Abbreviations used in the text 本詞典略語表（詳見M1頁）

abbr	abbreviation	i e	which is to say	*prep*	preposition(al)
adj, adjj	adjective(s)	illus	illustration	*pres p*	present participle
adv, advv	adverb(s)	imper	imperative	*pres t*	present tense
adv part	adverbial particle	impers	impersonal	*pron*	pronoun
affirm	affirmative(ly)	*indef art*	indefinite article	*pt*	past tense
anom fin	anomalous finite	inf	infinitive	RC	Roman Catholic
attrib	attributive(ly)	*int*	interjection	reflex	reflexive
aux	auxiliary	interr	interrogative	*rel*	relative
[C]	countable noun	intrans	intransitive	sb	somebody
Cf, cf	compare	Lat	Latin	Scot	Scottish
collect	collective(ly)	L*c*	length about	*sing*	singular
comp	comparative	masc	masculine	sth	something
conj	conjunction	*n, nn*	noun(s)	*suff*	suffix
def art	definite article	neg	negative(ly)	superl	superlative
demonstr	demonstrative	opp	opposite	trans	transitive
e g	for example	P	proprietary name	[U]	uncountable noun
esp	especially	*part adj*	participial adjective	US	America(n)
etc	and the others	pers	person	usu	usual(ly)
F	French	*pers pron*	personal pronoun	*v, vv*	verb(s)
fem	feminine	phr	phrase	[VP]	Verb Pattern
G	German	*pl*	plural	*vi*	verb intransitive
GB	British/Britain	*poss*	possessive	*vt*	verb transitive
Gk	Greek	*pp*	past participle	⇨	look at
H*c*	height about	pred	predicative(ly)	♂	male
I	Italian	*pref*	prefix	♀	female

Specialist English registers
專門名詞

accounts
aerospace
algebra (alg)
anatomy (anat)
architecture (archit)
arithmetic (arith)
art
astronomy (astron)
ballet
biblical
biology (biol)
book-keeping
botany (bot)
business
chemistry (chem)
cinema
commerce (comm)
computers (comp)
cricket
ecclesiastical (eccles)
engineering (eng)
electricity (electr)
farming
finance (fin)
football
gambling
geology (geol)
geometry (geom)
grammar (gram)
history (hist)
journalism
legal
linguistics (ling)
mathematics (maths)
mechanics (mech)
medical (med)
meteorology (met)
military (mil)
music
mythology (myth)
nautical (naut)
pathology (path)
philosophy (phil)
phonetics (phon)
photography (photo)
physics (phys)
physiology (physiol)
politics (pol)
psychology (psych)
racing
radio telegraphy (radio)
rugby
science
sport
tennis
theatre
trigonometry (trig)
zoology (zool)

Stylistic values
字格標準

archaic
colloquial (colloq)
dated
derogatory (derog)
dialect (dial)
emotive (emot)
emphatic (emph)
euphemistic (euphem)
facetious (facet)
figurative (fig)
formal
humorous (hum)
ironical (ironic)
jocular (joc)
laudatory (laud)
literally (lit)
literary (liter)
modern use (mod use)
old use
pejorative (pej)
poetic (poet)
proverb (prov)
rare
rhetorical (rhet)
slang (sl)
vulgar (vulg)
⚠ taboo

牛津現代高級英漢雙解詞典

OXFORD ADVANCED LEARNER'S ENGLISH - CHINESE DICTIONARY

Revised Third Edition 第三版

原著
A S Hornby

主編
張芳杰

編輯
劉錫炳　、林炳錚　　滕以魯
陳永昭　　張先信

啓思

啓思出版有限公司

This new bilingual (English-Chinese) edition
first published 1984
Twenty-four impression 1992

此新英漢版第一次印刷1984
第二十四次印刷1992

ISBN 0 19 583755 X (paperback平裝版)
ISBN 0 19 583768 1 (hardback精裝版)
ISBN 0 19 584984 5 (flexi-cover膠面精裝版)
ISBN 0 19 585341 5 (bible paper
in flexi-cover 膠面精裝聖經紙版)

Published by arrangement with Tung Hua Book Company; this bilingual (English-Chinese) edition based on *Oxford Advanced Learner's Dictionary of Current English Revised Third Edition* originally published by Oxford University Press, Walton Street, Oxford, England

Published by Keys Publishing Company Ltd., Warwick House, Quarry Bay, Hong Kong.

此英漢版由香港鰂魚涌和域大厦
啓思出版有限公司出版

The publishers are grateful to the following for permission to reproduce the photographs:

本詞典內之圖片及複製版權蒙下列各機構等提供，謹此致謝。

Aerofilms Ltd; The Associatd Press Ltd; Atkin, Grant & Lang Ltd; The Australian High Commission; Babcock Weitz; Barnaby's Picture Library; The British Aircraft Corporation; The British Leyland Motor Corporation Ltd; The British Oxygen Co Ltd; The British Petroleum Co Ltd; British Rail; The British Tourist Authority; Camera Press Ltd; The Canadian High Commission; J Allan Cash Ltd; The Controller of Her Majesty's Stationery Office (British Crown Copyright); Coventry Climax Engines Ltd; De Beers Ltd; Arnold Dolmetsch Ltd; The Electricity Council of Great Britain; Fox Photos Ltd; Gillette Industries Ltd; Gravity-Randall Ltd; The Greek State Tourist Office; Will Green Ltd; John M Henderson & Co Ltd; The International Harvester Co Ltd; The Japanese Embassy; Jarrold & Sons Ltd; Kelvin Hughes; The Keystone Press Agency Ltd; Kodak Ltd; Quentin Lloyd; The London Museum; Madame Tussaud's Ltd; The Mansell Collection; Massey-Ferguson (UK) Ltd; Messerschmitt-Bölkow-Blohm; Myford Ltd; The National Cash Register Co Ltd; The National Portrait Gallery, London; James Neill (Sheffield) Ltd; The New Charing Cross Hospital, London; The Novosti Press Agency; Philips Electrical Ltd; Pifco Ltd; The Rev C E Pocknee; The Post Office; The Progress Gyroscope Co Ltd; Prout Catamarans; Pye TVT; The Radio Times Hulton Picture Library; Rana Båtfabrikk; Ransomes, Sims & Jeffries Ltd; Record-Marples-Ridgway Ltd; The Royal National Institute for the Blind; St George's Hospital Medical School, London; The Science Museum, London (British Crown Copyright); Walter Scott (Bradford) Ltd; Scottish Aviation Ltd; Shure Electronics Ltd; The Singer Co Ltd; Thomas Smith & Sons (Rodley) Ltd; Spear & Jackson Ltd; The Sport & General Press Agency Ltd; Stanley Tools Ltd; Steinway & Sons; John Topham Ltd; The Trustees of the British Museum; The Trustees of the British Museum (Natural History); The Trustees of the Wallace Collection, London; The Union-Castle Mail Steamship Co Ltd; The United States Information Service; Vespa Scooters; Vickers Ltd; The Victoria & Albert Museum, London (British Crown Copyright); Wilkinson Sword Ltd; Wolf Electric Tools Ltd; Carl Zeiss Ltd; Mr Man Shek Hay.

序　言

Oxford Advanced Learner's Dictionary of Current English　於1963年二版問世後，因適合讀者需要，較諸第一版更受歡迎。爲求精進完善，主編郝恩貝(A. S. Hornby)先生在數年後又着手修訂的工作，於1974年推出了第三版。三版曾對二版作大幅度的修訂，不僅增添約四分之一的新字或定義，納入流行的美語及科技方面的新詞，而且重新處理過原有字條的定義和例句。此外還增加動詞類型，改進注音，加强用法說明，並充實附錄。整個言之，三版與二版間的變動不遜於二版之於一版，此種修訂，尤以常用的動詞爲甚。

三版問世後不久，東華書局的主人卓鑫淼先生即邀約我和部分同仁共同擔任重新編譯的工作。我們邀請了劉錫炳先生、林炳錚先生、滕以魯先生、陳永昭先生、張先信先生負責編輯。他們五位不但都是中英文造詣很深的專家，翻譯經驗豐富，而且都曾參與過二版的編輯工作。他們於教學之餘，再次參加這項工作，謹此誌謝。我們從1975年開始，約三年而脫稿。然而實際的工作卻延續了三四年，原因是 Oxford Advanced Learner's Dictionary 第三版在1974年出版後，屢經再版，至1982年已是第十六次再版。於1980年第十一次再版時，並曾作大幅度修訂，重新排版。爲配合時效，修訂後的資料自倫敦寄來後，我們經過迻譯再補充在原稿內，如此往返費時，也是本辭典遲未問世的原因之一。

本詞典歷經七載始出版的另一原因是東華卓鑫淼先生處事的態度。他爲人嚴謹，做事認眞負責，故對校對工作要求極爲嚴格，希望精益求精，將錯誤減少至最低。他特別邀請張先信先生主持校補工作，另請鄭瑞玲女士和張惠鎮女士擔任助理編輯，他們共同整理原稿，統一體例，發掘問題，加注 Kenyon and Knott 音標，鄭瑞玲女士並負責人名地名之編譯。Oxford Advanced Learner's Dictionary 新版中疏誤之處，我們均徵得原編者的同意，一一予以訂正。我們特別感謝東華編輯部同仁吳叠彬、梁屛仙、吳錦玲、潘蓮丹、譚遠祥、陳玉梅、王嘉芊、徐秀姬、陳麗玲、潘憲政、孫曉賢、徐中秀、戴茉莉等在四年多的校對過程中所作的努力，他們備極辛勞，對整個詞典反覆精心校對，並提供許多寶貴意見，對本詞典貢獻良多。

我們也很感謝東華書局的總編輯徐萬善先生，他爲本詞典的聯絡與協調工作，經常奔波。此外東華編輯部的工作同仁芮黎華、許明月、林秀愛、許桂香、孫麗雲、呂德敏、蕭怡貞、繆瑜英、林淸娟、陳麗俐、王素美、劉四貴等均參加了剪貼原稿工作，也頗辛苦，在此一併致謝。

在本詞典的誕生過程中，我們仍本信實負責的原則，各項問題的處理，儘量做到一絲不苟，往往花費三五日尋求解決一個小小疑難。誠如二版序言中所稱：「一個編輯英漢字典的人所遭遇的各種困煩，我們大部份都遭遇到了，而且我們有時覺得比在編輯其他英漢字典的時候，受到更多的束縛限制。」我們相信已盡最大的努力，但是疏漏之處，在所難免，尙希海內外讀者不吝指正。

張　芳　杰

Contents 目錄

Contributors

General Editor
A S Hornby
with
A P Cowie

Pronunciation
Professor A C Gimson
Dr S M Ramsaran

Specialist Editors
Dr L Todd
S Murison-Bowie

Illustrations
Roger Gorringe
Carl James
Richard Lewington
Sean Milne
Colin Newman
Vyvyan Thomas
David Woodroffe

Acknowledgements

I continue to be indebted to correspondents in many parts of the world for calling attention to occasional misprints and errors, and for suggestions on possible additions. These suggestions have been carefully considered and acted on where I felt in agreement with them.

Professor V Gatenby and Mr H Wakefield shared the work of compiling the first edition (1942). The value of their contributions remains, although these were extensively revised and added to in the second edition (1963) and in this third edition.

I pay tribute to the editors of the English Language Teaching Department of the Oxford University Press, especially Christina Ruse and Jonathan Price, and to the staff of the computer type-setting section, for their work on the text of this edition.

A S HORNBY

General preface

This is a completely revised, up-dated and re-set impression of the third edition. It combines the traditions of the Oxford Dictionaries with the language-teaching skills of A S Hornby. It provides the student or teacher of the English language with the most practically useful and comprehensive record of the language as it is spoken and written today.

There are four new features of this revised impression:

1 A simple but detailed *Introduction*, which not only explains what is in the Dictionary, but also suggests how the Dictionary can be used.
2 A phonetic interpretation and transcription by Professor A C Gimson, editor of the *English Pronouncing Dictionary*.
3 An Appendix on *Punctuation*, explaining how all the English punctuation marks are used.
4 A *Key to the verb patterns* inside the back cover, for constant easy reference.

Preface to the phonetic information

In this revised impression, the representation of pronunciation differs somewhat from that shown previously. The phonetic notation now conforms to that to be found in the majority of important English dictionaries used by non-native learners of English, and in particular to the latest (14th) edition of the *English Pronouncing Dictionary* (Dent, 1977). As a consequence, the length mark associated with certain vowels has been restored, though in strict phonological terms this mark may be considered redundant if the chosen vowel symbols distinguish qualitative differences. Nevertheless, the reactions of users of the Dictionary have suggested that an indication of length is widely held to be pedagogically useful, there being many occasions when quantitative as well as qualitative features provide significant cues to meaning. In addition, the simple vertical primary stress mark has been restored in place of the previous slanting mark, which was judged by many to be too readily suggestive of a specific tone.

The pronunciations recommended differ little from those shown previously. However, certain highly-elided forms have been replaced by others of a more careful style, judged to be more useful for even the advanced learner of English. Similarly, the marking of syllabic consonants in non-final positions has been abandoned, an expanded solution involving the insertion of a weak vowel being preferred.

The task of making these and other changes has been shared between my colleague Dr S M Ramsaran and myself.

A C GIMSON
University College London

誌　謝

世界許多地區的讀者，曾致書指出本詞典偶有印刷錯誤和疏漏之處，並建議可能增添之處，謹此仍舊向他們表示謝意。他們的建議均經過審愼考慮，其中本人同意之處，均已按照建議處理。

蓋登貝教授與威克斐爾德先生都曾分擔第一版（1942）的編輯工作。本詞典雖經第二版（1963）以及本版（第三版）大幅度的修訂和增添，他倆寶貴的貢獻依然存在。

爲本版之問世，我很感謝牛津大學出版社英語教學部的編輯，特別是克麗絲蒂娜・露絲和詹納桑・普萊斯以及電腦排版部的工作同仁。

郝恩貝

總　序

這是一部經完全修訂後，最新的、重新排版過的第三版詞典。本詞典兼容牛津詞典的傳統及郝恩貝先生之語言教學技巧，可提供英語教學的學生或教師最實用的、綜合性的今日英語說和寫的記錄。

本修訂版本有四種特色：

一、簡明而詳盡的說明，不僅說明本詞典的內容，並且指出其用途。

二、由「英語發音字典」編輯吉慕生教授作發音上的說明及注音。

三、附錄標點使用法，說明所有英文標點符號之用途。

四、封底內頁備有「動詞類型例釋」，以便易於經常參考。

發音說明

本修訂版中讀音的表示與以往者略有不同。其發音符號與非以英語爲母語的外國學習者使用的大多數重要英文字典一致，尤其符合最新版（十四版）的「英語發音字典」(Dent, 1977)。因此，我們又採用了與某些母音有關的長音符號，儘管就嚴格的語音學觀點而言，如果這些母音符號辨別音質方面之不同時，此種長音符號可能被認爲冗贅。雖然如此，本詞典讀者的反應建議中，曾提出長音符號在教學上普遍被認爲是有用的，因爲在許多情況中，音量和音質的特色表示對字義有不同的提示。此外，我們又恢復了簡單的垂直重音符號，以代替以前使用的斜線重音符號，由於許多人覺得斜線重音符號極易被視作表示一特殊的音調。

本版採用的發音方法則無異於以往。雖然如此，鑒於對甚至高級的學習者都比較有用，某些常被省略母音或音節的形式已由經過更審愼處理後的形式代替。同樣的，不是位於字尾的音節子音符號亦被廢除，整個的解決辦法是插入一弱母音代替。

以上修訂工作以及其他變更皆由我的同事羅慕蘭博士和我共同擔任。

吉慕生

倫敦大學

Key to entries 字目例釋

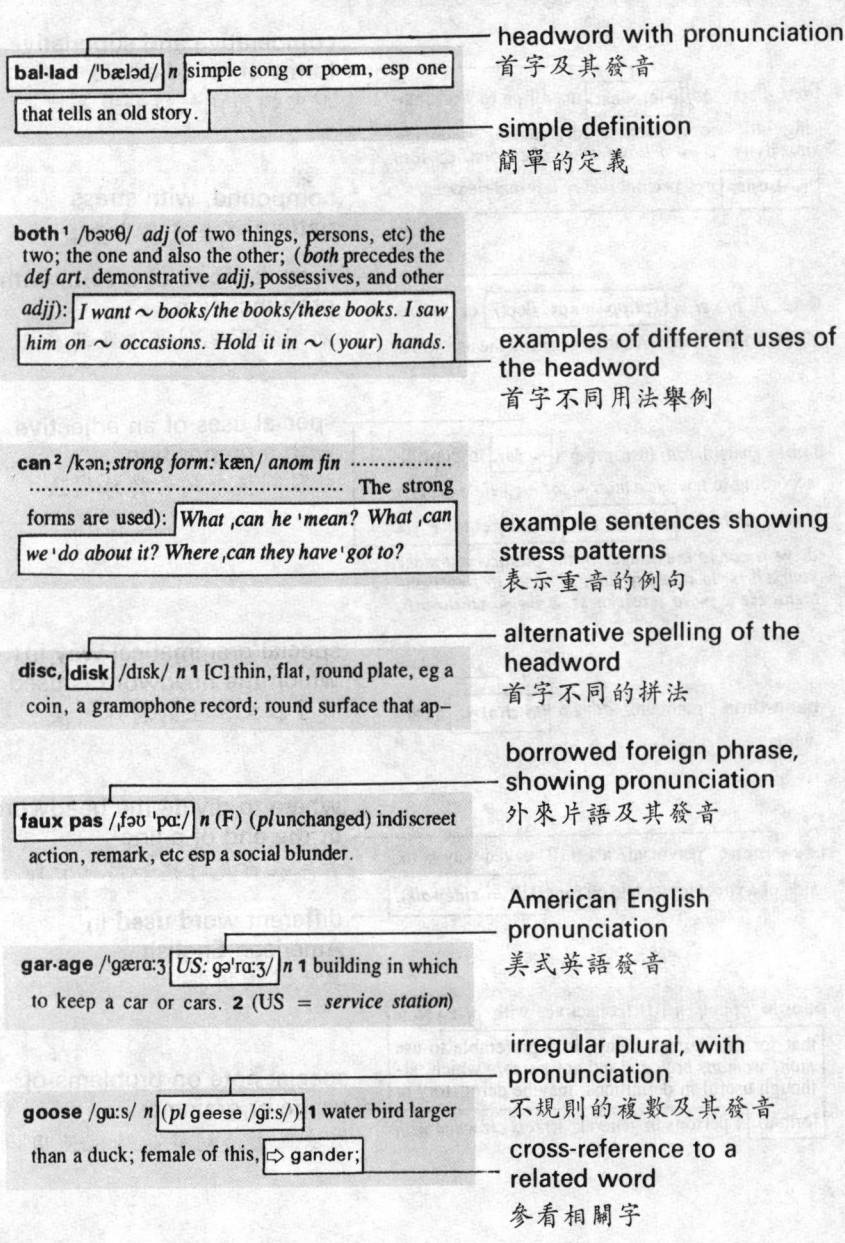

bal·lad /ˈbæləd/ *n* simple song or poem, esp one that tells an old story.

headword with pronunciation
首字及其發音

simple definition
簡單的定義

both[1] /bəʊθ/ *adj* (of two things, persons, etc) the two; the one and also the other; (*both* precedes the *def art*, demonstrative *adjj*, possessives, and other *adjj*): *I want ~ books/the books/these books. I saw him on ~ occasions. Hold it in ~ (your) hands.*

examples of different uses of the headword
首字不同用法舉例

can[2] /kən; *strong form:* kæn/ *anom fin* .... The strong forms are used): *What ˌcan he ˈmean? What ˌcan we ˈdo about it? Where ˌcan they have ˈgot to?*

example sentences showing stress patterns
表示重音的例句

disc, disk /dɪsk/ *n* **1** [C] thin, flat, round plate, eg a coin, a gramophone record; round surface that ap–

alternative spelling of the headword
首字不同的拼法

faux pas /ˌfəʊ ˈpɑː/ *n* (F) (*pl* unchanged) indiscreet action, remark, etc esp a social blunder.

borrowed foreign phrase, showing pronunciation
外來片語及其發音

gar·age /ˈgærɑːʒ *US:* gəˈrɑːʒ/ *n* **1** building in which to keep a car or cars. **2** (US = *service station*)

American English pronunciation
美式英語發音

goose /guːs/ *n* (*pl* **geese** /giːs/) **1** water bird larger than a duck; female of this, ⇨ **gander**;

irregular plural, with pronunciation
不規則的複數及其發音

cross-reference to a related word
參看相關字

hon·our[2] (US = **honor**) /ˈɒnə(r)/ *vt* [VP6A] **1** respect highly, feel honour for; confer honour on:

American English spelling
美式英語拼法

lazy /ˈleɪzɪ/ *adj* (-ier, -iest) unwilling to work; doing little work; suitable for, causing, inducing, inactivity: *a ~ fellow; a ~ afternoon.* ⇨ idle. **ˈ~-bones** *n* ~ person. **lazi·ly** *adv* **lazi·ness** *n*

comparative and superlative forms of an adjective
形容詞的比較級和最高級

compound, with stress pattern 複合字及其重音

leap /li:p/ *vi, vt* (*pt, pp* **leapt** /lept/ or **leaped** /li:pt/) **1** [VP2A,C,3A] jump (*jump* is the usu word;

irregular form of a verb, with pronunciation
動詞的不規則變化及其發音

li·able /ˈlaɪəbl/ *adj* (usu *pred*) **1** *~ for,* responsible according to law: *Is a man ~ for his wife's debts in your country?* **2** ***be ~ to sth,*** be subject to: *If you drive a car to the danger of the public, you make yourself ~ to a heavy fine, or even to imprisonment. He is ~ to seasickness.* **3 *be ~ to do sth,***

special uses of an adjective with a preposition
形容詞接介詞的特殊用法

mean·time /ˈmi:ntaɪm/ *adv, n* ***(in the) ~,*** meanwhile.

special grammatical way in which the headword is used
首字在文法上的特殊用法

pave|ment /ˈpeɪvmənt/ *n* **1** (GB) paved way at the side of a street for people on foot (US = *sidewalk*).

where to divide the headword at the end of a line
首字在行尾時應如何分音節

different word used in American English
美式英語用語

people /ˈpi:pl/ *n* [U] (collective, with *pl v.* Note that for one human being, it is preferable to use *man, woman, boy, girl* and not *person*, which, although useful in definitions, may be derogatory or formal). **1** persons in general: *streets crowded with*

special note on problems of usage or grammar
用法或文法問題的特殊說明

numbered headwords with the same spelling 以號碼表示的拼法相同的首字

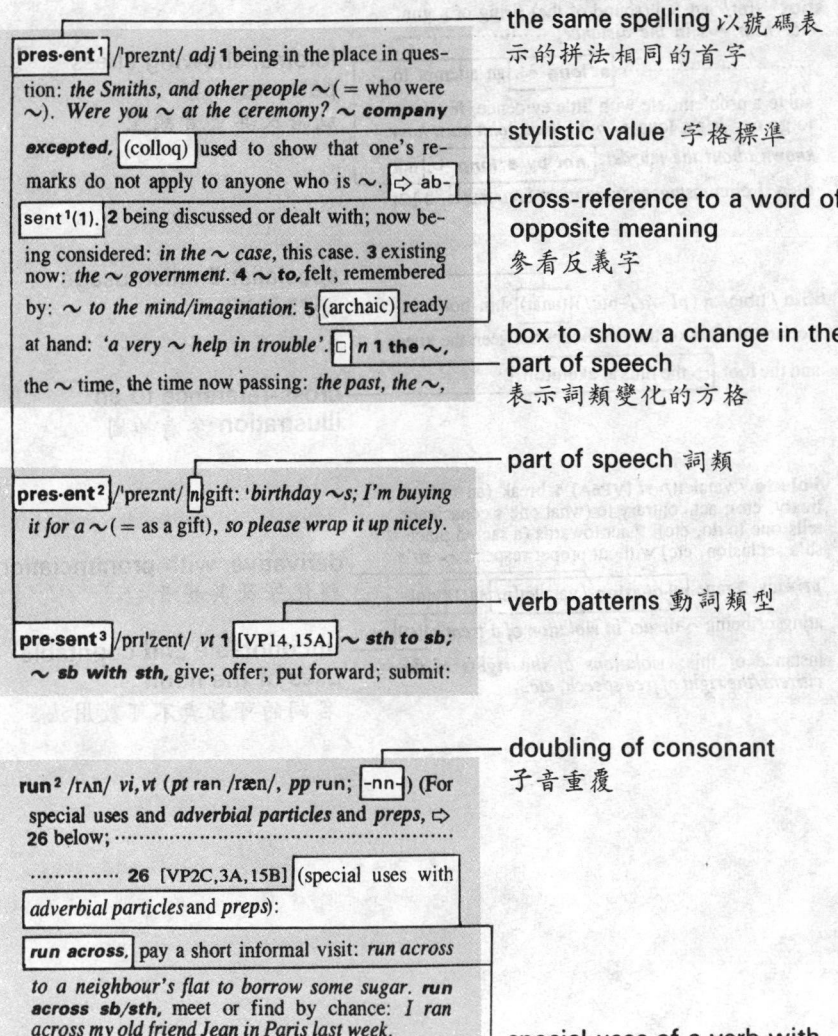

pres·ent[1] /ˈpreznt/ *adj* **1** being in the place in question: *the Smiths, and other people* ~ (= who were ~). *Were you* ~ *at the ceremony?* ~ ***company excepted,*** (colloq) used to show that one's remarks do not apply to anyone who is ~. ⇨ absent[1](1). **2** being discussed or dealt with; now being considered: *in the* ~ *case*, this case. **3** existing now: *the* ~ *government*. **4** ~ ***to,*** felt, remembered by: ~ *to the mind/imagination*. **5** (archaic) ready at hand: *'a very* ~ *help in trouble'*. □ *n* **1 the** ~, the ~ time, the time now passing: *the past, the* ~,

stylistic value 字格標準

cross-reference to a word of opposite meaning 參看反義字

box to show a change in the part of speech 表示詞類變化的方格

part of speech 詞類

pres·ent[2] /ˈpreznt/ *n* gift: *'birthday* ~*s; I'm buying it for a* ~ (= as a gift), *so please wrap it up nicely.*

verb patterns 動詞類型

pre·sent[3] /prɪˈzent/ *vt* **1** [VP14,15A] ~ ***sth to sb;*** ~ ***sb with sth,*** give; offer; put forward; submit:

doubling of consonant 子音重覆

run[2] /rʌn/ *vi,vt* (*pt* ran /ræn/, *pp* run; -nn-) (For special uses and *adverbial particles* and *preps,* ⇨ **26** below; ···

··············· **26** [VP2C,3A,15B] (special uses with *adverbial particles* and *preps*):

run across, pay a short informal visit: *run across to a neighbour's flat to borrow some sugar.* ***run across sb/sth,*** meet or find by chance: *I ran across my old friend Jean in Paris last week.*

run after sb/sth, (**a**) try to catch: *The dog was running after a rabbit.* (**b**) seek the society of; go after in order to get the attention of: *She runs after every good-looking man in the village.*

run against sb, compete with him by running in a race; (esp US) compete with him (for an elected office).

special uses of a verb with adverbial particles and prepositions 動詞與副詞接語及介詞連用的特殊用法

shot[1] /ʃɒt/ *n* **1** [C] (sound of the) firing of a gun, etc: *hear ~s in the distance;* ....

.... ***a 'long ~,*** an attempt to solve a problem, etc with little evidence, few facts to go on: *It's a long ~ but I think John must have known about the murder.* ***ˌnot by a 'long ~,*** not even if circumstances were most favourable. **3** [C]

idioms, showing stress patterns
成語及其重音類型

tibia /ˈtɪbɪə/ *n* (*pl* ~e /-bri:/) (anat) shin-bone; inner and thicker of the two bones between the knee and the foot. ⇨ the illus at **skeleton**.

specialist English usage
專門用語

cross-reference to an illustration 參看插圖

vi·ol·ate /ˈvaɪəleɪt/ *vt* [VP6A] **1** break (an oath, a treaty, etc); act contrary to (what one's conscience tells one to do, etc). **2** act towards (a sacred place, sb's seclusion, etc) without proper respect: *~ sb's privacy.* **3** rape. **vi·ol·ation** /ˌvaɪəˈleɪʃn/ *n* [U] violating or being ~d: *act in violation of a treaty;* [C] instance of this: *violations of the rights of the citizens/the right of free speech, etc.*

derivative, with pronunciation
轉化字及其發音

uncountable and countable uses of the noun
名詞的可數與不可數用法

Using the Dictionary
本詞典用法說明

Who is this Dictionary for?
本詞典的對象

This is a Dictionary that has been specially prepared for the learner of the English language. All its parts have been designed and put together to give the learner the most *practical* help in developing the three language skills: speaking, writing, and reading.

本詞典特爲學習英語者所編。各部分皆經設計和安排，在培養說、寫、讀三種語言技能上，給予學習者最實用的協助。

This is a Dictionary for the learner of English who has mastered the rules of English grammar and pronunciation, and has acquired a vocabulary that enables him to read and understand English of moderate difficulty. It is for the learner who wants to develop further his knowledge of how English words, compounds, and idiomatic expressions are used, what they mean, how they are pronounced, and how they are spelt.

使用本詞典者應已熟諳英文文法和讀法的規則，並已掌握一部分字彙，使其在閱讀和瞭解英文方面不太感到困難。本詞典可供學習者進一步瞭解英語單字、複合字以及成語的用法、意義、讀法和拼法。

What is in this Dictionary?
本詞典的內容

The Introduction 緒論

The Introduction has 3 aspects. 緒論包括三方面。

1 It explains, in simple, clear language, all the different parts that go to make up the entries for the words in the Dictionary. It also contains examples of all these different parts of a dictionary entry.
以簡易明晰的語言說明構成本詞典所列各字目之不同部分，並包含一個字目所有不同部分的例子。

2 It contains useful information about *spelling* (for example, how to spell the plurals of nouns), about *pronunciation* (for example, how to pronounce the inflections of nouns, verbs and adjectives), about *grammar* (for example, how to use a 'phrasal verb' like ***take off***) and about *style* (for example, how to use idioms and proverbs).
包括拼法(如名詞複數形式的拼法)、發音(如名詞、動詞及形容詞語尾變化的讀法)、文法(例如像 take off 等動詞片語的用法)，以及字格(如成語和諺語的用法)等有用的說明。

3 It has 4 important lists, which the learner will find constantly useful: (i) Verb patterns (p xxxvi); (ii) The forms of the anomalous verbs (eg *can, could*) (p li); (iii) The strong and weak spoken forms of common words (eg *and, from*) (p li); (iv) The written and spoken forms of the common English contractions (eg *we're, wasn't*) (p liv).
包括四種重要的表，學習者隨時都會發現它們很有用處：(i)動詞類型(xxxvi 頁)；(ii)變則動詞(如 can, could) 的形式(li 頁)；(iii)常用字(如 and, from)的强弱讀法(li頁)；(iv)常用英文縮寫式(如 we're, wasn't)的寫法和讀法(liv頁)。

The Dictionary 本詞典

This is a Dictionary of the English Language as it is written and spoken today by educated British men and women. It lists words, compound words and idiomatic expressions that the learner is likely to come across in everyday English speech, in official and informal writing, and in the literature of the 20th and 19th centuries. For all the listed items there is information on (i) spelling, (ii) pronunciation, (iii) grammatical use, (iv) meaning (or meanings). In addition, there are examples showing their use in current English. Guidance is also given, wherever necessary or helpful, on difficult points of meaning, spelling and pronunciation. All special American English spellings and pronunciations are given.

本詞典中的英語爲今日英國受過教育的男女所寫和說者。本詞典所列之單字、複合字及成語，學習者很可能在日常的談話，正式或非正式的寫作以及二十世紀和十九世紀的文學作品中接觸到。對於所列各字目，在拼法、發音、文法、意義等方面均有所說明。此外，尚有例句說明它們在當代英語中的用法。有必要或幫助時，凡是在字義、拼法和發音方面比較困難的地方也有所指引。美式英語的特殊拼法和發音均一一列出。

The Illustrations 插圖

There are a large number of illustrations, because a drawing is often a more useful way of showing a meaning than a written explanation. Many of these illustrations are found in groups, for example, *insects*, *wild cats* and *flowers*. Others are of systems that have many related parts, for example, *the respiratory system*, *the eye*, *the motor-car*, *football*. The learner is guided by a cross-reference from a word that is illustrated to the page where the illustration is found.

由於圖畫往往較文字解釋更能表示一意義，本詞典備有大量插圖。這些插圖有很多是成類出現的，例如 insects, wild cats 及 flowers 的插圖。有些插圖表明具有許多相關部分的某些系統，例如 the respiratory system, the eye, the motor-car, football 的插圖。學習者可自一字之參看部分找出插圖之所在。

The Appendices 附錄

There are 12 Appendices at the end of the book, containing useful information for the learner of English. There are 3 that the learner is particularly recommended to use:

本詞典末尾有十二個附錄，供給學習英語者有用的知識。其中有三個特別介紹給學習者使用：

Appendix 3 *Affixes.* These are the small items of the language that are used to build up many English words. They are divided into *prefixes*, which come at the beginning of a word (for example *ex-*, *extra-*, and *under-*, as in *ex-president*, *extra-thin*, and *underestimate*), and *suffixes*, which come at the end of a word (for example *-ee*, *-ish*, *-ize*, as in *employee*, *childish* and *criticize*). Notes on how these affixes are used to form words, their pronunciations, and examples of their use, are also given.

附錄三接語。接語是英語中形成許多英文單字的小項目，分作字首（例如 ex-president, extra-thin 和 underestimate 中之 ex-, extra- 和 under-）及字尾（例如 employee, childish 和 criticize 中之 -ee, -ish, -ize）。有關接語之構成單字，讀音及用法舉例均有註明。

Appendix 4 *Numerical Expressions.* This is a unique and comprehensive guide on how to use numbers and expressions that contain numbers. For example, there are sections on how to express *distance*, *temperature*, *sports scores*, *the time*, *the date*, *amounts of money* and *telephone numbers.* Notes on pronunciation, and many examples of usage, are also given.

附錄四數字表達法。本附錄爲一獨特的綜合性指南，說明如何表達數字和含有數字的詞句。比方說，本附錄各部分分別說明如何表達距離、溫度、運動分數、時間、日期、金錢數量以及電話號碼等。讀音與許多用法的實例也都列出來了。

Appendix 9 *Punctuation.* This is a detailed guide, with examples, on how to use all the English punctuation marks, for example *the comma, the colon, quotation marks, parentheses, the apostrophe.* There are also sections on the punctuation of *Abbreviations*, *Conversation*, *Quotations* and *Letters.*

附錄九標點使用法。本附錄對英文標點符號如逗點、冒號、引號、圓括弧、省略或所有格符號等的用法舉實例詳加說明。此外，尚有關於略語、會話、引句、書信等項目的標點用法的說明。

How is this Dictionary to be used?
本詞典的用途

There are two chief ways in which the Dictionary can be used.
本詞典有兩種主要用途。

1 It can be used to help the learner *understand* the meanings of words, compounds and idioms, when he meets them for the first time in spoken or written English.
用以幫助學習者初次聽到或看到某些單字、複合字及成語時瞭解它們的意思。

2 It can also help the learner to *use* words correctly in sentences of his own, (i) by giving their spelling and pronunciation, (ii) by showing their grammatical patterns and forms, (iii) by indicating (through examples) the contexts in which they are generally used.
也可幫助學習者造句時藉下列三種方式正確運用字詞：(i)表明拼法和讀音，(ii)表明文法的型式，(iii)(以例句)表明字詞在上下文中一般的用法。

If this *Introduction* is carefully studied, the user will come to understand the many different features of English words which are covered in the Dictionary. He will then be able to use the Dictionary regularly and successfully in reading, writing and speaking English.
使用者如能仔細閱讀本緒論，將會瞭解本詞典內英文字的許多不同特色，進而能在讀、寫、說英語方面經常和成功地使用本詞典。

The user of the Dictionary should also work carefully through the companion Practice Book, *Use Your Dictionary*. By doing all the exercises in *Use Your Dictionary*, the learner will increase his understanding of what is contained in the Dictionary, and of how it can be fully used.
本詞典的使用者亦應仔細閱讀另一手册‘利用你的詞典’。在把‘利用你的詞典’中所有的練習做完後，將會進一步瞭解本詞典的內容以及如何充分予以利用。

Finding words and meanings
查單字和字義

How to find a word in the Dictionary
如何查單字

A headword 首字

In the Dictionary the words explained are arranged in alphabetical order and printed in **bold** type. They are called *headwords*. The information explaining the meanings and uses of a headword is called an *entry*. Sometimes two or more headwords have the same spelling. These are numbered, for example **die**[1], **die**[2]. These headwords have the same spelling but they either have different meanings or they are different parts of speech.
本詞典所解釋的字均按照字母順序排列，並以黑體字排印，這些字稱作首字。對首字的意義和用法所作的解釋稱作字目。有時兩個或兩個以上的首字拼法一樣，它們均標有號碼，例如 die[1], die[2]。這些首字雖然拼法相同，但不是含義不同，便是屬於不同的詞類。

When you meet a word for the first time, in a book or paper, you will often find that its spelling is not the same as the headword to which it belongs, and which you need to refer to. This may be because it is the plural form of a *noun* (for example, *boxes*, *oxen*, *phenomena*). In the case of these three examples, the headword that you need to look up is the singular form of the nouns (**box**, **ox**, **phenomenon**) and you should refer to that. Note, however, that when a plural is very irregular (for example *brethren*), it will have an entry of its own.
當你在書籍或文件中初次遇到一字時，你時常會發現它的拼法與其所屬而且是你需要參考的首字不同。這種情形可能因爲它是一個名詞的複數式(如 boxes, oxen, phenomena)。在上述三例中，你需要查閱的首字應是那些名詞的單數式(box, ox, phenomenon)。但是要注意，當一複數式很不規則時(如 brethren)，它會單獨列爲一個字目。

Sometimes, too, you will meet the irregular past tense or past participle forms of *verbs* (for example *sprang*, *sprung*, or *bore*, *borne*, or *spoke, spoken*). In all these cases, the headwords are the infinitives (**spring**, **bear**, **speak**), and those are the words to look up. To help you, though, the Dictionary has special entries for all of the irregular forms *sprang*, *sprung*, etc and these refer you to the full entries for the verbs:

有時你也會遇到動詞不規則的過去式或過去分詞 (例如 sprang, sprung, 或 bore, borne, 或 spoke, spoken)。在這種情況下,首字爲不定詞(spring, bear, speak),亦卽需要查閱者。不過,爲幫助學習者起見,本詞典特地將sprang, sprung 等不規則的動詞形式列爲字目,並說明應該參考的不定詞字目:

sprang. . . *pt* of spring³.
sprung. . . *pp* of spring³.

Note, too, that if you meet the comparative (*faster*) or superlative (*fastest*) of an adjective (here, *fast*), it is the headword **fast** that you must refer to. Once again, irregular forms, such as *better* or *best*, have their own entries.

另外亦請注意,如果遇到形容詞(如 fast)的比較級(faster) 或最高級(fastest)時,則必須查首字 fast。此外如 better 或 best 等不規則形式,也都單獨列爲字目。

A derivative 轉化字

A *derivative* is a word formed by adding an ending (called a *suffix*) to a headword, for example *-able*, *-ness*, *-ance*, *-ly*, *-ment*, as in *acceptable*, *dryness*, *acceptance*, *yearly*, *amazement*. Derivatives are printed in **bold** type, and are listed alphabetically at the end of an entry. Some may be written **~·ness**, **~·ly**, **~·ment**, etc (where the tilde ~ represents the headword). Others are printed in full because the spelling has changed, for example **amazing**, **mag·nifi·cence**. (⇨ Appendix 3 for a list and explanation of endings such as *-able*, *-ness*, etc.)

轉化字係由首字加字尾(suffix)而成,例如 acceptable, dryness, acceptance, yearly, amazement 中之 -able, -ness, -ance, -ly, -ment。所有的轉化字均以黑體字排印,並按字母順序排列,置於字目末尾。有些轉化字印作 ~·ness, ~·ly, ~·ment 等(以波浪號~代表首字)。有些轉化字由於拼法改變而整個字印出,例如 amazing, magnificence。(有關 -able, -ness 等字尾的說明,請參看附錄三。)

Sometimes a derivative of a word has its own separate entry. This may be because its spelling is very different: compare **adhere** with its derivative **adhesion**. It may also be because its meaning is very different. For example, the derivative **scarcely** has a quite different meaning from that of its parent word **scarce**.

有時一個字的轉化字會單獨列爲一個字目，這可能是因爲拼法上有很大的差別:請比較 adhere 及其轉化字 adhesion。也可能是因爲字義上有很大的差別,譬如轉化字 scarcely 與其母字 scarce 的意義就大不相同。

A compound 複合字

A *compound* is a word formed by adding another word to a headword. It is written as one word (**nightdress**), or as two words separated by a hyphen (**night-time**), or as two separate words (**night life**). The same compound may be found, in different books, newspapers, notices etc, written sometimes with a hyphen, sometimes as one word, sometimes as two words. Compare, for example, **head-master**, **headmaster**, **head master**. This indicates that there is no general agreement amongst the users of the language about how that compound is written. The form given in the Dictionary is the most common in modern British English usage. Compounds are printed in **bold** type, and are listed alphabetically at the end of an entry, but before derivatives. In the longer entries, they are placed at the end of the numbered sections to whose meanings they are most closely related.

複合字係以首字加另一字而成。有時寫成一個字(nightdress); 有時寫成兩個字，中間以連字號分開(night-time)；有時單獨寫成兩個字 (night life)。在不同的書、報紙、公告等中，同一複合字可能以不同形式出現：有時中間加有連字號，有時寫成一個字，有時寫成兩個字(例如 head-master, headmaster, head master)。這表示英語的使用者對於該複合字的寫法意見並不一致。本詞典所列的形式爲現代英國英語用法中最常見者。複合字係以黑體字印出，並按字母順序排列於字目末尾，但在轉化字之前。在較長的字目中，複合字則排在意義上與其關係最爲密切那一項的末尾。

An idiom 成語

An *idiom* (also called an *idiomatic expression*) is a phrase or sentence of two or more words that has a special meaning of its own. Idioms are printed in ***bold italic*** type, and are listed alphabetically at the end of an entry, but before both compounds and derivatives. In the longer entries, they are placed at the end of the numbered sections to whose meanings they are most closely related. To find an idiom, look for it in the entry for the most important word in the phrase or sentence (usually a *noun*, *verb* or *adjective*). For example, ***pick holes in*** is found in the entry for **hole**; ***get hold of the wrong end of the stick*** is found in the entry for **stick**. (⇨ *Using idiomatic English* on page xxxiii of this Introduction.)

成語 (亦稱慣用語) 爲本身有其特殊含義且由兩個或兩個以上的字構成的片語或句子。成語係以黑斜體字排印，依字母順序排列於字目末尾，但在複合字與轉化字之前。在較長的字目中，成語則排在意義上與其關係最密切那一項的末尾。查一個成語時，先找該片語或句子中最重要的一個字的字目(通常爲一名詞，動詞或形容詞)，例如 pick holes in 可在 hole 的字目下查出；get hold of the wrong end of the stick 可在 stick 的字目下查出。(請參看本緒論 xxxiii 頁之‘怎樣用成語’。)

A verb with a particle or a preposition 與副詞接語或介詞連用的動詞

English contains many phrases made up of a *verb* and an *adverbial particle*, for example ***go back***, ***run away***, ***take sth down***, or of a *verb* and a *preposition*, for example, ***go through sth***, ***run into sb***, ***take after sb***. Many of these phrases are idiomatic, and are printed and listed in the same way as other idioms.

英語中有許多片語是由動詞與副詞接語組成，如 go back, run away, take sth down, 或由動詞與介詞組成，如 go through sth, run into sb, take after sb。這類片語有很多是習慣用法，它們排印和排列的方式與其他的成語相同。

In the entries for the very common verbs like **go**, **make**, **put**, **take**, these verbal phrases are all gathered together in alphabetical order at the end of the verb's entry. They are called 'special uses with *adverbial particles* and *prepositions*'. For example, at the end of the entry for the verb **take** you will find ***take after sb***, ***take sth apart***, ***take (away) from sth***, ***take sth back***, etc. (⇨ *How to use a verb with the correct adverbial particle or preposition* on page xxx of this Introduction.)

在那些很常用的動詞如 go, make, put, take 等的字目中，這類動詞片語全按字母順序集中排列在該動詞字目的末尾，稱作‘與副詞接語和介詞連用的特殊用法’。例如在動詞 take 這個字目的末尾，你會發現 take after sb, take sth apart, take (away) from sth, take sth back 等。(請參看本緒論 xxx 頁之‘怎樣正確使用與副詞接語或介詞連用的動詞’。)

When you meet a *verb + particle* in speech or writing, it may take one of several forms. Compare *He took down the curtains; He took the curtains down; He took them down.* These are different ways of using ***take sth down*** and this is the phrase you should look up in the Dictionary. On the other hand, *go through John's pockets, go through them* are the two possible ways of using the *verb+preposition* ***go through sth***, and that is the form which should be looked up.

當你在談話或寫作中遇到'動詞＋副詞接語'時,它可能以不同形式出現。比較He took down the curtains; He took the curtains down; He took them down。這三個句子便是使用片語 take sth down 的不同方式,這也就是你在本詞典中應該查的片語。在另一方面, go through John's pockets, go through them 便是使用'動詞＋介詞' go through sth 的兩種可能的方式,而 go through sth 就是你應該查的形式。

How to find the meaning of a word 怎樣查字義

Definition numbers 定義的編號

Many entries are divided into sections numbered in bold type, i.e. **1**, **2**, **3**, **4** etc. These numbers show the different meanings or usages that the headword has. For example, the verb **decorate** has three meanings: **1** to adorn, to make attractive. **2** to give a building paint, plaster, wallpaper, carpets, etc. **3** to award someone a medal. Definitions are listed in order of meanings from the most common or most simple to the most rare or most complicated.

有許多字目分成若干項,分別用黑體字 1, 2, 3, 4 等予以編號。這些號碼表示首字所具有的各種意義或用法。譬如動詞 decorate 有三種意義: 1 裝飾;美化。2 裝修(房屋);油漆(房屋);(給房屋)塗灰泥,糊壁紙,鋪地毯等。3 授勳;頒獎。各定義係按意義的順序排列,從最常用或最簡單的用法到最少用或最複雜的用法。

If you are faced with **decorate** used with one of these meanings you will want to have some way of deciding which of the numbered definitions is the right one. This is one of those occasions when the *example phrases and sentences* will prove of great value. Suppose that you have this sentence in front of you: *Two airmen were decorated for their heroism.* This will suggest that meaning **3** is the right one, as the sentence closely resembles the example provided in the entry: *Several soldiers were decorated for bravery.* It is by matching the sentence you have with the example sentences in the Dictionary entry that you are able to decide which definition is the right one.

當你碰到 decorate 一字用到其中的一種意義時,你會希望有某種方法來決定在那些編號的定義中,哪一個最合適。這正是本詞典所收例句極具價值的時候。假若你面前有這樣一個句子: Two airmen were decorated for their heroism, 這個句子將提醒你第3義最合適,因爲它和字目中的例句 Several soldiers were decorated for bravery 很相近。唯有將你面前的句子和本詞典字目中的例句相配,你才能够決定哪一個定義最合適。

Example phrases and sentences 例句

These form a very large and very important part of the Dictionary. They follow the definitions in *italic* type. They are included for 7 reasons:

本詞典所收例句佔很大篇幅,而且是很重要的一部分。例句都接在定義後面,以斜體排印。本詞典所收例句,有七項理由:

1 They show how the headword, derivative, compound or idiomatic expression is used in different sentence patterns.
表示首字、轉化字、複合字或成語如何用於不同的句型中。

2 They show the kinds of style or context in which the word or phrase is usually used. They include the words or sorts of words that the headword is usually used with. For example, at **sensational**(2) there is *a sensational writer/newspaper;* at **sense**(4) there is *have no sense of shame; a sense of one's own importance/responsibility.*
表明字或片語通常所用的各種文體或上下文。並且舉出通常與首字用在一起的各類字詞。例如,在 sensation 的第2義有 a sensational writer/newspaper 一例;在 sense 的第4義有 have no sense of shame; a sense of one's own importance/responsibility 等例。

3 They often include information on where to put the stress when using the headword in a phrase or sentence. For example, at **failure**(3) there is *ˈheart failure; ˈengine failures.*

時常標明首字用在片語或句中時重音的所在,例如 failure 第3義中之 ˈheart failure; ˈengine failures。

4 They teach the writing conventions of correct punctuation and the use of capital letters, because many of the examples are full, correctly written and punctuated sentences.

教導如何使用正確標點和大寫字母等寫作常規,因爲許多例句皆爲完整且有正確標點的句子。

5 They help you to decide whether you have found the correct definition.

幫助讀者決定是否已經找到正確的定義。

6 They help you to check that you have understood the meaning of the word or phrase.

幫助讀者核對是否已經瞭解某字或片語的意義。

7 They help you to make your own sentences using the word or phrase.

幫助讀者利用某字或片語造句。

The large box □
正方格

Many headwords can be used as more than one part of speech. For example, the word **picture** can be used as a *noun* or a *verb*; the word **welcome** as a *noun*, a *verb* or an *adjective*; the word **last¹** as an *adjective*, an *adverb* or a *noun*. These different sections within an entry are divided from one another by a large box □.

許多首字可用作一種以上的詞類, 例如 picture 可用作名詞或動詞; welcome 可用作名詞、動詞或形容詞; last¹ 可用作形容詞、副詞或名詞。一字目下的不同詞類係以正方格□彼此隔開。

The small box ▭
長方格

Sometimes a compound or a derivative of a headword can be used as more than one part of speech. For example, in the entry for **white**, the compound word **whitewash** can be used as a *noun* or a *verb*; in the entry for **alcohol**, the derivative **alcoholic** can be used as an *adjective* or a *noun*. These different sections, in the part of an entry that deals with compounds or derivatives, are divided from one another by the small box ▭.

一個首字的複合字或轉化字有時可用作一種以上的詞類,例如在 white 字目中,複合字 whitewash 可用作名詞或動詞;在 alcohol 字目中,轉化字 alcoholic 可用作形容詞或名詞。複合字或轉化字的不同詞類係以長方格▭彼此隔開。

The tilde ~
波浪號

If a headword has more than three letters, to save space the symbol called the *tilde* ~ is used in place of the letters of the headword in example phrases and sentences, derivatives, compounds and idioms. For example, in the entry for **fresh**, you will find the example phrase ~ **paint**, the derivative **~·en**, the compound **ˈ~·water**, and the idiom ***break ~ ground***. The tilde will be found useful for 2 reasons:

當首字的字母多於三個時,爲了節省篇幅,在例句、轉化字、複合字及成語中,用一個波浪號~代替首字的字母。例如在 fresh 字目中,你會發現例句 ~ paint, 轉化字 ~·en, 複合字 ˈ~·water, 以及成語 break ~ ground 等。有兩種理由說明波浪號的功用:

1 The tilde draws your attention immediately to how the word (or the derivative or compound formed from the word) is used in example phrases and sentences.

波浪號立卽引你注意該字(其轉化字或複合字)怎樣用於例句中。

2 The tilde makes it easy for you to see how an ending is used to form a derivative. For example, at **dull** there is **~·y**, at **star** there is **~ry**, at **grit** there is **~ty**. If the spelling of a headword is

changed when forming a derivative, this is shown very clearly because the tilde is *not* used. For example, at **pretty** there is **prettily**.

波浪號可幫助你看出怎樣用一個語尾形成一轉化字,例如 dull 一字有 ~y, star 一字有 ~ry, grit 一字有 ~ty。如果首字形成轉化字拼法有所改變時,也有十分明顯的表示,因爲此種情況不用波浪號,而將轉化字完全拼出來。例如 pretty 一字有 prettily。

The slant mark / and brackets ( ) 斜線和括弧

The slant mark / is used in example phrases and sentences, compounds and idioms, to show an *alternative* word or phrase. For example, in ***as mad as a March hare / as a hatter***, the slant mark means that this idiom can be used in either of the forms ***as mad as a March hare*** or ***as mad as a hatter***.

斜線/用於例句、複合字和成語中,表示另一可選擇的字或片語。例如在 as mad as a March hare / as a hatter 中,斜線表示該成語可作 as mad as a March hare, 亦可作 as mad as a hatter。

Brackets ( ) are used to show an *optional* word or phrase. For example, in ***make (both) ends meet***, the brackets mean that this idiom can be used in either of the forms ***make ends meet*** or ***make both ends meet***.

括弧( )用來表示一個可選擇的字或片語。例如在 make (both) ends meet 中,括弧表示這個成語可作 make ends meet 或 make both ends meet。

Sometimes both the slant and the brackets are used in the same phrase. For example, ***on (an / the) average*** means that the forms ***on average***, ***on an average*** or ***on the average*** can be used.

斜線和括弧有時用於同一片語中。例如 on (an / the) average 則表示 on average, on an average, 或 on the average 皆可用。

When a slant mark or brackets are used in an idiom, it is important to notice that the alternative word shown by the slant, or the optional word shown by the brackets, is the *only* alternative or optional word that may be used in the idiom.

當斜線或括弧用在一個成語中時,千萬要注意的是,斜線或括弧所表示的可選擇的字,是唯一可用於該成語中另一可選擇的字。

The use of the slant mark and of brackets in idioms is very important because it teaches the learner that many English idioms do not have fixed forms, and therefore that many idioms cannot be learnt by heart as one simple unit.

在成語中使用斜線和括弧是十分重要的,因爲這可以讓學習者知道,有許多英文成語並無固定的形式,故而不能當作一個單純的單位去默記。

The abbreviations *sb* and *sth* 縮寫式 sb 與 sth

The abbreviations *sb* and *sth* are used in idioms. *sb* stands for 'someone', *sth* stands for 'something'. *sb* means that only a word that refers to a *person* can be used in that place in the idiom. *sth* means that only a word that refers to a *thing* (or an *animal*) can be used in that place. *sb / sth* means that a word that refers to either a person or a thing can be used.

縮寫式 sb 和 sth 用於成語中。sb 代表 'Someone', sth 代表 'something'。sb 表示在該成語的那個位置只可用一個指人的字, sth 表示那個位置只能用一個指事物(或動物)的字。sb / sth 則表示指人或事物的字都可以用在那個位置。

Cross-references 前後參看

A cross-reference is an item in an entry using the sign ⇨. It is a way of guiding you from one part of the Dictionary to another. There are three sorts of cross-references:

在字目中前後參看係以符號⇨表示,可引導你參考本詞典的另一部分。前後參看的方式有三種:

1 The first sort guides you to a word or phrase.

第一種是參看一個字或片語。

➪ finger means 'look at the entry for the word **finger**'.
➪ finger 表示'參看 finger 字目'。
➪ fire[1](6) means 'look at meaning number 6 in the entry for the word **fire[1]**'.
➪ fire[1](6) 表示'參看 fire[1] 第6義'。
➪ *first name* at first[1](2) means 'look at the compound *first name* at meaning number 2 in the entry for **first[1]**'.
➪ first name at first[1](2)表示'參看 first[1] 第2義中複合字 first name'。

2 The second sort guides you to an illustration.
第二種是參看一插圖。
➪ the illus at mouth means 'look at the illustration that appears with the entry for the word **mouth**'.
➪ the illus at mouth 表示'參看 mouth 之插圖'。

3 The third sort guides you to one of the 10 Appendices at the back of the book.
第三種是參看本詞典後面十個附錄之一。
➪ App 9 means 'look at Appendix number 9'.
➪ App 9 表示'參看附錄九'。

British and American English
英式與美式英語

Special British or American meanings, or comments on British or American usage, are given using the signs (GB) or (US). For example:
特殊的英國或美國字義，或是對英國或美國用法的說明，均以(英)或(美)表示之。例如:

check[2] . . . **5** (US) cheque. (美)支票。
knock sb up, . . . (GB colloq) waken or rouse him by knocking at his door. (英俗)敲門喚醒某人。
sure . . . **3** (colloq, esp US) certainly. (俗,尤美)當然。

Writing English
寫英文

How to check the spelling of a word
怎樣查看一字的拼法

In order to learn how to spell a word you must find it in the Dictionary. It is important to know the alphabet well. You should be able to judge quickly whether any word comes before or after another one. Remember that if the first letters of two words are the same, you must look at the next letters to decide where to find the words in the Dictionary. In **care** and **cart** 'e' comes before 't' in the alphabet, so **care** comes before **cart** in the Dictionary.

爲了學習一字的拼法,你必須查閱本詞典。重要的是要熟悉字母,你應該能迅速判斷某字是在另一字之前或後。記住如果兩個字的前幾個字母相同,你必須看後面的字母來決定這兩個字在本詞典中的位置。在 care 和 cart 兩個字中,按字母順序 e 在 t 之前,因此在本詞典裡 care 在 cart 之前。

How to find a word on any page of the Dictionary
怎樣在本詞典任何一頁查單字

To help you quickly find a word in the Dictionary, the *first* and *last* headword are printed together in large bold type in the top left-hand or right-hand corner of that page. These two words are divided by a slant mark, for example **hold/home.** Suppose you want to check the spelling of the word **holiday.** Since it comes alphabetically between **hold** and **home**, immediately you see **hold/home** at the top of the page you know that that is the page where **holiday** is to be found.

爲了幫助你在本詞典中迅速地找到某字,在每一頁的左上角或右上角均以大型黑體字印有該頁的第一和最末一個字。這兩個字以斜線分開,例如 hold/home。假若你要查 holiday 的拼法,由於依照字母順序它在 hold 與 home 之間,在你一發現頁上角的 hold/home, 你便知道 holiday 就在這一頁。

How to spell the plural of a noun 怎樣拼名詞的複數

The plural of a noun is formed by adding *-s* to the end of the noun. For example *boat*, plural *boats*; *apple*, plural *apples*; *idea*, plural *ideas*. But if the noun ends in *-s*, *-z*, *-x*, *-ch* or *-sh*, then the plural is formed by adding *-es* to the noun. For example *bus*, plural *buses*; *box*, plural *boxes*; *dish*, plural *dishes*.

名詞的複數是由名詞字尾加 -s 形成,例如 boat, boats; apple, apples; idea, ideas. 但是當一名詞的字尾是 -s, -z, -x, -ch, 或 -sh 時,其複數則由該名詞加 -es 而形成,例如 bus, buses; box, boxes; dish, dishes.

How to spell the plural of a noun ending in *-y* 怎樣把字尾爲-y的名詞拼成複數

Nouns ending in *-y*, if the *-y* is preceded by a consonant, form the plural by changing the *-y* into *-ies*. For example *city*, plural *cities*. If the *-y* is preceded by a vowel, the plural is *-ys*. For example *monkey*, plural *monkeys*. This spelling information is given in the Dictionary for all nouns ending in *-y*.

字尾爲 -y 的名詞, -y 前若爲一子音,複數將 -y 變作 -ies, 例如 city, cities。-y 前若爲母音,複數爲 -ys, 例如 monkey, monkeys。這種拼法用於本詞典中所有字尾爲 -y 的名詞。

How to spell the plural of a noun ending in *-o* 怎樣把字尾爲-o的名詞拼成複數

Some nouns that end in *-o* add *-s* to form the plural. For example *piano*, plural *pianos*. Some add *-es* to form the plural. For example *tomato*, plural *tomatoes*. Some add either *-s* or *-es*. For example *volcano*, plural *volcanos* or *volcanoes*. This spelling information is given in the Dictionary for all nouns ending in *-o*.

有些字尾爲 -o 的名詞,其複數爲加 -s, 例如 piano, pianos。有些加 -es 形成複數,例如 tomato, tomatoes。還有一些則加 -s 或 -es 均可,例如 volcano, volcanos 或 volcanoes。這種拼法用於本詞典中所有字尾爲 -o 的名詞。

How to spell the forms of a verb 怎樣拼動詞

The third person present singular of a verb is formed by adding *-s* to the end of the verb. For example *fit*, *it fits*; *write*, *she writes*; *see*, *he sees*. But if the verb ends in *-s*, *-z*, *-x*, *-ch* or *-sh*, then the third person present singular is formed by adding *-es* to the verb. For example *miss*, *she misses*; *mix*, *it mixes*; *touch*, *he touches*.

第三人稱、現在式、單數的動詞需加 -s, 例如 fit, it fits; write, she writes; see, he sees。但是在動詞的字尾是 -s, -z, -x, -ch, 或 -sh 時,第三人稱、現在式、單數的動詞需加 -es, 例如 miss, she misses; mix, it mixes; touch, he touches.

The past tense and the past participle of a verb are formed by adding *-ed* to the end of the verb. For example *pull*, *pulled*; *push*, *pushed*; *follow*, *followed*. But if the verb ends in *-e* or *-ee*, then the past tense and past participle are formed by adding *-d* to the end of the verb. For example *smile*, *smiled*; *agree*, *agreed*.

動詞的過去式和過去分詞是在字尾加 -ed 形成, 例如 pull, pulled; push, pushed; follow, followed。但當動詞的字尾是 -e 或 -ee 時,其過去式和過去分詞則加 -d 卽可,例如 smile, smiled; agree, agreed.

The present participle of a verb is formed by adding *-ing* to the end of the verb. For example *think*, *thinking*; *go*, *going*; *be*, *being*; *see*, *seeing*. But if the verb ends in a 'silent' *-e*, then the present participle is formed by dropping this *-e* from the end of the verb and then adding *-ing*. For example *love*, *loving*; *owe*, *owing*; *tire*, *tiring*.

動詞的現在分詞是在字尾加 -ing 形成,例如 think, thinking; go, going; be, being; see, seeing。但當動詞字尾的 -e 不發音時,其現在分詞是將 -e 去掉後再加 -ing, 例如 love, loving; owe, owing; tire, tiring。

How to spell the forms of a verb ending in *-y* 怎樣拼字尾爲-y的動詞

Verbs that end in *-y* form the past tense and the past participle by changing the *-y* into *-ied*. For example *carry*, past tense and past participle *carried*. This spelling information is given in the Dictionary for all verbs that end in *-y*.

字尾爲 -y 的動詞,其過去式與過去分詞是將 -y 變作 -ied, 例如 carry, 其過去式及過去分詞爲 carried。這種拼法用於本詞典所有字尾爲 -y 的動詞。

The third person present singular of verbs ending in *-y* is formed by changing the *-y* to *-ies.* For example *you carry*, but *she carries.*

字尾是 -y 的動詞,其第三人稱、現在式、單數係將 -y 變作 -ies, 例如 you carry, she carries。

The present participle of verbs ending in *-y* is formed by adding *-ing* to the end of the verb. For example *carry*, present participle *carrying.*

字尾爲 -y 的動詞,其現在分詞是加 -ing, 例如 carry, carrying。

Doubled consonants 重複子音

Many verbs that end with a single consonant have this letter repeated in the spelling for the present and past participles and the past tense. For example, *drop* has *dropping* and *dropped.* In the same way, some adjectives repeat the last consonant in the spelling for the comparative and superlative. For example, *hot* has *hotter* and *hottest.* If the consonant is doubled, the Dictionary shows this by printing the repeated letter in brackets, for example, **drop** (-pp-); **hot** (-tt-). (⇨ *How American English is written*, below.)

許多以單一子音爲字尾的動詞,在形成現在和過去分詞以及過去式時,需重複該一子音,例如 drop, dropping, dropped。同樣的,有些形容詞的比較級和最高級亦需重複字尾的子音,例如 hot, hotter, hottest。本詞典內重複子音處皆以括弧表示,例如 drop (-pp-); hot (-tt-)。(參看下列'怎樣寫美式英文'。)

How to divide a word when writing or typing 寫作或打字時怎樣斷字

When writing or typing it is sometimes necessary to divide a word at the end of the line because there is not enough space for the complete word. This division is always shown by adding a hyphen(-) immediately after the first part of the divided word at the end of the line. Many people prefer not to divide words at all (especially when writing by hand), but if you do, here are three considerations to help you.

寫作或打字時,由於行尾的篇幅不够容納一個完整的字,有時需要斷字。這種斷字總是在行尾斷字的第一部份後面加一連字號(-)。許多人不願意斷字(尤其在手寫時),但假若你需要斷字時,下列三點可供你參考。

1 By syllable 按照音節

This means dividing the word into syllables or units of sound. For example, the word **kind** has one syllable, **kind•ly** has two, **un•kind•ly** has three and **un•kind•li•ness** has four.

即依照音節或發音單位斷字,例如 kind 有一個音節, kind·ly 有兩個音節, un·kind·ly 有三個音節,un·kind·li·ness 有四個音節。

2 By structure 按照結構

This means dividing the word into the smaller units of meaning from which the word is built up. It may have a beginning (a prefix) such as *anti-*, *dis-*, *un-*, etc (as in **anti•sep•tic**, **dis•ap•pear**, **un•able**) or an ending (a suffix) such as *-age*, *-able*, *-fully* (as in **post•age**, **agree•able**, **grate•fully**).

即依照一個字結構上較小的意義單位來斷字。一個字的開始可能是 anti-, dis-, un- 之類的字首(如 anti·sep·tic, dis·ap·pear, un·able),也可能是 -age, -able, -fully 之類的字尾(如 post·age, agree·able, grate·fully)。

3 By meaning 按照意義

This means deciding whether each part of the divided word can be understood or spoken so that the complete word is easily recognized from the two parts. For example, it may be a compound word made up of two different words, such as *spot* and *light* in **spot•light**.

即視斷字後的每一部分是否代表一個意義或可以讀出,以便從斷字後的兩部分容易地辨識全字,例如複合字 spot·light 一字係由二字組成,可分作 spot 和 light。

All three considerations must be used to decide whether and where you can divide a word. Here are six useful rules to help you:

以上三點可用來決定是否要斷字、在何處斷字，下面六項規則可以幫助你：

1 Never divide a word within a syllable.
不可在一個音節之內斷字。

2 Never divide an ending (a suffix) of two syllables such as *-able*, *-ably*, *-fully*.
由兩個音節組成的字尾，如 -able, -ably, -fully 等，不可斷字。

3 With the exception of *-ly*, never divide a word so that an ending of two letters such as *-ed*, *-er*, *-ic* begins the next line.
除了 -ly 例外，不可將兩個字母的字尾如 -ed, -er, -ic 等置於下一行之首。

4 Never divide a word so that one of the parts is a single letter.
不可在斷字之後讓其中一部分只剩下一個字母。

5 Never divide a word of one syllable.
單音節的字不能斷字。

6 Never divide a word of less than five letters.
未超過五個字母的字不能斷字。

The bold dot . 黑點

The recommended places of word-division are given in the Dictionary for all headwords, derivatives and compounds. A bold dot (·) is printed where division is recommended, for example **sep·ar·ate**; **~·ly**. This means that these divisions are all possible:
本詞典中所有的首字、轉化字及複合字皆註明了斷字之處，註明的方式是以一個黑點(·)分隔，例如 sep·ar·ate; ～·ly。亦即說明下列各種情況皆可斷字：

sep- arate	*separ- ate*	*separate- ly*

How American English is written 怎樣寫美式英文

When American spelling is different from British English, it is given in the Dictionary in brackets immediately after the headword, for example
當美式英文的拼法與英式不同時，本詞典就把美式拼法放在括弧裡，緊接在首字後面，例如

col·our (US = **color**), **py·ja·mas** (US = **pa·ja·mas**).

The main differences in spelling are:
英美拼法上主要的不同處如下：

British 英	**American 美**
-our (*honour*)	-or (*honor*)
-re (*centre*)	-er (*center*)
-ogue (*dialogue*)	-og (*dialog*)
-ence (*defence*)	-ense (*defense*)
-ize (*realize*) -ise (*realise*)	-ize (*realize*)
ae (*anaemia*)	e (*anemia*)

Sometimes American English spelling does not double the consonant at the end of a word, while British English spelling does, especially when the consonant is an 'l'. For example, *travel* has (GB) *travelling* and *traveller*, and (US) *traveling* and *traveler*. The Dictionary tells you these facts by putting (-ll-; US -l-) in the entry.
有時美式英文的拼法中不重複字尾的子音，而英式則重複，尤其當子音爲 'l' 時，例如關於 travel 一字，英國拼法有 travelling 和 traveller, 美式則爲 traveling 和 traveler。關於這方面的說明，本詞典是在字目下以(-ll-; US -l-)列出。

Speaking English
說 英 語

How a word is pronounced 怎樣讀一個字

In written English one letter can often be pronounced in different ways. For example, the letter *a* is pronounced differently in *hat*, *pass*, *came*, *water*, *dare*, *ago*. Phonetic spelling is a way of writing a word so that one symbol always represents only one sound. Two words may be spelt differently in ordinary spelling, but if they sound the same, then the phonetic spelling is the same. For example, *key* and *quay* have the same phonetic spelling /kiː/. Each headword and derivative has a phonetic spelling after the ordinary spelling. Inside the cover of the Dictionary there is a list of all the letters (*phonetic symbols*) used in the phonetic spelling.

英文中一個字母常作不同的發音。譬如 a 這個字母在 hat, pass, came, water, dare, ago 等字中卽有不同的讀法。音標中一個符號代表一個音。在一般拼法中兩個字雖然拼法不同,但如果它們發音相同,其音標是一樣的,例如 key 和 quay 這兩個字的音標都是 /kiː/。每一個字首和轉化字在其一般拼法後都有一個音標。在本詞典封面內頁有一個表,說明音標中所用的全部字母(注音符號)。

Models of pronunciation
讀音的模式

A British English pronunciation is given for each word, and, in those cases where there is a marked difference, the American version is also shown. The British English form is that which has been called *Received Pronunciation* or *General British*. The forms recommended correspond to those given in the *English Pronouncing Dictionary* (Dent), but the pronunciation shown may not always be that which appears first in *EPD*. Where there is a choice between several acceptable forms, that form is selected which is likely to be easiest for learners. The American pronunciation given is that which is widely acceptable in the United States and has been called *General American*.

本詞典中每一個字所注的都是英國讀音,但是在遇到英美讀音有顯著差別時,也加注了美式讀法。英式讀法卽稱作'公認的讀法'或'一般的英國讀法'。本詞典所採用者與'英語發音字典(Dent)'一致,但是所注的讀音並不一定永遠採取'英語發音字典'中字目下第一個出現者。遇到有幾種公認的讀法可供選擇時,我們總是選擇學習者最容易讀的一個。美式讀音係採取美國普遍採用者,稱作'一般的美國讀法'。

In spoken British English an *r* at the end of a written word (either as the final letter or in an *re* ending as in *fire*) is not sounded unless another word that begins with a vowel sound follows in the same sentence. For example, the *r* is not heard in *His car was sold* but it is heard in *His car isn't old*. To show this, words which end in *r* or *re* have (r) at the end of the phonetic spelling in the dictionary, for example **car** /kɑː(r)/.

當一個字的字尾是 r (最後一個字母是 r 或者像 fire 中的 re),英國的讀法是不將 r 音讀出,除非句中其後接的字係以母音開始。例如在 His car was sold 句中 r 卽不發音,但在 His car isn't old 句中則發音。本詞典中係在音標的末尾以(r)表示字尾是 r 或 re 之字的發音,例如 car /kɑː(r)/。

How American English is pronounced
怎樣讀美式英語

Whenever Americans pronounce a word in a very different way from British speakers, the Dictionary gives the phonetic spelling of the American pronunciation after the British one, for example **half** /hɑːf *US:* hæf/; **address** /əˈdres *US:* ˈædres/. If only part of the pronunciation changes, only that part is given for the American pronunciation in order to save space, for example **attitude** /ˈætɪtjuːd *US:* -tuːd/.

每當一個字的美式讀法與英式讀法差別很大時,本詞典則在英式讀法後面加注美式讀法,例如 half /hɑːf *US:* hæf/; address /əˈdres *US:* ˈædres/。如果只有部分的讀音改變,爲節省篇幅起見,僅將該部分的美式讀法注出,例如 attitude /ˈætɪtjuːd *US:* -tuːd/。

American English forms are shown with the same phonetic symbols as are used for British English. However, particularly in the case of vowels, the same symbol will often mean somewhat different qualities in the British and American varieties. For example, in American English, the /ɒ/ in *hot* is similar to the British English /ɑː/ sound, and the /ʌ/ of *cut* is similar to a stressed /ə/ sound.

美式英語是以英式所用的同樣的音標注出。雖然如此,特別是母音,同一音標在英式和美式英語變化中往往表示略微不同的性質。例如美式英語 hot 中之 /ɒ/ 音與英式的 /ɑː/ 音相似, cut 中之 /ʌ/ 音與重讀的 /ə/ 音相似。

There is one difference between British and American pronunciation that is *not* given in the Dictionary. This is the use of the /r/ sound in American English in words where British English does not use it, for example in the words **arm** and **poor**. The British pronunciations of these words are /ɑːm/ and /pʊə(r)/ (the symbol (r) is explained in *Models of Pronunciation* above); the American pronunciations are /ɑːrm/ and /pʊər/. The rule to follow in the case of the /r/ sound in American English is to sound the /r/ *whenever* it occurs in the spelling of a word.

英式和美式讀音上有一點不同處本詞典未加註明,就是關於 /r/ 音的問題,美式讀法發音,英式不發音,例如 arm 和 poor。這兩個字英國讀作 /ɑːm/ 和 /pʊə(r)/((r) 的用法在上列 '讀音的模式' 中曾有說明),美國讀作 /ɑːrm/ 和 /pʊər/。(r)音在美式英語中讀法的規則就是每當它在拼字中出現時都發音。

Syllabic consonants 音節子音

The consonants /n/ and /l/ often form a syllable by themselves, ie without a vowel, especially at the end of words. Thus, when *sudden, middle*, *nation*, *final*, for instance, are shown as /ˈsʌdn/, /ˈmɪdl/, /ˈneɪʃn/, /ˈfaɪnl/, this means that /n/ and /l/ are syllabic. But syllabic /n/ and /l/ may also occur before a vowel within a word. When this happens, /ən/ and /əl/ are usually given in the Dictionary, representing an equally acceptable pronunciation which many learners may find easier. Thus we have *final* /ˈfaɪnl/ and *finally* /ˈfaɪnəlɪ/, where /-əl-/ may be said as a syllabic /l/ if preferred (so that in any case it is distinct from *finely* /ˈfaɪnlɪ/).

/n/ 和 /l/ 這兩個子音在無母音的情況下,尤其是在字尾時,常單獨形成一個音節。因此,當 sudden, middle, nation, final 注成 /ˈsʌdn/, /ˈmɪdl/, /ˈneɪʃn/, /ˈfaɪnl/ 時,卽表示 /n/ 和 /l/ 是自成音節的。但是自成音節的 /n/ 和 /l/ 在字中也可能位於一個母音之前。遇到這種情形,本詞典通常把它們注成 /ən/ 和 /əl/, 這是一種同樣公認的讀音,也是學習者較易接受的讀音。因此,我們把 final 注成 /ˈfaɪnl/, 把 finally 注成 /ˈfaɪnəlɪ/; 如果願意的話,可以把此處的 /-əl/ 稱作自成音節的 /l/ (以便在必要時能與 finely /ˈfaɪnlɪ/ 有所不同)。

How a word is stressed 怎樣讀字的重音

When a word has more than one syllable, one of them is spoken with more force than the rest. This force is called *stress*, and the syllable which is stressed is shown with the stress-mark /ˈ/ before it in the Dictionary. For example, *any* /ˈenɪ/ has a stress on the first syllable, *depend* /dɪˈpend/ has a stress on the second syllable.

當一個字有一個以上的音節時,其中一個音節讀起來較其他的音節有力。這種力卽稱作重音,有重音的音節在本詞典中是在它的前面加一重音符號 /ˈ/ 來表示,例如 any /ˈenɪ/ 的重音在第一音節, depend /dɪˈpend/ 的重音在第二音節。

In some words, usually long ones, other syllables may also be spoken with more force than the rest, but with a stress that is not as strong as for those syllables marked /ˈ/. The stress-mark /ˌ/ is used to show this.

在有些通常較長的字中,尙有其他的音節讀起來又較其餘者有力,但不若以 /ˈ/ 標示者有力,我們以 /ˌ/ 表示這種音節。

So, /ˈ/ is used to show the strongest or *primary* stress, and /ˌ/ is used to show the less strong or *secondary* stress, as in **pronunciation** /prəˌnʌnsɪˈeɪʃn/.

因此, /ˈ/ 是用來表示最强的或主重音, /ˌ/ 則表示次重音,例如 pronunciation /prəˌnʌnsɪˈeɪʃn/。

How a two-word compound is stressed 怎樣讀兩個字組成的複合字的重音

A compound that is made up of two separately written words, for example **national park**, is normally spoken with the strong stress in the second word: **ˌnational ˈpark**. If a compound does not have stress marks indicated, then it follows this normal pattern. Sometimes, however, a compound is spoken with the strong stress on the first word, for example **ˈpost office**. In this case, the stress mark is always shown.

由兩個單字組成的複合字,例如 national park, 其主重音通常是在第二個字:

ˌnational ˈpark。未標出重音的複合字卽遵照這種正常的方式去讀。然而,有時複合字的主重音是在第一個字,例如 ˈpost office, 此種情形重音總會標出。

How an idiom is stressed 怎樣讀成語的重音

One of the words in any idiom is always spoken with more force than the other words. Normally, this stressed word is the last 'important' word in that idiom, that is, the last word that is either a *noun*, a *verb*, an *adjective* or an *adverb*. For example, in the idiom ***separate the sheep from the goats***, the word *goats* carries the strong stress, because it is the last important word (in this case a *noun*) in the idiom. In the idiom ***play fast and loose with*** the word *loose* carries the strong stress, because it is the last *adverb* in the idiom.

無論任何成語,其中總有一個字的讀音較其他的字有力。通常有重音的字是成語中最後一個 '重要的' 字,這個字不是名詞、動詞、形容詞就是副詞。例如,在 separate the sheep from the goats 一成語中,重音在 goats 一字,因爲它是該成語中最後一個重要的字(在此爲一名詞)。在 play fast and loose with 一成語中,重音在 loose, 因爲它是本成語最後一個副詞。

In some idioms, however, a word that comes before the last important word in the idiom carries the strong stress. In this case, the word that is stressed is always shown with a stress mark. For example, ***at ˈany rate*** and ***for the ˈmost part***.

然而在有些成語中,重讀的字是在最後一個重要的字之前。在此情形,重讀的字總標有重音,例如 at ˈany rate 和 for the ˈmost part.

How an inflection is pronounced 怎樣讀字尾變化

An *inflection* is the changed form a word takes when it is used in a particular grammatical way, for example, in the plural (*sky*, *skies*), in the past tense (*smile*, *smiled*), in the comparative (*wild*, *wilder*). Inflections are usually made by changing the ending of a word.

字形變化卽是一個字在文法上有特殊用法時其形式上的變化,例如用於複數 (sky, skies), 用於過去式 (smile, smiled), 用於比較級 (wild, wilder)。字形變化通常是由改變一個字的字尾而成。

The plural of nouns, and the third person singular present of verbs
名詞的複數與動詞的第三人稱、單數、現在式

1 If the final sound of the noun's singular or the verb's infinitive is a *vowel* or /b, d, g, v, ð, m, n, ŋ, l/, the ending is formed by the addition of /-z/. For example *city* /ˈsɪtɪ/, *cities* /ˈsɪtɪz/; *ring* /rɪŋ/, *rings* /rɪŋz/.

名詞的單數或動詞的不定詞的尾音若是母音或 /b, d, g, v, ð, m, n, ŋ, l/, 則接尾爲 /-z/。例如: city /ˈsɪtɪ/, cities /ˈsɪtɪz/; ring /rɪŋ/, rings /rɪŋz/。

2 If the final sound of the noun's singular or the verb's infinitive is /p, t, k, f, θ/, the ending is formed by the addition of /-s/. For example *work* /wɜ:k/, *works* /wɜ:ks/.

名詞的單數或動詞的不定詞的尾音若是 /p, t, k, f, θ/, 則接尾爲 /-s/。例如: work /wɜ:k/, works /wɜ:ks/.

3 If the final sound of the noun's singular or the verb's infinitive is /s, z, ʃ, ʒ, tʃ, dʒ/, the ending is formed by the addition of /-ɪz/. For example *match* /mætʃ/, *matches* /ˈmætʃɪz/.

名詞的單數或動詞的不定詞的尾音若是 /s, z, ʃ, ʒ, tʃ, dʒ/, 則接尾爲/-ɪz/。例如: match /mætʃ/, matches /ˈmætʃɪz/。

The past tense and past participle of verbs
動詞的過去式與過去分詞

1 If the final sound of the verb's infinitive is a *vowel* or /b, g, v, ð, z, ʒ, dʒ, m, n, ŋ, l/, the past tense and the past participle are formed

by the addition of /-d/. For example ***hurry*** /ˈhʌrɪ/, ***hurried*** /ˈhʌrɪd/; ***judge*** /dʒʌdʒ/, ***judged*** /dʒʌdʒd/.

動詞的不定詞的尾音若爲母音或 /b, g, v, ð, z, ʒ, dʒ, m, n, ŋ, l/, 過去式和過去分詞則加 /-d/。例如: hurry /ˈhʌrɪ/, hurried /ˈhʌrɪd/; judge /dʒʌdʒ/, judged /dʒʌdʒd/。

2 If the final sound of the verb's infinitive is /p, k, f, θ, s, ʃ, tʃ/, the past tense and the past participle are formed by the addition of /-t/. For example *stop* /stɒp/, *stopped* /stɒpt/.

動詞的不定詞的尾音若爲 /p, k, f, θ, s, ʃ, tʃ/, 過去式和過去分詞則加 /-t/。例如: stop /stɒp/, stopped /stɒpt/。

3 If the final sound of the verb's infinitive is /t, d/, the past tense and the past participle are formed by the addition of /-ɪd/. For example *paint* /peɪnt/, *painted* /ˈpeɪntɪd/.

動詞的不定詞的尾音若爲 /t, d/, 過去式和過去分詞則加 /-ɪd/。例如: paint /peɪnt/, painted /ˈpeɪntɪd/。

The comparative and superlative of adjectives
形容詞的比較級與最高級

1 The comparative is formed by the addition of /-ə(r)/ to the final sound of the adjective. For example ***high*** /haɪ/, ***higher*** /ˈhaɪə(r)/; ***wild*** /waɪld/, ***wilder*** /ˈwaɪldə(r)/.

比較級是在形容詞的尾音後面加 /-ə(r)/。例如: high /haɪ/, higher /ˈhaɪə(r)/; wild /waɪld/, wilder /ˈwaɪldə(r)/。

2 The superlative is formed by the addition of /-ɪst/ to the final sound of the adjective. For example *low* /ləʊ/, *lowest* /ˈləʊɪst/; *green* /gri:n/, *greenest* /ˈgri:nɪst/.

最高級是在形容詞的尾音後面加 /-ɪst/。例如: low /ləʊ/, lowest /ˈləʊɪst/; green /gri:n/, greenest /ˈgri:nɪst/。

In the Dictionary, phonetic spelling is given for inflections only if the forms do not follow the ordinary rules, for example, the plural of **basis**: bases /ˈbeɪsi:z/; the past tense of **read**: read /red/; the comparative of **young**: younger /ˈjʌŋgə(r)/.

在本詞典中,如字尾變化的形式未遵照通常的規則,則標示其注音,例如 basis 的複數: bases /ˈbeɪsi:z/; read 的過去式: read /red/; young 的比較級: younger /ˈjʌŋgə(r)/。

How a derivative is pronounced
怎樣讀轉化字

Most derivatives are formed by adding a *suffix* to the end of a word. The pronunciation of these suffixes is given in the special list of prefixes and suffixes found in Appendix 3, pages 1379-1382. These derivatives are pronounced simply by saying the suffix after the word. For example, the adverb **slowly** /ˈsləʊlɪ/ is made by joining the word **slow** /sləʊ/ to the suffix *-ly* /lɪ/.

大多數的轉化字是在一字的末尾加一字尾而成。這些字尾的讀音均列在本詞典附錄三字首與字尾一表之中(1379–1382頁)。這些轉化字的讀音只是將本字讀出再將字尾讀出即可,例如副詞 slowly /ˈsləʊlɪ/ 即由 slow /sləʊ/ 加上字尾 -ly /lɪ/ 而成。

However, whenever there is doubt about how a suffix or a derivative is pronounced, the phonetic spelling is given. For example **mouthful** /-fʊl/, **regretful** /-fl/. Also, if a change of stress is caused by adding a suffix to a word, then the pronunciation of the derivative is given in full, for example, **photograph** /ˈfəʊtəgrɑ:f/, but **photographer** /fəˈtɒgrəfə(r)/, **photographic** /ˌfəʊtəˈgræfɪk/.

然而,字尾與轉化字在讀法上有任何疑問時,均加以注音。例如: mouthful /-fʊl/, regretful /-fl/。同時,如一字由於加字尾而重音改變時,則將該轉化字的讀音全部注出,例如: photograph 讀做 /ˈfəʊtəgrɑ:f/, 但是 photographer 則讀做 /fəˈtɒgrəfə(r)/, photographic 則讀做 /ˌfəʊtəˈgræfɪk/。

How French words are pronounced in English
怎樣用英語發音讀法語

Some French words used in English are completely anglicized (ie no longer considered to be foreign words, and given a completely English pronunciation), for example *café* /ˈkæfeɪ/, *restaurant* /ˈrestrɒnt/. There are other French words and phrases which are still regarded as foreign but which are normally given a completely English pronunciation, for example *à la carte* /ˌɑː lɑː ˈkɑːt/, *table d'hôte* /ˌtɑːbl ˈdəʊt/. A difficulty arises with the pronunciation of French nasalized vowels, as in *salon*, *en route*. Native speakers of English use different pronunciations in such cases, varying from total anglicization to a more or less successful imitation of the French. This Dictionary gives the anglicized form, /ˈsælɒn/, /ˌɒn ˈruːt/.

英語中所用的法國字,有些已完全英語化(卽不再被認爲是外國字,並且完全照英語發音),例如 café /ˈkæfeɪ/, restaurant /ˈrestrɒnt/。雖然還有些法國字和片語仍舊被當作外國語,但它們通常完全注成英語發音,例如 à la carte /ˌɑː lɑː ˈkɑːt/, table d'hôte /ˌtɑːbl ˈdəʊt/。困難發生在以鼻音發出的法語母音,如 salon, en route 等中者。遇到這種情形，英國人用不同的讀音，有的用完全英語化的讀音，有的相當成功地模仿法語讀音。本詞典所注的是英語化的讀音，如 /ˈsælɒn/, /ˌɑn ˈruːt/。

Grammar
文　法

Irregular forms of nouns, verbs and adjectives
名詞、動詞和形容詞的不規則形式

An *irregular* form of a word is one that is not made in the normal (or *regular*) way. For example, the normal way of forming the plural of an English noun in writing is to add *-s* or *-es*, and the normal way of forming a past tense or past participle of a verb is to add *-d* or *-ed*. Whenever a form is made in any other way, then this is given (together with the pronunciation if necessary), at the beginning of the entry. For example, **axis** /ˈæksɪs/ *n* (*pl* axes /ˈæksiːz/); **choose** /tʃuːz/ *vt, vi* (*pt* chose /tʃəʊz/, *pp* chosen /ˈtʃəʊzn/); **bad** /bæd/ *adj* (worse, worst).

一個字之不規則形式卽不是以正常(或規則)的方式形成的字。譬如,形成英文名詞的複數的正常方式是加 -s 或 -es, 形成動詞的過去式或過去分詞的正常方式是加 -d 或 -ed。凡是以別的方式形成的形式,本詞典均在字目之首列出(必要時並加注音)。例如: axis /ˈæksɪs/ *n* (*pl* axes/ˈæksiːz/); choose /tʃuːz/ *vt, vi* (*pt* chose /tʃəʊz/, *pp* chosen /ˈtʃəʊzn/); bad /bæd/ *adj* (worse, worst)。

Comparative and superlative forms of adjectives
形容詞的比較級和最高級

The comparative and superlative forms of all adjectives of two or more syllables are made by using the words *more* and *most* before the adjective. For example, the comparative form of *interesting* is *more interesting*; the superlative form of *pleasant* is *most pleasant*.

所有兩個或兩個以上音節的形容詞,其比較級和最高級的形式是在前面加 more 和 most, 例如 interesting 的比較級是 more interesting, pleasant 的最高級是 most pleasant。

All adjectives of one syllable, and many adjectives of two syllables, make the comparative and superlative forms by adding *-r, -st* or *-er, -est* or *-ier, -iest* to the end of the adjective. For example, the comparative forms of *gentle*, *cold* and *happy* are *gentler*, *colder* and *happier*; the superlative forms are *gentlest*, *coldest* and *happiest*. In the Dictionary, an adjective that has a comparative and superlative form of this sort has (-r, -st) or (-er, -est) or (-ier, -iest) printed in the entry.

所有單音節和許多兩個音節的形容詞,其比較級和最高級的形式是在形容詞字尾加 -r, -st, 或 -er, -est, 或 -ier, -iest。例如 gentle, cold 和 happy 的比較級是 gentler, colder 和 happier; 最高級爲 gentlest, coldest 和 happiest。在本詞典中,有此種比較級和最高級的形容詞,均在字目下加有 (-r, -st) 或 (-er, -est) 或 (-ier, -iest)。

grammar

Countable and uncountable nouns 可數與不可數的名詞

The correct use of the *noun* is a very important but difficult skill to acquire when learning English. For example, some nouns can be used in the plural form, while others cannot. In addition, many nouns have several meanings, some of which may have a plural form, and some of which may not. This Dictionary gives the learner special help in this area, by the use of the symbols [C], [U] or [C, U] in an entry for a noun.

在學習英文過程中，名詞的正確用法是十分重要但也很難學到的技巧。例如有些名詞可以用作複數，有些則不可以。此外，許多名詞有好幾種意義，用作某些意義可作複數，有些意義則不可以。關於這一方面，本詞典特別在名詞字目下以[C], [U]或[C, U]等符號註明，以幫助學習者。

[C] means that the noun has both a singular and a plural form. It can be used in the singular with *a*, *an*, *another* (*a bottle*, *an apple*, *another boy*), in the plural with *many* (*many bottles*) and in the singular or plural with numbers (*one apple*, *six apples*). Nouns that can be used in these ways are *countable*. [C] in the entry tells you this. When no information is given in a noun entry, it is an obvious countable noun.

[C] 表示一名詞具有單數和複數形式，單數時可與 a, an, another 連用(如 a bottle, an apple, another boy)，複數時可與many 連用(如 many bottles)，此外不論單複數均可與數字連用(如 one apple, six apples)。可以這樣用的名詞是'可數的'，字目中的[C]即告訴你這一點。如果字目中沒有註明，則表示它是個明顯的可數名詞。

[U] means that the noun does not have a plural form. It can be used in the singular with words like *some*, *enough*, *much*, *more* (*some information*, *enough money*, *much noise*). It cannot be used with *a*, *an*, *another*, or with *many*, or with numbers. Nouns that are used in this way are *uncountable*. [U] in the entry tells you this.

[U]表示一名詞沒有複數的形式。其單數形可與 some, enough, much, more 等連用(如 some information, enough money, much noise)，但不可與 a, an, another, many 或數字連用。像這樣用的名詞是'不可數的'，字目中的[U]即告訴你這一點。

[C, U] means that the noun can be used either as countable or uncountable. For example, *coffee* is used as [C] in *Two coffees, please*, and as [U] in *Have some more coffee*.

[C, U] 表示一名詞可用作可數名詞，也可用作不可數名詞。例如coffee一字在 Two coffees, please 中是可數的，在 Have some more coffee 中則是不可數的。

Some nouns (or some meanings of some nouns) are only used with the definite article *the*, or only with the indefinite article *a/an*. The Dictionary shows this by putting *the* or *a/an*+the noun in **bold** type at the beginning of the definition. For example **the sun, a sleep**.

有些名詞(或有些名詞中的某些意義)僅可與定冠詞 the 連用，或僅可與不定冠詞 a 或 an 連用。這種情形，本詞典係在定義的開頭以黑體排印的 'the 或 a/an+名詞' 表示之，例如 **the sun, a sleep**。

How to use a verb with the correct adverbial particle or preposition 怎樣用一個與正確的副詞接語或介詞連用的動詞

Phrases like ***take off*** (a *verb* with an *adverbial particle*), ***go with*** (a *verb* with a *preposition*), and ***make up to*** (a *verb* with both an *adverbial particle* and a *preposition*) are very important in English because they are so common. They are treated with special care in the Dictionary. The correct particle or preposition is printed with the verb in ***bold italic*** type in the entry so that you can find it easily.

像 take off (動詞與副詞接語)，go with (動詞與介詞)，和 make up to (動詞與副詞接語及介詞)等片語，由於十分普通，在英文中是非常重要的。它們在本詞典中均經過特別處理。正確的副詞接語或介詞和動詞是以黑斜體排印，以便讀者易於查閱。

It is important to know why the dictionary uses the brackets ( ) and the slant/in providing this information. Brackets ( ) round a preposition or particle mean that the verb can be used with or without it. For example, ***prepare (for)*** can be used as in *prepare a meal*, or as in *prepare for an examination.* A slant / means that you can choose any of the words listed to make a sentence. For example, ***move along / down / up*** shows that *move along the bus, move down the bus, move up the bus* are all correct.

要瞭解何以本詞典在處理上述片語時使用括弧( )和斜線 / 是重要的。括弧表示動詞可與括弧中的介詞或副詞接語連用，也可以不與其連用。例如 prepare (for) 可用於 prepare a meal 或 prepare for an examination。斜線表示你可選擇任何一個以斜線隔開的字來造句。例如 move along / down / up 表示 move along the bus, move down the bus, move up the bus 都是對的。

It is also important to know why and how the words *sb* (somebody) and *sth* (something) are used in these phrases.

要瞭解何以及如何在這些片語中使用 sb (somebody) 和 sth (something) 也是重要的。

Consider the phrases ***take off*** (*verb + particle*). This is found in the dictionary in both the forms ***take off*** and ***take sth off. take off*** means that the phrase can be used without an object, for example *The aeroplane took off.* ***take sth off*** means that the phrase can be used with an object (in this case a thing), for example *She took her hat off* or *She took off her hat.*

試以 take off (動詞＋副詞接語)一片語爲例。在本詞典內有 take off 和 take sth off 兩種形式。take off 表示這個片語後面沒有受詞，例如 The aeroplane took off。take sth off 表示這個片語後面可接受詞(在此爲物)，例如 She took her hat off 或 She took off her hat。

Consider the phrase ***go with*** (*verb + preposition*). This is found in the dictionary only in the form ***go with sb / sth***. This means that the phrase must be used with an object (in this case either a person or a thing) after the preposition, for example *Paul went with* (= accompanied) *Peter to Rome*, or *Your shirt doesn't go with* (= match) *your trousers.*

再以 go with (動詞＋介詞)爲例，在本詞典中有 go with sb / sth 的形式，意思是說這個片語必須在介詞後接一受詞(在此爲人或物皆可)，例如：Paul went with (= accompanied) Peter to Rome, 或 Your shirt doesn't go with (= match) your trousers。

You will notice that some verbs (*get, give, go,* etc) are used with a large number of prepositions and particles. Because many of these combinations (for example ***make up***) have a large number of meanings, you will find a section at the end of each of these verb entries called 'special uses with *adverbial particles* and *prepositions*'. In this section, these combinations are listed in bold italic type in alphabetical order (***make after***, ***make at***, ***make away***, ***make for***, etc).

你會發現有些動詞(get, give, go 等)與許多介詞和副詞接語連用。由於很多這種結成的片語(如 make up)有許多意義，你在這些動詞字目的末尾會發現有一個項目，稱作'與副詞接語和介詞連用的特殊用法'。在此項目下，這些片語是按照字母順序(make after, make at, make away, make for 等)以黑斜體排印的。

How to use an adjective with the correct preposition
怎樣用一個與正確的介詞連用的形容詞

Many adjectives in English must, or may, be followed by a preposition, for example ***conversant with*** (where the preposition must be used), and ***distinct from*** (where *from* is optional). To help the learner to form correct sentences using these adjectives, the prepositions are included in bold print at the beginning of the entry. For example,

英文中很多形容詞必須或可能跟介詞連用，例如 conversant with (此處必須跟介詞 with)和 distinct from (from 可用可不用)。爲了幫助學習者用這些形容詞造出正確的句子，這些介詞是以黑斜體排印，列於字目之首，例如：

conversant . . . *adj* ~ ***with.***
distinct . . . *adj* ~ ***(from).***

Note that brackets ( ) are used when the preposition is optional.
注意：括弧( )表示介詞可用亦可不用。

Style 字格

How to choose the words that the headword usually combines with 怎樣選擇通常與首字連用的字

Speaking and writing correct English is not only a matter of pronunciation, spelling or grammar. You must also know the kinds of context in which the headword is normally used. The example phrases and sentences are especially valuable in this respect, because they show the words (or kinds of words) that the headword often combines with. For example, at **regular**(1) there is *regular teeth/features*; at **regular**(2) there is *regular hours/habits*; at **regulate**(1) there is *regulate one's conduct/expenditure*; at **regulate**(2) there is *regulate a clock* and *regulate speed.*

說和寫純正的英語不僅是發音、拼法或文法方面的問題，你還得知道首字通常所用的種種上下文。在這方面本詞典中的例句特別有價值，因爲它們指出那些常與首字連用的字(或各種字)。例如在 regular 的第1義中有 regular teeth/features; 在 regular 的第2義中有 regular hours/habits; 在 regulate 的第1義中有 regulate one's conduct/expenditure; 在 regulate的第2義中有 regulate a clock 和 regulate speed 等。

The learner wishing to make up sentences of his own will find examples containing the slant/particularly useful. For example, *inspired poets/artists* and *inspire sb with hope/enthusiasm/confidence.* He can compose different sentences using those alternatives; but they will also help him to guess other words that can be used. For example, *inspired musicians/dancers/painters* and *inspire sb with new faith/passion/devotion.*

學習者在自己造句時會發現那些有斜線的例子特別有用，例如inspired poets/artists 與 inspire sb with hope/enthusiasm/confidence 等。他可以利用那些選擇造成不同的句子，而且它們也會幫助他去猜想其他可用的字，譬如 inspired musicians/dancers/painters 與 inspire sb with new faith/passion/devotion 等。

How to use the more usual or more suitable word 怎樣用較常用或較適當的字

You should also be confident that the kind or style of English you are using is right in that particular context: that it is not too *formal* or *colloquial*, that it will not offend the listener or reader, or that it is not *dated* (old-fashioned), or *archaic* (no longer used). To help you, there is information in an entry when the word is to be used only in a particular style or context. For example, formal words are not used in everyday conversation, or in letters to friends and relations; while colloquial words are not used in business letters, or in conversation with a person whom you do not know well or who is your superior.

你也應該有把握，你所用的那種英文在某種特殊場合是正確的：它不會太正式或太口語化，它不會冒犯聽者或讀者，它不是過時用語或古語。爲了幫助你，當一個字要用在特殊標準或場合時，在字目下都有說明。例如正式的字不用於日常談話或寫給朋友親戚的書信中，另方面口語用的字不用於商業信函或是對不熟悉的人或尊長的談話中。

Sometimes the Dictionary will warn you that a word is both a *dated* word and a *slang* word (dated sl), or both a *modern* word and a *colloquial* word (modern colloq).

有時本詞典會警告你某一字既是過時用語也是俚語(過時俚語)，或者既是現代用語也是口語(現代俗語)。

Sometimes the Dictionary will tell you what the more usual word is, particularly in entries for *formal* or *dated* vocabulary.

有時本詞典會告訴你那些是較常用的字，尤其是在正式的或過時的字目中。

Remember that *slang* vocabulary is not popular for very long and that such words should only be used if you are sure that they are not dated, that they will sound quite natural when you use them, and that they will not cause offence.

要記住俚語不會流行很久，祇有在你確實知道它們並未過時，使用時聽起來十分自然，而且不會得罪人的情況下方可使用俚語。

How to use specialist English words 怎樣用英文專門術語

Some words are used only by a group of speakers or writers because of the work they do, the way they live, the activity they are enjoying, the subject they are studying, etc. These are 'specialist' areas such as *business, science, law, sport, music, medicine*, etc. Trying to use specialist words outside the contexts where they belong can make your English seem unnatural. To help you, the Dictionary gives the specialist English area in brackets at the beginning of the explanation of the meaning.

某一類說話者或作者由於工作關係、生活方式、喜愛的活動以及學習的科目等只用到某些字。這些字都屬於'專門的'領域，如商業、科學、法律、運動、音樂、醫學等。在不適當的場合用專門術語會使你的英文顯得不自然。為了幫助你，本詞典特將專門術語的領域置於括弧中，放在字義解釋的前頭。

How to use idiomatic English 怎樣用成語

An important sign of a person who has learnt English from a native-speaker (or a person who has a native-speaker's command of the language) is his knowledge of the meaning and correct use of expressions such as ***make up one's mind***, ***be all ears***, ***with all one's heart***, etc. These are called *idioms* or *idiomatic expressions*. They are groups of two or more words which must be learnt as a whole because the meaning of the expression may be different from the meanings of its parts. An example is ***hit the nail on the head***, which means 'guess right'. In the Dictionary, these expressions are printed in ***bold italic*** type.

一個已經從以英語為母語的人(或運用英語的能力相當於以英語為母語的人)那裡學會英語的人的重要徵象是，他能够瞭解並且正確運用像 make up one's mind, be all ears, with all one's heart 之類的片語。這些片語稱作成語或習慣用語。它們係由兩個或兩個以上的字組成，這些字必須當作一個整體來學，因為整個成語的意義可能和成語各部分的意義不同。例如 hit the nail on the head 這個成語的意思是'說中'。在本詞典中，成語是用黑斜體排印。

Like the style for verbs with prepositions or particles (which are themselves types of idioms), brackets are used for words which can be omitted, as in ***make (both) ends meet*** and slants for alternatives as in ***begin/start at the wrong end***. When there are no brackets or slants, the expression cannot be changed. For example, the idiom ***have an ear to the ground*** cannot be changed to *have a head to the ground* or *have an ear to the floor*. But the idiom ***bear/keep something in mind*** can be either *bear something in mind* or *keep something in mind*.

像處理動詞與介詞或副詞接語連用的動詞(它們本身卽為成語類型)一樣，可以省略的字都加有括弧，如 make (both) ends meet。可以選擇的字都用斜線隔開，如 begin/start at the wrong end。如果沒有括弧或斜線，則表示這個成語不可變更，例如 have an ear to the ground 不能改作 have a head to the ground 或 have an ear to the floor，但是 bear/keep something in mind 可作 bear something in mind 或 keep something in mind。

An exception to this is when ***etc*** is used after two or more words that are divided from one another by the slant mark. This means that *only words of a similar sort* to the words that are given (divided by the slant mark) may be used in the idiom. For example, the idiom ***be pushing thirty/forty, etc,*** means that only number words that express someone's age in years may be used in this idiom.

對上述者有一種例外的情況，卽當 etc 用於以斜線隔開的兩個或兩個以上的字後面時。這表示'祇有和列出的字(卽斜線隔開者)相似的字'可用於該成語中。例如 be pushing thirty/forty, etc, 表示祇有指年齡的數字可用在這個成語中。

When two or more idioms are divided from one another by a semicolon ***(;)***, this means that the idioms *have the same meaning*. For example, ***take it from me*** and ***take my word for it***, which are listed together, separated only by a semicolon ***(;)***, in the entry for the verb **take**, have the same meaning, 'believe me when I say'.

當兩個或兩個以上的成語用分號(;)隔開時，這表示這些成語'意義相同。'例如 take it from me 和 take my word for it 並列在 take 字目下,用分號隔開,它們的意義相同,即'相信我的話'。

Native speakers use these expressions naturally and unconsciously. You will need to learn them before using them. The more you use them, the more they will become a natural part of your English. Unless you use them, your English will always be 'foreign'. But you must be very careful not to use the idioms you know too often, and not to use them one after another in the same sentence, or in sentence after sentence. An idiom must be used with care and thought, only when your meaning can best be expressed with the idiom's special 'strengh', 'flavour' or 'style'.

以英語爲母語的人用這些成語時是自然的和不知不覺的。你則需要在運用以前先學習。你用得越多,它們便越會成爲你的英文中自然的一部分。如果你不用它們,你的英文將永遠是'外國的'。但是你必須很小心,不要太常使用你會用的成語,不要在同一句中一個接一個,或一句連一句的使用成語。運用成語必須小心和愼重,衹有在以成語的特殊'力量'、'風味'或'文體'最能表達你的意思時,才去用它。

Proverbs 諺語

You should note that *proverbs* are seldom used in ordinay speech or writing. Although the native speaker knows the meaning of most English proverbs, he will actually use one rarely, and then only when he is wanting to be humorous, or by referring to the proverb in an indirect way (for example by quoting only half of it), or by introducing it by saying something like 'You know what they say, . . .' or 'As the old saying goes, . . .' The reason is this. English proverbs are phrases or sentences containing advice, warning or truth. Although they are expressed in striking language, in their meanings they are rather obvious remarks to make about human experience. They are thought of as the sort of remark that would be made by someone who is rather dull, someone who cannot express in his own words what he thinks or feels, but who has to borrow a proverb from the language to do this. A *proverb*, a *cliché*, a *truism*, a *hackneyed phrase*, and a *trite remark* are all the sorts of expressions that someone who wants to express himself clearly, carefully and honestly will try to avoid.

你應注意諺語很少用於一般談話或寫作中。雖然以英語爲母語的人懂得大部分英文諺語的意思,但他極少去用一個諺語,即使是用也衹有在他想要幽默,或間接提到某一諺語(譬如僅提及一半),或者在說以前加上一種像'你知道人們都這樣說…'或'俗話說…'等套語之後再用。原因是這樣。英文諺語都是含有忠告、警告或眞理的片語或句子。雖然它們係由予人印象深刻的語言表達出來,但就其含義而言,它們都是些有關人世經驗的頗爲明顯的話。一般人認爲用諺語的人頭腦遲鈍,不能以自己的話表達其思想或感受,而必須借用諺語。一個想清晰地,愼重地和誠實地表達自己的人應避免用諺語、老套、老生常談以及陳腔濫調。

The sign ⚠ 標號

Some words in the Dictionary are followed by the sign ⚠. These are *taboo* words. They are words used when the speaker wishes to swear, or be indecent, or be offensive. They are all words that are likely to cause embarrassment or anger if they are used in the wrong situation. The learner of English is strongly advised to avoid using them.

本詞典中有些字後面有標號⚠。這些是應該避諱的字。想要咒駡或粗鄙無禮的人才用這些字。用在不當的情況它們多半會導致困窘或憤怒。學習英語的人最好盡量避免使用它們。

Verb patterns
動詞類型

For anyone who is learning to speak or write correct English, the most important word in a sentence is the *verb*. For this reason the compilers of the Dictionary have paid particular attention to *verb patterns*. These show the learner how to use verbs to form correct sentences.

對於任何學着說或寫正確英語的人而言，一個句子中最重要的一個字便是動詞。因是之故，本詞典的編輯們特別注意動詞的類型。這些動詞類型告訴學習者怎樣用動詞造正確的句子。

A person learning English as a foreign language may be tempted to form sentences by *analogy*. For example, he hears or sees such sentences as *Please tell me the meaning* and *Please show me the way* (an indirect object followed by a direct object). By analogy he forms the incorrect sentence **Please explain me the meaning* (instead of *Please explain the meaning to me*). He hears or sees such sentences as *I intend to come*, *I propose to come*, and *I want to come*, and by analogy he forms the incorrect sentences as **I suggest to come* (instead of *I suggest that I should come*). He hears or sees such sentences as *I asked him to come*, *I told him to come*, and *I wanted him to come*, and by analogy he forms such incorrect sentences as **I proposed him to come* and **I suggested him to come* (instead of *I proposed/suggested that he should come*). He notes that *He began to talk about the matter* means the same as *He began talking about the matter* and supposes, wrongly, that *He stopped to talk about the matter* means the same as *He stopped talking about the matter*.

把英語當作外國語去學習的人可能會受到誘惑，用'類推'的方式造句。譬如他聽到或看到 Please tell me the meaning 和 Please show me the way (間接受詞後跟直接受詞)這種句子，就會以此類推，造出 *Please explain me the meaning 這個錯誤的句子(正確者應為 Please explain the meaning to me)。他聽到或看到 I intend to come, I propose to come, I want to come 等句子，就會以此類推，造出 *I suggest to come 這個錯誤的句子(正確者應為 I suggest that I should come)。他聽到或看到 I asked him to come, I told him to come, 以及 I wanted him to come 等句，就會以此類推，造出 *I proposed him to come 和 *I suggested him to come 等錯誤的句子(正確者應為 I proposed/suggested that he should come)。他注意到 He began to talk about the matter 與 He began talking about the matter 的意思一樣，因而誤以為 He stopped to talk about the matter 與 He stopped talking about the matter 的意義是相同的。

To help the learner to avoid such mistakes, the compilers of the Dictionary have provided a set of tables (on pages xxxvi–li) in which various Verb Patterns are set out with examples. Each pattern has a numbered code (for example, [VP5], [VP6A], [VP21]), and this provides a link between the tables and the verb entries in the Dictionary, because every verb entry has its own code (or several codes if there are several meanings).

為了幫助學習者避免這種錯誤，本詞典的編輯提供了一系列的表(xxxvi–li 頁)，列出各種動詞類型和例句。每一類型都有一個標號(例如[VP5],[VP6A],[VP21])，由於動詞字目下也有類型標號(如有數種意義時就有數種標號)，這樣可使本詞典的動詞類型表與動詞字目之間互相連繫。

A few examples will show how the learner can refer from the [VP] codes in entries to the [VP] tables in the Introduction. One of the patterns given in the Dictionary for **congratulate** is [VP14], and this verb is also used in one of the examples in the [VP] table for [VP14]: *We congratulated him on his success.* The pattern provided for the second meaning of **consider** is [VP6A]. If the learner turns to that table he will find several examples based on that pattern, for example *We all enjoyed the film.* This will help him to form a correct sentence with **consider** in [VP6A], for example *He considered the problem.*

舉幾個例可以說明學習者怎樣從字目的標號去參考緒論中的動詞類型表。譬如 congratulate 一字在本詞典有[VP14]之標號,而在動詞類型表[VP14]中亦有其例句: We congratulated him on his success。又如 consider 的第2義有[VP6A]一型,如果學習者參看動詞類型表,他會發現這一類型有幾個例句,如 We all enjoyed the film 等,這會幫助他用 consider 根據[VP6A]造出一正確的句子,例如: He considered the problem。

Sometimes extra information is given in an entry to help the learner to learn the right pattern. For example, in the entry for **absolve**, he will find the verb + preposition ~ ***(from)***, placed after the codes [VP6A, 14]. This shows that the verb can be used as in *absolve a man from a vow*. In the entry for **accede** there are the codes [VP2A, 3A], followed by ~ ***(to)***, showing that the verb may be used as in *accede to a proposal*.

有時在字目中有額外的說明幫助學習者學得正確的句型。例如在 absolve 字目中,標號 [VP6A, 14] 後有動詞加介詞 ~ (from) 之說明,這表示這個動詞可以用於 absolve a man from a vow。在 accede 字目中,標號 [VP2A, 3A] 後有 ~ (to) 之說明,表示這個動詞可以用於 accede to a proposal。

It is important to note that the learner is not expected to memorize these verb patterns. They are a simple reference system, a practical tool to guide the learner who wants to form correct sentences. They are a way of helping the learner who will benefit from a list of the grammatical rules that underlie the different sorts of example sentences that are given in the entries for verbs.

要注意我們不是要學習者去熟記這些動詞類型, 這一點是重要的。它們是簡單的參考系統, 是引導想要造出正確句子的學習者一項實際的工具。它們是幫助學習者的一種方法,使他從動詞字目下各種不同的例句所呈現的一系列文法規則當中獲益。

A full treatment of these verb patterns is found in *Guide to Patterns and Usage in English*, by A S Hornby (Oxford University Press).

這些動詞類型的詳細說明見於郝恩貝所著'英文句型及用法指南'一書(牛津大學出版社出版)。

Note: The use of the asterisk * indicates that the phrase or sentence is an example of *incorrect* usage.

注意:星號 * 表示該片語或句子爲錯誤的用法。

[VP1]
動詞第一型

This pattern is for the verb *be*. The subject complement may be a noun, a pronoun, an adjective, an adjective phrase (eg a prepositional group). There may be an adverbial adjunct or an infinitive phrase.

此型使用於動詞 be。主詞補語可能是名詞、代名詞、形容詞、形容詞片語(例如介詞形成者),也可能是副詞修飾語或不定詞片語。

Subject + BE	subject complement／adjunct
1 *This is* 這是一本書。	*a book.*
2 *This suitcase is* 這個衣箱是我的。	*mine.*
3 *The children are* 孩子們睡着了。	*asleep.*
4 *This book is* 這本書是給你的。	*for you.*
5 *This is* 這就是我工作的地方。	*where I work.*

There are variations with introductory *there／it*.
there／it 用於句首時有變化。

There／It + BE	subject
1 *There was* 有一大羣人。	*a large crowd.*
2 *It was impossible* 再走遠些是不可能了。	*to go further.*
3 *It was a pity* 天氣這樣壞是遺憾的事。	*the weather was so bad.*

[VP2A] 動詞第二型 A組

This pattern is for verbs which may be used without a complement. Such verbs are called complete intransitive verbs. Adjuncts are possible but not essential.

用於此型的動詞後面可以不接補語。此類動詞稱作完全不及物動詞。可以與修飾語連用,但不是必須的。

Subject	*vi*
1 *We all* 我們都呼吸,飲水和吃東西。	*breathe, drink and eat.*
2 *The moon* 月亮升起了。	*rose.*
3 *A period of political unrest* 隨後是一段政治不安時期。	*followed.*

There are variations with introductory *there／it.*
there／it 用於句首時有變化。

1 *There followed* 隨後是很長一段政治不安時期。	*a long period of political unrest.*
2 *It doesn't matter* 我們現在或是晚些動身都沒有關係。	*whether we start now or later.*

That-clauses are possible after *seem, appear, happen, chance* and *follow.*
在 seem, appear, happen, chance 和 follow 後可用 that 子句。

1 *It seemed* 那一天似乎永遠也過不完。	(*that*) *the day would never end.*
2 *It so chanced／happened* 她來訪時適逢我們不在家。	(*that*) *we were out when she called.*
3 *It doesn't follow* 這並不能斷定他們是夫妻。	(*that*) *they are husband and wife.*

[VP2B] 動詞第二型 B組

Verbs in this pattern are used with an adverbial adjunct of distance, duration, weight, cost, etc. *For* may occur before adverbials of distance and duration. An indirect object may occur after *cost, last* and *take* (meaning 'require').

此型動詞與表示距離、持續時間、重量、價值等的副詞修飾語連用。在 cost, last 和 take (作 '需要' 解) 後面可以用間接受詞。

Subject + *vi*	(*for*) + adverbial adjunct
1 *We walked* 我們步行了五哩。	(*for*) *five miles.*
2 *The meeting lasted* 會議開了兩小時。	(*for*) *two hours.*
3 *The book cost* (*me*) 這本書花了(我) 1.20 鎊。	*£1.20.*
4 *This box weighs* 這個箱子重五公斤。	*five kilos.*

[VP2C] 動詞第二型 C組

Many intransitive verbs are used with an adverbial adjunct (including an adverbial particle alone, or an adverbial particle followed by a preposition).

許多不及物動詞與副詞修飾語(包括單獨的副詞接語,或副詞接語跟一介詞)連用。

Subject + *vi*	adverbial adjunct
1 *Go* 走開！	*away!*
2 *Please come* 請進來。	*in.*
3 *I'll soon catch* 我很快就會追上你。	*up with you.*
4 *It's getting* 快到半夜了。	*on for midnight.*
5 *It looks* 好像要下雨的樣子。	*like rain / as if it were going to rain.*

[VP2D] 動詞第二型 D組

Verbs in this pattern are followed by an adjective, a noun or, in the case of a reflexive verb, a pronoun. Inchoative verbs (eg *become, come, get*) and verbs of the senses (eg *smell, taste, feel*) are among the many verbs used in this pattern.

此型動詞後接一形容詞,名詞或代名詞(如爲反身動詞時)。表始動詞(如 become, come, get),知覺動詞(如 smell, taste, feel),以及許多其他動詞用於此型。

Subject + *vi*	adjective / noun / pronoun
1 *Her dreams have come* 她的夢想實現了。	*true.*
2 *The fire has burnt* 火勢減弱了。	*low.*
3 *She married* 她早婚。	*young.*
4 *He died* 他死時爲一百萬富翁。	*a millionaire.*
5 *Later he became* 他後來成爲一個賣藝人。	*an acrobat.*
6 *You're not looking* 你看來有點異樣。	*yourself.*

[VP2E] 動詞第二型 E組

In this pattern the predicative adjunct is a present participle.

在此型中述詞的修飾語是現在分詞。

Subject + *vi*	present participle
1 *She lay* 她躺着向我微笑。	*smiling at me.*
2 *Do you like to go* 你喜歡跳舞嗎？	*dancing?*
3 *The children came* 孩子們跑着過來接我們。	*running to meet us.*

[VP3A] 動詞第三型 A組

Verbs in this pattern are followed by a preposition and its object (which may be a noun, pronoun, gerund, phrase, or clause). The verb and preposition function as a unit.

用於此型的動詞後跟一介詞及其受詞(受詞可能是名詞、代名詞、動名詞、片語或子句)。動詞和介詞作爲一個單位。

Subject + *vi*	preposition + noun / pronoun
1 *You may rely* 你可以信賴那個人(他的謹慎,他是謹慎的)。	*on that man / his discretion / his being discreet.*
2 *Can I count* 我能指望你的幫助嗎？	*on your help?*
3 *What has happened* 他們怎麼樣了？	*to them?*

An infinitive phrase may follow the noun/pronoun.
名詞或代名詞後可接不定詞片語。

1 *We're waiting* *for our new car to be delivered.*
我們正等着我們的新車送來。
2 *I rely* *on you to be discreet.*
我信賴你的謹慎。
3 *She pleaded* *with the judge to have mercy.*
她向法官求情。

[VP3B] 動詞第三型 B組

The preposition is omitted before a *that*-clause, thus producing the same word order as in [VP9] (for transitive verbs).
介詞在 that 子句前省略，故與動詞第九型(及物動詞之一型)的詞序相同。

He insisted on his innocence. [VP3A]
He insisted that he was innocent. [VP3B]
Cf *He declared that he was innocent.* [VP9]

The preposition may be retained if its object is a dependent question, or if a preceding 'preposition + *it*' construction is used.
如遇受詞是一附屬問句或前面有'介詞 + it'之結構時，介詞可以保留。

Subject + *vi*	(preposition (+ *it*))	clause
1 *I agree* 我同意這是一項錯誤。		*that it was a mistake.*
2 *You must see* 你必須注意這一類的事情決不可以再發生。	*(to it)*	*that this sort of thing never occurs again.*
3 *I hesitated* 我對於是否接受你的提議猶豫不定。	*(about)*	*whether to accept your offer.*
4 *Have you decided* 你決定了到那裡去度假嗎？	*(upon)*	*where you will go for your holidays?*
5 *Don't worry* 不要為了這筆錢是怎樣遺失的而煩惱。	*(about)*	*how the money was lost.*

[VP4A] 動詞第四型 A組

In this pattern the verb is followed by a *to*-infinitive of purpose, outcome, or result.
此型動詞後接一表示目的或結果的不定詞。

Subject + *vi*	*to*-infinitive
1 *We stopped* 我們停下來休息。	*to rest/to have a rest.*
2 *How did you come* 你如何認識她的？	*to know her?*
3 *Will he live* 他會活到九十歲嗎？	*to be ninety?*
4 *Someone has called* 有人來拜訪你。	*to see you.*

[VP4B] 動詞第四型 B組

The infinitive may be equivalent to a co-ordinate clause.
不定詞相當於對等子句。

Subject + *vi*	*to*-infinitive
1 *He awoke* 他醒來發現房子着火了。	*to find the house on fire.*
2 *The good old days have gone* 美好的往日已去，永不復回。	*never to return.*
3 *Electronic music has clearly come* 電子音樂顯然已來臨。	*to stay.*

4 *He looked round* — *to see the door slowly opening.*
他回頭觀望,發現門慢慢打開了。

[VP4C] 動試第四型 C組

The infinitive adjunct is used after some verbs which, in [VP3A], are used with prepositions.
有些動詞後接不定詞修飾語,這些動詞用於動詞第三型A組時,是與介詞連用。
Don't trouble/bother about that.
Don't trouble/bother to meet me.

Subject + *vi*	*to*-infinitive
1 *She hesitated* 她有些不願告訴任何人。	*to tell anyone.*
2 *She was longing* 她渴望再見到她的家人。	*to see her family again.*
3 *He agreed* 他答應卽刻就來。	*to come at once.*

[VP4D] 動詞第四型 D組

The verbs *seem* and *appear* are used in this pattern. If the infinitive is *be* with an adjective or noun as complement, *to be* may be omitted (unless the adjective is one that is used only predicatively, as in [VP4E]).
動詞 seem 和 appear 用於此型。如果不定詞是 be, 並以形容詞或名詞作補語,則 to be 可以省略(除非該形容詞僅作敍述用法,如動詞第四型E組)。

Subject + SEEM/APPEAR	(*to be*) + adjective/noun
1 *He seemed* 他似乎對這消息感到驚訝。	(*to be*) *surprised at the news.*
2 *This seems* 這似乎是一件嚴重的事。	(*to be*) *a serious matter.*
3 *I seem* 我好像玩得不快樂。	(*to be*) *unable to enjoy myself.*

There is a variation of this pattern with introductory *it*, when the subject is an infinitive or gerund, or a clause.
如遇 it 作句首,此型有一變化,主詞爲一不定詞、動名詞或子句。

It + SEEM/APPEAR	adjective/noun	subject
1 *It seemed* 再試一次似乎是合理的。	*reasonable*	*to try again.*
2 *It seems* 浪費掉所有那些食物似乎是一憾事。	*a pity*	*to waste all that food.*
3 *It doesn't seem* 繼續下去好像沒有什麼用處。	*much use*	*going on.*
4 *It appears* 我們好像不大可能準時到達了。	*unlikely*	*that we'll arrive on time.*

[VP4E] 動詞第四型 E組

If the adjective after *seem/appear* is used only predicatively (eg *awake, asleep, afraid*), *to be* is obligatory. *Happen* and *chance* are also used in this pattern.
如果seem和appear後面的形容詞僅作敍述用法(例如awake, asleep, afraid), to be 則不可省略。happen 和 chance 也用於此型。

Subject + SEEM/APPEAR HAPPEN/CHANCE	*to*-infinitive
1 *The baby seems* 這嬰兒好像睡着了。	*to be asleep/to be sleeping.*
2 *My enquiries seem* 我的質詢似乎引起了怨恨。	*to have been resented.*
3 *She happened* 我往訪時她湊巧不在家。	*to be out when I called.*

4 *We chanced* 我們在公園裡偶遇。	*to meet in the park.*
5 *There seems* 好像有錯誤。	*to have been some mistake.*

[VP4F] 動詞第四型 F組 The finites of *be* are used with a *to*-infinitive to convey a variety of meanings, ⇨*be*[4] (3).
限定動詞 be 與不定詞連用時可表達不同的意義(參看 be[4] 第3義)。

Subject + BE	*to*-infinitive
1 *We're* 我們打算在五月裡結婚。	*to be married in May.*
2 *At what time am I* 要我什麼時候來？	*to come?*
3 *How am I* 我怎麼可能償還我的債務呢？	*to pay my debts?*

[VP5] 動詞第五型 In this pattern the auxiliary verbs or anomalous finites *will/would, shall/should, can/could, must, dare, need* are followed by a bare infinitive (ie without *to*). The phrases *had better, had/would rather* and *would sooner* fit into this pattern.
此型中的助動詞或變則定動詞 will/would, shall/should, can/could, must, dare, need 等後跟省去 to 的不定詞。片語如 had better, had/would rather 和 would sooner 也適合此型。

Subject + anomalous finite	infinitive
1 *You may* 你現在可以走了。	*leave now.*
2 *You needn't* 你不必等。	*wait.*
3 *You'll* 你會在那個盒子裡找到它。	*find it in that box.*
4 *I didn't dare* 我不敢告訴任何人。	*tell anyone.*
5 *You'd better* 你最好立刻動身。	*start at once.*

[VP6A] 動詞第六型 A組 The verbs in this pattern have a noun or pronoun as direct object. Conversion to the passive voice is possible.
此型中的動詞有一名詞或代名詞作直接受詞。可能變成被動語態。

Subject + *vt*	noun/pronoun
1 *Did you enjoy* 你喜歡那部電影嗎？	*the film?*
2 *We all had* 我們都玩得愉快。	*a good time.*
3 *Everyone likes* 每個人都喜歡她。	*her.*

[VP6B] 動詞第六型 B組 The verbs in this pattern have a noun or pronoun as direct object, but conversion to the passive voice is not possible. *Have*, meaning 'possess/take/eat/drink', follows this pattern. Reflexive verbs, and verbs with cognate objects, follow this pattern.
此型中的動詞有一名詞或代名詞作直接受詞，但不可能變成被動語態。Have (作'有,吃,飲' 解) 用於此型。反身動詞以及同源受詞的動詞亦用於此型。

Subject + *vt*	noun/pronoun
1 *Have you had* 你吃過早飯了嗎？	*breakfast yet?*

2 *She has* 她有綠色的眼睛。	*green eyes.*
3 *Have you hurt* 你傷到自己了嗎？	*yourself?*
4 *She smiled* 她微笑以示謝意。	*her thanks.*
5 *He dreamed* 他做了一個非常怪的夢。	*a very odd dream.*

[VP6C] 動詞第六型 C組

In this pattern the object is a gerund, not replaceable by a *to*-infinitive.
此型中的受詞是動名詞，不可用不定詞代替。

Subject + *vt*	gerund
1 *She enjoys* 她喜愛打網球。	*playing tennis.*
2 *Have you finished* 你的話講完沒有？	*talking?*
3 *I resent* 我怨恨這般無禮地對我說話。	*being spoken to so rudely.*

[VP6D] 動詞第六型 D組

In this pattern the object is a gerund. This may be replaced by a *to*-infinitive. For the difference between *like swimming* and *like to swim*, see the notes on [VP6D] in *Guide to Patterns and Usage.*
此型中的受詞爲動名詞，也可用不定詞代替。至於 like swimming 與 like to swim 含義之不同，請參閱 '英文句型及用法指南' 動詞第六型 D 組。

Subject + *vt*	gerund
1 *She loves* 她愛好看電影。	*going to the cinema.*
2 *I'll continue* 只要我健康良好，我就要繼續工作。	*working while my health is good.*
3 *He began* 他開始談論他那些聰明的孩子。	*talking about his clever children.*

[VP6E] 動詞第六型 E組

After *need, want* (= need) and *won't/wouldn't bear*, the gerund is equivalent to a passive infinitive.
在 need, want (= need) 及 won't/wouldn't bear 後，動名詞相當於被動的不定詞。

Subject + NEED/WANT/BEAR	gerund
1 *He'll need* 他需要人照顧。	*looking after* (= to be looked after).
2 *My shoes want* 我的鞋子需要修補。	*mending* (= to be mended).
3 *His language wouldn't bear* 他的話不堪重述。	*repeating* (= was too bad to be repeated).

[VP7A] 動詞第七型 A組

In this pattern the object of the verb is a *to*-infinitive. (For intransitive verbs with the same word order, see [VP4].)
此型中動詞的受詞爲不定詞。(關於用同樣詞序的不及物動詞，請參看動詞第四型。)

Subject + *vt*	(*not*) + *to*-infinitive
1 *Do they want* 他們想去嗎？	*to go?*
2 *He pretended* 他假裝沒有看見我。	*not to see me.*

3 *We hope/expect/intend* 我們希望(盼望,想要)攀登埃佛勒斯峯。	*to climb Mount Everest.*
4 *I forgot/remembered* 我忘記(並未忘記)爲你寄信。	*to post your letters.*

[VP7B] 動詞第七型 B組

Ought, and the finites of *have* in this pattern indicate obligation. In colloquial style *have got to* is more usual than *have to.*
ought 和 限定動詞 have 用於此型,表示義務。在口語中 have got to 較 have to 常用。

Subject + HAVE/OUGHT	(*not*) + *to*-infinitive
1 *Do you often have* 你時常必須加班工作嗎?	*to work overtime?*
2 *You don't have* 你還不需要離開,對嗎?	*to leave yet, do you?*
3 *You ought* 你不應該把你的錢浪費在那方面。	*not to waste your money there.*

[VP8] 動詞第八型

In this pattern the object of the verb is an interrogative pronoun or adverb (except *why* or *whether*), followed by a *to*-infinitive.
此型中動詞的受詞爲疑問代名詞或副詞(why 或 whether 例外),後面跟不定詞。

Subject + *vt*	interrogative pronoun/adverb + *to*-infinitive
1 *Do you know/see* 你知道怎樣做了嗎?	*how to do it?*
2 *I couldn't decide* 我不能決定下一步做什麼。	*what to do next.*
3 *I've discovered* 我已發現到那裡可以找到他。	*where to find him.*
4 *You must learn* 你必須學會何時予人忠告以及何時保持沈默。	*when to give advice and when to be silent.*

[VP9] 動詞第九型

The object of the verb is a *that*-clause. *That* is often omitted, except after more formal verbs (eg *decide, intend*).
動詞的受詞是一 that 子句。除非在較正式的動詞(如 decide, intend)後, that 常被省略。

Subject + *vt*	*that*-clause
1 *I suppose* 我認爲你快要離開了。	*you'll be leaving soon.*
2 *I wish* 請你不要打岔。	*you wouldn't interrupt.*
3 *Do you think* 你想會下雨嗎?	*it'll rain?*
4 *The workers decided* 工人們決定繼續罷工。	*that they would go on strike.*
5 *We intended* 我們打算邀請約翰。	*that John should be invited.*

[VP10] 動詞第十型

In this pattern the object of the verb is a dependent clause or question. The clause is introduced by a relative adverb or pronoun, *what,* or *whether/if.*
此型中動詞的受詞是一附屬子句或問句。子句係由關係副詞或代名詞、 what 或 whether/if 所引導。

Subject + *vt*	dependent clause/question
1 *Does anyone know* 有人知道這事是怎樣發生的嗎?	*how it happened?*
2 *Come and see* 來看我做了些什麼!	*what I've done!*

3 *I wonder* *whether/if he'll come.*
我想知道他是否要來。
4 *She asked* *why I was late.*
她問我爲何遲到。

[VP11]
動詞第十一型

The verb is followed by a noun or pronoun and a *that*-clause.
動詞後跟一名詞或代名詞和 that 子句。

Subject + *vt*	noun/pronoun	*that*-clause
1 *He warned* 他警告我們那些道路是覆蓋着冰的。	*us*	*that the roads were icy.*
2 *I convinced* 我說服了警察我是無罪的。	*the policeman*	*that I was innocent.*
3 *We satisfied* 我們確信計畫可以實行。	*ourselves*	*that the plan would work.*

[VP12A]
動詞第十二型
A組

The verb is followed by an indirect object (IO) and a direct object (DO). The indirect object is equivalent to a prepositional object with *to*, as in [VP13A].
動詞後跟一間接受詞(IO)與一直接受詞(DO)。間接受詞相當於介詞to加受詞,如動詞第十三型A組所示。

Subject + *vt*	IO	DO
1 *Won't you lend* 你不願意把你的汽車借給他嗎?	*him*	*your car?*
2 *He doesn't owe* 他什麼東西也沒有欠我。	*me*	*anything.*
3 *He denied/grudged* 她要什麼他便給她什麼。	*her*	*nothing.*

[VP12B]
動詞第十二型
B組

In this pattern the indirect object is equivalent to a prepositional object with *for*, as in [VP13B].
此型中的間接受詞相當於介詞 for 加受詞,如動詞第十三型 B 組所示。

Subject + *vt*	IO	DO
1 *She made* 她爲自己做了一件新裝。	*herself*	*a new dress.*
2 *Will you do* 你願意幫我一個忙嗎?	*me*	*a favour?*
3 *She cooked* 她爲她的丈夫煎了些臘腸。	*her husband*	*some sausages.*

[VP12C]
動詞第十二型
C組

Verbs in this pattern are rarely or never convertible to [VP13]. The labels IO and DO are not used.
此型中的動詞極少或永不可變爲第十三型。IO 和 DO 兩個標示不用在此型。

Subject + *vt*	noun/pronoun	noun/pronoun
1 *Ask* 問他的姓名。	*him*	*his name.*
2 *I envy* 我羡慕你那座美好的花園。	*you*	*your fine garden.*
3 *He struck* 他給了那門一個重擊。	*the door*	*a heavy blow.*

[VP13A]
動詞第十三型
A組

In this pattern the verb is followed by a direct object, the preposition *to*, and the prepositional object. It is convertible to [VP12A].
此型動詞後跟一直接受詞,介詞 to 及其受詞。此型可變爲動詞第十二型 A 組。

Subject + *vt*	DO	*to* + noun/pronoun
1 *She told* 她把這消息告訴了村子裡的每一個人。	*the news*	*to everyone in the village.*

2 *He sold* 他把他的舊汽車賣給了他的一個隣居。	*his old car*	*to one of his neighbours.*
3 *I've sent* 我已給我每一位家人寄出了禮物。	*presents*	*to everyone in my family.*

[VP13B]
動詞第十三型B組

In this pattern the preposition is *for*. It is convertible to [VP12B].
此型中的介詞是 for, 可變爲動詞第十二型 B 組。

Subject + *vt*	DO	*for* + noun/pronoun
1 *She made* 她爲她的女兒做了一件新裝。	*a new dress*	*for her daughter.*
2 *Will you do* 你願意幫我一個朋友的忙嗎？	*a favour*	*for a friend of mine?*
3 *Can you cash* 你能爲我將這張支票兌現嗎？	*this cheque*	*for me?*

[VP14]
動詞第十四型

In this pattern the verb is followed by a direct object and a preposition and its object. This pattern is not convertible to [VP12], as are [VP13A] and [VP13B], 'Give something to somebody' [VP12A] may be converted to 'Give somebody something' [VP13A]. 'Explain something to somebody' cannot be converted to '*Explain somebody something'.

此型中的動詞後跟一直接受詞與一介詞及其受詞。此型不像動詞第十三型A組和B組一樣可以變爲動詞第十二型。'Give something to somebody' (動詞第十二型 A 組)可以變作 'Give somebody something' (動詞第十三型 A 組)。'Explain something to somebody' 則不可以變作 '*Explain somebody something'。

The preposition is linked to the verb and they must be learnt together, eg 'congratulate somebody *on* something', 'compare one thing *to/with* another'. In [VP15] however the prepositional phrase is variable, eg 'put something *on/under the table, in the drawer*'.

介詞和動詞相連接,必須一起學習,例如 'congratulate somebody *on* something', 'compare one thing *to/with* another'。然而在動詞第十五型A組中介詞片語可以變化,例如 'put something *on/under the table, in the drawer*'。

Subject + *vt*	DO	prep	noun
1 *We congratulated* 我們向他祝賀他的成功。	*him*	*on*	*his success.*
2 *Compare* 把這副本與原件比較一下。	*the copy*	*with*	*the original.*
3 *He compared* 他把心臟比作唧筒。	*the heart*	*to*	*a pump.*
4 *I explained* 我把我的困難解釋給他聽。	*my difficulty*	*to*	*him.*

Variations are possible. If the DO is long, the prepositional phrase may precede it. Introductory *it* may be used when there is an infinitive phrase or a clause.

此型可以變化。如果直接受詞很長, 介詞片語可置於其前。遇有不定詞片語或子句時,可用具有引導作用的 it。

Subject + *vt*	prep + noun	DO
1 *I explained* 我把不可能答應他的請求解釋給他聽。	*to him*	*the impossibility of granting his request.*
2 *I must leave it* 我必須要你自己決定你是否應該提出辭職。	*to your own judgement*	*to decide whether you should offer your resignation.*

Compare: 比較:	Subject + *vt*	DO	prep + noun
	1 *I explained* 我向他解釋這問題。	*the problem*	*to him.*
	2 *I must leave* 我應該讓你來決定。	*the decision*	*to you.*

[VP15A]
動詞第十五型
A組

In [VP15A] the DO is followed by an adverbial phrase of place, duration, distance, etc which is obligatory. 'I read the book' [VP6] is a complete sentence, but '*I put the book' is not. *Put* needs an adjunct. eg 'I put the book *down/away/on the shelf*. With verbs marked [VP 15A] the adverbial is a prepositional phrase, which is variable (unlike VP14]).

在動詞第十五型 A 組中,直接受詞後面必須跟一表示地點、時間、距離等的副詞片語。'I read the book' (動詞第六型)是一完整的句子,而 '*I put the book' 則否。put 需要一修飾語,例如 'I put the book *down/away/on the shelf*'。標號第十五型 A 組的動詞後面的副詞片語卽介詞片語,並可以變化(不似動詞第十四型)。

Subject + *vt*	DO	adverbial phrase
1 *Don't let the child put* 不要讓孩子把頭伸出車窗外(伸入塑膠袋裡)。	*his head*	*out of the car window/into the plastic bag.*
2 *The secretary showed* 秘書引我到門口(進入接待室)。	*me*	*to the door/into the reception room.*
3 *Please put* 請把這些文件放在桌上(那個卷檔裡,我的手提箱裡)。	*these papers*	*on that desk/in that file/in my briefcase.*

[VP15B]
動詞第十五型
B組

In this pattern adverbial particles are used. When the DO is a personal pronoun, the adverbial particle follows. When the DO is a noun or noun phrase, the adverbial particle may either follow or precede. If the DO is long, the adverbial particle usually precedes.

副詞接語用於此型中。當直接受詞爲一人稱代名詞時,副詞接語在其後。當直接受詞爲一名詞或名詞片語時,副詞接語在其前後均可。如果直接受詞很長,副詞接語通常在其前。

Subject + *vt*	DO	adverbial particle
1 *Take* 把它們(你的鞋子)脫掉。	*them/your shoes*	*off.*
2 *Don't throw* 不要把它(那頂舊帽子)丟掉。	*it/that old hat*	*away.*
3 *Did you wind* 你(給鐘)上絃了嗎?	*it/the clock*	*up?*

Subject + *vt*	adverbial particle	DO
1 *Lock* 把你所有的貴重物品都鎖起來。	*up*	*all your valuables.*
2 *She gave* 她把她所有的舊衣服都送給別人了。	*away*	*all her old clothes.*
3 *Don't forget to switch* 不要忘記關掉樓下所有房間裡的燈。	*off*	*the lights in all the rooms downstairs.*

[VP16A]
動詞第十六型
A組

In this pattern there is an adverbial adjunct which is an infinitive phrase. This may be introduced by *in order to* or *so as to*. [VP16A] is to be distinguished from [VP17] (with the same word order).

此型中的副詞修飾語爲不定詞片語,亦可由 in order to 或 so as to 引導。動詞第十六型A組有別於動詞第十七型(詞序雖相同)。

Cf 參較: *I sent* *Tom* *to buy some fruit.* [VP16A]
我差湯姆去買些水果。(動詞第十六型A組)
I want *Tom* *to buy some fruit.* [VP17]
我要湯姆去買些水果。(動詞第十七型)

In [VP16A] the infinitive is one of purpose or intended result. In [VP17] the infinitive is part of the direct object.
動詞第十六型A組中的不定詞表示目的或意欲的結果,動詞第十七型中的不定詞是直接受詞的一部分。

Subject + *vt*	DO	*to*-infinitive
1 *He brought*	*his brother*	*to see me.*
他帶他兄弟來看我。		
2 *He opened*	*the door*	*to let the cat out.*
他打開門讓猫出去。		
3 *They left*	*me*	*to do all the dirty work.*
他們讓我做所有骯髒的工作。		

[VP16B] 動詞第十六型B組 The DO is followed by a noun introduced by *as* or *like*, or a clause introduced by *as if or as though.*
直接受詞後跟一由as或like引導的名詞,或者由as if或as though引導的子句。

Subject + *vt*	DO	*as/like* + noun *as if/though* + clause
1 *I can't see*	*myself*	*as a pop singer.*
我無法想像自己做了流行歌曲歌手以後是什麼樣子。		
2 *Her parents spoilt*	*her*	*as a child.*
她的父母像小孩子般寵壞了她。		
3 *He carries*	*himself*	*like a soldier.*
他的舉止像個軍人。		
4 *You mustn't treat*	*your wife*	*as if she were a servant.*
你不可以像對待僕人般對待你的妻子。		

[VP17] 動詞第十七型 In this pattern the verb is followed by a noun or pronoun and a *to*-infinitive. The noun/pronoun + *to*-infinitive is the object of the verb.
此型中動詞後跟一名詞或代名詞及一不定詞。名詞或代名詞及不定詞爲動詞的受詞。

Subject + *vt*	noun/pronoun	(*not*) + *to*-infinitive
1 *He likes*	*his wife*	*to dress colourfully.*
他喜歡他的妻子衣著華麗。		
2 *They warned*	*us*	*not to be late.*
他們警告我們不要遲到。		
3 *Do you want/wish*	*me*	*to stay?*
你要(希望)我留下來嗎?		

[VP18A] 動詞第十八型A組 In this pattern the verb is used with a noun or pronoun and a bare infinitive. The verbs indicate physical perceptions. These verbs are also used in [VP19]. [VP18] indicates completed activity and [VP19] activity in progress.
此型中的動詞與一名詞或代名詞及一省去 to 的不定詞連用。這些動詞表示身體上的感覺,亦可用於動詞第十九型。動詞第十八型表示完整的動作,動詞第十九型表示進行中的動作。

Subject + *vt*	noun/pronoun	infinitive
1 *Did you see/notice*	*anyone*	*leave the house?*
你看見(留意到)任何人離開那房屋嗎?		
2 *We felt*	*the house*	*shake.*
我們覺得房子在搖動。		
3 *I once heard*	*her*	*sing the part of Aida.*
我一度聽她唱過阿依達一角。		

[VP18B] 動詞第十八型 B組

A small number of verbs which do not indicate physical perceptions are used in this pattern. *Make* and *let* are examples. Compare *force/compel* and *allow/permit*, which are used in [VP17].

少數不表示身體上的感覺的動詞用於此型。make 和 let 卽爲其例。比較用於動詞第十七型的 force/compel 及 allow/permit:

Please let *me* *go.* [VP18B]
Please allow/permit *me* *to go.* [VP17]

Subject + *vt*	noun/pronoun	infinitive
1 *What makes* 什麼使你這樣想？	*you*	*think so?*
2 *Let* 讓我走！	*me*	*go!*
3 *I've never known* 我從不知道他的行爲這樣壞。	*him*	*behave so badly before.*

[VP18C] 動詞第十八型 C組

Have is used in this pattern when it means 'wish', 'experience' or 'cause'.

Have 表示 '要','經歷' 或 '使' 時,用於此型。

Subject + HAVE	noun/pronoun	infinitive
1 *What would you have* 你要我做什麼？	*me*	*do?*
2 *Have* 請把客人帶進來。	*the visitors*	*shown in, please.*
3 *I had* 昨天我遭遇到一件可怕的事。	*a frightening thing*	*happen to me yesterday.*
4 *We often have* 我們時常讓朋友在星期日來訪。	*our friends*	*visit us on Sundays.*

[VP19A] 動詞第十九型 A組

The verb is followed by a noun or pronoun and a present participle. The verbs indicate physical perceptions and are those used in [VP18A].

動詞後跟一名詞或代名詞及一現在分詞。這些動詞表示身體上的感覺,亦卽用於動詞第十八型A組中者。

Subject + *vt*	noun/pronoun	present participle
1 *Can you smell* 你能聞到有東西在燃燒嗎？	*something*	*burning?*
2 *She could feel* 她可以感覺到她的心在猛跳。	*her heart*	*beating wildly.*
3 *Did you notice* 你注意到有人站在大門口嗎？	*anyone*	*standing at the gate?*
4 *Didn't you hear* 你沒有聽見我敲門嗎？	*me*	*knocking?*

[VP19B] 動詞第十九型 B組

This pattern is used for some verbs which do not indicate physical perceptions.

此型用於一些不表示身體感覺的動詞。

Subject + *vt*	noun/pronoun	present participle
1 *I found* 我發現約翰在書桌邊工作。	*John*	*working at his desk.*
2 *They left* 他們讓我在外面等。	*me*	*waiting outside.*
3 *This set* 此事使我思考。	*me*	*thinking.*
4 *Please start* 請讓鐘走動。	*the clock*	*going.*
5 *He soon had* 他很快使得他們都大笑起來。	*them all*	*laughing.*

[VP19C] 動詞第十九型C組

In this pattern the noun or pronoun is followed by the *-ing* form of a verb, and this may be either the present participle or the gerund, depending upon whether it is preceded by a noun or pronoun, or a possessive. For fuller notes, see [VP19C] in *Guide to Patterns and Usage*.
此型中的名詞或代名詞後跟一動詞加 ing 的形式,此一形式或爲現在分詞或爲動名詞,要視其前爲一名詞或代名詞,或一所有格而定。較詳細的說明請參看‘英文句型及用法指南’中‘動詞第十九型C組’。

Subject + *vt*	noun/pronoun/possessive	*-ing* form of the verb
1 *I can't understand*	*him/his*	*behaving so foolishly.*
我不明白何以他的行爲如此愚蠢。		
2 *Can you imagine*	*me/my*	*being so stupid?*
你能想像我是如此愚蠢嗎?		
3 *Does this justify*	*you/your*	*taking legal action?*
這便是你要起訴的理由嗎?		
4 *I can't remember*	*my parents/their*	*ever being unkind to me.*
我不記得我的父母(他們)曾對我不好。		
5 *I admire*	*Tom('s)/him/his*	*standing his ground.*
我欽佩湯姆(他,他的)堅持立場。		

[VP20] 動詞第二十型

In this pattern the verb is followed by a noun or pronoun, an interrogative adverb (except *why*) or pronoun, and a *to*-infinitive. The pattern may be compared to [VP12A].
此型中的動詞後跟一名詞或代名詞,一疑問副詞(why 除外)或代名詞,及一不定詞。此型可與動詞第十二型A組作比較。

Tell	*me*	*your name.* [VP12A]
Tell	*me*	*what to call you.* [VP20]

Subject + *vt*	noun/pronoun	interrogative + *to*-infinitive
1 *I showed*	*them*	*how to do it.*
我演示給他們看如何做這件事。		
2 *Tell*	*him*	*where to put it.*
告訴他把它放在那裡。		
3 *Ask*	*your teacher*	*how to pronounce the word.*
問你的老師怎樣讀這個字。		

[VP21] 動詞第二十一型

This pattern is similar to [VP20]. An interrogative clause follows the noun or pronoun.
此型與動詞第二十型相似。疑問子句跟在名詞或代名詞後。

Subject + *vt*	noun/pronoun	interrogative clause
1 *Tell*	*me*	*what your name is.*
告訴我你的姓名。		
2 *Ask*	*him*	*where he put it.*
問問他,他把它放在那裡。		
3 *Show*	*me*	*what you have in your pockets.*
把你口袋裡的東西拿給我看。		

[VP22] 動詞第二十二型

The DO is followed by an adjective which indicates result or manner.
直接受詞後跟一表示結果或方式的形容詞。

Subject + *vt*	DO	adjective
1 *We painted*	*the ceiling*	*green.*
我們把天花板漆成了綠色。		
2 *The sun keeps*	*us*	*warm.*
太陽保持我們溫暖。		
3 *The mud made*	*walking*	*difficult.*
泥濘使行走困難。		

[VP23] 動詞第二十三型

The DO is followed by a noun (the object complement).
直接受詞後跟一名詞(受詞補語)。

Subject + *vt*	DO	noun
1 *They made*	*Newton*	*President of the Royal Society.*
他們舉牛頓爲皇家學會主席。		
2 *They named*	*the baby*	*Richard.*
他們替那嬰兒取名爲理查。		
3 *They usually call*	*him*	*Dick.*
他們平常叫他狄克。		

[VP24A] 動詞第二十四型 A組

The DO is followed by a past participle.
直接受詞後跟一過去分詞。

Subject + *vt*	DO	past participle
1 *You must make*	*your views*	*known.*
你必須使你的意見讓大家知道。		
2 *Have you ever heard*	*this opera*	*sung in Italian?*
你曾聽過這歌劇用義大利語唱出嗎?		
3 *We want*	*the work*	*finished by Saturday.*
我們要這工作在星期六以前完成。		

[VP24B] 動詞第二十四型 B組

Have is used in this pattern to indicate what the subject of the sentence experiences, undergoes, or suffers (as in Nos 1 and 2), or what is held or possessed (as in No 3).
have 用於此型表示句中主詞的經驗或經歷(如第1, 2句),或擁有之物(如第3句)。

Subject + HAVE	DO	past participle
1 *King Charles had*	*his head*	*cut off.*
查理王被人斬首。		
2 *I've recently had*	*my appendix*	*removed.*
我最近把闌尾割掉了。		
3 *They have*	*scarcely any money*	*saved for their old age.*
他們幾乎沒有儲蓄什麼錢以養老。		

[VP24C] 動詞第二十四型 C組

Have and *get* are used in this pattern meaning 'cause to be'.
have 和 get 用於此型表示'使成爲'。

Subject + HAVE/GET	DO	past participle
1 *Can we have/get*	*the programme*	*changed?*
我們能將計畫變更嗎?		
2 *Please have/get*	*these letters*	*translated into English.*
請把這些信件譯成英文。		
3 *I'll have/get*	*the matter*	*seen to.*
我會處理這件事。		

[VP25] 動詞第二十五型

The DO is followed by *to be* (often omitted) and an adjective or a noun. In spoken English [VP9] (ie with a *that*-clause) is preferred.
直接受詞後跟 to be (常被省略)與一形容詞或名詞。口語中則較常用動詞第九型(卽與一 that 子句連用)。

Subject + *vt*	DO	(*to be*) + adjective/noun
1 *Most people considered*	*him*	(*to be*) *innocent.*
大多數人認爲他是無罪的。		
2 *They all felt*	*the plan*	*to be unwise.*
他們都覺得這個計畫不智。		
3 *I've always found*	*Jonathan*	*friendly/a good friend.*
我一直覺得强納生很友善(是個好朋友)。		

4 *In Britain we presume* *a man* (*to be*) *innocent until he is proved guilty.*

在英國我們假定一個人在證實有罪以前是無罪的。

For 1, *Most people considered that he was innocent* [VP9] is more usual. Introductory *it* is used if, instead of a noun, there is a clause, infinitive phrase, etc.
關於第1句, Most people considered that he was innocent (動詞第九型) 較常用。遇有不是名詞,而是子句,不定詞片語等時,前面用 it。

Cf 參較: *Do you consider long hair for men strange?*
你認為男人留長髮奇怪嗎？
Do you consider it strange for men to let their hair grow long?
你認為男人把頭髮留得很長奇怪嗎？

Anomalous verbs
變則動詞

Some of the verbs in the Dictionary carry the description *anomalous verb* (abbreviated *anom v*), or *anomalous finite* (abbreviated *anom fin*). A verb is an *anomalous finite* if it forms its negative by adding the word *not* (or its contraction *-n't*) after the verb. For example, the negative of *must* is *must not* or *mustn't*. All the forms of the English anomalous verbs are set out in the table below.
本詞典中有些動詞附有 anomalous verb (變則動詞, 略作 anom v) 或 anomalous finite (變則定動詞,略作 anom fin) 的說明。如果一個動詞的否定形式是在它的後面加 not (或縮寫式 -n't),此一動詞便是變則定動詞。玆將英文變則動詞所有的形式列於下表。

Non-finite forms 無限式			Finite forms 有限式	
Infinitive 不定詞	Present Participle 現在分詞	Past Participle 過去分詞	Present Tense 現在式	Past Tense 過去式
be	*being*	*been*	*am, is, are*	*was, were*
have	*having*	*had*	*have, has*	*had*
do	*doing*	*done*	*do, does*	*did*
—	—	—	*shall*	*should*
—	—	—	*will*	*would*
—	—	—	*can*	*could*
—	—	—	*may*	*might*
—	—	—	*must*	—
—	—	—	*ought*	—
—	—	—	*need*	—
—	—	—	*dare*	—
—	—	—	—	*used*

Strong and weak forms
強式和弱式

The words listed below all have two or more different pronunciations: a *strong* form and one or more *weak* forms. It is the weak forms which occur most frequently in connected speech. For example, *from* is /frəm/ in *He ˌcomes from ˈSpain*.
下列各字都有兩種或兩種以上不同的讀法:一種强式讀法及一種或一種以上弱式讀法。弱式讀法最常出現在連貫性的談話中,例如在 He ˌcomes from ˈSpain 一句中的 from 讀作 /frəm/。

The strong form occurs when a word is said in isolation, or when it is given special emphasis in connected speech. For instance, *from* is /frɒm/ in *This ˌpresent's not 'from John; it's 'for him.* In addition, when prepositions and auxiliary verbs come at the end of a clause they generally take their strong form, whether or not they are stressed. For example, *ˌWhere do you 'come from?* has /frɒm/ (*not* /frəm/).

强式讀法出現在一個字單獨說出或在連貫性的談話中特別被强調時。例如在This ˌpresent's not 'from John; it's 'for him 一句中的 from 讀作 /frɒm/。此外，當介詞和助動詞位於一子句末尾時，不論是否重讀，通常都是强式。例如 ˌWhere do you 'come from? 一句中的 from 讀作 /frɒm/ (不是 /frəm/)。

The words below are very common in ordinary speech, and it is only by understanding the different forms and using them correctly that the learner will develop a mastery of natural, conversational English.

下列各字在一般談話中很常用，學習者必須瞭解這些不同的形式而且正確地使用它們，方能精通自然的會話式的英語。

	STRONG FORM 强式	WEAK FORM 弱式	NOTES ON THE WEAK FORM 弱式的註解
DETERMINER 限定詞			
a	/eɪ/	/ə/	
an	/æn/	/ən/	
his	/hɪz/	/ɪz/	Not used to begin a sentence 不用於句首
our	/'aʊə(r)/	/ɑ:(r)/	
some	/sʌm/	/səm/	Used only when *some* means 'an undefined amount or number of' 僅用於當 some 表示'未指明的量或數'時
the	/ði:/	/ðə/, /ðɪ/	/ðɪ/ before vowels 母音前讀作 /ðɪ/
your	/jɔ:(r)/	/jə(r)/	
CONJUNCTION 連接詞			
and	/ænd/	/ən/	
as	/æz/	/əz/	
but	/bʌt/	/bət/	
than	/ðæn/	/ðən/	
that	/ðæt/	/ðət/	Also used when *that* is a relative pronoun 亦用於 that 作關係代名詞
PREPOSITION 介詞			
at	/æt/	/ət/	
for	/fɔ:(r)/	/fə(r)/, /fr/	/fr/ before vowels 母音前讀作 /fr/
from	/frɒm/	/frəm/	
of	/ɒv/	/əv/	
to	/tu:/	/tə/	Not used before vowels 不用在母音前
PRONOUN 代名詞			
he	/hi:/	/i:/	Not used to begin a sentence 不用於句首
her	/hɜ:(r)/	/ɜ:(r)/, /ə(r)/	Not used to begin a sentence; /ə(r)/ in rapid speech 不用於句首；說話急促時讀作 /ə(r)/
him	/hɪm/	/ɪm/	
them	/ðem/	/ðəm/	
us	/ʌs/	/əs/	

	STRONG FORM 强式	WEAK FORM 弱式	NOTES ON THE WEAK FORM 弱式的註解
VERB 動詞			
am	/æm/	/əm/	
are	/ɑː(r)/	/ə(r)/	
can	/kæn/	/kən/	
do	/duː/	/də/	Not used before vowels 不用於母音前
does	/dʌz/	/dəz/	
had	/hæd/	/həd/, /əd/	Auxiliary use only; /həd/ used to begin a sentence 僅用作助動詞; /həd/ 用於句首
has	/hæz/	/həz/, /əz/, /z/, /s/	Auxiliary use only; /əz/ used after the consonants /s, z, ʃ, ʒ, tʃ, dʒ/; /həz/ used to begin a sentence 僅用作助動詞; /əz/ 用在子音 /s, z, ʃ, ʒ, tʃ, dʒ/ 之後; /həz/ 用於句首
have	/hæv/	/həv/, /əv/	Auxiliary use only; /həv/ used to begin a sentence 僅用作助動詞; /həv/ 用於句首
is	/ɪz/	/z/, /s/	Not used to begin or end a sentence 不用於句首或句尾
must	/mʌst/	/məst/	
shall	/ʃæl/	/ʃəl/	
was	/wɒz/	/wəz/	
were	/wɜː(r)/	/wə(r)/	
will	/wɪl/	/əl/	Not used to begin or end a sentence 不用於句首或句尾
would	/wʊd/	/əd/	Not used to begin or end a sentence 不用於句首或句尾

Contractions
縮寫式

In English there are a number of contractions of words which are used in speech, and in writing which reproduces spoken language, for example drama, direct speech in novels and short stories, personal letters. It is important that the learner should learn and make use of these contracted forms if he wants his English to sound natural.
英文中有許多縮寫的字用在談話裡以及敍述談話的寫作中，例如戲劇、小說和短篇故事中的直接談話、私人信件等。如果學習者想要他的英語聽來自然，學習并運用這些縮寫式是重要的。

When contractions are written, the two words are shortened by omitting one or two letters and joining the words together. The letters that are omitted are represented by an apostrophe (').
寫縮寫式時，是將兩個字省去一兩個字母後連接起來。省略的字母用省略號 (') 來表示。

When contractions are spoken, the two words are shortened by omitting some sounds and pronouncing the two words as one.
說縮寫式時，是將兩個字省略某些音後讀作一個字。

PERSONAL PRONOUN + VERB

I'm	/aɪm/	I am
I've	/aɪv/	I have
I'll	/aɪl/	I shall; I will
she'll	/ʃiːl/	she will
she'd	/ʃiːd/	she would; she had

contractions

PERSONAL PRONOUN + VERB

I'd	/aɪd/	I would; I had	*it's*	/ɪts/	it is; it has
			it'll	/ˈɪtl/	it will
you're	/jʊə(r)/	you are			
you've	/ju:v/	you have	*we're*	/wɪə(r)/	we are
you'll	/ju:l/	you will	*we've*	/wi:v/	we have
you'd	/ju:d/	you would; you had	*we'll*	/wi:l/	we shall; we will
			we'd	/wi:d/	we would; we had
he's	/hi:z/	he is; he has			
he'll	/hi:l/	he will	*they're*	/ˈðeɪə(r)/	they are
he'd	/hi:d/	he would; he had	*they've*	/ðeɪv/	they have
			they'll	/ðeɪl/	they will
she's	/ʃi:z/	she is; she has	*they'd*	/ðeɪd/	they would; they had

VERB + NOT

aren't	/ɑ:nt/	are not	*mayn't*	/ˈmeɪənt/	may not
can't	/kɑ:nt/	cannot	*mightn't*	/ˈmaɪtnt/	might not
couldn't	/ˈkʊdnt/	could not	*mustn't*	/ˈmʌsnt/	must not
daren't	/deənt/	dare not	*needn't*	/ˈni:dnt/	need not
didn't	/ˈdɪdnt/	did not	*oughtn't*	/ˈɔ:tnt/	ought not
doesn't	/ˈdʌznt/	does not	*shan't*	/ʃɑ:nt/	shall not
don't	/dəʊnt/	do not	*shouldn't*	/ˈʃʊdnt/	should not
hasn't	/ˈhæznt/	has not	*wasn't*	/ˈwɒznt/	was not
haven't	/ˈhævnt/	have not	*weren't*	/wɜ:nt/	were not
hadn't	/ˈhædnt/	had not	*won't*	/wəʊnt/	will not
isn't	/ˈɪznt/	is not	*wouldn't*	/ˈwʊdnt/	would not

OTHER COMMON CONTRACTIONS

here's	/hɪəz/	here is	*what's*	/wɒts/	what is?
how's	/haʊz/	how is?	*when's*	/wenz/	when is?
that'd	/ˈðætəd/	that would	*where's*	/weəz/	where is?
that'll	/ˈðætl/	that will	*who'd*	/hu:d/	who would?
that's	/ðæts/	that is	*who'll*	/hu:l/	who will?
there's	/ðeəz/	there is	*who's*	/hu:z/	who is?
what'll	/ˈwɒtl/	what will			

Phonetic systems used

兩種注音法

In the Key to phonetic symbols (facing page) two lists of symbols are provided. The first, headed 'Jones', represents the British English accent known as *Received Pronunciation* or *General British*; the second, headed 'Kenyon & Knott', represents the American English accent known as *General American*.

在下頁的音標例釋中，列出兩種注音法：基於'公認的讀法'或'一般的英國讀法'的 Jones 音標、和基於'一般的美國讀法'的 Kenyon & Knott 音標。

In the text of the dictionary, the first transcription given after each headword refers to the Jones system, and is followed by a semi-colon. The second refers to the Kenyon & Knott system.

本詞典內字目所注的音標，第一個是 Jones 音標，第二個是 Kenyon & Knott 音標。

In cases where American pronunciation differs from British, the Jones system for British pronunciation is given first, followed by the American pronunciation in both the Jones and Kenyon & Knott systems.

若英式和美式讀法有差別，首先用 Jones 音標注出英式讀法，後面再加註Jones 和 Kenyon & Knott 音標的美式讀法。

Key to phonetic symbols 音標例釋

Vowels and diphthongs 母音與雙母音

Symbol 符號 Jones	Kenyon & Knott	Example 範例	Symbol 符號 Jones	Kenyon & Knott	Example 範例
iː	i	see /siː ; si/	ʌ	ʌ	cup /kʌp ; kʌp/
ɪ	ɪ	sit /sɪt ; sɪt/	ɜː	ɝ	fur /fɜː(r) ; fɝ/
e	ɛ	ten /ten ; tɛn/	ə	ə	ago /əˈɡəʊ ; əˈɡo/
æ	æ	hat /hæt ; hæt/		ɚ	never /ˈnevə(r) ; ˈnɛvɚ/
ɑː	ɑr	arm /ɑːm ; ɑrm/	eɪ	e	page /peɪdʒ ; pedʒ/
	ɑ	palm /pɑːm ; pɑm/	əʊ	o	home /həʊm ; hom/
	æ	ask /ɑːsk ; æsk/	aɪ	aɪ	five /faɪv ; faɪv/
ɒ	ɑ	got /ɡɒt ; ɡɑt/	aʊ	aʊ	now /naʊ ; naʊ/
	ɔ	long /lɒŋ ; lɔŋ/	ɔɪ	ɔɪ	join /dʒɔɪn ; dʒɔɪn/
ɔː	ɔ	saw /sɔː ; sɔ/	ɪə	ɪr	near /nɪə(r) ; nɪr/
	ɔr	born /bɔːn ; bɔrn/	eə	ɛr	hair /heə(r) ; hɛr/
ʊ	ʊ	put /pʊt ; pʊt/	ʊə	ʊr	pure /pjʊə(r) ; pjʊr/
uː	u	too /tuː ; tu/			

Consonants 子音

Symbol 符號 Jones	Kenyon & Knott	Example 範例	Symbol 符號 Jones	Kenyon & Knott	Example 範例
p	p	pen /pen ; pɛn/	s	s	so /səʊ ; so/
b	b	bad /bæd ; bæd/	z	z	zoo /zuː ; zu/
t	t	tea /tiː ; ti/	ʃ	ʃ	she /ʃiː ; ʃi/
d	d	did /dɪd ; dɪd/	ʒ	ʒ	vision /ˈvɪʒn ; ˈvɪʒən/
k	k	cat /kæt ; kæt/	h	h	how /haʊ ; haʊ/
ɡ	ɡ	got /ɡɒt ; ɡɑt/	m	m	man /mæn ; mæn/
tʃ	tʃ	chin /tʃɪn ; tʃɪn/	n	n	no /nəʊ ; no/
dʒ	dʒ	June /dʒuːn ; dʒun/	ŋ	ŋ	sing /sɪŋ ; sɪŋ/
f	f	fall /fɔːl ; fɔl/	l	l	leg /leɡ ; lɛɡ/
v	v	voice /vɔɪs ; vɔɪs/	r	r	red /red ; rɛd/
θ	θ	thin /θɪn ; θɪn/	j	j	yes /jes ; jɛs/
ð	ð	then /ðen ; ðɛn/	w	w	wet /wet ; wɛt/
				hw	what /wɒt ; hwɑt/

/ˈ/ or /ˈ/ represents *primary stress* as in **about** /əˈbaʊt ; əˈbaʊt/
/ˈ/ 代表 Jones 音標的重音，/ˈ/ 代表 K.K. 音標的重音，如 about /əˈbaʊt ; əˈbaʊt/ 中之重音。
/ˌ/ or /ˏ/ represents *secondary stress* as in **academic** /ˌækəˈdemɪk ; ˏækəˈdɛmɪk/
/ˌ/ 代表 Jones 音標的次重音，/ˏ/ 代表 K.K. 音標的次重音，如 academic /ˌækəˈdemɪk ; ˏækəˈdɛmɪk/ 中之次重音。

(r) An 'r' in parentheses is heard in British pronunciation when it is immediately followed by a word, or a suffix, beginning with a vowel. Otherwise it is omitted. In American pronunciation no 'r' of the phonetic spelling or of the ordinary spelling is omitted.
在英式發音中，(r) 後面緊跟的字或接尾語以母音開始時，則 r 音應該讀出，否則就省略。在美式發音中，音標或普通拼字中的 r 音不能省略。

/-/ Hyphens preceding and/or following parts of a repeated transcription indicate that only the repeated part changes.
在部分之重複注音前面或後面所接的短劃，表示只有重複的部分有變化。

⇨ the Introduction for a full explanation of the phonetic information.
有關發音之詳細說明，請參看緒論。
Note that in the introductory pages of this dictionary, up to this page, for simplicity only the Jones phonetic system is used in the examples.
本頁之前的緒論和其他解釋，只採用 Jones 音標於例子中，以免混亂。

Abbreviations used in the text
本詞典略語表

abbr	abbreviation	(略)	略語
adj, adjj	adjective(s)	(形)	形容詞
adv, advv	adverb(s)	(副)	副詞
adv part	adverbial particle	(副接)	副詞接語
affirm	affirmative(ly)	(肯定)	肯定的(地)
anom fin	anomalous finite	(變定)	變則定動詞
attrib	attributive(ly)	(形容用法)	形容用法
aux	auxiliary	(助)	助動詞
[C]	countable noun	(可數)	可數名詞
Cf, cf	compare	(參較)	參較
collect	collective(ly)	(集合用法)	集合用法
comp	comparative	(比較級)	比較級
conj	conjunction	(連)	連接詞
def art	definite article	(定冠)	定冠詞
demonstr	demonstrative	(指示)	指示詞
e g	for example	(例如)	例如
esp	especially	(尤指)	尤指
etc	and the others	(等)	等等
F	French	(法)	法國的,法語
fem	feminine	(陰)	陰性的
G	German	(德)	德國的,德語
GB	British／Britain	(英)	英國的,英國用法
Gk	Greek	(希)	希臘的,希臘語
H*c*	height about	(高約)	高度約爲
I	Italian	(義)	義大利的,義大利語
i e	which is to say	(意卽)	意卽
illus	illustration	(插圖)	插圖
imper	imperative	(祈使)	祈使法
impers	impersonal	(無人稱)	無人稱的用法
indef art	indefinite article	(不定冠)	不定冠詞
inf	infinitive	(不定詞)	不定詞
int	interjection	(感)	感嘆詞
interr	interrogative	(疑問)	疑問的
intrans	intransitive	(不及物)	不及物的
Lat	Latin	(拉)	拉丁語
L*c*	length about	(長約)	長度約爲
masc	masculine	(陽)	陽性的
n, nn	noun(s)	(名)	名詞
neg	negative(ly)	(否定)	否定的(地)
opp	opposite	(相反)	相反的,相反字
P	proprietary name	(商標)	專利商標名
part adj	participial adjective	(分形)	分詞形容詞
pers	person	(人稱)	人稱
pers pron	personal pronoun	(人稱代)	人稱代名詞
phr	phrase	(片語)	片語
pl	plural	(複)	複數(的)
poss	possessive	(所有)	所有格的
pp	past participle	(過去分詞)	過去分詞
pred	predicative(ly)	(敍述用法)	敍述用法
pref	prefix	(字首)	字首
prep	preposition(al)	(介詞)	介詞,介系詞,介詞的
pres p	present participle	(現在分詞)	現在分詞
pres t	present tense	(現在)	現在式
pron	pronoun	(代)	代名詞

pt	past tense	(過去)	過去式
RC	Roman Catholic	(天主教)	天主教
reflex	reflexive	(反身)	反身的,反身式
rel	relative	(關係)	關係詞
sb	somebody	(某人)	某人
Scot	Scottish	(蘇)	蘇格蘭的,蘇格蘭語
sing	singular	(單)	單數(的)
sth	something	(某事物)	某物或某事
suff	suffix	(字尾)	字尾
superl	superlative	(最高)	最高級
trans	transitive	(及物)	及物的
[U]	uncountable noun	(不可數)	不可數名詞
US	America(n)	(美)	美國(的)
usu	usual(ly)	(通常)	通常的(地)
v, *vv*	verb(s)	(動)	動詞
[VP]	Verb Pattern	(動型)	動詞類型
vi	verb intransitive	(不及物動詞)	不及物動詞
vt	verb transitive	(及物動詞)	及物動詞
⇨	look at	(參看)	參看
♂	male	(男性)	男性(的)
♀	female	(女性)	女性(的)

Specialist English registers + abbreviations used
專門名詞及其略語

accounts	帳目
aerospace	太空
algebra (alg)	代數學(代數)
anatomy (anat)	解剖學(解剖)
architecture (archit)	建築學(建築)
arithmetic (arith)	算術(算術)
art	藝術
astronomy (astron)	天文學(天文)
ballet	芭蕾舞
biblical	聖經的,聖經中的(聖經)
biology (biol)	生物學(生物)
book-keeping	簿記
botany (bot)	植物學(植物)
business	貿易(貿)
chemistry (chem)	化學(化學)
cinema	電影
commerce (comm)	商業(商)
computers (comp)	電子計算機(計算機)
cricket	板球戲
ecclesiastical (eccles)	教會的(教會)
engineering (eng)	工程學(工程)
electricity (electr)	電學(電)
farming	農業
finance (fin)	財政學(財政)
football	足球
gambling	賭博
geology (geol)	地質學(地質)
geometry (geom)	幾何學(幾何)
grammar (gram)	文法(文法)
history (hist)	歷史(史)
journalism	新聞學
legal	法律

Abbreviations used in the text

linguistics (ling)	語言學(語言)
mathematics (maths)	數學(數學)
mechanics (mech)	機械學(機械)
medical (med)	醫學的(醫)
meteorology (met)	氣象學(氣象)
military (mil)	軍語(軍)
music	音樂
mythology (myth)	神話
nautical (naut)	航海的(航海)
pathology (path)	病理學(病理)
philosophy (phil)	哲學(哲)
phonetics (phon)	語音學(語音)
photography (photo)	攝影術(攝影)
physics (phys)	物理學(物理)
physiology (physiol)	生理學(生理)
politics (pol)	政治學(政治)
psychology (psych)	心理學(心理)
racing	賽馬,賽車
radio telegraphy (radio)	無線電報(無線電)
rugby	橄欖球
science	科學
sport	運動
tennis	網球
theatre	戲劇
trigonometry (trig)	三角學(三角)
zoology (zool)	動物學(動物)

Stylistic values
字格標準

archaic	古語(古)
colloquial (colloq)	俗語,口語(俗)
dated	過時用語
derogatory (derog)	貶抑語(貶)
dialect (dial)	方言(方)
emotive (emot)	情感的(情感)
emphatic (emph)	强勢語
euphemistic (euphem)	委婉語
facetious (facet)	玩笑語
figurative (fig)	比喻用法(喻)
formal	正式用語
humorous (hum)	詼諧語(諧)
ironical (ironic)	反語的,反語用法(反語)
jocular (joc)	戲謔語(謔)
laudatory (laud)	讚美語(讚)
literally (lit)	按照字面(字面)
literary (liter)	文學的(文)
modern use (mod use)	現代用法
old use	舊用法
pejorative (pej)	輕蔑語(蔑)
poetic (poet)	詩中用語(詩)
proverb (prov)	諺語(諺)
rare	罕用的(罕)
rhetorical (rhet)	修辭學的(修辭)
slang (sl)	俚語(俚)
vulgar (vulg)	粗鄙用語(鄙)
⚠ taboo	避諱語(諱)

Aa

A¹, a /eɪ ; e/ (*pl* A's, a's /eɪz ; ez/) the first letter of the English alphabet: 英文字母的第一個字母: *He knows the subject from A to Z,* knows it thoroughly. 他精通此一科目(從頭到尾徹底了解)。**A1** /ˌeɪ ˈwʌn ; ˈeˈwʌn/ **(a)** (of ships) classified as first class. (指船舶)列爲第一等的。⇨ Lloyd's. **(b)** (colloq) excellent: (俗)高級的; 頭等的; 極佳的: *an A1 dinner;* 頭等餐; *feeling A1,* in excellent health. 感覺健康極佳。

a² /ə ; ə; *strong form:* eɪ ; e/, **an** /ən ; ən; *strong form:* æn ; æn/ *indef art* **1** one: 一個: *I said ˈa train was coming, not ˈthe train.* 我是說'一輛火車'正駛來,不是'那輛火車'。*I have a pen* (*pl some pens*). 我有一枝筆(複數用 some pens)。*Have you a pen* (*pl any pens*)? 你有一枝筆(複數用 any pens)嗎? Cf 參較 *some, any, several, a few* with *pl nn.* **2** (used in the pattern ***a*** + *adj* or *pron* of number and quantity): (用於 a+adj 或 pron 的句型中,表示數與量): *a lot of money;* 很多錢; *a great many friends;* 很多朋友; *a few books;* 幾本書; *a little more.* 再多一點。**3** (with possessives): (與所有格名詞或代名詞連用): *a friend of my father's,* one of my father's friends; 我父親的一個朋友; *a book of John's,* one of John's books. 約翰的一本書。**4** (used in the pattern ***many / such / what*** + ***a***): (用於 many/such/what+a 的句型中): *Many a man would be glad of the opportunity / such an opportunity.* 許多人都會對這機會(這樣一個機會)感到高興。*What an opportunity you missed!* 你失去了多麼好的一個機會呵! **5** (used in the pattern ***half*** + ***a*** + *n*): (用於 half+a+n 的句型中): *half a dozen;* 半打; *half an hour;* 半小時; (before 1971) *half a crown,* the sum of 2s 6d. (1971年以前)半克郎(等於二先令六辨士之錢數)。Cf 參較 *a half-crown,* former coin worth 2s 6d (= $12\frac{1}{2}$p). 半克郎(昔日面值二先令六辨士的硬幣)(= $12\frac{1}{2}$ 辨士)。**6** (used in the pattern ***as / how / so / too*** + *adj* + ***a***): (用於 as/how/so/too+adj+a 的句型中): *He's not so big a fool as he looks.* 他並不是像他表面上看起來那樣的一個大傻瓜。*She's as clever a girl as you can wish to meet.* 她就是那種你希望遇見的聰明女孩子。*It's too difficult a book for me.* 對我來說,這是一本非常難的書。**7** that which is called; any; every (no *article* in *pl*): 所謂的;任何的;每一(複數不用冠詞): *A horse is an animal.* 馬是動物。Cf 參較 *Horses are animals.* **8** (When two objects, articles, etc naturally go together and are thought of as a unit, the *indef art* is not repeated): (當兩件物品等具有自然連帶關係,且被認爲是一個單位時,不須重複不定冠詞): *a cup and saucer;* 一副杯碟; *a knife and fork.* 一副刀叉。**9** (used with a person's name, and the title *Mr, Mrs,* etc to indicate that the person is perhaps unknown to the person addressed): (與人名及 Mr, Mrs 等稱號或頭銜連用,表示此人可能爲對方所不認識): *A Mr White has called.* 有一位懷特先生來訪過(或來過電話)。*A Mrs Green is asking to see you.* 有一位格林太太要見你。**10** one like: 像…的一個(人或物): *He thinks he's a Napoleon,* a man like Napoleon. 他認爲他是一個像拿破崙一樣的人物。**11** ***of / at a,*** (in some phrases) the same: (用於某些片語中)相同的;同一的: *They're all of a size.* 它們都是同樣大小的(全是同號的)。*Carry them three at a time.* 每次搬三件。***Birds of a feather flock together,*** (prov) people of the same kind like to be together. (諺)物以類聚。**12** (used distributively): (作分配語用): *twice a month;* 每月二次; *20p a pound;* 每磅二十辨士; *50p an hour;* 每小時五十辨士; *sixty miles an hour.* 每小時六十哩。

aback /əˈbæk ; əˈbæk/ *adv* backwards. 向後地;後退地。***be ˌtaken aˈback,*** be startled, disconcerted. 吃驚;驚慌。

aba·cus /ˈæbəkəs ; ˈæbəkəs/ (*pl* -cuses /-kəsɪz ; -kəˌsɪz/ or -ci /ˈæbəsaɪ ; ˈæbəˌsaɪ/) *n* frame with beads or balls sliding on rods, for teaching numbers to children, or (still in the East) for calculating; early form of digital computer. 算盤(木框內有珠或球可在細桿上滑動,用以教兒童算術,或仍用於東方作算具者);早期的數位計算機。

an abacus

abaft /əˈbɑːft *US:* əˈbæft ; əˈbæft/ *adv, prep* (naut) at, in, toward, the stern half of a ship; nearer the stern than; behind. (航海)在船尾;向船尾;較…更接近船尾;在後。

aban·don¹ /əˈbændən ; əˈbændən/ *vt* **1** [VP6A] go away from, not intending to return to; forsake: 拋棄;遺棄: *The order was given to ~ ship,* for all on board to leave the (sinking) ship. 下令棄船(命令船上所有的人員離開下沉中的船)。*The cruel man ~ed his wife and child.* 那個狠心的男人遺棄了他的妻兒。**2** [VP6A] give up: 放棄: *They ~ed the attempt,* stopped trying. 他們放棄嘗試。*They had ~ed all hope,* no longer had any hope. 他們已經放棄了一切希望(不再存有任何希望)。*The new engine design had to be ~ed for lack of financial support.* 因缺乏經費支持,不得不放棄新引擎的設計。**3** [VP14] ~ ***oneself to,*** give oneself up completely to, eg passions, impulses: 縱情;恣意;耽溺: *He ~ed himself to despair.* 他陷於絕望;他自暴自棄。**~ed** *part adj* **1** given up to bad ways; depraved; profligate: 耽於惡習的;墮落的;放縱的;恣意的: *You ~ed wretch!* 你這個惡棍! **2** deserted; forsaken. 被遺棄的;被拋棄的。**~·ment** *n* [U].

aban·don² /əˈbændən ; əˈbændən/ *n* [U] careless freedom, as when one gives way to impulses: 放任;放縱;縱情;狂放: *waving their arms with ~.* 盡情地揮搖著他們的手臂。

abase /əˈbeɪs ; əˈbes/ *vt* [VP6B] ~ ***oneself,*** humiliate or degrade oneself: 屈辱;自貶: *~ oneself so far as to do sth,* lower oneself in dignity to the extent of doing sth. 自貶身份至做某事的地步。**~·ment** *n* [U].

abash /əˈbæʃ ; əˈbæʃ/ *vt* [VP6A] (passive only) cause to feel self-conscious or embarrassed: (僅用於被動語態)使感覺不自然;使侷促不安;使困窘;使感到尷尬: *The poor man stood / felt ~ed at this display of wealth,* was confused, not knowing what to do or say. 那個窮人面對着這番財富的炫耀,感到惶惑不知所措。

abate /əˈbeɪt ; əˈbet/ *vt, vi* **1** [VP6A, 2A] (liter) (of winds, storms, floods, pain, etc) make or become less: (文)(指風,暴風雨,洪水,疼痛等)減少;減小;減退: *The ship sailed when the storm ~d.* 這船在暴風雨減弱時起航。**2** [VP6A] (legal) bring to an end; abolish: (法律)廢除;廢止: *We must ~ the smoke nuisance in our big cities.* 我們必須消除我們大城市裡討厭的煙氣。 **~·ment** *n* [U] abating; decrease. 減少;減小;減退;廢除;廢止。

ab·at·toir /ˈæbətwɑː(r) *US:* ˌæbəˈtwɑːr ; ˌæbəˈtwɑr/ *n* slaughter-house (for cattle, sheep, etc). (宰牛羊等的)屠宰場。

abbé /ˈæbeɪ *US:* ˌæˈbeɪ ; ˈæbe/ *n* (courtesy title for a) French priest, esp one without official duties. 法國傳教士(尤指無公務者);法國教士之尊稱;神父。

ab·bess /ˈæbes ; ˈæbɪs/ *n* woman (*Mother Superior*) at the head of a convent or nunnery. 女修道院院長。

ab·bey /ˈæbɪ ; ˈæbɪ/ *n* (*pl* -beys) **1** building(s) in which men (*monks*) or women (*nuns*) live as a community in the service of God. 修道院(修士或修女修道之所)。 **2** the whole number of monks or nuns in an ~. 修道院中全體修士或修女。 **3** church or house which was once an ~ or part of an ~. (曾爲修道院或修道院之一部份的)大教堂或大宅第。 **the A~**, often used of Westminster A~, London. (常用以指)倫敦西敏寺。

ab·bot /ˈæbət ; ˈæbət/ *n* man (*Father Superior*) at the head of the monks in an abbey or monastery. 修道院院長;方丈;住持。

ab·brevi·ate /əˈbriːvɪeɪt ; əˈbrivɪˌet/ *vt* [VP6A, 14] shorten (a word, title, etc): 將(字,銜稱等)縮短: ~ *January to Jan.* 將 January 縮寫爲 Jan。⇨ abridge. **ab·brevi·ation** /əˌbriːvɪˈeɪʃn ; əˌbrivɪˈeʃən/ *n* **1** [U] abbreviating or being ~d. 縮寫;縮短。 **2** [C] shortened form (esp of a word). (尤指字的)縮寫式。⇨ App 2, 9. 參看附錄二,九。

ABC /ˌeɪ biː ˈsiː ; ˈeˈbiˈsi/ *n* **1** the letters A to Z of the (Roman) alphabet. 從A到Z的(羅馬或拉丁)字母。 **2** simplest facts of a subject, to be learnt first. (一門學科的)基本要素;(初學者必學的)基本知識;初步;入門。

ab·di·cate /ˈæbdɪkeɪt ; ˈæbdəˌket/ *vt, vi* **1** [VP6A] give up, renounce, a high office, authority or control, responsibility. 放棄(高職位,權柄或統治,職責)。 **2** [VP2A] give up the throne: 放棄王位;退位;遜位: *King Edward VIII ~d in 1936 and was created Duke of Windsor.* 英王愛德華八世於 1936 年放棄王位並受封爲溫莎公爵。 **ab·di·ca·tion** /ˌæbdɪˈkeɪʃn ; ˌæbdəˈkeʃən/ *n* **1** [U] abdicating. 放棄權位、職責等;放棄王位;退位;遜位。 **2** [C] instance of this. 放棄權位、職責、王位等的實例。

ab·do·men /ˈæbdəmən ; ˈæbdəmən/ *n* **1** (colloq 俗 = *belly*) part of the body that includes the stomach and bowels. 腹部(包括腸胃)。⇨ the illus at trunk. 參看 trunk 之插圖。 **2** last of the three divisions of an insect, spider, etc. (昆蟲,蜘蛛等之)腹部(即其身體三部份中之最後一部份)。⇨ the illus at insect. 參看 insect 之插圖。

ab·domi·nal /æbˈdɒmɪnl ; æbˈdɑmənl/ *adj* in, of, for, the abdomen: 腹部中的;腹部的: ~ *pains;* 腹痛;肚子痛; *an ~ operation.* 腹部手術。⇨ intestinal.

ab·duct /æbˈdʌkt ; æbˈdʌkt/ *vt* [VP6A] take or lead (esp a woman or child) away unlawfully, by force or fraud. 綁架;誘拐(尤指婦女或小孩)。⇨ kidnap. **ab·duc·tion** /æbˈdʌkʃn ; æbˈdʌkʃən/ *n*

abeam /əˈbiːm ; əˈbim/ *adv* (naut) on a line at a right angle to the length of a ship or aircraft: (航海)在與船身(或航空器機身)成直角的線上;在正橫;舷向: *The lighthouse was ~ of the ship.* 燈塔正對着船的舷側。

abed /əˈbed ; əˈbɛd/ *adv* (old use) in bed. (舊用法)在床上。

ab·er·ra·tion /ˌæbəˈreɪʃn ; ˌæbəˈreʃən/ *n* **1** [U] (usu fig) straying away from the right path, from what is normal: (通常作喻)離正道;失常;錯亂;越軌;差: *stealing sth in a moment of ~.* 一時糊塗偷了東西。 **2** [C] instance of this; defect: 失常之行爲或實例;過失: *The delay was caused by an ~ in the computer.* 那次延擱係因電腦誤差所致。 **ab·er·rant** /æˈberənt ; æbˈɛrənt/ *adj* straying away from what is normal, expected or usual; not true to type. 離正道的;失常的;錯亂的;越軌的;差的。

abet /əˈbet ; əˈbɛt/ *vt* (-tt-) [VP6A, 14] (legal) help (sb) (*in* doing wrong); encourage (vice, crime): (法律)幫助(某人)(爲非作歹);教唆;唆使: ~ *sb in a crime.* 教唆某人犯罪。 ***aid and ~ sb,*** (legal) be an accomplice in his wrongdoing. (法律)與某人爲共犯。

abey·ance /əˈbeɪəns ; əˈbeəns/ *n* [U] (formal) condition of not being in force or in use for a time: (正式用語)暫時無效;暫緩: *The question is in ~,* is suspended, eg until more information is obtained. 這問題暫時擱置(例如,待獲得較多資料時再行研究)。 ***fall/go into ~,*** (legal) (of a law, rule, custom, etc) be suspended; be no longer observed. (法律)(指法令,規則,習俗等)失效;不再爲大家所遵行;中止。

ab·hor /əbˈhɔː(r) ; əbˈhɔr/ *vt* (-rr-) [VP6A] think of with hatred and disgust; detest: 憎恨;厭惡: ~ *cruelty to animals.* 憎恨虐待動物。 **~·rence** /əbˈhɒrəns *US:* -ˈhɔːr- ; əbˈhɔrəns/ *n* [U] hatred and disgust: 憎恨;厭惡: *hold sth in ~rence;* 憎恨某事物; *his ~rence of flattery.* 他對於諂媚之憎惡。 **~·rent** /əbˈhɒrənt *US:* -ˈhɔːr- ; əbˈhɔrənt/ *adj* hateful; causing horror (*to* sb, *to* his feelings). 可恨的;可惡的(與 to 連用,後接某人或其感情)。

abide /əˈbaɪd ; əˈbaɪd/ *vt, vi* (*pt, pp* (1,2,4) ~d, (3) abode /əˈbəʊd ; əˈbod/) **1** [VP3A] ~ ***by,*** (formal) be faithful to; keep: (正式用語)忠於;遵守: ~ *by a promise/decision.* 遵守諾言(決定)。 *I ~ by* (colloq 'stick to') *what I said.* (等於俗語的 I stick to what I said) 我堅守我所說的話。 *You'll have to ~ by the consequences,* endure them. (Used only of undesirable consequences.) 你將必須忍受其後果。(僅用於指不良之後果。) **2** [VP6A] (esp with *can't* or *couldn't*) endure; bear: (尤與 can't 或 couldn't 連用)忍耐;忍受: *She can't ~ that man.* 她無法忍受那個人。 **3** [VP2C] (in old or liter use) rest, remain, stay: (舊用法或文學用語)停留;居留;逗留: ~ *at/in a place;* 居留於某地; ~ *with sb.* 與某人同住。 **4** [VP6A] (liter) wait for: (文)等待: ~ *the event;* 等待事件之發生; ~ *sb's coming.* 等待某人到來。 **abid·ing** *adj* (liter) never-ending; lasting. (文)永無終止的;永恆的。

abil·ity /əˈbɪlətɪ ; əˈbɪlətɪ/ *n* **1** [U] (potential) capacity or power (to do sth physical or mental): (從事體力或心智方面之事務的)能力;潛力: *to the best of my ~,* as well as I can. 盡我的能力。 *I do not doubt your ~ to do the work.* 我不懷疑你有擔任這項工作的能力。 **2** [U] cleverness; intelligence: 聰明;智慧;才智: *a man of great ~.* 極有才智的人。 **3** [C] (*pl* -ties) special natural power to do sth well; talent: 才能;才幹: *a man of many abilities.* 有多方面才能的人。

ab initio /ˌæb ɪˈnɪʃɪəʊ ; ˈæbɪˈnɪʃɪˌo/ *adv* (Lat) from the beginning. (拉)從頭。

ab·ject /ˈæbdʒekt ; ˈæbdʒɛkt/ *adj* **1** (of conditions) wretched; miserable: (指境況)悲慘的;難堪的;可憐的: *living in ~ poverty.* 生活赤貧。 **2** (of persons, their actions, behaviour) degraded; deserving contempt because cowardly or self-abasing: (指人,動作,行爲)下流的;下賤的;卑鄙的;(因怯懦或自貶而)可鄙的: ~ *behaviour;* 卑鄙的行爲; *an ~ apology.* 低聲下氣的道歉;求饒。 **~·ly** *adv* **ab·jec·tion** /æbˈdʒekʃn ; æbˈdʒɛkʃən/ *n*

ab·jure /əbˈdʒʊə(r) ; əbˈdʒʊr/ *vt* [VP6A] (formal) promise or swear solemnly on oath or in public to give up, eg a belief, a right, evil ways: (正式用語)承諾或宣誓放棄某種信仰、權利、惡習等: ~ *one's religion.* 誓言放棄其宗教信仰。 **ab·jur·ation** /ˌæbdʒʊəˈreɪʃn ; ˌæbdʒʊˈreʃən/ *n* [U] abjuring; state of having been ~d; [C] action of this: 誓棄;誓絕;宣誓放棄之行爲: *an abjuration of faith.* 放棄信仰。

ab·la·tive /ˈæblətɪv ; ˈæblətɪv/ *adj, n* (gram) name

of a form in Latin nouns indicating an agent, instrument or cause. (文法)奪格(拉丁文名詞表示動作者,工具或原因的格)；奪格的。**the ～ case,** ⇨ case¹(3).

ab·laut /ˈæblaʊt ; ˈɑblaʊt/ *n* (ling) systematic vowel changes in verb forms of Indo-European languages (as in *drive, drove, driven*). (語言)母音變換 (印歐語系之語言中，母音之有系統的變換，例如 drive, drove, driven 中各母音之變換)。

ablaze /əˈbleɪz ; əˈblez/ *pred adj, adv* **1** on fire, in a blaze: 着火；燃燒；熾燃: *set it ～.* 點火燒之。*The whole building was soon ～.* 整個建築物不一會就全燒起來了。 **2** (fig) shining; bright; excited: (喻)光輝明亮的;激動的: *The streets were ～ with lights.* 各街道燈火輝煌。*Her face was ～ with anger.* 她怒容滿面。

able /ˈeɪbl ; ˈebl̩/ *adj* **1** *be ～ to do sth,* have the power, means or opportunity to do sth: 有能力、辦法或機會做某事；能: *Shall／Will you be ～ to come?* 你能來嗎？ *You are better ～ to do it than I am.* 你比我更有能力擔任此事。⇨ can², could. **2** (-r, -st) clever; capable; having or showing knowledge or skill: 聰明的;能幹的;有本事的: *an ～ lawyer;* 精明的律師； *an ～ speech;* 一篇表現睿智的演說； *the ～st／most ～ man I know.* 我所認識最有才幹的人。**ˌ～-ˈbodied** /-ˈbɒdɪd ; -ˈbɑdɪd/ *adj* physically strong. 身體强壯的。**ˌ～ ˈseaman, ˌ～-ˌbodied ˈseaman** *n* (GB abbr 英略 = AB) seaman trained and certified for all duties. (受過訓練並獲證明能承擔各種任務的)一等水手;二等水兵。**ably** /ˈeɪblɪ ; ˈeblɪ/ *adv* in an ～ manner. 精明幹練地;能幹地。

ab·lu·tion /əˈbluːʃn ; əbˈluʃən/ *n* (usu *pl*) (formal) ceremonial washing of the hands or the body, esp as an act of religion: (通常用複數) (正式用語) 洗手禮；淨體禮(尤指宗教上者): *perform one's ～s,* (often joc or fac) wash oneself. (常作諧或玩笑語) 沐浴。

ab·ne·ga·tion /ˌæbnɪˈgeɪʃn ; ˌæbnɪˈgeʃən/ *n* [U] (formal) self-denial; (often 常作 **ˌself-ˈ～**) self-sacrifice. (正式用語)克己;自制;自我犧牲。

ab·nor·mal /æbˈnɔːml ; æbˈnɔrml̩/ *adj* different, often in an undesirable way, from what is normal, ordinary or expected. 不正常的; 反常的; 變態的。**～·ly** *adv* **～·ity** /ˌæbnɔːˈmælətɪ ; ˌæbnɔrˈmælətɪ/ *n* [U] quality of being ～; [C] (*pl* -ties) sth that is ～. 不正常;反常;變態(性)；反常或變態的事物。

Abo /ˈæbəʊ ; ˈæbo/ *n* (*pl* Abos) ⚠ (derog) (諱,貶) = Aborigine.

aboard /əˈbɔːd ; əˈbord/ *adv, prep* on (to) or in(to) a ship, aircraft, or (US) a train or motor-coach: 在(向)船上,飛機上,或(美)火車或公共汽車上: *It's time to go ～.* 是上船(機,車等)的時候了。 *All ～!* (ie Go or come ～.) 請各位上船(飛機等)！ *Welcome ～!* (eg as a greeting by a stewardess on an aircraft.) 歡迎各位搭乘本飛機(船等)！ (例如空中小姐對旅客所作的歡迎語。)

abode¹ /əˈbəʊd ; əˈbod/ *n* **1** (old or liter use) house; dwelling-place: (舊用法或文學用語) 房屋;住所: *take up one's ～ with one's parents-in-law,* go and live with them. (男)與岳父母同住;(女)與翁姑同住。 **2** (legal) (法律) *place of ～,* domicile. 住所。***of／with no fixed ～,*** having no fixed dwelling-place. 無固定住所。

abode² /əˈbəʊd ; əˈbod/ *pt, pp* of abide.

abol·ish /əˈbɒlɪʃ ; əˈbɑlɪʃ/ *vt* [VP6A] put an end to, do away with, eg war, slavery, an old custom. 廢止; 廢除; 革除 (例如戰爭,奴役,舊習俗)。**abol·ition** /ˌæbəˈlɪʃn ; ˌæbəˈlɪʃən/ *n* [U] ～ing or being ～ed (esp used, in the 18th and 19th cc, of Negro slavery). 廢止;廢除;(尤用以指十八及十九世紀之)黑奴制度的廢除。 **abol·ition·ist** /ˌæbəˈlɪʃənɪst ; ˌæbəˈlɪʃənɪst/ *n* (esp) person who wished to ～ Negro slavery. 廢止論者;(尤指)主張廢除黑奴制度者。

A-bomb /ˈeɪ bɒm ; ˈeˌbɑm/ *n* ⇨ atomic.

abom·in·able /əˈbɒmɪnəbl ; əˈbɑmnəbl̩/ *adj* **1** causing hatred and disgust (*to* sb). 可憎惡的(與 to 連用，後接某人)。 **2** (colloq) unpleasant; bad: (俗)令人不愉快的;惡劣的: *～ weather／food.* 惡劣的天氣(食物)。**～ ˈsnowman,** = yeti. **abom·in·ably** /-əblɪ ; -əblɪ/ *adv*

abom·in·ate /əˈbɒmɪneɪt ; əˈbɑməˌnet/ *vt* [VP6A, C] detest; feel hatred or disgust for; (colloq) dislike. 憎惡; 厭惡; (俗)不喜歡。 **abom·in·ation** /əˌbɒmɪˈneɪʃn ; əˌbɑməˈneʃən/ **1** [U] horror and disgust: 憎惡;厭惡: *hold sth in abomination.* 憎惡某事物。 **2** [C] sth that arouses horror and disgust (*to* sb). 令人憎惡之事物(與 to 連用,後接某人)。

abo·rig·inal /ˌæbəˈrɪdʒənl ; ˌæbəˈrɪdʒənl̩/ *adj* (of races of people, living creatures, etc) belonging to, existing in, a region from earliest times, or from the time when the region was first known. (指人類種族，生物等) 從最早期就屬於或存在於某一地區的;當某一地區初爲人所知時就屬於或存在於該地區的;土著的。□ *n* ～ inhabitant, plant, etc of a region. (某地區之) 土著; 土人; 土產植物等。 **abo·rig·ines** /ˌæbəˈrɪdʒəniːz ; ˌæbəˈrɪdʒəˌniz/ *n pl* **the ～,** the ～ inhabitants. 土著;土人。**Abo·rig·ine** /ˌæbəˈrɪdʒənɪ ; ˌæbəˈrɪdʒəˌni/ *n* Australian ～ person. 澳洲土人。

abort /əˈbɔːt ; əˈbɔrt/ *vt, vi* [VP6A, 2A] come to nothing; miscarry; terminate prematurely: (使)成空;(使)失敗;(使)不能達到預期效果；早期終止；頓挫；(使)流產: *～ a space mission,* cancel it in space, eg because of mechanical trouble. 使一太空任務不能如期完成(例如因機械故障而取消)。

abor·tion /əˈbɔːʃn ; əˈbɔrʃən/ *n* **1** [U] (legal) expulsion of the foetus from the womb during the first 28 weeks of pregnancy; helping or causing this: (法律)流產(於開始懷孕至二十八週中,胎兒自子宮中排出)；小產;使流產;墮胎: *A～ was formerly a crime in Britain.* 以前在英國墮胎是一種犯罪行爲。 **2** [C] instance of this; miscarriage of birth: 流產之實例;小產;墮胎: *have／procure an ～.* 流產;墮胎。 **3** [C] creature produced by ～; dwarfed or misshapen creature; (fig) plan, effort, etc that has failed to develop. 流產兒;矮小或畸形之生物;(喻)未能發展的計畫、努力等。 **～·ist** /-ɪst ; -ɪst/ *n* person who brings about an ～; person who favours and supports legal ～. 墮胎者;打胎者;贊成合法墮胎者。

abort·ive /əˈbɔːtɪv ; əˈbɔrtɪv/ *adj* coming to nothing; unsuccessful; arrested in development: 成空的; 未成功的;失敗的;發育不全的; 進展受阻礙的;頓挫的: *plans that proved ～;* 終歸失敗的計畫; *an ～ rebellion.* 一次流產的叛變。**～·ly** *adv*

abound /əˈbaʊnd ; əˈbaʊnd/ *vi* [VP3A] ***～ in／with,*** have, exist, in great numbers or quantities: 大量具有;大量存在;富於: *The river ～s in fish.* 這條河有大量的魚。*Fish ～ in the river.* 魚類大量地生存於這條河中。*The hut ～ed with vermin.* 這棚屋有極多的蟲子(蚤,蝨等)。*Vermin ～ed in the hut.* 蟲子大量地生長在這棚屋中。

about¹ /əˈbaʊt ; əˈbaʊt/ *adv of degree* (contrasted with *just* or *exactly*) a little more or less than; a little before or after: (與 just 或 exactly 相對)比…稍多或稍少;在…的稍前或稍後;大約;前後;左右: *～ as high as that tree;* 大約像那棵樹那樣高; *for ～ three miles;* 大約三哩; *～ six o'clock;* 六點鐘左右; *on or ～ the fifth of May.* 在五月五日或其前後。*I've had just ～ enough* (colloq understatement for 'quite enough'). 我已經差不多夠了(俗,是'十分夠了'語氣較輕的說法)。*It's ～ time you stopped being so rude* (colloq understatement for 'quite time'). 是你停止粗野行爲的時候了(俗,是'現在應該'語氣較輕的說法)。 ***That's ～ (the size of) it,*** (colloq) That is how I assess it, how I see it. (俗) (大小)差不多了;大致如此(如我所估計或所看到的)。

about² /əˈbaʊt ; əˈbaʊt/ *adv part* (may usu be replaced by *around* in 1, 2 and 3) (第 1, 2, 3 義通常可由 around 代替) **1** (with *vv* of movement) here and there, in no particular direction: (與表示動向的動詞連用) 到處; 無固定方向: *The children were rushing ～.* 小孩子們到處亂闖。*The boys were* *climbing ~ on the rocks.* 男孩們在岩石上亂爬。*Don't drop cigarette ash ~.* 勿亂彈煙灰。*Don't leave waste paper and empty bottles ~ in the park.* 不要在公園中到處丟棄廢紙及空瓶。*He's taking Jane ~ a lot these days,* eg to dances, cinemas, theatres. 他近來帶着珍到處去玩(例如參加舞會,看電影,看戲)。**2** (with other *vv*, indicating position, etc): (與其他動詞連用,表示位置等): *There were books lying ~ on the floor/people sitting ~ on the grass.* 有些書散置在地板上(有些人坐在草地各處)。**3** (with *be*): (與 be 連用): *There was no one ~,* no one to be seen. 附近見不到一個人。*There's a lot of influenza ~,* many people have it. 附近有很多人患流行性感冒。***be (out and) ~,*** be able to get out, work, etc after eg an illness. 能出外,工作等(例如病後復元)。***be up and ~,*** be out of bed and active. 起床走動。**4** ***bring sth ~,*** ⇨ bring(6). ***come ~,*** ⇨ come(16). **5** facing round; in the opposite direction: 向後轉;朝相反的方向: *It's the wrong way ~.* 方向錯了,剛相反。*A~ turn!* (GB) (英), *A~ face!* (US) (美), (mil commands) turn round to face the other way. (軍,口令)向後轉!ˌ**~-ˈface** *vi* turn and face the other way. 向後轉。□ *n* complete reversal of views, actions, etc: (觀點,行爲等的)大轉變: *He did a complete ~-face.* 他作了一個一百八十度的大轉變。**6** (of two or more persons or groups) (指兩個或兩個以上的人,或指兩組或多組) ***take turns ~; (do sth) turn and turn ~,*** ⇨ turn¹(4).

about³ /əˈbaʊt ; əˈbaʊt/ *prep* (may usu be replaced by *around* or *round* in 1, 2 and 3) (第1, 2, 3 義通常可用 around或 round代替) **1** (with *vv* of movement) here and there, in no particular direction: (與表示動向的動詞連用)到處;在…各處: *walking ~ the town;* 在市內到處走; *travelling ~ the world.* 環遊世界。**2** (with other *vv*, indicating position, state, etc): (與其他動詞連用,表示位置、狀況等): *idle men standing ~ on street corners;* 在街角上到處站立的閒人; *books and papers lying ~ the room.* 零亂散置於室內的書籍和文件。*I haven't any money ~ me,* ie with me, in my pockets. 我身上沒有帶錢。**3** near to: 在…近處;在附近: *I dropped the key somewhere ~ here.* 我把鑰匙掉在這附近某個地方了。**4** concerning; regarding; in connection with: 關於;有關: *He is careless ~ his personal appearance.* 他不關心他自己的儀表。*What do you know ~ him?* 關於他,你知道些什麼? *What is he so angry ~?* 他爲何事如此發怒? *Tell me all ~ it.* 告訴我有關此事的一切。***How/What ~...,*** used to ask for information, to make a suggestion or to get sb's opinion: …怎麼樣(用以詢問消息,提供建議或徵詢意見): *What ~ his qualifications for the position?* 他擔任此職的學經歷如何? *How ~ going to France for our holidays?* 我們到法國去度假如何? **5** concerned or occupied with: 從事;忙於: *What are you ~?* (= colloq 'up to?'). 你在做什麼? (等於口語的 'up to?')。*And while you're ~ it...,* while you're doing that.... 在你做那事的時候…。*Mind what you're ~,* Be careful what you do. 注意你所做的事;小心。***go/set ~ sth,*** deal with it: 做某事;從事: *Do you know how to go ~ it,* deal with the task? 你知道如何做這事嗎? **6** round (which is now more usu preferred): 在周圍;圍繞着(現在比較常用 round): *the fields ~ Oxford.* 在牛津四周的田野。*She hung ~ his shoulders.* 她伏在他的肩膀上。*He has his wits ~ him,* ⇨ wit. 他很機警。**7** ***~ to*** + *inf*, on the point of (doing sth), just going to (do sth): 卽將;正要: *As I was ~ to say, when you interrupted me....* 我正要說的時候,你插嘴了。*He was ~ to start.* 他卽將動身。

above¹ /əˈbʌv ; əˈbʌv/ *adv* (contrasted with *below¹*, *under¹* (1) and *underneath*) (與 below¹, under¹(1) 及 underneath 相對) **1** at a higher point; overhead; on high: 在較高處;在頭頂上空;在上面;在高處: *My bedroom is just ~.* 我的臥室就在上面。*Seen from ~, the fields looked like a geometrical pattern.* 從高處看下來,那些農田像是幾何圖案。*A voice from ~ shouted a welcome.* 從上面傳來大叫歡迎的聲音。**2** earlier (in a book, article, etc): (書籍,文章等的)前文;上文: *As was stated ~...;* 如上所述…; *See the statement ~/the ~ statement.* 見前文;見上文。**3** in Heaven: 在天上: *the Powers ~,* the heavenly powers. 上天神明。ˌ**~ ˈboard** *adv* without deception or concealment; honourably. 無欺騙或蒙蔽地;光明正大地。□ *pred adj* frank; open. 坦白的;公開的;磊落的。⇨ underhand. ˌ**~-ˈmentioned,** ˌ**~-ˈnamed** *adjj* mentioned, named, ~ (or earlier) in this book, article, etc. (在本書,本文等中)上述的;前述的。

above² /əˈbʌv ; əˈbʌv/ *prep* (contrasted with *below²*, *under²* and *underneath;* ~ may sometimes be replaced by *over* or *beyond*) (與 below², under² 及 underneath 相對; above 有時可用 over 或 beyond 替換) **1** higher than: 高於;在…之上: *The sun rose ~ the horizon.* 太陽升到地平線之上。*We were flying ~ the clouds.* 我們飛行在雲層之上。Cf 參較 We flew *over/across* the Sahara. 我們飛越過撒哈拉大沙漠。*The water came ~ our knees.* 水深達膝部以上。*A captain in the Navy ranks ~ a captain in the Army.* 海軍的 captain (上校)階級高於陸軍的 captain (上尉)。**2** greater in number, price, weight, etc: (數目)大於;(價錢)高於;(重量)超過: *The temperature has been ~ the average recently.* 近來的氣溫一直比平均溫度高。*There is nothing in this shop ~/over fifty cents.* 這個店裡沒有一樣東西價錢超過五角。*It weighs ~/over ten tons.* 它的重量超過十噸。*Applicants must be ~/over the age of 21.* 申請人年齡必須超過二十一歲。**3** more than: 多於;較…更爲: *A soldier should value honour ~ life.* 軍人應視榮譽重於生命。***~ all,*** more than anything else. 最重要者;尤其。***over and ~,*** in addition to. 除…外。**4** too great, good, difficult, etc for: (因太偉大,太好,太難等而)不做;不爲;不屑;對…太困難;超過…之能力: *If you want to learn, you must not be ~ asking* (= not be too proud to ask) *questions.* 你如果要想學習,就不要恥於發問。*He is ~ meanness and deceit,* does not show meanness or practise deceit. 他不至於做卑鄙和欺騙的事情。*This book is ~* (now more usu *beyond*) *me,* too difficult for me. 這本書對我是太難了(今比較常用 beyond 代替 above)。**5** out of reach of (because too great, good, etc): (因太偉大,奇佳等而)超越;超出…的範圍: *His heroism was ~/beyond all praise.* 他的英勇讚揚不盡。*His conduct has always been ~ suspicion.* 他的行爲一直無可置疑。**6** (various uses): (其他各種用法): *the waterfall ~* (= up stream from) *the bridge;* 在橋上游的瀑布; *live ~/beyond one's means,* in a style too expensive for one's income; 生活奢侈,所費超過其收入; *be ~ oneself,* in high spirits; 興高采烈; *get ~ oneself,* become conceited, too self-satisfied and lacking in self-control. 得意忘形;趾高氣揚。*She married ~ her station,* married sb from a higher social class. 她和一個社會階級比她高的男人結婚。

ab·ra·ca·dabra /ˌæbrəkəˈdæbrə ; ˌæbrəkəˈdæbrə/ *n* [U] magic jargon; gibberish. 符咒;咒語;莫名其妙的話;胡言亂語。

abrade /əˈbreɪd ; əˈbred/ *vt* [VP6A] rub or scrape off, wear away (skin, etc) by friction or hard rubbing. 擦掉;磨損(表皮等);刮除。

ab·rasion /əˈbreɪʒn ; əˈbreʒən/ *n* [U] rubbing, scraping, or wearing off; [C] area where sth has been worn or scraped away: 擦掉;擦傷;刮除;磨損;磨損之處;擦傷之處: *an ~ of the skin.* 皮膚之擦傷處。

ab·ras·ive /əˈbreɪsɪv ; əˈbresɪv/ *n* [U] substance (eg *emery*) used for rubbing or grinding down surfaces; [C] particular type of ~. 磨料(摩擦表面用的材料,如金剛砂);某種磨料。□ *adj* causing abrasion; (fig) harsh, rough: (導致)擦傷的;(引起)磨損的;(喻)粗糙的: *an ~ voice/character.* 粗厲的聲音(粗魯的人)。

abreast /əˈbrest ; əˈbrɛst/ *adv* (of persons, ships, etc) on a level, side by side, and facing the same way: (指人，船等) 並肩; 並排; 並列; 並駛: *walking three ~;* 三人並肩行走; *warships in line ~.* 成直線並駛編隊的戰艦。**be/keep ~ (of/with),** level with, not behind: 與…並進; 不落後: *You should read the newspapers to keep ~ of the times,* to be informed of the latest events, ideas, discoveries, etc. 你必須看報，以便跟上時代 (讀報才能知道最新發生的事件、新概念、新發現等)。

abridge /əˈbrɪdʒ ; əˈbrɪdʒ/ *vt* [VP6A] make shorter, esp by using fewer words: 刪節; 節略: *an ~d edition of 'David Copperfield';* '塊肉餘生錄' 之節本; shorten (an interview, the time sth lasts). 縮短 (會談，某事物持續之時間)。⇨ abbreviate. **~·ment, abridg·ment** *n* [U] abridging; [C] sth, eg a book, that is ~d. 刪節; 節略; 經刪節的東西; (書等之) 節本。

abroad /əˈbrɔːd ; əˈbrɔd/ *adv* **1** in or to a foreign country or countries; away from one's own country: 在國外; 到國外; 出國: *be/go/live/travel ~;* 在外國 (出國; 旅居國外; 在國外旅行); *visitors who have come from ~.* 從外國 (或海外) 來的遊客。*Do you like it ~/being ~?* 你喜歡在外國生活嗎? **2** far and wide; everywhere: 遍佈; 廣佈; 到處: *There's a rumour ~ that...,* People are saying that.... 謠言四播說是…。**3** (old use) out of doors: (舊用法) 戶外; 室外: *You were ~ early this morning.* 你今天一大早就到戶外去了。

ab·ro·gate /ˈæbrəgeɪt ; ˈæbrəˌget/ *vt* [VP6A] (formal) repeal or annul by authority. (正式用語) 廢止; 廢除。**ab·ro·ga·tion** /ˌæbrəˈgeɪʃn ; ˌæbrəˈgeʃən/ *n*

abrupt /əˈbrʌpt ; əˈbrʌpt/ *adj* **1** unexpectedly sudden: 突然的; 意外的: *The road is full of ~ turns.* 這條路有很多急彎。**2** (of speech, writing, behaviour) rough; brusque; disconnected: (指言語，寫作，行爲) 粗魯的; 唐突的; 不連貫的: *a man with an ~ manner,* ie rather impolite, gruff, blunt; 舉止粗魯的人; *an ~ style,* eg of speaking or writing. 不連貫的方式 (如說話或寫作)。**3** (of a slope) steep. (指斜坡) 陡峭的。**~·ly** *adv* **~·ness** *n*

ab·scess /ˈæbses ; ˈæbˌsɛs/ *n* [C] collection of thick yellowish-white liquid (called *pus*) formed in a cavity in the body: 膿腫; 膿瘍: *~es on the gums.* 齒齦上的膿腫。

ab·scond /əbˈskɒnd ; æbˈskɑnd/ *vi* [VP2A, 3A] **~ (with) (from),** go away suddenly, secretly, and aware of having done wrong, esp to avoid arrest. 潛逃; 逃亡。

ab·sence /ˈæbsəns ; ˈæbsn̩s/ *n* **1** [U] being away (*from*): 缺席; 不在; 離開 (與 from 連用): *~ from school;* 曠課; 缺課; *during his ~ in America,* while he was there. 在他離開此地到美國去的期間。*In the ~ of the Manager* (ie while he is away) *Mr X is in charge of the business.* 經理不在的期間，由某先生管理業務。**leave of ~,** ⇨ leave²(1). **2** [C] occasion or time of being away: 一次缺席; 不在的時間: *numerous ~s from school;* 無數次的曠課; *a long ~;* 離開很久; *after an ~ of three months.* 在離開了三個月之後。**3** [U] lack; non-existence: 缺乏; 不存在: *in the ~ of definite information.* 在缺乏確定消息的情形下。*Cold is the ~ of heat.* 冷就是缺乏熱。**4 ~ of mind,** absent-mindedness (⇨ below). 心不在焉; 神不守舍 (參看下條)。

ab·sent¹ /ˈæbsənt ; ˈæbsn̩t/ *adj* **1 ~ (from),** not present (at): 缺…; 曠…: *~ from school/work.* 曠課 (曠工)。**2** lost in thought; abstracted: 迷茫於沉思中的; 茫然的; 恍惚的: *When I spoke to him he looked at me in an ~ way but did not answer.* 當我跟他說話時，他茫然地望着我而不答話。**~·ly** *adv* (rare) (罕) = ~-mindedly. **ˌ~-ˈminded** *adj* so deep or far away in thought that one is unaware of what one is doing, what is happening around one, etc. 心不在焉的; 茫然的; 恍惚的。**~-mind·ed·ly** *adv* **~-minded·ness** *n*

ab·sent² /əbˈsent ; æbˈsɛnt/ *vt* [VP6B, 14] **~ oneself (from),** stay away (from): 離開; 不在 (與 from 連用): *Why did you ~ yourself (from school) yesterday?* 你昨天爲什麼不來 (上學)?

ab·sen·tee /ˌæbsənˈtiː ; ˌæbsn̩ˈti/ *n* person who is absent. 缺席者; 曠課者; 曠職者; 不在者; 在外者。**~ landlord,** land or house owner who habitually lives away from the place he owns. 不住在產權所在地的地主或房主; 遙領地主。**~·ism** /-ɪzəm ; -ˌɪzəm/ *n* [U] habitual failure to be present, eg the practice of being absent from work or regular duty frequently and without good reason. 時常的缺席 (例如無緣無故的時常曠工或曠職)。

ab·sinthe, ab·sinth /ˈæbsɪnθ ; ˈæbsɪnθ/ *n* [U] bitter, green alcoholic drink made with wormwood and other herbs. 苦艾酒。

ab·so·lute /ˈæbsəluːt ; ˈæbsəˌlut/ *adj* **1** complete; perfect: 完全的: *A child usually has ~ trust in its mother.* 小孩通常完全信任其母親。*When giving evidence in a law court, we must tell the ~ truth.* 在法庭作證時，我們必須完全照實說。**2** unlimited; having complete or arbitrary power: 無限制的; 有絕對權力的; 有獨裁權的; 專制的: *An ~ ruler need not ask anyone for permission to do anything.* 一個有絕對權力的統治者做任何事都不必徵得任何人的同意。**3** real; undoubted: 眞實的; 無疑的: *It is an ~ fact.* 那是絕對的事實。*He must not be punished unless you have ~ proof of his guilt.* 他不可受懲罰，除非你有確實的證據證明他有罪。**4** unconditional; unqualified: 無條件的: *An ~ promise must be kept whatever happens.* 無條件的諾言無論在任何情形下都必須遵守。**5** not relative; not dependent on or measured by other things. 非相對的; 非基於他物或以他物來衡量的; 絕對的。**~ zero,** lowest temperature theoretically possible, = −273·15°C. 絕對零度 (理論上的最低溫度，等於攝氏零下 273·15 度)。⇨ App 5. 參看附錄五。**~·ly** *adv* **1** completely: 完全地: *~ly impossible;* 絕對不可能; *~ly right.* 完全對。**2** unconditionally: 無條件地: *He refused ~ly.* 他說什麼都不答應。**3** /ˌæbsəˈluːtlɪ ; ˌæbsəˈlutlɪ/ (colloq, in answer to a question, or as a comment) quite so; certainly. (俗，作爲對一問題的回答或評語) 十分對; 對極了; 當然。**ab·so·lut·ism** /ˈæbsəluːtɪzəm ; ˈæbsəlutˌɪzəm/ *n* (pol) ~(2) government; despotism. (政治) 專制政治; 專制主義。

ab·sol·ution /ˌæbsəˈluːʃn ; ˌæbsəˈluʃən/ *n* [U] (RC Church) freeing (esp by a priest in the sacrament of penance) from the consequences of sin: (天主教) (尤指神父在告解中之) 赦罪: *grant, pronounce ~ from sin.* 赦罪。⇨ penance.

ab·solve /əbˈzɒlv ; æbˈsɑlv/ *vt* [VP6A, 14] **~ (from),** declare free (from sin, guilt, a promise, duty, etc): 宣佈赦免 (罪過); 免除 (履行諾言，責任等): *I ~ you from all blame/from your vows.* 我讓你免受一切責難 (我解除你的誓約)。

ab·sorb /əbˈsɔːb ; əbˈsɔrb/ *vt* **1** [VP6A] take or suck in, eg a liquid; take in, eg heat, light, (fig) knowledge, etc: 吸收 (如液體，熱，光等); (喻) 吸收 (知識等): *Paper that ~s ink is called blotting-paper.* 吸收墨水的紙稱爲吸墨紙。*Dry sand ~s water.* 乾沙吸收水份。*The clever boy ~ed all the knowledge his teachers could give him.* 那聰明的男孩把他老師所能教他的知識都吸收了。**2** [VP6A] use up much of the attention, interest or time of: 吸引…的注意力或興趣; 耗費…的時間; 使全神貫注; 使專心: *His business ~s him.* 他的業務使他全神貫注。*He is completely ~ed in his business.* 他完全專心於他的業務。*He was ~ed in a book.* 他全神貫注於一本書。**~·ent** /-ənt ; -ənt/ *adj, n* (substance) capable of ~ing: 能吸收的 (物質); 有吸收力的 (物質); 吸水的 (物質): *~ent cotton wool.* 吸水脫脂棉。**ab·sorp·tion** /əbˈsɔːpʃn ; əbˈsɔrpʃən/ *n* [U] ~ing or being ~ed; engrossment: 吸收; 專注: *Complete absorption in sport interfered with his studies.* 全心專注於運動妨碍了他的學業。

ab·stain /əbˈsteɪn ; əbˈsten/ *vi* [VP3A, 2A] ~

(from), hold oneself back, refrain: 戒除;禁絶: *His doctor told him to ~ from beer and wine.* 他的醫生告訴他要戒酒。*At the last election he ~ed (from voting).* 上次選舉他棄權(沒投票)。**~er** *n* person who ~s, esp *total ~er,* one who never takes alcoholic drinks. 戒除者;禁絶者;(尤指)絶對戒酒的人。

ab·stemi·ous /əb'sti:mɪəs ; æb'stimɪəs/ *adj* sparing or moderate, esp in taking food and drink; frugal: (尤指在飲食方面)有節制的;節儉的: *~ habits;* 節制飲食的習慣; *an ~ meal.* 節儉的一餐。**~·ly** *adv* **~·ness** *n*

ab·sten·tion /əb'stenʃn ; æb'stɛnʃən/ *n* [U] ~ *(from)*, abstaining, esp not using one's vote at an election, etc; [C] instance of this: 戒除;(尤指選舉投票等的)棄權;棄權的實例: *six votes for, three against and two ~s.* 六票贊成,三票反對,兩票棄權。

ab·sti·nence /'æbstɪnəns ; 'æbstənəns/ *n* [U] ~ *(from)*, abstaining, eg from food, enjoyment, esp alcoholic drink. (對食物,享樂,尤指飲酒之)禁戒;戒除。**,total '~**, refraining completely from alcoholic drink. 絶對戒酒。

ab·stract¹ /'æbstrækt ; 'æbstrækt/ *adj* **1** separated from what is real or concrete; thought of separately from facts, objects or particular examples: 抽象的: *A flower is beautiful, but beauty itself is ~.* 花是美的,但美的本身是抽象的。**,~ 'art,** art which does not represent objects, scenes, etc in an obvious way, but abstracts and isolates features of reality. 抽象藝術(不以顯明的手法表現景物,而只擷取實物特色的一種藝術)。⇨ realism(1). **,~ 'noun,** (gram) one that is the name of a quality or state, eg *length, goodness, virtue.* (文法)抽象名詞(某一種性質或狀態之名稱,例如長度、善良、美德)。**2** *in the ~,* regarded in an ideal or theoretical way. 從抽象的(即概念的或理論的)方面看;觀念上;理論上。

ab·stract² /əb'strækt ; æb'strækt/ *vt* [VP6A,14] ~ *(from)*, take out; separate: 提煉出;取出;抽出: *~ metal from ore;* 從礦砂提煉金屬; (colloq) steal: (俗)竊取;偷: *~ a wallet from sb's pocket.* 從某人口袋中扒走皮夾。**~ed** *adj* not paying attention; withdrawn in thought. 心不在焉的;另有所思的;出神的。**~·ed·ly** *adv* in an absent-minded way. 心不在焉地;出神地。

ab·stract³ /'æbstrækt ; 'æbstrækt/ *n* [C] short account, eg of the chief points of a piece of writing, a book, speech, etc: (文章,書籍,演說等的)摘要: *an ~ of a sermon.* 一篇佈道詞的摘要。

ab·strac·tion /əb'strækʃn ; æb'strækʃən/ *n* **1** [U] abstracting or being abstracted. 提煉;取出;抽出。**2** [U] absent-mindedness: 心不在焉;出神: *in a moment of ~;* 一時心不在焉; *with an air of ~.* 帶着心不在焉的神態。**3** [C] visionary idea; idea of a quality apart from its material accompaniments: 幻想;抽象的概念: *Whiteness is an ~.* 白是一種抽象的概念。*Don't lose yourself in ~s,* ie keep a firm hold on reality. 不要沉迷在幻想中(意卽要緊緊地把握住現實)。**4** [U] formation of such an idea or ideas. 抽象概念之形成;抽象。

ab·struse /əb'stru:s ; æb'strus/ *adj* whose meaning or answer is hidden or difficult to understand; profound. 深奧的;難懂的。**~·ly** *adv* **~·ness** *n*

ab·surd /əb'sɜ:d;əb'sɝd/ *adj* unreasonable; foolish; ridiculous: 不合理的;愚蠢的;可笑的;荒謬的: *What an ~ suggestion!* 多麼荒謬的一個建議! *It was ~ of you to suggest such a thing.* 你竟提議這樣的一件事,眞可笑。**~·ly** *adv* **~·ity** *n* (*pl* -ties) **1** [U] state of being ~; unreasonableness. 不合理;愚蠢;可笑;荒謬。**2** [C] ~ act or statement. 荒謬之行爲或言詞;荒唐話。

abun·dance /ə'bʌndəns ; ə'bʌndəns/ *n* **1** [U] great plenty: 豐富;充裕: *food and drink in ~;* 豐富的飲食; *live in ~,* have plenty of those things that make life enjoyable. 過着豐衣足食的生活。**2** (with *indef art*) quantity that is more than enough: (與不定冠詞連用)豐富之量;很多: *an ~ of good things.* 很多的好東西。

abun·dant /ə'bʌndənt ; ə'bʌndənt/ *adj* **1** more than enough; plentiful: 很多的;豐富的;充裕的: *We have ~ proof of his guilt.* 我們有充分的證據證明他有罪。**2** *~ in,* rich in; well supplied with: 富於;富有…: *a land ~ in minerals* (*with an abundance of* or *abounding in* are more usu). 礦產豐富的土地(較常用 with an abundance of 或 abounding in)。**~·ly** *adv*: *I've made my views ~ly clear.* 我已充分說明了我的觀點。

abuse¹ /ə'bju:s ; ə'bjus/ *n* **1** [U] ~ *(of)*, wrong use; [C] instance of this: 濫用;妄用;濫用或妄用之實例: *an ~ of trust.* 辜負別人的信任。**2** [C] unjust custom or practice that has become established: 不正當的習俗;惡習;弊端: *remedy an ~;* 矯正一項惡習; *put an end to ~s.* 廢止不正當的習俗。**3** [U] angry or violent attack in words; bad language; cursing: 怒罵;辱罵;咒罵: *greet sb with a stream of ~;* 一見某人就破口大罵; *shower ~ on sb.* 大罵某人。

abuse² /ə'bju:z ; ə'bjuz/ *vt* [VP6A] **1** make a bad or wrong use of: 濫用;妄用;誤用: *Don't ~ your authority/the confidence they have placed in you.* 不要濫用你的威信(辜負他們對你的信任)。**2** say severe, cruel or unjust things to sb or about sb. 辱罵;詆毀;講(某人)的壞話。**3** (old use) ill-treat. (舊用法)虐待。**4** (old use, esp in the passive) deceive: (舊用法,尤用於被動語態)欺騙: *She has been much ~d.* 她老是受騙。

abus·ive /ə'bju:sɪv ; ə'bjusɪv/ *adj* using, containing, insults and curses: 辱罵的;詛咒的: *use ~ language to sb;* 咒罵某人; *become ~,* begin to insult and curse. 開始罵人。**~·ly** *adv*

abut /ə'bʌt ; ə'bʌt/ *vi* (-tt-) [VP3A] ~ *on,* (of land) have a common boundary with; border on. (指土地)與…接界;與…毗連。**~·ment** *n* (eng) structure that bears the weight of a bridge or an arch. (工程)橋台;橋座(托架橋或拱的結構)。

abysm /ə'bɪzəm ; ə'bɪzəm/ *n* [C] (poet) abyss. (詩)深淵。

abys·mal /ə'bɪzməl ; ə'bɪzml/ *adj* (esp fig and colloq) bottomless; extreme: (尤用於喻及俗)無底的;極端的: *~ ignorance,* (colloq) complete absence of knowledge. (俗)極端的無知。**~·ly** *adv*

abyss /ə'bɪs ; ə'bɪs/ *n* hole so deep as to appear bottomless: 深淵: (fig) (喻) *the ~ of despair.* 絶望的深淵。**the ~**, hell, or the lower world. 地獄;陰間。

aca·cia /ə'keɪʃə ; ə'keʃə/ *n* [C] **1** (sorts of) tree from which gum is obtained. 相思樹(屬)(可從其提取樹膠)。**2** (*false ~* or *locust tree*) (sorts of) similar tree grown as an ornament in parks and gardens. 洋槐(栽植於公園及花園中作裝飾用)。

aca·demic /,ækə'demɪk ; ,ækə'dɛmɪk/ *adj* **1** of teaching, studying; of schools, colleges, etc; scholarly, literary or classical (contrasted with technical or scientific): 學術的;學校的;學者的;文學的或古典作品的(與技術的或科學的相對): *~ subjects;* 學校裡的科目; *the ~ year,* (usu Oct to June in GB and US). 學年(在英國及美國,通常是自十月至次年六月)。**~ freedom,** liberty to teach and to discuss problems without outside, eg Government, interference. 學術自由(教學及討論問題而不受外力,如政府等,干擾之自由)。**2** too much concerned with theory and logic; not sufficiently practical: 過於注重理論與邏輯的;不够實際的: *The question/issue is ~,* is of no practical consequence. 此問題過於注重理論。**3** of an academy: 高等學府的;專科學校的: *~ rank/costume.* 大專教師之等級(學位服)。□ *n* [C] university teacher; professional scholar. 大學教師;專業學者。**aca·demi·cally** /-klɪ ; -klɪ/ *adv*

aca·dem·icals /,ækə'demɪklz ; ,ækə'dɛməklz/ *n pl* academic costume (cap and gown), as worn on ceremonial occasions. 學位服(典禮時所穿着的學位帽與學位袍)。

acad·emy /ə'kædəmɪ ; ə'kædəmɪ/ *n* (*pl* -mies) **1**

school for higher learning, usu for a special purpose: 高等學府；專科學校: *a 'naval/'military ~;* 海軍 (陸軍) 官校; *an ˌ~ of 'music;* 音樂學院; *a 'riding/'fencing ~.* 騎術 (擊劍) 學校。 **2** society of distinguished scholars; society for cultivating art, literature, etc, of which membership is an honour: 高等學術團體；學會: *The Royal A~ of Arts.* (英國) 皇家藝術學會。 **aca·dem·ician** /əˌkædə'mɪʃn *US:* ˌækədə'mɪʃn ; əˌkædə'mɪʃən/ *n* member of an ~(2), eg of the Royal A~ in GB or of the French A~. 學術團體之會員；學會會員 (例如英國皇家藝術學會或法國翰林院之會員)；院士。

ac·cede /ək'si:d ; æk'sid/ *vi* [VP2A, 3A] **~ *(to)*,** (formal) (正式用語) **1** assent or agree, eg to a request or proposal. 允諾；同意；贊成 (某一要求或建議)。 **2** take up or succeed to, eg an office, a post, a position of authority. 就職；即位；繼承 (王位)。

ac·cel·er·ando /ækˌselə'rændəʊ ; ækˌsɛlə'rændo/ *n, adv, adj* (music) (direction for) increasing speed gradually. (音樂) 漸快速度；逐漸加快速度地 (的)。 ⇨ rallentando.

ac·cel·er·ate /ək'seləreɪt ; æk'sɛləˌret/ *vt, vi* **1** [VP6A] increase the speed of; cause to move faster or happen earlier. 加快…之速度；使加速；催促。 **2** [VP2A] (of a motion or process) become faster. (指運動或程序) 變快；加速。 **ac·cel·er·ation** /əkˌselə'reɪʃn ; ækˌsɛlə'reʃən/ *n* [U] making or being made quicker; rate of increase of speed per unit of time: 加速；加速度；加速率: *a car with good acceleration.* 加速性能良好的汽車。

ac·cel·er·ator /ək'seləreɪtə(r) ; æk'sɛləˌretɚ/ *n* **1** device, eg the pedal in a car, for controlling speed. 加速裝置 (例如汽車等中之油門踏板)；加速器。⇨ the illus at motor. 參看 motor 之挿圖。 **2** (phys) device for accelerating particles or nuclei, also called (colloq) an 'atom-smasher'. (物理) 加速器 (俗稱 '核粒子加速器')。

ac·cent /'æksənt *US:* 'æksent ; 'æksɛnt/ *n* [C] **1** prominence (by means of stress or intonation) given to a syllable: (藉重讀或音調所加於一音節上的) 重音: *In the word 'today' the ~ is on the second syllable.* today 一字之重音在第二音節。 **2** mark or symbol, usu above a letter, used in writing and printing to indicate the quality of a vowel sound or syllabic stress. 重音符號 (通常標在字母上方，用於書寫或印刷中，以表示母音性質或重音節)。 ⇨ acute(5), circumflex and grave[3]. **3** [sometimes 有時候爲 U] individual, local or national way of pronouncing: (個人、地方或民族的) 口音；腔調；土腔: *a Cockney ~;* 倫敦東區的口音; *speaking English with a foreign ~;* 說英語帶外國腔調; *speak without an ~.* 說話不帶地方口音。 **4** (*pl*) way of speaking which indicates a particular quality, etc: (複) 說話的語氣；聲調；語調: *in the tender ~s of love.* 以情意綿綿的語調。 **5** (colloq) emphasis given to some aspect of a display, performance, etc: (俗) (加於展示，表演等某一方面的) 强調；着重；重點: *At this year's Motor Show the ~ is on sports cars.* 今年的汽車展覽會重點在跑車。 □ *vt* /æk'sent ; 'æksɛnt/ [VP6A] pronounce with an ~; put emphasis on (a syllable or word); make prominent or conspicuous. 以重音讀出；重讀 (某一音節或字)；强調；使顯著。

ac·cen·tu·ate /ək'sentʃʊeɪt ; æk'sɛntʃʊˌet/ *vt* [VP6A] give more force or importance to; draw attention to. 加重；强調。 **ac·cen·tu·ation** /əkˌsentʃʊ'eɪʃn ; ækˌsɛntʃʊ'eʃən/ *n*

ac·cept /ək'sept ; ək'sɛpt/ *vt, vi* [VP6A, 9, 16B, 2A] **1** (consent to) receive (sth offered): 接受；答應 (別人所提供的事物): *~ a gift/an invitation.* 接受禮物 (邀請)。 *He asked her to marry him and she ~ed him/his proposal.* 他請求她嫁給他，她答應了他 (他的求婚)。 *I cannot ~ your apology.* 我不能接受你的道歉。 **2** agree; recognize; regard with favour or approval: 同意；認可；贊同: *I ~ that the change may take some time.* 我同意改變頗費時日。 *It is an ~ed truth/fact,* sth that everyone believes. 這是大家所公認的眞理 (事實)。 **3** (comm) take responsibility for: (商) 承受…的責任；承兌: *~ a bill of exchange;* 承兌滙票; *~ delivery of goods.* 負責送貨。 **~·able** /-əbl ; -əbl̩/ *adj* worth ~ing; welcome: 可接受的；受歡迎的: *if this proposal is ~able to you.* 如果你覺得這個建議可以接受的話。 **ac·cepta·bil·ity** /əkˌseptə'bɪlətɪ ; əkˌsɛptə'bɪlətɪ/ *n* **ac·cept·ance** /-əns ; -əns/ *n* [U] **1** ~ing or being ~ed. 接受；答應；同意；認可。 **2** approval; favourable reception: 贊同；嘉納: *The proposal met with/found general ~ance.* 這建議得到普遍的贊同。 **3** (comm) agreement to pay; (legal) contract, bill of exchange, which has been offered and ~ed. (商) 承兌；認付；(法律) 經提出且被接受的合約；已認付的票據。 **ac·cep·ta·tion** /ˌæksep'teɪʃn ; ˌæksɛp'teʃən/ *n* generally ~ed meaning of a word or expression. 公認的字義。

ac·cess /'ækses ; 'æksɛs/ *n* [U] **1** way (in) to a place: 通入之路；通路: *easy/difficult of ~;* 易 (難) 進入的；易 (難) 接近的; (attrib) (形容用法) *good ~ roads,* roads giving good ~. 良好的通路。 *The only ~ to the farmhouse is across the fields.* 到達那農舍的唯一通路是穿過田間。 **'~-road,** (US) slip-road, ⇨ slip²(8). (美) 叉道。 **2 ~ *to*,** right, opportunity or means of reaching, using or approaching: 接觸，使用或接近的權利，機會或方法: *Students must have ~ to good books.* 學生必須有機會讀到好書。 *Only high officials had ~ to the Emperor.* 只有高級官員可以接近皇帝。 **3 *an ~ of*,** (old use) attack (of fever, etc); sudden attack, outburst (of anger, rage, despair, etc). (舊用法) (身體發燒等之) 發作；(憤怒，絕望等之) 突然發作；爆發。 **~·ible** /ək'sesəbl ; æk'sɛsəbl̩/ *adj* **~ *(to)*,** able to be reached, used, visited, etc: 可接近的；可進入的；可用的；可參觀的: *facts that are ~ible to all;* 人人可得參考的事實資料; *a collection of paintings not ~ible to the public;* 公衆無法看到的一批收藏的畫; that can be influenced by: 可被…影響的: *a man who is not ~ible to argument.* 不爲辯論所影響的人。 **ac·ces·si·bil·ity** /əkˌsesə'bɪlətɪ ; ækˌsɛsə'bɪlətɪ/ *n* [U].

ac·ces·sary /ək'sesərɪ ; æk'sɛsərɪ/ *n* (*pl* -ries), *pred adj* (= US 美 *accessory*(1)) (legal) person who helps in any act, esp a crime: (法律) 幫手；(尤指) 從犯；幫兇的；從犯的: *an ~ to a crime;* 一件犯罪案的從犯; *He was made ~ to the crime.* 他被人利用，成爲這件犯罪案的從犯。 ***~ before/after the fact,*** ⇨ fact(1).

ac·ces·sion /æk'seʃn ; æk'sɛʃən/ *n* **~ *to*,** **1** [U] reaching a rank, position or state: 達到某一地位或狀態: *the Queen's ~ to the throne;* 女王之即位; *on his ~ to the estate/to manhood.* 在他承繼產業 (到達成年) 的時候。 **2** [U] addition; increase; [C] example of this: 增加；添加；增加之實例: *recent ~s to the school library;* 學校圖書館最近增添的數批新書; *the ~ of new members to a political party.* 某政黨之增加新黨員。

ac·ces·sory /ək'sesərɪ ; æk'sɛsərɪ/ *n* (*pl* -ries) **1** = accessary. **2** sth extra, helpful, useful, but not an essential part of: 附件；附屬品: *the accessories of a bicycle,* eg the lamp, a pump; 脚踏車的附件 (如車燈，打氣筒); *the accessories of a woman's dress,* eg gloves, a handbag. 一件女裝的配件 (如手套，手提包)。

ac·ci·dence /'æksɪdəns ; 'æksədəns/ *n* [U] (gram) that part of grammar which deals with meaningful differences in the form of a word, eg *have, has, had; foot, feet,* etc. The more usu term is now *morphology.* (文法) 語形變化；字形變化 (如 have, has, had; foot, feet 等；今較常用 morphology)。 ⇨ syntax.

ac·ci·dent /'æksɪdənt ; 'æksədənt/ *n* **1** [C] sth that happens without a cause that can be seen at once, usu sth unfortunate and undesirable: 意外事

A

件;不測;禍事;事故: *There have been many railway ~s this year.* 今年發生了許多次火車車禍。*He was killed in a road/motoring ~.* 他在一次車禍中死亡。*There has been an ~ to....* …發生過一次意外。***A~s will happen,*** (prov) Some unfortunate events must be accepted as inevitable. (諺)意外事故難免會發生。***meet with/have an ~,*** experience one: 遭遇意外事故: *I had a slight ~ on the way to work this morning.* 我今晨在上班途中遭遇一件小小的意外事故。**'~-prone,** ⇨ prone. **2** [U] chance; fortune: 機遇;命運: *by ~ of birth.* 生來就是;由於出生的身世。***by ~,*** by chance: 偶然;意外地: *You might cut yourself by ~; you would not cut yourself on purpose.* 你可能意外地割傷自己;你不會故意割傷自己。***without ~,*** safely. 安全地;無恙地。**'~ insurance,** against injury, damage or death which is the result of an ~. 意外保險。

ac·ci·den·tal /ˌæksɪˈdentl; ˌæksəˈdɛntl/ *adj* happening unexpectedly and by chance: 偶然的;意外的: *an ~ meeting with a friend.* 偶然遇到一位朋友。**~·ly** /-təlɪ; -tlɪ/ *adv*

ac·claim /əˈkleɪm; əˈklem/ *vt* **1** [VP6A, 16B] welcome with shouts of approval; applaud loudly: 歡呼;喝采;稱讚: *~ the winner of a race;* 向賽跑得勝者歡呼; *~ sb as a great actor.* 喝采稱讚某人爲偉大的演員。**2** [VP23] make (sb) ruler, salute (sb) by ~ing: 歡呼以擁立(某人)爲統治者;向(某人)歡呼致敬: *They ~ed him King.* 他們歡呼擁立他爲國王。□ *n* [U] applause; approval: 歡呼;喝采;贊同: *The play received great critical ~.* 該劇大受激賞(極獲好評)。

ac·cla·ma·tion /ˌækləˈmeɪʃn; ˌækləˈmeʃən/ *n* **1** [U] loud and enthusiastic approval of a proposal, etc: (對提議等之)高聲而熱烈的贊同: *elected/carried by ~,* without voting. (不經過投票表決而)被全體一致口頭推選(通過)。**2** (usu *pl*) shouts or applause of welcome, acceptance: (通常用複數)歡呼;喝采: *the ~s of the crowd.* 群衆的歡呼。

ac·cli·mate /ˈæklɪmeɪt; ˈækləˌmet/ *vt, vi* = acclimatize. **ac·cli·ma·tion** /ˌæklaɪˈmeɪʃn; ˌækləˈmeʃən/ *n*

ac·cli·mat·ize /əˈklaɪmətaɪz; əˈklaɪməˌtaɪz/ *vt, vi* [VP14, 2A] ~ ***(to),*** get (oneself, animals, plants, etc) used to a new climate, or (fig) to a new environment, new conditions, etc: 使(自己,動物,植物等)習慣於新的氣候; (使)服水土; (喻)(使)適應新環境: *You will soon get ~d.* 你很快就會適應的。**ac·cli·mat·iz·ation** /əˌklaɪmətaɪˈzeɪʃn *US:* -tɪˈz-; əˌklaɪmətəˈzeʃən/ *n*

ac·cliv·ity /əˈklɪvətɪ; əˈklɪvətɪ/ *n* (*pl* -ties) [C] upward slope. 向上的斜坡。⇨ declivity.

ac·col·ade /ˈækəleɪd *US:* ˌækəˈleɪd; ˌækəˈled/ *n* [C] **1** bestowal of a knighthood by a tap on the shoulder with the flat of a sword. 爵位之授與(以劍面在肩上輕拍一下)。**2** (fig) praise; approval: (喻)讚頌;贊成: *the ~s of the literary critics.* 文學批評家的讚美。

ac·com·mo·date /əˈkɒmədeɪt; əˈkɑməˌdet/ *vt* [VP6A, 14] **1** have, provide, lodging for: 供給住宿: *This hotel can ~ 600 guests.* 這旅館可供六百位客人住宿。**2** ~ ***sb (with sth),*** grant sth to sb; do sb a favour: 答應某人(某件事);加惠於某人;幫某人一個忙: *The bank will ~ you with a loan.* 銀行將貸給你一筆款。**3** ~ ***sth to,*** change sth so that it fits with or is in harmony with (sth else): 使某事物配合(其他事物);修改某事物俾能與…調和;使適應: *I will ~ my plans to yours.* 我將修改我的計畫以配合你的計畫。**ac·com·mo·dat·ing** *adj* willing to oblige others; easy to deal with. 樂於助人的;隨和的。

ac·com·mo·da·tion /əˌkɒməˈdeɪʃn; əˌkɑməˈdeʃən/ *n* **1** [U] (GB) furnished, unfurnished room(s), eg in a flat, house, hostel or in a hotel, etc: (英)房間(泛指公寓,一般房屋,招待所或旅館等中,有或無傢具設備的房間): *Wanted, ~ for a married couple with small child, in London,* eg as in a newspaper advertisement. 徵租,倫敦市內,供夫婦及一小孩之房間(如報紙上之廣告)。*Hotel ~ was scarce during the Olympic Games.* 在世運會期間,旅館房間很難找。**2** (*pl*, US) lodgings; room(s) and food. (複,美)住所;膳宿。**3** [C] sth that helps; sth for convenience. 有益之物;便利的設備。**an '~ ladder,** (attrib) a portable one hung from the side of a ship. (形容用法)舷梯(掛於船舷之可移動的梯子)。**4** [U] (formal) compromise; settlement or adjustment (of one thing *to* another); [C] example of this: (正式用語)和解;調解;適應;調節(與 to 連用);調解或調節之實例: *come to an ~,* reach a compromise, eg in a dispute. 達成和解(如對某一爭端)。⇨ agreement.

ac·com·pani·ment /əˈkʌmpənɪmənt; əˈkʌmpənɪmənt/ *n* [C] **1** sth that naturally or often goes with another thing: 伴隨物;與之俱來的事物: *Disease is often an ~ of famine.* 疾病常隨飢饉而來。**2** (music) (usu) instrumental part to support a voice, choir or solo instrument: (音樂)(通常指對獨唱,合唱或獨奏樂器之)伴奏: *a song with a piano ~.* 由鋼琴伴奏之歌。**ac·com·pan·ist** /əˈkʌmpənɪst; əˈkʌmpənɪst/ *n* person who plays a musical ~. 伴奏者。

ac·com·pany /əˈkʌmpənɪ; əˈkʌmpənɪ/ *vt* (*pt, pp* -nied) [VP6A, 14] **1** go with: 伴隨;陪伴;跟隨: *Warships will ~ the convoy across the Atlantic.* 戰艦將護送該船隊過大西洋。*He was accompanied by his secretary.* 他有秘書隨行。**2** attend; characterize: 帶有;以…爲其特徵: *fever accompanied with delirium;* 帶囈語的發燒; *lightning accompanied with thunder.* 帶雷的閃電;雷電交作。**3** occur or do at the same time as: 與…同時發生或做出: *~ one's words with blows.* 一邊說一邊動拳頭。**4** (music) play an accompaniment to: (音樂)爲…伴奏: *The singer was accompanied at the piano by Gerald Moore.* 該歌唱者由吉樂爾德・穆爾鋼琴伴奏。

ac·com·plice /əˈkʌmplɪs *US:* əˈkɒm-; əˈkɑmplɪs/ *n* [C] helper or companion (*in*, esp, wrongdoing). 從犯;幫兇;同謀者(與 in 連用,尤指做壞事)。

ac·com·plish /əˈkʌmplɪʃ *US:* əˈkɒm-; əˈkɑmplɪʃ/ *vt* [VP6A] perform; succeed in doing; finish successfully: 實行;完成;成功地做完: *~ a task;* 完成一件工作; *a man who will never ~ anything.* 永遠一事無成的人。***an ~ed fact,*** sth already done. 既成事實。**~ed** *adj* clever; skilled (*in*): 技巧的;熟練的;精於…的(後接 in): *an ~ed dancer;* 舞技高超的舞者; well trained or educated in such social arts as conversation, art and music: 在談話,繪畫及音樂等社交藝術方面受過良好的訓練或教育的;善社交而多才多藝的: *an ~ed young lady.* 一位善社交而多才多藝的淑女。**~·ment** *n* **1** [U] completion; finishing: 完成: *the ~ment of their aims;* 他們目標之完成; *difficult of ~ment.* 難以完成。**2** [C] sth ~ed, esp sth well done. 完成之事;成就;成績。**3** [C] skill in a social or domestic art: (社交或家事方面的)才藝;教養;技藝: *Among her ~ments were dancing, playing the piano, sewing and cooking.* 她的才藝包括舞蹈,彈鋼琴,縫紉及烹飪。

ac·cord¹ /əˈkɔːd; əˈkɔrd/ *n* **1** [U] ***of one's own ~,*** without being asked or forced; willingly. 自願地;自動地。***in/out of ~ (with),*** in/out of harmony (with), agreeing/not agreeing with. (與…)(不)一致。***with one ~,*** everybody consenting. 全體一致。**2** [C] treaty, agreement (*between* countries; *with* a country). (兩國之間或與他國所訂的)條約;協定(與 between 或 with 連用)。

ac·cord² /əˈkɔːd; əˈkɔrd/ *vi, vt* **1** [VP2A, 2C, 3A] ~ ***(with),*** match, agree (with); be in agreement or harmony (with): (與…)相配合;一致;符合: *His behaviour and his principles do not ~ (well together).* 他的行爲與他的原則不符合。*His behaviour does not ~ with his principles.* 他的行爲不合他的原則。*What you say does not ~ with the previous evidence.* 你所說的與以前的證據不一致。**2** [VP13A,

12A] (formal style) give; grant: (正式文體)給與;贈與;賜與: ~ *sb permission;* 允許某人; ~ *permission to sb.* 允許某人。*He was ~ed a warm welcome.* 他受到熱烈的歡迎。

ac·cord·ance /ə'kɔːdəns ; ə'kɔrdṇs/ *n* ***in ~ with,*** in agreement or conformity with: 依照;根據: *in ~ with your wishes;* 根據你的願望; *in ~ with custom／the regulations.* 依照慣例(規章)。

ac·cord·ing /ə'kɔːdɪŋ ; ə'kɔrdɪŋ/ **1** ***~ as,*** *conj* in proportion as; in a manner that depends upon: 依照;根據: *You will be praised or blamed ~ as your work is good or bad.* 你將依照你工作成績的好壞而受到獎懲。 **2** ***~ to,*** *prep* **(a)** on the authority of: 根據: *A~ to the Bible, God created the world in six days.* 根據聖經所載,上帝在六天之內創造了世界。 **(b)** in a degree in proportion to: 視…而定: *He will be punished ~ to the seriousness of his crime.* 他所受的懲罰將視其犯罪的嚴重性而定。 **(c)** in a manner consistent with: 按照;依照: *The books are placed on the shelves ~ to authors.* 這些書按照作者的順序擺在書架上。 **~·ly** *adv* **1** for that reason; therefore. 因此;所以;於是。 **2** as the (stated) circumstances suggest: 按照(所說的)情形: *I have told you the circumstances, so you must act ~ly.* 我已經告訴你一切情況,所以你必須按照我所說的辦理。

ac·cord·ion /ə'kɔːdɪən ; ə'kɔrdɪən/ *n* (also 亦作 **piano** ~) portable musical instrument with a bellows, metal reeds and a keyboard; (attrib) having narrow folds like the bellows of an ~: 手風琴(一種手提型樂器,有風箱,金屬簧及鍵盤);(形容用法)像手風琴或其摺箱般有細褶的: ~ *pleats in a skirt.* 裙子上像手風琴摺箱般的細摺。

ac·cost /ə'kɒst *US:* ə'kɔːst ; ə'kɔst/ *vt* [VP6A] go up to and speak to first, esp a stranger in a public place; (of a prostitute) solicit: 走上前與之(尤指與公共場所之陌生人)攀談;(指妓女)勾搭;拉客;乞求: *I was ~ed by a beggar／a prostitute.* 一個乞丐(妓女)向我乞討(勾搭)。

ac·couche·ment /ə'kuːʃmɒŋ ; əkuʃmã/ *n* (F) lying in; confinement; childbirth. (法)分娩;坐蓐;生產。 ⇨ *lie in* at lie²(1).

ac·count¹ /ə'kaʊnt ; ə'kaʊnt/ *n* **1** [C] (comm) statement of money (to be) paid or received (for goods, services, etc): (商)帳目;帳;帳戶: *I have an ~ with the Midland Bank,* keep my money with that Bank, pay my debts, etc by means of cheques from that Bank, etc. 我在米德蘭銀行開有戶頭(存款於該銀行,開該行支票付款等)。***open an ~; open a bank／post office, etc ~,*** start to keep one's money at a bank, etc. 開戶頭;開一銀行(郵局等)戶頭(開始在銀行,郵局等中存款)。*ask a shop／shopkeeper／store to* ***put sth down to one's ~,*** ask him to note the price of what is bought, for payment later. 請店鋪(店東,商店)將某貨物記在自己的帳上。***settle one's ~ (with),*** pay what one owes (to a tradesman, etc); (fig) avenge oneself for an injury, etc. (向商人等)結清欠帳;結帳;清帳;(喻)報復;報一箭之仇。***send in／render an ~,*** send a written statement of what is owed. 送帳單。Hence, 由此產生, **ˌ~ 'rendered,** an ~ previously sent in but not yet paid. 先行提出而尚未付清之帳單;交驗帳。***balance／square ~s (with sb),*** receive or pay the difference between debit and credit; (fig) remove moral grievances between people by giving or taking punishment. (與某人) 結清帳目;(喻) (與某人)將恩恩怨怨作一了斷。**'budget ~,** (with a shop) one used for buying goods, paying bills, etc by making regular payments to the shop; (with a bank) special ~ with a bank which makes regular deductions for bills paid. 預算帳戶(在一商店中所開的帳戶,以購買貨物、付帳等,定期付款給該商店;或指在一銀行中所開的特別帳戶,該銀行定期從其存款中扣除已代付之費用)。**'current ~, de'posit ~, 'joint ~, 'private ~, 'savings ~,** ⇨ current¹(3), deposit²(1), joint¹, private(1) and save¹. **2** (archaic) counting; calculation. (古)計算。***money of ~,*** used of sums of money, not of coins or banknotes. 計算貨幣;虛位通貨(指錢數,不指硬幣或鈔票)。⇨ guinea. **3** (*sing* only) benefit; profit: (只用單數)利益: *invest one's money to good ~.* 將錢投資以獲高利。***turn／put sth to (good) ~,*** use money, abilities, talent, etc profitably: 對某事物善加利用(如有利地利用金錢,能力,才能等): *He turned／put his knowledge of Spanish to good ~.* 他善加利用他對西班牙語文的知識。***work on one's own ~,*** for one's own purposes and profit, and at one's own risk. 爲一己的目的及利益打算,且自行負責。 **4** [U] ***call／bring sb to ~,*** require him to justify or explain his conduct; state that he is answerable for sth. 叫某人解釋其行爲的理由;責問;質問。 **5** [C] ***give a good ~ of oneself,*** do well; act in a way that brings credit, eg by defeating opponents in contests. 大顯身手(例如在比賽中擊敗對手)。 **6** [C] report; description; narrative: 報告;敍述: *Don't always believe newspaper ~s of events.* 不要老是相信報紙的報導。***by one's own ~,*** according to what one oneself says. 據…自己說。***by／from all ~s,*** according to what everybody, all the papers, etc say. 人人(所有的報紙等)都如此說。 **7** [U] estimation. 估計;價值;考慮。***be (reckoned) of some／small ~,*** be (considered) of some／low value. (被認爲)有相當價值(無甚價值)。***take sth into ~; take ~ of sth,*** note or consider it; pay attention to it. 對某事物加以考慮;對某事加以注意。***leave sth out of ~; take no ~ of sth,*** pay no attention to it. 對某事物不予注意;對某事物不予考慮。 **8** [U] reason; cause. 理由;原因。***on ~ of,*** because of. 因爲。***on this／that ~,*** for this／that reason: 爲了這個(那個)緣故: *He's angry on that ~.* 爲了那個緣故他很生氣。*Don't stay away on ~ of John／on John's ~.* 爲了約翰,不要離開。***on no ~; not on any ~,*** in no case; not for any reason: 決不;切莫: *Don't on any ~ leave the baby alone in the house.* 切不可將嬰兒獨自留在家裏。

ac·count² /ə'kaʊnt ; ə'kaʊnt/ *vt, vi* **1** [VP3A] ***~ for,*** **(a)** serve as an explanation of; explain the cause of: 解釋;說明: *His illness ~s for his absence.* 他因爲生病,所以才缺席。*Ah, that ~s for it!* 呵,原來是這麼一回事! *He has been asked to ~ for his conduct,* explain why he acted as he did. 他被要求解釋他的行爲(說明他何以如此)。 ***There's no ~ing for tastes,*** We cannot explain why people have different likes and dislikes. 人的好惡是無法解釋的。 **(b)** give a reckoning of (money that has been entrusted to one): 報帳: *The boy has to ~ (to his parents) for the money they give him for school expenses.* 該男孩必須(向他父母親)報帳,說明他們所給他學雜費的支出細目。 **(c)** destroy; kill; capture: 摧毀;殺死;捕獲: *We ~ed for a fine brace of partridges.* 我們獵獲了一對很好的鷓鴣。 **2** [VP25] consider: 認爲;視爲: *In English law a man is ~ed innocent until he is proved guilty.* 在英國法律上,一個人未被證實有罪之前,被視爲清白的。 **~·able** /-əbl ; -əbḷ/ *adj* ***~able (to sb) (for sth),*** responsible; expected to give an explanation: 對某人(某事)負責;對…應加以說明: *I'll hold you ~able.* 我將唯你是問。*A madman is not ~able for his actions.* 瘋子對自己的行爲沒有責任。

ac·count·ancy /ə'kaʊntənsɪ ; ə'kaʊntənsɪ/ *n* [U] profession of an accountant. 會計師或會計之職業。

ac·count·ant /ə'kaʊntənt ; ə'kaʊntənt/ *n* [C] (in GB) person whose profession is to keep and examine business accounts¹. (英) 會計師;會計。**chartered ~,** (abbr 略作 **CA**) ⇨ charter *v*(1) (US 美 = **certified public ~,** abbr 略作 **CPA**).

ac·coutre·ments (US = **ac·cou·ter·ments**) /ə'kuːtəmənts ; ə'kutəmənts/ *n pl* equipment; trappings; (mil) soldier's kit excluding clothes and weapons. 裝備;裝飾物;(軍)(軍服及武器以外的)配備。

A

ac·credit /əˈkredɪt ; əˈkrɛdɪt/ *vt* [VP14] (usu passive) (通常用被動語態) **1** appoint or send (sb) as an ambassador, with official letters of introduction: 委派(某人)出任大使: *He was ~ed to/at Lisbon.* 他奉派出任駐里斯本大使。 **2** = credit². **~ed** *part adj* officially recognized (person); generally accepted (belief, opinion, etc); guaranteed to be of an approved quality. 官方認可的(人);普遍接受的(信仰,意見等);保證品質良好的。

ac·cretion /əˈkri:ʃn ; əˈkriʃən/ *n* **1** [U] increase by organic addition or growth; the growing of separate things into one. 生長;累積;黏連;長合。 **2** [C] sth added; sth resulting from ~. 增加物;生長部份;長合物。

ac·crue /əˈkru: ; əˈkru/ *vi* [VP2A, 3A] **~ *(to sb) (from sth),*** come as a natural growth or development: 自然增長或產生: *If you keep your money in the Savings Bank, interest ~s.* 如果你把錢存在儲蓄銀行裏,就會自然生息。 *A~d interest is interest due, but not yet paid or received.* 應計利息是到期利息,不過尙未付出或領取。

ac·cu·mu·late /əˈkju:mjʊleɪt ; əˈkjumjəˌlet/ *vt, vi* [VP6A, 2A] make or become greater in number or quantity; come or gather together; heap up: 累積;積聚;堆積: *By buying ten books every month, he soon ~d a library.* 他每月買十本書,不久就積聚了一批藏書。 *Dust soon ~s if the rooms are not swept.* 房間如果不打掃,灰塵不久就堆積起來了。 *By working hard you may ~ a fortune.* 努力工作你就可以積蓄一筆財產。

ac·cu·mu·la·tion /əˌkju:mjʊˈleɪʃn ; əˌkjumjəˈleʃən/ *n* **1** [U] accumulating; collection: 累積;積聚;收集: *the ~ of money/useful knowledge.* 金錢(有用知識)的積聚。 **2** [C] material, etc accumulated: 聚積物;堆積物;收集物: *an ~ of books/evidence/rubbish.* 收集的一批書籍(一堆證據,一堆垃圾)。 **ac·cu·mu·lat·ive** /əˈkju:mjʊlətɪv *US:* -leɪtɪv ; əˈkjumjəˌletɪv/ *adj* arising from ~; growing by a succession of additions. 積聚起來的;累積起來的。

ac·cu·mu·la·tor /əˈkjumjʊleɪtə(r) ; əˈkjumjəˌletɚ/ *n* [C] **1** (GB) storage battery, eg for a motor vehicle: (英)(汽車等的)蓄電池: *charge/discharge an ~,* cause a current to flow into/out of it. 使蓄電池充電(放電)。 **2** (in a computer) device which stores numbers and progressively adds numbers. (電腦中之)累積器(貯積及累計數字的裝置)。

ac·cu·rate /ˈækjərət ; ˈækjərɪt/ *adj* **1** careful and exact: 精確的: *be ~ in one's work/in what one says;* 作事(說話)精確; *quick and ~ at figures;* 計算迅速而精確; *take ~ aim.* 瞄準精確。 **2** free from error: 正確無誤的;準確的: *~ scales.* 準確的秤。 *Clocks in railway stations should be ~.* 火車站的鐘應該準確。 **~·ly** *adv* **ac·cu·racy** /ˈækjərəsɪ ; ˈækjərəsɪ/ *n* [U] exactness; correctness. 精確;正確;準確。

ac·cursed /əˈkɜ:sɪd ; əˈkɝsɪd/, **ac·curst** /əˈkɜ:st ; əˈkɝst/ *adj* (poetic) under a curse; detestable hateful. (詩)被詛咒的;可厭的;可恨的。

ac·cu·sa·tion /ˌækju:ˈzeɪʃn ; ˌækjəˈzeʃən/ *n* **1** [U] accusing or being accused. 非難;譴責;控訴;被非難;被控訴。 **2** [C] charge of doing wrong, of having broken the law: 控告: *bring an ~ of theft against sb;* 控告某人竊盜; *be under an ~ of theft.* 被控竊盜。

ac·cus·ative /əˈkju:zətɪv ; əˈkjuzətɪv/ *adj, n* (gram) (of the) form of a word when it is the direct object of a verb or preposition. (文法)受格(用作動詞或介詞的直接受詞之字的一種形式);受格的。 **the ~ case,** ⇨ case¹(3).

ac·cuse /əˈkju:z ; əˈkjuz/ *vt* [VP6A, 14] **~ *sb (of sth),*** say that (sb) has done wrong, broken the law, is to be blamed: 控告某人(犯某項罪);控訴;告發;非難;譴責: *~ sb of theft/cowardice;* 控告某人竊盜(責備某人怯懦); *be ~d of sth.* 被控犯某罪。 **the ~d,** the person(s) charged in a criminal case. (刑案中的)被告。 **ac·cuser** *n* **ac·cus·ing·ly** /əˈkju:zɪŋlɪ ; əˈkjuzɪŋlɪ/ *adv* in an accusing manner: 以控訴或譴責的態度: *He pointed accusingly at me.* 他以譴責的態度指着我。

ac·cus·tom /əˈkʌstəm ; əˈkʌstəm/ *vt* [VP14] **~ *(oneself) to,*** make used to: 使習慣於: *When he became a soldier, he had to ~ himself to long marches.* 當他當兵的時候,他不得不使自己習慣於長途行軍。 ***become/be ~ed to,*** become/be used to: 習慣於: *The boy soon became ~ed to hard work and poor food.* 那男孩不久就習慣於苦工及劣食了。 *This is not the kind of treatment I am ~ed to,* not the kind I usually receive. 這不是我所習慣的那種待遇。 **~ed** *part adj* usual; habitual: 通常的;慣常的: *in his ~ed seat.* 坐在他通常的座位上。

ace /eɪs ; es/ *n* [C] **1** the one on dice, on (playing-) cards or dominoes (⇨ these words); card so marked: (骰子,紙牌或骨牌上的)么點(參看 dice, card, domino 各字);么點牌: *the ~ of spades.* 黑桃牌之么點;黑桃愛斯。 ***an ace in the hole,*** (US sl, from the game of poker) sth held in reserve, likely to turn failure into success. (美俚,源於撲克牌戲)保留着用以轉敗爲勝之事物;扭轉乾坤之王牌。 **2** (colloq) person who is first-rate or expert at sth, esp an airman or a driver of racing cars. (俗)第一流人才或專家;(尤指)第一流飛行員或賽車駕駛員;能手。 **3** ***within an ace of,*** failing, escaping, by a narrow margin: 差一點;幾乎: *within an ace of death/of being killed.* 死裡逃生(險些喪命)。

acerb·ity /əˈsɜ:bətɪ ; əˈsɝbətɪ/ *n* **1** [U] (formal) bitterness of speech, manner, temper. (正式用語)(言語,態度,性情之)刻薄;尖刻。 **2** [C] (*pl* -ties) instance of this; bitter remark, etc. 刻薄之實例;尖刻的言語;刻薄話;嚴苛的態度等。

acetic /əˈsi:tɪk ; əˈsitɪk/ *adj* of vinegar or ~ acid. 醋的;醋酸的。 **ˌ~ ˈacid,** the acid contained in vinegar. 醋酸。 **acet·ate** /ˈæsɪteɪt ; ˈæsəˌtet/ *n* salt of ~ acid: 醋酸鹽: *acetate silk,* artificial silk made from cellulose acetate. 醋酸人造絲(醋酸纖維素製成之人造絲)。

acety·lene /əˈsetəli:n ; əˈsɛtḷˌin/ *n* [U] (chem) colourless gas **(C_2H_2)** which burns with a bright light, used in carbide lamps and for welding and cutting metal. (化學)乙炔;電石氣(一種無色氣體,分子式 C_2H_2,燃燒時發出明亮的光,用於電石氣燈及鎔接或切斷金屬)。 ⇨ oxyacetylene.

ache /eɪk ; ek/ *n* [C] (*sing,* with or without the *indef art*) dull continuous pain: (單數時可與不定冠詞連用,不用不定冠詞亦可)疼痛: *have ~s and pains all over.* 周身疼痛。(~ is only combined with *back, ear, head, heart, stomach, tummy* and *tooth,* as in *back~.* For other parts of the body *a pain/~ in my/his/the foot, etc* is used): (ache 僅與 back, ear, head, heart, stomach, tummy, tooth 等字結合,如 backache; 身體其他部分之疼痛則用 pain 或 ache 表示,例如 a pain (or ache) in my (his or the) foot): *have a ˈhead~;* 頭痛; *suffer from ˈback~s/from (the) ˈtooth~.* 背(牙)痛。 **ˈheart~,** ⇨ heart(7). □ *vi* **1** [VP2A] have a steady or continuous dull pain: 隱隱作痛;持續地痛: *My head ~s/is aching.* 我頭痛。 *After climbing the mountain, he ~d all over.* 爬山以後,他渾身疼痛。 *It makes my heart ~,* makes me sad. 它使我痛心。 **2** [VP3A, 4A] **~ *(for),*** have a longing: 渴望: *His heart ~ed for her.* 他的心苦念著她。 *He was aching for home.* 他渴望回家。 *He ~d to be free.* 他渴望自由。

achieve /əˈtʃi:v ; əˈtʃiv/ *vt* [VP6A] **1** complete; accomplish; get (sth) done: 完成;達成;成就: *He will never ~ anything,* will not do anything successfully. 他永不會有所成就。 *I've ~d only half of what I hoped to do.* 我僅完成了我所希望完成的一半。 **2** gain or reach by effort: 藉努力而獲得或達到: *~ one's purpose;* 達到目的; *~ success/distinction in public life.* 爲公衆服務(或擔任公職)獲得成功(殊榮)。 **achiev·able** /-əbl ; -əbḷ/ *adj* that can be ~d. 可完

成的;可達到的。~·**ment** *n* **1** [U] achieving: 完成;達成: *the ~ment of an undertaking/of one's aims;* 任務的完成 (某人目標的達到); *impossible of ~ment;* 不可能完成的; *an ~ment test* (of skills, etc). (技巧等的)成就測驗。 **2** [C] sth ~d; sth done successfully, with effort and skill: 成就;成績;功業;功績: *The inventor was rewarded by the Government for his scientific ~ments.* 該發明家由於他在科學上的成就受到政府的獎勵。

Achilles /ə'kɪli:z ; ə'kɪliz/ *n* **the heel of ~; ~' heel,** (fig) small but weak or vulnerable point, eg in sb's character: (喩) (某人之個性等中的) 弱點: *Spelling is my ~' heel.* 拼字是我的弱點。

acid[1] /'æsɪd ; 'æsɪd/ *adj* **1** sour; sharp to the taste: 酸的;酸味的: *A lemon is an ~ fruit.* 檸檬是酸的水果。 *Vinegar has an ~ taste.* 醋有酸味。 **'~ drops,** sweets of boiled sugar with an ~ flavour. 酸糖 (一種用糖熬成而帶酸味的糖果)。 **2** (fig) sharp; sarcastic: (喩) 尖酸刻薄的;譏諷的: *an ~ wit;* 譏諷的機智; *~ remarks.* 刻薄話。

acid[2] /'æsɪd ; 'æsɪd/ *n* **1** [U] (chem) substance that contains hydrogen, which may be replaced by a metal to form a salt: (化學) 酸 (所含之氫能被金屬取代而成爲鹽類之物質): *Vinegar contains acetic ~.* 醋含有醋酸。 *H_2SO_4 stands for sulphuric ~;* H_2SO_4 代表硫酸; [C] example of this: 酸類: *Some ~s burn holes in wood and cloth.* 有些酸類物質能在木料及布帛上燒成洞。~ **test** *n* (fig) test that gives conclusive proof of the value or worth of sth. 酸性試驗; (喩) (足以證明某事物之價值的) 決定性的考驗。 **2** [U] (sl) (俚) = **LSD.** ⇨ App 2. 參看附錄二。~·**ify** /ə'sɪdɪfaɪ ; ə'sɪdə,faɪ/ *vt, vi* (*pt, pp* -fied) [VP6A, 2A] make or become ~. 使變酸;變酸;酸化。~·**ity** /ə'sɪdətɪ ; ə'sɪdətɪ/ *n* [U] state or quality of being ~. 酸味;酸性。~**ic** /ə'sɪdɪk ; ə'sɪdɪk/ *adj* ~**u·lated** /ə'sɪdjʊleɪtɪd *US:* -ɪdʒʊl- ; ə'sɪdʒə,letɪd/ *adj* made slightly ~. 帶酸味的;微酸的。~**u·lous** /ə'sɪdjʊləs *US:* -dʒʊl- ; ə'sɪdʒələs/ *adj* (lit or fig) somewhat sour in taste or manner; sharp; bitter: (字面或喩) 微酸的;壞脾氣的;乖戾的;尖刻的: *an ~ulous drink/tone of voice.* 微酸的酒(尖刻的聲調)。

ack-ack /ˌæk 'æk ; 'æk'æk/ *n* (mil sl) anti-aircraft gun/fire, etc. (軍俚) 高射砲 (砲火等)。

ac·knowl·edge /ək'nɒlɪdʒ ; ək'nɑlɪdʒ/ *vt* **1** [VP 6A, C, 9, 24A] confess; admit the truth, existence or reality of: 供認;承認: *He refused to ~ defeat/that he was defeated.* 他拒絕承認失敗 (被擊敗)。*He would not ~ his mistake.* 他不會認錯。*He won't ~ himself beaten.* 他將不承認自己被打敗。*He ~d having been frightened.* 他承認受驚。 *Does he ~ the signature,* agree or admit that it is his? 他承認那是他的簽字嗎? [VP25] (liter style): (文言體): *We praise Thee, O God, we ~ Thee to be the Lord.* 我們讚美你,呵上帝,我們承認你是主。 [VP16B] *Stephen ~d Henry as his heir,* recognized his claim to be heir. 史蒂芬認可亨利爲他的繼承人。 [VP25] *They all ~d him master,* agreed that he was their master. 他們一致承認他是主人。 **2** [VP6A] report that one has received (sth): 說明已收到(某物): *~ (receipt of) a letter.* 說明已收到一封來信。 **3** [VP6A] express thanks for: 表示感謝;爲…致謝: *We must not fail to ~ his services to the town.* 我們必須感謝他對本市的貢獻。 *We should always ~ gifts promptly.* 我們收到禮物應立卽致謝。 **4** [VP6A] indicate that one recognizes (sb) by giving a greeting, a smile, a nod of the head, etc: (以問候語,微笑,點頭等)表示認識(某人);向(某人)打招呼: *I passed her in the street but she didn't even ~ me when I smiled.* 我在街上遇到她,可是當我向她微笑時,她連招呼都沒有向我打一下。~·**ment, ac·knowl·edg·ment** *n* **1** [U] act of acknowledging: 承認;致謝;感謝: *We are sending you a small sum of money in ~ment of your valuable help.* 玆奉上薄款對閣下之鼎力相助聊表謝意。 **2** [C] sth given or done to ~ sth: 藉以表示收到或感謝之物;收悉通知或回報;收條;回帖: *We have had no ~ment of our letter,* no reply. 我們尙未收到回信。 *This basket of fruit is a slight ~ment of your kindness.* 這一籃水果是用來對你的恩惠略表謝意。

acme /'ækmɪ ; 'ækmɪ/ *n* **the ~,** summit; highest point of development; point of perfection: 頂點;極點;極致: *the ~ of his desires/skill.* 他的慾望(技藝)的頂點。

acne /'æknɪ ; 'æknɪ/ *n* [U] disease (common among adolescents) in which there are pimples and blackheads on the face and neck. 痤瘡;粉刺(青年人普遍的一種皮膚病,在面部及頸部長丘疹及黑頭粉刺)。

aco·lyte /'ækəlaɪt ; 'ækə,laɪt/ *n* person who helps a priest in some religious services, esp the celebration of Mass. 教士或僧侶在舉行宗教儀式時(尤指領彌撒時)的助手。

ac·on·ite /'ækənaɪt ; 'ækə,naɪt/ *n* (bot) (sorts of) plant with blue or purple flowers; monkshood; drug from the dried poisonous root of one of these kinds, used to slow down the action of the heart. (植物) 附子;烏頭(開藍或紫花之一屬植物);烏頭素(由此屬植物之毒根所提煉之藥物,用以減緩心臟的活動)。

acorn /'eɪkɔ:n ; 'ekən/ *n* seed or fruit of the oak tree. 橡子;橡實。⇨ the illus at tree. 參看 tree 之插圖。 **'~-cup** *n* cuplike holder of an ~. 橡實殼斗。

acous·tic /ə'ku:stɪk ; ə'kustɪk/ *adj* of sound, the science of sound and the sense of hearing. 聲音的;聲學的;音響學的;聽覺的。 □ *n* [C] studio, hall, etc from the consideration of its ~s (⇨ 2 below): 具有某種音響效果的錄音室、大廳等 (參看下列第 2 義): *Try recording the music in a better ~.* 試在傳音性較好的廳裡錄該音樂。 **acous·tics** *n* **1** (with *sing v*) the scientific study of sound. (用單數動詞) 聲學;音響學。 **2** (with *pl v*) the physical properties of sound; the properties of a hall, etc, that make it good, poor, etc for hearing music, speeches, etc: (用複數動詞) 聲音的物理性質; (大廳等之) 傳音性 (使演講,音樂演奏等的收聽效果良好,不良等): *The ~s of the new concert hall are excellent.* 這新音樂廳的傳音性極佳。

ac·quaint /ə'kweɪnt ; ə'kwent/ *vt* [VP14] **1 ~ sb/oneself with,** make familiar with, reveal to: 使某人(自己)熟悉於…;使明白;使通曉: *~ sb with the facts of the case;* 使某人知道該事件之詳情; *~ oneself/become ~ed/make oneself ~ed with one's new duties.* 使自己明白自己的新職責。 **2 be ~ed (with sb),** have met (sb) personally: 與(某人)見過面;認識;熟識: *I am not ~ed with the lady.* 我不認識那位女士。*We are not ~ed.* 我們(彼此)不認識。

ac·quaint·ance /ə'kweɪntəns ; ə'kwentəns/ *n* **1** [U] knowledge or information gained through experience: 從經驗獲得的知識;習知: *He has some ~ with German, but does not speak it fluently.* 他略懂一點德文,但說得不流利。***have a bowing/nodding ~ with,*** have some ~ with (a person, a subject). 與(某人)爲點頭之交;對(某學科)略知一二。***make sb's ~, make the ~ of sb,*** get to know sb, eg by being introduced. 與某人結識(如經過介紹)。***(up)on (further) ~,*** when known for a (further) period of time. 經過(較久)一段時間的認識。 **2** [C] person with whom one is acquainted; person whom one knows (less intimately than a friend): 相識的人(不如朋友那樣親密): *He has a wide circle of ~s.* 他交際極廣。 **3** (older English, collective): (在舊式英語中用作集合名詞): *He has a wide ~,* many ~s. 他交際廣闊(認識很多人)。~·**ship** /-ʃɪp ; -,ʃɪp/ *n* (circle of) ~s(2). 所有相識者;交際圈。

ac·quiesce /ˌækwɪ'es ; ,ækwɪ'ɛs/ *vi* **1** [VP2A] agree; accept silently or without protest. 同意;默認;默許;順從。 **2** [VP3A] **~ in,** accept an arrangement, a conclusion, etc without protest: 不提抗議地接受(安排,結論等);勉强同意: *Her parents will never ~ in such an unsuitable marriage.* 她的父母決不會同意這門不適宜的婚事。 **ac·qui·es·cence** /ˌækwɪ'esns ; ,ækwɪ'ɛsns/ *n* (act of) acquiescing.

同意;默認;默許;順從。**ac·qui·es·cent** /-ˈesnt ; -ˈɛsn̩t/ *adj* disposed to ～. 同意的;默認的;默許的;順從的。

ac·quire /əˈkwaɪə(r) ; əˈkwaɪr/ *vt* [VP6A] gain by skill or ability, by one's own efforts or behaviour: (由技術，能力，努力或行爲而) 獲得;得到: *～ a good knowledge of English／a reputation for dishonesty／a taste for brandy.* 熟諳英文(蒙上不誠實臭名;養成喝白蘭地酒的嗜好)。 ***an ～d taste,*** one that comes when one has experimented with sth and, in the end, comes to like it: 習得的(非天生的)嗜好: *Retsina* (= the resin-flavoured Gk wine) *is an ～d taste for British people.* 英國人喝瑞星娜酒(以樹脂作香料的希臘葡萄酒) 是一種習得的嗜好。 **～·ment** *n* **1** [U] acquisition (now the more usu word). 獲得;得到 (今較常用 acquisition)。 **2** [C] accomplishment(3) (now the more usu word). 才藝;教養;技藝(今較常用 accomplishment)。

ac·qui·si·tion /ˌækwɪˈzɪʃn ; ˌækwəˈzɪʃən/ *n* **1** [U] acquiring: 獲得;得到: *He devotes his time to the ～ of knowledge.* 他把時間都花在求知上。 **2** [C] sth acquired: 獲得物;添加物: *my most recent ～s,* eg books I have bought recently. 我最近增添的東西(例如新近才買的書籍)。 *Mr A will be a valuable ～ to* (= a valuable new member of) *the teaching staff of our school.* A先生將是本校教員陣容中的一支生力軍。

ac·quis·itive /əˈkwɪzətɪv ; əˈkwɪzətɪv/ *adj* fond of, in the habit of, acquiring: 好求得的;好獲取的: *～ of new ideas.* 好求新知。 **the ～ society,** that values the possession of more and more material things. 物慾橫流的社會 (重視擁有更多更多的物質享受)。

ac·quit /əˈkwɪt ; əˈkwɪt/ *vt* (-tt-) **1** [VP6A, 14] ***～ sb (of／on sth),*** give a legal decision that (sb) is not guilty, eg of an offence: 宣告某人無罪(如對某一罪狀): *He was ～ted of the crime／～ted on two of the charges.* 他被宣告無罪(他被指控的罪狀其中有兩項被宣告無罪)。 **2** [VP16B] conduct (oneself): 持(身);行爲: *He ～ted himself well／like a hero.* 他行爲端正(所作所爲如英雄)。 **～·tal** /əˈkwɪtl ; əˈkwɪtl̩/ *n* [U] judgement that a person is not guilty: 無罪的判決: *a sentence of ～tal;* 判決無罪; [C] instance of this: 判決無罪的實例: *three convictions and two ～tals.* 三人宣判有罪,兩人判決無罪。

acre /ˈeɪkə(r) ; ˈekɚ/ *n* [C] measure of land, 4840 sq yds or about 4000 sq metres. 英畝;噉(＝4,840平方碼,約4,000平方公尺)。 **God's ～,** churchyard (for burials). 教堂墓地。 **～·age** /ˈeɪkərɪdʒ ; ˈekərɪdʒ/ *n* [U] area of land measured in ～s: 以英畝計算之土地面積;英畝數;噉數: *What is the ～age of the London parks?* 倫敦各公園共佔地多少英畝?

ac·rid /ˈækrɪd ; ˈækrɪd/ *adj* (of smell or taste) sharp; biting: (指氣味或味道)辛辣的;難聞的: *the ～ smell of burning feathers;* 燒焦羽毛之難聞氣味; (fig) bitter in temper or manner. (喻) (性情或態度)尖刻的。

ac·ri·mony /ˈækrɪmənɪ *US:* -məʊnɪ ; ˈækrəˌmonɪ/ *n* [U] (formal) bitterness of temper, manner, language. (正式用語) (性情,態度,言語的) 尖刻;刻薄。 **ac·ri·moni·ous** /ˌækrɪˈməʊnɪəs ; ˌækrəˈmonɪəs/ *adj* (of arguments, quarrels, words) bitter. (指辯論,爭論,言詞)尖刻的;刻薄的;劇烈的。

ac·ro·bat /ˈækrəbæt ; ˈækrəˌbæt/ *n* person who can perform difficult or unusual physical acts with skill, eg on a tightrope or trapeze. 特技表演者;賣藝者;走鋼絲者;走索者;空中飛人。**～ic** /ˌækrəˈbætɪk ; ˌækrəˈbætɪk/ *adj* of or like an ～: 特技表演的;賣藝人的;似賣藝人的: *～ic feats.* 賣藝人的技藝。 **～·ics** *n pl* (used with *sing v*) ～ic tricks or feats: (用單數動詞)特技;江湖技藝: *aircraft ～ics.* 飛行特技。

ac·ro·nym /ˈækrənɪm ; ˈækrənɪm/ *n* [C] word formed from the initial letters of a name, eg **NASA** /ˈnæsə ; ˈnæsə/, National Aeronautics and Space Administration. 字首組字 (由一名稱之各字首字母所組成的字，例如 NASA, 係由 National Aeronautics and Space Administration 國家航空及太空總署之字首所組成)。 ⇨ App 2. 參看附錄二。

acrop·olis /əˈkrɒpəlɪs ; əˈkrɑpəlɪs/ *n* fortified part of a Gk city in ancient times, esp **the A～,** that of Athens. 古希臘城市用以據守的城堡;衞城;(尤指)雅典之衞城。

across¹ /əˈkrɒs *US:* əˈkrɔːs ; əˈkrɔs/ *adv* (used with *vv* in the senses of the *prep*): (與動詞連用,意義同介詞): *Can you swim ～?* 你能游到對岸去嗎? *Will you row me ～?* 你願意把我划到對岸去嗎? *I helped the blind man ～.* 我幫助那盲人走過街。 *Come ～ to my office this afternoon.* 今天下午到我辦公室來。*The river is half a mile ～,* = wide. 這河面寬半英里。 ***～ from,*** (US) opposite: (美)在…的對面: *The bank is just ～ from the school.* 銀行就在學校的對面。

across² /əˈkrɒs *US:* əˈkrɔːs ; əˈkrɔs/ *prep* **1** from one side to the other side of: 從…的一邊到另一邊;橫過: *walk ～ the street;* 走過街; *draw a line ～ a sheet of paper;* 在一張紙上畫一條橫線; *a bridge ～ the river;* 橫跨河上的一座橋; *row sb ～ a lake.* 划船送某人過湖。 ***ˌ～-the-ˈboard,*** including all groups, members, etc esp in an occupation or industry: (尤指在某一職業或產業中)包括各團體,全體會員等的;全面的: *an ～-the-board wage increase.* 工資的全面提高。 **2** on the other side of: 在…的另一邊: *My house is just ～ the street.* 我的房子就在街對面。 *We shall soon be ～ the Channel.* 我們不久卽將渡過海峽了。*He addressed me from ～ the room.* 他從房間的另一邊向我講話。 **3** so as to form a cross; so as to cross or intersect: 作十字形;交叉: *He sat with his arms ～ his chest.* 他兩臂交叉在胸前坐着。*The two lines pass ～ each other at right angles.* 這兩條線成直角相交。 **4** (with *vv*) ⇨ come(16), drop²(13), get(17), put¹(11) and run²(26).

acros·tic /əˈkrɒstɪk *US:* -ˈkrɔːs- ; əˈkrɔstɪk/ *n* word puzzle, word arrangement, in which the first, or the first and last, letters of the lines make a word or words. 離合字謎;離合體詩(數行詩句之首字母,或其首尾字母能聯合成字者)。

acryl·ic /əˈkrɪlɪk ; əˈkrɪlɪk/ *n* (comm) (商) **ˌ～ ˈfibre,** (kinds of) synthetic fibre used for making dress materials, etc. 壓克力纖維(用以製衣料等之數種合成纖維)。 **ˌ～ ˈresin,** (kinds of) transparent colourless plastic widely used in industry, eg for plastic lenses, aircraft windows. 壓克力塑膠(數種透明無色的塑膠,工業上使用極廣,如製鏡片,飛機窗等)。

act¹ /ækt ; ækt/ *n* [C] **1** sth done: 行爲;舉動: *To kick a cat is a cruel act.* 踢貓是殘忍的行爲。*It is an act of kindness to help a blind man across the street.* 幫助盲人過街是慈善的行爲。 **Acts (of the Apostles),** (NT) accounts of the missionary work of the Apostles. (新約)使徒行傳。 **2** process of, instant of, doing; action. 行動;行動之際。 ***(catch sb) in the (very) act (of doing sth),*** while performing the action: 正當其從事(某種行爲)之際;當場(抓住某人): *The thief was caught in the act of breaking into the house.* 那賊潛入房舍之際當場被捕獲。 *In the act of* (= While) *picking up the ball, he slipped and fell.* 正當其拾球之際,他失足跌倒。 **Act of God,** sth which is the result of uncontrollable natural forces, eg storms, floods,

acrobats

earthquakes. 天災;不可抗力 (如風暴,洪水,地震)。⇨ also grace(3). **3** law made by a legislative body: (立法機構所立的)法案: *an Act of Parliament;* (英國)議院的法案; *the Acts of Congress.* (美國)國會的法案。 **4** main division of a play: (戲劇的)一幕: *a play in five acts;* 一個五幕劇; *Hamlet, Act 1, Scene 3.* 哈姆雷特第一幕第三場。⇨ scene(5). **5** one of a series of short performances in a programme: 節目單上之一項短的表演;節目: *a circus/variety act.* 馬戲表演(綜藝表演)中的一項節目。 **6** (colloq) pretence: (俗) 佯裝: *Don't take him seriously—it's just an ~.* 不要把他看得太認眞—他祇是假裝那樣而已。 ***put on an act,*** (colloq) pretend; behave in an affected way (to get one's own way, etc). (俗)假裝;裝模作樣。

act² /ækt ; ækt/ *vi, vt* **1** [VP2A, 3A] perform actions, do sth: 行動;採取行動;做某事: *The time for talking is past; we must act at once.* 空談的時候已經過去了;我們必須立刻行動。 *The girl's life was saved because the doctors acted so promptly.* 那女孩的生命由於醫生們行動迅速而得以挽救。*You have acted* (= behaved) *generously.* 你表現得很慷慨。 ***act (up)on*** (*a suggestion/sb's advice/an order*), do what is suggested, advised, etc. 按照(建議,某人的忠告,命令)行事。 **2** [VP2A, 3A] do what is required; function normally: 起作用;操作正常: *The brakes wouldn't act, so there was an accident.* 煞車失靈,故發生車禍。*The pump is not acting well,* not performing its proper function. 泵(抽水機)不大靈光了。***act (up)on,*** have an effect (up)on: 對…起作用; 對…有功效: *This medicine acts on the heart/the bowels.* 這藥品對心臟(腸)有功效。 **3** [VP2A, C, 3A] perform in a professional or official capacity: (以專業人員或官員身分)執行職務: *The police refused to act,* would not interfere. 警方拒絕干預。***act as,*** be, perform, as an interpreter, mediator, etc. 充任;擔任(譯員,調解人等)。***act for/on behalf of,*** represent (sb) as a solicitor, barrister in a legal case: (如訟案中的律師)代表;代理: *A solicitor acts for his clients.* 律師代表他的當事人。 **4** [VP2A, C, 6A] take part in a play on the stage; take the part of, eg a character in a play or cinema film, or in real life: 參加舞臺劇演出;演戲; 扮演 (戲劇,電影,或現實生活中的一個角色): *Who is acting* (*the part of*) *Hamlet?* 是誰扮演哈姆雷特(這個角色)? *She acts well.* 她戲演得很好。*Don't act the fool/ass/idiot,* don't behave foolishly. 不要當傻瓜(愚人,獃子)。 *Browning's plays won't act,* are not suitable for the stage. 布朗寧的戲劇不宜上演。*She's not really crying; she's only acting* (= pretending) *in order to gain your sympathy.* 她並非眞哭;她不過是假裝哭以獲得你的同情。[VP15B] ***act sth out,*** perform actions which represent, and may help to release, the fears, inhibitions, etc of a neurotic person. 動作化(指神經過敏者以動作表達或舒解內心的恐懼,壓抑等)。 ***act up,*** (colloq) behave badly so as to attract attention; cause pain, irritation, annoyance by functioning badly: (俗)行爲惡劣以引人注意;因功能不良而引起疼痛,不適,煩惱;調皮;搗蛋: *My leg/car/TV, etc has been acting* (now more usu *playing*) *up all week.* 我的腿(車子,電視機等)整個星期來一直跟我搗蛋(今較常用 playing up)。

act·ing /ˈæktɪŋ ; ˈæktɪŋ/ *adj* doing the duties of another person for a time: 代理的;代行的: *the A~ Manager/Headmaster;* 代經理(校長); *A~ Captain.* 代船長。□ *n* [U] (art of) performing in a play for the theatre, cinema, TV, etc: 演技;演戲: *She did a lot of ~ while she was at college.* 她在大學時代演過很多次戲。 **ˈ~ copy,** (of a script) one for the use of an actor or actress. (指劇本原稿)演員用的脚本。

ac·tin·ism /ˈæktɪnɪzəm ; ˈæktɪn,ɪzəm/ *n* [U] property of light rays that produces chemical activity and changes (as in photographic films). 光化性 (光線的一種性質,能引起化學作用及變化,如對照相軟片所發生的作用)。**ac·tinic** /ækˈtɪnɪk ; ækˈtɪnɪk/ *adj* of ~: 光化性的: *actinic rays,* component of the sun's radiation. (有)光化性射線(太陽輻射線的成分)。

ac·tion /ˈækʃn ; ˈækʃən/ *n* **1** [U] process of doing things; movement; (way of) using energy, influence, etc: 行動;動作;做法;作用: *The time has come for ~,* We must act now. 行動的時候到了。*A man of ~ is not content just to talk.* 講求行動的人不以空談爲滿足。***bring/call sth into ~,*** cause it to operate. 使起作用;使生效;使操作。 ***put/set sth in ~,*** cause it to start acting. 實行;開動。***put sth out of ~,*** stop it working; make it unfit for use. 使停止工作或活動;使不適用。 ***take ~,*** begin to act. 開始行動;採取行動。**ˈ~ painting,** form of abstract painting in which paint is splashed, dribbled, etc on to the canvas. 一種抽象畫(作畫時以濺,潑,滴等手法着顏料於畫布上);潑墨畫。 **2** [C] thing done; act: 所作之事;行爲:*We shall judge you by your ~s, not by your promises.* 我們將憑你的作爲,而不以你的諾言來評判你。*She is impulsive in her ~s,* does things impulsively. 她做事很衝動。 ***A~s speak louder than words,*** Doing sth is more convincing than talking about it. 行動比言論有力。 **3** [C] **(a)** mechanism of a piano, gun or other instrument. (鋼琴,槍砲或其他器械的)機械裝置。 **(b)** manner of bodily movement, eg of a horse when jumping, of an athlete. 姿勢;姿態(例如馬跳躍時,運動員等所表現者)。 **4** [C] legal process. 訴訟。***bring an ~ against sb,*** seek judgement against him in a law court. 向法院提起訴訟控告某人。 **5** [U] fighting between bodies of troops, between warships, etc: (軍隊或兵艦等之間的)戰鬥行動: *go into ~,* start fighting; 開始戰鬥; *killed in ~;* 陣亡; [C] instance of this: 戰鬥行動的實例: *break off the ~,* stop fighting. 停止戰鬥。**ˈ~ stations,** (mil) positions to which soldiers, etc go when fighting is expected to begin. (軍) (卽將開始作戰時各士兵所應就的)作戰崗位。**~·able** /-əbl ; -əbl̩/ *adj* giving just cause for legal ~. 可控訴的。

ac·ti·vate /ˈæktɪveɪt ; ˈæktə,vet/ *vt* [VP6A] make active; (chem) accelerate a reaction in, eg by heat; (phys) cause radiation from. 使活潑;使活動;(化學)加速…之反應(如藉加熱等); 活化; (物理)引起輻射;賦與射能。 **ac·ti·va·tion** /ˌæktɪˈveɪʃn ; ˌæktəˈveʃən/ *n*

ac·tive /ˈæktɪv ; ˈæktɪv/ *adj* **1** doing things; able to do things; in the habit of doing things; energetic; characterized by activity: 做事的;能做事的;慣於做事的;精力充沛的;活動的;活躍的;靈活的;積極的: *He's over 90 and not very ~.* 他已九十多歲,不太活動了。*A boy with an ~ brain will be more successful than a dull boy.* 頭腦靈活的男孩將比遲鈍的男孩有出息。*Mount Vesuvius is an ~ volcano,* is one that erupts. 維蘇威山是一個活火山。*She has an ~* (= lively) *imagination.* 她有靈活的想像力。 *He takes an ~ part in school affairs.* 他積極參加學校裡的活動。***on ~ service,*** (Navy, Army, Air Force) (GB) engaged in actual military service, esp in fighting during a war; (US) on full duty, not in the reserves. (海,陸,空軍) (英)服現役;(尤指)戰時參與戰鬥;(美)服現役。***under ~ consideration,*** being considered or canvassed. 考慮中;在徹底討論中。 **2** (gram) (文法) **the ~ (voice), (a)** form of a *v phrase* not containing *be* + *pp*, as in: *He was driving.* Cf *He was being driven.* 主動語態(不含 be + pp 的動詞片語形式,如在 He was driving 句中,動詞片語 was driving 卽是主動語態;在 He was being driven 句中, was being driven 則爲被動語態)。⇨ passive. **(b)** sentence containing a *vt* in which the *n* or *pron* preceding the *v*, and agreeing with it (the grammatical subject), refers to the doer of the action, ie the agent: *The children finished the cake* (active). Cf *The cake was finished by the children* (passive). 主動句(含一及物動詞的句子,

A

句中的名詞或代名詞位於動詞之前，數、人稱等與動詞一致，爲文法上之主詞，且爲動作的做出者，卽行爲者：如The children finished the cake 卽是主動句；The cake was finished by the children 卽是被動句）。～·ly *adv*

ac·tiv·ist /ˈæktɪvɪst ; ˈæktɪvɪst/ *n* [C] person taking an active part, eg in a political movement. 積極參與者（如參與政治運動者）。

ac·tiv·ity /ækˈtɪvətɪ ; ækˈtɪvətɪ/ *n* (*pl* -ties) **1** [U] being active or lively: 活動性；活力：*When a man is over 70, his time of full ～ is usually past.* 當人活到七十以後，他的充滿活力的時期通常都已過去了。 **2** [C] thing (to be) done; occupation: 所做或待做的事情；活動：*Classroom activities are things done by pupils in the classroom; outdoor activities are things done outside.* 教室活動是學生們在教室裏所作的事情；戶外活動是在室外所做的事情。*My numerous activities leave me little leisure.* 繁多的事務使我一點空閒也沒有。

ac·tor /ˈæktə(r) ; ˈæktɚ/ *n* **1** man who acts on the stage, TV or in films. （舞臺，電視或電影）男演員。 **2** person who takes part in a notable event, etc. 參加要事的角色。

ac·tress /ˈæktrɪs;ˈæktrɪs/ *n* woman actor(1). 女演員。

ac·tual /ˈæktʃʊəl ; ˈæktʃʊəl/ *adj* existing in fact; real: 實在的；眞實的；確實的；實際的：*It's an ～ fact; I haven't invented or imagined it.* 這是眞實的事實；並不是我捏造或想像出來的。*Can you give me the ～ figures,* the real figures, not an estimate or a guess? 你能給我確實的數字嗎（不要單是估計或猜測）？*What is the ～ position of affairs?* 事情的實際情況如何？～·ly /ˈæktʃʊlɪ ; ˈæktʃʊəlɪ/ *adv* **1** in ～ fact; really: 實際地；實在地：*the political party ～ly in power.* 實際掌握政權的政黨；執政黨。*He looks honest, but ～ly he's a rogue.* 他外表忠厚，但實際是個流氓。 **2** strange or surprising as it may seem: 居然；眞地：*He ～ly expected me to do his work for him!* 他眞地想要我替他做他的事！*He not only ran in the race; he ～ly won it!* 他不但參加了賽跑，並且居然跑贏了。～·**ity** /ˌæktʃʊˈælətɪ ; ˌæktʃʊˈælətɪ/ *n* (*pl* -ties) **1** [U] ～ existence; reality. 實際；眞實。 **2** [C, usu *pl*] ～ conditions or facts; realities. （通常用複數）實際情況；眞正的事實。

ac·tu·ary /ˈæktʃʊərɪ *US:* -tʃʊerɪ ; ˈæktʃʊˌɛrɪ/ *n* (*pl* -ries) expert who calculates insurance premiums (by studying rates of mortality, frequency of fires, thefts, accidents, etc). 保險公司的核計員（負責研究死亡率，火災、竊盜、意外事件等的出事率，而核計保險費率者）；理賠員。**ac·tu·ar·ial** /ˌæktʃʊˈeərɪəl ; ˌæktʃʊˈɛrɪəl/ *adj* of an ～ or his work. 保險公司核計員的；理賠員的；保險核計的。

ac·tu·ate /ˈæktʃʊeɪt ; ˈæktʃʊˌet/ *vt* [VP6A] (formal) cause to act: （正式用語）使活動；使行動：*A great statesman is ～d by love of his country, not by love of power.* 一個偉大政治家的行動係基於愛國，而非基於愛權。

acu·ity /əˈkjuːətɪ ; əˈkjuətɪ/ *n* [U] (formal) acuteness. （正式用語）尖銳；銳利；敏銳。

acu·men /əˈkjuːmen ; əˈkjumɪn/ *n* [U] sharpness and accuracy of judgement; ability to understand clearly: 敏銳及正確的判斷力；清晰的瞭解力；聰明才智：*business ～.* 善理事務的才智；生意眼。

acu·punc·ture /ˈækjʊpʌŋktʃə(r) ; ˈækjʊˌpʌŋktʃɚ/ *n* [U] (med) pricking or puncturing of the living tissues of the human body with fine needles to cure disease, to relieve pain and as a local anaesthetic. （醫）針灸；針刺法；針術（用細針在人體生機組織上穿刺，藉以治病，減除疼痛，並作局部麻醉）。

acute /əˈkjuːt ; əˈkjut/ *adj* **1** (of the senses, sensations, intellect) keen, sharp, quick: （指五官，感覺，智力）深刻的；劇烈的；敏銳的：*Dogs have an ～ sense of smell.* 狗有敏銳的嗅覺。*Our anxiety became more ～.* 我們的焦慮越來越厲害。*He felt ～ remorse for his wrongdoing.* 他對於他所做的壞事深深地感到懊悔。*A bad tooth can cause ～ pain.* 一顆壞牙齒會引起劇痛。*He is an ～ observer.* 他是一個敏銳的觀察者。 **2** (of diseases) coming sharply to a crisis: （指疾病）急性的：*The patient has reached the ～ stage of the disease,* the brief period during which the disease is severe and at a turning point. 該患者已經到達了此病的急性期。*Pneumonia is an ～ disease,* one that comes quickly to a turning-point. 肺炎是一種急性病。⇨ chronic. **3** (of sounds) high; shrill. （指聲音）高音的；尖銳的。 **4** ～ **angle**, angle of less than 90°. 銳角（小於 90° 之角）。⇨ the illus at angle. 參看 angle 之插圖。 **5** ～ **accent**, mark over a vowel (ʹ), as over *e* in *café*. 尖音記號（標於母音上者，例如 café 中母音 e 上的 ʹ）。～·**ly** *adv* ～·**ness** *n*

ad /æd ; æd/ *n* [C] (colloq abbr for) advertisement: （俗）廣告（爲 advertisement 之略）：*'Want ads'*, in newspapers, etc. （報紙等上的）'求才廣告'。

ad·age /ˈædɪdʒ ; ˈædɪdʒ/ *n* [C] old and wise saying; proverb. 古訓；俗諺。

adagio /əˈdɑːdʒɪəʊ ; əˈdɑdʒo/ *n* (*pl* -gios /-dʒɪəʊz ; -dʒoz/) *adj, adv* (music) (passage played) gracefully and in slow time. （音樂）慢板；慢板速度的樂章或樂曲；慢板的（地）。

Adam /ˈædəm ; ˈædəm/ *n* ˌ～'s ˈ**apple**, part that projects in the front of the throat, esp in men, and moves up and down when one speaks. 喉結（尤指男人咽喉前面之突出部份，於說話時上下移動）。⇨ the illus at head. 參看 head 之插圖。***the old*** ～, (facet) the immoral, selfish side of human nature. （玩笑語）人性邪惡的一面；本性；私慾。***not know sb from*** ～, not know him at all. 與某人從未謀面；與某人素不相識。⇨ know(2).

ada·mant /ˈædəmənt ; ˈædəˌmænt/ *n* [C] kind of stone that, it is said, cannot be cut or broken. 硬石（據說是一種不能被切割或敲碎的石頭）。□ *pred adj* unyielding; firm in purpose: 不讓步的；固執的；堅定不移的：*He was ～ to their pleas.* 他毫不爲他們的請求所動。*On this point I am ～,* Nothing can change my decision. 關於這一點，我是堅決的。*I only wish he were less ～.* 但願他不那麽固執。**ada·man·tine** /ˌædəˈmæntaɪn ; ˌædəˈmæntɪn/ *adj* unyielding; inflexible. 不讓步的；不屈不撓的；堅定不移的。

adapt /əˈdæpt ; əˈdæpt/ *vt* [VP6A, 14] make suitable for a new use, need, situation, etc: 使適應；使配合；改編；改寫：*When you go to a new country, you must ～ yourself to new manners and customs.* 當你到一個新的國家時，你必須使自己適應新的風俗習慣。*Difficult books are sometimes ～ed for use in schools.* 艱難的書籍有時被改寫，以便適用於學校。*This book is ～ed to the needs of beginners／～ed for beginners.* 本書經過改寫以適合初學者的需要。*The play has been ～ed from the French,* ie translated and changed to suit English audiences. 此劇係由法文本編譯而成（以應英國觀衆的需要）。*Novels are often ～ed for the stage, television and radio.* 小說常被改編爲舞台劇本，電視劇及廣播劇脚本。～**er**, ～**or** /-tə(r) ; -tɚ/ *nn* person who ～s sth; device that enables sth to be used for a purpose, or in a way, different from that for which it was designed, eg a fitting for taking electric current from an outlet so that more than one piece of apparatus may be used. 使某事物適合新需要的人；改造者；改編者；使某物適合新需要的裝置；接頭；配合件；轉接器；承接管。～·**able** /-əbl ; -əbl̩/ *adj* able to ～ oneself; able to be ～ed: 能適應的；可改編的：*an ～able man,* one who can ～ himself to circumstances, etc. 能適應環境的人。～·**a·bil·ity** /əˌdæptəˈbɪlətɪ ; əˌdæptəˈbɪlətɪ/ *n* [U] power of ～ing or being ～ed. 適應力；適應性。**ad·ap·ta·tion** /ˌædæpˈteɪʃn ; ˌædəpˈteʃən/ *n* ***～ation (of sth) (for／to sth)***, **1** [U] state of being ～ed; ～ing. 適應；改編；改作。 **2** [C] sth made by ～ing: 經改造而成的東西；改編成的作品：*an ～ation (of a novel) for the stage／for broadcasting.* （由小說）改編的舞台劇本（廣播劇脚本）。

add /æd ; æd/ *vt, vi* **1** [VP6A, 14] ***add sth (to sth)***, join, unite, put (one thing together with another): 加;增加;加添: *If you add 5 and/to 5 you get 10.* 五加五得十。*The house has been added to from time to time,* new rooms, etc have been built on to it. 這棟房子曾經一再的擴建。*If the tea is too strong, add some hot water.* 如果茶太濃,再加點開水。**'adding-machine** *n* machine for calculating mechanically. 加數機。 **2** [VP6A, 9] say further; go on to say: 又說;繼續說: *'and I hope you'll come early,' he added.* 他接着又說,'並且我希望你早點來。' *She added that....* 她接着又說…。 **3** [VP15B, 3A, 2C] (special uses with *adverbial particles* and *preps*): (與副詞接語及介詞連用之特殊用法):

add sth in, include. 包括;將某事物加進去。

add to, increase: 增加: *This adds to our difficulties.* 這會增加我們的困難。

add sth together, combine two or more things. 將某些事物結合起來;湊合在一起。

add sth up, find the sum of: 求…的總數;加起來: *add up a column of figures;* 將一列數字加起來; *add up ten figures;* 將十個數目加起來; *add them up.* 求它們的總和。

add up (to), **(a)** give as a result, when joined: 加起來總和是: *The figures add up to 365.* 這些數目加起來總和是365。**(b)** (colloq) mean; indicate; amount to: (俗)含義是;表示;等於;總而言之: *All that this adds up to is that you don't want to help, so why not say so at once?* 總而言之,你不想幫忙,那麼,爲何不立即明說呢? **(c)** (colloq) make sense; be plausible: (俗)有意義;講得通: *It just doesn't add up.* 這簡直沒有意義。

ad·den·dum /ə'dendəm; ə'dɛndəm/ *n* (*pl* -da /-də; -də/) thing (omitted) that is to be added. 補遺;補編。

ad·der /'ædə(r); 'ædɚ/ *n* viper; any of several small poisonous snakes common in Europe, Africa (eg the *puff-~*) and Asia. 蝮蛇;蝰蛇(產於歐,非,亞洲的小毒蛇,如產於非洲之鼓腹蝰)。⇨ the illus at snake. 參看 snake 之插圖。

ad·dict /ə'dɪkt; ə'dɪkt/ *vt* (usu passive) (通常用於被動語態) ***be ~ed to,*** be given to, habitually or compulsively: 耽溺於;嗜好: *He is ~ed to alcohol/smoking/lying/study/drugs.* 他嗜好喝酒(抽煙,說謊,讀書,麻醉藥)。□ *n* /'ædɪkt; 'ædɪkt/ person who is ~ed, esp to sth harmful: 耽溺於某種(尤指危害身體)嗜好的人: *a 'drug ~.* 有毒癮之人;有藥癮者。**ad·dic·tion** /ə'dɪkʃn; ə'dɪkʃən/ *n* [U] being ~ed; [C] instance of this. 癮;耽溺;癖好;嗜好。**ad·dic·tive** /ə'dɪktɪv; ə'dɪktɪv/ *adj* causing ~ion: 引起嗜好的;會令人上癮的: *~ive drugs.* 引人上癮的麻醉藥。

ad·di·tion /ə'dɪʃn; ə'dɪʃən/ *n* **1** [U] process of adding: 加: *The sign + stands for ~.* + 號代表加。***in ~ (to),*** as well (as). 加之;又;除…之外;並且。**2** [C] sth added or joined: 增加物: *They've just had an ~ to the family,* another child. 他們家裏剛又增加了一口。*He will be a useful ~ to the staff of the school,* a useful new teacher. 他將是該校教員中新增加的有用的一員。**~al** /-ʃənl; -ʃənḷ/ *adj* extra; added: 外加的;附加的;另加的: *~al charges.* 外加的費用。**~·ally** /-ʃənəlɪ; -ʃənḷɪ/ *adv*

ad·di·tive /'ædɪtɪv; 'ædətɪv/ *n* [C] substance added in small amounts for a special purpose: 爲某一特殊目的而加入的少量物質;添加劑: *food ~s,* eg to add colour; 食品添加劑; *petrol ~s,* eg to reduce engine knocking. 汽油添加劑(如減少引擎爆震者)。

addle /'ædl; 'ædḷ/ *adj* (usu in compounds) confused; muddled. (通常用於複合字中)糊塗的;混淆不清的。**'~-brained, '~-pated** /-peɪtɪd; -'petɪd/ *adjj* having confused ideas. 頭腦不清的;糊塗的。**'~-head,** *n* person with confused ideas. 頭腦不清的人;糊塗蛋。□ *vt, vi* **1** [VP6A] confuse: 使糊塗;攪昏: *~ one's head/brains.* 攪昏某人的頭腦。**2** [VP2A] (of eggs) become rotten: (指蛋)變腐壞: *~d eggs.* 壞蛋。

ad·dress[1] /ə'dres *US:* 'ædres; ə'drɛs/ *n* **1** details of where a person may be found and where letters, etc may be delivered: 通訊處;住址: *What's your home/business ~?* 你的住宅(辦公)地址爲何? *Let me know if you change your ~.* 假若你變更通訊處,請通知我。**2** speech or talk (to an audience). (對聽衆的)演說;談話。**ˌpublic '~ system,** system using microphones, loudspeakers, etc for amplifying speeches. 播講系統;擴音系統(利用麥克風,揚聲器等,使演說的聲音放大)。**3** [U] (old use) manner or behaviour, esp in conversation: (舊用法)態度;行爲;(尤指)談吐風度: *a man of pleasing ~.* 談吐風度優雅的人。**4** [U] ***form of ~,*** style of written or spoken communication: (通信或交談中的)稱呼: *polite forms of ~.* 客氣的稱呼形式。**5** (*pl*) (old use) polite attentions or courtship: (複)(舊用法)慇懃;求愛: *pay one's ~es to a lady,* seek to win her hand in marriage; 追求一女子; *reject sb's ~es,* show that one does not welcome sb's wishes to be friendly. 不接受某人的慇懃。**~ee** /ˌædre'siː; ˌædrɛs'i/ *n* person to whom sth is ~ed(2). 收件人。**A~o·graph** /ə'dresəʊgrɑːf *US:* -græf; ə'drɛsəˌgræf/ *n* (P) machine for printing ~es(1) on circulars, etc. (商標)姓名住址印刷機(用以印刷姓名住址於函件等)。

ad·dress[2] /ə'dres; ə'drɛs/ *vt* **1** [VP6A, 16B] make a speech to; speak to, using a title: 向…發表演說;向…說話;稱呼: *Mr Green will now ~ the meeting.* 現在由格林先生向大會演說。*Don't ~ me as Colonel'; I'm only a major.* 不要稱呼我爲上校;我只不過是少校。**2** [VP6A] write a destination on (with the name of the person to whom sth is to be delivered): 在…上寫收件人的姓名地址: *The letter was wrongly ~ed.* 這封信的地址寫錯了。**3** [VP14] ~ ***sth to,*** send (a remark, complaint, etc) to: 向…提出(評論,訴願等): *Please ~ all enquiries to this office.* 一切查詢請向本辦公室提出。*Please ~ complaints to the manager, not to me.* 請把訴願向經理提出,不要向我提出。**4** [VP14] ~ ***oneself to,*** (formal) (正式用語) work at, apply oneself to, be busy with (a task, etc): 從事於;忙着做: *It's time we ~ed ourselves to the business in hand,* time we got busy with the business we are here for. 是動手做我們手上的事情的時候了。

ad·duce /ə'djuːs *US:* ə'duːs; ə'djus/ *vt* [VP6A] (formal) put forward) as proof, as an example): (正式用語)(作爲證據或例子而)提出;舉出: *~ reasons/proof/authority.* 舉出理由(證據,根據)。

ad·en·oids /'ædɪnɔɪdz *US:* -dən-; 'ædṇˌɔɪdz/ *n pl* (anat) soft, sponge-like growth between the back of the nose and the throat, in some cases making breathing and speech difficult: (解剖)腺樣增殖體(生長於鼻後與喉之間的海綿狀柔軟瘤腫,有時可致呼吸及說話困難): *have one's ~ out,* ie by a surgical operation. 動手術把腺樣增殖體割掉。*She's got ~,* (colloq) is suffering from inflammation of the ~. (俗)她患了腺樣增殖體炎。⇨ the illus at head. 參看 head之插圖。**ad·en·oidal** /ˌædɪ'nɔɪdl; ˌædṇ'ɔɪdḷ/ *adj* of the ~: 腺樣增殖體的: *an adenoidal youth,* one suffering from diseased ~. 患腺樣增殖的年輕人。

adept /'ædept; 'ædɛpt/ *adj* expert, skilled (*in* sth; *at* or *in* doing sth). 長於…的;善於…的;精於…的(與 in 連用,後接名詞;與 in 或 at 連用,後接動名詞)。□ *n* expert: 擅長者;專家: *I'm not an ~ in photography.* 我並非攝影專家。

ad·equate /'ædɪkwət; 'ædəkwɪt/ *adj* satisfactory; sufficient; satisfying a requirement: 令人滿意的;適當的;足够的;符合要求的: *£10 a week is not ~ to support a family* 十鎊一週不足以維持一個家庭。*Are you getting an ~ wage for the work you're doing?* 你目前工作的待遇是否令你滿意? **~·ly** *adv* **ad·equacy** /'ædɪkwəsɪ; 'ædəkwəsɪ/ *n* [U] state of being ~: 適當;足够;勝任: *He often doubts his adequacy as a husband and father.* 他常常懷疑自己是否是一個够格的丈夫及父親。

ad·here /əd'hɪə(r); əd'hɪr/ *vi* [VP2A, 3A] ~ ***(to),*** (formal) (正式用語) **1** stick fast (to): 黏着;

附着（與 to 連用）: *Glue and paste are used to make one surface ~ to another.* 膠水和漿糊是用以黏合一個表面與另一表面的。**2** remain faithful (to); support firmly: 忠於（與 to 連用）;堅持: ~ *to one's plans／to an opinion／to a political party／to a promise.* 堅持計畫（堅持意見;忠於政黨;堅守諾言）。*We decided to ~ to the programme.* 我們決定堅持這項計畫。(Cf 參較 *depart from*). **ad·her·ence** /-rəns ; -rəns/ *n*: *adherence to a plan.* 堅持計畫。

ad·her·ent /əd'hɪərənt ; əd'hɪrənt/ *n* supporter (of a party, etc, but not necessarily a member): 支持者; 擁護者（爲政黨之擁護者不一定爲其黨員）: *The proposal is gaining more and more ~s.* 該建議正得到越來越多的支持者。

ad·hesion /əd'hi:ʒn ; əd'hiʒən/ *n* **1** [U] adhering; being or becoming attached or united. 黏合;黏附; 結合; 附着（力）。 **2** [U] support: 支持; 擁護: *give one's ~ to a plan.* 對某一項計畫予以支持。**3** [U] (path) joining together of tissues in the body, eg after an injury; [C] instance of this: （病理）體內組織之黏連（如於受傷後）; 此種黏連的實例: *painful ~s resulting from a wound that did not heal.* 因傷口未癒而引起的疼痛的黏連。

ad·hes·ive /əd'hi:sɪv ; əd'hisɪv/ *adj* having the property of sticking: 有黏性的: ~ *tape／plaster.* 黏帶;膠布（絆創膏;黏膏）。□ *n* [C, U] ~substance, eg *gum.* 有黏着性之物（如樹膠）。

ad hoc /ˌæd 'hɒk ; 'æd'hɑk/ *adj, adv* (Lat) arranged for a particular purpose; not pre-arranged; informal: （拉）爲某一目的而安排的;特別的;非預先安排的;非正式的:*an ~ committee meeting.*特別召開的委員會議。

adieu /ə'dju: *US:* ə'du: ; ə'dju/ *n, int* (*pl* -s or -x /ə'dju:z *US:* ə'du:z ; ə'djuz/) (F) goodbye: （法）再會;再見: *bid sb ~;* 向某人告別; *make one's ~／~s,* say goodbye. 告別;辭行。

ad in·fi·nitum /ˌæd ˌɪnfɪ'naɪtəm ; 'ædˌɪnfə'naɪtəm/ *adv* (Lat) without limit; for ever. （拉）無限地;永恆地;以至無窮。

ad inter·im /ˌæd 'ɪntərɪm ; 'æd'ɪntərɪm/ *adj, adv* (Lat) in the meantime. （拉）其間;在那個期間;臨時的;過渡的。

adi·pose /'ædɪpəʊs ; 'ædəˌpos/ *adj* of animal fat; fatty: 脂肪的;多脂肪的: ~ *tissue.* 脂肪組織。

ad·jac·ent /ə'dʒeɪsnt ; ə'dʒesn̩t/ *adj* next (*to*), lying near (*to*) but not necessarily touching: 毗連的; 接近的; 隣近的（不一定相接觸，與 to 連用）: ~ *rooms;* 相連的房間; ~ *angles,* ⇨ the illus at angle. 隣角（參看 angle 之插圖）。*The house ~ to the church is the vicarage.* 那棟毗隣教堂的房子是牧師住宅。

ad·jec·tive /'ædʒɪktɪv ; 'ædʒɪktɪv/ *n* (gram) word that names a quality, or that defines or limits a noun. （文法）形容詞。 **ad·jec·tival** /ˌædʒɪk'taɪvl ; ˌædʒɪk'taɪvl/ *adj* of or like an ~: 形容詞的;似形容詞的: *an adjectival phrase／clause.* 形容詞片語（子句）。

ad·join /ə'dʒɔɪn ; ə'dʒɔɪn/ *vt, vi* [VP6A, 2A] ~ ***(to),*** be next or nearest to: 臨近;隣近;接近;毗連: *The playing-field ~s the school.* 運動場臨近學校。*The two houses ~.* 這兩棟房屋相毗連。**~·ing** *part adj*: *~ing bedrooms.* 毗連的臥室。

ad·journ /ə'dʒɜ:n ; ə'dʒɝn/ *vt, vi* **1** [VP6A] break off, eg proceedings of a meeting, etc for a time: 使（會議等）停止一個時期;使休會: *The meeting was ~ed for a week／until the following week.* 會議休會一星期（下星期復會）。**2** [VP2C] (of a meeting, etc) be broken off in this way: （指會議等）休會: *The meeting ~ed at five o'clock.* 會議於五點鐘休會。**3** [VP2A, C] (colloq, of persons who have met together) （俗,指聚在一起的人們） **(a)** break off proceedings and separate. 停止活動而分手。**(b)** go to another place: 到另外一個地方去: *When dinner was over they ~ed to the sitting-room.* 當宴席完畢時,他們都到客廳裡去了。**~·ment** *n* ~ing or being ~ed. 休會;散會。

ad·judge /ə'dʒʌdʒ ; ə'dʒʌdʒ/ *vt* **1** [VP25, 9] decide officially, by law: 宣判;判定: ~ *sb* (*to be*) *guilty;* 宣判某人有罪; ~ *that a man is insane.* 判定某人精神不正常。 **2** [VP14] award: 判給;斷與: ~ *land and property to sb;* 將土地及財產判與某人; ~ *a prize／legal damages to sb.* 將獎賞（法定損害賠償）判歸某人。

ad·ju·di·cate /ə'dʒu:dɪkeɪt ; ə'dʒudɪˌket/ *vt, vi* **1** [VP6A, 14] (of a judge or court) give a judgement or decision upon: （指法官或法庭）判決;裁判: *~ a claim for damages.* 裁定一項損害賠償的要求。**2** [VP2A, 3A] sit in judgement in order to decide: 裁判;裁決: ~ (*up*) *on a question.* 裁決一個問題。 **3** [VP25] declare (sb to be): 宣布;宣判（某人是）: ~ *sb bankrupt.* 宣判某人破產。**ad·ju·di·ca·tion** /əˌdʒu:dɪ'keɪʃn ; əˌdʒudɪ'keʃən/ *n* **ad·ju·di·ca·tor** /-tə(r) ; -tɚ/ *n* judge; member of a jury, eg in a musical competition. 審判官;裁判;評判員（如音樂比賽中者）。

ad·junct /'ædʒʌŋkt ; 'ædʒʌŋkt/ *n* **1** sth extra but subordinate. 附加物;附屬物。 **2** (gram) word(s) or phrase added to qualify or define another word in a sentence. （文法）附屬語;修飾語（加在句中用以修飾其他字詞者）。

ad·jure /ə'dʒʊə(r) ; ə'dʒʊr/ *vt* [VP17] (formal) ask (sb) earnestly or solemnly; require (sb) to do sth as though on oath or under penalty: （正式用語）懇求（某人）;以發誓的方式要求（某人）做某事: *I ~ you to tell the truth.* 我懇求你說實話。 **ad·jur·ation** /ˌædʒʊə'reɪʃn ; ˌædʒʊ'reʃən/ *n* [U] adjuring; [C] earnest or solemn request. 懇求;誠懇或鄭重的請求。

ad·just /ə'dʒʌst ; ə'dʒʌst/ *vt* [VP6A,14] ~ ***oneself／sth (to),*** set right; put in order; regulate; make suitable or convenient for use: 調整;調節;使適用;使便於使用: *The body ~s itself to changes in temperature.* 身體能自行調節以適應氣溫變化。*You can't see well through a telescope unless it is ~ed correctly to your sight.* 除非你把望遠鏡準確地調節到適合你的視力,否則你就看不清楚。*She will have to ~ herself to new conditions,* change her ways of living, thinking, etc. 她將必須使自己能適應新的環境。*Please do not ~ your sets,* warning on a TV screen that the controls need not be changed. 請不要調整你的電視機（電視螢光幕上的提示,請勿變換電視機的頻道）。*You should ~ your expenditure to your income.* 你必須量入爲出（調節你的費用以配合你的收入）。**ˌwell-'~ed,** (psych) in harmonious relations with other persons: （心理）與他人保持和諧關係的;善於順應的: *a well-~ed child.* 與他人和諧相處的小孩。**~·able** /-əbl ; -əbl/ *adj* that can be ~ed. 可調節的;可調整的。**~·er** *n* (comm) person from an insurance company whose business it is to settle amounts due when claims are made, eg for loss. （商）保險公司調解員（其工作是,當投保人提出如損失賠償要求時,由其出面協商決定適當的賠償金額）。**~·ment** *n* **1** [U] ~ing; settling of, eg insurance, claims; [C] act of ~ing. 調節;調整;（保險、主張等之）調解。**2** [C] means of ~ing sth; part of an apparatus for ~ing sth. 調節器;調整具。

ad·ju·tant /'ædʒʊtənt ; 'ædʒətənt/ *n* **1** (mil) army officer responsible for general administration and discipline in a battalion. （軍）負責一營中之一般行政及風紀的陸軍軍官;副官。 **2** (also 亦作 ~ **bird**) large Indian stork. （印度產之）大鸛。

ad lib /ˌæd 'lɪb ; æd'lɪb/ *adv* (abbr of *ad libitum*) (colloq) freely; without restraint. （爲 ad libitum 之略）（俗）自由地;隨意;無限制地。 **ad-lib** *vi* (-bb-) [VP2A] (colloq) improvise, eg by making additions to one's part in a play. （俗）卽席而作（如在一劇中對其所扮演角色之台詞予以增加）;臨時穿插。□ *attrib adj* made by ad-libbing: 卽席而作的;臨時穿插的: *ad-lib comments.* 卽席而作的評論。

ad libitum /ˌæd 'lɪbɪtəm ; 'æd'lɪbɪtəm/ *adv* (Lat; 拉; abbr 略作 *ad lib*) (music) (to be) performed with omissions as desired. （音樂）任意;聽便。⇨ obbligato(1).

ad·man /'æd mæn ; 'ædˌmæn/ *n* (colloq) man who composes commercial advertisements. （俗）製作商業廣告的人。

ad·mass /ˈædmæs ; ˈædmæs/ *n* [U] that part of the public easily influenced by the mass media. 易受大衆傳播工具所左右的民衆。⇨ media.

ad·min·is·ter /ədˈmɪnɪstə(r) ; ədˈmɪnəstɚ/ *vt, vi* **1** [VP6A] control, manage, look after business affairs, a household, etc: 管理;處理;照料;治理(商務,家務等): *~ a country,* govern it. 治理國家。 **2** [VP6A, 14] apply; put into operation; hand out; give: 執行;實施;給與;施與: *~ the law;* 執法; *~ punishment to sb;* 予某人以懲罰; *~ relief/help to people who are suffering from floods;* 對水災災民施以救濟(救助); *~ a severe blow to the enemy;* 予敵人一記嚴重的打擊; *~ justice,* do the work of a judge. 審判;執法。 **3** [VP6A, 14] cause to take: 使作(誓言);使接受: *~ the last sacraments,* ie to a dying man. 行臨終的聖餐禮(即使垂死之人領最後的聖餐)。*The oath was ~ed to him.* 他受命宣誓。 **4** *~ to,* ⇨ minister².

ad·min·is·tra·tion /ədˌmɪnɪˈstreɪʃn ; ədˌmɪnəˈstreʃən/ *n* **1** [U] management of affairs, etc, esp public affairs, government policy, etc. (事務等,尤指公共事務,國家政策等之)管理;經營。 **2** [C] (often 常作 A~) (esp US) that part of the Government which manages public affairs: (尤美)中央政府的行政部門;中央政府;內閣: *Successive A~s failed to solve the country's problems.* 歷屆政府均未能解決該國的問題。 **3** [U] the administering of justice, an oath, a sacrament, relief, a remedy, a punishment. 執法;宣誓;行聖餐禮;救濟;用藥;懲罰。⇨ ministration.

ad·min·is·tra·tive /ədˈmɪnɪstrətɪv *US:* -streɪtɪv ; ədˈmɪnəˌstretɪv/ *adj* of the management of affairs; of an administration(2): 管理的;行政的: *an ~ post;* 行政的職位; *lacking in ~ ability.* 缺乏行政能力。

ad·min·is·tra·tor /ədˈmɪnɪstreɪtə(r) ; ədˈmɪnəˌstretɚ/ *n* person who administers; person with ability to organize; (legal) person officially appointed to manage the property of others, to take charge of an estate, etc. 管理者;具組織才能的人;(法律)(官方指定管理他人財產,或負責某一地產等的)財產管理人。

ad·mir·able /ˈædmərəbl ; ˈædmərəbḷ/ *adj* excellent; causing admiration. 極佳的;令人欽佩的。 **ad·mir·ably** /-əblɪ ; -əblɪ/ *adv*

ad·miral /ˈædmərəl ; ˈædmərəl/ *n* officer in command of a country's warships, or of a fleet or squadron; naval rank above vice-~ and below (GB) ~ of the fleet or (US) fleet ~. 艦(戰)隊司令;海軍上將(海軍軍階,在海軍中將之上,海軍元帥之下)。 **~·ty** /ˈædmərəltɪ ; ˈædmərəltɪ/ *n* **1** office of ~. 海軍上將或艦隊司令之職務。 **2** that branch of Government which controls the Navy. 海軍部。 **the A~ty,** (GB) headquarters of the naval administration. (英)海軍部之總司令部(指所在地)。 **ˌCourt of ˈA~ty,** court for deciding law questions concerning shipping. 海事法庭。

ad·mir·ation /ˌædməˈreɪʃn ; ˌædməˈreʃən/ *n* [U] **1** feeling of pleasure, satisfaction, respect or, formerly, wonder: 讚賞;讚美;欽佩;(昔時)驚奇: *She speaks English so well that her friends are filled with ~.* 她英語說得好極了,她的朋友皆讚美不已。*Everyone cried out in ~.* 人人皆驚呼讚嘆。*We were lost in ~ of the scenery.* 我們沈醉在美麗的風景中。*My ~ for your skill is great.* 我對你的技巧非常欽佩。 **2** (*sing* with *def art*) object that arouses ~. (單數與定冠詞連用)令人讚賞的對象。

ad·mire /ədˈmaɪə(r) ; ədˈmaɪr/ *vt* [VP6A] **1** look at with pleasure or satisfaction; have a high regard for: 讚賞;欽佩;羨慕: *Come and ~ the view!* 快來欣賞這風景!*Visitors to Britain usually ~ our policemen.* 來英國的遊客通常讚佩我們的警察。 **2** express admiration of: 表示讚美;誇獎: *Don't forget to ~ the baby.* 不要忘記誇獎那嬰兒。 **ad·mirer** *n* person who ~s; man who finds a woman attractive: 讚美者;羨慕者;愛慕某一女子的男人: *Mary and her many ~s.* 瑪莉和許多愛慕她的男人。 **ad·mir·ing** *adj* showing or feeling admiration: 表示或感覺讚賞的;讚美的;羨慕的: *admiring glances;* (表示)讚賞的目光; *an admiring crowd.* 讚賞的群衆。 **ad·mir·ing·ly** *adv*

ad·miss·ible /ədˈmɪsəbl ; ədˈmɪsəbḷ/ *adj* **1** (legal) that can be allowed as judicial proof: (法律)可被採納爲法庭之證據的: *~ evidence.* 法庭可採納的證據。 **2** (formal) that can be allowed or considered. (正式用語)可被容許的;可被考慮的。 **ad·missi·bil·ity** /ədˌmɪsəˈbɪlətɪ ; ədˌmɪsəˈbɪlətɪ/ *n* [U].

ad·mis·sion /ədˈmɪʃn ; ədˈmɪʃən/ *n* **1** [U] admitting, being admitted, to a society, a school, a building such as a theatre, a museum, etc; fee, charge or condition for this: (入會,入學,入場,如戲院,博物館等的)許可;入會費;門票: *A~ to the school is by examination only.* 就讀該校必須通過考試。*Price of ~, 10p.* 門票價,十辨士。*A~ free.* 不收門票。 **2** [C] statement admitting sth; confession or acknowledgement: 承認某事之陳述;供認: *make an ~ of guilt;* 認罪; *an ~ that one has done wrong.* 承認做了錯事。*To resign now would be an ~ of failure.* 現在辭職等於承認失敗。 ***by/on his own ~,*** as he himself admitted. 如他自己所承認的。

ad·mit /ədˈmɪt ; ədˈmɪt/ *vt, vi* (-tt-) **1** [VP6A, 14] ***~ sb/sth (into/in),*** allow (sb or sth) to enter; let in: 許可(人或物)進入;讓…進入: *The servant opened the door and ~ted me (into the house).* 僕人打開門讓我進入(到屋裏去)。*Only one hundred boys are ~ted to the school each year.* 該校每年只收一百名男生。*I ordered that he was not to be ~ted.* 我下令不許他進來。*Children not ~ted.* 禁止兒童入場。*The windows are small and do not ~ enough light and air.* 窗戶都很小,不能使足够的光線和空氣進入屋內。 **2** [VP6A] (of enclosed spaces) have room enough for: (指範圍之內的場所)可容納: *The harbour ~s large liners and cargo boats.* 該港口可停泊大型郵輪和貨輪。*The theatre is small and ~s only 300 people.* 該戲院很小,只能容納三百人。 **3** [VP6A] acknowledge, confess, accept, as true or valid: 採信;認可;認爲有效: *~ a claim/an assumption.* 認可一項權利(採信某一假定)。 **4** [VP6A, C, 9, 14, 25] acknowledge; confess: 承認;供認: *The accused man ~ted his guilt.* 被告承認了他的罪行。*I ~ my mistake/that I was mistaken.* 我承認我的錯誤(我錯了)。*He ~ted having done wrong.* 他承認做了錯事。*You must ~ the task to be difficult* (more usu, 較常用, *that the task is difficult*). 你得承認這工作是困難的。*It is generally ~ted that...,* Most people acknowledge or agree that.... 一般認爲…;咸認…。 **5** [VP3A] ***~ of,*** (formal) leave room for: (正式用語)容許;有…的餘地: *The words ~ of* (= can have) *no other meaning.* 這些字句不容許有別的意義。*It ~s of no excuse,* There can be no excuse for it. 這是無容辯解的。 ***~ to,*** make an acknowledgement; confess: 承認;供認: *I must ~ to feeling ashamed of my conduct.* 我必須承認我對自己的行爲感到慚愧。 **~·ted·ly** /ədˈmɪtɪdlɪ ; ədˈmɪtɪdlɪ/ *adv* **1** without denial; by general admission: 無可否認地;公認地: *He is ~tedly an atheist.* 他無可否認地是一個無神論者。 **2** (usu in initial position) = 'I acknowledge, agree': (通常用於句首)我承認;我同意: *A~tedly I've never actually been there.* 我承認我從未實際到過那裏。

ad·mit·tance /ədˈmɪtns ; ədˈmɪtṇs/ *n* [U] act of admitting, being admitted (esp to a place that is not public); right of entry: 許可進入(尤指非公共場所);進入的權利;入場許可: *I called at his house but was refused ~,* was not allowed to enter. 我到他家去拜訪他,但被拒絕進門。*No ~ except on business.* 非公莫入;閒人免進。

ad·mix /ædˈmɪks ; ædˈmɪks/ *vt, vi* [VP6A, 2A] mix; become mixed; add as an ingredient. 混合;羼雜。

ad·mix·ture /ædˈmɪkstʃə(r) ; ædˈmɪkstʃɚ/ *n* (formal) (正式用語) = mixture.

ad·mon·ish /ədˈmɒnɪʃ ; ədˈmɑnɪʃ/ *vt* [VP6A, 14] (formal) give a mild warning or a gentle reproof to: (正式用語)婉轉警告;勸告;輕責;訓誡: *The teacher*

~*ed the boys for being lazy/*~*ed them against smoking.* 老師訓誡學生們不可懶惰(抽煙)。**ad·mo·ni·tion** /ˌædməˈnɪʃn ; ˌædməˈnɪʃən/ *n* [U] ~ing; warning; [C] instance of this. 勸告;輕責;訓誡;警告。**ad·moni·tory** /ədˈmɒnɪtrɪ *US:* -tɔːrɪ ; ədˈmɑnəˌtorɪ/ *adj* containing admonition: 勸告的;輕責的;訓誡的;警告的: *an admonitory letter.* 訓誡信。

ad nauseam /ˌæd ˈnɔːzɪæm ; ˈædˈnɔʃɪˌæm/ *adv* (Lat) to the point of being disgusted; (colloq) to a degree so as to cause annoyance, eg because of length or repetition. (拉)令人厭煩地;(俗)至令人厭煩的程度(如因冗長或重覆)。

ado /əˈduː ; əˈdu/ *n* [U] (archaic) fuss; trouble and excitement: (古)無謂的紛擾;張惶: *Without more/much/further ado, he signed the agreement.* 他很乾脆地簽了約。

adobe /əˈdəʊbɪ ; əˈdobɪ/ *n* [U] sun-dried brick (not fired in a kiln), of clay and straw: 由黏土與稻草混雜經太陽晒乾(未經窰中燒過)的磚;土坯: (attrib)(形容用法) *an* ~ *house.* 土坯屋。

adobe houses

ado·les·cence /ˌædəˈlesns ; ˌædl̩ˈɛsns/ *n* [U] period of life between childhood and maturity; growth during this period. 青年期(介於孩童與成年之間的時期);青年期的發育成長;青春。**ado·les·cent** /-ˈlesnt ; -l̩ˈɛsn̩t/ *adj, n* (person) growing up from childhood (age 12 or 13 to 18). 青年;少年;青年期(十二、三歲至十八歲)的。

adopt /əˈdɒpt ; əˈdɑpt/ *vt* [VP6A] **1** take (sb) into one's family as a relation, esp as a son or daughter, with legal guardianship: 以合法監護人的身份將(某人)收入家中爲親屬; (尤指)收養(某人)爲養子或養女: *As they had no children of their own, they ~ed an orphan.* 他們沒有親生兒女,就收養了一個孤兒。⇨ foster. **2** take, eg an idea or custom, and use: 採納;採取(意見,風俗等);採用: *European dress has been ~ed by people in many parts of the world.* 歐洲服式爲世界許多地方的人們所採用。 **3** accept, eg a report or recommendation: 接受(報告,建議等): *Congress ~ed the new measures.* 國會通過了新的議案。**adop·tion** /əˈdɒpʃn ; əˈdɑpʃən/ *n* ~ing or being ~ed: 收養;採納;採取;採用;接受: *the country of his ~ion.* 他所歸化的國家。**adop·tive** *adj* taken by ~ion: 收養的;採取的: *his ~ive parents.* 他的養父及養母。

adore /əˈdɔː(r) ; əˈdɔr/ *vt* **1** [VP6A] worship (God); love deeply and respect highly. 崇拜(上帝);敬愛;愛慕。 **2** [VP6A, C] (colloq; not in progressive tenses) like very much: (俗,不用於進行式)極爲喜愛: *The baby ~s being tickled.* 那嬰孩極喜歡被胳肢。**ador·able** /-əbl ; -əbl/ *adj* lovable; delightful. 可愛的。**ador·ably** /-əblɪ ; -əblɪ/ *adv* **ador·ation** /ˌædəˈreɪʃn ; ˌædəˈreʃən/ *n* [U] worship; love: 崇拜;敬愛: *his adoration for Jane.* 他對珍的愛慕。**adorer** *n* person who ~s (sb). 崇拜者;敬愛(某人)者;愛慕者。**ador·ing** *adj* showing love: 表示愛慕的: *adoring looks.* 愛慕的神情。**ador·ing·ly** *adv*

adorn /əˈdɔːn ; əˈdɔrn/ *vt* [VP6A, 14] add beauty or ornament(s) to; decorate (oneself *with* jewels, etc); add distinction to. 裝飾;佩戴(珠寶等,與 with 連用);增加…的優美。~**·ment** *n* [U] ~ing; [C] sth used for ~ing; ornament; decoration. 裝飾;裝飾物;裝飾品。

ad·renal /əˈdriːnl ; ædˈrinl̩/ *adj* (anat) of or near the kidneys: (解剖)腎的;腎旁的: ~ *glands.* 腎上腺。

ad·ren·alin /əˈdrenəlɪn ; ædˈrɛnl̩ɪn/ *n* [U] (med) hormones secreted by the adrenal glands, prepared as a substance used in the treatment of heart failure, etc. (醫)腎上腺素;副腎素(由腎上腺所分泌出的荷爾蒙,經調製以用作治療心臟衰弱等之藥物)。

adrift /əˈdrɪft ; əˈdrɪft/ *adv, pred adj* (of ships and boats) afloat, not under control and driven by wind and water; loose: (指船)失去控制而隨風及水流漂浮(的);漂流(的);漂失(的): *cut a boat ~ from its moorings;* 切斷繫索使小船漂離繫船處; (fig) at the mercy of circumstances: (喻)任由環境安排;漂泊: *turn sb ~,* send him away, eg from home, without money or means of livelihood. 將某人(自家庭等)逐出使其過漂泊無依的生活。

adroit /əˈdrɔɪt ; əˈdrɔɪt/ *adj* ~ ***(at/in),*** clever; skilful; ingenious or resourceful when dealing with problems. 巧的;熟練的;機敏的; (處理問題時)能臨機應變的。~**·ly** *adv* ~**·ness** *n*

adu·la·tion /ˌædjʊˈleɪʃn *US:* -dʒʊˈl- ; ˌædʒəˈleʃən/ *n* [U] (the giving of) excessive praise or respect, esp to win favour. 諂媚;奉承;逢迎;拍馬。

adult /ˈædʌlt ; əˈdʌlt/ *adj* grown to full size or strength; (of persons) intellectually and emotionally mature. 發育成熟的;(指人)智慧及感情上已成熟的;成年的。□ *n* person or animal grown to full size and strength; (legal) person old enough to vote, marry, etc: 發育成熟的人或動物;(法律)成人(已到達投票,結婚等年齡的成年人): *education for ~s;* 成人教育; ~ *education.* 成人教育。~**·hood** /-hʊd ; -hʊd/ *n* the state of being ~. 成年。

adul·ter·ate /əˈdʌltəreɪt ; əˈdʌltəˌret/ *vt* [VP6A, 14] make impure, make poorer in quality, by adding sth of less value: 攙雜劣質物於…;以低級品攙進: *~d milk,* milk with water added. 攙水牛奶。**adul·ter·ant** /əˈdʌltərənt ; əˈdʌltərənt/ *n* sth used for adulterating. 用以攙雜的劣質物;攙雜物。**adul·ter·ation** /əˌdʌltəˈreɪʃn ; əˌdʌltəˈreʃən/ *n*

adul·tery /əˈdʌltərɪ ; əˈdʌltərɪ/ *n* [U] voluntary sexual intercourse of a married person with sb who is not the person to whom he or she is married; [C] (*pl* -ries) instance of this. 通姦;通姦之實例。**adul·terer** /əˈdʌltərə(r) ; əˈdʌltərə/ *n* man who commits ~. 犯通姦罪的男人;姦夫。**adul·ter·ess** /əˈdʌltərɪs ; əˈdʌltərɪs/ *n* woman who commits ~. 犯通姦罪的女人;姦婦;淫婦。**adul·ter·ous** /əˈdʌltərəs ; əˈdʌltərəs/ *adj* of ~. 通姦的。

ad·um·brate /ˈædʌmbreɪt ; ædˈʌmbret/ *vt* [VP6A] (formal) indicate vaguely or briefly; foreshadow (a coming event). (正式用語)約略暗示;預示。

ad valorem /ˌæd vəˈlɔːrəm ; ˌædvəˈlɔrəm/ *adv* (Lat) (of taxes) in proportion to the estimated value of the goods. (拉)(指稅)從價課稅;按值計稅;照價。

ad·vance[1] /ədˈvɑːns *US:* -ˈvæns ; ədˈvæns/ *n* **1** [U] forward movement; progress; [C] instance of this: 前進;陞進;進步;進步等之實例: *With the ~ of old age, he could no longer do the work well.* 因爲年事日高,他已不能再把工作做得很好了。 *Science has made great ~s during the last fifty years.* 科學在過去五十年內有很大的進步。*The country's industrial ~ has been remarkable.* 此國的工業進步是很驚人的。*Has there been an ~ in civilization during the 20th century?* 在二十世紀裡文明有進步嗎? ***in ~ (of),*** before(hand): 事前;在前;預先: *Send your luggage in ~,* before you yourself leave. 將行李預先交寄(即在你動身之前)。 *It's unwise to spend your income in ~.* 把你的收入預先花掉是不智之舉。*Galileo's ideas were (well) in ~ of the age in which he lived.* 伽利略的思想(大爲)超越了他生活的時代。 **2** (attrib use) in ~: (形容用法)事前的;預先的;在前的: *an ~ copy of a new book,* one supplied before publication; (正式發行前所供給的)新書樣本; *an ~ party,* party, eg of explorers, soldiers, sent in ~; (探險隊,軍隊等的)先頭部隊;先遣部隊; *have ~ notice*, eg of sb's arrival. 獲得事先通知(如某人之抵達)。 **3** [C] money paid before it is due, or for work only partially completed. 預付款。 ,~ '**booking,** reservation (of a room in a hotel, a seat in a theatre, etc) in ~ of the time when it is needed. (旅館房間,戲院座位等的)預定。

ad·vance² /əd'vɑ:ns *US:* -'væns ; əd'væns/ *vi, vt* **1** [VP2A, B, 3A] come or go forward: 前進: *Our troops have ~d two miles.* 我們的部隊已前進了兩哩。*He ~d (up) on me in a threatening manner.* 他以威脅的姿態向我走來。*Has civilization ~d during this century?* 文明在本世紀裡有所進步嗎? *The forces of the enemy ~d against us.* 敵軍向着我們推進。 **2** [VP2A] (of costs, values, prices) rise: (指費用,價值,物價)上漲: *Stock market prices/Property values continue to ~.* 股票市場價格(不動產價值)繼續上漲。 **3** [VP6A, 14] move, put or help forward: 向前移;提前;提出;提陞;促進: *The date of the meeting was ~d from the 10th to the 3rd of June.* 開會日期由六月十日提前到三日。 ⇨ postpone. *May I ~ my opinion on the matter?* 我可以提出我對於這事的意見嗎? *He worked so well that he was soon ~d* (= promoted) *to the position of manager.* 他工作非常努力,所以不久就被提陞到經理的職位了。*Such behaviour is not likely to ~ your interests.* 這種行爲不會增進你的利益。 **4** [VP6A] increase, raise (prices) (= colloq, 俗, *put up*): 增加;提高(物價): *The shopkeepers ~d their prices.* 店主們抬高物價。 **5** [VP12A, 13A] pay (money) before the due date: 預付(錢): *He asked his employer to ~ him a month's salary.* 他要求僱主先付他一個月的薪水。*The banks often ~ money to farmers for seed and fertilizer.* 銀行常貸款給農民購買種子及肥料。**ad·vanced** *part adj* far on in life or progress, etc: 年高的;程度高的;高深的: *~d in years*, very old; 年事已高的;非常老的; *~d courses of study.* 高級課程。*The professor is engaged in ~d studies.* 該教授正從事高深的學術研究。 ⇨ elementary. *He has ~d ideas*, ideas that are new and not generally accepted. 他有前進的思想(即尙未爲一般人所接受的新思想)。**~d level** (abbr 略作 **A level**) (of examinations of the General Certificate of Education) securing admission, in GB, to a college or university. 高等(指普通教育文憑考試,在英國可獲得學院或大學之入學許可)。 **~·ment** *n* [U] promotion; preferment; improvement: 擢陞;促進;改進;進步: *The aim of a university should be the ~ment of learning.* 大學的目標應該是促進學術的發展。

ad·van·tage /əd'vɑ:ntɪdʒ *US:* -'væn- ; əd'væntɪdʒ/ *n* **1** [C] sth useful or helpful, sth likely to bring success, esp in competition: 益處;便利;優點;(尤指競爭中的)優勢: *the ~s of a good education.* 良好教育的益處。*Living in a big town has many ~s, such as good schools, libraries and theatres.* 住在大都市裡有許多優點,例如好學校、圖書館及戲院。***have/gain/win an ~ (over); give sb an ~ (over),*** (have, give, etc) a better position or opportunity: 佔(獲得,贏得,給某人)優勢(後接 over): *Tom's university education gave him an ~ over boys who had not been to a university.* 湯姆的大學教育使他較未上大學的男孩子佔優勢。 ***have the ~ of sb,*** know sb or sth that he does not know. 較某人有利;比某人強(知其所不知)。 **2** [U] benefit; profit: 利益: *He gained little ~ from his visit to London.* 他遊歷倫敦獲益甚少。***take ~ of sb,*** deceive him, play a trick on him. 欺騙某人;捉弄某人。***take (full) ~ of sth,*** use it profitably, for one's own benefit: (充分)利用某事物: *He always takes full ~ of the mistakes made by his rivals.* 他總是充分利用他的對手所犯的錯誤。***to ~,*** in a way that enables sth to be seen, used, etc in the best way: 更加;越發有效地: *The painting is seen to better ~ from a distance.* 這幅畫從遠處看更顯眼。*You should lay out your money* (= decide how to spend or invest it) *to the best ~.* 你應該以最有效的方式來利用你的錢(決定如何花用或投資)。***be/prove to sb's ~,*** be profitable or helpful to him. 對某人有利;有助於某人。***turn sth to ~,*** make the most of it; use it profitably. 儘量利用某事物。 **3** (tennis) the first point scored after deuce. (網球)平手以後所得到的第一分。 □ *vt* [VP6A] benefit. 對…有利。

ad·van·tage·ous /,ædvən'teɪdʒəs ; ,ædvən'tedʒəs/ *adj* profitable; helpful. 有利的;有益的。**~·ly** *adv*

ad·vent /'ædvənt ; 'ædvɛnt/ *n* **1** (usu *sing* with *def art*) coming or arrival (of an important development, season, etc): (通常單數與定冠詞連用)來到;來臨(指重要發展,節期等): *Since the ~ of atomic power, there have been great changes in industry.* 自從原子動力問世之後,工業方面起了很大的改變。 **2** **A~,** (eccles) the coming of Christ; the season (with four Sundays) before Christmas Day. (教會)耶穌之降臨;降臨節(聖誕節前包括四個星期日之時期)。 **3** the second coming of Christ at the Last Judgement. 最後審判日耶穌之再臨。 **Ad·vent·ist** /'ædvəntɪst *US:* əd'ventɪst ; 'ædvɛntɪst/ *n* person who believes that Christ's second coming and the end of the world are near. 相信耶穌之再臨及世界末日已近的人。

ad·ven·ti·tious /,ædven'tɪʃəs ; ,ædvɛn'tɪʃəs/ *adj* (formal) coming by chance; accidental: (正式用語)偶然的: *~ aid.* 偶然的幫助。

ad·ven·ture /əd'ventʃə(r) ; əd'vɛntʃɚ/ *n* **1** [C] strange or unusual happening, esp an exciting or dangerous journey or activity: 奇遇;冒險的經歷: *A flight in an aeroplane used to be quite an ~.* 從前乘飛機飛行是相當冒險的事。 *The explorer told the boys about his ~s in the Arctic.* 那探險家把他在北極的奇遇講給那些男孩子聽。**~ playground,** playground with large wooden, metal, etc materials and structures for children to play with, in or on. 兒童遊樂場;兒童樂園。 **2** [U] risk; danger, eg in travel and exploration: 冒險: *fond of ~;* 喜愛冒險; *a story of ~;* 冒險故事; *Robin Hood lived a life of ~.* 羅賓漢過著冒險的生活。□ *vt* = venture (the usu word 通常用此字). **ad·ven·turer** *n* **1** person who seeks ~. 冒險者。 **2** person who is ready to make a profit for himself by risky or unscrupulous methods. 冒險圖利者;投機者。**ad·ven·tur·ess** /-ɪs ; -ɪs/ *n* woman ~r, esp one who is ready to use guile to obtain benefits. 女冒險者;(尤指)以詐欺手段冒險圖利之女人;女投機者。 **ad·ven·tur·ous** /-əs ; -əs/ *adj* **1** fond of, eager for, ~s. 喜冒險的。 **2** full of danger and excitement: 充滿危險和刺激的: *an adventurous voyage.* 驚險的航行。**~·some** /-səm ; -səm/ *adj* (rare or liter) (罕或文) = adventurous.

ad·verb /'ædvɜ:b ; 'ædvɝb/ *n* (gram) word that answers questions with *how, when, where* and modifies *vv, adjj* and other *advv*, etc, eg *soon, here, well, quickly.* (文法)副詞(用以回答 how, when, where 之問句,及修飾動詞,形容詞及其他副詞等之字,如 soon, here, well, quickly)。**ad·verb·ial** /æd'vɜ:bɪəl ; əd'vɝbɪəl/ *adj* of the nature of an ~. 副詞性質的。□ *n* ~ or ~ial phrase. 副詞;副詞(性質的)片語。**ad·verbi·ally** /æd'vɜ:bɪəlɪ ; əd'vɝbɪəlɪ/ *adv*

ad·ver·sary /'ædvəsərɪ *US:* -serɪ ; 'ædvɚ,sɛrɪ/ *n* (*pl* -ries) enemy; opponent (in any kind of contest). (任何比賽或競爭中的)敵手;對手。

ad·verse /'ædvɜ:s ; əd'vɝs/ *adj* unfavourable; contrary or hostile (*to*): 不利的;反對的;敵對的(與 to 連用): *~ weather conditions;* 惡劣的天候; *~ winds,* eg for a sailing-ship; 逆風(例如對帆船而言者); *developments ~ to our interests.* 與我們利益相反的發展。**~·ly** *adv*

ad·ver·sity /əd'vɜ:sətɪ ; əd'vɝsətɪ/ *n* (*pl* -ties). **1** [U] condition of adverse fortune; trouble: 逆境;厄運;患難;艱難: *be patient/cheerful in ~.* 在逆境中具堅忍(振奮)的精神;逆來順受。*A brave man smiles in the face of ~.* 一個勇敢的人臨難不懼。 **2** [C] misfortune; affliction. 不幸;災難;禍患。

ad·vert¹ /əd'vɜ:t ; əd'vɜt/ *vi* [VP3A] (formal) (正式用語) ~ ***to,*** refer to (in speech or writing): (在談話或寫作中)論及;談到: ~ *to a problem.* 談到一個問題。

ad·vert² /'ædvɜ:t ; 'ædvɜt/ *n* (GB colloq abbr for) advertisement(2). (英,俗) 廣告 (爲 advertisement 第2義之略)。

ad·ver·tise /'ædvətaɪz ; 'ædvɚ,taɪz/ *vt, vi* [VP6A, 2A, 3A] make known to people (by printing notices in newspapers, etc or by other means, eg TV): 爲…做廣告;登廣告: ~ *one's goods;* 爲其貨品做廣告; ~ *in all the newspapers;* 在所有的報紙上登廣告; ~ *for an assistant in the local newspapers,* announce that one wishes to engage an assistant. 在本地報紙上登廣告徵求助手。**ad·ver·tiser** *n* person who ~s. 登廣告者;做廣告者。 **~·ment** /əd'vɜ:tɪsmənt *US:* ˌædvər'taɪzmənt ; ˌædvɚ'taɪzmənt/ *n* **1** [U] advertising: 做廣告;登廣告: (attrib) (形容用法) *the ~ment manager,* eg of a newspaper. (如報社的)廣告部經理。*A~ment helps to sell goods.* 登廣告有助於銷路。 **2** [C] public announcement (in the press, TV, etc): 廣告;告白;啓事: *If you want to sell your piano, put an ~ in the newspaper.* 如果你要賣掉你的鋼琴,可在報紙上登一則廣告。⇨ commercial *n.*

ad·vice /əd'vaɪs ; əd'vaɪs/ *n* **1** [U] (informed) opinion about what to do, how to behave: 勸告;忠告;建議: *You won't get well unless you follow your doctor's ~.* 如果你不遵守醫生的囑咐,你將不會痊癒。*If you take my ~ and study hard, you'll pass the examination.* 如果你聽我的勸告用功讀書,你就會考及格。*You should take legal ~,* consult a lawyer. 你應該就教於律師。***act on sb's ~,*** do what he suggests. 照某人的建議去做;依勸告行事。***(give sb) a piece/bit/word/few words of ~,*** (give) an opinion about what to do, etc. (給某人)一項建議(一項勸告,幾句忠告)。 **2** [C] (comm) (usu *pl*) news from a distance, esp commercial: (商) (通常用複數)遠地來的消息;(尤指)行情: *~s from our Tokyo branch.* 從我們東京分公司來的消息。**'~-note, letter of ~,** (comm) formal notice of delivery of goods, a business call, etc. (商)正式通知(關於貨物之寄運,業務之接洽等)。

ad·vis·able /əd'vaɪzəbl ; əd'vaɪzəbl/ *adj* wise; sensible; to be advised or recommended: 明智的;合理的;適當的;可行的: *Do you think it ~ to wait?* 你認爲應該等候嗎? **ad·visa·bil·ity** /əd,vaɪzə'bɪlətɪ ; əd,vaɪzə'bɪlətɪ/ *n* [U].

ad·vise /əd'vaɪz ; əd'vaɪz/ *vt, vi* **1** [VP6A, C, 17, 20, 21, 14] give advice to; recommend: 勸告;忠告;建議: *The doctor ~d a complete rest.* 醫生勸告要完全休息。*What do you ~ me to do?* 你看我該怎麼辦? *Please ~ me whether I should accept the offer.* 請你指示我是否該接受此項提議。*We ~d an early start/their starting early/them to start early.* 我們建議早點開始(他們早點開始)。 *Her father ~d her against marrying in haste.* 她的父親勸告她不要匆匆結婚。*Who is the best man to ~ me on this question?* 關於這個問題,誰是我的最好顧問? **2** [VP 6A, 21, 14] (comm) inform; notify: (商)通知: *Please ~ us when the goods are dispatched/~ us of the dispatch of the goods.* 貨物交運時請通知我們(請將貨物交運情形通知我們)。 **3** [VP3A] ~ ***with (sb),*** (old use) consult; take counsel with. (舊用法)就教於(某人);與(某人)商量。 **ad·viser** *n* person who gives advice, esp one who is habitually consulted: 顧問;指導者: *~r to the Government.* 政府的顧問。**ad·vised** *adj* (old use) considered; carefully thought out; deliberate. (舊用法)考慮過的;仔細想出的;故意的。***ill ~d,*** unwise; injudicious. 不智的;欠考慮的。***well ~d,*** wise; judicious. 明智的;考慮周到的。 **ad·vis·ed·ly** /əd'vaɪzɪdlɪ ; əd'vaɪzɪdlɪ/ *adv* after careful thought. 經仔細考慮後。**ad·vis·ory** /əd'vaɪzərɪ ; əd'vaɪzərɪ/ *adj* of advice; having the power to ~: 勸告的;忠告的;有權進言的;供諮詢的;顧問的: *an advisory committee/council/panel.* 諮詢委員會(顧問會議;顧問小組)。

ad·vo·cate /'ædvəkət ; 'ædvəkɪt/ *n* **1** person who speaks in favour of sb or sth (esp a cause): 提倡者;倡導者;擁護者 (尤指對某一主義或目標言): *an ~ of equal pay for men and women.* 提倡男女同酬者。 **2** (legal) person who does this professionally in a court of law in Scotland (= *barrister* in England and Wales). (法律) (蘇格蘭法庭上的)辯護士(相當於英格蘭和威爾斯的 barrister);律師。**the Faculty of A~s,** the Scots Bar. 蘇格蘭律師公會。**Lord A~,** principal law officer in Scotland. (蘇格蘭的)檢察長。□ *vt* /'ædvəkeɪt ; 'ædvə,ket/ [VP6A, C] support; speak publicly in support of: 提倡;主張: *Do you ~ keeping all children at school till the age of sixteen?* 你主張將義務教育延長至十六歲嗎? **ad·vo·cacy** /'ædvəkəsɪ ; 'ædvəkəsɪ/ *n* [U] pleading in support (*of* a cause or sb). 主張;支持;提倡;擁護(一主義或某人)。

adze, adz /ædz ; ædz/ *n* carpenter's tool (with a blade at right angles to the handle) for cutting or shaping wood. 錛子;橫口斧(木工工具)。

aegis, egis /'i:dʒɪs ; 'idʒɪs/ *n* protection; sponsorship. 保護;支持。***under the ~ of,*** with the patronage or support of. 在…的保護或支持下。

aeon, eon /'i:ən ; 'iən/ *n* [C] period of time too long to be measured. 永世;億萬年 (極長而無法計算的時期)。

aer·ate /'eəreɪt ; 'eə,ret/ *vt* [VP6A] charge (a liquid) with air or gas; expose to the chemical purifying action of air: 充氣於(液體);暴露於空氣淨化作用中;灌氣: ~ *the soil by digging.* 挖掘使土壤暴露於空氣淨化作用。*Blood is ~d in the lungs.* 血液在肺部與氧結合。**aer·ation** /eə'reɪʃn ; ,eə'reʃən/ *n*

aer·ial /'eərɪəl ; e'ɪrɪəl/ *adj* **1** existing in, moving through, the air: 存在空氣中的;由空中經過的;空中的;航空的: *an ~ railway/ropeway,* a system of overhead suspension for transport. 高架鐵道(架空索道)。 **2** (archaic) of or like air; immaterial. (古)空氣的;似空氣的;虛幻的;無形的。□ *n* that part of a radio or TV system which receives or sends out signals, usu a wire or rod, or number of wires or rods (US 美 = *antenna*). (無線電或電視的)天線。

aerie, aery, eyrie, eyry /'eərɪ ; 'ɛrɪ/ *n* eagle's nest; nest of other birds of prey which are built high up among rocks; eagle's brood. 鷹巢;(高築於岩石中的)肉食鳥的鳥巢;一窩鷹雛。

aero·bat·ics /ˌeərə'bætɪks ; ˌɛrə'bætɪks/ *n* (*sing v*) [U] the performance of acrobatic feats by airmen, eg flying upside down. (用單數動詞) (飛行員所表演的)特技飛行(例如翻身飛行)。

aero·drome /'eərədrəʊm ; 'ɛrə,drom/ *n* (US = *airdrome*) (dated) ground for the arrival and departure and servicing of aircraft, with hangars, workshops, etc (*airfield* and *airport* are the more usu words). (過時用語) 飛機場 (今較常用 airfield 和 airport)。

aero·dy·nam·ics /ˌeərəʊdaɪ'næmɪks ; ˌɛrodaɪ'næmɪks/ *n pl* (*sing v*) [U] science dealing with the flow of air and the motion of aircraft, bullets, etc through air. (用單數動詞)氣體動力學。

aero·naut /'eərənɔ:t ; 'ɛrə,nɔt/ *n* person who pilots or travels in a balloon, airship or other aircraft. 輕氣球、飛艇或其他航空器之駕駛員或乘客。

aero·naut·ics /ˌeərə'nɔ:tɪks ; ˌɛrə'nɔtɪks/ *n* (*sing v*) [U] science and practice of aviation (the more usu word). (用單數動詞)航空學(較常用 aviation)。

aero·plane /'eərəpleɪn ; 'ɛrə,plen/ *n* (US=*airplane*) heavier-than-air flying machine with one or more engines. 飛機。⇨ *aircraft, airliner* at air¹(7).

aero·sol /'eərəsɒl *US:* -sɔ:l ; 'ɛrə,sɑl/ *n* [U] dispersion of fine solid or liquid particles, eg of scent, paint, insecticide, detergent, released (in a mist) by pressure from a container with compressed gas from a valve; [C] (P) the container itself.

(香水,油漆,殺蟲劑,清潔劑等的) 霧狀噴洒;噴霧; (商標) 噴霧罐;噴霧器。

aero·space /ˈeərəʊspeɪs ; ˈɛrə,spes/ *n* the earth's atmosphere and the space beyond, considered as area available to air- or space-craft: 地球大氣層及其外面的空間;太空: *the ~ industry.* 太空工業。

aer·tex /ˈeəteks ; ˈɛrtɛks/ *n* (P) kind of loosely woven textile material (as used for underwear). (商標) 一種鬆織的紡織品 (用以製內衣等)。

aery /ˈeərɪ ; ˈɛrɪ/ *n* ⇨ aerie.

aes·thete, es·thete /ˈiːsθiːt *US:* ˈesθiːt ; ˈɛsθit/ *n* person who has or claims to have great love of and understanding of what is beautiful, esp in the arts. 審美家 (尤指對藝術方面)。

aes·thetic, es·thetic /iːsˈθetɪk *US:* es- ; ɛsˈθɛtɪk/ *adj* of the appreciation of the beautiful, esp in the arts; (of persons) having such appreciation: (尤指有關藝術之) 審美的; (指人) 有審美能力的: *~ standards.* 審美標準。□ *n* [U] particular set of ~ principles: 美學原理; 審美論: *the ~ to which he remained faithful.* 他仍然堅守的審美原則。**aes·thet·ical, es·thet·ical** /-kl ; -kl/ *adj* = aesthetic. **aes·thet·ically** /-klɪ ; -klɪ/ *adv* **aes·thet·ics, es·thet·ics** *n* (*sing v*) [U] branch of philosophy which tries to make clear the laws and principles of beauty (contrasted with morality and utility). (用單數動詞) 審美學;美學 (哲學中的一門,研究美之法則及原理;與 morality 及 utility 相對)。

aether /ˈiːθə(r) ; ˈiθə/ *n* ⇨ ether.

aeti·ol·ogy /ˌiːtɪˈɒlədʒɪ ; ˌitɪˈɑlədʒɪ/ ⇨ etiology.

afar /əˈfɑː(r) ; əˈfɑr/ *adv* (poet) far off or away. (詩) 遠;遙遙地。***from ~,*** from a distance. 從遠處。

af·fable /ˈæfəbl ; ˈæfəbl̩/ *adj* polite and friendly; pleasant and easy to talk to: 有禮而友善的;和藹可親的;友善而易與交談的: *~ to everybody;* 對每個人都和藹可親; *an ~ reply.* 謙虛的回答。**af·fably** /-əblɪ ; -əblɪ/ *adv* **affa·bil·ity** /ˌæfəˈbɪlətɪ ; ˌæfəˈbɪlətɪ/ *n* quality of being ~ (*to* or *towards*). 和藹可親;謙虛有禮 (與 to 或 towards 連用)。

af·fair /əˈfeə(r) ; əˈfɛr/ *n* [C] **1** concern; sth (to be) done; business: 事;事務;職務;業務: *That's my ~, not yours.* 那是我的事,不是你的事。 **2** (*pl*) business of any kind; day-to-day concerns of organization, etc: (複) 任何種類的事務; (機關等的) 業務: *A prime minister is kept busy with ~s of state,* the task of government. 首相爲政務忙碌。*When he asked me how much I earned, I told him to mind his own ~s,* not to ask questions about my business, etc. 當他問我賺多少錢的時候,我告訴他少管閒事。*We can't afford a holiday in the present state of ~s,* while things remain as they are now. 在目前的情形下,我們無法去度假。**Secretary of State for Foreign／Home／Welsh, etc A~s,** titles of Government Ministers in GB. (英國政府的) 外交 (內政,威爾斯事務等) 部長。 **3** ***have an ~ (with sb),*** have an emotional (and sexual) relationship with sb to whom one is not married: 與 (某人,指非配偶) 發生愛情 (及性) 關係; (與某人) 私通: *The doctor, they say, is having an ~ with the rector's wife.* 據説那醫生和校長夫人私通。***~ of honour,*** duel. 決鬪。 **4** (colloq) occurrence; event; object: (俗) 事件;東西;物件: *The railway accident was a terrible ~.* 那次火車車禍是一可怕事件。*Her hat was a wonderful ~.* 她的帽子是一件絕妙之物。*What a ramshackle ~ your old car is!* 你的老爺車眞爛!

af·fect¹ /əˈfekt ; əˈfɛkt/ *vt* [VP6A] **1** have an influence or impression on; act on: 影響: *The climate ~ed his health,* injured it. 氣候影響 (損害) 了他的健康。*Some plants are quickly ~ed by cold.* 有些植物對寒冷很敏感。*Will the changes in taxation ~ you personally,* Will you have to pay more (or less) in taxes? 稅法的變更將會影響到你個人嗎? *The rise in the price of bread will ~ us all.* 麪包售價上漲,我們大家都會受影響。 **2** move the feelings of: 感動: *He was much ~ed by the sad news.* 這個悽愴的消息使他十分難過。*His death ~ed us deeply.* 他的死亡使我們深爲感慨。 **3** (of diseases) attack; cause a particular condition in: (指疾病) 侵襲: *The left lung is ~ed,* eg by cancer, tuberculosis. 左肺受到感染 (如被癌症或結核病)。 **4** ***well／ill ~ed (towards),*** well／ill disposed (the more usu word) or inclined (towards). (對…) 有好 (惡) 感 (較常用 disposed)。**~·ing** *adj* moving or touching (the feelings): 感人的;動人的: *an ~ing sight.* 感人的情景。**~·ing·ly** *adv* tenderly; pathetically. 動人地;哀惋地。

af·fect² /əˈfekt ; əˈfɛkt/ *vt* **1** [VP6A, 7A] pretend to have or feel (ignorance, indifference); pretend (to do, etc): 裝作;佯爲;假裝: *She ~s an American accent.* 她裝出美國腔調。*He ~ed not to hear me.* 他假裝沒聽見我。 **2** [VP6A] have a liking for and use (esp for ostentation): 愛用;愛穿;愛好 (尤指爲了誇耀): *He ~s long and learned words,* uses them instead of short and simple words. 他愛用長而艱澀的字 (不用短而簡單的字)。*She ~s bright colours,* wears brightly coloured clothes, etc. 她愛穿顏色鮮艷的衣服。**~ed** *adj* pretended; not natural or genuine: 矯飾的;造作的;不自然的;虛僞的: *an ~ed politeness;* 虛僞的禮貌; *~ed manners;* 矯揉造作的舉止; *with an ~ed cheerfulness;* 强作高興; *written in an ~ed style,* showing a liking for an artificial style. 以堆砌雕琢的文體寫成的。

af·fec·ta·tion /ˌæfekˈteɪʃn ; ˌæfɪkˈteʃən/ *n* **1** [U] behaviour that is not natural or genuine: 矯飾的行爲;不自然的行爲;虛僞的行爲: *Keep clear of all ~,* Do not behave unnaturally; 請摒除一切矯飾; [C] instance of this: 行爲矯飾或虛僞的實例: *Her little ~s annoyed me.* 她那些做作的小動作使我厭煩。 **2** [C] pretence (made on purpose, for effect): (故意的,爲引人注意的) 假裝;虛飾;做作: *an ~ of interest／indifference／ignorance.* 假裝有興趣 (冷淡,不知)。

af·fec·tion /əˈfekʃn ; əˈfɛkʃən/ *n* **1** [U] kindly feeling; love: 親愛;愛: *Every mother has ~ for／feels ~ toward her children* 每個母親都愛她的孩子。*He is held in great ~,* is much loved. 他極爲大家所愛戴。 **2** [U or *pl*] ***gain／win sb's ~(s),*** win the love of. 獲 (贏) 得某人的愛。 **3** [C] (old use) disease; unhealthy condition: (舊用法) 病;疾病;患病: *an ~ of the throat.* 喉嚨痛。

af·fec·tion·ate /əˈfekʃənət ; əˈfɛkʃənɪt/ *adj* loving; fond; showing love (*to* sb): 親愛的;摯愛的;示愛的 (與 to 連用,後接某人): *an ~ wife;* 溫柔體貼的妻子; *~ looks.* 表示親愛的神情。**~·ly** *adv* ***Yours ~ly,*** used at the close of a letter, eg from a man to his sister. 書信末尾簽名前的客氣語 (如一個男人寫給他姐姐或妹妹的信中所用者)。

af·fi·ance /əˈfaɪəns ; əˈfaɪəns/ *vt* [VP6A] (usu passive; liter or old use) promise in marriage: (通常用被動語態) (文或舊用法) 許諾結婚;訂婚;定親;定聘: *be ~d to (sb),* be engaged to marry him／her. 與 (某人) 訂婚;爲某人之未婚妻 (或未婚夫)。

af·fi·da·vit /ˌæfɪˈdeɪvɪt ; ˌæfəˈdevɪt/ *n* (legal) written statement, made on oath, (to be) used as legal proof or evidence: (法律) 宣誓書;口供書 (用作法定證據者): *swear／make／take an ~.* 立宣誓書。

af·fili·ate /əˈfɪlɪeɪt ; əˈfɪlɪ,et/ *vt, vi* [VP6A, 14, 2A] ***~ (to／with),*** (of a society or institution, or a member) enter into association: (指團體,機構或會員) 加盟;入會: *The College is ~d to the University.* 該學院附屬於該大學。*Is the Mineworkers' Union ~d with the TUC?* (英國) 礦工工會是附屬於勞工聯會的嗎?

af·fili·ation /əˌfɪlɪˈeɪʃn ; əˌfɪlɪˈeʃən/ *n* [U] affiliating or being affiliated; [C] connection made by affiliating. 加盟;入會;加入;聯營。**ˈ~ order,** (GB, legal) order made by a magistrate, determining the paternity of an illegitimate child and requiring the father to contribute towards its support. (英,法律) 父子關係認定令 (判定私生子之父,以便要求其

贍養）。

af·fin·ity /əˈfɪnətɪ ; əˈfɪnətɪ/ *n* (*pl* -ties) ~ ***(between/to/for),*** **1** [C] close connection, structural resemblance (between animals and plants, languages, etc) (or of one thing to/with another). 密切關係；構造相似(與 between 連用，指動植物、語言等之間者；與 to 或 with 連用，指一物對另一物言)；類緣。 **2** [U] relationship; [C] relation (by marriage); similarity of character suggesting relationship. 關係；姻親關係；(顯示可能有關係之)性格之相似。 **3** [C] strong liking or attraction: 强烈的愛好或吸引力：*She feels a strong ~ to/for him.* 她感到他對她具有强烈的吸引力。 **4** chemical or physical attraction: (化學或物理上的)親和力：*the ~ of common salt for water.* 食鹽與水之親和力。

af·firm /əˈfɜːm ; əˈfɝm/ *vt, vi* **1** [VP6A, 9, 14] declare positively: 肯定；斷言：*~ the truth of a statement/~ that it is true;* 斷言某項陳述的確實性；*~ to sb that....* 向某人斷言…。⇨ deny. **2** [VP2A] (legal) (of a person who has conscientious objections to swearing on the Bible) declare solemnly but not on oath. (法律)(指寧可本着良心不願憑聖經發誓之人)鄭重陳述。 **~·ation** /ˌæfəˈmeɪʃn ; ˌæfəˈmeʃən/ *n* **1** [U] ~ing. 肯定；斷言。 **2** [C] sth ~ed; (legal) declaration made by ~ing(2). 證實之事；(法律)(本着良心不經宣誓而作的)鄭重陳述。 **~·ative** /əˈfɜːmətɪv ; əˈfɝmətɪv/ *adj, n* (answering) 'yes': 肯定的；肯定：*an ~ative answer.* 肯定的回答。*The answer is the ~ative,* is 'Yes'. 回答是肯定的。⇨ negative(1).

af·fix[1] /əˈfɪks ; əˈfɪks/ *vt* [VP6A, 14] ~ ***sth (to),*** (formal) fix; fasten; attach: (正式用語)使固定；結牢；附加：*~ a seal/stamp to a document;* 在文件上加蓋印信；add in writing: 加寫；添寫：*~ your signature to an agreement.* 加添簽字於合約上。

af·fix[2] /ˈæfɪks ; ˈæfɪks/ *n* suffix or prefix, eg *-ly, -able, un-, co-.* 接語(接尾語或接頭語，例如 -ly, -able, un-, co-)。⇨ App 3. 參看附錄三。

af·fla·tus /əˈfleɪtəs ; əˈfletəs/ *n* [U] (formal) divine revelation; inspiration. (正式用語)神感；靈感。

af·flict /əˈflɪkt ; əˈflɪkt/ *vt* [VP6A, 14] cause bodily or mental trouble to: 使身體受痛苦；使苦惱：*~ed with rheumatism;* 爲風濕症所苦；*feel much ~ed at/by the news.* 爲此消息感到很難過。

af·flic·tion /əˈflɪkʃn ; əˈflɪkʃən/ *n* **1** [U] suffering; distress: 痛苦；苦難：*help people in ~.* 幫助苦難的人們。 **2** [C] cause or occasion of suffering: 痛苦之因；痛苦之事：*the ~s of old age,* eg deafness, blindness. 老年之苦(如聾、盲等)。

af·flu·ence /ˈæfluəns ; ˈæfluəns/ *n* [U] wealth; abundance: 富裕；豐富：*living in ~;* 生活富裕；*rise to ~,* become wealthy. 發財。

af·flu·ent[1] /ˈæfluənt ; ˈæfluənt/ *adj* wealthy; abundant: 富裕的；豐富的：*in ~ circumstances.* 在富裕的環境中。**the ~ society,** society which is prosperous and whose members are concerned with material improvement. 富裕繁榮的社會(人們均關切物質享受的改善)。

af·flu·ent[2] /ˈæfluənt ; ˈæfluənt/ *n* [C] stream flowing into a larger one (*tributary* is the usu word). 支流(通常用 tributary)。

af·ford /əˈfɔːd ; əˈfɔrd/ *vt* **1** [VP6A, 7A] (usu with *can/could, be able to*) spare or find enough time or money for: (通常與can, could, be able to連用)省出或找到足够的時間或金錢去(做某事)；力足以；…得起：*We can't ~ a holiday/can't ~ to go away this summer.* 今年夏天我們無法度假(抽不出時間去度假)。*Are you able to ~ the time for a holiday?* 你能抽出時間去度假嗎？ **2** [VP7A] (with *can/could*) run a risk by doing sth: (與 can 或 could 連用)冒…之險：*I can't ~ to neglect my work.* 我不能疏忽我的工作。*She couldn't ~ to displease her boss.* 她得罪不起她的上司。 **3** [VP12A, 13A, 6A] (formal) provide; give: (正式用語)供給；給與：*The trees ~ a pleasant shade.* 這些樹造成涼蔭。*It will ~ me great pleasure to have dinner with you.* 與你共餐將是我的一大樂事。

af·for·est /əˈfɒrɪst *US:* əˈfɔːr- ; əˈfɔrɪst/ *vt* [VP6A] make into forest land. 使成爲林地；造林於。 **af·for·est·ation** /əˌfɒrɪˈsteɪʃn *US:* əˌfɔːr- ; əˌfɑrɛsˈteʃən/ *n*: *~ation projects,* projects for planting large areas with trees. 造林計畫。

af·fran·chise /əˈfræntʃaɪz ; əˈfrænˌtʃaɪz/ *vt* [VP6A] free from servitude. 解除…之勞役；恢復…之自由。

af·fray /əˈfreɪ ; əˈfre/ *n* [C] fight in a public place, causing or likely to cause a disturbance of the peace: 在公共場所打架滋擾安寧：*The men were charged with causing an ~.* 那些人被控滋擾公共安寧。

af·front /əˈfrʌnt ; əˈfrʌnt/ *vt* [VP6A] insult on purpose; hurt sb's feelings or self-respect, esp in public: 故意侮辱；當衆使難堪：*feel ~ed at having one's word doubted.* 因自己的話受人懷疑而感到難堪。□ *n* [C] public insult; deliberate show of disrespect: 公然侮辱；故意表示不敬：*an ~ to his pride;* 對他自尊心的侮辱；*suffer an ~;* 受辱；*offer an ~ to sb.* 對某人加以侮辱。

afield /əˈfiːld ; əˈfild/ *adv* far away from home; to or at a distance: 遠離家鄉地；至遠方；在遠處；離鄉背井：*Don't go too far ~.* 不要走得太遠。

afire /əˈfaɪə(r) ; əˈfaɪr/ *pred adj* (poet) on fire. (詩)着火的。

aflame /əˈfleɪm ; əˈflem/ *pred adj* (poet) in flames; burning; red as if burning: (詩)着火的；燃燒中的；紅似火的：(fig) (喻) *~ with passion.* 怒火中燒；熱情如火。*The autumn woods were ~ with colour.* 那片秋林紅似火。

afloat /əˈfləʊt ; əˈflot/ *pred adj* **1** floating; borne up, carried along, on air or water: 飄浮在水中或空中的：*The ship stuck fast on the rocks and we couldn't get it ~ again.* 船牢牢地擱淺在礁石上，我們無法使它再浮起來。 **2** at sea; on board ship: 在海上的；在船上的：*life ~,* the life of a sailor. 海上生涯；水手生涯。 **3** awash; flooded. 爲海浪所冲打的；爲水所淹的。 **4** (business) started; solvent: (貿)開張的；新開的；有償付能力的：*get a new periodical ~,* launch it. 創辦一種新期刊。 **5** (of stories, rumours) current; in circulation. (指傳說，謠言)傳播各處的；流傳的。

afoot /əˈfʊt ; əˈfʊt/ *pred adj* **1** in progress or operation; being prepared: 在進行中的；在準備中的：*There's mischief ~.* 有人在準備搗亂。*There's a scheme ~ to improve the roads.* 有人在計畫改善道路。 **2** (old use) on foot; walking. (舊用法)步行的。

afore /əˈfɔː(r) ; əˈfɔr/ *adv, prep* (naut) before. (航海)在前。~ **the mast,** as an unlicensed seaman with quarters in the forecastle. 在船桅前(如無照之船員居於船首甲板下之水手艙)。 **ˈ~·said** *pron, adj* (legal) (that has been) said or mentioned before. (法律)前述(的)；上述(的)。 **ˈ~·thought,** ⇨ malice.

a fortiori /ˌeɪ ˌfɔːtɪˈɔːraɪ ; ˈeˌfɔrʃɪˈoraɪ/ *adv* (Lat) by a more convincing argument. (拉丁)更不用說；何況；更加。

afoul /əˈfaʊl ; əˈfaʊl/ *adv* ***run/fall ~ of,*** (more usu *run/fall foul of*) come into collision with; get mixed up with. (較常用 run/fall foul of) 與…衝突；與…糾纏在一起。

afraid /əˈfreɪd ; əˈfred/ *pred adj* **1** ~ ***(of),*** frightened (of): 害怕；畏懼：*There's nothing to be ~ of.* 沒有什麼好害怕的。*Are you ~ of snakes?* 你怕蛇嗎？ **2** ~ ***of... gerund;*** ~ ***that,*** doubtful or anxious about consequences: 恐怕：*I was ~ of hurting his feelings/that I might hurt his feelings.* 我恐怕傷了他的感情。*She was ~ of waking her husband,* didn't want to wake him, perhaps because he was ill or in need of sleep. 她怕吵醒了她的丈夫(或因他丈夫生病，或因他需要睡眠)。 **3** ~ ***to... inf,*** worried, filled with apprehension: 擔心；不敢：*She was ~ to wake her husband,* feared that he might be angry with her. 她不敢吵醒她的丈夫(怕他可能爲此而生她的氣)。*Don't be ~* (= Don't hesitate) *to* *ask for my help.* 不要擔心(儘管)向我求助。 **4 ~ (that),** (*that* usu omitted) (a polite formula used with a statement that may be unwelcome): (與 that 連用,但通常省略掉;要說的話可能不受歡迎時用的客套話): *I'm ~ (that) we shall be late.* 我恐怕我們將會遲到。*We missed the last train, I'm ~.* 恐怕我們已經錯過最後一班火車了。*I'm ~ I can't help.* 我恐怕無能相助。

afresh /əˈfreʃ; əˈfrɛʃ/ *adv* again; in a new way: 再;重新: *Let's start ~.* 讓我們重新開始。

Af·ri·can /ˈæfrɪkən; ˈæfrɪkən/ *n, adj* (indigenous inhabitant) of Africa. 非洲的;非洲人;非洲土人。

Af·ri·kaans /ˌæfrɪˈkɑːns; ˌæfrɪˈkɑnz/ *n* language developed from Dutch, one of the two official European languages in the Republic of South Africa. 阿非利康士語(南非共和國所用的兩種官方歐語之一,係由荷蘭語發展而成)。□ *adj* of this language or the people who speak it. 阿非利康士語的;說阿非利康士語之人的。**Afri·kaner** /-ˈkɑːnə(r); -ˈkɑnɚ/ *n, adj* (of) a native ~ speaker. 說阿非利康士語之人(的)。

Afro- /ˈæfrəʊ; ˈæfro/ *pref* (in compounds) of Africa or Africans: (用於複合字中)非洲的: *an A~-hairstyle.* 非洲式髮型。**ˌ~-ˈAsian** *adj* of Africa and Asia. 亞非的。**ˌ~-Aˈmerican** *n* American of African descent. 非裔美國人。**ˌ~-ˈwig** *n* wig in the style of hairdressing of some African women. 非洲式假髮(仿若干非洲女人所梳髮型的假髮)。

aft /ɑːft *US:* æft; æft/ *adv* (naut) at or near the stern of a ship, ⇨ the illus at ship: (航海)在船尾;近船尾(參看 ship 之插圖): *go aft;* 到船尾去; *fore and aft,* ⇨ fore. 從船頭到船尾。

after¹ /ˈɑːftə(r) *US:* ˈæf-; ˈæftɚ/ *adj* (attrib only) (僅作形容用法) **1** later; following: 以後的;往後的;隨後的: *in ~ years.* 在往後的幾年裡。**2** (naut) toward the stern of a ship: (航海)向船尾的: *the ˈ~ cabin;* 後艙;較近船尾的房艙; *the ˈ~ mast.* 後桅。

after² /ˈɑːftə(r) *US:* ˈæf-; ˈæftɚ/ *adv* later in time; behind in place: 以後;後來;在後: *He fell ill on Monday and died three days ~* (*later* is more usu). 他於星期一生病,三天以後就死了 (later 較常用)。*What comes ~?* 後來怎麼樣? *Soon ~* (*afterwards* is more usu), *he went to live in Wales.* 不久以後,他就到威爾斯去定居了 (afterwards 較常用)。

after³ /ˈɑːftə(r) *US:* ˈæf-; ˈæftɚ/ *conj* at or during a time later than: (指時間)在…之後: *I arrived ~ he (had) left.* 我在他離開以後到達。*I shall arrive ~ you leave/have left.* 我將在你離開以後到達。

after⁴ /ˈɑːftə(r) *US:* ˈæf-; ˈæftɚ/ *prep* **1** following in time; later than: (指時間)在…以後; …以後: *~ dinner;* 餐後; *~ dark;* 天黑以後; *~ two o'clock;* 兩點鐘以後; *soon/shortly ~ six.* 剛過六點鐘不久。Cf 參較 a little *before* six. *~ that,* then; next; 然後; *the day ~ tomorrow;* 後天; *the week ~ next;* 下下禮拜; (US) (美) *half ~* (GB 英 = *past*) *seven.* 七時半。 **2** next in order to; following: (指順序)在…後面: *Put the direct object ~ the verb.* 把直接受詞放在動詞後面。*'Against' comes ~ 'again' in the dictionary.* 在字典中 against 列於 again 之後。**3** behind: 在…後面: *Shut the door ~ you when you leave the room.* 你離開房間時,請隨手關門。 **4** in view of; as a result of: 鑒於;由於: *I shall never speak to him again ~ what he has said about me.* 由於他說了那些有關我的話,我將永遠不再跟他說話。 **5 ~ all, (a)** in spite of all: 雖然;儘管: *A~ all my care, it was broken.* 雖然我已盡量小心,仍然把它打破了。**(b)** nevertheless: 依然: *He failed ~ all*, in spite of all that had been done, etc. 他畢竟還是失敗了(雖然已盡了一切努力)。 **6** (in the pattern: *n ~ n*, indicating succession): (用於 *n ~ n* 之句型中,表示連續): *day ~ day;* 日復一日;一天一天地; *week ~ week;* 一星期一星期地; *time ~ time,* repeatedly, very often; 一次又一次地;屢次; *shot ~ shot.* 一槍接一槍地。***one (damned) thing ~ another,*** succession of unpleasant happenings, etc. 一連串不愉快的事件。 **7** (indicating manner) in the style of; in imitation of: (指方式)有…之風;倣照: *a painting ~ Rembrandt;* 一幅模倣命布蘭特的畫; ***(do sth) ~ a fashion; a man ~ my own heart,*** ⇨ fashion(1), heart(2). **8** (with *vv*, indicating pursuit, search, inquiry): (與動詞連用,表示追趕,搜尋,詢問): *The policeman ran ~ the thief.* 警察追趕竊賊。*Did they inquire ~ me,* ask for news of me? 他們有沒有問到我? ***be/get ~ sb,*** look for, in order to reprimand, punish, etc according to context: (為了給予申斥、處罰等而)尋找某人: *The police are ~ him.* 警方正在捉拿他。*They'll be ~ you if you steal apples from this orchard.* 如果你從這果園裡偷走蘋果,他們將會到處抓你。⇨ *look ~, name sb ~, take ~,* at look¹(7), name²(1) and take(16). **9** (Irish usage) preceding a gerund, making an equivalent of a perfect tense: (愛爾蘭用法) 置於動名詞前造成與完成式相等的結構: *He's ~ drinking,* has been drinking. 他一直在飲酒。

after- /ˈɑːftə(r) *US:* ˈæf-; ˈæftɚ/ *pref* second or later. 第二;後來;隨後。**ˈ~·care** *n* further treatment given to a person or class of persons, eg sb who has been ill or offenders discharged from prison. 後護法(對病人的病後照顧);恢復期護養;(對犯人出獄後的)適應輔導;就業輔導。**ˈ~·damp** *n* poisonous mixture of gases after the explosion of firedamp in a coal-mine. 炸後濁氣(煤礦坑內沼氣爆炸後所形成之有毒混合氣體)。**ˈ~-effect** *n* effect that occurs afterwards, eg a delayed effect of a drug used medically. (藥物等的)後作用;後效。**ˈ~·glow** *n* glow in the sky after sunset. (夕陽的)餘暉;晚霞;夕照。**(the) ˈ~·life** *n* **(a)** the life believed to follow death. (有人相信的)死後的生活;來世。**(b)** the later part of sb's lifetime (esp after a particular event). (尤指某一特殊事件後的)晚年;餘年;後半輩子。**ˈ~·math** /-mæθ; -mæθ/ *n* (of grass) crop from a second growth (after the hay harvest); (fig) outcome; consequence: (割後第二次長出的)再生草;(喻)結果;後果;餘波: *Misery is usually the ~math of war.* 苦難通常是戰後餘殃。**ˈ~·thought** *n* [U] reflection afterwards; [C] thought that comes afterwards. 回想;反省;事後才想起來的主意;事後聰明。

after·noon /ˌɑːftəˈnuːn *US:* ˈæf-; ˌæftɚˈnun/ *n* [U, C] time between morning and evening: 下午: *in/during the ~;* 在下午; *this/yesterday/tomorrow ~;* 今天(昨天,明天)下午; *every ~;* 每天下午; *on Sunday ~;* 在星期日下午; *on the ~ of May 1st;* 在五月一日的下午; *one ~ last week;* 上星期的一個下午; *on several ~s;* 在幾個下午; (attrib) (形容用法) *an ~ sleep/concert.* 午睡(午後演奏會)。

afters /ˈɑːftəz *US:* ˈæf-; ˈæftɚz/ *n pl* (colloq) last (usu sweet) course at a meal: (俗)餐席的最後一道菜(通常為甜點): *What's for ~? Is it fruit and custard?* 最後一道菜是什麼?是水果和乳蛋糕嗎?

after·wards /ˈɑːftəwədz *US:* ˈæf-; ˈæftɚwɚdz/ *adv* after; later. 以後;後來。

again /əˈgen; əˈgɛn/ *adv* **1** once more: 再一次;再: *If you fail the first time, try ~.* 如果你第一次失敗了,再試一次。*Say it ~, please.* 請再說一遍。*Do you think she will marry ~,* remarry? 你認為她將會再婚嗎? *You must type this letter ~,* retype it. 你必須把這封信重打一次。***now and ~,*** occasionally. 偶爾;間或。***~ and ~; time and (time) ~,*** repeatedly; very often. 一再;屢次地;再三。***(the) same ~,*** formula for re-ordering, eg a drink. 再來同樣的(為再點酒類等的套語)。 **2** (with *not, never*) any more: (與 not, never 連用)再: *This must never happen ~.* 這樣的事情以後不可再度發生。*Don't do that ~.* 別再做那種事。 **3** to or in the original condition, position, etc: 恢復原狀: *You'll soon be well ~.* 你不久就會康復。*He was glad to be home ~.* 他能夠再回到家裡感到高興。*You won't get the money back ~,* won't regain it. 你不會得回那筆錢。***be oneself ~,*** be restored to a normal (physical or mental) condition. (指身體或精神)恢復常態。 **4** ***as many/much*** ~, **(a)** the same number/quantity. 同樣數目(分量)。 **(b)** twice as many/much; the same in addition. 加一倍;多一倍。 ***half as many/much/long, etc*** ~, half as many/much, etc in addition. 加多(長等)一半。 **5** (often preceded by *and* or *and then*) furthermore, besides: (常用於 and 或 and then 之後)再者;此外;而且: *Then ~, I feel doubtful whether....* 再者,我感到懷疑是否…。

against /əˈgenst ; əˈgɛnst/ *prep* **1** (indicating opposition): (表示相反): *Public opinion was ~ the proposal.* 輿論反對此建議。Cf 參較 *for, in favour of. We were rowing ~ the current.* 我們逆水划船。Cf 參較 *with. It was a race ~ time,* an attempt to finish before a certain time, before a possible happening, etc. 那是一項爭取時間的努力(趕工,趕時間之意)。*She was married ~ her will.* 她違反本意而結婚。*Is there a law ~ spitting in the streets in this country?* 在這個國家裡,有法律禁止當街吐痰嗎? *His appearance is ~ him,* is such that people are unlikely to favour or support him. 他的儀表於他不利。**2** (with *vv* indicating protest): (與動詞連用,表示反對): *vote/cry out/write/raise one's voice ~ a proposal.* 投票(高呼,撰文,提高嗓音呼喊)反對一項提議。**3** (with *vv*, to indicate collision or impact): (與動詞連用,表示衝突或碰撞): *The rain was beating ~ the windows.* 雨點拍打在窗戶上。*He hit his head ~ the wall in the dark cellar.* 他的頭在黑暗的地窖中撞到了牆。⇨ *run against* at run¹(18). **4** in contrast to: 襯托;相映;對照: *The pine trees were black ~ the morning sky.* 在早晨天空的映照下,那些松樹是黑的。 **5** in preparation for; in anticipation of: 防備;預防: *take precautions ~ fire;* 採取防火措施; *an injection ~ rabies;* 狂犬病預防針; *save money ~ a rainy day,* (prov) for a time of possible need. (諺)儲蓄金錢,以備不時之需;未雨綢繆。**6** (indicating support or close proximity): (表示支持或緊靠): *Place the ladder ~ the tree.* 把梯子靠在樹上。*Put the piano with its back ~ the wall.* 把鋼琴的後背緊靠牆放。*He was leaning ~ a post.* 他倚靠在一根柱子上。**7** ***over*** ~, **(a)** facing, opposite to. 面對;相對。**(b)** (fig) in contrast with, in addition to. (喻)與…相比;除…之外。

agape /əˈgeɪp ; əˈgep/ *pred adj* (facet) with the mouth wide open (owing to wonder, surprise, or a yawn). (玩笑語)(因驚奇,驚愕或打呵欠而)大張着口;目瞪口呆。

agar-agar /ˌeɪgɑːr ˈeɪgɑː(r) *US:* ˌɑːg- ˈɑːg- ; ˈegɑr-ˈegɑr/ *n* [U] (jelly-like substance prepared from) seaweed. 石花菜;洋菜(用石花菜製成的一種膠狀食品)。

ag·ate /ˈægət ; ˈægɪt/ *n* (sorts of) very hard stone, a form of silica, with bands or patches of colour. 瑪瑙。

agave /əˈgeɪvɪ *US:* əˈgɑːvɪ ; əˈgevɪ/ *n* (bot) (kinds of) tropical fleshy-leaved plant (including *sisal*), cultivated for their fibres and as a source of intoxicating drinks, eg *pulque.* (植物)龍舌蘭。

age¹ /eɪdʒ ; edʒ/ *n* **1** [C] length of time a person has lived or a thing has existed: 年齡;年紀;年歲: *What's his age,* How old is he? 他多大年紀? *Their ages are 4, 7 and 9.* 他們的年齡是四歲,七歲和九歲。*At what age do children start school in your country?* 在你們國家,兒童幾歲開始上學? *What's the age of that old church?* 那座老教堂有多少年了? *When I was your age....* 當我像你這樣年紀時…。*I have a son your age,* a son the same age as you. 我有一個像你這樣年紀的兒子。*She ought to be earning her own living at her age,* She's old enough now to do this. 在她這樣的年紀,她應該自力謀生了。***be/come of age,*** be/become old enough to be responsible in law. 成年。⇨ *age of consent* at consent. ***be of an age,*** reach a stage in life when one ought to do sth: 到達該作某事的年齡: *He's of an age when he ought to be settling down,* eg get a good job, marry. 他已到了安定下來的年齡了(比如說成家立業) ***over age,*** having passed a certain age or age limit: 超過了某一年齡或某種年齡限制: *He won't be called up for military service; he's over age.* 他不會被徵召入伍;他已超過役齡。⇨ *age limit* at limit¹. ***under age,*** too young; not yet of age. 太年輕;未達規定年齡;未成年。ˈ**age-bracket** *n* period of life between two specified ages, eg between 20 and 30. 年齡分類;年齡範圍(例如二十歲至三十歲間)。ˈ**age-group** *n* number of persons of the same age. 同齡的一群人。 **2** [U] later part of life (contrasted with *youth*): 老年;晚年(與 youth 相對): *His back was bent with age.* 他的背因年老而傴僂。*If we could have the strength of youth and the wisdom of age,....* 假使我們能够有青年的體力和老年的智慧,…。**3** [C] great or long period of time, with special characteristics or events: (具有某特徵或特殊事件的)時代: *the age of machinery;* 機器時代; *the atomic age;* 原子時代; *the Elizabethan Age,* the time of Queen Elizabeth I of England (1558-1603). 伊利莎白時代(英國女王伊利莎白一世在位時期, 1558-1603)。⇨ *golden age, middle age, the Middle Ages, the Stone Age* at golden(2), middle(3), stone(1). **4** [C] (colloq) very long time: (俗)很長時間;很久: *We've been waiting an age/for ages.* 我們已經等候很久了。

age² /eɪdʒ ; edʒ/ *vt, vi* (*pres part* ageing or aging, *pp* aged /eɪdʒd ; edʒd/) [VP6A, 2A, C] (cause to) grow old: (使)變老: *He's ag(e)ing fast.* 他老得很快。*I found him greatly aged,* looking much older. 我發現他老得多了。 **aged** /eɪdʒd ; edʒd/ *pred adj* of the age of: …歲的: *a boy aged ten.* 十歲的男孩。□ *attrib adj* /ˈeɪdʒɪd ; ˈedʒɪd/ very old: 很老的;年老的: *an aged man;* 老人; *the poor and the aged,* those who are poor and old. 貧者及老者。ˈ**aging, ˈage·ing** *n* [U] process of growing old; changes that occur as the result of the passing of time. 變老的過程;因時間過去而發生的變化。ˈ**age·less** *adj* eternal; always young; not affected by time. 永恆的;永遠年輕的;不爲時間所影響的。ˈ**age-long** *adj* lasting for centuries; handed down the ages. 延續幾世紀的;源遠流長的。ˌ**age-ˈold** *adj* that has been known, practised, etc for a long time: 久爲人所知,所施行等的;古老的: *age-old customs/ceremonies.* 古老的習俗(禮儀)。

agency /ˈeɪdʒənsɪ ; ˈedʒənsɪ/ *n* (*pl* -cies) **1** business, place of business, of an agent(1): 經銷;代辦;代理;經銷處;代理處: *The Company has agencies in all parts of Africa.* 該公司在非洲各地均有代理店。*He found a job through an employment ~.* 他經由職業介紹所找到一個工作。*Not all travel agencies are reliable.* 並非所有旅行社都是可靠的。 **2** [U] ***the ~ of,*** the operation, action of: 動作;作用;工具;媒介;力量: *Rocks are worn smooth through the ~ of water.* 岩石由於水的作用而變得光光。*He obtained a position in a government office through/by the ~ (= with the help or influence) of friends.* 他藉助於朋友的力量在政府機關裡獲得了一個職位。

agenda /əˈdʒendə ; əˈdʒɛndə/ *n* [C] **1** (list of) things to be done, business to be discussed, eg by a committee: (委員會等的)待辦事項或待討論事務(表);議程: *the next item on the ~;* 議程上的次一項目; *item No 5 on the ~.* 議程上的第五項。**2** (comp) set of operations which form a procedure for solving a problem. (電腦)解決某一問題的一套作業程序。

agent /ˈeɪdʒənt ; ˈedʒənt/ *n* **1** person who acts for, or who manages the business affairs of, another or others: 代理人;代理商;代辦人;經紀人: *a ˈhouse-~,* one who buys, sells, lets and rents houses for the owners; 房產經紀人(代人買賣、租讓房屋者); *a ˈliterary ~,* one who helps authors to find a publisher; 著作經紀人(幫助作家找出版商者); *a ˈshipping or ˈforwarding ~,* one who sends goods by rail, sea, road, etc for merchants, manufacturers, etc. 貨運商(代商人、製造商等經由鐵路、海運、公路等運送貨品者)。ˈ**law ~,** (in Scotland) solicitor. (蘇格蘭之)律師;法律顧問。⇨ free¹(3), secret(1). **2** person used to achieve sth, to get a result; (science) substance, natural phenomenon, etc producing an effect:用以獲得某事物或某一結果的人;行爲者;動作者;作用者;(科學)產生某種效果的物質;自然力;媒劑;動因: *Rain and frost are natural ~s that wear away rocks.* 雨和霜都是磨蝕岩石的自然力。

agent pro·voca·teur /ˌæʒɒn prəˌvɒkəˈtɜː(r) ; ˌɑˈʒɑ̃ˌprɔˌvɔˌkaˈtɝ/ *n* (*pl* agents provocateurs, pronunciation unchanged) (複數發音不變) (F) person employed to find suspected criminals or offenders by tempting them to commit an offence openly. (法) 受雇誘使嫌疑犯公然犯罪以便加以逮捕之秘密偵探。

ag·glom·er·ate /əˈglɒməreɪt ; əˈglɑməˌret/ *vt, vi* [VP6A, 2A] gather, collect, into a mass. 聚結;結塊;成團;凝聚。□ *adj* /əˈglɒmərət ; əˈglɑmərɪt/ collected into, forming or growing into, a mass. 聚結成塊的;凝結成團的。**ag·glom·er·ation** /əˌglɒməˈreɪʃn ; əˌglɑməˈreʃən/ *n* [U] action of agglomerating; [C] (esp untidy) heap or collection of ~d objects, eg a sprawl of untidy suburbs. 聚結;結塊;成團;凝聚;聚集成的一堆 (尤指不整齊者,例如大城市不規則向外延伸而造成的不整齊的郊區)。

ag·glu·tin·ate /əˈgluːtɪneɪt ; əˈglutn̩ˌet/ *vt, vi* [VP 6A, 2A] join together as with glue; combine. (使) 黏合;膠合;膠着;結合。**ag·glu·ti·nat·ive** /əˈgluːtɪnətɪv *US:* -tənetɪv ; əˈglutn̩ˌetɪv/ *adj* (of languages) that combine simple words into compounds without change of form or loss of meaning. (指語言) 膠着的 (指某些語言可以由簡單的字不變其形或義而連綴組成複雜之結合語的現象)。

ag·grand·ize /əˈgrændaɪz ; ˈægrənˌdaɪz/ *vt* [VP6A] (formal) increase (in power, rank, wealth, importance). (正式用語) 增加 (權力,階級,財富,重要性)。**ag·grand·ize·ment** /əˈgrændɪzmənt ; əˈgrændɪzmənt/ *n*: *a man bent on personal ~.* 專心致力於擴充個人權勢財富的人。

ag·gra·vate /ˈægrəveɪt ; ˈægrəˌvet/ *vt* [VP6A] **1** make worse or more serious: 使惡化;使更嚴重: *~ an illness/offence.* 加重病勢(罪過)。**2** (colloq) irritate; exasperate: (俗)激怒;惹: *He ~s her beyond endurance.* 他使她怒不可遏。*How aggravating*, annoying! 多麼可惱呵! **ag·gra·va·tion** /ˌægrəˈveɪʃn ; ˌægrəˈveʃən/ *n* [U] aggravating or being ~d; [C] sth that ~s. 增劇;惡化;使惡化之事物。

ag·gre·gate /ˈægrɪgeɪt ; ˈægrɪˌget/ *vt, vi* **1** [VP6A, 2A] bring or come together in a mass. 聚集;聚集成團;凝結。**2** [VP2E] amount to (specified total). 總計;合計爲(某一總數);計達。□ *n* /ˈægrɪgət ; ˈægrɪgɪt/ **1** total obtained by addition; mass or amount brought together. 合計;總數;總量;聚合體。***in the ~,*** as a whole; collectively. 總計;合計;總共。**2** materials (sand, gravel, etc) mixed with cement to make concrete. 骨材(與水泥混合成混凝土的材料,如沙,礫石等)。**ag·gre·ga·tion** /ˌægrɪˈgeɪʃn ; ˌægrɪˈgeʃən/ *n* [U] number of separate things, materials, brought together into a mass or group. (由個別事物聚合而成的)集合體;聚集;集團。

ag·gres·sion /əˈgreʃn ; əˈgrɛʃən/ *n* **1** [U] unprovoked hostility, often beginning a quarrel or war: 侵略;攻擊;啓釁: *It was difficult to decide which country was guilty of ~ (on/upon the other).* 很難判定那一國犯侵略(他國)之罪。**2** [C] instance of this. 侵略或攻擊之實例。

ag·gres·sive /əˈgresɪv ; əˈgrɛsɪv/ *adj* **1** quarrelsome; disposed to attack: 好與人爭吵的;性好攻擊的: *an ~ man;* 好與人爭吵的人; *a man with an ~ disposition.* 性好攻擊他人之人。**2** offensive; of or for attack: 攻擊性的;侵略的: *~ weapons.* 攻擊性的武器。**3** pushing; not afraid of resistance: 有闖勁的;不怕阻力的: *A man who goes from door to door selling things has to be ~ if he wants to succeed.* 沿門兜售貨物的人要想成功,必須要有闖勁。**~·ly** *adv* **~·ness** *n* **ag·gres·sor** /-sə(r) ; -sɚ/ *n* person, country, making an ~ attack: 侵略者;攻擊者;侵略國: (attrib) (形容用法) *the aggressor nation.* 侵略國。

ag·grieve /əˈgriːv ; əˈgriv/ *vt* (usu passive) grieve: (通常用被動語態)使苦惱; 使悲傷: *be ~d.* 感到痛心;悲傷。***feel (oneself) much ~d (at/over sth),*** feel that one has been treated unjustly; be hurt in one's feelings. (爲了某事)覺得受了委屈;覺得感情受了傷害。

ag·gro /ˈægrəʊ ; ˈægro/ *n* [U] (GB sl) aggression as shown by gangs of teenagers towards other gangs, racial minorities, etc. (英俚)少年幫派對其他幫派、少數種族等的啓釁行爲。

aghast /əˈgɑːst *US:* əˈgæst ; əˈgæst/ *pred adj* filled with fear or surprise: 吃驚的;嚇呆的: *He stood ~ at the terrible sight.* 他被那個可怕的景象嚇呆了。

agile /ˈædʒaɪl *US:* ˈædʒl ; ˈædʒəl/ *adj* (of living things) quick-moving; active. (指有生命的東西)敏捷的;靈活的;活潑的。**~·ly** *adv* **agil·ity** /əˈdʒɪlətɪ ; əˈdʒɪlətɪ/ *n* [U].

agin /əˈgɪn ; əˈgɪn/ *prep* (used jocularly for) against, (謔)反對, eg in: 例如: *~ the government.* 反對政府。

ag·ing *n* = ageing. ⇨ age².

agi·tate /ˈædʒɪteɪt ; ˈædʒəˌtet/ *vt, vi* **1** [VP6A] move or shake (a liquid); stir up (the surface of a liquid). 搖動(液體);攪動(液體的表面)。**2** [VP 6A] disturb; cause anxiety to (a person, his mind or feelings): 擾亂;激動;使煩亂: *She was deeply ~d until she learnt that her husband was among the survivors.* 她十分焦急,直到她聽說她的丈夫在生還者之列,她才放心。*He was ~d about his wife's health.* 他爲妻子的健康擔憂。**3** [VP3A] ***~ for,*** argue publicly in favour of, take part in a campaign for: 煽動;鼓動;鼓吹: *~ for the repeal of a law;* 鼓吹廢止某項法律; *workers who ~d for higher wages.* 鼓動加薪的工人。**agi·tated** *part adj* troubled. 煩惱的;焦慮的。**agi·tat·ing** *part adj* causing anxiety. 令人焦慮的。**agi·ta·tion** /ˌædʒɪˈteɪʃn ; ˌædʒəˈteʃən/ *n* **1** [U] moving or shaking (of a liquid). (對液體之)搖動;攪動。**2** [U] excitement of the mind or feelings; anxiety: 激動;煩亂;心焦;憂慮: *She was in a state of agitation.* 她處於激動的狀態中。**3** [C, U] discussion or debate (for the purpose of bringing about a change); [U] social or political unrest or trouble caused by such discussion: (爲改革而作的)討論或辯論;鼓吹(改革);煽動;(因受鼓動而引起的社會或政治的)不安;騷動: *Small shopkeepers carried on a long agitation against the big department stores.* 小本商人進行了很久的激辯,反對大百貨公司。**agi·ta·tor** /-tə(r) ; -tɚ/ *n* person who ~s, esp politically. 鼓動者;(尤指政治方面的)煽動者。

aglow /əˈgləʊ ; əˈglo/ *pred adj* **1** bright with colour; in a glow: 發光彩的;發紅光的: *The sky was ~ with the setting sun.* 天空因夕陽映照而發紅光。**2** (of persons) showing warmth from exercise or excitement: (指人)(因運動或興奮而)發熱的: *~ with pleasure;* 因高興而發熱; shining: 發光的: *a face ~ with health.* 因健康而紅光滿面。

ag·nail /ˈægneɪl ; ˈægˌnel/ *n* [U] torn skin at the base of a finger nail. 逆剝;爪刺(爪甲基部的逆刺皮)。

ag·nos·tic /ægˈnɒstɪk ; ægˈnɑstɪk/ *n* person who believes that nothing can be known about God or of anything except material things. (對於神或物質以外的事物持)不可知論者。□ *adj* of this belief. 不可知論的。**ag·nos·ti·cism** /ægˈnɒstɪsɪzəm ; ægˈnɑstəˌsɪzəm/ *n* [U] this belief. 不可知論。

ago /əˈgəʊ ; əˈgo/ *adv* (used to indicate time measured back to a point in the past; always placed after the word or words it modifies; used with the simple *pt*): (用以指從現在倒算到過去某一點之時間;永遠置於所修飾之字或詞之後;與簡單過去式連用)…以前: *The train left a few minutes ago/not long ago.* 火車在幾分鐘(不久)以前開走了。*That was many years/a long while ago.* 那是許多年(很久)以

前的事了。*How long ago is it that you last saw her?* 你上一次看見她是多久以前的事？*I met Mary no longer ago than* (= as recently as) *last Sunday.* 我就在上個星期天還遇見過瑪莉。*It was seven years ago that my brother died.* 我哥哥(弟弟)是七年以前死的。Cf 參較 It *is* seven years *since* my brother died. 我哥哥(弟弟)去世於今已七年了。

agog /ə'gɒg ; ə'gag/ *pred adj* eager; excited: 渴望的；急切的；興奮的；激動的：*~ for news;* 渴望聽到消息；*~ to hear the news.* 急着要聽那消息。*The whole village was ~.* 全村的人都很興奮。*His unexpected return set the town ~,* eg was the cause of many rumours about the reasons for his return. 他意外的回來驚動了全鎮的人(例如紛紛揣測他何以回來)。

ag·ony /'ægənɪ ; 'ægənɪ/ *n* (*pl* -nies) [U, C] great pain or suffering (of mind or body): (精神或肉體上的)極大的痛苦：*She looked on in ~ at her child's sufferings.* 她在旁痛苦地看着她的孩子受苦。*I've suffered agonies/have been in agonies with toothache.* 我受到牙痛之苦。*He was in an ~ of remorse.* 他處於悔恨的痛苦中。'**~ column,** newspaper column with advertisements for news of missing friends, etc. (報紙上的)尋人廣告欄(刊載尋友等之廣告者)。***pile on the ~,*** (colloq) (俗) ⇨ pile³(1). **ag·on·ized** /'ægənaɪzd ; 'ægə,naɪzd/ *adj* expressing ~: 表示痛苦的：*agonized shrieks.* 痛苦的尖叫聲。**ag·on·iz·ing** /'ægənaɪzɪŋ; 'ægə,naɪzɪŋ/ *adj* causing ~.引起痛苦的。

agora /'ægərə ; 'ægərə/ *n* (in ancient Greece) (place of) assembly; market-place. (古希臘之)民衆大會(場)；市場。**~·phobia** /,ægərə'fəʊbɪə ; ,ægərə'fobɪə/ *n* [U] fear of (crossing) open spaces. 空曠恐怖；廣場恐怖；空室恐怖。

agrar·ian /ə'greərɪən ; ə'grɛrɪən/ *adj* of land (esp farmland) or land ownership: 土地的；(尤指)農地的；土地所有權的：*~ laws/problems/reforms/disputes.* 土地法(問題,改革,糾紛)。

agree /ə'griː ; ə'gri/ *vi, vt* **1** [VP2A, 3A, B] ***~ (to),*** say 'Yes'; consent: 同意；答應；允諾：*I asked him to help me and he ~d.* 我請他幫忙，他答應了。*Mary's father has ~d to her marrying John.* 瑪莉的父親已同意她嫁給約翰。*He ~d to my proposal.* 他已同意我的提議。**2** [VP3A,B,4C,7A] (also with an *inf* or a *that*-clause without a *prep*) be of the same opinion(s); be in harmony (*with* sb *on/about* sth, *as to* how to do sth, etc): (亦與不定詞或 that 子句連用而不用介系詞)同意；意見一致(後接 with 某人，on 或 about 某事物，as to 如何做某事等)：*we ~d to start early.* 我們同意早動身。*I hope you will ~ with me that our teacher's advice is excellent.* 我希望你會同意我的意見，認爲我們的老師的勸告好極了。*We all ~d on the terms.* 我們大家都同意這些條件。*We ~d on an early start/on making an early start/that we should start early/to start early.* 我們同意早動身。*We met at the ~d time,* at the time we had ~d on. 我們在約好的時間碰面了。*We are* (= have) *all ~d on finding the accused man innocent.* 我們大家一致認爲被告無罪。*We are all ~d that the proposal is a good one.* 我們大家一致認爲這是一項好的提議。*We could not ~* (*as to*) *how it should be done.* 關於這事應如何做法，我們大家意見不能一致。*Have you ~d about the price yet?* 關於價錢你們的意見已經一致了嗎？ **3** [VP2A, C] (of two or more persons) be happy together; get on well with one another (without arguing, etc): (指兩個以上的人)合得來；和睦相處；意氣相投：*We shall never ~.* 我們將永不會合得來。*Why can't you children ~* (*together*)? 你們小孩子爲什麼不能在一起和諧相處呢？ **4** [VP3A] ***~ (with),*** match, conform (with): 與…相配；與…符合：*Your story ~s with what I had already heard.* 你所說的跟我所聽到的相符。*This bill does not ~ with your original estimate,* the two are different. 這帳單與你原來的估計不符合。**5** [VP3A] ***~ with,*** suit, eg the health or constitution of: 適宜於…的健康或體質：*The climate doesn't ~ with me.* 這氣候對我不相宜。*The mussels I had for lunch haven't ~d with me,* have upset my stomach. 我中餐所吃的淡菜不合我的胃口。 **6** [VP3A] ***~ with,*** (gram) correspond in number, person, etc with: (文法)(在數，人稱等方面)與…一致：*The verb ~s with its subject in number and person.* 動詞的數和人稱與其主詞一致。 **7** [VP6A] (of figures, accounts, proposals, etc) accept or approve (as being correct): 認可(數字，帳目，提議等)：*The Inspector of Taxes has ~d your return of income.* 稅務稽查員已經認可你的所得稅申報表。

agree·able /ə'griːəbl ; ə'griəbḷ/ *adj* **1** pleasing; giving pleasure: 令人喜悅的；令人愉快的；宜人的：*She has an ~ voice.* 她的聲音悅耳。**2** ready to agree: 準備同意的；欣然同意的：*Are you ~ to the proposal?* 你能同意這提議嗎？*I'm ~ to doing what you suggest.* 我同意照你的建議去做。**agree·ably** /-əblɪ ; -əblɪ/ *adv*: 喜悅地；愉快地：*I was agreeably surprised,* surprised and pleased. 我又驚又喜。

agree·ment /ə'griːmənt ; ə'grimənt/ *n* **1** [U] having the same opinion(s); thinking in the same way: 同意；意見一致：*We are in ~ on that point.* 關於那一點我們的意見一致。*I'm quite in ~ with what you say.* 我十分同意你所說的話。*There is no ~ upon/about what should be done.* 應該怎麼辦，大家意見不一。**2** [C] arrangement or understanding (spoken or written) made by two or more persons, groups, business companies, governments, etc: (兩個以上的人，團體，公司，政府等所做口頭或書面的)協議；協定；合同；合約：*sign an ~;* 簽訂合約；*an ~ to rent a house.* 租屋契約。***come to/arrive at/make/reach an ~ (with sb),*** reach an understanding. (與某人)達成協議；商定。

ag·ri·cul·ture /'ægrɪkʌltʃə(r) ; 'ægrɪ,kʌltʃɚ/ *n* [U] science or practice of farming; cultivation of the soil. 農學；農業；農事；農耕。**ag·ri·cul·tural** /,ægrɪ'kʌltʃərəl ; ,ægrɪ'kʌltʃərəl/ *adj* of ~: 農業的：*agricultural workers.* 農業工人；農業工作者。

aground /ə'graʊnd ; ə'graʊnd/ *adv, pred adj* (of ships) touching the bottom in shallow water: (指船)擱淺：*The ship went ~/was fast ~/ran ~.* 該船擱淺(不能動)了。

ague /'eɪgjuː ; 'egju/ *n* [U, C] fever. 發熱；熱病。

ah /ɑː ; ɑ/ *int* cry of surprise, pity, etc. 啊(表示驚愕，憐憫等之感歎詞)。

aha /ɑː'hɑː ; ɑ'hɑ/ *int* cry of surprise, triumph, satisfaction, etc, according to context. 啊哈(表示驚愕，勝利，滿足等之感歎詞，視上下文而定)。

ahead /ə'hed ; ə'hɛd/ *adv* ***~ (of),*** in front; in advance: 在前面；在前頭：*Tom was a quick walker and soon got ~ of the others.* 湯姆是一個健步者，不久就走到別人前頭去了。*He ran on ~.* 他跑在前面。*Standard time in Turkey is two hours ~ of Greenwich Mean Time.* 土耳其的標準時間，比格林尼治標準時間早兩小時。***Full speed ~!*** Go forward at full speed! 全速前進！***go ~,*** **(a)** make progress: 進步；進行：*Things are going ~.* 一切事情都在進行。**(b)** (colloq, also 亦作 ***fire ~***) continue (with what you're about to say or do). (俗)(指你正要說的話或正要做的事)繼續下去。***in line ~,*** (of warships) moving forward, anchored, in a column or file. (指軍艦)成縱列前進或停泊。***look ~,*** (fig) think of and prepare for future needs. (喻)爲未來着想或打算；未雨綢繆。

ahem /ə'hem ; ə'hɛm/ *int* (usu spelling form of the) noise made when clearing the throat; noise made to give a slight warning or to call sb's attention. 啊哼(清喉嚨的聲音；表示小小的警告或促使某人注意的聲音)。

ahoy /ə'hɔɪ ; ə'hɔɪ/ *int* greeting or warning cry used by seamen. 啊荷；喂(水手所用打招呼或警告的喊聲)。

aid /eɪd ; ed/ *vt* [VP6A, 17, 14] help: 幫助；援助：*aid one another;* 彼此幫助；*aid sb to do sth;* 幫助某人做某事；*aid sb with money.* 以金錢幫助某人。□ *n* **1** [U] help: 幫助；援助：*aid programmes,* those designed to give help, eg to developing countries.

援助計畫(例如對開發中國家的援助)。*He came to my aid*, came to help me. 他來幫助我。*What is the collection in aid of*, What is the money to be used for? 所募集的款子將作何用途？ ⇨ first¹(2), legal. **2** [C] sth that helps. 有助之物。**visual aids**, pictures, films, film-strips, etc used in teaching. 視覺教具(如圖片,影片,幻燈片等)。 **ˈhearing-aid**, appliance that helps a deaf person to hear. (聾者所用的)助聽器。

aide-de-camp /ˌeɪd də ˈkɒm *US:* ˈkæmp ; ˈeddəˈkæmp/ *n* (*pl* aides-de-camp pronunciation unchanged) naval or military officer who helps a superior by carrying orders, etc. (複數發音不變)副官;侍從軍官。

aide-mémoire /ˌeɪd memˈwɑː(r) ; ˌedˌmemˈwɑr/ *n* **1** (in diplomacy) memorandum. (外交)備忘錄。**2** document, list etc to remind sb of sth. 備忘之文件、名單等。

aigrette, aigret /ˈeɪgret *US:* ˌeɪˈgret ; ˈegrɛt/ *n* tuft of feathers worn as an ornament on the head; spray of gems or jewels in imitation of this. 用做頭飾的羽毛;羽毛狀珠寶首飾。

ail /eɪl ; el/ *vt, vi* **1** [VP6A] (old use) trouble: (舊用法)使煩惱;使苦惱: *What ails him*, What's wrong with him, What's troubling him? 什麼事使他煩惱？他有什麼煩惱？ **2** [VP2A,B] be ill: 生病;有病: *The children are always ailing*, always in poor health. 孩子們總是生病。

aileron /ˈeɪlərɒn ; ˈeləˌrɑn/ *n* hinged part of the wing of an aircraft that helps to balance the aircraft and control ascent and descent. (飛機翼上幫助平衡飛機及控制昇降的) 副翼。⇨ the illus at aircraft. 參看 aircraft 之挿圖。

ail·ment /ˈeɪlmənt ; ˈelmənt/ *n* [C] illness. 疾病;恙。

aim¹ /eɪm ; em/ *vt, vi* **1** [VP6A, 14, 2A] ***aim (at)***, **(a)** point (a gun, etc) towards: 以(槍砲等)對準;瞄準: *aim a gun at sb.* 以槍瞄準某人。*He aimed (his gun) at the lion, fired and missed.* 他瞄準那獅子,放槍,未打中。**(b)** send, direct, eg a blow, object (*at* sb or sth): (對着…)打去;擲去(與at連用): *Tom got angry with his brother and aimed a heavy book at his head.* 湯姆對他的哥哥(弟弟)發怒,拿起一本厚書向他的頭擲去。(fig) (喻) *My remarks were not aimed at you.* 我的話不是對你而發。 **2** [VP3A, *aim at doing sth;* US 美 VP4A, *aim to do sth*] have as a plan or intention: 計畫;打算;以…爲目標: *Harry aims at becoming／to become a doctor.* 哈利立志要做醫生。*What are you aiming at?* 你的意向如何？

aim² /eɪm ; em/ *n* **1** [U] act of aiming, eg with a gun: (以槍等)對準;瞄準: *Take careful aim at the target.* 仔細瞄準靶子。*He missed his aim*, did not hit the target. 他未擊中標的。 **2** [C] purpose; object: 目標;目的: *What's your aim in life*, what do you want to do or be? 你的人生目標是什麼？ *He has only one aim in life—to be a millionaire.* 他只有一個人生目標──成爲百萬富翁。 **aim·less** *adj* having no purpose: 無目標的;無目的的: *an aimless life／task／journey.* 無目的的生活(工作,旅行)。**aim·less·ly** *adv*: 無目的地: *wandering aimlessly about the town.* 在鎮上無目的地遊逛。

ain't /eɪnt ; ent/ (vulg) contracted form of *are／is／am not*, and *have／has not*: (鄙) 爲 are not, is not, am not, have not, 及 has not 的縮體: *I ~ going.* 我不去。*We ~ got any.* 我們一點也沒有。

air¹ /eə(r) ; ɛr/ *n* **1** [U] the mixture of gases that surrounds the earth and which we breathe: 空氣: *Let's go out and have some fresh air.* 我們出去吸點新鮮空氣吧。***in the air***, **(a)** uncertain: 不定的;未定的: *My plans are still quite in the air.* 我的計畫還未定案。**(b)** (of opinions, etc) spreading about: (指意見等)傳播的;散佈的: *There are rumours in the air that....* 有謠言傳說…。**(c)** (mil) uncovered, unprotected: (軍) 無掩蔽的;無掩護的: *Their left flank was left in the air.* 他們的左翼無掩護。***clear the air***, **(a)** make the air (in a room, etc) fresh again. 使(室內等之)空氣恢復新鮮。**(b)** (fig) get rid of suspicion, doubt, etc by giving facts, etc. (喻)提出事實等以澄清疑慮。⇨ also castle, hot(8). **2** [U] the atmosphere as a place for aircraft to fly in; (attrib) of flying, aircraft, etc: 大氣;(形容用法)飛行的;飛機的;航空的: *air freight／transport／travel.* 空運貨物(航空運輸,乘飛機旅行)。***by air***, in an aircraft: 乘飛機;以空運: *travel by air;* 乘飛機旅行; *send goods by air.* 以航空運貨。 **3** [U] (radio) (無線電) ***on the air***, broadcasting: 廣播: *Radio Lichtenburg is on the air 24 hours a day.* 利克田堡廣播電台全天二十四小時廣播。***off the air***, not broadcasting. 停止廣播。***come／go on the air***, start broadcasting. 開始廣播。***come／go off the air***, stop broadcasting. 停止廣播。*Why has that station gone off the air?* 那個電台爲什麼停止廣播？ **4** [C] (liter, naut) breeze, light wind. (文,航海)微風。 **5** [C] (old use) tune, melody. (舊用法)歌調;曲調;旋律。 **6** [C] **(a)** appearance; manner: 容貌;外表;態度: *He has an air of importance*, seems to be, looks, important. 他有一種很了不起的樣子。*The house has an air of comfort.* 這房子看起來像很舒適的樣子。**(b)** (usu *pl*) (通常用複數) ***give oneself／put on airs***, behave in an unnatural way in the hope of impressing people. 擺架子;裝腔作勢。***airs and graces***, foolish, exaggerated ways of behaving. 裝腔作勢。 **7** (compounds and attrib uses) (複合字及形容用法) **ˈair·bed** *n* mattress inflated with air. 氣床墊。**ˈair-bladder** *n* (in animals and plants, esp seaweed) bladder filled with air. (動物及植物,尤指海藻體內之)鰾;氣胞。**ˈair·borne** *adj* **(a)** transported by air. 空運的。**(b)** (of an aircraft) having taken off; in flight: (指飛機)已起飛的;飛行中的: *We were soon airborne.* 我們不久就升空了。**(c)** (of troops) specially trained for air operations: (指軍隊)受特別訓練以適於空中活動的;空降的: *an airborne division.* 空降師。**ˈair-brake** *n* brake worked by compressed air. (空)氣煞車;風軔。**ˌAir (ˌChief) ˈMarshal, ˌAir ˈCommodore** *nn* highest ranks in the RAF. (英國皇家空軍)空軍大元帥;空軍代將。**ˈair-conditioned** *adj* (of a room, building, railway coach, etc) supplied with air that is purified and kept at a certain temperature and degree of humidity. (指房間,建築物,火車車廂等)裝有空氣調節設備的;有冷氣設備的。**ˈair-conditioning** *n* this process. 空氣調節。**ˌair-ˈcooled** *adj* cooled by a current of air. 空氣冷却的。**ˈair cover** *n* force of aircraft used to protect a military or naval operation, eg an invasion. 空中掩護(掩護陸海軍作戰的空軍掩護機羣,如在進襲時使用者)。**ˈair·craft** *n* (*sing* or collective *pl*) aeroplane(s); airship(s). (單數或集合複數) 航空器;飛機;飛艇;飛船。⇨ the illus at the end of air¹. 參看 air¹ 末尾之挿圖。 **ˈair·craft car·rier** *n* ship built to carry aircraft, with a long, wide deck for taking off and landing. 航空母艦。**ˈair·craft·man** /-mən ; -mən/ *n* lowest non-commissioned rank in the RAF. (英國皇家空軍)空軍兵。**ˈair·crew** *n* crew of an aircraft. 空勤人員 (一架飛機上的全體飛行人員)。**ˈair cushion** *n* one inflated with air. 氣墊;氣褥;氣枕。**ˈair-cushion vehicle** *n* vehicle or craft of the hovercraft type. 氣墊式船或車。⇨ the illus at hovercraft. 參看 hovercraft 之挿圖。 **ˈair·drome** *n* (US) aerodrome. (美)飛機場。**ˈair drop** *n* dropping (of men, supplies) by parachutes from aircraft. (部隊,人員,供應品之) 空降;空投。**ˈair duct** *n* device, eg in an aircraft or a ship's cabin, for directing a flow of air for the comfort of passengers. 通風設備(飛機、船艙等中爲旅客舒適而裝置之導氣管)。**ˈair·field** *n* area of open, level ground, with hangars, workshops, offices, etc for operations of (esp military) aircraft. 飛機場(尤指軍用機場)。**ˈair·flow** *n* flow of air over the surfaces of an aircraft in flight. 氣流(通過飛行中之飛機表面的空氣之流動)。**(an／the) ˈair force** *n* (with *sing* or *pl* *v*) (與單數或複數動詞連用) the part of a country's military forces that is organized for fighting in aircraft: 空軍: (GB) (英) *the Royal Air Force* (*RAF*). 皇家空軍。'**air·frame** *n* complete structure of an aircraft without the engine(s). 飛機構架(不包括引擎)。'**air gun** *n* gun in which compressed air is used to propel the charge. 氣槍。'**air hostess** *n* stewardess in an airliner. (服務於客機中的)空中小姐。'**air letter** *n* sheet of light paper (to be) folded and sent, without an envelope, cheaply by airmail. 航空郵簡。'**air lift** *n* large-scale transport of persons or supplies by air, esp in an emergency. (尤指緊急時期之) 人員或物資的大規模空運; 空中補給;空運。'**air·line** *n* regular service of aircraft for public use. 航空公司。'**air·liner** *n* passenger-carrying aircraft. 航空公司的客機;班機。'**air lock** *n* **(a)** (bubble of air in a pipe causing) stoppage in the flow of liquid. 使管中液體停止流動的氣泡; 由此氣泡引起的液體的停止流動;氣鎖;氣閘。**(b)** compartment with air-tight doors at each end. 氣密室; 不通空氣的小室。'**air·mail** *n* [U] mail (to be) carried by air: 航空郵件: '*airmail edition*, (of newspapers, periodicals) printed on thin light paper for sending by airmail. (指報紙,期刊) (用薄而輕之紙印刷以便航寄之)航空版。'**air·man** /-mən; -mən/ *n* man who flies in an aircraft as a member of the crew, esp a pilot; (RAF) man of any rank up to and including a Warrant Officer. 空勤組員;(尤指)駕駛員; (英國皇家空軍)准尉或准尉以下任何一級的空軍士兵。ˌ**air-'minded** *adj* looking upon flying as a normal and necessary method of transport. 贊成航空運輸的;熱心航空事業的。'**air pillow** *n* air cushion. 氣墊;氣褥;氣枕。'**air·plane** *n* (US) aeroplane. (美) 飛機。'**air pocket** *n* atmospheric condition (partial vacuum) causing an aircraft to drop some distance: 氣穴; 氣潭; 氣阱(大氣中的一種半眞空狀態,可使飛機突然下墜一段距離者): *We had a bumpy flight because of air pockets.* 我們的飛行甚爲顚簸,因爲遇到了一些氣穴。'**air·port** *n* public flying ground for commercial use by airliners. 民航飛機場; 航空站。'**air-pump** *n* pump for exhausting a vessel of its air. 排氣唧筒;抽氣機。'**air raid** *n* attack by aircraft that drop bombs; 空襲; (attrib, with hyphen): (形容用法,加連字號): *air-raid warnings/precautions;* 空襲警報 (預防措施); *air-raid warden*, person in charge of air-raid precautions. (應付空襲之)防護團員;民防隊員。'**air rifle** *n* = air gun. '**air·screw** *n* aircraft propeller. 飛機之推進器;螺旋槳。⇨ the illus at screw. 參看 screw 之插圖。ˌ**air-ˌsea 'rescue** *n* organization for, work of, rescuing airmen and passengers from the sea, eg by the use of motor-boats or helicopters. 空海救護隊; 空海救護 (在海上用汽艇或直昇機等救助失事飛機的機員及乘客)。'**air-shaft** *n* passage for air into a mine. (礦坑的)通風井。'**air·ship** *n* gas-filled flying-machine with engine(s). 飛艇; 氣艇。⇨ balloon, dirigible. '**air space** *n* part of the earth's atmosphere above a country: 空域;領空: *violation of our air space by military aircraft.* 軍機之侵犯我們的領空。'**air speed** *n* speed of an aircraft relative to the air through which it is moving. 空速(航空器經過空氣之速度)。'**air-strip** *n* strip of ground for the use of aircraft, esp one made for use in war or in an emergency. 起落地帶(尤指戰時或緊急時期所開闢的臨時狹長跑道)。'**air terminal** *n* terminus (in a town or city centre) to or from which passengers, etc travel to or from an airport. (城市中心區的) 航空站 (爲旅客往返於飛機場之間的集散處)。'**air·tight** *adj* not allowing air to enter or escape. 不透氣的;氣密的;密閉的。ˌ**air-to-'air** *adj* (of missiles) fired from one aircraft against another. (指飛彈)空對空的。ˌ**air-to-'ground** *adj* fired from an aircraft to hit a target on the ground. 空對地的。'**air umbrella** *n* = air cover. '**air·way** *n* route regularly followed by airliners; (*pl*) company operating a service of airliners: (民航班機所經常航行的) 航空線; (複)航空公司: *British Airways.* 英國航空公司。'**air·woman** *n* (WRAF) woman of any rank up to and including a Warrant Officer. (英國皇家空軍婦女隊)准尉以下各級之空軍女士兵。'**air-worthy** *adj* (of aircraft) fit to fly; in good working order. (指飛機)適航的; 適於飛行的; 機械運

aircraft

LIGHT AIRCRAFT

COMBAT AIRCRAFT (jet-fighter and bomber)

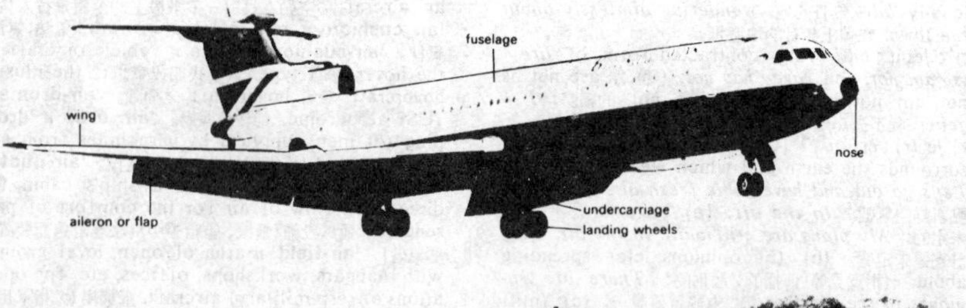

AIRLINER

轉情況良好的。'**air·worthi·ness** *n*

air² /eə(r) ; ɛr/ *vt* [VP6A] **1** put (clothing, bedding, etc) into the open air or into a warm place to make it quite dry: (將衣服、被褥等置於戶外或熱的處所)吹風;晾乾;晒乾: *The mattress needs to be aired.* 這個床墊需要拿出去晾一晾。 **2** let air into (a room, etc). 讓空氣進入 (房間等); 使通風。 **3** cause others to know (one's opinions, a grievance, etc): 誇示;炫耀;使人知道(自己的意見,寃屈等): *He likes to air his knowledge,* let people see how much he knows. 他喜歡炫耀他的知識。 **air·ing** /'eərɪŋ ; 'ɛrɪŋ/ *n*: *give sth an airing,* expose it to the air or to a fire; 將某物晾晒或置於火旁烘烤; *go for an airing, take the children for an airing,* out in the fresh air. 到外面散步,帶小孩子們出去散散步。 **'airing-cupboard** *n* warmed cupboard in which to keep bed-linen, towels, etc. (貯藏被褥,浴巾等之)暖橱。

Aire·dale /'eədeɪl ; 'ɛr,del/ *n* large rough-coated terrier (kind of dog). 一種粗毛大狗。

air·less /'eəlɪs ; 'ɛrlɪs/ *adj* **1** not having enough fresh air; stuffy: 無充分新鮮空氣的; 空氣不流通的; 通風不良的: *an ~ room.* 空氣不流通的房間。 **2** (of the weather) calm; still: (指天氣) 無風的; 平靜的: *Isn't it ~ this evening!* 今天晚上的天氣不是很平靜嗎!

airy /'eərɪ ; 'ɛrɪ/ *adj* **1** having plenty of fresh air moving through it: 空氣流通的: *a nice ~ room.* 一個空氣流通的好房間。 **2** of or like air; immaterial. 空氣的; 似空氣的; 無實質的。 **3** not sincere; superficial: 不誠懇的; 表面的; 虛僞的: *~ promises,* unlikely to be kept; 虛僞的允諾; *an ~ manner,* careless and light-hearted. 無憂無慮而愉快的樣子。 **air·ily** /'eərəlɪ ; 'ɛrəlɪ/ *adv*

aisle /aɪl ; aɪl/ *n* **1** passage in a church, esp one that is divided by a row of columns from the nave; (in a small church) passage between rows of pews (= seats). 教堂中之走廊(尤指與正廳隔以柱列者);(小教堂中兩排座位之間的)通道。⇨ the illus at church. 參看 church 之插圖。 **2** (US) passage between any rows of seats, eg in a theatre or railway coach; any long and narrow passageway. (美) (兩排座位之間的) 通道 (如戲院或火車車廂中者);任何狹長的通道。

aitch /eɪtʃ ; etʃ/ *n* the letter H. 英文字母H。 ***drop one's ~s,*** fail to utter the sound /h/ at the beginning of a word, eg by saying *'at* for *hat.* 未能發 /h/ 音(例如, 將 hat 發成 'at 音)。 **'~-bone** *n* (cut of beef over the) bone of the rump. 牛之臀骨; (指從牛之臀骨上切下之)臀骨肉。

ajar /ə'dʒɑː(r) ; ə'dʒɑr/ *pred adj* (of doors) slightly open. (指門) 半開; 微開。

akim·bo /ə'kɪmbəʊ ; ə'kɪmbo/ *adv* ***with arms ~,*** with the hands on the hips and elbows bent outwards. 兩手叉腰。

akin /ə'kɪn ; ə'kɪn/ *pred adj* ***~ (to),*** of similar character; like: 同性質的; 類似的: *Pity is often ~ to love.* 憐憫常近乎愛。

ala·bas·ter /'æləbɑːstə(r) *US:* -bæs- ; 'ælə,bæstə/ *n* [U] soft, white stone like marble in appearance, used for ornaments. 雪花石膏 (望之似大理石之軟質白石,用做裝飾品)。□ *adj* like ~ in smoothness and whiteness. 似雪花石膏的;光滑白潤的。

à la carte /,ɑː lɑː 'kɑːt ; ,ɑlə'kɑrt/ *adv* (F) (of meals) ordered from a list, course by course, not at a fixed price for the complete meal (as for *table d'hôte*). (法) (指在餐館裡吃飯) 從菜單上點菜 (爲客飯,和菜或定餐之對)。

alack /ə'læk ; ə'læk/ *int* (old use) cry of regret or sorrow. (舊用法) 表示惋惜或悲傷的感歎詞。

alac·rity /ə'lækrətɪ ; ə'lækrətɪ/ *n* [U] eager and cheerful readiness. 欣然且樂意的敏捷之狀; 爽快。

à la mode /,ɑːlɑː'məʊd ; ,ɑlə'mod/ *adv* (F) according to the latest fashion, ideas, etc; (US) served with ice-cream: (法) 按照最時興的樣式、觀念等;時髦地; (美) (指甜點) 加上或附有冰淇淋: *apple pie ~.* 蘋果餅加冰淇淋。

alarm /ə'lɑːm ; ə'lɑrm/ *n* **1** [C] (sound or signal giving a) warning of danger; apparatus used to give such a warning: 警報;警報之聲音或訊號;警報器: *a 'fire ~.* 火警警報。 ***give/raise/sound the ~,*** ring a bell or in other ways send out a warning signal. 搖警報器;發警報(如敲鐘等)。 **'~(-clock)** *n* clock that can be set to ring a bell or sound a buzzer at a fixed time to waken a sleeping person: 鬧鐘: *set the ~(-clock) for six o'clock.* 把鬧鐘定在六點上。 **2** [U] fear and excitement caused by the expectation of danger: 驚慌;恐慌: *He jumped up in ~.* 他驚慌地跳了起來。 *I hope you didn't take/feel ~ at the news.* 我希望你沒有因爲聽到那個消息而感到驚慌。□ *vt* [VP6A] give a warning or feeling of danger to; cause anxiety to: 警告;使驚駭;使恐慌;使憂慮: *The noise of the shot ~ed hundreds of birds.* 槍聲驚動了千百隻鳥。 *Everybody was ~ed at the news that war might break out.* 人人聽到了戰事可能爆發的消息都感到恐慌。 **~·ing** *part adj* causing ~. 驚人的;嚇人的。 **~·ist** /-ɪst ; -ɪst/ *adj, n* (person) raising ~s with little cause. 大驚小怪的(人)。

alas /ə'læs ; ə'læs/ *int* cry of sorrow or regret. 唉; 哎呀(表示悲哀或惋惜的感歎詞)。

alb /ælb ; ælb/ *n* white vestment reaching to the feet, worn by some Christian priests at ceremonies. (某些基督教牧師或天主教神父在典禮時所穿的長及足部之)白袍。⇨ the illus at vestment. 參看 vestment 之插圖。

al·ba·tross /'ælbətrɒs ; 'ælbə,trɔs/ *n* large, white, web-footed seabird, common in the Pacific and Southern Oceans. 信天翁 (白色蹼足大海鳥, 常見於太平洋及南半球各海洋)。⇨ the illus at water. 參看 water 之插圖。

al·beit /,ɔːl'biːɪt ; ɔl'biɪt/ *conj* (formal) though(1). (正式用語)雖然。

al·bino /æl'biːnəʊ *US:* -'baɪ- ; æl'baɪno/ *n* (*pl* ~s /-nəʊz ; -noz/) animal or human being born without natural colouring matter in the skin and hair (which are white) and the eyes (which are pink). 白公; 白化病者(生來其皮膚、毛髮及眼睛卽缺乏天然色素之動物或人,膚髮呈白色,眼睛呈粉紅色)。

al·bum /'ælbəm ; 'ælbəm/ *n* **1** blank book in which a collection of photographs, autographs, postage stamps, etc can be kept. 相片簿;簽名紀念册;集郵册(等)。 **2** holder for a set of discs; long-playing record with several pieces by the same musician(s), singer(s). (裝一套唱片,某音樂家之演奏專輯,某歌星之歌輯之)唱片簿;唱片集。

al·bu·men /'ælbjʊmɪn ; æl'bjumən/ *n* [U] **1** white of egg. 蛋白。 **2** substance as in white of egg, part of animal and vegetable matter. 蛋白質。

al·chem·ist /'ælkɪmɪst ; 'ælkəmɪst/ *n* person who studied or practised alchemy. 煉金術士。

al·chemy /'ælkɪmɪ ; 'ælkəmɪ/ *n* [U] chemistry of the Middle Ages, the chief aim of which was to discover how to change ordinary metals into gold. (中古時代企圖將普通金屬變成金的)煉金術。

al·co·hol /'ælkəhɒl *US:* -hɔːl ; 'ælkə,hɔl/ *n* **1** [U] (pure, colourless liquid present in) such drinks as beer, wine, brandy, whisky. 酒精(存在於各種酒類,如啤酒,葡萄酒,白蘭地,威士忌等中之純淨無色液體);酒。 **2** [U, C] (chem) large group of compounds of the same type as ~(1). (化學) (乙)醇。 **~ic** /,ælkə'hɒlɪk *US:* -'hɔːl- ; ,ælkə'hɔlɪk/ *adj* of or containing ~. 酒精的;含酒精的。□ *n* person addicted to ~ic drink. 酒精中毒者;酗酒者。 **~·ism** /-ɪzəm ; -,ɪzəm/ *n* [U] addiction to ~ic drink; diseased condition caused by this. 酗酒;酒精中毒。

al·cove /'ælkəʊv ; 'ælkov/ *n* recess; partially enclosed extension of a room, often occupied by a bed or by seats; similar space within a garden enclosure. 壁凹 (大房間內之凹形小室, 常置床或椅於此);(花園中似凹室之)小亭。

al·der /'ɔːldə(r) ; 'ɔldə/ *n* tree of the birch family, usu growing in marshy places. 赤楊(樺樹屬,通常生長於沼澤地帶)。

al·der·man /ˈɔːldəmən ; ˈɔldɚmən/ *n* (*pl* -men /-mən ; -mən/) senior member of a city or borough council in England and Ireland, next in rank to a mayor, elected by fellow councillors. (英格蘭及愛爾蘭之) 市議會之長老議員 (階級次於市長,由其他議員所選出者)。**~ic** /ˌɔːldəˈmænɪk ; ˌɔldɚˈmænɪk/ *adj*

ale /eɪl ; el/ *n* [U] (GB) (kind of) beer; (英) (一種) 啤酒; (old use) (舊用法) = beer. ⇨ also ginger. **ˈale-house** *n* (old name for) public house. 酒館 (爲 public house 之舊名)。

alee /əˈliː ; əˈli/ *adv, pred adj* (naut) at, on, towards, the lee or sheltered side of a ship. (航海) 在或向(船之)背風之一邊;向下風。

alert /əˈlɜːt ; əˈlɝt/ *adj* watchful; fully awake; lively: 留心的;警覺的;清醒的;機警的;靈活的: *~ in answering questions.* 留心回答問題。□ *n* **1 on the ~,** on the look-out (*for* sth, *against* an attack, etc, *to do* sth). 注意;提防;小心(後接 for 某事物, against 攻擊等或不定詞)。 **2** [C] (period of) watchfulness under enemy attack, esp an air raid. 警戒;警報(尤指空襲警報);空襲警報期間。 **3** [C] notice to stand ready: 促使準備妥當的通知: *They received the ~ at 10 am.* 他們上午十時接到通知,要他們準備妥當。□ *vt* [VP6A] put (troops, etc) on the ~. 命令(部隊等)警戒。 **~·ly** *adv* **~·ness** *n* being ~ or prompt (*in* doing sth). 機警;機敏(與 in 連用,後接動名詞)。

alex·an·drine /ˌælɪgˈzændraɪn ; ˌælɪgˈzændrɪn/ *n* (of verse rhythm) iambic line of six feet or twelve syllables. (詩律)六音步或十二音節之抑揚格詩行;亞歷山大詩行。

alexia /əˈleksɪə ; əˈlɛksɪə/ *n* [U] (path) disease in which cerebral lesions cause inability to read (popularly called 'word blindness'). (病理) 失讀症 (由於腦損害所導致之不會認字, 俗稱'字盲')。 **alexic** /əˈleksɪk ; əˈlɛksɪk/ *adj* of ~: 失讀症的: *alexic children.* 患失讀症的小孩。

al·falfa /ˌælˈfælfə ; ælˈfælfə/ *n* [U] (US) (美) = lucerne.

al·fresco /ˌælˈfreskəʊ ; ælˈfrɛsko/ *adj, adv* (of meals) in the open air; out of doors: (指餐食) 露天的(地);在戶外(的): *an ~ lunch;* 露天午餐; *lunching ~.* 在戶外吃午餐。

alga /ˈælgə ; ˈælgə/ *n* (*pl* algae /ˈældʒiː;ˈældʒi/) (bot) water plant of very simple structure. (植物)海藻。

al·ge·bra /ˈældʒɪbrə ; ˈældʒəbrə/ *n* branch of mathematics in which signs and letters are used to represent quantities. 代數學; 代數。 **~ic** /ˌældʒɪˈbreɪɪk ; ˌældʒəˈbre·ɪk/, **~·ical** /-kl ; -kəl/ *adj* of ~. 代數學的。 **~·ic·ally** /-klɪ ; -klɪ/ *adv*

alias /ˈeɪlɪəs ; ˈelɪəs/ *n* (*pl* ~es /-sɪz ; -sɪz/) name by which a person is called on other occasions: 別名; 化名; 假名: *The criminal had several ~es.* 該罪犯有數個化名。□ *adv* also called. 亦稱;又名。

alibi /ˈælɪbaɪ ; ˈæləˌbaɪ/ *n* (*pl* ~s /-baɪz ; -baɪz/) **1** (legal) plea that one was in another place at the time of an alleged act, esp a crime: (法律) 當時不在現場(尤指犯罪現場)之申辯: *The accused man was able to establish / prove an ~.* 該被告能够證明他當時不在現場。 **2** (colloq) excuse (for failure, etc). (俗) (失敗等之) 藉口;口實;託詞。

alien /ˈeɪlɪən ; ˈeljən/ *n* (legal or official use) foreigner who is not a subject of the country in which he lives: (法律或官方用語) 外僑: *An Englishman is an ~ in the United States.* 英國人在美國便是外國人。□ *adj* **1** foreign: 外國的: *an ~ environment.* 外國的環境。 **2 ~ (to),** differing in nature or character: 不同性質的: *These principles are ~ to our religion.* 這些原則性質上與我們的宗教相異。 **3** contrary or opposed (*to*): 相反的(與 to 連用): *Cruelty was quite ~ to his nature.* 殘忍與他的天性完全相反。

alien·ate /ˈeɪlɪəneɪt ; ˈeljənˌet/ *vt* [VP6A, 14] **1 ~ sb (from),** estrange; cause (sb previously friendly) to become unfriendly or indifferent (by unpopular or distasteful actions): 離間; 使不和; 使疏遠: *The Prime Minister's policy ~d many of his followers.* 首相的政策使許多擁護他的人疏遠了他。 *At various times artists have felt ~d from society,* felt shut out from society. 歷代藝術家都有與世隔離之感。 **2** transfer ownership of (property): 轉移(財產)的所有權;讓渡: *Enemy property is often ~d in time of war,* ie seized by the Government. 在戰時敵產常被(政府)沒收。 **alien·ation** /ˌeɪlɪəˈneɪʃn ; ˌeljənˈeʃən/ *n* alienating or being ~d; estrangement; (theatre) critical detachment (of actors and audience) from, emotional non-involvement in, problems presented by a drama. 離間;疏遠; (所有權之) 轉移; 讓渡; (戲劇) (演員與觀衆對劇中呈現之問題所持之) 超然態度。

alien·ist /ˈeɪlɪənɪst ; ˈeljənɪst/ *n* **1** (US) expert on the mental competence of witnesses in a law court. (美) 鑑定出庭之證人其心智是否能適任作證之專家。 **2** (old use) specialist in mental illness (now called a *psychiatrist*). (舊用法)精神病醫生;精神病學家(現稱作 psychiatrist)。

alight[1] /əˈlaɪt ; əˈlaɪt/ *pred adj* on fire; lighted up: 燃燒的; 發光亮的: *The sticks were damp and wouldn't catch ~.* 那些柴枝是潮濕的, 點燃不起來。 (fig) (喻) *Their faces were ~* (= bright, cheerful) *with happiness.* 他們的臉煥發着快樂的光彩。

alight[2] /əˈlaɪt ; əˈlaɪt/ *vi* [VP2A, 3A] **1** get down (*from* a horse, bus, etc). 下(馬,公共汽車等,與 from 連用)。 **2** (of a bird) come down from the air and settle (*on* a branch, etc). (指鳥) 落(於枝頭等, 與 on 連用)。 **3 ~ on,** (formal) (fig) find by chance. (正式用語) (喻) 偶然發現;碰見。

align /əˈlaɪn ; əˈlaɪn/ *vt, vi* **1** [VP6A, 2A] arrange in a line; bring into line (esp three or more points into a straight line); eg of soldiers, form in line: 排成一條直線; (尤指) 使(三點或更多的點)成一直線; (士兵等) 排成一行: *~ the sights of a rifle.* 將步槍瞄準(使照門, 準星成一直線)。 **2** [VP14, 3A] bring, come, into agreement, close co-operation, etc (*with*): 使一致; 與…一致; 使密切合作; 與…密切合作(與 with 連用): *They ~ed themselves with us.* 他們已與我們密切合作。 **~·ment** *n* [C, U] (an) arrangement in a straight line: 排成直線: *The desks are in / out of ~ment.* 桌子(沒有)排成直行。 *There was a new ~ment of European powers,* a new grouping (colloq, 俗稱, *line-up*) of powers. 歐洲列強間有一新的聯盟。

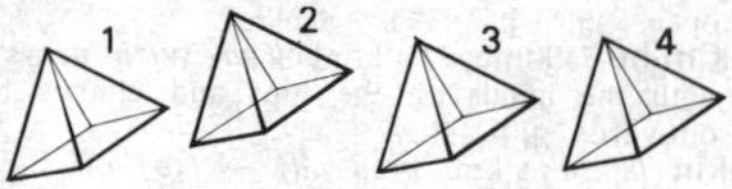

No 2 is out of alignment

alike /əˈlaɪk ; əˈlaɪk/ *pred adj* similar; like one another: 相似的;同樣的: *The two sisters are very much ~.* 這兩姐妹非常相像。 *All music is ~ to him,* He has no ear for music, cannot distinguish one kind from other kinds. 所有的音樂對他都一樣(他對音樂沒有欣賞力,對各種音樂不能加以辨別)。 □ *adv* in the same way: 以同樣方式: *treat everybody ~;* 以同樣方式對待每一個人; the same: 同樣地: *summer and winter ~.* 夏季和冬季都一樣。

ali·men·tary /ˌælɪˈmentərɪ ; ˌæləˈmɛntərɪ/ *adj* of food and digestion. 食物及消化的。 **the ~ canal,** parts of the body through which food passes (from the mouth to the anus). 消化管; 消化道(食物自口腔至肛門所經之管道)。

ali·mony /ˈælɪmənɪ *US:* -məʊnɪ ; ˈæləˌmonɪ/ *n* [U] money allowance (to be) paid by a man to his wife, or former wife, by a judge's order, eg after a legal separation or divorce. (經法院判決分居或離婚後男方對女方所付之) 贍養費。

alive /əˈlaɪv ; əˈlaɪv/ *pred adj* **1** living: 活的;在世的: *Who's the greatest man ~?* 當今最偉大的人物是誰？*You wouldn't like to be buried ~.* 你不會喜歡被活埋的。**2** in force; in existence: 有效力的;實施中的;存在的: *If a claim is kept ~, it is more likely to be recognized.* 如果把對於一項權利的要求持續下去,它就更可能被承認。*An awareness of the dangers of air-pollution should be kept ~ by the press and TV.* 報紙及電視應經常提醒人們注意空氣污染的危險。**3 ~ to,** conscious or aware of: 覺察;曉得: *He is fully ~ to the dangers of the situation/public opinion.* 他完全明白事態(輿論)的危險。**4** active; lively: 活潑的;活動的: *He is very much ~.* 他非常活潑。***Look ~!*** Hurry up! Get busy! 趕快！加油！**5 ~ with,** full of (living or moving things): 充滿(活的或動的東西): *The lake was ~ with fish.* 湖內充滿了魚。

al·kali /ˈælkəlaɪ ; ˈælkəˌlaɪ/ *n* (*pl* ~s /-laɪz ; -laɪz/) (chem) one of a number of substances (such as soda, potash, ammonia) that combine with acids to form salts. (化) 鹼(與酸化合成鹽之物質,如蘇打,鉀,氨是)。**al·ka·line** /ˈælkəlaɪn ; ˈælkəˌlaɪn/ *adj* of ~s: 鹼的;鹼性的: *soil of alkaline peat.* 鹼性泥炭土。

all[1] /ɔːl ; ɔl/ *adj* **1** (with *pl nn*) the whole number of; (with *sing* material or abstract *nn*) the whole extent or amount of; (followed by the *def art*, demonstratives, possessives, and cardinal numbers): (與複數名詞連用)全數的;所有的;(與單數的物質或抽象名詞連用)整個的; 全量的; (後接定冠詞,指示詞,所有格字及基數): *All horses are animals but not all animals are horses.* 所有的馬都是動物,但並非所有的動物都是馬。*All five men/All five of them are hard workers.* 他們五個人都是肯苦幹的人。*All you boys need to work harder.* 你們所有的男孩必須多用功。*You've had all the fun and I've had all the hard work.* 所有的玩樂都歸你享受了,而所有的苦工都歸我做了。*He has lived all his life in London.* 他一生都住在倫敦。***of ˈall people,*** specially; particularly: 特別地: *Of all people he should be the last to complain,* there is a strong reason why he shouldn't. 所有的人中,他最不該發牢騷。*Why ask ˈme to help, of ˈall people?* I am the least likely person to be able to help, or the person to whom the speaker has the least right to apply for help. 天下那麼多人,爲什麼偏偏找我幫忙？(我是最幫不上忙或是最不應該幫忙的人。) ***of all the idiots/nitwits,*** an expression of annoyance with sb who has behaved foolishly. 大笨蛋(對行爲愚蠢的人表示惱怒之詞)。***on all fours,*** ⇨ four. **2** *He spent all (of) that year* (= the whole of that year) *in London.* 他那一整年都消磨在倫敦。⇨ whole(3). **3** (Cf *all* and *every*. *All* suggests the whole; *every* points to each member of a group individually): (參較 all 和 every。all 指整個全體; every 個別地指一群中的每一個份子): *All (of) the boys enjoyed themselves.* 所有的男孩子都很快樂。Cf 參較 *Every one of the boys enjoyed himself.* 男孩子中每一個人都很快樂。**4 *with all speed/haste,*** the utmost possible. 盡速;盡力;盡可能;盡快。**5** any: 任何: *beyond all doubt/argument/question,* there can't be any doubt, etc. 毫無疑問(無可置辯;毫無問題)。*He hates all* (= any) *criticism of his work.* 他不喜歡任何對於他的工作(著作)的批評。**6 ˌAll ˈFools' Day,** 1 Apr; 愚人節;萬愚節(四月一日); **ˌAll ˈHallows', ˌAll ˈSaints, Day,** 1 Nov; 萬聖節(十一月一日); **ˌAll ˈSouls' Day,** 2 Nov. 萬靈節(十一月二日)。

the alimentary canal

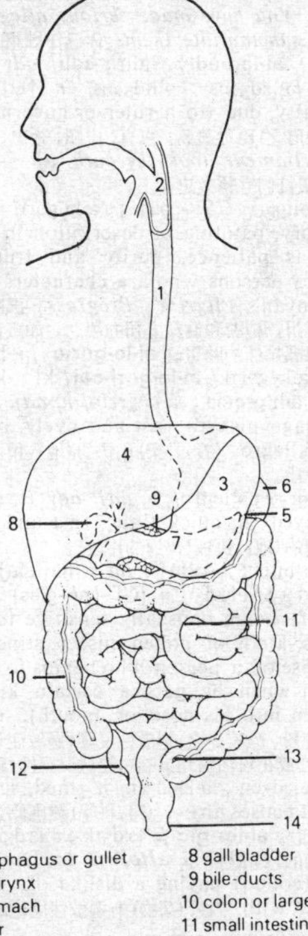

1 esophagus or gullet
2 pharynx
3 stomach
4 liver
5 pancreas
6 spleen
7 duodenum
8 gall bladder
9 bile-ducts
10 colon or large intestine
11 small intestine
12 vermiform appendix
13 rectum
14 anus

all[2] /ɔːl ; ɔl/ *adv* **1** quite; entirely: 十分;完全: *They were dressed all in black.* 他們全身穿着黑衣服。Cf 參較 *They were all dressed* (= All of them were dressed) *in black.* 他們大家都穿着黑衣服。*Your hands are all tar,* (colloq) covered with tar. (俗)你的雙手滿是柏油。*She was all* (colloq 俗 = greatly) *excited.* 她非常興奮。***be all about sth,*** (colloq) be concerned with it. (俗)關心某事物。***all alone,*** **(a)** not in the company of others. 獨自一人。**(b)** without the help and company of other persons. 獨力;自力。***all along,*** **(a)** for the whole length of: 沿着…的整個長度: *There are trees all along the road.* 整條路的兩旁都種有樹。**(b)** (colloq) all the time; from the start: (俗)自始至終;從開始起一直: *But I knew that all along!* 但是我一開始就知道此事！***all clear,*** ⇨ clear[1](5). ***all for,*** (colloq) strongly in favour of; anxious to have, etc: (俗)極其贊成;急於要有(等): *I'm all for accepting the offer.* 我極其贊成接受該項提議。***all the same,*** yet, nevertheless. 仍然;依然。***all the same to,*** a matter not causing inconvenience to; a matter of indifference to: 對於…沒有引起什麼不便;對…無所謂: *If it's all the same to you...;* 如果它對你沒有什麼不便的話…; *It's all the same to me whether you go or stay.* 不論你是去還是留,對我皆無所謂。***all one to,*** a matter of indifference to: 對…都是一樣;對…無所謂: *Do as you like; it's all one to me.* 隨便你怎麼做,對我都是一樣。***all in,*** **(a)** (colloq) exhausted: (俗)筋疲力竭的: *He was all in at the end of the race.* 賽跑結束時他已筋疲力竭。**(b)** (*all-in*) inclusive of everything: 包括一切的: *an all-in price;* 包括一切的價格; *all-in wrestling,* with no restrictions about methods or holds. 方法或抱、握等不加限制的角力。***all-out,*** (colloq) using all possible strength, energy, etc: (俗)全力以赴的: *He was going all out/was making an all-out effort.* 他正全力以赴。***all over,*** **(a)** in every part of: 遍及…的每一部份: *He has travelled all over the world.* 他曾旅行全世界各地。**(b)** at an end. 結束;完了。***all right,*** (US) (美)

al·right **(a)** satisfactory, satisfactorily; safe and sound; in good order: 滿意的(地);安然無恙的;情況良好的: *Are you feeling all right?* 你覺得還好嗎? **(b)** (as a response to a suggestion, etc) Yes, I consent. (作爲對於建議等的回答)好的(我同意)。***all there,*** (colloq) having one's wits about one; mentally alert. (俗)精明的;機敏的。***not all there,*** (colloq) not quite sane; mentally deficient. (俗)頭腦不很清楚的;心智不健全的。***all told,*** altogether; as the total: 一共;合計: *There were six people all told* (= in all). 總共有六個人。***all up (with),*** at an end, over (with): 結束;完了: *It's all up with him now,* He's likely to be ruined, to die, etc. 他現在一切都完了。 **2** ***all the*** + *comp adj,* much; so much: (用於 'all the + 比較級形容詞' 之句型中)更加;愈爲: *You'll be all the better for a holiday.* 度一次假,對你會更有好處。

all³ /ɔ:l ; ɔl/ *n* ***my/his/their, etc all,*** all that I/he/they, etc possess, value most, etc: 我(他,他們等)所有的,所最寶貴的一切: *We must stake our all in this struggle.* 我們必須傾所有的一切於此一鬥爭之中。*He had lost his all.* 他已失去了所有的一切。

all⁴ /ɔ:l ; ɔl/ (in compounds) (用於複合字中) **1** (prefixed to many *adjj* and *pres participles*) in the highest degree; without limit: (接在許多形容詞及現在分詞的前端)極;最;無限的: *ˌall-ˈmerciful;* 極慈悲的; *ˌall-ˈpowerful;* 有無限權力的;全能的; *ˌall-emˈbracing.* 包羅萬象的;包括一切的。 **2** **ˌall-ˈmains** *attrib adj* (of a radio receiver) adaptable to all voltages: (指收音機)可調節以適用於各種電壓的: *an all-mains set.* 一架可調節以適用於各種電壓的收音機。**ˌall-ˈround** *adj* having ability in many different ways: 多才多藝的;門門皆通的: *an all-round sportsman,* good at many different games and sports. 擅長多種運動的運動家。Hence,由此產生, **ˌall-ˈrounder** *n* ***an ˌall-ˌstar ˈcast,*** (for a play, etc) one with star performers for all the chief parts. 大堆頭明星陣容(一齣戲等的全部要角均由大牌明星擔任的鑽石陣容)。***ˌall-ˌtime ˈhigh/ˈlow*** *n* (colloq) highest/lowest figure, level, etc on record. (俗)空前最高(最低)記錄;記錄上所列的最高(最低)數字,水準等。***ˌall-ˌup ˈweight,*** total weight of an aircraft, including crew, passengers, cargo, when in the air. (飛機在空中的)全重(包括機上人員,乘客,貨物等)。

all⁵ /ɔ:l ; ɔl/ *pron* **1** everything: 所有的一切: *He wanted all or nothing.* 他要麼就全要,要麼就全不要。 **2** ***all of,*** every one, the whole: 每一個;全體;整個: *All of us want to go.* 我們全體都想去。*Take all of it.* 把所有的都拿去。 **3** (used in apposition, in the same way as *both* and *each*): (用於同位格,與both和each之用法相同): *We all want to go.* 我們大家都想去。*Take it all.* 把整個都拿去。*They were all broken.* 它們全被打破了。**4** (followed by a relative clause, *that* being omitted): (後接關係子句,that被省略): *All I want is peace and quiet.* 我所要的只是和平與安靜。*He took all there was.* 他把所有的全拿去了。 **5** (in prepositional phrases): (用於介詞片語中): ***above all,*** ⇨ above²(3). ***after all,*** ⇨ after⁴(5). ***(not) at all,*** /əˈtɔ:l ; əˈtɔl/ (not) in any way, in the least degree: 根本(不);全然(毫無);最少程度(毫不): *if you are at all worried;* 如果你有任何焦慮的話; *not at all suitable for the post.* 完全不適於此一職位。***Not at all,*** polite formula in answer to an expression of thanks. (回答對方表示感謝的客套話)別客氣。Cf 參較 US (美): You're welcome. ***for all*** (*his wealth/great learning*), in spite of. 雖然;儘管(他很有錢;學識淵博)。***for all I know/care, etc,*** (used to show ignorance or indifference): (表示不知情或不關心)誰知道;亦未可知(與我何干等): *He may be dead for all I know.* 他可能死了,也未可知。***in all,*** ⇨ in²(13). ***and all,*** as well; including: 連同;包括: *The dog ate the whole rabbit, head, bones and all.* 狗把整隻兔子,連頭及骨頭,都吃掉了。***once (and) for all,*** now and for the last or only time. 這是最後或唯一的一次;只此一次;決不再重複;斷然。***It was all I/he, etc could do not to*** (*laugh, etc*), I/he, etc could hardly refrain from (laughing, etc). 我(他等)已盡了最大努力忍住不(笑等)(意即我幾乎忍不住要笑等)。***all in all,*** of supreme or exclusive importance, interest, etc: 極其重要的;重於一切的;最關心的;最愛的: *They were all in all to each other.* 他們互相極爲關切(親愛)。***(taking it) all in all,*** considering everything. 從各方面考慮;就整個而言。***not as/so*** + *adj/adv* + ***as all that,*** to that extent; in that degree: 沒有…到那個程度: *It's not so difficult as all that,* as is suggested, supposed, etc. 它並非困難到那種程度。***not all that*** + *adj/adv,* (colloq or vulg): (俗或鄙)並不算: *It isn't all that cheap,* not cheap if all things are considered. 並不便宜(如果仔細算算的話)。

Allah /ˈælə ; ˈælɔ/ *n* name of God among Muslims. 阿拉(回教的上帝)。

al·lay /əˈleɪ ; əˈle/ *vt* (*pt, pp* -layed) [VP6A] make sth (eg pain, trouble, excitement, fears) less. 減輕;緩和(痛苦,煩擾,興奮,恐懼等)。

al·lege /əˈledʒ ; əˈlɛdʒ/ *vt* [VP6A, 9] declare; put forward, esp as a reason or excuse, in support of a claim or in denial of a charge: 宣稱;(作爲理由或託辭以支持一項主張或否認某一指控而)提出;供述: *In your statement you* ~ *that the accused man was seen at the scene of the crime.* 在你的口供中,你供述曾經看到被告在犯罪現場。*The statement* ~*d to have been made by the accused is clearly untrue.* 那份被認爲是被告所作的口供顯然不確實。*An* ~*d thief,* person who is declared to be a thief. 被認爲是竊賊的人;盜竊嫌疑犯。**al·le·ga·tion** /ˌælɪˈgeɪʃn ; ˌæləˈgeʃən/ *n* [U] alleging; [C] statement, esp one made without proof: 宣稱;聲稱;(尤指無證據的)供述;空言;辯解: *You have made serious allegations, but can you substantiate them?* 你已作鄭重的供述,但你能證實嗎? **al·leg·edly** /-ɪdlɪ ; -ɪdlɪ/ *adv*

al·le·giance /əˈli:dʒəns ; əˈlidʒəns/ *n* [U] duty, support, loyalty, due (to a ruler or government): (對統治者或政府之)臣從義務;忠貞;忠順;效忠: *Members of Parliament took the oath of* ~ *to the Queen.* 國會議員們宣誓效忠女王。

al·le·gory /ˈælɪgərɪ *US:* -gɔ:rɪ ; ˈæləˌgorɪ/ *n* [C] (*pl* -ries) story, painting or description in which ideas such as patience, purity and truth are symbolized by persons who are characters in the story, eg Bunyan's *Pilgrim's Progress.* 諷喻;寓言(以人物代表忍耐,純潔和眞誠之類的觀念,如班揚的'天路歷程'卽是);諷喻性的圖畫。**al·le·goric** /ˌælɪˈgɒrɪk *US:*-ˈgɔ:r- ; ˌæləˈgɔrɪk/, **al·le·gori·cal** /-kl ; -kəl/ *adj*

al·le·gretto /ˌælɪˈgretəʊ ; ˌæləˈgreto/ *n, adj, adv* (I; music) (passage played) fast and lively, but not so brisk as allegro. (義;音樂)稍快的(地);稍快板;小快板;稍快的片段。

al·legro /əˈleɪgrəʊ ; əˈlegro/ *n, adj, adv* (I; music) (passage played) in quick time; fast and lively. (義;音樂)快速的(地);快板;快速的片段。

al·le·luia /ˌælɪˈlu:jə ; ˌæləˈlujə/ *int* = hallelujah.

al·lergy /ˈælədʒɪ ; ˈælədʒɪ/ *n* [C] (*pl* -gies) (med) (condition of) being unusually sensitive to particular foods, kinds of pollen, insect stings, etc (as in the case of a person who begins to suffer from asthma when he gets a certain kind of dust or pollen into his nose or mouth). (醫)(對於某些食物、花粉、蟲咬等之)過敏性反應;過敏症(例如有人吸入某種灰塵或花粉卽引起氣喘);變態反應性;變應性。**al·ler·gen** /ˈælədʒen ; ˈæləˌdʒɛn/ *n* (med, science) anything that causes an ~. (醫,科學)變應原(任何引起變應性的東西)。**al·ler·gic** /əˈlɜ:dʒɪk ; əˈlɝdʒɪk/ *adj* of ~. 變應性的;過敏性的。***allergic to,*** having an ~ to (sth); (colloq) having a dislike of; unable to get on well with. 對於(某物)有過敏性反應的;(俗)厭惡;與…不能融洽相處。

al·levi·ate /əˈli:vɪeɪt ; əˈlivɪˌet/ *vt* [VP6A] make (pain, suffering) less or easier to bear. 使(痛苦)減輕或易於忍受;使緩和。**al·levi·ation** /əˌli:vɪˈeɪʃn ;

ə͵livɪˈeʃən/ *n*

al·ley /ˈælɪ ; ˈælɪ/ *n* [C] (*pl* ~s) (also 亦作 ˈ**~·way**) **1** narrow passage between houses or other buildings (often a narrow street in a slum quarter). 小巷;弄;胡同(常爲貧民區的狹窄街道)。 ˌ**blind** ˈ**~**, ~ closed at one end; (fig) occupation, eg that of an errand boy, that does not teach a trade or lead to a profession. 死巷;死胡同;(喻)不能學得一種技能或導向專業的職業;沒有前途的職業(如差役)。 **2** path or walk in a garden or park. (花園或公園中的)小徑。 **3** narrow enclosure for such games as bowls and skittles. 保齡球及九柱戲之球道或球場。

al·liance /əˈlaɪəns ; əˈlaɪəns/ *n* **1** [U] association or connection. 聯合。 ***in ~ (with),*** joined or united (with). (與…)聯合。 **2** [C] union of persons, families, eg by marriage, or states (by treaty): 聯結; 聯姻; 聯盟; 同盟: *enter into an ~ with a country.* 與某國結爲同盟國。

al·lied /əˈlaɪd ; əˈlaɪd/ ⇨ ally.

al·li·ga·tor /ˈælɪgeɪtə(r) ; ˈælə͵getɚ/ *n* reptile (like a crocodile but with a shorter snout) living in the lakes and rivers of southeastern US, ⇨ the illus at reptile; leather made from its skin. (一種產於美國東南部之河或湖中之)短吻鱷(參看 reptile 之挿圖);短吻鱷之皮製成之革。 ~ **pear,** avocado. 鱷梨(一種梨狀熱帶果實)。

al·li·ter·ation /ə͵lɪtəˈreɪʃn ; ə͵lɪtəˈreʃən/ *n* [U] repetition of the first sound or letter of a succession of words, eg *safe and sound; apt ~'s artful aid.* 頭韻(卽連續數字之起頭音或字母之重複,例如: safe and sound; apt ~'s artful aid)。 **al·lit·er·ative** /əˈlɪtrətɪv *US:* -təreɪtɪv ; əˈlɪtə͵retɪv/ *adj* **al·lit·er·ative·ly** *adv*

al·lo·cate /ˈæləkeɪt ; ˈælə͵ket/ *vt* [VP6A, 14] ~ ***(to/for),*** give, put on one side, as a share or for a purpose: 分配;配給;撥出: *~ duties to sb;* 分配職務給某人; *~ a sum of money among several persons;* 把一筆款子分配給幾個人; *~ a sum of money to education.* 撥出一筆款子作爲教育經費。 **al·lo·ca·tion** /ˌæləˈkeɪʃn ; ͵æləˈkeʃən/ *n* **1** [U] allocating or distributing. 分配;配給。 **2** [C] ~ ***(to/for),*** sth ~d or assigned (to or for a purpose, etc). 所分配之事物(與 to 或 for 連用,後接某一目的)。

al·lot /əˈlɒt ; əˈlɑt/ *vt* (-tt-) [VP6A, 12A, 13A, 14] ~ ***sth (to),*** make a distribution of; decide a person's share of: 分配;攤派: *~ sth to sb for a purpose;* 爲了某種目的而將某事物分配給某人; *~ duties (to sb).* 分配職務(給某人)。 *Can we do the work within the time they have ~ted (to) us?* 我們能在他們所分配給我們的時間內把工作做完嗎? *They were ~ted a house to live in.* 他們配得一幢房子住。 **~·ment** *n* **1** [U] division; distribution (of shares). 分配;配給。 **2** [C] part or share, esp (in GB) small area of public land rented as a vegetable garden. 所配得的一份;(尤指英國)租來作爲菜園用的一小塊公地。

allow /əˈlaʊ ; əˈlaʊ/ *vt, vi* **1** [VP6A, C, 17, 15B] permit: 允許;許可: *Smoking is not ~ed here.* 此處禁止吸煙。 *No dogs ~ed,* It is forbidden to bring dogs into this place (building, park, etc). 禁止攜狗入內(指建築物,公園等)。 *Please ~ me to carry your bag.* 請讓我替你拿你的提包。 *She is not ~ed out after dark.* 她在天黑之後不准外出。 **2** [VP12A, 13A, 14] give, let (sb or sth) have; agree to give: 給;讓…得到;同意給予: *How much money does your father ~ you for books?* 你的父親給你多少錢買書? *He ~s his wife £100 a year for clothes.* 他每年給他妻子一百鎊購買衣服。 *She ~ed her imagination full play,* did nothing to control it. 她讓她的想像力盡量發揮。 *The bank ~s 5 per cent interest on deposits.* 銀行對存款給五厘(年)息。 *We can ~* (=take off, deduct) *5 per cent for cash payment.* 付現款我們可以打九五折。 **3** [VP6A] (legal) agree that sth is right or just: (法律)同意其爲正當: *The judge ~ed the claim.* 法官同意該項主張爲正當。 **4** [VP25, 9] admit (now the more usu word): 承認(今較常用 admit): *We must ~ him to be a genius/~ that he is a genius.* 我們必須承認他是一個天才。 **5** [VP3A] ~ ***for,*** take into consideration: 考慮到;顧慮到;體諒;連…算在內: *It will take thirty minutes to get to the station, ~ing for traffic delays.* 到車站去將需要三十分鐘,連路上交通的躭擱都算在內。 ~ ***of,*** admit of (now more usu): 容許(今較常用admit of): *The situation ~s of no delay.* 情勢不容許延誤;刻不容緩。 **~·able** /-əbl ; -əbl̩/ *adj* that is or can be ~ed (by law, the rules, etc). (法律,規則等)所許可的;可承認的。

allow·ance /əˈlaʊəns ; əˈlaʊəns/ *n* **1** [C] sum of money, amount of sth, allowed to sb: 津貼;特別經費;所允許給予之量: *a dress ~ of £70 a year.* 一年七十鎊的製裝津貼。 *The Director has an entertainment ~,* money for entertaining important customers, etc. 董事有一筆交際費(用以招待重要主顧等)。 **2** [C] (comm, fin) deduction or discount. (商,財政)折扣。 **3** (*sing* or *pl*) ***make ~(s) for,*** allow for, ⇨ allow (5): (單或複)考慮到;顧慮到;體諒: *We must make ~(s) for his youth,* remember that he is young, and not be too severe, etc. 我們必須體諒他年輕。

alloy /ˈælɔɪ ; ˈælɔɪ/ *n* [C, U] mixture of metals, esp a metal of low value mixed with a metal of higher value: 合金;齊;(尤指)與較貴重金屬混合之賤金屬: (used attrib) (形容用法) ~ *steel.* 合金鋼(非純鋼)。 □ *vt* /əˈlɔɪ ; əˈlɔɪ/ [VP6A] mix (one metal) with a metal or metals of lower value; (fig) spoil; impair. 混合較賤金屬於(某種金屬);(喻)使變質;損害。

all·spice /ˈɔːlspaɪs ; ˈɔl͵spaɪs/ *n* [U] spice made from the dried berries of a W Indian tree called the pimento. (西印度群島所產之)甜胡椒;甘椒。

allude /əˈluːd ; əˈljud/ *vi* [VP3A] ~ ***to,*** refer (indirectly) to; mention (now the more usu word): 提及;暗示;說到(今較常用 mention): *In your remarks you ~ to certain sinister developments.* 在你所說的話中你暗示若干不祥的發展。

allure /əˈlʊə(r) ; əˈlʊr/ *vt* [VP6A, 14, 17] tempt; entice; lure (now the more usu word). 引誘;吸引;誘惑(今較常用 lure)。 □ *n* [C, U] (liter) power to ~; fascination. (文)誘惑力;魔力。 **allur·ing** *part adj* charming; fascinating. 迷人的;誘惑人的。 **~·ment** *n* [C, U] that which ~s; charm, attraction (now the more usu words). 有誘惑力之事物;魔力;吸引力(今較常用 charm 或 attraction)。

al·lu·sion /əˈluːʒn ; əˈluʒən/ *n* [C] ~ ***(to),*** indirect reference to: 間接提及;暗示;暗指;典故: *His speeches are full of classical ~s which few people understand.* 他的演說中用了很多鮮爲人知的典故。 *That man has a glass eye but he doesn't like people to make any ~ to it.* 那個人有一隻假眼,但他不喜歡人以任何方式間接地提到它。 **al·lus·ive** /əˈluːsɪv ; əˈlusɪv/ *adj* containing ~s. 含暗示的;含典故的。

al·luv·ial /əˈluːvɪəl ; əˈluvɪəl/ *adj* made of sand, earth, etc, left by rivers or floods: 沖積的;淤積的: *~ soil/deposits.* 沖積土(礦藏)。

ally /əˈlaɪ ; əˈlaɪ/ *vt* (*pt, pp* -lied) **1** [VP14] ~ ***(oneself) with/to,*** unite by treaty, marriage, etc: (使自己)與…聯盟; 聯姻: *Great Britain was allied with the United States in both World Wars;* 在兩次世界大戰中,英國都是與美國聯盟;Hence: 由此產生: *the Allied* /ˈælaɪd ; əˈlaɪd/ *Powers.* 同盟國。 **2** ***allied to,*** (of things) connected with: (指事物)與…有關係;與…同屬一系;與…相類似: *The English language is allied to the German language.* 英語與德語屬於同一語系。 □ *n* /ˈælaɪ ; ˈælaɪ/ (*pl* -lies) person, state, etc, allied to another; person who gives help or support. 同盟者;聯盟者;盟國;盟邦;盟友。

Alma Mater /ˌælmə ˈmɑːtə(r) ; ˈælməˈmetɚ/ *n* (Lat) name used for the university or school that a person attended; (US) school song or anthem. (拉)母校;(美)校歌。

al·ma·nac /ˈɔːlmənæk ; ˈɔlmə͵næk/ *n* annual book or calendar of months and days, with information about the sun, moon, tides, anniversaries, etc. 曆

書;天文年曆(內包括關於日,月,潮汐,紀念日等之說明);年鑑。

al·mighty /ɔːlˈmaɪtɪ ; ɔlˈmaɪtɪ/ *adj* having all power; powerful beyond measure, 萬能的;全能的;有無限權力的, esp 尤用於 *A~ God.* 全能的上帝。□ *n* **the A~,** God. 全能者(上帝)。

almond /ˈɑːmənd ; ˈɑmənd/ *n* (nut inside the) hard seed (*stone-fruit*) of a tree allied to the peach and plum: 杏核;杏仁: *ground ~s,* ~ nuts ground to powder; 杏仁粉; *shelled ~s,* ~ nuts removed from the shell or hard cover. 杏仁。**ˌ~-ˈeyed** *adj* having eyes that appear to slant upwards and become narrower. 杏眼的;眼向上斜而呈狹長形的。

almoner /ˈɑːmənə(r) *US:* ˈælm- ; ˈælmənɚ/ *n* **1** (formerly) official who distributed money and help to the poor. (昔時)賑濟員(負責發救濟金等給貧困者)。 **2** (GB) hospital official in charge of social service work for patients. (英)公立醫院中爲病人服務之社會工作員。

al·most /ˈɔːlməʊst ; ɔlˈmost/ *adv* **1** (with *vv, advv, adjj, nn;* replaceable by *nearly*): (與動詞,副詞,形容詞,名詞連用;可與 nearly 通用)幾乎;差一點就;差不多: *He slipped and ~ fell.* 他滑了一下,幾乎跌倒。*That's a mistake he ~ always makes.* 那是一個他幾乎經常犯的錯誤。*Dinner's ~ ready.* 晚餐差不多已經預備好了。*It's ~ time to start.* 差不多是開始的時候了。 **2** (with *no, none, nothing, never,* not replaceable by *nearly;* often replaced by *hardly* or *scarcely* with *any*): (與 no, none, nothing, never 連用,不可與 nearly 通用;常可與 hardly any 或 scarcely any 通用)幾乎;差不多: *A~ no one* (= Hardly anyone) *believed her.* 幾乎沒有一個人相信她。*The speaker said ~ nothing* (=scarcely anything) *worth listening to.* 那發言者所說的話幾乎沒有一句值得聽的。

alms /ɑːmz ; ɑmz/ *n* (*sing* or *pl*) money, clothes, food, etc given to the poor: (單或複)救濟金;救濟品(衣服、食物等): *give ~ to sb;* 給予某人救濟; *ask/beg (an) ~ of sb.* 向某人請求救濟。**ˈ~-box** *n* 救濟箱。**ˈ~-giving** *n* 施捨;賙濟。**ˈ~-house** *n* (old use) house, founded by charity, in which poor people, no longer able to earn money, may live without paying rent. (舊用法)救濟院;貧民院;濟貧院(爲慈善機關所設,收容窮困而無力謀生者)。

aloe /ˈæləʊ; ˈælo/ *n* **1** plant with thick, sharp-pointed leaves. 蘆薈。**2** (also 亦作 **bitter ~s**) juice from this plant, used in medicine. 蘆薈油(用於醫藥)。

aloft /əˈlɒft *US:* əˈlɔːft ; əˈlɔft/ *adv* high up, esp at the masthead of a ship, or up in the rigging. 在高處;(尤指)在桅桿頂上;在帆桅纜索上面。

alone /əˈləʊn ; əˈlon/ *pred adj, adv* ⇨ lonely. **1** (= *by oneself/itself*) without the company or help of others or other things: 獨自的(地);孤獨的(地);獨力的(地);單獨的(地): *He likes living ~,* by himself. 他喜歡孤獨生活。*The house stands on the hillside all ~,* with no other houses near it. 那房子孤零零地座落在山坡上。*You can't lift the piano ~,* without help. 你不能獨力抬起那鋼琴。*His silence ~ is proof of his guilt.* 單是他的沈默就是他犯罪的證明。 **2** (following a *n* or *pron*) and no other: (跟於名詞或代名詞之後)只有;唯有;沒有別人: *Smith ~* (= Smith and no one else) *knows what happened.* 只有史密斯知道發生了什麼事。*You ~* (=You and no other person) *can help me in this task.* 只有你能幫助我做這件事。 **3** (in the *pred,* with *in*): (在述語中與 in 連用): *We are not ~ in thinking* (=not the only persons who think) *that....* 並非只有我們認爲…。 **4** ***let ~,*** without referring to or considering: 遑論;至於…更不必說了: *He cannot find money for necessities, let ~ such luxuries as wine and tobacco.* 他連生活必需品都無錢購買,更不必說菸酒等奢侈品了。***let/leave sb/sth ~,*** abstain from touching, moving, interfering with: 不動,不碰或不干涉某人或某事物;聽其自然: *You had better leave that dog ~; it will bite you if you tease it.* 你最好不要去惹那隻狗;如果你捉弄它,它會咬你的。***let well ~,*** do not go further than what is already satisfactory. 不要畫蛇添足。

along /əˈlɒŋ *US:* əˈlɔːŋ ; əˈlɔŋ/ *adv* **1** (used with *vv* to indicate onward movement, often with the same sense as *on*): (與動詞連用,表示向前移動,常與 on 同義): *Come ~!* 來吧!跟我來吧! *The dog was running ~ behind its master.* 那狗跟在它的主人後面跑着。***Move ~ please!*** eg a request by a policeman to people who are holding up the movement of others. 請向前走動!(例如警察對阻礙他人前進的人所做的請求。) **2** (used, as are *over, across, up, down,* in informal requests): (用於非正式請求中,同 over, across, up, down): *Come ~ and see me some time.* 有空的時候過來看我。 **3** ***all ~,*** ⇨ all²(1). ***get ~,*** ⇨ get(17). □ *prep* **1** from one end of to the other end of; through any part of the length of: 沿着;循: *We walked ~ the road.* 我們沿着路走。*There are trees all ~ the river banks.* 沿河兩岸皆植有樹木。*Pass ~ the bus please!* (a request that passengers should move on so as to leave the entrance clear). 請向車裏面走!(對車上乘客的請求,俾上下車的乘客不致於在入口處受阻)。 **2** ***~ here,*** in this direction. 朝這方向。 **~·side** /əˌlɒŋˈsaɪd ; əˈlɔŋˈsaɪd/ *adv, prep* close to, parallel with, the side of (a ship, pier, wharf). 傍靠;沿着或靠着(船,碼頭)的旁邊。

aloof /əˈluːf ; əˈluf/ *adv* apart. 遠離地;分離地。***stand/hold/keep (oneself) ~ (from),*** keep away from, take no part in sth: 站得遠遠的;不接近(某物);不參與(某事): *Buyers are holding ~,* making no offers to buy. 購買者都裹足不前。□ *adj* cool; remote (by nature): 冷漠的;疏遠的: *I find him rather ~.* 我發現他頗爲冷漠。 *He's a very ~ character.* 他是個冷漠的怪人。 **~·ness** *n*

aloud /əˈlaʊd ; əˈlaud/ *adv* **1** in a voice loud enough to be heard, not in a whisper: 出聲地(俾能聽得到): *Please read the story ~.* 請誦讀這個故事。**2** loudly, so as to be heard at a distance: 高聲地(俾遠處能聽得到): *He called ~ for help.* 他高聲喊叫求救。

alp /ælp ; ælp/ *n* **1** high mountain, esp one of those (**the Alps**) between France and Italy. 高山;高峯(尤指屬於法義邊境之阿爾卑斯山脈者)。 **2** (in Switzerland) green pasture-land on a mountain-side. (瑞士境內)山坡上的牧場。

al·paca /ælˈpækə ; ælˈpækə/ *n* **1** [C] sheep-like animal, kind of llama, of Peru. 羊駝(產於秘魯)。 **2** [U] (cloth made from) its wool, often mixed with silk or cotton: 羊駝毛;羊駝毛織物(常混有絲或棉);羊駝呢: *an ~ coat.* 羊駝呢外衣。

alpen·stock /ˈælpənstɒk ; ˈælpɪnˌstɑk/ *n* long, iron-tipped stick used in climbing mountains. 登山手杖(長而有鐵頭者)。

al·pha /ˈælfə ; ˈælfə/ *n* the first letter (A, α) in the Gk alphabet: 希臘字母的第一個字母: ***A~ and Omega,*** the beginning and the end. 首尾;始終。⇨ App 4. 參看附錄四。 **ˈ~ particle,** helium nucleus given off by a radio-active substance. 阿爾伐質點(放射性物質所放出的氦原子核)。***~ plus,*** (of marks in an examination) very good indeed. (考試記分)甲上。

al·pha·bet /ˈælfəbet ; ˈælfəˌbɛt/ *n* the letters used in writing a language, arranged in order: (用以拼寫一種語言並按次序排列的全部)字母: *the Greek ~;* 希臘字母; the ABC. 基本知識;初步;入門。⇨ App 4. 參看附錄四。 **~·i·cal** /ˌælfəˈbetɪkl ; ˌælfəˈbɛtɪkḷ/ *adj* in the order of the ~: 按字母順序的: *The words in a dictionary are in ~ical order.* 字典中的單字係按字母順序排列的。 **~·i·cally** /-klɪ ; -klɪ/ *adv*

al·pine /ˈælpaɪn ; ˈælpaɪn/ *adj* of the Alps; of alps: 阿爾卑斯山脈的;高山的;高峯的: *~ plants;* 高山植物; *an ~ hut.* 高山茅舍。 **al·pin·ist** /ˈælpɪnɪst ; ˈælpɪnɪst/ *n* ~ climber. 登阿爾卑斯山者;登高山者。

al·ready /ɔːlˈredɪ ; ɔlˈrɛdɪ/ *adv* (usu with *v,* but may be placed elsewhere for emphasis) (通常與動詞連用,但也可以放在別處以加强語氣) **1** by this/

that time: 已經;業已: *The postman has ~ been/ has been ~.* 郵差已經來過了。*When I called, Tom was ~ dressed.* 當我去他家的時候,湯姆已經穿好衣服了。 **2** (Cf *yet* which usu replaces *already* in neg and interr sentences. In neg and interr sentences *already* is used to show surprise.): (參較 yet, 在否定及疑問句中,通常以 yet 替換 already; 在否定及疑問句中用 already 是表示驚奇): *Have you had breakfast ~?* 你已經吃過早餐了嗎? *Is it 10 o'clock ~?* 已經十點鐘了嗎? *You're not leaving us ~, are you?* 你不會這麼早就要離開我們吧,是不是? **3** previously; before now: 早已;曾經: *I've been there ~, so I don't want to go again.* 我早已到過那裡了,所以我不想再去。

al·right /ɔːlˈraɪt ; ɔlˈraɪt/ =all right, ⇨ all²(1).

Al·sa·tian /ælˈseɪʃn ; ælˈseʃən/ *n* (US 美=*German shepherd*) large breed of dog, like a wolf, often trained for police work. 一種大狼狗(常予以訓練使擔任警犬任務)。⇨ the illus at dog. 參看 dog 之插圖。

also /ˈɔːlsəʊ ; ˈɔlso/ *adv* too; besides; as well. (In spoken English, *too* and *as well* are often preferred to *also*. *Also* in an affirm sentence is replaced by *either* in a neg sentence.): 也;亦;並且(在口語中, too 及 as well 常較 also 爲佳。在肯定句中之 also, 在否定句中換爲 either): *Tom has been to Canada. Harry has ~ been to Canada.* 湯姆曾去過加拿大。哈利亦曾去過加拿大。*Cf* 參較 *Tom has not been to Brazil. Harry has not been to Brazil, either.* 湯姆沒有去過巴西。哈利也沒有去過巴西。***not only...but ~,*** both...and: 不但…而且: *He not only read the book but ~ remembered what he had read.* 他不但讀過此書,並且記得所讀的內容。**ˈ~-ran** *n* (racing) horse not among the first three at the winning post; (fig) unsuccessful person in a contest. (賽馬)落選之馬;(喩)(競賽中)落選之人;敗北者。

al·tar /ˈɔːltə(r) ; ˈɔltɚ/ *n* **1** raised place (flat-topped table or platform) on which offerings are made to a god. (置祭品於神前的)祭壇。 **2** (in Christian churches) the Communion table, ⇨ the illus at church. (基督教中)聖餐桌;神壇(參看 church 之插圖)。***lead (a woman) to the ~,*** marry her. 與(某女)結婚(字面意義爲:領某女至神壇)。**ˈ~-piece** *n* painting or sculpture placed behind an ~. 祭壇後方所置之圖畫或彫刻。

al·ter /ˈɔːltə(r) ; ˈɔltɚ/ *vt, vi* [VP6A, 2A] make or become different; change in character, appearance, etc: 改變;更改;變更;修改(指性格,外貌等): *The ship ~ed course.* 該船改變航路。*That ~s matters/ the case,* makes the situation different. 那就要使情勢改觀。*These clothes are too large; they must be ~ed.* 這些衣服太大,必須加以修改。*He has ~ed a great deal since I saw him a year ago.* 自從我在一年前見他以後,他已改變了很多。**~·able** /-əbl ; -əbl/ *adj* that ~s or that can be ~ed. 可改變的;可修改的。**~·ation** /ˌɔːltəˈreɪʃn ; ˌɔltəˈreʃən/ *n* [U] ~ing; making a change; [C] act of changing; change that is the result of ~ing: 改變;更改;變更;修改: *There isn't much ~ation in the village; it's almost the same as it was twenty years ago.* 村中沒有多少改變;它幾乎和二十年前是一樣的。*For making ~ations to a suit of clothes, £1.20.* 修改一套衣服,工資一鎊二十辨士。

al·ter·ca·tion /ˌɔːltəˈkeɪʃn ; ˌɔltɚˈkeʃən/ *n* (formal) [U] quarrelling; [C] quarrel; noisy argument. (正式用語)口角;爭論;爭辯;爭吵。

al·ter ego /ˌæltər ˈegəʊ *US:* ˈiːgəʊ ; ˈæltɚˈigo/ *n* (Lat) one's other self; very intimate friend. (拉)他我;另一個我;密友;至交。

al·ter·nate¹ /ɔːlˈtɜːnət ; ˈɔltɚnɪt/ *adj* **1** (of things of two kinds) by turns, first the one and then the other: (指兩種事物)輪流的;交替的: *~ laughter and tears.* 時笑時哭;又哭又笑。*Tom and Harry do the work on ~ days,* eg Tom on Monday, Harry on Tuesday, Tom on Wednesday, etc. 湯姆與哈利隔日輪流做這工作。 **2** (of leaves along a stem) not opposite. (指沿莖之葉)互生的(並非對生的)。**~·ly** *adv*

al·ter·nate² /ˈɔːltəneɪt ; ˈɔltɚˌnet/ *vt, vi* **1** [VP6A, 14] arrange or perform by turns; cause to take place, appear, one after the other: 輪流;使交替發生或出現: *He ~d kindness with severity,* was kind, then severe, then kind again, etc. 他時而仁慈時而嚴厲(恩威並施)。*Most farmers ~ crops.* 大多數的農人實行輪種(輪替種植不同的作物,以保持土壤之肥沃性)。⇨ rotation(2). **2** [VP3A] ~ ***between,*** pass from one state, etc to a second, then back to the first, etc: 一下子…一下子…: *He ~d between high spirits and low spirits.* 他一下子高興一下子沮喪。~ ***with,*** come one after the other, by turns: 輪流出現;交替;交互發生: *Wet days ~d with fine days.* 雨天與晴天交替更迭。**ˌalternating ˈcurrent,** current that reverses its direction at regular intervals, the cycle being repeated continuously, the number of complete cycles per second being known as the *frequency.* 交流;交流電。⇨ direct¹(5). **al·ter·na·tion** /ˌɔːltəˈneɪʃn ; ˌɔltɚˈneʃən/ *n*

al·ter·na·tive /ɔːlˈtɜːnətɪv ; ɔlˈtɝnətɪv/ *adj* (of two things) that may be had, used, etc in place of sth else: 二者任擇其一的;另一個可選擇的;選擇性的: *'Either' and 'or' are ~ conjunctions.* Either 和 or 都是選擇性的連接詞。*There are ~ answers to x^2 =16* (ie x=+4 or x=−4). '*x* 的二次方等於十六'有兩個可能的答案(卽 *x* 等於正 4 或負 4)。□ *n* [C] **1** choice between two things: 二者擇一;二者之一;變通辦法;選擇餘地: *You have the ~ of working hard and being successful or of not working hard and being unsuccessful.* 你有兩種選擇: 努力工作而成功或不努力工作而失敗。*Is there no ~ to what you propose?* 你的提議沒有變通的餘地嗎? **2** one of more than two possibilities. 數種可能之一。**~·ly** *adv* as an ~: 作爲一個代替的辦法;替換地: *a fine of £10 or ~ly six weeks imprisonment.* 罰鍰十鎊或者易爲六星期的徒刑。

altho /ɔːlˈðəʊ ; ɔlˈðo/ (US spelling for) although. although 之美國拼法。

al·though /ɔːlˈðəʊ ; ɔlˈðo/ *conj* ⇨ though.

al·tim·eter /ˈæltɪmiːtə(r) *US:* ˌælˈtɪmɪtər ; ælˈtɪmətɚ/ *n* barometer, eg as used in aircraft, for showing height above sea-level. 高度測量器;高度表(如用於飛機中者)。

al·ti·tude /ˈæltɪtjuːd *US:* -tuːd ; ˈæltəˌtjud/ *n* **1** (not of living things) height, esp above sea-level. (非生物之)高度;(尤指)海拔。 **2** (usu *pl*) place high above sea-level: (通常用複數)高處;海拔甚高的地方: *It is difficult to breathe at these ~s.* 在這些高的地方呼吸感到困難。 **3** (astron) angular distance of a celestial object above the horizon. (天文)地平緯度(天體在地平上之角距)。

alto /ˈæltəʊ ; ˈælto/ *n* (*pl* ~s /-təʊz ; -toz/) **1** (musical part for, a person having a) male singing voice between tenor and treble; counter tenor; female voice of similar range (*contralto*). 中音;中音部;唱中音者;女低音。 **2** instrument with the same range: 中音樂器: *~-saxophone.* 中音薩克管。

al·to·gether /ˌɔːltəˈgeðə(r) ; ˌɔltəˈgɛðɚ/ *adv* **1** entirely; wholly: 完全地;全部地: *I don't ~ agree with him.* 我不完全同意他。*It's ~ out of the question.* 那是完全不可能的。 **2** (of a total quantity) taken as a whole: (指總數量)總計: *You owe me £3 ~.* 你一共欠我三鎊。 **3** (modifying a complete sentence) on the whole; considering everything: (修飾全句)從整體看來;總而言之: *The weather was bad and the trains were crowded—~, it wasn't a very satisfactory excursion.* 天氣惡劣,火車又擠——總之,不是一次很滿意的郊遊。

al·tru·ism /ˈæltruːɪzəm ; ˈæltruˌɪzəm/ *n* [U] principle of considering the well-being and happiness of others first; unselfishness; [C] instance of this. 利他主義(卽一切以他人之幸福爲前提);利他;利他的實例。**al·tru·ist** /ˈæltruːɪst ; ˈæltruɪst/ *n* person who follows ~. 利他主義者。**al·tru·is·tic** /ˌæltruːˈɪstɪk ; ˌæltruˈɪstɪk/ *adj* **al·tru·is·ti·cally** /-klɪ ; -klɪ/ *adv*

alum /ˈæləm ; ˈæləm/ *n* [U] white mineral salt, used medically, in dyeing, etc. 明礬;白礬(用於醫藥,染色等)。

alu·min·ium /ˌæljʊˈmɪnɪəm ; ˌæljəˈmɪnɪəm/ (US = **alu·mi·num** /əˈluːmɪnəm ; əˈlumɪnəm/) *n* [U] light white metal (symbol **Al**) extracted chiefly from bauxite, used for making hard, light alloys for cooking utensils, electrical apparatus, etc. 鋁(白色輕金屬,符號爲 Al,主要由鐵鋁氧石提煉而來,用於製硬而輕的合金炊具,電器等)。

alumna /əˈlʌmnə ; əˈlʌmnə/ *n* (*pl* ~e /-niː ; -ni/) (US) girl or woman who was a pupil or student of a school, college or university. (美)女校友;女畢業生。

alum·nus /əˈlʌmnəs ; əˈlʌmnəs/ *n* (*pl* -ni /-naɪ ; -naɪ/) (US) boy or man who was a pupil or student of a school, college or university. (美)男校友;男畢業生。

al·veolar /ælˈvɪələ(r) ; ælˈviələ/ *n, adj* (phon) (consonant) made by the tongue against the gum behind the upper front teeth, eg /t, d, s/. (語音)齒齦音(用舌頂住上齒齦而發出的子音如 t, d, s 音);齒齦的。

al·ways /ˈɔːlweɪz ; ˈɔlwez/ *adv* **1** at all times; without exception: 永遠地;無例外地;總是: *The sun ~ rises in the east.* 太陽總是在東方升起。(*Always* may be modified by *almost, nearly* or *not.*) (Always 可以被 almost, nearly 或 not 修飾。) *He's nearly ~ at home in the evening.* 他晚上差不多總在家。Cf 參較 *not ~* and *hardly ever. I'm not ~ at home on Sundays,* ie I'm occasionally away from home. 我星期日不一定總在家(卽偶然也會不在家)。*I'm hardly ever* (=very seldom) *at home on Sundays.* 我星期日幾乎從不(卽極少)在家。 **2** (usu with the continuous tenses) again and again; repeatedly: (通常與進行式連用)再三地;累次地;總是: *He was ~ asking for money.* 他老是要錢。*Why are you ~ finding fault?* 你爲什麼總是吹毛求疵?

am /*after 'I':* m ; m; *otherwise:* əm ; əm; *strong form:* æm ; æm/ ⇨ be¹.

amah /ˈɑːmə ; ˈɑmə/ *n* (in the East) nursemaid; maidservant. (在東方各國)阿媽;老媽子;奶媽;女傭。

amain /əˈmeɪn ; əˈmen/ *adv* (old use, or poet) (舊用法或詩) **1** violently. 猛烈地;激烈地。 **2** in haste. 急忙地;匆促地。

amal·gam /əˈmælgəm ; əˈmælgəm/ *n* **1** alloy of mercury. 汞合金;汞齊。 **2** soft mixture, eg one used for filling holes in decayed teeth. 任何軟的混合物(如塡補齲齒用的齒科汞合金)。

amal·ga·mate /əˈmælgəmeɪt ; əˈmælgəˌmet/ *vt, vi* [VP6A, 2A] (of classes, societies, races of people, business companies) mix; combine; unite. (指階級,社會,民族,公司)混合;聯合;合倂。**amal·ga·ma·tion** /əˌmælgəˈmeɪʃn ; əˌmælgəˈmeʃən/ *n* [U] mixing; combining. [C] combination; union. 混合;聯合;合倂。

am·anu·en·sis /əˌmænjʊˈensɪs ; əˌmænjʊˈɛnsɪs/ *n* (*pl* -ses /-siːz ; -siz/) person who writes from dictation or copies what sb else has written. 筆記者;抄錄者;書記;文書。

ama·ryl·lis /ˌæməˈrɪlɪs ; ˌæməˈrɪlɪs/ *n* (kinds of) lily-like plant growing from a bulb. 宮人草。

amass /əˈmæs ; əˈmæs/ *vt* [VP6A] pile or heap up, collect: 聚積: *~ riches/a fortune.* 聚積財富(財產)。

ama·teur /ˈæmətə(r) ; ˈæməˌtʃʊr/ *n* person who paints pictures, performs music, acts in plays, etc, for the love of it, not for money; person playing a game, taking part in sports, etc, without receiving payment: 業餘從事者(指由於愛好,不是爲了賺錢,而從事繪畫、演奏音樂、演戲等的人): (attrib) (形容用法) *an ~ painter/photographer.* 業餘畫家(攝影家)。⇨ professional. **~·ish** /-rɪʃ ; -rɪʃ/ *adj* inexpert; imperfect. 不熟練的;不完善的。 **~·ism** /-ɪzəm ; -ɪzm̩/ *n*

ama·tory /ˈæmətərɪ *US:* -tɔːrɪ ; ˈæməˌtorɪ/ *adj* (formal) of or causing (esp sexual) love; of lovers; of making love. (正式用語)愛情(尤指性愛)的;引起愛情(性愛)的;愛人的;戀愛的;做愛的。

amaze /əˈmeɪz ; əˈmez/ *vt* [VP6A] fill with great surprise or wonder: 使大爲驚異;使驚愕;使愕然: *You ~ me!* 你使我大爲驚異! *I was ~d at the news/~d to hear that....* 我聽到這個消息(聽到…)大爲吃驚。**amaz·ing** *part adj* **amaz·ing·ly** *adv*: *He's doing amazingly well.* 他做得非常(令人驚訝之)好。**~·ment** *n* [U]: *I heard with ~ment that....* 我聽到…大爲吃驚。*His ~ment at the news was immense.* 他聽到這項消息極爲吃驚。*He looked at me in ~ment.* 他驚奇地望着我。

Ama·zon /ˈæməzən *US:* -zɒn ; ˈæməˌzɑn/ *n* **1** (in old Gk stories) female warrior. (古希臘傳說中之)女戰士;女勇士。 **2** (small *a*) tall, vigorous woman. (a 小寫)高大强壯的女人。

am·bas·sa·dor /æmˈbæsədə(r) ; æmˈbæsədə/ *n* **1** minister representing the Government of his country in a foreign country: (駐外國的)大使: *the British A~ to Greece.* 英國駐希臘大使。 **2** (often 常作 *A~ Extraordinary*) minister sent by the Government of one State to the Government of another on a special mission. 專使;特使。 **3** authorized representative. 經授權指派的代表。 **am·bas·sa·dress** /æmˈbæsədrɪs ; æmˈbæsədrɪs/ *n* female ~. 女大使;女特使;女代表。**~·ial** /æmˌbæsəˈdɔːrɪəl ; æmˌbæsəˈdorɪəl/ *adj* ⇨ diplomat, embassy.

am·ber /ˈæmbə(r) ; ˈæmbə/ *n* [U] hard, clear yellowish-brown gum used for making ornaments, etc; its colour (seen in traffic lights between red and green). 琥珀;琥珀色(黃褐色)。

am·ber·gris /ˈæmbəgriːs *US:* -grɪs ; ˈæmbəˌgris/ *n* [U] wax-like substance present in the intestines of whales and found floating in tropical seas, used as a fixative in perfumes. 鯨糞;龍涎香(用做香水之固定劑)。

am·bi·dex·trous /ˌæmbɪˈdekstrəs ; ˌæmbəˈdɛkstrəs/ *adj* able to use the left hand or the right equally well. 兩手均可靈巧使用的。

am·bi·ence /ˈæmbɪəns ; ˈæmbɪəns/ *n* environment; atmosphere. 環境;四圍的情況;氣氛。

am·bi·ent /ˈæmbɪənt ; ˈæmbɪənt/ *adj* (formal) (of air, etc) on all sides; surrounding. (正式用語)(指空氣等)環繞四周的;周圍的。

am·bi·guity /ˌæmbɪˈgjuːətɪ ; ˌæmbɪˈgjuətɪ/ *n* (*pl* -ties) **1** [U] state of being ambiguous. 意義含糊。 **2** [C] expression, etc that can have more than one meaning: 有兩種以上意義的辭句;意義含糊的話: *Let's clear up the ~ in this paragraph.* 讓我們把這一段中意義含糊的辭句解說明白。

am·bigu·ous /æmˈbɪgjʊəs ; æmˈbɪgjʊəs/ *adj* **1** having more than one meaning: 意義含糊的;有兩種以上之意義的: *'More' is ~ in 'Ask me more difficult questions.'* 在 'Ask me more difficult questions' 一句中,'more' 一字的意義含糊。 **2** of uncertain meaning or intention: 意向不明的;曖昧的: *He gave me an ~ glance.* 他意向不明的看了我一眼。**~·ly** *adv*

am·bit /ˈæmbɪt ; ˈæmbɪt/ *n* (often *pl*) bounds; extent; range of power or authority. (常用複數)界限;範圍;權力的範圍。

am·bi·tion /æmˈbɪʃn ; æmˈbɪʃən/ *n* **1** [U] strong desire (*to be* or *do* sth, *for* sth): 野心;雄心;志氣(與不定詞或 for 連用,後接某事物): *A boy who is filled with ~ usually works hard.* 一個充滿雄心的男孩通常很用功。*His ~ to become prime minister is likely to be realized.* 他要做首相的雄心可能會實現。 **2** [C] particular desire of this kind: 某項特別的野心或志向;抱負: *He has great ~s.* 他胸懷大志。 **3** [C] object of such a desire: 希望達到的目標;抱負: *achieve one's ~(s).* 達到個人所希望的目標。

am·bi·tious /æmˈbɪʃəs ; æmˈbɪʃəs/ *adj* **1** full of ambition: 充滿野心的;雄心勃勃的: *an ~ boy;* 有野心的男孩子; *~ for fame;* 有成名之野心(熱中功名)

的; ~ *for one's children;* 對兒女懷有熱切的期望; ~ *to succeed in life.* 立志要出人頭地。 **2** showing or needing ambition: 顯示或需要雄心的;抱負不凡的: ~ *plans;* 顯示出雄心的計畫(野心很大的計畫); *an ~ attempt.* 抱負不凡的嘗試。 **~·ly** *adv*

am·biva·lent /æm'bɪvələnt ; æm'bɪvələnt/ *adj* having either or both of two contrary or similar values, meanings, etc. 具有兩種相反或類似之價值、意義等的;兼具兩種互相衝突之感情的;情緒矛盾的。 **am·biva·lence** /-ləns ; -ləns/ *n*

amble /'æmbl ; 'æmbḷ/ *vi* [VP2A, C] (of a horse) move along without hurrying, lifting the two feet on one side together; (of a person) ride or walk at an easy pace. (指馬)以緩步行走(同側之兩足同時舉起); (指人)騎馬或走路緩緩而行。 □ *n* slow, easy, pace: 緩步;慢步: *He was coming along at an ~.* 他以緩慢的步子走來。

am·bro·sia /æm'brəuzɪə *US:* -əuʒə ; æm'broʒɪə/ *n* [U] (Gk myth) the food of the gods; anything that has a delightful taste or smell. (希神)神的食物;任何美味佳餚。

am·bu·lance /'æmbjuləns ; 'æmbjələns/ *n* closed vehicle for carrying people who are ill, wounded in war or hurt in accidents. 救護車(運送病人,傷兵或災禍受傷者之車)。

am·bus·cade /ˌæmbə'skeɪd ; ˌæmbəs'ked/ *n, vt* = ambush.

am·bush /'æmbuʃ ; 'æmbuʃ/ *n* [C,U] (the placing of) troops, etc, waiting to make a surprise attack: 埋伏(以備突擊);伏兵: *fall into an ~;* 中伏;遭遇埋伏; *be attacked from (an) ~.* 遭伏兵狙擊。 ***lie/wait in ~ (for),*** be hidden waiting to attack. 埋伏(以突擊)。 □ *vt* [VP6A] attack from such a position. 埋伏並突擊。

ameba /ə'mi:bə ; ə'mibə/ *n* = amoeba.

ameer /ə'mɪə(r) ; ə'mɪr/ *n* = amir.

ameli·or·ate /ə'mi:lɪəreɪt ; ə'miljəˌret/ *vt, vi* [VP6A, 2A] (formal) (cause to) become better. (正式用語)改善;改良;變好。 **ameli·or·ation** /əˌmi:lɪə'reɪʃn ; əˌmiljə'reʃən/ *n*

amen /ɑ:'men *US:* eɪ'men ; 'e'mɛn/ *int* (eccles) word used at the end of a prayer or hymn and meaning 'May it be so'. (教會)阿們(祈禱或頌詩終了時之語,意為'心願如此')。

amen·able /ə'mi:nəbl ; ə'minəbḷ/ *adj* ***~ (to),*** **1** (of persons) responsive; willing to be guided or controlled: (指人)易受感動的;願受指導或控制的;願服從的: *~ to kindness/advice/reason.* 易受仁慈感動(願接受勸告;通達情理)的。 *Do you find your wife ~?* 你覺得你的太太很順從嗎? **2** (legal) (of persons) responsible (*to*); in a position where one must do certain things or be punished for not doing them: (法律)(指人)有責任的;應負責任的(與 to 連用);有服從義務的: *We are all ~ to the law.* 我們都應該服從法律。 **3** (of cases, situations) able to be tested or dealt with: (指情形,情勢)可測驗的;可處理的;可解決的: *The case is not ~ to ordinary rules.* 這情形不是按普通規則所能處理的。

amend /ə'mend ; ə'mɛnd/ *vt, vi* **1** [VP6A, 2A] make or become better; improve; free from faults or errors: 改善;改良;改正: *He'll have to ~ his style of living.* 他將必須改善生活方式。 **2** [VP6A] make changes in the wording of a rule, a proposed law, etc. 修正(規則,提案等)。 **~·able** /-əbl ; -əbḷ/ *adj* **~·ment** *n* [U] ~ing; [C] change proposed or made (*to* a rule, regulation, etc). 改善;改良;改正;修正(與 to 連用,後接某項規則,條例等)。

amends /ə'mendz ; ə'mɛndz/ *n pl* ***make ~/all possible ~ (to sb) (for sth),*** give compensation: (為某事)(對某人)賠償;補償;賠罪: *make ~ to sb for an injury.* 賠償某人所受的傷害。

amen·ity /ə'mi:nətɪ ; ə'mɛnətɪ/ *n* (*pl* -ties) **1** (*pl*) things, circumstances, surroundings, that make life easy or pleasant: (複)使人愉快的事物,環境等: *an exchange of amenities,* of courtesies, polite expressions; 寒暄; *a town with many amenities,* eg a park, a public library, playing fields; 有許多休閒去處(如公園,公共圖書館,運動場)的城鎮; *the amenities offered by a Bank,* eg the provision of travel cheques, payment of standing orders. 銀行所提供便利客戶之措施(例如旅行支票之準備,定期滙票之付款等)。 **2** (*sing*) pleasantness: (單)爽適;宜人: *the ~ of the climate.* 氣候之宜人。

Amer·ica /ə'merɪkə ; ə'mɛrɪkə/ *n* the United States of ~. 美國。

Ameri·can /ə'merɪkən ; ə'mɛrɪkən/ *adj* of N or S America, esp the US. (北或南)美洲的;(尤指)美國的。 **'~ organ,** small organ with reeds but no pipes. 美國風琴(一種有簧無管之小型風琴)。 **'~ plan,** (at hotels) system of charges including room, all meals and service. 美國式旅館計帳法(包括房間,三餐及服務費)。 □ *n* native or inhabitant of America; citizen of the US. 美國人;美國居民;美國公民。 **~·ism** /-ɪzəm ; -ɪzəm/ *n* [C] word or phrase typical of ~ English; [U] loyalty to the US or to things typically ~. 美國英語所特有之字詞;對於美國或美國所特有之事物的忠誠;美國精神。

am·ethyst /'æmɪθɪst ; 'æməθɪst/ *n* precious stone, purple or violet. 紫晶;紫水晶。

ami·able /'eɪmɪəbl ; 'emɪəbḷ/ *adj* good-tempered; kind-hearted; easy and pleasant to talk to: 好脾氣的;仁慈的;友善的;和藹的;親切的: *I've always found him a most ~ fellow.* 我總覺得他是一位非常親切的人。 **amia·bil·ity** /ˌeɪmɪə'bɪlətɪ ; ˌemɪə'bɪlətɪ/ *n* **1** [U] friendliness. 友善;和藹;親切。 **2** (*pl*) (-ties) friendly remarks: (複)親切的談話: *after a few amiabilities.* 說過幾句客套話之後。 **ami·ably** /-əblɪ ; -əblɪ/ *adv*

amic·able /'æmɪkəbl ; 'æmɪkəbḷ/ *adj* peaceable; done in a friendly way: 和平的;溫和的;和善的;友好的: *When countries cannot settle a dispute in an ~ way, they should settle it by arbitration.* 當國與國間不能和平解決一項爭端時,他們應由仲裁加以解決。 **amica·bil·ity** /ˌæmɪkə'bɪlətɪ ; ˌæmɪkə'bɪlətɪ/ *n* **amic·ably** /-əblɪ ; -əblɪ/ *adv: live together amicably,* peacefully, in a friendly way. 友好地生活在一起。

amid /ə'mɪd ; ə'mɪd/, **amidst** /ə'mɪdst ; ə'mɪdst/ *preps* (poet) among; in or into the middle of. (詩)在…之中;在…之間。

amid·ships /ə'mɪdʃɪps ; ə'mɪdʃɪps/ *adv* (naut) half-way between the bows and stern of a ship: (航海)在船之中部: *Our cabin is ~.* 我們的艙位在船的中腰。

amir, ameer, emir /ə'mɪə(r) ; ə'mɪr/ *n* title used by some Muslim rulers. 若干回教國家統治者的稱號。

amiss /ə'mɪs ; ə'mɪs/ *pred adj, adv* wrong(ly); out of order: 誤;差錯(地);有毛病的: *There's not much ~ with it.* 它沒有多大毛病。 *Nothing comes ~ to him,* (colloq) He's ready to welcome, is able to use, anything that comes to him. (俗)什麼對他都是好的。 ***take sth ~,*** take offence at it, be hurt in one's feelings: (因為某事而)見怪;生氣: *Don't take it ~ if I point out your errors.* 假若我指出你的錯誤,請勿見怪。

am·ity /'æmətɪ ; 'æmətɪ/ *n* [U] friendship; friendly relations (between persons or countries): 友善;和好;友好;(人與人或國與國間的)友好關係: *live in ~ with sb;* 與某人和好相處; *a treaty of ~.* 友好條約。

am·me·ter /'æmɪtə(r) ; 'æmˌmitɚ/ *n* meter that measures electric current in amperes. 安培計;電表。

am·mo·nia /ə'məunɪə ; ə'monjə/ *n* [U] strong, colourless gas (**NH_3**) with a sharp smell, used in refrigeration and for the manufacture of explosives and fertilizers; solution of this gas in water. 阿摩尼亞;氨(強烈無色氣體,符號為 NH_3,味極臭,用於冷却,製造炸藥和肥料);阿摩尼亞水;氨水。 **am·mo·ni·ated** /ə'məunɪeɪtɪd ; ə'monɪˌetɪd/ *adj* combined with ~. 與氨化合的。

am·mon·ite /'æmənaɪt ; 'æməˌnaɪt/ *n* coiled shell of an extinct mollusc. 菊石(已絕跡之鸚鵡螺的盤繞形堅殼)。

am·mu·ni·tion /ˌæmju'nɪʃn ; ˌæmjə'nɪʃən/ *n* [U]

military stores, esp of explosives (shells, bombs, etc) to be used against the enemy. 軍火;彈藥。

am·nesia /æm'ni:zɪə *US:* -'ni:ʒə ; æm'niʒɪə/ *n* [U] (path) partial or total loss of memory. (病理)記憶缺失;健忘。

am·nesty /'æmnəstɪ ; 'æm,nɛstɪ/ *n* (*pl* -ties) [C] general pardon, esp for offences against the State: 大赦(尤指對內亂罪犯而言): *The rebels returned home under an ~.* 叛徒們被特赦釋放回家。

amoeba /ə'mi:bə ; ə'mibə/ *n* (*pl* ~s or ~e /-bi: ; -bi/) (zool) simple microscopic form of living matter, found in water, soil and animal parasites, always changing shape and too small to be seen except with the help of a microscope. (動物)阿米巴; 變形蟲(極微小之單細胞生物,生存於水、土壤及寄生蟲中,隨時改變形狀,除用顯微鏡外,肉眼不能看見)。 **amoebic** /ə'mi:bɪk ; ə'mibɪk/ *adj* of, caused by, amoebae: 阿米巴的;爲阿米巴所引起的: *amoebic dysentery.* 阿米巴痢疾;變形蟲痢疾。

amok /ə'mɒk ; ə'mʌk/ *adv* (also 亦作 **amuck**) ***run ~***, run about wildly and act violently. 橫衝直撞而且行爲兇暴。

among /ə'mʌŋ ; ə'mʌŋ/, **amongst** /ə'mʌŋst ; ə'mʌŋst/ *preps* **1** (showing position) surrounded by; in the middle of: (表示位置)被…所環繞;在…中間: *a village ~ the hills;* 岡巒環繞的村莊; *sitting ~ her children;* 坐在她的孩子們的中間; *hiding ~ the bushes.* 隱藏在樹叢中間。(Note that the *n* or *pron* after *among* must be *pl*) (注意 among 後面的名詞或代名詞必須是複數) Cf 參較 Switzerland is situated *between* France, Italy, Austria and W Germany. **2** (also with a *pl n* or *pron*, or a collective *n*, to show inclusion, association, connection): (亦與複數名詞或代名詞,或集合名詞連用,表示包括在內,有連帶關係)在…之中: *You are only one ~ many who need help.* 你不過是許多需要幫助的人之一。*A~ those present were the Prime Minister, the Bishop of Barchester and Mrs Proudie.* 到場的人士中有首相,巴撒斯特之主教及蒲勞狄夫人。 *I saw him ~ the crowd.* 我看見他在人群之中。 **3** (followed by a superl) one of: (後接最高級形容詞)…之一: *Leeds is ~ the largest industrial towns in England.* 里玆是英國最大工業城市之一。 **4** (indicating division, distribution, possession or joint activity to, for or by more than two persons): (表示涉及二人以上之劃分,分配,所有,聯合活動): *He divided his property ~ his sons.* 他把他的財產分給他的兒子們。*You must settle the matter ~ yourselves.* 你們必須自行解決此事。*They had less than £10 ~ them,* all of them together had less than £10. 他們的錢全部加起來不到十鎊。⇨ between²(7). **5** (after a *prep*): (用於介詞之後): *Choose one from ~ these.* 從這些中間選一個。

amoral /,eɪ'mɒrəl *US:* -'mɔ:rəl ; e'mɔrəl/ *adj* non-moral; not concerned with morals. 非道德的;與道德無關的。

am·or·ous /'æmərəs ; 'æmərəs/ *adj* easily moved to love; showing love; of (esp sexual) love: 多情的;易戀愛的;表示愛情的;愛情的;(尤指)性愛的;色情的: *~ looks;* 脈脈含情的表情; *an ~ young man;* 多情的青年; *~ poetry.* 情詩。 **~·ly** *adv*

amor·phous /ə'mɔ:fəs ; ə'mɔrfəs/ *adj* having no definite shape or form. 無定形的。

amor·tize /ə'mɔ:taɪz *US:* 'æmərt- ; 'æmɚ,taɪz/ *vt* [VP6A] (legal) end (a debt) by setting aside money regularly for future payments. (法律)經常按時撥出一筆金錢藉以逐漸分期清償(債務);攤還。⇨ *sinking fund* at sinking. **amor·ti·za·tion** /ə,mɔ:tɪ'zeɪʃn *US:* ,æmərtɪ- ; ,æmɚtə'zeʃən/ *n*

amount /ə'maʊnt ; ə'maunt/ *vi* [VP3A] **~ to**, add up to; be equal to: 總計;共達;等於: *His debts ~ to £5000.* 他的債務共達五千鎊。*What he said ~ed to very little indeed,* didn't mean much, wasn't important. 他所說的話並不重要。*Riding on a bus without paying the fare ~s to* (= is the same thing as) *cheating the bus company.* 乘公共汽車不付車資等於欺騙公共汽車公司。*It ~s to this, that...,* It means that.... 那就是說…。□ *n* **1** total; whole: 總額;總數: *He owed me £100 but could pay only half that ~,* could only pay £50. 他欠我一百鎊,但是只能償還總數的一半(即五十鎊)。 **2** [C] quantity; 數量: *A large ~ of money is spent on tobacco every year.* 每年都要花費大量金錢在於草上。*There is still quite an ~ of prejudice against him.* 人們對他尙有相當大的偏見。 **any ~ of**, large quantity: 大量: *He has any ~ of money,* is very rich. 他的錢不可數計(極富有之意)。 ***in large/small, etc ~s***, large/small, etc quantities at a time. 大量地;大宗地;大批地(小額地等)。

amour /ə'mʊə(r) ; ə'mʊr/ *n* [C] (facet) love affair: (玩笑語)戀愛: *Don't bore us with accounts of your ~s.* 不要老講你的戀愛史來煩我們。

amour-propre /,æmʊə 'prɒprə ; ,amur'prɔpr/ *n* (F) self-respect; self-esteem. (法)自尊;自重;自負。

amp /æmp ; æmp/ *n* (abbr) (略) = ampere.

am·pere /'æmpeə(r) *US:* 'æmpɪər ; 'æmpɪr/ *n* unit for measuring electric current. 安培(計算電流之單位)。

am·pheta·mine /æm'fetəmi:n ; æm'fɛtə,min/ *n* [C, U] (med) (trade name 商標名 *Benzedrine*) (variety of) drug used medically, eg for slimming, and by drug addicts seeking euphoria. (醫)安非他命(用於減肥或有毒癮者尋求精神欣快之藥物)。

am·phib·ian /æm'fɪbɪən ; æm'fɪbɪən/ *n* **1** animal able to live both on land and in water, eg a frog. 兩棲動物(如青蛙)。 **2** aircraft designed to

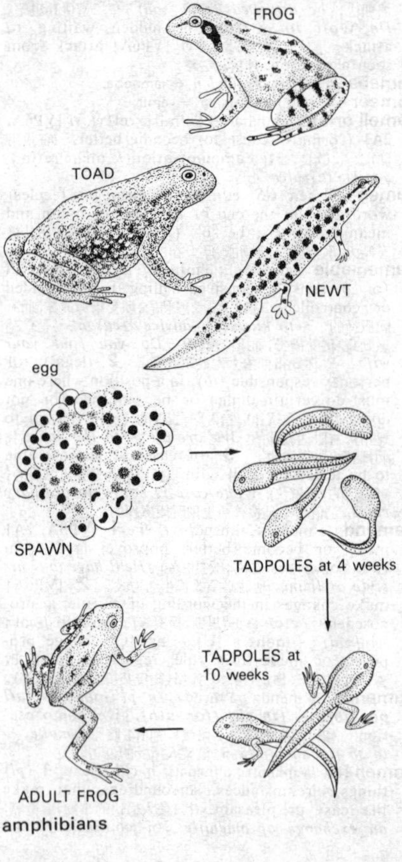

amphibians

take off from and alight on either land or water. 兩棲飛機；水陸兩用飛機。 **3** flat-bottomed vehicle able to move in water and on land: 水陸兩用之平底車輛: (attrib) (形容用法) ~ *tank*. 水陸兩用戰車。

am·phibi·ous /æm'fɪbɪəs ; æm'fɪbɪəs/ *adj* adapted for both land and water: 水陸兩棲的；水陸兩用的: ~ *vehicles,* vehicles that can cross rivers, etc as well as move on land; 兩棲車輛；水陸兩用車輛; ~ *operations,* military operations in which land forces use ~ vehicles when making an invasion from the sea. (陸軍部隊使用兩棲車輛自海上進攻的)兩棲作戰。

amphi·theatre (US = **-ter**) /'æmfɪθɪətə(r) ; 'æmfə,θiətə/ *n* **1** round or oval unroofed building with rows of seats rising behind and above each other round an open space used for public games and amusements. 四周有階梯式座位之露天圓形(或橢圓形)競技場或劇場。 **2** (not US) rows of seats similarly arranged in a half-circle in a theatre. (不用於美)戲院中之半圓形階梯式座位。 **3** (*natural* ~) level space with hills rising on all sides. 四面被小山環繞之一塊平地。

an amphitheatre

am·phora /'æmfərə ; 'æmfərə/ *n* (*pl* ~s or ~e /-riː ; -,ri/) two-handled jar, used in ancient Greece and Rome for holding wine or oil. (古希臘和羅馬用以盛酒或油的)雙柄瓶；雙耳瓶。

ample /'æmpl ; 'æmpl/ *adj* (-r, -st) **1** large-sized; with plenty of space: 大的；廣大的: *This new car has an ~ boot.* 這部新車有一很寬大的行李廂。*There's ~ room for the children on the back seat.* 後座很寬敞足以容納孩子們。 **2** plentiful: 充足的；豐富的: *He has ~ resources,* is wealthy. 他很富裕。 **3** sufficient; quite enough: 足够的；充足的: *£5 will be ~ for my needs.* 五鎊將足够應付我的需要了。**am·ply** /'æmplɪ ; 'æmplɪ/ *adv*: *amply supplied with money,* having more than is needed; 有充足的經費(已超過需要)； *amply rewarded,* well rewarded. 受到豐富的報酬。

am·plify /'æmplɪfaɪ ; 'æmplə,faɪ/ *vt* (*pt, pp* -fied) [VP6A] **1** make larger or fuller, esp give fuller information, more details, etc, about: 擴大；放大；擴充；詳述: ~ *a story/an account.* 詳述故事(將一項敍述作詳細的陳述)。 **2** increase the strength of (voltage or current, etc). 增强(電壓或電流等)。 **am·pli·fi·ca·tion** /,æmplɪfɪ'keɪʃn ; ,æmpləfə'keʃən/ *n* **am·pli·fier** /'æmplɪfaɪə(r) ; 'æmplə,faɪə/ *n* appliance for ~ing. 放大器；擴音器；擴大器；增幅器。

am·pli·tude /'æmplɪtjuːd *US:* -tuːd ; 'æmplə,tjud/ *n* [U] (formal) breadth; largeness; abundance. (正式用語)廣濶；廣大；豐富；充裕。

am·poule (US also **am·pule**) /'æmpuːl ; 'æmpul/ *n* small container, esp for a hypodermic injection. 安瓿(裝一次用量之皮下注射液的小玻璃管)；腹罇；壺腹狀玻管。

am·pu·tate /'æmpjʊteɪt ; 'æmpjə,tet/ *vt* [VP6A] cut off, eg an arm, a leg, by surgery. (以外科手術)截斷(臂，腿等)；切除。 **am·pu·ta·tion** /,æmpjʊ'teɪʃn ; ,æmpjə'teʃən/ *n*

amuck /ə'mʌk ; ə'mʌk/ *adv* ⇨ amok.

amu·let /'æmjʊlɪt ; 'æmjəlɪt/ *n* sth worn in the belief or hope that it will protect the wearer (*against* evil, etc). 護身符；驅邪物。

amuse /ə'mjuːz ; ə'mjuz/ *vt* [VP6A] **1** make time pass pleasantly for: 娛樂；使快樂: *The boys ~d themselves (by) drawing caricatures of their teacher.* 男孩子們畫他們老師的漫畫像以取樂。 *Keep the baby ~d with these toys.* 用這些玩具使嬰兒高興。 **2** make (sb) laugh or smile: 使(某人)笑: *His foolish mistakes ~d all of us.* 他的愚笨的錯誤使我們都發笑。*The children were ~d at/by the story-teller's jokes.* 小孩子們聽了說故事者的笑話，覺得很好笑。*We were ~d to learn that....* 我們獲悉…覺得好笑。**amus·ing** *part adj* causing laughter or smiles: 好笑的；有趣的；引人發笑的: *an amusing story/story-teller.* 好笑的故事(引人發笑的說故事者)。 **~·ment** *n* **1** [U] state of being ~d: 娛樂；快樂: *She couldn't hide her ~ment at his foolish mistake.* 她看到他的愚笨的錯誤，隱藏不住想笑的心情。*To the great ~ment of everybody, the actor's beard fell off.* 使每個人都感到極其好笑的是那演員的鬍鬚掉下來了。*He looked at me in ~ment.* 他很感興趣地望着我。 **2** [C] sth that makes time pass pleasantly: 提供娛樂或消遣的事物；娛樂品；遊樂場所: *There are plenty of ~ments here—cinemas, theatres, concerts, football matches, and so on.* 這裡有很多娛樂——電影院，戲院，音樂會，足球比賽等等。 **'~ment arcade,** room or hall containing pin-tables, gambling machines, etc, esp in large towns, seaside resorts, etc. 遊樂室；遊樂廳(內設彈球臺，賓果機等，尤指在大城鎮，海濱勝地等中者)。**'~ment park/grounds,** place with swings, roundabouts, shooting galleries, and other means of amusing oneself. 兒童樂園；遊樂場 (設有鞦韆，旋轉木馬，打靶場及其他遊樂設備)。 ***places of ~ment,*** cinemas, theatres, etc. 娛樂場所(如電影院，戲院等)。***do sth for ~ment,*** do it as a means of passing time pleasantly, not for a serious purpose. 爲消遣而做某事。

an[1] /ən ; ən; *strong form:* æn ; æn/ *indef art* ⇨ a[2].

an[2] /æn ; æn/ *conj* (old use) if. (舊用法)假若；假使。

anach·ron·ism /ə'nækrənɪzəm ; ə'nækrə,nɪzəm/ *n* [C] **1** mistake in dating sth; sth out of date now or in a description of past events: 年代錯誤；時代錯誤；過時之事物；對過去事件之敘述中與當時的時代不符的事物: *In the sentence 'Julius Caesar looked at his wrist-watch and lifted the telephone receiver' there are two ~s.* 在'凱撒看看他的手錶，拿起電話聽筒'這句話中，有兩項與時代不符的事物。 **2** person, custom, attitude, etc regarded (unfavourably) as out of date: 被視爲過時(不合時宜)的人，習俗，態度等: *Most young people in Britain regard Tory politicians who shoot grouse in Scotland as dreadful ~s.* 大多數的英國青年認爲在蘇格蘭射獵松雞的保守黨政要是討厭的老古董。 **anach·ron·is·tic** /ə,nækrə'nɪstɪk ; ə,nækrə'nɪstɪk/ *adj*

ana·conda /,ænə'kɒndə ; ,ænə'kɑndə/ *n* large snake of tropical S America, esp the kind that crushes its prey. 南美洲的一種熱帶大蟒蛇(尤指能捲死其所捕獲之動物者)。

anae·mia (US = **ane·mia**) /ə'niːmɪə ; ə'nimɪə/ *n* [U] lack of enough blood; poor condition of the blood, causing paleness. 貧血；貧血症。**anaemic** (US = **anemic**) /ə'niːmɪk ; ə'nimɪk/ *adj* suffering from ~. 患貧血症的。

an·aes·thesia (US = **an·es·thesia**) /,ænɪs'θiːzɪə *US:* -'θiːʒə ; ,ænəs'θiʒə/ *n* [U] state of being unable to feel (pain, heat, cold, etc); branch of chemistry concerned with substances producing this state. (對痛，熱，冷等之)感覺缺失；麻木；麻醉；麻醉法；麻醉劑學(化學中之一門)。 **an·aes·thetic** (US = **an·es·thetic**) /,ænɪs'θetɪk ; ,ænəs'θɛtɪk/ *n* [C] substance (eg ether, chloroform), technique, that produces ~: 麻醉藥；麻醉劑(如醚，氯仿)；麻醉術: *under an anaesthetic.* 在麻醉狀態中。 **general anaesthetic,** one affecting the whole body, usu administered in hospital. 全身麻醉藥(通常在醫院中施用者)。 **local anaesthetic,** one administered by injection and affecting only part of the body, eg into the gums by a dentist. 局部麻醉藥(藉注射

使身體局部痲醉,如牙醫注射入齒齦中者)。**an·aes·the·tize** (US = **an·es·the·tize**) /ə'ni:sθətaɪz ; ə'nɛsθə,taɪz/ *vt* [VP6A] make insensible to pain, etc. 使痲醉;施以痲醉劑。**an·aes·the·tist** (US = **an·es·the·tist**) /ə'ni:sθətɪst ; ə'nɛsθətɪst/ *n* person trained to administer anaesthetics. 痲醉師;痲醉士。

ana·gram /'ænəgræm ; 'ænəgræm/ *n* word made by changing the order of the letters in another word (eg plum—lump): 變位字(經變動另一字中字母順序而成之字,例如 plum—lump): *Let's play ～s,* make words of this kind. 我們來玩變位字遊戲。

anal /'eɪnl;'enl̩/ *adj* (anat) of the anus. (解剖) 肛門的。

ana·lects /'ænəlekts ; 'ænə,lɛkts/ (also **ana·lecta** /,ænə'lektə ; ,ænə'lɛktə/) *n pl* collection of pieces of literature: 文選;語錄;選集: *Confucian ～.* 論語。

an·al·gesia /,ænæl'dʒi:zɪə *US:* -ʒə ; ,ænæl'dʒizɪə/ *n* [U] (med) absence of, condition of not feeling, pain. (醫) 痛覺缺失;無痛。**an·al·gesic** /,ænæl'dʒi:sɪk ; ,ænæl'dʒizɪk/ *n* substance, eg an ointment which relieves pain. 止痛藥;鎮痛藥(如止痛軟膏)。

anal·og·ous /ə'næləgəs ; ə'næləgəs/ *adj* ***～ (with),*** similar or parallel (to): 相似的;(與…)類似的: *The two processes are not ～ (with each other).* 這兩種過程(彼此)不相似。 **～·ly** *adv*

ana·logue (also **-log**) /'ænəlɒg *US:* -lɔ:g ; 'ænl̩,ɔg/ *n* **1** sth that is similar to another thing: 類似物: *meat ～,* artificial prepared substitute for meat (usu of soya beans). 人造肉(通常以黃豆加工製成)。 **2** **'～ computer** *n* one which can perform operations on numbers, the numbers being represented by some physical quantity or electrical signal. 類比計算機。⇨ *digital computer* at digit.

anal·ogy /ə'nælədʒɪ ; ə'nælədʒɪ/ *n* (*pl* -gies) **1** [C] partial likeness or agreement. 比喻;相似;類似。 ***draw an ～ between,*** describe the similarities: 在…之間作比喻: *The teacher drew an ～ between the human heart and a pump.* 教師打了一個比喻,把人的心臟比做唧筒。 **2** [U] ***by／from ～; on the ～ of,*** by a process of reasoning between parallel cases: 用類推法;根據…類推: *argue by ～;* 用類推法辯論; *argument by／from ～.* 用類推法所作之議論。

ana·lyse (US = **-lyze**) /'ænəlaɪz ; 'ænl̩,aɪz/ *vt* [VP6A] **1** examine (sth) in order to learn what it is made up of: 分析(某事物)以發現其構造的成分: *If we ～ water, we find that it is made up of two parts of hydrogen and one part of oxygen.* 如果我們分析水,我們就會發現它是由二分氫一分氧構成的。 **2** (gram) split up (a sentence) into its grammatical parts. (文法) 分析(句子)以尋出其文法成分。 **3** study or examine in order to learn about: 分析研究: *The leader tried to ～ the causes of our failure.* 領袖試圖分析研究我們失敗的原因。 **4** = psycho～.

analy·sis /ə'næləsɪs ; ə'næləsɪs/ *n* (*pl* -yses /-əsi:z ; -ə,siz/) **1** [U] (eg of a book, a character, a situation) separation into parts possibly with comment and judgement: (對某一部書,性格,情況等之)分析(可能附帶評判): *critical ～ of literary texts;* 對文學作品本文的批評分析; *expert ～ of market trends,* ie of how prices, sales, etc are likely to go; 專家對市場趨勢所作的分析; [C] instance of this; statement of the result of doing this. 分析的實例;分析結果的說明。⇨ synthesis. **2** = psycho～. **ana·lytic** /,ænə'lɪtɪk ; ,ænl̩'ɪtɪk/, **-i·cal** /-kl ; -kl̩/ *adj* of ～; using ～. 分析的;用分析法的。**ana·lyti·cally** /-klɪ ; -klɪ/ *adv*

ana·lyst /'ænəlɪst ; 'ænl̩ɪst/ *n* **1** person skilled in making (esp chemical) analyses: 分析家;(尤指)化學分析家: *a food ～.* 食物分析家。 **2** = psycho～.

ana·lyze ⇨ analyse.

ana·paest (US = **-pest**) /'ænəpi:st *US:* -pest ; 'ænə,pɛst/ *n* (of verse rhythm) foot consisting of two unaccented syllables followed by one accented syllable, (⏑⏑—) as in eg 'I am 'mon／arch of 'all／I sur'vey'. (指詩律) 抑抑揚格(由兩個輕音節後跟一個重音節組成之音步,例如 'I am 'mon／arch of 'all／I sur'vey')。**ana·paes·tic,** (US = **-pestic**) /,ænə'pi:stɪk *US:* -'pest- ; ,ænə'pɛstɪk/ *adj*

an·archy /'ænəkɪ ; 'ænəkɪ/ *n* [U] absence of government or control; disorder; confusion. 無政府狀態;無秩序;混亂。**an·arch·ism** /-ɪzəm ; -ɪzəm/ *n* [U] political theory that government and laws are undesirable. 無政府主義(認爲不需要政府與法律之政治理論)。**an·arch·ist** /-ɪst ; -ɪst/ *n* person who favours ～; person who wishes to overthrow all established governments. 無政府主義者。**an·archic** /ə'nɑ:kɪk ; æn'ɑrkɪk/ *adj* **an·archi·cally** /-klɪ ; -klɪ/ *adv*

anath·ema /ə'næθəmə ; ə'næθəmə/ *n* **1** (eccles) formal declaration of the Church, excommunicating sb or condemning sth as evil. (教會) 教會的正式聲明(將某人逐出教會或宣布某事物爲邪惡者)。 **2** sth that is detested. 極令人討厭之事物。 **～·tize** /ə'næθəmətaɪz ; ə'næθəmə,taɪz/ *vt, vi* curse. 詛咒。

anat·omy /ə'nætəmɪ ; ə'nætəmɪ/ *n* [U] science of the structure of animal bodies; study of their structures by separation into parts. 解剖學;解剖。**ana·tomi·cal** /,ænə'tɒmɪkl;,ænə'tɑmɪkl̩/ *adj* **anat·om·ist** /-ɪst ; -ɪst/ *n* person who dissects corpses; person who studies or teaches ～. 解剖屍體者;解剖學家。

an·ces·tor /'ænsestə(r) ; 'ænsɛstɚ/ *n* any one of those persons from whom one is descended, esp one more remote than a grandparent: 祖先; 祖宗(尤指祖父母或外祖父母以上者)。 **～ worship,** the worship of one's ～s as spirits or gods. 祭祖。**an·ces·tress** /-trɪs ; -trɪs/ *n* woman ～. 女祖先;女祖宗。**an·ces·tral** /æn'sestrəl ; æn'sɛstrəl/ *adj* belonging to, having come from, one's ～s: 祖先的;祖宗傳下的: *his ancestral home.* 他的祖居。**an·ces·try** /'ænsestrɪ ; 'ænsɛstrɪ/ *n* (*pl* -ries) line of ～s. 祖先;祖系。

an·chor /'æŋkə(r) ; 'æŋkɚ/ *n* heavy piece of iron with a ring at one end, to which a cable is fastened, used for keeping a ship fast to the sea bottom or a balloon to the ground; anything that gives stability or security. (繫船或汽球用的) 錨;予人穩定或安全感之事物; 藉以支持或依靠之物。 ***let go／drop／cast the ～,*** lower it. 下錨。***weigh ～,*** raise it. 起錨。***come to ～; bring (a ship) to ～,*** stop sailing and lower the ～. 錨泊;下錨;將(船隻)停航並下錨。***lie／ride／be at ～,*** be made fast and held safe by the ～. 停泊妥當;停泊着。**～·man** /-mən ; -mən/, one who co-ordinates the work of a group of persons who work together, eg in a radio or TV studio. 協調員(協調一工作組之工作者);(廣播電台或電視台新聞節目等中之)主播。□ *vt, vi* [VP6A] make (a ship) secure with an ～; [VP2A] lower an ～. 下錨以使(船)停泊穩定;下錨。 **～·age** /-rɪdʒ ; -rɪdʒ/ *n* place where ships may ～ safely. 船隻可安全停泊之處所;錨地;泊地。

an·chor·ite /'æŋkəraɪt ; 'æŋkə,raɪt/ *n* hermit. 隱士;隱居者。

an·chovy /'æntʃəvɪ ; 'æntʃəvɪ/ *n* (*pl* -vies) small fish of the herring family; it has a strong flavour and is used for sauces, etc: 鯷類魚; 鱒魚: (attrib) (形容用法) *～ paste／sauce.* 鯷魚醬(鱒魚汁)。

ancient /'eɪnʃənt ; 'enʃənt/ *adj* **1** belonging to times long past: 古代的; 遠古的: *～ Rome and Greece;* 古羅馬及希臘; *the ～s,* the civilized people who lived long ago. 古人;古代的文明人。 **2** (often hum) very old: (常作詼諧用語) 舊式的; 很舊的: *an ～-looking hat.* 一頂樣子很舊的帽子。

an·cil·lary /æn'sɪlərɪ *US:* 'ænsəlerɪ ; 'ænsə,lɛrɪ/ *adj* **1** helping, providing a service to those carrying on the main business of an enterprise: 輔助的: *The transport corps is ～ to the infantry.* 運輸隊是步兵的輔助部隊。 **2** subordinate (*to*): 附屬的: *～ roads／undertakings／industries.* 附屬道路(事業,工業)。

and /*usu forms:* ən, ənd ; ən, ənd; (*after* t, d, f, v, θ, ð, s, z, ʃ, ʒ) *often* n; n; *strong form:* ænd ; ænd/ *conj* **1** (connecting words, clauses, sentences): (連接單字,子句,句子)和,及;與: *a table and four chairs;* 一張桌子和四把椅子; *learning to read and write.* 學習讀和寫。(When two *nn* stand for things or persons closely connected, the determining word is not repeated before the second *n*): (當兩個名詞代表互有密切關係之物或人時,第二個名詞前之指定詞不要重複): *a knife and fork.* 一副刀叉。Cf 參較 a knife and a spoon; 一把刀及一把湯匙; *my father and mother.* 我的父母。Cf 參較 my father and my uncle. 我的父親和我的叔父。 **2** (Note *twenty-five* but *five and twenty*, sometimes used in telling the time): (注意: twenty-five 亦可寫成 five and twenty, 後者有時用以指鐘點): *five and twenty to six.* 五點三十五分。 **3** (In constructions replacing an *if*-clause): (用於代替'假設'子句的構造中): *Work hard and you will pass* (=If you work hard, you will pass) *the examination.* 你若是用功讀書,就會考及格。 **4** (indicating intensive repetition or continuation): (表示加强語意的重複或連續不斷之意): *for hours and hours;* 許多許多小時; *for miles and miles;* 很多很多哩; *better and better.* 愈來愈好。*We knocked and knocked,* continued to knock. 我們敲了又敲(繼續不斷地敲門)。 **5** (colloq) to: (俗) = to: *Try and come early.* 儘量早來。*Go and buy one.* 去買一個。

an·dante /ænˈdæntɪ ; ænˈdæntɪ/ *n, adj, adv* (I; music) (piece of music to be played) in moderately slow time. (義;音樂)以適度緩慢的拍子(來演奏的樂曲);用中慢板的;行板。

and·iron /ˈændaɪən ; ˈænd,aɪɚn/ *n* iron support (usu one of a pair) for holding logs in a fireplace. 柴架 (壁爐中用以支架木柴之鐵架,通常指一對柴架中之一隻)。Also called 亦稱作 *firedog.*

an·ec·dote /ˈænɪkdəʊt ; ˈænɪk,dot/ *n* short, usu amusing, story about some real person or event. 軼事;趣聞(關於眞人眞事之小趣事)。

ane·mia, ane·mic ⇨ anaemia, anaemic.

anem·om·eter /ˌænɪˈmɒmɪtə(r) ; ˌænəˈmɑmətɚ/ *n* [C] (met) instrument for measuring the force and velocity of the wind. (氣象)風速表;風力計(測定風力及風速之儀器)。

anem·one /əˈnemənɪ ; əˈnɛmə,ni/ *n* **1** (bot) (also called 亦稱 *wind-flower*) small star-shaped woodland flower; cultivated varieties of this flower. (植物)白頭翁(生長於森林地帶之星狀小花);秋牡丹(白頭翁之園藝變種)。 **2** ˈ**sea** ~, popular name of a creature living in the sea, having a tube-like body with tentacles. 海葵(一種海生動物之通俗名稱,有帶鬚之管狀軀體)。

an anemone

a sea anemone

anent /əˈnent ; əˈnɛnt/ *prep* (old use, or Scot) concerning; about. (舊用法,或蘇格蘭語)關於。

an·er·oid /ˈænərɔɪd ; ˈænə,rɔɪd/ *adj, n* ~ **(barometer),** one that measures air-pressure by the action of air on the elastic lid of a box partly exhausted of air. 不用液體的;無液晴雨表;空盒氣壓表。

an·es·thesia *n* ⇨ anaesthesia.

anew /əˈnjuː *US:* əˈnuː ; əˈnju/ *adv* again; in a new or different way. 重新;再一次;以一種新的或不同的方式。

angel /ˈeɪndʒl ; ˈendʒəl/ *n* **1** (esp in Christian belief) messenger from God (usu shown in pictures as a human being in white with wings). (尤指基督教所相信之) 天使 (在圖畫中通常作人形,穿白衣,有翼)。 **2** lovely or innocent person. 可愛或純潔的人。 **3** (as a compliment to sb who is kind, thoughtful, etc): (對仁慈,體貼等之人的恭維語): *Thanks, you're an ~!* 謝謝,你眞是個大好人! **~ic** /ænˈdʒelɪk ; ænˈdʒɛlɪk/ *adj* of or like an ~. 天使的;如天使的。**~i·cally** /-klɪ ; -klɪ/ *adv*

an·gelica /ænˈdʒelɪkə ; ænˈdʒɛlɪkə/ *n* [U] sweet-smelling plant, esp the kind used in cooking and medicine; its stem, boiled in sugar. 羌活;白芷(一種有甜味之植物,用於烹調及醫藥);白芷根之蜜餞。

an·gelus /ˈændʒɪləs ; ˈændʒələs/ *n* (also 亦作 **A~**) (bell rung in RC churches at morning, noon and sunset to call people to recite) prayer to the Virgin Mary. (天主教在早晨,中午及日落時所敲之)奉告祈禱鐘;奉告祈禱。

anger /ˈæŋgə(r) ; ˈæŋgɚ/ *n* [U] the strong feeling that comes when one has been wronged or insulted, or when one sees cruelty or injustice; the feeling that makes people want to quarrel or fight: 怒;忿怒: *filled with ~ at what he saw;* 對於他所見到的事感到憤怒; *speak in ~;* 忿怒地說話; *do sth in a moment of ~.* 在一時的忿怒之下做出某事。□ *vt* [VP6A] fill (sb) with ~; make angry: 使(某人)發怒;激怒: *He is easily ~ed.* 他容易被激怒。

an·gina pec·toris /ænˌdʒaɪnə ˈpektərɪs ; ænˈdʒaɪnə ˈpɛktərɪs/ *n* (Lat) (path) heart disease marked by sharp pain in the chest. (拉) (病理)心絞痛;胸氣塞;狹心症。

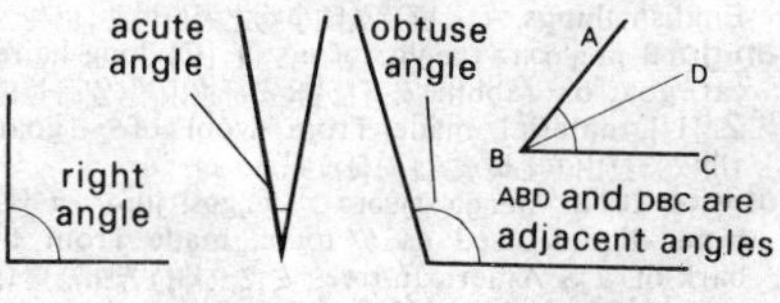

angles

angle¹ /ˈæŋgl ; ˈæŋgl/ *n* **1** space between two lines or surfaces that meet. 角;隅。ˈ**~-dozer** *n* mechanical scraper used for levelling roads or ground surfaces. (用以弄平路面或地面的) 斜鏟推土機。⇨ bulldozer. ˈ**~-iron** *n* L-shaped length of iron or steel used to strengthen a framework. (用以加强構架之L形的)角鐵。ˈ**~-park** *vt, vi* park a vehicle at an angle to the side of the roadway, etc: 與馬路等邊側成一角度停放汽車: *cars ~-parked as close as herringbones.* 停放在馬路邊側彼此密接如鯡魚骨般的汽車。 **2** (fig) point of view: (喩)觀點;看法;角度: *Try looking at the affair from a different ~.* 試從不同的角度來看這件事。*What ~ are you writing the story from?* 你是從何種觀點來寫這故事? □ *vt* [VP6A] *~ the news,* present it to the public in a particular way (usu to suit the bias of the writer or his employer). 從某一特殊觀點報導新聞(通常爲迎合報導者或其僱主之偏見);歪曲報導新聞。

angle² /ˈæŋgl ; ˈæŋgl/ *vi* [VP2A, 3A] **1** fish (for trout, etc) with a rod, line, hook and bait. 釣(魚)。 **2** ~ ***for,*** (fig) use tricks, hints, etc in order to get sth: (喩)使用手腕,暗示等以求獲得某物;引誘;謀取: *~ for compliments;* 求取旁人的讚譽; *~ for an invitation to a party.* 設法讓人邀請參加某宴會。**ang·ler** /ˈæŋglə(r) ; ˈæŋglɚ/ *n* person who ~s. 釣(魚)者。Cf 參較 *fisherman* using nets, etc. 漁夫;漁人(用網等捕魚者)。**ang·ling** *n* [U] (art, sport of) fishing with a rod. 釣魚;釣魚術;垂釣。

Ang·li·can /ˈæŋglɪkən ; ˈæŋglɪkən/ *n, adj* (member)

of the Church of England. 英國國教的；英國國教徒。

ang·li·cize /ˈæŋglɪsaɪz ; ˈæŋgləˌsaɪz/ *vt* [VP6A] make English or like English: 使成爲英文；英語化；英國化：～ *a French word.* 使一法文字成爲英文字。 **ang·li·cism** /ˈæŋglɪsɪzəm ; ˈæŋgləˌsɪzəm/ *n* English way of saying sth. 英語語風；英國人的說法。

Anglo- /ˌæŋgləʊ ; ˈæŋglo/ *pref* English: 英國的：*～-French relations*, between GB and France. 英法關係。ˌ**～-ˈCatholic** *n, adj* (member) of the party in the Anglican Church that insists upon its unbroken connection with the early Christian Church and that objects to being called Protestant. 英國國教高教會派（堅持其與早期基督教繼續不斷的關係，並反對被稱爲新教派）的；英國國教高教會派之教徒。ˌ**～-ˈIndian** *n, adj* **(a)** (person) of British birth, living or having lived, in India. 英國出生而居於印度的（人）。**(b)** (person) of mixed British and Indian blood; Eurasian. 英印混血的（人）。ˌ**～-ˈSaxon** *n, adj* (person) of English descent; one of the group of people who settled in England (from NW Europe) before the Norman Conquest; their language (also called *Old English*). 英國人（的）；盎格魯撒克遜人（在諾爾曼人征服英國之前自歐洲西北部移居英格蘭者）；盎格魯撒克遜語（亦稱古英語）。

Anglo·mania /ˌæŋgləʊˈmeɪnɪə ; ˌæŋgləˈmenɪə/ *n* excessive love of and admiration for English customs, etc. 對於英國事物之過份喜愛與讚賞；英國狂。

Anglo·phile /ˈæŋgləʊfaɪl ; ˈæŋgləˌfaɪl/ (also **-phil** /-fɪl ; -fɪl/) *n* person who loves England or English things. 親英者；醉心於英國事物者。

Anglo·phobe /ˈæŋgləʊfəʊb ; ˈæŋgləˌfob/ *n* person who hates or fears England or English things. 憎惡或恐懼英國或英國事物的人；仇英者。

Anglo·phobia /ˌæŋgləʊˈfəʊbɪə ; ˌæŋgləˈfobɪə/ *n* excessive hatred or fear of England and of English things. 對英國及英國事物之過份憎惡；仇英。

an·gora /æŋˈgɔːrə ; æŋˈgɔrə/ *n* **1** [C] long-haired cat, goat or rabbit. 安哥拉貓；安哥拉山羊；安哥拉兔。**2** [U] material made from wool of ～ goats. (用安哥拉山羊毛織成之) 安哥拉呢。

an·gos·tura /ˌæŋgəˈstjʊərə ; ˌæŋgəsˈtjʊrə/ *n* [U] bitter liquid, used as a tonic, made from the bark of a S American tree. 安戈士都拉苦味補藥（用產於南美洲之一種樹皮調製成的苦味液）。

angry /ˈæŋgrɪ ; ˈæŋgrɪ/ *adj* (-ier, -iest) **1** filled with anger (*with* sb, *at* what sb does or says, *about* sth): 忿怒的；發怒的；生氣的（後接 with 某人，at 某人之言行，about 某事）：*He was ～ at being kept waiting.* 他因久候而生氣。*He was ～ with himself for having made such a foolish mistake.* 他因犯如此愚蠢的錯誤而氣惱自己。*He will be ～ to learn* (= when he learns) *that you have disobeyed his orders.* 他得知你違背他的命令，將會生氣的。**2** (of a cut, sore, wound) red; inflamed. (指刀傷，瘡，傷口) 發紅的；發炎的；紅腫的。**3** (of the sea, sky, clouds) stormy; threatening. (指海，天，雲) 狂風暴雨的；狂烈的；翻騰的。**ang·ri·ly** /-əlɪ ; -əlɪ/ *adv*

angst /æŋst ; ɑŋst/ *n* [U] (G) feeling of anxiety (eg caused by considering the state of world affairs). (德) 焦慮；恐怖（如因考慮世界局勢所引起者）。

an·guish /ˈæŋgwɪʃ ; ˈæŋgwɪʃ/ *n* [U] severe suffering (esp of mind): (尤指心理上的) 劇烈痛苦；苦惱；苦悶：*She was in ～ until she knew that her husband's life had been saved.* 她心裡一直很痛苦，直到她知道她丈夫的生命已經得救才放心。**～ed** *adj* expressing ～: 表現痛苦的；顯得苦惱的：*～ed looks.* 痛苦的表情。

angu·lar /ˈæŋgjʊlə(r) ; ˈæŋgjələ/ *adj* **1** having angles or sharp corners. 有角的；有尖角的。**2** (of persons) with the shape of the bones showing under the skin; (of a person's nature, etc) rather stiff and awkward: (指人) 骨瘦如柴的；瘦削的；(指人的性情等) 執拗的；不圓滑的；不靈活的：*an ～ gait.* 僵挺的步態。**～·ity** /ˌæŋgjʊˈlærətɪ ; ˌæŋgjəˈlærətɪ/ *n* (*pl* -ties).

ani·line /ˈænɪliːn *US:* ˈænəlɪn ; ˈænḷˌin/ *n* substance obtained chemically from coal-tar, used in the manufacture of dyes, drugs, etc. 苯胺（用化學方法自煤焦油中提出的物質，用於製造染料、藥品等）。

ani·mad·vert /ˌænɪmædˈvɜːt ; ˌænəmædˈvɝt/ *vi* [VP 3A] *～ (on)*, (formal) make (esp critical) remarks (about sb's conduct). (正式用語) 批評；指謫；非難。**ani·mad·version** /ˌænɪmædˈvɜːʃn *US:* -ʒn ; ˌænəmædˈvɝʒən/ *n* criticism. 批評；指謫；非難。

ani·mal /ˈænɪml ; ˈænəmḷ/ *n* **1** living thing that can feel and move about. Men, dogs, birds, flies, fish and snakes are all ～s. 動物（如人，狗，鳥，蠅，魚，蛇等皆是）。**the ˈ～ kingdom**, one of three divisions (the others being *vegetable* and *mineral*). 動物界（博物學上三種類別之一，其他二界爲植物界及礦物界）。⇨ the illus at ape, bird, cat, dog, domestic, fish, insect, large, reptile, sea, small. 參看 ape, bird, cat, dog, domestic, fish, insect, large, reptile, sea, small 之插圖。**2** four-footed ～ (eg a dog or a horse): 獸；四足動物（如狗，馬等）：～ *husbandry*, the breeding of cattle, sheep, horses, etc. 畜牧業（牛，羊，馬等的飼養）。**3** ～ other than man. 除人以外的動物。**4** (used attrib) of the physical, not spiritual, side of man: (形容用法) 人之肉體（非精神）方面的：～ *needs*, eg food; 肉體上的需要（如食物）；～ *desires.* 肉慾。**～ spirits**, natural light-heartedness. 天生的愉快精神。**～·cule** /ˌænɪˈmælkjuːl ; ˌænəˈmælkjʊl/ *n* microscopically small ～. 微生動物。

ani·mate /ˈænɪmət ; ˈænəmɪt/ *adj* living; lively. 有生命的；活的；生氣勃勃的。□ *vt* /ˈænɪmeɪt ; ˈænəmet/ [VP6A, 14] **～ *sb/sth (to/with sth)***, give life to; make lively; inspire: 賦予生命；鼓舞；使活潑；使有生氣：*A smile ～d her face.* 笑容使她的臉上平添無限生氣。*There was an ～d discussion.* 有一場熱烈的討論。*The news ～d us to greater efforts/with greater enthusiasm.* 這消息鼓勵我們作更大的努力（激起我們更大的狂熱）。*All his life this great man was ～d by a passion for truth and justice.* 這個偉人畢生熱愛眞理和正義。ˌ**～d carˈtoon**, cinema film made by photographing a series of drawings. 卡通影片。**ani·ma·tion** /ˌænɪˈmeɪʃn ; ˌænəˈmeʃən/ *n* [U] (esp) liveliness; ardour. (尤指) 活潑；有生氣；熱心。

ani·mism /ˈænɪmɪzəm ; ˈænəˌmɪzəm/ *n* [U] belief that all objects (trees, stones, the wind, etc) have souls. 萬物（樹，石，風等）有靈論；泛靈信仰。

ani·mos·ity /ˌænɪˈmɒsətɪ ; ˌænəˈmɑsətɪ/ *n* [U] **～ *(against/towards/between)***, strong dislike, active enmity; [C] (*pl* -ties) instance of this. 憎惡；仇恨；敵意；仇視；此種情緒之實例。

ani·mus /ˈænɪməs ; ˈænəməs/ *n* [U] animosity; (with *indef art*) instance of this: 憎惡；仇恨；敵意；仇視；(與不定冠詞連用) 此種情緒之實例：*an ～ against me.* 對我的一種仇視。

an·ise /ˈænɪs ; ˈænɪs/ *n* plant with sweet-smelling seeds. 大茴香。**ani·seed** /ˈænɪsiːd ; ˈænɪˌsid/ *n* [U] seed of ～, used for flavouring. 大茴香子（調味用）。

ankle /ˈæŋkl ; ˈæŋkḷ/ *n* joint connecting the foot with the leg; thin part of the leg between this joint and the calf. 踝；脚脖子。⇨ the illus at leg. 參看 leg 之插圖。ˈ**～ socks**, short ones just covering the ～s. 僅蓋住脚脖子的短襪。**ank·let** /ˈæŋklɪt ; ˈæŋklɪt/ *n* ornament for the ～. 踝飾；脚鐲。

anna /ˈænə ; ˈænə/ *n* former copper coin in Pakistan and in India, a sixteenth part of a rupee. 安那（巴基斯坦及印度往昔之一種銅幣，等於一盧比之十六分之一）。

an·nals /ˈænlz ; ˈænḷz/ *n pl* story of events year by year; record of new knowledge or discoveries written year by year; yearly record of the work of a learned society. 編年史；(新知識或新發現之) 紀年表；年鑑；(學會之) 年報。**an·nal·ist** /ˈænəlɪst ; ˈænḷɪst/ *n* writer of ～. 編年史作者；紀年表作者；年報編輯人。

an·neal /əˈniːl ; əˈnil/ *vt* [VP6A] cool (metals, glass, etc) very slowly after heating, in order to toughen and temper. 加熱於(金屬,玻璃等)然後緩緩冷却,使之韌化;退火。

an·nex[1] /əˈneks ; əˈnɛks/ *vt* [VP6A, 14] **1** take possession of (territory, etc). 併吞;霸佔(領土等)。**2** ~ *(to)*, add or join (sth) (as an extra part *to* sth). 合併(某物)(作爲另外某物之附屬部份,與to連用,後接另外的某物)。**~·ation** /ˌænekˈseɪʃn ; ˌænɛksˈeʃən/ *n* [U] ~ing; [C] instance of this, that which is ~ed. 併吞;合併;併吞或合併之實例;合併地;附加物。

an·nex[2] /ˈænəks ; ˈænɛks/ (also **an·nexe**) *n* [C] **1** smaller building added to, or situated near, a larger one: 增添之較小建築;附屬建築物;擴建部份;別館: *an ~ to a hotel.* 旅館之附屬建築物(或指擴建部份)。**2** addition (*to* a document). (文件之)附件(與 to 連用)。

an·ni·hi·late /əˈnaɪəleɪt ; əˈnaɪəˌlet/ *vt* [VP6A] destroy completely; end the existence of (eg an army, a fleet): 徹底消滅;毀滅;殲滅;摧毁(如軍隊,艦隊): *The invasion force was ~d.* 入侵的部隊被殲滅了。(fig) (喩) *Radio communication has ~d space.* 無線電通訊已消除了空間的隔閡。**an·ni·hi·la·tion** /əˌnaɪəˈleɪʃn ; əˌnaɪəˈleʃən/ *n* [U] complete destruction (of military or naval forces, etc). 徹底消滅;殲滅;摧毁(指陸海軍等)。

an·ni·ver·sary /ˌænɪˈvɜːsərɪ ; ˌænəˈvɝsərɪ/ *n* [C] (*pl* -ries) yearly return of the date of an event; celebration of this: 週年紀念日;週年紀念: *my wedding ~;* 我的結婚週年紀念; *the ~ of Shakespeare's birth;* 莎士比亞誕辰紀念日; *an ~ dinner,* one held to celebrate an ~. 週年紀念餐會。

Anno Domini /ˌænəʊ ˈdɒmɪnaɪ ; ˈæno ˈdɑməˌnaɪ/ (Lat) (abbr 略作 **AD** /ˌeɪ ˈdiː ; ˈeˈdi/) in the year of our Lord: (拉)公元;西元;耶穌紀元後: *in* AD *250,* 250 years after the birth of Jesus. 於公元250年。⇨ *before Christ* (BC) at before[3]; ⇨ BC in App 2. 參看附錄二之 BC。

an·no·tate /ˈænəteɪt ; ˈænoˌtet/ *vt* [VP6A] add notes (to a book, etc) explaining difficulties, giving opinions, etc: 給(書等)作註釋: *an ~d text／version.* 加有註釋的本文(譯本)。**an·no·ta·tion** /ˌænəˈteɪʃn ; ˌænoˈteʃən/ *n* [U] annotating; [C] note or comment. 註釋;註解。

an·nounce /əˈnaʊns ; əˈnaʊns/ *vt* [VP6A, 9, 14] **1** make known: 宣布;通告;發表: *Mr Green ~d (to his friends) his engagement to Miss White.* 格林先生(向他的朋友們)宣布他與懷特小姐訂婚。*It has been ~d that Mr Green and Miss White will be married in May.* 格林先生與懷特小姐已宣布將於五月結婚。*The book was ~d as in preparation.* 根據預告該書正在印刷中。*The Government ~d that the danger was past.* 政府宣布危險業已過去。**2** make known the arrival of: 通報;宣告…的來臨: *The secretary ~d Mr and Mrs Brown,* spoke their names as they entered. 秘書通報布朗夫婦已到(卽在他們進入時報出他們的姓名)。**3** say that sb is about to speak, sing, etc (eg in a TV programme). (如在電視節目中)報告某人卽將發表談話,歌唱等。**~·ment** *n* [C] sth said, written, or printed to make known what has happened or (more often) what will happen: 通告;布告;告示: *a broadcast ~ment.* 廣播之通告。*An ~ment will be made next week.* 下週將發出一項通告。*A~ments of deaths, marriages and births appear in the newspapers.* 死亡,結婚,出生等各種啓事均可見於報紙上。**an·noun·cer** *n* (esp) person who ~s speakers, singers, etc in a radio or TV broadcast. 報告員;(尤指)廣播員;播音員;無線電廣播或電視之節目主持人。

an·noy /əˈnɔɪ ; əˈnɔɪ/ *vt* [VP6A esp in passive] ***be ~ed with sb／at sth／about sth,*** irritate; make rather angry: (尤用於被動語態)打攪;煩擾;使煩惱;使頗爲生氣: *He was ~ed with his wife because the dinner was badly cooked.* 他對他的妻子感到生氣,因那頓飯做得不好。*I felt ~ed when he refused to help.* 當他拒絕幫忙時,我覺得有點生氣。*Do stop ~ing your father!* 別再煩你父親了! *He was ~ed to learn that the train would be delayed.* 他聽說火車要誤點,心裡感到煩惱。*He felt／got／was ~ed with the boy for being so stupid／was ~ed at the boy's stupidity.* 他爲了這孩子如此的愚笨而感到煩惱。**~·ing** *part adj*: *It's ~ing to miss a train.* 趕不上火車是煩人的事。*How ~ing!* 眞討厭!煩死人! *The ~ing thing about it is that...,* What causes trouble or irritation is that.... 討厭的是…; 麻煩的是…。**~·ance** /-əns ; -əns/ *n* **1** [U] vexation; being ~ed: 煩厭;煩惱: *with a look of ~ance;* 帶着煩惱的表情; *much to our ~ance;* 十分使我們討厭地; *subject a person to ~ance,* worry him. 使某人受騷擾。**2** [C] sth that ~s: 可厭之事;煩惱之事: *All these little ~ances did not spoil her sweet temper.* 這一切小小的煩擾並未損及她的好脾氣。

an·nual /ˈænjʊəl ; ˈænjʊəl/ *adj* **1** coming or happening every year. 一年一次的。**2** lasting for only one year or season. 一年生的;僅持續一年或一季的。**3** of one year: 一年的: *his ~ income;* 他每年的收入; *the ~ production.* 年產量。□ *n* **1** plant that lives for one year or season. 一年生植物;一季生植物。ˌ**hardy** ˈ**~,** (joc) event, etc which often recurs (and is considered tiresome or monotonous). (謔)一再發生的事件(被認爲是麻煩或單調沒趣者)。**2** book, etc that appears under the same title but with new contents every year. 年鑑;年刊;年報。**~·ly** *adv*

an·nu·ity /əˈnjuːətɪ *US:* -ˈnuː- ; əˈnuətɪ/ *n* [C] (*pl* -ties) fixed sum of money paid to sb yearly as income during his lifetime; form of insurance to provide such a regular, annual income. 年金;養老金;養老金保險。**an·nui·tant** /əˈnjuːɪtənt *US:* -ˈnuː- ; əˈnuətənt/ *n* person who receives an ~. 領年金者;領養老金者。

an·nul /əˈnʌl ; əˈnʌl/ *vt* (-ll-) [VP6A] put an end to, eg an agreement, a law, etc; declare (that sth, eg a marriage, is) invalid, of no effect. 廢止(契約,法律等);取消(婚姻等);宣告無效。**~·ment** *n*

an·nu·lar /ˈænjʊlə(r) ; ˈænjələr/ *adj* (rare) ring-like. (罕)環狀的;如環的。

an·nun·ci·ate /əˈnʌnsɪeɪt ; əˈnʌnʃɪˌet/ *vt* [VP6A] (formal) announce; proclaim. (正式用語)宣布;宣告。

an·nun·ci·ation /əˌnʌnsɪˈeɪʃn ; əˌnʌnsɪˈeʃən/ *n* **the A~,** (eccles) the announcement by the angel Gabriel to Mary that she was to be the mother of Jesus Christ; festival that commemorates this, 25 Mar. (教會)天使加百列向聖母馬利亞奉告她將生耶穌;天使報喜;天使報喜節(三月廿五日)。

an·ode /ˈænəʊd ; ˈænod/ *n* (electr) (電) (US also called 美亦稱 *plate*) **1** positively charged electrode (from which current enters). 陽極;正極。⇨ cathode. **2** negative terminal of a battery. 電池的陰極接頭。

ano·dyne /ˈænədaɪn ; ˈænəˌdaɪn/ *n, adj* (medicine, drug) able to lessen pain; (sth) able to give comfort to the mind. 止痛的;止痛藥;鎭痛藥;能給予心靈以安慰的(事物)。

anoint /əˈnɔɪnt ; əˈnɔɪnt/ *vt* [VP6A, 23, 14] apply oil or ointment to (esp as a religious ceremony): 塗油;搽油;塗膏(尤指作爲一種宗教儀式而爲者): *~ sb with oil.* 將油塗在某人身上。*The Lord ~ed thee King over Israel* (⇨ I Sam 15 : 17). 耶和華膏你作以色列的王 (參看舊約聖經撒母耳記上第 15 章第 17 節)。**~·ment** *n*

anom·al·ous /əˈnɒmələs ; əˈnɑmələs/ *adj* irregular; different in some way from what is normal. 不規則的;變則的。**~ verb,** verb that forms its interr and neg without the helping verb *do* (eg *must, ought*). 變則動詞(指不用助動詞 do 而能構成疑問式及否定式之動詞,如 must, ought 是)。**~·ly** *adv* **anom·aly** /əˈnɒməlɪ ; əˈnɑməlɪ/ *n* (*pl* -lies) ~ thing: 反常之事物;異例: *A bird that cannot fly is an anomaly.* 一隻不會飛的鳥是一個異例。

anon[1] /əˈnɒn ; əˈnɑn/ *adv* (old use) soon. (舊用法)不久;未幾。***ever and ~,*** every now and then. 時

時地;不時地。

anon² /ə'nɒn ; ə'nɑn/ (in footnotes, etc) short for *by an anonymous author.* (用於註脚等中)爲未具名作家所作;作者不詳(爲 by an anonymous author 之略)。

ano·nym·ity /ˌænə'nɪmətɪ ; ˏænə'nɪmətɪ/ *n* [U] state of being anonymous. 無名;匿名;作者不明。

anony·mous /ə'nɒnɪməs ; ə'nɑnəməs/ *adj* without a name, or with a name that is not made known: 無名的;不具名的;匿名的: *an ~ letter,* not signed; 匿名信; *an ~ gift,* from sb whose name is not known; 由無名氏送的贈品; *an author who remains ~.* 一直不具名的作家。~·**ly** *adv*

anoph·eles /ə'nɒfɪliːz ; ə'nɑfəˏliz/ *n* (kinds of) mosquito, esp the kinds that spread malaria. 蚊;(尤指)瘧蚊;斑翅蚊。⇨ the illus at insect. 參看 insect 之插圖。

an·or·ak /'ænəræk ; 'ɑnəˏrɑk/ *n* [C] jacket with a hood attached, worn as protection against rain, wind and cold; wind-cheater. (禦雨、風、寒,附有風帽的)防風夾克。

an·other /ə'nʌðə(r) ; ə'nʌðɚ/ *pron, adj* ⇨ other. **1** an additional (one): 再一;又一: *Will you have ~ cup of tea?* 你要再喝一杯茶嗎? *Where shall we be in ~ ten years,* ten years from now? 再過十年我們的情況將變成什麼樣子? *I don't like this hat; please show me ~ (one).* 我不喜歡這頂帽子;請再給我拿一頂看看。 **2** a similar (one): 相似的(一個);類似的(一個): *This young man is very clever; he may be ~ Edison,* an inventor as clever as Edison. 這個年輕人很聰明;他可能成爲另一個愛廸生(如愛廸生一樣聰明的發明家)。 **3** a different (one): 不同的(一個);另一個: *We can do that ~ time.* 我們可以下一次再做。*That's quite ~ matter.* 那完全是另一回事。*Taking one thing／year, etc with ~,* on the whole, taking the average (of good and bad, etc). 大體而言;平均說來。**one ~,** ⇨ one³(3).

answer¹ /'ɑːnsə(r) *US:* 'æn- ; 'ænsɚ/ *n* ~ ***(to),*** **1** sth done in return; reply: (對…的)回答;答覆;答辯: *Have you had an ~ to your letter?* 你的信是否已有回信? *She gave no ~,* said nothing in return. 她沒有回答。*I have a complete ~ to the accusation,* can prove that it was wrongly made. 對於該項控告我能證明其全屬子虛。***in ~ (to),*** as a reply (to): 作爲對於…的回答;應…之請求: *in ~ to your letter.* 應來函之請求。*The doctor came at once in ~ to my telephone call.* 醫生應我電話之請求而立卽到來。 **2** solution; result of working with figures, etc: 答案;解答: *The ~ to* 3×17 *is* 51. 3×17 的答案是 51。***have／know all the ~s,*** know, or believe one knows, a great deal about sth. 對某事物知之甚詳。

answer² /'ɑːnsə(r) *US:* 'æn- ; 'ænsɚ/ *vt, vi* **1** [VP6A, 9, 12A, 2A] say, write or do, sth in return (to): (用口說,筆寫或行動)答覆;回答: *~ a question;* 回答一個問題; *~ the teacher.* 回答老師。*He ~ed nothing.* 他沒有回答。*What shall I ~?* 我將怎樣回答呢? *Have you ~ed his letter?* 你回了他的信嗎? *He ~ed that he knew nothing about it.* 他答覆說關於此事他一無所知。*No one ~ed.* 沒有一個人回答。*No one was able to ~ him a word* (⇨ Matt 22:46). 沒有一個人能回答一言(參看新約聖經馬太福音第22章第46節)。*A~ me this question.* 回答我這個問題。***~ the door／the bell,*** go to the door when sb has knocked or rung the bell. 應門(有人敲門或按門鈴時前往開門)。***~ the telephone,*** pick up the receiver and ~ the caller. 聽電話;接電話。[VP2C, 15B] ***~ (sb) back,*** ~ impolitely, interrupt, esp when being corrected or scolded. (尤指在被糾正或受斥責時)回嘴;還口。 **2** [VP6A] fulfil; be suitable or satisfactory for: 符合;適合: *Will this ~ your purpose?* 這將符合你的目的嗎? **3** [VP2A] succeed; be satisfactory: 成功;令人滿意:*This plan has not ~ed; we must find a better one.* 這個計畫未成功;我們必須另立一個更好的計畫。 **4** [VP3A] ~ ***to the name of,*** (of a pet animal) have the name of: (指畜養以供玩賞的動物)名叫: *The dog ~s to the name of Spot.* 這狗名叫小花。***~ to a description,*** correspond to it, be as described: 與所述相符: *He doesn't ~ to the description of the missing man that appeared in the newspapers.* 他與報紙上對失踪之人的描述不相符。 **5** [VP6A, 3A] ~ ***(to) the helm,*** (of a ship) change course when the helm is moved: (指船)能隨舵轉向:*The ship no longer ~s the helm,* cannot be steered. 此船已不能隨舵轉向(卽舵已失靈,不能駕駛了)。 **6** [VP3A] ~ ***for,*** be responsible for: 對…負責;擔保: *I can't ~ for his honesty,* cannot guarantee that he is honest. 我不能保證他誠實。*I will ~ for it* (= promise) *that the next one will be better.* 我可以保證下一個會好些。*You will have to ~ for* (= suffer for) *your wrongdoing one day.* 你總有一天會因爲做壞事而得到報應的。*He has a lot to ~ for,* is responsible for, to be blamed for, many things. 他有很多的事情要負責(應受責備)。~·**able** /-əbl ; -əbl̩/ *adj* **1** that can be ~ed. 可回答的;可答覆的。 **2** (*pred* only) responsible (*to* sb *for* sth). (僅作敍述用法)應負責的(與 to 連用,後接某人;與 for 連用,後接某事)。

ant /ænt ; ænt/ *n* small insect, proverbial for industry, that lives in highly organized societies. 螞蟻。⇨ the illus at insect. 參看 insect 之插圖。**'ant-eater** *n* name of various animals that live on ants. 食蟻獸。**'ant-hill** *n* pile of earth, etc, over an underground nest of ants; cone-shaped nest of white ants. 蟻丘;蟻垤;蟻塚。**ˌwhite 'ant** *n* white ant-like insect (termite) that destroys wood, etc by eating it. 白蟻(能毀壞木料等)。

an·tag·on·ism /æn'tægənɪzəm ; æn'tægəˏnɪzəm/ *n* [C, U] (instance of) active opposition: 對抗;敵對;對立: *the ~ between the two men;* 該二人之間的對立; *feel a strong ~ for／toward sb,* find oneself strongly opposed to him. 與某人相敵對。

an·tag·on·ist /æn'tægənɪst ; æn'tægəˏnɪst/ *n* person struggling against another; opponent. 敵對者;對立者;對手;敵手。

an·tag·on·is·tic /ænˌtægə'nɪstɪk ; ænˏtægə'nɪstɪk/ *adj* ~ ***(to),*** **1** hostile; opposed; contrary. 反對的;對立的。 **2** (of forces) acting against each other. (指力量)互相反對的;敵對的;互相抵制的。 **an·tag·on·is·ti·cally** /-klɪ ; -klɪ/ *adv*

an·tag·on·ize /æn'tægənaɪz ; æn'tægəˏnaɪz/ *vt* [VP6A] make an enemy of (sb); irritate into conflict: 反對;敵對;與(某人)爲敵;激怒使起爭執: *I advise you not to ~ him.* 我勸你別與他爲敵。

ant·arc·tic /æn'tɑːktɪk ; ænt'ɑrktɪk/ *adj* of the south polar regions. 南極的。**the ˌA~ 'Circle,** the line of latitude 66½°S. 南極圈(卽南緯66度半線)。

ante¹ /'æntɪ ; 'æntɪ/ *n* stake in the game of poker that a player must put down after looking at his cards or before he can draw new cards. (賭撲克牌時,看過手中牌後,或尙未發新牌前所下的)賭注;進牌金。***raise the ~,*** increase one's stake (or contribution to sth). 加大賭注;增加捐獻。

ante² /'æntɪ ; 'æntɪ/ *pref* before: 在…之前: *~nuptial,* before marriage. 在結婚之前的;婚前的。

ante·ced·ent /ˌæntɪ'siːdnt ; ˏæntə'sidn̩t/ *adj* ~ ***(to),*** (formal) previous (to). (正式用語)在…之前的。□ *n* **1** preceding event or circumstance. 前事;前情。 **2** (*pl*) ancestors; past history of a person or persons. (複)祖先;身世;經歷;人之過去的歷史。 **3** (gram) noun, clause or sentence, to which a following pronoun or adverb refers. (文法)先行詞。**ante·ced·ence** /-ns ; -n̩s/ *n* priority. 在前;佔先。

ante·cham·ber /'æntɪtʃeɪmbə(r) ; 'æntɪˏtʃembɚ/ *n* room leading into a large room or hall. (後連正廳之)前廳;前堂(用作來賓接待室)。

ante·date /ˌæntɪ'deɪt ; 'æntɪˏdet/ *vt* [VP6A] **1** put a date on, eg a letter, document, etc, earlier than the true one; give an earlier date than the true one to (an event). 在(信函,文件等)上面填寫較實際日期爲早的日期; 以較實際發生日期爲早之日期來記載(某事件)。 **2** come before in time: 發生時間在…

之前: *This event ~s the arrival of Columbus by several centuries.*這事件發生在哥倫布到達之前數世紀。

ante·di·luvian /ˌæntɪdɪˈluːvɪən ; ˌæntɪdɪˈljuvɪən/ *adj* of, suitable for, the time before the Flood, (Genesis); old-fashioned; out of date. (創世記所述之) 洪水時代以前的; 太古的; 古式的; 過時的。 □ *n* old-fashioned person. 守舊之人。

ante·lope /ˈæntɪləʊp ; ˈæntḷˌop/ *n* deer-like, fast-running animal with thin legs. 羚羊。⇨ the illus at large. 參看 large 之挿圖。

ante mer·id·iem /ˌæntɪ məˈrɪdɪəm ; ˈæntɪməˈrɪdɪˌɛm/ (Lat) (abbr 略作 **am**) time between midnight and noon: (拉)午前;上午: *7.30 am.* 上午七時半。⇨ *pm* at post meridiem; ⇨ App 4(6). 參看附錄四之六。

ante·na·tal /ˌæntɪˈneɪtl ; ˌæntɪˈnetḷ/ *adj* existing or occurring before birth; pre-natal: 存在或發生在出生以前的;誕生前的;產前的: ~ *clinics,* for pregnant women. 孕婦診療所;產前診所。

an·tenna /ænˈtenə ; ænˈtɛnə/ *n* (*pl* ~e /-niː ; -ni/) **1** jointed organ found in pairs on the heads of insects and crustaceans, used for feeling, etc. (昆蟲及甲殼動物的) 觸角;觸鬚。⇨ the illus at insect. 參看 insect 之挿圖。 **2** (*pl* also 亦作 ~s) (esp US) (kind of) radio or TV aerial. (尤美) (無線電或電視的) 天線。

ante·nup·tial /ˌæntɪˈnʌpʃl ; ˌæntɪˈnʌpʃəl/ *adj* before marriage: 婚前的: *an ~ contract.* 婚約。

ante·pen·ul·ti·mate /ˌæntɪpɪˈnʌltɪmət ; ˌæntɪpɪˈnʌltəmɪt/ *adj* last but two: 倒數第三的: *the ~ syllable.* 倒數第三音節。

an·ter·ior /ænˈtɪərɪə(r) ; ænˈtɪrɪə/ *adj* (formal) coming before (in time or position). (正式用語) (時間或位置) 在…前的。

ante·room /ˈæntɪrʊm *US:* -ruːm ; ˈæntɪˌrum/ *n* antechamber; waiting-room. 前廳;前堂;接待室。

an·them /ˈænθəm ; ˈænθəm/ *n* musical composition, usu for choir and organ, to be sung in churches. 教堂中合唱的歌曲 (通常供唱詩班及風琴之用); 聖歌。 ˌ**national** ˈ~, song or hymn of a country, eg 'God Save the Queen'. 國歌 (例如英國國歌'天佑吾王')。

an·ther /ˈænθə(r) ; ˈænθə/ *n* (bot) part of the stamen containing pollen. (植物) 雄蕊之花粉囊;花葯。⇨ the illus at flower. 參看 flower 之挿圖。

an·thol·ogy /ænˈθɒlədʒɪ ; ænˈθɑlədʒɪ/ *n* [C] (*pl* -gies) collection of poems or pieces of prose, or of both, by different writers, or a selection from the work of one writer. 詩集;文集;詩文集;文選;詩選 (作者爲一人或多人均可)。

an·thra·cite /ˈænθrəsaɪt ; ˈænθrəˌsaɪt/ *n* [U] very hard form of coal that burns with little smoke or flame. 無煙煤。

an·thrax /ˈænθræks ; ˈænθræks/ *n* [U] infectious, often fatal, disease of sheep and cattle that may be transmitted to human beings. 癰;炭疽;脾脫疽。

an·thro·poid /ˈænθrəpɔɪd ; ˈænθrəˌpɔɪd/ *adj* man-like. 似人類的。□ *n* ~ animal, esp an ape, eg a gorilla. 似人類之動物; (尤指) 猿類 (如大猩猩)。

an·thro·pol·ogy /ˌænθrəˈpɒlədʒɪ ; ˌænθrəˈpɑlədʒɪ/ *n* [U] science of man, esp of the beginnings, development, customs and beliefs of mankind. 人類學 (研究人類的起源、發展、習俗及信仰之科學)。 **an·thro·pol·ogist** /ˌænθrəˈpɒlədʒɪst ; ˌænθrəˈpɑlədʒɪst/ *n* expert in ~. 人類學家。 **an·thro·po·logi·cal** /ˌænθrəpəˈlɒdʒɪkl ; ˌænθrəpəˈlɑdʒɪkḷ/ *adj*

anti- /ˌæntɪ *US:* ˌæntaɪ ; ˈæntaɪ/ *pref* against: 反對; 抵抗;排斥: ˌ*~-balˈlistic;* 反彈道的; ˌ*~-ˈclerical;* 反聖職的;反對教士干預政治的; ˌ*~-ˈchristian,* opposed to Christianity. 反基督教的。

anti-air·craft /ˌæntɪ ˈeəkrɑːft *US:* -kræft ; ˌæntɪˈɛrˌkræft/ *adj* used against enemy aircraft: 用以對抗敵機的;防空的;對空的: ~ *guns.* 高射砲。

anti·biotic /ˌæntɪbaɪˈɒtɪk ; ˌæntɪbaɪˈɑtɪk/ *n, adj* (med) (substance, eg *penicillin*) produced by moulds and bacteria, capable of destroying or preventing the growth of bacteria. (醫) 抗生的;抗生藥;抗生素 (如盤尼西林)。

anti·body /ˈæntɪbɒdɪ ; ˈæntɪˌbɑdɪ/ *n* [C] (*pl* -dies) (physiol) (kinds of) substance formed in the blood tending to inhibit or destroy harmful bacteria, etc. (生理) 抗體(血液中所形成之可抑制或消滅有害細菌等之各種物質)。

an·tic /ˈæntɪk ; ˈæntɪk/ *n* (usu *pl*) grotesque movement, step, attitude, intended to amuse, eg by a clown at a circus; queer behaviour. (通常用複數) 滑稽的動作、脚步或姿態 (如馬戲團小丑所作以娛來賓者); 古怪的行爲。

an·tici·pate /ænˈtɪsɪpeɪt ; ænˈtɪsəˌpet/ *vt* [VP6A, C, 9] **1** do, make use of, before the right or natural time: 過早做;過早使用: *Don't ~ your income,* order goods, etc before you receive your income. 不要預先用掉你的收入 (如在未領得收入之前即先定購貨物等)。 **2** do sth before sb else does it: 在旁人未做之前先做某事;先人一着;占先: *It is said that Columbus discovered America, but he was probably ~d by sailors from Norway who reached Labrador 500 years earlier.* 大家都說哥倫布發現美洲,但是在早他五百年前,或許就有挪威航海者先他而到達了拉布拉多。 **3** see what needs doing, what is likely to happen, etc and do what is necessary: 預見必須做或將發生之事,並採取必要的措施;事前處理;預先準備: *He tries to ~ all my needs,* satisfy them before I mention them. 他設法將我所需的一切東西預爲準備。 *A good general tries to ~ the enemy's movements.* 一個優秀的將領常設法預知敵軍的行動,並加以應付。 **4** expect (which is the more usu word): 盼望;期望;預期 (expect 較常用): *We don't ~ much trouble.* 我們不希望有太多的麻煩。 *The directors ~d a fall in demand/that demand would fall.* 董事們預期(貨物的)需求會降低。 **an·tici·pa·tory** /ænˌtɪsɪˈpeɪtərɪ ; ænˈtɪsəpəˌtorɪ/ *adj*

an·tici·pa·tion /ænˌtɪsɪˈpeɪʃn ; ænˌtɪsəˈpeʃən/ *n* [C, U] ***(in) ~ (of),*** action of anticipating; sth anticipated: 預料; 預測; 預期; 預期之事物; 事前行爲: *We bought an extra supply of coal in ~ of a cold winter.* 我們多買了一些煤,以防寒冬。 *Thanking you in ~,* in advance and expecting you to do what I have asked. 謹先致謝。

anti-cli·max /ˌæntɪ ˈklaɪmæks ; ˌæntɪˈklaɪmæks/ *n* [C] sudden fall from sth noble, serious, important, sensible, etc; descent that contrasts with a previous rise. 高潮突降;漸降。

anti-clock·wise /ˌæntɪ ˈklɒkwaɪz ; ˌæntɪˈklɑkwaɪz/ *adv* in the direction opposite to the movements of the hands of a clock. 反時針方向地。

anti·cyc·lone /ˌæntɪˈsaɪkləʊn ; ˌæntɪˈsaɪklon/ *n* [C] (met) area in which atmospheric pressure is high compared with that of surrounding areas, with an outward flow of air; the area is characterized by quiet, settled weather. (氣象) 反氣旋;逆旋風;高氣壓圈。⇨ depression(4).

anti·dote /ˈæntɪdəʊt ; ˈæntɪˌdot/ *n* [C] medicine used against a poison, or to prevent a disease from having an effect: 解毒藥; 抗毒藥: *an ~ against/for/to snakebite.* 蛇咬解毒藥。

anti·freeze /ˈæntɪfriːz ; ˌæntɪˈfriz/ *n* [U] substance (usu a liquid) added to another liquid to lower its freezing point, eg as used in the radiator of a motor vehicle. 防凍劑(通常爲液體,加於另一種液體中以減低其冰點,例如加於汽車冷却器之中者)。

anti-hero /ˈæntɪ hɪərəʊ ; ˌæntɪˈhɪro/ *n* (*pl* ~es /-rəʊz ; -roz/) (in fiction and drama) protagonist lacking the traditional characteristics of a hero, such as courage and dignity. (小說與戲劇中之) 非英雄主角(缺乏傳統之英雄氣質,如勇氣及威嚴)。

anti·knock /ˌæntɪˈnɒk ; ˌæntɪˈnɑk/ *n* [U] substance added to the fuel in a motor-car engine to reduce noise. 防爆劑(加於汽車引擎燃料中以防止爆音者)。⇨ knock²(3).

anti·log·ar·ithm /ˌæntɪˈlɒgərɪðəm *US:* -ˈlɔːg- ;

ˌæntɪˈlɔgəˌrɪðəm/ *n* number to which a logarithm belongs: 反對數: *1000, 100 and 10 are the ~s of 3, 2 and 1.* 1000, 100, 10 是 3, 2, 1 的反對數。

anti·ma·cas·sar /ˌæntɪməˈkæsə(r) ; ˌæntɪməˈkæsɚ/ *n* covering to protect the back or arm of a chair or sofa from grease-marks. (椅子或沙發之靠背或扶手處防油汚用之)罩布。

anti·mony /ˈæntɪmənɪ *US:* -məʊnɪ ; ˈæntəˌmonɪ/ *n* [U] easily broken silvery white metal, (symbol **Sb**) used in alloys, esp metal for type¹(3). 銻(易碎之銀白色金屬,化學符號 Sb, 用於合金,尤用以製鉛字之合金)。

an·tipa·thy /ænˈtɪpəθɪ ; ænˈtɪpəθɪ/ *n* ~ ***(to/towards/against) (between** two persons),* [U] strong and decided dislike; [C] (*pl* -thies) instance or object of this: 反感;惡感;憎惡;反感之實例;反感的對象;討厭的事物: *feel/show a strong/marked ~ to a place/against sb.* 對於某地(某人)有强烈(顯著)的反感。 **anti·pa·thetic** /ˌæntɪpəˈθetɪk ; ænˌtɪpəˈθɛtɪk/ *adj*

anti-per·son·nel /ˌæntɪ ˌpɜːsəˈnel ; ˌæntɪˌpɝsəˈnɛl/ *adj* (usu of mines²(3)) designed to kill or wound human beings (not to destroy vehicles). (通常指地雷)用來殺傷人而非用來毁壞車輛的;殺傷性的。

an·tipo·des /ænˈtɪpədiːz ; ænˈtɪpəˌdiz/ *n pl* (usu 通常作 **the** ~) (two) place(s) on the opposite sides of the earth, esp the region opposite our own. 對蹠之地(地球上相反之二地區); (尤指) 與我們自己地區相反之地區。

anti·quar·ian /ˌæntɪˈkweərɪən ; ˌæntɪˈkwɛrɪən/ *adj* connected with the study, collection or sale of antiquities: 與研究、收藏或售賣古物有關的: *an ~ bookseller.* 售賣古書的商人。□ *n* antiquary. 研究、收藏或售賣古物之人;古物蒐集家。

anti·quary /ˈæntɪkwərɪ *US:* -kwerɪ ; ˈæntɪˌkwɛrɪ/ *n* (*pl* -ries) person who studies, collects or sells, antiquities. 研究、收藏或售賣古物之人;古物蒐集家。

anti·quated /ˈæntɪkweɪtɪd ; ˈæntəˌkwetɪd/ *adj* obsolete; out of date; (of persons) having old-fashioned ideas and ways. 已廢棄的;過時的;(指人)有舊式思想或氣派的。

an·tique /ænˈtiːk ; ænˈtik/ *adj* belonging to the distant past; existing since old times; in the style of past times. 古代的;自古卽存在的;古風的。□ *n* [C] material (eg a piece of furniture, a work of art) of a past period (in GB at least 50 years old, in US 100 years). 古物;古董;古藝術品(屬於以往時代的東西,如家俱、藝術作品等。在英國,至少爲五十年以上者; 在美國,一百年以上者)。 **the** ~, ~ style in art. 古代藝術風格。Cf 參較 *second-hand*, usu of things more recent. 舊的;二手貨的(通常指比較近期的東西)。

an·tiquity /ænˈtɪkwətɪ ; ænˈtɪkwətɪ/ *n* **1** [U] old times, esp before the Middle Ages; great age: 古代; 古老(尤指中世紀以前者); 古遠: *the heroes of ~;* 古代的英雄; *a city of great ~,* eg Athens; 古城(如雅典); *in remote ~.* 在遠古時代。 **2** (*pl* -ties) buildings, ruins, works of art, remaining from ancient times: 古建築物;古廢墟;古藝術品;古蹟;古物: *Greek and Roman antiquities.* 希臘羅馬之古蹟。

an·tir·rhi·num /ˌæntɪˈraɪnəm ; ˌæntɪˈraɪnəm/ *n* (*pl* ~s) (bot) genus of plants; snapdragon. (植物)金魚草。

anti-Sem·ite /ˌæntɪ ˈsiːmaɪt *US:* ˈsem- ; ˌæntɪˈsɛmaɪt/ *n, adj* (person) prejudiced against Jews, hating Jews. 對猶太人存有偏見或懷恨的(人);反猶太的(人)。 **anti-Sem·itic** /ˌæntɪ sɪˈmɪtɪk ; ˌæntɪsəˈmɪtɪk/ *adj* **anti-Semi·tism** /ˌæntɪˈsemətɪzm ; ˌæntɪˈsɛməˌtɪzəm/ *n* 反猶太主義。

anti·sep·tic /ˌæntɪˈseptɪk ; ˌæntəˈsɛptɪk/ *n, adj* (chemical substance) preventing a wound, etc from becoming septic, esp by destroying germs. 防腐劑;消毒劑;防腐的;有消毒力的。

anti·social /ˌæntɪˈsəʊʃl ; ˌæntɪˈsoʃəl/ *adj* **1** opposed to social laws or to organized societies. 反對社會律或有組織之社會的;反社會的。 **2** likely, tending, to interfere with or spoil public amenities: 想要,傾向於擾亂或破壞公共遊樂場所的;違反公益的: *It is ~ to leave litter in public places/to play a transistor in public.* 在公共場所留下零亂雜物(在群衆中收聽電晶體收音機)是違反公益的。 **3** not sociable. 不喜社交的。

anti·tank /ˌæntɪˈtæŋk ; ˌæntɪˈtæŋk/ *attrib adj* for use against military tanks: 反戰車的;防戰車的: *~ guns/ditches.* 反戰車砲(防戰車壕)。

an·tith·esis /ænˈtɪθəsɪs ; ænˈtɪθəsɪs/ *n* (*pl* -ses /-siːz ; -siz/) **1** [U] direct opposite (*of, to*). 正相反(與 of 或 to 連用)。 **2** [U] opposition (*of* one thing *to* another, *between* two things); [C] instance of this; contrast of ideas vividly expressed, as in 'Give me liberty, or give me death'. 相反;反對;對照(後接 of 一事物 to 另一事物, between 二事物); (修辭學上的)反襯; 對比(如'不自由,毋寧死')。 **anti·thetic** /ˌæntɪˈθetɪk ; ˌæntɪˈθɛtɪk/, **anti·theti·cal** /-ɪkl ; -ɪkl̩/ *adj* **anti·theti·cally** /-klɪ ; -klɪ/ *adv*

anti·toxin /ˌæntɪˈtɒksɪn ; ˌæntɪˈtɑksɪn/ *n* substance (usu a serum) able to counteract a toxin or disease. 抗毒素;抗毒血清。

anti·trade /ˌæntɪˈtreɪd ; ˈæntɪˌtred/ *adj* '~ **wind**, wind that blows in the opposite direction to a trade wind. 反貿易風;反信風。□ *n* (usu *pl*) ~ wind. (通常用複數)反貿易風;反信風。

ant·ler /ˈæntlə(r) ; ˈæntlɚ/ *n* branched horn; branch of a horn (of a stag or other deer). 分枝的獸角;鹿角的一枝。⇨ the illus at large. 參看 large 之插圖。

an·to·nym /ˈæntənɪm ; ˈæntəˌnɪm/ *n* [C] word that is contrary in meaning to another: 反義字: *Hot is the ~ of cold.* 熱是冷的反義字。⇨ synonym.

anus /ˈeɪnəs ; ˈenəs/ *n* (anat) opening at the end of the alimentary canal, through which waste matter passes out. (解剖)肛門。⇨ the illus at alimentary. 參看 alimentary 之插圖。

an·vil /ˈænvɪl ; ˈænvɪl/ *n* **1** large, heavy block of iron on which a smith hammers heated metal into shape. 鐵砧。 **2** (anat) bone in the ear. (解剖)砧骨。⇨ the illus at ear. 參看 ear 之插圖。

anxiety /æŋˈzaɪətɪ ; æŋˈzaɪətɪ/ *n* **1** [U] emotional condition in which there is fear and uncertainty about the future: 憂慮;焦慮;惶惶不安: *We waited with ~ for news of her safe arrival.* 我們焦慮地等待她安全到達的消息。*Tom's foolish behaviour caused his parents great ~.* 湯姆的愚行引起他的父母極大的不安。 **2** [C] (*pl* -ties) instance of such a feeling: 憂慮或不安之實例: *All these anxieties made him look pale and tired.* 這一切的憂慮使他面色蒼白且有倦容。*The Budget statement removed all anxieties about higher taxes.* 預算表消除了一切關於增稅的憂慮。 **3** [U] keen desire: 渴望;切望: *~ for knowledge;* 切望獲得知識; *his ~ to please his employers.* 他急欲討好僱主的切望。

anxious /ˈæŋkʃəs ; ˈæŋkʃəs/ *adj* **1** ~ ***(about/at/for),*** feeling anxiety; troubled: 憂慮的; 焦慮的;擔心的;不安的: *I am very ~ about my son's health.* 我極爲擔心我兒子的健康。*He is ~ for/about her safety/at her non-arrival.* 他擔心她的安全(因她未到達而憂慮)。 **2** causing anxiety: 引起憂慮的;令人擔心的: *We have had an ~ time.* 我們一直焦慮着。*His illness has been a very ~ business,* has caused us anxiety. 他的病是件極令人擔心的事。 **3** ~ ***to/for/about/that,*** strongly wishing: 渴望;切望: *He was ~ to meet you/~ for his brother to meet you.* 他渴望會見你(渴望他的兄弟會見你)。*We were ~ that help should be sent promptly/~ for help to be sent.* 我們渴望立卽派人救助。 **~·ly** *adv*

any¹ /ˈenɪ ; ˈɛnɪ/ *adj* **1** ⇨ some¹(1) (in neg and interr sentences, and in clauses of condition, etc). (用於否定句、疑問句及條件子句等)。 **2** (in affirm sentences, with negation implied, eg with a *v* such as *'prevent'*, after the *prep 'without'*, after such *advv* as *'hardly'*): (用於肯定句中具有否定的含義,例如與動詞 prevent 連用,在介系詞 without 之後,在副詞

hardly 等之後): *We did the work without any difficulty.* 我們毫無困難地做了這工作。*I have hardly any leisure nowadays.* 我這些日子幾乎毫無閒暇。*Please try to prevent any loss while the goods are on the way.* 貨物在運送途中請儘量防止任何損失。**3** (usu stressed; usu in affirm sentences) no matter which: (通常重讀;通常用於肯定句中)任何;無論哪一: *Come any day you like.* 隨便哪一天來都可以。*You will find me at my desk at any hour of the day,* at all times. 你會發現在一天之中的任何時刻我都在桌旁工作。*We must find an excuse, any excuse will do.* 我們必須要找一個藉口,任何藉口都可以。**4** ***in 'any case,*** whatever happens, whatever the circumstances may be. 無論如何。***at 'any rate,*** at least. 至少。**5** (colloq; used in affirm and neg sentences, with *sing* common *nn* for *a(n)* or *one*): (俗;用於肯定及否定句中,與單數普通名詞連用,代替 a, an 或 one): *This bucket is useless—it hasn't any handle.* 這個桶沒有用了——連個把手都沒有。

any² /'enɪ; 'ɛnɪ/ *adv of degree* (used in neg, interr and conditional sentences, in contexts where negation or doubt is indicated or implied, and with comparatives. Cf the similar use of *no* and *none.*) (用於否定、疑問及條件句中,顯示或暗示有否定或疑問意味之上下文中,及與比較級字連用。參較 no 及 none 之類似用法。) at all; in any degree: 絲毫;任何程度: *Is your father any better?* 你父親好些了嗎? *They were too tired to go any further.* 他們疲倦得一點也不能再往前走了。*The children didn't behave any too well,* ie they behaved rather badly. 這些孩子的行爲不太好。*If it's any good/use, I'll buy it.* 若是它有任何好處(用處),我就買它。***(not) any the better/the worse (for),*** (not) at all better/worse for: (絲毫沒有)因…而好(壞)一點;(絲毫沒有)受…的影響: *He got wet through in the rain yesterday but isn't any the worse for it,* has not suffered in any way. 他昨天被雨淋濕透了,可是絲毫未受影響。

any³ /'enɪ; 'ɛnɪ/ *pron* ⇨ some².

any·body /'enɪbɒdɪ; 'ɛnɪ,bɑdɪ/ *n, pron* **1** (in neg, interr, etc sentences: 用於否定、疑問等句中: ⇨ somebody, someone). **2** (in affirm sentences) no matter who: (用於肯定句中)無論誰;任何人: *A~ will tell you where the bus stop is.* 無論誰都會告訴你公共汽車站在哪裡。*A~ who saw the accident is asked to communicate with the police.* 任何親眼看見該禍事發生者,請與警方取得連絡。*That's ~'s guess,* (colloq) is quite uncertain. (俗)那是相當靠不住。***~ else,*** ⇨ else. **3** person of importance: 重要人物: *You must work harder if you wish to be ~.* 如果你想要成爲重要人物,你必須更加努力。*Was she ~ before her marriage,* Had she any social position? 她在結婚前有什麼社會地位嗎? *He'll never be ~.* 他永遠不會成器的。

any·how /'enɪhaʊ; 'ɛnɪ,haʊ/ *adv* **1** in any possible way; by any possible means: 以任何可能的方法;無論怎樣: *The house was empty and I couldn't get in ~.* 屋子裡沒有人,我無論怎樣都進不去。**2** carelessly; without order: 不仔細地;馬馬虎虎地;雜亂無章地: *The work was done all ~.* 這工作做得很馬虎。**3** (*adv* or *conj*) in any case; at any rate: 無論如何;至少: *A~, you can try,* even if there's not much chance of success. 至少你可以試試(縱然沒有多少成功的機會)。*It's too late now, ~.* 無論怎樣,現在已經太遲了。

any·one /'enɪwʌn; 'ɛnɪ,wʌn/ *n, pron* = anybody.

any·place /'enɪpleɪs; 'ɛnɪ,ples/ *adv* (esp in US) (尤用於美國) = anywhere.

any·thing /'enɪθɪŋ; 'ɛnɪ,θɪŋ/ *n, pron* **1** (in neg, interr, etc sentences: 用於否定,疑問等句中: ⇨ something) (note the position of the *adj*): (注意形容詞的位置): *Has ~ unusual happened?* 有什麼不平常的事發生嗎? **2** no matter what: 無論什麼: *I want something to eat; ~ will do.* 我想要點東西吃;無論什麼都可以。***be ~ but,*** be definitely not: 絕對不: *He's ~ but mad.* 他一點也不生氣。**3** (used adverbially to intensify a meaning): (作副詞用,加强某一意義): *The thief ran like ~ when he saw the policeman.* 那賊看見了警察跑得像什麼似的。***(as) easy as ~,*** (colloq) very easy. (俗)容易得很。

any·way /'enɪweɪ; 'ɛnɪ,we/ *adv* = anyhow(3).

any·where /'enɪweə(r) *US:* -hweər; 'ɛnɪ,hwɛr/ *adv* **1** (in neg, interr, etc sentences: 用於否定,疑問等句中: ⇨ somewhere) (note the use of ~ with post-adjuncts): (注意此字與後位附加語的連用法): *I'll go ~ (that) you suggest.* 你建議我到哪兒去,我就到哪兒去。*Are we going ~ (in) particular?* 我們要到什麼特定的地方去嗎?(意即:有沒有一定的目標?) **2** (used as a *prep* object): (用作介系詞之受詞): *That leaves me without ~ to keep all my books.* 這樣一來,我連一點可以放這些書籍的地方也沒有了。**3** no matter where: 無論何處;任何地方: *Put the box down ~.* 把盒子放下來,任何地方都可以。*We'll go ~ you like.* 你愛往哪兒去,我們就往哪兒去。

aorta /eɪ'ɔːtə; e'ɔrtə/ *n* chief blood-vessel through which blood is carried from the left side of the heart. 大動脈;主動脈。⇨ the illus at respiratory. 參看 respiratory 之挿圖。

apace /ə'peɪs; ə'pes/ *adv* (old use, or liter) quickly: (舊用法或文)快地;急速地: *Ill news spreads ~.* 壞消息傳得快(壞事傳千里)。

apache /ə'pæʃ; ə'pɑʃ/ *n* (in Paris) hooligan; rough. (在巴黎)街頭上的流氓或不良少年;太保;阿飛。

apa·nage (also **ap·pan·age**) /'æpənɪdʒ; 'æpənɪdʒ/ *n* [U] **1** natural accompaniment; sth that necessarily goes with sth else. 屬性;從屬物。**2** property, etc coming to sb because of birth or office. 由世襲或職位所得的財產等;封地;俸祿。

apart /ə'pɑːt; ə'pɑrt/ *adv* **1** distant: 遠離地;遠隔地: *The two houses are 500 metres ~.* 這兩棟房子相距五百公尺。*The negotiators are still miles ~,* show no signs of agreeing. 談判者之間仍有相當的距離(無協議的跡象)。**2** to or on one side: 向一邊;在一邊: *He took me ~ in order to speak to me alone.* 他把我拉到一邊,以便跟我單獨說話。*Why does she hold herself ~,* ie not mix with other people? 她爲什麼落落寡合(與他人格格不入)? ***joking/jesting ~,*** speaking seriously. 非開玩笑;說正經話。***set/put (sth/sb) ~ (from),*** put (it) on one side; reserve it; make (sb) (appear) special: 儲備;保留(某事物);使(某人)(顯得)特殊: *His far-sightedness set him ~ from most of his contemporaries.* 他的遠見使他顯得與其同輩的人迥然不同。**3** separate(ly): 分開;分離: *I can't get these two things ~.* 我分不開這兩樣東西。*He was standing with his feet wide ~.* 他兩足大開而立。***~ from,*** independently of; leaving on one side: 除開;除…以外: *~ from these reasons.* 除了這些理由以外。***tell/know two things or persons ~,*** distinguish one from the other. 能分辨兩種東西或兩個人。⇨ come(16), pull²(7), take¹(16).

apart·heid /ə'pɑːtheɪt; ə'pɑrthet/ *n* (S Africa) (policy of) racial segregation; separate development of Europeans and non-Europeans. (南非洲)種族隔離(政策);歐洲人與非歐洲人之分別發展。

apart·ment /ə'pɑːtmənt; ə'pɑrtmənt/ *n* **1** single room in a house. 房間。**2** (*pl*) set of rooms, furnished or unfurnished, either owned or rented by the week or month, eg for a holiday at the seaside. (複)套房(指有設備或無設備者,或爲私人產業或爲按週或按月計租,如供海濱度假者)。**3** (US) set of rooms in a large building (called *an '~ house*), usu on the same floor. (美)公寓(稱爲 apartment house 的大樓中的一套房間,通常在同一層樓)。(US ~ = GB *flat;* US ~ *house* = GB *block of flats;* US ~ *hotel* = GB *service flats.*) (美國的 apartment 等於英國的 flat; 美國的 apartment house 等於英國的 block of flats; 美國的 apartment hotel 等於英國的 service flats。) ⇨ tenement.

apa·thy /'æpəθɪ; 'æpəθɪ/ *n* [U] absence of sympathy or interest; indifference (*towards*). 不同情;無興趣;冷淡;淡漠;漠不關心(與 towards 連用)。**apa-**

apes and monkeys

thetic /ˌæpəˈθetɪk ; ˌæpəˈθɛtɪk/ *adj* showing or having ~. 不同情的;無興趣的;冷淡的;淡漠的。**apa·theti·cally** /-klɪ ; -klɪ/ *adv*

ape /eɪp ; ep/ *n* **1** tailless monkey (*gorilla, chimpanzee, orang-outang, gibbon*). 猿(包括大猩猩,黑猩猩,長臂猿等)。**2** person who mimics others: 模倣他人者: *play the ape,* mimic. 模倣。**3** (colloq) clumsy, ill-bred person. (俗)笨拙而無教養的人;粗野之人。□ *vt* imitate (sb's behaviour, etc). 模倣(某人之行爲等)。

aperi·ent /əˈpɪərɪənt ; əˈpɪrɪənt/ *n, adj* (formal) laxative. (正式用語)通便的;輕瀉的;通便劑;輕瀉藥。

aperi·tif /əˈperətɪf *US:* əˌperəˈtiːf ; aperiˈtif/ *n* [C] alcoholic drink, (eg *vermouth*) taken before a meal. 飯前酒;開胃酒(如 vermouth)。

ap·er·ture /ˈæpətʃə(r) ; ˈæpətʃɚ/ *n* opening, esp one that admits light, eg to a camera lens. 孔;隙;洞(尤指通光線者,如照相機之光孔)。

apex /ˈeɪpeks; ˈepɛks/ *n* (*pl* ~es or apices /ˈeɪpɪsiːz; ˈæpɪˌsiz/) top or highest point: 頂點;最高點;峯;尖頂: *the ~ of a triangle;* 三角形之頂點; *at the ~ of his career/fortunes.* 他的事業(運氣)的極盛時期。

apha·sia /əˈfeɪzɪə *US:* -ʒə ; əˈfeʒə/ *n* [U] (path) loss of ability to use speech or to understand speech (as the result of brain injury). (病理)(由於腦部受傷害而致之)運用或瞭解語言能力的喪失;失語症。

aphid /ˈeɪfɪd ; ˈefɪd/ *n* = aphis.

aphis /ˈeɪfɪs ; ˈefɪs/ *n* (*pl* aphides /ˈeɪfɪdiːz ; ˈæfɪˌdiz/) very small insect that lives by sucking juices from plants; plant louse. 蚜蟲(靠吸取植物汁液而生存之小蟲)。

aph·or·ism /ˈæfərɪzəm ; ˈæfəˌrɪzəm/ *n* [C] short, wise saying; maxim. 格言;警語。

aph·ro·dis·iac /ˌæfrəˈdɪzɪæk ; ˌæfrəˈdɪzɪˌæk/ *n, adj* [C, U] (substance, drug) exciting sexual desire and activity. 催慾的;壯陽的;壯陽藥;春藥。

api·ary /ˈeɪpɪərɪ *US:* -ɪerɪ ; ˈepɪˌɛrɪ/ *n* (*pl* -ries) place with a number of hives where bees are kept. 養蜂場;蜂房。**api·ar·ist** /ˈeɪpɪərɪst ; ˈepɪərɪst/ *n* person who keeps bees. 養蜂者。**api·cul·ture** /ˈeɪpɪkʌltʃə(r) ; ˈepɪˌkʌltʃɚ/ *n* bee-keeping. 養蜂。

apiece /əˈpiːs ; əˈpis/ *adv* to, for or by, each one of a group: 每個;每件;每人: *They cost a penny ~,* each. 它們的價錢是每個一辨士。

apish /ˈeɪpɪʃ ; ˈepɪʃ/ *adj* of or like an ape; foolishly imitative. 猿的;似猿的;愚蠢地模倣的。

aplomb /əˈplɒm ; əˈplɑm/ *n* [U] self-confidence; assurance (in speech or behaviour): 自信;(言語或行爲上的)沉着;鎮定;泰然自若: *He answered with perfect ~.* 他沉着地回答。

apoca·lypse /əˈpɒkəlɪps ; əˈpɑkəˌlɪps/ *n* revelation (esp of knowledge from God). 启示;(尤指)天啓。**the A~**, the last book in the Bible, recording the revelation to St John. 啓示錄(聖經之最後一卷,記載聖約翰所得之天啓)。 ⇨ App 10. 參看附錄十。**apoca·lyp·tic** /əˌpɒkəˈlɪptɪk ; əˌpɑkəˈlɪptɪk/ *adj* of or like an ~ or the A~. 啓示的; 天啓的; 似啓示的; 似天啓的;啓示錄的。

Apoc·ry·pha /əˈpɒkrɪfə ; əˈpɑkrəfə/ *n pl* (with *sing v*) those books of the Old Testament that are considered of doubtful authorship by the Jews and were excluded from the Bible at the time of the Reformation. (與單數動詞連用)(舊約聖經中猶太人認爲作者可疑,在宗教改革時被刪除的)僞經。 ⇨ App 10. 參看附錄十。**apoc·ry·phal** /əˈpɒkrɪfl ; əˈpɑkrəfəl/ *adj* of doubtful authority or authorship. 作者可疑的;眞僞不明的。

apo·gee /ˈæpədʒiː ; ˈæpəˌdʒi/ *n* **1** (astron) position (in the orbit of the moon or any planet) when it is at its greatest distance from the earth. (天文)遠地點(月球或任何行星軌道上距離地球最遠之點)。**2** (fig) highest point. (喻)最高點;極點。

apolo·getic /əˌpɒləˈdʒetɪk ; əˌpɑləˈdʒɛtɪk/ *adj* making an apology; expressing regret; excusing a fault or failure: 道歉的;表示歉意的;辯解過失的: *He was ~ about/for arriving late.* 他爲遲到而表示抱歉。*He wrote an ~ letter.* 他寫了一封道歉信。**apolo·geti·cally** /-klɪ ; -klɪ/ *adv* **apolo·get·ics** *n* (usu with *sing v*) the art or practice of explaining or justifying a religious belief, political creed, etc. (通常與單數動詞連用)(對宗教信仰,政治信條等的)辯證術。**apolo·gist** /əˈpɒlədʒɪst ; əˈpɑlədʒɪst/ *n* person who engages in ~s. 辯證者。

apolo·gize /əˈpɒlədʒaɪz ; əˈpɑləˌdʒaɪz/ *vi* [VP2A,

3A] ~ ***(to sb) (for sth),*** make an apology; say one is sorry: 道歉: *You must ~ to your sister for being so rude.* 你太無禮,必須向你姐姐(妹妹)道歉。

apol·ogy /əˈpɒlədʒɪ; əˈpɑlədʒɪ/ *n* (*pl* -gies) **1** [C] ~ ***(to sb) (for sth),*** statement of regret (for doing wrong, being impolite, hurting sb's feelings): 道歉;謝罪: *offer/make/accept/refuse an ~;* 表示(從事,接受,拒絕)道歉; *offer sb an ~;* 向某人道歉; *make one's apologies* (*to sb*), eg for being late, for not being able to come. (向某人)致歉意(如因遲到,因事不能來等)。**2** [C] explanation or defence (of beliefs, etc). (信仰等之)辯證;辯護。⇨ apologetics. **3** ***an ~ for,*** a poor specimen of, eg a dinner/letter. 爲…之勉强的代替物;爲…之低劣的樣品(如勉强算是一餐飯,勉强算是一封信);權充。

apo·phthegm, apo·thegm /ˈæpəθem; ˈæpə,θɛm/ *n* [C] short, pointed or forceful, saying. 箴言;格言;警語。

apo·plexy /ˈæpəpleksɪ; ˈæpə,plɛksɪ/ *n* [U] loss of power to feel, move, think, usu caused by injury to blood-vessels in the brain. 中風(因腦血管受傷而引起的昏迷狀態)。**apo·plec·tic** /ˌæpəˈplektɪk; ,æpəˈplɛktɪk/ *adj* connected with, causing ~; suffering from ~: 有關中風的;引起中風的;患中風的: *an apoplectic stroke/fit;* 中風發作;中風; (colloq) red in the face; easily made angry. (俗)紅臉的;易怒的。

apos·tasy /əˈpɒstəsɪ; əˈpɑstəsɪ/ *n* [U] giving up one's beliefs or faith; turning away from one's religion; [C] (*pl* -sies) instance of this. 放棄信仰;叛教;脫黨;變節。**apos·tate** /əˈpɒsteɪt; əˈpɑstet/ *n, adj* (person) guilty of ~. 叛教者;脫黨者;叛教的;脫黨的;變節的。

a pos·teri·ori /ˌeɪ ˌpɒsterɪˈɔːraɪ; ˈepɑs,tɪrɪˈɔraɪ/ *adv, adj phrase* (Lat) (reasoning) from effects to causes, eg saying, *'The boys are tired so they must have walked a long way'.* (拉)由結果推定其原因地(的);歸納地(的)(例如說'孩子們很疲乏,所以他們一定走了很長的路')。⇨ a priori.

apostle /əˈpɒsl; əˈpɑsl/ *n* **1** one of the twelve men (**the Twelve A~s**) chosen by Jesus to spread his teaching; missionary of the early Christian Church, eg St Paul, the A~ to the Gentiles. 使徒(耶穌所選十二門徒中之一;早期基督教之傳教士,如聖保羅即爲在異教徒中傳教之使徒)。**2** leader or teacher of reform, of a new faith or movement. 倡導改革,新教或新運動之人;倡導者;導師。**apos·tolic** /ˌæpəˈstɒlɪk; ,æpəsˈtɑlɪk/ *adj* **1** of the ~s(1) or the times when they lived. 耶穌之使徒的;耶穌使徒時代的。**2** of the Pope. 教皇的;教宗的。

apos·trophe¹ /əˈpɒstrəfɪ; əˈpɑstrəfɪ/ *n* the sign' used to show omission of letter(s) or number(s), (as in *can't, I'm, '05,* for *cannot, I am, 1905*), for the possessive (as in *boy's, boys'*), and for the plurals of letters (as in *There are two l's in 'Bell'*). 符號(')︰用作省略號(表示字母或數字之省略,如 can't = cannot, I'm = I am, '05 = 1905),或用作所有格符號(如 boy's, boys'),或用於構成字母的複數形(如 Bell 中有兩個 l 字母,以 two l's 表示之)。⇨ App 9. 參看附錄九。

apos·trophe² /əˈpɒstrəfɪ; əˈpɑstrəfɪ/ *n* passage in a public speech, in a poem, etc addressed to a particular person (who may be dead or absent). 演說或詩歌等中專對某已死亡或不在場之人所說的一段話;頓呼語。**apos·tro·phize** /əˈpɒstrəfaɪz; əˈpɑstrə,faɪz/ *vt* make an ~ to. 對…作頓呼語。

apoth·ecary /əˈpɒθɪkərɪ *US:* -kerɪ; əˈpɑθə,kɛrɪ/ *n* (*pl* -ries) (old use, but still in Scot) person who prepares and sells medicines and medical goods. (舊用法,但今仍用於蘇格蘭)賣藥者;藥劑師。**apothecaries' weight,** ⇨ App 5. 參看附錄五。

apo·thegm ⇨ apophthegm.

apothe·osis /əˌpɒθɪˈəʊsɪs; ə,pɑθɪˈosɪs/ *n* (*pl* -ses /-siːz; -siz/) **1** (of a human being) making or becoming a god or a saint: (指人)奉爲神聖;成神;成聖;神聖化: *the ~ of a Roman Emperor.* 羅馬皇帝之神聖化。**2** release from earthly life. 脫離現世的生命;解脫。**3** glorification; glorified ideal. 尊崇;頌讚;被頌讚的理想。

ap·pal (US also **ap·pall**) /əˈpɔːl; əˈpɔl/ *vt* (-ll-) [VP6A] fill with fear or terror; dismay; shock deeply: 驚嚇;使驚駭: *They were ~led at the news.* 他們被這消息嚇壞了。**~·ling** *adj:* 駭人的;可怕的: *When will this ~ling war end?* 這可怕的戰爭何時方可結束? **~·ling·ly** *adv*

ap·pa·nage ⇨ apanage.

ap·par·atus /ˌæpəˈreɪtəs *US:* -ˈrætəs; ,æpəˈretəs/ *n* [C] (*pl* ~es) (rarely *pl;* sometimes ***a piece of ~***). (罕用複數;有時用 a piece of ~)。**1** set of instruments or other mechanical appliances put together for a purpose: 一套儀器;一套器械;裝置: *a heating ~,* eg for supplying steam heat throughout a building. 暖氣裝置。**2** bodily organs by which natural processes are carried on: (身體內之)器官: *Your digestive ~ takes the food you eat and changes it so that it can be used to build up the body.* 你的消化器官把你所吃的食物消化、吸收,用以增進身體的健康。

ap·parel /əˈpærəl; əˈpærəl/ *n* [U] (old use, or liter) dress; clothing. (舊用法或文)衣服;服裝。□ *vt* (-ll-; US -l-) dress; clothe. 穿以衣服;穿著。

ap·par·ent /əˈpærənt; əˈpærənt/ *adj* **1** clearly seen or understood: 顯然的;明白的: *It was ~ to all of us...,* We all saw clearly...; …這對我們大家是顯而易見的; *as will soon become ~,* as you will soon see. 不久你即可明白。**2** seeming; according to appearances: 外表的;表面的: *in spite of her ~ indifference,* although she seemed to be indifferent. 儘管她表面上顯得冷淡。**~·ly** *adv*

ap·par·ition /ˌæpəˈrɪʃn; ,æpəˈrɪʃən/ *n* [C] the coming into view, esp of a ghost or the spirit of a dead person. 出現;(尤指)幽靈或鬼魂的出現。

ap·peal /əˈpiːl; əˈpil/ *vi* [VP2A, 3A] ~ ***(to sb) (against/for/from sth),*** **1** make an earnest request: 懇求;懇請: *The prisoner ~ed to the judge for mercy.* 囚犯懇求法官開恩。*At Christmas people ~ to us to help the poor.* 聖誕節期間人們呼籲我們捐助貧窮的人們。**2** (legal) take a question (to a higher court, etc) for rehearing and a new decision: (法律)(向上級法院)上訴: *~ to another court;* 向另一法院上訴; *~ against a decision;* 不服判決而上訴; *~ from a judgement.* 不服裁判而上訴。**3** go (to sb) for a decision: 請求(某人)決定;聽取(某人的)意見;訴諸: (football, etc) (足球賽等中) *~ to the linesman;* 聽取巡邊員的決定; *~ against the referee's decision;* 不服裁判的判決; (cricket) (板球) *The captain ~ed against the light,* said the light was too poor for further play. 隊長對光線提出異議(認爲光線太差不宜繼續比賽)。**4** attract; move the feelings of: 有吸引力;引起興趣: *Bright colours ~ to small children.* 鮮艷的色彩能吸引小孩。*Do these paintings ~ to you?* 你對這些畫感興趣嗎? □ *n* **1** ***an ~ for,*** an earnest call for: 懇求;呼籲: *make an ~ for help.* 懇求援助。**2** [C] (legal) act of ~ing(2): (法律)上訴: *an ~ to a higher court;* 向上級法院的上訴; *an ~ from a decision;* 不服判決而上訴; *to lodge an ~;* 提起上訴; [U] *to give notice of ~;* 告知上訴; *acquittal on ~.* 經上訴後平反(獲判無罪開釋)。**3** [C] (esp in sport) act of ~ing: (尤用於運動比賽中)請求決定;聽取意見: *an ~ to the referee.* 請求裁判員的裁決。**4** [U] interest; (power of) attraction: 引起興趣的力量;吸引力: *That sort of music hasn't much ~ for me/has lost its ~.* 那種音樂引不起我多大興趣(已經失去了它的吸引力)。**5** [U] supplication: 乞求;哀求: *with a look of ~ on her face,* asking for help or sympathy. 她的臉上帶着乞求(幫助或同情)的表情。**~·ing** *adj* **1** moving; touching the feelings or sympathy. 感動人的;哀求的。**2** attractive. 動人的;有吸引力的。**~·ing·ly** *adv*

ap·pear /əˈpɪə(r); əˈpɪr/ *vi* **1** [VP2A, C] come

into view, become visible: 出現；呈現: *When we reached the top of the hill, the town ~ed below us.* 當我們到達山頂時，市鎮就呈現在我們的脚下。*The ship ~ed on the horizon.* 船出現在水平線上。 **2** [VP2A, C] arrive: 到；抵達: *He promised to be here at four but didn't ~ until six.* 他答應在四點鐘來這裡，可是到六點鐘才到達。 **3** [VP2A,C] **(a)** (of an actor, singer, lecturer, etc) come before the public: (指演員、歌唱者、演講者等)出場；登台: *He has ~ed in every large concert hall in Europe.* 他曾在歐洲各大音樂廳演唱。**(b)** (of a book) be published: (指書)出版；發表: *When will your new novel ~?* 你的新小說將於何時出版？ **(c)** (legal) present oneself publicly: (法律)到庭；出庭: *The defendant failed to ~ before the court.* 被告未到庭。 **4** [VP2A, 4D, E] seem: 似乎；顯得；好像: *Why does she ~ so sad?* 她爲何顯得如此悲傷？*He ~s to have many friends.* 他似乎有很多朋友。*You don't want to ~ a fool,* to look like a fool. 你不要顯得像個傻子似的。*The house ~ed (to be) deserted.* 那房子看樣子好像是沒有人住的。*It would ~ that his intention was／His intention ~s to have been to arrive yesterday.* 他似乎原來打算昨天到達。*There ~s to have been a mistake.* 看起來曾有錯誤。*So it ~s.* 似乎是如此。*It ~s not.* 看起來並非如此。*It ~s to me that.../It begins to ~ that...,* It looks as though.... 在我看起來似乎…(看起來似乎…)。

ap·pear·ance /ə'pɪərəns ; ə'pɪrəns/ *n* [C] **1** act of appearing: 出現；出場；到場；出庭: *make an ~;* 露面；出庭; *make one's first ~,* (of an actor, singer, etc) appear in public for the first time. (指演員、歌唱者等)初次登台。***put in an ~,*** show oneself, attend (a meeting, party, etc): 到場；出席: *I don't want to go to the garden party but I'd better put in an ~.* 我本來不想參加那個園遊會，不過我最好還是去一下。 **2** that which shows or can be seen; what sth or sb appears to be: 外表；外觀；容貌: *The child had the ~ of being* (= looked as if it were) *half starved.* 那孩子看起來似乎在半飢餓狀態。*She has a slightly foreign ~.* 她看起來有點像外國人。*We mustn't judge by ~s,* by what can be seen outside, by outward looks. 我們不可以根據外貌判斷；不可以貌取人。***keep up ~s,*** maintain an outward show (in order to hide what one does not wish people to see, eg by buying smart clothes and spending little on food, etc). 虛飾外表；顧全面子；撐場面；打腫臉充胖子(例如購買華麗衣服而吃飯花錢很少等)。***in ~,*** so far as ~ is concerned; outwardly: 就外表而論；外表上看起來: *In ~ it is a strong building.* 外表上看起來這建築物很堅固。***to／by／from all ~(s),*** so far as can be seen: 就所能見及者而論；顯然: *He was to all ~(s) dead.* 他顯然已死。

ap·pease /ə'pi:z ; ə'piz/ *vt* [VP6A] make quiet or calm: 使平息；安撫: *~ sb's anger;* 平息某人的怒氣； *~ sb's curiosity／hunger.* 滿足某人之好奇心(充飢)。 **~·ment** *n* [U] appeasing, eg by making concessions to potential enemies. 平息；安撫；綏靖(例如對可能之敵人作讓步)；姑息。

ap·pel·lant /ə'pelənt; ə'pɛlənt/ *adj* (legal) concerned with appeals. (法律)上訴的。□ *n* (legal) person who appeals to a higher court. (法律)上訴人。

ap·pel·la·tion /ˌæpə'leɪʃn ; ˌæpə'leʃən/ *n* [C] (formal) name or title; system of names. (正式用語)名稱；稱呼；稱號；命名。

ap·pend /ə'pend ; ə'pɛnd/ *vt* [VP6A, 14] ***~ sth (to),*** (formal) add in writing or in print; add (sth) at the end: (正式用語)附加；添加；在後面增補: *~ a clause to a treaty;* 在條約上附加一項條款； *~ a seal or signature to a document.* 在文件上加蓋印信或簽署。

ap·pend·age /ə'pendɪdʒ ; ə'pɛndɪdʒ/ *n* [C] sth added to, fastened to or forming a natural part of, a larger thing. 附加物；附屬物；附屬部份；生成或固有的部份。

ap·pen·dix /ə'pendɪks ; ə'pɛndɪks/ *n* **1** [C] (*pl* -dices /-dɪsi:z ; -də,siz/) sth added, esp at the end of a book. 附加物；(尤指書末之)附錄。 **2** [C] (*pl* also 複數亦作 ~es) small out-growth on the surface of a bodily organ, esp (**'vermiform ~**) a wormlike appendage of the large intestine. 盲腸(尤指闌尾)。⇨ the illus at alimentary. 參看 alimentary 之插圖。**ap·pen·di·ci·tis** /əˌpendɪ'saɪtɪs ; əˌpɛndə'saɪtɪs/ *n* [U] diseased condition of the vermiform ~, requiring in many cases a surgical operation. 闌尾炎(俗稱盲腸炎)。**ap·pen·dec·tomy** /ˌæpen'dektəmɪ ; ˌæpən'dɛktəmɪ/ *n* (*pl* -mies) removal by surgery of the vermiform ~. 闌尾切除術。

ap·per·tain /ˌæpə'teɪn ; ˌæpə'ten/ *vi* [VP3A] ***~ to,*** (formal) belong to as a right; be appropriate: (正式用語)作爲一種權利而屬於；專屬: *the duties ~ing to his office.* 他的職位所應盡的責任。

ap·pe·tite /'æpɪtaɪt ; 'æpə,taɪt/ *n* [U] physical desire (esp *for* food): 欲望；(尤指)食慾: *She is suffering from lack of ~.* 她食慾不振。*If you eat a lot of chocolate before supper, it will spoil／take away your ~,* prevent you from enjoying your supper. 你如果在餐前吃很多巧克力，就會吃不下晚飯了。(fig) (喻) *He had no ~ for the fight.* 他失去鬥志。[C] instance of such a desire: 有食慾之實例: *The long walk gave him a good ~.* 長時間的走路使他食慾旺盛。**ap·pe·tizer** /'æpɪtaɪzə(r) ; 'æpə,taɪzə/ *n* sth done (eg a walk) or served (eg olives, a short alcoholic drink) in order to stimulate the ~. 增進食慾之事(如步行)；開胃的飲料或食物(如橄欖，少許的酒)；開胃品；開胃藥。**ap·pe·tiz·ing** *adj* pleasing to, exciting, the ~: 引起欲望或食慾的；促進食慾的；開胃的: *an appetizing smell from the kitchen.* 從厨房來的令人垂涎的味道。

ap·plaud /ə'plɔ:d ; ə'plɔd/ *vi, vt* **1** [VP6A, 2A, B] show approval (of) by clapping the hands: 鼓掌；藉鼓掌表示讚許: *The audience ~ed (the singer) for five minutes.* 聽衆(對歌唱者)鼓掌達五分鐘。*He was loudly ~ed.* 他受到熱烈的掌聲。**2** express approval of: 贊成；讚許: *I ~ your decision.* 我贊成你的決定。

ap·plause /ə'plɔ:z ; ə'plɔz/ *n* [U] loud approval; hand-clapping: 熱烈稱讚；喝采；鼓掌: *greeted with ~;* 受到熱烈的讚許; *win the ~ of the audience.* 贏得聽衆的掌聲。

apple /'æpl ; 'æpl/ *n* (tree with) round fruit with firm juicy flesh and skin that is green, red or yellow when the fruit is ripe. 蘋果；蘋果樹。⇨ the illus at fruit. 參看 fruit 之插圖。***the ~ of one's eye,*** sb or sth dearly loved. 極受珍愛之人或物；掌上明珠。***~ of discord,*** cause of quarrel. 爭吵的原因。***upset the／sb's '~-cart,*** spoil the／his plans. 破壞(某人之)計畫。***in ˌ~-ˌpie 'order,*** in perfect order, with everything in the right place. 井然有序。**'~-jack** *n* (US) brandy distilled from fermented cider. (美)蘋果白蘭地(由蒸餾發酵的蘋果汁而成)。**ˌ~ 'sauce,** (US = **'~-sauce**) *n* **(a)** sliced ~s stewed. 蘋果醬。 **(b)** (US colloq) nonsense; insincere flattery. (美俗)胡說；假意的恭維；奉承。**Adam's ~,** ⇨ Adam.

ap·pli·ance /ə'plaɪəns ; ə'plaɪəns/ *n* [C] instrument or apparatus: 工具；器械；器具；用具: *an ~ for rescuing sailors from a wrecked ship,* eg a rope that can be fired from a gun; 拯救海上遇難船員之救生器具(如可自槍中射出之繩索)； *household ~s,* eg a washing-machine, a food-mixer. 家庭器具(如洗衣機，食物拌合器等)。

ap·pli·cable /'æplɪkəbl ; 'æplɪkəbl̩/ *adj* ***~ (to),*** that can be applied; that is suitable and proper: 適用的；適當的；合適的: *Is the rule ~ to this case?* 該規則適用於這種情形嗎？

ap·pli·cant /'æplɪkənt ; 'æpləkənt/ *n* ***~ (for),*** person who applies (esp for a position): 申請人；請求者；(尤指)求職者: *As the wages were low, there were no ~s for the job.* 因爲工資低，沒有人申請這個工作。

ap·pli·ca·tion /ˌæplɪˈkeɪʃn ; ˌæpləˈkeʃən/ *n* **1** [U] **~ (to sb) (for sth),** making of a request: 申請; 請求: *A list of new books may be had on ~ to the publishers;* 新書目錄可向出版者索取; [C] request (esp in writing): 申請書;請求書: *The manager received twenty ~s for the position.* 經理收到了二十件求職申請書。*We made an ~ to the court for an enquiry.* 我們曾請求法院調查。 **ˈ~ form,** form to be filled in when applying for sth. 申請表格。 **2** [U] **~ (of sth) (to sth),** putting one thing on to another: 塗敷(某物於另一物上): *This oil is for external ~ only,* to be used only on the surface; 此油僅供外敷用; [C] substance used: 塗敷物;塗料;塗藥: *The doctor ordered an ~ of ice to the forehead.* 醫生吩咐敷冰於額上。 *Both cold and hot ~s are used to help people who are in pain.* 冷敷與熱敷均用於減輕疼痛。 **3** [U] **~ (of sth) (to sth),** bringing a rule to bear on a case; putting to practical use: 應用;運用: *the ~ of the rule to this case;* 把該規則應用於此一情形; *the ~ of a discovery/a new process, etc to industry.* 新發現(新方法等)之應用於工業。 **4** [U] effort; attention: 努力;注意: *If you show ~ in your studies* (= If you work hard) *you will succeed.* 如果你在功課上努力,你就會成功。*My work demands close ~,* ie I have to concentrate my thoughts on it. 我的工作需要聚精會神。

ap·plied ⇨ apply.

ap·pli·qué /æˈpliːkeɪ *US:* ˌæplɪˈkeɪ ; ˌæplɪˈke/ *n* [U] (esp in dress-making) ornamental work made of one kind of material, or material of one colour, applied to the surface of another. (尤指洋裁之)貼花(用不同的布料或不同顏色的布料加於服裝上的花飾)。 □ *vt* ornament in this way. 以貼花裝飾。

ap·ply /əˈplaɪ ; əˈplaɪ/ *vt, vi* (*pt, pp* -lied) **1** [VP2C, 3A] **~ (to sb) (for sth),** (formally) ask for: (正式)請求;申請: *~ to the Consul for a visa.* 向領事申請簽證。*You may ~ in person or by letter.* 你親自或通信申請均可。 **2** [VP6A, 14] lay one thing on or in another; cause (sth) to serve a purpose by doing this: 置一物於另一物上或中;應用;使用;貼用;敷塗: *~ a plaster to a cut;* 貼膏藥於割傷處; *~ the brakes* (of a motor vehicle, etc); 使用(汽車等之)刹車; (fig) (喻) *We intend to ~ economic sanctions.* 我們計畫施以經濟制裁。 **3** [VP6A, 3A] **~ (to sth),** (cause to) have a bearing (on); concern: (使)與…有關係;適用: *The rule cannot be applied in every case.* 這規則並非適用於所有的情形。*What I have said does not ~ to you.* 我所說的話與你無關。 **4** [VP14] **~ oneself/one's mind/one's energies (to sth/to doing sth),** concentrate one's thoughts, etc on a task, give all one's energy and attention to: 集中精力(做某事);全神貫注於: *~ your mind to your work.* 專心於你的工作。*We must ~ our energies to finding a solution.* 我們必須全力想出一個解決的辦法。 **5** [VP14] make practical use of (research, a discovery): 將(研究,發現)作實際應用;實際應用: *We can ~ his findings in new developments.* 我們可將他的調查結果應用於新發展中。 **ap·plied** *part adj* put to practical use: 應用的;實用的: *applied mathematics,* eg as used in engineering; 應用數學(如用於工程學中者); *applied art,* eg as used in textile designs, for pottery, etc. 實用美術(如用於織物圖案,陶器畫等者)。

ap·point /əˈpɔɪnt ; əˈpɔɪnt/ *vt* **1** [VP6A, 14, 16A] **~ sth (for sth),** choose, decide, fix (a time/date, etc): 定;決定;指定(時間,日期等): *The time ~ed for the meeting was 8.30pm.* 開會所定的時間是晚上八時三十分。 *We must ~ a time to meet again/a time for the next meeting.* 我們必須定出一個時間再集會(定出下次的會期)。 **2** [VP6A, 14, 16A, 23, 25] **~ sb (to sth),** choose for a post; set up by choosing members: 選派,指派,委派,任命(某人擔任某職位); 選定會員以組成: *They ~ed White (to be) manager.* 他們委派懷特爲經理。*Smith was ~ed to the vacant post.* 史密斯被派就那空缺。*The newly-~ed officials are all experts.* 那些新派任的官員全是專家老手。*We must ~ a committee.* 我們必須選派委員以組成一委員會。 **3** [VP9] (formal or older use) give orders: (正式用語或舊用法)下令;命令: *~ that sth shall be done.* 下令做某事。 **4 well/badly ~ed,** well/badly equipped. 設備好(壞)的。 **~ee** /əpɔɪnˈtiː ; əˌpɔɪnˈti/ *n* person ~ed to an office or position. 被派任者;被委派者;被指定人。

ap·point·ment /əˈpɔɪntmənt ; əˈpɔɪntmənt/ *n* **1** [U] appointing: 約定;任用;委派: *meet sb by ~,* after fixing a time and place. 經約定時間地點而會見某人。 **2** [C] arrangement to meet sb: 約會: *make/fix an ~ with sb;* 與某人約會; *keep/break an ~.* 踐約(失約)。 *I have an ~ with my dentist at 3pm.* 我已約定下午三時去看牙醫。 **3** [C] position or office: 職務;職位: *get a good ~ in a business firm;* 在一商行獲得一好職位; *an ~ as manager.* 擔任經理的職位。 **4** (*pl*) equipment; furniture. (複)設備;傢具。

ap·por·tion /əˈpɔːʃn ; əˈpɔrʃən/ *vt* [VP6A, 12B, 13B, 14] **~ (among/to),** divide; distribute; give as a share: 分;分配;分派: *I have ~ed you different duties each day of the week.* 我已把一週中每天的不同工作分派給你。*This sum of money is to be ~ed among the six boys.* 這筆錢將分配給這六個男孩子。

ap·po·site /ˈæpəzɪt ; ˈæpəzɪt/ *adj* strikingly appropriate for a purpose or occasion: 顯然適當的;適切的: *an ~ remark.* 適當的言論。 **~·ly** *adv*

ap·po·si·tion /ˌæpəˈzɪʃn ; ˌæpəˈzɪʃən/ *n* [U] (gram) addition of one word or group of words to another as an explanation: (文法)同位; 同格: *In the sentence, 'Herr Müller, our new teacher, is a German',* teacher *is in ~ to* Müller; teacher *and* Müller *are in ~.* 在 Herr Müller, our new teacher, is a German (米勒先生,我們的新老師,是德國人)一句中, teacher 是 Müller 的同位語; teacher 和 Müller 同位。

ap·praise /əˈpreɪz ; əˈprez/ *vt* [VP6A] fix a price for; say what sth is worth: 估計;估價;評價;鑑定: *~ the ability of one's pupils;* 鑑定其學生之能力; *~ property* (*at a certain sum*) *for taxation.* 估計財產之價值以爲課稅之依據。 **ap·prai·sal** /əˈpreɪzl ; əˈprezl̩/ *n* valuation. 估計;估價;評價。

ap·preci·able /əˈpriːʃəbl ; əˈpriʃɪəbl̩/ *adj* that can be seen, measured or felt: 可看見的;可測量的;可感到的: *an ~ change in the temperature.* 可感到的氣溫變化。 **ap·preci·ably** /-əblɪ ; -əblɪ/ *adv*

ap·preci·ate /əˈpriːʃɪeɪt ; əˈpriʃɪˌet/ *vt, vi* **1** [VP6A] judge rightly the value of; understand and enjoy: 正確地判斷…的價值;瞭解並欣賞;鑑賞: *You can't ~ English poetry unless you understand its rhythm.* 你若不懂英詩的韻律, 就不能欣賞英詩。*We all ~ a holiday after a year of hard work.* 經過一年之辛苦工作之後,我們大家都能領略假期的樂趣。 **2** [VP6A] put a high value on: 重視;寶貴;激賞: *We greatly ~ all your help.* 我們非常感激你的一切幫助。 **3** [VP2B] (of land, goods, etc) increase in value: (指土地,貨物等)價值增高;增值: *The land has ~d greatly since the new railway was built.* 自從新鐵路築成以後,這塊地的價值大爲增高。 **4** [VP6A, 9, 10] realize and understand: 了解: *I ~ your anxiety about your son's illness.* 我了解你爲兒子生病而憂慮的心情。

ap·preci·ation /əˌpriːʃɪˈeɪʃn ; əˌpriʃɪˈeʃən/ *n* **1** [C, U] (statement giving) judgement, valuation: 鑑識; 判斷; 評價; 欣賞; 評論; 批評: *Write an ~ of a new symphony.* 寫一篇評論一首新交響樂的文章。*She showed little or no ~ of good music.* 她對於好音樂毫無欣賞的能力。 **2** [U] proper understanding and recognition: 適切的瞭解與認知;激賞;感激: *in sincere ~ of your valuable help.* 對於你寶貴的幫助由衷感激。 **3** [U] rise in value, eg of land, business shares. (如土地,股票等之)增值;漲價。 **ap·preci·ative** /əˈpriːʃɪətɪv ; əˈpriʃɪˌetɪv/ *adj* feeling or showing ~(2): 欣賞的;表現出欣賞能力的;賞識的;

感激的: *an appreciative audience;* 有欣賞能力的聽衆; *appreciative of kindness.* 感激恩惠。**ap·preci·ative·ly** /əˈpriːʃjətɪvlɪ ; əˈpriʃɪˌetɪvlɪ/ *adv*

ap·pre·hend /ˌæprɪˈhend ; ˌæprɪˈhɛnd/ *vt* **1** [VP6A, 9] (old use) understand: (舊用法)了解;明瞭: *You are, I ~, ready to....* 我明瞭你已準備…。 **2** [VP6A, 9] (formal) fear: (正式用語)憂慮恐懼: *Do you ~ any difficulty / that there will be any difficulty?* 你怕有困難嗎? **3** [VP6A] (legal) arrest, seize: (法律)逮捕: *~ a thief.* 捕賊。**ap·pre·hen·sible** /ˌæprɪˈhensəbl ; ˌæprɪˈhɛnsəbl̩/ *adj* capable of being ~ed(1). 可了解的;可明瞭的。

ap·pre·hen·sion /ˌæprɪˈhenʃn ; ˌæprɪˈhɛnʃən/ *n* **1** [U] grasping (of ideas); understanding: 了解; 明瞭: *quick / slow of ~.* 悟性好(不好)。 **2** [C,U] fear; unhappy feeling about the future: 恐懼;憂慮: *feel ~ for sb's safety;* 爲某人之安全擔憂; *filled with ~;* 內心充滿憂慮; *entertain an ~ of failure.* 心中害怕失敗。 **3** (legal) seizing: (法律)逮捕: *the ~ of a thief / deserter.* 逮捕竊賊(逃亡者)。

ap·pre·hen·sive /ˌæprɪˈhensɪv ; ˌæprɪˈhɛnsɪv/ *adj* uneasy; worried: 不安的; 擔心的; 憂慮的: *~ of further defeats;* 擔心再失敗; *~ for sb's safety;* 爲某人之安全擔心; *~ that sb will be hurt.* 擔心某人會受到傷害。

ap·pren·tice /əˈprentɪs ; əˈprɛntɪs/ *n* learner of a trade who has agreed to work for a number of years in return for being taught. 學徒;徒弟。□ *vt* [VP6A,14] *~ (to),* bind as an ~: 使爲學徒: *The boy was ~d to a carpenter.* 那孩子被送到木匠那裏做學徒。**~·ship** /-tɪʃɪp ; -tɪsˌʃɪp/ *n* (time of) being an ~: 做學徒;學藝;學徒身份;學徒期間: *serve one's ~ship (with sb).* (跟某人)當學徒。

ap·prise /əˈpraɪz ; əˈpraɪz/ *vt* [VP14] *~ of,* (formal) inform: (正式用語)通知;報告: *be ~d of sb's intentions;* 獲悉某人的意圖; *be ~d that....* 已獲悉…。

ap·pro /ˈæprəʊ ; ˈæpro/ *n* **on ~,** (comm sl) on approval: (商俚)看貨後再做決定: *goods on ~,* to be returned if not satisfactory. 看貨後再做決定之貨物(如不滿意可以退還)。

ap·proach /əˈprəʊtʃ ; əˈprotʃ/ *vt, vi* **1** [VP6A, 2A] come near(er) (to): 走近;接近: *A boy of eighteen is ~ing manhood.* 十八歲的男孩快接近成年。 *As winter ~ed the weather became colder.* 因爲冬天漸近,天氣變得冷些了。(fig) (喻) *Few writers can even ~ Shakespeare in greatness.* 很少作家比得上莎士比亞的偉大。 **2** [VP6A] go to (sb) with a request or offer: 與(某人)接洽或交涉: *When is the best time to ~ my employer about an increase in salary?* 何時最適合與我的雇主交涉增加薪水? *He is rather difficult to ~,* It is not easy to get on friendly terms with him. 他是個不易接近的人。□ *n* **1** [U] act of ~ing: 漸近;接近: *The enemy ran away at our ~.* 當我們漸近的時候,敵人就逃竄了。 ***easy / difficult of ~,*** **(a)** (of a place) easy / difficult to get to. (指地方)容易(不易)到達的。**(b)** (of a person) easy / difficult to meet and talk to. (指人)容易(不易)接近的。***make ~es to sb,*** **(a)** try to obtain his interest, attract his attention. 設法博得某人的好感,或引起他的注意; 親近某人。**(b)** offer, try, to enter into personal relations with (eg of a man who wants intimate friendship with a girl or woman). (指欲與某女子建立親密友誼之男人等)設法與…搭上關係。 **2** [C] approximation: 近似;接近: *an ~ to perfection.* 接近完善。 **3** [C] way, path, road: 通路;引道: *All the ~es to the Palace were guarded by soldiers.* 所有通至王宮的道路都有士兵防守。**~·able** /-əbl ; -əbl̩/ *adj* (of a person or place) that can be ~ed; accessible. (指人)可親近的; (指地方)可到達的。

ap·pro·ba·tion /ˌæprəˈbeɪʃn ; ˌæprəˈbeʃən/ *n* [U] (formal) approval; sanction. (正式用語)許可;批准;讚許。

ap·pro·pri·ate¹ /əˈprəʊprɪət ; əˈpropriɪt/ *adj* ***~ (for / to sth),*** suited to; in keeping with: (對某事物)適當的;適合於…的;與…一致的: *Sports clothes are not ~ for a formal wedding.* 運動衣不適合於正式婚禮。*Write in a style ~ to your subject.* 以適合於你主題的文體來寫。**~·ly** *adv*

ap·pro·pri·ate² /əˈprəʊprɪeɪt ; əˈpropriˌet/ *vt* [VP6A, 14] **1** put on one side for a special purpose: 撥(款等)做某種特殊用途: *£20000 has been ~d for the new school buildings.* 已撥款兩萬鎊爲建築新校舍之用。 **2** take and use as one's own: 擅用;私用;挪用;竊用: *He often ~s my ideas.* 他時常剽竊我的見解。**ap·pro·pri·ation** /əˌprəʊprɪˈeɪʃn ; əˌpropriˈeʃən/ *n* **1** [U] appropriating or being ~d; [C] instance of this. 撥款;撥用;擅用;挪用;竊用;剽竊。 **2** [C] sth, esp a sum of money, that is ~d: 被撥用或擅用之物; (尤指)所撥之款: *make an appropriation for payment of debts;* 撥一筆款清償債務; *Senate A~s Committee,* (US) one which deals with funds for defence, welfare, etc. (美)參議院撥款委員會(負責防衛,福利等專款之劃撥)。

ap·pro·val /əˈpruːvl ; əˈpruvl̩/ *n* [U] feeling, showing or saying, that one is satisfied, that sth is right, that one agrees to sth: 贊成;認可;同意;批准: *Your plans have my ~.* 你的計畫我贊成。*Does what I have done meet with your ~?* 我所做的你贊成嗎? *She gave a nod of ~ / nodded her ~.* 她點頭表示同意。***goods on ~,*** to be returned if not satisfactory. 不滿意包換之貨物。

ap·prove /əˈpruːv ; əˈpruv/ *vt, vi* **1** [VP3A] ***~ of sth / sb,*** give one's approval of: 贊成;同意;認可;批准: *Her father will never ~ of her marriage to you.* 她父親永不會同意她和你結婚。*I cannot support a policy of which I have never ~d.* 我不能支持一項我所從未贊成的政策。 **2** [VP6A] confirm; agree to: 同意;認可;通過: *The minutes (of the meeting) were read and ~d.* (會議)紀錄經宣讀通過。*The expenditure has been ~d.* 該筆費用已獲通過。**ˈ~d school,** (GB) boarding school for training and educating children under 17 who are sent there by magistrates for juvenile offences or because in need of care and protection. (US 美 = *reformatory, reform school*). (英)少年罪犯教養院;少年感化院。**ap·prov·ing·ly** *adv*

ap·proxi·mate¹ /əˈprɒksɪmət ; əˈprɑksəmɪt/ *adj* ***~ (to),*** very near correct; about right: 極近於…的; 大約正確的;大概的: *a sum of money ~ to what will be needed.* 一筆極接近所需數目的款子。*The ~ area of my land is half an acre.* 我的土地的面積大概爲半畝。**~·ly** *adv*

ap·proxi·mate² /əˈprɒksɪmeɪt ; əˈprɑksəˌmet/ *vi, vt* **1** [VP3A] ***~ to,*** come near to (esp in quality or number): 近;接近(尤指在質或數方面): *His description of the event ~d to the truth but there were a few inaccuracies.* 他對於這件事的描述很接近於事實, 但仍有幾處不正確的地方。 **2** [VP6A, 3A] bring or come near to. 使接近;接近。**ap·proxi·ma·tion** /əˌprɒksɪˈmeɪʃn ; əˌprɑksəˈmeʃən/ *n* [C] almost correct amount or estimate; [U] being or getting near (in number or quality). 差不多正確的量或估計;概算;接近;近似值。

ap·pur·ten·ance /əˈpɜːtɪnəns ; əˈpɝtnəns/ *n* (usu *pl*) (legal) sth that belongs to or usu goes with another thing: (通常用複數) (法律)附屬物;從物;從屬權利: *the house and its ~s,* the lesser rights and privileges that go with ownership of the house. 房屋之所有權及其從屬權利。

après-ski /ˌæpreɪ ˈskiː ; ˌæpreˈski/ *attrib adj* of the evening period after skiing: 滑雪後之晚間的: *~ fun and games;* 滑雪後晚間之娛樂遊戲; *~ clothes.* 滑雪後之晚裝。

apri·cot /ˈeɪprɪkɒt ; ˈeprɪˌkɑt/ *n* (tree with) round, orange-yellow or orange-red fruit with soft flesh and a hard stone-like seed; colour of this fruit when ripe. 杏;杏樹;杏黃色。

April /ˈeɪprəl ; ˈeprəl/ *n* fourth month of the year. 四月。**ˌ~ ˈfool,** person who is hoaxed on ˌAll

'Fools' Day (1 April). 四月愚人(四月一日愚人節被人所愚弄的人)。

a priori /ˌeɪ praɪˈɔːraɪ ; ˈepraɪˈoraɪ/ *adv, adj* (Lat) (reasoning) from cause to effect, eg saying, *'The boys have walked a long way so they must be tired.'* (拉丁) 自原因推及結果地 (的); 演繹地 (的) (例如: '孩子們走了很多路，所以他們一定累了。') ⇨ a posteriori.

apron /ˈeɪprən ; ˈeprən/ *n* **1** loose garment worn over the front part of the body to keep clothes clean; any similar covering. 圍裙;圍腰布。 ***tied to his mother's/wife's ˈ~-strings,*** too long or too much under her control. 深受母親(妻子)所操縱或支配的。 **2** hard-surfaced (tarmac, concrete, etc) area on an air-field, used for manoeuvring and (un)loading aircraft. 停機坪(飛機場上用以調配飛機或裝卸貨物的一塊鋪有柏油或混凝土等的地方)。 **3** **ˈ~ stage,** (in some theatres) part of the stage jutting out into the audience. 舞台前部(在某些劇院中,舞台伸向觀衆席之部份)。⇨ proscenium.

apro·pos /ˌæprəˈpəʊ ; ˌæprəˈpo/ *adv, pred adj* to the purpose; well suited (to what is being said or done): 與目的切合地(的); (與正在說的或做的)適當地(的);切題地(的): *His suggestion is very much ~.* 他的建議非常適當。 ***~ of*** *prep* concerning, with reference to. 關於;至於;就…而論。

apse /æps ; æps/ *n* semi-circular or many-sided recess, with an arched or domed roof, esp at the east end of a church. 建築物之半圓形或多邊形的凹室(頂爲拱形或圓形,尤指在教堂之東端者); 半圓形殿。⇨ the illus at church. 參看 church 之挿圖。

apt /æpt ; æpt/ *adj* (-er, -est) **1** ***apt (at doing sth),*** quick-witted: (做某事)聰明的;敏捷的: *one of my aptest pupils;* 我的最聰明的學生之一; *very apt at picking up a new subject.* 極敏於學習新科目。 **2** to the point; well suited: 切題的;恰當的;適切的;適當的: *an apt remark.* 適當的言論。 **3** ***apt to do sth,*** having a tendency, likely to do sth: 有…的傾向;易於: *Cast iron is apt to break.* 生鐵易於斷折。 *He's a clever boy but apt to get into mischief.* 他是個聰明的孩子,但是好搗亂。 **apt·ly** *adv* suitably, justly. 合適地;適當地。 **apt·ness** *n*

ap·ti·tude /ˈæptɪtjuːd *US:* -tuːd ; ˈæptəˌtjud/ *n* [U] ***~ (for),*** natural or acquired talent: 資質;才能: *He shows some ~ for languages.* 他表現出學習語言的才能。 [C] particular talent: 某種才能: *He has a singular ~ for dealing with a crisis.* 他有處理危機的奇才。 **ˈ~ test,** test to discover and assess skills. 性向測驗。

aqua·lung /ˈækwəlʌŋ ; ˈækwəˌlʌŋ/ *n* (P) breathing unit (face mask, valve unit and cylinder(s) of compressed air or oxygen) used for underwater swimming or diving. (商標)水肺(潛水者所用的面具,活門及氧氣筒)。⇨ the illus at frogman. 參看 frogman 之挿圖。

aqua·mar·ine /ˌækwəməˈriːn ; ˌækwəməˈrin/ *n* [C,U] bluish-green (jewel). 水藍寶石;藍晶;藍綠色。

aqua·naut /ˈækwənɔːt ; ˈækwəˌnɔt/ *n* person trained to live for a long period, in a structure submerged in the sea, to study marine life, etc. 海底人(受過訓練能長時間生活在置於海中之構造物中,以硏究海洋生物等)。

aqua·plane /ˈækwəpleɪn ; ˈækwəˌplen/ *n* board on which a person stands while being pulled along by a fast motor-boat. 滑水板(由快艇牽引供人乘立之板,係水上運動器具)。□ *vi* ride on such a board. 乘滑水板作滑水運動。

aquar·ium /əˈkweərɪəm ; əˈkwɛrɪəm/ *n* (*pl* -s, -ria /-rɪə ; -rɪə/) (building with an) artificial pond or tank for keeping and showing living fish and water plants. 水族館;蓄魚池;養魚缸。

Aquar·ius /əˈkweərɪəs ; əˈkwɛrɪəs/ *n* the eleventh sign of the zodiac. 寶瓶宮(黃道十二宮中的第十一宮)。⇨ the illus at zodiac. 參看 zodiac 之挿圖。

aqua·tic /əˈkwætɪk ; əˈkwætɪk/ *adj* **1** (of plants, animals, etc) growing or living in or near water. (指植物,動物等) 水生的; 生長或棲於水中(或水邊)的。 **2** (of sports) taking place on or in water, eg rowing, swimming. (指運動)水上的; 在水上或水中舉行的(如划船,游泳)。

aqua·tint /ˈækwətɪnt ; ˈækwəˌtɪnt/ *n* [U] process of etching on copper, the picture being made by letting acid bite into a plate covered with a layer of resin dust; [C] picture made in this way. 銅版蝕鏤法 (利用酸性腐蝕作用刻畫於覆有一層樹脂的銅版之方法);以此種方法蝕鏤之圖畫。

aqua·vit /ˈækwəvɪt ; ˈækwəvɪt/ *n* [U] strong Scandinavian liquor flavoured with caraway seed. 一種北歐烈酒(用葛縷子之子作爲香料)。

aque·duct /ˈækwɪdʌkt ; ˈækwɪˌdʌkt/ *n* artificial channel for supplying water, esp one built of stone or brick and higher than the surrounding land. 輸水道; 水道橋 (人工水道,尤指用石或磚造成而高於周圍陸地者)。

an aqueduct

aque·ous /ˈeɪkwɪəs ; ˈekwɪəs/ *adj* of or like water: 水的;似水的: *an ~ solution.* 水溶液。

aqui·line /ˈækwɪlaɪn ; ˈækwəˌlaɪn/ *adj* of or like an eagle: 鷹的; 似鷹的: *an ~ nose,* hooked like an eagle's beak. 鷹鉤鼻子。

Arab /ˈærəb ; ˈærəb/ *n* name applied to any of those Semitic people who speak Arabic and claim descent from the inhabitants of the Arabian Peninsula who, in the 7th c, were conquerors of N Africa, Syria and Mesopotamia: 阿拉伯人: *the military conquests of the ~s;* 阿拉伯人藉軍事行動所畧取之土地; *the ~ League.* 阿拉伯聯盟。

ara·besque /ˌærəˈbesk ; ˌærəˈbɛsk/ *n* [C] (art) elaborate design of leaves, branches, scrolls, etc; (ballet) pose of a dancer on one leg, the other stretched backwards. (藝術)一種由葉,枝,渦卷等圖形組成之精細的圖案;阿拉伯花紋;(芭蕾) 一種舞姿 (單脚直立,另一脚向後伸直的姿勢)。

Ara·bian /əˈreɪbɪən ; əˈrebɪən/ *n, adj* (person) of (Saudi) Arabia or the Arabs. (沙烏地)阿拉伯的;(沙烏地) 阿拉伯人(的)。 **the ~ Nights,** famous stories of the Arabs in ancient times. 天方夜譚(古代阿拉伯人的著名故事)。 **the ~ camel,** the dromedary. 阿拉伯駱駝;單峯駱駝。

Ara·bic /ˈærəbɪk ; ˈærəbɪk/ *adj* of the Arabs. 阿拉伯人的。 **~ numerals,** the signs 0, 1, 2, 3, etc. 阿拉伯數字。⇨ App 4. 參看附錄四。□ *n* language of the Arabs. 阿拉伯語文。

Ara·bist /ˈærəbɪst ; ˈærəbɪst/ *n* student or specialist in Arabic culture, language, affairs, etc. 阿拉伯學者;阿拉伯專家(研究阿拉伯文化,語言,事務等)。

ar·able /ˈærəbl ; ˈærəbl̩/ *adj* (of land) suitable for ploughing; usually ploughed. (指土地)可耕的;適於耕種的;經常被耕作的。

arach·nid /əˈræknɪd ; əˈræknɪd/ *n* (zool) member of the genus including spiders, scorpions and mites. (動物)蜘蛛類節肢動物(包括蜘蛛,蠍及小蝨)。

ar·bi·ter /ˈɑːbɪtə(r) ; ˈɑrbɪtɚ/ *n* **1** ***~ (of),*** person with complete control (of sth): (對某事物)有完全控制力之人;主宰者;裁決者: *the sole ~ of their destinies.* 他們的命運的唯一主宰。 **2** = arbitrator.

ar·bitra·ment /ɑːˈbɪtrəmənt ; ɑrˈbɪtrəmənt/ *n* [U] (formal) deciding of a dispute by an arbiter; [C] decision made by an arbiter. (正式用語) 仲裁; 調停;仲裁人所作之決定。

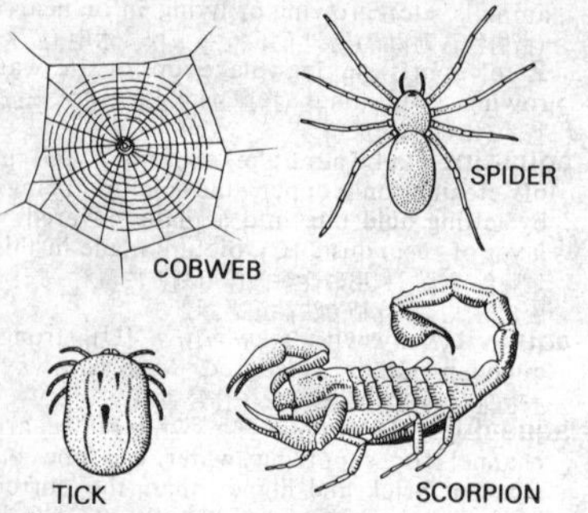

arachnids

ar·bit·rary /ˈɑːbɪtrərɪ *US:* -trerɪ ; ˈɑrbəˌtrerɪ/ *adj* **1** based on opinion or impulse only, not on reason. 僅依據意見或衝動而非基於理性的;武斷的。 **2** dictatorial; using despotic power. 獨裁的;專制的;專橫的。

ar·bi·trate /ˈɑːbɪtreɪt ; ˈɑrbəˌtret/ *vt, vi* [VP6A, 2A] ~ ***(between),*** decide by arbitration; judge between two parties to a dispute (usu at the request of the two parties): 由仲裁決定;仲裁;公斷(通常係應爭執中之雙方之請求而作裁判): *Mr X has been asked to ~ the dispute/to ~ between the employers and their workers.* 某先生已被邀請仲裁此項糾紛(仲裁雇主與工人之間的紛爭)。 *If countries would always ~ their quarrels, wars could be avoided.* 假若各國都願意由仲裁解決他們的紛爭,戰爭就可以避免了。

ar·bi·tra·tion /ˌɑːbɪˈtreɪʃn ; ˌɑrbəˈtreʃən/ *n* [U] (attempt at a) settlement of a dispute by the decision of a person or persons chosen and accepted as judges or umpires: 仲裁;公斷: *refer a wage dispute to ~;* 將一項工資爭執提請仲裁。 *submit a claim for ~;* 將一項紛爭提請仲裁; [C] instance of such a settlement. 仲裁之實例。 ***go to ~,*** arbitrate: 提請仲裁: *The Union agreed to go to ~,* ie for a settlement of their claims. 聯合王國(指 1706 年英格蘭與蘇格蘭的合併)同意提請仲裁解決。

ar·bi·tra·tor /ˈɑːbɪtreɪtə(r) ; ˈɑrbəˌtretɚ/ *n* (legal) arbiter; person appointed by two parties to settle a dispute. (法律)仲裁者;公斷人。

ar·bor ⇨ arbour.

ar·bor·eal /ɑːˈbɔːrɪəl ; ɑrˈbɔrɪəl/ *adj* (formal) of, living in, connected with trees: (正式用語)樹的;棲於樹上的; 關於樹的: ~ *animals,* eg squirrels, monkeys. 棲於樹上的動物(如松鼠,猴等)。

ar·bour (US = **ar·bor**) /ˈɑːbə(r) ; ˈɑrbɚ/ *n* shady place among trees, esp one made in a garden, with climbing plants growing over a framework. 樹木中之蔭處;花園中之藤架;涼亭。

arc /ɑːk ; ɑrk/ *n* part of the circumference of a circle or other curved line. 弧(圓周或曲線之一部份)。 ⇨ the illus at circle. 參看 circle 之插圖。 **ˈarc-lamp, ˈarc-light** *nn* brilliant light produced by electric current flowing across a space between two carbon rods. 弧光燈;弧光(由電流通過兩碳棒間之空處所產生之光亮)。

ar·cade /ɑːˈkeɪd ; ɑrˈked/ *n* covered passage, usu with an arched roof, eg a passage with shops or market stalls along one or both sides; covered market. 騎樓; 連環拱廊(通常有拱形頂蓋, 尤指其一側或兩側有商店或攤位之街道; 拱廊市場。 **aˈmusement ~,** ⇨ amusement.

Ar·cad·ian /ɑːˈkeɪdɪən ; ɑrˈkedɪən/ *adj* of an ideal rustic simplicity; simple and innocent. 一種理想鄉村之簡樸的; 淳樸的。 □ *n* person with ~ tastes. 淳樸之人。

ar·cane /ɑːˈkeɪn ; ɑrˈken/ *adj* secret; mysterious. 秘密的;神秘的。

arch[1] /ɑːtʃ ; ɑrtʃ/ *n* **1** curved structure supporting the weight of what is above it, as in bridges, aqueducts, gateways, etc. 拱(支持上面之重量的弓形構造,如見於橋梁,引水道,大門等者)。 ⇨ the illus at aqueduct, church. 參看 aqueduct, church 之插圖。 **2** (also 亦作 **ˈ~·way**) passageway under an ~, built as an ornament or gateway: 拱門;拱形牌坊: *a triumphal ~.* 凱旋門。 **3** any curve in the shape of an ~, eg the curved under-part of the foot, ⇨ the illus at leg; a structure for supporting climbing roses, etc. 任何拱形之曲部(例如足穹, 參看 leg 之插圖); (用以支持攀緣之玫瑰等之)拱架。 □ *vt, vi* **1** [VP6A] form into an ~: 使彎成拱形: *The cat ~ed its back when it saw the dog.* 貓見到狗卽拱其背。 *Horses ~ their necks.* 馬拱其頸。 **2** [VP2C] be like an ~: 成拱狀;成弓形: *The trees ~ over the river.* 這些樹的枝葉成弓形遮覆河上。

arch[2] /ɑːtʃ ; ɑrtʃ/ *attrib adj* mischievous in an innocent or playful way (esp of women and children): 頑皮的;調皮的;嬉戲的(尤指婦女及兒童): *an ~ glance/smile.* 調皮的一瞥(一笑)。 **~·ly** *adv*

arch- /ɑːtʃ ; ɑrtʃ/ *pref* chief; notable; extreme: 主要;顯著;極;首;大: ˌ~-ˈ*enemy.* 大敵;主敵。

ar·chae·ol·ogy (also **ar·che·ol-**) /ˌɑːkɪˈɒlədʒɪ ; ˌɑrkɪˈɑlədʒɪ/ *n* [U] study of ancient things, esp remains of prehistoric times, eg tombs, buried cities. 考古學(研究古物,尤其是史前時代之遺物,如墳墓,湮滅之古城等)。 **ar·chae·ologi·cal** /ˌɑːkɪəˈlɒdʒɪkl ; ˌɑrkɪəˈlɑdʒɪkḷ/ *adj* of ~. 考古學的。 **ar·chae·ol·ogist** /ˌɑːkɪˈɒlədʒɪst ; ˌɑrkɪˈɑlədʒɪst/ *n* expert in ~. 考古學家。

ar·chaic /ɑːˈkeɪɪk ; ɑrˈkeɪk/ *adj* **1** (of eg a word in a language) not now used except for special purposes. (指某一語言之某字等)除特殊情形外現已不用的;古的;已不通用的。 **2** of ancient times. 古代的。 **ar·cha·ism** /ˈɑːkeɪɪzəm ; ˈɑrkɪˌɪzəm/ *n* [C] ~ word or expression; [U] use or imitation of what is ~. 古字;古語;古字古語之使用或模倣;古風;古體。

arch·angel /ˈɑːkeɪndʒl ; ˈɑrkˈendʒəl/ *n* angel of high rank. 天使長;大天使。

arch·bishop /ˌɑːtʃˈbɪʃəp ; ˈɑrtʃˈbɪʃəp/ *n* chief bishop. 大主教。 **~·ric** *n* position or rank of an ~; church district governed by an ~. 大主教之職銜;大主教之轄區。

arch·deacon /ˌɑːtʃˈdiːkən ; ˈɑrtʃˈdikən/ *n* (in the C of E) priest next below a bishop, superintending rural deans. (英國國教)副主教(負責監督鄉村教會執事者)。 **~·ry** *n* (*pl* -ries) position, rank, residence, of an ~. 副主教之職位、住宅。

arch·dio·cese /ˌɑːtʃˈdaɪəsɪs ; ˈɑrtʃˈdaɪəˌsis/ *n* diocese of an archbishop. 大主教教區。

arch·duke /ˌɑːtʃˈdjuːk *US:* -ˈduːk ; ˈɑrtʃˈdjuk/ *n* (title given to) son or nephew of former Emperors of Austria. 大公;大公爵(昔日奧國皇太子或皇侄之頭銜)。

archer /ˈɑːtʃə(r) ; ˈɑrtʃɚ/ *n* person who shoots with a bow and arrows. 弓箭手。 **arch·ery** /ˈɑːtʃərɪ ; ˈɑrtʃərɪ/ *n* [U] (art of) shooting with a bow and arrows. 射箭術;射箭;箭藝。

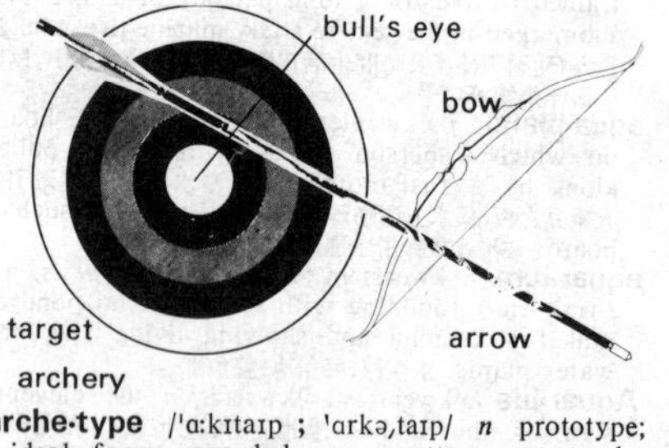

archery

arche·type /ˈɑːkɪtaɪp ; ˈɑrkəˌtaɪp/ *n* prototype; ideal form regarded as a pattern not to be changed. 原型;理想型。 **arche·typal** /ˌɑːkɪˈtaɪpl ;

ˈɑrkɪˈtaɪpḷ/ *adj*

archi·man·drite /ˌɑːkɪˈmændraɪt ; ˌɑrkɪˈmændraɪt/ *n* head of a monastery in the Gk Orthodox Church. 希臘正教之修道院長。

archi·pel·ago /ˌɑːkɪˈpeləgəʊ ; ˌɑrkəˈpɛləˌgo/ *n* (*pl* ~s, ~es /-gəʊz ; -goz/) (sea with a) group of many islands. 群島;有群島之海;多島海。

archi·tect /ˈɑːkɪtekt ; ˈɑrkəˌtɛkt/ *n* person who designs (and supervises the construction of) buildings, etc. 建築師。

archi·tec·ture /ˈɑːkɪtektʃə(r) ; ˈɑrkəˌtɛktʃɚ/ *n* [U] art and science of building; design or style of building(s). 建築學;建築術;建築之設計或式樣。**archi·tec·tural** /ˌɑːkɪˈtektʃərəl ; ˌɑrkəˈtɛktʃərəl/ *adj* of ~: 建築學(術)的: *the architectural beauties of a city.* 某城中的設計優美的建築物。

ar·chives /ˈɑːkaɪvz ; ˈɑrkaɪvz/ *n pl* (place for keeping) public or government records; other historical records. 檔案;檔案保管處;歷史性的記錄或文件。**archi·vist** /ˈɑːkɪvɪst ; ˈɑrkəvɪst/ *n* person in charge of ~. 檔案保管人。

arch·way /ˈɑːtʃweɪ ; ˈɑrtʃˌwe/ *n* ⇨ arch¹(2).

arc·tic /ˈɑːktɪk ; ˈɑrktɪk/ *adj* of the north polar regions: 北極的: *the A~ Ocean;* 北冰洋; *~ weather,* very cold weather. 嚴寒的天氣。**the ˌA~ ˈCircle,** the line of latitude 66½°N. 北極圈 (卽北緯六十六度半線)。

ar·dent /ˈɑːdnt ; ˈɑrdṇt/ *adj* full of ardour: 熱心的;熱情的: *~ supporters of the new movement.* 新運動的熱烈擁護者。**~·ly** *adv*

ar·dour (US = **-dor**) /ˈɑːdə(r) ; ˈɑrdɚ/ *n* **~ (for),** [C, U] warm emotion; enthusiasm. 熱情;熱心。

ar·du·ous /ˈɑːdjʊəs *US:* -dʒʊ- ; ˈɑrdʒʊəs/ *adj* **1** (of work) needing and using up much energy. (指工作)費力的;艱鉅的。**2** (of a road, etc) steep; hard to climb. (指道路等)陡峭的;難登的。**~·ly** *adv*

are¹ /ə(r) ; ɚ ; *strong form:* ɑː(r) ; ɑr/ ⇨ be¹.

are² /ɑː(r) ; ɛr/ *n* metric unit of area, = 100 square metres. 公畝(公制面積單位，等於一百平方公尺)。⇨ App 5. 參看附錄五。

area /ˈeərɪə ; ˈɛrɪə/ *n* **1** [U] surface measure: 面積: *If a room measures 3×5 metres, its ~ is 15 square metres/it is 15 square metres in ~.* 假若一個房間是三公尺寬五公尺長，它的面積就是十五平方公尺。[C] instance of this measurement. 面積之實例。⇨ App 5. 參看附錄五。**2** [C] region of the earth's surface: 地區: *desert ~s of North Africa;* 北非洲的沙漠地區; *the postal ~s* (more usu 較常用 *districts*) *into which London is divided.* 倫敦所劃的郵遞區。**3** [C] (fig) scope or range of activity: (喩)活動的區域; 範圍;領域: *the ~ of finance.* 財政(金融)範圍。*The ~s of disagreement were clearly indicated at the Board Meeting,* The subjects on which members of the Board disagreed became clear. 在委員會的會議中意見不一致的地方變得很明顯。**4** [C] small courtyard giving light to the windows of basement rooms, eg kitchen, scullery, in an old-fashioned town house, usu with stone steps from the street pavement: 地下室小庭院(英國舊式城市房屋之供光線給地下室窗戶,如廚房，碗碟洗滌室之小庭院，通常有石階可通街上人行道): *sitting on the ~ steps.* 坐在地下室庭院的石階上。

areca /ˈærɪkə ; ˈærɪkə/ *n* kind of palm-tree from which areca-nut (betel-nut) is obtained. 檳榔樹。⇨ betel.

arena /əˈriːnə ; əˈrinə/ *n* (*pl* ~s) central part, for games and fights, of a Roman amphitheatre, ⇨ the illus at amphitheatre; (fig) any scene of competition or struggle: 古羅馬圓形劇場中央供比賽及打鬥之處; 比武場; 鬥技場 (參看 amphitheatre 之插圖); (喩)任何競爭或角逐之場所; 舞台: *the ~ of politics.* 政治舞台。

aren't /ɑːnt ; ɑrnt/ = are not: *aren't I?* = am I not? 不是我嗎?

arête /æˈreɪt ; æˈret/ *n* (F) (esp of mountains in Switzerland) sharp ridge. (法) (尤指瑞士境內之山的)險峻山脊;峻嶺。⇨ the illus at mountain. 參看 mountain 之插圖。

ar·gent /ˈɑːdʒənt ; ˈɑrdʒənt/ *n, adj* (in heraldry and poetry) silver (colour). (紋章及詩)銀(的);銀色(的)。

ar·gon /ˈɑːgɒn ; ˈɑrgɑn/ *n* [U] chemically inactive gas (symbol **Ar**), present in the atmosphere (0·8 per cent), used in some kinds of electric lamps. 氬(化學性不活潑之氣體,化學符號 Ar,存在於大氣中,佔百分之零點八,用於某些種電燈中)。

Ar·go·naut /ˈɑːgənɔːt ; ˈɑrgəˌnɔt/ *n* (myth) one of the heroes who sailed in the ship Argo /ˈɑːgəʊ ; ˈɑrgo/ with Jason in search of the Golden Fleece. (神話)與 Jason 同乘 Argo 號船尋找金羊毛之英雄之一。

ar·gosy /ˈɑːgəsɪ ; ˈɑrgəsɪ/ *n* (*pl* -sies) (poet) large merchant ship, esp one with valuable cargo. (詩)大商船(尤指載有貴重貨物者)。

ar·got /ˈɑːgəʊ ; ˈɑrgo/ *n* [U] jargon; slang. 隱語;暗語;黑話;俚語。

ar·gue /ˈɑːgjuː ; ˈɑrgju/ *vi, vt* **1** [VP2A, C, 3A] **~ *(with sb) (about/over sth),*** express disagreement; quarrel: 表示不同意;(與某人)爭論(某事);爭吵: *Don't ~ with me; my decision is final.* 不要跟我爭論;我的決定是最後的了。*Why are they always ~ing?* 爲什麼他們總是在爭論? **2** [VP2A, 3A, 9] **~ *(for/against/that...),*** maintain a case, give reasons (in support of, for, against, esp with the aim of persuading sb): 堅持; 提出理由(以支持或反對,尤指以說服某人爲目的者);爭辯: *He ~s soundly.* 他爭辯得很有道理。*You can ~ either way, for or against.* 你可以在正反兩面擇一辯護。*He was arguing that poverty may be a blessing.* 他主張貧窮是福。**3** [VP14] **~ *sb into/out of doing sth,*** persuade by giving reasons: (提出理由以) 說服某人做 (不做)某事: *They tried to ~ him into joining them.* 他們試圖說服他參加他們。**4** [VP6A] debate: 討論;辯論: *The lawyers ~d the case for hours.* 律師們辯論該案件達數小時之久。**ar·gu·able** /ˈɑːgjʊəbl ; ˈɑrgjʊəbḷ/ *adj* that can be ~d about. 可爭論的;可討論的; 可辯論的。**ar·gu·ably** /-əblɪ ; -əblɪ/ *adv*

ar·gu·ment /ˈɑːgjʊmənt ; ˈɑrgjəmənt/ *n* **1** [C] ***an ~ (with sb) (about/over sth),*** (perhaps heated) disagreement; quarrel: (與某人的) (關於某事的) 意見不合;爭論;爭吵: *endless ~s about money;* 有關金錢的永遠沒完的爭論; *an ~ with the referee.* 與裁判員之爭論。**2** [U] reasoned discussion: 討論;辯論;論據: *It is beyond ~ that...;* …是無可置辯的; [C] ***an ~ (for/against),*** instance of this: (贊成,反對的)論據: *an ~ for not gambling.* 反對賭博的論據。*I have no wish to engage in (an) ~ with you.* 我不想跟你辯論。**3** [C] summary of the subject matter of a book, etc. (一本書等的)摘要;概要。**ar·gu·men·ta·tive** /ˌɑːgjʊˈmentətɪv ; ˌɑrgjəˈmɛntətɪv/ *adj* fond of arguing(1). 好爭論的;愛辯論的。

ar·gu·men·ta·tion /ˌɑːgjʊmenˈteɪʃn ; ˌɑrgjəmɛnˈteʃən/ *n* [U] process of arguing; debate. 辯論法;辯論;論爭;論證。

Ar·gus /ˈɑːgəs ; ˈɑrgəs/ *n* (GK myth) monster with a hundred eyes. (希神)百眼巨人。**ˌ~-ˈeyed** *adj* observant; vigilant. 善於觀察的;機警的;警醒的。

aria /ˈɑːrɪə ; ˈɑrɪə/ *n* (*pl* ~s) song for a single voice (esp in 18th c operas and oratorios). (尤指十八世紀歌劇及聖樂中之)獨唱曲;咏嘆調;抒情調。

arid /ˈærɪd ; ˈærɪd/ *adj* **1** (of soil, land) dry, barren; (of climate, regions) having not enough rainfall to support vegetation. (指土壤,土地)乾燥的;不生草木的;不毛的; (指氣候,地區) 乾旱的;雨量稀少的。**2** (fig) uninteresting. (喩)無趣味的;枯燥的。**arid·ity** /əˈrɪdətɪ ; əˈrɪdətɪ/ *n* [U] dryness. 乾燥;枯燥。

Aries /ˈeəriːz ; ˈɛriz/ *n* the Ram, the first sign of the zodiac. 白羊宮(黃道帶之第一宮)。⇨ the illus at zodiac. 參看 zodiac 之插圖。

aright /əˈraɪt ; əˈraɪt/ *adv* (archaic) rightly: (古)對;不錯;正確地: *if I heard ~.* 假如我聽得不錯的話。(Before a *pp* use *rightly,* as in *to be rightly in-*

formed.) (在過去分詞之前用 rightly,如 to be rightly informed. 得到正確的消息。)

arise /ə'raɪz ; ə'raɪz/ *vi* (*pt* arose /ə'rəʊz ; ə'roz/, *pp* arisen /ə'rɪzn ; ə'rɪzṇ/) **1** [VP2A] come into existence; come to notice; present itself: 發生;出現;呈現;起: *A new difficulty has ~n.* 一項新的困難發生了。*If the need should ~...;* 假若有必要的話…; *Before they could start a mist arose.* 在他們出發之前,起了霧。 **2** [VP3A] ~ ***from,*** result from: 產生: *Serious obligations may ~ from the proposed clause.* 由這項提議的條款可能產生一些重大的責任。 **3** [VP2A] (old use) get up; stand up. (舊用法)起身;起來;起立。

ar·is·toc·racy /ˌærɪ'stɒkrəsɪ ; ˌærə'stakrəsɪ/ *n* (*pl* -cies) **1** [U] government by persons of the highest social rank; [C] country or state with such a government. 貴族政治;實行貴族政治的國家。 **2** [C] ruling body of nobles; the social class from which these nobles come. 貴族統治集團;貴族階級。 **3** [C] best representatives in any class: (集合用法,任何階級之)最優秀代表;第一流的人物: *an ~ of talent.* 第一流的人才。

ar·is·to·crat /'ærɪstəkræt *US:* ə'rɪst- ; ə'rɪstəˌkræt/ *n* member of the class of nobles; person of noble birth. 貴族階級之一員;出身貴族的人;貴族。**~ic** /ˌærɪstə'krætɪk *US:* əˌrɪstə- ; əˌrɪstə'krætɪk/ *adj* of the aristocracy; having the ways and manners of an ~: 貴族的;貴族政治的;有貴族氣派的: *with an ~ic bearing.* 擧止態度有貴族氣質的。**~i·cally** /-klɪ ; -klɪ/ *adv*

arith·me·tic /ə'rɪθmətɪk ; ə'rɪθməˌtɪk/ *n* [U] science of numbers; working with numbers. 算術;計算。 **ar·ith·meti·cal** /ˌærɪθ'metɪkl ; ˌærɪθ'mɛtɪkḷ/ *adj* of ~. 算術的。 **~al progression,** series of numbers showing an increase, or decrease, by a quantity that is always the same, eg 1, 2, 3, etc, or 7, 5, 3, etc. 算術級數;等差級數。 **arith·metician** /əˌrɪθmə'tɪʃn ; əˌrɪθmə'tɪʃən/ *n* expert in ~. 精於算術的人;算術家。

ark /ɑːk ; ɑrk/ *n* (in the Bible) (聖經) **1** covered ship in which Noah and his family were saved from the Flood. (世界大洪水時期挪亞及其家人所乘藉以保全性命之有篷的)方舟。 **2** **Ark of the Covenant,** wooden chest in which writings of Jewish law were kept. 聖約櫃(保藏猶太法刻文之木櫃)。

arm¹ /ɑːm ; ɑrm/ *n* **1** either of the two upper limbs of the human body, from the shoulder to the hand: 臂: *She was carrying a child in her arms.* 她懷中抱着一個孩子。*He was carrying a book under his arm,* between the arm and the body. 他腋下挾着一本書。*She had a basket on her arm,* with the handle supported on her arm. 她手臂上掛着一個籃子。***baby/child/infant in arms,*** child too young to walk. 懷抱中的嬰兒;尚不會走路的小孩。(*hold, carry sth*) ***at arm's length,*** with the arm fully extended. 伸直手臂(執持某物)。***keep sb at arm's length,*** (fig) avoid becoming familiar with him. (喻)避免與某人親近;與某人保持距離。(*welcome sb/sth*) ***with open arms,*** warmly, with enthusiasm. 熱烈地;熱情地(歡迎某人,某事物)。***walk ˌarm-in-'arm,*** (of two persons) walk side by side, with the arm of one round the arm of the other. (指二人)挽臂而行。 **'arm-band** *n* armlet. 袖帶。 **'arm·chair** *n* chair with supports for the arms. 有扶手的椅子。**'armchair critic,** person who offers criticism but is not actively involved. 安坐於扶手椅中的批評家(對所批評之作品涉獵未深而提出批評意見者)。 **'arm-hole** *n* hole (in a shirt, jacket, etc) through which the arm is put. (襯衫,夾克等之)袖孔。**'arm·let** /-lɪt ; -lɪt/ *n* band (of cloth, etc) worn round the arm (on a sleeve). 袖帶。 **'arm·pit** *n* hollow under the arm near the shoulder. 腋窩;胳肢窩。 **2** sleeve: 袖子: *The arms of this coat are too long.* 這件外衣的袖子太長。 **3** large branch of a tree. (樹的)大枝。 **4** sth shaped like or suggesting an arm: 形狀似臂之物: *an arm of the sea;* 海灣; *the arms of a chair.* 椅子的扶手。 **5** (fig) (喻) ***the (long) arm of the law,*** the authority or power of the law. 法律之權威或力量;法網恢恢。**arm·ful** /'ɑːmfʊl ; 'ɑrmˌfʊl/ *n* as much as one arm, or both arms, can hold: (兩臂或一臂)一抱之量: *carrying in books by the armful.* 抱進一抱的書。

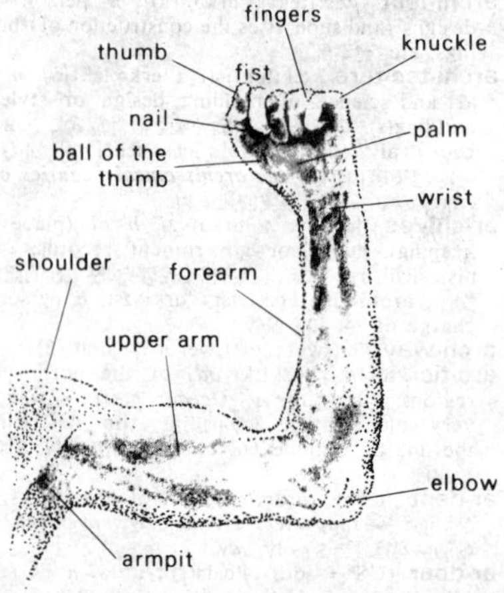

the arm and the hand

arm² /ɑːm ; ɑrm/ *n* branch or division of a country's armed forces: 兵種;兵科: *the infantry arm;* 步兵; *the air arm.* 空軍。

arm³ /ɑːm ; ɑrm/ *vt, vi* [VP6A, 14, 2A] ***arm (with),*** supply, fit, weapons and armour; prepare for war: 供以或配備武器及甲冑;裝備;備戰: *a warship armed with nuclear weapons;* 有核子武器裝備的戰艦; *armed with a big stick;* 持大棍作爲武器; (fig) (喻) *armed with patience/with answers to all questions.* 準備忍耐(回答一切問題)。*Their former enemy is arming again* (= rearming). 他們往昔的敵人正在重整軍備。 **the armed forces/services,** the army, navy and air force. 陸海空三軍。**armed neutrality,** policy of remaining neutral but prepared for defence against aggression. 武裝中立。

ar·mada /ɑː'mɑːdə ; ɑr'mɑdə/ *n* great fleet of warships, esp **the A~,** the fleet sent by King Philip II of Spain against England in 1588. 艦隊;(尤指)無敵艦隊 (the Armada, 1588 年西班牙國王菲力普二世派征英國之艦隊)。

ar·ma·dillo /ˌɑːmə'dɪləʊ ; ˌɑrmə'dɪlo/ *n* (*pl* ~s /-ləʊz ; -loz/) small burrowing animal of S America, with a body covered with a shell of bony plates, and the habit of rolling itself up into a ball when attacked. 犰狳(產於南美洲之穴居小動物;身體覆有骨質堅甲,遇敵能縮成球狀)。⇨ the illus at small. 參看 small 之插圖。

Ar·ma·ged·don /ˌɑːmə'gedn ; ˌɑrmə'gɛdṇ/ *n* **1** (biblical) (scene of) the last battle to be fought between the forces of good and evil, prophesied to happen at the end of time. (聖經)預言將在世界末日發生的善與惡的最後決戰;善與惡決戰的戰場。 ⇨ Rev 16: 16. 參看新約啓示錄第 16 章 16 節。 **2** (fig) any similar dramatic conflict. (喻)任何類似的戲劇性戰爭;大決戰。

ar·ma·ment /'ɑːməmənt ; 'ɑrməmənt/ *n* **1** (usu *pl*) military forces and their equipment; navy, army, air force. (通常用複數)全體軍隊及其配備;軍備;武備;海陸空軍。 **2** (usu *pl*) weapons, esp the large guns on a warship, military tank, etc: (通常用複數)武器;(尤指戰艦,戰車等上之)大砲: *the '~s industry.* 武器工業。 **3** [U] process of getting military forces equipped; preparation for war. 武裝;備戰。

ar·ma·ture /ˈɑ:mətʃʊə(r) ; ˈɑrmətʃɚ/ *n* (electr) that part of a dynamo which rotates in a magnetic field and in which the current is developed; coil(s) of an electric motor. (電) (發電機中之)電動子;電樞;電動馬達之線圈。

ar·mis·tice /ˈɑ:mɪstɪs ; ˈɑrməstɪs/ *n* agreement during a war or battle to stop fighting for a time. 休戰;停戰;休戰協定。**ˈA～ Day**, 11 Nov, kept as the anniversary of the ～ that ended fighting in the First World War (US 美=*Veterans' Day*). 第一次世界大戰休戰紀念日(十一月十一日)。⇨ remembrance.

ar·moire /ˈɑ:mwɑ:(r) *US:* ɑ:mˈwɑ:r ; ɑrˈmwɑr/ *n* [C] large cabinet or wardrobe. 大型的櫥櫃;大衣櫥;大衣櫃。

ar·mor ⇨ armour.

ar·mor·ial /ɑ:ˈmɔ:rɪəl ; ɑrˈmɔrɪəl/ *adj* of heraldry; of coats of arms. 紋章的;盾徽的。⇨ arms(2): ～ *bearings*, a coat of arms. 盾形紋章;盾徽。

ar·mour (US = **ar·mor**) /ˈɑ:mə(r) ; ˈɑrmɚ/ *n* [U] **1** defensive covering, usu metal, for the body, worn in fighting: 甲冑;盔甲: *a suit of* ～. 一套盔甲。**2** metal covering (steel plates, etc) for warships, tanks, motor vehicles, etc. (戰艦,戰車,汽車等之)裝甲;鋼甲;鐵甲。 **3** (collective) tanks, motor vehicles, etc protected with ～. (集合用法)裝甲車輛。**ˈ～-plate** *n* sheet of metal used as ～. 裝甲鋼板。**～ed** *part adj* **1** covered or protected with ～: 裝甲的: *an ～ed cruiser/car*. 裝甲巡洋艦(汽車)。**2** equipped with tanks, vehicles, guns, etc, that are protected with ～: 配有裝甲車輛及武器的: *an ～ed column/division, etc.* 裝甲縱隊(師等)。**～er** *n* **1** manufacturer or repairer of arms and ～. 製造或修理兵器及甲冑者。**2** man in charge of firearms. 軍械保管人。 **～y** /ˈɑ:mərɪ ; ˈɑrmərɪ/ *n* (*pl* -ries) place where arms are kept. 軍械庫。

arms /ɑ:mz ; ɑrmz/ *n pl* **1** weapons (note, *fire-arm*, used in the *sing* form): 武器;兵器(注意: fire-arm 用單數): (attrib) (形容用法) *an ～ depot*. 軍械庫。*The soldiers had plenty of ～ and ammunition.* 士兵們有充足的武器和彈藥。**ˈ～-race,** competition among nations on military strength. (各國間的) 軍備競爭。**ˈfire-～,** those requiring explosives. 火器;槍砲。**ˈsmall ～,** fire-～ that can be carried by hand, eg revolvers, rifles, light machine-guns. 輕武器(指可用手携帶者,如手槍,步槍,輕機槍)。***lay down (one's) ～,*** stop fighting. 放下武器;停戰。***take up ～; rise up in ～,*** (liter or fig) get ready to fight (*against*). (文或喻)拿起武器;武裝起來;準備作戰(與 against 連用)。***under ～,*** provided with weapons and ready to fight. 配備武器並準備作戰;在備戰狀態。***(be) up in ～ (about/over),*** (usu fig) be protesting vigorously. (通常作比喻用法)激烈反抗;强烈抗議。**2** (heraldry) pictorial design used by a noble family, town, university, etc. (紋章)紋章;徽章(代表貴族,城鎮,大學等之圖案徽誌)。**ˌcoat of ˈ～,** such a design, eg on a shield. 盾形紋章;盾徽。⇨ the illus at armour. 參看 armour 之插圖。

army /ˈɑ:mɪ ; ˈɑrmɪ/ *n* (*pl* -mies) **1 *(an/the)* ～,** (with *sing* or *pl v*) the part of a country's military forces that is organized for fighting on land: (與單數或複數動詞連用)(一國之)陸軍: *an ～ of 100,000 soldiers;* 十萬陸軍; *be in the ～,* be a soldier; 服兵役;當兵; *go into/join the ～,* become a soldier. 從軍。**ˈ～ corps** *n* main subdivision of an ～. 軍。**ˈ～ list** *n* official list of commissioned officers. 陸軍現役軍官名册。**2** organized body of persons: 協會;社;團體: *the Salvation A～;* 救世軍; large number: 大隊;大群: *an ～ of workmen/officials/ants.* 大群工人(官員,螞蟻)。

ar·nica /ˈɑ:nɪkə ; ˈɑrnɪkə/ *n* [U] medical substance (made from a plant) used for healing bruises and sprains. 山金車酊劑(用一種菊科植物山金車調製成的藥酒,用以醫療瘀傷及扭傷)。

aroma /əˈrəʊmə ; əˈromə/ *n* **1** sweet smell, fragrance: 香味;香氣;芬芳: *the ～ of a cigar.* 雪茄之

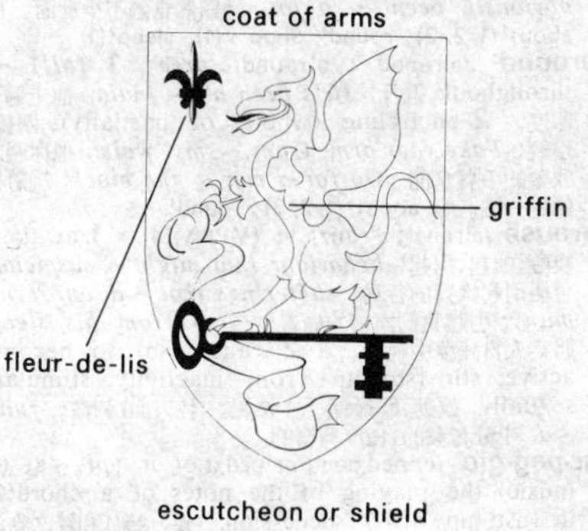

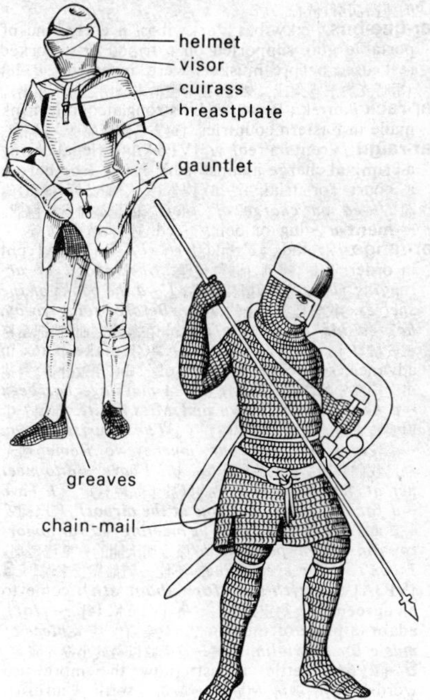

armour

芳香。**2** (fig) quality or surrounding atmosphere considered typical: (喻)韻味;情趣;氣氛;氣派: *the ～ of wealth.* 財富的氣派。**aro·matic** /ˌærəˈmætɪk ; ˌærəˈmætɪk/ *adj* fragrant; spicy: 芳香的;有香味的: *the ～tic bark of the cinnamon tree.* 肉桂樹之芳香樹皮。

arose /əˈrəʊz ; əˈroz/ *pt* of arise.

around¹ /əˈraʊnd ; əˈraund/ *adv* **1 *(all)* ～,** on every side; in every direction; here and there: 在四周;在周圍;到處;四方: *From all ～ we heard the laughter of children.* 我們到處都聽見兒童的笑聲。*Don't leave your clothes lying ～.* 不要把你的衣服到處放。**2** (colloq) not far away (in place or time): (俗) (空間或時間)不遠;在近處;不久: *I'll be ～ if you should want me.* 你如需要我,我就在附近。*I'll be seeing you ～, I expect.* 希望不久再見到你。**have been ～,** have travelled widely, have had experience of life and the world: 曾四處旅遊;有生活和處世經驗: *She's* *obviously been ~ a lot.* 她顯然見過不少世面。➪ about²(1, 2, 3), round², shop v(1), sleep²(1).

around² /əˈraʊnd ; əˈraʊnd/ *prep* **1** ***(all)*** **~,** throughout: 遍及: *He's been all ~ India.* 他走遍了印度。 **2** encircling (wholly or partially): 圍繞; 環繞: *Take your arm from ~ my waist.* 把你圍着我腰的手臂拿開。*Go for a run ~ the block.* 繞着街區跑一圈。➪ about³(1, 2, 3), round⁴.

arouse /əˈraʊz ; əˈraʊz/ *vt* [VP6A,14] **1** awaken: 喚醒;喚起;引起: *behaviour that might ~ suspicion;* 可能引起嫌疑的行爲; *sufferings that ~d our sympathy;* 引起我們同情的痛苦; *~ sb from his sleep.* 將某人自睡夢中喚醒。 **2** cause (sb) to become active; stir (sb) up from inactivity; stimulate sexually: 鼓動;鼓舞;激起;激勵;(性方面)刺激: *fully ~d.* 十分奮發的;極度興奮的。

ar·peg·gio /ɑːˈpedʒɪəʊ ; ɑrˈpɛdʒɪˌo/ *n* (*pl* ~s) (I; music) the playing of the notes of a chord(2) in (usu upwards) succession. (義;音樂)和音之急速的連續演奏;琶音。

ar·que·bus /ˈɑːkwɪbəs ; ˈɑrkwɪbəs/ *n* early kind of portable gun, supported on a tripod or a forked rest, used before muskets were invented. 火繩槍(用時支於三脚架或叉架上,在滑膛槍未發明之前所用者)。

ar·rack /ˈærək ; ˈærək/ *n* [U] strong alcoholic drink made in Eastern countries. (東方各國所釀造之)燒酒。

ar·raign /əˈreɪn ; əˈren/ *vt* [VP6A,14] (legal) bring a criminal charge against (sb); bring (sb) before a court for trial: (法律)控告(某人)犯某罪;提訊;傳訊: *~ed on charge of theft.* 因竊盜嫌疑被傳訊。 **~·ment** *n* ~ing or being ~ed. 控告;被控;責難。

ar·range /əˈreɪndʒ ; əˈrendʒ/ *vt, vi* **1** [VP6A] put in order: 安排;排列;佈置;整理: *She's good at arranging flowers.* 她擅長插花。*I ~d the books on the shelves.* 我整理書架上的書籍。*Before going away, he ~d his business affairs.* 在離開之前,他把業務都安排好了。 **2** [VP6A,15A,3A,4C] make plans in advance, see to the details of sth: 預做計畫;對某事之細節妥加注意;籌備;辦妥: *A marriage has been ~d between Mr Brown and Miss White.* 布朗先生與懷特小姐的婚禮已經籌備好了。*The Tourist Bureau ~d everything for our journey to Rome.* 觀光局爲我們到羅馬去的旅行籌備一切。*I have ~d to meet her at ten o'clock.* 我已約好於十點鐘見她。*I have ~d for a car to meet you at the airport.* 我已備妥一部車子到飛機場來接你。*The meeting ~d for tomorrow has been postponed.* 原定明天開的會業已延期。*I can't ~ for everything.* 不能一切都靠我來辦。 **3** [VP3A] **~ *(with sb) (for/about sth),*** come to an agreement. 約定;商定。 **4** [VP6A, 14] **~ *(for),*** adapt (a piece of music): 改寫(樂曲): *~ a piece of music for the violin.* 改寫一首樂曲以適於小提琴演奏。 **5** [VP6A] settle, adjust (now the more usu words): 解決;調解;使協調(今較常用 settle 或 adjust): *Mrs White often has to ~ disputes/differences between the two boys.* 懷特太太時常得調解這兩個孩子間的爭論。

ar·range·ment /əˈreɪndʒmənt ; əˈrendʒmənt/ *n* **1** [U] putting in order; arranging or being arranged: 安排;排列;佈置;整理: *The ~ of the furniture in our new house took a long time.* 在我們新房子裏佈置傢具花了很長的時間。 **2** (*pl*) plans; preparations: (複)計畫;籌備;準備: *Have you made ~s for your journey to Scotland?* 你已準備好了到蘇格蘭去旅行嗎?*I'll make ~s for somebody to meet you/for you to be met at the airport.* 我將設法派個人到飛機場去接你。 **3** [U] agreement; settlement: 同意;約定;解決: *The price of the house is a matter for ~,* is a matter to be settled by discussion. 此屋的價錢可以商談決定。*We can come to some sort of ~ over expenses.* 關於費用,我們可以獲致某種程度的協議。 **4** [C] result or manner of arranging: 安排、排列、佈置、整理的結果或方式: *an ~* (eg of orchestral music) *for the piano.* (如由管絃樂)改寫的鋼琴曲。*I have an ~ by which I can cash my cheques at banks everywhere in Britain.* 我有一種安排使我的支票可在英國各地銀行兌到現金。

ar·rant /ˈærənt ; ˈærənt/ *adj* (always of sth or sb bad) in the highest degree: (總是指壞的事或人)絕頂的;極端的;最大的: *an ~ liar/knave/dunce/hypocrite/rogue;* 第一號說謊者(騙子,愚人,僞君子,惡徒); *~ nonsense.* 最無意義的胡說。

ar·ras /ˈærəs ; ˈærəs/ *n* tapestry, esp the kind formerly hung on the walls of rooms. 花氈(尤指昔時裝飾牆壁之掛氈)。

ar·ray /əˈreɪ ; əˈre/ *vt* [VP6A, 15A] (liter) (文) **1** place (esp armed forces, troops) in order for battle: 佈署(軍隊等)以備作戰;列陣: *The Duke and his men ~ed themselves against the King,* took up arms against the King. 公爵及其部屬以武力反抗國王。 **2** dress: 穿着;盛裝: *~ed in ceremonial robes;* 穿着禮服; *~ed like a queen.* 盛裝如皇后。□ *n* (liter) (文) **1** order: 陣式: *troops in battle ~.* 列成戰陣的軍隊。 **2** clothes: 服裝: *in holiday ~;* 穿着假日服裝; *in bridal ~.* 穿着新娘禮服。 **3** **~ *(of),*** display: (陳列之)一大批;一系列: *a fine ~ of tools;* 一大批上選的工具; *an imposing ~ of statistics.* 一系列堂皇的統計數字。

ar·rears /əˈrɪəz ; əˈrɪrz/ *n pl* **1** money that is owing and that ought to have been paid: 欠債;應付而未付之款: *~ of rent/wages.* 欠租(工資)。***be in/fall into ~ (with),*** be late in paying. 拖欠。Cf 參較 *be behindhand with.* **2** work still waiting to be done: 尚待完成之工作: *~ of correspondence,* letters waiting to be answered. 待覆之信件。

ar·rest /əˈrest ; əˈrɛst/ *vt* [VP6A] **1** put a stop to (a process or movement): 阻止;妨礙(一種進展或運動): *Poor food ~s the natural growth of children.* 粗劣食物妨礙兒童的自然生長。 **2** catch (sb's attention): 吸引(某人的注意): *The bright colours of the flowers ~ed the child's attention.* 花卉之鮮艷顏色引起了那個小孩的注意。 **3** seize (sb) by the authority of the law: 依法逮捕;拘捕: *The police ~ed the thief and put him in prison.* 警察將該賊逮捕收押。□ *n* act of ~ing (a wrongdoer, etc): 逮捕;拘捕: *The police made several ~s.* 警方逮捕數人。***under ~,*** held as a prisoner. 被拘禁。***be/place/put/under ~,*** be/be made a prisoner: 被收押;被拘禁;成爲囚犯: *The officer was put under ~.* 該軍官被拘禁起來了。 **~er** *n* **ˈ~er hook,** device for reducing the speed of aircraft as they land on the deck of an aircraft carrier. 攔截鈎(飛機降落航空母艦之甲板上時用以減低其速度之裝置)。 **~·ing** *adj* striking; likely to hold the attention. 顯著的;有趣的;引人注目的。

ar·rière pensée /ˌærɪeə ˈpɒnseɪ *US:* pɒnˈseɪ ; ˌaˌrjɛrˌpɑ̃ˈse/ *n* (F) ulterior motive; mental reservation. (法)隱秘未表明的動機;隱而未宣的思想;心事。

ar·ri·val /əˈraɪvl ; əˈraɪvl̩/ *n* **1** [U] act of arriving: 到達;抵達: *on ~ home;* 在到家的時候; *on his ~;* 在他到達的時候; *waiting for the ~ of news;* 等待消息到達; *to await ~,* (on a letter, parcel, etc) to be kept until the addressee arrives. (書於信封,包裹等上面)等待收信(件)人前來領取。 **2** [C] sb or sth that arrives: 到達之人或物: *There are several new ~s at the hotel.* 旅館裏到了幾個新客人。*The new ~* (colloq = The newborn child) *is a boy.* (俗)新生兒是個男孩。

ar·rive /əˈraɪv ; əˈraɪv/ *vi* [VP2A, C, 3A] **1** reach a place, esp the end of a journey: 到達;抵達某地(尤指旅程的終點): *~ home;* 到家; *~ at a port;* 到達港口; *~ in harbour.* 抵達港內。 **2** come: 到;來: *At last the day ~d.* 那一天終於到了。*Her baby ~d* (= was born) *yesterday.* 她的嬰兒昨天出生了。 **3** **~ *at,*** reach (a decision, a price, the age of 40, manhood, etc). 達成(決議);談妥(價錢);活到(四十歲);到達(成年)等。 **4** establish one's position or reputation. 成功;成名。

ar·ro·gant /ˈærəgənt ; ˈærəgənt/ *adj* behaving in a proud, superior manner; (of behaviour, etc) showing too much pride in oneself and too little consideration for others: 傲慢的;自大的;(指行爲等)目中無人的;妄自尊大的: *speaking in an ~ tone.* 用傲慢的口吻說話。**~·ly** *adv* **ar·ro·gance** /-əns; -əns/ *n* [U].

ar·ro·gate /ˈærəgeɪt; ˈærəˌget/ *vt* [VP14] (formal) (正式用語) **1** ~ **to oneself,** claim or take without right: 冒稱;妄稱;擅取: *He ~d to himself the dignity of a chair,* claimed to be a university professor (although he was only a lecturer). 他冒稱自己爲大學教授(雖然他不過是個講師)。 **2** attribute unjustly; ascribe: 無理地認爲…是屬於;歸因於: *Don't ~ evil motives to me.* 不要向我栽誣。

ar·row /ˈærəʊ; ˈæro/ *n* **1** thin, pointed stick (to be) shot from a bow. 箭;矢。⇨ the illus at archery. 參看 archery 之插圖。 **2** mark or sign (→) used to show direction or position, eg on a map or as a road sign. 箭頭記號(→)(用以指示方向或位置,如地圖上或作路標用者)。 **ˈ~·head** *n* pointed end of an ~. 箭頭;鏃。

ar·row·root /ˈærəʊruːt; ˈæroˌrut/ *n* [U] starchy food made from the powdered root of a plant. 葛根粉所製之糊狀食品。

arse /ɑːs; ɑrs/ (US = **ass** /æs; æs/) *n* (⚠, not in polite use) buttocks; anus. (諱,不禮貌用語)臀部;屁股;肛門。*silly ~,* fool. 傻瓜;笨蛋。**ˈ~·hole** (US = **ˈass·hole**) *n* anus. 肛門。

ar·senal /ˈɑːsənl; ˈɑrsṇəl/ *n* building(s) where weapons and ammunition are made or stored; (fig) reserve of strength. 兵工廠;軍火庫;(喻)力量的貯存。

ar·senic /ˈɑːsnɪk; ˈɑrsṇɪk/ *n* [U] (chem) brittle, steel-grey crystalline chemical element (symbol **As**), used in glass-making, dyes, etc; white mineral compound of ~, a violent poison. (化)砷;砒素(性脆,鋼灰色之結晶形化學元素,化學符號 As, 用於製造玻璃,染料等);砒霜(砷之白色無機化合物,有劇烈毒性)。

ar·son /ˈɑːsn; ˈɑrsṇ/ *n* [U] act of setting sth on fire intentionally and unlawfully, eg another person's property or one's own with the purpose of claiming under an insurance policy. 縱火;放火(指非法有意之放火,如對他人財物之放火,或對自己財物之放火以領取保險金者)。

art¹ /ɑːt; ɑrt/ *n* **1** [U] the creation or expression of what is beautiful, esp in visual form; fine skill or aptitude in such expression: 美的事物(尤指肉眼可見者)的創造或表現;藝術: *the art of the Renaissance;* 文藝復興時期的藝術; *children's art;* 兒童藝術; *the art of landscape painting.* 風景畫的藝術。*The story is developed with great art.* 那故事非常技巧地展開。**the ˌfine ˈarts,** drawing, painting, sculpture, architecture, music, ballet. 美術(包括繪畫,彫刻,建築,音樂,芭蕾舞)。**a ˌwork of ˈart,** a fine painting, piece of sculpture, etc. 美術品;藝術品。**an ˈart gallery,** one for the display of works of art. 美術陳列館;藝術館。**an ˈart school,** one at which the arts of painting, etc are taught. 藝術專科學校。 **2** [C] sth in which imagination and personal taste are more important than exact measurement and calculation: 想像力及個人鑑賞力比精確計算更爲重要的事情;人文學科: *History and literature are among the arts/the arts subjects* (contrasted with science/science subjects). 歷史及文學均屬於人文科學(人文學科)(別於科學或科學學科)。*Teaching/Public speaking is an art.* 教學(演說)是人文學科。**ˌBachelor/ˌMaster of ˈArts,** (abbr 略作 **BA/MA**) person who has passed the examination and fulfilled other conditions for the award of a university degree in this branch of learning. 文科學士(碩士)。**3** [U] cunning; trickery; [C] trick: 詭計;詐術;手段;巧計;策術: *In spite of all her arts, the young man was not attracted to her.* 雖然她用盡了手段,那青年仍不爲她所動。**the black art,** magic (used for evil purposes). 魔術;妖術(作邪惡之用途者)。**4** (attrib) relating to art(1); of artistic design: (形容用法)藝術的;藝術設計的: *an ˈart historian/critic;* 藝術史家(批評家); *art needlework/pottery.* 藝術刺繡(陶器)。

art² /ɑːt; ɑrt/ *v* (*pres t* form of *be*) (archaic) used with *thou*: (古) be 的現在式,與 thou 連用: *thou art,* you are. 你是。

ar·te·fact ⇨ artifact.

ar·ter·ial /ɑːˈtɪərɪəl; ɑrˈtɪrɪəl/ *adj* of or like an artery: 動脈的;似動脈的: *~ blood;* 動脈血; *~ roads,* important main roads; 幹道;幹線; *~ railways/traffic.* 鐵路幹線(交通幹道)。

ar·terio·scler·osis /ɑːˌtɪərɪəʊskləˈrəʊsɪs; ɑrˈtɪrɪˌosklɪˈrosɪs/ *n* [U] chronic disease with the hardening of the arteries, hindering blood circulation. 動脈硬化。

ar·tery /ˈɑːtərɪ; ˈɑrtərɪ/ *n* (*pl* -ries) **1** one of the tubes carrying blood from the heart to all parts of the body. 動脈。⇨ the illus at respiratory. 參看 respiratory 之插圖。 **2** main road or river; chief channel in a system of communications, etc: 主要道路或河流;幹道;幹線;主流: *arteries of traffic.* 交通幹道。

ar·tesian /ɑːˈtiːzɪən *US:* -iːʒn; ɑrˈtiʒən/ *adj* **~ well,** perpendicular well producing a constant supply of water rising to the surface without pumping. 噴水井;自流井;鑽井。

art·ful /ˈɑːtfl; ˈɑrtfəl/ *adj* cunning, deceitful; clever in getting what one wants. 狡猾的;詐騙的;詭計多端的。**~ly** /-fəlɪ; -fəlɪ/ *adv* **~·ness** *n*

ar·thri·tis /ɑːˈθraɪtɪs; ɑrˈθraɪtɪs/ *n* [U] inflammation of a joint or joints; gout. 關節炎。**ar·thri·tic** /ɑːˈθrɪtɪk; ɑrˈθrɪtɪk/ *adj*

ar·ti·choke /ˈɑːtɪtʃəʊk; ˈɑrtɪˌtʃok/ *n* **1 globe ~,** plant like a large thistle, with a flowering head of thick, leaf-like scales used as a vegetable. 朝鮮薊(花頭可作蔬菜)。⇨ the illus at vegetable. 參看 vegetable 之插圖。 **2 Jerusalem ~,** plant like a sunflower, with tuberous roots used as a vegetable. 菊芋(似向日葵,其塊根可作蔬菜)。

ar·ticle /ˈɑːtɪkl; ˈɑrtɪkl/ *n* [C] **1** particular or separate thing: 物件;物品: *~s of clothing,* eg shirts, coats; 衣物(如襯衫,外衣); *toilet ~s,* eg soap, toothpaste. 盥洗用的物品(如肥皂,牙膏)。 **2** piece of writing, complete in itself, in a newspaper or other periodical. (報紙或雜誌所刊載的)文章;論文;專論。**ˌleading ˈ~,** (in a newspaper) ~ expressing the views of the editor(s). 報紙的社論。 **3** (legal) separate clause or item in an agreement: (法律)(契約的)條款;條目: *~s of apprenticeship/employment.* 學徒(雇用)契約的條款。 **4** (gram) (文法) **definite ~,** 'the'. 定冠詞(卽 the)。**indefinite ~,** 'a', 'an'. 不定冠詞(卽 a, an)。□ *vt* bind, eg an apprentice by ~s(3): 使(學徒等)受協議條款約束: *an ~d clerk.* 受協議條款約束的職員。

ar·ticu·late¹ /ɑːˈtɪkjʊlət; ɑrˈtɪkjəlɪt/ *adj* **1** (of speech) in which the separate sounds and words are clear. (指言語)發音清晰的。 **2** (of a person) able to put thoughts and feelings into clear speech: (指人)能用清晰之言語表達思想感情的: *That man is not very ~.* 那人口齒不太伶俐。 **3** jointed. 有關節相連的;連節的。**~·ly** *adv*

ar·ticu·late² /ɑːˈtɪkjʊleɪt; ɑrˈtɪkjəˌlet/ *vt,vi* **1** [VP6A, 2C] say (words) distinctly; speak (distinctly). 清楚地說出;說話;說話清晰。 **2** [VP15A, 2C] connect by joints: 以關節連接: *bones that ~/are ~d with others.* 以關節與其他骨骼相連的骨骼。**an ~d vehicle,** having parts joined in a flexible manner, eg a tractor flexibly joined to the part that carries the load. 掛接車(如一牽引機掛接一載貨之車架所成者)。

ar·ticu·la·tion /ɑːˌtɪkjʊˈleɪʃn; ɑrˌtɪkjəˈleʃən/ *n* [U] **1** production of speech sounds: 發音;讀音: *The speaker's ideas were good but his ~ was poor.* 這位演說者的思想很好,但是發音很差。**2** (connection by a) joint. 關節;由關節結合。

ar·ti·fact, ar·te·fact /ˈɑːtɪfækt; ˈɑrtɪˌfækt/ *n* [C] artificial product; something made by human being(s), esp a simple tool or weapon of archaeological interest. 人工製品(尤指出於考古興趣的簡單

工具或武器)。

ar·ti·fice /ˈɑːtɪfɪs ; ˈɑrtəfɪs/ *n* **1** [C] skilful way of doing sth. 技術;技巧。 **2** [U] cunning; ingenuity; trickery; [C] trick. 詭計;巧計;詐術;手段;策略。

ar·ti·fi·cer /ɑːˈtɪfɪsə(r) ; ɑrˈtɪfəsɚ/ *n* skilled workman. 技術工人;技工。**engine-room ~**, (rank in the Navy of a) skilled mechanic. (海軍之)輪機室技術士。

ar·ti·fi·cial /ˌɑːtɪˈfɪʃl ; ˌɑrtəˈfɪʃəl/ *adj* not natural or real; made by the art of man: 非天然的;非眞實的;人造的: ~ *flowers/teeth/light;* 人造花(假牙;人造光); ~ *silk,* (old name for) rayon; 人造絲(現稱 rayon); ~ *manures,* chemical manures (not dung); 人造肥料;化學肥料;人工堆肥(非糞尿); ~ *tears,* not caused by genuine sorrow; 假眼淚; ~ *manners,* affected, not natural manners. 做作的態度。 ~ **respiration**, method of forcing air into the lungs, eg to a man nearly drowned. 人工呼吸。⇨ also insemination. **ar·ti·fi·ci·ally** /-ʃəlɪ ; -ʃəlɪ/ *adv*

ar·til·lery /ɑːˈtɪlərɪ ; ɑrˈtɪlərɪ/ *n* [U] big guns (mounted on wheels, etc); branch of an army that uses these. 大砲;砲兵。

ar·ti·san /ˌɑːtɪˈzæn *US:* ˈɑːtɪzn ; ˈɑrtəzn̩/ *n* skilled workman in industry or trade; mechanic.工匠;技工。

art·ist /ˈɑːtɪst ; ˈɑrtɪst/ *n* **1** person who practises one of the fine arts, esp painting. 藝術家;(尤指)畫家。 **2** person who does sth with skill and good taste: 擅長做某事之人: *an ~ in words.* 擅長寫作者。

art·iste /ɑːˈtiːst ; ɑrˈtist/ *n* professional singer, actor, dancer, etc. 藝人(職業性的歌唱家,演員,舞蹈家等)。

ar·tis·tic /ɑːˈtɪstɪk ; ɑrˈtɪstɪk/ *adj* **1** done with skill and good taste, esp in the arts; able to appreciate what is beautiful. 以在藝術方面的技巧與鑑賞力做成的;有審美能力的。 **2** having or showing good taste. 高尙的;高雅的。 **3** of art or artists. 藝術的;藝術家的。 **ar·tis·ti·cally** /-klɪ ; -klɪ/ *adv*

art·istry /ˈɑːtɪstrɪ ; ˈɑrtɪstrɪ/ *n* [U] artistic skill or work; qualities of taste and skill possessed by an artist. 藝術技巧;藝術工作;藝術家的修養與技巧。

art·less /ˈɑːtlɪs ; ˈɑrtlɪs/ *adj* (contrasted with *artful*) natural; simple; innocent: (與 artful 相對)自然的;單純的;天眞爛漫的: *as ~ as a child of 5.* 天眞似五歲的孩童。**~·ly** *adv* **~·ness** *n*

arty /ˈɑːtɪ ; ˈɑrtɪ/ *adj* (colloq) pretending or falsely claiming to be artistic. (俗)假裝具有藝術修養與技巧的; 附庸風雅的。 **ˌ~-ˈcrafty**, (colloq) of, using, making, handmade articles, esp in a way that is considered affected. (俗)手工品(尤指冒牌貨)的; 使用手工品的;製造手工品的。

arum /ˈeərəm ; ˈɛrəm/ *n* **~ lily**, tall white lily. 白星海芋。

Aryan /ˈeərɪən ; ˈɛrɪən/ *adj* of the family of languages called Indo-European, ie related to Sanskrit, Persian, Greek, Latin and the Germanic and Slavonic languages; of a race using an ~ language. 亞利安語系(卽印歐語系,包括梵文、波斯文、希臘文、拉丁文、日耳曼語系及斯拉夫語系)的; 說亞利安語之民族的。 □ *n* person whose mother tongue is one of the ~ languages; (popular sense, now discredited) person of Germanic or Scandinavian ancestry. 說亞利安語之一的人;亞利安人。

as¹ /əz ; əz; *strong form:* æz ; æz/ *adv* (followed by *as, conj*) in the same degree: (後接連接詞 as)一樣;一般: *I'm as tall as you.* 我和你一般高。*Is it as difficult as they say it is?* 那是不是像他們所說的一樣困難? (In a neg sentence *as* is often replaced by *so*): (在否定句裡,常以 so 代替 as): *It's not so difficult as I expected.* 它並不如我所預料的那樣難。

as² /əz ; əz; *strong form:* æz ; æz/ *conj* **1** when; while: 當…之時: *I saw him as he was getting off the bus.* 當他下公共汽車時,我看見了他。*As a child, he lived in India.* 他小的時候居住在印度。 *As he grew older he became less active.* 當他年老的時候,他變得不活躍了。 **2** (expressing reason) since; seeing that: (表示理由)因爲;旣然: *As he wasn't ready in time, we went without him.* 因他未及時準備好,我們沒有等他就先走了。 **3** (in comparisons of equality, in the patterns: 以下列型式用於平等的比較: *as+adj/adv+as; not as/so+adj/adv as*): *I want a box twice as large as this.* 我要一個有這個兩倍大的箱子。 *It isn't as/so big as you think it is.* 它並沒有你所想像的那麼大。(Used in numerous proverbial phrases): (用於很多的諺語中): *as easy as ABC;* 極爲容易; *as heavy as lead.* 像鉛一樣的重。(Note the *pronouns* in these examples): (注意這些例句中的代名詞): *You hate him as much as I,* ie as much as I hate him; 你恨他像我恨他一樣的深; *You hate him as much as me,* ie as much as you hate me. 你恨他像恨我一樣的深。(When there is no ambiguity, the object form of the *pronoun* is used in speech): (如果意義不會含混不明的話,在說話中用代名詞的受詞形式): *At your age, you can't expect to play football as/so well as me* (= as I do). 在你這樣的年齡,你不能期望足球踢得跟我一樣好。 **4** (introducing a concessive clause, usu replaceable by a construction with *although*): (引導讓步子句,通常與 although 起首的子句通用): **(a)** (with an *adj* or *adv*): (與形容詞或副詞連用): *I know some of the family secrets, young as I am,* although I am young. 我雖然很小,可是我知道我家中的一些秘密。 *Much as I like you* (= Although I like you much), *I will not marry you.* 我雖然很喜歡你,可是不願與你結婚。**(b)** (with *vv*, esp *may, might, will, would*): (與動詞連用,尤與 may, might, will, would 連用): *Try as he would* (= Although he tried, However hard he tried), *he could not lift the rock.* 他雖然盡了最大努力,仍舊搬不動那塊石頭。 **5** (introducing adverbial clauses of manner) in the way in which: (引導表示狀態的副詞子句)如;像: *Do as I do.* 照我的樣子做。*Do it as I do it.* 照我的樣子做這件事。 *Leave it as it is.* 保持原狀,不要動它。 **6** (introducing a complement of manner) like: (引導表示狀態的補足語)如;像;似: *Why is he dressed as a woman?* 他爲什麼打扮得像個女人? **7** (used to avoid repetition in the predicate): (用以避免述語部份的重複): *Harry is unusually tall, as are his brothers,* and his brothers are also unusually tall. 哈利也像他的兄弟們一樣,身材奇高。 **8** in the capacity or character of: 作爲…(某種身分);當做;視爲: *He was respected both as a judge and as a man.* 大家尊崇他是位好法官,同時也尊崇他是個好人。*Looking at Napoleon as a statesman, not as a soldier....* 把拿破崙當做政治家,而不當做軍人來看…。 **9** (used in [VP16B] after *regard, view, represent, treat, acknowledge*, and *vv* similar in meaning but not after *consider,* to introduce a predicative): (用於regard, view, represent, treat, acknowledge及類似意義的動詞之後,但不用於 consider 之後,引導一個用於述語中的名詞或形容詞): *Most people regarded him* (=looked upon him) *as a fool.* 大多數人認爲他是個愚人。Cf 參較 Most people *considered him (to be)* a fool. 大多數人認爲他是個愚人。 *Do you treat all men as your equals?* 你是否把所有的人都當做與你平等的人看待? **10** (used to introduce illustrations or examples; usu preceded by *such;* replaceable by *for instance, for example* or *like*): (用以引述例證;通常跟在 such 後面;與 for instance, for example 或 like通用): *Countries in the north of Europe, such as Finland, Norway, Sweden,....* 北歐各國,如芬蘭、挪威、瑞典…。 **11** ***as if; as though,*** (introducing a clause of manner, with a *pt* in the clause): (引導表示狀態的子句,子句內用過去式): *He talks as if he knew all about it.* 他說話的口氣好像他全部都已經知道了。*He looks as if he had seen a ghost.* 他看起來好像看見了鬼似的。 *It isn't as though he were poor.* 看起來他不像貧窮的樣子。(followed by a *to*-infinitive): (後接帶 to 的不定詞): *He opened his lips as if to say something.* 他張開嘴好像要說什麼。 **12** ***ˈas for,*** with reference to (sometimes suggesting indifference or contempt): 至於(有時暗示不關心或輕視): *As for you, I never want to see you here again.* 至於你,我再也不想在這裏見到你。

'as to, about; concerning (better avoided except when the words following *as to* are shifted to the beginning of a sentence for prominence): 關於;至於(最好避免用此語,除非將整個片語移至句首,以加强其語氣): *As to your brother, I will deal with him later;* 至於你哥哥(弟弟),我以後再對付他; (with a gerund) *As to accepting their demand,....* (與動名詞連用)至於接受他們的要求,...。 **13** (used as a *conj* to introduce relative clauses, chiefly after *same* and *such*): (用作連接詞,引導關係子句,主要用於 same 及such之後): *Such women as knew Tom* (=Those women who knew him) *thought he was charming.* 認識湯姆的女人都認爲他很有魅力。 *Such women as Tom knew* (= Those women whom Tom knew) *thought he was charming.* 湯姆所認識的女人都認爲他很有魅力。 *You must show my wife the same respect as you show me,* the respect that you show me. 你必須尊敬我的妻,像你尊敬我一樣。 *We drove out of the town by the same road as we had entered by.* 我們沿着我們進城的同一道路開車出城。 **14** (introducing a non-defining relative clause, the antecedent being inferred): (引導一個非限制性的關係子句,無顯著先行詞): *Cyprus, as* (= which fact) *you all know, is in the Mediterranean.* 塞浦路斯島,你們大家都知道,是在地中海。 *To shut your eyes to facts, as many of you do, is foolish.* 故意不去正視事實,如你們很多人都那樣做的,乃是愚蠢的行爲。 **15** **'so as to, (a)** (introducing an infinitive of purpose): (引導表示目的的不定詞) 以便; 俾: *He stood up so as to* (=in order to) *see better.* 他站起來,以便看清楚些。 **(b)** (introducing an infinitive of manner): (引導表示狀態的不定詞): *It is foolish to behave so as to annoy* (=in ways that annoy) *your neighbours.* 做出那種足以打擾你的鄰居的行爲乃是愚蠢的。 **16** ***as good as,*** the same thing as: 像…一樣;幾乎等於: *Will he be as good as his word?* Will he do what he promised? 他是否會言行一致(言而有信)? *He's as good as dead,* almost dead, sure to die soon. 他跟死了一樣(很快就會死了)。 **17** ***as/so long as,*** **(a)** on condition that: 祇要: *You can go where you like so long as you get back before dark.* 你可以隨意到那裏去,祇要你在天黑以前返回。 **(b)** while: 在…的時候: *You shall never enter this house as long as I live in it.* 在我住在這裏的時候,你永遠不許進入這屋子。 **18** ***as much,*** so; (what really amounts to) that: 如此;實際和那個一樣: *I thought as much.* 我亦作如此想。 **19** ***as far as,*** ⇨ far²(2). ***as such; such as,*** ⇨ such *pron.* **20** ***(just) as soon; as soon as (not),*** ⇨ soon (3, 5). ***as well (as),*** ⇨ well²(8).

as·bes·tos /æz'bestɒs ; æs'bɛstəs/ *n* [U] soft, fibrous, grey, mineral substance that can be made into fire-proof fabrics or solid sheeting and used as a heat-insulating material. 石棉(可製成耐火織物及用作隔熱材料)。

as·cend /ə'send ; ə'sɛnd/ *vt, vi* **1** [VP6A, 2A, C] go or come up (a mountain, river, etc): 攀登(山); 往(河的)上(游)走;登上;上昇: *We watched the mists ~ing from the valley.* 我們看着霧由山谷昇起。 *The path ~s here.* 路由此處轉向上坡。 **2** *~ **the throne,*** become king or queen. 登王座;卽王位。

as·cend·ancy, -ency /ə'sendənsɪ; ə'sɛndənsɪ/ *n* [U] (position of) having power. 有權;權勢;優勢;權勢或優勢之地位。 ***gain/have the ~ (over sb)***: 獲得(具有) (超越某人的) 權勢或優勢: *He has the ~ over his rivals/his party.* 他獲得壓倒其敵手(其同夥)的優勢。

as·cend·ant, -ent /ə'sendənt ; ə'sɛndənt/ *n* ***in the ~,*** rising in power and influence. 權勢日隆的。

as·cen·sion /ə'senʃn ; ə'sɛnʃən/ *n* act of ascending. 昇高;上昇;往上。 **the A~,** the departure of Jesus from the earth, on the fortieth day after the Resurrection. 耶穌(復活後第四十日之)昇天。

as·cent /ə'sent ; ə'sɛnt/ *n* [C] act of ascending; way up; upward movement: 上昇;上行;上坡路;向上之運動: *The ~ of the mountain was not difficult.* 上這山不難。 *I have never made an ~* (=have never been up) *in a balloon.* 我從來沒有乘過氣球昇空。 *The last part of the ~ is steep.* 最後一段上坡路甚陡。

as·cer·tain /ˌæsə'teɪn ; ˌæsɚ'ten/ *vt* [VP6A, 9, 8, 10, 17] find out (in order to be certain about); get to know: 探出眞相;確實知道;探知: *~ the facts;* 探知事實眞相; *~ that the news is true;* 確知消息是實; *~ whether the train stops at X;* 探詢清楚火車是否在某地停; *~ what really happened.* 探查事情發生的眞相。 **~·able** /-əbl ; -əbḷ/ *adj* that can be ~ed. 可探知的;可弄清楚的。

as·cetic /ə'setɪk ; ə'sɛtɪk/ *adj* self-denying; austere; leading a life of severe self-discipline. 克己的;苦行的;過嚴格自律之生活的;修道的。 □ *n* person who (often for religious reasons) leads a severely simple life without ordinary pleasures. 修道者;苦行者。 **as·ceti·cally** /-klɪ ; -klɪ/ *adv* **as·ceti·cism** /ə'setɪsɪzəm ; ə'sɛtəˌsɪzəm/ *n*

as·cor·bic /ə'skɔːbɪk ; ə'skɔrbɪk/ *adj* *~* **acid,** (also known as *vitamin C*) vitamin found in citrus fruits and vegetable products, used against scurvy. 抗壞血酸(卽維他命C)。

as·cribe /ə'skraɪb ; ə'skraɪb/ *vt* [VP14] *~* ***to,*** **1** consider to be the cause, origin, reason or author, of: 認爲是…的原因,根源,理由或著作者;歸功於;歸咎於;歸因於: *He ~d his failure to bad luck.* 他把他的失敗歸咎於運氣不好。 *This play has been ~d to Shakespeare,* it has been said that Shakespeare was the author. 這個劇被認爲是莎士比亞所作。 **2** consider as belonging to: 認爲…屬於: *~ a wrong meaning to a word.* 將一字詮釋錯誤。 **as·crib·able** /-əbl ; -əbḷ/ *adj* that can be ~d: 可歸因於…的: *His quick recovery is ascribable to his sound constitution.* 他的迅速康復歸功於他的健全體質。 **as·crip·tion** /ə'skrɪpʃn ; əs'krɪpʃən/ *n* ascribing: 歸功;歸咎;歸因;歸與;歸屬: *The ascription of this work to Schubert may be false.* 認爲這樂曲是舒伯特的作品可能是錯的。

as·dic /'æzdɪk ; 'æzdɪk/ *n* device using reflected sound-waves, for detecting submarines, etc. 潛艇(等)探索器(利用聲波反射的一種);反潛儀。

asep·tic /ˌeɪ'septɪk ; ə'sɛptɪk/ *adj* (of wounds, dressings, etc) free from bacteria; surgically clean. (指傷口,繃帶等) 無菌的;外科手術上乾淨的。 **asep·sis** /ˌeɪ'sepsɪs ; ə'sɛpsɪs/ *n* [U] ~ condition. 無菌;無毒。

asex·ual /ˌeɪ'sekʃʊəl ; e'sɛkʃʊəl/ *adj* **1** without sex or sex organs: 無性的; 非性的; 無性器官的: *~ reproduction.* 無性生殖。 **2** (of a person) showing no interest in sexual relations. (指人)缺乏性慾的。 **~·ity** /eɪˌsekʃʊ'ælətɪ ; eˌsɛkʃʊ'ælətɪ/ *n*

ash¹ /æʃ ; æʃ/ *n* forest-tree with silver-grey bark and hard, tough wood; [U] wood of this tree. 秦皮;梣;梣木。 **'ash-key** *n* winged seed of the ash. 秦皮樹之翅果。 ⇨ the illus at tree. 參看 tree 之插圖。

ash² /æʃ ; æʃ/ *n* [U or *pl,* but not with numerals] (不可數名詞,或用複數,但不與數字連用) **1** powder that remains after sth has burnt: 灰燼;灰: *Don't drop cigarette ash on the carpet.* 不要讓香煙灰落在地毯上。 *Remove the ash(es) from the stove once a day.* 火爐裏面的灰每天清除一次。 *The house was burnt to ashes.* 房子燒成灰燼了。 **2** (*pl*) the burnt (= cremated) remains of a human body. (複)骨灰。 **Ash Wednesday,** first day of Lent. 灰星期三(四旬齋的第一日)。 **'ash-bin, 'ash-can** *nn* (esp US 尤美; ⇨ dustbin) large rigid receptacle for ashes, cinders, kitchen waste, etc. 垃圾箱。 **'ash-pan** *n* tray (in a fireplace, stove, etc) into which ashes drop from a fire. (壁爐,火爐等下面之)盛灰盤。 **'ash-tray** *n* small (metal, glass, etc) receptacle for tobacco ash. (金屬,玻璃等製之)煙灰盤;煙灰碟;煙灰缸。

ashamed /ə'ʃeɪmd ; ə'ʃemd/ *pred adj* *~* ***(of/that/to do sth),*** feeling shame: 感到羞恥的;慚愧的: *You should be ~ of yourself/of what you have done.* 你應(對自己所做之事)感到慚愧。 *He was/felt ~ to ask for help.* 他恥於向人求助。 *He felt ~ that* *he had done/of having done so little.* 他因爲做的事情太少而感到慚愧。*I feel ~ for you,* on your account, as if I were you. 我替你覺得可羞。**asham·ed·ly** /ə'ʃeɪmɪdlɪ ; ə'ʃemɪdlɪ/ *adv*

ashen /'æʃn ; 'æʃən/ *adj* of ashes; pale; ash-coloured: 灰燼的;灰白的;灰色的: *His face turned ~ at the news.* 他聽到這消息就臉色發白。

ashore /ə'ʃɔ:(r) ; ə'ʃɔr/ *adv* on, on to, the shore. 在岸上;向岸上;到岸上。***go ~,*** (of a sailor, etc) leave a ship to go on land. (指水手等) 離船上岸;登岸。***run/be driven ~,*** (of a ship) be forced to the shore, eg by bad weather. (指船) 如被惡劣天氣迫向岸上;被吹到岸上;擱淺。

ashy /'æʃɪ ; 'æʃɪ/ *adj* of or like ashes; covered with ashes; ash-coloured, pale. 灰燼的;似灰的;覆蓋着灰的;灰色的;灰白的。

Asian /'eɪʃn *US:* 'eɪʒn ; 'eʒən/ *n, adj* (native) of Asia. 亞洲的;亞洲人。

Asi·atic /ˌeɪʃɪ'ætɪk *US:* ˌeɪʒɪ- ; ˌeʒɪ'ætɪk/ *n, adj* (native) of Asia (*Asian* is the preferred word). 亞洲的;亞洲人 (Asian 爲較常用字)。

aside /ə'saɪd ; ə'saɪd/ *adv* on or to one side: 在一邊;向一邊: *He laid the book ~,* put it down and stopped reading it. 他丟開書(不讀了)。*We turned ~* (= away) *from the main road.* 我們離開大路向旁邊轉彎。*The decision/verdict was set ~,* made of no effect. 決議(判決) 被擱置(不生效)。*Please put this ~ for me,* reserve it. 請把這個替我保留起來。*Joking ~,* ie speaking seriously,.... 並非開玩笑(說正經話)...。□ *n* [C] words spoken ~, esp (on the stage) words that other persons (on the stage) are supposed not to hear. 旁白(只說給觀衆聽,而認爲臺上其他的人不會聽見的臺詞)。

as·in·ine /'æsɪnaɪn ; 'æsn̩ˌaɪn/ *adj* **1** of asses. 驢的。**2** (colloq) stupid. (俗) 愚笨的。

ask /ɑ:sk *US:* æsk ; æsk/ *vt, vi* (*pt, pp* asked) **1** [VP6A, 12C, 14 often with the indirect object omitted in 12C] call for an answer to; request information or service: (動詞第十二型C中的間接受詞常被省略) 問;詢問;要求;請求: *Did you ask the price?* 你問了價錢嗎? *Ask (him) his name.* 問(他)他的名字。*May I ask (you) a question?* 我可以問(你)一個問題嗎? *Have I asked too much of you/asked you for too much?* 我向你要求的太多嗎?*You asked of me more than you asked of the others.* 你向我要求的比你向別人要求的爲多。*He asked a favour of me.* 他請我幫個忙。*We must ask him about it.* 我們必須向他問個究竟。*He asked me for help.* 他請求我幫忙。[VP8, 20] *I will ask (him) how to get there.* 我將問問(他)怎樣到達那裏。*Did you ask (her) which to buy?* 你是否問過(她)買哪一個? [VP10, 21] *They asked (me) what my name was, where I came from, and why I had come.* 他們問(我)我的名字叫什麼,我從那裏來及我爲何事而來。*Please ask (her) when she will be back.* 請去問問她將於何時回來。[VP3A] ***ask after,*** ask for information about: 詢問;問候: *He asked after you/your health.* 他問候你(身體好) **2** [VP6A, 17, 15B, 3A] invite: 邀請;邀約: *We asked him to come again.* 我們邀請他再來。*I've been asked (out) to dinner.* 我已被請(外出)吃飯。*Mr Brown is at the door; shall I ask him in?* 布朗先生在門口;我可以請他進來嗎?***ask for trouble,*** (colloq) (俗) ***ask for it,*** behave in such a way that trouble is likely; invite trouble. 自找麻煩;惹麻煩。**3** [VP7A, 9, 17, 10] request to be allowed: 請求准許: *I must ask you to excuse me/ask to be excused.* 我必須請求你原諒我(請求原諒)。*He asked permission to get up.* 他請求准許起牀。*He asked to get up/that/if he might get up.* 他請求起牀(他請求是否可以起牀)。**4** [VP6A, 12C, 14] demand as a price: 要價;討價: *He asked (me) £25 a month as rent for that house.* 那棟房子,他(向我)要二十五鎊一月的租金。*You're asking too much.* 你要價太高。*What are they asking for the house?* 那棟房子他們要價多少? **5** ***ask the banns,*** (old use; now usu *put up* or *publish*) publish them. (舊用法;今通常用 put up 或 publish) 公佈結婚預告。

askance /ə'skæns ; ə'skæns/ *adv* (only in 只用於) ***look ~ at sb/sth,*** look at with suspicion. 以猜疑的心情看(某人或某事物);側目而視。

askew /ə'skju: ; ə'skju/ *adv, pred adj* out of the straight or usual (level) position: 歪斜地;歪斜的: *hang a picture ~;* 斜掛一幅畫; *have one's hat on ~;* 歪戴帽; *cut a plank ~,* aslant. 斜劈一塊木板。

ask·ing /'ɑ:skɪŋ ; 'æskɪŋ/ *n* ***for the ~,*** by requesting: 經索取;經要求: *You may have it/It's yours for the ~,* You have only to ask for it and it will be given to you. 如經索取就會給你。

aslant /ə'slɑ:nt *US:* ə'slænt ; ə'slænt/ *adv, prep* in a slanting direction (*to*): 斜地;成斜角地(與to連用);斜過: *The wrecked coach lay ~ the railway track.* 失事破毀的客車廂斜躺在鐵軌上。

asleep /ə'sli:p ; ə'slip/ *adv, pred adj* **1** sleeping: 睡;睡着(的): *He was fast ~.* 他睡得很熟。*He fell/dropped ~ during the sermon.* 他在聽講道時睡着了。**2** (of the arms or legs) without feeling (as when under pressure). (指四肢) 麻木(的);麻痺(的) (如受壓迫時)。

asp[1] /æsp ; æsp/ *n* = aspen.

asp[2] /æsp ; æsp/ *n* (zool) small poisonous snake of Egypt and Libya. (動物) (產於埃及和利比亞之) 小毒蛇。

as·para·gus /ə'spærəgəs ; ə'spærəgəs/ *n* [U] plant whose young shoots are cooked and eaten as a vegetable; the shoots. 石刁柏;蘆筍。

as·pect /'æspekt ; 'æspɛkt/ *n* **1** look or appearance (of a person or thing): 外貌;外觀;容貌: *a man of fierce ~;* 面目猙獰之人; *a man with a serious ~.* 外貌嚴肅之人。**2** front that faces a particular direction: (面對某一方向之) 正面: *a house with a southern ~.* 面朝南的房子。**3** (fig) particular part: (喻)特殊部分: *study every ~ of a subject,* study it thoroughly. 研究一個題目的每一方面;徹底研究它。**4** (gram) verb form which relates activity to passage of time. (文法) 相;態(敘述活動與時間經過之關係的動詞形式)。**as·pec·tual** /æ'spektʃʊəl ; æ'spɛktʃʊəl/ *adj: There is an ~ual difference between 'I saw him* cross *the road' and 'I saw him* cross*ing the road'.* 在 'I saw him *cross* the road' 與 'I saw him *crossing* the road' 兩句中 cross 和 crossing 間有相的不同。

as·pen /'æspən ; 'æspɪn/ *n* kind of poplar tree with leaves that move in the slightest wind. 白楊(其樹葉在最輕微之風中即行飄舞)。

as·per·ity /æ'sperətɪ ; æs'pɛrətɪ/ *n* (*pl* -ties) (formal) (正式用語) **1** [U] roughness; harshness (of manner); severity (of weather): 粗糙;(態度)粗暴;(氣候)酷烈: *speak with ~.* 粗暴地說。**2** (with *pl*) instance of one of these qualities: (用複數) 此種性質之實例: *the asperities of winter in Labrador;* 拉布拉多冬天之嚴寒; *an exchange of asperities,* eg of hard or bitter words. 互以粗暴刻薄的言語相對。

as·perse /ə'spɜ:s ; ə'spɝs/ *vt* [VP6A] (formal) slander; say false or unkind things about: (正式用語) 誹謗;中傷;破壞(名譽): *~ sb's good name/honour/reputation.* 誹謗某人的好聲譽(榮譽,名譽)。**as·per·sion** /ə'spɜ:ʃn *US:* -ʒn ; ə'spɝʒən/ *n* (only in 只用於) ***cast aspersions (up)on sb/sb's honour, etc,*** slander him; say false things about him. 對某人(某人之名譽等)加以誹謗。

as·phalt /'æsfælt *US:* -fɔ:lt ; 'æsfɔlt/ *n* [U] black, sticky substance like coal-tar used for making roofs, etc waterproof, and mixed with gravel or crushed rock, for making road surfaces. (地) 瀝青;柏油(用以塗屋頂等以防漏,並與碎石混合鋪路)。□ *vt* [VP6A] surface (a road) with ~. 以瀝青鋪(路)。

as·pho·del /'æsfədel ; 'æsfəˌdɛl/ *n* **1** sort of lily. 日光蘭;水仙花。**2** (poet) immortal flower of the Gk Elysium (home of the dead). (詩) (希臘神話中極樂世界之) 常春花。

as·phyxia /æs'fɪksɪə ; æs'fɪksɪə/ *n* [U] condition

caused by lack of enough air in the lungs; suffocation. 窒息狀態;窒息。**as·phyxi·ate** /æsˈfɪksɪeɪt ; æsˈfɪksɪˌet/ *vt* [VP6A] make ill, cause the death of, through lack of sufficient air in the lungs: 使窒息;悶死: *The men in the coal-mine were ~ted by bad gas.* 煤礦坑裡的工人們爲惡氣所窒息。 **as·phyxi·ation** /æsˌfɪksɪˈeɪʃn ; æsˌfɪksɪˈeʃən/ *n* [U] = asphyxia; suffocation. 窒息。

as·pic /ˈæspɪk ; ˈæspɪk/ *n* [U] clear meat jelly: (肉類)凍子: *chicken in ~.* 雞肉凍子。

as·pi·dis·tra /ˌæspɪˈdɪstrə ; ˌæspɪˈdɪstrə/ *n* (*pl* ~s) plant with broad, pointed leaves, usually grown as a house plant. 蜘蛛抱蛋;葉蘭。

as·pir·ant /əˈspaɪərənt ; əˈspaɪrənt/ *n* ~ ***(to／after),*** person who is ambitious for fame, etc: 有抱負者;熱望者;希求者: *an ~ to high office.* 求高職者。

as·pir·ate[1] /ˈæspərət ; ˈæspərɪt/ *n* (phon) the sound of 'h'; sound with an 'h' in it: (語音)聲門擦音 'h'; 送氣音: *Mind your ~s,* be careful to make the 'h' sounds where necessary. 注意你的 'h' 的發音。

as·pir·ate[2] /ˈæspəreɪt ; ˈæspəˌret/ *vt* (phon) say with an 'h' sound: (語音)帶着 'h' 音說出;把…發成送氣音: *The 'h' in 'honour' is not ~d.* 'honour'中之'h'不發音。

as·pir·ation /ˌæspəˈreɪʃn ; ˌæspəˈreʃən/ *n* [C, U] **1** ~ ***(for／after);*** ~ ***(to do／be),*** aspiring; desire: 願望;希望;渴望;熱望: *his ~s for fame;* 他的求名之心願; *his ~ to be an actor;* 他想做演員的願望; *the ~s of the developing countries.* 開發中國家的願望。 **2** aspirating. 發送氣音。

as·pire /əˈspaɪə(r) ; əˈspaɪr/ *vi* [VP3A, 4A] be filled with high ambition: 有抱負; 有雄心; 立志; 熱望: *~ after knowledge;* 立志求知識; *~ to fame;* 立志成名; *~ to become an author.* 熱望成爲作家。

as·pirin /ˈæsprɪn *US:* -pər- ; ˈæspərɪn/ *n* [U] (P) medicine used to relieve pain and reduce fever; [C] tablet or measure of this: (商標)阿司匹靈(止痛退燒藥);阿司匹靈藥片: *Take two ~s for a headache.* 吃兩片阿司匹靈治頭痛。

ass[1] /æs ; æs/ *n* **1** animal of the horse family with long ears and a tuft at the end of its tail; donkey; stupid person. 驢;愚人;傻瓜;笨蛋。 **2** ***make an ass of oneself,*** behave stupidly so that one is ridiculed. 行爲愚蠢因而受人嘲弄;弄出笑話來。

ass[2] /æs ; æs/ *n* (US vulg) (美鄙) = arse.

as·sa·gai /ˈæsəgaɪ ; ˈæsəˌgaɪ/ *n* = assegai.

as·sail /əˈseɪl ; əˈsel/ *vt* [VP6A, 14] ~ ***(with),*** attack violently; pester: 猛擊;痛擊;困擾: *~ sb with questions／insults;* 對某人加以質問(侮辱); *be ~ed with doubts.* 爲疑惑所困擾。**~·able** /-əbl ; -əbḷ/ *adj* that can be attacked. 可攻擊的。**~·ant** /-ənt ; -ənt/ *n* attacker. 攻擊者。

as·sas·sin /əˈsæsɪn *US:* -sn ; əˈsæsɪn/ *n* person, often one hired by others, who assassinates. 暗殺者; 刺客(常爲受人所雇者)。 **~·ate** /əˈsæsɪneɪt *US:* -sən- ; əˈsæsṇˌet/ *vt* [VP6A] kill sb (esp an important politician, ruler) violently and treacherously, for political reasons. 暗殺; 行刺(尤指政治要人,統治者)。 **~·ation** /əˌsæsɪˈneɪʃn *US:* əˌsæsənˈeɪʃn ; əˌsæsṇˈeʃən/ *n* [U] murder of this kind; [C] instance of this. 暗殺;行刺。

as·sault /əˈsɔːlt ; əˈsɔlt/ *n* ~ ***(on／upon),*** violent and sudden attack: 猛烈而突然之攻擊: *They made an ~ on the enemy's positions.* 他們突襲敵人的陣地。 *The sonic boom was an ~ on our nerves.* 飛機的聲爆是對我們神經的突擊。 *The enemy's positions were taken by ~.* 敵人的陣地被攻陷。 ***~ and battery,*** (legal) beating or hitting sb. (法律)毆打某人。 **ˈ~ craft** *n* portable boat with an outboard motor, used for making attacks across rivers, etc. 攻擊舟(馬達裝於船外,渡水攻敵用之輕便突擊艇)。 □ *vt* [VP6A] make an ~ on; attack (eg a fortress) by a sudden rush. 襲擊;突襲(堡壘等)。

as·say /əˈseɪ ; əˈse/ *n* [C] ~ ***(of),*** test of the fineness, purity, or quality (of precious metals, ores, etc): (檢驗貴金屬、礦苗等之精度,純度或品質所作之)化驗;分析: *make an ~ of an ore.* 分析礦苗以測其含礦度。□ *vt* **1** [VP6A] test, eg the purity of a metal, analyse, eg an ore, etc. 化驗(金屬之純度);分析(礦苗等)。 **2** ~ ***(to do sth),*** [VP6A, 7A] (old use) attempt, eg sth difficult. (舊用法)嘗試(困難之事)。

as·se·gai /ˈæsəgaɪ ; ˈæsəˌgaɪ/ *n* throwing-spear with a wooden haft, used by S African tribes. (南非洲部族所用之)木柄標槍。

as·sem·blage /əˈsemblɪdʒ ; əˈsɛmblɪdʒ/ *n* **1** [U] bringing or coming together; assembly (now the usu word): 集合; 組合; 裝置; 裝配(現通常用 assembly): *the ~ of parts of a machine.* 機器零件的裝配。 **2** [C] collection of things or (joc) persons. 聚集之物; (謔)聚集的人群;會衆。

as·semble /əˈsembl ; əˈsɛmbḷ/ *vt, vi* **1** [VP6A,2A] gather together; collect: 集合; 聚集: *The pupils ~d／were ~d in the school hall.* 學生們在學校禮堂中集合。**2** [VP6A] fit or put together (the parts of): 配合;裝配(…之零件): *~ a watch／car.* 裝配錶(汽車)。

as·sem·bly /əˈsemblɪ ; əˈsɛmblɪ/ *n* (*pl* -lies) **1** [C] number of persons who have come together, esp a meeting of law-makers: 聚集在一起的一群人;集會;(尤指立法者之)會議: *the Legislative A~;* 立法會議; *the school ~,* the daily ~ of pupils and staff. 學校集會 (學生與教職員的每日集會)。 **ˈ~ room(s),** public hall in which meetings, balls, etc take place. 公共會堂(供集會、舉行舞會等)。 **2 ˈ~ hall,** one where a school meets for prayers, etc; workshop where parts of large machines, eg aircraft, are put together. 學校聚會堂 (供祈禱等聚會用之場所); (裝配大型機器,如飛機等之) 裝配場。**ˈ~ line,** stage of mass production in which parts of a machine, vehicle, etc move along for progressive ~. 裝配線(大量生產過程中將各部份零件逐步裝配成爲機器、車輛等之階段)。**3** military call, by drum or bugle, for soldiers to assemble. (軍中之)集合鼓;集合號。

as·sent /əˈsent ; əˈsɛnt/ *n* ~ ***(to),*** official agreement, eg to a proposal; (royal) agreement (to a bill passed by Parliament). 官方同意(如某項建議); 國王的同意(議會所通過的法案);批准;認可。***by common ~,*** everybody agreeing. 一致贊成。***with one ~,*** unanimously; nobody opposing. 一致 (通過); 無異議。 ⇨ accord[1] (1), dissent. □ *vi* [VP2A, 3A] ~ ***(to),*** give agreement (eg to a proposal). 同意; 贊成(與 to 連用,後接一項建議等)。

as·sert /əˈsɜːt ; əˈsɝt/ *vt* **1** [VP6A] make a claim to, eg one's rights. 維護;辯護;要求 (自己的權利等); 主張。 **2** [VP6A, 9, 25] declare: 宣稱;斷言;聲明: *~ one's innocence／that one is innocent;* 聲明自己的清白(自己是清白的); *~ sth to be true.* 斷言某事是眞實的。 *~ **oneself,*** display authority, self-confidence. 表現自己的權威與自信;自作主張;堅持己見。

as·ser·tion /əˈsɜːʃn ; əˈsɝʃən/ *n* **1** [U] insisting upon the recognition of one's rights: 堅持要求承認自己的權利;斷言: *self-~.* 堅持己見。 **2** [C] strong statement; claim: 强硬的聲明;要求;主張: *make an ~.* 作强硬的聲明。

as·sert·ive /əˈsɜːtɪv ; əˈsɝtɪv/ *adj* having or showing positive assurance: 斷然的;確然無疑的: *speaking in an ~ tone.* 以斷然的口氣說。**~·ly** *adv*

as·sess /əˈses ; əˈsɛs/ *vt* [VP6A, 14] **1** decide or fix the amount of (eg a tax or a fine): 估定(稅額或罰款)的數額: *Damages were ~ed at £100.* 損失額估計爲一百鎊。 **2** appraise; fix or decide the value of (eg property), the amount of (eg income), for purposes of taxation; (fig) test the value of: 估計; 估定 (財產)之價值,(收入等)之數字(以作課稅之根據); (喻)評定…的價值; 評估: *~ a speech at its true worth.* 評定演說之眞正價值。 **~·ment** *n* [U] ~ing; [C] amount ~ed. 估計; 評估; 所估計之數額。**~·or** /-sə(r) ; -sə/ *n* **1** person who ~es property, income, taxes, etc. (財產、收入、稅款等之)估計員;估稅員。 **2** person who advises a judge, magistrate or official committee, etc on technical matters. (輔助法官,地方官,官廳委員會等解決技術問題

之)顧問;陪審推事。

as·set /ˈæset; ˈæsɛt/ *n* **1** (usu *pl*) anything owned by a person, company, etc that has money value and that may be sold to pay debts. (通常用複數)財產;資產。 ⇨ liability. **2** valuable or useful quality or skill: 有價值的或有用的性質或技能: *Good health is a great ~.* 良好的健康極爲可貴。

as·sev·er·ate /əˈsevəreɪt; əˈsɛvəˌret/ *vt* [VP6A, 9] (formal) assert solemnly: (正式用語)(鄭重地)宣稱;聲明: *~ one's innocence/that one is innocent.* 鄭重聲明自己的清白(自己是清白的)。 **as·sev·er·ation** /əˌsevəˈreɪʃn; əˌsɛvəˈreʃən/ *n*

as·si·du·ity /ˌæsɪˈdjuːətɪ *US:* -ˈduː-; ˌæsəˈdjuətɪ, -ˈdu-/ *n* **1** [U] constant and careful attention to what one is doing: 專心致志;勤勉不懈: *He plans everything with unfailing ~.* 他孜孜不倦地計畫每一件事。 **2** (*pl* -ties) constant attentions (*to*). 慇懃的照料;周到的關懷(與 to 連用)。

as·sidu·ous /əˈsɪdjʊəs *US:* -dʒʊəs; əˈsɪdʒʊəs/ *adj* diligent; persevering: 勤勉的;努力的;有毅力的: *~ in his duties.* 勤勉於他的職守。 **~·ly** *adv*

as·sign /əˈsaɪn; əˈsaɪn/ *vt* **1** [VP13A, 12A] *~ sth (to sb/sth),* give for use or enjoyment, or as a share or part in a distribution, eg of work, duty: 分配;分派(工作、任務等給某人): *Those rooms have been ~ed to us.* 那些房間已經分配給我們。 *Your teacher ~s you work to be done at home.* 你的老師會分配家庭作業給你。 **2** [VP13A, B] name, put forward as a time, place, reason, etc: 指定(時間、地點);提出(理由等): *Has a day been ~ed for the trial?* 審訊日期是否已定? *Can one ~ a cause to these events?* 誰能指出這些事件的起因嗎? **3** [VP13B, 17] *~ sb (to/to do),* appoint, name: 指派;選派: *A~ your best man to the job.* 選派你最好的人擔任那工作。 *Two pupils were ~ed to sweep the classroom.* 兩個學生被指派打掃教室。 **4** [VP14] *~ to,* (legal) transfer property, rights, etc. (法律)轉讓(財產,權利等);讓與;過戶給。 **~·able** /-əbl; -əbl̩/ *adj* that can be attributed or ~ed: 可分派的;可指定的;可歸因於…的: *~able to several causes.* 可歸於數種原因的。 **~·ment** *n* [U] ~ing; [C] that which is ~ed. 分配;分派;所分派之事物。

as·sig·na·tion /ˌæsɪgˈneɪʃn; ˌæsɪgˈneʃən/ *n* [C] appointment, eg of a time and place for a furtive meeting between lovers. 約會;(情侶間秘密的)幽會。

as·simi·late /əˈsɪməleɪt; əˈsɪml̩ˌet/ *vt, vi* **1** [VP6A, 2A] absorb (food) into the body (after digestion); be thus absorbed: 將(消化後之食物)吸收於身體中;(消化後之食物)被吸收: *We ~ some kinds of food more easily than others.* 我們對於某些種類的食物比較容易吸收。 *Some kinds of food ~ easily.* 有些種類的食物易被吸收。 **2** [VP6A, 2A] (allow people to) become part of another social group or state: 同化: *The USA has ~d people from many countries,* has absorbed them, so that they are Americans. 美國同化了來自許多國家的人。 **3** [VP6A] absorb, eg ideas, knowledge. 吸收(觀念,知識)。 **4** [VP3A] *~ to,* make or become like. 同化;使變成一樣;變成一樣。 **as·simi·la·tion** /əˌsɪməˈleɪʃn; əˌsɪml̩ˈeʃən/ *n* [U] assimilating or being ~d. 吸收;同化;吸收作用;同化作用。

as·sist /əˈsɪst; əˈsɪst/ *vt, vi* [VP6A, 17, 14, 2A, 3A] *~ (sb) (with sth/in doing sth/to do sth),* (formal) help: (正式用語)幫助(某人)(做某事);援助: *~ (sb) with the form-filling;* 幫助(某人)填表; *~ sb to fill in the forms.* 幫助某人填寫表格。 *Two men are ~ing the police in their enquiries,* are answering questions which may lead to the arrest of the criminal(s), or perhaps their own arrest as the criminals. 兩個男人在答覆警方的詢問。 **~·ance** /-əns; -əns/ *n* [U] help: 幫助;援助: *give/lend/render ~ance (to sb);* (對某人)予以援助;施以援手; *come to sb's ~ance;* 援助某人; *be of ~ance (to sb).* 幫助;援助(某人)。 **~·ant** /-ənt; -ənt/ *n* helper: 助手;副手;助理: *an ~ant to the Manager;* 副經理; 協理; *~ant master,* in a school; (學校中的)助教; *a ˈshop-~ant,* one who serves customers. 店員。

as·size /əˈsaɪz; əˈsaɪz/ *n* **1** [U] trial by a judge and jury. 審訊;審判。 **2** (*pl*) (until 1971) sessions held periodically in every English County to try civil and criminal cases before High Court Judges: (複)(此制度一直施行到1971年止)(英國高等法院法官定期至各郡審判案件之) 巡廻審判庭期;巡廻審判: (attrib, *sing*) (形容用法,單數) *courts of ~;* 巡廻審判法庭; *judges on ~;* 巡廻審判法官; *~ towns.* 巡廻審判城市。 ⇨ *Crown Court* at court¹(1) for the new system.

as·so·ci·ate¹ /əˈsəʊʃɪət; əˈsoʃɪɪt/ *adj* joined in function or dignity: 夥同的;副的: *an ~ judge.* 陪審推事。 □ *n* person who has been joined with others *in* work, business or crime; person given certain limited rights in an association; companion. 同事;同僚;同人;共犯;(會社之)準會員;同件;夥件。

as·so·ci·ate² /əˈsəʊʃɪeɪt; əˈsoʃɪˌet/ *vt, vi* *~ with,* **1** [VP14] join or connect: 聯合;結夥;結交;聯繫: *~ oneself with sb in a business undertaking;* 與某人合夥經商; *~ one thing with another.* 將一事(物)與另一事(物)聯繫在一起。 *We ~ Egypt with the Nile.* 我們想起埃及就想起尼羅河。 *I don't wish to ~ myself with what has been said,* don't want anyone to think that I have a part in it, or approve of it. 我不希望任何人以爲我自己與所說過的事有任何關聯(或以爲我贊成此事)。 **2** [VP3A] be often in the company of: 與…常在一起;結交;與…爲友: *Don't ~ with dishonest boys.* 勿與不誠實的男孩爲友。

as·so·ci·ation /əˌsəʊsɪˈeɪʃn; əˌsosɪˈeʃən/ *n* **1** [U] *~ (with),* associating; being associated; companionship: 聯合;結交;結合: *I benefited much from my ~ with him/from our ~.* 我與他結交獲益良多。 *His English benefited through his long ~ with British children.* 由於他長期與英國兒童接觸,使他的英語得以長進。 *in ~ (with),* together (with). 與…在一起;與…聯合,結交或有關連。 **2** [C] group of persons joined together for some common purpose: 協會;社團;會社: *the ˈAutomobile A~;* 汽車協會; *the ˌYoung Men's ˈChristian A~.* 基督教青年會。 **3** *ˌA~ ˈfootball,* (common abbr 普通略作 *soccer*) game in which two teams of eleven players use a spherical ball that must not be touched with the hands except by the goalkeeper or when throwing in. 英式足球(每隊十一人,用圓球,除門將或自邊線發球外,不可以手觸球者)。 ⇨ the illus at foot. 參看 foot 之挿圖。 **4** connection (of ideas). (觀念的)聯想。

as·son·ance /ˈæsənəns; ˈæsənəns/ *n* agreement between stressed vowels in two words, but not in the following consonants, as in *sharper* and *garter.* 半韻;半諧音(卽兩字間只有重讀的母音相同,而其後之子音不相同,如 sharper 與 garter 是)。

as·sorted /əˈsɔːtɪd; əˈsɔrtɪd/ *part adj* **1** of various sorts; mixed: 各種各樣的;各色俱備的;混合的;什錦的: *a pound of ~ toffees,* toffees of different kinds, mixed together. 一磅什錦太妃糖。 **2** matched, suited, one to another: 配合的;合適的: *an ill-~ couple,* husband and wife who get on badly. 一對怨偶(相處不好的夫妻)。 **as·sort·ment** /əˈsɔːtmənt; əˈsɔrtmənt/ *n* ~ collection of different examples of one class or of several classes: 屬於一類或數類的各色物品之集合: *This shop has a good assortment of goods to choose from.* 此店各色貨物俱備,任君選擇。

as·suage /əˈsweɪdʒ; əˈswedʒ/ *vt* [VP6A] make (sth, eg pain, suffering, feelings, desire) less. 減輕(痛苦);緩和(情緒或慾望);鎭定;平息。

as·sume /əˈsjuːm *US:* əˈsuːm; əˈsum/ *vt* **1** [VP6A, 9, 25] take as true before there is proof: (在未證實前)假定;以爲: *You ~ his innocence/him to be innocent/that he is innocent before hearing the evidence against him.* 在未聽到對他不利的證言之前,你假定他是無罪的。 *He's not such a fool as you ~d*

(= supposed) *him to be.* 他並非如你所以爲的那樣愚蠢。*Assuming this to be true....* 假定這是眞的…。⇨ presume(1). **2** [VP6A] take up; undertake: 擔任;承當: *~ the direction of a business;* 負責主持一項業務; *~ office;* 就職; *~ the reins of government,* begin to govern. 開始執政。 **3** [VP6A] take upon or for oneself sth not genuine or sincere: 假裝;佯作;冒用: *~ a look of innocence;* 裝作無辜的樣子; *~ a new name.* 用新名字;用化名。

as·sump·tion /əˈsʌmpʃn; əˈsʌmpʃən/ *n* **1** [C] sth taken for granted; sth supposed but not proved: 視爲當然之事; 所假定而未經證實之事: *Their ~ that the war would end quickly was proved wrong.* 他們認爲戰事會迅速結束的看法證明是錯誤的。***on the ~ that,*** accepting it to be true that.... 假定…。 **2** [C] ***~ of,*** the act of assuming(2): 擔任;承當: *his ~ of office/power/the presidency.* 他的就職(當權,就任大學校長)。 **3** [C] ***~ of,*** the adopting of a manner, etc which is not genuine: 假裝;作態: *with an ~ of indifference,* pretending not to be interested. 裝作冷淡的樣子。 **4 the A~,** reception into Heaven in bodily form of the Virgin Mary; Church feast commemorating this. 聖母昇天;聖母昇天節。

as·sur·ance /əˈʃuərəns; əˈʃurəns/ *n* **1** [U] (often 常作 *self-~*) confidence in oneself; belief and trust in one's own powers: 自信; 把握; 胸有成竹: *He answered all the questions with ~.* 他有把握地回答了所有的問題。*A businessman, to be successful, should act with perfect (self-)assurance.* 一個企業家要想成功,做事應該有十足的(自)信心。 **2** [C] promise; statement made to give confidence: 承諾;擔保;保證: *He gave me a definite ~ that the repairs would be finished by Friday.* 他給我確切保證星期五以前修理好。 **3** [U] (chiefly GB) insurance on sth that is certain: (主用於英國) (對於確知不可避免之事之)保險: *'life ~,* because death is certain. 人壽保險(因爲死亡是不可避免的)。⇨ insurance. **4** [U] impudence (the much more usu word). 厚顏;無恥(impudence 遠較 assurance 常用)。 **5** ***~ (in),*** [U] certainty; confidence (the much more usu word). 確信;信心 (confidence 遠較 assurance 常用)。***make ~ doubly sure,*** remove all possible doubt. 掃除一切可能的疑慮;做到萬無一失。

as·sure /əˈʃuə(r); əˈʃur/ *vt* **1** [VP11] say positively, with confidence: 斷然地說; 有信心地說: *I ~ you (that) there's no danger.* 我向你保證沒有危險。 **2** [VP11, 14] cause (sb) to be sure, to feel certain: 使 (某人) 相信; 使確信: *We tried to ~ the nervous old lady that flying was safe.* 我們盡力說服那緊張的老婦人,使她相信乘飛機是安全的。 *He ~d me of his readiness to help.* 他使我相信他願意幫忙。 **3** [VP6A] ensure (the more usu word): 獲得; 保證得到(ensure 爲較常用字): *Nothing can ~ permanent happiness.* 沒有東西能擔保永久的幸福。 **4** [VP6A] insure, esp against the death of sb or oneself. 保險(尤指人壽保險)。**as·sured** *part adj* sure; confident. 確信的;深信的。***rest ~d (that),*** feel confident (that). (對…)放心。 **as·sur·ed·ly** /əˈʃuərɪdlɪ; əˈʃurɪdlɪ/ *adv* surely; confidently. 一定地;深信地。

as·ter /ˈæstə(r); ˈæstɚ/ *n* garden plant with flowers that have white, pink or purple petals round a yellow centre. 紫菀(園藝植物,花瓣爲白色、粉紅或紫色,花心爲黃色)。

as·ter·isk /ˈæstərɪsk; ˈæstə,rɪsk/ *n* the mark *, used to call attention to something, eg a footnote, or to show that letters are omitted, as in *Mr J***s,* for *Mr Jones.* 星號;星標(用以指示應注意之事物,如註脚,或表示有字母被省略,如以 Mr J***s 代表 Mr Jones)。

astern /əˈstɜːn; əˈstɝn/ *adv* **1** in or at the stern of a ship. 在船尾。⇨ the illus at ship. 參看 ship 之插圖。 **2** backward: 向後: *Full speed ~!* 全速後退! **3** ***fall ~ (of),*** fall behind (another ship). 落於(另一船)之後。

as·ter·oid /ˈæstərɔɪd; ˈæstə,rɔɪd/ *n* [C] any of many small planets between the orbits of Mars and Jupiter. 小行星 (火星與木星軌道間之許多小行星之任一)。⇨ the illus at planet. 參看 planet 之挿圖。

asthma /ˈæsmə *US:* ˈæzmə; ˈæzmə/ *n* [U] chronic chest disease marked by difficulty in breathing. 氣喘;氣喘病。**asth·matic** /æsˈmætɪk *US:* æz-; æzˈmætɪk/ *adj* suffering from ~; of ~. 氣喘的;患氣喘病的;氣喘病的。

astig·ma·tism /əˈstɪgmətɪzəm; əˈstɪgmə,tɪzəm/ *n* [U] defect in an eye or lens that prevents correct focusing. (指眼)亂視;散光;(指透鏡)像散性;像散現象。 **as·tig·matic** /ˌæstɪgˈmætɪk; ˌæstɪgˈmætɪk/ *adj*

astir /əˈstɜː(r); əˈstɝ/ *adv, pred adj* **1** in motion; in a state of excitement: 在活動中;在騷動狀態中: *The whole village was ~ when news came that the Queen was coming.* 聽到女王要來的消息,全村爲之騷動。 **2** (dated) out of bed and about: (過時用語)起床到處走動: *You're ~ early this morning.* 你今天早晨起得很早。

as·ton·ish /əˈstɒnɪʃ; əˈstɑnɪʃ/ *vt* [VP6A] surprise greatly: 使大爲驚異;使驚駭;使驚愕: *The news ~ed everybody.* 這消息令人人感到驚愕。*You look ~ed at the news.* 你對這消息似乎感到驚異。*I was ~ed to see him there.* 我在那裏見到他,感到驚異。*I am ~ed that he didn't come.* 他沒有來,使我感到驚異。**~·ing** *part adj* very surprising: 非常驚人的;極可驚的: *It is ~ing to me that he should be absent.* 他竟會缺席,使我感到驚訝。 **~·ment** *n* [U] great surprise: 大驚奇;驚愕;驚異: *I heard to my ~ment that...;* 我聽到…甚感驚愕; *He looked at me in ~ment.* 他驚奇地望着我。

astound /əˈstaund; əˈstaund/ *vt* [VP6A] overcome with surprise; shock. 使大受驚駭;震驚。

as·tra·khan /ˌæstrəˈkæn *US:* ˈæstrəkən; ˈæstrəkən/ *n* [U] skin of young lambs with wool in tight little curls: 羔皮; 小羊皮 (其毛捲成小圈者): (used attrib) (形容用法) *an ~ coat/cap.* 羔皮大衣(帽)。

as·tral /ˈæstrəl; ˈæstrəl/ *adj* of or from the stars. 星的;從星上來的。

astray /əˈstreɪ; əˈstre/ *adv, pred adj* out of, off, the right path, esp (fig) into wrongdoing: 迷途; 離正路;(尤指,喩) 入歧途: *The boy was led ~ by bad companions.* 那個男孩被壞同伴引入歧途。

astride /əˈstraɪd; əˈstraɪd/ *adv, pred adj, prep* with one leg on each side (of): 兩腿分開(而騎);跨騎: *riding ~;* 跨騎; *sitting ~ his father's knee.* 騎坐在他父親的膝上。

as·trin·gent /əˈstrɪndʒənt; əˈstrɪndʒənt/ *n* (kind of) substance that shrinks soft tissues and contracts blood-vessels, thus checking the flow of blood. 收斂劑(可收縮柔軟之組織,並可收縮血管以止血者)。□ *adj* of or like an ~; (fig) harsh; severe. 收斂劑的;似收斂劑的; 收斂性的; (喩)嚴厲的; 嚴酷的。**as·trin·gency** /əˈstrɪndʒənsɪ; əˈstrɪndʒənsɪ/ *n*

as·tro·dome /ˈæstrədəum; ˈæstrə,dom/ *n* small, transparent observation dome on the top of the fuselage of an aircraft, used by the navigator. 天文航行艙(機身頂部供領航員觀測用的透明小圓頂)。

as·tro·labe /ˈæstrəleɪb; ˈæstrə,leb/ *n* instrument used in the Middle Ages to determine the height of the sun, etc. 星盤(中古時期用以測定太陽等高度的一種觀象儀)。⇨ sextant.

as·trol·ogy /əˈstrɒlədʒɪ; əˈstrɑlədʒɪ/ *n* [U] art of observing the positions of the stars in the belief that they influence human affairs. 占星術。**as·trol·oger** /-dʒə(r); -dʒɚ/ *n* expert in ~. 占星家。**as·tro·logi·cal** /ˌæstrəˈlɒdʒɪkl; ˌæstrəˈlɑdʒɪkl/ *adj*

as·tro·naut /ˈæstrənɔːt; ˈæstrə,nɔt/ *n* person who travels in a spacecraft. 太空人; 乘太空船旅行的人。**~·ics** /ˌæstrəˈnɔːtɪks; ˌæstrəˈnɔtɪks/ *n* (*sing v*) (用單數動詞) science and technology of travel through outer space. 太空航行學。

as·tron·omy /əˈstrɒnəmɪ; əˈstrɑnəmɪ/ *n* [U] science of the sun, moon, stars and planets. 天文學。**as·tron·omer** *n* student of, authority on, ~. 天文學者;天文學家。**as·tro·nomi·cal** /ˌæstrəˈnɒmɪkl; ˌæstrə'nɑmɪkl̩/ *adj* of the study of ~; (colloq; of a quantity) very large: 天文學的; (俗; 指數量) 極大的: *an astronomical amount.* 極大的數量。

as·tro·phys·ics /ˌæstrəʊ'fɪzɪks ; ˌæstro'fɪzɪks/ *n* (*sing v*) science of the chemical and physical conditions of the stars. (用單數動詞) 天體物理學。

as·tute /ə'stju:t *US:* ə'stu:t ; ə'stjut/ *adj* **1** quick at seeing how to gain an advantage. 敏於看出如何獲得利益的; 狡黠的。 **2** shrewd; clever: 精明的; 聰明的: *an ~ lawyer/businessman.* 精明的律師(商人)。 **~·ly** *adv* **~·ness** *n*

asun·der /ə'sʌndə(r) ; ə'sʌndɚ/ *adv* (liter) (文) **1** (of two or more things) apart: (指兩件或兩件以上之事物) 分開; 分離; 分散: *Parents and children were driven ~* (= separated) *by the war.* 父母與子女因戰事而分散。 **2** into pieces: 成碎片: *tear sth ~.* 將某物撕碎。

asy·lum /ə'saɪləm ; ə'saɪləm/ *n* **1** [U] refuge; safety; protection from persecution, etc: 庇護; 安全; 避難: *ask for political ~;* 請求政治庇護; [C] place where this is found or given. 庇護所; 避難所。 **2** [C] (formerly) institution where mentally ill people were cared for, now called a *mental home/hospital/institution.* (昔時) 瘋人院; 精神病院 (現稱 mental home, mental hospital 或 mental institution)。

at /ət ; ət; *strong form:* æt ; æt/ *prep* **1** (place and direction) (指地方與方向) **(a)** (indicating the place in or near which sth or sb was, is or will be): (指某人或某物所在之處，或在其附近): *at his office;* 在他的辦公室; *at my uncle's;* 在我叔父家; *at the station.* 在車站。 Cf 參較 *in* for countries and large towns, and places important to the speaker. in 用於國家和大城市，以及對說話者甚爲重要的地方。 **(b)** (towards; in the direction of): (向; 朝着): *look at sth/sb;* 朝着某物(某人)看; *shoot/aim a gun at sth;* 對着某物射擊(以槍瞄準某物); *rush at the enemy;* 向敵人衝去; *laugh/growl at sb/sth;* 嘲笑某人或某事物(對着某人或某事物咆哮); *throw sth at sb,* ie intending to hit him, ⇨ *throw to* at throw¹(1); 對準某人投擲某物(意欲擊中他); *talk at sb,* ie make an indirect attack on him, ⇨ *talk to* at talk²(1). 暗指某人而說; 暗諷(即間接攻擊某人)。 **(c)** (indicating an attempt to get or reach sth, an uncompleted or imperfect action): (指試圖得到或觸及某物，一種未完成或不完全的動作): *The drowning man clutched at the oar,* tried to seize it. 那溺水的人欲抓住槳(但尚未抓住)。 *He had to guess at the meaning.* 他不得不猜測那意思。 **(d)** (indicating distance): (指距離): *hold sth at arm's length.* 與某物保持距離。 *It looks better at a distance.* 它在遠處看起來更好。 **(e)** (indicating a point of entrance or exit) through; by: (指入口或出口處) 經過; 經由: *What the teacher says often goes in (at) one ear and out (at) the other.* 老師所說的話常左耳進右耳出。 **2** (time and order) (指時間及順序) **(a)** (indicating a point of time): (指時間之一點): *at 2 o'clock;* 在兩點鐘的時候; *at sunset;* 在日落的時候; *at any moment;* 在任何時刻; *at this (point),* when this happened. 當此事發生時。 **(b)** (of age): (指年齡): *He left school at (the age of) 15.* 他在十五歲時離開學校。 **(c)** (indicating order): (指順序): *at the third attempt;* 在第三次嘗試的時候; *at first;* 首先; 起初; *at last.* 最後; 終於。 **(d)** (indicating frequency): (指次數多寡): *at (all) times;* 有時候(無論何時; 總是); *at regular intervals.* 在每隔一定時間。 **3** (activity, state, manner) (指活動，情況，狀態，方式) **(a)** (indicating occupation): (指所做之事): *at work;* 在工作; *at play.* 在遊戲。 *What is he at now,* What is he doing? 他現在在做什麼? ˌ**hard 'at it,** working hard. 正在努力工作。 **(b)** (after *adjj*): (用於形容詞之後): *busy at his tasks;* 忙着做他的事; *good at translation.* 擅長翻譯。 **(c)** (state, condition): (指狀態，情況): *at war/peace;* 在戰(平)時; *at leisure.* 在閒暇時。 **(d)** (manner): (指方式，樣態): *at a gallop;* 以奔馳的步子; *finish something at a sitting,* ie during one continuous period of activity. 一口氣做完某事。 **4** (rate or degree, value, cost) (指速率或程度，價值，價錢) **(a)** (rate): (指速率): *at full speed;* 以全速; *at a snail's pace.* 以蝸牛的速度; 緩慢地。 **(b)** (value, cost, etc): (指價值，價錢等): *at immense cost;* 花極大的代價; *sell sth at a loss;* 虧本出售某物; *buy articles at 20p and sell them at 25p.* 以每件二十辨士之價購入貨品，以每件二十五辨士之價售出。 **(c)** (with *superl*): (與最高級形容詞或副詞連用): *at its/his/their, etc best;* 在它的(他的，他們的等) 最佳情況中; *at least;* 至少; 最少; *at (the) worst.* 卽使壞到極點。 **5** (cause) (指原因) **(a)** (after *vv*): (用於動詞之後): *The pupils marvelled at the extent of their teacher's knowledge.* 學生們對於其老師知識範圍之廣感到驚奇。 **(b)** (after *adjj* and *pp's*): (用於形容詞及過去分詞之後): *impatient at the delay;* 對於躭誤的情形感到不耐煩; *delighted at the idea of going to England.* 一想到要去英國就感到高興。 ⇨ also *n* entries for *at hand, at last, be in at the death* and others.

ata·brine /'ætəbri:n ; 'ætəbrin/ *n* [U] (P) bitter-tasting, anti-malarial drug. (商標) 瘧滌平; 阿的平 (一種苦味的治療瘧疾的藥)。

ata·vism /'ætəvɪzəm ; 'ætəˌvɪzəm/ *n* reappearance in a person of a characteristic or quality that has not shown itself for several or many generations. (人之特徵或性格的) 隔代遺傳; 祖型再現; 返祖遺傳; 返祖性。 ⇨ reversion, throwback. **ata·vis·tic** /ˌætə'vɪstɪk ; ˌætə'vɪstɪk/ *adj*

ate /et *US:* eɪt ; et/ *pt* of eat.

atel·ier /æ'telɪeɪ *US:* ˌætl'jeɪ ; 'ætl̩ˌje/ *n* (F) workshop; studio. (法) 工作室; 畫室。

athe·ism /'eɪθɪɪzəm ; 'eθɪˌɪzəm/ *n* [U] belief that there is no God. 無神論。 **athe·ist** /'eɪθɪɪst ; 'eθɪɪst/ *n* person who believes that there is no Cod. 無神論者。 **athe·is·tic** /ˌeɪθɪ'ɪstɪk ; ˌeθɪ'ɪstɪk/ *adj* of ~ or atheists. 無神論(者)的。

athirst /ə'θɜ:st ; ə'θɝst/ *pred adj* ~ ***(for),*** (liter) thirsty, eager (for news, etc). (文) 渴的; 渴望的 (與 for 連用，後接消息等)。

ath·lete /'æθli:t ; 'æθlit/ *n* person trained for competing in physical exercises and outdoor games, eg a person good at running, jumping, swimming, boxing. 運動選手; 運動員 (如擅長跑，跳，游泳，拳擊者)。

ath·letic /æθ'letɪk ; æθ'lɛtɪk/ *adj* **1** of athletes. 運動員的。 **2** physically strong, with well-balanced proportions between the trunk and limbs: 體格健美的; 體格强健而軀幹與四肢之比例勻稱的: *an ~-looking young man.* 一個體格健美的年輕人。

ath·let·ics /æθ'letɪks ; æθ'lɛtɪks/ *n pl* (usu with *sing v*) practice of physical exercises and sports, esp competitions in running, jumping, etc. (通常用單數動詞) 運動 (各項體育運動之總稱，尤指跑、跳等之競賽); 競技。

at-home /ət'həʊm ; ət'hom/ ⇨ home¹(1).

athwart /ə'θwɔ:t ; ə'θwɔrt/ *adv, prep* ~ ***(of),*** (naut) from one side to the other side. (航海) 橫越; 從(…之)一邊至另一邊。

atishoo /ə'tɪʃu: ; ə'tɪʃu/ *int* (hum) spelling form used to indicate a sneeze. (諧) 阿嚏 (卽打噴嚏)。

at·las /'ætləs ; 'ætləs/ *n* book of maps. 地圖集; 地圖。

at·mos·phere /'ætməsfɪə(r) ; 'ætməsˌfɪr/ *n* **1** [U] esp 尤指 **the** ~, mixture of gases surrounding the earth. 大氣; (繞於地球四周之) 空氣。 **2** [U] air in any place. (任何地方之) 空氣。 **3** [C] feeling, eg of good, evil, that the mind receives from a place, conditions, etc: 對於某一地方、情況等所得到的印象或感覺; 氣氛: *There is an ~ of peace and calm in the country quite different from the ~ of a big city.* 在鄉間有一種和平寧靜之氣氛，與大城市的氣氛截然不同。

at·mos·pheric /ˌætməs'ferɪk ; ˌætməs'fɛrɪk/ *adj* of, connected with, the atmosphere: 大氣的; 關於大氣的: *~ conditions.* 大氣的情況。 ˌ~ **'pressure,** pressure at a point due to the weight of the column of air above that point, about $14\frac{1}{2}$ lb or

6.6 kg per square inch at sea level. 大氣壓力(在海平面,每平方吋約 $14\frac{1}{2}$ 磅或6.6公斤)。**at·mos·pher·ics** *n pl* electrical discharges that occur in the atmosphere and cause crackling sounds in radio receivers. (能使收音機發生雜音之)天電。

atoll /ˈætɒl ; ˈætɑl/ *n* ring-shaped coral reef(s) almost or entirely enclosing a lagoon. 環狀珊瑚島(幾乎或完全圍繞着一礁湖);環礁。

an atoll

atom /ˈætəm ; ˈætəm/ *n* **1** smallest unit of an element that can take part in a chemical change: 原子 (元素中能參加化學變化之最小單位): *A molecule of water* (H_2O) *is made up of two ~s of hydrogen and one ~ of oxygen.* 一分子的水是由二氫原子和一氧原子構成的。 ⇨ electron, neutron, nucleus, proton. **ˈ~ bomb,** = atomic bomb. **2** very small bit: 微粒;極小之物: *blow sth to ~s,* destroy it by explosion. 將某物炸得粉碎(藉爆炸而毀掉它)。*There's not an ~ of truth* (= no truth at all) *in what he said.* 他所說的話根本不是眞的。

atomic /əˈtɒmɪk ; əˈtɑmɪk/ *adj* of an atom, or atoms. 原子的。 **ˈ~ bomb,** bomb of which the destructive power comes from the release of ~ energy in the shortest possible time. 原子彈。 **ˌ~ ˈenergy,** energy obtained as the result of nuclear fission. 原子能。 **ˌ~ ˈpile,** ⇨ reactor. 原子爐。 **ˌ~ ˈweight,** weight of an atom of an element expressed on a scale in which an atom of oxygen is 16. 原子量。⇨ nuclear.

at·om·ize /ˈætəmaɪz ; ˈætəmˌaɪz/ *vt* reduce to atoms. 使成原子;使成微粒如霧狀。 **~r** *n* device for producing a fine spray, eg of perfume. 噴霧器(例如噴香水者)。

atonal /eɪˈtəʊnl ; eˈtonl/ *adj* (music) not conforming to any system of key or mode. (音樂)無調的;不合任何音調系統的。 **~·ity** /ˌeɪtəʊˈnælətɪ ; ˌetoˈnælətɪ/ *n*

atone /əˈtəʊn ; əˈton/ *vi* [VP2A, 3A] **~ *(for),*** make repayment: 彌補;補償;贖罪: *~ (for) a fault by doing sth.* 藉做某事以彌補過失。*How can I ~ for hurting your feelings?* 我怎樣才能補償傷你感情之過呢? *How can I ~?* 我如何能贖罪? **~·ment** *n* [U] atoning: 彌補;補償;贖罪: *make ~ment for a fault.* 彌補過失;贖罪。 **the A~ment,** the sufferings and death of Jesus. 耶穌爲替世人贖罪所受之苦及死。

atop /əˈtɒp ; əˈtɑp/ *adv* **~ *(of),*** (US) on top (of). (美)在(…之)頂上。

at·ra·bil·ious /ˌætrəˈbɪlɪəs ; ˌætrəˈbɪljəs/ *adj* (rare) melancholy; acrimonious. (罕)憂鬱的;壞脾氣的;刻薄的。

atro·cious /əˈtrəʊʃəs ; əˈtroʃəs/ *adj* **1** very wicked or cruel: 極惡毒的;兇暴的;殘忍的: *an ~ crime.* 兇暴的罪行。 **2** (colloq) very bad: (俗)極壞的;極惡劣的: *an ~ dinner;* 極壞的一餐; *~ weather.* 極惡劣的天氣。 **~·ly** *adv*

atroc·ity /əˈtrɒsətɪ ; əˈtrɑsətɪ/ *n* [U] wickedness; [C] (*pl* -ties) wicked or cruel act: 惡毒;殘暴的行爲: *the atrocities of which the enemy forces were guilty.* 敵軍所犯的暴行。

atro·phy /ˈætrəfɪ ; ˈætrəfɪ/ *n* [U] wasting away (of the body or part of it, or (fig) of a moral quality). (指身體或其一部)萎縮;(喻,指道德)淪喪。□ *vt, vi* [VP6A] cause ~ in; [VP2A, B] suffer ~. 使萎縮;萎縮。

atta·boy /ˌætəˈbɔɪ ; ˈætəbɔɪ/ *int* (US colloq) (expressing encouragement or admiration) Bravo! (美,俗)(表示鼓勵或讚美)好極了!好小子!

at·tach /əˈtætʃ ; əˈtætʃ/ *vt, vi* **1** [VP14] **~ *sth (to sth),*** fasten or join: 附上;加上;貼上;繫上: *~ labels to the luggage;* 將標籤繫在行李上; *~ a document to a letter;* 將文件附在信中; *the sample ~ed to the letter;* 隨函附送的樣品; *a house with a garage ~ed.* 附有車房的房子。*A~ed you will find / A~ed please find...,* (business style) You will find, ~ed to this letter.... (商業函件型式)隨函附上…,請查收。 **2** [VP14] **~ *oneself to,*** join eg as a junior, and perhaps unwelcome, member: 參加;加入(作一資淺或許不受歡迎的會員等): *~ oneself to a political party / to a travelling circus.* 加入某一政黨(巡廻馬戲團)。 **3** ***be ~ed to,*** be bound to by love or affection: 爲愛或感情所束縛;愛慕;依戀: *She is deeply ~ed to her young brother.* 她深愛她的幼弟。 *He is foolishly ~ed to old customs.* 他愚昧地執着於舊習俗。 **4** [VP14] **~ *sth to sth,*** consider to have; connect with: 認爲有;使與…相關聯: *Do you ~ much importance to what he says?* 你認爲他所說的話有很大的重要性嗎? **5** [VP3A] **~ *to,*** go with, be joined to: 伴隨;(與…)相關聯: *No suspicion / blame ~es to him,* He cannot be suspected / blamed. 他無可懷疑(責備)之處。 **6** [VP6A] (legal) seize by legal authority: (法律)依法扣留;逮捕;拘留;查封: *Part of his salary was ~ed by shopkeepers to whom he owed money.* 他的一部份薪水被店主們依法扣下來償付他所欠他們的債務。 **7** ***~ed to,*** (mil) appointed to another unit for specialist duties: (軍)被派遣至另一單位擔任特定任務的;配屬的: *a gunnery officer ~ed to an infantry regiment.* 派遣至步兵團擔任特定任務之射擊軍官。 **~·ment** *n* **1** [U] act of ~ing or joining; being ~ed. 附着;附屬;附帶。 **2** [C] sth ~ed, esp an accessory ~ed to sth larger. 附屬物;附件。 **3** [C] affection; friendship: 情感;深情;友愛: *have an ~ment for sb.* 對某人有深情。 **4** legal seizing of goods, etc. (依法)扣留;查封(貨物等)。 **5** ***on ~ment to,*** (temporarily) appointed to. (暫時)配屬…。

at·taché /əˈtæʃeɪ *US:* ˌætəˈʃeɪ ; ˌætəˈʃe/ *n* person who is attached to the staff of an ambassador: (大使館的)隨員;館員: *the naval / military / press ~.* 海軍武官(陸軍武官;新聞參事)。 **~ case** /əˈtæʃɪ keɪs ; əˈtæʃɪ kes/ *n* small, flat, rectangular box or holder for documents. 小型公文包。

at·tack /əˈtæk ; əˈtæk/ *n* **1** [C] violent attempt to hurt, overcome, defeat: 攻擊;進攻;攻打: *make an ~ upon the enemy;* 向敵人進攻; [U] *The enemy came under ~.* 敵人受到攻擊。*A~ is said to be the best form of defence.* 常言道,攻擊是最好的防禦。 **2** [C] adverse criticism in speech or writing: (言語或文字的)攻擊;抨擊: *a strong ~ against / on the Government's policy.* 對政府政策猛烈的抨擊。 **3** [C] start, occurence, eg of disease: (疾病等之)發作;侵襲: *an ~ of fever;* 發燒; *a ˈliver ~;* 肝病突發; *a ˈheart ~,* pain in the region of the heart, with irregular beating. 心臟病發作。 **4** [U] way of beginning an activity, eg playing the violin, playing a stroke in cricket. 着手的方式;開始的手法(例如拉提琴,在板球中之一擊)。□ *vt* [VP6A] make an ~ upon: 攻擊;進攻;抨擊;侵襲: *~ the enemy;* 攻擊敵人; *~ the Prime Minister's proposals;* 抨擊首相的提議; *a disease that ~s children.* 侵襲兒童的疾病。*Rust ~s metals.* 銹能侵蝕金屬。 **~er** *n* person who ~s. 攻擊者;進攻者;抨擊者。

at·tain /əˈteɪn ; əˈten/ *vt, vi* **1** [VP6A] succeed in doing or getting: 達到;成就;實現;遂(願): *~ one's hopes / object / the end one has in view.* 實現其希望(達到其目的;實現所抱的目標)。 **2** [VP3A] **~ *to,*** reach, arrive at: 到達;至;得到: *~ to perfection / power / prosperity;* 到達完美(權力,繁榮)之境; *~ to man's estate,* reach manhood. 到達成年。 **~·able** /-əbl ; -əbl̩/ *adj* that can be ~ed: 可達到的;可得

到的: *The goal is not yet ~able.* 該目標目前尚無法達到。**~·ment** *n* **1** [U] act of ~ing: 達到;得到: *easy/difficult/impossible of ~ment,* easy, etc to ~; 容易(不易,不可能)達到的; *for the ~ment of* (= in order to ~) *his purpose.* 爲了達到他的目的。**2** [C] (usu *pl*) sth ~ed; skill or accomplishment in some branch of knowledge, etc: (通常用複數) 成就;造詣: *legal/linguistic ~ments;* 法學(語言學)上的成就; *a scholar of the highest ~ments.* 造詣極高的學者。

at·tain·der /ə'teɪndə(r) ; ə'tendɚ/ *n* (legal) forfeiture of property and civil rights following sentence of death or outlawry. (法律) (宣判死刑或放逐後所致之) 沒收財產及褫奪公權。**Bill of A~,** Parliamentary Bill imposing this penalty without trial. 褫奪公權之議案 (强制此種刑罰而不經受審之國會議案)。

at·tar /'ætə(r) ; 'ætɚ/ *n* [U] *~ of roses,* perfume from rose petals. 玫瑰油(用玫瑰花瓣所製之香油);玫瑰香水。

at·tempt /ə'tempt ; ə'tɛmpt/ *vt* **1** [VP7A, 6A] make a start at doing sth; try: 開始做;試做;嘗試;企圖: *The prisoners ~ed to escape/an escape but failed.* 囚犯們企圖逃獄,但是失敗了。*You have ~ed* (= made a start at performing) *a difficult task.* 你開始了一項艱難的工作。*Don't ~ impossibilities,* Don't try to do impossible things. 不要試做不可能的事情。**2** [VP6A] *~ sb's life,* (old use) try to kill him. (舊用法) 意圖謀害某人的性命。□ *n* [C] **1** ***~ to do sth; ~ at doing sth,*** ~ing; effort to do sth: 嘗試做某事;企圖做某事: *They made no ~ to escape/at escaping.* 他們未曾企圖脫逃。*His first ~ at English composition was poor.* 他第一次作的英文作文很差。*They failed in all their ~s to climb the mountain.* 他們攀登該山的一切嘗試都失敗了。**2** ***~ at,*** sth not very well done: 未做成功之事: *Her ~ at a Christmas cake had to be thrown away.* 她的聖誕蛋糕做得不好,只好丢掉。**3** ***~ on/upon,*** attack on: 攻擊;襲擊: *make an ~ on sb's life;* 謀害某人的性命; *an ~ on the world speed record.* 打破世界速度記錄的嘗試。

at·tend /ə'tend ; ə'tɛnd/ *vi, vt* **1** [VP3A, 2A] ***~ (to),*** give care and thought (to): 注意;用心;照顧: *~ to one's work;* 用心從事自己的工作; *~ to what sb is saying,* listen carefully; 注意聽某人的說話; *~ to the wants of customers,* try to supply them. 照應顧客的需要;照顧生意。*Are you being ~ed to?* (in a shop) Is anyone serving you? (在商店中) 有店員照應你嗎? *You're not ~ing,* not listening, not paying attention. 你沒有在注意聽。**2** [VP6A, 3A] ***~ (on/upon),*** wait on; serve; look after: 侍候;看護;照料: *Which doctor is ~ing you,* giving you medical care? 哪一個醫生爲你看病? *The patient has three nurses ~ing (on) him.* 那病人有三位護士看護他。*She has many servants ~ing upon her.* 她有許多僕人侍候她。*He had the honour of ~ing upon the Prince.* 他有幸能侍候王子。**3** [VP6A] go to; be present at: 到場;出席;參加;上(學): *~ school/church;* 上學(教堂); *~ a meeting/lecture.* 出席會議(聽演講)。*The lectures were well ~ed,* there were good audiences. 該項演講聽的人很多。**4** [VP6A] (formal) accompany: (正式用語) 伴隨: *a method that is ~ed by some risk.* 帶有相當冒險性的方法。*Our plans were ~ed with great difficulties.* 我們的計畫遇到很大的困難。*May good luck ~ you!* (formal) May you have good luck! (正式用語) 祝君幸運!

at·tend·ance /ə'tendəns ; ə'tɛndəns/ *n* **1** [U] ***in ~ (on/upon),*** act of attending (2): 侍候;看護;照料: *Major X was in ~ upon the Queen.* 某少校擔任女王的侍衞。*Now that the patient is out of danger, the doctor is no longer in ~.* 既然病人已經脫離險境,醫生就不再照料他了。⇨ dance²(2). **2** [C, U] (time of) being present, at school etc: 出席;到校等之次數: *The boy was given a prize for regular ~,* for attending school regularly. 那男孩獲頒全勤獎(從未缺課)。*How many ~s has he made?* 他出席了幾次? *Is ~ at school compulsory?* 到校上課是硬性規定的嗎? **3** [C] (with *adjj*) number of persons present: (與形容詞連用) 出席的人數: *There was a large ~ at church this morning.* 今天早上教堂中做禮拜的人很多。

at·tend·ant /ə'tendənt ; ə'tɛndənt/ *n* **1** servant or companion. 僕役;侍從。**2** *medical ~,* doctor. 醫生。**3** (*pl*) persons who accompany an important person: (複) (要人的) 隨從人員: *the Prince and his ~s.* 王子及其隨從人員。□ *adj* **1** accompanying: 伴隨的;隨之同來的: *famine and its ~ diseases,* the diseases that result from famine; 饑荒及隨之而來的疾病; *old age and its ~ evils,* eg deafness. 老年及其伴隨的疾患(如耳聾)。**2** waiting upon: 隨侍的;侍候的: *an ~ nurse.* 隨侍護士;特別護士。

at·ten·tion /ə'tenʃn ; ə'tɛnʃən/ *n* **1** [U] act of directing one's thoughts to sth: 注意;專心: *Pay ~ to what you're doing,* Don't let your thoughts wander. 注意你在做的事。*A teacher must know how to secure the ~ of his pupils.* 一個老師必須知道如何使學生專心上課。*No ~ was paid to my advice,* no one took it. 沒有一個人聽從我的勸告。*Give your whole ~ to what you are doing,* ie think of nothing else. 把全部注意力用於你所做的事。*He called/invited my ~ to some new evidence,* asked me to examine it. 他要我注意檢查新的證據。*He shouted to attract ~,* to make people notice him. 他高聲喊叫以引起別人的注意。*A~, Mr Roberts,* (in comm or official correspondence) This letter, memorandum, etc is to be dealt with by Mr Roberts. (用於商業信件或公函中) 本信件,便函等由羅伯次先生承辦。**2** (often *pl*) kind or polite act: (常用複數) 慇懃;厚待: *They showed the old lady numerous little ~s,* were kind and helpful in numerous ways. 他們對那老太太慇懃款待,無微不至。*A pretty girl usually receives more ~(s) than a plain girl,* finds men more willing to do things for her. 一個漂亮的女孩通常比一個不漂亮的女孩得到較多 (男子所獻) 的慇懃。***pay one's ~s to a lady,*** (dated) court her, be polite and kind in the hope of winning her affections. (過時用語) 向某女士獻慇懃;追求某女士。**3** [U] (mil) drill position in which a man stands straight and still: (軍) 立正之姿勢: *come to/stand at ~;* 立正; (as a military command): (用作軍隊之口令): *A~!* 立正! (shortened to 略作 *'shun* /ʃʌn ; ʃʌn/).

at·tent·ive /ə'tentɪv ; ə'tɛntɪv/ *adj* ***~ (to),*** giving or paying attention: 注意的;留心的;專心的;慇懃的;關懷的: *A speaker likes to have an ~ audience.* 演說者喜歡聽衆專心聽。*Please be more ~ to your studies.* 請多用點心讀書。*A good host is ~ to (the needs of) his guests.* 好主人留心客人(的需要)。*She was always ~ to her young brother.* 她總是注意照料她的幼弟。**~·ly** *adv*: *They listened ~ly to the teacher.* 他們專心聽老師(講話)。

at·tenu·ate /ə'tenjʊeɪt ; ə'tɛnjʊˌet/ *vt* [VP6A] (formal) make thin or slender; weaken; reduce. (正式用語) 使變細;使變弱;使變薄;減少。

at·test /ə'test ; ə'tɛst/ *vt, vi* **1** [VP6A] be or give clear proof of: 證明;是…的明證: *The man's ability was ~ed by his rapid promotion,* His promotion was proof of his ability. 那人的能力由於他的迅速陞遷而得到證明(他的迅速擢升是他能幹的證明)。*These papers ~ the fact that....* 這些文件證明了這個事實…。***~ a signature,*** make it legal by witnessing it. 見證簽字(簽自己之名於另一簽名之旁,以證明簽名屬實而使生法律效力)。**ˌ~ed 'milk/'cattle,** certified free of disease, esp tuberculosis. 經檢驗合格的牛奶(經證明無病,尤指無結核病,的牛)。**2** [VP6A] declare on oath; put (a person) on oath; cause (sb) to declare solemnly: 宣誓說出;使發誓;使鄭重宣佈: *I have said nothing that I am not ready to ~,* to say on oath. 我說的話句句屬實,皆可立誓爲證。**3** [VP2A] enrol for military service (by taking the oath of allegiance). (宣誓) 入伍;從軍。**4** [VP3A] ***~ to,***

bear witness to: 爲…作證: *feats which ~ to his strength of will.* 證明他堅强意志的功績。

at·tic /ˈætɪk ; ˈætɪk/ *n* space within the roof of a house: 屋頂下的小室;頂樓;閣樓: *two small rooms in the ~.* 頂樓的兩個小房間。

At·tic /ˈætɪk ; ˈætɪk/ *adj* of ancient Athens or Attica. 雅典的;阿提喀(古希臘之一地區,其首府爲雅典)的。

at·tire /əˈtaɪə(r) ; əˈtaɪr/ *n* [U] (liter or poet) dress: (文或詩)服裝: *in holiday ~.* 穿著假日的服裝。□ *vt* [VP6A] (dated) dress: (過時用語) 穿着: *~d in white/satin.* 穿着白色的(緞製的)衣服。

at·ti·tude /ˈætɪtjuːd *US:* -tuːd ; ˈætəˌtjud/ *n* [C] **1** manner of placing or holding the body: 姿勢;姿態: *He stood there in a threatening ~.* 他以威脅的姿態站在那裏。***strike an ~,*** suddenly and dramatically take up an ~. 突然而戲劇性地擺出一種姿態;裝模作樣。 **2** way of feeling, thinking or behaving: 態度;意見;看法: *What is your ~ towards this question,* What do you think about it, how do you propose to act? 你對這問題的態度如何?*We must maintain a firm ~,* not show signs of weakness. 我們必須保持堅定的態度。**at·ti·tu·din·ize** /ˌætɪˈtjuːdɪnaɪz *US:* -ˈtuːdən- ; ˌætəˈtjudnˌaɪz/ *vi* [VP2A] strike ~s; speak, write, behave in an affected way. 突然而戲劇性地做出一種姿態;裝模作樣;以矯飾的態度說話、寫作或做出行爲;矯揉造作。

at·tor·ney /əˈtɜːnɪ ; əˈtɝnɪ/ *n* (*pl* ~s) **1** person with legal authority to act for another in business or law: (在法律上有權代理他人辦理業務或訴訟之)代理人: *letter/warrant of ~,* written authority by which a person appoints another to act for him; (委託他人代理之)委託書; *power of ~,* authority so given. 受委託代理之權;委託權。 **2** ˌ**A~ ˈGeneral,** **(a)** legal officer with authority to act in all cases in which the State is a party, usu *district ~.* 首席檢察官;檢察長(通常爲地方檢察官)。**(b)** (US, in some States) public prosecutor. (美,某些州的)檢察官。 **3** solicitor. 律師。

at·tract /əˈtrækt ; əˈtrækt/ *vt* [VP6A] **1** pull towards (by unseen force): 吸引: *A magnet ~s steel.* 磁石吸引鋼。 **2** get the attention of; arouse interest or pleasure in: 引起…之注意或興趣: *Bright colours ~ babies.* 鮮艷的顏色可引起嬰孩的注意。*Bright lights ~ moths.* 亮光可招引燈蛾。*He shouted to ~ attention.* 他高聲喊叫以引起他人注意。*Do you feel ~ed to her,* Do you like her? 你感到她對你有吸引力嗎?

at·trac·tion /əˈtrækʃn ; əˈtrækʃən/ *n* **1** [U] power of pulling towards: 吸引力: *The ~ of the moon for the earth causes the tides.* 月球對地球的吸引力造成潮汐。 *He cannot resist the ~ of the sea on a hot day/of a pretty girl.* 他無法抗拒熱天裏海的(漂亮女郎的)吸引力。*The cinema has little ~ for some people.* 電影對某些人沒有什麼吸引力。 **2** [C] that which attracts: 吸引人的事物: *the ~s of a big city,* eg theatres, concerts, cinemas, fine shops. 大城市之誘人之處(例如戲院,音樂會,電影院,漂亮的商店)。

at·tract·ive /əˈtræktɪv ; əˈtræktɪv/ *adj* having the power to attract; pleasing: 有吸引力的;動人的;誘人的: *a most ~ girl*; 非常誘人的女郎; *goods offered at ~ prices.* 標價低廉誘人的貨品。**~·ly** *adv*

at·tribute[1] /əˈtrɪbjuːt ; əˈtrɪbjʊt/ *vt* [VP14] ~ ***to,*** consider as a quality of, as being the result of, as coming from: 認爲是…的屬性,是…的結果或來自…;歸於;歸因於: *He ~s wisdom to his teachers,* thinks they have wisdom. 他認爲他的老師都很有智慧。*He ~s his success to hard work,* says that his success is the result of hard work. 他認爲他的成功係由努力而來。*This comedy has been ~d to Shakespeare,* it has been said that Shakespeare was the author. 這個喜劇據說爲莎士比亞所作。 **at·trib·u·table** /əˈtrɪbjʊtəbl ; əˈtrɪbjʊtəbl̩/ *adj* that can be ~d (*to*). 可歸(因)於…的(與 to 連用)。**at·tri·bu·tion** /ˌætrɪˈbjuːʃn ; ˌætrəˈbjuʃən/ *n* [U] act of attributing (*to*); [C] that which is ~d. 歸屬;歸因;所歸屬之事物。

at·tribute[2] /ˈætrɪbjuːt ; ˈætrəˌbjut/ *n* [C] **1** quality looked upon as naturally or necessarily belonging to sb or sth: 性質;品性;屬性;本性: *Mercy is an ~ of God.* 寬恕是上帝的本性。*Politeness is an ~ of a gentleman.* 彬彬有禮是紳士的本色。 **2** material object recognized as a symbol of a person or his position: (被認爲代表某人或其地位的)象徵: *The crown is an ~ of kingship.* 王冠是王位的象徵。

at·tribu·tive /əˈtrɪbjʊtɪv ; əˈtrɪbjətɪv/ *adj* ~ **adjective,** naming a quality and used with the noun as in '*old* man', '*red* hair', and contrasted with predicative. 屬性形容詞(指出一種性質,並與名詞連用,如 *old* man, *red* hair 是,與 predicative 相對)。**~·ly** *adv*

at·tri·tion /əˈtrɪʃn ; əˈtrɪʃən/ *n* [U] wearing away by rubbing: 消耗; 消磨; 磨損: *war of ~,* war in which each side waits for the other to wear itself out. 消耗戰。

at·tune /əˈtjuːn *US:* əˈtuːn ; əˈtjun/ *vt* [VP14] ~ ***to,*** bring into harmony or agreement with: 使調和;使一致;使適合: *hearts ~d to worship;* 適合禮拜之心情; make used to: 使習慣於: *ears ~d to the sound of gunfire.* 習慣於砲聲的耳朵。

au·ber·gine /ˈəʊbəʒiːn ; ˈobɚˌʒin/ *n* [C] fruit of the eggplant, used as a vegetable. 茄子。⇨ the illus at vegetable. 參看 vegetable 之插圖。

au·brie·tia /ɔːˈbriːʃə ; ɔˈbriʃə/ *n* (kinds of) spring-flowering dwarf perennial grown on stone walls, rockeries, etc. (數種)十字花科植物(春季開花之矮小的多年生植物,生長於石牆、假山等之上)。

au·burn /ˈɔːbən ; ˈɔbɚn/ *adj* (usu of hair) reddish-brown. (通常指頭髮)赤褐色的;棗紅色的。

auc·tion /ˈɔːkʃn ; ˈɔkʃən/ *n* [C, U] public sale at which goods are sold to the persons making the highest bids or offers: 拍賣: *sale by ~;* 拍賣; *ˈ~-sale;* 拍賣; *sell goods by ~;* 拍賣貨物; *put sth up to/for ~;* 將某物交付拍賣; *attend all the local ~s;* 本地所有各次拍賣全都到場; *~ bridge,* ⇨ bridge[2]. □ *vt* [VP6A, 15B] ~ ***(off),*** sell by ~. 拍賣。**~·eer** /ˌɔːkʃəˈnɪə(r) ; ˌɔkʃənˈɪr/ *n* person who conducts an ~. 拍賣人。

aud·acious /ɔːˈdeɪʃəs ; ɔˈdeʃəs/ *adj* **1** daring; bold. 大膽的;勇敢的。 **2** foolishly bold. 愚勇的。 **3** impudent. 厚顏的;無恥的。**~·ly** *adv* **aud·ac·ity** /ɔːˈdæsətɪ ; ɔˈdæsətɪ/ *n*

aud·ible /ˈɔːdəbl ; ˈɔdəbl/ *adj* loud enough to be heard: 可聽見的;聽得見的: *in a scarcely ~ voice.* 以幾乎聽不見的聲音。*The speaker was scarcely ~,* could be heard only with difficulty. 那演說者的聲音小得幾乎聽不見。**aud·ibly** /-əblɪ ; -əblɪ/ *adv* **audi·bil·ity** *n* /ˌɔːdəˈbɪlətɪ ; ˌɔdəˈbɪlətɪ/ *n* capacity for being heard. 可聽見的程度;能聽度;可聞度。

audi·ence /ˈɔːdɪəns ; ˈɔdɪəns/ *n* **1** gathering of persons for the purpose of hearing a speaker, singer, etc: (集合在一起的)聽衆;觀衆: *There was a large ~ in the theatre.* 戲院中的觀衆很多。*He has addressed large ~s all over England.* 他曾在英國各地向大群的聽衆演說。 **2** persons within hearing, whether they are together or not: 在聽得見的範圍內的人(無論是否集合在一起): *A broadcaster may have an ~ of several million.* 廣播演說者可能有幾百萬的聽衆。 **3** (of a book) readers: (書的)讀者。*His book has reached a wide ~.* 他的書已擁有廣大的讀者。 **4** formal interview given by a ruler, the Pope, etc: (統治者,教宗等所准許的)謁見;覲見: *The Pope granted him an ~.* 教宗准許他謁見。*The Prime Minister was received in ~ by the Queen.* 首相被女王召見。

audio- /ˌɔːdɪəʊ ; ˈɔdɪˌo/ *pref* of hearing. 聽。ˌ**~-visual ˈaids,** teaching aids such as record players and film projectors. 視聽教具(如唱機及放映機等)。ˌ**~-lingual ˈmethods,** teaching methods making use of a language laboratory, tape recorders, etc. 耳聽口說教學法(利用語言實驗室、錄音機等)。ˌ**~ ˈfrequency,** (radio) frequency which, when converted into sound waves by a loudspeaker, can be heard. (無線電)成音頻率;音頻。

au·dit /ˈɔːdɪt ; ˈɔdɪt/ *n* official examination of accounts to see that they are in order. 帳目稽核;查帳。□ *vt* [VP6A] examine, eg accounts, officially. 稽核(帳目等)。

aud·ition /ɔːˈdɪʃn ; ɔˈdɪʃən/ *n* **1** [C] trial hearing to test the voice of a singer, speaker, etc who is applying for employment or of an actor wishing to take part in a play. (對於歌唱者、演說者求職時或演員欲扮演劇中角色時的)試聽。**2** [U] power of hearing; listening. 聽力;聽。□ *vt* [VP6A] give an ~ to. 試聽。

au·di·tor /ˈɔːdɪtə(r) ; ˈɔdɪtɚ/ *n* **1** listener to a speaker, etc. (演說者等的)聽者。 **2** person who audits. 查帳員;審計員;稽核員。

au·di·tor·ium /ˌɔːdɪˈtɔːrɪəm ; ˌɔdəˈtorɪəm/ *n* (*pl* ~s) building, or part of a building, in which an audience sits. 會堂;禮堂;演講廳;音樂廳。

au·di·tory /ˈɔːdɪtrɪ *US:* -tɔːrɪ ; ˈɔdəˌtorɪ/ *adj* of the sense of hearing: 聽覺的: *the ~ nerve.* 聽(覺)神經。➪ the illus at ear. 參看 ear 之插圖。

au fait /ˌəʊ ˈfeɪ ; oˈfe/ *pred adj* (F) instructed: (法)熟諳; 精通: *put sb ~ of sth,* instruct him about it. 教某人使之精通某事。

au fond /ˌəʊ ˈfɒn ; ˌoˈfɔ̃/ *adv* (F) basically. (法)基本上;根本地。

au·ger /ˈɔːgə(r) ; ˈɔgɚ/ *n* carpenter's tool for boring large holes in wood, with a handle at right angles; instrument for boring in soil. (鑽木或鑽土用的)螺旋鑽。➪ the illus at tool. 參看 tool 之插圖。

aught /ɔːt ; ɔt/ *n* (archaic) anything: (古)任何事物: *for ~ I know/care,* used to indicate that the speaker does not know/care at all. 我根本不知道(在乎)。

aug·ment /ɔːgˈment ; ɔgˈmɛnt/ *vt, vi* [VP6A, 2A] make or become greater; increase: 增大;增加: *~ one's income by writing short stories.* 藉寫短篇小說而增加其收入。 **aug·men·ta·tion** /ˌɔːgmenˈteɪʃn ; ˌɔgmɛnˈteʃən/ *n* [U] ~ing or being ~ed; [C] sth added. 增大;增加;增加之物。

au·gur /ˈɔːgə(r) ; ˈɔgɚ/ *n* (in ancient Rome) religious official who claimed to foretell future events by omens from the entrails of birds, etc. (古羅馬)教會中之占兆官(據稱能根據鳥之內臟等之徵兆預卜吉凶)。□ *vi, vt* [VP6A, 2A] foretell, be a sign of: 預兆;預示: *Does this news ~ war?* 這消息預示將有戰爭嗎? *~ **well/ill (for sb/sth),*** be a good/bad sign for the future, for us. 預示(某人或某事之)吉(凶)兆。 **~y** /ˈɔːgjʊrɪ ; ˈɔgjərɪ/ *n* (*pl* -ries) [C] omen; sign. 徵兆;預兆。

au·gust /ɔːˈgʌst ; ɔˈgʌst/ *adj* majestic; causing feelings of respect or awe. 威嚴的;令人敬畏的。

Au·gust /ˈɔːgəst ; ˈɔgəst/ *n* the eighth month. 八月。

Au·gust·an /ɔːˈgʌstən ; ɔˈgʌstən/ *adj* of the best period of Latin literature; classical; of the period of English Literature including Dryden, Pope and Swift. 拉丁文學之全盛時期的;古典的;英國文學全盛時期(包括 Dryden, Pope 及 Swift 之時代)的。

auk /ɔːk ; ɔk/ *n* northern seabird, with short wings used in swimming.海雀(北方海鳥,有用以游水的短翅)。

auld lang syne /ˌɔːld læŋ ˈsaɪn ; ˌold læŋ ˈsaɪn/ (Scot, name of song) good times long ago. (蘇,歌曲名)美好的往昔。

aunt /ɑːnt *US:* ænt ; ænt/ *n* sister of one's father or mother; wife of one's uncle. 姑母;姨母;嬸母;伯母;舅母。ˌ**A~ ˈSally,** wooden model of a woman's head, at which sticks are thrown, at fairs, etc; (fig) object, person, widely abused. 木頭模型的女人頭(市集等中之一種娛樂遊戲,玩者以木棒向之投擲);(喻)衆矢之的;廣受人指責的人或對象。**aun·tie, aun·ty** /ˈɑːntɪ *US:* ˈæntɪ ; ˈæntɪ/ *n* (familiar for) aunt. aunt 之暱稱。

au pair /ˌəʊ ˈpeə(r) ; oˈpɛr/ *n* (F) (in GB) girl from overseas who, in return for light household duties, receives board and lodging, and facilities for study. (法)(在英國)作輕鬆家務以換得食宿及學習環境的海外女子。

aura /ˈɔːrə ; ˈɔrə/ *n* atmosphere surrounding a person or object and thought to come from him or it: (環繞於某人或某物之四周且被認爲係發自該人或物之)氣氛;氛圍;氣息: *There seemed to be an ~ of holiness about the Indian saint.* 在那印度聖人的四周似乎有一種神聖的氣氛。

au·ral /ˈɔːrəl ; ˈɔrəl/ *adj* of the organs of hearing: 聽覺器官的;耳的: *an ~ surgeon.* 耳科外科醫生。

aure·ole /ˈɔːrɪəʊl ; ˈɔrɪˌol/ *n* halo. 光輪;光環;華蓋。

au re·voir /ˌəʊ rəˈvwɑː(r) ; ˌorəˈvɔr/ *int* (F) till we meet again; goodbye. (法)再見;再會。

aur·icle /ˈɔːrɪkl ; ˈɔrɪkl/ *n* **1** the external part of the ear. 外耳;耳郭。➪ the illus at ear. 參看 ear 之插圖。**2** either of the two upper cavities of the heart. 心耳(心臟上方的兩穴之一)。➪ the illus at respiratory. 參看 respiratory 之插圖。

aur·icu·lar /ɔːˈrɪkjʊlə(r) ; ɔˈrɪkjəlɚ/ *adj* of or near the ear: 耳的;近耳的: *~ confession,* made privately in the ear, eg of a priest. 耳語招供;秘密告解(對教士之私下供認)。

aur·if·er·ous /ɔːˈrɪfərəs ; ɔˈrɪfərəs/ *adj* yielding gold. 含金的;產金的。

aur·ora /ɔːˈrɔːrə ; ɔˈrorə/ *n* **1 A~,** Roman goddess of dawn. (羅馬神話中的)黎明女神。 **2 ~ bor·ea·lis** /ɔːˌrɔːrə ˌbɔːrɪˈeɪlɪs ; ɔˈrorə ˌborɪˈælɪs/ *n* display of coloured light, in streamers and bands, mainly red and green, seen in the sky in the regions of the North Pole; also called *Northern Lights.* 北極光(北極區上空所見之帶狀彩色射光,主要爲紅色和綠色;亦稱 Northern Lights)。**~ aus·tra·lis** /ɔːˌrɔːrə ɒˈstreɪlɪs ; ˈɔrorə ɔsˈtrelɪs/ *n* similar display seen in the southern hemisphere.南極光(南半球所見之類似射光)。

aus·pices /ˈɔːspɪsɪz ; ˈɔspɪsɪz/ *n pl* ***under (the) ~ (of),*** helped and favoured by: 由…主辦或贊助的: *under favourable ~,* with the omens in one's favour, with favourable prospects. 吉利地;順遂地。

aus·pi·cious /ɔːˈspɪʃəs ; ɔˈspɪʃəs/ *adj* showing signs, giving promise, of future success; favourable; prosperous. 前途光明的;吉利的;興隆的。**~·ly** *adv*

Aus·sie /ˈɒzɪ ; ˈɔsɪ/ *n* (sl) Australian. (俚)澳洲人。

aus·tere /ɔːˈstɪə(r) ; ɔˈstɪr/ *adj* **1** (of a person, his behaviour) severely moral and strict. (指人或其行爲)嚴肅不苟的;嚴峻的。**2** (of a way of living, of places, styles) simple and plain; without ornament or comfort. (指生活方式、地方、文體)質樸的;樸素無華的。**~·ly** *adv* **aus·ter·ity** /ɔːˈsterətɪ ; ɔˈstɛrətɪ/ *n* (*pl* -ties) **1** [U] quality of being ~. 嚴肅;嚴峻;樸素;質樸。**2** (*pl*) ~ practices, eg fasting, living in a cell, for religious reasons. (複)(爲宗教理由的)苦修;苦行(如齋戒;居於密室等)。

aut·archy /ˈɔːtɑːkɪ; ˈɔtɑrkɪ/ *n* [C, U] (country under) absolute sovereignty. 獨裁;專制;獨裁或專制的國家。

aut·arky /ˈɔːtɑːkɪ ; ˈɔtɑrkɪ/ *n* [U] self-sufficiency, esp of a State in its economy. (尤指一國)自給自足;經濟獨立。

auth·en·tic /ɔːˈθentɪk ; ɔˈθɛntɪk/ *adj* genuine; known to be true: 眞實的;可信的;可靠的: *~ news;* 可靠消息; *an ~ signature.* 眞的簽字。**auth·en·ti·cally** /-klɪ; -klɪ/ *adv* **~·ity** /ˌɔːθənˈtɪsətɪ ; ˌɔθənˈtɪsətɪ/ *n* [U] quality of being ~: 眞實;眞確;可靠: *feel confident of the ~ity of a signature.* 深信一個簽名之眞確。

auth·en·ti·cate /ɔːˈθentɪkeɪt ; ɔˈθɛntɪˌket/ *vt* [VP6A] prove to be genuine; prove beyond doubt the origin, authorship, etc of. 證明…爲眞;證明…之來源、作者等無訛;鑑定。**auth·en·ti·ca·tion** /ɔːˌθentɪˈkeɪʃn ; ɔˌθɛntɪˈkeʃən/ *n* [U] authenticating. 證明爲眞;鑑定。

author /ˈɔːθə(r) ; ˈɔθɚ/ *n* **1** writer of a book, play, etc: (書,劇本等之)著作者;著作家: *Dickens is his favourite ~.* 狄更斯是他最喜愛的作家。 **2** person who creates or begins sth: 創造者; 創始者: *God, the A~ of our being.* 上帝,我們生命的創造者。**~·ess**

/ˈɔːθərɪs ; ˈɔθəɪs/ *n* woman ~. 女作家。**~·ship** /-ʃɪp ; -ʃɪp/ *n* [U] **1** occupation of an ~: 寫作生涯；著作業：*It's risky to take to ~ship* (= begin to write books) *for a living.* 靠寫作爲生是冒險的。 **2** origin of a book, etc: (書等的)來源，作者等：*Nothing is known of the ~ship of the book,* about who wrote it. 此書作者爲誰不得而知。

auth·ori·tar·ian /ɔːˌθɒrɪˈteərɪən ; əˌθɔrəˈtɛrɪən/ *adj* supporting or requiring obedience to authority, esp that of the State, contrasted with individual liberty. 主張或要求服從(尤指政府之)權力(與個人自由相對)的；權力主義者的。□ *n* supporter of this principle. 權力主義者。**~·ism** /-ɪzəm ; -ˌɪzəm/ *n*

auth·ori·tat·ive /ɔːˈθɒrɪtətɪv *US:* -teɪtɪv ; əˈθɔrəˌtetɪv/ *adj* **1** having, given with, authority: 有權力的；賦有權力的；有權威的：~ *orders.* 必須服從的命令。 **2** having an air of authority; commanding: 具有一種權威之神態的；命令式的：*in an ~ manner;* 以命令的方式；*speaking in ~ tones.* 以命令式的口吻說。 **3** that can be trusted because from a reliable source: 權威的；來源可靠的；可信的：*an ~ report;* 可信的報告；*~ information;* 可靠的消息；*from an ~ source.* 來自權威方面的。**~·ly** *adv*

auth·or·ity /ɔːˈθɒrətɪ ; əˈθɔrətɪ/ *n* (*pl* -ties) **1** [U] power or right to give orders and make others obey: 權力；權威；權勢；威信：*The problem of how to cope with ~,* eg wrongdoers with the police, children with parents. 如何應付權威的問題(例如爲非作歹者之應付警方，孩子們之應付父母親)。*An officer has/exercises ~ over the soldiers under him.* 軍官有(行使)權力指揮其屬下士兵。*Who is in ~ here?* 誰是這裏的主管？*He has made his ~ felt,* caused people to realize that he has power to make them obey. 他已使人們感到他的權威(使人們明白他有權使他們服從)。***under the ~ of; under sb's ~,*** responsible(1) to: 對…負責；受…管理：*These boys are under the ~ of their teacher/under his ~.* 這些男孩受他們的老師的(他的)管教。 **2** [U] ***~ (for sth/to do sth),*** right given to sb: 賦予某人(做某事)之權：*Only the treasurer has ~ to make payments.* 只有出納員才有權付款。*He had the ~ of the Governor for what he did.* 他所做之事曾得省主席(州長或總督)之授權。 **3** [U] person or (*pl*) group of persons having ~: 掌權之人；(複)掌權的一群人；當局：*the City, Municipal, County, etc authorities;* 市(郡等)政府當局；*the health authorities;* 衛生當局；*the ˌAtomic ˈEnergy A~.* 原子能管理委員會。 **4** [C, U] person with special knowledge; book, etc that supplies reliable information or evidence: 具有特殊知識之人；提供可靠資料或證據的書籍等；權威；權威著作：*He is a great ~ on phonetics.* 他是語音學方面的權威。*The 'Oxford English Dictionary' is the best ~ on English words.* '牛津英文大字典'是關於英文字的最高權威著作。 *What is your ~ for that statement?* 你那句話有何根據？*You should quote your authorities,* give the titles of books, etc, names of persons, etc used as sources for facts. 你應該註明出處。

auth·or·ize /ˈɔːθəraɪz ; ˈɔθəˌraɪz/ *vt* **1** [VP17] give authority to: 授權與；委託代理：*I have ~d him to act for me while I am abroad.* 我已委託他在我出國期間代理我的業務。 **2** [VP6A] give authority for: 批准；許可：*The Finance Committee ~d the spending of £10000 on a new sports ground.* 財政委員會批准用一萬鎊建一個新運動場。*This payment has not been ~d.* 這筆付款尚未獲批准。**ˌA~d ˈVersion,** (common abbr 普通略作 **AV**) the English translation of the Bible, first published 1611. 聖經英譯之欽定本(最初出版於 1611 年)。**auth·or·iz·ation** /ˌɔːθəraɪˈzeɪʃn *US:* -rɪˈz- ; ˌɔθərəˈzeʃən/ *n* [U] authorizing; giving legal right (*to do* sth, *for* sth); the right given. 授權；委託(與不定詞或 for 連用，後接某事物)；所授之權。

aut·ism /ˈɔːtɪzəm ; ˈɔtɪzəm/ *n* [U] (psych) severe form of mental illness in children. (心理)孤獨癖；孤獨性；自閉(小孩的心理病態)。**aut·is·tic** /ɔːˈtɪstɪk ; ɔˈtɪstɪk/ *adj* of ~: 孤獨癖的；孤獨性的；自閉的：*autistic children.* 孤獨癖的小孩。

auto /ˈɔːtəʊ ; ˈɔto/ *n* (US colloq abbr of) automobile. (美俗)汽車(爲 automobile 之略)。

auto- /ˈɔːtəʊ ; ˈɔto/ *pref* (in compounds) self-, by oneself; independent(ly): (用於複合字中) 自己；自身；自行：*~-intoxication,* poisoning by substances produced within the body. 自身中毒；自體中毒。**ˈ~-changer,** device (on a record-player) that plays a number of discs in succession without attention. (唱機上的)自動換片裝置。

au·to·bahn /ˈɔːtəbɑːn ; ˈɔtəˌbɑn/ *n* (*pl* ~s or (G) ~en /-nən ; -nən/) (G) (德) = motorway.

auto·bi·ogra·phy /ˌɔːtəbaɪˈɒgrəfɪ ; ˌɔtəbaɪˈɑgrəfɪ/ *n* (*pl* -phies) **1** [C] story of a person's life written by himself. 自傳。 **2** [U] the art and practice of this sort of writing. 自傳作法；自傳寫作。**auto·bio·graphic** /ˌɔːtəbaɪəˈgræfɪk ; ˌɔtəˌbaɪəˈgræfɪk/, **auto·bio·graphi·cal** /-ɪkl ; -ɪkl̩/ *adjj* of, engaged in, ~. 自傳的；從事寫作自傳的。

au·toc·racy /ɔːˈtɒkrəsɪ ; ɔˈtɑkrəsɪ/ *n* (*pl* -cies) **1** [U] government by a ruler who has unlimited power. 獨裁政治；專制政治。 **2** [C] (country with a) government of this kind. 獨裁政府；獨裁國家。

au·to·crat /ˈɔːtəkræt ; ˈɔtəˌkræt/ *n* ruler with unlimited power; person who requires things to be done without considering the wishes of others. 獨裁者；專制者；專橫霸道的人。**~ic** /ˌɔːtəˈkrætɪk ; ˌɔtəˈkrætɪk/ *adj* of or like an ~: 獨裁者的；專制的；專橫的：*Don't be so ~ic,* Don't behave as if you were an ~. 不要這樣專橫。**auto·crati·cally** /-klɪ ; -klɪ/ *adv*

au·to-da-fé /ˌɔːtəʊ dɑː ˈfeɪ *US:* ˌaʊtəʊ də ; ˌɔtodəˈfe/ *n* (*pl* autos-da-fé /ˌɔːtəʊz *US:* ˌaʊtəʊz ; ˌɔtoz-/) trial and sentence of a heretic by the Inquisition; carrying out of the sentence, esp by burning. 宗教法庭對異教徒之審判；上述判決之執行(尤指將異教徒焚斃)。

au·to·giro, -gyro /ˌɔːtəʊˈdʒaɪərəʊ ; ˌɔtoˈdʒaɪro/ *n* (P) early form of helicopter with a propeller in front and rotors above. (商標)旋翼機(直昇飛機之前身，推進器在前方，水平旋翼在上方)。

au·to·graph /ˈɔːtəgrɑːf *US:* -græf ; ˈɔtəˌgræf/ *n* person's own handwriting, esp his signature: 親筆；(尤指)親筆簽名：ˈ~ *book/album,* one in which signatures, eg of famous persons, are collected. 請人(如名人)簽名留念的簽名册。□ *vt* [VP6A] write one's name on or in: 簽名於：*a book ~ed by the author;* 作者親自簽名的書；*an ~ed photograph.* 簽名照片。

au·to·mat /ˈɔːtəmæt ; ˈɔtəˌmæt/ *n* (US) restaurant at which food and drink are obtained, by the customers themselves, from coin-operated closed compartments. (美)使用自動售賣機的餐館。

au·to·mate /ˈɔːtəmeɪt ; ˈɔtəˌmet/ *vt* (science, comm) convert to, control by, automation. (科學，商)使自動化；使自動操作；使自動作業。

au·to·matic /ˌɔːtəˈmætɪk ; ˌɔtəˈmætɪk/ *adj* **1** self-acting; self-moving; (of a machine) able to work or be worked without attention: 自動的；(指機器)不需人照料而能自行操作的：*an ~ pilot,* (on an aircraft) maintaining altitude, course, etc; (飛機上的)自動駕駛儀(保持高度、航線等)；*~ gear-change* (in a motor-vehicle); (汽車中的)自動變換排檔；*~ weapons,* weapons that continue firing until pressure on the trigger is released. 自動武器(扣着扳機卽繼續發射的武器)。 **2** (of actions) done without thought; unconscious: (指動作)無意識的；不自覺的：*Breathing is ~.* 呼吸是無意識的動作。□ *n* small ~ firearm. 小型自動武器。**au·to·mati·cally** /-klɪ ; -klɪ/ *adv*

au·to·ma·tion /ˌɔːtəˈmeɪʃn ; ˌɔtəˈmeʃən/ *n* [U] (use of) methods and machines to save human labour. 節省人力的方法與機器；節省人力的方法與機器的使用；自動化作業。

au·toma·ton /ˌɔːˈtɒmətən *US:* -tɒn ; ɔˈtɑməˌtɑn/ *n* (*pl* ~s, -ta /-tə ; -tə/) person who appears to act involuntarily or without active intelligence; robot. 動作像機械或不善運用智力的人；機械式的人；機器人。

au·to·mo·bile /ˈɔːtəməbiːl *US:* ˌɔːtəməˈbiːl ; ˈɔtəməˌbil/ *n* (esp US) motor-car. (尤美)汽車。

au·ton·omous /ɔːˈtɒnəməs ; ɔˈtɑnəməs/ *adj* (of states) self-governing; free. (指州或邦等)自治的；自主的；自由的。**au·ton·omy** /ɔːˈtɒnəmɪ ; ɔˈtɑnəmɪ/ *n* (*pl* -mies) [U, C] (right of) self-government; freedom. 自治；自治權；自由。

au·topsy /ˈɔːtɒpsɪ ; ˈɔtɑpsɪ/ *n* (*pl* -sies) [C] (med) postmortem examination of a body (by cutting it open) to learn the cause of death. (醫)屍體剖檢(以追查死因)。⇨ biopsy.

au·to·strada /ˌaʊtəʊˈstrɑːdə;ˌautoˈstrɑdɑ/ *n* (*pl* ~s, (I) -de /-ˈstrɑːdeɪ ; -ˈstrɑde/) (I) (義) = motorway.

au·tumn /ˈɔːtəm ; ˈɔtəm/ *n* [C] (US 美 = *fall*) third season of the year, between summer and winter (Sept, Oct and Nov in the northern hemisphere): 秋；秋天；秋季: *in* ~; 在秋季；秋天裏；*in the ~ of 1980;* 在1980年之秋；*in (the) early/late ~;* 在初(晚)秋；(fig) (喻) *in the ~ of his life;* 在他的垂暮(開始衰老)之年；(attrib) (形容用法) *~ weather/fashions.* 秋天的天氣(秋季的款式)。 **au·tum·nal** /ɔːˈtʌmnəl ; ɔˈtʌmnl/ *adj* of ~. 秋的；秋天的；秋季的。

aux·ili·ary /ɔːgˈzɪlɪərɪ ; ɔgˈzɪljərɪ/ *adj* helping; supporting: 輔助的；幫助的: *~ troops;* 輔助部隊；*an ~ verb* (eg *is* in *He is working; has* in *He has gone*). 助動詞(例如 He is working 中的 is, He has gone 中的 has, 均爲助動詞)。□ *n* (*pl* -ries) **1** ~ verb. 助動詞。 **2** (usu *pl*) ~ troops (esp troops hired from a foreign or allied country, eg in the Roman Empire in ancient times). (通常用複數)輔助部隊；(尤指如古羅馬帝國所僱傭的)外籍輔助部隊。

avail /əˈveɪl ; əˈvel/ *vt, vi* **1** [VP14] ***~ oneself of,*** make use of, profit by, take advantage of: 利用: *You should ~ yourself of every opportunity to practise speaking English.* 你應該利用每一個機會練習說英語。 **2** [VP2A, 3A] (liter) be of value or help: (文)有價值；有幫助；有用: *Money does not ~ on a desert island.* 金錢在荒島上沒有用處。*Nothing ~ed against the storm.* 無一物可用以抵禦暴風雨。□ *n* ***of no/little ~,*** not helpful; not effective: 無助的；無效的；無用的: *His intervention was of little ~.* 他的調停無效。***without ~; to no ~,*** without result; unsuccessfully: 無結果；無效；不成功地: *We pulled him out of the river and tried to revive him, but to no ~.* 我們把他從河裏拉出來，並試圖使他恢復知覺，但是不成功。*Of what ~ is it to...,* What use is it to...? …有什麼益處？

avail·able /əˈveɪləbl ; əˈveləbl/ *adj* ***~ (for)*** **1** (of objects) able to be used; that may be obtained: (指物)可用的；有效的；可獲得的: *These tickets are ~ for one month only.* 這些票的有效期只有一個月。*The book you ordered is not ~.* 你訂購的那本書沒有貨。 **2** (of persons) able to be present: (指人)能出席的: *Are you ~ (for a meeting) tomorrow morning?* 你明天上午能出席(會議)嗎？ **avail·abil·ity** /əˌveɪləˈbɪlətɪ ; əˌveləˈbɪlətɪ/ *n* [U]

ava·lanche /ˈævəlɑːnʃ *US:* -læntʃ ; ˈævlˌæntʃ/ *n* great mass of snow and ice at a high altitude, caused by its own weight to slide down a mountain side, often carrying with it thousands of tons of rock, and sometimes destroying forests, houses, etc in its path: 雪崩(大量冰雪因自身之重量自高山崩落，常携帶巨量岩石，可毀壞森林、房舍等): (fig) (喻) *an ~ of words/letters/questions.* 滔滔不絕的言辭(如雪片飛來的信件；一湧而至的問題)。

avant-garde /ˌævɒn ˈgɑːd ; ˌavɑnˈgard/ *n* (F) vanguard of an army; (fig) radical leader(s) of any movement (in art, drama, literature, etc): (法)先鋒；前鋒；(喻)(藝術，戲劇，文學等之)激進派；先驅；前衛派: (attrib) (形容用法) *~ writers/artists.* 前衛派作家(藝術家)。

av·ar·ice /ˈævərɪs ; ˈævərɪs/ *n* [U] greed (for money or possessions); great eagerness to get or keep. 貪婪；貪心。 **av·ar·icious** /ˌævəˈrɪʃəs ; ˌævəˈrɪʃəs/ *adj* ***~ (of),*** greedy (of money, power, etc). 貪婪的；貪心的；貪求的。 **av·ar·icious·ly** *adv*

avast /əˈvɑːst *US:* əˈvæst ; əˈvæst/ *int* (naut) Stop! (航海)停住！

ava·tar /ˌævəˈtɑː(r) ; ˌævəˈtɑr/ *n* (Hindu myth) (descent to earth of a) deity in human or animal form. (印度神話)(化身作凡人或動物之)天神；天神下凡。

avaunt /əˈvɔːnt ; əˈvɔnt/ *int* (old use) Begone; Go away! (舊用法)走開！去！

avenge /əˈvendʒ ; əˈvɛndʒ/ *vt* [VP6A, 14] get or take vengeance for: 爲…報仇；報復: *~ an insult;* 爲受辱而報復； *~ oneself/be ~d on an enemy (for* an injury, etc). (爲傷害等)向仇敵報復。*He ~d his father's death upon the murderer,* punished the murderer. 他報了殺父之仇(卽已懲兇)。 **aven·ger** *n*

av·enue /ˈævənjuː *US:* -nuː ; ˈævəˌnu/ *n* **1** road with trees on each side, esp the private road going up to a large country house. 兩側有樹的道路(尤指通往大莊園的私人道路)。 **2** wide street with buildings on one or both sides. (城市中一側或兩側建築物林立的)大道；大馬路。 **3** ***~ (to),*** (fig) way (to some object or aim): (喻)(達到某種目的或目標的)方法；途徑: *~s to success/promotion.* 成功(晉陞)的途徑。

aver /əˈvɜː(r) ; əˈvɝ/ *vt* (-rr-) [VP6A, 9] ***~ (that),*** (old use) state positively (that sth is true). (舊用法)斷言；確言(某事爲眞實)。

av·er·age /ˈævərɪdʒ ; ˈævərɪdʒ/ *n* **1** [C] result of adding several quantities together and dividing the total by the number of quantities: 平均數: *The ~ of 4, 5 and 9 is 6.* 4, 5, 9 的平均數是 6。 **2** [U] standard or level regarded as ordinary or usual: 一般的水準；平均標準；平常的標準: *Tom's work at school is above (the) ~, Harry's is below (the) ~ and Jim's is about up to (the) ~.* 湯姆在校的功課在一般水準之上，哈利的功課在一般水準之下，吉姆的功課接近一般水準。 ***on (an/the) ~,*** according to the ~: 根據平均標準；平均而言: *On (an/the) ~, there are twenty boys present every day.* 平均說來，每天有二十個男生出席。□ *adj* **1** found by making an ~: 平均的: *The ~ age of the boys in this class is fifteen.* 本班男生的平均年齡是十五歲。*What's the ~ temperature in this town in August?* 本市八月裏的平均氣溫是多少？ **2** of the ordinary or usual standard: 一般標準的；普通的；平常的: *boys of ~ intelligence;* 智力平常的男生；*men of ~ ability.* 能力普通的人。□ *vt, vi* **1** [VP6A] find the ~ of: 求…的平均數: *If you ~ 7, 14 and 6, you get 9.* 如果你求 7, 14 和 6 的平均數，得 9。 **2** [VP2B] amount to as an ~; do as an ~: 平均達到(數目)；平均做；平均分配: *~ 200 miles a day during a journey.* 旅程中平均每天行 200 哩。*The rainfall ~s 36 inches a year.* 雨量平均每年達 36 吋。

averse /əˈvɜːs ; əˈvɝs/ *adj* ***~ from/to,*** opposed, disinclined: 反對的；嫌惡的；不願的: *He is ~ to hard work.* 他嫌惡繁重的工作。*We are ~ from taking action.* 我們不願採取行動。

aver·sion /əˈvɜːʃn *US:* -ʒn ; əˈvɝʒən/ *n* **1** [C, U] ***~ to,*** strong dislike: 厭惡；嫌惡: *He has a strong ~ to getting up early.* 他非常厭惡早起。*He took an ~ to me.* 他討厭我。*Do you feel any ~ to hard study?* 你討厭用功讀書嗎？ **2** [C] sth or sb disliked. 討厭之事物或人。 **pet ~,** sth specially disliked. 特別討厭的事物。

avert /əˈvɜːt ; əˈvɝt/ *vt* **1** [VP14] ***~ (from),*** turn away (one's eyes, thoughts, etc): 轉移(眼睛，思想等): *~ one's eyes/gaze from a terrible spectacle.* 轉開眼睛不看可怕的景象。 **2** [VP6A] prevent, avoid: 防止；避免: *~ an accident;* 避免災禍；*~ suspicion;* 避免嫌疑；*~ failure by hard work.* 努力工作以免失敗。

avi·ary /ˈeɪvɪərɪ *US:* -vɪerɪ ; ˈevɪˌɛrɪ/ *n* (*pl* -ries) place for keeping birds, eg in a zoo. 大鳥籠;鳥舍(如動物園中者)。

avi·ation /ˌeɪvɪˈeɪʃn ; ˌevɪˈeʃən/ *n* [U] (art and science of) flying in aircraft. 航空;飛行;航空術;航空學。ˈ~ **spirit**, high-octane motor spirit used in aircraft engines. 航空用酒精(含高辛烷,用於飛機引擎者)。 **avi·ator** /ˈeɪvɪeɪtə(r) ; ˈevɪˌetɚ/ *n* airman (now usu *pilot* or *captain*) who controls an aircraft, airship or balloon. 航空員;飛行員;(飛機、飛艇或氣球之)駕駛員(今常用 pilot 或 captain)。

avid /ˈævɪd ; ˈævɪd/ *adj* ~ **for**, eager, greedy: 熱望的;貪求的;貪圖的: ~ *for fame/applause.* 熱望名聲(渴望受讚賞)的。~**·ly** *adv* ~**·ity** /əˈvɪdətɪ ; əˈvɪdətɪ/ *n* [U] eagerness: 渴望;熱切: *He accepted the offer with ~ity.* 他熱切地採納了該項建議。

avo·cado /ˌævəˈkɑːdəʊ ; ˌɑvəˈkɑdo/ *n* (*pl* ~s /-dəʊz ; -doz/) (also 亦作 *alligator pear*) pear-shaped tropical fruit. 鱷梨(一種梨狀之熱帶水果)。 ⇨ the illus at fruit. 參看 fruit 之插圖。

avo·ca·tion /ˌævəˈkeɪʃn ; ˌævəˈkeʃən/ *n* (formal) occupation that is not a person's ordinary business. (正式用語)副業;業餘的愛好。

avoid /əˈvɔɪd ; əˈvɔɪd/ *vt* [VP6A, C] keep or get away from; escape: 避免;避開;逃避: *Try to ~ danger.* 盡力避免危險。*We only just ~ed an accident.* 我們倖免於一場災禍。*You can hardly ~ meeting her if you both work in the same office.* 如果你們兩人在同一個辦公室做事,你幾乎免不了要遇見她。~**·able** /-əbl ; -əbl/ *adj* that can be ~ed. 可避免的。~**·ance** /-əns ; -n̩s/ *n* [U] act of ~ing: 避免;避開;逃避: *the ~ance of bad companions;* 避免不良友伴; *~ance of taxation,* eg by not buying taxed goods such as tobacco and wine. 避稅(如不買有稅的貨物,如菸酒)。

avoir·du·pois /ˌævədəˈpɔɪz ; ˌævɚdəˈpɔɪz/ *n* system of weights used, before metrication, in most English-speaking countries (1 pound = 16 ounces), used for all goods except precious metals and stones, and medicines. 常衡(改用十進制前大多數英語國家所用之衡制,一磅等於十六兩,除貴金屬、寶石、藥品外,一切貨物均適用)。 ⇨ App 5. 參看附錄五。

avouch /əˈvaʊtʃ ; əˈvaʊtʃ/ *vt, vi* [VP6A, 9, 3A] (liter; now rare) assert; guarantee: (文;今罕用)確言;擔保;保證: ~ (*for*) *sth.* 保證某事物。

avow /əˈvaʊ ; əˈvaʊ/ *vt* [VP6A, 25 reflex VP25 用反身式] (formal) admit; declare openly: (正式用語)承認;公開宣佈: ~ *a fault.* 承認錯誤。 *He ~ed himself* (*to be*) *a Christian.* 他公開宣佈他是基督教徒。 ~**al** /-əl ; -əl/ *n* [U] free and open confession; [C] instance of this: 坦白承認;公開表示: *make an ~al of one's sentiments.* 公開表示自己的看法。 ~**·ed·ly** /əˈvaʊɪdlɪ ; əˈvaʊɪdlɪ/ *adv* by confession; openly: 自認地;公開地: *He was ~edly in the wrong.* 他自認錯誤。

avun·cu·lar /əˈvʌŋkjʊlə(r) ; əˈvʌŋkjəlɚ/ *adj* (joc) of or like an uncle (esp a benevolent uncle). (謔)伯父或叔父(尤指仁慈者)的;如伯(叔)父的。

await /əˈweɪt ; əˈwet/ *vt* [VP6A] **1** (of persons) wait for: (指人)等候: *I ~ your instructions.* 我等候你的指示。 **2** be in store for; be waiting for: 準備以待;等待: *A hearty welcome ~s you.* 熱烈的歡迎等待着你。*Death ~s all men.* 死亡等待着所有的人。

awake[1] /əˈweɪk ; əˈwek/ *vi* (*pt* awoke /əˈwəʊk ; əˈwok/, *pp* (rare) (罕) awoken or ~d) **1** [VP2A] = wake. (*awake* is preferred for the fig uses, intrans, and *awaken* for the fig uses, trans). (在比喻用法中, awake 以作 *vi* 較佳, awaken 以作 *vt* 較佳)。 **2** [VP3A] ~ **to**, become conscious of, realize: 覺醒;醒悟;覺悟;覺察;領會: *He awoke to his opportunities.* 他覺察到他的機會。*You must ~ to the fact* (= You must realize) *that failure will mean disgrace.* 你必須覺悟到失敗即是恥辱這一事實。*When he awoke to his surroundings...*, realized where he was.... 當他明白了他所處的環境時…。[VP4B] *He awoke to find himself famous,* learnt, the next day, that he was famous. 他一覺醒來,發現自己已經成名。

awake[2] /əˈweɪk ; əˈwek/ *pred adj* roused from sleep: 被喚醒的;醒著的: *Is he ~ or asleep?* 他是醒着還是睡着? ~ **to**, aware of: 知曉;覺察: *be ~ to what is going on/to a danger/to one's own interests.* 瞭解正在進行中的事(危險,自身的利益)。

awaken /əˈweɪkən ; əˈwekən/ *vt* **1** [VP6A] = awake (*awaken* is preferred for fig uses, trans). (awaken 在比喻用法中以作 *vt* 較佳)。 **2** [VP14] ~ **sb to sth**, make sb aware of: 使某人知道;喚起某人: ~ *sb to a sense of his responsibility/to a sense of shame.* 喚起某人的責任感(羞恥之心)。~**·ing** /əˈweɪknɪŋ ; əˈwekənɪŋ/ *n* act of becoming aware, of realizing, esp sth unpleasant: 覺醒;覺悟;明白(尤指不愉快之事物): *It was a rude ~ing when he was told that he was to be dismissed for inefficiency.* 當他聽說他將因工作效率低而被革職時,他才猛然覺悟。

award /əˈwɔːd ; əˈwɔrd/ *vt* [VP6A, 12A, 13A] give or grant (by official decision): 頒發;授與;賞給: *He was ~ed the first prize.* 他得到第一獎。*The judge ~ed her £200 as damages.* 法官判給她二百鎊作爲賠償損失費。*The gold medal was ~ed to Mr Brown for his fine show of vegetables.* 布朗先生因其優異的蔬菜展覽而獲得金質獎章。□ *n* [C] **1** decision made by a judge or arbitrator. (法官,評判員或仲裁人所作的)決定;決斷。 **2** sth given as the result of such a decision, eg a prize in a competition: 經過決定而贈與之物(例如比賽之獎品): *His horse was given the highest ~ at the show.* 他的馬在展覽會中得到最高獎。 **3** money granted to a student at a university, etc. (給予大學生等的)助學金。

aware /əˈweə(r) ; əˈwɛr/ *pred adj* ~ **of/that**, having knowledge or realization: 知道的;明白的;覺察的;意識到的: *Are you ~ that you're sitting on my hat?* 你可知道你坐在我的帽子上嗎? *We are fully ~ of the gravity of the situation.* 我們十分明白情勢的嚴重性。*Without being ~ of it....* 不曾覺察(留意)到它…。*I was not ~* (*of*) *how deeply he had felt the death of his mother.* 我不知道他對他母親之去世多麼傷感。~**·ness** *n* [U].

awash /əˈwɒʃ ; əˈwɑʃ/ *pred adj* washed over by, level with, the waves: 爲海浪所沖打的;與海浪平齊的: *rocks ~ at high tide.* 在漲潮時爲海浪所沖打的岩石。*The ship's deck was ~.* 此船的甲板與浪頭平齊。

away /əˈweɪ ; əˈwe/ *adv part* **1** to or at a distance (from the place, person, etc in question): 向遠處;在遠處(離開所說之地方、人等): *The sea is two miles ~.* 海離此地兩哩遠。*The shops are only a few minutes' walk ~.* 商店離此只有幾分鐘的步行路程。*Is our next football match at home or ~,* on our ground or on the ground of our opponents? 下一場足球賽是在我們的球場舉行還是在對方的球場舉行? *It's an ~ match.* 這是一場在對方球場舉行的比賽。*Take these things ~,* remove them. 把這些東西拿開。*Keep the baby ~ from the fire.* 不要讓小孩走近火爐。*Don't look ~* (ie in a different direction) *while I'm taking your photograph.* 在我給你拍照的時候,不要看別處。 **2** ~ **with...**, (used in verbless exclamations): (用於無動詞的驚嘆句): *A~ with them!* Take them ~! 把他們帶走! **3** continuously; constantly: 繼續不斷地;經常地: *He was working ~.* 他在不斷地工作中。 *He was laughing/muttering/grumbling ~.* 他一直在笑(喃喃自語,發牢騷)。 ⇨ grumble(1), laugh(2), mutter. **4** (used with *vv* to indicate loss, lessening, weakening, exhaustion): (與動詞連用,表示損失,減少,變弱,耗盡): *The water has all boiled ~,* There is no water left. 水完全熬乾了。 ⇨ blaze[2](4), boil[2](4), die[2](6), explain(2), melt(1). **5** (in phrases): (用於片語中): ***far and ~***, very much: 遠較;大爲: *This is far and ~ better.* 這個好得很多。 ***out and ~***, beyond comparison: 無與倫比地;超過其他地: *This is out and ~ the best.* 這個是最好的。 ***right/straight ~***, at once, without delay. 立刻;立即。

awe[1] /ɔː ; ɔ/ *n* [U] respect combined with fear and

reverence: 敬畏: *He had a feeling of awe as he was taken before the judge.* 當他被帶到法官面前，他有一種敬畏之感。*Savages often live in awe of nature.* 未開化的人常對自然存敬畏之心。*The lazy boy stood in awe of his stern teacher.* 那個懶惰的男孩畏懼他那位嚴厲的老師。**'awe-inspiring** *adj* filling with awe: 令人敬畏的: *an awe-inspiring sight.* 令人敬畏的景象。 **'awe-stricken, 'awe-struck** *adjj* suddenly filled with awe. 充滿敬畏的;畏懼的;害怕的。**'awe•some** /-səm ; -səm/ *adj* causing awe. 引起敬畏的;令人畏懼的。

awe² /ɔː ; ɔ/ *vt* [VP6A, 14] **awe (into),** strike with awe, fill with awe: 使敬畏;使畏懼;威嚇;嚇倒: *I was awed by his solemn words.* 我被他的嚴肅之詞嚇住了。*He awed them into obedience.* 他把他們嚇得服從了。*The children were awed into silence.* 孩子們被嚇得不敢做聲了。

aweigh /əˈweɪ ; əˈwe/ *adv* (naut, of an anchor) hanging just clear of the sea bottom. (航海,指錨) 剛離海底而懸着地。

aw•ful /ˈɔːfl ; ˈɔfl/ *adj* **1** terrible; dreadful: 可怕的: *He died an ~ death.* 他死得可怕。*His sufferings were ~ to behold.* 他的痛苦看起來令人可怕。 **2** (colloq, intensive) very bad; very great; extreme of its kind: (俗, 强勢語) 極壞的; 極其的; 非常的; 極端的: *What an ~ nuisance!* 討厭極了! *What ~ handwriting/weather!* 多麼壞的書法(天氣)! **~ly** /ˈɔːflɪ ; ˈɔflɪ/ *adv* (chiefly colloq) very (much): (主用於口語) 極爲;非常: *It has been ~ly hot this week.* 這個禮拜天氣一直很炎熱。*I'm ~ly sorry.* 我非常抱歉。*Thanks ~ly.* 非常感謝。

awhile /əˈwaɪl *US:* əˈhwaɪl ; əˈhwaɪl/ *adv* for a short time: 一會兒;片刻;少頃: *Stay ~.* 請逗留片刻。

awk•ward /ˈɔːkwəd ; ˈɔkwəd/ *adj* **1** (of objects, places) not well designed for use; (of circumstances, etc) likely to cause inconvenience or difficulty: (指物件,地方) 設計不良而使用起來不方便的; (指環境等) 可能引起不便或困難的: *This is an ~ staircase.* 這個樓梯不便上下。*This is an ~ corner; there have been several road accidents here.* 這是一個不好轉彎的拐角;這裏曾發生過幾次車禍。*The handle of this teapot has an ~ shape.* 這個茶壺柄的形狀不好用。*The meeting was at 9 o'clock, which was an ~ time for many people.* 會定在九點鐘開,這對於許多人是一個不方便的時間。*It's ~ that Brown should be unable to play in our team this week.* 很糟糕,布朗本星期不能參加我隊比賽。 ***an ~ customer,*** (colloq) person or animal difficult or dangerous to deal with. (俗) 難以應付之人或動物;危險之人或動物。 **2** (of living things) clumsy; having little skill: (指生物) 笨拙的; 無技巧的; 不熟練的; 不靈活的: *The child is still ~ with his knife and fork.* 這小孩還不大會用刀叉。*Some animals are ~ on land but able to move easily in the water.* 有些動物在陸地上不靈活,但在水中却能活動自如。**the '~ age,** years when adolescents are lacking in self-confidence. 尷尬的年齡(缺乏自信心的青春初期)。 **3** embarrassed: 困窘的;侷促不安的: *an ~ silence/pause.* 困窘的寂靜(停頓)。**~•ly** *adv* **~•ness** *n*

awl /ɔːl ; ɔl/ *n* small pointed tool for making holes, esp in leather or wood. 錐子 (尤指用以在皮革或木頭上鑽孔者)。 ⇨ the illus at tool. 參看 tool 之插圖。

awn•ing /ˈɔːnɪŋ ; ˈɔnɪŋ/ *n* canvas covering (against rain or sun), eg over a ship's deck, over or before doors or windows. 帆布篷;雨篷;遮日篷;遮陽(如用於輪船甲板或門窗之上者);天遮。

awoke ⇨ awake.

awry /əˈraɪ ; əˈraɪ/ *adv, pred adj* crooked(ly): wrong(ly): 扭;曲;斜;歪;錯誤: *Our plans have gone ~,* have gone wrong. 我們的計畫出岔子了。

ax, axe /æks ; æks/ *n* (*pl* axes /ˈæksɪz ; ˈæksɪz/) tool for felling trees or splitting wood, ⇨ the illus at tool: 斧(砍樹、劈木的工具;參看 tool 之插圖): *apply the axe to public expenditure,* reduce its cost by economies, etc. (藉節省等) 削減公家的經費。 ***,have an 'axe to grind,*** (fig) have private interests to serve. (喩) 懷有私心;別有企圖。***get the axe,*** (colloq) be dismissed from one's job. (俗) 被革職;被開除。 □ *vt* [VP6A] (colloq) reduce, eg costs, public services; dismiss: (俗) 減少;削減(成本,公共設施等);開除: *He's just been axed,* ie to save money. 他剛被解雇(爲了節省開支)。

ax•iom /ˈæksɪəm ; ˈæksɪəm/ *n* statement accepted as true without proof or argument. 公理(無須證明或無可辯論者)。**axio•matic** /ˌæksɪəˈmætɪk ; ˌæksɪəˈmætɪk/ *adj* of the nature of an ~; clear and evident without proof: 具有公理之性質的;無須證明卽可明白的: *It is ~atic that a whole is greater than any of its parts.* 整體大於其任何一部份,是不待證明卽可明白的。

axis /ˈæksɪs ; ˈæksɪs/ *n* (*pl* axes /ˈæksiːz ; ˈæksiz/) **1** line round which a turning object spins. (旋轉物體所繞以旋轉之) 軸。**the earth's ~,** the imaginary line joining the North and South Poles through the centre of the earth, on which the earth rotates once in twenty-four hours. 地軸(通過地心連接南北兩極之假想線,地球以此爲中心每二十四小時旋轉一週)。 **2** line that divides a regular figure into two symmetrical parts, eg the diameter of a circle. 軸線(將一正的圖形分爲兩個勻稱部分之平分線,如圓之直徑)。 **3** political connection (not always an alliance) between two or more states: (兩個或兩個以上國家之) 政治聯合(不一定是聯盟); 軸心: *the Berlin—Rome—Tokyo A~* (before 1939); (1939年以前之) 德、義、日軸心國; *A~ powers.* 軸心列强。

axle /ˈæksl ; ˈæksl/ *n* **1** rod upon or with which a wheel turns. 輪軸。 **2** bar or rod that passes through the centres of a pair of wheels: (通過兩輪中心之) 車軸: *the back ~ of a bus.* 公共汽車之後車軸。

ayah /ˈaɪə ; ˈɑjə/ *n* (In India and Pakistan) native nursemaid; lady's maid-servant. (在印度及巴基斯坦,由本地人充任之) 奶媽;保姆;(夫人之)女侍。

Aya•tol•lah /ˌaɪəˈtɒlə ; ˌaɪəˈtɑlə/ *n* title of various senior Muslim leaders in Iran. 伊朗資深回教領袖之尊稱。⇨ Imam.

aye¹, ay /aɪ ; aɪ/ *int, adv* (Scot and regional) yes; (naval) usual reply to an order: (蘇格蘭及方言) 是的; 對; 不錯; (海軍) 是(答覆命令的通常用語): *,Aye, 'aye, sir!* 是,是,長官! □ *n* vote or person supporting a proposal: 贊成某一建議的票或人: *The ayes have it,* Those for it are in the majority. 贊成者佔多數;大多數通過。

aye² /eɪ ; e/ *adv* (old use) always: (舊用法) 永遠;永久: *for ~.* 永遠地;永久地。

aza•lea /əˈzeɪlɪə ; əˈzeljə/ *n* (kinds of) flowering shrub of the rhododendron genus. 杜鵑花。

azi•muth /ˈæzɪməθ ; ˈæzəməθ/ *n* (astron) angular distance extending from the zenith to the horizon; (surveying) angle measured clockwise from the south or north. (天文) 地平經度; (測量) 方位角。

az•ure /ˈæʒə(r) ; ˈæʒɚ/ *adj, n* (poet) bright blue: (詩) 碧藍(的); 蔚藍(的): *an ~ sky.* 碧藍的天空。

Bb

B, b /biː ; bi/ (*pl* B's, b's /biːz ; biz/) the second letter of the English alphabet. 英文字母的第二個字母。

baa /bɑː ; bæː/ *n* cry of a sheep or lamb. 羊叫聲; 咩。 □ *vi* (baaing, baaed or baa'd /bɑːd ; bæːd/) make this cry; bleat. (羊) 叫。 **'~-lamb** *n* child's word for a sheep or lamb. (兒語) 羊。

B

baas /bɑːs ; bɑs/ *n* (S Africa) boss. (南非)主人;老板。

babble /ˈbæbl ; ˈbæbl̩/ *vi, vt* **1** [VP2A, B, C] talk in a way that is difficult to understand; make sounds like a baby; (of streams, etc) murmur. 說話模糊不清;發聲如嬰孩;牙牙學語;(指流水等)作潺潺聲。 **2** [VP6A, 15B] ~ ***(out)***, repeat foolishly; tell (a secret): 嘮叨;多嘴;洩漏(秘密): ~ *(out) nonsense/secrets*. 胡說(洩漏秘密)。 □ *n* [U] **1** childish or foolish talk; confused talk not clearly to be understood (as when many people are talking at once). 無意義的話;聽不清的話(如許多人同時談話)。 **2** gentle sound of water flowing over stones, etc. (流水經過石上所作的)潺潺之聲。 **bab·bler** /ˈbæblə(r) ; ˈbæbl̩ɚ/ *n* person who ~s, esp one who tells secrets. 嘮叨者;多嘴者;(尤指)洩漏秘密者。

babe /beɪb ; beb/ *n* **1** (liter) baby. (文)嬰兒。 **2** inexperienced and easily deceived person. 無經驗而易受欺騙之人。 **3** (US sl) girl or young woman. (美俚)女子;少女;小妞;妮子。

babel /ˈbeɪbl ; ˈbebl̩/ *n* **1 the Tower of B~,** tower built to reach heaven. (Gen 11). 巴別塔(古代巴比倫建築未成之通天塔,見創世紀 11 章)。 **2** (*sing* with *indef art*) scene of noisy and confused talking: (單數與不定冠詞連用) 鬧哄哄的情景;人聲嘈雜的地方: *What a ~!* 多麼嘈雜呵! *A ~ of voices could be heard from the schoolroom.* 可以聽見教室裏一陣嘈雜的聲音。

ba·boo, babu /ˈbɑːbuː ; ˈbɑbu/ *n* (as Hindu title) Mr; Hindu gentleman; Hindu clerk; (old use, pej) Hindu affecting English speech and manners. 先生(印度人對男子之尊稱);印度紳士;(會寫英文之)印度書記;(舊用法,蔑)愛用英語及英國習俗的印度人。

ba·boon /bəˈbuːn *US:* bæ- ; bæˈbun/ *n* large monkey (of Africa and southern Asia) with a dog-like face. 狒狒(一種大猴子,產於非洲及亞洲南部,面似狗)。 ⇨ the illus at ape. 參看 ape 之挿圖。

baby /ˈbeɪbɪ ; ˈbebɪ/ *n* (*pl* -bies) **1** very young child: 嬰兒;嬰孩;小兒: *She has a* ˌ*~ˈboy/ˈgirl.* 她有一個小男孩(女孩)。 *Which of you is the ~* (= the youngest member) *of the family?* 你們哪一個是全家最小的? ***(be left) carrying/holding/to carry/to hold the ~,*** (colloq) be left responsible for sth one does not wish to be responsible for (because of its difficulty or distastefulness). (俗)被促使擔任不願擔任的事情(因其爲困難或可厭之事)。 **ˈ~ carriage,** (US) pram. (美)嬰兒車。 **ˈ~-faced,** looking much younger than one's age. 娃娃臉的。 **ˈ~-farmer,** (often pej) woman who contracts to keep (esp unwanted) babies. (常爲輕蔑語)受約看護嬰孩(尤指不想要的嬰孩)的女人;代人育嬰的女人。 **ˈ~-minder,** woman paid to look after a ~ for long periods (eg while the mother is out working). 受雇長期照料嬰兒的女人(例如當母親外出工作時);保姆。 **ˈ~-sit·ter,** person paid to look after a ~ for a short time (eg while its parents are at the cinema). 臨時受雇照料嬰兒的人(例如當父母去看電影時)。 Hence, 由此產生, **ˈ~-sit** *vi*, **ˈ~-sit·ting** *n* **ˈ~-talk** *n* kind of speech used by or to babies with distorted vocabulary and syntax. 小兒語(嬰兒所說或對嬰兒說的言語,其單字及句法均異於常型)。 **2** (used attrib) very small of its kind: (形容用法)特小的;小型的: *a ~ car,* a small motor-car. 小型汽車。~ **ˈgrand,** small grand piano. 小型平臺鋼琴。 **3** (sl) girl; sweetheart. (俚)女郎;愛人。□ *vt* [VP6A] (colloq) treat like a ~: (俗)當嬰兒看待: *Don't ~ the boy!* 別把那男孩當嬰兒看待! **ˈ~·hood** *n* state of being a ~; time when one is a ~. 嬰兒期;嬰兒時代。 **~·ish** *adj* of or like a ~: 嬰兒的;如嬰兒的;幼稚的: *~ish behaviour.* 幼稚的行爲。

bac·ca·laur·eate /ˌbækəˈlɔːrɪət ; ˌbækəˈlɔrɪɪt/ *n* [C] **1** last secondary school examination in France. 法國中學結業考試。 **2** university degree of Bachelor. 學士學位。

bac·ca·rat /ˈbækərɑː ; ˌbækəˈrɑ/ *n* [U] gambling game with playing cards. 一種紙牌賭博。

bac·cha·nal /ˈbækənl ; ˈbækənl̩/ *adj* **1** of or like Bacchus /ˈbækəs ; ˈbækəs/ (the GK god of wine) or his rites. 屬於或像希臘酒神巴克斯或其崇拜儀式的。 **2** wild, excited, drunken: 狂歡暴飲的: *a ~ feast.* 狂歡暴飲的宴會。 □ *n* **1** follower of Bacchus; drunken reveller. 酒神巴克斯之信徒;狂飲作樂者。 **2** dance or song in honour of Bacchus; merrymaking. 酒神舞;酒神歌;作樂。**bac·cha·na·lian** /ˌbækəˈneɪlɪən ; ˌbækəˈnelɪən/ *adj* of ~s; noisy and drunken. 酒徒的;發酒瘋的;狂飲作樂的。

baccy /ˈbækɪ ; ˈbækɪ/ *n* [U] (colloq) tobacco. (俗)菸草。

bach·elor /ˈbætʃələ(r) ; ˈbætʃələ/ *n* **1** unmarried man, ⇨ spinster; (attrib) of, suitable for, an unmarried person: 未婚男子;單身漢;(形容用法)單身漢的;適宜於單身漢的: *a ~* (= independent unmarried) *girl;* 自食其力的未婚女子;*~ flats.* 單身公寓。 **2** (man or woman who has taken the) first university degree: (大學畢業所得的)學士學位; 學士(不分男女): *B~ of Arts/Science.* 文(理)學士。

ba·cil·lus /bəˈsɪləs ; bəˈsɪləs/ *n* (*pl* -cilli /-ˈsɪlaɪ ; -ˈsɪlaɪ/) rod-shaped bacterium, esp one of the types that cause disease. 桿狀細菌;(尤指能致病之)桿菌。

back[1] /bæk ; bæk/ *n* **1** (of the human body) surface of the body from the neck to the buttocks; spine, ⇨ the illus at skeleton: (指人體)背部(自頸項至臀部之背後部份);背脊(參看 skeleton 之挿圖): *If you lie on your ~, you can look up at the sky.* 如果你仰臥着,你就可以觀天。 *He slipped and fell on his ~.* 他仰天滑倒。 ***at the ~ of sb; at sb's ~,*** giving him support or protection: 支持或保護某人: *He knows that he has the head of the Department at his ~,* that the head is ready to support him. 他知道他有系主任支持他。 Cf 參較 *back sb up.* ***do/say sth behind sb's ~,*** without his knowledge (always in connection with sth unpleasant, such as slander). 在某人背後做(說)某事物(總與不愉快之事有關,如誹謗)。 ***break one's ~,*** fracture or dislocate one's spine; (fig) work (too) strenuously. 折斷脊椎骨;(喻)拼命工作;工作過於努力。 ***break the ~ of sth*** (eg a piece of work), finish the hardest or larger part of it. 完成某事物(如一件工作)最艱難的部份或其大部份。 ***get off sb's ~,*** stop being a burden or hindrance. 不再爲某人之累贅。 ***give sb a ~; make a ~ for sb,*** bend down in the game of leapfrog, or to enable sb to climb on one's ~ in order to get over a wall, etc. (在跳蛙遊戲中)彎下腰供人自背上跳越(或讓人爬上其背以翻越牆等)。 ***be glad to see the ~ of sb,*** feel pleased to see him go away. 因某人走開而高興。 ***be with/have one's ~ to the wall,*** be in a difficult position, forced to defend oneself. 處於困境;被迫自衞。 ***be on one's ~,*** (esp) be ill in bed. (尤指)臥病在床。 ***put one's ~ into sth,*** work at it with all one's energy. 盡全力爲之;全力以赴。 ***put/get sb's ~ up,*** make him angry. 觸怒某人;使之生氣。 ***turn one's ~ on sb,*** turn away from him in an impolite way; avoid, shun, him. 掉頭不理睬某人;避開某人。 **2** upper surface of an animal's body: 動物的脊背: *Fasten the saddle on the horse's ~.* 將鞍縛於馬背上。 **3** that part of a chair or seat on which a person's ~ rests. 椅或座位的靠背。 **4** (contrasted with *front*) that surface of an object that is less used, less visible or important: (與 front 相對)物體之較不常用、較不常見或較不重要之一面;背面;反面: *the ~ of one's hand,* with the nails and knuckles. 手背(有指甲及指節之面)。*You can't cut with the ~ of the knife.* 你無法用刀背切割。*You can't see the ~ of your head.* 你看不見自己的後腦袋。*You write the address on the front of an envelope, not on the ~.* 你把地址寫在信封的正面,不寫在信封的背面。 **5** (contrasted with *front*) that part of a thing that is farthest from the front: (與 front 相對)離前面最遠之處;後面: *a room at the ~ of the house;* 房屋內靠後面的一個房間;*a garden at* *the ~ of a house.* 房屋後面的花園;後花園。**the B~s,** lawns and grounds (on the River Cam) of some Cambridge colleges. 劍橋大學之某些學院的草地和校園(在肯河沿岸者)。 **6** ***break her ~,*** (of a ship) break in two. (指船)斷爲兩截。 **7** **('full-)~; ('half-)~,** (football, etc) player whose position is between the halfway line and the goal line. (足球等)(後)衛;(前)衛。⇨ the illus at football. 參看 football 之揷圖。

back² /bæk ; bæk/ *adv part* **1** (contrasted with *forward*) to or at the rear; away from the front or the centre: (與 forward 相對)往後面;在後面;離開前面或中央: *Stand ~, please!* 請退後! *The police held the crowd ~.* 警察攔住群衆不許向前。*Fasten the curtains ~.* 把窗簾拉開繫牢。*Sit ~ in your chair and be comfortable.* 靠着椅背坐,舒服舒服。*The house stands ~* (ie at some distance) *from the road.* 那房子離大路有一段距離。***go ~ (up)on/from one's word,*** fail to keep a promise. 食言;不守信。***(in) ~ of,*** (US colloq) behind: (美俗)在…後面: *the houses ~ of the church.* 教堂後面的房子。**2** in(to) an earlier position or condition: 在(至)先前的位置或情況: *Put the dictionary ~ on the shelf.* 把字典放回書架上。*Throw the ball ~ to me.* 把球擲還給我。*Call that boy ~.* 把那個男孩叫回來。*We shall be ~* (= home again) *before dark.* 我們將在天黑以前回來。*Shall we walk ~ or ride ~?* 我們是走路回去呢,還是坐車回去? *How far is it there and ~?* 到那裏來回有多遠? *My brother is just ~* (ie has just returned home) *from Paris.* 我哥哥(弟弟)剛從巴黎回來。*The company is now ~ on its feet,* has re-established itself after a period of financial, etc difficulties. 該公司現在又穩定下來了(如經過一段時期的財務困難等)。***~ and forth*** ⇨ forth. **3** in return: 還報: *If I hit you, would you hit me ~?* 如果我打你,你會不會還手? *Don't answer ~,* Don't retort or argue. 不要回嘴。*When can you pay ~* (=repay) *the money you borrowed?* 你何時能歸還你所借的錢? ***have/get one's 'own ~ (on sb),*** (colloq) have one's revenge. (俗)(向某人)報復。 **4** (of time) ago; into the past: (指時間)以前;溯至過去: *some few years ~;* 好些年以前; *far ~ in the Middle Ages.* 遠溯至中古時代。

back³ /bæk ; bæk/ *vt, vi* **1** [VP6A, 15A, 2A, C] go or cause to go ~ward(1): 後退;使後退: *The horse ~ed suddenly.* 馬忽然向後退。*He ~ed the car into/out of the garage.* 他把汽車倒退着駛入(出)停車間。*The wind ~ed,* changed gradually in an anti-clockwise direction (eg from E through NE to N). 風向逐漸倒轉(卽循着反時鐘方向轉,例如自東風轉爲東北風,再轉爲北風)。⇨ veer. ***~ the oars; ~ water,*** use the oars to reverse a boat's forward motion. 划槳使船後退。 **2** [VP6A, 15B] ***~ (up),*** support: 支持;擁護: *~ a friend in an argument or quarrel;* 在辯論或爭論中支持朋友; *~ up an argument.* 支持一論據。Hence, 由此產生, **'~-up** *n* (colloq) support; spare¹. (俗)支持;備件。***~ a bill/note,*** endorse it as a promise to pay money if necessary. 背書(在票據背面簽名,表示承諾必要時卽行付款)。 **3** [VP6A] bet money on (a horse, a greyhound): 下賭注於(某一匹馬或某一條跑狗): *The favourite was heavily ~ed,* Much money was bet on its winning the race. 大家對那匹熱門馬下了重注(賭其將爲得勝者)。 **4** [VP2C] ***~ 'down (from),*** give up a claim, etc: 放棄要求等: *I see he has ~ed down from the position he took last week.* 我看他已放棄了他上星期所採取的立場。Hence, 由此產生, **'~-down** *n.* ***~ off,*** give up a claim. 放棄要求。***~ out (of),*** withdraw (from a promise or undertaking): 食言;打退堂鼓: *He promised to help and then ~ed out.* 他答應幫忙,後來却食言了。*He's trying to ~ out of his bargain,* escape from the agreement. 他在設法不履行合約規定。 **5** [VP6A] put or be a lining to; put on as a surface at the ~: 加裏襯於;作爲…的裏襯;加於…的背面: *~ed with sheet iron.* 背面包上一層鐵皮。 **6** [VP6A, 3A] ***~ (on) (to),*** be situated at the ~ of: 位於…的後面: *Our garden ~s theirs.* 我們花園在他們的花園後面。*Their house ~s on (to) our garden.* 他們的房子在我們花園的背後。**~er** *n* **1** person who ~s a horse. 賽馬中的下注者。 **2** person who gives support or help (eg to a political movement); person who gives financial support to an undertaking. 支持者;擁護者(如擁護某一政治運動);贊助者(對某一事業予以財務上的支持者)。**~·ing** *n* **1** [U] help; support; [C] body of supporters: 贊助;支持;支持者之集團;贊助團;後臺: *The new leader has a large ~ing.* 此新領袖有大批的支持者。 **2** [U] material used to form a thing's ~ or support. 用作某物之後背或支撑物的材料;襯料;支材。 **3** [U, C] (pop music) musical accompaniment to a singer: (流行音樂)流行歌曲的伴奏: *vocal/instrumental ~ing.* 聲部(樂器)伴奏。

back⁴ /bæk ; bæk/ (used attrib, and in compounds, with references to the articles on the *n, adv part* and *v* above) (以上述名詞、副詞接語及動詞各義作形容用法,並用於複合字中) **1** ⇨ back¹(1, 2). **'~-ache** *n* [U, C] ache or pain in the ~. 背痛。**'~-band** *n* strap over a horse's cart-saddle, supporting the shafts of a cart or carriage. (馬車鞍上的附搭於馬背上用以支持車轅之)背帶。**'~·bone** *n* **(a)** line of bones down the middle of the ~, from the skull to the hips; spine, spinal column, ⇨ the illus at skeleton; (fig) chief support: 脊骨;脊柱(參看 skeleton 之挿圖);(喩)主要支持力;主幹;中堅份子: *Such men are the ~bone of the country.* 這種人才是國家的中堅份子。**(b)** [U] (fig) strength; firmness: (喩)剛强;堅毅: *He hasn't enough ~bone,* is weak in character. 他不够堅强。**(c)** ***to the ~bone,*** (fig) completely; in every way: (喩)徹頭徹尾地;道道地地: *He's British to the ~bone.* 他是道道地地的英國人。**'~-break·ing** *adj* (of work) exhausting. (指工作)費力的;累人的。 **2** ⇨ back¹(4, 5). **,~-'hand(ed)** *adj*: *~hand blow/stroke,* one that is delivered with the ~ of the hand turned outwards, or in a direction different from what is usual or expected. (用手背)反掌或反向的打擊;反手擊。⇨ forehand. Hence, 由此產生, (fig) (喩): *a ~handed compliment,* one that is ambiguous (eg suggesting sarcasm). 挖苦或含義不明的恭維。**'~·scratcher** *n* **(a)** device with claws on a long handle for scratching the ~ (when there is an irritation, etc). 痲姑爪(長柄,一端有爪,背癢時用以抓背的器具,有些地方叫'不求人')。 **(b)** flatterer. 諂媚者。⇨ scratch *v*(5). **'~-stroke** *n* **(a)** [U] swimming stroke done on the ~, rotating the arms alternately. 仰泳。**(b)** [C] ~-handed stroke. 反掌或反向的打擊;反手擊。**'~·sword** *n* sword with only one cutting edge. 單刄劍;大砍刀。 **3** ⇨ back¹(5) and back²(1). ***,~-to-'~,*** (of housing) of two rows of terrace houses, often separated by a narrow alley, with the ~s facing. (指房屋)背靠背的(指兩排連棟式的房屋,通常由一小巷隔開,兩排房屋之後面均朝小巷)。**,~-'bench(er)** *n* (person occupying) one of the seats in the House of Commons (or other law-making body) used by those members, who, because they do not or have not held office, are not entitled to a front-bench seat. 在英國下議院或其他議會中之後排座席;在英國下議院或其他議會中,坐於後排座位之議員(因其非爲,或不曾爲,政府官員,故不得坐於前排座位)。⇨ bench(1). **'~-blocks** *n pl* (in Australia) areas of land a long way from a railway, river, the sea-coast, etc and thinly populated. (澳洲)距離鐵路、河道、海岸等均甚遠且人口稀少之地區;偏僻地區。**'~·board** *n* movable board at the ~ of a cart. (馬車後面可以移動的)後板;背板。**'~·cloth** *n* painted cloth hung at the ~ of a stage in a theatre, as part of the scenery. (戲臺後面所掛的)背景幕;天幕。**,~-'door** *n* door at the ~ of a house or other building; (attrib, fig) secret or indirect; clandestine: 後門;(形容用法,喻)秘密的;間接的;幕後的;暗中的: *~door influence.* 幕後的勢力。ˈ**~·drop** *n* = ~cloth. ˈ**~·ground** *n* **(a)** that part of a view, scene (and, fig, a description) that serves as a setting for the chief objects, persons, etc. 背景;(喻)襯托性敍述。⇨ foreground. **(b)** person's past experiences, education, environment. 個人的學經歷與環境;背景。 **(c)** contemporary condition(s): 當時的情況;時代背景: *the social and political ~ground;* 當時社會及政治的情況; (comm) details necessary to an understanding of company business: (商)了解公司業務所必需的細節: *B~ground information will be supplied at the Board meeting.* 公司業務的詳細資料將於開董事會時提供。**(d)** ***(be/keep/stay) in the ~ground,*** away from publicity; hidden. 在(保持在)幕後。**(e)** **~ground music/effects, etc,** music, etc that accompanies dialogue, action, etc (eg in a radio or TV programme or a cinema film) but is not essential to the story, etc. (無線電廣播、電視節目或電影中,配合對話、動作等,而並非故事內容等所不可缺少的)配樂(音響效果等)。**~·less** *adj* (of a dress), not covering the ~; cut to the waist at the ~: (指女裝)無背的;露背的;背部底開到腰的: *a ~less gown.* 露背禮服。ˈ**~·most** *adj* farthest from the front. 最後面的。ˈ**~·room** *n* room at the ~ of a building: 位於建築物後部的房間;後房: ***~room boys,*** (colloq) scientists, engineers, research workers in offices and laboratories. (俗)辦公室或實驗室中的科學家、工程師或研究工作人員。ˌ**~·ˈseat** *n* seat at the ~. 後座。***take a ~seat,*** (fig) behave as if one were unimportant; humble oneself. (喻)謙遜;自謙。ˌ**~-seat ˈdriver,** passenger (in a car) who corrects or advises the driver. 後座駕駛員(坐在車中改正或勸告駕駛員的乘客)。ˈ**~·side** *n* (colloq) buttocks: (俗)臀部; 屁股: *give sb a kick on the ~side.* 踢某人屁股一下。ˌ**~·ˈstage** *adv* **(a)** behind the scenes (in a theatre): (戲院中)在後臺;至後臺: *I was taken ~stage by the leading actor.* 我被主角帶到後臺。**(b)** (attrib) (形容用法): *~stage life,* of actors and actresses when not on the stage. (演員的)後臺生活 (即非演戲時的私生活)。ˌ**~·ˈstair** *adj* secret; underhand: 秘密的;暗中的: *~stair influence.* 秘密勢力;暗中的影響力。ˌ**~·ˈstairs** *n* staircase from servants' quarters: (通至僕人住處的)後樓梯: (attrib) (形容用法) *~stairs gossip,* ie among servants. 僕人們的閒話。ˈ**~·stays** *n pl* (naut) set of ropes from the mast-head to the sides of a ship, sloping towards the stern. (航海)(自桅頂牽引至船側並向船尾斜下之)後拉索。ˈ**~·wash** *n* movement of water going away in waves, esp the rush of water behind a ship; (fig) unpleasant after-effects of sth done. 回浪(往遠處移動之波浪,尤指輪船等後面所攪起者); 水之反濺; (喻)完成某事物後所留下不愉快的後效;餘波。ˈ**~·water** *n* **(a)** part of a river not reached by its current, where the water does not flow. 死水;滯水(河流中水流不經過之處,此處之水不流動)。**(b)** (fig) place, condition of mind, untouched by events, progress, etc: (喻)窮鄉僻壤;思想停滯: *living in an intellectual ~water,* untouched by new ideas, etc. 生活於智力沉滯的狀態之中。ˈ**~·woods** *n pl* uncleared forest land; (fig) culturally backward area. 偏僻的莽林地區;(喻)文化落後地區。ˈ**~·woods·man** /-mən; -mən/ *n* (*pl* -men) man who lives in the ~woods; (fig) old-fashioned person. 居於偏僻的莽林地區之人;(喻)守舊的人。~ ˈ**yard** *n* (esp of terraced houses) (usu paved) area at the ~ of a house: 後院(房屋後面的空地,通常是加工鋪過的,尤指一排房屋之後院): *The dustbin is kept in the ~ yard.* 垃圾箱是放在後院裡。 **4** ⇨ back²(2). to an earlier point in time; to a former place. 至先前的時間;至原先的位置。ˌ**~·ˈdate** *vt* date ~ to a time in the past: 追溯至(過去某時): *The wage increases are to be ~dated to the first of January.* 工資的增加將追溯至元月一日。 ˌ**~·ˈfire** *n* (sound caused by the) too early explosion of gas in an internal combustion engine, causing the piston to move in the wrong direction. (內燃機氣缸內爆發過早致使活塞倒行之)逆火;逆火所引起的聲響。□ *vi* produce, make the sound of, a ~fire; (fig) produce an unexpected or undesired result: 發生逆火; 發出逆火的聲響; (喻) 產生意外或不良的後果: *The plot ~fired.* 該秘密計畫產生了不良的後果。ˈ**~-formation** *n* [U, C] (process of making a) word that appears to be the root of a longer word (eg *televise,* from *television*). 反造字(根據一個較長的字,反造出一個看來似乎為其字根之字,例如根據 television 反造出 televise); 反造法。ˈ**~·log** *n* accumulation of work or business (eg arrears of unfulfilled orders) not yet attended to. 積壓之待辦事項(如訂貨之遲未發出)。ˈ**~ num·ber** *n* **(a)** issue of a periodical of an earlier date, not now on sale. 過期的期刊(市面上已不賣的); 舊雜誌。**(b)** (fig, colloq) out-of-date or old-fashioned method, thing, person, etc. (喻,俗)過時或舊式的方法,事物,人等;老古董;落伍的觀念。 ˈ**~ pay / rent / taxes, etc,** *n* pay, etc in arrears; pay, etc that is overdue. 過期未付的款(房租,稅等)。ˌ**~·ˈpedal** *vi* (on a bicycle, etc) pedal ~wards; (fig) retreat hurriedly from sth stated or promised. (在腳踏車等上)倒踩腳踏板; (喻) 匆忙取消所說的或所答應的某事物。 ˌ**~-ˈslide** *vi* [VP2A] fall back from good ways into bad old ways of living; lose interest in religious practice, morality, etc. 從良好的生活方式恢復到以往的不良的方式;故態復萌; 對教規、道德等失去興趣;墮落;退步。 ˌ**~·ˈspace** *vi* move the carriage of a typewriter ~ one or more spaces by pressing the key (called 稱作 the ˈ*~spacer key*) used for this purpose. 按退格鍵使打字機的滾筒倒退一格或數格。 **5** ⇨ back²(3). in return; in reply. 還報;回答。ˈ**~-bite** *vt, vi* slander the reputation of (sb who is absent); speak slanderously about an absent person. 背後詆毀(某人)的名譽;誹謗;背後說人壞話;中傷。Hence, 由此產生,ˈ**~·biter** *n* person who ~bites. 背後說人壞話的人;誹謗者。 ˈ**~·chat** *n* [U] (colloq) (exchange of) impertinent remarks: (俗)惡言;粗魯的話;惡言相向: *I want none of your ~chat.* 不可對我說這種粗魯的話。ˈ**~·lash** *n* [U] **(a)** excessive movement caused by loose connections between mechanical parts (often causing ~ward movement). 反撞;齒隙(由於機器零件間連接的鬆弛而引起激烈運動,常導致反向運動)。 **(b)** (fig) antagonistic reaction (esp in social or race relations). (喻)敵對反應(尤指社會或種族關係中者)。ˈ**~·talk** *n* [U] = ~chat. 惡言;粗話;惡言反駁。

back·gam·mon /bækˈgæmən *US:* ˈbæk- ; ˈbækˌgæmən/ *n* [U] game for two players, played on a special double board with draughts and dice. 西洋雙陸棋戲。

back·sheesh ⇨ baksheesh.

back·ward /ˈbækwəd ; ˈbækwəˑd/ *adj* **1** towards the back or the starting-point: 向後的;倒着的: *a ~ glance/movement;* 向後的一看(動作); *a ~ flow of water.* 水之倒流。 **2** having made, making, less than the usual or normal progress: 進步遲緩的;落後的: *This part of the country is still ~; there are no railways or roads and no electricity.* 這個國家的這個地區仍甚落後; 沒有鐵道或公路,也沒有電力。*Because of his long illness, Tom is ~ in his studies.* 湯姆因久病所以功課落後。Cf 參較 *well up in. Spring is ~ this year.* 今年春天來得較遲。 **3** shy; reluctant; hesitant: 羞怯的;畏縮的;遲疑的: *Although he is clever, he is ~ in giving his views.* 他雖然很聰明,却不善發表他的意見。□ *adv* **~(s)** **1** away from one's front; towards the back: 向後;向背後: *He looked ~(s) over his shoulder.* 他回頭向後看。**2** with the back or the end first: 倒退着: *It's not easy to walk ~(s).* 倒退着走路不容易。*Can you say the alphabet ~(s),* ie ZYXWV, etc? 你能倒唸英文的二十六個字母嗎? ***know sth ~(s),*** know it perfectly; be quite familiar with it. 完全瞭解某事物;熟諳某事物。***~(s) and forward(s),*** first in one direction and then in the other: 來回地;往返地: *travelling ~(s) and forward(s) between London and the south coast.* 往返於倫敦和南海岸之間。Cf 參較 *back and forth; to and fro.*

bacon /ˈbeɪkən ; ˈbekən/ *n* [U] salted or smoked meat from the back or sides of a pig. 醃的或薰的猪肉(係猪之脊肋部份)。***bring home the ~,*** (sl) succeed in one's undertaking. (俚)獲得成功。***save one's ~,*** (colloq) escape death, injury, punishment. (俗)死裡逃生;倖免於難;免於受罰。

bac·ter·ium /bækˈtɪərɪəm ; bækˈtɪrɪəm/ *n* (*pl* -ria /-rɪə ; -rɪə/) (kinds of) simplest and smallest form of plant life, existing in air, water and soil, and in living and dead creatures and plants, essential to animal life and sometimes a cause of disease. 細菌。**bac·ter·ial** /-rɪəl ; -rɪəl/ *adj* of bacteria: 細菌的: *bacterial contamination.* 細菌感染。**bac·teri·ol·ogy** /bækˌtɪərɪˈɒlədʒɪ ; ˈbækˌtɪrɪˈɑlədʒɪ/ *n* science or study of bacteria. 細菌學。**bac·teri·ol·ogist** /-dʒɪst ; -dʒɪst/ *n* student of, expert in, bacteriology. 細菌學者;細菌學家。

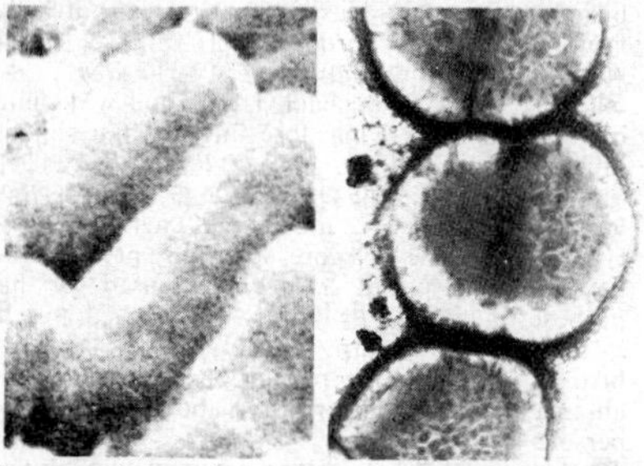

bacteria (seen through a microscope)

bad[1] /bæd ; bæd/ *adj* (worse, worst) **1** wicked, evil, immoral: 壞的;邪惡的;不道德的: *It is bad to steal.* 偷竊是壞事。*He leads a bad life.* 他過着邪惡的生活。***act in bad faith,*** dishonestly, insincerely. 行爲詭詐或不誠實。***a bad egg / hat / lot,*** (dated sl) morally unreliable person. (過時俚語)壞蛋。***call sb bad names,*** insult him. 辱罵某人。***bad language,*** swear-words; (the use of) obscene or profane words merely to insult or for emphasis. 詛咒;粗話;咒罵語;咒罵語之使用。**bad word,** swear-word. 咒罵語。 **2** unpleasant; disagreeable; unwelcome: 令人不愉快的;令人討厭的;不受歡迎的: *We've had some bad news.* 我們得到了一些壞消息。*What bad weather we're having!* 多麼可厭的天氣呵! *There's a bad smell here.* 這裡有股惡臭。*The way he was sacked created a bad odour,* (fig) created unpleasant feelings. (喻)他被解雇的方式留下了不愉快的感覺。 **3** (of things that are in themselves undesirable) notable; noticeable; serious: (指不好的事物)顯著的;嚴重的: *That was a bad mistake.* 那是一項大錯。*He's had a bad accident.* 他遭遇了一場嚴重的災禍。*There's been a bad falling-off in attendance.* 出席的人大爲減少。 **4** inferior; worthless; incorrect; of poor quality: 劣等的;無價值的;不正確的;劣質的: *His pronunciation is bad.* 他的發音很差。*He speaks bad English.* 他說的英語很差勁。*What a bad drawing!* 多糟的畫啊! *You can't take photographs if the light is bad.* 如果光線壞,你就不能照相。***be in a bad way,*** be very ill or unfortunate; be in trouble or difficulty. 病重;遭遇極大不幸;在困境中。***be in bad (with),*** (US colloq) be in disfavour: (美俗)失寵(於);受(…的)輕視: *He's in bad with the boss.* 他失寵於其上司。***go from bad to worse,*** become seriously worse. 越來越壞;每況愈下。***with bad grace,*** showing unwillingness. 不願意地;勉强地。***not (so) bad,*** (colloq understatement) quite good. (俗,含蓄說法)不壞;不錯。***not half bad,*** very good. 很好。**a bad business / job,** (colloq) an unfortunate affair. (俗)不幸的事。**bad debt,** one unlikely to be paid. 不可能償還的債務;倒帳;呆帳。 **ˈbad-lands** (US) barren, infertile regions. (美)貧瘠不毛地區。**bad law,** one that cannot be sustained or held to be valid. 不能證明其爲正確的定律;錯誤的定律。**bad shot,** (fig) wrong guess. (喻)誤猜。 **5** not able to be eaten; rotten: 不可食用的;腐壞的: *bad eggs / meat.* 腐壞的蛋(肉)。***go bad,*** become unfit to eat: (食物)變壞: *Don't let that fish go bad—put it in the fridge.* 不要讓那條魚變壞了—把牠放到冰箱裡。 **6** ***bad for,*** hurtful or injurious for; unsuitable for: 有害於;不適宜於: *Smoking is bad for the health.* 吸煙有害健康。*Very small print is bad for the eyes.* 印刷的字體太小對眼睛有害。 *It's bad for him to live alone.* 他不宜獨居。 **7** in ill health, diseased: 健康情況不佳的;有病的: *a bad* (= sore) *finger;* 痛的手指; *a bad leg,* causing pain; 會痛的腿; (colloq) (俗) *She feels bad today.* 她今天感覺不舒服。***be taken bad,*** (colloq) fall ill; become more ill: (俗)生病;病重: *She was taken bad during the night.* 她晚上病倒了。 **8** (colloq) unfortunate: (俗)不幸的: *It's too bad she's so ill.* 她病得這樣厲害,太不幸了。 **9** (colloq) sorry; bothered: (俗)抱憾的;感到不安的: *I feel so bad about not being able to help you.* 未能相助極感不安。**bad·ly** *adv* (worse, worst) (Cf 參較 *well, better, best.*) **1** in a bad manner; roughly; untidily, etc: 壞地;粗陋地;雜亂地;不整齊地: *badly made / dressed / wounded.* 粗製濫造的(服裝不整的;傷得很厲害的)。 **2** by much: 大大地: *badly beaten at football;* 在足球賽中大敗; *badly in need of repair.* 亟須修理。 **3** (with *want, need*) very much: (與 want, need 連用)非常地: *She wants it badly.* 她非常想要它。**4** ***badly off,*** poor. 窮的。***badly off for,*** in need of. 需要。**bad·ness** *n* quality of being bad: 壞;惡劣: *the badness of the weather / climate.* 天氣(氣候)之惡劣。

bad[2] /bæd ; bæd/ *n* [U] that which is bad: 壞的或惡劣的事物: *take the bad with the good,* take bad fortune with good fortune. 壞運與好運都要接受(逆來亦須順受)。***go to the bad,*** become completely immoral; become ruined. 墮落;自毀。***to the bad,*** (accounts) in loss: (帳目)虧損;負債: *I am £50 to the bad,* have lost £50 as the result (of the deal, etc). 我虧損五十鎊(由於交易等的結果)。

bade /bæd ; bæd/ ⇨ bid[1](4).

badge /bædʒ ; bædʒ/ *n* **1** sth worn (usu a design on cloth or made of metal) to show a person's occupation, rank, etc or membership of a society. 徽章;證章(通常爲布或金屬製成,上有圖案,表示職業、階級等,或會員身份)。 **2** (fig) sth that shows a quality or condition: (喻)象徵;代表: *Chains are a ~ of slavery.* 鐐銬爲奴隸之象徵。

badger[1] /ˈbædʒə(r) ; ˈbædʒɚ/ *n* small, grey animal living in holes in the earth and going about at night. 獾(灰色小動物,居於地洞中,夜出活動)。⇨ the illus at small. 參看 small 之插圖。

badger[2] /ˈbædʒə(r) ; ˈbædʒɚ/ *vt* [VP6A, 14, 16A] ***~ sb (with questions, etc) / (for sth) / (into doing sth),*** worry or tease: 煩擾;鬧着: *Tom has been ~ing his uncle to buy him a camera.* 湯姆一直鬧着要他叔父給他買一架照相機。*I was ~ed into doing what she wanted.* 我被鬧得照着她所要求的做了。

ba·di·nage /ˈbædɪnɑːʒ *US:* ˌbædənˈɑːʒ ; ˈbædnɪdʒ/ *n* [U] banter. 嘲弄;戲謔;開玩笑;打趣;揶揄。

bad·min·ton /ˈbædmɪntən ; ˈbædmɪntən/ *n* game played with rackets and shuttlecocks across a high, narrow net. 羽毛球戲。

baffle[1] /ˈbæfl ; ˈbæfl̩/ *vt* [VP6A] puzzle; prevent (sb) from doing sth; be too difficult to do, understand, etc: 困惑;阻止(某人)做某事;難住;難倒: *One of the examination questions ~d me com-*

pletely. 有道試題把我完全難住了。*They were ~d in their attempt.* 他們的企圖受挫。*The scene ~d all description,* could not be described. 那情景筆墨難以形容。

baffle[2] /ˈbæfl ; ˈbæfl̩/ *n* plate, board, screen or other device, used to hinder or control the flow of a gas, a liquid or sound through an inlet or outlet. (阻礙或控制氣體、液體或聲音流進流出之)障板；阻板；折流板。

bag[1] /bæg ; bæg/ *n* **1** container made of flexible material (paper, cloth, leather) with an opening at the top, used for carrying things from place to place: (紙、布、皮革所製之)袋子；提袋；提包: *ˈshopping-bag;* 購物袋; *ˈtravelling-bag;* 旅行袋; *ˈhandbag;* 女用手提包; *ˈkitbag;* (軍人、水手或旅行者之)背包；背袋；行李袋; *ˈtool-bag;* 工具袋; *ˈmailbag,* (運送郵件用的)郵袋，⇨ these words. 參看各該字。***bag and baggage,*** with all one's belongings (used esp of sb who is expelled). 帶着全部財產(尤指被驅逐之人)。***a bag of bones,*** a very thin person or animal. 很瘦的人或動物；瘦皮猴。***let the cat out of the bag,*** tell a secret (without intending to do so). (無意中)洩露秘密。***pack one's bags,*** pack (for a journey). 整理行裝(準備旅行)。***the whole bag of tricks,*** (colloq) everything needed for a purpose; the whole lot. (俗)爲某一目的所需要的一切東西；全部法寶。 **2** (= *game-bag*) a llthe birds, animals, etc shot or caught: 獵獲的全部飛禽走獸: *They secured a good bag.* 他們獵獲了很多鳥獸。***be in the bag,*** (colloq) (of results, outcomes, etc) be as desired: (俗)(指結果、結局等)將如所願；穩操勝算；十拿九穩；一定成功: *The election is in the bag.* 這場選擧我們將穩操勝算。 **3** ***bags of,*** (sl) plenty of: (俚)充足的；很多的: *There's bags of room.* 空間很大。*He has bags of money.* 他有很多錢。 **4** ***bags under the eyes,*** (colloq) puffiness under the eyes (eg from lack of sleep). (俗)腫眼泡；眼睛下面的鼓脹(例如因缺乏睡眠所致)。 **5** ***old bag,*** (colloq) fussy, unattractive, boring woman. (俗)愛挑剔，不漂亮，令人厭煩的女人。

bag[2] /bæg ; bæg/ *vt, vi* (-gg-) **1** [VP6A, 15B] put into a bag or bags: 裝入袋中: *to bag (up) wheat.* 把小麥裝入袋中。 **2** [VP6A] (of sportsmen) kill or catch: (指獵人)獵獲: *They bagged nothing except a couple of rabbits.* 他們僅僅獵獲兩隻兎子。 **3** [VP6A] (colloq) take (sb else's property, etc without permission, but not intending to steal): (俗)擅自取用(他人之物，但非存心偸竊)；順手牽羊: *Who has bagged my matches?* 誰把我的火柴拿去了？ *She bagged* (= occupied, sat in) *the most comfortable chair.* 她逕自坐上最舒服的椅子。*Try to bag an empty table,* secure one (eg in a crowded restaurant). 想辦法弄一張空桌子(例如在擁擠的餐館中)。 **4** [VP2A, C] hang loosely, looking like a cloth bag: 鬆弛地懸垂(如布袋狀): *trousers that bag at the knees.* 在膝蓋處特別寬鬆的褲子。

baga·telle /ˌbægəˈtel ; ˌbægəˈtɛl/ *n* **1** [U] kind of game like billiards, played on a board with holes instead of pockets. 一種彈子戲(枱板上有洞而無袋者)。 **2** [C] (often 常作 ***a mere ~***) sth small and of no importance. 小事物；不重要之事物。 **3** [C] musical trifle. 音樂小品；簡易短曲。

bag·gage /ˈbægɪdʒ ; ˈbægɪdʒ/ *n* [U] **1** (more usu, except in US, *luggage*) all the bags, trunks, etc with which a person travels. (除美國外，較常用 luggage) 行李(旅行時所攜帶之全部袋、箱等)。 **ˈ~ room,** (US) left luggage office. (美)行李寄存處。 **2** tents, bedding, equipment, etc, of an army: (軍隊之)輜重: *ˈ~ animals, ˈ~ train, etc,* animals, carts, trucks, etc, carrying ~. 運輸重的牲口、車輛等。 **3** (dated) (playfully) saucy girl: (過時用語)(謔)調皮的女孩子: *You little ~!* 你這調皮的小丫頭！

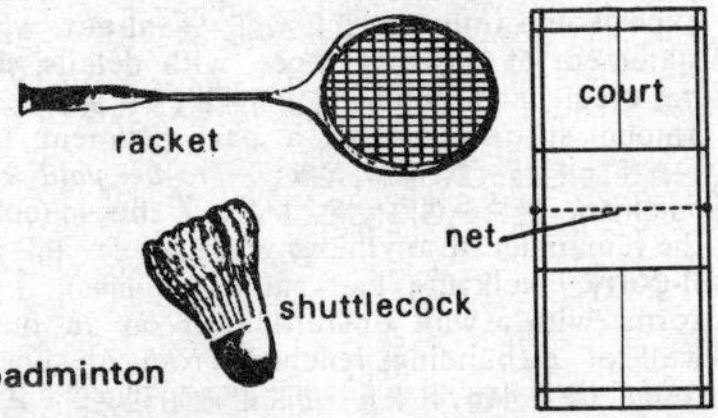

badminton

baggy /ˈbægɪ ; ˈbægɪ/ *adj* hanging in loose folds: 寬鬆而下垂的；寬鬆如袋的: *trousers ~ at the knees;* 膝部特別寬鬆的褲子; *~ skin under the eyes.* 眼睛下面鬆弛的皮膚。

bagnio /ˈbɑːnɪəʊ ; ˈbænjo/ *n* (old use) (舊用法) **1** prison. 牢獄。 **2** brothel. 妓院。

bag·pipe /ˈbægpaɪp ; ˈbægˌpaɪp/ *n* (often 常作 **the ~s**) musical instrument with air stored in a bag of wind held under one arm and pressed out through pipes in which there are reeds. 風笛(一種樂器，吹奏者一隻臂下的風袋中所貯藏的空氣，經由有簧的管中壓出)。⇨ the illus at kilt. 參看 kilt 之插圖。

bags /bægz ; bægz/ *n pl* (colloq) trousers: (俗)褲子: *Oxford ~.* 褲管寬鬆的褲子。⇨ debag.

bah /bɑː ; bɑ/ *int* used as a sign of contempt. 呸(表示鄙視的感歎語)。

bail[1] /beɪl ; bel/ *n* [U] sum of money demanded by a law court, paid by or for a person accused of wrongdoing, as security that he will appear for his trial, until which time he is allowed to go free. (被告或替被告付與法院以保證按時到庭應訊之)保釋金。***go/put in/stand ~ (for sb),*** pay money to secure his freedom in this way. (繳保釋金)保釋(某人)。***(be) out on ~,*** free after payment of ~. 在保釋中。***forfeit one's ~,*** fail to appear for trial. 經保釋在外而不按時到庭應訊。***refuse ~,*** (of a judge) refuse to accept ~ and give freedom to a prisoner. (指法官)不准保釋。***surrender to one's ~,*** appear for trial after being out on ~. 經保釋在外後如期到庭應訊。□ *vt* [VP15B] **~ sb out,** obtain his freedom until trial by payment of ~. 把某人保釋出來。**~ee** /ˌbeɪˈliː ; ˈbelˈi/ *n* (legal) person to whom permission is given to have the goods of another (eg a laundry which accepts goods for washing or dry-cleaning). (法律)受託人(獲准收取他人貨物者，例如接受衣物作水洗或乾洗之洗衣店)。 **~·ment** *n* (legal) delivery of goods to a ~ee. (法律)託交(貨物之託交給受託人)；委託。**~or** /ˈbeɪlɔː(r) ; ˌbelˈɔr/ *n* (legal) one who delivers goods to a ~ee. (法律)寄託人；委託人(將貨物託交給受託人者)。

bail[2] /beɪl ; bel/ *n* (cricket) either of the two cross pieces over the three stumps. (板球)門柱上之橫木。⇨ the illus at cricket. 參看 cricket 之插圖。

bail[3] /beɪl ; bel/ *vt, vi* **1** [VP6A, 15B, 2A, C] ***~ (out),*** throw water out of a boat with buckets, etc: 用桶等將船內之水舀出: *~ing water (out);* 將船內的水舀出; *~ing (out) the boat.* 舀出船內之水。 **2** (sometimes used for) (有時等於) bale[2].

bailey /ˈbeɪlɪ ; ˈbelɪ/ *n* outer wall of a castle; courtyard of a castle enclosed by strong walls. (中古城堡之)外牆；城堡外庭(城堡中四周有堅壁圍繞之庭院)。 **Old B~,** London Central Criminal Court. 倫敦中央刑事法庭。

Bailey bridge /ˈbeɪlɪ brɪdʒ ; ˈbelɪ brɪdʒ/ *n* bridge (in prefabricated sections) designed for speedy assembly, used for spanning rivers, etc. 倍力橋(橋身各部預先鑄好，可迅速組合以供跨越河流等)。⇨ the illus at bridge. 參看 bridge 之插圖。

bail·iff /ˈbeɪlɪf ; ˈbelɪf/ *n* **1** law officer who helps a sheriff. 州或郡之副司法官。 **2** landowner's agent or manager. 地主之代理人或管理人。

bairn /beən ; bɛrn/ *n* (Scot and N England) child. (用於蘇格蘭及英格蘭北部)小孩。

bait[1] /beɪt ; bet/ *n* **1** food, or sth made in imitation, put on a hook to catch fish, or in nets, traps, etc to attract prey: (掛於釣鈎上以釣魚或置於網中、陷穽等內以引誘獵物之)餌: *The fish took/swallowed/rose to/nibbled at the ~.* 魚食(吞,向上游至,咬)餌。**live ~,** small fish used as ~ to catch large fish. 活餌(作餌用的小魚,用以釣大魚者)。**2** (fig) sth that allures or tempts. (喻)引誘物;誘惑物;餌。***rise to the ~,*** succumb to temptation. 受誘惑;上鈎。

B

bait² /beɪt ; bet/ *vt, vi* **1** [VP6A] put food, real or imitation, (on a hook, etc) to catch fish, etc: 置餌於(鈎等上以捕魚等): *~ a hook with a worm.* 置蚯蚓於鈎上以爲餌。**2** [VP6A, 2A] give food to (horses on a journey); (of horses) take food. 在旅途中餵(馬);(指馬)吃草料。**3** [VP6A] worry (a chained animal) by making dogs attack it: 使狗騷擾(被鏈鎖住之動物): *'bear-~ing;* 以狗逗熊戲; *'bull-~ing;* 以狗逗牛戲; *~ a bear with dogs.* 以狗逗熊。**4** [VP6A] torment (sb) by making cruel or insulting remarks.以辱罵之辭折磨(某人);奚落(某人)。

baize /beɪz ; bez/ *n* [U] thick woollen cloth, usu green, used for covering (tables, etc): (做桌布等用,通常爲綠色之)厚毛呢: *a '~-covered door;* 以厚毛呢覆蓋着的門; *green ~ for the billiard-table.* 鋪彈子枱用的綠色厚毛呢。

bake /beɪk ; bek/ *vt, vi* [VP6A, 22, 2A, C] **1** cook, be cooked, by dry heat in an oven: (在爐中)烤;烘;焙: *~ bread/cakes;* 烘麵包(糕餅); *~d beans.* 烘豆。*The bread is baking/being ~d.* 麵包在爐中烘着。**2** make or become hard by heating: 烤硬;燒硬: *The sun ~d the ground hard.* 太陽將地晒得堅硬。*Bricks and earthenware articles are ~d in kilns.* 磚及各種陶器是在窰中燒成的。**3** be warmed or tanned: 晒熱;晒黑: *We are baking in the sun.* 我們在晒太陽。**ˌhalf-'~d** *adj* (colloq) half-witted; lacking in experience or common sense: (俗)愚蠢的;缺乏經驗或常識的;未成熟的: *half-~d ideas;* 愚蠢的思想; *a half-~d prophet.* 缺乏經驗的預言者。**ˌbaking-'hot** *adj* very hot: 炙熱的;極熱的: *a baking-hot day.* 炎熱的一日。**'baking-powder** *n* mixture of powders used to make bubbles of gas in cakes, etc and so cause them to be light. (製糕餅等用以使其鬆軟的) 醱粉。**baker** *n* person who ~s bread, etc. 烘製麵包等的人;麵包師傅。**~r's dozen,** thirteen. 麵包師之'打'(十三個,較普通之'打'多一個)。**bak·ery** /'beɪkərɪ ; 'bekərɪ/ *n* (*pl* -ries) place where bread is ~d for many people. 麵包廠;麵包店。

bake·lite /'beɪkəlaɪt ; 'bekəˌlaɪt/ *n* [U] (P) synthetic resin compound as formerly used for old fountain pens, trays, telephones, etc. (商標)膠木;電木(合成樹脂化合物,昔時用以製自來水筆,托盤,電話機等)。

bak·sheesh /'bækʃiːʃ ; 'bækʃiʃ/ *n* [U] (in the Middle East) money given as a tip or as alms: (用於中東)小費;小帳;救濟金: *The porter expects ~ from you.* 那脚夫期待你付小費。

bala·laika /ˌbælə'laɪkə ; ˌbælə'laɪkə/ *n* (*pl* ~s) guitar-like musical instrument (triangular, with three strings), popular in Russia and other countries in eastern Europe. 巴拉拉卡琴(流行於俄國及其他東歐國家之一種類似吉他的三角形的三絃琴)。⇨ the illus at string. 參看 string 之插圖。

bal·ance¹ /'bæləns ; 'bæləns/ *vt, vi* **1** [VP6A, 14] weigh (a question, etc); compare (two objects, plans, etc) (in order to judge the relative weight, value, etc). 衡量(問題等);權衡(二物品,計畫等)(以判定輕重、價值等)。**2** [VP6A,15A] keep or put (sth, oneself) in a state of balance: 保持平衡;使平衡;使均衡: *Can you ~ a stick on the end of your nose?* 你能把一根棍子放在鼻尖上使之保持平衡嗎? *How long can you ~ (yourself) on one foot?* 你用一隻脚能站立好久? **3** [VP6A] (accounts) compare debits and credits and record the sum needed to make them equal. (帳目)結帳;平衡。***~ the budget,*** arrange for income and expenditure to be equal. 平衡預算(使收支能相抵)。[VP2A] (of the two sides of a balance-sheet) be equal: (指資產負債表上借貸雙方)相抵;平衡: *My accounts ~.* 我的帳收支相抵。**4** ***a ~d diet,*** one with the quantity and variety of food needed for good health. (維持健康所需的包括各種食物及其正確數量之)均衡飲食。

a balance

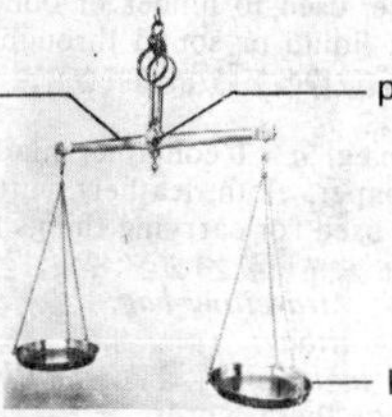

bal·ance² /'bæləns ; 'bæləns/ *n* **1** apparatus for weighing, with a central pivot, beam and two scales or pans. 天平;秤。***be/hang in the ~,*** (fig, of a result) be still uncertain: (喻,指結果)仍不一定;尚未可知;懸置未決: *For a long time his fate was in the ~.* 他的命運很久不能確定。**2** regulating apparatus of a watch or clock. (鐘錶內的)調整器;平衡器。**'~-wheel** *n* wheel, in a watch, that regulates the beat. (錶內的)平衡輪;擺輪。**3** [U] condition of being steady; condition that exists when two opposing forces are equal. 平衡狀態;均勢狀態。**checks and ~s,** ⇨ check²(1). ***hold the ~,*** have the power to decide. 有決定之權。***in the ~,*** undecided. 尚未決定的;懸而未決的。***keep one's ~,*** keep steady, remain upright: 保持平衡;保持直立: *A small child has to learn to keep its ~ before it can walk far.* 小孩在能走遠以前,必先學會保持平衡。*Don't get excited; keep your ~,* (fig) keep calm. (喻)不要衝動;保持冷靜。***lose one's ~,*** become unsteady; fall; (fig) be upset mentally: 失去平衡;傾倒;(喻)心緒紊亂: *He was surrounded by so many dangers that he lost his ~,* became nervous and upset. 他爲如此之多的危險所環繞,故心緒甚爲紊亂。***throw sb off his ~,*** upset him; cause him to fall. 使某人心情紊亂;使某人跌倒。**~ of power,** condition in which no one country or group of countries is much stronger than another. (國際間的)勢力均衡狀態。**4** [U] (in art) harmony of design and proportion: (藝術)構圖與比例之調和;調諧: *a picture lacking in ~.* 構圖與比例不調和的圖畫。**5** (accounts) difference between two columns of an account (money received and money paid out, etc). (帳目)借貸雙方的差額;收支差額;結餘。***on ~,*** taking everything into consideration. 將一切情形都考慮到。***strike a ~ (between...),*** find this difference; (fig) reach a solution or adjustment considered to be fair to all; (fig) compromise; find a middle course. 結算帳目;(喻)尋出公平的解決辦法;(喻)採折衷辦法;取中庸之道。**~ of payments,** statement (for a stated period) of the total payments to foreign countries (for imports, outflow of capital and gold) and the total receipts from foreign countries (for exports, inflow of capital and gold). 國際收支平衡表(說明在某一段期間內爲進口,資本和黃金的外流而付給外國的及爲出口,資本和黃金的流入而收自外國的全部款項)。**~ of trade,** difference in value between exports and imports. 貿易差額。**'~-sheet,** written statement of this difference, with details, showing credit and debit. 借貸對照表;資產負債表。**6** amount still owed after a part payment: (付過一部份款後之)欠款;餘額;尾款: *~ to be paid within one week.* 應於一週內付清之尾款。**7** **the ~,** (colloq) the remainder of anything; what is left. (俗)剩餘。

bal·cony /'bælkənɪ ; 'bælkənɪ/ *n* (*pl* -nies) **1** platform (with a wall or rail) built on an outside wall of a building, reached from an upstairs room. (築於外牆,與樓上一房間相通的)陽臺。**2** (in a theatre or concert hall) series of rows of seats above floor-level and (usu) rising one above the other. (US 美 = *gallery*). (戲院或音樂廳裏的)樓座(通常其座椅一排比一排高)。**bal·conied** *adj* having a ~ or balconies: 有陽臺的: *a balconied house.* 有陽臺的房子。

bald /bɔ:ld ; bɔld/ *adj* (-er, -est) **1** (of men) having no or not much hair on the scalp; (of animals) hairless; (of birds) featherless; (of trees) leafless; (of land, hills, etc) without trees or bushes. (指男人) 禿頭的 (頭頂全部或部份無髮)；(指動物) 無毛的；(指鳥類) 無羽毛的；(指樹木) 無葉的；(指土地,山丘等) 無草木的。 **2** (fig) dull; without ornament: (喻)單調的;枯燥的;無裝飾的: *a ~ style of writing;* 單調的文體；*a ~ statement of the facts,* one that gives the facts in an uninteresting way. 枯燥無味的事實陳述。 **3** '**~-head,** '**~-pate** *n* man with a ~ head. 禿頭頂的人。***go at it*** ˌ**~-'*headed,*** (colloq) attack or deal with it in a reckless manner, using all one's energy. (俗)不顧一切地盡全力去應付；硬幹；硬拚。**~·ly** *adv* (always fig): (總是作比喻用)：*speaking ~ly; to put it ~ly,* plainly, without trying to soften what one says. 直言不諱地說。**~·ness** *n*

bal·der·dash /'bɔ:ldədæʃ ; 'bɔldɚˌdæʃ/ *n* [U] foolish or meaningless talk or writing. 胡言亂語；無意義的話(或文字)。

bal·dric /'bɔ:ldrɪk ; 'bɔldrɪk/ *n* belt (passing over the right shoulder to the left hip) for a sword, bugle, horn, etc. (經過右肩至左股用以佩帶劍、號角等之) 佩帶；肩帶。

bale[1] /beɪl ; bel/ *n* [C] heap of material pressed together and tied with rope or wire: 用繩索或鐵絲緊紮在一起的一堆材料；包；捆：*~s of cloth,* (usu packed in canvas); 布捆(通常用帆布包裝)； *~s of hay,* (tied in string). 乾草捆(用繩子紮者)。□ *vt* [VP6A] make into, pack in, ~s: 使成捆；包裝成捆: *to ~ hay.* 捆乾草。

bale[2] /beɪl ; bel/ *vt* = bail[3](2). ***~ out (of),*** (of an airman) jump with a parachute from a damaged aircraft or an aircraft out of control. (指飛行員) 自損壞或失靈之飛機中跳傘降落。

bale[3] /beɪl ; bel/ *n* (old use, liter) evil. (舊用法,文)邪惡。**~·ful** /-fʊl ; -fəl/ *adj* evil; sinister, harmful: 邪惡的；兇惡的，有害的：*~ful looks／influences.* 兇惡的面容(惡勢力)。**~·fully** /-fʊlɪ ; -fəlɪ/ *adv*

balk, baulk[1] /bɔ:k ; bɔk/ *n* **1** thick, roughly squared beam of wood. 方木材；樑木。 **2** hindrance; obstacle; cause of delay. 阻碍；障碍；妨碍；遲延之原因。

balk, baulk[2] /bɔ:k ; bɔk/ *vt, vi* **1** [VP6A, 14] purposely get in the way of: 故意妨碍；阻碍；阻止：*~ sb's plans,* prevent him from carrying them out; 阻止某人的計畫(使不能實現)； *~ sb of his prey,* prevent him from getting it; 故意妨碍某人使其捕不着獵物；*be ~ed in one's purpose.* 受到妨碍達不到目的。 **2** [VP2A, 3A] ***~ (at),*** (eg of a horse) refuse to go forward; hesitate: (指馬等) 拒絕向前走；猶豫：*The horse ~ed at the high hedge.* 馬在高樹籬前面停蹄不前。*Her husband ~ed at the expense of the plans she had made.* 她丈夫對她的計畫中所需要的經費感到猶豫。

ball[1] /bɔ:l ; bɔl/ *n* **1** any solid or hollow sphere as used in games (*'base~, 'foot~, 'tennis-~, 'cricket-~,* etc). (棒球、足球、網球、板球等遊戲中所用之實心的或空心的) 球。⇨ the illus at these *nn.* 參看各名詞之插圖。***be on the ~,*** be alert, competent (in what one is doing). 小心謹愼、勝任愉快地從事(正在做的事)。***have the ~ at one's feet,*** have a good chance of attaining success. 有成功的好機會。***keep the ~ rolling,*** keep the conversation, etc going. 使談話等持續不斷。***play ~,*** (colloq) co-operate: (俗)合作: *The management refused to play ~.* 經理部拒絕合作。***start／set the ~ rolling,*** start sth, esp conversation, going. 開始；(尤指)開始談話。***The ~ is in his, etc court／with him, etc,*** The next move (in talks, etc) is his, etc. (在談話等中)下一個該輪到他(等)了。**three ~s,** pawnbroker's sign. 三球(當舖標記)。ˌ**~-'bearing(s),** bearings(5) in which friction is lessened by the use of small steel ~s; (*sing*) one of these ~s. 球軸承；滾珠軸承；(單) (滾珠軸承中之一粒) 鋼珠。 '**~(-)cock** *n* device which regulates the supply of water in a tank or cistern by means of a floating ~ which shuts or opens a valve as the water rises and falls. 球旋塞 (水箱中當水升降時藉水面浮球關閉或開啓活門以調節供水之裝置)。'**~-pen,** ˌ**~·point-'pen,** pen in which the ink flows round a ~-bearing that rotates on contact with the paper. 原子筆 (一種筆,在寫字時墨水沿着接觸紙面之旋轉小鋼珠流出)。 **2** (cricket) single delivery of the ~ by the bowler. (板球) 投手所投之一球。 ***no ~,*** delivery that breaks the rules; 犯規之投球；(baseball) any strike or throw: (棒球)任何一擊或一投: *a foul ~;* 界外球；(football) movement of the ~ by a player: (足球)傳球: *send over a high ~.* 傳一個高吊球。 **3** material gathered, rolled or wound, into a round mass: 聚成(滾成或纏成)球形之物: *a ~ of wool／string;* 一團毛線(線繩)；*a 'snow~;* 雪球；*a 'meat~,* of minced meat. (用碎肉團成的)肉丸子。 **4** metal missile to be fired from a gun: 砲彈；彈丸：*'cannon-~,* (old fashioned, cf *shell*). 砲彈(舊式用語，參較 shell)。'**~-cartridge,** one containing a bullet (contrasted with *blank cartridge*). 實彈(與 blank cartridge 相對)。 **5** round part: 圓形部份: *the ~ of the thumb,* near the palm, ⇨ the illus at arm; 大拇指之近手掌部份(參看 arm 之插圖)；*the ~ of the foot,* near the base of the big toe, ⇨ the illus at leg. 脚掌近大拇趾根部份(參看 leg 之插圖)。 **6** ⚠ (sl) testicle. (諱) (俚) 睪丸。 □ *int* ⚠ **~s!** (sl) Nonsense! (諱) (俚) 胡說！ □ *vi, vt* **1** form into a ~: 形成球形: *The snow ~ed under the horse's feet.* 雪在馬蹄下積成球形。 **2** wind or squeeze into a ~. 纏繞或捏成球形。 **3** ***~s sth up,*** (sl) make a mess of it. (俚)將某事物弄成一團糟。Hence, 由此產生，**~s-up** *n* mess. 雜亂。

ball[2] /bɔ:l ; bɔl/ *n* social gathering for dancing, with an organized programme, and (often) special entertainment. (節目事先安排好並常附有特別表演之) 舞會。'**~-dress,** woman's frock to be worn at ~s. 婦女於參加舞會時所穿之長禮服。 '**~·room,** large room for ~s. 跳舞廳。

bal·lad /'bæləd ; 'bæləd/ *n* simple song or poem, esp one that tells an old story. 民歌；民謠；(尤指) 敍事歌。

bal·lade /bæ'lɑ:d ; bə'lɑd/ *n* [C] **1** poem of one or more stanzas, each with 7, 8 or 10 lines, each ending with the same refrain line, followed by an envoy. 聯韻詩(通常爲三節，每節七行、八行或十行，每節皆以同一重疊句收尾，最後爲煞尾的短節)。**2** musical composition of a romantic nature. 浪漫曲；敍事曲。

bal·last /'bæləst ; 'bæləst/ *n* [U] **1** heavy material (eg rock, iron, sand) loaded into a ship to keep it steady. (船中所裝用以保持平衡之) 壓艙物(如石、鐵、砂)。***in ~,*** carrying ~ only. 僅裝壓艙物的。**2** sand or other material carried in a balloon, to be thrown out to make the balloon go higher. 壓載物(輕氣球所携，於欲使氣球昇得更高時可以拋棄之砂或其他物質)。 **3** (fig) mental stability. (喻)心理之穩定。 **4** gravel, crushed rock, etc used to make a foundation for a road, esp a railway. (鋪路基，尤指鋪鐵道道床，所用的)碎石。 □ *vt* [VP6A] supply with ~. 供應壓艙物、壓載物或碎石。

bal·ler·ina /ˌbælə'ri:nə ; ˌbælə'rinə/ *n* (*pl* ~s) (I) woman ballet-dancer, esp one who takes one of the chief classical roles. (義) 芭蕾舞女演員；(尤指) 芭蕾舞女主角。

bal·let /'bæleɪ ; 'bæle/ *n* **1** [C] dramatic performance, without dialogue or singing, illustrating a story by a group of dancers. 芭蕾舞劇(無對話，無歌唱，由一群舞者以動作敍述故事之表演)。 **2** [U] the dancers: 芭蕾舞劇演員之總稱: *a member* *of the* ～. 芭蕾舞團之一演員。 **3** [U] **the** ～, this kind of stage performance as an art. 芭蕾舞藝術。 '～**-dancer**, person who dances in ～s. 芭蕾舞劇演員。 '～**-skirt**, short skirt worn by a ～-dancer. 芭蕾舞裙(跳芭蕾舞者所穿之短裙)。

bal·lis·tic /bə'lɪstɪk ; bæ'lɪstɪk/ *adj* of projectiles: 拋射物的;彈道的: *intercontinental* ～ *missile* **(ICBM)**, long-range rocket for use in war. 洲際彈道飛彈(略作 ICBM)。 **bal·lis·tics** *n* (usu with *sing v*) study, science, of projectiles. (通常與單數動詞連用)彈道學。

bal·locks /'bɒləks ; 'bɑləks/ *n pl* ⚠ (vulg) (諱) (鄙) **1** testicles. 睪丸。 **2** nonsense. 胡說。

bal·loon /bə'lu:n ; bə'lun/ *n* **1** bag or envelope filled with air, or with gas lighter than air: 氣球: *captive* ～, one moored to the ground. 固定在地上的氣球; 繫留氣球。 '～ **barrage**, barrier of steel cables, supported by captive ～s, intended to give protection against low-flying enemy aircraft. 繫留氣球幕;氣球阻塞幕(用氣球支懸於空中以對抗低飛敵機之鋼絲障碍物)。 '**barrage** ～, one of these captive ～s. 阻塞氣球;障礙氣球。 **hot-'air** ～, apparatus for travel in the air with a basket or car (for the passengers, etc) suspended beneath a large bag of hot gas. 熱氣氣球(在充滿熱氣體的大袋下懸掛一籃或座艙以供人乘坐的航空器)。 '～ **tyre**, low-pressure pneumatic tyre of great width. 寬型之低壓充氣輪胎。 **2** (in a strip cartoon, etc) outline for dialogue, exclamations, etc. (連環漫畫等中供寫出對話,呼喊等的)氣球狀線圈。 □ *vi* [VP2A, C] swell out like a ～. 膨脹如氣球。 ～**·ist** *n* person who goes up in ～s. 乘氣球者。

balloons

bal·lot /'bælət ; 'bælət/ *n* **1** [C] piece of paper (also 亦作 '～*-paper*), ticket or ball, used in secret voting; [U] secret voting; [C] instance of this. (秘密投票所用之)選舉票(用紙製者,亦有用球者);秘密投票。 ***take a*** ～, decide by voting. 投票決定。 **2** votes so recorded. 投票總數。 '～**-box**, box into which ～-papers are dropped by voters. 投票箱;票匭。 □ *vi* [VP2A, 3A] ～ ***(for)***, give a vote; draw lots. 投票;投(…一)票;抽籤;拈鬮。

bally /'bælɪ ; 'bælɪ/ *adj, adv* (GB dated sl, euphem for *bloody*(3)) (used to show the speaker's strong feelings of like or dislike, etc): (英,過時俚語,為 bloody(3) 之委婉語) 甚; 很; 極(用以表示說話者極度之喜愛或憎惡): *What a* ～ *nuisance!* 多麼令人討厭呵！可厭透了！

bally·hoo /ˌbælɪ'hu: *US:* 'bælɪhu: ; 'bælɪˌhu/ *n* [U] (colloq) (俗) **1** noisy publicity or advertising; vulgar or misleading ways of attracting attention. 大吹大擂;大肆宣傳。 **2** uproar. 喧囂;叫鬧。

balm /bɑ:m ; bɑm/ *n* [U] **1** sweet-smelling oil or ointment obtained from certain kinds of trees, used for soothing pain or healing. (取自某些種樹中,用以止痛或療傷之)香油;香膏;香膠。 **2** (fig) that which gives peace of mind; consolation. (喻)慰藉物;慰藉;安慰。 ～**y** *adj* **1** (of air) soft and warm. (指空氣)溫暖的;暖和的。 **2** healing; fragrant. 能治療的;芳香的。 **3** (sl) (俚) = barmy.

bal·oney /bə'ləʊnɪ ; bə'lonɪ/ *n* = boloney.

balsa /'bɔ:lsə ; 'bɔlsə/ *n* [C, U] (light-weight wood of a) tropical American tree; raft of floats fastened to a framework: 白塞樹(產於熱帶美洲); 白塞木(白塞樹的輕質木材); (用白塞木紮於架上而成的)筏: (attrib) (形容用法) *a* ～ *raft*. 白塞木筏。

bal·sam /'bɔ:lsəm ; 'bɔlsəm/ *n* **1** = balm(1). **2** tree yielding balm. 香油樹;香膏樹;香膠樹。 **3** flowering plant grown in gardens. 鳳仙花。

bal·us·ter /'bæləstə(r) ; 'bæləstə/ *n* one of the upright posts supporting a handrail; (*pl*) banisters. 扶手欄杆的支柱; (複) 樓梯外側之扶手欄杆。

bal·us·trade /ˌbælə'streɪd ; ˌbælə'stred/ *n* row of balusters with the stonework or woodwork that joins them on top, round a balcony, terrace, flat roof, etc. (圍繞於陽台、平台、平屋頂等之)欄杆。

bam·bino /bæm'bi:nəʊ ; bæm'bino/ *n* (*pl* ～s) (I) (義) **1** baby. 嬰孩;嬰兒。 **2** representation in art of the infant Jesus. 耶穌幼時之像。

bam·boo /bæm'bu: ; bæm'bu/ *n* [U] tall plant with hard, hollow, jointed stems, of the grass family; [C] (*pl* ～s) stem, used as a stick or support. 竹;竹竿;竹棍。

bam·boozle /bæm'bu:zl ; bæm'buzl̩/ *vt* (colloq) (俗) [VP6A, 14] **1** mystify: 使困惑;使迷惑: *You can't* ～ *me.* 你不能使我迷惑。 **2** ～ ***sb (into／out of) (doing) (sth)***, trick, cheat him. 哄某人使(不)做某事;欺騙某人。

ban /bæn ; bæn/ *vt* (-nn-) **1** [VP6A] order with authority that sth must not be done, said, etc: 下令禁止;查禁: *a ban-the-bomb demonstration*, one calling for nuclear disarmament. 要求裁減核子武器之示威。 *The play was banned by the censor.* 該劇本被新聞檢查員查禁。 **2** [VP6A, 14] ～ ***sb (from) (doing) (sth)***, order with authority that sb may not do sth: 禁止(某人做某事): *He was* ～*ned from (attending) the meeting.* 他被禁止出席該會議。 □ *n* (also 亦作 '～**ning-order**) order that bans sth／sb: 禁令: *under a ban*, banned. 被查禁;被禁止。

ba·nal /bə'nɑ:l *US:* 'beɪnl ; 'benl/ *adj* commonplace; uninteresting: 平凡的;無趣味的: ～ *remarks.* 平凡的話。 ～**·ity** /bə'nælətɪ ; bə'nælətɪ/ *n* [U] quality of being ～; [C] (*pl* -ties) ～ remark, etc: 平凡;無趣;平凡的話等: *conversation that was chiefly* ～*ities.* 內容大半平凡的談話。

ba·nana /bə'nɑ:nə *US:* bə'nænə ; bə'nænə/ *n* [C] long, thick-skinned (yellow when ripe) fruit growing in bunches on the ～-tree in tropical and semi-tropical countries. 香蕉(產於熱帶及亞熱帶之長形水果,成串生長,果皮厚,成熟時變黃色)。 ⇨ the illus at fruit. 參看 fruit 之插圖。 ⇨ plantain¹.

band /bænd ; bænd/ *n* **1** flat, thin strip of material, esp for fastening things together or for placing round an object to strengthen it: 帶;箍: *iron* ～*s round a barrel;* 箍於桶外之鐵箍; *papers kept together with a rubber* ～. 用橡皮圈束在一起之文件。 '～**-saw** *n* (eng) machine-driven saw consisting of an endless steel belt. (工程)帶鋸(機器推動的鋸,由一條鋼環帶所組成)。 **2** flat, thin strip of material forming part of an article of clothing: (構成衣服一部份之)扁平的薄條帶: *Some shirts have a 'neck*～ *and two 'wrist*～*s.* 有些襯衫有一個領子和兩個袖口。 **3** strip or line, different from the rest in colour or design, on sth: (顏色或圖案與其餘部份不同之)條紋;條飾: *a white plate with a blue* ～ *round the edge.* 有一道藍邊的白盤。 **4** group of persons doing sth together under a leader and with a common purpose: 一隊;一組;一夥;一幫: *a* ～ *of robbers／*

fugitives/revellers. 一夥强盜(逃亡者，宴樂者)。 **5** group of persons who play music together, eg of wind-instrument performers (often 常作 *brass* ~): 樂隊；軍樂隊；管樂隊: *the ˌRegimental ˈB~;* 團部軍樂隊；*a ˈdance ~;* 舞蹈之伴奏樂隊；*a ˈjazz ~;* 爵士樂隊；*a ˈsteel ~.* 鋼鐵油桶樂隊(千里達等加勒比海國家特有之樂隊，以截成各種高度之油桶爲打樂器)。 **ˈ~·master** /ˈbændmɑːstə(r) ; ˈbændˌmæstɚ/ *n* conductor of a ~. 樂隊指揮。 **ˈ~s·man** /-mən ; -mən/ *n* (*pl* -men) member of a ~. 樂隊隊員。 **ˈ~·stand** /ˈbændstænd ; ˈbændˌstænd/ *n* raised platform usu roofed, for a ~ playing in the open air. (通常有頂之)露天音樂演奏臺。 **ˈ~·wagon** *n* wagon carrying the ~ heading a march or procession (esp of a political party). (爲遊行隊伍開道的)樂隊車(尤指屬於政黨之遊行隊伍者)。 ***climb/jump on/aboard the ~wagon,*** join in what seems likely to be a successful enterprise. 加入大有成功希望之事業。 **6** (radio; short for *ˈwave-~*) range of frequencies that may be tuned in together: (無線電; wave-band 之略)頻帶; 波段: *the 19-metre ~.* 十九公尺之頻帶。 □ *vt, vi* **1** [VP6A] put a ~, strip or line on. 加帶或條紋於…之上；用帶綁紮。 **2** [VP15B, 14, 2C] ~ ***together/with,*** unite in a group: 結夥; 結隊; 結合: ~ *people together;* 把人們結合起來；~ *with others to do sth.* 夥同他人做某事。*They ~ed together to protest.* 他們聯合抗議。

ban·dage /ˈbændɪdʒ ; ˈbændɪdʒ/ *n* strip of material for binding round a wound or injury, or for blindfolding sb. (包紮傷口之)繃帶；蒙眼巾。□ *vt* [VP6A, 15B] ~ ***(up),*** tie up with a ~: 用繃帶包紮；縛以繃帶: ~ *(up) a boy's leg;* 用繃帶將一男孩之腿包紮起來；*a man with a ~d hand.* 一隻手包了繃帶的人。

band-aid /ˈbændeɪd ; ˈbændˌed/ *n* [C, U] (P) (US) type of plaster(3). (商標)(美)一種橡皮膏；一種絆創膏。

ban·danna /bænˈdænə ; bænˈdænə/ *n* brightly coloured square of material with red or yellow spots, usu worn round the neck. (顏色鮮艷，帶紅色或黃色斑點，通常用以圍脖子的)方巾；絲巾。

band·box /ˈbændbɒks ; ˈbændˌbɑks/ *n* light, cardboard box for millinery: (裝女帽等之輕的)硬紙盒: *She looks as if she had just come out of a ~,* She looks extremely smart and neat. 她看起來極爲整潔漂亮。

ban·deau /ˈbændəʊ *US:* -ˈdəʊ ; bænˈdo/ *n* (*pl* -deaux /-dəʊz *US:* -ˈdəʊz ; -ˈdoz/) band for keeping a woman's hair in place. (女用之)束髮帶。

ban·dit /ˈbændɪt ; ˈbændɪt/ *n* robber, one of an armed band (eg of brigands attacking travellers in forests or mountains or, today, banks and offices). 土匪；强盜；刼匪。 **~ry** *n* [U] activity of ~s. 匪盜之行爲。

ban·do·leer, ban·do·lier /ˌbændəˈlɪə(r) ; ˌbændəˈlɪr/ *n* shoulder-belt with pockets for cartridges. (背於肩上之)子彈帶。

bandy[1] /ˈbændɪ ; ˈbændɪ/ *vt* (*pt, pp* -died) [VP6A, 14, 15B] exchange (words, blows). 爭吵；互毆。 ***have one's name bandied about,*** be talked about in an unfavourable way, be a subject for gossip. 受人批評；遭人物議。~ ***a story about,*** pass it from person to person. 傳播是非。~ ***words with sb,*** exchange remarks quickly, esp when quarrelling. 與某人爭吵。

bandy[2] /ˈbændɪ ; ˈbændɪ/ *adj* (of the legs) curving outwards at the knees. (指腿)膝部向外彎曲的。 **ˈ~-legged** *adj* (of persons or animals) having ~ legs. (指人或動物)有膝部外彎之腿的。

bane /beɪn ; ben/ *n* [U] **1** (only in compounds) poison: (僅用於複合字中)毒藥: *ˈrat's-~.* 毒鼠藥；殺鼠藥。 **2** cause of ruin or trouble: 禍根；禍害；麻煩的起因；累贅: *Drink was the ~ of his life.* 酒是毁他一生的禍根。 *He has been the ~ of my life,* caused me constant trouble and anxiety. 他是我一生的累贅。 **~·ful** /-fʊl ; -fəl/ *adj* evil: 不良的；有害的: *a ~ful influence.* 不良的影響。 **~·fully** /-fʊlɪ ; -fəlɪ/ *adv*

bang[1] /bæŋ ; bæŋ/ *n* violent blow; sudden, loud noise: 猛擊；猛撞；碰撞的聲音；突然的巨響；砰: *He fell and got a nasty ~ on the head.* 他跌了一跤，頭碰得很厲害。 *He always shuts the door with a ~.* 他關門總是砰然一聲。*The firework went off with a ~.* 煙火砰一聲射出了。 ***go (off) with a ~,*** (GB colloq) (英俗)；***go (over) with a ~,*** (US colloq) (美俗) (of a performance, etc) be successful, be greatly liked. (指表演等)極爲成功；大受歡迎。□ *vt, vi* **1** [VP6A, 15B, 2A, C] hit violently; give a ~ to; shut with a noise: 猛擊；砰然而擊；砰然關上: *He ~ed at the door.* 他砰砰地用力敲門。*He was ~ing on the door with his fist.* 他用拳頭猛敲門。*He ~ed his fist on the table.* 他用拳頭捶打桌子。*She ~ed the keys of the piano.* 她用力敲鋼琴鍵。*The teacher tried to ~ grammar into the heads of his pupils.* 那老師想把文法硬塞入學生的腦中。*Don't ~ the lid down.* 不要將蓋子砰然蓋上。*He ~ed the box down on the floor.* 他砰然一聲將盒子摔在地上。*A door was ~ing somewhere.* 什麼地方有一扇門砰然作響。*The door ~ed shut.* 門砰然一聲關上。 **2** [VP2A, C] make a loud noise: 發巨響；作噼啪聲；作隆隆聲: *The fireworks ~ed.* 煙火發出巨響。*The guns ~ed away.* 槍砲不斷地發出巨響。*We were ~ing away* (= firing continuously) *at the enemy.* 我們砰砰地不斷向敵人射擊。*Tell the children to stop ~ing about,* being noisy. 告訴孩子們不要到處弄出聲響。□ *adv, int: go ~,* burst with a loud noise; 發出砰然或轟然一聲巨響; ~ *in the middle,* exactly in the middle; 恰恰在中間；在正當中; *come ~ up* (= violently) *against sth.* 重重地碰撞在某物上。

bang[2] /bæŋ ; bæŋ/ *vt* cut (the front hair) squarely across the forehead: 將(額前髮)剪成劉海(即橫着剪齊): *She wears her hair ~ed.* 她的頭髮留有劉海。□ *n* [C] fringe of ~ed hair. 劉海型之前額垂髮。

banger /ˈbæŋə(r) ; ˈbæŋɚ/ *n* (sl) (俚) **1** sausage. 臘腸；香腸。 **2** noisy firework. (發巨響的)爆竹。 **3** old dilapidated car. 破爛的老爺車。

bangle /ˈbæŋgl ; ˈbæŋgl/ *n* ornamental rigid band worn round the arm or ankle. 手鐲；脚鐲。

ban·ian, ban·yan /ˈbænɪən ; ˈbænjən/ *n* **1** Hindu trader. 印度商人。 **2** (also 亦作 **ˈ~-tree**) Indian fig, whose branches come down to the ground and take root. 榕樹(樹枝垂至地上即可生根)。

ban·ish /ˈbænɪʃ ; ˈbænɪʃ/ *vt* [VP6A, 14] **1** ~ ***(from),*** send away, esp out of the country, as a punishment: 放逐；(尤指)驅逐出境: *He was ~ed from the realm.* 他被驅逐出境。 **2** put away from, out of (the mind): (自腦中)驅除；排除；忘却: ~ *care.* 消除煩憂。 **~·ment** *n* [U] state of being ~ed: 被放逐或驅除的狀態: *go into ~ment.* 被驅逐出境；被放逐。

ban·is·ter /ˈbænɪstə(r) ; ˈbænɪstɚ/ *n* post supporting the handrail of a staircase; (*pl*) posts and handrail together. 支持樓梯扶手的支柱；(複)樓梯的扶手及欄杆。

banjo /ˈbændʒəʊ ; ˈbændʒo/ *n* (*pl* ~s, ~es) musical instrument played by plucking the strings with the fingers. 班究琴。⇨ the illus at string. 參看 string 之插圖。

bank[1] /bæŋk ; bæŋk/ *n* [C] **1** land along each side of a river or canal; ground near a river: 河岸: *A river flows between its ~s.* 河水在兩岸之間流。*His house is on the south ~ of the river.* 他的房子是在河的南岸。 **2** sloping land or earth, often forming a border or division: 斜坡；土堤；埂(常構成一條界線或區分線): *low ~s of earth between rice-fields.* 稻田與稻田之間的低矮的田埂。*There were flowers growing on the ~s on each side of the country lanes.* 鄉村小道兩側之斜坡上長有花。 **3** (also 亦作 **ˈsand·~**) part of the sea-bed higher than its surroundings, but covered with enough water for ships except at low tide; (mining) coal-face. (海中的)淺灘;沙洲;(採礦)煤層中的採掘面。**4** flat-topped mass of cloud, snow, etc esp one formed by the wind: 狀似堤岸之雲堆、雪堆等(尤指爲風所吹成者): *The sun went down behind a ~ of clouds.* 太陽在雲堤後面落下去了。 **5** artificial slope made to enable a car to go round a curve with less risk. 公路上在彎路處便於汽車轉彎所作之傾斜面。

bank[2] /bæŋk ; bæŋk/ *vt, vi* **1** [VP6A, 15B, 2C] **~ *up*, (a)** make or form into ~s, ⇨ 4 above: 形成堤狀;(使)堆積(參看上列第4義): *The snow has ~ed up.* 雪已堆成了雪堤。 **(b)** stop water (of a river, etc) from flowing by making a ~ of earth, mud, etc. 築堤防堵(河等之)水。**(c)** heap up (the fire in a fireplace or furnace) with coal-dust, etc so that the fire burns slowly for a long time. 以煤灰等堆在(爐火)上,使其燃燒得慢,維持得久;封(爐火)。 **2** [VP2A] (of a motor-car or aircraft) travel with one side higher than the other (eg when turning). (指汽車或飛機)傾斜行進或飛行(如在轉彎時)。

bank[3] /bæŋk ; bæŋk/ *n* **1** establishment for keeping money and valuables safely, the money being paid out on the customer's order (by means of cheques). 銀行。 **the B~,** the B~ of England, which is used by the British Government; 英國國家銀行;英格蘭銀行; *have money in the ~,* have savings; 銀行中有存款; **'~** *clerk,* clerk working in a ~. 銀行辦事員。 **'~-bill** *n* bill drawn by one ~ upon another ~. 銀行滙票。 **'~-book** *n* (also 亦作 *'pass-book*) book containing a record of a customer's account. 銀行存摺。 **'~ draft,** = *~bill.* **,~ 'holiday** *n* (GB) one of those days (not Sundays) on which ~s are closed by law, usu kept as general holidays (eg Good Friday, Easter Monday, Christmas Day); (US) any weekday on which ~s are closed. (英)(除星期日以外的)法定銀行假日(如耶穌受難節,復活節之次日,聖誕節);(美)任何星期日以外之銀行假日。 **'~-note** *n* piece of paper money issued by a ~. (銀行所發行的)鈔票。**'~-rate** *n* rate at which the B~ of England (or other national ~) will discount bills, ⇨ bill[3](5). 英國國家銀行(或其他國家銀行)之票據貼現率。 **'~-roll** *n* roll of paper money. 鈔票捲。 **2** (gambling) sum of money held by the keeper of the gaming table, from which he pays his losses. (賭博)莊家的賭本。 ***break the ~,*** (eg at Monte Carlo) win all this money. (例如在蒙地卡羅)贏得莊家的全部賭本。 **3** (place for storing) reserve supplies. 儲備之供應品;儲蓄所;庫。 **'blood ~** *n* place where blood or blood plasma is stored for use in hospitals, etc. 血庫(儲備血液或血漿以供醫院等使用的地方)。

bank[4] /bæŋk ; bæŋk/ *vt, vi* **1** [VP6A] place (money) in a bank[3](1): 存(款)於銀行: *He ~s half his salary every month.* 他將每月薪水的一半存於銀行。 **2** [VP3A] **~ *(with)*,** keep money in a bank: 在銀行中有存款: *Who do you ~ with,* With what firm of bankers do you keep your money? 你在哪一家銀行存款? *Where do you ~?* 你在何處(哪一家銀行)存款? **3** [VP3A] **~ *on/upon*,** base one's hopes on: 指望;依靠: *I'm ~ing on your help.* 我指望着你的幫助。 **~er** *n* person who owns, is a partner in, or is a governor or director of, a bank[3](1); (gambling) keeper of a bank[3](2). 銀行家;經營銀行業務者;(賭場)莊家。 **'~er's card,** card (issued by a bank) that guarantees the payment of a customer's cheque (up to a certain amount). 銀行保證卡(保證替顧客支付高達某一數額之支票)。 **,~er's 'order,** = *standing order.* ⇨ standing(1).. **~ing** *n* [U] the business of keeping a bank[3](1): 銀行業: *choose ~ing as a career;* 選擇銀行業爲職業; *~ing hours,* eg 10am to 3.30pm. 銀行營業時間(如上午十時至下午三時半)。

bank[5] /bæŋk ; bæŋk/ *n* **1** row of keys, switches, etc: 一排鍵;鍵座;一排開關: *a three-~/four-~ typewriter.* 一架三排鍵(四排鍵)之打字機。 **2** bench for rowers in a galley(1). (古希臘羅馬戰艦中)划手坐的長橈。 **3** row of cylinders (in an engine). (引擎中的)汽缸排列。

bank·rupt /ˈbæŋkrʌpt ; ˈbæŋkrʌpt/ *n* (legal) person judged by a law court to be unable to pay his debts in full, his property being distributed for the benefit of his creditors. (法律)(經法院宣告之)破產者(即無力償清債務,以其財產分配給債權人)。□ *adj* **1** unable to pay one's debts. 無力還債的;破產的。 ***go ~,*** become ~, insolvent. 無力還債;破產。 **2 ~ *in/of*,** completely without: 完全缺乏: *The newspapers accused the Government of being ~ in ideas.* 報紙指控政府完全缺乏主意。□ *vt* [VP6A] make ~. 使破產。 **~cy** /ˈbæŋkrəpsɪ ; ˈbæŋkrʌptsɪ/ *n* [U] ~ condition; [C] (*pl* -cies) instance of this: 破產;倒閉: *There were ten ~cies in the town last year.* 本市去年有十家破產。

ban·ner /ˈbænə(r) ; ˈbænɚ/ *n* **1** flag (now chiefly fig): 旗幟(現主要作比喻用法): *the ~ of freedom.* 自由的旗幟。 ***under the ~ (of)*,** belonging to, supporting (a particular faith or movement). 在…的旗幟下(卽屬於或擁護某一信仰或運動)。 **2** flag or announcement, usu on two poles, carried in (eg religious or political) processions, making known principles, slogans, etc. 書有標語或口號之大旗(通常用兩根竿子擧起,執於宗敎或政治遊行的行列中)。 **~ headline,** (in a newspaper) prominent headline in large type. (報紙中)大號字體的顯著標題。

ban·nis·ter *n* = banister.

ban·nock /ˈbænək ; ˈbænək/ *n* (Scot and N England) flat, oatmeal, home-made loaf. (蘇格蘭及北英格蘭)用燕麥片自製的一種薄餅。

banns /bænz ; bænz/ *n pl* public announcement in church that two persons are to be married: (敎堂裏的)結婚預告: *put up/publish the ~;* 公佈結婚預告; *have one's ~ called.* 請求公佈結婚預告。 ***forbid the ~,*** declare opposition to a proposed marriage. 宣佈反對所預告之婚姻。

ban·quet /ˈbæŋkwɪt ; ˈbæŋkwɪt/ *n* elaborate meal, usu for a special event, at which speeches are made: (通常爲某一特殊事件所擧行之)正式宴會(會中並有演講者): *a 'wedding ~.* 結婚喜宴。□ *vt, vi* [VP 6A] give a ~ to (sb); [VP2A] take part in a ~; feast. 宴請(某人);參加宴會;飲宴。

ban·shee /bænˈʃiː *US:* ˈbænʃiː ; ˈbænʃi/ *n* (Ireland and the Scottish Highlands) spirit whose cry is said to mean that there will be a death in the house where the cry is heard. (愛爾蘭及蘇格蘭高地)(據說誰家聽到其哭聲就預示誰家將有人死亡之)妖精。

bant /bænt ; bænt/ *vi* [VP2A] (dated) adopt a diet designed to reduce weight (*slim* and *reduce* are the usu words). (過時用語)節食以減輕體重(通常用slim及reduce)。 **~·ing** *n* treatment of obesity by this means. 磐汀氏療法;節食減肥法。

ban·tam /ˈbæntəm ; ˈbæntəm/ *n* **1** small-sized kind of domestic fowl, esp the cock, which is a fighter. 一種矮小的鷄(尤指公鷄,被畜作鬥鷄)。 **2** boxer between 112 and 118 lb. 雛量級拳擊手(體重自112磅至118磅之間者)。

ban·ter /ˈbæntə(r) ; ˈbæntɚ/ *vt, vi* [VP6A, 2A] tease in a playful way (by joking talk). 嘲弄;戲謔;開玩笑。□ *n* [U] good-humoured teasing. 嘲弄;戲謔;開玩笑。 **~·ing** *adj* **~·ing·ly** *adv*

Ban·tu /bænˈtuː *US:* ˈbæntuː ; ˈbænˈtu/ *adj, n* (member) of a group of related Central and S African peoples; of their languages. 班圖人(居於非洲中部及南部);班圖語;班圖人的;班圖語的。

ban·yan *n* = banian.

bao·bab /ˈbeɪəbæb *US:* ˈbaʊbæb ; ˈbeo,bæb/ *n* tree of tropical Africa with a trunk that grows to an enormous size. 猢猻麵(產於熱帶非洲之一種巨樹)。

bap·tism /ˈbæptɪzəm; ˈbæptɪzəm/ *n* **1** [U] ceremony of sprinkling sb with, or immersing sb in, water, accepting him as a member of the Christian Church and (usu) giving him a name or names (in addition to the family name); [C] instance of this: 浸禮;洗禮(洒水於某人或將某人浸於水中,以示准許其爲基督教徒,通常並授予教名);浸禮或洗禮之實例: *There were six ~s at this church last week.* 此教堂於上週曾爲六人施洗禮。 **2** (fig) first experience of a new kind of life: (喻)一種新生活的初次經驗: *a soldier's ~ of fire,* his first experience of warfare. 一兵士初次臨戰之經驗。 **bap·tis·mal** /bæp'tɪzməl ; bæp'tɪzml/ *adj* of ~: 洗禮的;浸禮的: *~al name/water/font.* 洗禮名(水,盆)。

Bap·tist /'bæptɪst ; 'bæptɪst/ *n, adj* (member) of the denomination of Christians who object to infant baptism and believe that baptism should be by immersion and at an age when a person is old enough to understand the meaning of the ceremony. 浸信會教友(反對嬰兒受洗,認爲洗禮應用浸水法施行,並且在一個人長大足以瞭解其意義時施行);浸信會的。

bap·tize /bæp'taɪz ; bæp'taɪz/ *vt* [VP6A, 23] give baptism to (sb): 給(某人)施洗禮: *He had been ~d a Roman Catholic.* 他曾受洗爲天主教徒。

bar¹ /bɑ:(r) ; bɑr/ *n* **1** long piece of hard, stiff material (eg metal, wood, soap, chocolate). 棒;條(如金屬、木、肥皂、巧克力糖)。 **2** rod or rail, rigid length of wood or metal, across a door, window or gate, or forming part of a grate (in a fireplace or furnace) or grid: 橫槓;門窗之閂;(爐架或鐵柵上的)鐵條: *He was placed behind prison bars,* put into a prison cell. 他被關在監牢裏。 **3** barrier (across a road) that could not be passed (in former times) until a sum of money (called a *toll*) was paid: (昔日橫在道路上俟納稅後始准通行之)障碍物;稅卡門: *a toll bar.* 稅卡門。 **4** bank or ridge of sand, etc across the mouth of a river or the entrance to a bay, deposited by currents or tides, often hindering navigation: (河口或海灣之入口處由於流水或潮汐所造成常妨碍航行的) 沙洲: *The ship crossed the bar safely.* 這船安全地渡過沙洲。 *We stuck fast on the bar.* 我們牢牢地擱淺在沙洲上。 **5** (fig) barrier or obstacle; sth that hinders or stops progress: (喻)障碍;阻碍物: *Poor health may be a bar to success in life.* 健康不佳可能成爲一生中事業成功的障碍。 *Poverty is not always a bar to happiness.* 貧窮不一定是幸福的障碍。 **6** narrow band (of colour, light, etc): (色、光等之)帶;條;紋: *As the sun went down, there was a bar of red across the western sky.* 日落時,西方天際有一道紅暉。 **7** strip of metal across the ribbon of (esp a military) medal to indicate either 獎章或勳章之飾帶上的金屬橫條,表示 **(a)** that the holder has received the same award twice, 佩帶者兩次獲得同樣的功勳, or **(b)** that he has served in a particular field of operations. 佩帶者曾參與某一戰區作戰。 **8** (in music) vertical line across the stave marking divisions of equal value in time; one of these divisions and the notes in it: (音樂) (樂譜上劃分各小節的) 小節線;小節: *the opening bars of the National Anthem.* 國歌開頭的數小節。 ⇨ the illus at notation. 參看 notation 之插圖。 **9** railing or barrier in a law court, separating the part where the business is carried on from the part for spectators: 法庭上將審訊場所與旁聽席隔開的欄杆: *be tried at (the) Bar,* be tried in open court, where everyone may see and hear, not secretly. 受公開審訊。 ***the prisoner at the bar,*** the accused person. 被告。 **10** (in Parliament) railing dividing off the space to which non-members are admitted (eg for examination by members); similar place in the US Senate, House of Representatives and State Legislatures. 英國國會中區劃非議員席之欄杆(即非議員席);(美國參議院、衆議院及州議會中的)非議員席。 **11** (fig) sth that can be compared to a judge or examiner: (喻)可比做法官或審問者之事物;制裁: *at the bar of public opinion;* 輿論的制裁; *the bar of conscience.* 良心的制裁。 **12 the Bar,** the profession of barrister; all those who have the right to act as barristers. 律師業;律師界。 ***be called to the Bar,*** be received as a member of the Bar. 被接受充當律師;獲得律師資格。 ***read for the Bar,*** study to become a barrister. 讀法律;習法。 **13** **(a)** (in an inn or public house) room, counter, where drinks (such as beer and spirits) are served: (客棧或酒館裏的) 酒吧間;賣酒櫃臺;吧臺;酒吧: *the Public Bar,* 大衆酒吧間, *the Private Bar,* for different classes of users. 私用酒吧間(供不同階級使用者)。 **(b)** (in a hotel, licensed restaurant or private house) room with such a counter. (旅館、有執照之餐館或私家之)酒吧間。 **'bar·maid** *n* woman who serves drinks at a bar(13). 酒吧女侍者。 **'bar·man** /-mən ; -mən/ *n* (*pl* -men) man who does this. 酒吧男侍者。 **'bar·ten·der** *n* barmaid or barman. 酒吧招待;酒吧侍者。 **14** counter at which meals, etc are served and also eaten: 飲食販賣部;簡便飲食櫃臺: *a 'milk bar;* 牛奶販賣部; *a quick-lunch bar.* 午間快餐櫃臺。

bar² /bɑ:(r) ; bɑr/ *vt* (-rr-) **1** [VP6A] fasten (a door, gate, etc) with a bar or bars¹(2). 閂(門等)。 **2** [VP15B] keep (sb) in or out: 把(某人)關在裏面或外面: *He barred himself in,* fastened doors, windows, etc so that no one could enter the building. 他把自己關在房子裏面(使外人不能進入)。 **3** [VP6A] obstruct: 擋塞;阻碍: *bar a road/path.* 擋住路。 *Soldiers barred the way and we couldn't go any farther.* 軍隊擋住路,我們不能再往前走。 **4** [VP6A, 14] ***bar (from),*** prohibit: 禁止: *bar sb from a competition,* order that he shall not take part. 禁止某人參加比賽。 [VP6C] (colloq) (俗): *She bars smoking in the drawing-room,* does not permit it. 她禁止在客廳裏吸烟。 *We bar playing cards for money.* 我們禁止玩紙牌賭錢。 [VP12C] *I will bar no honest man my house,* will let any honest man visit my house. 我不阻止任何誠實的人到我家裏來。 **5** [VP6A] (usu passive) mark with a stripe or stripes: (通常用被動語態)飾以條紋: *a sky barred with clouds.* 有條狀雲的天空。

bar³ /bɑ:(r) ; bɑr/, **bar·ring** /'bɑ:rɪŋ ; 'bɑrɪŋ/ *prep* (colloq) except: (俗)除…以外;除非;若無: *We shall arrive at noon barring accidents,* unless there are accidents. 若無意外事件發生,我們將於中午到達。 ***bar none,*** without exception. 無例外。 ***bar one,*** except one. 有一例外。

bar⁴ /bɑ:(r) ; bɑr/ *n* large Mediterranean fish. 一種地中海大魚。

barb /bɑ:b ; bɑrb/ *n* back-turning or back-curving point of an arrow, spear, fish-hook, etc. (箭、矛、魚鈎等上的)倒刺;倒鈎。 **~ed** *adj* having a ~ or ~s. 有倒刺的;有倒鈎的。 **~ed wire,** wire with short, sharp points, used for fences, etc: 有鐵蒺藜之鐵絲: *~ed wire entanglements,* for defensive purposes in war. (戰爭中作防衞用的) 有鐵蒺藜之鐵絲網;有刺鐵絲網。

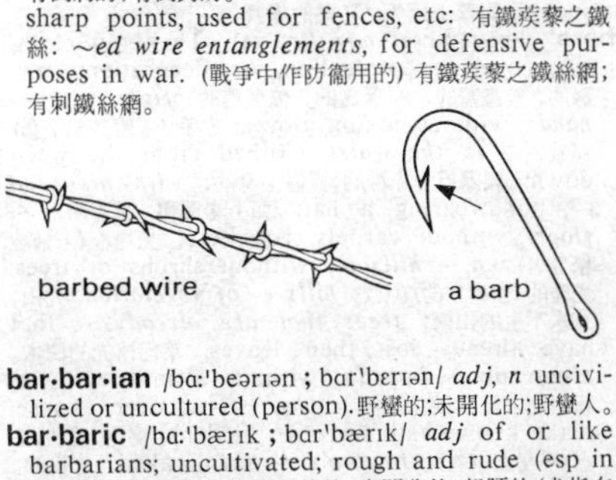

bar·bar·ian /bɑ:'beərɪən ; bɑr'bɛrɪən/ *adj, n* uncivilized or uncultured (person). 野蠻的;未開化的;野蠻人。

bar·baric /bɑ:'bærɪk ; bɑr'bærɪk/ *adj* of or like barbarians; uncultivated; rough and rude (esp in art and taste): 野蠻民族的;未開化的;粗陋的(尤指在藝術與欣賞力方面): *the ~ splendour of Attila's court.* 阿提拉宮廷的粗俗的華麗。

bar·bar·ism /'bɑ:bərɪzəm ; 'bɑrbə,rɪzəm/ *n* **1** [U] state of being uncivilized, ignorant, or rude: 未開化、無知識或粗野的狀態;野蠻: *living in ~.* 生活於

未開化狀態的。 **2** [C] instance of this; (esp) misuse of language by mixing foreign or vulgar words into talk or writing. 野蠻的實例；(尤指)濫用文字(於談話或寫作中攙入外國語或粗鄙字眼)。

bar·bar·ity /bɑːˈbærətɪ ; bɑrˈbærətɪ/ *n* [U] savage cruelty; [C] (*pl* -ties) instance of this: 殘忍；殘酷；無人道: *the barbarities of modern warfare*, eg the bombing of towns, sinking of passenger liners. 現代戰爭之殘酷(如轟炸城市，擊沉客輪)。

B

bar·bar·ize /ˈbɑːbəraɪz ; ˈbɑrbə,raɪz/ *vt* [VP6A] make barbarous. 使變粗野；使變野蠻；使言語蕪雜。

bar·bar·ous /ˈbɑːbərəs ; ˈbɑrbərəs/ *adj* uncivilized; cruel; savage; unrefined in taste, conduct, or habits. 未開化的；殘忍的；殘酷的；野蠻的；(趣味、行爲或習慣)粗俗的。 **~·ly** *adv*

bar·be·cue /ˈbɑːbɪkjuː ; ˈbɑrbɪ,kju/ *n* grill, iron framework, for cooking an animal whole; ox, pig, etc roasted whole; (outdoor) social occasion at which meat cooked over a charcoal fire is eaten. (炙烤整隻動物的)鐵烤架；炙烤的整隻牛、豬等；(戶外的)烤肉野餐。□ *vt* roast (meat, etc) in this way. 烤(肉等)。

bar·bel /ˈbɑːbl ; ˈbɑrbl̩/ *n* large European freshwater fish. 白魚(歐洲產之大淡水魚)。

bar·ber /ˈbɑːbə(r) ; ˈbɑrbɚ/ *n* person whose trade is shaving and cutting men's hair (cf 參較 *hairdresser*, for both men and women). (給男人理髮修面的)理髮師；理髮匠。 **~'s pole,** pole painted in coloured spirals and used as a sign. 理髮店招牌柱(漆有彩色螺旋紋者)。 **'~'s shop,** (US 美 = **'~ shop**) place where a ~ does his work. 理髮店；理髮廳。

bar·bi·can /ˈbɑːbɪkən ; ˈbɑrbɪkən/ *n* fortified building, esp a double tower over a gate or bridge, used in olden times as an outer defence to a city or castle. (古代城堡之)外堡；門首或橋頭之望樓；碉樓。

bar·bi·tone /ˈbɑːbɪtəʊn ; ˈbɑrbɪ,ton/ *n* [U] drug used to soothe the nerves and cause sleep; veronal. 巴比東(一種有鎮定神經及安眠作用的藥物)。

bar·bitu·rate /bɑːˈbɪtjʊrət ; ,bɑrˈbɪtjuret/ *n* [C, U] (chem) (kinds of) organic compound with a (possibly dangerous) soporific effect; pill for settling the nerves or inducing sleep. (化學)巴比妥酸鹽(有機化合物，具催眠之效，可能導致危險)；巴比妥酸鹽藥片(鎮定劑或催眠劑)。

bar·ca·role, bar·ca·rolle /,bɑːkəˈrəʊl ; ˈbɑrkə,rol/ *n* song of Venetian gondoliers. 威尼斯船夫歌。

bard /bɑːd ; bɑrd/ *n* **1** (esp Celtic) minstrel. (尤指古代克爾特族之)遊唱詩人。 **2** (liter) poet: (文)詩人: *the ~ of Avon*, Shakespeare. 亞芬河畔之詩人(指莎士比亞)。 **bar·dic** *adj* of ~s or their songs. 遊唱詩人或其詩歌的。 **bar·dol·atry** /bɑːˈdɒlətrɪ ; bɑrˈdɑlətrɪ/ *n* [U] enthusiastic admiration of Shakespeare. 對莎士比亞之狂熱的崇拜。

bare[1] /beə(r) ; bɛr/ *adj* (-r, -st) **1** without clothing, covering, protection, or decoration: 無衣服的；無遮蓋的；無保護的；無裝飾的: *fight with ~ hands*, without boxing gloves; 赤手(未帶拳擊手套)而戰; *~ to the waist*, clothed from the waist down; 腰際以上赤裸的；裸露上身的; *with his head ~*, not wearing a hat; 頭上未戴帽；光着頭; *~ floors*, without carpets, rugs, etc; 光地板(未鋪地毯等者); *a ~ hillside*, without shrubs or trees; 光禿的(無樹木的)山坡; *hills ~ of vegetation;* 禿山；草木不生的山巒; *trees that are already ~*, that have already lost their leaves. 葉已落光的樹木。 ***sleep on ~ boards,*** without a mattress, etc. 睡在硬木板上(無褥墊等)。 ***lay ~,*** uncover, expose, make known (sth secret or hidden). 揭露；揭發；暴露(隱秘之事物)。 ***in one's ~ skin,*** naked. 赤裸的。 **'~·back** *adv* (of a horse) without a saddle: (指馬)無鞍地；光背地: *ride ~back.* 騎無鞍之馬。 **,~-'backed** *adj* having the back ~. 無鞍的；光背的。□ *adv* = ~back. **'~·faced** *adj* insolent; shameless; undisguised: 侮慢的；無恥的；無掩飾的；簡直的；公然的: *It's ~faced robbery to ask £15 for such an old bicycle!* 這樣一輛舊脚踏車索價十五鎊，這簡直是搶刼！ **~·faced·ly** *adv* **'~·foot** *adv* without shoes and stockings: 赤足地；光着脚地: *be／go／walk ~foot.* 赤足(而行)。 **,~-'footed** *adj* with ~ feet. 赤足的；光着脚的。□ *adv* = ~foot. 赤足地。 **,~-'headed** *adj* with a ~ head; not wearing a hat. 光着頭的；未戴帽的。 **,~-'legged** *adj* with the legs ~; not wearing stockings. 光着腿的；未穿長襪的。 **2** empty or almost empty: 空的；幾乎是空的: *a room ~ of furniture;* 幾乎沒有傢具的房間; *a larder ~ of food;* 幾乎沒有食物的食物儲藏室; *~ shelves.* 幾乎沒有書的書架(或幾乎沒有東西擺在上面的架子)。*The garden looked ~ in winter*, had few or no flowers. 花園在冬天裏幾乎沒有花草。 **3** not more than; mere: 最起碼的；僅够的；僅僅的: *the ~ necessities of life*, things needed merely to keep alive; 最起碼的生活必需品; *earn a ~ living*, only just enough money to live on; 賺的錢僅足餬口; *approved by a ~ majority*, a very small one; 經勉勉强强的多數票通過; *a ~ possibility*, a mere or very slight one. 絕無僅有的可能性。 **~·ly** *adv* **1** in a ~ way: 赤裸裸地；空乏地: *~ly furnished rooms*, with little furniture. 幾乎沒有傢具的房間。 **2** only just; scarcely: 僅僅；僅只；幾乎不；幾乎沒有: *We ~ly had time to catch the train.* 我們僅有勉强可以趕上火車的時間。 *He can ~ly read and write.* 他僅粗通文字而已(勉强能讀能寫)。 *I ~ly know her.* 我與她僅只認識而已。 **~·ness** *n* ~ state. 赤裸；空乏；無裝飾。

bare[2] /beə(r) ; bɛr/ *vt* [VP6A] uncover; reveal: 揭露；去除…的覆蓋物；揭開: *~ one's head*, take one's hat off; 脫去帽子; *~ the end of a wire*, strip off the covering of rubber, etc (before making an electrical connection). (在連接電線之前)剝去電線端上包覆之橡皮等。 ***~ one's heart,*** make known one's deepest feelings. 說出眞心話；表露眞情。 ***~ its teeth,*** (of an animal) show its teeth in anger. (指動物憤怒時)齜牙。

bar·gain /ˈbɑːgɪn ; ˈbɑrgɪn/ *n* **1** agreement to buy, sell or exchange sth, made after discussion; (in industry) agreement between management and labour over wages, hours, etc; sth obtained as the result of such an agreement. (經過談判以後所作買賣或交換之)協議；(在工業中，勞資雙方有關工資、工時等的)協議；由此項協議所得之事物。 ***A ~'s a ~,*** When an agreement has been made, it must be kept. 旣經達成協議，就必得遵守。 ***drive a hard ~,*** try to force an agreement favourable to oneself. 試圖使對方同意有利自己的協議。 ***a good／bad ~,*** one that favours／does not favour oneself. 佔便宜的(吃虧的)交易。 ***into the ~,*** as well; in addition; moreover. 另外；此外；加之。 ***make／strike a ~ (with sb) (over sth),*** reach agreement. (與某人)(有關某事)達成協議。 **'~·ing position,** (in a debate, etc) state of affairs, arrangements, etc: (討論等中之)事態、安排等的情況；協商境況: *The Foreign Secretary was in a good／bad ~ing position in his dealings with his opposite number in France*, was in a favourable／unfavourable position when negotiating. 在與法國方面地位相當的官員(指法國外交部長)談判中，英國外相處於有利(不利)的協商地位。 **2** sth offered, sold or bought cheap: 索價便宜、賣得便宜或買得便宜的貨物: *a '~ sale*, sale of goods at reduced prices; 大減價; *'~-basement*, lowest floor of a shop, where goods are offered at reduced prices; 地下室廉價部; *'~-counter*, counter at which ~s are displayed or sold; 犧牲品櫃臺(展示並出售廉價品的櫃臺)；廉價部; *~ price*, low price; 廉價；特價; *'~-hunter*, person looking for ~s. 尋找便宜貨的人。□ *vi, vt* **1** [VP2A, 3A] *~ (with sb) (for sth),* talk for the purpose of reaching an agreement (about buying or selling sth, doing a piece of work, etc): (與某人)(爲某事物)討價還價；講價；談條件；談判: *We ~ed with the farmer for a supply of milk and butter.* 我們與那農夫講價，欲購買一批牛奶和白塔油。 **2** [VP3A] ***~ about,*** = ~ over. ***~ for,***

be ready or willing to accept or agree to: 願意接受或同意;預料;期待: *I didn't ~ for John arriving so soon,* was surprised by this, didn't expect it. 我沒有想到約翰會這麼快到達。***get more than one ~s for,*** (colloq) be unpleasantly surprised at the consequences. (俗)結果出乎預料之外(不愉快地感到驚奇)。***~ over sth,*** ~ with sb for sth. 與人協議某事。 **3** [VP9] make a condition: 提出條件: *The men ~ed that they should not have to work on Saturday afternoons.* 工人們提出條件謂他們不應於星期六下午還要工作。 **4** [VP15B] ***~ away,*** give up in return for sth; sacrifice: 放棄…以求獲得另外的某物;犧牲;賤賣: *~ away one's freedom,* give it up in return for some advantage or other. 犧牲其自由(以求獲得某種利益)。

barge[1] /bɑ:dʒ ; bɑrdʒ/ *n* **1** large flat-bottomed boat for carrying goods and people on rivers and canals, in harbours, etc with or without sails, towed by a tug or horse; similar boat with its own engine. 駁船(河上或港內載運客貨的大平底船,或有帆或無帆,以拖船或馬匹拖之);本身裝有引擎的類似的船。 **2** warship's boat, for the use of the officers. 戰艦上高級軍官之座艇。 **3** large rowing-boat for ceremonial occasions. 慶典用的大划艇。 **'~-pole** *n* long pole used for guiding a ~. 駁船之撐篙。***I wouldn't touch it with a ~-pole,*** I dislike or distrust it extremely. 我非常厭惡(不信任)它。

barge[2] /bɑ:dʒ ; bɑrdʒ/ *vi* (colloq) (俗) **1** [VP3A] ***~ into/against,*** rush or bump heavily into/against (sb or sth). 衝撞; 碰撞 (某人或某物)。 **2** [VP2C, 3A] ***~ about,*** move clumsily, without proper control of one's movements or without care (for persons or things). 笨拙地走動(對自己的動作沒有適當的控制,或不顧其他之人或物);亂碰亂闖。***~ in/into,*** intrude; make one's way in, interrupt, rudely: 闖入;打擾;打斷: *Stop barging into our conversation.* 不要打斷我們的談話。

bar·gee /bɑ:'dʒi: ; ˌbɑr'dʒi/ *n* master or member of the crew of a barge. 駁船的船主;駁船船夫。***swear like a ~,*** swear forcibly, and with a great variety of swear-words. 咒罵得很厲害;滿口骯髒字眼。

bari·tone /'bærɪtəʊn ; 'bærəˌton/ *n* male voice between tenor and bass. 男中音。

bar·ium /'beərɪəm ; 'bɛrɪəm/ *n* [U] **1** soft, silvery-white metal (symbol **Ba**) of which the compounds are used in industry. 鋇(銀白色軟金屬,化學符號Ba, 其化合物用於工業)。 **2** chemical substance (~ sulphate) introduced into the intestines before an X-ray photograph of them is taken. 鋇灌腸劑(硫酸鋇,在X光照腸之前,引入腸內之化學物質)。

bark[1] /bɑ:k ; bɑrk/ *n* [U] outer covering or skin on the trunks, boughs and branches of trees. 樹皮。⇨ the illus at tree. 參看 tree 之插圖。□ *vt* [VP6A] **1** take the ~ off (a tree). 剝去(樹)的皮。 **2** scrape the skin off (one's knuckles, shin, knee, etc) (by falling against sth, etc). (因跌跤等)擦破(指節、外脛、膝蓋等)之皮。

bark[2] /bɑ:k ; bɑrk/ *n* the cry made by dogs and foxes; (fig) sound of gunfire, or of a cough. 狗及狐狸的叫聲;吠聲;(喻)砲火聲;咳嗽聲。***His ~ is worse than his bite,*** He is bad-tempered but not dangerous or (fig) malicious. 他的脾氣很壞,但心地不惡。□ *vi, vt* **1** [VP2A, C, 3A] (of dogs, etc) give a ~ or ~s: (指狗等)吠叫: *The dog ~s at strangers.* 狗對陌生人吠叫。***~ up the wrong tree,*** (fig) direct one's complaint, accusation, etc wrongly. (喻)弄錯了抱怨、控訴等的對象。 **2** [VP6A, 15B] say (sth) in a sharp, commanding voice: 以嚴厲而威嚴的聲音說出;咆哮着說出;吼叫: *The officer ~ed out his orders.* 軍官以嚴厲而威嚴的聲音發出命令。*'Come here!' he ~ed (out).* '來這裏!'他吼叫着。

bark[3], **barque** /bɑ:k ; bɑrk/ *n* **1** sailing-ship with 3 to 5 masts and sails. 三桅(四桅或五桅)帆船。 **2** (poet) any ship or boat. (詩)船;小船。

barker /'bɑ:kə(r) ; 'bɑrkɚ/ *n* (colloq) (俗) **1** person who stands outside a booth in a travelling show, or outside a shop, talking loudly to advertise the show, goods, etc. (雜耍戲棚外或店鋪門外之) 宣傳員;招徠顧客者。 **2** (sl) pistol. (俚)手槍。

bar·ley /'bɑ:lɪ ; 'bɑrlɪ/ *n* [U] grass-like plant and its seed (called grain), used for food and for making beer and whisky. 大麥(用作食物,並釀造啤酒及威士忌酒)。⇨ the illus at cereal. 參看 cereal 之插圖。**'~-corn** *n* [U] grain of ~; (colloq) malt liquor. 大麥之實;大麥粒;(俗)麥芽酒。**pearl ~** *n* ~ grain made smaller by grinding. 眞珠麥(由大麥碾成之圓形顆粒)。**'~-sugar** *n* [U] solid sweet substance, made from pure sugar. 大麥糖(用純糖所製之糖果)。**'~-water** *n* [U] drink made by boiling pearl ~ in water and then straining it. 眞珠麥汁(用水煮眞珠麥,然後再將眞珠麥濾除而成之飲料)。

barm /bɑ:m ; bɑrm/ *n* [U] yeast. 酵母;酵素。

barmy /'bɑ:mɪ ; 'bɑrmɪ/ *adj* (GB colloq) wrong in the head; foolish. (英俗)精神不正常的;愚癡的。

barn /bɑ:n ; bɑrn/ *n* **1** covered building for storing hay, grain, etc on a farm. (農莊上儲藏乾草、穀物等的)穀倉。**'~ dance** *n* kind of rustic dance. 穀倉舞(一種農村舞)。**'~-door** *n* large door of a ~; (colloq fig) target too large to miss. 穀倉大門;(俗,喻)過大而不會打不中的目標。**ˌ~-'door fowl** *n* ordinary kind of fowl kept on farms. (農莊上所養的)普通家禽。**'~-storm** *vi* (US) travel rapidly through the country making political speeches, presenting plays, etc. (美) 旅行鄉間作政治性演講,演出戲劇等;在鄉間作巡廻演出。Hence, 由此產生, **'~-stormer** *n* person who does this. 在鄉間作旅行演說者;在鄉間作巡廻演出的藝人。**'~-yard** *n* = farmyard. **2** (contemptuous) any large, plain building: (輕蔑語)大而簡陋的房舍: *What a ~ of a house!* 這棟房屋簡直像穀倉! **3** (US) building for sheltering cattle or horses; depot for trams, buses, etc. (美)牛馬房;(電車、公共汽車等之)車庫;停車場。

bar·nacle /'bɑ:nəkl ; 'bɑrnəkl̩/ *n* small sea-animal that fastens itself to objects under water, rocks, the bottoms of ships, the timbers of wharves, etc. 藤壺(附於水面下之物體、岩石、船底、碼頭木柱等之小甲殼動物)。

ba·rom·eter /bə'rɒmɪtə(r) ; bə'rɑmətɚ/ *n* instrument for measuring the pressure of the atmosphere, used for forecasting the weather and measuring height above sea-level; (fig) something which forecasts changes or fluctuations (eg in public opinion, market prices). 氣壓計;晴雨表;海拔計;(喻)預言改變或波動之事物(例如在輿論、市價等方面)。 **baro·met·ric** /ˌbærə'metrɪk ; ˌbærə'mɛtrɪk/ *adj*

bar·on /'bærən ; 'bærən/ *n* **1** (in GB) nobleman; lowest rank of Peer (called *Lord* —); holder of the non-British title (called *Baron* —). (在英國)貴族;男爵(稱爲 Lord —); 他國男爵爵位之持有者(稱爲 Baron —)。 **2** (orig US) great industrial leader: (起源於美國)工業巨子;大王: *oil ~s;* 石油大王; *beer ~s.* 啤酒大王。**'~·age** /-ɪdʒ ; -ɪdʒ/ *n* the ~s collectively; book with a list of these Peers. 貴族(集合用法);貴族名册。**~·ess** /'bærənɪs ; 'bærənɪs/ *n* ~'s wife; woman holding the rank of a ~ in her own right. 男爵夫人;女男爵。 **bar·o·nial** /bə'rəʊnɪəl ; bə'ronɪəl/ *adj* of, suitable for, ~s. 男爵的;適於男爵的。**bar·ony** /'bærənɪ ; 'bærənɪ/ *n* rank of a ~: 男爵的爵位: *confer a ~y on sb,* make him a ~. 將男爵爵位授與某人。

bar·onet /'bærənɪt ; 'bærənɪt/ *n* member of the lowest hereditary titled order, lower in rank than a baron but above a knight; shortened to *Bart,* added to the name, as *Sir John Williams, Bart.* 從男爵 (最下級世襲爵位的貴族, 階級在 baron 之下 knight 之上;簡稱 Bart, 加在姓名之後, 如 Sir John Williams, Bart)。**~cy** /'bærənɪtsɪ ; 'bærənɪtsɪ/ *n* rank, title, of a ~. 從男爵之爵位及頭銜。

ba·roque /bə'rɒk *US:* -əʊk ; bə'rok/ *n, adj* (of the) florid or extravagant style in the arts (esp archi-a barque

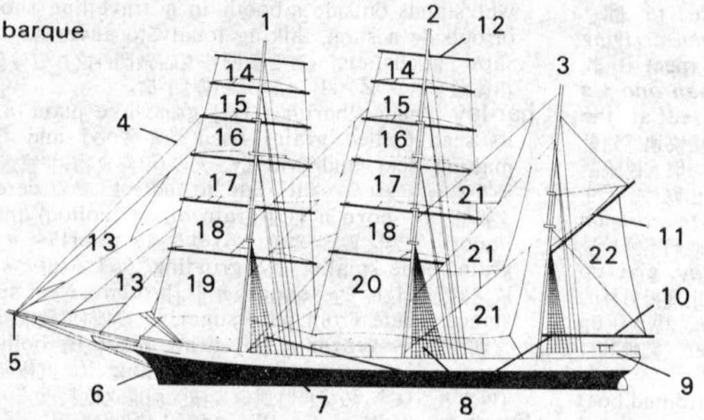

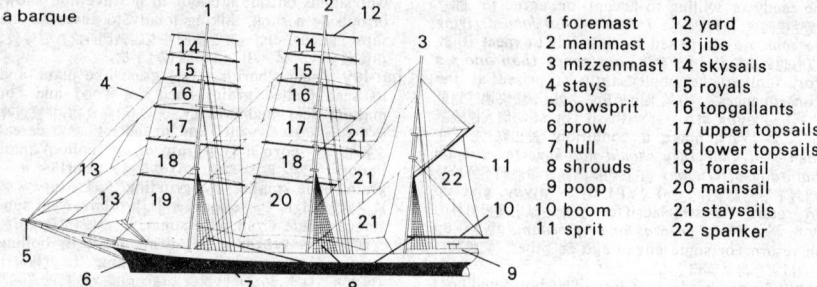

1 foremast
2 mainmast
3 mizzenmast
4 stays
5 bowsprit
6 prow
7 hull
8 shrouds
9 poop
10 boom
11 sprit
12 yard
13 jibs
14 skysails
15 royals
16 topgallants
17 upper topsails
18 lower topsails
19 foresail
20 mainsail
21 staysails
22 spanker

tecture) in Europe in the 17th and 18th cc. 巴洛克式(十七及十八世紀歐洲藝術過份裝飾之型式,尤指建築方面);巴洛克式的。

ba·rouche /bəˈruːʃ ; bəˈruʃ/ *n* four-wheeled carriage, pulled by horses, with two seats facing each other and a folding top, for four occupants and a driver. 一種四輪大馬車(有兩個對面座位及一可折疊之頂篷,可供四客及一車夫乘坐)。

barque /bɑːk ; bɑrk/ *n* ⇨ bark³.

bar·rack¹ /ˈbærək ; ˈbærək/ *n* **1** (usu *pl* with *indef art* and *sing v*) large building(s) for soldiers to live in: (常作複數,與不定冠詞和單數動詞連用) 兵營;營房: *The ~s are / is quite new.* 那(些)營房相當新。 **2** any building of plain or ugly appearance. 外表簡陋的房舍。

bar·rack² /ˈbærək ; ˈbærək/ *vt, vi* [VP6A, 2A] jeer at; make cries of protest against (eg slow play in a cricket match). 嘲笑;叫囂以示抗議(如對板球比賽之緩慢動作等)。 **~·ing** *n* slow clapping, etc. 喝倒采(如緩慢的拍掌等)。

bar·ra·cuda /ˌbærəˈkuːdə ; ˌbærəˈkudə/ *n* large, fierce Caribbean sea-fish. 梭子魚(加勒比海產之兇猛大海魚)。

bar·rage /ˈbærɑːʒ *US:* bəˈrɑːʒ ; ˈbɑrɪdʒ, bəˈrɑʒ/ *n* [C] **1** artificial obstacle built across a river (not across a valley) for storing water to be diverted into canals for irrigation (as on the Nile and the Indus). (攔河,非攔谷,所築用以蓄水導入渠溝,作灌溉用之) 堰壩(如尼羅河及印度河上所築者)。 ⇨ dam. **2** (mil) barrier made by heavy, continuous gunfire directed onto a given area. (軍)彈幕(針對某一地區不斷發射猛烈砲火所造成的障礙)。 **3** *balloon ~; ~ balloon,* ⇨ balloon. 繫留氣球幕。

barred /bɑːd ; bɑrd/ *pt, pp* of bar².

bar·rel /ˈbærəl ; ˈbærəl/ *n* **1** round container, made of wooden staves with bands or hoops, or of plastic; the amount that a ~ holds. (用木頭或塑膠做的)桶;一桶之量。 ˌ**~-roofed ˈvault** *n* (semi-) cylindrical roof. (半)圓筒形屋頂。 **2** metal tube of a rifle, revolver or pistol. 槍管;砲筒。 ⇨ the illus at rifle. 參看 rifle 之插圖。 **3** part of a fountain pen that holds the ink. (自來水筆中的)儲墨管。 **4** ˈ**~-organ** *n* instrument from which music is produced by turning a handle and so causing a cylinder to act mechanically on keys; usu played by a man who goes round the streets, playing it for money. 手風琴;筒風琴(搖動琴柄,使滾筒轉動,打擊琴鍵以發音;奏者常在街頭演奏,以求賞錢)。 □ *vt* (-ll-) put in a ~ or ~s. 裝入桶中。 **~led** *part adj* stored in a ~: 儲於桶中的: *~led beer.* 桶裝的啤酒。

bar·ren /ˈbærən ; ˈbærən/ *adj* **1** (of land) not good enough to produce crops. (指土地)貧瘠的;不長五穀的。 **2** (of plants, trees) not producing fruit or seeds. (指草木)不結果的;不結實的。 **3** (of women, animals) unable to have young ones. (指婦人,動物)不生育的;不孕的。 **4** (fig) without value, interest, or result: (喻)無價值、趣味或結果的: *a ~ subject / discussion;* 無價值(或無趣味)的題目(討論); *an attempt that was ~ of results.* 無結果的嘗試。 **~·ness** *n*

bar·ri·cade /ˌbærɪˈkeɪd ; ˌbærəˈked/ *n* barrier of objects (eg trees, carts, overturned or burnt-out cars, barrels) made across or in front of something as a defence. (利用樹木、馬車、倒翻或燒毀的汽車、木桶等橫攔或置於某物之前,作爲防衞用的)阻絕障礙物;路障。 □ *vt* [VP6A, 15B] *~ (in / off),* block (a street, etc) with a ~: 以阻絕障礙物阻塞(街道等): *They ~d themselves in.* 他們設置臨時障礙物,自己躲在裡面。

bar·rier /ˈbærɪə(r) ; ˈbærɪɚ/ *n* **1** sth (eg a wall, rail, fence, turnstile) that prevents, hinders or controls, progress or movement: 障礙物;阻礙物;控制進展或活動之物(如牆、柵、籬、十字轉門): *The Sahara Desert is a natural ~ that separates North and Central Africa.* 撒哈拉沙漠是北非洲與中非洲之間的天然屏障。 *Show your ticket at the ~,* eg in a railway station. 在柵門口(如在火車站者)繳驗你的票。 ⇨ also crash¹(1), half(3), heat¹(5) and sound²(3). **2** (fig) hindrance: (喻)障礙;阻礙: *Poor health and lack of money may both be ~s to educational progress.* 健康不佳和沒有錢都可以成爲教育進步的障礙。

bar·ring /ˈbɑːrɪŋ ; ˈbɑrɪŋ/ *prep* excluding. 除…以外。 ⇨ bar³.

bar·ris·ter /ˈbærɪstə(r) ; ˈbærɪstɚ/ *n* (in England) lawyer who has the right to speak and argue as an advocate in higher law courts. (用於英國)(可在高等法院出庭的)律師。 ⇨ advocate, solicitor, counsel.

bar·row¹ /ˈbærəʊ ; ˈbæro/ *n* **1** = wheel-~. **2** (also 亦作 ˈ*hand-~,* ˈ*coster's ~*) small cart with two wheels, pulled or pushed by hand. 兩輪手推車。 ˈ**~-boy / -man** /-mæn ; -mæn/ *n* costermonger. 沿街推車叫賣水果、蔬菜等之小販。 **3** (also 亦作 *luggage-~*) metal frame with two wheels used by porters for luggage (at railway-stations, in hotels, etc). (火車站、旅館等內搬運工人所用之)行李運送車。

bar·row² /ˈbærəʊ ; ˈbæro/ *n* mound, dating from prehistoric times, built over a burial ground. (史前時代的)古墳;古墓;塚。 ⇨ tumulus.

bar·ter /ˈbɑːtə(r) ; ˈbɑrtɚ/ *vt, vi* [VP15B, 14, 2A] *~ (with sb / for sth); ~ sth away,* exchange (goods, property, etc) (for other goods, etc): (以貨)易貨;物物交換: *~ wheat for machinery;* 以小麥交換機器; (fig) (喻) *~ away one's rights / honour / freedom.* (爲某種利益而)出賣自己的權利(榮譽,自由)。 □ *n* [U] exchange made in this way. 以貨易貨;物物交換。 **~·er** *n*

ba·salt /ˈbæsɔːlt *US:* bəˈsɔːlt ; bəˈsɔlt/ *n* [U] sorts of dark-coloured rock of volcanic origin. 玄武岩(由火山岩漿所形成之暗色岩石)。

bas·cule /ˈbæskjuːl ; ˈbæskjul/ *n* ˈ**~ bridge,** (eng) kind of drawbridge of which the two halves can be raised and lowered with counter-weights. (工程)跳開式吊橋;活動橋(橋身之兩半截可藉平衡重量同時起落)。

base¹ /beɪs ; bes/ *n* **1** lowest part of anything, esp the part on which sth rests or is supported: 底;根基;基礎: *the ~ of a pillar,* ⇨ the illus at column. 柱基(參看 column 之插圖)。 ˈ**~·board** *n* (US)

bases

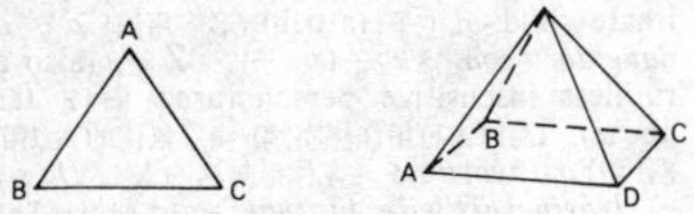

skirting-board. (美)踢脚板;壁脚板。 **2** (geom) line or surface on which a figure stands or can stand: (幾何)底邊;底面: *BC is the ~ of the triangle ABC.* BC 是三角形 ABC 之底邊。 *ABCD is the ~ of the pyramid.* ABCD 是角錐體的底面。 **3** (chem) substance capable of combining with an acid to form a salt; substance into which other things are mixed. (化學)鹽基;鹼(可與酸化合成鹽);(混合物之)主要成分。 **4** place at which armed forces, expeditions, etc have their stores, hospitals, etc: (軍隊,探險隊等之)基地;根據地: *a 'naval ~;* 海軍基地; *an 'air ~;* 空軍基地; *a ~ of operations;* 作戰根據地; *a ~ camp,* eg for an Everest expedition. 基地營帳(如埃佛勒斯峯探險隊者)。 **5** (maths) the number (usu 10) which is the starting point for a logarithmic system. (數學)(對數之)底(通常爲 10)。 **6** (~ball) one of four stations or positions. (棒球)壘。 ***get to first ~,*** (US; fig) take a successful first step towards achieving sth. (美;喻)邁向成功之路的第一步;初步成功。 **~ hit** *n* hit on which a player gets to first ~. 一壘安打(擊球者能上第一壘之一擊)。 **~·less** *adj* without cause or foundation: 無原因的;無緣無故的;無根據的: *~less fears.* 無緣無故的恐懼。

base[2] /beɪs ; bes/ *vt* [VP14] ***~ sth on/upon,*** build or place; use as a basis for: 建於…之上;以…爲根據: *Direct taxation is usually ~d upon income.* 直接稅通常以收入爲根據。 *I ~ my hopes on the news we had yesterday.* 我的希望是以我們昨天所得到的消息爲根據。

base[3] /beɪs ; bes/ *adj* **1** (-r, -st) (of persons, their behaviour, thoughts, etc) dishonourable: (指人,其行爲、思想等)卑鄙的: *acting from ~ motives.* 動機卑鄙的行爲。 **2 ~ metals,** non-precious metals. 賤金屬。 **~ coin,** mixed with inferior metals. 攙有賤金屬之硬幣。

base·ball /ˈbeɪsbɔːl ; ˈbesˌbɔl/ *n* national game of the US, played with a bat and ball, by two teams of nine players each, on a field with four bases[1](6). 棒球戲;棒球(美國之全國性運動,兩隊各九人,球場有四壘)。

base·ment /ˈbeɪsmənt ; ˈbesmənt/ *n* lowest part of a building, partly or wholly below ground level; inhabited room(s) in this part. 地下室(建築物之最下部份,一部份或全部在地面之下); 地下層有人居住的房間。

bases **1** /ˈbeɪsiːz ; ˈbesiz/ *pl* of basis. **2** /ˈbeɪsɪz ; ˈbesɪz/ *pl* of base[1].

bash /bæʃ ; bæʃ/ *vt* [VP6A, 15A, B] strike heavily so as to break or injure: 猛擊(以致擊破或擊傷); 痛擊: *~ in the lid of a box;* 將盒蓋子打陷進去; *~ sb on the head with a golf club;* 用高爾夫球棍猛打某人的頭; *~ one's head against sth in the dark.* 在黑暗中將頭碰在某物上。 □ *n* violent blow or knock: 猛擊;痛擊;重擊: *give sb a ~ on the nose.* 猛擊某人的鼻子。 ***have a ~ at sth,*** (sl) attempt it. (俚)嘗試某事。

bash·ful /ˈbæʃfl ; ˈbæʃfəl/ *adj* shy. 害羞的;羞怯的。 **~ly** /-fəlɪ ; -fəlɪ/ *adv*

basic /ˈbeɪsɪk ; ˈbesɪk/ *adj* of or at the base or foundation; fundamental: 基礎的; 基本的; 根本的: *the ~ processes of arithmetic,* eg adding, subtraction, multiplying; 算術的基本方法(如加法、減法、乘法); *the ~ vocabulary of a language,* the words that must be known. 一種語言的基本字彙(卽必須認識之字)。 **B~ English,** artificial, simplified form of English. 基本英語 (人爲之簡化英語)。 **~ slag** *n* fertilizer containing phosphates. 含有磷酸鹽之肥料; 鹼性熔渣。 **ba·si·cally** /-klɪ ; -klɪ/ *adv* fundamentally. 基本上;根本上。

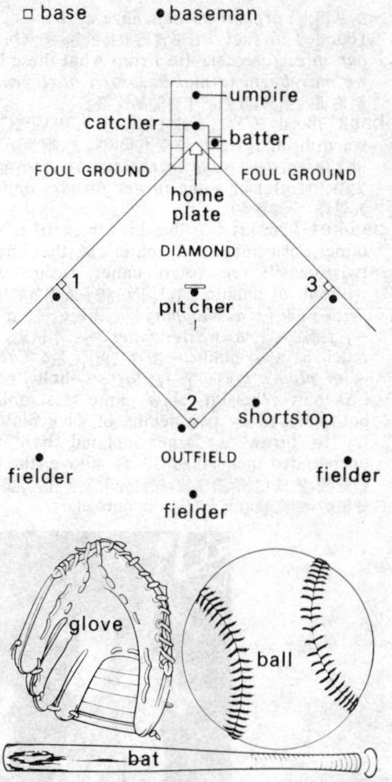

baseball

basil /ˈbæzl ; ˈbæzl̩/ *n* [U] sweet-smelling plant like mint, used in cooking. 羅勒;紫蘇(味香如薄荷,用於烹調)。

ba·sil·ica /bəˈzɪlɪkə ; bəˈsɪlɪkə/ *n* oblong hall with a double row of columns and an apse at one end (used in ancient Rome as a law court); building of this type used as a church: (古羅馬用作法庭之)長方形會堂; 長方形教堂: *the ~ of St Peter's in Rome.* 羅馬之聖彼得教堂。

bas·il·isk /ˈbæsɪlɪsk ; ˈbæsəˌlɪsk/ *n* **1** small American lizard with a hollow crest that can swell up with air. 美洲小蜥蜴(有中空之冠,能充氣而膨脹)。 **2** fabulous reptile able to cause death by its look or breath. 傳說中其目光或氣息可致人於死之怪爬蟲。

basin /ˈbeɪsn ; ˈbesn̩/ *n* **1** round, open dish of metal, pottery, etc for holding liquids; contents of a ~. (金屬、陶瓷等製之)盆;一盆之量。 ⇨ wash-~. **2** bowl for preparing or serving food in. (煮或盛食物之)碗。 **3** hollow place where water collects (eg a stone structure at the base of a fountain, a deep pool at the base of a waterfall). 水滙聚之凹形處所;(噴泉下之)盛水池;(瀑布下之)深水潭。 **4** deep part of a harbour that is almost surrounded by land; dock with gates that control the inflow and outflow of water. 港灣內幾全爲陸地所圍繞之深水處;有閘門控制水流出入之船塢;船渠。 **5** area of country drained by a river and its tributaries: (河流之)流域;盆地: *the Thames ~.* 泰晤士河流域。

basis /ˈbeɪsɪs ; ˈbesɪs/ *n* (*pl* bases /ˈbeɪsiːz ; ˈbesiz/) **1** substance into which others are mixed; most important part of a mixture. (混合物之)主要成分。 **2** foundation (usu fig): 基礎(通常作比喻用法): *the ~ of morality;* 道德的基礎; *on a solid ~;* 在堅實

的基礎上；*arguments that have a firm* ～, that are founded in facts. 有事實爲根據的論據。*On the* ～ *of our sales forecasts* (ie From what these indicate) *we may begin to make a profit next year.* 基於我們售貨的預測，我們明年將開始賺錢。

bask /bɑːsk *US:* bæsk；bæsk/ *vi* [VP2C] enjoy warmth and light: 享受溫暖與陽光；曬太陽：*sitting in the garden,* ～*ing in the sunshine;* 坐在花園裡曬太陽；(fig) (喻) ～*ing in her favour／approval.* 沐其恩澤(受其嘉許)。

B

bas·ket /ˈbɑːskɪt *US:* ˈbæskɪt；ˈbæskɪt/ *n* **1** container, usu made of materials that bend and twist easily (eg osiers, canes, rushes) with or without a handle: (以柳條、籐子或藺草等編製之)籃子；筐子；簍子：*a* ˈ*shopping* ～*;* 購物籃子；*a* ˈ*clothes* ～*;* 衣服籃子；*a waste-*ˈ*paper* ～. 字紙簍。 **2** as much as a ～ holds: 一籃(筐、簍)之量：*They ate a* ～ *of plums.* 他們吃了一籃李子。**～·ball** /ˈbɑːskɪtbɔːl *US:* ˈbæs-；ˈbæskɪtˌbɔl/ *n* game (resembling netball), played by two teams of five players who try to throw a large inflated ball into an open-ended net fixed 10 ft above the ground. 籃球戲；籃球(似落網球戲，球員分兩隊各五人，競相投球入球籃中，籃高離地面十呎)。⇨ netball.

basketball

bas-relief /ˌbæs rɪˈliːf；ˌbɑrɪˈlif/ *n* [U] (= *low relief*) form of art in which a flat surface of metal or stone is cut away so that a design or picture stands out as on a coin but often to a greater degree; [C] example of this. (於金屬或石頭的平面所作之)半浮雕；淺浮雕(如硬幣上之圖像，但常更爲突出)。⇨ the illus at church. 參看 church 之插圖。

bass[1] /bæs；bæs/ *n* (*pl* unchanged) (zool) kinds of fish (perch) used as food, caught in rivers, lakes and in the sea. (複數不變)(動物)鱸魚類(可食，在河、湖及海中均可捕得)。

bass[2] /beɪs；bes/ *adj* deep-sounding; low in tone. 聲音低沉的；音調低的。□ *n* lowest part in music (voice and instruments); singer or instrument with lowest notes: 音樂(人聲及樂器)之低音部；低音部之歌者或樂器：ˌ～*-clariˈnet;* 低音豎笛；ˌ～ ˈ*drum,* ⇨ the illus at percussion; 低音鼓；大鼓(參看 percussion 之插圖)；ˌ*double-*ˈ～, ⇨ the illus at string; 低音提琴(參看 string 之插圖)；ˌ～ˈ*clef,* ⇨ the illus at notation. 低音譜號(參看 notation 之插圖)。

bass[3] /bæs；bæs/ *n* [U] inner fibrous bark of the lime-tree, used for weaving baskets, mats, etc and for tying plants. 菩提樹之纖維質的內皮(用作編織籃、蓆等及綑綁植物)。

Bass /bæs；bæs/ *n* (P) beer made by the brewers named Bass. (商標)巴斯啤酒(由釀造者 Bass 而得名)。

bas·si·net /ˌbæsɪˈnet；ˌbæsəˈnɛt/ *n* baby's cradle or carriage made of woven wicker, with a hood. (用柳條編製，上有篷蓋的)小兒搖籃或推車。

bas·soon /bəˈsuːn；bæˈsun/ *n* musical wind-instrument with double reeds, made of wood, giving very low notes. 低音管；巴頌管(一種低音的雙簧木管樂器)。⇨ the illus at brass. 參看 brass 之插圖。

bast /bæst；bæst/ *n* [U] **1** = bass[3]. **2** other fibrous barks (eg raffia) used for tying and weaving. 可用作縛結和編織之他種纖維質內皮(例如拉菲亞棕櫚樹纖維)；韌皮。

bas·tard /ˈbɑːstəd *US:* ˈbæs-；ˈbæstəd/ *n* **1** illegitimate child: 私生子：(attrib) (形容用法) *a* ～ *child／daughter／son.* 私生子(女，子)。 **2** ⚠ (also as *int*) ruthless insensitive person (used as a term of abuse): (諱)(亦可用作感嘆詞)殘忍無情的人(用作責罵語)：*You heartless* ～*!* 你這無情的人！ *He's a real* ～, *leaving his wife in that way;* 他眞狠心，像那樣離開了他的妻子；(also, not abusively, friendly colloq): (亦可作表示友善的口語，無咒罵之含意)：*Harry, you old* ～*! Fancy meeting you here!* 哈利，你這老傢伙！想不到在這裡遇見你！ **3** ⚠ unfortunate fellow: (諱)不幸的人：*Poor* ～*! He's been sacked and he won't find another job very easily;* 可憐的傢伙！他已經被解雇了，而且很難再找到另一個工作；(also of an unfortunate incident, state, etc): (亦用以指不幸的事件，情況等)：*this* ～ *of a headache／essay.* 這討厭的頭痛(論文)。 **4** (usu attrib) (of things) not genuine or authentic; spurious. (通常作形容用法)(指事物)贋的；不眞實的；不可靠的；假的；僞造的。ˈ**～·ize** *vt* **1** prove to be, pronounce as a ～. 證實爲私生子；宣佈爲私生子；認定爲私生子。**2** make spurious: 使成爲贋品；使爲僞造；使不實：*a* ～*ized account of what happened.* 對所發生事故的不實報告。**～y** *n* (legal) illegitimacy: (法律)私生：*a* ～*y order,* one (made by a magistrate) for the support of an illegitimate by its father (now called a *maintenance order*). 贍養令；扶養令(地方法官的判令，某私生子應由其生父扶養，今稱爲 maintenance order)。

baste[1] /beɪst；best/ *vt* [VP6A, 15B] (in making clothes, etc) sew pieces together with long temporary stitches (so that adjustments are possible afterwards). (在製衣等中)疏縫；大縫；假縫(以長針脚將剪塊暫時縫合，以便以後修改)。

baste[2] /beɪst；best/ *vt* [VP6A] ～ *meat,* pour over it the fat, juices, etc which come from it during cooking. 煮肉時將肉所熬出的油脂、肉汁等澆於肉上。

baste[3] /beɪst；best/ *vt* [VP6A] thrash; beat. 鞭打；痛打。

bas·ti·nado /ˌbæstɪˈnɑːdəʊ；ˌbæstəˈnedo/ *n* (*pl* ～es) caning on the soles of the feet. 蹠刑(打脚掌的一種刑罰)。□ *vt* [VP6A] punish by caning in this way. 施以蹠刑。

bas·tion /ˈbæstɪən；ˈbæstʃən/ *n* (often five-sided) part of a fortification that stands out from the rest; (fig) military stronghold near hostile territory; (fig) sth preserved from destruction or change. 稜堡(防禦工事之突出部份，常有五面)；堡壘突角；(喻)臨近敵境之軍事據點；(喻)未被破壞或改變之物。

bat[1] /bæt；bæt/ *n* small mouse-like animal that flies at night and feeds on fruit and insects. 蝙蝠(體小如鼠之動物，於夜間飛翔，食水果及昆蟲)。⇨ the illus at small. 參看 small 之插圖。***have bats in the belfry,*** (sl) be eccentric, have queer ideas. (俚)古怪的；思想古怪的。***as blind as a bat,*** unable to see, not seeing, clearly. 半瞎的；目力不行的。

bat[2] /bæt；bæt/ *n* **1** shaped wooden implement for striking the ball in games, esp cricket and baseball. (板球戲中所用的)球板；(棒球戲中所用之)球棒。⇨ the illus at these entries. 參看 cricket 及 baseball 之插圖。***carry one's bat,*** (cricket) be 'not out' at the end of the innings. (板球)在一局結束時未被判出局。***do sth off one's own bat,*** (fig) do it without help. (喻)自己做(不要人幫忙)。 **2** = batsman: 擊球員：*He's a useful bat.* 他是個優異的擊球員。□ *vi, vt* (-tt-) **1** [VP2A, B, C] use a bat: 使用球棒；執棒：*Green batted (for) two hours,* was at the wicket for two hours. 格林執棒兩小時。 **2** [VP6A] hit (with a bat). (用棒)擊；打擊。**bats·man** /-smən；-smən/ *n* (*pl* -men) **1** (cricket) player who bats: (板球)擊球員：*He's a good batsman but no good as a bowler.* 他是個好擊球員，但不是個好投手。**2** (aviation) man who uses a pair of bats (like those used in table-tennis) to guide an aircraft as and after it touches down (eg on the deck of an aircraft-carrier). (航空)(航空母艦

等上手持兩板如乒乓球拍以) 指揮飛機降落者。

bat[3] /bæt ; bæt/ *n* ***go off at a terrific/rare bat,*** (sl) at a fast rate. (俚) 非常迅速地離去；急速而行。

bat[4] /bæt ; bæt/ *vt* (-tt-) (sl) wink. (俚) 霎(眼)。***not bat an eyelid,*** **(a)** not sleep at all. 未曾闔眼。**(b)** not show any surprise. 完全不露驚愕之色。

batch /bætʃ ; bætʃ/ *n* **1** number of loaves, cakes, etc baked together: 一次所烘的若干個麪包、糕餅等；一爐: *baked in ~es of twenty.* 每爐烘二十個。 **2** number of persons or things receiving attention as a group: (人或物之) 一批: *a ~ of letters to be answered;* 尚待回覆之一批信件; *a ~ of recruits for the army.* 一批陸軍的新兵。

bate /beɪt ; bet/ *vt* = abate. ***with ~d breath,*** with the voice lowered to a whisper (in expectancy, anxiety, etc). 低聲地；屏息地 (如在期望或焦慮時)。

bath /bɑːθ *US:* bæθ ; bæθ/ *n* (*pl* ~s /bɑːðz *US:* bæðz ; bæðz/) **1** washing of the body, esp by putting oneself completely in water: 沐浴；洗澡: *I shall have a hot ~ and go to bed.* 我將洗個熱水澡，然後睡覺。*He takes a cold ~ every morning.* 他每天早晨洗冷水澡。 **'~·robe** *n* loose-fitting robe worn before and after taking a ~. (沐浴前後所穿之) 浴袍。 **2** water for a ~: 洗澡水: *Your ~ is ready.* 你的洗澡水預備好了。 **'~·tub** *n* (usu *bath* in GB except in trade use) large (usu oblong) vessel (of fibre-glass, porcelain or metal) in which ~s are taken. 浴盆；澡盆；浴缸 (玻璃纖維，瓷質或金屬製成，通常爲長方形。在英國，除非商業用語，通常稱 bath)。 **'~·room** *n* room in which there is a ~tub (and usu a wash-hand-basin): 浴室 (內有浴盆，通常還有洗臉盆): *Every room in the hotel has a private ~-room,* ie its own ~room. 這旅館裏的每一個房間都附有私用浴室。 **3** (container for) liquid in which sth is washed or dipped (in chemical and industrial processes): (化學或工業程序中) 用以浸洗某物之液體；盛此液體之器皿；浸盤: *an 'oil ~,* (for parts of a machine); (浸洗機器零件之) 油池; *a 'hypo ~,* (photography). (洗相片用之) 定影藥液浸盤。 **4** (*pl*) place where one can bath or swim: (複) 澡堂；游泳池: *public swimming ~s;* 公共游泳池; *the Turkish ~s.* 土耳其式的澡堂。 □ *vt, vi* [VP6A, 2A] give a ~ to: 給…洗澡: *~ the baby;* 給嬰兒洗澡; take a bath: 洗澡: *I ~ every night.* 我每天晚上洗澡。

Bath /bɑːθ *US:* bæθ ; bæθ/ *n* (town in W England, with hot mineral springs). 巴斯 (英格蘭西部市鎮，有溫泉)。 **ˌ~-'chair** *n* three-wheeled chair for an invalid, pushed or pulled by hand. (供殘廢者一人坐，用手推或拉之有三個輪子的) 輪椅。

bathe /beɪð ; beð/ *vt, vi* **1** [VP6A] apply water to; soak in water; put in water: 用水洗；浸洗；置於水中: *The doctor told him to ~ his eyes twice a day.* 醫生要他每天洗眼兩次。*The nurse ~d the wound.* 護士洗傷口。 **2** ***be ~d in,*** be made wet or bright all over: 浸濕；發光亮: *Her face was ~d in tears.* 她以淚洗面。*The countryside was ~d in brilliant sunshine.* 這一片鄉野爲明亮的陽光所普照。*He was ~d in sweat.* 他滿身汗水淋漓。 ⇨ also sun(4). **3** [VP2A] go into the sea, a river, lake, etc for sport, swimming, to get cool, etc. 到海裏、河或湖裏做運動、游泳或泡水取涼等。 □ *n* act of swimming in the sea, a river, lake, etc: (在海裏、河裏或湖裏) 游泳: *We had an enjoyable ~ before breakfast.* 我們在早餐前作了一次舒服的游泳。*Let's go for a ~.* 我們游泳去吧。 Cf 參較 *have/take a bath.* **bather** /ˈbeɪðə(r) ; ˈbeðɚ/ *n*

bath·ing /ˈbeɪðɪŋ ; ˈbeðɪŋ/ *n* act or practice of going into the sea, etc: 海(河、湖)水浴；游泳: *The ~ here is safe,* It is safe to swim here. 在這裏游泳是安全的。*He's fond of ~.* 他喜歡游泳。*There have been many fatal ~ accidents here,* Many bathers have been drowned here. 這裏曾有許多游水者遭滅頂之禍。 **'~-cap** *n* cap to cover a woman's hair while in the water. (女用) 游泳帽。 **'~-costume/suit** *n* garment worn for swimming (cf 參較 *bikini, swimming-trunks*). 游泳衣。 **'~-machine** *n* cabin on wheels, pulled down to the water's edge and (formerly) used by bathers for dressing and undressing. (昔時，可以拖至水邊的) 游泳者更衣車。

bathos /ˈbeɪθɒs ; ˈbeθɑs/ *n* [U] (rhet) sudden change (in writing or speech) from what is deeply moving or sublime to what is foolish or unimportant. (修辭) (在寫作或演說中由深刻動人或莊嚴突然轉至詼諧或瑣細的) 突降法。

bathy·sphere /ˈbæθɪsfɪə(r) ; ˈbæθɪˌsfɪr/ *n* large, strongly built, hollow sphere that can be lowered to great depths in the sea, for observation of marine life. (觀察海洋生物之) 深海潛水箱。

ba·tik /bəˈtiːk ; ˈbɑtik/ *n* [U] method (originally in Java) of printing coloured designs on textiles by waxing the parts not to be dyed; [C] example of such a fabric. 蠟染法 (創始於爪哇之一種印花布染印法，將不欲染色之處，以蠟塗之)；蠟染印花布料。

ba·tiste /bæˈtiːst ; bæˈtist/ *n* [U] fine thin linen or cotton cloth. 上等細麻布或棉布。

bat·man /ˈbætmən ; ˈbætmən/ *n* (*pl* -men /-mən ; -mən/) (GB mil) army officer's personal servant. (英軍) 勤務兵；馬弁。

baton /ˈbætən *US:* bəˈtɒn ; bæˈtɑn/ *n* **1** policeman's short, thick stick, used as a weapon: (警察用作武器的) 警棍: *The police made a ~ charge,* drove the crowd back by using their ~s. 警察用警棍將群衆驅退。 **2** short, thin stick used by the conductor of a band or an orchestra. (樂隊指揮所用的) 指揮棒。 **3** staff of office: 官杖；司令杖: *a Field-Marshal's ~.* 陸軍元帥的司令杖。

bats /bæts ; bæts/ *pred adj* (sl) mad; eccentric. (俚) 瘋癲的；古怪的。 ⇨ also bat[1].

bat·tal·ion /bəˈtælɪən ; bəˈtæljən/ *n* army unit made up of several companies and forming part of a regiment or brigade. (陸軍之) 營 (由數連組成，構成一團或一旅之一部份)。

bat·ten[1] /ˈbætn ; ˈbætn̩/ *n* long board, esp one used to keep other boards in place, or to which other boards are nailed; (on a ship) strip of wood or metal used to fasten down covers or tarpaulins over a hatch. (固定木板所用之) 板條；夾板；木條；艙口壓條 (船艙上用以釘牢蓋子或防水布之木條或金屬條)。 □ *vt* [VP6A, 15B] ***~ sth (down),*** make secure with ~s: 釘板條或壓條以固定；釘板條使堅固: *~ down the hatches.* 釘上艙口壓條封閉艙口。

bat·ten[2] /ˈbætn ; ˈbætn̩/ *vi* [VP3A] ***~ on/upon,*** thrive, grow fat on (esp at the expense of others, or so as to injure others). 藉…以成長、發達或長肥 (尤指損及他人者)。

bat·ter[1] /ˈbætə(r) ; ˈbætɚ/ *vt, vi* [VP6A, 15A, B, 2C] strike hard and often; beat out of shape: 搗；搥打；擊；打得不成形: *The heavy waves ~ed the wrecked ship to pieces.* 巨浪將破船沖擊成碎片。*Let's ~ the door down.* 我們把門擊破吧。*Someone was ~ing (away) at the door.* 有人在用力敲門。*He was driving a badly ~ed old car and wearing a ~ed old hat.* 他駕着一輛舊破車，戴着一頂舊破帽。 **'~·ing ram** *n* /-tərɪŋ ; -tərɪŋ/ (mil) big, heavy log with an iron head used in olden times for ~ing down walls. (軍) 古代戰爭中用以擊牆或破城門，一端裝有鐵頭之巨大圓木；破城槌。

bat·ter[2] /ˈbætə(r) ; ˈbætɚ/ *n* [U] beaten mixture of flour, eggs, milk, etc for cooking. 麪粉、蛋、牛奶等和成用以調製糕點之糊狀物。

bat·tery /ˈbætərɪ ; ˈbætərɪ/ *n* (*pl* -ries) **1** army unit of big guns, with men and vehicles. 陸軍之砲兵連 (包括大砲，人員及車輛)。 **2** group of big guns on a warship, or for coastal defence. 軍艦上的砲組；海岸上的防禦砲臺。 **3** portable cell for supplying electricity: 電池；電瓶: *a 'car ~.* 汽車用之電瓶。*This transistor has four small batteries.* 這部電晶體收音機中有四個小電池。 ⇨ cell(3). **4** set of similar utensils or instruments used together: (器皿或用具之) 一套；一組: *a ~ of lenses/ovens.* 一

套鏡片 (一組烤爐)。 **5** ***assault and ~,*** (legal) attack upon or threatening touch (to sb). (法律) 毆打。 **6** series of boxes, etc in which hens are kept for laying eggs or for fattening. 養鷄房(用以放置母鷄的成排小隔間，以便讓母鷄生蛋或將之養肥)；鷄屋；鷄舍。 ˌ~ ˈ**farm** *n* farm for hens kept in batteries. 養雞場。ˈ~ **hen** *n* hen kept in a ~. 養在養雞房中的母雞。➪ *free-range* at free[1](3).

bat·ting /ˈbætɪŋ ; ˈbætɪŋ/ *n* [U] cotton wool in flat wads. 棉絮。

battle /ˈbætl ; ˈbætl̩/ *n* **1** [C] fight, esp between organized and armed forces (armies, navies, aircraft); (fig) any struggle: (有組織的武裝部隊,如陸、海或空軍之間的) 戰爭; 戰役; 戰鬥; 交戰; (喻) 鬥爭; 奮鬥: *the ~ of life.* 人生的奮鬥。 **2** [U] victory; success: 勝利;成功: *The ~ is to the strong,* The strong are likely to win. 勝利屬於强者。*Youth is half the ~,* Youthful strength brings likelihood of success. 年輕是成功的一半(青年的活力帶來成功的可能)。**3** [U] *die in ~,* die fighting. 戰死;陣亡。***give/offer ~,*** show readiness to fight. 挑戰。***refuse ~,*** refuse to fight. 拒絕應戰。□ *vi* [VP3A] ~ ***(with/against sth) (for sth),*** struggle: (與某事物) (爲某事物) 作戰; 奮鬥: *battling against adversity.* 與逆境奮鬥。*They ~d with the winds and waves.* 他們與風浪搏鬥。ˈ**~-axe** *n* **(a)** heavy axe with a long handle, formerly used as a weapon. (昔時用作武器的) 戰斧。**(b)** (colloq) domineering and assertive woman. (俗) 專橫的女人。ˈ**~-cruiser** *n* large fast cruiser with heavy guns and lighter armour than a ~-ship. 戰鬥巡洋艦。ˈ**~-dress** *n* soldier's uniform of belted blouse and trousers. 戰地服裝(軍人制服,衣褲皆用帶子束起)。ˈ**~·field** *n* place where a ~ is or was fought. 戰場。ˈ**~·ground** *n* ~field. 戰場。ˈ**~·ship** *n* large kind of warship, with big guns and heavy armour. 主力艦;戰艦。

battle·dore /ˈbætldɔː(r) ; ˈbætl̩ˌdɔr/ *n* bat or small racket used in the game called ~ and shuttlecock. (毽子戲中所用的) 打毽板。➪ the illus at badminton. 參看 badminton 之挿圖。

battle·ments /ˈbætlmənts ; ˈbætl̩mənts/ *n pl* flat roof of a tower or castle enclosed by parapets with openings through which to shoot. (碉堡上的) 城垛; 雉堞; 鋸壁。

bat·tue /bæˈtuː ; bæˈtu/ *n* [C] driving of game[1](6) (by beating bushes, etc) towards the sportsmen; occasion when this is done. 趕獵 (用打灌木樹叢等方法,將獵物驅趕向獵人); 趕獵時機。

batty /ˈbætɪ ; ˈbætɪ/ *adj* (sl) (of a person) crazy; slightly mad. (俚) (指人) 瘋狂的; 精神略微不正常的。➪ bats.

bauble /ˈbɔːbl ; ˈbɔbl̩/ *n* pretty, bright and pleasing ornament of little value. 美觀而無價值之飾物。

baulk /bɔːk ; bɔk/ ➪ balk.

baux·ite /ˈbɔːksaɪt ; ˈbɔksaɪt/ *n* [U] clay-like substance from which aluminium is obtained. 水礬土 (提鍊鋁之原料)。

baw·bee /ˈbɔːbiː ; ˈbɔbi/ *n* (Scot) halfpenny. (蘇) 半辨士。

bawd /bɔːd ; bɔd/ *n* (old use) woman who keeps a brothel. (舊用法) 開妓院的女人; 鴇母。 **~y** *adj* (of talk, persons) vulgar; humorously coarse: (指談話,人) 粗鄙的; 詼諧粗俗的; 猥褻的: *~y talk/stories;* 詼諧粗俗的談話 (猥褻的故事); *a ~y old man.* 粗鄙的老人。□ *n* ~y talk, etc. 詼諧粗俗的談話; 猥褻話。 **~·ily** *adv*

bawl /bɔːl ; bɔl/ *vt, vi* [VP6A, 15A, 2C, 3A] shout or cry loudly: 大叫; 大喊: *He ~ed out a curse.* 他大聲咒罵。*He ~ed to me across the street.* 他從街對面向我喊叫。*The frightened child ~ed for help.* 那受驚的小孩大叫求助。 ~ ***sb out,*** (US, sl) scold severely. (美,俚) 嚴厲責駡某人。

bay[1] /beɪ ; be/ *n* **1** (also 亦作 ˈ*bay-tree,* ˈ*bay laurel*) kind of tree or shrub with leaves that are used in cooking and are spicy when crushed. 月桂樹 (葉搗爛作香料,用於調味)。 **2 bays,** ˈ**bay-wreath,** laurel wreath given in olden times to poets and heroes, victors in war and athletic contests; (fig) honour; glory. 桂冠(古代用以奬飾詩人及英雄、戰爭或運動比賽之得勝者); (喻) 榮譽; 光榮。 **3 bay rum,** hair lotion, made from the leaves of a W Indian tree. 貝蘭髮水(用西印度群島之一種樹葉製成的頭髮香水)。

bay[2] /beɪ ; be/ *n* part of the sea or of a large lake, enclosed by a wide curve of the shore: 海灣; 大湖邊似海灣之部份: *the Bay of Biscay;* 比斯開灣; *Hudson Bay.* 哈得孫灣。

bay[3] /beɪ ; be/ *n* **1** compartment between columns and pillars that divide a building into regular parts. (建築物支柱與支柱間的) 間格。 **2** extensions of a room beyond the line of one or two of its walls; recess. 房間向外凸出之部份; 壁凹。 ˌ**bay ˈwindow,** window, usu with glass on three sides, built in such a recess. 凸窗 (通常三面有玻璃, 建於牆壁之凸出部份)。➪ the illus at window. 參看 window 之插圖。 **3** side-line and platform in a railway station, used as a starting-point and terminus for local trains, separate from the main lines. (火車站之與主線分開用作本地列車起站及終站的) 側線及月臺; 引進軌道及月臺。 **4** compartment in the fuselage of an aircraft: (飛機機身中的) 隔間; 隔室: *the* ˈ*bomb bay;* 飛機中的炸彈艙; part of a warship, college campus, etc for those who are ill or injured: (戰艦、大學等供傷患療養之) 醫務室; 醫療中心: *the* ˈ*sick-bay;* 醫務室; 醫療中心; compartment in a warehouse, barn etc for storing things: 倉庫、穀倉等中之隔間; 倉房: *Put the equipment in No 3 bay.* 把裝備放在第三號倉房。

bay[4] /beɪ ; be/ *n* deep bark, esp of hounds while hunting. (尤指出獵時的獵犬的) 低沉的吠聲。 ***at bay,*** (of a hunted animal) forced to face its attackers and show defiance; (fig) in a desperate position, compelled to struggle fiercely. (指被獵逐之獸) 被迫作困獸之鬥; (喻) 處於絕望之境, 被迫作困獸之鬥。***keep/hold sb at bay,*** keep an enemy, etc at a distance; prevent him from coming too near. 阻止敵人等使之不能前進; 不讓敵人接近。 ***bring*** *(a stag, an enemy)* ***to bay,*** force (it, him) to make a final resistance; come to close quarters so that escape is impossible. 圍困 (牡鹿, 敵人); 迫使做最後的抵抗; 迫近使之無法脫逃。□ *vi* [VP2A] (esp of large dogs, hounds) bark with a deep note, esp continuously, when hunting. (尤指大狗, 獵犬) 發出低沉的吠聲 (尤指狩獵時連續地發出)。

bay[5] /beɪ ; be/ *adj, n* reddish-brown (horse): 紅棕色的 (馬); 赤褐色的 (馬): *He was riding a dark bay.* 他騎着一匹深赤褐色的馬。

bay·onet /ˈbeɪənɪt ; ˈbeənɪt/ *n* dagger-like blade that can be fixed to the muzzle of a rifle and used in hand-to-hand fighting. 刺刀 (可裝於步槍槍口上, 用於白刃戰)。□ *vt* [VP6A] stab with a ~. 用刺刀刺。

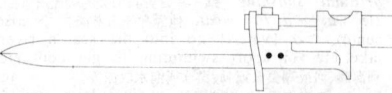

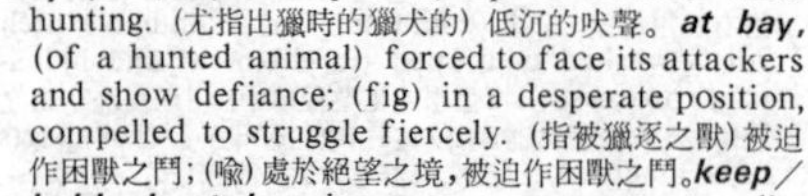

a bayonet

bayou /ˈbaɪuː ; ˈbaɪu/ *n* (in N America) marshy offshoot of a river. (北美洲境內河流之) 多沼澤的支流。

ba·zaar /bəˈzɑː(r) ; bəˈzɑr/ *n* **1** (in Iran, India and other Eastern countries) street of workshops and shops; that part of a town where the markets and shopping streets are. (伊朗、印度及其他東方國家之) 工場及商店集中之街道; (城市中的) 市場及商業區。 **2** (in GB, US) shop for the sale of cheap goods of great variety. (英國及美國之) 雜貨店。 **3** (place where there is a) sale of goods for charitable purposes: (爲慈善目的而舉行的) 義賣; 慈善義賣場: *a* *church* ~. 由教堂主辦的慈善義賣。

ba·zoo·ka /bəˈzuːkə ; bəˈzukə/ *n* (*pl* ~s) portable weapon for firing armour-piercing rockets. (輕便可携帶,威力能穿甲之) 火箭炮。

be[1] /biː ; bi/ *vi* (*pres t* am /*after 'I'*: m; m; *otherwise:* əm ; əm; *strong form:* æm ; æm/, is /z ; z; *but* s ; s *after* p, t, k, f, θ, *strong form:* ɪz ; ɪz/, are /ə(r) ; ɚ; *strong form:* ɑː(r) ; ɑr/; *pt* was /wəz ; wəz; *strong form:* wɒz ; wɑz/, were /wə(r) ; wɚ; *strong form:* wɜː(r) ; wɝ/; contracted forms, I'm /aɪm ; aɪm/, he's /hiːz ; hiz/, she's /ʃiːz ; ʃiz/, it's /ɪts ; ɪts/, we're /wɪə(r) ; wɪr/, you're /jʊə(r) ; jʊr/, they're /ðeə(r) ; ðer/; neg isn't /ˈɪznt ; ˈɪzn̩t/, aren't /ɑːnt ; ɑrnt/, wasn't /ˈwɒznt ; ˈwɑzn̩t/, weren't /wɜːnt ; wɝnt/; *Am I not* is contracted to *aren't I* /ˈɑːnt aɪ *US:* ˈænt ; ɑrnt aɪ/; *pres p* being /ˈbiːɪŋ ; ˈbiɪŋ/; *pp* been /biːn *US:* bɪn ; bɪn/) [VP1] (linking *v* (or *copula*), between the subject and various complements) (連繫動詞(或爲連繫詞),在主詞與各種補足詞之間) **1** (with a *n* or *pron*, identifying or asking about the subject): (與名詞或代名詞連用,示明或詢及主詞爲何): *Today is Monday.* 今天是星期一。*Peter is a teacher/a Catholic.* 彼得是一個教師(天主教徒)。*Who is that?* (那)是誰? *It's me/him/her/the postman.* 是我(他,她,郵差)。 **2** (with an *adj* or a *prep*, indicating a quality, an attribute): (與形容詞或介詞連用,表明性質或屬性): *The world is round.* 地球是圓的。*He is ten years old.* 他十歲了。*Short skirts are in/out of fashion.* 短裙正流行(不流行了)。⇨ fashionable, unfashionable. **3** (with a *prep* or *adverbial particle*, indicating a place): (與介詞或副詞接語連用,表示地方): *The lamp is on the table.* 那燈在桌上。*John's out in the garden.* 約翰在外頭花園裏。*Mary's upstairs.* 瑪莉在樓上。*The station is a mile away.* 車站距此一哩遠。 **4** (with a *n* or a *prep*, indicating possession, actual or intended): (與名詞或介詞連用,表實際所有或意欲據有): *The money's not yours, it's John's.* 那筆錢不是你的,是約翰的。*The parcel is for you.* 那包裹是寄給你的。

be[2] /biː ; bi/ *vi* ⇨ be[1] [VP1] (linking *v*, indicating a change from one quality, place, etc to another): (連繫動詞,表示從某種性質、某一地方等改變爲另一性質、另一地方等): *He wants to be* (= become) *a fireman when he grows up.* 他長大時要當消防隊隊員。*Give me a pound, and the skirt is* (= will be) *yours.* 給我一鎊,那條裙子就是你的。*You can be* (= get) *there in five minutes.* 你於五分鐘內就會到達該處。*Once more he was* (= again became) *the old John we used to know.* 他再一次變成我們所熟識的老約翰。*Suddenly his face was* (= became) *scarlet.* 突然間他的臉變紅。

be[3] /biː ; bi/ *vi* ⇨ be[1] [VP1] **1** (with introductory *there*): (與開端的there連用): *There's a bus-stop down the road.* 沿路下去有個公共汽車招呼站。*There were six of us.* 我們共有六個人。*There are some stamps in that drawer.* 那個抽屜裏有些郵票。*There's a letter for you,* A letter has come for you. 有一封給你的信。(Cf 參較 *One of the letters is for you.* 信件中有一封是給你的。) **2** (also with introductory *there*, meaning 'exist'): (亦與開端的 there 連用,表'存在'之意): *There is a God.* 有一個上帝 (上帝是存在的)。*For there to be life there must be air and water.* 有生物 (存在) 的地方必定有空氣和水(存在)。 **3** go; come (esp the *pp* been): 去;來(尤用過去分詞 been): *I've been to see* (= have paid a visit to) *my uncle.* 我去看過我的叔父了。*Have you ever been to Cairo?* 你到過開羅嗎? *He has been to Paris.* 他曾到過巴黎。(Cf 參較 *He's gone to Paris,* ie is now either in Paris or on the way there. 他到巴黎去了(卽現在巴黎,或在往巴黎的路上)。) *Has the postman been* (ie called) *yet?* 郵差已來過了嗎? **4** ***the ˌbe-all and ˈend-all (of sth),*** the most important part (of it). (某事物之)最重要的部分。 ***been and...,*** (vulg or hum) (used to indicate surprise, protest, etc): (鄙或諧) (用以表示驚異、抗議等): *You've been and bought a new hat!* 你竟買了一頂新帽子! *Who's been and taken my dictionary?* 誰把我的字典拿去了? ***for the time being,*** until some other arrangement. 暫時。⇨ also being. ***the...-to-be,*** the future...: 未來的…;準…: *the bride/mother-to-be.* 未來的新娘;準新娘(未來的母親)。**ˈwould-be** *adj* who wishes to be or imagines himself to be: 志願做…的;想像自己是…的;自以爲是…的: *a would-be poet.* 自以爲是詩人的人;有志爲詩人的人。**might-have-been** *n* [C] past possibility. 已經過去的可能之事。

be[4] /biː ; bi/ *aux v* ⇨ be[1] **1** (used with *pres p* to form the progressive or continuous tenses): (與現在分詞連用,構成進行式): *They are/were reading.* 他們正在看書。*I shall be seeing him soon.* 我不久就可見到他了。*What have you been doing this week?* 你這個星期以來在幹什麼? **2** (used with a *pp* to form the passive voice): (與過去分詞連用,構成被動語態): *He was killed in the war.* 他在戰爭中陣亡。*Where were they made?* 它們是在哪裏製造的? *He is to be pitied.* 他是可憐憫的。 **3** [VP4F] (used with a *to*-infinitive) (與帶 to 的不定詞連用) **(a)** (equivalent to *must* or *ought*, to indicate duty, necessity, etc): (等於 must 或 ought, 表示責任或必要等): *I am to inform you* (= I have been told to inform you) *that....* 我受託通知你…。*You are* (= ought, deserve) *to be congratulated.* 你該(值得)受祝賀。**(b)** intention: 意願;打算: *They are to be married in May.* 他們打算於五月裏結婚。**(c)** possibility: 可能性: *The book was not to be* (=could not be) *found.* 那書根本找不到了。**(d)** a supposition or unreal condition: 假設;非眞實情況: *If I were to tell you/Were I to tell you...;* 假使我告訴了你…; *If it were to rain* (=If it rained) *tomorrow....* 如果明天下雨…。**(e)** (chiefly *pt*) destiny: (主用過去式) 命運: *He was never to see his wife and family again,* Although he did not know this at the time, he did not see them again. 他從那時起就再也見不到他的妻子兒女了(雖然他當時並不知道,但是以後沒有再看見他們)。**(f)** mutual arrangement: 互相的約定: *We are to be married in May.* 我們定於五月裏結婚。*Every member of the party was to pay his own expenses.* 參加餐會者各人須自付餐費。**(g)** the expressed wish of another person: 他人所表示的願望: *At what time am I* (=do you want me) *to be there?* 我應於(你要我)何時到達那兒? **(h)** purpose: 目的: *The telegram was to say that she had been delayed.* 電報上要說的是她已因故延遲。

be- /bɪ- ; bɪ-/ *pref* **1** all over; in every direction 全面;到處;遍 **(a)** (making *vv* from *vv*): (由動詞構成動詞): *besmear*, smear all over (with sth). 搽;塗。**(b)** (making *vv* from *nn*): (由名詞構成動詞): *bedew*, cover with dew. 以露水沾濕。 **2** (making an intransitive *v* transitive): (使不及物動詞變爲及物動詞): *bemoan.* 悲悼;慟哭。Cf 參較 *bemoan one's fate,* moan about one's fate. 自嘆命苦。**3** (making *adjj* in *-ed* from *nn*) wearing: (由名詞加 -ed 構成形容詞) 戴…的: *bewigged;* 戴假髮的; covered with: 蓋以…的: *bejewelled.* 滿飾珠寶的。**4** (intensifying): (加强語氣): *begrudge;* 嫉妒; *belabour.* 毆打;打擊。

beach /biːtʃ ; bitʃ/ *n* shore between high- and low-water mark, covered with sand or water-worn pebbles. 海濱;海灘;水濱。**ˈ~ ball** *n* very large light-weight one used for games on the ~. 海灘上玩遊戲用的輕而大的球。**ˈ~ buggy** *n* small motorized vehicle, used for racing on waste ground, beaches, etc. 海灘車(一種用來在荒地、海灘等上作比賽用之小汽車)。**ˈ~·comber** /-kəʊmə(r) ; -ˌkomɚ/ *n* **(a)** long wave rolling in from the sea. 由海上滾向海濱的長浪;長卷浪。**(b)** man who makes a poor living on the waterfront in ports in the Pacific. 太平洋各港口碼頭區的貧苦謀生者。**ˈ~·head** *n* fortified position established on a ~ by an invading army. (登陸部隊所建之)灘頭陣地。⇨ bridgehead. **ˈ~·wear** *n* [U] clothes for sunbathing, swimming, playing games, etc on the ~. 在海濱日光浴、游泳、遊戲

等所穿之衣著;海灘裝。□ *vt* [VP6A] push or pull (a boat, a ship) up on to the shore or ～. 將(船)推或拖至岸邊或海灘。

bea·con /ˈbiːkən ; ˈbikən/ *n* **1** (old use 舊用法; also 亦作 ˈ**～-fire**) fire lit on a hill-top as a signal. (燃於山巔作爲信號之)烽火。 **2** light on a hill or mountain, or on the coast, on rocks, etc to give warning of danger or for the guidance of ships, etc. (設於山上、海岸或岩石上等以警告有危險或引導船隻航行之)信號燈。 **3** (also 亦作 ˈ**～-light**) fixed lantern to warn or guide ships; flashing light to warn aircraft of high mountains, etc. (警告或引導航船之)陸上標燈;(警告飛機該處有高山等之)信標光;燈標。 **4** (in GB) seven-foot high post with a lamp, used to indicate a street-crossing for pedestrians: (在英國)指路燈(燈柱高七呎，用以指示行人可於該處穿越馬路): *flashing ～* or *Belisha* /bəˈliːʃə ; bəˈliʃə/ *～*, one with a light that flashes, to warn motorists that pedestrians have priority over wheeled traffic. 表示行人有權較車輛優先通過之閃光燈。 **5** (US) (美) = beam(4).

bead /biːd ; bid/ *n* **1** small ball of wood, glass, etc with a hole through it, for threading with others on a string or wire; (*pl*) necklace of ～s. (有孔可穿於線上之木質或玻璃質等的)小珠子;(複)珠子項鍊;念珠。 **2** ***tell one's ～s,*** (old use) say one's prayers (while counting ～s on a rosary). (舊用法)(數念珠而)禱告。 **3** drop of liquid: 水珠;滴: *His face was covered with ～s of sweat.* 他滿臉汗珠。 **～·ing** *n* wooden strip with a pattern of ～s, used for ornament; similar pattern on stonework; lace trimmings, etc with ～s on the threads. 有小珠花樣的木條(用作裝飾);石造物上類似的花樣;串珠花邊。

beadle /ˈbiːdl ; ˈbidl̩/ *n* (formerly) parish officer who helped the priest by keeping order in church, giving out money to the poor, etc. (昔時)教區助理員(負責協助牧師維持教堂秩序，發放賑款給貧民等)。

beady /ˈbiːdɪ ; ˈbidɪ/ *adj* (of eyes) small, round and bright. (指眼睛)小，圓而明亮的。

beagle /ˈbiːgl ; ˈbigl̩/ *n* small, short-legged hound used for hunting hares when those who take part are on foot, not on horse-back. 一種獵兔用的短腿小獵犬(獵者步行，非騎馬)。 **beag·ling** /-glɪŋ ; -gl̩ɪŋ/ *n* hunting hares with ～s. 帶這種小獵犬獵兔。

beak[1] /biːk ; bik/ *n* **1** hard, horny part of bird's mouth, esp when curved. 鳥喙;鳥嘴(指前端之堅硬角質部份，尤指彎曲者)。⇨ the illus at prey. 參看 prey 之插圖。 **2** ram at the prow of a warship in ancient times. (古代戰艦前端之)撞角;鐵嘴。

beak[2] /biːk ; bik/ *n* **1** (sl) magistrate: (俚)地方官: *brought up before the ～.* 被告到官廳裏。 **2** (old use; sl) schoolmaster. (舊用法;俚)校長;教員。

beaker /ˈbiːkə(r) ; ˈbikɚ/ *n* **1** open glass vessel with a lip (as used for chemical experiments, etc). 有唇之大敞口杯(如作化學實驗等用之燒杯)。 **2** (liter or archaic) large drinking vessel; goblet. (文或古)大酒杯。 **3** plastic vessel, shaped like and used as a drinking glass. 塑膠杯。

beam /biːm ; bim/ *n* **1** long horizontal piece of squared timber, or of steel, light alloy, concrete, supported at both ends, used to carry the weight of a building, etc. (建築物中的)橫梁;桁(方木材，或爲鋼、輕合金、混凝土所製成)。 **2** horizontal cross-timber in a ship, joining the sides and supporting the deck(s); the greatest width of a ship, ⇨ the illus at ship. 船梁(船上連接兩舷並支持甲板之橫木);船寬(參看 ship 之插圖)。 ***on／off the port／starboard ～,*** on／at a distance from either side. 在(遠離)左(右)舷。 ***on her ˌ～-ˈends,*** (of a ship) lying over to one side; almost capsizing. (指船)傾向一邊;幾至傾覆。 ***be on one's ˌ～-ˈends,*** (of a person) at the end of one's financial resources; destitute; (指人)經濟拮据的;窮困的。 ***broad in the ～,*** (colloq, of a person) wide and stocky. (俗，指人)矮胖而且臀部寬闊的。 **3** **(a)** crosspiece of a balance, from which the scales hang. 天平的橫桿。⇨ the illus at balance. 參看 balance 之插圖。 **(b)** chief piece of timber in an old-style plough, to which the share is fastened. (舊式犂的)犂柄。 **4** **(a)** ray or stream of light (eg from a lamp or lighthouse, the sun or moon); (fig) bright look or smile, showing happiness, etc: (發自燈、燈塔或日月等之)光柱;(喻)高興的表情或微笑: *with a ～ of delight.* 帶着一種高興的表情。 **(b)** directed electromagnetic waves: 定向電磁波: *the ～ system*, by which short waves are directed to a specific target. 無線電短波定向播送法(將短波向某一特定方向放送之方法)。 **(c)** radio signal used to direct an aircraft on its course. 指導飛機航道的無線電信號;領航信號。 ***on／off the ～,*** (of an aircraft) following／not following the radio ～; (colloq) on the right／wrong track; behaving in a way likely／unlikely to be right. (指飛機)依從(未依從)領航信號;(俗)在常軌上(入歧途);行爲(不)正當。□ *vt, vi* **1** [VP2C] (of the sun, etc) send out light and warmth; (fig) smile happily and cheerfully: (指太陽等)發出光與熱;放射;(喻)高興地微笑: *～ing on his friends;* 對他的朋友高興地微笑; *～ing with satisfaction.* 滿意地微笑着。 **2** [VP6A, 14] ***～ sth (to),*** (telegraphy) broadcast (a message, radio programme, etc) in a particular direction: (電信)向某一特定方向播送(電信、廣播節目等): *～ed from Britain to S America.* 從英國向南美洲播送的。

bean /biːn ; bin/ *n* **1** (any of several plants bearing) seed in long pods (all used as vegetables): 豆子;豆類(均用作蔬菜者);豆科植物: *broad ～s,* 蠶豆, ˈ*kidney ～s,* 菜豆, ˈ*soya ～s.* 大豆。⇨ the illus at vegetable. 參看 vegetable 之插圖。 ˈ**～·stalk** *n* stalk of tall-growing varieties of ～. 豆莖;豆萁。 **2** seed similar in shape of other plants (esp ˈ*coffee-～s,* also called *berries*). 其他植物所產豆狀之實(尤指咖啡豆，亦稱 berries)。 **3** (sl uses) (俚語用法) ***be without／not have a ～,*** be without any money. 身無分文;一文不名。 ***full of ～s,*** lively; in high spirits or vigour. 有生氣的;活力充沛的;愉快的;高興的。 ***give sb ～s,*** punish or scold him. 處罰某人;責罵某人。 ***old ～,*** (dated sl, as a familiar form of address) old boy／fellow. (過時俚語，用作親密的稱呼)老友;老兄。 ***spill the ～s,*** give away information, esp sth not intended to be made known. 洩漏消息(尤指不欲人知的事);洩漏秘密。 ˈ**～-feast; beano** /ˈbiːnəʊ ; ˈbino/ *nn* (dated colloq) feast; celebration; jolly time. (過時俗語)宴會;慶祝;歡樂時刻。

bears

bear[1] /beə(r) ; bɛr/ *n* **1** large, heavy animal with thick fur. 熊。⇨ cub, whelp. ˈ**～·skin** *n* tall military headdress of black fur (worn by the Brigade of Guards in Britain). (英國近衞旅士兵所戴之)黑色皮高帽。 **2** rough, clumsy ill-mannered person. 粗鄙之人;鹵莽之人。 **3** ***the Great／Little B～,*** names of two constellations in the northern hemisphere. 大(小)熊星座。 **4** (stock exchange) person who sells stock for future delivery hoping before then to buy it cheap. (股票市場)空頭業者(抛售股票，希圖於交割前再以低價補進者)。⇨ bull[1](3).

~ish *adj* rough; clumsy. 粗暴的;笨拙的。

bear² /beə(r) ; bɛr/ *vt, vi* (*pt* bore /bɔ:(r) ; bɔr/, *pp* borne /bɔ:n ; bɔrn/) **1** [VP6A, 15B] carry: 攜帶;負荷;負載: *~ a heavy load.* 負重擔。~ **away,** (now usu 今常用 *carry off*): *~ away the palm,* excel in competition, by winning a prize, etc; 在比賽中獲勝(如贏得獎品等); *~ away* (ie win) *the prize.* 得獎。 **2** [VP6A] have; show: 有;顯示: *~ the marks/signs/traces of blows/wounds/punishment;* 有拳打(創傷,處罰)的痕跡; *a document that ~s your signature;* 有你的簽名的文件; *~ arms,* be provided with weapons; 持有武器;從軍; *~ no/some/not much/little resemblance to sb or sth.* 與某人或某事物沒有(有點,沒有太多,幾乎沒有)相似之處。 **3** [VP6A] have; be known by: 有;以…爲人所知: *~ a good character;* 有良好的品格; *a family that bore an ancient and honoured name.* 名門世家。 **4** [VP16B] **~ oneself,** (a) carry oneself in a specified way: 舉止: *He ~s himself like a soldier,* stands, walks, etc like one. 他舉止(站立、步行等)似軍人。(b) behave; conduct oneself: 行爲;處己;持身: *He bore himself with dignity in these difficult circumstances.* 他在這種困難的環境中表現出高尚的品格。 **5** [VP14, 12C] **~ (against/towards),** have in the heart or mind: 心懷: *~ a grudge against sb;* 對某人懷恨在心; *~ no malice towards sb; ~ sb no malice;* 對某人毫無惡意; *the love/hatred she bore him,* felt towards him. 她對他所懷的愛(恨)。 **6** [VP6A, 14, 11] bring; provide. 帶給;供給。~ **a hand,** help. 幫助;助一臂之力。~ **witness (to sth),** (fig) provide evidence; speak in support: (喻)提出證明;做證: *actions that ~ witness to his courage.* 證明他有勇氣的行爲。*Will you ~ witness (for me) that I am innocent?* 你願爲我做證證明我是無辜的嗎? **~ false witness (against sb),** give false evidence. 做(不利於某人的)僞證。 **7** [VP6A, 2A] support; sustain: 支持;負擔: *The ice is too thin to ~ your weight.* 這冰太薄了,支持不住你的重量。*The ice doesn't ~ yet.* 這冰還支持不住。*Who will ~ the responsibility/expense?* 誰將負擔這個責任(費用)? **8** [VP6A, 6D, 7A, 17] (usu with *can/could,* and esp in neg and interr) endure; tolerate; put up with: (通常與 can, could 連用,尤用於否定及疑問句) 忍耐;忍受;容忍: *I can't ~ (the sight of) that old man.* 我不能忍受(看見)那老人。*The pain was almost more than he could ~.* 那疼痛幾乎使他受不了。*There's no ~ing* (=It's impossible to ~) *such rude fellows.* 這種粗魯的人令人無法忍受。*She couldn't ~ to see animals treated cruelly.* 她不忍見動物受虐待。*She can't ~ to be laughed at/can't ~ being laughed at.* 她不能忍受被取笑。 **9** [VP6E] be fit for: 適宜於;堪: *His language won't ~ repeating.* 他的話不堪重述。*Your joke will ~ repeating,* is amusing enough to be heard again. 你的笑話百聽不厭。 **10** [VP6A, 12C] give birth to: 生產(孩子): *~ a child.* 產一嬰孩。*She has borne him six sons.* 她已爲他生了六個兒子。Cf 參較 *born: The eldest son was born in 1932.* 長子生於1932年。 **11** [VP2C] **~ (to the),** (of direction) turn, incline: (指方向)轉;傾斜: *When you reach the top of the hill, ~ (to the) right.* 當你到達山頂時,向右轉。 **12** [VP15B, 2C, 3A] (with *adverbial particles* and *preps*): (與副詞接語及介詞連用):

bear down, overcome; defeat: 克服;擊敗: *~ down the enemy;* 擊敗敵人; *~ down all resistance.* 克服一切阻力。**~ down on/upon,** (esp of a ship, car) move quickly towards. (尤指船、車)向…急速前進;逼近;衝向。

be borne 'in on/upon sb, (of sb) be made to realize: 使(某人)了解;完全認知: *The terrible truth was borne in on him,* he had to realize it. 他不得不相信這可怕的眞相。*It was gradually borne in on me that...,* The idea that...was one that I gradually had to accept. 我不得不漸漸相信…。

bear on/upon, have relation to, have influence on, be relevant to: 與…有關係;對…有影響: *How does this ~ upon the problem?* 這個與該問題有何關係? *These are matters that ~ upon the welfare of the community.* 這些都是與社會福利有關的問題。

bring to ~ on/upon, make (sth) relate to, have influence on: 使(某事物)與…有關;使對…有所影響;將(某事物)施於…: *bring all one's energies to ~ upon a task;* 將全副精力用於一項工作; *bring pressure to ~ on sb.* 對某人施以壓力。**~ hard/heavily/severely, etc on/upon,** be a burden on: 成爲…之重擔: *Taxation ~s heavily on all classes in Britain.* 捐稅使英國各階層均感受壓迫。

bear (sth or sb) out, confirm (sth); support (sb): 證實(某事);爲(某人)作證: *~ out a statement.* 證實一項陳述。*John will ~ me out/~ out what I've said.* 約翰將會爲我(我所說的話)作證。

bear up (against/under sth), be strong in the face of (sorrow, etc): (處於悲傷等之境)鼓起勇氣;堅强起來;不頹喪: *He bore up well against all these misfortunes.* 他在這一切不幸之中表現得很堅强。*Tell her to ~ up,* to have courage, not give way. 告訴她鼓起勇氣吧。

bear with sb, treat him patiently or indulgently: 耐心對待;寬縱對待;忍受: *If you will ~ with me* (ie listen patiently to me) *a little longer....* 如果你再耐心地聽我說一會兒…。

bear·able /'beərəbl ; 'bɛrəbl/ *adj* (from 源自 bear²(8)) that can be borne or endured. 可忍受的;忍得住的;可容忍的。

beard¹ /bɪəd ; bɪrd/ *n* **1** hair of the lower part of the face (excluding the moustache): 鬍鬚;髯(不包括髭): *a man with a ~;* 留鬍子的人; *a week's (growth of) ~;* 一星期未剃的鬍子; similar growth of hair on an animal: (動物的)鬍子: *a billy-goat's ~.* 雄山羊的鬍子。 **2** ~-like sheath on the grain of barley, oats, etc. (大麥、燕麥等的)芒。**~ed** *adj* having a ~. 有鬍子的。**~·less** *adj* having no ~: 無鬍鬚的: *a ~less youth.* 無鬍鬚的青年。

beard² /bɪəd ; bɪrd/ *vt* [VP6A] defy openly, oppose: 公然反抗;反對: *~ the lion in his den,* (fig) defy sb in his own stronghold. (喻)入虎穴取虎子;進入某人的老窩與之對抗;奮不顧身與其周旋。

bearer /'beərə(r) ; 'bɛrɚ/ *n* **1** person who brings a letter or message: 送信人;信差: *the ~ of good news;* 傳送好消息的人; *the ~ of this letter.* 持此信的人。 **2** person who helps to carry a coffin to a grave, who carries a stretcher, flag, etc. 抬棺者;扛棺人;柩夫;擔架夫;掌旗者。 **3** person employed to carry sth. 搬運夫;挑夫。 **4** person who presents, at a bank, a cheque payable on demand. 即期支票持票人。 **'~ bonds** *n pl* bonds, interest on which is payable to the ~, the owner's name not being written on them. 不記名債券(利息付與持票人)。 **5** (with *adjj*) plant, tree, etc that produces fruit, crops, etc: (與形容詞連用)結果實的植物、樹木等: *a good/poor ~.* 結果實多(不多)的樹;收穫多(不多)的作物。

bear·ing /'beərɪŋ ; 'bɛrɪŋ/ *n* **1** [U] way of behaving; way of standing, walking, etc: 行爲之方式;舉止;態度;(站立,步行等之)姿態: *a man of noble/soldierly ~.* 舉止高貴(像軍人)的人。*His kindly ~ caused all the children to like him.* 他那種和藹的態度使所有的孩子都喜歡他。 ⇨ bear²(4). **2** [C, U] relation, aspect: 關係;方面: *We must consider the question in all its ~s.* 我們必須從各方面考慮這個問題。*What he said has no/not much ~ on* (ie is not connected with) *the subject.* 他所說的話與本題沒有(沒有多大)關係。 ⇨ bear²(12). **3** [U] possibility of being endured; endurance: 可忍耐的限度;忍耐: *His conduct was beyond (all) ~.* 他的行爲令人忍無可忍。 ⇨ bear²(8). **4** [C] direction in which a place, etc, lies (as measured, eg in degrees): (一個地方等所處之) 方位; 方向(如用度數測量者): *take a compass ~ on a lighthouse;* 用羅盤測

度燈塔之方位; (*pl*) relative position; direction. (複)相對的位置;方向。***get / take one's ~s,*** find the direction of a ship's course; find one's position by looking round for landmarks, etc. 查明船的航行方向;環顧四周尋找陸標等以確定自己的位置。***lose / be out of one's ~s,*** be lost; (fig) be puzzled. 迷途;迷失方向; (喻)不知所措; 惶惑。 **5** (usu *pl*) (in a machine) device that supports moving parts and reduces friction: (通常用複數) (機器中之) 軸承 (承受各運轉部分並減少摩擦): *ball / roller ~s.* 滾珠 (滾子) 軸承。 **6** [U] (of a tree, etc): (指樹等): *in full ~,* producing fruit well. 盛產果實的。⇨ child-~.

bear·ish /ˈbeərɪʃ ; ˈbɛrɪʃ/ *adj* ⇨ bear[1].

beast /bi:st ; bist/ *n* **1** four-footed animal (*animal* is the usu word; *beast* is used in fables). 四足動物; 獸。(animal 是通常用字; beast 用於寓言中)。 **2** (farming) cow or bullock; animal for riding or driving. (農) 牛; 供騎乘或驅使的動物; 牲畜; 牛馬。 **3** cruel or disgusting person. 殘忍或令人厭惡的人; 兇惡的人。 **4** (reproachfully or playfully) person who behaves badly: (責備或戲謔語) 行爲令人厭惡的人: *They hate that ~ of a foreman!* (eg of a foreman who is very strict). 他們恨那可惡的工頭 (例如極嚴厲的工頭)。 **~·ly** *adj* **1** like a ~ or its ways; unfit for human use. 似獸的;獸性的;不適宜於人類使用的。 **2** (colloq) nasty: (俗) 可厭的;惡劣的: *What ~ly weather!* 多麼惡劣的天氣! ▭ *adv* (colloq; used to intensify *adjj* and *advv* used in a bad sense) very; unpleasantly: (俗;用以加强含壞意味的形容詞及副詞) 非常;極;令人不快地: *He was ~ly drunk.* 他喝得爛醉。⇨ jolly. *It was ~ly cold.* 那天冷極了。**~·li·ness** /-lɪnɪs ; -lɪnɪs/ *n* [U]

beat[1] /bi:t ; bit/ *vt, vi* (*pt* beat, *pp* ~en /ˈbi:tn ; ˈbitn̩/) **1** [VP6A, 14, 2A, C] hit repeatedly (esp with a stick): (尤指用棍棒) 連續地擊打: *She was ~ing the carpet / ~ing the dust out of the carpet.* 她正在用棒子敲打地毯 (把地毯上的灰打落下來)。 *He was ~ing a drum.* 他正在打鼓。*We heard the drums ~ing / being ~en.* 我們聽見打鼓的聲音。*The boy was ~en until he was black and blue,* covered with bruises. 那男孩被打得青一塊紫一塊。*The hunters had to ~ a way through the undergrowth,* make a path by forcing the branches, etc down. 獵人們不得不在灌木叢中開出一條路。 *Somebody was ~ing at / upon the door.* 有人在敲門。***~ one's brains,*** ⇨ brain(4). ***~ a retreat,*** give the signal (by drum) to retreat; (fig) go back, retire. 鳴鼓撤退;倉皇撤退; (喻) 打退堂鼓;放棄。 ***~ the woods,*** go into them to drive out game (for sport, shooting). 入叢林中驅出獵物 (以爲運動,或以便獵射)。 **~·ing** *n* **(a)** punishment, esp by hitting repeatedly: 處罰; (尤指) 接連地打: *give sb / get a good ~ing.* 痛打某人 (挨一頓痛打)。 **(b)** (colloq) defeat: (俗) 擊敗;失敗: *Our team got a sound ~ing.* 我們的隊遭到慘敗。 **2** [VP2C] (of the sun, rain, wind, etc) strike: (指太陽、雨、風等) 射;打;吹: *The rain was ~ing against the windows.* 雨打在窗戶上。 **3** [VP6A, 14] mix thoroughly and let air into by using a fork or similar utensil: 攪拌;打鬆: *~ eggs;* 打蛋 (使蛋白蛋黃混合); *~ cream* (to a froth); 攪乳脂 (使成泡沫); *~ flour and eggs, etc,* (to a paste). 攪拌麪粉、鷄蛋等使成糊狀。 ⇨ whip[2](2). **4** [VP6A, 22, 15B] hammer, change the shape of by blows: 鎚打使變形: *~ sth flat;* 將某物鎚薄; *~ out gold,* hammer it flat; 將金鎚薄; *~ the door in,* break in by hammering down the door. 破門而入。 **5** [VP6A, 14, 15A] defeat; do better than: 擊敗;優於;勝過: *Our army was ~en.* 我們的陸軍被打敗了。*I'll ~ you to the top of that hill,* race you and get there first. 我們來比賽跑到山頂,我將贏你。*He ~ me at chess.* 他下棋贏了我。***~ the record,*** break the record, make a new and better record. 打破紀錄;創新紀錄。 **6** [VP6A] be too difficult for; perplex: 難倒;使困惑: *That problem has ~en me.* 那個問題把我難倒了。 **7** [VP6A, 14, 2A, 3A] move up and down regularly: 拍 (翅); 鼓 (翼); 有規律地上下動: *The bird was ~ing its wings against the sides of the cage.* 那隻鳥鼓動它的翅膀拍打籠子的側邊。*His heart was still ~ing.* 他的心臟仍在跳動。 *Her heart was ~ing with joy.* 她的心因高興而猛跳。 ***~ time,*** measure time (in music) by making regular movements (with the hands, etc). (在音樂中,用手等) 打拍子。 **8** (various uses): (各種用法): ***~ about the bush,*** approach a subject without coming to the point. 兜圈子;不直接談正題。***dead ~,*** tired out. 疲倦極了。***~ it,*** (sl) go away. (俚) 走開。 **9** [VP2C, 15B] (with *adverbial particles* and *preps*): (與副詞接語及介詞連用):

beat down (on), 照射;吹;打: *The sun was ~ing down on our heads,* shining with great heat. 太陽直射在我們的頭頂上。***~ sb / sth down***: 使某人降低索價;殺價: *He wanted £800 for the car but I ~ him down* (= made him lower his price) *to £600.* 那部車他索價八百鎊,但我把他的價錢殺到六百鎊。*I ~ down his price,* made him lower it. 我壓低他的價錢。*The wheat had been ~en down* (= flattened) *by the rain.* 麥禾已被雨打倒了。

beat sb / sth off, 擊退: *The attacker / attack was ~en off,* repulsed. 攻擊者 (攻勢) 被擊退了。

beat sth out, 撲滅 (火); 敲出 (曲子): *The dry grass caught fire, but we ~ it out,* extinguished the fire by ~ing the burning grass. 乾草着了火,但是我們把它撲滅了。*He ~ out* (=drummed) *a tune on a tin can.* 他在洋鐵罐上敲出一首曲子。

beat sb up, 痛打;毒打: *He was badly ~en up* (= beaten severely with cudgels, etc) *in a back alley.* 他在後巷裡被人毒打。***~ sth up (into / to),*** mix thoroughly and let air into by using a fork or other utensil: 攪拌並打鬆某些東西 (使成爲…): *~ the mixture up to a creamy consistency;* 將這混合物打鬆到像乳脂的濃度; *~ the flour and eggs (up) to a paste.* 攪拌麪粉及鷄蛋使成麪團。

beat[2] /bi:t ; bit/ *n* **1** regular repeated stroke, or sound of this: 有規律的敲擊 (聲): *We heard the ~ of a drum.* 我們聽見擊鼓聲。 *His heart ~s were getting weaker.* 他的心跳逐漸微弱。 **2** recurring emphasis marking rhythm in music or poetry. 音樂或詩中標明節奏之重覆的强音;節拍。 **3** route over which sb goes regularly; appointed course of a sentinel or policeman: 某人常走之路;哨兵或警察之規定的巡邏路線: *The policeman was on his ~,* on the route he was ordered to patrol. 那警察在執行巡邏任務。***be off / out of one's ~,*** (fig) be doing sth with which one is not familiar, sth different from one's usual work, etc. (喻) 做自己不熟悉的事;做非本行的工作。

beat[3] /bi:t ; bit/ *attrib adj* of or like beatniks: (似) beatniks 的: *the ~ generation.* 反傳統的一代。▭ *n* = beatnik.

beaten /ˈbi:tn ; ˈbitn̩/ *adj* (esp) (尤指) **1** shaped by beating: 鎚成的: *~ silver.* 銀箔。 **2** (of a path) worn hard by use: (指道路) 很多人走過的;久經踐踏的: *a well-~ path.* 很多人走過的路。***go off / keep to the ~ track,*** do sth / not do anything unusual. 做 (不做任何) 越出常軌的事。

beater /ˈbi:tə(r) ; ˈbitə/ *n* **1** utensil used for beating, such as: 打或攪的器具,如: **ˈcarpet-~,** 打地毯的器具, **ˈegg-~.** 打蛋器;攪蛋器。 **2** man employed to drive birds, etc to those waiting with guns to shoot them. 被雇用驅趕鳥類等至獵人近處以便獵射之人;追獵夫。

bea·tif·ic /bɪəˈtɪfɪk ; ˌbiəˈtɪfɪk/ *adj* showing great happiness; making blessed. 極快樂的;祝福的。

be·atify /bɪˈætɪfaɪ ; bɪˈætəˌfaɪ/ *vt* [VP6A] (in the R C church) announce that a dead person is among the Blessed (ie those who will live for ever with God in a state of supreme happiness). (天主教) 爲死者宣福; 宣佈死者升天;行宣福禮。 **be·ati·fi·ca·tion** /bɪˌætɪfɪˈkeɪʃn ; bɪˌætəfəˈkeʃən/ *n* ~ing or being beatified; first step before canonization. 宣福;封爲聖徒之第一步。⇨ canonize.

be·ati·tude /bɪˈætɪtju:d *US*: -tu:d ; bɪˈætəˌtjud/ *n*

[U] great happiness; blessedness. 至福;全福;天福。**The B~s,** Christ's sermon on blessedness (in the Bible, Matt 5:3-11). 登山寶訓(耶穌論福所講的福音,在聖經中馬太福音第5章第3至11節)。

beat·nik /'bi:tnɪk ; 'bitnɪk/ *n* (1950's) person adopting unconventional manners and dress as a defiant protest against current morality and as a means of self-expression. 比特尼克(1950年代以怪異之行爲及服裝公然反抗當時之道德,藉以表現自我之人)。Cf 參較 *hippy,* a later word.

beau /bəʊ ; bo/ *n* (*pl* ~x /bəʊz ; boz/) **1** (old use) rather old man who is greatly interested in the fashion of his clothes. (舊用法)年紀相當大卻非常講究衣着樣式之男人。**2** (now usu fac) man who pays great attention to women. (今常作玩笑語)對女人獻慇懃者。**3** (now usu fac) girl's admirer or lover. (今常作玩笑語)女子之求愛者;情郎;愛人。**4** ~ **ideal,** one's idea of what is most excellent or beautiful. 至善;至美;典型。**the ~ monde** /ˌbəʊ 'mɔ:nd ; bo'mand/ (F) fashionable society. (法)上流社會。

Beau·jolais /'bəʊʒəleɪ *US:* ˌbəʊʒə'leɪ ; ˌboʒə'le/ *n* [U] (F) light wine (usu red) of Burgundy. (法)法國中部勃艮地所產的淡葡萄酒(通常爲紅色)。

beau·te·ous /'bju:tɪəs ; 'bjutɪəs/ *adj* (poet) beautiful. (詩)美的;美麗的。

beau·tician /bju:'tɪʃn ; bju'tɪʃən/ *n* person who runs a beauty-parlour. 經營美容院者。

beau·ti·ful /'bju:tɪfl ; 'bjutəfəl/ *adj* giving pleasure or delight to the mind or senses: 美的;美麗的;美觀的;令人生美感的: *a ~ face/flower/voice;* 美麗的面龐(花朵,嗓音); *~ weather/music.* 悅人的天氣(音樂)。**~ly** /-flɪ ; -fəlɪ/ *adv* in a ~ manner: 美地;美好地: *She sings ~ly.* 她唱歌唱得美極了。*That will do ~ly,* will be most satisfactory. 那樣好極了。**beau·tify** /'bju:tɪfaɪ ; 'bjutəˌfaɪ/ *vt* [VP6A] make ~. 使美麗;美化。

beauty /'bju:tɪ ; 'bjutɪ/ *n* **1** [U] combination of qualities that give pleasure to the senses (esp the eye and ear) or to the moral sense or the intellect: 美;美好(令視覺、聽覺、是非感或智力發生美感之各種性質之綜合): *Everyone must admire the ~ of a tropical sunset/a mother's love.* 每個人必定會讚嘆熱帶日落(母愛)之美。***B~ is only skin deep,*** (prov) We must not judge by outward appearance only. (諺)美貌是膚淺的(我們不可僅以貌取人)。**2** [C] (*pl* -ties) person, thing, specimen, feature, characteristic, that is beautiful or particularly good: 美麗或美好的人、物、樣品或特性: *Isn't she a ~!* 她眞是個美人! *Her smile is one of her beauties.* 她的笑靨是她的美點之一。*Look at this rose—isn't it a ~!* 請看這朵玫瑰花——它豈不是美的化身! *I'm always finding new beauties in Shakespeare's poetry.* 我經常在莎士比亞的詩中發現新的美點。*That's the ~ of it,* the point that gives satisfaction. 那是它美的所在(令人滿意之點)。**'~-parlour** *n* establishment (now usu 今通常作 *'~-salon*) in which women receive treatment (of the skin, hair, etc) to increase their ~. (婦女)美容院。**'~ queen** *n* girl voted the most beautiful in a ~ contest. (選美會中經投票選出的)后。**'~-salon,** = ~-parlour. **'~-sleep** *n* sleep before midnight. 午夜前之睡眠。**'~-spot** *n* **1** place with beautiful scenery. 名勝;美景。**2** birthmark or artificial patch on the face, said to heighten ~. (臉上的)美人痣(或爲天生,或由化粧而成)。

bea·ver¹ /'bi:və(r) ; 'bivɚ/ *n* **1** fur-coated animal that lives both on land and in water, with strong teeth with which it cuts down trees and makes dams across rivers. 海狸(一種水陸兩棲的毛皮動物,有堅齒,可以啃倒樹木,並可以築堰橫過河流)。⇨ the illus at small. 參看 small 之插圖。**2** [U] its fur. 海狸皮。**3** [U] heavy woollen cloth that looks like ~ fur. 似海狸皮之厚羊毛呢。**4** [C] high hat made of ~ fur, formerly worn by men. (昔日男人所戴之)高頂海狸皮帽。

bea·ver² /'bi:və(r) ; 'bivɚ/ *n* (on the helmet worn by soldiers in olden times) movable lower part that guarded the lips and chin. (昔時軍人所戴連在頭盔上之)半面罩(可移動,用以遮臉之下部)。

bea·ver³ /'bi:və(r) ; 'bivɚ/ *vi* [VP2A, C] ~ ***away (at sth),*** (colloq) work hard. (俗)努力工作;辛苦工作。

be·bop /'bi:bɒp ; 'bibap/ = bop.

be·calmed /bɪ'kɑ:md ; bɪ'kamd/ *pred adj* (of a sailing-ship) stopped because there is no wind. (指帆船)因無風而停止前進的。

be·came *pt* of become.

be·cause /bɪ'kɒz ; bɪ'kɔz/ *conj* **1** for the reason that: 因爲: *I did it ~ they asked me to do it.* 我做這事是因爲他們要我做。*Just ~ I don't complain, you mustn't suppose that I'm satisfied.* 你不可只因爲我不發怨言就以爲我滿意了。(Note that when the reason is obvious, or is thought to be known, it is preferable to use *as,* or a construction with *so:* 注意:如果理由是明顯的,或者被認爲是已知的,則以用 as 或有 so 的句法爲佳: *As it's raining, you'd better take a taxi. It's raining so you'd better take a taxi.* 既然在下雨,你最好乘計程車。After the noun *reason, that* is preferred to ~: 在名詞 reason 的後面,用 that 較用 because 爲佳: *The reason why we were late is that...* 我們遲到的原因是…) **2** ~ ***of,*** *prep* by reason of; on account of: 因爲: *B~ of his bad leg, he couldn't walk so fast as the others.* 因爲他的腿有毛病,他不能跟別的人走得一樣快。*I said nothing about it, ~ of his wife('s) being there.* 因爲他的妻子在那裡,我對這事一字未提。

beck¹ /bek ; bɛk/ *n* (N England) mountain stream or brook. (英格蘭北部)山澗;山溪。

beck² /bek ; bɛk/ *n* movement of the head, hand or arm, as a signal or sign, used only in: 作爲信號或示意的點頭或招手(僅用於以下成語中): ***be at sb's ~ and call,*** be bound to obey his orders, to come and go, all the time. 聽某人命令;受某人指揮;聽某人差遣。***have sb at one's ~ and call,*** have sb always waiting to obey one's orders. 使某人隨時聽其命令或受其指揮。

beckon /'bekən ; 'bɛkən/ *vt, vi* [VP6A,15B,16A,2A] call sb's attention by a movement of the hand or arm, usu to show that he is to come nearer or to follow: 招手令他人走近或跟着來: *He ~ed (to) me to follow.* 他向我招手要我跟他去。*He ~ed me on/in.* 他向我招手要我繼續前進(進去)。

be·come /bɪ'kʌm ; bɪ'kʌm/ *vi, vt* (*pt* became /bɪ'keɪm ; bɪ'kem/, *pp* become) **1** [VP2D] come or grow to be; begin to be: 變爲;成爲: *He became a doctor.* 他成爲醫生。*He has ~ a famous man.* 他已成爲名人。*The custom has now ~ a rule.* 那習俗現已變爲成規。*He has ~ accustomed to his new duties.* 他對他的新職務已經習慣了。*It's becoming much more expensive to travel abroad.* 現在出國旅行的費用貴得多了。**2** [VP3A] ~ ***of,*** happen to: (命運等)降臨;使遭遇: *What will ~ of the children if their father dies?* 如果他們的父親死了,這些孩子的遭遇將怎樣呢? *I don't know what has ~ of him.* 我不知道他的遭遇如何。**3** [VP6A] be well suited to: 適合: *Her new hat ~s her.* 她的新帽子很適合她。**4** [VP6A] be right or fitting; befit: 與…相稱;適宜;適於: *He used language* (eg insulting language) *that does not ~ a man of his education.* 他所用的字眼與一個受過他這樣的教育的人不相稱。**be·com·ing** *adj* ***becoming (to),*** **1** (of dress, etc) well suited to the wearer: (指衣服等)適於穿戴者的: *a becoming hat/dress/style of hair-dressing.* 合適的帽子(服裝、髮型)。**2** suitable, appropriate: 合適的;適宜的: *with a modesty becoming to his low rank.* 以一種適於其低微階級的謙卑。**be·com·ing·ly** *adv*

bed¹ /bed ; bɛd/ *n* **1** piece of furniture, or other arrangement, on which to sleep (Note omission and use of the articles): 牀(注意冠詞的省略及使用): *go to bed;* 就寢;睡覺; *be in bed;* 臥;睡; *get into/out of bed;* 上(起)牀; *put the children to bed;* 安置孩

子們睡覺; *sit on the bed;* 坐在牀上; *find a bed for sb;* 爲某人安置牀鋪; (fig) love-making: (喻) 做愛: *He thinks of nothing but bed.* 他什麼都不想,只想到做愛。**single bed,** for one person. 單人牀。**double bed,** for two persons: 雙人牀: *I want a room with two single beds/a double bed.* 我要一間有兩張單人牀 (一張雙人牀) 的房間。 **twin beds,** two exactly similar single beds. 兩張形式大小完全相同的單人牀。**spare bed(room),** one that is kept for an occasional visitor. 留給偶然來訪的客人住宿的空牀; 客房。**bed and board,** food and lodging; entertainment (at an inn, etc). 食宿;款待(在旅館等)。***make the beds,*** put the bed-clothes (sheets, blankets, etc) in order, ready for use. 整理牀鋪;鋪牀。***As you make your bed so you must lie on it,*** (prov) you must accept the consequences of your acts. (諺) 自作自受。***He got out of bed on the wrong side,*** said of sb who is bad-tempered for the day. 他今天脾氣不好。***take to/keep to one's bed,*** stay in bed because of illness. 臥病。**2** mattress: 牀墊: *a feather bed;* 鴨(鵝)絨牀墊; *a spring-bed.* 彈簧牀墊。 **3** flat base on which sth rests: 基座; 底座: *The machine rests on a bed of concrete.* 那機器安裝在水泥的基座上。 **4** bottom of the sea, a river, lake, etc; layer of rock, stone, etc, as a foundation for a road or railway; layer of clay, rock, etc, below the surface soil: 海底;河牀;湖底;公路或鐵路之路基;(地面下之)地層: *If you dig here, you will find a bed of clay.* 如果你在這裡挖掘,你可以發現黏土層。**'bed-rock,** solid rock below the soil, found at different depths in different places; (fig) ultimate facts or principles on which a theory, etc, is based: (地面下之)地盤岩;(喻)理論等所依據之基本事實或原理: *reach/get down to bed-rock.* 窮根究底。**5** garden plot, piece of ground (for flowers, vegetables, etc): 花圃;菜圃;苗牀: *'seed-bed;* 苗牀; *'onion-bed;* 洋葱圃; *'flower beds.* 花圃。 **6** (compounds) (複合字) **'bed-bug** *n* wingless, blood-sucking insect. 臭蟲。**'bed-clothes** *n pl* sheets, blankets, etc for a bed. 牀褥;被褥;鋪蓋(指被單、毯等)。**'bed-fellow** *n* person with whom one shares a bed; (fig) companion. 同牀者;共牀人;(喻)夥伴;友伴。**'bed-pan** *n* vessel for waste matter from the body, used by an invalid in bed. (病人在牀上用的)便盆;便器。**'bed•post** *n* upright support of a bedstead (esp the old-fashioned sort). 牀柱(尤指舊式者)。**'bed-ridden** *adj* confined to bed by weakness or old age. 因體弱或年老而長久臥牀的; 臥牀不起的; 纏綿病榻的。**'bed-roll** *n* portable roll of bedding (eg as used by campers). (如露營者等所用之可携帶的)鋪蓋捲。**'bed•room** */with -dr- as in 'dry', not separated as in 'head-room'* 本字中的 dr 應像 dry 中的 dr 那樣讀音,不能像 head-room 中那樣分開來讀/ *n* room for sleeping in. 寢室;臥室;臥房。**'bed•side** *n* side of (esp a sick person's) bed: (尤指病人的)牀側: *Dr Green has a good bedside manner,* is tactful, knows how to fill his patients with confidence in himself; 格林醫師很會對待病人(很機智,知道如何使其病人信任醫生); (attrib) (形容用法) *bedside table;* 牀側小儿; *bedside books.* 置于牀側以便閱讀的書籍。**bed•'sit(ter)** (colloq for) **ˌbed•'sitting-room** *n* room used (eg by students, single persons away from home) for both living in and sleeping in. (爲 bedsitting-room 的俗語) (供離家的學生或單身者居住之)坐臥兩用房間;寢室、起居室兩用之房間。**'bed•sore** *n* sore on the back, etc of an invalid, caused by lying in bed for a long time. (因久臥病榻在背部等處所引起的)褥瘡。 **'bed•spread** *n* covering spread over a bed during the day. 牀罩。**'bed•stead** *n* framework of wood and metal to support the mattress. 牀架。**'bed•time** *n* time for going to bed: 就寢時間: *His usual bedtime is eleven o'clock.* 他平常就寢的時間是十一點鐘。

bed² /bed ; bɛd/ *vt* (-dd-) [VP6A, 15A, B] **1** ***bed (in/out),*** plant (seedlings, etc): 種植(幼苗等): *He was bedding out some young cabbage plants.* 他正在種植包心菜幼苗。 *He bedded the seedlings (in).* 他種植幼苗。 **2** ***bed (in),*** place or fix in a foundation: 置於基座中使固定; 嵌入: *Bricks and stones are bedded in mortar or concrete.* 磚石用灰泥或混凝土砌起來。*The bullet bedded itself in* (= went deep into) *the wall.* 子彈深入於牆中。*Heavy guns have to be bedded (in) before they will fire accurately.* 重砲必須安置穩固,然後才會發射準確。 **3** ***bed down,*** provide with a bed or bedding: 供以床或鋪蓋: *bed down a horse,* provide it with straw, etc on which to rest; 爲馬鋪稻草等供其休息; *bed down a soldier/traveller, etc.* 供應鋪蓋給士兵(旅行者等)。**-bed•ded,** having the specified type or number of bed(s): 有…牀的: *a single-/double-/twin-bedded room.* 一個有一張單人牀(一張雙人牀,兩張單人牀)的房間。 **'bed•ding** *n* [U] **1** bed-clothes, eg blankets. 牀褥;被褥;鋪蓋(毯子等)。 **2** straw, etc, for animals to sleep on. 墊草(供牲畜睡臥的稻草等)。

be•daubed /bɪ'dɔ:bd ; bɪ'dɔbd/ *pred adj* ~ ***with,*** smeared (with sth dirty, wet, sticky, etc). (被污穢、潮濕或黏性等之物)弄髒的;污染的。

bed•ding /'bedɪŋ ; 'bɛdɪŋ/ *n* [U] ⇨ bed².

be•decked /bɪ'dekt ; bɪ'dɛkt/ *pred adj* ~ ***with,*** adorned, decorated (with flowers, jewels, etc). 以(花卉、珠寶等)裝飾或點綴的。

be•dev•il /bɪ'devl ; bɪ'dɛvḷ/ *vt* (-ll-, US: -l-) (usu passive) confuse; complicate: (通常用被動語態) 蠱惑; 迷惑;使複雜: *The issue is ~led by Smith's refusal to co-operate with us.* 該問題由於史密斯拒絕跟我們合作而變爲複雜。**~•ment** *n*

be•dewed /bɪ'dju:d *US:* -'du:d ; bɪ'djud/ *pred adj* ~ ***with,*** (liter) sprinkled with, made wet with: (文)爲…所沾濕的;爲…所洒濕的: *a face ~ with tears.* 爲眼淚沾濕的面龐。

be•dimmed /bɪ'dɪmd ; bɪ'dɪmd/ *pred adj* ~ ***with,*** (liter) (of the eyes, mind) made dim: (文)(指眼,心)模糊的;矇矓的: *eyes ~ with tears;* 矇矓的淚眼; *a mind ~ with sorrow.* 因憂傷而心亂如麻。

bed•lam /'bedləm ; 'bɛdləm/ *n* **1** (old use) asylum for mad people. (舊用法) 瘋人院。**2** scene of noisy confusion: 鬧哄哄的地方; 喧鬧的地方: *When the teacher was called away the classroom was a regular ~.* 當老師被叫走的時候,教室便喧鬧不堪。

Bed•ouin, Bed•uin /'beduɪn ; 'bɛduɪn/ *n* (*pl* unchanged) nomadic Arab of the desert. (複數不變) 遊牧於沙漠中之阿拉伯人。

be•drag•gled /bɪ'drægld ; bɪ'drægḷd/ *pred adj* (esp of clothing) made wet or dirty by rain, mud, etc. (尤指衣服)被雨、泥等弄濕或弄髒的。

bee /bi: ; bi/ *n* **1** small, four-winged, stinging insect that produces wax and honey after gathering nectar from flowers. 蜜蜂。⇨ the illus at insect. 參看 insect 之插圖。***have a bee in one's bonnet,*** be obsessed by an idea. 老想著某一個念頭。***make a 'bee-line for,*** go towards by the shortest way, go quickly towards. 取捷徑前往;迅速前往。**'bee•hive** *n* ⇨ hive(1). **2** (chiefly US) meeting for combined work and amusement (esp of neighbours and friends). (主用於美國) (尤指鄰居和朋友們)爲了合力完成某事或舉辦娛樂活動所作之集會。**'spelling bee,** competition in spelling. 拼字比賽。

beech /bi:tʃ ; bitʃ/ *n* [C] forest tree with smooth bark and shiny dark-green leaves and small triangular nuts; [U] its wood. 山毛櫸;椈(樹皮光滑,葉深綠有光澤,結三角形之小堅果); 其木材; 椈木。 **'~mast** *n* [U] ~ nuts. 椈實;椈子。

beef /bi:f ; bif/ *n* **1** [U] flesh of an ox, bull or cow, used as meat. (食用)牛肉。**'~ cattle,** bred and reared for ~. 肉牛(飼養以供肉食的牛)。⇨ dairy cattle. **~ tea,** stewed juice from ~ (for people who are ill). (病人所吃的)牛肉汁。 **'~•steak** *n* ⇨ steak. **'~•eater** *n* yeoman of the guard; one of the warders of the Tower of London, dressed as in the days of the Tudor kings. 英王的衛士；倫敦塔之獄吏(仍着都鐸王朝時代服裝)。 **2** [U] (in men) muscle: (男子之)肌肉；膂力： *He's got plenty of* ～. 他的肌肉很結實(或膂力很足)。 **3** [C] (*pl* beeves /bi:vz ; bivz/) fattened ox, considered as food. (養肥作爲食用之)肉牛。 □ *vi* (sl) complain: (俚)發牢騷；抱怨： *Stop* ～*ing so much!* 別再發這麼多的牢騷！ **～y** *adj* (of a person) well covered with flesh; strong. (指人)結實的；强壯的。

been ⇨ be¹.

beep /bi:p ; bip/ *n* repeated signal (as during a phone conversation, indicating that it is being recorded). 嗶嗶聲(如在電話通話中，表示被記錄之信號)。

beer /bɪə(r) ; bɪr/ *n* [U] alcoholic drink made from malt and flavoured with hops; other drinks made from roots, etc: 啤酒(用麥芽釀造，加入蛇麻子使帶苦味)；用植物之根等所製的其他飲料： ˌ*ginger*-ˈ～, 薑汁啤酒(一種不含酒精之飲料)，ˈ*nettle*-～. 蕁麻啤酒。***small*** **～**, sth trifling and unimportant: 微不足道和不重要的事物： *He thinks no small* ～ *of himself*, has a high opinion of himself. 他自視甚高。**～y** *adj* like ～ in taste or smell; (eg of a person) smelling of ～. 味道或氣味似啤酒的；(指人等)有啤酒味的。

bees·wax /ˈbi:zwæks ; ˈbizˌwæks/ *n* [U] wax made by bees for honeycomb, used for polishing wood. 蜂蠟(蜜蜂爲築蜂巢所製之蠟質物，可用爲木材添加光澤)。 □ *vt* polish with ～. 用蜂蠟打光。

beet /bi:t ; bit/ *n* sorts of plant with a sweet root. 甜菜(其根甜)。 ˈ**red ～**, used as a vegetable, esp in salads. 紅甜菜(作蔬菜用，尤用於拌生菜)。 ˈ**white ～**, used for making sugar. 白甜菜(用於製糖)。ˌ**～ˈsugar**, sugar made from ～s, identical with cane sugar. 甜菜糖；蘿蔔糖(與蔗糖完全相同)。 ˈ**～·root** /ˈbi:tru:t ; ˈbitˌrut *with* tr *as in 'try'* 本字中之 tr 讀做 try 中之 tr/ *n* [C, U] root of ～; red ～. 甜菜根；紅甜菜。

beetle¹ /ˈbi:tl ; ˈbitl/ *n* tool with a heavy head and handle, used for crushing, ramming and smoothing. 槌；大槌。

beetle² /ˈbi:tl ; ˈbitl/ *n* insect with hard, shiny wing-covers. 甲蟲。⇨ the illus at insect. 參看 insect 之插圖。

beetle³ /ˈbi:tl ; ˈbitl/ *vi* [VP2A] overhang; project: 突出；凸出懸垂： *beetling cliffs.* 懸崖。 ˈ**～-browed** *adj* having shaggy or projecting eyebrows. 眉毛蓬鬆或突出的。

beeves ⇨ beef(3).

be·fall /bɪˈfɔ:l ; bɪˈfɔl/ *vt, vi* (*pt* befell /bɪˈfel ; bɪˈfɛl/ *pp* befallen /bɪˈfɔ:lən ; bɪˈfɔlən/) [VP6A, 2A] (used only in the 3rd person) (old use) happen (to): (僅用於第三人稱) (舊用法) 發生；降臨；使遭遇： *What has* ～*en him?* 他發生了什麼事？

be·fit /bɪˈfɪt ; bɪˈfɪt/ *vt* (-tt-) [VP6A] (used only in 3rd person) (formal) be fitted for; be right and suitable for: (僅用於第三人稱) (正式用語)適宜；相當；對於…係適當的： *It does not* ～ *a man in your position to....* 在你這樣地位的人不應當…。**～·ting** *adj* right and proper. 適當的；應當的。 **～·ting·ly** *adv*

be·fogged /bɪˈfɒgd *US:* -ˈfɔ:gd ; bɪˈfɑgd/ *pred adj* (fig, of a person) puzzled; muddle-headed. (喻，指人)被困惑的；頭腦不清的；迷迷糊糊的。

be·fore¹ /bɪˈfɔ:(r) ; bɪˈfɔr/ *adv* **1** (contrasted with *afterwards*) at an earlier time; in the past; already: (與 afterwards 相對)從前；過去；已經： *I've seen that film* ～. 我從前看過那部影片。 *It had been fine the day* ～, the previous day. (那天) 前一天的天氣很好。 *You should have told me so* ～, earlier. 你早就應該告訴我。 *That happened long* ～, a long time earlier. 那是很久以前發生的。 **2** (of space or position): (指空間或位置)： *They have gone on* ～, in advance. 他們走到前面去了。

be·fore² /bɪˈfɔ:(r) ; bɪˈfɔr/ *conj* (contrasted with *after*) previous to the time when: (與 after 相對)在…以前(指時間)： *I must finish my work* ～ *I go home.* 我在回家以前，必須把我的工作做完。 *Do it now* ～ *you forget.* 現在就做，免得忘記了。 *It will be five years* ～ *we meet again* (note the use of the *present t* here). 五年以後我們才能再見(注意 meet 用現在式)。 Cf 參較 We *shall not meet again* until five years from now. 自現在起，五年內我們不能再見。

be·fore³ /bɪˈfɔ:(r) ; bɪˈfɔr/ *prep* **1** (contrasted with *after*) earlier than: (與 after 相對)在…以前(指時間)： *the day* ～ *yesterday;* 前天； *the year* ～ *last;* 前年； *two days* ～ *Christmas;* 聖誕節前兩天； ～ *the holidays;* 在假日以前； *since* ～ *the war;* 從戰前以來； ～ *now／then;* 在此(那)以前； ～ *long,* soon. 不久。 **～ Christ** (abbr 略作 **BC**): 公元前；耶穌降生以前： *in 55* BC, 55 years before the birth of Christ. 公元前 55 年。 **2** (contrasted with *after*) in front of (esp with reference to order or arrangement): (與 after 相對)在…之前(尤指順序或排列)： *B comes* ～ *C.* B 在 C 之前。 *Ladies* ～ *gentlemen,* ladies first. 女士們優先。 *Your name comes* ～ *mine on the list.* 名單上你的名字在我之前。 **3** (contrasted with *behind*) in front of (with reference to position). (與 behind 相對)在…之前(指位置)。(Except in a few phrases *in front of* is preferred to *before* in this sense, 除了在少數幾個片語中外，用 in front of 表示此義較 before 爲佳，eg 例如 There are some trees *in front of* the house. 房子的前面有一些樹。) ***carry all* ～ *one,*** be successful in everything one attempts. 所謀無不成功；萬事如意。 ***sail* ～ *the mast,*** as an ordinary seaman, not as an officer. 爲普通水手，非爲高級船員；爲水兵，非爲軍官。 ***sail* ～ *the wind,*** with the wind behind. 乘風而航；順風而駛。 **4** in the presence of; face to face with: 在…的面前；與…面對面： *He was brought* ～ *the judge.* 他被帶到法官面前。 *Don't hesitate to speak out* ～ *everyone* (ie in public) *about the way you've been treated.* 盡量向大家說出你所受待遇的情形。 **5** rather than; in preference to: 寧…而不…；而不： *Death* ～ *dishonour.* 寧死不受辱。

be·fore·hand /bɪˈfɔ:hænd ; bɪˈforˌhænd/ *adv* earlier; before¹(1): 較早；先前；預先： *I knew what he would need, so I made preparations* ～, in advance, in readiness. 我早知道他需要什麼，所以我預先做好了準備。 *Please let me know* ～. 請預先通知我。 *You ought to have told me* ～. 你早該在事前告訴我。 □ *pred adj* **～ *(with),*** early; in advance: 早的；預先的： *When you go on a journey, it's a good thing to be* ～ *with your packing.* 你出門旅行的時候最好預先把行李包裝好。 *She's always* ～ *with the rent,* pays it, or is ready to pay it, before it is due. 她的房租總是未到期就先付(或準備付)。

be·foul /bɪˈfaʊl ; bɪˈfaʊl/ *vt* (liter) make dirty. (文)弄髒；染污。

be·friend /bɪˈfrend ; bɪˈfrɛnd/ *vt* [VP6A] make a friend of; be kind and helpful to (esp sb younger and needing help). 與…成爲朋友；扶助；照顧(尤指對年輕需要幫助者)。

beg /beg ; bɛg/ *vt, vi* (-gg-) **1** [VP6A, 2A, C, 3A, 14] ***beg (for) (sth) (from／of sb),*** ask for (food, money, clothes, etc); make a living by asking for money (in the streets, etc): 乞求(食物，金錢，衣服等)；(在街上等)行乞；乞討： *He begged a meal.* 他乞討一餐飯。 *He was so poor that he had to beg (for) his bread.* 他非常貧窮，所以不得不乞食。 *He made a living by begging from the rich.* 他依靠向富人行乞爲生。 ***a begging letter,*** one that asks for help, esp money. 求援信(尤指金錢方面的資助)。 **2** [VP6A, 7A, 17, 9, 2C, 14] **～ *(sth) (of sb),*** ask earnestly, or with deep feeling: 懇求；拜託： *beg a favour of sb,* ask him to help to do sth; 懇求某人幫忙； *beg (of) sb to do sth.* 懇求某人做某事。 *They begged us not to punish them.* 他們懇求我們不要處罰他們。 *I beg (of) you not to take any risks.* 我懇求你不要冒險。 *I begged (of) him to stay／that he would stay.* 我懇求他不要走。 *The children begged to come with us／that they might come with us.* 孩子們懇求要與我們同來。 ***beg the question,*** assume (usu unjustifiably) the truth of the matter that is in question. 以討論中之問題爲論據;以未證實的假定爲論據;狡辯;詭辯。***go begging,*** (of things) be unwanted: (指物) 無人要的: *If these things are going begging* (= if nobody wants them), *I'll take them.* 如果這些東西沒人要,我就要了。***beg off,*** ask to be excused: 懇求免除責罰或責任等: *He promised to come and help but has since begged off.* 他本來答應來幫忙,卻一直找藉口,說是不能來。***beg sb off,*** ask that sb may be excused or forgiven. 爲某人求情;請求原諒某人。⇨ pardon. **3** [VP7A] take the liberty of (saying or doing sth): 冒昧;失禮;請原諒(說或做某事): *I beg to differ.* 對不起,本人有不同的意見。*I beg to state / observe, etc that....* 敬啓者(鄙意以爲)…。

be·gad /bɪˈgæd ; bɪˈgæd/ *int* (old use) by God! (舊用法) 誓必!

be·gan ⇨ begin.

be·get /bɪˈget ; bɪˈgɛt/ *vt* (-tt-) (*pt* begot /bɪˈgɒt ; bɪˈgɑt/, old use begat /bɪˈgæt ; bɪˈgæt/, *pp* begotten /bɪˈgɒtn ; bɪˈgɑtn̩/) [VP6A] **1** (archaic) give existence to (as father): (古) (以父親的身份) 給予生命;生(子): (Bible) (聖經) *Abraham begat Isaac.* 亞伯拉罕生以撒。*The only begotten of the Father,* the only Son of God the Father. 聖父的獨生子。**2** (liter) be the cause of: (文) 爲…之起因或根源: *War ~s misery and ruin.* 戰爭爲苦難與毀滅的根源。**~·ter** *n* one who ~s. 給予生命者;父。

beg·gar /ˈbegə(r) ; ˈbɛgɚ/ *n* **1** (also 亦作 **ˈ~man, ˈ~woman**) person who lives by begging, eg for money, food; poor person. 乞丐;窮人。***B~s can't be choosers,*** must take whatever is offered them. 乞丐無選擇(施者給什麼,他們就得拿什麼)。**2** person who begs for others, for charities, etc: (爲他人或慈善機構等) 勸募者: *He's a good ~,* successful in collecting money for charity, etc. 他是個善於勸募的人(如替慈善機構募捐等)。**3** (colloq; playful or friendly use) person; fellow: (俗;戲謔或友善用語) 人;傢伙: *You lucky ~!* 你這幸運的傢伙! □ *vt* **1** [VP6A] make poor, ruin: 使窮;毀滅: *You'll ~ your family if you spend so much money on drink.* 如果你花這麼多的錢喝酒,你的家將陷於貧困。**2** ***~ description,*** make words seem poor and inadequate: 筆墨難以形容: *The scenery ~ed description.* 那風景之美筆墨難以形容。**~·ly** *adj* very poor; mean; deserving contempt: 貧乏的;少得可憐的;卑賤的;令人輕蔑的: *What a ~ly salary to offer me!* 給我的薪資實在少得可憐! **~y** *n* [U] extreme poverty: 極端的窮困; 赤貧: *He complained that taxation was reducing him to ~y.* 他抱怨說捐稅使他陷於赤貧。

be·gin /bɪˈgɪn ; bɪˈgɪn/ *vt, vi* (-nn-, *pt* began /bɪˈgæn ; bɪˈgæn/, *pp* begun /bɪˈgʌn ; bɪˈgʌn/) (For notes on the use of *begin* and *start,* ⇨ start.) (關於 begin 與 start 之用法,參看 start。) **1** [VP6A, 2A, C] start: 開始: *When did you ~ English,* learn your first Engilsh words? 你什麼時候開始學英文的? *It's time to ~ work.* 是開始工作的時候了。*We shall ~ the meeting at seven o'clock.* 我們將於七點鐘開始開會。*The meeting will ~ at seven o'clock.* 會議將於七點鐘開始。*He has begun a new book,* is reading (or writing) the first few pages. 他已開始讀(或寫)一本新書。**~ *(on),*** [VP3A the *v* being understood 其後之動詞可了解] *He has begun on* (= is reading, writing) *a new book.* 他已開始(讀,寫)一本新書。*Has he begun (on) another bottle,* begun to drink another bottle? 他已開始(喝)另一瓶酒了嗎? **2** [VP7A, 6D] (used of activities and states that come into existence. The *inf* is preferred when the *pred* denotes a state of mind or a mental activity): (用於開始發生的動作和狀態。當述詞所指爲心理狀態或精神活動時,以用不定詞爲佳): *She began to feel dizzy / afraid.* 她開始感覺眩暈(害怕)。*I'm ~ning to understand.* 我漸漸懂得了。*I began to think you were never coming.* 我開始覺得你永遠不會來了。(The *inf* is preferred when the grammatical subject is lifeless, not a person): (當文法上之主詞爲無生命之物而非人時,用不定詞爲佳): *The plaster was ~ning to fall from the walls.* 牆上的灰泥開始脫落。*The barometer began to fall.* 氣壓計開始下降。*The water is ~ning to boil.* 水逐漸沸騰。*The snow began to melt when the sun came out.* 太陽出來時,雪就開始融化。(Either the *inf* or the *gerund* is used when the grammatical subject is a person and when the *pred* indicates an activity or process, not a state. Alternatives are given in the examples. Note that if *begin* is used in one of the progressive tenses, an *inf* follows, not a *gerund*): (當文法上之主詞是人,述詞所指是活動或過程,而非某種狀態時,不定詞或動名詞均可用。兩種用法於例句中舉出。注意: 在進行式中, begin 之後用不定詞,不用動名詞): *When did you begin learning / to learn German?* 你什麼時候開始學德文的? *She began crying / to cry.* 她開始哭泣。*It began raining / to rain.* (那時)開始下雨了。*It is ~ning to rain* (not *~ning raining*). 開始下雨了(勿用 beginning raining)。**3** ***~ at,*** start from: 從…開始: *Today we ~ at page 30, line 12.* 今天我們從第 30 頁第 12 行開始。***to ~ with,*** in the first place: 首先;第一點: *We can't give Smith the position; to ~ with, he's too young; secondly, I want my son to have the job.* 我們不能給史密斯這個職位;第一,他太年輕;其次,我想要我的兒子擔任這個工作。***~ life as,*** start one's life or career as: 開始…的生涯: *He began life as a builder's labourer.* 他開始了做建築工人的生涯。***~ the world,*** (old use; liter) start in life, enter upon one's career. (舊用法;文) 開始謀生;踏入社會。**~·ner** *n* (esp) person still learning and without much experience. (尤指) 初學者;無經驗者。**~·ning** *n* starting point: 開始;開端;起點: *I've read the book from ~ning to end.* 我已把這書從頭到尾讀完了。*When learning a foreign language, it's important to make a good ~ning.* 學外國語,打一個良好的基礎是重要的。*Did democracy have its ~nings in Athens?* 民主制度是源於雅典嗎?

be·gone /bɪˈgɒn *US:* -ˈgɔːn ; bɪˈgɔn/ *v* (imper only) (liter) go away (stronger than 'Go!'): (僅用於祈使句) (文) 走開;去你的; 滾蛋 (語氣較 'Go!' 强): *B~!* 滾蛋! *B~, dull care!* 隱憂,離去吧! ⇨ also woe~.

be·gonia /bɪˈgəʊnɪə ; bɪˈgonjə/ *n* [C] garden plant with brightly coloured leaves and flowers. 秋海棠(葉與花的顏色鮮艷)。

be·gorra /bɪˈgɒrə ; bɪˈgɑrə/ *int* (Irish form of) by God! by God! 之愛爾蘭語形式。

be·got, be·got·ten ⇨ beget.

be·grimed /bɪˈgraɪmd ; bɪˈgraɪmd/ *pred adj* made grimy: 汚穢的;被弄髒的: *hands ~ with oil and dirt.* 爲油及汚物弄髒的手。

be·grudge /bɪˈgrʌdʒ ; bɪˈgrʌdʒ/ *vt* (intensive form of *grudge*) [VP13A, 12A, 6C] feel or show dissatisfaction or envy at: (爲 grudge 之强式語) 對…不滿; 嫉妒; 妒恨; 羡慕: *No one ~s you your good fortune.* 沒有人嫉妒你的好運氣。*We don't ~ your going to Italy.* 我們不羡慕你到義大利去。

be·guile /bɪˈgaɪl ; bɪˈgaɪl/ *vt* **1** [VP6A, 14] ***~ sb (into),*** cheat, deceive: 欺騙;誘騙: *They were ~d into forming an unwise alliance.* 他們受騙而組成一不智的結盟。**2** [VP6A, 14] ***~ (with),*** cause (time, etc) to pass pleasantly: 使(時間等) 過得愉快;消遣;消磨: *Our journey was ~d with pleasant talk.* 我們在旅行中,以輕鬆的談話爲消遣。**3** [VP6A, 14] ***~ (with),*** amuse: 使娛樂: *We ~d the children with fairy tales.* 我們講童話故事以娛孩子們。

be·gum /ˈbeɪgəm ; ˈbigəm/ *n* Muslim princess or lady of high rank. (回教之) 公主;貴婦。

be·gun ⇨ begin.

be·half /bɪˈhɑːf *US:* -ˈhæf ; bɪˈhæf/ *n* ***in ~ of,*** (US) in the interest of. (美) 爲了…的利益。***on ~ of,*** for, in the interest of, on account of, as the representative of. 爲了…的緣故;爲了…的利益;代表。***on my / his / our / John's, etc ~,*** for me / him / us / John, etc: 代表(爲了)我(他,我們,約翰等): *On ~ of* *my colleagues and myself*, speaking for them and me. 茲代表我的同事和我自己。*Don't be uneasy on my* ~, about me. 不要爲我擔心。

be·have /bɪˈheɪv ; bɪˈhev/ *vi, reflex* **1** [VP2A, C, 6B] act; conduct oneself: 行爲;舉止: *He has ~d shamefully towards his wife*, has treated her in a shameful way. 他以可恥的態度對待他的妻子。*Can't you make your little boy ~ (himself)*, show good manners, be polite? 你不能教你的小孩學點禮貌(或規矩些)嗎? *The troops ~d gallantly under fire.* 部隊在砲火下表現得很英勇。 **2** [VP2A, C] (of machines, etc) work; function: (指機器等)工作;運轉;開動: *How's your new car behaving?* 你的新車跑得如何? **be·haved** *adj* (in compounds) (用於複合字中) **ˌwell-/ˌbadly-ˈ~d**, behaving well/badly. 行爲良好(惡劣)的。*What badly ~d children!* 多麼頑劣的小孩啊!

be·hav·iour (US = **-ior**) /bɪˈheɪvɪə(r) ; bɪˈhevjɚ/ *n* [U] way of behaving, manners (good or bad); treatment shown towards others: 行爲;舉止;品行;待人的態度: *His ~ towards me shows that he does not like me.* 他對我的態度顯示他不喜歡我。*Tom won a prize for good ~ at school.* 湯姆在學校裏得到品行優良獎。***be on one's best ~***, take great care to behave well. 非常小心以表現良好的行爲;行爲檢點;很守規矩。***put sb on his best ~***, advise or warn him to behave well. 勸導某人使表現良好的行爲。**~·ism** /-ɪzəm ; -ˌɪzəm/ *n* [U] (psych) doctrine that all human actions could, if full knowledge were available, be analysed into stimulus and response. (心理)行爲主義(認爲一切人類的行爲,如果有充分的了解,均可分析爲刺激與反應)。 **~·ist** /-ɪst ; -ɪst/ *n* believer in this doctrine. 行爲主義者。

be·head /bɪˈhed ; bɪˈhɛd/ *vt* [VP6A] cut off the head of (as a punishment). 斬…之首;砍…之頭(作爲一種刑罰)。

be·held ⇨ behold.

be·hest /bɪˈhest ; bɪˈhɛst/ *n* (old use; only in) (舊用法;僅用於) ***at sb's ~***, on sb's orders: 受某人的指揮;遵照某人的吩咐: *at the King's ~*. 聽命於王。

be·hind[1] /bɪˈhaɪnd ; bɪˈhaɪnd/ *adv* (contrasted with *ahead* or *in front*) (與 ahead 或 in front 相對) **1** in the rear: 在後: *The dog was running ~*. 狗跟在後面跑。*The others are a long way ~*. 其他的人落在後面很遠。*The enemy attacked us from ~*. 敵人從後面向我們進攻。***fall/lag ~***, fail to keep up: 跟不上;落後;落伍: *Keith was tired and fell ~*. 基斯疲倦了,所以落後。***stay/remain ~***, stay after others have left. (別人都走了)留下來不走;留在後面。**2** ***be ~ with/in***, be in arrears with: 積壓;積欠: *Are you ~ with your work/studies, etc*, Have you done less than you ought to have done? 你有積壓的(卽該做而未做的)工作(功課等)嗎? *He was ~ in his payments*, had not made payments (eg of rent) when they were due. 他未如期付出欠款(如欠租)。

be·hind[2] /bɪˈhaɪnd ; bɪˈhaɪnd/ *n* (colloq) buttocks: (俗)屁股;臀部: *He kicked the boy's ~*. 他踢那男孩的屁股。*He fell on his ~*. 他摔了一個屁股墩兒(他向後跌倒,屁股着地)。

be·hind[3] /bɪˈhaɪnd ; bɪˈhaɪnd/ *prep* **1** (contrasted with *in front of*) to the rear of: (與 in front of 相對)在…的後面: *The boy was hiding ~ a tree.* 那男孩躲在一棵樹的後面。*Come out from ~ the door.* 從門後面出來。*There is an orchard ~ the house.* 房子的後面有一個果樹園。*The sun was ~* (= hidden by) *the clouds.* 太陽被雲遮住了。*Walk close ~ me.* 緊跟着我的後面走。*He put the idea ~ him*, (fig) refused to consider it. (喻)他對這主意不予考慮。⇨ also back[1](1), scene(6) and leave[1](3). **2** (contrasted with *ahead of*) not having made so much progress as: (與 ahead of 相對)較…落後;進步的情形不如: *~ other boys of his age;* 不如同年齡的其他孩子; *a country far ~ its neighbours.* 遠比其鄰國落後的一個國家。*Mary is ~ the other girls in sewing.* 瑪莉在縫紉方面不如別的女孩子。**3** ***leave ~***, leave remaining after: 留於身後;走後留下: *He left nothing but debts ~ him.* 他除留下一堆債務外,別無他物。*The storm left a trail of destruction ~ it.* 暴風雨所經過之處留下瘡痍滿目。 **4** ***be ~ one***, (of time) be in the past: (指時間)成爲過去: *My schooldays are far ~ me.* 我的學生時代早已成爲過去。***~ time; ~ the time***, ⇨ time[1](3, 10). **5** ***be/lie ~ sth***, be the cause of, explanation for, it: 是…的原因;是…的說明: *What's ~ Guy's strange behaviour?* 蓋那種奇怪行爲的原因是什麼? *B~ her harsh remarks lay a guilty and unhappy spirit.* 她的厲聲談話說明了內心的愧疚和不快樂。

be·hind·hand /bɪˈhaɪndhænd ; bɪˈhaɪndˌhænd/ *pred adj* **1** ***be/get ~ (with/in)***, be in arrears: 拖欠;拖延;延擱: *be ~ with the rent;* 欠租; *get ~ in one's work.* 拖延工作。 **2** late; after others: 遲延;落後: *He did not want to be ~ in generosity*, later than others in being generous. 他在慷慨方面不欲後人。

be·hold /bɪˈhəʊld ; bɪˈhold/ *vt* (*pt, pp* beheld /bɪˈheld ; bɪˈhɛld/) [VP6A] (old or liter use) take notice; see (esp sth unusual or striking). (舊用法或文學用語)注意;看(尤指不尋常或可驚的事)。 **lo and ~**, ⇨ lo. **~er** *n* spectator. 觀者;看者。

be·holden /bɪˈhəʊldən ; bɪˈholdən/ *pred adj* ***~ (to)***, under an obligation; owing thanks: (對…)感激的;銘感的: *We are much ~ to you for your help.* 我們對於你的幫助深爲感激。

be·hove /bɪˈhəʊv ; bɪˈhov/ (US = **be·hoove** /bɪˈhuːv ; bɪˈhuv/) *vt* (impers) (無人稱) ***it ~s one to do sth***, (old formal use) it is right or necessary for one to do sth: (爲舊時正式用語)某人做…是應當或必須的: *It ~s you to*, It is your duty to, You ought to.... 你應當…。*It does not ~ you to*, You must not or ought not to.... 你不應當…。

beige /beɪʒ ; beʒ/ *n* [U] colour of sandstone (brown, brownish grey or greyish yellow); soft fabric of undyed and unbleached wool. 沙岩的顏色(卽棕色,棕灰色或灰黃色);(原毛未經染色及漂白織成的)本色軟呢。

be·ing /ˈbiːɪŋ ; ˈbiɪŋ/ *n* **1** [U] existence. 存在;生存。***bring/call sth into ~***, cause it to have reality or existence. 使產生;實現。***come into ~***, begin to exist: 開始存在;發生;產生: *We do not know when this world came into ~*. 我們不知道這個世界是何時開始存在的。***in ~***, existing. 現存的;現有的。**2** [C] living creature. 生物。**human ~**, human creature: 人: *Men, women and children are human ~s.* 男人、女人和兒童都是人。**3 the Supreme B~**, God. 上帝。

be·jew·elled (US = **-eled**) /bɪˈdʒuːəld ; bɪˈdʒuəld/ *part adj* decorated, adorned, with jewels. 飾以珠寶的。

be·labour (US = **-bor**) /bɪˈleɪbə(r) ; bɪˈlebɚ/ *vt* [VP6A] (archaic) beat hard, give hard blows to: (古)痛打;重擊: *The robbers ~ed him soundly.* 強盜們把他毒打了一頓。

be·lated /bɪˈleɪtɪd ; bɪˈletɪd/ *adj* **1** coming very late or too late: 來得太遲的;誤期的: *a ~ apology/explanation.* 過時的道歉(解釋)。**2** (old use) overtaken by darkness: (舊用法)日暮時尚在途中的: *The ~ travellers lost their way in the forest.* 日暮時尚在途中的旅客在森林中迷了路。**~·ly** *adv*

be·lay /bɪˈleɪ ; bɪˈle/ *vt* [VP6A] (naut and mountaineering) make secure (a rope) round sth or sb. (航海與登山)將(繩)繫繞於某物或某人之上。**beˈlay·ing-pin** *n* fixed wooden or iron pin or cleat for ~ing. 繫索栓(用以繫繩之木樁或鐵樁)。□ *n* turn of a rope in ~ing. (繫繩於栓上時)繩索之一繞。

belch /beltʃ ; bɛltʃ/ *vt, vi* **1** [VP6A, 15B] ***~ (out)***, send, eg smoke, flames, out: 噴出;冒出(烟、火等): *A volcano ~es out smoke and ashes.* 火山噴出煙及灰燼。**2** [VP2A] send out gas from the stomach noisily through the mouth. 打嗝。□ *n* act or sound of ~ing; sth ~ed out (eg a burst of flame from a furnace). 噴出;冒出;打嗝(聲);噴出物;冒出

物(如由爐中冒出的火焰)。

bel·dam, bel·dame /ˈbeldəm ; ˈbɛldəm/ *n* (old use) old, esp bad-tempered, woman. (舊用法)老太婆(尤指壞脾氣的)。

be·leaguer /bɪˈli:gə(r) ; bɪˈligɚ/ *vt* [VP6A] besiege. 圍攻;圍困。

bel·fry /ˈbelfrɪ ; ˈbɛlfrɪ/ *n* tower for bells; part of a church tower in which bells hang. 鐘樓;(教堂裏的)鐘塔。⇨ the illus at church. 參看 church 之插圖。***bats in the ~***, ⇨ bat[1].

be·lie /bɪˈlaɪ ; bɪˈlaɪ/ *vt* [VP6A] **1** give a wrong or untrue idea of: 使人對於…得到一個錯誤或不實的觀念;掩飾;使人誤會;給人錯覺: *His cheerful appearance ~d his feelings.* 他歡愉的外表掩飾了他的情緒。 **2** fail to justify or be equal to (what is hoped for or promised). 使失望;辜負。

be·lief /bɪˈli:f ; bɪˈlif/ *n* **1** [U] ***~ (in)***, the feeling that sth is real and true; trust; confidence: 相信;信心;信任;信仰: *I haven't much ~ in his honesty,* cannot feel sure that he is honest. 我對他的誠實沒有太大的信心。*He had no great ~ in his doctor,* had little confidence that his doctor could cure him. 他不太信任他的醫生。*He has lost his ~ in God,* no longer accepts the existence of God as true. 他已不相信上帝(不相信上帝的存在)。*It is my ~ that,* I feel confident that.... 我相信…。***in the ~ that***, feeling confident that: 相信: *He came to me in the ~ that I could help him.* 他到我這裏來,相信我能幫助他。***to the best of my ~***, in my genuine opinion. 我深信。**2** [C] sth accepted as true or real; sth taught as part of a religion; religion: 所相信的事物;作爲宗教之一部份而傳授的東西;信念;信條;教條: *the ~s of the Christian Church.* 基督教之教條。

be·lieve /bɪˈli:v ; bɪˈliv/ *vt, vi* **1** [VP6A, 9, 10, 25] feel sure of the truth of sth, that sb is telling the truth; be of the opinion (that): 相信(事物的眞實性,人的誠實);認爲(可與名詞子句連用): *I ~ that man.* 我相信那個人。*I ~ what that man says.* 我相信那個人所說的話。*People used to ~ (that) the world was flat.* 人們從前認爲地球是扁平的。*They ~d him to be/ ~d (that) he was insane.* 他們認爲他是瘋了。*I ~ it to have been a mistake.* 我相信這是一個錯誤。*Nobody will ~ what difficulty there has been over this question/how difficult this question has been.* 沒有人會相信這個問題曾經是那麼困難。*Will they be ready tomorrow? Yes, I ~ so. No, I ~ not.* 他們明天會準備好嗎?會的,我相信會。不會,我相信不會。***~ (you) me***, I assure you. 請(你)相信我;我向你保證;不騙你。**2** [VP3A] ***~ in***, **(a)** have trust in: 相信;信任;信賴: *I ~ in that man.* 我信任那個人。**(b)** feel sure of the existence of: 相信…的存在: *~ in God.* 相信上帝的存在。**(c)** feel sure of the value or worth of: 相信…之價值: *He ~s in getting plenty of exercise.* 他相信充分的運動必有益處。*He ~s in old-fashioned remedies.* 他相信舊式的藥方有效。 **3** ***make ~***, pretend: 假裝;假扮: *The boys made ~ that they were/made ~ to be explorers in the African forests.* 孩子們假裝是非洲森林中的探險者。Hence, 由此產生, **ˈmake-~** *n*: *Don't be frightened, it's all make-~,* is all pretence. 不要害怕,這全是假裝的。 **be·liever** *n* person who ~s, esp a person with religious faith. 相信者;(尤指)信教者;信徒。 **be·liev·able** *adj* that can be ~d. 可信的。 **be·liev·ing** *n* ***seeing is believing***, you may ~ sth if you see it. 眼見是實(百聞不如一見)。

be·like /bɪˈlaɪk ; bɪˈlaɪk/ *adv* (old use) possibly. (舊用法)可能地。

be·little /bɪˈlɪtl ; bɪˈlɪtḷ/ *vt* [VP6A] cause to seem unimportant or of small value: 輕視;藐視;貶抑: *Don't ~ yourself,* be too modest about your abilities, etc. 不要小看你自己。

bell /bel ; bɛl/ *n* **1** hollow vessel of cast metal, usu shaped like a cup, that makes a ringing sound when struck (usu by a tongue or clapper inside the ~ or, in an electric ~, by a small hammer). 鐘;鈴;電鈴。***~, book and candle***, ecclesiastical curse of excommunication. 鐘書燭(逐出教門的教會咒語)。***as sound as a ~***, (fig) in first-rate condition. (喩)處於極佳情況。***ring a ~***, (colloq) recall to memory sth half forgotten. (俗)令人回憶起一件幾乎遺忘的事。 **2** (naut) time signal in the form of a bell rung from one to eight times every half hour, eg: (航海)報時鐘(每半小時敲一次,每次敲一至八擊): *eight ~s,* 12, 4 or 8 o'clock; 八擊鐘(十二時,四時或八時); *four ~s,* 2, 6 or 10 o'clock. 四擊鐘(二時,六時或十時)。 **3** **ˈ~-boy, ˈ~-hop** *n* (US) boy or man employed in a hotel to carry luggage, messages, etc. (美)(受雇於旅館中爲旅客搬送行李,送信等的)男侍者;服務生。⇨ buttons(4) (GB). **ˈ~-bottomed** *adj* (of trousers) made very wide at the bottom of the leg (eg as worn by some sailors). (指褲子)褲管下部非常寬大的(如有些水手所穿者);喇叭形的。**ˈ~-bottoms** *n pl* trousers made this way. 喇叭褲。**ˈ~-buoy** *n* buoy with a ~ that is made to ring by the movement of the waves. (利用波浪的力量擊發鈴聲之)鈴浮標。**ˈ~-flower** *n* any plant of the genus *campanula*. 山小菜屬植物;吊鐘花。**ˈ~-founder** *n* person whose trade is the casting of ~s. 鑄鐘者。**ˈ~-foundry** *n* place where large ~s (for churches, etc) are cast. 教堂等所用之巨鐘的鑄造場。**ˈ~-metal** *n* [U] alloy of copper and tin used for making ~s. 鐘銅;青銅(用以鑄鐘之銅與錫之合金)。 **ˈ~-push** *n* button pressed to ring an electric ~. 電鈴之按鈕。 **ˈ~-ringer** *n* person who rings church ~s. 教堂之敲鐘人。**ˈ~-tent** *n* ~-shaped tent. 鐘形帳篷。**ˈ~-wether** *n* leading male sheep of a flock, with a ~ on its neck; (fig) ringleader. 頸間繫鈴以帶領羊群之公羊;鈴羊;帶頭羊;(喩)(暴亂等之)首領;魁首。□ *vt* ***~ the cat***, (prov) do something dangerous in order to save others (from the fable of the mouse that suggested fastening a ~ round the cat's neck). (諺)冒險救人(源出伊索寓言,老鼠建議在貓頸上繫鈴的故事)。

bella·donna /ˌbeləˈdɒnə ; ˌbɛləˈdɑnə/ *n* (drug prepared from) poisonous plant with red flowers and black berries. 顚茄;莨菪(一種有毒植物,開紅花,結黑漿果);顚茄製劑。

belle /bel ; bɛl/ *n* beautiful girl or woman: 美女;美婦;美人: *the ~ of the ball,* the most beautiful woman present. 舞會之花(舞會中最美的女人)。

belles-lettres /ˌbel ˈletrə ; bɛlˈlɛtrə/ *n pl* (with *sing v*) (F) literary studies and writings (contrasted with commercial, technical, scientific, etc). (與單數動詞連用)(法)純文學;純文藝(以別於商業、專門技術、科學等之著作)。

bel·li·cose /ˈbelɪkəʊs ; ˈbɛləˌkos/ *adj* (liter) inclined to fighting; anxious to fight. (文)好戰的;好打鬥的。

-bel·lied /-belɪd ; -bɛlɪd/ ⇨ belly.

bel·liger·ency /bɪˈlɪdʒərənsɪ ; bəˈlɪdʒərənsɪ/ *n* [U] being warlike; state of being at war. 好戰;交戰狀態。

bel·liger·ent /bɪˈlɪdʒərənt ; bəˈlɪdʒərənt/ *adj, n* (person, nation, etc) waging war: 交戰的(人、國等): *the ~ Powers,* those that are waging war. 交戰國。

bel·low /ˈbeləʊ ; ˈbɛlo/ *vi, vt* **1** [VP2A] make a loud, deep noise (like a bull); roar; shout: (牛等)吼叫;咆哮;大叫: *He ~ed before the dentist had even started.* 牙醫還未動手他就大叫起來。 **2** [VP6A, 15B] ***~ (out)***, utter loudly or angrily: 大聲發出;怒吼: *They ~ed out a drinking song.* 他們大聲吼叫着唱飲酒歌。

bel·lows /ˈbeləʊz ; ˈbɛloz/ *n pl* ***a pair of ~***, sometimes 有時作 ***a ~*** **1** apparatus for blowing air into a fire, eg in a forge. 風箱(鼓風入火之器具,如鍛鐵爐所用者)。 **2** apparatus for forcing air through the pipes of an organ, eg in a church. 風琴之風箱。

belly[1] /ˈbelɪ ; ˈbɛlɪ/ *n* **1** (colloq) abdomen. (俗)肚子;腹部。**ˈ~-flop** *n* (colloq) clumsy dive, landing in the water on the front of the body. (俗)腹部先接觸水面之笨拙跳水。**ˈ~-laugh** *n* loud, coarse laugh. 粗魯的高聲大笑。□ *vi* give such a laugh. 粗魯地高聲

大笑。 **2** the stomach: 胃: *with an empty* ~, hungry. 餓着肚子。 **'~-ache** *n* (colloq) pain in the stomach or bowels. (俗)胃痛;腹痛。 ▭ *vi* (colloq) grumble or complain bitterly, esp without good reason. (俗)(尤指無理地)發怨言;發牢騷。 **'~ button** *n* (colloq) navel. (俗)肚臍。 **3** bulging part (concave or convex) of anything, eg the surface of a violin across which the strings pass. 任何東西鼓出(或凹入)如肚狀的部份(如提琴之腹板,即支弦之部份)。 **'~ landing** *n* landing made on the hull of an aircraft (when the under-carriage fails to operate). (當飛機起落架失靈時所作之)機腹着陸降落。Hence, 由此產生, **'~-land** *vi* **-bellied** *adj*: 有…肚子的: *ˌbig-'bellied,* having a big ~. (有)大肚子的。 **~·ful** /-fʊl ; -ˌfʊl/ *n* as much as one wants of anything: 所需要之量;充分: *He's had his ~ful of fighting,* doesn't want any more. 他已打過癮了(不想再打了)。

belly² /'belɪ ; 'bɛlɪ/ *vi, vt* [VP6A,15B,2A,C] ~ ***(out),*** (cause to) swell out: (使)鼓起;(使)張滿: *The wind bellied (out) the sails.* 風使帆張滿。*The sails bellied (out).* 帆張滿。

be·long /bɪ'lɒŋ *US:* -'lɔːŋ ; bə'lɔŋ/ *vi* **1** [VP3A] ~ ***to,*** **(a)** be the property of: 屬於;爲…之財產: *These books* ~ *to me,* are mine. 這些書是我的。 **(b)** be a member of, be connected with: 爲…之一員;已加入: *Which club do you* ~ *to?* 你是哪一個俱樂部的會員? **2** [VP2C] have as a right or proper place: 有一個適當的地位或位置; 應該在(某處): *Do you* ~ *here,* live here? 你在這裡居住嗎? *Does this item of expenditure* ~ *under the head of office expenses,* is it rightly placed there? 此項開支是否該列在辦公費項下? **~·ings** *n pl* movable possessions (not land, buildings, a business, etc): 動產;財物(非指土地、建築物、企業等): *personal ~ings;* 個人所有的動產; *I hope you've left none of your ~ings in the hotel.* 我希望你沒有把你的財物遺忘在旅館裡。

be·loved /bɪ'lʌvd ; bɪ'lʌvd/ *pp, pred adj* dearly loved: 深愛的; 鍾愛的: ~ *by all;* 深受大家愛戴的; ~ *of all who knew her.* 被所有認識她的人所鍾愛。 ▭ *adj, n* /bɪ'lʌvɪd ; bɪ'lʌvɪd/ (person) dearly loved; darling: 所深愛的(人);愛人: *his* ~ *wife.* 他的愛妻。

be·low¹ /bɪ'ləʊ ; bə'lo/ *adv* (contrasted with *above¹*; 與 above¹ 相對; also ⇨ under¹, underneath, over¹ (2)) **1** (sometimes used after *from,* as if it were a *n*) at or to a lower level: (有時用於 from 之後,似爲名詞)在較低之處;向低處: *From the hilltop we saw the blue ocean* ~. 從山頂上我們看見了下面的藍色海洋。*The people in the rooms* ~ *are very noisy.* 樓下房間裡的人非常吵。*We heard voices from* ~. 我們聽見有人聲來自下面。 ***be/go* ~,** (in a ship) be/go ~ deck in (to) a cabin, saloon, etc. 在艙內(下艙裡去)。 **2** at the foot of a page, etc; later (in a book, article, etc): 在頁底;在(書籍、文章等之)較後部份: *see paragraph six* ~. 見下面第六段。*Please affix your signature* ~. 請在下面簽名。 **3** ***down* ~,** in the lower part of a building, in a ship's hold, etc (according to context). 在建築物、船艙等的較低部份(視上下文而定);在下面。 ***here* ~,** on earth. 在人世間。

be·low² /bɪ'ləʊ ; bə'lo/ *prep* (contrasted with *above²*; also ⇨ under², over² (2); *below* can sometimes, but not always, be replaced by *under*; when *under* is possible, it is given in the examples) (與 above² 相對; below 有時可與 under 通用,但並非永遠如此;可與 under 通用時,已在例句中標明) **1** lower than: 在…下面;低於: *Skirts this year reach just* ~ *the knees.* 今年的裙子剛及膝蓋下面。*When the sun sets it goes* ~ *the horizon.* 太陽下山時就會落到地平線下面去。*Shall I write my name on, above or* ~ *the line?* 我應該把名字寫在線上,線的上方,還是線的下面? *The temperature was five degrees* ~ *freezing-point.* 氣溫是冰點下五度。*There is nothing* ~ */under 50p,* costing less than this. 沒有一樣東西價錢在五十辨士以下。*The Dead Sea is* ~ *sea level.* 死海的海面低於海平面。*A captain in the army ranks* ~ *a captain in the Navy.* 陸軍的 captain (上尉)其階級低於海軍的 captain (上校)。*Your work is* ~ *the average.* 你的工作(成績)在一般水準之下。 *He can't be much* ~ */under sixty,* ie years of age. 他的年齡不可能比六十歲小很多。 ⇨ also belt(1), mark¹(8). **2** down stream from: 在…之下游: *a few yards* ~ *the bridge.* 在橋下游數碼之處。 **3** ***(speak)* ~ *one's breath*** (more usu 較常用 *under*), in a whisper. 低聲地(說話)。 **4** (replaceable by *beneath*) unworthy of: (可與 beneath 通用)與…不相稱;不值得: ~ *one's dignity.* 有損其尊嚴。

belt /belt ; bɛlt/ *n* **1** adjustable band or strip of cloth, leather, etc worn round the waist or over one shoulder to support or keep in place clothes or weapons, or, like a corset, to support the abdomen: 帶子; 布帶; 皮帶; 腰帶; 肩帶; 背帶; 吊帶; 腹帶: *He ate so much that he had to loosen his* ~ *two holes.* 他吃得太多,不得不把腰帶放鬆兩個洞。 ***hit below the* ~,** give an unfair blow, fight unfairly. 打擊對方腰帶以下的部份(按拳擊規則係犯規行爲);做不公正的打擊;玩卑鄙手段。 ***tighten one's* ~,** ⇨ tight. **2** endless strap, used to connect wheels and so drive machinery. (連接機輪以帶動機器之)皮帶;調革。 **'fan-belt,** in the engine of a car. (汽車引擎內的)風扇皮帶。 **3** any wide strip or band, surrounding area, etc. 任何廣闊之長條或周圍地區等;地帶。 **the com'muter belt,** residential area outside a large town, eg London, from which people commute to and from work. 通勤地區(大城市,如倫敦,四周之住宅區,居民每日通勤至大城市上班工作)。 **the 'Cotton ~,** (US) area in which cotton is extensively grown. (美)棉花地帶(廣泛種植棉花之地區)。 **'green ~,** area of grassland, parks, etc, round a town. 綠色地帶(環繞一城市之草地、公園等地區)。▭ *vt, vi* **1** [VP6A,15B] fasten with a ~: 以帶繫住: *The officer ~ed his sword on.* 那軍官用帶將劍佩上。 **2** [VP6A] thrash with a ~; (colloq) strike with the fist(s): 用皮帶打;(俗)拳打;毆打;揍: *If you don't shut up, I'll* ~ *you.* 你再不閉嘴,我要揍你。 **~·ing** *n*: *give the boy a good ~ing,* thrash him well. 用皮帶把那孩子狠打一頓。 **3** [VP2C,3A] ~ ***along,*** (colloq) move fast. (俗)行動迅速。 **4** [VP15B] ~ ***out,*** (colloq) sing loudly and forcefully: (俗)大聲用力唱: *No one can* ~ *out those old songs like she can.* 沒有人能像她一樣高聲唱出那些老歌。 **5** [VP2C] ~ ***up,*** (sl) stop talking. (俚)別講話。

be·moan /bɪ'məʊn ; bɪ'mon/ *vt* [VP6A] (poet) moan for; show great sorrow for: (詩)爲…而悲痛或慟哭; 爲…而表示極大之憂傷; 悲嘆: ~ *one's sad fate;* 自嘆命苦; *~ing the loss of all her money.* 悲痛她全部錢財的損失。

be·mused /bɪ'mjuːzd ; bɪ'mjuzd/ *pred adj* preoccupied; confused, bewildered. 恍惚的;發獃的;困惑的。

ben¹ /ben ; bɛn/ *n* (Scot) inner room (usu of a two-roomed house). (蘇)(通常指兩房間房屋之)後房。

ben² /ben ; bɛn/ *n* (Scot) mountain peak (used with names as *Ben Nevis*). (蘇)山峯(通常與峯名連用,例如 Ben Nevis 納維斯峯)。

bench /bentʃ ; bɛntʃ/ *n* **1** long seat of wood or stone, eg in a public park, or across a rowing-boat; (in the House of Commons) seat occupied by certain classes of members. 長櫈;板櫈;石櫈(如公園中或橫置於划艇中者); (下議院中) 某些類議員的席位。 **'back-~es,** for members not entitled to a front ~. 後排席位(無資格坐前排席位之議員的席位)。 **'cross-~es,** for independent members who do not vote with either of the two main political parties. 橫席位;中立議員席位(投票時不附和兩大政黨之任何一方面的獨立份子的席位)。 **'front-~es,** reserved for ministers or ex-ministers. 前排席位(爲內閣大臣或前任內閣大臣所保留的席位)。Hence, 由此產生, **ˌback-/ˌcross-/ˌfront-'bencher,** one of the above people. 後排席位(橫席位,前排席位)之人。 **the 'Treasury B~,** for Ministers. 內閣大臣席;國務大臣席。 **'~ seat,** (in a car) seat (for 2 or 3 persons) extending the width of the car. (汽車中的)橫排座位(供二人或三人坐者)。⇨ bucket seat. **2** [U] (collective, with *def art*, often **the B~**) judges; magistrates; judge's seat or office; law court. (集合用法,與定冠詞連用,常作 the Bench)法官;行政司法官;法官的席位或職位;法院。 ***be raised to the B~,*** be made a judge or a bishop. 被陞任爲法官或主教。 **the ˌKing's／ˌQueen's ˈB~ (Division),** of the High Court of Justice. (高等法院之)王座庭。 **3** work-table at which a shoemaker, carpenter, etc, works. (鞋匠、木匠等之)工作檯。

bend[1] /bend ; bɛnd/ *vt, vi* (*pt, pp* bent /bent ; bɛnt/) **1** [VP6A, 15A, B] cause (sth rigid) to be out of a straight line or surface; force into a curve or angle: 使(僵硬的東西)彎曲;使成弧形或一角度: *It isn't easy to ~ a bar of iron.* 使鐵棒彎曲不容易。 *He heated the iron rod and bent it into a right angle.* 他將鐵桿燒熱,然後將之彎成直角。 *B~ the end of the wire up／down／back.* 將金屬線端彎上來(下去,回來)。 *Rheumatism prevents him from ~ing his back.* 風濕痛使他不能彎腰。 *Her head was bent over her book.* 她埋頭讀書。 ***~ the knee (to),*** (rhet) bow, pray. (修辭)(向…)屈膝;屈服;祈禱;懇求。 ***on ~ed knees,*** (liter) kneeling; in an attitude of prayer or entreaty. (文)屈膝的;跪下的;以祈禱或懇求之態度。 ***~ a rule,*** (colloq) interpret it loosely (to suit the circumstances). (俗)(爲適應情況)從寬解釋一法令;通權達變。 **2** [VP2A, C] become curved or angular; bow; stoop: 彎曲;彎腰;屈身: *The branches were ~ing (down) with the weight of the fruit.* 樹枝被果實的重量壓得彎曲(下來)了。*The branch bent but didn't break when the boy climbed on to it.* 當那男孩爬上樹枝時,樹枝彎曲了,但是沒有斷。*Can you ~ down and touch your toes without ~ing your knees?* 你能彎下腰,不屈膝而觸着你的足趾嗎? *The tall man bent forward to listen to the little girl.* 那高個子彎下身來聽那小女孩的話。 *Sit up straight: don't ~ over your desk.* 坐端正:不要趴在桌子上。 *The river ~s* (= turns) *several times before reaching the sea.* 這條河轉了好幾個彎才流入海中。 *The road ~s to the left here.* 路在此向左彎。 **3** [VP15A] direct: 使朝向: *It's time for us to ~ our steps homeward,* turn towards home. 是我們歸去的時候了。 *All eyes were bent on me,* Every one was looking at me. 大家都在看我。 *She stood there with eyes bent on the ground,* looking down. 她站在那裏,眼睛看着地。*He couldn't ~ his mind* (=give his attention) *to his studies.* 他不能够專心於他的功課。 **4** [VP2C, 14] ***~ (sb) to,*** submit: 屈服;順從: *~ to sb's will;* 順從某人的意志; make (sb) submit: 使(某人)屈服或順從: *~ sb to one's will.* 使某人順從其意志。 **5** [VP6A] curve (a bow) in order to string it: 屈(弓)以上弦;張(弓);開(弓): *None of the suitors could ~ the bow of Odysseus.* 沒有一個求婚者能拉得動奧德修斯的弓。 **6** ***be bent on,*** have the mind set on, have as a fixed purpose: 專心致志於: *He is bent on mastering English,* determined to learn it thoroughly. 他專心致志於學通英文。*He is bent on mischief,* has plans to do sth mischievous. 他打算搗鬼。 **bent** *pred adj* (sl) dishonest; corrupt; mad. (俚)不誠實的;不道德的;瘋狂的。

bend[2] /bend ; bɛnd/ *n* **1** curve or turn: 轉彎;彎: *a sharp ~ in the road.* 路上的一個急彎。 ***round the bend,*** (sl) mad. (俚)發瘋的。 **2** sailor's knot (in a rope). (繩索之)水手結。**3 the ~s,** (colloq) pains in the joints, caused by working in compressed air, eg in a caisson(2). (俗)潛水夫病(在壓縮空氣中工作所引起的關節痛)。

be·neath /bɪˈniːθ ; brˈniθ/ *prep, adv* **1** (old use, or liter) below, under(neath). (舊用法或文)在(…)下面;在(…)底下。 **2** not worthy of: 不值得;與…不相稱: *His accusations are ~ contempt／notice,* should be ignored. 他的指控不值一提。*It is ~ you to complain,* unworthy of you to do so. 你犯不上抱怨。

ben·edick /ˈbenɪdɪk ; ˈbɛnəˌdɪk/ (US = **ben·e·dict**) /ˈbenɪdɪkt ; ˈbɛnəˌdɪkt/ *n* recently married man, esp one who has been a bachelor for many years. 新婚的男人(尤指曾經過着多年的獨身生活者)。

Bene·dic·tine /ˌbenɪˈdɪktɪn ; ˌbɛnəˈdɪktɪn/ *n, adj* **1** [C] (monk or nun) of the religious order founded in AD 529 by St Benedict. 班尼狄克教派的(該教派係由 St Benedict 創於公元 529 年);班尼狄克教派之修士或修女。 **2** [U] /-tiːn ; -tin/ liqueur made by monks of this order. 此派修士所釀造的一種甜酒。

bene·dic·tion /ˌbenɪˈdɪkʃn ; ˌbɛnəˈdɪkʃən/ *n* blessing (esp one given by a priest at the end of a church service): 祝福;祝禱(尤指教士在禮拜結束時所作者): *pronounce the ~.* 祝禱。

bene·fac·tion /ˌbenɪˈfækʃn ; ˌbɛnəˈfækʃən/ *n* [U] doing good; [C] good deed (esp the giving of money for charity); charitable gift: 行善;善行(尤指捐款給慈善事業);爲慈善目的所作之捐贈: *That man's ~s now amount to £10000.* 那個人的慈善捐款現已達一萬鎊。

bene·fac·tor /ˈbenɪfæktə(r) ; ˈbɛnəˌfæktɚ/ *n* person who has given friendly help, esp financial help, to a school, hospital or charitable institution. 幫助者;恩人;(尤指學校、醫院或慈善機關的)捐助者。 **bene·fac·tress** /ˈbenɪfæktrɪs ; ˈbɛnəˌfæktrɪs/ *n* woman ~. 女恩人;女捐助者。

bene·fice /ˈbenɪfɪs ; ˈbɛnəfɪs/ *n* income-producing property (called 稱作 a *church living*) held by a priest or clergyman (esp a vicar or rector). 神父或牧師(尤指教區牧師)所享有的教產;聖俸。 **bene·ficed** /-fɪst ; -ˌfɪst/ *adj* having a ~: 享有聖俸的: *a ~d clergyman.* 享有聖俸的牧師。

be·nefi·cence /bɪˈnefɪsns ; bəˈnɛfəsns/ *n* [U] (formal) doing good; active kindness. (正式用語)行善;善行;善事;德行;恩惠。 **be·nefi·cent** /bɪˈnefɪsnt ; bəˈnɛfəsnt/ *adj* (formal) doing good; kind. (正式用語)行善的;慈善的;仁慈的。

bene·fi·cial /ˌbenɪˈfɪʃl ; ˌbɛnəˈfɪʃəl/ *adj* (formal) having good effect; helpful: (正式用語)有益處的;有幫助的: *Fresh air and good food are ~ to the health.* 新鮮空氣和優良食物有益於健康。 *I hope your holiday will be ~,* do you good. 我希望你的假期會對你有益。 **~·ly** *adv*

bene·fi·ci·ary /ˌbenɪˈfɪʃərɪ *US:* -ˈfɪʃɪerɪ ; ˌbɛnəˈfɪʃərɪ/ *n* [C] (*pl* -ries) person who receives a benefit, esp one who receives money, property, etc under a will (at sb's death). 受益人;受惠人(尤指按死者遺囑承受遺產者)。

bene·fit /ˈbenɪfɪt ; ˈbɛnəfɪt/ *n* **1** [U] advantage; profit; help: 利益;益處;裨益;幫助: *Did you get much ~ from your holiday,* did you feel better afterwards? 你的假期是否對你有很大的益處? *The book wasn't of much ~ to me,* didn't help me much. 這本書對我沒有多大益處。*The money is to be used for the ~ of the poor,* to help poor people. 該款將用以救助貧困。 *It was done for your ~,* to help you. 這事情是爲了你的利益而做的。***give sb the ~ of the doubt,*** assume that he is innocent because there is insufficient evidence that he is guilty. 因無充分的證據證明某人有罪而假定其無罪;對某人之嫌疑作善意解釋。 ~ ***in kind,*** ⇨ kind[2](4). **ˈ~ performance／concert／match,** theatrical performance／concert／cricket or football match, etc, money for which is for the ~ of a charity, a particular player, etc. (爲慈善事業,或某一演員、球員等籌款的)義演(慈善音樂會,義賽)。 **2** [C] act of kindness; favour; advantage: 善行;恩惠;利益: *the ~s of a good education;* 良好教育的利益; *the ~s we receive from our parents and teachers.* 我們所受之於父母及師長的恩惠。 **3** [C] allowance of money to which a person is entitled as a citizen or as a member of an insurance society, etc: (以公民或投保人等身份而有資格領取之)救濟金;保險給付;津貼: *medical／unemployment／sickness ~s.* 醫療(失業,疾病)津貼。 □ *vt, vi* **1** [VP6A] do good to:

有益於;對…有益: *The new railway will ~ the district.* 新鐵路對於該地區將有裨益。*The sea air will ~ you.* 海上的空氣將對你有益。 **2** [VP3A] **~ from/by,** receive ~ from/by: 得益於;自…獲益: *You will ~ by a holiday.* 度假將有益於你。

ben·ev·ol·ence /bɪˈnevələns ; bəˈnɛvələns/ *n* [U] wish to do good; activity in doing good: 仁心;善行;善舉: *His ~ made it possible for many poor boys to attend college.* 他的善行使許多貧苦的男孩能够上大學。

ben·ev·ol·ent /bɪˈnevələnt ; bəˈnɛvələnt/ *adj* **~ to/towards,** kind and helpful. 仁慈的;慈善的;樂善好施的。**~·ly** *adv*

be·nighted /bɪˈnaɪtɪd ; bɪˈnaɪtɪd/ *part adj* **1** (liter or old use) without the light of knowledge; in moral darkness. (文或舊用法)愚昧無知的;蒙昧的。 **2** (old use, of travellers) overtaken by darkness. (舊用法,指旅行者)天黑仍在趕路的。

be·nign /bɪˈnaɪn ; bɪˈnaɪn/ *adj* **1** (of persons) kind and gentle. (指人)和藹可親的;慈祥的。 **2** (of soil, climate) mild, favourable. (指土壤,氣候)溫和的;有利的。 **3** (of a disease, tumour) not dangerous. (指病,瘤)無危險的;良性的。⇨ malignant(2). **~·ly** *adv*

be·nig·nant /bɪˈnɪgnənt ; bɪˈnɪgnənt/ *adj* (formal) kind, gracious. (正式用語)仁慈的;親切的。 **~·ly** *adv*

be·nig·nity /bɪˈnɪgnətɪ ; bɪˈnɪgnətɪ/ *n* (formal) [U] kindness of heart; [C] kind act, favour. (正式用語)仁心;仁慈;善行;善舉。

beni·son /ˈbenɪzn ; ˈbɛnɪzn/ *n* [C] (old use) blessing. (舊用法)幸福;祝福;神的恩典。

bent[1] /bent ; bɛnt/ *n* **~ (for),** inclination or aptitude; natural skill in and liking: (對…的)傾向;愛好: *She has a ~ for sewing/music.* 她生性愛好縫紉(音樂)。 ***follow one's ~,*** do what one is interested in and what one enjoys doing. 隨自己之所好;隨心所欲。 ***to the top of one's ~,*** to one's heart's desire. 盡心;盡量;盡情。

bent[2] ⇨ bend[1] esp (6).

be·numbed /bɪˈnʌmd ; bɪˈnʌmd/ *pred adj* made numb; with all feelings taken away: 麻木的;無感覺的;僵的: *My fingers were ~ with cold.* 我的手指凍僵了。

Ben·ze·drine /ˈbenzədri:n ; ˈbɛnzədrɪn/ *n* (P) brand of amphetamine. (商標)苯齊特林。

ben·zene /ˈbenzi:n ; ˈbɛnzin/ *n* [U] colourless liquid (C_6H_6) obtained from petroleum and coal-tar, used in the manufacture of numerous chemical products. 苯(無色液體,分子式 C_6H_6,自石油及煤溚中提出,用以製造很多種的化學產品)。

ben·zine /ˈbenzi:n ; ˈbɛnzin/ *n* [U] colourless liquid (mixture of hydrocarbons) obtained from mineral oil, used for cleaning, etc. 輕油精;石油精;奔散油(無色液體,爲碳氫族混合物,自礦物油中提出,用作清潔劑等)。

ben·zol /ˈbenzɒl *US:* -zɔ:l ; ˈbɛnzol/ *n* [U] = benzene.

be·queath /bɪˈkwi:ð ; bɪˈkwið/ *vt* [VP6A, 12A, 13A] **~ (to),** **1** arrange (by making a will) to give (property, etc to sb) at death: (立遺囑)贈與(財產等);遺贈;遺留: *He has ~ed me his gold watch.* 他已將他的金錶遺贈給我。 **2** (fig) hand down to those who come after: (喻)傳給後代: *discoveries ~ed to us by the scientists of the last century.* 前一世紀的科學家傳給我們的種種發現。

be·quest /bɪˈkwest ; bɪˈkwɛst/ *n* **1** [U] bequeathing. 遺贈; 遺留; 傳與。 **2** [C] sth bequeathed: 遺產;遺留物;遺贈物;傳給後代之物: *He left ~s of money to all his servants.* 他對所有的僕人都遺贈了一些金錢。

be·rate /bɪˈreɪt ; bɪˈret/ *vt* [VP6A] scold sharply. 嚴責;痛罵。

be·reave /bɪˈri:v ; bəˈriv/ *vt* (*pt, pp* bereft /bɪˈreft ; bəˈrɛft/ or bereaved; usu bereft in (1) and bereaved in (2)) (過去式及過去分詞爲 bereft 或 bereaved, 通常第 1 義用 bereft, 第 2 義用 bereaved) [VP14] **~ of,** **1** rob or dispossess (of sth immaterial): 奪去;剝奪;使喪失(指無形物): *bereft of hope,* without hope; 失去希望的; *bereft of reason,* mad. 失去理智(瘋狂)的。*Indignation bereft him of speech,* took away his power to speak. 他氣憤得說不出話來。 **2** (of death) leave sad by taking away (a relation, etc): (指死亡)使痛失(親屬等): *the accident that ~d him of his wife and child;* 使他痛失妻兒的禍事; *the ~d husband,* the man whose wife had died. 喪妻之人。**~·ment** *n* [U] being ~d; loss by death: 喪失親人;喪親之痛: *We all sympathize with you in your ~ment;* 我們皆同情你的喪親之痛; [C] instance of this: 親人喪亡之實例: *Owing to a recent ~ment she did not attend the concert.* 因爲她最近有親人喪亡,所以她沒有參加音樂會。

be·reft ⇨ bereave.

be·ret /ˈbereɪ *US:* bəˈreɪ ; bəˈre/ *n* flat, round cap of felt or cloth, worn with sports and holiday clothes, and as military head-dress. 一種扁圓帽(爲絨質或布質,配運動衫或假日服裝戴之,亦作軍帽)。

berg /bɜ:g ; bɝg/ *n* = iceberg.

beri-beri /ˌberɪ ˈberɪ ; ˈbɛrɪˈbɛrɪ/ *n* [U] disease, common in oriental and tropical countries, caused by lack of vitamins, etc, essential to health. (常見於東方及熱帶國家,因缺乏維護健康所必需的維他命等而引起之)脚氣病。

berry /ˈberɪ ; ˈbɛrɪ/ *n* (*pl* -ries) **1** small seedy fruit: 漿果;莓: *holly berries;* 冬青果; *straw~;* 草莓; *black~;* 黑莓; *rasp~.* 藨莓。⇨ the illus at fruit. 參看 fruit 之插圖。 **2** coffee bean. 咖啡實;咖啡豆。

ber·serk /bəˈsɜ:k ; ˈbɝsɝk/ *pred adj* **be/go/send sb ~,** be, go, cause sb to go uncontrollably wild: 發狂(使某人發狂): *He suddenly went ~ with rage.* 他突然狂怒。

berth /bɜ:θ ; bɝθ/ *n* **1** sleeping-place in a train, a ship or an aircraft. (火車、輪船或飛機上的)鋪位;臥鋪。 **2** place at a wharf where a ship can be tied up; place for a ship to swing at anchor. (碼頭上供船隻)碇泊的地方;可以有餘地供船廻轉的碇泊處。 ***give a wide ~ to,*** (fig) keep well away from, at a safe distance from. (喻)避開;遠避(與…保持安全的距離)。 **3** (dated colloq) job. (過時俗語)差事;職位。 ***find a snug ~,*** an easy or pleasant job. 找個輕鬆愉快的工作。□ *vt, vi* **1** [VP15A, 2C] (naut) find, have, a sleeping-place (for): (航海)(爲某人)安置鋪位(與 for 連用);佔有鋪位: *Six passengers can be ~ed amidships.* 在船中部有六個客人的鋪位。 **2** [VP6A] moor (a ship) in harbour, tie up (a ship) at a wharf, etc. 碇泊(船隻)於港口或碼頭。

beryl /ˈberəl ; ˈbɛrəl/ *n* precious stone (usu green). 綠寶石;綠玉。

be·seech /bɪˈsi:tʃ ; bɪˈsitʃ/ *vt* (*pt, pp* besought /bɪˈsɔ:t ; bɪˈsɔt/) [VP6A, 17, 11, 13B] (old use, or liter) ask earnestly or urgently: (舊用法或文)懇求;祈求;央求: *He besought an interview.* 他懇求面談。 *The prisoner besought the judge to be merciful/besought him for mercy.* 囚犯懇求法官寬赦。 *Spare him, I ~ you.* 赦免他,我懇求你。**~·ing** *adj* (of a person's look, tone of voice, etc) entreating, appealing. (指人的表情、語調等)懇求的; 乞求的; 哀求的。**~·ing·ly** *adv*

be·seem /bɪˈsi:m ; bɪˈsim/ *vt* (liter, old use) (only impers, in the 3rd person) be fitting or suitable: (文,舊用法;僅用於第三人稱之無人稱)適合;適宜: *It ill ~s you to refuse,* It is not fitting that you should refuse. 你不宜拒絕。

be·set /bɪˈset ; bɪˈsɛt/ *vt* (-tt-, *pt, pp* beset) [VP6A] close in on all sides, have on all sides: 包圍;圍困: *the temptations that ~ young people,* by which they are faced on all sides; 圍繞在年輕人身旁的種種誘惑; *a problem ~ with difficulties;* 困難重重的問題; *~ by doubts,* troubled by doubts. 爲疑竇所困擾的。**~·ting sin,** sin that most frequently tempts a person: 易犯的罪惡: *His ~ting sin is laziness.* 他所易犯的毛病就是懶惰。

be·shrew /bɪˈʃru: ; bɪˈʃru/ *vt* (archaic): (古): *B~ me!* May evil fall upon me! 願災禍降臨在我身上!

be·side /bɪˈsaɪd ; bɪˈsaɪd/ *prep* **1** at the side of;

close to: 在…的旁邊；在…的近旁：*Come and sit ~ me.* 來坐在我的身邊。*She would like to live ~ the sea,* at the sea-side. 她想住在海邊。 **2** compared with: 與…比較起來：*You're quite tall ~ your sister.* 與你姐姐(妹妹)相比，你是相當高的了。 **set ~,** put against; compare with: 與…相比：*There's no one to set ~ him as a general.* 作爲一個將軍，他是無與倫比的。 **3 ~ the point / mark / question,** wide of, having nothing to do with (what is being discussed, etc). 離題；與本題無關。 **4 ~ oneself,** at the end of one's self-control: 發狂；忘形：*He was ~ himself with joy / anger.* 他高興(憤怒)得發狂。

be·sides /bɪˈsaɪdz ; bɪˈsaɪdz/ *adv* moreover; also: 再者；加之；而且：*I don't like that new dictionary; ~, it's too expensive.* 我不喜歡那本新字典；而且，它也太貴。*It's too late to go for a walk now; ~, it's beginning to rain.* 現在出去散步已經太晚；再者，天又下雨了。□ *prep* in addition to; as well as: 除…之外：*I have three other hats ~ this.* 除了這頂之外，我還有三頂別的帽子。*There were five of us ~ John,* not including John. 除約翰之外，我們還有五人。*He hadn't time to prepare his lecture, ~ which, he was unwell.* 他沒有時間預備講稿，除此而外，他的身體也不大舒服。

be·siege /bɪˈsiːdʒ ; bɪˈsidʒ/ *vt* **1** [VP6A] surround (a place) with armed forces and keep them there; attack from all sides: 圍攻；包圍；圍困：*Troy was ~d by the Greeks for ten years.* 特洛伊城被希臘人圍困達十年。 **2** [VP14] **~ with,** crowd round (with requests, etc): 擁集在…的周圍；紛紛向…提出(請求等)：*The teacher was ~d with questions and requests from her pupils.* 學生們紛紛向那老師提出問題和請求。 **be·sieger** *n*

be·smear /bɪˈsmɪə(r) ; bɪˈsmɪr/ *vt* **~ with,** smear all over, eg with grease. (以油等)抹遍；塗遍。

be·smirch /bɪˈsmɜːtʃ ; bɪˈsmɝtʃ/ *vt* make dirty: 弄髒；染污：(fig) (喻) *His reputation was ~ed.* 他的名譽受損。

be·som /ˈbiːzəm ; ˈbizəm/ *n* broom made by tying a bundle of twigs to a long handle. 箒；掃把。

be·sot·ted /bɪˈsɒtɪd ; bɪˈsɑtɪd/ *part adj* **~ by / with,** stupefied (by alcoholic drink, drugs, love, etc). (因飲酒、服藥、沉溺於愛情等而)昏瞶糊塗的。

be·sought ⇨ beseech.

be·spangled /bɪˈspæŋgld ; bɪˈspæŋgḷd/ *pred adj* **~ with,** covered, decorated, with spangles. 飾以閃爍發光之小金屬片等的。

be·spat·tered /bɪˈspætəd ; bɪˈspætɚd/ *pred adj* **~ with,** covered with spots of mud, etc. 爲(污泥等)所覆蓋的；濺污的。

be·speak /bɪˈspiːk ; bɪˈspik/ *vt* (*pt* bespoke /bɪˈspəʊk ; bɪˈspok/, *pp* bespoke or bespoken /bɪˈspəʊkən ; bɪˈspokən/) **1** [VP6A] (old use) order in advance; engage or reserve (a table in a restaurant, a room in a hotel). (舊用法)預約；預定(餐館座位、旅館房間)。 **bespoke shoemaker / tailor,** one who makes goods to order (contrasted with a seller of ready-made shoes, etc). 專做定貨的鞋匠(裁縫)(以別於賣現成之鞋、衣者)。 ⇨ *custom-built* at custom(5). **2** [VP6A, 25] (formal) be evidence of: (正式用語)顯示；表示：*His polite manners ~ the gentleman.* 他的彬彬有禮的態度顯示他是個紳士。

best[1] /best ; bɛst/ *adj* (independent *superl*; 獨立最高級；⇨ good, better) of the most excellent kind: 最好的；最佳的；最優的：*the ~ poetry / poets;* 最好的詩(最優秀的詩人)；*the ~ dinner I have ever had;* 我所吃過的最好的一餐；*the ~* (= quickest, most convenient, etc) *way from London to Paris.* 由倫敦至巴黎最好的(即最快、最方便等的)走法。 **the ˈ~ part of,** most of; the greater part of: 大半的；大部份的：*I've been waiting the ~ part of an hour.* 我已等候大半個鐘頭了。 **the ~ thing to do,** that which is most likely to bring about the desired result. 最好的辦法；最上策。 **make the ~ use of one's time / gifts / opportunities, etc,** use one's time, etc in the most useful way. 盡量善爲利用自己的時間(天賦，機會等)。 **put one's ˈ~ foot forward,** ⇨ foot(1). **with the ˈ~ will in the world,** even making every effort to be fair, etc. 盡最大努力做到公平等。 **ˌ~ ˈman,** bridegroom's friend, supporting him at his wedding. 男儐相。

best[2] /best ; bɛst/ *adv* (independent *superl;* 獨立最高級；⇨ well, better) **1** in the most excellent way: 最好；最優；最佳：*He works ~ in the morning.* 他在早晨工作成績最好。*She was the ~-dressed woman in the village.* 她是村中衣著最漂亮的女人。 **as ~ one may / can,** in the ~ way possible to one. 盡力。 **think ~,** judge to be the ~ way of acting: 認爲最好：*Do as you think ~.* 你認爲怎麼好就怎麼做。 **2** most: 最；極：*He is the ~-hated man in the village.* 他是村中最爲人所憎恨的人。 **ˌ~-ˈseller** *n* book that is sold in very large numbers: 暢銷書：*His new novel is one of the season's ~-sellers.* 他的新小說是本季的暢銷書之一。 **3 had ~,** = had better. ⇨ better[2](2).

best[3] /best ; bɛst/ *pron* (independent *superl;* 獨立最高級；⇨ better[3]) the outstanding person, thing, etc among several; the most excellent part, aspect, of sth: 傑出的人或物；佼佼者；最好的東西；(物之)最佳部份；最好的一面：*He's the ~ of husbands,* is distinguished among husbands for good qualities. 他是一個傑出的丈夫。*We're the ~ of friends,* very close friends. 我們都是非常要好的朋友。 **be all for the ~,** be good in the end (although not at first seeming to be good). 終歸會是好的或幸運的(雖然最初似乎並非如此)。 **do sth all for the ~,** act with good intentions (although it may not seem so). 懷着善意做某事(雖在表面看起來也許並不如此)。 **be / dress in one's (Sunday) ~,** wear one's finest clothes: 穿着最漂亮的衣服；盛裝：*They were (dressed) in their ~ for the wedding.* 他們均盛裝參加該婚禮。 **All the ~!** (used when parting from sb) With warmest wishes! (與某人分別時的祝語)一切順利！萬事如意！ **the ˈ~ of it / the joke, etc,** the amusing part (of what happened): (發生之事中的)有趣部份；最佳處；最妙處：*And the ~ of it / the ~ part of it was that....* 最妙的是…。 **at ~,** taking the most hopeful view: 持着最樂觀的看法；充其量：*We can't arrive before Friday at ~.* 即使作最樂觀的估計，我們也不能在星期五以前到達。 **at its / their / his, etc ~,** in the ~ condition: 處於最佳狀態；處於顚峯狀態；在全盛期中：*The garden is at its best this month,* looking most beautiful. 本月份那花園看起來最漂亮(百花盛開時期)。*He was at his ~ yesterday evening and kept us all amused,* talked in his most amusing way. 他昨天晚上表現出最佳的談吐，使我們大家一直都很開心。 **(even) at the ˈ~ of times,** (even) when circumstances are most favourable. (甚至)在情勢最有利的時候。 **have / get the ~ of it / of the fight / quarrel / deal / bargain, etc,** win; gain the advantage. (在打鬪、爭論等中)得勝；贏；(在交易等中)獲利。 **have / get the ~ of everything,** enjoy the ~ food, housing, etc. 享受最好的食物、居所等；樣樣稱心如意。 **with the ~,** as well as anyone: 不比任何人差；不遜於他人：*Although he's nearly fifty, he can still play tennis with the ~.* 他雖然已近五十歲了，打起網球來却不比任何人差。 **with the ˈ~ of intentions,** intending only to help. 好心好意地。 **do one's ~ / the ~ one can,** do one's utmost. 盡全力；盡量。 **(do sth) to the ~ of one's ability / power,** use all one's ability / power when doing it. 全力以赴。 **make the ~ of a bad job / business,** do what one can, in spite of failure, misfortune, etc. 盡自己之所能去應付失敗或不幸等；善處逆境。 **make the ~ of one's way home,** return home as quickly as possible, in spite of difficulties. 不顧一切困難，以最快速度回家；儘快回家。 **make the ~ of things,** be contented (although things are not satisfactory). 感覺滿足(雖然事態並不令人滿意)。 **to the ~ of my knowl-**

edge/belief/recollection, so far as I know/believe/recollect (though my knowledge, etc may be imperfect). 就我所知(相信,記憶)。

best[4] /best; bɛst/ *vt* [VP6A] (colloq) get the better of; defeat. (俗)勝過;打敗。

bes·tial /ˈbestɪəl; ˈbɛstʃəl/ *adj* of or like a beast; brutish; savage. 獸類的;似獸類的;獸性的;殘忍的;野蠻的。**~ly** *adv* **bes·ti·al·ity** /ˌbestɪˈælətɪ; ˌbɛstʃɪˈælətɪ/ *n* (*pl* -ties) [U] quality of being ~; [C] ~ or brutal act. 獸性;殘忍;野蠻;獸行;殘忍或野蠻之行爲。

bes·ti·ary /ˈbestɪərɪ *US:* -tɪerɪ; ˈbɛstɪˌɛrɪ/ *n* medieval collection of moral stories about animals. 中世紀的動物寓言集。

be·stir /bɪˈstɜː(r); bɪˈstɝ/ *vt* (-rr-) [VP6A, 17] ~ ***oneself,*** (old use or joc) busy oneself, be active. (舊用法或謔)奮發;振作。

be·stow /bɪˈstəʊ; bɪˈsto/ *vt* **1** [VP6A, 14] ~ ***(on/upon),*** give as an offering: 給與;授予;賜贈: ~ *an honour/a title on sb;* 給與某人一項榮譽(頭銜); *the praise that has been ~ed upon him.* 他所受到的讚譽。 **2** [VP6A] (old use) put, place. (舊用法)放;置。**~al** *n* ~ing. 授予;贈與;放置。

be·strew /bɪˈstruː; bɪˈstru/ *vt* (*pt* ~ed, *pp* bestrewn /-ˈstruːn; -ˈstrun/ or ~ed) [VP6A, 14] ~ ***(with),*** (poet) strew (a surface); scatter (things) about. (詩)(以…)撒布於(表面);拋撒(某物)於各處。

be·stride /bɪˈstraɪd; bɪˈstraɪd/ *vt* (*pt* bestrode /bɪˈstrəʊd; bɪˈstrod/, *pp* bestridden /bɪˈstrɪdn; bɪˈstrɪdn̩/, bestrid /bɪˈstrɪd; bɪˈstrɪd/, bestrode) [VP 6A] (formal) sit, stand, with one leg on each side of: (正式用語)跨;跨坐;跨立;騎乘: ~ *a horse/chair/bidet/ditch/fence,* etc; 騎馬(兩腿分開跨坐椅上;跨坐在坐浴桶上;跨在溝上;騎在牆上); (fig) dominate: (喻)統治: *Caesar bestrode the Roman Empire.* 凱撒統治羅馬帝國。⇨ astride.

bet /bet; bɛt/ *vt, vi* (-tt-, *pt, pp* bet or betted) [VP9, 11, 12C, 2A, 3A] **1** ***bet on sth, bet (sb) that…,*** risk money on a race or on some other event of which the result is doubtful: 打賭(某事,如賽馬或其他結果不一定之事);與(某人)打賭…;賭: *He bet me a pound that Hyperion would win.* 他認爲亥伯龍會贏,與我賭一鎊。*It's foolish to bet on horses.* 爲賽馬打賭是愚蠢的。*Do you ever bet?* 你曾與人打賭嗎? **2** (colloq uses): (口語用法): *I bet,* I'm certain; 我敢打賭;我有把握;我確信; *you bet,* you may be certain. 的確;當然。□ *n* [C] agreement to risk money, etc on an event of which the result is doubtful; the money, etc offered: 賭;打賭;賭金;賭注: *make a bet;* 打賭; *win/lose a bet;* 賭贏(輸); *accept/take up a bet.* 接受打賭;同意與人打賭。

beta /ˈbiːtə *US:* ˈbeɪtə; ˈbetə/ *n* second letter (B, β) of the Greek alphabet. 希臘字母的第二個字母。⇨ App 4. 參看附錄四。

be·take /bɪˈteɪk; bɪˈtek/ *vt* (*pt* betook /bɪˈtʊk; bɪˈtʊk/, *pp* betaken /bɪˈteɪkən; bɪˈtekən/) [VP14, reflex 與反身代名詞連用] ~ ***oneself to,*** (old use) go to, apply oneself to. (舊用法)赴;去;專心於;致力於。

betel /ˈbiːtl; ˈbitl̩/ *n* leaf which is wrapped round bits of areca-nut and used by some Indians for chewing. 蒟醬之葉(印度人用以包檳榔而嚼之)。ˈ~ **nut,** areca-nut. 檳榔。

bête noire /ˌbeɪt ˈnwɑː(r); ˈbetˈnwɑr/ *n* (F) thing or person one dislikes greatly. (法)爲人所極其厭惡之事物或人。

bethel /ˈbeθl; ˈbɛθəl/ *n* nonconformist chapel; (esp US) chapel for seamen. 非英國國教徒之禮拜堂;(尤美)海員之禮拜堂。

be·think /bɪˈθɪŋk; bɪˈθɪŋk/ *vt* (*pt, pp* bethought /bɪˈθɔːt; bɪˈθɔt/) [VP11, 14, 17, 20, 21] ~ ***oneself (of),*** (old use) reflect, consider. (舊用法)思考;考慮。

be·tide /bɪˈtaɪd; bɪˈtaɪd/ *vt* (only in) (僅用於) ***woe ~ him/you, etc (if…),*** may misfortune come to him/you, etc (if…). (假使…)但願他(你等)遭遇不幸;願天降災於他(你等)。

be·times /bɪˈtaɪmz; bɪˈtaɪmz/ *adv* (old use) early; in good time: (舊用法)早;及時: *We must be up ~ tomorrow.* 我們明天必須早起。

be·token /bɪˈtəʊkən; bɪˈtokən/ *vt* [VP6A] (old use) indicate, suggest: (舊用法)指示;表示;預示: *Those black clouds ~ rain.* 那些烏雲預示有雨。

be·took ⇨ betake.

be·tray /bɪˈtreɪ; bɪˈtre/ *vt* **1** [VP6A] be disloyal to; act deceitfully towards: 不忠於;背叛;欺騙: *He ~ed his principles.* 他違背了他的原則。 **2** [VP6A, 14] ~ ***(to),*** give away or make known or sell treacherously: 出賣;陷害: *Judas ~ed Jesus to his enemies.* 猶大將耶穌出賣給他的敵人。 **3** [VP6A] allow (a secret) to become known, either by accident or on purpose. (無意或有意)洩露(秘密)。 **4** [VP6A, 25] be or give a sign of, show: 暴露;顯示: *The boy's face ~ed the fact that he had been eating jam.* 那男孩的臉顯示他吃過果醬。*His accent at once ~ed the fact that he was/~ed him to be a foreigner.* 他的口音立刻顯示出他是一個外國人。~ ***oneself,*** show what one really is, etc: 暴露出眞實身份: *He had a good disguise, but as soon as he spoke he ~ed himself,* ie he was recognized by his voice. 他僞裝得很好,但是他一說話就露出馬脚了(他的聲音使別人認出了他是誰)。 **~al** /bɪˈtreɪəl; bɪˈtreəl/ *n* [U] ~ing or being ~ed; [C] instance of this. 背叛;出賣;陷害;洩露;暴露。**~er** *n*

be·troth /bɪˈtrəʊð; bɪˈtrɔθ/ *vt* (old formal use) ~ ***to,*** [VP6A, 14] engage (a woman) in contract of marriage (usu in *pp*): (舊時正式用語)給(一女子)訂親;許配(通常用過去分詞): *His daughter was ~ed to a banker.* 他的女兒與一銀行家訂婚。**~ed** *n* person engaged to be married. 已訂婚者。**~al** *n* engagement (the usual word) to be married. 訂婚;婚約(engagement 爲常用字)。

bet·ter[1] /ˈbetə(r); ˈbɛtɚ/ *adj* (independent *comp;* 獨立比較級; ⇨ good, best) **1** *This is good but that is ~.* 這個很好,但是那個更好。*He's a ~ man than his brother.* 他的爲人比他哥哥(弟弟)好。~ ***than one's word,*** more generous than one's promise. 所做的超過所說的;比所許諾的更爲慷慨。 ***(do sth) against one's ~ judgement,*** despite feeling that it may be unwise. 知其不可爲(而爲之)。***no ~ than,*** practically the same as: 實際等於;簡直是: *He's no ~ than a beggar,* is, in spite of appearances, etc, almost a beggar. (他雖然外表不似乞丐)他實際等於一個乞丐。***be no ~ than she should be,*** (old use) be a woman of low regard or easy virtue. (舊用法)是個不正經的女人。⇨ virtue(2). ***the ~ part of,*** the larger part of: 大部份的;大半的: *Discretion is the ~ part of valour,* ⇨ discretion(1). 愼重卽勇過半矣。 ***see ~ days,*** be not so poor or unfortunate as at present: 不像目前之貧苦或潦倒;享受過富裕的生活;曾經得意過: *He has seen ~ days.* 他曾經得意過(並非像現在這樣貧窮或潦倒)。***one's ~ feelings,*** one's moral nature. 高尚的本性;良心;天良。***his ~ half,*** (colloq) his wife. (俗)他的妻子。 **2** (of health) recovering from illness (often contrasted with *ill* and related to *well*): (指健康)好些的;情況較佳的;康復的(常與 ill 相對,與 well 有關): *The patient is ~ today but is still not well enough to get up.* 病人今天好些,但仍不能起床。*I'm quite ~ now,* am fully recovered. 我現在已完全康復了。

bet·ter[2] /ˈbetə(r); ˈbɛtɚ/ *adv* (independent *comp;* 獨立比較級; ⇨ well, best) **1** *The ~* (= The more) *I know her the more I admire her abilities.* 我對她認識愈深,愈欽佩她的本領。*You would write ~ if you had a good pen.* 假如你有一枝好筆,你的字會寫得好些。*You play tennis ~ than I do.* 你網球打得比我好。*You'll like it ~* (= more) *when you understand it more.* 當你多瞭解它一些,你就會更喜歡它。***be ~ off,*** richer; more comfortable. 更富有;更舒服。***be ~ off without,*** happier; more at ease: 若無…更爲快樂;無…更爲舒適或安逸: *We'd be ~ off without all that din from the chil-*

dren's room. 若是沒有孩子房間裏傳來的嘈雜聲,我們會更爲舒適。**know ~, (a)** be wise or experienced enough not to do sth: 具有充分智慧或經驗而不去做某事;知道…是不對的: *You ought to know ~ than to go out without an overcoat on such a cold day.* 你不應糊塗到在這樣的冷天出去不穿大衣。**(b)** refuse to accept a statement (because one knows it is not true): 不相信某一句話(因爲知其不實): *He says he didn't cheat, but I know ~,* feel sure that he did. 他說他沒有欺騙,但是我不相信(我確信他欺騙)。**think (all) the ~ of sb,** have a higher opinion of him: 對某人更爲欽佩: *I shall think all the ~ of you after seeing you bear these misfortunes so bravely.* 看到你如此勇敢地忍受這些不幸事故,我將對你更加欽佩。**think ~ of sth/of doing sth,** decide, after thought, not to do it. 經再思而後決定作罷(不做某事)。 **2** (used in 用於 [VP5]) **had ~,** would find it more suitable, more to your advantage, etc: 最好(勸告或建議用語): *You had ~ mind your own business.* 你最好只管你自己的事(別管他人的事)。*You'd ~ not say that,* I advise you not to say that. 你最好別提那件事。*I had ~ begin by explaining...,* It will be useful if I begin by...; 我最好在開始的時候先解釋…; *Hadn't you ~ take an umbrella?* 你不覺得帶把傘比較好嗎?

bet·ter³ /ˈbetə(r) ; ˈbɛtɚ/ *n* **one's (elders and) ~s,** older, wiser, more experienced people: 自己的長輩;比自己年長者;比自己更明智或更有經驗的人們;勝於己者: *Don't ignore the advice of your elders and ~s.* 不要忽視長者的忠告。Cf 參較 *superior,* as in: *He's my superior at chess.* 他的棋藝比我强。**get the ~ of sb or sth,** overcome; defeat; win (an argument, etc): 克服(某事);勝過;打敗(某人);贏得(辯論等): *His shyness got the ~ of him,* he was overcome by shyness, was too shy to speak out. 他非常害羞;他害羞得不敢說話。*She always gets the ~ of these quarrels.* 在這一類的爭吵中她總是贏過別人。**for ~ (or) for worse,** in both good and bad fortune. 不論是好是歹;好也罷,歹也罷。Cf 參較 *for good or ill.*

bet·ter⁴ /ˈbetə(r) ; ˈbɛtɚ/ *vt* **1** [VP6A] improve; do better than: 改善;改良;改進;比…做得更好: *The Government hopes to ~ the conditions of the peasants.* 政府希望改善農民生活情況。*Your work last year was good; I hope you will ~ it, this year.* 你去年的成績不錯,希望你今年能百尺竿頭更進一步。**2 ~ oneself,** get a ~ position, higher wages, etc. 陞調;高陞;獲得加薪。**~·ment** *n* [U] making or becoming ~. 改善;改良;改進。

bet·ter⁵, bet·tor /ˈbetə(r) ; ˈbɛtɚ/ *n* person who bets; punter (the more usu word). 打賭者;下賭注的人(punter 爲較常用字)。

be·tween¹ /bɪˈtwiːn ; bəˈtwin/ *adv* ***(in)* ~,** in(to) a place or time that is before the one (place or time) but after the other: 介於其間的地方或時間;在其間: *We visited the Museum in the morning and the Art Gallery later, with a hurried lunch ~.* 我們上午參觀博物館,後來又參觀藝術館,中間匆匆地吃了一頓午餐。**far ~,** at wide intervals. 有很寬的間隔;彼此相距很遠。**few and far ~,** few and widely scattered or separate: 稀疏零落彼此相距很遠: *In this part of Canada houses are few and far ~.* 在加拿大這一帶,房屋稀少而彼此相距甚遠。

be·tween² /bɪˈtwiːn ; bəˈtwin/ *prep* **1** (of place) (指地點) *The letter B comes ~ A and C,* ie *after* A but *before* C. 字母B在A與C之間(卽在A之後但在C之前)。*The Mediterranean Sea is ~ Europe and Africa.* 地中海在歐洲與非洲之間。*A river flows ~ its banks.* 河在兩岸之間流。(*Between* usu involves only two limits, but when boundaries are concerned, there may be more than two limits. Between 通常僅牽涉兩個界限,但當牽涉到邊界時,則可能有兩個以上的界限。*Switzerland lies ~ France, Italy, Austria and Germany.* 瑞士位於法國、義大利、奧地利及德國之間。⇨ among.) **2** (of order, rank, etc): (指順序、階級等): *An army major ranks ~ a captain and a colonel.* 陸軍少校的階級在上尉與中校之間。 **3** (of time): (指時間): ~ *the two world wars;* 在兩次世界大戰之間; ~ *1 o'clock and 2 o'clock;* 在一點鐘與兩點鐘之間; ~ *youth and middle age.* 在青年與中年之間。**4** (of distance, amount, etc): (指距離、數量等): ~ *five and six miles;* 在五哩與六哩之間; ~ *thirty and forty tons;* 在三十噸與四十噸之間; ~ *5p and 10p;* 在五辨士與十辨士之間; ~ *freezing-point and boiling-point.* 在冰點與沸點之間。**5** (of movement) to and from: (指移動)來往於;往返於: *This liner sails ~ Southampton and New York.* 這艘班輪來往航行於南安普敦與紐約之間。**6** (showing connection): (表示關聯): *after all there has been ~ us,* in view of our past friendship, the experiences we have shared, etc. 鑒於過去我們之間的關係(指友誼或共同經歷等)。**There is ˌno ˈlove lost ~ them,** They dislike each other. 他們之間毫無愛情可言(互相憎惡)。**There's nothing to choose ~ them,** They are (both or all) alike. 它們之間無可選擇(它們兩個或全都一樣)。**7** (to show sharing; used of two only): (表示分享;僅用於二者): *Divide/Share the money ~ you.* 你們二人平分這錢。**~ ourselves; ~ you, me and the gatepost; ~ you and me,** in confidence. 當作秘密;勿爲外人道。**8** (to show combination, used of two, or more than two to show several and independent relationships): (表示連合,用於二者或二者以上,表示個別和獨立的關係): *The first five batsmen scored 253 runs ~ them.* 頭五個擊球員共得253分。*We* (two or more) *saved up for a year and bought a second-hand car ~ us.* 我們(二人或更多人)積蓄了一年,合夥買了一輛舊汽車。*B~ them* (ie as the result of their combined efforts) *they soon finished the work.* 他們大家一齊動手,不久就把工作完成了。**9 ~ sth and sth,** with these things combined: 由於…和…的原因: *B~ astonishment and despair she hardly knew what to do.* 在驚駭與絕望的雙重打擊下,她簡直不知怎麼辦。*My time is fully taken up ~ writing and lecturing.* 我的時間全用在寫作與演講上面。**10** (showing relationship): (表示關係): *the relation ~ teacher and pupil;* 師生關係; *the distinction ~ right and wrong;* 是非的區別; *a comparison ~ two things;* 兩件事物的比較; *quarrels/wars/ill-feeling/rivalries/friendships, etc ~ nations.* 國與國之間的不和(戰爭,惡感,競爭,友好等)。

be·twixt /bɪˈtwɪkst ; bəˈtwɪkst/ *prep, adv* (old or liter use) (舊用法或文) = between. **~ and between,** (colloq) in an intermediate state; neither one thing nor the other. (俗)處於中間的狀態;既非此亦非彼。

bevel /ˈbevl ; ˈbɛvl/ *n* sloping edge; surface with such a slope, eg at the side of a picture frame or a sheet of plate-glass. 有斜度的邊緣;斜面(如在鏡框或玻璃板之邊緣上者)。ˈ**~ gear,** either of a pair of gears with ~led teeth surfaces. 斜齒輪。□ *vt* (-ll-, US = -l-) give a sloping edge to. 將…之邊緣作成斜角邊;使有斜邊。

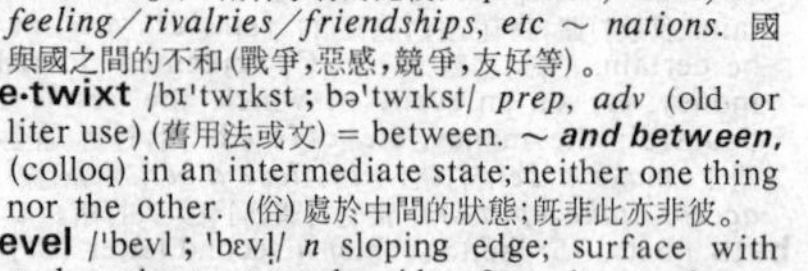

bevels

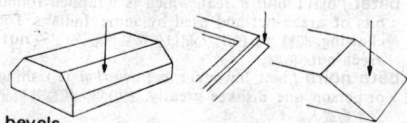

bev·er·age /ˈbevərɪdʒ ; ˈbɛvrɪdʒ/ *n* [C] (formal) any sort of drink except water, eg milk, tea, wine, beer. (正式用語)飲料(指除水以外之任何一種可飲用之液體,例如牛奶、茶、酒、啤酒)。

bevy /ˈbevɪ ; ˈbɛvɪ/ *n* **1** company or gathering. 一群。**2** flock (*of* birds, esp quail). 一群(鳥,尤指鵪鶉,與 of 連用)。

be·wail /bɪˈweɪl ; bɪˈwel/ *vt* [VP6A] (poet) express sorrow over; mourn for. (詩)因…而悲傷;哀痛;哀傷。

be·ware /bɪˈweə(r) ; bɪˈwɛr/ *vi, vt* [VP2A, 3A, 10

in the imperative and infinitive only 僅用於祈使句及不定詞] **~ (of)**, be on guard, take care: 小心;當心;注意;提防: *B~ of the dog!* 當心那隻狗! *B~ of pickpockets!* 謹防扒手! *B~ (of) how you attempt it.* 小心注意你應該怎樣去嘗試它。*B~, sir, (of) what you do.* 先生,請注意你自己的行爲。

be·wil·der /bɪˈwɪldə(r) ; bɪˈwɪldɚ/ *vt* [VP6A] puzzle; confuse: 使迷惑;使手足無措;使着慌;使昏亂;使糊塗;使發楞: *The old woman from the country was ~ed by the crowds and traffic in the big city.* 那鄉下老婆子看到大城市裏的人羣及車輛就楞住了。*Tom was ~ed by the examination questions.* 湯姆被考試題目難住了。**~·ing** *adj* that ~s: 使迷惑的;使手足無措的;使發楞的: *find sth ~ing.* 發現某事很爲難。**~·ment** *n* [U] state of being ~ed: 迷惑;昏亂;糊塗;發楞: *He looked at me in open-mouthed ~ment.* 他張大着嘴迷惑地看著我。

be·witch /bɪˈwɪtʃ ; bɪˈwɪtʃ/ *vt* [VP6A] **1** work magic on; put a magic spell on: 對…施妖術;蠱惑;迷惑: *The old woman ~ed the cows so that they gave no milk.* 那老婆子對那些母牛施妖術,使牠們擠不出牛奶。**2** charm; delight very much: 迷(人);使銷魂;使着迷;使極爲快樂: *She danced so well that she ~ed all the young men.* 她的舞姿極爲美妙,使所有在場的年輕小夥子都着了迷。**~·ing** *adj* that ~es: 迷人的;銷魂的: *a ~ing smile.* 迷人的微笑。**~·ing·ly** *adv*: 迷人地; 銷魂地: *She smiled at him ~ingly.* 她迷人地對他微笑。

bey /beɪ ; be/ *n* (Turkish word meaning) governor: (土耳其語)總督;長官;省長: *the Bey of Tunis.* 突尼斯總督。

be·yond[1] /bɪˈjɒnd ; bɪˈjɑnd/ *adv* at or to a distance; farther on: 在遠處;至遠處;再往前去: *India and the lands ~.* 印度及印度那邊的國家。*What is ~?* 再往前面是什麼?

be·yond[2] /bɪˈjɒnd ; bɪˈjɑnd/ *prep* **1** at, on or to, the farther side of: 在或向…的那一邊;越過: *The house is ~ the bridge.* 房屋在橋的那一邊。*Don't go ~ the town boundary.* 不要走出市界。*We saw peak ~ peak*, a succession of peaks. 我們看見重重的山峯。**2** (of time) later than: (指時間)超過;晚於: *Don't stay out ~ (after* is the more usu word) *10 o'clock.* 不要在外面停留到十點鐘以後還不回家(after 較常用)。*He never sees ~ the present.* 他從未看到將來。**3** surpassing, exceeding; out of reach of: 超出;出乎;爲…所不能及: *Your work is ~ all praise*, so good that it cannot be praised enough. 你的作品叫人讚揚不盡。*We succeeded ~ our hopes*, were more successful than we had hoped to be. 我們獲得如此之成功,是我們始料所不及的。*That's going ~ a joke*, passes the limits of what is reasonable as a joke. 那樣開玩笑是太過火了。*He lives ~ his income*, spends more than he earns. 他的生活入不敷出。*It's quite ~ me*, is more than I can understand. 這我完全不懂。**4** (in neg and interr) except: (用於否定及疑問句)除…以外: *He has nothing ~ his pension.* 他除了養老金之外毫無積蓄。

be·zique /bɪˈziːk ; bəˈzik/ *n* [U] card-game for two or four players. (二人或四人玩的)一種紙牌戲。

bhang /bæŋ ; bæŋ/ *n* (kind of) narcotic made from hemp. 一種用大麻製成的麻醉藥;印度大麻。

bi- /ˌbaɪ ; baɪ/ *pref* **1** appearing twice (in the period given): (在某一段時期中)出現兩次的: *ˌbi-ˈmonthly;* 每月兩次的(地); *bi-annual.* 每年兩次的。**2** lasting for two, appearing every two: 延續二…的;每二…出現一次的;每隔一…發生一次的: *biennial.* 二年生的;兩年一次的。**3** having two: 有二…的: *bilateral;* 有兩邊的;雙邊的; *bilingual;* 用兩種文字寫成的;會說兩種語言的(人); *biped;* 兩足動物; *biplane.* 雙翼飛機。**4** in two ways; doubly: 以兩種方式;兩面;雙: *bi-concave.* 雙凹鏡。

bias /ˈbaɪəs ; ˈbaɪəs/ *n* **1** leaning of the mind towards or away from sth; predisposition: 偏見;成見;偏愛;傾向;癖性: *He has a ~ towards/against the plan*, is in favour of it/opposed to it without having full knowledge of it. 他對此計畫有偏愛(有成見)。*He is without ~*, is impartial, unprejudiced. 他不偏不倚(公正,無偏見)。**2** ***cut on the ~***, (dress-making, etc) cut across, slantingly. (裁縫等)斜裁。**3** (esp of a ball in the game of bowls) tendency to swerve; the weighting causing this tendency. (尤指滾木球戲中的球)突然轉向的趨勢;歪曲的球路;造成歪曲球路的重力。□ *vt* (*pt, pp* ~ed or ~sed) [VP6A, 14] ***~ (towards/against)***, give a ~ to; influence (usu unfairly): 使存偏見;以偏見影響;使傾向一方: *The government used newspapers and the radio to ~ the opinions of the people.* 政府利用報紙及廣播左右人民的輿論。*He is ~(s)ed towards/against the plan*, is prejudiced. 他對該計畫有偏愛(偏見)。*He's clearly ~(s)ed.* 他顯然有成見。

bib[1] /bɪb ; bɪb/ *n* **1** piece of cloth tied under a child's chin. (繫於嬰兒下頦底下的)圍嘴;圍脖。**bib and tucker**, ⇨ tucker. **2** upper part of an apron. 圍裙的上部。

bib[2] /bɪb ; bɪb/ *vi* (-bb-) drink too much or too often (rare except in *wine-bibbing, wine-bibber*). 喝得太多;太常喝(罕用字,除非用於複合字wine-bibbing豪飲, wine-bibber 豪飲者)。

Bible /ˈbaɪbl ; ˈbaɪbl̩/ *n* sacred writings of the Jews and the Christian Church. 聖經(猶太人及基督教的聖書)。**ˈ~ puncher**, (colloq) evangelical preacher. (俗)福音傳道者;牧師。**bib·li·cal** /ˈbɪblɪkl ; ˈbɪblɪkl̩/ *adj* of, concerning, contained in, the ~: 聖經的;有關聖經的;聖經中的: *ˈbiblical style*, the style used in (esp the Authorized Version of) the ~. 聖經體裁(尤指欽定譯本者)。

bib·li·ogra·phy /ˌbɪblɪˈɒgrəfɪ ; ˌbɪblɪˈɑgrəfɪ/ *n* **1** [C] (*pl* -phies) list of books and writings of one author or about one subject. (某一作家的)著作目錄;(關於某一學科或題目的)書目。**2** [U] study of the authorship, editions, etc of books. 目錄學(研究書籍之作者、版本等)。**bib·li·ogra·pher** /ˌbɪblɪˈɒgrəfə(r) ; ˌbɪblɪˈɑgrəfɚ/ *n* person who writes or studies bibliographies. 著作目錄編纂者;研究目錄學者;書誌學者。

bib·lio·phile /ˈbɪblɪəfaɪl ; ˈbɪblɪəˌfaɪl/ *n* person who loves and collects books. 珍藏書籍者。

bibu·lous /ˈbɪbjʊləs ; ˈbɪbjələs/ *adj* (joc) fond of much alcoholic drink. (諧)嗜酒的;好飲酒的。

bi·cam·eral /ˌbaɪˈkæmərəl ; baɪˈkæmərəl/ *adj* (of a legislature) having two chambers, eg House of Commons, House of Lords. (指立法機關)有兩個議院(例如下議院,上議院)的;兩院制的。

bi·car·bon·ate /ˌbaɪˈkɑːbənət ; baɪˈkɑrbənɪt/ *n* [U] acid salt of carbonic acid. 酸式碳酸鹽。**~ of soda** (= *sodium ~*) **($NaHCO_3$)**, used in cooking and in medicine. 碳酸氫鈉;小蘇打(用於烹飪及醫藥)。

bi·cen·ten·ary /ˌbaɪsenˈtiːnərɪ *US:* -ˈsentənerɪ ; baɪˈsɛntəˌnɛrɪ/ *n* (celebration of the) 200th anniversary of an event. 二百周年;二百周年紀念。

bi·cen·ten·nial /ˌbaɪsenˈtenɪəl ; ˌbaɪsɛnˈtɛnɪəl/ *adj* **1** happening once in 200 years. 每二百年一次的。**2** lasting for 200 years. 延續二百年的。**3** of a 200th anniversary. 二百周年的。□ *n* 200th anniversary. 二百周年。

bi·ceps /ˈbaɪseps ; ˈbaɪsɛps/ *n* (*pl* unchanged) large muscle in the front part of the upper arm: (複數不變)(上臂前面之)二頭肌: *His ~ is/are impressive.* 他的二頭肌予人深刻的印象。

bicker /ˈbɪkə(r) ; ˈbɪkɚ/ *vi* [VP2A,C,3A] ***~ (with sb) (over/about sth)***, quarrel about sth unimportant: (與某人)(爲某事)吵嘴;爭吵(有關瑣細或不重要的小事): *Stop ~ing!* 別再吵嘴了!

bi·cycle /ˈbaɪsɪkl; ˈbaɪˌsɪkl̩/ *n* two-wheeled machine for riding on, propelled by using pedals. 脚踏車;自行車。□ *vi* (usu shortened to 通常略作 *cycle* /ˈsaɪkl ; ˈsaɪkl̩/) [VP2A, C] ride a ~. 騎脚踏車。

bid[1] /bɪd ; bɪd/ *vt, vi* (-dd-) **1** (*pt, pp* bid) [VP6A, 14, 2A, 3A] ***bid (for)***, (at an auction sale) make an offer of money; offer (a certain price): (在拍賣場所)出價;出(價): *Will anyone bid £5 for this*

a bicycle

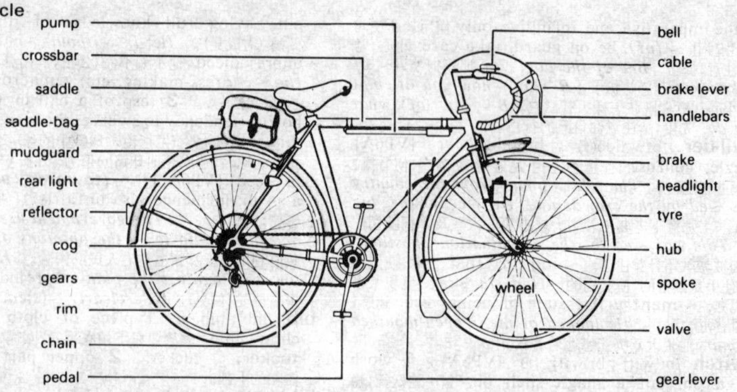

painting? 有人出五鎊買這幅畫嗎？ *Mr X bid £20 for the horse so I bid £21.* 某先生出二十鎊買這匹馬,所以我出二十一鎊。*Is nobody else going to bid?* 再沒有別人出價了嗎？ *What shall I bid?* 我要出多少價錢呢？ *I hoped to get the house but a rich man was bidding against me,* offering higher prices. 我本來想買那棟房子，可是一個有錢人出了更高的價。⇨ outbid. *The politicians are bidding for popular support,* making offers, eg of tax reductions, in order to get support from the public. 那些政客競相發表動人的諾言(如減稅),以爭取民衆的支持。***bid up,*** [VP15B] make the price higher by offering more money: 喊出高價藉以提高價格; 哄抬…之價格: *The goods were bid up far beyond their real value.* 這些貨物的價格被哄高得遠超出它們的實在價值。 **2** (*pt, pp* bid) [VP3A] ***bid for,*** (colloq) attempt to attain: (俗)期望達到;尋求: *The army bid for power and succeeded.* 陸軍希望增强實力並且如願以償。**3** (*pt, pp* bid) [VP2A, 3A] ***bid on,*** (US) state a price (for doing sth); put in a tender for: (美)提出價格(承做某事);投標: *The firm decided to bid on the new bridge.* 該商行決定投標承建這座新橋。 ⇨ tender³. **4** (old use) (*pt* bade /bæd ; bæd/, *pp* bidden /ˈbɪdn ; ˈbɪdn̩/, bid) [VP17, 18B] **(a)** command; tell: (舊用法)命令;吩咐: *He bade me (to) come in.* 他令我進來。*Do as you are bid.* 照你所受到的吩咐做。*Soldiers must do as they are bidden.* 軍人必須服從命令。*Bid him come in.* 叫他進來。**(b)** invite: 邀請: *the bidden guests;* 所請之客人; *bid sb to a wedding.* 邀請某人參加婚禮。 **(c)** [VP12A, 13A] say (as a greeting, etc): 說(問候的話等): *bid farewell* (=say goodbye) *to sb;* 向某人道別; *bid sb good morning.* 向某人問候早安。 **5** ***bid fair to,*** seem likely to: 很有可能: *Our plan bids fair to succeed.* 我們的計畫很有可能會成功。***bid defiance to,*** (old use) announce that one defies (the enemy, etc). (舊用法)宣佈對抗或蔑視(敵人等)。**6** (cards, bridge) make a bid: (牌戲,橋牌戲)叫牌: *bid 2 hearts.* 叫二紅心。⇨ bid²(4). **ˈbid·dable** *adj* (colloq) docile; ready to obey. (俗)溫順的;順從的;聽話的。**bid·ding** *n* [U] **1** command. 命令。***do sb's bidding,*** do what he commands. 服從某人的命令;照某人所吩咐的做。**2** act of offering a price at an auction sale: (在拍賣場所)出價: *Bidding was brisk,* There were many bids, quickly made. 出價很峭(即多而迅速)。**3** (at cards) the making of bids(4). (紙牌戲)叫牌。**bid·der** *n* person who bids. 出價者;投標人;叫牌者。

bid² /bɪd ; bɪd/ *n* **1** (at an auction sale) offer of a price: (在拍賣場所)出價: *Are there no bids for this very fine painting?* 沒有人出價買這張極美的畫嗎？ *Will no one make a higher/further bid?* 再沒有人出更高的價嗎？ **2** (US) statement of price for a piece of work, etc: (美)投標(承建工程等): *Bids were invited for the construction of a swimming-pool.* 招標建造游泳池。 ⇨ tender³. **3** ***make a bid for,*** (colloq) try to obtain: (俗)力求獲得;爭取: *make a bid for power/popular support.* 爭取權力(民衆的支持)。**4** (card games, esp bridge) statement of the number of tricks a player proposes to win: (紙牌戲,尤指橋牌)叫牌: *a bid of 2 hearts/3 no-trumps;* 叫二紅心(三無王); *raise the bid.* 提高叫牌。

bide /baɪd ; baɪd/ *vt* (liter; old use) abide. (文;舊用法)等待。(rare except in) (罕,僅用於) ~ ***one's time,*** wait for a favourable opportunity. 等待良機。

bidet /ˈbiːdeɪ *US:* biːˈdeɪ ; biˈde/ *n* (F) raised narrow bath (to be straddled) for washing the genitals and bottom. (法)(供跨坐以沖洗生殖器及臀部的)坐浴桶;坐浴盆。

bi·en·nial /baɪˈenɪəl ; baɪˈɛnɪəl/ *adj* lasting for two years; happening every alternate year. 持續二年的;二年生的;每隔一年發生的。□ *n* plant that lives two years and has flowers and seeds in the second year. 二年生的植物。**~·ly** *adv*

bier /bɪə(r) ; bɪr/ *n* movable wooden stand for a coffin or a dead body. 棺架;屍架。

biff /bɪf ; bɪf/ *n* (sl) sharp blow. (俚)猛擊。□ *vt* (sl) strike: (俚)打;擊: ~ *sb on the nose.* 打某人的鼻子。

bi·focal /ˌbaɪˈfəʊkl ; baɪˈfokl̩/ *adj* (esp of lenses in spectacles for the eyes) designed for both distant and near vision. (尤指眼鏡片)視遠景及近物兩用的;雙焦點的;雙光的。**bi·focals** *n pl* spectacles with ~ lenses. 雙光眼鏡。

bi·fur·cate /ˈbaɪfəkeɪt ; ˈbaɪfɚˌket/ *vt, vi* [VP6A, 2A] (formal) (of roads, rivers, boughs of trees, etc) divide into two branches, etc; fork. (正式用語)(指道路、河流、樹枝等)分爲兩支;分叉。□ *adj* (also 亦作 ~**d**) forked. 分爲兩支的;分叉的。**bi·fur·ca·tion** /ˌbaɪfəˈkeɪʃn ; ˌbaɪfɚˈkeʃən/ *n*

big /bɪg ; bɪg/ *adj* (-gg-) (antonym 反義字 *little;* cf 參較 *large,* and *small*) of large size, extent, capacity, importance, etc. 大的;廣大的;容量大的;重大的。 ***get/grow too big for one's boots,*** (colloq) become conceited. (俗)自大;自誇;妄自尊大。***have big ideas,*** be ambitious. 有野心;有抱負。***talk big,*** boast. 說大話;自誇;吹牛。**ˈbig bug** *n* (sl) (俚) ⇨ bug(4). **ˌbig ˈbusiness,** commerce on a ~ financial scale. 大企業。 **big game,** ⇨ game¹(6). **big end** *n* (eng) part of a connecting shaft that bears on a crankshaft. (工程)連軸之承接曲柄軸的部份。 **big noise** *n* (sl) (俚) ⇨ noise. **ˈbig shot** *n* (sl) (俚) ⇨ shot¹(8). **ˈbig stick,** = ~ shot. **the ˈbig time,** (sl) highest level. (俚)最高標準;第一流。 **ˈbig·wig** *n* (sl) important person. (俚)要人;大亨。

big·amy /ˈbɪgəmɪ ; ˈbɪgəmɪ/ *n* [U] having two wives or husbands living. 重婚(一夫二妻或一妻二夫)。**ˈbig·am·ous** /ˈbɪgəməs ; ˈbɪgəməs/ *adj* guilty of, involving, ~: 犯重婚罪的;涉及重婚的: *a bigamous marriage.* 重婚的婚姻。**ˈbig·am·ist** /ˈbɪgəmɪst ;

'bɪgəmɪst/ *n* person guilty of ～. 犯重婚罪者。

bight /baɪt ; baɪt/ *n* **1** loop made in a rope. 繩子所繞成的圈;繩圈。 **2** curve in a coast, larger than, or with not so much curve as, a bay. 灣浦(海岸線之彎曲部份,較海灣寬大,或其彎曲度不如海灣那樣大)。

bigot /'bɪgət ; 'bɪgət/ *n* person who holds strongly to an opinion or belief in defiance of reason or argument. (執着某一見解或信仰而不可理喻的)頑固者;盲信者。**～ed** /-ɪd ; -ɪd/ *adj* intolerant and narrow-minded (in religion, etc). (對宗教等)頑固的;偏執的。**～ry** /-rɪ ; -rɪ/ *n* [U] state of being ～ed; [C] act, etc, of a ～. 頑固;固執;固執之行爲等。

bi·jou /'bi:ʒu: ; 'biʒu/ *n* (F) jewel. (法)珠寶。□ *adj* small and elegant: 小巧玲瓏的: ～ *villas.* 小巧的別墅。

bike /baɪk ; baɪk/ *n, vi* (colloq and common abbr for) bicycle. (俗)(騎)脚踏車;(騎)自行車(bicycle之略)。

bi·kini /bɪ'ki:nɪ ; bɪ'kinɪ/ *n* scanty two-piece garment (bra and briefs) worn by girls and women for swimming and sun-bathing: 比基尼裝(一種既短又窄的兩件式女泳裝): ～ *top* (= bra); 比基尼上裝; ～ *briefs*, ⇨ briefs. 比基尼短褲。

bi·lab·ial /ˌbaɪ'leɪbɪəl ; baɪ'lebɪəl/ *adj, n* (phon) (consonant) pronounced with both lips, eg /b, p, m, w/. (語音)由雙唇發出的; 雙唇的; 雙唇子音(如 /b, p, m, w/ 等子音是)。

bi·lat·eral /ˌbaɪ'lætərəl ; baɪ'lætərəl/ *adj* of, on, with two sides; (legal) (of an agreement, etc) made between two (persons, governments). 兩邊的;在兩邊的;有兩邊的;(法律)(指協定等)雙邊的;由二人或兩個政府所訂立的。**～·ly** *adv* **～·ism** /-ɪzəm ; -ɪzm/ *n* principle based upon ～ agreements, esp of trade and financial agreements between countries. (尤指兩國間之商務及金融協定)基於雙邊協議的原則;互惠主義。

bil·berry /'bɪlbərɪ *US:* -berɪ ; 'bɪlˌbɛrɪ/ *n* (*pl* -ries) fruit of a dwarf hardy shrub growing on heaths, etc in N Europe (also called 亦稱作 *blaeberry, whortleberry*). 覆盆子(一種漿果,產於北歐)。

bile /baɪl ; baɪl/ *n* [U] brownish-yellow bitter liquid produced by the liver to help in digesting food; (med) disorder of the ～; (fig) peevishness, bad temper. 膽汁; (醫)膽病; (喻)脾氣乖戾。 **'～-duct,** (anat) tube carrying ～ to the duodenum. (解剖)輸膽管(將膽汁輸往十二指腸之管道)。⇨ the illus at alimentary. 參看 alimentary 之插圖。

bilge /bɪldʒ ; bɪldʒ/ *n* [U] **1** almost flat part of a ship's bottom, inside or outside; (also 亦作 **'～-water**) the dirty water that collects in a ship's ～. 舭(船底內部或外部的平坦部份);舭污水(積於船底的污水)。 **2** (sl) foolish or worthless talk or writing. (俚)無聊的談話或文章。

bil·har·zia /ˌbɪl'hɑ:zɪə ; bɪl'hɑrzɪə/ *n* tropical disease caused by parasites, flatworms in the blood and bladder. 血吸蟲病(由血液及膀胱中之寄生蟲,絛蟲所引起的一種熱帶病)。

bi·lin·gual /baɪ'lɪŋgwəl; baɪ'lɪŋgwəl/ *adj* **1** speaking, using, two languages (esp when these are learnt together in childhood): 能說兩種語言的(尤指幼年時代同時學會者);採用兩種語言的: *a* ～ *country*, one in which two languages are used officially. 併用兩種語言爲官方語言的國家; 雙語言國家。 **2** written, printed, in two languages: 用兩種文字寫成或印成的;兩種文字對照的: *a* ～ *dictionary.* 兩種文字對照的字典;雙解字典。□ *n* ～ person. 能說兩種語言的人。

bil·ious /'bɪlɪəs ; 'bɪljəs/ *adj* **1** caused by too much bile: 因膽汁過多而引起的: *a* ～ *complaint/headache/attack;* 膽汁過多症(偏頭痛; 膽病發作); suffering from such complaints: 患膽汁症的;患膽病的:～ *patients.* 患膽汁症的病人。 **2** peevish; taking a gloomy view of life. 性情乖戾的;悲觀的。**～·ness** *n*

bilk /bɪlk ; bɪlk/ *vt* [VP6A, 14] **～ *sb (out) of,*** escape paying money to; cheat (esp by running away): 逃避付帳給;欺騙(尤指藉逃走而達到欺騙目的者): *He* ～*ed us out of the money.* 他把我們的錢騙走了。

bill[1] /bɪl ; bɪl/ *n* (also 亦作 **'～·hook**) long-handled tool with a curved blade used for cutting off branches of trees. (砍斷樹枝用的)長柄彎刃之刀;鉤刀。

bill[2] /bɪl ; bɪl/ *n* horny part of the mouth of some birds. 鳥喙(鳥嘴之角質部份)。⇨ the illus at bird. 參看 bird 之插圖。□ *vi* (of doves) stroke ～ with ～. (指鴿子)接嘴;觸嘴。***～ and coo,*** (fig) exchange caresses. (喻)互相撫愛。

bill[3] /bɪl ; bɪl/ *n* **1** written statement of charges for goods delivered or services rendered: 帳單;發票: *It's wrong to leave a hotel without paying all your ～s.* 未付清帳而離開旅社是不對的。 *There are some ～s to pay/to be paid.* 有些帳要付。⇨ estimate[2], quotation(3). ***foot the ～,*** ⇨ foot[2]. **2** written or printed notice, poster, placard: 招貼;廣告;海報;通告: *a theatre/concert ～,* giving information about a play, concert, etc. 戲院(音樂會)之節目單或海報。***fill/fit the ～,*** be, do, all that is required or expected. 合乎要求;做所期望的一切。***head/top the ～,*** be advertised at the head of the list, in large type, etc. 領銜主演;掛頭牌。 **～ of fare,** list of dishes to be served at a hotel, restaurant, etc; menu. (旅館、餐館等的)菜單。 **'～·board** *n* (US) structure for the display of advertisements, eg at the roadside (GB 英 = *hoarding*). (美)(路旁等處張貼廣告的)廣告牌。 **'～-poster, '～-sticker** *nn* person who pastes up ～s or placards (on walls, hoardings, etc). 張貼廣告、海報等者。 **3** (legal) proposed law, to be discussed by a parliament (and called an *Act* when passed). (法律)(向國會提出待討論的)議案(通過後卽稱爲法案Act)。 **4** (US) banknote: (美)鈔票: *a ten-dollar ～.* 一張十元的鈔票。 **'～·fold** *n* (US) wallet for banknotes. (美)錢夾; 鈔票夾; 皮夾子。 **5 B～ of Exchange,** order to a bank to pay a sum of money on a given date. 票據;滙票。**～s payable,** ～s of exchange due for payment by the holder. 應付票據。**～s receivable,** such ～s due for payment to the holder. 應收票據。 **6** certificate. 證明書。**～ of entry,** (comm) certificate from the Customs to indicate final clearance of imported goods. (商)入港申報書(海關所發給,表明進口貨品各項手續均已辦妥)。**～ of health,** (naut) certificate regarding infectious disease in a ship's crew. (航海)船員的檢疫證書。***clean ～ of health,*** **(a)** one certifying that there is no such disease. 無疫情的檢疫證書;無病的健康證書。 **(b)** (fig) assurance of good health. (喻)優良證明;有利於某事物之報告。 **～ of lading,** ⇨ lading. **～ of quantities,** ⇨ quantity(4). **～ of sale,** ⇨ sale(1). □ *vt* **1** [VP6A] make known by means of ～s(2) or placards; announce, put, in a programme: 貼傳單、廣告以通告; 在節目單中宣佈; 置於節目單中: *Olivier was ～ed to appear as Lear,* It was announced that he would play the part of Lear. 奧立佛經宣佈將飾演李爾王。 **2** [VP14] **～ *sb for sth,*** submit a ～(1) to: 爲某事物送帳單給某人: ～ *a client for services rendered.* 爲所提供的服務送帳單給客戶。

bil·let[1] /'bɪlɪt ; 'bɪlɪt/ *n* **1** place (usu a private house) where soldiers are boarded and lodged: 營舍(軍隊食宿處,常指民房): *The troops are in ～s,* in ordinary homes, not in camp or barracks. 軍隊住宿於民房中(非軍營中)。 **2** (colloq) appointment or situation; job: (俗)職業;職位;差事: *a soft/cushy ～,* one not needing much effort. 輕鬆的差事。□ *vt* [VP6A, 14] **～ *(on),*** place (troops) in ～s: 安置(軍隊)於住宿之處: ～ *soldiers on sb/on a town/on the villagers.* 指定士兵住於某人之家(鎮上,村民的房屋中)。

bil·let[2] /'bɪlɪt ; 'bɪlɪt/ *n* thick piece of firewood. 粗木柴。

bil·let-doux /ˌbɪleɪ 'du: ; 'bɪlɪ'du/ *n* (*pl* billets-doux, pronunciation unchanged) (複數發音不變) (F) (joc) love-letter. (法)(謔)情書。

bill·hook /'bɪlhʊk ; 'bɪlhʊk/ *n* ⇨ bill[1].

bil·liards /'bɪlɪədz ; 'bɪljədz/ *n* (with *sing v*) game played with small, hard, heavy balls and long tapering sticks (called *cues*) on an oblong, cloth-covered table: (用單數動詞)彈子戲;撞球戲(打彈子用的球桿叫 cue): *play ~;* 打彈子;敲桿; *have a game of ~.* 打一桿彈子。*B~ is played by women as well as by men.* 彈子戲男女都玩。**'billiard-player／-room／-table／-marker** *nn* (*sing* in compounds 在複合字中用單數). 打彈子者(彈子房;彈子檯;彈子記分員)。

bil·lings·gate /ˈbɪlɪŋzgeɪt ; ˈbɪlɪŋz,get/ *n* [U] (from the name of a London fish-market) abusive language full of swear-words. (源出於倫敦一魚市名)下流話;粗鄙語。

bil·lion /ˈbɪlɪən ; ˈbɪljən/ *n* (GB) million millions or 10^{12}; (US) thousand millions or 10^{9}. (英)萬億; (美)十億。⇨ App 4. 參看附錄四。

bil·low /ˈbɪləʊ ; ˈbɪlo/ *n* (liter) great wave; (*pl*, poet) the sea; (fig) anything that sweeps along like a great wave. (文)巨浪;(複,詩)海;(喻)如巨浪般橫滾而來之物。□ *vi* [VP2C] rise or roll like waves: 如巨浪般洶湧奔騰: *The flames ~ed over the prairie.* 大火像浪濤一般滾過原野。**~y** *adj* rising or moving like ~s. 洶湧奔騰如巨浪的。

billy /ˈbɪlɪ ; ˈbɪlɪ/ *n* [C] (*pl* -lies) (esp in Australia) tin can (sometimes called a *billy-can*) with a lid and a wire handle, used as a kettle or cooking pot, esp in camping out. (尤用於澳洲)燒水煮飯用的洋鐵罐(尤指露營時所用者,有時稱 billy-can)。

billy-goat /ˈbɪlɪ gəʊt ; ˈbɪlɪ,got/ *n* male goat. 雄山羊。⇨ nanny-goat.

billy-(h)o /ˈbɪlɪ (h)əʊ ; ˈbɪlɪ (h)o/ *n* (dated sl) (過時俚語) ***like ~,*** vigorously: 有力地;强烈地;猛烈地: *raining／fighting like ~.* 雨下得很大(猛烈戰鬥)。

bil·tong /ˈbɪltɒŋ ; ˈbɪl,tɑŋ/ *n* [U] (in S Africa) sun-dried salted meat cut into strips. (在南非洲)乾鹹肉條。

bi·met·al·lism /,baɪˈmetəlɪzəm; baɪˈmɛtḷ,ɪzəm/ *n* [U] system of having two metals, eg gold and silver, with a fixed ratio to each other as legal tender. 複本位幣制(如金銀二本位制,在二者之間保持一定之兌換率)。**bi·met·al·lic** /,baɪmɪˈtælɪk ; ,baɪməˈtælɪk/ *adj*

bin /bɪn ; bɪn/ *n* large rigid container or enclosed space, usu with a lid, for storing coal, grain, flour, bread, etc: (貯藏煤、穀、麵粉、麵包等,通常有蓋之)箱或倉: *'dustbin,* bin for rubbish, ashes, etc; 垃圾箱; *'litter bin.* 雜物箱。

bi·nary /ˈbaɪnərɪ ; ˈbaɪnərɪ/ *adj* of or involving a pair or pairs: 一雙的;一對的;二;雙;複: *a '~ system,* (astron) two stars revolving round a common centre or one round the other. (天文)雙星系統(二星球繞一共同中心而轉,或一星球繞另一星球而轉)。*the ~ scale,* (maths) with two digits, 0 and 1, as the base of the notation: (數學)二進位法(用二個數字,0和1,作爲記法之基礎):

1	2	3	4	5	6	7	8	9	10
1	10	11	100	101	110	111	1000	1001	1010

bind /baɪnd ; baɪnd/ *vt, vi* (*pt, pp* bound /baʊnd ; baʊnd/) **1** [VP6A, 15B, 14] ***~ (to); ~ (together) (with),*** tie or fasten, with rope, etc: (以繩等)束;縛;綑;綁;紮: *They bound his legs (together) so that he shouldn't escape.* 他們把他的兩腿綁起來使他不能逃跑。*Joan of Arc was bound to the stake and burnt to death.* 聖女貞德被綁在火刑柱上燒死。*The prisoner was bound hand and foot,* His arms and legs were tied. 那囚犯手足被綁。(fig) (喻): *Commerce ~s the two countries together.* 貿易把這兩國連結起來(使關係密切)。*We are bound to him by gratitude／by a close friendship.* 我們對他有感激之情(有親密的友情)。**2** [VP6A, 14] ***~ (with),*** secure the edge of sth with tape, braid, etc: (用帶子、花邊等)緄(邊);鑲(邊): *~ the edge of a carpet,* to prevent fraying; 給地毯緄邊(以防磨損); *~ the cuffs of a jacket with leather.* 在短外衣的袖口緄皮邊。**3** [VP6A, 15B] ***~ (up),*** tie or wind sth round: 包紮: *~ up a wound.* 包紮傷口。*Before sweeping the house she bound up her hair in a large handkerchief.* 在打掃房屋之前,她把她的頭髮用一條大手帕包起來。**4** [VP6A, 15A, B] ***~ (up),*** fasten (sheets of paper) into a cover: 裝訂: *~ a*

a pair of binoculars

book; 裝訂一本書; *a well-bound book;* 一本裝訂優良的書; *bound in leather;* 皮面精裝的; *~ up two books into one volume.* 將兩本書裝訂成一冊。[VP2A in *progressive tenses* only 僅用於進行式] *The new impression is ~ing,* is being bound. 新版本正在裝訂中。**5** [VP6A, 15B, 2A] ***~ (up／together),*** hold or stick together in a solid mass: (使)結成硬塊;(使)凝固: *Frost ~s the soil.* 霜使土壤凝結。*The ground is frost-bound,* frozen hard. 地面被霜凝結了。*Clay ~s* (= becomes hard) *when it is baked.* 黏土被烘即行固結。*Stones bound together with cement make good roads.* 石頭與水泥黏結在一起可以建造好道路。*Some kinds of food ~ the bowels／are ~ing,* cause constipation. 有些種類的食物會引起便秘。**6** [VP17A, 14, 15B, 16B] ***~ sb to do sth／to sth,*** hold (sb) (by legal agreement, a promise, or under penalty) to a certain course of action: (因契約、允諾或處以懲罰而)使(某人)負有義務;使必須;使應當: *~ sb to pay a debt;* 使某人必須償債; *~ sb to secrecy,* make him promise to keep sth secret. 使某人答應守密。***~ oneself to do sth,*** promise, undertake, guarantee, to do it. 答應、許諾、保證做某事。***~ sb over*** (to keep the peace, etc), order that he must appear before the judge again (if he fails to keep the peace, etc). 令某人具結必須再出庭(如果他妨碍治安等)。***~ sb over (as an apprentice) (to sb),*** make an agreement that he shall be one: 立約使某人爲(某人之)學徒: *The boy was bound over as an apprentice to a carpenter.* 那男孩經立約爲一木匠之學徒。**7** [VP2A] (dated sl) complain; carp: (過時俚語)抱怨;吹毛求疵: *Oh, do stop ~ing!* 哦,別再埋怨了! **8** ⇨ bound[5] for special uses of the *pp.* 過去分詞之特殊用法參看 bound[5]。**~er** *n* **1** person who ~s, esp *a 'book-~er.* 包紮者;綑綁東西的人;緄邊者;(尤指)裝訂書籍者。**2** thing that ties or holds things together, eg a machine, or part of a machine, that cuts and ~s grain; loose cover for unbound magazines; substance such as cement or bitumen for joining things. 用以綁縛或接合之物;紮結器(如刈禾紮結機,或刈禾機之刈禾並紮結成綑之部份);(不裝訂之雜誌之)活頁封面;起黏固作用之物(如水泥或瀝青)。**'~·ery** *n* place where books are bound. 裝訂廠;裝訂所。**~·ing** *adj* ***be ~ing on／upon,*** ~(6) or oblige sb to do sth: 有約束力的;有束縛力的: *an agreement that is ~ing on／upon all parties.* 對於各方面均有拘束力的協定。⇨ also bind(5). □ *n* [C, U] (esp) (尤指) **1** book-cover. 書籍的封皮。**2** strip, braid, etc for protecting an edge or a seam (of a garment, etc). (保護衣邊或衣縫等的)花邊;緄條。

bind·weed /ˈbaɪndwiːd ; ˈbaɪnd,wid/ *n* [U] kinds of wild convolvulus. 旋花屬的野生植物。

bine /baɪn ; baɪn/ *n* flexible stem of various kinds of climbing plants, eg hops. (攀緣植物,例如蛇麻草之軟而彎曲的)蔓;莖;藤。

binge /bɪndʒ ; bɪndʒ/ *n* (sl) ***have a ~; go on the ~,*** drink and make merry. (俚)飲酒作樂。

bingo /ˈbɪŋgəʊ ; ˈbɪŋgo/ *n* [U] popular gambling game, played with cards on which numbered squares are covered as the numbers are called at random: 賓果遊戲: (attrib) (形容用法) *~ halls.* 賓果廳(玩賓果遊戲的大廳)。

bin·nacle /ˈbɪnəkl ; ˈbɪnəkḷ/ *n* (naut) non-magnetic stand for a ship's compass (usu in front of the helm). (航海)羅盤架;羅經箱(無磁性,通常在舵輪的前方)。

bin·ocu·lars /bɪˈnɒkjʊləz ; baɪˈnɑkjələ˞z/ *n pl* field-glasses; instrument with lenses for both eyes, making distant objects seem nearer. 雙筒望遠鏡。

bi·nomial /baɪˈnəʊmɪəl ; baɪˈnomɪəl/ *adj* (maths) made up of two numbers or algebraic expressions joined by + or − (eg a^2-3b). (數學)二項的;二項式的(例如 a^2-3b)。

bio·chem·is·try /ˌbaɪəʊˈkemɪstrɪ ; ˌbaɪoˈkɛmɪstrɪ/ *n* [U] chemistry of living organisms. 生物化學。

bio·de·grad·able /ˌbaɪəʊdɪˈgreɪdəbl ; ˌbaɪodɪˈgredəbl/ *adj* (of substances) that can be broken down by bacteria: (指物質)可被細菌破壞的: *Are plastic bags indestructible or ~?* 塑膠袋是不可毀滅的或是可被細菌破壞的？

bi·ogra·phy /baɪˈɒgrəfɪ ; baɪˈɑgrəfɪ/ *n* **1** [C] person's life-history written by another. 傳記。**2** [U] branch of literature dealing with the lives of persons. 傳記文學。**bi·ogra·pher** /baɪˈɒgrəfə(r) ; baɪˈɑgrəfə˞/ *n* person who writes a ~. 傳記作者。**bio·graphic, -i·cal** /ˌbaɪəˈgræfɪk, -ɪkl ; ˌbaɪəˈgræfɪk, -ɪkl/ *adj* of ~. 傳記的。

bi·ol·ogy /baɪˈɒlədʒɪ ; baɪˈɑlədʒɪ/ *n* [U] science of the physical life of animals (= *zoology*) and plants (= *botany*). 生物學。**bi·ol·ogist** /baɪˈɒlədʒɪst ; baɪˈɑlədʒɪst/ *n* student of, expert in, ~. 生物學者;生物學家。**bio·logi·cal** /ˌbaɪəˈlɒdʒɪkl ; ˌbaɪəˈlɑdʒɪkl/ *adj* of ~: 生物學的: *a biological laboratory/experiment.* 生物實驗室(實驗)。**bioˌlogical ˈwarfare,** deliberate use of bacteria to spread disease. 生物戰;細菌戰。

bi·opsy /ˈbaɪɒpsɪ ; ˈbaɪɑpsɪ/ *n* (*pl* -sies) [C] (med) removal and examination of tissue or fluid from a living body. (醫)活體檢視;活組織檢查。⇨ autopsy.

bio·scope /ˈbaɪəskəʊp ; ˈbaɪəˌskop/ *n* (S Africa) cinema. (南非)電影放映機。

bi·par·ti·san /ˌbaɪpɑːtɪˈzæn *US:* ˌbaɪˈpɑːrtɪzn ; baɪˈpɑrtəzn/ *adj* of, supported by, consisting of, two otherwise opposed (esp political) parties: 兩黨的;兩黨所支持的;由兩黨所組成的: *a ~ foreign policy.* 兩黨同支持的外交政策。

bi·ped /ˈbaɪped ; ˈbaɪpɛd/ *n* animal with only two feet. 兩足動物。

bi·plane /ˈbaɪpleɪn ; ˈbaɪˌplen/ *n* aircraft with two pairs of wings, one above the other. 雙翼飛機。

birch /bɜːtʃ ; bɝtʃ/ *n* **1** [C] (kinds of) forest tree growing in northern countries; it has smooth bark and slender branches. 樺樹;赤楊;樺類樹(產於北方國家,皮光滑,枝細長)。**2** [U] its wood, eg as used for making canoes. 樺木。**3** [C] (also 亦作 **ˈ~-rod**) bundle of ~ twigs tied together and used formerly for punishing schoolboys. (從前用以體罰學童的)樺樹條。□ *vt* [VP6A] punish with a ~-rod. 用樺樹條體罰。

bird /bɜːd ; bɝd/ *n* **1** feathered creature with two legs and two wings, usu able to fly. 鳥;禽類。⇨ the illus below and at fowl, prey, rare, water. 參看附圖以及 fowl, prey, rare, water 之插圖。***A ~ in the hand is worth two in the bush,*** (prov) Sth which one has, though small, is better than sth larger, which one has not. (諺)手中的一隻鳥勝過枝頭上的兩隻鳥(實際所有之物,其値雖小,猶勝無把握獲得之價値較大之物)。***(strictly) for the ~s,*** (sl) bad; worthless. (俚)(毫)無價値的;(毫)無用處的。***get the ~,*** (sl) be hissed, scorned or rejected. (俚)被人發噓聲;被鬨;被蔑視;被棄。***give sb the ~,*** (sl) hiss, scorn or reject him. (俚)對某人發噓聲;輕視或棄絕某人。***kill two ~s with one stone,*** achieve two aims at once. 一石二鳥;一箭雙鵰;一舉兩得。**ˈ~-cage** *n* cage for a ~ or ~s. 鳥籠。**ˈ~-fancier** *n* person who knows about, collects, breeds or sells ~s. 懂鳥者;養鳥者;鳥商。**ˈ~-lime** *n* sticky substance put on branches to catch ~s. (塗於樹枝上以捕鳥的)黏鳥膠。**ˌ~'s-ˌeye ˈview** *n* wide view seen from high up; (fig) general survey of a subject. 鳥瞰;(喻)(某一科目之)概覽。**ˈ~-nesting** *n* hunting for birds' nests (to get the eggs). 獵鳥巢(以取蛋)。**ˈ~-watch** *vi* [VP2A] study birds in their natural state; 研究鳥類之自然狀態; hence, 由此產生, **ˈ~-watcher** *n* person who does this; 研究鳥類之自然狀態者; hence, 由此產生, **ˈ~-watching** *n* [U]. ⇨ also feather¹, passage(1), prey. **2** (colloq) person: (俗)人: *an odd/wise ~;* 一個怪人(聰明人); *a cunning old ~.* 一個狡猾的老傢伙。**3** (GB sl) young woman. (英俚)年輕的女郎;小妞。

bir·etta /bɪˈretə ; bəˈrɛtə/ *n* [C] (*pl* ~s) square cap worn by RC and some Anglican priests. (天主教及某些英國國教僧侶所戴的)四角帽;法冠。

biro /ˈbaɪərəʊ ; ˈbaɪro/ *n* [C] (*pl* ~s) (P) (kind of) ball-pen. (商標)一種原子筆;拜樂牌原子筆。

birth /bɜːθ ; bɝθ/ *n* **1** [U] (process of) being born, coming into the world; [C] instance of this: 出生;出世;誕生: *The baby weighed seven pounds at ~,* when it was born. 那嬰兒生下來七磅重。*The boy has been delicate from (his) ~,* has been weak in health since he was born. 那男孩從生下來一直身體很弱。*Cats sometimes have four or five young at a ~.* 貓有時一窩生四隻或五隻小貓。*There were 167 more ~s than deaths in the town last year.* 此鎮去年出生者較死亡者多一百六十七人。***give ~ to,*** bring into the world; (fig) produce: 生產(嬰兒); (喩)產生;造成: *give ~ to a child/a poem/a dispute.* 生小孩(作出一首詩;造成紛爭)。**2** [U] origin, descent: 起源;血統;出身: *She is Russian by ~ and British by marriage.* 她原是俄國人,但嫁給英國人(而成了英國人)。***be of good ~,*** (old use) come of an acceptable family. (舊用法)出身高尙門第。**ˈ~-control** *n* [U] (method of) preventing unwanted conception(2). 節制生育(法)。**ˈ~·day** *n* (anniversary of the) day of one's ~. 生日;生日紀念。**ˈ~·mark** *n* mark on the body at or from ~. 胎記;胎痣。**ˈ~·place** *n* house or district in which one was born. 出生的房子;出生地;誕生地。**ˈ~·rate** *n* number of ~s in one year for every 1000 persons. 出生率(每年每一千人中之嬰兒出生數目)。**ˈ~·right** *n* any of various rights, privileges and properties to which a person has a right as a member of his family, a citizen of his country, etc. (對於各種權利、特權和財產的)與生俱來的權利;生爲某家庭之一份子或某國之公民應享之權利;生得權。

bis·cuit /ˈbɪskɪt ; ˈbɪskɪt/ *n* [C] **1** flat, thin, crisp cake of many kinds, sweetened or unsweetened. 餅乾。***take the ~,*** (sl) be the best/worst at something; be surprising. (俚)成爲前所未見或前所未聞之最好(最壞)事物;令人驚訝。**2** (US) bread dough baked in small shapes. (美)小點心。**3** light-brown. 淡棕色;淺褐色。

bi·sect /baɪˈsekt ; baɪˈsɛkt/ *vt* [VP6A] cut or divide into two (usu equal) parts. 切或分爲(通常相等的)兩分。**bi·sec·tion** /baɪˈsekʃn ; baɪˈsɛkʃən/ *n* [U] division into two (equal) parts. 分而爲二;二等分。

bi·sex·ual /ˌbaɪˈsekʃʊəl ; baɪˈsɛkʃʊəl/ *adj* of two sexes; having both male and female sexual organs; sexually attracted to either sex. 兩性的;兼具雌雄兩性性器官的;對男女兩性均感興趣的;陰陽的。□ *n* individual showing one of these characteristics. 陰陽人;兩性體。**~·ity** /ˌbaɪsekʃʊˈælətɪ ; ˌbaɪsɛkʃʊˈælətɪ/ *n* [U] condition of being ~. 兼具兩性;雌雄同體。

bishop /ˈbɪʃəp ; ˈbɪʃəp/ *n* **1** Christian clergyman of high rank who organizes the work of the Church in a city or district. 主教(主管一城市或一教區之教務)。⇨ the illus at vestment. 參看 vestment 之插圖。⇨ diocese. **~·ric** /-rɪk ; -rɪk/ *n* office of a ~; district under a ~. 主教職;主教轄區。**2** chess piece, ⇨ the illus at chess. 主教(西洋棋中的一棋子,參看 chess 之插圖)。

bis·muth /ˈbɪzməθ ; ˈbɪzməθ/ *n* [U] reddish-white metal (symbol **Bi**), used in alloys; compound of this used medically, eg for stomach troubles. 鉍(帶紅之白色金屬,化學符號 Bi,用於合金;鉍的化合物作醫藥用,如治療胃病)。

bi·son /ˈbaɪsn ; ˈbaɪsn̩/ *n* (*pl* unchanged) (複數不變) European wild ox; American buffalo. 歐洲的野牛；美洲野牛。⇨ the illus at large. 參看 large 之挿圖。

bis·tro /ˈbiːstrəʊ ; ˈbɪstro/ *n* [C] (*pl* ~s) small, cheap restaurant; (in France) small bar¹(13) or nightclub. 小餐館；(法國之)小酒吧；小型夜總會。

bit¹ /bɪt ; bɪt/ *n* **1** mouth-piece (metalbar) forming part of a horse's bridle. 馬嚼子；馬銜。⇨ the illus at harness. 參看 harness 之挿圖。***take the bit between one's teeth,*** (of a horse) run away out of control; (fig) apply oneself to sth difficult or risky or distasteful. (指馬)脫繮逃跑；(喩)集中精力去做艱難、冒險或討厭之事。 **2** part of a tool that cuts or grips when twisted; tool for boring or drilling holes, fitted into a *drill* or a *brace*. 工具之切割或抓的部份；(鑽子的)鑽頭；錐。⇨ the illus at drill, brace. 參看 drill, brace 之挿圖。

bit² /bɪt ; bɪt/ *n* **1** small piece of anything: 一小塊；一點點: *He took some paper and a few bits of wood and soon made a fire.* 他拿了一些紙和幾片木頭，不久就生了一堆火。*He ate every bit of* (= all) *his dinner.* 他把他的一份晚餐吃得光光。*He has saved a nice bit* (= a good sum) *of money.* 他已積蓄了相當數目的一筆錢。***bit by bit,*** slowly, gradually. 一點一點地；慢慢地；逐漸地。***a bit at a time,*** by degrees. 一步一步地；逐漸地。***every bit as (good, etc),*** equally (good, etc). 同等地(好等)。***do one's bit,*** perform one's share of a task; give as much help as is expected of one. 做分內之事；盡力幫助。***wait a bit,*** a short time. 等一會兒。***a bit,*** rather: 相當地；有點: *She's feeling a bit tired.* 她覺得有點疲倦。***a bit of a,*** rather a: 相當地: *He's a bit of a coward.* 他是相當膽小的。***a bit of all right,*** (GB sl) very fine. (英俚)很不錯。***not a bit,*** not at all; not in the least: 一點也不；毫不: *He's not a bit better.* 他一點也沒有好。*He doesn't care a bit.* 他一點也不在乎。*It's not a bit of use,* It's quite useless. 它一點用處也沒有。***not a bit of it,*** not at all (used as a strong denial): 一點也沒有；毫不(用作强烈的否認): *You'd think she'd be tired after such a long journey, but not a bit of it!* 你會以爲在這樣一次長途旅行之後她會疲倦，可是一點也不(她一點也不會感到疲倦)。***pull/cut/tear sth to bits,*** into small pieces. 將某物扯(切，撕)成碎塊。***go/come to bits,*** into small pieces. 成爲碎塊；變成碎片。 **2** (used colloq, like *piece,* with *news, advice, luck*): (俗，同 piece，與 news, advice, luck 連用): *a bit of good advice.* 一個忠告。 **3 (a)** small coin: 小錢幣: *threepenny bit,* (former) coin (GB) worth threepence. (昔時英國之)三辨士的錢幣。**(b)** (US) 12½ cents. (美)一角二分半。 **4** (colloq, esp US) area common to a group of subjects, attitudes, etc: (俗，尤美)一組題目、看法等的共同領域: *She couldn't accept the whole drug-culture bit.* 她無法接受吸毒之風氣。

bit³ /bɪt ; bɪt/ *n* (comp) unit of information expressed as a choice between two possibilities. (電腦)位元；數元。

bit⁴ /bɪt ; bɪt/ ⇨ bite¹

bitch /bɪtʃ ; bɪtʃ/ *n* **1** female dog, fox, otter or wolf. 母狗；母狐；母獺；母狼。 **2** ⚠ (derog sl) spiteful woman. (諱)(貶俚)惡毒的女人；壞女人；潑婦。□ *vi* [VP2A] (colloq) complain in a sour way; speak spitefully to or about sb or sth. (俗)尖刻地發牢騷；不懷好意地搬弄是非。**~y** *adj* (colloq) spiteful. (俗)惡意的。

bite¹ /baɪt ; baɪt/ *vt, vi* (*pt* bit /bɪt ; bɪt/, *pp* bitten /ˈbɪtn ; ˈbɪtn̩/). **1** [VP6A, 15B, 2A, 3A] ***~ (into),*** cut into with the teeth: 咬: *The dog bit me in the leg.* 那狗咬了我的腿。*Does your dog ~,* is it in the habit of biting people? 你的狗咬人嗎？*He bit into the peach.* 他咬那桃子。***~ at sth,*** try to get it with the teeth; snap at. 用牙去咬某物(以圖得到它)。***~ off,*** cut off with the teeth: 咬下來: *He bit off a large piece of the apple.* 他咬下一大塊蘋果。***~ off more than one can chew,*** attempt too much. 貪多嚼不爛(從事太多的工作，而無力完成)。***(have) sth to ~ on,*** sth to get one's teeth into; (fig) sth definite to do, examine, etc. (有)可咬的東西；(喩)(有)明確可爲、可查等的事物；(有)可資把持之東西。***~ the dust,*** (colloq) (fig) fall to the ground; be killed. (俗)(喩)倒下；被殺；陣亡。***~ one's lips,*** try to conceal one's anger or annoyance. 咬唇以圖掩飾憤怒或厭惡。***once bitten twice shy,*** (prov) a person who has been cheated, hurt, etc is likely to be cautious aftérwards. (諺)一回上當二回乖；上一次當學一次乖。***the biter bitten,*** the person who intended to cheat was himself cheated. 欲騙人者反而被人騙；害人反害己。 **2** [VP6A] **(a)** (of fleas, mosquitoes, etc) sting: (指跳蚤、蚊子等)咬；叮: *He was badly bitten by the mosquitoes.* 他被蚊子咬得很厲害。**(b)** (of fish) accept the bait: (指魚)吃餌；上鉤: *The fish wouldn't ~.* 這些魚不肯吃餌。*I tried to sell him my old car but he wouldn't ~,* (fig) would not consider the .suggestion. (喩)我試圖把我的舊車賣給他，但他不肯上鈎(不予考慮)。 **3** [VP6A, 2A, 3A] ***~ (into),*** cause a smarting pain to; injure: 使感覺劇痛；刺痛；傷害: *His fingers were bitten by the frost/*

small land birds

were frost-bitten. 他的手指凍傷了。*Mustard and pepper ~ the tongue.* 芥末和胡椒粉刺痛舌頭。*Strong acids ~ (into) metals,* make holes in them. 强酸能腐蝕金屬。 **4** [VP6A, 2A] take strong hold of; grip: 緊握；抓緊：*The rails were covered with ice and the wheels did not ~.* 鐵軌上面覆蓋着冰，車輪卡不住軌(不能前行)。**bit·ing** *adj* sharp; cutting: 尖刻的；刺痛的：*a biting wind;* 刺骨的寒風；*biting words.* 尖刻的話。**bit·ing·ly** *adv*

bite² /baɪt ; baɪt/ *n* **1** act of biting: 咬：*eating sth at one ~.* 一口將某物吃下。 **2** injury resulting from a ~ or sting: 咬傷；叮：*His face was covered with insect ~s.* 他滿臉都是蚊蚋的咬傷。 **3** piece cut off by biting. 咬下的一塊。 **4** (colloq) food to eat: (俗)食物：*I haven't had a ~ since morning,* have eaten nothing. 我從早晨到現在一口東西都未吃過。 **5** taking bait from a hook by fish: 魚之吞餌；上鈎：*He had been fishing all morning but hadn't had a ~.* 他釣了一上午的魚，但沒有魚上鈎。 **6** [U] sharpness; sting: 尖刻；刺痛：*There's a ~ in the air this morning.* 今天早晨有點寒風刺骨。 **7** [U] grip; hold: 緊抓；緊握：*a file／screw with plenty of ~.* 銳利的銼子(扭得牢的螺絲釘)。

bit·ten /ˈbɪtn ; ˈbɪtn̩/ ⇨ bite¹.

bit·ter /ˈbɪtə(r) ; ˈbɪtɚ/ *adj* **1** tasting like beer or unsweetened coffee. 味道似啤酒或未加糖之咖啡的；苦的。 **ˌ~-ˈsweet** *adj* sweet but with a ~ taste at the end; (fig) pleasant but with a mixture of sth unpleasant. 甜的但最後帶苦味的；甜中帶苦的；(喻)樂中帶苦的。 **2** unwelcome to the mind; hard to bear; causing sorrow: 難過的；難以忍受的；引起悲傷的；痛苦的：*~ hardships／experiences.* 難以忍受的艱辛(痛苦的經歷)。*His failure to pass the examination was a ~ disappointment.* 他考試失敗是一件極令人失望的事。 ***a ~ pill to swallow,*** sth unpleasant to accept. 苦藥丸；勉强接受的苦事。 **3** filled with, showing, caused by, envy, hate, remorse, or disappointment: 充滿或顯示嫉妒、憎恨、懊悔或失望之情緒的；由上述情緒所引起的：*~ quarrels／words／enemies／reproaches／tears.* 厲害的爭吵(怨言；死敵；苛責；傷心淚)。 **4** piercingly cold: 寒冷刺骨的：*a ~ wind.* 刺骨的寒風。 **5** ***to the ~ end,*** until all that is possible has been done: (奮鬥)到底；拚命：*fight to the ~ end.* 戰鬥到底。□ *n* **1** bitterness. 苦。 ***take the ~ with the sweet,*** accept misfortune as well as good fortune. 甘與苦都接受；不僅接受幸運，也要接受不幸。Cf 參較 *take the rough with the smooth,* which is more usu. 不快意的和快意的事同要接受(爲較常用之成語)。 **2** [U] ~ beer, ie heavily flavoured with hops: 苦啤酒：*a pint of ~.* 一品脫苦啤酒。 **3** (*pl*) liquor made from herbs, fruits, etc taken to help digestion or used to flavour gin, etc: (複)苦味藥酒(用藥草、果實等浸製成，飲之能幫助消化，或加於杜松子酒中以增味)：*orange ~s;* 柑桔藥酒；*gin and ~s.* 杜松子藥酒。 **~·ly** *adv* **~·ness** *n*

bit·tern /ˈbɪtən ; ˈbɪtɚn/ *n* any of several kinds of wading birds that live on marshes, esp the kind known for its booming note. 麻鳽(生活於沼澤地帶之數種涉禽，尤指能發低沉之鳴聲者)。⇨ the illus at water. 參看 water 之插圖。

bitu·men /ˈbɪtjʊmən ; bɪˈtjumən/ *n* [U] black, sticky substance (from petroleum), used for making roads, etc; mineral pitch; asphalt. 瀝青；地瀝青。 **bit·umi·nous** /bɪˈtjuːmɪnəs *US:* -ˈtuː- ; bɪˈtjumənəs/ *adj* containing ~ or tar: 含瀝青的：*bituminous coal,* burning with smoky yellow flames. 瀝青炭；瀝青煤(燃燒時發出含濃煙之黃色火焰)。

bi·valve /ˈbaɪvælv ; ˈbaɪˌvælv/ *n* (zool) mollusc with a hinged double shell, eg an oyster, a mussel, a clam. (動物)雙殼貝類；瓣鰓類(如蠔、貽貝、蛤等)。

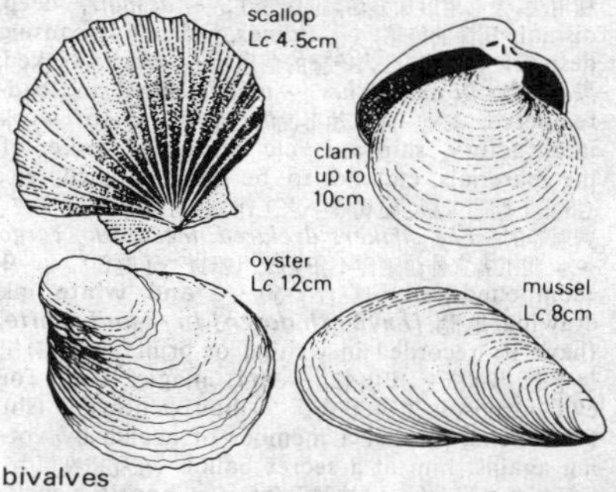

bivalves

biv·ouac /ˈbɪvʊæk ; ˈbɪvʊˌæk/ *n* soldiers' temporary camp without tents or other cover. (士兵之臨時的)野營(無篷帳或其他遮蓋)；露天營地。□ *vi* (*pt, pp* bivouacked) [VP2A] make a ~; stay in a ~. 紮野營；露宿於野營中。

biz /bɪz ; bɪz/ *n* (sl) (俚) = business: *Good biz!* Well done! 做得好！ **ˈshow·biz,** (sl) (providing and managing) popular entertainment. (俚)(籌備及安排)一般之娛樂及餘興節目。

bi·zarre /bɪˈzɑː(r) ; bɪˈzɑr/ *adj* grotesque; odd. 古怪的;怪異的;奇異的。

bi·zonal /ˌbaɪˈzəʊnl ; baɪˈzonḷ/ *adj* of two zones. 兩區的。

blab /blæb ; blæb/ *vt, vi* (-bb-) [VP6A, 15B, 2A] (colloq) talk foolishly or indiscreetly: (俗) 胡扯;亂談: *Don't ~!* 不要胡扯! ***~ (out),*** tèll (a secret): 洩漏(秘密): *~ out a secret.* 洩漏秘密。

blab·ber /ˈblæbə(r) ; ˈblæbɚ/ *vt, vi* = blab. **ˈ~-mouth** *n* person who ~s. 亂講話的人;洩密者。

black /blæk ; blæk/ *adj* (-er, -est) **1** without light or almost without light; the colour of this printing-ink; opposite to white. 黑暗的;黑色的;黑的。***be ~ and blue,*** covered with bruises. 遍佈青一塊、紫一塊的傷痕。***~ in the face,*** dark red or purple (with anger or because of making great efforts). (因發怒或使勁而) 臉色發紅或發紫; 臉色發青。***be in sb's ~ book(s),*** ⇨ book¹(6). ***look ~ at sb; give sb a ~ look,*** look at him angrily. 怒視某人。***not so ~ as one is painted,*** not so bad as one is said to be. 不像傳聞那麼壞。**2** (various uses, mostly to intensify the meaning of the *n*): (各種用法,大都用以加强名詞的意義): *~ despair,* deep, dismal; 深深的絶望; *~ tidings,* sad news, causing despair; 壞消息;令人絶望的消息; *~ deeds,* wicked; 黑心的事; *in one of his ~ moods,* silent and bad-tempered. 在他一陣默然不悅的心情中。**3** (of work in a factory, shipyard, etc during a strike; of the materials, etc) not to be done, handled, etc: (指罷工期間工廠、船塢等中之工作; 指材料等)不予完成、處理等的: *The strikers declared the work/cargo ~.* 罷工者宣佈該工作不予完成 (船貨不予處理)。**4** (compounds, etc) (複合字等) **~ and white,** ink drawing. 墨畫。***(have sth down) in ~ and white,*** (have it) recorded in writing or print. (把某事)記錄下來;寫在紙上;印出來。**~ art,** magic, used for evil purposes. 魔術;妖術。**ˈ~·ball** *vt* prevent (sb) from being elected a member of a club by voting against him at a secret ballot. (在秘密投票中)投反對票以阻止(某人)被選爲會員。**ˈ~-beetle** *n* cockroach. 蟑螂。**ˈ~·berry** /ˈblækbərɪ *US:* -berɪ ; ˈblækˌbɛrɪ/ *n* (*pl* -ries) small berry, ~ when ripe, growing wild on bushes (called *brambles*): 黑莓(一種小漿果,成熟時呈黑色,野生於稱爲懸鈎子之灌木上): *go ~berrying* /-berɪɪŋ ; -bɛrɪɪŋ/, go out gathering ~berries. 出去採黑莓。⇨ the illus at fruit. 參看 fruit 之挿圖。**ˈ~·bird** *n* common European songbird. 山烏類(一種常見於歐洲之鳴禽)。**ˈ~-board** *n* board used in schools for writing and drawing on with chalk. 黑板。**ˌ~ ˈbox** *n* device for recording information about the performance of an aircraft. 黑盒(記錄飛機作業資料的裝置)。**ˌ~ ˈcoffee** *n* coffee without milk, usu strong. 純咖啡;黑咖啡(不加牛奶之咖啡,通常很濃)。**ˌ~ ˈcomedy** *n* (theatre) comedy with a tragic element or basic pessimism, usu heavily ironical. (戲劇)有悲劇或悲觀成分的喜劇(通常富於諷刺性)。cf 參較 *sick joke.* **the ˈB~ Country,** the smoky, industrial area in Staffordshire and Warwickshire. 在斯塔福郡及瓦立克郡之煙霧瀰漫的工廠區域。**ˌ~·ˈcur·rant** *n* kind of currant with ~ fruit. 黑醋栗。⇨ currant(2). **the ˌ~ ˈflag,** flag formerly used by pirates (sea-robbers); flag once used at prisons as a signal that a murderer had been executed by hanging. 黑旗(從前爲海盜所用者,亦曾用於監獄,表示有殺人犯被處絞刑)。**ˌ~ ˈfrost** *n* hard frost without rime. 黑霜; 嚴霜。**ˈ~·guard** /ˈblægɑːd ; ˈblægɚd/ *n* person who is quite without honour; scoundrel. 下流的人;無賴;流氓。▭ *vt* call (sb) a ~guard; use very bad language about or to (sb). 罵(某人)下流;辱罵(某人)。**ˈ~·guard·ly** /ˈblægədlɪ ; ˈblægɚdlɪ/ *adj* dishonest and immoral: 卑鄙的;下流的: *a ~guardly trick.* 卑鄙的手段。**ˈ~·head** *n* (kind of) pimple on the skin, the top being ~. 尖頭呈黑色之丘疹;黑頭粉刺。**ˌ~ ˈhole** *n* (astron) region in space from which no matter or radiation (eg light) can escape. (天文)黑洞(太空中一區域,不會放出任何物質或輻射,如光等)。**ˌ~ ˈice** *n* ice, esp on a road surface, which is almost invisible and dangerous to drive on. 黑冰(尤指路面上所結之幾乎看不見的冰,駕車於其上有危險)。**ˌ~-ˈlead** *n* [U] soft, grey-black solid (plumbago, or graphite) used for lead pencils, polishing and as a lubricant. 石墨;黑鉛(用於製鉛筆心,打光及作潤滑劑)。▭ *vt* polish, eg a fireplace, with ~-lead. 用石墨打光(壁爐等)。**ˈ~·leg** *n* person who offers to work when the regular workers are on strike. 在正式工人罷工期間自求做工者; 不參加罷工的工人。▭ *vi, vt* (-gg-) act as ~leg; betray (fellow workers) by doing this. 在罷工期間背棄(其他工人)而自行上工。**ˈ~·list** *n* list of persons who are considered dangerous or who are to be punished. 黑名單(內列被認爲係危險人物或應受懲罰者)。▭ *vt* enter the name of (sb) on a ~list. 把(某人)列入黑名單。**ˌ~ ˈmagic** *n* witchcraft. 魔術;妖術。**ˈ~·mail** *vt, n* [U] (force sb to make a) payment of money for not making known sth discreditable about him. 敲詐;勒索;敲詐或勒索之款。Hence, 由此產生,**ˈ~·mailer** *n* person who does this. 敲詐者;勒索者。**ˌ~ Maˈria** /məˈraɪə ; məˈraɪə/ *n* van for taking prisoners from and to jail. 囚車。**ˌ~ ˈmark** *n* (fig) mark(4) of bad conduct, failure, etc: (喻)行爲不良、失敗等之污點: *Her continual lateness was a ~ mark against her promotion.* 她不斷的遲到是不利於她升職的一個污點。**ˌ~ ˈmarket** *n* unlawful buying and selling of goods, currencies, etc that are officially controlled; place where such trading is carried on. 黑市交易(對於官方控制之貨物、貨幣等之非法買賣);黑市;進行黑市交易之場所。**ˌ~ ˌmarkeˈteer** /ˌmɑːkɪˈtɪə(r) ; ˌmɑrkəˈtɪr/ *n* person carrying on this trade. 經營黑市交易者;黑市黃牛。**ˌ~ ˈmass** *n* travesty of the RC Mass, for Satan instead of God. 黑彌撒(冒瀆的模倣天主教之彌撒,所讚頌者是撒旦,而非上帝)。**ˈ~·out** *n* **(a)** (during wartime) the keeping of all buildings, etc, dark (by curtains, etc, in windows, by having no street-lighting, etc) in order to prevent any light being seen, esp from the air. (戰時之)燈火管制(尤指爲防空襲而實施者)。**(b)** temporary complete failure of the memory or consciousness; (esp flying) temporary blindness caused by a sudden turn or a change in speed. 暫時的喪失記憶或知覺;(尤指)黑暈(飛行中因突然轉向或改變速度所致的暫時性失明)。**(c)** extinguishing of all lights on the stage of a theatre, eg for a change of scenery. 舞臺上之熄燈(如爲換佈景)。▭ ***~ out*** *vt, vi* [VP15B, 2A] cause a ~out ((a) and (c) above); lose one's memory, etc, temporarily. 實施燈火管制;熄去舞臺上的全部燈光; 熄燈; 暫時失去記憶等。**ˌB~ ˈPanther** *n* (US, 1960's) member of a militant B~ Power group. 黑豹黨黨徒 (美國黑人 1960 年代黑權運動中之戰鬥份子)。**ˌB~ ˈPower** *n* (US, 1960's) militant movement for civil rights for Negroes. 黑權運動(美國 1960 年代爭取黑人民權之戰鬥運動)。**ˌ~ ˈpudding** *n* sausage made of blood, suet, barley, etc. (用血、板油、大麥等製成的)黑香腸。**ˌB~ ˈSash** *n* (S Africa) women's anti-apartheid organization. (南非)黑帶組織 (反對種族隔離制度之婦女組織)。**ˌ~ ˈsheep** *n* good-for-nothing person. 無用的人;名譽很壞的人;害群之馬;敗家子。**ˈB~·shirt** *n* member of the former Italian Fascist party. (昔之)義大利黑衫黨(法西斯黨)黨員。**ˈ~·smith** *n* man who makes and repairs things of iron, esp a shoer of horses. 鐵匠;(尤指)馬蹄鐵匠。**ˈ~ spot** *n* place (eg on a road) where accidents often happen. (道路等之)常發生意外之處。**ˈ~·thorn** *n* thorny shrub which has white blossom before the leaves appear and purple fruit (*sloe*) like a small plum. 櫻屬的一種有刺灌木(在未發葉前開白花,其果實稱作 sloe, 呈紫色,似小李子)。**ˌ~·water ˈfever** *n* tropical disease with bloody urine. 黑水熱;黑尿熱(帶血尿之一種熱帶病)。□ *n* **1** [U] ~

colour: 黑色: *He was dressed in* ~, in ~ clothes. 他穿着黑色衣服。 **2** [U] ~ paint or dye. 黑色顏料或染料。 **3** [C] particle of soot. 煤烟之微粒。 **4** [C] Negro (formerly derog, but now widely used). 黑人(從前爲貶抑語,但今已廣泛使用)。 **5 the** ~, credit side of business accounts. (帳目之)貸方。 ***be in/get into the*** ~, have/get assets that exceed liabilities. 有贏餘。 ⇨ red *n*(4). □ *vt* [VP6A] **1** make ~, polish (boots, etc), with blacking. 使變黑;用鞋油擦(靴等)。 **2** declare ~(3): 宣佈…不予完成或處理: *The strikers ~ed the ship/the cargo.* 罷工者宣佈不完成那艘船(不處理船貨)。 ~ ***out***, ⇨ ~out above.

black·a·moor /ˈblækəmʊə(r) ; ˈblækəˌmʊr/ *n* (old use, hum or derog) black person. (舊用法,諧或貶)黑人。

blacken /ˈblækən ; ˈblækən/ *vt, vi* **1** [VP6A, 2A] make or become black. 使黑;變黑。 **2** [VP6A] ~ ***(sb's name)***, speak evil of (sb's character). 說(某人的)壞話;毀謗。

black·ing /ˈblækɪŋ ; ˈblækɪŋ/ *n* [U] black paste or liquid for polishing shoes (now usu 今通常作 *shoe polish*). 黑色鞋油。

blad·der /ˈblædə(r) ; ˈblædɚ/ *n* **1** bag of skin in which urine collects in human and animal bodies. 膀胱。 ⇨ the illus at kidney. 參看 kidney 之挿圖。 **2** such a bag, or a bag of rubber, etc, that can be filled with air, eg the rubber ~ in a football. 可充氣之囊袋或橡皮囊袋(如足球內之球膽)。

blade /bleɪd ; bled/ *n* **1** flattened cutting part of a knife, sword, chisel, etc: (刀、劍、鑿等的)刄: *a pocket-knife with two ~s;* (可摺合的)雙刄小刀; *a packet of five razor ~s.* 一包五片的刮鬍刀刀片。 ⇨ the illus at razor. 參看 razor 之挿圖。 **2** sword; swordsman. 劍;劍術家;劍手。 **3** flat wide part of an oar (the part that goes into the water), bat, propeller, etc. 槳葉; (板球棒等的)擊球板; 螺旋槳葉(等)。 **4** flat, long, narrow leaf, esp of grass and cereals (wheat, barley, etc). (扁平而狹長之)草葉;葉片;葉身;(小麥、大麥等之)禾葉。

blae·berry /ˈbleɪbərɪ *US:* -berɪ; ˈblebərɪ/ *n* = bilberry.

blah /blɑː ; blɑ/ *n* [U] (colloq) high-sounding but meaningless talk or writing. (俗)浮誇而無意義的談話或文章;胡說。

blame /bleɪm ; blem/ *vt* [VP6A,14] ~ ***sb (for sth);*** ~ ***sth on sb***, fix on sb the responsibility for sth done (badly or wrongly) or not done: 責備;歸咎(某事於某人): *Bad workmen often ~ their tools.* 拙劣的工人常常怪他們的工具不好。 *He ~d his teacher for his failure.* 他把他的失敗歸咎於他的老師。 *He ~d his failure on his teacher.* 他把他的失敗歸咎於他的老師。 *I have nothing to ~ myself for.* 我沒有什麼可責怪自己的。 ***be to*** ~, deserve censure: 應受譴責;應負責任: *Who is to ~ for starting the fire,* Whom have we to find fault with? 火災之引起應由誰負其咎? *I am in no way to ~,* am not in any way responsible. 怎麼說我都不應負其責。 □ *n* [U] **1** responsibility for sth done (badly or wrongly) or not done: 對已做或未做之事所應負的責任;過失;咎: *Where does the ~ lie for our failure,* Who or what is responsible? 我們的失敗應歸咎何人(或何事)? ***bear/take the ~ (for sth)***, take the responsibility. (對某事)負責; 負咎。 ***put/lay the ~ on sb (for sth)***, make him responsible. (將某事)歸咎於某人。 **2** finding fault: 責難;非難;挑剔;指摘: *If you don't do the work well, you will incur ~,* people will find fault. 如果你不把工作做好,你將會招人責難。 ~**·less** *adj* free from ~ or faults; innocent: 無可責備的; 無過失的: *I am ~less in this matter.* 在這件事中,我是無過失的。 ~**·less·ly** *adv* ~**·worthy** /ˈbleɪmwɜːðɪ ; ˈblemˌwɝðɪ/ *adj* deserving ~. 應受責備的。

blanch /blɑːntʃ *US:* blæntʃ ; blæntʃ/ *vt, vi* [VP6A, 2A] make or become pale or white, eg by taking the skin off almonds, by not letting light get to plants; make or become pale with fear, cold, etc. 使變白(如將杏仁皮剝去或不讓光線射及植物); 變白; (因恐懼、寒冷等而)使變蒼白;變蒼白。

blanc·mange /bləˈmɒnʒ ; bləˈmɑnʒ/ *n* [C, U] jelly made in a mould with milk: 用牛奶在模型中製成的一種膠狀點心: ~ ***powder***, mixture of powdered milk, powdered gelatine, etc to make kinds of ~. 製此種點心之粉(係奶粉、膠粉等之混合物)。

bland /blænd ; blænd/ *adj* **1** gentle or polite in manner or talk (usu in order to ingratiate oneself). (通常指爲了予人好印象而) 態度或談話溫文有禮的。 **2** (of air, food, drink) mild; comforting. (指空氣、食物、飲料)溫和的;使人舒適的。 **3** featureless; uninteresting. 無特色的;枯燥無味的;不動人的。 ~**·ly** *adv* ~**·ness** *n*

bland·ish·ment /ˈblændɪʃmənt ; ˈblændɪʃmənt/ *n* (usu *pl*) (formal) soft and gentle ways and speech intended to make sb do sth; flattery; coaxing. (通常用複數)(正式用語)爲誘使某人做某事而表現的溫和態度與言語;諂媚;哄誘。

blank /blæŋk ; blæŋk/ *adj* **1** (of paper, parts of a document, etc) with nothing written, printed or drawn on it: (指紙,部分文件等)空白的;未寫字、印字或畫圖的: *a ~ sheet of paper;* 一張白紙; *a ~ page/space.* 空白的一頁(一塊空白)。 ˌ~ **ˈbill**, Bill of Exchange on which the name of the person to be paid is not stated. 不記名滙票(受款人姓名未寫明者)。 ˌ~ **ˈcheque**, one with the amount left for the payee to fill in. (金額由受款人自行塡寫的)空白支票。 ***give sb a ~ cheque***, (fig) full power to act as he thinks best. (喩)請某人全權處理。 **2** empty; without interest or expression: 茫然的;空虛的;無興趣的;無表情的: *There was a ~ look on his face,* He seemed not to be interested, not to understand, etc. 他的臉上毫無表情。 *He looked ~,* puzzled. 他看起來似感困惑。 *His future looks ~,* seems to be empty and dull. 他的前途似很黯淡。 *My mind went ~,* I could not recall things, esp things I needed to be aware of. 我心中茫然(腦中一片空白,什麼都忘了)。 ˌ~ **ˈcartridge**, with a charge of powder, but no bullet. 空包彈(有火藥而無彈丸的子彈)。 ˌ~ **ˈverse**, (usu lines of ten syllables) without rhyme. 無韻詩(通常一行十個音節)。 ˌ~ **ˈwall**, one with no door, window or other opening. 無門窗或洞孔的牆。 ***come up against a ~ wall***, (fig) be unable to find support, information, etc. (喩)碰壁(未能覓得支援、資料等)。 □ *n* **1** space left empty or to be filled (in sth printed or written): (表格等中的)空白處;空格: *In a telegraph form there are ~s for the name and address, the message, etc.* 在電報紙上有塡寫姓名、住址、電文等的空格。 *When Tom was doing his French translation, he left ~s for all the words he did not know.* 湯姆翻譯法文時把所有不認識的字都空下來。 **2** lottery ticket that does not win a prize. 未中獎的獎券。 ***draw a*** ~, get nothing (after hoping to win or find sth). 抽空籤;希望贏而未贏;希望找到而未找到。 **3** empty surface; emptiness: 空白的表面;空虛: *His mind/memory was a complete ~,* he could remember nothing. 他的記憶完全是一片空白(什麼都記不得了)。 *The death of her husband in the war left a big ~ in her life.* 她的丈夫在戰爭中死去了,使她覺得一切均茫然空虛。 **4** [C, U] ~ cartridge: 空彈;空包彈: *They fired twenty rounds of ~/twenty ~s.* 他們放了二十發的空彈。 ~**·ly** *adv*

blan·ket /ˈblæŋkɪt ; ˈblæŋkɪt/ *n* **1** thick, woollen covering used on beds, or for keeping a horse warm in a stable, etc: 毛毯;氈子: (fig) (喩) *a ~ of snow.* 一片白雪。 ***wet*** ~, (colloq) person who, by being gloomy himself, prevents others from enjoying themselves. (俗)自己不快活也不容別人快活的人;掃興的人。 **2** (used attrib) covering all cases or classes: (形容用法)包括一切情形或種類的;綜合的;總括的: *a ~ (= comprehensive) insurance policy;* 統保保險單;全險保單; ~ *instructions*, intended to provide for everything. 總括的指示。□ *vt* [VP6A, 14] ~ ***(in/with),*** cover thickly: 厚厚地蓋着…;濃密地彌漫着…: *The valley was ~ed with fog.* 濃霧彌漫着山谷。

blare /bleə(r) ; blɛr/ *n* [U] sound or noise (of trumpets or horns): (喇叭或號角之)響聲: *the ~ of a brass band.* 銅管樂隊的奏鳴聲。□ *vi, vt* **1** [VP2A, C] ~ ***(out),*** make such sounds: 發出喇叭或號角之響聲: *The trumpets ~d out.* 喇叭齊鳴。**2** [VP15B] ~ ***out,*** produce with such sounds; utter loudly: 以喇叭或號角之響聲發出;高聲地說: *The band ~d out a current hit.* 樂隊響亮地奏出流行歌曲。*He ~d out a warning.* 他高聲發出警告。

blar·ney /'blɑ:nɪ ; 'blɑrnɪ/ *n* [U] *vt, vi* (dated use) the kind of talk that flatters and deceives people: (過時用語)奉承的話; 甜言蜜語; 諂媚; 奉承: *Not so much of your ~!* 不要再奉承了!

blasé /'blɑ:zeɪ *US:* blɑ:'zeɪ ; blɑ'ze/ *adj* ~ ***(about),*** not showing signs of enjoying (sth) or being pleased (about sth): 對(某事物)不感興趣的;厭倦的: *~ about her success.* 對她的成功不感興趣。

blas·pheme /blæs'fi:m ; blæs'fim/ *vi, vt* [VP2A,6A] speak in an irreverent way about God and sacred things; use violent language about (sb or sth): 對於神及神聖的事物說不恭敬的話;褻瀆(神祇); 辱罵; 謾罵(某人或某事物): *~ the name of God.* 褻瀆神的名。**~r** *n* person who ~s. 對神出言不敬者;褻瀆神祇者;罵人者;謾罵者。**blas·phem·ous** /'blæsfəməs ; 'blæsfɪməs/ *adj* (of persons) using blasphemy; (of language) containing blasphemy. (指人)對神出言不敬的; (指用字) 含有不敬神祇的話的; 褻瀆神祇的。**blas·phem·ous·ly** *adv* **blas·phemy** /'blæsfəmɪ ; 'blæsfɪmɪ/ *n* [U] contemptuous or irreverent talk about God and sacred things; [C] instance of this. 對神及神聖事物不敬的話;褻瀆神祇的話;褻瀆神祇。

blast /blɑ:st *US:* blæst ; blæst/ *n* **1** strong, sudden rush of wind: 一陣突然的强風: *A ~ of hot air came from the furnace.* 一股熱氣自火爐吹來。*When the window was opened an icy ~ came into the room.* 當窗子打開時,一陣冰冷的風吹入房間。**2** (often [U]) strong rush of air or gas spreading outwards from an explosion: (由爆炸而引起的)爆震: *Thousands of windows were broken by ~ during the air raids.* 在空襲期間,成千累萬的窗戶都被爆炸所引起的爆震震破了。'**~-off,** ⇨ blast *v* (3). **3** stream of air used to intensify the heat in a furnace, etc. 向火爐等輸進之風(以增强火力)。***at full ~,*** (colloq) with the maximum activity. (俗)全力地;全速地。***in/out of ~,*** (of a furnace) working/not working. (指火爐)正在輸風而旺盛燃燒着(不在輸風而停歇着)。'**~-furnace** *n* furnace for melting iron ore by forcing into it a current of heated air. 鼓風爐;熔鐵爐。**4** sound made by a wind-instrument: 管樂器奏出的聲音: *The hunter blew a ~ on his horn.* 獵人吹出一陣號角聲。*The ship sounded a prolonged ~ on the siren.* 輪船發出一陣長長的汽笛聲。**5** quantity of explosive (eg dynamite) used at one time (eg in a quarry). (如在採石場)爆炸一次所用之炸藥量。□ *vt, vi* **1** [VP6A, 2A] blow up (rocks, etc) with explosives: (用炸藥)炸破 (岩石等); 炸毀; 炸開: *Danger! B~ing in progress!* 危險!爆炸在進行中! **2** [VP6A] cause (sth) to come to nothing; shrivel; injure: 毀滅;使枯萎;損害: *blossom ~ed by frost.* 爲霜所凍壞的花朵。*The tree had been ~ed by lightning.* 樹爲雷電所殛毀。*His hopes were ~ed.* 他的一切希望都破滅了。**3** [VP15B, 2C] ~ ***off,*** (of spacecraft, etc) force, be forced, upwards by expanding gases. (指太空船等)發射;上升;升空。Hence, 由此產生, '**~-off** *n* (time of) launching of such a spacecraft: (太空船等的)發射;升空;發射時間;升空時間: *the count-down to ~-off.* 倒數秒數至發射的時刻。**4** [VP6A] (sl) reproach sb severely: (俚)嚴責;苛責: *be ~ed by one's boss;* 被其上司嚴責; *get a ~ing from sb.* 爲某人所嚴責。**5** (in curses, with *May God* understood) (用於咒罵語中, May God 二字省略)。*B~ it/you!* 該死!活該!**~ed** /'blɑ:stɪd *US:* 'blæ-;'blæstɪd/ *attrib adj* (in curses) damnable. (用於咒罵語中)可詛咒的;該死的。

bla·tant /'bleɪtnt ; 'bletn̩t/ *adj* noisy and rough; attracting attention in a vulgar and shameless way; too obvious. 喧嘩的;吵鬧的;以粗俗而厚顏的方式引人注意的;太明顯的。**~·ly** *adv*

blather /'blæðə(r) ; 'blæðɚ/ *n, v* ⇨ blether.

blaze¹ /bleɪz ; blez/ *n* [C] **1** bright flame or fire: 火焰;火光: *We could see the ~ of a cheerful fire through the window.* 我們可以從窗戶看見融融爐火的火焰。*I put some wood on the fire and it soon burst into a ~,* began to burn brightly. 我放些木柴在火上,它不久就發出火焰來了。**2** fire; burning building(s): 火災;燃燒中的建築物: *It took the firemen two hours to put the ~ out.* 消防隊隊員花了兩小時才將火撲滅。**3** (*pl*) (sl) hell: (複)(俚)地獄: *Go to ~s!* 該死! *He was working like ~s,* working furiously. 他正在拚命地工作。**4** glow of colour; bright light: 光彩;光輝;光明;明亮: *The red tulips made a ~ of colour in the garden.* 紅色鬱金香花在花園中發出一片紅光。*The main street of the town is a ~ of light(s) in the evening.* 城裏的大街在晚間呈現一片輝煌的燈光。**5** violent outburst: 爆發;突發: *in a ~ of anger.* 勃然大怒。

blaze² /bleɪz ; blez/ *vi, vt* **1** [VP2A, C] burn with flame: 發出火焰而燃燒; 熾燃: *There was a fire blazing on the hearth.* 壁爐中的火正熊熊地燃燒着。*When the firemen arrived the whole building was blazing.* 救火人員到達的時候,整座建築物正熾烈地燃燒着。~ ***up,*** burst into flames. 熾烈地燃燒起來;冒出火焰。**2** [VP2A, C] be bright with colour; shine brightly or with warmth: 發光彩;光輝地照耀;和煦地照耀: *The garden was blazing with colour.* 花園中五彩繽紛。*The sun ~d down on us.* 陽光直射在我們身上。**3** [VP2A, C] burst out with strong feeling: 爆發出激烈的情緒;發怒: *He was blazing with anger/indignation.* 他勃然大怒。**4** [VP 2C, 15B] ~ ***away,*** fire continuously with rifles, etc: (用步槍等)不斷地射擊: *They ~d away at the enemy.* 他們不斷地向敵人射擊。*He ~d away all his ammunition.* 他把他所有的彈藥一口氣打光了。**blazing** *adj*: *a blazing fire;* 熾燃的火; (fig) conspicuous: (喻)顯然的: *a blazing indiscretion;* 顯然的輕率; (foxhunting) (獵狐) *a blazing* (= very strong) *scent.* 强烈的臭味。

blaze³ /bleɪz ; blez/ *n* white mark on a horse's or an ox's face; mark made on a tree by cutting the bark. 馬或牛面部的白斑;刻在樹上的記號。□ *vt* [VP6A] mark (a tree) by cutting off part of the bark. 在(樹上)刻出記號。~ ***a trail,*** mark trees to show a path through a forest; (fig) do sth for the first time and show others how to do it. 在森林中的樹上刻記號以指示路徑;(喻)做開路先鋒;領導。

blaze⁴ /bleɪz ; blez/ *vt* [VP6A, 15B] ~ ***(abroad),*** make known far and wide: 傳播;廣佈: *~ the news (abroad).* 傳播新聞。

blazer /'bleɪzə(r) ; 'blezɚ/ *n* loose-fitting jacket (sometimes in the colours of a school, club, team, etc) for informal wear. 一種寬鬆的外衣(所用之顏色有時係代表某一學校、會社、球隊等,爲非正式場合之服裝)。

bla·zon /'bleɪzn ; 'blezn̩/ *n* coat of arms, esp on a shield. 紋章(尤指盾形紋徽上者)。⇨ the illus at armour. 參看 armour 之插圖。□ *vt* = blaze⁴. **~ry** *n* bright display. 誇示;炫示。

bleach /bli:tʃ ; blitʃ/ *vt, vi* [VP6A, 2A] make or become white (by chemical action or sunlight): (藉化學作用或陽光)漂白;變白: *~ linen;* 漂白麻布; *bones of animals ~ing on the desert sand.* 在沙漠上變白的動物骨頭。'**~ing-powder** *n* (eg chloride of lime) substance used to remove colour from dyed materials. 漂白粉。□ *n* chemical for ~ing and sterilizing: 漂白劑;消毒劑: *household ~.* 家用漂白劑。

bleach·ers /ˈbliːtʃəz ; ˈblitʃɚz/ *n pl* (US) unroofed seats/planks at sports grounds. (美)運動場的露天(木板)看臺。

bleak /bliːk ; blik/ *adj* **1** (of the weather) cold and cheerless; (of a place) bare, swept by cold winds: (指天氣)陰冷的;寒冷的;(指地方)荒涼的;空曠而蕭瑟的: *a ~ hillside.* 荒涼的山坡。 **2** (fig) dreary: (喻)陰鬱的;黯淡的;淒涼的: *~ prospects.* 黯淡的前途。 **~·ly** *adv*

bleary /ˈblɪərɪ ; ˈblɪrɪ/ *adj* dim; blurred. 朦朧的;模糊不清的。 **ˌ~-ˈeyed** /ˌblɪərɪˈaɪd ; ˈblɪrɪˌaɪd/ *adj* having ~ eyes: 眼睛朦朧的: *He got out of bed all ~-eyed.* 他睡眼惺忪的下了床。

bleat /bliːt ; blit/ *n* cry of a sheep, goat or calf. 羊叫聲;小牛叫聲。□ *vi, vt* [VP2A] make a cry of this kind; [VP6A, 15B] **~ *(out),*** speak, say (sth) feebly: 作羊或小牛叫聲;以微弱的聲音說(話): *He ~ed (out) a complaint.* 他以微弱的聲音申訴。

bleed /bliːd ; blid/ *vi, vt* (*pt, pp* bled /bled ; blɛd/) **1** [VP2A, C] lose, send out, blood: 流血;失血: *If you cut your finger it will ~.* 如果你割破手指,它會流血。*He was slowly ~ing to death.* 他正慢慢流血而死。 **2** [VP2A, C, 3A simple tenses only 僅用簡單時式] **~ *(for),*** feel great distress: 悲痛;傷心: *Our hearts ~ for homeless people during this cold winter.* 我們的心爲在這嚴冬中無家可歸的人而悲傷。 **3** [VP6A] draw blood from: 自…抽血;放血: *Doctors used to ~ people when they were ill.* 昔時人們病了,醫生常爲他們放血。 **4** [VP6A, 14] force (sb) to pay money unjustly: 勒索;敲詐: *The blackmailers bled him for £500.* 敲詐者向他强索五百鎊。 **5** [VP2A] (of a plant, tree, etc) lose sap or juice. (指植物、樹木等)流漿汁;流出樹液。

bleep /bliːp ; blip/ *n* high-pitched sound or signal sent out by radio, used eg as a summoning or warning device. 無線電所發送出的高音調的聲音或信號(用以傳喚或警告等)。□ *vi* emit such sounds. 發出此種聲響。

blem·ish /ˈblemɪʃ ; ˈblɛmɪʃ/ *n* [C, U] mark, etc that spoils the beauty or perfection of sb or sth; moral defect: 汚點;缺點;瑕疵: *without ~,* faultless. 無瑕疵的。□ *vt* [VP6A] spoil the perfection of. 損害…之完美。

blench /blentʃ ; blɛntʃ/ *vi* [VP2A] make a quick movement of fear. 因恐懼而突然一動;畏縮。

blend /blend ; blɛnd/ *vt, vi* (*pt, pp* ~ed or, liter, blent /blent ; blɛnt/) **1** [VP6A] mix together, esp sorts of tea, tobacco, spirits, etc, to get a certain quality: 混合(尤指混合各種茶、菸草、酒等以求得到某種品質): *~ed whisky.* 混合威士忌。 *A grocer used to need to know how to ~ tea.* 雜貨商以往都必須知道如何混合茶葉。 *Our coffees* (ie varieties of coffee) *are carefully ~ed.* 我們的各種咖啡都是經仔細地攙混製成的。 **2** [VP2A, 3A] mix, form a mixture: 溶合;成爲混合物: *Oil and water do not ~.* 油與水不相溶合。 *Oil does not ~ with water.* 油不溶於水。 **3** [VP2A] go well together; have no sharp or unpleasant contrast; (esp of colours) pass by degrees into each other: 調和;(尤指顏色)融合: *These two colours ~ well.* 這兩種顏色融合得很好。 *How well their voices ~!* 他們的聲音配合得眞好! □ *n* [C] mixture made of various sorts (of tea, tobacco, etc): 不同種類之(茶、煙草等的)混合物: *This coffee is a ~ of Java and Brazil.* 這咖啡是由爪哇咖啡和巴西咖啡混調成的。

blent ⇨ blend.

bless /bles ; blɛs/ *vt* (*pt, pp* ~ed /blest ; blɛst/ and blest, as in (6) below) [VP6A] **1** ask God's favour for: 求神賜福於;祝福: *They brought the children to Jesus and he ~ed them.* 他們把孩子帶到耶穌的面前,耶穌就求神賜福他們。 *The priest ~ed the people/the crops.* 牧師祝福人們(祝豐收)。 **2** wish happiness or favour to: 祝福: *B~ you, my boy!* 祝福你,我的孩子! **3** consecrate; make sacred or holy: 使化爲神聖: *bread ~ed at the altar.* 奉獻於祭壇之麵包。 **4 *be ~ed with,*** be fortunate in having: 在…方面有福氣;很幸運地享有: *I am not greatly ~ed with worldly goods,* am not rich. 我沒有很多財產(並不富有)。 *May you always be ~ed with good health.* 願你永遠享有健康之福。 **5** call (God) holy: 稱(上帝)爲神聖;頌揚: *'We praise Thee, we ~ Thee.'* '我們讚美你,我們稱你爲聖。' *'We ~ Thy Holy Name.'* '我們稱你的名爲聖。' **6** (colloq, in exclamations, expressing surprise): (俗,用於感歎句中表示驚奇): *B~ me!* 哎呀! *B~ my soul!* 哎呀! *Well, I'm blest!* 哎呀! *I'm blest if I know!* ie I don't know at all. 我一點也不知道呀! **~ed** /ˈblesɪd ; ˈblɛsɪd/ *adj* **1** holy, sacred. 神聖的。 **the B~ed Virgin,** the mother of Jesus. 聖母(耶穌之母)。 **the B~ed Sacrament,** Holy Communion. 聖餐。 **2** fortunate: 有福的;幸福的;幸運的: *B~ed are the poor in spirit.* 虛心的人有福了。 **3 the B~ed,** those who are with God in paradise. 與上帝同在天堂中的聖徒們。 **4** (sl, mild swearing) cursed: (俚,溫和的咒罵語)受天罰的;受詛咒的: *I've broken the whole ~ed lot.* 我把那鬼東西全打破了。 **~ed·ness** /ˈblesɪdnɪs ; blɛsɪdnɪs/ *n* [U] happiness. 幸福;福祉。 **~·ing** *n* **1** the favour of God; prayer for God's favour; thanks to God before or after a meal: 神恩;向神祈福的禱告;餐前或餐後向神表示感謝的祈禱: *ask a ~ing.* 祈禱。 ⇨ grace(5). **2** sth that one is glad of; sth that brings comfort or happiness: 可喜的事;爲人帶來安適或幸福的事: *What a ~ing it is you didn't get caught in the storm yesterday!* 昨天你未受到暴風雨的襲擊眞是幸運! ***a ~ing in disguise,*** sth that seems unfortunate, but that is seen later to be fortunate. 起初似乎爲不幸而後來轉變爲幸運之事;塞翁失馬。

blether /ˈbleðə(r) ; ˈblɛðɚ/, **blather** /ˈblæðə(r) ; ˈblæðɚ/ *n* [U] foolish talk. 愚蠢的談話;廢話;胡說亂道。□ *vi* [VP2A, C] talk nonsense. 說廢話;胡說;胡扯。

blew /bluː ; blu/ ⇨ blow¹.

blight /blaɪt ; blaɪt/ *n* **1** [U] (sorts of) plant disease; mildew. 植物萎菌病;霉;黴。 **2** [C] evil influence of obscure origin: (根源不明的)壞影響;挫折;打擊: *a ~ upon his hopes.* 對於他的希望的一個打擊。□ *vt* [VP6A] be a ~ on: 破壞;挫折;打擊: *His hopes were ~ed.* 他的希望破滅了。 *Her life was ~ed by constant illness.* 她的一生因病魔的經常纏繞而被摧殘了。 **~er** *n* (dated sl) (過時俚語) **1** annoying person. 可厭的人。 **2** fellow: 人;傢伙: *You lucky ~er!* 你這個幸運兒!

Blighty /ˈblaɪtɪ ; ˈblaɪtɪ/ *n* (GB 1st world war sl) home (during service abroad). (第一次大戰時英俚)(在國外服役期間所稱的)老家;英國本土。 ***a ~ wound,*** one severe enough for a soldier to be returned to GB. 須送回英國本土治療的重傷。

bli·mey /ˈblaɪmɪ ; ˈblaɪmɪ/ *int* (vulg) expressing surprise. (鄙)哎呀!嘖嘖!(表示驚訝之詞)。

blimp /blɪmp ; blɪmp/ *n* **1** small non-rigid airship. 非硬式小飛艇。 **2 (Colonel) B~,** pompous-looking reactionary person. 裝模作樣的頑固保守的人。

blind¹ /blaɪnd ; blaɪnd/ *adj* **1** without the power to see: 盲目的;瞎的: *Tom helped the ~ man across the road.* 湯姆幫助瞎子過街。 *He is ~ in the right eye.* 他的右眼瞎了。 ***turn a/one's ~ eye to sth,*** pretend not to see it. 裝做未看見;對…睜隻眼閉隻眼。 **~ spot,** point on the retina insensible to light; (fig) inability to recognize, understand or sympathize with sth. 盲點(視網膜上對光線無感覺之點);(喻)無能力認識、瞭解或同情某事物。 **2 ~ *(to),*** unable to see effects, to judge or understand well: 缺乏眼光、判斷力或了解力: *Mothers are sometimes ~ to the faults of their children.* 做母親的有時不能覺察孩子們的過錯。 *A man would be ~ not to see that difficulty.* 連那個困難都看不出來的人一定是瞎了眼。 **3** reckless; thoughtless: 鹵莽的;輕率的;不審愼的: *In his ~ haste he almost ran into the river.* 他匆匆忙忙地幾乎跑到河裡去了。 **4** not ruled by purpose: 無目的的: *Some people think that the world* *is governed by* ~ *forces.* 有些人認爲這個世界受着無目的的力量所支配。 **5** (sl) drunk (also 亦作 ~ *drunk*). (俚)醉酒的。 **6** ~ **alley,** ⇨ alley(1). ~ **date,** ⇨ date¹(4). ~ **flying,** navigation, eg in cloud, fog, with the aid of instruments only. 盲目飛行(指在黑暗中或雲霧中僅靠儀器飛行)。 ~ **turning,** (in a road) one that cannot easily be seen by drivers. 公路上不易爲駕車者看清楚的轉彎處。 ˌ~-ˌ**man's** ˈ**buff** *n* game in which one player, who is blindfolded, tries to catch and identify one of the others who push him about. 捉迷藏遊戲。

blind² /blaɪnd ; blaɪnd/ *vt* [VP6A, 14] ~ **sb (to),** make ~; (fig) take away the power of judgement: 使盲;使失明;使瞎;(喻)使失去判斷力: *a* ~*ing light.* 令人目眩的强光。 *The soldier had been* ~*ed in the war.* 那兵業已在戰爭中雙目失明了。*His feelings for her* ~*ed him to her faults.* 他對她的感情使他看不見她的缺點。 ~**·ers** *n pl* (US) (美) = blinkers. ~**·ly** *adv* ~**·ness** *n*

blind³ /blaɪnd ; blaɪnd/ *n* [C] **1** roll of cloth (usu strong linen) fixed on a roller and pulled down to cover a window (US 美 = *window-shade*): (布質捲軸式的)窗簾;遮陽: *pull down/lower, draw up/raise the* ~*s.* 拉下(放下,捲起,扯起)窗簾。 **2** (fig) deception: (喻)欺騙;欺瞞;詭計: *It was only a* ~, sth intended to hide the reality. 它只是一種欺瞞的手法。 **3** (US) hide¹ *n.* (美)(攝影者等用以觀察野生動物,鳥類等之)隱藏處。

blind·fold /ˈblaɪndfəʊld ; ˈblaɪndˌfold/ *vt* [VP6A] cover the eyes of (sb) with a bandage so that he cannot see. 用一塊布蒙住(某人)的眼睛使之不能見物;使看不見。□ *n* [C] such a cover. 蒙眼布;眼罩。□ *adj* with the eyes bandaged, covered with a handkerchief, etc. 眼睛被蒙住的。

blink /blɪŋk ; blɪŋk/ *vi, vt* **1** [VP2A, C, 6A, 15B] shut and open the eyes quickly: 眨眼;霎眼: ~ *the eyes;* 眨眼睛;~ *away a tear.* 眨掉眼淚。 **2** [VP6A] ~ **the fact that,** (fig) refuse to consider; ignore: (喻)不考慮…的事實;忽視…的事實: *There's no* ~*ing the fact that....* 我們不能忽視…之事實。 **3** [VP2C] (of lights, esp when in the distance) come and go; shine in an unsteady way: (指燈光,尤指遠處者)閃爍不定: *We saw the lights of a steamer* ~*ing on the horizon.* 我們看見一艘輪船上的燈光在地平線上閃爍着。□ *n* [C] instance of ~ing. 眨眼;霎眼;閃爍。 ~**·ing** *adj* (colloq euphem for) bloody(3): (俗,委婉語)極度的;非常的: *It's a* ~*ing nuisance.* 那眞是極度令人厭惡之事。

blink·ers /ˈblɪŋkəz;ˈblɪŋkɚz/ *n pl* (US 美 = *blinders*) leather squares to prevent a horse from seeing sideways. 馬眼罩(皮製方塊,置於馬眼之兩旁使不能看兩側)。 ⇨ the illus at harness. 參看 harness 之插圖。

blip /blɪp ; blɪp/ *n* spot of light on a radar screen. 雷達幕上的光點。

bliss /blɪs ; blɪs/ *n* [U] perfect happiness; great joy. 福氣;極大的快樂。 ~**·ful** /-fʊl ; -fəl/ *adj* ~**·fully** /-fʊlɪ ; -fəlɪ/ *adv*

blis·ter /ˈblɪstə(r) ; ˈblɪstɚ/ *n* [C] **1** small bag-like swelling under the skin, filled with liquid (caused by rubbing, burning, etc): (皮膚因摩擦、灼燒等而起之)水泡: *If your shoes are too tight, you may get* ~*s on your feet.* 如果你的鞋太緊,(你的)脚上就可能起水泡。 **2** similar swelling on the surface of metal, painted or varnished wood, a plant, etc. (金屬表面、木器外表之油漆、植物表皮等所起之)浮泡。□ *vt, vi* [VP6A, 2A] cause, get, a ~ or ~s on: 起泡;使起泡: *He is not used to manual work and his hands* ~ *easily.* 他不慣於用手工作,他的手容易起泡。 *The hot sun has* ~*ed the paint on the door.* 炎陽晒得門上的油漆都起了泡。

blithe, blithe·some /blaɪð, -səm ; blaɪð, -səm/ *adj* (chiefly poet) gay and joyous. (主要用於詩中)快樂的;快活的;愉快的。 ~**·ly** *adv*

blith·er·ing /ˈblɪðərɪŋ ; ˈblɪðərɪŋ/ *adj* (colloq) utter; contemptible (esp in): (俗)完全的;全然的;卑劣的(尤用於): ~ *idiot.* 大傻瓜。

blitz /blɪts ; blɪts/ *n* rapid, violent attack (esp from the air). 閃電式的猛烈襲擊;閃擊(尤指由空軍從事者)。□ *vt* [VP6A] damage or destroy in this way (esp in *pp*): 以閃擊方式摧毁(尤用過去分詞): ~*ed areas/towns,* destroyed by bombing during air-raids. 在空襲中被炸毁的地區(市鎭)。

bliz·zard /ˈblɪzəd ; ˈblɪzɚd/ *n* [C] violent and heavy snowstorm. 大風雪;暴風雪。

bloated /ˈbləʊtɪd ; ˈblotɪd/ *adj* swollen; fat and large in an unhealthy way: 臃腫的;過於肥胖的: *a* ~ *face;* 臃腫的臉; *a fat, ugly man,* ~ *with over-eating;* 一個肥胖陋醜男人,因吃得過多而臃腫不堪;(fig) (喻) ~ *with pride,* puffed up with pride. 趾高氣揚的;驕氣十足的。

bloater /ˈbləʊtə(r) ; ˈblotɚ/ *n* kind of salted and smoked herring: 鹽醃而又烟薰的鯡魚: ~ *paste,* paste made from ~s. 醃薰鯡魚醬。 ⇨ kipper.

blob /blɒb ; blɑb/ *n* drop of liquid, eg paint; small round mass, eg of wax; spot of colour. 一滴(如油漆);一小圓塊(如臘丸);(顏色之)斑點。

bloc /blɒk ; blɑk/ *n* combination of parties, groups, states, etc with a special interest: 爲了某種特殊利益而結合的政黨、團體、國家等之集團: *the sterling* ~, those countries with currencies related to sterling. 英鎊集團(使用之貨幣與英鎊有關之國家)。

block¹ /blɒk ; blɑk/ *n* **1** large, solid piece of wood, stone, etc: (木、石等之)大塊: *A butcher cuts up his meat on a large* ~ *of wood.* 屠夫在一個大木墩上切肉。 *The* ~*s of stone in the Pyramids are five or six feet high.* 金字塔上的石塊有五、六呎高。*The statue is to be carved out of a* ~ *of marble.* 石像將由一大塊大理石雕成。 *Children play with building* ~*s,* cubes of wood put together to make toy houses, etc. 兒童們玩(堆砌玩具房子等的)積木。 ⇨ chip(1). **2** main part of a petrol engine, consisting of the cylinders and valves. 汽油動力機的主要部分(包括汽缸及閥)。 **3 the** ~, (in olden times) large piece of wood on which a person put his neck to have his head cut off as a punishment. 古時死刑犯斬首時用以放頭之大木塊;斷頭臺。 ***go/be sent to the*** ~, to death in this way. 上(被送上)斷頭臺;被處斬。 **4** shaped piece of wood on which hats are moulded. 帽楦。 **5** pulley, or system of pulleys, in a case (often ~ ***and tackle***). 滑車;滑輪;(常作 block and tackle) 滑車組。 **6** piece of wood or metal with designs, etc, cut (engraved) on it for printing. 木刻板;(金屬製之)蝕刻版;印版。 **7** mass of buildings (shops, offices, apartments, etc) joined together; (esp US) area of buildings bounded by four streets; the length of one side of such an area: 接連在一起的一片建築物(如商店、辦公室、公寓等);(尤美)四面臨街的一片建築物;街區;街區一邊之長度(卽兩條街間的距離): *To reach the post-office, walk two* ~*s east and then turn left.* 要到郵局去,請向東走兩個街區,然後向左轉。 ~**·buster** /ˈblɒkbʌstə(r) ; ˈblɑkˌbʌstɚ/ *n* powerful explosive to demolish buildings; (fig) forceful person or thing bringing about a sudden effect, eg in a dispute. 可摧毁建築物的强力爆炸物;(喻)引起突然效果的人或物(例如在辯論中)。 **8** division of seats in a theatre, concert hall, etc; large quantity of shares in a business. (戲院、音樂廳等)座位區;某一企業之大宗股份。 **9** obstruction; sth that makes movement or flow difficult or impossible: 阻礙;障礙物;阻塞;阻塞物: *There was a* ~ *in the pipe and the water couldn't flow away.* 管子內有阻塞物,水不能流走。 ˈ**road** ~, barrier across a road at which documents, etc are checked. 路卡(橫設於道路上的障礙物,作爲檢查文件等的關卡)。 ˈ**traffic** ~, (usu 通常作 *traffic jam*) large number of buses, cars, vans, trams, etc held up and unable to move on. 交通阻塞(大批的車輛被阻塞於途中不能前進)。 **10** ˈ~ **grant,** fixed and non-recurring subsidy. 固定且不再發的補助金。 ˌ~ ˈ**capitals**/ˈ**letters**/ˈ**writing,** with each letter separate and in capitals: 正楷大寫字母;正楷大寫字體: *Write your name in ~ letters.* 請用正楷大寫字母寫你的名字。 **11** (cricket) spot on which a batsman rests his bat before playing a ball. (板球)擊球員在擊球前置放球板之處。**12** (sl) (person's) head: (俚)(人的)頭: *I'll knock your ~ off!* 我將把你擺平!

block² /blɒk ; blɑk/ *vt* **1** [VP6A, 15B] ~ *(up)*, make movement difficult or impossible in (by sth being in the way); obstruct: 阻礙;阻塞;堵塞: *All roads were ~ed by the heavy snowfall.* 所有道路均爲大雪所阻塞。*They ~ed up* (=entirely covered) *the entrance to the cave with big rocks.* 他們用巨石將洞口全部堵塞起來了。*My cold gave me a ~ed-up nose.* 傷風使我鼻塞。 **2** [VP6A] obstruct (progress); make (action) difficult or impossible: 阻止(進行);使(行動)困難或不可能: *The general succeeded in ~ing the enemy's plans.* 這位將軍成功地阻擋住了敵軍的企圖。**3** [VP6A] (chiefly in *pp*) restrict the use or expenditure of (currency, assets, etc): (主要用過去分詞)限制(通貨、資產等)之使用或花費;封鎖;凍結: *~ed sterling.* 凍結的英鎊。**4** [VP6A] shape (eg hats) on a ~. (用木楦)使(帽等)成形。⇨ block¹(4). **5** ~ *in/out*, make a rough sketch or plan of the general arrangement (of objects in a drawing, etc). 畫略圖;打草樣。 **6** (cricket) stop (the ball) with the bat (kept upright in front of the wicket). (板球)在三柱門前將球板擧直以擋(球)。

block·ade /blɒˈkeɪd ; blɑˈked/ *n* the enclosing or surrounding of a place, eg by armies or warships, to keep goods or people from entering or leaving. (使用陸軍或海軍) 封鎖 (某一地區,使貨物或人民不能出入)。***run the ~,*** evade and get through the forces that are surrounding a place. 偷越封鎖線;突破封鎖;偷渡。 ***raise the ~,*** end it. 解除封鎖。 **ˈ~-runner** *n* ship, etc that gets through or past a ~. 偷越封鎖線的船隻等;偷渡者。 □ *vt* [VP6A] make a ~ around, eg a town, fort, etc. 封鎖(城鎮、要塞等)。

block·age /ˈblɒkɪdʒ ; ˈblɑkɪdʒ/ *n* [C] state of being blocked; sth that blocks: 被阻塞住之狀態;阻塞;堵塞;阻塞物: *There's a ~ in the drain-pipe.* 排水管內有阻塞物。

block·head /ˈblɒkhed ; ˈblɑkˌhɛd/ *n* slow and stupid person. 笨頭笨腦的人;呆笨的人。

block·house /ˈblɒkhaʊs ; ˈblɑkˌhaʊs/ *n* military strongpoint with openings through which to shoot. 碉堡。

bloke /bləʊk ; blok/ *n* (sl) man. (俚)男人;傢伙。

blond /blɒnd ; blɑnd/ *n, adj* (man) having fair¹(5) complexion and hair. 白膚金髮的(男人)。

blonde /blɒnd ; blɑnd/ *n, adj* (woman) blond. 白膚金髮的(女人)。

blood¹ /blʌd ; blʌd/ *n* [U] **1** red liquid flowing throughout the body of man and the higher animals: 血;血液: *The soldiers shed their ~* (= died) *for their country.* 將士們爲國捐軀。 *It was more than flesh and ~* (= human nature) *could stand.* 那是非血肉之軀(人性)所能忍受的。*He gave his ~ to help his sister,* gave ~ to be injected into his sister after a surgical operation or an accident. 他輸血給他的姊姊(妹妹)以救助她 (如手術過後或意外受傷後)。 ***infuse new ~ (into sth),*** (fig) revive business, etc by introducing new talent. (喩)引進新血輪(引進新的人才以重振事業等);補充生力軍。 ***let ~,*** draw off ~ from a vein. (外科)放血。⇨ 7 below. 參看下列第7義。 **2** passion; temper: 情緒;忿怒;脾氣: *His ~ is up,* he is angry, filled with passion. 他發脾氣了。*His ~ ran cold,* he was filled with terror or horror. 他嚇得魂不附體。 ***(kill sb) in cold ~,*** when one is not feeling angry or excited; deliberately. 非一時衝動地;蓄意地(殺死某人)。 ***make bad ~ between persons,*** cause them to feel ill will towards one another. 在二人之間挑撥感情;挑撥離間。 ***make one's ˈ~ boil,*** make one very angry. 使人非常憤怒。 ***make one's ˈ~ run cold,*** fill one with fear or horror. 使其感到恐懼或恐怖。 **3** relationships; family: 親屬;血親;血族;血統: *They are of the same ~,* have ancestors in common. 他們是同宗。 **ˌblue ˈ~** *n* aristocratic descent. 貴族血統;高貴門第。***of the (royal) ~,*** of royal family. 皇族的;皇家的。***one's (own) flesh and ~,*** one's relations. 某人之直系血親;親屬。***B~ is thicker than water,*** (prov) The ties of family relationship are real. (諺)血濃於水;疏不間親(親屬關係才是眞的)。 **ˈ~ feud** *n* deadly feud between families. (兩家族間不共戴天的)夙仇;世仇。 **ˈ~-relation** *n* person related by ~, not by marriage. 血親;骨肉。 **4** ***~ and iron,*** (fig) relentless use of force. (喩)鐵血政策;濫用武力。 **5** [C] (old colloq use) man of fashion; rich, pleasure-loving young man. (舊俗語用法)花花公子;紈袴子。 **6** ***~ and thunder*** *attrib adj* (of stories, dramas) melodramatic; full of exciting incidents. (指小說、戲劇)鬧劇性的;充滿刺激性情節的。 **7** (compounds) (複合字) **ˈ~ bank** *n* ⇨ bank³(3). **ˈ~-bath** *n* large-scale slaughter, eg in battle, or during a revolution. (如戰鬥中或革命期中之)大屠殺。 **ˈ~ brother,** one who swears to treat another as a brother (perhaps by the symbolic act of mixing his ~ with the other person). 歃血盟誓的兄弟;拜把兄弟。 **ˈ~ count** *n* (counting of the) number of red and white corpuscles in a certain volume of ~. 血球數 (某一定量血液中所含之紅血球及白血球之數目);血球計數。 **ˈ~-curdling** *adj* sending feelings of horror through the body. 使人毛骨悚然的。 **ˈ~-donor** *n* person who gives ~ for ~ transfusions. 捐血者。 **ˈ~-group/type** *n* any of several distinct classes of human ~. 血屬;血型。 **ˌ~-ˈheat** *n* the normal temperature of human ~ (about 98·5°F, 37°C). 人體的正常體溫(約爲華氏 98.5 度,攝氏 37 度)。 **ˈ~·hound** *n* large dog able to trace a person by scent. 一種大警犬(能靠嗅覺追踪人跡)。⇨ the illus at dog. 參看 dog 之插圖。 **ˈ~-letting** *n* surgical drawing off of some of a patient's ~. 放血(用外科手術放出病人若干血液)。 **ˈ~·lust,** desire for killing sb. 殺人慾。 **ˈ~-money** *n* money obtained at the cost of a life, eg received by a murderer for killing someone or as a reward for betraying sb who is to be put to death. 血腥錢(如受雇殺人所得之錢,或出賣他人使被處死刑所得之報酬)。 **ˈ~-poisoning** *n* condition that results when poisonous germs enter the ~, esp through a cut or wound. 血中毒;血毒症。 **ˈ~ pressure** *n* the force exerted by ~ within the arteries. 血壓。 **ˌ~ ˈred,** having the colour of ~. 血紅色的。 **ˈ~·shed** *n* killing or wounding of people; putting to death: 流血;殺傷;殺人: *There was great ~shed in Paris during the years after the Revolution in 1789.* 在 1789 年大革命後的幾年中,巴黎有很多的流血事件。 **ˈ~·shot** *adj* (of the white of the eyes) red. (指眼白)充血的;充滿血絲的。 **ˈ~-sports** *n pl* outdoor sports in which animals or birds are killed. 狩獵。 **ˈ~·stained** *adj* **(a)** stained with ~: 血污的;沾有血跡的: *a ~-stained shirt.* 沾有血跡的襯衫。**(b)** disgraced by ~shed. 血腥的;因殺傷過人而不名譽的。 **ˈ~·stock** *n* (collective) thoroughbred horses. (集合用法)純種馬。 **ˈ~·sucker** *n* **(a)** creature that sucks ~, esp a leech. 吸血蟲;(尤指)水蛭。 **(b)** (fig) person who unjustly forces another or others to give him as much money as possible. (喩)剝削他人之人;吸血鬼。 **ˈ~·thirsty** *adj* cruel and eager to take life; taking pleasure in killing. 殘忍的;嗜殺的。 **ˈ~-thirsti·ness** *n* **ˈ~-transfusion** *n* transfer of ~ (originally taken) from the veins of one person to those of another. 輸血(將血液由一人之靜脈抽出並輸入另一人之靜脈中)。 **ˈ~-vessel** *n* tube (vein or artery) through which ~ flows in the body. 血管。⇨ the illus at respiratory. 參看 respiratory 之插圖。 **~·less** *adj* **1** without ~shed: 未發生流血事件的;不流血的: *a ~less victory.* 不流血的勝利。 **2** pale; unfeeling and coldhearted. 無血色的;蒼白的;

無情的；冷酷的。～**·less·ly** *adv*

blood² /blʌd；blʌd/ *vt* [VP6A] allow the first taste of ～ to (foxhounds, etc). 讓(獵狐犬等)初次嘗血的味道。

bloody /'blʌdɪ；'blʌdɪ/ *adj* **1** bleeding; covered with blood: 流血的；血汚的：*a ～ nose.* 流血的鼻子。 **2** with much bloodshed: 傷亡很重的；流血很多的：*a ～ battle.* 傷亡慘重的戰役。 **3** (vulg intensive): (鄙，强勢語)：*What a ～ shame!* 多麼大的一項恥辱啊！ (derog) (貶) *You're a ～ fool!* 你這個大傻瓜！ (laud) (讚) *You're a ～ genius!* 你眞是個鬼才！ ,**～-'minded,** (sl) obstructive; unwilling to co-operate. (俚)存心阻撓的；不願合作的。□ *adv* (vulg sl): (鄙俚)：*Not ～ likely!* (= not a tall likely). 根本不可能的！ ～ ***well,*** (vulg sl) certainly. (鄙俚)無疑地；確定地。

bloom /blu:m；blum/ *n* **1** [C] flower, esp of plants admired chiefly for their flowers (eg roses, tulips, chrysanthemums). 花 (尤指憑其花而受人讚賞之植物的花，如玫瑰花，鬱金香，菊花)。***in ～,*** (of plants) flowering: (指花草)在開花中：*The tulips are in full ～ now.* 鬱金香現正盛開。Cf 參較 *in blossom* for shrubs and trees. in blossom 用於灌木及樹木。 **2** [U] (time of) greatest beauty or perfection: 青春；茂盛(時期)：*She was in the ～ of youth.* 她正在青春時期。 **3** [U] covering of fine dust or powder on plums, grapes, etc when they are at their best. 李子、葡萄等成熟時表面所生的一層霜粉；粉衣。***take the ～ off sth,*** cause it to seem stale. 使某物顯得陳舊。□ *vi* [VP2A, C] **1** be in flower; bear flowers: 開花：*The roses have been ～ing all summer.* 這些玫瑰整個夏天一直都在開花。 **2** (fig) be in full beauty and perfection. (喻)在青春美貌時期；在完美時期；在旺盛時期。**～·ing** *adj* **1** (in the senses of the *v*) 開花的；青春美貌的；完美的；旺盛的。 **2** /'blʊmɪŋ；'blumɪŋ/ (colloq euphem for *bloody*(3)): (俗，bloody 第 3 義之委婉語)極端的；非常的：*You ～ing idiot!* 你這個大白癡！

bloomer /'blu:mə(r)；'blumɚ/ *n* (sl) blunder: (俚)錯誤；謬誤：*He made a tremendous ～.* 他犯了一次大錯。

bloom·ers /'blu:məz；'blumɚz/ *n pl* loose garment covering each leg to the knee and hanging from the waist, formerly worn by girls and women for games, cycling, etc, with or without a skirt. (昔時婦女在運動、騎車等時所穿長及膝部之)燈籠褲(有的帶裙子，有的不帶裙子)。

blos·som /'blɒsəm；'blɑsəm/ *n* [C] flower, esp of a fruit-tree; [U] mass of flowers on a bush or tree. 花(尤指果樹之花)；(樹上的)花叢；花簇；花團。⇨ the illus at flower. 參看 flower 之插圖。***in ～,*** (of bushes and trees) having flowers: (指樹木)在開花中的：*The apple-trees are in ～.* 蘋果樹正在開花。⇨ bloom(1). □ *vi* **1** [VP2A] open into flowers: 開花：*The cherry-trees will ～ next month.* 櫻桃樹將於下月開花。 **2** [VP2C] **～ *out,*** develop: 發展：*He ～ed out as a first-rate athlete.* 他鍛鍊成爲第一流的運動員。

blot /blɒt；blɑt/ *n* **1** mark caused by ink spilt on paper. (墨水濺在紙上的)汚點；墨水點。 **2** fault; disgrace; sth that takes away from the beauty or goodness of sth: 缺點；瑕疵：*a ～ on his character;* 他的品格上的一個缺點；*a ～ on the landscape,* eg an ugly building or advertisement. 破壞天然風景的一個景象 (如一座醜陋的建築物或廣告)。□ *vt* (-tt-) **1** [VP6A] make a ～ or ～s on (paper with ink). 在(紙上)弄上墨水點。***～ one's copy-book,*** (colloq) do sth that spoils one's good record. (俗)做有損聲譽的事。 **2** [VP6A] dry up (wet ink) with ～ting-paper. 用吸墨紙吸乾(墨水)。 **'～·ting-paper** *n* absorbent paper used to dry up wet ink quickly. (使墨水快乾之) 吸墨紙。 **3** [VP15B] ～ ***out,*** **(a)** make a ～ over (words that have been written): 將(已寫之字)塗掉：*Several words in his letter had been ～ted out.* 他的信中有幾個字被塗掉了。 **(b)** hide from view: 遮蔽：*The mist came down and ～ted out the view.* 霧降下來把風景遮住了。**(c)** destroy, exterminate (enemies, etc). 摧毀；消滅(敵人等)。 **～·ter** *n* **1** book containing sheets of writing-paper interleaved with sheets of ～ting-paper. (每頁附有吸墨紙之)一本寫字紙；記事簿。**police ～ter,** (US) book in which the police enter records, eg of lost and found articles, missing persons. (美)警局記事簿(警察用以登記失物、被找到之物、失踪者等之記錄簿)。 **2** piece or pad of ～ting-paper. 吸墨紙；吸墨具。

blotch /blɒtʃ；blɑtʃ/ *n* large, discoloured mark, usu irregular in shape (eg on the skin, or of ink on paper). (皮膚上的)大塊斑點；(紙上的)墨水汚跡。

blotto /'blɒtəʊ；'blɑto/ *pred adj* (sl) fuddled or intoxicated with alcoholic drink. (俚)酩酊大醉的。

blouse /blaʊz *US:* blaʊs；blaʊs/ *n* **1** outer garment from neck to waist, worn by women and girls (US 美 = *shirtwaist*). (婦女所穿從頸部到腰際之)短衫。 **2** loose-fitting garment, often with a belt at the waist, worn by some workmen. (工人所穿通常腰部有束帶之)寬鬆上衣。 **3** tunic as worn by some sailors and soldiers. (水手，士兵所穿之)緊身上衣；軍便服上衣。

blow¹ /bləʊ；blo/ *vi, vt* (*pt* blew /blu:；blu/, *pp* blown /bləʊn；blon/, or, (11) below, ～ed) **1** [VP2A, C] (with *air, wind,* or *it* as the subject) move along, flow as a current of air: (用 air, wind, 或 it 作主詞)吹；刮；吹動：*It was ～ing hard,* there was a strong wind. 風正刮得很厲害。*It was ～ing a gale／～ing great guns,* there was a (violent) gale. 正在刮大風(狂風)。*The wind was ～ing round the street-corners.* 風正吹過街角。*It's ～ing up for rain,* the wind seems likely to bring rain soon. 風刮起來了，似乎就要有雨(山雨欲來風滿樓)。 **2** [VP15A, B] (of the wind) cause to move: (指風)刮走；吹動：*The wind blew my hat off.* 風把我的帽子吹落了。*I was almost ～n over by the wind.* 我幾乎被風吹倒了。*The ship was ～n out of its course／on to the rocks.* 船被風吹離航線(吹上礁石)。*The wind blew the papers out of my hand.* 風把我手裏的文件吹走了。[VP12A] ***It's an ill wind that ～s nobody any good,*** ⇨ ill(2). **3** [VP2C, E] (of objects, etc) be moved or carried by the wind or other air current: (指物件等)被風或其他氣流吹動；被吹走：*My hat blew off.* 我的帽子被風吹掉了。*The door blew open.* 門被風吹開了。*The dust has ～n into the house.* 灰塵被風吹進房子裏了。 **4** [VP6A,15B,2C] send or force a strong current of air upon, into or through: 吹氣於；充氣於：～ (*on*) *one's food* (to cool it); 將食物吹涼；～ *the dust off a book;* 將書上灰塵吹掉；～(*up*) *the fire,* make it burn better (eg by using a pair of bellows). (用風箱等)吹火(使燃燒旺盛)。～ ***hot and cold,*** (fig) vacillate. (喩) 猶疑不決；躊躇。～ ***one's nose,*** in order to clear it. 擤鼻涕。 **5** [VP6A] make by ～ing: 吹成；吹出：～ *bubbles,* by sending air through a pipe with soapy water, etc; 吹泡泡；shape by ～ing: 吹出(某種形狀)：～ *glass,* by sending a current of air into molten glass. 吹製玻璃器。 **6** [VP6A] use (sth) to produce a current of air: 使用(某物)以產生氣流：～ *bellows;* 扇風箱；work the bellows of: 操作…之風箱：～ *an organ.* 操作風琴之風箱。 **7** [VP6A, 2A] produce sound from (a trumpet, etc) by sending air into it; (of a wind-instrument, etc) produce sound: 吹奏(喇叭等)；(指管樂器等)發出聲音：*The referee blew his whistle.* 裁判鳴笛。*Stop work when the whistle ～s.* 汽笛一響就停止工作。*The huntsman blew his horn.* 獵人吹他的號角。*We heard the bugles ～ing.* 我們聽見吹號。 **8** [VP2A] breathe hard and quickly: 喘息；喘氣：*The old man was puffing and ～ing when he got to the top of the hill.* 那老人到達山頂時，喘息不已。 **9** [VP2A] (of whales) force up a stream of air and water: (指鯨)噴起一股空氣與水：*There she ～s!* There is the fountain sent up by the whale! 鯨魚在那邊噴

水！ **10** [VP2A,C,6A,15B] ~ ***(out),*** (of a fuse) melt because the electric current is too strong; cause to do this: (指保險絲)爲過强的電流所燒斷;燒斷: *The fuse has ~n.* 保險絲燒斷了。*The fuse blew out.* 保險絲斷了。*Don't ~ (out) the fuse.* 不要把保險絲燒斷。**11** (sl uses) spend (money) recklessly or extravagantly: (俚)一擲千金;揮(金)如土;濫花(錢): *~ £10 on a dinner with a girl friend.* 花十鎊同女友吃一頓飯。⇨ blue³. *B~ the expense,* Don't worry about it. 盡量花錢吧(不要擔心)。*I'll be ~ed if.../B~ed if I will...,* I will certainly not.... 我決不…;如果…我不是人。*Well, I'm ~ed!* (indicating surprise). (表示驚愕之語)眞該死！***~ one's top,*** lose one's temper; explode into angry words, etc. 發脾氣;發怒而罵人。**12** (compounds from the *v*) (由動詞各義而形成之複合字) **'~-dry** *vt* [VP6A] dry (sth, esp hair) by passing a current of warm air over (it). (用熱風)吹乾(頭髮等)。**'~·fly** *n* common meat fly. 大蒼蠅;琉璃蠅。**'~·hole** *n* **(a)** opening for air, smoke, etc, in a tunnel. (隧道中的)通風孔。**(b)** hole (in rocks, etc near the seashore) through which air and water are forced by rising tides. (海岸附近岩石等中的) 氣穴 (漲潮所驅迫的空氣與水可從中通過者)。**'~·lamp, '~torch** *nn* lamp for directing an intensely hot flame on to a surface. 噴燈。**'~·pipe** *n* **(a)** tube for increasing the heat of a flame by forcing air into it. 吹風管;吹管。**(b)** tube through which some primitive people ~ poisoned darts. (某些原始部族用以發射毒矢的) 吹箭筒;吹矢槍。**13** [VP2C,3A,15B] (special uses with *adverbial particles* and *preps*): (與副詞接語及介詞連用之特殊用法):

blow back, (of gas in a tube, etc) explode. (指導管中的煤氣等)爆炸。Hence, 由此產生, **'~·back** *n* explosion of gas in a tube, etc. 煤氣在導管等中的爆炸。

blow in/into, (colloq) arrive noisily, cheerfully, etc: (俗)喧嘩、高興等地來臨: *The door opened and John blew in/blew into the room.* 門一開約翰嘻嘻哈哈地進入房間裏來。

blow off steam, release tension by arguing, being noisy, etc: 藉辯論,吵吵鬧鬧等以解除情緒的緊張: *Parents must let children ~ off steam sometimes.* 做父母的有時必須讓孩子們吵吵鬧鬧,發洩發洩。

blow out; ~ sth out, (be) put out by ~ing: 吹滅;吹熄;被吹熄: *The candle was ~n out by the wind.* 蠟燭被風吹滅了。*The flame blew out.* 火焰被吹熄了。***~ itself out,*** exhaust itself: 歇息;停止: *The gale had ~n itself out.* 大風已經停止吹刮了。***~ one's brains out,*** kill oneself by shooting in the head. 以槍彈射入腦部自殺。**'~·out** *n* **(a)** sudden (often violent) escape of air, steam, etc; (esp) bursting of a tyre. 漏氣;噴氣;(尤指)輪胎爆裂。**(b)** ~ing out of an electric fuse. (電線保險絲)燒斷。**(c)** (sl) abundant meal; feast. (俚)豐盛的餐食;盛宴。

blow over, pass by; be forgotten: 過去;被忘記;平息: *The storm/scandal will soon ~ over.* 暴風雨(醜聞)不久就會平息。

blow up, **(a)** explode: 爆炸: *The barrel of gunpowder blew up.* 火藥桶爆炸了。**(b)** arise: 起;發生: *A storm is ~ing up.* 暴風雨來了。**(c)** lose one's temper; work up to a crisis: 發脾氣;逐漸接近危機: *I'm sorry I blew up at you.* 抱歉,對你發了脾氣。***~ sb up,*** (colloq) scold severely: (俗) 嚴厲責備某人: *The teacher blew John up for not doing his homework.* 老師嚴責約翰未做家庭作業。Hence, 由此產生, **ˌ~·ing-ˈup** *n* scolding. 罵;責備。***~ sth up,*** **(a)** break or destroy by explosion: 炸開;炸毀;炸斷: *The soldiers blew up the bridge.* 士兵們炸斷了那座橋。**(b)** inflate with air or gas: 使充氣;打氣: *~ up a tyre.* 給輪胎打氣。**(c)** enlarge greatly: 大幅放大: *~ up a photograph.* 大幅放大一張照片。Hence, 由此產生, **'~-up** *n* greatly enlarged photograph: 巨幅照片: *The men in the procession carried ~-ups of their leader.* 遊行隊伍中的人們都舉着他們領袖的巨幅照片。**(d)** exaggerate: 誇大: *His abilities have been greatly ~n up by the newspapers.* 報紙極力誇大了他的才能。

blow² /bləʊ; blo/ *n* blowing: 吹; 吹風: *Give your nose a good ~,* clear it thoroughly. 把你的鼻子擤乾淨。***have/go for a ~,*** go outdoors for fresh air. 到戶外去吹吹風(吸點新鮮空氣)。

blow³ /bləʊ; blo/ *n* **1** hard stroke (given with the hand, a stick, etc): (用拳、棒等之) 打;擊;捶打;毆打: *He struck his enemy a heavy ~ on the head.* 他在他敵人的頭上予以重重的一擊。***at one ~; at a (single) ~,*** in a single effort: 一擊;一舉;一下子: *I killed six flies at a ~.* 我一下子打死了六隻蒼蠅。***come to ~s; exchange ~s,*** fight. 打架;互毆。***get a ~ in,*** succeed in placing a ~. 擊中。***strike a ~ for,*** perform a single act of support for; struggle for. 作支持或擁護…之舉動;爲…而奮鬥。***without striking a ~,*** without having to fight. 不經戰鬥;兵不血刃。***a ~-by-~ account,*** a detailed account (eg of a boxing match). (拳擊比賽等之) 詳細敍述;詳盡報導。**2** shock; disaster: 突然的打擊;災禍;不幸: *His wife's death was a great ~ to him.* 他的妻之死對他是一大打擊。*It was a ~ to our hopes.* 這對我們的希望是一大打擊。

blow⁴ /bləʊ; blo/ *vi* (*pp* ~n /bləʊn; blon/) (chiefly in *pp* as) (主用過去分詞，例如) *full-blown roses,* wide open, with petals about to fall. 盛開的玫瑰花(花瓣卽將掉落的)。*She has a complexion like a new-blown rose,* a delicate pink complexion. 她的膚色像初開的玫瑰花(淡粉紅色)。

blower /ˈbləʊə(r); ˈbloɚ/ *n* **1** apparatus for forcing air, etc into or through sth. 吹風器;鼓風器。**2** person who makes things by blowing (eg *a 'glass-~*) or who pumps air into sth (eg *an 'organ-~*). 吹製…者 (如吹製玻璃器之工人); 充氣於某物的人; 充氣者 (如操作風琴風箱的人)。**3** (colloq) speaking-tube; (GB sl) telephone: (俗)通話管; (英俚)電話: *Get Jones on the ~ for me.* 請找瓊斯來接電話。

blown /bləʊn; blon/ *pp* of blow¹. ⇨ also blow⁴. □ *adj* breathless (as the result of effort). 喘息的;喘不過氣來的。

blowzy /ˈblaʊzɪ; ˈblaʊzɪ/ *adj* (usu of a woman) red-faced, dirty-looking and untidily dressed. (通常指女人)紅臉、髒兮兮、而且衣服不整的;邋遢的。

blub·ber¹ /ˈblʌbə(r); ˈblʌbɚ/ *n* [U] fat of whales and other sea-animals from which oil is obtained. 鯨脂;其他海生動物之脂肪。

blub·ber² /ˈblʌbə(r); ˈblʌbɚ/ *vi, vt* [VP2A] weep noisily; 號啕大哭; [VP15B] ***~ (sth) out,*** say with sobs. 哭泣着訴說(某事);哭訴。

bludgeon /ˈblʌdʒən; ˈblʌdʒən/ *n* short, thick stick with a heavy end, used as a weapon. 大頭短棒(作武器用)。□ *vt* [VP6A,14] strike repeatedly with a ~: 用大頭棒連打: *He had been ~ed to death.* 他被大頭棒連打致死。***~ sb into doing sth,*** (fig) compel him to do it. (喻)强迫某人做某事。

blue¹ /bluː; blu/ *adj* (-r, -st) coloured like the sky on a clear day or the deep sea when the sun is shining: 藍色的;蔚藍的;青色的: *~ eyes.* 藍色的眼睛。*His face was ~ with cold.* 他凍得臉發青。**ˌ~ ˈblood(ed)** *adj, n* (of) aristocratic birth. 出身貴族(的)。**ˌ~ ˈchips,** (fin) industrial shares considered valuable because of past records. (財政) (因以往業績而被視爲有價值的)優良股票。**ˌ~ ˈfilm,** obscene film. 色情影片。**ˌ~ ˈjokes,** improper jokes. 猥褻的笑話。**ˌB~ ˈPeter,** ~ flag with a white square in the centre, used to show that a ship is about to sail. 啓航旗(中央有白色方塊的藍旗,懸以表示船隻卽將出航)。**ˌ~ ˈribbon,** sign of great distinction: 藍帶;榮譽之標誌: *the ~ ribbon of the Atlantic,* held by the liner that has the record for the fastest crossing. 大西洋之藍帶獎(頒給保有横渡大西洋最快紀錄之班輪者)。***look ~,*** (colloq) be sad or depressed. (俗)面容沮喪;面有憂色。***(Things are) looking ~,*** depressing. (情勢)不樂觀。***once in a ~ moon,*** very rarely. 非常少地。

blue² /bluː; blu/ *n* **1** ~ colour: 藍色;青色: *dressed*

in ～; 穿着藍色衣服; *Oxford* ～, dark ～; 深藍色; *Cambridge* ～, light ～. 淺藍色。 **2** (the) sky. 青天;藍天。 ***appear／come out of the* ～,** unexpectedly. 爆出冷門;意外地出現。 ***a bolt from the* ～,** sth quite unexpected. 晴天霹靂;意外之事。 **3 *win／get one's* ～ *(for sth),*** (at Oxford or Cambridge University) gain the right to wear a ～ cap, scarf etc because one has represented the University in a sport: (在牛津或劍橋大學)曾代表學校參加運動會等之學生所獲戴藍帽、圍藍圍巾等之特權; 獲得藍色榮譽: *She got her* ～ *for tennis.* 她因爲打網球而獲得藍色榮譽。Hence, 由此產生, person with this right: 獲得藍色榮譽之人: *He's a rowing* ～. 他是獲得藍色榮譽的划船隊員。 **4** (poet) (the) sea. (詩)海。 **5 *a true* ～,** a loyal member (of a political party, esp the Conservative). 忠實份子 (指政黨黨員，尤指保守黨)。 **6** (*pl*) (dances, dance tunes, for) haunting jazz melodies originally of Negroes in the southern US. (複) 布魯斯(源出於美國南部黑人中之抑鬱難忘的爵士曲調);哀歌; 藍調; 布魯斯舞; 布魯斯舞曲。 **the** ～**s,** (colloq) condition of being sad, melancholy. (俗) 憂鬱;沮喪;不樂。 **7** (compounds) (複合字) **'～·bell** *n* (Scotland and N England) = harebell; (S England) wild hyacinth with ～ or white flowers growing in moist places and flowering in spring. (蘇格蘭及英格蘭北部) 山小菜; 藍鈴花 (= harebell); (英格蘭南部) 野風信子 (生長於潮濕地帶，春天開藍花或白花)。 **'～ book** *n* book published by the Government containing a report. 藍皮書 (政府所發表之報告書)。 **'～·bottle** *n* meat fly or blowfly. 青蠅;大蒼蠅; 琉璃蠅。 **,～-'collar** *adj* of workers in factories, etc, who wear overalls (contrasted with *white-collar* workers). 藍領的(用以指工廠等中穿着工作褲之工人;與白領階級相對); 藍領階級的。 **'～-jacket** *n* seaman in the Navy. 海軍戰士;水兵。 **,～-'pencil** *vt* mark, censor, with a ～ pencil. 用藍色鉛筆作記號，刪改(稿件)。 **'～-print** *n* photographic print, white on ～ paper, usu for building plans; (fig) plan, scheme: (影印的白字藍底,通常爲建築設計用的) 藍圖; 建築藍圖; (喻) 計畫; 方案: (attrib) (形容用法) *the* ～*print stage.* 設計階段;籌畫時期。 **'～-stock·ing** *n* woman who is regarded as having superior literary tastes and intellectual interests. 被認爲具有高度文學修養及知識趣味之女性;女學者。 **blu·ish** /'blu:ɪʃ; 'bluɪʃ/ *adj* tending towards ～: 帶藍色的;帶青色的: *bluish green.* 藍綠色。

blue[3] /blu: ; blu/ *vt* **1** make blue. 使成藍色。 **2** ～ ***one's money,*** (sl) spend it recklessly. (俚) 亂用錢; 胡亂花錢。

bluff[1] /blʌf ; blʌf/ *n* headland with a broad and very steep face. 伸入海中之懸崖絕壁。□ *adj* **1** (of headlands, cliffs, a ship's bows) with a broad, perpendicular front. (指懸崖絕壁、船首) 陡峭的; 前面寬而垂直的。 **2** (of a person, his manner, etc) abrupt; rough but honest and kind, simple and good-natured. (指人、其態度等) 率直的; 坦誠的; 直爽的。 **～·ly** *adv* **～·ness** *n*

bluff[2] /blʌf ; blʌf/ *vt, vi* [VP6A,14,15B,2A] deceive sb by pretending. 假裝而騙(人); 虛張聲勢以嚇(人); 詐騙。 ～ ***sb into doing sth,*** lead sb to do sth or believe sth by deceiving him: 騙某人做(或相信)某事;恫嚇某人使做某事: *They were* ～*ed into supposing we were ill prepared.* 他們受騙以爲我們沒有好好準備。 ～ ***it out,*** survive a difficult situation by pretence. 藉假裝以度過困境。 ～ ***one's way out of sth,*** escape from a situation by pretence. 藉假裝以逃脫某種情況。□ *n* [U,C] deception of this kind; (the use of) threats that are intended to get results without being carried out. 詐騙; 虛張聲勢。 ***call sb's* ～,** invite him to do what he threatened to do. 挑激虛張聲勢之人實際做出他所恫嚇的話。 **～er** *n* person who tries to ～ people. 虛張聲勢以騙人者; 嚇唬人者; 詐騙者。

blun·der /'blʌndə(r) ; 'blʌndɚ/ *vi, vt* **1** [VP2A, C, 3A] move about uncertainly, as if blind: 瞎闖; 亂闖: ～ *into a wall.* 瞎闖碰着了牆壁。 **2** [VP2A] make foolish mistakes: 犯大錯: *Our leaders have* ～*ed again.* 我們的領導階層又犯了大錯。 □ *n* [C] stupid or careless mistake. 大錯; 愚笨或粗心的錯誤。 **～er** *n* person who commits a ～. 犯大錯之人。

blun·der·buss /'blʌndəbʌs ; 'blʌndɚ,bʌs/ *n* old-fashioned gun with a wide mouth, firing many bullets or small shot at once at short range. 老式大口徑的短程散彈槍。

blunt /blʌnt ; blʌnt/ *adj* (-er, -est) **1** without a point or sharp edge: 不尖的; 不利的; 鈍的: *a* ～ *knife.* 鈍刀。 **2** (of a person, what he says) plain; not troubling to be polite: (指人,所說的話) 直率的; 直言的; 不客氣的: *He's a* ～ *man.* 他是個直率的人。 *The* ～ *fact is that....* 不可隱諱的事實是…。□ *vt* [VP6A] make ～: 使鈍: *If you try to cut stone with a knife, you will* ～ *the edge.* 如果你試以刀砍石，你就會把刀刃弄鈍。 **～·ly** *adv*: *to speak* ～*ly,* plainly, without ceremony. 直率地說; 坦白地說; 不客氣地說。 **～·ness** *n*

blur /blɜ:(r) ; blɝ/ *n* **1** dirty spot or mark; smear of ink. 污點; 污跡; 墨水跡。 **2** confused or indistinct effect: 模糊不清的現象; 一片模糊: *If, when you try to read small print, you see only a* ～, *you probably need glasses.* 如果你在看小字書報的時候,你只看見一片模糊,那麼你很可能需要戴眼鏡了。□ *vt, vi* (-rr-) [VP6A, 2A] make a dirty mark or smear on (sth); make or become unclear, confused in appearance: 弄污; 弄上污點; 使模糊不清; 變得模糊不清: *Tears* ～*red her eyes.* 淚水使她眼睛模糊。 *Mists* ～*red the view.* 霧使風景模糊。 *The writing was* ～*red.* 字跡被弄得模糊不清。 *Rain* ～*red the windows of our car.* 雨水使我們的車窗模糊了。

blurb /blɜ:b ; blɝb/ *n* publisher's description of the contents of a book, printed on the paper jacket, etc. 出版商對書籍內容之說明 (印在書的外封皮等處)。

blurt /blɜ:t ; blɝt/ *vt* [VP15B] ～ ***sth out,*** tell sth, eg a secret, suddenly, often thoughtlessly. 脫口說出某事 (如秘密)。

blush /blʌʃ ; blʌʃ/ *vi* **1** [VP2A, C, 3A] become red (in the face) from shame or confusion: (因羞愧或尷尬而) 臉紅; 赧顏: *She* ～*ed for／with shame.* 她因羞愧而臉紅。 *She* ～*ed at the thought of....* 她一想起…就臉紅。 *He* ～*ed as red as a peony.* 他的臉紅得像一朵牡丹花。 **2** [VP4B] (fig) be ashamed: (喻) 羞於; 慚愧: ～ *to confess that....* 羞於承認…。□ *n* **1** reddening of the face, eg from shame, etc: 臉紅; 赧顏: *She turned away to hide her* ～*es.* 她轉過身去掩飾她的臉紅。 **2** (old use) glimpse: (舊用法) 一瞥: *at first* ～, at the first look. 初見之; 乍看時。 **～·ing** *adj* **～·ing·ly** *adv*

blus·ter /'blʌstə(r) ; 'blʌstɚ/ *vi, vt* **1** [VP2A, C] (of the wind, waves, etc) storm; be rough or violent. (指風、浪等) 猛襲; 狂作; 狂吹。 **2** [VP2A] (of persons) act and speak in a forceful but rather unsteady, often rather boastful way. (指人) 咆哮; 恫嚇。 **3** [VP15B] ～ ***out,*** utter in this way: 咆哮而言: ～ *out threats.* 咆哮地說出恫嚇的話。□ *n* [U] **1** noise of violent wind or waves. (狂風或大浪之) 咆哮聲; 吼嘯聲。 **2** ～ing talk and behaviour; noisy threats. 咆哮之言行; 恫嚇。 **～y** *adj* (of the weather) rough and blowy. (指天氣) 刮大風的; 狂風大作的。

bo(h) /bəʊ ; bo/ *int* ⇨ boo.

boa /'bəʊə ; 'boə/ *n* **1** (also 亦作 **'boa-constrictor**) large non-poisonous snake that kills by crushing its prey. 蟒蛇 (無毒之巨蛇，能絞殺其捕獲物以食之)。 ⇨ the illus at snake. 參看 snake 之插圖。 **2** (also 亦作 **'feather-boa**) feather stole (formerly) worn by women. (昔時) 婦女所用之羽毛披肩。

boar /bɔ:(r) ; bɔr/ *n* **1** wild male pig. 雄野豬。 **2** uncastrated male domestic pig. 未去勢的雄豬。⇨ hog, sow[1].

board[1] /bɔ:d ; bɔrd/ *n* **1** long, thin, flat piece of wood with squared edges, used in building walls, floors, boats, ship's decks, etc. (用作牆壁、地板、船

身、甲板等之)木板。 **2** flat piece of wood or other material for a special purpose, sometimes bare, sometimes covered with cloth, leather, etc: (木質或其他材料,作爲某種特殊用途,有時包着布,皮革等之)板子;牌子: *'sign~;* 招牌; *'notice~;* 公告牌; *a 'diving-~.* 跳水板。 **3** flat surface with patterns, etc on which games, eg chess, are played.、做遊戲用,上有圖案、格子等的平板;棋盤。 ⇨ the illus at chess. 參看 chess 之挿圖。 **4** (from the ~s that form the stage of a theatre) (由搭成戲臺之木板而來) **the ~s,** the theatre: 戲院;劇場: *on the ~s,* employed as an actor; on the stage. 當演員;在戲臺上。 **5** (from the ~s that form the deck of a ship) (由作甲板之木板而來) ***on ~,*** in a ship. 在船上。 ***go on ~,*** go on to a ship or into an airliner (in US, also of trains). 上船;上飛機;(在美國亦指)上火車。 ***go by the ~,*** (of masts, etc) fall over the ship's side; (fig, of plans, hopes, etc) be given up or abandoned; fail completely. (指帆檣等)折斷落到船外;(喻,指計畫,希望的)被放棄;完全失敗。 **6** (from the idea of *table,* used for gambling). (由作賭博之桌子而來) ***above ~,*** openly, without deception. 公開地;無欺騙地。 ***sweep the ~,*** win all the cards or the money staked; (fig) be completely successful. 賭博時贏了賭桌上所有的牌或賭注;(喻)完全成功。 **7** (from the idea of *table*) council-table; councillors; committee; group of persons controlling a business, or a government department: (由桌子的意義而來) 會議桌;議員們;委員會;理事會;董事會;掌管一項事務或政府部門的一批人員: *the 'B~ of 'Governors,* eg of a school; (學校等的)董事會; *the ˌB~ of 'Trade;* 貿易委員會; *Local 'Government B~;* 地方政府的官員們; *'School B~,* (in England until 1902) controlling elementary schools known as *'b~-schools;* (英國在 1902 年以前管理小學 board-schools 的) 教育委員會; *a Se'lection B~,* one that selects from applicants or candidates. 選拔委員會。 ***ˌacross-the-'~,*** ⇨ across²(1). **8** [U] food served at table, esp meals supplied by the week or month (eg at a lodging-house) or as part payment for service: 伙食;膳食: *The hotel porter gets £40 a week and free ~.* 旅館服務生每週工資四十鎊並供膳食。 *B~ and lodging £45 weekly.* 膳宿費每週四十五鎊。 **9** thick, stiff paper, sometimes cloth-covered, used for book covers: (做書封面用,有時並包以布之)硬紙板: *bound in cloth ~s.* 布面精裝的。 ⇨ also card~, paste~. **10** (compounds) (複合字) **'~-room** *n* room in which meetings (of a B~ of Directors, etc) are held. (董事會等之)會議室。 **'~walk** *n* (US) promenade, originally made of planks, esp along a beach. (美)(原爲用木板裝成的,尤指沿着海灘的)散步道。

board² /bɔːd ; bɔrd/ *vt, vi* **1** [VP6A, 15B] make or cover with boards(1): 用木板做;用木板覆蓋: *~ up a window;* 將窗戶用木板蓋住; *~ (over) the stern of a boat,* cover it with boards to make a deck. 將船之尾部鋪上木板(以便做成甲板)。 *The floor was ~ed.* 地板上加鋪了木板。 **2** (⇨ board¹(8)) [VP6A, 3A, 2C] ***~ (at sth/with sb),*** get (from), supply (with), meals for a fixed weekly/monthly etc payment: (按週,按月等)包飯;搭伙;寄膳;寄食: *Mrs Jones makes a living by ~ing students.* 瓊斯太太靠給學生們包飯謀生。 *Jim ~s at 'The Willows'/with Mrs Jones.* 吉姆在'柳屋'(瓊斯太太家)寄膳。 ***~ out,*** take meals at a different place from that in which one lives. 不在住的地方吃飯。 **3** [VP6A] get on or into (a ship, train, plane, bus, etc). 上(船、火車、飛機、公共汽車等)。 **~er** *n* **1** person who ~s(2) with sb. 寄膳者;搭伙者。 **2** boy or girl at a ~ing-school (⇨ below). 寄宿學校的學生(男或女) (參看下列 boarding-school). **~ing** *n* [U] **1** structure of ~s(1). 用木板建造之物。 **2** the providing or receiving of ~¹(8). 供膳;包飯;寄膳。 **'~ing-card** *n* card allowing one to ~(3) (esp) a ship or plane. 乘船證;登機證。 **'~ing-house** *n* private house that provides ~¹(8) and lodging. 供給膳宿的私人房子;供膳食之宿舍;寄宿舍。 **'~ing-school** *n* school where pupils receive ~¹(8) and lodging as well as lessons. (供學生膳宿之)寄宿學校。

boast /bəʊst ; bost/ *n* [C] **1** words used in praise of oneself, one's acts, belongings, etc: 自誇之詞;自誇;自吹自擂: *It was the enemy's ~ that they could never be defeated.* 敵人稱他們永不打敗仗,係自誇之詞。 **2** cause for satisfaction; sth of which one may rightly be proud: 足以自負、自傲或自豪之事: *It was his ~ that he had never failed in an examination.* 他考試從來不失敗乃是他足以自傲之事。 □ *vt, vi* **1** [VP2A, 3A, B] ***~ (of/about),*** make a ~ or ~s: 自誇;自吹自擂: *He ~s of being/~s that he is the best tennis-player in the town.* 他自誇是全市最好的網球選手。 *That's nothing to ~ of.* 那沒有什麼好誇耀的。 *He often ~s to his neighbours about the successes of his children.* 他常常向鄰人誇耀他的孩子們的成就。 **2** [VP6A] possess with pride: 很可自豪地擁有: *Our school ~s a fine swimming-pool.* 我們的學校很可自豪地擁有一個完善的游泳池。 **~er** *n* person who ~s. 自誇者;自詡者;大言者。 **~·ful** /-fʊl ; -ˌfəl/ *adj* (of persons) fond of ~ing; (of words, etc) full of self-praise. (指人)好自誇的;(指言辭等)充滿自誇的。 **~·fully** /-fəlɪ ; -fəlɪ/ *adv*

boat /bəʊt ; bot/ *n* **1** small open vessel for travelling in on water, esp the kind moved with oars (*'rowing ~*), sails (*'sailing ~*), or petrol or oil engines (*'motor-~*); also used of fishing-vessels and small steamers: 無篷的小船;(尤指)用槳划之船;帆船;(用汽油引擎之)汽艇;(亦指)漁船;小汽船: *We crossed the river by ~/in a ~.* 我們乘船渡河。 *B~s for hire—£2 an hour.* 遊船出租—每小時兩鎊。 ***be (all) in the same ~,*** have the same dangers to face. (大家)處於同一境遇(尤指危險的境遇);同舟共濟。 ***burn one's ~s,*** do sth that makes it impossible to retreat, to change one's plans, etc. 破釜沈舟;斷絕退路。 ***take to the ~s,*** (of the crew and passengers of a ship) use the ship's ~s to escape, eg when the ship is sinking. (指船上的船員與乘客在船遇難下沈時)用救生艇逃生。 **'~-hook** *n* long pole for fending off or holding a ~, eg at a landing-stage. (撐船用之一端有鈎的)鈎篙。 **'~-house** *n* shed in which ~s are stored. 船庫(存放船之棚子)。 **'~·man** /-mən ; -mən/ *n* (*pl* ~men) man who rows or sails a small ~ for pay; man from whom rowing-~s may be hired. (划艇上的)船伕;出租划艇的人。 **'~-race** *n* race between rowing-~s. 划船比賽。 **'~-train** *n* train that takes people to or from a passenger ship, eg between London and Dover. 與郵船聯運之火車(如倫敦與多佛之間者)。 ⇨ ferry, house¹(7), life(14), mail²(1). **2** ~-shaped dish used at table for gravy or sauce. (餐桌上用以盛調味汁之)船形碟子。 □ *vi* [VP2A, C] travel in a ~, esp for pleasure: 乘船旅行;(尤指)乘遊艇遊玩: *We ~ed down the river.* 我們乘船順水而行。 ***go ~ing,*** go out (esp in a rowing-~) for pleasure. 去划船(取樂)。

boater /'bəʊtə(r) ; 'botə/ *n* hard straw hat (formerly worn in summer for boating). (昔時在夏天划船時所戴之)硬草帽。

boat·swain /'bəʊsn ; 'bosn/ *n* senior seaman who controls the work of other seamen and is in charge of a ship's rigging, boats, anchors, etc. (船上的)水手長;(管理其他水手之工作及索具、船上小艇、錨等之)資深水手;帆纜士官長。

bob¹ /bɒb ; bɑb/ *vi* (-bb-) [VP2C] **1** move up and down: 上下地動: *The cork on his fishing-line was bobbing on the water.* 他釣絲上的浮子在水面上下急動。 ***bob up,*** (fig) carry on again; reappear: (喻)繼續;再出現: *That fellow bobs up like a cork,* cannot be 'kept down', always becomes active again after being in trouble, etc. 那個人百折不回(經過患難以後立刻又振作起來)。 *That question often bobs up* (*crops up* is more usu), is often asked.

那個問題常被提起 (crops up 較常用)。 **2** ***bob to sb,*** also [VP6A] ***bob a curtsy,*** curtsy. 向某人行屈膝鞠躬禮。□ *n* quick up and down movement; curtsy. 上下來回的疾動;屈膝鞠躬禮。

bob² /bɒb ; bɑb/ *vt* (-bb-) (dated) cut (a woman's or girl's hair) so that it hangs loosely and short of the shoulders: (過時用語)將(女人的頭髮)剪短(至耳根處): *She wears her hair bobbed.* 她留著短髮。*I shall have my hair bobbed.* 我將要把我的頭髮剪短。□ *n* bobbed hair. 剪短之髮型;短髮。

bob³ /bɒb ; bɑb/ *n* (*pl* unchanged; sl) former British coin, called 'shilling' (replaced by the 5p coin). (複數不變; 俚)昔時英國之一種硬幣 (稱爲'先令', 後爲五辨士之硬幣所取代)。

bob·bin /ˈbɒbɪn ; ˈbɑbɪn/ *n* small roller or spool for holding thread, yarn, wire, etc in a machine. 線軸;(纏繞鋼絲等之)軸心。

bobby /ˈbɒbɪ ; ˈbɑbɪ/ *n* (GB colloq) policeman. (英俗)警察。

bobby pin /ˈbɒbɪ pɪn ; ˈbɑbɪ pɪn/ *n* (US) tight metal hair clip. (美)一種很緊的金屬髮夾。

bobby-socks, -sox /ˈbɒbɪ sɒks ; ˈbɑbɪˌsɑks/ *n pl* (US, comm) girls' ankle socks. (美,商)女短襪。

bobby-soxer /ˈbɒbɪ sɒksə(r) ; ˈbɑbɪˌsɑksɚ/ *n* (US sl during the 1940's) teenage or adolescent girl. (1940年代之美國俚語)十幾歲的姑娘;少女。

bobo·link /ˈbɒbəlɪŋk ; ˈbɑblˌɪŋk/ *n* N American songbird. 食米鳥(北美產之鳴禽)。

bob·sled, bob·sleigh /ˈbɒbsled, -sleɪ ; ˈbɑbˌslɛd, -sle/ *n* **1** sleigh made by joining two short sleighs, used in tobogganing. 連橇;長橇。 **2** large, long sleigh with brake and steering wheel, used for racing. (有制動器及方向盤,供比賽用之)大連橇。

a racing bobsleigh

bob·tail /ˈbɒbteɪl ; ˈbɑbˌtel/ *n* (horse or dog with a) docked tail. 尾巴剪短之馬或狗; 剪短之尾巴。 ***the rag-tag and ~,*** the rabble. 賤民。

bode /bəʊd ; bod/ *vt, vi* (old use or poet) (舊用法或詩) **1** [VP12B, 13B] be a sign of; foretell: 預兆; 預示: *This ~s us no good.* 這個對於我們不是吉兆。 **2** ***~ well/ill for,*** be of good/bad promise for: 預示有好的(不好的)前途: *His idle habits ~ ill for his future,* suggest that his future career will be a failure. 他的懶惰習慣預示他將來不會有好的前途。 **bod·ing** *n* feeling of coming evil. 對於將臨之禍事的預感;惡兆。

bod·ice /ˈbɒdɪs ; ˈbɑdɪs/ *n* close-fitting part of a woman's dress or of an under-garment from the shoulders to the waist. 女裝上半之緊身部份;女人緊身胸衣。

-bodied /-bɒdɪd ; -bɑdɪd/ *adj* (with *adjj*): (與形容詞連用): *ˈbig-~, ˈstrong-~,* having a big/strong body; 身體魁梧的;身體强壯的; *able-~,* ⇨ able

bod·ily /ˈbɒdəlɪ ; ˈbɑdḷɪ/ *adj* of or in the human body or physical nature: (人類之) 身體的;肉體的: *supply a person's ~ wants* (eg food); 供給某人身體的需要(如食物); ~ (= physical) *assault.* 身體的攻擊。□ *adv* **1** as a whole or mass; completely: 全部; 全體;整個;完全地: *The audience rose ~* (= everyone rose at the same moment) *to cheer the speaker.* 聽衆全體一致起立向演說者歡呼。 *The building was transported ~* (= as a whole, without being pulled down) *one hundred yards down the street.* 那建築物整座(未拆毀)被沿街移動了一百碼。 **2** in person; in the body. 親自;親身。

bod·kin /ˈbɒdkɪn ; ˈbɑdkɪn/ *n* blunt, thick needle with a large eye (used for drawing tape, etc through a hem). 不尖有大眼之粗針(用以拉帶子等穿過衣邊)。

body /ˈbɒdɪ ; ˈbɑdɪ/ *n* (*pl* -dies) **1** The whole physical structure of a man or animal: (人或動物的)身體;軀體;肉體: *We wear clothes to keep our bodies warm.* 我們穿衣以保持身體溫暖。⇨ the illus at arm, head, leg, skeleton, trunk. 參看 arm, head, leg, skeleton, trunk 之挿圖。 ⇨ mind, soul, spirit. ***keep ~ and soul together,*** remain alive: 維持生存;活命;苟延殘喘: *He earns scarcely enough to keep ~ and soul together.* 他所賺的錢幾乎不够維持溫飽。 **2** dead ~; corpse: 死屍;屍體;遺骸;遺體: *His ~ was brought back to England for burial.* 他的遺體被運回英國埋葬。 **3** main portion of a man or animal without the head, arms and legs: (人或動物的)軀幹部;軀體(頭和四肢除外): *He received one wound in the left leg and another in the ~.* 他左腿受了一處傷,軀體也受了一處傷。 **4** main part of a structure: 建造物之主要部份: *the ~ of a motor-car;* 汽車的車身; *the ~ of a concert hall,* the central part where the seats are. 音樂會堂中座位所在的中央部份。 **5** group of persons who do sth together or who are united in some way: (共同從事某種工作之) 團體; (爲某種原因而結合在一起的)人群; 隊伍: *Large bodies of unemployed men marched through the streets demanding work.* 一群群的失業者在街上遊行要求工作。*The affairs of the school are managed by the Governing B~.* 學校的事務由行政部門處理。*A legislative ~ is a group of persons who make laws.* 立法團體就是一群制訂法律的人。**the ˌ~ ˈpolitic,** ⇨ politic(3). ***in a ~,*** all together; as a whole: 全體;全部;整個: *The staff resigned in a ~.* 全體職員總辭職。 **6** (colloq) person; human being: (俗)人: *She's a nice old ~.* 她是一個很好的老人。(in compounds): (用於複合字中) : *every~, any~, some-~, no~.* 每個人,任何人,某人,無人。 **7** mass, quantity, collection: 團; 量; 聚集: *A lake is a ~ of water.* 湖是一潭水。 *He has a large ~ of facts to prove his statements.* 他搜集了很多事實以證明他的言論。 **8** distinct piece of matter: 物體: *the heavenly bodies,* the sun, moon and stars; 天體(即日、月、星辰); *a foreign ~* (= a speck of dirt) *in the eye.* 眼中之異物。 **9** [U] (of wine, etc) full, strong quality: (指酒等)濃郁的品質: *wine of good ~.* 十分濃郁的酒。 **10** (compounds) (複合字) **ˈ~·guard** *n* group of men (sometimes a single man) guarding an important person. (重要人物的)侍衛; 衞隊; 保鑣(有時指一人)。 **ˈ~ language** *n* interpreting the way sb sits, stands, moves etc as expressing his feelings. 身體語言(根據某人坐,站,行動等之方式來解釋他所表達之感情)。**ˈ~-snatcher** *n* (formerly) person who (illegally) dug up corpses and sold them for dissection. (昔時)掘墓盜屍(出售作解剖研究)者。**ˈ~-work** *n* [U] main outside structure of a motor vehicle. 汽車的外殼;車身。

Boer /bɔː(r) ; bor/ *n* (old use) South African of Dutch descent; Afrikaner. (舊用法)荷裔南非人;波爾人。□ *adj* (old use) of Dutch South Africa; Afrikaans. (舊用法) 荷屬南非洲的; 南非荷蘭語的。 **~ war,** between the ~s and the British (1899–1902). 波爾戰爭(1899年至1902年波爾人與英國人之間的戰爭)。

bof·fin /ˈbɒfɪn ; ˈbɑfɪn/ *n* (sl) technician or scientist (esp one engaged in research). (俚)(尤指從事研究工作之)技師或科學家。

bog /bɒg ; bɑg/ *n* **1** (area of) soft, wet, spongy ground (chiefly decayed or decaying vegetable matter). 沼澤; 沼澤區 (地面主要爲腐朽的植物)。 **2** (vulg sl) latrine. (鄙俚)厠所;毛坑。□ *vt, vi* (-gg-) [VP15B, 2C] ~ ***down,*** (cause to) be stuck fast, unable to make progress: (使)陷於泥淖;(使)陷入困

境: *The tanks (got) ~ged down in the mud.* 戰車陷於泥淖中不能前進。 *Our discussions have ~ged down.* 我們的討論僵住了(無法進展)。 **boggy** /ˈbɒgɪ; ˈbɑgɪ/ *adj* (of land) soft and wet. (指土地)軟而濕的;沼澤性的。

bo·gey¹ ⇨ bogy.

bo·gey² /ˈbəʊgɪ; ˈbogɪ/ *n* (golf) score that a good player makes for a hole (or the whole course) and that other players try to equal. (高爾夫球)(以高手爲標準所定的某一洞或全場的)標準桿數。⇨ par¹(2).

boggle /ˈbɒgl; ˈbɑgl̩/ *vi* [VP2A, 3A] ~ ***(at sth)***, be unwilling, hesitate; be alarmed, amazed: 對某事畏縮不前;猶豫;吃驚;受驚: *The mind/imagination ~s (at the idea).* 心中(想像中)(對那種想法)感到吃驚。

bo·gie /ˈbəʊgɪ; ˈbogɪ/ *n* (also 亦作 **bogey, bogy**) **1** trolley. 臺車。 **2** four-wheeled undercarriage fitted under (the end of) a railway engine or wagon to enable it to go round curves. 置於火車引擎或貨車(的末端)底下用以幫助轉彎之四輪車盤;轉向車。

bo·gus /ˈbəʊgəs; ˈbogəs/ *adj* sham; counterfeit. 假的;偽造的;贋造的。

bogy, bo·gey /ˈbəʊgɪ; ˈbogɪ/ *n* (*pl* -gies, -geys) evil spirit; sb or sth that causes fear. 妖怪;使人害怕的人或物;怪物。

bo·he·mi·an /bəʊˈhiːmɪən; boˈhimɪən/ *n, adj* (person) not living in ways considered socially normal or conventional. 生活方式不正常或不合習俗的(人);放蕩不羈的(人)。

boil¹ /bɔɪl; bɔɪl/ *n* hard (usu red, often painful) poisoned swelling under the skin, which bursts when ripe. 疔瘡;癤子(皮下所生之硬腫毒,通常呈紅色,常常很痛,化膿時會潰裂)。

boil² /bɔɪl; bɔɪl/ *vi, vt* **1** [VP2A,B,C,D] (of water or other liquid, also of the vessel that contains it and of what is in the water) reach the temperature at which change to gas occurs; bubble up: (指水或其他液體,亦指盛液體之器皿及水中之物)沸騰;(水)開: *When water ~s it changes into steam.* 水沸騰時就變成蒸汽。 *The kettle is ~ing.* 壺裏的水開了。 *The potatoes are ~ing.* 馬鈴薯在煮着。 *Don't let the kettle ~ dry.* 不要讓壺裏的水煮乾了。 *Let the vegetables ~ gently.* 把蔬菜用慢火煮着。 ***keep the pot ~ing***, (fig) earn or otherwise find enough money for food, etc. (喻)維持生活; 糊口。 ˈ**~ing-point** *n* temperature at which a liquid ~s. (液體的)沸點。 **~ing hot**, (colloq) very hot: (俗)極炎熱的: *a ~ing hot day.* 極炎熱的一日。 **2** [VP2A, C] (of the sea, of a person's feelings, etc) be agitated like ~ing water: (指海等)洶湧;(指感情等)激昂: *The boat was swallowed up by the ~ing waves.* 船被洶湧的浪濤吞沒。 *He was ~ing (over) with indignation.* 他怒氣冲冲。 *Cruelty to animals makes her blood ~.* 虐待動物使她極爲憤怒。 **3** [VP6A, 22] cause water or other liquid to ~; cook in ~ing water: 使(水或其他液體)沸騰;用開水煮: *We ~ eggs, fish and vegetables.* 我們烹煮蛋、魚及蔬菜。 *Please ~ my egg for three minutes.* 請把我的蛋煮三分鐘。 *I like my eggs ~ed hard.* 我喜歡吃煮老的蛋。 *My brother prefers soft-~ed eggs.* 我的哥哥(弟弟)喜歡吃煮嫩一點的蛋。 **4** [VP2C,15B] ~ ***away***, **(a)** continue to ~: 繼續沸騰: *The kettle was ~ing away merrily on the fire.* 壺裏的水在火上沸騰不已。 **(b)** ~ until nothing remains: 煮乾;燒乾: *The water had all ~ed away and the kettle was empty.* 水完全燒乾了,壺也空了。 ~ ***down***, be reduced in quantity: 在數量上減少: *It all ~s down to this...*, (colloq) The essence (of the statement, proposal, etc) is.... (俗)(指陳述、建議等)其要點就是…。 ~ ***sth down***, make less by ~ing; (fig) condense: 將某物煮濃;(喻)濃縮;縮短;摘要: ~ *down a long article to two hundred words*, make a précis of it. 將一篇長文濃縮到二百個字。 ~ ***over***, boil and flow over the side of a vessel: 沸騰而溢出: *The milk had ~ed over.* 牛奶已沸騰得溢出來了。 □ *n* **the ~**, ~ing point: 沸點: ***be on the ~***, be ~ing. 在沸點;在沸騰中。 ***bring sth to the ~***, heat it until it ~s. 將某物煮至沸騰。 ***come to the ~***, begin to ~. 開始沸騰。

boiler /ˈbɔɪlə(r); ˈbɔɪlɚ/ *n* **1** metal container in which water, etc is heated, eg for producing steam in an engine; tank forming part of a kitchen range for supplying hot water; tank for heating water for a laundry. 鍋爐;汽鍋;熱水器;燒水壺。 ˈ**~·suit** *n* one-piece garment, overalls, for rough or dirty work. (做粗工或髒工作時所穿的)上衣連褲的工作服。 **2** person whose trade is boiling sth: 以煮物爲業者: *a* ˈ*soap-~.* 製造肥皂者。

bois·ter·ous /ˈbɔɪstərəs; ˈbɔɪstərəs/ *adj* rough, violent: 狂暴的;猛烈的: ~ *weather;* 狂風暴雨的天氣; *a ~ wind/sea;* 暴風(波濤洶湧的海); (of a person, his behaviour) noisy and cheerful. (指人,其行爲)喧鬧的;鬧嚷的。 **~·ly** *adv*

bold /bəʊld; bold/ *adj* (-er, -est) **1** without, showing no, fear; enterprising. 無畏的;大膽的;勇敢的;有進取心的。 ***be/make so ~ as to do sth***, allow oneself to do it: 容許自己做某事;不揣冒昧做某事: *If I may be so ~ as to...*, If I may venture or presume to.... 我不揣冒昧…。 ***make ~ with sth***, (more usu 較常用 *make free with*) take the liberty of using it. 擅自使用(某物)。 **a ~ front**, ⇨ front(4). **2** without feelings of shame; immodest. 無恥的;無禮的。 ***as ~ as brass***, impudent. 厚顏的。 **3** well marked; clear: 輪廓清楚的: *the ~ outline of a mountain;* 一座山之清晰輪廓; *a ~ headland;* 輪廓清楚的海岬; *a painting made with a few ~* (=free and vigorous) *strokes of the brush.* 一幅由幾筆遒勁的筆觸畫成的畫。 **~·ly** *adv* **~·ness** *n*

bole /bəʊl; bol/ *n* trunk of a tree. 樹幹。

bol·ero /bəˈleərəʊ; boˈlɛro/ *n* [C] (*pl* ~s) **1** (music for a) Spanish dance. 西班牙舞;西班牙舞曲。 **2** /ˈbɒlərəʊ; boˈlɛro/ short jacket with no front fastening. (前面不開鈕的)短上衣。

boll /bəʊl; bol/ *n* round seed-vessel (of cotton and flax). (棉及亞麻之)圓蒴;莢殼。⇨ the illus at cotton. 參看 cotton 之插圖。 ˌ~ ˈ**weevil** /ˈwiːvl; ˈwivl̩/ *n* small destructive insect that infests cotton-plants. 棉蟲(侵害棉禾之小昆蟲)。

bol·lard /ˈbɒləd; ˈbɑlɚd/ *n* **1** upright post (usu of iron) on a quay or a ship's deck for making ropes secure. (碼頭上的)繫船樁;(甲板上的)繫纜樁。 **2** protective post on a traffic island, or a roadway, sometimes with an arrow to direct traffic. (馬路安全島上或車道上的)保護樁(有時上有箭號以指示交通)。

bol·locks /ˈbɒləks; ˈbɑləks/ *n pl* ⚠(諱)=ballocks.

bo·loney /bəˈləʊnɪ; bəˈlonɪ/ *n* [U] (US sl) nonsense; humbug. (美俚)胡說八道;胡扯。

Bol·she·vik /ˈbɒlʃəvɪk; ˈbɑlʃəˌvɪk/ *n* (hist) follower of the revolutionary Marxist party that came to power in Russia in 1917; (colloq) supporter of the system of government by soviets; (colloq) person favouring Marxism or Communism. (史)布爾什維克(1917年取得政權之蘇俄共產黨之擁護者);(俗)支持蘇維埃專政者;(俗)贊成馬克思主義或共產主義者。

bol·shy /ˈbɒlʃɪ; ˈbɑlʃɪ/ *adj* (sl) rebellious; stubborn. (俚)反叛的;反抗的;頑固的;頑强的。

bol·ster¹ /ˈbəʊlstə(r); ˈbolstɚ/ *n* long under-pillow for the head of a bed. (床頭上的)長枕墊。

bol·ster² /ˈbəʊlstə(r); ˈbolstɚ/ *vt* [VP6A, 15B] ~ ***(up)***, support; give (greatly needed, often undeserved) support to, eg a cause, theory, etc, that would otherwise fail. 支持;支援;對於(不支持就會失敗的運動、學說等)給予(極需要的,常爲不應得的)援助。

bolt¹ /bəʊlt; bolt/ *n* **1** metal fastening for a door or window, consisting of a sliding pin or rod and a staple into which it fits. (金屬的)門閂;窗閂。 **2** metal pin with a head at one end and a thread (as on a screw) at the other, used with a nut for holding things together. 帶帽的螺絲釘;螺栓。 **3** (old use) short heavy arrow shot from a crossbow. (舊用法)粗短的箭;矢。 ***shoot one's (last) ~***, make one's last effort. 盡其最後努力。**4** discharge of lightning. 閃電;霹靂。⇨ blue[2](2); ⇨ *thunder~* at thunder(1). **5** (as a measure of cloth, canvas, etc) roll (as it comes from the loom). (做爲布匹等從織布機上取下時之度量)一疋;一捲。□ *vt, vi* [VP6A, 15B, 2A] fasten with a ~(1): 用門閂住: *~ the doors and windows;* 將門窗閂住; *~ sb in,* shut him in by ~ing the door(s); 把(某人)關在屋裏; *~ sb out,* keep him out by ~ing the door(s). 將某人關在門外。*The door ~s on the inside.* 這門要從裏面閂。

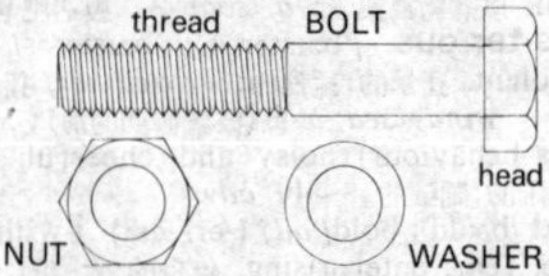

a bolt

bolt[2] /bəʊlt ; bolt/ *vi, vt* **1** [VP2A, C] run away quickly; (esp of a horse) run off out of control: 急逃;(尤指馬)突跑;狂奔: *As soon as I came downstairs the burglar ~ed through the back door.* 我一下樓來,竊賊就從後門飛奔而逃。**2** [VP6A] swallow (food) quickly: 匆匆吞嚥(食物): *We ~ed a few mouthfuls of food and hurried on.* 我們匆匆吞了幾口食物,就趕着繼續前進。**3** [VP2A] (of plants) grow quickly upwards and go to seed. (指植物)迅速成長並結實。□ *n* act of running away. 逃跑;逃走。***make a ~ for it,*** run off quickly (usu to escape from sth). 急忙逃走(通常係逃避某事物)。**'~-hole** *n* hole or burrow into which to ~ for safety. 逃入以躲避危險之洞穴。

bolt[3] /bəʊlt ; bolt/ *vt* [VP6A] sift (flour). 篩(麵粉)。

bolt[4] /bəʊlt ; bolt/ *adv* ***~ upright,*** (of sb's posture) quite upright. (指某人的姿勢)挺直的;直立的。

bomb /bɒm ; bɑm/ *n* hollow metal ball or shell filled either with explosive for causing destruction or with smoke, gas, or incendiary material, eg dropped from aircraft; (old use) hand-grenade. 炸彈(中空之金屬球或殼,內充破壞性之爆炸物,或產生煙霧、毒氣或燃燒性之物質,如從飛機上投下者);(舊用法)手榴彈。***go like a ~,*** (sl) be very efficient, successful, etc: (俚)非常有效、成功等: *My new car goes like a ~.* 我的新車跑得棒極了。**'~ bay** *n* compartment (in an aircraft) for holding ~s. (飛機中的)炸彈艙。**'~-disposal squad,** squad for removing unexploded ~s and making them harmless. 炸彈處理小組(移除並銷燬未爆炸之炸彈的小組)。**'~-proof** *adj* giving protection against exploding ~s: 不怕轟炸的;炸不破的;能防炸彈的: *a ~-proof shelter.* 防空避難室。**'~·shell** *n* (fig) sth that comes as a great surprise and shock. (喻)令人大爲震驚的意外事件。**'~-sight** *n* device (in an aircraft) for aiming ~s. (飛機中的)轟炸瞄準器。**'~-site** *n* area (in a town) devastated by ~s: (城市中)被炸彈炸燬的地區: *a car park on a ~-site.* 被炸燬地區上的停車場。□ *vt, vi* **1** [VP6A,15B] attack with ~s; drop ~s on. 轟炸。***~ out,*** drive out (of buildings, etc) with ~s: 以炸彈(自建築物等中)趕出: *~ed out families/factories.* 被炸彈趕出的家庭(工廠)。**2** [VP15B,2C] ***~ up,*** load (an aircraft) with ~s. 裝載炸彈於(飛機)中;裝載炸彈。**~er** /'bɒmə(r) ; 'bɑmə/ *n* aircraft used for ~ing, ⇨ the illus at aircraft; soldier trained in ~ing. 轟炸機(參看 aircraft 之插圖);轟炸員。

bom·bard /bɒm'bɑːd ; bɑm'bɑrd/ *vt* [VP6A, 14] ***~ (with),*** attack with shells from big guns; (fig) worry with questions, requests, complaints, etc; (nuclear physics) send a stream of high-speed particles against (an atom, etc). 砲轟;(喻)(以問題、要求、指摘等)困擾;質問;轟擊;(核子物理學)(放出一股高速粒子)撞擊(原子等)。**~·ment** *n* ~ing or being ~ed: 砲轟;轟擊: *after a long ~ment.* 經過長時間之轟擊之後。

bom·bar·dier /ˌbɒmbə'dɪə(r) ; ˌbɑmbə'dɪr/ *n* (in an artillery regiment) non-commissioned officer below a sergeant. (砲兵團中之)砲兵下士。

bom·bast /'bɒmbæst ; 'bɑmbæst/ *n* [U] insincere, high-sounding talk. 誇大之辭;高調。**bom·bas·tic** /bɒm'bæstɪk ; bɑm'bæstɪk/ *adj* (of a person, his talk, behaviour) promising much but not likely to do much; using fine high-sounding words. (指人、其言行)浮誇的;口氣大的;唱高調的。**bom·bas·ti·cally** /-klɪ ; -klɪ/ *adv*

bona fide /ˌbəʊnə 'faɪdɪ ; 'bonə'faɪdɪ/ *adj, adv* (Lat) genuine(ly); sincere(ly); in good faith: (拉)眞正的(地);眞誠的(地);誠實的(地): (comm) (商) *a ~ buyer.* 老實的購買者。**bona fides** /ˌbəʊnə 'faɪdɪz ; 'bonə'faɪdiz/ *n* (legal) honest intention; sincerity. (法律)誠意;眞誠。

bon·anza /bə'nænzə ; bo'nænzə/ *n* [C] (*pl* ~s) (US) sth, eg a gold-mine, an oil-well, that is prospering greatly; (attrib) bringing good luck and prosperity: (美)產量旺盛的金礦、油井等;富礦帶;大爲興隆的事物; (形容用法)帶來幸運及興隆的: *a ~ year.* 幸運發財的一年。

bon·bon /'bɒnbɒn ; 'bɑnˌbɑn/ *n* sweet; sth made of sugar in a fancy shape, etc. 一種糖果。

bond /bɒnd ; bɑnd/ *n* **1** agreement or engagement that a person is bound to observe, esp one that has force in law; document, signed and sealed, containing such an agreement. 契約;合同;票據;保結;此等文件: ***enter into a ~ with sb,*** agree to make a ~ with sb. 與某人訂契約。***His word is as good as his ~,*** He is so honest that his spoken promise is as reliable as a written agreement. 他說的話有信用(與他的契約一樣有效)。**2** printed paper issued by a government or a corporation acknowledging that money has been lent to it and will be paid back with interest. (政府或公司發行的)債票;債券;公債;公司債券。**'~-holder** *n* person holding ~s. 債券持有人。**3** sth that joins or unites (usu fig): 連結物;束縛物(通常作比喻用): *the ~(s) of affection.* 感情的聯繫。*Common tastes form a ~ between the two men,* They are friends because they are interested in the same things. 共同的愛好使這兩人結交爲朋友。**4** the state of being joined: 連結;結合: *Press the surfaces together to ensure a good, firm ~.* 將面與面緊壓在一起俾使牢固黏合。**5** (*pl*) prisoner's chains: (複)鐐銬;桎梏: *in ~s,* held as a prisoner or as a slave; 被囚禁;被奴役; *burst one's ~s,* win freedom. 掙脫枷鎖;贏得自由。**6** (comm) (商) ***in ~,*** (of goods) in a Customs warehouse (until duties are paid). (指貨物) 被扣留在海關的堆棧中 (待納稅後始可取出)。*place goods in/take goods out of ~.* 將貨物扣留在海關堆棧中以待納稅(納稅後自海關堆棧中取出貨物)。□ *vt* [VP6A] **1** put (goods) into a Customs warehouse. 海關扣留(貨物)(置於堆棧中)。***~ed goods,*** imported and placed in ~ until duty is paid. 被海關扣留的進口貨。***a ~ed warehouse,*** one in which goods are stored until duties are paid. 海關扣留貨物所用的堆棧。**2** join securely (with glue, etc). (用膠等)黏合。

bond- /bɒnd- ; bɑnd-/ *pref* in slavery, not free: 被奴役的;不自由的: *'~man, 'bonds-man* /-mən ; -mən/; 奴隸;奴僕; *'~maid;* 女奴; *'~servant;* 奴僕;奴隸; *'~slave.* 奴隸。

bond·age /'bɒndɪdʒ ; 'bɑndɪdʒ/ *n* [U] slavery, servitude: 奴役;束縛: *in hopeless ~ to his master.* 永爲主人之奴隸(無獲自由之希望)。

bone /bəʊn ; bon/ *n* **1** [C] one of the parts that make up the framework (ie skeleton) of an animal's body. (動物身體內的)骨;骨頭。⇨ the illus at skeleton. 參看 skeleton 之插圖。*This fish has a lot of ~s in it.* 這種魚骨頭很多。*No ~s broken, I hope,* I hope you have not hurt yourself. 我希望你未受傷。***~ of contention,*** subject of dispute. 爭論的題目。***feel in one's ~s that,*** feel certain that. 確有把握。***have a '~ to pick with sb,*** have sth to argue or complain about. 與某人有爭執或抱怨。

make no ~s about (doing) sth, not hesitate about it, do it without scruple: 毫不猶豫地做某事; 毫無顧忌地做某事: *They dismissed him and made no ~s about it.* 他們毫不猶豫地把他開革了。***(frozen) to the ~,*** completely, in a penetrating way. (寒凍)入骨;刺骨;刻骨。***will not make old ~s,*** will not live long. 不會活得很久。 **2** [U] hard substance of which ~s are made: 骨質物: *Buttons are sometimes made of ~.* 鈕扣有時用骨質物製成。*He's all skin and ~,* is very thin. 他骨瘦如柴。 **3** (*pl*, old use) castanets; dice. (複, 舊用法)響板; 骰子。 **4** (compounds). (複合字)。ˌ~ ˈ**dry** *adj* quite dry. 極乾燥的。ˈ**~-head** *n* (sl) stupid person. (俚)愚蠢的人; 呆頭呆腦的人;笨蛋。ˌ**~-ˈidle/-ˈlazy** *adj* completely idle. 懶到極點的。ˈ**~·meal** *n* fertilizer of crushed and powdered ~s. 骨粉(肥料)。ˈ**~-setter** *n* person who sets broken ~s. 接骨專家。ˈ**~·shaker** *n* (colloq) old bicycle without rubber tyres; old, shaky bus, car or cart. (俗)無橡皮輪胎之老式脚踏車;破舊顛簸的公車、汽車或馬車。ˌ**big-/ˌstrong-ˈ~d** *adj* having big/strong ~s. 骨骼大(强壯)的。□ *vt* [VP6A] **1** take ~s out of (a chicken, a piece of meat, etc). 取出(鷄、肉塊等之)骨頭;去…之骨。 **2** (old use) put ~s into (eg a corset). (舊用法)裝骨架於(如婦女用的束腹)。 **3** (sl) steal. (俚)偷竊。 **4** *~ up on* (a subject), (sl) study hard. (俚)鑽研(一門學科)。

boner /ˈbəunə(r); ˈbonɚ/ *n* (US sl) blunder. (美俚)大錯。

bon·fire /ˈbɒnfaɪə(r) ; ˈbɑnˌfaɪr/ *n* large fire made outdoors either to celebrate some event or to burn up dead leaves, rubbish, etc: 在戶外所擧之火(或爲慶祝某事,或爲焚燬枯葉、垃圾等);祝火;營火: ***make a ~ of,*** get rid of. 燒掉;焚燬;淸除。

bongo /ˈbɒŋgəu ; ˈbɑŋgo/ *n* (*pl* ~s) ˈ**~ (drum),** small drum played with the hands, usu one of a pair. 一種用手敲打之小鼓。⇨ the illus at percussion. 參看 percussion 之插圖。

bon·homie /ˈbɒnəmɪ ; ˌbɑnəˈmi/ *n* [U] (F) bluff, hearty pleasantness of manner. (法)坦誠;和善;親切;溫和;和藹。

bo·nito /bəˈni:təu ; bəˈnito/ *n* large kinds of tunny of the Atlantic Ocean, esp the striped tunny. 鰹(產於大西洋,尤指有條紋者)。

bon·kers /ˈbɒŋkəz ; ˈbɑŋkɚz/ *pred adj* ***(stark, raving) ~,*** (sl) raving mad; completely insane. (俚)瘋狂的。

bon mot /ˌbɒn ˈməu ; ˌbɑn ˈmo/ *n* (*pl* bons mots /ˈməuz ; ˈmoz/) witty saying or remark. 珠璣妙語; 雋語。

bon·net /ˈbɒnɪt ; ˈbɑnɪt/ *n* **1** small, round headdress without a hard brim, usu tied under the chin. (通常用帶繫於頷下之) 無邊小圓軟帽。 **2** soft, flat cap worn by men in Scotland and by soldiers in some regiments. (蘇格蘭男子及某些團的軍人所戴之)扁平軟帽。 **3** protective cover of various sorts, eg over a chimney, or (US 美 = *hood*) over the engine of a motor-car. 各種保護性的覆蓋物(如蓋於烟囱上者或汽車引擎的蓋子)。⇨ the illus at motor. 參看 motor 之插圖。

bonny /ˈbɒnɪ ; ˈbɑnɪ/ *adj* (Scot) (蘇) **1** attractive, fine. 可愛的;美好的。**2** healthy looking; with a glow of health: 健美的;容光煥發的: *a ~ baby;* 健美的嬰兒; *her ~ face.* 她那容光煥發的面龐。**bon·nily** *adj*

bo·nus /ˈbəunəs ; ˈbonəs/ *n* (*pl* ~es) payment in addition to what is usual, necessary or expected, eg an extra dividend to stockholders of a business company; (insurance) a share of profits to policy-holders, or an extra payment to workers: (分給股東的)額外利息;紅利;(保險)(分配給投保人的)餘利;額外優給;(工資以外的) 獎金; 津貼: *cost-of-ˈliving ~,* addition to wages or salaries because of rising prices. (因物價上漲所給薪資以外的) 生活補助金。**no ˈclaims ~,** percentage reduction in an insurance premium (for a motor vehicle) if claims are not made. (汽車保險之)未要求賠償之保險費之折扣優待。

bony /ˈbəunɪ ; ˈbonɪ/ *adj* (-ier, -iest) **1** full of bones: 多骨的: *a ~ fish,* eg a herring. 多骨的魚(如鯡)。 **2** having big or prominent bones: 骨骼大的;骨骼突出的: *a tall, ~ man.* 一個高而骨骼突出的人。 **3** with little flesh: 肉少的;瘦的: *~ fingers.* 瘦的手指。

boo /bu: ; bu/ (also 亦作 **bo, boh** /bəu ; bo/) *int* sound made to show disapproval or contempt; exclamation used to surprise or startle: 呸(表示不贊成或輕蔑之聲);令人驚愕的驚叫;嚇人的聲音: *He can't say boo to a goose,* is timid. 他膽子很小(對一隻鵝也不敢叫 boo)。□ *vt, vi* [VP6A, 15A, 2A] make such sounds: 發輕蔑之聲;發噓聲;發驚叫聲: *The speaker was booed off the platform.* 演說者被噓下臺來了。*The crowd booed and hooted.* 群衆發出輕蔑的叫囂聲。

boob[1] /bu:b ; bub/ *n* **1** = booby. **2** (colloq) silly mistake. (俗)愚蠢的錯。□ *vi* (colloq) make a silly mistake. (俗)犯愚蠢的錯。

boob[2] /bu:b ; bub/ *n* (sl) woman's breast. (俚)(女人的)奶子。

booby /ˈbu:bɪ ; ˈbubɪ/ *n* silly or stupid person. 傻瓜;呆子;笨蛋。ˈ**~ prize** *n* prize given as a joke to the person who is last in a race or competition. (賽跑或競賽之)末名奬(意在善意的開玩笑);倒數第一奬。ˈ**~-trap** *n* sth balanced on the top of a door so that it will fall on the first person to pass through; (mil) apparently harmless object that will kill or injure sb when picked up or interfered with. 置於門頂讓人開門經過卽落於其頭上之物; (軍)詭雷(看似無害,但一經撿拾或搬弄卽可殺傷人)。

boogie /ˈbu:gɪ *US:* ˈbʊgɪ ; ˈbʊgɪ/ (also 亦作 **boogie-woogie** /-ˈwu:gɪ *US:* -ˈwʊgɪ ; -ˈwʊgɪ/ *n* [C, U] (instance of) highly rhythmic variety of blues[2](6). 布吉舞曲(一種極富節奏之布魯斯舞曲);布吉舞。

book[1] /bʊk ; bʊk/ *n* **1** number of sheets of paper, either printed or blank, fastened together in a cover; literary composition that would fill such a set of sheets: 書;書籍;簿本;文字著作: *write a ~.* 寫一本書。 **2 the B~,** the Bible: 聖經: *swear on the B~,* take an oath. 對聖經發誓。 **3** main division of a large treatise or poem or the Bible: (大部著作之)卷;篇: *the B~ of Genesis.* (聖經之)創世記篇。 **4** packet of similar items fastened together, eg postage stamps, bus tickets, matches. (郵票、車票等的)本;(火柴等的)包。 **5** record of bets. 賽馬賭注紀錄。⇨ ~maker in 8 below. 參看下列第 8 義之 bookmaker. ***make/keep a ~ (on),*** take bets, etc. 接受賭注;下賭注;打賭。***not suit one's ~,*** not be convenient. 對某人不方便;不合某人之意。 **6** (*pl*) business accounts, records, etc: (複)商業帳册,紀錄等: *The firm has full order ~s,* orders for goods. 該商行有完整的訂貨紀錄。***be in sb's good/bad/black ~s,*** have/not have his favour or approval. 爲某人所(不)寵信。***bring sb to ~ (for sth),*** require him to explain his conduct. 要求某人解釋其行爲;斥責。 **7** libretto (of an opera). (歌劇之) 唱詞脚本。 **8** (compounds): (複合字): ˈ**~·case** *n* piece of furniture with shelves for ~s. 書架。ˈ**~·club** *n* organization that sells ~s at a discount to members who agree to buy a minimum number. 讀書會;讀書俱樂部(以折扣價格售書給會員,而會員則答應每期最少應買若干本書)。ˈ**~-ends** *n pl* pair of props used to keep ~s upright, eg on a table. (一對)書夾; 書擋; 書靠。ˈ**~-keeper** *n* person who keeps accounts, eg of a business, public office. 記帳員;簿記員。ˈ**~-keep·ing** *n* (art of) keeping (business) accounts. 簿記;記帳。ˈ**~·maker** *n* person whose business is taking bets on horse-races. 以賭賽馬爲業者。ˈ**~-mark(er)** *n* sth placed between the pages of a ~ to mark the place. 書籤。ˈ**~·mobile** /-məubi:l ; -ˈmobl̩/ *n* (US) truck equipped as a mobile ~ store or lending library. (美)(以貨車裝成的)流動書店;流動圖書館。ˈ**~·seller** *n* person who sells ~s retail. 書店老闆;書商。ˈ**~·stall** *n* stall, kiosk, etc at which ~s, newspapers, etc are shown for sale outdoors, in a railway station, a hotel lobby, etc (US 美 = *newsstand*). (車站、旅館休息室

等處之) 書報攤。'~ **token** *n* ⇨ token. '~•**worm** *n* small maggot that eats holes in ~s; (fig) person who is very fond of reading ~s. 書蟲;蠹魚;(喻) 書呆子;極愛讀書者。

book² /bʊk ; bʊk/ *vt* [VP6A] **1** write down (orders, etc) in a notebook; (of the police) record a charge against (sb): 記載(訂貨單等)於帳册中;(指警察)登記對(某人)之控告: *be ~ed for exceeding the speed limit.* 因超速駕車而被登記。**2** give or receive an order for, eg seats at a theatre, tickets for a journey; engage (sb) as a speaker, entertainer, etc: 定(座);定(票);接受定(座)或定(票);聘請(某人)爲演說者、表演者等: *Seats (for the theatre) can be ~ed from 10 am to 6pm.* (戲院之) 定座時間自上午十時起至下午六時止。*Have you ~ed your passage to New York*, arranged for a cabin? 你到紐約去的船艙位定好了嗎? *Can I ~ (a ticket) through to Naples?* 我可以買一張直達那不勒斯的票嗎? ***(fully) ~ed up,*** (of a restaurant, theatre, etc) no more tables, seats, available; (of a lecturer, singer, etc) unable to accept further engagements. (指餐館、戲院等)已滿座;(指演說者、歌星等)演出時間已排滿;無空擋;無法再接節目。'~•**ing clerk** *n* person who sells tickets, eg at a railway station. (火車站等之)售票員。'~•**ing office** *n* office for the sale of tickets (for travel). (車站等之)售票處;票房。'~•**able** /-əbl ; -əbl/ *adj* (of seats, etc) that can be reserved: (指座位等) 可預定的: *all seats ~able in advance.* 可預定之所有座位。

bookie /'bʊkɪ ; 'bʊkɪ/ *n* (colloq) bookmaker. (俗) 賭賽馬爲業者。⇨ book¹(8).

book•ish /'bʊkɪʃ ; 'bʊkɪʃ/ *adj* of books and studies: 書的;讀書的: *a ~ person,* one who gives much time to reading; 花很多時間讀書的人;好讀書的人; *~ expressions,* found in books but not colloquial; 書中的(非口語的)辭句;迂腐的辭句; *a ~ style,* literary, not colloquial. 文縐縐的 (非口語的)文體。~-**ness** *n*

book•let /'bʊklɪt ; 'bʊklɪt/ *n* thin book, usu in paper covers. 小册子(通常用紙面)。

boom¹ /bu:m ; bum/ *n* **1** long spar used to keep the bottom of a sail stretched out. 帆之下桁。⇨ the illus at barque. 參看 barque 之挿圖。**2 derrick ~,** pole fastened to a derrick crane, used for (un-)loading cargo. (船上裝卸貨物起重用的)吊桿。**3** heavy chain, mass of floating logs, etc held in position across a river or harbour entrance, eg as a defence in time of war, or to prevent logs from floating away. 橫攔於河中或港口之大鐵鍊或一批浮木(於戰時禦敵用,或用以阻攔圓木漂走);筏堰。**4** long, movable arm for a microphone. (掛麥克風用)活動長桿(臂)。

boom² /bu:m ; bum/ *vt, vi* **1** [VP2A, C] (of big guns, the wind, an organ) make deep, hollow, or resonant sounds. (指大砲、風、風琴)發出隆隆或轟轟的聲音。**2 ~ *out,*** [VP15B] utter in a deep voice: 用低沉的聲音說出: *~ing out Shakespearian verses.* 用低沉的聲音讀出莎士比亞的詩句。□ *n* deep, hollow sound: 低沉的聲音: *the ~ of the guns/surf;* 大砲(海浪)的隆隆聲; *a sonic ~.* 音爆(飛機飛行速度超過音速時所發生的爆炸聲)。

boom³ /bu:m ; bum/ *n* [C] sudden increase in trade activity, esp a time when money is being made quickly. 商業之突趨繁榮;(尤指)可以迅速發財的商業繁榮時期;景氣。⇨ slump. '~ **town** *n* town showing sudden growth and prosperity. 高速成長繁榮中的城市;新興城市。□ *vi* [VP2A, C] have a ~; become well known and successful: 突趨繁榮;聲名大噪: *Business is ~ing.* 商業突趨繁榮。*Jones is ~ing as a novelist,* becoming famous. 作爲一個小說家,瓊斯的聲譽日隆。

boom•er•ang /'bu:məræŋ ; 'buməˌræŋ/ *n* curved stick of hard wood (used by Australian Aborigines), which can be thrown so that, if it fails to hit anything, it returns to the thrower; (fig) argument or proposal that comes back and harms its author. (澳洲土人所用的)曲形硬木飛鏢(此種飛鏢若未擊中目標,卽返回投擲者原處);(喻)損及原倡議人之辯論或提案。

boon¹ /bu:n ; bun/ *n* **1** (liter) request; favour: (文)要求;恩惠: *ask a ~ of sb;* 請求某人賜惠; *grant a ~.* 施恩;施惠。**2** advantage; blessing, comfort: 益處;恩賜;恩物: *Parks are a great ~ to people in big cities.* 公園是大都市居民的恩物。*A vacuum cleaner is a tremendous ~ to busy housewives.* 眞空吸塵器是忙碌家庭主婦的大恩物。

boon² /bu:n ; bun/ *adj* (only in) (僅用於) **~ companion,** jolly, congenial, companion. 好朋友;良伴。

boor /bʊə(r) ; bʊr/ *n* rough, ill-mannered person. 舉止粗魯的人。~•**ish** /-ɪʃ ; -ɪʃ/ *adj* of or like a~. 舉止粗魯的。~•**ish•ly** *adv* ~•**ish•ness** *n*

boost /bu:st ; bust/ *vt* [VP6A] give (sb or sth) a push up; increase the value, reputation, etc of (sb or sth): 將(某人或某物) 向上推;推起;舉起;爲(某人或某事物)吹噓;捧: *Seeing him there ~ed my morale.* 看到他在那邊提高了我的士氣 (使我精神振作)。□ *n* [C] act of ~ing; being ~ed. (被)推起;(被)舉起;(被)捧起。~**er** *n* **1** thing that ~s: 幫助推起之物;聲援;後援: *His work got a welcome ~.* 他的工作獲得令人欣喜的後援。'~**er rocket** *n* rocket used to give initial speed to a missile, after which it drops and leaves the missile to continue under its own power. (給予飛彈初速之)增力火箭(初速產生以後,增力火箭脫落,飛彈靠其本身之動力繼續前進)。**2** '~**er (injection),** supplementary dose of vaccine to strengthen the effect of an earlier dose; extra dose of morphine, etc (by drug addicts). (加强前次疫苗注射效力之)輔助注射;(毒癮者之嗎啡等的)額外劑量。

boot¹ /bu:t ; but/ *n* **1** outer covering for the foot and ankle, made of leather or rubber. 長靴;皮靴;膠套靴。⇨ shoe. **high ~s,** reaching to the knee. (及膝的)長統靴。***die with one's ~s on; die in one's ~s,*** not in bed; die while still working, etc. 橫死;暴斃;死於非命;在工作時死亡。***get the ~,*** (sl) be dismissed, be kicked out. (俚)被開革;被解雇。***give sb the ~,*** (sl) dismiss him from his job. (俚)開革某人;解雇某人。***lick sb's ~s,*** behave in a servile way. 舐某人的靴;巴結某人;奉承某人。***put the ~ in,*** (sl) kick sb, eg in a brawl; (fig) be ruthless. (俚)(在爭吵等中)踢某人;(喻)殘忍的;無情的。'~•**lace** *n* string or leather strip for ~s. 皮靴帶。**2** (GB) place for luggage in a coach or at the back of a motor-car (US 美 = *trunk*). (英)(客車中或小汽車之後部)放行李的地方。□ *vt* [VP6A, 15A, B] kick. 踢。~ ***sb/sth out (of),*** (sl) get rid of (from); dismiss, expel (from): (俚)除去;解雇;趕出: *He was ~ed out of the house.* 他被趕出屋外。~**ed** *adj* wearing ~s: 穿靴的: *~ed and spurred,* ready for a journey. 穿着靴子並裝有馬刺的(整裝待發,準備好旅行的)。

boot² /bu:t ; but/ *n* ***to ~,*** in addition, as well. 並且;加之;而且。

boot³ /bu:t ; but/ *vt* (old use, usu with *it*): (舊用法,通常與 it 連用): *What ~s it to..., that...,* what use is it to..., that...? (後接不定詞或名詞子句)…有何益? ***It little ~s to; It ~s not to,*** It is of little/no avail to. (後接不定詞)…無甚(毫無)益處。

bootee /bu:'ti: ; bu'ti/ *n* [C] (*pl* ~s) infant's knitted wool boot; kind of warmly lined boot for women. 小兒的毛線鞋;女用暖靴。

booth /bu:ð *US:* bu:θ ; buθ/ *n* **1** shelter of boards, canvas or other light materials, esp one where goods are sold at a market or a fair. (木板、帆布或其他輕便材料所搭成的)棚子;(尤指市場或商展會之)攤棚;攤位。**2** enclosure for a public telephone. 公用電話亭。⇨ kiosk. **3** '**polling ~,** place for voting at elections. (選舉時投票所間隔起來的)投票處。'**listening ~,** (in a shop) enclosure where customers may listen to records. (商店中顧客試聽唱片的)試聽間。

boot•leg /'bu:tleg ; 'butˌlɛg/ *vt* make, transport or

sell illicit alcoholic drinks: 釀造,偷運或販賣私酒: (attrib) (形容用法) ~ *liquor.* 私酒。**~·ger** /-legə(r); -ˌlɛgɚ/ *n* person who does this. 釀造,偷運或販賣私酒者。

boot·less /ˈbu:tlɪs; ˈbutlɪs/ *adj* (liter) useless; unavailing. (文)無用的;無益的。

booty /ˈbu:tɪ; ˈbutɪ/ *n* [U] things taken by robbers or captured from the enemy in war (and usu to be divided among those who take them). (强盜之)刼掠物;贓物;(戰爭時自敵人手中所獲之)擄獲物;戰利品(通常分給擄獲者)。

booze /bu:z; buz/ *vi* [VP2A, C] ~ ***(up)***, (colloq) drink alcoholic liquor, esp in excess. (俗)飲酒;狂飲;暴飲。Hence, 由此產生, **ˈ~-up**, *n* [C] occasion of heavy drinking: 酒宴;酒會: *go on/have a ~-up.* 舉行酒宴。□ *n* [U] (colloq) alcoholic drink. (俗)酒。***go/be on the ~***, start/be in a period of heavy drinking. 狂飲;暴飲。**~r** *n* one who ~s; (sl) pub. 飲酒者;暴飲者;酒徒;(俚)酒館。**boozy** *adj*

bop /bɒp; bɑp/ *n* (1940s) [U] style of jazz with a strong beat; [U, C] dancing/dance to this. (1940年代之)巴卜(一種節拍强勁有力之爵士樂); (隨着此種爵士樂所跳之)巴卜舞。□ *vi* [VP2A] dance to this. 跳巴卜舞。

bo-peep /ˌbəʊˈpi:p; boˈpip/ *n* [U] game of hiding and suddenly showing oneself to a baby. 躲藏起來然後突然出現以逗小孩之遊戲;躲貓貓遊戲。

bor·acic /bəˈræsɪk; boˈræsɪk/ *adj* of borax: 硼砂的: ~ *acid*, boric acid, ⇨ boric. 硼酸。

bor·age /ˈbɒrɪdʒ *US:* ˈbɔ:rɪdʒ; ˈbɔrɪdʒ/ *n* [U] blue-flowered, hairy-leaved plant of which the leaves are used as a seasoning. 琉璃苣(藍花毛葉植物,其葉用作調味料)。

borax /ˈbɔ:ræks; ˈborəks/ *n* white powder used to make porcelain enamels, in glass manufacture and other industries, and for cleaning. 硼砂(白色粉末,用於製瓷釉、製玻璃及其他工業,並可作清潔劑)。

Bor·deaux /bɔ:ˈdəʊ; bɔrˈdo/ *n* [U] (F) (often attrib) wine from the ~ area of France; claret. (法)(常作形容用法)(法國波爾多地區產的)紅葡萄酒。

bor·der /ˈbɔ:də(r); ˈbɔrdɚ/ *n* **1** edge; part near the edge of sth: 邊緣;邊際: *We camped on the ~ of a lake.* 我們在湖邊紮營。*A woman's handkerchief may have a lace ~.* 女人的手帕可能有花邊。*There is a ~ of flowers round the lawn.* 草坪的四周有花圍繞。**2** (land near the) line dividing two states or countries: 邊界;邊境;國界;國境: *The criminal escaped over the ~.* 罪犯逃過了邊界。(attrib): (形容用法): *a ~ town;* 邊境的市鎮; *~ incidents*, eg small fights between armed forces of two neighbouring states. 兩國間邊界武裝部隊的小衝突; 邊界事件。**the B~**, (esp) that between England and Scotland. (尤指英格蘭與蘇格蘭之間的)邊界。**ˈ~·land** /-lænd; -ˌlænd/ *n* **(a)** district on either side of a ~ or boundary. 邊區;邊疆;邊境。**(b)** (*sing* with *def art*, and attrib) condition between: (單數與定冠詞連用,並作形容用法) 介於二者之間的狀態: *the ~-land between sleeping and waking.* 半醒半睡之混然狀態。**ˈ~·line** *n* line that marks a ~. (兩國等之間的)界線;國境線。**~line case** *n* one that is dubious, eg sb who may or may not pass an examination. 難以確定的兩可情形(例如某人的考試可能及格也可能不及格)。□ *vt, vi* **1** [VP6A] put or be a ~ to: 加邊界線於;爲…之邊界線: *Our garden is ~ed by a stream.* 我們的花園瀕臨一條小河。**2** [VP3A] ***~ on/upon***, be next to: 毗連;接界: *My land ~s (up)on yours.* 我的土地與你的土地接界。*The park ~s on the shores of the lake.* 公園毗連湖濱。**3** [VP3A] ***~ on/upon***, resemble; be almost the same as: 近似;幾乎是: *The proposal ~s upon the absurd.* 該提議近乎可笑。**~er** *n* person living on or near a frontier, esp that between England and Scotland. 邊境居民(尤指居於英格蘭與蘇格蘭之邊境者)。

bore¹ /bɔ:(r); bor/ *vt, vi* [VP6A, 14, 15A] make a narrow, round deep hole in sth with a revolving tool; make (a hole, one's way) by doing this or by digging out soil, etc: 鑽(孔);開鑿;掘地洞(或隧道)而前進: *~ a hole in wood;* 於木中鑽孔; *~ a well;* 鑽井; *~ a tunnel through a mountain;* 開鑿隧道通過一座山; *animals* (eg moles) *that ~ their way under the ground.* 在地下掘地洞前進之動物(如鼹鼠)。□ *n* **1** (also 亦作 **ˈ~-hole**) hole made by boring, eg to find water. 鑽孔;鑿孔(如尋水等在地下所鑿者);鑽探孔。**2** hollow inside of a gun barrel; its diameter. 槍膛;槍砲的膛徑或口徑。**borer** *n* (kind of) insect that ~s. 會鑽孔的昆蟲。

bore² /bɔ:(r); bor/ *vt* [VP6A] make (sb) feel tired by being dull or tedious: 令(人)厭煩: *I hope you're not getting ~d listening to me.* 我希望你聽我說話不覺厭煩。*I've heard all that man's stories before; they ~ me/he ~s me.* 那個人所講的事我都聽過;使我煩死了。***~ sb to death/tears***, ~ him intensely. 煩死了某人。□ *n* [C] person or thing that ~s. 令人生厭之人或事物。**bor·ing** *adj*: *a boring evening.* 一個百無聊賴的晚上。**~·dom** /-dəm; -dəm/ *n* [U] state of being ~d. 厭煩;厭倦。

bore³ /bɔ:(r); bor/ *n* [C] high tidal wave, often many feet high, that advances up a narrow estuary. 海嘯;進入海口之高潮(常達很多呎高);激潮。

bore⁴ /bɔ:(r); bor/ *pt* of bear.

boric /ˈbɔ:rɪk; ˈbɔrɪk/ *adj* ~ **acid**, used as an antiseptic and a preservative. 硼酸(用作消毒及防腐劑)。

born /bɔ:n; bɔrn/ one of the *pp's* of bear. bear 之過去分詞之一。**1** ***be ~***, come into the world by birth. 出生;出世。***~ with a silver spoon in one's mouth***, ⇨ silver(1). **2** (with a complement) destined to be: (與補足語連用)生而爲;命中註定: *He was ~ a poet.* 他天生是個詩人。*He was ~ to be hanged.* 他命中註定要受絞刑。**3** (attrib) by natural ability: (形容用法)有天才的;天生的: *a ~ orator.* 天才演說家。

borne /bɔ:n; born/ *pp* of bear (except of birth). bear (除"出生"之義外)之過去分詞。⇨ bear²(10, 12).

boron /ˈbɔ:rɒn; ˈborɑn/ *n* [U] non-metallic element (symbol **B**). 硼(非金屬元素,化學符號 B)。

bor·ough /ˈbʌrə *US:* -rəʊ; ˈbɝo/ *n* **1** (England) town, or part of a town, that sends one or more members to Parliament; town with a municipal corporation and rights of self-government conferred by royal charter. (英國)國會中有代表之市鎮或市區;享有皇授自治權之市鎮。**2** (US) any one of the five administrative units of New York City. (美)紐約市五個行政區中的一區。

bor·row /ˈbɒrəʊ; ˈbɑro/ *vt* [VP6A, 14] ~ ***(from)***, **1** get sth, or the use of sth, on the understanding that it is to be returned: 借來;借入;(向某人)借;借用: *May I ~ your pen?* 我可借用你的鋼筆嗎? *Don't ~ books from me — ~ them from the library!* 不要向我借書——去圖書館借吧! *He fell into the river and had to go home in ~ed clothes.* 他跌入河中,所以不得不穿借來的衣服回家。*Some people are good at ~ing but bad at giving back.* 有些人只曉得借,不曉得還。⇨ lend. **2** take and use as one's own: 擅自借用;抄襲;剽竊: *~ sb's ideas/methods.* 剽竊某人的想法(方法)。**~er** *n* person who ~s. 借入者;借用者;剽竊者。

borsch /bɔ:ʃ; bɔrʃ/ (US = **borscht** /bɔ:ʃt; bɔrʃt/) *n* [U] (kinds of) Eastern European soup, esp of beetroot. 羅宋湯(東歐之數種湯,尤指加甜菜根者)。

bor·stal /ˈbɔ:stl; ˈbɔrstəl/ *n* ~ **(institution)**, place where young offenders live and receive training designed to reform them. 少年犯感化院或管訓所。

bortsch /bɔ:tʃ; bɔrtʃ/ *n* = borsch.

bor·zoi /ˈbɔ:zɔɪ; ˈbɔrzɔɪ/ *n* Russian wolf-hound. 俄國獵狼犬。

bosh /bɒʃ; bɑʃ/ *n, int* nonsense. 胡說;無意義的話。

bosky /ˈbɒskɪ; ˈbɑskɪ/ *adj* (liter) (of land) covered with trees and bushes. (文)(指土地)被草木所覆蔽的。

bo'sn /ˈbəʊsn; ˈbosn/ ⇨ boatswain.

bosom /ˈbʊzəm; ˈbʊzəm/ *n* [C] **1** (old use) person's chest; woman's breasts; part of dress covering this. (舊用法)胸;(女人的)乳房;(衣服的)胸部。 **2** centre or inmost part, where one feels joy or sorrow; 內心;衷心;胸懷; (attrib) (形容用法) ***a ~ friend,*** one who is dear and close. 知己的朋友;心腹之交。 **3** midst: 中間: *in the ~ of one's family.* 在家屬之中;與家屬在一起。

boss[1] /bɒs ; bɔs/ *n* [C] (colloq) superior; person who controls or gives orders to workers: (俗)上司;老板;工頭: *Who's the ~ in this house,* Is the husband or the wife in control? 誰是這一家之主(是先生還是太太當家)? □ *vt* [VP6A, 15B] be the ~ of; give orders to: 指揮;控制;管: *He wants to ~ the show,* to make all the arrangements. 他想指揮一切。***~ sb about/around,*** order sb here and there. 指揮某人使其團團轉。**~y** *adj* (-ier, -iest) fond of ~ing, fond of giving orders. 愛管事的;跋扈的;喜專權的。

boss[2] /bɒs ; bɔs/ *n* round metal knob or stud on a shield or as an ornament. 盾上的金屬圓形突起物;突起之圓形金屬裝飾。

boss[3] /bɒs ; bɔs/ *n* (sl) (also亦作 **'~ shot**) bad shot or guess; bungle: (俚)未中的射擊; 未中的猜測; 拙劣的工作: *make a ~ shot at sth;* 嘗試做某事而未成功; *make a ~ of sth.* 把某事弄得一團糟。**'~-eyed** *adj* (sl) blind in one eye; cross-eyed. (俚)一隻眼瞎的;獨眼的;斜眼的。

bo'sun /'bəʊsn ; 'bosn̩/ ⇨ boatswain.

bot·any /'bɒtənɪ ; 'bɑtn̩ɪ/ *n* [U] science of the structure of plants. 植物學。**bot·an·ical** /bə'tænɪkl ; bo'tænɪkl̩/ *adj* of ~. 植物學的。**botanical gardens,** park where plants and trees are grown for scientific study. 植物園。**bot·an·ist** /'bɒtənɪst ; 'bɑtn̩ɪst/ *n* student of or expert in ~. 植物學者。**bot·an·ize** /'bɒtənaɪz ; 'bɑtn̩ˌaɪz/ *vi* go out studying and collecting wild plants. 到野外研究並採集植物;實地研究植物。

botch /bɒtʃ ; bɑtʃ/ *vt* [VP6A, 15B] ***~ sth (up),*** repair badly; spoil by poor, clumsy work: 修補得不好;因技術拙劣而弄壞: *a ~ed piece of work.* 技術拙劣的工作。□ *n* piece of clumsy, badly done work: 技術拙劣的工作: *make a ~ of sth;* 把某事搞得一團糟; clumsy patch[1](1). 笨拙的修補。**~er** *n* person who ~es work. 技術拙劣的工人。

both[1] /bəʊθ ; boθ/ *adj* (of two things, persons, etc) the two; the one and also the other (*both* precedes the *def art,* demonstrative *adjj,* possessives, and other *adjj*): (指兩件事物,兩個人等)二者…都;兩者…都 (both 用於定冠詞,指示形容詞,所有格形容詞及代名詞,及其他形容詞之前): *I want ~ books/the books/these books.* (這)兩本書我都要。*I saw him on ~ occasions.* 在那兩個場合我都看到了他。*Hold it in ~ (your) hands.* 用兩隻手拿着。*B~ his younger brothers are in the army.* 他的兩個弟弟均在服兵役。*You can't have it ~ ways,* must decide on one or the other. 你不能魚與熊掌兩者得兼(必須決定其中之一)。Cf 參較 *both* and *neither*: *B~ these books are useful.* 這兩本書都有用處。*Neither of these books is useful.* 這兩本書都沒有用處。Cf 參較 *both* and *each*: *There are shops on ~ sides of the street.* 街的兩邊都有商店。*There is a butcher's shop on each side of the street.* 街的每一邊都有一家肉店。

both[2] /bəʊθ ; boθ/ *adv* ***~... and,*** not only... but also: 不但…而且: *Queen Anne is ~ dead and buried.* 安女王已經死了,而且埋葬了。*He is remarkable for ~ his intelligence and his skill.* 他不但智慧高,而且技術好。*He is ~ a soldier and a poet.* 他不但是個軍人,而且是個詩人。

both[3] /bəʊθ ; boθ/ *pron* **1** the two; not only the one but also the other: 二者;兩者都: *B~ are good.* 二者都好。*B~ of them are good.* 他們兩人都好。Cf 參較 *both* and *neither*: *B~ of us want to go.* 我們兩人都想去。*Neither of us wants to go.* 我們兩人都不想去。 **2** (used in apposition, in the same way as *each* and *all*): (用於同位格,與 each 及 all 用法同): *We ~ want to go.* 我們兩人都想去。*They are ~ useful.* 它們二者都有用。*Take them ~.* 把二者都拿去。*You must ~ work harder.* 你們二人都必須要用功些。

bother /'bɒðə(r) ; 'bɑðɚ/ *vt, vi* **1** [VP6A, 14, 16A, 3A] be or cause trouble to; worry: 打擾;攪擾;煩擾: *Tell the children to stop ~ing their father.* 告訴孩子們不要再攪擾他們的父親。*Don't ~ me with foolish questions.* 不要拿傻問題來煩擾我。*That man is always ~ing me to lend him money.* 那個人老是來鬧着要我借錢給他。***~ (oneself/one's head) (about),*** be/feel anxious about: 焦慮;為…而操心或焦急: *It's not important; don't ~ your head about it.* 這是不重要的事; 不要為此心焦。*We needn't ~ (about) when it happened.* 我們不必操心那是何時發生的。**2** [VP3A, 4C, 2A] ***~ (about),*** take trouble: 麻煩: *Don't ~ about getting/~ to get dinner for me today; I'll eat out.* 今天不要麻煩為我預備飯了;我要在外頭吃。 **3** (used as an exclamation of impatience or annoyance): (用作表示不耐煩或厭惡的感歎詞): *Oh, ~ (it)!* 呵,真討厭! *B~ the flies!* 討厭的蒼蠅! *Oh, ~ you!* 呵,討厭你! □ *n* **1** [U] worry, trouble: 焦慮;麻煩: *Did you have much ~ (in) finding the house?* 你是否費了很大麻煩才找到那房子? *It will be no ~ (to me),* won't involve much work or inconvenience. (對於我)它不會有什麼麻煩(不會太費事或不方便)。*We had quite a lot of ~ (in) getting here because of the fog.* 因為有霧,所以我們費了很大的事才找到這兒來。*Don't put yourself to any ~,* inconvenience yourself. 不要跟你自己找麻煩。 **2** (with *indef art*) sb or sth that gives trouble: (與不定冠詞連用)令人焦慮,厭煩或引起麻煩的人或事物: *His lazy son is quite a ~ to him.* 他那個懶惰的兒子,對他是一件很傷腦筋的事。*This drawer won't shut; isn't it a ~!* 這個抽屜關不上;豈不討厭! **~·ation** /ˌbɒðə'reɪʃn ; ˌbɑðə'reʃən/ *int* What a nuisance! 真討厭! **'~·some** /-səm ; -səm/ *adj* causing ~; troublesome or annoying. 令人焦慮的;麻煩的;可厭的。

bottle /'bɒtl ; 'bɑtl̩/ *n* container, usu made of glass and with a narrow neck, for milk, beer, wine, medicine, ink, etc; the contents of a ~: (盛牛奶、啤酒、酒、藥水、墨水等,通常爲玻璃製的)瓶子;瓶中所裝之物;一瓶之量: *Mary drinks two ~s of milk a day.* 瑪莉每天喝兩瓶牛奶。**'~-fed; *brought up on the ~,*** (of a child) given milk from a feeding ~, not fed from its mother's breast. (指小兒)吃牛奶(非母奶)長大的。***too fond of the ~,*** of alcoholic drinks. 嗜酒如命。**ˌ~-'green** *adj* dark green. 深綠色的; 墨綠色的。 **'~-neck** *n* **(a)** narrow strip of road, between two wide parts, where traffic is slowed down or held up. 瓶頸路段(兩段寬敞道路間的狹窄部份,交通緩慢阻滯)。**(b)** that part of a manufacturing process, etc, where production is slowed down (eg by shortage of materials). 瓶頸(工業生產過程等中影響生產速率的部份,如因缺乏原料等)。□ *vt* [VP6A] put into, store in, ~s: 裝於瓶中;盛於瓶中;瓶裝: *~ fruit.* 將水果裝於瓶中。***~ up,*** [VP15B] (fig) hold in, keep under control, eg anger. (喻)抑制;控制(憤怒等)。

bot·tom /'bɒtəm ; 'bɑtəm/ *n* **1** lowest part of anything, inside or outside: 底;底部(內側或外側): *There are some tea-leaves in the ~ of the cup.* 杯底有一些茶葉。*He fell to the ~ of the well.* 他掉到井底去了。*We were glad to reach the ~ (= foot) of the mountain.* 我們很高興到達了山脚下。*Notes are sometimes printed at the ~ (= foot) of the page.* 註解有時印在頁底。 **2** part farthest from the front or more important part: 距離前邊或較重要部份最遠的部份;後部;尾部: *at the ~ of the garden;* 在花園的盡頭; less honourable end of a table, class, etc: 末席;末座;末位: *The poor relations were seated at the ~ of the long table.* 窮親戚們被排在長形餐桌的末座。 **3** bed of the sea, a lake, river, etc: 海底;湖底;河床: *The ship went to the ~,* sank. 船沉入水底了。*The lake is deep and a swimmer cannot touch ~,* touch the bed of the lake with his toes.

湖水很深，游泳者探不到底。**4** seat (of a chair); part of the body on which a person sits; buttocks: (椅之)坐的部份；屁股: *This chair needs a new ~.* 這把椅子的座面需要換新。*She smacked the child's ~.* 她揍孩子的屁股。**5** horizontal part of a ship near the keel: 船底: *The ship was found floating ~ upwards.* 該船被發現底朝天漂流着。**6** foundation: 基礎；根基；根源: *We must get to the ~ of this mystery,* find out how it began. 我們必須探查出這個謎的究竟。*Who's at the ~ of this business,* Who's responsible? 到底誰是這個企業的主持人？ **7** (fig uses): (比喻用法): *The ~ has fallen out of the market,* Trade has fallen to a very low level. 商業已落到極低的水準 (景況不好)。***at ~,*** in essential character: 根本上；基本上；實際上: *He's a good fellow at ~.* 他本質上是個好人。***from the ~ of my heart,*** genuinely, deeply. 眞誠地；誠摯地；衷心地。***knock the ~ out of (an argument, etc,)*** prove that it is worthless. 打破(一論點等)的根基；推翻(一論點等)；證明(一論點等)無價值。**8** (attrib) lowest, last: (形容用法) 最低的；最後的: *Put the book on the ~ shelf.* 把書放在最下層的架子上。*What's your ~ price?* 你們的最低價是多少？ *Who's the ~ boy of the class?* 該班的末名男生是誰？ ⇨ also gear(1), rock¹(6). □ *vi* ***~ out,*** (economics) reach a low level and remain there: (經濟)降到並停留在最低標準: *The value of our oil shares on the Stock Market has now ~ed out,* ie from now on can only rise, not fall further. 在證券市場上我們的石油股票的價值已經降到最低標準。**~·less** *adj* very deep: 極深的；無底的: *a ~less pit.* 無底的坑。

botu·lism /ˈbɒtjʊlɪzəm ; ˈbɑtʃəˌlɪzəm/ *n* [U] type of food poisoning. 臘腸毒菌病(一種食物中毒)。

bou·doir /ˈbuːdwɑː(r) ; buˈdwɑr/ *n* woman's private sitting-room or dressing-room. (婦人的)閨房。

bou·gain·vil·lea /ˌbuːgənˈvɪlɪə ; ˌbugənˈvɪlɪə/ *n* tropical climbing shrub with tiny flowers surrounded by red, purple, etc bracts. 九重葛(一種熱帶灌木，開小花，花之四周圍繞着紅、紫等色之苞葉)。

bough /baʊ ; baʊ/ *n* large branch coming from the trunk of a tree. 較粗大之樹枝；粗枝。⇨ the illus at tree. 參看 tree 之插圖。

bought /bɔːt ; bɔt/ *pt, pp* of buy.

bouil·lon /ˈbuːjɒn ; ˈbuljɑn/ *n* [U] (F) clear thin soup or broth. (法) 稀薄的肉湯；清燉肉湯。⇨ stock¹(9).

boul·der /ˈbəʊldə(r) ; ˈboldɚ/ *n* large piece of rock, large stone, esp one that has been rounded by water or weather. 大石頭(尤指因水或風雨的侵蝕而變圓者)。

boul·evard /ˈbuːləvɑːd *US:* ˈbʊl- ; ˈbuləˌvɑrd/ *n* (F) wide city street, often with trees on each side. (法)大馬路；大道(兩旁常植有樹木)；林蔭大道。

bounce /baʊns ; baʊns/ *vi, vt* **1** [VP2A, 6A] (of a ball, etc) (cause to) spring or jump back when sent against sth hard: (指球等)(使)遇堅硬物而跳回；彈回: *A rubber ball ~s well.* 橡皮球的彈力好。*The ball ~ed over the wall.* 球跳過牆去了。*She was bouncing a ball.* 她在拍球。**~ *back,*** [VP2C] (fig) recover jauntily from a setback. (喻)得意地從挫折中扳回優勢。**2** [VP2C, 6A] (cause to) move up and down violently or noisily; rush noisily or speedily: (使)跳上跳下；亂衝亂撞: *The boy was bouncing (up and down) on the bed.* 那男孩在床上蹦跳。*He ~d into/out of the room.* 他猛然衝進(出)房間。*She ~d out of her chair.* 她自椅子上跳了起來。*The old car ~d along the bad roads.* 這輛舊車在壞路上顛簸而行。**3** [VP2A] (colloq) (of a cheque) be returned by a bank as worthless: (俗)(指支票)被銀行退票: *Don't worry—my cheque won't ~.* 別擔心——我的支票不會退票的。□ *n* **1** [C] (of a ball) bouncing: (指球)跳回；彈回；反彈: *catch the ball on the ~.* 在球跳起來的時候把它抓住。**2** [U] (of a person) liveliness. (指人)活力。**bouncer** *n* = *chucker-out,* ⇨ chuck¹(1). **bounc·ing** *adj* (colloq) (of a person) strong and healthy. (俗)(指人)健壯的。

bound¹ /baʊnd ; baʊnd/ *n* (usu *pl*) limit: (通常用複數)範圍；界限；止境: *It is beyond the ~s of human knowledge,* Man can know nothing about it. 那是超出人類知識範圍以外的。*There are no ~s to his ambition.* 他的野心是無止境的。*Please keep within the ~s of reason,* do not say foolish things, attempt impracticable things. 請勿越出理智的範圍(不要說愚蠢的話，不要做不能做的事)。*He sets no ~s to his desires.* 他放縱他的欲望。*Is it within the ~s of probability?* 這件事是在可能的範圍以內嗎？ ***out of ~s,*** outside the limits of areas that one is allowed to enter: 禁止入內: *Most of the bars had been placed out of ~s to troops.* 大多數的酒吧都已被列爲禁止軍人進入之地。(US 美 = *off limits*).

bound² /baʊnd ; baʊnd/ *vt* [VP6A, usu passive] limit (lit, fig); set bounds to; be the boundary of: (常用被動語態) 限制 (字面或喩)；定…之界限；爲…之界限: *England is ~ed on the north by Scotland.* 英格蘭北界蘇格蘭。

bound³ /baʊnd ; baʊnd/ *vi* [VP2A, C, 4A] jump, spring, bounce; move or run in jumping movements: 跳；躍；彈回；跳着跑；躍進: *The ball struck the wall and ~ed back to me.* 球碰着牆又向我彈回來。*His heart ~ed with joy.* 他內心歡喜若狂。*His dog came ~ing to meet him.* 他的狗跳躍着來迎接他。*Big rocks were ~ing down the hillside.* 巨石由山坡上滾滾而下。□ *n* jumping movement upward or forward: 跳躍；躍進: *at one ~;* 一跳；一躍; *hit a ball on the ~* (or *rebound* /ˈriːbaʊnd ; ˈriˌbaʊnd/), after it has hit the ground and is in the air again. 在球跳起來的時候擊之。***by leaps and ~s,*** (fig) very rapidly. (喩)極迅速地；急速地。

bound⁴ /baʊnd ; baʊnd/ *part adj* ***~ (for),*** ready to start, having started, in the direction of: 準備啓程前往…；在赴…途中: *Where are you ~ (for),* Where are you going to? 你往哪裏去？ *The ship is ~ for Finland.* 此船係開往芬蘭。*If a British ship is going away from Britain, she is outward ~; if she is returning to Britain, she is homeward ~.* 英國船如果離開英國他往，就是外航；如果是回英國，就是回航。

bound⁵ /baʊnd ; baʊnd/ *pp* of bind. ***~ to do sth,*** **(a)** certain to: 一定: *He hasn't got any money—so he's ~ to turn up sooner or later.* 他沒有錢——所以，他遲早一定會出現的。**(b)** obliged to: 必須: *I'm ~ to visit my grandmother every week.* 我必須每個禮拜去看祖母。**~ *'up in,*** much interested in, very busy with: 埋頭於；專心於；忙於: *He is ~ up in his work.* 他埋頭於他的工作。**~ *'up with,*** closely connected with: 與…有密切關係: *The welfare of the individual is ~ up with the welfare of the community.* 個人的福祉與社會福祉有密切的關係。

bound·ary /ˈbaʊndrɪ ; ˈbaʊndərɪ/ *n* (*pl* -ries) **1** line that marks a limit; dividing line: 分界線；邊界；界限；範圍: *This stream forms a ~ between my land and his.* 這條小河構成我的地與他的地之間的分界線。*A ~ dispute is a quarrel about where a ~ is or ought to be.* 邊界糾紛就是關於界線在何處或應在何處之紛爭。*If something is beyond the ~ of human knowledge, man can know nothing about it.* 如果某事是超出人類之知識範圍以外，人類對它就一無所知。**2** (cricket) hit to or over the ~, scoring 4 or 6 runs. (板球)擊至(或擊過)邊線(可獲四分或六分)。

boun·den /ˈbaʊndən ; ˈbaʊndən/ *adj* (only in) (僅用於) ***my ~ duty,*** (archaic) what my conscience tells me I must do. (古)我的良心要我必須做的事；我的本分。

bounder /ˈbaʊndə(r) ; ˈbaʊndɚ/ *n* (GB dated colloq) untrustworthy, ill-bred person. (英過時俗)不足信賴的人；無良好教養的人；粗魯的人。

bound·less /ˈbaʊndlɪs ; ˈbaʊndlɪs/ *adj* without limits: 無限的；無窮的: *his ~ generosity.* 他的無限的慷慨。**~·ly** *adv*

boun·te·ous /ˈbaʊntɪəs ; ˈbaʊntɪəs/ *adj* (liter) generous; giving or given freely; abundant: (文)慷慨

的;豐富的: *a ~ harvest.* 豐收。**~·ly** *adv*

boun·ti·ful /ˈbaʊntɪfl ; ˈbaʊntəfəl/ *adj* (liter) bounteous. (文)慷慨的;豐富的。**ˈ~·ly** /-fəlɪ ; -flɪ/ *adv*

bounty /ˈbaʊntɪ ; ˈbaʊntɪ/ *n* (*pl* -ties) **1** [U] (formal) freedom in giving; generosity. (正式用語)慷慨;好施。**2** [C] (formal) sth given out of kindness (esp to the poor). (正式用語)(尤指對窮人之)施捨(物); 施與。**3** [C] reward or payment offered (usu by a government) to encourage sb to do sth (eg increase production of goods, kill dangerous wild animals). 獎金(通常由政府所提供以鼓勵某人做某事者,如增加貨物生產,捕殺危險野獸等)。

bou·quet /bʊˈkeɪ ; buˈke/ *n* **1** bunch of flowers (to be) carried in the hand. (持於手中的)花束。**2** perfume of wine. 酒之香味。

bour·bon /ˈbɜːbən ; ˈbʊrbən/ *n* [U] kinds of whisky distilled (in the US) from maize and rye. (美)波旁酒(用玉蜀黍和裸麥釀造的一種威士忌酒)。

bour·geois /ˈbʊəʒwɑː *US:* ˌbʊərˈʒwɑː ; bʊrˈʒwɑ/ *n, adj* (person) of the class that owns property or engages in trade; (pej) (person) concerned chiefly with material prosperity and social status. 布爾喬亞;(擁有資產或經商的)中產階級的(人);(蔑)熱中於物質榮華及社會地位的(人);有中產階級習氣的(人)。**the ~ie** /ˌbʊəʒwɑːˈziː ; ˌbʊrʒwɑˈzi/ *n* persons of this class, collectively. (集合用法)布爾喬亞階級;中產階級。

bourn /bʊən ; born/ *n* (old use) stream. (舊用法)小河;溪。

bourn(e) /bʊən ; born/ *n* (old use) boundary; limit; goal. (舊用法)分界線;界限;終點;目的地;目標。

bourse /bʊəs ; bʊrs/ *n* foreign stock exchange (esp that of Paris). 外國證券交易所;(尤指)巴黎證券交易所。⇨ stock¹(5).

bout /baʊt ; baʊt/ *n* **1** period of exercise, work or other activity: (運動、工作或其他活動之)一回;一次;一番: *a ˈwrestling ~;* 摔角之一回合; *a ~ of fighting;* 一場戰鬥; *a ˈdrinking ~.* 一次飲宴。**2** fit (of illness): (疾病的)發作: *a ~ of influenza;* 一次流行性感冒; *bad coughing ~s.* 一陣陣的劇烈咳嗽。

bou·tique /buːˈtiːk ; buˈtik/ *n* small shop selling articles (clothes, cosmetics, hats, etc) of the latest fashion. 經售最新流行服飾(如服裝、化粧品、帽子等)的小商店; 精品店。

bov·ine /ˈbəʊvaɪn ; ˈbovaɪn/ *adj* of, like, an ox: 牛的;如牛的: *~ stupidity.* 像牛一樣的愚笨。

bov·ril /ˈbɒvrɪl ; ˈbɑvrɪl/ *n* [U] (P) meat extract used like beef tea. (商標)保衞爾牛肉汁。

bow¹ /bəʊ ; bo/ *n* **1** piece of wood curved by a tight string, used for shooting arrows. (射箭用的)弓。⇨ the illus at archer. 參看 archer 之插圖。***have two strings to one's bow,*** have more than one plan, more resources than one. 有不止一個計畫;有幾個辦法。**2** rod of wood with horse-hair stretched from end to end, used for playing the violin, etc. (奏小提琴等用的)弓。⇨ the illus at string. 參看 string 之挿圖。**3** curve; rainbow. 彎形;弓形;虹。**4** knot made with a loop or loops; ribbon, etc, tied in this way: 蝴蝶結;結成蝴蝶結之帶子等: *Tie your shoelaces in a bow.* 把你的鞋帶結成蝴蝶結。*She had a bow of pink ribbon in her hair.* 她的頭髮上有一個用粉紅綢帶打的蝴蝶結。**ˌbow-ˈlegged** *adj* with the legs curved outwards at the knees; bandy. 腿之膝部向外彎曲的; 弓形腿的。**ˌbow ˈlegs** *n pl* such legs. 弓形腿;膝外翻。**ˌbow ˈtie** *n* necktie made into a bow. 蝶形領結。**ˈbow·man** /-mən ; -mən/ *n* (*pl* -men) archer. 弓箭(射)手。□ *vt* use a bow on (a violin, etc). 用弓拉(小提琴等)。**bow·ing** *n*: *The violinist's bowing is excellent.* 這位小提琴家的弓法極佳。

bow² /baʊ ; baʊ/ *vi, vt* **1** [VP2A, C, 6A, 3A] bend the head or body (as a sign of respect or as a greeting, or in submission, or to indicate assent); bend (the head or body): 鞠躬;頷首(表示尊敬、招呼、恭謹或應允);俯(首);彎(身): *I raised my hat to her and she bowed in return.* 我向她舉帽示禮,她鞠躬答禮。*They bowed down to the idol.* 他們向偶像鞠躬致敬。*They bowed their heads in prayer.* 他們低頭禱告。*He bowed before the shrine.* 他在神龕前鞠躬示敬。*He bowed his thanks,* expressed his thanks by bowing. 他鞠躬致謝。[VP15B] ***bow sb in,*** receive a visitor with low bows. 鞠躬以迎某人入內。[VP15B] ***bow sb out,*** bow low to sb as he leaves. 鞠躬恭送某人。***bow oneself out,*** bow as one goes out. 鞠躬告別(而出)。[VP2C, 15A, B] ***bow (oneself) out (of),*** dissociate, disengage: 脫離;退出: *I'm bowing out of this scheme —I think it's a big mistake.* 我正要退出這個計畫—我認爲那是個大錯誤。***bow to sb's opinion, etc,*** submit to it. 服從某人的意見(等)。***have a bowing acquaintance with,*** ⇨ acquaintance. **2** [VP6A, 15B, usu passive] bend: (通常用被動語態)使彎曲: *His father is bowed with age.* 他的父親因年高而彎腰駝背。*The branches were bowed down with the weight of the snow.* 樹枝被積雪的重量壓彎了。□ *n* bending of the head or body (in greeting, etc): 鞠躬;頷首;點頭(打招呼、表示禮節等): *He answered with a low bow.* 他深深一鞠躬表示回答。*He made his bow to the company and left the room.* 他向在座的人們鞠躬後離開房間。

bow³ /baʊ ; baʊ/ *n* **1** (often *pl*) front or forward end of a boat or ship from where it begins to curve. (常用複數)船首;船頭(翹高的部份);艏。***on/off the (port, starboard) bow,*** said of objects within 45° of the point right ahead. (指物體)在船首前面左右45度的弧內(在左舷的前方,在右舷的前方)。⇨ the illus at ship. 參看 ship 之插圖。**2** (in a rowing-boat) oarsman nearest the bow. (在划艇上)最靠近船首之划槳者。⇨ stroke.

Bow Bells /ˌbəʊ ˈbelz ; ˈbo ˈbɛlz/ *n pl* the bells of Bow Church, London. 倫敦 Bow 教堂之鐘。***born within the sound of ~,*** (said of a true Cockney) born in the City of London. 出生於倫敦市區內(指眞正的倫敦人而言)。

bowd·ler·ize /ˈbaʊdləraɪz ; ˈbaʊdləˌraɪz/ *vt* take out of (a book, etc) words, scenes, etc that might be considered improper, unsuitable for young readers, etc. 刪除(書等)不適宜於少年讀者等之猥褻鄙俗的字句,場景等。

bowel /ˈbaʊəl ; ˈbaʊəl/ *n* **1** (usu *pl* except in medical use and when attrib) division of the food canal below the stomach; intestine: (除用於醫學或用作形容詞外通常用複數)腸;腸部: *a ~ complaint.* 腸部疾病;泄瀉。*Keep your ~s open,* don't become constipated. 保持大便暢通。⇨ the illus at alimentary. 參看 alimentary 之插圖。**2** (always *pl*) innermost part: (總是用複數)最內的部份;中心;核心: *in the ~s of the earth,* deep underground. 在地下之深處。

bower /ˈbaʊə(r) ; ˈbaʊə˞/ *n* **1** summer-house in a garden; shady place under trees or climbing plants. 花園裏的涼亭;樹蔭處。**2** (liter) boudoir. (文)(婦人的)閨房。

bowie knife /ˈbəʊɪ naɪf ; ˈboɪ naɪf/ *n* long knife with a blade that is double-edged at the point, used as a weapon. 一種尖端兩面有刄,作武器用的長刀。

bowl¹ /bəʊl ; bol/ *n* **1** deep, round, hollow dish; contents of such a dish: 碗;缽;碗裏所盛之物: *She ate three ~s of rice;* 她吃了三碗米飯; (compounds): (複合字): *ˈfinger-~,* 洗指缽, *ˈsalad-~,* 裝生菜的碗, *ˈsugar-~.* 裝糖的碗。**2** sth shaped like a ~: 碗形物: *the ~ of a spoon.* 湯匙之盛湯部份。*He filled the ~ of his pipe,* put tobacco into it. 他裝滿了煙斗。*The electric light bulb is in an alabaster ~.* 這電燈泡裝在一個雪花石膏似的燈罩裏。**3** (esp US) amphitheatre (for open-air concerts, etc): (尤美)(供露天音樂會等演出之)露天圓形劇場: *The Hollywood B~.* 好萊塢露天圓形劇場。

bowl² /bəʊl ; bol/ *n* **1** heavy, wooden or composition ball made so that it rolls with a bias. 滾木球戲用之沉重的木球(木質或合成物質做成,滾動時球路略微彎曲)。**2** (*pl*) game played with these balls:

(複)滾木球戲;保齡球: *have a game of ~s;* 玩一場滾木球戲; *play (at) ~s.* 玩滾木球戲。

bowl³ /bəʊl ; bol/ *vi, vt* **1** [VP2A] play bowls. 玩滾木球戲。⇨ bowl²(2). **'~·ing-green** *n* area of fine, smooth grass for playing bowls. 玩滾木球戲之草坪。**'~·ing alley** *n* level area of wood, used for skittles, ninepins and tenpins. (撞柱戲、九柱戲及十柱戲中所用的木質的)球道。 **2** [VP2A, 6A] (cricket) send a ball to the batsman: (板球)投(球): *Smith ~ed ten overs.* 史密斯連投了十次球。⇨ over³. **~ (out),** [VP6A, 15B] dismiss (a batsman) by hitting the wicket or knocking the bails off: 因擊中三柱門或擊落柱上橫木而迫使(擊球員)退場; 使出局: *The first two batsmen were ~ed (out).* 頭兩個擊球員被判出局了。 **3 ~ along,** [VP2C] go quickly and smoothly on wheels: (車輛)輕快地行駛: *Our car ~ed along over the smooth roads.* 我們的車子在平滑的路上輕快地前行。 **4 ~ sb over,** [VP 15B] **(a)** knock down. 擊倒(某人)。**(b)** make helpless, overcome: 使狼狽; 使不知所措; 使驚呆; 使崩潰: *He was ~ed over by the news.* 這消息使他不知所措。*Her impudence ~ed me over,* left me speechless with surprise. 她的厚顏使我大爲吃驚。

bowler¹ /'bəʊlə(r) ; 'bolɚ/ *n* **1** person who plays bowls²(2). 玩滾木球戲者。 **2** person who bowls in cricket. (板球戲之)投球手。

bowler² /'bəʊlə(r) ; 'bolɚ/ *n* (also 亦作 ,~ 'hat) hard, rounded, usu black hat. 一種硬的圓頂禮帽(通常爲黑色)。

bow·line /'bəʊlɪn ; 'bolɪn/ *n* (also 亦作 '~ knot) simple but secure knot used by sailors, climbers, etc. 單結套(水手,攀登者等所用之一種簡單而極牢固之索結)。⇨ the illus at knot. 參看 knot 之挿圖。

bowls/ bəʊlz ; bolz/ *n* ⇨ bowl²(2).

bow·man /'bəʊmən ; 'bomən/ *n* (*pl* -men) archer. 弓箭射手。⇨ bow¹(1).

bow·sprit /'bəʊsprɪt ; 'baʊ,sprɪt/ *n* spar that extends from a ship's stem, to which ropes that support sails, etc are fastened. 第一斜桅;艏斜桅;牙檣(自艏材延伸出用以拴帆索之短木)。⇨ the illus at barque. 參看 barque 之挿圖。

bow win·dow /,bəʊ 'wɪndəʊ ; 'bo 'wɪndo/ *n* curved bay window. 弓形窗;凸窗。⇨ the illus at window. 參看 window 之挿圖。

bow-wow /,baʊ 'waʊ ; 'baʊ'waʊ/ *int* imitation of a dog's bark. 模擬之犬吠聲。□ *n* /'baʊ waʊ ; 'baʊ-'waʊ/ (young child's word for a) dog. (兒語)狗。

box¹ /bɒks ; bɑks/ *n* **1** container, usu with a lid, made of wood, cardboard, plastic, metal, etc used for holding solids: 盒;匣;箱: *a box of matches;* 一盒火柴; *a 'tool-box.* 工具匣;工具箱。 *Pack the books in a wooden box.* 把書籍裝在木箱中。**'box-kite** *n* kite made in the form of a box (or two boxes) of light material. 箱形風箏。**'box-number** *n* number used in a newspaper advertisement as an address to which answers may be sent (and forwarded from the newspaper office). 報紙廣告中爲便於讀者與登廣告者通訊所用之代替住址的編號。**PO Box No** *n* number used as part of an address to which letters, etc may be directed. 郵政信箱號碼。⇨ also call-box, Christmas-box, letter-box, money-box, pillar-box. **2** separate compartment, with seats for several persons, in a theatre, concert hall, etc. (戲院、音樂廳等之)包廂。**'box-office** *n* office for booking seats in a theatre, concert hall, etc: (戲院、音樂廳等之)售票處;票房: *The play was a box-office success,* a financial success. 該劇演出成功(指賣座好,票房記錄高)。 **3** compartment in a law court for a special purpose: 法庭之特別席位: *'jury-box;* 陪審團席; *'witness-box.* 證人席。 **4** small hut or shelter, eg for a sentry or railway signalman. 小亭;哨亭;(鐵路上的)信號員亭。 **5** separate compartment in a stable or railway truck for a horse. 馬廐或火車貨車廂中一馬所佔之小間隔;馬欄。 **6** raised seat for the driver of a carriage(1) or coach(1). (馬車上之)馭者座。**box·ful** /-fʊl ; -,fʊl/ *n* full box¹(1) (*of* sth). 一盒;一箱(與 of 連用,後接某物)。□ *vt* [VP6A] put into a box. 裝於盒中;裝箱。 **box sb/sth up,** [VP15B] shut up in a small space. 將某人關在(置某物於)一個小空間裏;幽禁某人。

box² /bɒks ; bɑks/ *vt, vi* [VP6A, 2A, 3A] ***box (with),*** fight (sb) with the fists, usu with thick gloves, for sport: 拳擊;與…拳擊: *Do you box,* Do you fight in this way? 你會拳擊嗎? ***box sb's ears,*** give him a blow with the open hand on the ear. 打(某人)一個耳光;摑。 **'box·ing-glove** *n* padded glove (one of a pair) for use in boxing. 拳擊手套。**'box·ing-match** *n* fight between two boxers. 拳擊比賽。□ *n* slap or blow with the open hand on the ear. 打耳光;掌頰;摑。**boxer** /'bɒksə(r) ; 'bɑksɚ/ *n* **1** person who boxes. 拳擊者;拳擊家;拳手。 **2** breed of dog (like a bulldog). 拳師犬(像鬥牛犬之一種猛犬)。**box·ing** *n* [U] organised sport of fist fighting. 拳擊。

box³ /bɒks ; bɑks/ *n* [U] **1** (kinds of) small, evergreen shrub, used in garden borders. 黃楊(常綠小灌木,用作花園的圍籬)。 **2** (also 亦作 **'box·wood**) wood of this shrub. 黃楊木。

Box·ing Day /'bɒksɪŋ deɪ ; 'bɑksɪŋ de/ *n* first weekday after Christmas Day. 聖誕節後的第一個週日。

boy /bɔɪ ; bɔɪ/ *n* **1** male child up to the age of 17 or 18. (十七、八歲以下之) 男孩; 男童。**'boy·friend,** favoured male companion of a girl or young woman. 男朋友(女孩子或年輕婦女所喜歡的男伴)。 **2** son (colloq, of any age): 兒子(俗,不限年齡): *He has two boys and one girl.* 他有兩個兒子一個女兒。 **3** *int* (US sl) expressing enthusiasm, relief, surprise, etc. (美俚)好傢伙(表示熱心、放心、驚訝等之感歎詞)。**'boy·hood** /-hʊd ; -hʊd/ *n* [U] time when one is/was a boy. 男孩時代;少男時代。**boy·ish** *adj* of, for, like, a boy. 男孩的;似男孩的。

boy·cott /'bɔɪkɒt ; 'bɔɪ,kɑt/ *vt* [VP6A] (join with others and) refuse to have anything to do with, to trade with (a person, business firm, country, etc); refuse to handle (goods, etc). (與他人、他公司、他國等聯合)拒絕與(某人、公司、國家等)來往、通商;拒絕買賣(貨物等);抵制;杯葛。□ *n* ~ing; treatment of this kind: 聯合抵制(貨物等);杯葛: *put sb/his shop/goods under a ~;* 聯合抵制某人(其商店,貨物); *put a ~ on sb, etc.* 聯合抵制某人等。

bra /brɑː ; brɑ/ *n* (colloq abbr of) brassière. (俗)奶罩(爲 brassière 之略)。

brace¹ /breɪs ; bres/ *n* **1** sth used to clasp, tighten or support, eg the roof or walls of a building. 鉤住、拉緊或支持(建築物之頂或牆壁等)之物。**2** revolving tool for holding another tool, eg a *bit* for boring holes, driving in screws, etc. (鑽子或螺絲起子之)曲柄。 **3** (*pl* unchanged) pair or couple (of dogs, game-birds): (複數不變) 一對 (狗、獵禽); 一雙: *five ~ of partridge.* 五對鷓鴣。**4** (*pl*) (US 美 =*suspenders*) straps passing over the shoulders, fastened to the front and back of trousers to keep them up. (複)吊褲帶;背帶(搭過兩肩之褲子背帶)。 **5** (often *pl*) appliance of bands and wires fastened to the teeth to correct their alignment. (常用複數)齒列矯正器。 **6** (printing) (印刷) ⇨ bracket(2).

a brace and bit

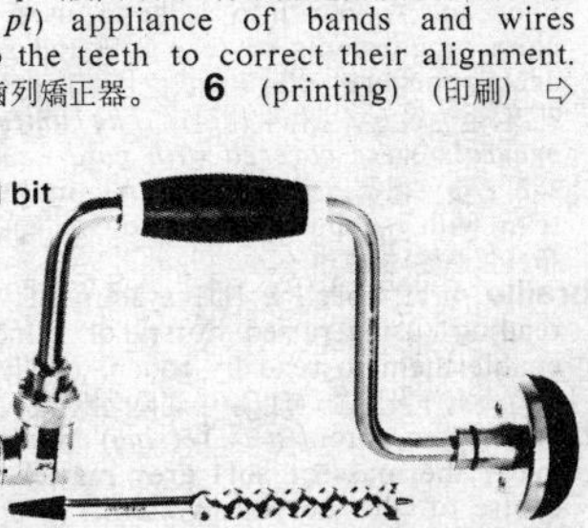

brace[2] /breɪs ; bres/ *vt* **1** [VP6A] support; give firmness to: 支持;使堅固;縛緊;撐牢;拉緊: *The struts are firmly ~d.* 那些支柱上得很牢靠。 **2** [VP6A, 15B, 16A] *~ (up),* steady oneself; stand firm: 使自己穩定或沉着;站穩;奮起;振作起來: *B~ up!* 打起精神來;振作起來! *He ~d himself to meet the blow.* 他振奮起來以接受打擊。 **3** (usu as *part adj* in *-ing*) enliven; stimulate: (通常作現在分詞形容詞用) 使活潑;使有生氣;激勵;鼓舞: *bracing air;* 令人精神爽快的空氣; *a bracing climate.* 宜人的氣候。

brace·let /ˈbreɪslɪt ; ˈbreslɪt/ *n* ornamental band or chain for the wrist or arm. 手鐲;臂鐲。

bracken /ˈbrækən ; ˈbrækən/ *n* [U] large fern that grows on hillsides, waste land, etc; mass of such fern. 蕨;羊齒(生於荒地及山坡等處);此種植物之一叢。

bracket /ˈbrækɪt ; ˈbrækɪt/ *n* **1** wood or metal support for a shelf; support on a wall for a gas or electric lamp. (釘於牆上之) 托架;撐架;(牆上所裝的) 煤氣燈架或電燈座。 **2** (printing, writing) any one of the paired marks () (*round ~s or parentheses*), [] (*square ~s*), {} (*braces*), used for enclosing words, figures etc to indicate separation from what precedes and follows. (印刷,書寫) 括弧(指圓括弧(),方括弧[ ],或大括弧{ }之任一)。 ⇨ App 9. 參看附錄九。 **3** grouping; classification: 類別;分類: *income ~,* eg of incomes from £3000 to £4500; 所得分類(例如所得自三千鎊至四千五百鎊之一類); *age ~,* eg 20 to 30 years of age. 年齡類別(例如二十歲至三十歲者)。 □ *vt* [VP6A, 15B] put inside, join with, ~s; put together to imply connection or equality: 置於括弧中;以括弧聯合;放在一起(以表示關聯或平等): *Jones and Smith were ~ed together at the top of the list.* 瓊斯與史密斯並列第一。

brack·ish /ˈbrækɪʃ ; ˈbrækɪʃ/ *adj* (of water) slightly salt; between salt and fresh water. (指水) 略有鹽味的;介於鹹水與淡水之間的。

bract /brækt ; brækt/ *n* [C] (bot) leaf-like part of a plant, often highly coloured, situated below a flower or cluster of flowers (as in bougainvillea, poinsettia). (植物) 苞;苞葉;花篦(植物之生長於花或花叢下之似葉部份,常呈鮮艷之顏色,如九重葛,聖誕紅者是)。

brad /bræd ; bræd/ *n* thin, flat nail with no head or a very small head. 無頭釘(或頭甚小者);曲頭釘;土釘。

brad·awl /ˈbrædɔːl ; ˈbrædˌɔl/ *n* small tool for piercing holes for brads or screws. 小錐子(用以鑽孔供上無頭釘或螺旋釘者)。 ⇨ the illus at tool. 參看 tool 之插圖。

brae /breɪ; bre/ *n* (Scot) slope; hillside. (蘇) 斜坡;山坡。

brag /bræg ; bræg/ *vi* (-gg-) *~ (of/about),* [VP2A, 3A] boast: 自誇;自吹;誇耀: *~ of what one has done.* 誇耀自己的作爲。 **brag·ging** *n* [U] **brag·gart** /ˈbrægət; ˈbrægɚt/ *n* person who ~s. 自誇者;大言者。

Brah·min /ˈbrɑːmɪn ; ˈbrɑmɪn/ *n* member of the highest Hindu priestly caste. 婆羅門(印度四大階級中之最高階級)的一員。

braid /breɪd ; bred/ *n* **1** [C] number of strands of hair woven together: 髮辮;辮子: *She wears her hair in ~s.* 她把她的頭髮編成辮子。 **2** [U] silk, linen, etc woven into a band, used for edging cloth or garments or (esp gold and silver ~) for decoration: (絲、亞麻等編成之) 辮帶;繐帶(用作衣布之花邊;金色銀色者尤作裝飾用): *The uniforms of the generals were covered with gold ~.* 將官的制服上裝飾着金色繐帶。 □ *vt* [VP6A] make into ~(s); trim with ~; put (hair) into ~s. 編成辮帶;飾以繐帶;將(頭髮)編成辮子。

braille /breɪl ; brel/ *n* [U] system of writing and reading (using raised dots) for blind people, to enable them to read by touch. (利用浮凸點之排列) 供盲人寫作及閱讀,可以用手觸摸之點字法。

brain /breɪn ; bren/ *n* **1** (*sing*) (in man and animals) the mass of soft grey matter in the head, centre of the nervous system: (單數) (人類或動物的) 腦(爲神經系統的中樞): *The human ~ is a complex organ.* 人類的腦是一複雜的器官。 *The creature's ~ weighs a quarter of a kilo.* 這動物的腦重四分之一公斤。 ⇨ the illus at head. 參看 head 之插圖。 **2** (colloq, usu *pl*) skull and brain(1) thought of together: (俗,通常用複數) 頭腦;腦袋: *He fell and dashed his ~s out on the rocks.* 他摔在岩石上,腦袋開了花。 ***blow out one's ~s,*** ⇨ blow[1](13). **3** (*pl*) animal's ~s, eaten as food: (複) (供作食物之動物的) 腦: *calf's/sheep's ~s.* 牛(羊)腦。 **4** (colloq, usu *sing*) mind; intellect: (俗,通常用單數) 心智;智力;智慧;腦筋;腦子: *have a good ~;* 有一副好腦筋;很聰明; *use one's ~(s).* 動腦筋;運用智慧。 ***beat/rack one's ~(s) (about sth),*** think very hard. (爲某事) 絞腦汁;苦思。 ***have sth*** (eg money, sex) ***on the ~,*** think constantly about it. 經常想着某事(如金錢、性問題等)。 ***tax one's ~,*** set oneself/be set a difficult mental task. 絞盡腦汁。 ***pick sb's ~(s),*** learn and use his ideas. 剽竊或抄襲某人的思想。 **5** [C] clever, brilliant person: 聰明卓越的人: *He's the ~ of the school staff.* 他是學校教職員的智囊。 **6** (compounds) (複合字) **'~-child** *n* original idea, etc attributed to a person or group. (某人或某一群人的) 腦力的產物(如創見等)。 **'~ drain** *n* ⇨ drain[1](2). **'~-fag** *n* (colloq) mental exhaustion: (俗) 精神疲勞;神經衰弱;腦衰竭: *suffering from ~-fag.* 患神經衰弱。 **'~ fever** *n* inflammation of the ~ 腦膜炎。 **'~-storm** *n* mental upset with uncontrolled emotion, eg weeping, and violence. 腦猝變;腦猝病(一種情緒不能控制,如哭泣及行爲暴烈的精神錯亂)。 **'~-teaser** *n* difficult problem; puzzle. 困難的問題;難題。 **'B~s Trust** *n* group of reputed experts giving advice, or answering questions put to them by members of an audience. (提供忠告,或答覆聽衆或觀衆所提出的問題的) 專家小組;智囊團。 **'~-washing** *n* process of forcing a person to reject old beliefs and accept new beliefs by use of extreme mental pressure, eg persistent questioning. 洗腦(使用極端的精神壓迫,如長時間的審問,以達到迫使某人放棄舊思想接受新思想之過程)。 **'~-wave** *n* (colloq) sudden inspiration or bright idea. (俗) 突然的靈感;靈機一動。 □ *vt* [VP6A] kill by a heavy blow on the head: 猛擊頭部以打死: *~ an ox.* 擊牛之頭以斃之。 **~·less** *adj* stupid. 無頭腦的;愚笨的。 **~y** *adj* (-ier, -iest) clever. 聰明的。

braise /breɪz ; brez/ *vt* [VP6A] cook (meat, vegetables) slowly in a covered pan or pot: 燉(肉、蔬菜);煨;燜: *~d beef/onions.* 燉牛肉(洋葱)。

brake[1] /breɪk ; brek/ *n* device for reducing speed or stopping motion, eg of a bicycle, motor-car, train, etc: (脚踏車、汽車、火車等之) 煞車;制動機: *put on/apply/* (colloq) (俗) *slam on the ~s;* 使用煞車;將車煞住; *act as a ~ upon* (*progress, initiative, etc*), hamper it; control it. 阻礙(進展,發動等);控制。 ⇨ the illus at motor 參看 motor 之插圖。 □ *vt, vi* [VP6A, 2A] put on the ~s: 煞車: *The driver ~d (his car) suddenly.* 駕駛者突然煞住(車子)。 **'~-man** /-mən ; -mən/ *n* (*pl* -men) (US) guard[1](5). (美) (火車之) 列車長。

brake[2] /breɪk ; brek/ *n* area or band of brushwood, thick undergrowth or bracken. 矮叢林區;叢林地帶。

brake[3] /breɪk ; brek/ *n* large wagon or open carriage pulled by one or more horses, and with

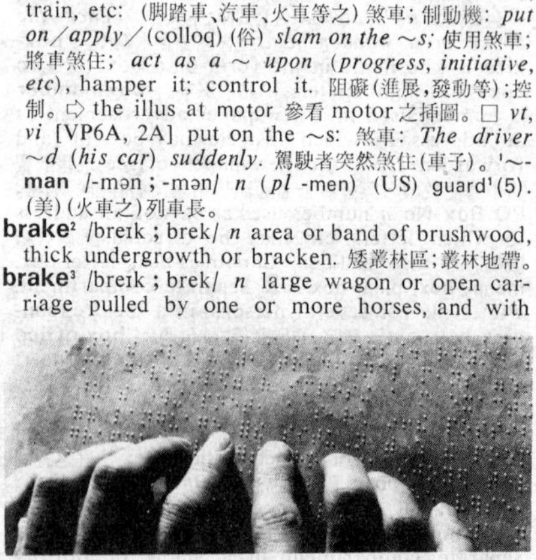

reading braille

facing side seats, formerly used for pleasure outings. 一種大馬車 (有篷或無篷,由一匹或數匹馬牽曳,兩邊有對面座位,從前用以出外遊玩)。⇨ shooting-brake.

bramble /ˈbræmbl ; ˈbræmbl/ *n* rough shrub with long prickly shoots; blackberry bush. 荆棘;懸鉤子;黑莓灌木叢。

bran /bræn ; bræn/ *n* [U] outer covering (husks) of grain (wheat, rye, etc) separated from flour by sifting. 糠;穀殼;麥麩。

branch /brɑːntʃ *US:* bræntʃ ; bræntʃ/ *n* **1** arm-like division of a tree, growing out from the trunk, or a bough, or another ~, ⇨ the illus at tree: 樹枝 (參看 tree 之挿圖): *He climbed up the tree and hid among the ~es.* 他爬上樹藏到樹枝裏面。 **2** (often attrib) division or subdivision of a river, road, railway, mountain range, etc; division or subdivision of a family, subject of knowledge, organization, etc: (常作形容用法) (河流的) 支流;(道路的)支路;(山脈的)支脈; (家族的)支系; (學術的)部門; (機構的)分支機構(等): *There is a ~ post office quite near.* 附近有一個郵局支局。*The bank has ~es in all parts of the country.* 該銀行在全國各地皆有分行。*English is a ~ of the Germanic family of languages.* 英語是日耳曼語系中的一支。***root and ~,*** ⇨ root¹(1). □ *vi* [VP2A, C] send out, divide into, ~es: 長出枝子;分枝;分叉: *The trees ~ (out) over the river.* 那些樹的枝子伸到河上去了。*The road ~es here.* 路在此分叉。 ***~ off,*** (of a car, road, train, etc) leave a main route and take a minor one. (指汽車、道路、火車等)離開幹道進入支線;分叉;分岐。 ***~ out,*** (of a person, business firm, etc) expand in a new direction, open new departments or lines of activities. (指人、商行等)向新的方向發展;創設新的部門或業務。**~y** *adj* with many ~es. 多枝的。

brand /brænd ; brænd/ *n* **1** trademark (painted or printed on boxes, tins, packets, etc); particular kind of goods with such a mark: (印於盒子、罐頭、包裝等上的)商標;牌子;某種牌子的貨物: *the best ~s of cigars;* 牌子最好的雪茄; *an excellent ~ of coffee.* 牌子極好的咖啡。ˌ**~-ˈnew** *adj* quite new (as if freshly stamped with a ~). 全新的(好似剛蓋上商標的);簇新的;嶄新的。 **2** piece of burning wood: 燃燒中的木頭: ***a ~ from the burning,*** person rescued from the consequences of sin; converted sinner. 從罪惡的淵藪中被救出的人;悛悔的罪人。**3** (also 亦作 ˈ**~·ing-iron**), iron used red-hot, for burning a mark into a surface; mark made in this way; (in olden times) mark burned on criminals, hence, (fig) mark of guilt or disgrace: (燒紅烙印用的)烙鐵;烙印;(古時)罪犯身上的烙印;(喻)犯罪或不名譽的標記: *the ~ of Cain,* of a murderer. 謀殺者的標記;殺人罪。**4** (poet) torch. (詩)火炬。□ *vt* [VP6A, 16B] **1** mark (cattle, goods, etc) with a ~: 打烙印於(牲畜等);印商標於(貨物): *On big farms cattle are usually ~ed.* 在大農場上,牲畜通常打有烙印。*Criminals used to be ~ed.* 罪犯從前是打有烙印的。(fig) (喻) *These frightful experiences are ~ed on his memory.* 這些可怕的經歷深深印入他的記憶。 **2** give (sb) a bad name: 指(某人)爲壞人;栽汚: *~ sb with infamy;* 破壞某人的名譽; *~ sb (as) a heretic.* 指某人爲異教徒。

bran·dish /ˈbrændɪʃ ; ˈbrændɪʃ/ *vt* [VP6A] wave about (to display, or before using): 炫耀地揮舞; (使用前)揮舞: *~ing a sword.* 揮劍。

brandy /ˈbrændɪ ; ˈbrændɪ/ *n* [C, U] strong alcoholic drink distilled from wine of grapes: 白蘭地酒: *two brandies and sodas,* two glasses of ~ mixed with soda water. 兩杯攙蘇打水的白蘭地酒。ˈ**~-ball** *n* kind of sweet. 白蘭地糖果 (糖果之一種)。ˈ**~-snap** *n* kind of gingerbread wafer. 一種有白蘭地味道之薑餅。

bran-new /ˌbrænˈnjuː ; ˈbrænˈnju/ *adj* = brand-new.

brash /bræʃ ; bræʃ/ *adj* (colloq) (俗) **1** saucy; cheeky. 莽撞的;無禮的。**2** hasty; rash. 鹵莽的;輕率的。

brass /brɑːs *US:* bræs ; bræs/ *n* **1** [U] bright yellow metal made by mixing copper and zinc: (由銅和鋅合成十分光亮的)黃銅: *~ rods/buttons;* 黃銅桿(扣子); *a ~ foundry.* 黃銅鑄造廠。***get down to ~ tacks,*** begin to talk, discuss, etc in plain, straightforward terms. 直截了當說、討論等;開門見山。ˌ**~ ˈhat,** (army sl) high-ranking officer. (軍俚) 高級軍官。ˌ**~ ˈplate,** oblong plate of ~, on a door or gate, with the name, trade, occupation, etc, eg as used by doctors, lawyers, business firms. (醫生、律師、商行等門外所懸掛刻有姓名、行業、職業等之長方形)銅牌。ˌ**top ˈ~,** (colloq, collective) high-ranking officers, managers, etc. (俗,集合用法)高級軍官;經理。**2** [U] (and *pl*) things made of ~, eg candlesticks, bowls, ornaments: (單數及複數均可) 黃銅製品; 黃銅器(如燭臺,碗,裝飾物): *clean/do the ~/the ~es.* 擦黃銅器。 **3 the ~,** (collective) (mus) musical instruments made of ~. (集合用法) (音樂) 銅管樂器。ˌ**~ ˈband,** band of musicians with ~ instruments. 管樂隊(卽軍樂隊)。 **4** [U] (GB sl) money. (英俚) 錢。 **5** [U] (sl) impudence. (俚)厚顏;無恥。⇨ brazen. **~y** *adj* (-ier, -iest) **1** like ~ in colour or sound. 黃銅色的;聲音如銅管樂器的。⇨ 3 above. 參看上列第3義。 **2** impudent. 厚顏的;無恥的。

bras·sard /ˈbræsɑːd ; ˈbræsɑrd/ *n* (arm-band bearing a) badge worn on the sleeve. 臂章;袖章;臂鎧。

brass·erie /ˈbræsərɪ ; ˌbræsˈri/ *n* beer-saloon or beer-garden (usu supplying food as well as drink). 啤酒店;啤酒園(通常並供應食物)。

brass·iere, ·ière /ˈbræsɪə(r) *US:* brəˈzɪər ; brəˈzɪr/ *n* (usu shortened to *bra*) woman's close-fitting support for the breasts. (通常略作 bra) (婦女用的) 胸罩;奶罩。

brat /bræt ; bræt/ *n* (derog) child. (貶) 小兒;乳臭未乾的小子。

bra·vado /brəˈvɑːdəʊ ; brəˈvɑdo/ *n* **1** [U] display of boldness or daring: 故作勇武;虛張聲勢: *do sth out of ~,* in order to display one's courage. 爲表現其勇武而做某事。 **2** [C] (*pl* ~es, ~s) instance of this. 故作勇武之實例。

brave /breɪv ; brev/ *adj* (-r, -st) **1** ready to face danger, pain or suffering; having no fear: 勇敢的;無畏的: *as ~ as a lion.* 勇如猛獅。*Be ~!* 勇敢些! *It was ~ of him to enter the burning building.* 他敢進入那燃燒着的房屋,眞是勇敢。 **2** needing courage: 需要勇氣的: *a ~ act.* 英勇的行爲。**3** (old use) fine and splendid: (舊用法) 艷麗的;華麗的;美好的: *this ~ new world.* 這美好的新世界。□ *n* (poet) American Indian warrior. (詩) 北美印第安勇士。□ *vt* [VP6A] face, go into, meet, without showing fear: 勇敢地面對、進入、從事、應付; 冒…之危險: *He had ~d death a hundred times.* 他出生入死達百次之多。*We decided to ~ the storm,* to go out in spite of the storm. 我們決定冒暴風雨出去。 ***~ it out,*** [VP15B] disregard, defy, suspicion or blame. 不顧猜疑或責難;硬幹下去。**~·ly** *adv* **brav·ery** /ˈbreɪvərɪ ; ˈbrevərɪ/ *n* [U] **1** courage; being ~. 英勇;勇敢;勇氣。 **2** (old use) splendour (of dress, etc): (舊用法) (服裝等的) 華麗: *decked out in all their ~ry.* 穿着他們最華麗的衣服。

bravo /ˌbrɑːˈvəʊ ; ˈbrɑvo/ *n, int* (*pl* ~es, ~s) (cry of approval) Well done! Excellent! (喝采聲)好極了!要得!

brawl /brɔːl ; brɔl/ *n* noisy quarrel or fight. 大聲的爭吵;吵鬧;吵架。□ *vi* [VP2A] quarrel noisily; take part in a ~; (of streams) flow noisily (over stones and rocks). 爭吵;吵鬧;吵架;(指溪流經過石上)淙淙而流。**~er** *n* person who takes part in a ~. 爭吵者;吵鬧者;吵架者。

brawn /brɔːn ; brɔn/ *n* [U] **1** muscle; strength. 肌肉;體力。 **2** (not US) meat (esp pork) cut up, spiced and pickled, and compressed. (非美語) (經過切塊及壓縮的) 醃肉; (尤指) 醃豬肉。**~y** *adj* (-ier, -iest) muscular: 肌肉多的;有力的;強壯的: *The miner has ~y arms.* 那礦工的胳臂很強壯。

bray /breɪ ; bre/ *n* cry of an ass; sound of a trum-

brass and woodwind instruments

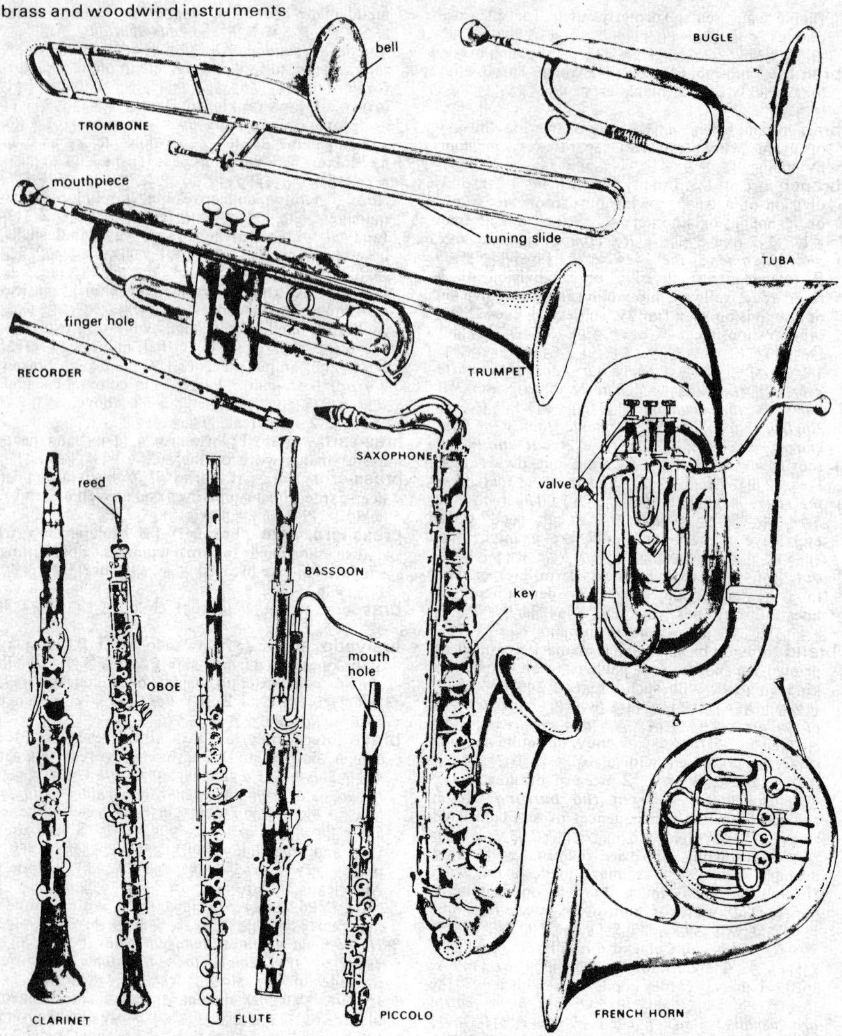

pet. 驢叫聲；小喇叭聲。□ *vi* [VP2A] make a cry or sound of this kind. 發此種聲音。

braze /breɪz ; brez/ *vt* [VP6A] solder with an alloy of brass and zinc. 以銅鋅合金銲接。

brazen /ˈbreɪzn ; ˈbrezn̩/ *adj* **1** made of brass; like brass: 黃銅製的；如黃銅的： *a* ~ (= hard-sounding) *voice;* 宏亮的聲音； *the ~ notes of a trumpet.* 小喇叭之響亮的聲音。 **2** (often 常作 **ˈ~-faced**) shameless. 厚顏的；無恥的。□ *vt* (only in) (僅用於) ~ ***it out,*** behave, in spite of having done wrong, as if one has nothing to be ashamed of. (雖已做錯仍)厚着臉皮幹下去。

braz·ier /ˈbreɪzɪə(r) ; ˈbreʒɚ/ *n* portable open metal framework (like a basket), usu on legs, for holding a charcoal or coal fire. (可移動，通常有脚架的)金屬炭盆；火盆。

breach /briːtʃ ; britʃ/ *n* **1** breaking or neglect (*of* a rule, duty, agreement, etc): 違犯；怠忽；破壞(與of連用，後接規則、職責、契約等)： *a ~ of the peace,* unlawful fighting in a public place, eg the streets; 在公共場所(如街頭)打架；妨害治安；騷動； *a ~ of contract* (in comm, etc); (商業上等之)違約(違反契約上的規定)； *a ~ of promise* (esp of a promise to marry); 背約；毀約(尤指婚約)； *a ~ of faith,* act of disloyalty; 不忠的行爲； *a ~ of confidence;* 洩密的行爲； *a ~ of security.* 違反安全的行爲。 **2** opening, esp one made in a defensive wall, etc by artillery, attacking forces, etc: 防禦工事等爲敵人炮火所穿之破洞；突破口： *step into/fill the ~,* come forward to help; 上前幫助； *throw/fling oneself into the ~,* help those who are in trouble or danger; 救人於危難之境；救人於水火之中； *stand in the ~,* bear the heaviest part of the attack; do most of the hard work. 承擔最猛烈的攻擊；獨當難局；做大部份的困難工作；挑重擔。 **3** broken place; gap: 破洞；缺口；裂縫；縫隙： *The sheep got out of the field after one of them had made a ~ in the hedge.*—隻羊在籬笆上弄了一個洞，所有的羊都從牧地跑走了。*The* *waves made a ~ in the sea wall.* 海浪在防波堤上衝出了一個缺口。 □ *vt* [VP6A] make a gap in, break through (a defensive wall, etc). 衝破;突破(防禦工事等)。

bread /bred ; brɛd/ *n* [U] food made by mixing flour with water and yeast, kneading, and baking in an oven: 麵包: *a loaf/slice/piece of ~;* 一條(片,塊)麵包; (sl) money: (俚)錢: *I'm only doing it for the ~.* 我純粹是爲了錢才做那件事的。 **~ and butter** /ˌbred n ˈbʌtə(r) ; ˈbrɛdṇˈbʌtɚ/, **(a)** slice(s) of ~ spread with butter. 塗有牛油的麵包片。 **~-and-butter letter,** one of thanks for hospitality. 多謝款待的謝函。 **(b)** (colloq) means of living: (俗)生計: *earn one's ~ and butter by writing.* 靠寫作謀生。 ***one's daily ~,*** one's means of living. 謀生之道; 每日的生計; 每日的食糧。 ***earn one's ~,*** make enough money to live on. 餬口;謀生。 ***know which side one's ~ is buttered,*** know where one may have advantages, where one's interest lies. 知道自己的利益所在;知道如何於己有利。 ***take the ˈ~ out of sb's mouth,*** take away his means of living, eg by business competition. 奪人之生計(如藉商業競爭);搶人家的飯碗。 **ˈ~·crumb** *n* [C] tiny bit of the inner part of a loaf, esp crumbled for use in cooking. 麵包屑;碎麵包(尤指弄碎而用於烹飪者)。 **ˈ~·fruit** *n* tree with starchy fruit, grown in the South Sea Islands and W Africa. 麵包樹 (果實含澱粉，產於南太平洋諸島及西非)。 **ˈ~-line** *n* line of people waiting for food given as charity or relief: 領麵包隊伍;領賑濟食糧或救濟品的隊伍: (fig) (喻) *on the ~line,* very poor. 極貧窮的;赤貧的。 **ˈ~·stuffs** *n pl* grain, flour. 製麵包的原料(麥、麵粉)。 **ˈ~·win·ner** *n* person who works to support a family. 負擔家庭生計者。

breadth /bretθ ; brɛdθ/ *n* [U] ⇨ broad¹(2). **1** distance or measure from side to side: 寬度;寬;闊: *ten feet in ~.* 十呎寬。⇨ hair(2). **2** largeness (of mind or view); boldness of effect (in music or art). 胸襟寬大; 氣量寬宏; (音樂或藝術之)雄渾。 **ˈ~·ways, ˈ~·wise** *adv* so that the broad side is in front. 橫(放);橫(置);橫着地。

break¹ /breɪk ; brek/ *vt, vi* (*pt* broke /brəʊk ; brok/ old Eng 古英語作 brake /breɪk ; brek/, *pp* broken /ˈbrəʊkən ; ˈbrokən/) **1** [VP6A, 15B, 2A, C] (of a whole thing) (cause to) go or come into two or more separate parts as the result of force, a blow or strain (but not by cutting): (指完整的東西) 打破; 擊破; 打斷;破碎; 破裂; 斷 (但非由切割所致): *When she dropped the teapot it broke.* 她把茶壺掉在地上打破了。*The boy fell from the tree and broke his leg.* 那男孩從樹上跌下,跌斷了腿。*Glass ~s easily.* 玻璃容易破碎。 *If you pull too hard you will ~ the rope.* 你如果太用力拉，就會把繩子拉斷。 *The string broke.* 繩子斷了。 ***~ into/to pieces; ~ in two, etc,*** (cause to) come or go into pieces, in two, etc parts: (使)成碎片;(使)破成兩半: *He broke the box into pieces.* 他把匣子打成粉碎。*When I hit the ball, my bat broke in two.* 當我擊球時,我的球棒斷成兩截。 **2** [VP6A, 15B, 2A, C] (of a part or parts) (cause to) be separate or discontinuous because of force or strain: (指部份) (使)分離;(使)斷折: *He broke a branch from the tree.* 他從樹上折下一枝樹枝。*The door-handle has broken off.* 門柄已經折斷。*A large part of it broke away,* came off. 它斷了一大塊。 ***~ sb/oneself of a habit,*** succeed in getting him/oneself to give it up. 使某人(自己)戒除一種習慣。 **3** [VP6A] make (sth) useless by injuring an essential part (of a machine, apparatus, etc): 損壞;破壞(機器等): *~ a clock/a sewing-machine.* 損壞一座鐘(一架縫紉機)。 **4** [VP 2D, 22] (with *adjj*): (與形容詞連用): ***~ ˈeven,*** make neither a profit nor a loss. 不賺也不虧;成和局;不分勝負。 ***~ ˈloose (from),*** get or become separate: 掙脫或脫離(鎖鍊等): *The dog has broken loose,* got free from its chain. 狗掙脫鎖鍊了。 *All hell has broken loose,* all the devils in hell have escaped; (fig) (used to describe a scene of confusion, eg a bombardment). 地獄裏所有的惡魔都逃出來了;(喻) (用以描寫混亂的情形,例如砲轟)。 ***~ sth open,*** get it open by using force: 用力打開;撬開: *~ open a safe/door/the lid of a desk.* 用力打開保險櫃(門,桌面)。 **5** [VP2A, C] (with various subjects): (與各種主詞連用): *The abscess/blister/bubble broke,* burst. 膿瘡(水泡,氣泡)破了。 *Day was beginning to ~,* daylight was beginning. 天開始亮了。⇨ daybreak. *His voice is beginning to ~,* change in quality as he reaches manhood. 他的聲音開始變粗了(長大成人的現象)。*She was filled with emotion and her voice broke,* She faltered, was unable to speak clearly because of emotion. 她激動得說不出話來。 *The storm broke,* began, burst into activity. 暴風雨驟然而來。 *The fine weather/The heat-wave/The frost broke,* The period of fine weather, etc ended after being settled. 好天氣(熱天氣,霜寒)(經過一段持續之後)突然轉變。 Cf 參較 How long will the fine weather *hold?* 這好天氣將會持續好久？ *The clouds broke* (= parted, showed an opening) *and the sun came through.* 雲開出一條縫隙,太陽就鑽出來了。 *The waves were ~ing* (= curling and falling) *over/on/against the rocks.* 浪濤沖擊着岩石。 *The sea was ~ing* (= sending waves that were ~ing) *on the beach/over the wrecked ship.* 海浪沖刷着海灘(破船的殘骸)。*The enemy broke* (= developed gaps in their lines, fell into confusion) *and fled.* 敵軍敗陣而逃。*When the bank broke* (= was unable to carry on business because of lack of funds), *many people were ruined.* 當銀行倒閉時,許多人都跟着破產了。*A good bowler can make the ball ~,* (in cricket) change from its course when it strikes the ground. (板球)好的球手能使球着地時改變方向。 **6** [VP6A] (with various objects): (與各種受詞連用): ***~ sb's back/neck/nose, etc,*** cause the bone(s) of the back, etc to be out of the right position. 擊斷某人的脊骨(頸項、鼻樑等)。 ⇨ back¹(1). ***~ the bank,*** exhaust its funds; win all the money that the person managing a gambling game has. 把莊家所有的錢都贏來;耗光莊家的賭本。 ***~ bounds,*** (mil) go out of bounds without permission or authority. (軍) 擅自進入禁止軍人進入之場所。 ***~ one's fall,*** weaken its effect, make it less violent. 減弱其摔跌之力。 ***~ the force of sth,*** reduce its force by bearing part of it: 減弱某物的力量: *The tall hedge ~s the force of the wind.* 高的樹籬能減弱風力。 ⇨ windbreak. ***~ fresh/new ground,*** (fig) start work at sth new. (喻)開闢新天地;開創新事業。 ***~ sb's heart,*** reduce him to despair. 令某人心碎; 令某人絕望。 ***~ a man,*** ruin him; compel him to reveal a secret, etc. 使某人破產; 毀滅某人; 迫使其吐露秘密。 ***~ the news,*** make it known. 洩漏消息。 ***~ the (bad) news (to sb),*** reveal the news in such a way that its effect is less of a shock. 用一點技巧(向某人)透露(壞)消息以便減輕聽者所受的打擊。 ***~ an officer,*** dismiss him, take his commission from him. 開除一軍官(免去他的軍職)。 ***~ a path/way,*** make one by pushing or beating aside obstacles. (清除障礙)開闢一條道路;打出一條路來。 ***~ prison/gaol,*** escape from, make one's way out of, prison. 越獄。 ***~ ranks,*** (of soldiers) leave the ranks without permission. (指士兵)(未獲准而)脫離隊伍。 ***~ a (Commonwealth/Olympic/World, etc) record,*** do better than it, make a new record. 打破 (大英國協,奧運,世界等的) 紀錄;締造新紀錄。 ***~ a set of books/china, etc,*** cause it to be incomplete by giving away or selling a part or parts of it. 拆散一套書籍(瓷器等)(如贈送或賣去一部份使之不能成套)。 ***~ the skin on one's elbow/knees/knuckles, etc,*** graze it, so as to cause bleeding. 擦破手肘(膝蓋、指節等)。 ***~ step,*** (of soldiers) stop marching rhythmically in step, eg to avoid excessive vibration on a weak bridge. (指士兵)改用便步走(例如在危橋上避免過分的震動)。**~ *a strike*,** end it by compelling the workers to submit. 迫使工人停止罷工。⇨ strike breaker. **~ *wind*,** expel wind from the bowels or stomach. 放屁。⇨ also code(3), cover²(5), ice¹(1). **7** [VP6A, 15A, B] train or discipline: 訓練;馴養: *~ a horse (in)*, bring it to a disciplined state: 馴馬: *a well-broken horse;* 馴良的馬; *~ a horse to harness/to the rein,* accustom it to wearing harness, etc. 馴馬使慣於戴馬具(韁繩)。**8** [VP6A, 15B] subdue, keep under, end by force: 壓倒;制服;控制;以武力使之結束: *~ sb's spirit/will;* 瓦解某人的精神(意志); *~ (down) the enemy's resistance;* 粉碎敵人的抵抗; *~ the power of the rebel leader.* 消滅叛亂首領的勢力。**9** [VP6A] act in opposition to; infringe: 違犯;違背;違反;侵犯;侵害: *~ the law/the rules/a regulation;* 違法(規,章); *~ a contract/an agreement;* 違背契約(協定); *~ the Sabbath,* do things on a Sunday that should not be done; 不守安息日(在星期天做不應該做的事); *~ one's word/a promise,* fail to keep a promise; 不守諾言;食言; *~ an appointment,* fail to keep it; 失約;爽約; *~ faith with sb,* betray or deceive him. 不忠於某人;欺騙某人。**10** [VP6A] interrupt or destroy the continuity of; end the operation or duration of: 使中止;使中斷;停止: *~ (the) silence,* end it, eg by speaking; 打破沈寂(如開始說話); *~ one's journey (at a place);* (在某地)中止其旅行; *~ the peace,* cause a disturbance; 破壞治安(引起騷動); *~ one's fast,* (old use) take food after going without, ⇨ breakfast; (舊用法)開齋;齋戒過後恢復進食; *~ short (a conversation, etc),* end it; 結束;終止(談話等); *a broken night's sleep,* one that is disturbed or interrupted. 一夜未能熟睡。**11** [VP15B, 2C, 3A] (special uses with *adverbial particles* and *preps*): (與副詞接語及介詞連用之特殊用法):

***break away (from)*,** go away suddenly or abruptly; give up (habits, modes of thought or belief): 突然走開或轉變方向;掙脫;脫逃;革除(習慣、思想方式或信仰): *The prisoner broke away* (= escaped after a struggle) *from his guards.* 囚犯自看守者手中掙脫。*Can't you ~ away from old habits?* 你不能戒除舊習慣嗎? *About twenty members of the Conservative Party have broken away* (= seceded). 大約有二十個保守黨黨員脫黨了。*There has been a ~-away from the Party.* 黨中有人脫黨。*One of the provinces has broken away to form a new State.* 諸省中有一省已經脫離而獨立成一新國家。

***break 'down*,** **(a)** collapse: 崩潰;瓦解: *His resistance will ~ down in time.* 他的抵抗終久是會瓦解的。*Our plans have broken down.* 我們的計畫已經失敗了。*Negotiations have broken down.* 談判已破裂。**(b)** become disabled or useless: (指機器等)出毛病;壞掉: *The car/engine/machinery broke down,* ie because of a mechanical fault. 汽車(發動機,機器)壞掉了。*That old broken-down bus is not worth £5.* 那輛破舊的公車值不了五鎊錢。**(c)** suffer a physical or mental weakening: 身體或精神衰弱: *His health broke down.* 他的身體變衰弱了。**(d)** be overcome by emotion, eg by bursting into tears: 情緒失去控制(如突然大哭): *She broke down when she heard the news, but quickly recovered.* 她聽到那消息就哭了起來,但很快就恢復過來了。**~ *sth down*,** **(a)** get (a door, wall, etc) down by battering it. 將(門,牆等)搗毀。**(b)** overthrow by force; suppress: 武力推翻;鎮壓: *~ down all resistance/opposition.* 鎮壓一切抵抗(反對)。**(c)** divide, analyse, classify (statistical material): 分析;分類(統計資料): *~ down expenditure,* give details of how money is spent. 列出開支細目。**(d)** change the chemical composition of: 分解…之化學成份: *Sugar and starch are broken down in the stomach.* 糖與澱粉在胃中被分解。**'~-down** *n.* **(a)** failure in machinery, etc: (機器等)壞掉;出毛病: *There was a ~down on the railway and trains were delayed.* 鐵路出了毛病,列車誤點了。*The earthquake has caused a ~down of communications.* 地震造成了交通電訊的中斷(交通與電訊設備的損壞)。Hence, 由此產生, **'~-down gang,** men called to repair or remove a train, etc that has been derailed, smashed, etc. (修理或清除出軌,撞毀等之火車等的)搶修大隊。**(b)** collapse; weakening: 不支;病倒;衰弱: *He's suffering from a nervous ~down.* 他正患神經衰弱。**(c)** statistical analysis: 統計分析;析列: *a ~down of expenditure.* 支出析列。

***break forth*,** (esp fig, of anger, indignation) burst out. (尤用於比喻,指怒氣)爆發;突發;迸發。

break in*,** enter a building by force: 強行進入房屋: *Burglars had broken in while we were away on holiday.* 我們出外度假時,小偷闖入屋內行竊。Hence, 由此產生, **'~-in** *n*: *The police are investigating a ~-in at the local bank.* 警方正在調查一件闖入當地銀行的竊案。**~ *sb (esp a horse) ***in*,** ⇨ 7 above; 參看上列第7義; train and discipline; accustom sb to a new routine. 使某人習慣於新的常規;訓練;(尤指)馴馬。**~ *in (up)on*,** disturb; interrupt: 打擾;打斷: *Please don't ~ in on our conversation.* 請不要打斷我們的談話。

***break into*,** **(a)** force one's way into (a building, etc): 強行進入;闖入(建築物等): *His house was broken into* (ie by burglars or thieves) *last week.* 他的房屋上星期曾有竊賊潛入。**(b)** burst suddenly into: 突然發出;突然開始: *~ (out) into a loud laugh/into loud curses/into song/into praises of sb.* 突然發出大笑(大聲詛咒,唱起歌來,稱讚某人)。**(c)** change one's method of movement suddenly: 突然改變步法: *~ into a run/trot/gallop.* 突然奔跑(疾走,飛奔)。**(d)** occupy, take up, undesirably: 侵佔: *Social duties ~ into my time/leisure.* 社交應酬侵佔了我的時間(閒暇)。**(e)** (of coins and notes): (指硬幣及鈔票): *~ into a pound note,* use one to pay for sth costing less than this sum: 用一鎊的鈔票支付不及一鎊之款額: *I can't pay you the 50p I owe you without ~ing into a £5 note.* 我要付你五十辨士的欠款,就得兌散一張五鎊的鈔票。**(f)** open and draw upon emergency supplies: 打開並提取緊急補給品: *The garrison broke into their reserves of ammunition.* 衛戍部隊啓用儲備的彈藥。

***break off*,** **(a)** stop speaking: 停止說話;中斷說話: *He broke off in the middle of a sentence.* 他一句話還未說完就中斷了。**(b)** pause; stop temporarily: 停頓;暫時停止: *Let's ~ off for half an hour and have some tea.* 讓我們小憩半小時喝點茶。**~ *(sth) off*,** **(a)** (cause to) separate (a part of sth): (使)斷折: *The mast broke off/was broken off.* 船桅斷了。**(b)** end abruptly: 突然斷絕;突然中止: *~ off relations (with sb);* (與某人)絕交; *~ off an engagement/conversation.* 解約(突然停止談話)。

***break out*,** ⇨ outbreak. (of fire, disease, war, rioting, violence) appear, start, suddenly: (指火災、疾病、戰爭、暴動、暴亂)突然發生: *A fire broke out during the night.* 夜間突然發生火警。*The quarrel broke out afresh.* 爭吵再度爆發。*Riots and disorders have broken out.* 暴動與騷亂已經發生了。**~ *out (of)*,** escape: 脫逃: *Several prisoners broke out of the jail.* 有幾個囚犯自獄中脫逃。**~ *out in*,** **(a)** suddenly become covered with: 突然佈滿: *His face broke out in pimples/a rash.* 他的臉突然間長出粉刺(紅疹)。*He broke out in a cold sweat,* was struck with fear. 他嚇得渾身出冷汗。**(b)** show sudden violence in speech or behaviour: (言語或行爲)突然激烈: *He broke out in a rage/in curses.* 他勃然大怒(破口大罵)。

***break through*,** make a way through (an enclosure, obstacles, etc): 突破(圍牆、障礙物等): *The enemy's defences were strong but our soldiers broke through.* 敵人的防線很堅強,但仍爲我軍所突破。*The sun broke through (the clouds).* 太陽鑽出(雲層)來了。**~ *through sth*,** overcome: 克服;征服;壓

倒: ～ *through a man's reserve.* 打破某人含蓄緘默的態度。Hence, 由此產生, ˈ**～·through** *n* **(a)** (mil) piercing (of the enemy's defences). (軍)(敵人防線的)突破。**(b)** major achievement, eg in technology: (科學技術等方面的) 主要成就;突破: *a ～through in cancer research.* 癌症研究的突破。

break up, **(a)** come to pieces; disintegrate: 破碎;碎裂;瓦解: *The ship was ～ing up on the rocks.* 船在礁石上撞毀了。*The gathering broke up in disorder.* 集會一哄而散。**(b)** (fig, of persons) go to pieces; become weak: (喻,指人)身體衰弱;變弱: *He broke up under the strain.* 他累垮了。**(c)** (of a school, etc) separate at the end of term for holidays: (指學校等)學期結束;放寒(暑)假: *When do you ～ ˈup?* 你們(的學校)何時放寒(暑)假? **(d)** (of a couple, a relationship) come to an end: (指婚姻或關係)結束: *The marriage is ～ing up.* 該婚姻瀕臨破裂。**(e)** divide: 分開: *Sentences ～ up into clauses.* 句子可分成若干子句。***～ sth up,*** **(a)** smash; demolish: 擊碎;搗毀: *～ up a box for firewood;* 搗毀一隻箱子當柴燒; *～ up an old ship for scrap metal.* 拆毀舊船當廢鐵。**(b)** (cause to) split, or divide: (使)分開; 分成: *～ up a piece of work (among several persons).* 分配一件工作(由數人擔任)。**(c)** (cause to) disperse: (使)分散;驅散: *The police broke up the crowd/meeting.* 警察驅散群衆(集會的人)。**(d)** bring to an end: 使結束;終止: *They broke up the alliance.* 他們終止了聯盟(或婚姻關係)。Hence, 由此產生, ˈ**～-up** *n* (end of a marriage, coalition, etc). (婚姻、聯盟等的)結束。**(e)** (esp of a period of fine weather) change for the worse; end: (尤指經過一段時期的好天氣之後)變壞;終止: *The weather is ～ing up.* 天氣變壞了。

break with, **(a)** end a friendship with: 與…絕交: *～ with an old friend.* 與老朋友絕交。**(b)** give up; make an end of: 放棄;結束: *～ with old habits;* 革除舊習慣; *～ with old ties,* eg when leaving a district. 斷絕舊關係(例如離開一個地區時)。

break² /breɪk ; brek/ *n* **1** breaking; broken place: 破裂;破口;裂口: *a ～ in the water mains.* 總輸水管之一破口。**2** [U] *～ of day* (= *day～*), dawn. 天亮;拂曉。**3** interval (in space of time): (一段時間中的)暫停;間歇: *a ～ in the conversation;* 談話中斷的時間; *an hour's ～ for lunch;* 一小時的暫停以進午餐; *the ˈtea-～,* eg in an office or factory; 飲茶時間(如在辦公室或工廠裏); *during a ～ at school,* during an interval between lessons. 在學校的下課時間內。***without a ～,*** continuously: 繼續不斷地;不休息地: *He has been writing since 2 o'clock without a ～.* 他從兩點鐘起一直不斷地在寫。**4** change, disturbance: 改變;變動: *a ～ in one's way of living;* 生活方式的改變; *a ～ in the weather.* 天氣的變化。**5** change of course of a cricket or tennis ball on first striking the ground: (板球或網球初觸地面時之)改向飛跳;曲球: *a leg ～,* (cricket) one that breaks to the left. (板球)左曲球。**6** (billiards) continuous score: (彈子戲)連續得分: *make a ～ of 450.* 連續得450分。**7** ***give sb a ～,*** (colloq) an opportunity (to make a new start or remedy an error). (俗)給予某人(改過自新的)機會。**8** (colloq) ***a bad ～,*** an unfortunate remark or ill-judged action; a piece of bad luck. (俗)失禮的話或不智的行動;不幸;倒霉。***a lucky ～,*** a piece of good fortune. 幸運的事。**9** (= *break-out*) (attempt to) escape (esp from prison). 脫逃;(尤指)逃獄;企圖脫逃。***(make a) break for it,*** escape. 脫逃;逃走。

break³ /breɪk ; brek/ *n* = brake³.

break·able /ˈbreɪkəbl ; ˈbrekəbl̩/ *adj* easily broken. 易破碎的。**break·ables** *n pl* ～ objects, eg glasses, cups and saucers. 易碎的物件(如玻璃杯,瓷杯,瓷碟)。

break·age /ˈbreɪkɪdʒ ; ˈbrekɪdʒ/ *n* **1** act of breaking. 破裂;破碎;破損。**2** place in, part of, sth that has been broken. 破裂處; 裂開部份。**3** (usu *pl*) broken articles; loss by breaking: (通常用複數)破損的物件;破毀的損失;破損: *The hotel allows £150 a year for ～s,* for the cost of broken dishes, glasses, etc. 該旅社每年備有150鎊的杯盤等損失費。

breaker /ˈbreɪkə(r) ; ˈbrekɚ/ *n* **1** large wave breaking into foam as it advances towards the shore; wave breaking against a rock, etc. 大浪衝岸後碎爲泡沫之浪花;衝擊於礁石等上之碎浪。**2** person or thing that breaks. 擊破者;軋碎機。ˈ**ice-～** *n* strongly built ship used to break up ice in harbours, etc. 破冰船(用以擊破海港等內之冰)。⇨ house～ and other similar compounds. 參看 housebreaker 及其他類似之複合字。

break·fast /ˈbrekfəst ; ˈbrɛkfəst/ *n* first meal of the day: 早餐;早點: *Have a good ～.* 早餐吃飽(或好)一點。*He hasn't eaten much ～.* 他早餐沒有吃多少。*They were having ～ when I arrived.* 我到達時,他們正在吃早餐。□ *vi* have ～. 吃早餐。

break·neck /ˈbreɪknek ; ˈbrekˌnɛk/ *adj* (usu) (通常作) ***at (a) ～ speed,*** at a dangerous speed. 以極危險的高速度。

break·water /ˈbreɪkwɔːtə(r) ; ˈbrekˌwɔtɚ/ *n* sth that breaks the force of waves, esp a structure built out into the sea to shelter (part of) a harbour. 減弱浪力之物;擋浪板;(尤指港口的)防波堤。

a breakwater

bream /briːm ; brim/ *n* (*pl* unchanged) (複數不變) **1** freshwater fish of the carp family. 鯛(一種鯉科之淡水魚)。**2** (also 亦作 ˈ**sea-～**) salt-water variety of this. 海鯛(一種鹹水魚,係淡水鯛之變種)。

breast /brest ; brɛst/ *n* **1** either of the milk-producing parts of a woman: (女人之)乳房: *a child at the ～;* 正在吃奶的嬰兒; *give a child the ～.* 哺乳嬰兒。⇨ suckle. **～·feed** *vi, vt* feed a baby from the breast; suckle. 餵奶;哺乳。ˈ**～-fed** *adj* (of a baby) fed with milk from the ～. (指嬰兒)人乳哺養的。Cf 參較 *bottle-fed.* **2** chest; upper front part of the human body, or of a garment covering this. (人體的)胸膛;胸部;衣服的胸部。ˈ**～ pocket** *n* one in the ～ of a jacket, etc. 上衣胸前的口袋。ˈ**～·stroke,** stroke (in swimming) in which both the arms are brought at the same time from in front of the head to the sides of the body. (游泳)俯泳(兩手同時自頭前向身體兩側之划法)。ˌ**～-ˈhigh** *adv* high as the ～: 高與胸齊地: *The wheat was ～-high.* 麥禾高與胸齊。ˌ**～-ˈdeep** *adv* deep enough to reach the ～: 深及胸部地: *In the middle of the stream the water was ～-deep.* 在溪流的中間,水深及胸。ˈ**～-plate** *n* piece of armour covering the ～. (盔甲之)護胸甲。⇨ the illus at armour. 參看 armour 之插圖。ˈ**～·work** *n* low wall, eg of earth, sandbags, stones, put up as a temporary defence. 胸牆(用泥土、沙袋、石頭等臨時構築之高及胸部的防禦工事)。**3** (fig) feelings; thoughts: (喻)感情; 思想;心情: *a troubled ～.* 心煩意亂。***make a clean ～ of,*** confess (wrong-doing, etc). 坦白承認(過失等)。**4** part of an animal corresponding to the human ～. (動物的) 胸部。□ *vt* [VP6A] present the ～(2) to, hence (fig), face, struggle with: 以胸抵抗;挺胸以當;(由此產生)(喻)面對;對付;與…搏鬥: *～ the waves.* 與波濤搏鬥。

breath /breθ ; brɛθ/ *n* **1** [U] air taken into and sent out of the lungs; [C] single act of taking in and sending air out: 呼吸之空氣;氣息;一次呼吸: *take a deep ～,* fill the lungs with air. 作一次深呼吸。***bad ～,*** with an unpleasant smell. 帶臭味的呼吸;呼氣很臭。***catch/hold one's ～,*** stop breathing for a moment (from fear, excitement, etc). (因恐懼、興奮等而)屏息。***get one's ~ (again/back)***, get back to the normal state. 恢復正常呼吸。***in the same ~***, at the same moment: 在同一時刻: *They are not to be mentioned in the same ~*, cannot be compared. 他們不可同日而語。***lose one's ~***, have difficulty in taking in ~, eg while running or working hard. (如因疾跑或工作辛苦而)喘不過氣來;喘息。***out of ~***, unable to take in ~ quickly enough. 喘不過氣來。***speak/say sth below/under one's ~***, in a whisper. 低聲地說某事。***take ~***, get enough ~ (after exertion): (努力之後)喘喘氣;歇息一會兒: *Half-way up the mountain we stopped to take ~*. 爬到半山時,我們停下來喘喘氣。***take sb's '~ away***, startle or surprise him. 使某人大爲吃驚。Hence, 由此產生, **'~-taking**, *adj* exciting; causing awe. 緊張刺激的;驚險的;令人敬畏的。***waste one's ~***, talk in vain. 白費唇舌。**'~ test** *n* test of the alcoholic contents of a person's ~. 呼吸試驗(試驗人之呼吸中的酒精含量)。**2** moving air; light breeze: 微風;輕風: *There wasn't a ~ of air/wind*, The air was quite still. 一絲微風都沒有。**3** (fig) suggestion (*of*): (喩)一絲痕跡;跡象: *not a ~ of suspicion/scandal*. 沒有一絲疑心(閒言閒語)。**~·less** *adj* **1** out of ~; panting; likely to cause shortness of ~: 喘不過氣來的;喘息的;可能引起喘息的: *in a ~less hurry;* 匆忙得喘不過氣來; *listening with ~less attention/in ~less expectation*, with the ~ held back (in concentration or excitement). 聚精會神地(抱着急切希望地)聽。**2** unstirred by wind: 無風的;空氣平靜的: *a ~less* (=calm) *evening*. 無風的夜晚。**~·less·ly** *adv*

breath·a·lyse /ˈbreθəlaɪz ; ˈbrɛθəlaɪz/ *vt* [VP6A] (GB) measure the amount of alcohol in a person's breath. (英)呼吸試驗(試驗某人呼吸中的酒精含量)。**~r** *n* instrument for breathalysing sb (usu used by the police on the driver of a car). 呼吸試驗器(警察通常用以試驗汽車駕駛人呼吸中的酒精含量)。

breathe /briːð ; brið/ *vi, vt* **1** [VP2A, C, 6A, 15B] take air into the lungs and send it out again: 呼吸: *~ in/out*. 吸入(呼出);吸(呼)氣。*He was breathing hard when he finished the race*. 他跑完賽跑時很費力地喘着氣。*We ~ air*. 我們呼吸空氣。*He ~d a sigh of relief*. 他放心地鬆了一口氣。*He's still breathing*, is still alive. 他還活着。***~ again; ~ freely (again)***, be at ease, be relieved (after exertion, excitement, fear, etc). (在努力、興奮、恐懼等之後)恢復常態;恢復平靜;安心;鬆一口氣。***~ down sb's neck***, ⇨ neck. **2** [VP6A] utter; send out, eg a scent, feeling: 說出;發出(氣味、感情等): *Don't ~ a word of this*, keep it secret. 不要走漏這個消息。**3** [VP6A] allow (a horse) to ~ gently and rest. 讓(馬)鬆一口氣休息休息。**breather** *n* **1** short pause for rest: 短時間的休息: *take/have a ~r*. 鬆一口氣休息休息。**2** short period of exercise: 短時間的運動: *go for a ~r*. 去運動運動。**breath·ing** *n* [U] **breath·ing-space** *n* time to ~; pause; rest. 喘氣的工夫;暫停;休息。

bred *pt, pp* of breed.

breech /briːtʃ ; britʃ/ *n* back part of a rifle or gun barrel, where the cartridge or shell is placed: (槍砲的) 後膛 (裝子彈或砲彈的地方): *a ˌ~-ˌloading ˈgun*, loaded at the ~, not through the muzzle. 由後膛裝彈的槍砲。**'~-block** *n* block of steel that closes the ~ of a gun. (槍砲之)閂鎖;槍砲閂。

breeches /ˈbrɪtʃɪz ; ˈbrɪtʃɪz/ *n pl* **1** **'knee-~**, garment fitting round the waist and below the knees. 長及膝蓋下之短褲。**'riding-~**, garment covering the hips and thighs, buttoned below the knee, worn by men and women for riding on horseback. 馬褲 (男女騎裝之短褲,膝下部份有鈕扣)。**2** (colloq) trousers; knickerbockers. (俗)褲;燈籠褲。***wear the ~***, (said of a woman) rule her husband. (指女人)駕馭丈夫。**'~-ˌbuoy** /ˈbriːtʃɪz- ; ˈbritʃɪz-/ *n* pair of canvas ~ fastened to a lifebuoy, pulled along a rope, used for saving life at sea. 短褲型之救生具。

breed /briːd ; brid/ *vt, vi* (*pt, pp* bred /bred ; brɛd/) **1** [VP6A] keep (animals, etc) for the purpose of producing young, esp by selection of parents: 飼養(牲畜等);(尤指)選種繁殖: *~ horses/cattle*. 養馬(牛)。**2** [VP2A] give birth to young; reproduce: 生育;繁殖: *Rabbits ~ quickly*. 兎子繁殖迅速。*Birds ~ in the spring*. 鳥類在春季繁殖。**3** [VP6A] train, educate, bring up: 訓練;教育;養育: *an Englishman born and bred;* 土生土長的英國人; *a well-bred boy*, one who has been trained to behave well. 一個教養良好的男孩子。***What's bred in the bone will come out in the flesh***, (prov) Hereditary characteristics always show themselves. (諺)遺傳的特質總會顯現出來的;龍生龍鳳生鳳,老鼠的兒子會打洞。**4** [VP6A] be the cause of: 引起;造成: *Dirt ~s disease*. 污穢引致疾病。*War ~s misery and ruin*. 戰爭造成苦難與災害。**~er** *n* **1** person who ~s animals. 畜養牲畜的人。**2** apparatus (reactor) that produces more radio-active material than is put into it. (放射物質)滋生反應器。**~·ing** *n* [U] **1** (in verbal senses): (照動詞意義): *the ~ing of horses;* 養馬; *the ~ing season for birds*. 鳥類的繁殖季節。**2** knowledge of how to behave resulting from training: (所受的)教養: *a man of good ~ing*. 教養良好的人。□ *n* [C] kind or variety (of animals, etc) with hereditary qualities: (牲畜等的)種: *a good ~ of cattle*. 良種牛。⇨ cross~, half-~.

breeze[1] /briːz ; briz/ *n* [C, U] wind, esp a soft, gentle wind: 和風;微風: *a land/sea ~*, one blowing from the land/sea at certain hours; 在一定時刻由大陸(海上)吹來的風;陸(海)風; *not much ~;* 很少的風; *not much of a ~;* 非常輕微的風; *spring ~s*. 春風。□ *vi* [VP2C] (colloq) ***~ in/out***, come in/go out in high spirits, or without warning, unexpectedly. (俗)飄然而來(去)(令人感到意外)。**breezy** *adj* **1** pleasantly windy: 輕風拂面的; 惠風和暢的: *breezy weather*. 惠風和暢的天氣。**2** swept by ~s: 微風掠過的;通風的: *a breezy corner*. 風涼的拐角處。**3** (of persons) jovial; lively; good-humoured. (指人)喜談笑的;樂天的;和氣的。**breez·ily** /ˈbriːzəlɪ ; ˈbrizɪlɪ/ *adv* **breezi·ness** /ˈbriːzɪnɪs ; ˈbrizɪnɪs/ *n*

breeze[2] /briːz ; briz/ *n* [U] (not US) small coal cinders. (不用於美國) 煤渣; 煤炭的餘燼。**'~ blocks**, light-weight concrete building blocks made of ~ and cement. (煤渣與水泥製成的)一種輕型水泥磚。

Bren /bren ; brɛn/ *n* (also亦作 **'~-gun**) light-weight, semiautomatic, light machine gun. 勃倫式半自動輕機槍。**'~ carrier** *n* small armoured vehicle that moves on tracks(5). 勃倫式(履帶)小戰車。

breth·ren /ˈbreðrən ; ˈbrɛðrən/ *n pl* (old use) brothers. (舊用法)兄弟們。

breve /briːv ; briv/ *n* (mus) note equal to two semibreves, now rarely used. (音樂)倍全音符;二全音符(現已少用)。⇨ the illus at notation. 參看notation 之挿圖。

bre·vet /ˈbrevɪt *US:* brɪˈvet ; brəˈvɛt/ *n* document that gives sb higher rank without corresponding increase in pay or authority: 加銜之公文(使某人晉級而不予加薪或提高其職權): *~ rank*, given by ~; 榮譽階級;加銜階級; *~ major*. 榮譽少校。

brevi·ary /ˈbriːvɪərɪ *US:* -ɪerɪ ; ˈbrivɪˌɛrɪ/ *n* (*pl* -ries) book with prayers to be said daily by priests etc of the RC Church. (天主教神父等所用的)每日祈禱書。

brev·ity /ˈbrevətɪ ; ˈbrɛvətɪ/ *n* [U] (formal) shortness (of statements, human life and other non-material things). (正式用語)簡潔;簡短;短暫(指言詞、人生及其他非物質事物)。

brew /bruː ; bru/ *vt, vi* **1** [VP6A] prepare (beer, tea, etc) by soaking or boiling grain, leaves, etc; [VP2A] make beer, etc. 釀(酒);泡(茶);調製;釀酒;調製飲料。**2** [VP6A] (fig) bring about; [VP2A, C] gather, be forming: (喩)造成;圖謀;聚集;形成;醞釀: *Those boys are ~ing mischief*. 那些男孩子正

圖謀搗亂。*A storm is ~ing*, gathering force. 暴風雨在形成中。*There's trouble ~ing between them*, They are likely to quarrel. 他們彼此之間正醞釀着不和。□ *n* result of ~ing; liquid made by ~ing: 釀造物;調製的飲料;所釀的酒: *the best ~s of beer;* 釀得最好的啤酒; *a good, strong ~ of tea.* 上好的濃茶。**~er** *n* person who ~s beer. 釀啤酒者。**~·ery** /ˈbrʊərɪ ; ˈbruərɪ/ *n* (*pl* -ries) building in which ~ing of beer is carried on. 啤酒廠。

briar /ˈbraɪə(r) ; ˈbraɪɚ/ *n* **1** [U] hard wood (root of a bush) used esp for making tobacco pipes. 石南根(尤用於製煙斗)。**2** [C] pipe made of this wood. 石南根煙斗。**3** = brier.

bribe /braɪb ; braɪb/ *n* [C] sth given, offered or promised to sb in order to influence or persuade him (often to do sth wrong) in favour of the giver: 賄賂: *offer/give/hand out/take ~s.* 送(收)賄賂。□ *vt* [VP6A, 17, 15A] offer, give, a ~ to: 送賄賂給;賄賂: *~ a judge/witness.* 賄賂法官(證人)。*The child was ~d to take the nasty medicine.* 那小孩被哄着吃難吃的藥。*He had been ~d into silence/~d to say nothing.* 他受到賄賂保持緘默。**bri·bable** /ˈbraɪbəbl ; ˈbraɪbəbl̩/ *adj* **bri·bery** /ˈbraɪbərɪ ; ˈbraɪbərɪ/ *n* [U] giving or taking of ~s. 賄賂;行賄;受賄。

bric-a-brac /ˈbrɪk ə bræk ; ˈbrɪkəˌbræk/ *n* [U] bits of old furniture, china, ornaments, etc, esp old and curious, of no great value. (不太值錢的)小古董;小古玩。

brick /brɪk ; brɪk/ *n* **1** [C, U] (usu rectangular block of) clay moulded and baked by fire or sun, used for building purposes: 磚: *a house made of red ~(s);* 一所紅磚造的房子; *a ~ wall.* 一道磚牆。***drop a ~,*** (colloq) do or say sth indiscreet. (俗)失言;失禮。***make ~s without straw,*** attempt a difficult and fruitless task. 做勞而無功的工作;爲無米之炊。**ˈ~·bat** *n* piece of ~, esp as a missile: 碎磚;磚塊(尤指作爲武器投擲用者): *The Minister collected a lot of ~bats,* (fig) much abuse. (喻)那部長備受各方的指責。**ˈ~-field, ˈ~·kiln** *n* field, kiln, in which ~s are made. 磚場;磚窰。**ˈ~·layer** *n* workman who builds with ~s. 磚匠;泥水匠。**ˈ~·work** *n* (part of a) structure made of ~. (建築工程中的)磚工;磚造部份。**2** child's rectangular block (usu of wood) used for building toy houses, etc. 積木(兒童玩具)。**3** ~-shaped block of sth, eg ice-cream. 形狀似磚的一塊東西(如冰淇淋磚)。**4** (colloq) generous or kind-hearted person: (俗)慷慨的人;好心的人: *You've behaved like a ~.* 你的行爲表現得像個好心的人。□ *vt* [VP15B] ***~ up/in,*** block (an opening) with ~s: 用磚堵住(洞口): *~ up a window.* 用磚將窗戶堵住。

bri·dal /ˈbraɪdl ; ˈbraɪdl/ *n* wedding-feast; wedding; (attrib) of a bride or wedding: 結婚之酒宴;婚禮; (形容用法)新娘的;婚禮的: *the ˈ~ party*, the bride and her attendants and friends. 新娘及其伴娘和朋友。

bride /braɪd ; braɪd/ *n* woman on her wedding-day; newly married woman. 新娘;新婚婦。**ˈ~·cake** *n* (old name for) wedding-cake. 結婚蛋糕; 喜餅(wedding-cake 之舊名)。

bride·groom /ˈbraɪdgrʊm ; ˈbraɪdˌgrum/ *n* man on his wedding-day; newly married man. 新郎;新婚的男子。

brides·maid /ˈbraɪdzmeɪd ; ˈbraɪdzˌmed/ *n* girl or young unmarried woman (usu one of several) attending a bride at her wedding. 女儐相;伴娘。Cf 參較 *best man* for the bridegroom. 新郎之男儐相。

bridge¹ /brɪdʒ ; brɪdʒ/ *n* **1** structure of wood, stone, brickwork, steel, concrete, etc, providing a way across a river, canal, railway, etc. 橋;橋樑。**ˈ~·head** *n* defensive post or area established on the enemy's side of a river, etc; (loosely) any military position occupied in the face of the enemy. (靠近敵人之)橋頭陣地;橋頭堡。⇨ beachhead. **2** platform over and across the deck of a ship for the use of the captain and officers. 船橋;艦橋(爲船長及高級船員等發號施令之場所)。**3** upper bony part of the nose. 鼻樑。**4** movable part over which the strings of a violin, etc are stretched. (小提琴等上繃弦的)琴馬; 琴橋。**5** device for keeping false teeth in place, fastened to natural teeth. 齒橋 (裝於眞牙上以固定假牙的金屬架子)。□ *vt* [VP6A] join by means of a ~; build a ~ over: 以橋連接;架橋於…上: *a ˈbridging loan*, loan (esp from a bank) to cover a period of

bridges

a pontoon bridge

a trestle bridge

a Bailey bridge

an arch bridge

a suspension bridge

a cantilever bridge

time, eg between the purchase of one house and the sale of another; 過渡貸款(尤指銀行的貸款,以過渡時期爲限，例如在購買新屋與售出舊屋之期間的貸款)；[VP15B] ~ ***over***, (fig) overcome (obstacles, etc): (喩)克服(障碍等)：~ *over difficulties.* 渡過難關。

bridge[2] /brɪdʒ ; brɪdʒ/ *n* [U] card game for four players in which one player looks on while his cards, placed face up on the table, are played by his partner. 橋牌戲(四人玩,其中一人,卽夢家,將牌攤於桌上,交由其夥伴支配出牌,自己則旁觀)。**'auction ~**, in which the right to name the trumps goes to the player who undertakes to make the highest score. (誰叫牌最高由誰決定王牌之)拍賣式橋牌戲。**'contract ~**, variety of auction ~ with penalties for failure to make the score. 合約式橋牌戲(上述橋牌之一種,若不能得到所叫之分數將受罰)。

bridle /ˈbraɪdl ; ˈbraɪdḷ/ *n* that part of a horse's harness that goes on its head, including the metal bit for the mouth, the straps and the reins. 馬籠頭(馬具之套在馬頭上的部份,包括口銜、轡及韁)。⇨ the illus at harness. 參看 harness 之挿圖。**'~-path, '~-road** *n* one fit for riders on horseback but not for cars, etc. 馬徑(適於騎馬不宜行車者)。□ *vt, vi* **1** [VP6A] put a ~ on (a horse). 套籠頭於(馬)。**2** [VP6A] (fig) control, check: (喩)控制；約束：*Try to ~ your passions.* 盡力控制你强烈的感情。**3** [VP2A, C] throw back the head and draw in the chin (showing pride, contempt, vanity, etc): 仰頭；昂首(表示驕傲、輕視、自大等)：~ *with anger;* 怒氣沖沖；~ *up;* 昂首；~ *at sb's remarks.* 輕視某人的言論。

brief[1] /bri:f ; brif/ *adj* (-er, -est) (of time, events, writing, speaking) lasting only for a short time: (指時間、事件、寫作、說話)暫時的；短的；簡短的；簡潔的：*to be ~*, to speak shortly. 簡而言之。⇨ brevity. ***in ~***, in a few words. 簡言之。**~·ly** *adv*

brief[2] /bri:f ; brif/ *n* **1** [C] summary of the facts of a case, drawn up for a barrister: (提供給律師的)案情摘要：*have plenty of ~s*, (of a barrister) be busy with professional work. (指律師)業務興旺，忙於案件。***hold a ~ for (sb)***, (fig) argue in support or favour of. (喩)爲…辯護；支持。***hold no ~ for***, (fig) not be prepared to support. (喩)不準備支持。**'~·case** *n* flat leather or plastic case, for documents, etc. (皮或塑膠製的供裝公文等的)公事包。**2** (also 亦作 **'~·ing**) information, instructions, advice, etc given in advance, eg to an aircraft crew before a combat mission. 簡報；任務提示(如對一組空勤人員出發執行戰鬥任務前所作者)。**3** (comm) instructions: (商)指示；說明：*My ~ did not include the buying of new materials.* 我的說明並不包括購買新材料。□ *vt* [VP6A] **1** instruct or employ (a barrister). 委託(律師)代理訴訟。**2** give a ~(2) to. 對…作任務提示。⇨ debrief. **3** (comm) summarize the facts, eg of a business programme: (商)摘要說明(例如有關業務計畫方面者)：*The Chairman will ~ the Board on the most recent developments.* 主席將向董事會摘要說明最近的發展。

briefs /bri:fs ; brifs/ *n pl* close-fitting pants without legs, held in position by an elastic waistband. (無褲腿,用鬆緊腰帶繫牢的貼身)短褲。

brier, briar /ˈbraɪə(r) ; ˈbraɪɚ/ *n* thorn-covered bush, esp the wild rose. 荊棘(尤指野薔薇)。

brig /brɪg ; brɪg/ *n* two-masted ship with square sails and an extra fore-and-aft sail on the mainmast. 一種雙桅船(帆爲方形,主桅上並另有縱帆)。⇨ the illus at barque. 參看 barque 之挿圖。

brig·ade /brɪˈgeɪd ; brɪˈged/ *n* **1** army unit, usu of three battalions, forming part of an army division; corresponding armoured unit. 旅(陸軍師的單位，通常包括三個營)；裝甲兵旅。**2** organized body of persons in uniform with special duties (eg **'fire-~**). 身著制服擔任特殊任務的團隊(如消防隊)。**Briga·dier** /ˌbrɪgəˈdɪə(r) ; ˌbrɪgəˈdɪr/ *n* (formerly 昔作 ˌ*Brigadier-ˈGeneral*) officer commanding a ~; army officer of rank between General and Colonel. 旅長；准將。

brig·and /ˈbrɪgənd ; ˈbrɪgənd/ *n* member of a band of robbers, esp a band that attacks travellers in forests or mountains. 强盜；土匪(尤指在山林中搶刼旅客爲生者)。

brig·an·tine /ˈbrɪgənti:n ; ˈbrɪgənˌtin/ *n* = brig.

bright /braɪt ; braɪt/ *adj* (-er, -est) **1** giving out or reflecting much light; shining: 光明的；發光的；明亮的：*Sunshine is ~.* 陽光是明亮的。*Polished steel is ~.* 磨光的鋼是發亮的。*The leaves on the trees are ~ green in spring.* 春天裏樹上的葉子是翠綠的。**2** cheerful and happy; lit up with joy or hope: 愉快的；高興的；樂觀的：~ *faces;* 高興的面容；*a ~ smile;* 愉快的微笑；*see the ~ side of things.* 對事物抱樂觀的態度。**3** quick-witted, clever: 聰明的；伶俐的：*A ~ boy learns quickly.* 聰明的孩子學得快。□ *adv* (chiefly with *shine*) (主要與 shine 連用) = ~ly. 光明地；光亮地。**~en** *vt, vi* [VP6A, 15B, 2A, C] ***~en up***, make or become ~er or lighter, more cheerful, etc: (使)更爲光明；(使)更爲愉快：*These flowers ~en the classroom.* 這些花朵使教室生輝。*The sky is ~ening.* 天正放晴。*His face ~ened up.* 他喜形於色。**~·ly** *adv* **~·ness** *n*

brill /brɪl ; brɪl/ *n* flat fish like a turbot. 一種鰈類之魚。

bril·liant /ˈbrɪlɪənt ; ˈbrɪljənt/ *adj* very bright; sparkling; splendid, causing admiration: 極明亮的；光輝燦爛的；令人欽佩或讚賞的：*a week of ~ sunshine;* 天氣晴朗的一週；*a ~ scientist;* 卓越的科學家；~ *jewels.* 燦爛的珠寶。**~·ly** *adv* **bril·liance** /ˈbrɪlɪəns ; ˈbrɪljəns/, **bril·liancy** /ˈbrɪlɪənsɪ ; ˈbrɪljənsɪ/ *nn* [U] radiance, splendour, intelligence. 光輝燦爛；顯赫；聰穎；才氣煥發。

bril·lian·tine /ˈbrɪlɪənti:n ; ˈbrɪljənˌtin/ *n* [U] cosmetic used to make the hair lie flat. (使頭髮柔順的)美髮油。

brim /brɪm ; brɪm/ *n* **1** edge of a cup, bowl, glass, etc: (杯、碗等的)邊：*full to the ~*, quite full. 滿盈的。**2** out-turned part (rim) of a hat, that gives shade. (帽的)邊。□ *vi* (-mm-) [VP2A,C] be full to the ~. 滿；盈。**~ *over***, be so full that some spills over the ~; 溢出；(fig) (喩) *~ming over with high spirits.* 興高采烈。**~·ful(l)** /ˈbrɪmˌfʊl ; ˈbrɪmˈfʊl/ *adj* full to the ~: 盈滿的；充滿的：*He is ~ful of new ideas.* 他有很多新的主意。

brim·stone /ˈbrɪmstəʊn ; ˈbrɪmˌston/ *n* [U] (old name for) sulphur. 硫黃石(硫黃之舊名)。

brindled /ˈbrɪndld ; ˈbrɪndḷd/ *adj* (esp of cows and cats) brown with streaks of another colour. (尤指牛及貓)棕色而有其他顏色之斑紋的。

brine /braɪn ; braɪn/ *n* [U] salt water, esp for pickling. (尤指浸醃菜之)鹽水。**briny** /ˈbraɪnɪ ; ˈbraɪnɪ/ *adj* salty. 鹽的；含鹽的；鹹的。□ *n* **the briny**, (colloq) the sea. (俗)海洋。

bring /brɪŋ ; brɪŋ/ *vt* (*pt, pp* brought /brɔ:t ; brɔt/) (For uses with *adverbial particles* and *preps*, ⇨ 6 below.) (與副詞接語及介詞連用之各種用法,參看下列第6義。) **1** ⇨ take [VP6A, 15B, 13A, B, 12A, B, C, 14] ~ ***(with)***, come carrying sth or accompanying sb: 拿來；取來；帶來(人或物)：*Take this empty box away and ~ me a full one.* 把這個空盒子拿走，給我拿個滿的來。*The soldiers came back ~ing ten prisoners (with them).* 士兵們帶着十個俘虜回來了。*B~ Mary to the party with you.* 帶瑪莉一道來參加宴會。*B~ one for me.* 拿一個給我。*B~ me one.* 給我拿一個來。**2** [VP6A, 19B, 12C, 14] cause to come; produce: 使來；帶來；引起；產生：*Spring ~s warm weather and flowers.* 春天帶來暖和的天氣和百花。*The sad news brought tears to her eyes.* 噩耗使她不禁流淚。*His writings ~ him £5000 a year.* 他的著作每年可使他獲得五千鎊。*A phone call brought him hurrying to Leeds.* 一通電話使他匆忙趕赴里茲。**3** [VP17] ~ ***sb/oneself to do sth***, persuade, induce, lead: 說服；引誘；引導：*They could not ~ themselves to believe the news.* 他們對這消

息覺得難以置信。*She couldn't ~ herself to speak about the matter.* 她鼓不起勇氣來談這事。*I wish I could ~ you to see the situation from my point of view.* 我眞希望能使你從我的觀點來看這情勢。 **4** [VP14] **~ against,** (legal) start, put forward: (法律)提起(訴訟)：~ *an action/charge/an accusation against sb.* 提起訴訟控告某人。 **5** (phrases) (片語) **~ sb to book,** ⇨ book[1](6); **~ sth to an end,** cause it to end; 使某事結束;了結某事; **~ sth home to sb,** ⇨ home[2](2); **~ low,** reduce to a low condition; 使(健康情況、財富或地位等)低落;降低;貶抑; **~ sth to light,** cause it to be visible or known; 使某事物可看得見;發現;發掘;公佈; **~ sth to mind;** 憶起某事; **~ sth to pass,** ⇨ pass[1](3); **~ sth into line/play,** ⇨ line[1](11), play[1](8); **~ sb to his senses,** ⇨ sense(2). **6** [VP15B] (special uses with *adverbial particles* and *preps*): (與副詞接語及介詞連用之特殊用法)：

bring about, **(a)** cause to happen: 引起;導致;致使: ~ *about a war/reforms/sb's ruin.* 引起戰爭(導致改革;致使某人破產)。**(b)** (naut) cause (a sailing-ship) to change direction: (航海)使(帆船)改向:*The helmsman brought us about.* 舵手使船改向。

bring back, **(a)** return: 歸還: *Please ~ back the book tomorrow;* 請於明天將書歸還; (with *indirect object*): (與間接受詞連用): *If you're going to the market, please ~ me back ten eggs.* 如果你要上市場,請給我帶十個蛋回來。**(b)** call to mind; cause to remember: 使記起;使回憶: *Your newsy letter brought back many memories.* 你那封帶來許多消息的信喚起了許多回憶。**(c)** restore; reintroduce: 使恢復;再導入: *How many MP's favour ~ing back capital punishment?* 有多少國會議員贊成恢復死刑？ **~ sb back to,** restore to: 復歸;使恢復: *Her stay among the mountains brought her back to health.* 她在山裏暫住使她恢復了健康。

bring sb/sth down, **(a)** cause to fall; cause to be down: 使落下;使跌下;使倒下: ~ *down a hostile aircraft,* shoot it down; 打落一架敵機; ~ *down prices,* lower them; 削價;減價; ~ *down* (= overthrow) *a tyrant.* 打倒暴君。**(b)** continue (records, etc) up to: 使(記錄)延續到…: *a new history of Europe, brought down to modern times,* ie made up to date. 一直寫到現代的一部新的歐洲史。**(c)** kill or wound: 打死;打傷;打倒: *He aimed, fired and brought down the antelope.* 他瞄準,射擊,打倒了那隻羚羊。**(d)** (football) cause (an opponent) to fall by fouling; (Rugby) tackle. (足球)犯規撞倒(對方); (橄欖球)擒抱。**(e)** (arith) transfer a digit from one part of a sum (from one column) to another: (算術)進位;退位: ~ *down the next two figures.* 將下兩位數字進位。**~ the 'house down/~ down the house,** ⇨ house(6). **~ down sb's wrath/fury on one's head,** cause it to be aimed at oneself. 使某人的怒氣發到自己頭上來。

bring sth forth, produce (fruit); give birth to (young ones): 結(果);生產(幼兒): *What will the future ~ forth?* 將來結果怎樣？

bring sth forward, **(a)** cause to be seen, discussed, etc: 提出(讓人看見或討論等):*Can you ~ forward* (= produce) *any proof of what you say?* 關於你所說的,你能提出證據嗎？ *Please ~ the matter forward at the next meeting.* 請將此一問題在下次會議提出討論。**(b)** advance: 提前: *The meeting has been brought forward from May 10 to May 3,* is to be a week earlier. 會期已自五月十日提前至五月三日。⇨ postpone. **(c)** (abbr 略作 **b/f**) (book-keeping) carry the total of a column of figures at the foot of one page to the top of the next page. (簿記)承前(將頁底一列數字之總和轉至下一頁之頁頂)。

bring sth/sb in, **(a)** yield; (of capital, investments, etc) produce as profit: 產生;(指本金,投資等)生(息);獲(利): *His orchards ~ (him) in £200 a year.* 他的果園每年獲利二百鎊。*He does odd jobs that ~ him in ten to twelve pounds a week.* 他做零工每週可賺十鎊至十二鎊。*This investment ~s (me) in 7½ per cent.* 此項投資(使我)可獲百分之七點五的盈利。**(b)** introduce: 介紹;引進: ~ *in a new fashion/a new topic.* 引進新式樣(提出新話題)。**(c)** introduce (legislation): 提出(立法): ~ *in a Bill on road safety.* 提出道路安全法案。**(d)** admit (as a partner, adviser, etc): 延聘(爲夥伴,顧問等):*They've brought in experts to advise on the scheme.* 他們已延聘專家對該計畫提供意見。**(e)** (of the police) arrest; ~ to a police station for questioning, etc: (指警方)逮捕;帶到派出所問話: *Two suspicious characters were brought in.* 兩個可疑人物被拘捕。**(f)** (of a jury) pronounce (a verdict): (指陪審團)宣(判): ~ *in a verdict of guilty.* 宣判有罪。

bring sth/sb off, **(a)** rescue (esp from a wrecked ship): 救助;拯救(尤指遭遇船難者): *The passengers and crew were brought off by the Deal lifeboat.* 乘客及船員均經 Deal 救生艇救起。**(b)** carry (an enterprise) to success; manage to do sth successfully: 經營成功;將(某事)做得很成功;終於達成任務: *It was a difficult task but we brought it off,* we succeeded. 那是一件困難的工作,但是我們終於達成任務。

bring sth/sb on, **(a)** lead to, (help to) produce: 引起;導致;促成: *He was out all day in the rain and this brought on a bad cold.* 他整天在外面淋雨,因此患了重感冒。**(b)** cause to develop or advance: 使發展或進步: *The fine weather is ~ing the crops on nicely.* 好天氣使農作物長得很好。**(c)** help (a pupil, learner, etc) to develop: 幫助(學生、學習者等)發展;教導;指導: *The coach is ~ing on some youngsters in the reserve team.* 教練正在指導預備隊的孩子們練球。

bring sth/sb out, **(a)** cause to appear, show clearly: 使顯現;闡釋;說明: ~ *out the meaning of a poem.* 闡明一首詩的意義。*The sunshine will ~ out the apple blossom,* cause it to open. 陽光將使蘋果花開放。**(b)** publish (a book, etc): 出版(書籍等): *When are the publishers ~ing out his new book?* 出版商何時出版他的新書？ **(c)** help to lose shyness or reserve: 幫助消除害羞心理或沉默寡言的態度: *She's a nice girl, but needs a lot of ~ing out.* 她是一個好女孩,但是需要多多勸導以消除害羞的心理。**(d)** call forth (a quality): 產生並使用(某一特質);發揮: *Danger ~s out the best in him.* 危險使他發揮出最優的才能。**(e)** cause to strike: 使罷工: *The shop-stewards brought out the foundrymen.* 工會的工廠代表使鑄造工人罷工。

bring sb over (to), (esp) convert (sb) (to a different way of thinking, to a cause, etc). 使(某人)改變;(尤指)使改變思想方式、主義等。

bring sb/sth round, **(a)** cause (sb) to regain consciousness after fainting: 使恢復知覺; 使甦醒: *Several girls fainted in the heat but they were soon brought round.* 有幾個女孩子在炎熱中昏倒,不過很快就被救醒了。**(b)** convert to one's views, etc: 使改變觀點等: *He wasn't keen on the plan, but we managed to ~ him round.* 他本來對該計畫沒有興趣,但我們終於使他改變過來了。**(c)** (naut) make a boat face the opposite way: (航海)使船對着相反的航向: *B~ her* (ie the boat) *round into the wind.* 使船逆風而駛。**~ sb/sth round to,** direct (discussion, etc) to sth new: 把(討論等)轉到新的話題上: *He brought the conversation round to his favourite subject.* 他把談話轉到他最喜歡的題目上。

bring sb through, save (sb who is ill): 挽救;治癒(病人): *He was very ill but good doctors and careful nursing brought him through,* restored him to health. 他的病很重,不過優良的醫生和悉心的看護挽救了他(使他恢復健康)。

bring sb/sth to, **(a)** = ~ round(a): 使復甦:*They brought the girl to with smelling salts.* 他們用嗅鹽使那女孩甦醒過來。*They brought her to.* 他們使她恢復知覺。**(b)** (naut) (cause to) stop: (航海)(使)停止航行: *The ship was brought to,* eg by the firing of a gun across her bows. 那艘船被迫停航

(如開砲射過其船首)。*The ship brought to,* came to a stop. 那艘船停止航行。

bring sb / sth under, **(a)** subdue; discipline: 制服;降服;控制: *The rebels were quickly brought under.* 叛徒們很快都被制服了。**(b)** include (within a category): 歸納;納入(某一範疇): *The various points to be dealt with can be brought under three main heads.* 尚待處理的各點可以歸納爲三大項目。

bring sb / sth up, **(a)** educate; rear: 教育;養育: *She has brought up five children.* 她養育了五個孩子。*If children are badly brought up they behave badly.* 如果孩子們的教養不好,他們的行爲就不好。**(b)** vomit: 嘔吐: *~ up one's dinner.* 吃的飯都吐出來了。**(c)** call attention to: 使注意到;引述: *These are facts that can always be brought up against you,* used as evidence against you. 這些事實永遠可以被引述做爲不利於你的證據。*These are matters that you can ~ up in committee.* 這些問題你可在委員會中提出。**(d)** (mil) summon to the front line: (軍)調至前線: *We need to ~ up more tanks.* 我們需要調更多的戰車來前線。**(e)** ~ for trial: 審訊: *He was brought up on a charge of drunken driving.* 他因酒醉駕車而受審。**(f)** cause to stop suddenly: 使突然停止: *His remarks brought me up short / sharp / with a jerk.* 他的話使我楞住了。***~ up the rear,*** come last (in a line): 排在(隊伍的)最後一個;殿後: *The cavalry brought up the rear of the column.* 縱隊的最後面是騎兵。***~ up at,*** (old use, esp of a ship) end a journey: (舊用法,尤指船)結束旅程;抵達終點: *The ship brought up at a port in Greece.* 該船抵達希臘某港。

brink /brɪŋk ; brɪŋk/ *n* **1** upper edge of a steep place, a sharp slope, etc; border (of water, esp when deep): 峭壁頂端的邊緣;瀕臨深水的陸地邊緣: *He stood shivering on the ~,* hesitating to plunge into the water. 他站在岸邊發抖(不敢躍入水中)。**2** (fig) edge of sth unknown, dangerous or exciting: (喻)(未知的、危險的或刺激性事物的)邊緣: *on the ~ of war / ruin / an exciting discovery.* 在戰爭(毀滅,大發現)的邊緣。*He's on the ~ of the grave,* will die soon. 他已瀕臨墳墓的邊緣(行將入土)。**~·manship** /ˈbrɪŋkmənʃɪp ; ˈbrɪŋkmən,ʃɪp/ *n* pursuit of a dangerous policy to the limits of safety. 冒險政策的施行(一直推行危險政策直到安全的極限)。

briny ⇨ brine.

bri·oche /briːˈɒʃ *US:* ˈbriːəʊʃ ; ˈbrioʃ/ *n* (F) piece of pastry baked in a circular shape. (法)奶油蛋捲。

bri·quette, bri·quet /brɪˈket ; brɪˈkɛt/ *n* block (brick- or egg-shaped) of compressed coal-dust. (用煤渣壓製的)煤餅;煤球。

brisk /brɪsk ; brɪsk/ *adj* (-er, -est) (of persons and movement) active; lively; quick-moving: (指人及動作)活躍的;活潑的;敏捷的: *a ~ walk;* 輕快的散步; *a ~ walker;* 走路輕快的人; *at a ~ pace;* 以輕快的步子; *a ~ demand for cotton goods.* 棉織品的暢銷。*Trade is ~.* 生意興隆。**~·ly** *adv*

bris·ket /ˈbrɪskɪt ; ˈbrɪskɪt/ *n* [U] breast of an animal, (sometimes eaten as a joint of meat). (獸類的)胸部;(供作食用的)胸肉。⇨ the illus at dog. 參看 dog 之插圖。

bristle /ˈbrɪsl ; ˈbrɪsl/ *n* one of the short stiff hairs on an animal; one of the short stiff hairs in a brush: (動物身上的)剛毛;鬃;刷子上的毛: *a toothbrush with stiff ~s.* 硬毛牙刷。□ *vi* **1** [VP2A,C] *~ (up),* (of hair) stand up, rise on end: (指毛髮)聳立;豎起: *The dog was angry and ~d up / its hair ~d.* 那狗發脾氣,毛都豎起來了。 **2** [VP2A, C] (fig) show rage, indignation, etc: (喻)表示憤怒等: *~ with anger.* 怒髮衝冠。 **3** *~ with,* have in large numbers (sth difficult, sth suggesting ~s): (如荊棘)叢生;(困難)重重: *The battle-front ~d with bayonets.* 戰線上刺刀林立。*The problem ~s with difficulties.* 這問題困難重重。**brist·ly** /ˈbrɪslɪ ; ˈbrɪslɪ/ *adj* like ~s; full of ~s; (of hair, etc) rough and coarse: 如剛毛的;多硬毛的;剛毛林立的;(指毛髮等)粗糙的: *She doesn't like his bristly moustache.* 她不喜歡他那刺人的鬍髭。*What a bristly, unshaven chin!* 沒有修鬍子的下巴多麼刺人呵!

Brit·ain /ˈbrɪtn ; ˈbrɪtən/ *n* (also 亦作 ,**Great ˈB~** 大不列顛) England, Wales and Scotland; 不列顛(包括英格蘭,威爾斯及蘇格蘭); *North B~,* Scotland. 北不列顛(即蘇格蘭)。**Bri·tan·nic** /brɪˈtænɪk ; brɪˈtænɪk/ *adj* of B~ 不列顛的 (chiefly in 主用於 *Her / His Britannic Majesty* 英(女)王陛下).

Brit·ish /ˈbrɪtɪʃ ; ˈbrɪtɪʃ/ *adj* **1** of the ancient Britons. 古不列顛人的。 **2** of Great Britain, the British Commonwealth or its inhabitants: 大不列顛的;英國的;大英國協的;英國人的: *the B~,* B~ people; 英國人民(總稱); *B~ citizenship;* 英國公民資格; *a Jamaican with a B~ passport.* 持有英國護照的牙買加人。**~er** *n*

Briton /ˈbrɪtn ; ˈbrɪtn̩/ *n* **1** one of the native inhabitants of S Britain at the time of the Roman invasion about 2000 years ago. 古不列顛人(約兩千年前羅馬人入侵時的英國南部土人)。 **2** (liter) native of Britain. (文)英國人。

brittle /ˈbrɪtl ; ˈbrɪtl̩/ *adj* hard but easily broken (eg coal, ice, glass): 脆的;易碎的(如煤、冰、玻璃): (fig) (喻) *He has a ~ temper,* quickly loses his temper. 他易發脾氣。

broach[1] /brəʊtʃ ; brotʃ/ *vt* [VP6A] make a hole in (a cask of liquor) and put in a tap in order to draw the wine, etc; (fig) begin discussion of (a topic). 鑿孔於(酒桶)並挿入活嘴以便汲酒; (喻)開始討論(題目)。

broach[2] /brəʊtʃ ; brotʃ/ *vi, vt* [VP2C, 15B] *~ to,* (naut) veer or cause (a ship) to veer so that its side is presented to the wind and waves. (航海)轉動(船首)使舷側面向風浪。

broad[1] /brɔːd ; brɔd/ *adj* (-er, -est) **1** wide, large across: 寬的; 濶的: *The river grows ~er as it nears the sea.* 河在愈接近海處愈寬。***~ in the beam,*** ⇨ beam(2). **2** (after a phrase indicating width) in breadth, from side to side: (用於指寬度的片語之後)寬: *a river fifty feet ~.* 一條五十呎寬的河。 **3** extending in various or all directions: 寬濶的;廣大的;遼濶的: *the ~ ocean;* 無際的海洋; *~ lands.* 遼濶的陸地。 **4** full and complete. 充足的;完全的。***in ~ daylight,*** when it is unmistakably light: 光天化日之下;大白天裏: *a bank raid in ~ daylight.* 光天化日之下的銀行搶刼。***give sb a ~ hint,*** a strong, unmistakable one. 給某人明顯的暗示。 **5** general, not minute or detailed: 概略的;粗略的;大概的: *a ~ distinction.* 大概的區別。***in ~ outline,*** without details. 概略地;粗枝大葉的。 **6** (of the mind and ideas) liberal; not kept within narrow limits: (指心理及思想)胸襟開濶的;寬宏大量的;氣量大的: *a man of ~ views,* a tolerant man. 對事寬大爲懷的人。**,~-ˈminded** /-ˈmaɪndɪd ; -ˈmaɪndɪd/ *adj* willing to listen sympathetically to the views of others even though one cannot agree with them; having a liberal and tolerant mind. 思想開明的;胸襟開濶的; 氣量寬宏的。 **7** (of speech) strongly marked, showing that the speaker is from a definite part of the country: (指言語)方音重的: *~ Scots;* 方音很重的蘇格蘭人; *a ~ accent.* 方音很重的口音。**8** improper; coarse: 不適當的;粗鄙的: *the ~ humour of Rabelais.* 拉伯雷之粗鄙的幽默。 **9** (phrase) (片語) ***It's as ~ as it is long,*** It's all the same, however you view the problem. 橫豎都一樣;怎麼看那問題全都一樣。 **10** (compounds, etc) (複合字等) **~ bean** *n* the common flattened variety, growing in large pods. 蠶豆。**B~ Church** *n* used of churchmen who do not insist upon dogma and doctrine. 不堅持教條的教派;廣教會派。**~·ly** *adv* **1** in a wide way. 廣闊地;廣大地。 **2** in a general way: 概略地;大概地: *~ly speaking,* speaking in a general way, without going into detail. 總而言之;概括地說。**~·ness** *n* = breadth (the usu word). (breadth 較常用)。 **~en** /ˈbrɔːdn ; ˈbrɔdn̩/ *vt, vi*

[VP6A, 15B, 2A, C] **~en (out)**, make or become ~(er): 使寬;變寬;放寬;拓寬: *His face ~ened (out) into a grin.* 他咧嘴而笑。

broad[2] /brɔ:d ; brɔd/ *n* the ~ part (*of* sth): (某物之)寬的部份(與 of 連用): *the ~ of the back.* 背部的寬處。**the B~s** *n pl* name used of wide stretches of water in Norfolk, used for boating holidays and barge traffic. 英國諾福克郡境內可供駕舟度假及航行平底駁船之大片的平靜水面。

broad·cast /'brɔ:dkɑ:st *US:* -kæst ; 'brɔd,kæst/ *vt, vi* (*pt, pp* broadcast or ~ed) **1** [VP6A] send out in all directions, esp by radio or TV: 廣播;(尤指經由無線電或電視)播送: ~ *the news/a speech/a concert.* 廣播(或播放)新聞(演說,音樂演奏)。 **2** [VP2A] speak, sing, perform music, etc for ~ing: 發表廣播(或電視)演說;廣播演唱(或演奏等);作電視演唱(或演奏等): *The Prime Minister will ~ this evening.* 首相將於今晚發表廣播(或作電視)演說。**3** [VP6A,2A] sow (seed) by scattering it, not by sowing it in drills, etc. 撒播(種子)。□ *n* (often attrib) ~ing; sth ~: (常作形容用法)廣播;播送;廣播的內容: *today's ~;* 今天的廣播節目; *a ~ of a football match.* 足球比賽之廣播。⇨ telecast. □ *adv* by ~ing: 用撒播的方式: *sow seed ~.* 撒種。**~·ing** *n, adj*: *the British B~ing Corporation*, the BBC; 英國廣播公司; *a '~ing station.* 廣播電臺。

broad·cloth /'brɔ:dklɒθ *US:* -klɔ:θ ; 'brɔd,klɔθ/ *n* [U] fine, smooth, double-width black cloth, formerly used for men's clothes. 一種雙幅的黑色布料(昔時用製男子服裝)。

broad·sheet /'brɔ:dʃi:t ; 'brɔd,ʃit/ *n* popular ballad or tract printed on one side only of a large sheet of paper (as formerly sold in the streets). 印在大幅紙張上(只印一面)的通俗歌謠或勸善文字(如昔時在街上出售者)。

broad·side /'brɔ:dsaɪd ; 'brɔd,saɪd/ *n* [C] **1** the whole of a ship's side above the water; (the firing on the same target of) all the guns on one side of a ship; (fig) strong attack of any kind made at one time against one person or group. 舷側(吃水線以上之全部船側);船舷一側所有的砲;偏舷齊放(船舷一側的所有各砲向同一目標齊發);(喻)對某一人或某團體所作之一次猛烈攻擊。 **2 ~ on (to)**, (of a ship) with one side presented to or facing: (指船)以側面對向: *a collision ~ on*, so that the ship's side collides with sth. 與舷側發生的碰撞。

broad·ways, broad·wise /'brɔ:dweɪz, -waɪz ; 'brɔd,wez, -waɪz/ *adv* in the direction of the breadth. 橫着;橫地。

bro·cade /brə'keɪd ; bro'ked/ *n* [C,U] woven material richly ornamented with designs (eg in raised gold or silver thread). (用金、銀線等織成之)錦緞;花緞。□ *vt* [VP6A] decorate (cloth) with raised patterns. 織成錦緞。

broc·coli /'brɒkəlɪ ; 'brɑkəlɪ/ *n* [C] hardy kind of cauliflower with numerous white or purple sprouts (flower-heads), each like a small cauliflower. 一種花椰菜;硬花甘藍。

bro·chure /'brəʊʃə(r) *US:* brəʊ'ʃʊər ; bro'ʃjʊr/ *n* short, usu descriptive, printed article in a paper cover; pamphlet: 小册子: *travel/holiday ~s.* 旅遊(度假)手册。

brogue[1] /brəʊg ; brog/ *n* strong, thick-soled, usu ornamented shoe for country wear. (通常爲帶有裝飾性小孔在鄉下穿的)結實的厚底皮鞋。

brogue[2] /brəʊg ; brog/ *n* regional way of speaking, esp the Irish way of speaking English. 土腔(尤指愛爾蘭人說英語之腔調)。

broil /brɔɪl ; brɔɪl/ *vt, vi* [VP6A,2A] cook, be cooked, by direct contact with fire or on a gridiron; grill; (fig) be very hot: 烤;燒;炙,在鐵架上烤(肉類);(喻)很熱;炙熱: *a ~ing day;* 炎熱的一日; *sit ~ing in the sun.* 坐着晒太陽。**~er** *n* bird, eg a chicken, killed at the age of 10 to 12 weeks and suitable for being ~ed or roasted, esp one reared in a shed or concrete building (and contrasted with a *free-range* bird), ⇨ battery(6). 適於燒烤的子鷄或嫩鷄(或指其他家禽,經飼養約十至十二星期,尤指養於鷄房中,而非養在空地上者)。

broke /brəʊk ; brok/ *attrib adj* **(stony/flat) ~**, (sl) penniless. (俚)身無分文;一文不名。

bro·ken /'brəʊkən ; 'brokən/ *pp* of break: *a ~ marriage*, one that has failed; 破裂的婚姻; *a ~ home*, one in which the parents have separated or are divorced, so that the children lack proper care, security, etc; 破裂的家庭(夫婦分居或離婚,因而孩子們缺少適當照顧者); ~ (= imperfect) *English;* 不流利的英語;蹩脚英語; *a ~ man*, a man reduced to despair; 絕望的人;精神頹喪的人; ~ (= uneven) *ground;* 崎嶇的地面; ~ (= disturbed, intermittent) *sleep;* 斷續的睡眠; ,~-'*hearted*, crushed by grief. 傷心的;斷腸的。

bro·ker /'brəʊkə(r) ; 'brokə/ *n* **1** person (eg '*stock-~*) who buys and sells (esp stocks and shares, bonds, etc) for others. (替人買賣股票,債券等之)掮客;經紀人。 **2** official licensed to sell the goods of sb unable to pay debts. 執行拍賣破產者財物之人員。**~·age** /'brəʊkərɪdʒ ; 'brokərɪdʒ/ *n* [U] ~'s commission for services. (掮客所收之)佣金;經紀費。

brolly /'brɒlɪ ; 'brɑlɪ/ *n* (colloq) umbrella. (俗)傘。

bro·mide /'brəʊmaɪd ; 'bromaɪd/ *n* **1** [U] chemical compound of bromine, eg potassium ~, esp as used in medicine to calm the nerves. 溴化物(如溴化鉀,尤指用作鎮靜劑者)。 **2** [C] (colloq) trite remark; dull, tiresome or boring person. (俗)庸俗或陳腐的話;遲鈍而令人厭倦的人。

bro·mine /'brəʊmi:n ; 'bromin/ *n* [U] non-metallic element (symbol **Br**), compounds of which are used in photographic and other chemicals. 溴(非金屬元素,化學符號Br,溴化物用於製攝影及其他化學藥品)。

bron·chi /'brɒŋkaɪ ; 'brɑŋkaɪ/ *n pl* (*sing* bron·chus /-kəs ; -kəs/) two main branches into which the windpipe divides before entering the lungs, also called *bronchial tubes.* 支氣管。⇨ the illus at respiratory. 參看 respiratory 之插圖。**~al** /'brɒŋkɪəl ; 'brɑŋkɪəl/ *adj* of or affecting the ~: 支氣管的;感染支氣管的: *bronchial asthma.* 支氣管性哮喘。**bron·chi·tic** /brɒŋ'kɪtɪk ; brɑn'kɪtɪk/ *adj* suffering from, prone to, bronchitis. 患支氣管炎的;易患支氣管炎的。 **bron·chi·tis** /brɒŋ'kaɪtɪs ; brɑn'kaɪtɪs/ *n* inflammation of the mucous membrane of the ~. 支氣管炎。

bronco /'brɒŋkəʊ ; 'brɑŋko/ *n* (*pl* -cos) wild or half-tamed horse of Western N America. 北美西部產之一種野馬。

bronze /brɒnz ; brɑnz/ *n* **1** [U] alloy of copper and tin: 青銅(銅與錫之合金): *a ~ statue;* 銅像; *a statue in ~.* 銅像。**the 'B~ Age**, period when men used tools and weapons made of ~(between the Stone Age and the Iron Age). 青銅器時代(介於石器時代與鐵器時代之間)。 **2** [U] colour of ~, reddish brown. 古銅色;赤褐色。 **3** [C] work of art, eg a vase, made of ~: 青銅器(作爲藝術品者,如花瓶): *a fine collection of ~s and ivories.* 所收藏之一批精緻的青銅器及象牙製品。□ *vt, vi* [VP6A, 2A] make or become ~ colour: (使)變成古銅色;(使)變成赤褐色: *faces ~d by the sun and wind.* 飽經日晒風吹之赤褐色的面孔。

brooch /brəʊtʃ ; brotʃ/ *n* ornamental pin for fastening or wearing on part of a woman's dress. (別於婦女服裝上的)花別針;胸針。

brood /bru:d ; brud/ *n* all the young birds hatched at one time in a nest; family of other egg-produced animals; (hum) young family of human beings. 一窩所孵的幼雛;其他卵生動物之一窩;(諧)一家裏的孩子們。 **'~-hen** *n* hen for breeding. 孵雛的母鷄。**'~-mare** *n* mare for breeding. 供繁殖之牝馬;傳種母馬。□ *vi* **1** [VP2A, C] (of a bird) sit on eggs to hatch them. (指禽類)(坐於卵上)孵雛;孵蛋。 **2** [VP3A] **~ (on/over)**, (fig) think about (troubles, etc) for a long time: (喻)沉思;思慮;憂思: *She sat there ~ing on whether life was worth living.* 她坐在那裏沉思人生是否值得活下去。 **~y** *adj* (of hens) wanting to ~; (colloq, of women) feeling the desire to have children; (fig, of persons) moody; depressed. (指母鷄)欲孵卵的; 要孵小鷄的; (俗,指女人)有生孩子之欲的; (喻,指人)憂鬱的; 沮喪的。

brook¹ /brʊk ; brʊk/ *n* small stream. 小河;溪流。

brook² /brʊk ; brʊk/ *vt* [VP6A, B] (formal) (usu in neg and interr) put up with; tolerate: (正式用語) (通常用於否定及疑問句中)忍受;容忍;耐;捱: *He cannot ~ interference/being interfered with.* 他不能忍受他人的干涉。

broom¹ /bru:m ; brum/ *n* [U] shrub with yellow or white flowers growing on sandy banks, etc. 金雀花(生於沙岸等處)。

broom² /bru:m ; brum/ *n* long-handled implement for sweeping floors, etc. 掃帚。 ***a new ~,*** (esp) a newly appointed official (who gets rid of old methods, traditions, etc): 新人; (尤指)新上任的官員(革除老法、舊傳統等者): (prov) (諺) *A new ~ sweeps clean.* 新官上任三把火。 **'~·stick** *n* handle of a broom (on which witches were said to ride through the air). 掃帚柄(傳說巫婆乘之飛行於空中)。

Bros ⇨ App 2. 參看附錄二。

broth /brɒθ ; brɔθ/ *n* [U] water in which meat has been boiled; this, flavoured and thickened with vegetables, etc, served as soup. 煮肉的清湯;肉湯(再加入蔬菜及調味品煮濃後供食者)。

brothel /'brɒθl ; 'brɔθəl/ *n* house at which prostitutes may be visited. 妓院。

brother /'brʌðə(r) ; 'brʌðɚ/ *n* **1** son of the same parents as another person: 兄弟: *my elder/younger ~;* 我的哥哥(弟弟); *the ~s Smith, the Smith ~s;* 史密斯兄弟們; *Smith Brothers* or (comm style) *Smith Bros.* 史密斯兄弟商店(商業型式作Smith Bros)。 **'~-in-law** /'brʌðər ɪn lɔ: ; 'brʌðərɪn,lɔ/ *n* (*pl* ~s-in-law) ~ of one's husband or wife; husband of one's sister. 夫或妻的兄弟; 大伯; 小叔; 內兄; 內弟; 姊夫; 妹夫。 **2** person united to others by membership of the same group, society, profession, etc; fellow member of a socialist organization, trade union, etc: 同道; 同人; 同行; 同業; 社會主義組織之一員; 同志; 公會會員(等): (esp attrib) (尤作形容用法) *a ~ doctor;* 加入公會的醫生; *~s in arms,* soldiers who are serving or have served together; (正在服役或已退役的)軍中同志; 袍澤; *~ officers,* in the same regiment. 同僚軍官。 **3** (*pl* brethren /'breðrən ; 'brɛðrɪn/) fellow member of a religious society. 同教會的教友。 **B~,** form of address: 稱呼形式: *B~ Luke.* 路克弟兄。 **'~·hood** /-hʊd ; -,hud/ *n* **1** [U] feeling of ~ for ~. 手足之情; 同胞之愛。 **2** [C] (members of an) association of men with common interests and aims, esp a religious society or socialist organization. 以共同興趣及目的而組成的團體(尤指宗教性或社會主義者); 同志會; 同道會; 全體同道。 **~·ly** *adj* of or like a ~('s): 兄弟的; 如兄弟的; 情同手足的: *~ly affection.* 手足之情。

brougham /'bru:əm ; 'bruəm/ *n* (19th c) four-wheeled closed carriage drawn by one horse. (十九世紀的)單馬有篷四輪馬車。

brought *pt, pp* of bring.

brou·haha /'bru:hɑ:hɑ: ; 'bruhɑhɑ/ *n* (dated colloq) fuss; excitement. (過時俗語)紛擾; 緊張; 興奮。

brow /braʊ ; braʊ/ *n* **1** (usu *pl*; 通常用複數; also 亦作 **'eye·~**) arch of hair above the eye: 眉; 眉毛: *knit one's ~s,* frown. 皺眉頭; 蹙額。 **2** forehead. 額。 ⇨ *highbrow* at high¹(12); *lowbrow* at low¹(13). **3** top of a slope; steep slope; overhanging edge. 坡頂; 陡坡; 懸崖。

brow·beat /'braʊbi:t ; 'braʊ,bit/ *vt* (*pt* browbeat, *pp* browbeaten) [VP6A, 14] ***~ (into doing sth),*** intimidate by shouting or looking stern at; bully: (以聲音或神情)威嚇(使做某事); 嚇唬: *~ sb into doing sth;* 威嚇某人做某事; *a poor, ~en little woman.* —個可憐的、被嚇倒的小婦人。

brown /braʊn ; braʊn/ *adj* (-er, -est), *n* colour of toasted bread, or coffee mixed with milk: 深黃色; 棕色; 褐色(烤過的麵包之色,或咖啡加牛奶後的顏色): *~ bread,* made with wholemeal flour; 黑麵包(以沒有去麩的麵粉製成者); *~ paper,* coarse kind used for parcels, etc; 棕色包裝紙; 牛皮紙; *~ sugar,* half refined. 紅糖。 ***in a ~ study,*** deep in thought; in a reverie. 在沉思冥想中。 **'~·stone** *n* [U] kinds of reddish-brown sandstone used for building. 一種赤褐色沙岩(用於建築)。 □ *vt, vi* [VP6A, 2A] make or become ~. (使)變成褐色。 ***,~ed 'off,*** (sl) bored; fed up. (俚)厭煩的; 忍受够了的。

brownie /'braʊnɪ ; 'braʊnɪ/ *n* **1** small, good-natured fairy or elf. 善良的小精靈。 **2 B~ (Guide),** (GB) junior member (age 8 to 11) of the Girl Guides. (英)幼年女童軍(八至十一歲)。

browse /braʊz ; braʊz/ *vi* [VP2A, C] **1** feed, as animals do (on grass, etc): (指動物)食; 嚙(草等): *cattle browsing in the fields.* 在田野中吃草的牛群。 **2** read (parts of a book or books) without any definite plan, for interest or enjoyment: 瀏覽(書籍); 隨便翻閱: *browsing among books in the public library.* 在公立圖書館中瀏覽各種書籍。 □ *n* (act, period, of) browsing: 瀏覽; 瀏覽的時間: *have a good ~.* 瀏覽很久的時間。

bruin /'bru:ɪn ; 'bruɪn/ *n* (pop name, eg in fairy tales, for) bear. (在童話等中之)熊的俗稱。

bruise /bru:z ; bruz/ *n* injury by a blow or knock to the body, or to a fruit, so that the skin is discoloured but not broken: (人體或水果由於打擊或碰撞使皮膚或果皮變色但未破裂之)挫傷; 碰傷; 瘀傷: *covered with ~s after falling off his bicycle.* 因從脚踏車上跌下而滿身受到挫傷。 □ *vt, vi* **1** [VP6A] cause a ~ or ~s to; batter, make dents in (wood or metal): 使受挫傷; 把(木頭或金屬)槌凹: *He fell and ~d his leg.* 他跌一跤挫傷了腿。 *Pack the peaches carefully so that they won't get ~d.* 小心包裝桃子,別讓它們碰傷或壓傷。 **2** [VP2A] show the effects of a blow or knock: 顯出挫傷或瘀傷的傷痕: *A child's flesh ~s easily.* 小孩的皮肉易顯出挫傷的瘀痕。 **bruiser** *n* tough, brutal boxer. 粗野殘酷的拳師。

bruit /bru:t ; brut/ *vt* [VP15B] ***~ abroad,*** (old use) spread (a rumour or report): (舊用法)傳佈(謠言或傳聞等): *~ it abroad,* spread the news everywhere. 傳遍各處。

brunch /brʌntʃ ; brʌntʃ/ *n* (colloq) late morning meal instead of breakfast and lunch. (俗)早午餐(代替早點及午餐者)。

bru·nette /bru:'net ; bru'nɛt/ *n* European with dark skin and dark-brown or black hair. 皮膚深色、頭髮呈深褐色或黑色的歐洲人。 ⇨ blond(e).

brunt /brʌnt ; brʌnt/ *n* chief stress or strain: 主要的壓力或拉力; 中心力量: *bear the ~ of an attack.* 承受攻擊的主力; 首當其衝。 *The main ~ of their criticism fell on us.* 他們批評的重點是針對着我們。

brush¹ /brʌʃ ; brʌʃ/ *n* **1** implement of bristles, hair, wire, etc fastened in wood, bone, or other material, used for scrubbing, sweeping, cleaning (eg *'tooth~, 'nail~*), or tidying the hair (*'hair~*); tuft of hair, etc set in a handle, used by painters and artists: (用鬃、髮、金屬絲等製之)刷子(如牙刷、指甲刷、髮刷); (畫家的)畫筆: *a 'paint-brush.* 畫筆。 **2** (act of) using a ~: 用刷子刷; 刷: *He gave his clothes a good ~,* used a ~ on them. 他把他的衣服好好地刷了一番。 ⇨ also *'~-up* at brush²(1). **3** fox's tail. 狐狸尾巴。 **4** [U] rough low-growing bushes; undergrowth: 矮灌木叢: *a ~ fire.* 矮灌木叢的大火。 ⇨ bush(2). **5** short, sharp fight or encounter: 小戰; 小衝突; 遭遇戰: *a ~ with the enemy.* 與敵人之遭遇戰。 **'~·wood** *n* [U] = brush(4). **'~-work** *n* artist's style or way of using a paint-~. 畫家的筆法。

brush² /brʌʃ ; brʌʃ/ *vt, vi* **1** [VP6A, 15B, 22] use a brush on; clean, polish, make tidy or smooth: 用

刷子刷;使清潔整齊等;刷清;刷亮;拂拭: ~ *your hat/clothes/shoes/hair/teeth;* 刷你的帽子(衣服,鞋子,頭髮,牙齒); ~ *sth clean.* 把某物刷乾淨。~ **sth away/off,** remove with a ~: 用刷子刷掉某物: *He ~ed away a fly from his nose,* used his hand to make the fly go away. 他用手趕走鼻子上的蒼蠅。*She ~ed the crumbs off the tablecloth.* 她刷掉枱布上的食品屑。~ **sth aside/away,** (fig) pay no or little attention to (difficulties, objections, etc). (喻)不理;不顧(困難、反對等)。~ **sb/sth off,** (colloq) reject, jilt; dismiss curtly: (俗)拒絕;拋棄;唐突地摒除: *He tries to get the girl to go out with him, but she always ~es him off.* 他試圖邀那女郎和他一起出去,但她總是拒絕他。Hence, 由此產生, '~**-off** *n* (colloq) rejection or dismissal: (俗)拒絕;摒棄: *She gave him the ~-off.* 她拒絕了他。~ **sth up,** use a ~ on: 刷某物: ~ *up the dust;* 把灰塵刷掉; (fig) study or practise (sth) in order to get back skill that has been lost: (喻)溫習;再練(俾能重獲業已荒疏的技術): *If you're going to France you'd better ~ up your French.* 如果你要到法國去,最好先溫習你的法文。Hence, 由此產生, '~**-up** *n: Give your French a ~-up.* 把你的法文溫習溫習。 **2** [VP2A, C, 6A] touch when passing: 擦過;掠過: *He ~ed past/by/(up) against me in a rude way.* 他粗魯地從我身邊擦過。*The leaves of the trees ~ed my face as I ran through the forest.* 當我從樹林中跑過時,樹葉在我的臉上掠過。 **3** [VP2C] ~ **off,** come off as the result of being ~ed: 被刷掉: *The mud will ~ off when it dries.* 泥土乾時可以刷掉。

brusque /bru:sk ; brʌsk/ *adj* (of speech or behaviour) rough and abrupt. (指語言或行爲)粗魯的;唐突的。~**·ly** *adj* ~**·ness** *n*

Brus·sels /'brʌslz ; 'brʌsḷz/ *n* (attrib) of or from ~ in Belgium: (形容用法)(比利時首都)布魯塞爾的;來自布魯塞爾的: ~ *lace/carpets.* 布魯塞爾花邊(地毯)。ˌ~ **'sprouts,** (plants with) buds growing thickly on the stem of a cabbage-like plant. 芽甘藍。⇨ the illus at vegetable. 參看 vegetable 之插圖。

brutal /'bru:tl ; 'brutḷ/ *adj* savage; cruel. 野蠻的;殘忍的。~**·ly** /-təlɪ ; -tḷɪ/ *adv* **bru·tal·ity** /bru:'tælətɪ ; bru'tælətɪ/ *n* [U] cruelty; savagery; [C] cruel or savage act. 殘忍;野蠻;殘忍或野蠻的行爲。'~**·ize** *vt* [VP6A] make ~: 使變殘忍;使野蠻: *Years of warfare had ~ized the troops.* 連年作戰使軍隊變得殘忍。

brute /bru:t ; brut/ *n* **1** animal (except man). 野獸。 **2** stupid, animal-like or cruel person. 愚蠢的人;人面獸心的人;殘忍的人。 **3** (attrib) animal-like; cruel and unthinking; unconscious or unreasoning; merely material: (形容用法)如野獸的;殘忍而無思想的;無意識的;無理性的;僅僅是物質的: ~ *force/strength,* 暴力(蠻力); ~ *matter.* 無生命之物;死物。 **brut·ish** /'bru:tɪʃ ; 'brutɪʃ/ *adj* of or like a ~: 野獸的;如野獸的: *brutish appetites.* 獸慾。 **brut·ish·ly** *adv*

bubble /'bʌbl ; 'bʌbḷ/ *n* **1** (in air) floating ball formed of liquid and containing air or gas: (浮於空氣中的)氣泡;泡: *soap ~s;* 肥皂泡; *blowing ~s.* 吹泡泡。 **2** (in liquid) ball of air or gas that rises to the surface, eg in boiling water, in sparkling wines. (從液體中浮於水面的)氣泡(如沸水、會冒泡的酒中者)。 **3** air-filled cavity in a solidified liquid, eg glass. 液體凝固後(如玻璃)內中存留的氣泡。 **4** (fig) visionary plan; idea, hope, etc that is not realized: (喻)幻想的計畫;無法實現的意念、希望等: *His ~ has burst.* 他的計畫(或希望)已成泡影(破滅了)。 **5** '~ **car** *n* small car with a transparent dome as roof. 泡泡車(車頂爲透明圓頂的小汽車)。'~ **gum** *n* chewing gum which can be blown into bubbles on the lips. 泡泡糖(可以吹成泡的口香糖)。□ *vi* [VP2A, C] send up ~s; rise in ~s; make the sound of ~s: 發出氣泡;起泡;發氣泡聲: *The water ~d up through the sand.* 水從沙中冒出氣泡。*She was bubbling over with joy/high spirits/laughter.* 她得意洋洋(高興,咯咯而笑)。 **bub·bly** /'bʌblɪ ; 'bʌblɪ/ *adj* full of ~s. 充滿泡沫的;多泡的。□ *n* (hum) champagne. (諧)香檳酒。

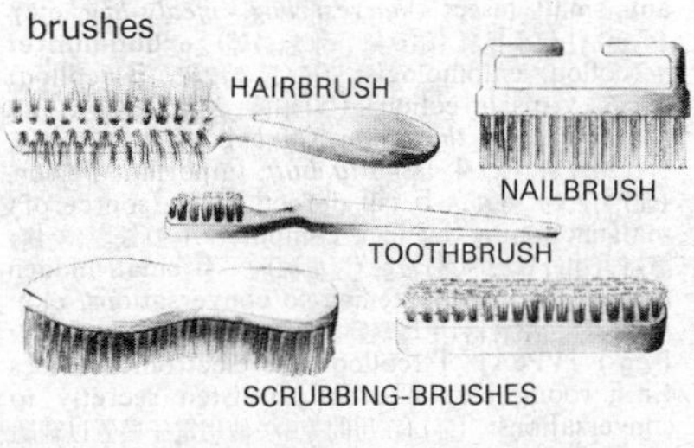

bu·bonic /bju:'bɒnɪk ; bju'bɑnɪk/ *adj* ~ **'plague,** contagious disease that spreads quickly (spread by rats, and marked by chills, fevers and swelling in the armpits and groin). 淋巴腺鼠疫(一種蔓延迅速的傳染病,由老鼠傳布,症狀爲發冷發熱,腋窩及鼠蹊腫大)。

buc·ca·neer /ˌbʌkə'nɪə(r) ; ˌbʌkə'nɪr/ *n* pirate; unscrupulous adventurer. 海盜;無顧忌的冒險者。

buck[1] /bʌk ; bʌk/ *n* **1** male of a deer, hare or rabbit. 牡鹿;雄兔。⇨ doe. '~**·skin** *n* [U] soft leather made from deerskin or goatskin, used for gloves, bags, etc. 鹿皮或羊皮所製成的柔軟皮革(用製手套、皮包等)。'~**·shot** *n* [U] large-size lead shot[1](4). 大型鉛彈;鹿彈。'~**·tooth** *n* (*pl* ~teeth) (usu upper) tooth that projects. (通常指上齒)獠牙;突出齒。 **2** (attrib) male. (形容用法)雄的。

buck[2] /bʌk ; bʌk/ *vi, vt* **1** [VP2A] (of a horse) jump up with the four feet together and the back arched; [VP6A] throw (the rider) to the ground by doing this. (指馬)四足離地拱背而跳躍;由此種跳躍而將(騎者)摔於地上。 **2** ~ **up,** [VP2C, esp in the *imperative* 尤用於祈使句] (colloq) hurry. (俗)趕快。~ **(sb) up,** [VP15B, 2C] make or become more vigorous or cheerful, ready for greater effort: (使)精神大振;鼓勵: *The good news ~ed us all up.* 這好消息使我們大家極爲興奮。*We were greatly ~ed up by the news.* 這消息令我們大爲振奮。

buck[3] /bʌk ; bʌk/ *n* (US sl) US dollar. (美俚)美元。

buck[4] /bʌk ; bʌk/ *n* **pass the ~ (to sb),** (sl) shift the responsibility (to). (俚)推諉責任(於某人)。**The ~ stops here,** The responsibility cannot be shifted further. 該責任不能再推諉了。

bucket[1] /'bʌkɪt ; 'bʌkɪt/ *n* **1** vessel of wood, metal, canvas, plastic, etc for holding or carrying water, milk, etc; (also 亦作 '~**·ful** /-fʊl ; -ˌfʊl/) the amount a ~ holds: (用木、金屬、帆布、塑膠等製成以盛或提水、牛奶等之)水桶;吊桶;一桶之量: *The rain was coming down in ~s,* was very heavy. 大雨傾盆。 **2** scoop of a dredging machine, grain-elevator, etc. (挖泥機、吊穀機等之)戽斗。 '~ **seat** *n* (in a car or aircraft) seat with a rounded back for one person (contrasted with a *bench* seat). (汽車或飛機中之)單人圓背座位(與 bench seat 相對)。

bucket[2] /'bʌkɪt ; 'bʌkɪt/ *vi* ride a horse hard. 拚命策馬飛奔;騎馬飛奔。

buckle /'bʌkl ; 'bʌkḷ/ *n* **1** metal, plastic or bone fastener, with one or more spikes made to go through a hole in a strap, etc, to keep sth in place. (皮帶等的)扣環。 **2** ornamental clasp on a shoe. 鞋上的裝飾性扣環。□ *vt, vi* **1** [VP6A, 15B] ~ **(on),** fasten with a ~: 以扣環扣住: ~ *a belt;* 扣起帶子; ~ *on a sword/one's armour.* 藉扣起扣環而佩帶劍(穿上甲冑)。 **2** [VP2C] (of a shoe, belt, etc) fasten (in a certain way). (指鞋、帶等)(以某種方式)結紮。 **3** [VP2C] ~ **to/down to** (*work, etc*), begin (work) in earnest: 開始認眞(工作等);努力從事: ~ *to a task.* 努力從事一項工作。*The sooner he ~s down to it, the better.* 他越早認眞開始做越好。 **4** [VP2A] (of metal work, etc) bend, become twisted, crumple up from strain or heat. (指金屬

品等因受壓力或熱力而)彎曲；扭曲；捲曲。

buck·ler /ˈbʌklə(r) ; ˈbʌklɚ/ *n* small round shield, usu held by a handle or worn on the arm. 小圓楯(通常有柄,或戴在臂上)。

buck·ram /ˈbʌkrəm ; ˈbʌkrəm/ *n* [U] stiff, rough cloth (esp as used for binding books). 硬粗布(尤指用於裝訂書籍者)。

buck·shot /ˈbʌkʃɒt ; ˈbʌk,ʃɑt/ ⇨ buck¹(1).

buck·wheat /ˈbʌkwi:t *US:* -hwi:t ; ˈbʌk,hwit/ *n* [U] (plant with) small triangular seed used for feeding horses and poultry. 蕎麥(用作馬及家禽飼料)。ˈ~ **flour,** flour made from this grain, used in US for breakfast cakes. 蕎麥麵粉(在美國用以製早餐糕餅)。

bu·colic /bju:ˈkɒlɪk ; bjuˈkɑlɪk/ *adj* of country life and farming, esp of shepherds: 農村生活的；(尤指)牧人的： ~ *verse.* 牧歌；田園詩。**bu·col·ics** *n pl* pastoral poems. 田園詩。

bud /bʌd ; bʌd/ *n* **1** leaf, flower or branch, at the beginning of its growth. (葉、花或枝初生時的)芽；苞；蓓蕾。***in bud,*** having buds or sending out buds: 正在發芽；含苞待放： *The trees are in bud.* 樹正在發芽。***nip sth in the bud,*** put an end to sth, eg a plot, while it is in the beginning stage. 趁某事尚未成熟卽行消滅之。 **2** partly opened flower. 初開的花。⇨ the illus at flower. 參看 flower 之插圖。□ *vi* (-dd-) put out buds. 發芽；萌芽；生芽。**bud·ding** *adj* beginning to develop: 發芽的；開始發展的；新進的： *a budding lawyer／poet.* 新進的律師(詩人)。

Bud·dhism /ˈbʊdɪzəm ; ˈbʊdɪzəm/ *n* the religion founded by Gautama /ˈgaʊtəmə ; ˈgɔtəmə/ or Siddhartha /sɪˈdɑ:tə ; sɪˈdɑrtə/ Buddha /ˈbʊdə ; ˈbʊdə/ (= teacher) in N India, in about the 6th c BC. 佛教(約於西元前六世紀,佛陀創始於印度北部之宗教)。**Bud·dhist** /ˈbʊdɪst ; ˈbʊdɪst/ *n* follower of Buddha. 佛教徒。

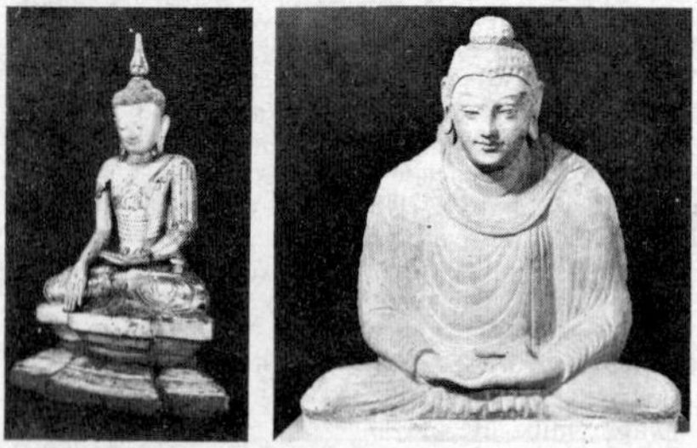

representations of Gautama Buddha

buddy /ˈbʌdɪ ; ˈbʌdɪ/ *n* (*pl* -dies) (sl, as a familiar form of address) chum; mate. (俚,對熟朋友的稱呼)老兄。

budge /bʌdʒ ; bʌdʒ/ *vt, vi* [VP6A, usu in *neg* and with *can, could*; 通常用於否定句中,與 can, could 連用; VP2A, C, usu in *neg* with *won't wouldn't* 通常用於否定句中,與 won't, wouldn't 連用] (cause to) move very little, make the slightest movement; (fig) (cause to) change a position or attitude: (使)稍微移動；(喩) (使)改變位置或態度： *I can't ~ it.* 我無法使它移動分毫。*It won't ~ an inch.* 它一點也不動。

bud·geri·gar /ˈbʌdʒərɪgɑ:(r) ; ˈbʌdʒərɪ,gɑr/ *n* Australian lovebird; kind of parakeet. 澳洲情鳥；一種小鸚鵡。⇨ the illus at rare. 參看 rare 之插圖。

budget /ˈbʌdʒɪt ; ˈbʌdʒɪt/ *n* [C] estimate of probable future income and expenditure, esp that made by a Government; similar estimate made by a business company, society, private person, etc. 預算(對於未來可能收支之估計,尤指政府之預算；亦指工商公司、團體、私人等之預算)。ˈ~ **account,** account with a bank maintained by monthly transfers from a current account, so that the Bank may pay regularly recurring expenses, eg gas, electricity, rates. 預算帳戶(在銀行開立之帳戶,由甲種存款帳戶中按月撥轉款項,使銀行可代付經常開支費用,如瓦斯、電費、稅)。ˈ~ **plan,** system of buying goods in (large) shops by making regular monthly payments to them. (大)商店之按月分期付款的銷貨方法。□ *vi* [VP3A] ~ ***for,*** allow or arrange for (in a ~): 爲…做預算： ~ *for the coming year.* 爲明年做預算。**~·ary** /ˈbʌdʒɪtərɪ *US:* -terɪ ; ˈbʌdʒɪ,tɛrɪ/ *adj* of a ~. 預算的。

budgie /ˈbʌdʒɪ ; ˈbʌdʒɪ/ *n* (colloq abbr for a) budgerigar. (俗)爲 budgerigar 之略。

buff /bʌf ; bʌf/ *n* [U] **1** thick, strong, soft leather. 厚而柔韌之皮革。 **2** dull yellow colour. 暗黃色。 **3** the bare skin, esp in: 不着衣飾的皮膚,尤用於： *stripped to the ~,* without clothing. 赤裸的。 **4** (US colloq) fan³, enthusiast. (美俗)迷；熱中者。□ *vt* polish (metal) with ~(1). 用此種皮革擦(金屬)使之光亮。

buf·falo /ˈbʌfələʊ ; ˈbʌfḷ,o/ *n* (*pl* ~s, US also ~es) kinds of large, usu wild ox in India, Asia, Europe and Africa; N American bison: (產於印度、亞洲、歐洲及非洲的)水牛；(北美洲之)野牛： *a herd of sixty ~s／~es.* 爲數六十頭之水牛群。

buf·fer¹ /ˈbʌfə(r) ; ˈbʌfɚ/ *n* apparatus (either spring-loaded or hydraulic) for lessening the effect of a blow or collision, eg on a railway engine or van. (利用彈簧或水力以減輕撞擊之)緩衝器(如裝於火車頭或貨車上者)。~ **state,** state situated between two or more powerful states, lessening the risk of war between them. (介於兩强國或數强國間以減少戰爭危險之)緩衝國。

buf·fer² /ˈbʌfə(r) ; ˈbʌfɚ/ *n* (sl, usu 通常作 **old** ~) old-fashioned or foolish man. (俚)老古板；愚人。

buf·fet¹ /ˈbʊfeɪ *US:* bəˈfeɪ ; buˈfe/ *n* counter where food and drink may be bought and consumed, eg in a railway station or (GB, in the ˈ~ *car*) on a train; sideboard or table from which food and drink are served, eg in a hotel: (火車站或英國火車餐車上之)飲食櫃臺；(旅館等中之)食物檯；餐檯： *cold ~,* (on a menu) cold cooked meat, etc; (菜單上)冷肉； ~ *supper,* meal served to guests who do not sit at a table. 自助(晚)餐。

buf·fet² /ˈbʌfɪt ; ˈbʌfɪt/ *n* blow, generally one given with the hand; (fig) misfortune; blow delivered by fate. (用手的)打擊；(喩)不幸；命運的打擊。□ *vt, vi* **1** [VP6A] give a ~ or ~s to: 予以一擊；打擊： *flowers ~ed by rain and wind;* 爲風雨所摧殘的花； *~ed by the waves／misfortunes.* 受浪濤(不幸)之打擊。 **2** [VP6A, 3A] (rare) contend (*with*): (罕) (與…)搏鬥；奮鬥；掙扎： ~ (*with*) *the waves.* 與浪濤搏鬥。

buf·foon /bəˈfu:n ; bʌˈfun/ *n* clown; jester. 丑角；滑稽演員。***play the ~,*** do and say foolish things to amuse others. 扮演小丑；做傻事說傻話以娛他人。**~·ery** /-ərɪ ; -ərɪ/ *n* [U] clowning; clown-like behaviour; (in *pl*) rough jokes and actions. 扮小丑；小丑行爲；(複數)粗俗的笑話和動作。

bug /bʌg ; bʌg/ *n* **1** small, flat, ill-smelling, blood-sucking insect that infests dirty houses and beds. 臭蟲(扁平吸血小蟲,出現在骯髒的房屋中及床上)。⇨ the illus at insect. 參看 insect 之插圖。 **2** (esp US) any small insect (ˈ*harvest bug,* ˈ*mealy-bug,* etc). (尤美)任何小昆蟲(如秋蚲、水蠟蟲等)。 ˈ**bug-hunter** *n* (colloq) entomologist. (俗)昆蟲學家。**3** (colloq) germ; virus infection: (俗)細菌；病菌；濾過性病毒傳染： *You've got the Asian 'flu bug.* 你染上了亞洲流行性感冒病毒。 **4** (sl) ***big bug,*** important person. (俚)大人物；要人。 **5** (sl) defect; snag; (source of) malfunctioning, eg in a computer. (俚)缺點；毛病；障碍；(如計算機等之)故障(之根源)。 **6** small hidden microphone (for listening to conversations, etc). 小型的隱密擴音器(用以竊聽談話等)；竊聽器。 □ *vt* (-gg-) [VP6A] **1** (colloq) use electronic devices (in a room, etc) in order to listen secretly to conversations: (俗)(在房間等中) 使用電子裝置以竊聽

談話；裝置竊聽器：ˈ*bugging devices*. 竊聽器。 **2** (US colloq) cause to make mistakes. (美俗)使犯錯。**3** (US sl) annoy: (美俚)打擾；煩擾： *That man really bugs me*. 那個人眞使我心煩。

buga·boo /ˈbʌgəbuː ; ˈbʌgəˌbu/ *n* source of annoyance or fear. 煩擾或恐懼的來源；令人煩擾或害怕的事物。

bug·bear /ˈbʌgbeə(r) ; ˈbʌgˌbɛr/ *n* sth feared or disliked, with or without good reason: (指有理由或無充分理由之)令人恐懼或討厭的事物： *the ~ of rising prices*. 令人討厭的高漲的物價。

bug·ger /ˈbʌgə(r) ; ˈbʌgɚ/ *n* **1** (legal) sodomite. (法律)鷄姦者。 **2** ⚠ used as a vulgar term of abuse: (諱)(粗鄙的罵人語)畜生；崽子： *You silly ~!* 你這傻崽子。 □ *vt, vi* [VP6A] commit ~y with. 鷄姦；犯鷄姦罪。 ***~ (it)!*** (int, used to express irritation, anger, etc.) (用以表示煩躁，憤怒等)該死！畜生！ ***~ off,*** (esp imper) go away. (尤用於祈使句中)走開。 ***~ sth up,*** spoil, ruin it. 弄壞；弄糟。Hence, 由此產生， ***~ed (up),*** spoilt, ruined. 弄壞的；弄糟的。 ˈ**~-all** *n* nothing. 沒什麼。**~y** *n* sodomy. 雞姦；獸姦。

buggy /ˈbʌgɪ ; ˈbʌgɪ/ *n* (*pl* -gies) **1** light carriage, pulled by one horse, for one or two persons: 輕便馬車(一馬拖拉，單座或雙座)：*the horse and ~ age*, period before motor vehicles came into use. (汽車問世前的)馬車時代。 **2** ˈ**beach ~,** ⇨ beach. **3** **(baby) ~,** (US) = pram. (美)嬰兒車。

bugle /ˈbjuːgl ; ˈbjugl̩/ *n* musical wind instrument of copper or brass (like a small trumpet but without keys or valves), used for military signals. 號角；銅號；軍號。 ⇨ the illus at brass. 參看 brass 之插圖。**bugler** *n* ~ blower. 吹號者；號手；號兵。

buhl /buːl ; bul/ *n* [U] furniture decoration of inlaid brass, tortoise-shell and ivory: 鑲有銅、龜殼及象牙的傢具裝飾： *a ~ cabinet*. 鑲嵌着銅、龜殼及象牙的橱櫃。

build[1] /bɪld ; bɪld/ *vt, vi* (*pt, pp* built /bɪlt ; bɪlt/) **1** [VP6A, 12B, 13B, 14] ***~ sth (of／out of),*** make by putting parts, materials, etc together (with what is made as the direct object): (用…)構築；建造；建築(以建造物作直接受詞)： *~ a house／railway*. 建造房屋(鐵路)。*Some birds ~ nests out of twigs*. 有些鳥類用小枝築巢。*The school is built of wood*. 該校校舍係木造。 *Mr Green is ~ing a garage for me／is ~ing me a garage*. 格林先生正替我造車房。 **2** [VP14] ***~ sth into,*** put parts together to form a whole (with the material as the direct object): 用(某物)建造成…(以材料作爲直接受詞)： *He has built these scraps of metal into a very strange-looking sculpture*. 他已將這些金屬碎片造成一尊奇形怪狀的雕塑品。 **3** [VP15B, 14] ***~ in／into,*** make (sth) form a firm and permanent part of sth larger; make (sth) a fixture: (在較大物體上)增建，添造，附加(固定而且永久之物)： *Ask the carpenter to ~ in some cupboards／to ~ some cupboards into the walls*. 請木匠在牆上嵌加幾個橱櫃。Hence, 由此產生， **built-in:** *a bedroom with built-in wardrobes;* 帶有壁橱的臥室； *a radio with a built-in aerial*. 帶有嵌入天線的收音機。 **4** [VP15B, 2C] ***~ up,*** **(a)** accumulate; form a block: 積聚；形成阻塞： *Traffic is ~ing up* (= The number of vehicles is increasing steadily) *along the roads to the coast*. 通往海邊的道路上的車輛在不斷增加。**(b)** come together (so as to increase or intensify): 結集；聚集(藉以增加或加强)： *One day your books will ~ up into a library*. 有一天你的書籍將會聚集成一座圖書館。 *Their pressure on the enemy is ~ing up*. 他們對敵人的壓力正逐漸加强。 ***~ sb／sth up,*** **(a)** try to increase sb's reputation (through publicity, praise): 試圖增加某人的信譽(如藉宣揚或讚美)： *Don't ~ me up too much—I may disappoint you*. 別把我捧上了天，我可能令你失望。 **(b)** make, acquire, steadily and gradually: 逐漸造成；逐漸獲得；建立： *He has built up a good business／a good reputation for his goods*. 他已經使他的生意興隆起來(建立起貨品優良的信譽)。 *He went on holiday and soon built up* (= strengthened) *his health*. 他去度一次假，很快就增進了他的健康。 **(c)** (passive and as *adj*) become covered with buildings: (用被動語態，並作形容詞用)到處都是建築物；蓋滿了房屋： *The district has been built up since I was last there*. 該區自從我上次去過以後已經蓋滿房屋。 Hence, 由此產生， ˈ**built-up areas**. 到處建滿房屋或其他建築物之區域。 **(d)** bring together (so as to increase or intensify): 集結(以增加或加强)： *They are ~ing up their military forces*. 他們在集結他們的軍隊。 Hence, 由此產生， ˈ**~-up** *n* **(a)** increase: 增加；加强： *a ~-up of forces／pressure*. 力量(壓力)的增加。**(b)** accumulation: 聚集；積聚： *a ~-up of traffic*. 交通阻塞。**(c)** flattering publicity, etc: 宣揚；讚揚；捧場： *the ~-up of a politician's image*. 提高某政客在人們心目中的地位。 *The press gave him a tremendous ~-up*. 報紙對他大大地捧了一番。 **5** [VP15B, 3A] ***~ on／upon,*** base (hopes, etc) on; rely on: 把(希望等)寄託於；依靠；依賴；指望： *Don't ~ too many hopes upon his helping you*. 別指望他會給予你幫助。*Don't ~ on his promises*. 不要指望他的諾言。 **6** (*pp* with *advv*): (過去分詞，與副詞連用)： *a well-built man*, a man whose body has good proportions; 體格勻稱的人； *solidly built*, having a solid frame(work). 構造堅固的。 **~er** *n* person who ~s, esp a contractor for ~ing houses; (fig) person who creates: 建築者；(尤指)營造商；(喻)創造者： *a great empire ~er*. 大帝國創立者。

build[2] /bɪld ; bɪld/ *n* [U] general shape or structure; (of the human body) general characteristics of shape and proportion: 大體的形狀或結構；(指人體)體格： *a man of powerful ~*. 體格强健的人。 *We are of the same ~*. 我們的體格是屬同一型的。

build·ing /ˈbɪldɪŋ ; ˈbɪldɪŋ/ *n* **1** [U] (art of) constructing houses, etc: 建築(術)： ˈ*~ operations;* 建築工作； ˈ***~ materials;*** 建築材料； ˈ***~ land,*** (to be) used for houses, etc. (可供)建築用之土地；建地。 ˈ**~ site,** an area of land on which an office-block, a house, etc is being built. (正在興建辦公大樓、房屋等的)工地。 ˈ**~-society,** organization for making loans to members who wish to build or buy a house, using funds supplied by its members. 建屋互助協會；建築合作社。 **2** [C] house or other structure: 房屋；建築物： *Houses, schools, churches, hotels, factories and sheds are all ~s*. 住宅、學校、教堂、旅館、工廠及棚屋均係建築物。

bulb /bʌlb ; bʌlb/ *n* **1** almost round, thick, underground stem, sending roots downwards and leaves upwards, of such plants as the lily, onion, tulip. (百合、洋葱、鬱金香等植物之生於地面下的)球莖。 **2** sth like a ~ in shape, esp an electric lamp or the swollen end of a glass tube, eg in a thermometer. 狀似植物球莖之物(尤指電燈燈泡、氣溫表等玻璃管下端之球狀部份)。 **bul·bous** /ˈbʌlbəs ; ˈbʌlbəs/ *adj* of or having or like a ~; growing from a ~. 球莖的；有球莖的；似球莖的；從球莖生長出來的。

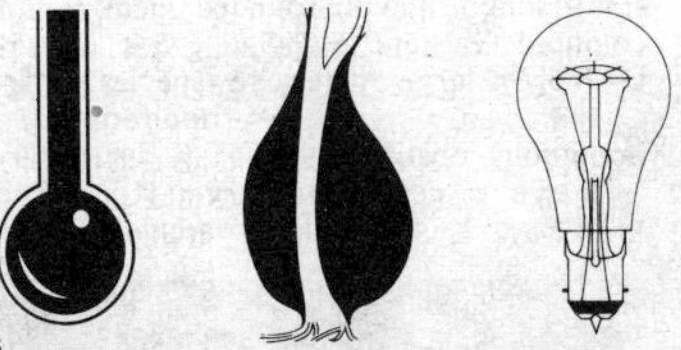

bulbs

bul·bul /ˈbʊlbʊl ; ˈbʊlbʊl/ *n* songbird of Asia and Africa. (亞洲及非洲的)一種鳴鳥。

bulge /bʌldʒ ; bʌldʒ/ *n* [C] irregular swelling; place where a swelling or curve shows; temporary increase in volume or numbers; (mil) salient. 不規則突起；鼓起；鼓起之處；體積或數目暫時的增加；膨脹；(軍)陣地之凸角。□ *vi, vt* [VP2A, C, 6A] (cause to) swell beyond the usual size; curve outwards: (使)

突起;脹大;膨脹;鼓起: *He ~d his pockets with apples.* 他把口袋裏裝滿蘋果,脹得鼓鼓的。*His pockets were bulging with apples.* 他的口袋裏因裝滿蘋果而脹得鼓鼓的。*He ~d his cheeks.* 他鼓起兩頰。

bulk /bʌlk ; bʌlk/ *n* [U] quantity, volume, esp when large. 量;大量;巨量;巨大的體積。***in ~,* (a)** in large amounts: 大量(地): *buy in ~;* 大量地買; *tankers to carry petroleum in ~.* 大量運輸石油的油船。**(b)** loose, not packed in boxes, tins, etc. 散裝的;未裝箱(罐等)的。***~ buying,*** purchase at one time of a very large quantity of goods, eg by the state during a war. 大批購買;整批購買。***the ~ of,*** the greater part or number of: 大半;大部: *He left the ~ of his property to his brother.* 他將大部財產遺留給他的胞弟。□ *vi* ***~ large,*** appear large or important. 顯得巨大或重要。 **~y** *adj* taking up much space; clumsy to move or carry. 佔地方的;笨重而不易搬移的。

bulk·head /ˈbʌlkhed ; ˈbʌlkˌhɛd/ *n* [C] water-tight division or dividing wall in a ship; similar division in a tunnel, etc. 船艙之不漏水的間隔或隔壁;艙壁;坑道等類似之隔壁;分壁。

bull¹ /bʊl ; bʊl/ *n* **1** uncastrated male of any animal of the ox family (⇨ cow): (未去勢的)公牛;牡牛: *a man with a neck like a ~* (*a* **ˈ~-neck**), with a thick neck. 一個粗脖子的人。***a ˌ~ in a ˈchina shop,*** person who is rough and clumsy where skill and care are needed. 動輒闖禍者;笨手笨脚的人;不能做精細工作者。***take the ~ by the horns,*** meet a difficulty boldly instead of trying to escape from it. 不畏艱難;毅然處斷難局。**ˈ~·fight** *n* fight between men and a ~ for public entertainment, as in Spain. 鬥牛(如風行於西班牙者)。**ˈ~·fighter** *n* **ˈ~·ring** *n* arena for ~fights. (圓形的)鬥牛場。**ˈ~·shit** *n* ⚠ (vulg sl) nonsense; foolish and exaggerated talk. (諱)(鄙俚)廢話;胡說。 **2** male of the whale, elephant and other large animals. 雄性的鯨、象和其他巨大動物。 **3** (Stock Exchange; ⇨ bear¹(4)) person who tries to raise prices with a view to selling at a profit: (股票市場)多頭業者(擡高股價以圖售出獲利者): *ˈ~ market,* with rising prices. 價格上漲的行情。 **4** (compounds) (複合字) **ˈ~·dog** *n* large, powerful breed of dog, with a short, thick neck, noted for its strong grip and its courage. 獥牛犬;牛頭犬(一種身體大而結實,頸粗短而善咬之猛犬)。⇨ the illus at dog. 參看 dog 之插圖。 **ˈ~·doze** *vt* [VP6A, 14] **(a)** remove earth, flatten obstacles with a ~-dozer. 用推土機移土或剷平障礙物;用推土機推平。**(b)** ***~doze sb into doing sth,*** force sb to do sth by using one's strength or by intimidating him. 用強力或恐嚇迫使某人做某事。 **~·dozer** /ˈbʊldəʊzə(r) ; ˈbʊlˌdozɚ/ *n* powerful tractor that pushes a broad steel blade or sheet in front, used for levelling land, shifting large quantities of earth, etc. 推土機(前面裝有一大塊鋼板,用以推平地面或移動大量泥土等)。 **ˈ~·finch** *n* small songbird with rounded beak and brightly coloured feathers. 照鶯(一種小鳴禽,圓喙,羽色鮮麗)。 **ˈ~·frog** *n* large American species of frog. 牛蛙(美洲產之一種大青蛙)。 **ˌ~-ˈheaded®** *adj* clumsy, impetuous, obstinate. 笨拙的;魯莽的;頑固的;頑强的。 **ˈ~'s-eye** *n* centre of target (for archers, etc). 靶心;鵠的。⇨ the illus at archery. 參看 archery

a bulldozer

之挿圖。 **ˌ~-ˈterrier** *n* cross between a ~dog and a terrier. 牛頭犬與㹴雜交所生之犬。

bull² /bʊl ; bʊl/ *n* official order or announcement from the Pope. 羅馬教皇之勅令或訓諭。

bull³ /bʊl ; bʊl/ *n* (also 亦作 **Irish ~**) foolish or amusing mistake in language, usu because there is a contradiction in terms 文字上的愚蠢或可笑的錯誤(通常因爲有邏輯上的矛盾) (eg 例如 'If you do not get this letter, please write and tell me' '如果你收不到這封信,請你寫信告訴我'): *It's a lot of ~,* nonsense. 胡說;一派胡言。

bul·let /ˈbʊlɪt ; ˈbʊlɪt/ *n* shaped piece of lead, usu coated with another metal, (to be) fired from a rifle or revolver. 子彈;槍彈。Cf 參較 *shells* fired from guns. ⇨ the illus at cartridge. 參看 cartridge 之挿圖。**ˈ~-headed** /-hedɪd ; -ˌhɛdɪd/ *adj* having a small, round head. 有小圓頭的。**ˈ~-proof** *adj* able to stop ~s: 能防子彈穿入的;防彈的: *a ~-proof jacket.* 防彈衣。

bull·etin /ˈbʊlətɪn ; ˈbʊlətɪn/ *n* **1** official statement of news: 公報;告示: *a ~ of news;* 新聞簡報; *a ˈnews ~.* 新聞快報。 **2** printed sheet with official news or announcements. 通告;公告。

bul·lion /ˈbʊlɪən ; ˈbʊljən/ *n* [U] gold or silver in bulk or bars, before manufacture. 金條;銀條;金塊;銀塊。

bul·lock /ˈbʊlək ; ˈbʊlək/ *n* **1** young bull. 小公牛。 **2** castrated bull. 閹牛。

bully¹ /ˈbʊlɪ ; ˈbʊlɪ/ *n* (*pl* -lies) person who uses his strength or power to frighten or hurt those who are weaker. 恃强凌弱者。□ *vt* [VP6A,14] ***~ sb (into doing sth),*** use strength, etc in this way to persuade sb to do sth. 威脅某人(做某事)。

bully² /ˈbʊlɪ ; ˈbʊlɪ/ *n* [U] (also 亦作 **ˈ~ beef**) tinned beef. 罐頭牛肉。

bully³ /ˈbʊlɪ ; ˈbʊlɪ/ *adj* (sl) fine; excellent: (俚)精美的;特佳的: *B~ for you!* Well done! 妙極了!棒透了!幹得好!

bully⁴ /ˈbʊlɪ ; ˈbʊlɪ/ *n* (hockey) way of putting the ball into play (beginning with two opposing players striking each others' sticks three times. (曲棍球) 開球 (開始時由敵對雙方各一人互擊球棍三次)。□ *vi* [VP2C] ***~ off,*** start to play in this way. (曲棍球)開始打球。

bul·rush /ˈbʊlrʌʃ ; ˈbʊlˌrʌʃ/ *n* [C] (kinds of) tall rush or reed with a thick velvety head. 蘆葦。

bul·wark /ˈbʊlwək ; ˈbʊlwɚk/ *n* **1** wall, esp one built of earth, against attack; earthwork; (fig) sth that defends or protects: 壁壘;堡壘;防禦工事;(喻)保衛或保護之物;屏藩;保障: *Law is the ~ of society,* gives us security. 法律是社會的保障。 **2** (usu *pl*) wall round (esp a sailing) ship's deck. (通常用複數) (尤指帆船)甲板上沿船殼之堅實圍牆;舷牆。

bum¹ /bʌm ; bʌm/ *n* (colloq) part of the body on which one sits; buttocks. (俗)臀;屁股。

bum² /bʌm ; bʌm/ (sl) *n* habitual beggar or loafer. (俚)職業乞丐;流浪者;無業遊民。□ *adj* of poor quality; worthless. 劣質的;無價值的。□ **1** *vi* (-mm-) [VP2C] ***~ around,*** loaf, wander about doing nothing. 遊蕩;遊手好閒。 **2** *vt* (-mm-) [VP6A, 14] ***~ sth (off/from sb),*** succeed in getting sb to give (usu reluctantly) sth to one: 乞討;(向某人)討得(某物): *He bummed a cigarette off me.* 他向我討了一支香煙。

bumble·bee /ˈbʌmbl biː ; ˈbʌmblˌbi/ *n* large kind of hairy bee with a loud hum. 大黄蜂;土蜂(體多毛,嗡聲很大)。

bum·boat /ˈbʌmbəʊt ; ˈbʌmˌbot/ *n* (naut) small boat carrying fresh provisions to ships lying offshore. (航海)運送新鮮食物至離岸停泊之船隻的小舟;販賣舟。

bump /bʌmp ; bʌmp/ *vt, vi* **1** [VP6A, 14, 3A] ***~ (against/into),*** come against with a blow or knock: 碰到;撞到;衝擊: *The room was dark and I ~ed (my head) against the door.* 房間內很黑,我(我的頭)碰着門了。*The blind man ~ed into me.* 那瞎子

撞了我個滿懷。*The car ~ed against the kerb/~ed into the car in front.* 那汽車撞在街道的邊石上(撞到了前面的車子)。~ ***against/on,*** hurt (one's head, etc) by striking it on sth. 碰傷(頭等)。 **2** [VP2C] move with a jerky, jolting motion (like a cart on a bad road): 顛簸而行(如車子在壞路上走): *The heavy bus ~ed along the rough mountain road.* 那沈重的客車在崎嶇的山路上顛簸而行。 **3** [VP15B] ~ ***sb off,*** (sl) murder him. (俚)謀殺某人。□ *adv* suddenly; violently: 突然地;劇烈地: *Our bus ran ~ into the wall.* 我們的客車猛撞在牆上。□ *n* **1** blow or knock; dull sound made by a blow (as when two things come together with force). 碰撞;撞擊;碰撞聲(如兩物互相猛撞時所發出的聲音)。 **2** swelling on the body caused by such a blow; natural bulge on the skull. 身體上因碰撞所起的腫塊;頭骨上的天然隆起。⇨ phrenology. **3** swelling on any surface. 任何腫塊或隆起。 **4** (jolt felt in an aircraft, caused by a) sudden change in air-pressure. (因氣壓突然改變在飛機中所感到的)顛簸;氣壓之突然改變。~**y** (-ier, -iest) *adj* with many ~s: 顛簸不堪的: *a ~y road/ride.* 顛簸不堪的道路(乘車旅行)。

bum·per[1] /ˈbʌmpə(r); ˈbʌmpɚ/ *n* fender (usu a horizontal bar) on a bus, motor-car, etc (front and rear), to lessen the effect of a collision, ⇨ the illus at motor; (車輛前後通常爲水平橫槓的)保險槓(參看 motor 之挿圖); (US) (美) = buffer[1].

bum·per[2] /ˈbʌmpə(r); ˈbʌmpɚ/ *n* **1** glass of wine, full to the brim. 滿滿的一杯酒。 **2** (attrib) sth unusually large or abundant: (形容用法)非常大或豐富之物: ~ *crops;* 結實纍纍的農作物; *a ~ harvest;* 豐收; *a ~ edition* (of a periodical). (期刊的)特大號。

bum·per[3] /ˈbʌmpə(r); ˈbʌmpɚ/ *n* (cricket) ball bowled that springs up high after striking the ground. (板球)反彈球。

bump·kin /ˈbʌmpkɪn; ˈbʌmpkɪn/ *n* awkward person with unpolished manners, esp from the country: 鄉下人;粗人: *a country ~.* 鄉巴佬。

bump·tious /ˈbʌmpʃəs; ˈbʌmpʃəs/ *adj* conceited; self-important: 高傲的;自大的: ~ *officials.* 高傲的官吏。~**·ly** *adv* ~**·ness** *n*

bun /bʌn; bʌn/ *n* **1** small, round, sweet cake, usu containing currants. 小而圓的甜麵包(通常含有葡萄乾)。 **2** ***in a bun,*** (of a woman's hair) twisted into a knot above the back of the neck. (指女人的頭髮)在腦後挽成一個髻。⇨ chignon.

bunch /bʌntʃ; bʌntʃ/ *n* **1** number of small, similar things naturally growing together: 串;簇(自然地生長在一起的一些相同的小東西): *a ~ of grapes/bananas.* 一串葡萄(香蕉)。 **2** collection of things of the same sort placed or fastened together: 束;捆(被放置或捆束在一起的同類物品): *a ~ of flowers/keys.* 一束花(一串鑰匙)。**3** (sl) mob; gang. (俚)暴民群衆;幫;夥。**4** ***the best of the ~,*** (colloq) the best or pick of the lot. (俗)一批中之最好的;精華。□ *vt, vi* [VP15B, 2A, C] ~ ***(up/together),*** form into a ~; come or bring together into a ~ or ~es, or in folds: 形成一串;聚成一簇;捆成一束: *Don't ~ up,* ie cluster together. 不要聚在一起。

bundle /ˈbʌndl; ˈbʌndl̩/ *n* number of articles fastened, tied, or wrapped together: 捆;束;紮;包;包裹: *a ~ of sticks/firewood;* 一捆棍子(柴);*a ~ of old rags.* 一捆破舊衣服。*The books were tied up in ~s of twenty.* 那些書被捆成二十本一捆。□ *vt, vi* **1** [VP15B] ~ ***up/together,*** make into a ~ or ~s: 捆紮;包紮: *We ~d everything up.* 我們把每件東西都捆紮起來了。 **2** [VP15A] put together in a confused heap; put away without order: 亂堆在一起: *We ~d everything into a drawer.* 我們把所有的東西都塞在一個抽屜裏。 **3** [VP15A,B,2C] send or go in a hurry or without ceremony: 匆匆遣走;匆匆離去: *They ~d him into a taxi.* 他們匆匆地把他推入一輛計程車。*His mother ~d him off to school.* 他母親趕緊打發他去上學。*They ~d off/out/away.* 他們匆匆離去。

bung /bʌŋ; bʌŋ/ *n* large (usu wooden, rubber, cork or plastic) stopper for closing a hole in a cask or barrel. (通常爲木、橡皮、軟木、塑膠製成,用以塞桶口之)塞子。□ *vt* [VP6A, 15B] ~ ***(up),*** put a ~ into (the hole in a cask). 用塞子塞住(桶口)。 ˈ~**-hole** *n* hole for filling a cask. 桶口。~***ed up,*** (of the nose) stopped up with mucus; (of drains) clogged with dirt. (指鼻)爲黏液塞住的;(指下水道)爲汚物塞住的。

bun·ga·low /ˈbʌŋgələʊ; ˈbʌŋgəˌlo/ *n* small house of only one storey; (in India) such a house surrounded by a large verandah. 單層屋;平房;(在印度)四周圍繞着大走廊的平房。**bun·ga·loid** /ˈbʌŋgəlɔɪd; ˈbʌŋgəˌlɔɪd/ *adj* of or like ~s: 平房的;似平房的: *bungaloid growth,* area of unsightly building development with many ~s. 平房地區(不雅觀地建着許多平房的建築發展地區)。

bungle /ˈbʌŋgl; ˈbʌŋgl̩/ *vt, vi* [VP6A, 2A] do (a piece of work) badly and clumsily; spoil (a task, etc) by lack of skill. 把(事情)做得一團糟;由於技術拙劣而把(事情)做壞。□ *n* ~d piece of work. 拙劣的工作。**bung·ler** /ˈbʌŋglə(r); ˈbʌŋglɚ/ *n* person who ~s. 工作拙劣的人。

bun·ion /ˈbʌnɪən; ˈbʌnjən/ *n* inflamed swelling, esp on the large joint of the big toe. 蹈囊炎腫。

bunk[1] /bʌŋk; bʌŋk/ *n* narrow bed fixed on the wall, eg of a cabin in a ship or in a train; sleeping-berth. (船艙或火車等上,固定於壁上的)床鋪;鋪位。~ ***beds,*** pair of single beds, one fixed above the other, usu for children. 雙層單人床(通常爲小孩所睡者)。

bunk[2] /bʌŋk; bʌŋk/ *vi* (GB sl) run away; play truant. (英俚)逃走;逃學。□ *n* ***do a ~,*** run away. 逃走。

bunk[3] /bʌŋk; bʌŋk/ *n* [U] abbr for bunkum. bunkum 之略。

bunker /ˈbʌŋkə(r); ˈbʌŋkɚ/ *n* **1** that part of a ship where coal or fuel oil is stored. (船上的)燃料儲存處;燃料艙。 **2** sandy hollow, made as an obstacle, on a golf-course. (高爾夫球場上人工造成作爲障碍之)沙窪。 **3** (mil) underground shelter, fortified point, of steel and concrete. (軍)(鋼筋混凝土構成的地下)重掩蓋掩體。□ *vt, vi* **1** [VP6A, 2A] fill a ship's ~s with fuel; (of a ship) obtain supplies of fuel. 裝燃料於燃料艙;(指船)獲得燃料補給。 **2** (usu passive) (通常用被動語態) ***be ~ed,*** get one's ball into a ~ at golf; (fig) be in difficulties. 打高爾夫球時球掉入沙窪;(喩)遭遇困難;陷入困境。

bun·kum /ˈbʌŋkəm; ˈbʌŋkəm/ *n* [U] (colloq) nonsense. (俗)胡說;廢話。

bunny /ˈbʌnɪ; ˈbʌnɪ/ *n* (*pl* -nies) (child's word) rabbit. (兒語)兔子。

Bun·sen /ˈbʌnsn; ˈbʌnsn̩/ *n* ˌ~ ˈ**burner,** burner for gas, with an air-valve for regulating the mixture of gas and air. 本生燈(一種煤氣燈,有通氣活瓣可以調節煤氣與空氣的混合量)。

bunt·ing /ˈbʌntɪŋ; ˈbʌntɪŋ/ *n* [U] (bright-coloured cloth used for making) flags and decorations (for use in streets and on buildings on festive occasions). 製旗幟等之色彩鮮艷的布;旗幟(節日用以裝飾街道及建築物者)。

buoy /bɔɪ; bɔɪ/ *n* **1** floating object, anchored

a bunch of keys

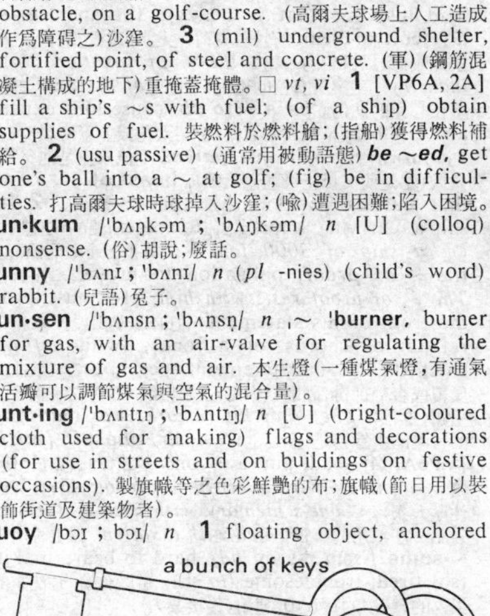

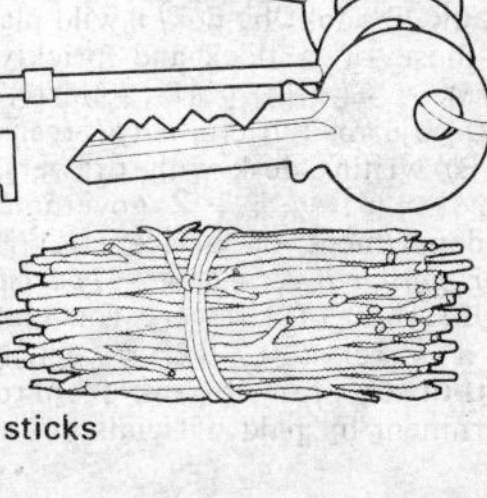

a bundle of sticks

to the bottom, used to show a navigable channel or to indicate reefs, submerged wrecks, etc. (固定於海底而漂浮於海面上,用以指示航道或礁石、海面下的沈船等之)浮標;浮筒。 **2** (also 亦作 **'life-~**) sth designed to keep a person afloat in the water, eg sth made of cork or sth that can be inflated with air. (用軟木或可充氣之材料製成的)救生圈。⇨ the illus at life. 參看 life 之挿圖。□ *vt* **1** [VP6A] mark the position of with a ~: 以浮標指示: *~ a wreck / channel.* 以浮標指示破船殘骸(航道)。 **2** [VP15B] *~ up,* keep afloat; (fig) keep up hopes, etc: 使漂浮;(喻)保持希望等;振作;鼓舞;支持: *~ed up with new hope.* 爲新希望所鼓舞。

buoy·ancy /'bɔɪənsɪ ; 'bɔɪənsɪ/ *n* [U] **1** power to float or keep things floating: 浮力: *Salt water has more ~ than fresh water.* 海水較淡水浮力爲大。 **2** (fig) lightness of spirits; power to recuperate; (of the stock market) tendency of prices to rise. (喻)快活;輕快的心情;恢復力;(指股票市場)上漲的趨勢;看漲的行情。

buoy·ant /'bɔɪənt ; 'bɔɪənt/ *adj* able to float or to keep things floating; (fig) light-hearted: 能漂浮的;有浮力的;(喻)心情愉快的; 快活的: *a ~ disposition;* 樂天的性情; springy: 有彈性的: *with a ~ step;* 一躍; (of the stock market, etc) maintaining high prices. (指股票市場等)維持高價的;盤高的。**~·ly** *adv*

bur, burr /bɜː(r) ; bɝ/ *n* (plant with a) seed-case or flower-head that clings to the hair or fur of animals; (fig) sth or sb that sticks like a ~, esp a person who forces his company on others and is hard to shake off. 其芒刺易附着於動物之毛上的種子殼或花頭;刺毬;芒刺;有芒刺之植物;(喻)易附着之物或人;(尤指)强與人同處而不易擺脫之人。

burble /'bɜːbl ; 'bɝbḷ/ *vi* make a gentle murmuring or bubbling sound: 作潺潺流水聲或起泡聲: *burbling with mirth.* 作歡笑聲。

bur·den /'bɜːdn ; 'bɝdṇ/ *n* **1** sth (to be) carried; load (esp one that is heavy); (lit and fig) sth difficult to bear: 負擔;負荷;(尤指)重擔;重負;(字面及比喩)難以擔負的事物: *the ~ of taxation (up)on industry;* 工業所負擔的重稅; *a ~ of sorrow / grief.* 壓在心頭的悲傷。***be a ~ to sb,*** cause him expense and trouble: 是某人的負擔(使某人花錢並惹麻煩): *He was always a ~ to his parents.* 他永遠是他父母的負擔(總是使父母花錢並惹麻煩)。**beast of ~,** animal that carries packs on its back. 馱獸。 **2** [U] ship's carrying capacity, tonnage: 船的載重量;噸位: *a ship of 3000 tons ~.* 載重三千噸的船。 **3** ***the ~ of proof,*** obligation to prove: 舉證責任: *The ~ of proof rests with him,* He must prove the truth of his statement. 他必須拿出證據來。 **4** refrain or chorus (of a song); (with *def art*) chief theme of a statement, speech, etc: (歌曲的)反覆或合唱部份;副歌;(與定冠詞連用)(聲明或演講等的)主題;主旨: *The ~ of his remarks was that....* 他的言論的主旨乃是…。□ *vt* ***~ sb / oneself (with),*** [VP6A, 14] load; put a ~ on: 裝載;加負擔於;使負擔: *~ oneself with a heavy overcoat;* 給自己加一件厚大衣; *~ one's memory with useless facts;* 勉强記一些無用的事實; *~ed with taxation.* 爲重稅所累。**~·some** /-səm ; -səm/ *adj* hard to bear; making (sb) tired; troublesome (*to* sb). 難以負擔的;沈重的;累人的;麻煩的(與 to 連用,後接某人)。

bur·dock /'bɜːdɒk ; 'bɝ,dɑk/ *n* wild plant with leaves like those of a dock and prickly flowerheads (*burrs*). 牛蒡(一種野生植物,葉似酸模之葉,花帶芒刺)。

bureau /'bjʊərəʊ ; 'bjʊro/ *n* (*pl* -reaux, /-rəʊz;-roz/) **1** (GB) writing desk with drawers. (英)有抽屜的寫字桌;寫字檯;辦公桌。 **2** government or municipal department or office: (政府機構)處; 局; 所: *,Infor'mation B~;* 新聞局; *'Tourist B~.* 觀光局。 **3** (US) chest of drawers for clothes, etc, usu with a mirror. (美)五斗櫃(通常附有鏡子)。

bureau·cracy /bjʊə'rɒkrəsɪ ; bjʊ'rɑkrəsɪ/ *n* [U] government by paid officials not elected by the people; officials who keep their positions whatever political party is in power; (over-)complicated system of administration; [C] (*pl* -cies) instance of this system of government; the officials as a body. 官僚政治(官吏係受僱用,而非民選者);官僚政客(無論任何政黨當權皆能保持其職位者);官僚政治制度;官僚作風;官吏的總稱。

bureau·crat /'bjʊərəkræt ; 'bjʊrə,kræt/ *n* (often pej) official who works in a bureau or government department, esp one who obeys the rules of his department without exercising much judgement. (常爲輕蔑語)官吏;官員;(尤指墨守成規而不大運用其判斷力的) 官僚。 **~ic** /,bjʊərə'krætɪk ; ,bjuro'krætɪk/ *adj* of or like a ~; too much attached to rules; carried on according to official rules and habits. 官僚的;官僚作風的;繁文縟節的;墨守成規的;公事公辦的。**~i·cally** /-ɪklɪ ; -ɪklɪ/ *adv*

burette /bjʊə'ret ; bjʊ'rɛt/ *n* graduated glass tube with a tap for measuring small quantities of liquid that are let out of it. 用以衡量少量液體的有刻度的玻璃管;滴定管;量管。

burg /bɜːg ; bɝg/ *n* (US colloq) town; city. (美俗)鎮;城;市。

bur·geon /'bɜːdʒən ; 'bɝdʒən/ *vi* (poet) put out leaves; begin to grow. (詩)發芽;萌芽;開始生長。

bur·ger /'bɜːgə(r);'bɝgɚ/ *n* (colloq) (俗) = hamburger.

burgh /'bʌrə ; bɝg/ *n* borough in Scotland. (蘇格蘭之)市鎮。

bur·gher /'bɜːgə(r) ; 'bɝgɚ/ *n* (old use) citizen (esp of a Dutch, Flemish or German town). (舊用法)(尤指荷蘭、法蘭德斯或德國市鎮之)市民;公民。

bur·glar /'bɜːglə(r) ; 'bɝglɚ/ *n* person who breaks into a house in order to steal. (闖入屋內行竊的)竊賊。**bur·glary** /'bɜːglərɪ ; 'bɝglərɪ/ *n* [U] crime of breaking into a house to steal; [C] (*pl* -ries) instance of this: 竊盜罪;竊案: *There have been numerous ~ies in this district recently.* 近來在這個區域內發生很多竊案。 **'~-alarm** *n* device to give warning of ~s. 防盜鈴。 **'~-proof** *adj* made so that ~s cannot break in or into. 防盜的。**burgle** /'bɜːgl ; 'bɝgḷ/ *vt, vi* [VP6A] break into (a building) to commit ~y; [VP2A] commit ~y. 闖入(建築物)行竊;竊盜;犯竊盜罪。**~i·ous** /bɜː'gleərɪəs ; bɝ'glɛrɪəs/ *adj* (legal) of ~y: (法律)竊盜的;竊盜罪的: *guilty of a ~ious attempt.* 犯企圖行竊罪。

burgo·mas·ter /'bɜːgəmɑːstə(r) *US:* -mæs- ; 'bɝgə,mæstɚ/ *n* mayor of a Dutch, Flemish or German town. (荷蘭、法蘭德斯或德國市鎮之)市長;鎮長。

Bur·gundy /'bɜːgəndɪ ; 'bɝgəndɪ/ *n* [U] kinds of (usu red) wine of Burgundy (in Central France). 勃艮地葡萄酒(法國中部勃艮地所產葡萄酒,通常爲紅色)。

burial /'berɪəl ; 'bɛrɪəl/ *n* [U] burying; [C] instance of this. 埋葬。 **'~-ground** *n* cemetery. 墓地。 **'B~ Service,** the religious ceremony at a funeral. (按宗教儀式所行的)葬禮。

burke /bɜːk ; bɝk/ *vt* [VP6A] avoid: 避免: *~ publicity / an issue;* 避免出風頭(避開一問題); suppress: 壓制;扣壓: *~ an inquiry.* 扣壓一調查案件。

bur·lap /'bɜːlæp ; 'bɝlæp/ *n* [U] coarse canvas (used for bags, wrappings, etc). 粗帆布(用以製袋、包布等)。

bur·lesque /bɜː'lesk ; bɚ'lɛsk/ *n* **1** [C] imitation, eg of a book, speech, person's behaviour, for the purpose of making fun of it or of amusing people. 模仿(書籍、演說、人的行爲等)以達諷刺或娛悅他人的目的。 **2** [U] amusing imitation or parody. 滑稽的模仿;遊戲詩文。 **3** (US) variety entertainment. (美)雜耍表演;綜藝節目。⇨ variety(5). **4** (as *adj* or attrib) intended as a ~. (作形容詞或形容用法)意在諷刺或娛悅他人的。□ *vt* [VP6A] make a ~ of; parody. 諷刺;滑稽地模仿。

burly /'bɜːlɪ ; 'bɝlɪ/ *adj* (of a person) big and strong; solidly built. (指人)魁梧的;强壯的;結實的。

burn[1] /bɜːn ; bɝn/ *n* (Scot) small stream. (蘇)小溪;小河。

burn[2] /bɜːn ; bɝn/ *vt, vi* (*pt, pp* burnt /bɜːnt ; bɝnt/

or 或作 burned /bɜːnd ; bɝnd/) (For uses with *adverbial particles* and *preps*, ⇨ 6 below.) (與副詞接語及介詞連用之用法，參看下列第6義。) **1** [VP6A] use for the purpose of lighting or heating: 燃燒(使發光或生熱): *Most large steamships now ~ oil instead of coal.* 現在大多數的大輪船都燒油而不燒煤。*This lamp ~s oil.* 這盞燈燒油。*We have ~t all our logs.* 我們所有的木柴都燒光了。 **2** [VP6A, 14] ~ *(to)*, damage, hurt, destroy by fire, heat or the action of acid: 燒毀;焚毀;燒傷;燒焦;燙傷;(被酸類)灼傷: *Be careful not to ~ the meat.* 小心不要把肉燒焦了。*The coffee is very hot, don't ~ your mouth.* 咖啡非常熱，不要燙着了你的嘴。 *You've ~t my toast to a cinder!* so that it is hard and black. 你把我的麵包烤焦了！*The child ~t itself/its fingers while playing with matches.* 那孩子玩火柴燒傷了自己(燒傷了自己的手指)。*Some acids are strong enough to ~ wood.* 有些酸類物酸性強得可以燒壞木頭。~ ***one's fingers***, ⇨ finger. **'~ing glass** *n* lens used to concentrate the sun's rays (to set fire to sth). (用以集中日光以取火的)凸透鏡;取火鏡。 **3** [VP2A, B, C] be on fire or alight; be capable of giving out light and heat: 燃燒;灼熱;發光;發亮;能發出光和熱: *Wood ~s easily.* 木頭容易燃燒。*Stone won't ~.* 石頭不會燃燒。*All the lights were ~ing.* 所有的燈都亮着。 **4** [VP6A] make by heat; heat (a material) to make (sth): 燒製;將(材料)加熱以製成(某物): ~ *bricks/lime/charcoal;* (在窰中)燒磚(燒製石灰;燒製木炭); ~ *clay to make bricks;* 燒黏土以製磚; ~ *a hole in a carpet*, eg by dropping a cigarette end. 把地毯燒一個洞(如因香烟頭落於其上)。 **5** [VP2A, C, 4A] be hurt or spoilt by fire or heat; scorch; be or feel warm or hot; (fig) be filled with strong feeling: 被燒壞;被燒傷;被燒焦;被晒黑;被晒傷;發燒;(喻)發火(怒);感情激動: *The milk/sauce has ~t.* 牛奶(調味汁)已燒焦。*She has a skin that ~s easily,* is quickly hurt by the sun. 她的皮膚易被晒傷。*Her cheeks were ~ing with shame.* 她的兩頰因羞愧而發燒。*They were ~ing to avenge the death of their leader.* 他們極爲激動要爲他們首領之死報仇。 **6** [VP15B, 2C] (special uses with *adverbial particles* and *preps*): (與副詞接語及介詞連用之特殊用法):

burn (sth) away, **(a)** continue to ~: 繼續燃燒: *The fire was ~ing away cheerfully.* 爐火融融。**(b)** make, become less, by ~ing; destroy, be destroyed, by ~ing: 因燃燒而消耗;燒毀;燒盡;燒掉: *Half the candle had ~t away.* 蠟燭已燒掉了一半。*An area of skin on his hand was ~t away.* 他手上的一塊皮膚被燒毀了。

burn (sth) down, be destroyed, destroy to the foundations, by fire: 燒毀;焚毀;燒光;燒盡: *The house (was) ~t down.* 該房子整幢燒掉了。~ ***(down) (low),*** ~ less brightly as the material ~s or the fuel is used. 因物質燃燒或燃料消耗而不如原先那樣明亮或旺盛:(燈燭等)燒殘;(燈火)將燒盡;火力減弱。

burn (sth) out, **(a)** become extinguished: 熄滅;燒完: *The fire ~t (itself) out.* 爐火熄滅了。**(b)** (of a rocket) use up its fuel. (指火箭)耗盡燃料;燃料用罄。**(c)** (of an electric motor, coil) stop working because high current has caused electrical ~ing. (指電動馬達,線圈)因高電流而燒壞。**(d)** (usu passive) be destroyed, be reduced to a shell, by fire; be gutted: (通常用被動語態)被焚毀只剩下一個空殼;內部被焚毀: *~t-out factories/tanks.* 內部被焚毀的工廠(戰車)。~ ***oneself out,*** ruin one's health by overwork, dissipation, etc. 因過度工作、生活放蕩等而毀了自己的健康。

burn (sth) up, **(a)** burst into flames, flare up: 迸出火光;燃燒旺盛: *Put some wood on the fire and make it ~ up.* 加點柴在爐火上,使它燒旺一點。 **(b)** consume, get rid of, by ~ing: 燒掉;焚化: *We ~t up all the garden rubbish.* 我們將花園中的垃圾全部焚化。 **(c)** (of a rocket, etc, re-entering the atmosphere from space) catch fire and be destroyed. (指火箭等,從太空重返大氣層時)着火燒毀。 **'~-up** *n* (GB sl) high-speed race on a public road between young people on motorcycles. (英俚)青年人駕機車在公路上彼此快速競逐。

burn[3] /bɜːn ; bɝn/ *n* **1** injury, mark, made by fire, heat or acid: (由火、熱或酸類物造成之)燒傷;灼傷: *He died of the ~s he received in the fire.* 他死於火災時所受到的灼傷。 **2** (aerospace) one firing of a rocket: (太空)火箭的一次發射: *a two-minute ~ to correct course to the moon.* 爲修正赴月球的航道所作之兩分鐘發射。

burner /'bɜːnə(r) ; 'bɝnɚ/ *n* **1** person who burns sth or makes sth by burning: 燒者;燒製者: *a 'charcoal-burner.* 燒製木炭者。**2** that part of a lamp, stove, etc from which the light or flame comes: (燈、爐等之)燈頭;燈心;爐心: *a four-~ oil-stove.* 有四個爐心的油爐。

burn·ing /'bɜːnɪŋ ; 'bɝnɪŋ/ *adj* **1** intense: 激烈的;强烈的: *a ~ thirst/desire.* 極度的渴(强烈的慾望)。**2** exciting; hotly debated: 使人激動的;被熱烈辯論的: *a ~ question.* 熱烈辯論的問題。 **3** notorious, scandalous: 不體面的;可恥的: *a ~ disgrace/shame.* 極爲可恥之事。

bur·nish /'bɜːnɪʃ ; 'bɝnɪʃ/ *vt, vi* [VP6A] polish (metal) by, or as if by, rubbing; [VP2A] take a polish: 擦亮(金屬);磨光;使光亮;被擦亮: *material that ~es well.* 容易擦亮的物質。

bur·nouse /bɜː'nuːs ; bɚ'nus/ *n* kind of cloak with a hood, worn by Arabs and Moors. (阿拉伯人和摩爾人所著之)連有兜帽之外衣。

burp /bɜːp ; bɝp/ *n* [C] (colloq) belch. (俗)打嗝。□ *vt, vi* [VP6A, 2A] (cause to) give a ~: (使)打嗝。~ *a baby.* 使嬰兒打嗝。

burr[1] *n* ⇨ bur.

burr[2] /bɜː(r) ; bɝ/ *n* **1** whirring sound made by parts of machines that turn quickly. (機器各部急速運轉所發的)轆轆聲。 **'~-drill** *n* one used by dentists. (牙醫用的)鑽孔器。 **2** marked pronunciation of 'r'; marked (rural) accent: 顯著的r音;顯著的(鄉村)口音: *speak with a soft West-country ~.* 說話帶些輕柔的西部鄉村口音。

bur·row /'bʌrəʊ ; 'bɝo/ *n* hole made in the ground (by foxes, rabbits, etc). (狐狸、兎子等在地下所掘的)洞穴。□ *vi, vt* [VP2A, C, 3A, 6A] ~ ***(into sth),*** dig (a ~); (fig) investigate (sth hidden). 掘(地洞);(喻)調查(隱藏的事物);探索;發掘。

bur·sar /'bɜːsə(r) ; 'bɝsɚ/ *n* **1** treasurer (esp of a college). (尤指大學內的)會計員。**2** (person holding a) scholarship at a university of Scotland, or a grant for continuation of studies: 蘇格蘭的大學獎學金或研究獎助金;此種獎學金或獎助金的享有人: *British Council ~s in Great Britain.* 英國文化協會在大不列顛所設的研究獎助金。 **~y** *n* **1** college ~'s office. (大學裏的)會計室。**2** scholarship; grant for continuation of studies. 獎學金;研究獎助金。

burst[1] /bɜːst ; bɝst/ *vi, vt* (*pt, pp* burst) (For uses with *adverbial particles* and *preps*, ⇨ 5 below.) (與副詞接語及介詞連用之用法參看下列第5義。) **1** [VP 2A] (of a bomb, shell, boiler, etc) fly or break violently apart from internal pressure; explode; (of river banks, a dam, an abscess, a boil) break outwards; (of a bubble) break; (of leaf and flower buds) open out. (指炸彈、砲彈、鍋爐等)爆炸;(指河岸、堤壩、膿瘡、疔瘡)決口;脹裂;穿頭;(指水泡)爆破;(指葉苞、花蕾)綻放。***be ~ing to,*** be eager to: 極欲;急於: *He was ~ing to tell us the news.* 他極欲告訴我們那消息。 **2** [VP6A, 22] cause to fly apart, explode, open suddenly, give way under pressure: 使爆破;使爆炸;使破口;擠破;脹破: ~ *a tyre/balloon;* 使輪胎(汽球)爆破; *We had to ~ the door open.* 我們不得不破門而入。*If you get much fatter you'll ~ your clothes.* 如果你再胖下去,你的衣服就要脹破了。*He ~ a blood-vessel,* suffered the ~ing of one; 他的一條血管破了。(fig) (喻) ~ *one's sides with laughing.* 笑破肚子。 **3** ~ ***(with),*** [VP2A, 3A] be full to overflowing; be able to contain with difficulty: 飽滿;滿盈;幾乎裝不下: *store-houses ~ing with grain;* 裝滿穀物的穀倉; *sacks ~ing with corn.* 裝滿玉蜀黍的大袋子。*They were ~ing with happiness/pride/excitement/impatience/health.* 他們樂不可支(滿懷驕傲,興奮,不耐煩,極爲健康)。**4** [VP2C] make a way or entry suddenly or by force: 突然闖過;强行進入: *He ~ into the room.* 他闖入室內。*The oil ~* (= gushed) *out of the ground.* 油從地下冒出。*The sun ~ through the clouds,* appeared through an opening in the clouds. 太陽從雲縫裏鑽出來。**5** [VP2C, 3A] (with *adverbial particles* and *preps*): (與副詞接語及介詞連用):

burst forth, ⇨ ~ out.

burst in (on/upon), (a) interrupt: 突然插嘴;打斷(談話): *Stop him ~ing in.* 別讓他打岔。*He ~ in upon our conversation.* 他打斷我們的談話。**(b)** appear or arrive suddenly: 突然出現或到達: *He'll be ~ing in on us at any moment.* 他隨時會出現在我們的面前。

burst into, (a) send out suddenly; break out into: 突然發出;迸發;爆發成: *The oil-stove upset and ~ into flames.* 油爐翻倒,立刻燃燒起來。**(b)** *~ into tears/laughter, etc,* suddenly begin to cry (laugh, etc); 突然大哭(大笑等); *~ into song,* begin to sing; 突然唱起歌來; *~ into angry speech,* begin to speak angrily. 大發雷霆。**(c)** *~ into bloom/blossom,* (of shrubs, trees) open out with blossom. (指灌木、樹木)開花。**(d)** *~ into view/sight,* (of a scene, spectacle) suddenly become visible. (指景象、奇觀)突然顯現。

burst on/upon, come suddenly or unexpectedly to: 突然或意外地出現於: *The view ~ upon our sight.* 那景象突然出現於我們的眼前。*The truth ~ upon him,* he suddenly realized it. 他突然領悟那道理。*The cries of the mob ~ upon our ears.* 暴徒們的叫囂突然傳到我們的耳邊。

burst out (into), exclaim; begin to speak: 大聲地說;咆哮地說: *'Why don't you behave?' he ~ out* (= ~ forth). '你爲什麼不規矩些?'他大聲地說。*He ~ out into threats.* 他突然大聲威脅。**~ out laughing/crying,** suddenly begin to laugh/cry. 突然大笑(大哭)。

burst² /bɜːst; bɜst/ *n* **1** bursting explosion: 爆炸;爆裂;破裂: *the ~ of a shell/bomb;* 砲彈(炸彈)之爆炸; *a ~ in the water main.* 在輸水總管上的一個裂口。**2** brief, violent effort: 短暫而猛烈的努力: *a ~ of energy/speed;* 一股勁(一陣高速); *work in sudden ~s.* 一陣一陣地努力工作。**3** outbreak: 爆發;迸發: *a ~ of applause/anger/tears;* 一陣喝采(發怒,眼淚); *a ~ of flame.* 一陣火焰。**4** short spurt: 一陣迸發: *a ~ of gunfire,* eg from a machine-gun. 砲火(如機槍)之一陣射擊。**5** ⇨ bust².

bur·then /ˈbɜːðən; ˈbɝðən/ *n, v* (liter) (文) = burden.

bur·ton /ˈbɜːtn; ˈbɝtn̩/ *n* beer brewed at Burton-on-Trent, Derbyshire. 波頓啤酒(英格蘭德貝郡,波頓城所釀製的啤酒)。**gone for a ~,** (GB sl) dead; missing. (英俚)死亡;失蹤。

bury /ˈberɪ; ˈbɛrɪ/ *vt* **1** [VP6A] place (a dead body) in the ground, in a grave or in the sea; (of a clergyman) perform the Burial Service over; (of relatives) lose by death: 埋葬(屍體);土葬;海葬;(指牧師或神父)爲…舉行葬禮;(指親屬)喪: *William Shakespeare is buried in the church at Stratford on Avon.* 莎士比亞埋葬在亞芬河畔斯特拉福市的教堂裏。*He was buried at sea.* 他被海葬了。*Poor old Joe—he's dead and buried.* 可憐的老喬——他已死亡並且埋葬了。*She has buried five husbands.* 她曾五度喪夫。**2** [VP6A, 22, 15A] put underground; cover with earth, leaves, etc; cover up and forget; hide from view: 埋藏於地下;以泥土、樹葉等遮蓋;遮蓋起來並且遺忘;隱藏;遮蔽;隱匿: *buried treasure.* 埋藏的財寶。*You wouldn't like to be buried alive.* 你不會喜歡被人活埋。*The dog buried the bone.* 狗將骨頭埋藏起來。*The end of the post was buried in the ground.* 柱子的末端埋在地下。*The house was half buried under snow.* 那房屋半截被埋在雪裏。*She buried* (= hid) *her face in her hands.* 她用雙手蒙住她的臉。**~ oneself in the country,** go to a place in the country where one will meet few people. 蟄居於鄉間;隱居於鄉間。**~ oneself in one's books/studies,** give all one's time and attention to them. 埋頭讀書(專心致力研究)。**be buried in thoughts/memories of the past, etc,** be deep in thought, etc, paying no attention to other things. 沉思(緬懷往事等)。**ˈ~ing-ground** *n* cemetery. 墓地;墳場。

bus /bʌs; bʌs/ *n* **1** (= *omnibus* which is now dated) public conveyance that travels along a fixed route and takes up and sets down passengers at fixed points: (行駛一定路線並且在一定地點上下乘客之)公共汽車(昔稱 omnibus): *Shall we walk or go by bus?* 我們是走路還是乘公共汽車?**miss the bus,** (colloq) be too late to use an opportunity. (俗)坐失良機。**ˈbus·man** /-mən; -mən/ *n* bus-driver. 公共汽車駕駛人。**ˌbusman's ˈholiday,** leisure time spent in the same kind of occupation as one's ordinary work. 應該休息而仍舊照常工作的假日。**ˈ~ stop** *n* fixed stopping place for buses. 公共汽車(招呼)站。**2** (sl) aeroplane; motor-car. (俚)飛機;汽車。□ *vi, vt* (-ss-) [VP2A, 6A] go, take, by bus; (esp US) transport children to their schools: 坐公共汽車去;以公共汽車運送;(尤美)以公共汽車送孩子們上學: *the bussing of children to achieve racial integration,* eg by taking children from white areas to schools in black areas and vice versa. 以公車送孩子上學以達成種族融合之目的(例如將白人區的孩子送至黑人區的學校就讀,或將黑人區的孩子送至白人區的學校就讀)。

busby /ˈbʌzbɪ; ˈbʌzbɪ/ *n* (*pl* -bies) fur cap worn for ceremonial parades by soldiers of some British regiments. (英國某些部隊於閱兵時所戴之)一種高頂皮軍帽。

bush /bʊʃ; bʊʃ/ *n* **1** [C] low-growing plant with several or many woody stems coming up from the root. Cf *tree,* with a single trunk: 灌木(多枝而無主幹的矮樹)(參較 tree,指有一主幹的喬木): *ˈrose-~;* 薔薇樹;玫瑰樹; *ˈfruit ~es,* eg currants, gooseberries. 灌木果樹叢(如紅醋栗、醋栗)。**2** [U] (often 常作 **the ~**) wild, uncultivated land, with or without trees or bushes, esp in Africa and Australia. (尤指非洲和澳洲的)未開墾的荒野。⇨ also telegraph. **ˈB~·man** /-mən; -mən/ *n* (*pl* -men) member of certain anciently settled tribes of West Southern Africa. 自古定居西南非洲的某些部落的土人。**~y** *adj* **1** covered with ~es. 灌木叢生的。**2** growing thickly; thick and rough: 密生的;叢生的: *~y eyebrows;* 濃眉; *a fox's ~y tail.* 狐狸的多毛的粗尾巴。

bushed /bʊʃt; bʊʃt/ *pred adj* (colloq) very tired. (俗)疲憊不堪的。

bushel /ˈbʊʃl; ˈbʊʃəl/ *n* (before metrication) measure for grain and fruit (8 gallons). 蒲式耳(採用十進制前的穀物及水果量名,等於八加侖)。⇨ App 5. 參看附錄五。**hide one's light under a ~,** be modest about one's abilities, good qualities, etc. 對於自己的能力、優點等持着謙遜態度;不露鋒芒。

busier, busiest, busily ⇨ busy.

busi·ness /ˈbɪznɪs; ˈbɪznɪs/ *n* **1** [U] buying and selling; commerce; trade: 買賣;生意;商業;貿易: *We do not do much ~ with them.* 我們跟他們沒有多少生意來往。*He's in the wool ~,* buys and sells wool. 他做羊毛生意。*He has set up in ~ as a bookseller.* 他在從事書籍的買賣。*He is in ~ for himself,* works on his own account, is not employed by others. 他自行經商(非受僱於他人)。*Which do you want to do, go into ~ or become a lawyer?* 你想幹哪一行:經商還是當律師?**on ~,** for the purpose of doing ~: 以辦公事爲目的;因公;有事: *Are you here on ~ or for pleasure?* 你在這裡辦公事還是遊玩?**ˈ~ address,**

address of one's shop, office, etc. 店鋪、辦公室等之地址;營業地址。Cf 參較 *home address.* '**~ hours,** hours during which ~ is done, eg 9am to 5pm. 營業時間(如上午九時至下午五時)。'**~-like** *adj* using, showing system, promptness, care, etc. 有系統的;迅速的;用心的;認眞的。'**~·man** /-mæn ; -,mæn/ *n* (*pl* -men) man who is engaged in buying and selling, etc. 商人;生意人;實業家;工商業家。 **2** [C] shop; commercial enterprise, etc: 商店;工商企業等: *He has a good ~ as a greengrocer.* 他開了一家很好的果菜商店。*He is the manager of three different ~es.* 他是三家商店的經理。*The newspapers advertise many small ~es for sale.* 報紙廣告登出有許多小商店要出讓。 **3** [U] task, duty, concern; what has to be done: 任務;責任;事務: *It is a teacher's ~ to help his pupils.* 幫助學生是教師的責任。*I will make it my ~* (= will undertake) *to see that the money is paid promptly.* 我要負責督促迅速付款。*That's no ~ of yours,* is something about which you need not or should not trouble. 那事與你無關。***get down to ~,*** start the work that must be done. 着手做必須做的事;言歸正傳。***mind one's own ~,*** attend to one's own duties and not interfere with those of others. 管自己的事;少管閒事。***mean ~,*** be in earnest. 當眞;說正經的(不是開玩笑)。***send sb about his ~,*** send him away and tell him not to interfere. 打發某人走開,叫他不要多管閒事。 **4** [U] right: 權利: *You have no ~ to do that.* 你無權那樣做。 **5** (with *indef art*) difficult matter: (與不定冠詞連用)難事: *What a ~ it is getting the children off to school!* 打發孩子們上學是多難的事啊! **6** (often contemptuous) affair; subject; device: (常含輕蔑意味)事情;題目;計策: *I'm sick of the whole ~,* tired of the affair. 我對這事情實在感到厭煩。 **7** (colloq): (俗): *the ~ end of a pin/a chisel, etc,* the sharp end, the end to be used. 針(鑿子等)之有尖(刃)的一端。 **8** [U] (theatre) action, facial expression, etc of the actors in interpreting their parts (as distinct from the words they speak). (戲劇)演員的動作、表情等;做功(以別於臺詞,道白)。

busker /'bʌskə(r) ; 'bʌskɚ/ *n* person who entertains people informally for money in public places, eg by singing or dancing to queues outside cinemas. (爲了賺錢而在公共場所作非正式的表演,如在電影院外面向排隊等候的人們唱歌或跳舞的)街頭藝人。

bust[1] /bʌst ; bʌst/ *n* **1** head and shoulders of a person cut in stone, or cast in bronze, gypsum, etc. (石彫、銅鑄或石膏塑的)半身像。 **2** woman's bosom; measurement round the bosom and back. 女人的胸部;胸圍尺寸。

bust[2] /bʌst ; bʌst/ *vt, vi* (sl for burst) (burst 之俚語) ~ *sth,* smash it. 擊碎某物。***go ~,*** fail; run out of money: 破產;缺錢: *The business went ~.* 這家商店破產了。□ *n* ***have a ~; go on the ~,*** a period of wild revelry. 縱情宴樂;縱飲。 '**~-up** *n* (sl) quarrel. (俚)爭吵。

bus·tard /'bʌstəd ; 'bʌstɚd/ *n* large, swift-running bird. 鴇(一種體大善跑之鳥)。

bus·ter[1] /'bʌstə(r) ; 'bʌstɚ/ *n* (in compounds) bomb or shell that wrecks completely: (用於複合字中)有徹底摧毀力之炸彈或砲彈: *'dam-~;* 能破壞水壩的炸彈; *'tank-~;* 能擊毀戰車的砲彈; *'block-~,* ie a bomb that may destroy a block of buildings. 能炸毀一街區建築物的炸彈。

bus·ter[2] /'bʌstə(r) ; 'bʌstɚ/ *n* (US sl, as a form of address) fellow (=GB 英 *mate*[1] 1). (美俚,稱呼語)老兄;老友。

bustle[1] /'bʌsl ; 'bʌsl̩/ *vi, vt* [VP2A, C, 15B] (cause to) move quickly and excitedly: (使)匆忙;忙碌;慌忙: *Tell him to ~,* hurry. 叫他趕快。*Everyone was bustling about/in and out,* appearing to be very busy. 人人都在匆匆忙忙地來來去去(進進出出)。*She ~d the children off to school.* 她匆匆地把孩子們打發上學。□ *n* [U] excited activity: 興奮的活動;匆忙;慌忙: *Everybody was in a ~.* 人人都很慌忙。*Why is there so much ~?* 爲什麼這樣忙亂?

bustle[2] /'bʌsl ; 'bʌsl̩/ *n* frame formerly used to puff out a woman's skirt at the back. (昔時女裙臀部的)裙撐。

busy /'bɪzɪ ; 'bɪzɪ/ *adj* (busier, busiest) **1** working; occupied; having much to do: 忙碌的;忙的: *The doctor is a ~ man.* 醫生是一位忙碌的人。*He was ~ with/at/over his work.* 他忙於工作。***be ~ doing sth,*** be in the process of doing it: 正忙於: *He was ~ getting ready for his journey.* 他正忙於準備旅行。***get ~,*** start: 開始: *You'd better get ~ eating.* 你最好開始吃。'**~·body** *n* (*pl* ~bodies) person who interferes in the affairs of other people, esp when his help is not wanted. 好管閒事的人;多事者。 **2** full of activity: 充滿活動的;繁忙的: *a ~ day;* 忙碌的一日; (of places) filled with active people, traffic, etc: (指地方)充滿活動的人群、車輛等;熱鬧的: *The shops are ~ before Christmas.* 商店在聖誕節前都很熱鬧。*This is one of the busiest underground stations in London.* 這是倫敦最熱鬧的地下車站之一。 **3** (of a telephone line) in use. (指電話線路)通話中的。□ *vt* [VP14, 6A] ***~ oneself (with); ~ oneself (by/in) doing sth,*** keep ~, occupy oneself with: 保持忙碌;使自己從事於…: *He busied himself with all sorts of little tasks.* 他忙於做各種小事。*She busied herself by tidying up her desk.* 她忙於收拾她的書桌。 **busi·ly** /'bɪzɪlɪ ; 'bɪzlɪ/ *adv* in a ~ way: 忙碌地: *busily engaged in doing sth.* 忙於做某事。

but[1] /bʌt ; bʌt/ *adv* only (now the usu word): 不過;只(此義今通常用 only): *We can but try.* 我們只能試一試。*He left but an hour ago.* 他不過一小時前才離去。*He's but a boy.* 他不過是一個孩子。***can not but+inf,*** (formal) = can only+*inf*: (正式用語)不得不;只好: *I cannot but think that…,* am compelled to…; 我不得不想…; *I could not but choose to go/I could not choose but go* (= had no alternative than to go). 我不得不去(我只好去)。*I cannot but admire* (= must admire, cannot help admiring) *your decision.* 我不得不欽佩你的決定。

but[2] /bət ; bət; *strong form:* bʌt ; bʌt/ *conj* **1** (coordinating): (對等用法): *Tom was not there but his brother was.* 湯姆不在那兒,但是他的哥哥(弟弟)在那兒。*We tried to do it but couldn't.* 我們試著做,但是做不到。*He's a hardworking but not very intelligent boy.* 他是個用功但不很聰明的孩子。 **2** (subordinating, with a neg implication): (附屬用法,有否定含義): *I never go past my old school but I think* (= without thinking) *of Mr Wilkins, the headmaster.* 每當我走過我的母校時,我都想起校長威爾金斯先生。*No man is so old but he may learn,* No man is too old to learn. 沒有人因爲太老而不能再學新的事物(活到老學到老)。*Never a month passes but she writes* (= in which she does not write) *to her old parents.* 她沒有一個月不給她年老的雙親寫信。

but[3] /bət ; bət; *strong form:* bʌt ; bʌt/ *prep* (The uses of *but* as a *prep* and as a *conj* are not always clearly to be distinguished. The subject forms of the *pers pronouns* are often used after *but* meaning 'except', as if it were a *conj.* The object forms are also used, as if *but* were a *prep*). (but 作爲介詞及連接詞的用法並非總能分得很清楚。在作 '除外' 解的 but 之後常用主格代名詞,這樣使 but 好像是個連接詞。也有用受格的,使 but 好似介詞)。(With negatives, eg *no one, none, nothing,* and interrogatives, eg *who,* and such words as *all, every one*) except, excluding: (與 no one, none, nothing 等否定詞連用;又與 who 等疑問詞連用;也與 all, every one 等字連用)除…外: *Nothing but disaster would come from such a plan.* 這個計畫只有招致災禍,別無益處。*They're all wrong but me.* 除我以外,他們全錯了。*None but the brave deserve the fair* (prov). (諺)只有英雄才配美人。*Who but Gloria would do such a thing?* 除了格洛瑞亞以外還有誰願意幹這種事? ***first/next/last but one/two/***

three: 第二(三，四)；第三(四，五)；倒數第二(三，四)：*Take the next turning but one* (= the second turning) *on your left.* 在你左方第二個轉彎處轉彎。*I live in the last house but two* (= the third house from the end) *in this street.* 我住在這條街上倒數第三家。*Smith was the last but one* (= second to last) *to arrive.* 史密斯是倒數第二個到達的。**'but for,** except for, without: 若非；要不是：*But for your help we should not have finished in time.* 要不是你幫忙，我們不會及時完工。*But for the rain* (= If it had not rained) *we should have had a pleasant journey.* 要不是下雨，我們那次旅行就愜意了。**'but that,** except that: 要不是爲了；若非：*He would have helped us but that* (= if it had not been for the fact that) *he was short of money at the time.* 要不是他那時候沒有錢，他會幫助我們的。***but then,*** on the other hand: 不過；在另一方面：*London is a noisy place, but then it's also the place where you get the best entertainment.* 倫敦是一個鬧市，不過另一方面它也是能給你最好娛樂的地方。

but[4] /bʌt ; bʌt/ *rel pron* (rare; formal) who/that do/does not: (罕；正式用語)其人(或該物)不：*There is not one of us but wishes* (= not one of us who does not wish) *to help you.* 我們中間沒有一人不願意幫助你。*There are few of us but* (= few of us who do not) *admire your determination.* 我們中間很少人不欽佩你的決心。

bu·tane /'bjuːteɪn ; 'bjuten/ *n* [U] gas produced from petroleum supplied in metal containers for use in houses, etc, where there is no piped supply of gas (for cooking, heating, lighting, etc). (無瓦斯管設備之家庭烹調、取暖、照明等所用之)鐵桶裝的煤氣；鋼瓶煤氣。

butch /bʊtʃ ; butʃ/ *adj* (colloq) (of a woman) having tendencies towards masculine behaviour and clothes; (of a man) exaggeratedly masculine. (俗) (指女人)行爲及服裝傾向男性化的；(指男人)過於男子氣的。□ *n* such a person. 傾向男性行爲及服裝的女人；過於男子氣的男人。

butcher /'bʊtʃə(r) ; 'butʃɚ/ *n* **1** person who kills, cuts up and sells animals for food. 屠夫；肉商。***~'s meat,*** meat excluding poultry, game and bacon; 屠宰商所賣的肉；鮮肉(不包括家禽、獵物及醃肉)；***the ~'s,*** the ~'s shop. 鮮肉店。**2** person who has caused unnecessary death, eg a general who wastes the lives of soldiers; person who kills savagely and needlessly. 造成不必要死亡的人(如無謂犧牲兵員之將領)；作野蠻及不必要屠殺的人；劊子手。□ *vt* [VP6A] kill violently, esp with a knife. (尤指用刀)殘殺；屠殺。**~y** *n* [U] **1** (attrib) ~'s trade: (形容用法)屠宰業：*He's in the ~y business.* 他是幹屠宰業的。**2** needless and cruel killing of people. 屠殺；殘殺(人類)。

but·ler /'bʌtlə(r) ; 'bʌtlɚ/ *n* head manservant (in charge of the wine-cellar, pantry, valuables, etc). 僕役長(管酒窖、食品室、貴重物品等)。

butt[1] /bʌt ; bʌt/ *n* **1** large cask for wine or ale. 大酒桶。**2** large barrel for storing rainwater, eg from roofs. 盛裝雨水(如自屋頂流下者)之大桶。

butt[2] /bʌt ; bʌt/ *n* **1** thicker (usu wooden) end (esp of a fishing-rod or rifle). 較粗的一端(通常爲木製)；(尤指)釣魚竿之柄；(步槍之)槍托。**2** unburned end of a smoked cigar or cigarette, or of a used candle. (雪茄、香煙或用過之蠟燭之)未燃燒之一端。

butt[3] /bʌt ; bʌt/ *n* **1** (usu *pl* with *def art*) shooting-range; the targets and the mound of earth behind them (used for practice in firing rifles). (通常用複數，並與定冠詞連用)靶場；(供練習步槍射擊用的)靶垜；靶子。**2** person who is a target for ridicule, jokes, etc: 成爲嘲笑對象的人：*He is the ~ of the whole school.* 他是全校的人所嘲笑的對象。

butt[4] /bʌt ; bʌt/ *vt, vi* **1** [VP6A, 15A] push with the head (as a goat does): 以頭牴(如山羊)；以頭撞：*~ someone in the stomach.* 以頭撞某人的腹部。**2** [VP2C] ***~ in,*** (colloq) force oneself into the conversation or company of others; interrupt sb: (俗)插嘴；介入；闖入；打擾：*May I ~ in?* 我可以打個岔嗎？ [VP3A] ***~ into,*** run into, head or front first. 以頭或正面碰撞。

but·ter /'bʌtə(r) ; 'bʌtɚ/ *n* [U] **1** fatty food substance made from cream by churning, used on bread, in cooking, etc: 奶油；白塔油；黃油：***~ will/would not melt in sb's mouth,*** he has a demure and innocent appearance. 一本正經的樣子。**'~·bean,** large, dried haricot ~. 大的乾扁豆。**'~-cup** *n* wild plant with yellow flowers. 金鳳花(開黃花的野生植物)。**'~·fin·gers** *n* person unable to hold things well, esp one unable to catch a ball. 拿東西拿不穩的人；(尤指)常失球的選手。**'~·milk** *n* liquid that remains after ~ has been separated from milk. 將奶油提出後的酸牛奶。**'~·scotch** *n* [U] sweet substance made by boiling sugar and ~ together. (用奶油與糖熬成的)奶油糖果。**2** substance similar to ~, made from other materials: 人造奶油(用其他物質製成之類似奶油的東西)：*cocoa ~;* 可可脂；*peanut ~.* 花生醬。□ *vt* **1** [VP6A] spread ~ on (esp bread); cook with ~. 塗奶油於(麵包等)；用奶油烹調。⇨ also bread. **2** [VP15B] ***~ sb up,*** flatter. 阿諛；諂媚。

but·ter·fly /'bʌtəflaɪ ; 'bʌtɚ,flaɪ/ *n* (*pl* -flies) insect with four wings, often brightly coloured, and feelers. 蝴蝶。**'~ (stroke)** *n* stroke used in swimming, both arms moving upward and outward at the same time as an up and down kick of the feet. 蝶泳(雙脚上下踢動時，雙臂同時向上並向外划)。

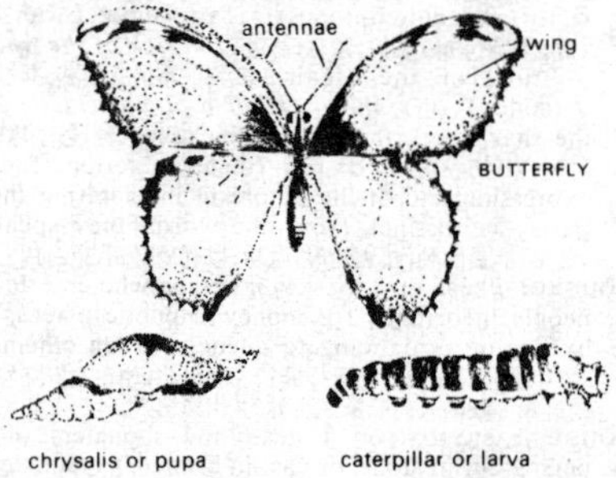

three stages in the life of a butterfly

but·tery /'bʌtərɪ ; 'bʌtrɪ/ *n* (*pl* -ries) (in some GB universities) place where provisions (bread, butter, ale) are kept and from which they are served. (在某些英國大學裏)放置及供應食物(麵包、奶油及啤酒)的處所。

but·tock /'bʌtək ; 'bʌtək/ *n* **1** either side of that part of the body on which a person sits: 臀(屁股之任一半)：*an injection of penicillin in the left ~.* 在左臀注射一針盤尼西林。**2** (*pl*) (複) **the ~s,** the rump, the bottom: 臀部；屁股：*a smack on the ~s.* 打在屁股上的一巴掌。⇨ the illus at leg. 參看 leg 之插圖。

but·ton /'bʌtn ; 'bʌtn̩/ *n* **1** small, usu round, bit of bone, metal, etc for fastening, on an article of clothing, or sewn on as an ornament. 鈕扣。**'~·hole** *n* hole through which a ~ is passed; flower worn in a ~hole (eg in the lapel of a jacket or coat). 鈕扣孔；戴於鈕扣孔上之花(如戴於男子外衣之翻領上面者)。□ *vt* [VP6A] hold sb by the ~hole (to get his attention). 抓住某人的鈕扣孔(以引起他的注意)。**'~·hook** *n* hook for pulling a ~ into place through a ~hole. (牽引鈕扣穿過扣孔之)搭鈕鉤；絆鉤。**'~·wood** *n* tall tree with a ~-shaped fruit, related to the sycamore; its wood. 篠懸木屬之植物(樹幹高，果實如鈕扣狀)；篠懸木。**2** small, round

~-like object, esp one that, when pushed, makes an electrical contact, eg for a bell: 鈕扣形之圓形小東西;鈕形物;(尤指開關電器之)按鈕(如按電鈴者)。*press / push / touch the ~.* 按電鈕。 **3** small, unopened mushroom. 未張開的小蘑菇。 **4** (*pl*) (colloq) boy wearing uniform, employed as a page in a club, hotel, etc. (複)(俗)俱樂部、旅館等處穿着制服的男侍役。⇨ bell-hop. □ *vt, vi* [VP6A, 15B, 2A] ~ ***(up/down)*** fasten with a ~ or ~s: (以鈕扣)扣;扣起;扣緊: ~ (*up*) *one's coat;* 扣起外衣的鈕扣; *a dress that ~s down the back.* 由背部扣鈕扣的女裝。*My collar won't ~ down,* I can't ~ it. 我的領子扣不起來。~ ***up,*** (colloq) complete safely, at last: (俗)終於順利完成: *That's that job ~ed up!* 也就是說,那項工作終於順利完成了! ˌ**~ed-ˈup,** *adj* (colloq) (of a person) silent and reserved. (俗)(指人)沉默寡言的。

but·tress /ˈbʌtrɪs ; ˈbʌtrɪs/ *n* support built against a wall, ⇨ the illus at church; (fig) prop; sth that supports: 撐牆;拱壁(參看 church 之插圖);(喻)支持物;支柱: *the ~es of society/the constitution.* 社會(憲法)的支柱。□ *vt* [VP6A, 15B] ~ ***(up),*** strengthen, hold up (by building a ~); (fig) support, strengthen: (築扶牆以)支撐;(喻)支持;加强: ~ *up an argument.* 支持一論點。

buxom /ˈbʌksəm ; ˈbʌksəm/ *adj* (of women) good-looking, healthy-looking and well covered with flesh. (指婦女)健美豐滿的。

buy /baɪ ; baɪ/ *vt, vi* (*pt, pp* bought /bɔːt ; bɔt/) **1** [VP6A, 15B, 12B, 13B, 2A, C] get in return for money, get by paying a price: 購買: *Can money buy happiness?* 金錢能買幸福嗎? *I bought this car from Chris.* 我從克里斯手中買得這輛汽車。*Buy one for me.* 給我買一個。*Buy me one.* 給我買一個。*I must buy myself a new shirt.* 我必須給我自己買件新襯衫。*He bought it for £2.* 他花了二鎊買它。*He bought them for/at 10p each.* 他以每個十辨士的價錢買下它們。*Prices are low—buy now!* 廉價出售——快來買吧! ***buy sth back:*** 再買回來: *He sold his house and then bought it back again.* 他把他的房子賣掉,然後又買回來了。***buy sth in,*** **(a)** buy a stock of: 買一大批: *buy in coal for the winter.* 買一大批煤過冬。**(b)** (at an auction sale) bid for and obtain (one's own goods) by offering a higher price than the highest offered by others (when other bids are considered too low). (在拍賣場)嫌他人出價過低,自己出較高的價錢買回(自己的貨物)。***buy sth off,*** get rid of (an unjust claim, a blackmailer) by making a payment. 付款擺脫(無理要求,勒索者)。***buy sb out,*** pay (sb) to give up a post, property, etc or a share in one's own business. 買通(某人)使放棄職位、財產等,或自己公司中的股份。***buy sb over,*** bribe or corrupt (sb). 賄賂(某人);向…行賄。***buy sth up,*** buy all or as much as possible of (sth). 全數買進;盡量收購(某物)。 **2** [VP6A] obtain at a sacrifice: 犧牲…以換得;換得: *He bought fame at the expense of his health and happiness.* 他犧牲了健康和幸福換得名譽。*Victory was dearly bought.* 勝利是以很高的代價換得的。□ *n* (colloq) purchase: (俗)購買;買得: *a good buy;* a bargain. 便宜的買賣;買得便宜的東西。**buyer** *n* person who buys. 購買者;採購者;買主。 **buyers' market,** state of affairs when goods are plentiful and money scarce, so that low prices favour buyers. 購買者市場(市場貨物充斥銀根緊峭,因而市價下跌有利於購買者的情況)。

buzz /bʌz ; bʌz/ *vi, vt* **1** [VP2A, C] make a humming sound (as of bees or machinery in rapid motion). 作嗡嗡聲(如蜜蜂);作營營聲(如疾速運轉中的機器)。 **2** [VP2C] move rapidly or excitedly: 急速或興奮地活動: ~ *about/around;* 匆匆忙忙地來來去去; *~ing along the road.* 沿路急急而行。~ ***off,*** (sl) go away. (俚)離去。 **3** [VP2A] (of the ears) be filled with a ~ing noise: (指耳)充滿嗡嗡之聲;鳴: *My ears began ~ing.* 我覺得耳鳴。 **4** [VP6A] (of an aircraft) fly near to or low over (another plane) in a threatening manner: (指飛機,以威脅的姿態)逼近或低飛掠過(另一架飛機): *Two fighters ~ed the airliner.* 兩架戰鬥機掠飛過那架客機。□ *n* humming (of bees or other insects); sound of people talking, of whirling machinery, etc. (蜜蜂或其他昆蟲的)嗡嗡聲;(機器轉動的)營營聲。***give sb a ~,*** (sl) make a telephone call to him. (俚)給某人打電話。**~er** *n* electrical device that produces a ~ (eg to signal time, a telephone call) when the current flows. 蜂音器(一種通過電流後發出嗡嗡聲的電鈴,用以報時、通知接電話等)。

buz·zard /ˈbʌzəd ; ˈbʌzɚd/ *n* kind of hawk. 鵟鵰。

by[1] /baɪ ; baɪ/ *adv part* **1** near: 在近旁;在附近: *He hid the money when nobody was by.* 當附近無人的時候,他把錢藏起來。**standby,** ⇨ stand[2] (10). **2** past: 從旁經過: *He hurried by without a word.* 他匆匆經過未說一句話。*Fame passed him by.* 他失去了成名的機會。*I can't get by,* can't pass. 我不能通過。*The time has/is gone by* (= is past) *when....* …的時代已經過去了。 **3** *lay/put/set sth by,* keep it, save it, for future use. 留作將來之用;儲藏以備用。 **4** (in phrases) (用於片語中) ***by and by,*** later on. 不久;不一會兒。***by the by(e), by the way,*** (used to introduce a new topic, or sth that has been forgotten). 且說;對了;順便提起(用以提出一個新的話題,或提起一件已經忘記的事)。***by and large,*** on the whole; taking everything into consideration. 大體而言;一般而論。

by[2] /baɪ ; baɪ/ *prep* **1** near; at or to the side of; beside: 靠近;在…近旁;在…旁邊;向…旁邊: *Come and sit by me/by my side.* 來坐在我的旁邊。*My house is by the river.* 我的家在河邊。*We had a day by the sea.* 我們在海邊過了一天。 ***by oneself,*** alone: 獨自地: *He went for a holiday (all) by himself.* 他獨自一人去度假。 ⇨ 12 below. 參看下列第 12 義。 ***have sth by one,*** have it handy, within easy reach: 手邊有某物;把某物放在伸手可及處: *It's useful to have a good dictionary by you when you're reading.* 當你在讀書的時候,手邊放一本好字典是很有用的。 ***stand by sb,*** support him. 支持某人。 **2** (in reading the cardinal points) towards: (方位讀法)偏向: *North by East,* one point towards the East from the North, ie between N and NNE; 正北偏東(即介於正北與北北東之間); *East by North,* one point North of East, ie between E and ENE. 正東偏北(即介於正東與東北東之間)。 ⇨ the illus at compass. 參看 compass 之插圖。 **3** (showing direction of movement) (= *by way of*) through, along, across, over: (表示移動的方向)通過;沿;橫過;越過: *We came by the fields, not by the roads.* 我們經由田間而來,不是由大路而來。 *Did you come by the nearest road?* 你是由最近的路來的嗎? *We travelled to Paris by Dover and Calais.* 我們經由多佛與加來而到巴黎。 **4** past: 經過: *I go by* (= I pass) *the post office every morning on my way to work.* 我每天早晨上班都經過郵局。*He walked by me without speaking.* 他從我身旁走過沒有說話。 **5** (of time, esp to indicate conditions and circumstances) during: (指時間,尤表示情況和環境)在…期間: *The enemy attacked by night.* 敵人乘夜間來襲。(emphasizing the circumstances—under cover of darkness, etc. 强調環境——在黑暗等的掩護下。Cf 參較 Everything was quiet *during* the night. 在夜間一切都是寂靜的。) *Do you prefer travelling by night or by day?* 你喜歡在夜間旅行,還是白天旅行? *We went for a sail on the lake by moonlight.* 我們在月光下去湖上泛舟。*It's no use trying to escape by daylight.* 在白晝想逃跑是辦不到的。 **6** (of time) as soon as; not later than; when (the time indicated) comes: (指時間)一到;不遲於;當(某時候)到了: *Can you finish the work by tomorrow?* 你能在明天以前把工作做完嗎? *He ought to be here by this time / by now.* 他此刻(現在)應該已經來到這裏了。*They were tired out by evening.* 他們到晚上疲倦極了。*By the time (that) you get there (that is* almost always omitted) *it will be dark.* 等到你到達那裏的時候，天會黑了(此種用法的 that 幾乎總被省略)。 **7** (to form adverbial phrases of time, length, weight, number): (形成時間、長度、重量、數目等之副詞片語): *rent a house by the year;* 按年租屋; *hire a bicycle by the day,* eg £5 for one day's use; 按日租脚踏車(例如:每日五鎊); *engage a clerk by the month;* 按月雇請辦事員; *pay a labourer by the day / the hour;* 按日(按小時)付工人工資; *sell cloth by the yard / coal by the ton / eggs by the dozen, etc;* 論碼賣布(論噸賣煤;論打賣蛋等); *freight charged by weight / volume;* 按重量(體積)算運費的(裝在車船上的)貨物; *a room 20 ft by 30 ft.* 長二十呎寬三十呎的房間。 **8** through the agency, means, or instrumentality of: 由於…之作用、方法或工具; 藉着;由;被: *The streets are lighted by electricity.* 街道用電照明。*This church was designed by Wren.* 這座教堂是列恩設計的。*He makes a living by teaching.* 他靠教書爲生。*He was shot by a sniper.* 他被狙擊兵擊斃。*The man was killed by a falling tree / by lightning.* 那人被倒下來的樹打死(被閃電殛斃)。(Note that *by lightning* is instrumentality, not instrument. 注意:'雷電' 係一種作用,非工具。Cf 參較 The rat was killed *by* Tom *with* a stick. 那隻老鼠被湯姆用棍打死。⇨ with(3).) **9** (indicating path or means of travel, transport, conveyance): (表示旅行、運輸等之路線、工具或方法): *travel by land / sea / air;* 由陸路(水路、航空)旅行; *by bus / car / boat, etc;* 乘公共汽車(汽車、船等); *send sth by post / hand.* 由郵局(專差)遞送某物。 **10** (indicating a part of the body that is touched, etc): (表被接觸等的身體之一部份): *take sb by the hand,* ie take his hand; 抓着某人的手; *seize sb by the hair;* 抓住某人的頭髮; *grab sb by the scruff of his neck.* 抓住某人的頸背。 **11** ***know / learn sth by heart,*** so that one can repeat it from memory. 諳記某事;牢記在心;能背出。***know sb by name / reputation / sight,*** know only his name, etc but not know him personally. 只知道某人的姓名(名聲,僅識某人之面)。 **12** (in adverbial phrases of manner) (用於表示方式或態度之副詞片語中): ***by accident / mistake,*** accidentally, not on purpose or intentionally. 由於意外(錯誤);非有意。***by chance / good fortune,*** as the result of chance or good fortune. 由於機遇(幸運)。***by oneself,*** without help. 親自;獨自;無他人幫助。⇨ 1 above. 參看上列第1義。 **13** in accordance with; in agreement with: 根據;依照: *by request of my employer;* 由於我的僱主的請求; *by your leave,* with your permission; 如果你許可的話;請原諒;恕我冒昧; *by (the terms of) Article 3 of the Treaty.* 根據條約之第3條(之條文)。 **14** according to: 根據;依據;按: *judging by appearances;* 就外表而論; *by rights,* rightly. 合理地;正當地;正確地。 *By my watch it is 2 o'clock.* 按我的錶,現在是兩點鐘。 *That's nothing to go by,* One should not form judgements by that. 那是不可作爲根據遽下斷語的。 **15** to the extent of: 至…之程度: *The bullet missed me by two inches.* 那槍彈差兩吋就擊中我。*It needs to be longer by two feet.* 它需要再長兩呎。*He's too clever by half,* much too smart. 他實在太聰明了。⇨ far²(2). **16** (in oaths) as surely as I believe in: (用於誓言中)如我對於…的信仰一樣地確然: *I swear by Almighty God that....* 我對着全能的神發誓…。*He swore by all that he held sacred that....* 他對着他所崇奉爲神聖的一切發誓…。 **17** (to express square or cubic measurement): (表示平方或立方的度量): *a carpet 30 metres by 20 metres.* 三十公尺長二十公尺寬的地毯。 **18** (arith) (to express division, = *divided by*): (算術)(表示除): *15 by 3 is / equals 5.* 15 除以 3 等於 5。

bye /baɪ; baɪ/ *n* **1** sth subordinate or incidental: 附屬物;附帶的東西: *by the bye.* 且說;對了;順便提起。⇨ by¹(4). **2** (cricket) run scored on a ball that passes the batsman and the wicket-keeper. (板球)球越過擊球手及守門員所得之分。

bye-bye /ˈbaɪ-baɪ; ˈbaɪˌbaɪ/ *n* (child's word for) sleep, bed: (兒語)睡覺;床鋪: *go to ~s* /ˈbaɪ baɪz; ˈbaɪˌbaɪz/. 去睡覺。□ *int* /ˌbaɪ ˈbaɪ; ˈbaɪˈbaɪ/ (colloq) goodbye. (俗)再見。

by-elec·tion /ˈbaɪ-ɪlekʃn; ˈbaɪɪˌlɛkʃən/ *n* election made necessary by the death or resignation of a member during the life of Parliament. (因國會議員任期未滿而死亡或辭職而必須舉行的)補選。⇨ general election.

by·gone /ˈbaɪgɒn *US:* -gɔːn; ˈbaɪˌgɔn/ *adj* past: 過去的;已往的: *in ~ days,* in the time now past. 在已往的日子;在過去的時代。□ *n* (*pl*) the past; past offences. (複)過去的事;過去的過錯。***Let ~s be ~s,*** Forgive and forget the past. 過去的事讓它過去吧;既往不咎。

by-law, bye-law /ˈbaɪlɔː; ˈbaɪˌlɔ/ *n* law or regulation made by a local, rather than a central, authority. 地方政府機關所制定的法規;地方法。

by-pass /ˈbaɪpɑːs *US:* -pæs; ˈbaɪˌpæs/ *n* new, wide road passing round a heavily populated urban area or village, to take through traffic. (環繞人口稠密之市區或鄉村藉以暢通車輛交通之)新闢的寬路;輔助道路。□ *vt* [VP6A] **1** provide with a ~: 在…外側闢一條道路: *~ a village / falls on a river.* 在鄉村外圍(環繞河上之瀑布)闢一條輔助道路。 **2** make a detour round (a town, etc): 繞道而過(市鎮等): (fig) (喻) *Let's ~ that proposal,* ignore it. 我們別理該項提議吧。

by·path /ˈbaɪpɑːθ *US:* -pæθ; ˈbaɪˌpæθ/ *n* less important or less direct path. 次要的小道;僻徑。

by·play /ˈbaɪpleɪ; ˈbaɪˌple/ *n* [U] (theatre) action apart from that of the main story; dumb-show of minor characters. (戲劇)與劇情無關的動作;配角的穿插動作。

by-prod·uct /ˈbaɪprɒdʌkt; ˈbaɪˌprɑdəkt/ *n* [C] substance obtained during the manufacture of some other substance: (製造某物時的)副產品: *Ammonia, coal-tar and coke are valuable ~s obtained in the manufacture of coal-gas.* 阿摩尼亞、煤焦油和焦炭都是製造煤氣時的重要副產品。

by-road /ˈbaɪrəʊd; ˈbaɪˌrod/ *n* side road; road that is not much used. 副道;旁道;僻路。

by·stander /ˈbaɪstændə(r); ˈbaɪˌstændɚ/ *n* person standing near but not taking part in an event or activity. 旁觀者;旁立而不參加活動者。*She was only an innocent ~.* 她只是一個無辜的旁觀者。

by-way /ˈbaɪweɪ; ˈbaɪˌwe/ *n* secondary or side road: 次要的道路;旁道: (fig) (喻) *~s of history / literature, etc,* less known departments of history, etc. 歷史(文學等)的冷僻部門。

by·word /ˈbaɪwɜːd; ˈbaɪˌwɝd/ *n* person, place, etc regarded and spoken of as a notable example (usu bad): (通常因惡事而)爲衆人所談論的人、地方等;笑柄;話柄: *She became the ~ of the village.* 她成了村中的話柄。*The place was a ~ for iniquity.* 此地以多罪惡之事出名。

Cc

C, c /siː; si/ (*pl* C's, c's /siːz; siz/) the third letter of the English alphabet; symbol for the Roman numeral 100, ⇨ App 4. 英文字母的第三個字母;羅馬數字表示100的符號(參看附錄四)。

cab /kæb; kæb/ *n* **1** vehicle (now usu motorised, = *taxicab*) that may be hired for short journeys: 出租汽車;計程車: *Shall we go by bus or take a cab?* 我們是乘公共汽車呢,還是乘出租汽車? **ˈcab·man**

/-mən ; -mən/ *n* (*pl* -men) driver of a cab. 計程車司機。 **'cab-rank** *n* row of cabs waiting to be hired. 待租的出租汽車所排成的行列。 **'cab·stand** *n* place where cabs are authorized to wait for customers. 經當局指定的出租汽車候客停車站。⇨ hansom; taxi. **2** part of a railway engine for the driver and fireman; part of a bus, lorry, etc for the driver. 火車機車內供司機及司爐所坐之處；(公共汽車、卡車等之)司機棲。

ca·bal /kə'bæl ; kə'bæl/ *n* (group of persons who carry on) secret intrigue (esp in politics). (尤指政治之)陰謀；陰謀集團。

cab·aret /'kæbəreɪ *US:* ˌkæbə'reɪ ; 'kæbəˌrɛt/ *n* (also 亦作 **'~ show**) entertainment (songs, dancing, etc) provided in a restaurant etc, while guests are at table. 餐館等中的歌舞表演。

cab·bage /'kæbɪdʒ ; 'kæbɪdʒ/ *n* [C] (kinds of) cultivated plant with a round head (often called the *heart*) of thick greenish-white or reddish-purple leaves, ⇨ the illus at vegetable; [U] these leaves cooked as a vegetable or eaten as salad, ⇨ coleslaw. 甘藍(俗稱包心菜或洋白菜)(參看 vegetable 之挿圖)；(作爲蔬菜烹煮吃的或作爲生菜吃的)甘藍菜葉。

cabby /'kæbɪ ; 'kæbɪ/ *n* (colloq) driver of a cab. (俗)出租汽車司機。

ca·ber /'keɪbə(r) ; 'kebə/ *n* trunk of a roughly trimmed young fir-tree tossed in games (in the Highlands of Scotland) as a trial of strength and skill: (蘇格蘭高地競技會中投擲以測驗臂力及技巧的)小樅樹幹: *toss the* ~. 投擲樅樹幹；投棒競力。

cabin /'kæbɪn ; 'kæbɪn/ *n* **1** room in a ship or aircraft, esp (in a ship) one for sleeping in. 船艙；飛機艙；(尤指)船上可以睡覺的房艙。 **'~ cruiser** *n* large motor-boat with a ~ or ~s. 有艙房設備的大遊艇。 **2** small, usu roughly made house (eg of logs); railway signal-box. (通常爲簡陋的)小屋；木屋；(鐵路的)信號房。

cabi·net /'kæbɪnɪt ; 'kæbənɪt/ *n* **1** piece of furniture with drawers or shelves for storing or displaying things: 有抽屜或格架以儲存或陳列物件之傢具；橱櫃: *a 'medicine* ~; 藥櫃; *a 'filing* ~, for storing letters, documents; 文件檔案櫃; *a 'china* ~, often with a glass front, for displaying ornamental china. 陳列裝飾性瓷器之玻璃橱。 **'~-maker** *n* skilled workman who makes fine furniture. 傢具木工；細木工。 **2** plastic, wooden or metal container for radio or record-playing equipment. 收音機或唱機之塑膠、木質或金屬外殼；箱。 **3** group of men (chief ministers of state) chosen by the head of the government (the prime minister in GB) to be responsible for government administration and policy. (政府最高首長，如英國的首相，所任命負責行政事務及國策的)內閣(包括各部會首長)。 **'C~ Minister**, one of these men. 內閣閣員。 **4** (old use) private room. (舊用法)私室。

cable /'keɪbl ; 'kebl̩/ *n* **1** [C, U] (length of) thick, strong rope (of fibre or wire strands), used for making ships fast; rope or chain of an anchor. (一截)繫船用的繩索或鐵索；錨索；錨鍊。 **2 '~('s)-length** *n* 100 fathoms, one-tenth of a nautical mile. 索(長度單位＝100噚，或$\frac{1}{10}$浬)。⇨ App 5. 參看附錄五。 **3** thick rope of wire strands for supporting a bridge, etc. (繫吊橋等的)金屬索；纜。 **'~-car, '~-railway**, one up a steep hillside, worked by a ~ and a stationary engine; funicular railway. (攀登陡坡之)纜車；索車；纜道車；纜索鐵路。 **4** protected bundle of insulated wires (laid underground or on the ocean bottom) for carrying messages by electric telegraph; message so carried (= ~gram). (用以通電報的)地下電纜；海底電纜；電報(由地下電纜等所傳送者)。 **5** insulated wires for conveying electric power overhead (⇨ the illus at pylon) or underground. (用以輸送電力的架空或地下)電纜(參看 pylon 之插圖)。 □ *vt, vi* [VP6A, 2A] send (a message), communicate, inform (sb) by ~(4). 打電報；與(某人)通電報；打電報通知(某人)。 **'~·gram** /'keɪblgræm ; 'kebl̩ˌgræm/ *n* ~d telegram. 海底電報；(有線)電報。

ca·boodle /kə'bu:dl ; kə'budl̩/ *n* (sl) ***the whole ~***, (of persons or things) all; the lot. (俚)(指人或物)全體；全部。

ca·boose /kə'bu:s ; kə'bus/ *n* **1** room on a ship's deck in which cooking is done. 船甲板上的厨房。 **2** (US) small van at the end of a freight train for the use of the train men. (美)(鐵路貨車尾部供車上人員用的)守車。

ca' canny /ˌkɑ: 'kænɪ ; kɑ'kænɪ/ *n* workers' policy of restricting output (by working slowly). (工人限制生產量之)怠工政策。

ca·cao /kə'kɑ:əʊ ; kə'keo/ *n* **1** (also 亦作 **'~-bean**) seed of a tropical tree from which cocoa and chocolate are made. 可可子(一種熱帶樹之種子，可製可可及巧克力)。 **2** (also 亦作 **'~-tree**) the tree. 可可樹。

cache /kæʃ ; kæʃ/ *n* (hiding-place for) food and stores left (eg by explorers) for later use. (探險者等)隱藏以供再來時用的食物及其他物品；此種隱藏所。 □ *vt* place in a ~. 置於隱藏所。

ca·chet /'kæʃeɪ *US:* kæ'ʃeɪ ; kæ'ʃe/ *n* distinguishing mark (to prove excellence, authenticity). (證明品質精良、眞正無僞之)標記；正字標記。

ca·chou /'kæʃu: *US:* kə'ʃu: ; kə'ʃu/ *n* scented sweet formerly used by smokers to disguise the odour of tobacco in the breath. (從前吸烟者用以掩蓋口中烟臭之)口香丸。

cackle /'kækl ; 'kækl̩/ *n* [U] noise made by a hen after laying an egg; [C] loud laugh; [U] foolish talk. (母鷄生蛋後的)咯咯叫聲；大笑；無意義的話。□ *vi* (of a hen) make this noise; (of a person) talk or laugh noisily. (指母鷄)咯咯叫；(指人)高聲談笑。 **cack·ler** *n*

ca·coph·ony /kæ'kɒfənɪ ; kæ'kɑfənɪ/ *n* loud, unpleasant mixture of sounds; discord(3). 不調和的聲音；刺耳的聲音。 **ca·coph·onous** /-nəs ; -nəs/ *adj*

cac·tus /'kæktəs ; 'kæktəs/ *n* (*pl* ~es, cacti /'kæktaɪ ; 'kæktaɪ/) (sorts of) plant from hot, dry climates with a thick, fleshy stem, usu with no leaves and covered with clusters of spines or prickles. 仙人掌。

cactuses

cad /kæd ; kæd/ *n* person guilty of or capable of dishonourable behaviour. 行爲下流的人；可能做卑鄙事的人；惡棍。 **cad·dish** /'kædɪʃ ; 'kædɪʃ/ *adj* of or like a cad: 下流人的；惡棍的；卑鄙的: *a caddish trick*. 卑鄙的手段。

ca·daver /kə'deɪvə(r) *US:* kə'dævər ; kə'dævə/ *n* corpse. 死屍。 **~·ous** /kə'dævərəs ; kə'dævərəs/ *adj* looking like a corpse; deadly pale. 看來像死屍的；面如死灰的；蒼白的。

caddy[1], caddie /'kædɪ ; 'kædɪ/ *n* (*pl* -dies) person who is paid to carry a golfer's clubs for him round the course. 在高爾夫球場上受僱替人背球棒之人；球童。

caddy[2] /'kædɪ ; 'kædɪ/ *n* small box for holding the dried leaves used for making tea. 茶葉罐。

ca·dence /'keɪdns ; 'kedn̩s/ *n* rhythm in sound; the rise and fall of the voice in speaking; (music) sequence of sounds moving towards a pause or an end. 韻律；節奏；步調；說話時聲調的抑揚頓挫；(音樂)

終止式。

ca·denza /kəˈdenzə ; kəˈdɛnzə/ *n* ornamental passage to be played by the soloist, usu near the end of a movement, in an instrumental concerto. 裝飾樂段（協奏曲中通常在近於一個樂章之尾部的技巧獨奏部份）。

ca·det /kəˈdet ; kəˈdɛt/ *n* **1** student at a naval, military or air force college. (陸、海、空軍之)軍校學生。ˈ~ **corps** *n* (at some GB schools) organization that gives military training to older boys. (某些英國中學之) 學生軍訓隊。 **2** young person under training for a profession: 受專業訓練中的年輕人: *ˈpolice ~s;* 警察訓練班的學員; *British Council ~s.* 在英國文化協會受專業訓練的年輕人。

cadge /kædʒ ; kædʒ/ *vt, vi* [VP6A, 14, 2A] ~ ***(from),*** beg; (try to) get by begging: 乞求;乞討;討得: *~ a meal from Auntie Ruby;* 向魯比姑媽討一頓飯吃; *be always cadging.* 老是向人討求。**cad·ger** *n* person who ~s; beggar. 乞討者;乞丐。

cad·mium /ˈkædmɪəm ; ˈkædmɪəm/ *n* [U] soft, silvery-white tin-like metal (symbol **Cd**). 鎘(性軟,銀白色,似錫之金屬,化學符號 Cd)。

cadre /ˈkɑːdə(r) *US:* ˈkædrɪ;ˈkædrɪ/ *n* **1** framework. 骨架;支架;骨幹。 **2** (mil) permanent establishment of a regiment, that can be expanded when necessary; hence, small group of important persons. (軍)(必要時可以擴充的)核心組織;(由此產生)重要幹部。

Caesar /ˈsiːzə(r) ; ˈsizɚ/ *n* title of the Roman emperors from Augustus to Hadrian; any Roman emperor. 古羅馬帝國(自 Augustus 至 Hadrian) 皇帝之稱號; 羅馬皇帝。 **~·ian** /sɪˈzeərɪən ; sɪˈzɛrɪən/ **(ˈsection/ˈbirth),** delivery of a child by cutting the walls of the abdomen and uterus. 剖腹取兒(術);帝王式切開術。

caesura /sɪˈzjʊərə *US:* -ˈʒʊərə ; sɪˈʒʊrə/ *n* point at which a pause naturally occurs in a line of verse. 一行詩中自然停頓的地方。

café /ˈkæfeɪ *US:* kæˈfeɪ ; kəˈfe/ *n* (in Europe) place where the public may buy and drink coffee, beer, wine, spirits, etc; (in GB) tea-shop, small restaurant at which meals (but not alcoholic drinks) may be bought. (在歐洲)咖啡館;酒店(可以購飲咖啡、啤酒、葡萄酒、烈酒等的地方);(在英國)茶館;小餐館(但不供應酒類)。**~-au-lait** /ˌkæfeɪ əʊ ˈleɪ; ˌkæfɪoˈle/ *n* (F) coffee with milk. (法)牛奶咖啡。

cafe·teria /ˌkæfɪˈtɪərɪə ; ˌkæfəˈtɪrɪə/ *n* restaurant at which customers collect their meals on trays at counters and carry them to tables. 自助餐廳。

caff /kæf ; kæf/ *n* (GB sl) (英俚) = café.

caf·feine /ˈkæfiːn ; ˈkæfiɪn/ *n* [U] organic compound in tea leaves and coffee beans, used in medicine. 茶精; 咖啡鹼(茶葉與咖啡豆中所含的有機化合物,用於醫藥)。

caf·tan /ˈkæftæn ; ˈkæftən/ *n* long tunic with a girdle at the waist, worn by men in the Near East; woman's loosely hanging long dress. 近東地區男人所穿之腰部束帶的長袍;長而鬆垂的女裝。

cage /keɪdʒ ; kedʒ/ *n* **1** framework, fixed or portable, with wires or bars, in which birds or animals may be kept. (畜養禽獸的)籠子;鳥籠;獸檻。 **2** camp for prisoners of war. 戰俘營。 **3** framework in which containers are lowered or raised in the shaft of a mine. (礦坑中的)升降機。□ *vt* [VP6A] put, keep, in a ~: 關入籠中: *a ~d bird.* 籠中鳥。

cagey /ˈkeɪdʒɪ ; ˈkedʒɪ/ *adj* (colloq) cautious about sharing confidences; uncommunicative; secretive. (俗)小心謹慎不洩露秘密的;守秘的。**cag·ily** *adv*

ca·goule /kəˈguːl ; kəˈgul/ *n* light, waterproof garment with a hood and long sleeves, worn over clothes for protection against rain. 有帽的長袖雨衣。

ca·hoots /kəˈhuːts ; kəˈhuts/ *n pl* ***be in ~ (with),*** (US sl) be planning sth (esp sth disreputable), be in league. (美俚)計畫某事(尤指不名譽之醜事);與…共謀;與…同夥。

cai·man, cay·man /ˈkeɪmən ; ˈkemən/ *n* S American reptile resembling an alligator. 南美鱷魚(似短吻鱷)。

cairn /keən ; kɛrn/ *n* pyramid-shaped heap of rough stones set up as a landmark or a memorial. (作爲界標或紀念碑之)角錐形石堆;石標。

cais·son /ˈkeɪsn ; ˈkesn̩/ *n* **1** chest or wagon for ammunition, usu attached to a big gun on wheels. (通常附於砲車後面的)彈藥箱;彈藥車。 **2** large watertight box or chamber in which men work under water (eg when building foundations): (工人在水面下工作,如建築橋基時,所乘之不漏水的)潛水箱;沉箱: *~ disease,* ⇨ bend²(3). 潛水夫病。

cai·tiff /ˈkeɪtɪf ; ˈketɪf/ *n* (old use) despicable or cowardly person. (舊用法)可鄙的人;懦夫。

ca·jole /kəˈdʒəʊl ; kəˈdʒol/ *vt* [VP6A, 14] ~ ***sb (into/out of doing sth),*** use flattery or deceit to persuade or soothe, or to get information, etc from sb. 以甜言蜜語哄騙(某人作或不作某事);(向某人)騙取(消息等)。**ca·jol·ery** *n*

cake /keɪk ; kek/ *n* **1** [C, U] sweet mixture of flour, eggs, butter, etc baked in an oven: (麵粉、鷄蛋、奶油等調和烘焙而成之)蛋糕;糕餅類: *an assortment of fancy ~s;* 形形色色漂亮的蛋糕; *a slice of ~,* ie of a large one that is cut into pieces. 一片蛋糕。 ***a piece of ~,*** (sl) sth very easy and pleasant. (俚)極其容易且使人愉快的事情。 ***(both) have one's cake and eat it,*** both preserve sth unchanged and allow it to change (ie an impossibility). 既想保有蛋糕,又想把它吃掉;想從事不可能的事情。 ***~s and ale,*** merry-making. 作樂;行樂。 ***(selling) like hot ~s,*** very fast. (像剛出爐的蛋糕一樣,銷售得)極快。 ***take the ~,*** (colloq) be the extreme example of sth, ⇨ biscuit(1). (俗)成爲極端的例子。 **2** [C] mixture of other kinds of food, usu compressed and cooked in a round or ornamental shape: 餅狀食物: *ˈfish-~s;* 魚餅; *ˈoat-~s.* 燕麥餅。 **3** [C] shaped piece of other materials or substances: (其他物質之成形的)一塊: *a ~ of soap/tobacco.* 一塊肥皂(菸草)。□ *vt, vi* [VP6A, 2A] coat thickly, become coated (*with* sth that becomes hard when dry); form into a thick hard mass: 覆以乾後會變硬之物質; 覆有乾硬的外層; 結成厚厚的硬塊: *His shoes were ~d with mud.* 他的鞋子黏着泥塊。

cala·bash /ˈkæləbæʃ ; ˈkæləˌbæʃ/ *n* (tree with) fruit or gourd of which the hard outer skin (or shell) is used as a container for liquids, grain, etc. 葫蘆(其堅硬之外殼可作液體、穀類等之盛器); 葫蘆樹。⇨ the illus at gourd. 參看 gourd 之插圖。

ca·lam·ity /kəˈlæmətɪ ; kəˈlæmətɪ/ *n* (*pl* -ties) great and serious misfortune or disaster (eg a big earthquake or flood, becoming blind, the loss of all one's money). 巨大而嚴重的不幸或災禍(如大地震或洪水,眼睛失明,損失全部的錢財)。**ca·lami·tous** /kəˈlæmɪtəs ; kəˈlæmətəs/ *adj* marked by, causing, ~ (*to*). 遭受災難的;引起災禍的(與 to 連用)。

cal·cify /ˈkælsɪfaɪ ; ˈkælsəˌfaɪ/ *vt, vi* [VP6A, 2A] change, be changed, into lime; harden by deposit of lime. (使)變成石灰;因積存石灰質而硬化;鈣化。

cal·cine /ˈkælsaɪn ; ˈkælsaɪn/ *vt, vi* [VP6A, 2A] make, be made, into quicklime or powder by roasting or burning; burn to ashes. 燒成生石灰或石灰粉;鍛燒;燒成灰。**cal·ci·na·tion** /ˌkælsɪˈneɪʃn ; ˌkælsɪˈneʃən/ *n* conversion of metals into their oxides by burning. 鍛燒金屬成氧化物;鍛燒;鍛。

cal·cium /ˈkælsɪəm ; ˈkælsɪəm/ *n* soft white metal (symbol **Ca**), the chemical basis of many compounds essential to life (occurs in bones and teeth, and forms part of limestone, marble and chalk). 鈣(軟性白色金屬元素,化學符號 Ca, 爲生命所必需之許多化合物的主要化學成分;存在於骨骼及牙齒中,並構成石灰石、大理石及白堊之一部份成分)。 ˌ~ ˈ**carbide** *n* compound of ~ and carbon **(CaC_2)**, used with water to make acetylene gas **(C_2H_2)**. 碳化鈣(加水可製乙炔卽電石氣)。~ **hydroxide** /haɪˈdrɒksaɪd;

haɪ'drɑksaɪd/ *n* slaked lime. 氫氧化鈣(熟石灰)。

cal·cu·lable /'kælkjʊləbl；'kælkjələbl/ *adj* that may be measured, reckoned or relied upon. 可計算的；可靠的。

cal·cu·late /'kælkjʊleɪt；'kælkjə,let/ *vt, vi* **1** [VP6A, 9, 8, 10, 2A] find out by working with numbers: 計算；算出: ～ *the cost of a journey.* 計算旅行費用。 *Astronomers can ～ when there will be eclipses of the sun and moon.* 天文學家可以算出何時發生日蝕及月蝕。 **'calculating machine** *n* one that works with numbers automatically. 計算機。 **2** ***be ～d to,*** be planned or designed to: 爲…而計畫或設計: *This advertisement is ～d to attract the attention of housewives.* 這個廣告是爲引起家庭主婦們的注意而設計的。 ***a ～d insult,*** said or done on purpose. 故意的侮辱。 **3** [VP3A] ～ ***on,*** (US) depend, bank (the usu words in GB) on: 依靠；依賴；指望(英國通常用 depend on 或 bank on): *We can't ～ on having fine weather for the sports meeting.* 我們不能指望有好天氣開運動會。 **4** [VP9] (US) suppose, believe. (美)認爲；覺得；相信。 **5** [VP9] weigh reasons, etc and be confident (*that* sth will happen, etc); estimate. 經考慮各種理由等而覺得有信心; 確信 (某事必然會發生等,後接由 that 引導之名詞子句)；估計。 **cal·cu·lat·ing** *adj* scheming; shrewd; crafty. 詭計多端的；精明的；狡猾的。 **cal·cu·la·tion** /,kælkjʊ'leɪʃən；,kælkjə'leʃən/ *n* [U] act of calculating; careful thought; [C] result of this: 計算; 考慮; 計算或考慮之結果: *After much calculation, they decided to give Phil the position of manager.* 經過愼重考慮後,他們決定給費爾經理的職位。 *I'm out in my calculations,* have made a mistake in them. 我計算(或考慮)錯了。 **cal·cu·la·tor** /-tə(r)；-tɚ/ *n* person who ～s; calculating machine. 計算者；計算機。

cal·cu·lus /'kælkjʊləs；'kælkjələs/ *n* (*pl* -li /-laɪ；-,laɪ/ or -luses /-ləsɪz；-ləsɪz/) **1** branch of mathematics divided into two parts, (**differential** ～ and **integral** ～), that deals with variable quantities, used to solve many mathematical problems. 微積分(數學之一部門,分爲微分與積分兩部份,研究變量,用以解決許多數學問題)。 **2** (med) stone in some part of the human body. (醫)(人體內的)結石。

cal·dron /'kɔːldrən；'kɔldrən/ *n* = cauldron.

cal·en·dar /'kælɪndə(r)；'kæləndɚ/ *n* **1** list of the days, weeks, months, of a particular year; list with dates that are important to certain groups of people. 日曆; 曆書; (某些團體用的) 行事曆。 **2** system by which time is divided into fixed periods, and marking the beginning and end of a year: 曆法；年曆法 (分一年時間爲若干固定單位之方法)。 *the Muslim ～;* 回教曆; *the Gregorian ～* (with every fourth year a leap year of 366 days). 格列高里曆法 (定每第四年爲閏年，卽366日)。 **,～ 'month** *n* month as marked on the ～ (contrasted with a lunar month of 28 days). 曆月(日曆上所劃分的月,與月球公轉週期之28日的太陰月有別)。

cal·en·der /'kælɪndə(r)；'kæləndɚ/ *n* roller-machine for pressing and smoothing cloth or paper. (用以壓光布與紙之)砑光機；壓光機；輪壓機。 □ *vt* [VP6A] put through a ～. 用砑光機壓光。

cal·ends, kal·ends /'kæləndz；'kæləndz/ *n pl* first of the month in the ancient Roman calendar. 古羅馬曆之朔日；初一。 ***on the Greek ～,*** never. 永遠沒有那一天；永不。

calf[1] /kɑːf *US:* kæf；kæf/ *n* **1** (*pl calves* /kɑːvz *US:* kævz；kævz/) young of the domestic cow, ⇨ the illus at domestic; young of the seal, whale and some other animals for the first year. 小牛；犢(參看 domestic 之插圖)；(一歲以內的)小海豹，小鯨或其他幼小的動物。 Cf 參較 *bull, cow, heifer, ox, steer.* ***cow in／with ～,*** pregnant cow. 懷孕的母牛。 **'～-love** *n* childish love affair; love of a young or inexperienced person. (少年男女間的)幼稚的戀愛。 **2** [U] (also 亦作 **'～ skin**) leather from the skin of a ～, esp as used in bookbinding and shoemaking. 小牛皮(尤指用以裝訂書籍及製皮鞋者)。

calf[2] /kɑːf *US:* kæf；kæf/ *n* (*pl* calves /kɑːvz *US:* kævz；kævz/) fleshy part of the back of the human leg, between the knee and the ankle. 腓；小腿(小腿後部膝與踝之間之多肉部份)。 ⇨ the illus at leg. 參看 leg 之挿圖。

cali·brate /'kælɪbreɪt；'kælə,bret/ *vt* [VP6A] determine or correct the calibre or scale of a thermometer, gauge or other graduated instrument. 測定或校準(溫度計、計量器或其他有刻度之儀器)之口徑或刻度。 **cali·bra·tion** /,kælɪ'breɪʃn；,kælɪ'breʃən/ *n* degree marks, etc on a measuring instrument. 計量器之度數記號等。

cal·ibre (US = **cali·ber**) /'kælɪbə(r)；'kæləbɚ/ *n* **1** [C] inside diameter of a tube／gun／barrel, etc. (管子、槍砲、桶等之)口徑；管徑；圓管內徑。 **2** [U] quality of mind or character; (person's) standing or importance: 才能；才幹；才具；(人之)地位或重要性: *a woman of high ～.* 很有才幹的女人；很有地位的女人。

cal·ico /'kælɪkəʊ；'kælə,ko/ *n* [U] cotton cloth, esp plain white cloth used for bed sheets, or with coloured designs printed on it, used for shirts, dresses, etc. 白洋布(如做床單用者)；印花布(用做襯衫，女裝等)。

cali·pers /'kælɪpəz；'kæləpɚz/ *n pl* (US) = callipers.

ca·liph, ca·lif /'keɪlɪf；'kelɪf/ *n* title once used by rulers who were descendants and successors of Muhammad; chief civil and religious Muslim ruler: 昔回教國家世襲之統治者(卽穆罕默德之後裔及繼承者)的稱號；回教國王兼教主: *the C～ of Baghdad.* 巴格達的國王兼教主。 **'～·ate** /'kælɪfeɪt；'kælɪ,fet/ *n* ～'s position and territory. 回教國王兼教主的職位及轄區。

cal·is·then·ics /,kælɪs'θenɪks；,kæləs'θenɪks/ *n pl* (US) = callisthenics.

calk[1] /kɔːk；kɔk/ *vt, n* [VP6A] (provide with a) sharp iron plate in a horse-shoe or boot to prevent slipping. (附於馬蹄鐵或皮靴上防滑之) 尖鐵片；釘尖鐵片於。

calk[2] /kɔːk；kɔk/ *vt* = caulk.

call[1] /kɔːl；kɔl/ *n* **1** shout; cry: 呼喊；喊叫: *a ～ for help.* 大呼求救。 *They came at my ～,* when I shouted to them. 他們應我喊叫而來。 ***within ～,*** within ～ing distance: 在呼喊聽得見的範圍內: *Please remain within ～,* close at hand. 請不要走遠(留在可以聽見呼喚的地方)。 **2** characteristic cry of a bird; military signal (on a bugle, etc). 鳥的特殊鳴聲；(軍隊的)號音。 **3** short visit (to sb's house, etc); short stop (at a place): (登某人之府等)拜訪；(在某地)小停: *pay a ～ on a friend.* 拜訪朋友。 *I have several ～s to make.* 我有幾處朋友要去拜訪。 *I must return their ～,* visit them because they visited me. 我必須回拜他們。 **port of ～,** one at which a ship stops for a short time. 船舶途中停靠之港口。 **4** message; summons; invitation: 信息；召喚；邀請: *telephone ～s.* 電話。 *I'll give you a ～.* 我會給你打電話。 *He felt the ～ of the sea,* i e to be a sailor. 他想去當海員。 **'～-box** *n* small cabin (in GB more usu called a 英國多稱爲 *telephone kiosk*) with a public telephone. 公用電話亭。 **'～-girl** *n* prostitute hired by telephone ～. 應召女郎(以電話連絡召喚之妓女)。 **5** demand for money (esp unpaid capital from company shareholders); claim of any kind: 要求付款(尤指公司股東未付之股金)；任何要求: *I have many ～s on my time.* 我有許多事情需要時間去做。 **'～-loan; '～-money; money on ～; money payable at／on ～,** money lent on condition that its return can be demanded without notice. 通知貸款；通知存(放)款。 **6** [U] (chiefly interr and neg) need; occasion: (主要用於疑問及否定句)需要；理由: *There's no ～ for you to worry.* 你沒有理由煩惱。 **7** player's right or turn to make a bid at bridge[2]; bid thus made: (橋牌)叫牌權；叫牌；所叫之牌: *Whose ～ is it?* 輪到誰叫牌？ *Was the last ～ two spades?*

剛叫的是二黑桃嗎？

call² /kɔ:l ; kɔl/ *vt, vi* (For special uses with *adverbial particles* and *preps*, ⇨ 9 below.) (與副詞接語及介詞連用的特殊用法，參看下列第9義。) **1** [VP2A, B, 3A] say sth in a loud voice; cry; speak or shout to attract attention: 大聲說話;喊;叫(以引起注意): *Why doesn't my son come when I ~?* 當我叫喚的時候,我的兒子爲何不來？ *I thought I heard somebody ~ing.* 我好像聽見有人在叫。 *She ~ed to her father for help.* 她向她的父親喊叫求救。 *I've been ~ing (for) ten minutes.* 我已叫了十分鐘了。~ **out,** cry or shout when needing help, or from surprise, pain, etc. (因需要救助,或因驚駭、疼痛等而)大叫。⇨ 9 below. 參看下列第9義。 **2** [VP2A, C, 3A, 4A] ~ ***(on sb / at a place),*** pay a short visit; go to sb's house / office etc; stop at: 拜訪;造訪;訪問;停於: *I ~ed on Mr Green.* 我拜訪了格林先生。*I ~ed at Mr Green's house.* 我曾至格林先生府上拜訪。 *I ~ed to see Mr Green.* 我曾往訪格林先生。*Mr Green was out when I ~ed.* 當我往訪時,格林先生不在家。 *A man has ~ed to read the gas meter.* 有人來抄煤氣錶。~ **for,** visit (a house, etc) to get sth, or to go somewhere with sb: 往人家等取某物或接某人同往某處: *A man ~s every Monday for old newspapers.* 有一個人每星期一來收舊報紙。 *I'll ~ for you at 6 o'clock.* 我六點鐘去接你。 **~er** *n* person who ~s on sb; visitor. 訪客;來訪者。 **3** [VP23] name; describe as: 爲…取名;把…稱做: *His name is Richard but we all ~ him Dick.* 他的名字是李查,但是我們都稱他狄克。*What are you going to ~ the baby?* 你將替嬰兒取什麼名字？ *He ~s himself a colonel,* claims that he has the right to this title. 他自稱爲上校。*You may ~ it what you like.* 你可以隨意把它叫什麼。⇨ also spade(1). ~ ***sb names,*** abuse or insult him. 詈罵某人。~ ***sth one's own,*** claim as one's own property: 稱某物爲自己的財產: *We have nothing that we can ~ our own.* 我們沒有一樣東西可以說是我們自己的財產。~ ***into being,*** create. 創造。~ ***it a day,*** ⇨ day(3). **4** [VP22, 23] consider; regard as: 認爲;視爲: *Do you ~ English an easy language?* 你認爲英文是一種容易的語文嗎？ *I ~ that a shame.* 我認爲那是一種恥辱。*I ~ that dishonest.* 我認爲那是不誠實的。 *Shall we ~ it five quid,* (colloq) settle the price, sum, etc at five pounds? (俗)我們就算作五鎊(指價錢、錢數等)好不好？ **5** [VP6A, 15B] summon; wake; send a message to: 召喚;請來;叫醒;傳喚;傳送信息: *Please ~ a doctor.* 請去請一位醫生。*Please ~ me* (= wake me up) *at 6 tomorrow morning.* 請在明天早晨六時叫醒我。 *The aircraft was ~ing* (ie sending radio signals to) *the control station at the airport.* 那飛機在(用無線電信號)呼叫飛機場的指揮臺。 *This is London ~ing,* is the BBC, London. 這裏是倫敦(英國廣播公司)播音。*The doctor was ~ed away to an accident.* 醫生被請去救治意外災害的受傷者。 *My brother ~ed me (up)* (= telephoned to me) *from Leeds last night.* 我的哥哥(弟弟)昨晚自里玆打電話給我。 [VP12B, 13B] (colloq): (俗): *Please ~ me a taxi / ~ a taxi for me.* 請替我叫部計程車。***be / feel ~ed to do sth,*** be / feel it to be one's duty to do it: 想做;應該做: *~ed to be a doctor / to practise medicine.* 想做醫生(行醫)。 **~·ing** *n* special duty; profession; occupation. 職業;行業。 **6** (special uses with *nouns*) (與名詞連用之特殊用法) ~ ***sb's bluff,*** ⇨ bluff². ~ ***a halt (to),*** say that it is time to halt: 命令停止: *~ a halt to gambling,* forbid it. 命令禁止賭博。~ ***a meeting,*** announce that one will be held and summon people to attend. 召集會議。~ ***the roll,*** ⇨ roll¹(4). ~ ***a strike,*** order workers to come out on strike. 發動罷工。 **7** (card-games) bid or make a demand. (紙牌)叫牌。⇨ call¹(7). **8** (phrases) (片語) ~ ***(sb) to account,*** ⇨ account¹(4). ~ ***attention to,*** require (sb) to give his attention to. 要求(某人)注意…。~ ***the banns,*** ⇨ banns. ***be ~ed to the Bar,*** ⇨ bar¹(12). ~ ***sth in / into question,*** declare that one has doubts about it. 宣稱對某事懷疑;對某事提出質問。~ ***sb / a meeting to order,*** ask for orderly behaviour, ask that attention should be paid to the rules. 請求某人(與會者)守秩序。 **9** [VP 15B, 3A] (special uses with *adverbial particles* and *preps*): (與副詞接語及介詞連用之特殊用法):

call by, (colloq) visit briefly (usu when passing the house, etc). (俗)短時間地拜訪;(通常指)順道拜訪。

call sb down, (US sl) reprimand him severely. (美俚)嚴厲斥責某人。~ ***sth down,*** invoke, ask for it: 祈求;要求;請求: *~ down curses on his head.* 求神降禍於他。

call for, demand, require: 要求;需要: *You must take such steps as seem (to be) ~ed for,* do what seems necessary. 你必須採取這些似乎必要的步驟。 *The occasion ~s for prompt action.* 情勢所迫,必須立卽採取行動。

call sth forth, **(a)** be the cause of: 引起;招致: *His behaviour ~ed forth numerous protests.* 他的行爲引起許多的抗議。 **(b)** produce and use: 鼓起;振作起: *You will have to ~ forth all your energy.* 你必須全力以赴。

call sth in, order or request the return of: 下令收回;請求收回: *The librarian has ~ed in all books.* 圖書館員業已通知收回全部書籍。*Gold coins were ~ed in by the Government.* 金幣已被政府下令收回。*He was so short of money that he had to ~ in the loans he had made.* 他非常缺錢,所以不得不收回他所借出的款子。

call sth off, **(a)** ~ away: 將…叫開: *Please ~ your dog off,* ~ to your dog so that it stops worrying me. 請把你的狗叫開。 **(b)** decide, give orders, to stop sth: 決定取消某事; 下令停止某事: *The strike / attack was ~ed off,* was either not started or was stopped. 罷工(攻擊)已取消(或已奉命停止)。 *You had better ~ the deal off,* not carry out what was agreed upon. 你最好取消這項交易。

call on / upon sb, **(a)** make a short visit to. 短暫地訪問;拜訪。⇨ 2 above. 參看上列第2義。 **(b)** ~ ***on / upon sb (to do sth),*** appeal to, invite, require him: 懇求;請求;邀請;要求: *I ~ed on* (= appealed to) *him to keep his promise.* 我懇求他遵守諾言。*I now ~ upon* (= invite) *Mr Grey to address the meeting.* 我現在請格雷先生向大會演講。*I feel ~ed upon* (= feel that I ought) *to warn you that....* 我覺得我應該警告你…。

call sb out, **(a)** summon, esp to an emergency: 召喚(尤指應付緊急事件): *The fire brigade was ~ed out twice yesterday.* 昨天消防隊被召喚兩次。*Troops had to be ~ed out.* (我們)不得不召來軍隊。 **(b)** instruct (workers) to come out on strike: 指示(工人)罷工: *The coal-miners were ~ed out by the Union officials.* 煤礦工人受工會職員指示而罷工。

call sth over, read (a list of names) to learn who is present. 點名;淸點(名單)。 **'~-over** *n* (also 亦作 **'roll-~**) reading of a list of names (eg in school, the army). 點名(如學校中或軍中)。

call sb / sth up, **(a)** telephone to: 打電話給: *I'll ~ you up this evening.* 我今晚將打電話給你。 **(b)** bring back to the mind: 使想起;使憶起: *~ up scenes of childhood.* 使回憶起童年時代的情景。 **(c)** summon for (military, etc) service: 徵召…服兵役等: *If war breaks out, we shall be ~ed up at once.* 倘若戰爭爆發,我們將立卽被徵召服役。 Hence, 由此產生, **'~-up** *n*

cal·ligra·phy /kə'lɪgrəfɪ ; kə'lɪgrəfɪ/ *n* [U] (art of) beautiful handwriting. 書法;美的字體。

cal·li·ope /kə'laɪəpɪ ; kə'laɪəpɪ/ *n* steam-organ; musical instrument with steam whistles played by pressing keys. 蒸汽風琴(一種按鍵而由各種汽笛發音之樂器)。

cal·li·pers /'kælɪpəz ; 'kæləpəz/ *n pl* **(pair of) ~, 1** instrument for measuring the diameter of round objects or the calibre of tubes, etc. (測量圓形物之直

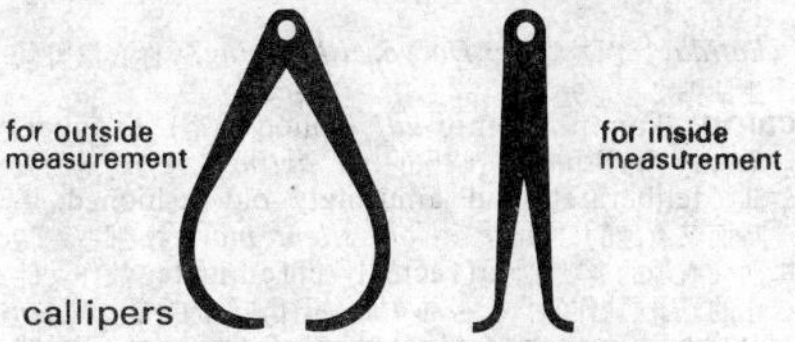

callipers

徑或圓管等口徑之)雙脚規;測徑器。 **2** metal supports attached to the legs of a disabled person to enable him to walk. 裝在殘廢者腿上助其行走的金屬架。

cal·lis·then·ics /ˌkælɪsˈθenɪks ; ˌkæləsˈθɛnɪks/ *n pl* (usu with a *sing v*) exercises designed to develop strong and graceful bodies. (通常與單數動詞連用) 柔軟體操;健身運動。

cal·los·ity /kæˈlɒsətɪ ; kəˈlɑsətɪ/ *n* (*pl* -ties) area of hardened thick skin; callus. 皮膚硬化的部分;胼胝。

cal·lous /ˈkæləs ; ˈkæləs/ *adj* **1** (of the skin) made hard (by rough work, etc). (指皮膚因操勞等而)結有硬塊的;結繭的;變硬的。**2** ~ ***(to)***, (fig) unfeeling; indifferent: (喩)無情的;無感覺的;冷淡的: *~ to insults/his employees/the suffering of others.* 對侮辱無感覺(對雇員無情;對別人的痛苦冷淡)。**~·ness** *n*

cal·low /ˈkæləʊ ; ˈkælo/ *adj* young; unfledged; inexperienced: 年幼的; 未生羽毛的; 無經驗的: *a ~ youth.* 一個無經驗的青年。**~·ness** *n*

cal·lus /ˈkæləs ; ˈkæləs/ *n* area of thick, hardened skin. 皮膚硬化的部分;胼胝。

calm /kɑːm ; kɑm/ *adj* (-er, -est) **1** (of the weather) quiet; not windy; (of the sea) still; without large waves. (指天氣) 平靜的; 無風的; (指海) 無風浪的。**2** not excited; untroubled; quiet: (心境)鎮定的;無憂慮的; 寧靜的: *keep ~.* 保持鎮定。□ *n* **a ~**, a time when everything is quiet and peaceful. 安靜太平的時候;平靜的時候。□ *vt, vi* [VP6A, 15B, 2C] **~ *(down)***, make or become ~: 使平靜;平息;靜下來: *C~ yourself!* 請你安靜(或鎮定)下來! *The sea ~ed down.* 海上風浪平息下來了。**~·ly** *adv* **~·ness** *n* ~ condition. 平靜;寧靜;安靜。

calo·mel /ˈkæləmel ; ˈkæləml̩/ *n* [U] white, tasteless, insoluble substance used as a purgative. 甘汞; 氯化亞汞(白色無味的不溶性物質,用作瀉藥)。

Calor gas /ˈkælə gæs ; ˈkælə gæs/ *n* [U] (P) butane. (商標)丁烷。

cal·orie /ˈkælərɪ ; ˈkælərɪ/ *n* unit of heat; unit of energy supplied by food: 卡路里;卡(熱量單位;食物所供給的能量單位): *An ounce of sugar supplies about 100 ~s.* 一兩糖可供給約一百卡熱。**cal·or·ific** /ˌkæləˈrɪfɪk ; ˌkæləˈrɪfɪk/ *adj* producing heat/energy: 生熱的;發熱的;生能的: *calorific value*, (of food or fuel) quantity of heat/energy produced by a given quantity. (食物或燃料之)熱量;能量。

cal·umny /ˈkæləmnɪ ; ˈkæləmnɪ/ *n* (*pl* -nies) (formal) [C] false statement about a person, made to damage his character; [U] slander. (正式用語)中傷他人人格的謊話;誹謗。**ca·lum·ni·ate** /kəˈlʌmnɪeɪt ; kəˈlʌmnɪˌet/ *vt* [VP6A] slander. 誹謗;中傷。

Cal·vary /ˈkælvərɪ ; ˈkælvərɪ/ *n* hill outside Jerusalem where Jesus was crucified; carved representation of the Crucifixion. 髑髏地(耶路撒冷近郊的一座小丘,耶穌在此被釘死在十字架上);(耶穌被釘死在十字架上的)受難像。

calve /kɑːv *US:* kæv ; kæv/ *vi* give birth to a calf. 產小牛。

Cal·vin·ism /ˈkælvɪnɪzəm ; ˈkælvɪnɪzəm/ *n* religious teaching of the French Protestant, John Calvin. 法國宗教改革家喀爾文之教義。**Cal·vin·ist** *n* follower of Calvin's teachings. 喀爾文教義之信徒;喀爾文派教徒。

ca·lyp·so /kəˈlɪpsəʊ ; kəˈlɪpso/ *n* (*pl* ~s /-səʊz ; -soz/) improvised song, as composed by West Indians, on a subject of current interest. 以時下事件爲主題所臨時製作的歌曲 (如西印度群島土人所作者); 加力騷。

ca·lyx /ˈkeɪlɪks ; ˈkelɪks/ *n* (*pl* ~es or calyces /ˈkeɪlɪsiːz ; ˈkelɪˌsiz/) ring of leaves (called *sepals*) forming the outer support of the petals of an unopened flower-bud. 植物的花萼(花蕾的花瓣外層的一圈小葉,稱爲 sepals 萼片)。⇨ the illus at flower. 參看 flower 之插圖。

cam /kæm ; kæm/ *n* projection on a wheel or shaft, designed to change circular motion into up-and-down or back-and-forth motion. 凸輪;鏗(輪或輪軸上的凸起設計,用以改變圓周運動爲上下或前後運動)。**cam·shaft** /ˈkæmʃɑːft *US:* -ʃæft ; ˈkæmˌʃæft/ *n* (eg in a car) shaft to which cams are attached. (汽車等之)凸輪軸。

cama·rad·erie /ˌkæməˈrɑːdərɪ *US:* -ˈræd- ; ˌkɑməˈrɑdərɪ/ *n* (F) [U] friendliness and mutual trust of comrades. (法)同志的友愛及互信;同志愛。

cam·ber /ˈkæmbə(r) ; ˈkæmbɚ/ *n* upwards slope (eg of a road surface) of a curve. (路面等之)彎路的向上傾斜;拱勢;側傾;翹曲;彎度。□ *vt, vi* (of a surface) have a ~; give a ~ to. (指表面)略爲拱起;使呈拱勢或側傾;(使)翹曲。

cam·bric /ˈkeɪmbrɪk ; ˈkembrɪk/ *n* [U] fine, thin cloth of cotton or linen. 一種細而薄之棉布或麻布。

came *pt* of come.

camel /ˈkæml ; ˈkæml̩/ *n* long-necked animal, with either one (*dromedary*) or two humps on its back, used in desert countries for riding and for carrying goods. 駱駝(一種長頸動物,背上有一或二駝峯,沙漠國家用以騎乘或載運貨物)。⇨ the illus at large. 參看 large 之插圖。**ˈ~-hair** *n* fine hair for making the brushes used by artists; soft, heavy cloth of this hair: 駝毛(用以製畫筆);駝絨(駝毛織成之柔軟的厚絨布): *a ~-hair coat.* 駝絨外衣。

ca·mel·lia /kəˈmiːlɪə ; kəˈmɛlɪə/ *n* evergreen shrub from China and Japan with shiny leaves and white, red or pink rose-like flowers; the flower. 山茶(原產於中國及日本之常青灌木,葉有光澤,開白、紅、或粉紅色玫瑰狀花);茶花。

Cam·em·bert /ˈkæməmbeə(r) ; ˈkæməmˌbɛr/ *n* (F) rich, soft cheese (of Normandy, France). (法)(產於諾曼第之) 濃味軟乾酪。

cameo /ˈkæmɪəʊ ; ˈkæmɪˌo/ *n* (*pl* ~s /-əʊz ; -oz/) **1** piece of hard stone with a raised design, often used as a jewel or ornament. 刻有不同顏色浮雕之硬石(用作寶石或裝飾品)。**2** short piece of writing or acting conveying the essential qualities of a person, place, event etc. (表現某人、某地、某事件等之特質之)短文;短劇。

cam·era /ˈkæmərə ; ˈkæmərə/ *n* **1** apparatus for taking still photographs or (**ˈfilm/ˈmovie ~**) moving pictures, or (**TˈV ~**) for receiving light images and transforming them for broadcasting live or for receiving on video tape. 照相機;電影攝影機 (film camera 或 movie camera); 電視攝影機 (TV camera)。**ˈ~-man** /-mæn ; -ˌmæn/ *n* (*pl* -men) person who operates a ~ for films or TV. 電影製片廠的攝影師;(電視廣播臺的)攝影機操作者。**2** *in ~*, (Lat) in the judge's private room, not in court; privately. (拉)在法官的私室裏(不在法庭上);私下地;秘密地。

cam·ion /ˈkæmɪən ; ˈkæmɪən/ *n* (F) low, four-wheeled truck; lorry. (法)一種低的四輪貨車;卡車。

camo·mile, chamo·mile /ˈkæməmaɪl ; ˈkæməˌmaɪl/ *n* [U] sweet-smelling plant with daisy-like flowers; the dried flowers and leaves used in medicine as a tonic. 甘菊(一種有香味的植物,花狀如雛菊);晒乾後之甘菊花及葉(醫藥上用作補劑)。

cam·ou·flage /ˈkæməflɑːʒ ; ˈkæməˌflɑʒ/ *n* [U] **1** that which makes it difficult to recognize the presence or real nature of sth: 掩飾;掩護(使難以認出某物之存在或眞實性質): *The white fur of the polar bear is a natural ~*, because the bear is not easily seen in the snow. 北極熊的白色毛皮是一種天然的掩護(因其在雪中不易被看見)。**2** (in war) the use of paint, netting, boughs of trees, smoke-screens, etc to deceive the enemy by giving a

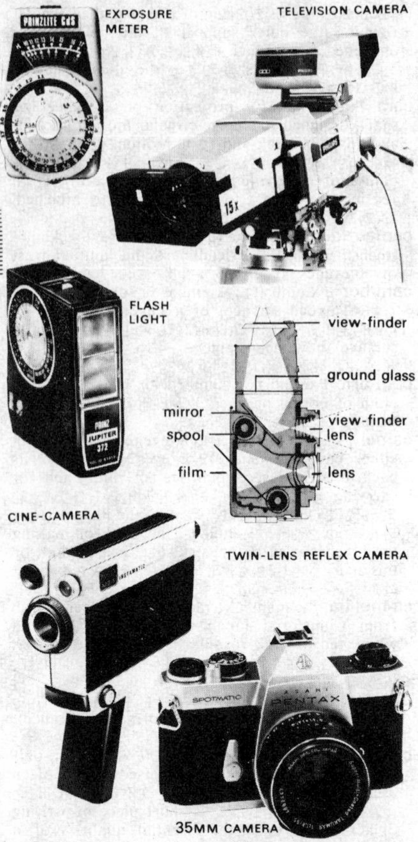

false appearance to things. (戰爭中)(用塗料、網子、樹枝、煙幕等)僞裝(以欺騙敵人)。□ *vt* [VP6A] try to conceal by means of ～. 掩護;僞裝。

camp[1] /kæmp ; kæmp/ *n* **1** place where people (eg people on holiday, soldiers, boy scouts, explorers) live in tents or huts for a time: (度假者、軍隊、童子軍、探險者等臨時搭帳篷所住的) 營地: *be in ～;* 在露營中; *pitch a ～;* 紮營; *strike/break up ～,* pack up (the tents, etc). 拔營。ˌ**～-'bed/-'chair/-'stool** *n* one that can be folded and carried easily. (可摺疊而便於携帶的)行軍床(摺椅;摺櫈)。 **'～-fire** *n* one of logs, etc, made in the open air. (在野外燃燒木頭等所做的) 營火。 **'～-follower** *n* person (not a soldier) who follows an army to sell goods or services. 跟隨軍隊販賣貨物或提供服務的人 (非軍人);隨營商販。⇨ also concentration ～. **2** number of people with the same ideas (esp on politics or religion): (尤指政治或宗教觀點相同的人所形成的)陣營;陣線: *You and I belong to different political ～s.* 你我屬於不同的政治陣營。*We're in the same ～,* are in agreement, are working together. 我們是志同道合(共同工作)的。 □ *vi* [VP2A, C] **～ *(out),*** make, live in, a ～: 紮營;宿營: *Where shall we ～ tonight?* 我們今晚將宿營何地? *They ～ed out in the woods.* 他們在樹林中宿營。***go ～ing,*** spend a holiday in tents, etc: 露營;在野外搭帳篷住宿(一種度假方式): *The boys have decided to go ～ing next summer.* 男孩們已決定明年夏天去露營(參加明年的夏令營)。**～er** *n* **～·ing** *n* (gerund) (動名詞) [U] *a ～ing holiday;* 露營假日; *Do you like ～ing?* 你喜歡野營生活嗎?

camp[2] /kæmp ; kæmp/ *adj* (colloq) (俗) exaggeratedly stylish: 過於時髦的: *～ acting;* 過於時髦的表演; deliberately and amusingly old-fashioned: 過時而又有趣的: *those ～ old silent movies;* 那些過時而又有趣的老默片; affectedly effeminate: 故作女性化的;矯揉造作的: *a ～ walk.* 矯揉造作的步態。□ *n* exaggeration and affectation of this sort. 過於時髦;矯揉造作。□ *vi, vt* **～ *(it up),*** behave in this way. 顯得過於時髦;顯得矯揉造作。

cam·paign /kæm'peɪn ; kæm'pen/ *n* [C] **1** group of military operations with a set purpose, usu in one area. 戰役(在某一地區所做一連串有固定目的的軍事行動)。 **2** series of planned activities to gain a special object: 運動(爲達到某一特殊目標所做的一連串有計畫的活動): *a political ～;* 競選活動; *an advertising ～;* 廣告活動; *a ～ to raise funds.* 募捐運動。□ *vi* [VP2A, 3A] take part in, go on, a ～. 參加某一戰役;參加運動;從事活動。**～er** *n* person who ～s or who ～ed: 參與某一戰役者;參加運動者;從事活動者: *He's an old ～er,* has much experience of adapting himself to circumstances. 他是一個老練者(富有經驗,能適應環境)。

cam·pa·nile /ˌkæmpə'ni:lɪ ; ˏkæmpə'nilɪ/ *n* bell tower, usu a separate building. 鐘樓(通常指獨立建造者)。

cam·pan·ula /kəm'pænjʊlə ; kæm'pænjʊlə/ *n* (kinds of) plant with bell-shaped flowers, usu blue or white. 山小菜屬;風輪草(花如鐘形,通常呈藍或白色)。

cam·phor /'kæmfə(r) ; 'kæmfɚ/ *n* [U] strong-smelling white substance used medically and in the manufacture of celluloid. 樟腦(有強味之白色物質,作藥用,或用以製賽璐珞)。**'～ ball** *n* small ball of ～, used to keep moths, etc out of clothes. 樟腦丸(用以驅除蛀蝕衣服之蟲等)。**～·ated** /'kæmfəreɪtɪd ; 'kæmfəˌretɪd/ *adj* containing ～: 含有樟腦的: *～ated oil.* 樟腦油。

cam·pion /'kæmpɪən ; 'kæmpɪən/ *n* [U] (kinds of) common flowering plant that grows wild on roadsides and in fields. 石竹科植物(常見之開花植物,長於路邊及田間);狗筋蔓。

cam·pus /'kæmpəs ; 'kæmpəs/ *n* (*pl* ～es /-pəsɪz ; -pəsɪz/) grounds of a school, college or university. (學校、學院或大學之)校區;校園;校苑。

can[1] /kæn ; kæn/ *n* **1** metal container, usu with a lid, for liquids, etc: (裝液體等,常帶有蓋之)金屬罐: *'oil-can,* 油罐, *'milk-can.* 牛奶罐。 ***carry the can (for sb),*** (sl) take the blame. (俚)(爲某人)背黑鍋;(代某人)受責。***(be) in the can,*** (of film, video-tape) exposed or recorded and stored ready for use. (指影片或電視錄影帶)已沖曬或錄影完畢存以備用。 **2** (formerly US but now also GB) tin-plated airtight container for food, drink etc; contents of such a container: (從前用於美國,現在亦用於英國)不透空氣的白鐵罐;罐頭(用以裝食物,飲料等);罐頭之內容: *a can of beer/peaches.* 一罐啤酒(桃子)。⇨tin. **3** (US sl) prison. (美俚)監獄;牢房。□ *vt* (-nn-) [VP6A] preserve (food, etc) by putting in a can(2) which is then hermetically sealed: 裝(食品等)於罐頭(然後密封以便長時間保存);罐裝: *canned fish;* 魚罐頭; *canned music,* (sl) music recorded on discs, etc. (俚)錄於唱片等上之音樂。**canned** /kænd ; kænd/ *adj* (US sl) drunk. (美俚)酒醉的。**can·nery** /'kænərɪ ; 'kænərɪ/ *n* place where food etc is canned. 罐頭工廠;裝罐工廠。

can[2] /kən ; kən; *strong form:* kæn ; kæn/ *anom fin* (*neg* cannot /'kænət ; 'kænɑt/ or can't /kɑ:nt *US:* kænt ; kænt/, *pt* could /kəd ; kəd; *strong form:* kʊd ; kʊd/, *neg* couldn't /'kʊdnt ; 'kʊdn̩t/) [VP5] **1** (indicating ability or capacity to do sth) be able to; know how to: (表示做某事之能力)能;會: *Can you lift this box?* 你能抬起這個箱子嗎? *I can't get the lid off.* 我打不開那蓋子。 *She can speak French.* 她會說法語。 (*Could* refers to ability or capacity in past time): (could 指從前能够): *She could read Latin and Greek when she was ten.* 當她十歲時就能讀拉丁文及希臘文。(*Could* is used in *if*- clauses to indicate a condition, expressed or implied): (could 用於假設子句中,表示明示或暗示的條件): *Could you lift that box* (ie now, if you tried)? (現在,如果你試一試)你能拿得起那只箱子嗎? *Could you have lifted that box* (ie if you had tried, eg yesterday)? (如果你試過的話,譬如說昨天) 你能拿得起那只箱子嗎? (Note that *could* is not used except in conditions, for an isolated achievement in past time. Instead, *be able to, manage to* or *succeed in* (*doing sth*) are preferred): (注意:除非用於條件中, could 不可以用來指過去的某一次成就,宜用be able to, manage to, 或 succeed in (doing sth)): *When the boat upset, they were able/managed to swim/succeeded in swimming to the bank* (not *they could swim to the bank* which is incorrect). 小船翻覆時,他們游泳抵達了岸上 (they could swim to the bank 是錯誤的)。 **2** (*Can* is used with *vv* of perception in place of the simple tenses, which are less usual. Nothing is added to the meaning.): (can 與感官動詞連用,代替簡單時式,且較簡單時式常用。意義上無任何差異。): *I can see a sail on the horizon.* 我看到海平線上有一帆船。*I can hear people talking in the next room.* 我聽見隔壁房內有人談話。(*Could* is used for past time): (could 用以表明過去時間): *We could hear someone singing in the bathroom.* 我們聽到有人在浴室唱歌。 *She said she could smell something burning.* 她說她聞到有東西燒着的味道。 **3** (*Can* is used, colloquial style, to indicate permission. The use of *may* is more formal. In reported speech, *could* is used after a *v* in the *pt*. *Could* may also replace *can* in a tentative request in question form): (can 用於口語中,表示許可。用 may 比較正式。在間接敍述句法中, could 用於過去時式之動詞之後。在問句中作試探性要求時, could 亦可代替 can): *You can* (= may) *go home now.* 你現在可以回家了。 *The children asked whether they could* (= might) *go for a swim.* 孩子們問他們是否可以去游泳。 *You can't travel first-class with a second-class ticket.* 你不可以拿二等票坐頭等位子旅行。*Put that cigarette out—you can't smoke near a petrol pump!* 把香煙熄掉——你不可以在靠近汽油泵(油幫浦)處抽煙! **4** (*Can/could* are used to indicate what is possible or likely): (can 或 could 用以表示可能性): *One of the prisoners escaped yesterday—he can/could* (= may) *be anywhere by now.* 昨天有一個囚犯逃走了——他目前可能躲在什麼地方。(*Can have* is used for past time): (can have 用以表示過去時間): *He's an hour late—he can have been delayed by fog, of course*, that's a possibility. 他遲到了一個鐘頭——當然,他可能是被霧所阻。 **5** (*Can/could* in questions (and esp with *what(ever), where, how*) indicate surprise, bewilderment, impatience, etc, according to context. The strong forms are used): (can 或 could 在問句中,尤其與 what, whatever, where, how 連用時,表示驚奇、困惑、不耐煩等,視其上下文而定。can 或 could 應重讀): *What ˌcan he ˈmean?* 他能有什麼用意? *What ˌcan we ˈdo about it?* 我們還能有什麼辦法? *Where ˌcan they have ˈgot to?* 他們還能上哪裏去? *How ˌcan/ˌcould you be so unˈkind?* 你怎能那樣無情? **6** (*Can/could* indicate what is considered characteristic, what sb or sth is considered capable of being or doing. Adverbials of frequency (eg *at times, sometimes*) often occur): (can 或 could 表示被視爲特性者,某人或某事物之能爲。常用表示次數之副詞,如 at times, sometimes): *Children can sometimes be very trying.* 孩子們有時非常討厭。 *It can be very cold here, even in May.* 此地卽使在五月裏也可能非常冷。*The Bay of Biscay can be very rough at times.* 比斯開灣時常風浪洶湧。*When I first knew her she could be very sarcastic, but she's more tolerant now.* 當我第一次認識她時,她是非常尖刻的,不過現在她是較爲寬容了。 **7** (*Could* is used to mean 'feel inclined to'): (could 用於指'想要'之意): *I could smack your face!* 我眞想摑你一巴掌! **8** (*Can* is used, colloquial style, with imperative force, meaning 'must'): (can 用於有命令意謂的口語中,表示'必須'): *Tell Mr Evans that he can come in now,* Tell him to come in. 叫艾文斯先生進來。 **9** (*Can/could* are used in polite requests; ⇨ will¹(3)): (can, could 用於禮貌的請求): *Do you think I could leave now/Could I leave now, do you think?* Please may I leave now? 請問我可以走了嗎? *Could you put out your cigarette, please?* Please put it out. 請把你的香煙熄掉好嗎?

Ca·na·dian /kəˈneɪdɪən ; kəˈnedɪən/ *n, adj* (native) of Canada. 加拿大人;加拿大的。

ca·nal /kəˈnæl ; kəˈnæl/ *n* **1** channel cut through land for use of boats or ships (eg **the Suez** /ˈsuːɪz ; ˈsuɛz/ **C∼**) or to carry water to fields for irrigation. (開鑿陸地以供行船的)運河(如蘇彝士運河);(引水灌溉田地的) 渠;圳。 ⇨ the illus at lock. 參看 lock 之插圖。 **ˈ∼ boat** *n* long, narrow boat, some of which are pulled by horses, used on ∼s. 行駛於運河的狹長形船(有些係用馬拖)。 **2** tube or pipe (or system of these) in a plant or animal body for food, air, etc: 管 (植物或動物體內通食物、空氣等的管道或一系列的通管): *the alimentary ∼.* 消化管。 ⇨ the illus at alimentary, ear. 參看 alimentary 及 ear 之插圖。 **∼·ize** /ˈkænəlaɪz ; kəˈnælaɪz/ *vt* [VP6A,14] make (a river) into a ∼ (by straightening, building locks, etc); (fig) direct; channel: 改造(河道,如改直河床、建設閘門等)使成爲運河; (喩)指導;引導;導向某一方向前進: *∼ize one's energies/efforts into charity work.* 致力於慈善事業。 **∼·iz·ation** /ˌkænəlaɪˈzeɪʃn *US:* -nəlɪˈz- ; kəˌnæləˈzeʃən/ *n*

can·apé /ˈkænəpeɪ *US:* ˌkænəˈpeɪ ; ˈkænəpɪ/ *n* (F) thin piece of bread or toast spread with seasoned fish, cheese, etc. (法)加有經過調味的魚、乾酪等之薄麵包片或烤麵包片。

ca·nard /kæˈnɑːd ; kəˈnɑrd/ *n* (F) false report. (法) 虛報;謊報。

ca·nary /kəˈneərɪ ; kəˈnɛrɪ/ *n* (*pl* -ries) **1** (also 亦作 **ˈ∼-bird**) small, yellow-feathered song-bird, usu kept in a cage; [U] its colour, light yellow. 金絲雀(黃羽毛小鳴禽,通常養於籠中);金絲雀之毛色(淺黃色)。 **2** (also 亦作 **ˈ∼-wine**) sweet white wine from the C∼ Islands. 加那利群島所產之白色甜葡萄酒。

ca·nasta /kəˈnæstə ; kəˈnæstə/ *n* card game for two to six players using two packs of cards. 卡納斯塔(一種二至六人玩之紙牌戲,使用兩副紙牌)。

can·can /ˈkænkæn ; ˈkænkæn/ *n* lively high-kicking dance performed by a group of women in long skirts. 康康舞(由一隊穿長裙之女人所演之活潑的高踢腿舞)。

can·cel /ˈkænsl ; ˈkænsl/ *vt, vi* (-ll-, US -l-) **1** [VP6A] cross out, draw a line through (words or figures); make a mark on (sth, eg postage stamps, to prevent re-use): 刪去;在(字或數字)的腰間畫一線表示消去;勾掉;註銷(某物,如郵票,以防再用): *∼led stamps.* 已註銷的郵票。 **2** [VP6A] say that sth already arranged or decided upon will not be done, will not take place, etc: 取消(已安排或決定的計畫等): *He ∼led his order for the goods,* said that he no longer wanted to receive them. 他取消貨物定購單(不想再要)。 *The sports meeting was ∼led.* 運動會已取消。 **3** [VP2C, 15B] *∼ out,* (arith) (of items from the numerator and denominator) equalize each other; (fig) neutralize, make up for, each other: (算術) (指分子及分母上的項目) 使相等;消去;相消;(喩)互相對消: *The arguments ∼ (each other) out.* 議論(互相)對消。 **∼·la·tion** /ˌkænsəˈleɪʃn ; ˌkænslˈeʃən/ *n* [U] ∼ling or being ∼led; [C] instance of this; mark(s) used in, made by, ∼ling (eg on postage stamps). 取消;刪去;勾掉;註銷;相消;註銷記號(如加於郵票上者)。

can·cer /ˈkænsə(r) ; ˈkænsə/ *n* [C, U] diseased

growth in the body, often causing death: 癌(身體內的毒瘤,常可致死): ~ *of the throat;* 喉癌; *'lung ~;* 肺癌; (fig) pernicious evil (eg in Society). (喻)(如社會之)害;罪惡。 **~·ous** /ˈkænsərəs ; ˈkænsərəs/ *adj* of or like ~; having ~. 癌症的;似癌症的;患癌症的。

Can·cer /ˈkænsə(r) ; ˈkænsɚ/ *n* **Tropic of ~,** the parallel of latitude 23½°N; fourth sign of the zodiac, ⇨ the illus at zodiac. 北回歸線;夏至線;巨蟹宮(參看 zodiac 之挿圖)。

can·de·la·brum /ˌkændɪˈlɑːbrəm ; ˌkændəˈlebrəm/ *n* (*pl* -bra /-brə ; -brə/) ornamental holder, with branches, for candles. 裝飾性的枝狀大燭臺。

can·did /ˈkændɪd ; ˈkændɪd/ *adj* **1** frank, straightforward: 坦白的;率直的: *I will be quite ~ with you: I think you acted foolishly.* 我要很坦白地對你說:我認爲你的行爲愚蠢。 **2 ~ camera,** small camera for taking informal or unposed photographs of people. 一種小型照相機(用以替人拍攝非正式或不必擺姿勢之照片者)。 **~·ly** *adv*

can·di·date /ˈkændɪdət *US:* -deɪt ; ˈkændəˌdet/ *n* **1** person who wishes, or who is put forward by others, to take an office or position (eg for election to Parliament): 候選人(如競選國會議員者): *The Labour ~ was elected.* 工黨候選人當選。 *He offered himself as a ~ for the post/job/position.* 他自薦爲該職位的候選人。 **2** person taking an examination. 參加考試者。 **can·di·da·ture** /ˈkændɪdətʃə(r) ; ˈkændədətʃɚ/ *n* being a ~(1). 候選人資格。

can·died ⇨ candy.

candle /ˈkændl ; ˈkændḷ/ *n* round stick of wax, etc with a wick through it, which is lit to burn with a light-giving flame. 蠟燭。 ***burn the ~ at both ends,*** use up too much energy; work very early and very late. 消耗太多的精力;清晨深夜都在工作;日夜趕工操勞過度。 ***can't/is not fit to hold a ~ to,*** is not to be compared to, is not nearly so good as. 不能與…相比;比不上。 ***The game is not worth the ~,*** is more trouble and expense than it is worth. 此事做起來得不償失(太麻煩,花費太大)。 **'~-light** *n* light of ~s: 燭光: *reading by ~light.* 在燭光下看書;秉燭夜讀。 **'~-power** *n* unit of light measurement: 燭光(量光度的單位): *a ten ~-power lamp.* 十燭光的燈。 **'~-stick** *n* holder for (usu) a single ~. 燭臺(通常指僅挿一支蠟燭者)。

can·dour (US = -dor) /ˈkændə(r) ; ˈkændɚ/ *n* [U] quality of being candid; saying freely what one thinks. 坦白;直率。

candy /ˈkændɪ ; ˈkændɪ/ *n* **1** (also 亦作 ˌ**sugar-'~**) [U] sugar made hard by repeated boilings; [C] (*pl* -dies) piece of this. 冰糖;冰糖塊。 **2** [C, U] (US only; GB = *sweet(s)*) (僅用於美國;等於英國的 sweet(s)) shaped piece(s) of cooked and flavoured sugar, syrup, etc usu with fruit juices, milk, nuts, etc added. 糖果(用糖、糖漿等加入調味料製成,形狀不一,通常並加入果汁、牛奶、果仁等)。 □ *vt, vi* **1** [VP6A] preserve (eg fruit) by boiling or cooking in sugar: 將(水果等)作成蜜餞: *candied plums/lemon peel.* 蜜餞李子(檸檬皮)。 **2** [VP2A] form into sugar crystals. 結晶成糖。

candy·tuft /ˈkændɪtʌft ; ˈkændɪˌtʌft/ *n* garden plant with flat tufts of white, pink or purple flowers. 蜀葵(園藝植物,花成扁平簇,呈白、粉紅或紫色)。

cane /keɪn ; ken/ *n* **1** long, hollow, jointed stem of tall reeds and grass-like plants (eg bamboo, sugar-~), either [U] collectively and as material for making furniture, etc or [C] of one stem or a length of it (eg used for supporting plants, as a walking-stick): 長而有節的莖(如竹子,甘蔗;作不可數名詞時爲集合稱,並指做傢具等的材料,作可數名詞時,指一截竹子或甘蔗、籐條,例如用以支持植物或作手杖者): *a chair with a ~ seat;* 有籐座的椅子; *raspberry ~s.* 覆盆子的新枝。 **'~ sugar** *n* sugar made from sugar-~, chemically the same as beet sugar. (甘蔗製成的)蔗糖(其化學成分與甜菜糖同)。 **2** length of ~ used as an instrument for punishing children by beating. (處罰兒童用的)籐鞭;籐條: ***get the ~,*** be punished with a ~. 吃籐條;挨打;受處罰。 □ *vt* [VP6A] punish with a ~(2). 用籐鞭責打。

ca·nine /ˈkeɪnaɪn ; ˈkenaɪn/ *adj* of, as of, a dog or dogs. 狗的;如狗的;似犬的。 **'~ tooth** *n* (in a human being) one of the four pointed teeth, one on each side of the four incisors, upper and lower. 犬齒(人的四顆尖齒之一,長在上下門牙的兩側)。 ⇨ the illus at mouth. 參看 mouth 之挿圖。

can·is·ter /ˈkænɪstə(r) ; ˈkænɪstɚ/ *n* **1** small box (usu metal) with a lid, used for holding tea, etc. 用以裝茶葉等之有蓋的小罐(通常爲金屬的);茶罐;茶筒。 **2** cylinder which, when thrown, or fired from a gun, bursts and scatters its contents: 霰彈筒(手扔或以槍砲發射,爆炸時其中破片等飛散): *a 'tear-gas ~.* 催淚毒氣彈筒。

can·ker /ˈkæŋkə(r) ; ˈkæŋkɚ/ *n* **1** [U] disease that destroys the wood of trees; disease that causes the formation of ulcers in the human mouth, in the ears of dogs and cats, etc. (傷害樹木的)癌腫病;(生於人口裏、貓狗等的耳朵裏的)口瘡;潰瘍。 **2** (fig) evil influence or tendency that causes decay. (喻)造成腐敗的惡劣影響或趨勢;積弊;弊害;弊病。 □ *vt* destroy by ~; be a ~ to. 以此種植物病害摧殘;使潰爛;使腐蝕;爲…腐敗之因;敗壞。 **~·ous** /ˈkæŋkərəs ; ˈkæŋkərəs/ *adj* of or like ~; causing ~. 此種病害的;像此種病害的;造成腐敗的。

canna /ˈkænə ; ˈkænə/ *n* plant with large, dark leaves and bright yellow, red or orange flowers; the flower. 曇華(葉大而色深,開鮮明的黃花、紅花或橘黃色花);曇華之花。

can·na·bis /ˈkænəbɪs ; ˈkænəbɪs/ *n* [U] Indian hemp, a drug also known as *hashish* and *marijuana,* smoked or chewed as an intoxicant. 印度大麻(藥用,亦稱 hashish 及 marijuana, 抽吸或咀嚼的一種麻醉劑,俗稱大麻煙)。 ⇨ hemp.

canned, can·nery ⇨ can².

can·ni·bal /ˈkænɪbl ; ˈkænəbḷ/ *n* person who eats human flesh; animal that eats its own kind; (attrib) of or like ~s: 食人肉的野人;食同類之肉的動物;(形容用法)(似)食人肉之野人的;食同類的: *a ~ feast.* 食人肉的宴會。 **~·ism** /ˈkænɪbəlɪzm ; ˈkænəbḷˌɪzəm/ *n* practice of eating the flesh of one's own kind. 食同類之肉的行爲或習俗;食人俗。 **~·is·tic** /ˌkænɪbəˈlɪstɪk ; ˌkænəbəlˈɪstɪk/ *adj* of or like ~s. (似)食人肉之野人的;吃同類的。 **~·ize** /ˈkænɪbəlaɪz ; ˈkænəbḷˌaɪz/ *vt* use (one of a number of similar machines, engines, etc) to provide spare parts for others. 使用(若干相似之機器、引擎等之一)供給其他機器之備用零件;拼修;拼配。

a cannon

can·non /ˈkænən ; ˈkænən/ *n* **1** (collective; *sing* often used instead of *pl*) large, heavy gun, fixed to the ground or to a guncarriage, esp the old kind that fired a solid ball of metal (called 稱作 a '~*ball*). (*Gun* and *shell* are the words used for the modern weapons). (集合稱,單數常用以代替複數)火砲;大砲(固定於地上或裝於砲車上,尤指舊式的發射實心金屬彈丸者)。(gun 與 shell 爲現代用字)。 **2** heavy, automatic gun, firing explosive shells, used in modern aircraft in war. 空用砲;機關砲(現代飛機在戰鬥中所使用之砲)。 **'~-fodder** *n* men regarded as expendable material in war. 在戰爭中被視爲消耗品或

犧牲品的兵員；砲灰。**~·ade** /ˌkænəˈneɪd ; ˌkænənˈed/ *n* continued firing of big guns. 大砲之連續轟擊。

can·not /ˈkænət ; ˈkænɑt/ ⇨ can².

canny /ˈkænɪ ; ˈkænɪ/ *adj* (-ier, -iest) not prepared to take unknown risks; shrewd, esp about money matters. 不準備冒不可知之危險的；謹愼的；精明的（尤指關於金錢的事情）。**can·nily** *adv*

ca·noe /kəˈnuː ; kəˈnu/ *n* light boat moved by one or more paddles. 用一隻或數隻槳划的輕舟；獨木舟。□ *vi* [VP2A, C] travel by ~. 乘此種輕舟旅行。**~·ist** *n* person who paddles a ~. 划獨木舟者；駕輕舟者。

canoeing

canon /ˈkænən ; ˈkænən/ *n* **1** ecclesiastical decree: 教會法規：~ *law*, church law. 教會法規。**2** general standard or principle by which sth is judged: 標準；準則：*the ~s of conduct/good taste.* 行爲（高尚趣味）的準則。**3** body of writings accepted as genuine; those books of the Bible accepted as genuine by the Christian Church: 正經；正典（基督教會所認爲聖經中之眞經部份）：*the ~ of Scripture;* 聖經之眞經；*the Chaucer ~.* 喬塞著作之眞本。**4** official list. 正式名單。**5** priest (with the title 頭銜爲 *the Rev Can*) who is one of a group with duties in a cathedral. 在大教堂中擔任職務的教士。⇨ chapter(3). **ca·noni·cal** /kəˈnɒnɪkl ; kəˈnɑnɪkḷ/ *adj* according to ~ law; authorized; regular: 依照教規的；審定的；正規的：*~ical books,* 正經；正典；*~ical dress*, ie of priests. 法衣（卽教士所著者）。

cañon /ˈkænjən ; ˈkænjən/ ⇨ canyon.

canon·ize /ˈkænənaɪz ; ˈkænənˌaɪz/ *vt* [VP6A] (RC Church) officially proclaim to be a saint(3); (colloq) authorize permanently. （天主教）正式宣布爲聖徒；（俗）永久認可。**canon·iz·ation** /ˌkænənaɪˈzeɪʃn *US:* -nɪˈz- ; ˌkænənəˈzeʃən/ *n* canonizing or being ~d. 正式宣布爲聖徒；永久認可。

can·opy /ˈkænəpɪ ; ˈkænəpɪ/ *n* (*pl* -pies) (usu cloth) covering above a bed, throne, etc or held (on poles) over a person; cover for the cockpit of an aircraft, ⇨ the illus at air¹; (fig) any overhanging covering: （通常爲布製）床、王座等上面之罩篷（或架於支柱上遮蓋在某人上空者）；雨遮；遮陽；天篷；（飛機之）座艙罩（參看 air¹ 之插圖）；（喻）任何懸於上空的篷罩；天幕：*the ~ of the heavens,* the sky; 蒼穹；*a ~ of leaves,* eg in a forest. （森林等中）樹葉所構成的天幕；林冠。

cant¹ /kænt ; kænt/ *n* [U] **1** insincere talk (esp implying false piety); hypocrisy. 虛僞之言（尤指假裝的虔敬）；僞善。**2** special talk, words, used by a class of people, a sect, etc; jargon: （某一階層、宗派等所用的）慣用語；隱語；術語；切口：*thieves' ~;* 盜賊用的暗語；黑話；(attrib)（形容用法）*a ~ phrase.* 隱語；術語。

cant² /kænt ; kænt/ *n* sloping or sideways surface or position. 傾斜；傾斜面。□ *vt, vi* [VP6A, 15B, 2A, C] give, have, a ~: （使）傾斜：*~ a boat for repairs.* 使船傾斜以便修理。

can't /kɑːnt *US:* kænt ; kænt/ = cannot, ⇨ can².

Can·tab /ˈkæntæb ; ˈkæntæb/ *adj* of Cambridge University. 英國劍橋大學的。

can·ta·loup, -loupe /ˈkæntəluːp ; ˈkæntḷˌop/ *n* kind of melon. 一種香瓜；甜瓜。

can·tank·er·ous /kænˈtæŋkərəs ; kænˈtæŋkərəs/ *adj* bad-tempered; quarrelsome. 壞脾氣的；好爭吵的。**~·ly** *adv*

can·tata /kænˈtɑːtə ; kænˈtɑtə/ *n* short musical work to be sung by soloists and a choir, usu a dramatic story, but not acted. 由獨唱者及合唱團演唱的短篇樂曲（通常有一齣戲劇性的故事，但無動作表演）；淸唱劇。⇨ oratorio, opera.

can·teen /kænˈtiːn ; kænˈtin/ *n* **1** place (esp in factories, offices, barracks) where food and drink are sold and meals bought and eaten. （尤指工廠、辦公處、軍營裏的）飲食部。**2** box or chest of table silver and cutlery (knives, forks, spoons): 餐具箱：*a ~ of cutlery.* 一箱餐具。**3** soldier's eating and drinking utensils. 軍人的飲食用具。

can·ter /ˈkæntə(r) ; ˈkæntɚ/ *n* (of a horse) easy gallop: （指馬）慢跑；小跑：*The horse won the race at a ~,* won easily. 那匹馬於比賽中輕易獲勝。□ *vt, vi* (cause to) gallop gently. （使）小跑；慢跑。

can·ticle /ˈkæntɪkl ; ˈkæntɪkḷ/ *n* short hymn, esp one taken from the Bible. 短的頌歌（尤指取自聖經者）。

can·ti·lever /ˈkæntɪliːvə(r) ; ˈkæntḷˌivɚ/ *n* long, large, armlike bracket extending from a wall or base (eg to support a balcony). （自牆或基座伸出以支持陽臺等之）懸臂；懸桁；肱梁。**'~ bridge** *n* one built on supports from which ~s extend and join. 懸臂橋（懸臂自支架伸出，彼此相接而築成的橋）。⇨ the illus at bridge. 參看 bridge 之插圖。

canto /ˈkæntəʊ ; ˈkænto/ *n* (*pl* ~s /-təʊz ; -toz/) chief division of a long poem. 長詩中的篇章。

can·ton /ˈkæntɒn ; ˈkæntṇ/ *n* subdivision of a country (esp of Switzerland). （尤指瑞士的）州；郡。

can·ton·ment /kænˈtuːnmənt *US:* -ˈtəʊn- ; kænˈtɑnmənt/ *n* permanent military station; place where soldiers live. 軍隊駐紮地；軍營。

can·tor /ˈkæntɔː(r) ; ˈkæntɔr/ *n* leader of the singing in a church or synagogue. （教堂或猶太教會堂唱詩班之）領導者。

Ca·nuck /kəˈnʊk ; kəˈnʌk/ *n* (US sl) French Canadian. （美俚）法裔加拿大人。

can·vas /ˈkænvəs ; ˈkænvəs/ *n* [U] strong, coarse cloth used for tents, sails, bags, etc and by artists for oil-paintings; [C] (piece of this for an) oil-painting. （用製帳篷、船帆、囊袋等之）帆布；油畫家所用的畫布；一張油畫布；油畫。***under ~,*** **(a)** (of soldiers, scouts, etc) living in tents. （指軍隊、童子軍等）住於帳篷中。**(b)** (of a ship) with sails spread. （指船）張帆的。

can·vass /ˈkænvəs ; ˈkænvəs/ *vt, vi* **1** [VP2A, 3A] ~ ***(for),*** go from person to person and ask for votes, orders for goods, subscriptions, etc or to learn about people's views on a question: 爲了向人拉票、兜售貨物、書報等或對某一問題作民意調查而奔走訪問：*He is ~ing for the Conservative candidate.* 他正在替保守黨候選人奔走拉票。**2** [VP6A] discuss thoroughly; examine by discussion: 徹底討論；藉討論以探究：*~ views/opinions.* 徹底討論某些意見。□ *n* ~ing. 奔走訪問；拉票；兜攬生意；調查；討論。

can·yon, cañon /ˈkænjən ; ˈkænjən/ *n* deep gorge (usu with a river flowing through it). 峽谷（通常有河流經過其中）。

cap /kæp ; kæp/ *n* **1** soft head-covering worn by boys and men, by some sailors and soldiers, without a brim, but often with a peak; special cap awarded to members of football teams, etc or worn to show rank: （男孩、男人及某些海軍及陸軍所戴之無邊但常有遮簷的）軟帽；（授與足球隊員等的）運動帽；（戴以表明階級的）制帽；法帽：*a cardinal's cap;* 紅衣主教法帽；academic head-dress with a flat top and a tassel: （平頂有帽縫的）學位帽：*wearing his cap and gown.* 穿戴他的學位服及學位帽。⇨ mortar-board. **2** indoor head-dress worn by nurses, and formerly by old women. 護士及從前老太婆在

室內所戴的頭飾。 **3** cap-like cover (eg on a milk bottle). 蓋子(如牛奶瓶蓋)。 **4 per'cussion cap,** small quantity of gunpowder in a wrapper of paper, etc, used as a detonator. 雷管;火帽(少量火藥包於紙等之中,用作起爆管)。 **5** (phrases) (片語) ***cap and bells,*** cap trimmed with bells, as formerly worn by jesters. 飾有小鈴之帽子(如從前弄臣所戴者)。 ***if the cap fits,*** if a person feels that the remark applies to him. 如果某人覺得這話適用於他;如果這話是恰當的。 ***cap in hand,*** humbly. 謙遜地;謙恭地。 ***set one's cap at sb,*** (of a girl or woman) try to attract as a suitor. (指婦女)逗引(某人)使之向她求婚。□ *vt* (-pp-) [VP6A] **1** put a cap on; cover the top of. 加帽於;蓋…之頂;把…蓋上蓋子。 **2** do or say sth better than (what sb else has done or said). 做得或說得優於(別人所做或所說的);勝過。 ***cap a story/joke,*** tell a more amusing one. 說一則更有趣的故事(笑話)。 **3** award (a player) a cap (as a member of a football team, etc): 授與(球員)隊員帽(認可爲某足球隊等之隊員): *He's been capped 36 times for England.* 他已經三十六次獲授帽爲英格蘭足球隊隊員。 (Scottish universities) confer a degree on. (蘇格蘭之大學)授予學位。

ca·pa·bil·ity /ˌkeɪpəˈbɪlətɪ ; ˌkepəˈbɪlətɪ/ *n* **1** [U] power (*of* doing things, *to do* things) ; fitness or capacity (*for* being improved, etc): 能力(指做某事的能力,與 of 連用,後接動名詞,亦可與不定詞連用);適宜或有可能 (如有可能改進等,與 for 連用,後接動名詞): *nuclear ~,* power, capacity, to wage nuclear war. 可發動核子戰爭的能力。 **2** (*pl*) (-ties) undeveloped faculties; qualities, etc, that can be developed: (複)尚未發展出來的才能;可以發展的性質等;潛能: *The boy has great capabilities.* 那男孩有很大的潛能。

ca·pable /ˈkeɪpəbl ; ˈkepəbl̩/ *adj* **1** gifted; able: 有天才的;有能力的;能幹的: *a very ~ doctor/nurse/teacher.* 極有能力的醫生(護士、教員)。 **2 ~ of, (a)** (of persons) having the power, ability or inclination: (指人)有某種能力或傾向的: *Show your teacher what you are ~ of,* Show him how well you can work. 向你的老師表現出你的才能。 *He's quite ~ of neglecting his duty,* is the sort of man who might do so. 他很可能會疏於職守。 *He's ~ of any crime.* 他能做得出任何犯罪的事。 **(b)** (of things, situations, etc) ready for; admitting of; open to: (指事物、情況等)可以…的;容許…的;易接受…的: *The situation is ~ of improvement.* 這情況可以改善。**ca·pably** *adv*

ca·pa·cious /kəˈpeɪʃəs ; kəˈpeʃəs/ *adj* able to hold much: 容量大的: *a ~ memory;* 能記憶很多事情的記憶力; *~ pockets.* 容量大的口袋。**~·ness** *n*

ca·pac·ity /kəˈpæsətɪ ; kəˈpæsətɪ/ *n* **1** [U] (and with *indef art*) ability to hold, contain, get hold of, learn things/qualities/ideas etc: (亦與不定冠詞連用) 容納力;學習力;理解力; 能量; 容量; 效能: *The hall has a seating ~ of 500,* has seats for 500 people. 此廳堂可坐五百人。*The theatre was filled to ~,* was quite full. 戲院客滿。*He has a mind of great ~,* a mind well able to grasp ideas. 他的理解力極强。 *This book is within the ~ of* (= can be understood by) *young readers.* 這本書是少年讀者可以瞭解的。*Some persons have more ~ for happiness* (= a greater power of experiencing happiness) *than others.* 有些人比別人更善於體驗幸福。 **2** [C] (*pl* -ties) position; character. 地位;身份;資格。 ***in one's ~ as,*** in one's position as being: 以…的身份: *I am your friend, but in my ~ as an officer of the law I must take you into custody.* 我是你的朋友,但是以執法人員的身份我必須逮捕你。

cap-à-pie /ˌkæp ə ˈpiː ; ˌkæpəˈpi/ *adv* **armed ~,** armed from head to foot, completely. 全副武裝地。

ca·pari·son /kəˈpærɪsn ; kəˈpærəsn̩/ *n* (often *pl*; old use) ornamental covering for a horse, or for a horse and the knight who rode it. (常用複數;舊用法)裝飾性的馬衣(遮蓋於馬身上或連馬帶騎馬武士一起遮蓋著)。□ *vt* put a ~ on (a horse). 以馬衣蓋於(馬)的身上。

cape¹ /keɪp ; kep/ *n* loose sleeveless garment, hanging from the shoulders. 披肩;短披風;短斗篷。

cape² /keɪp ; kep/ *n* high point of land going out into the sea; headland. 伸入海中的尖形高地;岬;海角。**the C~,** (S Africa) the C~ of Good Hope; C~ Province. (南非)好望角;角省。

ca·per¹ /ˈkeɪpə(r) ; ˈkepɚ/ *vi* jump about playfully. 跳躍嬉戲。□ *n* ***cut a ~/~s,*** jump about merrily; act foolishly or fantastically. 跳躍嬉戲;蹦蹦跳跳;做出愚蠢或怪誕的行爲。

ca·per² /ˈkeɪpə(r) ; ˈkepɚ/ *n* prickly shrub; (*pl*) pickled flower-buds of this shrub, used to make ~ sauce. 續隨子(有刺灌木);(複)醃泡的續隨子花蕾(用以製續隨子醬)。

cap·il·lary /kəˈpɪlərɪ *US:* ˈkæpəlerɪ ; ˈkæpl̩ˌɛrɪ/ *n* (*pl* -ries) tube with a hair-like diameter (eg joining the arteries and veins), ⇨ the illus at respiratory: 毛細管(如連接動脈和靜脈的微血管,參看 respiratory 之插圖): (attrib) (形容用法) ~ *attraction,* attraction of the kind that causes blotting-paper to absorb ink, or oil to rise through the wick of an oil lamp. 毛細管作用;毛管引力(使吸墨紙能吸墨水,或油能升上燈芯的作用)。

capi·tal¹ /ˈkæpɪtl ; ˈkæpətl/ *n* (often attrib) (常作形容用法) **1** town or city where the government of a country, state or province is carried on: 國都;首都;首府(中央或地方政府所在地): *Toronto is the ~ of Ontario.* 多倫多是安大略省的首府。 *London, Paris and Rome are ~ cities.* 倫敦、巴黎和羅馬都是國家首都。 **2** (of letters of the alphabet) not small: (指字母)大寫; 大寫的: *The pronoun 'I' is written and printed with a ~ letter.* 代名詞 'I' 用大寫字母寫或印刷。*Write your name in ~ letters/in ~s.* 用大寫字母寫你的名字。 **3** head, top part, of a column. 柱冠;柱頭。⇨ the illus at column. 參看 column 之插圖。□ *adj* **1** punishable by death: 可處死刑的: *~ offences.* 死罪。 **2** (dated colloq) excellent, first-rate: (過時俗語) 極好的;上等的: *He made a ~ speech.* 他做了一次極好的演講。 *What a ~ idea!* 眞是一個妙主意!

capi·tal² /ˈkæpɪtl ; ˈkæpətl̩/ *n* [U] wealth/money/property that may be used for the production of more wealth; money with which a business, etc is started (eg for building or buying factories, buying machinery). 資本;資金(可用以生產更多財富的財產;用以建立企業如建造或購買廠房、機器的錢)。**~ expenditure,** money spent on equipment, building, etc. 資本支出 (如購置設備,房屋等)。 **~ gain,** profit made from the sale of investments or property. 資本利得(出售投資物或不動產所獲之利得)。**~ goods,** goods used to produce other goods. 資本財(用以生產其他貨品之物)。**~ levy,** taking by the State of a part of all the private wealth in the country. 資本課稅;資本特徵(由國家徵收國內全部私有財產的一部分)。**ˈfixed ~,** machinery, buildings, etc. 固定資本(指機器,建築物等)。 **ˈfloating ~,** ~ goods. 流動資本(= capital goods)。***a ~ of,*** ~ valued at. 值…的資本。 ***make ~ of sth,*** use it to one's own advantage. 利用。

capi·tal·ism /ˈkæpɪtəlɪzəm ; ˈkæpətl̩ˌɪzəm/ *n* [U] economic system in which a country's trade and industry are organized and controlled by the owners of capital², the chief elements being competition, profit, supply and demand. 資本主義(一種全國工商業皆由資本家組織及控制之經濟體系,其要素爲競爭、牟利、供應及需求)。 ⇨ socialism. **capi·tal·ist** *n* **1** person who controls much capital². 資本家。 **2** person who supports ~. 資本主義者。□ *adj* of, supporting ~: 資本主義的: *a capitalist economy.* 資本主義經濟制度。 **capi·tal·is·tic** /ˌkæpɪtəˈlɪstɪk ; ˌkæpɪtl̩ˈɪstɪk/ *adj*

capi·tal·ize /ˈkæpɪtəlaɪz ; ˈkæpətl̩ˌaɪz/ *vt, vi* **1** [VP

6A] write or print with a capital letter. 用大寫字母書寫或印刷。**2** [VP6A] convert into, use as, capital²; (fig) take advantage of; use to one's advantage or profit. 轉作資本;用作資本;資本化;(喻)利用;用以牟利。**3** [VP3A] ~ *on*, profit by; exploit: 由於…而獲益;利用: *~ on the errors of a rival firm.* 由於敵對公司的錯誤而獲益。**capi·tal·iz·ation** /ˌkæpɪtəlaɪˈzeɪʃn *US:* -ɪˈzeɪʃn ; ˌkæpətḷəˈzeʃən/ *n*

capi·ta·tion /ˌkæpɪˈteɪʃn ; ˌkæpəˈteʃən/ *n* (reckoning of) tax, fee, charge or grant of an equal sum per person. (計算)人頭稅;丁稅;人口稅;按人均攤;按人均分的補助費(每人數目相等)。

Capi·tol /ˈkæpɪtl ; ˈkæpətḷ/ *n* building in which the United States Congress meets. 美國國會大廈。

ca·pitu·late /kəˈpɪtʃʊleɪt ; kəˈpɪtʃəˌlet/ *vi* [VP2A] surrender (on stated conditions). (按照提出的條件)投降。**ca·pitu·la·tion** /kəˌpɪtʃʊˈleɪʃn ; kəˌpɪtʃəˈleʃən/ *n* [U] surrendering (on stated conditions). (有條件的)投降。

ca·pon /ˈkeɪpən *US:* -pɒn ; ˈkepɑn/ *n* cock (male domestic fowl) castrated and fattened for eating. 閹鷄(養肥供食用者);肉鷄。

ca·price /kəˈpriːs ; kəˈpris/ *n* **1** (often sudden) change of mind or behaviour that has no obvious cause; tendency to change suddenly without apparent cause. 反覆無常;多變(無明顯理由而突然改變心意或行爲);善變。**2** piece of music in a lively, irregular style. (音樂)奇想曲;隨想曲;異想曲。

ca·pri·cious /kəˈprɪʃəs ; kəˈprɪʃəs/ *adj* often changing; irregular; unreliable; guided by caprice: 多變的;不可靠的;反覆無常的;無明顯理由而突然改變心意或行爲的: *a ~ breeze,* often or suddenly changing in direction. (時常或突然改變方向的)多變的風。**~·ly** *adv*

Cap·ri·corn /ˈkæprɪkɔːn ; ˈkæprɪˌkɔrn/ *n* **Tropic of ~,** the parallel of latitude $23\frac{1}{2}°$ S; tenth sign of the zodiac, ⇨ the illus at zodiac. 南回歸線;磨羯宮(十二宮中的第十宮,參看 zodiac 之插圖)。

cap·si·cum /ˈkæpsɪkəm ; ˈkæpsɪkəm/ *n* kinds of plant with seed-pods containing hot-tasting seeds; such pods prepared for use in cooking, etc. 番椒屬;番椒(俗名辣椒或大椒)。⇨ cayenne, pepper(2).

cap·size /kæpˈsaɪz ; kæpˈsaɪz/ *vt, vi* [VP6A, 2A] (esp of a boat in the water) (cause to) overturn, upset. (尤指水中的船)(使)傾覆;翻。

cap·stan /ˈkæpstən ; ˈkæpstən/ *n* upright barrel-like object turned (formerly) by men who walk round it pushing horizontal levers, or (more usu today) by steam, etc, power, used for raising anchors, sails, etc and for pulling a ship to a wharf, etc. 絞盤;起錨機(從前由人繞四周走並推動水平桿以旋轉之,或如今日更常見者,以蒸汽等動力旋轉之,用以起錨、張帆及拖船至碼頭等)。

a space-capsule

cap·sule /ˈkæpsjuːl *US:* ˈkæpsl ; ˈkæpsḷ/ *n* **1** seed-case that opens when the seeds are ripe. (植物的)蒴;莢(當種子成熟時卽行裂開)。**2** tiny container (eg for a dose of medicine, often soluble). (裝一劑藥物,常會溶化的)膠囊。**3** (recoverable or non-recoverable) receptacle (for scientific instruments, or an astronaut) which can be ejected from a spacecraft. (可從太空船彈射出的)太空艙(有的可收回,有的不能收回,內載科學儀器或太空人)。

cap·tain /ˈkæptɪn ; ˈkæptɪn/ *n* **1** leader or chief commander: 隊長;官長: *the ~ of a ship/fire-brigade/football or cricket team.* 船長;艦長(消防隊長;足球隊或板球隊長)。**2** (in the army) officer (below a major and above a lieutenant) who commands a company; (in the navy) officer below an admiral and above a commander. 陸軍上尉(在少校之下,中尉之上,統率一連);海軍上校(在將官之下,中校之上)。□ *vt* [VP6A] act as ~ of (a football team, etc). 擔任(足球隊等之)隊長。

cap·tion /ˈkæpʃn ; ˈkæpʃən/ *n* short title or heading of an article in a periodical, etc; words printed with a photograph or illustration, etc; word(s) on a movie film to establish the scene of the story, etc (eg Dover 1940). (雜誌等中文章的)標題;題目;(附於照片、插圖等上的)說明文字;(電影片上確立故事景地等的)文字說明(例如:多佛市 1940 年)。Cf 參較 *sub-titles.*

cap·tious /ˈkæpʃəs ; ˈkæpʃəs/ *adj* (formal) (fond of) finding fault, making protests, etc esp about unimportant points. (正式用語)好找人之錯的;好吹毛求疵的;好抗議的(尤其關於不重要的事情)。**~·ly** *adv*

cap·ti·vate /ˈkæptɪveɪt ; ˈkæptəˌvet/ *vt* [VP6A] capture the fancy of; fascinate: 使迷惑;使着迷: *He was ~d by Helen/~d with her charm.* 他爲海倫(爲她的美色)所迷。

cap·tive /ˈkæptɪv ; ˈkæptɪv/ *n, adj* **1** (person, animal) taken prisoner, kept as a prisoner. 俘虜;被俘虜的(人);被捕獲的(動物)。***be taken/hold sb ~,*** take or keep him prisoner. 被俘虜;被捕獲(俘虜某人)。ˌ**~ balˈloon,** one that is held to the ground by a cable. 用繩索繫於地面上的氣球;繫留氣球。**2** ˌ**~ ˈaudience,** one that cannot get away easily and is, therefore, open to persuasion (eg schoolchildren watching TV). 俘虜聽衆;俘虜觀衆(無法輕易離開者,故易受誘服,如觀看電視的學童)。**cap·tiv·ity** /kæpˈtɪvətɪ ; kæpˈtɪvətɪ/ *n* [U] state of being held ~: 被俘虜的狀態;囚禁: *Some birds will not sing in captivity.* 有的鳥被關住就不肯鳴叫。

cap·tor /ˈkæptə(r) ; ˈkæptɚ/ *n* person who takes sb captive. 俘虜者;捕獲者。

cap·ture /ˈkæptʃə(r) ; ˈkæptʃɚ/ *vt* [VP6A] make a prisoner of; take or obtain as a prize by force, trickery, skill, etc: 俘虜;捕獲;斬獲;騙得;巧取: *Our army ~d 500 of the enemy.* 我軍俘虜敵軍五百人。*The police have not ~d the thief yet.* 警方尚未將該盜賊捕獲。*This advertisement will ~ the attention of readers everywhere.* 這個廣告將可引起各處讀者的注意。□ *n* [U] act of capturing: 俘虜;捕獲;斬獲: *the ~ of a thief;* 一竊賊之捕獲; [C] thing that is ~d. 被捕獲之物;戰利品。

car /kɑː(r) ; kɑr/ *n* **1** motor-car. 汽車。⇨ the illus at motor. 參看 motor 之插圖。ˈ**car-ferry** *n* ferry (sea or air) for taking cars (eg across the English Channel). 車輛渡船;載汽車過渡之飛機(如渡英吉利海峽者)。ˈ**car-port** *n* open-sided shelter for a motor vehicle. (有頂無牆之)汽車棚。**2** (on a railway train) (in GB) coach: (英國)火車車廂;客車: ˈ*dining-car;* 餐車; ˈ*sleeping-car;* 臥車; (in US also) wagon for goods: (美國亦指)貨車: ˈ*freight-car* (GB 英 = ˈ*goods-wagon*). 貨車。**3** that part of a balloon, airship or lift (US 美 = *elevator*) used by passengers. (氣球,飛艇之載人的)座艙;(電梯的)座廂。**4** (poet) wheeled vehicle; chariot: (詩)有輪的車子;馬車;古代戰車: *the car of the sun-god.* 日神的車子(指太陽)。

ca·rafe /kəˈræf ; kəˈræf/ *n* water-bottle, or decanter for wine, for use at table. (餐桌上用的)水瓶;酒瓶。

cara·mel /ˈkærəmel ; ˈkærəmḷ/ *n* **1** [U] burnt sugar used for colouring and flavouring. 焦糖(用以着色和調味)。**2** [C] small, shaped piece of sticky boiled sugar; sweetmeat. 一種有黏性的糖果。

cara·pace /ˈkærəpeɪs ; ˈkærəˌpes/ *n* shell on the back of a tortoise and crustaceans. (龜或其他甲殼動物的)甲殼。⇨ the illus at crustacean, reptile. 參看 crustacean 及 reptile 之插圖。

carat /ˈkærət ; ˈkærət/ *n* **1** unit of weight (= 200 milligrams or about three and one-fifth grains) for precious stones. 克拉(寶石重量的單位,等於 200 公絲或 3⅓ 喱左右)。⇨ App 5. 參看附錄五。 **2** (US = *karat*) measure of the purity of gold, pure gold being 24 ~s: 開(金的純度的度量名,純金爲二十四開): *a gold ring of 20 ~s,* ie 20 parts gold, 4 parts alloy. 一只二十開的金戒指(卽二十分金,四分合金)。

cara·van /ˈkærəvæn ; ˈkærəˌvæn/ *n* **1** company of persons (eg pilgrims, merchants) making a journey together for safety, usu across desert country. (朝聖者、經商者等經過沙漠時爲安全計所組成的)旅行隊;商隊。 **2** covered cart or wagon used for living in, eg by Gypsies or people on holiday, esp (today) the kind pulled behind a motor vehicle. 有蓋頂可供居住的篷車(如吉普賽人或度假遊客所住者); (尤指今日拖行於汽車後面的) 拖車。⇨ also trailer at trail. **~·ning** *n* (the practice of) taking holidays in a ~. 在篷車或拖車中度假。 **~·sary, ~·serai** /ˌkærəˈvænsərɪ, -səraɪ ; ˌkærəˈvænsərɪ, -səˌraɪ/ *n* inn with a large inner courtyard where ~s put up in Eastern countries. (在東方國家)有大庭院可供旅行隊或車隊投宿的旅店;商棧。

cara·way /ˈkærəweɪ ; ˈkærəˌwe/ *n* plant with spicy seeds used to flavour bread, cakes, etc. 葛縷子(其子味香,用以爲麵包、糕餅等增味)。

car·bide /ˈkɑːbaɪd ; ˈkɑrbaɪd/ *n* compound of carbon. 碳化物。⇨ calcium.

car·bine /ˈkɑːbaɪn ; ˈkɑrbaɪn/ *n* short rifle (originally for soldiers on horseback). 卡賓槍(原爲騎兵所用的短來福槍)。

carbo·hy·drate /ˌkɑːbəʊˈhaɪdreɪt ; ˌkɑrboˈhaɪdret/ *n* [C, U] (kinds of) organic compound including sugars and starches; (*pl*) starchy foods, considered to be fattening. 醣(有機化合物,包括糖與澱粉);碳水化合物;(複)澱粉質食物(被認爲使人體發胖者)。

car·bolic acid /kɑːˌbɒlɪk ˈæsɪd ; kɑrˈbɑlɪk ˈæsɪd/ *n* [U] strong-smelling, powerful liquid used as an antiseptic and disinfectant. 石碳酸;酚(味烈强力藥水,用作防腐劑和消毒劑)。

car·bon /ˈkɑːbən ; ˈkɑrbən/ *n* **1** [U] non-metallic element (symbol **C**) that occurs in all living matter, in its pure form as diamonds and graphite and in an impure form in coal and charcoal. 碳(非金屬元素,化學符號C, 存在於一切生物體內,純碳物如鑽石及石墨,不純之碳存在於煤及木炭)。 **ˈ~ black** *n* black powder obtained by partly burning oil, wood, etc. (部份燃燒油、木材等而得之)黑煙末。 **ˈ~ dating,** method of dating prehistoric objects by measuring the decay of a radioactive isotope of ~. 碳鑑定法(測量碳的放射同位素之衰變以鑑定史前古物之年代的方法)。 **2** [C] stick or pencil of ~ used in an electric arc-lamp. 碳精棒(用於電弧光燈)。 **3** [U, C] (also 亦作 **ˈ~-paper**) (sheet of) thin paper coated with coloured matter, used between sheets of writing paper for taking copies. 複寫紙。 **4** [C] (also 亦作 **~ copy**) copy made by the use of ~-paper. 複寫本;副本。 **5** **ˌ~ diˈoxide** *n* gas (CO_2) produced by animal bodies and breathed out from the lungs; synthetic version of this used in eg canned beers and soft drinks, to give fizz. 二氧化碳(動物體內所產生的氣體,自肺中呼出);合成之二氧化碳(用於罐頭啤酒及不含酒精的飲料等中,使起泡及發嘶聲)。 **ˌ~ monˈoxide** *n* poisonous gas (**CO**) produced when ~ burns, present in the exhaust gas of petrol engines and after explosions in coal mines. 一氧化碳(由碳燃燒所產生之有毒氣體,存在於用汽油的發動機所排出的廢氣中,及發生爆炸後的煤礦坑中)。 **~·ated** /ˈkɑːbəneɪtɪd ; ˈkɑrbəˌnetɪd/ *adj* containing ~ dioxide: 含二氧化碳的: *~ed beverages.* 含二氧化碳的飲料。 **~·if·er·ous** /ˌkɑːbəˈnɪfərəs ; ˌkɑrbəˈnɪfərəs/ *adj* (geol) producing coal: (地質)產煤的;產炭的: *~-iferous strata.* 石炭層;煤層。 **~·ize** *vt* [VP6A] convert into ~ by burning. 燒成碳;碳化。 **~·iz·ation** /ˌkɑːbənaɪˈzeɪʃn *US:* -nɪˈz- ; ˌkɑrbənɪˈzeʃən/ *n*

car·bonic acid /kɑːˌbɒnɪk ˈæsɪd ; kɑrˈbɑnɪk ˈæsɪd/ *n* [U] carbon dioxide dissolved in water (eg

a caravan of camels

a gypsy caravan

a modern caravan

caravans

giving the sharp taste to soda water). 碳酸(溶解於水之二氧化碳,如使汽水有辛辣味道者)。

car·bor·un·dum /ˌkɑːbəˈrʌndəm ; ˌkɑrbəˈrʌndəm/ *n* (P) hard compound of carbon and silicon, used for polishing and grinding. (商標)碳化矽;金剛砂(用作磨擦材料)。

car·boy /ˈkɑːbɔɪ ; ˈkɑrbɔɪ/ *n* large, round glass or plastic bottle, usu enclosed in basketwork or a crate to protect it from being broken. 大而圓的玻璃瓶或塑膠瓶(通常套於柳條或木套中防破損);罈。

car·buncle /ˈkɑːbʌŋkl ; ˈkɑrbʌŋkl/ *n* **1** bright-red jewel. 鮮紅玉;紅寶石。 **2** red (usu painful) inflamed swelling under the skin. 癰(通常感到疼痛的皮下紅色炎腫)。

car·bu·ret·tor (US = **-retor**) /ˌkɑːbjʊˈretə(r) *US:* ˈkɑːrbəreɪtər ; ˈkɑrbəˌretɚ/ *n* that part of an internal combustion engine in which petrol and air are mixed to make an explosive mixture. (內燃機中的)汽化器(汽油與空氣在其中混合以製成有爆炸性的混合物)。

car·cass, car·case /ˈkɑːkəs ; ˈkɑrkəs/ *n* **1** dead body of an animal (esp one prepared for cutting up as meat): 動物的屍體(尤指其肉將被切開供食用者): *~ meat,* meat from a ~ (contrasted with tinned or corned meat). 鮮肉 (以別於罐頭肉或醃肉)。 **2** (contemptuous) human body. (蔑)人類之屍體;屍首。 **3** = shell(2).

card¹ /kɑːd ; kɑrd/ *n* **1** (usu small, oblong-shaped) piece of stiff paper or thin cardboard, as used for various purposes, (通常爲長方形之小)卡片(用硬紙或薄紙板製成,作各種用途), eg 例如 *a ˈvisiting-~* (US 美 *ˈcalling ~*), with a person's name, etc on it; 名片; *ˈChristmas／New ˈYear／ˈBirthday ~s,* sent with greetings at Christmas, etc; 聖誕(賀年,生日)卡片; *ˈrecord ~,* one for keeping records, notes, etc, and stored in a box or drawer; (裝於箱匣或抽屜中之)紀錄卡; *~ index,* index on ~s. 卡片式索引。 **~-carrying member** *n* registered member of a group, political party, trade union, etc. 已登記的會員(黨員、工會會員等)。 **ˈ~ vote** *n* vote taken at a trade union meeting at which each delegate has a ~ representing a certain number of workers.

卡片投票(工會的投票，因每一代表有一卡片，代表某一數目之工人，故名)。**2** programme for a race meeting or game, with details, and space for marking results: 賽跑或比賽場合(印有詳情介紹並留有空白以紀錄結果)之節目單: *a 'score ~,* eg for cricket. 記分卡(如用於板球比賽者)。**3** (esp) one of the 52 cards (often *'playing-~*) used for various games (canasta, bridge, poker, etc) and for telling fortunes. 紙牌；(尤指一副五十二張的)撲克牌(常作playing-card, 可用以玩各種遊戲，如 canasta、橋牌、撲克等及算命)。***have a ~ up one's sleeve,*** have a secret plan in reserve. 藏有密計；有錦囊妙計。***hold/keep one's ~s close to one's chest,*** ⇨ chest(2). ***make a ~,*** take a trick (⇨ trick(5)) with it. 以一牌而贏一磴。***on the ~s,*** (from fortune-telling by ~s) likely or possible. (源於用紙牌算命)可能的。***one's best/strongest ~,*** one's strongest argument, best way of getting what one wants. 某人之王牌(即最有力的論據，達到目的的最佳方法)；絕招；妙策。***play one's ~s well,*** do one's business cleverly, with good judgement. 做事精明；處理得當而有見地。***play a sure/safe/doubtful ~,*** use a plan or expedient that is sure, etc. 採用萬全的(穩妥的，靠不住的)辦法。***put one's ~s on the table,*** make one's plans, intentions, etc, known. 攤牌(明白表示出其計畫、意向等)。**'~-sharper** *n* person who makes a living by swindling at ~ games. 以紙牌騙賭爲生者；郎中；老千。**4** (hum) person who is queer or amusing. (諧)怪人；有趣的人。

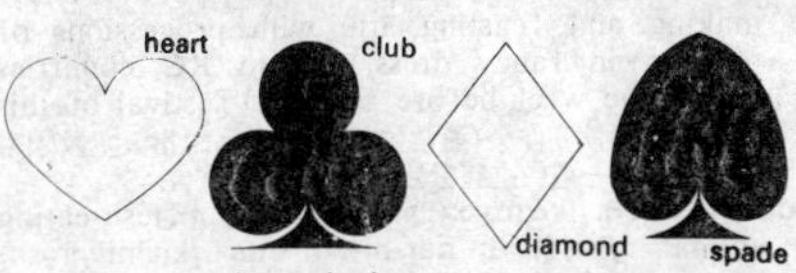

playing-card symbols

card² /kɑːd ; kɑrd/ *n* toothed instrument, wire brush, for combing or cleaning wool, hemp etc. (梳理羊毛、大麻等的)梳子；鋼絲刷。□ *vt* clean or comb with such an instrument. 用此種工具梳理。

car·da·mom /'kɑːdəməm ; 'kɑrdəməm/ *n* [U] aromatic spice from seed-capsules of various East Indian plants. 小豆蔻(東印度群島所產數種植物之種子莢所製的香料)。

card·board /'kɑːdbɔːd ; 'kɑrd,bord/ *n* [U] thick, stiff kind of paper or pasteboard, used for making boxes, binding books, etc. 厚硬紙板(用以製盒子、裝訂書籍等)。

car·diac /'kɑːdɪæk ; 'kɑrdɪ,æk/ *adj* of the heart: 心臟的: *~ muscle;* 心肌；*~ symptoms,* ie of heart disease. 心臟病症狀。

car·di·gan /'kɑːdɪgən ; 'kɑrdɪgən/ *n* knitted collarless woollen jacket that buttons up the front, made with sleeves. (胸前用鈕扣開合的對襟長袖無領的)羊毛衣；羊毛衫。

car·di·nal /'kɑːdɪnl ; 'kɑrdṇəl/ *adj* chief; most important; on which sth depends: 主要的；最重要的；某事物所依賴的；基本的: *the ~ virtues.* 四種基本的美德。**~ numbers,** eg 5, 6, 7 (contrasted with *ordinal numbers,* eg 5th, 6th, 7th); 基數(如五、六、七，以別於序數第五、第六、第七)；*the ~ points,* of the compass (N, S, E and W). 羅盤上的基本方位(即北、南、東、西)；基點。⇨ the illus at compass. 參看 compass 之挿圖。□ *n* bishop in the RC Church who is able to participate in the election of a Pope. (天主教的)紅衣主教；樞機主教(有權選舉教皇者)。

care¹ /keə(r) ; kɛr/ *n* **1** [U] serious attention or thought; watchfulness; pains: 審愼的注意或思索；小心；用心；謹愼: *You should take more ~ over your work.* 你應當對你的工作更加用心。*This is made of glass, so take ~ not to break it.* 這是玻璃做的，所以小心不要把它打破了。*Glass, with ~!* eg as a warning when goods are sent by rail. 玻璃，請小心！(如書於交鐵路運輸之貨物箱上，以爲警告者)。*Take ~ (that) you don't get run over when you cross the street.* 當你穿越街道時，小心不要被車子撞倒。*Do your work with more ~.* 你要更加小心做事。(Used with the *indef art*): (與不定冠詞連用): *Have a ~* (= Take ~), be cautious. 小心；注意。**2** [U] protection; charge; responsibility: 保護；照料；管理；責任: *The child was left in its sister's ~.* 這小孩留給他姐姐照料。*The library is under the ~ of Mr Grey.* 圖書館由格雷先生管理。*I will leave this in your ~,* leave you responsible for it. 我將把此事交由你負責。**~ of,** (often written 常寫作 **c/o**) used in addresses before the name of the person(s) to whose house, office, etc a letter is sent. 由…轉交(書於信封等上被託請轉信件人姓名之前)。**Child C~ officer** *n* (in GB but no longer current, now *social worker*) person appointed to look after children who are homeless or whose parents are neglectful, etc. 小孩保護官(昔時英國之官員，今稱社會工作人員，被指派照顧無家可歸或父母疏於照料的孩童)。***take into ~,*** (of such an officer) take (a child lacking proper ~) to an institution. (指上述之官員)將(缺乏適當照料的孩童)送到孤兒院或教養院。***take ~ of,*** (colloq) deal with, be responsible for. (俗)處理；負責。**'~·taker** *n* person paid to take ~ of a building during the owner's absence; (US 美 = *janitor*) person in charge of the upkeep of a public building such as a school or of a private building such as a block of flats. (房主不在時)受雇替房主看管房屋之人；(公共建築如學校或私人公寓等之)管理員。**~-taker Government,** administration that continues in office until a new one is formed to take over its work. 看守政府(在新內閣未組成前繼續執行政務之內閣)。**3** [U] worry; anxiety; troubled state of mind caused by doubt or fear: 憂慮；焦慮；疑慮；疑懼；操心；擔憂: *free from ~.* 無憂無慮。*C~ had made him look ten years older.* 憂慮已使他顯得老了十歲。**'~·free** *adj* showing no worry; cheerful. 無憂無慮的；逍遙自在的；快樂的。**'~·laden, '~·worn** *adjj* showing worry; troubled. 憂心忡忡的；操心勞碌的。**4** [C] (usu *pl*) cause of sorrow and anxiety: (通常用複數)憂慮之因；可憂慮的事: *He was rich and free from ~s of every kind.* 他很富有，又無任何可憂慮之事。*He was poor and troubled by the ~s of a large family.* 他貧窮又爲衆多的子女所累。

care² /keə(r) ; kɛr/ *vi* **1** [VP2A, 3A, B] (with *prep* usu omitted before a clause) (在子句前面，通常省去介系詞) ~ ***(about),*** feel interest, anxiety or sorrow: (對…)感到關切、操心或憂慮: *He failed in the examination but I don't think he ~s very much/he doesn't seem to ~.* 他雖然考試不及格，但我認爲他並不大在乎(他似乎並不在乎)。*He doesn't ~ much (about) what happens to me.* 他不太關心我所發生的事。*He doesn't ~ what they say.* 他不管他們怎麼說。*I don't ~ who you are/how soon you leave.* 我不管你是誰(我不在乎你多快離開)。*He doesn't ~ a damn,* is not in the least interested, worried, etc. 他一點也不在乎。*Who ~s?* 誰在乎？**2** [VP3A] ***~ for,*** like (to have): 喜歡；想要: *Would you ~ for a drink?* 你想喝一杯嗎？*I shouldn't ~ for that man to be my doctor.* 我不要那個人替我看病。*He doesn't much ~ for television.* 他不太想看電視。**3** [VP3A] ***~ for,*** have a taste for; like: 愛好；喜愛: *Do you ~ for modern music?* 你愛聽現代音樂嗎？**4** [VP3A] ***~ for,*** look after; provide food, money, shelter, etc: 照顧；養活: *Who will ~ for the children if their mother dies?* 如果這些孩子的母親死了，誰將照顧他們？*The State must ~ for the families of soldiers killed in the war.* 國家必須照料陣亡軍人家屬的生活。**5** [VP4C] like; be willing or desirous (inter and neg only): 想；願意；欲望(僅用於疑問句及否定句): *Would you ~ to go for a walk?* 你想去散散步嗎？*I don't ~ to be seen in his company.* 我不願被人看見同他一起。

ca·reen /kə'riːn ; kə'rin/ *vt, vi* **1** [VP6A] turn (a ship) on one side for cleaning, repairing, etc. 使(船)傾側(以便清潔、修理等)。**2** [VP6A, 2A] (cause to) tilt, lean over to one side. (使)傾側。

ca·reer /kə'rɪə(r) ; kə'rɪr/ *n* **1** [C] progress through life; development and progress of a party／principle etc: 一生的經歷；(黨派、主義等的)發展和進步: *We can learn much by reading about the ~s of great men.* 閱讀偉人一生經歷的作品可獲很多心得。 **2** [C] way of making a living; profession: 謀生之道；職業: *Should all ~s be open to women,* Should women be allowed to enter all occupations? 各行各業是否均應容許婦女參與？(attrib) professional: (形容用法)職業性的: *a ~ diplomat;* 職業外交家; *a '~ girl,* (esp) one who prefers a ~ to marriage.職業婦女(尤指喜歡工作勝過結婚者)。**3** [U] quick or violent forward movement: 飛躍；猛進: *in full ~,* at full speed; 全速進行; *stop (sb) in mid ~.* 使(某人)中途停住。□ *vi* [VP2C, 3A] ~ ***about／along／past／through, etc,*** rush wildly. 飛奔；急馳。**~·ist** *n* person whose chief interest is personal advancement in his profession. 主要興趣在於達到個人的陞遷或發跡的人。

care·ful /'keəfl ; 'kɛrfəl/ *adj* **1** (pred) (敍述用法) ***be ~ (about／of),*** (of a person) taking care; cautious; thinking of, paying attention to, what one does, says, etc: (指人)小心的；當心的；仔細的；審愼的: *Be ~ not to break the eggs.* 小心不要打破雞蛋。*Be ~ (about／of) what you do／what you say／where you go／how you carry it etc.* 對你所做的事(所說的話，到何處去，怎樣拿它等)要小心。*Be more ~ with your work.* 對你的工作要更加注意。*Be ~ of your health.* 小心你的健康。**2** done with, showing, care: 小心做出的；顯示小心或審愼的: *~ guidance／a ~ guide;* 小心的指導(審愼的嚮導); *a ~ piece of work;* 精細的作品; *a ~ examination of the facts.* 對於事實所作仔細的調查。**~·ly** /-fəlɪ ; -fəlɪ/ *adv* **~·ness** *n*

care·less /'keəlɪs ; 'kɛrlɪs/ *adj* **1** (of a person) not taking care; thoughtless: (指人)不小心的；不謹愼的；粗心的: *He is ~ about leaving the door unlocked when he goes to bed.* 他粗心大意睡前忘記門門。*A ~ driver is a danger to the public.* 粗心的駕駛員對於公衆是一種危險。**2** done or made without care: 不用心或不仔細做成的: *a ~ mistake.* 粗心的錯誤。 **3** (liter) light-hearted; gay: (文)無憂無慮的；快活的: *~ little songbirds.* 快活的小鳴禽。**4** ***~ of,*** (liter) unconcerned about; uncomplainingly accepting: (文)不在乎的；不抱怨地接受的: *He is ~ of his reputation.* 他不在乎他的名聲。*The soldiers were ~ of hardship.* 那些軍人不在乎苦。**~·ly** *adv* **~·ness** *n: a piece of ~ness,* a ~ act. 一次粗心的行爲。

ca·ress /kə'res ; kə'rɛs/ *n* [C] loving or affectionate touch or light stroke. 撫愛；撫摸。□ *vt* [VP6A] give a ~ or ~es to. 撫愛；撫摸。**~·ing** *adj* showing love. 示愛的。**~·ing·ly** *adv*

caret /'kærət ; 'kærət/ *n* mark (‸) used (eg in correcting proofs) to show, in writing or print, where sth is to be inserted. (如校對時用的)脫字記號；加字記號(‸)。

cargo /'kɑːgəʊ ; 'kɑrgo/ *n* (*pl* ~es, US also ~s /-gəʊz ; -goz/) [C, U] goods carried in a ship, aircraft or other vehicle: (船上、飛機或其他車輛所載的)貨物: *a '~ ship／plane.* 貨輪(運輸機)。Cf 參較 *goods／freight train.*

cari·bou /'kærɪbuː ; 'kærə,bu/ *n* (*pl* ~s or, collective *pl* 集合複數 ~) N American reindeer. (北美洲產的)馴鹿。

cari·ca·ture /'kærɪkətjʊə(r) ; 'kærɪkətʃɚ/ *n* **1** [C] picture of sb or sth, imitation of a person's voice, behaviour, etc, stressing certain features, to amuse or ridicule. 諷刺畫；漫畫；對某人之聲音、行爲等的模倣(藉强調某些特徵以引人發笑或予以嘲弄)。 **2** [C] art of doing this. 諷刺畫之藝術；諷刺性的滑稽模倣術。□ *vt* [VP6A] make, give, a ~ of. 爲…作諷刺畫；對…作諷刺性的滑稽模倣。**cari·ca·tur·ist** *n* expert in ~. 諷刺畫家；諷刺性的滑稽模倣者。

car·ies /'keəriːz ; 'kɛriz/ *n* [U] (med) decay (of bones or teeth): (醫)齲；骨瘍；骨疽: *dental ~.* 齲齒。**cari·ous** /'keərɪəs ; 'kɛrɪəs/ *adj* (of bone) affected with ~. (指骨)患骨疽的。

car·il·lon /kə'rɪljən *US:* 'kærəlɒn ; 'kærə,lɑn/ *n* set of bells in a tower on which tunes may be played by some kind of mechanism (eg a keyboard). (可用機械，如鍵盤，奏出曲調的)排鐘；鐘琴。

Car·mel·ite /'kɑːməlaɪt ; 'kɑrml̩,aɪt/ *n, adj* (friar or nun) of the religious order founded in 1155. (創始於 1155 年之) 卡米爾敎派的；卡米爾敎派之修道士或修女；白袍苦行僧。

car·mine /'kɑːmaɪn ; 'kɑrmɪn/ *n, adj* deep red (colour or colouring matter). 深紅的(顏色，色素)；洋紅；胭脂紅。

car·nage /'kɑːnɪdʒ ; 'kɑrnɪdʒ/ *n* [U] (liter) killing of many people: (文)大屠殺；殘殺(人類): *a scene of ~,* eg a battlefield. 殘殺的場所(如戰場)。

car·nal /'kɑːnl ; 'kɑrnəl/ *adj* (formal) of the body or flesh; sensual (opposite to *spiritual*): (正式用語)肉體的；感官的(爲spiritual之相反字)：*~ desires.* 肉慾。**~·ly** *adv*

car·na·tion /kɑː'neɪʃn ; kɑr'neʃən/ *n* garden plant with sweet-smelling white, pink or red flowers; the flower. 紅茂草(亦稱作荷蘭石竹，園藝植物，開白色、粉紅色或紅色的香花)；紅茂草之花；康乃馨。

car·ni·val /'kɑːnɪvl ; 'kɑrnəvl̩/ *n* [U] public merry-making and feasting, usu with processions of persons in fancy dress, esp in RC countries during the week before Lent; [C] festival of this kind. 公衆飲宴作樂(通常並有化裝遊行，尤指天主敎國家在四旬齋前一週內之狂歡)；狂歡節；嘉年華會。

car·ni·vore /'kɑːnɪvɔː(r) ; 'kɑrnə,vor/ *n* flesh-eating animal. 食肉動物。 **car·ni·vor·ous** /kɑː'nɪvərəs ; kɑr'nɪvərəs/ *adj* flesh-eating. 食肉的。

carol /'kærəl ; 'kærəl/ *n* song of joy or praise, esp a Christmas hymn: 歡樂或讚美之歌；(尤指)聖誕頌歌: *'~ singers,* singers who visit people's houses at Christmas to sing ~s (and usu to collect money for charity). (聖誕節挨戶唱聖誕頌歌的)頌歌隊(通常作慈善募款)。□ *vi, vt* (-ll-, in US also -l-) sing joyfully; celebrate with ~s. 歡樂地唱；唱頌歌以慶祝；歌頌。**~·ler** *n*

ca·rouse /kə'raʊz ; kə'raʊz/ *vi* [VP2A] drink heavily and be merry (at a noisy meal, party etc). (在喧鬧的宴會等) 狂飲作樂。 **ca·rousal** /kə'raʊzl ; kə'raʊzl̩/ *n* noisy drinking-party or revelry. 喧鬧的飲宴或狂歡。

carp[1] /kɑːp ; kɑrp/ *n* (*pl* unchanged) large fresh-water fish that lives in lakes and ponds. (複數不變)鯉魚(產於湖泊及養於池中之大淡水魚)。

carp[2] /kɑːp ; kɑrp/ *vi* [VP2A, 3A] ***~ (at),*** make unnecessary complaints about small matters: 吹毛求疵；找小錯；挑小毛病: *a ~ing tongue;* 愛找碴兒的嘴; *~ing criticism.* 吹毛求疵的批評。*She's always ~ing at her husband.* 她老是挑她丈夫的小毛病。

car·pal /'kɑːpl ; 'kɑrpl̩/ *adj* (anat) of the wrist. (解剖)腕的。□ *n* (anat) bone in the wrist, ⇨ the illus at skeleton. (解剖)腕骨(參看 skeleton 之插圖)。

car·pen·ter /'kɑːpɪntə(r) ; 'kɑrpəntɚ/ *n* workman who makes and repairs (esp) the wooden parts of buildings and other structures of wood. 木匠。⇨ joiner. **car·pen·try** /-trɪ ; -trɪ/ *n* [U] work of a ~. 木工；木作。

car·pet /'kɑːpɪt ; 'kɑrpɪt/ *n* [C] **1** thick covering for floors or stairs, usu of wool, hair or synthetic fibres, often with a pattern or designs woven into it. 地毯(通常以羊毛、獸毛或合成纖維織成，並常織有各種圖案)。***on the ~,*** (colloq) being reprimanded. (俗)受責罰；受責備；挨罵。 ***sweep sth under the ~,*** hide, ignore, sth, in order to delay action, escape blame, etc. 隱藏、不理某事物以期拖延行動、逃

避受責等。 ˈ~-bag *n* (old fashioned) travelling bag made of ~. (舊式之)毯製之旅行手提包。ˈ~-**bag·ger** *n* (US) person, during the American Civil War (1861-5), from northern USA who went to the South to seek financial or political advantage. (美)1861年至1865年南北戰爭期中赴南方尋求金錢或政治利益的北方人。 ˈ~-**knight** *n* soldier who has not seen active service, stay-at-home soldier; ladies' man. 未參加過實地作戰之軍人;守在家裏的軍人;喜與女人廝混的男人。ˈ~-**slippers** *n pl* (old-fashioned) kind of soft slippers with uppers of woollen cloth. 一種(舊式的)毛布爲面的軟拖鞋。ˈ~-**sweeper** *n* device with revolving brush(es) for sweeping ~s and rugs. (有旋轉刷的)掃毯器。 **2** sth suggesting a ~: 毯狀物;像地毯般的覆蓋物: *a ~ of moss*, eg in a garden. 一層(如地毯般的)青苔。□ *vt* [VP6A] **1** cover (as) with a ~: (如)以地毯覆蓋: *to ~ the stairs;* 將樓梯鋪上地毯; *a lawn ~ed with fallen leaves.* 蓋着一層落葉的草地。**2** (sl) reprimand: (俚)申斥;責罵: *He's been ~ed.* 他挨了罵。

car·riage /ˈkærɪdʒ; ˈkærɪdʒ/ *n* **1** [C] vehicle, esp one with four wheels, pulled by a horse or horses, for carrying people: 車;(尤指一或數匹馬拉的載人的)四輪馬車: *a ~ and pair*, one pulled by two horses. 兩匹馬拉的馬車。 ⇨ coach¹. ˈ~·**way** *n* (part of a) road used by vehicles: 車道: *Cars must not park on the ~way.* 汽車不可停在車道上。 ˌ**dual** ˈ~-**way**, road divided down the centre (by a barrier, a strip of pavement or grass) for traffic in each direction (US 美 = *divided highway*). 雙車道公路(路之中央由柵欄、砌石或草坪分開,兩邊車輛各向一方行駛)。 **2** [C] wheeled vehicle for passengers on a railway train (US 美 = *car*); coach: (鐵路列車的)客車廂;客車: *The first class ~s are in front.* 頭等車廂在前面。 **3** [U] (cost of) carrying of goods from place to place. 貨物運費;貨運。 ~ ***forward***, cost of ~ to be paid by the receiver. 運費由收貨人負擔。~ ***free/paid***, ~ free to the receiver/paid by the sender. (收貨人)免付運費;運費已付。 **4** [C] wheeled support on which a heavy object may move or be moved (eg a *gun ~*); moving part of a machine, changing the position of other parts (eg the roller of a typewriter). (可用以移動重物的)有輪支架(例如砲架);軌運器(機器之活動的部份,可以改變其他部份之位置者,如打字機之滾筒)。 **5** (*sing* only) manner of holding the head or the body (when walking, etc): (僅用單數)儀態;姿勢;舉止: *She has a graceful ~*, She stands and walks gracefully. 她舉止優雅。⇨ carry(8).

a carriage

car·rier /ˈkærɪə(r); ˈkærɪɚ/ *n* **1** person or company that carries goods or people for payment (eg a railway, shipping or aircraft company). 運貨人;貨運公司(如鐵路、輪船或航空公司);運輸業者。 **2** support for luggage, etc fixed to a bicycle, motor-car, etc. (裝於脚踏車、汽車等之)置物架;行李架;貨架。 **3** person, animal, etc that carries or transmits a disease without himself or itself suffering from it. 菌郵(攜帶或傳染疾病而其本身不受感染之人或動物等);帶菌者。 **4** vehicle, ship, etc used for the transport of troops, aircraft, tanks, etc. 運輸軍隊、飛機、戰車等之車輛、艦艇等。⇨ aircraft-~, Bren-~, troop-~. **5** ˈ~-**bag** *n* strong paper or plastic bag with hand grips for eg carrying away purchases from shops. 裝貨袋(如用以裝購買物自商店中帶走的手提厚紙袋或塑膠袋)。 ˈ~-**pigeon** *n* pigeon used to carry messages because it can find its way home from a distant place. 傳信鴿。

car·rion /ˈkærɪən; ˈkærɪən/ *n* [U] dead and decaying flesh. 腐肉。ˈ~-**crow**, crow that lives on ~ and small animals. 食腐肉及小動物之烏鴉。

car·rot /ˈkærət; ˈkærət/ *n* (plant with) yellow or orange-red root used as a vegetable, ⇨ the illus at vegetable. 胡蘿蔔(根部黃色或橘紅色,作蔬菜食用;參看 vegetable 之插圖)。 ***the stick and the ~***, threats and bribes. 威脅利誘。 ***hold out/offer a ~ to sb***, entice by offering a reward or advantage. 許以報酬或利益以誘惑某人;利誘某人。 ~**y** *adj* (esp of hair) orange-red. (尤指頭髮)橘紅色的。

carry¹ /ˈkærɪ; ˈkærɪ/ *vt, vi* (*pt, pp* carried) (For uses with *adverbial particles* and *preps*, ⇨ 11 below.) (與副詞接語及介詞連用之用法,參看下列第11義。) **1** [VP6A 15A, B] support the weight of and move from place to place; take a person, a message, etc from one place to another: 攜帶;搬運;傳送;將(人、信息等)由甲地運送至乙地: *He was ~ing a box on his shoulder.* 他的肩上扛着一隻箱子。 *She was ~ing the baby in her arms.* 她懷中抱着嬰兒。 *Railways and ships ~ goods.* 鐵路及船舶運輸貨物。 *He carried* (= went round and told) *the news to everyone in the village.* 他將消息傳告村中每一個人。 *He ran off as fast as his legs could ~ him*, as fast as he could run. 他儘快飛奔而去。*This bicycle has carried me 500 miles.* 這部脚踏車已載我跑了五百哩路。*How far will five gallons of petrol ~ you?* 五加侖汽油可(載你)跑多少路? *Some kinds of seeds are carried by the wind for great distances.* 有些種類的種子藉風力送到遠的地方。*The raft was carried by ocean currents to a small island.* 該筏被大洋的水流飄送至一小島。*A spy carries his life in his hands*, takes the risk of death. 間諜隨時有死亡的危險。 ˈ~-**cot** *n* light cot with handles (but no wheels) for ~ing a baby. (輕便有把手,但無輪子的)嬰兒床。 **2** [VP6A, 15A] have with one; wear; possess: 帶着;穿着;有: *Do you always ~ an umbrella?* 你總是帶傘嗎? *Ought the police to be allowed to ~ fire-arms?* 警察應被准許攜帶武器嗎? *I never ~ much money with me.* 我身邊從來不帶很多錢。*Can you ~ all these figures in your head*, remember them without writing them down? 你能僅憑腦筋記得所有這些數字嗎? *The wound left a scar that he will ~ with him to the grave*, that will remain for life. 那傷口給他留下了一個一輩子也去不掉的疤痕。**3** [VP6A] support: 支持;支撐: *These pillars ~ the weight of the roof.* 這些柱子支撐屋頂的重量。*The girders are carried on trestles.* 這些大梁是由支架撐着。 **4** [VP6A] involve; entail; have as a result: 含有;具有;使負擔;有某種後果: *The loan carries* $3\frac{1}{2}$*% interest.* 該貸款負擔百分之三點五的利息。 *That argument does not ~ conviction*, is not convincing. 該論據不能令人折服。*Power carries responsibility with it.* 權力本身亦含有責任。 *His word/promise carries weight*, is influential. 他的話(承諾)具有分量(有影響力)。**5** [VP6A,15A] (of pipes, wires, etc) conduct; take: (指管子、金屬絲等)輸送;傳導: *The oil is carried across the desert in pipe-lines.* 石油用管子送過沙漠。*Copper carries electricity.* 銅能傳電。 **6** [VP15A] make longer; extend; take (to a specified point, in a specified direction, etc): 使延長;伸展;使延伸(至某一點、向某一方向等): *~ a fence round a field;* 延伸籬笆使圍起一塊地; *~ pipes under a street;* 將管子從街道下面延伸; *~ a joke too far*, be no longer amusing. 把一則笑話說得太長(不再有趣)。 *Don't ~ modesty too far.* 不要謙虛得過份。 **7** [VP 6A, 15A] win; capture; persuade; overcome: 贏得;奪得;說服;克服: *The soldiers rushed forward and carried the enemy's position.* 士兵們衝上去奪得敵人的陣地。*He carried his audience with him*, won their sympathy and agreement. 他博得了聽衆的贊同。*The* *bill/motion/resolution was carried*, there were more votes for it than against it. 該提案(動議,決議)業經表決通過。 ~ ***the day***, be victorious. 得勝;勝利。 ~ ***everything before one***, be completely successful. 萬事如意;完全成功。 ~ ***one's point***, win approval for it. 意見獲得贊同。 **8** [VP6A, 15A, 16B] hold oneself/one's head/one's body in a specified way: (使自己、頭部、身體)做出某種姿勢或體態: *He carries himself like a soldier*, stands and walks like one. 他的擧止行動像個軍人。*She carries herself badly*, eg by slouching or stooping. 她的體態欠佳(懶散或彎腰駝背)。 **9** [VP2B, C] (of guns) send a shell, etc a certain distance; (of missiles, sounds, voices, etc) have the power to go to: (指槍砲)將(砲彈等)射至某一距離;(指發射物、聲音、語音等)能達及;能射至;能傳至: *Our guns do not ~ far enough.* 我們的砲射程不够遠。*The sound of the guns carried many miles.* 槍砲的聲音傳至許多哩遠。*The shot carried 200 metres.* 那子彈射至二百公尺遠。*A public speaker must have a voice that carries well.* 演說家必須有很遠都能聽到的(洪亮的)嗓音。 **10** [VP6A] (of a newspaper, etc) print in its pages: (指報紙等)登載;刊出: *a newspaper that carries several pages of advertisements.* 登載有數版廣告的一份報紙。 **11** [VP15B, 2C] (with *adverbial particles* and *preps*): (與副詞接語及介詞連用):

carry sb/sth away, **(a)** (usu passive) cause to lose self-control: (通常用被動語態)使失去自我控制力;使失去理智: *He was carried away by his enthusiasm*, was so enthusiastic that he was unable to judge calmly, etc. 他因太熱情而失去理智。**(b)** (naut) lose (masts, etc) by breaking: (航海)因折斷而失去(桅等): *The ship's masts were carried away during the storm.* 該船的帆檣在暴風雨中全被折斷。

carry sb back, take back in the memory: 使憶起: *an incident that carried me back to my schooldays*, caused me to recall them. 一件使我憶起學生時代的偶然事件。

carry sth forward, (comm, book-keeping) transfer (a total of figures on a page) to the head of a new column or page. (商,簿記)將(一頁的總數)轉記於另一頁或另一欄的開頭;延後;結轉;過次。

carry sth off, win: 贏得: *Tom carried off all the school prizes.* 湯姆把學校裡的獎品都得來了。~ ***it/sth off (well)***, succeed in a difficult situation; cover a mistake, etc. 在困難環境中獲得成功;將錯誤等掩飾起來。

carry (sth) on, **(a)** conduct; manage: 進行;經營: *Rising costs made it hard to ~ on the business.* 上漲的成本使生意難做。 *It's difficult to ~ on a conversation at a noisy party.* 在喧鬧的宴會中談話困難。**(b)** talk volubly and complainingly; behave strangely or suspiciously: 滔滔不絕而帶牢騷地談話;行爲奇特或令人起疑: *How she does ~ on!* 她眞是滔滔不絕,牢騷滿腹! *Did you notice how they were ~ing on?* 你注意到他們的行爲多奇怪嗎?Hence, 由此產生, **~ings-on** *n pl*: *Such queer carryings-on next door*, such queer happenings! 隔壁鄰家居然發生了如此奇怪的事情! ~ ***on (with)***, continue (doing sth): 繼續(做某事): *C~ on (with your work).* 繼續做(你的工作)。*They decided to ~ on in spite of the weather.* 不管天氣如何他們決定繼續做下去。~ ***on (an affair) (with)***, (often suggesting disapproval) flirt with; have a love affair with: (常表示不贊許)調情;與…談愛: *His wife is ~ing on with the postman.* 他的妻子正在和郵差調情。***(sth) to ~ on with***, (sth) (to do or use) for the time being: 暫時使用(某物);湊合着用(某物): *I can't give you all you need, but here's £5 to ~ on/be ~ing on with.* 我不能給你所需的一切,不過這裡是五鎊錢供你暫時之用。

carry sth out, **(a)** do as required or specified; fulfil; complete: 實行;完成: *~ out a promise/threat/plan/instruction.* 實踐諾言(實行威脅;實現計畫;完成命令)。**(b)** perform; conduct: 進行: *~ out experiments/tests.* 進行試驗。

carry sb/sth through, **(a)** help (through difficulties, etc): 幫助(度過難關等): *Their courage will ~ them through.* 他們的勇氣將會使他們度過難關。**(b)** complete; fulfil: 完成: *Having made a promise, you must ~ it through.* 既已許下承諾,你必須完成它(履行)。

carry² /ˈkærɪ; ˈkærɪ/ *n* **1** range of a gun, etc; distance that a shell, etc, goes. (槍砲等之)射程;子彈等所能達到之距離。 **2** portage; act of carrying boat, setc, from one river or lake to another; place where this must be done. 兩水路間之陸上運送;水陸聯運;將船隻等自甲河(湖)運至乙河(湖);此種聯運地點。

cart /kɑːt; kɑrt/ *n* two-wheeled vehicle pulled by a horse. 二輪單馬車。 ⇨ also hand~. ***be in the ~***, (sl) be in an awkward or losing position. (俚)處於困厄或失利的地位。 ***put the ~ before the horse***, do or put things in the wrong order, take the effect for the cause (eg by saying 'I was lazy because I didn't study'). 做事本末倒置;倒果爲因(如說'我很懶惰因爲我沒有讀書')。 ***turn ˈ~-wheels***, turn somersaults sideways. 側身翻觔斗。 **ˈ~-horse** *n* strong horse for heavy work. 擔任重工作的壯馬。 **ˈ~-load** *n* as much as a ~ holds: 一馬車所載之量: *a ~-load of manure.* 一馬車肥料。 **ˈ~-road/-track**, rough unmetalled road. 未鋪碎石的不平道路。 □ *vt* [VP6A, 15B] **1** carry in a ~: 用馬車裝運: *~ing hay;* 用馬車運乾草; *~ away the rubbish.* 用馬車將垃圾運走。 **2** (colloq) carry in the hands, etc: (俗)用手等攜帶;隨身帶: *Have you really got to ~ these parcels around for the rest of the day?* 在今天其餘的時間裡你眞的非要帶著這些包裹到處走不可嗎? **~·age** /ˈkɑːtɪdʒ; ˈkɑrtɪdʒ/ *n* [U] (cost of) carting. 馬車裝運(費)。**~er** *n* man whose work is driving ~s; carrier(1). 馬車伕;運貨人;貨運公司;運輸業者。

a cart

carte blanche /ˌkɑːt ˈblɒnʃ; ˈkɑrtˈblɑnʃ/ *n* (F) full authority or freedom (to use one's own judgement about how to proceed, etc). (法)全權;自由處理權(運用自己的判斷力以決定如何進行等之權)。

car·tel /kɑːˈtel; ˈkɑrtḷ/ *n* (comm) combination of traders, manufacturers, etc to control output, marketing, prices of goods, etc. (商)卡特爾;同業聯盟(工商業者之聯合組織,以便控制生產量、銷售及貨價等)。

car·ti·lage /ˈkɑːtɪlɪdʒ; ˈkɑrtḷɪdʒ/ *n* [C, U] (structure, part, of) tough, white tissue attached to the joints, in animal bodies; gristle. (動物體內連於關節上的)軟骨;軟骨結構。 **car·ti·lagi·nous** /ˌkɑːtɪˈlædʒɪnəs; ˌkɑrtḷˈædʒənəs/ *adj* of or like ~. 軟骨的;如軟骨的。

car·togra·pher /kɑːˈtɒɡrəfə(r); kɑrˈtɑɡrəfɚ/ *n* person who makes maps and charts. 繪製圖表者;繪圖員。 **car·togra·phy** /kɑːˈtɒɡrəfɪ; kɑrˈtɑɡrəfɪ/ *n* [U] the drawing of maps and charts. 繪製圖表;製圖法;製圖學。

car·ton /ˈkɑːtn; ˈkɑrtn̩/ *n* cardboard box for holding goods: (裝貨物的)紙板盒: *a ~ of 200 cigarettes*, with 10 packets of 20. 一條香煙(共十包,每包二十支)。

car·toon /kɑːˈtuːn; kɑrˈtun/ *n* **1** drawing dealing with current (esp political) events in an amusing or satirical way. 卡通;漫畫(以時事,尤指政治事件,爲題材所作之風趣或諷刺圖畫)。 **2** full-size preliminary drawing on paper, used as a model for a painting, a tapestry, a fresco, a mosaic, etc. 底圖;草圖

(作畫、織錦、壁畫、鑲嵌細工等所用畫於紙上的大樣)。 **3** (= *animated* ~) cinema film made by photographing a series of drawings: 卡通影片(由拍攝一連串之圖畫所製成之活動影片): *a Walt Disney* ~. 一部華德・狄斯耐製作的卡通影片。 □ *vt* represent (a person, etc) in a ~. 以漫畫畫(人物等)。 **~·ist** *n* person who draws ~s(1). 漫畫家。

car·tridge /ˈkɑːtrɪdʒ ; ˈkartrɪdʒ/ *n* **1** case (of metal, cardboard, etc) containing explosive (for blasting), or explosive with bullet or shot (for firing from a rifle or shot gun). 子彈(彈殼由金屬或紙板等製成,內裝火藥,起爆炸作用);彈筒(內裝火藥,並帶彈頭,自步槍或砲中發射)。 ⇨ blank *n*(4). **ˈ~-belt** *n* one with sockets for holding ~s. 子彈帶。 **ˈ~-paper, (a)** paper for making ~ cases. 彈筒紙(製彈筒用的厚紙板)。 **(b)** thick white paper for pencil and ink drawings. (鉛筆畫或墨水畫用的)厚白紙。 **2** detachable head of a pick-up (on a record-player), holding the stylus. (唱機之)唱頭(裝置唱針的部份)。 **3** (US) cassette. (美)卡式錄音帶盒;卡式膠捲盒。

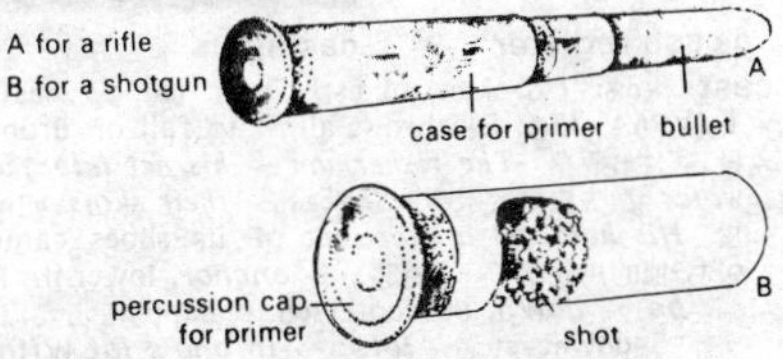

cartridges

carve /kɑːv ; karv/ *vt, vi* **1** [VP6A, 14, 15B] form (sth) by cutting away material from a piece of wood or stone: 雕刻;用木頭或石頭雕成(某物): ~ *a statue out of wood/a statue in oak;* 雕刻一座木(橡木)像; *a figure ~d from marble;* 大理石雕像; ~ *out a career for oneself,* (fig) achieve one by great effort. (喻)爲自己創立一番事業。 **2** [VP6A,15A] inscribe by cutting on a surface: (在物之表面上)刻字;銘刻: ~ *one's initials on a tree trunk;* 將其姓名之起首字母刻於樹幹上; ~ *an inscription on a bench.* 將題字刻於長櫈上。 **3** [VP6A, 15B] cut up (cooked meat) into pieces or slices at or for the table: 將(煮熟的肉)切成塊或片以便食用: ~ *a leg of mutton/a turkey.* 將羊腿(火鷄)切開以便食用。 **ˈcarving-knife/-fork** *n* knife, fork, used for carving meat. (餐桌上用的)切肉刀、叉。 **carver** *n* carving-knife; person who ~s; (*pl*) carving-knife and fork. 切肉刀;切肉的人;(複)切肉刀叉。 **carv·ing** *n* sth ~d in wood, etc. (木等之)雕刻品。 ⇨ sculptor, sculpture.

cary·atid /ˌkærɪˈætɪd ; ˌkærɪˈætɪd/ *n* (archit) draped statue of a female figure used as a support (eg a pillar) in a building. (建築)女像柱。

cas·cade /kæˈskeɪd ; kæsˈked/ *n* waterfall; one section of a large, broken waterfall; wave-like fall of lace, cloth, etc. 瀑布;大瀑布之一支;分段瀑布;花邊、布等作波狀之下垂;波狀花邊。 □ *vi* fall like a ~. 如瀑布落下。

case[1] /keɪs ; kes/ *n* **1** instance or example of the occurrence of sth; actual state of affairs; circumstances or special conditions relating to a person or thing; (med) person suffering from a disease; instance of a diseased condition: 事例;實情;與某人或某事物有關的環境或特殊情況;(醫)病人;病例;病案: *Is it the* ~ (= Is it true) *that you have lost all your money?* 你的錢全部都損失了,是眞的嗎? *No, that's not the* ~, is not true. 不,那不是事情的眞相。 *If that's the* ~ (= If the situation is as stated or suggested), *you'll have to work much harder.* 如果情形是那樣的話,你將必須更加努力工作。 *I can't make an exception in your* ~, for you and not for others. 我不能爲你破例。 *Such being the* ~ (= In view of, Because of, these facts, etc), *you can't go away.* 既然如此,你不能離開。 *It's a clear* ~ *of cheating,* is clear that cheating has taken place. 這顯然是欺騙。 *There were five* ~*s of* (= five persons suffering from) *influenza.* 有五起患流行性感冒的病案。 *The worst* ~*s were sent to hospital.* 最嚴重的病人被送到醫院去了。 ***a* ~ *in point,*** ⇨ point[1](9). ***(just) in* ~,** if it should happen that; because of a possibility: 若;如果;萬一: *It may rain—you'd better take an umbrella (just) in* ~. 可能會下雨——你最好帶一把雨傘,以防萬一。 *In* ~ *I forget, please remind me of my promise.* 如果我忘記了,請提醒我我的諾言。 ***in* ~ *of,*** in the event of: 若;如果;萬一: *In* ~ *of fire, ring the alarm bell.* 萬一失火的話,請按警鈴。 ***in ˈany* ~,** whatever happens or may have happened. 無論如何。 ***in ˈno* ~,** in no circumstances. 決不。 ***in ˈthis/ˈthat* ~,** if this/that happens, has happened, should happen. 若是這樣(那樣)的話。 **ˈ~-book** *n* record kept by a professional man (eg a doctor) of ~s dealt with. (專業人員,如醫生之)病歷簿;個案紀錄簿;事例集。 **ˌ~-ˈhistory** *n* record of the history of sb suffering from a disease, social or mental trouble, etc. (病人的)病歷;個案歷史。 **ˈ~·work** *n* work involving personal study of individuals or families with social problems. (涉及社會問題之個人或家庭的)個案研究工作。 **2** (legal) question to be decided in a law court; the facts, arguments, etc, used on one side in a law court: (法律)案件;訟案;訴訟之一方所陳述之事實、理由等: *the* ~ *for the defendant,* the statement of facts, etc in his favour. 有利被告之案情的陳述。 *When will the* ~ *come before the Court?* 該案將於何時開庭審訊? *State your* ~, Give the facts and arguments in your favour. 述說對你有利的事實和論點。 *He has a strong* ~. 他有充足的理由可爲自己辯護。 ***make out a* ~ *(for),*** give arguments in favour (of) (sb, doing sth). (爲某人,爲作某事)提供有利的論點。 ***make out one's* ~,** prove that one is right. 證明自己有理。 **ˈ~-law** *n* law based on decisions made by judges. 判例法。 **3** (gram) (change in the) form of a noun or pronoun that shows its relation to another word: (文法)格(名詞或代名詞表示與他字之關係的形式或其變化): *The first person singular personal pronoun in English has two* ~ *forms:* 'I' (*subject* ~), *and* 'me' (*object* ~). 英文裡的第一人稱單數代名詞有兩個格的形式: I (主格)和 me (受格)。

case[2] /keɪs ; kes/ *n* **1** box, bag, covering, container: 盒;袋;套;箱: *ˈpacking-~,* large box in which goods are packed; 貨物包裝箱; *glass* ~, for the display of specimens, etc (eg in a museum); 玻璃匣、橱等(如博物館中展覽標本等者); *a ˈwatch* ~; 錶殼; *a ˈjewel* ~, lined with velvet for keeping jewels in; (有絲絨襯裡的)珠寶盒子; *a ˈseed* ~, on a plant, in which the seeds ripen; (植物的)種子莢; *a ˈpillow-~,* of cloth for covering a pillow; 枕頭套; *a ˈdressing-~,* a bag for hair-brushes, combs, razors, etc. (裝髮刷、梳子、刮鬍刀等之)梳妝盒;化粧袋。 ⇨ also suit~, book~. **ˌ~-ˈhardened** *adj* (fig) made callous by experience. (喻)由於經驗多而變得硬心腸或無感情的;老於世故而冷酷無情的。 **2** (printing): (印刷): *upper* ~, capital letters; 大寫字母; *lower* ~, small letters. 小寫字母。 □ *vt* [VP6A] enclose in a ~ or casing; encase. 置於箱或匣中;裝盒;裝箱。

casein /ˈkeɪsiːn ; ˈkesɪɪn/ *n* [U] body-building food (protein) present in milk and forming the basis of cheese. 酪蛋白;酪素。

case·ment /ˈkeɪsmənt ; ˈkesmənt/ *n* window that opens outwards or inwards like a door, not up or down or from side to side, ⇨ sash window and the illus at window; (poet) window. (像門一樣向外或向內開之)門式窗(非上下推或左右拉者,參看 window 之插圖);(詩)窗。

cash /kæʃ ; kæʃ/ *n* [U] **1** money in coin or notes:

現款;現金;現鈔: *I have no ~ with me—may I pay by cheque?* 我沒有帶現款──我可以付支票嗎? *We sell goods for ~ only—we don't give credit.* 我們售貨只收現金──不予賒帳。 '**~ crops** *n* crops (eg coffee, sisal) to be sold for ~ (contrasted with *subsistence crops* such as millet, beans, grown for use by the growers). 售現農作物(爲出售換得現金而栽種的農作物,例如咖啡、西沙爾蔴,與 subsistence crops 相對)。'**~ desk,** desk or counter (in a shop, etc) where payments (by ~ or cheque) are made. 櫃臺(商店等中付帳之處)。 '**~ dispenser,** machine (outside some banks) which, by the use of a personal coded card, dispenses ~. (有些銀行外面所陳設的利用個人號碼卡而取錢的)自動付款機。**~ down; ~ on delivery,** payment on delivery of the goods. 交貨收款;貨到付款。⇨ credit¹(1). '**~ price** *n* price for immediate payment. 現金售價。**~ register** *n* ~ box with a device for recording and storing ~ received. 現金收入紀錄機;收銀機。**~ and 'carry store** *n* one where goods are sold (usu at lower prices) for ~ payment if the buyer takes them away with him. 現賣現帶商店(購買者付現款卽帶走所購貨物的商店,通常價格較廉)。 **2** money in any form: 錢;款子: *be short of ~;* 缺錢; *be rolling in ~;* 極爲富有; *out of ~,* without money. 沒錢。□ *vt, vi* **1** [VP6A, 12B, 13B] give or get ~ for: 兌現;兌付;付現: *~ a cheque.* 兌現一張支票。 *Can you ~ this cheque for me/~ me a cheque?* 你能將這張支票兌換現金給我嗎? **2** [VP2C] **~ in (on),** take advantage (of); benefit (from): 利用;從…中獲利: *shopkeepers who ~ in on shortages by putting up prices.* 因貨量不足藉提高價錢以獲利的店主們。 **~·able** /-əbl ; -əbḷ/ *adj* that can be ~ed. 可兌現的;可兌換現金的。

ca·shew /'kæʃuː ; kə'ʃu/ *n* (tropical American tree with) small kidney-shaped nut. 檟如樹(一種熱帶美洲樹);都咸子(此樹之腎狀小堅果);腰果。

cash·ier¹ /kæ'ʃɪə(r) ; kæ'ʃɪr/ *n* person who receives and pays out money in a bank, store, hotel, restaurant, etc. (銀行、商店、旅館、餐廳等中之)出納員。

cash·ier² /kə'ʃɪə(r) ; kæ'ʃɪr/ *vt* [VP6A] dismiss (eg an officer) with dishonour and disgrace. 革除(軍官等)之職;撤職。

cash·mere /kæʃ'mɪə(r) ; 'kæʃmɪr/ *n* [U] fine soft wool of Kashmir goats of Asia: 開斯米(亞洲喀什米爾山羊之細軟羊毛): *a ~ shawl.* 開斯米圍巾。

cas·ing /'keɪsɪŋ ; 'kesɪŋ/ *n* covering; protective wrapping: 匣;套;鞘;封殼;盒;保護性的外罩: *copper wire with a ~ of rubber;* 包有膠皮的銅絲; *~s for sausages.* 製香腸的腸衣。

ca·sino /kə'siːnəʊ ; kə'sino/ *n* (*pl* ~s) public room or building for gambling and other amusements. (供賭博及其他娛樂之)娛樂場;俱樂部。

cask /kɑːsk *US:* kæsk ; kæsk/ *n* barrel for liquids: (裝液體之)桶: *a ~ of cider;* 一桶蘋果酒; amount that a ~ holds. 一桶所裝之量。

cas·ket /'kɑːskɪt *US:* 'kæskɪt ; 'kæskɪt/ *n* **1** small box to hold letters, jewels, cremated ashes, etc. (收藏信件、珠寶、骨灰等之)小箱。 **2** (US) coffin. (美)棺;柩。

cas·sava /kə'sɑːvə ; kə'sɑvə/ *n* [U] tropical plant with starchy roots from which tapioca is extracted. 參茨(熱帶植物,根含澱粉質);木薯。 ⇨ the illus at vegetable. 參看 vegetable 之插圖。

cas·ser·ole /'kæsərəʊl ; 'kæsə,rol/ *n* covered and heat-proof dish in which food is cooked and then served at table; food so cooked: 烤鍋(有蓋的耐熱淺鍋,食品置於其中烤煮,然後連鍋端上餐桌);砂鍋;焙盤;用烤鍋等所做之食物: *a ~ of lamb.* 羊肉砂鍋。

cas·sette /kə'set ; kə'sɛt/ *n* [C] (US 美 = *cartridge*) container for magnetic tape (for use with a ~ tape-recorder) or for photographic film (to be fitted into a camera). 卡式錄音帶盒(配合卡式錄音機用者);卡式膠捲盒(裝於攝影機中用者)。⇨ the illus at tape. 參看 tape 之插圖。

cas·sock /'kæsək ; 'kæsək/ *n* long, close-fitting outer garment, worn by some priests. (某些教士所穿之)緊身長外衣;法衣。 ⇨ the illus at vestment. 參看 vestment 之插圖。

cas·so·wary /'kæsəweərɪ ; 'kæsə,wɛrɪ/ *n* (*pl* -ries) large bird of SE Asia, unable to fly, similar to, but smaller than, an emu. 食火雞(一種東南亞產之大鳥,不能飛,似鴯鶓,但較小)。 ⇨ the illus at rare. 參看 rare 之插圖。

a cash register

castanets

cast¹ /kɑːst *US:* kæst ; kæst/ *vt, vi* (*pt, pp* cast) **1** [VP6A, 15A, B] throw; allow to fall or drop: 投;擲;拋;脫落: *The fisherman ~ his net into the water.* 漁夫撒網於水中。 *Snakes ~ their skins.* 蛇蛻皮。 *His horse ~ a shoe,* one of its shoes came off. 他的馬脫落了一隻蹄鐵。 **~ anchor,** lower it. 下錨。 **be ~ down,** be depressed, unhappy. 沮喪;不樂。 ⇨ downcast. **~ lots; ~ in one's lot with,** ⇨ lot²(1, 3). **~ a vote,** give a vote. 投票。 **~·ing vote** *n* one given (eg by the chairman) to decide a question when votes on each side are equal. 決定票(例如當雙方票數相等時由主席所投之一票)。 **~ sth in sb's teeth,** ⇨ tooth(1). **2** [VP6A, 15A, 2C] turn or send in a particular direction: 轉向或送至某一特定方向;投射: *~ one's eye over sth,* look at, examine, it; 看看(查看)某物; *~ a gloom/shadow on sth,* make it seem gloomy, depressing; 在某件事上投下一片陰影(使其看起來令人愁悶、沮喪); *~ a new light on a problem, etc,* make it clearer, easier to understand; 使某一問題等更明白,更易於了解; *~ a rather wary glance at sb,* look at him warily; 機警地看了某人一眼; *~ a slur on someone's reputation,* say things to damage it. 中傷某人的名譽。 **~ about for,** (anxiously) look for, try to find (eg *allies, excuses*). 焦急地尋找(盟友,藉口等)。 **3** [VP6A] pour (liquid metal) into a mould; make (eg a statue *in* bronze, etc) in this way: 澆(液化金屬)於模中;鑄造(銅像等,與 in 連用): *a figure ~ in bronze.* 青銅鑄成的人像。 **~ iron** *n* iron in a hard, brittle form, made by shaping in moulds after melting the ore in a blast furnace, and usually converted into wrought iron or steel before being used. 生鐵;鑄鐵(鐵砂在鼓風爐中熔化後經注於模中所形成之堅而脆之鐵塊,在使用前通常再鍊成鍛鐵或鋼)。Hence, 由此產生, '**~-iron** *adj* **(a)** made of ~ iron. 鑄鐵造的。 **(b)** (fig) hard; untiring; unyielding: (喻)堅强的;不懈的;不屈不撓的: *a man with a ~-iron will/constitution.* 意志堅强(體格强壯)的人。 **4** [VP6A, 15B] **~ up,** add, calculate (more usu *add up* or *tot up*): 加起;計算(較常用 add up 或 tot up): *~ up a column of figures.* 加起一欄數字。 **5** [VP15B, 2C] **~ (sb/sth) aside,** (= *cast off,* (b)) abandon; throw away as useless or unwanted. 拋棄;因其無用或不需要而丟棄某物。 **~ (sth) off, (a)** unloose (a boat) and let go. 解纜;放(船)。 **(b)** (fig) abandon; throw away as unwanted. (喻)拋棄;丟棄。Hence, 由此產生, **,~-off 'clothes; '~-offs** *n pl* clothes that the owner will not wear again. 不要的衣服;不再穿的衣服;被丟棄的衣服。 **~ off,** (knitting) remove the last row of stitches from the needles. (編織)收針。 **~ on,** (knitting) make the first row of stitches. (編織)起針。 **6**

[VP6A] give (an actor) a part in a play: 派(演員)擔任戲中角色: *He was ~ for the part of Hamlet.* 他被派扮演哈姆雷特的角色。**~·ing** *n* [C] sth shaped by being poured in a mould (eg a wheel or axle), ⇨ 3 above. 鑄造之物(如車輪或車軸);鑄件;鑄品(參看上列第3義)。

cast² /kɑːst *US:* kæst ; kæst/ *n* **1** act of throwing (eg a net or fishing line): 投;擲;拋(如漁網或釣絲): *stake everything on a single ~ of the dice.* 孤注一擲。 **2** sth made by casting(3) or by pressing soft material into a mould: 鑄造物;模造物: *His leg was in a plaster ~.* 他的腿打了石膏。 **3** mould where metal is poured or where soft material is pressed. (鑄金屬之)模子;內型;(壓製軟質物之)模型。 **4** set of actors in a play; the distribution of the parts among these actors: (一齣戲的)演員陣容;演員角色分配: *a play with an all-star ~.* 全由名角演出的一齣戲。 **5** type or quality: 類型;特質: *~ of features;* 面貌; *~ of mind.* 性情;脾氣。 **6** (of the eyes) slight squint. (指眼)斜視。

cas·ta·nets /ˌkæstəˈnets ; ˌkæstəˈnɛts/ *n pl* instruments of hardwood or ivory used in pairs on the fingers to make rattling sounds as a rhythm for dancing. 響板(用硬木或象牙製之二片板,繫於手指上,互擊而發出咯咯聲,作爲舞蹈的節奏)。⇨ the illus at cash. 參看 cash 之插圖。

cast·away /ˈkɑːstəweɪ *US:* ˈkæst- ; ˈkæstəˌwe/ *n* shipwrecked person, esp one reaching a strange country or lonely island. 乘船遇難之人(尤指漂流至異鄉或孤島者)。

caste /kɑːst *US:* kæst ; kæst/ *n* one of the Hindu hereditary social classes; any exclusive social class; [U] this system. 印度之世襲的社會階級之一;任何排他的社會階級;此種階級制度。***lose ~ with/among,*** lose the right to be respected; come down in social rank. 失去被尊敬的社會地位;階級地位降低。

cas·tel·lated /ˈkæstəleɪtɪd ; ˈkæstəˌletɪd/ *adj* having turrets or battlements (like a castle). (似城堡之)有角樓或城垛的;有雉堞的。

cas·ti·gate /ˈkæstɪgeɪt ; ˈkæstəˌget/ *vt* [VP6A] punish severely with blows or by criticizing. 痛毆;嚴懲;苛評。**cas·ti·ga·tion** /ˌkæstɪˈgeɪʃn ; ˌkæstəˈgeʃən/ *n* [C, U] (instance of) severe punishment. 嚴懲;嚴懲之實例。

castle /ˈkɑːsl *US:* ˈkæsl ; ˈkæsl̩/ *n* large building or group of buildings fortified against attack, esp as in olden times; house that was once such a fortified building; piece (also called 亦稱 *rook*) used in the game of chess, ⇨ the illus at chess. 城堡;堡壘;古堡;原爲城堡之房舍;(西洋棋中之)城形棋子(參看 chess 之插圖)。***~s in the air; ~s in Spain,*** day-dreams; plans or hopes that are unlikely to be realized. 白日夢;不可能實現的計畫或希望;空中樓閣。***an Englishman's house is his ~,*** his place of refuge and safety. 一個英國人的住宅就是他的避難所。□ *vi* (chess) move the king sideways two squares towards the ~ and place the ~ on the square the king moved across. (西洋棋)將王向着城堡橫移二格,並將城堡放於王所移越過的空格中。

cas·tor, cas·ter /ˈkɑːstə(r) *US:* ˈkæs- ; ˈkæstɚ/ *n* **1** wheel (on a swivel) fixed to each leg of a piece of furniture (so that it may be turned and moved easily). 脚輪(裝於傢具腿部旋轉座上,以便於轉動及移動者)。 **2** bottle or metal pot, with holes in the top, for sugar, salt, etc. 裝糖、鹽等頂端有孔之小瓶;調味瓶。ˈ**~ sugar** *n* white, finely powdered sugar. 細白糖。

cas·tor oil /ˌkɑːstər ˈɔɪl *US:* ˈkæstər ɔɪl ; ˈkæstɚ ɔɪl/ *n* [U] thick, yellowish oil, made from beans of the ~ plant, used as a purgative. 蓖麻油(帶黃色之濃油,自蓖麻子取出,用作瀉劑)。

cas·trate /kæˈstreɪt *US:* ˈkæstreɪt ; ˈkæstret/ *vt* [VP6A] remove the sex glands of (a male animal); make (a male animal) useless for breeding purposes. 割去(雄性動物)之性腺;閹割;去勢(使不能生殖)。**cas·tra·tion** /kæˈstreɪʃn ; kæsˈtreʃən/ *n* castrating. 閹割;去勢。

cas·ual /ˈkæʒʊəl ; ˈkæʒʊəl/ *adj* **1** happening by chance: 偶然的;不意的: *a ~ meeting.* 偶然的相會。 **2** careless; undesigned; unmethodical; informal: 不小心的;無心的;馬虎的;疏忽的;隨便的: *a ~ glance;* 不經心的一瞥; *clothes for ~ wear,* for informal occasions, holidays, etc. 便服;便裝。*She's a very ~ person,* eg is careless and thoughtless about the convenience of others. 她是一個極疏忽(如不顧他人方便)的人。 **3** irregular; not continued: 非經常的;非長期的: *earn a living by ~ labour;* 靠做短工爲生; *~ labourers,* not permanently engaged by one employer. 零工;短工(非由一主人永久僱用者)。**~·ly** *adv*

casu·alty /ˈkæʒʊəltɪ ; ˈkæʒʊəltɪ/ *n* [C] **1** accident, esp one involving loss of life. 意外;(尤指有人死亡的)災禍。 **2** soldier or sailor who is killed, wounded or missing; person killed or seriously injured in an accident: 傷亡或失踪的陸海軍戰士;意外災禍中的傷亡者;傷亡: *The enemy suffered heavy casualties.* 敵人傷亡慘重。*C~ lists were published the day after the train accident.* 傷亡名單在火車意外事件發生後的第二天就公佈了。ˈ**C~ Ward/Department** *n* part of a hospital to which persons injured, eg in road accidents, are taken for urgent treatment. 狩傷病室;急診室(醫院中的一個部門,收容並急診車禍等中之傷者)。

casu·ist /ˈkæzjʊɪst ; ˈkæʒʊɪst/ *n* expert in ~ry. 詭辯家。**~ry** /-rɪ ; -rɪ/ *n* [U] judgement of right and wrong by reference to theories, social conventions, etc, (often with false but clever reasoning); [C] false but clever argument used in this way. (引述理論、社會習俗慣例所作之似是而非的)詭辯;曲解。**casu·is·tic, -ti·cal** /ˌkæzjʊˈɪstɪk, -tɪkl ; ˌkæʒʊˈɪstɪk, -tɪkl̩/ *adj* of or like ~ry. 詭辯的;曲解的。

casus belli /ˌkeɪsəs ˈbelaɪ ; ˈkesəsˈbɛlaɪ/ *n* (Lat) act that is held to justify war. (拉)開戰理由。

cat /kæt ; kæt/ *n* **1** small, domestic, fur-covered animal often kept as a pet, to catch mice, etc; (= ˈ**wild cat**) any animal of the group that includes tigers, lions, panthers and leopards. 貓(家庭養馴之小毛皮動物,常養作寵物、養以捕鼠等);貓科動物(包括虎、獅、美洲豹及豹)。***bell the cat,*** ⇨ bell *vt.* ***let the cat out of the bag,*** ⇨ bag¹(1). ***like a cat on hot bricks,*** very nervous or jumpy. 似熱磚上的貓;似熱鍋上的螞蟻;緊張而激動的。***put/set the cat among the pigeons,*** cause alarm and confusion. 製造緊張及混亂。***wait for the cat to jump; see which way the cat jumps,*** refuse to give advice, make plans, etc, until one sees what other people are thinking and doing. 觀望形勢(在未獲悉別人的想法和做法之前拒作忠告、計畫等)。ˌ***cat-and-ˈdog life,*** one full of quarrels. 經常吵鬧的生活。 **2** (short for係下字之略) ˌ**cat-o'-ˈnine-tails** *n* whip with many knotted cords, formerly used for punishing wrong-doers. 九尾鞭(從前用以懲罰犯罪者)。***room to swing a cat in,*** just enough space. 剛好够的空間。 **3** (compounds, etc) (複合字等) ˈ**cat burglar** *n* one who enters a building by climbing up walls, rainpipes, etc. (攀登牆、簷水管等而潛入屋內的)竊賊。ˈ**cat·call** *n, v* (make a) loud, shrill whistle expressing disapproval (eg at a political meeting). (發出)響亮而尖銳的口哨聲(表示不贊成,如在政治集會場合所發出者)。ˈ**cat·fish** *n* large fish without scales, with feelers around the mouth. 鯰魚(無鱗大魚,口之周圍有觸鬚)。ˈ**cat-nap,** ˈ**cat-sleep** *n* short sleep (in a chair, etc, not in bed). (在椅等之中而非在床上之)小睡;假寐。ˌ**cat's ˈcradle** *n* children's game with a length of string looped over the fingers of both hands and transferred between the fingers of two players. 翻線戲;翻罟;翻絞絞;編花籃(二人玩之兒童遊戲,用一根線套於兩手之手指間,玩者彼此互翻套

some wild cats

換)。**'cat's eye** *n* reflector stud placed in roadways to guide traffic in darkness or on the rear of a vehicle (eg a bicycle). (裝於路上以便於黑暗中指示交通或裝於車輛如脚踏車等後部的) 反光鈕。**'cat's paw** *n* person who is used as a tool by another. 被他人利用爲工具之人。**'cat suit** *n* woman's or child's close-fitting one-piece garment for the whole body. (女人或兒童之上下身連成一片的)緊身衣。**'cat-walk** *n* narrow footway along a bridge, or through a mass of machinery, engines, etc. 沿橋樑之步行小道;機器、引擎等中間的甬道。

cata·clysm /'kætəklɪzəm ; 'kætə,klɪzəm/ *n* [C] sudden and violent change (eg a flood, an earthquake, a great war, a political or social revolution). 突然而劇烈的變動(如洪水、地震、大戰、政治的或社會的革命)。**cata·clys·mic** /ˌkætə'klɪzmɪk ; ,kætə'klɪzmɪk/ *adj*

cata·combs /'kætəku:mz ; 'kætə,komz/ *n pl* series of underground galleries with openings along the sides for the burial of the dead (as in ancient Rome). (如古羅馬之)地下墓穴;陵寢。

cata·falque /'kætəfælk ; 'kætə,fælk/ *n* decorated stand or stage for a coffin at a funeral. 靈柩臺(葬禮時用以置棺材者)。

cata·lepsy /'kætəlepsɪ ; 'kætə,lɛpsɪ/ *n* [U] disease in which the sufferer has periods when he loses consciousness and sensation and his muscles become rigid. 强直性昏厥;類癇症(患者時而有一陣失去知覺,肌肉亦變得僵硬)。**cata·lep·tic** /ˌkætə'leptɪk ; ,kætə'lɛptɪk/ *adj* of, having, ~. 類癇症的;患類癇症的。□ *n* person who has ~. 類癇症患者。

cata·logue (US also **catalog**) /'kætəlɒg *US:* -lɔ:g ; 'kætl̩,ɔg/ *n* list of names/places/goods etc, in a special order: (人名、地名、貨物等之)目錄;概覽;一覽表: *a library* ~. 圖書館之圖書目錄。□ *vt* [VP6A] make a ~ of; put in a ~. 編列目錄;列入目錄。

ca·talpa /kə'tælpə ; kə'tælpə/ *n* (kinds of) tree with heart-shaped leaves and trumpet-shaped flowers. 梓屬樹;黃金樹(葉如心狀,開喇叭狀花)。

ca·ta·ly·sis /kə'tæləsɪs ; kə'tæləsɪs/ *n* the process of aiding or speeding up a chemical process by a substance that does not itself undergo any change. 觸媒作用;催化作用;接觸反應 (一種本身不起變化的物質所幫助或促進化學變化之程序)。 **cata·lyst** /'kætəlɪst ; 'kætl̩ɪst/ *n* [C] substance that causes ~; (fig) sb or sth that helps to bring about a change. 觸媒;催化劑;(喩)促使改變之人或事物。**cata·lyt·ic** /ˌkætə'lɪtɪk ; ,kætl̩'ɪtɪk/ *adj* of ~; causing ~. 觸媒的;起觸媒作用的;催化的。

cata·maran /ˌkætəmə'ræn ; ,kætəmə'ræn/ *n* boat with twin hulls; two boats or canoes fastened side by side (as used in the South Seas). 一種雙船身的小艇;(兩隻船並側而繫結在一起之)雙身船(如用於南洋者)。

cat·a·pult /'kætəpʌlt ; 'kætə,pʌlt/ *n* **1** Y-shaped stick with a piece of elastic, for shooting stones, etc from; (in ancient times) machine for throwing heavy stones in war. 彈弓(由一根叉木及一條橡皮製成,用以發射石子等);彈弩(古代戰爭中用以投擲大石頭之機械)。 **2** apparatus for launching aircraft without a runway (eg from the deck of a carrier). (不需跑道而發射飛機起飛之)飛機彈射器(如於航空母艦甲板上所用者)。□ *vt* launch (aircraft) with a ~; shoot (as) from a ~. 用彈射器彈射(飛機)升空;(如)用彈弓發射;彈射。

cata·ract /'kætərækt ; 'kætə,rækt/ *n* [C] **1** large, steep waterfall. 大而陡的瀑布。 **2** (path) disease of the eye, in which the lens slowly clouds over, obscuring sight. (病理)白內障(水晶體生翳而遮蔽視線之眼疾)。⇨ the illus at eye. 參看 eye 之插圖。

ca·tarrh /kə'tɑ:(r) ; kə'tɑr/ *n* [U] inflamation of the mucous membrane, esp of the nose and throat, causing flow of liquid, as when one has a cold; this liquid. 加答兒;黏膜炎(尤指鼻喉之黏膜炎,可引致流出液體,如傷風時之現象);加答兒液。

ca·tas·trophe /kə'tæstrəfɪ ; kə'tæstrəfɪ/ *n* [C] sudden happening that causes great suffering and destruction(eg a flood, earthquake, fire). (驟然而來造成極大苦難及毀滅之)大災害;異常的災禍(如洪水、地震、火災等)。**cata·strophic** /ˌkætə'strɒfɪk ; ,kætə'strɑfɪk/ *adj*

catch[1] /kætʃ ; kætʃ/ *vt, vi* (*pt, pp* caught /kɔ:t ; kɔt/) **1** [VP6A] stop (sth that is in motion) (eg by getting hold of it with the hands, by holding out sth into which it may come): 捕捉(運動中的物體);(用手等)捉住;(用袋狀物等)捕住: *I threw the ball to him and he caught it.* 我將球拋給他,他接住

a catamaran

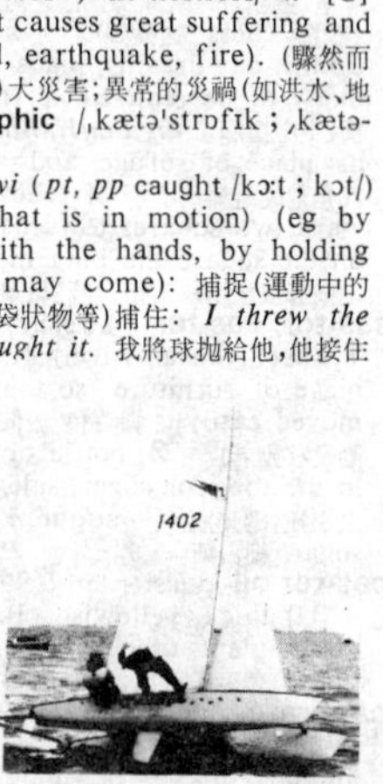

了。*The dog caught the bit of meat in its mouth.* 那狗用嘴接住了那塊肉。[VP15B] ~ ***sb out,*** (cricket) dismiss a batsman by ~ing the ball he has struck before it touches the ground. (板球)在球觸地之前捕住球而迫使(擊球員)出場;接殺出局。⇨ also 3 below. 亦參看下列第 3 義。 **2** [VP6A] capture; seize; intercept: 捕獲;捉住;攫取;攔截: ~ *a rat in a trap;* 用捕鼠機捕住一隻鼠; ~ *a thief.* 捉住一個賊。*How many fish did you ~?* 你捕到了幾條魚? *Cats ~ mice.* 貓捕鼠。*I caught him* (= met him and stopped him) *just as he was leaving the house.* 我在他正要出門的時候攔住了他。 **3** [VP6A, 19B, 14, 15B, 22] come unexpectedly upon (sb) doing sth (esp sth wrong); surprise or detect: 撞見(某人)做某事(尤指壞事);當場破獲;發覺: *I caught the boys stealing apples from my garden.* 我撞見那些孩子們偷我園中的蘋果。*You won't ~ me* (= There's no likelihood of my being discovered) *doing that again!* 你將不會再發現我做那事! ~ ***sb at it;*** ~ ***sb in the act (of doing sth),*** come upon him while he is actually doing it: 當場抓住;撞見某人做某事: *Just let me ~ you at it again* (—then there'll be trouble)! 你要是再讓我逮到的話(——就有你好看了)! ~ ***sb out,*** detect him making a mistake. 發現某人做錯事(犯過)。~ ***sb napping,*** ⇨ nap[1]. **4** [VP6A] be in time for: 及時趕到;趕上: ~ *a train/the bus, etc;* 趕上火車(公共汽車等); ~ *the post,* post letters before the box is emptied by the postman. 趕上郵局的一班收信時刻(在郵差從郵筒取信之前投遞)。 **5** [VP15B, 2C] ~ ***sb up;*** ~ ***up (with sb),*** **(a)** come up to sb who is going in the same direction; overtake: 趕上向同一方向行進之人;趕上某人: *Go on in front, I'll soon ~ you up/~ up (with you).* 你在前面走,我一會兒就會趕上你。**(b)** do all the work that has not yet been done: 趕做未做完的工作;趕工: *Tom was away from school for a month so now he's got to work hard to ~ up with the rest of the class.* 湯姆有一個月未到校上課,所以他現在必須努力用功,好趕上班裏其他的同學。 **6** [VP6A, 2A, 3A, 14, 15A] ~ ***(in/on),*** (cause to) become fixed or prevented from moving; (cause to) be entangled: (使)絆住;(使)纏住;掛住: *The nail caught her dress.* 釘子鉤住了她的衣服。*Her dress caught on a nail.* 她的衣服被釘子鉤住了。*I caught my fingers in the door,* trapped them between the door and the doorpost. 我的手指被夾在門縫中了(門與門柱的中間)。*This bolt doesn't ~,* cannot be fastened. 這個門閂閂不住了。*The latch has caught,* stuck fast. 這門閂拔不出來了。*The car was caught between two lorries.* 那部汽車被兩輛貨車夾在中間。*He caught his foot on a tree root and stumbled.* 他的一隻脚被樹根絆住,因而跌倒。 **7** [VP6A] get (the meaning of sth); hear (the sound of sth); receive (punishment, etc): 懂得;了解(某事物的意義);聽見(某物的聲音);受到(處罰等): *I don't quite ~ your meaning.* 我不十分懂你的意思。*I didn't ~ the end of the sentence.* 我未聽見那句話的末尾。 *I don't quite ~* (= fully understand) *the idea.* 我不十分明白那意思。[VP2C] ~ ***on (to sth),*** understand. 明白。~ ***it,*** be scolded, punished, hit, etc: 挨罵;受罰;被打中: *You'll ~ it if you're not careful!* 你若是不小心就會挨罵的! *He caught it* (=was hit) *right in the eye.* 他的眼睛被打個正著。 ~ ***sb's attention/fancy,*** succeed in getting it. 引起某人的注意(迎合某人的心意)。~ ***sb's eye,*** look at him to attract his attention when he looks in your direction. 注視某人以引起他的注意。Hence, 由此產生, **'eye-~ing** *adj* ⇨ eye[1](3). ~ ***sight/a glimpse of,*** see for a short time. 一眼看見;一瞥。 **8** [VP6A] become infected with: 染患;罹患: ~ *a disease/a fever;* 患病(發燒); ~ *a cold.* 患感冒;傷風。 **9** [VP3A] ~ ***at,*** try to grasp: 試圖抓住;想把握住: *A drowning man will ~ at a straw.* 快要溺死的人連一根稻草也要設法抓住。*He will ~ at* (= take eagerly) *any opportunity of practising his English.* 他會把握住任何機會練習他的英文。⇨ clutch[1]. [VP15B] ~ ***up,*** grasp; seize: 把握;抓;搶: ~ *up a loose end of rope.* 抓住繩子未繫牢的一端。*They were caught up* (fig, carried away) *in the wave of enthusiasm.* (喻)他們被熱情的浪潮冲昏了頭。[VP15A] ~ ***hold of,*** seize, grab. 握住;攫取。 **10** ~ ***(fire),*** begin to burn: 着火;燒着: *The wood soon caught (fire).* 那木頭不一會兒就燒着了。 **11** [VP6A, 12C, 15A] hit: 打;擊: ~ *sb a blow.* 打某人一拳。*She caught him one* (= gave him a blow) *on the cheek.* 她打了他一記耳光。 **12** ~ ***one's breath,*** fail to breathe regularly for a moment (from surprise, etc). (因吃驚等)暫時不能規律地呼吸;屏息。**'~-crop** *n* quick-growing crop (eg lettuce) grown between rows of other crops. (種植於其他作物行間生長迅速的)間作(如萵苣菜)。**'~·penny** *adj* designed or intended merely to get sales: 僅爲賺錢而設計的;以賺錢爲目的的: *a book with a ~penny title.* 其書名僅爲賺錢而設計的一本書。**'~·word** *n* **1** word placed so as to draw attention to an article, eg the subject of a paragraph; first or last word of a page in a dictionary, printed above the columns. 標字(用以引起注意一篇文章,如一段文章的主題;印於字典之每一欄上方的每一頁的首字及末字)。 **2** phrase or slogan in frequent current use. 流行的口號;標語。 **~er** *n* (baseball) player who stands behind the batter to ~ the ball thrown by the pitcher. (棒球)(立於打擊手之後以接投手投來之球的)捕手。 **~·ing** *adj* (esp of diseases) infectious. (尤指疾病)傳染性的。 **~y** *adj* **1** (of a tune, etc) easily remembered. (指曲調等)容易記憶的。 **2** tricky, deceptive. 騙人的;引人上當的。

catch[2] /kætʃ ; kætʃ/ *n* **1** act of catching (esp a ball): 捕捉(尤指接球): *That was a difficult ~.* 那是一個難接的球(但已接住)。 **2** that which is caught or worth ~ing: 所捕獲或值得捕獲之物: *a fine ~ of fish.* 捕獲的魚很多。*He's a good ~ for some young woman,* is a good man to get as a husband. 他是少女結婚的好對象。 **3** sth intended to trick or deceive; cunning question or device: 引人上當的事物;使人容易答錯的問題;詭詐: *There's a ~ in it somewhere.* 這裏面有詭詐。*Does the teacher ever include ~ questions in examination papers?* 老師在試卷中出過令人迷惑的問題嗎? **4** device for fastening or securing a lock, door, etc. (使鎖、門等牢固的)搭鈕;鎖環;掛鈎;彈簧梢。⇨ the illus at latch. 參看 latch 之挿圖。 **5** song for a number of voices starting one after another. 數部輪唱曲。

catch·ment /'kætʃmənt ; 'kætʃmənt/ *n* **'~(-area)** land from which a river or reservoir draws its rainfall (also **'~-basin**); (fig) area(s) from which central body draws its members, eg a school its pupils, a hospital its patients; [U] amount of rainfall, etc caught. 集水區域;集水盆地;(喻)人員集結區(如學區,醫療區); 集聚之雨量。

catch·up /'kætʃəp ; 'kætʃəp/ *n* = ketchup.

cat·echism /'kætɪkɪzəm ; 'kætəˌkɪzəm/ *n* [U] instruction (esp about religion) by question and answer; [C] number, succession of questions and answers designed for this purpose: 問答教學法(尤指教義之傳授);爲達此目的而設計的一連串的問答;教義問答教本: *put a person through his ~,* question him closely. 詳細詰問某人。

cat·echize /'kætɪkaɪz ; 'kætəˌkaɪz/ *vt* [VP6A] teach or examine by asking many questions. 用問答法教學或考試。

cat·egori·cal /ˌkætɪ'gɒrɪkl *US:* -gɔːr- ; ˌkætə'gɔrɪkl/ *adj* (of a statement) unconditional; absolute; detailed; explicit. (指陳述)無條件的;絕對的;詳細的;明顯的。**~ly** /-ɪklɪ ; -ɪklɪ/ *adv*

cat·egory /'kætɪgərɪ *US:* -gɔːrɪ ; 'kætəˌgorɪ/ *n* (*pl* -ries) division or class in a complete system or grouping. (整個系統或組合中的)部門;種類;範疇。**cat·egor·ize** /'kætɪgəraɪz ; 'kætəgəˌraɪz/ *vt* [VP6A] place in a ~. 置於某一部門中;分門別類。

cater /'keɪtə(r) ; 'ketə/ *vi* **1** [VP3A] ~ ***for,*** provide food: 備辦食物: *Weddings and parties ~ed for,* The advertiser will supply food for weddings, etc. 包辦婚禮及宴會酒席(廣告文字)。 **2** [VP3A] ~ ***for/to,*** make provision *for*, supply what is desired or required *to*; pander *to*: 提供;迎合: *TV programmes usually ~ for all tastes.* 電視通常提供各種不同趣味的娛樂節目。*Some tabloid newspapers ~ to low tastes.* 有些小型報紙迎合低級趣味。**~er** *n* person who provides meals, etc brought from outside, to clubs, homes, etc; owner or manager of a hotel, restaurant, etc. 包辦酒席或餐食者(將之送至俱樂部、家庭等處);旅館、餐館等之老闆或經理。

cat·er·pil·lar /ˈkætəpɪlə(r) ; ˈkætɚˌpɪlɚ/ *n* **1** larva of a butterfly or moth, ⇨ the illus at butterfly. 蠋;蝶或蛾的幼蟲;毛蟲 (參看 butterfly 之挿圖)。 **2** endless belt passing over toothed wheels, used to give vehicles, tanks, etc, a good grip on soft or uneven surfaces: (套於帶齒車輪上以便在軟地或不平之地行走,如戰車等之)環帶;履帶;防滑帶: ~ *tractor,* one fitted with such belts. 環帶牽引車(農場用)。

cat·er·waul /ˈkætəwɔːl ; ˈkætɚˌwɔl/ *vi, n* (make a) cat's howling cry. (發出)貓叫春的聲音。

cat·gut /ˈkætgʌt ; ˈkætˌgʌt/ *n* [U] material used for the strings of violins, tennis rackets, etc (made by twisting the intestines of sheep and other animals). (用以做小提琴弦、網球拍等之)羊腸筋;腸線(用羊腸或其他動物之腸絞成)。

ca·thar·sis /kəˈθɑːsɪs ; kəˈθarsɪs/ *n* (*pl* -arses /-siːz ; -siz/) **1** [C, U] (med) emptying of the bowels. (醫)導瀉;通便。 **2** outlet for strong emotion (eg as given by the drama, or by a willing account of deep feelings given to another person). 强烈情緒的發抒;滌除作用(由觀劇或向他人敍述自己的深刻情緒,而使自己的感情得到發抒)。**ca·thar·tic** /kəˈθɑːtɪk; kəˈθartɪk/ *n* (med), *adj* (substance) giving ~. (醫)緩瀉劑;通便的;導瀉的;發抒感情的。

ca·the·dral /kəˈθiːdrəl ; kəˈθidrəl/ *n* chief church in a diocese, in which is the bishop's throne, under the charge of a dean. (內設主教聖座而由首席牧師主持的)總教堂;大教堂;主教座堂。

cath·ode /ˈkæθəʊd;ˈkæθod/ *n* **1** negative electrode in the form of a filament which, when hot, releases negative electrons which are attracted towards the (positive) anode. 陰電極(燈絲形,受熱時,放出爲陽電極所吸引的陰電子)。 **2** negative terminal of a battery. (電池的)陰極。 ˌ~ ˈ**ray** *n* invisible stream of electrons from the ~ in a vacuum tube (as used in radar, television, etc), called *a* ˌ~ ˈ*ray tube*. 陰極射線(眞空管中由陰極放出肉眼不能見的電子流,此種眞空管用於雷達、電視等,稱爲陰極射線管)。

cath·olic /ˈkæθəlɪk;ˈkæθəlɪk/ *adj* **1** liberal; general; including many or most things: 寬大的;普遍的;廣泛的: *a man with ~ tastes and interests;* 興趣廣泛的人;*~ in his sympathies.* 他富有同情心。 **2 the C~ Church,** the whole body of Christians. 基督教徒之總稱。**Roman C~** *n, adj* (member) of the Church that has the Pope as its chief bishop. 天主教(的);天主教徒(的)。⇨ Pope, Protestant, Roman(3). **Ca·tholicism** /kəˈθɒləsɪzm;kəˈθaləˌsɪzəm/ *n* teaching, beliefs, etc, of the Roman Catholic Church. 天主教之教義、信仰等。**cath·ol·ic·ity** /ˌkæθəˈlɪsətɪ ; ˌkæθəˈlɪsətɪ/ *n* [U] quality of being ~(1). 普遍性;廣泛性;寬大。

cat·kin /ˈkætkɪn ; ˈkætkɪn/ *n* [C] tuft of soft, downy flowers hanging down from twigs of such trees as willows and birches. (垂於柳樹及樺樹枝頭之)帳毛花穗;葇荑花序;柳絮。

cat·sup /ˈkætsəp ; ˈkætsəp/ *n* = ketchup.

cat·tish, cat·ty /ˈkætɪʃ, ˈkætɪ ; ˈkætɪʃ, ˈkætɪ/ *adj* (esp) sly and spiteful. (尤指)狡猾的;惡意的。**cat·ti·ness** *n*

cattle /ˈkætl ; ˈkætl̩/ *n pl* oxen (bulls, bullocks, cows): 牛的總稱: *twenty head of ~.* 二十頭牛。*C~ were allowed to graze on the village common.* 牛被允許在村中的公地上吃草。ˈ**~-cake** *n* [U] food fed to ~, made from various materials. 牛餅(用各種材料製成的牛的飼料)。

Cau·casian /kɔːˈkeɪzɪən *US:* kɔːˈkeɪʒn ; kɔˈkeʒən/ *n, adj* (member) of the Indo-European group of people. 高加索人;白種人;高加索人的;白種人的。

cau·cus /ˈkɔːkəs ; ˈkɔkəs/ *n* (meeting of the) organization committee of a political party (making plans, decisions, etc). (政黨中負責設計、決策等之)組織委員會(或其會議)。

caught /kɔːt ; kɔt/ *pt, pp* of catch.

caul /kɔːl ; kɔl/ *n* (physiol) thin skin enclosing a foetus, part of which, when covering a baby's head, was once thought to be a charm against drowning. (生理)胎膜(昔時認爲覆於初生嬰兒頭上之部分能防止溺斃)。

caul·dron /ˈkɔːldrən ; ˈkɔldrən/ *n* large, deep, open pot in which things are boiled. 大而深的敞口鍋;釜。

cauli·flower /ˈkɒlɪflaʊə(r) *US:* ˈkɔːlɪ- ; ˈkɔləˌflaʊɚ/ *n* [C, U] (cabbage-like plant with a) large, white flower-head, used as a vegetable. 花椰菜;菜花。⇨ the illus at vegetable. 參看 vegetable 之挿圖。

caulk /kɔːk ; kɔk/ *vt* [VP6A] make (joins between planks, etc) tight with fibre or a sticky substance. (用纖維或黏性物)使(木板等之間的連接處)嚴密不透水;填隙。

causal /ˈkɔːzl ; ˈkɔzl̩/ *adj* of cause and effect; of, expressing, cause. 因果的;原因的;表示原因的。**~·ity** /kɔːˈzælətɪ ; kɔˈzælətɪ/ *n* [U] relation of cause and effect; the principle that nothing can happen without a cause: 因果關係;事必有因之原理;因果律: *the law of ~ity,* eg cause always precedes effect. 因果律(如先因後果)。**cau·sa·tion** /kɔːˈzeɪʃn ; kɔˈzeʃən/ *n* [U] ~ity; causing or being caused. 因果關係;起因;造因。**cau·sa·tive** /ˈkɔːzətɪv ; ˈkɔzətɪv/ *adj* acting as, expressing, cause. 爲…之起因的;表示原因的。

cause /kɔːz ; kɔz/ *n* **1** [C, U] that which produces an effect; thing, event, person, etc, that makes sth happen: 原因;導致某事發生之物、事、人等;起因;緣由: *The ~ of the fire was carelessness.* 起火的原因是不謹愼。*We can't get rid of war until we get rid of the ~s of war.* 我們不能消滅戰爭,除非我們先消滅戰爭的起因。 **2** [U] reason: 理由: *There is no ~ for anxiety.* 沒有理由要焦慮。*You have no ~ for complaint/no ~ to complain.* 你沒有理由抱怨。*Don't stay away without good ~.* 不要無故缺席或離開。 **3** [C] purpose for which efforts are being made: 努力的目的;主義;目標;道: *work in/for a good ~;* 爲高尚的目標而工作; *fight in the ~ of justice.* 爲正義而戰。***make common ~ with sb,*** help and support him (in a political, social, etc movement). (在政治、社會等運動中)幫助並支持某人。 □ *vt* [VP6A, 17, 12A, 13A] be the ~ of; make happen: 引起;致令;使發生;爲…之因: *What ~s the tides?* 潮汐的原因爲何? *What ~d his death?* 他的死因爲何? *You've ~d trouble to all of us.* 你給我們大家都惹來了麻煩。 *This has ~d us much anxiety.* 這事使我們極爲擔心。*What ~d the plants to die?* (*What made them die* is more usual.) 那些植物係死於何種原因? (What made them die 較常用。) *He ~d the prisoners to be put to death.* (*He had them put to death* is more usual.) 他使囚犯們被處死。(He had them put to death 較常用。) **~-less** *adj* without any natural or known ~. 無緣無故的;無自然或已知之理由的。

caus·erie /ˈkəʊzərɪ ; ˌkozəˈri/ *n* informal discussion. 非正式的討論;閒談;漫談;隨筆。

cause·way /ˈkɔːzweɪ ; ˈkɔzˌwe/ *n* raised road or footpath, esp across wet land or swamp. (尤指濕地或沼澤中的)堤道;砌道。

caus·tic /ˈkɔːstɪk ; ˈkɔstɪk/ *adj* **1** able to burn or destroy by chemical action. 腐蝕性的;苛性的。~ **soda** *n* (*Sodium Hydroxide* /haɪˈdrɒksaɪd ; haɪˈdraksaɪd/ **NaOH**) corrosive chemical substance used in the manufacture of soap. (用以製肥皂之)苛性鈉。 **2** (fig) biting; sarcastic: (喩)刻薄的;譏諷

的: ~ *remarks;* 刻薄話; *a ~ manner.* 譏諷的態度。 **caus·ti·cally** /-klɪ ; -klɪ/ *adv*

cau·ter·ize /ˈkɔːtəraɪz ; ˈkɔtəˌraɪz/ *vt* [VP6A] burn (eg a poisoned wound, a snake-bite) with a caustic substance or with a hot iron (to destroy infection). (用腐蝕性物質或烙鐵)炙燒;燒灼(如中毒傷口、蛇咬)以消毒;烙。

cau·tion /ˈkɔːʃn ; ˈkɔʃən/ *n* **1** [U] taking care; paying attention (to avoid danger or making mistakes): 小心;謹慎(以免危險或犯錯): *When crossing a busy street we must use ~.* 穿越熱鬧的街道時,我們必須小心。 **2** [C] warning words: 警告;提醒注意的話: *A sign with 'DANGER!' on it is a ~.* 書有'危險'的牌子就是一個警告。 *The judge gave the prisoner a ~ and set him free.* 法官警告那犯人一番就把他釋放了。 **3** (*sing* with *indef art*) (sl) person whose appearance, behaviour or conversation causes amusement. (單數與不定冠詞連用)(俚)外貌、行動或談話使人發噱的人。□ *vt* [VP6A, 17, 14] ~ ***(against),*** give a ~ to: 予以警告: *I ~ed him against being late.* 我曾警告他不要遲到。 *We were ~ed not to drive fast.* 我們曾受警告勿開快車。 *The judge ~ed the prisoner,* warned and reproved him. 法官警告並責備那犯人。 **~·ary** /ˈkɔːʃənrɪ *US:* ˈkɔːʃənerɪ ; ˈkɔʃənˌɛrɪ/ *adj* conveying advice or warning: 表達忠告或警告的: *~ary tales.* 警世的故事。

cau·tious /ˈkɔːʃəs ; ˈkɔʃəs/ *adj* having or showing caution: 小心的;謹愼的: *~ about / of giving offence;* 愼防得罪人; *~ not to give offence.* 小心不得罪人。 **~·ly** *adv*

cav·al·cade /ˌkævlˈkeɪd ; ˌkævl̩ˈked/ *n* [C] company or procession of persons on horseback or in carriages. 一隊騎馬或坐馬車的人;一隊人馬;馬車行列。

cava·lier /ˌkævəˈlɪə(r) ; ˌkævəˈlɪr/ *n* **1** (old use) horseman or knight. (舊用法)騎士;武士。 **2** (in the Civil War, England, 17th c) supporter of Charles I. (十七世紀英國內戰中)擁護查理一世者;保王黨人。□ *adj* (of a person) without due seriousness; offhand; discourteous. (指人)隨便的;不禮貌的;失禮的。 **~·ly** *adv*

cav·alry /ˈkævlrɪ ; ˈkævl̩rɪ/ *n* (usu with *pl v*, collective) soldiers who fight on horseback: (通常與複數動詞連用,集合用法) 騎兵; 騎兵部隊: (attrib) (形容用法) *~ soldier / officer.* 騎兵(騎兵軍官)。

cave /keɪv ; kev/ *n* hollow place in the side of a cliff or hill; large natural hollow under the ground. (山崖邊的)穴洞; (地下的)天然大穴洞。 **ˈ~-dweller** *n* person living in a ~, esp in prehistoric times. (尤指史前時代之)穴居者。 **ˈ~·man** /-mæn ; -mæn/ *n* (*pl* -men) ~ dweller; (colloq) man of primitive instincts and behaviour. 穴居者;(俗)有原始人本能及行爲之人;野蠻人;粗野的人。□ *vi, vt* [VP2C, 15B] ***~ in,*** (cause to) fall in, give way to pressure: (使)凹陷;塌陷;陷落: *The roof of the tunnel ~d in.* 隧道的頂塌陷了。Hence, 由此產生, **ˈ~-in** *n*

ca·veat /ˈkeɪvɪæt ; ˈkevɪˌæt/ *n* **1** (legal) process to suspend proceedings. (法律)中止訴訟程序之申請。 **2** (formal) qualification; proviso: (正式用語)條件;限制: *put in / enter a ~ (against).* 申請中止(對…之)訴訟。

cav·ern /ˈkævən ; ˈkævən/ *n* (liter) cave. (文)洞穴。 **~·ous** *adj* like a ~; full of ~s; (of a person's eyes) deepset. 如洞穴的;多洞穴的;(指人的眼睛)深陷的。

caviar, cavi·are /ˈkævɪɑː(r) ; ˌkævɪˈɑr/ *n* [U] pickled roe (eggs) of the sturgeon or certain other large fish. (鱣魚或某些其他大魚魚子所做的)魚子醬。 ***~ to the general,*** too fine or delicate to be appreciated by ordinary people. 過於高雅因而不能爲一般人所欣賞;曲高和寡。

cavil /ˈkævl ; ˈkævl̩/ *vi* (-ll-, US also -l-) [VP2A, 3A] ***~ (at),*** (formal) make unnecessary complaints against, find fault with. (正式用語)無端指摘;(對…)吹毛求疵。

cav·ity /ˈkævətɪ ; ˈkævətɪ/ *n* (*pl* -ties) empty space; small hole, within a solid body: (固體物中的)洞;腔;窩: *a ~ in a tooth;* 齒腔;齲齒或蛀牙所造之洞; *~ walls,* hollow, to provide insulation. 空壁(起絕緣作用的中空的牆壁)。

ca·vort /kəˈvɔːt ; kəˈvɔrt/ *vi* (colloq) prance or jump about like an excited horse. (俗)(像一匹受刺激的馬般地)跳躍;騰躍。

caw /kɔː ; kɔ/ *n* cry of a raven, rook or crow. 烏鴉的叫聲。□ *vi, vt* **1** [VP2A] make this cry. (烏鴉)叫;發出烏鴉的叫聲;哇哇地叫。 **2** [VP15B] ***caw out,*** utter in a cawing tone. 用似烏鴉叫的聲調說出;哇哇地說出。

cay·enne /keɪˈen ; kaɪˈɛn/ *n* (also 亦作 ~ /ˈkeɪen ; ˈkaɪɛn/ **ˈpepper**) [U] very hot kind of red pepper. 一種極辣的紅辣椒。

cay·man ⇨ caiman.

cease /siːs ; sis/ *vt, vi* [VP6A, D, 7A, 2A, 3A] ***~ (from),*** (formal) come or bring to an end; stop (the more usual word): (正式用語)停止;中止 (stop 較常用): *C~ fire* (=stop shooting)*!* 停止射擊! *The old German Empire ~d to exist in 1918.* 舊德意志帝國於 1918 年滅亡。 *The factory has ~d making bicycles.* 該工廠已停止製造脚踏車。 *Since he ~d (from) working,....* 他既然已停止不再工作,…。 **ˌ~-ˈfire** *n* signal to stop firing (guns); truce. 停火(戰)信號;休戰。□ *n* (only in) (僅用於) ***without ~,*** incessantly. 不斷地;不停地。 **~·less** *adj* never ending. 永不休止的。 **~·less·ly** *adv*

cedar /ˈsiːdə(r) ; ˈsidə/ *n* [C] evergreen tree with hard, red, sweet-smelling wood used for making boxes, pencils, fences, etc; [U] the wood: 西洋杉;香柏(一種常綠樹,木質甚堅,紅色,有香味,用製盒子、鉛筆、籬笆等);香柏木: *a ~ cigar box.* 香柏木雪茄烟盒。

cede /siːd ; sid/ *vt* [VP6A, 14] ***~ (to),*** give up (rights, land, etc to another state, etc). 割讓;讓(權利、土地等)給(另一國家等)。

ce·dilla /sɪˈdɪlə ; sɪˈdɪlə/ *n* mark put under the c (ç) in the spelling of some French, Spanish and Portuguese words (as in *façade*) to show that the sound is /s/. (某些法文、西班牙文及葡萄牙文字中)字母c下面的一撇 (ç) (如 façade, 以表示該字母 c 讀作 /s/)。

ceil·ing /ˈsiːlɪŋ ; ˈsilɪŋ/ *n* **1** top inner surface of a room. 天花板;平頂。 **2** cloud level; highest (practicable) level (to be) reached by an aircraft: 雲幕高度;一架飛機所(能)飛的最高限度;升限: *an aircraft with a ~ of 20 000 ft.* 一架能飛兩萬呎高的飛機。 **3** maximum height, limit or level: 最高限度;最高度: *price ~s;* 最高的限價; *wage ~s.* 最高的工資。

cel·an·dine /ˈseləndaɪn ; ˈsɛlənˌdaɪn/ *n* small, wild plant with yellow flowers. 白屈菜(小野生菜,開黃花)。

cel·ebrant /ˈselɪbrənt ; ˈsɛləbrənt/ *n* priest who leads the service of the Mass. 天主教主領彌撒之神父。

cel·ebrate /ˈselɪbreɪt ; ˈsɛləˌbret/ *vt* [VP6A, but with the *direct object* sometimes to be understood] (屬動詞 6A 型,但直接受詞有時省略) **1** do sth to show that a day or an event is important, or an occasion for rejoicing: 慶祝;祝賀: *~ Christmas / one's birthday / a wedding anniversary / a victory;* 慶祝聖誕節(某人的生日,結婚紀念日,勝利); *~ Mass,* lead the ceremony of the Eucharist. 主領彌撒。 *It's your birthday tomorrow, so we must celebrate (it).* 明天是你的生日,所以我們必須慶祝(它)。 **2** praise and honour: 褒揚;讚揚;稱頌: *The names of many heroes are ~d by the poets.* 許多英雄的名字爲詩人所歌頌。 **cel·ebrated** (*pp* as *adj*) famous: (過去分詞作形容詞用)著名的: *a ~d painter;* 一位著名的畫家; *~d for its hot springs;* 以其溫泉著稱的; *~d as a hot spring resort.* 以溫泉勝地著稱。 **cel·ebra·tion** /ˌselɪˈbreɪʃn ; ˌsɛləˈbreʃən/ *n* [C, U] (the act of, an occasion of) celebrating. 慶祝(之活動或場合);慶祝會;慶典。 **ce·leb·rity** /sɪˈlebrətɪ ; səˈlɛbrətɪ/ *n* **1** [U] being ~d; fame and honour. 著名;名望;名聲。 **2** [C] (*pl* -ties) ~d person: 名人;聞人: *all the celebrities of the London theatre,* all the famous actors and actresses performing in

London. 倫敦戲劇界所有的名人(指在倫敦演戲之所有著名的男女演員)。

ce·ler·ity /sɪ'lerətɪ ; 'sələrətɪ/ *n* [U] (formal) quickness. (正式用語)敏捷;迅速。

cel·ery /'selərɪ ; 'sɛlərɪ/ *n* [U] garden plant of which the stems are eaten raw as salad or cooked as a vegetable: 芹菜(莖可生吃或熟吃): *a bunch/stick/head of ~*; 一束(一根、一棵)芹菜; *~ soup*. 芹菜湯。

ce·les·tial /sɪ'lestɪəl *US:* -tʃl ; sə'lɛstʃəl/ *adj* **1** of the sky; of heaven: 天空的;天上的: *~ bodies*, eg the sun and the stars; 天體(如太陽及星辰); *~ joys*. 天堂之樂。 **2** divinely good or beautiful. 極美的;極佳的。

celi·bacy /'selɪbəsɪ ; 'sɛləbəsɪ/ *n* [U] state of living unmarried, esp as a religious obligation. 獨身;獨身狀態;獨身生活(尤指出於宗教上之承諾者)。**celi·bate** /'selɪbət ; 'sɛləbɪt/ *n* [C] unmarried person (esp a priest who has taken a vow not to marry). 獨身者(尤指發誓不結婚的神父)。

cell /sel ; sɛl/ *n* **1** small room for one person (esp in a prison or a monastery). 供一人住的小室;(尤指監獄裏的)小囚房;(修道院裏的)密室。 **2** compartment in a larger structure, esp in a honeycomb. 較大結構物中的小間隔;(尤指蜂巢中的)小蜂窩。 ⇨ the illus at honeycomb. 參看 honeycomb 之插圖。 **3** unit of an apparatus for producing electric current by chemical action, eg of metal plates in acid, often part of a battery. 電池(通常以金屬片置於酸中,藉化學作用產生電流的裝置,通常為 battery 之一部份)。 **4** microscopic unit of living matter enclosing a nucleus with self-producing genes. (生物的) 細胞 (包含一細胞核,帶有自生能力的遺傳因子)。 **5** (of persons) centre or nucleus of (usu revolutionary) political activity: (指人) (通常指革命的) 政治活動小組: ***communist ~s in an industrial town***. 共產黨在一工業城中的活動小組。

cel·lar /'selə(r) ; 'sɛlɚ/ *n* underground room for storing coal, wine, etc; (person's) store of wine. 貯藏煤、酒等的地下室;地窖;(某人)所貯藏的酒。 **~·age** /'selərɪdʒ ; 'sɛlərɪdʒ/ *n* amount of ~ space; charge for storing sth in a ~. 地窖的容積;藏物於地窖中的貯藏費。

cello /'tʃeləʊ ; 'tʃɛlo/ *n* (*pl* ~s) bass violin, held between the player's knees, ⇨ the illus at string. 大提琴;低音提琴(參看 string 之插圖)。 **cel·list** /'tʃelɪst ; 'tʃɛlɪst/ *n* ~ player. 大提琴手。

cel·lo·phane /'seləfeɪn ; 'sɛlə,fen/ *n* [U] (P) thin, moistureproof, transparent material used for wrapping and packing. (商標) (包裝用之薄而防濕的透明的)玻璃紙。

cel·lu·lar /'seljʊlə(r) ; 'sɛljəlɚ/ *adj* **1** consisting of cells (4): 由細胞組成的: *~ tissue*. 細胞組織。 **2** (of textile materials) loosely woven: (指織物) 鬆織的: *~ shirts*. 鬆織布料做成的襯衫。

cel·lu·loid /'seljʊlɔɪd ; 'sɛljə,lɔɪd/ *n* [U] (P) flammable plastic substance used for making toys, toilet articles, etc (and formerly for photographic film). (商標) 賽璐珞 (一種易著火的可塑物質,用以製玩具、化粧用具等,昔時用以製照相底片)。

cel·lu·lose /'seljʊləʊs ; 'sɛljə,los/ *n* [U] **1** structural tissue that forms the chief part of all plants and trees, and hence of paper and many textile fibres; wood fibre. 細胞膜質(構成一切花草、樹木以及紙和織物纖維之主要部分的結構組織); 纖維素; 纖維質。 **2** (popularly, for ,~ '*acetate*) plastic substance used for many industrial purposes (eg explosives, ornaments, toughened glass). (cellulose acetate 的俗稱) 醋酸纖維素(作許多工業用途的可塑物質,如製炸藥、裝飾品、韌玻璃)。

Celsius /'selsɪəs ; 'sɛlsɪəs/ *n* (of thermometers) (指溫度計) = centigrade.

Celt /kelt *US:* selt ; sɛlt/ *n* member of the last group of immigrants to settle in Britain before the coming of the Anglo-Saxons; (loosely) one of the Irish, Welsh, Gaelic or Breton people today. 克爾特人 (亦譯作塞爾特人;在盎格魯撒克遜人來到之前,最後一批移民而定居於英國的人;廣義指現今之愛爾蘭人,威爾斯人,蓋爾人或不列塔尼人)。 **~ic** *n, adj* (language) of the ~s. 克爾特人的;克爾特語。

ce·ment /sɪ'ment ; sə'mɛnt/ *n* [U] **1** grey powder (made by burning lime and clay) which, after being wetted, becomes hard like stone and is used for building, etc. 水門汀;水泥(用石灰及黏土燒製成之灰色粉末,加水即變堅硬如石,用以蓋房子等)。⇨ concrete. '**~-mixer** *n* revolving drum in which ~ is mixed with other material to make concrete. 水泥混合機;混凝土混合機 (旋轉的鼓形容器,水泥在其中與其他物質拌合而成混凝土)。 **2** any similar soft substance that sets firm, used for filling holes (eg in the teeth), or for joining things. 用以填洞,如填於牙齒中,或黏接物件之任何能凝固之類似水泥的軟物質;堊質;接合劑。 □ *vt* [VP6A, 15B] put ~ on or in; join with ~; (fig) strengthen; unite firmly: 加水泥於;用堊質填;用接合劑黏接; (喻) 加强;團結;使強固: *~ a friendship*. 鞏固友誼。

cem·etery /'semətrɪ *US:* 'seməterɪ ; 'sɛmə,tɛrɪ/ *n* (*pl* -ries) area of land, not a churchyard, used for burials. 墓地(非指毗連教堂者);公墓。

ceno·taph /'senətɑ:f *US:* -tæf ; 'sɛnə,tæf/ *n* monument put up in memory of a person or persons buried elsewhere. (為葬於別處之死者所立之)紀念碑。

cen·ser /'sensə(r) ; 'sɛnsɚ/ *n* vessel in which incense is burnt in churches. (教堂中之)香爐。

cen·sor /'sensə(r) ; 'sɛnsɚ/ *n* **1** official with authority to examine letters, books, periodicals, plays, films, etc and to cut out anything regarded as immoral or in other ways undesirable, or, in time of war, helpful to the enemy. 新聞檢查員(有權檢查信件、書籍、期刊、劇本、影片等並刪去其中被認為不道德或在其他方面不當,或在戰時有利於敵方之部份)。 **2** (ancient Rome) officer who prepared a register or census of citizens and supervized public morals. (古羅馬之) 監察官 (負責登記及調查市民並監督公眾道德行為者)。 □ *vt* [VP6A] examine, cut out, parts of (a book, etc); act as a ~. 檢查並刪剪(書籍等)之部份。 **~·ship** /-ʃɪp ; -,ʃɪp/ *n* function or duties of a ~. 新聞檢查員的職責;新聞書刊等之檢查。

cen·sori·ous /sen'sɔ:rɪəs ; sɛn'sorɪəs/ *adj* fault-finding; severely critical: 吹毛求疵的;嚴苛批評的: *~ of one's neighbours*. 嚴苛批評鄰居的。

cen·sure /'senʃə(r) ; 'sɛnʃɚ/ *vt* [VP6A, 14] **~ sb *(for)***, criticize unfavourably for: (為某事)批評某人;責難;非難;責備: *~ sb for being lazy*. 責備某人懶惰。□ *n* [U] rebuke; disapproval: 責備;責難;非難;不贊成: *pass a vote of ~ (on sb)*; 通過(對某人的)不信任投票; *lay oneself open to public ~*; 給人以責難的口實; [C] expression of disapproval: 非難的言詞: *a review containing unfair ~s of a new book*. 對某一新書肆意攻訐的一篇評論。

cen·sus /'sensəs ; 'sɛnsəs/ *n* (*pl* ~es) official counting of the population. (官方的) 人口統計; 人口調查; 戶口調查。

cent /sent ; sɛnt/ *n* the 100th part of a US dollar and many other metric units of currency; metal coin of this value. 一分錢(美金一元或其他十進制貨幣單位之百分之一);價值一分錢的硬幣。 ***per ~***, (%) in, by or for, every 100. 百分率;百分之…。 ***(agree, etc) one hundred per ~***, completely. 百分之百地(贊成,同意等);完全地。

cen·taur /'sentɔ:(r) ; 'sɛntɔr/ *n* (Gk myth) fabulous creature, half man and half horse. (希神)半人半馬怪物。⇨ the illus at Minotaur. 參看 Minotaur之插圖。

cen·ten·ar·ian /,sentɪ'neərɪən ; ,sɛntə'nɛrɪən/ *n, adj* (person who is) 100 or more years old. 一百歲或百歲以上的(老人);人瑞。

cen·ten·ary /sen'ti:nərɪ *US:* 'sentənerɪ ; 'sɛntə,nɛrɪ/ *adj, n* (*pl* -ries) (having to do with a) period of 100 years; 100th anniversary. 一百年(的);百年紀念。

cen·ten·nial /sen'tenɪəl ; sɛn'tɛnɪəl/ *adj, n* = cen-

tenary. **~·ly** /-nɪəlɪ ; -nɪəlɪ/ *adv*
cen·ter /'sentə(r) ; 'sɛntɚ/ *n* (US) = centre.
centi- /'sentɪ ; 'sɛntɪ/ *pref* one-hundredth part of: 表"百分之一"之義: *~gram,* 公毫(百分之一克), *~metre.* 公分(百分之一米)。⇨ App 5. 參看附錄五。
cen·ti·grade /'sentɪgreɪd ; 'sɛntə,gred/ *adj* in or of the temperature scale that has 100 degrees between the freezing-point and the boiling-point of water: 攝氏寒暑表(自水之冰點至沸點爲100度)的: *the ~ thermometer;* 攝氏寒暑表; 攝氏溫度計; *100° ~* (100°C). 攝氏100度。⇨ Fahrenheit and App 5. 參看 Fahrenheit 及附錄五。
cen·time /'sɒnti:m ; 'sɑntim/ *n* the 100th part of a franc. 生丁(一法郎之百分之一)。
cen·ti·pede /'sentɪpi:d ; 'sɛntə,pid/ *n* small insect-like crawling creature with a long, thin body, numerous joints, and a pair of feet at each joint. 蜈蚣(似昆蟲之爬行小動物,體細長,多節,每節有足一對)。
cen·tral /'sentrəl ; 'sɛntrəl/ *adj* **1** of, at, from or near, the centre: 中央的;中心的;在中心的;自中心的;近中心的: *My house is very ~,* is in or near the middle of the town. 我的家非常近市中心區。**~ heating,** method of warming a building by steam, hot air or water in pipes from a ~ source. 中央系統供暖(大建築物內用管將蒸汽、熱空氣或熱水自中心處輸至各部份之供暖方法);中央系統暖氣設備。 **2** chief; most important: 主要的;最重要的: *the ~ idea of an argument;* 一項議論的主要思想; *the ~ figures* (= the chief persons) *in a novel.* 小說的中心人物。**the ~ government** *n* that of the whole country. (全國的)中央政府。□ *n* (US) telephone exchange. (美)電話總機。**~·ly** /'sentrəlɪ ; 'sɛntrəlɪ/ *adv*
cen·tral·ize /'sentrəlaɪz ; 'sɛntrəl,aɪz/ *vt, vi* [VP6A, 2A] bring to the centre; come, put, bring, under central control: 集於中央;由中央統一管理;實行中央集權: *~ the administration of the coal mines.* 統一管理所有煤礦。 **cen·tral·iz·ation** /,sentrəlaɪ'zeɪʃn *US:* -lɪ'z- ; ,sɛntrələ'zeʃən/ *n*
centre (US = **center**) /'sentə(r) ; 'sɛntɚ/ *n* **1** middle part or point: 中心;中央;中心點: *the ~ of London;* 倫敦市的中心; *the ~ of a circle.* 圓心。⇨ the illus at circle. 參看 circle 之插圖。**~ of gravity,** that point in an object about which the weight is evenly balanced in any position. (物體的)重心。 **'~-bit,** tool for boring holes in wood. 三叉鑽頭。⇨ brace. **'~-board,** movable board that can be raised or lowered through a slot in the keel of a sailing-boat to prevent drifting to leeward. 垂板龍骨;船中板(帆船中可穿過龍骨上的槽而上升或放下之活動船板,以防船向下風漂流)。 **'~-piece,** ornament for the ~ of a table, ceiling, etc; (fig) most important part. (餐桌、天花板等的)中心裝飾;(喻)最重要部分。 **2** place of great activity, esp one to which people are attracted from surrounding districts or from which they go out: 活動極其繁多之地方;(尤指很多人來往的)中心區: *the 'shopping ~ of a town;* 一城市的購物中心區; *a ~ of commerce.* 商業中心。 **3** person or thing that attracts interest, attention etc: 引人興趣、注意的中心人物或事物: *She loves to be the ~ of interest.* 她喜歡成爲引人注意的中心人物。 **4** that which occupies a middle position, eg in politics, persons with moderate views, between two extremes. (政治上的)中立派;(兩極端之間的)中間派。□ *vt, vi* **1** [VP6A, 15A] place in, pass to, come to, be at, the ~: 置於中央;傳至中央;集中;在中央: *The defender ~d the ball.* 守衛者將球傳至中央。 **2** [VP3A, 14] *~ on/upon,* focus, fix, on: 集中於: *Our thoughts ~ upon/are ~d upon one idea.* 我們的思想集中於一個觀念。
cen·tri·fu·gal /sen'trɪfjugl ; sɛn'trɪfjugḷ/ *adj* moving, tending to move, away from the centre or axis: 離心的: *~ force,* the force which causes a body spinning round a centre to tend to fly off. 離心力(使繞一中心旋轉之物體有飛脫之勢的力量)。**cen·tri·fuge** /'sentrɪfju:dʒ ; 'sɛntrə,fjudʒ/ *n* (mech) ~ machine, eg for separating small solid particles in a liquid by rotating motion. (機械)離心分離機(例如藉旋轉使液體中之小固體粒子分離之機器)。
cen·tri·pe·tal /sen'trɪpɪtl ; sɛn'trɪpətḷ/ *adj* tending towards the centre or axis. 向心的;向軸心的。
cen·tur·ion /sen'tʃuərɪən *US:* -'tuər- ; sɛn'tjurɪən/ *n* (in ancient Rome) leader of a unit of 100 soldiers. (古羅馬的)百夫長(一隊一百名士兵的隊長)。
cen·tury /'sentʃərɪ ; 'sɛntʃərɪ/ *n* [C] (*pl* -ries) **1** 100 years. 一百年。 **2** one of the periods of 100 years before or since the birth of Jesus Christ: 世紀(指耶穌基督出生前或後每一百年之期間): *in the 20th ~,* AD 1900-1999. 在二十世紀中(卽自西元1900年至1999年)。 **3** (cricket) 100 runs made by a batsman in one innings: (板球)(擊球員在一局所得的)百分: *make/score a ~.* 得百分。
ce·ramic /sɪ'ræmɪk ; sə'ræmɪk/ *adj* of the art of pottery. 製陶術的。**ce·ram·ics** *n* **1** (*sing v*) art of making and decorating pottery. (用單數動詞)陶器製法;製陶術;陶藝。 **2** (*pl v*) articles made of porcelain, clay, etc. (用複數動詞)陶瓷製品。
cer·eal /'sɪərɪəl ; 'sɪrɪəl/ *n* (usu *pl*) any kind of grain used for food: (通常用複數)作食物用的任何穀物: *~ grasses,* eg wheat, rye, barley; 穀類禾本植物(如小麥、裸麥、大麥); food prepared from ~s: 用穀類調製成的食物: *'breakfast ~s.* 作爲早餐的麥粥。
cer·ebral /'serəbrəl *US:* sə'ri:brəl ; 'sɛrəbrəl/ *adj* **1** of the brain: 大腦的;腦的: *~ haemorrhage;* 腦出血;腦溢血; *~ palsy.* 腦麻痺;大腦性癱瘓。⇨ spastic. **2** intellectual; excluding the emotions. 智力的;智慧的;理智的。
cer·ebra·tion /,serɪ'breɪʃn ; ,sɛrə'breʃən/ *n* [U] (formal) working of the brain; thinking. (正式用語)大腦活動;思想;思考。
cer·emo·nial /,serɪ'məunɪəl ; ,sɛrə'monɪəl/ *adj* formal; as used for ceremonies: 正式的;用於典禮或儀式的: *~ dress.* 禮服。□ *n* [C, U] special order of ceremony, formality, for a special event, etc: 特殊的禮儀: *the ~s of religion.* 宗教禮儀。**~·ly** *adv*
cer·emo·ni·ous /,serɪ'məunɪəs ; ,sɛrə'monɪəs/ *adj* fond of, marked by, ceremony or formality. 好禮的;講究禮儀的;顯示禮儀的;隆重的。**~·ly** *adv*
cer·e·mo·ny /'serɪmənɪ *US:* -məunɪ ; 'sɛrə,monɪ/ *n* (*pl* -nies) **1** [C] special act(s), religious service, etc on an occasion such as a wedding, funeral,

cereals

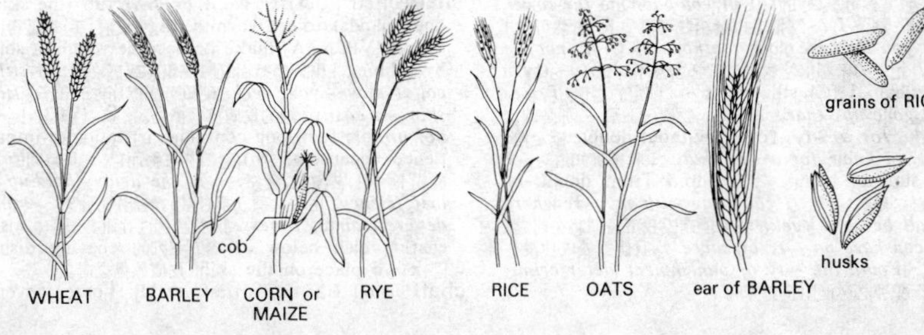

the opening of a new public building, etc. 典禮;儀式(如爲結婚、送葬、新公共建築物開幕等場合所擧行者)。ˌ**Master of ˈCeremonies** *n* person in charge of such formal proceedings. 司儀。 **2** [U] behaviour required by social customs, esp among officials, people of a special group, etc: (社會風俗所要求的) 禮節;禮貌 (尤指行於官員、特殊團體人士等之間者): *There's no need for ~ between friends.* 朋友之間不必拘禮。*There's too much ~ on official occasions.* 在正式的場合禮節太多。 ***stand on ~***, pay great attention to rules of behaviour: 極注意禮節;拘於禮節: *Please don't stand on ~*, please be natural and easy. 請勿拘禮;請不要客氣。

ce·rise /səˈriːz *US:* -iːs ; səˈriz/ *adj, n* (of a) light, clear red. 鮮紅色(的)。

cert /sɜːt ; sɝt/ *n* (sl) sth looked upon as certain to happen or that certainly has happened: (俚) 被認爲一定會發生之事;確已發生之事: *a dead ~*, an absolute certainty. 絕對確實的事情。

cer·tain /ˈsɜːtn ; ˈsɝtn̩/ *adj* **1** (pred only) settled; of which there is no doubt: (僅作敘述用法) 確定的;無疑的: *It is ~ that two and two make four.* 二加二得四是確定無疑的。 **2** (pred only) (僅作敘述用法) ***~ (that...); ~ (of/about); ~ to do sth***, convinced; having no doubt; confident: 確信的;無疑惑的;深信的: *I'm ~ (that) he saw me.* 我確信他看見了我。*I'm not ~ (of) who he is/where he went, etc.* 我不敢確說他是誰(他到哪裏去了,等)。 *You can be ~ of success.* 你一定會成功。*Are you ~ of/about that?* 你對那事確信無疑嗎? *He is ~ to come*, there is no doubt that he will come. 他一定會來。***for ~***, without doubt: 無疑地;確定地: *I cannot say for ~* (= with complete confidence) *when he will arrive.* 我不敢確定地說他將於何時到達。*I don't know for ~*, have no definite knowledge. 我不確切知道。***make ~***, **(a)** inquire in order to be ~: 弄清楚;弄明白;弄確實: *I think there's a train at 8.20 but you ought to make ~.* 我想在八點二十分有一班火車,不過你應該問清楚。 **(b)** do sth in order to be assured: 採取行動以便確有把握: *I'll go to the theatre and make ~ of our seats*, eg by reserving them in advance. 我要到戲院去把我們的座位訂好 (以便有把握到開演時有座位)。 **3** assured; reliable; sure to come or happen: 有把握的;可靠的;一定會來到或發生的: *There is no ~ cure for this disease.* 此病沒有可靠的治療藥物。*The soldier faced ~ death.* 那個士兵勇敢地面對必然來臨的死亡。 **4** (attrib only) not named, stated or described, although it is possible to do so: (僅作形容用法) (雖可指明或說明而) 未指明的;未說明的;某: *for a ~ reason;* 爲了某種理由; *on ~ conditions;* 附帶某些條件; *a ~ person I met yesterday;* 我昨天遇到的某一個人; *a person of a ~ age* (usu = *middle-aged*). 某一年齡的人(通常指中年人)。 **5** (attrib only) some, but not much: (僅作形容用法) 一些;一點;少許;多少: *There was a ~ coldness in her attitude towards me.* 她對我的態度有一點冷淡。*There is a ~ pleasure in pointing out other people's errors.* 指出他人的錯誤多少有點樂趣。 **~·ly** *adv* **1** without doubt: 無疑地;確定地: *He will ~ly die if you don't get a doctor.* 如果你請不到醫生,他一定會死的。 ⇨ surely. **2** (in answer to questions) yes: (用於回答問題) 當然可以;好的: *Will you pass me the towel, please? C~ly!* 請把毛巾遞給我可以嗎? 當然可以! *Will you lend me your toothbrush? C~ly not* (= No)! 把你的牙刷借給我可以嗎?當然不可以! **~·ty** *n* (*pl* -ties) **1** [C] sth that is ~: 確定的事情: *Prices have gone up—that's a ~ty.* 物價已上漲——那是確定的事情。 ***for a ~ty***, for ~, without doubt: 確定地;無疑地: *I know for a ~ty that....* 我確實知道…。 **2** [U] state of being ~; freedom from doubt: 確知;確信;確實;必然: *I can't say with any ~ty where I shall be next week.* 我不能確說我下星期將在何處。*We can have no ~ty of success.* 我們對於成功沒有把握。*Would the ~ty of punishment deter criminals?* 犯罪必懲能阻止犯罪嗎?

cer·ti·fi·able /ˌsɜːtɪˈfaɪəbl ; ˈsɝtəˌfaɪəbl̩/ *adj* that can be certified: 可證明的: *a ~ lunatic*, a person who can be certified by a doctor as insane. 可由醫生出具證明之精神錯亂者。

cer·ti·fi·cate /səˈtɪfɪkət ; səˈtɪfəkɪt/ *n* written or printed statement, made by sb in authority, that may be used as proof or evidence of sth: (由有關方面所出具的) 證明書: *a ˈbirth/ˈmarriage ~;* 出生(結婚)證書; *a ˈhealth ~*, from a doctor; (醫生所出具的) 健康證明書; *~ of origin*, (comm) document stating the country or origin of imported goods. (商) (進口貨品之) 原產地證明書。□ *vt* provide with a ~. 授證書予…。 **cer·ti·fi·cated** /-keɪtɪd ; -ˌketɪd/ *adj* having the right or authority to do sth as the result of obtaining a ~: 領有證書的;合格的: *~d teachers*, who have obtained teaching diplomas (now called 今稱作 *qualified teachers*). 檢定合格教員。 **cer·ti·fi·ca·tion** /ˌsɜːtɪfɪˈkeɪʃn ; ˌsɝtəfəˈkeʃən/ *n* [U] act of certifying; state of being certified; [C] that which certifies. 證明;被證明;證明書。

cer·tify /ˈsɜːtɪfaɪ ; ˈsɝtəˌfaɪ/ *vt, vi* **1** [VP6A,9,16B,25] declare (usu by giving a certificate) that one is certain of sth, that sth is true, correct, in order: (通常以出具證明書) 證明 (某事物是眞實、正確、合格的): *I ~ (that) this is a true copy of....* 玆證明本件確係…之副本。 *I ~ this as/to be a true copy of....* 玆證明本件確係…之副本。 *He was certified (as) insane*, The doctor(s) wrote a certificate declaring that he was insane. 他已由醫生出具證明書證明爲精神錯亂。 *The accounts were certified (as) correct.* 帳目業經查核證明無誤。 **certified cheque**, cheque the value of which is guaranteed by the bank. 保付支票(款額由銀行擔保之支票)。 **2** [VP3A] ***~ to sth***, attest it: 證明或保證某事物: *~ to sb's character*, declare that one is satisfied that it is reliable, etc. 證明某人之品格良好。

cer·ti·tude /ˈsɜːtɪtjuːd *US:* -tuːd ; ˈsɝtəˌtjud/ *n* [U] (formal) certainty (the more usu word). (正式用語) 確知;確信;確實;必然 (certainty 爲較常用字)。

ceru·lean /sɪˈruːlɪən ; səˈrulɪən/ *adj* (formal) sky-blue. (正式用語) 天藍色的;蔚藍色的。

cer·vix /ˈsɜːvɪks ; ˈsɝvɪks/ *n* (*pl* cervices /ˈsɜːvɪsiːz ; səˈvaɪsiz/ or ~es) (anat) narrow part of the womb. (解剖) 子宮頸。⇨ the illus at reproduce. 參看 reproduce 之插圖。 **cer·vi·cal** /sɜːˈvaɪkl *US:* ˈsɜːvɪkl ; ˈsɝvɪkl̩/ *adj* of the ~: 子宮頸的: *cervical smear*, smear taken from the ~, to test for cancer. 子宮頸塗片(取自子宮頸之塗片,用以檢驗子宮癌者)。

Cesar·ean = Caesarean.

ces·sa·tion /seˈseɪʃn ; sɛˈseʃən/ *n* [U] (formal) ceasing: (正式用語) 停止;中止;中斷: *the ~ of hostilities.* 戰爭的停止。

ces·sion /ˈseʃn ; ˈsɛʃən/ *n* [U] act of ceding (giving up lands, rights, etc by agreement); [C] sth ceded. 讓與;割讓土地;放棄權利;讓與或放棄之事物。

cess·pit /ˈsespɪt ; ˈsɛsˌpɪt/, **cess·pool** /ˈsespuːl ; ˈsɛsˌpul/ *nn* (usu covered) hole, pit or underground tank into which drains (esp for sewage) empty; (fig) filthy place. (通常有蓋之) 容納汚水的洞、坑或地下池;汚水池;汚水滲坑;糞坑;化糞池;(喻) 骯髒的地方;汚穢的場所。

chafe /tʃeɪf ; tʃef/ *vi, vt* **1** [VP6A] rub (the skin, one's hands) to get warmth. 摩擦(皮膚、手)以獲得溫暖。 **2** [VP2A,6A] make or become rough or sore by rubbing: 由於摩擦而(使)變粗糙或感疼痛: *A stiff collar may ~ your neck.* 硬領可能擦痛你的頸子。*Her skin ~s easily.* 她的皮膚容易擦傷。 **3** [VP3A] ***~ at/under***, feel long-continued irritation or impatience (because of sth): (因某事物而) 感到長時間的惱怒或不耐煩;被激怒;發怒: *~ at the delay/hold-up/inefficiency;* 由於此項耽誤(停頓,無能)而惱怒; *~ under restraints/illness.* 因受制(生病)而心煩。⇨ also chafing dish below. 亦參看下列的 chafing dish。 □ *n* ~d place on the skin. 皮膚擦傷之處。

chaff¹ /tʃɑːf *US:* tʃæf ; tʃæf/ *n* [U] **1** outer covering (husks) of grain, removed before the grain is used as human food. (穀物在食用前所去掉的)穀殼;糠。 **2** hay or straw cut up as food for cattle. (切碎作牛馬飼料用的)乾草;草料;秣。□ *vt* [VP6A] cut up (hay, straw). 切(乾草、稻草)。

chaff[2] /tʃɑːf *US:* tʃæf ; tʃæf/ *n* [U] good-humoured teasing or joking. 打趣;開玩笑。□ *vt, vi* [VP2A, C, 6A, 15A] make good-humoured fun (of): 打趣;開玩笑: ～ *sb about sth.* 爲某事開某人的玩笑。

chaf·finch /ˈtʃæfɪntʃ ; ˈtʃæfɪntʃ/ *n* small European song-bird. 鶸類;磧鶸(歐洲產小鳴鳥)。

chaf·ing dish /ˈtʃeɪfɪŋ dɪʃ ; ˈtʃefɪŋ dɪʃ/ *n* vessel with a heater under it, used at table for cooking food or keeping it warm. (餐桌上所用,下面附有火爐,用以煮或保持食物溫熱的)火鍋。

chag·rin /ˈʃægrɪn *US:* ʃəˈgriːn ; ʃəˈgrɪn/ *n* [U] feeling of disappointment or annoyance (at having failed, made a mistake, etc): (因失敗、犯錯等所生的)失望或厭煩之感;惱怒;懊惱: *Much to his ～, he did not win the race.* 他在賽跑中未能得勝使他大爲懊惱。□ *vt* [VP6A] (usu passive) affect with ～: (通常用被動語態)使懊惱;使煩悶: *be/feel ～ed at/by.* 因…而感煩悶。

chain /tʃeɪn ; tʃen/ *n* **1** flexible line of connected rings or links for connecting, continuing, restraining, ornamenting, etc, ⇨ the illus at bicycle; (*pl*) fetters of this kind, used for prisoners. (由若干圈環連接而成之可彎曲的)鏈子;鏈條(用以連接、接續、限制、裝飾等)(參看 bicycle 之挿圖);(複)(用於囚犯的)鐐銬。***in ～s,*** kept as a prisoner or slave. 被囚禁;爲奴隸。 **2** number of connected things, events, etc: 一系列;一連串(事物、事件等): *a ～ of mountains/ideas/events/proof.* 山脈(一系列的觀念;一連串的事件;一系列的證據)。 **3** measure of length (66 ft). 測鏈(長度單位,等於 66 呎)。⇨ App 5. 參看附錄五。**4** (compounds) (複合字) **ˈ～-armour/-mail,** armour made of metal rings linked together. 用金屬圈連接成的甲胄;鎖子甲。⇨ the illus at armour. 參看 armour 之挿圖。 **ˈ～-gang,** gang of convicts fastened together with ～s while at work outside their prison. 用鐵鏈繫在一起在監獄外面做工的一群囚犯。**ˈ～-letter,** letter of which the recipient is asked to make copies to be sent to other persons, who will do the same. 連鎖書信(要求收信人照抄若干份轉寄他人,而他人又同樣抄寄他人者)。**ˈ～ reaction,** chemical change forming products that themselves cause more changes so that the process is repeated again and again (as in the atomic bomb). 連鎖反應(變化之產物能引起更多變化之一連串化學反應,如原子彈中者)。 **ˈ～-smoker,** person who smokes cigarettes in continuous succession. 一支接一支地抽香煙的人。**ˈ～-stitch,** kind of sewing in which each stitch makes a loop through which the next stitch is taken. (每一針脚打一個圈由次一針脚穿入之)鏈形縫法;連鎖針脚。 **ˈ～-store,** one of many retail shops owned and controlled by the same company. 連鎖商店(由同一公司所經營管理的許多零售商店之一)。□ *vt* [VP6A,15A,B] make fast with a ～ or ～s: 用鐵鏈鎖住: *The prisoners were ～ed to the wall.* 囚犯們被鐵鏈鎖在牆上。*C～ up your dog.* 把你的狗用鏈子拴起來。

chair /tʃeə(r) ; tʃɛr/ *n* **1** separate movable seat for one person, usu with a back and in some cases with arms (*arm～*): 椅子(通常有靠背,有時並有扶手,卽 armchair): *Won't you take a ～,* sit down? 你不坐嗎? **ˈ～-lift** *n* aerial ropeway with seats for carrying persons up and down mountain slopes, etc. (運送人上下山坡之)空中吊椅。Cf 參較 *ski-lift.* ⇨ also electric, sedan. **2** [U] ***the ～,*** seat, office, of a person who presides at a meeting. (主持會議之)主席的席位或職位。 ***be in/take the ～,*** preside. 就任主席;主持開會。***leave the ～,*** end the proceedings. 閉會;結束會議。 **3** position of professor: 教授的職位;講座: *the C～ of Philosophy.* 哲學講座。□ *vt* [VP6A] **1** place in a ～, raise up and carry (sb who has won a contest): 置於椅中或轎中,舉起,並抬着走(指對於比賽中的得勝者): *The newly elected MP was ～ed by his supporters.* 那新當選的國會議員被支持他的人們用椅子抬着遊行。**2** preside over: 主持(會議): *～ a meeting.* 主持會議。 **ˈ～·man** /-mən ; -mən/ *n* (*pl* -men) person presiding at a meeting; president of a company or a committee: (主持開會的)主席;(公司之)董事長;(委員會之)主任委員: *～man's report,* annual report of a company, signed by the ～man and presented at the annual general meeting. (公司於年會中由董事長簽名提出之)年度報告。

chaise /ʃeɪz ; ʃez/ *n* low, two- or four-wheeled horse-carriage (formerly) used by people driving for pleasure. 一種二輪或四輪的低馬車(昔時供人駕駛以爲娛樂者)。**ˌ～ ˈlongue** /lɒŋ *US:* lɔːŋ; lɔŋg/ *n* (*pl* ～s longues, pronunciation unchanged 複數發音不變) (F) kind of long, low chair, with an arm at one side only, for lying on. (法)(一側有扶手的)躺椅。

chalet /ˈʃæleɪ ; ʃæˈle/ *n* Swiss mountain hut built of wood and with sharply sloping and overhanging roof; summer cottage built in the same style; small hut in a holiday camp, etc. 瑞士山中屋頂極爲傾斜而懸垂之木屋;同形式的夏季別墅;假期營地之小屋等。

chal·ice /ˈtʃælɪs ; ˈtʃælɪs/ *n* wine-cup, esp that used for the Eucharist. 酒杯;(尤指)聖餐杯。

chalices

chalk /tʃɔːk ; tʃɔk/ *n* **1** [U] soft, white, natural substance (a kind of limestone) used for making lime. 白堊(軟性白色天然物質,係石灰石之一種,用以製石灰)。**ˈ～·pit** *n* one from which ～ is dug. 白堊坑(挖掘白堊的坑洞)。 **2** [C, U] this material, or a material similar in texture, white or coloured, made into sticks for writing and drawing. (用白堊或類似物質製成之白色或彩色的)粉筆。⇨ blackboard. **3** ***as different as ～ and cheese; as like as ～ (is) to cheese,*** essentially unlike. 根本不同;實質不同。***by a ˈlong ～,*** by far, by much. (差得)很遠;…得多。 □ *vt* write, draw, mark, with ～; whiten with ～. 用白堊或粉筆寫、畫、作記號;用白堊塗白。 [VP15B] ～ ***sth up,*** write a score or record. 記分;記錄;記下。 **～y** *adj* of, containing, like, ～. 白堊的;含白堊的;似白堊的。

chal·lenge /ˈtʃælɪndʒ ; ˈtʃælɪndʒ/ *n* **1** invitation or call to play a game, run a race, have a fight, etc to see who is better, stronger, etc. 邀請比賽(以較量高低);挑戰(以定强弱等)。 **2** order given by a sentry to stop and explain who one is: (哨兵令人止步並說明身份的)口令: *'Who goes there?' is the ～.* '甚麼人?'便是哨兵的口令。□ *vt* [VP6A, 17, 14] ～ ***(to),*** give, send, be, a ～ to; ask for facts (to support a statement, etc): 向…挑戰;要求提出事實(以證明一項陳述等);提出異議;質問: *～ sb to a duel;* 向某人要求決鬥; *～ sb to fight;* 向某人挑戰; *～ sb's right to do sth;* 對某人作某事的權利提出異議; *～ a juryman,* (legal) object to his being a member of the jury. (法律)對一陪審員的身份提出異議(反對其爲陪審員)。**chal·lenger** *n* one who ～s. 挑戰者;質問者;詰難者。

cham·ber /ˈtʃeɪmbə(r) ; ˈtʃembɚ/ *n* **1** (old use) room, esp a bedroom. (舊用法)房間;室;(尤指)臥室。 **ˈ～ concert,** concert of ～ music. 室內樂演奏會。**ˌ～ of ˈhorrors,** place where gruesome objects are displayed. 展示恐怖物品的房間。 '~·**maid,** housemaid who keeps bedrooms in order (now chiefly in hotels). 清理臥室的女僕;(今主用以指旅館中)清理房間的女服務生。'~ **music,** music for a small number of players (eg a string quartet). 室內樂(由少數人演奏的音樂,例如弦樂四重奏)。'~-**pot,** vessel for urine, used in a bedroom. (臥室中所用之)尿壺;夜壺。 **2** (*pl*) judge's room for hearing cases that need not be taken into court; (not US) set of rooms in a large building to live in or to use as offices. (複) 法官辦公室; 內庭 (法官審訊不須上法庭之案件的小室); (不用於美國)大廈中供居住或辦公的一套房間。 **3** (hall used by a) group of legislators (eg in US, the Senate and the House of Representatives), often distinguished as the *'Upper C~* and the *'Lower C~*. 國會中的議院 (常分爲上議院及下議院, 如美國之參議院及衆議院);議院中的全體議員。 **4** offices of barristers, etc esp in the Inns of Court. 律師事務室(尤指倫敦之四法學協會中者)。 **5** group of persons organized for purposes of trade: 爲貿易目的所組織的團體: *a C~ of Commerce.* 商會。 **6** enclosed or walled space in the body of an animal or plant: (動植物體內的)窩;穴;室: *a ~ of the heart,* ⇨ auricle, ventricle; 心腔; similar cavity in some kinds of machinery; enclosed space in a gun (where a shell or cartridge is laid). (某些機器內部之)室;(槍砲之)藥室;彈膛。

cham·ber·lain /'tʃeɪmbəlɪn ; 'tʃembəlɪn/ *n* (old use) officer who manages the household of a king, noble, etc. (舊用法) (國王或貴族家中的)管家。

cha·me·leon /kə'miːlɪən ; kə'miliən/ *n* small long-tongued lizard whose colour changes according to its background, ⇨ the illus at reptile; person who changes his voice, manner, etc to match his surroundings. 變色蜥蜴; 避役 (能隨背景而變色的長舌小蜥蜴) (參看 reptile 之挿圖);能配合環境而改變聲音、態度等的人;善變的人。

chammy-leather /'ʃæmɪ leðə(r) ; 'ʃæmɪ 'lɛðɚ/ *n* = chamois-leather.

cham·ois /'ʃæmwɑː *US:* 'ʃæmɪ ; 'ʃæmɪ/ *n* small goat-like animal that lives in the high mountains of Europe and SW Asia. 臆羚(歐洲及亞洲西南部高山所產之小羚羊)。 ~-**leather** /'ʃæmɪ leðə(r) ; 'ʃæmɪ 'lɛðɚ/ *n* soft leather from the skin of goats and sheep. 雪米皮;麂皮;油鞣革(用山羊及綿羊皮所製的軟皮革)。

chamo·mile *n* (US) = camomile.

champ[1] /tʃæmp ; tʃæmp/ *vt, vi* [VP6A, 2A, C, 4A] **1** (of horses) bite (food, the bit) noisily. (指馬)大聲地嚼(食物,銜鐵)。 **2** (fig) show impatience: (喻)表示不耐煩: *~ with rage.* 大發雷霆;因憤怒而顯示忍無可忍之狀。 *The boys were ~ing to start/~ing at the bit.* 孩子們急於要出發(極不願受拘束)。

champ[2] /tʃæmp ; tʃæmp/ *n* (colloq abbr of) champion(2). (俗)冠軍(champion 之略)。

cham·pagne /ʃæm'peɪn ; ʃæm'pen/ *n* (kinds of) white sparkling (because charged with gas) French wine. 香檳酒(法國產之因充有氣體而起泡的白色葡萄酒)。

cham·pion /'tʃæmpɪən ; 'tʃæmpɪən/ *n*. **1** person who fights, argues or speaks in support of another or of a cause: 爲支持他人或某項運動而奮鬪、辯論或演說的人;支持者;贊助者;擁護者;提倡者;鬥士: *a ~ of free speech/of woman's rights.* 爲言論自由(女權)而奮鬪的人。 **2** person, team, animal, etc taking the first place in a competition: 冠軍(比賽中獲得第一名之個人、團體或動物): *a boxing/swimming/tennis, etc ~;* 拳擊(游泳、網球等)冠軍;(attrib): (形容用法): *the ~ team;* 冠軍隊; *the ~ horse.* (賽馬中獲得冠軍之)頭馬。□ *adj, adv* (colloq) splendid(ly): (俗)極好的(地): *That's ~!* 好極了! □ *vt* [VP6A] support; defend. 支持;衛護。~·**ship** /-ʃɪp ; -ˌʃɪp/ *n* [U] act of ~ing; [C] position of being, or competition to decide, a ~: 擁護;支持;衛護;優勝;冠軍的地位;冠軍賽;錦標賽: *to win a world swimming ~ship.* 贏得世界游泳冠軍。

chance[1] /tʃɑːns *US:* tʃæns ; tʃæns/ *n* **1** [U] the happening of events without any cause that can be seen or understood; the way things happen; fortune or luck: 事件之發生無可見或可瞭解之原因;機會;偶然;幸運;運氣: *Let's leave it to ~.* 我們就讓它聽其自然(聽憑機會)吧。 *Let ~ decide.* 聽憑機會決定吧。 ***by ~,*** by accident, not by design or on purpose. 偶然地;非預謀或故意地。 ***game of ~,*** one that is decided by luck, not by skill. 憑機會而不憑本領之遊戲。 ***take one's ~,*** trust to luck, take whatever happens to come. 碰運氣;冒險。 **2** [C,U] possibility: 可能性: *He has no ~/not much ~/a poor ~ of winning.* 他沒有可能(沒有多少可能,只有微小的可能)會贏。 *I've had no ~ to get away/of getting away.* 我一直沒有機會脫身。 *What ~ of success is there?* 成功的可能性如何? *What is our ~/are our ~s of succeeding?* 我們成功的可能性如何? *What are the ~s that we shall succeed?* 我們成功的可能性如何? *The ~s are a hundred to one against you,* It's most unlikely that you will succeed. 你只有百分之一成功的可能。 *If, by any ~,..., If, by some ~ or other...,* If it so happens that.... 如果湊巧…;萬一…。 ***on the (off) ~ that/of doing sth,*** in view of the possibility, in the hope: 也許能够(做到某事);希望能够(做某事);指望: *I'll call at his office on the ~ that I'll see/of seeing him before he leaves.* 我將到辦公室去訪他,希望能在他下班前見到他。 **3** [C] opportunity; occasion when success seems very probable: 機會;成功可能性極大的機遇: *This was the ~ he had been waiting for.* 那正是他一直在等待的機會。 *It's the ~ of a lifetime,* a favourable opportunity that is unlikely ever to come again. 這是一生中難得再遇到的機會。 ***stand a good/fair ~ (of...),*** have a fair prospect (of sth). 大(頗)有…希望。 **the ˌmain '~** *n* opportunity of making money: 賺錢的機會: *He always has an eye to the main ~,* sees when money can be made. 他總在注意賺錢的機會。 **4** (attrib) coming or happening by ~(1): (形容用法)偶然的: *a ~ meeting;* 偶然的相遇; *a ~ companion.* 萍水相逢的友伴。

chance[2] /tʃɑːns *US:* tʃæns ; tʃæns/ *vi, vt* **1** [VP3A] ***~ on/upon,*** find or meet by chance. 偶然發現;偶然遇到。[VP4E, 2A, after *it* 用於 it 之後] happen by chance: 偶然發生;恰巧: *I ~d to be there.* 我恰巧在那裏。 *It ~d that I was out/I ~d to be out when he called.* 他來訪時適逢我不在家。 **2** [VP6A, C] take a risk, 冒險, esp (尤用於) ***~ it; ~ one's arm,*** (colloq) take a chance of success although failure is probable. (俗)雖極可能失敗而仍然試圖獲得成功;冒險一試。

chan·cel /'tʃɑːnsl *US:* 'tʃænsl ; 'tʃænsl̩/ *n* eastern part of a church, round the altar, used by the priest(s) and choir. 聖壇(教堂中靠東端繞着聖壇的部份,爲神父或牧師及唱詩班所在的地方)。⇨ the illus at church. 參看 church 之挿圖。

chan·cel·lery /'tʃɑːnsəlrɪ *US:* 'tʃæns- ; 'tʃænsələrɪ/ *n* (*pl* -ries) **1** chancellor's position, department or residence. 大臣的職位、部、府或官邸。 **2** place of business of an embassy, legation or consulate. 大使館、公使館或領事館的辦公處。

chan·cel·lor /'tʃɑːnsələ(r) *US:* 'tʃæns- ; 'tʃænsəlɚ/ *n* **1** (in some countries, eg W Germany) chief minister of state. (某些國家,如西德)總理; 首相; 國務大臣。 **2** (of some universities) titular head or president (the duties being performed by the Vice-C~) (某些大學的) 名義上的校長 (其職務由副校長負責)。 **3** (GB) chief secretary of an embassy. (英) (大使館的) 一等秘書。 **4** State or law official of various kinds: 大臣; 法官: *the Lord C~ of England, the Lord High C~,* the highest judge (and chairman of the House of Lords); 英國的大法官(最高之法官,兼上議院議長); *the C~ of the Exchequer.* 財政大臣。

chan·cery /'tʃɑːnsərɪ *US:* 'tʃæns- ; 'tʃænsərɪ/ *n* (*pl* -ries) **1** (GB) Lord Chancellor's division of the

High Court of Justice. (英)大法官廳(高等法院中之一部份)。***ward in ~,*** person (usu a *minor* (*n*)) whose affairs are in the charge of the Lord Chancellor (eg because of the death of the ward's parents). 受大法官監護的人(如未成年孤兒)。**2** (US) court of equity for those cases with no remedy in common law. (美)衡平法院(處理習慣法不能解決之案件)。**3** office of public records. 檔案處。**4** = chancellery(2).

chancy /ˈtʃɑːnsɪ *US:* ˈtʃænsɪ ; ˈtʃænsɪ/ *adj* (colloq) risky; uncertain. (俗)冒險的;不可靠的。

chan·de·lier /ˌʃændəˈlɪə(r) ; ˌʃændḷˈɪr/ *n* ornamental branched holder (usu hanging from the ceiling) for a number of lights. 裝飾性的燈架(有分枝,通常懸於天花板上,可裝數枝燈者);枝形吊燈架。

chan·dler /ˈtʃɑːndlə(r) *US:* ˈtʃænd- ; ˈtʃændlɚ/ *n* **1** person who makes or sells candles, oil, soap, paint, etc. 製造或販賣蠟燭、油類、肥皂、漆等之商人。**2** ***ship's ~,*** dealer in canvas, ropes and other supplies for ships. 販賣船上用具(如帆布、索具等)之商人。

change¹ /tʃeɪndʒ ; tʃendʒ/ *vt, vi* **1** [VP6A,14,2A] ~ ***(from/out of) (to/into); ~ (for),*** leave one place and go to, enter, another; take off sth and put sth else on: 換(掉);換(上);更換;更(衣);改換: *I must ~ these trousers—they've got oil on them.* 我必須換條褲子——褲子上沾了油。*It won't take me five minutes to ~,* to put on different clothes. 我換衣服不需要五分鐘。*He ~d out of his overalls (and into a suit).* 他換掉了工作褲(換上了一套西服)。*He ~ed his overalls (for a suit).* 他脫下工作褲(換上一套西服。*We seldom ~ for dinner,* eg seldom ~ into formal evening dress. 我們很少爲了進晚餐而換上晚禮服。*I've ~d my address,* moved to a different house, flat, etc. 我的住址改變了。*The house has ~d hands several times,* has been bought and sold several times. 此屋曾數度易手(易主)。~ ***(trains),*** leave one train and get into another during a journey: 換火車(在旅程中由甲車轉至乙車): *~ (trains) at Crewe for Stockport.* 在克儒換火車前往史塔克波特。*Where do we ~?* 我們在哪裏換車? *All ~!* (a cry heard at stations when a train is going no further). 所有旅客一律換車!(在火車站當一列車不再前進時所聽到的報告聲)。~ ***up/down,*** (motoring) change to a higher/lower gear. (汽車駕駛)改爲高(低)擋。**2** [VP6A,14] ***~ sth (for/into sth else),*** give and receive in return: 兌換;互換;付出(某物)並收回(他物): *Can you ~ this five-pound note,* give me notes and/or coins of smaller denominations? 你能兌換這張五鎊的鈔票(換成小額鈔票或硬幣)嗎? *He ~d his Italian money before leaving Rome.* 他在離開羅馬前已將義大利錢幣兌換掉了。*Shall we ~ seats?* 我們換換座位好不好? *I ~d places with her.* 我與她互換位置。*He ~d his car for a foreign make.* 他換了一部外國廠牌的車。**3** [VP6A, 14, 2A, C] ~ ***(from) (into/to),*** make or become different: (使)變成不同的;改變;變化: *That has ~d my ideas.* 那使我變了主意。*My plans have ~d.* 我的計畫已經改變了。*Caterpillars ~ into butterflies or moths.* 毛蟲會變成蝴蝶或蛾。*The traffic lights ~d from red to green.* 那交通指示燈從紅色變成綠色。*You've ~d since I last saw you.* 自從我上次見你以後你已變了。~ ***over (from) (to),*** abandon an old system and take up a new one: 從(舊的)變成(新的): *the country has ~ed over from military to democratic rule.* 該國已從軍政變成憲政。Hence, 由此產生, **ˈ~-over** *n.* ~ ***one's mind,*** decide on a new plan, have a new opinion, etc. 改變主意。~ ***one's note/tune,*** become more humble, sad, etc. 改變態度(變得更爲謙卑、憂愁等)。~ ***step,*** (when marching with a group) march so that the other foot is keeping time (eg with the beat of a drum). (在團體行軍時)換步(以便使另一足合着節拍,如踏着鼓音)。**~·able** *adj* likely to alter; often altering; able to be ~d: 易變的;常變的;能被改變的: *~able weather;* 多變的天氣; *a ~able sort of person,* one whose moods often ~. 喜怒無常的人;善變的人。**~·able·ness** *n*

change² /tʃeɪndʒ ; tʃendʒ/ *n* **1** [C] changed or different condition(s); sth used in place of another or others; move from one place to another: 變化後的情況;不同的情況;代替物;從一地移至另一地;換車: *a welcome ~ from town to country life.* 令人舒暢的從城市生活改變到鄉村生活的情況。*We have a new house—it's a great ~ for the better.* 我們有了一棟新房子——一切變得好多了。*Take a ~ of clothes with you,* extra clothes to ~ into. 帶一套換洗的衣服。*He had to make a quick ~* (ie of trains) *at Crewe.* 他不得不在克儒匆忙換車(如換另一列車)。 ***a ~ of air/climate,*** eg a holiday away from home. 換換空氣(氣候)(例如離家度假)。***ring the ~s,*** ⇨ ring²(11). **2** [U] money in small(er) units; money that is the difference between the price or cost of sth and the sum offered in payment: (較)小額貨幣;零錢;(購物付款後)找回的錢: *Can you give me ~ for a one-pound note?* 你能替我換一鎊零錢嗎? *I have no small ~,* no coins of small value. 我沒有零錢。*Don't leave your ~ on the shop counter!* 不要把你找回的錢遺忘在店中的櫃臺上! ***get no ~ out of (sb),*** (colloq) get no help, information or advantage from. (俗)從(某人)處得不到幫助或消息;無法從其得到好處;在…身上無利可圖;拿(他)沒辦法。**3** [C, U] alteration; changing: 改變;變化;變更: *C~ is not necessarily a good thing in itself.* 改變,其本身並不一定都是好的。*We shall have to make a ~ in the programme.* 我們勢必將節目內容變動一下。*Let's hope there will be a ~ in the weather.* 但願天氣會變好。***for a ~,*** for the sake of variety; to be different from one's routine: 爲求變化起見;爲了與日常生活有所不同: *I usually have breakfast at 7.30, but during the holidays I'm having it at 8.30 for a ~.* 我通常七點半吃早餐,但在假期中我八時半吃早餐,爲的是變化變化。~ ***of life,*** = menopause. **~·ful** /-fʊl ; -fəl/ *adj* continually changing; likely to change. 不斷改變的;易變的;多變的。**ˈ~·less** *adj* unchanging. 不變的。

change·ling /ˈtʃeɪndʒlɪŋ ; ˈtʃendʒlɪŋ/ *n* child secretly substituted for another in infancy, esp (in old stories) a strange, ugly or stupid child left by fairies in place of one they have stolen. 調包兒(被秘密換入的嬰兒,尤指舊傳說中由神仙在偷走一個小孩後所留下的一個又怪又醜又笨的孩子)。

chan·nel /ˈtʃænl ; ˈtʃænḷ/ *n* **1** stretch of water joining two seas: (連接兩海的)海峽: *the English C~,* between France and England. 英吉利海峽(在法國與英國之間)。**2** natural or artificial bed of a stream of water; passage along which a liquid may flow. (天然或人工的)河床;水道;溝渠;槽。**3** deeper part of a waterway: 水道之較深處;航道: *The ~ is marked by buoys.* 航道有浮標標示。*Keep to the ~—the river is shallow at the sides.* 照着航道走——河的兩旁水淺。**4** (fig) any way by which news, ideas, etc may travel: (喻)(消息、意思等傳播的)途徑;路線;方法: *He has secret ~s of information.* 他有秘密的消息來源。***through the usual ~s,*** by the usual means of communication (between persons, groups, etc): 經由通常的途徑(指經由人與人間、團體與團體間等通常的溝通): *A debate on this question can be arranged through the usual ~s,* eg, in Parliament, through the leaders of political parties. 對此問題的辯論可循通常的途徑予以安排(例如在國會中,經由各政黨的領袖)。**5** (radio, TV) band of frequencies within which signals from a transmitter must be kept (to prevent interference from other transmitters). (無線電、電視)波段;波道;頻道(自發射臺所發出的電波爲了避免受其他發射台的干擾所必須遵守的頻率帶)。□ *vt* (-ll-, US also -l-) [VP6A, 14] **1** form a ~ or ~s in, cut out (a way): 形成河床;沖出(一條路): *The river had ~led its way through the soft rock.* 河水已在鬆軟的岩石中沖成一條河床。**2** cause to go through a ~ or ~s. 使經

過某種路線前進;引導。

chant /tʃɑːnt *US:* tʃænt ; tʃænt/ *n* [C] often-repeated tune to which psalms and canticles are fitted; several syllables or words to one note. (讚美詩及頌歌中所用之)常重覆的曲調;用同一音調唱出的幾個音節或字。⇨ hymn. □ *vi, vt* [VP2A, 6A] sing; sing a ~; use a singing note (eg for a prayer in Church): 唱歌;重覆地唱;用唱歌的調子(如教堂做禱告者): ~ *sb's praises*, (fig) praise constantly. (喻)不斷地稱讚;歌頌。

chantey, chanty /ˈʃæntɪ ; ˈʃæntɪ/ *n* (US) = shanty².

chaos /ˈkeɪɒs ; ˈkeɑs/ *n* [U] complete absence of order or shape; confusion: 完全無秩序或不整齊;紛亂;混亂;一團糟: *The room was in a state of ~ when the burglars had left.* 竊賊離去後,室內紊亂不堪。**cha·otic** /keɪˈɒtɪk ; keˈɑtɪk/ *adj* in a state of ~; confused. 無秩序的;混亂的;亂七八糟的。**cha·oti·cally** /keɪˈɒtɪklɪ ; keˈɑtɪklɪ/ *adv*

chap¹ /tʃæp ; tʃæp/ *vt, vi* (-pp-) **1** [VP2A] (of the skin) become sore, rough, cracked: (指皮膚)發痛;變粗糙;破裂: *My skin soon ~s in cold weather.* 我的皮膚在冷天裏很快就會破裂。 **2** [VP6A] cause to become cracked or rough: 使皸裂或變粗糙: *hands and face ~ped by the cold.* 因寒凍而皸裂的手和臉。□ *n* crack, esp in the skin. (尤指皮膚上的)裂口。

chap² /tʃæp ; tʃæp/ *n* (also 亦作 *chop*) (*pl*) jaws, esp of animals; cheeks. (複)(動物的)顎;頰。 **ˈ~·fallen** *adj* dispirited, dejected. 沮喪的;失望的。

chap³ /tʃæp ; tʃæp/ *n* (colloq) man; boy; fellow. (俗)人;小伙子;傢伙。

chapel /ˈtʃæpl ; ˈtʃæpḷ/ *n* **1** place (not a parish church) used for Christian worship, eg in a large private house, school, prison, etc. (大私宅、學校、監獄等處所附屬的)基督教禮拜堂(非教區教堂)。 **2** small place within a Christian church, used for private prayer, with an altar, and usually named (eg a ˈ*Lady C~*, one dedicated to Mary, the mother of Jesus). (大教堂裏的)小禮拜堂(用作個人禮拜之所,有祭壇,通常另有名稱,如 '聖母禮拜堂' 係奉獻給聖母瑪利亞者)。⇨ the illus at church. 參看 church 之插圖。 **3** (GB; obsolescent use) place of worship used by those who do not belong to the established (Anglican) Church of England: (英;逐漸廢用)非國教教徒之禮拜堂;自由教堂: *the Methodist ~.* 美以美會禮拜堂。*Are you church or ~,* Do you belong to the Church of England or to one of the Free Churches? 你是國教徒還是自由教徒? ⇨ free¹(3). **ˈ~·goer** /-gəʊə(r) ; -goɚ/ *n* nonconformist (contrasted with a member of the Church of England). 自由教徒(與英國國教徒相對);非國教徒。**4** [U] service held in a ~(1, 3): 基督教禮拜堂或自由教堂的禮拜式: *go to ~.* 到自由教堂做禮拜。

chap·er·on /ˈʃæpərəʊn ; ˈʃæpəˌron/ *n* married or elderly person (usu a woman) in charge of a girl or young unmarried woman on social occasions. 陪未婚少女上社交場所之已婚或較年長的人(通常爲婦人);女伴;陪媼。□ *vt* [VP6A] act as a ~ to. 作…之陪媼;陪伴。

chap·fallen /ˈtʃæpfɔːlən ; ˈtʃæpˌfɔlən/ *adj* ⇨ chap².

chap·lain /ˈtʃæplɪn ; ˈtʃæplɪn/ *n* priest or clergyman, esp in the navy, army or air force, or officiating in a chapel(1). 海、陸、空軍之隨營牧師;軍中傳教士;主持非教區教堂之禮拜的牧師。⇨ padre. **~·cy** /-sɪ ; -sɪ/ *n* function, area or house of a ~. 隨營牧師等之職責、轄區或住宅。

chap·let /ˈtʃæplɪt ; ˈtʃæplɪt/ *n* wreath (of leaves, flowers, jewels, etc) for the head; string of beads (a short rosary) for counting prayers. 用枝葉、花、珠寶等編成戴在頭上的花圈;花冠;祈禱時計數用的念珠(較短珠串)。

chap·man /ˈtʃæpmən ; ˈtʃæpmən/ *n* (*pl* -men) (old use) pedlar. (舊用法)販夫;小販。

chap·ter /ˈtʃæptə(r) ; ˈtʃæptɚ/ *n* **1** (usu numbered) main division of a book. (書的)章;篇(通常有編號)。 **~ *of accidents*,** number of misfortunes closely following one another. 接踵而來的災禍。 **~ *and verse*,** exact reference to a passage, etc or authority (*for* a statement, etc) for. (一段話等之)確實的出處;精確引證;典故(與 for 連用)。 **2** period; epoch: 時期;時代: *the most brilliant ~ in the history of the French court.* 法國王朝史上最光輝的時代。 **3** (general meeting of the) whole number of canons of a cathedral church, or the members of a monastery or convent. 大教堂的全體教士(大會);修道院或女修道院的全體修士(大會)。 **ˈ~-house** *n* building used for such meetings. 教士或修士大會會堂。

char¹ /tʃɑː(r) ; tʃɑr/ *vt, vi* (-rr-) [VP6A, 2A] (of a surface) make or become black by burning: (指表面)燒焦;燒黑: *~red wood.* 木炭。

char² /tʃɑː(r) ; tʃɑr/ *vi* (-rr-) do the cleaning of offices, houses, etc with payment by the hour or the day: 替辦公室、私宅等做打掃清潔之臨時工作(按小時或按日計酬): *go out ~ring.* 出去做打掃清潔之零工。□ *n* = ~woman. 替人打掃清潔之女工。 **ˈ~·lady, ˈ~·woman** *nn* woman who earns money by ~ring, paid by the hour or the day. (按小時或按日計酬)替人打掃清潔之女工。

char³ /tʃɑː(r) ; tʃɑr/ *n* [U] (GB sl) tea: (英俚)茶: *a cup of ~.* 一杯茶。

char-à-banc, char·a·banc /ˈʃærəbæŋ; ˈʃærəˌbæŋk/ *n* (not US) (now usu called 現通常稱做 *coach*) single-decked motor-coach with all seats facing forward, used for pleasure trips. (不用於美國)(座位一律向前之)單層遊覽汽車。

char·ac·ter /ˈkærəktə(r) ; ˈkærɪktɚ/ *n* **1** [U] (of a person, community, race, etc) mental or moral nature; mental or moral qualities that make one person, race, etc different from others: (指個人、社會、民族等之)天性;性情;性格;特質;個性: *a woman of fine/strong/noble, etc ~;* 性情很好(個性很强,氣質高貴等)之女人; *the ~ of Julius Cæsar/of the French.* 朱利阿斯•西撒(法國民族)的性格。***in/out of ~***, appropriate/inappropriate to the actions, etc known to be in accord with a person's ~. (指行爲等)合(不合)於個性。**2** [U] moral strength: 道德的力量;品格: *a man of ~.* 有品格的人。*Should ~ building be the chief aim of education?* 品格的培養應該是教育的主要目的嗎? **3** [U] all those qualities that make a thing, place, etc what it is and different from others: (事物、地方等與其他不同之)特點;特質;特徵;特性: *the ~ of the desert areas of N Africa.* 北非洲沙漠地區之特質。 **4** [C] person who is well known: 出名的人;聞人: *a public ~;* 社會知名之士; person in a novel, play, etc: (小說、戲劇等中的)角色;人物: *the ~s in the novels of Charles Dickens;* 狄更斯小說中的人物; person who is in some ways unusual: 某些方面不平常的人: *He's quite a ~,* has peculiarities of his own, is not an average or typical sort of person. 他是個很特殊的人物。 **ˈ~ actor** *n* one who specialises in portraying unusual or eccentric people. 性格演員(善於飾演奇特人物之演員)。 **5** [C] (old use) description of a person's abilities and qualities, esp in a letter by an employer, that may be used when applying for a job (*testimonial* is now the usu word). (舊用法)僱主對於僱員之能力和品行所出的證明信(可用以另外求職者;現通常用 testimonial)。 **6** [C] reputation: 名譽: *He has gained the ~ of a miser.* 他博得了一個守財奴之名。 **7** [C] letter, sign, mark, etc used in a system of writing or printing: 文字;字母: *Greek/Chinese, etc ~s.* 希臘字母(漢字等)。**~·is·tic** /ˌkærəktəˈrɪstɪk ; ˌkærɪktəˈrɪstɪk/ *adj* forming part of, showing, the ~ of: 構成…的性格之一部份的;表明…的性格的;性格中所特有的;特別的: *with his ~istic enthusiasm.* 以他所特有的熱心。*It's ~istic of him,* It's what people would expect him to do, because of his ~. 那是他的特殊作風。□ *n* [C] special mark or quality: 特點;特質;特性;特色;特徵: *What are the ~istics that distinguish the Chinese from* *the Japanese?* 中國人與日本人不同的特質是什麼？ **~·is·ti·cally** /ˌkærəktəˈrɪstɪklɪ ; ˌkærɪktəˈrɪstɪkḷɪ/ *adv* **ˈ~·ize** *vt* [VP6A] show the ~ of; give ~ to; mark in a special way: 顯示…之特徵；賦予…特徵；以特別的方式標明: *Your work is ~ized by lack of attention to detail.* 你的工作的特點是不注意細節。*The camel is ~ized by the ability to go for long periods without water.* 駱駝的特點是能夠長期行走而不喝水。 **~·less** *adj* without ~; undistinguished; ordinary. 無特點的；無特色的；不出衆的；平常的。

cha·rade /ʃəˈrɑːd *US:* -ˈreɪd ; ʃəˈred/ *n* [C] episode in a game in which a word is guessed by the onlookers after the word itself, and each syllable of it in turn, have been suggested by acting a little play; (*pl*, with sing *v*) this game; (fig) action of no or sham significance; pretence. 比手畫脚猜字遊戲的謎面（藉短短的表演暗示一字及其每一音節然後令觀者猜係何字）；(複)（與單數動詞連用）比手畫脚猜字遊戲；(喻)無意義的行爲；虛僞的行為；假裝。

char·coal /ˈtʃɑːkəʊl ; ˈtʃɑrˌkol/ *n* [U] black substance, used as fuel, as a filtering material and for drawing, made by burning wood slowly in an oven with little air: 木炭（將木材置於爐中悶燒而成之黑色物質，用作燃料、過濾材料及作畫）: *a bale/stick/piece, etc of ~.* 一綑（根，塊等）木炭。 **ˈ~-burner** *n* person who makes ~; stove, etc in which ~ is used as the fuel. 燒製木炭者；木炭爐。

chard /tʃɑːd ; tʃɑrd/ *n* (often 常作 *Swiss ~*) variety of beet of which the leaves are used as a vegetable. 其葉可當作蔬菜食用之一種甜菜。

charge¹ /tʃɑːdʒ ; tʃɑrdʒ/ *n* **1** accusation; statement that a person has done wrong, esp that he has broken a law: 指控；控告（尤指控告某人犯法者）: *arrested on a ~ of theft.* 因偷竊的罪名而被捕。 ***bring a ~ (of sth) against sb,*** accuse him (of a crime, etc). 控告某人（犯某種罪等）。 ***face a ~ (of sth),*** have to answer it in court: 必須出庭（爲某事）作答辯: *He faces serious ~s.* 他必須到庭應付嚴重的控告。 ***lay sth to sb's ~,*** bring an accusation of sth against him. 爲某事控告某人。 **ˈ~-sheet** *n* record of cases kept in a police station. 警察局的檔案；案件記錄。 **2** sudden and violent attack at high speed (by soldiers, wild animals, a football player, etc). （指軍隊、野獸、足球隊隊員等所做之）迅速突襲；突然猛攻；衝鋒。 **3** price asked for goods or services: 索取之價錢（指貨價）；（因服務而索取的）費用: *hotel ~s.* 旅館費用。 **ˈ~-account** *n* (US) credit account. (美)賒帳。 ⇨ credit¹(1). **4** amount of powder, etc (to be) used in a gun or for causing an explosion; amount of electricity (to be) put into an accumulator, contained in a substance, etc: 槍砲發一彈或爆炸一次所用的火藥等；儲於蓄電池內或某物質等中所含的電量；電荷；充電: *a positive/negative ~.* 正電荷；陽電荷（負電荷；陰電荷）。 **5** [C] work given to sb as a duty; thing or person given or entrusted to sb to be taken care of; [U] responsibility; trust: 交與某人的工作責任；託付某人照料的事務或人；責任；委託: *This ward of the hospital is in/under the ~ of Dr Green.* 本醫院的這間病房是由格林醫生負責。 *I hope you'll never become a ~ on the public,* ie become a pauper, to be supported at public expense. 我希望你永遠不會變成受公衆照料的人（變成赤貧而須由公家賙濟）。 ***put sb/be in ~ (of),*** be (put) in a position of responsibility (for): (使)負責管理: *Mary was (put) in ~ of the baby.* 瑪莉負責照料這個嬰兒。 *Who's in ~ here?* 這裏是誰負責？ ***put sb/be in sb's ~,*** be (put) in his care: (使)由…負責管理: *The baby was (put) in Mary's ~.* 這個嬰兒是由瑪莉負責照料。 ***give sb in ~,*** give him up to the police. 將某人交付警方。 ***take ~ of,*** become responsible for. 負責管理。 **6** directions; instructions: 命令；指示: *the judge's ~ to the jury,* instructions concerning their duty (in reaching a verdict). 法官對於陪審團（裁決案件）的職責所做的指示。

charge² /tʃɑːdʒ ; tʃɑrdʒ/ *vt, vi* **1** [VP6A, 14] ~ ***sb (with),*** accuse; bring a charge(1) against: 指控；控告（某人做某事）: *He was ~d with murder.* 他被控告謀殺。 *He ~d me with neglecting my duty.* 他指控我疏忽職責。 **2** [VP6A, 2A, C] make a charge (2) against; rush forward and attack: 突襲；猛攻；衝鋒；向前衝進並攻擊: *Our soldiers ~d the enemy.* 我軍向敵軍猛攻。 *One of our strikers* (ie in a game of football) *was violently ~d by the defender.* （指足球賽中）我們的前鋒之一受到（對方）後衛的猛襲。 *The wounded lion suddenly ~d at me.* 那隻被擊傷的獅子突然向我衝襲。 **3** [VP2B, 14] ~ ***(for),*** ask as a price; ask in payment: 索價；要價: *He ~d (me) fifty pence (for it).* （這件東西）他（向我）索價五十辨士。 *How much do you ~ for mending a pair of shoes?* 你補一雙鞋要多少錢？ **4** [VP14, 15A, B] ~ ***to; ~ up; ~ up to,*** make a record of (as a debt): 記帳: *Please ~ these purchases to my account.* 請將這些購貨價款記在我的帳上。 **5** [VP6A, 2A] load (a gun); fill, put a charge(4) into: 裝彈藥於（槍砲）；充電於: *~ an accumulator.* 充電於蓄電池。 *Electrons are negatively ~d with electricity; protons are positively ~d.* 電子是帶負（陰）電荷；質子是帶正（陽）電荷。 **6** [VP14] ~ ***with,*** give as a task or duty; give into sb's care: 交付責任；交…負責照料: *He was ~d with an important mission.* 他被交付重要使命。 *He ~d himself with* (= undertook) *the task of keeping the club's accounts in order.* 他負起替協會管帳的責任。 **7** [VP6A, 17] (esp of a judge, or person in authority) command; instruct: （尤指法官或主管）命令；指示；訓令: *I ~ you not to forget what I have said.* 我命令你不要忘記我所說的話。 *The judge ~d the jury,* gave them directions about how to perform their duty. 法官訓示陪審團（指示他們如何執行職務）。

charge·able /ˈtʃɑːdʒəbl ; ˈtʃɑrdʒəbḷ/ *adj* **1** that can be, is liable to be, charged: 可被控告的；可能遭受控告的: *If you steal, you are ~ with theft.* 如果你偷竊，你就會被控竊盜罪。 **2** ~ ***on/to*** (comm) that may be added (to an account): (商)可記在（帳上）的: *sums ~ to a reserve;* 可記入準備金項下的款項; that may be made an expense: 可報帳的: *Costs of repairs are ~ on the owner of the building.* 修繕費可向房東報帳。

chargé d'affaires /ˌʃɑːʒeɪ dæˈfeə(r) ; ʃɑrˈʒedæˈfɛr/ *n* (*pl* chargés d'affaires, pronunciation unchanged 複數讀音不變) official who takes the place of an ambassador or minister when the ambassador, etc is absent from his post. 代辦（大使或公使公出時的代理者）。

charger¹ /ˈtʃɑːdʒə(r) ; ˈtʃɑrdʒɚ/ *n* (old use) army officer's horse. (舊用法)（陸軍軍官的）戰馬。

charger² /ˈtʃɑːdʒə(r) ; ˈtʃɑrdʒɚ/ *n* (old use) large, flat dish; platter. (舊用法)大淺盤。

char·iot /ˈtʃærɪət ; ˈtʃærɪət/ *n* open, two-wheeled, horse-drawn carriage, used in ancient times in fighting and racing. （古代作戰和比賽用的）兩輪無篷馬車。 **char·io·teer** /ˌtʃærɪəˈtɪə(r) ; ˌtʃærɪətˈɪr/ *n* driver of a ~. 駕駛此種馬車者。

cha·ris·ma /kəˈrɪzmə ; kəˈrɪzmə/ *n* **1** (theology) spiritual grace. (神學)上帝的恩賜（如治病的能力等）。 **2** capacity to inspire devotion and enthusiasm. 激勵忠誠及熱情的才能。 **char·is·matic** /ˌkærɪzˈmætɪk ; ˌkærɪzˈmætɪk/ *adj*

chari·table /ˈtʃærɪtəbl ; ˈtʃærətəbḷ/ *adj* showing, having, charity (*to*); for charity: 表示慈善的；有慈善心的（與 to 連用）；爲慈善的: *~ institutions,* for helping poor or suffering or needy people; 慈善機關（救濟貧困及受難者）; *~ to all men.* 對所有的人表示慈悲。 **ˈchari·tably** /-blɪ ; -blɪ/ *adv*

char·ity /ˈtʃærətɪ ; ˈtʃærətɪ/ *n* **1** [U] willingness to judge other persons with kindness; neighbourly love: 寬厚；仁恕；博愛；慈悲: *judge other people with ~.* 寬厚待人；仁恕待人。 *C~ begins at home,* (prov) A person's first duty is to help the members of his own family. (諺)慈善始於家庭(意謂一個人的首要責任是照顧自己的家屬)。 **2** (kindness in giving) help to the poor; money, food, etc so given. 慈善;施與;賙濟;救濟金;賙濟品;施捨之食物等。***live on/off ~,*** live by accepting money etc from others. 靠賙濟過日子。 **3** [C] (*pl* -ties) society or organization for serving those in need: 慈善團體: *He left all his money to charities,* to charitable institutions. 他把所有的錢都捐給了慈善團體。

chari·vari /ˌʃɑːrɪˈvɑːrɪ *US:* ˌʃɪvəˈriː ; ʃəˌrɪvəˈri/ *n* [U] hubbub; medley of noises and voices. 嘈雜;喧囂;騷鬧。

char·lady /ˈtʃɑːleɪdɪ ; ˈtʃɑrˌledɪ/ *n* (*pl* -ladies) charwoman. 做零工的女傭。⇨ char²

char·la·tan /ˈʃɑːlətən ; ˈʃɑrlətn̩/ *n* person who claims to have more skill, knowledge or ability than he really has, esp one who pretends to have medical knowledge. 冒充內行者;(尤指)冒充醫生者;江湖郎中;江湖醫生。

Charles·ton /ˈtʃɑːlstən ; ˈtʃɑrlztən/ *n* fast dance with side kicks from the knee (popular in the 1920's). 却爾斯登舞(一種快速的舞蹈,膝向外側踢,流行於 1920 年代)。

char·lock /ˈtʃɑːlɒk ; ˈtʃɑrlək/ *n* wild mustard, a weed with yellow flowers. 野芥菜(一種開黃花之野草)。

charm /tʃɑːm ; tʃɑrm/ *n* **1** [U] attractiveness; power to give pleasure; [C] pleasing quality or feature: 吸引力;給人快感之能力;可愛的性質或特點;魅力;魔力: *Her ~ of manner made her very popular.* 她的風度之優雅使她極受大家歡迎。*He fell a victim to her ~s,* her beauty, her attractive ways, etc. 他爲她的姿色所傾倒。 **2** [C] sth believed to have magic power, good or bad: 被認爲具有(善或惡)魔力之物;符咒: *under a ~,* influenced in a magic way; 着魔的; *~s against evil spirits;* 能驅除惡魔之符咒; *a ~ to bring good luck,* eg a trinket worn on the body. 可帶來福氣之物(如戴於身上的小飾物);吉祥物。***work like a ~,*** with complete success. 完全成功的工作(或作品)。□ *vt, vi* **1** [VP6A, 2A] attract; give pleasure to: 吸引;給與快感;使陶醉;使欣賞;迷人: *Does goodness ~ more than beauty?* 良善是否較美色更能使人欣賞? *We were ~ed with the scenery.* 我們陶醉在風景中。*I'm ~ed* (*pleased* is more usu 較常用 pleased) *to meet you* (used as a polite formula). 幸會,幸會(客套話)。 **2** [VP6A, 15A] use magic on; influence or protect as if by magic: 施魔術於;似以魔力影響或保護: *He's had a ~ed life,* has escaped dangers, as if protected by magic. 他的性命似有神力保護;他有吉星高照(使他得以避開危險)。*She ~ed away his sorrow,* caused him to forget his troubles. 她驅走了他的悲傷。**~·ing** *adj* delightful: 嫵媚的;迷人的: *a ~ing young lady.* 嫵媚的少女。**~·ing·ly** *adv* **~er** *n* (usu joc) young man or woman with ~. (通常爲謔)迷人的青年男子或女子。**ˈsnake ~er** *n* person able to ~(2) snakes. 玩蛇者;弄蛇者。

char·nel house /ˈtʃɑːnl haʊs ; ˈtʃɑrnl̩ haʊs/ *n* place where dead human bodies or bones are stored. 存放死人屍體或骸骨之所;藏骸所;積骨堂。

chart /tʃɑːt ; tʃɑrt/ *n* **1** map used by sailors, showing the coasts, depth of the sea, position of rocks, lighthouses, etc. (水手所用,標示海岸線、海洋深度、礁石、燈塔等之位置的)航海圖。**2** sheet of paper with information, in the form of curves, diagrams, etc (about such things as the weather, prices, business conditions, etc): (以曲線、圖解等表示氣象、物價、商情等資料之) 圖表: *a ˈweather/ˈtemperature ~.* 氣象(溫度)圖表。□ *vt* [VP6A] make a ~ of; show on a ~. 製成圖表;以圖表表示。

char·ter /ˈtʃɑːtə(r) ; ˈtʃɑrtɚ/ *n* **1** (written or printed statement of) rights, permission to do sth, esp from a ruler or government (eg to a town, city or university). (由統治者或政府發給城鎮或大學等的)特許狀;營業執照;特權;特許;憲章。 **2** hiring or engagement (of an aircraft, a ship, etc): 包租(飛機、船等);包機;包船: *a ˈ~ flight.* 包機。*C~s of oil-tankers may be by time or for the voyage.* 油輪的包租可以按時間計費或按航程計費。□ *vt* [VP6A] **1** give a ~ to; grant a privilege to. 發給特許狀;給與特權。**ˌ~ed acˈcountant,** (in GB) member of the Institute of Accountants (which has a royal ~). (英)會計師(獲有皇家特許狀,爲會計師協會之會員)。 **2** hire or engage a ship, an aircraft, etc for an agreed time, purpose and payment: (議定時間、用途及價款)包租(船、飛機等): *travel in a ~ed aircraft.* 乘包機旅行。**ˈ~-party** *n* (comm) agreement between a shipowner and merchant for the use of a ship. (商)包船租約(商人向船主租船所立的租約);租船契約。

Chart·ism /ˈtʃɑːtɪzəm ; ˈtʃɑrtɪzəm/ *n* early 19th c working-class movement for social and industrial reform. (十九世紀早期致力於社會和工業改革的)民權運動。**Chart·ist** /-ɪst ; -ɪst/ *n*

char·treuse /ʃɑːˈtrɜːz *US:* -ˈtruːz ; ʃɑrˈtrəz/ *n* (kinds of) liqueur (green, yellow) made by Carthusian /kɑːˈθjuːzɪən *US:* -ˈθuːʒn ; kɑrˈθjuʒən/ monks (of an austere monastic order founded in S France in 1086). 蕁蔴酒(1086 年創於法國南部之卡爾特苦行修道團的僧侶所造之綠色或黃色酒)。

char·woman /ˈtʃɑːwʊmən ; ˈtʃɑrˌwʊmən/ *n* ⇨ char².

chary /ˈtʃeərɪ ; ˈtʃɛrɪ/ *adj* ***~ (of),*** cautious, wary, careful: 小心的;謹慎的;注意的: *~ of catching cold;* 當心受涼; *a teacher who is ~ of giving praise,* who seldom praises his pupils. 不輕易稱讚學生的教師。**char·ily** *adv*

Cha·ryb·dis /kəˈrɪbdɪs ; kəˈrɪbdɪs/ *n* ⇨ Scylla.

chase¹ /tʃeɪs ; tʃes/ *vt, vi* **1** [VP6A, 3A, 15A, B] ***~ (after),*** run after in order to capture, kill, overtake or drive away: 追捕;追擊;追趕;驅逐: *Dogs like to ~ rabbits.* 狗喜歡追趕兎子。*C~ that dog out of the garden.* 把那條狗趕出花園去。*The letter had been chasing after him for weeks,* eg had been following him from place to place during his travels. 此信已追踪他數星期(如當他在旅行中由甲地追至乙地,又由乙地追至丙地等)。*This'll ~ away the blues!* 這將把憂鬱驅散! **2** [VP2C] (colloq) hurry; rush: (俗)趕快;急跑: *The children all ~d off after the procession.* 孩子們紛紛跑去跟隨遊行的隊伍。□ *n* act of chasing: 追趕;追逐: *After a long ~, we caught the thief.* 經過很久的追趕,我們終於捉住了那個小偷。***give ~ (to),*** run after; start in pursuit (of). 追逐;追趕;追擊。***in ~ of sb/sth,*** pursuing, running after. 追逐或追趕某人(某物)。***(go on) a ˌwild ˈgoose ~,*** (embark on) a search, expedition, etc that can have no success. (從事)不會成功的搜索,探險等;(從事)勞而無功的事。**chaser** *n* (in compounds) person or thing that ~s; (colloq) drink taken after another, eg a mild after a strong: (用於複合字中) 追踪或追擊之人或物; (俗)酒後所飲之酒或飲料(例如烈性酒飲過後再飲淡性酒): *whisky with beer ~rs.* 威士忌之後再飲啤酒。

chase² /tʃeɪs ; tʃes/ *vt* [VP6A] cut patterns or designs on (metal or other hard material); engrave: 刻圖於(金屬或其他硬材料);雕鏤: *~d silver.* 雕花銀器。

chasm /ˈkæzəm ; ˈkæzəm/ *n* deep opening or crack in the ground; abyss; gorge; (fig) wide difference (of feeling or interests, *between* persons, groups, nations, etc). (地上的)深坑或裂縫;罅隙;深淵;峽;(喻)(個人、團體或國家等之間感情或利害的)分歧;衝突;裂痕(與 between 連用)。

chas·sis /ˈʃæsɪ ; ˈʃæsɪ/ *n* (*pl* spelling unchanged, but pronounced 複數拼法不變,但讀作 /ˈʃæsɪz ; ˈʃæsɪz/) base framework of a motor-vehicle, radio or TV, on which the body and working parts are mounted. (汽車,收音機或電視機的)底盤。

chaste /tʃeɪst ; tʃest/ *adj* **1** virtuous in word, thought and deed; (esp) abstaining from promiscuous or all sexual intercourse. (言語、思想及行爲)有德行的;純潔的;(尤指)不亂交的;貞潔的。 **2** (of style, taste) simple; without ornament; pure. (指風格、嗜

好)簡單的;樸實無華的;純樸的。~**•ly** *adv*

chas•ten /ˈtʃeɪsn; ˈtʃesn̩/ *vt* [VP6A] **1** punish in order to correct; discipline. 懲戒;磨鍊。 **2** make chaste(2). 使純樸。

chas•tise /tʃæˈstaɪz; tʃæsˈtaɪz/ *vt* [VP6A] punish severely. 嚴懲;責罰。~**•ment** *n* [U] punishment. 懲戒;懲罰。

chas•tity /ˈtʃæstətɪ; ˈtʃæstətɪ/ *n* [U] state of being chaste. 純潔;貞節;純樸。

chas•uble /ˈtʃæzjʊbl; ˈtʃæzjʊbl̩/ *n* (eccles) loose, sleeveless garment worn over all other vestments by a priest at the Eucharist. (教會)十字褡(神父行聖餐禮時所著,罩於所有其他衣服之外的寬鬆無袖長袍)。⇨ the illus at vestment. 參看 vestment 之插圖。

chat /tʃæt; tʃæt/ *n* [C] friendly talk (usu about unimportant things): 閒談;聊天: *I had a long ~ with him.* 我與他閒談了很久。□ *vi, vt* (-tt-) **1** [VP2A,C] have a ~: 閒談;聊天: *They were ~ting (away) in the corner.* 他們在屋角裏閒聊。 **2** [VP15B] ~ ***sb up,*** (colloq) ~ to in order to win friendship, or for fun: (俗) (爲獲得友誼或取樂)與某人聊天: *~ up a pretty barmaid.* 與可愛的酒吧女侍聊天。~**ty** *adj* fond of ~ting. 喜好閒談的。

châ•teau /ˈʃætəʊ; ʃæˈto/ *n* (*pl* ~x /-təʊz; -toz/) castle or large country house in France. (法國的)古堡;鄉間大莊園;別墅。

a chateau

chat•el•aine /ˈʃætəleɪn; ˈʃætl̩ˌen/ *n* (old use) set of short chains fastened to a woman's belt for carrying keys, etc; mistress of a large country house or castle. (舊用法)繫於婦人腰帶上以懸掛鑰匙等之短鍊子;大別墅或古堡的女主人。

chat•tel /ˈtʃætl; ˈtʃætl̩/ *n* (legal) article of personal movable property (eg a chair, a motor-car, a horse): (法律)動產(如椅子、汽車、馬匹): *a person's goods and ~s.* 一個人所有的雜物用品。

chat•ter /ˈtʃætə(r); ˈtʃætɚ/ *vi* [VP2A, C] **1** (of a person) talk quickly or foolishly; talk too much. (指人)嘮叨;喋喋不休。 **2** (of the cries of monkeys and some birds, of typewriter keys, of a person's upper and lower teeth striking together from cold or fear) make quick, indistinct sounds. (指猴子和某些鳥類的叫聲,打字機的字鍵,人的牙齒因寒冷或恐懼而碰擊在一起) 發出迅速而不清晰的聲響;格格作響。□ *n* [U] sounds of the kind noted above: 上述的各種聲音: *the ~ of sparrows/children.* 麻雀的啁啾聲(兒童們的喋喋話聲)。ˈ~**•box,** person who ~s, esp a small child. 話匣子;碎嘴子;喋喋不休之人(尤指小兒)。

chauf•feur /ˈʃəʊfə(r) *US:* ʃəʊˈfɜːr; ˈʃofɚ/ *n* man paid to drive a privately-owned motor-car. 受僱駕駛私人汽車之司機。 **chauf•feuse** /ˈʃəʊfɜːz *US:* ʃəʊˈfɜːz; ˌʃoˈfɜz/ *n* woman ~. 受僱駕駛私人汽車的女司機。

chau•vin•ism /ˈʃəʊvɪnɪzəm; ˈʃovɪnˌɪzəm/ *n* [U] unreasoning enthusiasm for (esp) the glory of one's own country. 沙文主義;(尤指)本國至上主義。 **chau•vin•ist** /-ɪst; -ɪst/ *n* person with such enthusiasm. 沙文主義者;本國至上主義者。 **male chauvinist; chauvinist male,** (mod use) man who believes that men are superior to women and acts accordingly. (現代用法)相信男子比女子優越並有所行動者; 大男人主義者。 **chau•vin•is•tic** /ˌʃəʊvɪˈnɪstɪk; ˌʃovɪˈnɪstɪk/ *adj* of ~ or chauvinists. 無理性的狂熱(者)的;偏激的愛國(者)的。

chaw /tʃɔː; tʃɔ/ *n, vt* (vulg) chew. (鄙)咀嚼。ˈ~-**bacon** *n* ignorant bumpkin. 無知的鄉巴佬。

cheap /tʃiːp; tʃip/ *adj* (-er, -est) **1** low in price; costing little money: 價低的;價廉的;花費少的: *the ~ seats in a theatre;* 戲院中票價低廉的座位; *travel by the ~est route;* 採取花錢最少的路線旅行; *~ tickets/trips,* at specially reduced fares; 特價票(旅行); (used as *adv*): (用作副詞): *buy/sell/get sth ~,* ie for a low price. 廉價買得(賣出;取得)某物。 ***go ~,*** be offered or bought for a low price: 廉價出售;便宜賣出: *Cauliflowers going ~—only 10p each!* 菜花便宜賣──十辨士一棵! ***on the ~,*** (colloq) for a low price: (俗)廉價地: *buy/sell/get sth on the ~.* 廉價買得(賣出,取得)某物。 **2** worth more than the cost; of good value for the money. 便宜的;花錢少而貨色好的;合算的。 **3** of poor quality: 品質低劣的: *~ and nasty.* 品質惡劣的。 ˈ~**•jack** *adj* ~ and shoddy. 質劣而冒充好貨的。 **4** shallow; insincere: 膚淺的;不眞誠的: *~ emotion;* 虛僞的感情; *~ flattery.* 假意奉承。 **5** ***feel ~,*** (colloq) feel ashamed. (俗)感覺慚愧。 ***hold sth ~,*** put a low value on it, despise it. 認爲某事物無甚價值;輕視某事物。 ***make oneself ~,*** behave so that one's reputation goes down. 做出自貶身價之行爲。~ **gibe** *n* unkind taunt. 辱罵。~**•ly** *adv* for a low price: 價廉地: *buy/sell/get sth ~ly.* 廉價買得(賣出,取得)某物。~**•ness** *n*

cheapen /ˈtʃiːpən; ˈtʃipən/ *vt, vi* [VP6A, 2A] make or become cheap; lower the price of: 貶損價値;降低…的價格;減價: *You mustn't ~ yourself,* behave so that you lower your reputation. 你不可自貶身價。

cheat /tʃiːt; tʃit/ *vi, vt* [VP6A,2A,C,14] ~ ***sb (out of sth);*** ~ ***(in/at sth),*** act in a dishonest way to win an advantage or profit: 欺騙;騙取(利益等): *~ the customs,* eg by not declaring dutiable goods; 蒙騙海關(如不報應完稅之貨物); *~ sb out of his money;* 騙取某人的錢; *~ at cards;* 玩紙牌時作弊; *~ in an examination.* 在考試中作弊。□ *n* person who ~s; dishonest trick. 騙子;騙徒;欺騙;欺詐;欺騙手段。

check[1] /tʃek; tʃɛk/ *vt, vi* **1** [VP6A, 15B, 2C] examine in order to learn whether sth is correct: 檢查;查證;核對(以查明是否正確): *~ a bill;* 核對帳單; *~ sb's statements.* 查證某人的陳述。 *Will you please ~ these figures?* 請檢查這些數字有無錯誤? ~ ***sth off,*** mark it as having been found correct. 做記號於某物上表示已核對無誤。 ~ ***sth up;*** ~ ***up on sth,*** (US 美= ~ ***sth out***) examine or compare it to learn whether it is correct. 檢查或核對某物(以查明是否正確)。 ~ ***up on sb,*** examine his credentials to see whether he is what he claims to be. 檢查某人的各種證明文件(以核證其所聲稱各項是否屬實)。 **2** [VP6A] hold back; restrain; cause to go slow or stop: 抑止; 控制; 阻止; 阻擋: *We have ~ed the enemy's advance.* 我們業已擋住敵軍的前進。 *He couldn't ~ his anger.* 他不能抑制他的憤怒。 *This extravagant spending must be ~ed.* 這種奢侈的花費必須停止。 **3** [VP6A] (chess) put in ~²(4). (下棋)攻王棋;將軍。 **4** [VP2C] ~ ***in (at),*** arrive and register at a hotel/a factory etc. 到達登記(指到達旅館,工廠等)。 ~ ***out (from),*** pay one's bill and leave (a hotel, supermarket etc): 付帳離開(旅館,超級市場等): ˈ*~-out time,* time at which a room must be vacated. 結帳遷出時間(過該時間要多算一天房錢)。 ˈ~**-out** *n* (esp) place (eg in a supermarket) where one pays the bill, wraps one's goods and leaves. (尤指超級市場等之) 付帳、包裝所購貨物並離開的地方;付款處。 **5** (US) [VP6A] get a ticket, a piece of wood, metal, etc that shows a right to sth (eg hat and coat at a theatre, luggage sent by train or left at a railway station): (美)寄存;託運(在戲院寄存衣帽,在火車站託運或寄存行李,並取得一個代表取件權的卡片、木牌或金屬製的號牌等): *Have you ~ed* (= got a ~²(3) for) *all your baggage?* 你所有的行李都已交運了嗎? ~**er** *n* person who ~s stores, orders, etc. 檢查存貨、定貨單等之人。

check² /tʃek ; tʃɛk/ *n* [U] **1** control; person or thing that checks or restrains: 控制;起控制、制止或阻止作用的人或物: *Wind acts as a ~ upon speed.* 風對於速度是一種阻力。*Our forces have met with a ~*, Their advance has been stopped, they have suffered a reverse. 我軍遭遇了阻遏。*We are keeping/holding the enemy in ~*, are preventing their advance. 我們正阻擋着敵人(使不能前進)。*I advise you to keep a ~ on* (= control) *your temper.* 我勸你要控制你的脾氣。ˌ**~s and 'balances** *n pl* (methods of) control or supervision by Government, or other authorities, to guard against misuse of power. 為預防濫用權力,政府或其他當局所施之控制或督導(的方法)。 **2** examination to make certain of accuracy; mark or tick (usu written ✓) to show that sth has been examined and proved to be correct: 檢查;查核;核對;表示業經檢查正確無誤之記號(通常寫作✓): *If we both add up the figures, your result will be a ~ on mine.* 如果我們兩人都加算這些數字,你的得數就可以跟我的核對。 **'~-list** *n* list of items, titles, etc, used in checking sth. 供核對用的清單或名冊。 **'~·out** *n* ⇨ check¹(4). **'~·point** *n* (esp) place where traffic is halted for inspection. 檢查處;檢查站(尤指停車以供檢查的地方)。**'~·up** *n* (esp a medical) examination made to certify sb/sth. 為證明某人或某事物所作的檢查;(尤指)身體檢查;體格檢查。 **3** receipt (bit of paper, piece of wood or metal with a number on it, etc) given in return for sth handed over to sb (eg a hat and coat at a theatre, luggage sent by train). (在戲院寄存衣帽、交火車運送行李等所取得之紙製、木製、或金屬製之)號碼牌。 **'~·room,** (US) left-luggage office. (美)行李寄存室。 **4** ***in ~,*** (chess) position of an opponent's king when it is exposed to direct attack. (下棋)敵方王棋受攻擊之位置;將軍。⇨ checkmate. **5** (US) = cheque. **'~·book,** (US) = chequebook. **6** (US) (美) = bill³(1): *I'll ask the waiter for my ~.* 我要叫侍者拿帳單來。

check³ /tʃek ; tʃɛk/ *n* **1** pattern of crossed lines forming squares (often of different shades or colours); cloth with such a pattern: (明暗或顏色不同之)方格花式;方格花布: *Which do you want for your new dress, a stripe or a ~?* 你要哪一種布做你的新衣,條子布還是方格布? **2** (attrib) (形容用法) *a ~ tablecloth;* 方格桌布; *a ~ pattern.* 方格花式。 **checked** /tʃekt ; tʃɛkt/ *adj* with a ~ pattern: 有方格花式的: *~ed material.* 方格花布料。

checker /'tʃekə(r) ; 'tʃɛkɚ/ *vt* (US) = chequer.

check·ers /'tʃekəz ; 'tʃɛkɚz/ *n* (US) (美) = draughts.

check·mate /'tʃekmeɪt ; 'tʃɛkˌmet/ *vt* [VP6A] **1** (chess) make a move that prevents the opponent's king from being moved away from a direct attack (and so win the game). (下棋)進攻敵方之王棋使無路可走因而獲勝;將死。⇨ check²(4). **2** obstruct and defeat (a person, his plans). 阻止並擊敗(某人,其計畫)。□ *n* complete defeat. 完全擊敗。

Ched·dar /'tʃedə(r) ; 'tʃɛdɚ/ *n* [U] kind of hard yellow cheese. 一種黃色硬乾酪。

cheek /tʃi:k ; tʃik/ *n* **1** either side of the face below the eye. 頰。⇨ the illus at head. 參看 head 之插圖。 ***~ by jowl,*** close together. 緊靠在一起。 ***turn the other ~,*** respond to violence with non-violence. 忍受暴力;忍受侮辱。⇨ Matt 5.39. 參看馬太福音第5章第39節。 **'~·bone** *n* the bone below the eye. 顴骨。 **tongue-in-~** ⇨ tongue. **2** [U] impudence; saucy talk or behaviour: 厚顏;失禮的話或行為: *He had the ~ to ask me to do his work for him!* 他居然有臉要我替他做他的工作! *No more of your ~!* 不要再這樣厚臉皮了!□ *vt* [VP6A] be impudent to: 對…無禮;頂撞: *Stop ~ing your mother!* 不要再頂撞你的母親! **-cheeked** *suffix* (with an *adj*): (與形容詞連用): ˌ*rosy-*ˌ*~ed 'boys,* boys with rosy ~s. 臉頰紅潤的男孩子們。 **~y** *adj* saucy; impudent. 失禮的;厚顏的。 **~·ily** *adv*

cheep /tʃi:p ; tʃip/ *vi, n* [VP2A, C] (make a) weak, shrill note (as young birds do). (發)輕微而尖銳的聲音(如雛鳥之唧唧聲或吱喳聲)。

cheer¹ /tʃɪə(r) ; tʃɪr/ *vt, vi* **1** [VP6A, 15B] ***~ sb (up),*** fill with gladness, hope, high spirits; comfort: (使某人)充滿歡喜、希望、高興;鼓舞;安慰: *Your visit has ~ed (up) the sick man.* 你的訪問(探病)使病人高興。*Everyone was ~ed by the good news.* 每個人皆為此好消息而高興。 **~·ing** *adj*: *That's ~ing news.* 那是令人興奮的消息。 **2** [VP2C] ***~ up,*** take comfort, become happy: 高興起來: *He ~ed up at once when I promised to help him.* 當我答應幫他的忙時,他立刻高興起來。 **3** [VP6A, 15B, 2A, C] ***~ (on),*** give shouts of joy, approval or encouragement to: 歡呼;喝采;高呼加油: *The speaker was loudly ~ed.* 演說者受到高聲的歡呼。*Everyone ~ed the news that the war was over.* 人人為戰爭結束的消息而歡呼。*The boys ~ed their football team.* 男孩子們為他們的足球隊加油。 **~·ing** *n* [U]: *The ~ing could be heard half a mile away.* 歡呼之聲半哩以外都可以聽得到。

cheer² /tʃɪə(r) ; tʃɪr/ *n* **1** [U] (old use) state of hope, gladness: (舊用法)振奮;高興;喜悅: *words of ~,* of encouragement. 鼓勵的話。 **2** [U] ***good ~,*** (old use) good food and drink. (舊用法)佳餚美酒。 **3** [C] shout of joy or encouragement: 歡呼;喝采: *give three ~s for,* cry or shout 'Hurrah!' three times. 向…歡呼三聲。 **'~-leader** *n* (US) one who leads organised cheering by a group or crowd. (美)啦啦隊隊長。 **4** (old use) (舊用法) *What ~?* How do you feel? 你好嗎? **5 C~s!** Word used when one drinks to sb's health, etc. 祝福!祝健康!乾杯(當舉杯祝某人健康等時的用字)

cheer·ful /'tʃɪəfl ; 'tʃɪrfəl/ *adj* **1** bringing or suggesting happiness: 令人高興的;快樂的;愉快的: *a ~ day/room/smile;* 令人高興的日子(房間,微笑); *~ conversation.* 愉快的談話。 **2** happy and contented; willing: 高興的;樂意的: *~ workers.* 高興的工人們。 **~·ly** /-fəlɪ ; -fəlɪ/ *adv* **~·ness** *n*

cheer·io /ˌtʃɪərɪ'əʊ ; 'tʃɪrɪˌo/ *int* (colloq) (俗) **1** (at parting) goodbye. (分手時)再見;再會。 **2** (not US; dated) (in drinking) To your health! (不用於美國;過時用語)(敬酒時)祝你健康!

cheer·less /'tʃɪəlɪs ; 'tʃɪrlɛs/ *adj* without comfort; gloomy; miserable: 無歡笑的;無慰藉的;陰鬱的;淒涼的: *a wet and ~ day;* 陰雨天; *a damp, cold and ~ room.* 潮濕,冰冷而陰森的房間。 **~·ly** *adv* **~·ness** *n*

cheery /'tʃɪərɪ ; 'tʃɪrɪ/ *adj* lively; genial; merry: 活潑的;歡樂的;愉快的: *a ~ smile/greeting.* 愉快的笑(歡迎)。 **cheer·ily** /'tʃɪərəlɪ ; 'tʃɪrəlɪ/ *adv*

cheese /tʃi:z ; tʃiz/ *n* [U] solid food made from milk curds; [C] shaped and wrapped portion or ball of this: (由凝乳製成的)乾酪;乳酪;乾酪塊;乾酪團: *two cream ~s.* 兩塊乾乳酪。 **'~-cake,** *n* **(a)** tart filled with a sweet mixture of curd, eggs, etc. 以凝乳、蛋等混合為餡之甜餅。 **(b)** (sl) displays of a shapely female body (in a photograph, advertisement, etc). (俚)(照片、廣告等中)女性胴體美之展示;半裸美女照。⇨ *pin-up* at pin²(1). **'~-cloth,** thin cotton cloth (gauze) put round some kinds of ~; similar (thicker) cloth used to make shirts, etc. 包某些乾酪用的紗布;一種類似而較厚的棉布(用以製襯衫等)。 **'~-paring,** excessive carefulness in the spending of money: 用錢過於謹慎(的);極為節儉(的);吝嗇(的): *~-paring economies.* 過於謹慎的節儉。

chee·tah /'tʃi:tə ; 'tʃitə/ *n* kind of wild cat of Africa, resembling a leopard, which can be trained to hunt deer. (一種非洲產、可以訓練來獵鹿的)獵豹。

chef /ʃef ; ʃɛf/ *n* head cook in a hotel, restaurant, etc. (旅館、餐廳等)廚師之領班;主廚。

chef-d'œuvre /ˌʃeɪ 'dɜ:vrə ; ʃɛ'dœvrə/ *n* (*pl* chefs-d'œuvre, pronunciation unchanged 複數讀音不變) (F) (person's) masterpiece. (法)(某人之)傑作;名著。

chemi·cal /'kemɪkl ; 'kɛmɪkḷ/ *adj* of, made by, chemistry: 化學的;經化學程序製成的: *~ warfare,* using poison gas, smoke, incendiary bombs, etc. 化學戰(使用毒氣、煙幕、燃燒彈等)。□ *n* (often *pl*) substance used in, or obtained by, chemistry. (常用複數) 化學藥品;化學產品 (用於化學或以化學方法製成之物質)。~**·ly** /-klɪ ; -klɪ/ *adv*

che·mise /ʃə'mi:z ; ʃə'miz/ *n* loose, long under-garment formerly worn by women and girls; loose beltless dress. 昔時婦女所穿之寬鬆內衣;無腰帶的寬鬆女衣。

chem·ist /'kemɪst ; 'kɛmɪst/ *n* **1** person trained or expert in chemistry. 化學家。 **2** (US 美 = *druggist*) pharmacist; person who prepares medicines (from prescriptions) and sells medical goods, toilet articles, etc: 藥劑師;藥商(根據藥方配藥並販賣藥品、化粧用品等): *~'s shop*, pharmacy. 藥店;藥房。

chem·is·try /'kemɪstrɪ ; 'kɛmɪstrɪ/ *n* [U] branch of science that deals with how substances are made up, how they (their elements) combine, how they act under different conditions. 化學(科學的一部門,研究物質之構成及其元素,其化合及其在不同情況下之作用)。

chemo·ther·apy /ˌkeməʊ'θerəpɪ ; ˌkɛmo'θɛrəpɪ/ *n* [U] treatment of disease by drugs that attack microbes. 化學療法(指使用藥物殺滅病菌的療法)。

che·nille /ʃə'ni:l ; ʃə'nil/ *n* velvety cord used for trimming dresses and furniture. (用以裝飾衣服及傢具之)絲絨線。

cheque /tʃek ; tʃɛk/ *n* (US = **check**) written order (usu on a printed form) to a bank to pay money: 支票(開向銀行取款之單據,通常爲排印好的固定形式): *a ~ for £10;* 一張十鎊的支票; *pay by ~.* 以支票付給。Cf 參較 *pay in cash.* 付現款。 **'~-book** *n* number of blank ~s bound together. 支票簿。 **'~ card,** = *banker's card.* ⇨ bank[4].

chequer /'tʃekə(r) ; 'tʃɛkɚ/ *vt* (US = **checker**) (usu passive) mark with a pattern of squares or patches of different colours or shades; (fig) mark by changes of good and bad fortune, etc: (通常用被動語態)使具有不同色彩或色度的方格花式;(喻)使交替遭遇好運與惡運等: *a lawn ~ed with sunlight and shade;* 陽光與樹蔭交錯的草坪; *a ~ed career,* full of ups and downs of fortune, with variety of incident. 飽經滄桑的一生;盛衰多變的一生。

cher·ish /'tʃerɪʃ ; 'tʃɛrɪʃ/ *vt* [VP6A] **1** care for tenderly. 珍愛;撫愛。**2** keep alive (hope, ambition, feelings, etc) in one's heart: 心中懷着(希望、志願、感情等): *For years she ~ed the hope that her husband might still be alive.* 許多年來,她一直懷着她的丈夫可能仍活在人世的希望。*Don't ~ the illusion that your father will always pay your debts.* 不要心存你父親會永遠替你償債的幻想。

che·root /ʃə'ru:t ; ʃə'rut/ *n* cigar with both ends open. 方頭的雪茄烟(卽無尖頭者)。

cherry /'tʃerɪ ; 'tʃɛrɪ/ *n* (*pl* -rries) (tree with) soft, small, round fruit, red, yellow or black when ripe and with a stone-like seed in the middle, ⇨ the illus at fruit; [U] the wood of this tree. 櫻桃(一種軟的小圓果,ㄏ熟時呈紅、黃或黑色,中心有堅硬果核 參看 fruit 之挿圖);櫻桃樹;櫻桃木。□ *adj* red: 紅色的: *~ lips.* 櫻唇。

cherub /'tʃerəb ; 'tʃɛrəb/ *n* **1** (*pl* ~s) small beautiful child; (in art) such a child with wings. 美麗的孩童;(藝術中)有翼的小天使。 **2** (*pl* ~im /'tʃerəbɪm ; 'tʃɛrjubɪm/) (biblical) one of the second highest order of angels. (聖經)二級天使。⇨ seraph. **che·ru·bic** /tʃɪ'ru:bɪk ; tʃə'rubɪk/ *adj* (esp) sweet and innocent looking; roundfaced. (尤指)甜美而天眞無邪的;圓臉的。

cher·vil /'tʃɜ:vɪl ; 'tʃɝvɪl/ *n* [U] garden herb used to flavour soups, salads, etc. 山蘿蔔(其嫩葉用於湯、沙拉等之調味)。

chess /tʃes ; tʃɛs/ *n* [U] game for two players with sixteen pieces each (each called a **'~·man** /-mæn ; -ˌmæn/), on a board with sixty-four squares (called a **'~-board**). 西洋棋(二人對奕,每人十六子,稱爲棋子,置於有六十四方格之盤上,稱爲棋盤)。

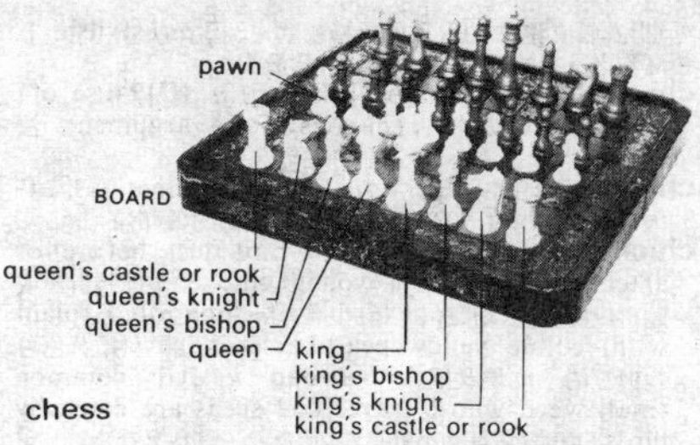

chess

chest /tʃest ; tʃɛst/ *n* **1** large, strong (usu wooden) box with a lid for storing, eg clothes, tools, money, medicine, tea, etc. (大而堅固,通常係木製之有蓋的)箱;大木箱(用以存放衣服、工具、錢財、醫藥、茶等)。 **ˌ~ of 'drawers,** large ~ with drawers for clothes. (裝衣服的)五屜櫃;衣櫃。 **2** (anat) upper front part of the body, enclosed by the ribs, containing the heart and lungs. (解剖)(人體的)胸部(外爲肋骨,內含心臟及肺)。⇨ the illus at trunk. 參看 trunk 之挿圖。 ***get sth off one's ~,*** (colloq) say sth one is anxious to say. (俗)傾吐胸中積悶;說出所要說的話。 ***hold/keep one's cards close to one's/the ~,*** be secretive. 善於保守秘密;秘而不宣的。 **3** (US) (funds of the) treasury of a public institution: (美)(公家機構的)金庫;經費;基金: *the community ~,* for charitable purposes. (用於慈善事業的)社會基金。

ches·ter·field /'tʃestəfi:ld ; 'tʃɛstɚˌfild/ *n* **1** single-breasted overcoat with a flap that covers the buttonholes. 單排扣並有蓋遮住扣眼之外衣。 **2** long padded couch with sides and a back. 有扶手及靠背之長沙發。

chest·nut /'tʃesnʌt ; 'tʃɛsnət/ *n* **1** [C, U] (sorts of, wood of) tree with smooth, bright reddish-brown nut; the nut of this tree (those of the Spanish or sweet ~ being edible). 栗樹(所結之栗子光滑而呈鮮明之紅褐色);栗木;栗子(西班牙栗樹或甜栗樹所結可食之栗子)。 ⇨ the illus at tree; 參看 tree 之挿圖; ⇨ horse(4). **2** colour of the nut. 栗子色;棗紅色。 **3** horse of this colour. 栗色馬;棗紅色馬。 **4** (colloq) story or joke that is too old or well known to be amusing. (俗)已不能再引起人興趣的陳腐的故事或笑話。

cheval glass /ʃə'væl glɑ:s *US:* -glæs ; ʃə'vælˌglæs/ *n* full-length mirror mounted on upright supports on which it can be tilted. 裝於直立的架上可以傾斜的全身鏡;穿衣鏡。

chev·ron /'ʃevrən ; 'ʃɛvrən/ *n* bent line or stripe (∨ or ∧) worn on the sleeve by soldiers, policemen, etc to show rank, etc. 軍人、警察等佩於袖上以代表階級等的臂章;(作∨或∧形的)袖章。

chew /tʃu: ; tʃu/ *vt, vi* **1** [VP6A,15B,2A,C] *~ (up),* work (food, etc) about between the teeth in order to crush it: 咀嚼(食物等): *C~ your food well before you swallow it.* 食物在吞嚥前要仔細咀嚼。 **'~ing-gum** *n* [U] sticky substance sweetened and flavoured for ~ing. 橡皮糖;口香糖。⇨ also bite[1](1) and cud. **2** [VP15B, 3A] *~ **sth over; ~ (up)on sth,*** (colloq) think over, consider. (俗)考慮;思量(某事)。 *~ **the rag,*** (dated sl) discuss matters (esp old grievances). (過時俚語)討論事情(尤指舊日的苦況);發牢騷。□ *n* act of ~ing; sth (to be) ~ed: 咀嚼;所(要)嚼之物: *a ~ of tobacco.* 一次所嚼之菸草;一塊嚼煙。

Chi·anti /kɪ'æntɪ ; kɪ'æntɪ/ *n* [U] dry red or white Italian wine. 一種無甜味的紅色或白色義大利葡萄酒。

chi·aro·scuro /kɪˌɑ:rə'skʊərəʊ ; kɪˌarə'skjʊro/ *n* (I) distribution of light and shade (esp in a painting). (義)(尤指圖畫中)明暗之配合;明暗對照法。

chic /ʃi:k ; ʃik/ *n* [U] (of clothes, their wearer) style that gives an air of sophisticated elegance.

(指衣服或穿衣者)高雅的風格或款式。□ *adj* stylish. 有高雅之風格的;漂亮的;時髦的;瀟洒的。

chi·can·ery /ʃɪˈkeɪnərɪ ; ʃɪˈkenərɪ/ *n* [U] (use of) legal trickery; [C] (*pl* -ries) false argument. 法律上的狡計;奸詐手段;詭辯;狡辯。

chi·chi /ˈʃiːʃiː ; ˈʃiˈʃi/ *adj* (colloq) pretentious; affected; vulgar. (俗)自命不凡的;矯飾的;鄙俗的。

chick /tʃɪk ; tʃɪk/ *n* **1** young bird just before or after hatching, esp a young chicken. 即將孵出或剛孵出的小鳥;幼雛;(尤指)小雞。ˈ**~·pea** *n* [C] (plant with) edible yellow pea-like seeds. 雛豆(結黃色可食似豆的子);埃及豆。ˈ**~·weed** *n* [U] common small weed whose leaves and seeds are eaten by birds. 蘩縷(常見之小野草,其葉及種子爲鳥之食物)。 **2** small child; (sl) girl. 嬰孩;小孩;(俚)女孩。

chicken /ˈtʃɪkɪn ; ˈtʃɪkɪn/ *n* **1** young bird, esp a young hen: 幼鳥;幼雛;(尤指)小母雞: *She's no ~*, (fig, sl) is no longer young. (喻,俚)她年紀不輕了。 ⇨ the illus at fowl. 參看 fowl 之挿圖。***(Don't) count one's ~s before they are hatched,*** (Don't) be too hopeful of one's chances of success, etc. (不要)蛋尚未孵出先數雞;(不要)對於成功等的可能性過於樂觀。ˈ**~·feed** *n* (fig, sl) sth of relatively small value. (喻,俚)價值極少的東西;微不足道的東西。ˌ**~-ˈhearted** /-hɑːtɪd ; -ˈhɑrtɪd/ *adj* lacking in courage. 無勇氣的;膽小的;怯懦的。ˈ**~·pox** *n* [U] disease (esp of children) accompanied by red spots on the skin. (尤爲兒童所患的)水痘。ˈ**~-run** *n* fenced-in area for ~s to run in. 雞欄(四周設圍供養雞的地方)。**2** [U] its flesh as food. 小雞肉;嫩雞肉。□ *pred adj* (sl) cowardly. (俚)膽小的;怯懦的。

chicle /ˈtʃɪkl ; ˈtʃɪkl̩/ *n* [U] chief ingredient of chewing-gum. 奇可樹液(製口香糖的主要原料)。

chic·ory /ˈtʃɪkərɪ ; ˈtʃɪkərɪ/ *n* [U] plant used as a vegetable and for salad, the root of which is roasted and made into a powder (used with or instead of coffee). 菊苣(可作蔬菜並可涼拌食之,其根經烘焙並製成粉,可與咖啡同用,或做咖啡之代用品)。⇨ the illus at vegetable. 參看 vegetable 之挿圖。

chide /tʃaɪd ; tʃaɪd/ *vt, vi* (*pt* chided /ˈtʃaɪdɪd ; ˈtʃaɪdɪd/ or chid /tʃɪd ; tʃɪd/, *pp* chided, chid or chidden /ˈtʃɪdn ; ˈtʃɪdn̩/) [VP6A, 14] ~ ***sb (for),*** (liter) scold; rebuke. (文)責駡;斥責。

chief /tʃiːf ; tʃif/ *n* **1** leader or ruler: 首領;酋長;頭目: *the ~ of the tribe.* 該部族之酋長。 **2** head of a department; highest official. 機關首長。***C~ of Staff,*** senior staff officer. 參謀長。***in ~,*** most of all, especially: 最要者;尤其: *for many reasons, and this one in ~.* 爲了許多理由,尤其這一點。**-in-ˈ~,** supreme: 最高的: *the Commander-in-~.* 統帥;總司令。□ *adj* (attrib only; no comp or superl) (僅作形容用法;無比較級或最高級) **1** principal; most important: 主要的;最重要的: *the ~ rivers of India;* 印度之主要的河流; *the ~ thing to remember.* 要記住的最重要事情。 **2** first in rank: 階級最高的: *the C~ Justice;* 審判長; *the ~ priest.* 祭司長。**~·ly** *adv* **1** above all; first of all. 尤要者;首要者。 **2** mostly; mainly: 大半;主要: *It is ~ly composed of....* 它主要係由…構成。

chief·tain /ˈtʃiːftən ; ˈtʃiftɪn/ *n* leader of a clan or tribe; chief. 族長;部落酋長;首長;首領。**~cy** /ˈtʃiːftənsɪ ; ˈtʃiftɪnsɪ/ *n* position or rank of a ~. 族長或酋長等的地位或階級。

chif·fon /ˈʃɪfɒn *US:* ʃɪˈfɒn ; ʃɪˈfɑn/ *n* [U] thin, transparent silk material used for scarves, veils, etc. 一種透明的絲織薄紗(用以製圍巾、面紗等)。

chif·fon·ier /ˌʃɪfəˈnɪə(r);ˌʃɪfəˈnɪr/ *n* **1** (GB) movable low cupboard with a flat top used as a table. (英)一種可移動之矮橱(其平頂可用作桌子)。 **2** (US) high chest of drawers (GB 英 = *tallboy*). (美)高衣橱。

chi·gnon /ˈʃiːnjɒn ; ˈʃinjɑn/ *n* (F) knot or roll of hair worn at the back of the head by women. (法)婦人梳於頭後之髮髻。

chil·blain /ˈtʃɪlbleɪn ; ˈtʃɪlˌblen/ *n* [C] painful swelling, esp on the hand or foot, caused by exposure to cold. (尤指手或脚上的)凍瘡。**~ed** /-eɪnd ; -end/ *adj* having ~s. 有凍瘡的;生凍瘡的。

child /tʃaɪld ; tʃaɪld/ *n* (*pl* children /ˈtʃɪldrən ; ˈtʃɪldrən/) unborn or newly born human being; boy or girl; son or daughter (of any age). 嬰兒;胎兒;小孩(男或女);孩子(子或女,不限年齡)。ˈ**~'s play,** sth very easily done. 極易做之事。***be with ~,*** (archaic) be pregnant. (古)懷孕。ˈ**~-bearing** *n* [U] giving birth to children: 生產小孩: *Ten years of ~-bearing exhausted her strength.* 生產小孩十年耗盡了她的體力。ˈ**~·birth** *n* [U] the process of giving birth to a ~: 分娩;生產(小孩): *She died in ~birth.* 她因生產而死。ˈ**~·hood** /-hʊd ; -ˌhʊd/ *n* [U] state of being a ~; time during which one is a ~: 幼年;兒童期;童年時代: *have a happy ~hood.* 有快樂的童年。***second ~hood,*** dotage (in extreme old age). 老耄;衰老。**~·ish** *adj* of, behaving like, suitable for, a ~; not suited to an adult: 兒童的;行爲如兒童的;適合於兒童的;幼稚的;不適合成年人的: *~ish games／arguments.* 小兒玩的遊戲(幼稚的論點)。 **~·less** *adj* having no child(ren): 無子女的: *a ~less couple.* 無子女的夫婦。ˈ**~·like** *adj* simple, innocent, frank. 率直的;純眞的;天眞無邪的。

chile, chili /ˈtʃɪlɪ ; ˈtʃɪlɪ/ *n* (US) = chilli.

chill /tʃɪl ; tʃɪl/ *n* **1** (*sing* only) unpleasant feeling of coldness: (僅用單數)由寒冷所引起不舒服的感覺;寒意: *There's quite a ~ in the air this morning.* 今天早晨的空氣頗有寒意。 *Take the ~ off the water,* warm it a little. 將這水熱一熱。 **2** (fig) (*sing* only) depressing influence; sth that causes a downhearted feeling: (喻)(僅用單數)掃興;沮喪;使人沮喪或掃興之事: *The bad news cast a ~ over the gathering.* 這個壞消息使聚會的人感到掃興。 **3** [C] illness caused by cold and damp, with shivering of the body: 由寒冷與潮濕所引起之疾病(身體有顫抖現象);寒慄;寒戰;感冒: *catch a ~.* 受寒。□ *adj* unpleasantly cold: 冷得使人不舒服的;寒冷的;冷酷的: *a ~ breeze;* 帶寒意的微風; *a ~ welcome.* 冷淡的歡迎。□ *vt, vi* [VP6A, 2A, C] make or become cold or cool: 使寒冷;變爲寒冷: *He was ~ed to the bone.* 他覺得寒冷徹骨。 *Don't ~ their enthusiasm.* 不要向他們的熱心潑冷水。**~ed beef,** beef preserved in cold storage at a moderately low temperature but not frozen. 冷藏牛肉(僅保持適當的低溫度,但未冰凍)。**~y** *adj* (-ier, -iest) **1** rather cold: 頗冷的;相當冷的;寒冷的: *a ~y room;* 寒冷的房間; *feel ~y.* 覺得寒冷。*It's rather ~y this morning.* 今天早晨相當冷。 **2** (fig) unfriendly: (喻)不友善的;冷淡的: *a ~y welcome;* 冷淡的歡迎; *~y politeness.* 冷淡的禮貌。

chilli, chilly, chile, chili /ˈtʃɪlɪ ; ˈtʃɪlɪ/ *n* (*pl* -ies) dried pod of red pepper (capsicum), often made into powder and used to give a hot flavour to sauces, etc. 乾辣椒(常磨成粉用以爲調味汁等添加辣味)。

chime /tʃaɪm ; tʃaɪm/ *n* (series of notes sounded by a) tuned set of bells: 鐘琴(一組樂鐘);管鐘;鐘琴所發出的樂音: *a ~ of bells;* 一組鐘琴; *ring the ~s;* 擊奏鐘琴; *listen to the ~s.* 聽鐘琴之樂聲。□ *vi, vt* **1** [VP6A, 15A, 2A, C] (of bells, a clock) make (bells) ring; ring (~s) on bells; show (the hour) by ringing: (指樂鐘、時鐘)鳴響;發鐘聲;鳴響報(時): *The bells／The ringers ~d out a tune.* 樂鐘(鳴鐘者)奏出曲調。 *The bells are chiming.* 樂鐘在響。 *The church clock ~d midnight.* 教堂裡的時鐘敲出午夜的時間。 **2** [VP2C] ~ ***in,*** break in on the talk of others, usu to express agreement: 當別人談話時突然挿嘴(通常表示同意): *'Of course,' he ~d in.* '當然',他突然挿嘴說。~ ***(in) with,*** be in agreement with; suit: 與…一致;適合: *I think your plans will ~ in with mine.* 我想你的計畫會與我的一致。

chim·era, chim·aera /kaɪˈmɪərə ; kəˈmɪrə/ *n* **1** (Gk myth) monster with a lion's head, a goat's body, and a serpent's tail. (希臘神話)凱米拉(獅頭、羊身、蛇尾之怪物)。 **2** horrible creature of the imagination. 想像中的可怕的怪物。 **3** (fig) wild or impossible idea or fancy. (喻)幻想;妄想;狂想。

chim·eri·cal /kaɪˈmerɪkl ; kəˈmɪrɪkl/ *adj* unreal; visionary: 非眞實的; 幻想的: *chimerical ideas / schemes.* 幻想的念頭(計謀)。

chim·ney /ˈtʃɪmnɪ ; ˈtʃɪmnɪ/ *n* **1** structure through which smoke from a fire is carried away through the wall or roof of a building. 煙囱;煙筒。 **ˈ~-breast** *n* projecting wall in a room that contains the ~. 煙囱凸肚牆(室內凸出的牆,裡面有煙囱)。**ˈ~ corner,** seat in an old-fashioned fireplace. 舊式壁爐邊的座位。 **ˈ~·piece** *n* = mantel. **ˈ~·pot** *n* pipe (earthenware or metal) fitted to the top of a ~. (陶製或金屬製的)煙囱頂管。**ˈ~·stack** *n* group of ~ tops. (包括數個煙道的)總煙囱。 **ˈ~-sweep(er)** *n* man who sweeps soot from ~s. 掃煙囱的人。 **2** glass tube that protects the flame of an oil-lamp from draughts. (油燈用以遮風的)玻璃燈罩。 **3** (mountaineering) narrow cleft or opening by which a cliff face may be climbed. (爬山術)懸崖表面可供爬山者攀登之窄狹的裂縫或缺口。 ⇨ the illus at mountain. 參看 mountain 之插圖。

chimneys

chimp /tʃɪmp ; tʃɪmp/ *n* (colloq abbr of) chimpanzee. (俗)爲 chimpanzee 之略。

chim·pan·zee /ˌtʃɪmpænˈziː ; ˌtʃɪmpænˈzi/ *n* African ape, smaller than a gorilla. 非洲人猿; 黑猩猩(較 gorilla 爲小)。⇨ the illus at ape. 參看 ape 之插圖。

chin /tʃɪn ; tʃɪn/ *n* part of the face below the mouth; front of the lower jaw. 下巴;下頷(面部之在嘴以下之部份,下顎之前端)。 ⇨ the illus at head. 參看 head 之插圖。 ***keep one's ˈ~ up,*** (colloq) show determination to face trouble without betraying fear or sorrow. (俗)表示決心應付困難而無畏。**ˈ~-strap** *n* strap (on a helmet) held on the ~. (頭盔上)套住下巴的皮帶。 **ˈ~-wagging** *n* (colloq) talking, gossiping. (俗)閒談;聊天。

china /ˈtʃaɪnə ; ˈtʃaɪnə/ *n* [U] baked and glazed fine white clay; (collective) articles (eg cups, saucers, plates) made from this. 陶瓷;(集合用法)瓷器(如杯、碟、盤)。**ˈ~-closet** *n* cupboard in which ~ is kept or displayed. 放置或展示瓷器杯皿的櫥櫃。 **ˈ~·ware** *n* [U] dishes, ornaments, etc made of ~ clay. 瓷器(如盤碟、裝飾品等)。

chin·chil·la /tʃɪnˈtʃɪlə ; tʃɪnˈtʃɪlə/ *n* [C] small S American animal that looks sth like a squirrel; [U] its soft grey fur. 南美洲產之栗鼠類(類似松鼠); 栗鼠之柔軟的灰色毛皮。

chine /tʃaɪn ; tʃaɪn/ *n* animal's backbone or part of it as a joint of meat. 動物的脊椎骨;脊肉;排骨肉。

chink[1] /tʃɪŋk ; tʃɪŋk/ *n* narrow opening or crack (eg between boards in the wall of a shed, through which the wind blows or through which one may peep). 縫隙;裂罅(如棚屋之牆板中間,風可以吹入,或可用以窺視者)。

chink[2] /tʃɪŋk ; tʃɪŋk/ *vt, vi* [VP6A,15B,2A,C] make the sound of coins, glasses, etc striking together; cause (coins, etc) to make such sounds. 發出硬幣、玻璃製品等碰擊時之叮噹聲;使(錢幣、玻璃製品等)發叮噹聲。 □ *n* ***a/the ~ (of),*** this sound: (碰擊硬幣、玻璃製品等所發出之)叮噹聲: *I heard the ~ of coins.* 我聽見錢幣碰擊的聲音。

chintz /tʃɪnts ; tʃɪnts/ *n* [U] kind of cotton cloth (usu glazed) with printed designs in colours, used for curtains, furniture covers, etc. 印花棉布(通常表面光滑,用製帷幔、傢具套等)。

chip /tʃɪp ; tʃɪp/ *n* **1** small piece cut or broken off (from wood, stone, china, glass, etc). (木、石、瓷、玻璃等之) 削片;破片;渣; 屑。 **ˈ~·board** *n* building material made from compressed ~s of waste wood, sawdust, etc and glue. 木渣板(用木屑、鋸屑等廢材連同膠緊壓而成的建材)。 ~ ***off/of the old block,*** son who is very like his father. 酷似其父之子。 ***have a ˈ~ on one's shoulder,*** have a defiant air, as if expecting and ready to accept a challenge; resent prejudice against oneself as (often incorrectly) perceived in other people. 像要跟人打架的樣子;氣勢洶洶; 憤恨別人對自己 (常爲不正確地)懷有偏見。 **2** strip cut from an apple, a potato, etc: (自蘋果、馬鈴薯等切下的細長的)條: *fish and ~s,* fried fish and potato ~s. 油炸的魚及馬鈴薯條。 **3** place (eg in a cup) from which a ~ has come. (如茶杯之)缺口。**4** thin strip cut from wood, palm-leaf, etc, used in making baskets, hats, etc: (編籃子、帽子等所用之) 薄木片條、棕葉片條等: (usu attrib) (通常作形容用法) ~ *bonnets;* 用上述材料所編之無邊女帽; ~ *baskets.* 用上述材料所編之籃子。 **5** flat plastic counter used as a money token (esp in gambling). (尤指賭錢用的塑膠製的) 籌碼。 ***have had one's ~s,*** (sl) one's last chance. (俚)再也沒有機會了。***(when) the ~s are down,*** (when) a crisis point is reached. (當) 危急關頭到臨。 □ *vt, vi* (-pp-) **1** [VP6A, 15A, 15B] ~ ***off/from,*** cut or break a piece: 切下或擊破一片: ~ *a piece off (the edge of a cup);* (在杯子的邊上)打破一塊; ~ *old paint from the side of a ship.* 自船側鏟去舊油漆。*All the plates have ~ped edges.* 所有的盤子邊上都有破損。 **2** [VP6A] make into ~s(2): 切成細條;切成薄片: *~ped potatoes.* 把馬鈴薯切成細長條。 **3** [VP2A] (of things) be easily broken at the edge: (指物件)邊緣容易破損: *These cups ~ if you are not careful.* 這些杯子,如果你不小心,邊緣容易破損。 **4** [VP2C] ~ ***in,*** (colloq) (俗) **(a)** interrupt; join in (a conversation). 插嘴; 加入(談話)。**(b)** contribute money (to a fund). 捐獻金錢(給某一基金)。 **5** [VP6A] shape (sth) by cutting the edge or surface (with an axe or a chisel). (用斧或鑿) 劈鑿(某物)的邊緣或表面使成某種形狀。**ˈ~·pings** *n pl* bits of stone, marble, etc made by ~ping: 劈鑿下來的碎石等;碎屑;破片: *ˈroad ~pings,* for making a road surface. 鋪路用的碎石。

chip·munk /ˈtʃɪpmʌŋk ; ˈtʃɪpmʌŋk/ *n* small, striped N American squirrel-like rodent. 金花鼠(北美洲所產有條紋似松鼠的齧齒小動物)。

Chip·pen·dale /ˈtʃɪpəndeɪl ; ˈtʃɪpənˌdel/ *n* light style of drawing-room furniture (18th c in England): 齊本德耳式 (十八世紀英國之客廳傢具的輕巧款式): ~ *chairs.* 齊本德耳式椅。

chi·rop·odist /kɪˈrɒpədɪst ; kaɪˈrɑpədɪst/ *n* person who is expert in the treatment of troubles of the feet and toenails. 足科醫生(專醫足及足趾甲之疾患)。 **chi·rop·ody** /kɪˈrɒpədɪ ; kaɪˈrɑpədɪ/ *n* [U] work of a ~. 足病的治療。

chiro·prac·tor /ˈkaɪərəʊpræktə(r) ; ˈkaɪrəˌpræktɚ/ *n* person who treats diseases by manipulating the joints (esp the spinal column). 按摩關節(尤指脊椎)以治病者;按脊術士。

chirp /tʃɜːp ; tʃɝp/ *vi, vt, n* [VP2A, C, 6A] (make) short, sharp note(s) or sound(s) (as of small birds or insects); utter in this way: (發)啁啾聲(如小鳥之鳴聲)或吱唧聲(如昆蟲鳴聲);以此種聲音說出: *the ~s of the sparrows/cicadas;* 麻雀之吱喳聲 (蟬之吱唧聲); *grasshoppers ~ing all day.* 終日唧唧而鳴的蚱蜢。

chirpy /ˈtʃɜːpɪ ; ˈtʃɝpɪ/ *adj* (colloq) lively, cheerful. (俗)活潑的;高興的。**chirp·ily** /ˈtʃɜːpɪlɪ ; ˈtʃɝpɪlɪ/ *adv* **chirpi·ness** *n*

chir·rup /ˈtʃɪrəp ; ˈtʃɪrəp/ *vt, vi, n* (make a) series of chirps. (發)連續的吱喳鳴聲。

chisel /ˈtʃɪzl ; ˈtʃɪzl/ *n* steel tool with a bevelled edge for shaping wood, stone or metal. 鑿子(修鑿木、石或金屬之有斜刃的鋼製工具)。 ⇨ the illus at tool. 參看 tool 之插圖。□ *vt* (-ll-, also -l- in US) [VP6A, 15B, 14] **1** cut or shape with a ~: 用鑿子鑿成某種形狀;鑿刻: *~led features,* (of a person's appearance) clear cut; well modelled. (指人的容貌)輪廓鮮明的五官。 **2** (colloq) cheat; swindle. (俗)欺騙;詐騙。**~·ler** /ˈtʃɪzələ(r) ; ˈtʃɪzlɚ/ *n* person who ~s(2). 騙子;騙徒。

chit¹ /tʃɪt ; tʃɪt/ *n* young child; young, small, slender woman (often used rather ˌcontemptuously): 幼兒;瘦小的少女(常含輕蔑之意): *a mere ˈ~ of a child;* 不過是一個小毛頭; *only a ˈ~ of a woman.* 只不過是一個黃毛丫頭。

chit² /tʃɪt ; tʃɪt/ *n* short note or letter; note of sum of money owed (eg for drinks, etc at a hotel). 短信;便條;欠款之單據;掛帳之單據(如旅館之酒帳等)。

chit-chat /ˈtʃɪt tʃæt ; ˈtʃɪtˌtʃæt/ *n* [U] light, informal conversation. 閒談;聊天。

chiv·al·ry /ˈʃɪvlrɪ ; ˈʃɪvl̩rɪ/ *n* [U] laws and customs (religious, moral and social) of the knights in the Middle Ages; the qualities that knights were expected to have (courage, honour, courtesy, loyalty, devotion to the weak and helpless, to the service of women). (中世紀的)武士制度(一種宗教的、道德的和社會的法律及習俗); 騎士道; 武士精神(包括勇敢、榮譽心、禮貌、忠貞、熱心幫助弱者及婦女)。**chiv·al·rous** /ˈʃɪvlrəs ; ˈʃɪvl̩rəs/ *adj* of, as of, the age of ~; of, as of, the knights of the Middle Ages; honourable; courteous. 武士時代的;中世紀之武士的;俠義的;可敬的;有禮貌的。

chive /tʃaɪv ; tʃaɪv/ *n* [U] small plant of the onion family, of which the slender leaves are used as a seasoning (in salads, etc). 蝦夷葱(葱屬小植物,其細長的葉子可以調味,用於沙拉等)。

chivy, chivvy /ˈtʃɪvɪ ; ˈtʃɪvɪ/ *vt* [VP15B] (colloq) *~ sb about/along/up,* pester; chase; harass. (俗)使某人苦惱;到處追逐某人;煩擾。

chlor·ide /ˈklɔːraɪd ; ˈkloraɪd/ *n* [U] (chem) compound of chlorine: (化)氯化物: *~ of lime/soda/potash.* 漂白粉(氯化鈉;氯化鉀)。

chlor·ine /ˈklɔːriːn ; ˈklorin/ *n* [U] (chem) greenish-yellow, bad-smelling poisonous gas (symbol **Cl**), obtained from common salt (= *sodium chloride*), used as a sterilizing agent and in industry. (化)氯(黃綠色有臭味毒氣,化學符號 Cl,自普通鹽即氯化鈉中提出,用作消毒劑及用於工業中)。 **chlor·in·ate** /ˈklɔːrɪneɪt ; ˈklorɪˌnet/ *vt* treat, sterilize, with ~: 以氯處理或消毒: *chlorinated water,* water purified from disease germs by this treatment. 以氯消毒過的水。**chlori·na·tion** /ˌklɔːrɪˈneɪʃn ; ˌklorɪˈneʃən/ *n*

chloro·form /ˈklɒrəfɔːm *US:* ˈklɔːr- ; ˈkloraˌfɔrm/ *n* [U] thin, colourless liquid formerly given, in the form of vapour, to make a person unconscious during a surgical operation. 氯仿;哥羅仿;三氯甲烷(稀薄無色液體,昔時經汽化用於外科手術作麻醉劑)。

chloro·phyll /ˈklɒrəfɪl *US:* ˈklɔːr- ; ˈkloraˌfɪl/ *n* [U] (bot) green colouring matter in the leaves of plants. (植)葉綠素。

chock /tʃɒk ; tʃɑk/ *n* block or wedge of wood used to prevent sth (eg a wheel, barrel, door) from moving. (防止某物如輪子、桶、門等移動所用之)墊木;輪檔。□ *vt* [VP6A, 15B] *~ (up),* **1** make fast with, support on, a ~ or ~s. 用墊木墊住使穩固;用楔子支持。 **2** (colloq) (俗): *a room ~ed up with furniture,* filled up with far too much furniture. 爲傢具所擁塞不堪的房間。 **ˈ~-full (of); ˌ~-a-ˈblock (with); ˌ~-a-ˌblock ˈfull (of),** *adjj* (pred) filled to the limit. (敍述用法)充滿的;塞滿的。

choc·olate /ˈtʃɒklət ; ˈtʃɔkəlɪt/ *n* **1** [U] substance (powder or slab) made from the crushed seeds of the cacao tree; drink made by mixing this with hot water or milk; [C, U] (colloq abbr 俗略作 **choc** /tʃɒk ; tʃɑk/) sweet substance made from this, usu sweetened and often flavoured: 巧克力(自磨碎之可可子中提取之物質,粉狀或塊狀); 由巧克力與熱水或牛奶混合的飲料;(由巧克力粉製成的)巧克力糖(通常加糖且常加香料): *a bar of ~;* 一塊巧克力糖; *a box of ~s;* 一盒巧克力糖; (attrib) (形容用法) *~ biscuit,* covered with ~; 覆有巧克力的餅乾; *~ cream,* sweet paste covered with ~. 奶油夾心巧克力。 **2** the colour of this substance, dark brown. 巧克力色;深褐色。**choc-ice** /ˈtʃɒkaɪs ; ˈtʃɑk aɪs/ *n* (colloq) slab of ice-cream coated with ~. (俗)外加一層巧克力的雪糕;巧克力雪糕。

choice /tʃɔɪs ; tʃɔɪs/ *n* **1** act of choosing: 選擇;挑選: *make a careful ~;* 細心選擇; *be careful in your ~;* 仔細從事選擇; *take your ~.* 隨你選擇。 **2** [U] right or possibility of choosing: 選擇的權利或可能: *I have no ~ in the matter,* cannot choose, must act in this way. 在這件事中我沒有選擇的餘地(必須這樣做)。 ***for ~,*** by preference; if one must select: 憑着喜愛;如果必須選擇: *I should take this one for ~.* 要選我就選這個。***Hobson's ~,*** no ~ at all because there is only one thing to take or do. 沒有選擇的餘地(因爲只有一樣事物可取或可做)。 **3** variety from which to choose: 備選的種類: *This shop has a large ~ of clothes.* 此店有甚多種類的衣服可供挑選。 **4** person or thing chosen: 所選擇的人或物: *This is my ~.* 這就是我所選的。□ *adj* carefully chosen; uncommonly good: 精選的;上等的: *~ fruit.* 上選的水果。

choir /ˈkwaɪə(r) ; kwaɪr/ *n* **1** company of persons trained to sing together, esp to lead the singing in church. 合唱團; (尤指教堂裡領導衆人唱詩的)唱詩班;聖樂隊。 **2** part of a church building for the ~. 教堂裏唱詩班的席位。⇨ the illus at church. 參看 church 之插圖。 **ˈ~-school** *n* grammar school (attached to or connected with a cathedral) for **ˈ~-boys.** 大教堂爲唱詩班的男童所附設的中學。

choke¹ /tʃəʊk ; tʃok/ *vi, vt* **1** [VP2A,3A] be unable to breathe because of sth in the windpipe, or because of emotion: 因某物塞住氣管或因感情激動而不能呼吸; 窒息; 有物哽於喉中: *~ over one's food;* 喉爲食物所哽; *~ with anger;* 怒氣哽喉; *~ to death.* 哽死。**2** [VP6A,14] *~ (with),* stop the breathing of, by pressing the windpipe from outside or blocking it up inside, or (of smoke, etc) by being unfit to breathe: 由外扼住或由內塞住氣管使不能呼吸; (指烟)因不適宜於呼吸而使人窒息;使悶氣: *~ the life out of sb.* 將某人扼斃。*The smoke almost ~d me.* 這烟幾乎使我窒息。 *Her voice was ~d with sobs.* 她因啜泣而不能成聲。 *Anger ~d his words.* 他因發怒而說不出話來。*He swallowed a plum-stone and was almost ~d,* ie to death. 他吞下了一個梅核幾乎哽死。 **3** [VP3A, 6A, 15B] *~ (up) (with),* fill, partly or completely, a passage, space, etc that is usually clear: 堵塞;阻塞;充塞(通道,空間等): *a chimney/drain ~d (up) with dirt.* 爲污物所堵塞的烟囱(排水管)。*The garden is ~d with weeds.* 花園中野草叢生。*Weeds have ~ed (up) the garden.* 野草長滿了花園。*The room was ~d up with useless old furniture.* 此房充塞着無用的舊傢具。 **4** [VP15B] ***~ sth back/down,*** hold or keep back/down: 忍住;抑制: *~ back one's tears/indignation;* 忍住眼淚(怒火); *~ down one's anger.* 抑制住憤怒。 ***~ sb off,*** (colloq) discourage him (from doing sth); reprimand him for doing sth wrong: (俗)勸阻某人做某事;申斥某人做錯事: *He got ~d off for being late.* 他因遲到而被申斥。 **ˈ~-damp,** carbon dioxide gas, left after an explosion in a coal-mine. 礦坑中爆炸後所留下的二氧化碳氣體。

choke² /tʃəʊk ; tʃok/ *n* valve in a petrol engine to control the intake of air: 汽油發動機內控制空氣進入的活門;阻流瓣;抗流器: *pull out the ~,* ie the ~ control. 拉阻流瓣。

choker /ˈtʃəʊkə(r) ; ˈtʃokɚ/ *n* **1** (hum) stiff, high collar; clerical collar. (諧)硬高領;神父的衣領。 **2** close-fitting necklace (eg of pearls) or scarf. 緊圍在脖子上的(珠寶)項鍊或圍巾。

chokey, choky /ˈtʃəʊkɪ ; ˈtʃokɪ/ *n* (GB; dated sl)

prison. (英;過時俚語)監牢;牢房。

choler /ˈkɒlə(r); ˈkɑlɚ/ *n* (old use, or poet, liter) anger. (舊用法或詩,文)憤怒。 **~ic** /ˈkɒlərɪk; ˈkɑlərɪk/ *adj* easily made angry; often angry. 易激怒的;常發怒的。

chol·era /ˈkɒlərə; ˈkɑlərə/ *n* [U] infectious and often fatal disease, common in hot countries, with vomiting and continual emptying of the bowels. 霍亂(一種傳染性且常爲致命的疾病,常發生於熱帶國家,病狀爲上吐下瀉)。

choose /tʃuːz; tʃuz/ *vt, vi* (*pt* chose /tʃəuz; tʃoz/, *pp* chosen /ˈtʃəuzn; ˈtʃozn̩/) **1** [VP6A, 16A, B, 23, 2A, C, 3A] **~ *(from/out of/between),*** pick out from a greater number; show what or which one wants by taking: (從多數中) 選擇; 挑選;選取: *She took a long time to ~ her new hat.* 她花了很久的時間挑選她的新帽子。 *The greedy boy chose the largest apple in the dish.* 那貪心的孩子挑選了盤中最大的一隻蘋果。 *There are only five to ~ from.* 只有五個可供選擇。 *C~ your friends carefully.* 審愼擇友。*You have chosen well.* 你選得好。*They chose me as their leader/to be their leader.* 他們選了我做他們的領袖。*I was chosen (as) leader.* 我被選爲領袖。 *He had to ~ between death and dishonour.* 他不得不在死亡和屈辱之間做一選擇。***There is nothing/not much/little to ~ between (two or more people or things),*** They are about equal, are equally good/bad, etc. 二者之間沒有什麼可選擇的餘地(意謂二者或二者以上的人或事物差不多相等,同樣地好或壞等)。 **2** [VP7A, 2A] decide; be pleased or determined: 決定;願意;下決心: *I do not ~ to be a candidate.* 我不願意競選。 *He chose to stay where he was.* 他決定停留在他原來的地方。*Do just as you ~,* whatever pleases you. 你願意怎麼做就怎麼做。 ***cannot ~ but,*** (liter) must, have to: (文) 不得不;必須: *He cannot ~ but obey.* 他不得不服從。

choosy, choosey /ˈtʃuːzɪ; ˈtʃuzɪ/ *adj* (-ier, -iest) (colloq, of persons) careful and cautious in choosing; difficult to please. (俗,指人)小心挑選的;挑三揀四的;難以取悅的;好挑剔的。

chop¹ /tʃɒp; tʃɑp/ *vt, vi* (-pp-) [VP6A, 15A, B] **~ *(up) (into),*** cut (into pieces) by blow(s) with an axe or other edged tool: (用斧或其他有刄的工具)砍;劈;剁: *He was ~ping wood,* cutting wood into sticks. 他在劈柴。*Meat is often ~ped up into cubes before being cooked.* 肉在烹煮之前常切成小塊。 *He ~ped a branch off the tree.* 他從樹上砍下一樹枝。 *I'm going to ~ that tree down.* 我要把那棵樹砍倒。 *We had to ~ a way* (= make a path by ~ping) *through the undergrowth.* 我們必須在矮樹林中砍伐出一條路來。[VP3A] **~ *at sth,*** aim a cutting blow at. 向某物砍去。

chop² /tʃɒp; tʃɑp/ *n* **1** chopping blow. 砍;劈。 **2** thick slice of meat with bone in it, (to be) cooked for one person. 供一人吃的一塊連骨的肉;一塊排骨肉。 **ˈ~-house** *n* (now usu 今通常稱 *steakhouse*) restaurant serving chops and steaks. 供應排骨肉及牛排的餐館;牛排館。 **3** ***be for/get the ~,*** be about to be/be killed or sacked². 卽將被殺或解雇;被殺或解雇。 **4** (boxing) short downward blow. (拳擊)向下的短擊。

chop³ /tʃɒp; tʃɑp/ *n* official seal or stamp; trademark; brand of goods; (colloq) quality. 官印;圖章;商標;貨物的牌子;(俗)品質。

chop⁴ /tʃɒp; tʃɑp/ *vi* (-pp-) **1** [VP2A] **~ *and change,*** (emphatic for *change*) be inconsistent: (change 之加强語)多變;善變: *He's always ~ping and changing,* always changing his opinions, plans, etc. 他總是朝秦暮楚 (總是改變意見、計畫等)。 **2** [VP 2C] **~ *about,*** (of the wind) change direction. (指風)改變方向。

chop⁵ /tʃɒp; tʃɑp/ *n* ⇨ chap².

chop-chop /ˌtʃɒp ˈtʃɒp; ˈtʃɑpˈtʃɑp/ *adv* (sl) quickly. (俚)快;迅速地。

chop·per¹ /ˈtʃɒpə(r); ˈtʃɑpɚ/ *n* heavy tool with a sharp edge for chopping meat, wood, etc. (砍肉、柴等之)刀或斧。⇨ the illus at tool. 參看 tool 之插圖。

chop·per² /ˈtʃɒpə(r); ˈtʃɑpɚ/ *n* (colloq) helicopter. (俗)直升飛機。

choppy /ˈtʃɒpɪ; ˈtʃɑpɪ/ *adj* (-ier, -iest) (of the sea) moving in short, broken irregular waves; (of the wind) continually changing. (指海)波濤洶湧的;(指風)不斷改變方向的。

chop·sticks /ˈtʃɒpstɪks; ˈtʃɑpˌstɪks/ *n pl* pair of tapering sticks (wood, ivory, etc) used by the Chinese and Japanese for lifting food (placed on the thinnest ends) to the mouth. 筷子(木、象牙等製,爲中國人及日本人進食的餐具,指一雙)。

chopsticks

chop suey /ˌtʃɒp ˈsuːɪ; ˈtʃɑpˈsuɪ/ *n* [U] dish of meat or chicken served with rice, onions, etc (as in a Chinese restaurant). 一盤附帶米飯、洋葱等之肉或鷄肉(如中國餐館所供應者);雜碎。

choral /ˈkɔːrəl; ˈkorəl/ *adj* of, for, sung by or together with, a choir: 唱詩班的;合唱的;唱詩班所唱的;與唱詩班合唱的: *a ˈ~ society;* 合唱會; *a ~ service;* 唱詩禮拜; *Beethoven's ~ symphony.* 貝多芬的合唱交響曲。

chorale /kəˈrɑːl; koˈrɑl/ *n* simple hymn tune, usu sung by the choir and congregation together. 通常由會衆與唱詩班合唱之簡單聖歌調。

chord /kɔːd; kɔrd/ *n* **1** straight line that joins two points on the circumference of a circle or the ends of an arc. 弦(連接圓周上任意兩點或一弧之兩端的直線)。⇨ the illus at circle. 參看 circle 之插圖。 **2** (music) combination of three or more notes sounded together in harmony. (音樂)和弦;和(諧)音。⇨ discord and also the illus at notation. 參看 notation 之挿圖。 **3** (now usu spelt 現常拼作 *cord*) (anat) string-like structure, as in the throat (*the vocal ~s*) or the back (*the spinal ~*). (解剖) 帶 (身體內的帶狀組織,如喉部之 vocal chords 聲帶,背部之 spinal chord 脊髓)。⇨ the illus at head. 參看 head 之插圖。 **4** string (of a harp, etc): (豎琴等的)弦: *touch the right ~,* (fig) appeal cleverly to emotion. (喻)巧妙地觸動情緒;扣人心弦。

chore /tʃɔː(r); tʃor/ *n* small duty or piece of work, esp an ordinary everyday task (in the home, on a farm, etc); unpleasant or tiring task. (家庭中、農場上等處之)雜務;雜事;零星的事務;(尤指)日常之普通工作;不愉快的工作;令人疲勞的工作。Cf 參較 *char.*

chor·eogra·phy /ˌkɒrɪˈɒgrəfɪ *US:* ˌkɔːr-; ˌkorɪˈɑgrəfɪ/ *n* [U] art of designing and specifying the steps of ballet. 芭蕾舞設計術。**chor·eogra·pher** *n*

chor·is·ter /ˈkɒrɪstə(r) *US:* ˈkɔːr-; ˈkɔrɪstɚ/ *n* member of a choir, esp a choir-boy. 合唱團員(尤指男童團員);唱詩班中的男童歌手。

chortle /ˈtʃɔːtl; ˈtʃɔrtl̩/ *vi, n* (give a) loud chuckle of glee. (發)咯咯笑聲;歡笑。

chorus /ˈkɔːrəs; ˈkorəs/ *n* **1** (music for a) group of singers. 合唱團;合唱曲。 **ˈ~-girl** *n* one of a group of girls who sing and dance in a musical play. 歌劇中擔任歌舞之女演員;歌舞團女團員。**2** (part of a) song for all to sing (after solo verses): (歌曲獨唱部份之後的)合唱部份: *Bill sang the verses and everybody joined in the ~.* 比爾唱獨唱部份,然後大家一起唱合唱部份。 **3** sth said or cried by many people together: 由許多人一起說出或喊出的話;異口同聲: *The proposal was greeted with a ~ of approval.* 該項提議獲得大家異口同聲的贊成。***in***

~, all together: 大家一起;共同: *sing/answer in* ~. 齊聲歌唱(回答)。⇨ unison. **4** (in old Gk drama) band of singers and dancers whose words and actions are a commentary on the events of the play. (古希臘戲劇中的)合唱歌舞隊(其唱詞及舞姿對劇情提供一種解釋)。 **5** (eg in Shakespeare's plays) actor who recites the prologue and epilogue. (如在莎士比亞的戲劇中)朗誦序詩及收場詩的演員。 □ *vt* sing, speak, in ~. 齊聲唱;齊聲說。

chose, chosen ⇨ choose.

chow /tʃaʊ; tʃaʊ/ *n* **1** dog of a Chinese breed. 一種中國狗。 **2** (sl) food. (俚)食物。

chow·der /ˈtʃaʊdə(r); ˈtʃaʊdɚ/ *n* (US) thick soup or stew of fish or clams with vegetables. (美)(魚或蛤與蔬菜同煮之)濃湯或燉菜。

Christ /kraɪst; kraɪst/ *n* title (= *anointed one*) given to Jesus, now used as part of (ie *Jesus* ~) or as an alternative to his name. 基督(加於耶穌的頭銜,意謂"受膏者",現與其名連用或互用)。 **ˈ~·like** *adj* of or like ~; showing the spirit of ~. 基督的;似基督的;表示出基督精神的。

christen /ˈkrɪsn; ˈkrɪsn̩/ *vt* [VP6A, 23] **1** receive into the Christian church by baptism; give a name to at the baptism. 施洗禮使成爲基督徒;在施洗禮時爲…取教名。*The child was ~ed Mary.* 此孩取教名瑪莉。 **2** give a name to (eg to a new ship when it is launched). 予以命名(例如當新船行下水禮時)。 **ˈ~·ing** *n* ceremony of baptizing or naming: 洗禮;命名典禮: *There were ten ~ings at this church last month.* 本教堂在上月之內曾爲十個嬰孩施洗禮。

Christen·dom /ˈkrɪsndəm; ˈkrɪsn̩dəm/ *n* all Christian people and Christian countries. 所有信基督教的人們及國家;基督教世界。

Chris·tian /ˈkrɪstʃən; ˈkrɪstʃən/ *adj* of Jesus and his teaching; of the religion, beliefs, church, etc based on this teaching. 耶穌基督及其教訓的;基督教及其信仰、教會等的。 **~ era,** time reckoned from the birth of Jesus. 耶穌紀元(自耶穌降生算起);西曆紀元。 **ˈ~ name,** name given at baptism. (在施洗禮時所取的)教名。Cf 參較 *family name.* **ˌ~ ˈScience,** church and religious system of healing through spiritual means. 基督教信仰醫療法(藉精神信仰的療病法)。 □ *n* person believing in the ~ religion. 基督教徒。 **Chris·ti·an·ity** /ˌkrɪstɪˈænətɪ; ˌkrɪstʃɪˈænətɪ/ *n* [U] the ~ faith or religion; being a ~; ~ character. 基督教;基督教的教義;做基督教徒;信基督教;基督教徒的性格。

Christ·mas /ˈkrɪsməs; ˈkrɪsməs/ *n* (also 亦作 **ˌ~ ˈDay**) yearly celebration of the birth of Jesus Christ, 25 Dec; the week beginning on 24 Dec: 聖誕節(耶穌誕生之紀念日,卽十二月廿五日); 聖誕節期(自十二月廿四日聖誕前夕起算之一週間): (attrib) (形容用法) *the ~ holidays.* 聖誕節假期。 **ˈ~-box** *n* (not US) money given for services during the year. (不用於美國)聖誕節時酬謝終年辛勞之賞金。 **ˈ~ card,** sent to friends at ~ to wish them 'A Merry ~ and a Happy New Year', etc. 聖誕卡。 **ˌFather ˈ~,** traditional figure who is supposed to give children gifts at ~ (= *Santa Claus*). 聖誕老人。 **ˈ~-tide/-time,** the ~ season. 聖誕節節期。 **ˈ~-tree** *n* small evergreen tree set up at ~ and decorated with tinsel, candles, presents, etc. 聖誕樹(豎立並裝飾着閃光之金屬絲片、蠟燭、禮物等之小常綠樹)。

chro·matic /krəʊˈmætɪk; kroˈmætɪk/ *adj* **1** of, in, colour(s): 顏色的;彩色的;五彩的: ~ *printing.* 彩色印刷。 **2** (music) of, having notes of the ~ scale, that is, the succession of semitones, twelve to the octave, normal in Western music. (音樂)半音的;半音音階(由連續的十二個半音組成)的。

chrome /krəʊm; krom/ *n* yellow pigment, colouring matter, obtained from chromium salts, used in paints, rubber, ceramics, etc. 鉻黃(取自鉻鹽之黃色顏料,用於油漆、橡皮、陶器等中)。 **ˈ~ steel** *n* alloy of steel and chromium. 鉻鋼(鋼與鉻的合金)。

chro·mium /ˈkrəʊmɪəm; ˈkromɪəm/ *n* [U] element (symbol **Cr**) used for plating taps, hardware, motor-car fittings, etc and in steel alloys (including stainless steel): 鉻(元素之一,化學符號Cr,用於電鍍龍頭、五金器具、汽車配件等,及用於鋼合金,包括不銹鋼): ~ *plating;* 鍍鉻; *ˌ~-ˌplated ˈfittings.* 鍍鉻的配件。

chro·mo·some /ˈkrəʊməsəʊm; ˈkroməˌsom/ *n* [C] (biol) one of the minute threads in every nucleus in animal and plant cells, carrying genes. (生物)染色體(每一動植物細胞核中所含的帶有遺傳因子的細絲之一)。

chro·nic /ˈkrɒnɪk; ˈkrɑnɪk/ *adj* **1** (of a disease or condition) continual, lasting for a long time: (指疾病或情況)延續性的;纏綿甚久的;慢性的: ~ *rheumatism;* 慢性的風濕症; *a ~ invalid,* a person with a ~ illness. 痼疾患者。⇨ acute(2). **2** (sl) intense; severe. (俚)緊張的; 嚴重的; 劇烈的。 **chro·ni·cally** /-klɪ; -klɪ/ *adv*

chron·icle /ˈkrɒnɪkl; ˈkrɑnɪkl̩/ *n* [C] record of events in the order of their happening. 編年史。 □ *vt* [VP6A] make a ~ of; record in a ~. 將…編爲編年史;載入編年史。

chro·no·logi·cal /ˌkrɒnəˈlɒdʒɪkl; ˌkrɑnəˈlɑdʒɪkl/ *adj* in order of time: 按時間順序的;按年代先後的: *Shakespeare's plays in ~ order,* in the order in which they were written. 按著作年代先後次序編輯的莎士比亞戲劇集。 **~ly** /-klɪ; -klɪ/ *adv*

chro·no·logy /krəˈnɒlədʒɪ; krəˈnɑlədʒɪ/ *n* [U] science of fixing dates; [C] (*pl* -gies) arrangement of events with dates; list or table showing this. 編年學;年代學;年代紀;年代表。

chro·no·meter /krəˈnɒmɪtə(r); krəˈnɑmətɚ/ *n* kind of watch that keeps very accurate time, esp as used for fixing longitude at sea. 精密時計(尤指用於海上測量經度者);天文鐘;船鐘;經線儀。

chry·sa·lis /ˈkrɪsəlɪs; ˈkrɪsl̩ɪs/ *n* (*pl* -lises /-lɪsɪz; -l̩ɪsɪz/) form taken by an insect during the torpid stage of its life (ie between the time when it creeps or crawls as a larva and the time when it flies as a moth, butterfly, etc); the sheath that covers it during this time. 金蛹(昆蟲生活史的第二階段,如蛾、蝶等之介於幼蟲爬行期與成蟲飛行期的階段); 繭(蛹之外殼)。⇨ the illus at butterfly. 參看 butterfly 之插圖。

chry·san·the·mum /krɪˈsænθəməm; krɪsˈænθəməm/ *n* (flower of) garden plant blooming in autumn and early winter. 菊;菊花(於秋季及初冬開花)。

chubby /ˈtʃʌbɪ; ˈtʃʌbɪ/ *adj* (-ier, -iest) plump: 豐滿的;圓胖的: ~ *cheeks;* 豐滿的兩頰; round-faced: 圓臉的: *a ~ child.* 圓臉的小孩。

chuck[1] /tʃʌk; tʃʌk/ *vt* (colloq) (俗) **1** [VP15A, B, 12A, 13A] throw: 投;拋;擲: ~ *away rubbish;* 拋棄垃圾; ~ *a drunken man out of a pub.* 把一個醉漢從酒店中推出去。 **ˌ~er-ˈout** *n* (sl) person whose duty it is to throw out troublesome people (from public-houses, political meetings, etc). (俚)負責驅逐在酒店、政治會議等中搗亂者之人; 打手; 保鏢。 **2** [VP6A, 15B] ~ ***(up),*** abandon, give up (in disgust): 拋棄;(因厭惡而)放棄: ~ *up one's job;* 放棄其職業; ~ *work.* 拋棄工作。*C~ it,* (sl) Stop doing that! (俚)停止!住手! **3** ***~ sb under the chin,*** touch him or her playfully with the back of the fist under the chin. 用拳背觸弄某人的下巴。 □ *n* ***the ~,*** (sl) dismissal from one's job: (俚)解雇;革職: *get the ~,* be dismissed; 被解雇; *give sb the ~,* dismiss him. 解雇某人。

chuck[2] /tʃʌk; tʃʌk/ *n* that part of a lathe which grips the work to be operated on or which grips the bit on a drill. 車床上能夾緊工作件以待操作或夾緊鑽頭的部份;夾頭;卡盤;招子;鑽軋頭。⇨ the illus at lathe. 參看 lathe 之插圖。

chuckle /ˈtʃʌkl; ˈtʃʌkl̩/ *n* low, quiet laugh with closed mouth (indicating satisfaction or amusement). 抿著嘴的輕笑(表示滿意或覺得有趣)。 □ *vi* [VP2A, C] laugh in this way: 抿著嘴輕笑: *He was chuckling to himself over what he was reading.* 他讀到有趣的地方就自個兒抿著嘴笑。

chuffed /tʃʌft ; tʃʌft/ *pred adj* (GB colloq) very pleased: (英俗)非常高興的: *be/feel/look ~.* 覺得(顯得)非常高興。

chug /tʃʌg ; tʃʌg/ *vi* (-gg-) [VP2C] make the muffled explosive sound (of an oil-engine or small petrol-engine running slowly): 發出(重油發動機或汽油發動機緩動時之)突突聲; 噗噗作響; 軋軋地響: *The boat ~ged along.* 船發着突突聲而行進。□ *n* this sound. 突突聲; 噗噗聲; 軋軋聲。

chuk·ker /ˈtʃʌkə(r) ; ˈtʃʌkɚ/ *n* (polo) one of the periods into which the game is divided. (馬球)一巡。

chum /tʃʌm ; tʃʌm/ *n* close friend (esp among boys): 密友; 至友(尤指男孩之間者): (Australia) (澳) *new ~*, new arrival; recent immigrant; 新到的人; 新移民; (US) room-mate. (美)同寢室者; 室友。□ *vi* (-mm-) [VP2C] **~ *up (with sb)***, form a friendship (with). (與某人)結爲密友。**~my** *adj* friendly; like a ~. 友善的; 親切的; 如密友的。

chump /tʃʌmp ; tʃʌmp/ *n* **1** short, thick block of wood. 短而厚的木塊。**2** thick piece of meat: 一塊厚厚的肉: *a ~ chop.* 一塊厚厚的排骨肉。**3** (sl) fool; blockhead. (俚)愚人; 笨蛋; 蠢貨。**4** (sl) head. (俚)頭。***off one's ~***, crazy. 發瘋的; 發狂的。

chunk /tʃʌŋk ; tʃʌŋk/ *n* thick, solid piece or lump cut off a loaf, a piece of meat/cheese etc. (自麵包、一塊肉、乾酪等切下的) 厚而密實的一塊; 一厚塊; 一大塊。**~y** *adj* (-ier, -iest) short and thick. 短而厚的; 粗短的。

church /tʃɜːtʃ ; tʃɝtʃ/ *n* **1** building for public Christian worship. 教堂。⇨ chapel. ˌ**~ ˈregister** *n* records of births, marriages and deaths in a parish. 教堂記錄(登記教區中之出生、婚姻及死亡之記錄)。ˈ**~·yard** *n* burial ground round a ~. 教堂墓地(教堂四周的墓地)。⇨ cemetery. **2** [U] service in such a building: 在教堂中的禮拜儀式: *What time does ~ begin?* 禮拜何時開始? *They're in/at ~*, attending a service. 他們在教堂中做禮拜。Cf 參較 *They're in the ~*, inside the building. 他們在教堂裏面。*How often do you go to ~?* 你多久去教堂做一次禮拜? ˈ**~·goer** /-gəʊə(r) ; -ˌgoɚ/ *n* person who attends ~ services regularly. 經常上教堂做禮拜的人。**3** [U] ***the C~ (of Christ)***, the whole body of Christians. 全體基督教徒。***the C~ of England***, England's official Protestant ~, founded in the 16th century by King Henry VIII. 英國國教(十六世紀英王亨利八世所創之新教); 英格蘭教會。***enter the C~***, become a minister¹(3) or monk/nun. 做牧師; 做修道士; 做修女。**~·war·den** *n* elected representative of a C~ of England parish, not a priest, who helps to manage the business, funds, etc of a ~. 英國國教每教區所選舉出的教會執事(非牧師,其職司爲協助管理教會事務、經費等)。

churl /tʃɜːl ; tʃɝl/ *n* bad-tempered person. 壞脾氣的人。**~·ish** *adj* bad-tempered; ill-bred. 壞脾氣的; 無教養的。**~·ish·ly** *adv*

churn /tʃɜːn ; tʃɝn/ *n* **1** tub in which cream is shaken or beaten to make butter. 在其中攪動乳脂以製成奶油之桶; 攪乳器。**2** (not US) very large can in which milk is carried from the farm. (不用於美國)自農場裝運牛奶之大罐。□ *vt, vi* **1** [VP6A] make (butter), beat and shake (cream) in a ~. 在攪乳器製(奶油); 攪(乳脂)。**2** [VP6A, 15B, 2A, C] **~ *(up)***, stir or move about violently: 劇烈地攪動: *The ship's propellers ~ed the waves to foam/~ed up the waves.* 輪船的推進器將海浪攪起泡沫。(fig) agitate the emotions. (喻)激動感情。***~ out***, produce in a mass: 大量生產: *~ out silly romantic novels.* 大量生產可笑的浪漫小說。

chute /ʃuːt ; ʃut/ *n* **1** long, narrow, steep slope down which things may slide (eg for coal, barrels, etc into a cellar, logs down a hillside, letters, refuse, etc from the upper storeys of a high building). 狹長而陡峭,物件可以在上面滑下之斜槽(例如將煤、酒桶等滑至地窖者,將圓木材滑至山坡下者,信件、垃圾等自高樓中滑下之管道); 滑運道; 導槽; 滑槽。**2** smooth, rapid fall of water over a slope. 斜坡上之平滑的急流。**3** (colloq abbr of) parachute. (俗)降落傘(爲 parachute 之略)。

chut·ney /ˈtʃʌtnɪ ; ˈtʃʌtnɪ/ *n* [U] hot-tasting mixture of fruit, peppers, etc eaten with curry, cold meat, etc. 水果辣椒等混合製成的辣醬(與咖哩、冷肉等合食)。

ci·cada /sɪˈkɑːdə ; sɪˈkedə/ *n* winged insect with transparent wings, the male of which chirps shrilly in hot, dry weather. 蟬(翅翼透明之昆蟲,雄者在乾燥的暑天發出尖銳的鳴聲)。⇨ the illus at insect. 參看 insect 之插圖。

ci·cala /sɪˈkɑːlə ; sɪˈkɑlə/ *n* = cicada.

cica·trice /ˈsɪkətrɪs ; ˈsɪkətrɪs/, **cica·trix** /ˈsɪkətrɪks ; ˈsɪkətrɪks/ *n* (*pl* -trices /-ˈtraɪsiːz ; -ˈtraɪsiz/) scar left by a healed wound. 傷痕; 傷疤。

cice·rone /ˌtʃɪtʃəˈrəʊnɪ ; ˌsɪsəˈronɪ/ *n* (*pl* -ni /-niː ; -ni/) (I) guide who understands and describes to sightseers places and objects of interest. (義)向遊客指點名勝古蹟之嚮導; 導遊。

cider /ˈsaɪdə(r) ; ˈsaɪdɚ/ *n* [U] fermented apple juice. 發酵的蘋果汁; 蘋果酒。ˈ**~-press** *n* machine for pressing juice from apples. 蘋果榨汁機。

cigar /sɪˈgɑː(r) ; sɪˈgɑr/ *n* tight roll of tobacco leaves with pointed end(s) for smoking. 雪茄煙(用煙葉捲緊,兩端或一端作尖形以便吸食之煙捲)。ˈ**~-shaped**, shaped like a cylinder with pointed ends. 兩頭尖之棒形的; 雪茄煙形的。

ciga·rette /ˌsɪgəˈret *US:* ˈsɪgəret ; ˌsɪgəˈrɛt, ˈsɪgəˌrɛt/ *n* roll of shredded tobacco enclosed in thin paper for smoking. 香煙; 紙煙(將煙絲捲於薄紙中供吸食之煙捲)。ˈ**~-case** *n* one in which a supply of ~s may be carried in the pocket or handbag. 香煙盒(裝香煙以便帶於口袋或手提包中)。ˈ**~-holder** *n* tube in which a ~ may be put for smoking. 煙嘴。ˈ**~-paper**, that used to make ~s. (捲香煙用的)煙紙。

cinch /sɪntʃ ; sɪntʃ/ *n* (US sl) something that is certain; something easy and sure. (美俚)有把握之事; 易做而有把握之事。

cin·chona /sɪŋˈkəʊnə ; sɪnˈkonə/ *n* tree from whose bark quinine is obtained. 金鷄納樹(自其樹皮可提取奎寧)。

cinc·ture /ˈsɪŋktʃə(r) ; ˈsɪŋktʃɚ/ *n* (liter) belt or girdle. (文)帶; 環帶。

cin·der /ˈsɪndə(r) ; ˈsɪndɚ/ *n* small piece of coal, wood, etc partly burned, no longer flaming, and not yet ash. 經部份燃燒,已無火焰但尚未成灰之煤渣、焦木塊等; 餘燼。***burnt to a ~***, (of a cake, etc) cooked so that it is hard and black. (指糕餅等)被烤焦; 被燒焦; 被燒糊。ˈ**~-track** *n* running track made with fine ~s. 用細煤渣鋪的跑道。

Cin·de·rella /ˌsɪndəˈrelə ; ˌsɪndəˈrɛlə/ *n* girl or woman whose attraction, merits, etc have not been recognized; (fig) sth long neglected. 魅力、優點等尚未爲人所識的女子; (喻)長期爲人所疏忽的事物。

cine- /ˈsɪnɪ ; ˈsɪnɪ/ *pref* form used for *cinema* in compounds. 電影 (用於複合字中)。ˈ**~-cam·era** *n* camera used for taking moving pictures. 電影攝影機。⇨ the illus at camera. 參看 camera 之插圖。ˈ**~-film** *n* film used in ~-cameras. 拍攝電影用的軟片; 電影膠片。ˈ**~-pro·jec·tor** *n* machine for showing ~-films on a screen. 電影放映機。

cin·ema /ˈsɪnəmə ; ˈsɪnəmə/ *n* **1** (not US) theatre in which films are shown. (不用於美國)電影院。**2** **(the) ~**, motion pictures as an art-form or an industry: 電影藝術; 電影事業: *Are you interested in (the) ~?* 你對電影(藝術)有興趣嗎? Cf 參較 *(the) drama.* **~·tic** /ˌsɪnəˈmætɪk ; ˌsɪnɪˈmætɪk/ *adj* of ~(2). 電影藝術的; 電影事業的。**~·to·graphy** /ˌsɪnəməˈtɒgrəfɪ ; ˌsɪnəməˈtɑgrəfɪ/ *n* [U] ~(2). 電影藝術; 電影事業。

cin·na·mon /ˈsɪnəmən ; ˈsɪnəmən/ *n* [U] spice from the inner bark of an E Indian tree, used in cooking; its colour, yellowish brown. 肉桂(自東印度群島一種樹之內皮取得的香料,用於烹調); 肉桂色; 黃褐色。

cinque·foil /ˈsɪŋkfɔɪl ; ˈsɪŋkˌfɔɪl/ *n* plant with

leaves divided into five parts and with small yellow flowers. 洋莓屬之植物(葉分五瓣,開小黃花)。

cipher, cypher /ˈsaɪfə(r) ; ˈsaɪfɚ/ *n* **1** the symbol 0, representing nought or zero. 零;0。 **2** any Arabic numeral, 1 to 9. 自1至9任何阿拉伯數字。 **3** (fig) person or thing of no importance. (喻)無重要性的人或物。 **4** (method of, key to) secret writing: 暗號;暗碼;譯解暗號或密碼的方法或解答: *a message in ~;* 密碼信; *a ~ key;* 密碼本;密碼解答; *the ˈ~ officer,* officer who codes and decodes messages. (擔任翻譯密碼之)譯電員。□ *vt, vi* **1** [VP6A] put into secret writing. 將…譯成密碼;用密碼寫。**2** [VP6A, 2A] (colloq) do arithmetical problems; add up, divide, etc; work out a problem in figures. (俗)做算術題;加減乘除;計算出數字上的問題。

circa /ˈsɜːkə ; ˈsɝkə/ *prep* (Lat, abbr *c, ca* or *circ*) about (with dates): (拉丁文,略作 c, ca 或 circ) 大約(與年代連用): *born ~ 150* BC. 生於西元前約150年。

circle /ˈsɜːkl ; ˈsɝkl̩/ *n* **1** (geom) space enclosed by a curved line, every point on which is the same distance from the centre; the line enclosing this space. (幾何)圓形空間;圓;圓周。⇨ also the illus at concentric. 亦參看 concentric 之插圖。 **2** sth round like a ~; ring: 圓形物;圈;環: *a ~ of trees / hills;* 一圈樹木(山丘); *standing in a ~.* 站成一個圓圈。 ***a vicious ~,*** ⇨ vicious. **3** block of seats in curved rows, one above the other, between the highest part (the gallery) and the floor (the stalls) of a theatre or hall. 電影院、劇院或音樂廳中的中樓座(介於最高樓座與地面座位之間,座位排成弧形,一排比一排高)。 **4** number of persons bound together by having the same or similar interests: 同道或同好的集團;(社會上的)…界;圈子: *in theatrical ~s,* among actors, etc; 在戲劇界(在演員等的圈子裏); *moving in fashionable ~s,* among those in fashionable society; 在上流社會中走動; *business ~s.* 工商界。*He has a large ~ of friends.* 他的交遊極廣。*They are newcomers to our ~.* 他們是我們這一行中的新進者。 **5** complete series: 循環;周而復始: *the ~ of the seasons,* the four seasons in succession. 四季的循環。***come full ~,*** end at the starting-point. 繞行一周(在起點終止)。□ *vt,vi* [VP6A, 2A, C] move in a ~; go round: 環繞;繞行;盤繞;盤旋: *The aircraft ~d (over) the landing-field.* 該飛機在起落場上空盤旋。 *Drake ~d the globe,* sailed round the world. 杜雷克航行地球一週。*The news ~d round,* was passed round. 該新聞被到處傳播。

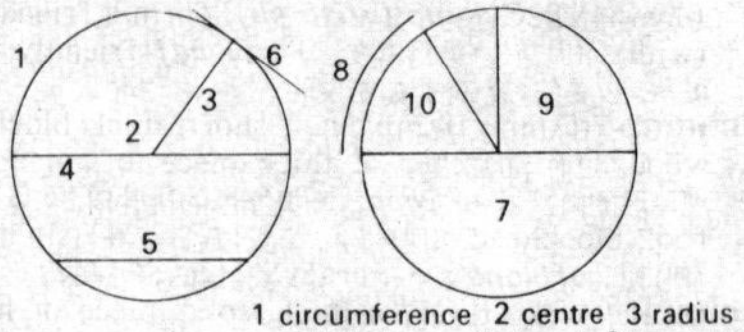

1 circumference 2 centre 3 radius
4 diameter 5 chord 6 tangent
7 semicircle 8 arc 9 quadrant
10 sector

parts of a circle

circ·let /ˈsɜːklɪt ; ˈsɝklɪt/ *n* round band (eg of gold or flowers) worn as an ornament on the head, neck or arm. 戴在頭、頸或手臂上做裝飾用的圈環(如金圈或花環)。

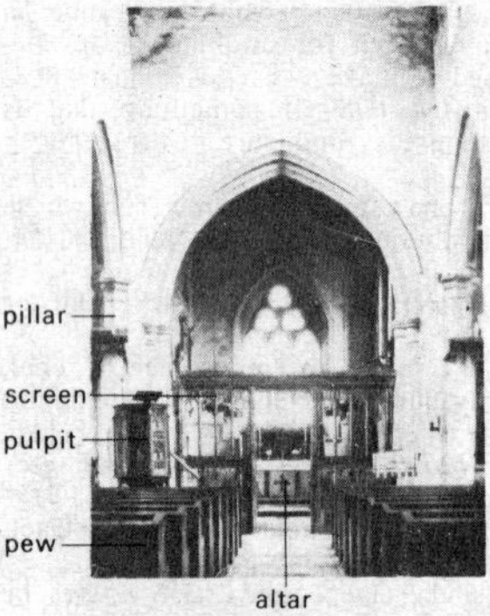

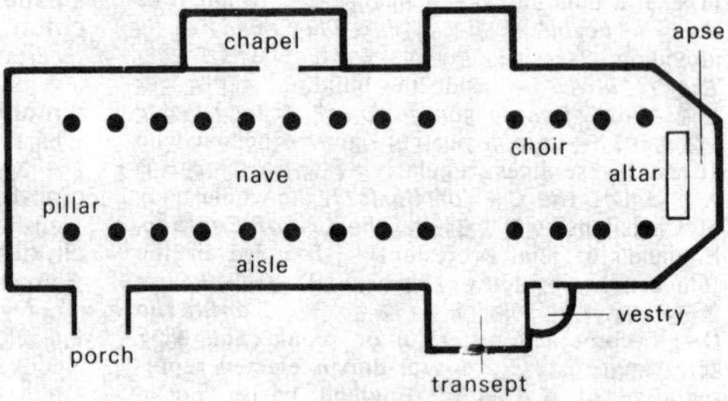

ORGAN

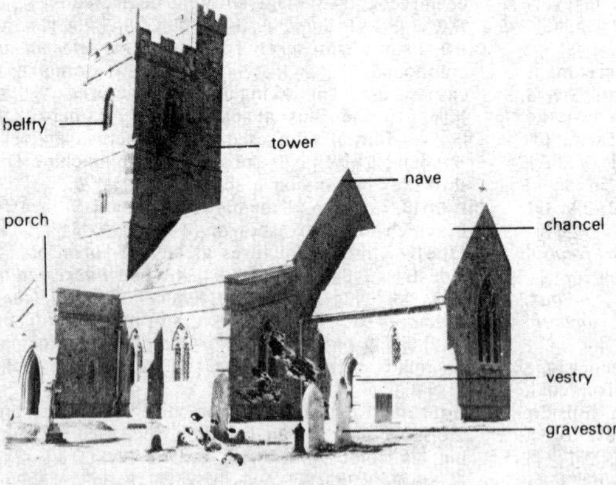

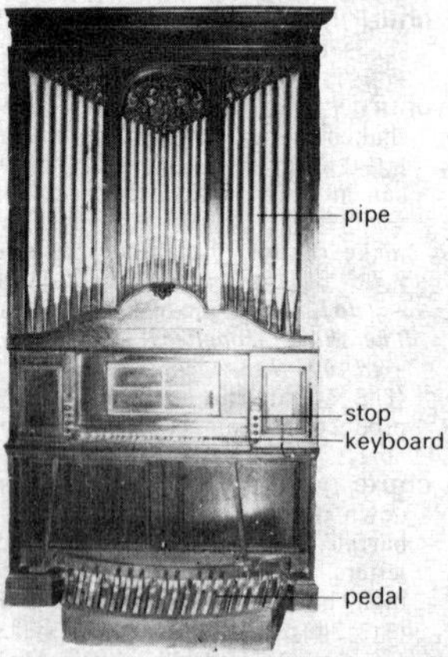

church architecture

cir·cuit /ˈsɜːkɪt ; ˈsɝkɪt/ *n* **1** journey round, ending where one began: 周遊;巡行一周;巡行;巡迴: *The ~ of the city walls is three miles.* 城牆周長三哩。 ***make a ~ of***, go round. 環行一周;巡視一周;巡迴;巡察。 **2** regular journey or itinerary made by judges and barristers to towns in England and Wales to county towns (*~ towns*) to hold courts to hear civil and criminal cases, replaced in 1972 by Crown Courts ⇨ court[1]. One of six areas in the country, each having a number of Crown Courts. 巡迴審判 (法官與律師們至英格蘭及威爾斯各城市及郡首邑審理民事及刑事案件之按時的巡迴旅程，自1972年爲 Crown Courts 所取代; 參看 court[1]);皇家法庭巡迴區(英國共分六區,每區均有若干皇家法庭)。 ***go on ~***, make this journey: 作巡迴審判: *Judges go on ~ for part of the year.'* 法官們每年用一部份的時間從事巡迴審判。 **3** chain of cinemas, theatres, etc under a single management: 某一企業下所經營的一系列的電影院、劇院等: *Some theatrical companies travel over regular ~s*, visit certain towns in succession. 有些劇團按照一定的路線前往某些市鎮作巡迴演出。 **4** closed path for an electrical current; apparatus with a sequence of conductors, transistors, etc for carrying an electric current: 電路(電流的通路,或裝設着一系列導體、電晶體等以傳導電流之全部裝置): ˈ*~ diagram*, one that shows the connections in such an apparatus. 電路圖。 **closed ~ (TV)**, ⇨ close[4](2). **short ~**, ⇨ short[1](1). **5** regional group of Methodist churches sharing preachers. 聘有共同傳道士之若干美以美會教堂的地區性集團。

cir·cu·itous /sɜːˈkjuːɪtəs ; sɚˈkjuɪtəs/ *adj* (formal) indirect; going a long way round: (正式用語)間接的;迂迴的: *a ~ route.* 迂迴的路線;繞圈子的路。

cir·cu·lar /ˈsɜːkjʊlə(r) ; ˈsɝkjələ/ *adj* round or curved in shape; moving round: 圓形的;弧形的;環繞而行的: *a ~ building;* 一座圓形的建築物; *the North C~ Road*, round the north of London, for through traffic; 倫敦北端的環市馬路(供經過倫敦中途不停之車輛行駛者); *a ~ tour/trip*, ending at the starting-point without visiting a place more than once. 環遊各地的旅行。 **~ letter** *n* one sent out to many persons. 寄與許多人傳閱的函件。 **~ saw** *n* disc-shaped saw that revolves by machinery. (由機件旋轉的)圓形鋸。 □ *n* printed letter, advertisement, announcement, etc of which many copies are made and distributed. 同式而印發許多份之函件、廣告、通告等;傳閱之文件;傳單。 **~·ize** /ˈsɜːkjʊləraɪz ; ˈsɝkjələˌraɪz/ *vt* [VP6A] send ~s to. 將傳閱文件送給;寄傳單給。

cir·cu·late /ˈsɜːkjʊleɪt ; ˈsɝkjəˌlet/ *vi, vt* **1** [VP2A, C] go round continuously; move from place to place freely: 流通;循環;傳播: *Blood ~s through the body.* 血在人體內循環。 *In many buildings hot water ~s through pipes to keep rooms warm.* 在許多建築物中,用熱水在管中循環的方法保持室內的溫暖。 *Bad news ~s quickly.* 壞消息傳播迅速。 *In times of prosperity money ~s quickly; during a depression it ~s slowly.* 在商業景氣的時期,錢流通得快;在商業蕭條的時期,錢流通得慢。 **circulating library**, one from which books may be borrowed, usu on payment of a subscription. 書籍可以借出的圖書館(通常要付租書費);流通圖書館。 **2** [VP6A] cause to ~: 傳播;散佈: *People who ~ false news are to be blamed.* 散佈流言者該受譴責。

BAS RELIEF

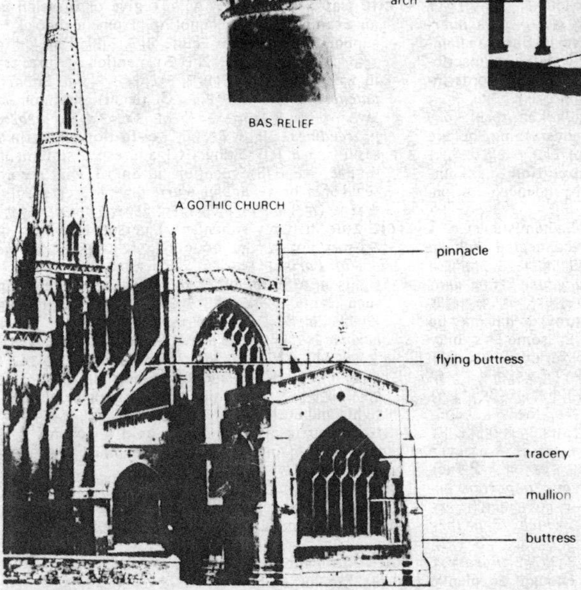

A GOTHIC CHURCH

GARGOYLE

cir·cu·la·tion /ˌsɜːkjʊˈleɪʃn ; ˌsɝkjəˈleʃən/ *n* **1** [U, C] circulating or being circulated, esp the movement of the blood from and to the heart: 循環(尤指血液出入心臟之運行): *He has (a) good/bad ~.* 他的血液循環很好(不良)。*The ~ of rumours is common in wartime.* 在戰時謠言的流傳是常事。**2** [U] state of being circulated: 流通;流動;發行: *Are there many forged banknotes in ~?* 有許多假鈔票在流通嗎? *That book has been withdrawn from ~,* cannot now be obtained. 該書業已停止發行(現在買不到了)。*When were the decimal coins put into ~?* 十進制硬幣何時發行的? **3** [C] number of copies of a newspaper or other periodical sold to the public: (報紙、期刊等的)發行數額: *a newspaper with a (daily) ~ of more than one million.* (每日)發行額超過一百萬份的報紙。

cir·cum·cise /ˈsɜːkəmsaɪz ; ˈsɝkəmˌsaɪz/ *vt* remove the foreskin of (a male) or the clitoris of (a female). 環割(男性)的包皮; 割除(女性)的陰蒂。**cir·cum·cision** /ˌsɜːkəmˈsɪʒn ; ˌsɝkəmˈsɪʒən/ *n* circumcising, esp (of males) as a religious rite among Jews and Muslims. 環割術;包皮環割;(尤指)割禮(猶太人及回教徒之割包皮,作爲一種宗教儀式)。

cir·cum·fer·ence /sɜːˈkʌmfərəns ; sɚˈkʌmfərəns/ *n* (geom) line that marks out a circle or other curved figure; distance round sth: (幾何)圓周;周圍長度: *The ~ of the earth is almost 25 000 miles.* 地球的周圍長度約爲二萬五千哩。⇨ the illus at circle. 參看 circle 之挿圖。

cir·cum·flex /ˈsɜːkəmfleks ; ˈsɝkəmˌflɛks/ *n* (also 亦作 ~ **accent**) mark placed over a vowel to indicate how it is to be sounded (as in French *rôle*). 置於母音上指示發音方法的符號(如法文 rôle 中之ˆ)。

cir·cum·lo·cu·tion /ˌsɜːkəmləˈkjuːʃn ; ˌsɝkəmloˈkjuʃən/ *n* [C, U] (instance of) saying in many words what may be said in few words. 迂廻說法;累贅句法;累贅的句子。

cir·cum·navi·gate /ˌsɜːkəmˈnævɪgeɪt ; ˌsɝkəmˈnævəˌget/ *vt* [VP6A] (formal) sail round (esp the world). (正式用語)環航(尤指世界)一周。**cir·cum·navi·ga·tion** /ˌsɜːkəmˌnævɪˈgeɪʃn ; ˌsɝkəmˌnævəˈgeʃən/ *n*

cir·cum·scribe /ˈsɜːkəmskraɪb ; ˌsɝkəmˈskraɪb/ *vt* [VP6A] (formal) draw a line round; mark the limit(s) of; narrow down, restrict: (正式用語)在周圍畫一條線;標出…的範圍或界限;限制: *~ one's interests.* 限制某人的愛好。**cir·cum·scrip·tion** /ˌsɜːkəmˈskrɪpʃn ; ˌsɝkəmˈskrɪpʃən/ *n* **1** [U] circumscribing or being ~d. 劃界限;限制。**2** [C] words inscribed round a coin. 錢幣周圍所刻的字。

cir·cum·spect /ˈsɜːkəmspekt ; ˈsɝkəmˌspɛkt/ *adj* paying careful attention to everything before taking action; cautious. 在採取行動之前考慮周詳的;愼審的。**~·ly** *adv* **cir·cum·spec·tion** /ˌsɜːkəmˈspekʃn ; ˌsɝkəmˈspɛkʃən/ *n* [U] prudence; caution. 謹愼;小心。

cir·cum·stance /ˈsɜːkəmstəns ; ˈsɝkəmˌstæns/ *n* **1** (usu *pl*) conditions, facts, etc connected with an event or person: (通常用複數)與某事件或某人有關的情況、事實等;環境;情勢: *Don't judge the crime until you know the ~s.* 在你未瞭解一切情況之前,勿對此罪行下判斷。***C~s alter cases,*** (prov) What may be good, wise, praiseworthy, etc in some ~s may be bad, foolish or blameworthy in other ~s. (諺)情勢改變事態;人的行爲須因時地制宜(在某種情勢下是好的、明智的、值得稱讚的,在別的情勢下也許是壞的、愚蠢的或該受責備的)。***in/under the ~s,*** the ~s being so; such being the state of affairs. 在此種情形下;情形既然如此。***in/under no ~s,*** never; whatever may happen. 決不;無論在何種情況下均不可。**2** fact or detail: 詳情;細節: *There is one important ~ you have not mentioned.* 還有一件重要的事實你沒有提到。*He has plenty of money, which is a fortunate ~.* 他有充足的錢,這是一件幸運的事。**3** (*pl*) financial condition: (複)經濟情形;境況: *in easy/good/flourishing ~s,* having enough or plenty of money; 在富裕的生活環境中; *in reduced/straitened ~s,* poor. 經濟拮据;貧困。**4** (*sing*) (used only in) (單數)(僅用於) **pomp and ~,** show and ceremony. 鋪張。

cir·cum·stan·tial /ˌsɜːkəmˈstænʃl ; ˌsɝkəmˈstænʃəl/ *adj* **1** (of a description) giving full details. (指描寫)周詳的;詳盡的。**2** (of evidence) based on, consisting of details that strongly suggest sth but do not provide direct proof. (指證據)根據情況的;間接的;旁(證);佐(證)。**~·ly** /-nʃəlɪ ; -nʃəlɪ/ *adv*

cir·cum·vent /ˌsɜːkəmˈvent ; ˌsɝkəmˈvɛnt/ *vt* [VP6A] (formal) prevent (a plan) from being carried out; find a way to get round (a law, rule, difficulty, etc). (正式用語)阻遏(計畫)實現; 設法規避(法律、規則、困難等)。**cir·cum·ven·tion** /ˌsɜːkəmˈvenʃn ; ˌsɝkəmˈvɛnʃən/ *n*

cir·cus /ˈsɜːkəs ; ˈsɝkəs/ *n* **1** (in ancient Rome) round or oval place with seats on all sides for public games. (古羅馬)四周有座位之圓形(或橢圓形)競技場。**2** (in modern times) a travelling show, usu given in a large tent (called *the big top*) of performing animals, clever horse-riding, etc; persons and animals giving such a show. (現代)馬戲表演(通常在大帳篷 'the big top' 內表演);馬戲團。**3** (esp in proper names) open space where a number of streets converge: (尤用於專有名詞中)數條街道會集的廣場: *Piccadilly C~,* in London. (倫敦的)比加得力廣場。

cir·rho·sis /sɪˈrəʊsɪs ; sɪˈrosɪs/ *n* [U] chronic (and often fatal) disease of the liver. 肝硬化(慢性且常爲致命的肝病)。

cir·rus /ˈsɪrəs ; ˈsɪrəs/ *n* type of cloud, high in the sky, delicate and feathery in appearance. (高空中纖細如羽毛狀的)卷雲。

cissy /ˈsɪsɪ ; ˈsɪsɪ/ *adj, n* = sissy.

cis·tern /ˈsɪstən ; ˈsɪstɚn/ *n* water tank, eg as above the bowl of a WC, or for storing water in a building, with pipes to taps on lower storeys. (抽水馬桶的)水箱;(有水管通往低層樓之龍頭的) 貯水槽;貯水池;水塔。

cita·del /ˈsɪtədəl ; ˈsɪtədl̩/ *n* fortress for protecting a town; (fig) place of refuge or safety. 護城碉堡;城砦;城堡;(喩)避難所;安全地點。

cite /saɪt ; saɪt/ *vt* [VP6A] **1** give or mention as an example (esp by quoting from a book, to support an argument, etc). 引述;引證;引用(某書中之字句,以證明論點等)。**2** (US) mention for bravery in war: (美) 因英勇作戰而予以褒揚: *~d in dispatches.* 在公報中被褒揚。**3** (legal) summon at law: (法律) 傳喚至法庭; 傳訊: *be ~d in divorce proceedings.* 因離婚案被傳訊。**ci·ta·tion** /saɪˈteɪʃn ; saɪˈteʃən/ *n* [U] citing; [C] sth, esp a statement, that is ~d; (US) mention in an official record (eg for a brave act in war). 引述;引證;條文;引用文;(美)(在公報中)褒揚;表揚(如爲作戰英勇事蹟);獎狀。

citi·zen /ˈsɪtɪzn ; ˈsɪtəzn̩/ *n* **1** person who lives in a town, not in the country: (城市中的)市民: *the ~s of Paris.* 巴黎市民。**2** person who has full rights in a State, either by birth or by gaining such rights: (一國中享有完全權利之)公民(或因出生在該國,或因取得此項權利): *immigrants who have become ~s of the United States,* 已成爲美國公民之外來移民, Cf 參較 *British subject;* 英國的臣民; *~ of the world,* cosmopolitan person. 世界之公民;無國家偏見之人。**'~·ship** /-ʃɪp ; -ˌʃɪp/ *n* being a ~; rights and duties of a ~. 公民資格;公民之權利和義務。

cit·ric /ˈsɪtrɪk ; ˈsɪtrɪk/ *adj* ~ **acid** *n* (chem) acid from such fruits as lemons and limes. (化學)(由檸檬和宜母子等水果中取出之)檸檬酸。

cit·ron /ˈsɪtrən ; ˈsɪtrən/ *n* (tree with) pale yellow fruit like a lemon but larger, less acid, and thicker skinned. 枸櫞;香櫞(淺黃色水果,似檸檬但較大,較不酸,皮亦較厚);香櫞樹。

cit·rous /ˈsɪtrəs ; ˈsɪtrəs/ *adj* of the citrus fruits. 柑橘屬水果的。

cit·rus /ˈsɪtrəs ; ˈsɪtrəs/ *n* (bot) genus of trees that includes the lemon, lime, citron, orange and grapefruit; (attrib) of these trees: (植物)柑橘屬(包括檸檬,宜母子,香櫞,柑橘及柚子等);(形容用法)柑橘屬的: ˈ~ *fruit.* 柑橘屬水果。

city /ˈsɪtɪ ; ˈsɪtɪ/ *n* (*pl* -ties) **1** large and important town; town given special rights in self-government (in GB by royal charter, in US by a charter from the State). 都市;城市;享有特別自治權之城市(此權在英國由皇家特許狀所賦予,在美國由州的特許狀所賦予)。 **the C~,** the oldest part of London, now the commercial and financial centre. 倫敦市之最古老的部份,現爲商業及金融中心。 **2** people living in a ~. 一城市的全體市民。 **3** (attrib): (形容用法): ˌ~ ˈ*centre,* central area of a city; 市中心區; ˌ~ ˈ*editor,* (GB) one who deals with financial news; (US) one in charge of local news; (英)財經新聞編輯;(美)地方新聞編輯;採訪主任; ˌ~ ˈ*hall,* building for transaction of the official business of a ~; 市政廳;市政府; *a* ˈ*C~ man,* engaged in commerce or finance; 經營商業或金融業的人; ~ *state,* city that is also an independent sovereign state (eg Athens in ancient times). 城邦(既爲城市,亦爲獨立自主之國家,如古代之雅典)。

civet /ˈsɪvɪt ; ˈsɪvɪt/ *n* **1** (also 亦作 ˈ**~-cat**) small spotted cat-like animal of Africa, Asia and Europe. 麝貓;靈貓;香貓(體小有斑點似貓之動物,產於非、亞、歐洲)。 **2** [U] strong-smelling substance from certain glands of this animal. 麝貓香(自麝貓之某種腺體中取出之極香的物質)。

civic /ˈsɪvɪk ; ˈsɪvɪk/ *adj* of the official life and affairs of a town or a citizen: 市政的;市民的;公民的: ~ *duties;* 公民的義務; ~ *pride;* 公民的自豪; *a ~ centre,* where the official buildings, eg the town hall, library, hospitals, etc, are grouped together. 市政中心(政府機關如市政廳、圖書館、醫院等集中之地)。 **civ·ics** *n pl* (*sing v*) study of city government, the rights and duties of citizens, etc. (用單數動詞)公民(研究市政、公民權利與義務等的課程)。

civ·ies /ˈsɪvɪz ; ˈsɪvɪz/ *n pl* (GB sl) civilian clothes. (英俚)普通人民穿的衣服;便服。

civil /ˈsɪvl ; ˈsɪvl̩/ *adj* **1** of human society; of people living together: 人類社會的;群居之人們的;公民的: *We all have ~ rights and ~ duties.* 我們都有公民的權利和義務。 ˌ**~ ˌdisoˈbedience,** organized refusal to obey the laws (esp as part of a political campaign). 人民之集體的拒絕遵守法律(尤指作爲一項政治運動之一部份者);非暴力抵抗。 ˌ**~ ˌengiˈneering,** the design and building of roads, railways, canals, docks, etc. 土木工程(設計及建築道路、鐵路、運河、碼頭等)。 ˌ**~ ˈlaw,** law dealing with private rights of citizens, not with crime. 民法(處理公民私有權利而非處理犯罪之法律)。 ˌ**~ ˈmarriage,** without religious ceremony but recognized by law. 未經宗教儀式但爲法律所認可之婚姻。 ˌ**~ ˈrights,** rights of a citizen to political, racial, legal, social freedom or equality. 公民權(公民所享有之對政治、種族、法律、社會之自由或平等之權利)。 ˌ**~ ˈrights movement,** organized movement aiming to secure for all citizens the enjoyment of constitutional rights. 公民權運動(爲所有公民爭取享有憲法上所制定的權利的有組織運動)。 ˌ**~ ˈwar,** war between two sides in the same country, eg in the US 1861-65, in Spain 1936-39. 內戰(同一國內兩派間之戰爭,例如 1861-65 美國之南北戰爭及 1936-39 西班牙之內戰)。 **2** not of the armed forces. 平民的(對軍人而言);非軍人的。 ˌ**C~ Deˈfence Corps,** organization to deal with results of attack (esp from the air). 民防隊;民衆防護團(尤指處理空襲善後者)。 ˌ**~ ˈservant,** official in the C~ Service. (政府裏的)文官;公務員。 **the** ˌ**C~ ˈService,** all government departments except the Navy, Army and Air Force. 政府的文職機關(卽除海、陸、空軍以外者)。 **3** politely helpful: 有禮貌和助益的: *The boy gave me a ~ answer.* 那男孩給我一個有禮貌而又有助益的回答。 *Can't you be ~?* 你不能有禮貌點嗎? *It was ~ of them to offer to help us.* 他們自動幫助我們眞令人感佩。 **4** ˈ**~ list,** (GB) allowance of money made by Parliament for the royal household and royal pensions. (英)國會撥給皇室作爲皇家年俸之專款;王室年金。 **~·ly** /ˈsɪvəlɪ ; ˈsɪvl̩ɪ/ *adv* politely. 有禮貌地。 **ci·vil·ity** /sɪˈvɪlətɪ ; səˈvɪlətɪ/ *n* [U] politeness (*to*); (*pl;* -ties) polite acts. (對人)有禮貌(與 to 連用);有禮貌的行爲。

ci·vil·ian /sɪˈvɪlɪən ; səˈvɪljən/ *n, adj* (person) not serving with the armed forces: 未在軍中服役的;平民的;平民: *I asked the soldier what he was in ~ life.* 我問那軍人他做平民時是幹什麼的。*He left the army and returned to ~ life.* 他離開軍隊恢復平民生活。 *In modern wars ~s as well as soldiers are killed.* 在現代戰爭中,平民和軍人一樣地喪命。

civi·li·za·tion /ˌsɪvɪlaɪˈzeɪʃn *US:* -əlɪˈz- ; ˌsɪvl̩əˈzeʃən/ *n* **1** [U] civilizing or being civilized; state of being civilized: 教化;開化;教導: *The ~ of mankind has taken thousands of years.* 人類的開化已經有幾千年。 **2** [C] system, stage of, social development: 文化;文明(社會進化的方式或階段): *the ~s of ancient Egypt, Babylon and Persia.* 古埃及、巴比侖和波斯的文化。**3** [U] civilized States collectively: (集合用法)文明世界;文明國家: *acts that horrified ~.* 令文明國家震驚的行爲。

civi·lize /ˈsɪvəlaɪz ; ˈsɪvl̩ˌaɪz/ *vt* [VP6A] **1** bring from a savage or ignorant condition to a higher one (by giving education in methods of government, moral teaching, etc). (藉教以治理方法、道德訓示等)使自野蠻或無知的狀態進入較高等的階段;教化;開化。 **2** improve and educate; refine the manners of: 使之進步並教育;教導: *Many a rough man has been ~d by his wife.* 許多粗野的男人都被妻子教好了。

civ·vies /ˈsɪvɪz ; ˈsɪvɪz/ *n pl* = civies.

Civvy Street /ˈsɪvɪ striːt ; ˈsɪvɪ ˈstrit/ *n* (GB sl) civilian life. (英俚)平民生活。

clack /klæk ; klæk/ *vi, n* (make the) short, sharp sound of objects struck together: (發出)短而尖銳的碰撞聲: *the ~ of her knitting needles;* 她編織毛線的針的畢剝聲; *~ing typewriters;* 噼哩啪啦響的打字機; *~ing tongues at the Women's Institute.* 婦女會館裏吱吱喳喳的說話聲。

clad /klæd ; klæd/ old *pp* of clothe: clothe 的舊式過去分詞: *poorly ~,* dressed in poor clothes; 衣著粗劣的; (poet): (詩): *hills ~ in verdure;* 覆滿葱綠樹木的丘陵; (in compounds): (用於複合字中): ˈ*steel-~;* 鋼面的; ˈ*iron-~.* 包着鐵皮的。

claim¹ /kleɪm ; klem/ *vt, vi* [VP6A, 7A, 9, 2A] **1** demand recognition that one is, or owns, or has a right to (sth): 要求承認某人之身份、所有權或對(某物)享有某種權利: *Does anyone ~ this umbrella?* 有沒有人認領這把傘? *Every citizen in a democratic country may ~ the protection of the law.* 一個民主國家的每一個公民都可以要求法律的保護。 *He ~ed to be the owner of/~ed that he owned the land.* 他要求承認爲該土地之所有人。 *Have you ~ed yet,* eg made a ~ under an insurance policy? 你提出要求了嗎(如按保險單上的約定提出某項要求)? **~ damages,** (legal) (法律) ⇨ damage. ⇨ also bonus. **2** assert; say that sth is a fact: 聲言;宣稱;說某事爲事實: *He ~ed to have/~ed that he had done the work without help.* 他聲言未得到幫助而完成了此工作。 *He ~ed to be the best tennis player in the school.* 他自稱是全校最佳的網球手。 **3** (of things) need; deserve: (指事物)需要;值得: *There are several matters that ~ my attention.* 有數樁事值得我注意。

claim² /kleɪm ; klem/ *n* **1** [C] assertion of a right; act of ~ing¹ (1): 要求承認其所有權或某種權利: *Does anyone make a ~ to* (but more usu *Does anyone ~*) *this purse,* say that it is his? 有沒有人認領這個錢包? (但較常用 Does anyone claim this purse?) *His ~ to own the house is invalid.* 他對該房產所有權的要求是無效的。 **lay ~ to,** demand (sth) as one's due: 宣稱(某物)應歸其所有: *If the land really belongs to you, why don't you lay ~ to it,* say so and try to get it? 假若這塊土地眞是屬於你的,你何不請求歸還產權? **2** [C] sum of money demanded under an insurance agreement (for loss, damage, etc): 根據保險合約所要求的賠款 (如因損失、損壞等): *make/put in a ~ (for sth)*. (因某物之損壞)提出賠償要求。**3** [U, C] right to ask for: 要求權;債權: *You have no ~ on my sympathies.* 你無權要求我同情。**4** [C] sth that is ~ed; piece of land (esp in a gold-bearing region) allotted to a miner: 所要求之物; (尤指產金礦的地區)分配給礦工的一塊地: *stake out a ~*, mark boundaries to assert ownership. 標出地界以維護所有權。 **'~·ant** /'kleɪmənt ; 'klemənt/ *n* person who makes a ~, esp in law. 要求者(尤指提出法律要求者)。

clair·voy·ance /kleə'vɔɪəns ; klɛr'vɔɪəns/ *n* [U] power of perceiving what is not present to the senses; exceptional insight. 對於非眼前事物的覺察力;超人的洞察力。⇨ telepathy. **clair·voy·ant** /kleə'vɔɪənt ; klɛr'vɔɪənt/ *n* person with such power. 有超人洞察力的人。

clam /klæm ; klæm/ *n* large shell-fish, with a shell in two halves, used for food. 蛤;蚌(殼分兩半之大貝類,用作食物)。⇨ the illus at bivalve. 參看 bivalve 之插圖。 **~·bake** /'klæmbeɪk ; 'klæm,bek/ *n* (US) seashore picnic at which ~s and other foods are baked. (美)烤蚌野餐(在海灘上烤蚌殼類及其他食物的野餐)。□ *vi* (-mm) **1** [VP2A] dig for, go out for, ~s. 掘蚌;拾蚌。**2** [VP2C] *~ up*, (colloq) (suddenly) become silent; refuse to speak. (俗)(突然)變爲沉默;拒絕說話。

clam·ber /'klæmbə(r) ; 'klæmbɚ/ *vi* [VP2C] climb with some difficulty, using the hands and feet: 攀爬;爬上;攀登: *~ up/over a wall.* 爬上(過)牆。□ *n* awkward or difficult climb. 麻煩的或艱難的攀登。

clammy /'klæmɪ ; 'klæmɪ/ *adj* (-ier, -iest) damp; moist; cold and sticky to the touch: 潮濕的;冷而黏的: *~ hands;* 又冷又黏的手; *a face ~ with sweat.* 汗濕的臉。 **clam·mi·ly** *adv*

clam·our (US = **clam·or**) /'klæmə(r) ; 'klæmɚ/ *n* [C, U] loud confused noise or shout, esp of people complaining angrily or making a demand. 喧鬧;叫囂;(尤指)群衆之憤怒或有所要求的呼喊。□ *vi, vt* [VP2A, C, 4A] make a ~: 喧鬧;叫囂;大聲呼喊: *The foolish people were ~ing for war.* 愚昧的人們叫囂着要求打仗。*The newspapers ~ed against the government's policy.* 報紙大聲疾呼反對政府的政策。*The troops were ~ing to go home.* 軍隊大聲喊着要回國。**clam·or·ous** /'klæmərəs ; 'klæmərəs/ *adj* noisy: 吵鬧的;叫喊的: *a clamorous mob.* 喧嚷的暴民。

clamp /klæmp ; klæmp/ *n* **1** appliance for holding things together tightly by means of a screw. 夾鉗。**2** band of iron, etc for strengthening or tightening. 釘夾;鐵箍;夾板;鐵馬釘。□ *vt, vi* **1** [VP6A, 15B] put a ~ or ~s on; put in a ~. 用螺絲鉗夾;置於螺絲鉗中;加鐵箍或置於鐵箍中。**2** [VP2C] *~ **down (on)**,* (colloq) put pressure on; exert pressure against (in order to stop sth): (俗)施壓力於;用力制止;箝制: *They ~ed down on the newspapers.* 他們施壓力制止報紙報導。Hence, 由此產生, **'~-down** *n*

clan /klæn ; klæn/ *n* large family group, as found in tribal communities, esp Scottish Highlanders with a common ancestor: 大家族;宗族;氏族(如見於部落社會者); (尤指) 同一祖宗的蘇格蘭高地人: *the Campbell ~.* 康伯爾氏宗族。

clan·des·tine /klæn'destɪn ; klæn'dɛstɪn/ *adj* (formal) secret; done secretly; kept secret: (正式用語)秘密的;秘密而做的;被保密的: *a ~ marriage.* 秘密的結婚。

clang /klæŋ ; klæŋ/ *vt, vi, n* [VP6A, 2A] (make a) loud ringing sound (eg a hammer striking an anvil): (使)(發出)玎璫聲;璫琅聲(如鐵錘擊鐵砧之聲): *The tramdriver ~ed his bell.* 電車司機踏鈴。*The ~ of the firebell alarmed the village.* 火警鈴的噹噹聲驚動了全村的人。 **~er** *n* (sl) (俚) ***drop a ~er,*** say sth indiscreet or embarrassing. 說出不得體或令人困窘的話。

clang·our (US = **clangor**) /'klæŋə(r) ; 'klæŋgɚ/ *n* continued clanging noise; series of clangs. 連續的玎璫聲。**clangor·ous** /'klæŋərəs ; 'klæŋgərəs/ *adj*

clank /klæŋk ; klæŋk/ *vt, vi, n* [VP6A, 2A] (make a) dull metallic sound (not so loud as a clang) (eg chains or knives striking together): (使)(發出)玎璫聲(較 clang 聲爲小,如鐵鍊或刀相擊之聲): *prisoners ~ing their chains.* 使鐐銬琅璫作響的囚犯。

clan·nish /'klænɪʃ ; 'klænɪʃ/ *adj* showing clan feeling; (of people) in the habit of supporting one another against outsiders. 表現宗族感情的;(指人們)習慣於團結排外的。 **~·ly** *adv*

clans·man /'klænzmən ; 'klænzmən/ *n* (*pl* -men) member of a clan. 同一宗族的人;族人。

clap¹ /klæp ; klæp/ *vt, vi* (-pp-) **1** [VP6A, 2A, B] show approval, applaud, by striking (often) the front part of the hands together: 鼓掌(表示贊成、讚許);拍(手): *When the violinist finished the audience ~ped for five minutes.* 當小提琴手演奏完時,聽衆鼓掌達五分鐘。*The baby ~ped its hands.* 那嬰孩在拍手。**2** [VP14] strike or slap lightly with the open hand, usu in a friendly way: (用手掌)輕拍(通常以友善的方式): *~ sb on the back.* 拍拍某人的背。**3** [VP15A, B] put quickly or energetically: 迅速有力地放置: *~ sb in prison;* 把某人投入獄中; *~ one's hat on;* 迅速用力地將帽戴上; *~ on sail,* spread more sail. 張多一點帆。 ***~ eyes on sb,*** (colloq, esp in neg) catch sight of: (俗,尤用於否定句中)看見;見到: *I haven't ~ped eyes on him since 1960.* 我從1960年以後就沒有見到過他。□ *n* **1** loud explosive noise (eg of thunder). 大的爆發聲;轟隆聲(例如雷聲)。**2** sound of the front of the hands brought together. (*Clapping* is the usu word for applause, not *claps*). 擊掌聲;拍手聲。(指鼓掌喝采通常用 clapping, 非 claps)。

clap² /klæp ; klæp/ *n* [U] **(the) ~,** (sl) venereal disease; (esp) gonorrhea. (俚)性病;(尤指)淋病。

clap·board /'klæpbɔːd *US:* 'klæbɔːrd ; 'klæbɚd/ *n* weather-board. (房屋外面的)牆面板;護牆板;魚鱗板;簷板。

clap·per /'klæpə(r) ; 'klæpɚ/ *n* tongue or striker of a bell; noisy hand rattle (used, for example, to scare birds from crops). (鐘鈴之)擊錘;鈴(鐘)舌;手搖之鳴響器(如用以嚇走田中之鳥者)。 **'~·board** *n* (filming) divided, hinged and marked board which is sharply closed to mark the start of filming. (電影)場記板(刻有標誌裝有鉸鏈的兩塊木板,拍擊以示攝影開始)。

clasped hands

a clamp

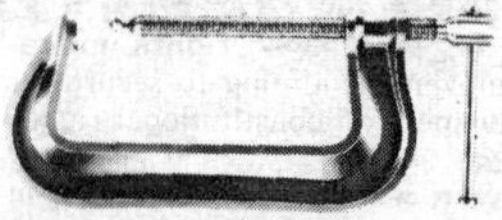

clap·trap /'klæptræp ; 'klæp,træp/ *n* [U] ideas, remarks, that are intended merely to attract attention or win applause; nonsense. 旨在引人注意或贏得喝采的主意或談話;噱頭;胡言亂語。

claque /klæk ; klæk/ *n* [C] number of persons hired to applaud at a theatre, concert, etc. 受雇在劇院、音樂會等中鼓掌捧場的人群。

claret /'klærət ; 'klærət/ *n* [U] (kind of) red table wine from Bordeaux; (also *adj*) its colour, dark red. (產於波爾多之)紅葡萄酒;(亦作形容詞用)此種酒之顏色;深紅色(的)。

clar·ify /'klærɪfaɪ ; 'klærə,faɪ/ *vt, vi* [VP6A, 2A]

make or become clear; make (a liquid, etc) free from impurities. 澄清;使明白;使(液體等)清潔(不含雜質)。 **clari·fi·ca·tion** /ˌklærɪfɪˈkeɪʃn ; ˌklærəfəˈkeʃən/ *n* [U] ~ing or being clarified. 澄清;闡明。

clari·net /ˌklærɪˈnet ; ˌklærəˈnɛt/ *n* musical wood-wind instrument, with finger holes and keys. 單簧管;豎笛。⇨ the illus at brass. 參看 brass 之插圖。~**·ist**, ~**·tist** *n* person who plays the ~. 吹奏豎笛者;豎笛手。

clar·ion /ˈklærɪən ; ˈklærɪən/ *n* loud, shrill call made to rouse and excite; (attrib) loud and clear: (有喚起或激勵作用的)響亮尖銳之聲;(形容用法) 響亮清澈的: *a ~ call;* 響亮的呼喚; *a ~ voice.* 響亮的嗓音。

clar·ity /ˈklærətɪ ; ˈklærətɪ/ *n* [U] clearness. 清楚;清澈;透明。

clash /klæʃ ; klæʃ/ *vi, vt* **1** [VP6A, 15B, 2A, C] make a loud, broken, confused noise (as when metal objects strike together): (使)發撞擊聲(如金屬物體互撞而發者);發鏗鏘之聲: *Their swords ~ed.* 他們的劍互擊而發鏗鏘之聲。*She ~ed the pans down on the stone floor.* 她把炒鍋噹啷一聲掉在石地上。*The cymbals ~ed.* 鐃鈸鳴擊而發響亮之聲。 **2** [VP2A, C] come suddenly together; meet in conflict: 互撞;互碰: *The two armies ~ed outside the town.* 兩軍在城外交鋒。 **3** [VP2A, C] (of events) interfere with each other because they are (to be) at the same time on the same date: (指事件)時間衝突(卽在同一日期的同一時刻): *It's a pity the two concerts ~, I want to go to both.* 可惜兩個音樂會時間衝突,我兩個都想去聽。**4** [VP3A, 2A, C] ~ ***(with)***, be in disagreement or at variance: (與…)不合;不一致: *I ~ed with him/We ~ed at the last meeting of the Council.* 在上一次議會的集會中我與他(我們)的意見不一致。*The colour of the curtains ~es with the colour of the carpet.* 窗簾的顏色與地毯的顏色不調和。*The date of your party ~es with another engagement.* 你的宴會的日期與另一約會相抵觸。□ *n* **1** ~ing noise: 撞擊聲;碰擊聲: *the ~ of weapons/of pots falling/of cymbals.* 武器互擊(鍋跌落,銅鈸)的響聲。**2** disagreement; conflict: 不合;不調和;衝突;抵觸: *a ~ of views/opinions/colours.* 見解(意見,色彩)不合。

clasp /klɑːsp *US:* klæsp ; klæsp/ *n* **1** device with two parts that fasten, used to keep together two things or two parts of one thing (eg the ends of a necklace or belt). (作扣子用的)鈎環;扣鈎;扣環(如用以扣住項鍊或腰帶的兩端者)。 **ˈ~-knife**, folding knife with a ~ for fixing the blade when open. (打開時有扣環可以固定刀刃的)折叠式小刀。 **2** bar of silver, etc on a medal-ribbon (with the name of the battle, campaign, etc at which the person to whom the medal was awarded was present). 勳表附飾;勳標(勳章飾帶上刻着受勳者所曾參加之戰役等名稱之銀質或其他質料扣桿)。 **3** firm hold (with the fingers or arm); handshake; embrace. (用手指或臂膀)緊握;握手;擁抱。□ *vt, vi* **1** [VP6A, 15A] hold tightly or closely: 緊握;緊抱: *~ed in each other's arms;* 互相緊緊擁抱; *~ sb by the hand.* 緊握住某人的手。*The thief was ~ing a knife in his hand.* 竊賊手中緊握着一把刀。~ ***hands***, shake hands with sb (showing more emotion than in the usual handshake). 緊緊地握手 (比普通的握手表示較多的感情)。~ ***one's hands***, press them together with the fingers interlaced: 將兩手手指互相交叉而握着: *with hands ~ed in prayer;* 在禱告時交叉屈指合掌; *with his hands ~ed behind him.* 他把兩手交叉握於背後。 **2** [VP6A, 15A] fasten with a clasp(1): 用鈎環扣住: *~ a bracelet round one's wrist.* 將手鐲扣戴在手腕上。 **3** [VP2A] *This bracelet won't ~,* cannot be ~ed. 這只手鐲扣不住。

class /klɑːs *US:* klæs ; klæs/ *n* **1** group having qualities of the same kind; kind, sort or division: 種;類;門類;類別;等級: *There used to be first-~, second-~ and third-~ carriages on the trains in Britain.* 英國火車從前分爲頭等、二等、三等車廂。 *The second highest division of the animal or vegetable kingdom is a ~.* 動植物的第二高類別叫綱。⇨ family, genus, order¹(15), phylum, species. *As an actor A is not in the same ~ with B,* is not so good as B. 作爲一個演員而論,甲不如乙。 **2** [U] system of ranks in society; caste system: (社會的)階級;階級制度: *It will be difficult to abolish ~;* 要廢除社會階級制度是很難的; (used attrib): (形容用法): *~ conflicts;* 社會階級間的衝突; *the ˈ~ struggle.* 階級鬥爭。 **ˈ~-conscious**, realizing one's ~ in society and the differences between social ~es. 有階級意識的 (覺察自己的社會階級及社會各階級之差別的)。 **ˈ~-feeling**, feeling of envy, etc of one ~ for another. 階級感(階級間互相嫉妒等之感覺)。 **ˌ~-ˈwarfare**, struggle, enmity, between ~es. 階級鬥爭。 **3** [C] all persons in one of these ranks: 所有同一階級的人: *Society may be divided into upper, middle and lower ~es.* 社會可分爲上層、中層和下層階級。 **4** group of persons taught together; their course of teaching. (學生的)班;級;課。 **ˈ~-fellow/-mate**, present or past member of the same ~: 同班同學: *Jim and I were ~-mates last term.* 吉姆和我上學期同班。 **ˈ~-room**, room where a ~ is taught. 教室。 **5** (US) group of pupils or students who enter school or college in the same year and leave together: (美)同年入學同年畢業之一班學生;級: *the ~ of 1973,* those who finished their school course in that year. 1973 級(此年畢業之一班學生)。 **6** all those men conscripted for service in the armed forces in a year: 同年徵召入伍的士兵: *the 1970 ~.* 1970 年次的役男。 **7** (not US) grade or merit after examination: (不用於美國) 考試成績之等第: *take a first/second-~ degree.* 考得第一 (第二) 等。 **ˈ~-list**, honours list issued by examiners. (由主試者公佈的)成績優異學生名單。 **8** (colloq; often attrib) distinction; excellence; style: (俗;常作形容用法)優秀;特優;卓越;風度;氣質: *He's a ~ tennis player.* 他是一個優秀的網球選手。*There's not much ~ about her.* 她沒有什麼氣質。 □ *vt* [VP6A, 14] place in a ~(1): 分入某類;歸類: *a ship ~ed A1;* 列爲頭等的船; *to ~ one thing with another.* 將甲物與乙物歸入一類。**~-less** *adj* without distinctions of ~(2): 無階級之分的: *Is a ~less society possible?* 一個無階級之分的社會是可能的嗎?

clas·sic /ˈklæsɪk ; ˈklæsɪk/ *adj* **1** of the highest quality; having a value or position recognized and unquestioned. 最佳的;最高等的;第一流的;具有公認而無可爭議之價值或地位的。 **2** of the standard of ancient Greek and Latin literature, art and culture. 古代希臘及羅馬文學、藝術和文化之標準的;古典的。 **3** with qualities like those of ~(2) art, ie simple, harmonious and restrained. 有古典藝術風格的(卽樸素的,調和的和嚴謹的)。 **4** famous because of a long history: 因歷史悠久而著名的: *a ~ event,* eg the Oxford and Cambridge boat race or the Derby. 因歷史悠久而著名的大賽會(如牛津大學與劍橋大學的划船競賽或英國大賽馬)。 **5** (of style in costume, etc) traditional; not new. (指服裝等的式樣)傳統的;非新式的。 □ *n* **1** writer, artist, book, etc of the highest class: 第一流的作家、藝術家、著作等: *Milton is a ~.* 密爾頓是第一流作家。*'Robinson Crusoe' is a ~.* '魯濱遜漂流記'是一部名著。**2** ancient Greek or Latin writer. 古希臘或羅馬的作家;古典作家。 **3 the ~s,** (literature of the) ancient languages of Greece and Rome. 古希臘、羅馬的文學或語文;古典文學;古典語文。**C~s,** university course in these subjects: (大學課程中的) 古典文學或古典語文: *He read ~s at Oxford.* 他在牛津大學攻讀古典文學。 **4** ~ event, ⇨ the *adj* 4 above. 歷史悠久的大事;傳統的大賽會(參看上列形容詞第 4 義)。

clas·si·cal /ˈklæsɪkl ; ˈklæsɪkl/ *adj* **1** in, of ancient Gk and Roman art and literature: 古希臘、羅馬之文學藝術的: *~ studies;* 古典文學藝術研究; *a ~ education;* 古典文學藝術的教育; *a ˈ~ scholar.* 精通

古典文學藝術的學者。 **2** of proved value because of having passed the test of time: 經過時間的考驗被證明爲有價值的: ~ *music*, usually taking traditional, well-defined form as a concerto, symphony, etc, eg of Haydn and Mozart. 古典音樂(通常爲協奏曲、交響曲等定義明確的傳統曲式,如海頓及莫扎特的作品)。 **3** simple and restrained; not over-ornamented. 古典式的;有古典之風格的(卽樸實、嚴謹而無華的)。 **~·ly** /-kəlɪ ; -klɪ/ *adv*

clas·si·cist /ˈklæsɪsɪst ; ˈklæsəsɪst/ *n* follower of classic style; classical scholar: 崇尚古典風格者;古典主義者;古典學者: *Milton was a* ~. 密爾頓是一位古典派作家。

clas·si·fi·ca·tion /ˌklæsɪfɪˈkeɪʃn ; ˌklæsəfəˈkeʃən/ *n* [U] classifying or being classified; [C] group into which sth is put. 分類;歸類;(某物所歸入的)類別;門類;種類。

clas·sify /ˈklæsɪfaɪ ; ˈklæsəˌfaɪ/ *vt* [VP6A] arrange in classes or groups; put into a class(1): 分類;歸類: *In a library books are usually classified by subjects.* 在圖書館裏,書籍通常是按科目分類。 **clas·si·fied** *adj* arranged in classes(1): 按種類分列的;分類的;類別的: *classified advertisements* (also, colloq, *classified ads*); 分類廣告(口語亦作 classified ads); *classified directory*, one in which the entries (eg of business firms) are entered in classes (eg builders, electricians, plumbers); 分類電話簿(如公司行號之按營業項目分類,如建築商、電工、鉛管工等); (US) put in a group that is officially secret: (美)歸入官方機密的;經保密區分的: *classified information*. 機密的資料。 **clas·si·fi·able** /ˈklæsɪfaɪəbl; ˈklæsəˌfaɪəbl̩/ *adj* that can be classified. 可分類的;可歸類的。

classy /ˈklɑːsɪ *US:* ˈklæsɪ ; ˈklæsɪ/ *adj* (-ier, -iest) (colloq) stylish; superior; upper-class. (俗)漂亮的;時髦的;優良的;上等的;頂呱呱的。

clat·ter /ˈklætə(r) ; ˈklætɚ/ *n* (*sing* only) (僅用單數) **1** long, continuous, resounding noise (as of hard things falling or knocking together): 長而連續的回響聲(如堅硬物體落地或互相碰撞的聲音): *the ~ of a horse's hoofs on a hard road;* 馬蹄在硬路上行走的踢踏聲; *the ~ of machinery;* 機器的轆轆聲; *the ~ of cutlery.* 刀、劍的碰擊聲。 **2** noisy talk: 喧嚷的談話: *The boys stopped their ~ when the teacher came into the classroom.* 當老師走進教室時,男生們停止喧嘩。 □ *vi, vt* [VP6A, 2A, C] make a ~(1): (使)發出長而連續的回響聲: *Pots and pans were ~ing in the kitchen.* 盆子鍋子在廚房裏碰擊作響。 *Don't ~ your knives and forks.* 不要讓你的刀叉碰擊出聲。 *Some of the dishes ~ed down during the earthquake.* 有些盤子在地震的時候嘩喇地落在地上。

clause /klɔːz ; klɔz/ *n* **1** (gram) component of a (complex) sentence, with its own subject and predicate, esp one doing the work of a noun, adjective or adverb: (文法)子句(構成(複雜)句子的一個成分,自有其主詞和述語,尤指其功用同名詞、形容詞或副詞者): *dependent/subordinate* ~. 附屬子句。 **2** (legal) complete paragraph in an agreement, legal document, etc. (法律)(契約、法律文件等之)條款。

claus·tro·pho·bia /ˌklɔːstrəˈfəʊbɪə ; ˌklɔstrəˈfobɪə/ *n* [U] morbid fear of confined places (eg a lift, cave or coal-mine). 幽閉恐怖(對於狹窄幽閉處所如電梯、洞穴或煤礦坑等的恐懼症)。

clavi·chord /ˈklævɪkɔːd ; ˈklævəˌkɔrd/ *n* stringed instrument with a keyboard, predecessor of the piano. 古鋼琴(有鍵盤之弦樂器,爲鋼琴之前身)。

clav·icle /ˈklævɪkl ; ˈklævəkl̩/ *n* (anat) collar-bone. (解剖)鎖骨。 ⇨ the illus at skeleton. 參看 skeleton 之插圖。

claw /klɔː ; klɔ/ *n* **1** one of the pointed nails on the feet of some animals, reptiles and birds; foot with such nails. (某些獸類、爬虫類及鳥類足上的)爪;有爪之足。 ⇨ the illus at bird. 參看 bird 之插圖。 **2** pincers of a shell-fish (eg a lobster). (甲殼類如龍蝦的)螯。 ⇨ the illus at crustacean. 參看 crustacean 之插圖。 **3** instrument or device like a ~ (eg a steel hook on a machine for lifting things). 似爪之工具(如吊物機之鋼抓鈎)。 **ˈ~-hammer** *n* hammer with one end of the head bent and divided for pulling nails out of wood. (一端略彎中間有縫可自木中拔釘之)羊角錘;拔釘錘。 □ *vi, vt* [VP3A, 6A, 15B] **~ at; ~ (back),** (try to) get hold of, pull, scratch, with ~s or hands. (用爪或手)抓;撕;扯;搔。 Hence, 由此產生, **ˈ~-back** *n* (colloq) regaining sth with effort and persistence. (俗)努力復得某事物。

clay /kleɪ ; kle/ *n* [U] stiff, sticky earth that becomes hard when baked; material from which bricks, pots, earthenware, etc are made: 黏土;陶土(經烘焙卽變硬,爲製磚、缽、陶器等之材料): (attrib) (形容用法) ~ *soil;* 黏質土壤;黏土; *a ~ pipe*, tobacco pipe made of white ~. 白黏土製的煙斗;陶製煙斗。 **~ey** /ˈkleɪɪ ; ˈkle·ɪ/ *adj* of, like, containing, covered with, ~. 黏土的;似黏土的;內含或覆蓋着黏土的。

clean[1] /kliːn ; klin/ *adj* (-er, -est) **1** free from dirt: 清潔的;無汚垢的: ~ *hands;* 清潔的手;清白; ~ *air*, free from smoke; 清潔(無烟)的空氣; *a ~ bomb*, atomic or hydrogen bomb that, it is claimed, explodes without fall-out. 淨彈(據稱爆炸後無原子塵之原子彈或氫彈)。 ⇨ fall²(14). *Keep the classroom* ~. 保持教室清潔。 *Wash it* ~. 把它洗乾淨。 **2** not yet used; fresh: 尙未用過的;新鮮的;乾淨的: *Put some* ~ (eg after having been washed) *sheets on the bed.* 鋪一些乾淨的(如剛洗過的)褥單在床上。 *Give me a ~ sheet of paper.* 給我一張沒有用過的紙。 **3** pure; innocent; free from wrong-doing or indecency: 純潔的;清白的;無犯過或下流行爲的;無前科的: *a ~ joke.* 一則乾淨(不下流)的笑話。 *You must lead a ~ life.* 你必須過純潔的生活。 *He has a ~ record*, is not known to have done wrong. 他的記錄清白(從無犯罪行爲)。 *Keep the party* ~, (colloq) Don't use bad language or tell improper stories. (俗)不要說下流的話或不道德的故事。 **4** well-formed; of good shape: 整齊的;好看的;形式美觀的: *a motor-car/ship with ~ lines.* 外貌美觀的汽車(船)。 ⇨ streamlined. **ˌ~-ˈlimbed** *adj* having well-shaped limbs. 四肢的樣子好看的;姿態優美的;手足勻稱的。 **5** even; regular; with a smooth edge or surface: 勻稱的;規則的;邊緣或表面光滑的: *A sharp knife makes a ~ cut.* 快刀切得乾淨俐落。 *C~ timber has no knots in it.* 光潔的木料沒有節疤。 **6** skilful; smart: 技術熟練的;乾淨俐落的: *a ~ boxer;* 技術熟練的拳擊手; (cricket) (板球) ~ *fielding;* 技巧的接球; *a ~ stroke/blow.* 乾淨俐落的一擊。 **7** having ~ habits: 有清潔習慣的;愛清潔的: *a ~ cat.* 愛清潔的貓。 **8** fit for food: 可食的: *~/un~ animals*, those that are/are not considered fit for food (by religious custom). (按宗教習俗)被認爲可食(不可食)的動物。 **9** thorough, complete. 徹底的;完全的。 ***make a ~ sweep of,*** ⇨ sweep¹(1). ⇨ also breast and slate(2). □ *adv* completely; entirely: 完全地;全然: *I ~ forgot about it.* 我完全忘記它了。 *The bullet went ~ through his shoulder.* 槍彈洞穿他的肩膀。 ***come ~,*** make a full confession. 全部供認。 **ˌ~-ˈbowled** *adj* (cricket) bowled with no possibility of doubt. (板球)毫無疑問地被振出場的。 **ˌ~-ˈcut** *adj* sharply and pleasingly outlined: 輪廓鮮明可愛的: *~-cut features.* 輪廓鮮明可愛的臉龐。 **ˌ~-ˈliving** *adj* chaste. 貞潔的。 **ˌ~-ˈshaven** *adj* with the hair of the face shaved off; not having a moustache or beard. 臉面修得乾淨的;不留鬍髭的。

clean[2] /kliːn ; klin/ *vt, vi* **1** [VP6A] make clean (of dirt, etc): 弄乾淨;使清潔(使無汚垢等): *Wash your hands and ~ your nails.* 洗你的手並把指甲弄乾淨。 *I must have this suit ~ed*, sent to the dry-cleaner's. 我必須把這套衣服送去(乾洗店)乾洗。 ⇨ dry¹(12). *C~ your shoes before you come into the houes*, ie remove the mud, etc. 在進入屋內以前請把鞋子弄乾淨。 ⇨ brush, polish. **2** [VP2A] *A porcelain sink ~s easily*, is easy to ~. 瓷水槽容易弄清潔。 **3** [VP15B, 2C] (special uses with *adverbial par-*

ticles and preps): (與副詞接語及介詞連用之特殊用法): **~ sth down,** ~ by brushing or wiping: 清掃;刷乾淨;擦乾淨: *~ down the walls.* 把牆上的塵土掃下。**~ sb out,** win or take all the money of: 贏得或取去…的全部金錢: *They really ~ed me out at Las Vegas,* I lost all my money gambling there. 我在拉斯維加斯把所有的錢全輸光了。**~ sth out,** ~ the inside of, remove dirt, dust, etc from: 打掃某物之內部;掃除某物上之塵土等: *It's time you ~ed out your bedroom.* 現在該是你打掃臥室的時候了。**be ~ed out,** (colloq) have no money left. (俗)一文不名。**~ up,** make clean or tidy; put in order: 打掃清潔或收拾整齊;整理: *You should always ~ up after a picnic,* burn wastepaper, collect litter, empty bottles, etc. 野餐過後你一定要收拾乾淨(燒掉廢紙,收拾雜物、空瓶等)。**~ sth up, (a)** get rid of criminal and immoral elements, etc: 清除罪犯和不道德的份子等;整頓(某事物): *The mayor has decided to ~ up the city,* end corruption, etc. 市長已決定要整頓市政(清除貪污等)。**(b)** (colloq) make money (as gain or profit). (俗)賺(錢);獲(利)。**'~-up** *n* (esp (process of) ending or reducing crime, corruption, etc. (尤指)清除或減少犯罪、腐化等;整頓。□ *n* ~ing: 清潔;打掃: *Give it a good ~,* ~ it well. 把它好好地清潔清潔。**~er** *n* person or thing that ~s; tool, machine, etc for ~ing; substance that removes dirt, stains, grease, etc: 做清潔工作的人或物;打掃清潔的工具、機器等;洗濯污垢、污漬、油漬等之物質;清潔器;吸塵器;清潔劑;洗滌劑: *send/take a suit to the (,dry) '~ers;* 把一套衣服送到(乾洗)洗衣店去; *'window-~er;* 擦窗門的工人; *'vacuum-~er.* 眞空吸塵器。

cleanly[1] /'klenlɪ ; 'klɛnlɪ/ *adj* (-ier, -iest) habitually clean; having clean habits: 經常乾淨的;有清潔習慣的;愛清潔的: *Are cats ~ animals?* 貓是愛清潔的動物嗎? **clean·li·ness** /'klenlɪnəs ; 'klɛnlɪnəs/ *n* [U] being clean. 乾淨;清潔。

cleanly[2] /'kli:nlɪ;'klinlɪ/ *adv* exactly; sharply; neatly: 正確地;清清楚楚地;乾淨俐落地;整潔地: *This knife doesn't cut ~.* 這把刀子切起來不俐落。*He caught the ball ~,* without fumbling. 他乾淨俐落地接住了那隻球。

cleanse /klenz ; klɛnz/ *vt* [VP6A] (formal or archaic) make thoroughly clean; make pure: (正式用語或古語)徹底清潔;使純潔;滌淨: *~ of/from sin.* 清除…的罪。**~r** *n* [C,U] substance that ~s (eg a synthetic detergent). 使徹底清潔的東西(如合成的清潔劑);洗滌劑。

clear[1] /klɪə(r) ; klɪr/ *adj* **1** easy to see through: 清亮的;清澈的;容易看穿的: *~ glass;* 透明的玻璃; *the ~ water of a mountain lake;* 清澈的高山湖水; free from cloud: 無雲的;晴朗的: *a ~ sky;* 晴朗無雲的天空; bright, pure: 光明的;純淨的: *a ~ light;* 亮光; *a ~ fire,* burning without much smoke; 明亮的火(沒有很多烟); distinct; easily seen: 清晰的;容易看清楚的: *a line of hills ~ in the morning sky;* 襯托在清晨天空中清晰可見的一排山巒; *a ~ photograph;* 照得很清楚的相片; *a ~ reflection in the water.* 映在水中清楚的倒影。**2** free from guilt or blame: 無愧疚的;清白的: *a ~ conscience,* knowledge that one is innocent. 清白的良心;問心無愧。**3** (of sounds, etc) easily heard; distinct; pure: (指聲音等)清晰可聞的;響亮的;清純的: *a ~ voice;* 嘹亮的嗓音; *the ~ note of a bell;* 清晰的鐘聲; *speak so that one's words are ~.* 咬字清楚地說。**4 ~ (about),** (of and to the mind) free from doubt or difficulty: (指心智和對於心智)明白無疑的;不難懂的: *a ~ thinker/statement.* 條理清晰的思想家(陳述)。*My memory is not ~ about/on that point.* 關於此點我的記憶已不清楚了。*It was ~ (to everyone) that the war would not end quickly.* 人人都明白戰爭不會很快結束。**make oneself/one's meaning ~,** make oneself understood: 使自己(自己的意思)讓人明白: *Now, do I make myself ~?* 現在,(你們)明白我了嗎? **,~-'headed,** having good understanding. 頭腦清楚的;理解力强的。**,~-'sighted,** able to see, think, understand well. 目力好的;有眼光的;有見識的。**5 ~ (of),** easy or safe to pass along; free from obstacles, dangers, etc: 通行容易或安全的;無障礙、危險等的: *Is the road ~?* 這條路暢通嗎? *The coast is ~,* (fig) There is no one about (so one can escape, etc). (喻)毫無阻礙(可以逃走等);可放心而為;是行動的好機會。*Is the sea ~ of ice yet?* 海上的浮冰消失了嗎? *The signal 'All ~' was sounded,* eg after an air raid, to inform people that the raiders had left. '解除'警報響過了(如在空襲過後通知人民敵機已去)。**'~·way** *n* (in GB) section of the public highway on which vehicles must not stop or park. (在英國)暢通道(公路車道上禁止行車停止或停放的一段道路)。**6 ~ (about),** confident; certain: 有把握的;確知的: *I want to be quite ~ on this point.* 關於這一點我要完全弄清楚。*I am not ~ as to what you expect me to do.* 我不明白你期望我做什麼。**7 ~ (of),** free (from debt, suspicion, a charge): 債務已清償的;嫌疑已釋除的;已證明無所控之罪的: *I wish I were ~ of debt.* 但願我的債已還清。*You are now ~ of suspicion.* 現在你的嫌疑已澄清。**8** complete: 完全的;整個的: *for three ~ days;* 整整三天; without limitations; with nothing (to be) deducted: 無限制的;不折不扣的;淨得的;十足的: *a ~ profit of £5;* 五鎊之淨利; *passed by a ~ majority of ten.* 以足足超過十票之多數通過。□ *n* **in the ~,** free from suspicion, danger, etc. 無嫌疑、危險等的。**~·ness** *n* [U] state of being ~; clarity: 清楚;明顯;清明度;晴朗;清澈: *the ~ness of the atmosphere;* 大氣之清明度; *~ness of vision.* 視力清楚;視力敏銳。

clear[2] /klɪə(r) ; klɪr/ *adv* **1** distinctly: 清楚地;明白地: *speak loud and ~.* 說話聲音響亮而清楚。**,~-'cut** *adv* well defined; distinct; having ~ outlines: 措詞清楚的;明顯的;輪廓清晰的: *~-cut ideas/plans.* 清楚的觀念(計畫)。**2** quite; completely: 十分地;完全地: *The prisoner got ~ away.* 該囚犯逃得無踪無影。**3 ~ (of),** apart; without touching; at or to a distance: 分離地;不接觸地;有距離地: *He jumped three inches ~ of the bar.* 他以超過三吋的高度跳過竿去。*Stand ~ of the gates of the lift.* 要與電梯門離開一些站着。**keep/stay ~ of,** avoid; have nothing to do with: 避開;不與…來往: *You should keep ~ of that fellow.* 你不應與那傢伙來往。*You should keep ~ of alcohol if you're driving.* 駕車時不應飲酒。

clear[3] /klɪə(r) ; klɪr/ *vt, vi* **1** [VP6A,14] **~ sth (of/from),** remove, get rid of, what is unwanted or unwelcome: 清除;清理: *~ the streets of snow/~ snow from the streets;* 清除街上的積雪; *~ a canal of obstructions/~ obstructions from a canal;* 清除運河中的障礙物; *~ a desk,* of papers, etc; 清理書桌(把文件等收拾起來); *~ the table,* after a meal; 收拾桌子(指餐後收拾餐桌上的餐具); *~ land of trees,* esp before cultivation; (尤指耕種前之)砍去樹木開拓土地; *~ one's mind of doubt;* 釋除心中的疑慮; *~ oneself (of a charge),* prove one's innocence. 證明自己無所控之罪嫌。**~ the air,** ⇨ air[1](1). **~ the decks (for action),** get a ship ready for a fight; (fig) make ready for any kind of struggle or activity. 清艦備戰(清除甲板上的障礙物以備作戰);(喻)準備奮鬪;(為任何活動)作準備。**~ one's throat,** eg by coughing. 清嗓子(如藉輕咳)。**2** [VP6A] get past or over without touching: 通過或越過而未觸及: *The winner ~ed six feet,* jumped this without touching the bar. 得勝者俐落地躍過六呎(高的橫桿)。*Can your horse ~ that hedge?* 你的馬能俐落地躍過那樹籬嗎? *Our car only just ~ed the gatepost.* 我們的汽車差一點就碰着門柱了。*Jack up that wheel until it ~s (= no longer rests on) the ground.* 用千斤頂將那個輪子頂起,直到它完全離地為止。**3** [VP6A] make as a net gain or profit: 淨賺;獲淨利: *~ £50;* 淨賺五十鎊; *~ expenses,* make enough money to cover them. 賺的錢足夠開銷。**4** [VP6A] get (a ship or its cargo) free by doing what is necessary (signing papers, paying dues, etc) on entering or leaving a port: 為(船或船貨)辦清手續(如簽署文件、繳納關稅等): ~

goods through customs, deal with requirements of the customs (eg by paying any necessary duties); 爲貨物辦清通過海關的手續(按照海關規定,如繳稅等); leave (a port) after doing this. 手續辦清駛離(港口);辦清結關手續出(港)。 **5** [VP6A] pass a cheque／bill of exchange etc through a clearing-house. 使支票(票據等)通過票據交換所。 **6** [VP15B, 2C] (special uses with *adverbial particles* and *preps*): (與副詞接語及介詞連用之特殊用法):
clear away, pass away: 消散;消失: *The clouds have ~ed away.* 雲已消散。 ***~ sth away,*** take away, get rid of: 拿去;收去;清除: *~ away the tea-things.* 把茶具收去。
clear off, (colloq, of a person) go away; get rid of: (俗,指人)離去;除去: *they ~ed off／we ~ed them off fast.* 他們離開了(我們迅速把他們打發了)。 ***~ sth off,*** get rid of, make an end of: 除去;清除;結束: *~ off a debt;* 清償債務; *~ off arrears of work.* 做完積壓的工作。
clear out, (colloq) go away; leave: (俗)離去;走開;溜走: *The police are after you, you'd better ~ out!* 警察在追踪你,你最好溜吧! ***~ sth out,*** empty; make clear by taking out the contents of: 使空;清除內含之物: *~ out a drain／a cupboard.* 清除水溝(食櫥)中的污物。 *All these hospital expenses have ~ed me out,* (colloq) have left me without money. (俗)所有這些醫院費用把我掏空了(花掉了我所有的錢)。
clear up, become clear: (天氣)變晴: *The weather／The sky is ~ing up.* 天氣變晴了(天空晴朗了)。 ***~ sth up,*** **(a)** put in order; make tidy: 清理某事物;整理: *C~ up your desk before you leave the office.* 在離開辦公室以前,請把你的桌子整理一下。 *Who's going to ~ up the mess?* 誰來負責清理這些亂七八糟的東西? **(b)** make clear; solve (a mystery, etc): 說明;解決;解明(神秘之事物等): *~ up a difficulty／misunderstanding.* 解決困難(澄清誤會)。

clear·ance /ˈklɪərəns ; ˈklɪrəns/ *n* **1** clearing up, removing, making tidy: 清理;清潔;清除: *a ~ sale,* a sale to clear out unwanted or superfluous stocks of goods. 出清存貨大減價。 *You've made a tremendous ~ in the flat,* made it tidy, etc by getting rid of what was unwanted. 你已把這公寓做了一番大掃除。 **2** [C, U] free space; space between, for moving past: 餘地;(某物經過另一物時兩者之間的)間隙;空間: *a ~ of only two feet,* eg for a ship moving through a canal. 僅有二呎的餘地(如通過運河之船兩側之餘地)。 *There is not much／not enough ~ for large lorries passing under this bridge.* 沒有足够的空間供大卡車在此橋下通過。 **3** (certificate of) clearing a ship, ⇨ clear³(4). (指進出港口船隻之)結關手續;結關單;結關證書;出(入)港執照。

clear·ing /ˈklɪərɪŋ ; ˈklɪrɪŋ/ *n* open space from which trees have been cleared in a forest. 森林中伐去一片樹木所成之空地。 **ˈ~-house,** office at which banks exchange cheques, etc and settle accounts, the balance being paid in cash. 票據交換所(各銀行在此交換支票等,結算帳目,差額付現)。

clear·ly /ˈklɪəlɪ ; ˈklɪrlɪ/ *adv* **1** distinctly: 清楚地;明白地: *speak ~;* 說話清楚; *state one's facts ~.* 把事實說明白。 *It is too dark to see ~.* 天太黑看不清楚。 **2** obviously; undoubtedly: 顯然地;無疑地: *'Was he mistaken?' 'C~.'* '他錯了嗎?''毫無疑問。'

cleat /kliːt ; klit/ *n* **1** strip of wood, etc fastened to a gangway, etc to prevent slipping. 釘於梯口等上以防滑倒之木條等。 **2** piece of wood, metal, etc bolted on to sth, on which ropes may be fastened (by winding). 固定在某物上可以栓繩之木樁(或金屬等製之樁);繫纜栓;繫索扣。 **3** piece of material fastened to the underside of a shoe or boot (eg for football) to prevent slipping. (貼於鞋或靴底上,如足球鞋底上的)防滑片。 **4** V-shaped wedge. 楔子;三角木。

cleav·age /ˈkliːvɪdʒ ; ˈklivɪdʒ/ *n* split or division; direction in which sth tends to split or divide; place where there is a split or cleft; (colloq) the cleft between a woman's breasts as seen above a low neckline of a dress. 劈開;劈裂;分裂;趨於劈裂的方向;裂開之處;裂痕;(俗)(女人兩乳房之間的)乳溝(穿低領女裝時所見者)。

cleave¹ /kliːv ; kliv/ *vt, vi* (*pt* clove /kləʊv ; klov/, cleft /kleft ; klɛft/ or cleaved /kliːvd ; klivd/, *pp* cloven /ˈkləʊvn ; ˈklovən/, cleft or cleaved) **1** [VP 6A, 22, 15A, B] cut into two (with a blow from a heavy axe, etc); split: (用大斧等)劈成兩半;使分裂: *~ a block of wood in two;* 將一木頭劈成兩半; *~ a man's head open with a sword.* 一劍劈開人頭。 **2** [VP2A] come apart; split: 裂開;分裂: *This wood ~s easily.* 這種木材容易起裂縫。 **3** [VP6A, 14] ***~ (through),*** make by cutting: 劈出;砍成: *~ one's way through the crowd;* 在人群中闢開一條路而前進; *~ a path through the jungle.* 在叢林中砍伐出一條路。 ***in a cleft stick,*** (fig) in a tight place where neither advance nor retreat is possible. (喻)處於進退兩難之境。 **ˌcleft ˈpalate** *n* malformation in the roof of the mouth because the two sides of the palate did not join before birth. 裂腭(上腭分爲兩半,係由先天發育不全而形成的一種口腔畸形)。 **ˌcloven ˈhoof** *n* divided hoof of an ox, a sheep, a goat (and a devil). 分趾蹄;偶蹄(如牛、羊、惡魔之蹄)。

cleave² /kliːv ; kliv/ *vi* (*pt* ~d or, old use, 舊用法, clave /kleɪv ; klev/, *pp* ~d) [VP3A] **~ *to,*** stick fast to; (fig) be faithful to. 固守;(喻)忠於。

cleaver /ˈkliːvə(r) ; ˈklivɚ/ *n* heavy knife used by a butcher for chopping up meat. 屠夫用以切肉的大砍刀。

clef /klef ; klɛf/ *n* (music) symbol placed at the beginning of a stave to show the pitch of the notes. (音樂)(置於譜表之首的)譜號;音部記號。 ⇨ the illus at notation. 參看 notation 之插圖。

cleft¹ /kleft ; klɛft/ *n* crack or split (eg in the ground or in rock); opening made by a cleavage. 裂痕;裂縫(例如地上或岩石中者);裂開;裂口。

cleft² /kleft ; klɛft/ *pt, pp* of cleave¹.

cle·ma·tis /ˈklemətɪs ; ˈklɛmətɪs/ *n* [U] (kinds of) climbing plant with white, yellow or purple flowers. 爭藤蘭;女萎屬(攀爬植物,開白、黃或紫色花);鐵線蓮。

clem·ency /ˈklemənsɪ ; ˈklɛmənsɪ/ *n* [U] (formal) mercy; mildness (of temper or weather). (正式用語)仁慈;溫和(指性情或天氣)。

clem·ent /ˈklemənt ; ˈklɛmənt/ *adj* (formal) showing mercy; (of the weather, a person's temper) mild. (正式用語)仁慈的;(指天氣或人的脾氣)溫和的。

clench /klentʃ ; klɛntʃ/ *vt* **1** [VP6A] press firmly together, close tightly: 緊握;緊閉: *~ one's teeth／jaws;* 咬緊牙關; *~ one's fingers／fist;* 緊握拳頭; *a ~ed-fist salute.* 握拳敬禮。 **2** [VP14] grasp firmly: 抓緊;抓牢: *~ sth in／with one's hand(s).* 用手抓緊某物。 **3** = clinch.

clere·story /ˈklɪəstɔːrɪ ; ˈklɪrˌstorɪ/ *n* (*pl* -ries) upper part of a wall in a large church, with windows in it above the aisle roofs. (大教堂內高於側廊之頂的)高窗(爲牆之連窗的上部)。 ⇨ the illus at church. 參看 church 之插圖。

clergy /ˈklɜːdʒɪ ; ˈklɝdʒɪ/ *n* (collective *n* with *pl v*) persons ordained as priests or ministers of the Christian Church: (集合名詞,用複數動詞)基督教會正式任命的神父或牧師;教士;聖職人員: *Thirty of the ~ were present at the ceremony.* 牧師有三十人參加典禮。 *The ~ are opposed to the plan.* 牧師們反對該計畫。 **ˈ~·man** /-mən ; -mən/ *n* (*pl* -men) (not used of a bishop) ordained minister, esp of the Church of England. (不用以指主教)正式任命的牧師(尤指英國國教者)。

cleric /ˈklerɪk ; ˈklɛrɪk/ *n* clergyman. 牧師;神父;教士;聖職人員。

cleri·cal /ˈklerɪkl ; ˈklɛrɪkl/ *adj* **1** of the clergy: 牧師的;神父的;教士的;聖職人員的: *~ dress;* 牧師服; *a ~ collar.* 神父的硬領。 **2** of, for, made by, a clerk or clerks(1): 辦事員的;書記的: *ˈ~ work;* 辦事員的工作; *a ~ error,* one made in copying or writing.

抄寫的錯誤;筆誤。

cleri·hew /ˈklerɪhjuː; ˈklɛrəhju/ *n* witty or nonsensical piece of verse, usu two rhyming couplets of varying length. 詼諧的或無意義的短詩(通常爲四行詩,每兩行押韻,每行長短不一)。

clerk /klɑːk *US:* klɜːrk; klɝk/ *n* **1** person employed in a bank, office, shop, etc to keep records and accounts, copy letters, etc: (銀行、辦公室、商店等所僱用的)辦事員; 書記(保管案卷、帳册、抄寫信件等): *a ˈbank ~;* 銀行辦事員; *a ˌcorreˈspondence ~.* 管來往信件的辦事員。**2** officer in charge of records, etc: 負責管理檔案等之官員: *the Town C~;* 市政府秘書; *the C~ to the Council,* (usu a lawyer); 議會秘書(通常爲律師); *~ of the works,* having charge of materials, etc for building done by contract. 工程管理員(掌管包工之建築材料者)。 **3** (US) shop-assistant; salesman or saleswoman. (美)商店的店員。 **4** (formal or legal): (正式或法律用語): *~ in holy orders,* clergyman. 牧師;神父;教士。 **5** lay officer of the church with various duties: 教會中非僧職的執事(管理雜務者): *the parish ~.* 教區執事。 **6** (old use) person who can read and write: (舊用法)能識字寫字的人: *I'm no great ~,* am not much good at writing. 我不大會寫字。□ *vi* (US only) work as a ~(3). (僅用於美國)做店員。

clever /ˈklevə(r); ˈklɛvɚ/ *adj* (-er, -est) **1** quick in learning and understanding things; skilful: 聰明的; 敏於學習和瞭解的; 伶俐的; 有技巧的: *He's ~ at arithmetic/at making excuses.* 他在算術(找藉口)方面很聰明。*How ~ of you to do that!* 你會做那個可眞聰明啊! *He's a ~ workman.* 他是個有技巧的工人。 **2** (of things done) showing ability and skill: (指做成之事物)顯示能力和技巧的: *a ~ speech/book.* 巧妙的演說(書)。 **3** nimble: 靈活的;敏捷的: *~ fingers.* 靈活的手指。 **4** smart: 機敏的;精明的: *He was too ~ for us,* he outwitted us. 他太精明了,我們鬥不過他。 **~·ly** *adv* **~·ness** *n*

clew /kluː; klu/ *n* (naut) metal loop attached to the lower corner of a sail; loop holding the strings of a hammock. (航海)附連於船帆下角的金屬環;吊床上穿繩用的金屬環。□ *vt* (also 亦作 *clue*) (naut) haul (a sail) up or down. (航海)扯(帆);上(帆);下(帆)。

cliché /ˈkliːʃeɪ *US:* kliːˈʃeɪ; kliˈʃe/ *n* [C] idea or expression that has been too much used and is now out-dated; stereotyped phrase: 陳腔濫調;陳腐的話;老套: *a ~-ridden newspaper article.* 滿篇陳腔濫調的報紙文章。

click[1] /klɪk; klɪk/ *vi, vt, n* [VP6A, 2A, C] (make, or cause to make, a) short, sharp sound (like that of a key turning in a lock): (發,使發)喀搭聲;滴答聲(似鑰匙開鎖之聲): *The door ~ed shut.* 門喀搭一聲關上了。*The soldier ~ed his heels and saluted.* 那兵兩足跟喀搭一聲立正敬禮。 *Some African languages contain several ~s,* ~ing sounds. 有些非洲語言充滿嘖嘖之音。

click[2] /klɪk; klɪk/ *vi* [VP2A] (sl; not US) strike up an acquaintance, become friends, at once. (俚;不用於美國)剛一認識就成了朋友;一見投緣。

cli·ent /ˈklaɪənt; ˈklaɪənt/ *n* **1** person who gets help or advice from a lawyer or any professional man: (律師或專門職業的)當事人;委託人: *a successful lawyer with hundreds of ~s.* 一個生意興隆、擁有數以百計委託人的律師。 **2** customer (at a shop). (商店的)顧客。 **cli·en·tele** /ˌkliːənˈtel *US:* ˌklaɪən-; ˌklaɪənˈtɛl/ *n* (collective) customers; patrons of a restaurant, theatre, etc. (集合用法)顧客;餐館、戲院等之老主顧。

cliff /klɪf; klɪf/ *n* steep face of rock, esp at the edge of the sea. 懸崖;峭壁;絕壁(尤指海邊者)。 **ˈ~-hanger** *n* episode in a story or contest of which the end is uncertain, so that the reader or spectator is held in suspense. 吊人胃口的故事情節或比賽(因結局不明而令讀者或觀衆疑慮者);懸疑。

cli·mac·ter·ic /klaɪˈmæktərɪk; klaɪˈmæktərɪk/ *n* critical turning-point in (the body's) physical development. 更年期;斷經期。

cli·mac·tic /klaɪˈmæktɪk; klaɪˈmæktɪk/ *adj* forming a climax. 形成高潮的。

cli·mate /ˈklaɪmɪt; ˈklaɪmɪt/ *n* **1** weather conditions of a place or area; conditions of temperature, rainfall, wind, etc. 氣候(某一地區之天氣狀況;溫度、雨量、風等之狀況)。 **2** area or region with certain weather conditions: 具有某種氣候之區域: *A drier ~ would be good for her health.* 氣候較乾爽的地區會對她的健康有益。 **3** prevailing condition: 普遍的情形;一般的趨勢: *the political ~;* 政壇上的一般情況; *~ of opinion,* general attitude of people to an aspect of life, policy, etc. 民意趨向(一般人民對於生活之某一方面、政策等之態度)。 **cli·mat·ic** /klaɪˈmætɪk; klaɪˈmætɪk/ *adj* of ~. 氣候的;具有某種氣候之地區的。**cli·mati·cally** /-klɪ; -klɪ/ *adv* **cli·ma·tol·ogy** /ˌklaɪməˈtɒlədʒɪ; ˌklaɪməˈtɑlədʒɪ/ *n* [U] science of ~. 氣候學。

cli·max /ˈklaɪmæks; ˈklaɪmæks/ *n* event, point, of greatest interest or intensity (eg in a story or drama): 頂點;極點;高潮(如故事或戲劇中最有趣或最緊張的地方): *bring matters to a ~;* 使事態發展到高潮; *work up to a ~;* 逐漸發展到頂點; *as a ~ to the day's entertainment.* 作爲一天遊藝活動之高潮。□ *vt, vi* bring or come to a ~. (使)達到頂點或高潮。

climb /klaɪm; klaɪm/ *vt, vi* [VP6A, 2A, C] go or get up (a tree, wall, rope, mountain, etc) or down; (of aircraft) go higher, gain height; (of plants) grow upwards by turning round a support, or with the support of tendrils, etc; rise by effort in social rank, position, etc: 攀登;攀爬;爬上(樹、牆、繩索、山等)或爬下;(指飛機)爬升;升高;(指植物)盤繞支架向上生長或藉卷鬚攀爬生長;因努力而在社會階級、職位等方面高陞: *~ a tree;* 爬樹; *~ up/down a tree;* 爬上(下)樹; *~ a wall;* 爬牆; *~ over a wall.* 爬過牆。*Monkeys ~ well.* 猴子善於攀爬。 **~ down,** (fig) admit that one has been mistaken, unreasonable, boastful, etc. (喻)自認錯誤、無理、誇大等;屈服;認輸;讓步。Hence, 由此產生, **ˈ~-down** *n* such an admission. 認錯;認輸;屈服;讓步。 **ˈ~·ing irons** *n* spikes (to be) fastened to the boots for ~ing trees, ice-slopes, etc. 繫於鞋底以便爬樹、爬冰坡等之鐵釘;攀樹器。□ *n* ~ing; place (to be) ~ed: 攀登;攀登之地;可攀登之地: *a hard ~.* 艱難的攀登。*Have you done that ~?* 你已攀登過那個地方嗎? **~er** *n* person who ~s; person who tries to advance socially; ~ing plant. 攀登者;爬山者;在社會中努力求高陞者;鑽求更高社會地位的人;攀緣植物。

clime /klaɪm; klaɪm/ *n* (poet) climate(2). (詩)具有某種氣候之地區。

clinch /klɪntʃ; klɪntʃ/ *vt, vi* **1** [VP6A] make (a nail or rivet) fast by hammering sideways the end that protrudes. 橫着鎚擊突出在外的釘頭以使(釘子)牢固;將釘頭敲彎或敲平以使(釘子)牢固。 **2** [VP6A] settle (a bargain, an argument) conclusively: 確定地解決或結束(交易、議論): *That ~es the argument,* ends all doubt. 那就澄清了這項議論(結束了一切疑問)。 **3** [VP2A] (boxing) come to grips, with one or both arms round the opponent's body: (拳擊)(以一臂或兩臂繞抱對方身體)扭在一起;互相扭住: *The boxers ~ed and the referee intervened.* 拳擊者互扭在一起,裁判加以阻止。□ *n* (boxing) the act, an instance, of ~ing: (拳擊)互相扭抱: *get into a ~;* 互相扭抱在一起; *break a ~;* 擺脫扭抱;將互扭在一起的兩人分開; (colloq) embrace. (俗)擁抱。 **~er** *n* (colloq) ~ing argument. (俗)決定性的議論。

cline /klaɪn; klaɪn/ *n* graded sequence of differences. 分類差異序列;族羣相。⇨ continuum.

cling /klɪŋ; klɪŋ/ *vi* (*pt, pp* clung /klʌŋ; klʌŋ/) [VP2C, 3A] **~ to/together,** hold tight; resist separation: 堅守;固執;抱緊;抓緊;堅拒分開: *~ to one's possessions;* 堅守自己的財產不肯放棄; *~ to a hope of being rescued.* 堅定地抱着獲救的希望。*They clung together when the time came to part.*

分離的時候到了，他們緊抱着不肯分開。*The ship clung to* (= did not go far from) *the coast.* 這船緊靠着海岸航行。*The child clung to its mother's skirt／garments.* 那孩子緊緊地抓着他媽媽的裙子(衣服)。*She's the ～ing sort,* is prone to depend upon others. 她是纏人不放那一型的女人(易於依附他人者)。'**～·ing clothes** *n* showing the shape or outline of the body or limbs. 緊箍在身上的衣服；曲線畢露的衣服。

cli·nic /'klɪnɪk ; 'klɪnɪk/ *n* **1** (part of a) hospital or institution where medical advice and treatment are given and where students are taught through observation of cases; teaching so given; class of students taught in this way. (供學生作臨床觀察的)教學醫院或醫療機構；臨床教學；接受臨床教學的一班學生。**2** medical establishment for a specified purpose: 診所；門診所：*a 'birth-control ～;* 節制生育診所；*an ˌante-'natal ～;* 產前診所；*an a'bortion ～.* 流產診所。

cli·ni·cal /'klɪnɪkl ; 'klɪnɪkl/ *adj* **1** (of medical teaching given) at the hospital bedside: (指醫科教學)臨床的；臨床教學的：*～ thermometer,* one for measuring the temperature of the body. 體溫計。**2** objective(2); uninvolved: 客觀的；未牽扯在內的：*～ judgement.* 客觀的判斷。

clink¹ /klɪŋk ; klɪŋk/ *vi, vt, n* [VP6A, 2A, C] (make, or cause to make the) sound of small bits of metal, glass, etc knocking together: (發出，使發出)小片金屬、玻璃等互相碰撞之聲音；玎玲聲：*the ～ of keys／glasses.* 鑰匙(玻璃杯)碰擊之玎玲聲。*They ～ed glasses,* brought their glasses together before drinking each other's health. 他們碰杯互祝健康。

clink² /klɪŋk ; klɪŋk/ *n* (sl) prison: (俚)監牢：*be in ～;* 坐牢；*be put in ～;* 被關入獄；*go to ～.* 入獄。

clinker /'klɪŋkə(r) ; 'klɪŋkɚ/ *n* [C, U] (piece of the) mass of rough, hard, slag-like material left in a stove, furnace, etc after coal has been burned. (煤在火爐、熔爐等中燃燒後所留下的)渣滓；熔渣；熔塊。

clinker-built /'klɪŋkə bɪlt ; 'klɪŋkɚˌbɪlt/ *adj* (of boats) made with the outside planks or metal plates overlapping downwards. (指船)外側之木板或金屬板向下叠接的；魚鱗叠接的。

clip¹ /klɪp ; klɪp/ *n* [C] **1** wire or metal device for holding things (eg papers) together. 金屬絲或金屬所製夾物之具(例如夾紙者)；夾子；廻紋針；兩脚針。**2** holder (with loops) for cartridges (to be used in a magazine rifle). (帶有圈套的)彈夾(用於裝彈夾之步槍中)。□ *vt, vi* (-pp-) [VP6A, 15B, 2C] put or keep together with a ～ or ～s: 用夾子夾在一起：*～ papers together;* 把文件夾在一起；*～ one paper to another.* 把一件文件跟另一件文件夾在一起。'**～-on** *adj* (attrib) that can be attached with a ～: (形容用法)可用夾子夾住的：*a ～-on tie／brooch.* 可用夾子夾戴的領帶(花別針)。

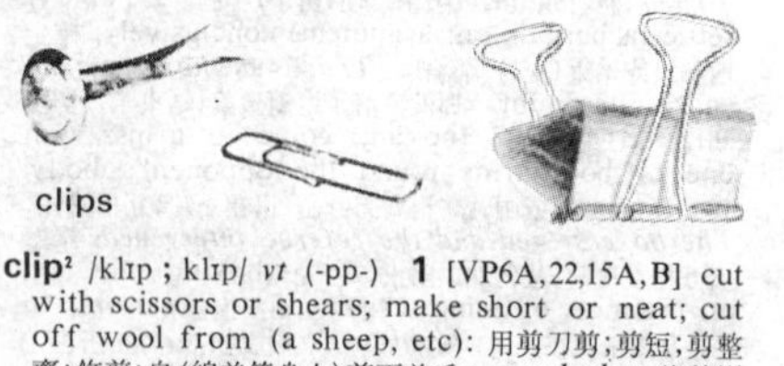

clips

clip² /klɪp ; klɪp/ *vt* (-pp-) **1** [VP6A, 22, 15A, B] cut with scissors or shears; make short or neat; cut off wool from (a sheep, etc): 用剪刀剪；剪短；剪整齊；修剪；自(綿羊等身上)剪下羊毛：*～ a hedge;* 修剪樹籬；*～ a bird's wings;* 剪短鳥翼；*～ sb's wings,* (fig) prevent him from doing what he is ambitious to do. (喻)阻止某人實現其野心；斷其双翼。*～ sth out (of),* remove by ～ping: (自…)剪下某物：*～ an article out of a newspaper.* 自報紙上剪下一篇文章；剪報。'**～-joint** *n* (US sl) club that overcharges; business that defrauds. (美俚)敲竹槓的俱樂部或夜總會；欺騙顧客的場所。**2** [VP6A] omit or abbreviate (esp the end of) sounds of (words). 省略或簡略(字)中之音(尤指尾音)。**3** [VP6A] punch a hole in (a bus, tram or train ticket). 在(公共汽車、電車或火車票)上剪洞。**4** (sl) hit or punch sharply: (俚)猛擊；猛打：*～ sb's ear;* 打某人的耳光；*～ sb on the jaw.* 打某人的下巴。□ *n* **1** operation of shearing. 剪羊毛的作業。**2** amount of wool cut from (a flock of) sheep at one time. 一次自(一羣)綿羊身上所剪下羊毛之量。**3** smart blow: 痛擊：*a ～ on the jaw.* 對下巴之一擊。**4** (US) fast speed. (美)高速。**～·ping** *n* (in verbal senses) (esp) sth ～ped off or out: (具有動詞之各種意義)(尤指)剪下之物：*newspaper ～pings.* 報紙之剪輯；剪報。

clip·per /'klɪpə(r) ; 'klɪpɚ/ *n* **1** ***(pair of) ～s,*** instrument for clipping: 修剪之工具；剪取器；剪刀：*'hair-～s;* 理髮剪；*'nail-～s.* 指甲刀。**2** sailing ship built for speed and used formerly esp in the tea-trade, ⇨ the illus at barque; (before jet aircraft) propeller-driven air-liner. (從前用於做茶葉生意之特建的)快速帆船(參看 barque 之插圖)；(噴射機問世前之)螺旋槳推進的客機。

clique /kli:k ; klik/ *n* group of persons united by common interests (esp in literature or art), members of which support each other and shut out others from their company. 由志同道合者(尤指文學藝術方面)所組成彼此輔助而排斥外人之派別；私黨；朋黨；派系；門閥。**cliquish** /'kli:kɪʃ ; 'klikɪʃ/ *adj* of or like a ～; tending to form a ～. 派別的；似派別的；有形成派別之趨向的。

clit·oris /'klɪtərɪs ; 'klaɪtərɪs/ *n* (anat) erectile organ at the upper end of the vulva, analogous to the penis. (解剖)陰蒂；陰核(女陰上端能勃起之器官，類似男人之陰莖)。

cloak /kləʊk ; klok/ *n* loose outer garment, without sleeves; (fig) sth used to hide or keep secret: 披風；斗篷；(喻)遮蓋物；掩飾物；掩護物：*use patriotism as a ～ for violence;* 利用愛國主義作爲暴動的掩飾；*under the ～ of darkness.* 在黑暗之掩護下。***～ and dagger,*** (used attrib) in the style of, concerning, espionage, melodramatic intrigue, etc. (形容用法)具有間諜、鬧劇式密謀等之風格的；有關間諜、鬧劇式密謀等的。'**～·room** *n* place where hats, coats, parcels, etc may be left for a short time (eg in a theatre or a railway station); (euphem) lavatory. (戲院或火車站臨時寄存衣帽、小包等之)衣帽間；寄物處；(婉)厠所。□ *vt* [VP6A] (chiefly fig) conceal (thoughts, purposes, etc). (主用作喻)掩藏(思想、目的等)。

clob·ber¹ /'klɒbə(r) ; 'klɑbɚ/ *vt* [VP6A] (sl) (俚) **1** strike violently and repeatedly; hurt badly: 連續猛擊；痛擊；嚴重傷害：*～ the taxpayer,* by heavy taxation. (以苛稅)整慘納稅人。**2** defeat thoroughly: 徹底打敗；打垮：*Our team got ～ed on Saturday.* 星期六我們的球隊慘敗了。

clob·ber² /'klɒbə(r) ; 'klɑbɚ/ *n* (GB sl) clothing; equipment. (英俚)衣服；裝備。

cloche /klɒʃ ; kloʃ/ *n* [C] **1** glass or clear plastic protection, placed in long rows over tender plants; (older use) bell-shaped glass cover for a plant. (成長排置於幼嫩植物之上藉以發生保護作用之)園藝玻璃罩或透明塑膠罩；(舊用法)(用於一棵植物之)鐘形玻璃罩。**2** woman's close-fitting hat. (緊套於頭上之)女帽。

clock¹ /klɒk ; klɑk/ *n* instrument (not carried or worn like a watch) for measuring and showing the time. 時鐘；鐘；時計(非掛錶或手錶)。***put the '～ back,*** **(a)** move the hands of the ～ back (eg when Summer Time ends). 將時鐘撥回(如於夏令時間終止時將時鐘撥回標準時間)。**(b)** (fig) take reactionary measures. (喻)開倒車。***work against the ～,*** work fast to finish before a certain time. 加速工作以爭取時間。***(work) round the ～,*** (work) all day and night. 日夜工作。Hence, 由此產生，**ˌround-the-'～,** (used attrib): (形容用法)：*a round-the-～ watch／guard on sth,* all day and night. 不分晝夜的監視(看守某物)。'**～-face／-dial,** surface of a ~ showing figures marking the hours, etc. (標明鐘點數字的)鐘面。~-'**golf**, game in which a golf-ball is putted on greens arranged in a circle. 草地高爾夫 (在圓形之草地上，輕擊高爾夫球之一種球戲)。'**~-tower**, tall structure (forming part of a building, eg a church) with a ~ high up on an outside wall. 鐘樓 (形成建築物之一部份，如教堂上者，其外牆上高懸一時鐘)。'**~-watching**, practice (of some workers) of thinking constantly of how soon work will end. (指某些工作者) 經常掛念着何時可以下班的習氣。'**~·wise**/ˌ**anti-'~·wise** *adj, adv* moving in a curve in the same direction as/in the direction opposite to that taken by the hands of a ~. 順時針(反時針)方向(旋轉)的(地)。'**~·work**, (often attrib) mechanism with wheels and springs like a ~: (常作形容用法) 有似時鐘之齒輪與發條的機械: *~-work toys;* 有發條與齒輪的玩具; *a ~work driven train;* 以發條推動的玩具火車; *with ~work precision;* 如鐘錶之精確地; *like ~work*, smoothly, without trouble. 順利地;無毛病地。□ *vt, vi* **1** [VP6A] measure the time of; do sth (eg run a race) in a measured period of time: 計…之時;在一段計算的時間內做某事(如賽跑): *He ~ed 9·6 seconds for the 100 metres.* 他一百公尺跑了九秒六。 **2** [VP2C, 15B] ***~ (sb) in/out; ~ (sb) on/off***, record/have recorded the time of (eg arrival/departure): 記錄…之時間(如到達或離去的時間): *Workers in this factory are required to ~ in and out.* 這個工廠裏的工人規定必須記錄到廠離廠(上下班)的時間。 **3** [VP6A] (GB sl) strike; hit: (英俚) 打;擊;揍: *If you don't shut up, I'll ~ you one.* 如果你不閉嘴，我可要揍你一頓。

clock[2] /klɒk; klɑk/ *n* design sewn or woven on the side of a sock or stocking, at the ankle. 在襪子側面的踝部所織繡的圖案;繡花。

clod /klɒd; klɑd/ *n* lump (of earth, clay, etc). (泥土、黏土等之)塊。'**~·hop·per** /-hɒpə(r); -ˌhɑpɚ/ *n* (derog) clumsy, heavy-footed person, esp a rough farm worker. (貶)笨拙而脚步沉重的人;(尤指)粗鄙的農夫;莊稼漢;鄉下佬。

clog[1] /klɒg; klɑg/ *n* **1** shoe with a wooden sole; shoe carved out of a block of wood. 木底鞋;木屐。'**~-dance** *n* dance in which the dancer wears ~s or wooden-soled shoes. 木屐舞(舞者穿着木屐)。 **2** block of wood fastened to the leg of an animal to prevent its straying; (fig) encumbrance: 縛於動物之腿部以防其走失之木塊;(喻)障礙物;累贅: *a ~ on his movements.* 加於他的行動的一種障礙。

clogs

clog[2] /klɒg; klɑg/ *vt, vi* (-gg-) [VP6A, 15B, 2A, C] ***~ (up)***, **1** (cause to) be or become blocked with waste matter, dirt, grease, etc so that movement, flow of liquid, etc is difficult or prevented: (使)被廢物、污物、油膩等塞住以致活動、液體流動等困難或受阻;阻礙;妨礙;阻塞: *pipes ~ged with dirt;* 爲污物所阻塞之管子; *machinery ~ged (up) with grease.* 因爲油脂太多而運轉不靈的機器。 **2** encumber; burden: 塞滿;堆滿: *Don't ~ (up) your memory with useless facts.* 不要使你的記憶中堆滿無益的事情。 **~gy** *adj* (-ier, -iest) lumpy; sticky. 多塊的;黏膩的。

cloi·sonné /klwɑːˈzɒneɪ *US:* ˌklɔɪzəˈneɪ; ˌklɔɪzəˈne/ *n* [U] enamel ware, in which the colours of the design are kept apart by thin metal strips. 景泰藍(一種搪瓷器，其圖案中之各種顏色係由細金屬條分開)。

clois·ter /ˈklɔɪstə(r); ˈklɔɪstɚ/ *n* **1** covered walk, usu on the sides of an open court or quadrangle, with a wall on the outer side and columns or arches on the inner side, esp within a convent, cathedral or college building. (修道院、大教堂或大學建築物之)廻廊(通常圍繞着一個院子，廊之外側有牆，內側有一排柱子或拱門);遊廊。⇨ the illus at church. 參看 church 之插圖。 **2** (life in a) convent or monastery. 修道院;修道院中之生活;寺院;僧侶之生活。 **the ~** *n* the seclusion of a convent, etc. 修道院之隱居生活。□ *vt* [VP6A] put in, live in, a ~(2): 置於修道院或寺院中;過修道生活: *live a ~ed life*, a life of seclusion. 過隱居生活。

clone /kləʊn; klon/ *n* (biol) (member of a) group of organisms or plants produced non-sexually from one ancestor. (生物)無性繁殖系(由一母體經無性生殖而繁生的一群生物或植物)。

close[1] /kləʊs; klos/ *adj* (-r, -st) **1** near (in space or time): 近的(指空間或時間): *fire at ~ range;* 在近距離射擊; *in ~ combat;* 白刃戰;肉搏; *in ~ proximity*, almost touching. 極爲接近。***a ~ call/thing***, almost an accident, disaster or failure. 險些兒造成意外、災禍或失敗的事。***a ~ shave***, (fig) a narrow escape from collision or accident. (喻)間不容髮的危險遭遇;幸免於難;僅以身免。'**~-up** *n* **(a)** photograph, esp as shown on a cinema or television screen, taken at ~ range and showing the subject on a large scale. 電影或電視在近距離所拍攝的放大鏡頭;特寫鏡頭。 **(b)** close view. 精密的觀察。 **2** with little or no space in between: 緊密的;密集的: *~ writing;* 寫得很密的文字; *material of ~ texture*, eg woven with the threads ~ together. 質地緊密的布料。 *The soldiers advanced in ~ order*, with little space between them. 士兵們成密集隊形前進。 **3** strict; severe; rigorous: 嚴格的;嚴密的;嚴厲的: *a ~ blockade/siege;* 嚴密的封鎖(包圍); *in ~ confinement;* 被嚴密監禁; *be (kept) under ~ arrest.* 被嚴密拘禁。***keep a ~ watch on sb***, watch him carefully. 嚴密看守某人。 **4** detailed; leaving no gaps or weak points; showing each step clearly: 詳盡的;精密的;無懈可擊的;精細的: *a ~ argument;* 周密(無懈可擊)的論點; *~ reasoning;* 精密的推理; *a ~ reasoner.* 精密的推理者。 **5** thorough; concentrated: 徹底的; 集中心思的; 專心的; 用心的: *after ~ consideration;* 經過徹底的考慮以後; *on ~r examination.* 經過進一步的考查。 *You must give me your ~ attention.* 你必須對我特別注意(你必須特別用心聽我所說的話)。 *Please make a ~ (= faithful and exact) translation.* 請作精確的翻譯。 **6** intimate: 親密的;親近的: *a ~ friend/friendship.* 親密的朋友(友誼)。 **7** restricted; limited: 有限制的: *a ~ scholarship*, open only to a restricted category of candidates. 限於給某類候選人之獎學金。 **8** (of competitions, games, their results) in which the competitors are almost equal: (指比賽、遊戲或其結果) 勢均力敵的;幾乎平手的: *a ~ contest/match/election/finish.* 勢均力敵的比賽(比賽，競選，結局)。 **9** (phonetics; of vowels) made with the tongue and the roof of the mouth fairly close together: (語音學; 指母音) 合口的 (舌與上顎相當接近的): *The English vowels /iː/ and /uː/ are ~.* 英語中的母音 /iː/ 和 /uː/ 是合口的。 **10** (also 亦作 ˌ**~-'fisted**) stingy; niggardly. 吝嗇的;手緊的。 **11** '**~ season**, time (the breeding season) during which the killing of certain wild birds and animals, and the catching of certain fish, is illegal. (禁止捕獵某些鳥獸或魚類的)禁獵期(即其繁殖時期)。 **12** (of the weather) stifling; (of a room, etc) unventilated; having little fresh air; (of the air) difficult to breathe because heavy: (指天氣)沉悶的;(指房間等)空氣不流通的;新鮮空氣少的;(指空氣)難以呼吸的;窒悶的: *Open the windows—this room/the air here is too ~.* 把窗戶打開——這房間(這裏的空氣)太悶了。 **13** concealed; secret; not in the habit of talking about one's affairs: 隱藏的;秘密的;不好談論自己的事情的:

keep/lie ~ for a while, keep one's whereabouts secret, not show oneself; 躲藏一些時候(將自己的行踪保守秘密,不露面); *keep sth ~,* say nothing about it, keep it secret; 將某事保守秘密; *be ~* (= secretive) *about sth,* 對某事保守秘密, Cf 參較 *keep sth to oneself.* **~·ly** *adv* in a ~ manner: 接近地;緊密地;嚴密地;密切地: *listen ~ly;* 細心地聽; *follow an argument ~ly;* 注意聆聽一項議論; *a ~ly contested election.* 旗鼓相當的競選。*She ~ly resembles her mother.* 她非常像她的母親。**~·ness** *n* being ~: 接近;緊密;嚴密;精密: *the ~ness of a resemblance/friendship/translation/pursuit.* 相似之極(友誼之親密;翻譯之精確;追趕之接近)。

close[2] /kləʊs ; klos/ *adv* in a close manner; near together; tightly: 接近地;靠近地;緊緊地: *follow ~ behind sb;* 緊跟在某人的後面; *stand/sit ~ against the wall;* 緊靠着牆壁而立(坐); *come ~r together;* 更靠近一點; *~ shut.* 密閉的。**~ at hand,** not far away. 在旁邊;在眼前。**~ by (sth); ~ to sth,** near (it): 在…的近旁: *He lives ~ by (the church).* 他住在附近(在教堂的附近)。*There's a bus-stop ~ to the school.* 在學校近旁有一公共汽車站。*The ship kept ~ to the coast.* 該船靠近海岸航行。**~ up (to sb/sth),** very near in space (to him/it): 靠近;貼靠: *Snuggle as ~ up to me as you can.* 盡量挨近我。**~ on/upon,** almost; very near to: 差不多;極靠近: *He is ~ upon sixty.* 他年近六十。*It was ~ upon midnight.* 那時已將近午夜。**sail ~ to the wind,** sail almost against the wind; (fig) almost break a law or a moral principle. 搶風(幾乎逆風)行駛; (喻)幾乎犯法或違反道德律。 **ˌ~-ˈcropped/ˈcut** *adj* (of hair, grass, etc) cut very short. (指頭髮、草等)剪得很短的。**ˌ~-ˈfitting** *adj* fitting ~ (to the body, etc): 緊貼(身體等)的; 緊身的: *a ~-fitting dress.* 一套緊身的女裝。**ˌ~-ˈgrained** *adj* (esp of wood) having a grain in which the lines in the pattern made by growth are ~ together (eg mahogany). (尤指木材)紋理細密的(如桃花心木)。**ˌ~-ˈhauled** *adj* (of a sailing-ship) with the sails set for sailing as nearly as possible in the direction from which the wind is blowing. (指帆船)迎風的;逆風的;搶風的;迎風行駛的。**ˌ~-ˈset** *adj* set, placed, ~ together: 緊靠在一起的: *~-set eyes/teeth.* 緊靠在一起的眼睛(牙齒)。

close[3] /kləʊs ; klos/ *n* **1** grounds round a cathedral, abbey or school, usu with its buildings (houses of the clergy, etc) round it. 大教堂、寺院或學校周圍的場地(通常其周圍有建築物,如牧師住宅等)。 **2** cul-de-sac. 死巷。

close[4] /kləʊz ; kloz/ *vt, vi* **1** [VP6A, 2A] shut: 閉;關;合起: *If you ~ your eyes, you can't see.* 如果你閉起眼,你就看不見。*Did you ~ all the doors and windows?* 你把所有的門窗都關了嗎? *This box/The lid of this box doesn't ~ properly,* The lid does not fit properly. 這箱子(這箱子的蓋子)關不攏。*Many flowers open in the morning and ~ at night.* 有許多花早晨開放晚上合起。 **~d book,** (fig) subject about which one knows nothing: (喻)完全不懂的學科: *Nuclear physics is a ~d book to most of us.* 核子物理學是我們大多數的人完全不懂的一門學科。 **2** [VP6A, 2A] be, declare, be declared, not open: 關閉;宣佈關閉;不開放: *This road is ~d to heavy motor traffic.* 此路禁止重型車輛通行。*The theatres have ~d for the summer.* 戲院已關閉歇暑。*It's Sunday, so the shops are ~d.* 今天是星期天,店鋪皆不開門。*Wednesday is early-closing day here,* the day on which shops ~ for a half-holiday. 星期三是這裏的店鋪提早打烊(休息半日)的日子。 *When is ˈclosing time,* the time at which shops, etc, stop doing business? 什麼時間關閉(如店鋪打烊)? *The inquiry was held behind/with ~d doors,* the public being excluded. 那次質詢係秘密進行(拒絕旁聽)。**ˌ~d ˈcircuit** *n* (in TV) circuit by which the current from the camera to the screen has its path along wires all the way (instead of being transmitted through the air): (電視)閉路(電流自電視攝影機至映像幕經由電線傳送而非經由空中傳送之電路): (attrib) (形容用法) *ˌ~d-ˌcircuit ˈtelevision.* 閉路電視。**ˌ~d ˈshop** *n* trade or profession, workshop, factory, establishment, etc in which employment is open only to members of an approved trade union. 只雇用工會會員之行業、工廠、企業等。 **3** [VP6A, 2A] bring or come to an end: 結束;終結: *~ a discussion;* 結束討論; *the closing days of the year;* 年終的數日; *the closing* (= last, final) *day for applications.* 申請(報名)截止之日。 *The chairman declared the discussion ~d.* 主席宣佈討論結束。*I want to ~ my account,* settle it by paying or receiving money that is due. 我想結帳(結清應付或應收之款)。**~ a deal,** complete it, by agreeing to the terms, etc. 完成一項交易;成交。**ˈclosing prices,** (comm) prices of shares quoted at a Stock-Exchange at the end of a day's business. (商)(股票交換所之某一天的)收盤股價。 **4** [VP6A, 2C] bring or come together by making less space or fewer spaces between: (使)靠緊;(使)靠攏(以減少其間距離): *~ the ranks;* 使行列靠攏; *~ up,* (of soldiers, etc) come ~r together in line or lines. (指士兵等)互相靠攏;排隊集合。 **5** [VP15B, 2A, 3A] (special uses with *adverbial particles* and *preps*): (與副詞接語及介詞連用的特殊用法):

close down, (a) (of a factory, business, etc) stop production, shut completely: (指工廠、商行等)關門;停業: *The factory (was) ~d down because of a lack of orders.* 該工廠因無人定貨而關門。**(b)** (of a broadcasting station) stop transmitting: (指廣播電臺)結束一次的廣播節目;停止播送: *It is midnight and we are now closing down.* 時間已到午夜,我們今天的各項廣播節目到此結束。Hence, 由此產生, **ˈ~-down** *n*

close in, *The days are closing in,* getting shorter. 白晝逐漸變短。**~ in on/upon, (a)** envelop: 包圍: *Darkness ~d in on us.* 暮色籠罩着我們(暮色四合)。**(b)** come near(er) and attack: 迫近並攻擊: *The enemy ~d in upon us.* 敵軍迫近並攻擊我們。

close with, (a) come within striking distance of (an enemy, etc). 與(敵軍等)短兵相接。 **(b)** accept (an offer); make a bargain with. 接受(建議、提供); 與…達成協議或交易。

close[5] /kləʊz ; kloz/ *n* (*sing* only) end (of a period of time); conclusion (of an activity, etc): (僅用單數)(一段時間的)末尾;(活動等之)結束: *at the ~ of the day;* 在黃昏時候; *towards the ~ of the 17th century;* 將近十七世紀末葉; *(at) (the) ~ of play,* (cricket) (at the) end of play for the day. (板球)(在)當天比賽結束的時候。*The day had reached its ~.* 天已黑。**draw/bring sth to a ~,** end. 結束(某事物)。

closet /ˈklɒzɪt ; ˈklɑzɪt/ *n* **1** (now chiefly US) small room for storing things. (現主美)儲藏物品之小房間;儲藏室。⇨ cupboard, storeroom. **2** (old use) small room for private interviews. (舊用法)秘密會談之小房間。 **3** (old use) watercloset. (舊用法)便所;廁所。⇨ water[1](7). □ *attrib adj* (colloq) acting only in private; not publicly known: (俗)私下活動的;祕密的: *I suspect he's a ~ fascist.* 我猜想他是個祕密活動的法西斯黨員。□ *vt* (usu passive) (通常用被動語態) **be ~ed with sb/together,** have a private meeting with: 與…密談;在一起密談: *He was ~ed with the manager/They were ~ed together for two hours.* 他與經理密談(他們在一起密談)了二小時。

clo·sure /ˈkləʊʒə(r) ; ˈkloʒə/ *n* **1** (US = cloture) [C, U] (in Parliament) device to end debate by taking a vote on a question: (英國國會中)投票表決問題以終止辯論的辦法: *apply the ~ to a debate;* 用投票表決法終止辯論; *move the ~.* 提議停止辯論付諸投票表決。⇨ guillotine. **2** [C] act of closing: 關閉;停業;終止: *pit ~s,* eg of coal-mines which are no longer economic. 關閉不再有經濟價值的礦坑(如煤礦)。

clot /klɒt ; klɑt/ *n* [C] **1** half-solid lump formed from liquid, esp blood. (液體,尤指血液所結的)凝塊;血塊。 **2** (dated schoolboy sl) idiot, fool. (過時學

童俚語)白癡;獃子。□ *vt, vi* (-tt-) [VP6A, 2A] form into ~s: 結塊: *~ted cream,* made by scalding it; 凝結的乳脂(將乳脂加熱煮沸而成); *~ted hair,* stuck together by dirt or blood, etc. 被汚垢或血液黏結成團的頭髮。

cloth /klɒθ *US:* klɔːθ ; klɔθ/ *n* (*pl* ~s /klɒθs *US:* klɔːðz ; klɔðz/) **1** [U] material made by weaving (cotton, wool, silk, linen, etc): (棉、羊毛、絲、麻等織的)布;布料;毛料;絲綢;麻布: *three yards of ~;* 三碼布; *a book with a ~ binding.* 布面精裝的書。**2** [C] piece of this material for special purpose: 作某種特殊用途的一塊布: *a 'floor~;* 擦地板布; *a 'dish~.* 洗碟布。**3** [U] profession as shown by the clothes worn: 以某種服裝所代表的行業: *the respect due to his ~.* 對他的職業應有的尊敬。**the ~,** the clergy. 傳教士。

clothe /kləʊð ; kloð/ *vt* (*pt, pp* clothed /kləʊðd ; kloðd/, old style clad /klæd ; klæd/) [VP6A] **1** wear clothes; put clothes on, supply clothes for: 穿衣服;給…穿衣服;供給…衣服: *warmly ~d;* 穿得暖的; *~d in wool.* 穿着毛料衣服的。*He has to work hard in order to ~ his family,* earn money for their clothes. 他必須辛苦工作賺錢替家裡的人買衣服。**2** (fig) express: (喩)表示;表達: *His sentiments were ~d in suitable language.* 他的感情藉適當的語言表達出來了。

clothes /kləʊðz *US:* kləʊz ; kloz/ *n pl* (no *sing;* not used with numerals) (無單數形,不與數字連用) **1** coverings for a person's body; dress: 衣服;服裝: *a baby in long ~;* 在襁褓中的嬰孩; *a '~-brush.* 衣刷。**2 'bed-~,** sheets, blankets, etc, for or on a bed. (床上的)被褥;被單、毯等。**'~-basket,** one for ~ which are to be, or have been, washed. (裝待洗或已洗之衣服的)衣籃。**'~-horse,** frame for airing ~ that have been washed and dried. 晾衣架(用以晾已洗淨並已絞乾之衣服者)。**'~-line,** rope (stretched between posts) on which ~ are hung to be dried after being washed. 曬衣繩(牽引於兩柱間,用以掛曬洗過之衣服者)。**'~-peg/-pin,** one used for fastening ~ to a ~-line. (用於曬衣繩上夾衣服之)衣夾。⇨ the illus at peg. 參看 peg 之插圖。

cloth·ier /'kləʊðɪə(r) ; 'kloðjɚ/ *n* dealer in cloth or clothes. 做布疋或衣服生意的人;布商;衣服商。

cloth·ing /'kləʊðɪŋ ; 'kloðɪŋ/ *n* [U] (collective) clothes: (集合用法)衣服: *articles of ~.* 衣物。

clo·ture /'kləʊtʃə(r) ; 'klotʃɚ/ *n* (US) = closure(1).

cloud /klaʊd ; klaʊd/ *n* **1** [C, U] (separate mass of) visible water vapour floating above the earth: 雲;雲層;雲團(飄浮於地球上空可以看得見的水蒸氣): *The top of the mountain was covered with/hidden under ~.* 山頂爲雲所覆蓋。*Large, black ~s announced a coming storm.* 大堆的烏雲預示着將臨的暴風雨。**'~-bank** *n* thick mass of low ~. 雲堤(低而密的雲團)。**'~-burst** *n* sudden and violent rainstorm. (突然的)暴雨;驟雨;豪雨。**'~-capped** *adj* (eg of mountains) having the top enveloped in ~. 頂部爲密雲所籠罩的(如高山)。**~-'cuckoo-land** *n* imaginary and ridiculously ideal place. 想像中的荒謬的理想地方。**2** mass of things in the air moving together: 飛掠而過的一大羣東西: *a ~ of arrows/insects/horsemen, etc.* 一陣密集的箭(一大群飛蟲,騎兵等)。**3** mass (*of* smoke, dust, sand, etc) in the air. 飛揚於空中之一陣(煙、塵、沙等,與 of 連用)。**4** vague patch on or in a liquid or a transparent object. (液體或透明物體中的)混濁的一塊;汚斑。**5** something that causes unhappiness or fear: 引起不愉快或恐懼之事物: *the ~s of war;* 戰雲; *a ~ of gloom.* 愁雲。***under a ~,*** out of favour, under suspicion, in disgrace. 失寵;受到懷疑;失體面。**6** (*pl*) (複) ***(have one's head) in the ~s,*** (fig) with one's thoughts far away, not paying attention (to one's surroundings, etc). (喩)心不在焉;沉入冥想;茫然。□ *vi, vt* [VP2A, C, 3A, 6A] ***~ (over),*** become, make, indistinct (as) through ~: (使)變得不清楚(如爲雲所蔽);(使)變模糊: *The sky ~ed over.* 天空佈滿了雲。*Her eyes were ~ed (over) with tears.* 她淚眼模糊(因兩眼蒙上一層淚水)。*All these troubles have ~ed his mind,* have affected his reason. 所有這些困難已使他理智不清。**~·less** *adj* free from ~s; clear: 無雲的;晴朗的: *a ~less sky.* 晴朗的天空。**~y** *adj* (-ier, -iest) **1** covered with ~s: 爲雲所遮蔽的;有雲的;陰的: *a ~y sky.* 陰天。**2** (esp of liquids) not clear. (尤指液體)不清的;混濁的。

clout /klaʊt ; klaʊt/ *n* **1** (colloq) blow or knock (on the head, etc, given with the hand). (俗)(用手)敲;打(頭等)。**2** (archaic) piece of old cloth used for housework, etc: (古)家庭中用以擦洗物件的一塊舊布;抹布: *a 'dish-~.* 洗碟布;洗碗布。**3** (archaic) article of clothing. (古)一件衣服;衣物。□ *vt* (colloq) hit: (俗)打;敲: *~ sb on the head.* 打某人的頭。

clove[1] ⇨ cleave[1].

clove[2] /kləʊv ; klov/ *n* dried, unopened flower-bud of a tropical tree, used as a spice. 丁香(一種熱帶樹)的乾花苞(用作香料或調味品)。**,oil of '~s,** oil extracted from ~s and used in medicine. 丁香花油(作藥物用)。

clove[3] /kləʊv ; klov/ *n* one of the small, separate sections of a compound bulb: (複合球莖之)一瓣;一片: *a ~ of garlic.* 一瓣蒜。

clove hitch /'kləʊv hɪtʃ ; 'klov hɪtʃ/ *n* knot for fastening a rope round a pole, etc. 丁香結;卷結(用以縛繩於竿柱等之結繩法)。⇨ the illus at knots. 參看 knots 之插圖。

clo·ven ⇨ cleave[1].

clo·ver /'kləʊvə(r) ; 'klovɚ/ *n* [U] low-growing plant with (usu) three leaves on each stalk, and purple, pink or white flowers, grown as food for cattle, etc. 三葉草;苜蓿(一種低矮植物,每一葉柄上通常只有三片葉子,開紫、粉紅或白花,用作牛等之飼料)。***be/live in ~,*** in great comfort and luxury. 生活安逸奢侈。**'~-leaf,** highway intersection with flyovers, etc forming the pattern of a four-leaved ~. 四葉苜蓿形交流道(有天橋等交叉呈四葉苜蓿形的公路交叉點)。**,four-leaf '~,** rare variety with four-leaved stalk, the finding of which is considered to be a good omen. 四葉苜蓿;幸運草(極稀少,如發現或認爲是好預兆)。

clown /klaʊn ; klaʊn/ *n* person (esp in a circus or pantomime) who makes a living by performing amusing or foolish tricks and antics; person acting like a ~; rude, clumsy man. (馬戲團或啞劇中靠玩笨把戲及滑稽動作爲生的)丑角;小丑;行動似小丑的人;粗魯、笨拙的人。□ *vi* [VP2A] behave like a ~: 扮演丑角;做出如小丑之行爲: *Stop all this ~ing.* 不要再耍小丑了。**~·ish** *adj* of or like a ~. 小丑的;丑角的;似小丑的。

cloy /klɔɪ ; klɔɪ/ *vt, vi* [VP6A, 2A] make or become distasteful by excess, sweetness, richness (of food, pleasure, etc); satiate: (對於食物、玩樂等)(使)因享受得過多,或因味太甜、太濃而生厭;吃膩;玩膩;厭膩: *~ed with pleasure;* 玩樂膩了; *~ the appetite by eating too much sweet food.* 因吃太多甜食而致食慾不佳。

club[1] /klʌb ; klʌb/ *n* **1** heavy stick with one thick end, used as a weapon. (一端較粗,用作武器之)棍;棒。**2** stick with a curved head for hitting the ball in golf and hockey. (一端有彎曲之頭的)高爾夫球棒;曲棍球棒。□ *vt* (-bb-) [VP6A, 14] hit with a ~: 用棍棒打擊: *He had been ~bed to death.* 他被棍棒打死。*They ~bed him with their rifles.* 他們用槍托打他。**,~-'foot** *n* foot that is (from birth) thick and badly formed. 天生特厚之畸形足。Hence, 由此產生, **,~-'footed** *adj*

club[2] /klʌb ; klʌb/ *n* one of the thirteen playing-cards with a black three-leaf design printed on it: 印有黑梅花(卽一黑色三葉狀圖案)之紙牌: *the ace/ten of ~s;* 梅花牌之么點(十點);梅花A(10); *play a small ~;* 打小點之梅花牌; *C~s are trumps.* 梅花是王牌。⇨the illus at card. 參看 card 之插圖。

club[3] /klʌb ; klʌb/ *n* society of persons who subscribe money to provide themselves with sport, social entertainment, or any other shared activity, sometimes in their own grounds, buildings, etc where meals and bedrooms are available; the rooms or building(s) used by such a society (also called a '**~house**). 會社;社團;俱樂部(各人納費供作體育運動或社交娛樂等,其會所並備有餐食及宿舍,有時各種活動即在所中舉行); 俱樂部所用的房屋; 會所 (亦作 clubhouse)。□ *vi* (-bb-) [VP2C] ~ ***together,*** join or act (together, with others) for a common purpose: 爲共同目的而結合或共同行動;聯合行動: *The villagers ~bed together to help the old pensioners whose house had been burnt down.* 全村的人聯合起來救助那些房子被燒燬的退休老人。 '**~·bable** /'klʌbəbl ; 'klʌbəbl/ *adj* fit for membership of a ~; sociable. 有資格加入會社爲會員的;好交際的。

cluck /klʌk ; klʌk/ *vi, n* [VP2A] (make the) noise made by a hen, eg when calling her chickens. (作)母雞的咯咯聲(如喚小雞時所發出者);咯咯叫。

clue /klu: ; klu/ *n* fact, idea, etc that suggests a possible answer to a problem: 線索;端倪(即對一問題提示可能之答案的事實、想法等): *get/find a ~ to a mystery.* 對某神秘事得到(找到)一條線索。 ***not have a ~,*** (colloq) be completely ignorant of, unable to understand or explain (what is in question). (俗)(對當前討論的問題)毫無頭緒;一無所知;完全不懂。

clump¹ /klʌmp ; klʌmp/ *n* group or cluster (*of* trees, shrubs or plants): (樹、灌木或花草之)叢;藪: *growing in ~s.* 叢生。□ *vt* plant in ~s. 成叢地種植。

clump² /klʌmp ; klʌmp/ *vi* [VP2A, C] tread heavily: 重踏脚步而行: ~ *about,* walk about putting the feet down heavily. 以沉重的脚步到處行走。

clumsy /'klʌmzɪ ; 'klʌmzɪ/ *adj* (-ier, -iest) **1** heavy and ungraceful in movement or construction; not well designed for its purpose: (行動或構造) 笨拙的; 笨重的; 設計與用途不很符合的: *The ~ workman put his elbow through the window and broke it.* 那笨拙的工人把肘拐伸入窗子,把它弄破了。*An axe would be a ~ tool to open a tin of jam with.* 斧頭用來開果醬罐頭是一種不合用的工具。 **2** tactless; unskilful: 不圓滑的; 缺乏技巧的: *a ~ apology/forgery;* 笨拙的辯解(僞造); *~ praise.* 不得體的讚揚。 **clum·sily** /-zəlɪ ; -zəlɪ/ *adv* **clum·si·ness** *n*

clung /klʌŋ ; klʌŋ/ *pt, pp* of cling.

clunk /klʌŋk ; klʌŋk/ *vi, n* (make the) dull sound of heavy metals etc striking together. (發出)金屬等之沉濁碰撃聲。

clus·ter /'klʌstə(r) ; 'klʌstə/ *n* **1** number of things of the same kind growing closely together: (指緊密地生長在一起的同類東西)叢;簇;束;串;團: *a ~ of flowers/berries/curls;* 一簇花(漿果,鬈髮); *hair growing in thick ~s.* 成叢生長的毛髮。 **2** number of persons, animals, objects, etc in a small, close group: (指人、動物、物件等)小群: *a ~ of bees/spectators/islands;* 一小群蜜蜂(觀衆,島嶼); *consonant ~s* (in phonetics, eg *str* in *strong*); 子音群 (語音學術語,如 strong 中之 str 是); *houses here and there in ~s.* 到處成簇集結的房屋。□ *vi* [VP2A, C, 3A] ~ ***(together) (round),*** be in, form, a close group round: 繞着…結集成群;繞着…叢生;圍集在…的四周: *roses ~ing (together) round the window.* 繞着窗戶叢生的玫瑰花。 *The village ~s round the church.* 村子的房屋圍集在教堂的四周。

clutch¹ /klʌtʃ ; klʌtʃ/ *vt, vi* [VP2A, 3A, 15A] ~ ***(at),*** seize; take hold of tightly with the hand(s); attempt to seize: 用手抓住;攫取;試圖抓住;捕捉: *He ~ed (at) the rope we threw to him.* 他抓住了(或試圖抓住)我們拋給他的繩索。 *A drowning man will ~ at a straw,* will make a last, desperate but hopeless attempt to be saved. 將要溺死的人連一根草也要去抓。 *Mary ~ed her doll to her breast.* 瑪莉把她的玩偶緊抱在懷裏。□ *n* **1** the act of ~ing: 抓;捕;握: *make a ~ at sth.* 向某物抓去。 **2** (esp in *pl*) control; power. (尤用複數)控制;掌握。 ***be in/out of the ~es of; get into/out of the ~es of,*** eg of moneylenders. 在(不在)…的控制中;陷入(擺脫)…(如放債者)的掌握。 **3** device, eg a pedal, in a machine or engine for connecting and disconnecting working parts: (機器或引擎中使工作機件接合或分離的)離合器;離合器踏板;齧合子: *let in/disengage/withdraw the ~;* 接合(分離,退離)離合器; *put the ~ in/out.* 接合(分離)離合器。*The ~ is in/out.* 離合器是接合的(分離的)。 ⇨ the illus at motor. 參看 motor 之挿圖。

clutch² /klʌtʃ ; klʌtʃ/ *n* set of eggs placed under a hen to hatch at one time; number of young chickens hatched from these. 母鷄一次所孵之鷄蛋;一次所孵出的小鷄數。

clut·ter /'klʌtə(r) ; 'klʌtə/ *vt* [VP6A, 15B] ~ ***(up),*** make untidy or confused by crowding: 使散亂;亂堆;亂塞: *a desk ~ed up with papers;* 堆滿散亂文件之寫字桌; *~ up a room with unnecessary furniture.* 將房間裏塞滿了不必要的傢具。□ *n* [C,U] untidy or confused state: 雜亂;零亂: *in a ~,* in disorder or confusion. 亂作一團;亂七八糟。 *Get rid of all this ~!* 快把這些亂糟糟的東西弄走!

co- /kəʊ ; ko/ *pref* together with (another or others): 與(他人)共同: *co-author;* 合著者; *co-heir;* 共同繼承人; *co-exist;* 共存; *co-belligerents.* 共同參戰國。

coach¹ /kəʊtʃ ; kotʃ/ *n* **1** four-wheeled carriage pulled by four or more horses, used to carry passengers and mail before railways were built ('*stage-~* and '*mail-~* for public use; '*state-~* used by a head of state on ceremonial occasions). 由四匹(或四匹以上)馬拉的四輪馬車(在鐵路築成以前用以載客和郵件, stage-coach 及 mail-coach 供一般人用; state-coach 供國家元首在典禮時用)。 ***drive a ~ and horses through (sth),*** defeat the intention of (a regulation, etc) by finding serious faults in its wording. 挑剔其文字上的嚴重錯誤以打擊(某一法規等)的意圖。 **2** (US 美 = *car*) railway carriage, often divided into compartments. 鐵路客車廂(常畫分爲若干小間)。 **3** (**'motor-~**) long-distance, single-decked motor-bus: 長途單層客運汽車: *travel by ~;* 乘長途汽車旅行; *a ~-tour of Europe;* 乘長途汽車旅行歐洲; *leave by ~ for Edinburgh.* 乘長途汽車往愛丁堡。 '**~-builder** *n* craftsman who builds the bodywork of motor vehicles. 打造汽車車身的工匠。

a state-coach

coach² /kəʊtʃ ; kotʃ/ *n* teacher, esp one who gives private lessons to prepare students for a public examination; person who trains athletes for contests: (爲學生準備參加考試之) 私人補習教師;(訓練運動員參加比賽的)教練: *a* '*baseball ~.* 棒球教練。□ *vt, vi* [VP6A, 14, 2A] teach or train: 教導;訓練: *~ sb for an exam;* 指導某人準備參加考試; *~ the crew for the boat race.* 訓練船員參加划船比賽。

co·agu·late /kəʊ'ægjʊleɪt ; ko'ægjəˌlet/ *vt, vi* [VP 6A,2A] (of liquids) change to a thick and solid state, as blood does in air. (指液體)凝結;凝固(如血液在空氣中凝結)。 **co·agu·lation** /kəʊˌægjʊ'leɪʃn ; koˌægjə'leʃən/ *n*

coal /kəʊl ; kol/ *n* [U] black mineral that burns and supplies heat, and from which ~-gas is made; [C] piece of this material, esp (*a live ~*) one that is burning: 煤(能燃燒生熱並可製煤氣之黑色礦物);煤塊(尤指正燃燒中者,稱爲 a live coal): *A hot ~ fell from the fire and burnt a hole in the* *carpet*. 火爐中掉出來一塊煤，把地毯燒了一個洞。***carry ~s to Newcastle***, take goods to a place where they are already plentiful. 運煤至產煤地；多此一舉。***heap ~s of fire on sb's head***, return good for evil and so induce remorse. 以德報怨而使人懊悔。**'~·face** *n* part of a ~ seam from which ~ is being cut. 煤層中的採掘面。**'~·field** *n* district in which ~ is mined. 煤礦區；煤田。**'~-gas** *n* the mixture of gases made by treating ~, used for lighting and heating. 煤氣(用煤製成的混合氣體，用以發光或加熱)。**'~-hole** *n* cellar for storing ~. 貯藏煤的地下室；地下煤庫。**'~-house** *n* shed for storing ~. 藏煤的簡陋小屋；煤庫。**'~-mine／-pit** *nn* mine from which ~ is dug. 煤礦(坑)。**'~-scuttle** *n* container for a supply of ~ near a fireside. (壁爐邊的)煤斗；煤桶。**'~-seam** *n* underground layer of ~. (地下的)煤層。**'~-tar** *n* [U] (sometimes 有時作 *'gas-tar*) thick, black, sticky substance produced when gas is made from ~. 煤溚；柏油；煤焦油(自煤中提取煤氣時所得之濃厚、黑色、黏性物質)。□ *vt, vi* [VP6A, 2A] put ~ (into a ship, etc); take in ~: 裝煤；加煤: *The ship called at Gibraltar to ~*. 該船停靠直布羅陀加煤。*Coaling (a ship) is a dirty job*. 加煤(於船)是一件髒的工作。**'~·ing-station** *n* port where ships can obtain supplies of ~. 輪船可以加煤的港口；加煤站。

co·alesce /ˌkəʊə'les ; ˌkoə'lɛs/ *vi* come together and unite into one substance, group, etc. 聯合；合併；結合。**co·ales·cence** /ˌkəʊə'lesns ; ˌkoə'lɛsns/ *n*

co·ali·tion /ˌkəʊə'lɪʃn ; ˌkoə'lɪʃən/ *n* [U] uniting; [C] union of political parties for a special purpose: 聯合；各政黨爲某一特殊目的所組的聯盟: *a ~ government;* 聯合政府; *the left-wing ~;* 左翼聯盟; *form a ~*. 組織聯盟。

coam·ing /'kəʊmɪŋ ; 'komɪŋ/ *n* raised rim round a ship's hatches to keep water out. 艙口緣圍(船艙口周圍防水流入之凸起邊緣)。

coarse /kɔːs ; kors/ *adj* (-r, -st) **1** (of material) not fine and small; rough and lumpy: (指質料)粗糙的；粗的: *~ sand／sugar;* 粗沙(糖); having a rough surface or texture: 表面或織地粗糙的: *a dress made of ~ cloth;* 粗布做的衣服; *a ~ skin／complexion*. 粗糙的皮膚(顏面)。**2** (of food) common; inferior: (指食物)普通的；粗劣的: *~ fish;* 肉粗的魚; *~ fishing*, eg for chub, roach, pike. 捕粗肉魚(如諸子鰷，斜齒鯿，梭子魚)。**3** vulgar; not delicate or refined: 粗魯的；粗俗的；不高雅的: *~ manners／language／words／laughter／jokes／tastes;* 粗魯的舉止(言語，話語，笑聲，笑話，嗜好); *~ of speech*. 說話粗魯的。**coarsen** /'kɔːsn ; 'korsn̩/ *vt, vi* [VP6A, 2A] make or become ~. (使)變粗糙；(使)變粗魯；(使)變粗俗。**~·ly** *adv* **~·ness** *n*

coast[1] /kəʊst ; kost/ *n* [C] land bordering the sea; seashore and land near it: 海岸；沿岸地區: *The ship was wrecked on the Kent ~*. 該船在肯特海岸觸礁。*There are numerous islands off the ~*. 在這海岸外有無數的島嶼。*The village is on the south ~*. 該村在南方海岸。**'~·guard** *n* officer on police duty on the ~ (to prevent or detect smuggling, report passing ships, etc). 海岸巡邏隊；水上警察(防止或緝查走私，報告經過船隻等)。**'~·line** *n* shoreline, esp with regard to its shape: 海岸線(尤指其形狀): *a rugged ~line*. 崎嶇的海岸線。**~al** /'kəʊstl ; 'kostl/ *adj* of the ~: 海岸的: *~al navigation*. 沿海岸的航行。**'~·wise** *adj, adv* along the ~. 沿海岸的(地)。

coast[2] /kəʊst ; kost/ *vi, vt* [VP2A, C, 3A, 6A] **1** ~ ***(along)***, go in, sail, a ship along the coast. 乘船沿海岸而航行。**2** ride or slide down a hill or slope without using power (eg along a road on a bicycle). 不用動力而自斜坡向下滑行(如騎脚踏車沿路滑下)。**~er** *n* **1** ship that sails from port to port along the coast. (來往於沿海各港埠之)沿海船；近海船。**2** small mat, etc (for a drinking-glass, etc) to protect a polished table, etc from drips or moisture. 茶杯墊子(墊於茶杯等下面以防滴水或水氣污損桌面油漆等)。

coat /kəʊt ; kot/ *n* **1** long outer garment with sleeves, buttoned in the front. (在前面扣合的有袖的)長外衣。⇨ over-~; *rain-~* at rain[1](1). ***turn one's ~***, change one's side or principles, desert one army or party and join the other. 改變立場或主義；背叛甲軍或甲黨而加入乙軍或乙黨；變節；改宗。**ˌ~ of 'arms**, ⇨ arms. **ˌ~ of 'mail**, piece of armour of metal rings or plate for the upper part of the body. (金屬圈或片製成保護上身的)甲冑。⇨ the illus at armour. 參看 armour 之插圖。**'~-tails** *n pl* divided tapering part of a *tail-~*, ⇨ tail(2). 燕尾服之尾。**2** jacket(1). 夾克。**3** any covering that can be compared to a garment, eg an animal's hair or wool. 被比做衣服之任何覆蓋物(如動物之毛或羊毛)。**4** layer of paint or other substance put on a surface at one time: 一層(一次塗於表面的油漆或其他物質): *The woodwork has had its final ~ of paint*. 木造部份已經塗過了最後一層油漆。□ *vt* [VP6A, 14] cover with a ~ or layer: 外加一層；覆以一層: *furniture ~ed with dust;* 上面覆一層灰塵的傢具; *~ pills with sugar*. 將藥丸加上糖衣。*Tinplate is made by ~ing sheets of iron with tin*. 洋鐵皮是在鐵皮上鍍一層錫製成的。**'~·ing** *n* **1** thin layer or covering: 薄層；薄皮: *two ~ings of wax*. 兩層薄蠟。**2** [U] cloth for ~s(1, 2). 外衣料；夾克料。

coatee /kəʊ'tiː ; ˌkot'i/ *n* short coat. 短外衣。

coax /kəʊks ; koks/ *vt, vi* [VP6A, 17, 15B, 14, 2A] ~ ***(from／into／out of)***, get sb or sth to do sth by kindness or patience: 以和善或耐性使某人或某物做某事；哄誘；勸誘: *~ a child to take its medicine;* 哄小孩吃藥; *~ a fire to burn;* 耐心使火燃燒起來；引火; *~ (up) the fire;* 耐心地設法使爐火燒旺(起來); *~ sb into／out of doing sth;* 哄某人做(不做)某事; *~ a smile from the baby*. 逗嬰孩一笑。**~·ing** *n* [U, C] being ~ed: (受)哄誘；(受)勸誘: *give sb a ~ing*. 勸誘某人。*He took a lot of ~ing before he agreed to take her to the theatre*. 經過很久的勸誘之後，他才答應帶她去看戲。**'~·ing·ly** *adv*

cob /kɒb ; kɑb/ *n* **1** male swan. 雄天鵝。**2** strong short-legged horse for riding. 供騎乘之强壯而腿短的馬。**3** (also 亦作 **'cob-nut**) large kind of hazelnut. 大榛實。**4** (also 亦作 **'corn-cob**) central part of an ear of maize on which the grain grows: 玉蜀黍的穗軸；玉米軸: *corn on the cob*. 尙未自穗軸上剝下的玉蜀黍。⇨ the illus at cereal. 參看 cereal 之插圖。

co·balt /'kəʊbɔːlt ; 'kobɔlt/ *n* hard silvery-white metal (symbol **Co**) used in many alloys; deep blue colouring matter made from its compounds, used to colour glass and ceramics. 鈷(堅硬的銀白色金屬，化學符號 Co，用於許多種合金)；用鈷化合物所製的深藍色顏料(用以加顏色於玻璃及陶器)；鈷藍。

cob·ber /'kɒbə(r) ; 'kɑbɚ/ *n* (Australia; colloq) fellow. (澳；俗)同伴；夥伴。

cobble[1] /'kɒbl ; 'kɑbl̩/ *n* (also 亦作 **'~-stone**) stone worn round and smooth by water and used for paving. 由水沖磨成圓而光滑的石頭(用以鋪路)；大礫石；鵝卵石。□ *vt* pave with these stones: 用圓石頭鋪(路): *~d streets*. 用圓石頭鋪成的街道。

cobble[2] /'kɒbl ; 'kɑbl̩/ *vt* [VP6A] mend, patch (esp shoes), or put together roughly. 補綴(尤指鞋)；粗劣地修補。

cob·bler /'kɒblə(r) ; 'kɑblɚ/ *n* **1** mender of shoes. (*'shoe-repairer* is now the usu word). 補鞋匠(現在通常用 shoe-repairer)。**2** clumsy workman. 笨拙的工人。**3** (US) type of pie. (美)一種餡餅。***a load of (old) ~s***, (GB sl) nonsense. (英俚)胡說；廢話。

co·bra /'kəʊbrə ; 'kobrə/ *n* poisonous snake of Asia and Africa. 眼鏡蛇(亞洲及非洲產之毒蛇)。⇨ the illus at snake. 參看 snake 之插圖。

cob·web /'kɒbweb ; 'kɑbˌwɛb/ *n* [C] fine network or single thread made by a spider. 蜘蛛網；蛛絲。⇨ the illus at arachnid. 參看 arachnid 之插圖。

Coca-Cola /ˌkəʊkə'kəʊlə ; ˌkokə'kolə/ *n* (P) popular non-alcoholic carbonated drink. (商標)可口可樂(流

行的非酒類充碳酸氣的飲料)。

co·caine /kəʊ'keɪn ; ko'ken/ *n* [U] product (from a shrub) used by doctors as a local anaesthetic, and also used as a stimulant by drug addicts. 古柯鹼 (由一種灌木中提取的產物，醫師們用之作局部麻醉劑，藥瘾者用之作興奮劑)。

cochi·neal /ˌkɒtʃɪ'ni:l ; ˌkatʃə'nil/ *n* [U] bright red colouring-matter made from the dried bodies of certain insects. 用某些昆蟲乾骸所製的鮮紅顏料；洋紅；胭脂紅。

coch·lea /'kɒklɪə ; 'kaklɪə/ *n* spiral-shaped part of the inner ear. 耳蝸(內耳之螺旋形部份)。⇨ the illus at ear. 參看 ear 之插圖。

cock¹ /kɒk ; kak/ *n* **1** (used alone) adult male bird of the domestic or farmyard fowl (US 美 = *rooster*) ⇨ the illus at fowl. (單獨用)公鷄；雄鷄(參看 fowl 之插圖)。**'~-crow** *n* early dawn. 天初亮；黎明；破曉；拂曉。**ˌ~-a-'hoop** *adj, adv* with boastful crowing; exultant(ly). 意氣揚揚的(地)；狂喜的(地)。**~-a-doodle-doo** /ˌkɒk ə ˌdu:dl'du: ; 'kakəˌdudl'du/ *n* the crow of the ~(1); child's name for a ~(1). 雄鷄的啼聲；喔喔；(兒語之)雄鷄。***ˌ~-and-'bull story,*** foolish story that one should not believe. 無稽之談。**'~-fighting** *n* fighting by game-~s as a sport for onlookers, ⇨ game¹(6). 鬥鷄遊戲(以供玩賞者)。***live like 'fighting-~s,*** live on the best possible food. 享受最佳的食物；過奢侈生活。***~ of the walk,*** person who dominates others. 某行業的首領；頭子；頭目。**2** (in compounds) male of other kinds of bird: (用於複合字中)別種鳥類的雄者: *'pea~;* 雄孔雀; *ˌ~-'sparrow;* 雄麻雀; *ˌ~-'robin.* 雄知更鳥。

cock² /kɒk ; kak/ *n* **1** tap and spout for controlling the flow of a liquid or a gas, eg from a pipe, barrel. (控制管、桶等中液體或氣體流出之)龍頭；活栓。**2** lever in a gun; position of this lever when it is raised and ready to be released by the trigger. (槍上的)擊鐵；擊鐵張開的位置(待扣扳機射擊)。***at half／full ~,*** half ready／quite ready to be fired. 擊鐵半(全)張；半(全)準備射擊。***go off at half ~,*** of schemes, ceremonies, etc, begin before the arrangements are complete. (指計畫、典禮等)尚未全部安排就緒卽行開始。**3** ⚠ (vulg sl) penis. (諱)(鄙俚)陰莖；鷄巴。

cock³ /kɒk ; kak/ *vt* [VP6A,15B] ~ ***(up),*** **1** turn upwards, cause to be erect (showing attention, inquiry, defiance, etc): 向上翹起；豎起；使直立(表示注意、詢問、輕蔑等): *The horse ~ed its ears.* 馬豎起耳朵。*The horse stopped with its ears ~ed up.* 馬停下來，耳朵豎着。*He ~ed his eye at me,* glanced or winked at me knowingly, or raised his eyebrow. 他對我使眼色。**ˌ~ed 'hat** *n* triangular hat, pointed front and back, worn with some uoiforms. 前後呈尖形的三角帽 (配合某種制服戴者)。***knock sb／sth into a ~ed hat,*** knock shapeless, or so that recognition is impossible; beat thoroughly. 將(某人或某物)打得不成樣子；將…弄得面目全非；徹底打敗。**2** [VP6A] raise the cock of (a gun) ready for firing. 扳起(槍)的擊鐵準備發射。⇨ cock²(2). **3** ~ ***up,*** (sl) make a mess of; upset: (俚)將…弄得一團糟；擾亂: *They completely ~ed up the arrangements for our holiday.* 他們把我們度假的計畫完全搞亂了。Hence, 由此產生，**'~-up** *n*

cock⁴ /kɒk ; kak/ *n* small, cone-shaped pile of straw or hay. 小的圓錐形乾草堆。□ *vt* pile (hay) in ~s. 將(乾草)堆成小的圓錐形堆。

cock·ade /kɒ'keɪd ; kak'ed/ *n* knot of ribbon worn on a hat as a badge. 結在帽上作爲徽章之帶結；帽章。

cocka·too /ˌkɒkə'tu: ; ˌkakə'tu/ *n* crested parrot. 美冠鸚鵡；白鸚。⇨ the illus at rare. 參看 rare 之插圖。

cock·chafer /'kɒktʃeɪfə(r) ; 'kakˌtʃefɚ/ *n* large beetle that flies with a loud whirring sound and is destructive to vegetation. 金龜子(飛起來帶響鬧的嗡嗡聲之大甲蟲，對植物有害)。

cocker /'kɒkə(r) ; 'kakɚ/ *n* breed of spaniel. 一種長毛垂耳之犬。

cock·erel /'kɒkərəl ; 'kakərəl/ *n* young cock¹(1), not more than one year old. (未滿一歲的)小公鷄。

cock-eyed /'kɒkaɪd ; 'kakˌaɪd/ *adj* (sl) (俚) **1** squinting; crooked; turned or twisted to one side. 斜眼的；彎曲的；向一邊歪扭的。**2** wild, ill-judged: 輕率而未予妥善判斷的: *a ~ scheme.* 輕率的計畫。

cock·horse /ˌkɒk'hɔ:s ; 'kak'hɔrs/ *n* ***ride a ~,*** (children's word) ride on horseback or on a rocking-horse. (小兒語)騎馬；騎搖動木馬。⇨ rock².

cockle /'kɒkl ; 'kakl/ *n* **1** edible shellfish; (also 亦作 **'~-shell**) its shell. 烏蛤；海扇(一種可食的貝類)；海扇殼。**2** small, shallow boat. 淺的小船；小舟。**3** ***(warm, delight, etc) the ~s of one's heart,*** one's feelings. (使)某人的情緒(振奮，愉快等)。

cock·ney /'kɒknɪ ; 'kaknɪ/ *adj, n* (characteristic of a) native of the East End of London: 倫敦東區人；倫敦東區人的個性: *a ~ accent;* 倫敦東區人的口音; *~ humour.* 倫敦東區人的幽默。

cock·pit /'kɒkpɪt ; 'kakˌpɪt/ *n* **1** enclosed space where game-cocks fought, ⇨ *cock-fighting* at cock¹(1); (fig) area where battles have often been fought: 鬥鷄場；(喩)屢經戰役的戰場: *Belgium, the ~ of Europe.* 比利時，歐洲的戰場。**2** compartment in a small aircraft for the pilot. 小型飛機的駕駛艙；座艙。Cf 參較 *flight deck* of an airliner; (客機的)駕駛室; driver's seat in a racing-car. (賽車的)駕駛座。⇨ the illus at air¹. 參看 air¹ 之插圖。

cock·roach /'kɒkrəʊtʃ ; 'kakˌrotʃ/ *n* large, dark-brown insect that comes out at night in kitchens and places where food is kept. 蟑螂(深褐色的大昆蟲，夜間外出，在廚房及置食物處覓食)。⇨ the illus at insect. 參看 insect 之插圖。

cocks·comb /'kɒkskəʊm ; 'kaksˌkom/ *n* **1** red crest of a cock¹(1). (雄鷄的)鷄冠。⇨ the illus at fowl. 參看 fowl 之插圖。**2** jester's cap. 丑角所戴的鷄冠帽。**3** plant with clusters of red or yellow feather-like flowers. 鷄冠花(開密集之紅色或黃色羽狀花之植物)。

cock·sure /ˌkɒk'ʃʊə(r) ; 'kak'ʃʊr/ *adj* presumptuously or offensively sure (*of* or *about* sth); confident. 自信得令人厭惡的；過於自信的(與 of 或 about 連用，後接某事)；確信的；深信的。

cock·tail /'kɒkteɪl ; 'kakˌtel/ *n* [C] **1** mixed alcoholic drink, esp one taken before a meal, eg gin and vermouth. 鷄尾酒(各種混合之酒，尤指飯前所飲者，如杜松子酒與苦艾酒混合者)。**2** mixture of fruit juices, or spiced tomato juice, served in a glass as an appetizer; quantity of crab meat or shrimps, similarly served. 混合果汁或加有香料之蕃茄汁(以杯進食，作爲開胃品)；(作爲開胃品的)蟹肉或蝦肉。**3** mixed fruit salad served in a glass. (置於杯中進食之)什錦水果沙拉。

cocky /'kɒkɪ ; 'kakɪ/ *adj* (-ier, -iest) (colloq) cocksure; pert; conceited. (俗)過於自信的；無禮的；自負的。

coco /'kəʊkəʊ ; 'koko/ *n* (also 亦作 **'~-palm, '~-nut palm**) tropical seaside palm-tree. (生於熱帶海濱之)椰子樹。**~·nut**/'kəʊkənʌt ; 'kokənət/ *n* large hard-shelled seed of this palm-tree, filled with milky juice and a solid white eatable lining from which oil is extracted; 椰子(外有硬殼，內有乳狀汁，殼內有一層白色可食的物質，卽椰子肉，可製椰子油)。⇨ copra. ⇨ the illus at palm. 參看 palm 之插圖。**ˌ~-nut 'matting,** made from the tough fibre of the ~nut's outer covering. (用椰子殼之堅韌的纖維製成之)棕蓆。

co·coa /'kəʊkəʊ ; 'koko/ *n* [U] powder of crushed cacao seeds; hot drink made from this with water or milk. (用可可子磨成的)可可粉；用可可粉與水或牛奶所製成的熱飲料；可可。

co·coon /kə'ku:n ; kə'kun/ *n* silky covering made by a caterpillar to protect itself while it is a chrysalis, esp that of the silkworm. 繭(毛蟲在作蛹時期結絲以保護自己的外殼)；(尤指)蠶繭。⇨ the illus at butterfly, silk. 參看 butterfly 及 silk 之插圖。□ *vt* [VP6A] protect by covering completely. 完全

蓋住以保護;封存。

co·cotte /kɒ'kɒt ; ko'kɑt/ *n* (F) (dated) fashionable prostitute. (法) (過時用語) 上流社會的娼妓;高級妓女。

cod¹ /kɒd ; kɑd/ *n* **1** [C] (*pl* unchanged) (複數不變) (also 亦作 **'cod·fish**) large sea fish. 鱈。 **2** [U] its flesh as food. 鱈魚肉(作爲食物者)。 **~-liver oil** /ˌkɒd lɪvər'ɔɪl ; ˌkɑdlɪvɚ'ɔɪl/ *n* [U] used as a medicine. 魚肝油(作藥物用)。

cod² /kɒd ; kɑd/ *vt, vi* (-dd-) [VP6A, 2A] (dated colloq) hoax; make a fool of: (過時俗語) 欺騙;愚弄: *You're codding (me)!* 你在騙人(騙我)!

coda /'kəʊdə ; 'kodə/ *n* passage (often elaborate in style) that completes a piece of music. (樂曲的) 尾聲(常爲加意雕琢之作)。

coddle /'kɒdl ; 'kɑdḷ/ *vt* [VP6A] **1** (also 亦作 **'molly-~**) treat with great care and tenderness; pamper: 嬌養;溺愛;寵愛;縱容: *~ a child because it is in poor health.* 嬌養一個孩子因其體弱。 **2** cook, eg eggs, in water just below boiling-point. 以僅低於沸點的溫度在水中煮(蛋等);軟煮。

code /kəʊd ; kod/ *n* [C] **1** collection of laws arranged in a system. 法典;法規;章程;規程。 **2** system of rules and principles that has been accepted by society or a class or group of people: (社會或某階層所遵守的) 禮法;規約;慣例;道德律: *a high moral ~;* 崇高的道德準則; *a ~ of honour.* 社交禮法;紳士淑女之道。 *You must live up to the ~ of the school,* accept its unwritten rules of honour and conduct. 你必須遵守學校的傳統規約。 **3** (also 亦作 [U]) system of signs used for secrecy or brevity, eg in wartime, or for economy in sending cables, or for a computer: 密碼(如在戰時用以保守機密者);(打電報或電腦中所用以求節時省字的) 電碼: *send a message in ~;* 用密碼發送消息; *a 'telegraph ~;* (電報之) 電碼; *a ~ telegram;* 密碼電報;電碼電報; *a ˌfive-'letter ~,* eg one in which BXYMA stands for a phrase or sentence. 五字母密碼(如 BXYMA 卽代表一片語或句子)。 ***break a ~,*** discover how to interpret a secret ~. 解密碼。 **the 'Morse ~,** using dots and dashes for letters and numerals. 摩爾斯電碼(用點及長畫代表字母和數字)。□ *vt* (also 亦作 **en~** /en'kəʊd ; ɛn'kod/) put in a ~(3); ⇨ decode. 編成密碼;譯成電碼。

co·deine /'kəʊdiːn ; 'kodɪˌin/ *n* [U] narcotic derived from opium. 可待因(自鴉片提製成的一種痲醉藥)。

co·dex /'kəʊdeks ; 'kodɛks/ *n* (*pl* codices /'kəʊdɪsiːz ; 'kodəˌsiz/) manuscript volume (esp of ancient texts). (尤指古代典籍之) 抄本。

codger /'kɒdʒə(r) ; 'kɑdʒɚ/ *n* (colloq) queer old person; fellow. (俗) 古怪的老人;老怪物;傢伙。

codi·ces ⇨ codex.

codi·cil /'kəʊdɪsɪl *US:* 'kɒdəsl ; 'kɑdəsl/ *n* appendix to a will, esp sth modifying or revoking part of it. 遺囑的附錄(尤指修改或取消遺囑之部份內容者);遺囑更改;遺囑附加條款。

codi·fy /'kəʊdɪfaɪ *US:* 'kɒdəfaɪ ; 'kɑdəˌfaɪ/ *vt* [VP6A] put into the form of a code(1): 編成法典;編纂: *~ the laws.* 編纂法典。 **codi·fi·ca·tion** /ˌkəʊdɪfɪ'keɪʃn *US:* ˌkɒd- ; ˌkɑdəfə'keʃən/ *n*

cod·ling /'kɒdlɪŋ ; 'kɑdlɪŋ/ *n* young codfish. 幼鱈。

cod·piece /'kɒdpiːs ; 'kɑdˌpis/ *n* (15th and 16th cc) bag or flap concealing the opening in the front of a man's close-fitting hose²(2). (十五及十六世紀男人緊身褲前面開口的) 遮袋或遮蓋。

co-ed /'kəʊ ed ; 'ko'ɛd/ *n* (US colloq) (girl or woman at a) co-educational school or college. (美俗) 男女合校的學校;男女合校中的女生。

co-edu·ca·tion /ˌkəʊ ˌedʒʊ'keɪʃn ; ˌkoɛdʒə'keʃən/ *n* [U] education of boys and girls together. 男女合校的教育;男女同校。 **~al** /-'keɪʃənl ; -'keʃənḷ/ *adj*

co-ef·fi·cient /ˌkəʊɪ'fɪʃnt ; ˌkoə'fɪʃənt/ *n* **1** (maths) number or symbol placed before and multiplying another quantity, known or unknown. (數學) 係數(置於已知或未知數之前表示相乘之數或符號)。(In *3xy*, 3 is the ~ of *xy*). (在 3xy 中, 3 是 xy 的係數)。 **2** (phys) multiplier that measures some property. (物理) 率;係數。

co·erce /kəʊ'ɜːs ; ko'ɝs/ *vt* [VP6A, 14] ***~ sb (into doing sth),*** use force to make sb obedient, etc; compel sb (to a course of action). 强迫某人(服從等);强迫某人(做某事)。 **co·ercion** /kəʊ'ɜːʃn *US:* -ʒn ; ko'ɝʃən/ *n* [U] coercing or being ~d; government by force: 强迫;被迫;强制;壓制: *He paid the money under coercion.* 他被迫付錢。 **co·ercive** /kəʊ'ɜːsɪv ; ko'ɝsɪv/ *adj* of coercion; using coercion: 强迫的;用强迫方法的: *coercive methods/measures.* 壓制方法(手段)。

co·eval /ˌkəʊ'iːvl ; ko'ivḷ/ *adj, n* ***~ (with),*** (person) of the same age; (person, things) existing at, lasting for, the same period of time. (與…) 同年齡的(人);同時期的(人、事物)。

co·exist /ˌkəʊɪg'zɪst ; ˌko·ɪg'zɪst/ *vi* [VP2A, 3A] ***~ (with),*** exist at the same time. (與…) 同時存在;共存。 **~·ence** /-təns ; -təns/ *n* [U] (esp) peaceful existence side by side of states with opposed political systems. (尤指政治制度相反的各國間之) 和平共存。

cof·fee /'kɒfɪ *US:* 'kɔːfɪ ; 'kɔfɪ/ *n* [U] bush or shrub with berries containing seeds (called *beans*) which, when roasted and ground to powder, are used by infusing with boiling water for making a drink; the seeds; the powder; [C, U] the drink: 咖啡樹(所結漿果內的子,稱咖啡豆,經焙炒磨成粉,加開水用以調製飲料);咖啡豆;咖啡子;咖啡粉;咖啡飲料;咖啡: *three black ~s,* three cups of ~ without milk; 三杯不加牛奶的咖啡; *white ~,* with milk. 加牛奶的咖啡。 **'~ bar** *n* small café serving ~ beverages and light refreshments. (供應咖啡飲料及小點心的) 小咖啡館。 **'~-house** *n* (formerly, in England) place frequented by literary men as a sort of club. (昔時英國) 文人常去聚談的似俱樂部的地方;咖啡屋。 **'~-mill** *n* device for grinding roasted ~-beans. 磨咖啡機。 **'~-stall** *n* movable stand selling hot ~ and food in the streets (esp at night). 街頭的流動咖啡攤(賣熱咖啡及食物,尤見於夜間)。

cof·fer /'kɒfə(r) ; 'kɔfɚ/ *n* **1** large, strong box, esp one for holding money or other valuables; (*pl*) place for storing valuables: (尤指裝金錢或其他貴重物品之) 大而堅固之箱;保險箱;(複) 儲藏貴重物品的地方;金庫;寶庫: *the ~s of a bank.* 銀行的金庫。 **2** ornamental panel in a ceiling, etc. (天花板等之) 飾板;鑲板。 **3** (also 亦作 **'~ dam**) caisson(2). 潛水箱;沈箱。

cof·fin /'kɒfɪn ; 'kɔfɪn/ *n* box or case for a dead person to be placed in and then buried. (安置和埋葬死人的) 棺材;柩。 ***drive a nail into sb's ~,*** do sth that will bring his death or ruin nearer. 做某事使某人提早死亡或使其事業提早崩潰。

cog /kɒg ; kɑg/ *n* one of a series of teeth on the rim of a wheel which transfers motion by locking into the teeth of a similar wheel. 輪齒;鈍齒(與相似的輪之輪齒扣合,可以傳遞動力)。 ⇨ the illus at bicycle, gear. 參看 bicycle, gear 之插圖。 ***be a cog in the machine,*** (fig) an unimportant part of a large enterprise. (喻) 爲大企業中不重要的部份。 **'cog-wheel** *n* toothed wheel. 鑲齒輪;嵌齒輪。

co·gent /'kəʊdʒənt ; 'kodʒənt/ *adj* (of arguments) strong and convincing. (指論據) 有力而令人信服的。 **co·gency** /'kəʊdʒənsɪ ; 'kodʒənsɪ/ *n* [U] force or strength (of arguments). (論據之) 力量;說服力。

cogi·tate /'kɒdʒɪteɪt ; 'kɑdʒəˌtet/ *vi, vt* [VP2A, 3A, 6A, 14] (formal or facet) meditate; think deeply: (正式用語或玩笑語) 愼思;沉思;思考: *~ upon sth;* 愼思某事; *~ mischief against sb.* 想壞主意害人。 **cogi·ta·tion** /ˌkɒdʒɪ'teɪʃn ; ˌkɑdʒə'teʃən/ *n* **1** [U] cogitating: 愼思;沉思;思考: *after much cogitation.* 經過長久的思考之後。 **2** (*pl*) thoughts; reflections. (複) 想法;看法。

cognac /'kɒnjæk ; 'konjæk/ *n* [U] fine French brandy. 上等的法國白蘭地酒。

cog·nate /'kɒgneɪt ; 'kɑgnet/ *adj* **1** ***~ (with),***

having the same source of origin: (與…)同根源的: *English, Dutch and German are ~ languages.* 英語,荷蘭語和德語是同源語言。 **2** related; having much in common: 互有關係的;有關聯的;有很多共同點的: *Physics and astronomy are ~ sciences.* 物理學和天文學是互有關聯的科學。□ *n* [C] word, etc that is ~ with another. 同源字;同源物。

cog·ni·tion /kɒg'nɪʃn ; kɑg'nɪʃən/ *n* [U] (phil) knowing; awareness (including sensation but excluding emotion). (哲學)認識;認知(包括感覺,但不包括感情)。

cog·ni·zance /'kɒgnɪzns ; 'kɑgnəzəns/ *n* [U] **1** (legal) being aware, having conscious knowledge (of sth). (法律)察覺;認識;知道。***take ~ of,*** become officially aware of. 正式獲知。**2** (right of) dealing with a matter legally or judicially. 依法審理;審理權;管轄權。***fall within/go beyond one's ~,*** be sth one can/cannot deal with. 歸(不歸)某人處理;在(不在)某人的管轄之內。**cog·ni·zant** /'kɒgnɪzənt ; 'kɑgnəzənt/ *adj* ~ ***of,*** (phil, legal) having knowledge, being fully aware of. (哲學,法律)認識的;知道的;知曉的。

cog·no·men /kɒg'nəʊmən ; kɑg'nomən/ *n* [C] (formal) (正式用語) **1** surname. 姓。 **2** descriptive nickname, eg *Rusty* or *Shorty*. (描繪某人特徵的)綽號(例如 Rusty 或 Shorty)。

co·habit /kəʊ'hæbɪt ; ko'hæbɪt/ *vi* (formal) (usu of an unmarried couple) live together. (正式用語)(通常指一對未婚的情侶)共同生活; 同居。 **co·habi·tation** /ˌkəʊhæbɪ'teɪʃn ; koˏhæbə'teʃən/ *n*

co·here /kəʊ'hɪə(r) ; ko'hɪr/ *vi* [VP2A] (formal) stick together; be or remain united; (of arguments, etc) be consistent. (正式用語)黏在一起;黏着;連結在一起; 凝結; (指論據等) 連貫; 前後一致。**co·her·ence** /ˌkəʊ'hɪərəns ; ko'hɪrəns/ *n* **co·her·en·cy** /-rənsɪ ; -rənsɪ/ *n* **co·her·ent** /-rənt ; -rənt/ *adj* **1** sticking together. 黏在一起的;結合在一起的。**2** consistent; (esp of speech, thought, ideas, reasoning) clear; easy to understand. 一致的;連貫的; (尤指言詞、思想、觀念、推理)清晰的;易懂的。**co·her·ent·ly** *adv*

co·he·sion /kəʊ'hi:ʒn ; ko'hiʒən/ *n* cohering; tendency to stick together; force with which molecules cohere. 附着;黏着;附着力;結合力;(分子的)內聚性;內聚力。 **co·he·sive** /kəʊ'hi:sɪv ; ko'hisɪv/ *adj* having the power of cohering; tending to cohere. 有附着力的;有內聚力的。

co·hort /'kəʊhɔ:t ; 'kohɔrt/ *n* **1** (in the ancient Roman armies) tenth part of a legion. (古羅馬軍隊)軍團的十分之一;大隊。 **2** number of persons banded together. 一隊(人)。

coif /kɔɪf ; kɔɪf/ *n* (old use) close-fitting cap covering the top, back and sides of the head. (舊用法) 一種覆蓋着頭頂、頭後及兩側之緊帽。

coif·feur /kwɑ:'fɜ:(r) ; ˏkwɑ'fɝ/ *n* (F) hairdresser. (法) (爲婦女理髮的)理髮師。

coif·fure /kwɑ:'fjʊə(r) ; kwɑ'fjʊr/ *n* style of hairdressing. 婦女的髮式;髮型。

coign /kɔɪn ; kɔɪn/ *n* ~ **of 'vantage** (formal, usu fig) place from which one has a good view of sth. (正式用語,通常用作喩)對於某事物能作仔細觀察的地方;有利的地位。

coil /kɔɪl ; kɔɪl/ *vt, vi* [VP6A, 15A, B, 2A, C] wind or twist into a continuous circular or spiral shape; curl round and round: 繞成盤狀;盤繞;纏繞;一圈一圈地捲起: *~ a rope.* 捲起繩索。*The snake ~ed (itself) round the branch/~ed itself up.* 那蛇盤繞在樹枝上(把身體盤繞起來)。□ *n* **1** sth ~ed; a single turn of sth ~ed: 盤繞之物;所盤繞之一圈: *the thick ~s of a python.* 蟒蛇所盤繞之重疊的圈圈。⇨ the illus at snake. 參看 snake 之插圖。 **2** length of wire wound in a spiral to conduct electric current. (用金屬線所繞成以傳導電流的)線圈。 **3** (colloq) an intra-uterine contraceptive device in the shape of a ~. (俗)(置於子宮中的)圈形避孕器。

coin /kɔɪn ; kɔɪn/ *n* [C, U] (piece of) metal money: (一枚)鑄幣;硬幣: *a small heap of ~s;* 一小堆硬幣; *gold and silver ~s;* 金幣和銀幣; *false ~,* imitation ~ in metal of low value. 用賤金屬所製的假錢;僞造的錢幣。***the other side of the ~,*** (fig) other aspect of the matter. (喩)事情的另一方面。***pay a man back in the same/his own ~,*** treat him as he has treated you. 他曾怎樣對待你,你也怎樣對待他;以其人之道還治其人之身。□ *vt* [VP6A] make (metal) into ~s; invent (esp a new word). 用(金屬)鑄造錢幣;創造;杜撰(尤指新字)。***be '~ing money,*** be making money fast, be making large profits. 迅速地發財;暴富;賺大錢。***to ~ a phrase,*** (ironic) to use a very well established idiom as if it were a new one. (反語)將一盛行已久的慣用語當作新鮮成語使用。**~·age** /'kɔɪnɪdʒ ; 'kɔɪnɪdʒ/ *n* **1** [U] making ~s; the ~s made; [C] system of ~s in use: 鑄造錢幣;所鑄之錢幣;通用的貨幣制度: *a decimal ~age.* 十進貨幣制度。 **2** [U] inventing (of a new word); [C] newly invented word. (新字的)創造;新創造的字。**~er** *n* maker of counterfeit ~s. 僞造錢幣者。

co·incide /ˌkəʊɪn'saɪd ; ˏko·ɪn'saɪd/ *vi* [VP2A, 3A] ~ ***(with),*** **1** (of two or more objects) correspond in area and outline. (指兩個或更多的物件)在面積與輪廓上相符合。 **2** (of events) happen at the same time; occupy the same period of time: (指事件)同時發生;佔同一時期;巧合: *They could not go to the theatre together because his free time never ~d with hers.* 他們無法一同去看戲,因爲他們的閑暇從來湊不到一起。 **3** (of ideas, etc) be in harmony or agreement: (指意見等)一致;協調: *The judges did not ~ in opinion.* 裁判們的意見不一致。*His tastes and habits ~ with those of his wife.* 他的嗜好和習慣與他妻子的恰好一致。

co·inci·dence /kəʊ'ɪnsɪdəns ; ko'ɪnsədəns/ *n* [U] the condition of coinciding; [C] instance of this, happening by chance: 同時發生;符合;巧合;巧合之事: *by a curious ~.* 剛好;湊巧;碰巧。*What a ~!* How curious, etc that these two events should come together! 多麼湊巧的事情啊! (這兩件事發生在同時,多麼巧啊!) **co·inci·dent** /-dənt ; -dənt/ *adj* coinciding. 同時發生的;一致的;巧合的。**co·inci·den·tal** /kəʊˌɪnsɪ'dentl ; koˏɪnsə'dɛntl/ *adj* of the nature of a, exhibiting ~. 巧合性的;巧合的。

coir /'kɔɪə(r) ; kɔɪr/ *n* fibre from coconut shells, used for making ropes, matting, etc. 椰子殼之纖維(用以製繩、蓆等)。

co·ition /kəʊ'ɪʃn ; ko'ɪʃən/ *n* = coitus.

co·itus /'kəʊɪtəs ; 'ko·ɪtəs/ *n* [U] (formal) sexual intercourse to the point of (mutual) orgasm between two human beings; the insertion of the penis into the vagina. (正式用語) (雙方) 達性慾高潮的性交;性交;交媾。

coke[1] /kəʊk ; kok/ *n* [U] rough, light substance that remains when gas has been taken out of coal by heating it in an oven, used as a fuel in stoves and furnaces. (將煤置於爐中加熱去掉煤氣後所剩餘的)焦炭;焦煤(作爲火爐或熔爐之燃料)。□ *vt* turn (coal) into ~. 將(煤)製成焦煤。

coke[2] /kəʊk ; kok/ *n* (P) (colloq abbr of) Coca-Cola. (商標) (俗)可口可樂 (Coca-Cola 之略)。

coke[3] /kəʊk ; kok/ *n* (sl) cocaine. (俚)古柯鹼。

coker·nut /'kəʊkənʌt ; 'kokɚˏnʌt/ *n* = coconut.

col /kɒl ; kɑl/ *n* depression or pass in a mountain range. (山脈中的)峽口;峽路;隘口。⇨ the illus at mountain. 參看 mountain 之插圖。

cola /'kəʊlə ; 'kolə/ *n* = kola

col·an·der, cul·len·der /'kʌləndə(r) ; 'kʌləndɚ/ *n* bowl-shaped vessel or dish with many small holes, used to drain off water from vegetables, etc in cooking. 濾鍋;濾盆(上有許多小孔,烹調時用以漏去蔬菜等中之水)。

cold[1] /kəʊld ; kold/ *adj* **1** of low temperature, esp when compared with the human body: 氣溫低的;寒冷的; 冷的 (尤指與人的體溫相比而言): *~ weather;* 寒冷的天氣; *a ~ wind;* 寒風;冷風; *feel ~;* 感覺冷;

a hotel with hot and ~ water in every bedroom. 每間房間都有冷熱水設備的旅館。 ***give sb the ~ shoulder,*** (fig) snub him; show distaste for his company. (喻)以冷淡態度對待某人;表示不歡迎某人。 Hence, 由此產生, ˌ**~-ˈshoulder** *vt* [VP6A] snub. 冷落;輕待。 ***have ~ feet,*** feel afraid or reluctant (to do sth involving risk or danger). 感覺害怕或遲疑(而不敢做冒險或危險的事)。 ***leave one ~,*** leave one unmoved, unimpressed. 未能打動某人的心,沒使其留下深刻印象。 ***(kill sb) in ~ blood; make one's ˈblood run ~,*** ⇨ blood¹. ***pour/throw ~ water on,*** ⇨ water¹(1). ˈ**~ chisel,** one for cutting soft metals while they are ~. 冷鏨(用以切割冷却之軟金屬的鏨子)。 ˌ**~ ˈcomfort,** poor consolation. 令人寒心的事。 ˈ**~ cream,** ointment for cleansing and softening the skin. 冷霜(清潔並滋潤皮膚的油膏)。 ˌ**~ ˈfront,** ⇨ front(7). ˌ**~ ˈmeat,** meat that has been cooked and cooled: (煮熟的)冷肉: *~ meat for supper.* 晚餐吃的冷肉。 ˌ**~ ˈsteel,** [U] cutting or stabbing weapon (eg a sword or bayonet contrasted with firearms). 砍或刺戳的武器(如劍或刺刀,以別於槍砲)。 ˌ**~ ˈturkey,** ⇨ turkey. ˌ**~ ˈwar,** struggle for superiority waged by hostile propaganda, economic measures, etc without actual fighting. 冷戰(藉宣傳、經濟措施等,而非藉實際戰鬥以獲得優勢)。 ˌ**~-ˈblooded** /-ˈblʌdɪd ; -ˈblʌdɪd/ *adj* **(a)** having blood that varies with the temperature (eg fish, reptiles). 冷血的;血液能隨溫度而改變的(如魚、爬蟲類)。 **(b)** (fig of persons, their actions) without feeling; pitiless. (喻)(指人,人之行為)無情的;無憐憫心的;冷酷的。 ˌ**~-ˈhearted** /-ˈhɑːtɪd ; -ˈhɑrtɪd/ *adj* without sympathy; indifferent. 無同情心的;冷漠的。 **2** (fig) (喻) **(a)** unkind; unfriendly: 冷淡的;不親熱的: *a ~ greeting/welcome, etc.* 冷淡的招呼(歡迎等)。 **(b)** sexually unresponsive. 性方面無反應的;性冷感的。 **3** (of colours) suggesting ~, eg grey and blue. (指顏色)令人感覺涼爽的(如灰色和藍色)。 **~·ly** *adv* **~·ness** *n* [U] state of being ~: 冷;寒冷: *Because of the ~ness of the weather, we stayed indoors.* 因為天氣寒冷,所以我們待在室內。

cold² /kəʊld ; kold/ *n* **1** [U] **(the) ~,** relative absence of heat; low temperature (esp in the atmosphere): 冷;寒冷;低溫度(尤指氣溫): *He was shivering with ~.* 他冷得直發抖。 *He disliked both the heat of summer and the ~ of winter.* 他既不喜歡夏天之熱,也不喜歡冬天之冷。 *Don't stay outside in the ~, come indoors by the fire.* 不要待在外面受寒,到室內火爐邊來。 ***(be left) out in the ~,*** (fig) (be) ignored or neglected. (喻)(被)冷落。 **2** [U] (phys) freezing-point of water or below. (物理)(水之)冰點或冰點以下: *five degrees of ~.* 冰點以下五度。 **3** [C, U] inflammation of the mucous membrane of the nose or throat: 傷風;感冒: *have a ~;* 患傷風;感冒; *catch (a) ~.* 受涼;感冒。 *Half the boys in the school were absent with ~s.* 半數的男生均因患感冒而缺席。

cole·slaw /ˈkəʊlslɔː ; ˈkolˌslɔ/ *n* [U] finely shredded dressed raw cabbage (as a salad). 切絲生拌的包心菜(作生菜食用)。

colic /ˈkɒlɪk ; ˈkɑlɪk/ *n* [U] severe pain in the stomach and bowels without diarrhoea. 腹部絞痛(但無腹瀉);疚痛。

co·li·tis /kəˈlaɪtɪs ; koˈlaɪtɪs/ *n* [U] (med) inflammation of the mucous membrane of the colon. (醫)結腸炎(結腸黏膜發炎)。

col·lab·or·ate /kəˈlæbəreɪt ; kəˈlæbəˌret/ *vi* **1** [VP2A, 3A] **~ *(on sth) (with sb),*** work in partnership, esp in literature or art: (尤指文學或藝術方面)(與某人)合著;合作(某作品): *~ on a biography with a friend.* 與一朋友合著一部傳記。 **2** [VP3A] ***~ with,*** work treasonably, esp with enemy forces occupying one's country. 做叛國的工作(尤指與佔領的敵軍合作);勾結(敵人);通敵。 **col·lab·or·ator** /kəˈlæbəreɪtə(r) ; kəˈlæbəˌretɚ/ *n* person who ~s(1, 2). 合著者;合作者;通敵者。 **col·lab·or·ation** /kəˌlæbəˈreɪʃn ; kəˌlæbəˈreʃən/ *n* [U] collaborating: 合著;合作;通敵: *working in collaboration with others.* 與別人合作。 **col·lab·or·ation·ist** /kəˌlæbəˈreɪʃənɪst ; kəˌlæbəˈreʃənɪst/ *n* person who ~s(2). 通敵者。

col·lage /ˈkɒlɑːʒ *US:* kəˈlɑːʒ ; kəˈlɑʒ/ *n* [U, C] (art) (picture made by an) unusual combination of bits of paper, cloth, photographs, metal etc. (藝術)(用紙片、碎布、照片、金屬等的)美術拼貼;拼貼畫。

col·lapse /kəˈlæps ; kəˈlæps/ *vi* [VP2A] **1** fall down or in; come or break to pieces suddenly: 倒塌;塌陷: *The weight of the snow on the roof caused the shed to ~.* 棚頂積雪的重量使得小棚倒塌。 *The roof ~d under the weight of the snow.* 屋頂因積雪的重壓而塌陷。 *If you cut the ropes of a tent, it will ~.* 如果你割斷帳蓬的繩索,它就會倒塌。 **2** lose physical strength, courage, mental powers, etc; break down: 失去體力、勇氣、心智能力等;病倒;頹喪;崩潰;瓦解: *If you work too hard you/your health may ~.* 如果你辛勞過度,你會病倒。 *Our plans will ~ unless we get more help.* 我們的計畫將會瓦解,除非我們能得到更多的幫助。 *The price of copper ~d,* dropped to a low level. 銅的價錢暴跌。 **3** (of apparatus) close or fold up. (指器械)摺疊。 **4** *vt* [VP6A] cause to ~: 使倒塌;使崩潰;使摺疊: *~ a canvas chair.* 將一帆布椅摺起。 □ *n* collapsing: 倒塌;崩潰;病倒;(價格之)暴跌: *the ~ of a table/tent/tower, etc;* 桌子(帳篷,塔等)的倒塌; (fig): (喻): *the ~ of their plans/hopes;* 他們的計畫(希望)的破滅; *suffer a nervous ~.* 精神崩潰。 **col·laps·ible, -able** /-səbl ; -səbl̩/ *adj* that can be ~d(4) (for packing, etc): 可摺疊(以便包裝等)的: *a collapsible boat/chair.* 可摺疊的小船(椅子)。

col·lar /ˈkɒlə(r) ; ˈkɑlɚ/ *n* **1** part of a garment that fits round the neck; turned-over neckband of a shirt, dress, etc: 衣領;領: *The wind was so cold that he turned his coat ~ up.* 風太冷了,所以他把外套的領子翻起來。 ***ˈblue/ˈwhite ~ workers,*** ⇨ blue, white. **2** separate article of clothing (linen, lace, etc) worn round the neck and fastened to a shirt or blouse. (可與襯衫或短上衣扣合,用亞麻布、花邊等做成的)假領;領飾。 ˈ**~ stud** *n* small button-like device for fastening a ~ to a shirt. 領扣(用以將衣領與襯衫扣合)。 **3** band of leather, etc put round the neck of a dog, horse or other animal. (狗、馬或其他動物頸間所繫,用皮革等做的)項圈。 ⇨ the illus at harness. 參看 harness 之插圖。 **4** metal band joining two pipes, rods or shafts, eg in a machine. (連結兩管、兩桿或機械之軸之)環管;軸環。 **5** ˈ**~·bone** *n* bone joining the shoulder and the breast-bone. (連接肩與胸骨的)鎖骨。 ⇨ the illus at skeleton. 參看 skeleton 之插圖。 □ *vt* [VP6A] **1** seize (sb) by the ~; take hold of roughly: 扭住(某人的)領子;抓住: *The policeman ~ed the thief.* 警察抓住那竊賊。 **2** (dated colloq) take without permission: (過時俗語)未得許可而拿走;擅取: *Who's ~ed my pen?* 誰把我的鋼筆拿去了?

col·late /kəˈleɪt ; kəˈlet/ *vt* [VP6A] make a careful comparison between (copies of texts, manuscripts, books, etc) to learn the differences between them: 詳細比較(若干本正文、原稿、書籍等)以尋出其間差別;對照;校勘: *~ a new edition with an earlier edition.* 將新版本與舊版本作詳細比較。

col·lat·eral /kəˈlætərəl ; kəˈlætərəl/ *adj* **1** secondary or subordinate but from the same source: 次要的;附屬的;附帶的(但係同一來源): *~ evidence;* 附屬證據; *~ security,* property, eg stocks or bonds, pledged as security for repayment of a loan. (保證歸還借款之)抵押品(如股票或債券)。 **2** descended from a common ancestor but in a different line, ie through different sons or daughters. (指親屬)旁系的(如兄弟姊妹之子女是)。 □ *n* [U] ~ security. 抵押品。

col·la·tion /kəˈleɪʃn ; kɑˈleʃən/ *n* [C] (formal) light meal, (usu 通常作 *cold ~*), often one served at a time different from usual meal times. (正式用語)(常指正餐時間以外所備的)便餐。

col·league /ˈkɒliːg ; ˈkɑlig/ *n* one of two or more persons working together and (usu) having similar rank and duties: (在一起工作,通常並有同等階級和職務的)同事;同僚: *the Prime Minister and his ~s*, the other members of the Cabinet. 首相及其同僚(即其內閣之閣員)。

col·lect¹ /kəˈlekt ; kəˈlɛkt/ *vt, vi* **1** [VP6A, 15B] **~ (up / together)**, bring or gather together; get from a number of persons or places: 收集;搜集;募集: *The teacher told the boys to ~ (up / together) all the waste paper lying about after the picnic and burn it.* 那老師告訴男學生們,在野餐以後把四處散置的廢紙撿集起來燒掉。*If he could ~ all the money people owe him, he would be a rich man.* 假使他能够把所有別人欠他的錢都要到手,他就會成爲一位富翁了。*A man who ~s taxes is called a tax-~or.* 收稅的人叫稅務員。 **2** [VP6A] obtain specimens of (books, stamps, etc), eg as a hobby or in order to study sth: 蒐集(書籍、郵票等)之樣品(例如作爲癖好或爲了研究): *~ foreign stamps / old china.* 蒐集外國郵票(古瓷器)。 **3** [VP2A, C] **~ (together)**, come together: 聚集;聚積: *A crowd soon ~s (together) when there's a street accident.* 當街頭發生意外事件的時候,立刻就有一群人聚集起來。 **4** [VP6A] fetch: 拿來;接來: *~ a child from school.* 自校中接回小孩。 **5** [VP6A] gather together, recover control of (one's thoughts, energies, oneself): 使(思想、精力)集中;使(心神)鎮定: *Before you begin to make a speech, you should ~ your thoughts and ideas.* 在你開始發表演說之前,你應當集中你的思想和意念。□ *adj, adv* (US comm) paid for on delivery: (美商)收到時即付款的(地);由收件人付款的(地): *a ~ telegram.* 收報人付款的電報。*I'll pay for the goods ~*, when they are delivered. 我收到貨時卽會付款。 **~ed** *adj* (esp of a person) calm; not distracted. (尤指人)鎮靜的;心思不亂的。 **~ed·ly** *adv*

col·lect² /ˈkɒlekt ; ˈkɑlɛkt/ *n* short prayer of the Church of Rome or the Church of England, to be read on certain appointed days. (天主教或英國國教之在某些指定的日子所念的)短祈禱文。

col·lec·tion /kəˈlekʃn ; kəˈlɛkʃən/ *n* **1** [U] collecting; [C] instance of this: 收集; 收取: *How many ~s of letters are there every day*, How often does the postman empty the boxes? 郵差每天收幾次信? **2** [C] group of objects that have been collected and that belong together: 蒐集品;收藏品(所收藏的同類物品): *a fine ~ of old swords / paintings / postage stamps.* 所收藏的一批珍貴的古劍(圖畫,郵票)。 **3** heap of materials or objects that have come together: 聚集在一起的東西;聚積物: *a ~ of dust / rubbish.* 一堆灰塵(垃圾)。 **4** [C] money collected at a meeting, a Church service, etc. (集會、禮拜等時候)所募集的捐款。***take (up) / make a ~***: *The ~ will be taken (up) / made after the sermon.* 在講道之後將作捐獻。

col·lec·tive /kəˈlektɪv ; kəˈlɛktɪv/ *adj* **1** of a group or society (of persons, nations, etc) as a whole: 群體的;社會的;共有的;集體的(指人、國家等): *~ leadership*, (emphasis on) government by a group rather than an individual; 集體領導(强調由一群人而非一個人所領導的政治); *~ ownership of the land / of means of production, etc*, by all citizens for the benefit of all; 土地(生產工具等)之集體所有權(爲全體公民所有並享用); *~ security*, security of a State or States against aggression by means of common military, etc preparedness. 集體安全(一國或數國爲抵抗侵略在軍事等方面所作之共同的防禦措施)。 **~ farm**, (eg in a Socialist State) one owned by the State and run by the workers for the benefit of all the citizens. 集體農場(如在社會主義國家中者,農場爲國家所有,爲工人所經營,利益歸全民所享)。 **2 ~ noun**, (gram) one that is singular in form but stands for many individuals, as *cattle, crowd, audience*: (文法)集合名詞(形式上是單數但實際上代表許多個體之名詞,如 cattle, crowd, audience): *In 'to catch fish', fish is a ~ noun.* 在 to catch fish 中, fish 是集合名詞。 **col·lec·tiv·ize** /kəˈlektɪvaɪz ; kəˈlɛktɪˌvaɪz/ *vt* [VP6A] change, eg farm lands, from private ownership to a system of State control. 變私有(如耕地)爲國有;使集體化。 **col·lec·tiv·iz·ation** /kəˌlektɪvaɪˈzeɪʃn *US:* -vɪˈz- ; kəˌlɛktəvəˈzeʃən/ *n*

col·lec·tor /kəˈlektə(r) ; kəˈlɛktə/ *n* person who collects: 收集者;蒐集者;收藏者: *a 'stamp-~;* 集郵者; *a 'tax-~;* 收稅人;稅務員; *a 'ticket-~*, eg at a railway station. (火車站等之)收票員。 **~'s item / piece**, article sought by ~s, eg a book, a piece of china or furniture, because of its beauty, rarity, etc. 收藏家所尋求之物(如珍貴的書籍、瓷器或傢具)。

col·leen /ˈkɒliːn ; ˈkɑlin/ *n* (Irish) young girl. (愛爾蘭語)少女。

col·lege /ˈkɒlɪdʒ ; ˈkɑlɪdʒ/ *n* **1** [C, U] school for higher or professional education; body of teachers and students forming part of a university; their building(s): 高等教育機關;專科學校;學院(爲大學之一部份,可指其師生全體,亦可指其建築物): *go to ~;* 讀大學;上大學; *be at ~;* 在大學求學; *a C~ of Agriculture / Pharmacy, etc;* 農(藥等)學院; *the Oxford and Cambridge ~s;* 牛津及劍橋諸學院; *Heads of C~s*, ⇨ for their titles Master¹(9), President, Principal, Provost, Rector, Warden. 大學之首長(其正式頭銜參看 Master¹(9), President, Principal, Provost, Rector, Warden)。 **2** [C] union of persons with common purposes and privileges: (有共同目的和特權的)學會;社團: *the C~ of Surgeons;* 外科醫師學會; *the C~ of Cardinals*, who elect and advise the Pope. 紅衣主教團(可選舉教宗並爲其顧問)。 **col·le·giate** /kəˈliːdʒɪət ; kəˈlidʒɪɪt/ *adj* of or like a ~ or ~ student: 專科學校的;學院的;大學的;大學生的: *collegiate life*, life in ~s and universities. 大學生活。

col·lide /kəˈlaɪd ; kəˈlaɪd/ *vi* [VP2A, C, 3A] **~ (with)**, **1** come together violently; meet and strike: 互撞;碰撞: *As the bus came round the corner, it ~d with a van.* 公共汽車在轉過街角時與一輛貨車互撞。*The bus and the van ~d.* 公共汽車與貨車互撞。*The ships ~d in the fog.* 船在濃霧中互撞。 **2** be opposed; be in conflict: 相反;衝突: *If the aims of two countries ~, there may be war* 如果兩國的目標衝突,就可能發生戰爭。

col·lie /ˈkɒlɪ ; ˈkɑlɪ/ *n* Scottish sheep-dog with shaggy hair. 蘇格蘭產之老毛牧羊犬。⇨ the illus at dog. 參看 dog 之插圖。

col·lier /ˈkɒlɪə(r) ; ˈkɑljə/ *n* **1** coal-miner. 煤礦工人。 **2** ship that carries coal as cargo. 運煤船。

col·liery /ˈkɒljərɪ ; ˈkɑljərɪ/ *n* (*pl* -ries) coal-mine (and the buildings, etc connected with it). 煤礦場(包括附屬建築物等)。

col·li·sion /kəˈlɪʒn ; kəˈlɪʒən/ *n* [U] colliding; [C] instance of this: 互撞;猛烈碰撞;互撞之實例;衝突;抵觸: *a head-on ~ between two buses;* 兩輛公共汽車迎面互撞; *a railway ~;* 火車撞車事件; *on (a) '~ course*, likely to collide. 可能互撞。 ***be in / come into ~ (with)***, have collided / collide (with): (與…)互撞: *The liner is reported to have been in ~ with an oil-tanker.* 據報導該客船與一油輪互撞。*The two ships were in / came into ~.* 兩船互撞。*People with revolutionary ideas may find themselves in ~ with the forces of the law*, get into trouble with the police. 抱有革命思想的人可能和執法的人發生衝突。

col·lo·cate /ˈkɒləkeɪt ; ˈkɑloˌket/ *vi* [VP2A, 3A] **~ (with)**, (of words) combine in a way characteristic of language: (指字)(按習慣用法與…)搭配;連用: *'Weak' ~s with 'tea' but 'feeble' does not.* weak 與 tea 連用而 feeble 則不能。 **col·lo·ca·tion** /ˌkɑləˈkeɪʃn ; ˌkɑloˈkeʃən/ *n* [C, U] coming together; collocating of words: (字之)配置;搭配;連用: *'Strong* *tea' and 'heavy drinker' are English collocations; so are 'by accident' and 'so as to'.* strong tea 與 heavy drinker 都是英語中習慣上的搭配；by accident 及 so as to 也是。

col·loquial /kəˈləʊkwɪəl ; kəˈlokwɪəl/ *adj* (of words, phrases, style) belonging to, suitable for, ordinary conversation; not formal or literary. (指字、辭、風格)屬於或適於日常會話的；非正式的；非文學性的；通俗的；口語的。**~·ly** *adv* **~·ism** *n* [C] ~ word or phrase. 俗字；俗語；口語說法。

col·lo·quy /ˈkɒləkwɪ ; ˈkɑləkwɪ/ *n* (*pl* -quies) [C, U] (formal) conversation: (正式用語) 談話；會談：*engage in ~ with sb.* 與某人會談。

col·lu·sion /kəˈluːʒn ; kəˈluʒən/ *n* [U] secret agreement or understanding for a deceitful or fraudulent purpose: 暗中串通；勾結；共謀(以騙人)：*act in ~ with sb;* 與某人暗中串通；*~ between persons who appear to be opposed to each other.* 二人表面佯裝互相反對而實際暗中勾結。**col·lus·ive** /kəˈluːsɪv ; kəˈlusɪv/ *adj*

colly·wobbles /ˈkɒlɪwɒblz ; ˈkɑlɪˌwɑbl̩z/ *n* (colloq) stomach-ache; slight feeling of fear (with nausea). (俗) 肚子痛；(有噁心的)輕微的害怕。

co·lon[1] /ˈkəʊlən ; ˈkolən/ *n* lower and greater part of the large intestine. 結腸(大腸下端之較大的部份)。⇨ the illus at alimentary. 參看 alimentary 之插圖。

co·lon[2] /ˈkəʊlən ; ˈkolən/ *n* punctuation mark (:) used in writing and printing (to direct special attention to what follows). 冒號(書寫及印刷中的標點符號，即(:)，以指示特別注意下列者)。⇨ App 9. 參看附錄九。

colo·nel /ˈkɜːnl ; ˈkɝnl̩/ *n* army officer above a lieutenant-~ and (in US) commanding a regiment; (abbr for) lieutenant-~. 陸軍上校(在中校之上，在美國統率一團軍隊)；陸軍中校 (lieutenant-colonel 之略稱)。

co·lo·nial /kəˈləʊnɪəl ; kəˈlonɪəl/ *adj* **1** of a colony or colonies(1). 殖民地的。**ˈC~ Office,** (GB) former State department in charge of colonies. (英) (昔日之)殖民部(專司殖民地事務)。**2** (esp US) in the style of architecture in the British colonies in N America before and during the Revolution. (尤美) (在美國革命以前或期中)北美洲英國殖民地之建築式的。□ *n* inhabitant of a colony(1), esp a descendant of those who colonized it. 殖民地居民；(尤指)殖民地開拓者之後裔。**~·ism** *n* [U] policy of having colonies(1) and keeping them dependent. 殖民政策；殖民主義。**~·ist** *n* supporter of ~ism; one who favours the retention of colonies(1). 支持殖民政策者；殖民主義者。

col·on·ist /ˈkɒlənɪst ; ˈkɑlənɪst/ *n* pioneer settler in a colony(1). 開拓新殖民地者。

col·on·ize /ˈkɒlənaɪz ; ˈkɑləˌnaɪz/ *vt* [VP6A] establish a colony in; establish as a colony: 開拓殖民地於；殖民於：*The ancient Greeks ~d many parts of the Mediterranean.* 古代希臘人在地中海區域開拓了許多殖民地。**col·on·iz·ation** /ˌkɒlənaɪˈzeɪʃn *US:* -nɪˈz- ; ˌkɑlənəˈzeʃən/ *n* [U] colonizing: 開拓殖民地；拓殖；殖民：*the colonization of N America by the British, Dutch and French.* 英國人，荷蘭人和法國人對北美洲之拓殖。**col·on·izer** *n* one who helps to establish a colony(1). 幫助建立殖民地的人；殖民地開拓者。

col·on·nade /ˌkɒləˈneɪd ; ˌkɑləˈned/ *n* row of columns(1) set (usu) at equal distances. (通常爲)距離相等的一列柱子；柱廊。⇨ the illus at column. 參看 column 之插圖。**col·on·naded** /ˌkɒləˈneɪdɪd ; ˌkɑləˈnedɪd/ *adj* having a ~. 有柱廊的。

col·ony /ˈkɒlənɪ ; ˈkɑlənɪ/ *n* (*pl* -nies) **1** country or territory settled by migrants from another country, and controlled by it. 殖民地(由某國移民所定居的國家或領土，且爲該國所控制者)。**2** group of people from another country, or of people with the same trade, profession or occupation, living together: 來自他國並生活在一起的一批人民；僑民；同行業並生活在一起的一群人：*the American ~ in Paris;* 在巴黎的美國僑民；*a ~ of artists,* eg one living in a place famous for its scenic beauty. 一群藝術家(如居於著名的風景優美之地者)。**3** (biol) number of animals or plants, living or growing together: (生物)羣居或生長在一起的若干動物或植物；羣體：*a ~ of ants.* 一窩螞蟻。

color (US) = colour.

col·ora·tura /ˌkɒlərəˈtʊərə ; ˌkʌlərəˈtjʊrə/ *n* [U] flowery or ornamental passages in vocal music; 歌曲中的華彩部份；華彩；花腔；(attrib) (形容用法)：*a ~ soprano.* 華彩女高音；花腔女高音。

co·los·sal /kəˈlɒsl ; kəˈlɑsl̩/ *adj* immense. 巨大的。

co·los·sus /kəˈlɒsəs ; kəˈlɑsəs/ *n* (*pl* -lossi /-ˈlɒsaɪ ; -ˈlɑsaɪ/, ~es /-ˈlɒsəsɪz ; -ˈlɑsəsɪz/) immense statue (esp of a man, much greater than life-size); immense person or personification of sth. 巨大的雕像(尤指大於眞人的人像)；巨人；某物之巨大的擬人像。

col·our[1] (US = **color**) /ˈkʌlə(r) ; ˈkʌlɚ/ *n* **1** [U] sensation produced in the eye by rays of decomposed light; [C] effect produced by a ray of light of a particular wavelength, or by a mixture of these: 顏色；色彩(白光分解以後之各種光線在眼中所產生的感覺；具有某種特定波長的光線或混合光線所產生的效果)：*~ films;* 彩色底片；彩色影片；*~ TV.* 彩色電視(機)。*Red, blue and yellow are ~s.* 紅、藍和黃都是顏色。*There isn't enough ~ in the picture.* 這幅畫中的色彩不够。**ˈ~-blind** *adj* unable to distinguish between certain ~s, or to see certain ~s. 色盲的(不能分辨或看不見某些顏色的)。**ˈ~ scheme** *n* scheme for combination of ~s in a design (eg for the furnishing and decoration of a room, the planting of a flower garden). 色彩設計(如房間內部裝潢的設計，花園中花卉種植的設計)。**ˈ~-wash** *n* coloured distemper. 彩色塗料。**2** [U] redness of the face: 面部的紅潤之色；血色：*She has very little ~,* has a pale face. 她面上幾無血色(面色蒼白)。***change ~,*** grow paler or redder than usual. 面部變色(變白或變紅)。***have a high ~,*** have a red complexion. 面部緋紅。***lose ~,*** become pale. 臉色變白；失色。***be/feel/look off ~,*** (colloq) be/seem unwell, in low spirits. (俗)氣色不好；神情沮喪。**3** (*pl*) materials used by artists; paint: (複) (畫家用的)顏料：*ˈwater-~s;* 水彩顏料；*ˈoil-~s;* 油畫顏料；⇨ oil, water; appearance produced by their use: 由於使用色彩所產生的外觀：*paint sth in bright/dark ~s,* (fig) make it appear favourable/unfavourable. (喻) 對某事物加以粉飾 (貶抑)；强調其光明 (黑暗) 面。***(see sth/appear) in its true ~s,*** as it really is. 看清某事物的眞相(原形畢露)。**4** [U] (of events, descriptions) appearance of reality or truth; pretext. (指事件、描寫)表面的眞實性；託辭。***give/lend ~ to,*** give an appearance of probability to: 使有某種跡象；使看起來有可能；使顯得可信：*His torn clothing gave ~ to his story that he had been attacked and robbed.* 他被撕破的衣服使他所說被襲擊和搶刼的事顯得可信。***give false ~ to,*** give a wrong character or tone to: 曲解；歪曲(事實眞相)：*Newspapers often give false ~ to the news they report,* twist the meaning to suit their aims. 報紙常常對其所報導的新聞加以曲解(以求配合其目的)。**5** ***local ~,*** (in literature) use of details to make a description of a place, scene or time realistic. (文學中的)地方色彩(利用細節使對某一地方、場面或時間的描寫有眞實感)。**6** (in music) [U] timbre, quality; variety of expression. (音樂) 音質；音色；表現法之變化。**7** (*pl*) ribbon, dress, cap, etc, worn as a symbol of a party, a club, a school, etc, or to show ownership of a race-horse, etc: (複)徽章；(代表黨派、會社、學校等之)有顏色的絲帶、制服、帽等；(代表賽跑馬匹之主人等的)色彩標識：*The owner of a horse is always glad to see his ~s get to the winning-post first,* to see his horse win a race. 馬主永遠高興看到戴着他的標識的馬最先到達終點。***get/win one's ~s,*** (at college, etc) be awarded a place in a sports team. (在大學等)被選爲某運動隊的隊員。

8 (*pl*) flag (of a ship); ensign or standard of a regiment: (複) 船旗；隊旗；軍旗: *salute the ~s;* 向軍旗敬禮; *serve with／join the ~s,* the Navy, Army or Air Force. (在海軍,陸軍或空軍) 服兵役 (從軍)。***come through／off with flying ~s,*** make a great success of sth. 凱旋；奏凱歌；大爲成功。***lower one's ~s,*** give up one's demands or position; surrender. 放棄要求或立場；讓步；投降。***nail one's ~s to the mast,*** make a decision, announce it, and show strong determination not to change it. 做了一項決定,宣佈出去,並且顯示堅强的決心,永不加以更改；宣揚永不改變的決心。***sail under false ~s,*** be a hypocrite or impostor. 打着假招牌騙人。***show one's true ~s,*** show what one really is. 露出眞面目。***stick to one's ~s,*** refuse to change one's opinion or party. 堅持自己的主張；不改其志；忠於其黨。 **9** [U] racial characteristic of skin ~. 代表種族特徵的膚色。**'~-bar,** legal and／or social distinction between different races. 膚色隔閡 (不同人種之間在法律上和社會上的差別地位)。**~·ful** /-fl ; -fəl/ *adj* full of ~; bright; gay; exciting; vivid, etc: 富有色彩的；鮮艷的；多采多姿的；生動的: *a ~ful scene;* 多采多姿的景色； *a ~ful style of writing;* 多采多姿的文體；生動的文體； *lead a ~ful life.* 過一種多采多姿 (富於刺激性) 的生活。**~·less** *adj* without ~; pale; (fig) lacking in interest, character, vividness: 無色的；蒼白的；(喻) 無趣味的；無特色的；不生動的: *a ~less style;* 不生動的文體； *leading a ~less existence.* 過着平淡的生活。

col·our[2] (US = **color**) /ˈkʌlə(r) ; ˈkʌlɚ/ *vt, vi* **1** [VP6A, 22] give colour to; put colour on: 染色；着色；塗顏色於: *~ a wall green.* 將牆壁塗爲綠色。**2** [VP2A, C] ~ ***(up),*** take on colour; blush: 變爲有色；變色；變紅: *The leaves have begun to ~,* to take on their autumn colours of yellow, brown, etc. 樹葉已開始變色 (變成秋天的黃、褐等色)。*The girl is so shy that she ~s (up) whenever a man speaks to her.* 那女孩非常害羞,每當一個男人跟她講話時,她就臉紅。 **3** [VP6A] change or misrepresent in some way: 渲染；歪曲: *News is often ~ed,* changed to suit the views of those who supply it or those who will read it. 新聞常被歪曲報導 (以符合報導者或讀者的觀點)。*Travellers' tales are often highly ~ed,* exaggerated. 旅行者的故事常是極爲誇大的。**~ed** *adj* **1** (in compounds) having the colour specified: (用於複合字中) 有某種顏色的: *'cream-~ed;* 奶油色的； *'flesh-~ed.* 肉色的。 **2** (of persons) partly of European descent; (esp) of the Negro race. (指人) 具有部分歐洲人血統的；有色人種的；(尤指) 黑種的。**(Cape) C~ed** *n* South African person of mixed race. 南非的混血種人。 **~·ing** *n* [U] sth that produces colour; face colour; style in which sth is ~ed; style in which an artist uses colour. 顏料；面色；着色的格調；(藝術家) 用色的風格；着色法；色調。

colt[1] /kəʊlt ; kolt/ *n* young horse (male) up to the age of 4 or 5, ⇨ filly; (四、五歲以下的) 雄駒；(fig) young man with little experience. (喻) 無經驗的年青人。**~·ish** /ˈkəʊltɪʃ ; ˈkoltɪʃ/ *adj* like a ~; frisky. 似小馬的；蹦蹦跳跳的；活潑的。

colt[2] /kəʊlt ; kolt/ *n* (P) (US) early type of revolver or pistol. (商標) (美) 卡爾特式手槍 (一種早期的左輪或手槍)。

col·ter /ˈkəʊltə(r) ; ˈkoltɚ/ (US) = coulter.

col·um·bine /ˈkɒləmbaɪn ; ˈkɑləm͵baɪn/ *n* garden plant with spur-shaped flowers and petals. 耬斗菜 (花及花瓣形似刺馬釘)。

col·umn /ˈkɒləm ; ˈkɑləm/ *n* **1** tall, upright pillar, usu of stone, either supporting or decorating part of a building, or standing alone as a monument. 柱；圓柱；石柱 (或用以支持屋頂,或用以裝飾建築物的一部份,或獨立作爲紀念碑)。 **2** sth shaped like or suggesting a ~: 柱狀物: *a ~ of smoke* (rising straight up); 向上直昇的煙柱； *the spinal ~,* the backbone; 脊椎骨；脊柱； *a ~ of mercury* (in a thermometer); (寒暑表中的) 水銀柱； *a refining ~,* one in which oil, heated to vapour, is refined into fuel oil, petrol, etc. 精煉柱 (原油在其中加熱蒸發,以提煉成燃油、汽油等)。 **3** vertical division of a printed page (eg of this page); or of a newspaper, occupied regularly by one subject: 直欄 (如本頁中者)；(報紙上經常爲一主題所佔用的) 專欄；欄: *the correspondence ~s of 'The Times';* '泰晤士報'上的通訊欄； *the advertising ~s.* 廣告欄。**4** series of numbers arranged under one another: 直式排列的一列數字；縱行: *add up a long ~ of figures.* 加起一長列的數字。 **5** line of ships following one another; deep arrangement of soldiers in short ranks, one behind the other. (艦隊的) 縱隊柱；行；(軍隊的) 縱隊 (橫排很短而縱深順次配置的隊形)。 **fifth ~,** ⇨ fifth. **col·um·nist** /ˈkɒləmnɪst ; ˈkɑləmɪst/ *n* journalist who regularly writes a ~ of miscellaneous news, political comment, etc for a newspaper. (爲報紙經常寫新聞雜拾、政治評論等的) 專欄作家。

coma /ˈkəʊmə ; ˈkomə/ *n* unnatural deep sleep usu from injury or illness. (通常因傷或病) 昏迷；昏厥；昏睡。***be in a ~; go into a ~,*** be in, pass into such a sleep. 陷於昏迷狀態。**~·tose** /ˈkəʊmətəʊs ; ˈkɑmə͵tos/ *adj* in a ~; unconscious. 在昏迷狀態中；不省人事的。

comb /kəʊm ; kom/ *n* **1** piece of metal, rubber, plastic, etc with teeth for cleaning the hair, making it tidy, keeping it in place, etc or as an ornament. 梳子 (由金屬、橡皮、塑膠等製成,有齒可以梳理頭髮使之整齊而不蓬亂,亦可作爲裝飾品)。 **2** part of a machine with a ~-like look or purpose, esp for tidying and straightening wool, cotton, etc for manufacture. 梳直羊毛、棉花等之機件中的梳狀部份；梳齒。 **3** wax structure made by bees for

columns

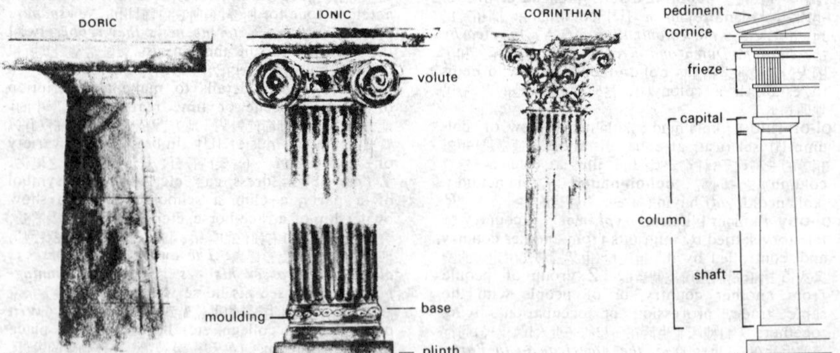

honey. 蜂房;蜂巢(蜜蜂爲產蜜而作的蠟質結構體)。⇨ honey~. **4** red fleshy crest of fowl. 鷄冠。⇨ cocks~. **5** crest of a large wave. (大浪的)浪頭;浪峯。□ *vt, vi* [VP6A, 15B] **1** use a ~ on (the hair). (用梳子)梳(頭髮)。 **2** prepare (wool, flax, etc) with ~s for manufacture. 梳理(羊毛、亞麻等)以供紡織。 **3** search thoroughly: 徹底搜查: *The police ~ed the whole city in their efforts to find the murderer.* 警方搜遍全市,以求找到兇手。 **4** **~ out,** (fig) take out (unwanted things, persons) from a group: (喻)(自團體中)去除(不需要的東西、人): *~ out a government department,* get rid of officials who are not really needed, who are inefficient, etc. 裁汰政府一部門中的冗員、無能者等。Hence, 由此產生, **'~-out** *n* act of getting rid of (unnecessary officials, etc). 淘汰;裁汰(冗員或無能者等)。 **5** [VP2C, 3A] **~ over,** (of a wave) break, curl: (指浪)湧起浪花;滾騰: *waves ~ing over the ship.* 濺至船上的海浪。

com·bat /'kɒmbæt ; 'kɑmbæt/ *n* fight; struggle: 戰鬥;鬥爭;搏鬥;奮鬥;打鬥: (attrib) (形容用法) *a ~ mission.* 戰鬥任務。 **single ~,** fight between two persons only. 一對一的打鬥。□ *vt, vi* [VP6A, 3A] **~ (against/with),** fight; struggle: 戰鬥;鬥爭;搏鬥;奮鬥;打鬥: *~ the enemy;* 與敵人搏鬥; *~ error;* 努力改正錯誤; *a ship ~ing with the wind and waves.* 與風浪搏鬥的船。 **~·ant** /'kɒmbətənt ; 'kɑmbətənt/ *adj* fighting. 戰鬥的;搏鬥的;奮鬥的。□ *n* one who fights: 戰鬥人員: *In modern wars both ~ants and non-~ants are killed in air attacks.* 在現代戰爭中,戰鬥員與非戰鬥員均有可能死於空襲中。 **~·ive** /'kɒmbətɪv ; kəm'bætɪv/ *adj* fond of fighting; ready to fight. 好戰的;好鬥的。 **~·ive·ly** *adv*

com·bi·na·tion /ˌkɒmbɪ'neɪʃn ; ˌkɑmbə'neʃən/ *n* **1** [U] joining or putting together; state of being joined: 聯合;結合;化合;合併;組合: *in ~ with;* 與…聯合在一起; *enter into ~ with;* 與…結合在一起; *every possible ~ and permutation,* every possible arrangement. 每一可能的組合及排列。 **2** [C] number of persons or things that are joined: 結合在一起的若干人或物;團體;組合物: *The college is supported by a ~ of income from endowments and fees from students.* 該學院的經費係由捐款收入及學生所繳的學費聯合支持的。 **'~ room,** (at Cambridge) common-room. (劍橋大學之)教授休息室;學生交誼廳。⇨ common¹(1). **3** [C] motor-bike with sidecar attached. 帶側車的機器脚踏車。 **4** (*pl*) one-piece undergarment covering body and legs. (複)衫褲連在一起的內衣。 **5** [C] formula, complicated arrangement, for the lock (= **'~-lock**) of a safe, strong-room, etc: 保險櫃、保險室等之保險鎖所用的暗碼: *How did the thieves learn the ~ used to open the safe?* 竊盜們如何曉得用以開保險櫃的暗碼?

com·bine¹ /kəm'baɪn ; kəm'baɪn/ *vt, vi* [VP6A, 14, 2A, 3A, 4A] **~ (with),** (cause to) join together; possess at the same time: (使)聯合;連接;結合;同時具有: *We can't always ~ work with pleasure.* 我們不能永遠在工作中享受到樂趣。 *Hydrogen and oxygen ~/Hydrogen ~s with oxygen to form water.* 氫與氧化合成水。 *Some films ~ education with recreation.* 有些影片使教育與娛樂融合在一起。 *Everything ~d against him,* Circumstances, etc made his task difficult or impossible. 一切情勢均對他不利。 **~d operations/exercises,** in which air, sea and land forces work together. 陸、海、空軍聯合作戰(演習)。

com·bine² /'kɒmbaɪn ; 'kɑmbaɪn/ *n* **1** group of persons, trading companies, etc joined for a purpose (such as controlling prices). (個人、貿易公司等爲某一目的,如控制物價,所組織的)團體;組合;聯營組織。 **2** (also 亦作 ˌ**~ 'harvester**) machine that both reaps and threshes (grain). (兼具收割及打穀功能的)聯合收穫機。

com·bust·ible /kəm'bʌstəbl ; kəm'bʌstəbl/ *adj* catching fire and burning easily; (fig, of people) excitable. 容易着火燃燒的;(喻,指人)易激動的;易怒的。□ *n* (usu *pl*) ~ material. (通常用複數)易燃物品。

com·bus·tion /kəm'bʌstʃən ; kəm'bʌstʃən/ *n* [U] process of burning; destruction by fire. 燃燒的過程;燒毀;焚毀;燃燒。⇨ spontaneous.

come /kʌm ; kʌm/ *vi* (*pt* came /keɪm ; kem/, *pp* come) (For uses with *adverbial particles* and *preps,* ⇨ 16 below). (與副詞接語及介詞連用之用法,參看下列第16義)。 **1** [VP2A, B, C, 3A] **~ (to/from) (with),** **(a)** move to be with sb, or to be at a place specified: 來(向說話的人移近);來到(某一地方): *C~ here!* 到這裡來! *Are you coming to my party?* 你來參加我的宴會嗎? *May I come to your party?* 我可以參加你的宴會嗎? *Who are you coming with?* 你同誰一起來? *I'll be coming with Keith.* 我將和基斯一起來。 *I've only ~ for an hour.* 我才來了一小時。 **(b)** arrive: 到達: *Help has ~.* 援助到了。 *They came to a river.* 他們來到了一條河邊。 *He's just ~ from Leeds.* 他剛從里玆來。 **(c)** [VP4A with infinitive of purpose, 與表示目的之不定詞連用, 3A] **~ (for),** move, travel, arrive: (爲…)行動,旅行,到來: *He has ~ here to work.* 他已來此工作。 *They've ~ all the way from London to look for jobs.* 他們老遠從倫敦來找工作。 *He's ~ to get/~ for his book.* 他已來取他的書。 *They've ~ for (= to get) me!* 他們爲我而來(他們來找我的,來接我的)! *C~ to see what I've done* (colloq 俗 *C~ and see what I've done,* ⇨ and(5)). 過來看我做了些什麼。 **(d)** [VP2E] (with a *pres p* to indicate two activities or states that occur together): (與現在分詞連用,表示發生在一起的兩個活動或情況): *The children came running (= ran) to meet us.* 孩子們跑着來迎接我們。 *He came hurrying (= hurried) to her bedside as soon as he heard she was ill.* 一聽到她生病了,他就趕着來到她的床邊。 *She came smiling/crying up to me.* 她笑着(哭着)來到我面前。 **2** [VP2C, E] **~ (into/onto/in/on, etc),** move into, etc the place where the speaker is: 進入(說話者的地方);來到(…地方): *C~ into the hallway out of the rain.* 到走廊裡來避雨。 *The train came puffing into the station.* 火車噴着煙駛入車站。 *Can you ~ out with me for a walk?* 你能跟我出來散散步嗎? *He came back to have a word with me.* 他回來跟我談談。 *The sunshine came streaming through the windows.* 陽光自窗戶射入。 **3** [VP3A] **(a)** **~ to sth,** reach; rise to; fall to (a particular level, figure, point): 到達;升至;降臨於;落至(某一水準、數字、點): *Your bill ~s to £20.* 你的帳單計達二十鎊。 *His earnings ~ to more than £5000 a year.* 他一年所賺的錢超過五千鎊。 **~ to much/little/nothing,** amount to much, etc: 很有(無甚、沒有)結果或作爲: *All his plans came to nothing,* had no result, no success. 他所有的計畫都歸失敗。 *He will never ~ to much,* will never be successful, etc. 他將來絕不會很有作爲。 **~ to this/that, etc,** reach the state of affairs indicated, or a particular state of affairs: 達到上下文所暗示的某種地步;達到某種情況: *What you say ~s to this,* means this. 你所說的話就是這個意思。 *When it ~s to helping his wife with the housework, John never*

a combine harvester

grumbles. 臨到約翰幫忙他太太做家事時,他從不會出怨言。*If it ~s to that...,* If that is the state of affairs.... 如果事已至此…。**(b)** (in fixed phrases) reach the state or condition indicated by the *nouns* for which there is often an equivalent *verb.* (用於固定片語中)達到片語中名詞所表明的情況,此等名詞常有意義相當的動詞。⇨ the *noun* entries. 參看以下各片語之名詞。**~ to an agreement,** agree. 達成協議。**~ to blows (with),** start fighting. 開始打架;(與…)互毆。**~ to a decision,** decide. 決定。**~ to an end,** end, finish. 終止;結束。**~ to fruition,** ripen, mature. 成熟。**~ to a halt/standstill,** stop. 停止;靜止。**~ to light,** become known; be revealed or discovered. 被知曉;被揭露;被發現;顯露。**~ to one's notice/attention,** be noticed. 被人注意;引人注意。**~ to one's senses/oneself, (a)** become conscious after fainting. (昏厥後) 恢復知覺;甦醒;復甦。**(b)** become sensible or normal after behaving foolishly. (行爲一度糊塗後) 恢復明智或正常。**~ to terms (with sb),** reach an agreement. (與某人)達成協議。**4** (used with *into* in numerous phrases) reach the state or condition indicated by the *nouns.* (與 into 連用於許多片語中)達到片語中名詞所表明的情況。⇨ the *nouns* in the phrases. 參看片語中的各名詞。**~ into blossom/bud/flower/leaf,** begin to have blossom, buds, etc. 開始開花(發芽,開花,發葉)。**~ into contact (with sb/sth),** meet sb, touch sth. (與某人)會面;接頭;(與某事物)接觸。**~ into focus,** be sharply defined; become prominent. 輪廓分明;變得明顯。**~ into money/a fortune/a legacy, etc,** receive, inherit it. 接受、承繼或獲得一筆金錢(財產,遺產等)。**~ into operation,** start to operate. 開始操作;開始軍事行動。**~ into one's own,** receive the credit, fame, etc that one deserves, what rightly belongs to one, etc. 得到其所應得(如榮譽、名譽等或屬其所有之物)。**~ into power,** (of a political party, etc) form the Government. (指政黨等)取得政權;組織政府。Cf 參較 *go into Opposition.* 成爲反對黨(在野黨)。**~ into sight/view,** appear. 出現;顯現。⇨ also collision, effect(1), *existence* at exist, fashion(2), force[1](5), line[1](11), open(*n*), play[1](8), possession(1), *prominence* at prominent, question[1](2), use[1](1). **5 ~ to sb (from sb),** be left, willed, to sb (by Will and Testament, on death): (某人死時經由遺囑)遺留或遺贈給某人: *He has a lot of money coming to him,* will receive it, eg when sb dies. 他將獲得一大筆遺贈的錢(例如當某人去世後)。*The farm came to him on his father's death.* 他父親去世時遺留給他那農場。**6 ~ to sb,** occur to, strike sb; befall sb: 發生在某人身上;使某人想起;降臨於某人: *The idea came* (= occurred) *to him in his bath.* 他在洗澡時想起那主意。*No harm will ~ to you if you're careful.* 只要你小心,你不會遭遇損害的。*He had it coming to him,* (sl used only of unpleasant events) what happened was fated, and probably deserved. (俚,僅用以指不愉快的事件,極可能是其所應得的)他活該有這樣的遭遇。**7** [VP4A] reach a point where one sees, understands, etc: 到達了明白、了解等之點: *He came to realize that he was mistaken.* 他終於明白他錯了。*He had ~ to see the problem in a new light.* 他終於對此問題獲得新的認識。*I have ~ to believe that...,* I now believe that.... 我現在相信…了。*When we ~ to know them better....* 等我們對他們認識清楚一點的時候…。**8** [VP4A] (usu with *how*) asking for an explanation or reason: (通常與 how 連用)要求解釋或說明理由: *How did you ~* (archaic 古, *How came you*) *to find out where she's living?* 你如何打聽到她住在哪裏? *How did you ~ to be so foolish?* 你爲什麼如此愚蠢? (*Now that I*) *~* (= happen) *to think of it....* (既然我)想到了它…。**How ~ (that),** (sl) How does/did sth happen: (俚)…是如何發生的;…是怎麼回事: *How ~ (that) you just sat there doing nothing?* 你只坐在那裏什麼事也沒做,是怎麼回事? **9** [VP2C] occur; be found; have as its place: 發生;出現;在: *May ~s between April and June.* 五月在四月與六月之間。*On what page does it ~?*它在哪一頁? *His resignation came as a surprise/It came as a surprise when he resigned.* 他的辭職令人驚異。**10** [VP2C, D] be; become; prove to be: 成爲;證實爲: *Your dream will one day ~ true,* be realized. 你的夢想將來有一天會實現。*It ~s easily with practice.* 一經練習,就很容易。*The handle has ~ loose.* 把柄鬆了。*It ~s cheaper if you buy things in bulk.* 大批購物會便宜些。*Everything will ~* (*all*) *right in the end.* 一切問題終會解決;一切困難終會過去。*That sort of thing ~s naturally to her,* she does it without having to learn or make an effort. 那種事情她不學自會。**be as clever/stupid, etc as they ~,** be very clever/stupid, etc. 非常聰明(愚蠢等)。**11** [VP2D] (with *part adjj* prefixed with *un-*, denoting undesirable conditions, etc) become: (與帶字首 un- 之分詞形容詞連用,表示不良的情況等)成爲;變成: *My shoelaces have ~ undone.* 我的鞋帶鬆開了。*The seam came unstitched.* 衣縫綻線了。*The flap of the envelope has ~ unstuck.* 信封口的黏膠不黏了。⇨ unstuck for a colloq use. 參看 unstuck 的口語用法。**12** [VP2D] (with a *n* or *adj,* usu with the *def art,* used adverbially as the nominal part of the predicate) (colloq) play the part of; behave, talk, etc as if one were (often with the suggestion of overdoing sth): (與通常加定冠詞之名詞或形容詞連用,作副詞用,爲述語的名詞部分) (俗) 擔任…之角色;行爲、談話等宛如(常暗示'做得過火'): *Don't ~ the bully/the high and mighty over me,* don't (try to) bully me. 不要想恃強欺侮我。*He tried to ~ the artful/virtuous over me,* impress me by being artful/virtuous. 他想對我耍手段 (他在我面前故作善良)。*That's coming it a bit strong,* is making an extravagant claim or assertion. 那做(要求或說)得太過火了一點。⇨ also the *noun* entry for *the heavy swell.* **13** (as a *to*-inf, used as a *pred adj*) future: (以不定詞形式,用作敍述形容詞)將來的;未來的: *in years to ~;* 在未來的年歲裏; *books to ~,* forthcoming books; 行將出版的書籍; *the life to ~,* life in the next world; 來生; *for some time to ~,* for a period of time in the future. 在將來的一段時期。**14** (colloq uses): (俗語用法): *two years ~ Christmas,* two years including the time from now to Christmas. 從過去的某時算起到下一個聖誕節的兩年間(包括從現在至聖誕節之一段期間)。*She will be 21 ~ May,* when May comes, ie next May. 她將於(明年或今年)五月滿二十一歲。*Mary is coming ten,* is in her tenth year, will be ten on her next birthday. 瑪莉快十歲了(到了她生日的那一天就滿十歲)。**15** [VP2A] (colloq) reach orgasm. (俗)達到性交高潮。**16** [VP2C, 3A] (special uses with *adverbial particles* and *preps*): (與副詞接語及介詞連用的特殊用法):

come about, happen: 發生: *It came about in this way.* 它就是這樣發生的。*How does it ~ about that...?* …是怎樣發生的? ⇨ 8 above. 參看上列第8義。

come across sb/sth, (a) find or meet by chance: 偶然發現或遇見某人(某物): *I came across this old brooch in a curio shop.* 我在一家古玩店裏偶然發現了這枝古老的扣花。**(b)** occur to: 出現於…中: *The thought came across my mind that...,* occurred to me.... …的想法出現於我的腦海中;我忽然想到…。Cf 參較 *It crossed my mind that....* **~ across (with),** (sl) pay (money owing); agree to give information. (俚)償付(欠款);同意提供消息或情報;同意說出。

come after sb, follow in pursuit of: 跟隨;追蹤;追捕: *The farmer came after the intruders with a big stick.* 那農夫拿着一根大棍子追捕侵入者。

come along, (a) (imper) try harder; make more effort: (祈使)再努力點;加緊努力: *C~ along, now—someone must know the answer!* 再想想看——一定有

人知道答案的！**(b)** progress: 進步: *The garden is coming along quite nicely.* 那花園越來越美。**(c)** appear; arrive: 出現;到達: *When the right opportunity ~s along, he'll take it.* 當良機到來時,他會抓住的。**(d)** (imper) hurry up; make haste: (祈使)快一點;趕快: *C~ along—we'll be late for the theatre!* 趕快——我們看戲要遲到了！

come apart, ~, fall, to pieces: 破掉;碎掉: *The teapot just came apart in my hands.* 那茶壺就在我手中破了。

come at sb/sth, **(a)** reach; get access to: 達到;接近;得到: *The truth is often difficult to ~ at* (*get at* is more usu). 事實眞相常常難獲知(較常用 get at)。**(b)** attack: 攻擊;襲擊: *The man came at me with a big stick.* 那人手持粗棍向我打來。Hence, 由此產生, **~-at-able** /ˌkʌmˈætəbl ; kʌmˈætəbl̩/ *adj* (colloq) accessible (*get-at-able* is more usu). (俗)可接近的;可獲得的(較常用 get-at-able)。

come away (from), become detached: (從…)脫落;掉下: *The light switch came away from the wall.* 電燈開關從牆上掉下來了。

come back, return; (of fashions) become popular again: 回來;(指時樣)再度流行: *Will ruffs ~ back?* 寬硬的縐領會再度流行嗎？***~ back at,*** retort; retaliate: 反駁;報復: *He came back at the speaker with some sharp questions.* 他以一些尖刻的問題反駁演說者。***~ back (to one),*** return to the memory: 重現於(某人的)記憶中: *Their names are all coming back to me now,* I'm beginning to remember them. 他們的名字,我現在都漸漸想起來了。Hence, 由此產生, **ˈ~-back** *n* **(a)** (eg of actors, politicians, sportsmen, etc) successful return to, reinstatement in, a former position: (如演員、從政者、運動員等的)恢復先前的地位;東山再起: *Can he stage a ~-back?* 他能夠東山再起嗎？**(b)** retort; repartee. 反駁;反擊。**(c)** redress; recompense (for a loss, etc): 補償;賠償(損失等): *If you're uninsured and you're burgled, you'll have no ~-back.* 如果你未投保而被小偷光顧,你將得不到賠償。

come before sb/sth, **(a)** be dealt with by: 被…討論: *The complaint will ~ before the United Nations Assembly next week.* 該項控訴將於下週提交聯合國大會討論。**(b)** have precedence over: 地位高於: *Baronets ~ before knights.* 從男爵的地位高於爵士。

come between, **(a)** interfere with a relationship: 干預;干擾: *It is not advisable to ~ between a man and his wife.* 干預別人夫妻間之事是不智的。**(b)** prevent sb from having sth: 阻撓某人不使其有某物或作某事;阻礙;阻止: *He never lets anything ~ between him and his evening paper.* 他從不讓任何事阻礙他看晚報。

come by sth, **(a)** obtain by effort; become possessed of: 努力獲得;獲有: *Was the money honestly ~ by?* 那錢的來路正當嗎？*Jobs were hard to ~ by.* 工作難求。**(b)** receive by accident or chance: 由於意外事件或偶然地受到: *How did you ~ by that cut on your wrist?* 你手腕上的割傷是怎麼來的？

come down, **(a)** collapse: 塌陷;崩潰: *The ceiling came down on our heads.* 天花板塌下來掉在我們的頭上。**(b)** (of rain, snow, hail) fall: (指雨、雪、雹)落下: *The rain came down in bucketfuls.* 大雨傾盆。**(c)** (of prices, temperature, etc) fall. (指物價、氣溫等)跌落;下落;下降。**(d)** ~ from a city or large town to a smaller locality: (從城市或大鎮)到較小的地方;下鄉: *She came down from Glasgow last year and settled in the village.* 她於去年從格拉斯哥下鄉來並定居在該村中。**(e)** (colloq) pay money: (俗)付錢;出手: *My rich uncle came down generously,* made a generous gift of money. 我那有錢的叔父出手大方(給了相當多的錢)。***~ down (from),*** leave university (esp Oxford or Cambridge): 大學畢業或肄業(尤指自牛津或劍橋大學): *His son has just ~ down from Oxford.* 他兒子剛自牛津大學畢業。***~ ˈdown in the world,*** lose social position; become poor. 失去社會地位;失勢;變窮;敗落。Hence, 由此產生, **ˈ~-down** *n* fall in social position; humiliation: (社會地位或聲望)衰落;低落;敗落;貶抑;屈辱: *He has had to sell his house and furniture—what a ~-down for him!* 他不得不賣掉房屋及傢具——對他該是多大的屈辱！***~ down in favour of sb/sth; ~ down on the side of sb/sth,*** decide to support: 決定支持;決心擁護: *He came down on the side of a more flexible trade policy.* 他決定支持比較有彈性的貿易政策。***~ down on sb,*** (colloq) rebuke severely: (俗)嚴責: *The headmaster came down on the boy like a ton of bricks.* 校長兇猛地對那男孩嚴加斥責。***~ down on sb for sth,*** demand payment of money owing: 向某人索還錢等: *Tradesmen came down on him for prompt settlement of his accounts.* 商人們要他迅速結帳。***~ down to,*** **(a)** reach to: 到達;垂及: *Her hair ~s down to her waist.* 她的頭髮下垂到腰部。**(b)** reduce to: 減少或降低至: *Your choices in the matter ~ down to these.* 有關此事你的選擇只限於這些。**(c)** (of traditions, etc) be handed down: (指傳統等)傳下;世代相傳: *legends that have ~ down to us,* ie from our ancestors. 自古相傳至今的傳說。***~ down to doing sth,*** be forced, eg by poverty, to do sth humiliating: (如因窮困等)被迫做屈辱的事: *He had ~ down to begging.* 他已淪爲乞丐。***~ down to earth,*** return to reality: 返回現實: *Now that his money has all been spent, he's had to ~ down to earth.* 既然他的錢已全部花掉了,他不得不回到現實(的生活)裏來。***~ down to it,*** examine the meaning, the essentials. 審查含義或要點。***~ down with,*** (colloq) contribute: (俗)捐獻: *I had to ~ down with £10 to her favourite charity.* 我不得不捐出十鎊來給她所喜歡的慈善事業。

come forward, **(a)** offer or present oneself: 自告奮勇;自願效勞: *Will no one ~ forward as a candidate?* 無人出來競選嗎？*No witness of the accident has ~ forward.* 沒有人出來做那意外事件的見證人。**(b)** (comm) become available: (商)可供銷售;可資運用: *the number of cattle coming forward for slaughter,* brought to market to be sold. 可供宰殺的肉牛數目。

come from, **(a)** (not with progressive tenses) have as a birthplace, place of origin, etc: (不用進行式)出生於;來自;源自: *He ~s from Kent.* 他是肯特郡人。*Much of the butter eaten in England ~s from New Zealand.* 英格蘭境內所食用的牛油有很多是來自紐西蘭。**(b)** = ~ of (b).

come home to, ⇨ home²(2).

come in, **(a)** (of the tide) rise: (指潮水)漲: *The tide is coming in.* 潮正在上漲。**(b)** become seasonable: 當令;上市: *When do oysters ~ in?* 蠔何時上市？**(c)** become fashionable: 開始流行: *When did women's trousers ~ in?* 婦女的長褲何時開始流行？**(d)** (of a batsman in cricket) take his stand at the wicket: (指板球戲中的擊球手)就其在三柱門旁之位置;上場: *When the next man came in,....* 當下一個擊球手上場的時候,…。**(e)** take a place in the result of a race: 在賽跑中得名次: *Which horse came in first?* 哪一匹馬跑第一名？**(f)** be elected; ~ into power: 當選;當權;執政;上臺: *If the Democrats ~ in,....* 假若民主黨上臺的話,…。**(g)** be received as income, etc: 作爲收入等而被收到: *There's not much money coming in at present.* 目前沒有多少錢收入。**(h)** have a part to play: 擔任職務: *Here is the plan of attack, and this is where you ~ in.* 這是攻擊計畫,此處是你的任務崗位。*Where do I ~ in,* (according to context) What is my share, How do I benefit, etc? (根據上下文)我的職務是什麼,我的好處在哪裏等？***~ in handy/useful (for sth),*** happen to be useful, serve a purpose: 偶然會有用;可能有用: *Don't throw it away—it may ~ in handy one day.* 不要把它丟掉——它有一天也許會有用處。***~ ˈin for,*** **(a)** receive (as an inheritance, a share, etc): 得到(遺產、一份等): *She has ~ in for a fortune.* 她得到了一筆財產。**(b)** attract; be the object of: 吸引;

爲…之對象;招致: *Their handling of the case has ~ in for a great deal of criticism.* 他們對該案件的處理已經招致了許多的批評。 ***~ in on,*** join; take part in: 加入;參加: *If you want to ~ in on the scheme, you must decide now.* 如果你要參加此計畫,你必須現在就作決定。

come into sth, ⇨ 4 above. 參看上列第4義。

come of, **(a)** be descended from: 爲…之後裔;出身於: *She ~s of an interesting family.* 她出身於有趣的家庭。**(b)** be the result of: 爲…之結果: *He promised his help, but I don't think anything will ~ of it.* 他答應幫忙,但我不認爲他的幫忙會有任何結果。*No harm can ~ of trying.* 試試無妨(不會有害)。 ***~ of age,*** ⇨ age[1](1).

come off, **(a)** take place: 發生;擧行: *The match didn't ~ off.* 比賽未擧行。*Did the proposed visit to Rome ever ~ off?* 所提議之羅馬之行實現了嗎? **(b)** (of plans, attempts) succeed: (指計畫、企圖)成功: *The experiment did not ~ off.* 這項實驗未成功。*The film doesn't quite ~ off.* 該影片不大成功。 **(c)** (of persons) fare; prosper; acquit oneself: (指人)進展;成就;行爲;表現: *They came off well/badly.* 他們表現得很好(壞);他們做得很成功(失敗)。*Who came off best,* who won? 誰獲勝? ***come off (sth),*** **(a)** become detached or separated (from): (從某物上)脫落;分離;掉下: *A button has ~ off my coat.* 我的外衣掉了一顆扣子。 *Please use lipstick that doesn't ~ off on the wineglasses.* 請用不會印在酒杯上的口紅。*When we came off the gold standard...,* abandoned it.... 當我們廢棄金本位制時…。**(b)** fall (from): (自…)跌下: *~ off a horse/bicycle.* 自馬(脚踏車)上跌下。*Don't ~ off!* 不要摔下來! **(c)** get down (from): (自…)下來: *C~ off that wall before you fall off (it).* 快下來,免得從牆上摔下來。⇨ also perch[2](2). **(d)** ***~ off it,*** (colloq, imper) stop pretending, or talking nonsense: (俗,祈使)別裝了;別吹了;別胡說八道;住口: *Oh, ~ off it! What do you know about horseracing?* 唉,別吹了!關於賽馬你懂什麼?

come on, **(a)** follow: 跟隨: *You go first, I'll ~ on later.* 你先去,我隨後就來。Hence, 由此產生, **'~-on** *n* (sl) lure; seductive action. (俚)誘惑;引誘。**(b)** (as a challenge): (作爲挑戰語): *C~ on! Let's race to the bottom of the hill.* 來吧!我們賽跑到山脚下。**(c)** make progress; develop: 進步;發展;發育: *How's your garden coming on?* 你的花園發展的情形如何? *The baby is coming on well.* 嬰兒的發育情形良好。 **(d)** (of rain, the seasons, night, illness, etc) start; arrive: (指雨、季、夜、病等)開始;來到: *Night/Darkness came on.* 夜色(黑暗)降臨。*The rain came on again worse than ever.* 雨又下了,較前更爲加劇。*He said he felt a cold coming on,* was beginning to suffer from a cold. 他說他感到有患感冒的跡象。**(e)** (of questions, lawsuits) arise for discussion: (指問題、訟案)被提出討論: *When does the case ~ on for trial,* When will the court deal with it? 該案何時開庭審訊? **(f)** (cricket, of a bowler) begin to bowl. (板球戲,指投手)開始投球。 **(g)** (of an actor) appear on the stage; (of a play) be performed: (指演員)登場;上場;(指劇本)上演: *'Macbeth' is coming on again next month.* '馬克白'下月將再度上演。 ***~ on to + inf,*** begin to: 開始: *It came on to rain.* 開始下雨。

come out, **(a)** appear; become visible: 出現;顯現: *The sun/stars came out.* 太陽(星星)出來了。*The buds/flowers are coming out,* are opening. 蓓蕾(花)綻放。**(b)** become known: (消息)傳出;(眞相)大白: *When the news came out....* 當消息傳出的時候…。*If the truth ever ~s out....* 如果事實眞相終會明白…。 **(c)** be published: 出版: *When will his new book ~ out?* 他的新著將於何時出版? **(d)** (of workmen) strike: (指工人)罷工: *The car workers have all ~ out again.* 汽車工人再度全體罷工。**(e)** (of details, etc in a photograph; of qualities) appear: (指相片上的細微處;指品質)顯現;表露: *You have ~ out well in that photograph,* It is a good likeness. 你的那張相片照得很好。 *His arrogance ~s out in every speech he makes.* 他的驕氣表露於他每一次的演講中。 **(f)** (of stains, etc) be removed: (指汚跡等)被除去: *These ink stains won't ~ out.* 這些墨水跡洗不掉。 **(g)** (of dyes, etc) fade; disappear: (指染料等)褪色;消失: *Will the colour ~ out if the material is washed?* 這料子經洗滌後會褪色嗎? **(h)** (of problems) be solved: (指問題)被解決: *I can't make this sum/equation ~ out,* can't solve it. 我算不出這個算術題(方程式)。**(i)** make a debut; (colloq) begin to live publicly as sth. 初入社交場合;(俗)出頭。**(j)** (of meaning, sense) become clear: (指意思,意義)變明白;顯明: *The meaning of the passage ~s out clearly in his interpretation.* 這一段文字的意義經他的解釋後就明白了。***~ out at,*** (of totals, averages, etc) amount to: (指總數、平均數等)達到: *The total ~s out at 756,* is 756. 總數達到756。***~ out first/last, etc,*** (in examinations) have a certain position: (在考試中)得第一名(最後一名等): *Tom came out first.* 湯姆(考試成績)名列第一。 ***~ out in,*** be partially covered in (pimples, a rash, etc): 部份覆蓋着(粉刺、疹等): *She's ~ out in spots!* 她身上出疹子了! ***~ out with,*** utter; say: 說出;道出: *He came out with a most extraordinary story/a string of oaths.* 他說出了一個非常驚人的故事(一連串的咒罵語)。

come over, **(a)** ~ from a distance: 從遠處來: *Won't you ~ over to England for a holiday?* 你不來英國度假嗎? **(b)** change sides or opinions: 改變立場或意見: *He will never ~ over to our side.* 他決不會改變立場參加我們這一邊。***~ over sb,*** (of feelings, influences) take possession of: (指感情、影響力)掌握住某人;佔據: *What has ~ over you,* Why have you changed in this way? 你爲什麼會變成這個樣子? *A fit of dizziness came over her,* She suddenly felt dizzy. 她突然感到暈眩。 ***~ over queer/funny/dizzy,*** (colloq) suffer a feeling of faintness/sickness/dizziness. (俗)感到頭暈(不適,暈眩)。

come round, **(a)** ~ by a circuitous route: 由迂曲的路線而來;走彎路: *The road was blocked so we had to ~ round by the fields.* 道路阻塞了,所以我們不得不由田間繞道而來。**(b)** pay an informal visit to: (非正式地)訪問: *Won't you ~ round and see me some time?* 什麼時候來看我好嗎? **(c)** recur: 再現;再來;再臨: *Christmas will soon ~ round,* be here again. 聖誕節不久又要來臨了。**(d)** change views, etc: 改變觀念、見解等: *He will never ~ round to our way of thinking,* change his views and adopt ours. 他決不會放棄他的觀點而採取我們的。 *He has ~ round,* has accepted / agreed. 他已接受(同意)。 **(e)** regain consciousness: 恢復知覺;甦醒: *Pour a jug of water on his face—he'll soon ~ round.* 澆一罐水在他的臉上,他馬上就會甦醒。**(f)** recover from ill temper, etc: 從壞脾氣等恢復過來: *Don't scold the boy; he'll ~ round in time.* 不要責罵那個男孩;他的壞脾氣終會過去的。

come through, **(a)** recover from a serious illness, from risk of injury: (從重病中)復元;(從遭遇受傷危險中)度過;脫險: *With such a weak heart, he was lucky to ~ through.* 他的心臟如此衰弱,竟能復元眞是幸運。*How did you manage to ~ through without even a scratch,* to escape even a slight injury? 你用什麼方法能够絲毫未受傷(安然脫險)? **(b)** arrive (by telephone, radio, etc): (經由電話、無線電等)到達;打通: *Listen—a message is just coming through.* 聽——電訊剛接通。**(c)** pass through official channels: 獲得官方批准: *Your posting has just ~ through: it's Hong Kong!* 你的派令剛下來:地點是香港! ***~ through sth,*** survive: 經歷…之後仍然活着: *He has ~ through two world wars,* has lived safely through them. 他身經兩次世界大戰。

come 'to, **(a)** recover consciousness; ⇨ come round(e). 恢復知覺;甦醒。**(b)** ***~ to sth,*** ⇨ 3 above. 參看上列第3義。

come under sth, **(a)** be classed among; be in

(a certain category, etc): 歸入(某一類等): *What heading does this ~ under?* 這個應歸入哪一項? **(b)** be subjected to: 受到: *~ under sb's notice/influence.* 受到某人的注意(影響)。

come up, **(a)** (of seed, herbaceous plants, etc) show above the ground: (指種子、草本植物等)長出地面: *The seeds/snowdrops haven't ~ up yet.* 種子(雪花草)尚未發出芽來。**(b)** arise; be put forward: 發生;被提出: *The question hasn't ~ up yet,* has not been raised or discussed. 問題尚未被提出或討論。*Her divorce case ~s up next month,* will be dealt with then. 她的離婚案件將於下月討論。**(c)** (colloq) be drawn (in a lottery): (俗)(在抽獎中)被抽中: *My sweepstake ticket came up; I won £100.* 我的馬票中獎了(號碼被抽出);我中了一百鎊。**(d)** occur; arise: 發生;出現: *We shall write to you if a vacancy ~s up.* 如果出缺我們會寫信給你。**(e)** rise in social position: 社會地位升高;出頭: *He came up the hard way,* succeeded through his own, unaided efforts. 他靠自己的努力而出人頭地。***~ up against,*** meet (difficulties, opposition). 對付;應付(困難、反對)。***~ up to,*** **(a)** reach: 達到;及於: *The water came up to my waist.* 水深及於我的腰部。**(b)** equal: 等於;達到: *Your work has not ~ up to my expectations/to the required standards.* 你的工作沒有達到我的期望(要求的標準)。***~ up with,*** **(a)** draw level with: 與…並行;趕上: *We came up with a party of hikers.* 我們趕上了一隊遠足者。**(b)** produce; find (a solution, an answer). 產生;發現(解決辦法,答案)。

come upon sb/sth, **(a)** attack by surprise; strike: 突襲;突臨: *the disaster that came upon them.* 突然降臨於他們的災禍。*Fear came upon us.* 我們突然感到害怕。**(b)** = come across (a).

com·edian /kə'mi:dɪən ; kə'midɪən/ *n* actor who plays comic parts in plays, broadcasts and TV; person who behaves in a comic way and who cannot be taken seriously. 戲劇、廣播或電視中擔任滑稽角色的演員;喜劇演員;行動滑稽的人;丑角。**com·edienne** /kə,mi:dɪ'en ; kə,midɪ'ɛn/ *n* female ~. 喜劇中的女演員;女丑角。

com·edy /'kɒmədɪ ; 'kɑmədɪ/ *n* **1** [U] branch of drama that deals with everyday life and humorous events: 喜劇(戲劇的一部門,描寫日常生活及可笑的事件): *He prefers ~ to tragedy;* 他比較喜歡喜劇而不大喜歡悲劇; [C] (*pl* -dies) play for the theatre, of a light, amusing kind. 輕鬆滑稽的舞臺劇;喜劇。**,musical '~,** such a play, with music, songs and dancing. 滑稽歌舞劇;歌舞喜劇。**2** [C, U] amusing activity or incident in real life: 眞實人生中有趣的事情;趣事;趣聞: *There's not much ~ in modern war.* 現代戰爭並不是好玩的事。

come·ly /'kʌmlɪ ; 'kʌmlɪ/ *adj* (-ier, -iest) (old use, usu of a person) pleasant to look at. (舊用法,通常指人)漂亮的;好看的。**come·li·ness** *n*

comer /'kʌmə(r) ; 'kʌmɚ/ *n* (chiefly in compounds) one who comes: (主用於複合字中)來的人;來者;到者: *the first ~;* 最先到達者; *the late-~s;* 遲到者;晚來的人; *all ~s.* 全體來到者。

com·est·ible /kə'mestəbl ; kə'mɛstəbl/ *n* (formal, usu *pl*) thing to eat. (正式用語,通常用複數)食物;食品。

comet /'kɒmɪt ; 'kɑmɪt/ *n* heavenly body (looking like a star with a bright centre and a less bright tail) that moves round the sun in an eccentric orbit. 彗星(爲一天體,看來像星,中心明亮而有較暗之尾,循離心軌道繞太陽旋轉)。

a comet

come·up·pance /kʌm'ʌpəns ; kʌm'ʌpəns/ *n* deserved punishment or misfortune: 應得的懲罰或災禍: *The tyrant President got his ~ when his country was invaded and conquered.* 當他的國家被攻克時,那位暴虐的總統得到了他應得的懲罰。

com·fit /'kʌmfɪt ; 'kʌmfɪt/ *n* (old use) sweetmeat; fruit (eg a plum) preserved in sugar. (舊用法)糖果;蜜餞(如梅子)。

com·fort /'kʌmfət ; 'kʌmfɚt/ *n* **1** [U] state of being free from suffering, anxiety, pain, etc; contentment; physical well-being: 舒服;舒適(無憂無慮無痛無苦的狀態);滿足;(身體的)安逸: *become fond of ~ as one grows old;* 人年紀大了就變得喜歡安逸; *living in great ~.* 生活極爲舒適。**2** [U] help or kindness to sb who is suffering: (對受痛苦者的)安慰;慰藉: *a few words of ~;* 幾句安慰的話; *news that brought ~ to all of us.* 令我們大家都感到安慰的消息。***cold ~,*** not much consolation. 無關痛癢的安慰。**3** [C] person or thing that brings relief or help: 帶來安慰的人或事物: *Your letters have been a great ~ to me.* 你的來信給了我很大的安慰。*It's a ~ to know that she is safe.* 知道她平安無事,是一項安慰。*The hotel has every modern ~/all modern ~s.* 這旅館中有各種現代設備。**'~ station,** (US) public lavatory. (美)公共厠所。□ *vt* [VP6A] give ~ to: 安慰;鼓舞: *~ those who are in trouble.* 安慰處於困境的人。*The child ran to its mother to be ~ed.* 那孩子跑到媽媽身邊俾得到安慰。**'~·less** *adj* without ~: 不舒適的: *a ~less room.* 不舒適的房間。

com·fort·able /'kʌmftəbl *US:* -fərt- ; 'kʌmfɚtəbl/ *adj* **1** giving comfort to the body: (使身體)舒適的;安逸的: *a ~ chair/bed.* 舒適的椅子(床)。**2** having or providing comfort: 享有或供給舒適的: *a ~ life/income.* 舒適的生活(相當豐富的收入)。**3** at ease; free from (excessive) pain, anxiety, etc: 舒暢的;無(過度)痛苦、憂慮等的: *to be/feel ~.* 感到舒適。*Make yourself ~!* 別客氣!**com·fort·ably** /-təblɪ ; -təblɪ/ *adv* in a ~ manner: 舒適地;安逸地;舒服地: *a car that holds six people comfortably.* 能够舒舒服服地供六人坐的汽車。***be comfortably off,*** have enough money to live in comfort. 生活富裕。

com·forter /'kʌmfətə(r) ; 'kʌmfɚtɚ/ *n* **1** person who comforts. 安慰者。**the C~,** (= *strengthener*) the Holy Spirit. 保惠師(聖靈)。**2** (GB) warm woollen scarf, worn round the neck. (英)暖和的羊毛圍巾。**3** (GB) teat of a baby's dummy (US 美 = *pacifier*). (英)奶嘴。**4** (US) quilt. (美)棉被。

com·frey /'kʌmfrɪ ; 'kʌmfrɪ/ *n* [U] tall wild plant with rough leaves and purple or white flowers. 紫草科植物(高莖野生植物,葉粗糙,開紫或白花)。

comfy /'kʌmfɪ ; 'kʌmfɪ/ *adj* (-ier, -iest) (colloq) comfortable. (俗)舒適的;安逸的;舒服的。

comic /'kɒmɪk ; 'kɑmɪk/ *adj* **1** causing people to laugh: 使人發笑的;滑稽的: *a ~ song;* 滑稽歌曲; intended to amuse: 娛樂性的: *~ strips,* strips of humorous drawings, as printed in newspapers, etc. (如報紙上所刊載的)連環漫畫。**2** of comedy: 喜劇的: *~ opera.* 喜歌劇。□ *n* **1** music-hall comedian. 雜耍戲院裏的滑稽演員。**2** (US 美 = '~ **book**) book or magazine containing stories etc in the form of drawings. 附有連環漫畫的書或雜誌;連環圖畫。

comi·cal /'kɒmɪkl ; 'kɑmɪkl/ *adj* amusing; odd: 有趣的;奇特的;古怪的: *a ~ old hat.* 古怪的舊帽。**~ly** /-klɪ ; -klɪ/ *adv*

coming /'kʌmɪŋ ; 'kʌmɪŋ/ *n* arrival: 來到;到達;抵達: *He believes in the Second C~,* the return of Jesus Christ when the world ends. 他相信世界末日時耶穌基督的再臨。□ *adj* which will come: 未來的;將來的: *in the ~ years;* 在未來的年歲裏; *the ~ generation.* 下一代。***a ~ man,*** a man who is likely to be important, famous, etc. 一個前程似錦的人(將成爲重要人物或將成名等)。

com·ity /'kɒmɪtɪ ; 'kɑmətɪ/ *n* [U] (formal) harmonious friendliness; courtesy. (正式用語)和睦;禮

讓;禮貌。~ **of nations**, friendly recognition, shown by one nation, of the laws, customs, etc of other nations. 國際間對於彼此之法律、風俗等的互相尊重;國際禮讓。

comma /ˈkɒmə ; ˈkɑmə/ *n* punctuation mark (,) to indicate a slight pause or break between parts of a sentence. 逗點(,)(用以表示句中各部份間之略微的停頓)。**inˌverted ˈ~s**, the marks (" ") or (' '). 引號(" "或' ')。⇨ App 9. 參看附錄九。

com·mand¹ /kəˈmɑːnd *US:* -ˈmænd ; kəˈmænd/ *vt, vi* **1** [VP6A, 17, 9, 2A] order (usu with the right to be obeyed): 命令(通常有使對方必須服從之權): *Do as I ~ (you)*. 照我的命令去做。*The officer ~ed his men to fire.* 那軍官命令其部下開火。*The pirate chief ~ed that the prisoners should be shot.* 海盜首領下令將俘虜槍殺。*God ~s and man obeys.* 上帝命令,人服從。**2** [VP6A, 2A] have authority over; be in control of: 統率;指揮: *The captain of a ship ~s all the officers and men.* 艦長統率艦上全體官兵。*Who ~s the army?* 誰指揮陸軍? *Who ~s here?* 這裏由誰指揮? **3** [VP6A] restrain; hold back; control (the more usu word): 抑制;克制;控制(較常用 control): *~ oneself / one's temper / one's passions.* 克制自己(自己的脾氣,自己的情感)。**4** [VP6A] be in a position to use; have at one's service: 可以使用;能够支配: *He ~s great sums of money*, is able to use them if he so wishes. 他可以支配大筆的款子。*A Minister of State ~s the services of many officials.* 國務大臣可以支配許多官員。**5** [VP6A] deserve and get: 應該得到並且得到;博得: *Great men ~ our respect.* 偉人受我們尊敬。*He ~s the sympathy of all who have heard the story of his sufferings.* 他的苦難遭遇博得所有聽衆的同情。**6** [VP6A] (of a place) be in a position that overlooks (and may control): (指地點)俯視(也可以控制): *The fort ~ed the entrance to the valley.* 該碉堡俯視(控制)山谷的入口。*The hill ~s a fine view*, a fine view can be obtained from the top. 此山俯覽一片美景。**~·ing** *adj* that ~s: 命令的;指揮的: *the ~ing officer;* 司令官;指揮官; *in a ~ing tone;* 以命令的口吻; *in a ~ing position.* 居於指揮的地位。

com·mand² /kəˈmɑːnd *US:* -ˈmænd ; kəˈmænd/ *n* **1** [C] order: 命令: *His ~s were quickly obeyed.* 他的命令很快就執行了。*Give your ~s in a loud, confident voice.* 以響亮自信的聲調發佈你的命令。***at the word of ~***, (mil) when the ~ is given. (軍)命令一發;當命令下達時。**2** [U] authority; power (to control): 權力;統率權;指揮權: *General X is in ~ of the army.* 某將軍統率陸軍。*The army is under the ~ of General X.* 陸軍由某將軍統率。*He has twenty men under his ~.* 他有二十人由他指揮。***have / take ~ of***, have / take authority: 指揮: *When the major was killed, the senior captain took ~ of the company.* 當少校陣亡時,全連由資深的上尉指揮。***do sth at / by sb's ~***, on his authority: 奉某人之命做某事: *It was done by the Queen's ~.* 此事係奉女王之命而行。***be at sb's ~***, ready to obey: 願受某人的指揮;聽某人的吩咐: *I am at your ~*, ready to obey you. 我願受你的指揮;我隨時聽候你的吩咐。**ˈ~ module**, part of a spacecraft carrying the crew and control equipment. 指揮艙(太空船裝載人員及控制裝備部分)。**~ performance**, (at a theatre) one given at the request of a head of State. (戲院中)應國家元首之請求而舉行的特別表演;御前表演。**3** [C] part of an army, air force, etc under separate ~: 由單獨指揮系統所轄的部分陸軍、空軍等;指揮部;部隊: *Western C~;* 西方部隊; *Bomber C~.* 轟炸指揮部。**4** [U] possession and mastery: 具有並能自由使用;支配: *He has (a) good ~ of the English language*, is able to use it well. 他精通英文。*He has no ~ over himself*, cannot control his feelings, temper, etc. 他不能克制自己(如情感、脾氣等)。*He offered me all the money at his ~*, all the money he controlled. 他把所有由他支配的錢都給我了。

com·man·dant /ˌkɒmənˈdænt ; ˌkɑmənˈdænt/ *n* commanding officer. 指揮官。

com·man·deer /ˌkɒmənˈdɪə(r) ; ˌkɑmənˈdɪr/ *vt* [VP6A] seize (horses, stores, buildings, etc) for military purposes under martial law. 在戒嚴令下徵用(馬匹、物資、建築物等)作爲軍用。

com·mander /kəˈmɑːndə(r) *US:* -ˈmæn- ; kəˈmændə/ *n* person in command: 司令官;指揮官;部隊長;隊長: *the ~ of the expedition;* 探險隊隊長; *C~, Lieuˌtenant-ˈC~*, naval officers (above lieutenant and below captain); 海軍中校;海軍少校; *Wing-C~*, rank in the RAF; 英國空軍中校; **ˌ~-in-ˈchief**, ~ of all the military forces of a State. (統率全國所有陸、海、空軍之)總司令。

com·mand·ment /kəˈmɑːndmənt *US:* -ˈmænd- ; kəˈmændmənt/ *n* divine command. 神的戒律;聖誡。**the Ten C~s**, the ten laws given by God to Moses. ⇨ Exod 20:1-17. 十誡(上帝授予摩西的十條戒律;參看舊約聖經出埃及記第 20 章第 1 至 17 節)。

com·mando /kəˈmɑːndəʊ *US:* -ˈmæn- ; kəˈmændo/ *n* (*pl* ~s or ~es) (member of a) body of men specially picked and trained for carrying out raids and making assaults. (特別挑選並加以訓練擔任突擊任務的)突擊隊(員)。

com·mem·or·ate /kəˈmeməreɪt ; kəˈmɛməˌret/ *vt* [VP6A] keep or honour the memory of (a person or event); (of things) be in memory of: 紀念(人或事件);(指事物)作爲對於…之紀念;慶祝: *Christmas ~s the birth of Christ.* 聖誕節紀念基督的降生。*A monument was built to ~ the victory.* 立一紀念碑以紀念勝利。**com·mem·or·ative** /kəˈmemərətɪv *US:* -ˈmeməreɪt- ; kəˈmɛməˌretɪv/ *adj* serving to ~: 作爲紀念用的;紀念的: *commemorative stamps / medals.* 紀念郵票(章)。

com·mem·or·ation /kəˌmeməˈreɪʃn ; kəˌmɛməˈreʃən/ *n* [U] act of commemorating: 紀念;慶祝: *in ~ of;* 紀念;慶祝; [C] (part of a) service in memory of a person or event. 紀念儀式;慶祝活動。

com·mence /kəˈmens ; kəˈmɛns/ *vt, vi* [VP6A, C, 2A, 3A] (formal) begin; start (the more usu words). (正式用語)開始(begin 和 start 爲較常用字)。**~·ment** *n* **1** beginning. 開始。**2** (in US universities, and at Cambridge and Dublin) ceremony at which degrees are conferred. (美國各大學、英國劍橋大學及愛爾蘭都柏林大學)學位授予典禮;畢業典禮。

com·mend /kəˈmend ; kəˈmɛnd/ *vt* **1** [VP6A, 14] ***~ sb (on / upon sth); ~ sb / sth (to sb)***, praise; speak favourably of: 稱讚;讚揚: *~ someone upon his good manners;* 稱讚某人有禮貌; *~ a man to his employers.* 向某人之雇主稱讚某人。*His work was highly ~ed.* 他的工作極受讚揚。**2** [VP14] ***~ sth to***, entrust for safekeeping to: 將某事物付託給…;信託;託…保管: *~ one's soul to God.* 將靈魂付託上帝。**3** [VP14] ***~ oneself / itself to***, be to the liking of; be acceptable to: 投…之所好;受…的歡迎;使感興趣: *This book does not ~ itself to me.* 我對這本書不感興趣。*Will the proposal ~ itself to the public?* 這建議會受大衆的歡迎嗎? **~·able** *adj* worthy of praise. 可稱讚的;值得讚揚的。**com·men·da·tion** /ˌkɒmenˈdeɪʃn ; ˌkɑmənˈdeʃən/ *n* [U] praise; approval. 稱讚;讚揚;贊成。

com·men·sur·able /kəˈmenʃərəbl ; kəˈmɛnʃərəbl/ *adj* ***~ (to / with)***, that can be measured by the same standard (as): 可以用同一標準衡量的;有公度的;有公比量的;相稱的;相當的: *Their achievements are not ~.* 他們的成就是不能相比的。

com·men·sur·ate /kəˈmenʃərət ; kəˈmɛnʃərɪt/ *adj* ***~ (to / with)***, in the right proportion (to): (與…)相當的;相稱的;成適當比例的: *Was the pay you received ~ with the work you did?* 你所得的薪資與你所作的工作相稱嗎?

com·ment /ˈkɒment ; ˈkɑmɛnt/ *n* [C, U] opinion given briefly in speech or writing about an event, or in explanation or criticism of sth: (對某事件用言語或文字所作簡短的)評論;(對某事之)說明;解釋;批

評: *Have you any ~(s) to make upon my story?* 你對於我的故事有沒有什麼意見? *Her strange behaviour caused a good deal of ~,* of talk, gossip, etc. 她奇怪的行爲引起了諸多議論。***No ~!*** I've nothing to say on this subject. 無可奉告(對於此問題我沒有什麼好說的)! □ *vi* [VP2A, 3A] ~ ***(on / upon),*** make ~s (on); give opinions. 發表(有關…的)意見或議論; 批評。

com·men·tary /ˈkɒməntrɪ *US:* -terɪ ; ˈkamən,tɛrɪ/ *n* (*pl* -ries) **1** collection of comments, eg on a book: 集註;註釋(如關於某書者): *a Bible ~.* 聖經集註。 **2** series of continuous comments (on an event): (關於某事件之)連續的評論或報導: *a broadcast ~ on a football match.* 一場足球賽的廣播報導。***a running ~,*** number of remarks following one another continuously while an event is taking place: (某一事件發生中的)現場轉播: *He kept up a running ~ on the race.* 他不斷地轉播比賽的實況。 **com·men·tate** /ˈkɒməntеɪt ; ˈkamən,tet/ *vi* [VP3A] ***commentate on,*** give a ~ on. 對…加以註釋,評論或報導。**com·men·ta·tor** /ˈkɒmənteɪtə(r) ; ˈkamən,tetə/ *n* eyewitness who gives a broadcast ~ on an event, eg a horse-race or football match; writer of a ~(1). 播報實況轉播(如賽馬或足球比賽)並兼作評論者;廣播評論家;撰寫評註者;評註家。

com·merce /ˈkɒmɜːs ; ˈkamɝs/ *n* [U] trade (esp between countries); the exchange and distribution of goods: 貿易;(尤指)國際貿易;商業;商務: *a Chamber of C~.* 商會。

com·mer·cial /kəˈmɜːʃl ; kəˈmɝʃəl/ *adj* of or for commerce: 商業的;商務的: *~ education;* 商業教育; *a ~ attitude.* 商業態度。~ **traveller,** person who travels with samples of goods to obtain orders. (攜帶貨樣至各地的) 旅行推銷員。 ~ **TV / radio,** financed by charges made for ~ advertising in programmes. 靠商業廣告維持的電視(無線電廣播)事業。~ **vehicles,** vans, lorries, etc, for the transport of goods. 商用車輛; 貨車(供搬運貨物用的有篷貨車、卡車等)。□ *n* [C] advertisement inserted in a TV or radio programme. 電視或無線電廣播節目中插入的廣告。**~ly** /-ʃəlɪ ; -ʃəlɪ/ *adv* **~·ize** /kəˈmɜːʃəlaɪz ; kəˈmɝʃəl,aɪz/ *vt* [VP6A] (try to) make money out of: 使商業化;(企圖)從…當中賺錢: *Is it wise to ~ize sport?* 將運動商業化是聰明的嗎?

com·mi·na·tion /ˌkɒmɪˈneɪʃn ; ˌkaməˈneʃən/ *n* [C, U] (formal) threatening of divine vengeance. (正式用語) 天譴的威嚇; 神罰的威嚇。**com·mina·tory** /ˈkɒmɪnətrɪ *US:* -tɔːrɪ ; ˈkamənə,torɪ/ *adj* threatening. 威脅的;恐嚇的。

com·mingle /kəˈmɪŋgl ; kəˈmɪŋgḷ/ *vt, vi* [VP6A,2A] mingle together. 混合;摻合;混雜。

com·miser·ate /kəˈmɪzəreɪt ; kəˈmɪzə,ret/ *vi* [VP3A] ~ ***with,*** feel, say that one feels, pity for: 感覺憐憫或同情; 表示憐憫或同情: *~ with a friend on his misfortunes.* 對朋友的不幸表示同情。 **com·miser·ation** /kəˌmɪzəˈreɪʃn ; kə,mɪzəˈreʃən/ *n* [C,U] (expression of) pity or sympathy (*for* sb). 憐憫或同情(的表示) (與 for 連用,後接某人)。

com·mis·sar /ˈkɒmɪsɑː(r) ; ˌkaməˈsar/ *n* **1** (formerly) head of a major Government Department of the USSR. (昔時蘇聯政府主要部門之)首長;人民委員。 **2** (formerly) political officer in the army of the USSR. (昔日蘇聯軍隊中之)政委。

com·mis·sar·iat /ˌkɒmɪˈseərɪət ; ˌkaməˈsɛrɪət/ *n* **1** (formerly) major Government Department of the USSR. (昔時蘇聯政府的) 人民委員部。 **2** (formerly) department that supplied food and other stores to troops. (昔時)軍需部(供應糧食及其他補給品給軍隊者)。 **3** food supply. 糧食補給。

com·mis·sary /ˈkɒmɪsərɪ *US:* -serɪ ; ˈkamə,sɛrɪ/ *n* (*pl* -ries) **1** (formal) deputy, delegate. (正式用語)代表。 **2** (formerly) officer responsible for supplying food to troops. (昔時)軍需官(負責軍中之糧食補給者)。,~ **ˈgeneral,** head of a commissariat(2). 軍需部部長。

com·mis·sion /kəˈmɪʃn ; kəˈmɪʃən/ *n* **1** [U] the giving of authority to sb to act for another; [C] instance of this; [C] action or piece of business that is done: 授權某人代辦;委託;所辦之事: *He has secured two ~s to design buildings for a local authority.* 他已承包兩起爲當地政府設計建築物的業務。 **2** [U] performance or committing (*of* crime). 犯(罪)。 **3** [C, U] payment to sb for selling goods, etc, rising in proportion to the results gained: (請人銷售貨物等,按獲利比例所付的)佣金;酬勞金;回扣: *He receives a ~ of 10 per cent on sales, as well as a salary.* 他按銷售數量收取百分之十的佣金,另外還有一份薪水。***on ~,*** drawing a percentage of the receipts: 抽佣金: *to sell goods on ~.* 按抽佣金辦法售貨。 **4** [C] official paper (called a *warrant*) giving authority; (esp) (in GB) warrant signed by the Sovereign appointing an officer in the armed services: 任官令;委任狀;(尤指英國由君主簽署的)軍職任命狀: *get / resign one's ~.* 獲得(辭去)軍職。 **5** [C] body of persons given the duty of making an inquiry and writing a report: 考察團;調查團(由若干人組成受命調查某事並作成報告之團體);委員會: *a Royal C~ to report on betting and gambling.* 由英王委派的調查賭博的委員會。 **6** group of people legally authorized to discharge a task. 合法受權執行某一任務的一群人。,**C~ of the ˈPeace,** Justices of the Peace collectively. (集合用法)保安官;治安法官。 **7** ***in ~,*** (eg of a ship) with crew and supplies complete; ready for sea. (指船隻等)人員及供應品均齊備的;已準備好即可出海的。 ***out of ~,*** kept in reserve; not in working order; (fig) not working, not available. 保留的;後備的;損壞了的;(喻)不能用的。□ *vt* [VP6A, 17] give a ~(1) to: 委託;請託: *~ an artist to paint a portrait;* 請畫家畫一張肖像; *be ~ed to buy books for a friend.* 受託替友人買書。 **com·mis·sioned** *adj* (of officers) holding rank by ~(4). (指軍官)經過委任保有官階的;受委任的。⇨ non-~ed.

com·mis·sion·aire /kəˌmɪʃəˈneə(r) ; kə,mɪʃənˈɛr/ *n* uniformed porter at the entrance to a cinema, theatre, hotel, large shop, etc. (電影院、戲院、旅館、大商店等大門口)著制服的侍者。

com·mis·sioner /kəˈmɪʃənə(r) ; kəˈmɪʃənə/ *n* **1** member of a commission(5, 6), esp one with particular duties: (尤指負有特殊任務之委員會、調查團或考察團的)委員: *the C~s of Inland Revenue,* who control Income Tax; 國內稅收監督官(管理所得稅者); *the Civil Service C~s,* who conduct the Civil Service examinations. 文官考試委員。 **2** person who has been given a commission(1): 受委託負某種責任的人: *a C~ for Oaths,* solicitor (given commission by the Lord Chancellor) before whom documents are sworn on oath. 宣誓公證人(受英國大法官之委託負責監視簽署文件者宣誓之律師)。 **3** representative of high rank: 高級代表: *the High C~ for Canada,* eg representing the Canadian Government in London; 加拿大高級代表(如代表加拿大政府駐倫敦者); *the British High C~ in Accra.* 駐阿克拉的英國高級代表。

com·mit /kəˈmɪt ; kəˈmɪt/ *vt* (-tt-) **1** [VP6A] perform (a crime, foolish act, etc): 犯(罪、錯等): *~ murder / suicide / an offence.* 犯謀殺罪(自殺;犯罪)。 **2** [VP14] ~ ***sb / sth to,*** entrust, give up, hand over to, for safe keeping or treatment: 交託;交付;移交(爲保管或處理): *~ a man to prison;* 將某人交付監禁; *~ a patient to a mental hospital;* 將病人交付精神病院; *~ sth to paper / to writing,* write it down. 將某事寫下來。*The body was ~ted to the flames,* was cremated. 屍體被火化。~ ***to memory,*** learn by heart. 牢記。~ ***a prisoner for trial,*** ~ him to prison for trial later. 將囚犯收押候審。 **3** [VP6A, 14, 16A] ~ ***oneself (to...),*** make oneself responsible; undertake: 承諾;答應負責;使自己負有責任: *He has ~ted himself to support his brother's children.* 他已答應負責養育他的姪子。

He refused to ~ himself by talking about the crime, refused to say anything because it might get him into trouble. 他對此犯罪案拒絶表示任何意見,以免自己受牽累。 **4** [VP6A, 14] (often reflex) pledge; bind (oneself): (常用反身式)保證;束縛(自己);使(自己)受約束: *I won't ~ myself to that course of action.* 我決不承諾採取彼項行動。⇨ uncommitted. **~·ment** *n* [U] being ~ted (2, 3, 4); [C] sth to which one has ~ted(3) oneself; promise; pledge; undertaking: 委託;所承諾之事;許諾;保證;承約: *If you have agreed to give a number of lectures, help to pay your brother's school expenses and give your sister £100 a year for clothes, you have quite a lot of ~ments.* 假如你已答應作若干次演講,又補助你弟弟的學費,又給你妹妹一年一百鎊的置裝費,那麼你就作了相當多的承諾。

com·mit·tee /kə'mɪtɪ ; kə'mɪtɪ/ *n* group of persons appointed (usu by a larger group) to attend to special business: (通常由較大的團體所委派以處理特殊事務的)委員會: *to attend a '~ meeting,* 參加委員會會議; *to be/sit on the ~;* 爲委員會之委員; *a Parliamentary C~,* one appointed by the House of Commons (or Lords) to examine a Bill. 英國國會中的調查委員會(由下議院或上議院指派組成,負責研究議案)。 *in ~,* functioning as (a member of) a ~. 執行委員會之職權;擔任委員。

com·mode /kə'məʊd ; kə'mod/ *n* **1** chest of drawers. 五斗櫥;衣櫃。 **2** piece of bedroom furniture to hold a chamber-pot. 臥室內置便溺器的傢具。

com·modi·ous /kə'məʊdɪəs ; kə'modɪəs/ *adj* having plenty of space for what is needed: 寬敞的;有充分的空間足供需要的: *a ~ house / cupboard.* 寬敞的房子(食櫥)。

com·mod·ity /kə'mɒdətɪ ; kə'mɑdətɪ/ *n* (*pl* -ties) [C] useful thing, esp an article of trade: 有用的物品;(尤指)商品: *household commodities,* eg pots and pans. 家庭用品(如鍋、盆)。

com·mo·dore /'kɒmədɔː(r) ; 'kɑmə,dor/ *n* naval officer having rank above a captain and below a rear-admiral; president of a yacht club; senior captain of a shipping line: 海軍代將(在上校之上少將之下);遊艇俱樂部主席;輪船公司的資深船長: *the ~ of the Cunard Line;* 寇納德輪船公司的資深船長; *Air C~,* officer in the Air Force. 空軍准將。

com·mon¹ /'kɒmən ; 'kɑmən/ *adj* **1** belonging to, used by, coming from, done by, affecting, all or nearly all members of a group or society: (爲團體或社會所有或幾乎所有之份子所) 共有的;公用的;共同的;共爲的;共受影響的: *The husband is French, the wife German, and the lodger Italian, but they have English as a ~ language,* they can all use English. 丈夫是法國人,妻子是德國人,房客是意大利人,但是英語是他們的共同語言。 *It is to the ~ advantage* (= to everyone's advantage) *that street traffic should be well controlled.* 街市上的交通應善加管理,這是爲了大家的利益。 **~ ground,** (fig) basis for argument accepted by persons in a dispute, etc. (喻) (辯論等之雙方所承認的)共同立論基礎。 **~ knowledge,** what is known to most persons, esp in a group: (尤指某一團體內)大多數人所知道之事: *It was ~ knowledge among bankers that....* …是銀行界人所共知之事。 Cf 參較 *general knowledge.* **'~ land,** land that belongs to, or may be used by, the community, esp in a village. (爲全社區,尤指全村,所共有或可共同使用的)公地。 ⇨ common²(1). **~ factor/multiple,** (maths) belonging to two or more quantities. (數學)公因子(公倍數)。 **~ law,** (in England) unwritten law developed from old customs, eg in Saxon and Danish times, and decisions made by judges. (英國由古代,如撒克遜和丹麥時代,的習慣及法官判例所發展成的)不成文法;習慣法。⇨ *statute law* at statute, and *case-law* at case¹(2). **~-law wife,** woman with whom a man lives, as if she were his wife, but without marrying her. 非正式太太 (與男人同居,却未辦正式婚姻手續的女人)。 **the C~ Market** *n* (officially *the European Economic Community*), economic, social and political association, established in 1958, of Belgium, France, Italy, Luxembourg, the Netherlands and West Germany, since enlarged in 1973 by the inclusion of Britain, Ireland and Denmark, with associate membership (for economic preferences) by other countries. 歐洲共同市場(正式名稱作 the European Economic Community, 於1958年由比利時、法國、意大利、盧森堡、荷蘭及西德所組成之經濟、社會及政治的聯盟,此後由於1973年英國、愛爾蘭共和國及丹麥之納入組織而擴大,尚有其他以經濟利益爲優先的準會員國家)。 **~ noun,** (gram) name that can be used for any member of a class, eg *book* or *knife.* (文法)普通名詞(可用以指同類事物之任何一個之名稱,如 book 或 knife)。 **a ~ nuisance,** an offence that is harmful to the community and for which there is legal remedy. 妨害治安行爲(有害於社會,法律並訂有制裁辦法者)。⇨ also cause and prayer. **'~-room,** room for use of the teachers or students at a school, college, etc. (中小學、大學等之)教師室;教授室;學生室。 **2** usual and ordinary; happening or found often and in many places: 普通的;常見的;常常發生的;到處可見的: *a ~ flower;* 常見的花; *a ~ experience.* 普通的經驗。 *Pine-trees are ~ in many parts of the world.* 松樹在世界上許多地方都很常見。 *Is this word in ~ use?* 這個字常用嗎? **the ~ man/people,** the ordinary or average citizen(s): 常人;普通人;老百姓: *The ~ man in every country wants peace.* 每一個國家的老百姓都想要和平。 **~ metre,** hymn stanza of 4 lines, with 8, 6, 8, 6 syllables. 普通韻律(讚美詩用之,四行一節,各行音節數目爲8,6,8,6)。 **~ sense,** practical good sense gained by experience of life, not by special study. 常識(由生活經驗得來,而非由特別研究得來的實用判斷力)。 **~ time/measure,** two or four beats in a bar. (音樂)普通拍子(每小節兩拍或四拍)。 **3** (colloq) (of persons, their behaviour and possessions) vulgar; of inferior quality or taste: (俗)(指人、其行爲及所有物)粗鄙的;劣等的;低級的: *~ manners;* 粗鄙的舉止; *speak with a ~ accent;* 以粗俗的口音說話; *a girl who looks ~/who wears ~ clothes.* 貌不美(穿粗劣衣服)的女子。 **~·ly** *adv* **1** usually: 通常地: *That very ~ly happens.* 那事極常發生。 *Thomas, ~ly called Tom.* 湯瑪斯,通常呼爲湯姆。 **2** in a ~(3) way: 粗鄙地;粗劣地: *~ly dressed.* 衣著粗劣的。

com·mon² /'kɒmən ; 'kɑmən/ *n* **1** [C] area (usu in or near a village) of unfenced grassland for all to use: (通常在村內或附近,無垣籬的)公用草地;村公園: *Saturday afternoon cricket on the village ~.* 星期六下午在村公園舉行的板球比賽。 **2** *in ~,* for or by all (of a group). (團體)共同的;公有的。 ***have in ~ (with),*** share (with): (與…)共有: *They have nothing in ~ with one another,* have no similar interests, etc. 他們彼此毫無共同之點(沒有同樣的興趣等)。 ***in ~ with,*** together with: 與…一起;與…一樣: *In ~ with* (= Like) *many people he prefers meat to fish.* 像許多人一樣,他喜歡肉而不喜歡魚。 ***out of the ~,*** unusual. 不平常的。

com·mon·alty /'kɒmənəltɪ ; 'kɑmənəltɪ/ *n* **the ~,** the common people (contrasted with the upper classes). 普通人民;平民(與高階層人士相對)。

com·moner /'kɒmənə(r) ; 'kɑmənɚ/ *n* one of the common people, not a member of the nobility. (一個)平民(非貴族)。

com·mon·place /'kɒmənpleɪs ; 'kɑmən,ples/ *adj* ordinary or usual: 平常的;平凡的;平庸的: *a ~ kind of man.* 一種平凡的人。□ *n* remark, event, etc that is ordinary or usual: 老生常談;平常的事: *conversation full of mere ~s.* 充滿老生常談的談話。 *Travel by air is now a ~.* 航空旅行現在是一件平常的事。

com·mons /'kɒmənz ; 'kɑmənz/ *n pl* **1 the ~,** (old use) the common people. (舊用法)平民。⇨ aristocracy, nobility. **the ˌHouse of 'C~,** assembly of those elected by the common people;

lower house of the British Parliament. (英國的)下議院(議員係由平民所選)。**2** provisions shared in common. 公用的食物。***be on short* ~,** not have enough to eat. 缺乏食物。

com·mon·wealth /'kɒmənwelθ ; 'kɑmən,wɛlθ/ *n* **1** State; group of States (eg *the C~ of Australia*) associating politically for their common good. 國家;(爲共同利益所組織的)聯邦(例如澳洲聯邦)。**2 the C~,** a free association of sovereign independent states (formerly colonies and dominions of GB) with their dependencies. 大英國協(若干昔爲英國殖民地及自治領而現爲獨立自主國家及其屬地的自由結合)。

com·mo·tion /kə'məʊʃn ; kə'moʃən/ *n* [U] noisy confusion; excitement; [C] instance of this; violent uprising or disturbance: 騷動;騷擾;暴動;暴亂: *You're making a great ~ about nothing.* 你簡直是在無理取鬧。

com·mu·nal /'kɒmjʊnl ; 'kɑmjʊnl/ *adj* **1** of or for a community: 社會的;公有的: ~ *disturbances*, eg in countries where there are antagonisms between people of different races and religions. 社會的動盪不安 (例如在某些國家人民間有種族和宗教的敵視)。**2** for common use; shared: 公用的;共用的: ~ *land/kitchens.* 公用的土地(共用的厨房)。

com·mune[1] /kə'mju:n ; kə'mjun/ *vi* [VP2C, 3A] **~ *(together)*; ~ *(with)*,** feel at one with; feel, be, in close touch with; talk with in an intimate way: (與…)感覺一致;(感覺)與…很親近;與…親密地交談: ~ *with nature/one's friends/God in prayer;* 與大自然合而爲一(與朋友親密交談;在禱告中與上帝作靈的溝通); *friends communing together.* 在一起親密交談的朋友。

com·mune[2] /'kɒmju:n ; 'kɑmjun/ *n* **1** (in France, Belgium, Italy, Spain) smallest territorial district for purposes of administration, with a mayor and council. (在法國、比利時、義大利、西班牙)最小的地方行政區(設市長及議會)。**2** organized group of people promoting local interests. 爲促進地方福利而組成的人民團體;福利社。**3** group of people living together and sharing property and responsibilities. 生活在一起、共有財產、分擔職責的一群人;公社。

com·muni·cable /kə'mju:nɪkəbl ; kə'mjunɪkəbl̩/ *adj* (of ideas, illness, etc) that can be communicated or imparted. (指觀念、疾病等)可溝通的;可傳染的。

com·muni·cant /kə'mju:nɪkənt ; kə'mjunɪkənt/ *n* **1** one who (regularly) receives Holy Communion. (按時)領受聖餐者。**2** informer (the more usu word). 報信者;通消息者 (informer 爲較常用字)。

com·muni·cate /kə'mju:nɪkeɪt ; kə'mjunə,ket/ *vt, vi* **1** [VP6A, 14] **~ *sth (to)*,** pass on (news, information, feelings, heat, motion, an illness, etc). 傳達(新聞、消息、感情);傳播(熱力);傳遞(運動);傳染(疾病)。**2** [VP3A] **~ *with*,** share or exchange (news, etc): 共有或交換(消息等);通信;通訊: *We can ~ with people in most parts of the world by telephone.* 我們可以藉電話與世界上大多數地區的人通訊。*Young people sometimes complain of not being able to ~ with their parents.* 年輕人有時抱怨無法與父母溝通思想。**3** [VP2A, 3A] **~ *(with)*,** (of rooms, gardens, roads, etc) be connected: (指房間、花園、道路等)互通;通連: *My garden ~s with the garden next door by means of a gate.* 我的花園與隔壁的花園有門相通。*We asked the hotel to let us have communicating rooms*, rooms with a connecting door. 我們向旅館要有門互通的房間。

com·muni·ca·tion /kə,mju:nɪ'keɪʃn ; kə,mjunə'keʃən/ *n* **1** [U] the act of communicating: 傳達;傳播;傳遞;傳染;通信: *Among the deaf and dumb ~ may be carried on by means of the finger alphabet.* 聾啞的人可以藉手語傳達意思。*Spitting in public places may lead to the ~ of disease.* 在公共場所吐痰可能導致疾病的傳染。*I'm in/I must get into ~ with him on this subject.* 關於這問題,我正(必須)與他交換意見。**2** [C] that which is communicated (eg news): 被傳播之事(如新聞);信息;消息: *This ~ is confidential.* 這消息是機密的。**3** [C, U] means of communicating; roads, railways, telephone or telegraph lines connecting places, radio and TV: 交通或通訊設備;(連絡各地的)公路、鐵路、電話或電報線;無線電;電視: *a world ~s network;* 世界性通訊網; *~ satellites;* 通訊人造衛星; *mass ~s media.* 大衆通訊媒介。*Telegraphic ~/~s between Amman and Baghdad has/have been restored.* 安曼與巴格達之間的電報通訊業已恢復。*All ~ with the north has been stopped by snowstorms.* 與北部的一切交通均爲風雪所阻。**'~ cord,** cord that passes along the length of a train inside the coaches, to be pulled (to stop the train) in an emergency. 火車廂內順着火車所裝,在發生緊急事件時拉之以通知利車之警鈴線。

com·muni·cat·ive /kə'mju:nɪkətɪv *US:* -keɪtɪv ; kə'mjunə,ketɪv/ *adj* ready and willing to talk and give information. 好說話的;直言的;不隱諱的。⇨ *reserved* at reserve[2].

com·mu·nion /kə'mju:nɪən ; kə'mjunjən/ *n* **1** [U] sharing in common; participation (*with*). 共有;同享;參與(與 with 連用)。**2** [U] exchange of thought and feelings; intercourse. (思想感情的)交通;靈的交通。***hold '~ with oneself*,** think deeply (esp about moral or religious problems). 深思;獨自思考(尤指關於道德或宗教的問題)。**self-~,** thinking about oneself. 自省;獨自深思。**3** [C] group of persons with the same religious beliefs: 由同一宗教信仰的人所構成的團體;教會;教派: *We belong to the same ~.* 我們屬於同一教會。**4 (Holy) C~,** (in the Christian Church) celebration of the Lord's Supper. 聖餐(基督教會紀念耶穌最後晚餐的儀式)。***go to C~*, (a)** attend church for this celebration. 參加聖餐禮。**(b)** receive the Eucharist. 領聖餐。

com·mu·niqué /kə'mju:nɪkeɪ ; kə,mjunə'ke/ *n* official announcement, eg as issued to the press. 公報;官報。

com·mu·nism /'kɒmjʊnɪzm ; 'kɑmjʊ,nɪzəm/ *n* [U] **1** ideology that proclaims the abolition of class oppression and exploitation, and the foundation of a society based on the common possession of the means of production and the equal distribution of goods. 共產主義(主張消除階級迫害及剝削,建立一個以共有生產工具及平均分配財貨爲基礎之社會的思想體系)。**2** (usu 通常作 **C~**) (colloq) political system in which the power is held by the Communist or Workers' Party, and the land and its resources, the means of production etc are under state control. (俗)共產制度(一種政治制度,由共產黨或工黨專政,土地及其資源、生產工具等均由政府控制)。**com·mu·nist** /'kɒmjʊnɪst ; 'kɑmjʊnɪst/ *n* believer in, supporter of, ~. 共產主義者;共產黨員(信仰或擁護共產主義者)。□ *adj* of ~. 共產主義的;共產主義者的。

com·mun·ity /kə'mju:nətɪ ; kə'mjunətɪ/ *n* (*pl* -ties) **1 the ~,** the people living in one place, district or country, considered as a whole: (由同住於一地、一地區或一國的人所構成的)社會;社區: *work for the good of the ~.* 爲社會利益而工作。**'~ centre,** building(s), etc where people meet for adult education classes, amateur dramatics, informal social intercourse, etc. 社區活動中心(民衆可以在此參加成人教育班,業餘戲劇公演,非正式社交活動等);公共會堂。**~ chest,** (US) welfare fund for helping people in distress. (美)社區(救濟窮困者的)福利基金。**2** [C] group of persons having the same religion, race, occupation, etc or with common interests: 由同宗教、同種族、同職業或其他共同利益的人所構成的團體: *a ~ of monks;* 一群和尚; *the Jewish ~ in London;* 住在倫敦的猶太僑民團體; *the European ~ in Karachi.* 住在喀拉蚩的歐洲僑民團體。**3** [U] condition of sharing, having things in common, being alike in some way: 共享;共有;共同;相同: *~ of race/religion/interests;* 種族(宗教,利益)的相同; *a ~ spirit*, shared feeling of membership. 團隊精神。***in* ~,** together. 一起;共同。**'~ singing,** organized singing in which all present take part. (所有在場的人一齊參加的) 大合唱。

com·mut·able /kə'mju:təbl ; kə'mjutəbl/ *adj* that can be exchanged or converted (*into/for*). 可交換的; 可改變的 (與 into 及 for 連用)。

com·mu·ta·tion /ˌkɒmju:'teɪʃn ; ˌkɑmju'teʃən/ *n* **1** [U] commuting; making one kind of payment instead of another, eg money instead of service. 折算; 折合償付; 代償 (如以金錢代償勞役)。 **2** [C] payment made in this way. 代償金。 **3** [C] reduced punishment: 減刑: *a ~ of the death sentence to life imprisonment.* 由死刑改爲無期徒刑的減刑。 **4** **~ ticket,** (US) season ticket. (美) 月季票。

com·mu·ta·tor /'kɒmju:teɪtə(r) ; 'kɑmjuˌtetɚ/ *n* device for altering the direction of an electric current. (改換電流方向的) 換向器; 整流器。

com·mute /kə'mju:t ; kə'mjut/ *vt, vi* **1** [VP6A, 14] **~ (into/for),** exchange one thing (esp one kind of payment) for another: 改換某物 (爲另一物); 折合 (以一物代替另一物, 尤指其償付方式): *~ one's pension;* 改換養老金的償付方式; *~ an annuity into/for a lump sum.* 將年金合算爲一總數, 一次付清。 **2** [VP6A, 14] **~ (to),** reduce the severity of a punishment: 減 (刑): *~ a death sentence (to one of life imprisonment).* 將死刑減刑 (爲無期徒刑)。 **3** [VP2A] travel regularly, eg by train or car, between one's work in a town and one's home in the country or suburbs. 通勤 (如搭乘火車或汽車, 經常往返於市區工作地點與鄉村或郊區住家之間)。 **com·muter** *n* person who ~s(3). 通勤者。

com·pact¹ /'kɒmpækt ; 'kɑmpækt/ *n* agreement between parties; contract; covenant. 合同; 合約; 契約; 協定。

com·pact² /kəm'pækt ; kəm'pækt/ *adj* closely packed together; neatly fitted; (of literary style) condensed. 包紮緊密的; 壓緊的; 緻密的; 恰好合適的; (指文體) 簡潔的。 □ *vt* (usu passive) join firmly together. (通常用被動語態) 緊密結合。 **~·ly** *adv* **~·ness** *n*

com·pact³ /'kɒmpækt ; 'kɑmpækt/ *n* small, flat container for face-powder (and often with a mirror), made for carrying in a woman's handbag. (婦女手提包中所帶的) 粉盒 (常附有照面鏡)。

com·pan·ion¹ /kəm'pænɪən ; kəm'pænjən/ *n* **1** person who goes with, or is often or always with, another: 同伴; 同行者; 伴侶 (時常或總是跟另一人在一起者): *my ~s on the journey.* 我的旅伴。 **2** person who shares in the work, pleasures, misfortunes, etc of another: 與另一人同工作、共遊樂或共患難等的人: *~s in arms,* fellow soldiers; 軍中同僚; 戰友; *~s in misfortune,* associated in it; 患難朋友; *a faithful ~ of 50 years,* eg said by a man speaking of his wife. 五十年的忠實伴侶 (如夫指其妻而言)。 **3** person with similar tastes, interests, etc: 同好者; 志趣相投者: *He's an excellent ~.* 他是一個極合得來的人。 *His brother is not much of a ~ for him.* 他哥哥 (弟弟) 與他志趣不甚相投。 **4** one of two or more things that go together; thing that matches another or is one of a pair: 成套物件之一; 成對物件之一: *Here's the glove for my left hand, but where's the ~?* 我左手的手套在這裏, 可是右手的在哪裏? (also attrib): (亦作形容用法): *the ~ volume(s).* 上册或下册; 成套書的一卷。 **5** person paid to keep another (usu old or ill) person company. 受雇陪伴老人或病人等的人。 **6** handbook or reference book: 手册; 參考書; 指南: *the Gardener's C~.* 園藝指南。 **7** **C~,** member of some Orders: 有某種勳位者: *C~ of the Bath.* 有巴斯勳位者。 ⇨ order¹(9). **~·able** *adj* friendly; sociable. 和善的; 友愛的; 友善的。 **~·ship** /-ʃɪp ; -ˌʃɪp/ *n* state of being ~s: 伴同; 同伴之誼: *enjoy sb's ~ship;* 樂與某人爲友; *a ~ship of many years.* 多年之交誼。

com·pan·ion² /kəm'pænɪən ; kəm'pænjən/ *n* (usu 通常作 **ˌ~·way**) staircase from the deck of a ship to the saloon or cabins. 艙梯 (由甲板通至交誼廳或船艙的梯子)。

com·pany /'kʌmpənɪ ; 'kʌmpənɪ/ *n* **1** [U] being together with another or others: 伴隨; 陪伴; 與他人在一起: *I shall be glad of your ~* (= to have you with me) *on the journey.* 我將很高興與你同行。 ***be good/poor/bad/excellent, etc ~,*** be a good, etc, companion(3). 與人很 (不很, 極等) 合得來的同伴。 ***for ~,*** to provide companionship: 作爲同伴; 陪伴: *I'll go with you as far as the station for ~.* 我將陪伴你到車站。 ***in ~ (with),*** together (with): (與…) 一同; 一起: *He came in ~ with a group of boys.* 他與一群男孩子同來。 *We went in ~.* 我們一起去的。 ***keep sb ~; keep ~ with sb,*** be or go with him: 陪伴某人: *He stayed at home to keep his wife ~.* 他留在家裏陪伴太太。 ***part ~ (with sb),*** ⇨ part²(1). **2** [U] group of persons; number of guests: 人群; 一群客人: *We're expecting ~* (= guests, visitors) *next week.* 我們下星期將有客人來訪。 *He's not well enough to receive a great deal of ~,* many visitors. 他的健康尚未十分恢復, 不能接見很多訪客。 ***sin in good ~,*** better men have done the same. 人非聖賢, 孰能無過。 **3** [U] persons with whom one spends one's time: 同伴; 伙伴; 友伴: *You may know a man by the ~ he keeps,* judge his character by his friends. 看他與什麼人來往, 你就可以知道他是個什麼樣的人。 *Don't get into/keep bad ~,* Don't become friendly with/mix with bad persons. 勿與壞人交往。 **4** (often 常作 **C~,** abbr 略作 **Co**) [C] (*pl* -nies) number of persons united for business or commerce: (由若干人組成經營商業的) 公司: *a steamship ~.* 輪船公司。 **a ˌLimited ˌLia'bility C~,** C~ whose partners are not named in the title: 有限責任公司; 商號上不列合夥人姓名的公司: *ˌT ˌS 'Smith & Co.* 史密斯公司 (及其合夥人)。 **5** number of persons working together: 一隊 (在一起工作的人): *a ~ of players,* actors who perform plays together; 一隊在一起演戲的演員; *a theatrical ~;* 劇團; 劇社; 戲班; *the ship's ~,* the crew. 船上的全體船員。 **6** subdivision of an infantry battalion, commanded by a captain or major. 連 (步兵營以下之單位, 由上尉或少校指揮)。

com·par·able /'kɒmpərəbl; 'kɑmpərəbl/ *adj* **~ (to/with),** that can be compared: 可與相比的; 可與比擬的: *The sets of figures are not ~.* 這兩組 (或這幾組) 數字是不能相比的。 *His achievements are ~ with the best.* 他的成績可與最優者相比。

com·para·tive /kəm'pærətɪv ; kəm'pærətɪv/ *adj* **1** having to do with comparison or comparing: 比較性的; 與比較有關的: *the ~ method of studying,* ie by finding out what is similar and different in two or more branches of knowledge; 比較研究法 (藉尋出二或多門學問間之異同, 以從事研究之方法); *~ religion;* 比較宗教; *~ linguistics.* 比較語言學。 **2** measured or judged by comparing: 比較而言的; 相當的: *living in ~ comfort,* eg comfortably compared with others, or with one's own life at an earlier period. 生活比較舒適的 (與他人或自己早期的生活比較起來算是舒適)。 **3** (gram) of or related to the form of adjectives and adverbs expressing 'more', (文法) (形容詞和副詞之) 比較級的, as in 如 *worse, harder, more difficult, more prettily.* □ *n* **~ degree:** 比較級: *'Better' is the ~ of 'good'.* better 是 good 的比較級。 **~·ly** *adv*

com·pare /kəm'peə(r) ; kəm'pɛr/ *vt, vi* **1** [VP6A, 14] **~ (with),** examine, judge to what extent persons or things are similar or not similar: 比較 (研究、評判人與人或事物與事物之間相同或相異之程度): *~ two translations;* 比較兩種譯文; *~ your translation with the model translation on the blackboard.* 將你的翻譯與黑板上的模範翻譯加以比較。 ***~ notes,*** exchange observations, ideas or opinions. 交換意見; 商量。 **2** [VP14] **~ to,** point out the likeness or relation between: 喻爲; 比擬 (指出其間的相似或關係): *Poets have ~d sleep to death.* 詩人一直把睡眠比作死亡。 *Mine cannot be ~d to yours,* is quite different. 我的與你的極不相同。 **3** [VP3A]

~ *with,* be ~ed with; bear comparison with: 與…比較;匹敵: *He cannot ~ with Shakespeare as a writer of tragedies,* is not nearly so great. 作爲一個悲劇作家,他無法與莎士比亞相比。*This cannot ~ with that,* no comparison is possible because they are so different. 這個與那個無法比較(因其完全不同)。 **4** (gram) form the comparative and superlative degrees (of adjectives and adverbs). (文法)構成(形容詞和副詞的)比較級和最高級。□ *n* (poet) comparison (but only in) (詩)比較(但僅用於) ***beyond/past/without ~:*** 無可比擬的;無匹敵的;無雙的: *She is lovely beyond ~,* so lovely that none can be ~d to her. 她的可愛是無與倫比的。

com·pari·son /kəmˈpærɪsn ; kəmˈpærəsn̩/ *n* **1** [U] ***by/in ~ (with),*** when compared (with): (與…)比較起來;相較;較之: *This one costs more but is cheaper by/in ~,* is plainly better value when you compare them and examine the quality, etc. 這件東西價錢貴一點,但是比較起來(比較其質料等)還是便宜。*The tallest buildings in London are small in ~ with those of New York.* 倫敦最高的建築物與紐約的比較起來,仍然很小。***the ~ of X and/with Y,*** the act of comparing X with Y. X與Y的比較;相比。 **2** [C] ***(make) a ~ between X and Y/of X to Y,*** (perform) an act of comparing; an instance of this: (X與Y間之)比較;比擬;相比;比喻: *It is often useful to make a ~ between two things.* 比較兩件事物常是有用的。*The ~ of the heart to a pump/between the heart and a pump has often been made.* 常有人將心臟比作幫浦。*There's no ~ between them,* They cannot be compared, one being clearly much better than the other. 兩者不可同日而語(因其相差懸殊)。***~s are odious,*** in this case it is unfair to make any ~. 在此情況下作比較是不公平的。 **3** ***bear/stand ~ with,*** be able to be compared favourably with: 比得上;不亞於: *That's a good dictionary, but it won't/can't stand ~ with this.* 那是一部好字典,但是還比不上這一本。 **4** ***degrees of ~,*** (gram) positive, comparative and superlative (of adjectives and adverbs), eg *good, better, best.* (文法)比較之級(指形容詞和副詞之原級、比較級及最高級,例如 good, better, best)。

com·part·ment /kəmˈpɑːtmənt ; kəmˈpɑrtmənt/ *n* one of several separate divisions of a structure, esp of a railway carriage or coach: (構造物之)隔間;(尤指鐵路客車等中的)小間;車室: *The first-class ~s are in front.* 頭等房間在前端。*The ship's hold is built in watertight ~s.* 船艙建造成許多水密艙區。 **com·part·men·tal·ize**/ ˌkɒmpɑːtˈmentəlaɪz ; ˌkəmpɑrtˈmɛntl̩ˌaɪz/ *vt* divide into ~s or categories. 分成隔間或部門;區劃。

com·pass¹ /ˈkʌmpəs ; ˈkʌmpəs/ *n* **1** **(magˈnetic) ~,** device with a needle that points to the magnetic north: 指南針;羅盤;羅經: *the points of the ~* (N, NE, E, SE, S, SW, W, NW, etc); 羅經上的方位(北、東北、東、東南、南、西南、西、西北等); similar device, eg 類似的裝置,例如 *a radio ~,* for determining direction. (用以指定方位的)電子羅經。 **2** (old use 舊用法 **pair of ~es**) **~(es),** V-shaped instrument with two arms joined by a hinge, used for drawing circles, measuring distances on a map or chart, etc. 兩脚規;圓規(一種V字形儀器,用以畫圓、量地圖或圖表上的距離等)。⇨ the illus at dividers. 參看 dividers 之插圖。 **3** extent; range: 範圍: *beyond the ~ of the human mind;* 超出人類智力的範圍; *outside the ~ (= range) of her voice.* 超出她的音域。

com·pass² /ˈkʌmpəs ; ˈkʌmpəs/ *vt* encompass (the more usu word). 圍繞;包圍(encompass 爲較常用字)。

com·pas·sion /kəmˈpæʃn ; kəmˈpæʃən/ *n* [U] pity; feeling for the sufferings of others, prompting one to give help: 憐憫;同情: *have/take ~ on sufferers;* 同情受苦者; *be filled with ~ for the refugees;* 對於難民們充滿了憐憫; *look at someone in/with ~;* 以憐憫的目光看某人; *give a man money out of ~.* 由於同情心而給人錢。 **~·ate** /kəmˈpæʃənət; kəmˈpæʃənɪt/ *adj* showing or feeling ~: 顯示同情心的;感覺憐憫的: *The soldier was granted ~ate leave,* given leave² (2), eg because personal affairs made necessary his presence at home. 該士兵請事假回家獲得准許。

com·pat·ible /kəmˈpætəbl ; kəmˈpætəbl̩/ *adj* ~ ***(with),*** (of ideas, arguments, principles, etc) suited (to), in accord (with), able to exist together (with): (指觀念、議論、原則等)適宜(於…)的;(與…)符合的;能共存的;相容的: *pleasure ~ with duty;* 與職責不背的行樂; *driving a car at a speed ~ with safety.* 以兼顧安全的速度駕車。 **com·pat·ibly** /-əblɪ ; -əblɪ/ *adv* **com·pati·bil·ity** /kəmˌpætəˈbɪlətɪ ; kəmˌpætəˈbɪlətɪ/ *n* [U] the state of being ~. 相合;相容;一致;可合性;不矛盾。

com·patriot /kəmˈpætrɪət *US:* -ˈpeɪt- ; kəmˈpetrɪət/ *n* person born in, or citizen of, the same country as another; fellow-countryman. 同國人;同胞(生於同國或爲同一國家公民的人)。

com·peer /ˈkɒmpɪə(r) ; kəmˈpɪr/ *n* person equal in rank or capacity. (地位或能力)相等的人;同志。

com·pel /kəmˈpel ; kəmˈpɛl/ *vt* (-ll-) **1** [VP17] ~ ***sb/sth to do sth,*** force (sb or sth to do sth); get, bring about, by force: 强迫;迫使(某人或某物做某事);强取;强致: *His conscience ~led him to confess.* 他的良心迫使他承認。*He was ~led by illness to resign.* 他因病被迫辭職。 **2** [VP14, 6A] ~ ***(from),*** obtain by pressure: 施壓力以獲得: *Can they ~ obedience from us,* force us to obey? 他們能强迫我們服從嗎?

com·pen·di·ous /kəmˈpendɪəs ; kəmˈpɛndɪəs/ *adj* (of authors, books, etc) giving much information briefly. (指作家、書籍等)簡要的;精簡的。

com·pen·dium /kəmˈpendɪəm ; kəmˈpɛndɪəm/ *n* concise and comprehensive account; summary. 簡明而廣泛的叙述;摘要;撮要;概要。

com·pen·sate /ˈkɒmpenseɪt ; ˈkɑmpənˌset/ *vt, vi* [VP6A, 14, 3A] ~ ***(sb) (for sth),*** make a suitable payment, give something to make up (*for* loss, injury, etc): 賠償;補償(損失、傷害等): *Do employers in your country ~ workers for injuries suffered at their work?* 貴國工人在工作時受傷,雇主是否予以賠償? *Nothing can ~ for the loss of one's health.* 失去健康是無可補償的事。 **com·pen·sa·tory** /kəmˈpensətərɪ *US:* -tɔːrɪ ; kəmˈpɛnsəˌtorɪ/ *adj* compensating. 賠償的;補償的;報償的。

com·pen·sa·tion /ˌkɒmpenˈseɪʃn ; ˌkɑmpənˈseʃən/ *n* [U] compensating; [C] sth given to compensate: 賠償;補償;賠償物: *He received £5000 in ~/by way of ~/as a ~ for the loss of his right hand.* 他失去右手,獲得五千鎊的賠償。

com·père /ˈkɒmpeə(r) ; ˈkɑmpɛr/ *n* (F) organizer

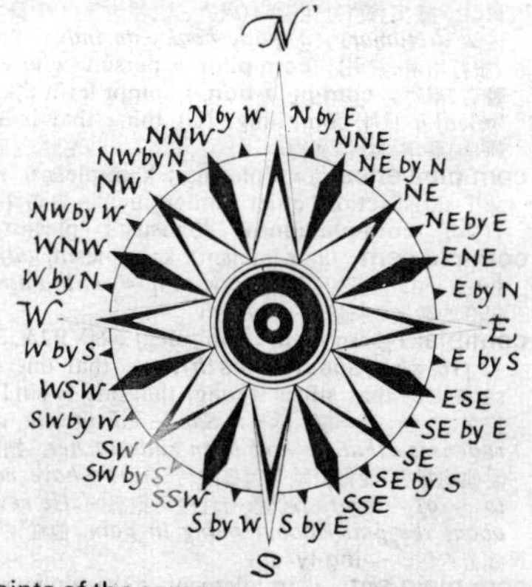

the points of the compass

of a cabaret or broadcast entertainment who introduces the performers, speakers, etc. (法) (餐館歌舞表演或廣播綜藝節目的) 安排並報告節目者；節目主持人 (介紹演員、演講者等)。□ *vt* act as ~ for. 爲…擔任安排並報告節目者；擔任…之節目主持人。

com·pete /kəm'piːt ; kəm'pit/ *vi* [VP2A, 3A] take part in a race, contest, examination, etc: (參加賽跑、比賽、考試等) 競爭；比賽: *to ~ in a race (against/with others, for a prize, for the first place, etc)*; 參加賽跑；(同別人，爲獎品，爲得第一名等) 競爭； *to ~ against/with other countries in trade.* 與別的國家在貿易上競爭。

com·pet·ence /'kɒmpɪtəns ; 'kɑmpətəns/ *n* **1** [U] being competent; ability: 稱職；勝任；能力: *his ~ in handling money/to handle money.* 他的理財 (處理金錢) 的能力。 **2** (usu 常作 **a ~**) income large enough for a person to live on in comfort: 足以使人過舒適生活的收入: *have/enjoy a small ~.* 有一筆足以過舒適生活的小收入。 **3** [U] (of a court, a magistrate) legal capacity: (指法庭、地方法官) 管轄權；權限: *business that is within/beyond the ~ of the court.* 在法院管轄權以內 (以外) 的業務。

com·pet·ent /'kɒmpɪtənt ; 'kɑmpətənt/ *adj* **1** (of persons) having ability, power, authority, skill, knowledge, etc (to do what is needed): (指人) 有能力、權力、權威、技能、知識等 (去做必須做之事) 的；能幹的；勝任的: *Is Miss X ~ in her work/~ as a teacher/~ to teach French?* 某小姐能勝任她的工作 (能任教員，能教法文) 嗎？ **2** (of qualities) sufficient, adequate: (指性質) 足够的；適當的: *Has she a ~ knowledge of French?* 她的法文知識够用嗎？ **~·ly** *adv*

com·pe·ti·tion /ˌkɒmpə'tɪʃn ; ˌkɑmpə'tɪʃən/ *n* **1** [U] competing; activity in which persons compete: 競爭；競賽；角逐；競爭的活動: *trade ~ between countries;* 國際間的貿易競爭； *keen ~ for a job.* 求職的激烈競爭。 *At the Olympic Games our representatives were in ~* (= were competing) *with the best swimmers from all parts of the world.* 在奧運會上，我們的代表曾與世界各地的最佳游泳選手角逐。 **2** [C] instance of competing; contest; meeting(s) at which skill, strength, knowledge, etc is tested: 比賽；(比賽技巧、體力、知識等的) 賽會: *boxing/chess ~s.* 拳擊 (西洋棋等) 比賽。

com·peti·tive /kəm'petətɪv ; kəm'pɛtətɪv/ *adj* in or for which there is competition: 競爭性的；比賽性的: *~ examinations for government posts.* 公職甄選考試。 *Our firm offers you ~ prices,* prices that compare favourably with those of other firms. 本店向你提出競爭性的價格 (比其他商店公道的價格)。

com·peti·tor /kəm'petɪtə(r) ; kəm'pɛtətɚ/ *n* person who competes. 競爭者；敵手。

com·pile /kəm'paɪl ; kəm'paɪl/ *vt* [VP6A] collect (information) and arrange (in a book, list, report, etc): 搜集 (資料) 並編輯 (成書、表、報告等)；編纂；編輯: *~ a dictionary/a guide-book/an index.* 編輯字典 (旅行指南，索引)。 **com·piler** *n* person who ~s. 編纂者；編輯。 **com·pi·la·tion** /ˌkɒmpɪ'leɪʃn ; ˌkɑmpɪ'leʃən/ *n* [U] compiling; [C] thing that is ~d. 編輯；編纂；編製；編纂物。

com·pla·cence /kəm'pleɪsns ; kəm'plesṇs/ *n* [U] self-satisfaction; quiet contentment. 自滿；得意；暗自滿足。 **com·pla·cency** /-'pleɪsnsɪ ; -'plesṇsɪ/ *n*

com·pla·cent /kəm'pleɪsnt ; kəm'plesṇt/ *adj* self-satisfied: 自滿的；得意的: *with a ~ smile/air.* 帶着得意的微笑 (神情)。 **~·ly** *adv*

com·plain /kəm'pleɪn ; kəm'plen/ *vi* [VP2A, 3A, B] ***~ (to sb) (about/of sth),*** say that one is not satisfied, that sth is wrong, that one is suffering: 抱怨；不滿；發牢騷；訴苦: *She ~ed to me of his rudeness/that he had been rude to her.* 她向我訴說他的粗魯 (他曾對她有粗魯的行爲)。 *We have nothing to ~ of/about.* 我們沒有什麼可抱怨的。 *He never ~s about the pain/about being in pain.* 他從來不爲那痛苦抱怨。 **~·ing·ly** *adv*

com·plain·ant /kəm'pleɪnənt ; kəm'plenənt/ *n* (legal) plaintiff. (法律) 原告。

com·plaint /kəm'pleɪnt ; kəm'plent/ *n* **1** [U] complaining; [C] statement of, grounds for, dissatisfaction: 抱怨；不滿；抱怨的話；不滿的理由；控訴: *You have no cause/grounds of/for ~.* 你沒有理由抱怨。 *Have you any ~s to make?* 你有什麼苦要訴嗎？ *Some children are full of ~s about their food.* 有些孩子滿口抱怨他們的食物不好。 *Why don't you lodge a ~ against your noisy neighbours?* 你爲何不控告你的喧囂的鄰居？ **2** [C] illness; disease: 疾病: *a heart/liver ~;* 心臟 (肝) 病； *childish ~s,* illnesses common among children. 小兒常患的疾病。

com·plais·ance /kəm'pleɪzns ; kəm'plezṇs/ *n* [U] easy-going habit of mind; readiness and willingness to do what pleases others: 隨遇而安的心理；樂於做出使旁人高興之事的意願；慇懃；順從: *do sth out of ~.* 爲獻慇懃而做某事。 **com·plais·ant** /-zənt ; -zṇt/ *adj* obliging; disposed to please: 慇懃的；順從的: *a complaisant husband.* 順從的丈夫。

com·ple·ment /'kɒmplɪmənt ; 'kɑmpləmənt/ *n* **1** that which makes sth complete; the full number or quantity needed: 補足物；補充物；所需要的全數或量；足數；足量: *the ship's ~,* the full number of officers and men. 船上的編制員額。 **2** (gram) word(s) esp *adjj* and *nn,* used after *vv* such as *be* and *become* and qualifying the subject: (文法) 補語；(尤指形容詞及名詞，用於 be 及 become 等動詞之後以形容主詞): *In the sentence 'I'm tired' tired is the ~.* 在 'I'm tired' 句中，tired 是補語。 **~·ary** /ˌkɒmplɪ'mentrɪ ; ˌkɑmplə'mɛntərɪ/ *adj* forming a ~. 補足的；補充的。 □ *vt* [VP6A] complete; form the ~ to. 補足；補充；爲…的補足物。

com·plete[1] /kəm'pliːt ; kəm'plit/ *adj* **1** having all its parts; whole: 完整的；完全的；全部的；整個的: *a ~ edition of Shakespeare's plays.* 莎士比亞戲劇全集。 **2** finished; ended: 完成的；結束的: *When will the work be ~?* 這項工作將於何時完成？ **3** thorough; in every way: 徹底的；完完全全的: *He's a ~ stranger to me.* 對我來說他完全是個陌生人。 *It was a ~ surprise to me,* I wasn't expecting it and hadn't even thought of it. 它對我完全是件意外的事 (我未預料到它，甚至未曾想到它)。 **~·ly** *adv* wholly; in every way: 完全地；徹底地: *~ly successful.* 完全成功。 **~·ness** *n*

com·plete[2] /kəm'pliːt ; kəm'plit/ *vt* [VP6A] finish; bring to an end; make perfect: 完成；使完善: *The railway is not ~d yet.* 鐵路尚未完工。 *I need one volume to ~ my set of Dickens.* 我只差一本書就可以有全套狄更斯作品了。

com·ple·tion /kəm'pliːʃn ; kəm'pliʃən/ *n* [U] act of completing; state of being complete: 完成；完工；完滿；完結；完全: *You may occupy the house on ~ of contract,* when the contract of sale has been completed. 買賣契約手續完成時，你就可以住進此屋。

com·plex[1] /'kɒmpleks *US:* kɒm'pleks ; kəm'plɛks/ *adj* made up of closely connected parts; difficult to understand or explain: 由許多密切聯繫的部份合成的；難以瞭解或解釋的；複雜的；複合的: *a ~ argument/proposal/situation;* 複雜的論據 (提議，情況)； *a ~ system of government;* 複雜的行政制度； *a ~ sentence,* (gram) one containing subordinate clauses. (文法) 複雜句 (包含附屬子句的句子)。 **~·ity** /kəm'pleksətɪ ; kəm'plɛksətɪ/ *n* [U] state of being ~; [C] (*pl* -ties) sth that is ~. 複雜的狀態；複雜之事物。

com·plex[2] /'kɒmpleks ; 'kɑmplɛks/ *n* [C] **1** complex whole; number of dissimilar parts intricately related: 複合體；複雜相關的一群相異的部份: *a building ~.* 綜合建築。 **2** (psych) (abnormal) mental state which is the result of past experiences or suppressed tendencies; (colloq) obsessive concern or fear: (心理學) 由於過去的經驗或被壓抑的性向所造成的 (不正常) 心理狀態；情結；感；(俗) 縈繞於心的憂慮或恐懼: *He has a ~ about his weight.* 他過分關心他的體重。 ⇨ *inferiority* at inferior, *superiority* at superior.

com·plexion /kəm'plekʃn ; kəm'plɛkʃən/ *n* [C] **1** natural colour, appearance, etc of the skin, esp of the face: (天然的)膚色;面色;面貌: *a good/dark/fair* ~. 姣好的(棕黑的; 白皙的)膚色。 **2** general character or aspect (of conduct, affairs, etc): (指行爲、事情等)一般表徵;一般形勢;外觀: *This victory changed the ~ of the war,* made the probable outcome different, gave hope of an early end, etc. 這一場勝仗使大戰形勢爲之改觀(使可能的結果發生變化,使之可望早日結束等)。

com·pli·ance /kəmˈplaɪəns ; kəmˈplaɪəns/ *n* [U] **1** action of complying: 順從;聽從;依從: *in ~ with your wishes,* as you wish(ed) us (to do). 順從你的願望;依你所願;遵囑。 **2** tendency to give way to others; unworthy submission. 順從他人的意向;卑屈。

com·pli·ant /kəmˈplaɪənt ; kəmˈplaɪənt/ *adj* ready or disposed to comply. 願意順從的;聽從的。

com·pli·cate /ˈkɒmplɪkeɪt ; ˈkɑmpləˌket/ *vt* [VP6A] make complex; make (sth) difficult to do or understand: 使複雜;使(某事物)難做或難懂: *This ~s matters.* 這把事情弄複雜了。**com·pli·cated** *adj* made up of many parts; difficult to do or understand: 複雜的;難做的;難懂的: *a ~d machine;* 複雜的機器; *~d business deals.* 複雜的商業交易。

com·pli·ca·tion /ˌkɒmplɪˈkeɪʃn ; ˌkɑmpləˈkeʃən/ *n* [C] **1** state of being complex, confused, difficult; sth that adds new difficulties: 複雜的狀態;混亂;困難;增加新困難的事物: *Here are further ~s to worry us.* 這裏還有更多的複雜的事情困擾我們。 **2** (med) new illness, or new development of an illness, that makes treatment more difficult: (醫)(增加治療困難的)新發病症或病情之新的發展;併發症: *influenza with ~s;* 流行性感冒帶併發症; *if no ~s set in.* 如果不發生併發症的話。

com·plic·ity /kəmˈplɪsətɪ ; kəmˈplɪsətɪ/ *n* [U] ~ *(in),* taking part with another person (in crime). (與另一人)共謀;串通。

com·pli·ment /ˈkɒmplɪmənt ; ˈkɑmpləmənt/ *n* [C] **1** expression of admiration, approval, etc, either in words or by action, eg by asking sb for his advice or opinions, or by imitating him. (以言語或行動做出之)恭維之表示;敬意;讚揚(例如向某人請教或效法他)。 ***pay sb a ~/pay a ~ to sb (on sth)***: (爲某事物)恭維某人: *They paid me a well-deserved ~.* 他們給了我極應得的讚揚。 **2** (*pl*) (formal) greetings: (複)(正式用語)問候;致意;道賀: *My ~s to your wife,* Please give her a greeting from me. 請代我向尊夫人致意。*With the ~s of the season,* phrase used at Christmas and the New Year. 恭祝聖誕,並賀年禧(聖誕節及新年期間的致意話)。 *With the author's/publisher's ~s,* phrase used when an author/publisher sends a gift of a book newly issued. 作者(出版者)敬贈(作者或出版者贈送新出版之書與他人時的客套語)。 □ *vt* /ˈkɒmplɪment ; ˈkɑmpləˌmɛnt/ [VP6A, 14] ~ ***sb (on sth),*** pay a ~ to: 恭維;稱讚: *I ~ed him on his skill.* 我稱讚他的技術。

com·pli·men·tary /ˌkɒmplɪˈmentrɪ ; ˌkɑmpləˈmɛntərɪ/ *adj* **1** expressing admiration, praise, etc. 恭維的;表示欽佩、讚美等的。 **2** given free, out of courtesy or kindness: (因禮貌或客氣而)免費贈送的: *a ~ ticket/copy of a book, etc.* 贈送的票(一冊書等)。

com·plin, com·pline /ˈkɒmplɪn ; ˈkɑmplɪn/ *n* (in RC and Anglo-Catholic ritual) last (church) service of the day. (天主教或英國國教高教會儀式)一日中的最後崇拜;晚禱。

com·ply /kəmˈplaɪ ; kəmˈplaɪ/ *vi* [VP2A, 3A] ~ *(with),* act in accordance (with a request, command, sb's wishes, etc): 依從;順從;聽從;服從(請求、命令、某人的願望等): *You must ~ with* (= obey) *the rules.* 你必須遵守規則。*He refused to ~.* 他拒絕服從。

com·po·nent /kəmˈpəʊnənt ; kəmˈponənt/ *adj* helping to form (a complete thing): 組成的;構成(全物)的: *~ parts.* 組成的各部分;組成件。□ *n* ~ part: 部分;成分: *the ~s of a camera lens.* 組成照相機鏡頭的各部分。

com·port /kəmˈpɔːt ; kəmˈpɔrt/ *vt, vi* (formal) (正式用語) **1** [VP15A] (usu reflex) behave; conduct: (通常用反身式)行爲;持(己);舉止: ~ *oneself with dignity.* 舉止莊重。 **2** [VP3A] ~ ***with,*** suit, be in harmony with: 適合;相稱;一致: *His conduct did not ~ with his position.* 他的舉止與他的地位不相稱。 **~·ment** *n*

com·pose /kəmˈpəʊz ; kəmˈpoz/ *vt, vi* **1** [VP6A] (of elements) make up, form: (指要素)組成;構成: *the parts that ~ the whole;* 組成全體的各部分; (usu in the passive) ***be ~d of,*** be made up of: (通常用被動語態)由…組成: *Water* (H_2O) *is ~d of hydrogen and oxygen.* 水由氫與氧化合而成。*Our party was ~d of teachers, pupils and their parents.* 我們這一夥由教員、學生及學生的父母組成。 **2** [VP6A, 2A] put together (words, ideas, musical notes, etc) in literary, musical, etc, form: 著作;作(曲等): ~ *a poem/a song/an opera/a speech.* 作詩(歌,歌劇,演講稿)。*He teaches music and also ~s,* writes music. 他教音樂,並且作曲。 **3** [VP6A] (printing) set up (type) to form words, paragraphs, pages, etc. (印刷)排(活字)成字、段、頁等。 ⇨ compositor. **4** [VP6A, 16A] get under control; calm: 控制;使鎮定;使安靜: ~ *one's thoughts/passions.* 鎮定思緒(情緒)。*She ~d herself to answer the letter.* 她鎮靜下來回信。*Try to ~ your features,* make yourself look calm. 盡量保持鎮靜的神色。 **com·posed** *adj* calm; with feelings under control. 鎮靜的;神情泰然的。**com·posed·ly** /kəmˈpəʊzɪdlɪ ; kəmˈpozɪdlɪ/ *adv* in a ~d manner. 鎮靜地;泰然地。

com·poser /kəmˈpəʊzə(r) ; kəmˈpozɚ/ *n* (esp) person who composes music. (尤指)作曲家。

com·pos·ite /ˈkɒmpəzɪt ; kəmˈpɑzɪt/ *adj* made up of different parts or materials: 由各種不同的部分或材料組成的;集成的;拼成的;綜合的: *a ~ illustration,* made by putting together two or more drawings, etc. 綜合圖說(集合若干圖片等而成的說明)。

com·po·si·tion /ˌkɒmpəˈzɪʃn ; ˌkɑmpəˈzɪʃən/ *n* **1** [U] act or art of composing, eg a piece of writing or music, type for printing, objects that will be included in a painting: 著作;作曲;排字;構圖: *He played a piano sonata of his own ~,* that he himself had composed. 他彈奏了一首自作的鋼琴奏鳴曲。 **2** [C] that which is composed, eg a poem, a book, a piece of music, an arrangement of objects to be painted or photographed; (esp) exercise in writing by one who is learning a language. 著作物;製作物(如詩、書、樂曲、繪畫或照相的構圖);(尤指學習語文者爲練習寫作而寫的)作文。 **3** [U] the parts of which sth is made up: (組成某物的)成分: *Scientists study the ~ of the soil.* 科學家研究土壤的成分。*He has a touch of madness in his ~,* There is an element of madness in him. 他生來就有點瘋瘋癲癲。 **4** [C] substance composed of more than one material, esp an artificial substance: (由多種材料尤指人造物質)合成之物;混合物;人造物: *~ floors.* 合成地板。

com·po·si·tor /kəmˈpɒzɪtə(r) ; kəmˈpɑzɪtɚ/ *n* skilled person who composes type for printing. 排字工人。

compos mentis /ˌkɒmpəs ˈmentɪs ; ˈkɑmpəsˈmɛntɪs/ *adj* (Lat) (colloq) sane: (拉丁)(俗)心理健全的;神智清楚的: *He's not quite ~,* is a little mad. 他的精神不十分健全(有點瘋狂)。

com·post /ˈkɒmpɒst ; ˈkɑmpost/ *n* [U] prepared mixture, esp of rotted organic matter, manure, etc, for use in horticulture. (由腐爛的有機物、糞便等混成用於園藝的)混合肥料;堆肥。□ *vt* [VP6A] make into ~; treat with ~. 製成堆肥;施以堆肥。

com·po·sure /kəmˈpəʊʒə(r) ; kəmˈpoʒɚ/ *n* [U] condition of being composed in mind; calmness (of mind or behaviour): 心神鎮靜;態度沉着;泰然自若: *behave with great ~.* 態度極爲鎮定。

com·pote /ˈkɒmpɒt ; ˈkɑmpot/ *n* [C, U] (dish of) fruit cooked with sugar and water. 一道蜜餞水果。

com·pound¹ /ˈkɒmpaʊnd ; ˈkɑmpaund/ *n, adj* **1**

(sth) made up of two or more combined parts: 複合的；結合的；合成的；複合物；化合物：*Common salt is a ~ of sodium and chlorine.* 食鹽是鈉和氯的化合物。**2** (gram) item composed of two or more parts, (written as one or two words, or joined by a hyphen), themselves usu words, (文法)複合字(由兩個或更多的部份合成，這些部份本身通常都是字，複合字寫作一字或二字，或由一連字號相連)，eg 例如 *'bus conductor.* ˌ~ **'sentence,** one containing two or more co-ordinate clauses (linked by *and, but,* etc). 複合句(含兩個或更多對等子句的句子，各子句間用 and, but 等連接)。**3** ˌ~**'interest,** interest on capital and on accumulated interest. 複利(本金利息加累積利息的利息)。ˌ~ **'fracture,** breaking of a bone complicated by an open wound in the skin. 哆開骨折；穿破骨折；複雜骨折。

com·pound² /kəm'paund ; kəm'paund/ *vt, vi* **1** [VP6A] mix together (to make sth new or different): 混合(以製新物或不同之物)；摻合；調合：~ *a medicine;* 配藥；*a cake ~ed of the best ingredients.* 用各種最好的材料調製成的糕餅。**2** [VP6A, 2A, 3A] **~ *(with sb) (for sth),*** settle (a quarrel, a debt) by mutual concession; come to terms: (由於互作讓步而)和解；解決(爭端、債務)；達成協議；談妥：*He ~ed with his creditors for a remission of what he owed.* 他與債權人談妥免除其債務。**3** [VP6A] add to, increase (an offence or injury) by causing another: (由於引起另一罪行或傷害而)加重(罪行或傷害)：*That simply ~s the offence.* 那只會加重罪過。

com·pound³ /'kɒmpaund ; 'kampaund/ *n* enclosed area with buildings, etc, eg a number of houses, a commercial or trading centre. 圍地(場內有建築物，如房屋等)；商業或貿易中心。

com·pre·hend /ˌkɒmprɪ'hend ; ˌkamprɪ'hɛnd/ *vt* [VP6A] **1** understand fully. 充分瞭解；領悟。**2** include. 包括；包含。

com·pre·hen·sible /ˌkɒmprɪ'hensəbl ; ˌkamprɪ'hɛnsəbl/ *adj* that can be understood fully: 可充分瞭解的：*a book that is ~ only to specialists.* 只有專家才可以瞭解的一本書。**com·pre·hen·si·bil·ity** /ˌkɒmprɪˌhensə'bɪlətɪ ; ˌkamprɪˌhɛnsə'bɪlətɪ/ *n*

com·pre·hen·sion /ˌkɒmprɪ'henʃn ; ˌkamprɪ'hɛnʃən/ *n* [U, C] **1** the mind's act or power of understanding: 理解；領會；理解力：*The problem is above/beyond my ~.* 這問題超出我的理解力以外。**2** exercise aimed at improving or testing one's understanding of a language (written or spoken). (對某種語言的文字或口語的)理解力練習；理解力測驗；閱讀測驗；聽力測驗。**3** power of including: 包含力；含蓄力：*a term of wide ~,* eg a word that includes many meanings, uses, etc. 包羅廣泛的名辭(例如一含義和用法甚多的字)。

com·pre·hen·sive /ˌkɒmprɪ'hensɪv ; ˌkamprɪ'hɛnsɪv/ *adj* that comprehends(2) much: 包羅廣泛的；綜合性的：*a ~ description/review of the term's work, etc;* 綜合性的描述(全學期功課的溫習等)；*a man with a ~ mind/grasp of ideas.* 富有理解力(對於各種觀念有廣泛之瞭解力)的人。'~ **(school),** large school that combines all types of secondary education, ie academic and technical. 綜合中學(一種包含學術及技能教育的大型中學)。**~·ly** *adv* **~·ness** *n*

com·press¹ /kəm'pres ; kəm'prɛs/ *vt* [VP6A, 14] **1** press together; get into a small(er) space: 緊壓；壓縮(以便置於較小之空間)：*~ed air;* 壓縮空氣；*~ cotton into bales.* 將棉花壓緊打包。**2** put (ideas, etc) into fewer words; condense. 扼要敘述；摘要敘述(要點等)。

com·press² /'kɒmpres ; 'kamprɛs/ *n* pad or cloth pressed on to a part of the body (to stop bleeding, reduce fever, etc): 貼在身上某部份(以止血、退熱等)之壓布；繃帶：*a cold/hot ~.* 冷(熱)壓布。

com·pres·sion /kəm'preʃn ; kəm'prɛʃən/ *n* [U] compressing; being compressed: 壓緊；壓縮：*~ of ideas.* 言簡意賅。

com·prise /kəm'praɪz ; kəm'praɪz/ *vt* [VP6A] be composed of; have as parts or members: 由…組成；包括；包含：*The committee ~s men of widely different views.* 委員會中包括意見極不相同的份子。*The force ~d two battalions and a battery.* 該部隊包含兩個步兵營及一個砲兵連。

com·pro·mise /'kɒmprəmaɪz ; 'kamprəˌmaɪz/ *n* [U] settlement of a dispute by which each side gives up sth it has asked for and neither side gets all it has asked for; [C] instance of this; settlement reached in this way: 由於彼此讓步而解決爭端；和解；妥協；折衷(每一方面放棄一部份要求，兩方面都不能得到全部所要求的)；折衷處理；折衷辦法：*The strike was not ended until they resorted to ~.* 罷工到雙方互相讓步才終止。*A ~ agreement was at last arrived at.* 一個折衷的協議終於達成。*Can we effect a ~?* 我們能想出一個折衷辦法嗎？□ *vt, vi* **1** [VP6A, 2A] settle a dispute, etc, by making a ~: 以折衷辦法解決爭端等：*if they agree to ~.* 如果他們同意折衷的話。**2** bring (sb, sth, oneself) under suspicion by unwise behaviour, etc: 由於不智的行爲等致使(某人、某事物、自己)受牽連；損害：*You will ~ yourself/your reputation if you spend all your time gambling.* 如果你終日賭博，你就會損害自己(你的名聲)。**3** imperil the safety of (by folly or rashness, etc): (由於愚昧或魯莽等而)危及…的安全：*The position of the army was ~d by the general's poor judgement.* 這支軍隊的陣地由於將軍不智的判斷而受危害。

comp·trol·ler /kən'trəulə(r) ; kən'trolɚ/ *n* (in some titles) controller: (在某些職銜中)主任；長；主計長；會計主任；審計長：~ *of accounts.* 審計長；審計官。

com·pul·sion /kəm'pʌlʃn ; kəm'pʌlʃən/ *n* [U] compelling or being compelled. 强迫；被迫。***under ~,*** because one must: 被迫；不得已：*A defeated country usually signs a treaty of peace under ~.* 戰敗國通常被迫簽訂和約。

com·pul·sive /kəm'pʌlsɪv ; kəm'pʌlsɪv/ *adj* having a tendency or the power to compel; caused by an obsession: 强迫性的；强制的；由於成見或頑念所引起的：*a ~ eater/TV viewer,* one who feels compelled to eat/watch TV; 强迫性食者(看電視者)(被縈繞心中的固執偏見所驅使而去吃東西或看電視者)；*a ~ liar,* one who lies repeatedly. 一再說謊的人。**~·ly** *adv*

com·pul·sory /kəm'pʌlsərɪ ; kəm'pʌlsərɪ/ *adj* that must be done; required: 必須做的；必修的；規定的；强迫的；義務的：*Is military service ~ in your country?* 在貴國，服兵役是義務的嗎？*Is English a ~ subject?* 英語是必修科嗎？**com·pul·sor·ily** /kəm'pʌlsərəlɪ ; kəm'pʌlsərəlɪ/ *adv*

com·punc·tion /kəm'pʌŋkʃn ; kəm'pʌŋkʃən/ *n* [U] uneasiness of conscience; feeling of regret for one's action: 良心的不安；(對於自己行爲的)懊悔；後悔；抱歉：*She kept me waiting without the slightest ~.* 她使我久候而絲毫沒有歉意。

com·pu·ta·tion /ˌkɒmpju'teɪʃn ; ˌkampjə'teʃən/ *n* [U] computing; [C] result of computing; calculation: 計算；計算的結果；估計：*It will cost £5000 at the lowest ~.* 根據最低的估計，它也要值五千鎊。*He has wealth beyond ~.* 他的財富無法估計。*Addition and division are forms of ~.* 加法和除法都是計算的方法。

com·pute /kəm'pju:t ; kəm'pjut/ *vt, vi* [VP6A, 14, 2A] **~ *(at),*** reckon; calculate: 計算；估計：*He ~d his losses at £50.* 他估計他的損失在五十鎊。*What is the ~d horse-power of the engine?* 這引擎的估計馬力是多少？

com·puter /kəm'pju:tə(r) ; kəm'pjutɚ/ *n* electronic device which stores information on eg magnetic tape, analyses it and produces information as required from the data on the tapes. 電子計算機；電腦(儲存資料於磁帶上等，將之加以分析，並能應需要提供所存之資料的電子裝置)。**~·ize** *vt* [VP6A] store (information) with or in a ~ or system of ~s; supply with a ~ or ~s. 用電子計算機儲存(資料)；

將(資料)存入電腦中；供以計算機；以電腦配備。

com·rade /'kɒmreɪd *US:* -ræd ; 'kɑmræd/ *n* **1** trusted companion; loyal friend: 可靠的友伴；忠實的朋友：*~s in arms*, fellow soldiers; 戰友；*~s in exile*, those who are exiled together. 同被放逐者。**2** fellow member of a trade union, a (left-wing) political party, etc. 工會的同人；(左翼政黨等的)同志。**~·ly** /'kɒmreɪdlɪ ; 'kɑmrædlɪ/ *adv* **~·ship** /'kɒmreɪdʃɪp ; 'kɑmræd,ʃɪp/ *n*

con[1] /kɒn ; kɑn/ *adv* ***pro and con***, for and against: 正反兩面地：*argue pro and con for hours.* 正反兩面辯論數小時。□ *n* ***the pros and cons***, the arguments for and against. 辯論的正反兩面理由。

con[2] /kɒn ; kɑn/ (sl) short for *confidence*, in attrib uses: (俚)(confidence 之略)(作形容用法)：*a con man;* 騙子；*the con game.* 騙術。⇨ confidence(3). □ *vt* (-nn-) [VP6A, 14] ***con sb (into doing sth)***, (colloq) swindle him after winning his confidence; persuade him to do sth in this way. (俗)取得某人信賴後再欺騙；騙某人(作某事)。

con·cat·ena·tion /kɒn,kætɪ'neɪʃn ; ,kɑnkætn̩'eʃən/ *n* [U] linking together; [C] series of things or events linked together. 連鎖；一連串的東西或事件。

con·cave /'kɒŋkeɪv ; kɑn'kev/ *adj* (of an outline or surface) curved inwards like the inner surface of a sphere or ball. (指輪廓或表面)凹的(如圓球之內面)。⇨ the illus at convex. 參看 convex 之挿圖。**con·cav·ity** /,kɒn'kævətɪ ; kɑn'kævətɪ/ *n* [U] ~ condition; [C] (*pl* -ties) ~ surface. 凹性；凹狀；凹面。

con·ceal /kən'si:l ; kən'sil/ *vt* [VP6A, 14] ***~ (from)***, hide; keep secret: 隱藏；隱匿；隱瞞：*~ sth from sb.* 隱藏或隱瞞某事物。*He tried to ~ the fact that....* 他企圖隱瞞…之事實。*C~ed turning*, (as a road sign) warning that a turning into a road is hidden from view, eg by bushes or trees. 蔭蔽彎路(公路路標，警告前面彎路爲樹林等所遮蔽)。**~·ment** *n* [U] act of ~ing; state of being ~ed: 隱藏；隱匿；躱藏；隱蔽：*stay in ~ment until the danger has passed.* 躱藏起來直到危險過去。

con·cede /kən'si:d ; kən'sid/ *vt* [VP6A, 9, 13A, 12A] admit; grant; allow: 承認；讓與；容許：*~ a point in an argument.* 在辯論中承認某點正確。*He ~d ten points to his opponent／~d him ten points*, ie in a game. (在比賽中)他讓他的對手十分。*They have ~d us the right to cross their land.* 他們已容許我們經過他們的土地。*You must ~ that I have tried hard.* 你必須承認我已盡力爲之。*We cannot ~ any of our territory*, allow another country to have it. 我們不能放棄一寸國土。

con·ceit /kən'si:t ; kən'sit/ *n* **1** [U] over-high opinion of, too much pride in, oneself or one's powers, abilities, etc: 對於自己或自己的能力等之過高的評價；自大；自負；自豪：*He's full of ~.* 他極其自負。***in one's own ~***, (old use) in one's own judgement. (舊用法)自認爲。***out of ~ with***, (old use) no longer pleased with. (舊用法)對…不再歡喜。**2** [C] humorous or witty thought or expression. 詼諧或機智的思想或辭句。**~ed** *adj* full of ~. 極其自負的。**~·ed·ly** /-ɪdlɪ ; -ɪdlɪ/ *adv*

con·ceive /kən'si:v ; kən'siv/ *vt, vi* **1** [VP6A, 10, 3A, 9, 14] ***~ (of)***, form (an idea, plan, etc) in the mind: 想出(一個主意、計畫等)；構思；想像：*Who first ~d the idea of filling bags with gas to make balloons?* 誰最先想到充氣體於袋中以製成汽球的？*I can't ~ why you allowed／can't ~ of your allowing the child to travel alone.* 我想不通你爲什麼讓那孩子獨自旅行。*I ~d that there must be some difficulties.* 我料想到一定有些困難。*Why have you ~d such a dislike for me?* 你爲什麼對我感到這樣厭惡？**2** [VP2A, 6A] (of a woman) become pregnant: (指女人)受孕；懷孕：*~ a child.* 懷孕。**con·ceiv·able** *adj* that can be ~d or believed: 可想像的；可相信的：*It is hardly conceivable (to me) that....* (我)簡直難以想像…。**con·ceiv·ably** /-əblɪ ; -əblɪ/ *adv*

con·cen·trate /'kɒnsntreɪt ; 'kɑnsn̩,tret/ *vt, vi* **1** [VP6A, 14, 2A] bring or come together at one point: 集中(於一點)；集合：*to ~ soldiers in a town.* 將軍隊集中於城內。*The troops were ordered to scatter and then ~ twenty miles to the south.* 這軍隊奉命解散，然後在南方二十哩處集合。**2** [VP14, 3A, 2A] ***~ (on／upon)***, focus one's attention on: 集中注意力於；專心於；注意：*You should ~ (your attention) on your work.* 你應該專心(集中你的注意力)於你的工作。*You'll solve the problem if you ~ upon it*, give all your attention to it. 如果你全神貫注，你會解決這問題。*I can't ~!* 我的注意力無法集中！**3** [VP6A] increase the strength of (a solution) by reducing its volume (eg by boiling it). (用蒸發方法)濃縮(溶液)。□ *n* product made by concentrating(3). 濃縮物；濃縮液。**con·cen·trated** *adj* **1** intense: 集中的；加强的：*~d hate;* 强烈的仇恨；*~d fire*, the firing of guns all aimed at one point. 集中一點而發射的砲火；集中射擊。**2** increased in strength or value by evaporation of liquid: 濃縮(藉蒸發液體而增强其力量或價值)的：*a ~d solution;* 濃縮溶液；*~d food.* 濃縮食物。

con·cen·tra·tion /,kɒnsn'treɪʃn ; ,kɑnsn̩'treʃən/ *n* **1** [C] that which is concentrated: 集中物；集結物：*~s of enemy troops.* 敵軍在數處之集結。**2** [U] concentrating or being concentrated on: 集合；集中：*a book that requires great ~;* 需要全神貫注才能讀得懂的書；*a child with little power of ~.* 注意力不能集中的小孩。**'~ camp**, place where civilian political prisoners or internees are brought together and confined. 集中營(集中監禁政治犯或被拘留者的地方)。

con·cen·tric /kən'sentrɪk ; kən'sɛntrɪk/ *adj* ***~ (with)***, (of circles) having a common centre. (指數個圓)同中心的；(與另一圓)同心的。

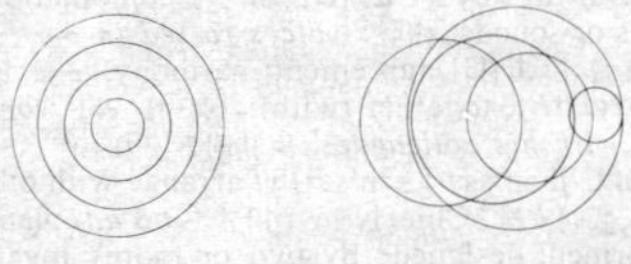

concentric circles　circles not concentric

con·cept /'kɒnsept ; 'kɑnsɛpt/ *n* [C] idea underlying a class of things; general notion. 一類事物的基本觀念；概念。

con·cep·tion /kən'sepʃn ; kən'sɛpʃən/ *n* **1** [U] conceiving of an idea or plan; [C] idea or plan that takes shape in the mind: 構思；構想；想像；想出的意念或計畫：*A good novelist needs great powers of ~.* 一個好的小說家需要極大的構思力。*I have no ~ of what you mean.* 我想不出你的意思是什麼。*An actor must have a clear ~ of the part he is to play.* 一個演員對他所要演的角色，必須要有一個淸楚的瞭解。**2** [U, C] conceiving(2); becoming pregnant. 懷孕；妊娠。**'~ control**, more precise, but less common, term for *birth-control.* 節制懷孕(爲 birth-control 之較精確名辭，但較不普遍)。

con·cern[1] /kən'sɜ:n ; kən'sɝn/ *vt* **1** [VP6A] have relation to; affect; be of importance to: 與…有關係；影響；對…有重要性：*Does this ~ me?* 這個與我有關係嗎？*Don't trouble about things that don't ~ you.* 不要操心與你無關的事。*He is said to have been ~ed in the crime*, to have had some connection with it. 據說他與此犯罪案有關連。*So／As far as I'm ~ed...*, so far as the matter is important to me, or affects me.... 就(此事與)我個人(的關係)而言…。*Where the children are ~ed...*, in matters where it is necessary to think of them.... 在與孩子們有關的事情方面…。***as ~s***, regarding. 關於。**2** [VP14] ***~ oneself with／in／about***, be busy with, interest oneself in. 忙於；從事；關心；關切。**3** [VP6A] (esp in the passive 尤用於被動語態 ***be ~ed about／for sb／sth***) worry; trouble; bother: 使擔憂；使煩惱；使操心：*Don't let my illness ~ you.* 不要爲我的

病擔憂。*Please don't be ~ed about me.* 請不要爲我操心。*We are all ~ed for/about her safety.* 我們大家都擔心着她的安全。**~·ing** *prep* about. 關於。

con·cern² /kən'sɜːn ; kən'sɝn/ *n* **1** [C] relation or connection; sth in which one is interested or which is important to one: 關係; 關連; 關心之事; (對某人)關係重大之事: *It's no ~ of mine,* I have nothing to do with it. 這事與我無關。*Mind your own ~s* (*business* is more usu), Don't interfere in other people's affairs. 管你自己的事(不要管別人的閒事) (business 較常用)。*What ~ is it of yours,* Why do you take an interest in it? 此事與你何干? (你爲何要介入?) **2** [C] business or undertaking: 營業;事務;業務: *The shop has now become a paying ~,* is making profits. 這商店現在已可賺錢了。***a going ~,*** one that is active and in operation, not merely planned. 已開始營業(活動等) (非僅計畫中之事而已)。**3** [C] share: 股份: *He has a ~ in the business,* is a part-owner. 他在這企業中有一股份(爲股東之一)。**4** [U] anxiety: 憂慮; 擔心: *filled with ~;* 滿懷憂慮; *look at sb in ~.* 擔心地看着某人。*There is some cause for ~ but no need for alarm.* 是有點令人憂慮,但不必驚慌。**~ed** /-'sɜːnd ; -'sɝnd/ *adj* anxious: 焦慮的;擔心的: *with a ~ed look.* 以焦慮的神情。**~·edly** /-'sɜːnɪdlɪ ; -'sɝnɪdlɪ/ *adv*

con·cert¹ /'kɒnsət ; 'kɑnsɝt/ *n* **1** [C] musical entertainment, esp one given in a public hall by players or singers. (在公共廳堂中由演奏者或歌唱者所舉行的)音樂會。~ **grand,** grand piano of the largest size, for ~s. (音樂會用的) 大型平臺鋼琴。**'~-hall,** hall for ~s. 音樂會堂;音樂廳。➪ music-hall. ***at ˌ~ 'pitch,*** (fig) in a state of full efficiency or readiness. (喻)在效率極高或準備極佳的狀態。➪ *keyed up* at key². **2** [U] ***in ~,*** combination of voices or sounds: 齊聲: *voices raised in ~.* 一起提高的聲音。**3** [U] agreement; harmony. 一致;協調。***in ~ (with),*** together (with): (與…)一起: *working in ~ with his colleagues.* 與其同事協力工作。

con·cert² /kən'sɜːt ; kən'sɝt/ *vt* arrange with others. 與他人共同安排。Chiefly in 主用於 **~ed** *adj* planned, performed, designed (by two or more) together: (由二人或更多的人)共同計畫、表演、設計的;一致的: *to take ~ed action;* 採取一致行動; *to make a ~ed attack.* 聯合攻擊。

con·cer·tina /ˌkɒnsə'tiːnə ; ˌkɑnsɚ'tinə/ *n* musical wind instrument consisting of a pair of bellows, held in the hands and played by pressing keys at each end. 六角形手風琴(由一對風箱構成,捧於手中,按兩端之鍵而奏的一種手風琴)。

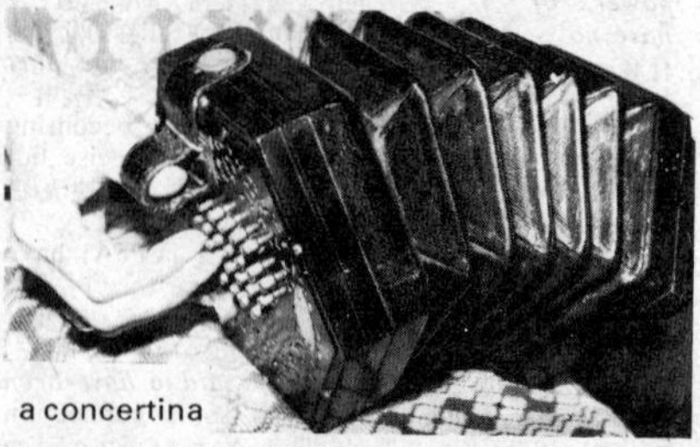

a concertina

con·certo /kən'tʃeətəʊ; kən'tʃɛrto/ *n* (*pl* ~s) musical composition for one or more solo instruments supported by an orchestra: 協奏曲 (供一件或數件樂器獨奏而由管弦樂隊配合之樂曲): *a 'piano ~;* 鋼琴協奏曲; *a ~ for two violins.* 雙小提琴協奏曲。

con·ces·sion /kən'seʃn ; kən'sɛʃən/ *n* **1** [U] conceding; [C] that which is conceded, esp after discussion, a difference of opinion, an argument, etc: 讓步; 妥協; (尤指)經過討論、異議、辯論等之後所作的讓步: *As a ~ to the public outcry, the Government reduced the tax on petrol.* 政府減低汽油稅作爲對民衆反對的讓步。**2** [C] (esp) right given by owner(s) of land, or by a Government, to do sth (eg take minerals from land): (尤指)由地主或政府許可的特權(如土地中的礦物開採權); 轉讓; 租讓: *oil/mining ~s.* 石油開採權(採礦權)。**con·ces·sive** /kən'sesɪv ; kən'sɛsɪv/ *adj* (gram) expressing ~: (文法)讓步的: *a concessive clause,* eg introduced by *as* or *although,* implying a contrast between circumstances, etc. 讓步子句 (以 as 或 although 等開始的子句, 含示情況等之差異)。**~·aire** /kənˌseʃə'neə(r) ; kənˌsɛʃən'ɛr/ *n* holder of a ~(2). 特許權所有人。

conch /kɒntʃ ; kɑŋk/ *n* shellfish with a large spiral shell. 海螺(有大螺旋貝殼)。➪ the illus at mollusc. 參看 mollusc 之插圖。**con·chol·ogy** /kɒŋ'kɒlədʒɪ ; kɑŋ'kɑlədʒɪ/ *n* [U] study of shells and shellfish. 介類學;貝類學。

con·ci·erge /ˌkɒnsɪ'eəʒ *US:* ˌkɒnsɪ'eərʒ ; ˌkɑnsɪ'ɛrʒ/ *n* (F) (in France, etc) door-keeper, porter (of a block of flats, etc). (法) (法國等地之公寓等的)看門人。

con·cili·ate /kən'sɪlɪeɪt ; kən'sɪlɪˌet/ *vt* [VP6A] win the support, goodwill or friendly feelings of; calm the anger of; soothe. 贏得…的支持、善意或友情;與…修好;平息…的怒氣;安慰;撫慰。**con·cili·atory** /kən'sɪlɪətərɪ *US:* -tɔːrɪ ; kən'sɪlɪəˌtorɪ/ *adj* intending to or likely to ~: 有助於或可能促進修好的: *a conciliatory act/gesture/spirit.* 修好的行動(姿態,精神)。

con·cili·ation /kənˌsɪlɪ'eɪʃn ; kənˌsɪlɪ'eʃən/ *n* [U] conciliating or being conciliated: 修好;安慰;調解: *The dispute in the engineering industry is being dealt with by a ~ board,* a group of persons who arbitrate, etc. 工程業的糾紛現由一調解委員會處理中。

con·cise /kən'saɪs ; kən'saɪs/ *adj* (of a person's speech or style of writing, etc) brief; giving much information in few words. (指某人的言語或文體等) 簡潔的;簡明的;用少數字傳達多量意思的。**~·ly** *adv* **~·ness** *n*

con·clave /'kɒnkleɪv ; 'kɑnklev/ *n* [C] private or secret meeting (eg of cardinals to elect a Pope). 秘密會議(如紅衣主教所開選舉教皇者)。***sit in ~,*** hold a secret meeting. 舉行秘密會議。

con·clude /kən'kluːd ; kən'klud/ *vt, vi* **1** [VP6A, 14, 2A, 3A] come or bring to an end; 結束: *to ~ a speech/a lecture.* 結束演說(學術演講)。*He ~d by saying that....* 他結束時說…。*The meeting ~d at 8 o'clock.* 會議在八點鐘結束。*The concert ~d with the National Anthem.* 音樂會最後演奏國歌而結束。**2** [VP6A, 14] ***~ sth (with sb),*** arrange; bring about: 安排;訂立;使成立: *Wales ~ed a treaty with Scotland.* 威爾斯與蘇格蘭訂立條約。**3** [VP9] arrive at a belief or opinion: 作結論: *The jury ~d, from the evidence, that the accused man was not guilty.* 陪審團依據證據作出結論, 認定被告無罪。**4** [VP7A] (esp US) decide, resolve (after discussion): (尤用於美國) (經討論後) 決定;決心: *We ~d not to go.* 我們(經討論後) 決定不去。

con·clusion /kən'kluːʒn ; kən'kluʒən/ *n* [C] **1** end: 結束;終結: *at the ~ of his speech;* 在他演說結束時; *bring a matter to a speedy ~.* 使事情迅速結束。***in ~,*** lastly. 最後地。**2** arranging; deciding; settling (*of*): 安排; 訂立; 決定; 解決 (與 of 連用): *the ~ of a peace treaty.* 和約的訂立。**3** belief or opinion which is the result of reasoning: 結論; 結語; 由推理的結果所得到的信念或意見: *come to/reach the ~ that...;* 得到以下的結論…; *to draw a ~ (from evidence, etc).* (由證據等) 獲得結論。***a foregone ~,*** something settled or decided in advance, not to be doubted. 早已確定的事;必然的結論;毫無疑問的事。**4** ***try ~s with,*** have a trial of skill with. 與…較量高低;與…一決勝負。

con·clus·ive /kən'kluːsɪv ; kən'klusɪv/ *adj* (of facts, evidence, etc) convincing; ending doubt: (指事實、證據等) 令人確信的; 確定的; 決定性的; 釋除疑問的: *~ evidence/proof of his guilt.* 關於他的罪行的決定性

的證據。~·ly *adv*

con·coct /kən'kɒkt ; kɑn'kɑkt/ *vt* [VP6A] **1** prepare by mixing together: 混合調製;配合: *to ~ a new kind of soup.* 調製一種新湯。 **2** invent (a story, an excuse, a plot for a novel, etc). 編造;捏造;虛構(故事、口實、小說情節等)。 **con·coc·tion** /kən'kɒkʃn ; kɑn'kɑkʃən/ *n* [U] ~ing; [C] sth that is ~ed. 配合;調製;虛構;調配之物;杜撰或捏造之事。

con·comi·tant /kən'kɒmɪtənt ; kɑn'kɑmətənt/ *adj* (formal) accompanying: (正式用語)伴隨的;隨…而至的: *~ circumstances.* 伴隨的情況。□ *n* [C] (usu *pl*) accompanying thing: (通常用複數)伴隨物: *the infirmities that are the ~s of old age.* 隨老年而至的虛弱。

con·cord /'kɒŋkɔ:d ; 'kɑŋkɔrd/ *n* **1** [U] agreement or harmony (between persons or things): (人與人或事物與事物之間的)一致;協調;和諧;和睦: *live in ~ (with...)*; (與…)和睦相處; [C] instance of this. 和睦之實例。 **2** (gram) [U] agreement between words in number, etc, eg between a *verb* and its subject in the present tense. (文法)(字與字之間單複數等的)一致(例如現在式中動詞與主詞間的一致)。

con·cord·ance /kən'kɔ:dəns ; kɑn'kɔrdn̩s/ *n* **1** [U] agreement. 一致;協調;和諧。 **2** [C] arrangement in ABC order of the important words used by an author or in a book: 著作家或書籍中所用之重要語詞索引(按字母順序排列): *a 'Bible ~;* 聖經語詞索引; *a 'Shakespeare ~.* 莎士比亞語詞索引。

con·cord·ant /kən'kɔ:dənt ; kɑn'kɔrdn̩t/ *adj* **~ *(with)***, agreeing, harmonious. (與…)一致的;協調的;和諧的。

con·cordat /kən'kɔ:dæt ; kɑn'kɔrdæt/ *n* agreement, eg between a State and the Church, for settlement of ecclesiastical affairs. 協定;協約(例如教會與政府間爲解決宗教事務所訂者)。

con·course /'kɒŋkɔ:s ; 'kɑnkors/ *n* **1** coming or moving together of things, persons, etc: (事物、人等的)滙聚;聚集;會合: *an unforeseen ~ of circumstances.* 不能預見的各種情況的湊合。 **2** place (usu not enclosed) where crowds come together; (esp US) large hall of a railway station. 群衆聚集的場所(通常爲空地);(尤美)火車站的大廳。

con·crete¹ /'kɒŋkri:t ; 'kɑnkrit/ *adj* **1** of material things; existing in material form; that can be touched, felt, etc: 實物的;具體存在的;有形的;可觸摸、感覺等的: *A lamp is ~ but its brightness is abstract.* 燈是具體的,但其光亮是抽象的。 **~ music,** composed of re-arranged recorded natural sounds. 實體音樂(將錄好之自然音響重新組合而成)。 **~ noun,** name of a thing, not of a quality. 具體名詞(非指性質之名詞)。 **2** definite; positive: 明確的;確定的;確實的;無問題的: *~ proposals/evidence/proof.* 確切的建議(證據,證明)。□ *n* [U] building material made by mixing cement with sand, gravel, etc: 混凝土;三合土(水泥與沙、碎石等混合成的建築材料): *roads surfaced with ~;* 混凝土路面的道路; *a ~ wall;* 混凝土牆; *a '~ mixer* (usu a revolving drum). 混凝土攪拌器(通常爲旋轉的圓鼓形容器)。□ *vt* [VP6A] cover with ~: 鋪以混凝土: *~ a road.* 以混凝土鋪路。~·ly *adv*

con·crete² /'kɒŋkri:t ; kɑn'krit/ *vi* [VP2A] form into a mass; solidify. 固結;凝固;凝結。 **con·cretion** /kən'kri:ʃn ; kɑn'kriʃən/ *n* [U] process of forming into a mass; [C] mass formed in this way. 凝固;凝結;凝結物。

con·cu·bine /'kɒŋkjʊbaɪn ; 'kɑŋkjʊ,baɪn/ *n* **1** (old use) woman who lives with a man as if she were his wife, without being lawfully married to him. (舊用法)姘婦(與男人同居,過夫婦生活,却未正式結婚之女人)。 **2** (in some countries, where polygamy is legal) lesser wife. (在某些容許一夫多妻的國家)妾;小老婆;姨太太。

con·cu·pis·cence /kən'kju:pɪsns ; kɑn'kjupəsn̩s/ *n* [U] (formal) sexual desire; lust. (正式用語)性慾;色慾。

con·cur /kən'kɜ:(r) ; kən'kɝ/ *vi* (-rr-) **1** [VP2A, 3A] **~ *(with sb) (in sth)***, agree in opinion: (與某人)(在某件事上)意見一致;同意: *I ~ with the speaker in condemning what has been done.* 我同意發言者對所做之事加以譴責。 **2** [VP4A] (of circumstances, etc) happen together: (指周遭的情況等)同時發生: *Everything ~red to produce a successful result.* 一切情況湊合起來產生一個圓滿的結果。 **~·rence** /kən'kʌrəns ; kən'kɝəns/ *n* [U, C] agreement; coming together: 同意;一致;協力;齊來;俱發: *a ~rence of ideas;* 意見一致; *~rence in helping to find homes for refugees.* 協力幫忙尋找安置難民的處所。

con·cur·rent /kən'kʌrənt ; kən'kɝənt/ *adj* concurring; existing together; co-operating. 同意的;一致的;同在的;合作的;協力的。~·ly *adv*

con·cuss /kən'kʌs ; kən'kʌs/ *vt* [VP6A] injure (the brain) by concussion. 使(腦)受震盪而傷害。

con·cus·sion /kən'kʌʃn ; kən'kʌʃən/ *n* [C, U] (an) injury (to the brain); (a) violent shaking or shock (as caused by a blow, knock or fall). (對腦部的)傷害;腦震盪;(由打擊或摔跌所造成的)劇烈震盪。

con·demn /kən'dem ; kən'dɛm/ *vt* **1** [VP6A, 14, 16B] **~ *(for)***, say that sb is, or has done, wrong or that sth is wrong, faulty or unfit for use: 責備;責難;譴責;指摘;指…爲不當: *We all ~ cruelty to children.* 我們大家一致譴責虐待兒童。 *Everyone ~ed his foolish behaviour.* 每個人都責備他的愚昧行爲。 *The newspapers ~ed the Prime Minister for....* 各報紙因爲…而責難首相。 *The meat was ~ed as unfit for human consumption.* 此肉被指爲不宜於人類食用。 *This old bridge is unsafe; it should be ~ed.* 這舊橋不安全,應予宣告不適用。 **2** [VP6A, 14] **~ *sb (to)***, (legal) give judgement against: (法律)判罪;處刑: *~ a murderer to life imprisonment.* 判兇手無期徒刑。 **~ed cell,** cell where a person ~ed to death is kept. 幽禁死刑犯之小室。 **3** [VP6A, 14, 17] **~ *sb (to sth/to do sth)***, doom, send, appoint (to sth unwelcome or painful): 註定,差遣,派遣(做或面對不愉快的或痛苦的事): *an unhappy housewife, ~ed to spend hours at the kitchen sink.* 註定要花很多時間做乏味家事的不快樂的主婦。 *He got well again, although the doctors had ~ed him*, said that he would not recover. 他又康復了,雖然醫生們曾經宣佈他的病已絕望。 **4** [VP6A] declare (smuggled goods, property, etc) to be forfeited: 宣告沒收;充公(走私的貨物、財產等): *Merchant ships captured in war were often ~ed*, taken from the owners without compensation. 在戰時所截獲的商船常被沒收。 **5** [VP6A] show conviction of guilt: 顯示有罪: *His looks ~ed him.* 他的神情顯示他有罪。 **con·dem·na·tion** /,kɒndem'neɪʃn ; ,kɑndɛm'neʃən/ *n* [U] ~ing or being ~ed. 責難;譴責;判罪;註定;沒收。

con·den·sa·tion /,kɒnden'seɪʃn ; ,kɑndɛn'seʃən/ *n* [U] condensing or being condensed: 濃縮;凝結;冷凝: *The ~ of milk*, by taking out most of the water; 牛乳之濃縮(去除其中大部份水分); *the ~ of steam to water;* 蒸氣之凝結爲水; [C, U] (mass of) drops of liquid formed when vapour condenses: (由水蒸氣凝結成的)水滴;凝塊: *A cloud is a ~ of vapour.* 雲就是水蒸氣凝結成的。

con·dense /kən'dens ; kən'dɛns/ *vt, vi* **1** [VP6A, 14, 2A, 3A] (of a liquid) (cause to) increase in density or strength, to become thicker: (指液體)(使)濃縮;凝縮: *to ~ milk;* 濃縮牛乳; *~ed milk;* 濃縮之牛乳;煉乳; (of a gas or vapour) (cause to) change to a liquid: (指氣體或水蒸氣)(使)凝結成液體: *Steam ~s/is ~d to water when it touches a cold surface;* 水蒸氣觸及冷的表面卽凝結成水; (of light) focus, concentrate (by passing through a lens). (指光線)集中;使(經過透鏡而)集中。 **2** [VP6A, 14] put into fewer words: 縮短(文章);摘要;作簡要的敍述: *a ~d account of an event.* 對某事件之簡要的敍述。

con·den·ser /kən'densə(r) ; kən'dɛnsɚ/ *n* apparatus for cooling vapour and condensing it to liquid; apparatus for receiving and accumulating static electricity; mirror or lens that concentrates light, eg in a film projector. (使水蒸汽凝結成水之) 冷凝器; (收受並蓄積靜電的) 電容器; (如用於電影放映機之) 聚光鏡; 聚光器。

con·de·scend /ˌkɒndɪ'send ; ˌkandɪ'sɛnd/ *vi* [VP2A, 3A, 4A] **~ to sb/sth; ~ to do sth, 1** (in a good sense) do sth, accept a position, etc that one's rank, merits, abilities, etc do not require one to do. (好的意思) 屈尊; 俯就 (做依照自己的地位、功名、能力等所不需要做的事)。 **2** (in a bad sense) stoop, lower oneself: (壞的意思) 屈身; 卑躬; 降低身份: *He occasionally ~ed to trickery/to take bribes.* 他偶爾也自貶身價從事欺詐 (接受賄賂)。 **3** behave graciously, but in a way that shows one's feeling of superiority: 態度雖親切却又顯出自己的優越感: *Mr Pigge sometimes ~s to help his wife with the housework.* 皮基先生有時以屈尊的姿態幫他的妻子做家事。*Mrs Drudge doesn't like being ~ed to.* 德拉基太太不喜歡旁人以屈尊的姿態對待她。 **~·ing** *adj* **~·ing·ly** *adv* **con·de·scen·sion** /ˌkɒndɪ'senʃn ; ˌkandɪ'sɛnʃən/ *n* [U] ~ing (all senses); [C] instance of this. 屈尊; 俯就; 屈身; 卑躬; 優越感。

con·dign /kən'daɪn ; kən'daɪn/ *adj* (formal) (of punishment, vengeance) severe and well deserved. (正式用語) (指懲罰、復仇) 嚴厲而應得的; 適當的。

con·di·ment /'kɒndɪmənt ; 'kandəmənt/ *n* [C, U] sth used to give flavour and relish to food, eg pepper, salt, spices. 調味品; 佐料 (如胡椒、鹽、香料)。

con·di·tion¹ /kən'dɪʃn ; kən'dɪʃən/ *n* **1** sth needed before sth else is possible; sth on which another thing depends: (在別的事物實現之前必需的) 條件; 要件: *Ability is one of the ~s of success in life.* 能力是人生中成功的條件之一。 *Her parents allowed her to go, but made it a ~ that she should get home before midnight.* 她的父母准許她去, 但是有一個條件, 就是她要在午夜以前回家。 ***on ~ (that),*** only if; provided (that): 只有在…的條件下; 設若: *You can go swimming on ~ (that) you don't go too far from the river bank.* 你只有在不遠離河岸的條件下才可以去游泳。 ***on 'this/'that/'no/'what ~:*** 在這種 (那種, 沒有的, 什麼) 情形下: *You must on no ~ tell him what has happened,* whatever he may say, do, ask, etc. 你無論在何種情形下都不可告訴他所發生的事。*On what ~ will you agree,* What is necessary before you agree? 你要在什麼條件之下才答應? **2** the present state of things; nature, quality, character of sth or sb: 目前的情況; (事物或人的) 狀況; 狀態: *The ~ of my health prevents me from working.* 我的健康情況不容許我工作。*The ship is not in a ~ to make a long voyage.* 此船的情況不宜於長程航行。 ***in good, etc ~,*** unspoiled, undamaged, etc: 情況良好等: *Everything arrived in good ~,* undamaged, fit for use. 一切均安全到達 (毫未受損)。 ***in no ~ (to),*** unable to because ill, old, etc: (因病、老等) 不能 (作某事): *He's in no ~ to travel,* is not well or strong enough. 他的健康情況不宜於旅行。 ***in/out of ~,*** in good/poor health; physically (un)fit: 健康良好 (不佳); 體況適合 (不適合): *I can't go climbing this summer: I'm out of ~.* 今年夏天我不能去爬山——我的健康不佳。 **3** (*pl*) circumstances: (複) 環境; 情形: *under existing/favourable ~s.* 在現有的 (有利的) 情形下。 **4** position in society: 社會地位: *persons of every ~/of all ~s.* 社會各階層的人。 **5** state of ill-health: 健康不良: *a heart/liver ~.* 心臟 (肝臟) 不良。

con·di·tion² /kən'dɪʃn ; kən'dɪʃən/ *vt* [VP6A] **1** determine; govern; regulate: 決定; 支配; 限制: *My expenditure is ~ed by my income.* 我的支出受我的收入限制。 **2** bring into a desired state or condition: 使達到所要求的情況: *We'll never ~ the workers to a willing acceptance of a wage freeze.* 我們永不能滿足工人使其心甘情願接受穩定的工資。 *ˌill-/ˌwell-'~ed;* 情況不佳 (良好); bring (dogs, horses, etc) into good physical condition: 使 (狗、馬等) 肥壯: *~ing powders,* for this purpose. 壯狗 (馬) 粉。 **con·di·tioned** *part adj* subject to certain provisions or conditions; having a specified condition: 受某種條件限制的; 有某種情況的: *air-~ed cinemas.* 裝有空氣調節設備的電影院。 **~ed reflex,** reflex action (one done normally in answer to a stimulus) that is a response, through practice or training, to a different stimulus not naturally connected with it. 條件反射; 制約反射 (經由練習或訓練的結果, 使對於非自然關聯的刺激產生某種反應的作用)。

con·di·tional /kən'dɪʃənl ; kən'dɪʃənl̩/ *adj* **~ (on/upon),** depending upon, containing, a condition: 依賴條件的; 含有條件的: *a ~ clause,* beginning with 'if' or 'unless'. 條件子句 (以 if 或 unless 起首的子句)。 *My promise to help you is ~ on your good behaviour.* 我答應幫助你, 要以你的品行優良爲條件。 **~·ly** /-ʃənəlɪ ; -ʃənlɪ/ *adv*

con·dole /kən'dəʊl ; kən'dol/ *vi* [VP3A] **~ with sb (on/upon sth),** express sympathy, regret, at a loss, misfortune, etc. (爲損失、不幸等) 表示同情、惋惜或悲悼; 慰問; 弔唁。 **con·dol·ence** /kən'dəʊləns ; kən'doləns/ *n* (often *pl*) expression of sympathy: (常用複數) 慰問的話; 弔詞: *Please accept my condolences.* 謹致慰問之意。

con·dom /'kɒndəm ; 'kandəm/ *n* protective sheath, ⇨ sheath(2). 保險套。

con·do·min·ium /ˌkɒndə'mɪnɪəm ; ˌkandə'mɪnɪəm/ *n* joint control of a State's affairs by two or more other States. (兩個或更多的國家對於另一國家之事務的) 共同管轄 (權)。

con·done /kən'dəʊn ; kən'don/ *vt* [VP6A, C] (of a person) overlook or forgive (an offence): (指人) 寬恕; 原諒; 宥恕 (旁人對不起他的事): *~ a husband's infidelity;* 宥恕丈夫的不忠; (of an act) atone for; make up for: (指行爲) 補償; 彌補: *good qualities that ~ his many shortcomings.* 可以彌補他的許多缺點的優點。 **con·do·na·tion** /ˌkɒndəʊ'neɪʃn ; ˌkando'neʃən/ *n*

con·dor /'kɒndɔː(r) ; 'kandɚ/ *n* large kind of vulture (in S America). (南美洲產之) 神鷹; 大兀鷹。

con·duce /kən'djuːs *US:* -'duːs ; kən'djus/ *vi* [VP3A] **~ to/towards,** (formal) contribute to; help to produce: (正式用語) 有助於; 導致; 幫助產生: *Does temperance ~ to good health?* 節制有助於健康嗎? **con·duc·ive** /kən'djuːsɪv *US:* -'duːs- ; kən'djusɪv/ *adj* **conducive to,** helping to produce: 有助於…的; 有益於…的: *Good health is conducive to happiness.* 健康有助於幸福。

con·duct¹ /'kɒndʌkt ; 'kandʌkt/ *n* [U] **1** behaviour (esp moral): 行爲; (尤指道德方面的) 品行; 操行: *good or bad ~;* 好的或壞的行爲; *the rules of ~.* 行爲的守則。 **2** manner of directing or managing affairs: 督導或處理事務的方式: *People were not at all satisfied with the ~ of the war,* the way in which the leaders were directing it. 人民完全不滿當局的作戰方式。

con·duct² /kən'dʌkt ; kən'dʌkt/ *vt, vi* **1** [VP6A, 14, 15A, B] lead or guide: 領導; 指導; 引導: *The Curator ~ed the visitors round the museum.* 館長領着遊客們在博物館中參觀。*Do you prefer ~ed tours or independent travel?* 你比較喜歡有嚮導的遊覽抑或獨自旅行? *The secretary ~ed me in/out.* 秘書領我進去 (出來)。*C~ her to the door!* 領她到門口! **2** [VP6A, 2A] control; direct; manage: 管理; 指揮; 處理: *to ~ a meeting/negotiations;* 主持會議 (談判); *If he ~s his business affairs in the careless way he ~s his private affairs, they must be in confusion.* 如果他處理公事也像他處理私事一樣的粗心, 那些事情一定會紊亂。*Who is ~ing (the orchestra) this evening?* 今晚由誰指揮 (管弦樂隊)? **3** [VP6A, 15A, 16A] (reflex, with *adv*) behave: (反身式, 與副詞連用) 持 (身); 行爲: *He ~s himself well.* 他行爲端正。 **4** [VP6A, 2A] (of substances) transmit; allow (heat, electric current) to pass along or through: (指物質) 傳導; 容許 (熱, 電流) 通過: *Copper ~s electricity better than other materials.* 銅傳電較

其他物質爲優。**con·duc·tion** /kən'dʌkʃn ; kən'dʌkʃən/ *n* [U] transmission or ~ing, eg of electric current along wires, of liquids through pipes, of heat by contact. 傳導(如電流經過電線);輸送(如液體經過管子);傳播(如熱由接觸傳播)。**con·duc·tive** /kən'dʌktɪv ; kən'dʌktɪv/ *adj* able to ~ (heat, electric current, etc). 能傳(熱、電流等)的;傳導性的。**con·duc·tiv·ity** /ˌkɒndʌk'tɪvətɪ ; ˌkɑndʌk'tɪvətɪ/ *n* (*pl* -ties) property or power of ~ing. 傳導性;傳導力。

con·duc·tor /kən'dʌktə(r) ; kən'dʌktɚ/ *n* **1** person who conducts esp one who conducts a group of singers, a band, an orchestra. 領導者;指導者;(尤指合唱團、管樂隊、管弦樂隊的)指揮。**2** person who collects fares on a bus or tram; (US) person in charge of passengers on a train. (公共汽車或電車上的)收票員;車掌;(美)(火車上的)管理員。⇨ guard (GB). **3** substance that conducts heat or electric current: (傳導熱或電流的)導體: ~ *rail*, rail (laid parallel to tracks) from which a locomotive picks up electric current. 導電軌條(與路軌平行設置,火車頭可由此接電)。**con·duc·tress** /kən'dʌktrɪs ; kən'dʌktres/ *n* woman ~ (on a bus, etc). (公共汽車等之)女收票員;車掌小姐。

con·duit /'kɒndɪt *US:* -duːɪt ; 'kɑndɪt/ *n* large pipe or waterway; tube enclosing insulated electric wires. 大管道;水道導管;(絕緣電線由其中通過的)線管。

cone /kəʊn ; kon/ *n* **1** solid body which narrows to a point from a round, flat base. 圓錐體(尖頂圓底之實體)。**2** sth of this shape whether solid or hollow, eg a ~-shaped basket hoisted as a storm signal, as an indication of road repairs, or an edible container for ice-cream. 圓錐形之物(無論實體或中空,如高懸作風暴信號或修路標記之錐形籃、用以盛冰淇淋之可食的圓錐形蛋捲)。**3** fruit of certain evergreen trees (fir, pine, cedar). 某些常綠樹(如樅、松、西洋杉)的毬果。⇨ the illus at tree. 參看 tree 之插圖。□ *vt* [VP15B] ~ ***off***, mark off with ~s: 用錐形信標標明: ~ *off a section of the motorway during repairs.* 用錐形信標標明在修理中的一段快車道。

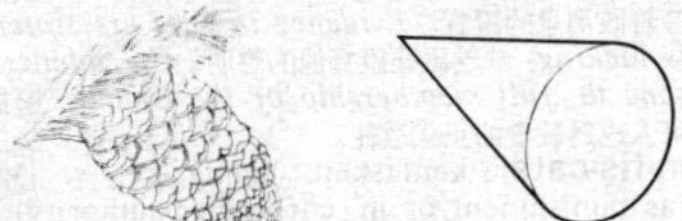

cones

co·ney *n* = cony.

con·fab /'kɒnfæb ; 'kɑnfæb/ *n, vi* (-bb-) (colloq abbr of *confabulation* or *confabulate*). (俗,爲 confabulate 或 confabulation 之略)。

con·fabu·late /ˌkən'fæbjʊleɪt ; kən'fæbjəˌlet/ *vi* [VP2A, 3A] ~ ***(with)***, have a confabulation. (與…)談話;閒談;會談。**con·fabu·la·tion** /kənˌfæbjʊ'leɪʃn ; kənˌfæbjə'leʃən/ *n* [C] friendly and private conversation. 友善的私下談話;閒談;會談。

con·fec·tion /kən'fekʃn ; kən'fɛkʃən/ *n* **1** [C] mixture of sweet things; sweet cake. 糖果;甜點。**2** [U] mixing; compounding. 混合;調和。**3** [C] (dress-making trade) stylish or fancy ready-made article of dress (usu for a woman). (製衣業)時麾或別緻的成衣(通常指女裝)。**~er** *n* person who makes and sells pastry, pies, cakes, etc. 製賣糖果、糕餅、點心等的商人。**~·ery** /kən'fekʃənərɪ *US:* -ʃənerɪ ; kən'fɛkʃənˌɛrɪ/ *n* [U] sweets, chocolates, cakes, pies, pastry, etc; [C] (*pl* -ries) (place of) business of a ~er. 糖果、糕餅等;糖果糕餅業(店)。

con·fed·er·acy /kən'fedərəsɪ ; kən'fɛdərəsɪ/ *n* (*pl* -cies) union of states, parties or persons: (州、黨或人的)聯盟;同盟: *the Southern C~*, the eleven States that separated from the Union (US, 1860–61) and brought about the Civil War. 美國南部邦聯(1860–1861 年間退出美利堅合衆國,因而導致美國內戰之南部十一州)。

con·fed·er·ate[1] /kən'fedərət ; kən'fɛdərɪt/ *adj* joined together by an agreement or treaty: 聯盟的;同盟的;邦盟的: *the C~ States of America.* 美國南部邦聯。⇨ above. 參看上條。□ *n* [C] **1** person or State joined with another or others. 與他人或他國結合的人或國;盟友;盟邦。**2** accomplice (in a plot, etc). (陰謀等的)共謀者;共犯;同夥;黨羽。

con·fed·er·ate[2] /kən'fedəreɪt ; kən'fɛdəˌret/ *vt, vi* [VP6A, 14, 2A, 3A] ~ ***(with)***, bring or come into alliance. (使)聯盟;(與…)同盟。**con·fed·er·ation** /kənˌfedə'reɪʃn ; kənˌfɛdə'reʃən/ *n* [U] confederating or being confederated; [C] alliance; league. 組織同盟;同盟;聯盟。

con·fer /kən'fɜː(r) ; kən'fɝ/ *vt, vi* (-rr-) **1** [VP14] ~ ***sth on/upon***, give or grant (a degree, title, favour): 授予(學位,頭銜,恩惠): *The Queen ~red knighthoods on several distinguished men.* 女王將爵士頭銜授予數位傑出人士。**2** [VP2A, 3A] ~ ***(with sb) (on/about sth)***, consult or discuss: (與某人)商談(有關某事);商議;討論: ~ *with one's lawyer.* 與律師商談。**~·ment** *n*

con·fer·ence /'kɒnfərəns ; 'kɑnfərəns/ *n* [C, U] (meeting for) discussion; exchange of views: 會談;商談;談判;會議: *The Director is in ~ now.* 主任現在正在開會。*Many international ~s have been held in Geneva.* 許多國際會議曾在日內瓦舉行。

con·fess /kən'fes ; kən'fɛs/ *vt, vi* **1** [VP6A, 9, 14, 2A, 3A, 3B, 25] ~ ***(to)***, say or admit (that one has done wrong); acknowledge: 認錯;招供;承認;供認: *He ~ed that he had stolen the money.* 他承認他偷了那筆錢。*The prisoner refused to ~. (his crime/to his crime).* 犯人拒絕招供。*She ~ed herself (to be) guilty.* 她自己承認有罪。*She ~ed to (having) a dread of spiders*, admitted that she was afraid of them. 她承認她害怕蜘蛛。**2** [VP6A, 2A, 3A] ~ ***(to)***, (esp in the RC Church) make known one's sins to a priest; (of a priest) listen to sb doing this: (尤指天主教)向神父認罪懺悔;告解;(指神父)聽某人告解: ~ *one's sins.* 認罪;悔罪。*The criminal ~ed to the priest.* 犯罪者向神父告解。*The priest ~ed the criminal.* 神父聽取那犯罪者告解。**~ed·ly** /-ɪdlɪ ; -ɪdlɪ/ *adv* as ~ed ; by one's own confession. 承認地;自認地;自白地。

con·fes·sion /kən'feʃn ; kən'fɛʃən/ *n* **1** [U] confessing; [C] instance of this: 承認;自認;自白;招供;供認;(天主教)告解;懺悔: *The accused man made a full ~.* 被告已全部供認。*On his own ~ he has taken part in the robbery.* 據他自己供認,他曾參與此搶案。*She is a Catholic and goes to ~ regularly.* 她是個天主教徒,經常去告解。*The priest is ready to hear ~s in Italian, French or English.* 那神父可以接受以義語、法語或英語告解。⇨ absolution, penance. **2** [C] declaration (of religious beliefs, or of principles of conduct, etc): 聲明;表白(指宗教信仰或行爲準則等): *a ~ of faith.* 宗教信仰之聲明。

con·fes·sional /kən'feʃənl ; kən'fɛʃənəl/ *n* private place (*stall*(4)) in a church where a priest sits to hear confessions: 懺悔室;告解所(教會中神父接受告解的秘室): *the secrets of the ~.* 在告解所中所吐露的隱情。

con·fes·sor /kən'fesə(r) ; kən'fɛsɚ/ *n* priest who has authority to hear confessions. 有權聽取告解的神父。

con·fetti /kən'fetɪ ; kən'fɛtɪ/ *n* (*pl; sing v*) small bits of coloured paper showered on people at weddings and carnivals. (複;用單數動詞)(婚禮及狂歡節撒擲在人身上的)五彩碎紙;紙米。

con·fi·dant /ˌkɒnfɪ'dænt ; ˌkɑnfə'dænt/ *n* person who is trusted with private affairs or secrets (esp about love affairs). (可以傾訴衷腸,尤其是戀愛方面之秘密的)密友;知己。

con·fide /kən'faɪd ; kən'faɪd/ *vt, vi* **1** [VP14] ~ ***to***, tell (a secret) to sb; give to be looked after; give (a task or duty) to sb: 向某人傾訴(秘密);交託給(某人)加以照料;交託(工作或職責)於某人: *He ~d his troubles to a friend.* 他向朋友傾訴煩惱事。*The children were ~d to the care of the ship's* *captain.* 孩子們被交託船長監護。*She~d to me that....* 她秘密告訴我…。 **2** [VP3A] ~ ***in,*** have trust or faith in: 信賴;信仰;信任: *Can I ~ in his honesty?* 我能信任他的誠實嗎？*There's no one here I can ~ in.* 這裏沒有一個我可以信賴的人。 **con·fid·ing** *adj* truthful; trusting: 誠實的; 易信賴人的: *The girl is of a confiding nature,* ready to trust others, unsuspicious. 這女孩天性易信賴他人。**con·fid·ing·ly** *adv*

con·fi·dence /ˈkɒnfɪdəns ; ˈkɑnfədəns/ *n* **1** [U] (act of) confiding in or to. 信賴;信任。***in strict ~,*** expecting sth to be kept secret: 期待對某事保秘: *I'm telling you this in strict ~.* 我告訴你此事係絶對的秘密(請你守密)。***take sb into one's ~,*** tell him one's secrets, etc. 告訴某人一己之秘密。 **2** [C] secret which is confided to sb: 向知己傾訴的秘密;知心話: *The two girls sat in a corner exchanging ~s about the young men they knew.* 那兩個女孩坐在角落裏互相秘密談論她們所認識的青年男子。 **3** [U] belief in oneself or others or in what is said, reported, etc; belief that one is right or that one is able to do sth: 信心(對自己或別人,或對所說、所報告等的);相信(自己是對的或自己能做某事);自信: *to have/lose ~ in sb;* 對某人有(失去)信心; *to put little/complete/no ~ in sb/sth;* 對某人(某事)無甚(完全有,毫無)信心; *Don't put too much ~ in what the newspapers say.* 不要過份相信報紙上所說的。*There is a lack of ~ in the government,* People do not feel that its policies are wise. 人民對政府缺乏信心(一般人覺得它的政策不智)。 *I hope he will justify my ~ in him/my ~ that he will do well.* 我希望他將會證明我對於他(對於他會做得好)的信心是對的。*The prisoner answered the questions with ~.* 那囚犯很有自信地回答問題。 **ˈ~ trick,** persuasion of a foolish person to entrust valuables to sb as a sign of ~(3). 信用欺騙(說服傻人以貴重物品相託付,作爲信任之表示,藉以騙財)。 **ˈ~ man/trickster** (also 亦作 **ˈcon-man**), one who swindles people in this way. 以此術騙取他人財物的人;金光黨歹徒。

con·fi·dent /ˈkɒnfɪdənt ; ˈkɑnfədənt/ *adj* ~ ***(of/that),*** feeling or showing confidence; certain: 感覺有信心的; 顯示信任的; 有把握的: *He feels ~ of passing/that he will pass the examination.* 他自信能考及格。*The little girl gave her mother a ~ smile.* 那小女孩向她母親作信賴的微笑。*We are ~ of success.* 我們有信心能成功。**~·ly** *adv*

con·fi·den·tial /ˌkɒnfɪˈdenʃl ; ˌkɑnfəˈdɛnʃəl/ *adj* **1** (to be kept) secret; given in confidence: 機密的;應被守秘密的: *~ information.* 機密消息。 **2** having the confidence of another or others: 獲他人信任的: *a ~ clerk/secretary.* 機要書記(秘書)。 **3** (of persons) inclined to give confidences: (指人)易於信任他人的: *Don't become too ~ with strangers.* 不要太信任陌生人。 **~·ity** /ˌkɒnfɪˌdenʃɪˈælətɪ ; ˌkɑnfɪˌdɛnʃɪˈælɪtɪ/ *n* **~·ly** /-ʃəlɪ ; -ʃəlɪ/ *adv*

con·figur·ation /kənˌfɪgjʊˈreɪʃn ; kənˌfɪgjəˈreʃən/ *n* [C] shape or outline; method of arrangement: 形狀;外貌;輪廓;構形; 形相; 排列方法: *the ~ of the earth's surface.* 地球表面的形狀。

con·fine /kənˈfaɪn ; kənˈfaɪn/ *vt* **1** [VP14] ~ ***to,*** keep or hold, restrict, within limits: 限制;限於範圍內: *I wish the speaker would ~ himself to the subject.* 我希望演說者不要離題。 *Please ~ your remarks to the subject we are debating.* 請你發言不要離開我們所討論的題目。 **2** [VP6A, 14] keep shut up: 關起來;禁閉: *Is it cruel to ~ a lark in a cage?* 將雲雀關在籠子裏是殘忍的嗎？*He is ~d to the house by illness.* 他受疾病的限制不能出門。 *I should hate to be ~d within the four walls of an office all day.* 我討厭終日被關在辦公室裏。**3** ***be ~d,*** (passive only) (old use) be in bed to give birth to a child: (僅用於被動語態)(舊用法)分娩: *She expects to be ~d next month.* 她預期下月分娩。**con·fined** *adj* (of space) limited; narrow; restricted. (指空間)有限的;狹窄的。**~·ment** *n* **1** [U] being ~d; imprisonment: 限制;監禁;禁閉;拘禁: *He was placed in ~ment,* in prison, in a mental hospital, etc. 他被監禁(坐牢,關在精神病院等)。*The prisoner was sentenced to three months' solitary ~ment.* 那囚犯被判處三個月的單獨監禁。 **2** [U] giving birth to a child; [C] instance of this: 分娩;分娩的實例: *Dr Spock has attended six ~ments this week.* 史波克醫生這一星期接了六次生。*When does she expect her ~ment?* 她預期何時分娩？

con·fines /ˈkɒnfaɪnz ; ˈkɑnfaɪnz/ *n pl* limits; borders; boundaries: 界限;境界;範圍;疆界: *beyond the ~ of human knowledge;* 超出人類知識的範圍;*within the ~ of this valley.* 在此山谷的範圍內。

con·firm /kənˈfɜːm ; kənˈfɝm/ *vt* [VP6A, 9] **1** make (power, ownership, opinions, rights, feelings, etc) firmer or stronger: 使(權力、所有權、意見、權利、感情等)更鞏固或堅强;證實: *Please ~ your telephone message by letter,* send a letter repeating the message. 請來信證實一下你在電話裡所說的話。*The report of an earthquake in Greece has now been ~ed,* We now know that the report was true. 希臘境內地震的報導現在已經證實。 *What you tell me ~s my suspicions.* 你告訴我的話證實了我的懷疑。 **2** ratify; agree definitely to (a treaty, an appointment, etc). 批准;認可(條約、任命等)。 **3** admit to full membership of the Christian Church: (教會)施堅振禮(使成爲正式教徒): *She was baptized when she was a month old and ~ed when she was thirteen.* 她在一個月大時受洗禮,在十三歲時受堅振禮。**con·firmed** *part adj* (esp) unlikely to change or be changed: (尤指)確定的;證實的;不會改變的: *a ~ed invalid,* one who is unlikely to be well again; 終身不會康復的病人;患痼疾的病人; *a ~ed drunkard,* one who cannot be cured of drunken habits; 飲酒成癖(永不能戒除)的人; *a ~ed report,* one that can be trusted. 可靠的報導。

con·fir·ma·tion /ˌkɒnfəˈmeɪʃn ; ˌkɑnfɚˈmeʃən/ *n* [C, U] ~ ***(of),*** confirming or being confirmed (all senses): 鞏固;强化;證實;批准;認可;(教會的)堅振禮: *We are waiting for ~ of the news.* 我們正在等着該消息的證實。*Evidence in ~ of his statements is lacking.* 缺乏證據證實他的聲明。*C~ admits persons to full membership of the Church.* 堅振禮許可人成爲教會的正式教徒。

con·fis·cate /ˈkɒnfɪskeɪt ; ˈkɑnfɪsˌket/ *vt* [VP6A] (as punishment or in enforcing authority) take possession of (private property) without compensation or payment: (作爲懲罰或執行權力)充公;沒收(私有財產): *If you try to smuggle goods into the country, they may be ~d by the Customs authorities.* 如果你企圖走私貨物進入國內,貨物可能被海關當局沒收。**con·fis·ca·tion** /ˌkɒnfɪˈskeɪʃn ; ˌkɑnfɪsˈkeʃən/ *n* [U] confiscating or being ~d; [C] instance of this: 充公;沒收;充公或沒收的實例: *numerous confiscations of obscene books.* 多次的沒收淫書。

con·fla·gra·tion /ˌkɒnfləˈgreɪʃn ; ˌkɑnfləˈgreʃən/ *n* [C] great and destructive fire, esp one that destroys buildings or forests. (尤指毀滅房屋或森林的)大火災。

con·flict¹ /ˈkɒnflɪkt ; ˈkɑnflɪkt/ *n* **1** [C] fight; struggle; quarrel: 戰鬪;鬪爭;爭執: *a wordy ~,* a bitter argument;舌戰; *a long-drawn-out ~ between employers and workers.* 勞資之間拖延甚久的爭執。 **2** [C, U] (of opinions, desires, etc) opposition; difference: (指意見,欲望等)相左; 衝突; 抵觸: *the ~ between duty and desire;* 責任與欲望的衝突; *a ~ of evidence;* 證據之互相抵觸; ***be in ~ (with),*** not agree (with): (與…)相衝突: *a statement that is in ~ with other evidence.* 與其他證據相衝突的陳述。

con·flict² /kənˈflɪkt ; kənˈflɪkt/ *vi* [VP2A, 3A] ~ ***(with),*** be in opposition or disagreement (with): (與…) 相反;抵觸;衝突: *Our accounts ~.* 我們的報導不一致。 *Their account of the causes of the war ~s with ours.* 他們對於戰爭起因的報導與我們的相反。

~·ing *adj*: *~ing views/passions/evidence.* 相反的意見(情慾,證據)。

con·flu·ence /ˈkɒnfluəns ; ˈkɑnfluəns/ *n* flowing together, esp a place where two rivers unite. 滙流;合流;(尤指)兩條河的合流點。**con·flu·ent** /ˈkɒnfluənt ; ˈkɑnfluənt/ *adj* flowing together; uniting. 滙流的;會合的。

con·form /kənˈfɔːm ; kənˈfɔrm/ *vi, vt* **1** [VP2A, 3A] ~ ***(to)***, be in agreement with, comply with (generally accepted rules, standards, etc): 符合;順從;遵守(一般所接受的規則、準則等): *You should ~ to the rules/to the wishes of others/to the usages of society/to the usages of the Established Church.* 你應該遵守規則(順從他人的願望,遵從社會習慣,遵守國教的習俗)。**2** [VP14] ~ ***to***, make similar to; adapt oneself to: 使相似;適應: *~ one's life to certain principles.* 使自己的生活符合某些準則。**~·able** *adj* obedient; submissive; in agreement. 服從的;順從的;一致的;符合的。

con·for·ma·tion /ˌkɒnfɔːˈmeɪʃn ; ˌkɑnfɔrˈmeʃən/ *n* way in which sth is formed; structure. 構造;結構;組成。

con·form·ist /kənˈfɔːmɪst ; kənˈfɔrmɪst/ *n* person who conforms; conventional person; (hist) person who followed the practices of the Church of England. 遵奉者;順從習俗者;(史)信奉英國國教者。⇨ *dissenter* at dissent², *nonconformist* at non-.

con·form·ity /kənˈfɔːmətɪ ; kənˈfɔrmətɪ/ *n* [U] **1** ~ ***(to)***, action, behaviour, in agreement with what is usual, accepted or required by custom, etc: 遵守;順從(社會習俗等)的行爲: *C~ to fashion* (=Having things of the latest fashions) *is not essential to the happiness of all women.* 順應時髦並非對於所有婦女的幸福都是必要的。**2** ***in ~ with***, in agreement with: 與…一致;符合: *in ~ with your request,* 按照你的要求。*Was his action in ~ with the law?* 他的行動是否合法?

con·found /kənˈfaʊnd ; kɑnˈfaʊnd/ *vt* **1** [VP6A] fill with, throw into, perplexity or confusion: 使困惑;使迷惑;使糊塗: *His behaviour amazed and ~ed her.* 他的行爲使她感到驚愕而困惑。*I was ~ed to hear that....* 我聽到…感到大惑不解。**2** [VP6A, 14] ~ ***(with)***, mix up, confuse (ideas, etc): 混淆;分不清(意念等): *Don't ~ the means with the ends.* 不要使手段與目的混淆不清。**3** [VP6A] (liter) defeat; overthrow (enemies, plans, etc). (文)擊敗;推翻(敵人,計畫等)。**4** [VP6A] (dated) used to express annoyance or anger: (過時用語)用以表示厭惡或忿怒: *C~ it!* 討厭!該死!*C~ you!* 天罰你!混蛋!**~ed** *part adj* (from 4 above; dated): (由上列第4義轉成;過時用語)討厭的: *You're a ~ed nuisance!* 你眞是個可厭的東西!**~·edly** /-ɪdlɪ ; -ɪdlɪ/ *adv* very: 非常;極: *~edly hot.* 極熱的。

con·frère /ˈkɒnfreə(r) ; ˈkɑnfrɛr/ *n* (F) fellow member of a profession, learned society, etc. (法)同仁;同志;(同一學術社團的)會員;社員。

con·front /kənˈfrʌnt ; kənˈfrʌnt/ *vt* **1** [VP14] ~ ***sb with***, bring face to face: 使面對: *The prisoner was ~ed with his accusers.* 那犯人被傳與告訴人對質。*When ~ed with the evidence of his guilt, he confessed at once.* 當面對着他的犯罪證據的時候,他立卽認罪。**2** [VP6A] be or come face to face with: 面對;面臨: *The difficulties that ~ us seem insuperable.* 我們所面臨的困難似乎是不可克服的。*A soldier has to ~ danger.* 軍人須面對危險。**3** [VP6A] be opposite to: 與…相對: *My house ~s his.* 我的家與他的家對門。

con·fron·ta·tion /ˌkɒnfrʌnˈteɪʃn ; ˌkɑnfrʌnˈteʃən/ *n* [C, U] (instance of) defiant opposition, of being face to face: 公然反對;面對;敵對: *the ~ between Israel and the Arab world.* 以色列與阿拉伯世界之間的敵對。

Con·fu·cian /kənˈfjuːʃn ; kənˈfjuʃən/ *adj, n* (follower) of Confucius. 孔子的;孔子的尊崇者。

con·fuse /kənˈfjuːz ; kənˈfjuz/ *vt* [VP6A, 14] ~ ***(with)***, **1** put into disorder; mix up in the mind: 使混亂;使糊塗: *They asked so many questions that they ~d me/I got ~d.* 他們問了許許多多的問題,把我弄糊塗了。**2** mistake one thing for another: 誤甲爲乙;弄混淆: *Don't ~ Austria with/and Australia.* 不要把奧國跟澳洲弄混淆了。**con·fus·ed·ly** /-ɪdlɪ ; -ɪdlɪ/ *adv* in a ~d manner. 混亂地;混淆地。

con·fusion /kənˈfjuːʒn ; kənˈfjuʒən/ *n* [U] being confused; disorder: 混亂;紛亂;混淆;無秩序: *He remained calm in the ~ of battle.* 他在戰事的混亂中保持鎮靜。*His unexpected arrival threw me into ~.* 他的突然光臨使我手忙脚亂。*Everything was in ~.* 一切都在混亂中。*There has been some ~ of names.* 有人把名字弄混了。

con·fute /kənˈfjuːt ; kənˈfjut/ *vt* [VP6A] prove (a person) to be wrong; show (an argument) to be false. 證明(某人或論點)是錯誤的;推翻;駁倒。**con·fu·ta·tion** /ˌkɒnfjuːˈteɪʃn ; ˌkɑnfjʊˈteʃən/ *n*

congé /ˈkɒnʒeɪ ; ˈkɑnʒe/ *n* **1** formal permission to depart: 正式許可離去: *give sb his ~.* 允許某人離去。**2** abrupt and unceremonious dismissal. (突然而不客氣的)革退;罷黜;撤職。

con·geal /kənˈdʒiːl ; kənˈdʒil/ *vt, vi* [VP6A,2A] make or become stiff or solid (esp as the effect of cold, or of the air on blood); thicken as if frozen: (使)凝固;凝結(尤指冷凍的結果或空氣對於血液之作用);變濃(如凍結然): *His blood was ~ed,* (fig) eg through fear. 他的血液都凝結起來了(喻,猶言被嚇呆了)。

con·gen·ial /kənˈdʒiːnɪəl ; kənˈdʒinjəl/ *adj* **1** (of persons) having the same or a similar nature, common interests, etc: (指人)有相同或相似的性情或興趣的;志趣相投的: *In this small village he found few persons ~ to him.* 在這小村中他發現很少人跟他志趣相投。**2** (of things, occupations, etc) in agreement with one's tastes, nature: (指事物、職業等)與某人的趣味、天性相合的;適意的;合意的: *a ~ climate;* 適意的氣候; *~ work.* 合意的工作。**~·ly** /-ɪəlɪ ; -jəlɪ/ *adv*

con·geni·tal /kənˈdʒenɪtl ; kənˈdʒɛnətl/ *adj* (of diseases, etc) present, belonging to one, from or before birth: (指疾病等)與生俱來的;先天的;天生的: *~ idiocy.* 先天性白癡。

con·ger /ˈkɒŋgə(r) ; ˈkɑŋgə/ *n* (also 亦作 ˌ~-ˈeel) ocean eel of large size. 海鰻(海生大鰻)。⇨ the illus at sea. 參看 sea 之插圖。

con·gested /kənˈdʒestɪd ; kənˈdʒɛstɪd/ *part adj* **1** too full; overcrowded: 過份充滿的;擁塞的;充塞的: *streets ~ with traffic;* 交通擁塞的街道; *~ areas of a large town.* 大城市中擁塞的區域。**2** (of parts of the body, eg the brain, the lungs) having an abnormal accumulation of blood. (指身體的某部,如腦、肺)充血的。

con·ges·tion /kənˈdʒestʃən ; kənˈdʒɛstʃən/ *n* [U] being congested: 充滿;擁塞;充塞;充血: *~ of the lungs;* 肺充血; *delayed by the ~ of traffic in town.* 爲城市中擁擠的交通所躭誤。

con·glom·er·ate¹ /kənˈglɒmərət ; kənˈglɑmərɪt/ *adj, n* (made up of a) number of things or parts come together in a mass (eg rock made up of small stones held together); (fig; comm) large corporation made up of many different firms). 由許多東西或部份聚成的;一團;一塊(如由小石頭聚結成的大石塊);礫岩(的);(喻;商)由許多公司組成的大公司;企業集團。

con·glom·er·ate² /kənˈglɒməreɪt ; kənˈglɑməˌret/ *vt, vi* [VP6A, 2A] collect into a mass. (使)聚結成一團或一塊。

con·glom·er·ation /kənˌglɒməˈreɪʃn ; kənˌglɑməˈreʃən/ *n* [U] conglomerating or being conglomerated; [C] mass of conglomerated things. 聚結;團;塊。

con·gratu·late /kənˈgrætʃʊleɪt ; kənˈgrætʃəˌlet/ *vt* [VP6A, 14] ~ ***sb (on/upon sth)***, **1** tell sb that one is pleased about sth happy or fortunate that has come to him: (爲某事)向(某人)道賀;祝賀;慶賀:

~ *sb on his marriage*. 向某人祝賀結婚。 **2** (reflex) consider oneself fortunate: (反身式) 自慶;私自慶幸: *I ~d myself on my escape/on having escaped unhurt*. 我能安然逃脫,深自慶幸。**con·gratu·la·tory** /kən'grætʃʊlətərɪ *US:* -tɔːrɪ ; kən'grætʃələ,torɪ/ *adj* that ~s: 祝賀的;慶賀的: *a congratulatory letter/telegram*. 祝賀信(電報);賀函;賀電。

con·gratu·la·tion /kən,grætʃʊ'leɪʃn ; kən,grætʃə-'leʃən/ *n* (often *pl*) words that congratulate: (常用複數) 祝賀辭: *offer a friend one's ~s on/upon his success*. 向朋友祝賀成功。

con·gre·gate /'kɒŋgrɪgeɪt ; 'kɑŋgrɪ,get/ *vi, vt* [VP6A, 2A, C] come or bring together: 集合;聚集: *People quickly ~d round the speaker*. 人們迅速地圍攏在演說者的四周。

con·gre·ga·tion /,kɒŋgrɪ'geɪʃn ; ,kɑŋgrɪ'geʃən/ *n* [U] congregating; [C] gathering of people; (esp) body of people (usu except the minister and choir) taking part in religious worship. 集合;人群;(尤指) 參加宗教禮拜式 (通常除牧師及唱詩班外) 的會衆。 **~al** *adj* of a ~. 群衆的;會衆的。 **C~al** *adj* of the Union of Free Churches in which individual churches manage their own affairs. 公理會(爲獨立教會之聯盟,各教會自行處理其事務)的。

con·gress /'kɒŋgres *US:* -grəs ; 'kɑŋgrəs/ *n* **1** [C] meeting, series of meetings, of representatives (of societies, etc) for discussion: (學術團體等的) 代表會議;討論會: *a medical ~;* 醫學會議;*the Church C~*. 教會代表會議。 **2** **C~**, law-making body eg of US; political party in India. 國會 (例如美國國會);國會黨 (印度的政黨)。 **'~·man** /-mən ; -mən/ *n* (*pl* -men) **'~·woman** *n* (*pl* -women) member of US C~. (美國) 國會議員;國會女議員。Cf 參較 senator. **con·gres·sional** /kən'greʃənl ; kən'grɛʃənl/ *adj* of a ~: 會議的;國會的: *~ional debates*. 大會中的辯論。

con·gru·ent /'kɒŋgrʊənt ; 'kɑŋgrʊənt/ *adj* **1** ~ ***(with)***, suitable; agreeing (with). 適合的;(與…)一致的。 **2** (geom) having the same size and shape: (幾何) 全等的: *~ triangles*. 全等三角形。

con·gru·ous /'kɒŋgrʊəs ; 'kɑŋgrʊəs/ *adj* ~ ***(with)***, (formal) fitting; proper; harmonious. (正式用語) 適合的;適當的;協調的。

conic /'kɒnɪk ; 'kɑnɪk/ *adj* of a cone: 圓錐體的: *~ sections*. 圓錐曲線;錐線。**coni·cal** /'kɒnɪkl ; 'kɑnɪkḷ/ *adj* cone-shaped. 圓錐形的。⇨ the illus at projection. 參看 projection 之挿圖。

coni·fer /'kɒnɪfə(r) ; 'konəfɚ/ *n* tree of the kind (eg *pine, fir*) that bears cones. 針葉樹 (結毬果之樹,如松、樅)。**co·nif·er·ous** /kə'nɪfərəs ; ko'nɪfərəs/ *adj* (of kinds of trees) that bear cones. 針葉樹的;結毬果的。

con·jec·ture /kən'dʒektʃə(r) ; kən'dʒɛktʃɚ/ *vi, vt* [VP6A, 9, 2A, 25] guess; put forward an opinion formed without facts as proof: 猜測;推測;臆測;推想;發表無事實爲證的意見: *It was just as I ~d*. 它正如我所猜測的。*May we ~ that...?* 我們可以推想…嗎? □ *n* [C,U] guess; guessing: 推測;猜測;猜想: *I was right in my ~s*. 我的猜想對了。*We had no facts, so were reduced to ~*. 我們沒有事實資料,所以只好猜測。 **con·jec·tural** /kən'dʒektʃərəl ; kən-'dʒɛktʃərəl/ *adj* involving ~; inclined to ~. 猜測的;好猜測的。

con·join /kən'dʒɔɪn ; kən'dʒɔɪn/ *vt, vi* [VP6A, 2A] (formal) join together; unite. (正式用語) 結合;連接;聯合。 **~t** /kən'dʒɔɪnt ; kən'dʒɔɪnt/ *adj* united; associated. 結合的;聯合的。**~t·ly** *adv*

con·ju·gal /'kɒndʒʊgl ; 'kɑndʒʊgḷ/ *adj* of marriage and wedded life; of husband and wife: 婚姻的;婚姻生活的;夫婦的: *~ happiness/affection/infidelity*. 婚姻之樂(夫婦之愛;對配偶不忠)。 **~·ly** /-gəlɪ ; -gḷɪ/ *adv*

con·ju·gate /'kɒndʒʊgeɪt ; 'kɑndʒə,get/ *vt, vi* **1** [VP6A] give the forms of (a verb) for number, tense, etc. 列擧(動詞)數、時態等的變形。 **2** [VP2A] (of a verb) have these forms. (指動詞) 有各種變形;變化。 **con·ju·ga·tion** /,kɒndʒʊ'geɪʃn ; ,kɑndʒə-'geʃən/ *n* [C, U] scheme or system of verb forms; [C] class of verbs ~d alike. 動詞變化的系統;動詞活用表;變形方式相同的一類動詞。

con·junc·tion /kən'dʒʌŋkʃn ; kən'dʒʌŋkʃən/ *n* **1** [C] (gram) word that joins other words, clauses, etc, eg *and, but, or*. (文法) 連接詞(連接字、子句等的字,例如 and, but, or 是)。 **2** [U] joining; state of being joined: 連接;連結;連接在一起: *the ~ of skill and imagination in planning a garden*. 計畫一座花園之技術與想像力的結合。***in ~ with***, together with. 連同。 **3** [C] combination (of events, etc): (指事件等) 湊合;結合: *an unusual ~ of circumstances*. 各種情況之非常的巧合。

con·junc·tiva /,kɒndʒʌŋk'taɪvə ; ,kɑndʒʌŋk'taɪvə/ *n* (anat) thin transparent membrane connecting the upper and lower inner eyelids, covering the cornea. (解剖) 結膜。⇨ the illus at eye. 參看 eye 之插圖。 **con·junc·ti·vitis** /kɒn,dʒʌŋktɪ'vaɪtɪs ; kən-,dʒʌŋktə'vaɪtɪs/ *n* [U] inflammation of the ~. 結膜炎。

con·junc·tive /kən'dʒʌŋktɪv ; kən'dʒʌŋktɪv/ *adj* serving to join; connective. 有連接作用的;連接性的。□ *n* ~ word. 連接字;連繫詞。

con·junc·ture /kən'dʒʌŋktʃə(r) ; kən'dʒʌŋktʃɚ/ *n* [C] combination of events or circumstances. 事件或情況的湊合;局面;時機。

con·jur·ation /,kɒndʒʊ'reɪʃn ; ,kɑndʒʊ'reʃən/ *n* [C] (formal) solemn appeal, incantation. (正式用語) 懇求;咒語;咒文。

con·jure /'kʌndʒə(r) ; 'kʌndʒɚ/ *vt, vi* **1** [VP2A, 15A] do clever tricks which appear magical, esp by quick movements of the hands: 玩魔術;(尤指以敏捷的手法) 變戲法;用戲法變出: *a conjuring trick;* 魔術;*~ a rabbit out of a hat*. 從帽子裏變出一隻兔子來。***a name to ~ with***, sb of great importance/influence. 極重要之人;極有影響力之人。 **2** [VP15B] ~ ***up***, cause to appear as if from nothing, or as a picture in the mind: 使從虛無中顯現; 使在腦中顯現如畫;想像;追憶: *~ up visions of the past;* 回憶過去的景象; compel (a spirit) to appear by invocation: 念咒召(鬼魂): *~ up the spirits of the dead;* 念咒召喚死者的靈魂;*~ up a meal*, produce it quickly. 像變魔術似地很快做出一頓飯菜。 **3** /kən'dʒʊə(r) ; kən'dʒʊr/ [VP17] (formal) appeal solemnly to: (正式用語) 懇求;哀求: *I ~ you not to betray me*. 我懇求你不要背棄我。**con·jurer, con·juror** /'kʌndʒərə(r) ; 'kʌndʒərɚ/ *n* person who performs conjuring tricks. 魔術師。⇨ 1 above. 參看上列第 1 義。

conk[1] /kɒŋk ; kɑŋk/ *n* (GB sl) nose. (英俚) 鼻。

conk[2] /kɒŋk ; kɑŋk/ *vi* ~ ***out***, (colloq) (of a machine) fail or give signs of failing: (俗) (指機器) 失靈;發生故障;有發生故障的跡象: *The engine's ~ing out*. 引擎快要發生故障了。

conker /'kɒŋkə(r);'kɑŋkɚ/ *n* (colloq) horse chestnut. (俗) 七葉樹;七葉樹之實。

con-man /'kɒn mæn ; 'kɑn ,mæn/ *n* ⇨ confidence(3).

con·nect /kə'nekt ; kə'nɛkt/ *vt, vi* **1** [VP6A, 15A, B, 14, 2A, 2C, 3A] ~ ***(up) (to/with)***, join, be joined (materially, by personal relationships, etc): 連接;連結 (在物質上,人事關係上等): *~ telephone subscribers;* 爲電話用戶接線; *~ (up) the cells of a battery (to/with one another)*. 連接電池組的各個電池。*The two towns are ~ed by a railway*. 這兩市鎮有鐵路相連。 *A railway ~s Oxford and Reading/~s Oxford to/with Reading*.牛津和瑞丁間有一鐵路相連。*Where does the cooker ~ with the gas-pipe?* 煤氣爐在何處與煤氣管銜接? *Mr Y has been ~ed with this firm since 1950*. Y 先生從 1950 年起就一直在此公司做事。*He is ~ed with the Smiths/He and the Smiths are ~ed by marriage*, ie his wife is a member of the Smith family. 他與史密斯家聯姻(娶史家小姐爲妻)。 *The 9.00am train from London ~s with the 12.05pm train at Crewe*, ie arrives at Crewe so as to enable passengers to continue their journeys by the 12.05 p m train. 上午九時自倫敦開出的列車在克魯與下午十二時五分的列車相銜接(長途乘客可在此換車)。 ***well ~ed,*** with relatives who are high in society, or who hold important positions, etc. 有優越的社會關係(有親屬或親戚在社會上居高位或要職)。 **2** [VP14] ~ ***(with),*** think of (different things or persons) as being related to each other: 聯想 (在思想中使不同的事物或人聯繫起來): *to ~ Malaya with rubber and tin.* 提到馬來亞就聯想到橡膠和錫。

con·nec·tion /kə'nekʃn ; kə'nɛkʃən/ *n* **1** [C, U] connecting or being connected; point where two things are connected; thing which connects: 連接；連結；連接點；連接物: *a bicycle pump ~.* 腳踏車打氣筒的接頭。*How long will the ~ of the new telephone take,* How long will it take to connect the house by telephone to the exchange? 新裝的電話機與總機接線需要好久的時間？*What is the ~ between the two ideas?* 這兩個意念之間有何關聯？ ***in this／that ~,*** with reference to this／that. 關於此(彼)點。 ***in ~ with,*** with reference to: 與…相連；關於: *The meeting is in ~ with a proposal to construct a new swimming-pool.* 該集會與建一個新的游泳池有關。 **2** [C] train, boat, etc timed to leave a station, port, etc soon after the arrival of another, enabling passengers to change from one to the other: (與另一到達的交通工具在時間上相連接以便旅客換乘的) 聯運列車、船等: *The train was late and I missed my ~.* 火車誤點了，我沒趕上聯運車(船)。 **3** [C] (collective noun) number of customers, clients, etc: (集合名詞) 商店的主顧；醫生的病家；律師的委託人；一批顧客: *He set up in business and soon had a good ~.* 他開業經商，很快就有相當多的顧客。 *This dressmaker has good ~s among the well-to-do women of the town.* 這個女裁縫在本鎮富家婦女之中擁有相當多的顧客。 **4** [C] number of people united in a religious organization: 結合於一宗教組織中的人們；教派: *the Methodist ~.* 美以美教派。

con·nect·ive /kə'nektɪv ; kə'nɛktɪv/ *adj* serving to connect. 有連接作用的。□ *n* (esp) word that connects (eg a conjunction). (尤指) 連接字(如連接詞)。

con·nex·ion /kə'nekʃn ; kə'nɛkʃən/ occasional GB spelling for *connection.* 偶而使用的 connection 的英國拼法。

con·ning tower /'kɒnɪŋ taʊə(r) ; 'kanɪŋ 'taʊɚ/ *n* (on a warship) superstructure from which steering, etc is directed (esp of a submarine on or near the surface). (戰艦上的) 指揮塔(尤指潛艇在水面上或近水面時的駕駛臺或瞭望塔)。

con·nive /kə'naɪv ; kə'naɪv/ *vi* [VP3A] ~ ***at,*** take no notice of (what is wrong, what ought to be opposed) (suggesting that tacit consent or approval is given): 假裝不見(應糾正或反對之事)；默許；縱容: *~ at an escape from prison.* 故縱逃獄。**con·niv·ance** /kə'naɪvəns ; kə'naɪvəns/ *n* [U] conniving (*at／in* a crime): 默許；縱容: *done with the connivance of／in connivance with....* 得到…的默許而做的。

con·nois·seur /ˌkɒnə'sɜ:(r) ; ˌkanə'sɝ/ *n* person with good judgement on matters in which taste (5) is needed: 鑑賞家；鑑定家；內行: *a ~ of painting／old porcelain／antique furniture／wine.* 名畫(古瓷，古老傢具，葡萄酒)鑑定家。

con·note /kə'nəʊt ; kə'not/ *vt* [VP6A] (of words) suggest in addition to the fundamental meaning: (指字) (除本義外) 含有…的意義；有…的含意: *The word 'Tropics' means the area between about 23° N and 23° S; it ~s heat.* Tropics 一字本義指約自北緯 23 度至南緯 23 度之間的地區；它含有炎熱的意義。 **con·no·ta·tion** /ˌkɒnə'teɪʃn ; ˌkanə'teʃən/ *n* [C] that which is ~d. 含蓄的意義；含意；內涵；包攝。

con·nu·bial /kə'nju:bɪəl *US:* -'nu:- ; kə'nubɪəl/ *adj* (formal) of marriage; of husband and wife. (正式用語) 婚姻的；夫婦的。

con·quer /'kɒŋkə(r) ; 'kɔŋkɚ/ *vt* [VP6A] **1** defeat or overcome enemies／bad habits, etc. 擊敗(敵人)；克服(惡習等)。 **2** take possession of by force: 藉武力佔領: *~ a country.* 征服一國。**~or** /'kɒŋkərə(r) ; 'kaŋkərɚ/ *n* one who ~s: 征服者；戰勝者: *William the C~or,* King William I of England. 征服者威廉(英王威廉一世的稱號)。

con·quest /'kɒŋkwest ; 'kaŋkwɛst/ *n* **1** [U] conquering (eg a country and its people): 征服(如一國及其人民): *the (Norman) C~,* of England by the Normans in 1066. 諾曼第人之征服英國(時爲1066年)。 **2** [C] sth got by conquering: 由征服所得之物；斬獲品；戰利品: *the Roman ~s in Africa.* 羅馬人在非洲的斬獲。 ***make a ~ (of),*** win the affections (of). 贏得(…的)愛情。

con·quista·dor /kɒn'kwɪstədɔ:(r) ; kan'kwɪstəˌdɔr/ *n* (16th c) one of the Spanish conquerors of Mexico and Peru. (十六世紀) 西班牙征服者(征服墨西哥與秘魯之西班牙人)。

con·san·guin·ity /ˌkɒnsæŋ'gwɪnətɪ ; ˌkansæŋ'gwɪnətɪ/ *n* [U] (formal) relationship by blood or birth: (正式用語) 血親關係；血緣；血親: *united by ties of ~.* 爲血緣關係所連繫。

con·science /'kɒnʃəns ; 'kanʃəns/ *n* [C, U] the consciousness within oneself of the choice one ought to make between right and wrong: 良心；天良；良知；道德心；是非心: *have a clear／guilty ~.* 問心無(有)愧。***have no ~,*** be as ready to do wrong as right. 沒有良心；失去良知。***(have sth) on one's ~,*** (feel) troubled about sth one has done, or failed to do. (因做了某事或未能做某事而感到) 內疚；受良心譴責。'~ ***money,*** money paid to rectify sth and ease one's ~ (esp when no other person knows that it is owing). 因良心不安所付的錢 (尤指所欠爲他人所不知者)。 '**~-smitten** /-smɪtn ; -ˌsmɪtn/ *adj* filled with remorse. 良心不安的；受良心譴責的。 ***for '~' sake,*** to satisfy one's ~. 爲求心之所安。***in all ~,*** (forms of emphatic declaration) surely; (colloq) by all that is fair: (加强語氣之宣言的套語) 當然；一定；確實地；(俗) 憑良心；公道地；公正地: *I cannot in all ~ agree.* 憑良心我不能贊成。 ***make sth／be a matter of ~,*** make sth／be a question which one's ~ must decide. 使某事成爲良心必須決定的問題；是有關良心的事。

con·scien·tious /ˌkɒnʃɪ'enʃəs ; ˌkanʃɪ'ɛnʃəs/ *adj* **1** (of persons) guided by one's sense of duty: (指人) 有責任心的; 負責的; 盡責的: *a '~ worker.* 盡責的工作者。 **~ objector,** person who objects to doing sth (esp serving in the armed forces) because he thinks it is morally wrong. 因覺違背道德而反對做某事(尤指服兵役)的人; 基於道德理由的拒絕者。 **2** (of actions) done carefully and honestly: (指行爲) 謹愼的；盡責的；本良心做的: *~ work.* 本良心做的工作。 **~·ly** *adv* **~·ness** *n*

con·scious /'kɒnʃəs ; 'kanʃəs/ *adj* **1** ~ ***(of／that),*** (pred use) awake; aware; knowing things because one is using the bodily senses and mental powers: (敍述用法) 清醒的; 明白的; 察覺的; (因用感官和腦力而) 知道的: *They were ~ of being／that they were being watched.* 他們知道有人在監視他們。*He was ~ of his guilt.* 他自知有罪。*Are you ~ (of) how people will regard such behaviour?* 你可知道人們對此種行爲作何觀感？ *A healthy man is not ~ of his breathing.* 健康的人對自己的呼吸無所感覺。*The old man was ~ to the last,* aware of what was happening round him until the moment he died. 那老人臨終仍甚清醒。 **2** (of actions, feelings, etc) realized by oneself: (指行動、感情等) 自覺的: *He spoke／acted with ~ superiority.* 他說話(舉止)帶着自覺的優越感。 **~·ly** *adv*

con·scious·ness /'kɒnʃəsnɪs ; 'kanʃəsnɪs/ *n* [U] **1** being conscious: 知覺；感覺: *We have no ~ during sleep.* 我們在睡眠時沒有知覺。*The blow caused him to lose ~.* 那一擊使他失去知覺。*He did not recover／regain ~ until two hours after the accident.* 他在禍事發生以後兩個小時才恢復知覺。 **2** all the ideas, thoughts, feelings, wishes, intentions, recollections, of a person or persons: 意識(指一人或衆人之所有的觀念、思想、感情、願望、意向、記憶): *the moral ~ of a political party.* 一政黨之道德意識。

con·script /kən'skrɪpt ; kən'skrɪpt/ *vt* [VP6A, 14]~ ***(into)***, compel (sb) by law to serve in the armed forces; summon for such service: 徵召(某人)服兵役;召集(服兵役): *~ed into the army.* 被徵召入陸軍服役。 ⇨ draft²(2). □ *n* /'kɒnskrɪpt ; 'kɑnskrɪpt/ person who is ~ed; 被徵召者; (attrib) (形容用法) ~ *soldiers.* 徵召的士兵們; 應徵部隊。 **con·scrip·tion** /kən'skrɪpʃn ; kən'skrɪpʃən/ *n* [U] ~ing (of men into the armed forces); taxation or confiscation of property (as a penalty or for war needs). 徵兵;(作爲處罰或因戰時需要)對於私有財產之課稅或徵用;徵用制度。

con·se·crate /'kɒnsɪkreɪt ; 'kɑnsɪ,kret/ *vt* [VP6A, 14, 23] ~ ***(to)***, set apart as sacred or for a special purpose; make sacred: 奉爲神聖;供獻(作爲特殊用途);奉獻;使成爲神聖: *to ~ one's life to the service of God/to the relief of suffering.* 奉獻自己的生命爲神服務(從事解除世人的苦難)。*The new church was ~d by the Bishop of Chester.* 新教堂的奉獻禮係由赤斯特的主教主持。*He was ~ed Archbishop last year.* 他於去年被奉爲大主教(任大主教之聖職)。

con·se·cra·tion /ˌkɒnsɪ'kreɪʃn ; ˌkɑnsɪ'kreʃən/ *n* [U] consecrating or being consecrated; [C] instance of this: 供獻;奉獻;神聖化;供獻或奉獻之實例: *the ~ of a church;* 教堂的奉獻; *the ~ of a bishop,* the ceremony at which a priest is made a bishop. 主教授職禮(由神父升任主教之典禮)。

con·secu·tive /kən'sekjʊtɪv ; kən'sɛkjətɪv/ *adj* following continuously; coming one after the other in regular order: 連續不斷的;接連而來的: *on five ~ days.* 連續五天。**~·ly** *adv*

con·sen·sus /kən'sensəs ; kən'sɛnsəs/ *n* [C, U] general agreement (*of* opinion, etc); collective opinion. (意見等的)共同一致;輿論。 ~ **politics**, the practice of basing policies on what will gain wide support. 輿論政治(以能够獲得大衆支持之事物爲施政方針之依據)。

con·sent /kən'sent ; kən'sɛnt/ *vi* [VP2A, 3A, 4C] ~ ***(to)***, give agreement or permission: 同意;答應;應允: *He ~ed to the proposal.* 他同意這提議。*Anne's father would not ~ to her marrying a foreigner.* 安的父親不會答應她嫁給外國人。□ *n* [U] ~ ***(to)***, agreement; permission: 同意; 答應; 許可: *He was chosen leader by general ~,* when everyone agreed. 他爲大家一致贊同選爲領袖。*Her parents refused their ~ to the marriage.* 她的父母不答應此椿婚事。*Silence gives ~,* If no one objects, it seems that ~ is given. 沉默卽是同意。 ***with one ~***, unanimously. 全體一致地。 **ˌage of '~**, age at which the law recognizes a person's responsibility for agreeing to sexual intercourse, a person's right to ~ to marry, etc. 承諾年齡(法律上許可一人有權同意與人發生性關係、婚姻有自主權等的年齡)。

con·se·quence /'kɒnsɪkwəns *US:* -kwens ; 'kɑnsə,kwɛns/ *n* **1** [C] that which follows or is brought about as the result or effect of sth: (某事的)後果;影響: *If you behave so foolishly you must be ready to take the ~s,* accept what happens as a result. 如果你這樣愚昧下去,你必須準備自食其果。***in ~ (of)***, as a result (of). 結果;因…而。 **2** [U] importance: 重要性: *It's of no ~.* 它無重要性。*Is it of any/much ~?* 它有任何(大的)重要性嗎? *He may be a man of ~* (= an important man, or a man of high rank) *in his own village, but he's nobody here.* 他在他自己的村中也許算是個要人,但在此地微不足道。

con·se·quent /'kɒnsɪkwənt ; 'kɑnsə,kwɛnt/ *adj* ~ ***on/upon***, (formal) following as a consequence: (正式用語)跟隨發生的;由…而起的: *the rise in prices ~ upon the failure of the crops.* 由於農作物歉收而引起的物價上漲。**~·ly** *adv*

conse·quen·tial /ˌkɒnsɪ'kwenʃl ; ˌkɑnsə'kwɛnʃəl/ *adj* **1** = consequent. **2** (of a person) self-important. (指人)自大的;自傲的;自以爲了不起的。 **~·ly** /-ʃəlɪ ; -ʃəlɪ/ *adv*

con·ser·vancy /kən'sɜːvənsɪ ; kən'sɝvənsɪ/ *n* (*pl* -cies) **1** [C] commission controlling a port, river, etc: (港口、河道等)管理委員會: *the Thames C~;* 泰晤士河管理委員會; *the Nature C~.* 自然資源管理委員會。 **2** [U] official conservation (of forests, etc). 政府(對於森林等)的保護。

con·ser·va·tion /ˌkɒnsə'veɪʃn ; ˌkɑnsə'veʃən/ *n* [U] preservation; prevention of loss, waste, damage, etc: 保護;保存(以免損失、浪費、損壞等): *the ~ of forests/waterpower etc;* 對於森林(水力等)的保護; *the ~ of energy,* the principle that the total quantity of energy in the universe never varies. 能量不滅律(宇宙間能源的總和永遠不變之定律)。

con·ser·va·tism /kən'sɜːvətɪzm ; kən'sɝvə,tɪzəm/ *n* [U] tendency to maintain a state of affairs (esp in politics) without great or sudden change; the principles of the Conservative Party in British politics. (尤指政治上主張維持現狀而不作大幅度或突然之改革的)保守性;保守主義;英國政界保守黨的政策。

con·ser·va·tive /kən'sɜːvətɪv ; kən'sɝvətɪv/ *adj* **1** opposed to (great or sudden) change: 反對(大幅度或突然)改革的;保守的;守舊的: *Old people are usually more ~ than young people.* 老年人通常較青年人爲保守。 **2 the 'C~ Party,** one of the main political parties in Great Britain. 保守黨(英國之一政黨)。⇨ *Labour* at labour(3), *Liberal* at liberal(4), *Socialist* at socialism. **3** cautious; moderate: 謹愼的;採中庸之道的: *a ~ estimate of one's future income.* 對於自己將來收入的保守的估計。□ *n* ~ person; member of the C~ Party. 守舊的人;保守者;保守黨黨員。 **~·ly** *adv*

con·ser·va·toire /kən'sɜːvətwɑː(r) ; kən,sɝvə'twɑr/ *n* (F) (esp in Europe) public school of music, drama etc. (法)(尤用於歐洲)音樂學校;戲劇學校等。

con·ser·va·tory /kən'sɜːvətrɪ *US:* -tɔːrɪ ; kən'sɝvə,tɔrɪ/ *n* (*pl* -ries) **1** building, or part of a building, with glass walls and roof in which plants are protected from cold. 溫室;花房(保護植物使免受寒凍的玻璃房子)。 **2** = conservatoire.

con·serve /kən'sɜːv ; kən'sɝv/ *vt* [VP6A] keep from change, loss or destruction: 保存;保全(以免變質或損毀): *~ one's strength/energies/health;* 保持實力(精力,健康); *~ fruit,* eg by making it into jam. 保藏水果使不變壞(例如將水果製成果醬)。□ *n* (usu *pl*) fruit preserved in sugar; jam. (通常用複數)蜜餞;果醬。

con·sider /kən'sɪdə(r) ; kən'sɪdɚ/ *vt* **1** [VP6A, C, 8, 10] think about: 考慮;思考: *Please ~ my suggestion.* 請考慮我的建議。*We are ~ing going to Canada.* 我們正考慮赴加拿大。*Have you ~ed how to get/how you could get there?* 你曾考慮到如何能到達那裏嗎? *Have you ever ~ed the fact that your pension will be inadequate?* 你曾經考慮過你的養老金將會不够(生活)嗎? ***one's ~ed opinion,*** one's opinion arrived at after some thought: (某人之)經過考慮後所得到的意見: *It's my ~ed opinion that you should resign.* 經過考慮後我的意見是你應該辭職。 **2** [VP6A] take into account; make allowances for: 顧慮;顧及;體諒: *We must ~ the feelings of other people.* 我們必須顧及他人的感情。 *You should ~ his youth.* 你應當體諒他的年輕。 ***all things ~ed,*** taking into account, thinking of, all the events, possibilities, etc. 綜合各項情勢而觀;把一切情形、可能等都考慮到。 **3** [VP25, 9] be of the opinion; regard as: 認爲;以爲;覺得: *They ~ed themselves very important.* 他們自以爲非常重要。*Do you ~ it wise to interfere?* 你覺得干預是明智的嗎? *He will be ~ed a weak leader.* 他會被認爲是個能力不足的領袖。*C~ yourself* (=You are) *under arrest.* 你是在拘禁中(別想逃走)。*We ~ that you are not to blame.* 我們認爲你不應受責(不是你的錯)。

con·sider·able /kən'sɪdərəbl ; kən'sɪdərəbḷ/ *adj*

great; much; important: 相當大的；相當多的；相當重要的：*a ～ income／distance;* 相當可觀的收入(相當遠的距離)；*bought at a ～ expense;* 花相當多的錢購買的；*a ～ man in local affairs.* 地方事務上相當重要的人物。**～·ably** /-əblɪ ; -əblɪ/ *adv* much; a great deal: 相當地；十分地：*It's considerably colder this morning.* 今天早晨冷得多。

con·sider·ate /kənˈsɪdərət ; kənˈsɪdərɪt/ *adj* **～ (of),** thoughtful (of the needs, etc, of others): 顧慮他人之需要等的；爲着他人着想的；體諒的；體貼的；顧慮週到的：*It was ～ of you not to play the piano while I was having a sleep.* 在我睡覺的時候你不彈鋼琴，眞是顧慮得週到。**～·ly** *adv* **～·ness** *n*

con·sider·ation /kənˌsɪdəˈreɪʃn ; kənˌsɪdəˈreʃən/ *n* **1** [U] act of considering, thinking about: 考慮；思考：*Please give the matter your careful ～.* 請對此事細加思考。*The proposals are still under ～.* 那些提議仍在考慮中。***leave sth out of ～,*** neglect or fail to consider it: 對某事未加考慮：*There is one important fact that has been left out of ～.* 有一重要事實未曾考慮到。***take sth into ～,*** (esp) make allowances for: 考慮到某事；(尤指)體諒；原諒；顧慮到：*When marking Tom's examination papers, the teacher took Tom's long illness into ～.* 在評閱到湯姆的考卷時，老師體諒到湯姆患了很久的病。 **2** [U] **～ (for),** quality of being considerate; thoughtful attention to the wishes, feelings, etc, of others: 體諒；顧慮；顧及他人的願望、感情等：*He has never shown much ～ for his wife's feelings.* 他從來不大顧及他妻子的情緒。***in ～ of; out of ～ for,*** considering(2). 體諒；顧及。 **3** [C] sth which must be thought about; fact, thing, etc thought of as a reason: 必須考慮的事；被當做理由的事實、事物等；因素：*Time is an important ～ in this case.* 在這件事中，時間是一個重要的因素。*Several ～s have influenced me in coming to a decision.* 好幾個因素影響我作決定。***on no ～,*** in no circumstances; in no case. 無論如何決不。 **4** [C] reward; payment: 報酬；酬資：*He's the sort of man who would do anything for a ～,* if he were paid to do it. 他是只要能獲報酬，什麼事都做得出來的那種人。 **5** [U] (rare use) importance: (罕用)重要性：*It's of no ～ at all.* 它一點也不重要。

con·sider·ing /kənˈsɪdərɪŋ ; kənˈsɪdərɪŋ/ *prep, adv* in view of; having regard to: 鑒於；就…而論：*She's very active, ～ her age.* 就她的年齡而論，她眞是非常活躍的。*You've done very well, ～,* ie in view of the circumstances, etc. 就目前情況等而言，你做得很好。

con·sign /kənˈsaɪn ; kənˈsaɪn/ *vt* **～ (to), 1** [VP6A, 14] send (goods, etc) for delivery: 寄遞；運送(貨物等)：*The goods have been ～ed by rail.* 貨物已交由鐵路運寄。 **2** [VP14] hand over, give up: 移交；交付：*～ a child to its uncle's care;* 將小孩交其叔父照顧；*～ one's soul to God.* 把心靈交給上帝；歸主。 **～ee** /ˌkɒnsaɪˈniː ; ˌkɑnsaɪˈni/ *n* person to whom sth is ～ed. 收件人；受付託者。 **～er, ～or** /-nər ; -nɚ/ *nn* person who ～s goods. 寄件人；發貨人。**～·ment** *n* [U] ～ing; [C] goods ～ed. 遞運；委託；所遞運的貨物；委託物。***on ～ment,*** with payment for goods to be made after they have been sold by the receiver: 以委託方式(待貨品售出後方付款給貨主)；以寄售方式：*take／send／ship goods on ～ment.* 以寄售方式接受(寄出，運寄)貨品。**ˈ～ment note,** one sent with a ～ment of goods. 發貨通知書。

con·sist /kənˈsɪst ; kənˈsɪst/ *vi* [VP3A] **1 ～ of,** (not in the progressive tenses) be made up of: (不用進行式)由…組成：*The committee ～s of ten members.* 委員會由十人組成。 **2 ～ in,** have as the chief or only element: 在於；以…爲主要或唯一因素：*The happiness of a country ～s in the freedom of its citizens.* 一國之幸福以其全民之自由爲首要。

con·sist·ence /kənˈsɪstəns ; kənˈsɪstəns/ *n* = consistency.

con·sist·ency /kənˈsɪstənsɪ ; kənˈsɪstənsɪ/ *n* **1** [U] the state of always being the same in thought, behaviour, etc; keeping to the same principles: (思想、行動等的永遠)一致；一貫；固守同樣的原則：*His actions lack ～.* 他的行動缺乏一貫性。 **2** [C, U] (*pl* -cies) degree of thickness, firmness or solidity (esp of a thick liquid, or of sth made by mixing with a liquid): 濃度；堅度；硬度；稠度(尤指濃稠液體或與液體混合物的濃度等)：*mix flour and milk to the right ～;* 混合麵粉和牛奶至適當的濃度；*mixtures of various consistencies.* 各種不同濃度的混合物。

con·sist·ent /kənˈsɪstənt ; kənˈsɪstənt/ *adj* **1** (of a person, his behaviour, principles, etc) conforming to a regular pattern or style; regular: (指人、其行爲、立身之道等)一致的；經常的；一貫的：*He's been a ～ friend to me.* 他是我歷久不渝的朋友。*The ideas in his various speeches are not ～.* 他在各項演說中所持的觀念不一致。 **2 ～ (with),** in agreement: (與…)一致；符合：*What you say now is not ～ with what you said last week.* 你現在所說的話與你上星期所說的話不相符合。**～·ly** *adv*

con·sis·tory /kənˈsɪstərɪ ; kənˈsɪstərɪ/ *n* (*pl* -ries) **C～(Court),** court of clergymen to deal with church business. (由教士組成以處理教會事務的)宗教法庭。

con·so·la·tion /ˌkɒnsəˈleɪʃn ; ˌkɑnsəˈleʃən/ *n* **1** [U] consoling or being consoled; sth that consoles: 安慰；慰藉；安慰物：*a few words of ～;* 幾句安慰的話；*a letter of ～.* 慰問信。**ˈ～ prize,** one given to a competitor who has just missed success or come last. (給予參加比賽未獲名次或得末名者的)精神獎。 **2** [C] circumstances or person that consoles: 令人安慰的情勢或人：*That's one ～.* 那是一件可以告慰的事。*Your company has been a great ～ to me.* 你能陪伴我對我是件極可安慰的事。

con·sola·tory /kənˈsɒlətərɪ *US:* -tɔːrɪ ; kənˈsɑləˌtorɪ/ *adj* comforting; intended to console: 安慰的；旨在安慰人的：*a ～ letter.* 慰問信。

con·sole[1] /kənˈsəʊl ; kənˈsol/ *vt* [VP6A, 14] give comfort or sympathy to (sb who is unhappy, disappointed, etc): 給予(愁苦者，失望者等)安慰或同情；慰問：*～ sb for a loss;* 安慰遭受損失的人；*～ oneself with the thought that it might have been worse.* 以情形沒有變得更壞而告慰自己。**con·sol·able** *adj* that can be ～d. 可安慰的。

con·sole[2] /ˈkɒnsəʊl ; ˈkɑnsol/ *n* **1** bracket to support a shelf. 板架的支架。**ˈ～ table,** narrow table held up by a bracket or brackets fixed to a wall. 用三角支架裝在牆壁上的狹枱。 **2** frame containing the keyboards, stops, etc of an organ. 風琴的操作部份(包括鍵盤，音栓等)。 **3** radio or TV cabinet made to stand on the floor (not a table model). 落地式收音機或電視機的外殼。 **4** panel for the controls of electronic or mechanical equipment. (電子或機械裝置的)控制盤。

con·soli·date /kənˈsɒlɪdeɪt ; kənˈsɑləˌdet/ *vt, vi* **1** [VP6A, 2A] make or become solid or strong: (使)鞏固；(使)堅强：*～ one's position／influence.* 鞏固其地位(勢力)。 **2** [VP6A] unite or combine into one: 團結；聯合；合併；統一：*～ debts／business companies／banks.* 合併債務(商行，銀行)。**～d annuities,** (also 亦稱 **consols** /ˈkɒnsɒlz ; ˈkɑnsɑlz/) Government securities of Great Britain, ～d in 1751 into a single stock. 英國政府(1751 年合併爲一)的統一公債。**C～d Fund** *n* fund from taxation, used for payment of interest on the national debt. 由稅收撥出的公債利息基金。

con·soli·da·tion /kənˌsɒlɪˈdeɪʃn ; kənˌsɑləˈdeʃən/ *n* [U] consolidating or being consolidated; [C] instance of this: 鞏固；團結；聯合；合併；統一：*successive ～s of the national debt.* 公債之歷次的合併。

con·sols /ˈkɒnsɒlz ; ˈkɑnsɑlz/ *n pl* consolidated annuities. 英國政府之統一公債。⇨ consolidate(2).

con·sommé /kənˈsɒmeɪ *US:* ˌkɒnsəˈmeɪ ; ˌkɑnsəˈme/ *n* (F) clear, meat soup. (法)清的肉湯。

con·son·ance /ˈkɒnsənəns ; ˈkɑnsənəns/ *n* [U] **1** agreement. 一致。 **2** harmony. 協調；和諧。

con·son·ant[1] /ˈkɒnsənənt ; ˈkɑnsənənt/ *n* [C] speech

sound produced by a complete or partial stoppage of the breath; letter of the alphabet or symbol (eg phonetic) for such a sound: *b, c, d, f,* etc. 子音；輔音(由完全阻塞或不完全阻塞呼氣所發的語音)；子音字母(如 b, c, d, f 等)；子音符號(如子音音標)。

con·son·ant² /ˈkɒnsənənt ; ˈkɑnsənənt/ *adj* (formal) **~ *with,*** harmonious: (正式用語)(與…)協調的；和諧的: *actions ~ with his beliefs;* 與其信仰一致的行動; *a position in the service ~ with your rank.* 與你的軍階相符合的軍職。**~ *to,*** agreeable: 一致的；符合的: *~ to reason.* 合理的。

con·sort¹ /ˈkɒnsɔːt ; ˈkɑnsɔrt/ *n* **1** husband or wife, esp of a ruler: 配偶；夫或妻(尤指君王之夫或妻): *the queen ~,* the king's wife; 王后; *the prince ~,* the reigning queen's husband. 女王的丈夫；王夫。**2** ship sailing with another (esp for safety during a war). (尤指戰時爲安全而)結伴航行的船隻。

con·sort² /kənˈsɔːt ; kənˈsɔrt/ *vi* [VP3A, 2C] **~ *with,*** **1** pass time in the company of: 陪伴；結交；交往: *~ with criminals／one's equals.* 與犯罪者(平輩)交往。**2** be in harmony, go well: 協調；一致；符合: *His practice does not ~ with his preaching,* He behaves in one way, but talks in another way. 他的言行不符。

con·sor·tium /kənˈsɔːtɪəm *US:* -ˈsɔːrʃɪəm ; kənˈsɔrʃɪəm/ *n* (*pl* -tia /-tɪə *US:* -ʃɪə ; -ʃɪə/) temporary co-operation of a number of powers, companies, banks, etc for a common purpose: (若干强國、大公司、銀行等爲一共同目的而臨時合作組成的)國際財團；國際銀行團；協會；聯營；協營: *the ~ of Upper Clyde shipbuilders.* 上克萊造船公司協營。

con·spec·tus /kənˈspektəs ; kənˈspɛktəs/ *n* (*pl* ~es /-ɪz ; -ɪz/) general view of a subject, scene, etc; synopsis (eg in the form of tables). (對於某一學科，地點等的)概覽；概要；大綱(如列成圖表者)。

con·spicu·ous /kənˈspɪkjʊəs ; kənˈspɪkjʊəs/ *adj* easily seen; attracting attention; remarkable: 顯而易見的；顯著的；引人注目的；值得注意的；特出的；出衆的: *~ for his bravery.* 以其英勇而受人注意。*Traffic signs should be ~.* 交通標誌應該顯明。***make oneself ~,*** attract attention by unusual behaviour, wearing unusual clothes, etc. 藉不尋常的行爲、穿著不尋常的衣服等而引人注目；標新立異出風頭。**~·ly** *adv* **~·ness** *n*

con·spir·acy /kənˈspɪrəsɪ ; kənˈspɪrəsɪ/ *n* [U] act of conspiring; [C] (*pl* -cies) plan made by conspiring: 陰謀；共謀；謀反: *a ~ to overthrow the Government;* 推翻政府的陰謀; *a ~ of silence,* an agreement not to talk publicly about sth. 緘默協定(同意不公開談論某事)。

con·spire /kənˈspaɪə(r) ; kənˈspaɪr/ *vi, vt* **1** [VP2A, 3A, 4A] ***~ (with) (against),*** make secret plans (with others, esp to do sth wrong): 陰謀；密謀；密商: *~ against the Government.* 陰謀反對政府。*His enemies ~d to ruin him.* 他的仇人密謀毀滅他。**2** [VP6A] plot: 陰謀；密謀: *~ sb's ruin.* 陰謀毀滅某人。**3** [VP4A] (of events) act together; combine: (指事件)合作；聯合；湊合: *events that ~d to bring about his downfall.* 湊合起來使他垮臺的各項事件。**con·spira·tor** /kənˈspɪrətə(r) ; kənˈspɪrətɚ/ *n* person who ~s. 陰謀者；共謀者；謀叛者。**con·spira·tor·ial** /kənˌspɪrəˈtɔːrɪəl ; kənˌspɪrəˈtɔrɪəl/ *adj* of conspirators or a conspiracy: 陰謀(者)的；共謀(者)的；謀叛(者)的: *with a conspiratorial air.* 帶着一種密謀的神情。

con·stable /ˈkʌnstəbl *US:* ˈkɒn- ; ˈkɑnstəbl/ *n* **1** (GB) **(poˈlice) ~,** policeman or policewoman of basic grade. (英)(階級最低之)警察；女警。**Chief C~,** head of the police force of a county, etc. (郡等的)警察局長。**special ~,** person who acts as a ~ on special occasions or for special duty. (在特殊場合或負有特殊任務的)臨時警察；特種警察。**2** (hist) principal officer in a royal household; governor of a royal castle, etc. (史)宮廷長官；皇室侍衛長；皇室城堡等的總管。**con·sta·bu·lary** /kənˈstæbjʊlərɪ *US:* -lerɪ ; kənˈstæbjəˌlɛrɪ/ *n* (*pl* -ries) organized body of police ~s; police force. 警察隊；保安隊。

con·stancy /ˈkɒnstənsɪ ; ˈkɑnstənsɪ/ *n* [U] quality of being firm, unchanging: 堅定不移；恒久不變: *~ of purpose.* 志向不變。

con·stant /ˈkɒnstənt ; ˈkɑnstənt/ *adj* **1** going on all the time; frequently recurring: 經常的；永恒的；屢見的；不斷的: *~ complaints.* 不斷的抱怨。**2** firm; faithful; unchanging: 堅定的；忠實的；不變的: *a ~ friend.* 忠實的朋友。*He has been ~ in his devotion to scientific studies.* 他堅毅地致力於科學的研究。□ *n* (maths, phys) number or quantity that does not vary. (數學，物理)常數；恒量；恒定。**~·ly** *adv* continuously; frequently. 經常地；不斷地；時常地。

con·stel·la·tion /ˌkɒnstəˈleɪʃn ; ˌkɑnstəˈleʃən/ *n* named group of fixed stars (eg *the Great Bear*); (fig) group. 業經命名的恒星羣；星座(如大熊星座)；(喻)羣體。

con·ster·na·tion /ˌkɒnstəˈneɪʃn ; ˌkɑnstɚˈneʃən/ *n* [U] surprise and fear; dismay: 驚愕；驚恐；驚慌: *filled with ~;* 充滿驚恐之情; *looking back in ~.* 驚慌地向後張望。

con·sti·pate /ˈkɒnstɪpeɪt ; ˈkɑnstəˌpet/ *vt* [VP6A] cause constipation: 使便秘: *to find some kinds of food constipating.* 發現某些食物會引起便秘。

con·sti·pated /ˈkɒnstɪpeɪtɪd ; ˈkɑnstəˌpetɪd/ *part adj* having bowels that can be emptied infrequently or only with difficulty. 便秘的。

con·sti·pa·tion /ˌkɒnstɪˈpeɪʃn ; ˌkɑnstəˈpeʃən/ *n* [U] difficult or infrequent emptying of the bowels. 便秘。

con·sti·tu·ency /kənˈstɪtjʊənsɪ ; kənˈstɪtʃʊənsɪ/ *n* (*pl* -cies) [C] (body of voters living in a) town or district that sends a representative to Parliament. 英國國會議員選舉區；居於一選舉區中的選民。

con·sti·tu·ent /kənˈstɪtjʊənt ; kənˈstɪtʃʊənt/ *adj* **1** having the power or right to make or alter a political constitution: 有權創制或修改憲法的: *a ~ assembly.* 立憲議會；國民代表大會。**2** forming or helping to make a whole: 組成的；構成的: *a ~ part.* 組成的成份。□ *n* **1** member of a constituency. 英國國會議員選舉區之選民。**2** component part: 成份；組分；組成物: *the ~s of happiness.* 幸福的要素。

con·sti·tute /ˈkɒnstɪtjuːt *US:* -tuːt ; ˈkɑnstəˌtjut/ *vt* **1** [VP23] give (sb) authority to hold (a position, etc): 任命(某人)擔任(某項職位等): *They ~d him chief adviser.* 他們委任他爲首席顧問。*What right have you to ~ yourself a judge of my conduct?* 你有何權自命爲我的行爲的評判人？ **2** [VP6A] establish; give legal authority to (a committee, etc). 成立；授給法之權與(委員會等)。**3** [VP6A] make up (a whole); amount to; be the components of: 組成(整體)；構成；爲…之成分: *Twelve months ~ a year.* 十二個月構成一年。*He is so ~d* (=His nature is such) *that he can accept unjust criticism without getting angry.* 他的性情天生如此，能受不公正的批評而不動怒。

con·sti·tu·tion /ˌkɒnstɪˈtjuːʃn *US:* -ˈtuːʃn ; ˌkɑnstəˈtjuʃən/ *n* **1** [C] system of government; laws and principles according to which a state is governed: 政治制度；憲法(治理一國所依據的法規): *Great Britain has an unwritten ~; the United States has a written ~.* 英國的憲法是不成文的；美國的憲法是成文的。**2** [C] general physical structure and condition of a person's body: 體格；體質: *Only people with strong ~s should climb in the Himalayas.* 只有體格强健的人才可以攀登喜馬拉雅山。**3** [C, U] general structure of a thing; act or manner of constituting: 物的一般構造；組織；任命、成立、授權或構成的行爲或方式: *the ~ of the solar spectrum;* 太陽光譜的構成; *the ~ of one's mind and character.* 某人之心理和性格的素質。

con·sti·tu·tional /ˌkɒnstɪˈtjuːʃənl *US:* -ˈtuː- ; ˌkɑnstəˈtjuʃənl/ *adj* **1** of a constitution (1): 憲法的；立憲的: *~ government;* 立憲政體; *a ~ ruler,* controlled or limited by a constitution; 立憲君主(受憲法控制或限制的君主)； *~ reform.* 憲法修改。⇨

absolute, *autocratic* at autocrat. **2** of a person's constitution(2): 體格的;體質的: *a ~ weakness.* 體格的虛弱。□ *n* (dated colloq) short walk for the health's sake: (過時俗語)爲健康目的所作的散步;健行: *go for/take a ~.* 散散步;作徒步健行。**~·ly** /-ʃənəlɪ; -ʃənḷɪ/ *adv* **~·ism** *n* [U] (belief in) ~ government or ~ principles. 立憲政體;立憲主義。**~·ist** *n* supporter of ~ principles. 立憲主義者。 **~·ize** /-ʃnəlaɪz; -ʃənḷaɪz/ *vt* make ~. 使實施立憲政體。

con·sti·tut·ive /kən'stɪtjʊtɪv; 'kanstə,tjutɪv/ *adj* constructive; formative; essential. 構成的; 組成的; 基本的;必要的。

con·strain /kən'streɪn; kən'stren/ *vt* [VP6A, 17] make (sb) do sth by using force or strong persuasion; (of conscience, inner forces) compel: 强迫;勉强(某人)做某事;(指良心、內在力量)驅使: *I feel ~ed to write and ask for your forgiveness.* 我不得不寫信請你原諒。**~ed** *part adj* (of voice, manner, etc) forced; uneasy; unnatural. (指聲音、態度等)勉强的;不自然的;做作的。**~·ed·ly** /-ɪdlɪ; -ɪdlɪ/ *adv*

con·straint /kən'streɪnt; kən'strent/ *n* [U] constraining or being constrained: 强迫;逼迫;迫使;勉强;拘束: *to act under ~*, because one is forced to do so; 受逼迫而行動; *to feel/show ~ in a person's presence,* to hold back one's natural feelings. 在某人面前感覺(表現)拘束。

con·strict /kən'strɪkt; kən'strɪkt/ *vt* [VP6A] make tight or smaller; cause (a vein or muscle) to become tight or narrow: 使緊或變小;使(靜脈或肌肉)收縮;壓縮;收緊: (fig) (喻) *a ~ed outlook,* one that is narrow or limited. 狹隘的看法。**con·stric·tion** /kən'strɪkʃn; kən'strɪkʃən/ *n* [U] ~ing; [C] feeling of being ~ed: 壓緊;收縮;壓迫的感覺: *a ~ion in the chest;* 胸部感到壓迫; [C] sth that ~s. 能壓緊或收縮之物。

con·struct /kən'strʌkt; kən'strʌkt/ *vt* [VP6A] build; put or fit together: 建築;建造;建立;構築: *to ~ a factory/an aircraft/a sentence/a theory;* 建工廠(造飛機;造句子;建立理論); *a well-~ed novel.* 結構很完善的小說。**~or** /-tə(r); -tɚ/ *n* person who ~s things: 建築者;建造者: *motor-car body ~ors.* 車體承造商。

con·struc·tion /kən'strʌkʃn; kən'strʌkʃən/ *n* **1** [U] act or manner of constructing; being constructed: 施工;構築;修築;建設: *the ~ of new roads.* 新道路的修築。*The new railway is still under ~/in the course of ~.* 新的鐵路尙在修築中。*The new factory is of very solid ~.* 那新工廠造得很堅固。**2** [C] sth constructed; structure; building. 建築物;構造物。**3** [C] meaning; sense in which words, statements, acts, etc are taken: 意義;(個人對於字、句、行爲等的)解釋: *Please do not put a wrong ~ on his action,* misunderstand its purpose. 請不要誤會他的行動的用意。*The sentence does not bear such a ~,* cannot be understood in that way. 這句話並不含有那樣的意思(不能那樣解釋)。⇨ construe. **4** [C] arrangement and relationships of words in a sentence: 字在句中的安排及字與字之間的關係;造句法: *This dictionary gives the meanings of words and also illustrates their ~s.* 本字典解釋字義,並且舉例說明字在句中的構造法。

con·struc·tive /kən'strʌktɪv; kən'strʌktɪv/ *adj* helping to construct; giving helpful suggestions: 建設性的;有裨益的;積極的: *~ criticism/proposals.* 建設性的批評(提議)。**~·ly** *adv*

con·strue /kən'stru:; kən'stru/ *vt, vi* **1** [VP6A, 2A] translate or explain the meaning of words, sentences, acts: 譯註;解釋;銓釋(字、句、行爲): *~ a passage from Homer.* 註釋荷馬著作的一段文字。*His remarks were wrongly ~d,* were misunderstood. 他的話被誤解了。**2** [VP6A] analyse (a sentence); combine (words with words) grammatically. 分析(句子);按文法連(字)造句。**3** [VP2A] be capable of being analysed: 可被分析: *This sentence won't ~.* 這個句子不可分析。

con·sub·stan·ti·ation /,kɒnsəb,stænʃɪ'eɪʃn; ,kansəb,stænʃɪ'eʃən/ *n* [U] doctrine that the body and blood of Christ co-exist with the bread and wine in the Eucharist. 聖體共在論(基督之聖體和聖血與聖餐中之麵包和葡萄酒共在的教義)。

con·sul /'kɒnsl; 'kansḷ/ *n* **1** State's agent living in a foreign town to help and protect his countrymen there. (派駐外國協助和保護僑民的)領事。**2** (in ancient Rome) either of the two Heads of the State before Rome became an Empire. (古羅馬變成帝國之前的)兩執政官之一。**3** any one of the three chief magistrates of the French Republic, 1799–1804. 1799 至 1804 年法蘭西共和國三個主要執政官之一。**~·ship** /-ʃɪp; -,ʃɪp/ *n* position of a ~; period of time during which a ~ holds his position. 領事或執政官的職位或任期。

con·su·lar /'kɒnsjʊlə(r) *US:* -səl-; 'kansḷɚ/ *adj* of a consul or his work. 領事的;執政官的;領事或執政官的職務的。

con·su·late /'kɒnsjʊlət *US:* -səl-; 'kansḷɪt/ *n* consul's position; offices of a consul(1); period of consular government in France. 領事或執政官的職位;領事館;法國的執政統治時期。

con·sult /kən'sʌlt; kən'sʌlt/ *vt, vi* **1** [VP6A, 14] go to a person, a book, etc for information, advice, opinion, etc: 向(人)求教;查閱(書籍等)以便尋得資料、參考意見等: *to ~ one's lawyer/a map/the dictionary;* 就教律師(查閱地圖;查字典); *a ~ing engineer,* one with special knowledge of one or more branches of engineering. 工程顧問;顧問工程師(具有一門或數門工程方面之特殊知識)。**2** [VP6A] (old use; *consider* is now preferred) take into consideration or account: (舊用法;今人喜用 consider) 考慮;顧及: *We must ~ his convenience,* cause him as little inconvenience as possible. 我們必須顧及他的方便。**3** [VP3A] **~ with,** discuss with: 商量;商議: *~ with one's partners.* 與合夥人商量。

con·sul·tant /kən'sʌltənt; kən'sʌltənt/ *n* person who gives expert advice (eg in medicine, surgery, business): 提供專家意見的人(如有關醫藥、外科、商業等方面者);顧問: (attrib) (形容用法) *a ~ surgeon;* 外科顧問醫師(不應診只提供專家意見的外科醫生); *a firm of ~s.* 顧問公司(供應專家作顧問的公司)。

con·sul·ta·tion /,kɒnsl'teɪʃn; ,kansḷ'teʃən/ *n* **1** [U] consulting or being consulted: 請教;就教;咨詢;商議: *in ~ with the director.* 與主任商議。**2** [C] meeting for consulting: 商量的會議; 協議會: *The doctors held a ~ to decide whether an operation was necessary.* 醫生們會診以決定是否需要動手術。

con·sult·ative /kən'sʌltətɪv; kən'sʌltətɪv/ *adj* of, for the purpose of, consulting: 供咨詢的;顧問的: *a ~ committee.* 顧問委員會。

con·sume /kən'sju:m *US:* -'su:m; kən'sum/ *vt, vi* **1** [VP6A] eat or drink. 食;飲。**2** [VP6A] use up; get to the end of; destroy by fire or wastefulness: 用盡;耗盡;被火或因浪費而毀滅;蕩盡: *~ all one's energies.* 耗盡其所有的精力。*The flames quickly ~d the wooden huts.* 火焰很快地吞滅了那些簡陋的木屋。*He soon ~d his fortune,* spent the money wastefully. 他不久就把他的財產揮霍殆盡。*He was ~d* (= filled) *with envy/hatred/greed.* 他心中充滿着嫉妬(仇恨,貪婪)。*This is time-consuming work,* work that takes up a lot of time. 這是一項費時的工作。**3** **~ away,** waste away. 喪失體力及健康;消瘦;憔悴。**con·sum·ing** *part adj* possessing or dominating: 佔有的;控制的;支配的: *consuming ambition.* 佔有的野心;支配的野心。

con·sumer /kən'sju:mə(r) *US:* -'su:-; kən'sumɚ/ *n* (opp to *producer*) person who uses goods. (爲 producer 之相反字)消費者;用戶。**~ goods,** those which directly satisfy human needs and desires (eg food and clothing) (opp to *capital goods,* eg factory equipment). 消費品;消費財(直接滿足人類需要及慾望的貨品,如食品和衣服,與 capital goods 相

對,如工廠設備)。～ **research,** market research, ⇨ market[1](4). 消費者調查;市場調查。～ **sales resistance,** unwillingness of people to buy a product. 消費者銷貨阻力;消費抵制。 **～·ism** /-ɪzəm ; -ɪzəm/ *n* [U] protection of ～s' interests. 消費者利益之保護。

con·sum·mate[1] /kən'sʌmət ; kən'sʌmɪt/ *adj* supremely skilled; perfect: 高度技巧的;完全的;完美的: *～ skill／taste.* 高超的技術(鑑賞力)。

con·sum·mate[2] /'kɒnsəmeɪt.; 'kɑnsə,met/ *vt* [VP6A] **1** accomplish; make perfect: 完成;使圓滿;使完善: *Her happiness was ～d when her father took her to Paris.* 當她父親帶她到巴黎時,她的快樂達到了極點。 **2** make complete (esp marriage by sexual intercourse). 使完全;(尤指)完婚;圓房。

con·sum·ma·tion /,kɒnsə'meɪʃn ; ,kɑnsə'meʃən/ *n* [C,U] action or point of completing, perfecting, or fulfilling: 完成;圓滿成功;成就: *the ～ of a life's work／one's ambitions／a marriage.* 畢生事業(志願,婚姻)的完成。

con·sump·tion /kən'sʌmpʃn ; kən'sʌmpʃən/ *n* [U] **1** using up, consuming (of food, energy, materials, etc); the quantity consumed: 用罄;消費(指食物、精力、物資等);消耗量: *The ～ of beer did not go down when the tax was raised.* 啤酒稅增高時,啤酒的消耗量却未降低。 **2** (popular name for) pulmonary tuberculosis. 癆病(肺結核的通俗名稱);肺病。

con·sump·tive /kən'sʌmptɪv ; kən'sʌmptɪv/ *adj* suffering from, having a tendency to, consumption(2). 患肺病的;有肺病之傾向的。□ *n* ～ person. 肺病患者。

con·tact /'kɒntækt ; 'kɑntækt/ *n* **1** [U] (state of) touching or communication; (process of) coming together, esp in: 接觸;傳達;交換意見;接觸或傳達的狀態;接觸的過程;(尤用於): ***be in／out of ～ (with); come／bring into ～ (with):*** (與…)在接觸中(停止接觸);接觸及(使接觸到);(使)與…交往: *Our troops are in ～ with the enemy.* 我們的部隊已與敵軍接觸。 *The opposing forces are now in／out of ～ (with each other).* 敵對的兩軍現正接觸中(現已停止接觸)。 *A steel cable came into ～ with an electric power line.* 一條鋼索觸到了電線。 *We can learn much by being brought into ～ with other minds／opposing opinions, etc.* 由於與他人交換意見(聽取反對意見等),我們可以學得很多東西。 ***make ～ (with),*** come into ～ (with), esp after searching, striving, etc: (尤指經過搜尋、努力等之後,與…)接觸;結識;交往: *I finally made ～ with him in Paris.* 我終於在巴黎與他連絡上了。 *We never really succeeded in making ～.* 我們從未眞正地結識。 *They made ～ by radio／made radio ～ with headquarters.* 他們用無線電與總部互通信息(與總部作無線電接觸)。 ***make／break ～,*** complete／interrupt an electric circuit. 接通(阻斷)電路。 **'～ lens,** one of thin plastic material made to fit closely over and in ～ with the eyeball to improve vision. 隱形眼鏡(薄的塑膠製成的鏡片,裝於眼球上,與眼球接觸,藉以增進視力)。 **2** [C] meeting with a person; person one has met or will meet: 與人接觸或會晤;所接觸或將會晤的人: *He made many useful social ～s while he was in Canada,* met people who could be useful to him. 在他留加拿大期間,他曾結識了許多有力的社會人士。 *Do you have any ～s in Rangoon?* 你在仰光有要會晤的人嗎? **3** [C] connection (for electric current); device for effecting this. (電流的)接觸;接觸器。 **4** [C] (med) person recently exposed to a contagious disease. (醫)接觸者(最近與傳染病接觸過的人)。□ *vt* [VP6A] get in ～ with (sb); reach (sb) (by message, telephone, etc): 與(某人)接觸;與(某人)會晤;(以訊息、電話等)與(某人)連繫: *Where can I ～ Jeff's wife?* 我在何處可以會晤傑夫的太太?

con·tagion /kən'teɪdʒən ; kən'tedʒən/ *n* [U] the spreading of disease by contact or close association; [C] disease that can be spread by contact; (fig) the spreading of ideas, false rumours, feelings, etc; [C] influence, etc that spreads: (疾病的)接觸傳染; 觸染; 接觸傳染病(可藉接觸而傳佈的疾病);觸染病;(喩)(思想、謠言、情緒等的)傳佈;蔓延;散播的影響力等: *A ～ of fear swept through the crowd.* 一種恐懼的感覺侵襲群衆。

con·tagious /kən'teɪdʒəs ; kən'tedʒəs/ *adj* **1** (of disease) spreading by contact: (指疾病)傳染性的;由接觸而傳染的;觸染的: *Scarlet fever is ～.* 猩紅熱是傳染性的。 **2** (of a person) in such a condition that he may spread disease. (指人)患傳染病的;可能傳染疾病的。 **3** (fig) spreading easily by example: (喩)容易引起同感的;有感染性的: *～ laughter／enthusiasm.* 使人想笑之笑聲(能激起熱心之熱心);感染性的笑聲(熱情)。 *Yawning is ～.* 打呵欠是有感染性的。 **～·ly** *adv*

con·tain /kən'teɪn ; kən'ten/ *vt* [VP6A] (not in the progressive tenses) (不用進行式) **1** have or hold within itself: 包含;含有: *The atlas ～s forty maps, including three of Great Britain.* 這地圖集含有四十幅地圖,包括三幅英國地圖在內。 *Whisky ～s a large percentage of alcohol.* 威士忌酒含有酒精的百分比甚高。 **2** be equal to: 等於: *A gallon ～s eight pints.* 一加侖等於八品脫。 **3** be capable of holding: 能容納;可盛;可裝: *How much does this bottle ～?* 這瓶子能裝多少? **4** keep feelings, enemy forces, etc under control, within limits: 控制(情緒、敵軍等);圍堵;牽制: *Can't you ～ your enthusiasm?* 你不能控制你的熱情嗎? *He couldn't ～ himself for joy,* was so happy that his feelings burst out. 他抑制不住他的歡樂之情。 *He couldn't ～ his wine,* was sick, became drunk, etc. 他不能控制他的酒量(病了,醉了等)。 *Has the cholera outbreak been ～ed,* prevented from spreading? 霍亂的發生已經被控制住(不再蔓延)了嗎? **5** (geom) form the boundary of: (幾何)構成…的邊界;圍;夾: *The angle ～ed by the lines A B and A C in the triangle A B C is a right angle.* 在三角形 *A B C* 中爲 *A B* 和 *A C* 兩邊所夾的角是直角。

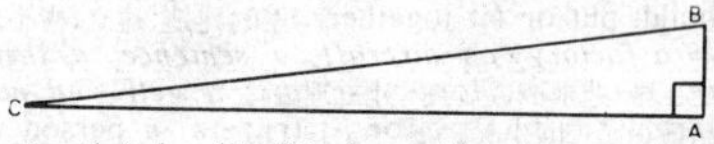

6 (maths) be divisible by, without a remainder: (數學)可被…除盡;可整除: *12 ～s 2, 3, 4 and 6.* 12 可被 2, 3, 4 和 6 除盡。 **～er** *n* **1** box, bottle, etc designed to ～ sth. 容器(箱、匣、瓶等)。 **2** large metal box or other sealed ～er for transport of goods by road, rail, sea or air: 貨櫃(公路、鐵路、海上或空中貨運用的大型金屬箱或其他密閉式的容器): *'～er crane,* large crane mounted on a gantry, used on quays, etc to move ～ers(2). 貨櫃起重機(碼頭等處裝於橋形臺架上用以裝卸貨櫃的大型起重機)。 *'～er train／liner,* one designed for such ～ers; 貨櫃列車(貨運班機); *'～er traffic;* 貨櫃交通; *'～er depot,* eg where ～ers are loaded and unloaded. 貨櫃站(裝卸貨櫃的地點)。 **～·ment** *n* [U] policy of preventing a State from extending its sphere of influence. (阻止一國家延伸其勢力範圍的)封鎖政策;圍堵政策。

con·tami·nate /kən'tæmɪneɪt ; kən'tæmə,net/ *vt* [VP6A] make dirty, impure or diseased (by touching, or adding sth impure): (由於接觸或加入汚物而)染汚;弄髒;汚損: *～d clothing,* eg by poison-gas or radioactive materials. (例如爲毒氣或放射性物質所)染汚的衣服。 *Flies ～ food.* 蒼蠅會染汚食物。 *His morals have been ～d by bad companions.* 他的品行已爲不良的友伴所敗壞。

con·tami·na·tion /kən,tæmɪ'neɪʃn ; kən,tæmə'neʃən/ *n* **1** [U] contaminating or being contaminated: 染汚;弄髒;沾染;汚損: *～ of the water supply.* 給水之汚染。 **2** [C] that which contaminates. 汚穢之物;可染汚他物之物。

con·temn /kən'tem ; kən'tɛm/ *vt* [VP6A] (liter) despise; disregard. (文)輕侮;蔑視。

con·tem·plate /'kɒntempleɪt ; 'kɑntəm,plet/ *vt, vi* **1** [VP6A] look at (with the eyes, or in the mind): 注視;熟視;沉思: *She stood contemplating her figure／herself in the mirror.* 她站着注視她(自

己)鏡中的身影。 **2** [VP6A, C, 19C] have in view as a purpose, intention or possibility: 在心中打算(作爲一種目的、意願或可能): *She was contemplating a visit to London.* 她正打算赴倫敦觀光。*I hope your mother does not ~ coming to stay with us.* 我希望你的母親不打算來與我們同住。*I do not ~ any opposition from him,* do not think this is likely or possible. 我想他不至於反對。 **3** [VP2A, 6A] meditate (esp as a religious practice). 瞑思(尤指宗教習慣上的)。

con·tem·pla·tion /ˌkɒntemˈpleɪʃn ; ˌkɑntəmˈpleʃən/ *n* [U] contemplating; deep thought; intention; expectation: 注視;默察;沉思;打算;希望;期待: *He sat there deep in ~.* 他坐在那兒沉思默想。

con·tem·pla·tive /kənˈtemplətɪv ; ˈkɑntəmˌpletɪv/ *adj* thoughtful; fond of contemplation; given up to religious contemplation. 多思想的;好深思的;專注於宗教思想的。

con·tem·por·aneous /kənˌtempəˈreɪnɪəs ; kənˌtɛmpəˈrenɪəs/ *adj* ~ ***(with),*** originating, existing, happening, during the same period of time: 起源、存在或發生於同一時期的;同期的;同時代的: *~ events.* 同時代的事件。 **~·ly** *adv*

con·tem·por·ary /kənˈtemprərɪ *US:* -ərerɪ ; kənˈtɛmpəˌrɛrɪ/ *adj* of the time or period to which reference is being made; belonging to the same time: 同時的;同時代的;屬於同一時期的: *a ~ record of events,* one made by persons living at that time; 該時代的人對該時代的事所作的記載; *furniture in ~ style,* of the present time (contrasted with period(2) furniture). 目前流行的式樣的傢具(與period furniture 相對)。*Dickens was ~ with Thackeray.* 狄更斯與薩克萊屬於同一時代。□ *n* (*pl* -ries) person ~ with another: 同時的人;同時代的人: *Jack and I were contemporaries at college.* 傑克與我同時讀大學。

con·tempt /kənˈtempt ; kənˈtɛmpt/ *n* [U] **1** condition of being looked down upon or despised: 被輕視;被蔑視;被鄙視: *to fall into ~ by foolish or bad behaviour.* 由於愚昧或不良的行爲而被鄙視。*Such behaviour will bring you into ~.* 這種行爲將使你遭受鄙視。 *A man who is cruel to his children should be held in ~.* 虐待自己孩子的人應受鄙視。 **2** mental attitude of despising: 輕視; 蔑視; 鄙視: *We feel ~ for liars.* 我們對於說謊者有鄙視的心理。 ***beneath ~: Such an accusation is beneath ~,*** not worth despising (because it is so ridiculous, etc). 這種控告不值得一顧。 **3** disregard or disrespect; total disregard: 藐視;不尊敬;完全不理: *in ~ of all rules and regulations.* 藐視一切規章。 *He rushed forward in ~ of danger.* 他完全不顧危險地往前衝。 *He showed his ~ of death by rushing at the enemy.* 他衝向敵人表現出不怕死的精神。 ***Familiarity breeds ~,*** (prov) (諺) ⇨ familiarity(1). ***ˌ~ of ˈcourt,*** disobedience to an order made by a court; disrespect shown to a judge. 不服從法庭的命令;輕蔑法官;藐視法庭。

con·tempt·ible /kənˈtemptəbl ; kənˈtɛmptəbl/ *adj* deserving or provoking contempt. 可鄙的;卑劣的。

con·temptu·ous /kənˈtemptʃʊəs ; kənˈtɛmptʃʊəs/ *adj* showing contempt: 顯示輕蔑的: *~ of public opinion.* 蔑視輿論。 **~·ly** *adv*

con·tend /kənˈtend ; kənˈtɛnd/ *vi, vt* **1** [VP3A] ~ ***with/against/for,*** struggle, be in rivalry or competition: 奮鬥;鬥爭;競爭: *~ing with difficulties;* 與困苦奮鬥; *~ing for a prize;* 爭取獎品; *~ing passions,* strong feelings of different kinds (eg pity, a sense of justice) that make decision difficult. 使人難做決定的矛盾的心情(如憐憫與正義感)。 **2** [VP9] argue, assert: 主張;力辯;斷言: *~ that the universe is expanding.* 斷言宇宙正在擴展中。 **~er** *n* competitor, rival, eg one who challenges the holder of a boxing title. 競爭者;敵手(如拳擊衛冕賽的挑戰者)。

con·tent¹ /kənˈtent ; kənˈtɛnt/ *adj* (not used attrib; ⇨ contented below) (不作形容用法;參看下列 contented) **1** ~ ***(with),*** not wanting more; satisfied with what one has: 滿足的;滿意的;不再想要更多的;滿於現狀的: *Are you ~ with your present salary?* 你對於你現在的薪水感覺滿意嗎？ *She is ~ with very little.* 她很容易滿足。 **2** ~ ***to do sth,*** willing or ready (to do sth): 願意做某事的: *I am ~ to remain where I am now.* 我願意保持現狀。*I should be well ~* (= quite pleased) *to do so.* 我很高興這樣做。□ *n* [U] condition of being satisfied: 滿意的狀態;滿足: *living in peace and ~.* 生活平靜滿足。 ***to one's heart's ~,*** to the extent that brings satisfaction. 心滿意足;盡情;盡歡。□ *vt* [VP6A, 14] ***~ sb/oneself (with),*** make ~; satisfy: 使滿意;使滿足: *There's no ~ing some people,* It's impossible to please or satisfy them. 欲使某些人滿意是不可能的。*As there's no butter we must ~ ourselves* (= be satisfied) *with dry bread.* 既然沒有奶油,我們只好吃乾麵包了。 **~ed** *adj* satisfied; showing or feeling ~: 滿意的;顯示或感到滿意的: *with a ~ed look/smile.* 帶滿意的表情(微笑)。 **~·ed·ly** *adv* **~·ment** *n* [U] state of being ~. 滿意;滿足。

con·tent² /ˈkɒntent ; ˈkɑntɛnt/ *n* **1** (*pl*) that which is contained in sth: (複)內容; 內部所有之物: *the ~s of a room/a book/a schoolboy's pockets, etc.* 房間內部的東西(書的內容;學童衣袋裏面的東西等)。 ***table of ~s,*** list of the matter in a book, periodical, etc. (書籍、雜誌等的)目錄;目次。 **2** (*sing* or *pl;* with *sing v*) the amount which a vessel will hold; capacity: (單或複;與單數動詞連用)(容器的)容量;容積: *the ~(s) of a barrel or cask.* 一桶的容積。 **3** (*sing*) substance; essential meaning (of a book, speech, etc as opposed to its form): (單)(書籍、演說等的)內容;要義(與其形式相對): *Do you approve of the ~ of the article/speech?* 你贊同此文(演說)的內容嗎？ **4** ***~ (of sth),*** (*sing;* preceded by a *n*) part (of it): (單;前有一名詞)(該名詞的)成分;含量: *a high fat ~;* 高度脂肪含量; *the silver ~ of a coin;* 一硬幣中銀的成分; *the sugar ~ of milk.* 牛奶中糖的成分。

con·ten·tion /kənˈtenʃn ; kənˈtɛnʃən/ *n* **1** [U] contending(2); quarrelling or disputing: 爭辯;爭論: *This is not a time for ~.* 這不是爭論的時候。 ⇨ bone. **2** [C] argument used in contending: 爭辯中所持的論點: *My ~ is that....* 我的論點是…。

con·ten·tious /kənˈtenʃəs ; kənˈtɛnʃəs/ *adj* quarrelsome; likely to cause contention: 好爭論的;可能引起爭論的: *a ~ clause in a treaty.* 條約中可引起爭論的條款。

con·termi·nous /kɒnˈtɜːmɪnəs ; kɑnˈtɝmənəs/ *adj* = coterminous.

con·test /kənˈtest ; kənˈtɛst/ *vt, vi* **1** [VP6A, 9] argue; debate; dispute: 爭辯;爭論;辯論;反駁: *~ a statement/point,* try to show that it is wrong; 反駁某陳述(論點); *~ sb's right/that sb has a right to do sth.* 對某人做某事之權表示異議。 **2** [VP3A] contend(1). 奮鬥;鬥爭;競爭。 **3** [VP6A] fight or compete for; try to win: 競爭以奪取;爭取: *~ a seat in Parliament.* 爭取國會席次。*The enemy ~ed every inch of the ground,* fought with determination not to retreat. 敵人寸土不退。□ *n* /ˈkɒntest ; ˈkɑntɛst/ [C] struggle; fight; competition: 鬥爭;競爭;比賽: *a keen ~ for the prize;* 對於獎品之激烈的競爭; *a ~ of skill;* 技能競賽; *a ˈspeed ~;* 速度競賽; (boxing) (拳擊) *a three-round featherweight ~.* 三回合之羽量級比賽。 **~ant** /kənˈtestənt ; kənˈtɛstənt/ *n* one who ~s. 奮鬥者;競爭者;比賽者。

con·text /ˈkɒntekst ; ˈkɑntɛkst/ *n* [C, U] **1** what comes before and after a word, phrase, statement, etc helping to fix the meaning: (字、辭、句等的前後可幫助確定其意義的)上下文: *Can't you guess the meaning of the word from the ~?* 你不能由上下文猜出此字的意義嗎？ *Don't quote my words out of ~,* eg so as to give a false impression of what I mean. 別把我所說的話斷章取義(曲解我的意思)。 **2** circumstances in which an event occurs. (某一事件發生的)環境;背景。 **con·tex·tual** /kənˈtekstʃʊəl ;

kən'tɛkstʃʊəl/ *adj* according to the ~. 依照上下文的；由上下文而定的。

con·ti·guity /ˌkɒntɪ'gjuːətɪ ; ˌkɑntɪ'gjuətɪ/ *n* [U] the state of being contiguous. 接觸；相鄰；鄰近。

con·tigu·ous /kən'tɪgjʊəs ; kən'tɪgjuəs/ *adj* ~ **to,** (formal) touching; neighbouring; near. (正式用語) 接觸的；相鄰的；接近的。**~·ly** *adv*

con·ti·nence /'kɒntɪnəns ; 'kɑntənəns/ *n* [U] self-control; self-restraint (esp of passions and desires). 自制；自律；節制(尤指激情及慾望)。

con·ti·nent[1] /'kɒntɪnənt ; 'kɑntənənt/ *n* one of the main land masses (Europe, Asia, Africa, etc). (歐、亞、非等)大洲之一；洲；大陸。**the C~,** (as used by people in GB) the mainland of Europe. (英國人所指的)歐洲大陸。**con·ti·nen·tal** /ˌkɒntɪ'nentl ; ˌkɑntə'nɛntl/ *adj* **1** belonging to, typical of, a ~: 屬於大陸的；大陸性的: *a ~al climate.* 大陸性的氣候。 **2** of the mainland of Europe: 歐洲大陸的: *~al wars / alliances.* 歐洲大陸的戰爭(聯盟)。 **~al breakfast,** one of coffee and bread only. 僅含咖啡和麵包的早餐。**~al Sunday,** as in Europe (with wider freedom for theatrical and other entertainments, sport, etc than formerly in GB). 歐洲大陸式的星期日(人們在戲院等處看綜藝表演、運動等比從前在英國國內享有較廣泛的自由)。□ *n* inhabitant of the mainland of Europe. 歐洲大陸人。

con·ti·nent[2] /'kɒntɪnənt ; 'kɑntənənt/ *adj* (formal) self-controlled; having control of one's feelings and (esp sexual) desires; (med) able to retain excretion voluntarily. (正式用語)自制的；自律的；有節制的(指節制情感與慾望，尤指性慾)；禁慾的；(醫)能自動抑制排泄物的。

con·tin·gency /kən'tɪndʒənsɪ ; kən'tɪndʒənsɪ/ *n* [U] uncertainty of occurrence; [C] (*pl* -cies) uncertain event; event that happens by chance; sth that may happen if sth else happens: 偶然性；偶發性；偶發事件；意外事件；偶然事故；可能附帶發生之事: *to be prepared for all contingencies;* 準備應付一切偶發事件; *a result that depends upon contingencies;* 依賴臨時情形方可決定的結果; (attrib) (形容用法) *~ arrangements / plans.* 為(預防發生)臨時事故而作的安排(計畫)。

con·tin·gent[1] /kən'tɪndʒənt ; kən'tɪndʒənt/ *adj* **1** uncertain; accidental: 偶然的；意外的；偶發的: *a ~ advantage.* 偶然的獲益。 **2 ~ *upon,*** dependent upon (sth that may or may not happen). 視(可能發生也可能不發生之某事)而定的；視當時情形而定的；不一定的；靠不住的。

con·tin·gent[2] /kən'tɪndʒənt ; kən'tɪndʒənt/ *n* [C] body of troops, number of ships, lent or supplied to form part of a larger force; group of persons forming part of a larger group. (借調或派遣加入大軍的)分遣隊；分遣艦隊；構成較大集團之一部分的一批人。

con·tin·ual /kən'tɪnjʊəl ; kən'tɪnjuəl/ *adj* going on all the time without stopping, or with only short breaks: 連續不斷的(或僅有短暫之間歇的)；不停的: *Aren't you tired of this ~ rain?* 你對於這不停的雨不覺得厭煩嗎？ **~·ly** *adv* again and again; without stopping. 屢次地；再三地；不斷地。

con·tin·uance /kən'tɪnjʊəns ; kən'tɪnjuəns/ *n* (*sing* only) (僅用單數) **1** time for which sth continues; duration (the more usu word): 繼續的期間；持續時間 (duration 為較常用字): *during the ~ of the war.* 在戰爭持續期間。 **2** remaining; staying: 停留；保持；持續: *a ~ of prosperity.* 繁榮的持續。

con·tinu·ation /kənˌtɪnjʊ'eɪʃn ; kənˌtɪnjʊ'eʃən/ *n* ~ ***(of),*** **1** [U] continuing; starting again after a stop: 繼續；連續；(停一段時間後的)再繼續: *C~ of study after the holidays was difficult at first.* 假期過後再繼續讀書在起初是困難的。 **2** [C] part, etc by which sth is continued: 連續的部份: *The May number of the magazine will contain a ~ of the story.* 本雜誌五月號將刊載該故事的續篇。

con·tinue /kən'tɪnjuː ; kən'tɪnju/ *vi, vt* **1** [VP2A, B, D, E, 6A, D, 7A] go farther; go on (being); go on (doing); stay at / in; remain at / in: 延伸；延續；繼續；仍舊: *The desert ~d as far as the eye could reach.* 沙漠向前延伸至視線的盡處。*How far does this road ~?* 這條路全長多少？通至何處？*I hope this wet weather will not ~.* 我希望這種雨天不會延續下去。*He hopes to ~ at school for another year.* 他希望再繼續求學一年。*The weather ~d calm.* 天氣仍然平靜。*He ~d to live with his parents after his marriage.* 他結婚後仍舊與其雙親同住。*How long will you ~ working?* 你將繼續工作多久？ *You must ~ your study of French.* 你必須繼續讀你的法文。 **2** [VP6A, 2A] start again after stopping: (中斷以後)再繼續；恢復: *The story will be ~d in next month's issue.* 這故事將於下月號續刊。*'Well,' he ~d, 'when we arrived...'* '後來,'他接着說,'當我們到達的時候…'。 **3** [VP14] retain (sb in office, etc): 使留任；挽留(某人): *The Colonial Secretary was ~d in office.* 殖民大臣留任。

con·ti·nu·ity /ˌkɒntɪ'njuːətɪ *US:* -'nuː- ; ˌkɑntə'nuətɪ/ *n* [U] **1** the state of being continuous: 連續；繼續；連續性: *There is no ~ of subject in a dictionary.* 字典沒有主題的連續性。 **2** (cinema, TV) scenario; arrangement of the parts of a story: (電影,電視)脚本；分景劇本；電影或電視故事之各部份的排列: *Films and TV programmes are often made out of ~,* eg a scene in the middle may be filmed before a scene near the beginning. 電影和電視節目的拍攝常不按照先後的次序(例如中段的一景也許較在前段的一景先行拍攝)。 **3** connecting comments, announcements, etc, made between the parts of a broadcast programme. 廣播節目各部份之間的插白；節目說明。

con·tinu·ous /kən'tɪnjʊəs ; kən'tɪnjuəs/ *adj* going on without a break: 連續不斷的；不停歇的: *~ performance, 1.00pm to 11.30pm,* eg at a cinema. 連續表演(或放映)：下午一時至十一時卅分。 **~ tense,** ⇨ progressive(1). **~·ly** *adv*

con·tinu·um /kən'tɪnjʊəm ; kən'tɪnjuəm/ *n* (*pl* -uums or -ua /-ʊə ; -ʊə/) **1** sth that is continuous. 連續之事物。 **2** graded sequence of differences. 分類差異序列；族群相。⇨ cline.

con·tort /kən'tɔːt ; kən'tɔrt/ *vt* [VP6A,14] force or twist out of the usual shape or appearance: 扭歪；使扭曲；使成奇形怪狀: *a face ~ed with pain;* 因痛苦而扭曲的面孔; (fig) (喻) *~ a word out of its ordinary meaning.* 曲解字義(不照其通常的意義解釋)。

con·tor·tion /kən'tɔːʃn ; kən'tɔrʃən/ *n* [U] contorting or being contorted (esp of the face or body); [C] instance of this; contorted condition: 扭歪；扭曲(尤指使面部或身體變成異樣)；扭歪或扭曲的狀況: *the ~s of an acrobat.* 賣藝人所做的軟功。**~·ist** /-ʃənɪst ; -ʃənɪst/ *n* acrobat clever at contorting his body. 擅長軟功的賣藝人。

con·tour /'kɒntʊə(r) ; 'kɑntʊr/ *n* [C] outline (of a coast, mountain range, etc); (on a map, design, etc) line separating differently coloured parts. (海岸、山脈等的)輪廓；周線；圍線；(地圖、圖案等)各着色區域間的區分線。**'~ line,** line (on a map) showing all points at the same height above sea-level. (地圖上表示所有海拔相同各點之)等高線。 **'~ map,** one with ~ lines at fixed intervals (eg of 25 metres). 等高線地圖(按固定間隔,如25公尺,以等高線繪製者)。**'~ ploughing,** ploughing in which furrows follow ~ lines (on a hillside, etc) to prevent soil erosion. 循等高線耕犂法(用於山坡上等處，以防雨水沖蝕土壤)。□ *vt* [VP6A] mark with ~ lines; make (a road) round the ~ of a hill. 繪以等高線；以等高線標明；順着山之起伏開闢(道路)。

contra- /'kɒntrə- ; 'kɑntrə-/ *pref* against. 反對。

contra·band /'kɒntrəbænd ; 'kɑntrəˌbænd/ *n* [U] bringing into, taking out of, a country goods contrary to the law; (trade in) goods so brought in or taken out. 走私(將貨物違法的運入或運出一國)；(買賣)私貨；違禁品。 **~ *of war,*** goods (eg ammunition) supplied by neutral countries to countries that are at war, which can be seized by any of the countries at war. 戰時違禁品(中立國運往交戰國並可由任一交戰國沒收的禁運品,如軍火)。(attrib)(形容用法)~ *goods;* 私貨;禁運品; ~ *trade.* 私貨之買賣;走私。

contra·bass /ˌkɒntrəˈbeɪs ; ˈkɑntrəˌbes/ *n* =double-bass.

contra·cep·tion /ˌkɒntrəˈsepʃn ; ˌkɑntrəˈsɛpʃən/ *n* [U] practice, method, of preventing or planning conception(2). 避孕;避孕法;計畫生育。**contra·cep·tive** /ˌkɒntrəˈseptɪv ; ˌkɑntrəˈsɛptɪv/ *n* [C] device or drug intended to prevent conception(2). 避孕器;避孕藥;避孕劑。□ *adj* preventing conception: 避孕的: *contraceptive pills/devices.* 避孕丸(器)。

con·tract[1] /ˈkɒntrækt ; ˈkɑntrækt/ *n* **1** [C] binding agreement (between persons, groups, states); agreement to supply goods, do work, etc at a fixed price. (個人、團體、國家間的)合約;合同;(按固定價格供應貨物或做工的)契約。***enter into/make a ~ (with sb) (for sth),*** make such an agreement. (與某人)(爲某事)訂立合約。***exchange ~s,*** eg for the purchase of a house. (如購買房屋成交時之)交換合約。***sign a ~,*** eg for the sale of land or buildings. 簽訂合約(如房地產買賣)。[U] (phrases in which no article is used): (不用冠詞之片語): *bind oneself by ~;* 立約保證; *work to be done by private ~;* 需包給私人做的工作; *work on ~;* 做包工; *breach of ~;* 違約; *conditions of ~;* 合約的條件; (attrib use) (形容用法) *~ price/date,* price, date, agreed to. 合約價格(日期)。**2** ˌ***~ ˈbridge,*** kind of bridge[2] in which only tricks bid[1](6) and won count towards game[1](4). 合約橋牌(只有所叫並贏得的磴數才計入每局所獲得的分數)。

con·tract[2] /kənˈtrækt ; kənˈtrækt/ *vt, vi* **1** [VP6A, 14, 4A] **~ *(with) (for),*** make a contract or agreement: (與某人)(爲某事或做某事而)訂立合約;訂契約;承包;承建;承購: *~ a marriage;* 締結婚姻;訂結婚約; *~ to build a bridge;* 立約承建橋樑; *~ with a firm for 1000 tons of cement;* 向某公司立約承購一千噸水泥; *~ an alliance with another country.* 與另一國成立聯盟。[VP2C] **~ *out (of),*** /ˌkɒntrækt ˈaʊt ; ˌkɑntrækt ˈaʊt/, reject, abandon, the terms of a contract: 廢棄合約的條件: *~ out of an agreement/alliance.* 廢棄合約(聯盟條約);廢約。**2** [VP6A] **~ *debts,*** become liable for them. 負債。**3** [VP6A] catch (an illness); form; acquire (eg bad habits). 染患(疾病);形成;獲得;染上(惡習等)。**~or** /-tə(r) ; -tə/ *n* person, business firm, that enters into ~s: 立契約的人或商店;包工;承包商: *engineering ~ors;* 工程承包商;營造商; *army ~ors.* 軍需品承包商。**con·trac·tual** /kənˈtræktʃʊəl ; kənˈtræktʃʊəl/ *adj* of (the nature of) a ~. 契約(性質)的。

con·tract[3] /kənˈtrækt ; kənˈtrækt/ *vt, vi* [VP6A, 14, 2A, C] **1** make or become smaller or shorter: 收縮;縮小;縮短: *Metals ~ as they become cool.* 金屬冷則收縮。*'I will' is ~ed to 'I'll'.* I will 縮寫成爲 I'll。**2** make or become tighter or narrower: 縮緊;縮窄: *to ~ a muscle;* 收縮肌肉; *to ~ the brows/forehead.* 皺眉頭(前額)。*The valley ~s as one goes up it.* 當人循山谷上行時,山谷漸狹。**~ible** *adj* that can be ~ed. 可收縮的;可縮小的。**con·trac·tile** /kənˈtræktaɪl *US:* -tl ; kənˈtræktl/ *adj* that can ~ or be ~ed: 可收縮的: *~ile wings,* eg of an insect, that can be folded over the body. (昆蟲等)可收摺於背上的翅翼。

con·trac·tion /kənˈtrækʃn ; kənˈtrækʃən/ *n* **1** [U] contracting or being contracted: 收縮;縮小: *the ~ of a muscle;* 肌肉的收縮; *the ~ of the mercury in a thermometer.* 水銀在寒暑表中的收縮。**2** [C] sth contracted; shortened form, as *can't* for *cannot.* 收縮之物;縮寫式(如 can't 爲 cannot 的縮寫式)。

con·tra·dict /ˌkɒntrəˈdɪkt ; ˌkɑntrəˈdɪkt/ *vt* [VP6A] **1** deny the truth of (sth said or written); deny (the words of a person): 否定(所說或所寫之事物)之眞實性;否定(某人所說的話);反駁;駁斥: *to ~ a statement.* 駁斥一項聲明。*Don't ~ me.* 不要反駁我。**2** (of facts, statements, etc) be contrary to: (指事實、陳述等)與…相矛盾、相抵觸、相反: *The reports ~ each other.* 這些報告互相矛盾。**con·tra·dic·tion** /ˌkɒntrəˈdɪkʃn ; ˌkɑntrəˈdɪkʃən/ *n* **1** [U] ~ing; [C] instance of this. 反駁;駁斥。**2** [U] absence of agreement. 不一致;矛盾。***be in ~ion with,*** =~: 否定…的眞實性;與…互相矛盾: *Your statements today are in ~ion with* (ie they ~) *what you said yesterday.* 你今天的聲明和你昨天所說的話互相矛盾。[C] instance of this. 否定的實例;相矛盾的實例。***a ~ion in terms,*** statement that includes words that ~ each other (eg *a generous miser*). 言辭上的矛盾(在一陳述中使用互相矛盾之字辭,如慷慨的守財奴)。**con·tra·dic·tory** /ˌkɒntrəˈdɪktərɪ ; ˌkɑntrəˈdɪktərɪ/ *adj* ~ing: 互相矛盾的: *~ory statements/reports.* 互相矛盾的陳述(報告)。

contra·dis·tinc·tion /ˌkɒntrədɪˈstɪŋkʃn ; ˌkɑntrədɪˈstɪŋkʃən/ *n* (formal) distinction by contrast: (正式用語)對比起來的不同;對照的區別: *the crossing of the Atlantic by air in a few hours, in ~ to the longer journey by sea.* 乘飛機只要數小時卽可橫渡大西洋,與乘船之漫長的航程不可同日而語。

contra·dis·tin·guish /ˌkɒntrədɪˈstɪŋgwɪʃ ; ˌkɑntrədɪˈstɪŋgwɪʃ/ *vt* [VP14] **~ *from,*** distinguish by contrast. 以對比的方式區別。

con·tralto /kənˈtræltəʊ ; kənˈtrælto/ (*pl* ~s /-təʊz ; -toz/) *n* lowest female voice; woman with, musical part to be sung by, such a voice. 女低音;女低音歌唱家;樂曲之女低音部份。

con·trap·tion /kənˈtræpʃn ; kənˈtræpʃən/ *n* (colloq) strange-looking apparatus or device. (俗)奇異的器械或裝置;稀奇的玩意兒。

contra·pun·tal /ˌkɒntrəˈpʌntl ; ˌkɑntrəˈpʌntl/ *adj* of or in counterpoint. (音樂)對位法的;對位的。

contra·riety /ˌkɒntrəˈraɪətɪ ; ˌkɑntrəˈraɪətɪ/ *n* (formal) [U] opposition or antagonism (in nature, quality or action); [C] (*pl* -ties) sth that is inconsistent or contrary: (正式用語)(本質、性質或行爲的)相反;對立;不一致或相反的事物: *contrarieties in nature.* 本質相反的事物。

con·trari·wise /ˈkɒntrərɪwaɪz ; ˈkɑntrɛrɪˌwaɪz/ *adv* **1** on the contrary. 相反地。**2** in the opposite way. 在相反的方面;以相反的方式。**3** /kənˈtreərɪwaɪz ; kənˈtrɛrɪwaɪz/ perversely; in a manner showing opposition. 倔强地;態度上表示反對地。

con·trary[1] /ˈkɒntrərɪ *US:* -trerɪ ; ˈkɑntrɛrɪ/ *adj* **1** opposite (in nature or tendency): (在性質或傾向上)相反的: *'Hot' and 'cold' are ~ terms.* 熱與冷係相反之詞。**2** (of the wind and weather) unfavourable (for sailing): (指風向和天氣)不利(於航行)的: *The ship was delayed by ~ winds.* 此船爲逆風所阻而延遲。**3** (/kənˈtreərɪ ; kənˈtrɛrɪ/) obstinate; self-willed. 頑固的;倔强的。**4** **~ *to,*** (compound *prep*) in opposition to; against: (複合介詞)反對;違反: *to act ~ to the rules;* 違規行事; *events that went ~ to my interests.* 與我不利的事件。*What you have done is ~ to the doctor's orders.* 你所做的與醫生的指示相反。*The result was ~ to expectation.* 結果與期望相反。**con·trar·ily** /ˈkɒntrərəlɪ *US:* -trerəlɪ ; ˈkɑntrɛrəlɪ/ *adv* in a ~ manner. 相反地;不利地;固執地;倔强地。**con·trari·ness** /-nɪs ; -nɪs/ *n* being ~. 相反;不利;固執;倔强。

con·trary[2] /ˈkɒntrərɪ *US:* -trerɪ ; ˈkɑntrɛrɪ/ *n* (*pl* -ries) **1** [U] ***the ~,*** opposite: 反面; 相反字: *The ~ of 'wet' is 'dry'.* '濕' 的相反字是 '乾'。***on the ~,*** phrase used to make a denial or contradiction more emphatic: 相反地(强調否定或反駁之辭): *'You've nothing to do now, I suppose.' —'On the ~, I have piles of work.'* '我想你現在沒有事可做了。'—'恰好相反,我有成堆的工作。' ***to the ~,*** to the opposite effect: 有相反的意思;相反的(地): *I will come on Monday unless you write to the ~,* telling me not to come. 我將於星期一來,除非你寫信叫我不要來。*I shall continue to believe it until I get proof to the ~,* proof that it is not true. 在我未得到相反的證據之前,我將繼續相信它。**2** [C] *by contraries,* **(a)** ~ to expectation: 與預期相違: *Many things in our lives go by contraries.* 我們一生之中有許多事情與願望相違。 **(b)** by way of opposition: 表相反之意;有相反之情形: *She said that dreams go by contraries,* eg that a dream about bad fortune may foretell good fortune. 她說夢境預兆相反的事(如夢見惡運可能預兆好運)。

con·trast¹ /kən'trɑ:st *US:* -'træst ; kən'træst/ *vt, vi* **1** [VP6A, 14] ~ ***(with/and),*** compare so that differences are made clear: 比較(某物與另一物)以明其相異之點;對比;比一比(…與…): *C~ these imported goods with/and the domestic product.* 把這些進口貨與國貨比比看(就知道它們的差別了)。 *It is interesting to ~ the two speakers.* 把那兩位演說者比一比,眞是有趣。 **2** [VP2C, 3A] ~ ***(with),*** show a difference when compared: 比較起來顯示出差別;成對照: *His actions ~ sharply with his promises.* 他的言行相差太遠(行動與許諾太不相符)。*His actions and his promises ~ sharply.* 他的言行相差太遠。

con·trast² /'kɒntrɑ:st *US:* -træst ; 'kɑntræst/ *n* **1** [U] the act of contrasting: 比較;對比;對照: *C~ may make something appear more beautiful than it is when seen alone.* 對比可使某物顯得比單獨看時更美。 **2** ~ ***(to/with);*** ~ ***(between/of),*** [C, U] difference which is clearly seen when unlike things are put together; sth showing such a difference:(不同之物擺在一起所現出的)明顯的差別;顯示明顯差別之物: *There is a remarkable ~ between the two brothers.* 這兩兄弟間有極顯著的差別。*The white walls make a ~ to/with the black carpet.* 白牆與黑毯構成了顯著的對比。*The ~ of light and shade is important in photography.* 明暗的對比在攝影術上是很重要的。***by/in ~ (with); in ~ (to),*** when a ~ is made (to/with): (與…)成對比: *His white hair was in sharp ~ to his dark skin.* 他的白頭髮與他的黑皮膚構成鮮明的對比。*Tom's marks* (eg 90 per cent) *by ~ with Harry's marks* (eg 35 per cent) *were excellent.* 湯姆的分數(例如 90 分)與哈利的分數(例如 35 分)比起來算是上乘的。

con·tra·vene /ˌkɒntrə'vi:n ; ˌkɑntrə'vin/ *vt* [VP6A] **1** act in opposition to; go against (a law, a custom). 違反;違犯(法律、習俗)。 **2** dispute, attack (a statement, a principle). 反駁;攻擊(陳述、原則)。 **3** (of things) conflict with; be out of harmony with. (指事物)抵觸;與…衝突;與…不協調。

con·tra·ven·tion /ˌkɒntrə'venʃn ; ˌkɑntrə'venʃən/ *n* [C, U] act of contravening (a law, etc). 違反;違犯(法律等)。***in ~ of sth,*** so as to break or violate it. 違犯規則。

contre·temps /'kɒntrətɒm ; kõtrə'tɑ̃/ *n* (*pl* unchanged) (複數不變) (F) unfortunate happening; unexpected hitch; setback. (法)不幸的事件;阻礙;挫折。

con·trib·ute /kən'trɪbju:t ; kən'trɪbjut/ *vt, vi* ~ ***(to),*** **1** [VP6A, 14, 2A, 3A] join with others in giving help, money, etc (*to* a common cause, *for* a purpose); give ideas, suggestions, etc: 捐贈;捐助(指出力、出錢等以協助公益事業;與 to 連用,後接運動;與 for 連用,後接目的);貢獻(意見、建議等): *~ food and clothing for the refugees;* 捐贈食物和衣服給難民; *~ to the Red Cross;* 捐助紅十字會; *~ new information on a scientific problem.* 對於一項科學問題貢獻新的知識。 **2** [VP3A] have a share in; help to bring about: 有助於;促成: *Drink ~d to his ruin.* 飲酒促成他的毀滅。 **3** [VP14, 3A] write (articles, etc) and send in: (爲…)寫(文章等);投稿: *Mr Green has ~d (poems) to the 'London Magazine' for several years.* 格林先生向'倫敦雜誌'投(詩)稿已有幾年了。 **con·tribu·tor** /-tə(r) ; -tə˞/ *n* person who ~s (money *to* a fund, articles *to* a periodical, etc). 捐助人;捐款者;投稿人(與 to 連用)。

con·tri·bu·tion /ˌkɒntrɪ'bju:ʃn ; ˌkɑntrə'bjuʃən/ *n* **1** [U] act of contributing; [C] sth contributed: 捐助;捐贈;貢獻;促成;投稿;捐助或貢獻之物;捐款;捐贈物;稿件: *~s to the relief fund.* 捐給救濟基金的捐款。*Do you consider ~s to the village funds a duty or a pleasure?* 你認爲捐款給村莊基金是義務還是樂事? *The editor is short of ~s for the May issue.* 編者缺乏稿件編五月號的雜誌。 **2** [C, U] compulsory payment. 强收的稅款。***lay under ~,*** require ~s from. 向…强收稅款。

con·tribu·tory /kən'trɪbjʊtrɪ *US:* -tɔ:rɪ ; kən'trɪbjəˌtorɪ/ *adj* **1** helping to bring about: 有助於…的;促成…的: *~ negligence,* eg that helped to cause an accident. 造成意外事件的疏忽。 **2** for which contributions are to be made: 待捐助的;靠捐助的: *a ˌ~ 'pension scheme.* 靠捐助的年金方案。

con·trite /'kɒntraɪt ; 'kɑntraɪt/ *adj* filled with, showing, deep sorrow for wrongdoing: 對於做錯的事深表懊悔的;痛悔前非的;悔罪的: *a ~ heart.* 悔罪的心。**~·ly** *adv*

con·tri·tion /kən'trɪʃn ; kən'trɪʃən/ *n* [U] deep sorrow (for sins, wrongdoing); repentance. (對於罪行、過失的)悔恨;痛悔;懺悔。

con·triv·ance /kən'traɪvəns ; kən'traɪvəns/ *n* **1** [U] act or manner of contriving: 發明;設計;設法: *the ~ by which botanists fertilize flowers to obtain hybrids.* 植物學家使花受粉而得到配種的發明。 **2** [U] capacity to invent: 發明的才能: *Some things are beyond human ~.* 有些東西是人類發明不出來的。 **3** [C] sth contrived; deceitful practice; invention or mechanical device: 想出的辦法;騙術;發明物;機械裝置: *a ~ to record both sides of a telephone conversation on magnetic tape.* 一種將電話中雙方的談話錄於磁帶上的機械裝置。

con·trive /kən'traɪv ; kən'traɪv/ *vt, vi* **1** [VP6A, 7A] invent; design; find a way of doing (sth), of causing (sth to happen): 發明;設計;想辦法;動腦筋: *to ~ a means of escape from prison;* 設法逃獄; *to ~ to live on a small income.* 設法靠着微薄的收入過活。*He ~d to make matters worse,* made them worse by his efforts, even though this was not his intention. 他想的辦法把事情弄得更糟了(雖然這並非他的原意)。*Can you ~* (= manage) *to be here early?* 你能設法早到這裏嗎? **2** [VP2A] (liter) manage successfully: (文)設法應付;設法完成: *She finds it difficult to ~* (= manage her housekeeping economically) *now that prices are rising every month.* 因爲物價每月上漲,使她覺得難以持家。 **con·triver** /kən'traɪvə(r) ; kən'traɪvə˞/ *n* (liter) one who ~s, esp one who manages household affairs: (文)設法者;(尤指)料理家務者: *His wife is a good ~r.* 他的妻子善理家務。

con·trol¹ /kən'trəʊl ; kən'trol/ *n* **1** [U] power or authority to direct, order, or restrain: 指揮、命令或限制的權力;管理;管轄;監督;支配;控制;克制;抑制: *children who lack parental ~,* who are not kept in order by parents. 缺乏父母管束的孩子們。***be in ~ (of),*** be in command, in charge. 握有(對…的)控制力;控制。***be/come/bring/get under ~,*** be, become, cause to be, under authority, under restraint, in order, working properly: 在(變成在,使在,置於)控制之下;(使)操作情況良好: *get flood waters under ~.* 使泛濫的洪水受到控制。***be/get out of ~,*** in a state where authority, etc is lost: 失去控制(不受控制);不能(不受)操縱: *The children are/have got out of ~.* 孩子們不聽管教。***have/get/keep ~ (over/of),*** have, get, keep authority, power, etc: (對…)有(得到,保有)權威、權力等;能控制: *a teacher who has no ~ over his class;* 不能維持教室秩序的教師; *get ~ over a horse,* make it obey. 能駕馭一匹馬;馴服一匹馬。***lose ~ (of),*** be unable to manage or contain: 不能駕馭或控制;失去對…的控制: *lose ~ of one's temper.* 不能抑制自己的脾氣。***take ~ (of),*** take authority: 管轄;管理;控制: *We must find someone to take overall ~ of this project.* 我們必須找個人來總攬這個計畫。 **2** [U] management; guidance: 管制;指導: *~ of traffic/traffic ~;* 交通管制; *~ of foreign exchange.* 外滙管制。 **'birth-~** *n* planning of the number of births, eg by the use of contraceptives. (藉

使用避孕器或避孕藥等的）節育。 **3** [C] means of regulating, restraining, keeping in order; check: 管理、限制、控制的手段: *Government ~s on trade and industry.* 政府對工商業的管制。*The chairman's power to veto a proposal is a ~ over what the committee may do.* 主席對於提議的否決權，是限制委員會權力的一種手段。 **4** [C] standard of comparison for results of an experiment: （鑑定實驗結果的）比較標準: *The tests were given to three groups, Group Two being used as a ~.* 受測驗者有三組，以第二組爲比較標準。*We must make more ~ experiments.* 我們必須多做有比較標準的實驗。 **5** (usu *pl*) means by which a machine, etc is operated or regulated: （通常用複數）（機器等的）操縱裝置: *the ~s of an aircraft,* for direction, altitude, etc; 飛機的操縱裝置（藉以控制方向、高度等）; *a car with dual ~s／a dual-~ car;* 一部雙操縱裝置的車子; *the ~s of a transistor radio,* eg the volume ~, regulating the volume of sound; 電晶體收音機的各種控制器（如音量控制器）; *the '~ tower of an airport,* for regulating air traffic. （航空站指揮飛機活動的）指揮塔；塔臺。 **6** [C] station at which cars taking part in a race may stop for overhaul, etc. （參加賽車的汽車可以停車接受檢修等的）檢修站。 **7** [C] (spiritualism) spirit actuating a medium(4). （招魂術）驅使靈媒的精靈。

con·trol² /kən'trəʊl ; kən'trol/ *vt* (-ll-) [VP6A] **1** have control, authority, power over: 控制；管理；支配；抑制；指揮: *to ~ one's temper／expenditure／a horse／oneself.* 控制自己的脾氣（開支，馬，自己）。**~ling interest** *n* (fin) holding of enough stock(5) of a company to ~ policy. （財政）擁有足以控制公司政策的股票；控制股權。 **2** regulate (prices, etc). 管制（物價等）。 **3** check; verify: 檢查；查驗: *to ~ the accounts.* 查帳。 **~·lable** *adj* that can be ~led. 可控制的。

con·trol·ler /kən'trəʊlə(r) ; kən'trolɚ/ *n* **1** (also 亦作 **comptroller**) person who controls expenditure and accounts. 會計長；主計官；主計員（管理開支及帳册的人）。 **2** person who controls or directs a department or division of a large organization: （大機關裏的）組、處主任: *~ of B B C Radio.* 英國廣播公司無線電組主任。

con·tro·ver·sial /ˌkɒntrə'vɜːʃl ; ˌkɑntrə'vɝʃəl/ *adj* likely to cause controversy: 可能引起爭論的: *a ~ speech;* 可能引起爭論的演說; (of persons) fond of controversy. （指人）好爭論的。 **~·ly** /-ʃəlɪ ; -ʃəlɪ/ *adv* **~·ist** *n* person who is fond of or good at controversy. 喜爭論者；善於爭論者。

con·tro·versy /'kɒntrəvɜːsɪ ; 'kɑntrəˌvɝsɪ/ *n* (*pl* -sies) [C, U] prolonged argument, esp over social, moral or political matters: 長期的爭論；（尤指關於社會、道德或政治問題的）論戰: *engage in (a) ~ with／against sb (on* or *about sth);* 與某人（關於某事）進行論戰; *a question that has given rise to much ~;* 曾經引起很多爭論的問題; *facts that are beyond ~,* that cannot be argued about. 無可置辯的事實。

con·tro·vert /ˌkɒntrə'vɜːt ; 'kɑntrəˌvɝt/ *vt* [VP6A] (formal) dispute about; deny; oppose. （正式用語）辯駁；否認；反對。

con·tu·ma·cious /ˌkɒntjuː'meɪʃəs ; ˌkɑntjʊ'meʃəs/ *adj* (formal) stubborn and rebellious; obstinate and disobedient. （正式用語）頑强的；抗命的。 **~·ly** *adv*

con·tu·macy /'kɒntjʊməsɪ *US:* kən'tuːməsɪ ; 'kɑntjʊməsɪ/ *n* [U] (formal) obstinate resistance; stubborn disobedience; [C] (*pl* -cies) instance of this. （正式用語）頑强；頑抗；抗命；堅不服從。

con·tu·melious /ˌkɒntjuː'miːlɪəs *US:* -tə'm- ; ˌkɑntjʊ'milɪəs/ *adj* (formal) insolent; opprobrious. （正式用語）侮慢的；無禮的；輕蔑的。 **~·ly** *adv*

con·tu·mely /'kɒntjuːmlɪ *US:* kən'tuːməlɪ ; 'kɑntjʊˌmɪlɪ/ *n* [U] (formal) abusive language or treatment; [C] instance of this; humiliating insult. （正式用語）侮辱的言語或態度；侮辱。

con·tuse /kən'tjuːz *US:* -'tuːz ; kən'tjuz/ *vt* [VP6A] (med) bruise; injure (part of the body) by a blow, without breaking the skin. （醫）挫傷；打傷；撞傷；打青（而不破皮）。 **con·tusion** /kən'tjuːʒn *US:* -'tuː- ; kən'tjuʒən/ *n* [C] bruise. 挫傷；打傷；撞傷；青腫。

co·nun·drum /kə'nʌndrəm ; kə'nʌndrəm/ *n* [C] puzzling question, esp one asked for fun; riddle. 難答的問題；難題（尤指爲好玩而問者）；謎語。

con·ur·ba·tion /ˌkɒnɜː'beɪʃn ; ˌkɑnɚ'beʃən/ *n* [C] area of large urban communities where towns, etc have spread and become joined beyond their administrative boundaries. 集合城市（由數市鎮等擴展連接而成的大都市區）。

con·va·lesce /ˌkɒnvə'les ; ˌkɑnvə'lɛs/ *vi* [VP2A] regain health and strength after an illness: 病後康復: *She is convalescing after a long illness.* 她在久病之後正康復中。 **con·va·les·cent** /ˌkɒnvə'lesnt ; ˌkɑnvə'lɛsn̩t/ *n, adj* (person who is) recovering from illness: 康復中的（病人）: *a ~nt hospital,* one for ~nts. 療養院。 **con·va·les·cence** /ˌkɒnvə'lesns ; ˌkɑnvə'lɛsn̩s/ *n* [U] gradual recovery of health and strength. 逐漸康復。

con·vec·tion /kən'vekʃn ; kən'vɛkʃən/ *n* [U] the conveying of heat from one part of a liquid or gas to another by the movement of heated substances. 熱的對流（藉受熱物質之運動作用，熱從液體或氣體之一部傳至他部之現象）。

con·vec·tor /kən'vektə(r) ; kən'vɛktɚ/ *n* apparatus (for heating a room, etc) by which air is warmed as it passes over hot surfaces. 環流機（一種使房間等溫暖之設備，能使空氣經過熱的表面而變熱）；換流器。

con·vene /kən'viːn ; kən'vin/ *vt, vi* **1** [VP6A] summon (persons) to come together; form (a meeting, etc): 召集（人們）；召開（會議等）: *~ the people／the meeting.* 召集人們（召開會議）。 **2** [VP2A] come together (for a meeting, council, etc). 集合（開會等）。 **con·vener** *n* member (of a society, etc) whose duty it is to ~ meetings. （社團等的）會議召集人。

con·veni·ence /kən'viːnɪəns ; kən'vinjəns/ *n* **1** [U] the quality of being convenient or suitable; freedom from difficulty or worry: 方便；合適；無困難；無憂慮: *I keep my reference books near my desk for ~.* 我把我的參考書籍放在我的寫字桌近旁以求方便。*The house was planned for ~, not for display,* ie planned so as to be easy to live and work in. 那房屋的設計是爲了方便，而非爲了排場。*Please send the goods at your earliest ~,* at the earliest time that does not give you trouble. 請將貨品儘速寄下。*Please do the work at your own ~,* how and when it best suits you. 這工作如何做，何時做，悉聽尊便。*It was a marriage of ~,* one in which material advantage was the chief consideration. 那是一項着眼於實利的婚姻。 **2** [C] appliance, device, arrangement, etc that is useful, helpful or convenient: 有用的、有益的或方便的用具、裝置、安排等: *It was a great ~ to have the doctor living near us.* 有醫生住在我們附近，極爲方便。*The house has all modern ~s,* eg central heating, hot water supply, points for electric current. 此屋具有所有現代化的設備（如中央暖氣、熱水供應、電源插座）。*The nearest public ~s* (=W C's, lavatories) *are in West Street.* 最近的公共厠所在西街。 ***make a ~ of sb,*** use his services unreasonably; take too much advantage of his good nature. 過份利用某人（利用他的熱心服務或詩良忠厚）；欺負老實人。 ***flag of ~,*** ⇨ flag¹. '~ **food** *n* [U, C] food (eg sold in a tin, packet, etc) that needs very little preparation. 便當。

con·veni·ent /kən'viːnɪənt ; kən'vinjənt/ *adj* ***~ (for),*** suitable; handy; serving to avoid trouble or difficulty; easy to get to or at: 合適的；方便的；使免麻煩或困難的；容易接近的: *Will it be ~ for you to start work tomorrow?* 明天開始工作對你方便嗎？*This is a ~ tool for the job.* 這對那工作是一種合適的工具。*Will the 3.50 train be ~ for you?* 三點五十分的火車對你方便嗎？*We must arrange a ~ time and place for the meeting.* 我們必須安排一個合適的時間和地點開會。 **~·ly** *adv* in a ~ manner: 方便地: *My house is ~ly near the bus stop.* 我的家離公車站近，

實在方便。

con·vent /ˈkɒnvənt *US:* -vent ; ˈkɑnvɛnt/ *n* **1** society of women (called 稱作 *nuns*) living apart from others in the service of God. (與塵世隔絕以侍奉上帝的)女修道會;修女會。⇨ monastery. ~ **(school)** *n* one run by nuns. 修女會所辦的學校。 **2** building(s) in which nuns live and work: 女修道院: *enter a* ~, become a nun. 當修女。

con·ven·ticle /kənˈventɪkl ; kənˈvɛntɪkl̩/ *n* (building used for) secret religious meetings. 秘密的宗教性集會;秘密的宗教性集會所。

con·ven·tion /kənˈvenʃn ; kənˈvɛnʃən/ *n* **1** [C] conference of members of a society, political party, etc devoted to a particular purpose (eg election of candidates); conference of persons in business, commerce, etc: (社團、政黨等爲某一特殊目的,如選舉候選人,所召開的) 大會; (商業界等人士所開的) 會議;年會: *the Democratic Party C*~. 民主黨大會。Cf 參較 *conference* in GB. **2** [C] agreement between States, rulers, etc (less formal than a treaty): (國家、君王等之間的) 協約;協定(不及條約正式): *the Geneva C~s,* about the treatment of prisoners of war, etc. (關於戰俘之待遇等的) 日內瓦協定。 **3** [U] general (usu tacit) consent (esp about forms of behaviour); [C] practice or custom based on general consent: 公認的標準(通常指大衆所默認者,尤指關於行爲者);慣例;常規;習俗: *When men wore hats,* ~ *required them to raise them when they met a woman they knew.* 當男人戴着帽時,社會的習俗要求他們在遇到他們所認識的女子時要舉帽示禮。*It is silly to be a slave to* ~*/to social* ~*s.* 做傳統習俗(社會習俗)的奴隸是不智的。 **4** [C] (in various card and board games, esp bridge) practice that is generally followed in bidding, leading cards, making an opening move in chess, etc. (在各種牌戲及下棋,尤指橋牌中,叫牌、出牌、下第一步棋等的)一般常規。

con·ven·tional /kənˈvenʃənl ; kənˈvɛnʃənl̩/ *adj* **1** based on convention (3,4): 根據慣例的: ~ *greetings;* 慣用的問候語; *a few* ~ *remarks.* 幾句老生常談的話。 **2** following what has been customary; traditional: 習俗的;傳統的: *a* ~ *design for a carpet;* 地毯上用的老式花樣; ~ *art;* 傳統的藝術; ~ *weapons,* ie excluding atomic bombs, etc; 傳統武器(不包括原子彈等); *a* ~ *power station,* using coal or oil as fuel (contrasted with heat from a nuclear reactor). 傳統發電廠(使用煤或油作燃料者,爲利用核子反應爐生熱爲動力之核子發電廠之對)。~**·ly** /-ʃənəlɪ ; -ʃnəlɪ/ *adv*

con·ven·tion·al·ity /kənˌvenʃəˈnælətɪ ; kənˌvɛnʃənˈælətɪ/ *n* **1** [U] conventional quality or character: 習俗性;傳統性;因襲;老式: *the* ~ *of the paintings at the Academy Exhibition.* 在英國皇家藝術學會所舉行之一年一度的美術展覽會上所展出之繪畫的傳統性。 **2** [C, U] (*pl* -ties) convention(3). 習俗;慣例。

con·verge /kənˈvɜːdʒ ; kənˈvɝdʒ/ *vi* [VP2A, 2C, 3A] ~ ***(at/on/upon)*** (of lines, moving objects, opinions) come towards each other and meet at a point; tend to do this: (指線條、運動的物體、意見)自四面八方向一點滙合;收斂;輻輳;聚集: *armies converging on the capital.* 自各方面向首都進發的大軍。*Parallel lines* ~ *at infinity.* 平行線永遠不會相交。 **con·ver·gence** /kənˈvɜːdʒəns ; kənˈvɝdʒəns/ *n* **con·ver·gent** *adj*

con·ver·sant /kənˈvɜːsnt ; ˈkɑnvəsn̩t/ *adj* ~ ***with,*** having a knowledge of: 具有關於…的知識;通達;憧得;熟諳: ~ *with all the rules.* 熟諳所有的規則。

con·ver·sa·tion /ˌkɒnvəˈseɪʃn ; ˌkɑnvəˈseʃən/ *n* [U] talking; [C] talk: 談話;會話;會談;交談: *I saw him in* ~ *with a friend.* 我看見他與朋友談話。*No* ~ *while I'm playing the piano, please.* 我在彈鋼琴的時候,請勿談話。*I've had several* ~*s with him.* 我已經和他談過幾次了。~**al** /-ʃənl ; -ʃənl̩/ *adj* (of words, etc) used in, characteristic of, ~; colloquial. (指字等)用於談話的;會話性質的;口語的;通俗的。

con·verse¹ /kənˈvɜːs ; kənˈvɝs/ *vi* [VP2A, C, 3A] ~ ***(with sb) (about/on sth),*** (formal) talk. (正式用語) 談話;談論。

con·verse² /ˈkɒnvɜːs ; ˈkɑnvɝs/ *n, adj* **1** (idea, statement which is) opposite (to another). 相反的(觀念、陳述);反;逆。 **2** (logic) form of words produced by transposing some of the words of another: (邏輯) 倒轉命題(調換一命題中數字所成之相反命題);反轉句;反轉語: *'He is happy but not rich' is the* ~ *of 'He is rich but not happy'.* '他樂而不富' 是'他富而不樂' 的反轉句。~**·ly** *adv*

con·verse³ /ˈkɒnvɜːs ; ˈkɑnvɝs/ *n* [U] (old use) conversation. (舊用法) 談話;談論;交談。

con·ver·sion /kənˈvɜːʃn *US:* -ʒn ; kənˈvɝʃən/ *n* [U] converting or being converted: 轉變;改變;轉化: *the* ~ *of cream into butter/of forest land into arable land/of pagans to Christianity;* 乳脂之變爲奶油(林地之變爲耕地;異教徒之變爲基督教徒); *the improper* ~ *of public funds to one's own use,* eg by a government official; 公款之非法移作私用(如政府官吏所爲者); [C] instance of ~: 轉變的實例: *many* ~*s to Buddhism;* 許多人的皈依佛教; *building firms which specialize in house* ~*s,* eg of large houses into flats. 專門改建房屋的建築公司(如將大房屋改建成公寓者)。

con·vert¹ /kənˈvɜːt ; kənˈvɝt/ *vt* [VP6A, 14] **1** ~ ***sth (from sth) (to/into sth),*** change (from one form, use, etc into another): 使(自一種形式、用途等)轉變(爲另一種): *to* ~ *rags into paper/securities into cash/pounds into francs;* 將破布變成紙(證券變成現款,英鎊換成法郎); ~ *club funds to one's own use,* use them unlawfully. 挪用會社基金。 **2** ~ ***sb (from sth) (to sth),*** cause him to change his beliefs, etc: 使人改變信仰等: *to* ~ *a man from atheism to Christianity.* 使某人由無神論改信基督教。 **3** (Rugby football) complete (a try) by kicking a goal. (橄欖球)將球踢入球門而完成(進球)。 ~**ed** *part adj* that has been ~ed: 改建的;改造的: *a* ~*ed mews,* stable(s) rebuilt, decorated, etc for use as a residence. 由馬廄改建成的住宅。

con·vert² /ˈkɒnvɜːt ; ˈkɑnvɝt/ *n* person converted, esp to a different religion (or from no religion), or to different principles: 改教者;改宗者;由不信教改爲信教者;皈依者;改主義者;改黨者: *a* ~ *to socialism.* 改信社會主義者。

con·vert·ible /kənˈvɜːtəbl ; kənˈvɝtəbl̩/ *adj* that can be converted: 可變換的;可改變的: *Banknotes are not usually* ~ *into gold nowadays.* 現今紙幣通常不能兌換爲黃金了。□ *n* (esp US) touring car with a folding or detachable roof. (尤美) 敞篷車 (車篷可摺疊起來或拆卸的旅行車)。**con·verti·bil·ity** /kənˌvɜːtəˈbɪlətɪ ; kənˌvɝtəˈbɪlətɪ/ *n*

con·vex /ˈkɒnveks ; ˈkɑnvɛks/ *adj* with the surface curved like the outside of a ball: 表面彎曲如球的外側的;凸起的: *a* ~ *lens.* 凸透鏡。⇨ concave. ~**·ly** *adv* ~**·ity** /kɒnˈveksətɪ ; kənˈvɛksətɪ/ *n* state of being ~. 凸;凸性。

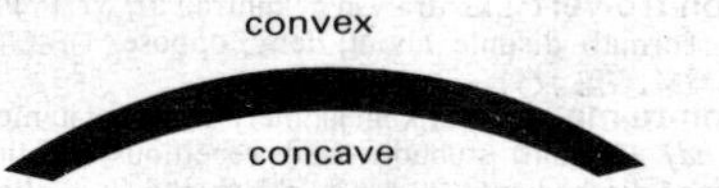

con·vey /kənˈveɪ ; kənˈve/ *vt* [VP6A, 14] **1** ~ ***(from) (to),*** take, carry: 運輸;運送: *Pipes* ~ *hot water from this boiler to every part of the building.* 水管將熱水自此燒水器輸送至大樓的每一部份。*This train* ~*s both passengers and goods.* 這班列車客貨均載。 **2** ~ ***(to sb),*** make known ideas, views, feelings, etc to another person: 傳達(意思、見解、感情等): *Words fail to* ~ *my meaning.* 言語不能表達我的意思。*This picture will* ~ *to you some idea of the beauty of the scenery.* 這幅畫可將那處風景的美麗向你傳達一二。 **3** ~ ***to,*** (legal) give full legal rights (in land or property): (法律) (將土地或產業經合法手續)讓與;轉讓: *The land was* ~*ed to his* *brother*. 此地已讓與他的兄弟。**~er, ~or** /-veɪə(r) ; -'veɚ/ *n* person or thing that ~s: 運送者;運輸裝置;運送機: *a 'coal ~er*. 運煤裝置;運煤設備。**'~er-belt,** (eg in a factory) flexible band or chain moving over wheels for ~ing packages, etc. (如工廠中的)運輸帶(裝於輪子上轉動以運送包裹等的帶或鏈)。

con·vey·ance /kən'veɪəns ; kən'veəns/ *n* **1** [U] conveying. 運輸;運送。**2** [C] sth which conveys; carriage or other vehicle. 運輸工具;車輛。**3** [C, U] (legal) (document) conveying property. (法律)財產讓與(證書)。**con·vey·ancer** *n* lawyer who prepares ~s. 辦理財產讓與的律師。

con·vict¹ /kən'vɪkt ; kən'vɪkt/ *vt* [VP6A, 14] **~ *sb (of sth)*, 1** cause (sb) to be certain that he has done wrong, made a mistake: 使(某人)確信自己有罪或有錯: *to ~ sb of his errors;* 使某人相信他自己所犯之錯; *to be ~ed of sin*. 確信自己有罪。⇨ convince. **2** (of a jury or a judge) declare in a law court that (sb) is guilty (*of* crime): (指陪審團或法官)宣告(某人)有罪(與 of 連用,後接罪行): *He was ~ed of murder*. 他被判謀殺罪。

con·vict² /'kɒnvɪkt ; 'kɑnvɪkt/ *n* person convicted of crime and undergoing punishment. (已定罪並在服刑中的)囚犯;監犯。

con·vic·tion /kən'vɪkʃn ; kən'vɪkʃən/ *n* **1** [U] the convicting of a person for a crime; [C] instance of this: 定罪;宣告有罪: *The ~ of the accused man surprised us*. 被告被判定有罪使我們吃驚。*There were five acquittals and six ~s*. 有五人宣判無罪,六人宣判有罪。**2** [U] the act of convincing, of bringing certainty to the mind. 使信服;使確信。***(not) carry ~***, (not) be convincing. (不能)令人相信。***be open to ~***, be ready to listen to evidence, etc that may convince one. 願意聽取可信之證據等;服理。**3** [C, U] firm or assured belief: 堅信;確信;深信: *I speak in the full ~ that...*, firmly convinced that.... 我深深相信…。*Do you always act up to your ~s*, do what you are convinced is right, just, etc? 你是否永遠行動與信仰一致(照你認爲對的、正當的去做)?

con·vince /kən'vɪns ; kən'vɪns/ *vt* [VP6A, 11, 14] **~ *sb (of sth/that...)***, make (sb) feel certain; cause (sb) to realize: 使(某人)信服;使(某人)明白: *I am ~d of his honesty/that he is honest*. 我深信他的誠實(他是誠實的)。*We couldn't ~ him of his mistake*. 我們無法使他明白他的錯。**con·vinc·ing** *adj* that ~s: 令人信服的: *a convincing speaker/argument*. 令人信服的演說家(論據)。**con·vin·cing·ly** *adv*: *to speak convincingly*. 說話能令人信服。**con·vinc·ible** /kən'vɪnsəbl ; kən'vɪnsəbl/ *adj* willing, ready, to be ~d. 可說服的;服理的。

con·viv·ial /kən'vɪvɪəl ; kən'vɪvɪəl/ *adj* **1** gay; fond of chatting, merry-making, drinking, etc: 歡樂的;好閒談、飲酒作樂等的: *~ companions*. 酒肉朋友。**2** marked by merry-making, etc: 有作樂之事的: *a ~ evening*. 作樂的一晚。**~·ly** /-ɪəlɪ ; -ɪəlɪ/ *adv* **~·ity** /kənˌvɪvɪ'ælətɪ ; kənˌvɪvɪ'ælətɪ/ *n* (*pl* -ties) [C, U] merry-making; being ~. 飲宴作樂;歡樂。

con·vo·ca·tion /ˌkɒnvə'keɪʃn ; ˌkɑnvə'keʃən/ *n* **1** [U] convoking; calling together. 召集;召開會議。**2** [C] legislative assembly of the Church of England, of graduates of some universities. (英國教會或某些大學畢業生的)評議會。

con·voke /kən'vəʊk ; kən'vok/ *vt* [VP6A] (formal) call together, summon (a meeting): (正式用語)召集;召開(會議): *to ~ Parliament*. 召開國會。

con·vol·uted /'kɒnvəlu:tɪd ; 'kɑnvəˌljutɪd/ *part adj* (zool, biol) coiled; twisted (eg a ram's horn); (fig) complicated and difficult: (動物,生物)盤繞的;廻旋狀的(如公羊角);(喻)複雜困難的: *a ~ argument*. 複雜錯綜的爭論。

con·vol·ution /ˌkɒnvə'lu:ʃn ; ˌkɑnvə'luʃən/ *n* [C] coil; twist: 盤旋;纏繞: *the ~s of a snake*. 蛇所盤繞的圈圈。

con·vol·vu·lus /kən'vɒlvjʊləs ; kən'vɑlvjələs/ *n* (*pl* ~es /-ləsɪz ; -ləsɪz/) kinds of twining plant including bindweed and morning-glory (with white, pink or blue flowers). 旋花植物(包括野生旋花植物及牽牛花,開白、粉紅或藍花)。

con·voy¹ /'kɒnvɔɪ ; kən'vɔɪ/ *vt* [VP6A] (esp of a warship) go with, escort (other ships) to protect (them): (尤指戰艦)護送(其他船隻);護衛;護航: *The troopships were ~ed across the Atlantic*. 運兵的船隻被護送渡過大西洋。

con·voy² /'kɒnvɔɪ ; 'kɑnvɔɪ/ *n* **1** [U] convoying or being convoyed; protection: 護送;護衛;護航: *The supply ships sailed under ~*. 補給船在護送之下航行。**2** [C] protecting force (of warships, troops, etc). 護航艦隊;護送部隊。**3** [C] ship, number of ships, under escort; supplies, etc under escort: 被護送之船隻或補給品等: *The ~ was attacked by submarines*. 被護送之船隻受到潛水艇的攻擊。

con·vulse /kən'vʌls ; kən'vʌls/ *vt* [VP6A] (usu in passive) cause violent movements or disturbances: (通常作被動語態)使劇烈震動;震撼;搖動;使起騷動;使不安: *~d with laughter/anger/toothache;* 大笑(震怒;牙齒劇痛); *a country that has often been ~d by earthquakes/civil war*. 常爲地震(內戰)所苦的國家。

con·vul·sion /kən'vʌlʃn ; kən'vʌlʃən/ *n* [C] **1** violent disturbance: 劇烈震動;震撼;動亂;騷動: *a ~ of nature*, eg an earthquake, 自然的動亂;天災(如地震); *civil ~s*, riots, etc; 內亂;人禍(如暴動等); *a political ~*, eg an attempt at revolution. 政治的騷動(如企圖革命)。**2** (usu *pl*) violent irregular movement of a limb or limbs, or of the body, caused by contraction of muscles: (通常用複數)(由肌肉收縮所造成四肢或身體的)痙攣;抽搐: *The child's ~s filled us with fear*. 那孩子的抽筋使我們害怕極了。**3** (*pl*) violent fit of laughter: (複)狂笑;大笑: *The story was so funny that we were all in ~s*. 那故事有趣極了,使我們大家都捧腹大笑。

con·vul·sive /kən'vʌlsɪv ; kən'vʌlsɪv/ *adj* violently disturbing; having or producing convulsions: 劇烈震動的;搖撼的;抽搐的;痙攣的: *~ movements*. 抽動。

cony, coney /'kəʊnɪ ; 'konɪ/ *n* (*pl* conies, coneys) **1** (US) rabbit. (美)家兔。**2** rabbit-skin, esp when dyed and prepared so as to resemble the fur of some other animal. 兔的毛皮(尤指經過染色及處理與其他動物之毛皮相似者)。

coo /ku: ; ku/ *vi, vt, n* (*pt, pp* cooed /ku:d ; kud/, *pres p* cooing) [VP2A] (make a) soft, murmuring sound (as of doves); [VP6A] say in a soft murmur: (作)鵠鵠聲(如鴿子);低聲說話;喁喁而言: *to coo one's words*. 低聲說話。⇨ bill².

cook /kʊk ; kʊk/ *vt, vi* **1** [VP6A, 2A, 12B, 13B] prepare (food) by heating (eg boiling, baking, roasting, frying). 烹調(如煮、焙、烤、炸);做飯;燒菜。***~ sb's goose***, ⇨ goose. **2** [VP2A] undergo ~ing: 受煮;經煮: *These apples ~ well*. 這種蘋果適於烹煮。**'~ing apple, pear, etc,** suitable for ~ing. 適於烹煮的蘋果,梨等。Cf 參較 *dessert/eating apples*. **3** [VP15B] **~ *up***, concoct, invent (a story, tale, etc): 編造;虛構;杜撰(故事、小說等): *Don't give me some ~ed-up yarn!* 不要說編造的故事給我聽! **4** [VP6A] tamper with; prepare fraudulently: 竄改;僞造: *~ the books/the accounts*, falsify them. 竄改書籍(帳目)。□ *n* person who ~s food. 廚子。**'~-book** *n* =cookery-book. **'~-house** *n* detached or outdoor kitchen (eg in a camp); ship's galley. 獨立的廚房;露天廚房(如露營時);船上的廚房。**~·ing** *n* [U] *'~ing lessons*. 烹飪課。

cooker /'kʊkə(r) ; 'kʊkɚ/ *n* **1** (esp in compounds, as *'oil-~, 'gas-~*) apparatus, stove, for cooking food. (煮飯做菜用的)炊具;鍋;爐(尤用於複合字中,如油爐、煤氣爐)。**2** kind of fruit, etc (esp apples, pears, plums) grown for cooking: 爲烹食而種植的果物(尤指蘋果、梨、李子): *These apples are good ~s*. 這些蘋果宜於煮食。Cf 參較 *dessert apples*, to be eaten uncooked. 點心蘋果(不經烹煮而食者)。

cook·ery /'kʊkərɪ ; 'kʊkərɪ/ *n* [U] art and practice of cooking. 烹調術;烹飪術;烹飪法。**'~-book,** one that deals with ~; book of cooking recipes. 烹飪書;食譜。

cooky, cookie /ˈkʊkɪ ; ˈkʊkɪ/ *n* (*pl* -kies) (Scot) small, flat, thin, sweet cake (esp home-made); (US) biscuit. (蘇)小甜餅(尤指自製者);(美)餅乾。

cool¹ /kuːl ; kul/ *adj* **1** between warm and cold: 涼的;微冷的;不熱的: ~ *autumn weather.* 秋涼天氣。*Let's sit in the shade and keep* ~. 我們坐到樹蔭下去涼爽涼爽吧。*The coffee's not* ~ *enough to drink.* 咖啡還未涼得能喝。 **2** providing or allowing a feeling between warm and cold: 涼爽的;涼快的: *a* ~ *room/dress.* 涼爽的房間(衣服)。 **3** calm; unexcited: 冷靜的;鎮定的: *Keep* ~*!* 保持鎮定！*He was always* ~ *in the face of danger.* 他面臨危險時總能保持鎮定。*He has a* ~ *head,* doesn't get agitated. 他有冷靜的頭腦(不激動,不慌張)。Hence, 由此產生, ˌ~-ˈ**headed** *adj* **4** impudent in a calm way; without shame: 厚顏的;無恥的: *What* ~ *behaviour—taking my lawn-mower without asking my permission!* 未得到我的許可就拿走我的刈草機 — 這是多麼可恥的行爲呵！ **5** (of behaviour) not showing interest or enthusiasm: (指行爲)冷淡的; 不感興趣的; 不熱心的: *They gave the prime minister a* ~ *reception.* 他們很冷淡地接待那位首相。***play it* ~,** (colloq) deal calmly with a situation; be relaxed. (俗)冷靜應付; 放輕鬆。 **6** (of sums of money, distances, etc) putting emphasis on the figure, and perhaps suggesting complacency: (指錢的數目、距離等)整整的; 不折不扣的: *My new car cost me a* ~ *thousand.* 我的新車整整花了我一千(鎊)。*He suggested that we should walk a* ~ *twenty miles farther.* 他建議我們至少再向前行二十哩。 **7** (US sl) pleasant; fine. (美俚)適意的;好的。□ *n* **1** (usu 通常作 **the** ~) ~ air or place; ~ness: 涼爽的空氣或地方;涼爽: *in the* ~ *of the evening;* 在傍晚涼爽的空氣中; *the* ~ *of the forest.* 林中的蔭涼處。 **2** [U] (colloq) composure. (俗)鎮靜;沉着;冷靜。***keep one's* ~,** remain calm, unworried. 保持鎮靜;不慌。**~·ly** /ˈkuːllɪ ; ˈkullɪ/ *adv* **~·ness** *n*

cool² /kuːl ; kul/ *vt, vi* [VP6A, 2A] make or become cool: (使)變涼;平息: *The rain has* ~*ed the air.* 雨已使空氣變涼。*Has his anger* ~*ed yet?* 他的怒氣平息了嗎？ [VP2C] **~ *down/off,*** (esp fig) become calm, less excited or enthusiastic: (尤用於比喻)變冷靜;變冷淡: *Her passion for me has* ~*ed down.* 她對我的熱情已漸冷淡。***a* ˌ~*ing* ˈ*off period,*** (in industrial disputes, etc) a compulsory delay (to ~ tempers) before a threatened strike. (勞資爭執等中，在可能發生罷工前强制實行之)冷靜期(讓情緒平靜下來)。 **~ *one's heels,*** be kept waiting: 等候; 久候: *Let him* ~ *his heels in the outer office—that will teach him to be more polite.* 讓他在外面的辦公室等候—那將教訓他以後要有禮貌。ˈ**~ing-tower** *n* large container used in industry to ~ hot water before re-using it. 冷却塔(工業中用以冷却熱水以備再度使用之大型容器)。

cool·ant /ˈkuːlənt ; ˈkulənt/ *n* [C, U] (kind of) fluid used for cooling (eg in nuclear reactors). 冷却劑(液態,如核子反應爐中者)。

cooler /ˈkuːlə(r) ; ˈkulɚ/ *n* container in which things are cooled: 冷却器: *a wine/butter* ~; 葡萄酒(奶油)冷却器; (sl) prison cell. (俚)監房;囚房。

coolie /ˈkuːlɪ ; ˈkulɪ/ *n* ⚠ (sl, derog) unskilled Asian labourer. (諱)(俚,貶)(亞洲的)苦力;力夫。

coon /kuːn ; kun/ *n* **1** raccoon. 浣熊。**2** ⚠ (sl, derog) Negro. (諱)(俚,貶)黑人。

coop /kuːp ; kup/ *n* cage, esp for hens with small chickens. 籠;(尤指爲帶著小鷄的母鷄而設置的)鷄籠;鷄舍。□ *vt* [VP6A, 15B] **~ *up,*** put in a ~; confine (a person): 關入籠中;拘禁(人): *How long are we going to stay* ~*ed up in here?* 我們要被困在此地多久？

co-op /ˈkəʊ ɒp ; koˈɑp/ *n* **the** ~, (colloq) the co-operative society (shop, store): (俗)合作社: *She does all her shopping at the* ~. 她一切東西都在合作社購買。

cooper /ˈkuːpə(r) ; ˈkupɚ/ *n* maker of tubs, barrels, casks, etc. 桶匠。

co-op·er·ate /kəʊˈɒpəreɪt ; koˈɑpəˌret/ *vi* [VP2A, 3A, 4A] ~ ***(with sb) (in doing/to do sth),*** work or act together in order to bring about a result: 合作;協力;相配合: ~ *with friends in starting a social club.* 與友人合作創立一交誼會。*Everything* ~*d to make our holiday a success.* 一切湊合起來使我們的假期圓滿過去。**co-op·er·ator** /-tə(r) ; -tɚ/ *n*

co-op·er·ation /kəʊˌɒpəˈreɪʃn ; koˌɑpəˈreʃən/ *n* [U] working or acting together for a common purpose. (爲一共同目的而)合作;協力。***in* ~ *with; with the* ~ *of,*** together with: 與…合作: *The workers, in* ~ *with the management, have increased output by 10 per cent.* 工人們與廠方合作已使生產量增加了百分之十。

co-op·er·ative /kəʊˈɒpərətɪv ; koˈɑpəˌretɪv/ *adj* of co-operation; willing to co-operate. 合作的;願意合作的。**a ~ society** *n* group of persons who co-operate, eg to buy machines and services for all to share, or to produce, buy and sell goods among themselves for mutual benefit, or to save and lend money. 合作社;信用合作社(如共同購買機器或僱工，或自行生產互相買賣共同獲利，或辦理儲蓄及貸款)。□ *n* (shop of a) ~ society; ~ group: 合作社; 合作商店; 合作機構: *agricultural* ~*s in India and China.* 印度及中國的農業合作社。

co-opt /kəʊ ˈɒpt ; koˈɑpt/ *vt* [VP6A, 14] (of a committee) add (a person) as a member by the votes of those who are already members: (指委員會)(由原有委員投票選舉而)增添(新委員): ~ *a new member on to the committee.* 投票增選該委員會的一名新委員。

co-or·di·nate¹ /ˌkəʊ ˈɔːdənət ; koˈɔrdnɪt/ *adj* equal in importance. (重要性)平等的; 同等的; 同格的。**~ clause,** (gram) clause in a compound sentence, equal in rank to, and often joined by a conjunction to, the other clause(s) in that sentence. (文法)對等子句(複合句中，與其他子句地位相等，且常由連接詞相連者)。⇨ subordinate. □ *n* ~ thing or person. 同等之物或人。**~·ly** *adv*

co-or·di·nate² /ˌkəʊ ˈɔːdɪneɪt ; koˈɔrdn̩ˌet/ *vt* [VP 6A] make co-ordinate; bring or put into proper relation: 使平等;使同等; 使有適當關聯; 調和; 使協調: *to* ~ *ideas;* 調和各項意見; *to* ~ *one's movements when swimming/*~ *the movements of the arms and legs.* 游泳時協調各部的動作(協調臂與腿的動作)。**co-or·di·na·tor** /-neɪtə(r) ; -netɚ/ *n* person who ~s. 協調人;調和者。

co-or·di·na·tion /ˌkəʊ ˌɔːdɪˈneɪʃn ; koˌɔrdn̩ˈeʃən/ *n* the act of co-ordinating; the state of being co-ordinate. 平等;同等;協調;調和;調整。

coot /kuːt ; kut/ *n* name of several kinds of swimming and diving birds. 大鷭(水鳥)。ˈ**bald** ~, *n* one with a white spot on the forehead. 禿頭大鷭(前額有白斑)。Hence, 由此產生, ***as bald as a* ~,** very bald. 頭頂光禿的。

cop¹ /kɒp ; kɑp/ *n* (sl) policeman. (俚)警察。

cop² /kɒp ; kɑp/ *vt, vi* (-pp-) (sl) (俚) **1** ***cop it,*** be punished. 受罰。 **2** [VP2C] ***cop out (of),*** abandon (an attempt, responsibility, etc). 放棄(嘗試、責任等)。Hence, 由此產生, ˈ**cop-out** *n* act of or excuse for copping out. 放棄嘗試或責任;放棄嘗試、責任等之藉口。□ *n* (sl) (俚) **1** capture. 捕獲。***it's a fair cop,*** I have/He has, etc been caught and arrested in the act of committing the offence. 我(他等)被當場逮捕。 **2** ***not much cop,*** nothing to value highly. 沒有什麼值得珍視;無甚價值。

co-part·ner /ˌkəʊ ˈpɑːtnə(r) ; koˈpɑrtnɚ/ *n* partner, eg an employee, who has a share in the profits of a business, etc in addition to his salary or wages. 合夥人 (如職工股東，除其薪資外並可分紅者)。**~·ship** /-ʃɪp ; -ˌʃɪp/ *n* system, practice, of having ~s in business or industry. (工商企業之)職工股東制度;勞資合夥。

cope¹ /kəʊp ; kop/ *n* long, loose cloak worn by clergy on some special occasions. 某些教士主禮時

所穿之長而寬大的披風。⇨ the illus at vestment. 參看 vestment 之挿圖。

cope² /kəup ; kop/ *vi* [VP2A, 3A] ~ ***(with)***, manage successfully; be equal to: (成功地)應付;對付;對抗: ~ *with difficulties.* 應付困難。

co·peck /ˈkəupek ; ˈkopɛk/ *n* (Russian coin worth) one-hundredth part of a rouble. 一盧布之百分之一;値百分之一盧布之蘇俄硬幣。

Co·per·ni·can /kəˈpɜːnɪkən ; koˈpɝnɪkən/ *adj* **the ~ system/theory,** of Copernicus, a Polish astronomer, that the planets, including the earth, move round the sun. 哥白尼系(學說)(哥白尼,波蘭天文學家,認爲行星,包括地球,繞太陽旋轉)。

cop·ing /ˈkəupɪŋ ; ˈkopɪŋ/ *n* (archit) line of (sometimes overhanging) stonework or brickwork on top of a wall. (建築)壓頂; 牆頂(牆上端有時作懸突狀的石工或磚工線)。 **ˈ~-stone** *n* (fig) final act, crowning, of a piece of work. (喩)一項工作之最後的潤色;完成一項工作之最後的行爲。

copi·ous /ˈkəupɪəs ; ˈkopɪəs/ *adj* plentiful: 豐富的: *a ~ supply;* 豐富的貯藏; *~ tears;* 很多的眼淚; (of a writer) writing much. (指作家)多產的。**~·ly** *adv*

cop·per¹ /ˈkɒpə(r) ; ˈkɑpɚ/ *n* **1** [U] common reddish-brown metal (symbol **Cu**): 銅(化學符號Cu): (attrib) (形容用法) ~ *wire/cable/alloy.* 銅線(纜,合金)。 **2** [C] coin made of ~ or a ~ alloy. 銅幣(用銅或其合金鑄成的硬幣)。 **3** [C] large vessel made of metal, esp one in which clothes are boiled. 金屬鍋(尤指煮衣用者)。⇨ boiler(1). **4 ~ beech** *n* kind of beech-tree with ~-coloured leaves. 銅榔(一種櫸樹,葉呈銅色)。 **ˌ~-ˈbottomed** *adj* **(a)** (of a ship) having the bottom plated with copper (and therefore seaworthy). (指船)銅皮包底的(因此是建造良好適於航行的)。**(b)** (fig) safe in every way: (喩)各方面均安全的;紮實的;牢靠的: *~-bottomed guarantees.* 牢靠的抵押品。 **ˈ~·head** *n* poisonous snake of the US. 銅頭蛇(產於美國的一種毒蛇)。 **~·ˈplate** *n* polished ~ plate on which designs, etc, are engraved: (刻有圖案等以便印刷的)銅版: **~·plate (hand)·writing** *n* ie cursive, neat and clear. 銅版字(清晰的草體字)。 **ˈ~·smith** *n* one who works in ~. 銅匠。□ *vt* (also亦作 **ˌ~-ˈbottom**) sheathe (a ship's bottom, etc) with ~. 以銅皮包(船底等)。

cop·per² /ˈkɒpə(r);ˈkɑpɚ/ *n* (sl) policeman. (俚)警察。

cop·pice /ˈkɒpɪs ; ˈkɑpɪs/ *n* [C] small woodland area of undergrowth and small trees (grown for periodical cutting, eg for bean and pea sticks). 一小片矮樹叢(可定期砍伐以作豆架等而種植者);矮林。

copra /ˈkɒprə ; ˈkɑprə/ *n* [U] dried kernels of coconuts, from which oil is extracted for making soap, etc. 乾椰子肉(可從其中搾油以製肥皂等)。

copse /kɒps ; kɑps/ *n* = coppice.

Copt /kɒpt ; kɑpt/ *n* one of the direct descendants of the ancient Egyptians (about one-tenth of the population of modern Egypt). 柯普特人(古埃及人的嫡系後裔,佔今埃及人口的十分之一)。 **Cop·tic** /ˈkɒptɪk ; ˈkɑptɪk/ *n* language used in the liturgy of the ~ic Church of Egypt and Ethiopia. 柯普特語(埃及與衣索比亞境內,柯普特教會禮拜式所用的語文)。□ *adj* of the ~s. 柯普特人的。

cop·ula /ˈkɒpjʊlə ; ˈkɑpjələ/ *n* (gram) verb form (eg the finites of *be* and *become*) that connects a subject and the complement. (文法)連繫詞(連接主詞與補足詞的動詞語形,例如be和become之有限式)。

copu·late /ˈkɒpjʊleɪt ; ˈkɑpjəˌlet/ *vi* [VP2A, 3A] ~ ***(with)***, (esp of animals) unite in sexual intercourse. (尤指動物)交配;交合;性交。**copu·la·tion** /ˌkɒpjʊˈleɪʃn ; ˌkɑpjəˈleʃən/ *n* act or process of copulating. 交配;交媾;性交。 **copu·lat·ive** /ˈkɒpjʊlətɪv ; ˈkɑpjəˌletɪv/ *adj* (formal) serving to connect. (正式用語)有連繫作用的。□ *n* (gram) word that connects (and which implies combination). (文法)連繫詞(含結合之意)。

copy¹ /ˈkɒpɪ ; ˈkɑpɪ/ *n* (*pl* -pies) **1** thing made to be like another; reproduction of a letter, picture, etc: 複製品;抄本;複本;謄本;(信件的)副本;加印之圖片;(影片之)拷貝: *Make three carbon copies of the letter.* 將此信打三份複寫本。 **rough ~,** the first (often imperfect) outline or draft of sth written or drawn. (寫作或繪畫的)草稿;草圖。 **fair ~,** the final form of sth written or drawn. 謄清之稿。 **ˈ~·book** *n* exercise book containing models of handwriting for learners to imitate: 習字帖;習字簿: *~book maxims,* commonplace maxims (as formerly found in ~books). 陳腐的格言(從前常見於習字帖中)。⇨ also blot. **ˈ~·cat** *n* (colloq) slavish imitator. (俗)毫無創造性的模倣者;文抄公。 **2** one example of a book, newspaper, etc of which many have been made: (書籍,報紙等印刷物之)一本;一份: *If you can't afford a new ~ of the book, perhaps you can find a secondhand ~.* 如果你買不起新的,你或許可以找得到一本舊的。 **3** [U] material to be sent to a printer: (送印刷廠的)原稿;底稿;稿子: *The printers are waiting for more ~.* 印刷廠正等着更多的稿子。*The fall of the Cabinet will make good ~,* will make exciting news for the journalists to write about. 內閣的垮臺將成爲大新聞。 **ˈ~ desk** *n* (US) desk in a newspaper office where ~ is edited and prepared for printing. (美)報館裏編輯稿件以備付印的辦公桌。 **ˈ~·writer** *n* person who writes advertising or publicity ~. 撰寫廣告文字者。

copy² /ˈkɒpɪ ; ˈkɑpɪ/ *vt, vi* **1** [VP6A, 15A, B] make a copy of: 抄寫;謄寫;複寫;製一份…的副本: ~ *notes (out of a book, etc) into a notebook;* 抄錄(某書等之)要點於筆記簿中; ~ *out a letter,* make a complete copy of it; 將信函抄一副本; ~ *sth down (from the blackboard).* 將…(自黑板上)抄下來。 **2** [VP6A] do, try to do, the same as; imitate: 摹倣;倣效: *You should ~ his good points, not his bad points.* 你應當倣效他的優點,不要倣效他的缺點。 **3** [VP2A] cheat by looking at a neighbour's paper, etc: 在考試中作弊,抄鄰座的答案等: *He was punished for ~ing during the examination.* 他因考試時抄鄰座答案而被罰。 **~·ist** /ˈkɒpɪɪst ; ˈkɑpɪɪst/ *n* person who copies or transcribes (eg old documents); imitator. (古舊文件等之)謄寫者;抄寫者;摹倣者。

copy·hold /ˈkɒpɪhəuld ; ˈkɑpɪˌhold/ *n* [U] (GB) the holding of land on conditions that were laid down in records of the manor; land held in this way. (英)根據領主册籍中的條件享有的土地權;憑劵管業;如此所享有的土地。~**er** *n* person holding land in this way. 憑劵管業者。

copy·right /ˈkɒpɪraɪt ; ˈkɑpɪˌraɪt/ *n* [U] sole legal right, held for a certain number of years, by the author or composer of a work, or by someone delegated by him, to print, publish, sell, broadcast, perform, film or record his work or any part of it; (attrib) protected by ~. 著作權;版權(著作家或作曲家,或由其所委託的代表,在一定年限以內對其著作物所獨享的法定權益,如印刷、出版、銷售、廣播、上演、拍片或錄音); (形容用法)受版權保護的; 有著作權的。□ *vt* secure ~ for (a book, etc). 取得(書等)的版權。

co·quetry /ˈkɒkɪtrɪ ; ˈkokɪtrɪ/ *n* [U] flirting; [C] (*pl* -ries) instance of this; flirtatious act. (女子向男子)賣弄風情;調情;調情行爲。

co·quette /kɒˈket ; koˈkɛt/ *n* girl or woman who flirts. 賣弄風情的女子。 **co·quet·tish** /kəuˈketɪʃ ; koˈkɛtɪʃ/ *adj* of or like a ~: 賣弄風情的: *coquettish smiles.* 賣弄風情的微笑。**co·quet·tish·ly** *adv*

cor·acle /ˈkɒrəkl ; ˈkɔrəkl/ *n* small, light boat made of wicker, covered with watertight material, used by fishermen on Welsh and Irish rivers and lakes. 一種用枝條編成外覆防水布等的輕便小舟 (威爾斯及愛爾蘭漁夫用於河川湖澤之上)。

coral /ˈkɒrəl *US:* ˈkɔːrəl ; ˈkɑrəl/ *n* **1** [U] hard, red, pink or white substance built on the sea bed by small creatures (*polyps*). 珊瑚(質堅呈紅、粉紅或白色的物質,產於海底,由小生物水螅所造成)。 **ˌ~ ˈisland,** one formed by the growth of ~. 珊瑚島。 **ˈ~-reef,**

accumulation of ~. (由珊瑚果積成的)珊瑚礁。⇨ the illus at atoll. 參看 atoll 之插圖。**2** [C] sea organism that makes this substance. (造成珊瑚的)珊瑚蟲。□ *adj* like ~ in colour; red or pink: 珊瑚色的;紅的;粉紅的: ~ *lips.* 粉紅色的唇。

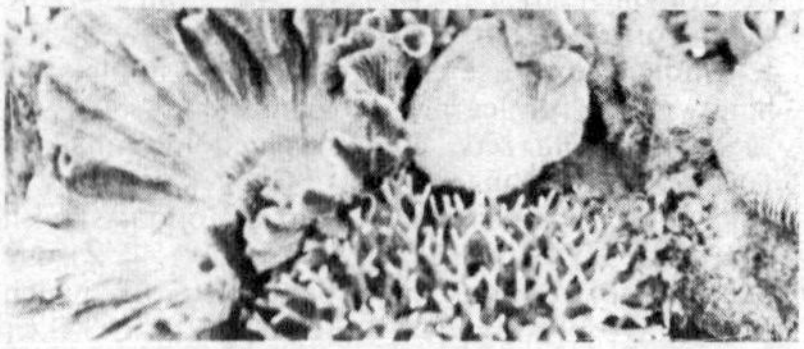

coral

cor an·glais /ˌkɔːr ˈɒŋgleɪ *US:* ɔːŋˈgleɪ, ˌkɔrɑŋˈgle/ *n* (music) woodwind instrument (tenor oboe). (音樂)英國管(一種雙簧木管樂器，又稱次中音木管)。⇨ the illus at brass. 參看 brass 之插圖。

cor·bel /ˈkɔːbl; ˈkɔrbl/ *n* (archit) stone or timber projection from a wall to support sth (eg a cornice, an arch). (建築)(自牆上伸出作支撐用的石質或木質)承材(如飛簷,拱);枕梁;牛腿。⇨ the illus at window. 參看 window 之插圖。

cord /kɔːd; kɔrd/ *n* **1** [C, U] (length of) twisted strands, thicker than string, thinner than rope. (一截)粗線;細線;索;帶。**2** [C] part of the body like a ~: 身體上的帶狀部份: *the spinal ~;* 脊髓; *the vocal ~s.* 聲帶。⇨ chord(3). **3** [C] measure of wood cut for fuel (usu 128 cubic ft). 量柴堆的體積單位(通常爲 128 立方呎)。□ *vt* put a ~ or ~s(1) round. 以繩索捆紮。

cord·age /ˈkɔːdɪdʒ; ˈkɔrdɪdʒ/ *n* [U] cords, ropes, etc, esp the rigging of a ship. 繩索的總稱;(尤指)船的纜索。

cor·dial /ˈkɔːdɪəl *US:* ˈkɔːrdʒəl; ˈkɔrdʒəl/ *adj* warm and sincere (in feeling, behaviour): (在感情或行爲上)熱誠的;懇摯的;誠懇的: *a ~ smile/welcome/handshake;* 熱誠的微笑(歡迎,握手); strongly felt: 深切感到的: ~ *dislike.* 深深的厭惡。□ *n* sweetened, invigorating liquor: 提神的甜酒: *lime juice ~.* 萊姆汁酒。**~·ly** /-dɪəlɪ *US:* -dʒəlɪ; -dʒəlɪ/ *adv* **~·ity** /ˌkɔːdɪˈælətɪ *US:* ˌkɔːrdʒɪ-; ˌkɔrdʒɪˈælətɪ/ *n* [U] quality of being ~; [C] (*pl* -ties) expression of ~ feeling. 熱誠;懇摯;熱誠的表示。

cor·dite /ˈkɔːdaɪt; ˈkɔrdaɪt/ *n* [U] smokeless explosive substance. 無煙火藥;拋射藥;柯達藥。

cor·don /ˈkɔːdn; ˈkɔrdn̩/ *n* [C] **1** line, ring, of police, soldiers, military posts, etc acting as guards: 由警察、士兵、哨崗等所構成的警戒線: *a sanitary ~,* a guarded line separating infected and uninfected districts. 衛生警戒線(隔絕傳染區與非傳染區的界線);防疫線。**2** fruit-tree with all its branches pruned back so that it grows as a single stem (usu against a wall or along wires). 剪去一切分枝僅留主幹的果樹(通常靠牆或沿金屬線生長者)。**3** ornamental ribbon of an Order[1](9) (usu worn across the shoulder). 代表勳位的飾帶(通常斜披於肩上);綬帶。**~ bleu** /ˌkɔːdɒn ˈblɜː; kɔrˈdɔ̃ˈblœ/, (F) award to a cook or restaurant for high quality cooking. (法)(爲其高超的烹飪手藝而頒給廚子或餐館的)優異獎。□ *vt* [VP15B] **~ *off,*** separate, keep at a distance, by means of a ~(1): 以警戒線隔離或阻擋: *The crowds were ~ed off by the police.* 群衆爲警察的警戒線所阻擋。

cords /kɔːdz; kɔrdz/ *n pl* (colloq abbr) corduroy trousers. (俗)棱紋布褲子(爲corduroy trousers之略)。

cor·du·roy /ˈkɔːdərɔɪ; ˌkɔrdəˈrɔɪ/ *n* **1** [U] thick coarse, strong cotton cloth with raised lines on it. 有棱紋之厚粗棉布;燈芯絨。**2** (*pl*) trousers made of this cloth. (複)棱紋布褲子。**3** **~ road,** one made of tree trunks laid across swampy land. (以樹幹置於低濕之地所築成的)木排路;木桿道。

core /kɔː(r); kor/ *n* **1** (usu hard) centre, with seeds, of such fruits as the apple and pear. (蘋果及梨等的)果心(通常堅硬,並含籽)。⇨ the illus at fruit. 參看 fruit 之插圖。**2** central or most important part of anything: 任何物之中心或最重要的部份;核心部份: *the ~ of an electro-magnet* (a bar of soft iron); 電磁鐵心(即構成電磁鐵之核心的一條輭鐵); *to get to the ~ of a subject.* 觸及論題的核心。***to the ~,*** right to the centre: 直至中心;透心: *rotten to the ~,* (lit or fig) completely bad. (字面或喻)爛透了的;壞透了的。*He is English to the ~,* completely English in manner, speech, dress, etc. 他是個道道地地的英國人(態度、說話、服裝等都是英國式的)。□ *vt* [VP6A] take out the ~ of: 去…的核心: *to ~ an apple.* 去蘋果的核心。

co-re·ligion·ist /ˌkəʊ rɪˈlɪdʒənɪst; ˌko-rɪˈlɪdʒənɪst/ *n* one of two or more persons who adhere to the same religion. 信奉同一宗教的人。

co-re·spon·dent /ˌkəʊ rɪˈspɒndənt; ˌko-rɪˈspɑndənt/ *n* (legal) person charged with adultery with the spouse (husband or wife) of the *respondent* (petitioner or plaintiff) in a divorce suit. (法律)在離婚案件中被控與原告之夫或妻通姦者;共同被告。

corgi /ˈkɔːgɪ; ˈkɔrgɪ/ *n* breed of small Welsh dog. 威爾斯產的一種小狗。

Co·rin·thian /kəˈrɪnθɪən; kəˈrɪnθɪən/ *n, adj* **1** (native) of Corinth /ˈkɒrɪnθ; ˈkɔrɪnθ/. 科林斯的;科林斯人。**2** (archit) of the most ornate of the three types of column(1) in ancient Greek architecture, with a decoration of leaves on the capital[1](3). (建築)科林斯式柱(古希臘建築最華麗的三種柱式之一,柱冠飾有葉形雕花)。⇨ the illus at column. 參看 column 之插圖。

cork /kɔːk; kɔrk/ *n* **1** [U] light, elastic, tough substance, the thick outer bark of the tree called the *~-oak;* (attrib) made of this material: 木栓層;軟木(輕,有彈性,堅靭,爲軟木橡樹的外層樹皮);(形容用法)軟木製的: *a ~ jacket.* 軟木製的背心(救生衣)。**2** [C] round piece of this material used as a stopper for a bottle: 軟木製的瓶塞;軟木塞: *to draw/pull out the ~.* 拔開軟木塞。**ˈ~-screw** *n* tool for drawing ~s from bottles. 起軟木塞的螺絲起子;瓶塞鑽。□ *vt* [VP6A, 15B] **~ *(up),*** stop with, or as with, a ~: (似)用軟木塞塞住: *to ~ a bottle;* 用軟木塞將瓶口塞住; (fig): (喻): *to ~ up one's feelings.* 抑制感情。**corked** *adj* (of wine) contaminated by decayed ~ or a bad ~: (指葡萄酒)被腐壞的軟木塞敗壞的: *~ed port.* 被腐壞軟木塞敗壞的紅葡萄酒。

cork·age /ˈkɔːkɪdʒ; ˈkɔrkɪdʒ/ *n* [U] charge made by a restaurant for serving wine not supplied by itself. (飯店對於非由其店中供應之酒所收取之)開瓶費。

corker /ˈkɔːkə(r); ˈkɔrkɚ/ *n* (dated sl) (過時俚語) **1** sth remarkable or astonishing. 不平常或驚人的事物。**2** unanswerable argument. 無法辯駁的論點。

corm /kɔːm; kɔrm/ *n* (bot) bulb-like swelling on the underground stem of a plant (eg a crocus or a gladiolus), from the top of which buds sprout. (植物)(植物如蕃紅花或劍蘭之生長於地下的)球莖。Cf 參較 *bulb* which has scales. 有鱗苞的球莖。

cor·mor·ant /ˈkɔːmərənt; ˈkɔrmərənt/ *n* large, long-necked seabird with a pouch under its beak for holding the fish it catches. 鸕鶿(大的長頸水鳥,喙下有囊可存所捕之魚)。⇨ the illus at water. 參看 water 之插圖。

corn[1] /kɔːn; kɔrn/ *n* **1** [U] (collective) (seed of) any of various grain plants, chiefly wheat, oats, rye and (esp US) maize; such plants while growing: (集合用法)穀類;五穀(主指小麥、大麥、燕麥、裸麥,在美國尤指玉蜀黍);穀禾: *a field of ~;* 一片穀類作物; *a ˈ~-field;* 穀田; *a sheaf of ~.* 一捆穀禾。⇨ the illus at cereal. 參看 cereal 之插圖。**ˈ~-cob,** thick, cylindrical part of an ear of maize, on which the grains grow. 玉蜀黍穗軸。**~ *on the cob,*** maize cooked and eaten in this form. 帶軸烹煮並食用的玉蜀黍。**ˈ~·crake** /-kreɪk; -ˌkrek/, common European bird, the male of which has a loud, harsh cry. 秧鷄 (歐洲常見之鳥，雄者鳴聲粗宏)。 **'~-exchange,** place where dealers in ~ do business. 糧食市場(糧食販做生意的地方)。**'~-flakes** *n pl* cereal of toasted maize flakes. 烘過的玉蜀黍片(用作食物)。**'~-flour** (US 美 **'~-starch**), flour made from maize, rice or other grains. 玉蜀黍、米或其他穀物所磨成的粉。**'~-flower,** name of various flowers growing wild in ~-fields, esp a blue-flowered kind (also grown in gardens). 矢車菊(野生於穀田中，尤指開藍花者，亦種於花園中)。**'C~ Laws,** (esp) laws in GB, repealed in 1846, regulating trade in ~. (尤指英國於 1846 年所廢除的)穀類貿易法令。**'~ pone** /-pəʊn ; -pon/, (US) baked or fried maize bread. (美)烤或煎的玉蜀黍粉製成的麵包。**'~-starch,** (US) ~flour. (美)玉蜀黍、米或其他穀物所磨成的粉。**2** [C] single grain (of wheat, pepper, etc). 穀粒;辣椒子。

corn² /kɔːn ; kɔrn/ *n* small area of hardened skin on the foot, esp on a toe, often with a painful centre and root. 鷄眼(一小塊硬化的皮膚,生於足部,尤指足趾上,常有疼痛的中心及根)。***tread on sb's ~s,*** (fig) hurt his feelings. (喻)觸及某人的傷心處;令某人傷心。

corn³ /kɔːn ; kɔrn/ *vt* preserve (meat) in salt: 用鹽醃(肉): *~ed beef*. 醃牛肉。

cor·nea /'kɔːnɪə ; 'kɔrnɪə/ *n* (anat) tough transparent part of the eyeball, covering the pupil and iris. (解剖)角膜(眼球的堅韌透明外膜，覆蓋著瞳孔及虹彩)。⇨ the illus at eye. 參看 eye 之挿圖。**~l** *adj* of the ~: 角膜的: *a ~l graft*. 角膜移植片。

cor·nel·ian /kɔː'niːlɪən ; kɔr'niljən/ *n* semi-precious stone, reddish, reddish-brown or white. 紅玉髓(次等寶石,紅色、紅褐色或白色)。

cor·ner /'kɔːnə(r) ; 'kɔrnɚ/ *n* **1** position (exterior or interior) of the angle where two lines, sides, edges or surfaces meet; angle enclosed by two walls, sides, etc that meet: 角;隅(兩線、邊或面相交之外部或內部之位置;或指兩牆、邊等所圍成之角落): *standing at a street ~;* 站在街角上; *a shop situated on/at the corner;* 位於街角的商店; *just round the ~,* (colloq) very near; (俗)一轉彎就是;非常近; *sitting in the ~ of the room.* 坐在屋內的一隅。***cut off a ~,*** go across, not round, it; take a short cut. 走直路;走近路(不經過轉角處)。***cut ~s,*** (of the driver of a motor vehicle) go across, not round them when travelling fast; (fig) simplify proceedings, ignore regulations, etc to get work done quickly: (指駕駛汽車者)小轉彎;斜切(當開快車時不繞角而斜切而行);(喻)簡化過程、忽視規則等使工作速成: *We've had to cut a few ~s to get your visa ready in time.* 我們必須簡化手續使你的護照簽證及時弄好。***drive sb into a ~,*** (fig) put him in a difficult situation from which escape is difficult. (喻)迫人入困境。***turn the ~,*** (fig) pass a critical point in an illness, a period of difficulty, etc. (喻)(在病中、困境等)度過危險期;脫險;度過難關。***be in a tight ~,*** in an awkward or difficult situation. 處於困境中。**'~-stone** *n* **(a)** stone that forms a ~ of the foundation of a building (often laid in position at a ceremony). 建築物的基石(常在奠基禮中下土)。**(b)** (fig) foundation: (喻)基礎: *Hard work was the ~stone of his success.* 努力工作是他成功的基礎。 **2** hidden, secret, or out-of-the-way place: 隱密處;偏僻處: *money hidden in odd ~s;* 藏在隱密難尋之處的錢; *hole-and-~ methods/transactions,* secret and underhand. 秘密而狡詐的方法(交易)。**3** region; quarter: 地區;區域: *to the four ~s of the earth.* 至世界各地;遍及四面八方。 **4** (comm) the buying up of all or as much as possible of the supply of an article of trade, a commodity, a stock, etc in order to secure a monopoly and control the price. (商)壟斷市場(買盡或盡量買進某項商品、貨物、股票等,以圖獨家壟斷而控制價格);囤積居奇。***make a ~ in sth,*** (eg the buying of wheat). 壟斷某物 (如收購小麥) 之市場。 **5** (Assoc football) (also 亦作 **'~-kick**) kick from the ~ of the field, allowed when the ball has been kicked by an opponent over his own goal-line. (英式足球)角球(自場角所罰之球,因對方球員將球自其球門線踢出場外而罰之)。□ *vt, vi* **1** [VP6A] force into a ~; put into a difficult position: 迫入角隅;逼入困境: *The escaped prisoner was ~ed at last.* 那逃犯終被迫入絕境，無法逃脫。*That question ~ed me.* 那問題把我難倒了。 **2** [VP6A] make a ~(4) in (wheat, etc): 壟斷(小麥等)市場: *~ the market.* 壟斷市場。**3** [VP2A] (of a vehicle, its driver) turn a ~ (on a road, etc): (指車輛、其駕駛人)(在路上等處)轉彎;拐角: *My new car ~s well,* remains stable when going round ~s. 我的新車轉彎時車行很穩。**~ed** *adj* (in compounds) having ~s: (用於複合字中)有角的: *a three-~ed hat.* 三角帽。

cor·net¹ /'kɔːnɪt ; 'kɔrnɪt/ *n* **1** small musical instrument of brass, like a trumpet. 短號;短喇叭。**2** piece of paper twisted into the shape of a cone, to hold sweets; cone-shaped container for ice-cream. 錐形紙袋(用以裝糖果);盛冰淇淋的錐形杯。

cor·net² /'kɔːnɪt ; 'kɔrnɪt/ *n* (in former times) officer in a troop of cavalry who carried the colours¹(8). (從前)騎兵隊的掌旗官。

cor·nice /'kɔːnɪs ; 'kɔrnɪs/ *n* (archit) projecting part, above the frieze, above a column, ⇨ the illus at column; ornamental moulding (eg in plaster) round the walls of a room, just below the ceiling; horizontal strip of carved wood or stone along an outside wall; overhanging mass of snow above a precipice. (建築)柱頂壁緣上方的突出部份;柱帶(參看 column 之挿圖);室內沿牆與天花板之間裝飾性的嵌線(如用灰泥做成者);壁帶;沿外牆之雕木或刻石飛簷;雪簷(凍結於懸崖上的懸垂的雪塊)。

cor·nu·co·pia /ˌkɔːnjʊ'kəʊpɪə ; ˌkɔrnə'kopɪə/ *n* ornamental horn shown in art as overflowing with flowers, fruit and corn; (myth) horn of plenty; (fig) abundant supply. 藝術品中所示裝滿花果和玉蜀黍之裝飾性的羊角;(神話)希臘神話中哺乳 Zeus 神的山羊角 (= horn of plenty); (喻)豐富;豐饒。

corny /'kɔːnɪ ; 'kɔrnɪ/ *adj* (-ier, -iest) (sl) hackneyed; often heard or repeated: (俚)陳腐的;陳舊的;老生常談的: *~ jokes/music.* 陳舊的笑話(音樂)。

co·rolla /kə'rɒlə ; kə'rɑlə/ *n* (bot) ring of petals forming the cup of a flower. (植物)花冠。⇨ the illus at flower. 參看 flower 之挿圖。

co·rol·lary /kə'rɒlərɪ *US:* 'kɒrəlerɪ ; 'kɔrəˌlɛrɪ/ *n* (*pl* -ries) [C] natural sequence or outcome of sth; sth self-evident after sth else has been proved. 自然的結果;(由已證明之事物所得的)推論;系定理。

co·rona /kə'rəʊnə ; kə'ronə/ *n* (*pl* ~s /-nəz ; -nəz/, ~e /-niː ; -ni/) ring of light seen round the sun or moon, eg during an eclipse. 日月週圍的光環(如日月蝕時所現者); 日冕; 日華; 月華。⇨ the illus at eclipse. 參看 eclipse 之挿圖。

cor·on·ary /'kɒrənrɪ *US:* 'kɔːrənerɪ ; 'kɔrəˌnɛrɪ/ *adj* (anat) of arteries supplying blood to the heart: (解剖)冠狀動脈的: *~ thrombosis,* formation of a clot in a ~ artery. 冠狀動脈栓塞。□ *n* (*pl* -ries) (colloq) attack of ~ thrombosis. (俗)冠狀動脈栓塞之發作。

cor·on·ation /ˌkɒrə'neɪʃn *US:* ˌkɔːr- ; ˌkɑrə'neʃən/ *n* ceremony of crowning a king, queen or other sovereign ruler: (王、女王或其他君主的)加冕禮: (attrib) (形容用法) *the queen's ~ robes.* 女王的加冕袍。

cor·oner /'kɒrənə(r) *US:* 'kɔːr- ; 'kɔrənɚ/ *n* official who inquires into the cause of any death thought to be from violent or unnatural causes: (調查死因的)驗屍官;法醫: *~'s inquest,* such an inquiry (held with a jury). 驗屍(會同陪審團)。

cor·onet /'kɒrənet *US:* 'kɔːr- ; 'kɔrənɪt/ *n* small crown worn by a peer or peeress; band of precious materials worn as (part of) a woman's head-dress; garland of flowers. (貴族所戴的)小冠冕;(作爲婦女頭飾的)珠寶帶;花環。

cor·poral¹ /'kɔːpərəl ; 'kɔrpərəl/ *adj* (formal) of

the human body. (正式用語) 人體的;身體的;肉體的。～ **punishment**, eg whipping, beating. 體罰(如鞭打)。

cor·poral² /ˈkɔːpərəl ; ˈkɔrpərəl/ *n* (army) non-commissioned officer (below a sergeant); (陸軍) 下士(階級低於中士); (navy): (海軍): *ship's ～*, one with police duties. 艦上下士(執行警衛任務的下士)。

cor·por·ate /ˈkɔːpərət ; ˈkɔrpərɪt/ *adj* **1** of or belonging to a corporation: 法人的;團體的;社團的;公司的;市自治體的;市政當局的: *～ property;* 社團財產; *～ bonds,* (Stock Exchange term for) bonds held by a group or company. 法人債券;公司債券(由一團體或公司所持有之債券)。 **2** of, shared by, members of a group of persons: 全體的;共同的: *～ responsibility/action.* 共同責任(行動)。 **3** united in one group: 結合成爲一個團體的: *a ～ body.* 法人組織。

cor·por·ation /ˌkɔːpəˈreɪʃn ; ˌkɔrpəˈreʃən/ *n* **1** group of persons elected to govern a town: 被選主持市政的一批人;市政當局: *the Mayor and ～;* 市長及全體市政當局; *the municipal ～;* 市自治體;市行政機關; (attrib) (形容用法) *the ～ tramways.* 市營電車。 **2** group of persons authorized to act as an individual, eg for business purposes: 法人(團體行動如一人者,如以貿易爲目的的團體);公司;社團: *In Great Britain the Electricity Authority and the National Coal Board are public ～s.* 在英國,電力管理處和國家煤礦管理處都是公法人。 **3** (US) limited liability company. (美)有限責任公司。 **4** (colloq) large belly. (俗)大肚子;大腹便便。

cor·por·eal /kɔːˈpɔːrɪəl ; kɔrˈporɪəl/ *adj* (formal) (正式用語) **1** of or for the body: 身體的: *～ needs,* eg food and drink. 身體的需要(如食物和飲料)。 **2** physical (contrasted with *spiritual*). 肉體的(與 spiritual 相對)。

corps /kɔː(r) ; kɔr/ *n* (*pl* corps /kɔːz ; kɔrz/) **1** one of the technical branches of an army: 陸軍中的特種部隊: *the ˌRoyal ˌArmy ˈMedical C～.* 英國皇家陸軍醫療隊。 **2** military force made up of two or more divisions. 軍(由兩師或兩師以上之兵力組成)。 **3** **～ de ballet** /ˌkɔː də ˈbæleɪ ; ˌkɔrdə bæˈle/ (F) company of dancers in a ballet. (法)芭蕾舞中的全體舞者。 **the Diploˈmatic C～; the C～ Diplomatique** /ˌkɔː ˌdɪpləmæˈtiːk ; kɔrˌdɪpləˌmæˈtik/ (F) all the ambassadors, ministers and attachés of foreign states at a capital or Court. (法) (駐於一國首都或宮廷的)各國外交使節團。

corpse /kɔːps ; kɔrps/ *n* dead body (esp of a human being). 屍體(尤指人類的)。⇨ carcass.

cor·pu·lent /ˈkɔːpjʊlənt ; ˈkɔrpjələnt/ *adj* (of a person or his body) fat and heavy. (指人或其身體) 肥胖的。**cor·pu·lence** /ˈkɔːpjʊləns ; ˈkɔrpjələns/ *n*

cor·pus /ˈkɔːpəs ; ˈkɔrpəs/ *n* (*pl* corpora /ˈkɔːpərə ; ˈkɔrpərə/) body, collection, esp of writings on a specified subject or of material for study (eg for linguists, a collection of examples of spoken and written usages). 身體;集體;(尤指某專題著作之)文集;全集;研究資料之集成(如語言學者所收集之口語及文字用法實例大全)。

cor·puscle /ˈkɔːpʌsl ; ˈkɔrpəsl̩/ *n* one of the red or white cells in the blood. 血球(紅血球或白血球之一)。

cor·ral /kəˈrɑːl *US:* -ˈræl ; kəˈræl/ *n* **1** enclosure for horses and cattle or the capture of wild animals. (關牛馬或捕野獸的)畜欄;獸柵。 **2** = laager. □ *vt* (-ll-) [VP6A] drive (cattle, etc) into, shut up in, a ～; form (wagons) into a ～. 驅(牛馬)入欄;關入畜欄;佈(篷車)成圓陣。

cor·rect¹ /kəˈrekt ; kəˈrɛkt/ *adj* **1** true; right: 正確的;對的: *a ～ answer;* 正確的答案; *the ～ time;* 正確的時刻; *～ in every particular.* 每一細節均正確。 **2** (of conduct, manners, dress, etc) proper; in accord with good taste or convention: (指行爲、禮貌、服裝等)合適的;高尚的;合禮儀的: *the ～ dress for a ceremony;* 典禮時應穿的禮服; *a very ～ young lady.* 儀態非常端莊的年輕女士。**～·ly** *adv* **～·ness** *n*

cor·rect² /kəˈrekt ; kəˈrɛkt/ *vt* [VP6A,14] **1** make right; take out mistakes from: 改正;修正;修改: *I ～ed my watch by the time signal.* 我照報時信號校正我的錶。*Please ～ my pronunciation.* 請改正我的發音。 **2** point out the faults of; punish: 告誡;懲戒: *～ a child for disobedience.* 懲戒小孩不聽話。

cor·rec·tion /kəˈrekʃn ; kəˈrɛkʃən/ *n* **1** [U] correcting: 校正;修改;矯正: *the ～ of schoolchildren's work.* 學童作業的批改。 ***speak under ～,*** speak while knowing that one may need to be corrected. 自知所說不一定對而發言。**house of ～,** (old name for a) prison. 監獄(舊稱)。 **2** [C] sth put in place of what is wrong: 所修改之處;改正的東西: *a written exercise with ～s in red ink.* 有紅墨水修改的筆寫練習。

cor·rec·ti·tude /kəˈrektɪtjuːd *US:* -tuːd ; kəˈrɛktəˌtjud/ *n* [U] (formal) correctness (esp of conduct, eg in diplomacy). (正式用語)端正(尤指外交方面等的行爲)。

cor·rect·ive /kəˈrektɪv ; kəˈrɛktɪv/ *n, adj* (sth) serving to correct: 有矯正作用的(事物): *～ training,* eg for juvenile delinquents. 感化教育(如施於少年罪犯者)。

cor·re·late /ˈkɒrəleɪt *US:* ˈkɔːr- ; ˈkɔrəˌlet/ *vt, vi* [VP6A, 14, 2A, 3A] ～ ***(with),*** have a mutual relation, bring (one thing) into such a relation (with another): (與…)有相互關係;使(一物)(與另一物)發生連繫: *Results in the natural sciences seldom ～ with those in history or art.* 自然科學的結果很少與歷史或藝術的結果有相互關係。*Research workers find it hard to ～ the two sets of figures/to ～ one set with the other.* 從事研究工作者發現很難使這兩組數字發生相互關係。

cor·re·la·tion /ˌkɒrəˈleɪʃn *US:* ˌkɔːr- ; ˌkɔrəˈleʃən/ *n* mutual relationship: 相互關係;關連;相關: *the ～ between climate and vegetation.* 氣候與植物的相互關係。

cor·rela·tive /kɒˈrelətɪv ; kəˈrɛlətɪv/ *n, adj* (word or thing) having a mutual relation: 有相互關係的(字或物): *'Either' and 'or' are ～ conjunctions.* Either 和 or 是相關連接詞。

cor·re·spond /ˌkɒrɪˈspɒnd *US:* ˌkɔːr- ; ˌkɔrəˈspɑnd/ *vi* [VP2A, 3A] **1** ～ ***(with),*** be in harmony: (與…)調和;符合: *The house exactly ～s with my needs.* 這房子恰好符合我的需要。*His actions do not ～ with his words.* 他的言行不符。 **2** ～ ***(to),*** be equal; be similar (in position, etc): 相等(於);(地位等)相似;相稱;相當;相配: *His expenses do not ～ to his income.* 他的花費與他的收入不相稱。*The American Congress ～s to the British Parliament.* 美國的國會相當於英國的議會。 **3** ～ ***(with),*** exchange letters. (與…)通信。**～·ing** *adj* that ～(s): 相當的;相同的: *Imports for 1–10 July this year are larger by 10 per cent than for the ～ing period last year.* 今年七月一日至十日的輸入量較去年同一期間超出百分之十。**～·ing·ly** *adv*

cor·re·spon·dence /ˌkɒrɪˈspɒndəns *US:* ˌkɔːr- ; ˌkɑrəˈspɑndəns/ *n* **1** [C, U] agreement; similarity: 相符;一致;相似: *There is not much ～ between their ideals and ours.* 他們的理想與我們的理想之間沒有多少相似之處。 **2** [U] letter-writing; letters: 通信;信件;書信: *I have been in ～ with him about the problem.* 關於這問題,我與他一直有書信往返。 *Is commercial ～ taught in the school?* 學校中是否教授商業尺牘? *He has a great deal of ～ to deal with.* 他有大批信件需要處理。ˈ**～ course,** course of academic study by posting essays, etc to one's tutor. 函授課程。

cor·re·spon·dent /ˌkɒrɪˈspɒndənt *US:* ˌkɔːr- ; ˌkɑrəˈspɑndənt/ *n* **1** person with whom one exchanges letters: 通信者: *He's a good/bad ～,* writes regularly/seldom. 他是個勤(懶)於寫信的人。 **2** person regularly contributing local news or special articles to a newspaper: 報紙通訊員;通訊記者(經常爲報紙報導地方新聞或撰寫特稿的人): *our Hong Kong ～;* 我們派駐香港的通訊員; *a foreign/war ～,* person writing reports from a foreign country/a war. 國外(戰地)通訊記者。 **3** (comm) person, firm, bank, etc which has regular business relations with another (esp in a foreign country). (商)(尤指與國外)有商務關係之個人、公司、銀行等;客戶。

cor·ri·dor /'kɒrɪdɔ:(r) *US:* 'kɔ:r- ; 'kɔrədɚ/ *n* long narrow passages from which doors open into rooms or compartments. 有門通至各房間的狹長通道;走廊。 **～s of power,** places where influence is unofficially exerted. 勢力走廊。 **'～ train,** one with coaches having ～s which open into compartments. 首尾有走廊相通的列車。

cor·rie /'kɒrɪ *US:* 'kɔ:rɪ ; 'kɔrɪ/ *n* [C] (Scot) round hollow in a hillside. (蘭)山邊的圓形窪地。

corri·gen·dum /ˌkɒrɪ'dʒendəm *US:* ˌkɔ:r- ; ˏkɔrɪ'dʒɛndəm/ *n* (*pl* -da /-də;-də/) thing to be corrected (esp in a printed book). (尤指出版之書籍中)需要改正之處。

cor·ri·gible /'kɒrɪdʒəbl *US:* 'kɔ:r- ; 'kɔrədʒəbl/ *adj* (formal) capable of being corrected; (of persons) submitting to correction. (正式用語)可改正的;(指人)尙可救藥的。

cor·rob·or·ate /kə'rɒbəreɪt ; kə'rɑbəˏret/ *vt* [VP6A] give support or certainty to (a statement, belief, theory, etc). 支持;證實(陳述、信仰、理論等)。 **cor·rob·or·at·ive** /kə'rɒbərətɪv *US:* -reɪtɪv ; kə'rɑbəˏretɪv/ *adj* tending to ～. 可確證的;可證實的。

cor·rob·or·ation /kəˌrɒbə'reɪʃn ; kəˏrɑbə'reʃən/ *n* [U] support or strengthening by further evidence; additional evidence: (以進一步的證據)確證;證實;進一步的證據: *in* ～ (*of*), giving further support (of). 爲(…之)確證。

cor·rode /kə'rəud ; kə'rod/ *vt, vi* [VP6A, 2A] wear away, destroy slowly by chemical action or disease; be worn away thus: (由於化學作用或疾病而)腐蝕;侵蝕;受損害;受損傷: *Rust ～s iron.* 銹能蝕鐵。 *Iron ～s easily.* 鐵易銹損。 **cor·rosion** /kə'rəuʒn ; kə'roʒən/ *n* [U] corroding or being ～d. 腐蝕;侵蝕;損害;受損。

cor·ros·ive /kə'rəusɪv ; kə'rosɪv/ *n, adj* (substance) that corrodes: 腐蝕性的(物質): *Rust and acids are ～.* 銹及酸類係腐蝕性的物質。

cor·ru·gate /'kɒrəgeɪt *US:* 'kɔ:r- ; 'kɔrəget/ *vt, vi* [VP6A, 2A] make into folds, wrinkles or furrows: (使)起皺紋;成波狀;使起褶: ～ *the forehead;* 皺額頭; *～d cardboard,* used for packing fragile goods; 波狀紙板(用以包裝容易破碎之貨物); *～d roads in tropical countries,* with a furrowed surface caused by weather and use. 熱帶國家因天氣及使用關係所造成的起伏不平的波狀道路。 **ˌ～d 'iron,** sheet iron made into folds, used for roofs, fences, etc. 波狀鐵皮(用作屋頂、藩籬等)。 **cor·ru·ga·tion** /ˌkɒrə'geɪʃn *US:* ˌkɔ:r- ; ˏkɔrə'geʃən/ *n* [C, U] fold(s); wrinkle(s). 皺紋;波紋;溝紋;波形;皺摺。

cor·rupt[1] /kə'rʌpt ; kə'rʌpt/ *adj* **1** (of persons, their actions) immoral; depraved; dishonest (esp through taking bribes): (指人、其行動)不道德的;腐化的;不誠實的(尤指貪汚受賄): ～ *practices,* (esp) the offering and accepting of bribes. 舞弊;(尤指)賄賂;行賄;受賄。 **2** impure: 不純潔的: ～ *air／blood.* 不純潔的空氣(血)。 **3** (of languages, texts, etc) debased by errors or alterations: (指語文、原文等)(因訛誤或塗改而)貶値的;敗壞的;轉訛的: *a ～ form of Latin.* 不標準的拉丁文。 **～·ly** *adv* **～·ness** *n*

cor·rupt[2] /kə'rʌpt ; kə'rʌpt/ *vt, vi* [VP6A, 2A] make or become corrupt: (使)腐敗;敗壞;行賄: *young persons whose morals have been ～ed;* 其品行已經敗壞的年輕人; *to ～ the electorate,* eg try to win their votes by bribing them. 向選民行賄(以圖拉票)。 *Does pornography ～?* 色情文學會使人腐化嗎? **～·ible** *adj* that can be ～ed: 可敗壞的; 可賄賂的: *～ible government officials.* 可賄賂的政府官吏。 **～·i·bil·ity** /kəˌrʌptə'bɪlətɪ ; kəˏrʌptə'bɪlətɪ/ *n*

cor·rup·tion /kə'rʌpʃn ; kə'rʌpʃən/ *n* [U] corrupting or being corrupt; decay: 腐敗;腐爛;腐化;敗壞: *the ～ of the body after death;* 死後身體的腐爛; *the ～ of a language;* 語文之被誤用; *officials who are proof against ～,* who cannot be bribed. 不貪汚腐化的官吏。

cor·sage /kɔ:'sɑ:ʒ ; kɔr'sɑʒ/ *n* upper part of a woman's dress (round the bust); (US) small bouquet of flowers to be worn on this part of the dress or at the waist. 女服的胸部;(美)飾於女服胸部或腰部的花束。

cor·sair /'kɔ:seə(r) ; 'kɔrsɛr/ *n* (hist) pirate or pirate ship, esp of N Africa, attacking ships of European countries. (史)海盜; 海盜船(尤指北非騷擾歐洲各國船隻者)。

corse /kɔ:s ; kɔrs/ *n* (archaic or poet) corpse. (古或詩)屍體。

corse·let, cors·let /'kɔ:slɪt ; 'kɔrslɪt/ *n* coat of armour, esp one covering the trunk only. 甲胄(尤指體甲)。

cor·set /'kɔ:sɪt ; 'kɔrsɪt/ *n* close-fitting reinforced undergarment confining the waist and hips, to shape the body to the current style (often named, in trade, a *foundation,* or *foundation garment*). 女用束腹(以保持腰及臀部之曲線者;商用名稱常作 foundation 或 foundation garment)。

cor·tege, cor·tège /kɔ:'teɪʒ ; kɔr'tɛʒ/ *n* (F) train of attendants; procession, eg at the funeral of a king or president. (法)侍從隊;扈從;行列(例如爲國王或總統送葬者)。

cor·tex /'kɔ:teks ; 'kɔrtɛks/ *n* (*pl* cortices /'kɔ:tɪsi:z ; 'kɔrtɪˏsiz/) outer shell or covering (eg the bark of a tree); outer layer of grey matter of the brain. 外殼;表皮層(如樹皮);(腦的)外層灰質;皮質。 **cor·ti·cal** /'kɔ:tɪkl ; 'kɔrtɪkl/ *adj* of the ～. 外殼的;皮層的;皮質的。

cor·ti·sone /'kɔ:tɪzəun ; 'kɔrtɪˏson/ *n* (P) [U] substance (a hormone from the adrenal gland) used medically in the treatment of arthritis and some allergies. (商標)可體松(取自腎上腺的一種荷爾蒙,醫學上用以治療關節炎及某些過敏症)。

co·run·dum /kə'rʌndəm ; kə'rʌndəm/ *n* hard crystallized mineral used chiefly in abrasive, in powder form (for polishing). 剛石(舊稱剛玉,一種堅硬的結晶礦石,主用於作磨料,呈粉狀,起磨光作用)。

cor·us·cate /'kɒrəskeɪt *US:* 'kɔ:r- ; 'kɔrəsˏket/ *vi* [VP2A] flash, sparkle: 閃光; 閃爍: *coruscating wit.* 煥發的機智。 **cor·us·ca·tion** /ˌkɒrə'skeɪʃn *US:* ˌkɔ:r- ; ˏkɔrəs'keʃən/ *n*

cor·vée /'kɔ:veɪ ; kɔr've/ *n* [C] (F) (in feudal times) day's unpaid work which had to be done by French peasants; (modern use) hard task or duty unwillingly performed. (法)(封建時代)法國農奴一天的强迫勞役;徭役;(現代用法)强迫勞役。

cor·vette /kɔ:'vet ; kɔr'vɛt/ *n* (old use) warship with sails and one tier of guns; (modern use) small fast warship designed for escorting merchant ships. (舊用法)裝單排砲位的帆艦;(現代用法)小型快速戰艦(爲擔任商船護航而設計者)。

cos[1] /kɒs ; kɑs/ *n* (kind of) long-leaved lettuce. (一種)長葉萵苣。

cos[2] /kɒs ; kɑs/ *n* (abbr of) cosine. (三角學)餘弦(cosine 之略)。

cos[3] /kəz ; kəz/ *conj* (colloq abbr of) because. (俗)因爲;爲了 (because 之略)。

cosh /kɒʃ ; kɑʃ/ *vt, n* (GB sl) (strike with a) length of lead pipe, rubber tubing filled with metal, etc. (英俚)一截鉛管或內充金屬等的橡皮管;短棍;用此種短棍打。

cosher /'kəuʃə(r) ; 'kɑʃɚ/ *adj, n* = kosher.

co-signa·tory /ˌkəu 'sɪgnətərɪ *US:* -tɔ:rɪ ; ko'sɪgnəˏtorɪ/ *adj, n* (*pl* -ries) (person) signing jointly with others. 共同簽字的(人);連署(者)。

co·sine /'kəusaɪn ; 'kosaɪn/ *n* (trig; abbr cos) sine of the complement of a given angle. (三角學;略作 cos) 餘弦(某角之餘角的正弦)。

cos·metic /kɒz'metɪk ; kɑz'mɛtɪk/ *adj, n* [C] (preparation, substance, esp one that adds colour) designed to make the skin or hair beautiful, eg *face-cream, lipstick*. 化粧用的;化粧品(尤指上色的,如面霜、口紅)。 ~ **surgery,** to restore or correct outward appearance. 整型外科手術。**cos·me·tician** /ˌkɒzməˈtɪʃn ; ˌkɑzməˈtɪʃən/ *n* person employed in the preparation or sale of ~s. 化粧品製作人; 化粧品販賣商。

cos·mic /ˈkɒzmɪk ; ˈkɑzmɪk/ *adj* of the whole universe or cosmos: 宇宙的: ~ **rays,** radiations that reach the earth from outer space. 宇宙射線(自外太空射至地球的輻射線)。

cos·mog·ony /kɒzˈmɒgənɪ ; kɑzˈmɑgənɪ/ *n* (*pl* -nies) (theory of) the origin, creation and evolution of the universe. 宇宙的起源及進化;宇宙起源論;宇宙進化論。

cos·mo·naut /ˈkɒzmənɔːt ; ˈkɑzməˌnɔt/ *n* = astronaut.

cos·mo·poli·tan /ˌkɒzməˈpɒlɪtən ; ˌkɑzməˈpɑlətn̩/ *adj* **1** of or from all, or many different parts of, the world: 屬於(或來自)全世界各地的;世界性的: *the ~ gatherings at the United Nations Assembly.* 聯合國大會之各種世界性集會。 **2** free from national prejudices because of wide experience of the world: 無國家偏見的;有四海一家之觀念的;世界主義的: *a statesman with a ~ outlook.* 有四海一家之胸襟的政治家。□ *n* ~(2) person. 無國家偏見者;世界主義者。

cos·mos¹ /ˈkɒzmɒs ; ˈkɑzməs/ *n* the universe, all space, considered as a well-ordered system (contrasted with *chaos*). 宇宙(被認爲係井然有序的整個空間,與 chaos 相對)。

cos·mos² /ˈkɒzmɒs ; ˈkɑzməs/ *n* garden plant with white, pink or purple flowers. 大波斯菊(園藝植物,開白、粉紅或紫花)。

cos·set /ˈkɒsɪt ; ˈkɑsɪt/ *vt* pamper. 溺愛;縱容。

cost¹ /kɒst *US:* kɔːst ; kɔst/ *vi* (*pt, pp* cost) [VP2B] (the adverbial adjunct indicating price, etc may be preceded by an indirect object; not used in the passive voice). (表示價錢等的副詞修飾語之前可置間接受詞;不用於被動語態)。 **1** be obtainable at the price of; require the payment of: 價值(若干);花(多少錢): *The house ~ him £15000.* 此屋花了他一萬五千鎊。*It ~s them £500 a year to run a car.* 使用一部小汽車每年花他們五百鎊。*It ~s too much.* 它的價錢太貴。*Compiling a dictionary ~s much time and patience.* 編一部字典花很多時間和耐性。**2** result in the loss of: 喪失;犧牲: *Careless driving may ~ you your life.* 粗心大意的駕車可能使你喪命。 **3** bring (injury or disadvantage): 使受損害;引起麻煩: *The boy's bad behaviour ~ his mother many sleepless nights.* 那孩子的不良行爲使他的母親許多夜睡不着。 **4** *vt* [VP6A] (*pt, pp* ~ed) (industry and comm) estimate the price to be charged for an article based on the expense of producing it. (工商業)按生產成本估計貨品應售價格。**~·ing** *n* [U] (industry) fixing of prices: (工業)作價;成本計算: *the ~ing department.* 成本計算部門。

cost² /kɒst *US:* kɔːst ; kɔst/ *n* **1** [C, U] price (to be) paid for a thing: 價錢;成本;費用: *the ~ of living;* 生活費用; *living ~s,* the general level of prices; 生活費用(物價的一般水準); *the ~-of-living index,* 生活費指數, ⇨ index(3); *the ~ price of an article,* the ~ of producing it or the price at which it may be bought wholesale, ⇨ retail; 貨品的成本價格;批發價(格); *to sell sth at ~,* ie at ~ price; 按批發價售賣某物;照成本賣。*He built his house without regard to ~,* without considering how much money would be needed. 他不計花錢多寡蓋房子。**ˈ~ accountant/clerk,** one who keeps a record of every item of expense in a business, etc. (工商企業的)成本會計員。**ˌcost-efˈfective** *adj* economical compared with money spent; 划算的; hence, 由此產生, **ˌcost-efˈfectiveness** *n* [U]. **2** [C, U *sing* only] that which is used, needed or given to obtain sth: (欲獲得某物所付的)代價: *The battle was won at (a) great ~ in human lives,* only after many soldiers had been killed. 犧牲了許多士兵的性命才換來這場戰役的勝利。 ***at ˈall ~s,*** whatever the ~ may be. 不惜任何代價;無論如何。 ***at the ~ of,*** at the loss or expense of: 喪失;犧牲: *He saved his son from drowning, but only at the ~ of his own life.* 他救了他兒子的命使免溺死,但却犧牲了他自己的生命。***count the ~,*** consider the risks, possible losses, etc before doing sth. 事前詳細盤算得失等。***to one's ~,*** to one's loss or disadvantage: 使某人遭受損失或不便: *Wasps' stings are serious, as I know to my ~,* as I know because of personal suffering from them. 我知道被黃蜂螫了是嚴重的事情,因爲我曾身受其害。 **3** (*pl*) (legal) expense of having sth settled in a law court: (複)(法律)訴訟費用: *pay a £25 fine and £7 ~s.* 繳二十五鎊罰金和七鎊訴訟費。

co-star /ˌkəʊ ˈstɑː(r) ; ˈkoˈstɑr/ *vi, vt* (-rr-) (journalism) (新聞) **1** [VP6A] present (one star(4)) as having equal status with another or others: 合演;聯合主演;使(一明星)與另一明星或其他明星聯合主演: *The film ~red Robert Redford.* 該影片由勞勃瑞福與其他明星聯合主演。 **2** [VP3A] ~ **with,** (of an actor or actress) appear as a star(4) with: (指演員)與…聯合主演: *Laurence Olivier ~s with Maggie Smith in this production.* 勞倫斯奧立佛與瑪姬史密斯在本劇中聯合主演。□ *n* /ˈkəʊstɑː(r) ; ˈkostɑr/ person who ~s. 合演者;聯合主演者。

cos·ter·monger /ˈkɒstəmʌŋgə(r) ; ˈkɑstɚˌmʌŋgɚ/ *n* person who sells fruit, vegetables, etc from a barrow in the street. 沿街推車叫賣水果、蔬菜等的小販。

cos·tive /ˈkɒstɪv ; ˈkɑstɪv/ *adj* (liter) constipated. (文)便秘的。

costly /ˈkɒstlɪ *US:* ˈkɔːst- ; ˈkɔstlɪ/ *adj* (-ier, -iest) of great value; costing much: 貴重的;昂貴的;造成嚴重損失的: *a ~ mistake,* one involving great loss or sacrifice. 造成重大損失或犧牲的錯誤。**cost·li·ness** *n*

cos·tume /ˈkɒstjuːm *US:* -tuːm ; ˈkɑstjum/ *n* **1** [U, C] style of dress: 服裝的式樣: *actors wearing historical ~,* clothes in the style of a period in the past; 穿着古裝的演員; *Scotsmen in Highland ~,* wearing the kilt, etc; 穿着蘇格蘭高地服裝(如褶疊短裙等)的蘇格蘭男子; *a ˈ~ piece/play,* one in which the actors wear historical ~. 古裝劇。**ˈ~ jewellery,** artificial jewellery. 戲裝用的珠寶;假珠寶。 **2** [C] (dated) woman's suit (short coat and skirt of the same material). (過時用語)女裝;女服(西裝式短上衣及裙子,上下係同一布料)。⇨ bathing. **cos·tumier** /kɒˈstjuːmɪə(r) *US:* -ˈstuː- ; kɑsˈtjumɪɚ/ *n* maker of, dealer in, ~s. 女裝商人(製作或販賣女裝者)。

cosy¹ /ˈkəʊzɪ ; ˈkozɪ/ *adj* (-ier, -iest) warm and comfortable: 溫暖而舒適的;安逸的: *a ~ little room.* 溫暖而舒適的小房間。**cosi·ly** *adv* **cosi·ness** *n*

cosy² /ˈkəʊzɪ ; ˈkozɪ/ *n* covering for a teapot, or an egg in an egg-cup. (茶壺或盛煮蛋的蛋杯的)暖蓋。

cot¹ /kɒt ; kɑt/ *n* **1** small, narrow, easily moved bed; bed for a young child (usu with sides to prevent the child from falling out) (US 美 = *crib*). 狹小而容易移動的床;小兒床(通常設有欄杆以防小兒跌出)。 **2** (US) camp bed; bunk bed on board ship. (美)(可摺叠而便於攜帶的)行軍床;(船上的)床鋪。

cot² /kɒt ; kɑt/ *n* **1** small building for sheltering animals: (養牲畜的)小棚;圈: *a sheep-cot.* 羊圈。 **2** (poet) cottage. (詩)茅舍;小屋。

cote /kəʊt ; kot/ *n* shed or shelter for domestic animals or birds: (養牲畜及家禽的)棚;圈;欄: *a ˈdove-~;* 鴿棚; *a ˈsheep-~.* 羊圈。

co-ten·ant /ˌkəʊ ˈtenənt ; koˈtɛnənt/ *n* joint tenant. 共同租地人;共同佃戶;合租人。

co·terie /ˈkəʊtərɪ ; ˈkotərɪ/ *n* group of persons associated by common interests, tastes, etc, esp one that tends to be exclusive: 由於共同興趣、嗜好等所形成的小集團(尤指有排他性者): *a literary ~.* 文人之小集團。

co·termi·nous /ˌkəʊˈtɜːmɪnəs ; koˈtɝmənəs/ *adj* having a common terminus or boundary. 共終點

的;共邊界的;毗連的;隣接的。

co·til·lion, co·til·ion /kəˈtɪlɪən ; koˈtɪljən/ *n* name of several kinds of lively French dance originated in the 18th c; music for these. 高替洋舞(源於十八世紀的數種活潑的法國舞);高替洋舞曲。

cot·tage /ˈkɒtɪdʒ ; ˈkatɪdʒ/ *n* small house, esp in the country: 茅舍;村舍;農舍: *farm labourers' ~s;* 農舍; house at a summer resort. (避暑勝地的)別墅。 **~ cheese**, soft, white kind, made from curds. (由凝乳製成的)鬆軟白乾酪。 **~ industry**, one that can be carried on in ~s, eg knitting, pottery, some kinds of weaving. 鄉村工藝(可在農舍裏做的手工,如編織、製陶器、某些種紡織)。

cot·tar, cot·ter /ˈkɒtə(r) ; ˈkatɚ/ *n* (Scot) man living in a cottage on a farm and working on the farm. (蘇)農事工人或佃農(住在農舍裏,在農場上工作)。

cot·ton /ˈkɒtn ; ˈkatn̩/ *n* [U] **1** soft, white fibrous substance round the seeds of the **ˈ~-plant,** used for making thread, cloth, etc: 棉花(棉花子周圍之柔軟的白色纖維物質,用以紡紗織布等): (attrib) (形容用法) *~ yarn;* 棉紗; *~ cloth;* 棉布; *~ goods.* 棉織品 **2** thread spun from ~ yarn: 棉線: *a ˌneedle and ˈ~.* 一根穿有棉線的針。 **ˈ~ batting** *n* (US) cotton-wool. (美)棉花;脫脂棉。 **ˈ~-cake,** cattle food made by pressing out oil from seeds of the ~-plant. 棉子餅(由棉子榨出其中之油壓成之,作牲畜飼料)。 **ˌ~ seed ˈoil,** oil obtained from ~ seed. 棉子油(由棉子中提取之油)。 **ˈ~-tail** *n* (US) rabbit. (美)家兔。 **ˌ~-ˈwool,** (GB) cleaned raw ~ or natural ~; absorbent ~ as used for padding, bandaging, etc. (英)棉花;原棉;生棉;脫脂棉(用作塡料、敷料等)。 □ *vi* **~ up (to),** (dated sl) make friendly advances (to). (過時俚語)(向…)親近;巴結。 **~ on (to),** (sl) understand. (俚)懂得。

a cotton-plant

coty·ledon /ˌkɒtɪˈliːdn ; ˌkatl̩ˈidn̩/ *n* (bot) first leaf growing from a seed. (植物)子葉(最初自種子中長出的葉)。

couch¹ /kaʊtʃ ; kaʊtʃ/ *n* **1** (liter) bed: (文)床;榻: *retire to one's ~.* 就寢。 **2** long bed-like seat for sitting on or lying on during the day: 長沙發(供晝間坐臥,似床之長椅): *studio-~.* 可以拉開來成爲整張床的長沙發。

couch² /kaʊtʃ ; kaʊtʃ/ *vt, vi* **1** [VP6A, 14] **~ (in),** (formal) put (a thought, etc, in words): (正式用語)措辭;(以話語或文字)表達(思想等): *The reply was ~ed in insolent terms.* 回答措辭蠻悍。 **2** [VP2A] (of animals) lie flat (either in hiding, or ready for a jump forward): (指動物)俯臥;蹲伏(或爲躲藏,或準備向前跳): *a deer ~ed on a grassy bank.* 蹲伏在草堤上的一隻鹿。 **3** [VP6A] lower (a spear or lance) to the position for attack. 平執;平握(槍矛等,作攻擊姿勢)。 **4** (*pp* only; liter or poet) reclining (as if) on a couch¹: (僅用過去分詞,文或詩)俯臥的: *~ed in slumber.* 俯臥而眠。

couch³, couch-grass /ˈkaʊtʃ (grɑːs *US:* græs) ; ˈkaʊtʃ (græs)/ *n* [U] kind of grass with long creeping roots. 茅草(生蔓延的長根)。

couch·ant /ˈkaʊtʃənt ; ˈkaʊtʃənt/ *adj* (heraldry, of animals in a coat of arms, etc) lying with the body resting on the legs and the head raised. (紋章,指盾形徽章等上的動物圖形)身體臥於四肢上而頭抬起的;昂首蹲伏的。

cou·chette /kuːˈʃet ; kaʊˈtʃɛt/ *n* (F) sleeping berth (in a railway compartment). (法)(火車上的)臥鋪。

cou·gar /ˈkuːgə(r) ; ˈkugɚ/ *n* large wild cat, also called a *puma.* 美洲豹(亦稱作 puma)。 ⇨ the illus at cat. 參看 cat 之插圖。

cough¹ /kɒf *US:* kɔːf ; kɔf/ *vi, vt* [VP2A, 15B] send out air from the lungs violently and noisily. 咳嗽。 **~ sb down,** (of an audience) prevent him by ~ing, from being heard. (指聽衆)以咳嗽的方式使演說者的話不被聽到。 **~ sth up,** get it out of the throat by ~ing; (fig, sl) say, produce (it) reluctantly. 咳出;(喻,俚)勉强說出某事;勉强交出或提出某物。

cough² /kɒf *US:* kɔːf ; kɔf/ *n* **1** act or sound of coughing: 咳嗽;咳嗽聲: *He gave me a warning ~.* 他以咳嗽警告我。 **2** condition, illness, that causes a person to cough often: 咳嗽病: *to have a bad ~;* 咳嗽得很厲害; *ˈ~-drop, ˈ~-lozenge,* taken to relieve a ~. 止咳藥片。

could /kʊd ; kʊd/, *weak form* /kəd ; kəd/ (neg 否定式 couldn't /ˈkʊdnt ; ˈkʊdn̩t/) *anom fin* 變則定動詞 *pt* of *can,* used in indirect speech in place of *can* if the main verb is *pt;* to express conditions, and to express occasional occurrence and inclination. can 之過去式,用於間接引用語中以代替 can, 假如其主要動詞爲過去式;亦可表示條件,以及偶然發生的事情和意向。 ⇨ can.

couldst /kʊdst ; kʊdst/ old form of *could,* used with *thou.* could 之古體,與 thou 連用。

coul·ter (US = **col·ter**) /ˈkəʊltə(r) ; ˈkoltɚ/ *n* iron blade fixed vertically in front of a plough share (to cut the soil before it is lifted and turned by the share). 犂頭鐵;犂刀(垂直裝於犂之前端以切入泥土而翻轉之)。

coun·cil /ˈkaʊnsl ; ˈkaʊnsl̩/ *n* group of persons appointed, elected or chosen to give advice, make rules, and carry out plans, manage affairs, etc, esp of government: 議會;政務會(由委派或選舉之議員組成,其任務爲提供意見、制定規章、實行計畫、處理公務等);會議: *a city/county ~;* 市(郡)議會; *the municipal ~;* 市議會; *to be/to meet in ~;* 舉行會議; *the C~ of the Republic,* upper house in the French legislature; 法國議會中的上議院; *a ~ of war,* assembly of officers called by the Commander-in-Chief, etc; (由總司令等所召集的)軍事會議;作戰會議; *the Privy C~.* 英國樞密院。 **ˈ~-board,** table at which members of a ~ sit. 會議桌。 **ˈ~-chamber,** in which a ~ meets. 會議室。 **ˈ~ estate,** housing estate built by a city, county, etc ~. 市(郡等)議會所建的房產。 ⇨ housing. **ˈ~ flat/house,** flat/house in a ~ estate. 議會所建的公寓(房屋)。

coun·cil·lor (US also **coun·cil·or**) /ˈkaʊnsələ(r) ; ˈkaʊnsl̩ɚ/ *n* member of a council. 議會議員。

coun·sel¹ /ˈkaʊnsl ; ˈkaʊnsl̩/ *n* **1** [U] (formal) advice; consultation; opinions; suggestions. (正式用語)勸告; 忠告; 意見; 建議。 **keep one's own ~,** keep one's views, plans, etc secret. 對於自已的意見、計畫等保守秘密。 **hold/take ~ with sb,** consult him. 聽取某人的意見;與…商量。 **take ~ together,** consult together. 共同商議。 **2** (with *indef art* or in *pl* but not with numerals): (與不定冠詞連用或用複數,但不與數字連用): *a ~/~s of perfection,* excellent advice that cannot be followed. 不能實現的理想建議。 **3** (*pl* unchanged) barrister, or group of barristers, giving advice in a law case: (複數不變)辯護律師;法律顧問: *when the jury had heard ~ on both sides,* the barristers for the prosecution and the defence. 當陪審團聽過了原告及被告雙方律師之辯護以後。 **ˌQueen's/ˌKing's ˈC~,** (abbr to 略作 **QC/KC**) barrister appointed to act for the State, higher in authority than other barristers. 王室律師(權位高於其他律師)。

coun·sel² /ˈkaʊnsl ; ˈkaʊnsl̩/ *vt* (-ll-, US also -l-) [VP6A, D, 17] advise; give counsel to: 勸告;向…建議: *to ~ an early start;* 建議早開始; *to ~ patience.*

勸告多忍耐。*Would you ~ our giving up/~ us to give up the plan?* 你會建議我們放棄這計畫嗎？

coun·sel·lor (US also **coun·sel·or**) /ˈkaʊnsələ(r); ˈkaʊnslɚ/ *n* adviser; (in Ireland and US) lawyer. 顧問;參事;(在愛爾蘭及美國)律師。

count¹ /kaʊnt; kaʊnt/ *vt, vi* **1** [VP2A, C, 3A] ~ ***(from) (to),*** say or name (eg the numerals) in order: 按順序數(數目等): *to ~ from 1 to 20.* 從一數到二十。*He can't ~ yet.* 他還不會數數目。**~·able** *adj* that can be ~ed. 可數的;可計算的。 **2** [VP6A] find the total of: 數一數(以便知其總數);計數: *Don't forget to ~ your change.* 不要忘記數一數找給你的零錢。*Have the votes been ~ed yet?* 選票計數了沒有？ **ˈ~·ing-house** *n* building or room where accounts are kept (eg in a bank). 會計室;帳房(例如銀行中者)。 **3** [VP6A, 14, 2A, C] include, be included, in the reckoning: (被)計算在內;在考慮之列: *fifty people, not ~ing the children.* 五十人,兒童不算。*That doesn't ~,* need not be considered or reckoned. 那個不必考慮。 **4** [VP25, 16B] consider (sth or sb) to be: 認(某物或某人)為;視為: *I ~ myself fortunate in being here.* 我能在這裏實在很幸運。*I ~ it a great honour to serve you.* 我認為能為你服務是很大的光榮。*I'm afraid we must ~ him as dead.* 恐怕我們得算他死了。 **5** [VP14, 15B, 3A, 2C] (special uses with *adverbial particles* and *prepositions*): (與副詞接語及介詞連用之特殊用法):

count against sb; ~ (sth) against sb, be considered, consider, to the disadvantage of: 認為(某事物)不利於某人;因(某事物)而低估某人: *His past record ~s against him.* 他以往的紀錄對他不利。*He is young and inexperienced, but please do not ~ that against him.* 他年輕而無經驗,但請不要因此而低估他。

count among sb/sth; ~ sb/st hamong sb/sth, be regarded, regard, as one of: 被認為(視為)…之一: *You ~/You are ~ed among my best friends.* 你可算是我的最好朋友之一。*I no longer ~ him among my friends.* 我不再認為他是我的朋友。

count down, ~ seconds backwards (eg 10, 9, 8, 7...) as when launching a rocket, etc into space. (如發射火箭等進入太空時)倒數秒(例如十、九、八、七…)。Hence, 由此產生, **ˈ~-down** *n*

(not) count for anything/nothing/much/little, (not) be of any/no etc worth or importance: 沒有(無甚)價值或重要性: *Knowledge without common sense ~s for little.* 有知識而無常識則無甚價值。*Such men do not ~ for anything.* 這種人無足輕重。

count sb/sth in, include: 包括;計及: *Go and see how many plates we have—but don't ~ in the cracked ones.* 去看看我們有多少個盤子——但不要算有裂紋的。*If you're all going to the pub for a drink, you can ~ me in,* I will certainly be one of the party. 如果你們全都要去酒館喝酒,把我算在內(我一定也要參加)。

count on/upon sb/sth, expect with confidence; rely upon: 指望;仰賴;依賴: *We ~ on your help/~ on you to help.* 我們仰賴你的幫助。*You had better not ~ on an increase in your salary this year.* 你今年最好不要指望加薪。

count sb/sth out, **(a)** ~ things (slowly), one by one: (慢慢地)一個一個地數東西: *The old lady ~ed out fifteen pence and passed it to the salesgirl.* 那老太婆慢吞吞地、一個一個地數了十五辨士然後交給女店員。**(b)** ~ up to ten over a boxer who has been knocked out: 在被擊倒的拳擊者上面從一數到十;判…被技術擊倒: *The referee ~ed him out in the first round.* 裁判判他在第一回合被技術擊倒。 **(c)** not include: 不包括;不計及: *If it's going to be a rowdy party, ~ me out,* I shall certainly not be there. 如果那是一個吵鬧的聚會,別把我算在內(我不會去)。~ ***the House out,*** (GB, House of Commons) ~ the members present and declare that, because enough members are not present, there must be an adjournment. (英國下議院)因清點出席人數不足而宣布延會。

count sth up, find the total of: 算出總數: *Just you ~ up the number of times he has failed to keep a promise!* 你算算看他總共失信多少次了！

count² /kaʊnt; kaʊnt/ *n* **1** [C] act of counting; number got by counting: 計算;計數;得數: *Four ~s were necessary before we were certain of the total.* 要計算四次,我們對於總和才有把握。***keep/lose ~ (of),*** be aware/fail to know how many there are (of): 曉得(不曉得)共有多少: *I've bought so many new books this year that I've lost ~ of them.* 我今年買的新書多得算不清。***take the ~; be out for the ~,*** (boxing) be counted out. (拳擊)被判被技術擊倒;被判失敗。⇨ count¹(5). **2** [U] account(7); notice (the more usu words): 重視;注意;顧慮 (account 及 notice 較常用): *to take no/some/any/not much, etc ~ of what people say.* 不(有一點,不太等)顧慮別人說什麼。 **3** [C] (legal) one of a number of things of which a person has been accused: (法律)被控告的各點之一;被控事項: *He was found guilty on all ~s.* 他被控各點均經認定有罪。

count³ /kaʊnt; kaʊnt/ *n* title of nobility in France, Italy, etc (but not in GB). 伯爵(貴族的頭銜,用於法、義等國,但不用於英國)。⇨ countess, earl.

coun·ten·ance¹ /ˈkaʊntɪnəns; ˈkaʊntənəns/ *n* (formal) (正式用語) **1** face, including its appearance and expression: 面容;面色: *a woman with a fierce ~;* 面目猙獰的女人; *to change ~,* change one's expression because of emotion. (因為情緒的關係而)改變面色。***keep one's ~,*** maintain one's composure (esp by not laughing). 保持鎮靜;不動聲色(尤指忍住不笑)。***put/stare sb out of ~,*** disconcert him, cause him to feel troubled or at fault (by looking at him steadily). (凝視某人)使侷促不安;使感到苦惱或茫然。 **2** [U] support; approval: 支持;贊成;鼓勵: *to give ~ to a person/a plan.* 支持某人(計畫)。

coun·ten·ance² /ˈkaʊntɪnəns; ˈkaʊntənəns/ *vt* [VP6A] give support or approval to: 支持;贊助;鼓勵: *to ~ a fraud.* 鼓勵欺騙。*We can never ~ a war of aggression.* 我們決不可鼓勵侵略戰爭。

counter¹ /ˈkaʊntə(r); ˈkaʊntɚ/ *n* table or flat surface on which goods are shown, customers served, in a shop or bank. (商店、銀行的)櫃臺。***under the ~,*** (of goods in shops) bought or sold surreptitiously, eg when they are scarce and difficult to obtain. (指商店中的貨物)暗中買賣的(如當缺貨不易購得時)。

counter² /ˈkaʊntə(r); ˈkaʊntɚ/ *n* **1** small (usu round) flat piece of metal, plastic, etc used for keeping count in games, etc; piece used in draughts(6), etc. 遊戲、牌戲等中用以記分的籌碼(通常為扁平之小圓形物,用金屬、塑膠等製成);(西洋象棋等中所用的)棋子。 **2** (in compounds) device for keeping count (in machinery, etc): (用於複合字中)機器等中的計算器;計數器: *ˈspeed-~;* 計速器; *ˌrevoˈlution-~.* 轉數器。

counter³ /ˈkaʊntə(r); ˈkaʊntɚ/ *adv* ~ ***to,*** contrary; in the opposite direction; in opposition: (與…)相反;(與…)方向相反;反對: *to act ~ to a person's wishes;* 違背某人的意願而行事; *requirements that run/go ~ to one's inclinations.* 與某人意向不合的要求。

counter⁴ /ˈkaʊntə(r); ˈkaʊntɚ/ *vt, vi* [VP6A, 14, 2A, 3A] ~ ***(with),*** oppose; meet an attack (with a return attack): 反對;反擊;還擊: *They ~ed our proposal with one of their own.* 他們提出一項建議以對抗我們的建議。*The champion ~ed with the right,* (boxing) parried a blow and returned it with a right-handed blow. (拳擊)衛冕者閃過一拳並還以右拳。

counter- /ˌkaʊntə(r); ˌkaʊntɚ/ *pref* **1** opposite in direction: 方向相反: *~-attraction;* 反引力; *~-productive.* 反生產的。 **2** made in answer to: 反還: *ˈ~-attack;* 反攻;反擊;還擊; *ˌ~-ˈespionage/-inˈtelligence.* 反間諜(情報)。 **3** corresponding: 對當的: *ˈ~part.* 互相對當的人或物;對手。

counter·act /ˌkaʊntərˈækt; ˌkaʊntɚˈækt/ *vt* [VP

6A] act against and make (action, force) of less or no effect: 抵消;抵抗;減少或消解(作用、力量): ~ *(the effects of) a poison/sb's bad influence.* 抵消毒物的作用 (某人之惡劣影響)。 **counter·action** /ˌkauntərˈækʃn ; ˌkauntɚˈækʃən/ *n* ~ing. 抵消;消解;反作用。

counter-at·tack /ˈkauntər ətæk ; ˈkauntərəˌtæk/ *n* attack made in reply to an attack by the enemy. 反攻;反擊: □ *vt, vi* make a. ~ (on). 反攻;反擊。

counter-at·trac·tion /ˌkauntər əˈtrækʃn ; ˌkauntərəˈtrækʃən/ *n* [C] rival attraction. 反引力。

counter·bal·ance /ˈkauntəˌbæləns; ˈkauntɚˌbæləns/ *n* [C] weight, force, equal to another and balancing it. (與另一重物或力量相等而與之平衡的)衡重體;平衡錘;平衡力。 □ *vt* /ˌkauntəˈbæləns ; ˌkauntɚˈbæləns/ [VP6A] act as a ~ to. 與…平衡;使平衡。

counter·blast /ˈkauntəblɑːst *US:* -blæst ; ˈkauntɚˌblæst/ *n* [C] violent reply. 猛烈的反擊;强硬的反駁。

counter·claim /ˈkauntəkleɪm ; ˈkauntɚˌklem/ *n* claim made in opposition to another claim: 反要求;反訴: *a ~ for damages,* by a defendant in a lawsuit. (訟案中之被告)反訴要求賠償損失。

counter-clock·wise /ˌkauntəˈklɒkwaɪz ; ˌkauntɚˈklɑkˌwaɪz/ *adv* = anti-clockwise (the more usu word). (anti-clockwise 較常用)。

counter-espion·age /ˌkauntərˈespɪənɑːʒ ; ˌkauntɚˈɛspɪənɪdʒ/ *n* [U] spying directed against the enemy's spying. 反間諜活動。

counter·feit /ˈkauntəfɪt ; ˈkauntɚfɪt/ *n, adj* (sth) made or done in imitation of another thing in order to deceive: 僞造的;仿造的;假裝的;贋品;僞造物: *~ money/jewels/grief.* 僞造錢幣(仿造珠寶;假裝悲傷)。 *This ten-dollar bill is a ~.* 這張十元券是僞鈔。 □ *vt* [VP6A] copy, imitate (coins, handwriting, etc) in order to deceive. 僞造;仿造(錢幣、筆跡等)。 **~er** *n* person who ~s. 僞造者;仿造者。

counter·foil /ˈkauntəfɔɪl ; ˈkauntɚˌfɔɪl/ *n* section of a cheque, receipt, etc kept by the sender as a record. (支票、收據等的)存根。 ⇨ stub(2).

counter-in·tel·li·gence /ˌkauntər ɪnˈtelɪdʒəns ; ˌkauntərɪnˈtɛlədʒəns/ *n* [U] =counter-espionage.

counter-ir·ri·tant /ˌkauntərˈɪrɪtənt ; ˌkauntɚˈɪrətənt/ *n* sth used to produce a surface irritation and in this way relieve a more deeply seated pain, eg rheumatism. 對抗刺激劑 (用以產生表層刺激之藥物,以減輕部位較深之痛楚,如風濕痛)。

counter·mand /ˌkauntəˈmɑːnd *US:* -ˈmænd ; ˌkauntɚˈmænd/ *vt* [VP6A] take back, cancel, a command already given. 撤回或取消(已發出之命令)。

counter·mine /ˈkauntəmaɪn ; ˈkauntɚˌmaɪn/ *n* (in war) mine (on land or sea) to counteract one of the enemy's; (fig) counterplot. (戰爭中)(佈於陸上或水中以使敵方所佈者先行爆發之) 反雷; 誘發地雷; 誘發水雷; (喻)反計;對抗策略。□ *vt, vi* oppose by ~s; make a ~. 以反佈雷抵抗;反佈雷。

counter·offer /ˈkauntərɒfə(r) ; ˈkauntɚˌɑfɚ/ *n* offer made in reply to an offer made by sb else. 反報價;還價。

counter·pane /ˈkauntəpeɪn ; ˈkauntɚˌpen/ *n* covering for a bed; bedspread. 床罩;床單。

counter·part /ˈkauntəpɑːt ; ˈkauntɚˌpɑrt/ *n* person or thing exactly like, or closely corresponding to, another. 與另一個完全相似或極爲相當的人或物;互相對當的人或物;配對者;對方;相對物。

counter·plot /ˈkauntəplɒt ; ˈkauntɚˌplɑt/ *n* plot made to defeat another plot. 反計(用以對付另一計謀之計謀);對抗策略。□ *vt, vi* (-tt-) make a ~ (against). 用反計(對抗);將計就計。

counter·point /ˈkauntəpɔɪnt ; ˈkauntɚˌpɔɪnt/ *n* (music) (音樂) **1** [C] melody added as an accompaniment to another melody. 對位;配合另一旋律之旋律。 **2** [U] art or method of adding melodies as accompaniment according to fixed rules. 對位法;旋律配合法。

counter·poise /ˈkauntəpɔɪz ; ˈkauntɚˌpɔɪz/ *n* **1** [C] weight used to balance another weight; force, power or influence that counterbalances another. 用以平衡另一重物之重物;秤錘;砝碼;平衡力;均衡力。 **2** [U] the condition of being in balance; equilibrium. 平衡;均衡。□ *vt* bring into, keep in, equilibrium. 使平衡;保持平衡。

counter-rev·ol·ution /ˌkauntəˌrevəˈluːʃn ; ˌkauntɚˌrɛvəˈluʃən/ *n* [U, C] political movement directed against a revolution. 反革命(對抗一項革命的政治運動)。 **~·ary** /-ˈluːʃənərɪ *US:* -nerɪ ; -ˈluʃənˌɛrɪ/ *adj* characteristic of a ~. 反革命的。 ▭ *n* (*pl* -ries) person engaged in ~(s). 從事反革命的人;反革命分子;反動分子。

counter·sign /ˈkauntəsaɪn ; ˈkauntɚˌsaɪn/ *n* [C] password; secret word(s) to be given, on demand, to a sentry before he allows sb to pass: 口令;答令(對答哨兵以便通過之暗語): *'Advance and give the ~'.* '向前來說出口令'。 □ *vt* [VP6A] add another signature to (a document) to give it authority. 加另一簽字於(文件)上以加强其效力;連署;副署;會簽。

counter·sink /ˈkauntəsɪŋk ; ˈkauntɚˌsɪŋk/ *vt* (*pt* -sank /-sæŋk ; -ˌsæŋk/, *pp* -sunk /-sʌŋk ; -ˌsʌŋk/) **1** enlarge the top of (a hole) so that the head of a screw or bolt fits in level with or below the surface. 加大 (孔洞) 的頂端以便螺絲釘或螺栓頭旋入而與表面平齊或低於表面; 鑽大(孔口)。 **2** sink (the head of a screw or bolt) in such an enlarged hole. 將(螺絲釘或螺栓頭)旋入此種加大之孔中。

counter·tenor /ˌkauntəˈtenə(r) ; ˌkauntɚˈtɛnɚ/ *n* (music) (part for an) (adult person with a) male voice higher than tenor; male alto. (音樂)上次中音(成人男聲之最高者);樂譜中的上次中音部;唱上次中音者。

counter·vail /ˈkauntəveɪl ; ˌkauntɚˈvel/ *vt, vi* **1** [VP6A] counterbalance. 使平衡。 **2** [VP2A] have equal or compensating power against: 抵銷;補償: *~ing duties*(3), to be paid (as part of a tariff) on imports on which a subsidy is paid in the exporting country. (對有出口津貼的進口貨所征收的)抵銷關稅。

count·ess /ˈkauntɪs ; ˈkauntɪs/ *n* wife or widow of a count or earl; woman to whom an earldom has descended. 伯爵夫人;女伯爵。

count·less /ˈkauntləs ; ˈkauntlɪs/ *adj* that cannot be counted (because too numerous). (因太多而)不能數的;無數的;數不盡的。

coun·tri·fied /ˈkʌntrɪfaɪd ; ˈkʌntrɪˌfaɪd/ *adj* rural; rustic; having the unsophisticated ways, habits, outlook, etc, of those who live in the country(4), not of towns. 鄉村的;有鄉村特色的;有鄉下人之單純方式、習慣、見解等的;純樸的;土氣的。

coun·try /ˈkʌntrɪ ; ˈkʌntrɪ/ *n* (*pl* -ries) **1** [C] land occupied by a nation: 國家;國土: *European countries.* 歐洲國家。 **2** [C] land of a person's birth or citizenship: 故鄉;祖國: *to return to one's own ~.* 返回故鄉。 **3** **the ~,** the people of a ~(1); the nation as a whole: 一國的人民; 全國: *Does the ~ want war?* 全體國人都要戰爭嗎? ***go to the ~,*** (GB) appeal to the public by a general election for the right to form a government(3). (英)舉行大選(要求全民普選以決定組閣之權)。 **4** **the ~,** land used for farming, land consisting of open spaces, etc; the contrary of town and suburb: 鄉間; 田野; 鄉野(與城市及城郊相對): *to live in the ~;* 居住於鄉間; *to spend a day in the ~.* 在鄉間度過一日。 **5** (used attrib) of or in the ~(4): (形容用法)鄉間的;鄉下的: *~ life;* 鄉間生活; *~ roads.* 鄉下的路。 **~ club,** club in the ~ or suburbs, where members may enjoy outdoor sports, etc. 鄉村俱樂部(會員可在此享受戶外運動等)。 **~ cousin,** (colloq) person who is unaccustomed to town life and ways. (俗) (不慣城市生活的)鄉巴佬; 鄉下老表。 **~ dance,** (esp GB) one in which couples are face to face in two long lines or face inwards from four sides. (尤指英國的)土風舞(由男女面對面排成兩長排或面向內排成四邊形而舞之)。 **~ gentleman,** man who owns land in the ~ and has a house there. 鄉紳(在鄉間擁有田地房產之人)。**~-house, ~-seat,** house of a ~ gentleman. 鄉紳的住宅;莊園。'**~ party,** political party supporting agricultural interests (against manufacturing interests). 農民黨(支持農民利益以對抗實業利益的政黨)。 **6** [U] (with attrib *adj*) area of land (esp considered with reference to its physical or geographical features): (與屬性形容詞連用)(帶有某種地形或地理特點的)曠野;地域;地帶: *We passed through miles of densely wooded ~.* 我們經過了許多哩茂密的森林地帶。*This is unknown ~ to me,* I have not been through it before (or, fig, This is a branch of learning, etc with which I am unfamiliar). 這地方我未曾到過;(或作喻)這門學問我不懂。

coun·try·man /'kʌntrɪmən ; 'kʌntrɪmən/, **coun·try·woman** /'kʌntrɪwʊmən ; 'kʌntrɪ,wʊmən/ *n* (*pl* -men, -women) **1** person living in the country(4). 鄉下人;鄉下女人。 **2** person of one's own (or a specified) country(1). 同國人;同胞;某國人。

coun·try·side /'kʌntrɪsaɪd ; 'kʌntrɪ,saɪd/ *n* [U] rural area(s) (contrasted with urban areas): 鄉村地區;鄉間(與市區相對): *The English ~ looks its best in May and June.* 英國的鄉村在五、六月間景色最美。*The preservation of the ~ is important.* 鄉村地區的保護是重要的。

county /'kaʊntɪ ; 'kaʊntɪ/ *n* **1** [C] division of GB, the largest unit of local government: 郡;州(英國的最大地方行政區域): *the ~ of Kent.* 肯特郡。**~ borough,** town having the right to send one or more representatives to Parliament and administrative powers similar to those of a ~ council. 行政自治市(有權自行選出一位或更多國會議員之城市,其行政權同郡議會)。 **~ council,** body of persons elected to govern a ~. 郡議會。**~ court,** local court for certain legal matters, eg recovery of debt. 郡法院(審判某些法律案件,如債務,之地方法院)。 **~ family,** family that has lived in a ~ for many generations and has an ancestral home in it. 郡中世家(許多代居於某郡內並有祖居在該郡的家族)。 **~ town,** (US 美 = ~ *seat*) chief town of a ~, where administration is carried on. 郡的首邑(郡政府所在地)。 **the home counties,** those round London. 倫敦四周的數郡。 **the ~,** (with *sing* or *pl v*) all the ~ families. (接單數或複數動詞)所有的郡中世家。 **2** (in US and other countries) subdivision of a State. (美國及其他國家之)郡;縣(州之下的行政區分)。 **3** (GB; pred use) of a ~ family: (英;敘述用法) 郡中世家的: *Are you ~?* 你世代都居於郡中嗎?

coup /ku: ; ku/ *n* (*pl* -s /ku:z ; kuz/) (F) sudden action taken to get power, obtain a desired result, etc: (法)(爲獲得權力、達到欲求的目的等所採取的)突然行動;猝然一擊;奇襲妙計: *He pulled off/made a great ~,* succeeded in what he attempted. 他大爲(一舉)成功。 **~ d'état** /ˌku: deɪ'tɑ: ; 'kude'tɑ/, violent or unconstitutional change in government. 政變(以暴力或不合憲法方式的改變政權)。**~ de grâce** /ˌku:də'grɑ:s *US:* 'græs ; kudə'grɑ:s/, finishing stroke. 最後(致命的)一擊。

coupé /'ku:peɪ *US:* ku:'peɪ ; ku'pe/ *n* (*pl* ~s /-peɪz ; -'pez/) **1** closed horse-drawn carriage with one inside seat for two people and an outside seat for the driver. 一種有篷的馬車(篷內一個座位可坐兩人,篷外有車夫座)。 **2** (US **coupe** /ku:p ; kup/) two-door motor-car for two people. (可容兩人之)雙門小轎車。

couple¹ /'kʌpl ; 'kʌpl̩/ *n* two persons or things, seen together or associated: 一對;一雙(在一起或互有關係的兩個人或物): *married ~s;* 夫婦; *courting ~s.* 對對情侶。*Ten ~s took the floor,* went out into the middle of the room to dance. 有十對下池跳舞。*He went out shooting and came back with a ~ of rabbits.* 他出去打獵,獵獲幾隻兔子回來。

couple² /'kʌpl ; 'kʌpl̩/ *vt, vi* **1** [VP6A, 14] fasten, join (two things) together: 連合或連接(二物): *to ~ two railway coaches.* 連接二節火車客車廂。 *The dining-car was ~d on at Crewe.* 餐車是在克魯掛上的。 *We ~ the name of Oxford with the idea of learning.* 我們將牛津之名與學術的觀念聯在一起。 **2** [VP6A, 2A] marry; [VP2A] (of animals) unite sexually; [VP2A] (of things) come together; unite. (和…)結婚;(指動物)交配;(指事物)關聯;聯合。

coup·let /'kʌplɪt ; 'kʌplɪt/ *n* two successive lines of verse, equal in length and with rhyme: 相連、同長度並押韻的兩行詩句; 對句: *a heroic ~,* with lines of five feet¹(6) and ten syllables. 英雄雙行體(每行各五音步十音節)。

coup·ling /'kʌplɪŋ ; 'kʌplɪŋ/ *n* [U] act of joining; [C] link, etc that joins two parts, esp two railway coaches or other vehicles. 連合;結合;接連;聯接器;耦合管;接箍;(尤指火車車廂或其他車輛的)掛鈎;車鈎。

cou·pon /'ku:pɒn ; 'kupɑn/ *n* ticket, part of a document, paper, bond, etc, which gives the holder the right to receive sth or do sth, eg a voucher given with a purchase to be exchanged for goods; entry form for a competition: 證明持有人有某種權利的卡片、條子、票、劵等(例如購物時所附贈以交換贈品的贈劵);參與競爭的登記單: *fill in the football ~s,* by forecasting results of matches. 填寫足球賽門票的附單(以預測比賽的結果)。

cour·age /'kʌrɪdʒ ; 'kɝɪdʒ/ *n* [U] bravery; quality that enables a person to control fear in the face of danger, pain, misfortune, etc. 勇敢;勇氣(使人能在危險、痛楚、不幸等之中有克制恐懼的精神力量): ***have the ~ of one's convictions,*** be brave enough to do what one feels to be right. 有勇氣去做自己認爲對的事。***not have the ~ (to do sth),*** not be brave enough. 沒勇氣…。***lose ~,*** become less brave. 失去勇氣。 ***take/pluck up/muster up/summon up ~,*** be brave. 鼓起勇氣。***take one's ~ in both hands,*** summon up one's ~ for sth needing to be done. 鼓起勇氣(做必須做的事)。

cou·rageous /kə'reɪdʒəs ; kə'redʒəs/ *adj* brave; fearless: 勇敢的;英勇的;無畏的: *It was ~ of him to oppose his chief.* 他敢反對他的上司,眞是勇敢。**~·ly** *adv*

cour·gette /kʊə'ʒet ; kʊr'ʒet/ *n* (US 美 = *zucchini*) small green marrow(3) eaten as a vegetable. 小胡瓜(作蔬菜食用的一種小而綠色的葫蘆科植物)。⇨ the illus at vegetable. 參看 vegetable 之插圖。

cour·ier /'kʊrɪə(r) ; 'kʊrɪɚ/ *n* **1** person who is paid to attend to details of travel (eg buying tickets, arranging for hotels, etc) and (sometimes) accompanying travellers. (受僱照料旅行事務如買票、訂旅館等,有時並陪伴旅客的)旅遊服務員。 **2** messenger carrying news or important government papers. 遞送新聞或重要官署文件的信差。

course¹ /kɔ:s ; kors/ *n* **1** [U] forward movement in space or time: (空間或時間的)前進;進行: *the ~ of life from the cradle to the grave;* 人生自搖籃至墓穴的旅程;從出生到死亡的人生旅程; *a river in its ~ to the sea;* 流向大海的河; *the ~ of events.* 世事的發展。 ***in ~ of,*** in process of: 在…過程中: *The railway is in ~ of construction,* being built. 鐵路正在修築中。 ***in due ~,*** in the natural order; at the normal time: 照自然的順序; 到適當的時候: *Sow the seed now and in due ~ you will have the flowers.* 現在就播種,到時候你就會有花。 ***in the ~ of,*** during: 在…期間: *in the ~ of the discussion;* 在討論期間; *in the ~ of conversation,* while we were talking; 在談話中; *in the ~ of centuries,* as the centuries pass. 經過數百年的期間。***in the (ordinary) ~ of nature/events/things,*** normally; as part of the normal or expected sequence of events. 照正常的情形; 依自然發展的常理。 ***in (the) ~ of time,*** at length; finally; when (enough) time has passed. 終於; 最後;總有一天。 **2** [C] direction taken by sth; line along which sth moves; line of action: (某事物的)進行方向; 所經之路; 行動方針: *a map that shows the ~s of the chief rivers;* 示明主要河流所經過之區域的地圖; (liter) (文) *the stars in their ~s.* 沿着軌道運行的星辰。*Our ~ was due north.* 我們的路線是向

正北。*The ~ of the argument suddenly changed,* went in a different direction. 辯論的方向忽然改變了。*What are the ~s open to us,* the ways in which we may proceed to act? 我們有些什麼路可走(即有些什麼辦法可以採取)? *He took to evil ~s,* formed bad ways of living. 他自甘墮落(耽於放蕩的生活)。***run/take its ~,*** develop as is normal; proceed to the usual end: 聽其自然發展;進行到通常的結局為止: *The disease must run its ~.* 這病一定要完全發作過後才會好。*The law must take its ~,* the lawyers cannot save you from punishment. 法律必循其道(律師也無法救你使你免於受罰)。*We can do nothing except let matters run/take their ~.* 我們除了一切聽其自然之外別無辦法。***(as) a matter of ~,*** (in) a way that one would expect to be or happen, for which no effort is needed: 當然之事;自然之事(如所預料必然發生而不需費力的事): *You needn't ask him to come; he'll come as a matter of ~.* 你不需要請求他來;他自然會來。*Some people take my help as a matter of ~,* expect to get it without asking for it (or even thanking me for it). 有些人把我對他們的幫助視為當然之事(認為他們不必要求我也應該幫助他們,甚至連謝也不謝)。***of ~,*** naturally; certainly: 自然;當然: *'Do you study hard?' 'Of ~ I do'.* '你用功讀書嗎?' '我當然用功。' ***on/off ~,*** in the right/wrong direction: 在正確(不正確)方向: *Our ship was blown off ~.* 我們的船被(風)吹離航道。 **3** [C] ground for golf: 高爾夫球場: *a 'golf-~;* 高爾夫球場; place for horse-races: 跑馬場: *a 'race-~.* 跑馬場。***stay the ~,*** (lit, fig) continue going until the end; not give up. (字面,喻)繼續進行至結局為止;貫徹到底;不放棄。 **4** [C] series of talks, treatments, etc: (談話、治療等的)一連串;連續: *a ~ of lectures/study/instruction;* 連續的講演(一門課程;一門教程); *a ~ of X-ray treatment/pills;* 連續的X光治療(藥丸治療); *the high-school ~.* 中學學程。 **5** [C] continuous layer of brick, stone, etc in a wall: (牆壁中磚、石等之連續的)層: *a 'damp~,* layer of slate or other material to prevent damp rising from the ground. (由一層石板或其他材料砌成以防止地上潮氣上升的)防濕層。 **6** [C] one of the several parts of a meal, eg soup, fish, dessert: 一道菜或點心: *a dinner of five ~s/a five-~ dinner;* 五道菜的正餐; *the main ~.* 主菜。 **7** (naut) sail fastened to the lowest yard of a mast. (航海)大橫帆(繫於最低帆桁者)。

course[2] /kɔːs ; kɔrs/ *vt, vi* **1** [VP6A, 2A] chase (esp hares) with dogs (greyhounds). 用獵犬追獵(尤指野兔)。**2** [VP2C] move quickly; (of liquids) run: 急行;(指液體)流動: *The blood ~d through his veins.* 血在他的血管中奔流。*Tears ~d down her cheeks.* 眼淚從她的兩頰流下。**cours·ing** /ˈkɔːsɪŋ ; ˈkorsɪŋ/ *n* sport of chasing hares with greyhounds (by sight, not scent). 用獵犬藉視覺而不藉嗅覺追趕野兔。

courser /ˈkɔːsə(r) ; ˈkorsɚ/ *n* (poet) swift horse. (詩)駿馬。

court[1] /kɔːt ; kɔrt/ *n* **1** [C] place where law-cases are held; the judges, magistrates, and other officers who administer justice: 法院;法庭;執法者(指法官及其他執法官員): *a ˌ~ of ˈlaw/a ˈlaw ~;* 法院; 法庭; *a '~-room;* 法庭; *a ~ of justice;* 法院; *a po'lice-~;* 警務法庭; *a (military or naval) ~ of inquiry,* one that deals with cases of indiscipline, etc. (陸軍或海軍的)偵訊法庭;調查庭(處理違紀等案件)。*The prisoner was brought to ~ for trial.* 那囚犯被提上法庭受審。*The judge ordered the ~ to be cleared,* ordered members of the public to leave. 法官令旁聽的群衆離開法庭。*The case was settled out of ~,* a settlement was reached that made it unnecessary for the case to be decided in ~. 該案在庭外和解(不必再由法庭裁判)。***be ruled/put out of ~; put oneself out of ~,*** do or say sth so that one is not entitled to be heard in ~. 訴訟不被受理;遭駁回。**~ of assize; ~ of quarter sessions,** ~s in England and Wales before 1971. 1971年以前的英格蘭及威爾斯法院。**Crown C~,** (since 1971) one that may sit anywhere in England and Wales for all cases above magistrates' ~ level (replacing the former assize and quarter sessions). 直轄法院(1971年以後取代上述的 ~ of assize 及 ~ of quarter sessions,可在英格蘭及威爾斯之任何地方開庭審判一切案件,權力在地方法院之上)。 **2** [U] residence of a sovereign; his family and officials, councillors, etc: 朝廷;宮廷: *The C~ of St James's,* the ~ of the British sovereign. 英國宮廷。*The C~ went into mourning when the Queen's uncle died.* 當女王的叔父逝世時,王宮服喪。***be presented at ~,*** make one's first appearance at a state reception at the sovereign's ~. 初次入朝覲見帝王;初次受帝王接見。***hold ~,*** ⇨ hold[1](12). **'~-card,** playing card with a king, queen or knave. 繪有王、后或侍衛的紙牌(即撲克牌中的K, Q 或 J)。 **3** [C] space marked out for certain games: 某些遊戲的場地: *a 'tennis-~.* 網球場。*Do you prefer grass ~s or hard ~s?* 你比較喜歡草地球場還是硬地球場? ⇨ the illus at tennis. 參看 tennis 之挿圖。 **4** (also 亦作 **'~·yard**) unroofed space with walls or buildings round it, eg in a college at Cambridge, in a castle or an old inn; the buildings round such a space. (四周由牆壁或建築物圍成的)庭院;大天井(如劍橋大學之學院內、古堡內或古客棧內者);天井周圍的建築物。 Cf 參較 *quadrangle* at Oxford. ⇨ close[3]. **5** [C] small enclosed yard of a house, usu opening off a street. 與街道相通的小院。 **6** [U] ***pay ~ to (a woman),*** (formal) try to win her affections. (正式用語)向女人獻慇懃求愛。

court[2] /kɔːt ; kɔrt/ *vt, vi* **1** [VP6A, 2A] try to win the affections of, with a view to marriage: 向…求愛;追求: *He had been ~ing Jane for six months.* 他追求珍已六個月之久。*There were several ~ing couples in the park.* 公園中有幾對談情說愛的男女。 **2** [VP6A] try to win or obtain: 設法贏得;設法獲得;懇求;乞求: *to ~ sb's approval/support;* 求某人贊成(支持); *to ~ applause.* 設法贏得喝采或稱讚。 **3** [VP 6A] act in such a way that one may meet or receive (sth disagreeable): 招惹;招致(不愉快之事): *to ~ defeat/danger/disaster.* 招致失敗(危險,災禍)。

cour·teous /ˈkɜːtɪəs ; ˈkɝtɪəs/ *adj* having, showing, good manners; polite and kind (*to*). 彬彬有禮的;謙恭的;客氣的(與 to 連用)。**~·ly** *adv*

court·esan /ˌkɔːtɪˈzæn *US:* ˈkɔːtɪzn ; ˈkortəzn/ *n* (in former times, esp in court(2) circles) refined or high-placed prostitute who (because of her beauty, wit, success) could limit the number of men to whom she gave herself. (昔時,尤指王公貴族中之)高雅或高等妓女(因其美色、才智或成就,僅接待少數男人)。

cour·tesy /ˈkɜːtəsɪ ; ˈkɝtəsɪ/ *n* **1** [U] courteous behaviour. 禮貌; 謙恭的態度。 **2** [C] (*pl* -sies) courteous act. 謙恭的行為。 **3 '~ title,** (GB) title of nobility having no legal validity. (英)禮貌上的貴族銜稱(實際上被稱呼者並未擁有該頭銜)。***by ~ of,*** by favour or permission, usu free of charge: 由於…的好意或許可(通常係免費): *a radio programme presented by ~ of....* 由…所提供的廣播節目。

court·ier /ˈkɔːtɪə(r) ; ˈkortɪɚ/ *n* person in attendance at the court of a sovereign: 朝臣(朝廷中的侍臣): *the King and his ~s.* 國王及其朝臣。

court·ly /ˈkɔːtlɪ ; ˈkortlɪ/ *adj* (-ier, -iest) polite and dignified. 謙和而威嚴的。**court·li·ness** *n*

court-mar·tial /ˌkɔːt ˈmɑːʃl ; ˈkortˈmɑrʃəl/ *n* (*pl* courts-martial) court for trying offences against military law; trial by ~. 軍事法庭(審訊違犯軍法案件);軍法審判。 □ *vt* [VP6A] (-ll-) try (sb) in a court of this kind. 在軍事法庭審訊(某人);以軍法審判。

court·ship /ˈkɔːtʃɪp ; ˈkortʃɪp/ *n* courting(1); [C] period during which this lasts: 求愛;追求;追求期間: *after a year's ~;* 經過了一年的追求; *after a brief ~.* 經過短時間的追求。

court·yard /ˈkɔːtjɑːd ; ˈkort,jard/ *n* = court[1](4).

cousin /ˈkʌzn ; ˈkʌzn̩/ *n* **first ~,** child of one's uncle or aunt. 堂兄弟；堂姐妹；表兄弟；表姐妹。**second ~,** child of one's parent's first ~. 遠房堂(表)兄弟姐妹。**~·ly** *adj* of, suitable for, ~s: (適合於)堂(表)兄弟姐妹的: *~ly affection.* 堂(表)兄弟姐妹之親情。

cove[1] /kəʊv ; kov/ *n* small bay[2]. 小海灣。

a cove

cove[2] /kəʊv ; kov/ *n* (GB, dated sl) person. (英，過時俚語)人。

coven /ˈkʌvn ; ˈkʌvən/ *n* assembly of witches. (女巫們的)集會。

cov·en·ant /ˈkʌvənənt ; ˈkʌvənənt/ *n* **1** (legal) formal agreement that is legally binding. (法律)(有法律約束力的正式)合約；契約；盟約。ˌ**deed of ˈ~,** written, signed and sealed agreement, usu concerning property. (經簽字並蓋章，通常爲有關房地產的)契據；契約書。 **2** undertaking to make regular payments to a charity, trust, etc. (爲慈善事業、信託財產等而定期付款的)承諾。□ *vt, vi* [VP6A, 7A, 9, 14, 3A] **~ *(with sb) (for sth),*** make a ~. 訂立契約。

Cov·en·try /ˈkɒvntrɪ ; ˈkɑvəntrɪ/ *n* town in Warwickshire, GB. 科芬特里 (英國瓦立克郡之一鎭)。***send a person to ~,*** refuse to associate with him (esp by not speaking to him). 拒絕與某人交往(尤指不與其交談)。

cover[1] /ˈkʌvə(r) ; ˈkʌvɚ/ *vt* [VP6A, 15A, B] **1** place (one substance or thing) over or in front of (another); hide or protect (sth) in this way; lie or extend over; occupy the surface of: 用東西蓋住；加蓋以藏匿或保護；遮蓋；遮蔽⋯的表面: *C~ the table with a cloth.* 在桌上鋪一塊枱布。 *Pull your skirt down and ~ your knees.* 把你的裙子拉下一點，遮住你的膝蓋。 *We shall ~ the seat of this old chair with chintz.* 我們將用印花布罩住這舊椅子的椅面。 *Snow ~ed the ground.* 雪蓋住地面。*The floods ~ed large areas on both banks of the river.* 洪水淹沒了河兩岸很大的區域。 *She ~ed her face in/with her hands.* 她以雙手掩面。*He laughed to ~* (= hide) *his nervousness.* 他大笑以掩飾其緊張的心情。 ***~ in,*** complete the ~ing of: 完全蓋起: *The grave was quickly ~ed in,* filled with earth. 墓穴很快就被泥土蓋滿。***~ over,*** spread sth over: 蓋住；覆蓋: *to ~ over a hole in a roof.* 蓋住屋頂漏洞。 ***~ up,*** wrap up, hide: 包裹；隱藏: *C~ yourself up well,* Put on warm clothes, etc. 衣服穿暖一點。*How can we ~ up our tracks/our mistakes?* 我們如何能掩藏住我們的踪跡(錯誤)？Hence, 由此產生，**~-up** *n* (fig, colloq) way of hiding: (喻，俗)掩飾或隱藏的方法: *a ~-up for her shyness.* 掩飾她害羞的方法。**~ed wagon** *n* (US) large wagon with an arched canvas roof, used by pioneers for travel across the prairies. (美)大篷車 (昔時拓荒者用以旅行於大草原之上的有弧形遮篷的大車)。 **2** ***be ~ed with,*** **(a)** have a great number or amount of: 有很多的: *trees ~ed with blossom/fruit;* 開滿花 (結滿果實)的樹; *roses ~ed with greenfly.* 生滿綠蚜蟲的玫瑰。**(b)** have as a natural coat: 天然生有(毛皮): *Cats are ~ed with fur and dogs are ~ed with hair.* 貓長着一身細毛，狗長着一身粗毛。**(c)** (of non-material things) be overcome by: (指精神或心靈)爲⋯所克服: *~ed with shame/confusion.* 不勝羞愧(惶惑)。 **3** sprinkle or strew with: 濺；灑；撒佈: *A taxi went by and ~ed us with mud.* 一輛計程車駛過去，濺了我們一身泥。*The wind blew from the desert and ~ed everything with sand.* 風從沙漠裏吹過來，使一切東西都覆蓋着一層沙。**4** (reflex) bring upon oneself: (反身)使自身滿載或蒙受: *~ oneself with glory/honour/disgrace.* 使自身感到光榮(獲得榮譽，蒙受羞恥)。 **5** protect: 保護；掩護；庇護: *He ~ed his wife from the man's blows with his own body.* 他以自己的身體掩護他的妻子，使不致受到那人的毆打。 *Warships ~ed the landing of the invading army,* fired their guns to keep the enemy at a distance, etc. 戰艦砲火掩護攻擊部隊登陸。*Are you ~ed* (= insured) *against fire and theft?* 你們是否已保火險及竊盜險？ **6** travel (a certain distance): 走(一段路程): *By sunset we had ~ed thirty miles.* 日落的時候，我們已走了三十哩。 **7** (of guns, fortresses, etc) command(6); dominate: (指大砲、堡壘等)砲火能及；射程能達到；能控制: *Our heavy artillery ~ed every possible approach to the town.* 我們的重砲砲火控制了通達鎮上的每一條路。 **8** keep a gun aimed at sb (so that he cannot shoot or escape): 以槍砲瞄準着某人(使其不能射擊或逃走): *C~ your man!* 瞄準你的敵人！ *Keep them ~ed!* 舉槍對着他們瞄準(不要中止)！ **9** (of money) be enough for: (指錢)够用；足敷: *£10 will ~ my needs for the journey.* 十鎊卽足够我的旅行費用。*We have only just ~ed our expenses,* made enough for our expenses, but no profit. 我們的收入僅够開支而已(無盈餘)。 **10** include; comprise; extend over; be adequate for: 包括；包羅；涵蓋；適用於: *Professor A's lectures ~ed the subject thoroughly.* A 教授的演講將這題目講得很透徹。 *His researches ~ed a wide field.* 他的研究範圍很廣。*This book does not fully ~ the subject,* does not deal with all aspects of it. 這本書對於這題目闡述不够詳盡。*Do the rules ~* (= Are they adequate for) *all possible cases?* 這些規則是否適用於所有可能的情形？ **11** (in games such as cricket and baseball) stand behind (a player) to stop balls that he may miss: (板球及棒球戲)立於(球手)後方以捕捉所失之球: *The short-stop ~ed second base.* 游擊手立於第二壘之後守球。 **12** (of a journalist) report (what is said and done at meetings, on public occasions, etc): (指新聞記者)採訪；報導(會議、公衆場合等之新聞): *~ the Labour Party's annual conference.* 採訪工黨年會新聞。**~·ing** *n* sth that ~s: 遮蓋物: *a leafy ~ing,* the trees. 樹木；樹蔭。□ *part adj* **~ing letter,** one sent with a document, or with goods, etc. 公文、貨物等的附函。

cover[2] /ˈkʌvə(r) ; ˈkʌvɚ/ *n* **1** thing that covers: 遮蓋物；蓋子；套子: *When the water boils, take the ~* (= lid) *from the pan.* 當水開了的時候，將鍋蓋揭開。*Some chairs are fitted with loose ~s.* 有些椅子裝着可以隨意取下和套上的套子。 **2** binding of a book, magazine, etc; either half of this: (書籍、雜誌等的)封面；殼面: *The book needs a new ~.* 這書需要裝個新封面。***from ~ to ~,*** from beginning to end: 從頭到尾: *The child read the book from ~ to ~.* 那孩子將書從頭讀到尾。**ˈ~ girl,** girl who poses for photographs to be used on the cover of a magazine. (雜誌的)封面女郎。 **3** wrapper or envelope. 封套；封皮。***under plain ~,*** in a parcel or envelope which has no indication of the firm, the contents, etc: 在未寫明商號、內容等之包裹或信封中: *The book of photographs of girls in the nude is being sent under plain ~.* 那本裸體女郎照片的書是用未寫明寄件商號及內容的信封郵寄的。 ***under separate ~,*** (comm) in a separate parcel or envelope: (商)在另一包裹或信封中；另行封寄: *We are sending the goods under separate ~.* 貨品我們將另行封寄。 **4** [U] place or area giving shelter or protection: 可以隱蔽的地方；躲避處；庇護所: *The land was flat* *and treeless and provided no ~ for the troops.* 該地平坦且無樹木，軍隊無法隱蔽。 ***take ~,*** place oneself where one is protected or concealed: 利用掩護物將自己隱藏起來；掩蔽: *There was nowhere where we could take ~,* eg from rain. 沒有一個我們可以躲避的地方(如避雨)。 ***under ~,*** sheltered. 在遮蔽之下；在保護之下。 **5** [U] woods or undergrowth protecting animals, etc. (隱藏動物等的)叢林。 ***break ~,*** (eg of a fox) come out of the undergrowth, etc. (指狐狸等)自所隱藏的樹叢中出來。 **6** [U] ***under ~ of,*** with a pretence of: 以…之名義；在…的僞裝下；以…爲藉口；假託…之名: *under ~ of friendship/religion;* 藉友誼(宗教)之名; *murders committed under ~ of patriotism.* 假藉愛國之口實所犯的謀殺罪行。 **7** [U] protection from attack: 保護(以免受攻擊)；掩護: *give ~.* 給予掩護。 **8** place laid at table for a meal: 餐桌上所佈置的席位: *C~s were laid for six.* 佈置了六個席位。 **'~ charge** *n* (in a restaurant) charge in addition to the cost of the food and drink. (餐館中飲食費用以外之)附加費；服務費。 **9** [U] (comm) money deposited to meet a liability or possible loss. (商)負債或虧損準備金。 **10** [U] insurance against loss, damage, etc: 損壞等之保險: *Does your policy provide adequate ~ against fire?* 你的保險單是否提供適當的火險？ **'~ note,** document from an insurance company to provide temporary ~ between the acceptance and issue of a policy. 臨時保單(保險公司所發給之文件，提供在接受投保至發給保單之期間的臨時保險)。

cover·age /ˈkʌvərɪdʒ ; ˈkʌvərɪdʒ/ *n* [U] covering of events, etc: 採訪新聞；新聞報導: *TV ~ of the election campaign,* eg by televising political meetings, interviews with candidates and voters. 競選活動的電視報導(如轉播政黨大會實況，訪問候選人及投票人等)。 ⇨ cover¹(12).

cover·let /ˈkʌvəlɪt ; ˈkʌvəˑlɪt/ *n* bedspread. 床單；床罩。

cov·ert¹ /ˈkʌvət ; ˈkʌvəˑt/ *adj* (half-)hidden; disguised: (半)掩藏的；掩飾的；暗地的: *~ glances/threats.* 偷偷的瞥視(暗地的威脅)。 **~·ly** *adv* ⇨ overt.

cov·ert² /ˈkʌvət ; ˈkʌvəˑt/ *n* area of thick undergrowth in which animals hide. 動物所隱藏的樹叢。 ***draw a ~,*** search it (for foxes, etc). 搜索樹叢(找尋狐狸等)。 ⇨ cover²(5).

covet /ˈkʌvɪt ; ˈkʌvɪt/ *vt* [VP6A] desire eagerly (esp sth that belongs to sb else). 垂涎；貪圖(尤指屬於他人的東西)。

covet·ous /ˈkʌvɪtəs ; ˈkʌvətəs/ *adj ~ (of),* eagerly desirous (esp of things belonging to sb else). 垂涎的；貪圖(尤指他人之物)的。 **~·ly** *adv* **~·ness** *n*

covey /ˈkʌvɪ ; ˈkʌvɪ/ *n* (*pl* ~s) brood, small flock of partridges. 一窩或一小群鷓鴣。

cow¹ /kaʊ ; kaʊ/ *n* fully grown female of any animal of the ox family, esp the domestic kind kept by farmers for producing milk, ⇨ the illus at domestic; also female elephant, rhinoceros, whale, etc. 母牛；牝牛；(尤指農人畜養以取其乳之)乳牛(參看 domestic 之挿圖)；(亦指)母象；母犀牛；母鯨(等)。 ⇨ bull¹(1), calf¹(1), heifer, steer¹. **'cow·bell,** bell hung round a cow's neck to indicate her whereabouts. 牛鈴(繫於牛頸上的鈴，用以指示其所在)。 **'cow·boy,** man (usu on horseback) who looks after cattle in the western parts of the US. 美國西部的牧人(通常騎於馬上照料牛群)；牛仔。 **'cow·catcher,** metal frame fastened to the front of a railway engine to push obstacles off the track. (火車機車前的) 排障裝置。 **'cow·hand, 'cow·herd,** person who looks after cattle at pasture. 牧牛者；牧人；牧童。 **'cow·hide,** leather (or a strip of leather as a whip) made from a cow's hide. 牛皮所製的皮革；牛皮鞭。 **'cow·house, 'cow·shed,** building in which cows are kept when not at pasture, or to which they are taken to be milked. 牛舍 (在未放牧時關牛的房舍，或擠牛奶的地方)。 **'cow·man** /-mən ; -mən/ (*pl* -men), man responsible for milking cows. 擠牛奶的工人。 **cow·skin,** (leather from the) skin of a cow. 牛皮；牛皮革。

cow² /kaʊ ; kaʊ/ *vt* [VP6A] frighten (sb) into submission: 恐嚇(某人)使屈服: *The child had a cowed look,* looked frightened because of threats of violence, etc. 那孩子(因受恐嚇等而)顯出畏懼的樣子。

cow·ard /ˈkaʊəd ; ˈkaʊəˑd/ *n* person unable to control his fear; person who runs away from danger. 膽小的人；膽怯者；懦夫。 ***turn ~,*** become a ~. 變成懦夫。 **~·ly** *adj* **1** not brave. 膽小的；怯懦的。 **2** contemptible; of or like a ~: 可鄙的；懦夫的: *a ~ly lie;* 可鄙的謊言; *~ly behaviour.* 懦夫的行爲。

cow·ard·ice /ˈkaʊədɪs ; ˈkaʊəˑdɪs/ *n* [U] feeling, way of behaviour, of a coward; faint-heartedness. 膽小；怯懦；卑怯。

cower /ˈkaʊə(r) ; ˈkaʊəˑ/ *vi* [VP2A, C] lower the body; crouch; shrink back from cold, misery, fear, shame: 屈縮身體；畏縮；退縮(因寒冷、痛苦、恐懼或羞恥): *The dog ~ed under the table when its master raised the whip.* 那條狗在主人揚起鞭子時縮到桌子下面去了。

cowl /kaʊl ; kaʊl/ *n* **1** long, loose gown (as worn by monks) with a hood that can be pulled over the head; the hood itself. (僧人等所穿) 連帶頭巾的寬鬆長袍；頭巾。 **2** metal cap for a chimney, ventilating pipe, etc, often made so as to revolve with the wind and improve the draught(1). 裝於煙囱、通風管等頂上可以隨風旋轉以利通風的罩子；通風帽。 **~·ing** *n* removable metal covering for an (aircraft) engine. 發動機整流罩(飛機等引擎的活動金屬罩)。

cow·pox /ˈkaʊpɒks ; ˈkaʊˌpɑks/ *n* contagious disease of cattle, caused by a virus which, when isolated, is the source of vaccine for smallpox. 牛痘(由於病毒所引起的一種牛的傳染病，此種病毒經過分離後即爲牛痘苗之來源)。

cow·rie /ˈkaʊrɪ ; ˈkaʊrɪ/ *n* (*pl* ~s) small shell formerly used as money in parts of Africa and Asia. 子安貝 (從前爲非洲及亞洲某些地區用作錢幣)。

cow·slip /ˈkaʊslɪp ; ˈkaʊˌslɪp/ *n* small plant with yellow flowers, growing wild in temperate countries. 野櫻草(開黃花，野生於溫帶國家)。

cox /kɒks ; kɑks/ *n* (colloq abbr of) coxswain. (俗)舵手 (coxswain 之略)。 □ *vt, vi* [VP6A, 2A] act as coxswain (of a rowing-boat): 做 (划船的) 舵手；掌舵: *The Oxford boat was coxed by....* 牛津大學的賽船由…人掌舵。

cox·comb /ˈkɒkskəʊm ; ˈkɑksˌkom/ *n* **1** vain, foolish person, esp one who pays too much attention to his clothes. 愛虛榮而糊塗的人；(尤指)特別注意衣著的人；花花公子。 **2** = cockscomb(2).

cox·swain /ˈkɒksn ; ˈkɑksn̩/ *n* person who steers a rowing-boat, esp in races; person in charge of a ship's boat and crew. 掌(尤指賽船之)舵的人；舵手；輪船上管理小艇及其水手的人；小艇長。 ⇨ the illus at eight. 參看 eight 之挿圖。

coy /kɔɪ ; kɔɪ/ *adj* (-er, -est) (esp of a girl) shy, modest; pretending to be shy; seeming more modest than one really is. (尤指女孩) 害羞的；嬌羞的；假裝害羞的；忸怩的。 **coy·ly** *adv* **coy·ness** *n*

coy·ote /kɔɪˈəʊt *US:* ˈkaɪəʊt ; kaɪˈot/ *n* prairie wolf of western N America. (北美洲西部大草原的)山狗；郊狼。

coypu /ˈkɔɪpuː ; ˈkɔɪpu/ *n* S American rodent with webbed hind feet, bred for its fur (*nutria fur*). 河鼠 (產於南美洲之齧齒動物，後足有蹼，畜養以取其毛皮)。 ⇨ nutria.

cozen /ˈkʌzn ; ˈkʌzn̩/ *vt* [VP6A,14] ***~ sb (out) of sth,*** (liter) defraud him of sth. (文)欺騙；詐騙；哄騙某人取得某物。 ***~ sb into doing sth,*** (liter) beguile him into it. (文)哄騙某人做某事。

cozy /ˈkəʊzɪ ; ˈkozɪ/ *adj* (US) (美) = cosy.

crab¹ /kræb ; kræb/ *n* [C] ten-legged shellfish; [U] its meat as food. 蟹；蟹肉(作爲食物者)。 ⇨ the illus at crustacean. 參看 crustacean 之挿圖。 ***catch a ~,*** (rowing) make a faulty stroke with one's oar. (划船)划錯一槳。

crab² /kræb ; kræb/ *n* (also 亦作 **'~-apple**) wild apple-tree; its hard, sour fruit. 野蘋果(樹);山楂(子樹)。

crab³ /kræb ; kræb/ *vi, vt* (-bb-) (colloq) complain; grumble; criticize. (俗)責難;抱怨;批評。

crab·bed /'kræbɪd ; 'kræbɪd/ *adj* **1** bad-tempered; easily irritated. 脾氣乖戾的; 易怒的。 **2** (of handwriting) difficult to read; (of writings, authors) difficult to understand. (指字跡)難辨認的;(指作品、作家)難懂的。

crack¹ /kræk ; kræk/ *n* **1 (a)** line of division where sth is broken, but not into separate parts: 罅裂; 裂縫: *a cup with bad ~s in it.* 裂得很厲害的茶杯。 *Don't go skating today—there are dangerous ~s in the ice.* 今天不要去溜冰，冰上有危險的裂縫。**(b)** narrow opening. 窄縫;小縫。***open sth a ~,*** open it very slightly. 將某物打開一點點。***the ~ of dawn,*** (colloq) daybreak. (俗) 破曉; 黎明。 **2** sudden, sharp noise (as of a rifle or whip, or sth breaking): 噼啪聲(如放槍、抽鞭或物件破碎的聲音): *the ~ of a pistol shot;* 手槍的射擊聲; *a ~ of thunder.* 雷聲。***the ~ of doom,*** the peal of thunder on the Day of Judgement. 世界末日的霹靂聲。 **3** sharp blow which can be heard: 聽得見響聲的重擊: *give sb/get a ~ on the head.* 對準某人頭部一擊(頭上挨了一擊)。 **4** (sl) (= *wise~*) lively, forceful, or cutting comment or retort, esp one that causes laughter. (俚) 俏皮話; 幽默的諷刺或反駁語。 **5** (sl) attempt. (俚)試圖;嘗試。***have a ~ at sth,*** try to do sth which is difficult. 嘗試做某件困難事。 **6** (attrib use) first-rate; very clever or expert: (形容用法)第一流的; 技藝高超的: *a ~ polo-player;* 第一流的馬球選手; *a ~ regiment.* 精銳的團; 勁旅。 *He's a ~ shot,* expert at using a rifle. 他是一位神槍手。 **7 '~-brained** *adj* crazy; foolish: 瘋狂的; 狂妄的;愚蠢的: *a ~-brained scheme.* 愚蠢的計謀。

crack² /kræk ; kræk/ *vt, vi* **1** [VP6A, 14, 2A, C] get or make a crack or cracks(1) in: 打裂;擊裂;破裂: *I can ~ it, but I can't break it.* 我能打裂它,但不能打碎它。 *You've ~ed the window.* 你把窗戶打裂了。 *The glass will ~ if you pour boiling water into it.* 這玻璃杯一倒滾開水進去就會破裂。 *He fell out of the window and ~ed his skull.* 他自窗戶上跌出去,把頭蓋骨跌裂了。 **2** [VP6A, 2A] make, cause to make, a crack or cracks(2): (使)發噼啪聲: *to ~ a whip/the joints of the fingers.* 抽鞭子(屈指節)使發響聲。 *The hunter's rifle ~ed and the deer fell dead.* 獵人的槍一響,鹿即倒地而死。*We heard a ~ing noise among the trees.* 我們聽見樹林中有噼啪聲。 ***~ open,*** open with a ~ing sound: 啪的一聲打開了: *~ open a safe.* 啪的一聲打開了保險箱。 **3** [VP2A] (of the voice) become harsh; (of a boy's voice when he is reaching puberty) undergo a change and become dissonant (*break* is more usu). (指嗓音) 變沙啞; (指男孩初達青春期) 變聲; 變嗓 (break 較常用)。 **4** [VP6A] decompose (petroleum) by using heat and pressure so as to change thick oils into thinner oils. 將(石油)加熱加壓,使自重油變成輕油; 裂解。Hence, 由此產生, **'~·ing plant.** 裂解工廠。 **5** (colloq and sl uses) (俚俗用法) ***~ down on sb/sth,*** take disciplinary action against: 處罰(某人,某事): *~ down on gambling.* 處罰賭博。 Hence, 由此產生, **'~-down** *n.* ***~ sb/sth up (to be sth),*** [VP15B] praise highly, or in an exaggerated way: (誇大地)讚揚;頌揚(某人或某事): *He's not so clever as he's ~ed up to be.* 他並不如人們所讚揚的那樣聰明。 ***~ up,*** **(a)** [VP2C] lose strength (in old age); suffer a mental collapse. (老年) 體力衰退; 精神崩潰。 Hence, 由此產生, **'~-up** *n* failure; breakdown. 失敗; 崩潰。 **(b)** [VP2C, 15B] (of a vehicle) (cause to) suffer damage, crash. (指車輛)(使)毀壞;撞毀。***~ a bottle,*** open one and drink the contents. 打開(酒)瓶喝(酒)。 ***~ a joke,*** make one. 說笑話。 ⇨ crack¹(4). ***get ~ing,*** get busy (with work waiting to be done). 趕工。

cracker /'krækə(r) ; 'krækɚ/ *n* **1** thin, flaky, dry biscuit (as eaten with cheese). 薄脆的餅乾 (如與乾酪同食者)。 **2** firework that makes cracking noises when set off: 爆竹;鞭炮: *The Chinese use ~s to frighten away evil spirits.* 中國人以鞭炮驅邪。 **'Christmas ~,** one made of brightly coloured paper, which explodes harmlessly when the ends are pulled. 用五彩花紙做成,兩端一拉即行爆炸(但不傷人)的紙炮。 **3** (*pl*, 複, also 亦作 **'nut-~s**) instrument for cracking nuts. 軋果殼鉗;胡桃鉗。

crackers /'krækəz ; 'krækɚz/ *pred adj* (GB sl) mad; crazy. (英俚)瘋狂的。

crackle /'krækl ; 'krækḷ/ *vi* [VP2A, C] make a series of small cracking sounds, as when one treads on dry twigs, or when dry sticks burn: 發連續不斷的細碎響聲 (如踐踏乾樹枝或乾柴燃燒時所發出者): *a crackling camp-fire.* 嗶嗶啪啪響的營火。*A cheerful wood fire was crackling in the sitting-room.* 熊熊的柴火在起居室爐中嗶啪作響。□ *n* [U] **1** small cracking sounds, as described above: 細碎的聲音;嗶啪聲: *the distant ~ of machine-gun fire.* 遠處的機槍聲。 **2** (also 亦作 **'~-china/~-ware**) china, etc covered with a network of what appear to be tiny cracks. 表面飾有細碎裂紋圖案的瓷器。

crack·ling /'kræklɪŋ ; 'kræklɪŋ/ *n* [U] **1** ⇨ crackle(1). **2** crisp, well-cooked skin of roast pork. (烤豬肉的)脆皮。

crack·pot /'krækpɒt ; 'kræk,pɑt/ *n* eccentric person with strange ideas: 有怪念頭的怪人; 狂想者: (attrib) (形容用法) *~ ideas.* 怪念頭;怪主意。

cracks·man /'kræksmən ; 'kræksmən/ *n* (*pl* -men) burglar. 竊賊;夜賊。

cradle /'kreɪdl ; 'kredḷ/ *n* **1** small, low bed sometimes mounted on rockers, for a newborn baby: (新生嬰兒用的)搖籃;搖床: *from/in the ~,* from/during infancy; 自(在)幼小時; *from the ~ to the grave,* from birth to death. 從生到死。 **2** (fig) place where sth is born or begins: (喻) 發源地;發祥地: *Greece, the ~ of Western culture.* 希臘,西方文化的發源地。 **3** framework resembling a ~ or which is used like a ~, eg a structure on which a ship is supported while being built or repaired; platform that can be moved up and down an outside wall by means of ropes and pulleys, used by workmen; part of a telephone apparatus on which the receiver rests. 形似搖籃之筐架; (造船或修船時) 承船的托架; (工人用繩索及滑輪操縱,可沿外牆) 昇降的平臺; 電話機的聽筒支架。□ *vt* [VP6A, 14] place, hold, in or as in a ~: (如)置於搖籃中: *~ a child in one's arms;* 將嬰孩抱於臂膀中; *~ the telephone receiver,* put it down. 放下電話聽筒。

craft /krɑːft *US:* kræft ; kræft/ *n* **1** [C] occupation, esp one in which skill in the use of the hands is needed; such a skill or technique: 職業; (尤指)手工業; 手藝; 工藝: *the potter's ~;* 陶器業; *to learn the ~ of the woodcarver;* 學習木雕的工藝; *a school for arts and ~s.* 工藝學校。Used in many compounds, 用於許多複合字中, as 如 **'needle·~, 'wood·~, 'handi·~, 'stage-~.** **2** (collective) those engaged in such an occupation, organized in a guild or union: (集合用法)同業;公會: *the ~ of masons;* 泥瓦匠公會; *the C~,* brotherhood of Freemasons. 互助會(的全體會員)。 **3** (*pl* unchanged) boat(s), ship(s): (複數不變)船;艇;艦: *a handy and useful little ~.* 輕便小艇。*The harbour was full of all kinds of ~/~ of all kinds.* 港內泊滿了各式各樣的船隻。 ⇨ *air~* at air¹(7), *space~* at space. **4** [U] cunning; trickery; skill in deceiving: 狡猾;詭計多端;欺騙的伎倆: *Be careful when you do business with that man: he's full of ~.* 與那人做生意你得小心,他詭計多端。 *He got it from me by ~.* 他用詭計從我這裏得到它的。 **~y** *adj* (-ier, -iest) full of ~(4): 詭計多端的;狡猾的: *a ~y politician;* 狡猾的政客; *as ~y as a fox.* 狡猾如狐狸。

~•ily *adv* ~i•ness *n*

crafts•man /ˈkrɑ:ftsmən *US:* ˈkræfts- ; ˈkræftsmən/ *n* (*pl* -men) skilled workman who practises a craft. 技工;工匠;精於一門工藝的匠人。**~•ship** /-ʃɪp ; -,ʃɪp/ *n* skilled workmanship. 精巧的技藝;手藝。

crag /kræg ; kræg/ *n* [C] high, steep, sharp or rugged mass of rock. 峭壁;危岩。**~•ged** /ˈkrægɪd ; ˈkrægɪd/ (poet) (詩), **~gy** (-ier, -iest) *adjj* having many ~s. 多峭壁的; 嶙峋的。**ˈcrags•man** /-mən ; -mən/ *n* (*pl* -men) one who is clever at climbing ~s. 善於攀登陡崖峭壁者。

crake /kreɪk ; krek/ *n* kinds of bird. 秧鷄。⇨ *corn-crake* at corn[1](1).

cram /kræm ; kræm/ *vt, vi* (-mm-) [VP6A, 14, 15B, 2A] **1** *~ (into); ~ (up) (with),* make too full; put, push, very much or too much into: 塡塞;勉强塞入: *to ~ food into one's mouth/~ up one's mouth with food;* 將食物塞入口中; *to ~ papers into a drawer;* 將文件塞入抽屜內; *an essay ~med with quotations.* 充滿引用句的文章。**2** fill the head with facts (for an examination): (爲考試而)做塡鴨式的敎學: *to ~ pupils;* 以塡鴨的方式敎學生; *to ~ up a subject,* commit facts to memory (without serious study). 强記一門功課(而不求甚解)。**,~-ˈfull** *adj, adv* as full as ~ming can make it. 塡飽;塞滿。**~•mer** *n* special school where students are ~med; teacher paid to ~ students for examinations; textbook designed for ~ming; student who ~s for examinations. 爲應付考試而實施塡鴨式敎學的補習班;爲應付考試而聘請的補習敎師;爲應付考試而編的敎科書;强記功課以應付考試的學生。

cramp[1] /kræmp ; kræmp/ *n* [U] sudden and painful tightening of the muscles, usu caused by cold or overwork, making movement difficult: 抽筋;痙攣(通常由寒冷或過勞而起,使活動困難): *writer's ~,* of the finger muscles. 書寫痙攣。*The swimmer was seized with ~ and had to be helped out of the water.* 游泳者忽然抽筋,因而不得不由他人救助出水。

cramp[2] /kræmp ; kræmp/ *vt* [VP6A] **1** keep in a narrow space; hinder or prevent the movement or growth of: 限制(於狹窄的空間);阻礙活動或生長: *All these difficulties ~ed his progress.* 所有這些困難阻礙了他的進步。***be ~ed for room/space etc,*** be without enough room etc. 沒有足够的空間等的。***~ one's style,*** (colloq) prevent one from doing sth as well as one could do it in more favourable circumstances. (俗)使某人不能發揮其才能。**2** cause to have, affect with, cramp[1]. 使抽筋。**3** fasten with a cramp[3]: 以鐵箍扣緊: *~ a beam.* 用鐵箍將樑緊扣。**cramped** *part adj* (of handwriting) with small letters close together and for this reason difficult to read. (指字跡)字母小而緊密的;(因此而)難辨認的。

cramp[3] /kræmp ; kræmp/ *n* **1** (also 亦作 **ˈ~-iron**) metal bar with the ends bent, used for holding together masonry or timbers. 鐵箍;鐵搭;鋼筋(用以固結石造物或木料)。**2** =clamp[1].

cram•pon /ˈkræmpɒn ; ˈkræmpən/ *n* (usu *pl*) iron plate with spikes, worn on shoes for walking or climbing on ice, rock etc. (通常用複數)(固定在鞋底上用以在冰上行走或攀爬岩石等的)尖鐵釘。

cran•berry /ˈkrænbərɪ *US:* -berɪ ; ˈkræn,bɛrɪ/ *n* (*pl* -ries) small, red, tart berry of a dwarf shrub, used for making jelly and sauce. 蔓越橘(一種矮小灌木所結之小紅酸莓,用以製果凍及果醬)。

crane[1] /kreɪn ; kren/ *n* **1** large wading bird with long legs and neck. 鶴(長腿長頸之大涉水鳥)。⇨ the illus at water. 參看 water 之插圖。**2** machine with a long arm that can be swung round, used for lifting and moving heavy weights. 起重機(有可以轉動之長臂,用以吊起及移動重物);吊車。

crane[2] /kreɪn ; kren/ *vt, vi* [VP6A, 16A, 2A, C] stretch (the neck); stretch the neck like a crane[1](1): 引(頸);(像鶴一樣)伸長脖子: *to ~ forward;* 將頭向前伸出; *to ~ one's neck to see sth.* 伸長脖子看東西。

crane-fly /ˈkreɪn flaɪ ; ˈkren flaɪ/ *n* (*pl* -flies) kind of fly with very long legs; daddy-long-legs. 一種長足之蠅;蚊姥。

cran•ial /ˈkreɪnɪəl ; ˈkrenɪəl/ *adj* (anat) of the skull. (解剖)頭蓋骨的。

cran•ium /ˈkreɪnɪəm ; ˈkrenɪəm/ *n* (anat) bony part of the head enclosing the brain; skull. (解剖)頭蓋骨;顱。⇨ the illus at head. 參看 head 之插圖。

crank[1] /kræŋk ; kræŋk/ *n* L-shaped arm and handle for transmitting rotary motion. (用以傳送旋轉動作的)曲柄。**ˈ~•shaft** *n* shaft that turns or is turned by a ~. (轉動或由曲柄轉動的) 機軸。□ *vt* [VP6A, 15B] ***~ (up),*** (of an engine) start, cause to start, by turning a ~. (指引擎)轉動曲柄以發動。

crank[2] /kræŋk ; kræŋk/ *n* person with fixed (and often strange) ideas, esp on one matter: (尤指對某一事)有怪誕成見的人;思想怪異的人: *a fresh air ~,* one who insists on having windows open, however cold, stormy, etc, it may be. 對於新鮮空氣有怪誕成見之人 (不管天氣多冷或是狂風暴雨仍堅持開窗)。**~y** *adj* (-ier, -iest) (of people) odd; eccentric; (of machines, etc) unsteady; unreliable. (指人)古怪的;任性的;(指機器等)不穩固的;不可靠的。

cranny /ˈkrænɪ ; ˈkrænɪ/ *n* (*pl* -nnies) small crack or opening, eg in a wall. (牆壁等上的) 縫隙;小孔。**cran•nied** *adj* full of crannies. 多縫隙的。

crap /kræp ; kræp/ *vi* (-pp-) ⚠ defecate. (諱)排便;拉屎。□ *n* ⚠ (諱) **1** [U] excrement. 糞;屎;排泄物。**2** [C] act of defecating: 排便;拉屎: *have a ~.* 大便;拉屎。**3** [U] (sl) nonsense; sth unpleasant or unwanted. (俚)笨話; 愚行;不愉快之事;無用之物。**~py** *adj* (sl) bad; worthless; unpleasant. (俚)不好的;無用的;不愉快的。

crape /kreɪp ; krep/ *n* [U] black silk or cotton material with a wrinkled surface (formerly used for mourning). 黑縐綢或縐紗(昔時用以表示哀悼)。⇨ crêpe.

craps /kræps ; kræps/ *n* (also 亦作 **ˈcrap-shooting**) [U] (US) gambling game played with two dice. (美)擲兩顆骰子的賭博。***shoot ~,*** play this game. 擲兩顆骰子(賭博)。

crash[1] /kræʃ ; kræʃ/ *n* **1** (noise made by a) violent fall, blow or breaking: 猛烈的墜落、打擊或破裂(所發的響聲): *The tree fell with a great ~.* 那樹嘩啦一聲倒下來。*His words were drowned in a ~ of thunder.* 他的話爲一聲響雷所淹蓋。*He was killed in an ˈair ~.* 他於飛機失事中喪生。**ˈ~ barrier,** fence, rail, wall, etc designed to keep people, vehicles, etc apart where there is danger (eg one in the centre of a motorway). 防撞柵欄(設置於快車道中央等危險地帶,以隔開行人、車輛等)。**ˈ~-dive** *n* sudden dive made by a submarine, eg to escape attack. 潛水艇所作的緊急下沉(如逃避攻擊)。□ *vi* dive in this way. 緊急下沉。**,~-ˈland** *vi, vt* (of aircraft) land, be landed, partly or wholly out of control, with a ~. (指飛機) (因部份或完全失去控制而)緊急降落;强迫着陸。Hence, 由此產生, **,crash-ˈlanding** *n* **ˈ~-helmet,** padded helmet worn to protect the head in case of a ~, eg by a motorcyclist. (機車騎士等所戴之)安全帽;護頭盔。**ˈ~ pad,** (sl) place to

cranes

sleep in an emergency. (俚)緊急時睡覺之處。'～ **programme**, one made with intensive efforts to achieve quick results. 全力以赴俾求速成的計畫;應急計畫。 **2** ruin; collapse (eg in trade, finance): (貿易,財政等之)毀滅;敗亡;破產;崩潰: *The great ～ on Wall Street in 1929 ruined international trade.* 1929 年華爾街的股市暴跌使國際間的貿易大爲蕭條。□ *adv* with a ～. 嘩啦一聲地。

crash² /kræʃ ; kræʃ/ *vt, vi* **1** [VP2A, C, 6A] fall or strike suddenly, violently, and noisily (esp of things that break): 猛跌或猛撞並帶破碎聲;撞碎;撞壞;墜毀: *The bus ～ed into a tree.* 公共汽車猛撞在一棵樹上。*The tree ～ed through the window.* 樹嘩啦一聲倒入窗內。*The dishes ～ed to the floor.* 那些盤子嘩啦一聲掉在地上。*The aircraft ～ed.* 那飛機墜毀了。 **2** [VP2A, C] force or break through violently: 衝入;闖進: *～ through a barrier;* 衝過障礙物; [VP6A] (sl) (俚) = *gatecrash.* ⇨ gate. **3** [VP2A] (of a business company, government, etc) come to ruin; meet disaster: (指商業公司、政府等)破產;垮臺: *His great financial scheme ～ed.* 他的大財政計畫失敗了。 **4** [VP6A] cause to ～: 使粉碎;毀壞: *to ～ a plane.* 使飛機撞毀。

crash³ /kræʃ ; kræʃ/ *n* [U] coarse linen cloth (as used for towels, etc). (用作毛巾等的)粗麻布。

crass /kræs ; kræs/ *adj* (of such qualities as ignorance, stupidity, etc) complete; very great. (指無知、愚笨等)完全的;非常的。

crate /kreɪt ; kret/ *n* **1** large framework of light boards or basketwork for goods in transport. (運貨用的)大板條箱;枝條編成的簍或籃。 **2** (sl) old, worn-out motor-car or aircraft. (俚)用久而破爛的汽車或飛機;老爺車;老爺機。□ *vt* put in a ～. 裝於板條箱等中。

cra·ter /ˈkreɪtə(r) ; ˈkretə/ *n* mouth of a volcano; hole in the ground made by the explosion of a bomb, shell, etc. 火山口;(炸彈、砲彈等在地上所炸成的)彈坑。 ～ **lake**, lake in the ～ of an extinct volcano. 火山湖(在死火山口所形成的湖泊)。

cra·vat /krəˈvæt ; krəˈvæt/ *n* piece of linen, lace, etc loosely folded and worn as a necktie. 鬆摺而繫於頸上作爲領帶的麻布等製的飾帶;舊式領帶。

crave /kreɪv ; krev/ *vt, vi* [VP6A,3A] *～ (for)*, ask earnestly for, have a strong desire for: 懇求;渴望;熱望: *to ～ (for) mercy／forgiveness;* 懇求寬恕(原諒); *to ～ for a drink.* 極欲飲水。 **crav·ing** /ˈkreɪvɪŋ ; ˈkrevɪŋ/ *n* [C] strong desire: 渴望;熱望: *a craving for strong drink.* 極欲喝烈酒。

cra·ven /ˈkreɪvn ; ˈkrevən/ *n, adj* (person who is) cowardly. 怯懦的;懦夫。

craw·fish /ˈkrɔːfɪʃ ; ˈkrɔˌfɪʃ/ *n* = crayfish.

crawl /krɔːl ; krɔl/ *vi* [VP2A, C] **1** move slowly, pulling the body along the ground or other surface (as worms and snakes do); (of human beings) move in this way, or on the hands and knees: 爬;爬行(如蟲類和蛇所爲);(指人)匍匐而行;爬行: *The wounded soldier ～ed into a shell-hole.* 那受傷的兵爬入一砲彈坑。 ～ **to sb**, (colloq) try to bring oneself into his favour. (俗)向某人拍馬屁;巴結。 **2** go very slowly: 徐緩而行: *Our train ～ed over the damaged bridge.* 我們的列車緩慢地開過受損的橋。 **3** be full of, covered with, things that ～: 充滿或覆滿爬行的東西: *The ground was ～ing with ants.* 地上爬滿了螞蟻。*The child's hair was ～ing with vermin.* 那孩子的頭髮生滿了蝨子。 **4** (of the flesh) feel as if covered with ～ing things: (指肌膚)起鷄皮疙瘩: *She says that the sight of snakes makes her flesh ～.* 她說她看見蛇就起鷄皮疙瘩。□ *n* **1 a** ～, ～ing movement: 爬行;緩慢而行: *Traffic in Oxford St was reduced to a ～ during the rush hours.* 牛津街的交通在上下班擁擠時刻簡直變成了緩慢的蠕動。 **'pub-～** *vi, n* visit(ing) and drink(ing) at several pubs in succession: 在數家酒館連續飲酒: *go pub-～ing;* 去酒館喝酒; *go on a pub-～.* 連續在幾家酒館喝酒。 **2 (the)** ～, high-speed swimming stroke with alternate circular arm movements and rapid leg kicks. 自由式游泳(以雙臂呈圓形交替的動作與急速的兩腿踢動形成的快速游泳法)。 **～er** *n* person or thing that ～s; (*pl*) overall garment made for a baby to ～ about in. 爬行之人或物;(複)幼兒所穿可以到處爬行的全身罩服。

cray·fish /ˈkreɪfɪʃ ; ˈkreˌfɪʃ/ *n* freshwater lobster-like shellfish. (淡水中的)小龍蝦。

crayon /ˈkreɪən ; ˈkreən/ *n* stick or pencil of soft coloured chalk, wax or charcoal. 有色的粉筆;蠟筆;炭筆。□ *vt* draw with ～s. 用蠟筆或炭筆畫。

craze /kreɪz ; krez/ *n* enthusiastic interest that may last for a comparatively short time; the object of such interest: 爲時短暫的濃厚興趣;一時的狂熱;此種狂熱的對象: *schoolboy ～s,* eg the making of paper darts as weapons; 學童們流行一時的狂熱興趣(如摺紙鏢); *the modern ～ for bingo.* 時下對賓果遊戲的狂熱。

crazed /kreɪzd ; krezd/ *adj* (also 亦作 **half-～**) wildly excited; mad: 極度興奮的;瘋狂的: *a ～ look／expression;* 瘋狂的神情(表情); *a half-～ prophet.* 瘋狂的預言者。

crazy /ˈkreɪzɪ ; ˈkrezɪ/ *adj* (-ier, -iest) **1** *～ (about)*, (colloq) wildly excited or enthusiastic: (俗)狂熱的;醉心的: *He is ～ about skiing.* 他醉心於滑雪。*I'm ～ about you, darling.* 親愛的,我愛你愛得發狂。 **2** suffering from mental disorder; foolish: 癲狂的;糊塗的: *You were ～ to lend that man your money.* 你把錢借給那個人,眞糊塗。 *It was ～ of you to let such a young girl drive your car.* 你讓這樣年輕的女孩駕你的車,眞糊塗。 **3** (of buildings, etc) unsafe; likely to collapse. (指建築物等)不安全的;可能坍塌的。 **4** (of quilts, pavements, etc) made up of irregularly shaped pieces fitted together: (指棉被、人行道等)由形狀不規則的塊子拼湊成的: *～ paving.* 用不規則的石塊拼湊成的人行道。 **craz·ily** *adv* **crazi·ness** *n*

creak /kriːk ; krik/ *n, vi* [VP2A] (make a) sound like that of an unoiled door-hinge, or badly-fitting floorboards when trodden on. (發)咯吱聲;嘰嘎聲(如轉動未上油的門鉸鍊或踏在鬆脫的地板上)。 **～y** *adj* (-ier, -iest) making ～ing sounds: 咯吱作響的: *～y stairs.* 咯吱作響的樓梯。 **～·ily** *adv*

cream /kriːm ; krim/ *n* [U] **1** fatty or oily part of milk which rises to the surface and can be made into butter. 乳脂;乳皮;奶酥(可製奶油)。 **2** kind of food containing or resembling ～: 含乳脂或似乳脂的食品: *～ cheese;* 乾乳酪; *ice-～;* 冰淇淋; *～ ices;* 冰淇淋; *chocolate ～;* 巧克力奶油; *～ buns.* 奶油小麵包。 **3** substance like ～ in appearance or consistency, used for polishing, as a cosmetic, etc: (似乳脂之物,用以擦亮或作化粧品用的)膏;霜;油: *'furniture ～;* 傢具油; *'shoe-～;* 鞋油; *'face-～;* 面霜; *'cold-～.* 冷霜。 **4** part of a liquid that gathers at the top: 液體之浮於面上的部份: *～ of tartar／lime.* 酒石(英)(石灰乳)。 **5** best part of anything: 精華;精粹: *the ～ of the crop;* 收成的精華; *the ～ of the story,* the most amusing part, the point of it. 故事的精采處。 **6** (attrib) yellowish-white: (形容用法)乳脂色;乳白色;淡黃色;米色: *～-laid／-wove paper,* smooth ～-coloured writing-paper. 光滑的淡黃色寫字紙。□ *vt* take ～ from (milk); make ～y; add ～ to: 撇去(牛奶)的乳脂;使成乳脂狀;加乳脂於: *～ed potatoes,* cooked so that they have the consistency of ～. 乳脂馬鈴薯(加乳脂煮熟的馬鈴薯)。 **～y** *adj* (-ier, -iest) smooth and rich like ～; containing much ～. 滑膩似乳脂的;含有多量乳脂的。 **～·ery** *n* (*pl* -ries) **1** place where milk, ～, butter, cheese, etc are sold. 賣乳品的商店。 **2** butter and cheese factory. 奶油及乾酪工廠。

crease /kriːs ; kris/ *n* **1** line made (on cloth, paper, etc) by crushing, folding or pressing: (由搓揉、摺叠、或壓緊而在布、紙等上所造成的)摺痕;皺摺: *～-resistant cloth,* which does not easily form into ～s. 不皺布料。 **2** (cricket) white line on the ground to mark the positions of certain players (bowlers, batsmen).

(板球)地上標識某些球員(投球者、擊球者)位置的白線。⇨ the illus at cricket. 參看 cricket 之插圖。□ *vt, vi* [VP6A, 2A] make a ~ or ~s in; fall into ~s; get ~s in: (使)起摺痕;起皺: *Pack the dresses so that they won't ~.* 把衣服裝起來,免得弄皺了。*This material ~s easily.* 這種料子容易皺。

cre·ate /kriː'eɪt ; krɪ'et/ *vt* **1** [VP6A] cause sth to exist; make (sth new or original): 創作;創造: *God ~d the world.* 上帝創造世界。*Dickens ~d many wonderful characters in his novels.* 狄更斯在他的小說中創造了許多奇妙的人物。**~ *a part,*** (of an actor) be the first to play it. (指演員)爲某角色的最初扮演者。 **2** [VP6A] give rise to; produce: 產生;製造: *His behaviour ~d a bad impression.* 他的行爲給人惡劣的印象。*Her appearance ~d a sensation.* 她的出現曾轟動一時。 **3** [VP23, 6A] invest (sb) with a rank: 封(某人)爵位; 任命: *He was ~d Baron of Bunthorp.* 他被封爲班紹浦男爵。 *Eight new peers were ~d.* 新封了八個貴族。

cre·ation /kriː'eɪʃn ; krɪ'eʃən/ *n* **1** [U] the act of creating: 創造: *the ~ of great works of art.* 偉大藝術作品的創造。*Economic conditions may be responsible for the ~ of social unrest.* 經濟狀況可能是產生社會不安的根源。*Is the ~ of new peers desirable?* 加封新的貴族是否必要? **2** [U] all created things: 一切被創造之物;萬物: *man, the lord of ~.* 人,萬物的主宰。**(the) C~,** the world or universe as created by God. (上帝所創造的)世界或宇宙。 **3** [C] production of the human intelligence, esp one in which imagination has a part: 人類智慧的產物;(尤指)想像的產物: *the ~s of poets, artists, composers and dramatists.* 詩人、藝術家、作曲家及劇作家的作品。*The women were wearing the newest ~s of the Paris dressmakers.* 婦女們穿着巴黎裁縫師的最新製作。

cre·ative /kriː'eɪtɪv ; krɪ'etɪv/ *adj* having power to create; of creation: 有創造力的;創造的: *useful and ~ work,* ie requiring intelligence and imagination, not merely mechanical skill. 有用的和創造性的工作(卽需要智慧與想像,而不僅是呆板的技術)。 **~·ly** *adv* **~·ness** *n*

cre·ator /kriː'eɪtə(r) ; krɪ'etɚ/ *n* one who creates. 創造者。**the C~,** God. 上帝。

crea·ture /'kriːtʃə(r) ; 'kritʃɚ/ *n* **1** living animal: 動物: *dumb ~s,* animals. 不能說話的下等動物;畜牲。 **2** (with an *adj*) living person: (與形容詞連用)人: *a lovely ~,* a beautiful person; 美麗的人; *a poor ~,* a contemptible person, or a person who is to be pitied; 可鄙的人;可憐的人; *a good ~,* a kind-hearted person. 善心人; 好心人。 **~ comforts,** material needs such as food and drink. 物質的需要(如飲食)。 **3** person who owes his position to another, esp one who is content to carry out another person's wishes without question: 依人爲生者;唯命是聽者;走狗: *mere ~s of the dictator.* 獨裁者的走狗。

crèche /kreɪʃ *US:* kreʃ ; kreʃ/ *n* **1** (GB) public nursery where babies are looked after while their mothers are at work. (英) (爲職業婦女所設的) 托兒所。 **2** (US) (美) = crib¹(3).

cre·dence /'kriːdns ; 'kridn̩s/ *n* [U] ***give/attach ~ to,*** (formal) believe (gossip, what is said, etc). (正式用語)相信(閒話、傳言等)。 ***letter of ~,*** letter of introduction. 介紹信。

cre·den·tials /krɪ'denʃlz ; krɪ'dɛnʃəlz/ *n pl* letters or papers showing that a person is what he claims to be: 證明身份、學經歷等的信件或文件: *His ~ were so satisfactory that he was given the post of manager.* 他的各項證件令人極爲滿意,因此給他經理的職位。

cred·ible /'kredəbl ; 'krɛdəbl̩/ *adj* that can be believed: 可信的;可靠的: *~ witnesses.* 可信的證人。 *It hardly seems ~,* seems almost impossible to believe. 它似乎是難以置信的。**cred·ibly** *adv* in a ~ manner: 可信地;確實地: *We are credibly informed that....* 我們獲得可靠的消息…。**credi·bil·ity** /ˌkredɪ'bɪlətɪ ; ˌkrɛdə'bɪlətɪ/ *n* [U] the ability to be believed in. 確實性;可信性。**credi'bility gap,** the difference between what sb says and what is considered to be true. 可信度(某人所說的話及其確實性之間的差異)。

credit¹ /'kredɪt ; 'krɛdɪt/ *n* **1** [U] belief of others that a person, business company, etc can pay debts, or will keep a promise to pay: (個人、公司等對於償債方面的)信用;信譽: *No ~ is given at this shop,* payment must be in cash. 這家商店概不賒欠。*His ~ is good for only £50.* 他的信用僅限於五十鎊。*If you're very rich, you can probably get unlimited ~.* 如果你是個很富有的人,你或許能獲得無限的信用。***buy/sell on ~,*** buy/sell goods, payment being made later. 賒買(賣)貨物。**'~ account,** (US 美 = *charge account*) account with a shop, store, etc under an agreement for payments at a later date (eg monthly or quarterly). 賒帳;欠帳(商店等記載顧客定期如按月或按季付款賒購貨物的帳目)。 **'~ card, (a)** card issued by a business firm enabling the holder to obtain goods and services on ~. 信用卡(由一公司行號所發行,持卡人可記帳先取得貨物或享受服務)。**(b)** card issued by a bank, allowing the holder to draw money from its branches and use its cheques in payment for goods and services, with a maximum for each occasion. 信用卡(銀行所發行,持卡之客戶可在各分行提款,且使用該行支票償付貨款及工資,但每筆款有一定的限額)。**'~ note,** (comm) one that gives ~ to a customer for goods returned or for overcharged goods. (商)信用票據。**'~ sales,** sales for which payment is made, by agreement, later. 賒售;賒賣(經同意先交貨後收款)。Cf 參較 *cash sales.* **ˌletter of '~,** letter from a bank to its agent(s) giving authority for credit to the holder. 信用狀(銀行發給其代理銀行,授權對持有人予以信任的函件)。**'~-worthy** *adj* accepted by tradesmen, hire-purchase companies, etc as safe for ~. 信用可靠的 (其信用安全爲商店、分期付款公司等所接受的)。Hence, 由此產生, **'~-worthiness** *n.* **2** [U] money shown as owned by a person, company, etc in a bank account: (銀行帳戶中的)存款: *How much have I standing to my ~?* 我的存款尙有多少? *You have a ~ balance of £250.* 你的存款餘額爲二百五十鎊。 **3** [C] sum of money advanced or loaned (by a bank, etc): (銀行等對客戶的)預付款;墊款;貸款: *The bank refused further ~s to the company.* 銀行拒絕再貸款給該公司。**'~ squeeze,** (government) policy of making it difficult to borrow money (eg by raising interest rates), as part of a policy against inflation. 緊縮貸款(如藉提高利率增加借款的困難,爲抵制通貨膨脹的一部分)。 **4** (bookkeeping) record of payments received: (簿記)貸方: *Does this item go among the ~s or the debits?* 這筆帳應記入貸方抑或借方? **'~-side,** right-hand side of an account for recording payment received. 貸方。⇨ debit. **5** [C] (US) entry on a record to show that a course of study has been completed: (美)(表示某一學科業已修畢的) 學分登記: *~s in history and geography;* 歷史與地理的學分; *a '~ course,* university course depending upon the number of grades and ~s received. 學分學科(根據所獲之等級及學分數目的大學學科)。**6** [U] honour, approval, good name or reputation: 光榮;榮譽;贊許;好名聲;名譽;名望;名氣: *a man of the highest ~.* 極有名望的人。***get/take ~ (for sth),*** get/take recognition, honour etc: 得到賞識;獲得榮譽;(爲…)而獲得聲譽: *Candidates will get additional ~* (ie marks) *for clearly labelled diagrams.* 參加考試者若有清晰標明的圖解將獲得加分。*It is dishonest to take ~ for work done by others.* 拿他人所完成的工作以謀個人的榮譽,是不誠實的。***give ~ (to sb) (for sth),*** give recognition, praise, approval: (爲某事)認可、稱讚或贊許(某人): *He's cleverer than I gave him ~ for,* than I thought. 他的聰明伶俐超過我所料想的。*I gave you ~ for being more sensible,* You are less sensible than I thought. 我未料到你會如此不懂事。*One must give ~ where it is due.* 該贊許的就得贊許。**7 *do sb ~; do ~ to sb; be/stand to sb's ~; reflect ~ on sb,*** add to his reputation: 增加某人的聲譽;成爲某人的光榮;使某人大有面子:*The work does you ~.* 這項工作是你的光榮。*His smart appearance does ~ to his tailors.* 他英俊的儀表使他的裁縫們的技藝益爲生色。*It is/stands greatly to your ~ that you have passed such a difficult examination.* 這樣難的考試你都考及格了,是你莫大的光榮。*His fluency in Arabic reflects great ~ on/is greatly to the ~ of his teacher.* 他說得一口流利的阿拉伯語,爲他的老師增光不少。***be a ~ to sb/sth,*** add to the good name of sb/sth: 增加某人(某事物)的聲譽: *The pupils are a ~ to their teacher/school.* 學生們爲他們的老師(學校)增光。**~s; '~ titles,** names, shown on a cinema or TV screen, of persons responsible for the acting, direction, production, etc. (電影銀幕或電視螢幕上所顯示的)演員、導演、製作人等的名單。 **8** [U] belief; trust; confidence: 相信;信託;信任: *The rumour is gaining ~.* 那謠言已漸爲人所相信。***lend ~ to,*** strengthen belief in: 加强對…之相信: *The latest news lends ~ to the earlier reports.* 最新的消息可證實早先的報導是可靠的。

credit² /'kredɪt ; 'krɛdɪt/ *vt* [VP6A, 14] ***~ sb/sth (with sth); ~ sth (to sb/sth),*** **(a)** believe that he/it has sth: 相信…具有…;信賴: *Until now I've always ~ed you with more sense.* 到現在爲止,我一直都相信你不至如此糊塗。 *The relics are ~ed with miraculous powers.* 這些遺骸被認爲具有神奇的力量。*Miraculous powers are ~ed to the relics.* 人們認爲這些遺骸具有神奇力量。**(b)** enter on the ~ side of an account: 記入貸方: *~ a customer with £8;* 在客戶的貸方記入八鎊; *~ £8 to a customer/an account.* 在客戶(帳目)的貸方記入八鎊。⇨ credit¹(4).

credi·table /'kredɪtəbl ; 'krɛdɪtəbl̩/ *adj* ***~ (to),*** that brings credit(6, 7, 8): 可稱讚的; 增加聲譽的; 可信的: *a ~ attempt;* 可稱讚的努力; *conduct that was very ~ to him.* 他的極可稱讚的品行。 **credi·tably** /'kredɪtəblɪ ; 'krɛdɪtəblɪ/ *adv*

credi·tor /'kredɪtə(r) ; 'krɛdɪtə/ *n* person to whom one owes money: 債主; 債權人: *run away from one's ~s.* 躲避債主。

credo /'kri:dəʊ ; 'krido/ *n* (*pl* ~s /-dəʊz ; -doz/) creed. 信條。

cre·du·lity /krɪ'dju:lətɪ *US:* -'du:- ; krə'dulətɪ/ *n* (*pl* -ties) [U, C] too great a readiness to believe things. 易信;輕信。

credu·lous /'kredjʊləs *US:* -dʒʊ- ; 'krɛdʒələs/ *adj* (too) ready to believe things: 易信的;輕信的: *~ people who accept all the promises of the politicians.* 易受政客們的許諾哄騙的人們。**~·ly** *adv*

creed /kri:d ; krid/ *n* [C] (system of) beliefs or opinions, esp on religious doctrine. (尤指宗教的)信條; 教條。**the C~,** short summary of Christian doctrine. 使徒的信條(基督教信條的精義)。

creek /kri:k ; krik/ *n* **1** (GB) narrow inlet of water on the sea-shore or in a river-bank. (英)海岸的小灣; 河邊的小溪。 **2** (N America) small river. (北美洲)小河;溪流。***be up the ~,*** (sl) be in difficulties. (俚)在困難中;在困境。

creel /kri:l ; kril/ *n* angler's wicker basket for carrying the fish he catches. 漁人用的柳條魚簍。

creep /kri:p ; krip/ *vi* (*pt, pp* crept /krept ; krɛpt/) [VP2A, B, C] **1** move along with the body close to the ground or floor; move slowly, quietly or secretly: 爬行(以身體緊貼地面移動); 緩慢地、無聲地或暗暗地移動; 匍匐; 蠕動: *The cat crept silently towards the bird.* 那隻貓一聲不響地爬向那隻鳥。*The thief crept along the corridor.* 那賊偷偷地在走廊上潛行。 **2** (of time, age, etc) come on gradually: (指時間、年齡等)不知不覺而來: *Old age ~s upon one unawares.* 不知不覺間老年就來臨了。 *A feeling of drowsiness crept over him.* 一種昏昏欲睡的感覺逐漸襲着他。 **3** (of plants, etc) grow along the ground, over the surface of a wall, etc: (指植物等)沿地面、牆壁的表面等而蔓延;攀爬: *Ivy had crept over the ruined castle walls.* 常春籐已爬滿了那荒堡殘垣。 **4** (of the flesh) have the feeling that things are ~ing over it (as the result of fear, repugnance, etc); (指肌膚)有蟲爬的感覺(如由於恐懼、嫌惡等之結果); 起鷄皮疙瘩: *The sight of the cold, damp prison cell, with rats running about, made her flesh ~.* 看見那冰冷陰濕的牢房,還有老鼠在裏面跑來跑去,使她起鷄皮疙瘩。⇨ crawl(4). □ *n* **1** (sl) despicable person who tries to win favour by doing small favours, snooping, etc. (俚)(藉施小惠、打小報告等以求取寵的)卑鄙小人。 **2** ***give sb the ~s,*** (colloq) cause the flesh to ~(4); cause distaste in sb. (俗)使某人皮膚感覺有如蟲爬(不寒而慄);使人厭惡。

creeper /'kri:pə(r) ; 'kripə/ *n* insect, bird, etc that creeps; plant that creeps along the ground, over rocks, walls, etc. 爬行的昆蟲、鳥等; 蔓延於地上、岩石上、牆上等處的植物;爬籐。

creepy /'kri:pɪ ; 'kripɪ/ *adj* (-ier, -iest) (colloq) having or causing a creeping of the flesh, ⇨ creep (4): (俗) 令人感覺皮膚上有蟲爬似的; 令人毛骨悚然的: *a ~ story.* 令人毛骨悚然的故事。

creepy-crawly /ˌkri:pɪ'krɔ:lɪ ; ˌkripɪ'krɔlɪ/ *n* (*pl* -ies) (colloq) creeping or crawling insect etc. (俗)爬行的昆蟲。

cre·mate /krɪ'meɪt ; 'krimet/ *vt* [VP6A] burn (a corpse) to ashes: 火葬;燒(屍)成灰: *He says he wants to be ~d, not buried.* 他說他(死後)要火葬,不要土葬。**cre·ma·tion** /krɪ'meɪʃn ; krɪ'meʃən/ *n* [U] cremating; [C] instance of this. 火葬。 **cre·ma·tor·ium** /ˌkremə'tɔ:rɪəm ; ˌkrɛmə'torɪəm/ *n* furnace, building, place, for the cremating of corpses. 焚屍爐;火葬場。**cre·ma·tory** /'kremətərɪ *US:* -tɔ:rɪ ; 'krimə,torɪ/ *n* (*pl* -ries) = crematorium.

crème de menthe /ˌkrem də 'mɒnθ ; krɛmdə'mɑ̃t/ *n* [U] (F) sweet, thick, green liqueur flavoured with peppermint. (法)一種帶薄荷味的甜、濃、綠酒。

cren·el·lated (US=**-el·ated**) /'krenəleɪtɪd ; 'krɛnl̩,etɪd/ *adj* having battlements. 有城垛的;有雉堞的;有槍眼的;有砲門的。

Cre·ole /'kri:əʊl ; 'kriol/ *n, adj* **1** (person) of pure European or mixed European and African descent in the West Indies, Spanish America or the old French or Spanish states of the Southern US. 生於西印度群島,西班牙美洲,或昔時美國南部法國或西班牙所屬各州的歐洲人或歐非混血兒 (的); 克里奧爾人 (的)。 **2** (of a) dialect of French, Spanish or English spoken by persons of mixed European and African descent in N and S America and the W Indies. 南北美洲和西印度群島之歐非混血人種所說的法國、西班牙或英國方言(的);克里奧語(的)。

creo·sote /'krɪəsəʊt ; 'kriə,sot/ *n* [U] **1** thick, brown, oily liquid obtained from coal-tar, used to preserve wood. 雜酚油(褐色濃油,取自煤溚,用以防護木料)。 **2** antiseptic obtained from wood-tar. (取自木溚之)防腐油。

crêpe, crepe /kreɪp ; krep/ *n* [U] **1** any crape that is not black. 縐綢;縐紗(非指黑紗)。⇨ crape. **2** ~ **rubber,** raw rubber pressed into blocks. It has a wrinkled surface and is used for the soles of shoes, etc. 縐紋膠(一種壓成塊狀的生膠,可做鞋底等用);縐(橡)膠。**3** ~ **paper,** thin paper with a wavy or wrinkled surface. 縐紋紙。

crepi·tate /'krepɪteɪt ; 'krɛpə,tet/ *vi* [VP2A] make a series of sharp, crackling sounds. 作一連串之小爆裂聲。**crepi·ta·tion** /ˌkrepɪ'teɪʃn ; ˌkrɛpə'teʃən/ *n* crepitating (sound). 此種爆裂(聲)。

crept ⇨ creep.

cre·pus·cu·lar /krɪ'pʌskjʊlə(r) ; krɪ'pʌskjələ/ *adj* (formal) of, seen, heard or active during, twilight. (正式用語)晨昏之際(可見,可聞或活動)的。

cres·cendo /krɪ'ʃendəʊ ; krə'ʃɛndo/ *n* (*pl* ~s

/-dəʊz ; -doz/), *adv, adj* (passage of music to be played, sth heard) with, of, increasing loudness; (fig) progress towards a climax. 音量漸强的(一節樂曲或聲音);(喻)漸趨高潮。⇨ diminuendo.

cres·cent /ˈkresnt ; ˈkrɛsn̩t/ *n* **1** (sth shaped like) the curve of the moon in the first quarter, ⇨ the illus at phase; row of houses in the form of a ~. 弦月;弦月狀之物;(參看 phase之挿圖);弦月狀之一排房屋。**2 the C~,** (fig) faith and religion of Islam: (喻)回教: *the Cross* (Christianity) *and the C~.* 基督教與回教。**3** (attrib) ~-shaped; increasing in size: (形容用法)弦月狀的;漸大的: *a ~ moon.* 弦月;蛾眉月。

cress /kres ; krɛs/ *n* [U] name of various plants, esp the kind with hot-tasting leaves (used in salads and sandwiches). 水芹;水堇(尤指葉味辣者,用於沙拉及三明治)。

crest /krest ; krɛst/ *n* **1** tuft of feathers on a bird's head; cock's comb. 鳥冠;鷄冠。⇨ the illus at fowl, water. 參看 fowl, water 之挿圖。**'~-fallen,** (fig) dejected, disappointed (at failure, etc). (喻)(因失敗等)沮喪的;垂頭喪氣的;受挫折的。**2** ~-like decoration formerly worn on the top of a helmet; (poet) helmet. 昔時頭盔頂上所戴之鷄冠狀裝飾物;(詩)盔。**3** design over the shield of a coat of arms, or used separately (eg on a seal, or on notepaper): 盾形紋章上端之飾章;單獨使用之飾章(例如用於印信或便箋上者): *the family ~,* one used by a family. 家族飾章。**4** top of a slope or hill; white top of a large wave. 斜坡或小山的頂;浪頭;浪峯。***on the ~ of a wave,*** (fig) at the most favourable moment of one's fortunes. (喻)在某人最得意的時刻。**~ed** *adj* having a ~(3): 有飾章的: *~ed note-paper;* 有飾章的信箋; (in compounds, as names of birds) *the golden-~ed wren.* (用於複合字中,作爲鳥類名稱)金冠鷦鷯。□ *vt, vi* reach, form into, a ~ of a hill/wave. 達到(山,浪)之頂;形成頂。

cre·ta·cious /krɪˈteɪʃəs ; krɪˈteʃəs/ *adj* (geol) of (the nature of) chalk: (地質)白堊(質)的: *the ~ age,* when chalk-rocks were formed. 白堊紀。

cre·tin /ˈkretɪn *US:* ˈkriːtn ; ˈkritɪn/ *n* deformed and mentally undeveloped person (diseased because of weakness of the thyroid gland). 畸形而低能者(因甲狀腺功能太弱而引起者);白癡;矮呆子。**~·ous** /ˈkretɪnəs *US:* ˈkriːt- ; ˈkritɪnəs/ *adj*

cre·tonne /ˈkretɒn ; krɪˈtɑn/ *n* [U] cotton cloth with printed designs, used for curtains, furniture covers, etc. (做窗簾、傢具套等之)印花棉布。

cre·vasse /krɪˈvæs ; krəˈvæs/ *n* deep, open crack, esp in ice on a glacier. (冰河等的)裂縫;破口。⇨ the illus at mountain. 參看 mountain 之挿圖。

crev·ice /ˈkrevɪs ; ˈkrɛvɪs/ *n* narrow opening or crack (in a rock, wall, etc). (岩石、牆等的)裂縫;罅隙。

crew¹ /kruː ; kru/ *n* **1** (collective noun) all the

a crescent

persons working on a ship, aircraft, train, etc. (集合名詞)船上,飛機或火車上全體工作人員。**'ground ~,** mechanics who service an aircraft on the ground. 地勤組(在地面修護飛機的機械士)。**2** group of persons working together; gang. 一群共同工作的人;幫;群。**'~-cut** *n* closely cropped style of hair-cut for men. 小平頭(男人的一種髮式)。**'~-neck** *n* style of round, close-fitting collar. 圓式緊衣領。□ *vi* act as ~ on a boat: 做賽艇工作人員: *Will you ~ for me in tomorrow's race?* 明天賽艇時你做我的助手好嗎?

crew² /kruː ; kru/ *pt* of crow².

crib¹ /krɪb ; krɪb/ *n* **1** wooden framework from which animals can pull out fodder; manger. (牲畜用的)秣槽;芻槽;食槽。**2** (US) bin or box for storing maize, salt, etc. (美)貯藏玉蜀黍、鹽等的箱或盒。**3** (US 美 = *crèche*) representation (eg in a church at Christmas) of the nativity. 耶穌誕生的圖畫或演示(例如聖誕節教堂內展出者)。**4** bed for a newborn baby. 嬰兒睡的小床。□ *vt* (-bb-) shut up in a small space. 關閉在狹小的地方。

crib² /krɪb ; krɪb/ *n* **1** sth copied dishonestly from the work of another. 抄襲他人的作品;剽竊之物。**2** word-for-word translation of a foreign text used by students of the language. (外語學生用的)逐字翻譯本。□ *vt, vi* (-bb-) use a ~(2); copy (another pupil's written work) dishonestly. 使用逐字翻譯本;抄襲(另一學生的作業)。

crib·bage /ˈkrɪbɪdʒ ; ˈkrɪbɪdʒ/ *n* [U] card-game for two, three or four persons, who use pegs and a board (**'~-board**) with peg-holes in it for keeping the score. 一種紙牌戲(二人、三人或四人遊戲,用木釘及有孔的木板記分)。

crick /krɪk ; krɪk/ *n* (usu 常作 **a ~**) stiff condition of the muscles of the neck or the back causing sudden, sharp pain: 頸或背部肌肉的痙攣(會引起劇痛): *to have/get a ~ in the neck.* 頸部發生痙攣;感覺頸項不能轉動。□ *vt* produce a ~ in: 引起痙攣: *to ~ one's neck/back.* 引起頸項(背部)痙攣。

cricket¹ /ˈkrɪkɪt ; ˈkrɪkɪt/ *n* small, brown jumping insect which makes a shrill noise by rubbing its front wings together: 蟋蟀(一種能跳躍的褐色小昆蟲,摩擦其翅可發尖銳的鳴聲): *the chirping of ~s.* 蟋蟀的唧唧鳴聲。⇨ the illus at insect. 參看 insect 之挿圖。

cricket

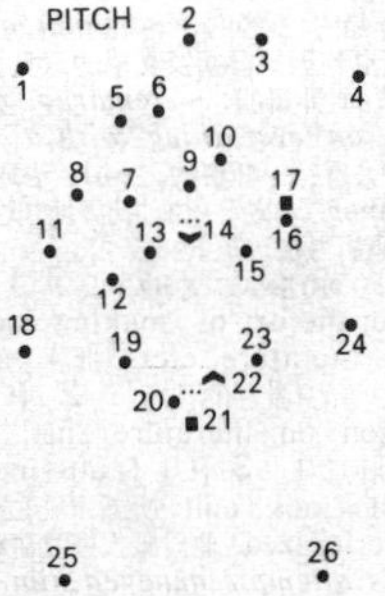

PLAYERS' POSITIONS

1 third man
2 long stop
3 deep fine leg
4 long leg
5 second slip
6 first slip
7 backward point
8 gully
9 wicket keeper
10 leg slip
11 cover point
12 short extra cover
13 silly mid-off
14 batsman
15 silly mid-on
16 square leg
17 umpire
18 extra cover
19 mid-off
20 bowler
21 umpire
22 batsman
23 mid-on
24 mid-wicket
25 long-off
26 long-on
... crease

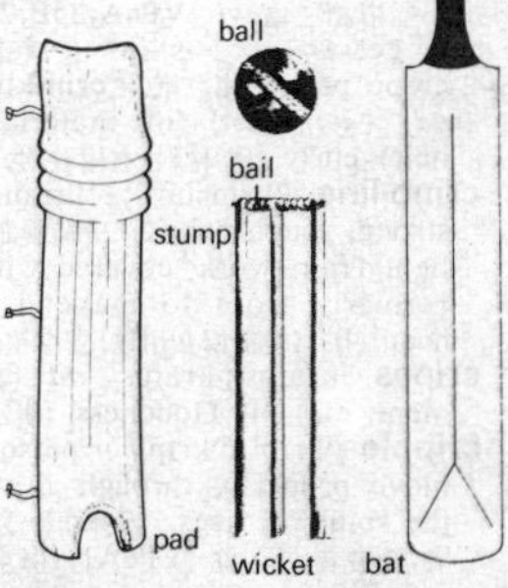

Note Although in fact only eleven men in addition to the batsmen and umpires are on the field at one time, they can be placed in any of these positions

cricket² /ˈkrɪkɪt; ˈkrɪkɪt/ *n* [U] ball game played on a grass field by two teams of eleven players each, with bats and wickets. 板球;板球戲(兩隊各十一人,以板及三柱門在草地上比賽)。 ***not* ~,** (colloq) unfair; unsportsmanlike. (俗)不公平的; 不合運動精神的。**~er** *n* ~ player. 板球選手;玩板球者。

cried /kraɪd; kraɪd/ ⇨ cry¹.

crier /ˈkraɪə(r); ˈkraɪɚ/ *n* **1** officer who makes public announcements in a court of law. (法庭上的)傳令員。ˌ**town-ˈ~,** (old use) man who goes round the streets to make proclamations and announcements. (舊用法) 沿街向市民傳告政令的人。**2** person (esp a young child) who cries(2) a lot. 好哭的人(尤指嬰兒)。

cries /kraɪz; kraɪz/ *prest* of cry¹; *pl* of cry².

cri·key /ˈkraɪkɪ; ˈkraɪkɪ/ *int* (colloq) exclamation of surprise. (俗)噯呀(表示驚訝的叫聲)。

crime /kraɪm; kraɪm/ *n* **1** [C] offence for which there is severe punishment by law; [U] such offences collectively; serious law-breaking: 爲法律所嚴懲的罪; 犯罪行爲; 嚴重的犯法: *to commit a serious ~;* 犯重罪; *the ~s of which he was proved guilty.* 他所犯的業已證明的罪行。*It is the business of the police to prevent and detect ~ and of the law courts to punish ~.* 防止及偵察犯罪是警察的職務而懲罰犯罪是法庭的責任。ˈ**~ fiction,** novels in which the detection of ~ is the chief interest. 描寫偵察犯罪爲主的小說; 偵探小說。**2** foolish or wrong act, not necessarily an offence against the law: 愚昧或錯誤的行爲(不一定是犯法的行爲): *It would be a ~ to send the boy out on such a cold, wet night.* 在這樣寒冷的雨夜把孩子遣出是不對的。**3** (in the army) serious breaking of the regulations (not necessarily an offence against civil law). (軍中)嚴重違犯軍紀;犯大過(不一定觸犯民法)。ˈ**~ sheet,** record of a soldier's offences. 犯軍紀的記錄。□ *vt* charge (a man) with, convict (a man) of, a military offence. 告或判(某人)違犯軍紀。

crimi·nal /ˈkrɪmɪnl; ˈkrɪmən̩l/ *adj* of crime: 犯罪的;犯法的: *a ~ act;* 犯罪的行爲; *a ~ offender;* 犯刑事罪者; *~ law.* 刑法。⇨ *civil law* at civil(1). □ *n* person who commits a crime or crimes. 犯罪者;罪犯。**~·ly** /-əlɪ; -l̩ɪ/ *adv*

crimi·nol·ogy /ˌkrɪmɪˈnɒlədʒɪ; ˌkrɪməˈnɑlədʒɪ/ *n* [U] the study of crime. 犯罪學。

crimp /krɪmp; krɪmp/ *vt* make (eg hair) wavy or curly (as with a hot iron). 使(髮等)捲曲(如用熱鐵棒)。

crim·son /ˈkrɪmzn; ˈkrɪmzn̩/ *adj, n* deep red. 深紅色(的)。□ *vt, vi* make or become ~. (使)變成深紅色。

cringe /krɪndʒ; krɪndʒ/ *vi* [VP2A, C] **1** ~ ***(at),*** move (the body) back or down in fear: (因恐懼而)退縮;畏縮: *The dog ~d at the sight of the whip.* 那狗看見鞭子就畏縮。**2** behave (towards a superior) in a way that shows lack of self-respect; be too humble: (對長上)表現卑躬屈膝的樣子;過分謙卑: *a cringing beggar;* 卑躬的乞丐; *to ~ to/before a policeman.* 對警察卑躬屈膝。

crinkle /ˈkrɪŋkl; ˈkrɪŋkl̩/ *n* small, narrow wrinkle (in material such as foil or paper). (箔或紙上的)小摺縐。□ *vt, vi* [VP6A, 15B, 2A, C] ~ ***(up),*** make or get a ~ or ~s in: (使)起縐紋: *~d paper,* eg crêpe paper. 縐紋紙。**crin·kly** /ˈkrɪŋklɪ; ˈkrɪŋklɪ/ *adj* (-ier, -iest) (of materials) having ~s; (of hair) curly. (指材料)有縐紋的;(指髮)捲曲的。

crino·line /ˈkrɪnəlɪn; ˈkrɪnl̩ɪn/ *n* **1** [U] stiff, strong, rough fabric. 一種硬而堅牢的粗布。**2** [C] light framework covered with stiff material, as formerly worn to make a skirt swell out; ⇨ hoop¹(1). (從前婦女用以)支撐裙子的襯架。

cripes /kraɪps; kraɪps/ *int* (expressing astonishment, etc) My Goodness! (表示驚異等)天啊！啊呀！

cripple /ˈkrɪpl; ˈkrɪpl̩/ *n* person unable to walk or move properly, through injury or weakness in the spine or legs. 因脊椎骨或腿受傷或發育不良而跛者;殘廢者。□ *vt* [VP6A] (lit, fig) make a ~ of; damage or weaken seriously: (字面,喻)使跛;使殘廢;嚴重地損壞或削弱: *~d soldiers;* 跛足的傷兵; *~d with rheumatism;* 因患風濕症而跛足的; *a ship that was ~d in a storm;* 在暴風雨中受到嚴重損壞的船; *activities ~d by lack of money.* 因缺乏經費而停頓的活動。

cri·sis /ˈkraɪsɪs; ˈkraɪsɪs/ *n* (*pl* crises /-siːz; -siz/) turning-point in illness, life, history, etc; time of difficulty, danger or anxiety about the future: (疾病、生命、歷史等之)轉捩點;艱苦危難的時期;危機;緊要關頭: *a financial ~.* 財政的危機。*Things are coming to/drawing to/reaching a ~.* 事情漸近緊要關頭。*We must bring things to a ~,* do sth to reach the state when a definite decision must be taken. 我們必須採取步驟促使事情達於決定階段。

crisp /krɪsp; krɪsp/ *adj* **1** (esp of food) hard, dry and easily broken: (尤指食物)脆的;酥的: *~ toast/biscuits.* 脆的烤麵包(餅乾)。*The snow was ~ underfoot.* 脚底下的雪踩起來是脆的。**2** (of the air, the weather) frosty, cold and dry: (指空氣,天氣)有霜氣的;寒冷而乾燥的: *the ~ air of an autumn morning.* 秋晨的霜氣。**3** (of hair) tightly curled. (指毛髮)捲得緊的。**4** (of style, manners) quick, precise and decided; showing no doubts or hesitation: (指風度、態度)乾脆的;明快的;斬釘截鐵的: *a man with a ~ manner of speaking.* 說話態度爽快的人。□ *n* (US 美 = *chip*) (also 亦作 **poˌtato ˈ~**) thin slice of potato, fried and dried (usu sold in bulk in packets). 炸馬鈴薯片(通常裝於小袋中售賣)。□ *vt, vi* make or become ~. (使)變酥脆;(使)變寒凍;(使)變捲緊;(使)變明快。**~·ly** *adv* **~·ness** *n*

criss·cross /ˈkrɪskrɒs *US:* -krɔːs; ˈkrɪsˌkrɔs/ *adj* with crossed lines: 線條互相交叉作十字狀的: *a ~ pattern/design.* 十字形圖案。□ *adv* crosswise. 互相交叉地。□ *vt, vi* move crosswise; mark with lines that cross. 交叉而行;以十字線標示。

cri·terion /kraɪˈtɪərɪən; kraɪˈtɪrɪən/ *n* (*pl* -ria /-rɪə; -rɪə/ or ~s) standard of judgement; principle by which sth is measured for value: 判斷的標準; 衡量某事物之價值的準則: *Success in money-making is not always a good ~ of real success in life.* 在賺錢方面的成功,不一定是人生事業眞正成功的一個好的準則。

critic /ˈkrɪtɪk; ˈkrɪtɪk/ *n* **1** person who forms and gives judgements, esp about literature, art, music, etc: (文學、藝術、音樂等的) 批評家: *music(al)/drama(tic)/literary, etc ~s.* 音樂(戲劇,文學等)批評家。**2** person who finds fault, points out mistakes, etc: 吹毛求疵者; 非難者: *I am my own most severe ~.* 我對自己要求非常嚴格。

criti·cal /ˈkrɪtɪkl; ˈkrɪtɪkl̩/ *adj* **1** of or at a crisis: 在危機期中的;緊要關頭的;轉捩點的: *We are at a ~ time in our history.* 我們正處於我們的歷史的危急時期。*The patient's condition is ~,* He is dangerously ill. 病人的情況甚危。*This is a ~ moment,* eg one when there will be a change for the better or the worse. 這是生死存亡的關頭。**2** of the work of a critic: 批評家之作品的;批評的: *~ opinions on art and literature.* 批評家對於藝術及文學的意見。**3** fault-finding: 吹毛求疵的;非難的: *~ remarks.* 吹毛求疵的評論。*She looks on everything with a ~ eye.* 她以吹毛求疵的眼光去看每一樣事物。**~·ly** /-ɪklɪ; -ɪklɪ/ *adv* in a ~ manner: 岌岌可危地;批評地;吹毛求疵地: *He is ~ly ill.* 他病得很沉重。

criti·cism /ˈkrɪtɪsɪzəm; ˈkrɪtəˌsɪzəm/ *n* **1** [U] the work of a critic; the art of making judgements (concerning art, literature, etc). 批評家的作品; 批評;(關於藝術、文學等的)批評的技巧。**2** [C] judgement or opinion on literature, art, etc. (對文學、藝術等的)批評意見。**3** [U] fault-finding; [C] remark, etc that finds fault: 吹毛求疵(之論): *He hates ~,* being criticized. 他討厭人家批評他。*Your frank ~s of his attempts annoyed him.* 你對於他的嘗試所作的坦白批評使他很生氣。

criti·cize /ˈkrɪtɪsaɪz; ˈkrɪtəˌsaɪz/ *vt, vi* [VP6A, 14, 2A] ~ ***(for),*** form and give a judgement of; find fault with: 批評;非難;吹毛求疵: *~ sb's work;* 批評

某人的作品; ~ *sb for doing/not doing sth.* 責備某人(未)做某事。

cri·tique /krɪˈtiːk ; krɪˈtik/ *n* [C] critical essay or review. 批評的文章;評論。

croak /krəʊk ; krok/ *n* deep, hoarse sound (as made by frogs or ravens). 蛙或烏鴉的叫聲;深沉的嗄聲。□ *vt, vi* **1** [VP2A, 6A, 15B] ~ ***(out)***, make this kind of sound; say (sth) in a ~ing voice; foretell (evil); express dismal views about the future. 發此種聲音; 說話聲如烏鴉叫; 以粗厲的聲音說(某事);預言(凶事);對於未來表示悲觀的看法。 **2** [VP 2A] (sl) die². (俚)死亡。

cro·chet /ˈkrəʊʃeɪ *US:* krəʊˈʃeɪ ; kroˈʃe/ *vt, vi* [VP 6A, 2A] make (needlework, eg a shawl) with a thread looped over others with the help of a small hooked needle (called a **ˈ~-hook**). 用鈎針(crochet-hook) 編織(披肩等)。 □ *n* [U] material (eg lace) made or being made in this way. 用鈎針編織的織物(如花邊)。

crock¹ /krɒk ; krɑk/ *n* pot or jar made of baked earth, eg for containing water; broken piece of such a pot: (裝水等的) 瓦罐; 瓦罐碎片: *Fill the bottom of the flower-pot with ~s for drainage.* 在花缽的底部塡以瓦罐碎片以便排水。

crock² /krɒk ; krɑk/ *n* (colloq) horse that has become old, weak and useless; person who cannot work well because of bad health, lameness, etc; very old motor vehicle, etc. (俗)老弱無用的馬;因健康不佳,跛足等而不善工作的人;極破舊的車輛等。 □ *vi, vt* [VP2C, 15B] ~ ***up***, become, cause to become, a ~: (使) 變爲無用; (使) 變衰弱: *This attack of influenza has ~ed me up.* 這一場流行性感冒使我衰弱得無法工作。*The poor man is ~ing up.* 那可憐的人漸漸無用了。

crock·ery /ˈkrɒkərɪ ; ˈkrɑkərɪ/ *n* [U] pots, plates, cups, dishes and other utensils (made of baked clay). 瓦器;陶器(如罐、盤、杯、碟等)。

croco·dile /ˈkrɒkədaɪl ; ˈkrɑkəˌdaɪl/ *n* **1** large river reptile with a long body and tail, covered with a hard skin. 鱷魚(河產爬虫,體及尾甚長,皮甚堅硬)。 ⇨ the illus at reptile. 參看 reptile 之插圖。 **ˈ~ tears** *n pl* insincere sorrow. 假悲傷。 **2** (GB colloq) school children walking in procession, two by two. (英俗)成雙列排隊而行的學童。

cro·cus /ˈkrəʊkəs ; ˈkrokəs/ *n* (*pl* ~es /-sɪz ; -sɪz/) (kind of) small plant growing from a corm, with coloured flowers early in spring. 番紅花(自球莖長出之小植物,花色不一,初春時開放)。

Croe·sus /ˈkriːsəs ; ˈkrisəs/ *n* (6th c BC) wealthy king in Asia Minor. 克里薩斯(西元前六世紀小亞細亞一富有之王)。**a ~**, very wealthy person. 大富翁。

croft /krɒft *US:* krɔːft ; krɔft/ *n* (GB) small, enclosed field; small farm. (英)圍起來的小塊地;小農場。 **~er** *n* person who rents or owns a small farm, esp a joint tenant of a divided farm in Scotland. 小農場佃戶或場主;(尤指)蘇格蘭小農場佃農。

crom·lech /ˈkrɒmlek ; ˈkrɑmlɛk/ *n* prehistoric structure of large flat stones laid horizontally on upright stones. (史前時代以扁平巨石平置於豎立石塊上之)大石碑坊。

crone /krəʊn ; kron/ *n* withered old woman. 乾癟的老太婆。

crony /ˈkrəʊnɪ ; ˈkronɪ/ *n* close friend; companion; close associate. 密友;同伴;親密的夥伴。

crook /krʊk ; krʊk/ *n* **1** stick or staff with a rounded hook at one end, esp such a stick used by a shepherd. 一端有彎鈎的棍杖(尤指牧羊人用者)。 ⇨ hook. **2** bend or curve, eg in a river or path. (河道或道路等的)彎處; 彎子。 **ˈ~-back(ed)**, hunchback(ed). 駝背(的)。 **3** (colloq) person who makes a living by dishonest or criminal means. (俗)騙徒;惡棍;流氓。 **4** ***on the ~***, (sl) dishonest(ly). (俚)狡詐的(地);詭譎的(地)。 □ *vt, vi* [VP6A, 2A] bend into the shape of a ~: 使彎曲: *to ~ one's finger/arm.* 屈指(臂)。

crooked /ˈkrʊkɪd ; ˈkrʊkɪd/ *adj* **1** not straight or level; twisted; bent: 不平直的; 扭曲的; 彎曲的: *a ~ lane.* 彎曲的小巷。 *You've got your hat on ~.* 你把帽子戴歪了。 **2** (of a person or his actions) dishonest; not straightforward. (指人或其行動)不誠實的;欺騙的;狡詐的。 **~·ly** *adv* **~·ness** *n*

croon /kruːn ; krun/ *vt, vi* [VP6A, 13A, 15A, 2C] hum or sing gently in a narrow range of notes: 輕哼; 低唱: *~ to oneself;* 獨自輕聲低唱; *~ a lullaby;* 輕唱搖籃曲;*~ the baby to sleep.* 輕唱以使嬰兒入睡。**~er** *n* (1930's and 1940's) person who ~s, esp a public entertainer who sings sentimental songs with a microphone held at the lips. (1930年代及1940年代)輕唱者(尤指對着擴音器唱感傷歌曲以娛聽衆者)。

crop¹ /krɒp ; krɑp/ *n* [C] **1** yearly (or season's) produce of grain, grass, fruit, etc; (*pl*) agricultural plants in the fields: (穀物、果類等)一年或一季的收穫;(複)田中的農作物: *the ˈpotato ~;* 馬鈴薯的產量; *a good ~ of rice;* 稻穀的豐收; *to get the ~s in;* 收割田中的穀物; (attrib) (形容用法) *~ failures.* 穀物收成不好。*The land is in/under ~,* being cultivated. 這塊土地種有作物。*The land is out of ~,* not being cultivated. 這塊土地未種作物。 **ˈ~-dusting**, dusting (eg from low-flying aircraft) of growing ~s with insecticide or fertiliser. (自低飛的飛機等)對農作物噴撒殺蟲劑或肥料。 **2** group of persons or thing, samount of anything, appearing or produced together: 一大堆(同時出現或產生的人、物、數量): *The Prime Minister's statement produced a ~ of questions.* 首相的聲明引起了一大堆問題。

crop² /krɒp ; krɑp/ *n* [C] **1** bag-like part of a bird's throat where food is broken up for digestion before passing into the stomach. 鳥的膆囊(食物在進入胃以前在此磨碎以便消化)。 ***neck and ~***, ⇨ neck. **2** handle of a whip; (also 亦作 **ˈhunting-~**) whip-handle with a loop instead of a lash. 鞭柄;帶皮圈而無皮條的鞭柄。 **3** very short hair-cut: 剪得極短的髮式;平頭: *You look as if you've had a prison ~,* had your hair cut very short, like men in prison. 你的頭髮看來剪得像牢裏的犯人一樣短。

crop³ /krɒp ; krɑp/ *vt, vi* (-pp-) **1** [VP6A, 22] (of animals) bite off the tops of (grass, plants, etc); graze: (指牲畜)咬去(青草、植物等)的尖端;吃青草: *The sheep had ~ped the grass short.* 羊群已將青草吃短。 **2** [VP6A, 22] cut short (a person's hair, a horse's tail or ears). 剪短 (人的頭髮, 馬的尾巴或耳朵)。 **3** [VP6A, 14] ~ ***(with)***, sow or plant: 播種; 種植: *to ~ ten acres with wheat.* 種植十畝地的小麥。 **4** [VP2A] bear a crop: 收穫: *The beans ~ped well this year.* 豆子今年豐收。⇨ crop¹(1). **5** [VP2C] ~ ***up/out***, (of rock, minerals) show up above the earth's surface. (指岩石,礦物)露出地面之上。⇨ outcrop. **6** [VP2C] ~ ***up***, appear or arise (esp unexpectedly): 出現或發生(尤指意外地): *All sorts of difficulties ~ped up.* 各種各樣的困難一齊都來了。 *The subject ~ped up in the course of conversation.* 談話時無意中談到了這個題目。

crop·per /ˈkrɒpə(r) ; ˈkrɑpɚ/ *n* **1** ***good/bad/heavy/light ~***, plant yielding a good etc crop: 結實或收成好(壞,多,少)的植物: *These peas are good ~s.* 這些豆子結實甚豐。 **2** person or thing that crops. 收穫者;收割機。⇨ *share-cropper* at share¹(1). **3** ***come a ~***, (colloq) have a fall; meet with failure (eg in an examination). (俗)跌倒;失敗(如考試不及格)。

cro·quet /ˈkrəʊkeɪ *US:* krəʊˈkeɪ ; kroˈke/ *n* [U] game played on short grass with wooden balls which are knocked with wooden mallets through hoops. 槌球遊戲(在短草地上玩,以木槌擊木球鑽小圈)。

cro·quette /krəʊˈket ; kroˈkɛt/ *n* [C] ball of minced meat, fish, potato etc, coated with bread-crumbs and cooked in fat. (以碎的肉,魚或馬鈴薯等外黏麵包屑而炸成之)炸肉丸;炸魚丸;炸馬鈴薯丸。

crore /krɔː(r) ; kror/ *n* (India and Pakistan) ten millions; one hundred lakhs (eg of rupees). (印度

及巴基斯坦)一千萬(盧比等)。

cro·sier, cro·zier /ˈkrəʊzɪə(r) *US:* -ʒər ; ˈkroʒɚ/ *n* bishop's staff, usu shaped like a shepherd's crook. 主教的權杖(通常作牧羊人的牧杖形)。⇨ the illus at vestment. 參看 vestment 之插圖。

cross¹ /krɒs *US:* krɔːs ; krɔs/ *n* **1** mark made by drawing one line across another, thus: ×, +: 十字形或叉形記號: *The place is marked on the map with a* ~. 該地在地圖上以十字記號標出。***make one's*** ~, put a ~ on a document instead of one's signature (as in former times by illiterate persons). 畫押;畫十字(如昔時文盲在文件上畫十字以代替簽名者)。**2** line or stroke forming part of a letter (eg the horizontal stroke on a 't'). 字母 (例如 t) 上的一橫。**3** stake or post with another piece of wood across it like T, † or X, as used in ancient times for crucifixion, esp **the C~**, that on which Christ died; model of this as a religious emblem; sth (esp a monument) in the form of a ~ (eg one in stone set up in the market-place of a village or town, called a **ˈmarket-~**); sign of a ~ made with the right hand as a religious act. 在木柱上另釘一塊橫木構成的十字架(如古代用作刑具者); (尤指)釘死耶穌的十字架;作爲宗教表記的十字架模型;十字形石碑(如立於村鎮市場者,稱爲 market-cross);用右手所畫的十字(係宗教行爲)。**4** (fig) suffering; affliction; burden of sorrow: (喻) 苦難; 痛苦; 磨難; 憂患: *to bear one's* ~; 忍受苦難; *to take up one's* ~, be ready to bear affliction or suffering. 準備忍受苦難。**5** emblem, in the form of a ~ or a star, (to be) worn by an order of knighthood; decoration for personal valour: (某等級爵士所戴的)十字徽章; (紀念英勇行爲的)十字勳章: *the Victoria C~;* 維多利亞十字勳章; *the Distinguished Service C~.* 服務優異十字勳章。**6** (place of) crossing. 交叉(處)。***cut on the*** ~, (dress-making) cut diagonally: (裁縫)斜地剪裁: *This skirt material was cut on the* ~, on the bias. 這裙子料是斜裁的。**7** offspring of animals or plants of different sorts or breeds: 異種動物或植物雜交所產生的混合種: *A mule is a* ~ *between a horse and an ass.* 騾係馬與驢交配所生的混合種。

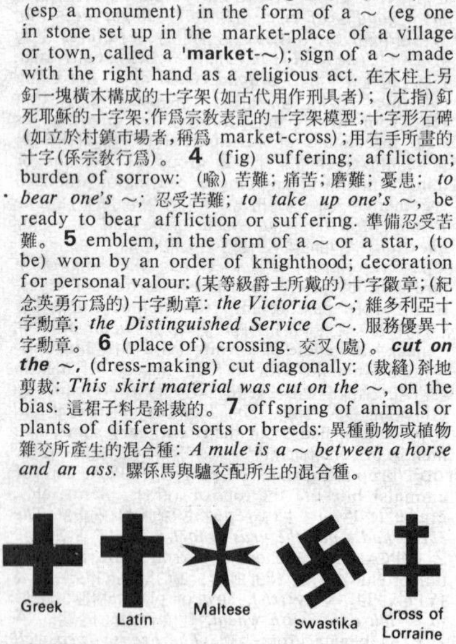

crosses

cross² /krɒs *US:* krɔːs ; krɔs/ *vt, vi* **1** [VP6A, 2A, C] ~ ***(from) (to)***, go across; pass from one side to the other side of: 橫過;越過;渡過: *to* ~ *a road/river/bridge/the sea/the Sahara, etc;* 橫越道路(河流,橋樑,海,撒哈拉沙漠等); *to* ~ *from Dover to Calais.* 自多佛橫渡海峽至加來。~ ***a person's path***, meet him: 遇見某人: *I hope I shall never* ~ *that man's path again.* 我希望我永不再遇見那個人。~ ***one's mind***, (of ideas, etc) occur to one: (指念頭等) 出現於腦中: *The idea has just* ~*ed my mind that....* 我剛才想到…。**2** [VP6A, 15A, B] ~ ***(off/out/through)***, draw a line or lines across or through (to cancel): 畫橫線於(以刪除): *Two of the words had been* ~*ed out.* 其中有兩個字被畫去了。*I* ~*ed his name off the list.* 我把他的名字從名單中剔除了。~ ***a cheque***, draw two lines across it so that payment can be made only through a bank. 畫兩條線於支票(表示僅能經由銀行兌現)。Hence, 由此產生, **ˌ~ed ˈcheque** *n* one that must be paid into a bank account, and cannot be cashed unless made out to 'self' or 'cash'. 畫線支票(必須存入戶頭,如未標明 'self' 或 'cash' 字樣不可兌現)。~ ***one's t's and dot one's i's***, (fig) be careful and exact. (喻)謹愼而嚴正。**3** [VP6A, 14] put or place across or over: 交叉: *to* ~ *one's legs;* 交叉兩腿; *to* ~ *one's arms on one's chest.* 交叉兩臂於胸前。~ ***sb's palm with silver***, give a coin to him (esp to a fortune-teller). 拿一枚銅錢給某人(尤指給算命者)。~ ***swords with sb***, fight or argue with him. 與某人交鋒;與某人辯論。***keep one's fingers*** ~***ed***, (fig) hope for the best, that nothing will happen to upset one's plans, etc. (喻)求神保佑一切順利;希望不要有意外事情妨礙計畫等。**4** ~ ***oneself***, make the sign of the cross on or over oneself as a religious act, to invoke God's protection, or as a sign of awe. 用右手在胸前畫十字(係宗教行爲,意爲求上帝保護或表示敬畏)。**5** [VP6A, 2A] (of persons travelling, letters in the post) meet and pass: (指行路的人,郵遞中的信件)互相在路上錯過: *We* ~*ed each other on the way.* 我們兩人在路上錯過去了。*Our letters* ~*ed in the post.* 我們的信件在郵局錯過。*Your letter* ~*ed mine in the post.* 你的信跟我的信在郵局中錯過。**~ed line**, interruption by mistake into a telephone connection. 電話岔線。**6** [VP6A] oppose or obstruct (sb, his plans, wishes, etc): 反對或阻礙 (某人,其計畫、意願等): *He was angry at having his plans* ~*ed.* 他因計畫受阻而忿怒。*He* ~*es me in everything.* 他處處與我作對。*He has been* ~*ed in love*, has failed to win the love of the woman he was in love with. 他在愛情上曾受挫折(未獲所愛之女人的垂青)。**7** [VP2A, 6A, 14] ~ ***(with)***, produce a cross(7) by mixing breeds; (cause to) interbreed; cross-fertilize (plants, etc). 使異種交配以產生混合種;使雜交;雜配(植物等)。⇨ crossbreed.

cross³ /krɒs *US:* krɔːs ; krɔs/ *adj* **1** (colloq) bad-tempered; easily or quickly showing anger: (俗)脾氣壞的; 易怒的: *Don't be* ~ *with the child for being late.* 不要對那遲到的孩子發脾氣。*I've never heard a* ~ *word from her lips.* 我從未聽到她說過一句發脾氣的話。*Don't pull the dog's tail, you'll make him* ~. 不要拉狗的尾巴,你會使牠發脾氣的。***as*** ~ ***as two sticks***, (colloq) very bad-tempered. (俗)脾氣乖戾的。**2** (of winds) contrary; opposed: (指風)相反的;逆的: *Strong* ~ *winds made it difficult for the yachts to leave harbour.* 强烈的逆風使那些小艇不易出港。**~·ly** *adv* **~·ness** *n*

cross·bar /ˈkrɒsbɑː(r) *US:* ˈkrɔːs- ; ˈkrɔsˌbɑr/ *n* bar going across, eg the bar joining the two upright posts of the goal (in football, etc) or the front and rear ends of a bicycle frame. 橫木;橫槓(例如足球門等之橫木或脚踏車之橫槓)。⇨ the illus at bicycle. 參看 bicycle 之插圖。

cross·beam /ˈkrɒsbiːm *US:* ˈkrɔːs- ; ˈkrɔsˌbim/ *n* beam placed across, esp one that supports parts of a structure; girder. 房屋的橫樑;橫桁;大樑。

cross·benches /ˈkrɒsbentʃɪz *US:* ˈkrɔːs- ; ˈkrɔsˌbɛntʃɪz/ *n pl* those benches in the House of Commons used by members who do not vote regularly with either the Government or the Opposition. (英國下議院不固定投政府票或反對票的)中立議員席。Hence, 由此產生, **crossbencher** *n* ⇨ bench.

cross·bones /ˈkrɒsbəʊnz *US:* ˈkrɔːs- ; ˈkrɔsˌbonz/ *n pl* (design of) two thigh bones laid across each other, usu under a skull, as an emblem of death (used as a warning of danger, and on the black flag once used by pirates). 通常畫於頭蓋骨下面象徵死亡的兩條交叉股骨; 此種圖形(用作危險的警告,昔時海盜亦用於黑旗上)。

cross·bow /ˈkrɒsbəʊ *US:* ˈkrɔːs- ; ˈkrɔsˌbo/ *n* old kind of bow placed across a grooved wooden support, used for shooting arrows, bolts, stones, etc. 十字弓;弩(一種舊式弓,橫置於有溝的木架上,以發射箭、矢、石等)。

cross·bred /ˈkrɒsbred *US:* ˈkrɔːs- ; ˈkrɔsˌbrɛd/ *adj* produced by crossing breeds: 由雜交所產生的;雜種的: ~ *sheep.* 雜種綿羊。

cross·breed /ˈkrɒsbriːd *US:* ˈkrɔːs- ; ˈkrɔsˌbrid/ *n* (in farming, etc) animal, plant, etc, produced by crossing different kinds. (在畜牧,農業等中)由雜交

所產的雜種(動物，植物等)。□ *vi, vt* [VP2A, 6A] produce in this way. (使)雜交；(使)異種交配。

cross-check /ˌkrɒs ˈtʃek *US:* ˌkrɔːs ; ˌkrɔs ˈtʃɛk/ *vt, vi* [VP6A, 2A] verify, eg a method, calculation, by using a different method, etc: (以不同方法等)查核；核對(某一方法或計算結果等)：*We ~ed the results twice.* 我們將結果核對了兩次。□ *n* verification of this sort: 以不同方法查核；核對：*We'd better do a ~ on these figures.* 我們最好核對一下這些數字。

cross·country /ˌkrɒsˈkʌntrɪ *US:* ˌkrɔːs- ; ˈkrɔs-ˌkʌntrɪ/ *adj, adv* across the country or fields, not along roads: 越野的(地)：*a ~ race.* 越野賽跑。

cross-cur·rent /ˈkrɒs kʌrənt *US:* ˈkrɔːs ; ˈkrɔs-ˌkɝənt/ *n* current flowing across another; (fig) body of opinion contrary to that of the majority (on sth of public interest). 交叉的水流；(喻)(對有關公益事件)與大多數人相反的意見。

cross·cut /ˈkrɒskʌt *US:* ˈkrɔːs- ; ˈkrɔs,kʌt/ *adj* (of a saw) with teeth designed for cutting across the grain of wood. (指鋸)有特種鋸齒而能橫木紋而鋸的；橫切的。□ *n* diagonal cut or path; short cut. 對角斜切；斜路；捷徑。

cross-division /ˌkrɒs dɪˈvɪʒn *US:* ˌkrɔːs ; ˈkrɔsdə-ˈvɪʒən/ *n* [U] division of a group according to more than one factor at the same time so that sub-divisions interrelate; [C] instance of this. 橫式區分(同時根據幾個因素劃分一團體,俾使再分成的部分有相互關係)；此種區分的實例。

crosse /krɒs *US:* krɔːs ; krɔs/ *n* kind of long-handled racquet used in lacrosse. 曲棍球棒。

cross-exam·ine /ˌkrɒs ɪgˈzæmɪn *US:* ˌkrɔːs ; ˈkrɔsɪgˈzæmɪn/ *vt* [VP6A] question closely, esp to test answers already given to someone else, as in a law court, by counsel, etc. 嚴密詢問；(尤指在法庭等中由辯護律師等就某人對他人所作之回答進行)盤問；盤詰。**cross-exam·iner** /-mɪnə(r);-mɪnɚ/ *n* **cross-exam·in·ation** /ˌkrɒs ɪgˌzæmɪˈneɪʃn *US:* ˌkrɔːs ; ˈkrɔsɪg,zæməˈneʃən/ *n*

cross·eyed /ˈkrɒsaɪd *US:* ˈkrɔːs- ; ˈkrɔsˈaɪd/ *adj* with one or both eyeballs turned towards the nose. 一眼球或二眼球向鼻子斜的；內斜視的；鬥雞眼的。

cross-fer·ti·lize /ˌkrɒs ˈfɜːtəlaɪz *US:* ˌkrɔːs ; ˈkrɔs-ˈfɝtḷ,aɪz/ *vt* (bot) carry pollen from the stamens of one plant to the pistil of another plant to produce hybrids. (植物)使異花受精(將異種雄蕊之花粉送至雌蕊受精以產生雜種)。**cross-fer·ti·li·za·tion** /ˌkrɒs-ˌfɜːtəlaɪˈzeɪʃn *US:* ˌkrɔːs ; ˈkrɔs,fɝtḷəˈzeʃən/ *n*

cross·fire /ˈkrɒsfaɪə(r) *US:* ˈkrɔːs- ; ˈkrɔs,faɪr/ *n* [U, C] (mil) firing of guns from two or more points so that the lines of fire cross; (fig) situation in which questions are put to sb from different persons. (軍)交叉射擊(自兩處或多處向同一目標射擊,以致砲火交錯)；(喻)(自不同人士對某人發出的)交相質問。

cross-grained /ˌkrɒs ˈgreɪnd *US:* ˌkrɔːs ; ˈkrɔs-ˈgrend/ *adj* **1** (of wood) with the grain in crossing directions. (指木材)紋理交錯的。**2** (fig) perverse; difficult to please or get on with. (喻)執拗的；難以取悅或相處的。

cross-head(·ing) /ˈkrɒs hed(ɪŋ) *US:* ˈkrɔːs ; ˈkrɔs-ˈhɛd(ɪŋ)/ *n* (in a newspaper, etc) heading within an article, dividing a column. (報紙等之)小標題(插在各段落之間)；子題。

cross-index /ˌkrɒs ˈɪndeks *US:* ˌkrɔːs ; ˈkrɔsˈɪndɛks/ *n, vt* [VP6A] (supply with) cross-reference. (供以)前後參看。

cross·ing /ˈkrɒsɪŋ *US:* ˈkrɔːs- ; ˈkrɔsɪŋ/ *n* **1** [U, C] the act of going across, esp by sea: 橫越(尤指渡海)：*We had a rough ~ from Dover to Calais.* 我們由多佛渡海至加來時,風浪很大。**2** [C] place where two roads, two railways, or (esp) a road and a railway cross. 十字路口；兩鐵道交叉處；(尤指)(鐵路與公路交叉處的)平交道。ˌ**level** ˈ**~**, one without a bridge (US 美 = *grade ~*). 平交道。**3 peˌdestrian/ˌzebra** ˈ**~**, place on a street where pedestrians are requested to cross (often marked by studs or white lines and sometimes by traffic lights operated by pedestrians) (US 美 = *crosswalk*). 行人穿越道(常以飾釘或白線表示,有時由行人操縱交通燈控制)；斑馬線。

cross·keys /ˌkrɒsˈkiːz *US:* ˌkrɔːs- ; ˈkrɔsˈkiz/ *n pl* (design of) crossed keys as Papal arms, and as an inn sign. 交叉鑰匙(圖形)(如教皇紋章或旅館招牌上的標記)。

cross-legged /ˌkrɒs ˈlegd *US:* ˌkrɔːs ; ˈkrɔsˈlɛgɪd, -ˈlɛgd/ *adv* (of a person sitting) with one leg placed across the other. (指坐着的人)兩腿交叉地。

cross·patch /ˈkrɒspætʃ *US:* ˈkrɔːs- ; ˈkrɔs,pætʃ/ *n* (colloq) cross, bad-tempered person. (俗)脾氣乖戾的人。

cross-piece /ˈkrɒs piːs *US:* ˈkrɔːs ; ˈkrɔs,pis/ *n* piece (of a structure) lying across another piece. (指構造物中)置於他物上的橫放物；橫檔。

cross-pur·poses /ˌkrɒs ˈpɜːpəsɪz *US:* ˌkrɔːs ; ˈkrɔsˈpɝpəsɪz/ *n pl* **be at ~,** (of two persons or groups) misunderstand one another; have different and conflicting purposes. (指二人或團體)互相誤解；持有不同而且衝突的目的。

cross-question /ˌkrɒs ˈkwestʃən *US:* ˌkrɔːs ; ˈkrɔsˈkwɛstʃən/ *vt* [VP6A] = cross-examine.

cross-ref·er·ence /ˌkrɒs ˈrefrəns *US:* ˌkrɔːs ; ˈkrɔsˈrɛfərəns/ *n* [C] reference from one part of a book, index, file, etc to another, for further information. 書中前後互相參看之處。

cross·road /ˈkrɒsrəʊd *US:* ˈkrɔːs- ; ˈkrɔs,rod/ *n* **1** road that crosses another. 交叉路。**2 a/the ~s,** (used with *sing v*) place where two roads meet and cross: (用單數動詞)十字路口：*We came to a ~s.* 我們走到一個十字路口。**3** ***at the ~s,*** (fig) at a critical turning-point (in life, etc). (喻)處於(人生等的)轉捩點。

cross-sec·tion /ˌkrɒs ˈsekʃn *US:* ˌkrɔːs ; ˈkrɔs-ˈsɛkʃən/ *n* [C] (drawing of a) piece or slice made by cutting across, eg a tree trunk; (fig) typical or representative sample of the whole: 橫切面(例如樹幹者)；橫切面之圖；(喻)(用以代表全體的)樣品；抽樣：*a ~ of the electors/the middle classes.* 選舉人(中產階級)的代表。

cross-stitch /ˈkrɒs stɪtʃ *US:* ˈkrɔːs ; ˈkrɔs,stɪtʃ/ *n* [C] stitch formed of two stitches that cross; [U] needlework in which this stitch is used. 十字針法；用十字針法編織的織物。

cross-talk /ˈkrɒs tɔːk *US:* ˈkrɔːs ; ˈkrɔs,tɔk/ *n* [U] (GB, colloq) rapid exchange of remarks, eg by comedians in a variety entertainment or in a quarrel; talk in which conversation is garbled, eg by crossed telephone lines. (英,俗)鬥嘴(例如雜技團中滑稽角色之插科或吵架時之對罵)；(電話中因線路交錯而由他處傳來的)片斷對話。

cross·trees /ˈkrɒstriːz *US:* ˈkrɔːs- ; ˈkrɔs,triz/ *n pl* two horizontal timbers bolted to a lower mast to support the mast above and to support ropes, etc. 桅頂橫桁(二平行木材,鬥於較低之桅頂以支持上端較高之桅及纜索等)。

cross·walk /ˈkrɒswɔːk *US:* ˈkrɔːs- ; ˈkrɔs,wɔk/ *n* ⇨ crossing(3).

cross·wind /ˈkrɒswɪnd *US:* ˈkrɔːs- ; ˈkrɔswɪnd/ *n* [C] wind blowing at right angles, eg to an aircraft's line of flight or to traffic on a motorway. 側風(例如成直角吹向一飛機的航線或在高速公路上行駛的車輛者)。

cross-wise /ˈkrɒs waɪz *US:* ˈkrɔːs ; ˈkrɔs,waɪz/ *adv* across; diagonally; in the form of a cross. 橫地；斜地；作十字狀地。

cross·word /ˈkrɒswɜːd *US:* ˈkrɔːs- ; ˈkrɔs,wɝd/ *n* (also 亦作 ˈ**~ puzzle**) puzzle in which words have to be written (from numbered clues) vertically (= clues *down*) and horizontally (= clues *across*) in spaces on a chequered square or oblong. 縱橫字謎(依號碼排列的提示,在一塊方陣或長方

陣之許多小方格內,按縱橫方向塡字的一種遊戲)。

crotch /krɒtʃ; krɑtʃ/ *n* **1** place where a branch forks from a tree: 樹的枝枒;樹叉: *The child was sitting in a ~ of a tree.* 那孩子坐在一個樹叉上。**2** place where a pair of trousers or a person's legs fork from the trunk. (褲子的)袴襠;(人體的)胯部。

crotchet /ˈkrɒtʃɪt; ˈkrɑtʃɪt/ *n* **1** (music) (US 美 = *quarter note*) black-headed note with stem (♩), half of a minim. (音樂)四分音符。⇨ the illus at notation. 參看 notation 之插圖。**2** strange, unreasonable idea. 不合理的奇思怪想。**~y** *adj* full of ~s(2); bad-tempered. 充滿奇思怪想的;脾氣壞的。

crouch /kraʊtʃ; kraʊtʃ/ *vi* [VP2A, C, 4A] **~ (down)**, lower the body with the limbs together (in fear or to hide, or, of animals, ready to spring). 蹲伏(四肢收縮,身體低下,因恐懼或欲隱藏,或指動物預備猛撲的姿勢)。□ *n* ~ing position. 蹲伏的姿勢。

croup[1] /kruːp; krup/ *n* [U] children's disease in which there is inflammation of the windpipe, with coughing and difficulty in breathing. 格魯布性喉頭炎;哮吼(兒童疾病,氣管發炎,有咳嗽及呼吸困難現象)。

croup[2] /kruːp; krup/ *n* rump or buttocks of certain animals. (某些動物之)臀部。⇨ the illus of *horse* at domestic. 參看 domestic 項下 horse 之插圖。

crou·pier /ˈkruːpɪeɪ *US:* -pɪər; ˈkrupɪɚ/ *n* person who rakes in the money at a gaming table and pays out winnings. 賭桌上收取及償付賭注的人。

crow[1] /krəʊ; kro/ *n* (kinds of) large, black bird with a harsh cry. 烏鴉。⇨ the illus at bird. 參看 bird 之插圖。⇨ also carrion, jackdaw, raven, rook[1]. ***as the ˈ~ flies***, in a straight line. 成直線地。**ˈ~'s-nest**, protected look-out platform fixed at the mast-head of a ship (eg a whaling ship) for the look-out man. 桅樓;瞭望台(例如捕鯨船桅頂供瞭望者所用者)。**ˈ~'s-feet** *n pl* network of little lines on the skin near the outer corners of a person's eyes. 魚尾紋(成人眼角外側附近皮膚上的皺紋)。

crow[2] /krəʊ; kro/ *vi* (*pt* crowed or (archaic) (古) crew /kruː; kru/, *pp* crowed) [VP2A, 3A] **1** (of a cock) make a loud, shrill cry. (指公鷄)啼;叫;喔喔。**2** (of a baby) make sounds showing happiness. (指嬰兒)發笑聲。**3 ~ (over)**, (of persons) express gleeful triumph: (指人)表示得意洋洋: *to ~ over an unsuccessful rival.* 面對失敗的敵手而得意洋洋。□ *n* ~ing sound. 公鷄的啼聲;嬰兒笑聲。

crow·bar /ˈkrəʊbɑː(r); ˈkroˌbɑr/ *n* straight iron bar, often with a forked end, used as a lever for moving heavy objects. 作爲槓桿移動重物的鐵棍;鐵撬;鐵梃;撬棍。

crowd /kraʊd; kraʊd/ *n* [C] **1** large number of people together, but without order or organization: 人群;群衆: *There were large ~s of people in the streets on New Year's Eve.* 除夕的街上有大批的人群。*He pushed his way through the ~.* 他從人群中擠過去。***(would) pass in a ~***, is not obviously unsatisfactory or defective. 還過得去;還不壞。**2 the ~**, the masses; people in general. 民衆;大衆。***follow/move with the ~***, be content to do what most people do. 從衆;跟大家一樣。**3** (colloq) company of persons associated in some way; set or clique of persons: (俗)一夥;一班;一幫: *I can't afford to go about with that ~; they're too extravagant.* 我沒有財力同那夥人打交道;他們太奢侈了。**4** large number (of things, usu without order): 一大批(指東西,通常是雜亂的): *a desk covered with a ~ of books and papers.* 雜亂地堆滿書籍和文件的寫字桌。□ *vi, vt* **1** [VP2B, C, 6A, 14, 15A, B] come together in a ~; fill (a space) with people: 群聚;擁擠;使擠滿: *~ a beach/square/hall.* 群聚於海濱(廣場,大廳)。*Now, don't all ~ together!* 不要統統擠在一起!**~ round**, form a circle (round): 圍攏;圍著: *People quickly ~ round when there is a street accident.* 街上發生意外事故時,人們很快地就圍了起來。*The pupils ~ed round the teacher to ask questions.* 學生們圍着老師問問題。***~ through/in/into, etc; ~ (sth) with***, (cause to) move through, etc in a ~; fill with: (使)擠過(擠入等);(使)充塞: *They ~ed through the gates into the stadium.* 他們擠過大門,進入運動場。*They ~ed the buses with passengers/~ed people into the buses.* 他們使公共汽車擠滿了乘客(使人們擠進公共汽車)。*Let's not ~ the room with furniture.* 我們不要在這房間裡擺設太多的傢具吧。*Memories ~ed in upon me,* came thick and fast into my mind. 往事一齊湧入我的腦海。***~ sb/sth out (of)***, keep out by ~ing: 將某人(某物)擠到(…的)外面: *There was an overflow meeting for those who were ~ed out,* unable to obtain admission. 爲被擠在外面的人(無法進入者)另外舉行了一個會。*Your contribution to the magazine was ~ed out,* There was no space for it. 你爲那雜誌所寫的稿件因稿擠而未被刊登。**2** (naut) ***~ on sail***, hoist many sails (so as to increase speed). (航海)揚起許多帆(以增航速)。**3** [VP6A] (colloq) put pressure on: (俗)施以壓力;逼迫: *Don't ~ me; give me time to think!* 不要逼我;給我時間讓我想想!**~ed** *part adj* having large numbers of people: 擠滿人群的;擁擠的: *~ed cities/trains/buses.* 擁擠的城市(火車,公共汽車)。

crown[1] /kraʊn; kraʊn/ *n* **1** ornamental headdress of gold, jewels, etc worn by a sovereign ruler; royal power: 王冕;皇冠(君主所戴以黃金、珠寶等製成者);王權;君權: *to wear the ~*, rule as a sovereign; 卽王位;爲王; *succeed to the ~*, become the sovereign ruler; 繼承王位;爲王; *an officer of the ~*, a State official; 國家的官吏; *a minister of the ~*, a Cabinet Minister; 內閣閣員; *a ~ appointment*, one made by the sovereign. 國王任命的差事。**C~ Colony**, one governed completely by Great Britain. 英國直轄殖民地。**~-land**, land that belongs to the C~. 屬於君主的土地;王室領地。**~ prince**, next in succession to the throne. 皇太子(王位繼承人)。**~ princess**, wife of a ~ prince. 皇太子之妃。**~ witness**, witness for the Prosecution in a criminal case. (刑事)原告方面的證人。**2** circle or wreath of flowers or leaves worn on the head, esp as a sign of victory, or as a reward: 榮冠;花冠(尤指象徵勝利或作爲獎賞者): *a martyr's ~.* 烈士的花冠。**3** British coin worth 25p, formerly 5 shillings. 英國硬幣(値25辨士,昔時値五先令)。**half a ~; a half~**, (until 1971) British coin worth 12½p. (1971年以前)英國硬幣(値12½辨士)。**4** top of the head or of a hat; part of a tooth that shows; (fig) perfection, completion: 頭頂;帽頂;齒冠(牙齒露於齦外的部分);(喻)完美;完善: *the ~ of one's labours;* 某人勞力之完滿成果(功成名就); *the ~ of the year,* the autumn, season of harvests. 秋季;收穫的季節。**5** ~-shaped ornament (eg a crest or badge). 冠狀飾物(例如飾章或徽章)。

crown[2] /kraʊn; kraʊn/ *vt* **1** [VP6A, 23] put a crown on (a king or queen): 爲(王或女王)加冕: *the ~ed heads* (= kings and queens) *of Europe.* 歐洲的帝王和女王。*They ~ed him king.* 他們爲他加冕(立之爲王)。**2** [VP6A, 14] **~ (with)**, reward with a crown; give honour to; reward: 賞以榮冠;褒獎;賞賜: *to be ~ed with victory;* 獲得勝利的榮譽; *efforts that were ~ed with success.* 如願以償的努力。**3** [VP6A, 14] **~ (with)**, be or have at the top of: 位於…之頂;頂上有: *The hill is ~ed with a wood.* 山頂上有森林。**4** [VP6A] put a happy finishing touch to: 對…做最後圓滿的潤飾: *to open a bottle of wine to ~ a feast.* 開一瓶葡萄酒使宴會圓滿結束。***to ~ (it) all***, to complete good/bad fortune, etc: 更妙(糟糕)的是;加之;尤其是: *It was raining, we had no umbrellas, and, to ~ all, we missed the last bus and had to walk home.* 下雨了,我們沒有帶傘,更糟糕的是我們誤了最後一班公共汽車,於是不得不步行回家。**5** [VP6A] put an artificial cover on a broken tooth. 鑲(牙)。⇨ crown[1](4). **~·ing** *part adj* (attrib only) (僅作形容用法) completing; making perfect: 使完善的;使完美的: *the ~ing touch to the evening's entertainment.* 使晚會圓滿的一項行動。*Her ~ing glory is her hair.* 她最美的地方是她的頭髮。

cro·zier /ˈkrəʊzɪə(r) *US:* -ʒər ; ˈkroʒɚ/ *n* = crosier.

cru·cial /ˈkruːʃl ; ˈkruʃəl/ *adj* decisive; critical: 決定性的;關係重大的: *the ~ test/question;* 決定性的測驗(問題); *at the ~ moment.* 在重要的關頭。**~·ly** /-ʃəlɪ ; -ʃəlɪ/ *adv*

cru·cible /ˈkruːsɪbl ; ˈkrusəbl̩/ *n* pot in which metals are melted; (fig) severe test or trial. (可鎔金屬的)坩堝;(喻)嚴厲的考驗。

cru·ci·fix /ˈkruːsɪfɪks ; ˈkrusə,fɪks/ *n* model of the Cross with the figure of Jesus on it. 有耶穌像的十字架模型;耶穌受難像。

cru·ci·fixion /ˌkruːsɪˈfɪkʃn ; ˌkrusəˈfɪkʃən/ *n* [U] putting to death, being put to death, on a cross (3); [C] instance of this. (被)釘死於十字架上。**the C~**, that of Jesus. 耶穌之被釘死於十字架。

cru·ci·form /ˈkruːsɪfɔːm ; ˈkrusə,fɔrm/ *adj* cross-shaped. 十字形的。

cru·cify /ˈkruːsɪfaɪ ; ˈkrusə,faɪ/ *vt* put to death by nailing or binding to a cross(3). 釘於十字架或綁於十字架以處死。

crud /krʌd ; krʌd/ *n* (GB sl) unpleasant person. (英俚)討厭的人。**~dy** *adj* unpleasant. 討厭的;使人不愉快的。

crude /kruːd ; krud/ *adj* **1** (of materials) in a natural state; not refined or manufactured: (指物質)原狀的;未提煉的;未加工製造的;粗糙的;生的: *~ oil,* petroleum; 原油(石油); *~ sugar;* 粗糖; *~ ore.* 原礦。**2** not having grace, taste or refinement: 粗鄙的;粗魯的: *~ manners.* 粗魯的舉止。**3** not finished properly; badly worked out: 粗製濫造的;不完善的: *~ schemes/methods/ideas;* 不完善的計畫(方法,思想); *~ paintings,* showing lack of skill; 技巧拙劣的繪畫; *~ facts,* presented in an undisguised way, with no attempt to make them less unpleasant; 赤裸裸(未加掩飾)的事實; *a ~ log cabin.* 簡陋的木屋。**~·ly** *adv*

crud·ity /ˈkruːdɪtɪ ; ˈkrudətɪ/ *n* [U] the state or quality of being crude; [C] (*pl* -ties) instance of this; crude act, remark, etc. 粗糙;粗野;粗魯;粗魯的行爲,言辭等。

cruel /ˈkrʊəl ; ˈkruəl/ *adj* (-ller, -llest) **1** (of persons) taking pleasure in the suffering of others; ready to give pain to others: (指人)殘忍的;殘暴的;以他人之受苦爲樂的;好虐待的: *a ~ master;* 殘暴的主人; *a man who is ~ to animals.* 虐待動物的人。*It was ~ of him to make the donkey carry such a heavy load.* 他讓那驢子馱這樣重的東西,眞是殘忍。**2** causing pain or suffering; showing indifference to the sufferings of others: 殘酷的;無情的: *a ~ blow/punishment/disease/war;* 殘酷的打擊(懲罰,疾病,戰爭); *in a ~* (= distressing) *predicament.* 在痛苦的折磨中。**~·ly** /ˈkrʊəlɪ ; ˈkruəlɪ/ *adv*

cruelty /ˈkrʊəltɪ ; ˈkruəltɪ/ *n* **1** [U] readiness to give pain or cause suffering to others; delight in this; cruel nature: 殘忍;殘暴;殘酷;殘忍的天性: *C~ to animals is severely punished in England.* 虐待動物在英國處罰很重。**2** [C] (*pl* -ties) cruel act. 殘暴的行爲。

cruet /ˈkruːɪt ; ˈkruɪt/ *n* **1** small glass bottle for vinegar or oil for use at table. 餐桌上用的裝醋或油類的小玻璃瓶;調味瓶。**2** (also 亦作 **ˈ~-stand**) stand for oil and vinegar ~s, and for mustard, chutney, etc. 置放油瓶,醋瓶,芥子醬瓶,調味醬瓶等的瓶架;五味瓶架;調味瓶架。

cruise /kruːz ; kruz/ *vi* [VP2A, C] **1** sail about, either for pleasure, or, in war, looking for enemy ships. 乘船巡遊(或爲遊樂,或爲搜尋敵艦);巡航。**2** (of cars, aircraft) travel at the speed (and of aircraft at the altitude) most economical of fuel, less than the top speed: (指汽車,飛機)以最省燃料的速度或高度(但不及最高速度)行進: *The car has a cruising speed of 50 miles an hour.* 該汽車之省油速度爲每小時五十哩。□ *n* cruising voyage: 乘船巡遊;巡航: *to go on/for a ~.* 乘船巡遊。*The liner is making a round-the-world ~ this year,* a pleasure voyage. 這艘客輪今年正在作環球航行。**cruiser** /ˈkruːzə(r) ; ˈkruzɚ/ *n* **1** fast warship. 巡洋艦。**2** **ˈcabin-~r**, motor-boat (with sleeping accommodation, etc) designed for pleasure ~s. 遊覽汽艇(供睡眠設備等)。

crumb /krʌm ; krʌm/ *n* **1** [C] very small piece of dry food, esp a bit of bread or cake rubbed off or dropped from a large piece: 乾食品的屑末;(尤指)麵包或糕餅屑: *sweep up the ~s;* 掃去食品屑; [U] soft, inner part of a loaf of bread. 麵包心。⇨ crust(1). **2** (fig) small amount: (喻)少許;少量: *a few ~s of information/comfort.* 少許的消息(安慰)。

crumble /ˈkrʌmbl ; ˈkrʌmbl̩/ *vt, vi* [VP6A, 2A, C] break, rub or fall into very small pieces: 弄碎;碎爲細屑: *to ~ one's bread,* rub it into crumbs; 將麵包弄成碎屑; *crumbling walls,* that are falling into ruin; 崩塌中的牆壁; *great empires that have ~d* (= decayed) *and fallen;* 已崩潰衰落的一些大帝國; (fig) (喻) *hopes that ~d to dust,* came to nothing. 成爲泡影的希望。

crum·bly /ˈkrʌmblɪ;ˈkrʌmblɪ/ *adj* easy to crumble. 易粉碎的。

crummy /ˈkrʌmɪ ; ˈkrʌmɪ/ *adj* (sl) bad; worthless; unpleasant. (俚)不好的;無用的;不愉快的: *a ~ party;* 不愉快的聚會; *feel ~,* ill. 覺得不舒服。

crum·pet /ˈkrʌmpɪt ; ˈkrʌmpɪt/ *n* (GB) (英) **1** flat, round, soft, unsweetened cake, usu toasted and eaten hot with butter spread on it. 一種鬆脆無甜味的圓餅(通常烤後趁熱塗奶油食之)。**2** (sl) head. (俚)頭。**3** (sl) sexually attractive girl or woman. (俚)性感的女郎或婦人。

crumple /ˈkrʌmpl ; ˈkrʌmpl̩/ *vt, vi* [VP6A, 15B, 2A, C] **1** press or crush into folds or creases: 壓皺;擠皺: *to ~ one's clothes,* eg by packing them carelessly. 把衣服壓皺(如因裝箱不小心所致)。**2** become full of folds or creases: 變得有許多摺皺: *Some kinds of material ~ more easily than others.* 有些料子比其他的料子易皺。*Do nylon sheets ~?* 尼龍床單會起皺嗎? **3** *~ up,* (lit, fig) crush; collapse: (字面,喻)壓碎;崩潰: *to ~ up a sheet of paper into a ball;* 將一張紙揉做一團; *to ~ up an opposing army.* 擊潰敵軍。*The wings of the aircraft ~d up.* 飛機的兩翼撞壞了。

crunch /krʌntʃ ; krʌntʃ/ *vt, vi* [VP6A, 2A, C] **1** crush noisily with the teeth when eating: 進食時用牙咬碎嘎扎作響: *The dog was ~ing a bone.* 那狗在啃一塊骨頭。*People who ~ peanuts in the cinema can be very annoying.* 在電影院裡剝食花生的人十分討厭。**2** crush, be crushed, noisily under one's feet, under wheels, etc: (被)踩碎或(被)碾碎而發碎裂聲: *The frozen snow ~ed under the wheels of our car.* 凍結了的雪在我們的汽車輪下發出碎裂聲。*Our feet ~ed the gravel.* 我們的脚踏在碎石上沙沙作響。□ *n* the act of ~ing; noise made by ~ing. 踩碎(聲);碾碎(聲)。***when it comes to the ~; when the ~ comes,*** (colloq) when the moment of crisis or decision is reached. (俗)當緊要關頭來臨時。

crup·per /ˈkrʌpə(r) ; ˈkrʌpɚ/ *n* leather strap fastened to the back of a saddle or harness and looped under the horse's tail; hindquarters of a horse. 連在馬鞍或輓具後邊兜過馬尾下的皮帶;馬的臀部。⇨ the illus at harness. 參看 harness 之挿圖。

cru·sade /kruːˈseɪd ; kruˈsed/ *n* **1** any one of the military expeditions made by the Christian rulers and people of Europe during the Middle Ages to recover the Holy Land from the Muslims. 十字軍(中世紀由基督教君主及歐洲人民組成向回教地區進攻以圖奪回聖地的遠征軍)。**2** any struggle or movement in support of sth believed to be good or against sth believed to be bad: 任何贊助善事或反對惡事的奮鬥或運動: *a ~ against bribery.* 反對授受賄賂運動。□ *vi* [VP2A, 3A] ***~ (for/against),***

take part in a ~. 參加某種運動(以贊助或反對)。 **cru·sader** *n* person taking part in a ~. 參加某種運動者;十字軍戰士。

crush[1] /krʌʃ ; krʌʃ/ *vt, vi* **1** [VP6A, 15A, B] press, be pressed, so that there is breaking or injury: (被)壓碎;(被)壓破;壓傷;使擠入: *Don't ~ this box; it has flowers in it.* 不要把這個盒子壓破了;裡面裝的有花。*Wine is made by ~ing grapes.* 葡萄酒是壓榨葡萄製成的。*Several people were ~ed to death as they tried to escape from the burning theatre.* 有幾個人欲自失火燃燒中的戲院裏逃出而被壓死了。*We can't ~ any more people into the hall; it's crowded already.* 我們再也不能讓任何人進入大廳了;裏面已經很擠了。**~ up,** make into powder by ~ing. 壓為粉末。**~ out (of),** force out by ~ing: 壓出;榨出: *to ~ out the juice from oranges.* 榨出橙汁。 **2** [VP6A, 15A, B, 2A, C] (cause to) become full of creases or irregular folds; lose shape: (使)起皺;(使)變形: *Her dresses were badly ~ed when she took them out of the suitcase.* 她把衣服從箱中取出時,衣服被壓皺得一塌糊塗。 *Some of the new synthetic dress materials do not ~.* 有些新式的人造衣料不會皺。 **3** [VP6A] subdue; overwhelm: 征服;制服;壓倒: *He was not satisfied until he had ~ed his enemies.* 他直到完全制服敵人後方才滿足。*Our hopes have been ~ed.* 我們的希望已破滅。*He smiled at her, but she ~ed him* (= made him feel abashed) *with a haughty look.* 他向她微笑,但她卻擺出一副傲慢神情使他難堪。 **4** [VP2C] (of persons) **~ in/into/through/past, etc,** press or push in, etc: (指人)擠入(過等): *They all tried to ~ into the front seats.* 他們大家都想擠到前排的座位去。[VP15A, B] (With cognate object) (與同源受詞連用) *We had to ~ our way through the crowd.* 我們不得不由人群中擠過去。 **~·ing** *adj* overwhelming: 壓倒的: *a ~ing defeat;* 大敗; in a manner intended to subdue or disconcert: 意欲降服對方或使對方不知所措的: *a ~ing reply.* 使無言以對的回答;使目瞪口呆的回答。 **~·ing·ly** *adv*

crush[2] /krʌʃ ; krʌʃ/ *n* **1 a/the ~,** crowd of people pressed together: 擁擠的人群: *There was a violent ~ at the gate into the stadium.* 運動場的大門口人群擁擠不堪。 **'~ barrier,** one erected to keep back crowds (eg along a pavement when crowds of people are expected). 阻攔人群的障礙物(例如置於預料有人群的人行道上者)。 **2** (colloq) crowded social gathering. (俗)擁擠的社交集會。 **3** (sl) (俚) **get/have a ~ on sb,** (usu of a young person) be, imagine oneself to be, in love with him. (通常指年輕人)迷戀;對…自作多情。 **4** [U] fruit drink made by pressing out juice (eg from oranges). 果汁飲料(例如橙汁)。

crust /krʌst ; krʌst/ *n* **1** [C, U] (piece of the) hard-baked surface of a loaf; outer covering (pastry) of a pie or tart. (一片)麵包皮;糕餅的麵製外殼。 **2** [C, U] hard surface: 硬殼: *a thin ~ of ice/frozen snow;* 一層薄冰(凍結的雪); *the earth's ~,* the outer portion. 地殼。 **3** hard deposit on the inside of a bottle of wine. 酒瓶內沉澱的渣。□ *vt, vi* [VP6A, 2A, C] **~ (over),** cover, become covered, with a ~; form into a ~: 以硬殼覆蓋;為硬殼覆蓋;結一層硬殼: *The snow ~ed over* (= froze hard on top) *during the night.* 雪在夜裏結了一層冰。

crus·ta·cean /krʌˈsteɪʃn ; krʌsˈteʃən/ *n* any of a numerous class of animals, mostly living in water (and popularly called *shellfish*) with a hard shell (eg *crabs, lobsters*). 甲殼類動物(大半生活於水中,俗稱貝類,例如蟹、龍蝦)。

crusted /ˈkrʌstɪd ; ˈkrʌstɪd/ *adj* **1** having a crust. 有外殼的;有硬殼的。 **2** ancient; venerable. 古老的;因古老而可敬的。 **3** fixed; engrained: 根深蒂固的;確立的: *~ prejudices/habits.* 根深蒂固的偏見(習慣)。

crusty /ˈkrʌstɪ ; ˈkrʌstɪ/ *adj* (-ier, -iest) **1** having a crust; hard like a crust: 有硬殼的;硬如殼的: *~ bread.* 硬麵包。 **2** (of persons, their behaviour) curt, harsh; quick to show irritation, etc. (指人,其行為)厲聲厲色的;脾氣暴躁的。

crutch /krʌtʃ ; krʌtʃ/ *n* **1** support used under the arm to help a lame person to walk: (跛足者腋下用的)拐杖: *a pair of ~es;* 一對拐杖; *to go about on ~es.* 靠拐杖行動。 **2** support that is like a ~ in shape or use; (fig) any moral support. 似拐杖之支持物;(喻)任何精神上的支持。 **3** crotch(2). 袴襠;胯部。

crux /krʌks ; krʌks/ *n* (*pl* ~es) part (of a problem) that is the most difficult to solve: 問題的關鍵;最難解決之處: *The ~ of the matter is this.* 問題的關鍵在此。

cry[1] /kraɪ ; kraɪ/ *vi, vt* (*pt, pp* cried) **1 cry (out),** [VP2A, B, C, 3A, 4A] (of persons, animals, birds) make (usu loud) sounds that express feelings (eg pain, fear) but not ideas, thoughts, etc: (指人、獸、禽)喊叫;號叫;鳴叫(如因痛楚、恐懼所發出者,僅表感情而不表思想等): *A baby can cry as soon as it is born.* 嬰兒一生下來就會哭。*He cried out with pain when the dentist pulled the tooth out.* 當牙醫為他拔牙時他痛得叫了起來。 **2** [VP2A, B, C, 3A, 6A, 15B] (of persons) weep; shed tears (with or without sounds): (指人)哭泣;啜泣: *The boy was crying because he had lost his money.* 那男孩因丟了錢而哭。*She was crying over her misfortunes.* 她為她的不幸遭遇而哭。 *She was crying for joy,* because she was happy. 她喜極而泣。*The child was crying for* (= because he wanted) *his mother.* 那孩子哭着要媽媽。*The boy was crying with pain/hunger.* 那男孩痛(餓)得哭起來。*She cried hot tears.* 她熱淚直下。**cry one's 'eyes/'heart out,** weep very bitterly. 痛哭。**cry oneself to sleep,** cry until one falls asleep. 哭到睡着了。**give sb sth to cry for/about,** punish him for crying without a good or obvious cause. 處罰某人無緣無故的哭。 **3** [VP6A, 14, 9, 2C, 3A, 4A] exclaim; call out loudly in words: 高聲喊叫;大聲說: *'Help! Help!' he cried.* '救命啊!救命啊!'他高聲叫喊。*The starving people cried to their chief for bread.* 那些飢餓的人向他們的首領喊着要麵包。*He cried for mercy.* 他喊着求饒。**cry for the moon,** demand sth impossible. 要求不可能的事物。 ⇨ shame(3). **4** [VP6A, 15A, B] announce for sale; make known by calling out: 叫賣;以叫喊使大家知道;高聲傳報: *to cry one's wares;* 叫賣貨物; *to cry the news all over the town.* 將新聞向鎮上各處高聲傳報。 **5 cry sth down,** suggest that it is worth little. 輕視某事物。**cry off,** withdraw from sth that one has undertaken: 打退堂鼓;打消原意: *I had promised to go, but had to cry off at the last moment.* 我本來答應要去,但最後不得不打消去意。 **cry sth up,** praise it highly. 極力讚揚某事物。

cry[2] /kraɪ ; kraɪ/ *n* (*pl* cries) **1** loud sound of fear, pain, grief, etc; loud, excited utterance of

crustaceans

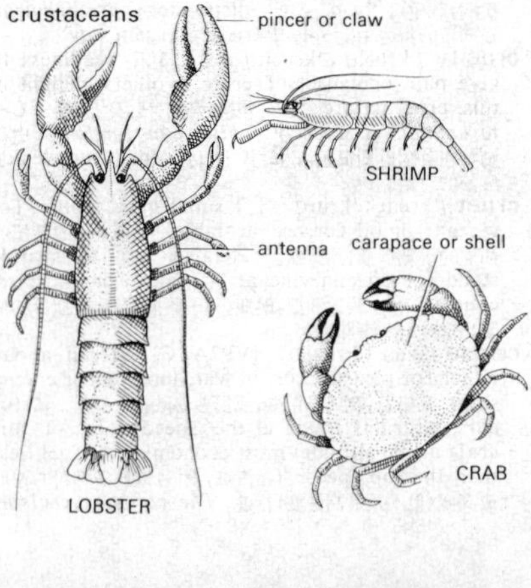

words: (因恐懼、痛苦、悲傷等)號叫;哭號;大叫;高喊: *a cry for help;* 求救的呼聲; *the cry of an animal in pain;* 動物痛楚的叫聲; *a cry of triumph;* 勝利的歡呼; *angry cries from the mob.* 暴民憤怒的叫嚣。*They set up/raised a cry of 'Traitor!'* 他們高喊'賣國賊!' ***a far/long cry from,*** a long way from; very different from: 遙遠的路途;極大的差別: *Being a junior clerk is a far cry from being one of the Directors.* 做小職員與做董事差別甚大。***in full cry,*** (of a pack of hounds) barking together as they pursue or hunt (an animal); (fig) eagerly attacking (sb). (指一群獵犬)一齊嗥叫着緊追(動物);(喻)猛烈攻擊(某人)。***much cry and little wool,*** (prov) much fuss with little result. (諺)大事紛擾而無甚結果;雷聲大而雨點小。***within cry (of),*** within hearing; near enough to hear a call. 在可以聽得到呼聲的地方。⇨ hue². **2** words spoken loudly to give information: 大聲傳報的消息: *the cry of the night watchman;* 守夜人的叫聲; call announcing sth for sale (by a person in the street): (街上小販的)叫賣聲: *the old (street) cries of London, eg 'Fresh Herrings'.* 倫敦街上舊有的叫賣聲,例如'鮮鯡'。⇨ crier(1). **3** watchword or phrase, used for a principle or cause: (代表主義或運動的)口號: *a 'war-cry;* (作戰時的)喊殺聲;(政黨等的)口號; *a 'battle-cry.* (作戰時的)吶喊;標語;口號。*'Asia for the Asians' was their cry.* '亞洲人的亞洲'是他們的口號。**4** fit of weeping: 一陣哭泣: *have a good cry,* find emotional relief by shedding tears. 盡情哭一場(以抒發鬱積的感情)。*Let her have her cry out,* let her weep until she becomes calm again. 讓她哭個痛快吧。**'cry-baby,** child who cries often or easily without good or apparent cause. 好哭的嬰兒(常無故而哭)。

cry·ing /ˈkraɪɪŋ ; ˈkraɪɪŋ/ *attrib adj* (esp of evils) demanding attention: (尤指惡事)需要注意的: *a ~ shame/evil/need.* 奇恥大辱(急待矯正的弊病;迫切的需要)。

crypt /krɪpt ; krɪpt/ *n* underground room, esp of a church. (尤指教堂的)地下室。

a church crypt

cryp·tic /ˈkrɪptɪk ; ˈkrɪptɪk/ *adj* secret; with a hidden meaning, or a meaning not easily seen: 祕密的;含有隱藏之意義的;意義深遠的: *a ~ remark.* 含義深遠的評語。**cryp·ti·cally** /-klɪ ; -klɪ/ *adv*

crypto- /ˌkrɪptəʊ ; ˌkrɪpto/ (in combination) hidden, secret: (用於複合字)隱藏的;祕密的: *a ˌ~-ˈfascist,* person who has fascist sympathies but does not make them public. 祕密同情法西斯黨的人。

crypto·gram /ˈkrɪptəgræm ; ˈkrɪptəˌgræm/ *n* [C] sth written in a secret code. 密碼文件。

crys·tal /ˈkrɪstl ; ˈkrɪstl̩/ *n* **1** [U] transparent, natural substance like quartz; [C] piece of this as an ornament: 水晶石;水晶製的裝飾品: *a necklace of ~s;* 水晶珠項鍊;(attrib) (形容用法) *~ ornaments;* 水晶製的裝飾品; *~ detector,* type used in early radio sets (called a '~ **set**). 晶體檢波器(用於早期晶體收音機'crystal set')。~ ***clear,*** entirely clear; (fig) completely understood. 完全透明的;(喻)極其明白的;十分清楚的。**'~-gazing,** looking into a ~ ball in an attempt to see future events pictured there. 水晶球占卜術(向水晶球裏窺視以期藉裏面所呈現的圖形測知未來的事情)。**2** [U] glassware of best quality, made into bowls, vases, vessels, etc: 品質最好的玻璃器皿(如碗、瓶、盤碟等): *The dining-table shone with silver and ~.* 餐桌上擺設的銀器和玻璃器琳琅滿目。**3** [C] (science) definite and regular shape taken naturally by the molecules of certain substances: (科學)(某些物質的分子自然形成的)結晶體: *sugar and salt ~s;* 糖和鹽的結晶體; *snow and ice ~s.* 雪和冰的結晶體。**4** (US) glass over the face of a watch. (美)錶面玻璃。

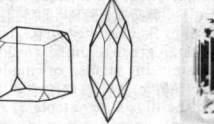

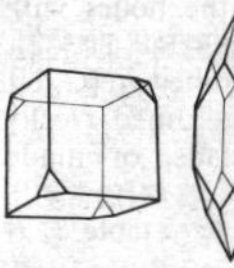

crystals

diamonds

crys·tal·line /ˈkrɪstəlaɪn ; ˈkrɪstl̩ɪn/ *adj* made of crystal(s); like crystal; very clear. 水晶製的;似水晶的;結晶質的;透明的。

crys·tal·lize /ˈkrɪstəlaɪz ; ˈkrɪstl̩ˌaɪz/ *vt, vi* **1** [VP 6A, 2A] form, cause to form, into crystals. 形成結晶體;使結晶。**2** [VP6A] cover (fruit, etc) with sugar-crystals: 將糖的結晶體覆於(水果等)上: *~d ginger.* 蜜餞的薑。**3** [VP6A, 2A] (fig, of ideas, plans) become, cause to be, clear and definite: (喻;指思想,計畫)(使)變得明確: *His vague ideas ~d into a definite plan.* 他那些模糊的概念變成一個明確的計畫。**crys·tal·li·za·tion** /ˌkrɪstəlaɪˈzeɪʃn *US:* -lɪˈz- ; ˌkrɪstl̩əˈzeʃən/ *n*

cub /kʌb ; kʌb/ *n* **1** young lion, bear, fox, tiger. 幼獅、熊、狐、虎。**cub reporter,** young and inexperienced newspaper reporter. 年輕無經驗的記者。**Cub (Scout),** member of the junior branch of the Scout Association. 幼童軍。**2** ill-mannered young man. 不懂規矩的年輕人。

cubby-hole /ˈkʌbɪ həʊl ; ˈkʌbɪˌhol/ *n* small enclosed space; snug place. 圍起來的小天地;舒適的地方。

cube /kjuːb ; kjub/ *n* **1** solid body having six equal square sides; block of something so shaped or similarly shaped. 正六面體;立方體;立方形物(塊)。**2** (maths) product of a number multiplied by itself twice: (數學)立方(某數的三乘冪或自乘兩次的積): *The ~ of 5* (5^3) *is* $5 \times 5 \times 5$ *(=125).* 5的立方就是 $5 \times 5 \times 5$ (= 125)。*The ~ root of 64* ($\sqrt[3]{64}$) *is 4* ($4 \times 4 \times 4$ =64). 64 的立方根是 4。□ *vt* [VP6A] multiply a number by itself twice: 以某數自乘二次;求立方: *10 ~d is 1000.* 10 的立方爲 1000。

cu·bic /ˈkjuːbɪk ; ˈkjubɪk/ *adj* having the shape of a cube; of a cube: 立方形的;立方體的: *one ~ metre,* volume of a cube whose edge is one metre; 一立方公尺(每邊各一公尺之立方體積); *~ content,* volume expressed in cubic measurement; 體積;容積; *a motor vehicle with a 2000cc capacity,* ie 2000 ~ centimetres. 一部排氣量爲兩千立方公分的汽車。

cu·bi·cal /ˈkjuːbɪkl ; ˈkjubɪkl̩/ *adj* = cubic.

cu·bicle /ˈkjuːbɪkl ; ˈkjubɪkl̩/ *n* small division of a larger room, walled or curtained to make a separate compartment, eg for sleeping in, or for (un)dressing at a swimming-pool. 大房間內以牆或幕隔成的小室(例如小寢室或游泳池旁之更衣室)。

cub·ism /ˈkjuːbɪzəm ; ˈkjubɪzəm/ *n* [U] style in art in which objects are represented so that they appear to be largely of geometrical shapes. 立體主義;立體派(所作繪畫中的物體似大半由幾何圖形構成)。**cub·ist** /ˈkjuːbɪst ; ˈkjubɪst/ *n* artist who practises ~. 立體派藝術家。

cu·bit /ˈkjuːbɪt ; ˈkjubɪt/ *n* old measure of length (18 to 22 inches or 45 to 56 centimetres). 腕尺(舊長度單位,約 18 至 22 吋或 45 至 56 公分)。

cuck·old /ˈkʌkəʊld ; ˈkʌkl̩d/ *n* (archaic) man whose wife has committed adultery. (古)妻子與人私通的

男人;戴綠帽子的男人。□ *vt* [VP6A] (of a man) make (another man) a ~ by seducing his wife; (of a woman) make (her husband) a ~. (指男人)勾引人妻使(他人)戴綠帽子; (指女人)與人私通使(其夫)戴綠帽子。

cuckoo /ˈkʊkuː; ˈkʊku/ *n* bird whose call is like its name, a migratory bird which reaches the British Isles in spring and lays its eggs in the nests of small birds. 布穀鳥;杜鵑(候鳥,春天到英國,產卵於小鳥之巢)。⇨ the illus at bird. 參看 bird 之插圖。**ˈ~-clock,** one that strikes the hours with notes like the call of a ~. 報時似布穀鳥叫的時鐘。

cu·cum·ber /ˈkjuːkʌmbə(r); ˈkjukʌmbɚ/ *n* [C, U] (creeping plant with) long, green-skinned fleshy fruit, usu sliced and eaten in salads, or made into pickle. 胡瓜; 黃瓜(藤類植物,長形,綠皮,通常切片做生菜食之,或製醃菜)。⇨ the illus at vegetable. 參看 vegetable 之插圖。***as cool as a ~,*** unexcited; self-possessed. 冷靜的;沉着的;不激動的。

cud /kʌd; kʌd/ *n* [U] food which oxen, etc bring back from the first stomach and chew again. (牛等自第一胃吐出之)反芻之食物。***chew the cud,*** (fig) reflect; ponder. (喻)反省;細思。

cuddle /ˈkʌdl; ˈkʌdl/ *vt, vi* [VP6A, 15B, 2C] **1** hold close and lovingly in one's arms: 撫愛地緊抱;摟抱: *The baby doesn't like being ~d herself, but she likes to ~ her doll.* 那嬰孩自己不喜歡被人摟抱,但她却喜歡摟抱她的洋娃娃。 **2** *~ up (to/together),* lie close and comfortably: 貼身而睡;蜷曲着身子: *They ~d up (together) under the blankets.* 他們擁睡在毯子下面。*She ~d up to him to get warm.* 她依偎着他以獲得溫暖。□ *n* act of cuddling; hug. 擁抱;摟抱。**~·some** /-səm; -səm/, **cuddly** /ˈkʌdlɪ; ˈkʌdlɪ/ *adjj* suitable for, inviting, cuddling: 適於摟抱的;令人欲摟抱的: *a nice cuddly teddy bear.* 可愛的令人欲摟抱的玩具熊。

cud·gel /ˈkʌdʒəl; ˈkʌdʒəl/ *vt, n* (-ll-; US also -l-) [VP6A] (hit with a) short, thick stick or club. 短棒;用短棒打擊。***take up the ~s for,*** (rhet) fight for; support strongly. (修辭)爲…而奮鬪; 極力支持。***~ one's brains,*** think hard on a difficult problem; try to think of sth one has forgotten. 苦思一難題;竭力回想已經忘記的事。

cue[1] /kjuː; kju/ *n* [C] **1** sth (eg the last words of an actor's speech) which shows when sb else is to do or say sth. 提示(例如演員臺詞的最後一句,暗示其他演員出臺或接話者)。 **2** hint about how to behave, what to do, etc: (關於如何行動或做什麼的)暗示: ***take one's cue from sb,*** observe what he does as a guide to one's own action. 看某人怎麼做就怎樣做。

cue[2] /kjuː; kju/ *n* billiard-player's long, tapering, leather-tipped rod, for striking the ball. (撞球戲)球桿(尖端包有皮革)。

cuff[1] /kʌf; kʌf/ *n* **1** end of a shirt or coat sleeve at the wrist. (襯衫或外衣的)袖口。***play it off the ~,*** (colloq) use one's wits in a situation for which one is unprepared. (俗)臨時利用機智。**ˈ~-links,** used for fastening ~s. 襯衫袖口的鏈扣。 **2** (US) turned-up fold at the bottom of a leg of a pair of trousers. (GB 英 = *turn-up*). (美)西裝褲脚的反褶部分。 **3** (*pl,* colloq) handcuffs. (複,俗)手銬。

cuff[2] /kʌf; kʌf/ *vt, n* [VP6A] (give sb a) light blow with the open hand. 以手輕拍或輕捶(某人)。

cuir·ass /kwɪˈræs; kwɪˈræs/ *n* piece of armour to protect the body, breastplate and plate for the back, fastened together. 胸甲(保護前胸後背的甲胄)。⇨ the illus at armour. 參看 armour 之插圖。**cuir·as·sier** /ˌkwɪrəˈsɪə(r); ˌkwɪrəˈsɪr/ *n* horse-soldier wearing a ~. 着胸甲的騎兵。

cui·sine /kwɪˈziːn; kwɪˈzin/ *n* [U] (F) (style of) cooking: (法)烹調(的方式): *French ~;* 法國式烹調; *a hotel where the ~ is excellent.* 菜餚特佳的旅館。

cul-de-sac /ˈkʌl də sæk; ˈkʌldəˈsæk/ *n* (F) street with an opening at one end only; blind alley. (法)僅有一端與外間相通的街道;死巷。

cu·li·nary /ˈkʌlɪnərɪ *US:* -nerɪ; ˈkjuləˌnerɪ/ *adj* of cooking or a kitchen: 烹調的;廚房的: *a ~ triumph,* a superbly cooked dish or meal; 烹調極佳的一道菜或一餐; *~ plants,* suitable for cooking. 適於烹調的植物;蔬菜。

cull /kʌl; kʌl/ *vt* [VP6A] pick (a flower); select: 採摘(花);揀選: *extracts ~ed from the best authors.* 名家著作精選。□ *n* sth that is ~ed (eg a hen that no longer lays well, picked out and killed for food). 剔除之物(例如不大生蛋而被挑出殺來吃的母鷄)。

cul·len·der /ˈkʌləndə(r); ˈkʌləndɚ/ *n* = colander.

cul·mi·nate /ˈkʌlmɪneɪt; ˈkʌlməˌnet/ *vi* [VP3A] *~ in,* (of efforts, hopes, careers, etc) reach the highest point: (指努力、希望、事業等)達於極點: *misfortunes that ~d in bankruptcy.* 終於導致破產的種種不幸。**cul·mi·na·tion** /ˌkʌlmɪˈneɪʃn; ˌkʌlməˈneʃən/ *n* highest point: 頂點;極點: *the culmination of his career.* 他的事業的頂點。

culp·able /ˈkʌlpəbl; ˈkʌlpəbl̩/ *adj* (legal) blameworthy; deserving punishment: (法律)該受責備的;應受懲罰的: *hold a person ~;* 認爲某人該受責備; *dismissed for ~ negligence,* wrongly neglecting to do sth. 因重大疏忽而被開革。**culp·ably** /ˈkʌlpəblɪ; ˈkʌlpəblɪ/ *adv* **cul·pa·bil·ity** /ˌkʌlpəˈbɪlətɪ; ˌkʌlpəˈbɪlətɪ/ *n*

cul·prit /ˈkʌlprɪt; ˈkʌlprɪt/ *n* person who has done wrong; offender. 犯過者;犯罪者。

cult /kʌlt; kʌlt/ *n* [C] **1** system of religious worship. 禮拜的儀式;崇祀。 **2** devotion to a person (esp a single deity) or practice: 對某人(尤指對一個神)或風尚的崇拜: *the ~ of archery;* 崇尚箭術; *the ~ of Browning.* 對布朗寧的崇拜。 **3** (group of persons devoted to a) popular fashion or craze: 時尚;崇拜某一時尚的一群人: (attrib) (形容用法) *a ˈ~ word,* one used because it is fashionable among members of such a group. 時髦的用語(崇拜某一時尚的人們所流行的用語)。

cul·ti·vable /ˈkʌltɪvəbl; ˈkʌltəvəbl̩/ *adj* that can be cultivated. 可耕種的;可培養的。

cul·ti·vate /ˈkʌltɪveɪt; ˈkʌltəˌvet/ *vt* [VP6A] **1** prepare (land) for crops by ploughing, etc; help (crops) to grow (eg by breaking up the soil around them, destroying weeds, etc). 耕種(田地);培植(禾物)(如翻土、除草等)。 **2** give care, thought, time, etc in order to develop sth: 培養;修養;花費心思、時間等以發展某事物: *to ~ the mind/sb's friendship.* 修養心性(培養與某人的友誼)。*He ~s* (= tries to win the good will of) *the sort of people who can be useful to him in his business.* 他培養對於他事業有用的人。**cul·ti·vated** *adj* (of a person) having good manners and education. (指人)舉止文雅的;有教養的。

cul·ti·va·tion /ˌkʌltɪˈveɪʃn; ˌkʌltəˈveʃən/ *n* [U] cultivating or being cultivated: 耕種;耕耘;開墾;培養;修養: *the ~ of the soil;* 耕田;犁地: *land that is under ~;* 耕種中的土地; *to bring land into ~;* 開墾荒地; *to allow land to go out of ~.* 讓地荒蕪。

cul·ti·va·tor /ˈkʌltɪveɪtə(r); ˈkʌltəˌvetɚ/ *n* person who cultivates; machine for breaking up ground, destroying weeds, etc. 耕種者;耕耘機。

cul·tural /ˈkʌltʃərəl; ˈkʌltʃərəl/ *adj* having to do with culture: 文化的;文明的: *~ studies,* eg art, literature; 與文化有關的學科(例如藝術、文學); *a ~ institute.* 文化研究所。

cul·ture /ˈkʌltʃə(r); ˈkʌltʃɚ/ *n* **1** [U] advanced development of the human powers; development of the body, mind and spirit by training and experience: 人類能力的高度發展;藉訓練與經驗而促成的身心的發展;(身體的)鍛鍊;(心性與精神的)修養: *Physical ~ is important, but we must not neglect the ~ of the mind.* 體格的鍛鍊是重要的,但是我們不可忽略心性的修養。 **2** [U] evidence of intellectual development (of arts, science, etc) in human society: 人類社會智力發展(指人文、科學等)的證據;文明;

文化: *He is a man of considerable ~.* 他是個文化修養很高的人。*Universities should be centres of ~.* 大學應該是文化的中心。**3** [U] state of intellectual development among a people; [C] particular form of intellectual development: 一個民族的智力發展狀況;某一特定形式的文化: *We owe much to Greek ~.* 我們得益於希臘文化之處甚多。*He has studied the ~s of Oriental countries.* 他曾研究東方各國的文化。**4** [U] all the arts, beliefs, social institutions, etc characteristic of a community, race, etc: 某一會社、種族等特有的文藝、信仰、風俗等: *the ~ of the Eskimos.* 愛斯基摩人的文化。**5** [U] cultivating; the rearing of bees, silkworms, etc: 培養;種植;栽培;(蜂、蠶等的)飼養: *He has five acres devoted to bulb ~,* to the growing of such flowers as daffodils and tulips. 他用五畝地專事栽培球根植物(如水仙花、鬱金香)。**6** [C] (biol) growth of bacteria (for medical or scientific study): (生物)細菌的培養(供醫學或科學研究): *a ~ of cholera germs.* 一次所培養的霍亂菌。**cul·tured** *adj* (of persons) cultivated; having ~ of the mind; (of tastes, interests, etc) refined. (指人)文雅的;有修養的;(指嗜好、興趣等)高尚的;優雅的。**'~d pearl,** pearl produced in an oyster shell into which a piece of grit has been introduced. 養珠(經人工將砂粒置於蠔殼內培養出來的珍珠)。

cul·vert /'kʌlvət ; 'kʌlvɚt/ *n* sewer or drain that crosses under a road, railway or embankment; channel for electrical cables under the ground. (穿過道路,鐵路或路堤的)下水道或陰溝;地下電纜道。

cum·ber /'kʌmbə(r) ; 'kʌmbɚ/ *vt* [VP6A, 14] ~ **(with),** hamper; burden: 阻礙;拖累: *~ oneself with an overcoat on a warm day;* 在暖和的日子穿大衣是個累贅; *~ed with parcels.* 被一些小包裹所拖累。

cum·ber·some /'kʌmbəsəm ; 'kʌmbɚsəm/ *adj* burdensome; heavy and awkward to carry: 沉重的;笨重而不便攜帶的: *A soldier today would find old-fashioned armour very ~.* 現代的士兵會覺得舊式的甲冑非常笨重。

cum·brous /'kʌmbrəs ; 'kʌmbrəs/ *adj* = cumbersome.

cum·mer·bund /'kʌməbʌnd ; 'kʌmɚˌbʌnd/ *n* sash worn round the waist. 圍腰之巾;腰巾。

cumu·lat·ive /'kju:mjʊlətɪv *US:* -leɪtɪv ; 'kjumjəˌletɪv/ *adj* increasing in amount by one addition after another. 累積的。

cumu·lus /'kju:mjʊləs ; 'kjumjələs/ *n* (*pl* -li /-laɪ ; -ˌlaɪ/), *adj* (cloud) made up of rounded masses on a flat base. 積雲(由圓形雲團所形成而且底部水平的雲層);由圓形雲團形成的。

cunei·form /'kju:nɪfɔ:m *US:* kju:'nɪəfɔ:rm ; kjʊ'niəˌfɔrm/ *adj* wedge-shaped: 楔形的: *~ characters,* as used in old Persian and Assyrian writing. 楔形文字(如古代波斯和亞述文中所用者)。

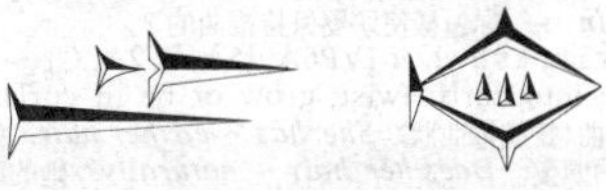

cuneiform characters

cun·ning¹ /'kʌnɪŋ ; 'kʌnɪŋ/ *adj* **1** clever at deceiving; showing this kind of cleverness: 善於欺騙的;狡猾的;奸詐的: *a ~ old fox;* 狡猾的老狐狸; *a ~ trick.* 詭計;狡計。**2** (old use) skilful: (舊用法)技術熟練的: *a ~ workman.* 技術熟練的工人。**3** (US) attractive; cute: (美)吸引人的;可愛的;動人的: *a ~ smile/baby/kitten.* 可愛的微笑(嬰兒,小貓)。**~·ly** *adv*

cun·ning² /'kʌnɪŋ ; 'kʌnɪŋ/ *n* [U] **1** quality of being cunning(1): 狡猾;奸詐: *The boy showed a great deal of ~ in getting what he wanted.* 那孩子在取得他所需要的東西的過程中,表現得極爲狡猾。**2** (old use) skill: (舊用法)技巧: *My hand has lost its ~.* 我的手已不靈活。

cunt /kʌnt ; kʌnt/ *n* ⚠ (諱) **1** vagina. 陰道。**2** female pudenda. 女性生殖器官之外部;陰部。**3** (vulg; sl) (by transference) woman or girl, regarded as a sexual object. (鄙;俚)(轉爲)女人或女郎(視爲性慾對象)。**4** (vulg; derog sl) despicable person. (鄙;貶俚)可鄙之人。

cup¹ /kʌp ; kʌp/ *n* **1** small porcelain bowl, usu with a handle, used with a saucer, for tea, coffee etc; contents of a cup: (通常有柄,用時帶碟的)瓷杯(用以裝茶,咖啡等);杯中所盛之物: *a 'teacup;* 茶杯; *a ˌcup and 'saucer;* 一套杯碟; *a ˌcup of 'coffee;* 一杯咖啡; *two cups of flour* (used as a measure in cooking). 兩杯麵粉(烹調時用作量器)。***not my cup of tea,*** (colloq) not what I like, not what suits me. (俗)不是我所喜歡的;不適合於我。**2** = chalice. **3** (fig) that which comes to a person; experience: (喻)命運;經歷;遭遇: *His cup of happiness was full.* 他享盡幸福。**4** vessel (usu of gold or silver) given as a prize in competitions. (比賽時贈爲獎品的)金杯;銀杯。**ˌcup-'final,** (football) final match to decide a competition. (足球)優勝杯決賽。**'cup-tie,** (football) match to eliminate teams competing for a cup. (足球)優勝杯淘汰賽。**5** (from *'wine cup*) wine. (由酒杯而來)酒。***in his cups,*** partly or wholly intoxicated. 醉酒(半醉或全醉)。**'cup-bearer,** official of a royal or nobleman's household who serves wine at banquets. (宮廷或貴族宅第宴會上的)司酒官;上酒者。**6** sth shaped like a cup: 杯形物: *the cup of a flower;* 花萼; *an 'egg-cup;* 盛一個煮蛋的小杯; *'acorn-cups;* 橡實殼斗; *the cups of a bra.* 胸罩之罩杯。**7** iced drink of wine, etc, usu flavoured: 加冰的酒等飲料(通常加有調味料): *'claret-cup;* 加冰的紅葡萄酒; *'cider-cup.* 加冰的蘋果汁。**cup·ful** /'kʌpfʊl ; 'kʌpˌfʊl/ *n* (*pl* cupfuls) as much as a cup will hold. 一杯之量。

cup² /kʌp ; kʌp/ *vt* (-pp-) [VP6A] **1** put into the shape of a cup: 做成杯狀: *to cup one's hands,* eg to catch a ball; 兩手做捧物狀(例如接球時); put round or over like a cup: 置於其四周或上方作杯狀: *with her chin cupped in her hand.* 她以手捧着她的下巴。**2** (archaic) perform the operation of cupping on (a person). (古)爲(某人)作杯吸手術。⇨ cupping below. 參看下列之 cupping。

cup·board /'kʌbəd ; 'kʌbɚd/ *n* set of shelves with doors, either built into a room as a fixture, or a separate piece of furniture, used for dishes, provisions, clothes, etc: (嵌於室內牆壁上或自成一件傢具之)櫥;碗櫥;食櫥;衣櫥: *a ˌkitchen-'~;* 碗櫥或食櫥; *a 'hanging-~,* one in which dresses, suits, etc may be hung on coat-hangers. 掛衣櫥(其中之衣服可掛於衣架上者)。Cf US 參較美 *china-closet, linen-closet.* **'~-love,** affection that is shown in the hope of getting sth by it (eg a child hoping for cake). 爲企圖得到某物所表示的親愛(例如小兒想吃糕餅時所表現者)。

Cu·pid /'kju:pɪd ; 'kjupɪd/ *n* Roman god of love; (picture or statue of a) beautiful boy (with wings and a bow and arrows) as symbol of love. 邱比特(羅馬的愛神);(有雙翼,手持弓箭,視爲愛的象徵的)美童;美童的像片或雕像。

cu·pid·ity /kju:'pɪdətɪ ; kjʊ'pɪdətɪ/ *n* [U] greed, esp for money or property. 貪婪;(尤指)貪財。

cu·pola /'kju:pələ ; 'kjupələ/ *n* small dome forming (part of) a roof; ceiling of a dome. 圓屋頂;圓屋頂的內面;穹窿天花板。

cuppa /'kʌpə ; 'kʌpə/ *n* (GB sl) cup of tea: (英俚)一杯茶: *What about a ~?* 來杯茶如何?

cup·ping /'kʌpɪŋ ; 'kʌpɪŋ/ *n* [U] (archaic) operation of drawing blood to or through the skin by creating a partial vacuum over the area by means of a glass cup (called a *'~-glass*). (古)藉玻璃吸杯(cupping-glass)在皮膚上造成局部眞空以吸聚或吸取血液的手術;杯術;吸器放血法。

cu·pric /'kju:prɪk ; 'kjuprɪk/ *adj* containing copper. 含銅的。

cu·pro-nickel /ˌkjuːprəʊˈnɪkl; ˌkjuproˈnɪkl̩/ *n* [U] alloy of copper and nickel used for making coins. 銅鎳合金(用以製硬幣)。

cur /kɜː(r); kɝ/ *n* bad-tempered or worthless dog (esp low-bred); cowardly or badly behaved man. 脾氣壞或無用之狗(尤指品種低賤者);懦夫;行爲卑劣者。

cur·able /ˈkjʊərəbl; ˈkjʊrəbl/ *adj* that can be cured. 可治療的; 可矯正的。 **cura·bil·ity** /ˌkjʊərəˈbɪlətɪ; ˌkjʊrəˈbɪlətɪ/ *n*

cura·çao, -çoa /ˌkjʊərəˈsəʊ *US:* -ˈsaʊ; ˌkjʊrəˈso/ *n* liqueur (sweet and syrupy) flavoured with peel of bitter oranges. (加苦橙皮味的)柑香酒。

cur·acy /ˈkjʊərəsɪ; ˈkjʊrəsɪ/ *n* (*pl* -cies) office or work of a curate. 副牧師的職位或職務。

curate /ˈkjʊərət; ˈkjʊrɪt/ *n* clergyman who helps a parish priest. 副牧師;助理牧師。

cura·tive /ˈkjʊərətɪv; ˈkjʊrətɪv/ *adj* helping to, able to, cure (disease or ill health): 幫助治療的;能治病的;醫療的: *the ~ value of sunshine and sea air.* 陽光與海邊的空氣的醫療價值。

cu·ra·tor /kjʊəˈreɪtə(r); kjʊˈretɚ/ *n* official in charge (esp of a museum or art gallery). (尤指博物館或藝術館之)館長。

curb /kɜːb; kɝb/ *n* **1** chain or leather strap passing under a horse's jaw, used to control it. 馬勒;馬銜索(兜於馬嘴下面以控制馬的鍊或皮帶)。⇨ the illus at harness. 參看 harness 之插圖。 **2** (fig) sth that holds one back or restrains: (喩)阻止物;抑制的東西: *put / keep a ~ on one's anger / passions.* 抑制自己的怒氣(激情)。 **3** = kerb. □ *vt* [VP6A] **1** control (a horse) by means of a ~. 藉馬勒以控制(馬)。 **2** keep (feelings, etc) under control: 抑制(感情等): *to ~ one's impatience.* 抑制自己的不耐煩。

curd /kɜːd; kɝd/ *n* **1** (often *pl*) thick, soft substance, almost solid, formed when milk turns sour, used to make cheese. (常用複數)凝乳(牛乳變酸時所凝結的物質,可用以製乳酪)。 **2** [U] (in compounds) substance resembling ~: (用於複合字中)似凝乳的物質: ˌ*lemon-ˈ~*, made from eggs, butter and sugar, flavoured with lemon. 檸檬乳糕(用鷄蛋、奶油和糖製成,加有檸檬味)。

curdle /ˈkɜːdl; ˈkɝdl/ *vi, vt* [VP6A, 2A] form, cause to form, into curds; become curd-like: (使)結成凝乳;變成凝乳狀: *The milk has ~d;* 牛奶已凝結; (fig uses): (比喩用法): *What a blood-curdling* (= horrifying) *yell!* 多麼令人心驚膽戰的號叫! *His blood ~d at the sight,* He was filled with horror. 他看見這景象就嚇呆了。

cure[1] /kjʊə(r); kjʊr/ *n* [C] **1** curing or being ~d(1): 治療;治癒: *The doctor cannot guarantee a ~.* 醫生不能保證治癒。*His ~ took six weeks.* 他的病花了六個星期才治好。 **2** substance or treatment which ~s(1): 治療的藥物;治療法: *Is there a certain ~ for cancer yet?* 迄今對癌症有無有效的治療法? *He has tried all sorts of ~s, but is still ill.* 他已試過各種藥物,但病仍未癒。*You need a ˈrest-~,* a holiday from your work. 你需要休假療養。 **3** spiritual charge(5): 聖職;傳教的職務: *to obtain / resign a ~,* a position as a priest. 就任(辭去)牧師的職務。

cure[2] /kjʊə(r); kjʊr/ *vt, vi* [VP6A, 14] **1** *~ sb (of sth); ~ sth,* bring (a person) back to health; provide and use successfully a remedy for a disease, ill health, suffering; get rid of (an evil): 使(人)恢復健康;治癒;治療(疾病,病患,痛苦);除祛(惡害): *to ~ a man of a disease;* 治癒某人的病; *to ~ an illness;* 治病; *to ~ poverty / drunkenness;* 消除貧困(矯正酒癖); *to ~ a child of bad habits;* 革除孩童的惡習; *to try to ~ social discontent at home by making war abroad.* 向外發動戰爭以安撫國內社會的不滿。 **ˈ~-all** *n* sth which, it is claimed, ~s all ills. 萬靈丹;萬靈藥。 **2** treat meat, fish, skin, tobacco, etc in order to keep it in good condition by salting, smoking, drying, etc: (用鹽醃,煙薰,乾燥等法)保存(肉,魚,皮革,菸草等): *well-~d bacon.* 醃得好的醃肉。

curé /ˈkjʊəreɪ *US:* kjʊˈreɪ; kjʊˈre/ *n* parish priest in France. 法國的教區牧師。

cur·few /ˈkɜːfjuː; ˈkɝfju/ *n* **1** (old use) ringing of a bell as a signal for lights to be put out and fires covered; bell for this; hour at which the bell was rung. (舊用法)晚間令人熄滅燈火的鐘聲;爲此所用的鐘;晚鐘;鳴晚鐘的時刻。 **2** (modern use) time or signal (under martial law) for people to remain indoors: (現代用法)(實施戒嚴期間)禁止外出的時間或信號;宵禁: *to impose a ~ on a town;* 在鎮上實施宵禁; *to lift / end the ~.* 解除宵禁。

curio /ˈkjʊərɪəʊ; ˈkjʊrɪˌo/ *n* (*pl* ~s) work of art of a strange or unusual character and valued for this reason. 古董;古玩;珍品。

curi·os·ity /ˌkjʊərɪˈɒsətɪ; ˌkjʊrɪˈɑsətɪ/ *n* **1** [U] being curious (1, 2): 好奇心;求知慾;好管閒事: *~ about / ~ to learn about distant lands;* 對於遠鄉異地的好奇心(求知慾); *to be dying of / burning with ~ to know what was happening.* 極欲(渴望)知道發生了什麼事。*He yielded to ~ and opened the letter addressed to his sister.* 他受好奇心的驅使,拆開了別人寫給他姊姊(妹妹)的信。 **2** [C] (*pl* -ties) curious(3) thing; strange or rare object. 珍奇的事物;珍品。

curi·ous /ˈkjʊərɪəs; ˈkjʊrɪəs/ *adj* **1** *~ (to do sth); ~ (about sth),* (in a good sense) eager (to learn / know, etc); interested (in sth): (用在好的意味上)好奇的;渴望知道的;對(某事)有興趣的: *~ about the origin of mankind.* 對人類的起源有興趣的。*I'm ~ to know what he said.* 我極想知道他說了什麼。*If a boy is ~, he is always asking questions.* 一個男孩若是好奇,就會經常發問。 **2** *~ (about sth),* meddlesome; having or showing too much interest in the affairs of others: 愛管閒事的;對他人之事過份感興趣的: *~ neighbours.* 愛管閒事的鄰居。*Don't ask so many ~ questions.* 不要問這麼多關於別人的問題。*Hide it where ~ eyes won't see it.* 把它藏在好事者的眼睛看不見的地方。*What is he so ~ about?* 他要打聽什麼人的閒事? **3** strange; unusual; hard to understand: 古怪的;不尋常的;難懂的: *What a ~ mistake!* 多麼奇怪的錯誤! *There was a ~ silence.* 有一種出乎尋常的沉寂。*Isn't he a ~-looking little man!* 他豈不是一個相貌奇特的矮人! **4** (rather old use) showing the result of care and attention: (頗舊用法)精細的;精工的: *a jewel of ~ workmanship.* 精工琢磨的珠寶。 **~·ly** *adv*

curl[1] /kɜːl; kɝl/ *n* **1** [C] sth naturally like or twisted into a shape like a spiral or the thread of a screw, esp a lock of hair of this shape: 天然或扭曲似螺紋之物;(尤指)鬈髮: *~s (of hair) falling over her shoulders;* 垂在她肩上的鬈髮; *hair falling in ~s over the shoulder;* 垂於肩上的鬈髮; *a ~ of smoke rising from a cigarette;* 自香煙升起的一縷輕煙; *the ~ of a wave;* 浪頭; *a ~ of the lips,* expressing scorn. 撇嘴(表示輕蔑)。 **2** [U] the state of being curly: 捲曲的狀態: *How do you keep your hair in ~?* 你怎樣使頭髮保持捲曲的?

curl[2] /kɜːl; kɝl/ *vt, vi* [VP6A, 15A, B, 2A, C] *~ (up),* make into curls; twist; grow or be in curls: 使捲曲;扭曲;長成捲曲狀: *She has ~ed her hair.* 她已捲過她的頭髮。*Does her hair ~ naturally?* 她的頭髮是天然捲曲的嗎? *The smoke from the camp fire ~ed upwards.* 煙自營火繚繞上升。*The frost made the young leaves ~* (*up*) / *~ed up the young leaves.* 嚴霜使嫩葉捲縮。*The dog ~ed* (*itself*) *up on the rug.* 狗蜷着身子臥在地毯上。 *~ (sb) up,* (cause to) collapse: (使)崩潰;(使)倒下: *The cricket ball hit him on the head and he ~ed up* (= fell to the ground) *at once.* 板球擊中他的頭部,他立即倒在地上。*She ~ed up* (*with laughter*) *at his joke.* 他的笑話使她笑彎了腰。*The blow ~ed him up completely.* 那一擊使他完全倒下。 **ˈ~·er,** small cylindrical object round which warmed or wet hair is wound to create a ~. (捲髮用的圓筒形)髮捲。 **ˈ~ing-tongs / -irons,** instruments (heated before use) for ~ing or straightening the hair. (使用前加熱的)燙髮鉗;捲髮

鉗。'~ing-pins, clips (used cold) for ~ing the hair. (不加熱的)捲髮夾子。

cur·lew /'kɜːljuː; 'kɝlu/ *n* wading bird with a long, slender, down-curved bill. 麻鷸(一種喙細長且下彎的涉禽)。⇨ the illus at water. 參看 water 之挿圖。

curl·ing /'kɜːlɪŋ; 'kɝlɪŋ/ *n* [U] Scottish game played on ice with heavy, flat-bottomed stones ('~-**stones**) with handles, sent along the ice towards a mark. 一種蘇格蘭的遊戲,在冰上將有柄、沉重而且平底的石頭(curling-stones)滑向某一目標。

curly /'kɜːlɪ; 'kɝlɪ/ *adj* (-ier, -iest) having curls; arranged in curls: 有捲髮的;捲曲的: *~ hair;* 鬈髮; *a '~-headed girl.* 頭髮捲曲的女孩。

cur·mudgeon /kɜː'mʌdʒən; kɚ'mʌdʒən/ *n* (colloq) bad-tempered or miserly person. (俗)脾氣壞或吝嗇的人。

cur·rant /'kʌrənt; 'kɝənt/ *n* **1** small, sweet, dried seedless grape (grown in Greece and neighbouring countries) used in buns, cakes, puddings, etc. 一種小的甜葡萄乾(產於希臘及其隣近各國,用以製小圓麵包、糕餅、布丁等)。 **2** (cultivated bush with) small black red or white juicy fruit growing in clusters. 紅醋栗(黑,紅或白色的多汁小果,簇生);紅醋栗樹(灌木)。

cur·rency /'kʌrənsɪ; 'kɝənsɪ/ *n* **1** [U] the state of being in common or general use: 流行;通用;流通: *Many slang words have short ~*, soon go out of use. 許多俚語流行不久就不再用了。*The rumour soon gained ~*, was repeated until many people were aware of it. 謠言不久就傳開了。***give ~ to***, make current(1); spread: 使流行;傳播: *Do not give ~ to idle gossip.* 不要傳播閒言。 **2** [C,U] (*pl* -cies) money that is actually in use in a country: (一國中實際通用的)貨幣: *a gold/paper ~;* 金(紙)幣; *foreign currencies;* 外幣; *a decimal ~.* 十進制貨幣。

cur·rent[1] /'kʌrənt; 'kɝənt/ *adj* **1** in common or general use; generally accepted: 通用的; 流行的; 通行的;公認的: *~ coin/money;* 通貨; *~ opinions/beliefs;* 許多人持有的意見(信仰); *words that are no longer ~.* 已不通行的字。 **2** now passing; of the present time: 現行的;現時的;現今的: *~ expenses/prices;* 經常費(時價); *the ~ issue of a magazine;* 雜誌之最近的一期; *the ~ year,* this year; 今年; *a newsreel showing ~ events.* 報導時事的新聞影片。 **3 ~ account**, (with a bank) one from which money may be drawn without previous notice. (在銀行的) 活期存款 (不需事先通知卽可提款)。⇨ *deposit account* at deposit[2](1), *savings account* at save[1]. **~ assets**, (comm) assets which are not fixed but which change in the course of business (eg amounts owing). (商)流動資產(非固定的資產,商業過程中可變動者,例如負債)。**~·ly** *adv* in a ~(1, 2) manner: 通行地; 流行地; 現今地; 最近地: *It is ~ly reported that....* 據最近報導…。

cur·rent[2] /'kʌrənt; 'kɝənt/ *n* **1** stream of water, air, gas, esp one flowing through slower moving or still water, etc: 流;水流;氣流;(尤指緩流或靜水中之)激流: *A cold ~ of air came in when the door was opened.* 門打開時進來了一股冷風。*Although he was a strong swimmer he was swept away by the ~ and was drowned.* 雖然他的泳術高强,但是他被激流捲走淹死了。*The warm ~s in the Atlantic influence the climate of Great Britain.* 大西洋中的暖流影響英國的氣候。 **2** flow of electricity through sth or along a wire or cable. (通過某物或沿線纜的)電流。⇨ alternate[2](2), direct[1](5). **3** course or movement (of events, opinions, thoughts, etc): (事件,意見,思想等的)動向;趨勢;潮流: *Nothing disturbs the peaceful ~ of her life.* 在她平靜的生活中,沒有任何的騷擾。*The government used the radio to influence the ~ of thought.* 政府利用無線電廣播影響思想的趨向。

cur·ricu·lum /kə'rɪkjʊləm; kə'rɪkjələm/ *n* (*pl* ~s or -la /-lə; -lə/) course of study in a school, college, etc. (學校,學院等所開的)課程。 **~ vitae** /'viːtaɪ; 'vaɪti/ (Lat) brief written account of one's past history (eg education, employment), used when applying for a job, etc (US 美 = *résumé*). (拉)履歷(求職等時所寫個人之學歷,經歷等)。

cur·rish /'kɜːrɪʃ; 'kɝɪʃ/ *adj* like a cur. 脾氣壞的;下賤的;卑怯的。**~·ly** *adv*

curry[1] /'kʌrɪ; 'kɝɪ/ *n* (*pl* -ries) [C, U] (dish of) meat, fish, eggs, etc cooked with hot-tasting spices: 用咖哩調製的肉,魚,蛋等;一道咖哩菜: *a chicken ~;* 咖哩鷄; *Madras curries;* 馬德拉斯咖哩菜; *to eat too much ~.* 吃太多咖哩調製的菜。**'~-powder**, mixture of spices for a ~ ground or beaten to a powder. 咖哩粉。□ *vt* prepare (food) with hot-tasting spices; flavour (food) with ~-powder: 用咖哩烹調(食物);加咖哩粉於(食物): *curried chicken.* 咖哩鷄。

curry[2] /'kʌrɪ; 'kɝɪ/ *vt* [VP6A] rub down and clean (a horse); prepare (tanned leather) by soaking, scraping, etc. 刷洗(馬);(用泡,刮等方法)製(革);硝(皮)。 ***~ favour (with sb)***, try to win favour or approval (by using flattery, etc). (藉諂媚等)求恩寵;曲意逢迎。

curse[1] /kɜːs; kɝs/ *n* **1** word, phrase or sentence calling for the punishment, injury or destruction of sth or sb. 詛咒(祈天懲罰,傷害或毀滅某物或某人)。***be under a ~***, suffer as the result of a ~. 因被詛咒而受災禍。***call down ~s (from Heaven) upon sb***, ask God or Heaven to punish him. 祈天降禍於某人。***lay sb under a ~***, make him suffer as the result of a ~. 使因被詛咒而受災禍。 **2** cause of misfortune or ruin: 禍因;禍源;爲禍之物: *Gambling is often a ~.* 賭博常是禍因。*The rabbits are a ~* (ie do a lot of damage to crops, etc) *in this part of the country.* 兔子在這一帶農村是一種禍害(卽損壞農作物等)。*His wealth proved a ~ to him.* 他的財富成爲他的禍因。 **3** word or words used in violent language expressing anger. 怒罵之詞。 **4 the ~**, (colloq) menses. (俗)月經。

curse[2] /kɜːs; kɝs/ *vt, vi* **1** [VP6A] use a curse against; use violent language against. 詛咒;咒罵;詈罵。 **2** [VP2A, 3A] **~ (at)**, utter curses: 口出惡言;咒罵: *to ~ and swear;* 口出惡言;*to ~ at fate.* 詛咒命運。 **3 *be ~d with***, suffer misfortune, trouble, etc because of: 因…而受害: *to be ~d with idle daughters/a violent temper.* 受了懶惰女兒(暴躁脾氣)的害。

cursed /'kɜːsɪd; 'kɝsɪd/ *adj* damnable; hateful (often used colloq merely to show annoyance): 該死的;可恨的;(俗)可厭的: *This work is a ~ nuisance.* 這工作極爲討厭。**~·ly** *adv*

cur·sive /'kɜːsɪv; 'kɝsɪv/ *adj* (of handwriting) with the letters rounded and joined together. (指書法)草書的;草體的。⇨ script.

cur·sory /'kɜːsərɪ; 'kɝsərɪ/ *adj* (of work, reading, etc) quick; hurried; done without attention to details: (指工作,閱讀等)匆促的;粗略的;不精細的;不注意細節的: *a ~ glance/inspection.* 匆匆的一瞥(檢查)。 **cur·sor·ily** /'kɜːsərəlɪ; 'kɝsərəlɪ/ *adv*

curst /kɜːst; kɝst/ *adj* = cursed.

curt /kɜːt; kɝt/ *adj* (of a speaker, his manner, what he says) short-spoken; hardly polite: (指說話者,其態度,所說的話)簡短的;禮貌不週的;唐突的: *to give sb a ~ answer;* 給某人一簡短的回答; *a ~ way of speaking.* 說話唐突。**~·ly** *adv* **~·ness** *n*

cur·tail /kɜː'teɪl; kɝ'tel/ *vt* [VP6A] make shorter than was at first planned; cut off a part of: (較最初計畫)縮短;縮減;提早結束: *to ~ a speech/one's holidays;* 提早結束演說(休假); *to ~ the allowance one has been making to sb,* give him less money. 減少給予某人的津貼。**~·ment** *n* [U, C] act or result of ~ing. 縮短;縮減;減少。

cur·tain /'kɜːtn; 'kɝtn/ *n* **1** piece of cloth or lace hung up at a window or door or (in former times) round a bed: 窗簾;門簾;(昔時圍於床四周的)帳帷: *Please draw the ~s,* pull them across the window(s). 請將窗簾拉上。***draw a ~ over sth,*** (fig) say no more about it. (喩)停止講某事;不再提某事。**'~-lecture,** (old use) wife's scolding of her husband in private (originally in bed after the bed-~s were drawn). (舊用法)妻子在私下對丈夫的責備(原指在床帷拉上的時候)。 **2** sheet of heavy material to draw or lower across the front of the stage in a theatre before and after each scene of a play: (戲台上在一景戲演出前後所啓閉的)幕: *The ~ rises/is raised,* The play/act begins. 啓幕(戲開演)。*The ~ falls,* The play/act ends. 落幕(戲演完)。**'~-call,** call (given by the audience) to an actor or actress to appear before the ~ for applause. (觀衆)要求演員出場謝幕(接受鼓掌)的呼聲。**'~-raiser,** short piece performed before the chief play. 開場戲(正戲前的短戲)。**'safety-~,** one that is fire-proof. 安全幕(防火者)。 **3** (various senses indicating cover or protection): (各種表示遮蔽或保護的意義): *A ~ of mist hid the view.* 一層薄霧遮住視線。*The troops went forward behind a ~ of fire* (gun-fire from their artillery). 軍隊在砲火掩護下前進。□ *vt* **1** [VP6A] furnish or cover with ~s: 裝以簾幕;以簾幕遮蓋: *~ed windows;* 有窗簾的窗戶; *enough material to ~ all the windows.* 足够爲所有窗子裝窗簾的布料。 **2** [VP15B] ~ ***off,*** separate or divide with a ~ or ~s: 用簾幕分隔: *to ~ off part of a room.* 用簾幕隔出房間的一部份。

curt·sey, curtsy /ˈkɜːtsɪ ; ˈkɝtsɪ/ *n* (*pl* ~s, -sies) gesture of respect (bending the knees) made by women and girls (eg to a queen): 婦女所行的屈膝禮(如對女王所行者): *to make/drop/bob a ~ (to sb).* (向某人)行屈膝禮。□ *vi* (*pt, pp* ~ed, curtsied) make a ~ (*to*). 行屈膝禮(與 to 連用)。

cur·va·ture /ˈkɜːvətʃə(r) *US:* -tʃʊər ; ˈkɝvətʃɚ/ *n* [U] curving; the state of being curved: 彎曲;屈曲;曲度: *to suffer from ~ of the spine;* 患脊椎骨彎曲症; *the ~ of the earth's surface.* 地球表面的曲度。

curve /kɜːv ; kɝv/ *n* line of which no part is straight and which changes direction without angles: 曲線;弧線;彎曲處: *a ~ in the road.* 彎路。*The driver of a car should not go round/take ~s at high speed.* 汽車駕駛人不應在高速下轉彎。□ *vt, vi* [VP6A, 2A] have, cause to have, the form of a ~: (使)成彎形: *The river ~s round the town.* 河水環繞市鎮。

cushion /ˈkʊʃn ; ˈkʊʃən/ *n* **1** small bag filled with feathers or other soft material (eg foam rubber), to make a seat more comfortable, or to kneel on, etc; sth soft and like a ~ in shape or function: 軟墊子;坐墊;椅墊(內裝羽毛或其他柔軟物質,如泡沫橡膠,以墊座位或跪時墊於膝下等); 形式或功用似軟墊之物。*a ~ of moss;* 一層青苔; *a 'pin-~;* (裁縫插針用的)針墊。*a ~ of air,* as for a hovercraft. 氣墊(如氣墊船之噴射引擎向下噴出之氣體所形成者)。 **2** soft, resilient lining on the inner sides of a billiard-table where the balls hit. 撞球枱邊緣內側碰球的有彈性的裡襯。□ *vt* [VP6A, 14] supply with ~s; protect from shock with ~s: 裝墊子;用墊子保護(以免碰撞): *~ed seats;* 有墊子的座位; (fig) protect from harmful changes: (喩)保護(以免受變動之害): *farmers who are ~ed against falls in prices,* eg by subsidies. 受保護(例如政府津貼)以免受物價下跌影響之農人。

cushy /ˈkʊʃɪ ; ˈkʊʃɪ/ *adj* (-ier, -iest) (sl) (of a job, etc) not requiring much effort: (俚)(指工作等)輕鬆的;不費力的: *get a ~ job in the Civil Service.* 在文職機關獲一輕鬆的工作。

cusp /kʌsp ; kʌsp/ *n* pointed end (esp of a leaf). 尖點;(尤指)葉的尖端。

cus·pi·dor /ˈkʌspɪdɔː(r) ; ˈkʌspəˌdɔr/ *n* (US) spittoon. (美)痰盂。

cuss /kʌs ; kʌs/ *n* (sl) (俚) **1** curse. 詛咒。***not give/care a ~,*** be quite unworried. 一點不在乎。***not worth a tinker's ~,*** quite worthless. 一文不值的。 **2** person: 人: *a queer old ~.* 老怪物。

cussed /ˈkʌsɪd ; ˈkʌsɪd/ *adj* (colloq) perverse; obstinate. (俗)剛愎的;固執的。**~·ly** *adv* **~·ness** *n*

cus·tard /ˈkʌstəd ; ˈkʌstɚd/ *n* [C, U] **(egg-)~,** (dish of) mixture of eggs and milk, sweetened and flavoured, baked or boiled; mixture of powdered eggs, etc **('~-powder)** prepared by adding sugar and milk to flavoured cornflour, eaten with fruit, pastry, etc. 乳蛋糕(亦作 egg-custard, 鷄蛋和牛奶混合加糖及味料經烘焙或烹煮製成的食品);一道乳蛋糕;乳蛋粉(亦作 custard-powder, 以糖和牛奶加含有味料的玉蜀黍粉製成,與水果、糕餅等共食)。

cus·tod·ian /kʌˈstəʊdɪən ; kʌsˈtodɪən/ *n* person who has custody of sth or sb; caretaker of a public building. 保管人;監護人;(公共建築物的)管理員。

cus·tody /ˈkʌstədɪ ; ˈkʌstədɪ/ *n* [U] **1** (duty of) caring for, guarding: 照顧;監護(的責任): *A father has the ~ of his children while they are young.* 孩子幼時,父親有監護之責。*When Mary's parents died, she was placed in the ~ of her aunt.* 瑪莉的父母去世以後,她就交由她的姑母照顧。*If you are going away for a long time you should leave your jewellery in safe ~,* eg with your bank. 如果你將離家很久,你應將珠寶飾物交付(銀行等)保管。 **2** imprisonment. 監禁。***(be) in ~,*** in prison (eg awaiting trial). 在羈押中(如候審)。***give sb into ~,*** hand him over to the police. 將某人交給警察。***take sb into ~,*** arrest him. 逮捕某人。

cus·tom /ˈkʌstəm ; ˈkʌstəm/ *n* **1** [U] usual and generally accepted behaviour among members of a social group: 風俗;習俗(某一社會團體各份子間通常一般公認的行爲方式): *Don't be a slave to ~,* Do not do things merely because most people do them and have always done them. 不要做習俗的奴隸(勿僅因大多數人如此做或經常如此做而亦如此做)。*It has become the ~* (= has become usual) *for our family to go to the seaside in summer.* 我們家在夏季常去海濱。 **2** [C] particular way of behaving which, because it has been long established, is observed by individuals and social groups: (個人的)習慣;(社會的)習俗;慣例: *Social ~s vary in different countries.* 社會風俗各國不同。*It was Tom's ~ to get up early and go for a walk before breakfast.* 湯姆的習慣是很早起床,並且在早餐以前散步。(Cf 參較 *habit,* a word that means sth that a person does regularly, and that he cannot easily give up. 指個人經常所做之事而不容易放棄者。) **3** [U] regular support given to a tradesman by those who buy his goods: (由於經常購買其貨物而給予經商者的)照顧;惠顧: *We should very much like to have your ~,* would like you to buy our goods. 我們竭誠歡迎你來光顧。*I shall withdraw my ~ from that shop,* not buy goods there in future. 我將不再照顧那家商店(卽不再購買他們的貨物)。 **4** (*pl*) taxes due to the government on goods imported into a country; import duties; department of government (*the C~s*) that collects such duties: (複)(由政府所徵收的)貨物進口稅;關稅;海關(作 the Customs): *How long will it take us to pass* (= get through) *the C~s?* 通過海關檢查要花我們多久時間? *The C~s formalities are simple.* 海關檢查的手續很簡單。**'~ house,** office (esp at a port) where ~s are collected. (尤指港口的)海關辦公處。**'~s union,** agreement by States on a common policy on tariffs. 關稅同盟(國際間對課征關稅之共同協定)。 **5** (attrib use only) made to order. (僅作形容用法)定製的。**ˌ~-ˈbuilt,** as specified by the buyer. 定製的;買主特定的。**ˌ~-ˈmade** *adj* (of clothes) made-to-measure; making things to order: (指衣服)定做的;專做定貨的: *~ tailors/shoemakers.* 專做定貨的裁縫(鞋匠)。⇨ *bespoke* at bespeak; *tailor-made* at tailor.

cus·tom·ary /ˈkʌstəmərɪ *US:* -merɪ ; ˈkʌstəmˌɛrɪ/ *adj* in agreement with, according to, custom(1, 2): 合於風俗或習慣的;根據風俗或習慣的: *Is it ~ for guests at hotels in your country to tip the waiters?* 在貴國住旅館的客人依慣例是否給侍者小費? *There was the ~ vote of thanks to the chairman.* 依照慣例向主席鼓掌致謝。**cus·tom·ar·ily** /ˈkʌstəmərəlɪ *US:*

ˌkʌstəˈmerəlɪ ; ˈkʌstəmˌɛrəlɪ/ *adv*

cus·tomer /ˈkʌstəmə(r) ; ˈkʌstəmə/ *n* **1** person who buys things, esp one who gives his custom(3) to a shop: 顧客;顧主;(尤指)經常照顧某商店者: *Mr X has lost some of his best ~s.* 某先生已喪失一部份最好的老顧客。 **2** (colloq) person or fellow, esp in: (俗)人;傢伙;漢子(尤用於): *a queer ~;* 怪人; *an awkward ~,* person who is difficult to deal with. 難纏的傢伙。

cut[1] /kʌt ; kʌt/ *vt, vi* (-tt-) (*pt, pp* cut) (For uses with *adverbial particles* and *preps* ⇨ 10 below; for uses with *adjj* ⇨ 7 below; for uses with *nouns* or *pronouns* ⇨ 6 below.) (與副詞接語和介詞連用參看下列第 10 義; 與形容詞連用參看下列第 7 義; 與名詞或代名詞連用參看下列第6義。) **1** [VP6A, 12B, 13B, 15A, 2A] make an opening, incision (with a sharp-edged instrument, eg a knife, a pair of scissors, or other edged tool); (用有刃的器具如刀,剪刀等)切開;割破; **(a)** make a mark, wound, in sth: 割傷: *He cut his face/himself while shaving.* 他在刮鬍子的時候把臉割傷了。⇨ *cut into sth* in 10 below. 參看下列第10義之 cut into sth。**(b)** sever; reap: 切斷; 收割: *Don't pluck the flowers; it's better to cut them.* 不要用手採花;最好用剪刀剪。 *Has the wheat been cut* (= harvested, reaped) *yet?* 小麥已經收割了嗎? **(c)** shorten: 剪短: *to cut one's nails;* 剪指甲; *to cut a hedge;* 修剪樹籬; *to have one's hair cut.* 理髮。Hence,由此產生, **ˈhair-cut** *n* ⇨ also *cut sth short* in 7 below. 亦參看下列第 7 義 之 cut sth short。**(d)** separate; remove from sth larger: 使分開;自較大部分切下: *Please cut a slice of cake for me/cut me a slice of cake.* 請切一塊蛋糕給我。*Cut yourself some pineapple.* 你自己切些鳳梨吃吧。*Cut some pineapple for your sister.* 給你姊姊(妹妹)切些鳳梨。*Two scenes/episodes were cut by the censor.* 兩個景(事件)被檢查員刪除了。⇨ also *cut off* and *cut out* in 10 below. 亦參看下列第 10 義之 cut off 及 cut out。**(e)** reduce sth by removing part: 減少: *Was your salary cut?* 你的薪水減少了嗎? *The new jet service cuts the travelling time by half.* 新噴射客機減少了一半旅行的時間。 ⇨ *cut down* in 10 below. 參看下列第 10 義之 cut down。 **(f)** divide into smaller pieces: 分成小塊: *Will you cut the cake?* ie into pieces. 請你切蛋糕好嗎? *If you'll cut the bread* (ie into slices), *we'll make toast.* 如果你切麵包,我們就來烤麵包。⇨ *cut up* in 10 below. 參看下列第 10 義之 cut up。 **(g)** divide, separate into two: 分割爲二: *Don't cut the string, untie the knots.* 不要剪斷那繩子,把繩結打開。 *The Minister cut the tape to open a new section of motorway.* 部長爲一段新完工的高速公路剪綵。 **(h)** make, fashion, by removing material with tools, machines, etc that cut: 割成;切成;挖成;雕成: *to cut steps in the ice;* 在冰上挖出踏脚之處; *to cut a tunnel through a hill;* 穿山挖一條隧道; *to cut a road up a hillside;* 挖一條路至山坡上; *to cut an inscription/one's initials.* 刻碑文(自己名字的爲首字母)。⇨ *cut out* in 10 below. 參看下列第 10 義之 cut out。 **2** [VP2A, C] **(a)** (of a sharp tool, instrument, etc) be suitable to use: (指鋒利的工具等)適於使用: *This knife does not cut well.* 這把刀切起來不利。**(b)** (of a material) be capable of being cut: (指原料)可被切,剪,刻等: *Sandstone cuts easily.* 沙岩很容易切開。 *This cloth is too narrow to cut well,* is narrow and difficult to cut into the shapes needed. 這塊布料太窄,不易裁成所需式樣。**3** [VP6A] (colloq) stay away from, be absent from (sth one ought to attend): (俗)缺席;不出席(應出席之場所): *to cut a class/a lecture.* 逃學;逃課。 **4** [VP6A] (of lines) cross: (指線條)相交: *Let the point where AB cuts CD be called E.* 假設 AB 線與 CD 線相交之點爲E。 **5** [VP6A] (sport, esp cricket, tennis, billiards) strike (a ball) so that it spins or is deflected; hit the edge of (a ball). (尤指板球,網球,撞球等)擊(球)使其迴旋;斜擊(一球); 削(球)。 **6** [VP6A] (used with *nouns* or *pronouns*) (與名詞或代名詞連用) ***cut the cards/pack,*** lift part of a pack of playing-cards lying face downwards and turn it up to decide sth (eg who is to deal, who are to be partners). 翻牌決定(自一副面向下的紙牌拿起一部分並翻轉來以決定誰發牌或與誰同夥)。***cut one's coat according to one's cloth,*** suit one's expenditure to one's income; not be too ambitious in one's plans. 量入爲出;不存奢望;不抱太大野心。 ***cut (off) a corner,*** go across, not round it. 走直路; 走近路(不經過轉角處)。***cut corners,*** (fig) take a short-cut. (喻)走捷徑。***cut a disc/record,*** record music, etc on to a gramophone record. 將音樂等錄於唱片上。***cut the ground from under sb/from under sb's feet,*** leave him in a weak or illogical position; destroy the foundation of his plan, argument, etc. 拆某人的台子;破壞某人的計畫、論據等的基礎。***cut no/not much ice (with sb),*** have little or no effect or influence (on him): (對某人)無作用或影響力。***cut one's losses,*** abandon a scheme that has caused financial losses before one loses too much. 及早放棄造成經濟損失的計畫以免遭受更大的損失。***cut a tooth,*** have a new tooth just begin to show itself above the gum. 長牙;生新牙(剛自牙肉中生出)。***cut one's teeth on sth,*** learn, gain experience, from: 自…獲取經驗: *There's a job for you to cut your teeth on.* 有一個使你增加經驗的工作。***cut both ways,*** (of an action or argument) have an effect both for and against. (指行動或論據)騎牆;兩面倒。⇨ also caper[1], dash[1](6), figure(5), Gordian. **7** [VP22] (with an *adj* as complement) (與作補語的形容詞連用) ***cut sb dead,*** pretend not to have seen; treat as a complete stranger: 佯裝未見某人;完全把某人當做陌生人看待: *She cut me dead in the street,* ignored me completely. 她在街上把我視若路人。 ***cut it fine,*** (colloq) leave oneself only the minimum of what is needed (esp time): (俗)只剩下最低限度;扣得很緊(尤指時間): *He cut it rather fine,* eg by reaching the station half a minute before his train was due to leave. 他把時間扣得太緊了(例如在火車開行前半分鐘才到達車站)。 ***cut sb/sth free (from),*** make or get free by cutting: 割斷繩索等以解脫: *He cut himself free from the ropes with which they had bound him.* 他割斷他們用以綁他的繩索而逃脫了。 ***cut sth/sb loose (from),*** make loose or separate by cutting: 割斷(繩索等)以解放: *cut loose a boat/cut a boat loose;* 割斷繩索以放開船; *cut oneself loose from one's family,* live an independent life. 離家自立謀生。***cut sth open,*** make an opening or split in: 使破;使裂: *He fell and cut his head open.* 他摔了一跤跌破了頭。***cut sth short,*** make shorter: 縮短;刪節: *to cut a long story short;* 把長的故事截短; 長話短說; *to cut short a person's remarks;* 打斷某人的話; *a career cut short by illness.* 因病半途而廢的事業。 **8** ***C~!*** (cinema; imper) Stop (shooting a scene)! (電影;祈使)停止(拍攝一鏡頭)! **9** (uses with the *pp*) (過去分詞的用法) ***cut and dried,*** (of opinions, etc) already formed and unlikely to be changed. (指意見等)已決定的;不大會改變的。**ˌcut ˈflowers,** flowers cut for decoration (contrasted with flowers growing in the garden, in pots, etc). (爲裝飾用而)剪下的花(與園中,盆中等長的花相對)。**ˌcut ˈglass,** glass with patterns and designs cut on it. 雕花玻璃。**ˌcut-ˈprice** *attrib adj* at a reduced price, and below those of rivals or those recommended by the manufacturers, etc. 削價的(指低於同業或廠商所定的價格的)。 **ˌcut-ˈrate** *attrib adj* = cut-price. **ˌcut toˈbacco,** shredded (contrasted with *cake* tobacco). 菸絲(與 cake tobacco 相對)。 **cut·ting** *part adj* **(a)** sharp; piercing: 銳利的;刺人的: *a cutting wind.* 刺骨的風。 **(b)** sarcastic; wounding: 譏刺的; 傷害的: *cutting remarks.* 傷感情的話。 **10** [VP3A, 15B, A, 2C] (uses with *adverbial particles* and *preps*): (與副

詞接語及介詞連用的用法):
cut across sth, **(a)** take a shorter route across (a field, etc). 取捷徑穿過(田地等)。**(b)** be contrary to: 與…相反: *Opinion on preserving the environment cut clean across normal political loyalties.*保護環境的意見與政治上普通的忠誠完全相反。 ***cut at sb/sth,*** aim a sharp blow at (eg with a sword or whip): (用刀劍或鞭等)對準…而猛擊: *cut at a hedge/a group of nettles with a stick.* 用棍棒對着樹籬(一簇蕁麻)猛擊。 ***cut sth away,*** remove by cutting: 割掉;砍去: *We cut away all the dead wood from the tree.* 我們把樹上所有的枯枝都砍去了。*The yacht was in danger of sinking until they cut away the broken mast and rigging.* 那遊艇有沉沒的危險,後來他們砍去那斷桅及纜索,危險方告消除。 ***cut sth back,*** **(a)** (of shrubs, bushes, etc) prune close to the stem. (指矮樹,灌木等)剪短(其枝葉)。**(b)** reduce: 減少;減低: *cut back production.* 減低生產。Hence, 由此產生, **'cut·back** *n* **(a)** reduction: 減少; 減低: *a cutback in expenditure.* 減少開銷。**(b)** flashback. (電影)倒叙。 ***cut sth/sb down,*** **(a)** cause to fall by cutting: 砍倒: *to cut down a tree.* 砍倒一樹。**(b)** kill or injure by striking with a sword or other edged weapon: (用刀劍或其他有刃武器)砍殺;殺傷: *He cut down his enemy.* 他殺傷了他的敵人。**(c)** deprive of life or health (by disease, etc): (爲疾病等)奪去生命或健康;病死;病倒: *He was cut down in the prime of manhood.* 他在壯年時期病死了。**(d)** reduce in quantity, amount, etc: 減少(數量等): *cut down expenses.* 減低用費。*I won't have a cigarette, thanks—I'm trying to cut down,* reduce the number of cigarettes I smoke. 謝謝,我不要抽煙——我正在設法減少抽煙量。**(e)** persuade (sb) to reduce a price, charge, etc: 說服(某人)減價等: *We managed to cut him down by £30.* 我們總算說服他把價錢減低了三十鎊。**(f)** reduce the length of: 減短: *cut down a pair of trousers,* eg for sb who is shorter. 改短褲脚(給較矮者穿)。*cut down an article to make it fit the space available,* in a periodical, etc. 刪節一篇文章使適合雜誌中有限的篇幅。 ***cut 'down on,*** reduce one's consumption of: 減少對…之消耗量: *He's trying to cut down on cigarettes and beer.* 他在設法減少吸香煙和飲啤酒的量。***cut sb down to size,*** (colloq) show him that he is not so important as he thinks he is: (俗)告訴某人他並不像他自己所想的那樣重要: *Some of these so-called experts really need cutting down to size.* 這些所謂專家當中有些眞需要讓他們知道他們並不像他們自己所想的那樣重要。
cut in (on), (of the driver of a motor vehicle, etc, who has overtaken another vehicle) return too soon to his own side of the road (with possibility of collision, etc): (指汽車等駕駛者,超車後)駛入原車道過急(可能與他車相撞等): *Accidents are often caused by drivers who cut in (on other cars).* 車禍常因駕駛者超車過急而造成。 ***cut sb in,*** (colloq) include sb in a (profitable) venture: (俗)讓某人加入(賺錢的)冒險事業: *If you'll contribute £500 we'll cut you in.* 如果你願意拿出五百鎊,我們就讓你入夥。***cut in (on)/into,*** interrupt (a conversation, etc): 打斷(談話等);插嘴: *Don't cut into the story/in on the conversation/in so rudely—let her finish.* 不要打斷這故事(打斷談話,那樣魯莽地插嘴)——讓她說完。***cut in half/two/three, etc; cut into halves/quarters/thirds, etc,*** divide: 切爲兩半(二,三,四等塊);分割: *The submarine was cut in half by a destroyer.* 那潛艇被一驅逐艦擊成兩半。*Cut the cable in two.* 將此纜截成兩段。*Cut the apples into halves.* 將這些蘋果各切爲兩半。
cut into sth, **(a)** make a cut in: 切開(某物): *Mary cut into her birthday cake and everybody clapped.* 瑪莉切開她的生日蛋糕,大家鼓掌慶賀。**(b)** interfere with: 妨礙: *All this extra homework cuts into his weekends,* leaves him less free time. 所有這些額外的課外作業使他在週末都沒有多少空閒。
cut sb/sth off (from), **(a)** remove (esp sth at an extremity) by cutting: 切去(尤指尖端部分): *Don't cut your fingers off!* 不要把你的手指切斷了! *Cut the chicken's head off.* 把鷄頭砍掉。*He cut off a metre of cloth from the roll.* 他自那捲布上剪下一公尺。**(b)** stop; interrupt; isolate: 停止;打斷;使孤立: *be cut off while talking by telephone;* 正在打電話時線路被切斷; *cut off the gas/electricity supply,* eg because of unpaid accounts; 切斷煤氣(電力)供應(如因未繳清欠款); *cut off an army from its base,* by getting in between; 切斷軍隊與基地的連絡; *cut off stragglers,* separate them from the main body and so capture them; 截住掉隊者(以便捕捉之); *be cut off from all possibility of help;* 被切斷一切受援助的可能; *towns cut off* (= isolated) *by floods;* 爲洪水所困困的市鎭; *cut off by the tide,* isolated on a rock, sandbank, etc by the incoming tide; 爲漲潮所困(如被孤立在岩石,沙灘等上); *cut off sb's supplies/a son's allowance,* no longer allow him to receive them; 切斷某人的供應來源(不再給兒子零用錢); *cut off sb with a shilling,* disinherit him (eg a son who has behaved badly) except for a small sum (to show that the act is deliberate). 留一先令剝奪某人之繼承權(例如兒子品行不良,僅留給他很少的一點錢,表示此舉是故意的)。***cut (off) a corner,*** ⇨ 6 above. 參看上列第6義。
cut out, stop functioning: 停止作用: *One of the aircraft's engines cut out.* 那架飛機的一個引擎失去作用。***cut sth out,*** **(a)** remove by cutting (eg from a periodical): (自刋物等)剪下; 切去: *That's an interesting article—I'll cut it out.* 那是篇有趣的文章——我要把它剪下來。**(b)** make by cutting: 剪成;砍成: *cut out a path through the jungle.* 在叢林中砍出一條路。**(c)** shape (a garment) by cutting the outlines of the parts on cloth: 剪裁(衣服): *cut out a dress.* 剪裁一件衣服。**(d)** (colloq) leave out; omit: (俗)刪去: *Let's cut out unimportant details.* 我們刪去不重要的細節吧。**(e)** (colloq) stop doing or using (sth): (俗)戒除;不用: *My doctor told me I must cut out tobacco,* stop smoking. 我的醫生說我必須戒煙。***cut sb out,*** defeat, eliminate (a rival, esp in competition for sth): 擊敗(對手,尤指在競爭中): *cut out all rivals for a girl's affections.* 擊敗所有情敵而贏得某女郎的愛情。***cut it/that out,*** (colloq, imper) stop fighting, squabbling, etc: (俗,祈使)停止打鬥、爭吵等: *Now just cut it out, you two!* 你兩個現在不要再吵(打)了! ***cut out (the) dead wood,*** (colloq) remove unnecessary or unproductive parts: (俗)除去不必要或不能生產部分: *There's a lot of dead wood to be cut out if the industry is to be efficient.* 如欲提高工業的效率,許多不必要之處應予消除。***(not) be cut out for,*** (not) have the qualities and abilities needed for: (無)有…所需要的才能: *He's not cut out for that sort of work.* 他沒有担任那種工作的才能。***have one's work cut out (for one),*** be faced with as much work as one can manage: 面對着足以佔用某人全部時間和精力的工作: *It's a big job; he'll have his work cut out for him to meet the dead-line.* 這是椿艱巨的工作;他得全力以赴,始能如期完成。**'cut-out** *n* **(a)** design, figure, etc (to be) cut out from paper, cardboard, etc. 由紙,紙板等剪下的圖案,圖形等。**(b)** (electr) device that interrupts or disconnects a circuit (eg to avoid too heavy a load). (電)斷流器(如避免過重負荷,截斷電流之設計);保險開關。
cut sb to the heart/quick, cause him pain or suffering: 使某人痛苦: *His ingratitude cut her to the heart.* 他的忘恩負義使她傷心。***cut sb/sth to pieces,*** destroy by cutting, by gunfire, etc: 切碎; 剪碎;(以砲火等)摧毀: *The enemy were cut to pieces.* 敵人被砲火摧毀。
cut sth/sb up, **(a)** cut into pieces: 切碎;剪碎: *cut up one's meat.* 將肉切碎。**(b)** destroy: 摧

毀;粉碎: *cut up the enemy's forces.* 摧毀敵人軍力。**(c)** (colloq, usu passive) cause mental suffering to: (俗,通常用被動語態)使傷心;使悲痛: *He was badly cut up by the news of his son's death.* 他得到兒子的死訊,極爲悲傷。*Don't be so cut up about it.* 不要爲此過於悲傷。**(d)** criticize adversely; point out the faults of: 苛評;嚴評: *His latest novel has been cut up by the reviewers.* 他最近的小說被評論家批評得體無完膚。***cut up (into),*** be capable of being cut up (into): 能被剪成;能被切成: *This piece of cloth will cut up into* (= has enough material in it for) *three suits.* 這塊布將可裁製三套衣服。***cut up (for),*** (colloq) be worth: (俗)有價值: *The old man cut up for ten thousand,* left £10 000 to be divided among his heirs. 那老人死後留下一萬英鎊(供繼承者去分)。***cut up rough,*** (sl) behave aggressively; be violent and aggressive: (俚)大發脾氣;大吵大鬧: *He'll cut up rough if you don't give him what he asked for.* 你要是不給他所要求的,他會大吵大鬧。

cut² /kʌt; kʌt/ *n* **1** act of cutting; stroke with a sword, whip, etc; result of such a stroke; opening made by a knife or other sharp-edged tool, etc: 切; 割; 刻; 鞭打; 砍; 砍傷; 用刀或其他利器所割的破口: *give a horse a cut across the flanks;* 在馬的側腹抽一鞭子; *a deep cut in the leg;* 腿上深入的割傷; *cuts on the face,* eg after shaving. 臉上的傷口(例如刮臉後)。 ***cut and thrust,*** (usu fig) vigorous argument, etc: (常喻)激烈的爭論等: *the cut and thrust of debate.* 辯論的激烈。 **2** reduction in size, amount, length, etc: 減少;減低;減短: *a cut in prices/salaries;* 減價(薪); *a cut in expenditure/production;* 減低開支(生產); *a power cut,* a reduction in the strength of electrical current, or a period for which current is cut off. 電力減弱;停電期間。 **3** a cutting out; part that is cut out: 剪去;剪去的部分: *There were several cuts in the film,* Parts of it had been cut out (eg by the film censors). 該影片有數處被剪去(如爲影片檢查員所剪)。*Where can we make a cut in this long article?* 我們能在甚麼地方把這篇長文刪掉一些嗎? **4** sth obtained by cutting: 切下或割下之物: *a nice cut of beef;* 一塊上好牛肉; *a cut off the joint,* a slice from a cooked joint of meat; 自烹調好的一大塊腿肉上切下的一塊; *this year's cut of wool,* the wool sheared from the sheep. 今年所剪的羊毛(總量)。 **5** style in which clothes, etc are made by cutting: 衣服等剪裁的式樣: *I don't like the cut of his trousers.* 我不喜歡他的褲子的式樣。 ⇨ jib¹(1). **6** (cricket, tennis) quick, sharp stroke: (板球,網球)快速而使球旋轉的一擊; 切球; 削球: *a cut to the boundary.* 向邊線切的一球。 **7** remark, etc that wounds a person's feelings: 傷人感情的話: *That remark was a cut at me,* was directed at me. 那句話是對我而發的。 **8** refusal to recognize a person: 裝做未見某人; 佯裝不識: *give sb a cut.* 毫不理睬某人。⇨ *cut sb dead* at cut¹(7). **9 *short cut,*** way across (from one place to another) that shortens the distance. 近路;捷徑。 **10 *a cut above,*** (colloq) rather superior to: (俗)頗優於;勝過;超過: *She's a cut above the other girls in the office,* is better educated, has wider interests, etc. 她在辦公室中較其他的女職員爲强 (教育程度較高,興趣範圍較廣等)。 *That's a cut above me,* above my range of interests, my abilities, etc. 那非我的興趣(能力等)所及。 **11** railway cutting; canal. 低於地面開鑿的鐵道路基; 運河河道。 ⇨ cutting(1). **12** block or plate on which a design, illustration, etc has been cut; picture, etc, made from such a block. 圖版;刻版;版畫。⇨ *woodcut* at wood(4).

cute /kjuːt; kjut/ *adj* (-r, -st) **1** sharp-witted; quick-thinking. 機敏的; 聰穎的。 **2** (US colloq) attractive; pretty and charming. (美俗)吸引人的; 俏麗的; 美麗而逗人喜歡的。**~·ly** *adv* **~·ness** *n*

cu·ticle /ˈkjuːtɪkl; ˈkjutɪkl/ *n* outer layer of hardened skin (esp at the base of a finger-nail or toe-nail). 表皮;外皮(尤指手指甲或脚指甲根部者)。

cut·lass /ˈkʌtləs; ˈkʌtləs/ *n* **1** (hist) sailor's short, one-edged sword with a slightly curved blade. (史)(水手所用)刀鋒略彎的單刃短刀。 **2** cutting tool (= *machete*) used by cacao-growers and copra-growers. 種植可可及乾椰子者所用的刀子。

cut·ler /ˈkʌtlə(r); ˈkʌtlɚ/ *n* man who makes and repairs knives and other cutting tools and instruments. 刀匠 (製造及修理各種刀具的人)。 **~y** *n* [U] trade of a ~; implements used at table (knives, forks, spoons, esp if made of stainless steel); things made or sold by ~s. 刀劍製造業;餐具(刀、叉、匙等,尤指不銹鋼製成者);刀劍等利器。

cut·let /ˈkʌtlɪt; ˈkʌtlɪt/ *n* slice of meat or fish for one person: (一人份)肉片或魚片: *a veal ~.* (一人份的)一塊小牛肉。

cut·purse /ˈkʌtpɜːs; ˈkʌtˌpɝs/ *n* (hist) pickpocket. (史)扒手。

cut·ter /ˈkʌtə(r); ˈkʌtɚ/ *n* **1** person or thing that cuts: 切割者;裁剪器;削切器: *a tailor's ~,* who cuts out cloth; 成衣店的裁衣師; *a 'wire-~.* 剪金屬線的器具。 **2** sailing-vessel with one mast; ship's boat, for use between ship and shore. 獨桅帆船;屬於大船而用於船岸之間的小艇。

cut-throat /ˈkʌtθrəʊt; ˈkʌtˌθrot/ *n* **1** murderer. 兇手;刺客。 **2** (attrib uses) ruthless, cruel: (形容用法)兇狠的;殘忍的: *~ competition,* likely to ruin the weaker competitors. 抗唸競爭(較弱之一方可能毀滅的競爭)。 *~* **razor,** one with no guard on the long blade. 無安全設備的剃刀。⇨ the illus at razor. 參看 razor 之挿圖。

cut·ting /ˈkʌtɪŋ; ˈkʌtɪŋ/ *n* **1** unroofed passage dug through the ground for a road, railway, canal, etc. 自山丘或地面開鑿出來的道路,鐵路,運河河床等;路塹。 **2** sth cut from a newspaper, etc and kept for reference: 自報紙等剪下的參考資料;剪報: *'press ~s.* 剪報。Cf 參較 US 美 *clipping.* **3** short piece of a plant, to be used for growing a new plant: 挿枝(自植物剪下供分栽的小枝): *chrysanthemum ~s;* 菊花挿枝; *to take a ~.* 剪枝(供挿栽)。 **4** [U] process of editing films, tape recordings, etc, by cutting out unwanted parts. 剪輯(電影片、錄音帶等剪去不需要部分的剪接工作)。 Hence, 由此產生, **'~-room,** room where this is done. 剪輯室。□ *part adj* (of words, etc) wounding the feelings, etc: (指言語等)傷感情的: *~ remarks.* 傷感情的話。

cut·tle·fish /ˈkʌtlfɪʃ; ˈkʌtlˌfɪʃ/ *n* sea-water animal with long arms (tentacles), which sends out a black liquid when attacked. 墨魚;烏賊(海產動物,有長觸手,受攻擊時能放出黑色液體)。⇨ the illus at mollusc. 參看 mollusc 之挿圖。

cut·worm /ˈkʌtwɜːm; ˈkʌtˌwɝm/ *n* caterpillar that eats through the stems of young plants level with the ground. 夜盜蟲;糖蛾的幼虫(能沿地面咬斷初生植物)。

cy·an·ide /ˈsaɪənaɪd; ˈsaɪəˌnaɪd/ *n* [U] poisonous compound substance: 氰化物(有毒的化合物): *potassium ~;* 氰化鉀; *sodium ~.* 氰化鈉。

cy·ber·net·ics /ˌsaɪbəˈnetɪks; ˌsaɪbɚˈnɛtɪks/ *n* (*sing v*) the science of communication and control in machines and animals (including man). (用單數動詞)神經機械學(研究機械和動物(包含人類)之資訊傳送及控制之科學)。**cy·ber·netic** *adj*

cyc·la·men /ˈsɪkləmən *US:* ˈsaɪk-; ˈsɪkləmən/ *n* kinds of plant, wild and cultivated, of the primrose family, with delicate, small flowers. 櫻草屬植物(野生及栽培,開細緻的小花)。

cycle /ˈsaɪkl; ˈsaɪkl/ *n* **1** series of events taking place in a regularly repeated order: 按一定規律重複發生的一連串事象;循環;週期;周: *the ~ of the seasons.* 四季的循環。 **2** complete set or series: 全集;全套;全本: *a song ~,* eg by Schubert; 聯篇歌曲(聯合若干短篇爲一題的歌集,如舒伯特所作者); *the Arthurian* /ɑːˈθjʊərɪən *US:* -ˈθʊər-; ɑrˈθjʊrɪən/ *~,* the stories of King Arthur and his knights. 亞瑟王和他的武士們的全套故事。**3** (short for) bicycle or motor-cycle. 兩輪或機器脚踏車(的簡稱)。□ *vi* [VP2A, B, C] ride a bicycle. 騎脚踏車。

cyc·lic /ˈsaɪklɪk ; ˈsaɪklɪk/ *adj* recurring in cycles. 循環的;有週期性的。

cyc·li·cal /ˈsaɪklɪkl ; ˈsaɪklɪkḷ/ *adj* = cyclic.

cyc·list /ˈsaɪklɪst ; ˈsaɪklɪst/ *n* person who rides a cycle. 騎脚踏車或機車者。

cyc·lone /ˈsaɪkləʊn ; ˈsaɪklon/ *n* violent wind rotating round a calm central area; violent windstorm. 氣旋 (中心平靜四周猛烈的風); 暴風; 旋風。**cyc·lonic** /saɪˈklɒnɪk ; saɪˈklɑnɪk/ *adj* of or like a ~. 氣旋(式)的;(似)暴風的。

cyclo·pae·dia /ˌsaɪkləˈpiːdɪə ; ˌsaɪkləˈpidɪə/ *n* = encyclopaedia.

Cyclo·pean /saɪˈkləʊpɪən ; ˌsaɪkləˈpiən/ *adj* of or like a Cyclops /ˈsaɪklɒps ; ˈsaɪklɑps/ (a one-eyed giant in Greek myth); huge; immense. (似)(希臘神話獨眼巨人)塞克拉普斯的;巨大的。

cyclo·style /ˈsaɪkləstaɪl ; ˈsaɪkləˌstaɪl/ *n* apparatus for printing copies from a stencil. 一種油印機。□ *vt* reproduce (copies) with this. 用此種油印機印刷(文件)。

cyclo·tron /ˈsaɪklətrɒn ; ˈsaɪkləˌtrɑn/ *n* apparatus used for producing heavy electric particles moving at high speed, used experimentally in nuclear research work. 迴旋加速器(用以產生高速運動之帶電重粒子,用於核子研究實驗)。

cyder /ˈsaɪdə(r) ; ˈsaɪdɚ/ *n* = cider.

cyg·net /ˈsɪgnɪt ; ˈsɪgnɪt/ *n* young swan. 小天鵝。

cyl·in·der /ˈsɪlɪndə(r) ; ˈsɪlɪndɚ/ *n* **1** solid or hollow body with equal, circular ends and regular, curving sides. 柱;圓筒;滾筒(實心或空心)。⇨ the illus here and at projection. 參看本條與 projection 之挿圖。**2** ~-shaped chamber (in an engine) in which gas or steam works a piston: 汽缸(引擎內汽油或蒸汽推動活塞之一圓形筒): *a six-~ engine/motor-car.* 有六個汽缸的引擎(汽車)。***(working) on all ~s,*** (colloq) with the maximum power or effort. (俗)盡全力(工作);傾全力。**cy·lin·dri·cal** /sɪˈlɪndrɪkl ; sɪˈlɪndrɪkḷ/ *adj* ~-shaped. 圓筒狀的。

cym·bal /ˈsɪmbl ; ˈsɪmbḷ/ *n* one of a pair of round brass plates struck together to make clanging sounds. 銅鈸;鐃鈸(一對互擊可以發響亮之聲音的圓盤形銅樂器之一)。⇨ the illus at percussion. 參看 percussion 之挿圖。

cynic /ˈsɪnɪk ; ˈsɪnɪk/ *n* person who sees little or no good in anything and who has no belief in human progress; person who shows this by sneering and being sarcastic. 憤世嫉俗者(對世間一切都看不順眼,不相信人類的進步);諷世者。**cyni·cism** /ˈsɪnɪsɪzm ; ˈsɪnəˌsɪzəm/ *n* [U] ~'s opinions or attitude of mind; [C] expression of this attitude. 憤世嫉俗的意見或態度;此種態度的表現;犬儒主義。

cyni·cal /ˈsɪnɪkl ; ˈsɪnɪkəl/ *adj* of or like a cynic; sneering or contemptuous: 憤世嫉俗的;嘲罵的;譏刺的: *a ~ smile/remark.* 嘲諷的笑容;冷笑(譏刺的話)。**~·ly** /-klɪ ; -klɪ/ *adv*

cyno·sure /ˌsɪnəˈzjʊə(r) *US:* ˈsaɪnʊəʃʊər ; ˈsaɪnəˌʃʊr/ *n* sth or sb that draws everyone's attention; centre of attraction. 引起衆人注視的事物或人;吸引人的地方。

cy·pher /ˈsaɪfə(r) ; ˈsaɪfɚ/ *n* = cipher.

cy·press /ˈsaɪprəs ; ˈsaɪprəs/ *n* (kinds of) tall, thin, cone-bearing evergreen tree with dark leaves and hard wood. 柏樹(高而細的常綠樹,葉深色,木堅,生毬果)。

Cyril·lic /sɪˈrɪlɪk ; sɪˈrɪlɪk/ *adj* **the ~ alphabet,** that used for Slavonic languages (eg Russian). 斯拉夫語(如俄語)所用的字母。

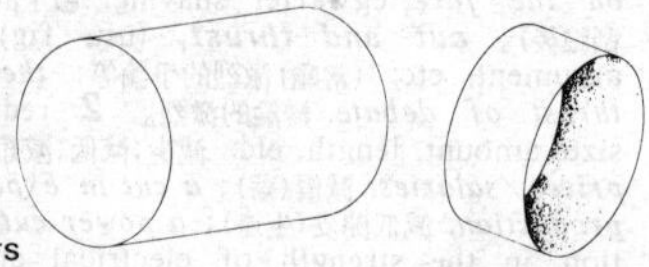

cylinders

cyst /sɪst ; sɪst/ *n* enclosed hollow organ in the body containing liquid matter. (身體內含有液體物質的)胞;囊;包囊。

czar /zɑː(r) ; zɑr/ *n* (also 亦作 **tsar**) emperor of Russia (before 1917). 沙皇(1917年以前俄國皇帝的稱號)。**czar·ina** /zɑːˈriːnə ; zɑˈrinə/ *n* Russian empress. 俄國的皇后或女王。

Czech /tʃek ; tʃɛk/ *n* member of a branch of the Slavs; their language. 捷克人(斯拉夫民族之一支);捷克語。

Dd

D, d /diː ; di/ (*pl* D's, d's /diːz ; diz/) the fourth letter of the English alphabet; Roman numeral for 500. 英文字母的第四個字母;羅馬數字的 500。**'d,** used for *had* or *would* (esp after *I, we, you, he, she, they, who*). 尤在 I, we, you, he, she, they, who 各字之後,'d 用以代替 had 或 would。

dab¹ /dæb ; dæb/ *vt, vi* (-bb-) [VP6A, 14, 15A, B, 2C, 3A] ~ ***(at),*** touch, put on, lightly and gently: 輕拍; 輕觸; 輕柔地塗敷: *dab one's eyes with a handkerchief;* 用手帕輕拭眼睛; *dab paint on a picture,* suggesting light, quick strokes of the brush. 以輕快的筆法作畫。*She was dabbing (at) her cheeks with a powder-puff.* 她以粉撲搽她的臉頰。□ *n* [C] **1** small quantity (of paint, etc) dabbed on. 輕輕塗上的少量(顏料等)。**2** slight tap; brief application of sth to a surface (without rubbing): 輕拍;輕觸(而不揉擦): *A dab with a sponge won't remove the dirt, you'll have to rub it.* 用海綿輕輕地吸,去不掉那污物,你必須用力擦。

dab² /dæb ; dæb/ *n* kind of flat-fish. 孫鰈(比目魚之一種)。

dab³ /dæb ; dæb/ *n* ~ **(hand),** (colloq) expert (at games, etc, at doing things): (俗)(運動的)健將;(做事的)能手: *She's a dab (hand) at tennis.* 她是網球健將。

dabble /ˈdæbl ; ˈdæbḷ/ *vt, vi* **1** [VP6A, 15A, B, 2C] splash (the hands, feet, etc) about in water; put in and out of water. 用(手,足等)濺水;玩水;戲水;使出入水中。**2** [VP3A] ~ *at/in* (art, politics, etc), engage in, study, as a hobby, not professionally. 業餘性地研究(藝術,政治等); 涉獵。**dab·bler** /ˈdæblə(r) ; ˈdæblɚ/ *n*

da capo /ˌdɑː ˈkɑːpəʊ ; dɑˈkɑpo/ (I, music) (as a direction) repeat from the beginning. (義,音樂)從頭再奏(作爲指引)。

dace /deɪs ; des/ *n* (*pl* unchanged) small freshwater fish. (複數不變)鰷魚(一種小淡水魚)。

dacha /ˈdætʃə ; ˈdɑtʃə/ *n* Russian country house or villa. 蘇俄鄉間邸宅或別墅。

dachs·hund /ˈdækshʊnd ; ˈdɑksˌhʊnd/ *n* small short-legged breed of dog. 一種短腿小狗。⇨ the illus at dog. 參看 dog 之挿圖。

da·coit /dəˈkɔɪt ; dəˈkɔɪt/ *n* member of a band of armed robbers (formerly, in India, Burma). (昔時印度,緬甸的)土匪;强盜。**~y** *n* (*pl* -ties) robbery by ~s. 土匪搶劫。

dac·tyl /ˈdæktɪl ; ˈdæktɪl/ *n* (prosody) metrical foot of one accented syllable followed by two unaccented syllables (韻律學) 揚抑抑格 (即一重音節後跟兩輕音節之音步), (—⏑⏑eg 如 *ˈtenderly*), as in: 又如: *ˈunder the/ˈblossom that/ˈhangs on the/ˈbough.* **~ic** /dækˈtɪlɪk ; dækˈtɪlɪk/ *adj*

dad /dæd ; dæd/ *n* (colloq) father. (俗)爸爸。

daddy /ˈdædɪ; ˈdædɪ/ *n* (*pl* -dies) child's word for 'father'. (兒語)爹爹;爸爸。ˌ**~-ˈlong·legs** *n* (popular name for the) crane-fly (a long-legged flying insect). 蚊姥(一種長腿會飛的昆蟲,爲crane-fly的俗稱)。

dado /ˈdeɪdəʊ; ˈdedo/ *n* (*pl* ~s, US ~es /-dəʊz; -doz/) lower part of a wall in a room, when this is different from the upper part in colour or material. 牆壁之底部(顏色或質料與牆壁上部者不同);護牆。

dae·mon /ˈdiːmən; ˈdimən/ *n* = demon.

daf·fo·dil /ˈdæfədɪl; ˈdæfədɪl/ *n* yellow flower with long narrow leaves growing from a bulb. 水仙花(花黃色,葉狹長,自球莖生出)。⇨ the illus at flower. 參看 flower 之插圖。

daft /dɑːft *US:* dæft; dæft/ *adj* (-er, -est) (colloq) silly; foolish; reckless. (俗)傻的;笨的;鹵莽的。**~·ly** *adv*

dag·ger /ˈdægə(r); ˈdægə/ *n* **1** short, pointed, two-edged knife used as a weapon. 短劍;匕首(短而尖的雙刃刀,用作武器)。***at ~s drawn (with sb)***, about to fight. 劍拔弩張;(與某人)卽將打起來。***look ~s at sb***, look with an expression of hatred and enmity. 對某人怒目而視。**2** (printing) mark of reference(†) (印刷)劍號(卽†,表示附註之記號)。

dago /ˈdeɪgəʊ; ˈdego/ *n* (*pl* ~s /-gəʊz; -goz/) ⚠ (sl, term of contempt for an) Italian, Spaniard or Portuguese. (諱)(俚,含輕蔑之意)義大利人;西班牙人;葡萄牙人。

da·guerreo·type /dəˈgerətaɪp; dəˈgɛrəˌtaɪp/ *n* photograph taken by an early photographic process. 用早期照像術所照的像。

dah·lia /ˈdeɪlɪə *US:* ˈdælɪə; ˈdæljə/ *n* garden plant with brightly coloured flowers, growing from tuberous roots. 天竺牡丹;大利花(園藝植物,花色鮮艷,自塊莖長出)。

Dail Eire·ann /ˌdɔɪl ˈeərən; ˈdɔɪlˈerən/ *n* legislative assembly of the Republic of Ireland. 愛爾蘭共和國之下議院。

daily /ˈdeɪlɪ; ˈdelɪ/ *adj, adv* happening, done, appearing, every day (or every weekday): 每日的(地);每週日的(地): *Most newspapers appear ~.* 大多數的報紙每日出版。*Thousands of people cross this bridge ~.* 每日有數以千計的人通過此橋。**~ dozen**, one's usual physical exercises. 每天都做的運動。***one's ~ bread***, one's necessary food, etc. 人必需的糧食;生計。□ *n* **1** newspaper published every weekday. 每週日出版的報紙;日報。**2** (colloq) person who is paid to do housework every weekday. (俗)每週日來做家事的工人。

dainty[1] /ˈdeɪntɪ; ˈdentɪ/ *adj* (-ier, -iest) **1** (of persons) pretty, neat and delicate(1, 3) in appearance and tastes: (指人)嬌美的;俏麗的;優雅的。*a ~ little lady.* 小巧玲瓏的女子。**2** (of persons and animals) rather difficult to please because of delicate tastes: (指人及動物)因嗜好甚高而難以取悅的;講究的;挑剔的: *She's ~ about her food.* 她對於飲食甚爲講究。*My cat is a ~ feeder.* 我的貓對於食物很挑剔。**3** (of things) pretty; delicate(3), easily injured or broken: (指物)美麗的;漂亮的;嬌嫩而易破損的: *~ cups and saucers;* 漂亮的杯盤; *~ spring flowers.* 嬌艷的春花。**4** (of food) delicate(8) and delicious. (指食物)味美的。**dain·tily** *adv* in a ~ manner: 優雅地;好看地;嬌艷地;講究地: *a daintily dressed young lady.* 衣著高雅的少女。**dainti·ness** *n*

dainty[2] /ˈdeɪntɪ; ˈdentɪ/ *n* (*pl* -ties) (usu *pl*) dainty morsel or dish of food: (通常作複數)美味的(少量)食物;珍餚: *There were dainties of every kind in the picnic basket.* 野餐籃裏有各種美味的食物。

dairy /ˈdeərɪ; ˈdɛrɪ/ *n* (*pl* -ries) **1** (part of a) building where milk is kept and milk products are made. 牛奶場;奶品場。ˈ**~-farm**, one that produces milk and butter. 奶品農場。**~·ing**, ˈ**~-farming**, the business of a ~-farm. 奶品製造業。ˈ**~ cattle**, cows raised to produce milk, not meat. 乳牛(爲產奶而非爲產肉所飼養者)。ˈ**~·maid**, woman who works in a ~. 奶品廠的女工。**2** shop where milk, butter, eggs, etc, are sold. 售牛奶、奶油、鷄蛋等的商店。ˈ**~·man** /-mən; -mən/ (*pl* -men) dealer in milk, etc. 牛奶商;奶品商。

dais /ˈdeɪɪs; ˈde·ɪs/ *n* (*pl* ~es /-sɪz; -sɪz/) platform (esp at the end of a hall) for a table, lectern etc. 講臺(尤指設於大廳之一端者,其上可置放桌子,講桌等)。

daisy /ˈdeɪzɪ; ˈdezɪ/ *n* (*pl* -sies) small white flower with a yellow centre, commonly growing wild; similar garden flower; other plants of various sorts (*Michaelmas ~*, etc) resembling it or of the same species. 雛菊;延命菊(黃心之小白花,通常野生);類似之園藝花卉;其他各種大小類似或同屬的花(如紫菀等)。***push up the daisies***, ⇨ push[2](9).

dale /deɪl; del/ *n* (esp in N England and in poetry) valley. (尤用於英格蘭北部及詩中)山谷。**dales·man** /ˈdeɪlzmən; ˈdelzmən/ *n* (*pl* -men) person who lives in the ~s (in N England). (英格蘭北部)山谷中的居民。

D

dal·li·ance /ˈdælɪəns; ˈdælɪəns/ *n* [U] trifling behaviour; flirting for amusement. 玩弄的行爲;調戲;調情。

dally /ˈdælɪ; ˈdælɪ/ *vi* **1** [VP2A, 3A] ~ ***(with)***, trifle; think idly about: 玩弄;戲弄;不愼重考慮;玩忽: *~ with an idea or proposal;* 不愼重考慮一項意見或建議; *~ with a woman's affections*, flirt with her. 玩弄女人的愛情(調戲她)。**2** [VP2A, 3A] ~ ***(over)***, waste time: 浪費時間: *Don't ~ over your work.* 不要浪費你工作的時間。

dal·ma·tian /ˌdælˈmeɪʃn; dælˈmeʃən/ *n* large, short-haired dog, white with dark spots. 一種短毛大狗(毛色白,帶有黑色斑點)。

dam[1] /dæm; dæm/ *n* **1** barrier built to keep back water and raise its level (eg to form a reservoir, or for hydroelectric power). 水壩;閘(擋住流水的去路以升高其水面,如構成蓄水庫或用作水力發電)。(Cf 參較 *barrage*, a barrier across a river, usu for irrigation purposes. 作灌溉用之水堰。) **2** reservoir formed by such a barrier. 水壩圍成的水庫。□ *vt* (-mm-) [VP6A, 15B] ~ ***(up)***, make a dam across (a narrow valley, etc); hold back by means of a dam; (fig) hold back: 攔(狹谷等)修築水壩;藉水壩攔阻;(喩)攔阻;抑制: *to dam up one's feelings/sb's eloquence.* 抑制其感情(阻止某人的雄辯)。

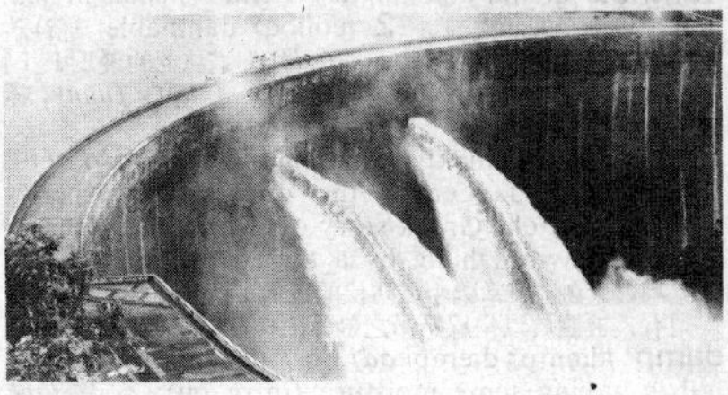

a dam

dam[2] /dæm; dæm/ *n* mother (of four-footed animals). (四足動物的)母獸。⇨ sire(3).

dam·age /ˈdæmɪdʒ; ˈdæmɪdʒ/ *n* **1** [U] ~ ***(to)***, harm or injury that causes loss of value: 損害;損毀(使失去價值): *The storm did great ~ to the crops.* 那次暴風雨對農作物造成極大的損害。*The insurance company will pay for the ~ to my car.* 保險公司將賠償我的汽車所受的損害。**2** (*pl*) (legal) money claimed from or paid by a person causing loss or injury: (複)(法律)損害賠償(向造成損害者索取或由其所付的賠償費): *He claimed £5000 ~s from his employers for the loss of his right arm while at work.* 他爲在工作時所喪失的右臂向雇主要求五千鎊的賠償費。**3** ***What's the ~?*** (colloq) What's the cost? (俗)値多少錢? □ *vt* [VP6A] cause ~(1) to: 使受損害;損壞: *furniture ~d by fire.* 爲火所損壞的傢具。

dam·as·cene /ˈdæməsiːn; ˈdæməˌsin/ *adj* of damask. 錦緞的；大馬色鋼的。□ *vt* work into damask steel. 製成大馬色鋼。

dam·ask /ˈdæməsk ; ˈdæməsk/ *n* [U] **1** silk or linen material with designs shown up by reflection of light: (由反光而顯示圖案的) 花緞；錦緞；織花麻布: (attrib) (形容用法) ~ *table-cloths;* 織花桌布；~ *silk.* 錦緞。 **2** steel with a pattern of wavy lines or with inlaid gold or silver: 大馬色鋼(帶波紋圖案或鑲有金銀): (attrib) (形容用法) ~ (or *damascene*) *steel.* 大馬色鋼。 **3** ˈ~ **rose,** variety originally brought from Damascus; its colour (bright pink). 粉紅色薔薇(原產於大馬士革)；粉紅薔薇色。

dame /deɪm ; dem/ *n* **1** (old use) woman, esp a married woman. (舊用法) 婦女 (尤指已婚者)。 **2** (title of a) woman who has been awarded the highest grade of an order¹(9): 英國獲有爵位的婦女；此種頭銜: *D~ Ellen Terry.* 愛琳·特里夫人。(Cf 參較 the title *Lady.*) **3** title as used eg in 作爲頭銜用於 **D~ Nature, D~ Fortune,** nature, fortune, personified. '自然', '幸運' 的人格化。 **4** (US, sl) woman. (美，俚) 女人。

damn /dæm ; dæm/ *vt* [VP6A] **1** (of God) condemn to everlasting torment. (指上帝) 使永遠受折磨；使永遠受罰；使下地獄。 **2** condemn; say that sth or sb is worthless, bad, etc: 譴責；指摘；說某物或某人無價值、壞等: *The book was ~ed by the critics.* 此書遭批評家指責。 **3** (colloq) (esp as *int*) used to express anger, annoyance, impatience, etc: (俗) (尤用作感嘆詞) 用以表示憤怒，厭煩，急躁等: *D~!* 該死！ *I'll be ~ed if I'll go,* I refuse to go. 我要是去就不是人(我絕不去)。*D~ it all!* 該死的！ *D~ you/your impudence!* 混帳！ □ *n* (colloq) **not give/care a ~,** not care at all. (俗) 一點也不在乎。 **not (be) worth a ~,** (be) worthless. 一文不值。□ *adj, adv* (colloq) (intensive): (俗，强勢語) 非常的(地): *Don't be ~ silly/a ~ fool.* 不要那麼傻(不要做個大傻瓜)。~ **well,** certainly. 必然；當然。

dam·nable /ˈdæmnəbl ; ˈdæmnəbl̩/ *adj* hateful; deserving to be damned; (colloq) very bad: 可恨的；可惡的；該受天罰的；(俗) 極壞的: ~ *weather.* 極惡劣的天氣。**dam·nab·ly** /ˈdæmnəblɪ ; ˈdæmnəblɪ/ *adv*

dam·na·tion /dæmˈneɪʃn ; dæmˈneʃən/ *n* [U] being damned; ruin: 遭天罰；毀滅: *to suffer eternal ~.* 受到永遠的懲罰。

damned /dæmd ; dæmd/ *adj* **1 the ~,** souls in hell. 在地獄中受罪的靈魂。 **2** (colloq) damnable: (俗) 該遭天罰的；該死的: *You ~ fool!* 你這該死的傻瓜！ □ *adv* (colloq) extremely: (俗) 極: ~ *hot/funny.* 極熱(可笑)的。

Damocles /ˈdæməkliːz ; ˈdæməˌkliz/ *n* **sword of ~,** threatened danger in the midst of prosperity (from the old Greek story of a man who feasted while a sword hung by a thread over him). 達摩克利茲之劍 (喻幸福中所隱伏的危機；源出於古希臘故事，謂有人被置於以一線懸吊之劍下而作飲宴之樂)。

damp¹ /dæmp ; dæmp/ *adj* (-er, -est) not thoroughly dry; having some moisture (in or on): 不完全乾燥的；潮濕的；有濕氣的: ~ *clothes;* 濕衣服; *to wipe a window with a ~ cloth.* 用濕布擦窗戶。*Don't sleep between ~ sheets.* 不要睡在潮濕的被褥中。~ **squib,** ⇨ squib. □ *n* [U] **1** state of being ~; ~ atmosphere; moisture on the surface of, or existing throughout, sth: 潮濕；濕氣；某物之表面或內部所含的水份: *The ~ rising from the ground caused the walls to stain badly.* 自地面上升的濕氣使牆壁沾上嚴重的污跡。 *Don't stay outside in the ~.* 不要停留在外面的潮濕空氣中。 ⇨ *~-course* at course¹(5). **2 cast/strike a ~ over,** (fig) cause dejection or unhappiness: (喻) 使沮喪或不快樂: *Their mother's illness cast a ~ over the celebrations.* 他們母親的病使他們在那些慶典中悶悶不樂。 **3** (also 亦作 ˈ**fire-~**) dangerous gas which may collect in coal-mines. (可能在煤礦內聚集的) 一種危險氣體；坑氣；沼氣；甲烷。~**·ish** *adj* rather ~. 相當潮濕的。~**·ly** *adv* ~**·ness** *n*

damp² /dæmp ; dæmp/ *vt, vi* **1** [VP6A] make damp(1): 使潮濕: *to ~ clothes before ironing them.* 在熨衣服前將衣服打濕。 **2** [VP6A] (also 亦作 ˈ**dampen**) make sad or dull: 使沮喪；使憂戚；使敗興: *Nothing could ~ his spirits.* 任何事都不能敗他的興。 **3** [VP15B] ~ **down,** make (a fire) burn more slowly (eg by heaping ashes on it, or by controlling the draught of air entering a stove, etc). 減弱(火勢) (如堆灰於其上，或控制通入爐等之中的氣流)。 **4** [VP2C] ~ **off,** (of young plants) rot and die because of excessive damp(1). (指幼苗) 因水份過多而爛死。

dampen /ˈdæmpən ; ˈdæmpən/ *vt* = damp²(2).

damper /ˈdæmpə(r) ; ˈdæmpɚ/ *n* **1** movable metal plate that regulates the flow of air into a fire in a stove or furnace. 爐喉調節閘 (火爐或鍋爐中用以控制通風量的金屬板)；氣閘。 **2** person or thing that checks or discourages. 控制或掃興的人或物。 ⇨ damp¹(2).

dam·sel /ˈdæmzl ; ˈdæmzl/ *n* (old use) girl; young unmarried woman. (舊用法) 閨女；未婚少女。

dam·son /ˈdæmzn ; ˈdæmzn̩/ *n* (tree producing) small dark-purple plum; dark-purple. 西洋李子(樹) (結深紫色小李子)；深紫色。

dance¹ /dɑːns *US:* dæns ; dæns/ *n* [C] **1** (series of) movements and steps in time with music; special form (eg a *waltz*), tune, piece of music, for such movements and steps: 跳舞；舞蹈；舞步(伴音樂而有節奏的步法)；某種形式的舞(如華爾茲舞)；舞曲；舞樂: *May I have the next ~,* Will you be my partner in the next ~? 下一支曲子可否請你與我共舞？ *Shall we join the ~,* go out among the dancers? 我們與大家齊舞好嗎？ **lead sb a (pretty) ~,** cause him a lot of trouble, make him follow from place to place. 使某人遭受許多麻煩；使某人到處跟隨。 **2** social gathering for dancing: 社交舞會: *to give a ~,* arrange for and invite persons to such a gathering. 舉行舞會。 **3** (attrib): (形容用法): ˈ~-*rhythm.* 舞步的節拍。ˈ~**-band/-orchestra** *nn* providing music for dancing. 奏舞曲的樂隊。ˈ~**-hall** *n* hall for public ~s, with a charge for admission. (收取門票的) 公共舞廳。⇨ *ballroom* at ball².

dance² /dɑːns *US:* dæns ; dæns/ *vi, vt* **1** [VP2A, C] move along in rhythmical steps, usu with music, either alone, or with a partner, or in a group: 跳舞；舞蹈(按照有節奏的步法移動，通常伴隨音樂，或個人舞，或與舞伴共舞，或團體共舞): *Will you ~ with me?* 你願和我共舞嗎？ *They went on dancing until after midnight.* 他們一直舞到午夜以後。 **2** [VP6A] perform (a named kind of such movements or the named (style of) music for it): 跳(某一種舞): *to ~ a waltz/a ballet/Swan Lake.* 跳華爾茲(芭蕾舞，天鵝湖)。*Is the polka often ~d nowadays?* 波爾卡舞現在還常有人跳嗎？ ~ **attendance upon sb,** follow him about, pay great attention to his wishes, etc. 小心侍候某人；亦步亦趨地奉承某人；迎合某人的心意。~ **to sb's tune,** obey him. 服從某人。**3** [VP2A, C] move in a lively way, quickly, up and down, etc: 跳躍；雀躍: *The leaves were dancing in the wind.* 樹葉隨風飄舞。 *She ~d for joy.* 她因快樂而跳躍。 *The sudden pain made him ~ up and down.* 突然的疼痛使他蹦跳不已。*Look at that boat dancing on the waves.* 看那隻隨波飄盪的船。 **4** [VP6A, 15A] cause to ~(3): 使跳躍: *to ~ a baby on one's knee.* 使嬰兒在膝上跳躍。 **dancer** *n* person who ~s: 舞蹈者；舞者: *a clever ~r;* 靈巧的舞者; person who ~s in public for pay. 職業舞者。⇨ ballerina, ballet-~r. **danc·ing** *part adj* who or that ~s: 跳舞的；跳躍的: *a ˌdancing ˈdervish.* 崇拜時身體迴旋舞動的回教苦修僧。 □ *n* (gerund) (動名詞) [U] **1** (attrib) (stress on the gerund): (形容用法) (在下列詞語中重音在動名詞): ˈ*dancing-master,* professional teacher of dancing; 職業舞蹈教師; ˈ*dancing-partner,* person with whom one (usu) ~s; (慣常的) 舞伴; ˈ*dancing-shoes,* light shoes for dancing. 舞鞋。 **2** (stress on the first element):（重音在前一字）: '*ballet-dancing;* 芭蕾舞; '*tap-dancing.* 踢踺舞。

dan·de·lion /ˈdændɪlaɪən ; ˈdændḷˌaɪən/ *n* small wild plant with bright yellow flowers and deeply notched leaves. 蒲公英(小野生植物,開鮮黃色花,葉邊有深的缺口)。

dan·der /ˈdændə(r) ; ˈdænd𝑎ɚ/ *n* (colloq, only in) (俗,僅用於) ***get sb's ~ up,*** make him angry. 激怒某人;觸怒某人。***get one's ~ up,*** become angry. 發怒;發脾氣。

dandle /ˈdændl ; ˈdændḷ/ *vt* [VP6A, 15A, B] move (eg a child) up and down on one's knee(s) or in the arms.在膝上或懷抱中將(嬰兒等)舉上放下以逗弄之。

dan·druff /ˈdændrʌf ; ˈdændrəf/ *n* [U] dead skin in small scales among the hair of the scalp; scurf. 頭髮間的頭皮屑;皮垢。

dandy[1] /ˈdændɪ ; ˈdændɪ/ *n* man who pays too much care to his clothes and personal appearance. 過份注意衣着和外表的男人; 花花公子。 **dan·di·fied** /ˈdændɪfaɪd ; ˈdændɪˌfaɪd/ *adj* dressed up, etc like a ~: 衣着等似花花公子的: *a dandified appearance.* 油頭粉面;花花公子的外表。

dandy[2] /ˈdændɪ ; ˈdændɪ/ *adj* (sl) excellent; first-rate:(俚)極佳的;第一流的;頭等的:*fine and ~.*極好的。

Dane /deɪn ; den/ *n* native of Denmark. 丹麥人。

dan·ger /ˈdeɪndʒə(r) ; ˈdendʒɚ/ *n* **1** [U] chance of suffering, liability to suffer, injury or loss of life: 危險(受害的機會;受害、受傷或喪命的可能): *D~—thin ice!* 危險!—薄冰! *Is there any ~ of fire?* 有遭火災的危險嗎? *In war a soldier's life is full of ~.* 在戰爭中,士兵的生命是充滿危險的。***at ~:*** *The signal* (on a railway line) *was at ~,* in the position giving a warning of ~. (鐵路線上的)信號標誌指在警告有危險的位置上。***in ~ (of):*** *His life was in ~.* 他有生命的危險。*He was in ~ of losing his life.* 他有喪命的危險。***out of ~:*** *He has been very ill, but the doctors say that he is now out of ~,* not likely to die. 他的病一直很沉重,但是醫生們說他現已脫離險境。 **'~ money,** extra pay for dangerous work. 危險工作的額外報酬。 **2** [C] sth or sb that may cause ~: 可能引起危險的物或人: *He looked round carefully for hidden ~s.* 他四周仔細察看有無隱伏的危險。*The wreck is a ~ to shipping.* 那遇難的船骸對於航運是個危險的東西。*That man is a ~ to society.* 那個人對於社會是個危險人物。

dan·ger·ous /ˈdeɪndʒərəs ; ˈdendʒərəs/ *adj* ***~ (to/for),*** likely to cause danger or be a danger: 可能引起危險的;(對…)有危險的: *a ~ bridge/journey/illness.* 危險的橋樑(旅程,疾病)。*The river is ~ for bathers.* 在這河裏游泳有危險。 *That dog looks ~,* looks as though it might attack people. 那隻狗看來危險(看來有咬人的可能)。**~·ly** *adv*

dangle /ˈdæŋgl ; ˈdæŋgḷ/ *vi, vt* **1** [VP2A, C, 6A, 15A] hang or swing loosely; carry (sth) so that it hangs or swings loosely: 懸吊着或擺動不定;攜帶(某物)使懸吊着或擺動不定: *a bunch of keys dangling at the end of a chain;* 在鍊子的一端懸吊着的一串鑰匙; *to ~ a toy in front of a baby;* 將玩具在嬰兒的面前搖擺; (fig) (喻) *to ~ bright prospects* (eg of wealth, a well-paid position) *before a man.* 用光明的遠景(如財富,高薪的職位)引誘某人。 **2** [VP2C] ***~ round/about,*** remain near (sb or sth) (as an admirer) hoping to obtain sth: 追隨(某人或某物)希望獲得某物: *She always has half a dozen men dangling round her.* 她總有五六個男人追求她。

Dan·iel /ˈdænɪəl ; ˈdænjəl/ *n* upright judge, ⇨ Dan 1 to 6; 正直的法官(參看舊約聖經但以理書1至6章); person of great wisdom, ⇨ Mer of Ven, 4: 1. 智慧極高的人(參看'威尼斯商人'第四幕第一景)。

Dan·ish /ˈdeɪnɪʃ ; ˈdenɪʃ/ *n, adj* (language) of Denmark or the Danes. 丹麥的;丹麥人的;丹麥語。

dank /dæŋk ; dæŋk/ *adj* (-er, -est) damp in an unpleasant or unhealthy way: 陰濕的(因而令人感覺不愉快或影響健康): *the ~ undergrowth of a forest;* 森林中陰濕的下層林叢; *a ~ and chilly cave.* 陰冷的洞穴。

daphne /ˈdæfnɪ ; ˈdæfnɪ/ *n* kinds of flowering shrub. 瑞香;月桂樹(數種開花的灌木)。

dap·per /ˈdæpə(r) ; ˈdæpɚ/ *adj* (usu of a small person) neat and smart in appearance; active in movement: (通常指矮小的人)整潔漂亮的;行動活潑的: *Isn't he a ~ little man!* 他豈不是一個短小而行動矯健的人!

dapple /ˈdæpl ; ˈdæpḷ/ *vt* [VP6A] (usu in *pp*) mark, become marked, with rounded patches of different colour or shades of colour, esp of an animal, or of sunlight and shadow: (通常用過去分詞)加以,或變成有,各種不同顏色或顏色深淺不同之圓形斑點(尤指動物,或指陽光與陰影): *~d deer;* 有圓形斑點之鹿; *a ~d horse;* 有圓形斑點之馬; *~d shade,* as when sunlight comes through the leaves of trees. (陽光通過樹葉間在樹下所形成)有點點陽光的樹蔭。 **,~-'grey** *adj, n* (horse) of grey with darker patches. 灰色而帶深灰色斑點的(馬)。

Darby and Joan /ˌdɑːbɪ ən ˈdʒəʊn ; ˈdɑrbɪ ən ˈdʒon/ *n* old and loving married couple: 恩愛老夫妻: *a ~ club,* one for old couples. 老夫妻俱樂部。

dare[1] /deə(r) ; dɛr/ *anom fin* (*pt* dared /deəd ; dɛrd/ or, less often, durst /dɜːst ; dɝst/) (*dare not* is abbr to *daren't* /deənt ; dɛrnt/, *3rd pers sing* is *dare,* not *dares*) (Used with an inf without *to,* chiefly in neg sentences, including those with *hardly, never* and *no one, nobody,* and in interr and conditional sentences, and in sentences to indicate doubt.) (dare not 縮寫爲 daren't, 第三人稱單數不加s)(與不帶to的不定詞連用,主要用於否定句,包括有 hardly, never, no one, nobody 的句子,此外尚用於疑問,條件和表示懷疑的句中) [VP5] have the courage, impudence or effrontery to: 敢;敢於;竟敢;膽敢: *Don't (you) ~ do that again!* 不要再這樣膽大妄爲! *I ~n't/don't ~ speak to him.* 我不敢和他談話。*I wonder whether he ~ try.* 我不知他是否敢於一試。 *No one/Nobody ~d ask him about his intentions.* 無人敢問他的意思是什麼。 *He will hardly/never ~ go there again.* 他幾乎不(永不)敢再去那兒了。*How ~ he say such rude things about me!* 他怎敢說出這樣對我不禮貌的話! ***I ~ say,*** It seems to me likely or possible: 我覺得很可能;我敢說: *I ~ say he'll come later.* 我敢說他過些時候會來的。

dare[2] /deə(r) ; dɛr/ *vt, vi* **1** [VP5, 4A] (with or without *to*) be brave enough to: (用或不用 to)敢;敢於: *He didn't ~ (to) go.* 他不敢去。*I wonder how he ~s (to) say such things.* 我奇怪他怎麼敢說這些話。 *I've never ~d (to) ask him.* 我一直不敢問他。 *They wouldn't ~ (to be so rude)!* 他們不敢(這樣不禮貌)! **2** [VP6A] take the risk of; face: 敢冒(危險);面對;不懼: *He will ~ any danger.* 他敢冒任何危險。 **3** [VP6A, 17] ***~ sb (to do sth),*** challenge; suggest that sb has not the courage or ability to do sth: 挑激;暗示某人無勇氣或能力做某事: *I ~ you to say that again!* 我諒你不敢再說那話! *He ~d me to jump from the bridge into the river.* 他挑激我,說我不敢自橋上跳下河。 *Go on, insult me! I ~ you!* 好,你侮辱我吧!我諒你也不敢! **'~-devil** *n* (often attrib) person who is foolishly bold or reckless: (常作形容用法) 蠻勇的人;冒失鬼;膽大鬼: *You ~-devil!* 你這個冒失鬼! *What a ~-devil fellow he is!* 他眞是個冒失的傢伙! □ *n* challenge. 挑激。 ***do sth for a ~,*** do sth because one is ~d(3) to do it. 因受挑激而做某事。

dar·ing /ˈdeərɪŋ ; ˈdɛrɪŋ/ *n* [U] adventurous courage; audacity: 冒險精神;勇敢;勇氣: *the ~ of the paratroops;* 傘兵部隊的冒險犯難精神; *lose one's ~.* 失去勇氣。□ *adj* brave; audacious: 勇敢的;大膽的: *a ~ robbery.* 大膽的搶劫。*What a ~ thing to do!* 這眞是件有膽量的人才敢做的事! **~·ly** *adv*

dark[1] /dɑːk ; dɑrk/ *n* [U] **1** absence of light: 黑暗;無光: *All the lights went out and we were left in the ~.* 所有的燈都熄了,我們陷入黑暗中。*Some children are afraid of the ~.* 有些小孩怕黑暗。*Don't*

D

leave me alone in the ~. 不要留下我一個人在黑暗中。***before/after ~,*** before/after the sun goes down: 日落天黑以前(後): *Try to get home before ~.* 盡量在天黑以前回家。*The place is so dangerous that we don't often go out after ~.* 這地方很危險，所以我們在天黑以後就不常出門。 **2** (fig) ignorance. (喻)愚昧；無知。***keep sb/be in the ~ (about sth),*** keep sb/be in ignorance: 把某人蒙在鼓裏；不讓某人知道(某事)；(對某事)毫不知情: *We were completely in the ~ about his movements.* 我們絲毫不知道他的行動。

dark[2] /dɑ:k ; dɑrk/ *adj* (-er, -est) **1** with no or very little light: 黑暗的: *a ~, moonless night;* 一個黑暗的，無月光的夜晚；*a ~ corner of the room.* 房間裏黑暗的角落。*It's getting too ~ to take photographs.* 天色太晚，不能照相。 **'~ lantern,** one that can have its light covered. 能將其光遮蔽的燈籠。 **'~-room,** one that can be made ~ for photographic work. (沖洗相片用的)暗房。 **2** (of colour) not reflecting much light; nearer black than white: (指顏色)深色的；暗色的: *a ~ dress/suit;* 深色的衣服(西裝)；*~ blue/green/brown;* 深藍(綠,褐)色；*~-brown eyes.* 深褐色的眼睛。 **3** (of the skin) not fair: (指皮膚)棕黑的: *a ~ complexion.* 棕黑的膚色。 **4** (fig) hidden, mysterious: (喻)隱藏的；神祕的: *a ~ secret,* one that is closely guarded. 嚴守的祕密。***keep it ~,*** keep a secret. 保守祕密。**the D~ Continent,** Africa (used of the time when most of it was unexplored and mysterious). 黑暗大陸；非洲(指非洲在從前大部份未開發因而帶神祕性的時代)。**a ~ horse,** race-horse with unexpected or unknown capabilities, (fig) person whose capabilities may be greater than they are known to be. 黑馬(賽馬會中出人意料之外得勝的馬)；(喻) 能力可能出人意外高強的人。 **5** hopeless; sad; cheerless: 無希望的；悲傷的；無精打采的: *Don't look on the ~ side of things.* 不要抱悲觀的態度觀察事物。 **6** unenlightened (morally or intellectually). (道德或智力) 未啓蒙的；未發展的。 **the D~ Ages,** (in European history) from the 6th to the 12th cc; (also) between the end of the Roman Empire (AD 476) and the close of the 10th c. (歐洲歷史上的)黑暗時代(自6世紀至12世紀；亦指自羅馬帝國衰亡，即西元476年，至10世紀末)。 **7** not clear to or in the mind: 意義不明的；不易瞭解的；曖昧的: *a ~ saying,* one that is obscure. 意義不明的話。 **~·ly** *adv* **~·ness** *n* [U] the state of being ~: 黑暗；晦暗: *The room was in complete ~ness.* 室內一片漆黑。

darken /'dɑ:kən ; 'dɑrkən/ *vt, vi* [VP6A, 2A] make or become dark. (使)變黑暗等。 ***~ sb's door,*** (facet) visit him. (玩笑語)拜訪某人。

Darkey, Darkie, Darky /'dɑ:kɪ ; 'dɑrkɪ/ *n* ⚠ (colloq) (offensive term for a) Negro or Negress. (諱)(俗)黑鬼(對黑人無禮貌的稱呼)。

dar·ling /'dɑ:lɪŋ ; 'dɑrlɪŋ/ *n* **1** person or object very much loved: 親愛的人；極可愛的人；寵愛之物: *She's a little ~.* 她是個極可愛的小孩！ *My ~!* 親愛的！ **2** (attrib, colloq) charming; delightful: (形容用法，俗)迷人的；可愛的；宜人的: *What a ~ little cottage!* 多麼宜人的小雅舍！

darn[1] /dɑ:n ; dɑrn/ *vt, vi* [VP6A, 2A] mend (esp sth knitted, eg a sock) by passing thread in and out and in two directions: 織補(編織物，如襪子): *My socks have been ~ed again and again.* 我的襪子已經一補再補。□ *n* place mended by ~ing. 織補之處。**~·ing** *n* (esp) things needing to be ~ed. (尤指) 需織補之物。 **'~ing-needle,** large sewing needle used for ~ing. 織補用的大針。

darn[2] /dɑ:n ; dɑrn/ *vt* [VP6A] (sl) damn(3): (俚)用以表示憤怒，厭煩，急躁等: *Well, I'll be ~ed.* 唉，我眞要煩死了。

dart[1] /dɑ:t ; dɑrt/ *n* [C] **1** quick, sudden, forward movement: 急速而突然的向前衝；急馳；飛奔: *The child made a sudden ~ across the road.* 那小孩突然衝過馬路。 **2** small, sharp missile (feathered and pointed), to be thrown at a target (marked with numbers for scoring) in the game called ~s. 飛鏢(小而尖銳的投擲物，尾端有羽毛，向目標投擲，標盤上有計分的數字，此種遊戲卽稱爲 darts)。

dart[2] /dɑ:t ; dɑrt/ *vi, vt* [VP2A, C, 6A, 15A, B] (cause to) move forward suddenly and quickly; send suddenly and quickly: (使)突然而急促地向前衝；飛奔；投擲；投射: *The deer ~ed away when it saw us.* 鹿看見我們就飛奔而逃。*The snake ~ed out its tongue.* 蛇吐出舌頭。*She ~ed an angry look at him.* 她向他投以憤怒的一瞥。 *Swallows were ~ing through the air.* 燕子飛鏢似地穿過空中。*She ~ed into the shop.* 她衝進店中。

dash[1] /dæʃ ; dæʃ/ *n* **1** [C] sudden rush; violent movement: 急奔；猛衝；突擊: *to make a ~ for shelter/freedom;* 急奔以尋求隱蔽(自由)； *to make a ~ at the enemy.* 向敵人突襲。***at a ~,*** quickly and smartly: 迅速而俐落地: *The cavalry rode off at a ~.* 騎兵隊急馳而去。 **2** (usu 通常作 **a/the ~ of**) (sound of) liquid striking sth or being thrown or struck: 冲擊或濺灑之液體(的聲音): *the ~ of the waves on the rocks;* 海浪在岩石上的冲擊聲； *the ~ of oars striking the water.* 搖槳擊水的聲音。*A ~ of cold water will revive a person who has fainted.* 潑灑冷水可使昏厥的人復甦。 **3** [C] small amount of sth added or mixed: (加入或混合的)少許；少量: *a ~ of pepper in the soup;* 加入湯中的少許胡椒；*water with a ~ of whisky in it;* 加入少許威士忌的水；*red with a ~ of blue.* 略帶藍色的紅色。 **4** [C] stroke of the pen or a mark (—) used in printing. 破折號。 ⇨ App 9. 參看附錄九。 **5 the ~,** short race, sprint: 短跑；短距離賽跑: *the 100-metres ~.* 一百米短跑。 **6** [U] (capacity for) vigorous action; energy: 活力；精力；幹勁: *an officer famous for his skill and ~.* 以幹練與幹勁聞名的軍官。 ***cut a ~,*** make a brilliant show (in appearance and behaviour). (在外表及行爲上) 大出風頭。 **'~·board,** **(a)** screen on the front part of a horse-drawn cart, wagon, etc to protect from mud splashed up from the road. (馬車等前部的)遮泥板(擋住自路上濺起的泥)。 **(b)** panel beneath the windscreen of a motor-car, with speedometer, various controls, etc. (汽車擋風玻璃下面，裝置速率表，各種控制器等的)儀表板。 ⇨ the illus at motor. 參看 motor 之插圖。

dash[2] /dæʃ ; dæʃ/ *vt, vi* **1** [VP6A, 15A, B, 2C] send or throw violently; move or be moved violently: 猛擲；猛撞；猛擊；猛衝: *The boat was ~ed against the rocks.* 那船猛撞在礁石上。*The huge waves ~ed over the rocks.* 掀天大浪冲擊在岩石上。 *The elephants ~ed through the undergrowth.* 那些大象急速衝過下層林叢。 *D~ a bucketful of water over this muddy floor.* 拿一桶水把這泥汚的地板冲洗一下。 *A motor-car ~ed past us/~ed mud all over us as it passed.* 一輛汽車自我們身邊飛馳而過(飛馳而過時，濺了我們滿身泥)。 ***~ sth off,*** write or draw sth quickly: 匆匆而寫或畫: *I must ~ off a few letters before I go out.* 我在出去以前必須趕寫幾封信。 **2** [VP6A] ***~ sb's hopes,*** destroy, discourage, them. 使某人的希望破滅。 **3** [VP6A] (colloq, used as a mild substitute for) Damn!: (俗)可惡！(咒罵語，較Damn語氣稍弱): *D~ it!* 可惡！ **~·ing** *adj* impetuous; lively; full of, showing, energy: 猛烈的；有生氣的；精力充沛的: *a ~ing cavalry charge;* 騎兵的猛攻； *a ~ing rider,* eg one who rides a horse boldly. 勇猛的騎馬者。**~·ing·ly** *adv*

das·tard /'dæstəd ; 'dæstəd/ *n* (old use) bully; coward who is brutal when there is no risk to himself. (舊用法)欺軟怕硬的懦夫(在無危險時却很兇)。 **~·ly** *adj* of or like a ~. 怯懦的；欺軟怕硬的。

data /'deɪtə ; 'detə/ *n pl* (*pl* of Lat *datum*) (拉丁文 datum 的複數形) **1** facts; things certainly known (and from which conclusions may be drawn): 事實資料；可據以下斷語的材料: *unless sufficient ~ are available.* 除非有充分的事實資料可以利用。 **2** (usu with *sing v*) information prepared for and operated on a computer programme: (通常與單數

動詞連用)供電腦程式使用的資料: *The ~ is ready for processing.* 資料已齊備,等待處理。 '~ **bank,** centre with a comprehensive file of computer ~. 資料庫(有包羅廣泛的電腦資料卷檔)。 ˌ~ '**processing,** the performing of operations on ~ to obtain information, solutions to problems, etc. 資料處理(電腦對資料的操作,以獲取情報,問題的答案等)。

date[1] /deɪt ; det/ *n* **1** statement of the time, day, month, year, one or all three of these, when sth happened or is to happen: (某事在過去發生或將來發生的)日期;年代;年月日: *D~ of birth, 20 April 1974;* 出生日期,1974年4月20日; *the ~ of the discovery of America by Columbus (1492).* 哥倫布發現美洲的年代(1492)。 *What's the ~ today?* 今天是幾月幾日? *Has the ~ for the meeting been fixed?* 開會的日期決定了嗎? '**~-line, (a)** (*International ~-line*) meridian 180° from Greenwich, east and west of which at any given time the calendar ~s differ by one day. 國際換日線(即距格林尼治 180 度之子午線,在此線以東及以西的地區,日曆上的日期永遠相差一日)。 **(b)** phrase giving the ~ and place of origin of an article in a periodical. 期刊中載明一篇文章出版日期和出處的文字。 **2** [U] period of time, eg one to which antiquities belong: (古物等所屬的)時代: *Many ruins of Roman ~* (= of the time of ancient Rome) *are to be seen in the south of France.* 許多古羅馬時代的遺跡可以在法國南部看到。 **3** (phrases) (片語) ***be/go ˌout of '~,*** be/become not modern: 過時的;陳舊的: *will denim jeans ever go out of ~?* 斜紋粗棉布牛仔褲會過時嗎? Hence, 由此產生, '**out-of-~** *adj: out-of-~ clothes/ideas/slang.* 過時的衣服(陳舊的觀念;已廢的俚語)。 ***be/bring sth ˌup to '~,*** **(a)** be/make it modern. (使)時新;(使)合於現代潮流。 **(b)** be/bring it up to the present time: (使)直到現在: *bring a catalogue up to ~.* 增訂目錄使包括最近的資料。 ⇨ update. Hence, 由此產生, '**up-to-~** *adj:* 時新的;現代的;直到現在的: *up-to-~ styles/methods/books.* 最新的式樣(方法,書)。 ***to ~,*** so far; until now: 到目前爲止: *There's no news to ~.* 到目前爲止還沒有消息。 **4** (colloq) social meeting arranged with sb at a certain time and place; appointment: (俗)(與某人定好時間和地點的)約會: *I've got a ~ with her tonight.* 我今天晚上和她有約會。 ˌ**blind '~,** arrangement to meet sb socially, having not met him before. 與從未晤面的人作社交約會。 **5** (by extension; colloq) companion of the other sex with whom ~s(4) are arranged. (引伸之義;俗)約會的異性友伴。 **~·less** *adj* endless; immemorial. 無盡的;古老至人所不能記憶的。

date[2] /deɪt ; det/ *vt, vi* **1** [VP6A] have or put a date(1) on: 加日期於: *Don't forget to ~ your letters.* 不要忘記在你的信上加日期。 *The letter is ~d from London, 24 May.* 此信係五月二十四日寄自倫敦。 **2** [VP6A] give a date(2) to: 鑑定(古物等)的時代: *to ~ old coins/sth found in an excavation.* 鑑定古幣(發掘物)的時代。 *That suit ~s you,* shows your age (because it is old-fashioned). 那套衣服顯示出你的年紀(因其老式的樣子)。 ⇨ 4 below. 參看下列第4義。 **3** [VP2C, 3A] ~ ***from/back to,*** have existed since: 自…時代存在至今: *The castle ~s back to the 14th century,* was built then. 此堡建於十四世紀。 *The prosperity of the family ~s from the war,* They became rich (eg by making munitions) during the war. 這家人的發迹始於大戰時期(如藉戰時製造軍火)。 **4** [VP2A] show signs of becoming out-of-date: 逐漸過時或變陳舊: *Isn't this textbook beginning to ~?* 這教本不是已漸漸陳舊了嗎? **5** [VP6A] make a date(4) with. 與…作社交約會。 **dated** *adj* out of fashion; (of words and phrases) used in the past but not now current. 過時的;陳舊的;(指字和片語)現已不再採用的。 **dat·able** *adj* that can be dated(2). 可鑑定時代的。

date[3] /deɪt ; det/ *n* small, brown, sweet, edible fruit of the date-palm, common in N Africa and SW Asia. (棗椰樹所結的)棗子(常見於北非及西南亞)。 ⇨ the illus at palm. 參看 palm 之插圖。

dat·ive /'deɪtɪv ; 'detɪv/ *n, adj* (gram) (in Latin and other inflected languages) (of the) form of a word showing that it is an indirect object of the verb; (in English, loosely used for) indirect object (eg *me* in 'Tell me your name'). (文法)與格;間接受格(拉丁語及其他曲折語的一種字形變化,表示其爲動詞的間接受詞); (英語中非嚴謹用法)間接受詞(如 Tell me your name 中的 me 即是)。 ⇨ case[1](3).

datum /'deɪtəm ; 'detəm/ *n* fact. 事實資料。 ⇨ data.

daub /dɔːb ; dɔb/ *vt, vi* **1** [VP6A, 14, 15A, B] put paint, clay, plaster, etc roughly on a surface: 在表面塗抹(油漆,泥,灰泥等): *to ~ plaster on a wall;* 塗灰泥於牆上; *to ~ a wall with paint.* 油漆牆壁。 *Don't ~ the paint on too thickly.* 不要把油漆塗得太厚。 **2** [VP6A, 2A] paint (pictures) without skill or artistry. 塗鴉式地繪(畫)。 **3** [VP6A, 14] make dirty: 弄髒: *trousers ~ed with paint.* 沾有油漆的褲子。 □ *n* **1** [C, U] (covering of) soft, sticky material, eg clay. 軟而黏的塗料(如黏土);塗抹。 **2** [C] badly painted picture. 拙劣的畫;塗鴉的作品。 **~er** *n* person who paints unskilfully. 拙劣的畫者。

daugh·ter /'dɔːtə(r) ; 'dɔtɚ/ *n* one's female child. 女兒。 **~-in-law** /'dɔːtər ɪn lɔː ; 'dɔtərɪnˌlɔ/ (*pl* **~s-in-law** /'dɔːtəz ɪn lɔː ; 'dɔtɚzɪnˌlɔ/) wife of one's son. 兒媳。 **~·ly** *adj* befitting a ~: 適於女兒的: *~ly affection.* 女兒對父母之愛。

daunt /dɔːnt ; dɔnt/ *vt* [VP6A] discourage: 挫折;使氣餒: *nothing ~ed,* not at all discouraged. 毫無懼色;毫不氣餒。

daunt·less /'dɔːntlɪs ; 'dɔntlɛs/ *adj* not daunted; persevering. 勇敢的;無畏的;勇往直前的。 **~·ly** *adv*

dau·phin /'dɔːfɪn ; 'dɔfɪn/ *n* title of the King of France's eldest son (from 1349 to 1830). (自1349至1830年間)法國皇太子的稱號。

dav·en·port /'dævnpɔːt ; 'dævənˌpɔrt/ *n* **1** (GB) piece of furniture with drawers and a hinged flap that opens so that it can be used as a writing-desk. (英)一種有抽屜並帶一塊木板以鉸鏈相連可以垂下或升起用做寫字枱的傢具;活動書桌。 **2** (US) long seat for two or three persons, with arms and a back. (美)有扶手及靠背的長沙發。 ⇨ settee.

davit /'dævɪt ; 'dævɪt/ *n* one of a pair of small cranes(2), curved at the top, for supporting, lowering and raising a ship's boat. 輪船上懸小艇的吊柱(頂端彎曲,可將小艇放下和拉起)。

daw /dɔː ; dɔ/ *n* = jackdaw.

dawdle /'dɔːdl ; 'dɔdḷ/ *vi, vt* [VP2A, C, 15B] ~ ***(away),*** be slow; waste time: 行動遲緩;虛擲時光;閒蕩: *Stop dawdling and do something useful!* 不要閒蕩了,做點有益的事吧! *Don't ~ away your time!* 不要虛擲光陰! *He's always dawdling.* 他老是閒着不做事。 **daw·dler** /'dɔːdlə(r) ; 'dɔdlɚ/ *n* person who ~s. 閒蕩不做事者。

dawn[1] /dɔːn ; dɔn/ *n* **1** [U, C] first light of day; daybreak: 天初亮;黎明;破曉: *We must start at ~.* 我們必須天一亮即動身。 *He works from ~ till dark.* 他自天亮工作到天黑。 *It's almost ~.* 天差不多要亮了。 **2** [U, C] (fig) beginning; birth: (喻)開始;發端;誕生: *the ~ of intelligence/love/civilization.* 智力(愛情,文明)的發端。 *The war ended and we looked forward to the ~ of happier days.* 大戰結束了,我們盼望較幸福日子的來臨。

dawn[2] /dɔːn ; dɔn/ *vi* **1** [VP2A] begin to grow light: 破曉;(天)初亮: *The day was just ~ing.* 天才開始亮。 **2** [VP2A, 3A] ~ ***(on/upon sb),*** begin to appear; grow clear (to the mind): 開始現出;變得(爲人所)明白: *The truth began to ~ upon him.* 他開始明白那道理。 *It has just ~ed on me that...,* I have just begun to realize that.... 我剛剛才明白…。

day /deɪ ; de/ *n* **1** [U] time between sunrise and sunset: 白晝;日間(自日出至日落);白天: *He has been working all day.* 他已工作了一整天。 *We travelled day and night/night and day without stopping.*

D

我們日夜不停的旅行。***before day,*** before daylight comes. 在天亮以前。***by day,*** during daylight: 晝間；日間；白天裏: *We travelled by day and stayed at hotels every night.* 我們白天旅行，每晚住旅館。***pass the time of day (with sb),*** exchange greetings (eg by saying 'Good morning'). (與某人)互道安好(如說'早安')。**2** [C] period of twenty-four hours (from midnight): 一日；一晝夜 (自午夜起二十四小時): *There are seven days in a week.* 一週有七日。*I saw Tom three days ago.* 我在三天前看見湯姆。*I shall see Mary in a few days' time,* a few days from now. 我再過幾天就要見到瑪莉了。*What day of the week is it? It's Monday.* 今天星期幾？今天星期一。***the day after tomorrow***: *If today is Wednesday, the day after tomorrow will be Friday.* 假若今天是星期三，後天就是星期五。***the day before yesterday***: *If today is Wednesday, the day before yesterday was Monday.* 假若今天是星期三，前天就是星期一。***this day week***: *If today is 1 May, this day week will be 8 May.* 假若今天是五月一日，下星期的今天就是五月八日。***this day fortnight***: *If today is 1 May, this day fortnight will be 15 May.* 假若今天是五月一日，兩星期後的今天就是五月十五日。***day after day; every day,*** for many days together. 日復一日；一天又一天；每日；一連許多天。***day in, day out,*** continuously. 一天又一天；連續不斷地。***from day to day; from one day to the next***: *No one can be certain about what will happen from day to day.* 沒有人能確知逐日會發生什麼事。***one day,*** on a day (past or future). (過去)某一天；(將來)有一天。***the other day,*** a few days ago. 前幾天；數天前。***some day,*** on some day in the future. 將來有一天；他日。***one of these days,*** (used in making a promise or a prophecy) before long. (用於許諾或預言)不久；過不了幾天。***one of those days,*** day of much misfortune. 不幸的日子。***that'll be the day,*** (ironic) that will never happen. (反語)那永遠不會發生。***if he's a day,*** (of age) at least: (指年齡)至少: *He's eighty if he's a day!* 他至少八十歲了！***not be one's day,*** day when things go badly for one. 倒霉的一天；不如意的一天。***to a/the day,*** exactly: 恰好；剛好: *three years ago to the/a day.* 一天不差恰好三年前。Note the omission of relatives after *day*: 注意 day 後面關係代名詞的省略: *the day (on which) I met you.* 我遇到你的那一天。*We shall have many days (on which) to talk things over.* 我們將有很多的日子可以討論一切。**3** the hours of the day given to work: 每日工作的小時數: *I've done a good day's work.* 我已做了足足一日的工作。*His working day is eight hours.* 他每天的工作時數是八小時。*They want a six-hour day and a five-day week.* 他們要求每日工作六小時，每週工作五日。*Most workers are paid weekly, but some are paid by the day.* 大多數的工人都是按週計酬，但也有一些按日計酬。***call it a day,*** decide that we have done enough (work) for one day: 認爲一日的工作量已够: *Let's call it a day,* stop. 這一天的工作够了，停工吧。***all in a/the day's work,*** all part of the normal routine. 每日所應做的事。***at the end of the day,*** when the work, etc is completed. 工作等完成時。***early/late in the day,*** (too) early/late. (太)早(遲)。**day 'off,** holiday. 假日。**day release,** permission for a worker to attend a college during a working day. 准許工人於工作日進大學進修。**4** (often *pl*) time; period: (常用複數)時代；時期: *in my school-days;* 在我的學生時代；*in his boyhood days;* 在他的幼年時代；*in the days of Queen Victoria;* 維多利亞女王時代；*in days of old/in olden days,* in former times; 在昔日；昔時；*in days to come,* in future times; 在未來的時代；*the men of other days,* of past times. 昔人；古人。**better days,** times when one was, or will be, richer, more prosperous, etc: (過去或未來)生活更富裕繁榮的日子: *Let's hope we'll soon see better days.* 希望我們不久能過好日子。***fall on evil days,*** suffer misfortune. 遭遇不幸。***the present day,*** the time we are now living in. 現代。Hence, 由此產生，**'present-day** *attrib adj*: *present-day* (= modern) *writers.* 現代作家。***(in) these days,*** nowadays. 如今；目下。***in those days,*** then. 在當時。***in this day and age,*** (cliché) in this present period. (陳辭)在今天這個時代。**5** (*sing* preceded by *his, her, their,* etc) lifetime; period of success, prosperity, power, etc: (單數，前用 his, her, their 等)一生；鼎盛時期: *Colonialism has had its day.* 殖民主義曾盛極一時。*She was a beauty in her day,* before she grew old. 她年輕的時候是個美人。***Every dog has its day,*** (prov) We all have good luck or a period of success at some time or other. (諺)人人都有一段走運的時期。***those were the days,*** (cliché) ie better times. (陳辭)那是在好時期；那才是好年頭。**6 the day,** contest: 競賽: *We've won/carried the day.* 我們獲勝了。*The day is ours.* 我們贏了。*We've lost the day.* 我們比賽輸了。**7** (used attrib, and in compounds) (形容用法，並用於複合字中) **'day bed,** bed or couch for daytime sleep or rest. 白天睡覺或休息的牀；睡椅。**'day-book,** (comm) book for record of sales as they take place, for transfer to a ledger. (商)流水帳；日記帳(買賣東西隨時的記錄，將來轉至總帳)。**'day-boy/girl,** one who attends school daily but sleeps at home. 通學生；走讀生(每日到校上課，晚上回家睡覺)。**'day-break** *n* [U] dawn. 拂曉；破曉；黎明。**ˌday 'care** *n* [U] care for small children, away from home, during the day: 托兒(白天替人照顧幼兒): *a 'day-care center.* 托兒所。**'day·dream** *n, vi* [VP2A] (think) pleasant thoughts. (作)白日夢。**'day-labourer,** one who is hired by the day. 按日計酬的雇工。**'day-long** *adj, adv* (lasting) for the whole day. 終日的(地)。**'day nursery,** place where small children may be left during the day. 日間托兒所。**ˌday re'lease** *n* [U] system of allowing employees off work (eg for one day per week) for educational purposes. (員工每週一日的)休假進修。**'day-return** *n* [C] return ticket (often at a reduced rate) available both ways on one day only. 限當天有效的來回票(通常票價較低)。**'day-school,** used as the opp of *boarding-school, evening school,* and *Sunday school.* 日校(用爲寄宿學校，夜校及主日學校之對)。**'day shift,** (workers working a) period during the day, esp in a mine. (尤指在礦場)白日工作的一段時間；日班；日班工人。**'day-spring,** (poet) dawn. (詩)拂曉；黎明。**'day-time,** day(1), 白晝；日間；白天，esp: 尤用於: *in the day-time.* 在日間；在白晝。

day·light /ˈdeɪlaɪt ; ˈdeˌlaɪt/ *n* [U] **1** light of day: 日光；日間: *Can we reach our destination in ~,* before it gets dark? 我們能在天黑以前到達目的地嗎？**~ robbery** *n* [U] **(a)** open cheating. 公開的欺騙。**(b)** high, unfair price(s). 過高的價錢。**~ saving** *n* [U] putting the hands of the clock forward so that darkness falls later. 日光節約(夏天將時鐘的針向前撥以使天晚一點黑)。⇨ *summer time* at summer. **2** dawn: 破曉；黎明: *leave/arrive before ~.* 在天亮以前啓程(到達)。

daze /deɪz ; dez/ *vt* [VP6A] make (sb) feel stupid or unable to think clearly: 使(某人)茫然或暈眩: *If someone gave you a heavy blow on the head, you would probably feel ~d.* 假使有人在你頭上猛敲一記，你就可能會感覺暈眩。*He looked ~d with drugs/was in a ~d state.* 他看樣子似因服藥物而致暈眩(在暈眩中)。□ *n* ***in a ~,*** in a bewildered condition. 在恍惚之中；不知所措。**dazed·ly** /ˈdeɪzɪdlɪ ; ˈdezɪdlɪ/ *adv* in a ~d manner. 恍惚地；迷迷糊糊地。

dazzle /ˈdæzl ; ˈdæzḷ/ *vt* [VP6A] make (sb) unable to see clearly or act normally because of too much light, brilliance, splendour, etc: 使(某人)因强光，絢爛，壯麗等而看不清楚或行動失常；使眼花；使目眩: *~d by bright lights;* 因强光而目眩；*dazzling sunshine/diamonds.* 眩目的陽光(鑽石)。□ *n* [U] glitter. 閃光；輝耀。

D-day /ˈdiː deɪ; ˈdiˌde/ *n* (code name for the) day (6 June 1944) on which British and American forces landed in N France, during the Second World War; unnamed day on which important work is to start. 二次世界大戰時英美盟軍在法國北部登陸的日子(1944年6月6日);該日的祕密代號;重大工作開始之日。

dea·con /ˈdiːkən; ˈdikən/ *n* minister or officer who has various duties in certain Christian churches (eg in the Church of England, below a bishop or priest; in nonconformist churches, a layman attending to secular affairs). 基督教會中的執事牧師或職員(如英國國教中,位於主教或牧師之下者;在獨立教會中職司非宗教事務之非聖職人員)。**~·ess** /ˈdiːkənɪs; ˈdikənɪs/ *n* woman with duties similar to a ~'s. 基督教會中的女執事或女職員。

dead /ded; dɛd/ *adj* **1** (of plants, animals, persons) no longer living: (指植物,動物,人)已死的;凋謝的: *~ flowers/leaves.* 凋謝的花(葉)。*The hunter fired and the tiger fell ~.* 獵人開槍,老虎倒地而亡。***D~ men tell no tales,*** (prov, used as an argument for killing sb whose knowledge of a secret may cause one loss or trouble). (諺) 死人洩露不了祕密(用作殺人滅口的理由)。***wait for a ~ man's shoes,*** wait for sb to die in order to step into his position. 等着某人死去以便接替他的職位。**the ~,** all those who have died or been killed: 死者(之全體): *to rise from the ~;* 死後復活; *the ~ and the wounded.* 死者及傷者。**~ march,** piece of slow, solemn music for a funeral. 送葬進行曲;悼喪進行曲。 **2** never having had life: 無生命的: *~ matter,* eg rock. 無生命的物質(如岩石)。 **3** without movement or activity: 無活動的: *in the ~ hours of the night,* when everything is quiet; 夜闌人靜的時刻; (as *n*) (用作名詞) *in the ~ of winter,* when there is no growth of vegetation, when the weather makes outdoor activity difficult, etc. 在隆冬時期(一切草木皆已死亡,因爲氣候關係戶外活動亦甚困難等)。 **~ end** *n* cul-de-sac. 死巷。***be at/come to/reach a ~ end,*** (fig) the stage from which further progress appears impossible. (喻)到達似乎不可能再有所進步的階段;陷入僵局;面臨絕境。⇨ 9 below. 參看下列第9義。 **4** (of languages, customs, etc) no longer used or observed. (指語言,習俗等)已不通用或通行的。**~ language,** eg ancient Greek. 死的語言(如古希臘語)。 **~ letter, (a)** regulation to which attention is no longer paid. 已成具文的規章;不再受人重視的規章。**(b)** letter kept by the post-office because the person to whom it is addressed has not claimed it and neither he nor the sender can be found. 郵局所保存無法投遞的信件。**5** (of the hands, etc) numbed, eg by cold; unable to feel anything: (指手等)麻木的(例如受凍);無感覺的: *~ fingers.* 被凍僵的手指。 **~ to,** unconscious of, hardened against: 對於…無感覺;感覺已麻木: *~ to all feelings of shame;* 對於羞恥全無感覺;不知羞恥; *~ to the world,* (fig) fast asleep. (喻)酣睡。 **6** complete; abrupt; exact: 全然的;突然的;精確的: *to come to a ~ stop;* 完全停頓下來; *runners on a ~ level,* running side by side; 並肩而跑者; *a ~ calm,* not even a breath of wind. 連一絲風也沒有的平靜狀態;死寂。***go into/be in a ~ faint,*** complete unconsciousness. 全然失去知覺。 **~ heat,** a race in which two or more runners reach the winning-post together. 有兩個或更多個賽跑選手同時到達終點的比賽。 **~ loss,** a complete loss, with no compensation; (sl, of a person) one who is of no help or use to anyone. 無可補償的損失;(俚,指人)無用的人。**the ~ centre,** the exact centre. 正中心。 **~ shot,** person who hits the target without fail; shot that goes to the exact point aimed at. 非常準確的射手或射擊。 **~ silence,** complete silence. 十分寂靜。**~ sleep,** a deep sleep (as if ~). 熟睡(睡得像死人一樣)。 **7** that can no longer be used: 已不可再用的: *a ~ match,* one that has been struck; 已擦過的火柴; *a ~ wire,* one through which electric current no longer passes. 不再通電的電線。*The telephone went ~,* did not transmit sounds. 電話沒有聲音了。 **8** (of sound) dull, heavy; (of colours) lacking brilliance; (cricket, tennis, etc) (of the surface of the ground) such that balls move slowly: (指聲音)鈍重的;(指色彩)不鮮明的;(板球,網球等)(指地面)崎嶇不平的;球在上面滾動得慢的: *a ~ pitch;* (板球)三柱門之間球滾動緩慢的場地; (of the ball, in various games) out of play. (指各種遊戲中的球)不合規則的;死(球)。 **9** (various uses) (各種用法) **ˈ~·line** *n* fixed limit of time for finishing a piece of work: 截止的期限: *meet a ~line,* do, finish sth by the time assigned for it. 在截止期限內做完某事。**~·pan** *adj* (colloq) (of a person's face, looks) showing no emotion. (俗)(指人的面孔,樣子)不動聲色的;無表情的。**~weight** *n* **1** (with *indef art*) heavy inert mass. (與不定冠詞連用)沉重的物體。 **2** (comm) ship's loaded weight, including fuel and cargo. (商)船之總載重量(包括燃料和貨物)。□ *adv* completely; absolutely; thoroughly: 完全地;絕對地;徹底地: *~ ˈbeat/ˈtired;* 疲倦已極; *~ ˈcertain/ˈsure;* 絕對相信;確信; *~ ˈdrunk,* so drunk as to be incapable; 爛醉如泥; *~ slow,* as slowly as possible; 盡可能的慢;極爲緩慢; *~ ahead,* directly ahead. 正前方。*The wind was ~ against us.* 風正對我們迎面吹來。*You're ~ right!* 你對極了! ***cut sb ~,*** ⇨ cut¹ (7).

deaden /ˈdedn; ˈdɛdn̩/ *vt* [VP6A] take away, deprive of, force, feeling, brightness: 除去;消除(力量,感情,亮度): *drugs to ~ the pain;* 止痛藥; *thick walls that ~ street noises;* 隔絕市街鬧聲的厚牆; *thick clothing that ~ed the force of the blow.* 減輕了所受打擊力的厚衣服。

dead·lock /ˈdedlɒk; ˈdɛdˌlɑk/ *n* [C, U] complete failure to reach agreement, to settle a quarrel or grievance: 處於僵局(完全不能達成協議,解決爭端或訴願的局面): *to reach ~;* 造成僵持狀態; *to be at/come to a total ~.* 處於僵持狀態。***break the ~,*** cause change in the blocked state. 打破僵局。

dead·ly /ˈdedlɪ; ˈdɛdlɪ/ *adj* (-ier, -iest) **1** causing, likely to cause, death: (可能)致死的;致命的: *~ weapons/poison.* 致命的武器(毒藥)。*Fog is one of the sailor's deadliest enemies.* 霧是水手的死敵之一。 **2** filled with hate: 充滿仇恨的: *~ enemies.* 深仇死敵。 **3** that may result in damnation: 可遭天罰的: *the seven ~ sins.* 七項可遭天罰的大罪。 **4** like that of death: 如死一般的: *a ~ paleness.* 如死人般的蒼白。 **5** (colloq) excessive: (俗)過度的: *~ determination.* 過份堅決。□ *adv* like that of death: 如死一般地: *~ pale;* 死人般地蒼白; (colloq) excessively: (俗)過度地: *~ serious.* 非常嚴重。

deaf /def; dɛf/ *adj* **1** unable to hear at all; unable to hear well: 聾的;聽力不佳的: *to become ~;* 變聾; *the ~ and dumb alphabet,* one in which signs made with the hands are used for letters or words; 聾啞人用的字母(以手勢代替文字者); 手語; *to be ~ in one ear.* 一隻耳聾。**ˈ~-aid** *n* hearing aid; small device, usu electronic, that helps a ~ person to hear. 助聽器(裝有電子設備以助聽覺的小器具)。 **ˌ~ ˈmute** *n* person who is ~ and dumb. 聾啞之人。 **2** unwilling to listen: 不願意聽的: *~ all advice/entreaty.* 不聽一切勸告(懇求)。*He turned a ~ ear to* (=refused to listen to) *our requests for help.* 他對我們的請求援助置之不理。**~·ness** *n*

deafen /ˈdefn; ˈdɛfən/ *vt* [VP6A] make so much noise that hearing is difficult or impossible: 震耳欲聾;鬧聲太大使不易聽清楚: *We were almost ~ed by the uproar.* 喧囂之聲使我們震耳欲聾。*There were ~ing cheers when the speaker finished.* 當演說者講完時,歡呼之聲震耳欲聾。

deal¹ /diːl; dil/ *n* (board of) fir or pine wood: 樅木或松木(板);杉板: (chiefly attrib) (主作形容用法) *~ furniture;* 樅木傢具; *a ~ table;* 樅木桌; *made of white ~.* 白樅木製的。

D

deal[2] /diːl ; dil/ *n* **a (good/great) ~ (of sth),** much; many: 大量;許多: *spend a good ~ of money;* 花很大一筆錢; *take a great ~ of trouble;* 費盡心力; *cause sb a ~ of anxiety;* 使某人非常憂慮; *have a great ~ of friends;* 有很多朋友; *be a good ~ better;* 好得多了; *see sb a great ~,* often. 常常見到某人。

deal[3] /diːl ; dil/ *vt, vi* (*pt, pp* dealt /delt ; dɛlt/) **1** [VP6A, 15B, 2A, 12A, 13A] **~ (out),** give out to a number of persons: 分配;配發(給若干人): *The money must be ~t out fairly.* 這筆錢必須公平分配。 *Who ~t the cards?* 誰發的牌? *He had been ~t four aces.* 他被分到四張么點牌。 *It is the duty of a judge to ~ out justice.* 公正執法是法官的職責。 **~ sb a blow; ~ a blow at/to sb, (a)** hit or strike him: 予某人打擊: *He ~t me a hard blow on the chin.* 他對準我的下巴用力一擊。 **(b)** (fig) hurt; upset: (喻)傷害;使不安: *The news ~t me a severe blow.* 那消息使我心緒煩亂。 **2** [VP3A] **~ in sth,** stock, sell: 經營;買賣: *a shop that ~s in goods of all sorts;* 經營各種貨物的商店; spend time on: 消磨時間於: *to ~ in gossip and slander.* 把時間用於論人是非和散布謠言。 **3** [VP3A] **~ with sb/at a place,** do business: 與…有生意往來: *Do you ~ with Smith, the butcher?* 你與肉商史密斯有生意來往嗎? *I've stopped ~ing at that shop—their prices are too high.* 我已不在那商店購物;他們的價錢太貴。 **4** [VP3A] **~ with, (a)** have relations with: 與…往來;與…相處: *That man is easy/difficult/impossible to ~ with.* 那人容易(不易,極難)相處。 **(b)** behave towards; treat: 對待;對付: *How would you ~ with an armed burglar?* 遇到持有武器的竊盜,你將如何對付? *What is the best way of ~ing with young criminals,* How can we make them into good citizens? 對付少年犯最好的辦法是什麼(如何使他們變成好公民)? **(c)** (of affairs) manage; attend to: (指事務)處理: *How shall we ~ with this problem?* 我們將如何處理這問題? **(d)** be about; be concerned with: 關於;有關: *a book ~ing with West Africa.* 關於西非的一本書。 **5 ~ well/badly by sb,** treat him well/badly (usu in passive): 善(虐)待某人(通常用於被動語態): *He has always ~t well by me.* 他一直對我很好。 *You've been badly ~t by.* 你受到了虐待。

deal[4] /diːl ; dil/ *n* [C] **1** (in games) distribution of playing cards: (遊戲)發紙牌: *It's your ~,* your turn to deal out the cards. 輪到你發牌。 ***a new ~,*** (originally 原指 ***the New D~***) programme of social and economic reform (in US); any new plan that is thought to be just or fair. 新政(美國社會經濟的改革計畫);任何被視爲公正或公平的新計畫。 **2** business transaction or agreement; (colloq) bargain: 成交;(俗)交易: *Well, it's a ~,* I agree to do business with you on those terms. 好的,這樣就算成交了。 *I'll do a ~ with you,* make a bargain. 我願與你做一項交易。 ***a fair/square ~,*** fair treatment. 公平的對待。 ***a raw/rough ~,*** harsh or unjust treatment. 粗野或不公平的對待。

dealer /ˈdiːlə(r) ; ˈdilɚ/ *n* **1** person who deals out playing-cards. 發牌者。 **2** trader: 商人;販子: *a ˈhorse-~;* 販馬商; *a ~ in* (=person who buys and sells) *stolen goods;* 買賣偷竊之贓物者; *a ˈcar ~.* 汽車商。 Cf 參較 *a coal merchant.*

deal·ing /ˈdiːlɪŋ ; ˈdilɪŋ/ *n* **1** [U] dealing out or distributing; behaviour towards others: 分配;分發;對待他人的態度: *He is well known for fair ~.* 他以公平待人著名。 **2** (*pl*) business relations: (複)交易;來往: *I've always found him honest in his ~s with me.* 在他與我的交易中,我一直覺得他很誠實。 *I advise you to have no ~s with that fellow.* 我勸你不要跟那個人來往。

dealt /delt ; dɛlt/ *pt, pp* of deal[3].

dean /diːn ; din/ *n* **1** clergyman at the head of a cathedral chapter. 大教堂全體教士的主持;主持牧師。 **2 rural ~,** clergyman who, under an archdeacon, is responsible for a number of parishes. 在副主教之下負責若干教區的牧師;鄉區牧師。 **3** (in some universities) person with authority to maintain discipline; head of a department of studies. (某些大學的)訓導長;系主任。 **4** = doyen. **~·ery** /ˈdiːnərɪ ; ˈdinərɪ/ *n* (*pl* -ries) office, house, of a ~; group of parishes under a rural ~. 大教堂主持牧師的辦公室或宅邸;受鄉區牧師管轄的諸教區。

dear /dɪə(r) ; dɪr/ *adj* (-er, -est) **1 ~ (to),** loved (by); lovable: 親愛的;可愛的: *Your mother is ~ to you.* 你的母親是你所愛的。 *What a ~ little child!* 多麼可愛的小孩! ***hold sth/sb ~,*** (formal) love very much. (正式用語)極愛某物或某人。 **2** used as a form of address (polite or ironical) in speech, and at the beginning of letters: 用作稱謂之詞(表示客氣或諷刺,用於說話及信函的開端);閣下: *My ~ Jones;* 親愛的瓊斯; *D~ Madam/Sir;* 女士(先生)大鑒;敬啓者; *D~ Mr Green.* 格林先生閣下。 **3** high in price; (of a shop) asking high prices: 昂貴的;(指商店)索價昂貴的: *Everything is getting ~er.* 一切都漲價了。 *That's a ~ shop.* 那是個索價高的商店。 **ˈ~ money,** (when loans are difficult to obtain) on which a high rate of interest must be paid. (貸款不易時)付高利借來的錢。 **4 ~ (to),** precious (to); greatly valued: (對…)貴重的;珍貴的: *He lost everything that was ~ to him.* 他失去了所珍貴的一切。 □ *adv* at a high cost: 高價地;昂貴地: *If you want to make money, you must buy cheap and sell ~.* 如果你想要賺錢,你必須賤買貴賣。 □ *n* **1** lovable person: 可愛的人: *Isn't she a ~!* 她豈不是個可愛的人兒! *Aren't they ~s!* 他們不是很可愛嗎! **2** (also 亦作 **~·est**) (used to address a person): (用作對人的稱呼): *'Come, my ~est.' 'Yes, ~';* '來吧,親愛的。' '來啦,親愛的'; (used with *indef art,* esp when coaxing sb): (與不定冠詞連用,尤用於哄某人時): *'Drink your milk up, Anne, there's a ~.'* '把你的牛奶喝完,安,這樣才是個乖寶寶。' □ *int* used to express surprise, impatience, wonder, dismay, etc: 作感嘆詞用,表示驚愕,不耐煩,奇怪,驚慌等: *Oh ~!* 天啊! *D~ me!* 我的天啊! **~·ly** *adv* **1** very much: 極;非常: *He would ~ly* (=earnestly) *love to see his mother again.* 他極想再見到他的母親。 *He loves his mother ~ly.* 他極愛他的母親。 **2** at great cost: 付出很大的代價;高價地: *Victory was ~ly bought,* eg when hundreds of soldiers were killed. 勝利的代價很高(如犧牲了數以百計的士兵的生命)。 **~·ness** *n* being ~; great cost. 親愛;昂貴。

dearth /dɜːθ ; dɝθ/ *n* **~ (of),** (*sing* only) scarcity; too small a supply: (僅用單數)稀少;缺乏: *in time of ~;* 在缺乏(糧食)時; *a ~ of food.* 缺乏糧食。 ⇨ shortage, a much commoner word. shortage 遠比 dearth 常用。

deary, dearie /ˈdɪərɪ ; ˈdɪrɪ/ *n* (colloq) dear one; darling (used esp by an older to a younger person, eg by a mother to address her child). (俗)親愛的人;親親;小寶貝(尤指長輩對晚輩,如母親對孩兒,的稱呼)。

death /deθ ; dɛθ/ *n* [C, U] (as shown in the examples) (如例句所示) **1** dying; ending of life: 死亡;斃命;逝世: *There have been several ~s from drowning here this summer.* 今夏這裡曾有數起溺斃的事。 *His mother's ~ was a great blow to him.* 他母親的去世對他是一大打擊。 ***at ~'s door,*** dying; in danger of ~. 在死亡的邊緣;有死亡的危險。 ***to ~,*** so that dying occurs: 致死: *Two children were burnt to ~ in the fire.* 大火中有兩個小孩被燒死。 *Don't work yourself to ~,* work so hard that you become ill and die. 不要工作得把你自己累死了。 ***bore sb to ~,*** bore him extremely. 使某人非常厭煩。 ***sick to ~ of sb/sth,*** extremely tired, bored, etc. 對某人或某事物厭極了。 **ˈ~-bed,** bed on which one dies: 臨死所臥之床: *The criminal made a ~-bed confession,* confessed his crimes while dying. 那罪犯臨死才懺悔。 **ˈ~-duties,** taxes (to be) paid on a person's property before it passes to his heir(s). 遺產稅(對死者遺產未遺留給繼承人前所徵的稅)。 **ˈ~'s head,** human skull (as an emblem of ~). 骷髏;骷髏像(用

作死亡的象徵)。'~-**rate**, yearly number of ~s per 1000 of population. 死亡率 (每年一千人中死亡的人數)。'~ **rattle** *n* unusual rattling sound in the throat of a dying person. 臨終前喉間發出的急促而不清楚的聲音。 **2** killing or being killed: 殺死;處死: *The murderer was sentenced to* ~, to be executed. 兇手被判死刑。 ***be in at the*** ~, (fox-hunting) see the fox killed; (fig) see the end of an enterprise, etc. (獵狐)親見狐被射死; (喻)親見企業等衰落。***put sb to*** ~, kill him; execute him. 將某人處死。***stone sb to*** ~, kill him by throwing stones at him. 用石頭將某人砸死。'~-**roll**, list of persons killed (in war, in an earthquake, etc). (戰爭,地震等的)死亡名單。'~-**trap**, place where persons are likely to be killed (eg one where many fatal traffic accidents occur); place, set of circumstances, where people lose their lives (eg a burning building with no means of escape). 有生命危險的處所(如曾經發生多次大車禍的地方); 使人遭難的場所(如無逃生設備的燃燒中的大樓)。 '~-**warrant**, official paper giving authority for the execution of a criminal, traitor, etc; (fig) sth which destroys prospects of life or happiness, ends an old custom, etc. (對罪犯,賣國賊等)死刑執行令;(喻)毁滅人生前途或幸福,或破除舊習俗等的事物。 **3** [U] state of being dead: 死亡的狀態: *eyes closed in* ~; 死後緊閉的兩眼; *united in* ~, eg of husband and wife in the same grave. 死後合葬 (如夫婦同葬一墓)。*D~ comes to all men.* 人皆有死。***(a fate) worse than*** ~, to be greatly dreaded. 比死亡更可怕的(命運)。 '~-**mask**, cast taken of a dead person's face. 照死者面孔所製的面型。⇨ the illus at mask. 參看 mask 之挿圖。 **4** ***be the ~ of sb***, be the cause of sb's ~: 爲某人的死因: *That old motor-bike will be the ~ of you one of these days*, you will have a fatal accident. 將來有一天,你的命會斷送在那輛舊機器脚踏車上。*Don't make me laugh so much; you'll be the ~ of me*, make me die of laughing. 不要使我笑得這麼厲害;你會使我笑死的。***catch one's ~ (of cold)***, (colloq) catch a cold that will be fatal. (俗)患感冒甚重,可能致死。'~-**blow**, blow that causes ~; (fig) shock from which recovery is impossible: 致命的一擊;(喻)致命的打擊: *a ~-blow to his hopes of success.* 對於他成功的希望之致命打擊。**the Black 'D~**, pestilence in Europe in the 14th c. 黑死病(歐洲十四世紀所流行的瘟疫)。 **5** (fig) destruction; end: (喻)毁滅;消滅: *the ~ of one's hopes/plans.* 希望(計畫)的破滅。

death·less /'deθlɪs ; 'dɛθlɪs/ *adj* never dying or forgotten; immortal: 不死的;不朽的;永恆的: *~ fame/glory.* 不朽的盛名(光榮)。

death·like /'deθlaɪk ; 'dɛθ,laɪk/ *adj* like that of death: 像死一般的: *a ~ silence.* 死一般的沉寂。

death·ly /'deθlɪ ; 'dɛθlɪ/ *adj* like death: 死一般的: *a ~ stillness.* 一片死寂。□ *adv* like death: 如死一般地: *~ pale.* 死人般地蒼白。

deb /deb ; dɛb/ *n* (abbr of) débutante. 爲 débutante 之略。

dé·bâcle /deɪ'bɑːkl ; de'bɑkl/ *n* (F) confused rush or stampede; sudden and great disaster; downfall. (法)大混亂;突然的大災難;崩潰。

de·bag /ˌdiː'bæg ; di'bæg/ *vt* (-gg-) [VP6A] forcibly take off the trousers from. 用力脫下…的褲子。

de·bar/ dɪ'bɑː(r) ; dɪ'bar/ *vt* (-rr-) [VP14]~ ***sb from***, shut out; prevent (sb) by a regulation (from doing or having sth): 排除;按法令褫奪(某人)的行爲權或所有權: *~ persons who have been convicted of crime from voting at elections.* 褫奪被判罪者的選舉投票權。

de·bark /dɪ'bɑːk ; dɪ'bark/ *vt, vi* **de·bark·ation** /ˌdiːbɑː'keɪʃn ; ˌdibar'keʃən/ *n* = disembark.

de·base /dɪ'beɪs ; dɪ'bes/ *vt* [VP6A] make lower in value, poorer in quality, character, etc: 貶低(價值,品質,品格等): *to ~ the coinage*, eg by reducing the percentage of silver. 減低鑄幣的成色 (如減低其含銀的百分率)。~·**ment** *n*

de·bat·able /dɪ'beɪtəbl ; dɪ'betəbl̩/ *adj* that can be debated or disputed; open to question: 可爭辯的; 成問題的: *~ ground.* 有爭議的土地;可爭辯之處。

de·bate /dɪ'beɪt ; dɪ'bet/ *n* [C, U] formal discussion, eg at a public meeting or in Parliament; contest between two speakers, or two groups of speakers, to show skill and ability in arguing: 正式討論(如公共集會或國會中者); 辯論; 辯論會(二人或二團體間,以示辯論的技巧和能力): *After a long ~ the bill was passed by the House of Commons and sent to the House of Lords.* 經過長久討論後,該議案在下議院中通過,並經送達上議院。 *After much ~ Harry was chosen captain of the football team.* 經過許多討論後,哈利被選爲足球隊長。 *Who opened the ~*, was the first to speak? 誰最先發言(開始辯論)? *The question under ~ was....* 在爭辯中的問題是…。□ *vt, vi* [VP6A, 8, 10, 2A, C] have a ~ about; take part in a ~; think over in order to decide: 正式討論;辯論;參加辯論;考慮以便決定: *to ~ (upon) a question with sb;* 與某人辯論一問題; *to ~ about sth;* 辯論某事; *a debating society.* 辯論社。 *We were debating whether to go to the mountains or to the seaside.* 我們正在辯論到底是去山上還是去海邊。**de·bater** *n* one who ~s. 辯論者。

de·bauch /dɪ'bɔːtʃ ; dɪ'bɔtʃ/ *vt* [VP6A] cause (sb) to lose virtue, to act immorally; turn (sb) away from good taste or judgement. 使(某人)行爲失檢或道德敗壞;使(某人)陷於低級趣味。□ *n* [C] occasion of excessive drinking, immoral behaviour, usu in company: 縱飲及行爲 放蕩的場合 (通常指與同伴在一起): *a drunken ~.* 縱飲作樂。~·**ery** /dɪ'bɔːtʃərɪ ; dɪ'bɔtʃərɪ/ *n* [U] intemperance and indulgence in sensual pleasures: 放縱及沉溺於聲色的享樂: *a life of ~ery;* 放蕩的生活; (*pl* -ries) instances or periods of this. 放蕩的實例或時期。~**ee** /dɪˌbɔː'tʃiː ; ˌdɛbɔ'tʃi/ *n* ~ed person. 放蕩者。

de·ben·ture /dɪ'bentʃə(r) ; dɪ'bɛntʃɚ/ *n* [C] (fin) certificate given by a business corporation, etc as a receipt for money lent at a fixed rate of interest until the principal(4) is repaid. (財政)債券(企業公司等所發行,言明一定的利息至本金還回時爲止)。

de·bili·tate /dɪ'bɪlɪteɪt ; dɪ'bɪlə,tet/ *vt* [VP6A] make (a person, his constitution) weak: 使(人,其體格)衰弱: *a debilitating climate.* 不宜人的氣候。

de·bil·ity /dɪ'bɪlətɪ ; dɪ'bɪlətɪ/ *n* [U] weakness (of health, purpose): (健康,決心的)衰弱;虛弱;軟弱: *After her long illness she is suffering from general ~.* 久病之後,她現在全身虛弱。

debit /'debɪt ; 'dɛbɪt/ *n* (book-keeping) entry (in an account) of a sum owing. (簿記) (帳簿中所記)負債的項目;借方金額。'~-**side**, lefthand side of an account, on which such entries are made. 借方(帳簿中左方記載借方金額之處)。⇨ credit¹(4). □ *vt* [VP6A, 14] ~ ***sth (against/to sb)***, put money on the ~ side (of sb's account): 將(一筆錢)記入(某人帳戶的)借方: *~ £5 against my account;* 在我的帳戶的借方記入五鎊; *~ £5 to me.* 在我的帳戶的借方記入五鎊。~ ***sb (with sth)***, give him a ~ (of money): 在某人的借方記入(一筆錢): *~ sb/sb's account with £5.* 在某人(某人帳戶)的借方記入五鎊。

deb·on·air /ˌdebə'neə(r) ; ˌdɛbə'nɛr/ *adj* cheerful; bright and light-hearted. 高興的;心情愉快的。

de·bouch /dɪ'baʊtʃ ; dɪ'buʃ/ *vt, vi* [VP6A, 2A] (cause to) emerge or issue. (使)出現或發出。

de·brief /ˌdiː'briːf ; di'brif/ *vt* [VP6A] question, examine, eg persons who have returned from a mission, etc, to obtain information. 向(任務完畢歸來人員等)詢問以獲取情報。⇨ brief².

de·bris, dé·bris /'deɪbriː; *US:* də'briː ; də'bri/ *n* [U] scattered broken pieces; wreckage: 散亂的碎片; 殘骸: *searching among the ~ after the explosion.* 爆炸後在碎片中搜尋。

debt /det ; dɛt/ *n* [C, U] payment which must be, but has not yet been, paid to sb; obligation: 必須付出而尚未付出的錢款;債;債務;人情債: *If I pay all*

D

my ~s I shall have no money left. 如果我償清了所有的債,我就一文錢不剩了。*I owe him a ~ of gratitude for all he has done for me.*我欠他一筆人情債因爲他曾幫我的忙。**be in/out of ~,** owe/not owe money. 欠(不欠)債。***get into/out of ~,*** reach a point where one owes/does not owe money: 欠(償)債: *It's much easier to get into ~ than to get out of ~.* 欠債容易償債難。**National D~** *n* money owed by the State to those who have lent it money. 公債(國家對人民所負的債)。⇨ bad¹(4), honour¹(2). **~or** /-tə(r) ; -tə/ *n* person who is in ~ to another. 負債者;債務人。

de·bug /ˌdiːˈbʌg ; diˈbʌg/ *vt* (-gg-) [VP6A] (colloq) search for and remove (possible causes of trouble, faults, errors, eg from a computer programme, engines on a production line). (俗)尋找並除去(可能導致麻煩,錯誤等的原因,例如自電腦作業或生產線之引擎中尋查者)。

de·bunk /diːˈbʌŋk ; diˈbʌŋk/ *vt* [VP6A] reveal the truth about (a person, idea, institution) by stripping away false sentiments, traditions, etc. 揭開虛僞的感情,傳統等以露出關於(人,觀念,習尚等)的眞相。

debut, début /ˈdeɪbjuː *US:* dɪˈbjuː ; dɪˈbju/ *n* (esp of a young woman) first appearance at adult parties and other social events; (of an actor, musician, etc) first appearance on a public stage: (尤指年輕女子)初次參加成人的宴會及其他社交場合;(指演員,音樂家等)初次登臺: *to make one's ~.* 初次登臺;初次參加社交活動。

debu·tante, déb- /ˈdebjuːtɑːnt ; ˌdɛbjʊˈtɑnt/ *n* young woman making her debut into high society. 初次參加上流社交場合的少女。

deca- /dekə ; dɛkə/ *pref* ten (in the metric system). (米突制中)十。

dec·ade /ˈdekeɪd ; ˈdɛked/ *n* period of ten years: 十年的期間: *the first ~ of the 20th century*, ie 1900–1909. 二十世紀的最初十年(1900–1909年)。

deca·dence /ˈdekədəns ; dɪˈkedn̩s/ *n* [U] falling to a lower level (in morals, art, literature, etc esp after a period at a high level). (道德,藝術,文學等經過極盛時期以後的)衰落;衰微;頹廢。

deca·dent /ˈdekədənt ; dɪˈkedənt/ *adj* in a state of decadence. 衰落的;衰微的;墮落的。□ *n* person in this state. 墮落者;頹廢者。

Deca·logue /ˈdekəlɒg *US:* -lɔːg ; ˈdɛkəˌlɔg/ *n* **the ~,** the Ten Commandments of Moses. 摩西的十誡。⇨ commandment; ⇨ Exod 20: 1-17. 參看舊約聖經出埃及記第20章1至17節。

de·camp /dɪˈkæmp ; dɪˈkæmp/ *vi* [VP2A, 3A] **~ *(with),*** go away suddenly (and often secretly). 突然(且時常祕密地)離開;逃亡。

de·cant /dɪˈkænt ; dɪˈkænt/ *vt* [VP6A] pour (wine, etc) from a bottle into another vessel slowly so as not to disturb the sediment. 慢慢地自瓶中將(酒等)倒於另一盛器中,使不致震動瓶中的沉澱物。**~er** *n* vessel, usu of decorated glass with a stopper, into which liquor is ~ed. 玻璃酒瓶(通常有塞子,用以盛去沉澱的酒)。

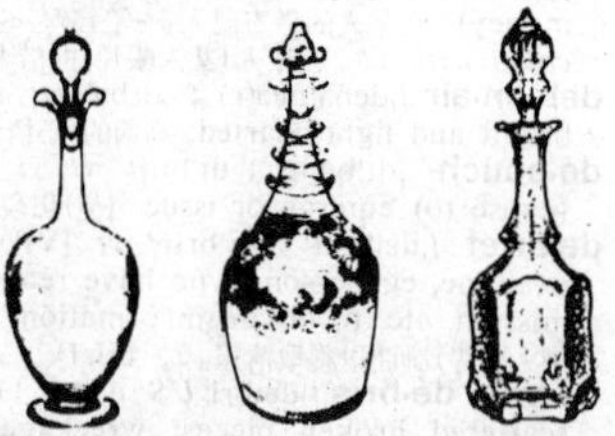

decanters

de·capi·tate /dɪˈkæpɪteɪt ; dɪˈkæpəˌtet/ *vt* [VP6A] behead (esp as a legal punishment). 斬首;殺頭(尤指作爲刑罰者)。 **de·capi·ta·tion** /dɪˌkæpɪˈteɪʃn ; dɪˌkæpəˈteʃən/ *n*

de·car·bon·ize /ˌdiːˈkɑːbənaɪz ; diˈkarbənˌaɪz/ *vt* remove carbon from, esp an internal combustion engine. 除去(內燃機等)的碳。

deca·syl·lable /ˈdekəsɪləbl ; ˈdɛkəˌsɪləbl̩/ *n* **deca·syl·labic** /ˌdekəsɪˈlæbɪk ; ˌdɛkəsɪˈlæbɪk/ *adj* (line) of ten syllables. 含十個音節的(一行詩)。

de·cay /dɪˈkeɪ ; dɪˈke/ *vi* [VP2A] go bad; lose power, health: 變壞;腐敗;衰落;衰敗;衰弱: *~ing teeth/vegetables.* 齲齒(腐爛的蔬菜)。*Our powers ~ in old age.* 我們的體力在老年時衰退。*What caused the Roman Empire to ~?* 羅馬帝國衰亡的原因何在? □ *n* [U] decaying: 變壞;腐敗;衰落;衰敗;衰弱: *the ~ of the teeth.* 牙齒的腐損。*The house is in ~.* 這房子已腐朽。*Old civilizations may fall into ~,* lose strength. 古老的文化可能衰落。

de·cease /dɪˈsiːs ; dɪˈsis/ *n* [U] (formal, legal) (a person's) death. (正式用語,法律)(人的)死亡。□ *vi* die. 死亡。**the ~d,** (formal, legal) person who has, persons who have, recently died. (正式用語,法律)死者;最近去世者。

de·ceit /dɪˈsiːt ; dɪˈsit/ *n* **1** [U] deceiving; causing a person to accept as true or genuine sth that is false: 欺騙;蒙騙: *She is incapable of ~,* would never tell lies, etc. 她是絕不會欺騙的。 **2** [C] lie; dishonest trick. 謊言;騙術。

de·ceit·ful /dɪˈsiːtfl ; dɪˈsitfəl/ *adj* **1** in the habit of deceiving: 慣於欺騙的: *No one can admire a ~ boy.* 沒有人會賞識愛騙人的男孩。 **2** intended to deceive; misleading in appearance, etc: 用以騙人的; 外表等使人發生錯誤想法的: *~ words/behaviour.* 騙人的話(行爲)。**~ly** /-fʊlɪ ; -fəlɪ/ *adv* **~·ness** *n*

de·ceive /dɪˈsiːv ; dɪˈsiv/ *vt* [VP6A, 14] ***~ (in/into),*** cause (sb) to believe sth that is false; play a trick on; mislead (on purpose): 使(某人)相信不眞實的事; 欺騙; 詐騙; (故意)使人有錯誤的想法: *You can't pass the examination without working hard, so don't ~ yourself.* 你不用功就不能考及格,所以不要自欺。*I've been ~d in you,* have found that you were not what I thought you were. 我對你感到失望(發覺你並非如我原來所想像的那樣)。*We were ~d into the belief/~d into believing that....* 我們被騙得相信…。**de·ceiver** /-və(r) ; -və/ *n* person who ~s. 騙徒;騙子;欺騙的人。**de·ceiv·ing·ly** *adv*

de·celer·ate /ˌdiːˈseləreɪt ; diˈsɛləˌret/ *vt, vi* (cause to) diminish speed. (使)減速。⇨ accelerate.

De·cem·ber /dɪˈsembə(r) ; dɪˈsɛmbə/ *n* twelfth month of the year. 十二月。

de·cency /ˈdiːsnsɪ ; ˈdisn̩sɪ/ *n* **1** [U] (the quality of) being decent; (regard for the) general opinion as to what is decent: 正當;適合;可敬;(合乎)一般人對於規矩和禮貌的看法: *an offence against ~,* eg appearing naked in public. 違犯社會行爲標準的事;可羞的事(如當衆裸體)。 **2** *(pl)* (複) **the decencies,** requirements of respectable behaviour in society: 社會所要求的可敬的行爲或標準;禮貌;規矩: *We must observe the decencies.* 我們必須遵守社會行爲標準。

de·cent /ˈdiːsnt ; ˈdisn̩t/ *adj* **1** right and suitable; respectful: 正當而合適的; 可敬的: *Put on some ~ clothes before you call on the Smiths.* 去拜訪史密斯家人的時候,應穿適當的衣服。*Poor people cannot always live in ~ conditions.* 窮人生活不能經常保持體面。 **2** modest; not likely to shock or embarrass others (the only sense for which *indecent* is the opposite): 文雅的;優雅的;不致使別人感覺可羞的(這是唯一與 indecent 相反的意義): *~ language and behaviour.* 高雅的談吐和行爲。*Never tell stories that are not ~.* 切勿講不雅的故事。 **3** (colloq) likeable; satisfactory: (俗)尚可的; 令人滿意的: *He's a very ~ fellow.* 他是個很規矩的人。*He gave us quite a ~ dinner.* 他請我們吃了一頓很不錯的飯。**~·ly** *adv* in a ~(1, 2) manner: 尙佳地;合規矩地;高雅地: *~ly dressed;* 穿着體面; *behave ~ly;* 行爲規矩; (colloq): (俗): *He's doing very ~ly,* eg making a good income. 他的境況尙佳(如收入不錯)。

de·cen·tra·lize /ˌdiːˈsentrəlaɪz ; diˈsɛntrəlˌaɪz/ *vt* [VP6A] give greater powers (for self-government, etc) to (places, branches, etc away from the centre). 分權(給予各地方,分支機構等較大的自治權等)。 **de·cen·tra·liz·ation** /ˌdiːˌsentrəlaɪˈzeɪʃn *US:* -lɪˈz-; ˌdisɛntrələˈzeʃən/ *n*

de·cep·tion /dɪˈsepʃn ; dɪˈsɛpʃən/ *n* **1** [U] deceiving; being deceived: 欺騙;詐騙;受騙: *to practise ~ on the public.* 欺瞞公衆耳目。 **2** [C] trick intended to deceive: 詐術;騙術;詭計: *a gross ~.* 粗鄙的騙術。

de·cep·tive /dɪˈseptɪv ; dɪˈsɛptɪv/ *adj* deceiving: 欺騙的;不實的: *Appearances are often ~*, Things are not always what they seem to be. 外表常是靠不住的。 **~·ly** *adv*

deci- /ˌdesɪ ; ˌdɛsɪ/ *pref* one-tenth (in the metric system). (米突制中)十分之一。

deci·bel /ˈdesɪbel ; ˈdɛsəˌbɛl/ *n* unit for measuring the relative loudness of sounds. 分貝(測音量大小的單位)。

de·cide /dɪˈsaɪd ; dɪˈsaɪd/ *vt, vi* **1** [VP6A, 14, 2A, 3A] settle (a question or a doubt); give a judgement (*between, for, in favour of, against*): 解決(問題或疑惑);判斷(與 between, for, in favour of, against 連用): *We ~d the question by experiment.* 我們用實驗解決那問題。*The judge ~d the case.* 法官對這個案子已做了判決。*It's difficult to ~ between the two.* 很難在這二者之間做一取捨;很難判定這二人的曲直。*The judge ~d for/in favour of/against the plaintiff.* 那法官的判決有利(有利,不利)於原告。 **2** [VP6A, 7A, 8, 9, 10, 3A] ***~ (on/against)***, think about and come to a conclusion; make up one's mind; resolve: 考慮並下一結論;下決心;決定: *The boy ~d not to/~d that he would not become a sailor.* 那男孩子決定將來不做海員。 *It has been ~d that the exhibition shall not be open on Sundays.* 經決定展覽會星期日不開放。*He could not ~ what to do/what he should do next.* 他不能決定該怎麼辦(下一步該怎麼辦)。*In the end she ~d on (buying)/~d to buy the green hat.* 最後她決定要(決定買)那綠色的帽子。 *We ~d against (going for)/~d not to go for a holiday in Wales.* 我們決定不要去威爾斯度假。 **3** [VP17] cause to ~(2): 使決定: *What ~d you to give up your job?* 什麼使你決定放棄你的職業? **de·cided** *part adj* **1** clear; definite: 清楚的;明確的;顯然的: *There is a ~d difference between them.* 他們之間有顯然的不同。*He's a man of ~d opinions.* 他是個很有主見的人。 **2** (of persons) having firm opinions; determined: (指人)有堅定之意見的;堅決的: *He's quite ~d about it.* 關於此事他的態度十分堅決。 **de·cid·ed·ly** *adv* definitely; undoubtedly: 明確地;無疑地: *answer ~dly,* 明確地答覆;*~dly better.* 顯然較佳。

de·cidu·ous /dɪˈsɪdjʊəs ; dɪˈsɪdʒʊəs/ *adj* (of trees) losing their leaves annually (esp in autumn). (指樹)每年(尤指秋季)落葉的。

deci·mal /ˈdesɪml ; ˈdɛsəml̩/ *adj* of tens or one-tenths: 十進的: *the ˈ~ system*, for money, weights, etc; 十進制(指貨幣,重量等); *a ~ fraction*, eg 0·091; 小數(如 0·091); *the ~ point*, the point in eg 15·61. 小數點(如15·61中之小數點)。**~·ize** *vt* [VP6A] express as a ~ fraction: 以小數表示: 1½ *~ized is* 1·5; 1½ 以小數表示爲 1·5; change to a ~ system: 改爲十進制: *~ize the currency.* 改貨幣爲十進制。**~·iz·ation** /ˌdesɪməlaɪˈzeɪʃn *US:* -lɪˈz- ; ˌdɛsəməlɪˈzeʃən/ *n*

deci·mate /ˈdesɪmeɪt ; ˈdɛsəˌmet/ *vt* [VP6A] kill or destroy a larger part of: 殺死或毀滅…的大部分: *a population ~d by disease.* 因病死亡佔大部分的人口。

de·cipher /dɪˈsaɪfə(r) ; dɪˈsaɪfɚ/ *vt* [VP6A] find the meaning of (sth written in cipher, bad handwriting, sth puzzling or difficult to understand). 解釋(密碼文字,潦草的筆跡,難懂的事物)。 **~·able** /dɪˈsaɪfrəbl ; dɪˈsaɪfərəbl/ *adj* that can be ~ed. 可解釋的;可闡明的。

de·ci·sion /dɪˈsɪʒn ; dɪˈsɪʒən/ *n* **1** [U] deciding; judging; [C] result of this; settlement of a question: 決定;判斷;問題的解決: *give a ~ on a case.* 判決一案件。 *Have they reached/come to/arrived at/taken/made a ~ yet?* 他們是否已有所決定? *His ~ to retire surprised all of us.* 他決定退休使我們大家都爲之一驚。 **2** [U] ability to decide and act accordingly; the quality of being decided(2): 決定及照決定行動的能力;堅定;決心;決斷: *A man who lacks ~* (=who hesitates, cannot decide questions) *cannot hold a position of responsibility.* 缺乏決斷力的人不能擔負重任。

de·cis·ive /dɪˈsaɪsɪv ; dɪˈsaɪsɪv/ *adj* **1** having a decided or definite outcome or result: 決定性的;有明確的結果的: *a ~ battle*, deciding which side wins the war. 一次決定性的戰役(決定那一方在整個戰爭中獲勝者)。 **2** showing decision(2); definite: 表示決心的;決定的;確定的: *He gave a ~ answer.* 他給了一個確定的回答。 **~·ly** *adv*

deck[1] /dek ; dɛk/ *n* **1** any of the floors of a ship, usu of wooden planks, in or above the hull: 船的甲板(通常係木板造,在船身的內部或上層): *My cabin is on E ~.* 我的艙位在E甲板。*Shall we go up on ~*, up (from a cabin, saloon, etc) on to the main (or promenade) ~? 我們(從艙中,大廳等)到主甲板(或散步甲板)上去好嗎? ⇨ the illus at ship. 參看 ship 之插圖。 ***clear the ~s***, ⇨ clear[3](1). **ˈ~ cabin**, one on an open ~, not one that is below the main ~. 甲板艙(主甲板以上的房艙)。 **ˈ~ chair**, collapsible chair of canvas, on a wooden or metal frame, used out of doors, eg in parks, the sea front, and on the ~s of ships. 用於戶外可折叠的帆布椅(有木或金屬架,例如用於公園,海濱,及輪船甲板上者)。 **ˈ~ hand**, member of a ship's crew who works on ~. 甲板上工作的海員。**ˈ~ officers**, the captain and mates (contrasted with the engineers). 艙面船員(指船長及大副,二副等,以別於輪機員)。**ˈ~ passenger**, one who does not use a cabin or the public rooms, but eats and sleeps on ~. 艙面乘客(不使用艙位或廳房而食宿均在甲板上者)。 **ˈ~ quoits** /kɔɪts ; kwɔɪts/, game played on a ~(1) in which a ring (*quoit*) is thrown. 甲板上玩的擲環套樁遊戲。 **2** any similar surface, eg the floor of a bus: 任何似甲板的一層(例如公共汽車的一層車廂): *the top ~ of a London bus.* 倫敦公共汽車的上層。 **3** (chiefly US) pack of playing-cards; (comm) collection of punched cards from a particular file. (主美)一副紙牌;(商)釘存文件中之一組卡片。**~·er** *n* (in compounds) having a specified number of ~s: (用於複合字中)有特定數目之甲板或層數的: *a three-~er ship;* 三層甲板的船; *a single-/double-~er bus;* 單(雙)層公共汽車; *a double-/triple-~er sandwich,* one with three/four layers of bread. 三(四)層的三明治。

deck[2] /dek ; dɛk/ *vt* [VP6A, 14, 15A] **1** ***~ (with/out in)***, decorate: 裝飾;點綴: *streets ~ed with flags.* 掛滿旗幟的街道。*She was ~ed out in her finest clothes.* 她穿着盛裝。 **2** cover, provide (a boat, ship) with a deck. 爲(船)裝甲板。

deckle-edged /ˌdekl ˈedʒd ; ˈdɛkl̩ˈɛdʒd/ *adj* (of some kinds of paper, eg hand-made notepaper) having untrimmed edges. (指某些紙,如手工製的信紙)毛邊的。

de·claim /dɪˈkleɪm ; dɪˈklem/ *vi, vt* **1** [VP2A, 3A] ***~ (against)***, speak with strong feeling; attack in words. 譴責;以言辭攻擊。 **2** [VP6A, 2A] speak in the manner of addressing an audience or reciting poetry; recite, eg a poem, rhetorically. 如演說或朗誦詩般說話;高聲演說;朗誦(詩歌等)。

dec·la·ma·tion /ˌdekləˈmeɪʃn ; ˌdɛkləˈmeʃən/ *n* [U] declaiming; [C] speech full of strong feeling; formal speech. 譴責;以言辭攻擊;激昂的演說;正式演說。 **de·clama·tory** /dɪˈklæmətərɪ *US:* -tɔːrɪ ; dɪˈklæməˌtorɪ/ *adj* of ~. 譴責的;演說的。

dec·lar·ation /ˌdekləˈreɪʃn ; ˌdɛkləˈreʃən/ *n* [U] declaring; [C] that which is declared: 宣布;宣言: *a ~ of war;* 宣戰; *the D~ of Independence*, that made by the N American colonies of Great Britain, on 4 July 1776, that they were politically independent; 獨立宣言(發表於1776年7月4日,英國的北美洲殖民地宣布獨立); *a ~ of income,* one (to be) made to the Inspector of Taxes. (向稅務稽查員所提出的)所得申報。

de·clare /dɪˈkleə(r) ; dɪˈklɛr/ *vt, vi* **1** [VP6A, 14, 25] make known clearly or formally; announce: 宣布;宣告;公告: *to ~ the results of an election.* 公告選舉結果。 *I ~ this meeting closed.* 我宣告散會。 ***~ (an innings closed),*** (cricket) (of the captain of the team) announce that the team will not continue batting although the innings is not finished: (板球)(指隊長)宣布該隊將不繼續擊球(雖然賽局未結束): *Australia ~d when the score reached 500.* 當積分達 500 分時,澳洲隊宣布不再繼續擊球。 ***~ trumps,*** (in bridge²) say which suit(5) will be played as trumps. (橋牌) 宣布王牌。 ***~ war (on/against),*** announce that a state of war exists. (對…)宣戰。 **2** [VP9, 25] say solemnly; say in order to show that one has no doubt: 鄭重地說;斷言;聲稱: *The accused man ~d that he was not guilty/~d himself innocent.* 被告人聲言他無罪(聲言他本人無罪)。 **3** [VP3A] ***~ for/against,*** say that one is/is not in favour of. 贊成(反對)。 **4** [VP6A] make a statement (to customs officials) of dutiable goods brought into a country, or (to a Tax Inspector) of one's income: (向海關官員)申報進口應納稅的貨物;(向稅務員)申報其收入額: *Have you anything to ~?* 你是否帶有應該報稅的東西? **5** (*int*) expressing surprise: (感嘆詞)表示驚愕: *Well, I ~!* 眞奇怪! **de·clar·able** /dɪˈkleərəbl ; dɪˈklɛrəbl/ *adj* that must be ~d(4). 必須申報納稅的。

de·class·ify /ˌdiːˈklæsɪfaɪ ; diˈklæsəˌfaɪ/ *vt* [VP6A] remove from a special class (esp sth hitherto secret): 公開(原屬祕密性的資料): *~ information concerning nuclear fission.* 公開原子分裂的秘密資料。 **de·class·ifi·ca·tion** /ˌdiːˌklæsɪfɪˈkeɪʃn ; ˈdiˌklæsəfəˈkeʃən/ *n*

de·clen·sion /dɪˈklenʃn ; dɪˈklɛnʃən/ *n* (gram) [U] varying the endings of *nouns, pronouns,* and *adjectives* according to their use in a sentence (eg in Latin), ⇨ case¹(3), decline¹(4); [C] class of words whose endings for different cases are alike. (文法) 名詞,代名詞及形容詞因其在句中(如拉丁文)之用法而生的字尾變化;各格字尾同形的一類字。

de·cli·na·tion /ˌdeklɪˈneɪʃn ; ˌdɛkləˈneʃən/ *n* deviation of the needle of a compass, E or W from the true north. 羅盤指針的偏差(卽偏東或偏西而非指正北);磁偏角。

de·cline¹ /dɪˈklaɪn ; dɪˈklaɪn/ *vt, vi* **1** [VP6A, 7A, 2A] say 'No' (to); refuse (sth offered): 辭謝;婉拒(邀請等);謝絕: *to ~ an invitation to dinner.* 辭謝吃飯的邀請。 *He ~d to discuss his plans with the newspaper men.* 他謝絕與新聞記者討論他的計畫。 **2** [VP2A, C] continue to become smaller, weaker, lower: 繼續變小,變弱,變低: *a declining birthrate;* 在下降中的出生率; *declining sales.* 銷售不景氣。 *His strength slowly ~d.* 他的體力漸衰。 *He spent his declining years* (= the years when, in old age, he was losing strength) *in the country.* 他在鄉間度過他的晚年。 **3** [VP2A] (of the sun) go down. (指太陽)落下。 **4** [VP6A] (gram) give the cases (ie the *declension*) of a word. (文法)列述(某字)之各種格位的字尾變化。⇨ case¹(3), inflect(1).

de·cline² /dɪˈklaɪn ; dɪˈklaɪn/ *n* [C] declining; gradual and continued loss of strength: 逐漸衰弱;衰落;衰敗: *the ~ of the Roman Empire;* 羅馬帝國的衰亡; *a ~ in prices/prosperity.* 物價的跌落(繁榮的逐漸衰退)。 ***fall into a ~,*** lose strength. 衰弱。 ***on the ~,*** declining. 衰落中;衰退中。

de·cliv·ity /dɪˈklɪvətɪ ; dɪˈklɪvətɪ/ *n* [C] (*pl* -ties) downward slope. 下傾的斜面。⇨ acclivity.

de·clutch /ˌdiːˈklʌtʃ ; diˈklʌtʃ/ *vi* [VP2A] disconnect the clutch (of a motor vehicle) in readiness for changing gear. 使(汽車)離合器分離以備更換排檔;放空檔。

de·code /ˌdiːˈkəʊd ; diˈkod/ *vt* [VP6A] decipher (sth written in code). 譯解(密碼文字)。⇨ encode. **de·coder** *n* (esp) device for translating data from one code to another. (尤指)翻譯密碼器(將一種密碼譯成另一種密碼的機器)。

de·coke /ˌdiːˈkəʊk ; diˈkok/ *vt* (colloq) (俗) = decarbonize.

dé·colleté /ˌdeɪˈkɒlteɪ *US:* -kɒlˈteɪ ; ˌdekɑlˈte/ *adj* (F) (of a gown, etc) leaving the neck and shoulders uncovered; (of a woman) wearing such a gown. (法)(指女子長服等)露出頸及肩部的;(指女人)穿著此種衣服的。

de·col·on·ize /ˌdiːˈkɒlənaɪz ; diˈkɑləˌnaɪz/ *vt* [VP6A] change from colonial to independent status. 使脫離殖民地的地位。 **de·col·on·iz·ation** /ˌdiːˌkɒlənaɪˈzeɪʃn *US:* -nɪˈz- ; ˌdiˌkɑlənəˈzeʃən/ *n*

de·com·pose /ˌdiːkəmˈpəʊz ; ˌdikəmˈpoz/ *vt, vi* **1** [VP6A] separate (a substance, light, etc) into its parts: 分解(物質,光線等)的成分: *A prism ~s light.* 三稜鏡可以分解光線。 **2** [VP6A, 2A] (cause to) become bad or rotten; decay. (使)腐爛。 **de·com·po·si·tion** /ˌdiːkɒmpəˈzɪʃn ; ˌdikɑmpəˈzɪʃən/ *n*

de·com·press /ˌdiːkəmˈpres ; ˌdikəmˈprɛs/ *vt* [VP6A] bring back (sb in compressed air, eg in a diving suit) to normal pressure; reduce compression in (sth). 解除(在壓縮空氣中,如潛水衣中,之人的)壓力;減低(某物)之壓力。 **de·com·pression** /ˌdiːkəmˈpreʃn ; ˌdikəmˈprɛʃən/ *n: a ~ion chamber.* 減壓室。

de·con·tami·nate /ˌdiːkənˈtæmɪneɪt ; ˌdikənˈtæməˌnet/ *vt* [VP6A] remove contamination from (eg what has been affected by poison-gas or radioactivity). 淨化;消毒(如感染毒氣或放射現象者)。 **de·con·tami·na·tion** /ˌdiːkənˌtæmɪˈneɪʃn ; ˌdikənˌtæməˈneʃən/ *n*

de·con·trol /ˌdiːkənˈtrəʊl ; ˌdikənˈtrol/ *vt* (-ll-) [VP6A] release from control (eg of trade by the Government during a war). 解除管制(如戰時政府對貿易的管制)。

dé·cor /ˈdeɪkɔː(r) *US:* deɪˈkɔːr ; deˈkɔr/ *n* all that makes up the general appearance, eg of a room or the stage of a theatre. 全部陳設(例如室內);(舞臺的)全套佈景。

dec·or·ate /ˈdekəreɪt ; ˈdɛkəˌret/ *vt* [VP6A, 14] **1** ***~ (with),*** put ornaments on; make (more) beautiful by placing adornments on or in: 裝飾;加裝飾品於…使之(更加)美麗: *to ~ a street with flags/the house with holly at Christmas.* 以旗幟裝飾街道(在聖誕節以冬青裝飾屋子)。 **2** paint, plaster, etc the outside of (a building); put paint, wallpaper, etc on the inside rooms of (a building). 塗油漆,灰泥等於(房屋)之外側;粉刷(房屋);油漆或糊紙於(室內牆壁);裝修(房屋)。 **3** ***~ (for),*** give (sb) a mark of distinction (eg a medal, an order): 授予(某人)殊榮(如獎章,勳位): *Several soldiers were ~d for bravery.* 數名士兵因英勇而獲獎。 **dec·or·ator** /-tə(r) ; -tə/ *n* workman who ~s(2): 裝飾房屋的工人;裝潢工人: *interior decorators.* 室內裝潢設計師。

dec·ora·tion /ˌdekəˈreɪʃn ; ˌdɛkəˈreʃən/ *n* **1** [U] decorating or being decorated. 裝飾。 **2** [C] sth used for decorating: 裝飾品: *Christmas ~s.* 聖誕節用的裝飾物品。 **3** [C] medal, ribbon, etc given and worn as an honour or award. (代表榮譽或獎勵的)獎章,勳綬等。

dec·or·ative /ˈdekərətɪv *US:* ˈdekəreɪtɪv ; ˈdɛkəˌretɪv/ *adj* suitable for decorating(1): 適於作裝飾品的;裝飾性的: *Holly, with its bright red berries, is very ~.* 冬青因有鮮紅的果子,極適於用作裝飾物。

dec·or·ous /ˈdekərəs ; ˈdɛkərəs/ *adj* polite; decent. 有禮貌的;高雅的。 **~·ly** *adv*

de·corum /dɪˈkɔːrəm ; dɪˈkɔrəm/ *n* **1** [U] right and proper behaviour, as required by social custom. 社會習俗所要求的正當而合禮的行爲;禮貌。 **2** (*pl*) requirements of polite society. (複)上流社會的禮節或慣例。

de·coy /ˈdiːkɔɪ ; dɪˈkɔɪ/ *n* **1** (real or imitation)

bird (eg a duck) or animal used to attract others so that they may be shot or caught; place designed for this purpose (eg a sheet of water with nets in which birds are trapped). 用以引誘別的鳥獸以便射殺或捕捉的眞鳥或假鳥(如野鴨),或眞動物或假動物;鳥媒;囮子;餌獸;誘捕鳥獸之預定場所(如設有捕禽鳥之網的水面)。**2** (fig) person or thing used to tempt sb into a position of danger. (喻)引誘某人使陷入險境的人或物。□ *vt* /dɪˈkɔɪ ; dɪˈkɔɪ/ [VP6A, 14] trick (sb or sth) into a place of danger by means of a ~: 以詭計引誘(某人或某物)使陷於危險的境地: *He had been ~ed across the frontier and arrested as a spy.* 他被引誘越過邊界,然後當做間諜被捕。

de·crease /dɪˈkri:s ; dɪˈkris/ *vt, vi* [VP6A, 2A] (cause to) become shorter, smaller, less: (使)縮短,變小,減少: *Your hunger ~s as you eat.* 你吃過東西以後就不餓了。*The population of the village has ~d by 150 to 500.* 該村的人口已減少 150, 只剩下 500人。□ *n* /ˈdi:kri:s ; ˈdikris/ [U] decreasing; [C] amount by which sth ~s: 減少;減少之量: *There has been a ~ in our imports this year.* 我們今年的輸入物品減少了。***on the ~,*** decreasing: 在減少中: *Is crime on the ~?* 犯罪案件是否在減少中?

de·cree /dɪˈkri: ; dɪˈkri/ *n* [C] **1** order given by a ruler or authority and having the force of a law: 君主或政府所下的具有法律效力的命令; 法令: *issue a ~;* 下令; *rule by ~.* 以法令統治。**2** judgement or decision of some law courts: 法院的判決: *a ~ of divorce.* 離婚判決。**~ nisi** /dɪˌkri: ˈnaɪsaɪ ; dɪˈkri ˈnaɪsaɪ/ *n* order for a divorce unless cause to the contrary is shown within a fixed period. 離婚之假判決;有條件的離婚判決(經一固定期間無異議方才執行)。□ *vt* [VP6A, 9] issue a ~; order by ~: 下令;發布命令: *It had been ~d that....* 業經下令…。*Fate ~d a surprise.* 命運註定一突然或意外之事。

de·crepit /dɪˈkrepɪt ; dɪˈkrɛpɪt/ *adj* made weak by old age or hard use: 老弱的; 衰老的: *a ~ horse.* 衰老的馬。**de·crepi·tude** /dɪˈkrepɪtju:d *US:* -tu:d ; dɪˈkrɛpɪtjud/ *n* [U] the state of being ~. 老弱;衰老。

de·cry /dɪˈkraɪ ; dɪˈkraɪ/ *vt* [VP6A] try, by speaking against sth, to make it seem less valuable, useful, etc; disapprove of. 責難;譴責;指出某事物的缺點以貶低其價值,效用等;不贊成。

dedi·cate /ˈdedɪkeɪt ; ˈdɛdəˌket/ *vt* [VP6A, 14] ~ ***(to),*** **1** give up, devote (one's time, energy, etc, to a noble cause or purpose): 奉獻;貢獻(時間,精力等以從事崇高的事業或目的): *He ~d his life to the service of his country.* 他獻身爲國服務。**2** devote with solemn ceremonies (to God, to a sacred use). 舉行莊嚴的儀式以奉獻(給神,作神聖的用途)。**3** (of an author) write (or print) a person's name at the beginning of a book (to show gratitude or friendship to). (指作者)將某人的名字寫或印在書的前端(以表示感謝或友誼)。**dedi·ca·tion** /ˌdedɪˈkeɪʃn ; ˌdɛdəˈkeʃən/ *n* [U] dedicating: 奉獻;貢獻: *the dedication of a church;* 教堂的奉獻; [C] words used in dedicating a book. 將一本書題獻某人所用的字句;題獻辭。

de·duce /dɪˈdju:s *US:* dɪˈdu:s ; dɪˈdjus/ *vt* [VP6A, 14, 9] ~ ***(from),*** arrive at (knowledge, a theory, etc) by reasoning; reach a conclusion: (根據事實)推理;推想;演繹出(知識,學說等);獲致結論: *If you saw a doctor leaving a house, you might ~ the fact that someone in the house was ill.* 假如你看見一個醫生離開一個人家,你就可以推想那家裡有人生病。

de·duct /dɪˈdʌkt ; dɪˈdʌkt/ *vt* [VP6A, 14] take away (an amount or part). 扣除;減除(一個數量或部分)。⇨ subtract for numbers. (數字的減除用subtract)。**~·ible** /dɪˈdʌktəbl ; dɪˈdʌktəbl̩/ *adj* that may be ~ed. 可扣除的;可減除的。

de·duc·tion /dɪˈdʌkʃn ; dɪˈdʌkʃən/ *n* **1** [U] deducting; [C] amount deducted: 扣除;扣除之量: *~s from pay for insurance and pension.* 自薪金中所扣除的保險費及退休金。**2** [U] deducing; [C] conclusion reached by reasoning from general laws to a particular case. 推論;演繹法;由一般法則推演到特殊事例所獲的結論。**de·duct·ive** /dɪˈdʌktɪv ; dɪˈdʌktɪv/ *adj* of, using, reasoning by, ~(2). 推論的;推斷的;用演繹法的。

deed /di:d ; did/ *n* **1** sth done; act: 所做的事;行爲;行動: *to be rewarded for one's good ~s.* 因所做的善事而得到報酬。*D~s are better than words when people are in need of help.* 當有人需要救助的時候,行動勝於言語。**2** (legal) written or printed signed agreement, esp about ownership or rights. (法律)(證明所有權或其他權力的)證書;契據。**ˌ~ of ˈcovenant,** ⇨ covenant(1). **ˈ~-box** *n* one in which legal ~s are stored. 契據箱。**ˈ~·poll** *n* legal ~ made by one person only. 一人立的契據。

deem /di:m ; dim/ *vt* [VP9, 25] (formal) believe; consider: (正式用語)相信;認爲: *He ~ed that it was/~ed it his duty to help.* 他認爲助人是他的責任。

deep¹ /di:p ; dip/ *adj* **1** going a long way down from the top: 深的: *a ~ well/river.* 深井(河)。⇨ shallow. **ˈ~-ˌsea, ˈ~-ˌwater,** *attrib adjj,* of the deeper parts of the sea, away from the coastal water: 深海的;遠離海岸的: *~-sea fishing.* 深海捕魚。***go (in) off the ˈ~ end,*** ⇨ end¹(1). ***in ~ water(s),*** (fig) in great difficulties, etc. (喻)在困境中。**2** going a long way from the surface or edge: 深長的: *a ~ shelf;* 深的板架; *a ~ wound;* 深的傷口; *a huge, ~-chested wrestler.* 一個高大而且胸部很厚的摔角家。**3** placed or extending down, back or in (with words to indicate extent): 置於深處的;縱深的(與表示程度的字連用): *a hole two feet ~;* 兩呎深的洞; *with his hands ~ in his pockets;* 兩手深藏在口袋裡; *water six feet ~;* 六呎深的水; *ankle-~ in mud;* 泥深及踝; *to be ~ in debt;* 深陷於債務中;債臺高築; *a plot of land 100 feet ~,* ie going back this distance from a street, road or other frontage. 縱深達一百呎的一塊土地(即自街道,馬路或其他前沿算起)。*The people were standing twenty ~ to see the Queen go past.* 民衆一層層站立共達二十層以觀看女王經過。**4** (of sounds) low: (指聲音)低沉的: *in a ~ voice;* 以低沉的聲調; *the ~ notes of a cello.* 大提琴之低沉的音調。**5** (of sleep) profound: (指睡眠)酣: *in a ~ sleep,* from which one is not easily awakened. 在酣睡中。**6** (of colours) strong; intense: (指顏色)深濃的: *a ~ red.* 深紅色。**7** brought from far down: 自深處發出來的: *a ~ sigh;* 深長的嘆息; strongly felt; coming from the heart: 强烈地感到的;來自內心的: *~ sorrow/feelings/sympathy.* 內心深處所感到的哀傷(感情,同情)。**8** ~ ***in,*** absorbed in; having all one's attention centred on: 專心的;全神貫注的: *~ in thought/study/a book.* 專心於思想(研究,一本書)。**9** (fig) difficult to understand or learn about: (喻)深奧的;難懂的;難瞭解的: *a ~ mystery;* 難瞭解的神秘事物; *a ~ secret;* 難瞭解的秘密; (of a person) artful; concealing his real feelings, motives, etc: (指人)詭計多端的;不使感情,動機等表露於外的: *He's a ~ one.* 他是個詭計多端的人。**10** (fig) going far; not superficial: (喻)深入的;不膚淺的: *~ learning;* 深奧的學問; *a man with ~ insight;* 具有深遠之見解的人; *a ~ thinker.* 深入的思想家。**~en** /ˈdi:pən ; ˈdipən/ *vt, vi* make or become ~. (使)變深。**~·ly** *adv* far; profoundly; intensely: 深遠地;深入地;深刻地;深厚地: *to bite ~ly;* 咬得很深; *He is ~ly interested in the subject.* 他對此門學科有濃厚的興趣。*She felt her mother's death ~ly.* 她對她母親的去世內心深感悲傷。**~·ness** *n*

deep² /di:p ; dip/ *adv* far down or in: 深深地: *We had to dig ~ to find water.* 我們必須挖得很深才能發現水。*He went on studying ~ into the night.* 他繼續讀到深夜。***Still waters run ~,*** (prov) said of a person whose real feelings, ideas, etc are not openly displayed. (諺)靜水流深;大智若愚;沈默者深謀(指感情,學識等不露於外的人)。**ˌ~-ˈfreeze** *vt* freeze (food) quickly in order to preserve it for long periods: 迅速冷凍(食物)以便長期保藏之;冷藏: *~-frozen fish.* 冷藏的魚。□ *n* special type of refrigerator (or a special part of an ordinary refrigerator) used for this purpose: 特別用於冷藏的電冰箱;普通電冰箱中之冷藏室: *put surplus fruit and vegetables in the ~-freeze.* 將剩餘的水果和蔬菜放在冷藏室中。ˌ~-ˈ**laid,** (of schemes, etc) secretly and carefully planned. (指方案等) 秘密而仔細計畫的。ˌ~-ˈ**mined,** (of coal) from ordinary coal-mines (contrasted with *open-cast;* ⇨ open¹(11)). (指煤)自普通煤礦坑中開採出來的(與 open-cast 相對)。ˌ~-ˈ**rooted,** not easily removed: 根深蒂固的;不易除去的: *his ~-rooted dislike of hard work.* 他對艱難工作根深蒂固的厭惡。ˌ~-ˈ**seated,** firmly established: 基礎鞏固的;根源深的: *The causes of the trouble are ~-seated.* 這毛病的根源很深。

D

deep³ /diːp ; dip/ *n* (poet) (詩) **the ~,** the sea. 海。

deer /dɪə(r) ; dɪr/ *n* (*pl* unchanged) (kinds of) graceful, quick-running animal, the male of which has horns. (複數不變) 鹿 (外形優雅,善跑,雄者有角)。⇨ the illus at large. 參看 large 之插圖。ˈ~**-skin,** (leather made of) ~'s skin. 鹿皮(革)。ˈ~**-stalker, (a)** sportsman who stalks ~. 以埋伏或偷襲法獵鹿者。**(b)** cloth cap with two peaks, one in front and the other behind. 有兩個遮簷(一在前,一在後)的布帽。ˈ~**-stalking,** sport of hunting ~ by approaching them stealthily or from concealment. 埋伏或偷襲獵鹿法。

de-esca·late /ˌdiːˈeskəleɪt ; diˈɛskəˌlet/ *vt* [VP6A] decrease the area or intensity of, eg a war. 減少(戰爭等)之區域或强度。 **de-esca·la·tion** /diːˌeskəˈleɪʃn ; diˌɛskəˈleʃən/ *n*

de·face /dɪˈfeɪs ; dɪˈfes/ *vt* [VP6A] spoil the appearance of (by marking or damaging the surface of); make engraved lettering (eg on a tombstone) illegible. 汚損或毀傷…的外表;使(墓碑等的)碑文不易辨認。~**·ment** *n* [U] defacing or being ~d; [C] sth that ~s. (被)毀損外表;毀損外表之物。

de facto /ˌdeɪ ˈfæktəʊ ; dɪˈfækto/ *adj, adv* (Lat) in fact, whether by right (*de jure*) or not: (拉丁) 事實上(的);實際上(不論合法與否)(的): *the ~ king.* 實際的國王。

de·fal·ca·tion /ˌdiːfælˈkeɪʃn ; ˌdifælˈkeʃən/ *n* [U] (legal) misappropriation of money entrusted to one; [C] instance of this; amount of money misappropriated. (法律) 挪用公款或委託金;所挪用的錢數。

de·fame /dɪˈfeɪm ; dɪˈfem/ *vt* [VP6A] attack the good reputation of; say evil things about. 破壞名譽;誹謗;中傷。**defa·ma·tion** /ˌdefəˈmeɪʃn ; ˌdɛfəˈmeʃən/ *n* [U] defaming or being ~d; harm done to sb's reputation. 誹謗;中傷;某人名譽所受的傷害。 **de·fama·tory** /dɪˈfæmətrɪ *US:* -tɔːrɪ ; dɪˈfæməˌtorɪ/ *adj* intended to ~: 以誹謗爲目的的: *defamatory statements.* 誹謗他人名譽的話。

de·fault¹ /dɪˈfɔːlt ; dɪˈfɔlt/ *n* [U] failure to act: 不負責;不到場;不還債: *to win a case／a game by ~,* because the other party／team／player does not appear. 因對方不到庭而勝訴 (不到場而贏得比賽)。***in ~ of,*** in the absence of; if (sth) is not to be obtained, does not take place, etc. 因爲沒有或缺乏…;倘若(某物)未獲得,未發生等。

de·fault² /dɪˈfɔːlt ; dɪˈfɔlt/ *vi* [VP2A] fail to perform a duty, or to appear (eg in a law court) when required to do so, or to pay a debt. 不負責;不到場;不到法庭應訊;不還債。~**er** *n* **1** person who ~s. 不負責,不到場或不還債者。**2** soldier guilty of a military offence. 觸犯軍紀的軍人。

de·feat /dɪˈfiːt ; dɪˈfit/ *vt* [VP6A] **1** overcome; win a victory over: 擊敗;勝過: *They were ~ed in their attempt to reach the top of the mountain.* 他們達到山巔的企圖未成功。 **2** bring to nothing; make useless; cause to fail: 使幻滅;使無用;使失敗: *Our hopes were ~ed.* 我們的希望幻滅了。□ *n* [U] ~ing or being ~ed: 擊敗;失敗: *a baseball team that has not yet suffered ~;* 還沒有輸過的棒球隊; [C] instance of this: 失敗的實例: *six victories and two ~s.* 六勝二敗。~**·ism** /-ɪzəm ; -ɪzəm/ *n* [U] attitude, conduct, use of arguments, based on expectations of ~. 失敗論;失敗主義(預期前途將失敗的態度,行爲,言論)。~**·ist** *n* person with such an attitude, etc. 失敗論者;失敗主義者。

de·fe·cate /ˈdefəkeɪt ; ˈdɛfəˌket/ *vi* [VP2A] (med) empty the bowels. (醫)通便。**def·eca·tion** /ˌdefəˈkeɪʃn ; ˌdɛfəˈkeʃən/ *n*

de·fect¹ /ˈdiːfekt ; dɪˈfɛkt/ *n* [C] fault; imperfection; shortcoming; sth lacking in completeness or perfection: 缺點; 短處; 美中不足: *~s in a system of education.* 教育制度上的缺點。

de·fect² /dɪˈfekt ; dɪˈfɛkt/ *vi* [VP2A, C, 3A] ~ ***(from) (to),*** desert one's country, one's allegiance, etc: 背叛;變節: *the soldier who ~ed from Ruritania to Lilliput,* eg by asking for political asylum. 從理想國投奔小人國的士兵(例如以求政治庇護)。**de·fec·tor** /-tə(r) ; -tɚ/ *n* person who ~s: 背叛者;變節者: *~ors from the Republican Party.* 背叛共和黨者。

de·fec·tion /dɪˈfekʃn ; dɪˈfɛkʃən/ *n* [U] falling away from loyalty to a political party (or its leader), religion or duty; [C] instance of this: 背叛政黨(或政黨領袖);脫黨;叛教;變節: *~s from the Socialist Party.* 自社會黨脫黨的事件。

de·fec·tive /dɪˈfektɪv ; dɪˈfɛktɪv/ *adj* having a defect or defects; imperfect: 有缺點的;不完善的: *~ in workmanship／moral sense;* 技藝(道德感)不高的; *mentally ~,* mentally subnormal; 低能的; *a ~ verb,* eg *must.* 變化不完全的動詞(例如 must)。~**·ly** *adv* ~**·ness** *n*

de·fence (US = **de·fense**) /dɪˈfens ; dɪˈfɛns/ *n* **1** [U] defending from attack; fighting against attack: 防禦;防衛;保衛戰: *money needed for national ~;* 國防所需要的經費; *to fight in ~ of one's country;* 爲保衛祖國而戰; *weapons of offence and ~* 攻擊與防衛的武器。*I never fight except in self-~.* 我除了自衞以外決不言戰。 **2** [C] sth used for defending or protecting; means of defending: 防禦物;防禦設備: *coastal ~s,* against attacks from the sea. 沿海防禦工事。*People used to build strong walls round their towns as a ~ against enemies.* 人們從前在城鎮四周築堅固 城牆以抵禦敵人。 *A thick overcoat is a good ~ against the cold.* 一件厚大衣足以禦寒。 **3** [C, U] (legal) argument(s) used to contest an accusation; the lawyer(s) acting for an accused person: (法律)被告人的答辯;被告人的辯護律師: *The accused man made no ~.* 被告未作答辯。*Counsel for the ~ put in a plea for mercy.* 被告人的辯護律師遞狀請求從輕處刑。*Counsel worked out a very convincing ~.* 辯護律師完成一甚有說服力的答辯。~**·less** *adj* having no ~; unable to defend oneself. 無防衛的;未設防的;不能自衛的。 ~**·less·ly** *adv* ~**·less·ness** *n*

de·fend /dɪˈfend ; dɪˈfɛnd/ *vt* [VP6A, 14] **1** ~ ***(against／from),*** guard; protect; make safe: 保護;防禦;保衛: *to ~ one's country against enemies;* 保衛祖國抵禦敵人; *to ~ sb from harm.* 保護某人使不受傷害。 *When the dog attacked me, I ~ed myself with a stick.* 當那狗向我攻擊時,我以手杖自衛。 **2** speak or write in support of: 以言語或文字替…辯護: ~ (= uphold) *a claim;* 支持一要求; ~ (= contest) *a lawsuit.* 爲一訴訟辯護。*He made a long speech ~ing his ideas.* 他發表一長篇的演說爲他的見解辯護。*You will need lawyers to ~ you.* 你將需要律師爲你辯護。~**er** *n* **1** person who ~s. 辯護者;保衛者。Note legal term at defence(3). 注意 defence(3) 的法律名詞。 **2** (in sport, eg football) player who guards his goal area against attacks from the other side. (足球等運動)守門;防守者。

de·fend·ant /dɪˈfendənt ; dɪˈfɛndənt/ *n* person against whom a legal action is brought. 被告;被告人。⇨ plaintiff.

de·fense /dɪˈfens ; dɪˈfɛns/ (US) ⇨ defence.

de·fens·ible /dɪˈfensəbl ; dɪˈfɛnsəbḷ/ *adj* able to be defended. 可保衛的;可防禦的;可辯護的。

de·fens·ive /dɪˈfensɪv ; dɪˈfɛnsɪv/ *adj* used for, intended for, defending: 防禦用的;防禦性的: *~ warfare/measures.* 防禦戰(措施)。*Whether a gun is a ~ or an offensive weapon may depend upon whether you're behind it or in front of it.* 大砲是防禦性武器還是攻擊性武器,可以根據你是在它的後面,還是在它的前面而定。□ *n* (usu 通常作) ***be/act on the ~***, be in a state/act from a position of defence. 處於防禦的狀態;採取守勢。**~·ly** *adv*

de·fer[1] /dɪˈfɜː(r) ; dɪˈfɝ/ *vt* (-rr-) [VP6A, C] put off to a later time; postpone: 延緩;展期: *a ~red telegram,* one sent later at a cheaper rate; 緩發電報(費用較低者); *a ~red annuity;* 緩發的年金; *to ~ one's departure for a week;* 延緩一星期離開; *to ~ making a decision;* 暫緩作決定; *payment on ~red terms,* ie by instalments after purchase. 分期付款。⇨ *on hirepurchase* at hire. **~·ment** *n*

de·fer[2] /dɪˈfɜː(r) ; dɪˈfɝ/ *vi* (-rr-) [VP3A] **~ *to***, give way; yield (often to show respect): 服從;順從(常表示尊敬): *to ~ to one's elders/to sb's opinions.* 順從長上(某人的意見)。

de·fer·ence /ˈdefərəns ; ˈdɛfərəns/ *n* [U] giving way to the wishes, accepting the opinions or judgements, of another or others; respect: 順從他人的意願;接受他人的意見或判斷;尊重: *to treat one's elders with ~;* 以恭順的態度對待長上; *to show ~ to a judge.* 對法官表示尊重。***in ~ to***, out of respect for. 尊重。**de·fer·en·tial** /ˌdefəˈrenʃl ; ˌdɛfəˈrɛnʃəl/ *adj* showing ~. 表示順從或尊重的。**de·fer·en·tially** /-ʃəlɪ ; -ʃəlɪ/ *adv*

de·fiance /dɪˈfaɪəns ; dɪˈfaɪəns/ *n* [U] open disobedience or resistance; refusal to recognize authority; defying. 公然反抗;蔑視權威;不顧;不尊重。***in ~ of***, showing contempt of or indifference to: 表示蔑視或不顧的: *to act in ~ of orders,* do sth one has been ordered not to do. 行動違抗命令。*He went swimming in the sea in ~ of the warning sign telling him not to.* 他不顧警告標誌而到那海中游泳。***bid ~ to***, challenge, offer to fight. 向…挑戰。***set sth at ~***, treat with contempt; challenge: 蔑視;挑戰: *If you set the law/public opinion at ~, you'll get into trouble.* 如果你蔑視法律(輿論),你將招致麻煩。

de·fiant /dɪˈfaɪənt ; dɪˈfaɪənt/ *adj* showing defiance; openly disobedient. 表示違抗的;公然不服從的。**~·ly** *adv*

de·fi·ciency /dɪˈfɪʃnsɪ ; dɪˈfɪʃənsɪ/ *n* (*pl* -cies) **1** [U] the state of being short of, less than, what is correct or needed; [C] instance of this: 缺乏;不足(正確或所需之數): *suffering from a ~ of food;* 受到食物不足的痛苦; *~ diseases,* caused by a ~ of sth, eg vitamins, in diet. 因食物中缺乏維他命等所引起的病症。 **2** [C] amount by which sth is short of what is correct or needed: 不足之數量(與正確或所需之數量間的差額): *a ~ of £5.* 短少五鎊。 **3** [C] sth imperfect: 缺點;不完美之處;缺陷: *Cosmetics do not always cover up the deficiencies of nature.* 化粧品有時亦不能遮蓋天生的缺陷。

de·fi·cient /dɪˈfɪʃnt ; dɪˈfɪʃənt/ *adj* not having enough of: 沒有足夠的;缺乏的: *~ in courage,* 缺乏勇氣的; *a mentally ~ person,* one who is mentally subnormal. 低能的人。

defi·cit /ˈdefɪsɪt ; ˈdɛfəsɪt/ *n* [C] amount by which sth, esp a sum of money, is too small; amount by which payments exceed receipts. (尤指錢款之)不足額;收支不平衡之數;虧絀;赤字。⇨ surplus.

de·file[1] /dɪˈfaɪl ; dɪˈfaɪl/ *vt* [VP6A] make dirty or impure: 弄髒;使不純潔: *rivers ~d by waste from factories.* 被工廠廢物所污染的河流。**~·ment** *n* [U] defiling or being ~d; pollution. 污染;玷污;(使)不潔。

de·file[2] /ˈdiːfaɪl ; dɪˈfaɪl/ *n* narrow way, gorge, through mountains. 山中的峽道;隘路。□ *vi* /dɪˈfaɪl ; dɪˈfaɪl/ (of troops) march in a single file or a narrow column. (指軍隊)成單行或縱隊行進。

de·fine /dɪˈfaɪn ; dɪˈfaɪn/ *vt* [VP6A] **1** state precisely the meaning of (eg words). 精確地解釋(字等)的意義;下定義。 **2** state or show clearly: 敘述明白;詳細說明;示明: *Please listen while I ~ your duties.* 請聽我詳細說明你的職務。*The powers of a judge are ~d by law.* 法官的權力法律有明文規定。*When boundaries between countries are not clearly ~d, there is usually trouble.* 國與國間的國界未明白劃定時,通常會發生糾紛。*The mountain was clearly ~d against the eastern sky.* 那山在東方天際的襯托下顯得輪廓分明。**de·fin·able** /-əbl ; -əbḷ/ *adj* that can be ~d. 可釋明其意義的;可下定義的;可詳細說明的。

defi·nite /ˈdefɪnət ; ˈdɛfənɪt/ *adj* clear; not doubtful or uncertain: 明白的;確定的;無疑的: *I want a ~ answer: 'Yes' or 'No'.* 我要一個明確的回答:'是'或'否'。*I want an appointment for a ~ time and place.* 我要一個有確定的時間和地點的約會。**~ 'article** *n* the word 'the'. 定冠詞(即 the)。**~·ly** /ˈdefɪnətlɪ ; ˈdɛfənɪtlɪ/ *adv* **1** in a ~ manner. 明確地;確切地。 **2** (colloq, in answer to a question) yes, certainly. (俗,用於回答問題)是的,一點不錯。

defi·ni·tion /ˌdefɪˈnɪʃn ; ˌdɛfəˈnɪʃən/ *n* **1** [U] defining; [C] statement that defines: 闡明;定義;界說: *To give a ~ of a word is more difficult than to give an illustration of its uses.* 給一個字下定義,較之舉例說明它的用法爲難。 **2** [U] clearness of outline; making or being distinct in outline; power of a lens (in a camera or telescope) to show clear outlines. 輪廓清楚;(使)輪廓鮮明;(照相機或望遠鏡中)透鏡之清晰度。

de·fini·tive /dɪˈfɪnətɪv ; dɪˈfɪnətɪv/ *adj* final; to be looked upon as decisive and without the need for, or possibility of, change or addition: 最後的;被認爲決定性的(而不需要或不可能加以改變或增添的): *a ~ offer/answer/edition of sb's poetry.* 最後的提議(明確的回答;某人之詩集的確定的版本)。

de·flate /dɪˈfleɪt ; dɪˈflet/ *vt* [VP6A] **1** make (a tyre, balloon, etc) smaller by letting out air or gas; (fig) lessen the conceit of: 放出(輪胎,氣球等)中的空氣或氣體;(喻)挫…之傲氣: *~ a pompous politician.* 挫一自大的政客的傲氣。 **2** /ˌdiːˈfleɪt ; dɪˈflet/ take action to reduce the amount of money in circulation in order to lower or keep steady the prices of salable goods. 採取行動緊縮通貨以降低或穩定物價。**de·fla·tion** /-eɪʃn ; -eʃən/ *n* [U] the action of deflating. 放出空氣;緊縮通貨以穩定物價。**de·fla·tion·ary** /ˌdiːˈfleɪʃnərɪ *US:* -nerɪ ; dɪˈfleʃənˌɛrɪ/ *adj* produced, designed or tending to produce monetary deflation: 用以緊縮通貨以降低或穩定物價的: *deflationary measures applied by the Chancellor.* 首相所採取的緊縮通貨以穩定物價的措施。⇨ inflate.

de·flect /dɪˈflekt ; dɪˈflɛkt/ *vt, vi* [VP6A, 14, 2A, 3A] **~ *(from)***, (cause to) turn aside (from): (使)偏斜;(使)轉向: *The bullet struck a wall and was ~ed from its course.* 那槍彈擊中牆壁,因而偏斜了。**de·flec·tion** /dɪˈflekʃn ; dɪˈflɛkʃən/ *n*

de·flower /diːˈflaʊə(r) ; dɪˈflaʊɚ/ *vt* (liter or old use) deprive of virginity; ravage; spoil. (文學或舊用法)奪去…的童貞;蹂躪;糟塌。

de·foli·ate /ˌdiːˈfəʊlɪeɪt ; dɪˈfolɪˌet/ *vt* [VP6A] destroy the leaves of: 毀去…的葉: *forests ~d by chemical means.* 用化學方法除去樹葉的森林。**de·foli·ation** /ˌdiːfəʊlɪˈeɪʃn ; dɪˌfolɪˈeʃən/ *n* **de·foli·ant** /ˌdiːˈfəʊlɪənt ; dɪˈfolɪənt/ *n* chemical used, eg by spraying, on vegetation to destroy the leaves. 用以毀去草木之葉的化學藥品(例如噴射劑)。

de·for·est /ˌdiːˈfɒrɪst *US:* -ˈfɔːr- ; dɪˈfɔrɪst/ *vt* (esp US) (尤美) = disafforest.

de·form /dɪˈfɔːm ; dɪˈfɔrm/ *vt* [VP6A] spoil the form or appearance of; put out of shape. 破壞…的外形或外表;使不成形;使成畸形。**de·formed** *part adj* (of the body, or a part of it; fig, of the mind) badly shaped; unnaturally shaped: (指身體或其一部;

喻，指心理)畸形的；形狀不自然的；不正常的：*The boy has a ~ed foot and cannot play games.* 那孩子有一隻腳畸形，不能玩遊戲。

de·form·ity /dɪˈfɔːmətɪ ; dɪˈfɔrmətɪ/ *n* [U] being deformed; [C] (*pl* -ties) deformed part (esp of the body). 畸形；(尤指身體的)畸形部份。

de·fraud /dɪˈfrɔːd ; dɪˈfrɔd/ *vt* [VP6A, 14] ~ ***(of)***, trick (sb) out of what is rightly his; get by fraud: 騙取(某人)的所有物；以騙術得到：~ *an author of his royalties by ignoring copyright.* 由漠視版權而騙得作者的版稅。

de·fray /dɪˈfreɪ ; dɪˈfre/ *vt* [VP6A] supply the money needed for sth; pay (the cost or expenses of sth). 供給爲某事所需要的錢；付給；支付(某事物的費用)。**~al** /dɪˈfreɪəl ; dɪˈfreəl/ *n* **~·ment** *n*

de·frock /ˌdiːˈfrɒk ; diˈfrɑk/ *vt* = unfrock.

de·frost /ˌdiːˈfrɒst *US:* ˌdiːˈfrɔːst ; diˈfrɔst/ *vt* [VP6A] remove, get rid of, ice or frost (eg in a refrigerator, on the windscreen of a motor-car). 除去(電冰箱中的，或汽車擋風玻璃上的)冰霜；除霜。**~er** *n* device that ~s. 除霜器；除霜裝置。

deft /deft ; dɛft/ *adj* quick and clever (esp with the fingers). (尤指用手指)敏捷的；靈巧的。**~·ly** *adv* **~·ness** *n*

de·funct /dɪˈfʌŋkt ; dɪˈfʌŋkt/ *adj* (of persons) dead; (of things, eg laws) extinct. (指人)死的；(指事物，如法律)廢絕的。**the ~**, (legal) the dead person (who is being discussed). (法律)(被討論中的)死者。

de·fuse /ˌdiːˈfjuːz ; diˈfjuz/ *vt* [VP6A] remove or render useless the fuse of, eg an unexploded bomb or shell; (fig) make calm; reduce the tension in: 拆除或毀去(未爆炸的炸彈或砲彈的)信管；(喻)使鎭定；減除緊張或不安：~ *a situation/crisis.* 減少一局勢(危機)之緊張。

defy /dɪˈfaɪ ; dɪˈfaɪ/ *vt* (*pt, pp* -fied) **1** [VP6A] resist openly; say that one is ready to fight. 公然反抗；聲言不惜以武力相對。**2** [VP6A] refuse to obey or show respect to: 不服從；不尊重；違抗：~*ing one's superiors.* 違抗長上。*If you ~ the law, you may find yourself in prison.* 如果你不服從法律，你就可能會坐牢。**3** [VP6A] offer difficulties that cannot be overcome: 有無法克服的困難：*The problem defied solution,* could not be solved. 這問題不能解決。*The door defied all attempts to open it.* 這門無論如何打不開。**4** [VP17] ~ ***sb to do sth***, call on sb to do sth that one believes he cannot or will not do: 挑激某人做某事(即相信他做不到或不願做)：*I ~ you to prove that I have cheated.* 我敢說你不能證明我曾欺騙。⇨ defiance.

de·gauss /ˌdiːˈgaʊs ; dɪˈgaʊs/ *vt* [VP6A] neutralize the magnetic field of, eg a TV screen. 中和…之磁場(例如電視之螢光幕)。

de·gen·er·ate /dɪˈdʒenəreɪt ; dɪˈdʒɛnəˌret/ *vi* [VP2A, 3A] ~ ***(into)***, pass from a state of goodness to a lower state by losing qualities which are considered normal and desirable: (由於失去被認爲是正常和優良的特質而)退步；墮落；腐化；惡化：*Thrift is desirable, but do not let it ~ into avarice.* 節儉是好的，但不要使它變成貪財。*He denied that the young men of toady were degenerating,* eg that they were becoming less hard-working, less intelligent, less honest, than those of earlier times. 他否認這一代的年輕人不如上一代(例如不如他們上一代努力、聰明、誠實)。□ *adj* /dɪˈdʒenərət ; dɪˈdʒɛnərɪt/ having lost qualities (physical, moral or mental) that are considered normal and desirable: 失去原有正常和良好之特質的(指身體、道德或心理上的)；退步的；墮落的；腐化的：*He didn't let riches and luxury make him ~.* 他並沒有讓財富及奢侈使他墮落。□ *n* /dɪˈdʒenərət ; dɪˈdʒɛnərɪt/ ~ person or animal. 退步的人；退化的動物。**de·gen·er·acy** /dɪˈdʒenərəsɪ ; dɪˈdʒɛnərəsɪ/ *n* [U] state or condition of being ~; process of degenerating. 退化；墮落；退步的過程。**de·gen·er·ation** /dɪˌdʒenəˈreɪʃn ; dɪˌdʒɛnəˈreʃən/ *n* [U] degenerating; the state of being ~d. 退化；墮落；腐化；惡化。

de·grade /dɪˈgreɪd ; dɪˈgred/ *vt* [VP6A] **1** reduce in rank or status. 降…的階級或職位。**2** cause (sb) to be less moral or less deserving of respect: 使(某人)道德墮落或不值得尊敬：*to ~ oneself by cheating and telling lies.* 因欺騙說謊而自甘墮落。**degra·da·tion** /ˌdegrəˈdeɪʃn ; ˌdɛgrəˈdeʃən/ *n* [U] degrading or being ~d: 降級；墮落：*a family living in degradation,* eg one that lives in slum conditions. 生活潦倒的家庭(如生活於貧苦的環境中者)。

de·gree /dɪˈgriː ; dɪˈgri/ *n* **1** unit of measurement for angles: 度(角的單位)：*an angle of ninety ~s,* (90°) a right angle; 90 度的角(卽直角)；*a ~ of latitude,* about 69 miles. 緯度的一度(約 69 哩)。**2** unit of measurement for temperature: 度(溫度的單位)：*Water freezes at 32 ~s Fahrenheit* (32°F) *or zero* (= *nought ~s*) *Centigrade* (0°C). 水在華氏 32 度或攝氏零度結冰。**3** [C, U] step or stage in a scale or process: 階段；程度：*The boys show various ~s of skill in their use of carpentry tools.* 孩子們對於木工用具的使用能力各有不同。*His work has reached a high ~ of excellence.* 他的作品已達爐火純青之境。*He was not in the slightest ~ interested,* was completely uninterested. 他絲毫不感覺興趣。***by ~s***, step by step; gradually: 一步一步地；逐漸地：*Their friendship by ~s grew into love.* 他們的友誼逐漸成長爲愛情。***to a ~***, (colloq) = to the highest ~: (俗)非常：*He is scrupulous to a ~.* 他非常謹愼。***to a high/the highest ~***, intensively; exceedingly: 非常；極：*He is vain to a high ~.* 他非常愛虛榮。***to what ~***, to what extent; how much: 達於何種程度；如何：*To what ~ are you interested in botany?* 你對於植物學的興趣達到何種程度？***first ~***, stage of seriousness: 嚴重階段：*first ~ burns;* 第一度灼傷；*first ~ murder.* 一級謀殺。***third ~***, severe and long examination (eg by the police) of an accused man to get information or a confession: 爲求犯人供白所作嚴厲而長時間的審問；刑求逼供；拷問：*Are third-~ methods used in your country?* 貴國使用刑求嗎？**4** [U] position in society: 社會地位：*persons of high ~.* 社會地位高的人。**5** academic title; rank or grade given by a university to one who has passed an examination: (大學授予通過考試者的)學位：*studying for a ~;* 讀學位；*the ~ of Master of Arts* (MA). 文學碩士。⇨ graduate, undergraduate. **6** (music) interval from one note to another on a stave. (音樂)階；音度。**7** (gram) one of the three forms of comparison of an *adj* or *adv*: (文法)形容詞或副詞比較的三種級之一：*~s of comparison.* 表示比較的各種級。*'Good', 'better' and 'best' are the positive, comparative and superlative ~s of 'good'.* good, better 及 best 是 good 的原級，比較級及最高級。*'Rich', 'richer' and 'richest' are the positive, comparative and superlative ~s of 'rich'.* rich, richer 及 richest 是 rich 的原級，比較級及最高級。

de·horn /ˌdiː ˈhɔːn ; diˈhɔrn/ *vt* [VP6A] remove the horns from (cattle). 除去(牛)的角。

de·hu·man·ize /ˌdiːˈhjuːmənaɪz ; diˈhjuməˌnaɪz/ *vt* [VP6A] take away human qualities from. 使失去人性。

de·hy·drate /ˌdiːˈhaɪdreɪt ; diˈhaɪdret/ *vt* [VP6A] deprive (a substance) of water or moisture: 去掉(物質)中的水份；使脫水：*~d vegetables/eggs,* often in powdered form. 脫水蔬菜(鷄蛋)(通常係粉狀)。

de-ice /ˌdiː ˈaɪs ; diˈaɪs/ *vt* [VP6A] free, eg the surfaces of an aircraft, from ice. 防止(如飛機的表面)結冰；除去…的冰。

de·ify /ˈdiːɪfaɪ ; ˈdiəˌfaɪ/ *vt* (*pt, pp* -fied) [VP6A] make a god of; worship as a god. 使成神；奉爲神。**de·ifi·ca·tion** /ˌdiːɪfɪˈkeɪʃn ; ˌdiəfəˈkeʃən/ *n* [U] ~ing or being deified: (被)奉爲神；神化：*the deification of a Roman emperor.* 羅馬皇帝之被奉爲神。

deign /deɪn ; den/ *vi* [VP4A] ~ ***to do sth***, condescend; be kind or gracious enough to: 屈尊；俯就：

He passed by without ~ing to look at me. 他走過時不屑看我一眼。

de·ism /ˈdiːɪzəm ; ˈdiɪzəm/ *n* belief in the existence of a Divine Being, but without acceptance of revelation or religious dogma. 自然神論; 理神論 (相信有神存在,但不相信神能對人有所啓示或宗教教條)。 **de·ist** /ˈdiːɪst ; ˈdiɪst/ *n* supporter of ~. 自然神論者;理神論者。⇨ theism.

de·ity /ˈdiːɪtɪ ; ˈdiətɪ/ *n* **1** [U] divine quality or nature; state of being a god or goddess. 神性。 **2** [C] (*pl* -ties) god or goddess: 神;女神: *Roman deities*, eg Neptune, Minerva. 羅馬諸神(如海神,司智慧等之女神)。 **the D~**, God. 神;上帝。

déjà vu /ˌdeɪʒɑːˈvjuː ; deʒɑˈvju/ *n* [U] (F) feeling that one remembers an event or scene that one has not experienced or seen before; (colloq) feeling that one has experienced sth too often. (法)記憶錯覺;(俗)對某事經歷次數太多的感覺。

de·ject /dɪˈdʒekt ; dɪˈdʒɛkt/ *vt* (usu in *pp*) make sad or gloomy: (通常用過去分詞) 使悲傷; 使沮喪: *Why is she looking so ~ed*, in such low spirits? 她爲什麼神情如此沮喪? **de·ject·ed·ly** *adv* **de·jec·tion** /dɪˈdʒekʃn ; dɪˈdʒɛkʃən/ *n* [U] ~ed state; low spirits: 憂戚;沮喪: *He left in ~.* 他怏怏而去。

de jure /ˌdeɪ ˈdʒʊərɪ ; diˈdʒʊrɪ/ *adj, adv* (Lat) by right; according to law: (拉) 合法的; 有權的; 依法: *the ~ king;* 合法的王; *king ~.* 合法的王。⇨ de facto.

dekko /ˈdekəʊ ; ˈdɛko/ *n* (sl) (俚) ***have a ~***, have a look (at sth). (對某物)看一眼。

de·lay /dɪˈleɪ ; dɪˈle/ *vt, vi* **1** [VP6A, 2A, B] make or be slow or late: 延遲;延緩: *Don't ~.* 不要拖延。*The train was ~ed (for) two hours.* 火車遲延兩小時。*I was ~ed by the traffic.* 我因交通擁擠而遲到。**~ed-action** *adj, n* operating after a lapse of time: 經過一段時期後始起作用(的): *a ~ed-action bomb*, with a device causing it to explode after a pre-determined interval. 定時炸彈。 **2** [VP6A, C] put off until later: 延期;展期: *We must ~ our journey until the weather improves.* 我們必須延緩旅行,等天氣好轉後再說。*Why have they ~ed opening the new school?* 他們爲什麼遲遲不讓那新學校開學? □ *n* **1** [U] ~ing or being ~ed: 遲延;延後;延期: *We must leave without ~.* 我們必須立刻離開。 **2** [C] instance of this; time of being ~ed: 遲延的事; 躭誤;遲延的時間: *after several ~s;* 經過數次展期以後; *after a ~ of three hours.* 經過三小時的躭誤以後。

de·lec·table /dɪˈlektəbl ; dɪˈlɛktəbl/ *adj* (liter) delightful; pleasant. (文)宜人的;令人愉快的。

de·lec·ta·tion /ˌdiːlekˈteɪʃn ; ˌdilɛkˈteʃən/ *n* [U] (liter, ironic) enjoyment; entertainment: (文,反語)享受;娛樂: *TV programmes suitable for the ~ of half-educated people.* 投合未受很多教育者所好的電視節目。

del·egacy /ˈdelɪgəsɪ ; ˈdɛlɪgəsɪ/ *n* (*pl* -cies) system of delegating; body of delegates. 代表制度;代表團。

del·egate¹ /ˈdelɪgət ; ˈdɛləˌget/ *n* person to whom sth is delegated (eg an elected representative sent to a conference or convention). (被選派參加會議等的)代表;受委託者。

del·egate² /ˈdelɪgeɪt ; ˈdɛləˌget/ *vt* [VP17, 14] ***~ (to)***, appoint and send (sb) as a representative to a meeting; entrust (duties, rights, etc to sb): 派遣(某人)爲代表(參加某會);付託(責任,權利等於某人): *to ~ sb to perform a task;* 請某人代表執行任務; *to ~ rights to a deputy.* 付託權利予代理人。**del·ega·tion** /ˌdelɪˈgeɪʃn ; ˌdɛləˈgeʃən/ *n* **1** [U] delegating or being delegated. 派代表;被派爲代表。 **2** [C] group of delegates. 代表團。

de·lete /dɪˈliːt ; dɪˈlit/ *vt* [VP6A, 14] ***~ (from)***, strike or take out (sth written or printed): 消去;刪除 (稿件或印刷物中的字句): *Several words had been ~d from the letter by the censor.* 那封信中有好幾個字被新聞檢查員刪去了。**de·le·tion** /dɪˈliːʃn ; dɪˈliʃən/ *n* [U] deleting; [C] sth deleted. 刪除;刪除之字句。

del·eteri·ous /ˌdelɪˈtɪərɪəs ; ˌdɛləˈtɪrɪəs/ *adj* (formal) harmful (to mind or body). (正式用語)有害(於身心)的。

delft /delft ; dɛlft/, (also 亦作 **delf** /delf ; dɛlf/, or 或作 **ˈ~-ware**) *n* [U] kind of glazed earthenware, usu with blue designs or decorations. 一種上釉的陶器(通常帶藍色圖案或花紋)。

de·lib·er·ate¹ /dɪˈlɪbərət ; dɪˈlɪbərɪt/ *adj* **1** done on purpose; intentional: 故意的;存心的: *a ~ lie/insult.* 存心的謊言(侮辱)。 **2** slow and cautious (in action, speech, etc): (行動,言語等)從容而謹慎的: *a ~ speech.* 從容而謹愼的演說。*He entered the room with ~ steps.* 他從容不迫地走進室內。**~·ly** *adv*

de·lib·er·ate² /dɪˈlɪbəreɪt ; dɪˈlɪbəˌret/ *vt, vi* [VP6A, 8, 10, 2A, 3A] ***~ (over/on/upon)***, consider, talk about, carefully: 仔細考慮; 研討; 商討: *We were deliberating what to do/how it might be done/whether to buy a new motor-car.* 我們在商討怎麼辦 (如何是好, 是否買一部新汽車)。*They're still deliberating over/upon the question.* 他們仍然在愼重考慮這問題。 **de·lib·er·ative** /dɪˈlɪbərətɪv *US:* -reɪtɪv ; dɪˈlɪbəˌretɪv/ *adj* for the purpose of deliberating: 以商討爲目的的: *a deliberative assembly.* 討論會。

de·lib·er·ation /dɪˌlɪbəˈreɪʃn ; dɪˌlɪbəˈreʃən/ *n* **1** [C, U] careful consideration and discussion; debate: 愼重考慮;商討;辯論: *After long ~, they decided....* 經過很久的商討以後,他們決定…。*What was the result of your ~(s)?* 你(們)考慮的結果如何? **2** [U] being deliberate(2); slowness of movement: 從容不迫;不慌不忙: *to speak/take aim/walk into a room with great ~.* 極爲從容地說話(瞄準,走進室內)。

deli·cacy /ˈdelɪkəsɪ ; ˈdɛləkəsɪ/ *n* (*pl* -cies) **1** [U] quality of being delicate (all senses): 精美;細緻;纖弱;微妙;優美;(顏色)柔和;(感官)靈敏;(儀器)精密;體貼;美味: *Everyone admired the ~ of her features*, their fineness and tenderness. 人人都噗賞她的花容月貌。*Because of the ~ of her skin* (=Because it is easily hurt by the sun), *she never sunbathes.* 因爲她的皮膚極爲細嫩(易爲陽光晒壞),所以她從不作日光浴。*The girl's ~* (= The fact that she is delicate in health) *has always worried her parents.* 那女孩之纖弱的體質一直使她的父母心焦。*The political situation is one of great ~*, requires careful handling. 目前的政治情勢是極微妙的 (需要小心處理)。*The violinist played with great ~*, with a very fine touch. 那小提琴家以極其優美的手法演奏。 **2** [C] delicate(8) kind of food: 珍饈;美味: *all the delicacies of the season.* 一切應時的珍饈美味。

deli·cate /ˈdelɪkət ; ˈdɛləkət/ *adj* **1** soft; tender; of fine or thin material: 柔軟的; 細嫩的; 纖細的: *as ~ as silk;* 柔滑如綢; *the ~ skin of a young girl.* 女孩之柔嫩的皮膚。 **2** fine; exquisite: 精緻的; 細膩的: *jewellery of ~ workmanship.* 精工鑲嵌的珠寶飾物。 **3** easily injured; becoming ill easily; needing great care: 易損的; 身體嬌弱的; 需要小心照料的: *~ china/plants;* 精緻而易損壞的瓷器(需要小心照料的植物); *a ~-looking child;* 看起來瘦弱的小孩; *in ~ health.* 身體嬌弱的。 **4** requiring careful treatment or skilful handling: 需要小心或技巧處理的: *a ~ surgical operation*, eg on sb's eyes. 精細的外科手術(如施於眼部者)。*The international situation is very ~ at present.* 目前的國際局勢極其微妙。 **5** (of colours) soft; not strong: (指顏色)柔和的;淡的;淺的: *a ~ shade of pink.* 淡粉紅色。 **6** (of the senses, of instruments) able to appreciate or indicate very small changes or differences: (指感官,儀器)能辨別或指示細微之變化或差別的; 靈敏的; 敏感的; 精密的: *a ~ sense of smell/touch;* 靈敏的嗅(觸)覺; *the ~ instruments needed by scientists*, eg for weighing or measuring. 科學家所需要的精密儀器(如用以稱量或度量者)。 **7** taking great care not to be immodest, not to hurt the feelings of others: 極其小心不使自己失禮,不傷人感情的;賢淑的;體貼的: *a ~ speech.* 得體的演說。 **8** (of food, its flavour) pleasing to

D

the taste and not strongly flavoured: (指食物,其味)美味的;清淡可口的: *Chicken is more ~ than beef.* 鷄肉比牛肉味美。*When people are ill they need ~ food.* 當人生病的時候,他們需要清淡可口的食物。*Some kinds of fish have a more ~ flavour than others.* 某些種類的魚,其味較他種魚類爲佳。~·**ly** *adv*

deli·ca·tessen /ˌdelɪkəˈtesn ; ˌdɛləkəˈtɛsn̩/ *n* [C, U] (shop selling) prepared foods ready for serving (esp cooked meat, smoked fish, pickles): 做熟售賣的菜餚(尤指煮熟的肉,燻魚,醃菜);熟食店: *The ~ (shop) closes at 5.30.* 熟食店五點半打烊。

de·li·cious /dɪˈlɪʃəs ; dɪˈlɪʃəs/ *adj* giving delight (esp to the senses of taste and smell, and to the sense of humour): 美味的;有香味的;堪玩味的(尤指使人在味覺,嗅覺及幽默感方面發生樂趣的): *a ~ cake.* 美味的糕餅。*Doesn't it smell ~!* 其味豈不美哉! *What a ~ joke!* 多麼有趣的笑話! ~·**ly** *adv*

D

de·light¹ /dɪˈlaɪt ; dɪˈlaɪt/ *n* **1** [U] great pleasure; joy: 欣喜;樂趣;高興;愉快: *to give ~ to sb.* 給予娛樂;使某人高興。*To his great ~ his novel was accepted for publication.* 他的小說被接受出版,使他極爲高興。***take ~ in,*** find pleasure in: 喜好;以…爲樂: *The naughty boy takes great ~ in pulling the cat's tail.* 那頑皮的男孩以拉貓的尾巴爲樂。 **2** [C] cause or source of great pleasure: 賞心樂事;嗜好: *Dancing is her chief ~.* 跳舞是她主要的嗜好。*He often thinks of the ~s of life in the country.* 他時常懷念鄉村生活的樂趣。~·**ful** /-fl ; -fəl/ *adj* giving ~ (*to*): 令人愉快的;可愛的(可與 to 連用): *a ~ful holiday.* 快樂的假日。~·**fully** /-fəlɪ ; -fəlɪ/ *adv*

de·light² /dɪˈlaɪt ; dɪˈlaɪt/ *vt, vi* **1** [VP6A] give great pleasure to; please greatly: 給予樂趣;使極爲喜悅;使非常高興: *Her singing ~ed everyone.* 她的歌唱使人人歡喜。 **2** (passive): (被動語態): *be ~ed,* be greatly pleased. 極爲高興。*I was ~ed to hear the news of your success/~ed at the news.../~ed that you were successful.* 我聽到你成功的消息極爲高興。 **3** [VP3A, 4C] ~ ***(in),*** take or find great pleasure: 引以爲樂;喜歡: *He ~s in teasing his young sister.* 他以逗弄他的小妹妹爲樂。*He ~s to prove his brother wrong.* 他很喜歡證明他的哥哥(弟弟)錯誤。

de·limit /diːˈlɪmɪt; dɪˈlɪmɪt/, **de·limi·tate** /diːˈlɪmɪteɪt; dɪˈlɪmɪˌtet/ *vt* [VP6A] determine the limits or boundaries of. 定…的界線;劃界線。**de·limi·ta·tion** /diːˌlɪmɪˈteɪʃn ; dɪˌlɪməˈteʃən/ *n* [C, U].

de·lin·eate /dɪˈlɪnɪeɪt ; dɪˈlɪnɪˌet/ *vt* [VP6A] (formal) show by drawing or by describing; portray. (正式用語)描畫;描繪;描寫。**de·lin·ea·tion** /dɪˌlɪnɪˈeɪʃn ; dɪˌlɪnɪˈeʃən/ *n* [C, U].

de·lin·quency /dɪˈlɪŋkwənsɪ ; dɪˈlɪŋkwənsɪ/ *n* **1** [U] wrong-doing; neglect of duty: 過失;失職;違法;犯罪: *the problem of juvenile ~,* wrong-doing by young persons. 少年犯罪問題。 **2** [C] (*pl* -cies) instance of this; misdeed. 罪行;惡行。

de·lin·quent /dɪˈlɪŋkwənt ; dɪˈlɪŋkwənt/ *n, adj* (person) doing wrong, failing to perform a duty. 犯過的(人);犯法的(人);失職的(人)。

deli·ques·cent /ˌdelɪˈkwesnt ; ˌdɛləˈkwɛsnt/ *adj* (chem) becoming liquid in air (by absorbing moisture). (化學)潮解(在空氣中吸收水份而溶解)的。

de·liri·ous /dɪˈlɪrɪəs ; dɪˈlɪrɪəs/ *adj* **1** suffering from delirium; wildly excited: 精神錯亂的;譫妄的;極激動的;發狂的: *The patient's temperature went up and he became ~.* 那病人的體溫昇高,變得胡言亂語。*The children were ~ with joy.* 孩子們欣喜若狂。 **2** showing the effects of delirium: 顯示精神錯亂的: *~ speech.* 狂語;譫語。~·**ly** *adv*

de·lirium /dɪˈlɪrɪəm ; dɪˈlɪrɪəm/ *n* [U] violent mental disturbance caused by illness, often accompanied by wild talk, esp during feverish illness; wild excitement. 譫妄(精神錯亂,常伴隨胡言亂語,尤指在發燒的病症中);發狂。ˌ~ ˈ**tremens** /ˈtriːmenz ; ˈtrimənz/ (usu 通常作 **d t(s)** /ˌdiː ˈtiː(z) ; diˈti(z)/), ~ caused by extreme alcoholism. 震戰性譫妄(因極度酒精中毒引起者);酒狂。

de·liver /dɪˈlɪvə(r) ; dɪˈlɪvə/ *vt* **1** [VP6A] take (letters, parcels, goods, etc) to houses, to the person(s) to whom they are addressed, to the buyer(s): 遞送(信件,包裹,貨物等)至收件處,收件人或購貨人;交付: *A postman is a man employed to ~ letters and parcels.* 郵差就是僱來投遞信件及包裹的人。*Did you ~ my message to your father?* 你已將我的信交給你父親了嗎? ~ ***the goods,*** (fig) do what is wanted. (喻)實踐諾言;不負所望。 **2** [VP14] ~ ***from,*** (old use) rescue, save, set free: (舊用法)拯救;解救;釋放: *May God ~ us from all evil.* 願上帝使我們脫離一切邪惡。 **3** [VP6A] give forth in words: 發言;陳述;發表(演說): *to ~ a sermon/a course of lectures;* 講道(講授一門功課); *to ~ oneself of an opinion.* 發表意見。 **4** [VP6A] (of a medical attendant, eg a midwife) help (a woman) in childbirth: (指醫護人員,如助產士)助產: *to be ~ed of a child,* give birth to one. 產一小孩。 **5** [VP6A, 15B] ~ ***(up/over) (to),*** surrender; give up; hand over: 交出;放棄;移交: *to ~ up stolen goods;* 交出贓物; *to ~ over one's property to one's son;* 將財產交付與兒子; *to ~ (up) a fortress to the enemy.* 將一要塞棄守與敵人。 **6** [VP6A] launch; aim; send against: 對準;予以: (fig) (喻) *to ~ a blow in the cause of freedom.* 予自由運動當頭一棒。~**er** *n* one who ~s; rescuer; saviour. 遞送者;交付者;拯救者;解救者;發言者;陳述者;演講者。

de·liver·ance /dɪˈlɪvərəns ; dɪˈlɪvərəns/ *n* **1** [U] ~ ***from,*** delivering(2); rescue; being set free. 拯救;救助;被釋放。 **2** [C] formal or emphatic statement of opinion. 正式的或强調的意見聲明;意見。

de·liv·ery /dɪˈlɪvərɪ ; dɪˈlɪvərɪ/ *n* **1** [U] delivering (of letters, goods, etc); [C] (*pl* -ries) periodical performance of this: 遞送(信,貨等);按時遞送: *We guarantee prompt ~ of goods.* 我們擔保送貨迅速。*How many deliveries are there in your town* (= How often does the postman deliver letters) *every week?* 你們的城裏每週送幾次信? ***on ~,*** at the time of ~. 送達時;交貨時。***take ~ of,*** receive: 收到: *When can you take ~ of the new car?* 你何時能收到新車? ˈ~ **note** *n* note, usu in duplicate, sent with goods, to be signed by the recipient. 交貨單(通常有副本,由收貨人簽名)。ˈ~ **truck** *n* (US) goods van. (美)貨車。 **2** (*sing* only) manner of speaking (in lectures, etc): (僅用單數)(演講等的)說話方式;演講的技術: *His speech was good, but his ~ was poor.* 他的演說內容很好,可是表達的技巧很差。

dell /del ; dɛl/ *n* small valley, usu with trees on its sides. 小山谷(通常兩側有樹木);幽谷。

de·louse /ˌdiːˈlaʊs ; diˈlaʊs/ *vt.* rid (sb or sth) of lice. 除去(某人或某物)身上的虱子。

Del·phic /ˈdelfɪk ; ˈdɛlfɪk/ *adj* of the oracle of Apollo /əˈpɒləʊ ; əˈpɑlo/ at Delphi (in ancient Greece); obscure; ambiguous. 阿波羅神在(古希臘)特耳非城所作之神諭的;含義不明的;意義模稜兩可的。

del·phin·ium /delˈfɪnɪəm ; dɛlˈfɪnɪəm/ *n* (kinds of) garden plant, usu with tall spikes of usu blue flowers. 飛燕草(數種園藝植物,通常生藍色的高大的穗狀花)。

delta /ˈdeltə ; ˈdɛltə/ *n* Greek letter *d,* ⇨ App 4; land (with alluvial deposits) in the shape of a capital ~ (Δ) at the mouth of a river between two or more branches: 希臘字母的第四個字母(Δ, δ)(參看附錄四);(在河口由數條支流沖積成的)三角洲: *the Nile D~;* 尼羅河三角洲; ˌ~-ˈ*winged,* (of aircraft) having ~-shaped wings. (指飛機)有三角翼的。

de·lude /dɪˈluːd ; dɪˈlud/ *vt* [VP6A, 14] ~ ***sb with sth/into doing sth,*** deceive; mislead (on purpose): 欺騙;(故意)使人有錯誤想法: *to ~ sb with promises one does not intend to keep;* 以不打算實現的諾言欺騙某人; *to ~ oneself with false hopes;* 以虛幻的希望自欺; *to ~ sb/oneself into believing that....* 欺騙某人(自己)使相信…。

del·uge /ˈdeljuːdʒ ; ˈdɛljudʒ/ *n* [C] **1** great flood; heavy rush of water; violent rainfall. 洪水;大水

災；暴雨。**the D~,** the flood at the time of Noah /ˈnəʊə ; ˈnoə/ ⇨ Gen 7. 挪亞時代的大洪水(參看舊約聖經創世紀第7章)。 **2** anything coming in a heavy rush: 如洪水湧至的事物: *a ~ of words/questions/protests.* 一連串的話(問題,抗議)。□ *vt* [VP6A, 14] ~ ***(with),*** flood; come down on (sb or sth) like a ~: 氾濫；如洪水湧至(某人或某物): *He was ~d with questions.* 他爲大堆的問題所困。

de·lusion /dɪˈluːʒn ; dɪˈluʒən/ *n* [U] deluding or being deluded; [C] false opinion or belief, esp one that may be a symptom of madness: 欺騙；被欺；幻念；幻想(尤指可能爲癲狂之病徵者): *to be under a ~/under the ~ that...;* 處於幻覺中(誤以爲…)；*to suffer from ~s.* 患幻想症。

de·lus·ive /dɪˈluːsɪv ; dɪˈlusɪv/ *adj* not real; deceptive. 非眞實的；虛幻的；令人發生錯覺的。**~·ly** *adv*

de luxe /dɪ ˈlʌks ; dɪˈlʊks/ *adj* (F) of very high quality, high standards of comfort, etc: (法)品質高超的；精美的；極舒適的；豪華的: *a ~ edition of a book.* 一書之精裝本。

delve /delv ; dɛlv/ *vt, vi* **1** [VP6A, 2A] (old use) dig. (舊用法) 挖掘。 **2** [VP3A] ~ ***into,*** make researches into: 鑽研；深入研究: *~ for information into old books;* 在古書中搜求資料；*to ~ into sb's past.* 深入調查某人的過去。

de·mag·net·ize /ˌdiːˈmægnɪtaɪz ; diˈmægnəˌtaɪz/ *vt* [VP6A] deprive of magnetic properties. 除去磁性。 **de·mag·net·iz·ation** /ˌdiːˌmægnɪtaɪˈzeɪʃn *US:* -tɪˈz- ; ˌdimægnətəˈzeʃən/ *n*

dema·gogue /ˈdeməgɒg *US:* -gɔːg ; ˈdɛməˌgɔg/ *n* political leader who tries, by speeches appealing to the feelings instead of to reason, to stir up the people. 用訴諸感情而非理智的演說以煽動民衆的政治領袖；煽動家。 **dema·gogy** /ˈdeməgɒgɪ ; ˈdɛməˌgodʒɪ/ *n* [U] principles and practices of a ~. 煽動；煽動性；煽動行爲。**dema·gogic** /ˌdeməˈgɒgɪk ; ˌdɛməˈgɑdʒɪk/ *adj* of or like a ~. 煽動家的；似煽動家的。

de·mand[1] /dɪˈmɑːnd *US:* -ˈmænd ; dɪˈmænd/ *n* ~ ***(for),*** **1** [C] act of demanding(1); sth demanded (1): 要求；所要求之物: *The workers' ~s* (eg for higher pay) *were refused by the employers.* 工人們的要求(如要求加薪)爲僱主所拒。 *It is impossible to satisfy all ~s.* 不可能滿足所有的要求。 *I have/People make many ~s on my time,* I am expected to do many things, etc. 我有許多事情要做。 *There have been ~s for the prime minister to resign/for his resignation/that he should resign.* 已有人要求首相辭職。***on ~,*** when demanded: 在要求時: *a cheque payable on ~.* 卽期(應付)支票。 **ˈ~ (note),** note that demands payment, eg of income tax. 繳款(如繳所得稅)通知。 **2** [U] (or with an *indef art* and *adj*) desire, by people ready to buy, employ, etc (for goods, services, etc): (或與不定冠詞及形容詞連用)(社會對於貨物,人才等的)需求；需要: *There is a great ~ for typists but a poor ~/not much ~ for clerks.* (目前社會上)極需要打字員,而不大需要書記。 *There is little ~ for these goods.* 這些貨物的需要量極小。*The ~ for fish this month exceeds the supply.* 本月的魚市供不應求。***in ~,*** wanted; popular: 需要的；受歡迎的: *His records are always in ~/are in constant ~.* 他的唱片一直很暢銷。

de·mand[2] /dɪˈmɑːnd *US:* -ˈmænd ; dɪˈmænd/ *vt* **1** [VP6A, 7A, 9] ask for (sth) as if ordering, or as if one has a right to: 要求(某事物): *~ an apology from sb.* 要求某人道歉。 *The gatekeeper ~ed my business,* asked what I wanted. 守門人問我有何事。 *The policeman ~ed his name and address/~ed to know where he lived.* 警察要求他說出姓名和住址(要求他說出住在何處)。 *He came to my house and ~ed help/~ed that I should help him.* 他來到我家並要求我幫助。 *He ~s that I shall tell him everything/~s to be told everything.* 他要求我告訴他一切。 **2** [VP6A] need; require: 需要；需求: *This sort of work ~s great patience.* 這種工作需要極大的耐性。 *Does the letter ~ an immediate answer,* Must it be answered at once? 此信需要立卽答覆嗎？

de·mar·cate /ˈdiːmɑːkeɪt ; dɪˈmarket/ *vt* [VP6A] mark or fix the limits of, eg a frontier. 劃範圍；劃界線(如邊界)。

de·mar·ca·tion /ˌdiːmɑːˈkeɪʃn ; ˌdimarˈkeʃən/ *n* [U] marking of a boundary or limit; separation: 劃界線；區分；劃分: *a line of ~;* 分界線; *~ problems in industry,* eg settling the kind of work to be done by workers in different trades. 工業上各部門工作範圍的劃分問題。

dé·marche /ˈdeɪmɑːʃ ; deˈmarʃ/ *n* (F) political step or proceeding; diplomatic representation (to a foreign government). (法) 政治上的步驟或手段；(駐外)外交代表。

de·mean /dɪˈmiːn ; dɪˈmin/ *vt* [VP6A] ~ ***oneself,*** lower oneself in dignity, social esteem. 自貶身份。

de·mean·our (US = **-or**) /dɪˈmiːnə(r) ; dɪˈminə/ *n* [U] way of behaving: 行爲；擧止；態度；風度: *I dislike his supercilious ~.* 我不喜歡他傲慢的態度。

de·mented /dɪˈmentɪd ; dɪˈmɛntɪd/ *adj* mad; (colloq) wild with worry: 瘋狂的；(俗)因憂慮而發狂的；精神錯亂的: *a poor, ~ creature.* 可憐的,精神錯亂的人。*She'll become ~ if you don't stop asking silly questions.* 假若你再不停止問傻問題,她會發瘋的。 **~·ly** *adv*

deme·rara /ˌdeməˈreərə ; ˌdɛməˈrærə/ *n* [U] ~ **sugar,** light brown raw cane sugar (from Guyana). (蓋亞那所產的)淡褐色蔗糖。

de·merit /diːˈmerɪt ; diˈmɛrɪt/ *n* [C] fault; defect. 過失；缺點。

de·mesne /dɪˈmeɪn ; dɪˈmen/ *n* [U] (legal) the holding of land as one's own property: (法律)土地的領有(作爲私產): *land held in ~;* 領有的地產; [C] landed estate held in this way, not let to tenants. 領有供自用(而非租給佃戶)的地產。

demi·god /ˈdemɪgɒd ; ˈdɛməˌgɑd/ *n* one who is partly divine and partly human; (in GK myth, etc) the son of a god and a mortal woman, eg *Hercules* /ˈhɜːkjʊliːz ; ˈhɝkjəˌliz/. 半神半人；(在希臘神話等中)天神與凡女所生之子(如海克力斯)。

demi·john /ˈdemɪdʒɒn ; ˈdɛməˌdʒɑn/ *n* large narrow-necked bottle, usu encased in wicker-work. 一種細頸大罎(通常套於柳條編的套中)。

de·mili·tar·ize /ˌdiːˈmɪlɪtəraɪz ; diˈmɪlətəˌraɪz/ *vt* [VP6A] (of a country, or part of it) require, by treaty or agreement, to have no military forces or installation in: (指國或國之一部)(按照條約或協定)解除武裝；廢除軍備: *a ~d zone.* 解除武裝的地區。

demi·monde /ˌdemɪˈmɔːnd ; ˈdɛmɪˌmand/ *n* **the ~,** (F) (class of society made up of) people on the fringe of respectable society. (法)位於高尙社會邊緣的人；此種人構成的社會階級。 **demi·mon·daine** /ˌdemɪmɔːnˈdeɪn ; ˌdɛmɪmanˈden/ *n* woman of this class. 位於高尙社會邊緣的婦女。

de·mise /dɪˈmaɪz ; dɪˈmaɪz/ *n* (legal) death. (法律)死亡。

de·mist /ˌdiːˈmɪst ; diˈmɪst/ *vt* remove the mist from, eg the windscreen of a motor vehicle. 擦去(汽車之擋風玻璃等)的霧水。 **~er** /-stə(r) ; -stə/ *n* device that ~s. 除霧器。

demo /ˈdeməʊ ; ˈdɛmo/ *n* [C] (colloq abbr for) demonstration(2). (俗)示威(爲 demonstration 之略)。

de·mob /ˌdiːˈmɒb ; diˈmɑb/ *vt* (-bb-) and *n* (GB colloq abbr for) *demobilize* and *demobilization*: (英俗)遣散；(使)復員(爲demobilize與demobilization之略): *When do you get ~bed/your ~?* 你何時可獲遣散？

de·mo·bil·ize /diːˈməʊbəlaɪz ; diˈmoblˌaɪz/ *vt* [VP 6A] release from military service. 遣散(兵員)；使(軍隊)復員。 **de·mo·bil·iz·ation** /dɪˌməʊbəlaɪˈzeɪʃn *US:* -lɪˈz- ; ˌdimoblə̩ˈzeʃən/ *n*

democ·racy /dɪˈmɒkrəsɪ ; dəˈmɑkrəsɪ/ *n* (*pl* -cies) **1** [C, U] (country with principles of) government

D

in which all adult citizens share through their elected representatives. 民主政治(由全體成年公民通過其所選舉的代表共同參與施政的政治制度);實行民主政治的國家。 **2** [C, U] (country with) government which encourages and allows rights of citizenship such as freedom of speech, religion, opinion and association, the assertion of the rule of law, majority rule, accompanied by respect for the rights of minorities. 民主政體(鼓勵並許可人民有各種公民權如言論、信仰、意見及集會結社之自由,主張法治,服從多數同時並尊重少數者之權利); 擁有民主政體的國家。 **3** [C, U] (society in which there is) treatment of each other by citizens as equals and with absence of class feeling: 公民互相平等待遇(的社會): *Is there more ~ in Australia than in Great Britain?* 在澳洲是否比英國更爲自由平等?

D

demo·crat /ˈdeməkræt ; ˈdɛmə͵kræt/ *n* **1** person who favours or supports democracy. 贊成或支持民主政治的人。 **2** **D~**, (US) member of the Democratic Party. (美)民主黨員。

demo·cratic /ˌdeməˈkrætɪk ; ͵dɛməˈkrætɪk/ *adj* **1** of, like, supporting, democracy (1, 2). 民主政治的; 民主政體的; 民主國家的; 類似或支持民主政治的。 **2** (esp) of, supporting, democracy(3); paying no or little attention to class divisions based on birth or wealth. (尤指)贊成人人平等的;不分貴賤的;不分貧富的。 **3** **the ˈD~ Party**, (US) one of the two main political parties. (美) 民主黨 (美國兩大政黨之一)。⇨ Republican. **demo·crati·cally** /-klɪ ; -klɪ/ *adv*

de·moc·ra·tize /dɪˈmɒkrətaɪz ; dəˈmɑkrə͵taɪz/ *vt* [VP6A] make democratic. 民主化; 平民化。 **de·moc·ra·tiz·ation** /dɪˌmɒkrətaɪˈzeɪʃn *US:* -tɪˈz- ; dɪ͵mɑkrətɪˈzeʃən/ *n*

dé·modé /ˌdeɪˈməʊdeɪ *US:* ˌdeɪməʊˈdeɪ ; ͵demoˈde/ *adj* (F) outmoded; out of fashion. (法)過時的;已不流行的;老式的。

de·mog·ra·phy /dɪˈmɒgrəfɪ ; dɪˈmɑgrəfɪ/ *n* [U] (study of) statistics of births, deaths, diseases, etc to show the condition of a community. 人口統計(包括出生、死亡、疾病等的統計,以示明社區狀況);人口統計學。 **demo·graphic** /ˌdeməˈgræfɪk ; ͵dimə-ˈgræfɪk/ *adj*

de·mol·ish /dɪˈmɒlɪʃ ; dɪˈmɑlɪʃ/ *vt* [VP6A] pull or tear down, eg old buildings; destroy, eg sb's argument; make an end of. 拆除(舊建築物等);推翻(某人的論據等); 毀壞; 破壞。 **demo·li·tion** /ˌdeməˈlɪʃn ; ͵dɛməˈlɪʃən/ *n* [U] ~ing or being ~ed; [C] instance of this. 拆除;推翻;毀壞;破壞。

de·mon /ˈdiːmən ; ˈdimən/ *n* evil, wicked or cruel supernatural being or spirit; (colloq) fierce or energetic person: 惡魔; 魔鬼; (俗)兇惡的或精力充沛的人: *a ~ bowler*, (cricket) very fast bowler. (板球)兇猛的投手。 *He's a ~ for work*, (colloq) works with great energy. (俗)他做起事來精力過人。 **~ic** /diːˈmɒnɪk ; diˈmɑnɪk/ *adj*

de·monet·ize /ˌdiːˈmʌnɪtaɪz ; diˈmɑnə͵taɪz/ *vt* deprive (a metal) of its value as currency; withdraw (a metal) from use as currency. 廢止(金屬)充作貨幣之價值; 停止(金屬) 充作貨幣。 **de·monet·iz·ation** /diːˌmʌnɪtaɪˈzeɪʃn *US:* -tɪˈz- ; di͵mɑnətɪˈzeʃən/ *n*

de·mon·iac /dɪˈməʊnɪæk ; dɪˈmonɪ͵æk/ *n, adj* (person who is) devilish, frenzied, fiercely energetic. 邪惡的(人);狂亂的(人);精力充沛的(人)。**~al** /ˌdiːmə-ˈnaɪəkl ; ͵diməˈnaɪəkḷ/ *adj* = ~. **~ally** /ˌdiːmə-ˈnaɪəklɪ ; ͵diməˈnaɪəklɪ/ *adv*

de·mon·strable /ˈdemənstrəbl ; ˈdɛmənstrəbḷ/ *adj* that can be demonstrated or logically proved. 可用證據或邏輯證明的。**de·mon·strably** /-blɪ ; -blɪ/ *adv* **de·mon·stra·bil·ity** /ˌdemənstrəˈbɪlɪtɪ ; ͵dɛmənstrəˈbɪlətɪ/ *n*

dem·on·strate /ˈdemənstreɪt ; ˈdɛmən͵stret/ *vt, vi* **1** [VP6A, 9] show clearly by giving proof(s) or example(s): 拿出證據或舉例證明;演示: *How would you ~ that the world is round?* 你如何證明世界是圓的? *The salesman ~d the new washing-machine*, showed how it was used. 那售貨員演示如何使用新式洗衣機。 **2** [VP2A, 3A] take part in a demonstration(2): 示威;參加示威運動: *The workers marched through the streets with flags and banners to ~ against the rising cost of living.* 工人們在街上遊行,手執旗幟示威抗議生活費用的高漲。

dem·on·stra·tion /ˌdemənˈstreɪʃn ; ͵dɛmənˈstreʃən/ *n* [C, U] **1** demonstrating(1): 證明;演示;示範: *to teach sth by ~;* 示範教學; *a ~ of affection*, eg when a child puts its arms round its mother's neck; 親愛的表示(如小孩用兩臂摟着母親的脖子); *a ~ of a new car*, to show how it works. 示範新式汽車的使用。 **2** public and organised display of opinion by a group, eg of workers, students. (工人,學生等之)示威運動。

de·mon·stra·tive /dɪˈmɒnstrətɪv ; dɪˈmɑnstrətɪv/ *adj* **1** (of persons) showing the feelings: (指人)表露出感情的: *Some children are more ~ than others*, readier to show affection, etc. 有些小孩比其他的小孩容易表露感情。 **2** marked by open expression of feelings: 將感情公然表露出來的: *~ behaviour.* 將感情表露出來的行爲。 **3** serving to point out; 指示的; esp (gram) (尤指文法上的) **͵~ ˈpronoun**, 指示代名詞 (*this, these, that, those*). **~·ly** *adv*

dem·on·stra·tor /ˈdemənstreɪtə(r) ; ˈdɛmən͵stretɚ/ *n* **1** person who demonstrates(2): 遊行示威者: *The ~s were dispersed by the police.* 遊行示威者爲警察所驅散。 **2** person who teaches or explains by demonstrating(1). 用演示法教學者;示範者。

de·moral·ize /dɪˈmɒrəlaɪz *US:* -ˈmɔːr- ; dɪˈmɔrəl-͵aɪz/ *vt* [VP6A] **1** hurt or weaken the morals of: 敗壞…的道德: *a boy who was ~d by bad companions.* 與壞人爲友而道德被敗壞的孩子。 **2** weaken the courage, confidence, self-discipline, etc of, eg an army. 消弱(軍隊等)的勇氣,自信,紀律等; 使士氣沮喪。⇨ morale. **de·moral·iz·ation** /dɪˌmɒrəlaɪ-ˈzeɪʃn *US:* -ˌmɔːrəlɪˈz- ; dɪ͵mɔrələˈzeʃən/ *n*

de·mote /ˌdiːˈməʊt ; dɪˈmot/ *vt* [VP6A] reduce to a lower rank or grade. 使降級。⇨ promote. **de·motion** /ˌdiːˈməʊʃn ; dɪˈmoʃən/ *n*

de·motic /dɪˈmɒtɪk ; diˈmɑtɪk/ *adj* of, used by, the common people: 民衆(用)的;通俗的: *~ Greek*, the colloquial form of modern Greek. 通俗的希臘語。

de·mur /dɪˈmɜː(r) ; dɪˈmɝ/ *vi* (-rr-) [VP2A, 3A] ~ ***(at/to)***, (formal) raise a doubt or an objection: (正式用語)提出異議;反對: *to ~ to a demand;* 對某項要求提出異議; *to ~ at working on Sundays.* 反對星期日上班。□ *n* [U] hesitation or objection: 躊躇; 猶豫;異議: (chiefly in) (主用於) *without ~*. 無異議。

de·mure /dɪˈmjʊə(r) ; dɪˈmjʊr/ *adj* quiet and serious: 嫻靜的;嚴肅的;端莊的: *a ~ young lady;* 嫻靜的少女; pretending to be, suggesting that one is, ~: 佯作或顯示嫻靜嚴肅的: *She gave him a ~ smile.* 她向他故作端莊(佯作嫻靜)的一笑。 **~·ly** *adv* **~·ness** *n*

den /den ; dɛn/ *n* **1** animal's hidden home, eg a cave. 獸穴(如山洞)。 **2** secret resort: 祕密之所;窟: *an opium den;* 鴉片烟窟; *a den of thieves.* 賊窩。 **3** (colloq) room in which a person works and studies without being disturbed. (俗) 私人的工作室或研究室。

den·ary /ˈdiːnərɪ ; ˈdɛnərɪ/ *adj* = decimal.

de·nation·al·ize /ˌdiːˈnæʃənəlaɪz ; diˈnæʃənḷ͵aɪz/ *vt* [VP6A] transfer (a nationalized industry, etc) to private ownership again. 使(國營工業等)復歸民營; 解除國有化。⇨ nationalize. **de·nation·al·iz·ation** /ˌdiːˌnæʃənəlaɪˈzeɪʃn *US:* -lɪˈz- ; di͵næʃənəlɪˈzeʃən/ *n*

de·natured /ˌdiːˈneɪtʃəd ; diˈnetʃɚd/ *adj* that has been made unfit for eating and drinking (but may still be used for other purposes): 被變成不適於飲食用的(但仍可作其他用途): *~ alcohol;* 變性酒精; having lost natural qualities: 已失去自然本質的: *~ rubber*, no longer elastic. 失去彈性的橡皮。

de·ni·able /dɪˈnaɪəbl ; dɪˈnaɪəbḷ/ *adj* that one can deny. 可否認的;可拒絕的;可反對的。

de·nial /dɪˈnaɪəl ; dɪˈnaɪəl/ *n* ~ ***(of)***, **1** [U] denying

(2, 3); [C] instance of this: 否認;拒絶一項要求: *the ~ of justice / a request for help.* 不予公平處理或待遇(拒絶他人之求助)。 **2** [C] statement that sth is not true: 否認某事爲事實的聲明: *the prisoner's repeated ~s of the charge brought against him.* 該囚犯對於被指控的罪名之再三的否認。⇨ *self-~* at self-

den·ier /ˈdenɪə(r) ; ˈdɛnɪr/ *n* unit of fineness for rayon, nylon and silk yarns: 丹尼爾(一種測量人造絲,尼龍和絲線細度的單位): *30-~ stockings.* 細度爲三十丹尼爾的長襪。

deni·grate /ˈdenɪgreɪt ; ˈdɛnəˌgret/ *vt* [VP6A] defame. 毀壞名譽。 **deni·gra·tion** /ˌdenɪˈgreɪʃn ; ˌdɛnəˈgreʃən/ *n*

denim /ˈdenɪm ; ˈdɛnəm/ *n* **1** [U] twilled cotton cloth (used for jeans, overalls, etc). 一種斜紋棉布(用以製牛仔褲,工作服等)。 **2** (*pl*) (colloq) jeans made from ~. (複)(俗)此種斜紋布製的牛仔褲。

deni·zen /ˈdenɪzn ; ˈdɛnəzn̩/ *n* person, kind of animal or plant, living or growing permanently in the district, etc mentioned: 永遠定居於某地區的人或動物;永遠生長在某地區的植物: *~s of the Arctic.* 恒生於北極地區的人或生物。

de·nomi·nate /dɪˈnɒmɪneɪt ; dɪˈnɑməˌnet/ *vt* [VP23] give a name to; call. 命名;取名。

de·nomi·na·tion /dɪˌnɒmɪˈneɪʃn ; dɪˌnɑməˈneʃən/ *n* [C] **1** name, esp one given to a class or religious group or sect: (尤指給予階級或教派的)名稱: *The Protestant ~s include the Methodists, Presbyterians and Baptists.* 新教會包括美以美會,長老會和浸信會。 **2** class or unit (in weight, length, numbers, money, etc): (重量,長度,數目,貨幣等之)單位或類別: *The US coin of the lowest ~ is the cent.* 美國錢幣的最低單位是分。 *We can reduce fractions to the same ~,* eg $\frac{1}{2}$, $\frac{5}{8}=\frac{8}{16}$, $\frac{10}{16}$. 我們可把分數化成同一分母(例如$\frac{1}{2}$, $\frac{5}{8}=\frac{8}{16}$, $\frac{10}{16}$)。 **~al** /-ˈneɪʃənl ; -ˈneʃənl̩/ *adj* of ~s(1): 各教派的: *~al schools.* 各教派的學校。

de·nomi·na·tor /dɪˈnɒmɪneɪtə(r) ; dɪˈnɑməˌnetɚ/ *n* number or quantity below the line in a fraction, eg 4 in $\frac{3}{4}$. 分母(分數線下的數目,例如 $\frac{3}{4}$ 中的 4)。

de·note /dɪˈnəʊt ; dɪˈnot/ *vt* **1** [VP6A] be the sign or symbol of; be the name of: 爲…之符號;爲…之名稱;代表;指: *In algebra the sign* x *usually ~s an unknown quantity.* 在代數學中,符號 x 通常代表一未知數。 **2** [VP6A, 9] indicate: 指示;指出: *The mark (‸) ~s a place of omission / ~s that something has been omitted.* 記號 (‸) 指示有脫漏的地方。

dé·noue·ment /ˌdeɪˈnuːmɔːŋ *US:* ˌdeɪnuːˈmɔːŋ ; deˈnumɑ̃/ *n* (F) final stage, where everything is made clear, in the development of the plot of a story, play, etc. (法)(小説,戲劇等)情節發展的最後階段;結局;收場。

de·nounce /dɪˈnaʊns ; dɪˈnaʊns/ *vt* **1** [VP6A, 16B] speak publicly against; give information against: 公開指摘;揭發;告發: *to ~ a heresy;* 公開指摘異端邪説; *to ~ sb as a spy.* 指某人爲奸細。 **2** [VP6A] give notice that one intends to end (a treaty or agreement). 通知廢止(條約或協定)。

dense /dens; dɛns/ *adj* (-r, -st) **1** (of liquids, vapour) not easily seen through: (指液體,蒸氣)不易透視的;濃密的: *a ~ fog;* 濃霧; *~ smoke.* 濃煙。 **2** (of people and things) crowded together in great numbers: (指人和物)密集的;稠密的: *a ~ crowd;* 擁擠的人群; *a ~ forest.* 茂密的森林。 **3** (colloq) stupid; having a mind that ideas can penetrate only with difficulty. (俗)愚鈍的;不易受教的。 **~·ly** *adv*: 濃密地: *a ~ly populated country;* 人口稠密的國家; *~ly wooded,* covered with trees growing close together. 林木茂密的。 **~·ness** *n*

den·sity /ˈdensətɪ ; ˈdɛnsətɪ/ *n* **1** [U] the quality of being dense: 濃密;稠密;密集: *the ~ of a forest / the fog / the population.* 森林的茂密(霧的濃密;人口的稠密)。 **2** [C, U] (*pl* -ties) (phys) relation of weight to volume. (物理)密度(重量與體積的關係)。

dent /dent ; dɛnt/ *n* hollow, depression, in a hard surface made by a blow or by pressure; (fig, colloq): (堅硬的表面上因受打擊或壓力所形成的)凹痕;凹陷;(喩,俗): *a ~ in one's pride.* 自尊心受到的創痕。 □ *vt, vi* **1** [VP6A] make a ~ or ~s in: 使凹陷;造成凹痕於: *a motor-car badly ~ed in a collision.* 在撞車中被撞凹得厲害的汽車。 **2** [VP2A] get ~s in: 被撞凹: *metal that ~s easily.* 易被撞凹的金屬。

den·tal /ˈdentl ; ˈdɛntl̩/ *adj* **1** of or for the teeth: 牙齒的;適於牙齒的: *a ~ plate,* a denture; 一副假牙; *a ~ surgeon.* 口腔外科醫師。 **2** (phon) with the tip of the tongue near or touching the upper front teeth: (語音)齒音的(以舌尖靠近或接觸上門牙): *~ sounds,* eg /θ, ð/. 齒音(例如 /θ, ð/)。

den·ti·frice /ˈdentɪfrɪs ; ˈdɛntəˌfrɪs/ *n* [U] tooth-powder or toothpaste (the usu words). 牙粉;牙膏(toothpowder 及 toothpaste 爲通常用語)。

den·tist /ˈdentɪst ; ˈdɛntɪst/ *n* person whose work is filling, cleaning, taking out teeth and fitting artificial teeth. 牙醫(其業務爲補牙、洗牙、拔牙及裝假牙)。 **~ry** /ˈdentɪstrɪ ; ˈdɛntɪstrɪ/ *n* [U] work of a ~. 牙醫術。

den·ture /ˈdentʃə(r) ; ˈdɛntʃɚ/ *n* [C] plate (fitted on the gums) of artificial teeth. (裝於齒齦上的)假牙。

de·nude /dɪˈnjuːd *US:* -ˈnuːd ; dɪˈnjud/ *vt* [VP6A, 14] ~ ***(of),*** **1** make bare; take away covering: 使裸露;取去其覆蓋物: *trees ~d of leaves;* 葉子落盡的禿樹; *hillsides ~d of trees.* 無樹木的禿山坡。 **2** deprive: 剝奪: *~d by his creditors of every penny he had.* 被債權人剝得分文不留。 **de·nud·ation** /ˌdiːnjuːˈdeɪʃn *US:* -nuː- ; ˌdinjuˈdeʃən/ *n*

de·nunci·ation /dɪˌnʌnsɪˈeɪʃn ; dɪˌnʌnsɪˈeʃən/ *n* [C, U] denouncing: 公開指摘;揭發;通知廢止: *the ~ of a traitor.* 揭發某人爲奸逆。

deny /dɪˈnaɪ ; dɪˈnaɪ/ *vt* **1** [VP6A, C, 9, 25] say that (sth) is not true: 否認(某事);不承認: *The accused man denied the charge.* 被告人不承認所控之罪。 *I ~ that the statement is true.* 我不承認這話是眞的。 *He denied this to be the case.* 他不承認情形是如此。 *He denied knowing anything about / denied any knowledge of their plans.* 他否認知悉他們的計畫。 *It cannot be denied that... / There is no ~ing the fact that...,* Everyone must admit that.... 不可否認的是…(我們必須承認…)。 ⇨ affirm. **2** [VP6A] say that one knows nothing about; disown; refuse to acknowledge: 否認知情;拒認: *He denied the signature,* said that it was not his. 他否認這是他的簽字。 *Peter denied Christ.* 彼得不認基督。 **3** [VP12A, 13A] say 'no' to a request; refuse to give (sth asked for or needed): 拒絶;不給(所請求或需要之物): *He denies himself / his wife nothing.* 他對自己(妻子)有求必應。 *He gave to his friends what he denied to his family.* 他寧贈朋友不與家人。 *She was angry at being denied admittance.* 她因被拒進入而發怒。

deo·dar /ˈdɪədɑː(r) ; ˈdiəˌdɑr/ *n* Himalayan cedar. 喜馬拉雅山所產之杉。

de·odor·ant /diːˈəʊdərənt ; diˈodərənt/ *n* substance that disguises or absorbs (esp body) odours. 防臭劑;除臭劑(尤指除體臭者)。

de·odor·ize /diːˈəʊdəraɪz ; diˈodəˌraɪz/ *vt* [VP6A] remove odour (esp bad smells) from. 除去…之氣味(尤指臭氣);防臭。

de·part /dɪˈpɑːt ; dɪˈpɑrt/ *vi* **1** [VP2A, 3A] ~ ***(from),*** go away; leave (esp in timetables, abbr **dep**): 離開;出發;開出(尤用於行車時刻表中,略作 dep): *dep Leeds 4.30 pm.* 下午四時三十分自里玆開出。⇨ arrive. **2** [VP3A] ~ ***from,*** behave in a way that differs from: 不按照;不遵守: *~ from routine / the usual procedure / old customs;* 不按照常規(通常手續,舊風俗)行事; *~ from the truth.* 違背眞理。 **3** ~ ***(from) this life,*** (archaic) die. (古)亡故;逝世。 **~ed** *part adj* bygone: 過去的;逝去的: *thinking of ~ed glories.* 懷念過去的光榮。□ *n* **the ~ed,** *(sing)* person who has recently died; (*pl*) those who have died: (單)最近亡故的人;(複)死者: *pray for the* *souls of the ~ed.* 爲死者的靈魂祈禱。

de·part·ment /dɪˈpɑːtmənt ; dɪˈpɑrtmənt/ *n* **1** one of several divisions of a government, business, shop, university, etc: (政府或商業機構中的)部門;(大學中的)系科: *the Education D~ / D~ of Education;* 教育部(系); *the shipping ~* (of a business firm); (商業公司的)發貨部; *the men's clothing ~* (in a large shop); (大商店中的)男裝部; *a '~ store,* a large shop where many kinds of goods are sold in different ~s. (貨物分門別類的)百貨公司。 **2** (F) administrative district. (法) 行政區。**~al** /ˌdiːpɑːtˈmentl ; dɪˌpɑrtˈmɛntl̩/ *adj* of a ~ (contrasted with the whole): 一個部門的(與整體相對): *~al duties / administration.* 各部門的職責(行政)。

de·par·ture /dɪˈpɑːtʃə(r) ; dɪˈpɑrtʃɚ/ *n* **~ *(from),*** **1** [U] departing; going away; [C] instance of this: 離開;離去;出發: *His ~ was unexpected.* 他的離去出人意外。*There are notices showing arrivals and ~s of trains near the booking-office.* 在售票處附近有公告說明火車到站及開出的時刻。*Which is the ~ platform,* that from which the train leaves? 哪一個月臺是開車月臺? **2** [C, U] turning away or aside; changing: 背馳;轉變;改變: *a ~ from old custom;* 不照舊俗行事; *a new ~ in physics,* eg the discovery of nuclear fission. 物理學上的新起點(如核子分裂之發現)。

de·pend /dɪˈpend ; dɪˈpɛnd/ *vi* [VP3A] **~ *on / upon,*** **1** (not in the progressive tenses) need, rely on (the support, etc of) in order to exist or to be true or to succeed: (不用於進行式)依賴;依靠(…的支持方可存在,成爲事實或成功): *Children ~ on their parents for food and clothing.* 小孩依賴他們的父母供給衣食。*Good health ~s upon good food, exercise and getting enough sleep.* 良好的健康仰賴良好的食物,運動和充足的睡眠。*He ~s on his pen for a living,* makes a living by writing. 他靠筆桿(卽寫作)爲生。 ***that ~s; it (all) ~s,*** (alone, or at the beginning of a sentence) the result ~s on sth else: 視情形而定(單獨使用或置於句首): *It ~s how you tackle the problem.* 那要看你如何應付這問題而定。 **2** trust; be certain about: 信賴;相信: *you can always ~ upon John to be there when he is needed.* 當你需要約翰的時候,你可永遠相信他一定在那兒。*You may ~ upon his coming / ~ upon it that he will want to come.* 你可相信(我敢說)他會來。*Can I ~ upon this railway guide or is it an old one?* 這火車時刻手册是可靠的,還是舊的? ***~ upon it,*** (at the beginning or end of a sentence) you can be quite certain: (用於句首或句尾)你可以完全相信;我敢說: *The strike will ruin the country, ~ upon it.* 這次罷工將使國家遭受嚴重損失,我敢說。**~·able** *adj* that may be ~ed upon. 可信賴的;可靠的。

de·pend·ant (also **-ent**) /dɪˈpendənt ; dɪˈpɛndənt/ *n* sb who depends upon another or others for a home, food, etc; servant. 依賴他人生活者;眷屬;僕從。⇨ dependent *adj.*

de·pend·ence /dɪˈpendəns ; dɪˈpɛndəns/ *n* **~ *on / upon,*** [U] **1** the state of depending; being supported by others: 依賴;依靠: *Why don't you find a job and end this ~ upon your parents?* 你爲何不找個職業,不要再依靠你的父母呢? **2** confident trust; reliance: 信賴;信任: *He's not a man you can put much ~ on,* you can't rely on him. 他不是個可靠的人。 **3** the state of being determined or conditioned by: 視…而定的狀態;受到限制的狀態: *the ~ of the crops upon the weather;* 作物之視天氣狀況而定; *drug ~.* 藥癮。

de·pend·ency /dɪˈpendənsɪ ; dɪˈpɛndənsɪ/ *n* (*pl* -cies) country governed or controlled by another: 屬地;附庸國: *The Hawaiian Islands are no longer a ~ of the USA.* 夏威夷群島不再是美國的屬地。

de·pend·ent /dɪˈpendənt ; dɪˈpɛndənt/ *n* = dependant. □ *adj* **~ *on / upon,*** depending: 依賴的;依靠的: *The man was out of work and ~ on his son's earnings.* 那人失業了,依賴其子之收入過活。*Promotion is ~ upon your record of success.* 晉級依據優良的考績。

de·pict /dɪˈpɪkt ; dɪˈpɪkt/ *vt* [VP6A] show in the form of a picture; describe in words: 描繪;描寫: *biblical scenes ~ed in tapestry.* 繡帷上所繡的聖經故事。 **de·pic·tion** /dɪˈpɪkʃn ; dɪˈpɪkʃən/ *n*

de·pila·tory /dɪˈpɪlətrɪ *US:* -tɔːrɪ ; dɪˈpɪləˌtorɪ/ *adj, n* (liquid, cream, etc) able to remove superfluous hair. 能除去多餘毛髮的;脫毛的;脫毛劑。

de·plane /ˌdiːˈpleɪn ; diˈplen/ *vi* (usu of troops, etc) disembark from an aircraft. (通常指軍隊等)下飛機。

de·plete /dɪˈpliːt ; dɪˈplit/ *vt* [VP6A, 14] **~ *(of),*** use up, empty until little or none remains: 用盡;使竭: *to ~ a lake of fish;* 將湖中之魚捕盡; *~d supplies.* 用盡的必需品。 **de·pletion** /dɪˈpliːʃn ; dɪˈpliʃən/ *n* [U] depleting or being ~d. 取盡;用盡。

de·plore /dɪˈplɔː(r) ; dɪˈplor/ *vt* [VP6A] show, say, that one is filled with sorrow or regret for; condemn. 表示爲…而悲痛或懊悔;指責。**de·plor·able** /dɪˈplɔːrəbl ; dɪˈplorəbl̩/ *adj* that is, or should be, ~d: 可悲的;可憐的;不幸的: *deplorable conduct;* 可悲的行爲; *a deplorable accident.* 悲慘的意外禍事。 **de·plor·ably** /-əblɪ ; -əblɪ/ *adv*

de·ploy /dɪˈplɔɪ ; dɪˈplɔɪ/ *vt, vi* [VP6A, 2A] (mil, of troops etc) (cause to) spread out, eg into line of battle; (fig) bring into action: (軍,指部隊等)(使)展開(成戰鬪隊形等);(喻)使開始活動或工作: *~ arguments.* 展開辯論。**~·ment** *n*

de·pon·ent /dɪˈpəʊnənt ; dɪˈponənt/ *n* (legal) person who gives written testimony for use in a law court. (法律)作書面證詞供法院使用的人;作證者。

de·popu·late /ˌdiːˈpɒpjʊleɪt ; diˈpɑpjəˌlet/ *vt* [VP6A] lessen the number of people living in a place: 減少(居住某地之)人口: *a country ~d by war / famine.* 因戰爭(饑荒)而人口減少的國家。 **de·popu·la·tion** /ˌdiːˌpɒpjʊˈleɪʃn ; ˌdipɑpjəˈleʃən/ *n*

de·port[1] /dɪˈpɔːt ; dɪˈport/ *vt* [VP6A] expel (an unwanted person) from a country: 驅逐(不受歡迎者)出境: *The spy was imprisoned for two years and then ~ed.* 那間諜經監禁兩年後被驅逐出境。**de·port·ation** /ˌdiːpɔːˈteɪʃn ; ˌdiporˈteʃən/ *n* [U] ~ing or being ~ed: 驅逐出境;被放逐: *Years ago criminals in England could be sentenced to ~ation to Australia.* 許多年前,英國的罪犯可能被判放逐至澳洲。**~ee** /ˌdiːpɔːˈtiː ; ˌdiporˈti/ *n* ~ed person. 被放逐者。

de·port[2] /dɪˈpɔːt ; dɪˈport/ *vt* [VP6A, 16B] (reflex, formal) behave: (用反身式,正式用語)行爲;持身;處己: *to ~ oneself with dignity.* 舉止莊重。**~·ment** *n* [U] behaviour; way of holding oneself in standing and walking: 行爲;舉止: *Young ladies used to have lessons in ~ment.* 少女們以前從師學習舉止行動的規矩。

de·pose /dɪˈpəʊz ; dɪˈpoz/ *vt, vi* **1** [VP6A] remove, esp a ruler such as a king, from a position of authority; dethrone. 迫使(君王等)下臺;廢除(王位等)。 **2** [VP3A, 9] **~ *(to + gerund),*** (legal) bear witness, give evidence, esp on oath in a law court: (法律)(尤指在法庭宣誓)作證: *to ~ that one saw...;* 誓證曾親見…; *to ~ to having seen....* 誓證曾親見…。 ⇨ deposition.

de·posit[1] /dɪˈpɒzɪt ; dɪˈpɑzɪt/ *vt* [VP6A] **1** lay or put down: 置;放下: *He ~ed the books on the desk.* 他將書籍放在寫字桌上。*Some insects ~ their eggs in the ground.* 有些昆蟲產卵於土中。 **2** put or store for safe-keeping: 存放;貯存;交與…保管: *to ~ money in a bank / papers with one's lawyer.* 將錢存於銀行(將文件交與律師保管)。 **3** make part payment of money that is or will be owed: 付定金;先付一部分: *We should like you to ~ a quarter of the price of the house.* 我們希望你能先付房價的四分之一。 **4** (esp of a liquid, a river) leave (a layer of matter on): (尤指液體,河流)沉澱;淤積: *When the Nile rises it ~s a layer of mud on the land.* 尼羅河漲水時在地上淤積一層泥。

de·posit[2] /dɪˈpɒzɪt ; dɪˈpɑzɪt/ *n* [C] **1** money that is deposited (2, 3): 存款;定金;定錢: *The shopkeeper* *promised to keep the goods for me if I left/paid/made a* ~. 店主答應，如果我付一點定錢，他就可將貨物替我保留下來。'~ **account**, money deposited in a bank, not to be withdrawn without notice, on which interest is payable. (需預先通知方可提取而且可以拿利息的)存款帳戶。⇨ *current account* at current¹(3). ***money on*** ~, money deposited in this way. 存款。'~ **safe**, safe in the strong-room of a bank, rented for the custody of valuables. 銀行保險庫內之保險箱 (可租用置放貴重物品者)。**2** layer of matter deposited(4): 沉澱物；淤積物: *A thick ~ of mud covered the fields after the floods went down.* 洪水過後，田地上蓋着一層厚厚的淤泥。**3** layer of solid matter left behind (often buried in the earth) after having been naturally accumulated: (天然積聚而成，通常埋藏於地下的)礦床；礦層: *Valuable new ~s of tin have been found in Bolivia.* 寶貴的新錫礦床已在玻利維亞發現。

de·posi·tion /ˌdepəˈzɪʃn ; ˌdɛpəˈzɪʃən/ *n* **1** [U] deposing from office; dethronement. 革職；廢王位。**2** [C] (legal) statement made on oath. (法律)經宣誓所作的證言。**3** [U] depositing, eg of mud. (泥等的)淤積；沉澱。

de·posi·tor /dɪˈpɒzɪtə(r) ; dɪˈpɑzɪtɚ/ *n* person who deposits, eg money in a bank. 寄託者；(存款於銀行等中的)存款者。

de·posi·tory /dɪˈpɒzɪtrɪ *US:* -tɔːrɪ ; dɪˈpɑzəˌtorɪ/ *n* (*pl* -ries) place where goods are deposited; storehouse. 存放貨物的地方；倉庫。

de·pot /ˈdepəʊ *US:* ˈdiːpəʊ ; ˈdipo/ *n* **1** storehouse, esp for military supplies; warehouse; place for storing vehicles (eg buses). 軍需庫；倉庫；庫房；(公共汽車等之)車庫。**2** (US) railway or bus station. (美)火車站；公共汽車站。

de·prave /dɪˈpreɪv ; dɪˈprev/ *vt* [VP6A] make morally bad; corrupt (usu in *pp*): 使道德敗壞；使腐敗(通常用過去分詞): *~d persons;* 墮落的人; *~d* (= vicious or perverted) *tastes.* 邪惡的嗜好。

de·prav·ity /dɪˈprævətɪ ; dɪˈprævətɪ/ *n* [U] depraved state; viciousness: 墮落；邪惡；腐敗: *sunk in ~;* 沉淪；墮落; [C] (*pl* -ties) vicious act. 邪惡的行爲。

dep·re·cate /ˈdeprəkeɪt ; ˈdɛprəˌket/ *vt* [VP6A, C] (formal) feel and express disapproval of: (正式用語)表示不贊成；反對: *Hasty action is to be ~d.* 草率行事應予反對。*He ~s changing the rules at present.* 他不贊成在目前改變規章。**dep·reca·tion** /ˌdeprəˈkeɪʃn ; ˌdɛprəˈkeʃən/ *n*

de·pre·ci·ate /dɪˈpriːʃɪeɪt ; dɪˈpriʃɪˌet/ *vt, vi* [VP6A, 2A] make or become less in value; say that (sth) has little value: (使)減低價值；(使)貶值；輕視；貶抑: *Shares in this company have ~d.* 這家公司的股票已貶值了。*Don't ~ my efforts to help.* 不要輕視我爲了幫忙所作的努力。**de·pre·ci·atory** /dɪˈpriːʃətərɪ *US:* -tɔːrɪ ; dɪˈpriʃɪəˌtorɪ/ *adj* tending to ~: 貶值的；輕視的；貶抑的: *depreciatory remarks about my work.* 對我的工作有所貶抑的話。**de·pre·ci·ation** /dɪˌpriːʃɪˈeɪʃn ; dɪˌpriʃɪˈeʃən/ *n* [U] lessening of value or estimation. 貶值；折舊；輕視。

dep·re·da·tion /ˌdeprəˈdeɪʃn ; ˌdɛprɪˈdeʃən/ *n* (usu *pl*) (formal) destruction or pillaging of property. (通常用複數)(正式用語)毀壞或刧掠財產。

de·press /dɪˈpres ; dɪˈprɛs/ *vt* [VP6A] **1** press, push or pull down: 壓下；推下；拉下: *to ~ a lever/the keys of a piano.* 壓下槓桿(鋼琴鍵)。ˌ~**ed** ˈ**classes**, classes of people who are prevented from rising, or unable to rise, socially or economically, eg by a rigid caste system. 受壓迫的階級；下層階級之人民(社會或經濟地位不能提高之人，如因受嚴格的階級制度所限制者)。**2** make sad, low in spirits: 使愁苦；使沮喪: *Wet weather always ~es her.* 雨天總使她愁苦。*The newspapers are full of ~ing news nowadays,* eg of war, crime, natural disasters, rising prices. 報紙如今充滿了令人憂愁的消息(例如戰爭，犯罪，天災，物價上漲)。**3** make less active; cause (prices) to be lower: 使不活潑；使跌價；使蕭條: *When business is ~ed there is usually an increase in unemployment.* 當商業蕭條時，通常失業就會增加。ˌ~**ed** ˈ**area**, part of a country where industry is ~ed (with consequent poverty and unemployment). 工商業蕭條(結果造成貧窮和失業)的地區。

de·press·ion /dɪˈpreʃn ; dɪˈprɛʃən/ *n* **1** [U] being depressed(2); low spirits: 愁苦；沮喪；抑鬱: *He commited suicide during a fit of ~.* 他一時想不開自殺了。**2** [C] hollow, sunk place, in the surface of sth, esp the ground: 表面(尤指地面)凹陷之處；窪穴；坑: *It rained heavily and every ~ in the bad road was soon filled with water.* 雨下得很大，不久那壞路上的每一坑凹都積滿了水。*The soldiers hid from the enemy in a slight ~.* 士兵們藏在一個淺坑裏躲過了敵人的視線。**3** [C] time when business is depressed(3). 商業蕭條的時期。**4** [C] lowering of atmospheric pressure; (esp) area of low barometric pressure; the system of winds round it: 氣壓降低；低氣壓；(尤指)低氣壓區域；低氣壓區域周圍的風: *a ~ over Iceland.* 冰島上空的低氣壓。

de·press·ive /dɪˈpresɪv ; dɪˈprɛsɪv/ *adj* tending to depress; of depression(1): 壓抑的；壓下的；不景氣的；沮喪的；抑鬱的: *~ financial measures;* 平抑物價的金融措施; *a ~ fit.* 一陣沮喪。□ *n* person tending to suffer from depression(1). 沮喪者；抑鬱者。

de·prive /dɪˈpraɪv ; dɪˈpraɪv/ *vt* [VP14] ~ ***of***, take away from; prevent from using or enjoying: 取走；剝奪；使喪失；使不能使用或享受: *trees that ~ a house of light.* 遮住房中光線的樹木。*What would a student do if he were ~d of his books?* 一個學生假若沒有了書籍，將怎麼辦？**de·prived** *adj* = underprivileged. **depri·va·tion** /ˌdeprɪˈveɪʃn ; ˌdɛprɪˈveʃən/ *n* [U] depriving or being ~d: 剝奪；奪去: *deprivation of one's rights as a citizen;* 某人公民權之被剝奪; [C] sth of which one is ~d. 被奪之物。

depth /depθ ; dɛpθ/ *n* **1** [C, U] being deep; distance from the top down, from the front to the back, from the surface inwards: 深；深度(自頂端而下，自前至後，自表面向內的距離): *What is the ~ of the well?* 此井深度若干？*Water was found at a ~ of 30 feet.* 水在三十呎深處被發現。*At what ~ is the wreck lying?* 破船殘骸在多深的水中？*The snow is three feet in ~.* 雪積三呎深。***in*** ~, thorough(ly): 徹底的(地): *explore a subject in ~;* 徹底探究一題目; *a study in ~.* 徹底的研究。***be/go/get out of one's*** ~, **(a)** be in/enter water too deep to stand in: 入水至不能立穩(即觸不到底或沒頂)的深度: *If you can't swim, don't go out of your ~.* 你如果不會游泳，不要到水太深的地方去。**(b)** (fig) attempt the study of sth that is too difficult: (喻)企圖研究過於難懂的事物: *When people start talking about nuclear physics I'm out of my ~.* 當人們談起核子物理學，我就茫無所知了。ˈ~-**bomb**/-**charge**, bomb used against a submarine, for explosion under water. 深水炸彈(在水中爆炸，以攻擊潛艇者)。**2** [C, U] deep learning, thought, feeling, etc: 深奧的學問，思想，感情等: *a book that shows scholarship and ~ of thought.* 顯示出學術及思想之深度的書。*She showed a ~ of feeling that surprised us.* 她表現出的强烈的感情令我們吃驚。**3** ***the*** ~**(s)**, deepest or most central part(s): 最深之處；最內部: *in the ~ of one's heart;* 在心的深處; *in the ~ of winter;* 在隆冬; *in the ~s of despair;* 在極度絕望中; *in the ~ of the country,* a long way from any town. 在窮鄉僻壤。

depu·ta·tion /ˌdepjʊˈteɪʃn ; ˌdɛpjəˈteʃən/ *n* group of representatives; number of persons given the right to act or speak for others. 代表團(被授權代表他人行爲或發言的若干人)。

de·pute /dɪˈpjuːt ; dɪˈpjut/ *vt* [VP14, 17] ~ ***sth to sb/sb to do sth***, give (one's work, authority, etc) to a substitute; give (another person) authority to act as one's representative. 將(工作，職權等)交與代理人；給予(某人)代表行事之權。

depu·tize /ˈdepjʊtaɪz ; ˈdɛpjəˌtaɪz/ *vi* [VP2A, 3A] ~ ***(for sb)***, act as deputy. (爲某人之)代表。

dep·uty /'depjʊtɪ ; 'dɛpjətɪ/ *n* (*pl* -ties) **1** person to whom work, authority, etc is deputed: 受託代理工作，職權等的人；代表；代理人: *I must find someone to act as* (*a*) ～ *for me during my absence.* 我必須找一個人，在我離開期間代理我的職務。 **2** (in some countries, eg France) member of a legislative assembly. (在某些國家，例如法國)議員。

de·rail /dɪ'reɪl ; di'rel/ *vt* [VP6A] cause (a train, etc) to run off the rails: 使(火車等)出軌: *The engine was ～ed.* 火車頭出軌了。 **～·ment** *n*

de·range /dɪ'reɪndʒ ; dɪ'rendʒ/ *vt* [VP6A] put out of working order; put into confusion; disturb: 使失去正常的作用或功能；使混亂；攪亂: *He is mentally ～d,* insane. 他精神錯亂了。 **～·ment** *n*

de·rate /ˌdiː'reɪt ; di'ret/ *vt* [VP6A] (GB) relieve (industries, etc) from a proportion of the local rates(3): (英)減低(工業等)的房地產稅: *the Derating Act, 1929.* 1929 年所制定的減低房地產稅法案。

derby[1] /'dɑːbɪ *US:* 'dɜːrbɪ ; 'dɝbɪ/ *n* **1 The D～,** annual horserace at Epsom, England. 在英國艾普孫所舉行一年一度的大賽馬。 **'D～ Day,** day of the race (in June). 舉行此項大賽馬的日子(在六月)。 **2** (US) any of several annual horseraces. (美)任何每年舉行的賽馬會。 **3** sporting contest. 運動比賽。 **local ～,** one between local teams. 地方運動比賽。

derby[2] /'dɜːrbɪ ; 'dɝbɪ/ *n* (US) bowler hat. (美)圓頂禮帽。

der·el·ict /'derəlɪkt ; 'dɛrəˌlɪkt/ *adj* abandoned; deserted and left to fall into ruin: 被棄的；被遺棄的: *a ～ house;* 被棄的房屋； *a ～ ship;* 棄船； *～ areas,* eg those made squalid by open-cast mining, gravel digging. 被棄地區(例如因地上開採礦物，掘砂礫後被棄置的污穢地區)。 **der·el·ic·tion** /ˌderə'lɪkʃn ; ˌdɛrə'lɪkʃən/ *n* [U] **1** making ～: 放棄；遺棄: *the dereliction caused by the armies of Genghis Khan.* 成吉思汗的軍隊造成的廢墟。**2** (wilful) neglect of duty. (故意的)怠忽職責。

de·requi·si·tion /ˌdiːˌrekwɪ'zɪʃn ; diˌrɛkwə'zɪʃən/ *vt* [VP6A] free (requisitioned property, etc). 退還(被徵用的財產等)。

de·re·strict /ˌdiːrɪ'strɪkt ; ˌdirɪ'strɪkt/ *vt* [VP6A] cancel a restriction upon: 解除限制: *～ a road,* remove a speed limit from it. 解除某路之行車速率限制。

de·ride /dɪ'raɪd ; dɪ'raɪd/ *vt* [VP6A, 16B] mock; laugh scornfully at: 嘲弄；嘲笑: *They ～d his efforts as childish.* 他們笑指他的努力爲幼稚。

de rigeur /də rɪ'gɜː(r) ; dəri'gœːr/ *pred adj* (F) required by etiquette or custom: (法)禮節或風俗上所需要的: *Evening dress is ～ at the Casino.* 晚禮服在娛樂場是禮節上所需要的。

de·rision /dɪ'rɪʒn ; dɪ'rɪʒən/ *n* [U] deriding or being derided; ridicule, mockery: 嘲弄；嘲笑；被嘲笑的事物；笑柄: *hold sb／sth in ～;* 嘲笑某人(某事物)； *be／become an object of ～;* 成爲嘲笑的對象； *make sb／sth an object of ～.* 使某人(某事物)成爲笑柄。

de·ris·ive /dɪ'raɪsɪv ; dɪ'raɪsɪv/ *adj* showing or deserving derision: 嘲笑的；嘲弄的；可笑的: *～ laughter;* 嘲弄的笑聲； *a ～ offer,* eg £100 for a car that is worth £1000. 可笑的出價(如出一百鎊欲買價值一千鎊的汽車)。

de·ris·ory /dɪ'raɪsərɪ ; dɪ'raɪsərɪ/ *adj* = derisive.

deri·va·tion /ˌderɪ'veɪʃn ; ˌdɛrə'veʃən/ *n* **1** [U] deriving or being derived; origin; descent: 引出；導出；根源；由來: *the ～ of words from Latin* 源於拉丁文之字的演變； *a word of Latin ～.* 源出於拉丁文之字。 **2** [C] first form and meaning of a word; statement of how a word was formed and how it changed: 字之最初的形義；字之起源及變化的說明: *to study the ～s of words.* 研究字的起源及變化。

de·riva·tive /dɪ'rɪvətɪv ; də'rɪvətɪv/ *adj, n* [C] (thing, word, substance) derived from another; not original or primitive: 由他物而來的(物件，物質)；由他字而來的(字)；非本來的；非原始的；轉來的；衍生物；轉化字；引申字: *'Assertion' is a ～ of 'assert'.* assertion 一字由 assert 轉化而來。

de·rive /dɪ'raɪv ; də'raɪv/ *vt, vi* **1** [VP14] **～ from,** (formal) get: (正式用語)得來；得到: *to ～ great pleasure from one's studies;* 自讀書研究獲得極大的樂趣； *medicine from which she has ～d little benefit.* 使她得益很少的藥物。 **2** [VP14, 3A] **～ from,** take／have as a starting-point, source or origin: 源出；起源: *Thousands of English words ～ from／are ～d from Latin.* 英文有成千上萬的字源出於拉丁文。

der·ma·tol·ogy /ˌdɜːmə'tɒlədʒɪ ; ˌdɝmə'tɑlədʒɪ/ *n* [U] medical study of the skin, its diseases, etc. 皮膚(病)學。 **der·ma·tol·ogist** /ˌdɜːmə'tɒlədʒɪst ; ˌdɝmə'tɑlədʒɪst/ *n* expert in ～. 皮膚(病)學家。

dero·gate /'derəgeɪt ; 'dɛrəˌget/ *vi* [VP3A] **～ from,** (formal) take away (a merit, good quality, right). (正式用語)取去；除去(功績、良好的品質、權利)。 **dero·ga·tion** /ˌderə'geɪʃn ; ˌdɛrə'geʃən/ *n* [U] lessening (*of* authority, dignity, reputation, etc). 減低(權威、尊嚴、名譽等，與 of 連用)。

de·roga·tory /dɪ'rɒgətrɪ *US:* -tɔːrɪ ; dɪ'rɑgəˌtorɪ/ *adj* (abbr *derog* used in this dictionary) (本字典中略作 derog) **～ (to),** tending to damage or take away from (one's credit, etc); insulting: 損毀或減低(人之榮譽等)的；侮蔑的；貶抑的: *remarks that are ～ to my reputation.* 有損我名譽的言論。 *Is the slang word 'cop' as ～ as 'pig' for 'policeman',* Are policemen likely to object to it as being insulting? 用俚語 cop 稱警察和用 pig 稱呼他們一樣會引起反感(會使警察因受辱而反對)嗎？

der·rick /'derɪk ; 'dɛrɪk/ *n* **1 ～ crane,** large crane for moving or lifting heavy weights, esp on a ship. (尤指船上的)起重機。 **2** (also 亦作 *oil-rig*) framework over an oil-well or bore-hole, to hold the drilling machinery, etc. (在油井或其他鑽孔上用以支持鑽具等的)鐵架塔。

derrick cranes

an oil derrick

der·ring-do /ˌderɪŋ 'duː ; 'dɛrɪŋ'du/ *n* [U] (old use) desperate courage: (舊用法)不顧危險的勇敢: *deeds of ～.* 不顧死活的勇敢行爲。

derv /dɜːv ; dɝv/ *n* [U] fuel oil for diesel engines (from *d*iesel *e*ngined *r*oad *v*ehicle). 柴油機所用的燃料油；柴油(原名由 *d*iesel *e*ngined *r*oad *v*ehicle 四字爲首字母拼成)。

der·vish /'dɜːvɪʃ ; 'dɝvɪʃ/ *n* member of an order of Muslim religious enthusiasts: (回教之)苦修僧人: *dancing ～es,* who engage in whirling dances; 崇拜時身體廻旋舞動的苦修僧人； *howling ～es,* who shout loudly. 高聲吼叫的苦修僧人。

de·sali·nate /ˌdiː'sælɪneɪt ; di'sæləˌnet/ *vt* [VP6A] = desalinize. **de·sali·na·tion** /ˌdiːˌsælɪ'neɪʃn ; ˌdisælə'neʃən/ *n*

de·sali·nize /ˌdiː'sælɪnaɪz ; di'sælɪˌnaɪz/ *vt* [VP6A] remove salt from (sea water or saline water). 除去(海水或鹽水中的)鹽分。 **de·salin·iz·ation** /ˌdiːˌsælɪnaɪ'zeɪʃn *US:* -nɪ'z- ; ˌdisæˌlɪnə'zeʃən/ *n*

de·salt /ˌdiː'sɔːlt ; di'sɔlt/ *vt* = desalinize.

de·scale /ˌdiː'skeɪl ; di'skel/ *vt* [VP6A] remove the scale from, eg the inside of boiler tubes. 除去(汽鍋管內等)的鍋垢或銹皮。

des·cant /'deskænt ; 'dɛskænt/ *n* (music) additional

independent accompaniment (often improvised) to a melody. (音樂)附加的獨立伴奏或伴唱旋律(常是即興而作的)。□ *vi* /dɪˈskænt ; dɛsˈkænt/ [VP3A] ～ ***on／upon***, **(a)** (music) sing or play a ～ on. (音樂)爲…唱或演奏獨立伴奏曲。**(b)** comment on, enlarge upon (a topic). 評論;評論(一題目)。

de·scend /dɪˈsend ; dɪˈsɛnd/ *vi, vt* **1** [VP2A, C, 6A] (formal) come or go down: (正式用語)下來;下去: *On turning the corner, we saw that the road ～ed steeply.* 在轉彎的時候,我們看見路陡然下斜。*The balloon ～ed in Poland.* 汽球落於波蘭境內。*He ～ed the stairs.* 他下樓。 **2** ***be ～ed from***, have as ancestors: 爲…的後裔: *According to the Bible, we are all ～ed from Adam.* 根據聖經,我們都是亞當的後裔。 **3** [VP2C] (of property, qualities, rights) pass (from father to son) by inheritance; come from earlier times. (指財產,氣質,權利)遺傳;傳代;由較早的時代傳下來。**4** [VP3A] ～ ***on／upon***, attack suddenly; (colloq) visit unexpectedly: 突擊;(俗)出其不意地拜訪: *The bandits ～ed upon the defenceless village.* 匪徒突擊無防禦的村莊。 **5** [VP3A] ～ ***to***, lower oneself to: 自貶身份;流於: *You would never ～ to fraud／cheating.* 你絕不至淪於欺騙。 **6** ***～ to particulars***, pass on (in an argument, etc) to details, eg after a general introduction to a subject. (在辯論等中介紹過題目的概要過後)進入詳細討論階段。**～ant** /-ənt;-ənt/ *n* person who is ～ed from (the person or persons named): 後裔;後代;子孫: *the ～ants of Queen Victoria.* 維多利亞女王的後裔。

de·scent /dɪˈsent ; dɪˈsɛnt/ *n* **1** [C, U] coming or going down: 下來;下去: *The land slopes to the sea by a gradual ～,* slopes gradually. 陸地逐漸向海傾斜下去。 *The ～ of the mountain took two hours.* 下山花了兩個小時。 **2** [U] ancestry: 祖先;祖籍: *of French ～*, having French ancestors; 祖籍法國; *Darwin's 'D～ of Man'*, ie his theory of evolution. 達爾文的'進化論'。*He traces his ～ from the Queen of Sheba.* 他追溯他的祖籍係出於希巴女王。 **3** [C] ～ ***on／upon***, sudden attack on; (colloq) unexpected visit to: 突襲;(俗)出其不意的拜訪: *The Danes made numerous ～s upon the English coast during the 10th century.* 在第10世紀中,丹麥人曾對英國沿海作無數次的突襲。**4** [U] handing down, eg of property, titles, qualities, etc by inheritance. (財產,名位,特質等)世代相傳。

de·scribe /dɪˈskraɪb ; dɪˈskraɪb/ *vt* **1** [VP6A, 14, 10, 16B] ～ ***(to／for)***, say what (sb or sth) is like; give a picture of in words: 描寫;(用語言文字)描繪;描述: *Words cannot ～ the beauty of the scene.* 此景之美非筆墨所能形容。*Can you ～ it to／for me?* 你能把它描述給我聽嗎? *Please ～ what you saw.* 請敘述所見。 **2** [VP16B] ～ ***as***, qualify; say that (sb or sth) has certain qualities: 形容;說(某人或某事物)有某種性質: *I hesitate to ～ him as really clever.* 我不願說他是眞正的聰明。*He ～s himself as a doctor.* 他自稱係醫生。**3** [VP6A] mark out, draw (esp a geometrical figure): 作圖;畫(尤指幾何圖形): *It is easy to ～ a circle if you have a pair of compasses.* 如果你有一副圓規,很容易畫一個圓。

de·scrip·tion /dɪˈskrɪpʃn ; dɪˈskrɪpʃən/ *n* **1** [U] describing; [C] picture in words: 描寫;描述;形容: *He's not very good at ～.* 他不太會描寫。*The scenery was beautiful beyond ～.* 這風景美得難以形容。*Can you give me a ～ of the thief?* 你能爲我描述一下那賊的模樣嗎? ⇨ answer²(4). **2** [C] (colloq) sort: (俗)種類;式樣: *The harbour was crowded with vessels of every ～.* 那港內充滿各式各樣的船隻。

de·scrip·tive /dɪˈskrɪptɪv ; dɪˈskrɪptɪv/ *adj* serving to describe; fond of describing: 描寫的;喜歡描寫的: *There is some excellent ～ writing* (eg descriptions of scenery) *in Hardy's novels.* 在哈代的小說中,有些極美的描寫(如描寫風景)。

des·cry /dɪˈskraɪ ; dɪˈskraɪ/ *vt* [VP6A] (formal) catch sight of; see (esp sth a long way off). (正式用語)察覺;發現;看見(尤指遠處之物)。

des·ecrate /ˈdesɪkreɪt ; ˈdɛsɪˌkret/ *vt* [VP6A] use (a sacred thing or place) in an unworthy or wicked way. 把(聖物或聖地)作俗用或惡用;褻瀆。 **des·ecra·tion** /ˌdesɪˈkreɪʃn ; ˌdɛsɪˈkreʃən/ *n* [U] desecrating or being ～d. 褻瀆;汚辱(聖物或聖地)。

de·seg·re·gate /ˌdiːˈsegrɪgeɪt;diˈsɛgrəget/ *vt* [VP6A] abolish (esp racial) segregation in: 廢除(尤指種族)隔離: ～ *schools in Alabama.* 消除阿拉巴馬州學校內的種族隔離。 **de·seg·re·ga·tion** /ˌdiːˌsegrɪˈgeɪʃn ; diˌsɛgrəˈgeʃən/ *n*

de·sen·si·tize /ˌdiːˈsensɪtaɪz ; diˈsɛnsəˌtaɪz/ *vt* [VP6A] render insensitive or less sensitive, eg to light or pain. 使無感覺;使較不敏感(如對光線或苦痛)。 **de·sen·si·tiz·ation** /ˌdiːˌsensɪtaɪˈzeɪʃn *US:* -tɪˈz- ; ˌdisɛnsətəˈzeʃən/ *n*

de·sert¹ /dɪˈzɜːt ; dɪˈzɝt/ *vt, vi* **1** [VP6A] leave; go away from: 離開;放棄;拋棄: *The village had been hurriedly ～ed, perhaps because bandits were in the district.* 全村的人都匆匆逃走了,或許因爲有土匪到達該地區。*The streets were ～ed,* no people were to be seen. 街上行人絕跡。*We sheltered from the storm in a ～ed hut,* one that had been abandoned. 我們在一個空無人住的茅屋裏躲暴風雨。**2** [VP6A] leave without help or support, esp in a wrong or cruel way: 背棄;遺棄不顧(尤指以不當或殘忍的方法): *He ～ed his wife and children and went abroad.* 他置妻子兒女於不顧,出國去了。*He has become so rude that his friends are ～ing him.* 他變得粗暴無禮,所以朋友們都不和他來往了。 **3** [VP6A, 2A] run away from; leave (esp service in a ship, the armed forces) without authority or permission: 潛逃;未經准假而離開(尤指船上,軍中的職守);逃亡;開小差: *A soldier who ～s his post in time of war is punished severely.* 在戰時逃兵的處罰很重。 **4** [VP6A] fail: 使失敗;使失望: *His courage／presence of mind ～ed him.* 他的勇氣(鎮靜功夫)盡失。 **～er** *n* person who ～s(3). 背棄者;潛逃者;(尤指)逃兵。 **de·ser·tion** /dɪˈzɜːʃn ; dɪˈzɝʃən/ *n* [C, U] (instance of) ～ing or being ～ed. 離開;放棄;背棄;遺棄;逃亡。

des·ert² /ˈdezət ; ˈdɛzɚt/ *n* [C, U] (large area of) barren land, waterless and treeless, often sand-covered: 沙漠(無水,無樹,常爲沙覆蓋的一大片不毛之地);荒地: *the Sahara D～.* 撒哈拉沙漠。□ *adj* **1** barren; uncultivated: 荒涼的;不毛的: *the ～ areas of N Africa.* 北非洲的荒漠地區。 **2** uninhabited: 無人居住的: *wrecked on a ～ island.* 在一荒島觸礁失事。

de·serts /dɪˈzɜːts ; dɪˈzɝts/ *n* (*pl*) what sb deserves: (複)某人應得的賞罰: *to be rewarded／punished according to one's ～,* 受到應得的獎賞(懲罰); *to get／meet with one's ～.* 得到應得的賞罰。

de·serve /dɪˈzɜːv ; dɪˈzɝv/ *vt, vi* (not used in the progressive tenses; 不用於進行式; ⇨ deserving.) **1** [VP6A, 7A] be entitled to (because of actions, conduct, qualities); merit: (因爲行爲,品行,才幹而)應該得到;值得: *Good work ～s good pay.* 好的工作應得好的報酬。*He certainly ～s to be sent to prison.* 他的確應該送去坐監牢。*These people ～ our help.* 這些人值得我們幫助。 **2** ***to ～ well／ill of***, to ～ to be well／badly treated by: 應該受到…之優(虐)待: *He ～s well of his country.* 他應得國家的優待。 **de·served** *adj* that ought to be given; just: 應得的: *～d punishment／reward／praise.* 應得的懲罰(報酬,讚美)。*His promotion wasn't ～d.* 他的陞遷是不應得的。 **de·serv·ed·ly** /dɪˈzɜːvɪdlɪ ; dɪˈzɝvɪdlɪ/ *adv* according to what is ～d; justly; rightly: 按功過應得地;當然應該地: *to be ～dly punished.* 罰得應該。

de·serv·ing /dɪˈzɜːvɪŋ ; dɪˈzɝvɪŋ/ *adj* ～ ***(of)***, having merit; worthy: 有功的;值得的: *to give money to a ～ cause;* 捐款給有價值的事業; *to be ～ of sympathy;* 值得同情的; *a ～ case,* a person who, because of his circumstances, etc, deserves interest, sympathy, help, etc. 因其環境等值得關心,同情或幫助的人。

dés·habillé /ˌdeɪzæˈbiːeɪ ; dəzabiˈje/ (F) (法) =

dishabille.

des·ic·cant /ˈdesɪkənt ; ˈdɛsəkənt/ *n* (US) substance used to absorb moisture. (美)乾燥劑。

des·ic·cate /ˈdesɪkeɪt ; ˈdɛsə͵ket/ *vt* [VP6A] dry out all the moisture from, esp solid food, to preserve it: 除去(固體食物等)的水份以保存之; 乾貯: *~d fruit/coconut.* 水果(椰子)乾。

de·sid·er·atum /dɪ͵zɪdəˈrɑːtəm ; dɪ͵sɪdəˈretəm/ *n* (*pl* -rata /-ˈrɑːtə ; -ˈretə/) sth felt to be lacking and needed. 感到缺乏或需要的東西。

de·sign /dɪˈzaɪn ; dɪˈzaɪn/ *n* **1** [C] drawing or outline from which sth may be made: 圖樣;設計圖樣: *~s for a dress/garden;* 服裝(花園)的設計圖樣; [U] art of making such drawings, etc: 設計製圖術: *a school of ~.* 設計製圖學校。 **2** [U] general arrangement or planning (of a picture, book, building, machine, etc): (圖畫,書籍,建築物,機器等的)設計;佈局;配置: *The building seats 2000 people, but is poor in ~.* 這建築物有二千人的座位,但設計很差。 *A machine of faulty ~ will not sell well.* 設計不良的機器銷路不會好。 **3** [C] pattern; arrangement of lines, shapes, details, as ornament, eg on a bowl or carpet: 圖案(線條,圖形,枝節的安排,作爲裝飾,如碗上或地毯上者): *a vase with a ~ of flowers on it.* 有花形圖案的花瓶。 **4** [C, U] purpose; intention; mental plan: 目的;意向;計畫: *Whether by accident or ~, he arrived too late to help us.* 無論是意外或故意,他到得太遲了,幫不上我們的忙。 *Was the world made by ~ or did it come into existence by chance?* 宇宙是按照計畫造成的,還是偶然產生的? ***have ~s on/against,*** intend (selfishly or evilly) to get possession of: (自私或不軌地)圖謀佔有或奪取: *That man has ~s on your money/your life;* 那人圖謀你的錢財(性命); (colloq) (俗) *He has ~s on that young girl,* wants to be intimate with her. 他想打那個年輕女郎的主意。 □ *vt, vi* **1** [VP6A] prepare a plan, sketch, etc (of sth to be made): 爲…畫圖樣: *~ a dress/garden.* 爲服裝(花園)畫圖樣。 **2** [VP2A, C] make ~s(1) from which sth will be made: 設計圖樣;設計圖案: *He ~s for a large firm of carpet manufacturers.* 他爲一家織造地毯的大公司設計圖案。 **3** [VP14, 16A, B] *~ for,* set apart, intend, plan: 留作專用;打算;計畫: *This course of study is ~ed to help those wishing to teach abroad.* 這門課程是爲幫助欲至國外教書的人而開的。 *This room was ~ed for the children/~ed as a children's playroom.* 這個房間預定留給孩子們用(留作孩子們的遊戲室)。 **~·ed·ly** /-ɪdlɪ ; -ɪdlɪ/ *adv* by ~(4); on purpose. 故意地;存心地。

des·ig·nate¹ /ˈdezɪgneɪt ; ˈdɛzɪgnɪt/ *adj* (placed after the *n*) appointed to an office (but not yet installed): (置於名詞之後)已受命(而尚未就職)的: *the bishop ~.* 已受命而尚未就職的主教。

des·ig·nate² /ˈdezɪgneɪt ; ˈdɛzɪg͵net/ *vt* **1** [VP6A] mark or point out clearly; give a name or title to: 標明;指明;命名: *to ~ boundaries.* 標明界限。 **2** [VP6A, 17, 16B] appoint to a position or office: 任命;指派: *He ~d Smith as his successor.* 他指定史密斯爲他的繼任人。

des·ig·na·tion /͵dezɪgˈneɪʃn ; ͵dɛzɪgˈneʃən/ *n* [U] appointing to an office; [C] name, title or description. 任命;委派;名義;頭銜。

de·sign·er /dɪˈzaɪnə(r) ; dɪˈzaɪnə/ *n* person who designs, eg machinery, dresses. (機器,服裝等的)設計人;製圖樣者。

de·sign·ing /dɪˈzaɪnɪŋ ; dɪˈzaɪnɪŋ/ *adj* artful and cunning; fond of intrigue. 狡猾的;詭譎的;喜好陰謀的。 □ *n* [U] art of making designs (for machinery, etc). (機器等的)設計術。

de·sir·able /dɪˈzaɪərəbl ; dɪˈzaɪrəbl/ *adj* to be desired; causing desire; worth having: 想要的;令人想望的;值得有的: *This ~ property to be sold or let,* as in a house-agent's advertisement. 優良房產出售或出租(房產經紀人的廣告)。 *It is most ~ that he should attend the conference.* 他能參加此項會議,是最好不過了。 **de·sir·abil·ity** /dɪ͵zaɪərəˈbɪlətɪ ; dɪ͵zaɪrəˈbɪlətɪ/ *n*

de·sire¹ /dɪˈzaɪə(r) ; dɪˈzaɪr/ *n* **1** [U] strong longing; strong sexual attraction; [C] instance of this; earnest wish: 慾望;殷望;渴望;情慾: *He has no/not much ~ for wealth.* 他對於財富無(無大)慾望。 *He works hard from a ~ to become rich.* 他因渴望致富而努力工作。 *He spoke about his country's ~ for friendly relations/that friendly relations should be established.* 他說明他的國家欲建立友好關係的願望。 *It is impossible to satisfy all their ~s.* 使他們所有的慾望都得到滿足是不可能的。 **2** (*sing*) request: (單)請求: *at the ~ of Her Majesty.* 根據女王的請求。 **3** [C] thing that is wished for: 所渴望得到之物: *I hope you will get all your heart's ~s,* all you wish for. 我希望你想得到的東西都能得到。

de·sire² /dɪˈzaɪə(r) ; dɪˈzaɪr/ *vt* [VP6A, 7A, 17, 9] **1** (formal) long for; wish; have a desire(1) for: (正式用語)渴望;願望;欲得到: *We all ~ happiness and health.* 我們都想得到幸福和健康。 *Our rooms at the hotel were all that could be ~d,* were quite satisfactory. 我們在旅館中所住的房間令我們滿意極了。 *What do you ~ me to do?* 你想要我做什麼? **2** (official style) request: (官方文體)請求: *It is ~d that this rule shall be brought to the attention of the staff.* 請轉知全體工作人員注意本條規章。

de·sir·ous /dɪˈzaɪərəs ; dɪˈzaɪrəs/ *adj* ***~ (of),*** (formal, official) feeling desire: (正式及官方用語)想望的;渴望的: *~ of peace;* 渴望和平的; *~ to do sth;* 渴望做某事; *~ that....* 渴望…。

de·sist /dɪˈzɪst ; dɪˈzɪst/ *vi* [VP2A, 3A] ***~ (from),*** (formal) cease: (正式用語)停止: *~ from gossiping.* 停止談閒話。

desk /desk ; dɛsk/ *n* **1** piece of furniture (not a table) with a flat or sloping top and drawers at which to read, write or do business, eg one for office or school use. 讀書寫字桌;書桌;辦公桌。 **2** reception desk, ⇨ reception(1): 接待處; 服務臺: *leave a message at the ~ (of the hotel).* 留信於(旅館之)服務臺。 **'~ clerk** *n* (US) reception clerk. (美)接待人員。

deso·late /ˈdesələt ; ˈdɛslɪt/ *adj* **1** (of a place) in a ruined, neglected state; (of land or a country) unlived in; unfit to live in; barren: (指地方)荒廢的; 荒蕪的; (指土地或國家)無人烟的;不適於居住的;不毛的: *a ~, wind-swept moorland area.* 荒涼而又多風的荒地。 **2** friendless; wretched; lonely and sad: 孤獨的;可憐的;淒涼的: *a ~-looking child;* 其狀堪憐的孩童; *a ~ life.* 淒涼的一生。 **~·ly** *adv* □ *vt* /ˈdesəleɪt ; ˈdɛsl͵et/ [VP6A] make ~. 使荒涼;使成廢墟;使淒慘。 **deso·la·tion** /͵desəˈleɪʃn ; ͵dɛslˈeʃən/ *n* [U] making or being ~: 荒涼;荒蕪: *the desolation caused by war.* 戰爭所造成的荒涼。

des·pair¹ /dɪˈspeə(r) ; dɪˈspɛr/ *n* [U] **1** the state of having lost all hope: 一切希望斷絕的情況;絕望: *Your stupidity will drive me to ~.* 你的愚笨將會使我絕望。 *He gave up the attempt in ~.* 絕望之餘,他放棄嘗試。 *He was filled with ~ when he read the examination questions.* 他一看到考試題目,就感到絕望了。 *The refugee's ~ of ever seeing his family again filled us with pity.* 那難民對於再也見不到他的家人所抱的絕望心情,令我們感到憐憫。 **2** ***be the ~ of,*** be sb or sth that causes loss of hope to: 成爲令人絕望的人或事物: *This boy is the ~ of all his teachers,* They no longer hope to teach him anything. 這孩子使他所有的老師都對他感到絕望。 *He is the ~ of all other pianists,* plays so well that they cannot hope to rival him. 他使所有其他的鋼琴家感到絕望(因其演奏技巧使他們望塵莫及)。

des·pair² /dɪˈspeə(r) ; dɪˈspɛr/ *vi* [VP2A, 3A] ***~ (of),*** be in ~ about: 絕望: *to ~ of success/of ever succeeding.* 毫無成功希望。 *His life was ~ed of,* All hope that he would live was lost. 已經完全沒有救活他的希望了。 **~·ing·ly** *adv*

des·patch /dɪˈspætʃ ; dɪˈspætʃ/ *n, vt* = dispatch.

des·per·ado /ˌdespəˈrɑːdəʊ ; ˏdɛspəˈredo/ *n* (*pl* ~es; US also ~s /-dəʊz ; -doz/) person ready to do any reckless or criminal act. 亡命之徒;暴徒。

des·per·ate /ˈdespərət ; ˈdɛspərɪt/ *adj* **1** (of a person) filled with despair and ready to do anything, regardless of danger: (指人)因絕望而不惜冒險的: *The prisoners became ~ in their attempts to escape.* 那些囚犯拚命企圖逃亡。 **2** lawless; violent: 不法的;兇暴的: *~ criminals.* 兇暴的罪犯。 **3** extremely serious or dangerous: 極嚴重或危險的: *The state of the country is ~.* 該國的情況極爲嚴重。 **4** giving little hope of success; tried when all else has failed: 甚少成功希望的;孤注一擲的: *~ remedies.* 甚少成功希望的補救方法。 **~·ly** *adv* **des·per·ation** /ˌdespəˈreɪʃn ; ˏdɛspəˈreʃən/ *n* [U] the state of being ~(1): 不顧一切的冒險;拚命: *The wretched people rose in desperation against their rulers.* 可憐的人們冒死起來反抗他們的統治者。*You'll drive me to desperation,* (colloq) fill me with despair, make me ready to do sth ~. (俗)你將使我絕望而走極端。

des·pic·able /dɪˈspɪkəbl ; ˈdɛspɪkəbl̩/ *adj* deserving to be despised; contemptible. 可鄙的;卑劣的。 **des·pic·ably** /-əblɪ ; -əblɪ/ *adv*

des·pise /dɪˈspaɪz ; dɪˈspaɪz/ *vt* [VP6A] feel contempt for; consider worthless: 鄙視;輕視;瞧不起: *Strike-breakers are ~d by their workmates.* 破壞罷工者爲同事者所鄙視。 *A dish of strawberries and cream is not to be ~d,* is very good and should not be refused. 一盤草莓和乳酪不算很差。

des·pite /dɪˈspaɪt ; dɪˈspaɪt/ *prep* in spite of: 不管;不顧: *~ what she says....* 不論她怎麼說…。 □ *n* (obsolescent) ***~ of; in ~ of,*** in spite of (which is now the usu phrase). (過時用語)不管;不顧(如今通常用 in spite of)。 **~·ful** /-fʊl ; -fəl/ *adj* (archaic) spiteful. (古)懷有惡意的。 **~·fully** /-fəlɪ ; -fəlɪ/ *adv*

de·spoil /dɪˈspɔɪl ; dɪˈspɔɪl/ *vt* [VP6A, 14] ~ ***sb (of),*** (liter) rob, plunder. (文)奪取;掠奪;搶劫。

de·spon·dency /dɪˈspɒndənsɪ ; dɪˈspɑndənsɪ/ *n* [U] loss of hope; melancholy: 失望; 沮喪; 意氣消沉: *to fall into ~.* 變得沮喪。 **de·spon·dent** /dɪˈspɒndənt ; dɪˈspɑndənt/ *adj* having or showing loss of hope: 感到失望的; 沮喪的; 消沉的: *Don't become despondent.* 不要灰心。 **de·spon·dent·ly** *adv*

des·pot /ˈdespɒt ; ˈdɛspət/ *n* ruler with unlimited powers, esp one who uses these powers wrongly or cruelly; tyrant. 擁有無限權力的專制統治者;暴君。 **~ic** /dɪˈspɒtɪk ; dɪˈspɑtɪk/ *adj* of or like a ~ or tyrant. 暴君(似)的。 **~·ism** /ˈdespətɪzəm ; ˈdɛspət-ˏɪzəm/ *n* [U] the rule of a ~; tyranny; [C] country ruled by a ~. 專制;暴政;專制國家。

des·sert /dɪˈzɜːt ; dɪˈzɝt/ *n* **1** course of fruit, etc, at the end of a meal: 正餐後的水果等: (attrib) (形容用法) *a '~ apple.* 一個餐後食用的蘋果。 **'~·spoon,** medium-sized spoon. 中匙(吃餐後食品用者)。 **'~-spoon·ful** /-fʊl ; -ˏfʊl/ *n* as much as a ~spoon will hold. 一中匙(之量)。 ⇨ *teaspoon* at tea, *tablespoon* at table. **2** (US) any sweet dish, eg pie, pudding, ice-cream, served at the end of a meal (GB 英 = *sweet, pudding*). (美)正餐後所上的甜點(如水果餅,布丁,冰淇淋)。

des·ti·na·tion /ˌdestɪˈneɪʃn ; ˏdɛstəˈneʃən/ *n* place to which sb or sth is going or is being sent. (某人或某物所去的或被運送的)目的地。

des·tine /ˈdestɪn ; ˈdɛstɪn/ *vt* [VP17, 14] (usu passive) ~ ***(for),*** set apart, decide or ordain in advance: (通常用被動語態)命中注定;預定: *He was a soldier's son and was ~d from birth for the army,* His father had decided, when the boy was born, that he should become a soldier. 他是軍人之子, 並且從生下來就注定 (爲其父所決定) 要做軍人。 *They were ~d never to meet again,* Fate had determined that they should never meet again. 他們命中注定將永不能再見。 *His hopes were ~d to be realized,* His hopes came true. 他的希望後來都實現了。

des·tiny /ˈdestɪnɪ ; ˈdɛstənɪ/ *n* **1** [U] power believed to control events: 命運(被相信爲主宰人事的力量): *the tricks played on human beings by ~.* 命運之神對人類的戲弄。 **2** [C] (*pl* -nies) that which happens to sb, thought of as determined in advance by fate: 定數;天命(認爲係命運所決定的遭遇): *It was his ~ to die in a foreign country, far from his family.* 天命要他死在異邦,遠離其家人。

des·ti·tute /ˈdestɪtjuːt *US:* -tuːt ; ˈdɛstəˏtjut/ *adj* **1** without food, clothes and other things necessary for life: 缺乏衣, 食及其他必需品的; 窮困的: *When Mr Hill died, his wife and children were left ~.* 當希爾先生去世的時候,他的妻子兒女皆陷於窮困。 **2** ***~ of,*** not having: 缺乏;沒有: *officials who are ~ of ordinary human feelings.* 缺乏同情心的官吏。 **des·ti·tu·tion** /ˌdestɪˈtjuːʃn *US:* -ˈtuːʃn ; ˏdɛstəˈtjuʃən/ *n* [U] being ~(1): 匱乏;窮困: *a war that brought desolation and destitution;* 帶來荒涼與窮困的戰爭; *reduced to destitution,* to complete poverty. 陷於赤貧之境。

de·stroy /dɪˈstrɔɪ ; dɪˈstrɔɪ/ *vt* [VP6A] break to pieces; make useless; put an end to: 毀滅;摧毀;毀壞;破壞: *Don't ~ that box—it may be useful.* 不要把那個盒子毀掉——它也許有用。 *The forest was ~ed by fire.* 森林爲大火所毀。 *All his hopes were ~ed.* 他的一切希望都破滅了。 **~er** *n* **1** person or thing that ~s. 毀壞者。 **2** small, fast warship for protecting larger warships or convoys of merchant-ships. (保護較大戰艦或商船隊的)驅逐艦。

de·struc·tible /dɪˈstrʌktəbl ; dɪˈstrʌktəbl̩/ *adj* that can be destroyed. 可破壞的;可毀滅的。 **de·struc·ti·bil·ity** /dɪˌstrʌktəˈbɪlətɪ ; dɪˏstrʌktəˈbɪlətɪ/ *n*

de·struc·tion /dɪˈstrʌkʃn ; dɪˈstrʌkʃən/ *n* [U] destroying or being destroyed: 破壞;毀壞;毀滅: *the ~ of a town by an earthquake;* 被地震所毀之市鎮; that which ruins or destroys: 毀滅之根源: *Gambling was his ~.* 賭博是他毀滅的根源。

de·struc·tive /dɪˈstrʌktɪv ; dɪˈstrʌktɪv/ *adj* causing destruction; fond of, in the habit of, destroying: 毀滅性的;喜好或習慣於破壞的: *a ~ storm;* 造成損害的暴風雨; *~ criticism.* 破壞性的批評。 *Are all small children ~?* 所有的小孩子都喜好破壞嗎? **~·ly** *adv* **~·ness** *n*

desue·tude /dɪˈsjuːɪtjuːd *US:* -tuːd ; ˈdɛswɪˏtjud/ *n* [U] (formal, esp in) (正式用語,尤用於) ***fall into ~,*** pass out of use: 已不用;廢止: *customs/fashions/words that have fallen into ~.* 已廢的習俗(時尚,字)。

des·ul·tory /ˈdesəltrɪ *US:* -tɔːrɪ ; ˈdɛsl̩ˏtorɪ/ *adj* without system, purpose; not continuous: 無系統或目的的;不連貫的: *~ reading.* 散漫的閱讀。

de·tach /dɪˈtætʃ ; dɪˈtætʃ/ *vt* **1** [VP6A, 14] ~ ***(from),*** unfasten and take apart; separate: 解開;拆開; 使分離: *to ~ a link from a chain/a coach from a train.* 將一環自一鏈條上取下(將車廂自一列車上分離)。 ⇨ attach. **2** [VP6A, 16A] (armed forces) send (a party of men, ships, etc) away from the main body: (部隊)派遣; 分遣(兵員, 船艦等): *A number of men were ~ed to guard the right flank.* 若干士兵被派遣保衛右翼。 **de·tached** *part adj* **1** (of the mind, opinions, etc) impartial; not influenced by others; (colloq) unemotional: (指心理,意見等)超然的;不受他人影響的;客觀的;(俗)冷靜的: *to take a ~ed view of an event.* 對某事件持超然的看法。 **2** (of a house) not joined to another on either side. (指房屋)左右不與其他房屋相連的;獨立的。 ⇨ *semi-~ed* at semi-. **~·able** /-əbl ; -əbl̩/ *adj* that can be ~ed: 可分開的;可分遣的: *a ~able lining in a coat.* 外衣內可取下的襯裏。

de·tach·ment /dɪˈtætʃmənt ; dɪˈtætʃmənt/ *n* **1** [U] detaching or being detached: 分開;分離: *the ~ of a key from a key-ring.* 鑰匙之自鑰匙環取下。 **2** [U] the state of being detached; being uninfluenced by surroundings, the opinions of others, etc; being indifferent and uninterested: 獨立;超然;不受環境或他人意見的影響;不偏不倚: *He answered with an air of ~.* 他以超然的神態回答。 **3** [C] group of men, ships, etc, detached(2) from a larger number (for a special duty, etc). 分遣隊(分遣擔任特殊任務等的部隊或艦隊等)。

de·tail¹ /ˈdiːteɪl *US:* dɪˈteɪl ; ˈditel/ *n* **1** [C] small, particular fact or item: 細節;瑣碎的事: *Please give me all the ~s.* 請讓我知道所有的細節。 *Don't omit a single ~.* 不要遺漏一點細節。 *Every ~ of her dress was perfect.* 她衣服上的每個小地方都很完美。 **2** [U] collection of such small facts or items. 細目;詳情。 ***go/enter into ~s; explain sth in ~,*** to give the facts, item by item. 詳細說明。 **3** [U] (in art) the smaller or less important parts considered as a whole: (藝術)枝節部分: *The composition of the picture is good but there is too much ~.* 這幅畫的構圖不錯,但是枝節太多。 **4** [C] = detachment(3).

de·tail² /ˈdiːteɪl *US:* dɪˈteɪl ; dɪˈtel/ *vt* **1** [VP6A, 14] ***~ (to/for),*** describe fully; give full ~s of: 詳細描寫或說明: *a ~ed description,* given with every detail; 詳細的描寫; *The characteristics of the machine are fully ~ed in our brochure.* 這機器的性能在我們的小册子內有詳細說明。 **2** [VP6A, 16A] appoint for special duty: 派遣擔任特殊任務: *Three soldiers were ~ed to guard the bridge.* 三個兵被派去守望那橋。 ⇨ detail¹(4).

de·tain /dɪˈteɪn ; dɪˈten/ *vt* [VP6A, 16A] keep waiting; keep back; prevent from leaving or going forward: 使等候;使延遲;阻止;躭擱;拘留: *He told his wife that he had been ~ed in the office by unexpected callers.* 他告訴他妻子他因爲臨時有人來訪而留在辦公室裏。 *This question need not ~ us long,* can be settled quickly. 這個問題不需要很久的時間解決(可以很快地解決)。 *The police ~ed the man to make further inquiries.* 警局拘留那人以便進一步偵訊。 **~ee** /ˌdiːteɪˈniː ; dɪˌteˈni/ *n* person who is ~ed (esp by the authorities, as one who is suspected of wrongdoing, political agitation, etc). 被拘留者(尤指因涉嫌犯罪,政治煽動等被當局拘留者)。

de·tect /dɪˈtekt ; dɪˈtɛkt/ *vt* [VP6A] discover (the existence or presence of sb or sth, the identity of sb guilty of wrongdoing): 查明;查出(某人或某物之存在或在場,犯罪者的姓名等): *The dentist could ~ no sign of decay in her teeth.* 牙醫在她的牙齒上找不出腐蝕的跡象。 *Can you ~ an escape of gas in this corner of the room?* 你能覺察出這屋角有煤氣漏出來嗎? **~·able** /-əbl ; -əbḷ/ *adj* that can be ~ed. 可查明的;可找出的。 **~or** /-tə(r) ; -tɚ/ *n* device for ~ing, eg changes of pressure, temperature or a radio signal. 探查器(例如測壓器,測溫器,檢波器等)。 **ˈlie-~or,** ⇨ lie¹.

de·tec·tion /dɪˈtekʃn ; dɪˈtɛkʃən/ *n* [U] detecting; discovering: 查明;查出;發現: *the ~ of crime.* 犯罪之查明。 *He tried to escape ~ by disguising himself as an old man.* 他喬裝成一老人,企圖逃過偵查者的耳目。

de·tec·tive /dɪˈtektɪv ; dɪˈtɛktɪv/ *n* person whose business it is to detect criminals. 偵探(以偵察犯罪者爲職業的人)。 **ˈ~ story/novel,** one in which the main interest is a puzzling crime and the process of solving it. 偵探小說(以一離奇的犯罪案件及其偵破經過爲主題的小說)。

dé·tente /ˌdeɪˈtɑːnt ; deˈtɑ̃t/ *n* [U] (F) easing of strained relations, esp between countries. (法)國際間緊張關係之緩和;低盪。

de·ten·tion /dɪˈtenʃn ; dɪˈtɛnʃən/ *n* [U] detaining or being detained, (eg a pupil in school after ordinary hours, as a punishment; a prisoner without a trial). 阻止;延遲;留置;拘留(例如令學生放學以後不得回家以爲處罰;受審前拘留的犯人)。

de·ter /dɪˈtɜː(r) ; dɪˈtɝ/ *vt* (-rr-) [VP6A, 14] ***~ (from),*** discourage, hinder (sb from doing sth): 使灰心;阻礙(某人做某事): *Failure did not ~ him from trying again.* 失敗並未使他灰心不再嘗試。 **~·rent** /dɪˈterənt *US:* -ˈtɜː- ; dɪˈtɝənt/ *adj, n* (thing) tending to, intended to, ~: 阻止性或用來阻止的(事物);防止的(物): *Do you believe that the hydrogen bomb is a ~rent,* that it will ~ countries from making war? 你相信氫彈能够防止戰爭嗎?

de·ter·gent /dɪˈtɜːdʒənt ; dɪˈtɝdʒənt/ *adj, n* (substance) that removes dirt, esp from the surface of things: 洗滌(劑);清潔(劑): *Most synthetic ~s are in the form of powder or liquid.* 大多數合成清潔劑都是製成粉狀或液狀。

de·terio·rate /dɪˈtɪərɪəreɪt ; dɪˈtɪrɪəˌret/ *vt, vi* [VP 6A, 2A] make or become of less value, or worse in quality: (使)變壞;(使)變質: *Leather quickly ~s in a hot, damp climate.* 皮革在熱而濕的氣候中極易變壞。 **de·terio·ra·tion** /dɪˌtɪərɪəˈreɪʃn ; dɪˌtɪrɪəˈreʃən/ *n*

de·ter·mi·nant /dɪˈtɜːmɪnənt ; dɪˈtɝmənənt/ *adj, n* determining or deciding (agent, factor, element, etc). 決定性的(人,事物,要素等)。

de·ter·mi·nate /dɪˈtɜːmɪnət ; dɪˈtɝmənɪt/ *adj* limited; definite; fixed. 有限的;確定的;固定的。

de·ter·mi·na·tion /dɪˌtɜːmɪˈneɪʃn ; dɪˌtɝməˈneʃən/ *n* [U] **1** ***~ of,*** determining or being determined; deciding: 決定: *The ~ of the meaning of a word is often difficult without a context.* 沒有上下文,決定一字的意義常常是件難事。 **2** ***~ of,*** calculation or finding out (of an amount, etc): 計算;測定(數量等): *the ~ of the amount of metal in a specimen of ore.* 礦砂樣品中所含金屬量的測定。 **3** ***~ (to do sth),*** firmness of purpose; resolution: 決心(做某事);決意;堅決: *his ~ to learn English;* 他要學英文的決心; *to carry out a plan with ~;* 堅決地實現一項計畫; *with an air of ~,* with a purposeful look. 帶有堅決的表情。

de·ter·mi·nat·ive /dɪˈtɜːmɪnətɪv *US:* -neɪtɪv ; dɪˈtɝməˌnetɪv/ *n, adj* (thing) having the power to direct, determine, limit; (gram) determiner. 有指示,決定或限制力的(事物);(文法)指定或限定其後之名詞的字;限定詞。

de·ter·mine /dɪˈtɜːmɪn ; dɪˈtɝmɪn/ *vt, vi* **1** [VP6A, 10] decide; fix precisely: 決定;確定: *to ~ the meaning of a word;* 決定一字的意義; *to ~ a date for a meeting.* 確定開會的日期。 **2** [VP6A] calculate; find out precisely: 測定;明確地找出: *to ~ the speed of light/the height of a mountain by trigonometry.* 測定光速(用三角學測定一山之高度)。 **3** [VP6A, 7A, 9, 8, 10, 3A] ***~ to do sth; ~ on/upon sth,*** decide firmly, resolve, make up one's mind: 下決心: *He ~d to learn Greek.* 他決心學希臘文。 *We ~d to start early/~d on an early start.* 我們決定早些動身。 *He has ~d on proving/~d to prove his friend's innocence.* 他決心爲他的朋友洗清罪名。 *Have they ~d where the new school will be built?* 他們決定了新學校的校址嗎? *He has ~d that nothing shall/will prevent him.* 他已決心不顧一切的阻礙。 *His future has not yet been ~d, but he may study medicine.* 他的未來尚未決定,不過他可能讀醫科。 **4** [VP17, 14] ***~ sb to do sth/against sth,*** cause to decide: 使決定: *What ~d you to accept the offer?* 什麼原因使你決定接受此項提議? *The news ~d him against further delay.* 此項消息使他決定不再拖延。 **5** [VP6A] be the fact that ~s: 作爲決定性的事實;(指事實)決定: *The size of your feet ~s the size of your shoes.* 你的脚的大小決定你的鞋子的大小。 *Do heredity and environment ~ a man's character?* 遺傳與環境可決定一個人的性格嗎? **de·ter·min·able** /-əbl ; -əbḷ/ *adj* that can be ~d. 可決定的。

de·ter·miner /dɪˈtɜːmɪnə(r) ; dɪˈtɝmɪnɚ/ *n* [C] (gram) word that determines or limits the noun that follows. (文法)指定或限定其後之名詞的字; 限定詞;指定詞。

de·ter·rent ⇨ deter.

de·test /dɪˈtest ; dɪˈtɛst/ *vt* [VP6A, C] hate strongly: 深恨;深惡;憎惡;極討厭: *to ~ dogs;* 極討厭狗; *to ~*

having to get up early. 極討厭不得不早起。**~·able** *adj* hateful; deserving to be hated. 可恨的;可厭惡的。**~·ably** /-əblɪ; -əblɪ/ *adv* **de·tes·ta·tion** /ˌdi:teˈsteɪʃn; ˌditɛsˈteʃən/ *n* [U] strong hatred; [C] sth that is strongly hated. 深恨;極厭惡;極可厭之事物。

de·throne /ˌdi:ˈθrəʊn; dɪˈθron/ *vt* [VP6A] remove (a ruler) from the throne, or (fig, a person) from a position of authority or influence. 迫使(君王)去位;(喩)使(當權者)下野或垮臺。**~·ment** *n*

det·on·ate /ˈdetəneɪt; ˈdɛtəˌnet/ *vt, vi* [VP6A, 2A] (cause to) explode with a loud noise. (使)轟然爆炸;起爆。**det·on·ator** /ˈdetəneɪtə(r); ˈdɛtəˌnetɚ/ *n* part of a bomb or shell that explodes first, causing the substance in the bomb, etc to explode. (炸彈或砲彈中的)起爆管;雷管。**det·on·ation** /ˌdetəˈneɪʃn; ˌdɛtəˈneʃən/ *n* explosion; noise of an explosion. 爆炸(聲)。

de·tour /ˈdi:tʊə(r) *US:* dɪˈtʊər; ˈditʊr/ *n* roundabout way, eg a way used when the main road is blocked; diversion: 迂迴路(如當幹道堵塞時所用者);轉向: *to make a ~.* 迂迴;繞道而行。□ *vt* [VP6A] make a ~. 迂迴;繞道而行。

de·tract /dɪˈtrækt; dɪˈtrækt/ *vi* [VP3A] **~ from,** take away (from the credit, value, etc, of): 減損(…之功績,價值等): *to ~ from sb's merit,* make it less. 減損某人的功績。**de·trac·tor** /-tə(r); -tɚ/ *n* person who ~s; person who tries to make sb's reputation, etc, smaller. 損毀某人之名譽者;貶抑者。**de·trac·tion** /dɪˈtrækʃn; dɪˈtrækʃən/ *n* ~ing; disparagement. 減損;貶抑。

de·train /ˌdi:ˈtreɪn; diˈtren/ *vt, vi* [VP6A, 2A] (of troops, etc) (cause to) get out of a train. (指軍隊等)(使)下火車。

de·tribal·ize /ˌdi:ˈtraɪbəlaɪz; diˈtraɪblˌaɪz/ *vt* [VP 6A] render (a person) no longer a member of a tribe; destroy the tribal customs of. 使(某人)脫離某部族;除去…的部族習俗。**de·tribal·iz·ation** /ˌdi:ˌtraɪbəlaɪˈzeɪʃn *US:* -lɪˈz-; diˌtraɪbəlɪˈzeʃən/ *n*

det·ri·ment /ˈdetrɪmənt; ˈdɛtrəmənt/ *n* [U] damage; harm: 損害;傷害: *I know nothing to his ~,* nothing against him. 我一點也不知道對他不利的事。**to the ~ of,** harming: 有害於: *He works long hours to the ~ of his health.* 他工作的時間過久,有害於他的健康。**det·ri·men·tal** /ˌdetrɪˈmentl; ˌdɛtrəˈmɛntl̩/ *adj* **~ (to),** harmful: 有害的;有損的: *activities that would be ~al to our interests.* 會損及我們利益的活動。**det·ri·men·tally** /-təlɪ; -tl̩ɪ/ *adv*

de·tri·tus /dɪˈtraɪtəs; dɪˈtraɪtəs/ *n* [U] matter, eg sand, silt, gravel, produced by wearing away (from rock, etc). 風化土礫(自岩石等脫落的碎砂石)。

de trop /də ˈtrəʊ; dəˈtro/ *pred adj* (F) in the way; not wanted; unwelcome. (法)擋路的;礙事的;不需要的;不受歡迎的。

deuce[1] /dju:s *US:* du:s; djus/ *n* **1** the two on playing cards or dice. (紙牌或骰子上的)二點。**2** (tennis) the score of 40 all, or five games each, after which either side must gain two successive points (or games) to win the match (or set). (網球)平手(兩方各獲40分或各勝五局,然後任何一方必須連獲二分方爲勝)。

deuce[2] /dju:s *US:* du:s; djus/ *n* **(the) ~,** (dated colloq, in exclamations of annoyance) the devil, bad luck. (過時俗語,表煩惱的感歎詞)鬼;倒霉;晦氣。**deuced** /ˈdju:st *US:* ˈdu:st; ˈdjust/ *adj* very great. 極大的;非常的。**deuced·ly** /ˈdju:sɪdlɪ *US:* ˈdu:-; ˈdjusɪdlɪ/ *adv* very. 非常地。

de·value /ˌdi:ˈvælju:; diˈvæljʊ/ (US also **de·val·u·ate** /ˌdi:ˈvæljʊeɪt; diˈvæljʊˌet/) *vt* [VP6A] make (the value of a currency) less (esp in terms of gold): 使(貨幣價值)貶值(尤指以金計算): *to ~ the dollar/pound.* 使美元(英鎊)貶值。**de·valu·ation** /ˌdi:ˌvæljʊˈeɪʃn; ˌdivæljʊˈeʃən/ *n* [U, C] (of currency) change to a new, lower fixed value. (指貨幣)貶值。

dev·as·tate /ˈdevəsteɪt; ˈdɛvəsˌtet/ *vt* [VP6A] ruin; make desolate: 毀壞;破壞;使荒涼;使成廢墟: *towns ~d by fire/floods/war.* 爲火災(洪水,戰爭)所毀壞的城鎮。**dev·as·ta·tion** /ˌdevəˈsteɪʃn; ˌdɛvəsˈteʃən/ *n* devastating or being ~d. 毀壞;破壞;成爲廢墟。

de·vel·op /dɪˈveləp; dɪˈvɛləp/ *vt, vi* **1** [VP6A, 2A, 3A] **~ (from) (into),** (cause to) grow larger, fuller or more mature, organized; (cause to) unfold: (使)成長;(使)發育;發展;開發: *Plants ~ from seeds.* 植物由種子發育而成。*A chicken ~s in the egg.* 鷄在卵中孕育。*We must ~ the natural resources of our country,* make the minerals, forests, etc available for use. 我們必須開發我們國家的天然資源(如使礦產,森林等成爲有用之物)。*The plot of the new novel gradually ~ed in the author's mind.* 那新小說的佈局在作者的頭腦中逐漸形成。**ˌ~ing ˈcountry,** one which is advancing to a higher (economic) state. 開發中的國家(經濟情況進步中的國家)。**2** [VP6A, 2A, C] (of sth not at first active or visible) come or bring into a state in which it is active or visible: (指起初不活動或看不見的東西)發展成爲活動性的或看得見的;出現;發生: *Symptoms of malaria ~ed,* appeared. 瘧疾的徵候出現了。*He ~ed a cough.* 他咳嗽起來了。**3** [VP6A, 2A] (photo) treat (an exposed film or plate) with chemicals so that the picture can be seen. (照相)冲洗;顯影(用化學藥品處理已曝光的底片使影像顯出)。**4** use (an area of land) for the building of houses (or shops, factories, etc) and so increase its value. 在(一塊土地)上建築房屋,商店,工廠等以增高其價值;利用(土地)。**~er** *n* person who, authority which, ~s land, etc; substance used to ~ films and plates. 開發或利用土地等的人或當局;(冲洗底片用的)顯影劑。

de·vel·op·ment /dɪˈveləpmənt; dɪˈvɛləpmənt/ *n* **1** [U] developing or being developed (all senses): 成長;發育;發展;開發;出現;發生;(照相之)冲洗;顯影;(土地之)利用: *He is engaged in the ~ of his business.* 他正從事於發展業務。*Which is more important, moral ~ or physical ~?* 道德培養與體格的培養那一樣較重要? *The ~ of photographic films requires a dark-room.* 冲洗照相底片需要暗房。*This land is ripe for ~,* for being developed(4). 這塊土地已達可以利用的成熟階段。**ˈ~ area,** one to which new industries are directed as a means of increasing employment. 新社區(欲建立新工業以增加就業機會之地區)。**2** [C] new stage which is the result of developing: 發展的新階段;新的發展: *the latest ~s in foreign affairs.* 外交上最近的發展。*We must await further ~s.* 我們必須等待進一步的發展。

de·vi·ant /ˈdi:vɪənt; ˈdivɪənt/ *n, adj* (person who is) different in moral and social standards from what is normal or customary. 道德與社會標準觀念不合常軌或慣例的(人)。

de·vi·ate /ˈdi:vɪeɪt; ˈdivɪˌet/ *vi* [VP3A] **~ from,** turn away, leave (what is usual, customary, right, etc): 離(常軌,慣例,正道等);不符合;有偏差: *to ~ from the truth/a rule/one's custom.* 與事實(規則,個人的習慣)不符合。

de·vi·ation /ˌdi:vɪˈeɪʃn; ˌdivɪˈeʃən/ *n* [U] **~ (from),** turning aside or away; difference: 逸出常軌;不符合;離正道;偏差: *~ from the rules;* 與規則不合; [C] instance or amount or degree of this: 偏差或不合的事例或程度: *slight ~s of the magnetic needle,* in a compass; (羅盤上)磁針之略微的偏差; *~s from the rules of syntax.* 不合造句規則之處。**~·ist** *n* person who deviates, esp from the principles of a social or political system. (背離某種社會或政治制度之原則的)異端份子; 偏差份子。**~·ism** /-ɪzəm; -ˌɪzəm/ *n*

de·vice /dɪˈvaɪs; dɪˈvaɪs/ *n* [C] **1** plan; scheme; trick: 計畫;策略;詭計: *a ~ to put the police off the scent.* 引誘警察追錯方向的詭計。**leave sb to his own ~s,** let him do as he wishes, without help or advice. 讓某人自行設法(不予幫助或建議)。**2** sth thought out, invented or adapted, for a special purpose: 爲某種特殊用途而設計,發明或改裝

的東西;裝置物: *a ~ for catching flies;* 捕捉蒼蠅的裝置; *a nuclear ~*, eg an atomic or hydrogen bomb. 核子裝置(如原子彈或氫彈)。 **3** sign, symbol or figure used in a decoration, eg a crest on a shield. 用於裝飾品上的圖案(如盾形徽章上端的飾章)。

devil[1] /'devl ; 'dɛvl/ *n* **1** the spirit of evil; wicked spirit; cruel or mischievous person. 惡魔;魔鬼;殘暴的人;惡人。 ***between the ~ and the deep (blue) sea,*** in a dilemma. 進退兩難;進退維谷。 ***give the ~ his due,*** be just, even to one who does not deserve much or who is unfriendly. 卽使對於惡人亦宜待以公平;一視同仁。 ***go to the ~!*** go away! 走開!滾開! ***play the ~ with,*** harm, ruin. 傷害;毀壞。 **the D~,** the supreme spirit of evil, Satan. 魔王;撒旦。 **~'s advocate,** sb who points out the faults of sb or sth so that there can be a full discussion. 指出某人或某事物之缺點而引起辯論的人;唱反調的人。 **2** (usu 通常作 ***poor*** ~) wretched or unfortunate person. 可憐或不幸的人。 **printer's ~,** (old use) errand-boy in a printing-office. (舊用法)印刷所的童僕或學徒。 **3** (colloq) used to give emphasis: (俗)(用以加强語氣): *what/who/why/where the ~...?* 到底什麼(誰,爲何,何處)…? *He has the ~ of a time,* ie according to context, a difficult, exciting, amusing, etc time. (意義視上下文而定)他處於極端(困難,興奮,歡娛等)之境。 *He was working/running like the ~*, very hard. 他拚命工作(跑)。 *There will be the ~ to pay,* trouble to be faced (as the result of sth done or said). (由於做某事或說某話)後果不堪設想。 **,~-may-'care** *adj* reckless. 不要命的;不顧一切的。

devil[2] /'devl ; 'dɛvl/ *vt, vi* (-ll-, US -l-) **1** [VP6A] grill with hot condiments: 加辛辣調味品燒烤: *~led kidneys / ham.* 加辛辣調味品的烤腰子(火腿)。 **2** [VP2A, 3A] ~ ***for,*** work (for a barrister). 做(律師的)助手;代(律師)工作。

devil·ish /'devəlɪʃ ; 'dɛvlɪʃ/ *adj* wicked; cruel: 惡毒的;殘忍的: *a ~ plot.* 惡毒的陰謀。□ *adv* (colloq) very: (俗)極;非常: *~ hot.* 極熱的。

devil·ment /'devlmənt ; 'dɛvlmənt/, **dev·ilry** /'devlrɪ ; 'dɛvlrɪ/ *nn* **1** [C] mischief: 惡作劇: *She's up to some ~ or other.* 她正忙於某種惡作劇。 **2** [U] high spirits: 高興: *full of ~.* 興高采烈。

de·vi·ous /'di:vɪəs ; 'divɪəs/ *adj* winding; roundabout; not straightforward: 彎曲的;迂迴的;不直的: *to take a ~ route to avoid busy streets;* 繞道而行以免經過鬧街; *to get rich by ~ (= cunning, underhand) ways.* 不以正道致富。 **~·ly** *adv* **~·ness** *n*

de·vise /dɪ'vaɪz ; dɪ'vaɪz/ *vt* **1** [VP6A, 8] think out; plan: 想出;計畫;設計;發明: *to ~ a scheme for making money;* 想辦法賺錢; *to ~ how to do sth.* 計畫如何進行某事。⇨ device. **2** [VP14] ~ ***to,*** (legal) leave (property) by will. (法律)遺囑將(財產)贈予。

de·vital·ize /,di:'vaɪtəlaɪz ; di'vaɪtl,aɪz/ *vt* [VP6A] take away strength and vigour from. 使失去活力。 **de·vital·iz·ation** /,di:,vaɪtəlaɪ'zeɪʃn *US:* -lɪ'z- ; di,vaɪtlə'zeʃən/ *n*

de·void /dɪ'vɔɪd ; dɪ'vɔɪd/ *adj* ~ ***of,*** without; empty of: 沒有;空虛;無: *~ of shame/sense.* 無恥(無見識)。

de·vol·ution /,di:və'lu:ʃn *US:* ,dev- ; ,dɛvə'luʃən/ *n* [U] deputing or delegating (of power or authority); decentralization. (權或權力之)轉移;移交;授予權力;地方分權。

de·volve /dɪ'vɒlv ; dɪ'valv/ *vi, vt* **1** [VP3A] ~ ***on/upon,*** (of work, duties) be transferred or passed to: (指工作或職務)被轉移或移交: *When the President is ill, his duties ~ upon the Vice-President.* 當總統生病時,其職務交由副總統代理。 **2** [VP6A, 14] ~ ***(to/upon),*** pass, transfer (work, duties, to sb). 傳遞;轉移;移交(工作,職務給某人)。

de·vote /dɪ'vəʊt ; dɪ'vot/ *vt* [VP14] ~ ***oneself/sth to,*** give up (oneself, one's time, energy, etc) to: 奉獻(自己,時間,精力等);致力於;專心;專門;獻身: *to ~ oneself to the cure of cancer/one's spare time to sport.* 致力於癌症的治療(以空閒的時間從事運動)。 **de·voted** *adj* very loving or loyal: 熱愛的;非常忠實的: *a ~d friend.* 忠實的朋友。 *She is ~d to her children.* 她摯愛她的子女。 **de·vot·ed·ly** *adv*

devo·tee /,devə'ti: ; ,dɛvə'ti/ *n* ~ ***(of),*** person who is devoted to sth: 專心的人;熱心者: *a ~ of sport/music;* 熱心運動(音樂)的人; zealous supporter (of a sect, etc). (對教派等)熱心支持者。⇨ votary.

de·vo·tion /dɪ'vəʊʃn ; dɪ'voʃən/ *n* **1** [U] ~ ***(for),*** deep, strong love: 深愛;摯愛;熱愛: *the ~ of a mother for her children.* 母親對子女的摯愛。 **2** [U] ~ ***(to),*** devoting or being devoted: 忠實;專心;熱心: *~ to duty;* 忠於職守; *a teacher's ~ to the cause of education.* 教師之對於教育事業的熱心。 **3** (*pl*) prayers: (複)祈禱: *The priest was at his ~s.* 祭司在祈禱。 **~al** /-'vəʊʃənl ; -'voʃənl/ *adj* of ~; used in ~s(3): 忠誠的;用於祈禱的: *~al literature,* for use in worship. 祈禱文獻。

de·vour /dɪ'vaʊə(r) ; dɪ'vaʊr/ *vt* [VP6A] **1** eat hungrily or greedily: 貪婪地吃;吞食: *The hungry boy ~ed his dinner.* 那飢餓的孩子狼吞虎嚥地吃飯。 (fig) (喻) *She ~ed the new detective story.* 她一口氣看完了那本新的偵探小說。 *The fire ~ed twenty square miles of forest.* 那場大火吞噬了二十平方哩的森林。 **2** ***be ~ed by*** (curiosity, anxiety, etc), be filled with, have all one's attention taken up by. 心中充滿(好奇,憂慮等);全部注意力爲…所吸引。

de·vout /dɪ'vaʊt ; dɪ'vaʊt/ *adj* **1** paying serious attention to religious duties: (對宗教)虔誠的;虔敬的: *a ~ old lady.* 虔誠的老太太。 **2** (of prayers, wishes, etc) deepfelt; sincere: (指祈禱,願望等)衷心的;熱誠的: *a ~ supporter;* 熱誠的支持者; *~ wishes for your success.* 衷心地祝你成功。 **~·ly** *adv* eagerly; sincerely. 熱心地;熱誠地。 **~·ness** *n*

dew /dju: *US:* du: ; dju/ *n* [U] tiny drops of moisture condensed on cool surfaces between evening and morning from water vapour in the air: 露;露水(空中的水蒸氣於夜間在涼冷的物體表面上所凝結的水珠): *The grass was wet with dew.* 草爲露水沾濕。 **'dew drop** *n* small drop of dew. 露珠。 **dewy** *adj* wet with dew. 爲露水沾濕的;帶露水的。

dew·lap /'dju:læp *US:* 'du:- ; 'dju,læp/ *n* fold of loose skin hanging down from the neck of an animal such as a cow or ox. (牛等)自喉部垂下的鬆皮;喉袋。

dex·ter·ity /dek'sterətɪ ; dɛks'tɛrətɪ/ *n* [U] skill, esp in handling things. 技巧;(尤指用手做事的)靈巧;靈活。

dex·ter·ous, dex·trous /'dekstrəs ; 'dɛkstərəs/ *adj* clever, skilful with the hands. 兩手靈巧的;善於用手的。 **~·ly** *adv*

dex·trose /'dekstrəʊz *US:* -əʊs ; 'dɛkstros/ *n* [U] form of glucose. 葡萄糖;右旋糖。

dho·ti /'dəʊtɪ ; 'dotɪ/ *n* loin-cloth as customarily worn by male Hindus. 印度男子習慣纏的腰布。

dhow /daʊ ; daʊ/ *n* single-masted ship, esp as used by Arab sailors for coastal voyages. 單桅帆船(尤指阿拉伯水手用於沿海航行者)。

dia·betes /,daɪə'bi:ti:z ; ,daɪə'bitɪs/ *n* [U] disease of the pancreas in which sugar and starchy foods cannot be properly absorbed. 糖尿病(對糖及澱粉食物不能適當吸收的胰臟病症)。

dia·betic /,daɪə'betɪk ; ,daɪə'bɛtɪk/ *adj* of diabetes. 糖尿病的。□ *n* person suffering from diabetes. 糖尿病患者。

dia·bolic /,daɪə'bɒlɪk ; ,daɪə'balɪk/ *adj* of or like a devil; very cruel or wicked. 惡魔(似)的;極殘忍或惡毒的。 **~al** /-kl ; -kl/ *adj* **dia·boli·cally** /-klɪ ; -klɪ/ *adv*

dia·critic /,daɪə'krɪtɪk ; ,daɪə'krɪtɪk/ *adj, n* (of a) mark (eg ´ ` ^ ¨), used in writing and printing to indicate different sounds of a letter. 加於字母上的變音符號(在印刷中用以表示字母之不同發音的記號,例如: ´ ` ^ ¨) (的)。 **~al** /-kl ; -kl/ *adj* =~.

dia·dem /'daɪədem ; 'daɪə,dɛm/ *n* crown, worn as a sign of royal power; wreath of flowers or leaves worn round the head. (象徵王權的)王冠;冕;

戴於頭上的花冠或葉冠。

di·aer·esis, di·er·esis /daɪˈerɪsɪs ; daɪˈɛrəsɪs/ *n* (*pl* -eses /-əsi:z ; -əˌsiz/) mark (as in *naïve*) placed over a vowel to show that it is sounded separately from a preceding vowel. 分音符(置於母音之上,以示其與前一母音分開發音,如 naïve 中之¨)。

di·ag·nose /ˈdaɪəgnəʊz *US:* -əʊs ; ˌdaɪəgˈnos/ *vt* [VP6A, 16B] determine the nature of (esp a disease) from observation of symptoms: 診斷(由觀察徵候而斷定疾病等的性質): *The doctor ~d the illness as diphtheria.* 醫生診斷該病爲白喉。

di·ag·nosis /ˌdaɪəgˈnəʊsɪs;ˌdaɪəgˈnosɪs/ *n* (*pl* -noses /-ˈnəʊsi:z ; -ˈnosiz/ [U] diagnosing; [C] (statement of the) result of this. 診斷;診斷的結果;診斷書。

di·ag·nos·tic /ˌdaɪəgˈnɒstɪk ; ˌdaɪəgˈnɑstɪk/ *adj* of diagnosis: 診斷的: *symptoms that were of little ~ value,* that were not very useful in determining the disease. 無甚診斷價值(無助於診斷)的徵候。

di·ag·onal /daɪˈægənl ; daɪˈægənl̩/ *n, adj* (straight line) going across a straight-sided figure, eg an oblong, from corner to corner; slanting; crossed by slanting lines. 直邊圖形(如長方形)的對角線;連接對角的;斜的;爲斜線所交叉的。⇨ the illus at quadrilateral. 參看 quadrilateral 之插圖。 **~·ly** /-nəlɪ ; -nl̩ɪ/ *adv*

dia·gram /ˈdaɪəgræm ; ˈdaɪəˌgræm/ *n* drawing, design or plan to explain or illustrate something: 圖解(作解釋或說明的圖表): *a ~ of a gear-box.* 齒輪箱的圖解。 **~·matic** /ˌdaɪəgrəˈmætɪk ; ˌdaɪəgrəˈmætɪk/, **~·mati·cal** /-kl ; -kl̩/ *adjj* **~·mati·cally** /-klɪ ; -klɪ/ *adv*

dial /ˈdaɪəl ; ˈdaɪəl/ *n* **1** face (of a clock or watch). 鐘面;錶面。 **2** marked face or flat plate with a pointer for measuring (weight, volume, pressure, consumption of gas, etc). 各種儀表(如計量重量,容量,壓力,耗油等)的標度盤;針面;盤面。 **3** plate, disc, etc on a radio set with names or numbers, showing wavelengths of broadcasting stations. 刻度盤(收音機上標示周率或電臺波長的盤面)。**4** part of an automatic telephone, with numbers and/or letters, used to make a connection. 自動電話機的撥號盤。□ *vt* (-ll-; US -l-) [VP6A] call by means of a telephone ~: 撥號碼打電話: *to ~ 01-2301212.* 撥 01-2301212。 **ˈ~ling code,** code of numbers for a telephone exchange to be ~led before the number of the person to whom the call is to be made: 電話區域號碼(交換地區號碼): *The ~ling code for the London area is 01.* 倫敦地區的電話區號是01。 **ˈ~ling tone,** the sound showing that one may proceed to ~ the number wanted. 表示可以撥號打電話的嗡嗡聲音。

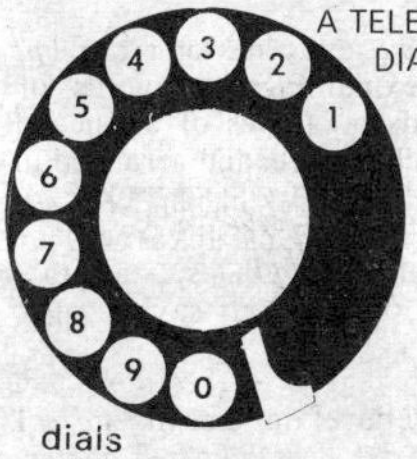
A TELEPHONE DIAL

A CLOCK DIAL

dials

dia·lect /ˈdaɪəlekt ; ˈdaɪəˌlɛkt/ *n* [C, U] form of a language (grammar, vocabulary and pronunciation) used in a part of a country or by a class of people: 方言;土話;某一階級之人說話的方式: *the Yorkshire ~;* 約克郡的方言; *a play written in ~;* 用方言寫的劇本; (attrib) (形容用法) *~ words/pronunciations.* 方言用字(發音)。 **~al** /ˌdaɪəˈlektl ; ˌdaɪəˈlɛktl/ *adj* of a ~ or ~s: 方言的;土話的: *~al differences between two counties.* 兩郡間方言的差異。

dia·lec·tic /ˌdaɪəˈlektɪk ; ˌdaɪəˈlɛktɪk/ *n* (also *pl* with *sing v*) critical analysis of mental processes; art of logical disputation. (亦作複數,用單數動詞)思維方法的評判分析;論理辯證法;辯證法。 **dia·lec·ti·cal** /-kl ; -kl̩/ *adj* of ~: 論理辯證法的;辯證法的: *the ~al conflict* (= the logical dispute) *between innovators and conservatives.* 革新者與保守人士間理論上的爭辯。 **ˌ~al maˈterialism,** theory developed principally by Marx, combining traditional *materialism*(1) with a critical analysis of *development* by the conflict between an original direction, its direct opposite and their unification. 辨證唯物論(主要爲馬克斯所提出之理論,係利用其正、反、合之間的矛盾,對傳統的唯物論加以批判)。⇨ Marxist. **dia·lec·tician** /ˌdaɪəlekˈtɪʃn ; ˌdaɪəlɛkˈtɪʃən/ *n* person skilled in ~. 論理學家;辯證學者。

dia·logue (US also **dia·log**) /ˈdaɪəlɒg *US:* -lɔ:g ; ˈdaɪəˌlɔg/ *n* **1** [U] (writing in the form of a) conversation or talk: 對話;用對話體寫的作品: *Plays are written in ~.* 戲劇用對話體寫。*There is some good descriptive writing in the novel, but the ~ is poor.* 這小說裏有些很好的描寫,但對話很差。**2** [C] exchange of views (between leaders, etc): (領導人物等間之)交換意見: *a ~ between the two Prime Ministers.* 兩位首相間之交換意見。 **3** [C] talk: 談話: *long ~s between two comedians.* 兩位喜劇演員間之冗長的對話。

di·am·eter /daɪˈæmɪtə(r) ; daɪˈæmətəʳ/ *n* measurement across any geometrical figure or body; (length of a) straight line drawn from side to side through the centre, esp of a circular, spherical or cylindrical form: 直徑(橫過任何幾何圖形或物體的度量;穿過圓心、球心、或圓柱中心、兩端及於週邊之直線或其長度);對徑;徑;倍: *the ~ of a tree-trunk;* 樹幹的直徑; *a lens that magnifies 20 ~s,* that makes an object look 20 times longer, wider, etc than it is, ⇨ the illus at circle. 放大二十倍的透鏡(參看 circle 之插圖)。

dia·metri·cally /ˌdaɪəˈmetrɪklɪ ; ˌdaɪəˈmɛtrɪkl̩ɪ/ *adv* completely; entirely: 完全地;全然地: *~ opposed views.* 完全相反的意見。

dia·mond /ˈdaɪəmənd ; ˈdaɪəmənd/ *n* **1** brilliant precious stone of pure carbon in crystallized form, the hardest substance known: 金鋼鑽;鑽石(由純碳結晶而成之燦爛寶石,係已知的最堅硬的物質): *a ring with a ~ in it;* 鑽石戒指; (attrib) (形容用法) *a ~ ring/necklace.* 鑽石戒指(項鍊)。⇨ the illus at crystal. 參看 crystal 之插圖。**~ wedding** *n* sixtieth anniversary of a wedding. 鑽石婚(結婚六十週年紀念)。**rough ~,** person with rough manners but a kind heart. 行動粗魯而心腸好的人。 **2** piece of this substance (often artificially made) as used in industry, or as a stylus for playing gramophone records. 工業用的金鋼鑽(常係人造品);唱機用的鑽石唱針。**3** figure with four equal sides whose angles are not right angles; this shape (as printed in red on playing-cards): 菱形(等邊而非直角的四邊形);紙牌上的紅方塊: *the ten of ~s.* 方塊牌的十點。⇨ the illus at card. 參看 card 之插圖。**4** (baseball) the space inside the lines that connect the bases. (棒球)內野(四壘連線之內的場地)。⇨ the illus at baseball. 參看 baseball 之插圖。

dia·per /ˈdaɪəpə(r) ; ˈdaɪəpəʳ/ *n* **1** (linen fabric with) geometric pattern of lines crossing to make diamond shapes which are shown up by reflection of light. 接連的菱形圖案(圖案由反光而顯出);有菱形圖案的格子麻布。**2** (US) napkin(2) for a baby. (美)嬰兒的尿布。

di·apha·nous /daɪˈæfənəs ; daɪˈæfənəs/ *adj* (of material for veils, dresses, etc) transparent; translucent. (指製面紗,女服等的布料)透明的;半透明的。

dia·phragm /ˈdaɪəfræm ; ˈdaɪəˌfræm/ *n* **1** internal wall of muscle between the chest and the abdomen. (胸腔與腹腔間的)橫膈膜。⇨ the illus at respiratory. 參看 respiratory 之插圖。 **2** arrangement of thin plates that control the inlet of light, eg through a camera lens. 控制光線的薄片裝置;照相機

鏡頭上的光圈。 **3** vibrating disc or cone in some instruments, eg a telephone receiver, a loudspeaker, producing sound-waves. (電話機受話器與擴音機等中產生聲波的)膜片。

di·ar·chy /ˈdaɪɑːkɪ ; ˈdaɪɑrkɪ/ *n* (*pl* -chies) government shared by two joint authorities or rulers. 兩頭政治(由兩個獨立的當政者或權力機構統治)。

di·ar·rhoea (also **di·ar·rhea**) /ˌdaɪəˈrɪə ; ˌdaɪəˈriə/ *n* [U] too frequent and too watery emptying of the bowels. 腹瀉;瀉肚子。

diary /ˈdaɪərɪ ; ˈdaɪərɪ/ *n* (*pl* -ries) (book for) daily record of events, thoughts, etc: 日記(對事件,思想等每日的記載);日記簿: *keep a* ~. 寫日記。 **dia·rist** /ˈdaɪərɪst ; ˈdaɪərɪst/ *n* person who keeps a diary. 寫日記的人。

Di·as·pora /daɪˈæspərə ; daɪˈæspərə/ *n* **the D~,** the dispersion of the Jews among the Gentiles after their period of exile (538 BC): (紀元前538年)猶太人被放逐後之散居世界各地非猶太人中: *People from every country of the* ~ *now live in Israel.* 散居世界各國的猶太人現在都住在以色列。

dia·tonic /ˌdaɪəˈtɒnɪk ; ˌdaɪəˈtɑnɪk/ *adj* (mus) of a key¹(9). (音樂)全音的。~ **scale** *n* = key¹(9).

dia·tribe /ˈdaɪətraɪb ; ˈdaɪəˌtraɪb/ *n* [C] ~ ***(against),*** bitter and violent attack in words. 怒罵;猛烈的抨擊。

dibble /ˈdɪbl ; ˈdɪbl̩/ *n* (also 亦作 **dib·ber** /ˈdɪbə(r) ; ˈdɪbɚ/) short wooden tool with a pointed end for making holes in the ground (for tubers, young plants, etc). (在地上挖洞以種植塊莖植物、幼苗等用的一端尖的)短木杵;點播器。 □ *vt* [VP15B] put (plants, etc, *in*) with a ~. 用短木杵或點播器挖洞栽種(幼苗等)(與 in 連用)。

dice /daɪs ; daɪs/ *n pl* (*sing* (formal) die or (colloq) dice) (其單數形式在正式用法中爲 die, 在口語中仍爲 dice) small cubes of wood, bone, etc marked with 1–6 spots, used in games of chance: 骰子(木質或骨質小六面體,每面刻有 1–6 個點數,用作賭具): *to play* ~. 擲骰子。***The die is cast,*** (prov) One's course is determined and cannot now be changed. (諺)已做決定,不能更改。(Note: except in this prov, *die* is rarely used. 'One of the dice' is preferred to 'a die'.) (注意:除此諺語外, die 現今罕用。用 one of the dice 較用 a die 爲妥當)。 **ˈ~-box** *n* deep, narrow box in which ~ are shaken and from which they are thrown. (搖擲骰子用的)骰子筒。□ *vi, vt* **1** [VP2A] play ~. 擲骰子。~ ***with death,*** (colloq) act dangerously and at the risk of death. (俗)冒死的危險。 **2** [VP6A] cut (food, eg carrots) into small cubes like ~. 將(胡蘿蔔等)切成似骰子的小方塊;將…切丁。

dicey /ˈdaɪsɪ ; ˈdaɪsɪ/ *adj* (colloq) risky; uncertain. (俗)冒險的;不確定的。

di·chot·omy /daɪˈkɒtəmɪ ; daɪˈkɑtəmɪ/ *n* (*pl* -mies) division into two (usu contradictory classes or mutually exclusive pairs): 兩分(通常指將互相矛盾的類別或互不相容的兩種東西分爲二): *the* ~ *of truth and falsehood.* 眞理與謊言的劃分。

dick·ens /ˈdɪkɪnz ; ˈdɪkɪnz/ *n* (colloq) used like devil and deuce: (俗)(與 devil 和 deuce 用法同): *'Who/What/Where the* ~...?' '到底是誰(什麼,何處)…?'

dicker /ˈdɪkə(r) ; ˈdɪkɚ/ *vi* (colloq) [VP2A, 3A] bargain or haggle (*with* sb, *for* sth). (俗)談生意;講價錢;(與 with 連用後接某人,與 for 連用後接某事物)。

dicky¹, dickey /ˈdɪkɪ ; ˈdɪkɪ/ *n* (colloq) (俗) **1** (also 亦作 **ˈ~-seat**) small, extra folding seat at the back of a two-seater motor-car. 供二人乘坐的汽車後部備用的摺叠小椅。 **2** false shirt-front. 假襯胸(襯衫的假胸)。 **3** **ˈ~-bird,** child's word for a bird. (兒語)鳥。

dicky² /ˈdɪkɪ ; ˈdɪkɪ/ *adj* (sl) unsound; weak: (俚)不健全的;脆弱的: *a* ~ *heart;* 脆弱的心; liable to break or fall. 易碎的;易跌落的。

Dic·ta·phone /ˈdɪktəfəʊn ; ˈdɪktəˌfon/ *n* (P) office machine that records words spoken into it and then reproduces them (for transcription, etc). (商標)(辦公室中用以錄話供以後抄寫等的)錄音機;口授留聲機。

dic·tate /dɪkˈteɪt *US:* ˈdɪkteɪt ; ˈdɪktet/ *vt, vi* **1** [VP6A, 2A, 14] ~ ***(to),*** say or read aloud (words to be written down by another or others): 大聲講或讀;口授(字句以供他人聽寫): *to* ~ *a letter to a secretary.* 向祕書口授信稿。 *The teacher* ~*d a passage to the class.* 教師讀一段文章要全班聽寫。 **2** [VP6A, 14] ~ ***(to),*** state with the force of authority: 指示;指定;指令: *to* ~ *terms to a defeated enemy.* 向戰敗的敵人指定條款。 **3** [VP3A] ~ ***to,*** order: 命令: *I won't be* ~*d to,* I refuse to accept orders from you. 我不接受你的命令。□ *n* /ˈdɪkteɪt ; ˈdɪktet/ (usu *pl*) direction or order (esp given by reason, conscience, etc): (通常用複數)指示;指令(尤指發自理智,良心等者): *the* ~*s of common sense.* 根據常識的判斷。 *Follow the* ~*s of your conscience,* Do what your conscience tells you to do. 遵照良心的指示(憑良心行事)。

dic·ta·tion /dɪkˈteɪʃn ; dɪkˈteʃən/ *n* **1** [U] dictating; being dictated to: 口授;聽寫;命令: *The pupils wrote at their teacher's* ~. 教師口授,學生聽寫。 **2** [C] passage, etc that is dictated. 口授聽寫的一段文字等。

dic·ta·tor /dɪkˈteɪtə(r) *US:* ˈdɪkteɪtər ; ˈdɪktetɚ/ *n* ruler who has absolute authority, esp one who has obtained such power by force or in an irregular way. 獨裁者(有絕對權力的統治者,尤指以武力或非常的手段獲此權力者)。 **~·ship** /-ʃɪp ; -ˌʃɪp/ *n* [C, U] (country with) government by a ~. 獨裁政治;獨裁國家。 **dic·ta·torial** /ˌdɪktəˈtɔːrɪəl ; ˌdɪktəˈtorɪəl/ *adj* of or like a ~: 獨裁者的; 似獨裁者的: ~*ial government;* 獨裁政治; overbearing; fond of giving orders: 盛氣凌人的;喜發號施令的: *his* ~*ial manner.* 他那種盛氣凌人的態度。 **dic·ta·tori·ally** /-əlɪ ; -əlɪ/ *adv*

dice **printer's dies**

dic·tion /ˈdɪkʃn ; ˈdɪkʃən/ *n* [U] choice and use of words; style or manner of speaking and writing. 用字;措辭;句法。

dic·tion·ary /ˈdɪkʃənrɪ *US:* -nerɪ ; ˈdɪkʃənˌɛrɪ/ *n* (*pl* -ries) book listing and explaining the words of a language, or the words or topics of a special subject, eg the Bible, architecture, and arranged in ABC order. 字典(將字按字母順序編列出並解釋字義者);詞典(解釋專門學科如聖經,建築學等之名詞或論題者)。

dic·tum /ˈdɪktəm ; ˈdɪktəm/ *n* (*pl* ~s, -ta /-tə ; -tə/) formal expression of opinion; saying. 正式發表的意見;格言。

did /dɪd ; dɪd/ ⇨ do.

di·dac·tic /dɪˈdæktɪk *US:* daɪ- ; daɪˈdæktɪk/ *adj* **1** intended to teach: 說教的;教訓的;教誨的: ~ *poetry.* 說教的詩。 **2** having the manner of a teacher: 表現教訓態度的: *A teacher should not be* ~ *outside the classroom.* 教師走出教室就不應再持教訓的態度。 **di·dac·ti·cally** /-klɪ ; -kl̩ɪ/ *adv*

diddle /ˈdɪdl ; ˈdɪdl̩/ *vt* [VP6A, 14] ~ ***sb (out of sth),*** (colloq) cheat. (俗)欺騙;詐欺。

die¹ /daɪ ; daɪ/ *n* **1** (*pl* dice) ⇨ dice. **2** (*pl* dies /daɪz ; daɪz/) block of hard metal with a design, etc cut in it, used for shaping coins, type¹(3), medals, etc or stamping paper, leather, etc so that designs stand out from the surface. 鑄錢幣,

獎章等刻有陰紋圖案的模子;在紙,皮革等上壓印凸紋圖案的鋼印模。'**die-cast** *adj* made by casting metal in a mould: 印模鑄造的: *die-cast toys*, eg small models of cars. 印模鑄造的玩具(如小汽車模型)。

die² /daɪ ; daɪ/ *vi* (*pt, pp* died, *pres part* dying) **1** [VP2A, C, D] come to the end of life; cease to live: 生命結束;死亡;死去: *Flowers soon die if they are left without water.* 花如不澆水,不久卽枯死。(Note the *preps*): (注意介詞): *to die of an illness/a disease/hunger/grief;* 死於疾病(疾病,飢餓,悲傷); *to die by violence;* 慘死;橫死; *to die by one's own hand*, ie commit suicide; 自殺; *to die from a wound;* 受傷不治而死; *to die for one's country;* 爲國捐軀; *to die through neglect;* 因疏忽而送命; *to die in battle;* 戰死; *to die happy/poor;* 在幸福(窮困)中死亡; *to die a beggar/a martyr.* 乞食(殉道)而死。 **2** (various phrases) (各種成語) ***die in one's bed,*** of old age or illness. 老死或病死;壽終正寢。***die with one's boots on,*** while still vigorous, while fighting. 橫死;暴斃;戰死。***die in the last ditch,*** fighting desperately to defend sth. 戰鬪到底。***die game,*** facing death bravely. 勇敢地面對死亡;至死不屈。***die hard,*** only after a struggle. 經一番掙扎方才死去;不易死去。 ⇨ 5 below. 參看下列第5義。***die in harness,*** while still at one's usual occupation, still working. 死在崗位上;殉職。 **3** [VP3A, 4C] ***be dying for sth/to do sth,*** have a strong wish: 有强烈的願望;渴望: *We're all dying for a drink.* 我們都渴得要死。*She's dying to know where you've been.* 她渴望知道你到哪裏去了。 **4** [VP2A, C] pass from human knowledge; be lost: 無人知曉;被遺忘: *His fame will never die.* 他的名聲將永垂不朽。*His secret died with him,* He died without telling it to anyone. 他的祕密至死未告訴他人。 **5** '**die-hard,** (often attrib) person who obstinately resists being compelled to do anything; politician who obstinately opposes new policies and fights hard in defence of old policies. (常作形容用法)死硬派;倔强的人(堅不屈服的人或堅決反對新政策而拚命衞護舊政策的從政者)。**6** [VP2C] (with various *adverbial particles*): (與各副詞接語連用): ***die away,*** lose strength, become faint or weak: 減低力量;漸消;漸弱: *The breeze died away.* 風漸息。*The noise died away.* 鬧聲漸消。

die back, (of plants) die down to the roots, which remain alive and send up shoots the next growing season: (指植物)莖死根不死(至下一季再發幼苗): *The dahlias died back when the frosts came.* 大利花打霜以後暫時枯萎。

die down, (of a fire in a fireplace, etc) burn with less heat; (of excitement, etc) become less violent; (of noise, etc) become less loud. (指爐火等)漸熄;(指騷動等)漸平息;(指鬧聲等)漸消失。

die off, die one by one: 先後死去;一一死去: *The leaves of this plant are dying off.* 這植物的葉子在凋落中。

die out, become extinct; come to a complete end: 死光;絶種: *With the death of the fifth earl, this old family had died out.* 隨着第五伯爵之死,這個老世家就絶後了。*Many old customs are gradually dying out.* 許多舊習俗都在日漸消失中。

di·er·esis /daɪ'erɪsɪs ; daɪ'ɛrəsɪs/ ⇨ diaeresis.

die·sel /'di:zl ; 'dizḷ/ *n* (attrib) (形容用法) **~-electric locomotive,** one that generates its own electric current from a ~ engine. 笛塞爾電動機車;柴油電力機車(由笛塞爾內燃機發電以行駛者)。'**~ engine,** oil-burning engine (as used for buses, locomotives) in which ignition is produced by the heat of suddenly compressed gas. 笛塞爾內燃機;柴油機(其發火係由突然受壓縮氣體的熱力產生,如用於公共汽車或火車機車中者)。'**~ oil,** heavy fuel oil. 柴油。

diet¹ /'daɪət ; 'daɪət/ *n* [C] **1** sort of food usually eaten (by a person, community, etc): (個人,社區等)通常所吃的食物: *the Japanese ~ of rice, vegetables and fish.* 日本人所常吃的食物: 米,蔬菜和魚。*Too rich a ~ (=* Too much rich food) *is not good for you.* 太油膩的食物對你不好。 **2** sort of food to which a person is limited, eg for medical reasons: 某人(因醫療的理由等)被限制食用的食物: *The doctor put her on a ~.* 醫生限制她的飲食。*No potatoes for me—I'm on a ~.* 不要給我馬鈴薯——我在吃規定的飲食。 □ *vt, vi* [VP6A, 2A] restrict (oneself, sb), be restricted, to a ~(2): 規定或限制(自己或他人)的飲食;實行節食: *She became so fat that she had to ~ herself.* 她長得太胖,所以不得不實行節食。*My doctor is ~ing me very strictly.* 我的醫生正極嚴格地限制我的飲食。*Is he still ~ing?* 他仍在節食嗎? **die·tary** /'daɪətərɪ *US:* -terɪ ; 'daɪə,tɛrɪ/ *adj* of ~: 限制飲食的: *~ary rules;* 飲食規則; *~ary taboos,* eg pork for Muslims. 飲食方面的禁忌(例如回教徒之不食豬肉)。**die·tet·ics** /,daɪə'tetɪks ; ,daɪə'tɛtɪks/ *n* (*sing v*) science of ~. (用單數動詞)飲食學;營養學。 **die·tician, die·titian** /,daɪə'tɪʃn ; ,daɪə'tɪʃən/ *n* expert in dietetics. 飲食學家;營養學家。

diet² /'daɪət ; 'daɪət/ *n* series of meetings for discussion of national, international or church affairs. 會議(包括一連串的集會,討論國內、國際或教會事務等)。

dif·fer /'dɪfə(r) ; 'dɪfɚ/ *vi* [VP2A, C, 3A] **1** ~ ***(from),*** be unlike; be distinguishable: 不同;有異: *The two brothers are like each other in appearance, but ~ widely in their tastes.* 這兩兄弟相貌相像,但趣味却大不相同。*French ~s from English in having gender for all nouns.* 法文與英文不同:法文所有的名詞都有性別。*Tastes ~,* Different people have different interests. 趣味人各不同。 **2** ~ ***from sb (about/on sth),*** disagree; have another opinion: 不同意;持異議: *I'm sorry to ~ from you about/on that question.* 對不起,關於那個問題我與你的看法不同。***agree to ~,*** give up the attempt to convince each other. 同意各持己見(不欲互相說服)。

dif·fer·ence /'dɪfrəns ; 'dɪfərəns/ *n* [C, U] ***~(between),*** **1** the state of being unlike: 不同;相異;差別: *the ~ between summer and winter.* 冬夏之別。**2** amount, degree, manner, in which things are unlike: 事物彼此不同的數額,程度或方式;差數;差別之處: *The ~ between 7 and 18 is 11.* 7與18的差數是11。*What a great ~ there is in the temperature today!* 今天的氣溫差別好大啊! *There are many ~s between the two languages.* 這兩種語言有許多不同之處。***split the ~,*** ⇨ split. **3** ***make a/some/no/any/not much/a great deal of ~,*** be of some/no, etc importance: 有(頗有,沒有,有何,沒有多大,有很大)重要性: *It won't make much ~ whether you go today or tomorrow.* 你今天去或明天去沒有多大關係。*Does that make any ~,* Is it important, need we consider it? 那是否有重要性? 我們是否需要考慮它? ***make a ~ between,*** treat differently. 差別對待。 **4** disagreement: 不同意;歧見: *Why can't you settle your ~s and be friends again?* 你們爲何不消除歧見而言歸於好?

dif·fer·ent /'dɪfrənt ; 'dɪfərənt/ *adj* **1** not the same: 不同的;相異的: *They are ~ people with the same name.* 他們名雖同而人互異。*The two boys are ~ in their tastes.* 這兩個孩子的興趣不同。*She is wearing a ~ dress every time I see her.* 我每次看見她,她都穿一件不同的衣服。**~ *from/to/*** (US) (美) ***than,*** 與…不同: *Your method is ~ from/to mine.* 你的方法與我的不同。(Note: **~ *than*** may be used when ~ is not immediately followed by its *prep*: 注意: different 後面未緊接介詞時可用 than: *How ~ life today is than what it was fifty years ago.* Cf 參較 *Life today is ~ from life fifty years ago,* where ~ is followed immediately by *from.* 此句中 different 後緊接介詞 from。) **2** separate; distinct: 分別的;各不相同的: *I called three ~ times, but he was out.* 我打了三次電話,他都不在家。*They are sold in ~ colours,* a variety of colours. 它們以各種不同的顏色出售。**~·ly** *adv*

dif·fer·en·tial /,dɪfə'renʃl ; ,dɪfə'rɛnʃəl/ *adj* **1** of, showing, depending on, a difference: 有分別的; 基於差別的: ~ *tariffs,* that differ according to circumstances. 差別的稅率 (根據情況不同而異)。⇨ calculus. **2** ~ **(gear),** arrangement of gears (in a motor-car, etc) that allows the rear wheels to turn at different speeds on curves. 差動(速)齒輪 (裝於汽車等中,使後輪在轉彎時以不同速度轉動)。□ *n* **(wage)~,** difference (expressed in a percentage) in wages between skilled and unskilled workers in the same industry: (在同一種工業內,技術工與非技術工之)工資差別(按百分比計算): *They opposed a flat increase for all workers because that would upset the wage ~.* 他們反對予所有的工人平等的加薪,因爲那樣就破壞了工資差別制度。

dif·fer·en·ti·ate /ˌdɪfəˈrenʃɪeɪt ; ˌdɪfəˈrɛnʃɪˌet/ *vt* **1** [VP6A, 14] ~ ***(from),*** see as different; show to be different: 區別;分別;辨別: *to ~ varieties of plants;* 辨別各種植物; *to ~ one variety from another.* 區別一種與另一種。*The report does not ~ the two aspects of the problem.* 此報告未能將問題的兩方面加以區別。*One aspect is not ~ed from the other.* 一方面未與另一方面區別。 **2** [VP3A] ~ ***between,*** treat as different: 差別對待: *It is wrong to ~ between pupils according to their family background.* 由於家庭背景而差別對待學生是不對的。 **dif·fer·en·ti·ation** /ˌdɪfərenʃɪˈeɪʃn ; ˌdɪfəˌrɛnʃɪˈeʃən/ *n*

dif·fi·cult /ˈdɪfɪkəlt ; ˈdɪfəkḷt/ *adj* **1** not easy; requiring effort, strength, skill or ability: 不容易的; 困難的;需要用力的;需要技巧或能力的: *a ~ problem / language.* 困難的問題(語言)。*He finds it ~ to stop smoking.* 他覺得戒煙是件難事。*The sound is ~ to pronounce.* 這個音不容易發。*It is a ~ sound to pronounce.* 它是一個難發的音。*The place is ~ to reach / ~ of access.* 那個處所不易到達。*He was placed in ~ circumstances.* 他被置於困境。 **2** (of persons) not easily pleased or satisfied; easily offended: (指人)不易取悅或滿足的;易惱怒的: *He's a ~ man to get on with.* 他是個不易相處的人。*The famous actress was being rather ~,* was causing trouble, eg to the other members of the cast, the producer. 那著名女伶相當難對付(使別的演員,製片人都感到麻煩)。*Please don't be so ~.* 請不要那樣彆扭。

dif·fi·culty /ˈdɪfɪkəltɪ ; ˈdɪfəˌkʌltɪ/ *n* **1** [U] the state or quality of being difficult: 困難; 艱難; 費力: *Do you have any ~ in understanding spoken English?* 你對於瞭解口語英文有無困難? *There was some ~ in getting everybody here in time.* 使每一個人都按時到達這裏曾經過相當的周折。*He did the work without ~ / without any / much ~.* 他毫不費力地做完那工作。*He did it, but with ~.* 他做是做到了,但頗爲費力。 **2** [C] (*pl* -ties) sth difficult, hard to do or understand: 難事;難做的事;難懂的事: *the difficulties of Greek syntax;* 希臘文造句法的困難之處; *to be working under difficulties,* in difficult circumstances; 在不利的環境中工作; *to be in financial difficulties,* short of money, in debt, etc. 處於經濟困難中(如缺錢,負債等)。*If you knew the difficulties I am in!* 你完全不知道我遭遇了何種困難! *Mary's father raised / made difficulties when she said she wanted to marry a poor school-teacher,* He objected to, opposed, the proposal. 瑪莉說她想嫁一個窮教員時,她父親提出了異議。

dif·fi·dent /ˈdɪfɪdənt ; ˈdɪfədənt/ *adj* not having, not showing, much belief in one's own abilities; lacking in self-confidence: 對自己的能力沒有信心的;缺乏自信心的: *to be ~ about doing sth;* 對於做某事缺乏自信心; *to speak in a ~ manner.* 說話沒有自信心的樣子。**~·ly** *adv* **dif·fi·dence** /-dəns ; -dəns/ *n* [U] being ~; shyness. 無自信心;羞怯。

dif·fract /dɪˈfrækt ; dɪˈfrækt/ *vt* [VP6A] break up (a beam of light) into a series of dark and light bands or the coloured bands of the spectrum. 分解(光線)使成爲明暗或七彩的光譜;使繞射。⇨ the illus at spectrum. 參看 spectrum 之插圖。 **dif·frac·tion** /dɪˈfrækʃn ; dɪˈfrækʃən/ *n*

dif·fuse¹ /dɪˈfjuːz ; dɪˈfjuz/ *vt, vi* **1** [VP6A] send out, spread, in every direction: 散佈;傳播;傳佈;漫射: *to ~ learning / knowledge / good humour / light / heat / a scent / an odour;* 傳播學問(知識,高興,光,熱,氣味); *~d lighting,* contrasted with direct lighting. 漫射燈光(與直射燈光相對)。 **2** [VP6A, 2A] (of gases and liquids) (cause to) mix slowly. (指氣體及液體)(使)慢慢混合;(使)擴散。 **dif·fu·sion** /dɪˈfjuːʒn ; dɪˈfjuʒən/ *n* [U] diffusing or being ~d: 散佈;傳播;漫射;擴散: *the diffusion of knowledge through books and lectures;* 知識經由書籍及演講的傳播; *the diffusion of gases and liquids,* their mixing without external force. 氣體和液體不經外力的自然混合。

dif·fuse² /dɪˈfjuːs ; dɪˈfjus/ *adj* **1** using too many words: 用字太多的;冗贅的: *a ~ writer / style.* 冗贅的作家(文體)。 **2** spread out; scattered: 散佈的;散播的;擴散的;漫射的: *~ light.* 漫射光。**~·ly** *adv* **~·ness** *n*

dig¹ /dɪɡ ; dɪɡ/ *vt, vi* (*pt, pp* dug /dʌɡ ; dʌɡ/) (-gg-) **1** [VP6A, 15B, 2C] use a tool (eg a spade), a machine, claws, etc to break up and move earth, etc; make a way (*through, into,* etc) by doing this; make (a hole, etc) by doing this; get (sth) by doing this: 用工具(如鐵鏟),機器,爪子等挖掘土地等;挖穿(與 through 連用);挖入(與 into 連用);挖(洞等);挖得;掘出: *It is difficult to dig the ground when it is frozen hard.* 地面凍硬時不易挖掘。*They are digging through the hill to make a tunnel / digging a tunnel through the hill.* 他們正在穿山鑿一隧道。*He dug a deep hole.* 他挖了一個深洞。*The soldiers were digging trenches.* 士兵們(那時)正在挖戰壕。 **2** [VP6A] (sl) enjoy; appreciate; understand; follow: (俚)喜歡;欣賞;瞭解;懂: *I don't dig modern jazz.* 我不欣賞現代爵士樂。 **3** [VP15B, 3A, 2C] (uses with *adverbial particles* and *preps*): (與副詞接語及介詞連用的用法):

dig in; dig into sth, serve oneself with food, begin eating, with appetite: 津津有味地進食;開始津津有味地吃: *dig into a pie.* 津津有味地吃一餡餅。*The food's here, so dig in!* 食物在這裏,開始吃罷! ***dig sth in,*** mix with the soil by digging: 混入土壤中: *The manure should be well dug in.* 肥料應該均勻地混入土壤中。 ***dig sth in; dig into sth,*** push, thrust, poke: 推;插入;刺: *to dig a fork into a pie / a potato.* 將叉子插入餡餅(洋芋)中。*The rider dug his spurs into the horse's flank / dug his spurs in.* 騎者以馬刺刺馬的側腹。 ***dig oneself in,*** **(a)** protect oneself by digging a trench, etc. 挖壕溝等以藏身。 **(b)** (fig, colloq) establish oneself securely (in a position, etc). (喻,俗)鞏固自己的職位等。 ***dig sb in the ribs,*** poke one's elbow in his ribs, eg to call attention to sth funny. 用肘拐觸某人的肋骨(如爲促其注意可笑的事物)。

dig sb / sth out (of sth), **(a)** get out by digging: 挖出;掘出;挖地而逼出: *They dug out the fox / dug the fox out of its hole.* 他們挖地逼出那狐狸(將狐狸自洞中逼出)。*He was buried by the avalanche and had to be dug out.* 他爲雪崩所埋,必須讓人挖出來。 **(b)** get by searching: 探索: *to dig information out of books and reports;* 自書中與報告中探索知識; *to dig out the truth.* 尋求實情。

dig sth up, **(a)** break up (land) by digging: 翻(土): *to dig up land for a new garden.* 翻土建一新花園。 **(b)** remove from the ground by digging: 自地上挖掉: *We dug the tree up by the roots.* 我們把那樹連根挖起。 **(c)** bring to light (what has been buried or hidden) by digging: 挖出(被湮埋之物): *An old Greek statue was dug up here last month.* 一尊古希臘雕像上個月在此地被挖出。 **(d)** (fig) (喻): *The newspapers love to dig up scandals.* 報紙喜歡揭露醜聞。

dig² /dɪɡ ; dɪɡ/ *n* **1** push or thrust: 推;戳;刺: *give sb a dig in the ribs.* 推推某人的肋骨。*That was a* *dig at me*, a remark directed against me. 那句話是對我而發的。 **2** site being excavated by archaeologists. 考古學家所挖掘的地點。 **3** (*pl*) (GB, colloq) lodgings: (複) (英,俗) 寄宿舍: *Are you living at home or in digs?* 你住在家裏還是住在寄宿舍？

di·gest[1] /ˈdaɪdʒest ; ˈdaɪdʒɛst/ *n* [C] short, condensed account; summary: 摘要;綱要: *a ~ of the week's news.* 一週新聞摘要。

di·gest[2] /dɪˈdʒest ; dəˈdʒɛst/ *vt, vi* [VP6A, 2A] **1** (of food) change, be changed, in the stomach and bowels, so that it can be used in the body: (指食物) 消化 (在胃腸中起變化以便身體吸收)；被消化: *Some foods ~/are ~ed more easily than others.* 某些食物較其他的食物易於消化。 **2** take into the mind; make part of one's knowledge; reduce (a mass of facts, etc) to order: 吸收於腦中;使成爲自己的知識的一部分; 將 (一堆事實等) 整理出系統; 透徹瞭解: *Have you ~ed everything that is important in the book?* 你是否已將書中每一要點透徹瞭解？ **~·ible** /dɪˈdʒestəbl ; dəˈdʒɛstəbl/ *adj* that can be ~ed. 可消化的。**~i·bil·ity** /dɪˌdʒestəˈbɪlətɪ ; dəˌdʒɛstəˈbɪlətɪ/ *n*

di·ges·tion /dɪˈdʒestʃən ; dəˈdʒɛstʃən/ *n* [U] digesting: 消化;吸收: *food that is easy/difficult of ~;* 易(難)於消化的食物; [C] power of digesting food: 消化力: *to have a poor/good ~.* 消化力弱(强)。

di·ges·tive /dɪˈdʒestɪv ; dəˈdʒɛstɪv/ *adj* of digestion (of food): 消化(食物)的: *suffer from ~ trouble.* 患消化系統的疾病。**the ˈ~ system**, the alimentary canal. 消化系統。

dig·ger /ˈdɪgə(r) ; ˈdɪgɚ/ *n* **1** (usu in compounds) person who digs: (通常用於複合字中)挖掘者: *ˈgold-~*, one who tries to find gold in a gold-field. 採金者;淘金者。 **2** mechanical excavator. 挖掘機。**3** (sl) Australian. (俚)澳洲人。

dig·ging /ˈdɪgɪŋ ; ˈdɪgɪŋ/ *n* [U] action of digging; [C] (often *pl*) place where men dig or search for metal, esp gold. 挖掘;(常用複數)採礦場(尤指金礦)。

digit /ˈdɪdʒɪt ; ˈdɪdʒɪt/ *n* **1** any one of the ten Arabic numerals 0 to 9: 阿拉伯數字: *The number 57306 contains five ~s.* 57306一數中含五個數字。**2** finger or toe. 手指;趾。**digi·tal** /ˈdɪdʒɪtl ; ˈdɪdʒɪtl/ *adj* of ~s. 數字的;指或趾的。**~al clock/watch**, one without hands, showing the time by ~s (eg 07.45) only. (沒有時針分針而用數字表示時間的)電子鐘(錶)。**~al computer**, one showing its calculations by ~s (binary or decimal). 數位計算機(以二進或十進數字表示計算結果者)。

dig·nify /ˈdɪgnɪfaɪ ; ˈdɪgnəˌfaɪ/ *vt* [VP6A, 14] ~ ***(with)***, cause to appear worthy or honourable; give dignity to: 使顯得有價值或可尊敬;使顯赫;使高貴: *to ~ a small collection of books by calling it a library/~ it with the name library.* 稱少數的藏書爲圖書館，以提高其身價。 **dig·ni·fied** *part adj* having or showing dignity: 可敬的; 高貴的: *a dignified old lady.* 高貴的老婦人。

dig·ni·tary /ˈdɪgnɪtərɪ *US:* -terɪ ; ˈdɪgnəˌtɛrɪ/ *n* (*pl* -ries) person holding a high office. 顯要人物;權貴。

dig·nity /ˈdɪgnətɪ ; ˈdɪgnətɪ/ *n* **1** [U] true worth; the quality that earns or deserves respect: 眞實價值;可尊敬的品格: *the ~ of labour.* 勞動的眞正價值;勞工神聖。*A man's ~ depends not upon his wealth or rank but upon his character.* 人的眞正價值不在財富或地位,而在品格。 **2** [U] calm and serious manner or style: 尊嚴;威嚴: *If you're afraid of losing your ~* (eg of being made to look foolish), *you can't expect to learn to speak a foreign language.* 如果你怕失去尊嚴，你就不能期望學會說一種外國話。***beneath one's ~***, below one's moral, social, etc standards: 有傷尊嚴;有失身份: *It is beneath your ~ to answer such a rude remark.* 回答這種粗野的話有傷你的尊嚴。***stand on/upon one's ~***, insist upon being treated with proper respect; refuse to do what one considers to be below one's moral, social, etc standards. 堅持禮遇;保持尊嚴(拒絕做有失身分的事)。 **3** [C] (*pl* -ties) high or honourable rank, port or title: 高位顯爵: *The Queen conferred the ~ of a peerage on him.* 女王授他以貴族身分。

di·graph /ˈdaɪgrɑːf *US:* -græf ; ˈdaɪgræf/ *n* two letters that represent a single sound (eg *sh* /ʃ/, *ea* /iː/ in *sheaf*). 代表單一語音的兩個字母(如 sheaf 中 sh 代表 /ʃ/ 音，ea 代表 /iː/ 音)。

di·gress /daɪˈgres;dəˈgrɛs/ *vi* [VP2A, 3A] ~ ***(from)***, (esp in speaking or writing) turn or wander away (from the main subject). (尤指演說或寫作時)離開(本題);轉入枝節。**di·gression** /daɪˈgreʃn ; dəˈgrɛʃən/ *n* [U] ~ing; [C] instance of this. 離題;轉入枝節。

digs /dɪgz ; dɪgz/ *n pl* (GB, colloq) lodgings. (英,俗)寄宿舍。

dike, dyke /daɪk ; daɪk/ *n* **1** ditch (for carrying away water from land). (排水的)溝。 **2** long wall of earth, etc (to keep back water and prevent flooding). 堤(阻水或防洪的長壁,以土等築成)。 **3** ⚠ (derog sl) (masculine) lesbian. (諱) (貶俚) (男性化之)同性戀女子。□ *vi, vt* [VP2A, 6A] make or provide with a ~ or ~s. 築堤。

a dike

dil·api·dated /dɪˈlæpɪdeɪtɪd ; dəˈlæpəˌdetɪd/ *adj* (of buildings, furniture, etc) falling to pieces; in a state of disrepair: (指建築物,傢具等)殘破的;失修的;倒塌的: *a ~-looking car;* 破爛不堪的汽車; *a ~ old house.* 殘破的古屋。**dil·api·da·tion** /dɪˌlæpɪˈdeɪʃn ; dəˌlæpəˈdeʃən/ *n* [U] being or becoming ~. 殘破不堪;失修倒塌。

di·late /daɪˈleɪt ; daɪˈlet/ *vi, vt* **1** [VP6A, 2A] (cause to) become wider, larger, further open: (使)擴大;膨脹;張大: *The pupils of your eyes ~ when you enter a dark room.* 當你進入暗室,你的眼睛的瞳孔就會擴大。*The horse ~d its nostrils.* 那馬張大牠的鼻孔。 **2** [VP3A] ~ ***upon***, (formal) speak or write comprehensively about: (正式用語)詳述(說或寫): *If there were time, I could ~ upon this subject.* 假如有時間,我可對此題目加以詳述。**di·la·tion** /ˌdaɪˈleɪʃn ; daɪˈleʃən/ *n* [U] dilating or being ~d. 擴大;膨脹;詳述。

dila·tory /ˈdɪlətərɪ *US:* -tɔːrɪ ; ˈdɪləˌtɔrɪ/ *adj* slow in acting; causing delay. 做事緩慢的;拖延的。

di·lemma /dɪˈlemə ; dəˈlɛmə/ *n* situation in which one has to choose between two things, two courses of action, etc both unfavourable or undesirable. 進退兩難之境;兩條路均不如意的困境。***be in/place sb in a ~***: 處(使處)於進退兩難之境: *You place me in something of a ~.* 你使我進退兩難。

dil·et·tante /ˌdɪlɪˈtæntɪ ; ˌdɪləˈtæntɪ/ *n* (*pl* ~s /-tiːz ; -tiz/ or -ti /-tiː ; -ti/) one who studies sth, but not seriously and not with real understanding. 研究某事物而不認眞且不甚瞭解的人。

dili·gence /ˈdɪlɪdʒəns ; ˈdɪlədʒəns/ *n* [U] ~ ***(in)***, steady effort; showing care and effort (in what one does). 勤勉;細心而用功。

dili·gent /ˈdɪlɪdʒənt ; ˈdɪlədʒənt/ *adj* ~ ***(in)***, hard-working; showing care and effort (in what one does). 勤勉的;努力的;細心而用功的。**~·ly** *adv*

dill /dɪl ; dɪl/ *n* herb with spicy seeds, eg as used for flavouring pickles. 蒔蘿(草本植物,子有香味,用作泡菜等之香料)。

dilly-dally /ˈdɪlɪ dælɪ ; ˈdɪlɪˌdælɪ/ *vi* [VP2A] dawdle; waste time (by not making up one's mind). (因猶豫不決而)浪費時間。

di·lute /daɪ'lju:t *US:* -'lu:t ; dɪ'lut/ *vt* [VP6A, 14] ~ ***(with),*** make (a liquid or colour) weaker or thinner (by adding water or other liquid): (加水等使液體或顏色)變稀;變淡;稀釋;沖淡: *to ~ wine with water;* 加水於酒以沖淡之; (fig) weaken the force of (by mixing): (喻)(由混合而)減弱…之力量: *to ~ skilled labour,* eg by employing a proportion of unskilled workers. 在熟練的工人中攙入不熟練的工人。□ *adj* (of acids, etc) weakened by diluting. (指酸液等) 稀釋的; 沖淡的; 攙水的。 **di·lu·tion** /daɪ-'lju:ʃn *US:* -'lu:- ; dɪ'luʃən/ *n* [U] diluting or being ~d; [C] sth that is ~d. 稀釋; 沖淡; 攙水;稀釋或沖淡之物。

dim /dɪm ; dɪm/ *adj* (-mmer, -mmest) **1** not bright; not clearly to be seen: 不亮的;看不清楚的;朦朧的;模糊的: *the dim light of a candle;* 微弱的燭光; *the dim outline of buildings on a dark night;* 在黑夜裏建築物之朦朧的輪廓; *dim memories/recollections of my childhood.* 對於兒時之模糊的記憶。 **2** (of the eyes, eyesight) not able to see clearly: (指眼睛,目力)看不清楚的: *eyes dim with tears.* 爲淚水所模糊的眼睛。*His eyesight is getting dim.* 他的目力逐漸模糊。***take a dim view of,*** (colloq) regard with disapproval or pessimism. (俗)對…不贊成或不抱樂觀。 **3** (colloq, of persons) lacking intelligence. (俗,指人)愚鈍的。□ *vt, vi* (-mm-) [VP6A, 2A] make or become dim: (使)變微弱、朦朧、模糊: *The light of a candle is dimmed by sunlight.* 燭光在太陽光下變得微弱。**dim·ly** *adv* in a dim manner: 模糊地;朦朧地: *a dimly lit room.* 燈光微弱的房間。 **dim·ness** *n*

dime /daɪm ; daɪm/ *n* coin of US and Canada worth ten cents. (美國及加拿大銀幣)一角。

di·men·sion /dɪ'menʃn ; də'mɛnʃən/ *n* **1** [U, C] measurement of any sort (breadth, length, thickness, height, etc): 任何一種度量(寬、長、厚、高等): *What are the ~s of the room?* 這房間的長、寬、高是多少? **2** (*pl*) size; extent: (複)大小;面積;體積;範圍;程度: *a building of great ~s;* 龐大的建築物; *the ~s of the problem.* 問題的範圍。 **3** (algebra) number of unknown quantities contained as factors in a product: (代數)維;次元(乘積之因子數): x^3, x^2y and *xyz are of three ~s.* x^3, x^2y, xyz 都是三次式。**~al** /-ʃənl ; -ʃənḷ/ *adj* having (a certain number of) ~s: …次元的: *two-/three-~al figures.* 二(三)次元的數字。**3D** /ˌθri: 'di: ; ˌθri'di/ (abbr of *three-~al*) (three-dimensional 之略) stereoscopic, giving the illusion of depth in perspective (as well as height and breadth). 立體的(給人不但有高、闊,且有深度的感覺)。

dim·in·ish /dɪ'mɪnɪʃ ; də'mɪnɪʃ/ *vt, vi* [VP6A, 2A] make or become less: (使)減少;縮小: *~ing food supplies;* 日漸減少的食品供應; *a war that seriously ~ed the country's wealth;* 使國家財富嚴重減少的戰爭; *a currency that has ~ed in value.* 已貶值的貨幣。

dim·inu·endo /dɪˌmɪnju'endəʊ ; dəˌmɪnju'ɛndo/ *n* (*pl* ~s /-dəʊz ; -doz/) [C] (music) gradual decrease in loudness: (音樂)聲音漸弱: *a sudden ~.* 聲音突然減弱。

dim·in·ution /ˌdɪmɪ'nju:ʃn *US:* -'nu:ʃn ; ˌdɪmə-'njuʃən/ *n* [U] diminishing or being diminished; [C] amount of this: 減少;縮小;減少量;縮小量: *to hope for a small ~ in taxes.* 希望稅捐略微減低。

dim·inu·tive /dɪ'mɪnjʊtɪv ; də'mɪnjətɪv/ *adj* **1** unusually or remarkably small. 較通常爲小的;小得多的。 **2** (gram, of a *suff*) indicating smallness. (文法,指字尾)表示'小'的。□ *n* word formed by the use of a *suff* of this kind, eg *streamlet,* a small stream, *lambkin,* a small lamb. 由此種字尾所構成的字(如 streamlet 小溪, lambkin 小羊)。

dim·ity /'dɪmɪtɪ ; 'dɪmətɪ/ *n* [U] (kinds of) cotton cloth woven with raised strips or designs, used for bedroom hangings, etc. (數種)有楞條或凸出之花樣的棉布(用製臥室帷幔等)。

dimple /'dɪmpl ; 'dɪmpḷ/ *n* small natural hollow in the chin or cheek (either permanent, or which appears eg when a person smiles); slight hollow on water (made eg by a breeze). 面頰上的酒窩;笑靨;風吹水面所起的漣漪。□ *vt, vi* [VP6A, 2A] make ~s on; form ~s. (使)現酒窩;(使)起漣漪。

din /dɪn ; dɪn/ *n* [U] (or **a din**) loud, confused noise that continues: 不斷的喧鬧聲; 嘈雜聲: *The children were making so much din/such a din that I couldn't study.* 孩子們吵鬧得非常厲害,我簡直不能讀書。*They made/kicked up such a din at the party.* 那次聚會中他們吵鬧得真兇。□ *vi, vt* (-nn-) **1** [VP2C] make a din: 喧囂;吵鬧;發嘈雜聲: *The cries of his tormentors were still dinning in his ears.* 那些折磨他的人的吼叫聲仍然在他的耳朵裡響個不停。 **2** ***din sth into sb,*** tell him again and again, in a forcible manner. 再三叮囑;三番五次地告誡。

dine /daɪn ; daɪn/ *vi, vt* **1** [VP2A] (formal) have dinner. (正式用語)吃飯;進餐。 ~ ***out,*** dine outside one's home (eg at the house of friends, or at a restaurant). 在外面吃飯(在朋友家或餐館吃飯)。 **2** [VP6A] give a dinner for: 設宴款待;請(客): *The great man was wined and ~d wherever he went,* People gave dinner-parties for him. 那大人物無論走到哪裏都受到酒宴招待。**'dining-car,** railway coach in which meals are served. (火車的)餐車。**'dining-room,** room in which meals are eaten. 餐廳;飯廳。 **'dining-table,** table used for eating on. 餐桌。

diner /'daɪnə(r) ; 'daɪnə/ *n* **1** person who dines. 吃飯者;進餐者。 **2** dining-car on a train. (火車的)餐車。 **3** (US) restaurant shaped like a ~(2). (美)外形似餐車般的餐館。

ding-dong /ˌdɪŋ 'dɒŋ ; 'dɪŋˌdɔŋ/ *n, adv* (with the) sound of bells striking repeatedly. (鐘反覆敲擊的)叮噹聲;叮叮噹噹地。 **a ~ struggle/battle,** one in which each of two contestants has the advantage alternately. 雙方互有勝敗的比賽;旗鼓相當的競爭。

din·ghy /'dɪŋgɪ ; 'dɪŋgɪ/ *n* (*pl* -ghies) (kinds of) small open boat; inflatable rubber boat (eg carried by an aircraft for use if forced down on water). 無篷小船;(飛機等攜帶以備迫降水上用的可以充氣的)橡皮艇。

dingle /'dɪŋgl ; 'dɪŋgḷ/ *n* deep dell, usu with trees. 深谷(通常有樹木)。

dingy /'dɪndʒɪ ; 'dɪndʒɪ/ *adj* (-ier, -iest) dirty-looking; not fresh or cheerful: 樣子骯髒的;不清爽的;昏暗的: *a ~ manufacturing town;* 骯髒的製造工業城鎮; *a ~ room in a ~ boarding-house.* 昏暗的寄宿舍中一個昏暗的房間。**ding·ily** *adv* **dingi·ness** *n*

dining /'daɪnɪŋ ; 'daɪnɪŋ/ ⇨ dine.

dinky /'dɪŋkɪ ; 'dɪŋkɪ/ *adj* (-ier, -iest) (GB, colloq) pretty; neat: (英,俗)漂亮的;整潔的;精緻的: *What a ~ little hat!* 多麼精緻的一頂小帽!

din·ner /'dɪnə(r) ; 'dɪnə/ *n* main meal of the day, whether eaten at midday or in the evening (note the *preps* and the use and omission of the articles): 一日間的主餐(無論中午吃或晚間吃。注意連用的介詞以及冠詞的使用和省略): *It's time for ~/'~-time.* 吃飯的時間到了。*Have you had* (US 美=*eaten*) *~ yet?* 你吃了飯沒有? *They were at ~/having ~ when I called.* 當我訪晤時,他們正在吃飯。*He ate too much ~.* 他飯吃得太多。*The ~ was badly served.* 飯菜上得不好。*Shall we give a ~* (= **'~-party**) *for her?* 我們需要爲她開一次宴會嗎? *Four ~s at £5 a head.* 四客飯,每客五鎊。*Shall we ask him to ~?* 我們要請他吃飯嗎? **'~-jacket,** black jacket worn by men in the evening for formal occasions. 男人在晚間正式場合所穿的黑色禮服。 (Cf *dress coat,* with tails, and US *tuxedo.*) (參較有燕尾之 dress coat, 及美國用之 tuxedo。) **'~-service, '~-set,** set of plates, dishes, etc for ~. 一套(杯盤碗碟等)餐具。

dino·saur /'daɪnəsɔ:(r) ; 'daɪnəˌsɔr/ *n* large extinct reptile. 恐龍(已絕跡的巨大爬蟲)。

dint /dɪnt ; dɪnt/ *n* **1** [C] =dent. **2** ***by ~ of,*** by means of: 由於;憑藉: *He succeeded by ~ of hard* *work.* 他憑苦幹而成功。

dio·cese /ˈdaɪəsɪs ; ˈdaɪəˌsis/ *n* bishop's district. (主教的)教區。**di·ocesan** /daɪˈɒsɪsn ; daɪˈɑsəsn̩/ *adj, n* (of a) ~. 教區(的)。

di·ox·ide /daɪˈɒksaɪd ; daɪˈɑksaɪd/ *n* (chem) oxide formed by combination of two atoms of oxygen and one atom of a metal or other element: (化學)二氧化物(二氧原子和一金屬或其他元素之原子的化合物): *carbon* ~, **(CO_2)**. 二氧化碳。

dip[1] /dɪp ; dɪp/ *vt, vi* (-pp-) **1** [VP6A, 14] ***dip in/into,*** put, lower, (sth) into a liquid: 將(某物)浸於液體中;沾: *to dip one's pen into the ink;* 將筆伸入墨水中(沾墨水); *to dip sheep,* immerse them in a liquid that disinfects them, kills vermin; 用消毒水洗羊(以消滅蚤蝨等); *to dip candles,* make them by dipping wick into melted fat; 用燭心沾融油以製蠟燭; *dip a garment,* put it in a liquid dye to change its colour. (浸於液體染料中)染衣服。**ˈdip-stick,** stick or rod (to be) dipped into a tank or other container to measure the depth of liquid in it (eg oil in the sump of an engine). 探條(伸入液體容器中以探測其中液體深度,如探測發動機貯油槽中的油所用者)。 **2** [VP3A] ***dip into,*** (fig): (喻): *to dip into one's purse,* spend money; 花錢; *to dip into the future,* try to imagine what it will be like; 預想未來的事情; *to dip into a book/an author, etc,* make a cursory study. 瀏覽一本書(一個作家的作品等)。 **3** [VP2A, C] go below a surface or level: 沉入;降至(某平面)以下:*The sun dipped below the horizon.* 太陽沉入地平線以下。*The birds rose and dipped in their flight.* 鳥上下飛翔。 **4** [VP6A, 2A] (cause to) go down and then up again: (使)一低一揚;降下復升起: *to dip a flag,* as a salute, eg to another ship; 行點旗禮(將旗下降復升起,以示向另一船敬禮); *to dip the headlights of a car,* lower their beams (in order not to dazzle the driver of another car). 使汽車前燈之光度減弱(以免使另一汽車的駕駛員目眩);打近燈。*The land dips gently to the south.* 地面向南方微弱傾斜。

dip[2] /dɪp ; dɪp/ *n* **1** [C] act of dipping, esp (colloq) quick bathe or swim: 浸;沾;(尤指,俗)短促的沐浴或游泳: *to have/take/go for a dip.* 作短促的沐浴(或游泳)。 **2** [U] cleansing liquid in which sheep are dipped. 洗羊的消毒水。 **3** [C] downward slope: 斜坡: *a dip in the road;* 路上的斜坡; *a dip among the hills.* 山中的斜坡。 **4** [U] position of a flag when it is dipped(4): 旗幟下降示敬的位置;點旗: *at the dip.* 在下降示敬的位置。

diph·theria /dɪfˈθɪərɪə ; dɪfˈθɪrɪə/ *n* [U] serious contagious disease of the throat causing difficulty in breathing. 白喉(喉部嚴重的傳染病,使呼吸困難)。

diph·thong /ˈdɪfθɒŋ *US:* -θɔːŋ ; ˈdɪfθɔŋ/ *n* union of two vowel sounds or (more usu *digraph*) vowel letters, eg the sounds /aɪ ; aɪ/ in *pipe* /paɪp ; paɪp/, the letters *ou* in *doubt.* 二重母音;雙元音(合讀一音的兩個母音);合讀一音的兩個母音字母 (digraph 較常用)。

di·ploma /dɪˈpləʊmə ; dɪˈplomə/ *n* [C] educational certificate of proficiency: 畢業證書;文憑: *a* ~ *in architecture.* 建築科系畢業證書。

di·plo·macy /dɪˈpləʊməsɪ ; dɪˈploməsɪ/ *n* [U] **1** management of a country's affairs by its agents abroad (ambassadors and ministers), and their direction by the Ministry of Foreign Affairs at home; skill in this. 外交;外交手段。 **2** art of, skill in, dealing with people so that business is done smoothly. (爲業務進行順利,對人的)交際手腕。

a dinosaur

diplo·mat /ˈdɪpləmæt ; ˈdɪpləˌmæt/ *n* **1** person engaged in diplomacy for his country (eg an ambassador). 外交官(例如大使)。 **2** person clever at dealing with people. 善於應付人者;善於辦交涉者。

diplo·matic /ˌdɪpləˈmætɪk ; ˌdɪpləˈmætɪk/ *adj* **1** of diplomacy: 外交的: *the ˈ~ service*(2); 外交界;外交官的總稱; *the ˈ~ corps/body,* all the ambassadors, ministers and their officers in the capital of a country. 外交使節團;一國首都的所有外交使節。 **2** tactful; having diplomacy(2): 圓通的;圓滑的;有交際手腕的: *a* ~ *answer;* 圓滑的答覆; *to be* ~ *in dealing with people.* 對人有交際手腕。**diplo·mati·cally** /-klɪ ; -klɪ/ *adv*

di·ploma·tist /dɪˈpləʊmətɪst ; dɪˈplomətɪst/ *n* = diplomat.

dip·per /ˈdɪpə(r) ; ˈdɪpɚ/ *n* **1** cup-shaped vessel with a long handle, for ladling out liquids. 有長柄的舀水杓。 **2** (US) **the Big D~, the Little D~,** groups of stars in the northern sky. (美)大熊星及小熊星之北斗七星。⇨ bear[1](3), plough(4).

dip·so·mania /ˌdɪpsəˈmeɪnɪə ; ˌdɪpsəˈmenɪə/ *n* [U] insatiable craving for alcoholic drink. 嗜酒狂。**dip·so·maniac** /ˌdɪpsəˈmeɪnɪæk ; ˌdɪpsəˈmenɪˌæk/ *n* person suffering from ~. 嗜酒狂患者。

dip·tych /ˈdɪptɪk ; ˈdɪptɪk/ *n* painting or carving, esp an altarpiece, on two hinged panels that can be closed like a book. (尤指祭壇上方或背後)似書般可折合的雙連畫或雕刻。

dire /ˈdaɪə(r) ; daɪr/ *adj* dreadful; terrible: 可怖的;可怕的: ~ *news;* 可怕的消息; extreme: 極度的: *to be in* ~ *need of help.* 非常需要幫助。

di·rect[1] /dɪˈrekt ; dəˈrɛkt/ *adj* **1** (going) straight; not curved or crooked; not turned aside: 直(進)的;不彎曲的;不曲折的: *in a* ~ *line;* 成一直線; *a* ~ *hit/shot,* not turned aside by hitting sth else first; 直接命中; *the* ~ *rays of the sun,* not reflected from sth. 太陽的直射光線。 **2** with nothing or no one in between; in an unbroken line: 直接的;直系的: *to be in* ~ *contact with sb;* 與某人直接連絡; *as a* ~ *result of this decision.* 此一決定之直接結果。*He's a* ~ *descendant of the Duke of Bumford.* 他是巴穆富公爵的直系子孫。 **3** straightforward; going straight to the point; frank; unhesitating: 直率的;直截了當的;坦白的;爽快的: *He has a* ~ *way of speaking/acting.* 他說話直率(做事直截了當)。*He made a* ~ *answer to the charges brought against him.* 他對於被指控的罪名做直率的答覆。 **4** exact, diametrical: 恰好的;全然的: *a* ~ *contradiction;* 完全矛盾; *the* ~ *opposite/contrary.* 正好相反。 **5** (various uses): (各種不同的用法): ~ **action,** use of strikes by workmen to get their demands. 直接行動(工人爲達到要求而從事罷工)。~ **current,** electric current flowing in one direction. 直流電。⇨ alternate. ~ **speech,** speaker's actual words. 直接敍述。⇨ indirect. **ˈ~ tax,** one levied on the person who pays it (eg income tax), not (eg purchase tax) on goods, etc. 直接稅(例如所得稅,而非購買稅等)。□ *adv* without interrupting a journey; without going by a roundabout way: 直接地;一直: *The train goes there* ~. 火車直達那裏。*He came* ~ *to London.* 他直接來到倫敦。⇨ directly. **~·ness** *n*

di·rect[2] /dɪˈrekt ; dəˈrɛkt/ *vt, vi* **1** [VP6A, 14] ~ ***sb (to),*** tell or show (sb) how to do sth, how to get somewhere: 指點;指示方向;指引:*Can you* ~ *me to the post office?* 你能指示我去郵局的路嗎? *They* ~*ed me wrongly.* 他們把我指引錯了。 **2** [VP6A, 14] ~ ***sth (to),*** address (a letter, parcel, etc): 書寫(信件,包裹等之)地址: *Shall I* ~ *the letter to his business address or to his home address?* 這封信我寫他的辦公地址還是他的住宅地址? **3** [VP14] ~ ***sth to sb,*** speak or write to: 對某人說…;寫…給某人: *My remarks were not* ~*ed to all of you.* 我的話並

非指你們全體說的。 **4** [VP6A] manage; control: 管理;支配;指揮;指導: *Who is ~ing the workmen?* 誰在指揮工人? *Who ~ed the film?* 誰導演這部影片的? ⇨ director. **5** [VP14] ~ ***to/towards,*** turn: 指向: *We ~ed our steps towards home.* 我們走向回家的路。 *Our energies must be ~ed towards higher productivity.* 我們必須努力謀求增產。 **6** [VP17, 9] order: 命令: *The officer ~ed his men to advance/that his men should advance.* 那軍官命令部下前進。

di·rec·tion /dɪˈrekʃn ; dəˈrɛkʃən/ *n* **1** [C] course taken by a moving person or thing; point towards which a person or thing looks or faces: 方向;方位: *Tom went off in one ~ and Harry in another ~.* 湯姆朝着一個方向去,哈利朝着另一個方向去。 *The aircraft was flying in a northerly ~.* 那飛機在向北飛行中。 *When the police arrived, the crowd scattered in all ~s.* 警察來時,群衆向四方散去。 (fig) (喩) *Reforms are needed in numerous ~s.* 許多方面需要改革。 ˈ**~-finder,** radio device that shows the ~ from which wireless signals are coming. 無線電定向儀; 探向器(指示無線電信號發來之方向者)。 **2** [U] ***have a good/poor sense of ~,*** be able/unable to determine well one's position with regard to one's surroundings when there are no known or visible landmarks. 有(無)方向感(在無可見的陸標處,能或不能決定自己的位置和周遭方位的能力)。 **3** (often *pl*) information or instructions about what to do, where to go, how to do sth, etc: (常用複數)說明;指引: *D~s about putting the parts together are printed on the card.* 組合各種零件的說明印在卡片上。 *He gave me full ~s to enable me to find his house.* 他對我詳細說明如何去他的家。 **4** (*pl*) address on or for a letter, parcel, etc: (複)(信件,包裹等上面之)地址: *The parcel was returned to the sender because the ~s were insufficient.* 這包裹因地址不詳細而退還寄件人。 **5** [U] management; control; guidance: 管理; 指揮; 指導: *~ of labour,* movement of workers from one area, or one kind of work, to another. 勞工管理(將工人自一地區轉至另一地區,或由一工作轉至另一工作)。 *He did the work under my ~.* 他在我的指導下做這事。 *She feels the need of ~,* wants sb to guide and advise her. 她感到需要有人指導她。 **~al** /-ʃənl ; -ʃənl̩/ *adj* of ~ in space (esp of radio signals transmitted over a narrow angle): 定向的(尤指關於無線電信號呈狹小的角度發送者): *a ~al aerial.* 定向天線。

di·rec·tive /dɪˈrektɪv ; dəˈrɛktɪv/ *n* [C] general or detailed instruction. 一般或詳細的指令;訓令。

di·rect·ly /dɪˈrektlɪ ; dəˈrɛktlɪ/ *adv* **1** in a direct manner: 直接地; 一直: *He was looking ~ at us.* 他直視着我們。 **2** at once; without delay: 卽刻; 立刻: *Come in ~.* 卽刻進來。 **3** in a short time: 不久: *I'll be there ~.* 我馬上就到那裏。 □ *conj* (colloq) as soon as: (俗)剛一…就;立卽: *D~ I had done it, I knew I had made a mistake.* 我剛一做完這事,就知道我做錯了。

di·rec·tor /dɪˈrektə(r) ; dəˈrɛktɚ/ *n* person who directs, esp one of a group (called **the Board of D~s**) who manage the affairs of a business company; (theatre, cinema, TV) person who supervises and instructs the actors and actresses, the camera crew, etc. 指導者;(尤指) 董事 (董事會稱作 the Board of Directors); (戲劇,電影或電視之)導演。 **~·ship** /-ʃɪp ; -ˌʃɪp/ *n* position of a company ~; time during which he holds his position. 董事之職;董事之任期。

di·rec·tor·ate /dɪˈrektərət ; dəˈrɛktərɪt/ *n* **1** office or position of a director. 指導者,董事或導演的職位。 **2** board of directors. 董事會。

di·rec·tory /dɪˈrektərɪ ; dəˈrɛktərɪ/ *n* (*pl* -ries) (book with a) list of persons, business firms, etc in a district; list of telephone subscribers (and usu addresses) in A B C order. 姓名住址錄;電話簿(按字母順序排列者)。

dire·ful /ˈdaɪəfl ; ˈdaɪrfəl/ *adj* (liter) dire; terrible. (文)可怕的; 可怖的; 悲慘的。 **~ly** /ˈdaɪəfəlɪ ; ˈdaɪrfəlɪ/ *adv*

dirge /dɜːdʒ ; dɝdʒ/ *n* song sung at a burial or for a dead person. 輓歌。

diri·gible /ˈdɪrɪdʒəbl ; ˈdɪrədʒəbl̩/ *n* [C] balloon (used as an airship) that can be steered; zeppelin. 可駕駛的氣球;飛船;飛艇。

dirk /dɜːk ; dɝk/ *n* kind of dagger. 一種短劍;匕首。

dirndl /ˈdɜːndl ; ˈdɝndl̩/ *n* full-skirted dress with a close-fitting bodice. 一種連裙的上半身爲緊身的女裝。

dirt /dɜːt ; dɝt/ *n* [U] **1** unclean matter (eg dust, soil, mud) esp when it is where it is not wanted (eg on the skin, clothes, in buildings): 汚穢物 (例如皮膚,衣服,建築物上的灰塵,泥土等): *His clothes were covered with ~.* 他的衣服上滿是髒東西。 *How can I get the ~ off the walls?* 我怎樣除掉牆上的髒東西? **2** loose earth or soil: 鬆土: *a ~ road,* (US) unpaved, not macadamized. (美)未經鋪修的道路;泥土路。 ***as cheap/common as ~,*** vulgar; low-class. 賤如糞土的;低級的。 ***fling/throw ~ at sb,*** say slanderous things about him. 誹謗某人。 ***treat sb like ~,*** treat him as if he were worthless. 輕待某人。 ˈ**~ farmer,** (US) one who does all his own work. (美)自耕農。ˌ**~-ˈcheap,** very cheap, almost valueless. 很賤的;幾乎毫無價值的。 ˈ**~-track,** one made of cinders, etc, (for eg motor-cycle races). (由泥土,煤渣等鋪成的)賽車跑道。 **3** unclean thought or talk. 骯髒的思想或言語。

dirty[1] /ˈdɜːtɪ ; ˈdɝtɪ/ *adj* (-ier, -iest) **1** not clean; covered with dirt: 汚穢的;髒的;覆滿汚穢物的: *~ hands/clothes;* 髒的手(衣服); causing one to be ~: 會把人弄髒的: *~ work.* 會把人弄髒的工作。 **2** (of the weather) rough; stormy: (指天氣)有暴風雨的: *I'm glad I haven't to go out on such a ~ night.* 我很高興,因爲在這樣一個暴風雨夜裏我不必外出。 **3** unclean in thought or talk; obscene: 思想或言語猥褻的;淫猥的: *scribble ~ words on lavatory walls.* 在厠所牆上亂寫猥褻的文字。 **4** (colloq) mean, dishonourable, underhand: (俗)卑鄙的;可恥的;欺瞞的: *play a ~ trick on sb,* play a mean trick on him; 以卑鄙的手段對付某人; *get/give sb a ~ look,* one of severe disapproval or disgust. 被(對某人)瞪一眼。 **dirt·ily** *adv*

dirty[2] /ˈdɜːtɪ ; ˈdɝtɪ/ *vt, vi* [VP6A, 2A] make or become dirty: 弄髒;變髒: *Don't ~ your new dress.* 不要弄髒你的新衣服。 *White gloves ~ easily.* 白手套易髒。

dis·abil·ity /ˌdɪsəˈbɪlətɪ ; ˌdɪsəˈbɪlətɪ/ *n* (*pl* -ties) **1** [U] state of being disabled; incapacity. 無能力; 失去能力。 **2** [C] sth that disables or disqualifies one: 使人無能力的事物;使人無資格的事物: *Mr Hill has a ~ and a pension from the government,* eg because he lost a leg while he was in the army. 希爾先生領有一筆政府發給的傷殘撫卹金(例如因其在軍中時斷過腿)。

dis·able /dɪsˈeɪbl ; dɪsˈebl̩/ *vt* [VP6A] make unable to do sth, esp take away the power of using the limbs: 使無能力;(尤指)使殘廢: *~d ex-service men,* former soldiers, crippled in war. 殘廢的退役軍人。 **~·ment** *n*

dis·abuse /ˌdɪsəˈbjuːz ; ˌdɪsəˈbjuz/ *vt* [VP6A, 14] ~ ***(of),*** (formal) free (sb, his mind) from false ideas; put (a person) right (in his ideas): (正式用語)使(某人,某人的心靈)免除虛妄的觀念; (在觀念上)矯正(某人);解惑;開導: *to ~ a man of silly prejudices.* 開導某人的愚妄的偏見。

dis·ad·van·tage /ˌdɪsədˈvɑːntɪdʒ *US:* -ˈvæn- ; ˌdɪsədˈvæntɪdʒ/ *n* **1** [C] unfavourable condition, sth that stands in the way of progress, success, etc: 不利的條件;妨礙進步、成功等的事物: *It is a ~ to be small when you're standing in a crowd to look at a football game.* 站在人群中看足球比賽時,身材矮小是一個不利的條件。 *His inability to speak English puts him at a ~ when he attends international conferences.* 他不會說英語,使他在參加國際會議時處於

不利的情況。**2** [U] loss; injury: 損失;傷害: *rumours to his* ~, that hurt his reputation, etc. 損害其名譽等的謠言。 **~·ous** /ˌdɪsˌædvənˈteɪdʒəs ; dɪsˌædvən-ˈtedʒəs/ *adj* **~ous (to),** causing a ~: 不利的: *in a ~ous place.* 處於不利的地位。 **~·ous·ly** *adv*

dis·af·fected /ˌdɪsəˈfektɪd ; ˌdɪsəˈfɛktɪd/ *adj* discontented; rebellious; disloyal. 不滿的;反叛的;不忠的。 **dis·af·fec·tion** /ˌdɪsəˈfekʃn ; ˌdɪsəˈfɛkʃən/ *n* [U] political discontent; disloyalty. 政治上的不滿;不忠;背叛。

dis·af·for·est /ˌdɪsəˈfɒrɪst *US:* -ˈfɔːr- ; ˌdɪsəˈfɑrɪst/ *vt* = disforest.

dis·agree /ˌdɪsəˈgriː ; ˌdɪsəˈgri/ *vi* **1** [VP2A, 3A] ~ ***(with),*** take a different view; have different opinions; not agree: 持不同的意見;意見不合;不同意;不一致: *Even friends sometimes* ~. 卽使是朋友,有時也會意見不合。 *I'm sorry to ~ with you/with your statement/with what you say.* 很抱歉,我不同意你的意見(你的聲明,你所說的話)。 *The reports from Rome ~ with those from Milan.* 來自羅馬的報導與來自米蘭的報導不一致。 **2** [VP3A] ~ ***with sb,*** (of food, climate) have bad effects on; prove unsuitable for: (指食物、氣候)對…有不良影響;不適宜: *The climate ~s with me.* 這氣候對我不適宜。 **~·able** /-əbl; -əbl/ *adj* unpleasant: 令人不愉快的: *~able weather;* 討厭的天氣; bad-tempered: 脾氣壞的: *a ~able fellow.* 一個脾氣壞的人。 **~·able·ness** *n* **~·ably** /-əblɪ; -əblɪ/ *adv*

dis·agree·ment /ˌdɪsəˈgriːmənt ; ˌdɪsəˈgrimənt/ *n* **1** [U] disagreeing; absence of agreement: 意見不合;不一致;不適合;不調合: *to be in ~ with sb or sth.* 與某人的意見不合或與某事物不調合。 **2** [C] instance of this; difference of opinion; slight quarrel: 意見不合的實例;爭論;小爭執: *~s between husbands and wives.* 夫妻間的小爭執。

dis·al·low /ˌdɪsəˈlaʊ ; ˌdɪsəˈlaʊ/ *vt* [VP6A] refuse to allow or accept as correct: 不准;不承認;不接受: *The judge ~ed the claim.* 法官駁回該要求。

dis·ap·pear /ˌdɪsəˈpɪə(r) ; ˌdɪsəˈpɪr/ *vi* [VP2A] go out of sight; be seen no more: 不見;消失: *Let's hope our difficulties will soon ~,* vanish. 希望我們的困難不久便可以消除。 *The snow soon ~ed,* melted. 雪很快地融化了。 **~·ance** /-rəns ; -rəns/ *n* ~ing. 不見;消失。

dis·ap·point /ˌdɪsəˈpɔɪnt ; ˌdɪsəˈpɔɪnt/ *vt* [VP6A] **1** fail to do or be equal to what is hoped for or expected: 使失望: *The book/match/meeting ~ed me.* 這本書(比賽,會議)令我失望。 *Please don't ~ me,* don't fail to do what you have promised. 請不要使我失望。 **2** prevent a hope, plan, etc from being realized: 阻礙(希望,計畫等)實現: *I'm sorry to ~ your expectations.* 我很抱歉使你的期望落空。 **~ed** *part adj* **~ed (in/at sth) (with sb),** sad at not getting what was hoped for, etc: 失望的;受挫折的: *We were ~ed/~ed to hear/~ed when we heard that you could not come.* 聽說你不能來,我們感到失望。 *I was ~ed at not finding/~ed not to find her at home.* 我發現她不在家,感到失望。 *We were ~ed in our hopes.* 我們的希望落空了。 *What are you looking so ~ed about?* 什麼事情使你顯得如此失望? *I'm ~ed with you.* 我對你感到失望。 **~·ed·ly** *adv* **~·ing** *adj* causing sb to be ~ed: 令人失望的: *The weather this summer has been ~ing.* 今年夏天的天氣一直令人失望。

dis·ap·point·ment /ˌdɪsəˈpɔɪntmənt ; ˌdɪsəˈpɔɪnt-mənt/ *n* **1** [U] being disappointed: 失望: *To her great ~, it rained on the day of the picnic.* 野餐的那一天下雨,使她大爲失望。 **2** [C] sb or sth that disappoints: 令人失望的人或物: *He had suffered many ~s in love,* Many women had not returned his love. 他在戀愛方面,曾經遭受多次失意。

dis·ap·pro·ba·tion /ˌdɪsˌæprəˈbeɪʃn ; ˌdɪsæprəˈbeʃən/ *n* (formal) [U] disapproval. (正式用語)不贊成。

dis·ap·prove /ˌdɪsəˈpruːv ; ˌdɪsəˈpruv/ *vi, vt* [VP2A, 3A, 6A] ~ ***(of),*** have, express, an unfavourable opinion: 不贊成: *She wants to train for the theatre but her parents ~/~ of her intentions.* 她想訓練自己做戲劇演員,但她的父母不贊成她的意圖。 **dis·ap·proval** /-ˈpruːvl ; -ˈpruvḷ/ *n* [U] disapproving: 不贊成: *He shook his head in disapproval,* to show that he ~ed. 他搖頭表示不贊成。 **dis·ap·prov·ing·ly** /-ɪŋlɪ ; -ɪŋlɪ/ *adv* in a way that shows disapproval: 不以爲然地: *When Mary lit a cigarette, her father looked at her disapprovingly.* 當瑪莉點起一支香煙時,她父親不以爲然地望着她。

dis·arm /dɪsˈɑːm ; dɪsˈɑrm/ *vi, vt* **1** [VP6A] take away weapons and other means of attack from: 繳械;解除…的武裝: *Five hundred rebels were captured and ~ed.* 五百名叛軍被俘並被繳械。 **2** [VP2A] (of nations) reduce the size of, give up the use of, armed forces: (指國家)裁減軍備: *It is difficult to persuade the Great Powers to* ~. 要說服列强裁軍是很困難的。 **3** [VP6A] make it difficult for sb to feel anger, suspicion, doubt: 消除某人之憤怒、猜忌或懷疑: *By frankly admitting that he was not a scholar, he ~ed criticism.* 他坦白承認他不是一位學者,因而消除了旁人對他的非議。 *I felt angry, but her smiles ~ed me.* 我很生氣,但她的微笑使我的怒氣消失了。 **dis·arma·ment** /dɪsˈɑːməmənt ; dɪs-ˈɑrməmənt/ *n* [U] ~ing or being ~ed(2): 裁減軍備: *~ament conferences;* 裁軍會議; *new proposals for ~ament.* 新的裁軍建議。

dis·ar·range /ˌdɪsəˈreɪndʒ ; ˌdɪsəˈrendʒ/ *vt* [VP6A] disturb; upset; put into disorder: 擾亂;使亂;使紊亂: *to ~ sb's plans/hair.* 擾亂某人之計畫(弄亂某人的頭髮)。 **~·ment** *n*

dis·ar·ray /ˌdɪsəˈreɪ; ˌdɪsəˈre/ *n, vt* [VP6A] (put into) disorder: (使)紊亂: *The troops were in ~.* 軍隊混亂。

dis·as·so·ci·ate /ˌdɪsəˈsəʊʃɪeɪt ; ˌdɪsəˈsoʃɪˌet/ *vt* [VP14] ~ ***from*** = dissociate.

dis·as·ter /dɪˈzɑːstə(r) *US:* -ˈzæs- ; dɪzˈæstɚ/ *n* **1** [C] great or sudden misfortune; terrible accident (eg a great flood or fire, an earthquake, a serious defeat in war, the loss of a large sum of money). 大災難;突然的災難;災禍(例如洪水或大火,地震,戰爭大敗,大量金錢之損失)。 **2** [U] great misfortune or suffering: 重大的不幸或災難: *a record of* ~. 災難的記錄。 **dis·as·trous** /dɪˈzɑːstrəs *US:* -ˈzæs- ; dɪz-ˈæstrəs/ *adj* causing ~: 招致災禍的: *disastrous floods;* 損失慘重的水災; *a defeat that was disastrous to the country.* 使國家蒙受災禍的失敗。 **dis·as·trous·ly** *adv*

dis·avow /ˌdɪsəˈvaʊ ; ˌdɪsəˈvaʊ/ *vt* [VP6A] (formal) deny belief in, approval or knowledge of: (正式用語)否認;不承認: *He ~ed my share in the plot.* 他否認我曾參與這項密謀。 **~al** /-ˈvaʊəl ; -ˈvaʊəl/ *n*

dis·band /dɪsˈbænd ; dɪsˈbænd/ *vt, vi* [VP6A, 2A] (of organized groups) break up: (指團體)解散;裁撤: *The army (was) ~ed when the war ended.* 戰事結束後,軍隊(被)裁撤了。 **~·ment** *n*

dis·be·lieve /ˌdɪsbɪˈliːv ; ˌdɪsbəˈliv/ *vt, vi* [VP6A, 2A, 3A] ~ ***in,*** refuse to believe (sb or sth); be unable or unwilling to believe in. 不肯相信(某人或某事);不能或不願相信。 **dis·be·lief** /ˌdɪsbɪˈliːf ; ˌdɪsbəˈlif/ *n* [U] lack of belief; refusal to believe. 不相信;不肯相信。

dis·bud /dɪsˈbʌd ; dɪsˈbʌd/ *vt* (-dd-) [VP6A] remove buds from (a plant, etc) (eg to get stronger or better shoots from those that are left). 摘去(草木等)之嫩芽(例如以使餘下部分長成較佳之新芽)。

dis·bur·den /dɪsˈbɜːdn ; dɪsˈbɝdṇ/ *vt* [VP6A, 14] ~ ***(of),*** (formal) relieve of a burden; unburden (the more usu word). (正式用語)卸除…的重負(unburden 爲較常用之字)。

dis·burse /dɪsˈbɜːs ; dɪsˈbɝs/ *vt, vi* [VP6A, 2A] pay out (money). 支付(錢)。 **~·ment** *n* [U] paying out (of money); [C] sum of money paid out. (金錢的)支付;付出之款;支出。

disc, disk /dɪsk ; dɪsk/ *n* **1** [C] thin, flat, round plate, eg a coin, a gramophone record; round surface that appears to be flat: 薄平的圓盤狀物(如銅幣、唱片);扁平的圓狀表面: *the sun's ~.* 日輪。'~ **brake,** brake which operates when a flat plate is brought into contact with another (rotating) plate at the centre of a (car) wheel. 圓盤煞車。'~ **harrow,** one with ~s instead of teeth. 圓盤耙(非帶齒者)。'~ **jockey,** radio or TV broadcaster who introduces performers and comments on records and tapes of (esp) light and popular music. 電臺或電視臺唱片音樂節目主持人。 **2** (anat) layer of cartilage between vertebrae. (解剖)椎間盤(脊椎骨間的一片軟骨)。**a slipped ~,** one that is slightly dislocated. 略微突出的椎間盤。

dis·card /dɪ'skɑ:d ; dɪs'kɑrd/ *vt* [VP6A] throw out or away; put aside, give up (sth useless or unwanted): 抛棄;放棄;摒棄;抛開(無用或不需要之物): *to ~ one's winter underclothing when the weather gets warm;* 天氣轉暖時抛開冬天穿的內衣; *to ~ old beliefs.* 摒棄舊信仰。□ /'dɪskɑ:d ; 'dɪskɑrd/ *n* card or cards ~ed in a card game. 被擲出的無用之牌。

dis·cern /dɪ'sɜ:n ; dɪ'zɝn/ *vt* [VP6A] see clearly (with the eyes or with the mind); (esp) see with an effort: (用目或用心)辨明(尤指努力以認清): *We ~ed the figure of a man clinging to the mast of the wrecked ship.* 我們看出有一人緊抱着破船的桅。 *It is often difficult to ~ the truth of an event from a newspaper report.* 要從報紙的報導去辨明一個事件的眞實性常是困難的。**~·ing** *adj* able to see and understand well. 眼光好的;有辨識力的。**~·ible** /-əbl ; -əbl/ *adj* that can be ~ed. 可辨明的。**~·ment** *n* [U] ~ing; ability to ~; keenness in judging, forming opinions. 辨明;眼力;辨認力;敏於判斷。

dis·charge[1] /'dɪstʃɑ:dʒ ; dɪs'tʃɑrdʒ/ *n* **1** [U] discharging or being discharged (all senses, the numbers refer to *discharge*[2]): 卸貨;放出;流出;發射;遣走;放行;償還;執行: *How long will the ~(1) of the cargo take?* 卸貨需要多久? *The ~(2) of water from the reservoir is carefully controlled.* 水庫的放水被愼重的控制着。 *After his ~(4) from the army, he emigrated to Canada.* 退役後,他移居加拿大。 *The prisoners were glad to get their ~(4).* 犯人們獲釋都很高興。 *He is faithful in the ~(5) of his duties.* 他忠於執行他的職守。 *Will £50 be enough for the ~(5) of your liabilities?* 五十鎊够不够還淸你的債務? **2** [U, C] that which is discharged: 放出物;流出物: *The wound hasn't healed—there's still some/a ~.* 這傷口尙未治好──仍然有東西流出來。

dis·charge[2] /dɪs'tʃɑ:dʒ ; dɪs'tʃɑrdʒ/ *vt, vi* [VP6A, 14] **1** unload (cargo from) a ship. 卸(船上之貨);自(船)上卸貨。 **2** give or send out (liquid, gas, electric current, etc): 放出;流出(液體、氣體、電流等): *Where do the sewers ~ their contents?* 陰溝裏的水流往哪裏? *The Nile ~s itself* (=flows) *into the Mediterranean.* 尼羅河注入地中海。 *Lightning is caused by clouds discharging electricity.* 閃電係由雲層放電所造成的。 *The wound is still discharging pus.* 這傷口仍在流膿。 **3** fire (a gun, etc); let fly (an arrow or other missile). 開(槍等);發射(箭或其他投射物)。 **4** send (sb) away; allow (sb) to leave: 遣走(某人);讓(某人)離去: *to ~ a patient from hospital.* 讓病人出院。 *The accused man was found not guilty and was ~d.* 這被告因無罪而被開釋。 *The members of the jury were ~d,* set free from their duties. 陪審員們被解除了職務。 **5** pay (a debt); perform (a duty): 償還(債務);執行(職責): *a ~d bankrupt,* man who, after being made bankrupt, has done what the court requires and is now free to act as he wishes. 債務消除的破產者(已履行法院規定之處置後可自由行動的破產者)。

dis·ciple /dɪ'saɪpl ; dɪ'saɪpḷ/ *n* follower of any leader of religious thought, art, learning, etc. 信徒;弟子。**the Twelve D~s,** the twelve personal followers of Jesus Christ. 耶穌十二門徒。

dis·ci·pli·nar·ian /ˌdɪsəplɪ'neərɪən ; ˌdɪsəplɪn'ɛrɪən/ *n* person able to maintain discipline(2): 維持紀律的人: *a good/strict/poor ~.* 能(嚴格,不能)維持紀律的人。 *He's no ~,* does not or cannot maintain discipline. 他不能維持紀律。

dis·ci·pline[1] /'dɪsɪplɪn ; 'dɪsəplɪn/ *n* **1** [U] training, esp of the mind and character, to produce self-control, habits of obedience, etc: 訓練(尤指頭腦和品行的訓練,以培養自制,服從的習慣等): *school ~;* 學校訓練; *military ~.* 軍事訓練。 **2** [U] the result of such training; order kept (eg among schoolchildren, soldiers): 上述訓練的結果;(學生,士兵等之)紀律;風紀: *The soldiers showed perfect ~ under the fire of the enemy.* 在敵人的砲火下,那些士兵表現了良好的紀律。 *The children were clever, but there was not much ~ in the school.* 那些孩子們很聰明,但學校裏缺少紀律。 **3** [C] set rules for conduct; method by which training may be given: 戒律;訓練方法: *Pronunciation drill and question and answer work are good ~s for learning a foreign language.* 發音練習和問答是學習外國語言的良好方法。 **4** [U] punishment. 懲罰。 **5** [C] branch of knowledge; subject of instruction. 學科;科目。**dis·ci·plin·ary** /'dɪsɪplɪnərɪ *US:* -nerɪ ; 'dɪsəplɪnˌɛrɪ/ *adj* of or for ~: 訓練的;紀律的;訓練方法的;懲罰的;學科的: *to take disciplinary measures;* 採取懲戒的措施; *disciplinary punishment.* 懲戒的處分。

dis·ci·pline[2] /'dɪsɪplɪn ; 'dɪsəˌplɪn/ *vt* [VP6A] apply discipline(1) to; train and control the mind and character of; punish: 訓練;訓導;薰陶;懲罰: *to ~ badly behaved children.* 懲罰行爲不良的兒童。

dis·claim /dɪs'kleɪm ; dɪs'klem/ *vt* [VP6A, C] say that one does not own, that one has no connection with: 否認有;否認與…有關: *to ~ responsibility for sth;* 否認對某事有責任; *to ~ all knowledge of an incident.* 否認對一事件知情。**~er** *n* statement that ~s: 否認的聲明: *to issue/send sb a ~er.* 發表(致某人)否認的聲明。

dis·close /dɪs'kləʊz ; dɪs'kloz/ *vt* [VP6A, 14] ~ ***(to),*** uncover; allow to be seen; make known: 揭發;使顯露;透露: *to refuse to ~ one's name and address;* 拒絕透露自己的姓名和住址; *to ~ a secret.* 揭發祕密。**dis·clos·ure** /dɪs'kləʊʒə(r) ; dɪs'kloʒɚ/ *n* [U] disclosing or being ~d; [C] that which is ~d (esp what has been kept secret). 揭發;顯露;被顯露的事物(尤指祕密)。

disco /'dɪskəʊ ; 'dɪsko/ *n* (colloq) (俗) = discotheque.

dis·col·our (US = **-lor**) /dɪs'kʌlə(r) ; dɪs'kʌlɚ/ *vt, vi* **1** [VP6A] change, spoil, the colour of: 使變色;使褪色;使變污: *walls ~ed by damp.* 被濕氣沾污的牆壁。 **2** [VP2A] become changed in colour: 變色;褪色: *materials that ~ in strong sunlight.* 遇强烈陽光而褪色的料子。**dis·col·our·ation** (US= **-lor-**) /dɪsˌkʌlə'reɪʃn ; ˌdɪskʌlə'reʃən/ *n* [U] ~ing or being ~ed; [C] ~ed place; stain. 變色;褪色;變污;變色之處;污點。

dis·com·fit /dɪs'kʌmfɪt ; dɪs'kʌmfɪt/ *vt* [VP6A] baffle; confuse; embarrass. 使困惑;使混亂;使窘迫。**dis·com·fi·ture** /dɪs'kʌmfɪtʃə(r) ; dɪs'kʌmfɪtʃɚ/ *n* [U] ~ing or being ~ed. 困惑;混亂;窘迫。

dis·com·fort /dɪs'kʌmfət ; dɪs'kʌmfɚt/ *n* **1** [U] absence of comfort; uneasiness of mind or body. 不適;不安。 **2** [C] sth that causes uneasiness; hardship: 令人不安適之物;困苦: *the ~s endured by explorers in the Antarctic.* 南極探險家忍受的艱難。

dis·com·mode /ˌdɪskə'məʊd ; ˌdɪskə'mod/ *vt* [VP6A] (formal) put (sb) to inconvenience. (正式用語)使(某人)不方便。

dis·com·pose /ˌdɪskəm'pəʊz ; ˌdɪskəm'poz/ *vt* [VP6A] disturb the composure of: 使不安;使煩亂: *Don't let their objections ~ you.* 不要讓他們的反對使你不安。 **dis·com·posure** /-əʊʒə(r) ; -oʒɚ/ *n* [U] state of being ~d. 不安;心情煩亂。

dis·con·cert /ˌdɪskən'sɜ:t ; ˌdɪskən'sɝt/ *vt* [VP6A] upset the calmness or self-possession of: 使不安;使慌亂: *The Manager was ~ed to discover that he had gone to the office without putting in his false* *teeth.* 經理發現他未戴假牙而來辦公室時感到很窘。

dis·con·nect /ˌdɪskəˈnekt ; ˌdɪskəˈnɛkt/ *vt* [VP6A, 14] ~ ***(from),*** detach from; take (two things) apart: 使分開;拆開(兩物): *You should ~ the TV set* (eg by pulling out the plug) *before you make adjustments inside it.* 你應將電視機的插頭拔掉,始可做內部的調整。 **~ed** *adj* (of speech or writing) having the ideas, etc badly connected. (指演說或寫作)無系統的;不連貫的。

dis·con·so·late /dɪsˈkɒnsələt ; dɪsˈkɑnsḷɪt/ *adj* unhappy at the loss of sth; without hope or comfort; inconsolable. (因失去某物而)不愉快的;無希望或安慰的;無法安慰的。 **~·ly** *adv*

dis·con·tent /ˌdɪskənˈtent ; ˌdɪskənˈtɛnt/ *n* [U] dissatisfaction; absence of contentment; [C] cause of this; grievance. 不滿意;不滿的原因;不滿。 □ *vt* [VP6A] (usu in the *pp*) make dissatisfied: (通常用過去分詞)使不滿意: *to be ~ed with one's job.* 對自己的工作不滿。 **~·ed·ly** /-ɪdlɪ ; -ɪdlɪ/ *adv*

dis·con·tinue /ˌdɪskənˈtɪnjuː ; ˌdɪskənˈtɪnjʊ/ *vt, vi* [VP6A, C, 2A] cease; give up; put an end to; come to an end: 停止;放棄;結束;中止: *I'm so busy that I shall have to ~* (*paying*) *these weekly visits.* 我太忙,故必須停止這些每週的往訪。 **dis·con·tinu·ance** /-ˈtɪnjʊəns ; -ˈtɪnjʊəns/ *n*

dis·con·tinu·ous /ˌdɪskənˈtɪnjʊəs ; ˌdɪskənˈtɪnjʊəs/ *adj* not continuous. 不繼續的;中斷的。

dis·cord /ˈdɪskɔːd ; ˈdɪskɔrd/ *n* **1** [U] disagreement; quarrelling: 不一致;爭吵: *What has brought ~ into the family*, caused its members to be quarrelsome? 甚麼事情使得這一家人爭吵? **2** [C] difference of opinion; dispute. 意見不和;爭論。 **3** [U] (music) lack of harmony between sounds, notes, etc sounded together; [C] instance of this, offending the ear; clashing sound that lacks harmony. (音樂)(聲音、音調等)不和諧;刺耳的聲音;嘈雜聲。 **dis·cor·dance** /dɪˈskɔːdəns ; dɪsˈkɔrdṇs/ *n* [U] want of harmony; disagreement. 不和諧;不一致。 **dis·cor·dant** /dɪˈskɔːdənt ; dɪsˈkɔrdṇt/ *adj* **1** not in agreement: 不一致的: *~ant opinions.* 不一致的意見。 **2** (of sounds) not harmonious; harsh: (指聲音)不和諧的;刺耳的: *the ~ant noises of motor-car horns.* 汽車喇叭的噪音。 **dis·cor·dant·ly** *adv*

dis·co·theque /ˈdɪskətek ; ˈdɪskətɛk/ *n* (colloq abbr 俗語略作 **disco** /ˈdɪskəʊ ; ˈdɪsko/) club or party where people dance to amplified recorded music played by a *disc jockey*. 由唱片伴奏的舞廳或舞會;狄斯可舞會。

dis·count[1] /ˈdɪskaʊnt ; ˈdɪskaʊnt/ *n* [C, U] amount of money which may be taken off the full price, eg of goods bought by shopkeepers for resale, of an account if paid promptly, of a bill of exchange not yet due for payment: 折扣(例如自下列情況中獲得者:批發的貨物,立即付現款,未到期的期票);貼現: *We give* (*a*) *10 per cent ~ for cash,* for prompt payment instead of payment at a later date. 現金付款,我們予以九折優待。 **ˈ~ broker** *n* (comm) broker who gets a fee for acting as an intermediary between buyers and sellers. (商)貼現掮客。 **ˈ~ house** *n* (comm) establishment which specializes in the ~ing of bills of exchange. (商)票據貼現所。 ⇨ discount[2] (1). ***at a ~,*** (of goods) not in demand; easily obtained; (fig) not in high esteem: (指貨物)無銷路的;易獲得的;(喻)不受重視的: *Is honesty at a ~ today?* 誠實在今天不受重視嗎?

dis·count[2] /dɪsˈkaʊnt *US:* ˈdɪskaʊnt ; ˈdɪskaʊnt/ *vt* [VP6A] **1** (comm) give or receive the present value of a bill of exchange not yet due. (商)貼現。 **2** refuse complete belief to a piece of news, a story, etc; allow for exaggeration: 不全部置信(一消息、故事等);認為有誇張之處: *You should ~ a great deal of what appears in the newspapers.* 你對報上的消息,要打一個大折扣。

dis·coun·ten·ance /dɪsˈkaʊntɪnəns ; dɪsˈkaʊntənəns/ *vt* [VP6A] (formal) refuse to approve of; discourage. (正式用語)不贊成;勸阻。

dis·cour·age /dɪˈskʌrɪdʒ ; dɪsˈkɝɪdʒ/ *vt* **1** [VP6A] lessen, take away, the courage or confidence of: 使氣餒;使沮喪: *Don't let one failure ~ you: try again.* 勿因一次失敗而氣餒,再試試看。 **2** [VP14] ***~ sb from doing sth,*** put difficulties in his way; make it seem not worth while; try to persuade him not to do it: 阻礙;使認為某事不值得做;勸阻: *We tried to ~ him from climbing the mountain without a guide.* 我們設法勸他無嚮導不要去爬山。 **~·ment** *n* [U] discouraging or being ~d; [C] sth that ~s. 挫折;氣餒;令人氣餒的事物;障礙。

dis·course /ˈdɪskɔːs ; ˈdɪskors/ *n* [C] speech; lecture; sermon; treatise. 演說;演講;講道;論文。 □ *vi* /dɪˈskɔːs ; dɪˈskors/ ***~ upon,*** (formal) talk, preach or lecture upon (usu at length). (正式用語)談論;講道;講述(通常為詳細地)。

dis·cour·teous /dɪsˈkɜːtɪəs ; dɪsˈkɝtɪəs/ *adj* not courteous; impolite: 不禮貌的;失禮的: *It was ~ of you to arrive late.* 你遲到是失禮的。 **~·ly** *adv* **dis·cour·tesy** /dɪsˈkɜːtəsɪ ; dɪsˈkɝtəsɪ/ *n* [U] impoliteness; [C] (*pl* -sies) impolite act. 失禮;失禮的行為。

dis·cover /dɪˈskʌvə(r) ; dɪˈskʌvɚ/ *vt* [VP6A, 9, 8, 10, 25] find out; get knowledge of, bring to view (sth existing but not yet known); realize (sth new or unexpected): 發現(存在而未為人知之物);發覺(新奇或意外之物): *Columbus ~ed America, but did not explore the new continent.* 哥倫布發現了美洲,但未探勘此新大陸。 *Harvey ~ed the circulation of the blood.* 哈維發現了血液的循環。 *It was never ~ed how he died.* 他是如何死去的,始終未被發現。 *I never ~ed how to start the engine.* 我從來不知道怎樣發動這引擎。 *We suddenly ~ed that it was too late to catch the train.* 我們突然發覺已來不及趕上火車了。 *We have ~ed him to be* (more usu 比較常用 *that he is*) *quite untrustworthy.* 我們已發覺他很不可靠。 **~er** *n* person who has made a ~y. 發現者;發覺者。

dis·covery /dɪˈskʌvərɪ ; dɪˈskʌvərɪ/ *n* **1** [U] discovering or being discovered: 發現;發覺: *a voyage of ~;* (企圖)有所發現的航海;探測航行; *the ~ of new chemical elements;* 新化學元素的發現; *the ~ by Franklin that lightning is electricity.* 富蘭克林之發現閃電即是電。 **2** [C] (*pl* -ries) sth that is discovered: 被發現之物: *He made wonderful scientific discoveries.* 他完成了驚人的科學發現。

dis·credit[1] /dɪsˈkredɪt ; dɪsˈkrɛdɪt/ *vt* [VP6A] refuse to believe or have confidence in; cause the truth, value or credit of sth or sb to seem doubtful: 不相信;不信任;懷疑;使(某事物或某人的眞情、價值或信譽)顯得可疑: *His theories were ~ed by scientists.* 他的理論受到科學家們的懷疑。 *The judge advised the jury to ~ the evidence of one of the witnesses.* 法官勸陪審員不要相信一位證人的證詞。

dis·credit[2] /dɪsˈkredɪt ; dɪsˈkrɛdɪt/ *n* **1** [U] loss of credit or reputation: 不名譽;丟面子: *If you continue to behave in this way, you will bring ~ upon yourself.* 如果你繼續做出這樣的行為,你會玷辱了你的名譽。 **2** ***a ~ to,*** person, thing, causing such loss to: 玷辱名譽的人或物: *a ~ to the school/to your family.* 破壞學校(家庭)名譽的人或物。 **3** [U] doubt; disbelief. 懷疑;不相信。 **~·able** /-əbl ; -əbḷ/ *adj* bringing ~: 不名譽的: *~able conduct.* 不名譽的行為。 **~·ably** /-əblɪ ; -əblɪ/ *adv*

dis·creet /dɪˈskriːt ; dɪˈskrit/ *adj* careful, tactful, in what one says and does; prudent: 謹慎的;有智慮的: *to maintain a ~ silence.* 保持愼重的沉默。 **~·ly** *adv*

dis·crep·ancy /dɪˈskrepənsɪ ; dɪˈskrɛpənsɪ/ *n* (*pl* -cies) [C, U] (of statements and accounts) difference; absence of agreement: (指言論和記述)不同;不符合: *There was* (*a*) *considerable ~/There were numerous discrepancies between the two accounts of the fighting.* 這兩段關於戰事的敘述頗有出入(有甚多不符之處)。

dis·crete /dɪˈskriːt ; dɪˈskrit/ *adj* discontinuous; individually distinct. 不連續的;分立的。 **~·ness** *n*

dis·cre·tion /dɪˈskreʃn ; dɪˈskrɛʃən/ *n* [U] **1** being discreet; prudence: 謹慎;顧慮周到: *You must show more ~ in choosing your friends.* 你擇友時須更加謹慎。***years/age of ~,*** the age at which one is fit to judge and decide for oneself. 責任年齡(自己可判斷事物的年齡)。***D~ is the better part of valour,*** (prov) used jokingly to excuse oneself for not taking unnecessary risks. (諺)慎重卽勇過半矣(爲不做無謂冒險的藉口,用以解嘲)。 **2** freedom to act according to one's own judgement, to do what seems right or best: 自由處理;自由決定: *Use your ~.* 由你自行決定。*It is within your own ~,* You are free to decide. 此事可由你自作決定。*You have full ~ to act.* 你可完全隨意行事。**~·ary** /dɪˈskreʃənərɪ *US:* -nerɪ ; dɪˈskrɛʃən,ɛrɪ/ *adj* having ~(2): 可自由處理的;可自由決定的: *an official with ~ary powers.* 有擅自處理權的官員。

dis·crimi·nate /dɪˈskrɪmɪneɪt ; dɪˈskrɪmə,net/ *vt, vi* **1** [VP14, 3A] ***~ one thing from another; ~ between two things,*** be, make, see, a difference between: 區別;辨別: *Can you ~ good books from bad/~ between good and bad books?* 你能區別好書和壞書嗎? **2** [VP2A, 3A] ***~ (against),*** treat differently; make distinctions: 以不同方式對待;歧視: *laws which do not ~ against anyone,* that treat all people in the same way. 不歧視任何人的法律(對所有人民一視同仁)。**dis·crimi·nat·ing** *adj* **1** able to see or make small differences: 有辨別力的: *a discriminating taste in literature.* 對文學的辨識鑑賞力。 **2** giving special or different treatment to certain people, countries, etc; differential(1): 對某些人民、國家等待遇不同的; 歧視的; 差別的: *discriminating tariffs/rates/duties.* 差別關稅(地方稅,國家稅)。

dis·crimi·na·tion /dɪˌskrɪmɪˈneɪʃn ; dɪ,skrɪməˈneʃən/ *n* [U] discriminating; ability to discriminate: 區別;辨別;差別待遇;歧視;辨別力: *Some people do not show much ~ in their choice of books.* 有些人看書不加選擇。*D~ against goods from foreign countries is usually done by means of tariffs.* 對外國貨的差別待遇通常藉關稅行之。*Is there racial ~ in your country?* 在你們的國家內有種族歧視嗎? **dis·crim·i·na·tory** /dɪˈskrɪmɪnətərɪ *US:* -tɔːrɪ ; dɪˈskrɪmənə,torɪ/ *adj* discriminating(2): 差別待遇的;歧視的: *discriminatory legislation.* 不公平的法律。

dis·cur·sive /dɪˈskɜːsɪv ; dɪˈskɝsɪv/ *adj* (of a person, what he says or does, his style) wandering from one point or subject to another. (指人,人的言行、文體)散漫的。**~·ly** *adv* **~·ness** *n*

dis·cus /ˈdɪskəs ; ˈdɪskəs/ *n* heavy, round plate of stone, metal or wood, thrown in ancient Roman and Greek athletic contests and in modern contests (eg the Olympic Games): 鐵餅(石頭、金屬或木製的重的圓形盤狀物,在古羅馬希臘運動會及現代運動會如世運會中投擲者): *the ~ throw,* name used for this contest. 擲鐵餅(此種比賽之名稱)。

throwing the discus

dis·cuss /dɪˈskʌs ; dɪˈskʌs/ *vt* [VP6A, 8, 10, 14] ~ ***(with),*** examine and argue about (a subject): 討論(題目);商討: *to ~ a question with sb;* 與某人討論一問題; *to ~ (with one's friends) what to do/how to do it/how something should be done.* (與友人)商討做何事(如何做一事)。

dis·cus·sion /dɪˈskʌʃn ; dɪˈskʌʃən/ *n* [U, C] discussing or being discussed; talk for the purpose of discussing: 討論;商討;議論: *after much ~;* 經詳細討論後; *after several long ~s.* 經數度長時間的討論後。*We had a long ~ about the question.* 關於該問題我們曾做長時間的討論。*When will the matter come up for ~?* 此事將於何時提出討論? ***under ~,*** being discussed: 在討論中: *The question is still under ~.* 這問題仍在討論中。

dis·dain /dɪsˈdeɪn ; dɪsˈden/ *vt* [VP6A, C, 7A] look on with contempt; think (it) dishonourable (to do sth); be too proud (to do sth): 輕視;藐視;不屑爲: *A good man should ~ flattery.* 好人應鄙視諂媚。*He ~ed to notice the insult.* 他不屑計較這侮辱。*He ~ed my offer of help.* 他輕視我的援助之意。□ *n* [U] contempt; scorn: 輕視;藐視: *No one likes to be treated with ~.* 沒有人喜歡受到輕視。**~·ful** /-fʊl ; -fəl/ *adj* showing ~: 表示輕視的; 藐視的: *~ful looks.* 輕視的樣子。**~·fully** /-fəlɪ ; -fəlɪ/ *adv*

dis·ease /dɪˈziːz ; dɪˈziz/ *n* [U] illness; disorder of body or mind or of plants; [C] particular kind of illness or disorder: 病;疾病;植物的病害;某種疾病: *The business of doctors is to prevent and cure ~.* 醫生的職務爲防止和治療疾病。*Measles, mumps and influenza are common ~s.* 痲疹、耳下腺炎和流行性感冒是普通的疾病。**dis·eased** /dɪˈziːzd ; dɪˈzizd/ *part adj* suffering from, injured by, ~: 有病的;爲疾病傷害的: *~d vines;* 有病害的葡萄樹; *~d in body and mind.* 身心有病的。

dis·em·bark /ˌdɪsɪmˈbɑːk ; ˌdɪsɪmˈbɑrk/ *vt, vi* [VP6A, 14, 2A, C] ~ ***(from),*** put, go, on shore (from a ship). (自船上)置於岸上;登岸;上岸。**dis·em·bar·ka·tion** /ˌdɪsembɑːˈkeɪʃn ; ˌdɪsɛmbɑrˈkeʃən/ *n*

dis·em·barrass /ˌdɪsɪmˈbærəs ; ˌdɪsɪmˈbærəs/ *vt* [VP14] ~ ***of,*** (formal) rid (sb, oneself) from embarrassment; rid (sb, oneself) of a burden: (正式用語)使(某人、自己)脫離困窘; 使(某人、自己)擺脫負擔: *to ~ oneself of a burden/charge/responsibility.* 使自己擺脫一負擔(責任)。**~·ment** *n*

dis·em·body /ˌdɪsɪmˈbɒdɪ ; ˌdɪsɪmˈbɑdɪ/ *vt* [VP6A] (chiefly in *pp*) separate, set free (the soul or spirit) from the body: (主要用過去分詞)使(靈魂或精神)脫離軀體: *a building haunted by a disembodied spirit.* 一所有幽靈出沒的建築物。

dis·em·bowel /ˌdɪsɪmˈbaʊəl ; ˌdɪsɪmˈbaʊəl/ *vt* (-ll-) (US also -l-) [VP6A] cut out the bowels of. 切腹取出…之腸。

dis·en·chant /ˌdɪsɪnˈtʃɑːnt *US:* -ˈtʃænt ; ˌdɪsɪnˈtʃænt/ *vt* [VP6A] free from enchantment or illusion: 使脫除魔力或幻想: *He is quite ~ed with the Tory Government.* 他對保守黨政府不再存有幻想。**~·ment** *n*

dis·en·cum·ber /ˌdɪsɪnˈkʌmbə(r) ; ˌdɪsɪnˈkʌmbɚ/ *vt* [VP6A, 14] ~ ***(from),*** (formal) free from encumbrance: (正式用語)使脫除障礙或負累: *~ed of his heavy responsibilities.* 卸下他的重責。

dis·en·franchise /ˌdɪsɪnˈfræntʃaɪz ; ˌdɪsɪnˈfræntʃaɪz/ *vt* = disfranchise.

dis·en·gage /ˌdɪsɪnˈgeɪdʒ ; ˌdɪsɪnˈgedʒ/ *vt, vi* [VP6A, 14, 2A, C] ~ ***(from),*** separate, detach (oneself or sth): 分開;使(自己或某物)脫離: *Two enemy battalions (were) ~d from the battle after suffering heavy casualties.* 在遭受嚴重傷亡後,敵人的兩營士兵脫離了戰鬪。**dis·en·gaged** *pp* (of a person) free from engagements: (指人)無約會的;空閒的: *If the Manager is ~d...,* if he is free.... 如果經理有空的話…。**~·ment** *n* (condition of) being ~d: 脫離;解脫: *the military and economic ~ment of the USA from SE Asia.* 美國在軍事和經濟上之脫離東南亞。

dis·en·tangle /ˌdɪsɪnˈtæŋgl ; ˌdɪsɪnˈtæŋgl/ *vt, vi* **1** [VP6A, 14] ~ ***(from),*** free from complications, tangles or confusion: 使脫除糾纏或混亂狀態: *to ~ truth from falsehood.* 分辨眞僞。 **2** [VP2A] unravel; become clear of tangles: 解開; 解開纏結: *This skein of wool won't ~,* cannot be ~d. 這一束毛線解不開了。**~·ment** *n*

dis·equi·lib·rium /ˌdɪsiːkwɪ'lɪbrɪəm ; dɪsˌikwə'lɪbrɪəm/ *n* [U] absence, loss, of equilibrium; instability. 不平衡;失去平衡;不穩定。

dis·es·tab·lish /ˌdɪsɪ'stæblɪʃ ; ˌdɪsə'stæblɪʃ/ *vt* [VP6A] end, break up, an established state of affairs, esp the constitutional connection between a national Church (eg the Church of England) and the State. 廢除既成狀態;(尤指)廢除國教(例如英國國教)制;使(教會)與政府分離。**~·ment** *n*

dis·favour (US = **-favor**) /ˌdɪs'feɪvə(r) ; dɪs'fevɚ/ *n* [U] state of being out of favour; disapproval: 不喜歡;不贊成: *to regard sth with ~;* 不贊成某事; *to be in ~;* 受冷遇; *to fall into ~;* 失寵; *to incur sb's ~.* 引起某人的反對。□ *vt* [VP6A] regard with ~; disapprove of. 不喜歡;不贊成。

dis·figure /dɪs'fɪgə(r) *US:* -gjər ; dɪs'fɪgjɚ/ *vt* [VP6A] spoil the appearance or shape of: 損毀…之外表或形狀: *beautiful scenery ~d by ugly advertising signs;* 被醜陋的廣告招牌損毀的美麗的風景; *a face ~d by a broken nose/an ugly scar.* 被殘缺的鼻子(難看的傷疤)所毀的面貌。**~·ment** *n* [U] disfiguring or being ~d; [C] sth that ~s. 損毀外表或形狀;損毀外表或形狀之物。

dis·for·est /dɪs'fɒrɪst *US:* -'fɔːr- ; dɪs'fɑrɪst/ *vt* [VP6A] clear (land) of forests. 砍伐(某地)之森林。

dis·fran·chise /dɪs'fræntʃaɪz ; dɪs'fræntʃaɪz/ *vt* [VP6A] deprive of rights of citizenship; (esp) deprive (a place) of the right to send a representative to parliament or (a citizen) of the right to vote for a parliamentary representative. 褫奪公權;(尤指)剝奪(某地或某人)之議員選舉權。**~·ment** /-'fræntʃɪzmənt ; -'fræntʃɪzmənt/ *n*

dis·gorge /dɪs'gɔːdʒ ; dɪs'gɔrdʒ/ *vt* [VP6A] throw up or out from, or as from, the throat; (fig) give up (esp sth taken wrongfully). 吐;吐出;(喻)放棄(尤指非法獲得之物)。

dis·grace¹ /dɪs'greɪs ; dɪs'gres/ *n* **1** [U] loss of respect, favour, reputation: 恥辱;不名譽;喪失體面: *A man who commits a crime and is sent to prison brings ~ on himself and his family.* 因犯罪而被關入監獄的人玷辱了自己和他的家族。*There need be no ~ in being poor.* 貧窮並不足爲恥。 ***be in ~,*** be in a state of having lost respect, etc: 處於不受他人尊重的狀態: *He told a lie and is in ~.* 他說謊而不受他人的尊重。**2** **a ~,** thing, state of affairs, person, that is a cause of shame or discredit: 招致恥辱的人或物: *These slums are a ~ to the city authorities.* 這些貧民窟爲市當局的恥辱。*The continued use of armed forces to settle disputes is a ~ to the rulers of all countries.* 不斷用武力解決糾紛實乃各國元首之恥。**~·ful** /-fl ; -fəl/ *adj* bringing or causing ~: 可恥的;不名譽的: *~ful behaviour.* 可恥的行爲。**~·fully** /-fəlɪ ; -fəlɪ/ *adv*: *to behave ~fully.* 行爲可恥。

dis·grace² /dɪs'greɪs ; dɪs'gres/ *vt* [VP6A] **1** bring disgrace on; be a disgrace to: 玷辱;使蒙羞: *Don't ~ the family name.* 勿玷辱家聲。 **2** put (sb) out of favour. 使(某人)不再受寵;使失寵。

dis·gruntled /dɪs'grʌntld ; dɪs'grʌntl̩d/ *adj* ***~ (at sth/with sb),*** discontented; in a bad mood. 不滿意的;不高興的。

dis·guise¹ /dɪs'gaɪz ; dɪs'gaɪz/ *vt* [VP6A, 16B] **1** change the appearance, etc of, in order to deceive or to hide the identity of: 僞裝;假扮: *He ~d his looks but he could not ~ his voice.* 他僞裝了他的外貌,但無法僞裝他的聲音。*He ~d himself as a woman/~d himself by wearing a wig.* 他假扮成一個女人(戴上假髮僞裝自己)。 **2** conceal; cover up: 隱藏;掩飾: *He ~d his sorrow beneath a cheerful appearance/by appearing cheerful.* 他以歡樂的外貌掩飾他的悲苦。*There is no disguising the fact that...,* The fact that... cannot be concealed. …的事實是無法掩飾的。

dis·guise² /dɪs'gaɪz ; dɪs'gaɪz/ *n* **1** [U] disguising; disguised condition: 僞裝;假扮;掩飾;僞裝或掩飾的狀態: *He went among the enemy in ~.* 他化裝混入敵人中。 *He went to the ball in the ~ of a clown.* 他假扮成一個小丑去參加舞會。**2** [C,U] dress, actions, manner, etc used for disguising: 用以僞裝的衣服、行動、態度等: *a clever ~.* 巧妙的僞裝。*He had tried all sorts of ~s.* 他嘗試過各種僞裝。*She made no ~ of her feelings,* did not hide them. 她不掩飾她的情感。

dis·gust¹ /dɪs'gʌst ; dɪs'gʌst/ *n* [U] ***~ (at sth/with sb),*** strong feeling of dislike or distaste (eg caused by a bad smell or taste, a horrible sight, evil conduct): 厭惡;嫌惡(例如由惡臭或惡味,可怕的景象,邪惡的行爲所引起者): *He turned away in ~.* 他厭惡地把臉轉開。*His ~ at the government's policy caused him to resign.* 他對政府的政策的厭惡促使他辭職。

dis·gust² /dɪs'gʌst ; dɪs'gʌst/ *vt* [VP6A] cause disgust in: 使人厭惡;使人嫌惡: *His behaviour ~ed everybody.* 他的行爲使每一個人都厭惡。 *We were ~ed at/by/with what we saw.* 我們討厭我們所看到的東西。**~·ing** *adj*: *~ing political opinions.* 令人厭惡的政見。**~·ing·ly** *adv*: *He is ~ingly* (colloq 俗 = extremely) *mean with his money.* 他對金錢極爲吝嗇(他對金錢的吝嗇令人憎惡)。**~·ed·ly** /-ɪdlɪ ; -ɪdlɪ/ *adv* with ~: 厭惡地: *He looked ~edly at the dirty room.* 他厭惡地望着那骯髒的房間。

dish¹ /dɪʃ ; dɪʃ/ *n* **1** shallow, flat-bottomed (often oval or oblong) vessel, of earthenware, glass, metal, etc from which food is served at table: 盤;碟: *a 'meat-~.* 盛肉盤。**~·ful** /-fʊl ; -ˌfʊl/ *n* as much as a ~ will contain. 一碟或一盤之量。 **2** **the ~es,** all the crockery (plates, bowls, cups and saucers, etc) used for a meal: 進餐時所用的全部盤碟杯碗等: *to wash up the ~es.* 將盤碟等洗好。**'~·cloth,** cloth for washing ~es, etc. 洗碗布;抹布。**'~·washer,** power-operated machine for washing dishes, cutlery, ect. 洗碟機。 **'~·water,** water in which ~es have been washed. 洗碗水。 **3** food brought to table on or in a ~: 盤中的食物;菜: *His favourite ~ is steak and kidney pie.* 他最喜愛的菜是牛排和腰子餅。 **4** ~-shaped object, esp a large concave reflector for the reception of radio-waves from outer space, or in radio telescopes, etc. 盤碟狀之物;(尤指用以接收太空的電波或用於無線電望遠鏡等中之大而凹形的)反射器。⇨ the illus at radio telescope. 參看 radio telescope 之插圖。 **5** (sl) attractive person: (俚)漂亮的人: *She's quite a ~.* 她眞漂亮。**~y** *adj* (-ier, -iest) (sl) (of a person) attractive. (俚)(指人)漂亮的;動人的。

dish² /dɪʃ ; dɪʃ/ *vt* **1** [VP15B] ***~ sth up,*** put on or into a ~ or ~es: 盛於盤碟中: *to ~ (up) the dinner,* get it ready for serving; 將飯菜盛於盤碟中準備開飯; (fig) prepare, serve up facts, arguments, etc: (喻)準備並提出(事實、論據等): *to ~ up the usual arguments in a new form.* 以新方式提出平常的論據。 ***~ sth out,*** distribute it. 分配。 **2** [VP6A] (colloq) upset; thwart: (俗)破壞;挫敗: *to ~ one's opponents.* 挫敗對手。*The scandal ~ed his hopes of being elected.* 毀謗破壞了他當選的希望。

dis·habille /ˌdɪsæ'biːl ; ˌdɪsə'bil/ *n* [U] (usu 通常用 ***in*** ~) (usu of a woman) the state of being negligently or partly dressed. (通常指婦女)衣著隨便;服裝不整。

dis·har·mony /dɪs'hɑːmənɪ ; dɪs'hɑrmənɪ/ *n* [U] lack of harmony; discord. 不和諧;不調和。**dis·har·moni·ous** /ˌdɪshɑː'məʊnɪəs ; ˌdɪshɑr'monɪəs/ *adj*

dis·hearten /dɪs'hɑːtn ; dɪs'hɑrtn̩/ *vt* [VP6A] cause to lose courage or confidence: 使沮喪;使氣餒: *Don't be ~ed by a single failure.* 勿因一次失敗而氣餒。

di·shev·elled (US = **-eled**) /dɪ'ʃevld ; dɪ'ʃevl̩d/ *adj* with the hair uncombed; (of the hair and clothes) in disorder; untidy. 頭髮蓬亂的;(指頭髮和衣服)散亂的;不整齊的。

dis·hon·est /dɪs'ɒnɪst ; dɪs'ɑnɪst/ *adj* not honest; intended to cheat, deceive or mislead. 不誠實的;欺騙的;欺詐的。**~·ly** *adv* **dis·hon·esty** /dɪs'ɒnɪstɪ ;

dɪs'ɑnɪstɪ/ *n* [U] being ~; [C] ~ act, etc. 不誠實；欺騙；欺騙的行爲等。

dis·hon·our (US = **-honor**) /dɪs'ɒnə(r)；dɪs'ɑnɚ/ *n* [U] **1** disgrace or shame; loss, absence, of honour and self-respect: 不名譽；恥辱: *to bring ~ on one's family.* 玷辱家聲。 **2** *a ~ to,* person or thing that brings ~ to: 不名譽的人或物: *He was a ~ to his regiment.* 他是他那一團的恥辱。 □ *vt* [VP6A] **1** bring shame, discredit, loss of honour on (sb or sth). 玷辱(某人或某物)。 **2** (of a bank) ~ *a cheque／bill of exchange,* refuse to pay money on it (because the bank's customer has not enough credit). (指銀行) 退票 (因顧客無足够存款而拒絶兌現)。 **~·able** /-əbl；-əbl̩/ *adj* without honour; shameful. 不名譽的；可耻的。 **~·ably** /-əblɪ；-əblɪ/ *adv*

dis·il·lusion /ˌdɪsɪ'lu:ʒn；ˏdɪsɪ'luʒən/ *vt* [VP6A] set free from mistaken beliefs: 使從錯誤信念中醒悟；使覺醒；使幻想破滅: *They had thought that the new colony would be a paradise, but they were soon ~ed.* 他們原以爲新殖民地是一個天堂，但不久便從這幻想中覺醒了。□ *n* [U] the state of being ~ed. 醒悟；覺醒。 **~·ment** *n* [U] freedom from illusions: 醒悟；幻想破滅: *in a state of complete ~(ment).* 徹底自幻想中醒悟。

dis·in·cen·tive /ˌdɪsɪn'sentɪv；ˏdɪsɪn'sɛntɪv/ *n* [C] act, measure, etc that tends to discourage efforts, production, etc: 使努力受挫，阻礙生產等的行動、措施等；阻力；障礙: *Is high taxation a ~ to members of the managerial class?* 高稅對經理人員的工作情緒有妨礙嗎？

dis·in·cli·na·tion /ˌdɪsɪnklɪ'neɪʃn；ˏdɪsɪnklə'neʃən/ *n* [U, C] ~ ***(for sth／to do sth),*** (usu with *indef art*) unwillingness: (通常與不定冠詞連用) 不願意: *Some schoolboys have a strong ~ for work.* 有些男學生極不願意工作。*His ~ to meet people worries his wife, who is very sociable.* 他的不喜與人接觸使他那位很愛交際的妻子煩惱。

dis·in·cline /ˌdɪsɪn'klaɪn；ˏdɪsɪn'klaɪn/ *vt* [VP17, 14] (usu passive) (通常用被動語態) ***be ~d for sth; be ~d to do sth,*** be reluctant or unwilling: 不願意: *He was ~d to help me.* 他不願幫助我。*The hot weather made him feel ~d for work.* 炎熱的天氣使他感到不願工作。

dis·in·fect /ˌdɪsɪn'fekt；ˏdɪsɪn'fɛkt/ *vt* [VP6A] make free from bacterial infection: 使免受細菌的傳染；消毒: *The house was ~ed after Tom had had scarlet fever.* 湯姆患過猩紅熱後，這房子曾經過消毒。 **dis·in·fec·tant** /ˌdɪsɪn'fektənt；ˏdɪsɪn'fɛktənt/ *adj, n* ~ing (chemical). 消毒的；消毒劑。 **dis·in·fec·tion** /ˌdɪsɪn'fekʃn；ˏdɪsɪn'fɛkʃən/ *n* [U] (act of) ~ing. 消毒；消毒作用。

dis·in·fest /ˌdɪsɪn'fest；ˏdɪsɪn'fɛst/ *vt* [VP6A] get rid of vermin. 消滅害蟲或害獸。 **dis·in·fes·ta·tion** /ˌdɪsɪnfe'steɪʃn；dɪsˏɪnfɛs'teʃən/ *n* [U]: *~ation officer,* person employed to get rid of vermin (eg a rat-catcher). 消滅害蟲或害獸(例如捕鼠)的官員。

dis·in·fla·tion /ˌdɪsɪn'fleɪʃn；ˏdɪsɪn'fleʃən/ *n* (process of) returning from a state of inflation to a stable or more normal level (in which prices, wages, etc do not vary much). 通貨緊縮(由通貨膨脹返回原來物價，工資等穩定或較正常的狀態)；通貨緊縮的過程。

dis·in·genu·ous /ˌdɪsɪn'dʒenjʊəs；ˏdɪsɪn'dʒɛnjʊəs/ *adj* (formal) insincere; not straightforward. (正式用語) 不眞誠的；不坦白的。 **~·ly** *adv* **~·ness** *n*

dis·in·herit /ˌdɪsɪn'herɪt；ˏdɪsɪn'hɛrɪt/ *vt* [VP6A] take away the right (of sb) to inherit. 剝奪(某人的)繼承權。 **dis·in·heri·tance** /ˌdɪsɪn'herɪtəns；ˏdɪsɪn'hɛrətəns/ *n* [U] (act of) ~ing. 剝奪繼承權。

dis·in·te·grate /dɪs'ɪntɪgreɪt；dɪs'ɪntəˏgret/ *vt, vi* [VP6A, 2A] (cause to) break up into small parts or pieces: (使)分裂成小塊: *rocks ~d by frost and rain.* 被霜和雨蝕裂成碎塊的岩石。 **dis·in·te·gra·tion** /dɪsˌɪntɪ'greɪʃn；dɪsˏɪntə'greʃən/ *n*

dis·inter /ˌdɪsɪn'tɜ:(r)；ˏdɪsɪn'tɝ/ *vt* (-rr-) [VP6A] (formal) dig up from the earth (eg from a grave). (正式用語) 自地中(如墳墓中)掘出。 **~·ment** *n*

dis·in·ter·ested /dɪs'ɪntrəstɪd；dɪs'ɪntərəstɪd/ *adj* not influenced by personal feelings or interests: 不爲個人情感或利害所影響的；公正無私的: *His action was not altogether ~.* 他的行動並不完全公正。 ⇨ uninterested. **~·ly** *adv* **~·ness** *n*

dis·joint /dɪs'dʒɔɪnt；dɪs'dʒɔɪnt/ *vt* [VP6A] separate at the joints; take to pieces: 自關節處拆開；拆散: *to ~ a chicken.* 自關節處切開一隻鷄。

dis·jointed /dɪs'dʒɔɪntɪd；dɪs'dʒɔɪntɪd/ *adj* (eg of speech and writing) not connected; incoherent. (指說話和寫作等) 不連貫的；無系統的。 **~·ly** *adv* **~·ness** *n*

dis·junc·tive /dɪs'dʒʌŋktɪv；dɪs'dʒʌŋktɪv/ *adj* ~ ***conjunction,*** (gram) one expressing opposition of or contrast between ideas (eg *either...or*). (文法) 反意連接詞(例如 either...or)。

disk *n* ⇨ disc.

dis·like /dɪs'laɪk；dɪs'laɪk/ *vt* [VP6A, C] not like: 不喜歡；厭惡: *to ~ getting up early／being disturbed.* 不喜歡早起 (受打擾)。 *If you behave like that, you'll get yourself ~d,* become unpopular. 如果你的行爲像那個樣子，你會使人厭惡。□ *n* [U, C] feeling of not liking; feeling against: 不喜歡；厭惡: *to have a ~ of／for cats;* 不喜歡貓; *to feel ~ for sb.* 不喜歡某人。 ***take a ~ to sb,*** begin to ~ him. 厭惡某人。 ***likes and ~s*** /'dɪslaɪks；'dɪslaɪks/, preferences and aversions: 喜愛和厭惡之物: *He has so many likes and ~s that he is difficult to please.* 他喜愛很多東西，也討厭很多東西，故而他是個難以取悅的人。

dis·lo·cate /'dɪsləkeɪt *US:* -ləʊk-；'dısloˏket/ *vt* [VP6A] **1** put (esp a bone in the body) out of position: (尤指身體之骨) 脫離原位；使脫臼: *He fell from his horse and ~d his collarbone.* 他從馬上跌下，而使鎖骨脫臼了。 **2** put traffic, machinery, business, etc out of order: 使(交通、機器、事務等)混亂: *Traffic was badly ~d by the heavy fall of snow.* 大雪使交通十分紊亂。 **dis·lo·ca·tion** /ˌdɪslə'keɪʃn *US:* -ləʊ'k-；ˏdɪslo'keʃən/*n* [U, C] dislocating or being ~d: 脫臼；混亂: *the dislocation of trade caused by the blocking of the canal.* 運河受阻引起的貿易混亂。

dis·lodge /dɪs'lɒdʒ；dɪs'lɑdʒ/ *vt* [VP6A, 14] ~ ***(from),*** move, force (sb or sth) from the place occupied: (自其佔有的位置) 移去或驅逐(人或物): *to ~ a stone from a building／the enemy from their positions.* 自一建築物移走一石(將敵人自陣地逐出)。 **~·ment** *n*

dis·loyal /dɪs'lɔɪəl；dɪs'lɔɪəl/ *adj* ~ ***to,*** not loyal to. 對…不忠的。 **~ly** /-'lɔɪəlɪ；-'lɔɪəlɪ/ *adv* **~·ty** /-'lɔɪəltɪ；-'lɔɪəltɪ/ *n* [U] ***~ty (to),*** being ~ (to); [C] (*pl* -ties) ~ act, etc. (對…) 不忠；不忠的行爲等。

dis·mal /'dɪzməl；'dɪzml̩/ *adj* sad, gloomy; miserable; comfortless: 悲哀的；陰鬱的；憂愁的；不愉快的: *~ weather;* 陰沉的天氣; *in a ~ voice.* 以憂鬱的聲音。 **~·ly** /'dɪzməlɪ；'dɪzml̩ɪ/ *adv*

dis·mantle /dɪs'mæntl；dɪs'mæntl̩/ *vt* [VP6A] **1** take away fittings, furnishings, etc from: 拆除…之裝備等: *The old warship was ~d,* Its guns, armour, engines, etc were taken out. 舊戰艦上的裝備(即槍砲、裝甲、發動機等)被拆除了。 **2** take to pieces: 拆散: *to ~ an engine.* 拆散一發動機。 **~·ment** *n* [U] dismantling (now the usu word). 拆除裝備；拆散(現在較常用 dismantling)。

dis·may /dɪs'meɪ；dɪs'me/ *n* [U] feeling of fear and discouragement: 驚慌；喪膽: *The news that the enemy were near filled／struck them with ~.* 敵人逼近的消息使他們驚慌。 *He looked at me in (blank) ~.* 他驚慌(茫然不知所措)地望着我。 □ *vt* [VP6A] fill with ~: 使驚慌: *We were ~ed at the news.* 聽到這消息，我們感到驚慌。

dis·mem·ber /dɪs'membə(r)；dɪs'mɛmbɚ/ *vt* [VP 6A] **1** tear or cut the limbs from: 割斷…的四肢；肢解: *Poor fellow! He was ~ed by a pack of wolves.*

可憐的傢伙！ 他被一群狼給肢解了。 **2** (fig) divide up (a country, etc). (喻)瓜分(國家等)。 ~**·ment** *n*

dis·miss /dɪsˈmɪs ; dɪsˈmɪs/ *vt* [VP6A, 14] ~ ***(from),*** **1** send away (from one's employment, from service): 解雇；撤職；開除；開革: *The servant was ~ed for being lazy and dishonest.* 這僕人因懶惰和不誠實而被解雇。*The officer was ~ed from the service for neglect of duty.* 這軍官因疏於職守而被撤職。 **2** allow to go: 使退去；解散: *The teacher ~ed his class when the bell rang.* 鈴聲響，老師就讓學生下課。 **3** put away from the mind; stop thinking or talking about: 自心中摒除；不再考慮或談論: *to ~ all thoughts of revenge.* 摒除一切報復的念頭。 **4** (cricket, of the team that is fielding) put a batsman/a team out: (板球，指防守的球隊)使(擊球員或球隊)出局: *The fast bowler ~ed Smith for ten runs.* 那位快速球投手在第十分時卽使史密斯出局。 ~**al** /-ˈmɪsl ; -ˈmɪsl/ *n* [U, C] ~ing or being ~ed: 解雇；撤職；解散；退去: *~al from the Navy.* 自海軍解職。

dis·mount /ˌdɪsˈmaʊnt ; dɪsˈmaʊnt/ *vi, vt* **1** [VP2A, 3A] ~ ***(from),*** get down (from sth on which one is riding): (自乘騎之物)下來: *to ~ from one's horse/bicycle.* 從馬上(脚踏車上)下來。 (Cf *alight* from a bus, taxi, tram or train.) (參較 alight 表示下公共汽車、計程車、電車或火車。) **2** [VP6A] remove (sth) from its mount: 自托架上移下(某物): *to ~ a gun* (from the gun-carriage). (自砲架)將砲卸下。 **3** [VP6A] cause to fall (from a horse, etc). 使(從馬上等)跌下。⇨ joust. ~**ed** *part adj* (of cavalry) fighting as infantry. (指騎兵部隊)似步兵般作戰的。

dis·obedi·ence /ˌdɪsəˈbiːdɪəns ; ˌdɪsəˈbidɪəns/ *n* [U] ~ ***(to),*** failure or refusal to obey: 不服從；違命: *acts of ~;* 違命的行動； *~ to orders.* 違抗命令。 **dis·obedi·ent** *adj* ~ ***(to),*** not obedient. 不服從的；違命的。 **dis·obedi·ent·ly** *adv*

dis·obey /ˌdɪsəˈbeɪ ; ˌdɪsəˈbe/ *vt, vi* [VP6A, 2A] pay no attention to orders; not obey a person, a law, etc. 不服從命令；違命；不服從(某人、法律等)。

dis·oblige /ˌdɪsəˈblaɪdʒ ; ˌdɪsəˈblaɪdʒ/ *vt* [VP6A] (formal) refuse to be helpful or to think about another person's wishes or needs: (正式用語)拒絕幫助；不考慮別人的願望或需要: *I'm sorry to ~ you, but last time I lent you money you did not repay me.* 我很抱歉不能幫助你，但上次我借錢給你，你沒有還我。

dis·order /dɪsˈɔːdə(r) ; dɪsˈɔrdɚ/ *n* **1** [U] absence of order; confusion: 無秩序；混亂: *The burglars left the room in great ~.* 竊賊將這房間弄得亂七八糟。*The enemy retreated in ~.* 敵人狼狽地退却。 **2** [U] absence of order caused by political troubles; [C] angry outburst of rioting caused by political troubles, etc: (政治糾紛引起的)騷動；騷亂: *Troops were called out to deal with the ~s in the capital.* 軍隊被召去鎮壓首都的騷亂。 **3** [C, U] disturbance of the normal working of the body or mind: 身心不適；疾病: *a ~ of the digestive system;* 消化系統的毛病； *suffering from mental ~;* 患精神病； *~s of the mind.* 精神方面的毛病。□ *vt* [VP6A] put into ~: 使紊亂: *a ~ed imagination/mind.* 紊亂的想像(心緒)。

dis·order·ly /dɪsˈɔːdəlɪ ; dɪsˈɔrdɚlɪ/ *adj* **1** in disorder: 無秩序的；混亂的: *a ~ room/desk.* 亂七八糟的房間(書桌)。 **2** causing disturbance; unruly; lawless: 造成混亂的；騷亂的；不守法的: *~ crowds;* 騷亂的群衆； *a ~ mob;* 騷亂的暴民； *~ behaviour.* 不守法的行爲。 **a ~ house,** a brothel or a place where illegal gambling is carried on. 敗壞風紀的場所；妓院；賭場。

dis·or·gan·ize /ˌdɪsˈɔːgənaɪz ; dɪsˈɔrgəˌnaɪz/ *vt* [VP 6A] throw into confusion; upset the working or system of: 使紊亂；破壞…的工作或組織: *The train service was ~d by fog.* 火車班次被霧攪亂了。 **dis·or·gan·iz·ation** /dɪsˌɔːgənaɪˈzeɪʃn *US:* -nɪˈz- ; dɪsˌɔrgənəˈzeʃən/ *n* [U].

dis·orien·tate /dɪsˈɔːrɪənteɪt ; dɪsˈɔrɪɛnˌtet/ (also, esp US) **dis·orient** /dɪsˈɔːrɪənt ; dɪsˈɔrɪˌɛnt/ *vt* [VP 6A] (lit, fig) confuse (sb) as to his bearings(4). (字面，喻)使(某人)迷失方向。

dis·own /dɪsˈəʊn ; dɪsˈon/ *vt* [VP6A] say that one does not know (sb or sth), that one has not, or no longer wishes to have, any connection with (sb or sth): 否認(某人或某物)；不承認與(某人或某物)有關係；聲明與(某人)脫離關係: *The boy was so wicked that his father ~ed him.* 這男孩太頑劣，所以他父親聲稱與他脫離父子關係。

dis·par·age /dɪˈspærɪdʒ ; dɪˈspærɪdʒ/ *vt* [VP6A] say things to suggest that (sb or sth) is of small value or importance. 貶抑；藐視。 ~**·ment** *n* **dis·par·ag·ing·ly** *adv* in a disparaging manner. 貶抑地；藐視地。

dis·par·ate /ˈdɪspərət ; ˈdɪspərɪt/ *adj* that cannot be compared in quality, amount, kind, etc; essentially different. (性質、數量、種類等)不可比較的；根本不同的。□ *n pl* things so unlike that comparison is impossible. 差異太大而無法比較之物。

dis·par·ity /dɪˈspærətɪ ; dɪsˈpærətɪ/ *n* [U] inequality; difference; [C] (*pl* -ties) instance or degree of this: 不等；不同；不等或不同的實例或程度: *~ in age/rank/position;* 年齡(階級，職位)之不同； *the disparities in the newspaper accounts of the accident.* 報紙對這事件之報導的不同。

dis·pas·sion·ate /dɪˈspæʃənət ; dɪsˈpæʃənɪt/ *adj* free from passion; not taking sides, not showing favour (in a quarrel, etc between others). 冷靜的；不偏私的；(對他人的爭執等)態度公平的。 ~**·ly** *adv* ~**·ness** *n*

dis·patch¹, des·patch /dɪˈspætʃ ; dɪˈspætʃ/ *n* **1** [U] dispatching or being dispatched (all senses): 派遣；發送；迅速結束；殺死；處死: *Please hurry up the ~ of these telegrams.* 請趕緊將這些電報發出去。 **2** [C] sth dispatched (1), esp, a government, military or newspaper report: 發送之物；(尤指)政府、軍事文電或新聞(電訊)報導: *London newspapers receive ~es from all parts of the world.* 倫敦的報紙收到世界各地發來的新聞電訊。*The soldier was mentioned in ~es,* had his name recorded in accounts of fighting, etc because of his bravery, etc. 發出的文件中提到了這個士兵(因其英勇的戰績等，在戰事報導中記載了他的姓名)。 ⇨ *citation* at cite. **'~-box,** one for official ~es. 公文遞送箱。 **'~-rider,** man who carries military ~es (usu on a motor-bike). 遞送軍事公文者(通常乘機器脚踏車)。 **3** [U] promptness; speed: 迅速；急速: *to act with ~.* 迅速行動。

dis·patch², des·patch /dɪˈspætʃ ; dɪˈspætʃ/ *vt* **1** [VP6A, 14] ~ ***(to),*** send off, to a destination, on a journey, for a special purpose: 派遣；發送: *to ~ letters/telegrams;* 發出信件(電報)； *to ~ a cruiser to the island to restore order.* 派一巡洋艦至該島以恢復秩序。 **2** [VP6A] finish, get through, business, a meal quickly. 迅速結束(事務，餐膳)。 **3** [VP6A] kill; give the death blow to: 殺死；處死: *The executioner quickly ~ed the condemned man.* 行刑者迅速將該犯處決了。

dis·pel /dɪˈspel ; dɪˈspɛl/ *vt* (-ll-) [VP6A] drive away; scatter: 驅逐；驅散: *The wind soon ~led the fog.* 風不久卽將霧驅散了。*How can we ~ their doubts and fears?* 我們如何才能消除他們的懷疑和恐懼？

dis·pens·able /dɪˈspensəbl ; dɪˈspɛnsəbl/ *adj* that can be done without; not necessary. 不必要的；不需要的。

dis·pens·ary /dɪˈspensərɪ ; dɪˈspɛnsərɪ/ *n* (*pl* -ries) place where medicines are dispensed (eg in a hospital). 發藥處(例如醫院中者)；藥局。

dis·pen·sa·tion /ˌdɪspenˈseɪʃn ; ˌdɪspənˈseʃən/ *n* **1** [U] the act of dispensing (1) or distributing: 分配；分給；施給: *the ~ of justice/charity/food.* 法律之執行(放賑；食物的分配)。 **2** [U] ordering or management, esp of the world by Providence; [C] sth arranged by Nature or Providence: 治理(尤指上帝對人世的治理)；造物主或上帝所安排的事物；天道；神意: *A bereavement* (eg the death of a very old person) *is sometimes called a ~ of Providence.* 親屬的喪亡(例如高齡者之去世)有時被稱作上天的安排。 **3** [C, U] permission to do sth that is usually forbidden, or not to do sth that is usually required, esp by ecclesiastical law: 特准;特免(尤指教規所禁止或規定者): *to be granted ~ from fasting during a journey.* 旅途中特免齋戒。 **4** [C] religious system prevalent at a period: 某一時代的宗教制度: *the Mosaic ~*, that of the time of Moses. 摩西時代的律法。

dis·pense /dɪˈspens ; dɪˈspɛns/ *vt, vi* **1** [VP6A, 14] **~ *(to)*,** deal out; distribute; administer: 分配;分給;施給: *to ~ charity/alms/one's favours to people;* 對人們放賑(施捨,施恩); (legal) (法律) *to ~ justice* (in law courts). (在法庭)執法。 **2** [VP6A] mix; prepare, give out (medicines): 配製並分發(藥物): *to ~ a prescription;* 照藥方配藥; *a dispensing chemist*, one qualified to do this. 藥劑師。 **3** [VP3A] **~ *with*, (a)** do without: 無需;不用;沒有也可以: *He is not yet well enough to ~ with the doctor's services.* 他尚未痊癒,仍需醫生的照看。 **(b)** render unnecessary: 使不必要;使多餘: *The new machinery ~s with hand-labour.* 新機器使手工成爲多餘。 **dis·penser** *n* **1** person who ~s, esp medicines. (尤指)配藥者;藥劑師。 **2** container from which sth can be withdrawn, ejected or otherwise obtained without removing a cover, lid, etc: 一種不需要拿開蓋子便可取物的容器: *a ~r for liquid soap/toilet powder/paper cups.* 免開蓋式肥皂水容器(撲粉盒,紙杯盒)。

dis·perse /dɪˈspɜːs ; dɪˈspɝs/ *vt, vi* [VP6A, 2A] (cause to) go in different directions; scatter: 驅散;散開: *The police ~d the crowd.* 警察驅散群衆。 *The crowd ~d when the police arrived.* 警察來時,群衆散開。 *The soldiers were ~d* (= stationed at different points) *along a wide front.* 兵士們散駐在廣闊的前線上。 *A prism ~s light*, breaks it up into its coloured rays. 三稜鏡可使光色散(使其散爲彩色光線)。 **dis·per·sal** /dɪˈspɜːsl ; dɪˈspɝsl̩/ *n* [U, C] dispersing or being ~d. 驅散;散開。 **dis·per·sion** /dɪˈspɜːʃn *US:* -ʒn ; dɪˈspɝʃən/ *n* = dispersal, esp of light. (尤指光的)色散。 **the Dispersion**, the Jews ~d among the Gentiles. 散居在異邦人中間的猶太人。 ⇨ Diaspora.

dis·pirit /dɪˈspɪrɪt ; dɪˈspɪrɪt/ *vt* [VP6A] discourage; dishearten (chiefly in *pp*): 使沮喪;使氣餒(主要用過去分詞): *to look ~ed.* 顯得神情沮喪。 **~·ed·ly** *adv*

dis·place /dɪsˈpleɪs ; dɪsˈples/ *vt* [VP6A] **1** put out of the right or usual position. 自正常位置移走;移置。 **ˌ~d ˈperson**, refugee left homeless, unable or unwilling to return to his own country. 不能或不願返國的難民。 **2** take the place of; put sth or sb else in the place of: 代替;替換: *The volunteers were ~d by a professional army.* 志願軍被正規軍替換。 *Tom has ~d Harry in Mary's affections.* 在瑪莉的感情上,湯姆已代替了哈利的位置。

dis·place·ment /dɪsˈpleɪsmənt ; dɪsˈplesmənt/ *n* **1** [U] displacing or being displaced: 移置;代替: *the ~ of human labour by machines.* 人力之被機器代替。 **2** [C] amount of water displaced by a solid body in it, or floating in it: 排水量: *a ship with a ~ of 10000 tons.* 一艘有一萬噸排水量的船。

dis·play¹ /dɪˈspleɪ ; dɪˈsple/ *vt* [VP6A] **1** show; place or spread out so that there is no difficulty in seeing: 展示;陳列: *Department stores ~ their goods in the windows.* 百貨公司將貨物陳列在櫥窗內。 *The peacock ~ed its fine tail feathers.* 那孔雀展示牠尾巴上美麗的羽毛。 **2** allow to be seen; show signs of having: 顯露;表現: *to ~ one's ignorance.* 顯示自己的無知。 *She ~ed no sign of emotion when she was told of her son's death.* 她聽到兒子去世的消息時並未顯得悲哀。

dis·play² /dɪˈspleɪ ; dɪˈsple/ *n* [C, U] displaying; show or exhibition: 展示;陳列;顯露;表現: *a fashion ~*, a showing of new styles in clothes, etc; 時裝等展覽; *a fine ~ of courage;* 勇氣的充分表現; *a ~ of bad temper;* 壞脾氣的表現; *to make a ~ of one's knowledge*, show what a lot one knows; 炫耀自己的知識; *to make a ~ of one's affection*, show great affection (whether genuine or not). 顯得非常親切(不論眞或假)。

dis·please /dɪsˈpliːz ; dɪsˈpliz/ *vt* [VP6A] not please; offend; annoy; make indignant or angry: 使不高興;觸怒;使厭煩;使生氣: *to ~ one's wife;* 使妻子不悅; *to be ~d with sb* (*for* doing sth); 對某人(因做某事)不高興; *to be ~d at sb's conduct.* 不滿某人的行爲。**dis·pleas·ing** *adj* **~ *(to)*,** not pleasing. 使人不高興的;令人不愉快的。 **dis·pleas·ing·ly** *adv*

dis·pleasure /dɪsˈpleʒə(r) ; dɪsˈplɛʒɚ/ *n* [U] displeased feeling; dissatisfaction: 不悅;不滿: *He incurred his father's ~.* 他引起他父親的不悅。 *He looked with ~ at the meal that was set before him.* 他不滿地望着擺在他面前的食物。

dis·port /dɪˈspɔːt ; dɪˈspɔrt/ *vt* [VP6A] **~ *oneself*,** (formal) play; amuse oneself, eg in the sea or in the sunshine. (正式用語)玩樂;(在海上或陽光下等)嬉戲。

dis·pos·able /dɪˈspəʊzəbl ; dɪˈspozəbl̩/ *adj* made so that it may be (easily) disposed of after use: 使用後易處理的;用後易處置的: *~ nappies/panties*, made of soft paper which disintegrates quickly in water. 用後易處置的尿布(短內褲)(用軟紙製成,棄於水中易碎裂者)。

dis·posal /dɪˈspəʊzl ; dɪˈspozl̩/ *n* [U] **~ *(of)*, 1** the act of disposing (1,2): 處理;處置;除去;布置: *the ~ of property*, eg by selling it, leaving it to sb in one's will; 財產的處理(如將其售賣,或照遺囑贈與某人); *the ~ of rubbish*, getting rid of it; 垃圾的清理; *a waste-~ unit*, kind of machine that shreds waste products so that they can be washed away down the drains; 廢物處理機(可將廢物弄碎,使其由溝中流走); *a bomb ~ squad*, group of men who, when unexploded bombs are found, try to make them harmless and remove them; 未爆彈清除隊(清除未爆炸的炸彈者); *the ~ of troops*, the method of using them, placing them in position, etc; 軍隊的部署; *the ~ of business affairs*, settling them. 業務的處理。 **2** control; management: 控制;支配: *In time of war the government must have entire ~ of all material resources.* 在戰時政府必須完全控制全國的物資。 ***at one's ~*,** to be used as one wishes: 任意使用: *He placed £50 at my ~.* 他留下五十鎊任我使用。 *My car is at your ~.* 我的車隨便你使用。

dis·pose /dɪˈspəʊz ; dɪˈspoz/ *vi, vt* **1** [VP3A] **~ *of*,** finish with; get rid of; deal with: 處理;除去;處置: *to ~ of rubbish.* 除去垃圾。 *He doesn't want to ~ of* (eg sell) *the land.* 他不想處理(例如賣掉)那塊地。 *I think we have ~d of all his arguments*, answered them, proved them unsound. 我認爲我們已答覆了他所有的論點(證明其不確)。 *The dictator soon ~d of his opponents*, eg by putting them in prison. 那獨裁者不久就把那些反對他的人清除了(例如將他們下獄)。 **2** [VP6A, 2A] place (persons, objects) in good order or in suitable positions: 置(人或物)於適當位置;布置: *The cruisers were ~d in line abreast.* 巡洋艦被布置爲横隊。 ***Man proposes, God ~s*,** (prov) Men may propose things, but God determines what shall happen. (諺)謀事在人,成事在天。 **3** [VP17] **~ *sb to do sth*,** (formal) make willing or ready: (正式用語)使願意或準備做某事: *Your news ~s me to believe that....* 你的消息使我相信…。 *The low salary did not ~ him to accept the position.* 菲薄的待遇使他不願接受這工作。 *I'm not ~d/don't feel ~d to help that lazy fellow.* 我不願意幫助那個懶惰的人。 ***be well/ill ~d (towards)*,** be/not be friendly and helpful: (對…)有好(惡)感;(對…)友善(不友善): *Most of the newspapers seem to be well ~d towards the new government.* 大多數的報紙似乎對新政府的態度友善。

dis·po·si·tion /ˌdɪspəˈzɪʃn ; ˌdɪspəˈzɪʃən/ *n* [C] **1**

arrangement; placing in order: 排列;布置: *the ~ of furniture in a room;* 房間內傢具的布置; *a clever ~ of troops.* 軍隊之巧妙的部署。 **2** person's natural qualities of mind and character: 性情;氣質: *a man with a cheerful ~;* 性情開朗的人; *a ~ to jealousy/to take offence easily.* 喜妒嫉(易發怒)的性情。 **3** inclination: 傾向: *There was a general ~ to leave early,* Most people seemed to wish to leave early. 大多數人似乎想早些動身。 **4** power of ordering and disposing: 支配權;處理權: *Who has the ~ of this property,* the power or authority to dispose of it? 誰有處置這項財產之權?

dis·pos·sess /ˌdɪspəˈzes ; ˌdɪspəˈzɛs/ *vt* [VP14] ~ ***sb of sth,*** take away (property, esp land) from; compel (sb) to give up (the house he occupies): 剝奪(某人的財產,尤指土地); 霸佔(某人之房屋): *The nobles were ~ed of their property after the Revolution.* 貴族們的財產於革命後被人强佔。**dis·pos·session** /ˌdɪspəˈzeʃn ; ˌdɪspəˈzɛʃən/ *n*

dis·proof /dɪsˈpruːf ; dɪsˈpruf/ *n* [U] disproving; [C] that which disproves; proof to the contrary. 證明爲誤;反證物;反證。

dis·pro·por·tion /ˌdɪsprəˈpɔːʃn ; ˌdɪsprəˈpɔrʃən/ *n* [U] the state of being out of proportion: 不均衡; 不相稱: *~ in age.* 年齡的不相稱。**~·ate** /-ˈpɔːʃənət ; -ˈpɔrʃənɪt/ *adj* ~ ***(to),*** out of proportion; relatively too large or small, etc: 不相稱的;比較而言過大或過小等的: *to give a ~ate amount of one's time to games;* 以過量的時間遊戲; *pay that is ~ate to the work done.* 與工作不相稱的待遇。**~·ate·ly** *adv*

dis·prove /ˌdɪsˈpruːv ; dɪsˈpruv/ *vt* [VP6A] prove to be wrong or false. 證明爲誤;證明爲僞。

dis·put·able /dɪˈspjuːtəbl ; dɪˈspjutəbl/ *adj* that may be disputed; questionable. 可能引起辯論的;有問題的。

dis·pu·tant /dɪˈspjuːtənt ; ˈdɪspjutənt/ *n* person who disputes. 辯論者;爭論者。

dis·pu·ta·tion /ˌdɪspjuːˈteɪʃn ; ˌdɪspjuˈteʃən/ *n* [U] disputing; [C] debate, controversy. 辯論;爭論。

dis·pu·ta·tious /ˌdɪspjuːˈteɪʃəs ; ˌdɪspjuˈteʃəs/ *adj* fond of disputing; inclined to dispute. 愛辯論的; 喜爭論的。**~·ly** *adv*

dis·pute[1] /dɪˈspjuːt ; dɪˈspjut/ *n* **1** [U] debate, argument. 辯論;爭論。***in ~***: *The matter in ~* (= being disputed) *is the ownership of a house.* 目下爭論的事是一所房子的所有權。***beyond/past (all) ~,*** unquestionably; undoubtedly: 無疑地: *This is beyond ~ the best book on the subject.* 這無疑是有關此問題最好的一本書。***in ~ with,*** engaged in a ~ with: 與…辯論;與…爭論: *The workers' union is in ~ with the management.* 工會與經理人員爭論。***without ~,*** without fear of contradiction. 不會引起反駁地。 **2** [C] quarrel; argument; controversy: 爭吵;爭辯;爭論: *There were many religious ~s in England during the 17th century.* 十七世紀在英國有許多宗教上的爭論。

dis·pute[2] /dɪˈspjuːt ; dɪˈspjut/ *vi, vt* **1** [VP2A, 3A] ~ ***(with/against sb),*** argue, debate, quarrel in words: (與某人)辯論;爭論: *Some people are always disputing.* 有些人總喜歡爭論。 **2** [VP6A, 8, 10] discuss, question the truth or validity of: 討論;懷疑…的眞實性或妥當性: *to ~ a statement/a claim/a decision.* 討論一聲明(要求,決策)的眞實性或妥當性。*The election result was ~d,* eg it was said that the votes had been counted wrongly. 選舉的結果引起異議(如據說選票被數錯)。*The will was ~d,* eg it was said that it had not been made in correct legal form. 這遺囑的眞實性受到懷疑(如據說係未經合法手續而立者)。*They were disputing whether to start at once or wait.* 他們討論是立刻開始還是等待。*They ~d (about) how to get the best results.* 他們討論如何獲得最佳結果。 **3** [VP6A] fight for, try to win: 爭奪;競爭: *Our team ~d the victory until the last minute of the game.* 我們的隊爭取勝利直到比賽的最後一分鐘。

dis·qual·ify /dɪsˈkwɒlɪfaɪ ; dɪsˈkwɑlə,faɪ/ *vt* [VP6A, 14] ~ ***sb (for sth/from doing sth),*** make unfit or unable: 使不適合;使不能;使不合格: *His weak eyesight disqualified him for military service.* 他的目力欠佳使他不能服兵役。*As he was a professional, he was disqualified from taking part in the Olympic Games.* 由於他是個職業運動員,他無資格參加世界運動會。 **dis·quali·fi·ca·tion** /dɪsˌkwɒlɪfɪˈkeɪʃn ; ˌdɪskwɑləfəˈkeʃən/ *n* [U] ~ing or being disqualified; [C] that which disqualifies. 不適合; 無能力;不合格;不合格的原因。

dis·quiet /dɪsˈkwaɪət ; dɪsˈkwaɪət/ *vt* [VP6A] make troubled, anxious, uneasy: 使不安;使煩亂: *~ed by rumours of war.* 由於戰爭的謠言而不安。 □ *n* [U] anxiety; troubled condition: 憂慮;不安: *The President's speech caused considerable ~ in some European capitals.* 總統的演說在歐洲的某些首都中引起很大的不安。 **~·ing** *adj* causing ~: 引起不安的: *~ing news.* 令人不安的消息。**~·ing·ly** *adv* in a way that causes ~: 引起不安地: *a ~ingly high percentage of errors in the examination papers.* 考卷中令人憂慮的百分比很高的錯誤。 **~·ude** /dɪsˈkwaɪətjuːd *US:* -tuːd ; dɪsˈkwaɪə,tjud/ *n* [U] state of ~; uneasiness. 憂慮;不安。

dis·qui·si·tion /ˌdɪskwɪˈzɪʃn ; ˌdɪskwəˈzɪʃən/ *n* [C] ~ ***on sth,*** long, elaborate speech or piece of writing. 精心做出的長篇演說或寫作; 專題演講; 專論。

dis·re·gard /ˌdɪsrɪˈɡɑːd ; ˌdɪsrɪˈɡɑrd/ *vt* [VP6A] pay no attention to; show no respect for: 不注意;忽視: *to ~ a warning/sb's objections to a proposal.* 不理一項警告(某人對一建議的反對)。□ *n* [U] inattention; indifference; neglect: 不注意;忽視;不理: *~ of a rule;* 忽視一規則; *~ for one's teachers.* 漠視老師。

dis·re·pair /ˌdɪsrɪˈpeə(r) ; ˌdɪsrɪˈpɛr/ *n* [U] the state of needing repair: 需要修理;失修: *The building was in bad ~,* in great need of being repaired. 這建築物急需修理。

dis·repu·table /dɪsˈrepjʊtəbl ; dɪsˈrɛpjətəbl/ *adj* having a bad reputation: 名譽不好的;聲名狼藉的: *~ bars and clubs;* 聲名狼藉的酒吧和俱樂部; not respectable in appearance: 外表不雅的: *a ~-looking fellow.* 外表不雅的人。 ~ ***to,*** reflecting badly on: 玷辱名聲的: *incidents ~ to his character as a priest.* 有損他做爲牧師的品格的事件。**dis·repu·tably** /-təblɪ ; -təblɪ/ *adv*

dis·re·pute /ˌdɪsrɪˈpjuːt ; ˌdɪsrɪˈpjut/ *n* [U] condition of being disreputable; discredit: 聲名狼藉;不名譽: *The hotel has fallen into ~,* no longer has a good reputation. 這旅館已名譽掃地了。

dis·re·spect /ˌdɪsrɪˈspekt ; ˌdɪsrɪˈspɛkt/ *n* [U] rudeness; want of respect: 無禮;不敬: *He meant no ~ by that remark,* did not intend to be impolite. 他說那句話並無不敬之意。 **~·ful** /-fʊl ; -fəl/ *adj* showing ~: 無禮的;不敬的: *to be ~ful to sb.* 對某人無禮。**~·fully** /-fʊlɪ ; -fəlɪ/ *adv*: *to speak ~fully of/about sb.* 無敬意地談論某人。

dis·robe /dɪsˈrəʊb ; dɪsˈrob/ *vi, vt* [VP6A, 2A] undress; take off (esp official or ceremonial robes): 脫衣(尤指官服或禮服): *The Queen ~d after the coronation ceremony.* 女王於加冕禮後脫去王袍。

dis·rupt /dɪsˈrʌpt ; dɪsˈrʌpt/ *vt* [VP6A] break up, split, separate by force a State, an empire, communications, other non-physical things: 分裂(國家, 帝國, 交通或其他無形之物): *Their quarrels seem likely to ~ the Coalition.* 他們的爭執似乎可能使聯盟分裂。**dis·rup·tion** /dɪsˈrʌpʃn ; dɪsˈrʌpʃən/ *n* [U] ~ing or being ~ed: 分裂;被分裂: *the ~ion of the Roman Empire.* 羅馬帝國的分裂。**dis·rup·tive** /dɪsˈrʌptɪv ; dɪsˈrʌptɪv/ *adj* causing ~ion: 造成分裂的: *~ive forces.* 造成分裂的力量;迸裂力。

dis·sat·is·fac·tion /ˌdɪsˌsætɪsˈfækʃn ; ˌdɪssætɪsˈfækʃən/ *n* [U] ~ ***(with sb/sth) (at doing sth),*** the state of being dissatisfied. 不滿。

dis·sat·isfy /dɪsˈsætɪsfaɪ ; dɪsˈsætɪs,faɪ/ *vt* [VP6A] (usu passive) fail to satisfy; make discontented. (通常用被動語態)使不滿;使不滿足。***be dissatisfied***

(with sb/sth)/(at doing sth): *to be dissatisfied with one's salary/at not getting a better salary.* 對薪金(不能獲較高薪金)不滿。

dis·sect /dɪ'sekt ; dɪ'sɛkt/ *vt* [VP6A] **1** cut up (parts of an animal body, plant, etc) in order to study its structure. 解剖(動植物各部)。 **2** (fig) examine (a theory, argument, etc) part by part, to judge its value. (喻)詳細研究或分析(學說,論據等)。 **dis·section** /dɪ'sekʃn ; dɪ'sɛkʃən/ *n* [U] ~ing or being ~ed; [C] (part of) sth that has been ~ed. 解剖;解剖體;詳細研究或分析;經過詳細研究或分析的事物。

dis·semble /dɪ'sembl ; dɪ'sɛmbḷ/ *vt, vi* [VP6A, 2A] (formal) speak, behave, so as to hide one's real feelings, thoughts, plans, etc, or give a wrong idea of them: (正式用語)以言語或行動掩飾(眞正情感,思想,計畫等,或令人對它們有一種錯誤的想法): *to ~ one's emotions.* 掩飾感情。 **dis·sem·bler** /-blə(r) ; -blɚ/ *n* person who ~s; deceiver. 以言語或行動做掩飾者;欺騙者。

dis·semi·nate /dɪ'semɪneɪt ; dɪ'sɛmə,net/ *vt* [VP6A] distribute or spread widely ideas, doctrines, etc. 傳播;散佈(思想,教義等)。 **dis·semi·na·tion** /dɪ,semɪ'neɪʃn ; dɪ,sɛmə'neʃən/ *n*

dis·sen·sion /dɪ'senʃn ; dɪ'sɛnʃən/ *n* [U] angry quarrelling; [C] angry quarrel: 紛爭;爭吵: *~(s) between rival groups in politics.* 敵對政黨間的紛爭。

dis·sent¹ /dɪ'sent ; dɪ'sɛnt/ *n* [U] dissenting; (expression of) disagreement: 意見不同;不從英國國教;不同意(的表示): *to express strong ~.* 表示極不贊同。

dis·sent² /dɪ'sent ; dɪ'sɛnt/ *vi* **1** [VP3A] ~ ***from,*** have a different opinion from; refuse to assent to: 與…意見不同;不同意: *I strongly ~ from what the last speaker has said.* 我十分不同意剛才這位發言者的話。 **2** [VP2A, 3A] ~ ***(from),*** (esp) refuse to accept the religious doctrine of the Church of England. (尤指)不從英國國教。 **~er** *n* (often *D~*) one who ~s (esp as in 2 above). 意見不同者;(常作大寫)不從英國國教者。

dis·ser·ta·tion /,dɪsə'teɪʃn ; ,dɪsɚ'teʃən/ *n* [C] long written or spoken account (eg as submitted for a higher university degree): 長篇論文或演說(例如爲獲得大學較高學位而提出者): *a ~ on/upon/concerning sth.* 關於某事物的長篇論文或演說。

dis·ser·vice /dɪs'sɜ:vɪs ; dɪs'sɝvɪs/ *n* [U, C] ***(a) ~ (to),*** harmful or unhelpful action: 有害的行動;損害: *to do sb a ~.* 損害某人。 *The spreading of such ideas is of great ~* (= is very harmful) *to the State.* 散播這種思想對國家極爲有害。

dis·sever /dɪ'sevə(r) ; dɪ'sɛvɚ/ *vt* [VP6A] sever. 切斷;割開。

dis·si·dent /'dɪsɪdənt ; 'dɪsədənt/ *adj* disagreeing. 意見不同的。 □ *n* person who disagrees; dissenter. 不同意者;意見不同者。 **dis·si·dence** /-dəns ; -dəns/ *n* [U] disagreement. 意見不同;持異議。

dis·simi·lar /dɪ'sɪmɪlə(r) ; dɪ'sɪmələ/ *adj* ~ ***(from/to),*** not the same; not similar: (與…)不相同的;不相似的: *people with ~ tastes.* 嗜好不同的人們。 **~·ity** /,dɪsɪmɪ'lærətɪ ; dɪ,sɪmə'lærətɪ/ *n* [U] lack of similarity; [C] (*pl* -ties) point of difference. 不相似; 不同之點。 **dis·sim·ili·tude** /,dɪsɪ'mɪlɪtju:d *US:* -tu:d ; ,dɪssɪ'mɪlə,tjud/ *n* ~ity; unlikeness. 不相同;不相似。

dis·simu·late /dɪ'sɪmjʊleɪt ; dɪ'sɪmjə,let/ *vt, vi* [VP6A, 2A] (formal) dissemble. (正式用語)以言語或行動掩飾。 **dis·simu·la·tion** /dɪ,sɪmjʊ'leɪʃn ; dɪ,sɪmjə'leʃən/ *n*

dis·si·pate /'dɪsɪpeɪt ; 'dɪsə,pet/ *vt, vi* **1** [VP6A, 2A] (cause to) disperse, go away: 驅散;消失: *to ~ fear/doubt/ignorance.* 消除恐懼(懷疑,愚昧)。 **2** [VP6A] waste (time, money) foolishly: 浪費(時間,金錢): *He soon ~d his fortune.* 他不久便將他的財產蕩盡了。 *Don't ~ your efforts.* 不要浪費你的精力。 **dis·si·pated** *part adj* given up to foolish and often harmful pleasures: 放蕩的; 閒遊浪蕩的: *to lead a ~d life;* 過放蕩的生活; *to fall into ~d ways.* 耽於閒遊浪蕩。

dis·si·pa·tion /,dɪsɪ'peɪʃn ; ,dɪsə'peʃən/ *n* [U] dissipating or being dissipated: 驅散;消散;浪費;放蕩: *a life of ~;* 放蕩的生活; *unwise ~ of one's energy.* 不智的浪費精力。

dis·so·ci·ate /dɪ'səʊʃɪeɪt ; dɪ'soʃɪ,et/ *vt* [VP6A, 14] ~ ***(from),*** separate (in thought, feeling); not associate with: (在思想,情感上)與…分離;與…無關係: *It is difficult to ~ the man from his position,* to think of the man without also thinking of his work and duties. 將一個人和他的職位分開來是困難的(想到某人便聯想到他的工作和職務)。 *A politician's public and private life should be ~d.* 從政者的公私生活應分開。 *I wish to ~ myself from what has just been said.* 我眞希望自己與剛才所說的話毫無關係。 **dis·so·cia·tion** /dɪ,səʊsɪ'eɪʃn ; dɪ,sosɪ'eʃən/ *n* [U] dissociating or being ~d: (思想,情感上的)分離;無關係。 *dissociation of ideas,* keeping them distinct. 將各種觀念分開。

dis·sol·uble /dɪ'sɒljʊbl ; dɪ'sɑljəbḷ/ *adj* that can be dissolved or disintegrated; (of non-material things) that can be annulled: 可溶解的;可解散的;(指無形物)可作廢的;可取消的: *Is marriage ~?* 婚姻是可以解除的嗎? **dis·solu·bil·ity** /dɪ,sɒljʊ'bɪlətɪ ; dɪ,sɑljə'bɪlətɪ/ *n*

dis·so·lute /'dɪsəlu:t *US:* -lu:t ; 'dɪsə,lut/ *adj* (of persons) given up to immoral conduct; (of behaviour, etc) evil; vicious: (指人)荒淫的;(指行爲等)邪惡的;放蕩的;不道德的: *to lead a ~ life;* 過荒淫的生活; *~ conduct.* 邪惡的行爲。 **~·ly** *adv*

dis·sol·ution /,dɪsə'lu:ʃn ; ,dɪsə'luʃən/ *n* [C, U] ~ ***(of),*** breaking up; undoing or ending (of a marriage, partnership, etc); (esp) ending of Parliament before a general election. 分解;解除(婚約,合夥關係等);(尤指)普選前國會之解散。

dis·solve /dɪ'zɒlv ; dɪ'zɑlv/ *vt, vi* **1** [VP6A] (of a liquid) soak into a solid so that the solid itself becomes liquid: (指液體)溶解: *Water ~s salt.* 水溶解鹽。 **2** [VP2A, 3A] ~ ***(in),*** (of a solid) become liquid as the result of being taken into a liquid: (指固體在液體中)溶解: *Salt ~s in water.* 鹽在水中溶解。 **3** [VP6A, 14] ~ ***(in),*** cause (a solid) to ~: 使(固體)溶解: *He ~d the salt in water.* 他使鹽在水中溶解。 **4** [VP2A, C] disappear; fade away: 消失;消散: *The view ~d in mist.* 那景色在霧中消失了。 **5** [VP6A, 2A] bring to, come to, an end: 結束: *to ~ a business partnership/a marriage/Parliament.* 結束商業上的合夥關係(解除婚約; 解散國會)。 *Parliament ~d.* 國會解散了。

dis·son·ance /'dɪsənəns ; 'dɪsənəns/ *n* [U] discord; [C] combination of notes that is discordant. 不和諧;不和諧的音調;不協和音。

dis·son·ant /'dɪsənənt ; 'dɪsənənt/ *adj* not harmonious; harsh in tone. 不和諧的;刺耳的。

dis·suade /dɪ'sweɪd ; dɪ'swed/ *vt* [VP6A, 14] ~ ***sb (from sth/from doing sth),*** advise against; (try to) turn (sb) away: 勸阻;勸戒(某人): *to ~ a friend from marrying.* 勸阻友人結婚。 **dis·sua·sion** /dɪ'sweɪʒn ; dɪ'sweʒən/ *n* [U].

dis·taff /'dɪstɑ:f *US:* -tæf ; 'dɪstæf/ *n* stick round which wool, flax, etc, is wound for spinning by hand. (手紡用的)纏線桿。 ***on the '~ side,*** on the mother's side of the family. 屬於母系的。

dis·tance /'dɪstəns ; 'dɪstəns/ *n* [C, U] **1** measure of space, between two points, places, etc; being far off: 距離;遠: *In the USA ~ is measured in miles, not in kilometres.* 在美國測量距離用英里,不用公里。 *The house stands on a hill and can be seen from a ~ of two miles,* from two miles away. 那房子在山頂上,從二哩外可以看到。 *The town is a great ~ off,* a long way off. 那城市很遙遠。 *My house is within easy walking ~ of the shops,* near enough for me to walk to them easily. 我家離商店很近,走幾步就到了。 ***at a ~,*** not too near. 不太近;在遠處。 ***in the ~,*** far away. 在遠處。 ***keep sb at a ~,*** refuse to let him become familiar; treat him with reserve. 不與某人親近;對某人保持相當距離。 ***keep one's ~,*** (fig) not be too friendly or familiar. (喻)不與親近。 ***no ~,*** near. 在近處。 ***some ~,*** fairly far away. 相當遠。 **long-~** *adj* **(a)** (of races, journeys, etc) covering an extensive length, area, etc: (指競賽、旅行等)長距離的: *long-~ runners.* 長距離的賽跑者。 **(b)** (of telephone calls) to/from a distant place. (指電話)長途的。 **middle-~** *adj* (of races, etc) covering a medium-size length or area. (指競賽等)中距離的。 **the middle-~** *n* that part of a view between the foreground and the background. 中景(前景與背景間)。 **2** space of time: 時間的距離: *to look back over a ~ of fifty years;* 回顧過去五十年的時間; *at this ~ of time.* 在如此長久的時間。□ *vt* [VP6A, 14] ~ ***(from),*** place or keep at a ~. 使遠離;不與…接近。

dis·tant /ˈdɪstənt ; ˈdɪstənt/ *adj* **1** ~ ***(from),*** far away in space or time: 遠離的;遠隔的;遙遠的: *The school is three miles ~ from the station.* 這學校距車站三哩。 *We had a ~ view of Mt Everest.* 我們遠眺埃佛勒斯峯。 **2** far off in family relationship: 親屬關係遠的;遠房的: *She is a ~ cousin of mine.* 她是我的一位遠房表妹。 **3** (of degree of similarity) not easily seen: (指相似程度)不易見的: *There is a ~ resemblance between the cousins.* 這兩位堂兄弟隱約相像。 **4** reserved; not showing familiarity: 冷淡的;不表示親近的: *Instead of stopping to speak, she passed by with only a ~ nod.* 她沒有停下來談話,祇冷淡的點一下頭走了過去。 **~·ly** *adv* in a ~ manner: 遠離地;遙遠地;遠房地;不易見地;冷淡地: *He is ~ly related to me.* 他是我的遠親。

dis·taste /dɪsˈteɪst ; dɪsˈtest/ *n* [U, C] ***(a) ~ (for),*** dislike; aversion: 厭惡;憎厭: *a ~ for hard work.* 討厭辛苦的工作。 *He turned away in ~.* 他厭惡地走開了。 **~·ful** /-fl ; -fəl/ *adj* ***~ful (to),*** disagreeable; unpleasant: 討厭的;令人不愉快的: *It is ~ful to me to have to say this, but....* 我必須這樣說使我很不愉快,但是…。 **~·fully** /-fəlɪ ; -fəlɪ/ *adv* **~·ful·ness** /-fəlnɪs ; -fəlnɪs/ *n*

dis·temper[1] /dɪˈstempə(r) ; dɪsˈtɛmpɚ/ *n* [U] (method of painting with) colouring matter (to be) mixed with water and brushed on walls and ceilings. 色膠(與水混合,用以塗刷牆壁和天花板的一種顏料);用色膠作畫的方法。□ *vt* [VP6A, 22] colour with ~: 用色膠粉刷: *We ~ed the walls green.* 我們用色膠將牆壁粉刷成綠色。

dis·temper[2] /dɪˈstempə(r) ; dɪsˈtɛmpɚ/ *n* [U] disease of dogs and some other animals, with coughing and weakness. 犬瘟熱(狗和某些其他動物所患的一種瘟熱病,有咳嗽及虛弱的現象)。

dis·tend /dɪˈstend ; dɪˈstɛnd/ *vt, vi* [VP6A, 2A] (cause to) swell out (by pressure from within): (使)擴張; (使)膨脹(由內部壓力所致): *a ~ed stomach/vein.* 擴張的胃(靜脈)。 **dis·ten·sion** (US = **-tion**) /dɪˈstenʃn ; dɪˈstɛnʃən/ *n* ~ing or being ~ed. 擴張;膨脹。

dis·til (US = **-till**) /dɪˈstɪl ; dɪˈstɪl/ *vt, vi* (-ll-) **1** [VP6A, 15B, 14] ~ ***sth (from sth); ~ sth off/out,*** change (a liquid) to vapour by heating, cool the vapour and collect the drops of liquid that condense from the vapour; purify (a liquid) thus; drive *out* or *off* impurities thus; make (whisky, essences) thus: 蒸餾(液體);用蒸餾法淨化(液體);用蒸餾法除去不純之物(與 out 或 off 連用);用蒸餾法製造(威士忌酒,香精等): *Salt water can be ~led and made into drinking water.* 鹹水可被蒸餾成爲飲用的水。 **2** [VP6A, 2A] fall, let fall, in drops: 滴下;使滴下: *flowers that ~ nectar.* 滴出花蜜的花。 **dis·til·la·tion** /ˌdɪstɪˈleɪʃn ; ˌdɪstḷˈeʃən/ *n* **1** [U] ~ling or being ~led: 蒸餾;由蒸餾法淨化或製造: *the ~lation of malted barley* (to make whisky). 蒸餾發芽的大麥(以製威士忌酒)。 **2** [C, U] substance obtained by ~ling. 蒸餾物。

dis·til·ler /dɪˈstɪlə(r) ; dɪˈstɪlɚ/ *n* person who distils (esp whisky). 蒸餾者(尤指以蒸餾法製造威士忌酒者)。 **dis·til·lery** /-lərɪ ; -lərɪ/ *n* (*pl* -ries) place where liquids (eg gin, whisky) are distilled. 蒸餾所;造酒廠。

dis·tinct /dɪˈstɪŋkt ; dɪˈstɪŋkt/ *adj* **1** easily heard, seen, understood; plain; clearly marked: 清楚的;明白的;明晰的;明顯的: *a ~ pronunciation.* 清晰的發音。 *The earth's shadow on the moon was quite ~.* 月球上的地球陰影是十分清晰的。 *There is a ~ improvement in her typing.* 她的打字有顯著的進步。 **2** ~ ***(from),*** different in kind; separate: 種類不同的;分開的: *Keep the two ideas ~, the one from the other.* 將這兩個觀念彼此分別清楚。 *Hares and rabbits are ~ animals.* 野兎和家兎是不同的動物。 **~·ly** *adv* in a ~ manner: 清楚地;清晰地;不同地: *to speak/remember ~ly.* 說話(記得)清楚。 **~·ness** *n*

dis·tinc·tion /dɪˈstɪŋkʃn ; dɪˈstɪŋkʃən/ *n* **1** [U] being, keeping things, different or distinct(2); distinguishing, being distinguished, as different; [C] instance of this: 種類不同;分別;區別: *The President shook hands with everyone, without ~ of rank.* 總統與每個人握手,不分階級。 *The ~s of birth* (= The different classes of society into which people are born) *are less important than they used to be.* 出身貴賤之分在今日不像往時那樣重要了。 *It is difficult to make exact ~s between all the meanings of a word.* 對一字的各種意義詳加區別是困難的。 ***a ~ without a difference,*** no real difference at all. 無差異的區別(假的區別)。 **2** [C] point of difference; that which makes one thing different from another: 不同之點;差別之處: *the ~ between poetry and prose.* 詩與散文之不同處。 **3** [U] quality of being superior, excellent, distinguished: 優越;卓越;非凡: *a writer/novel of ~.* 卓越的作家(小說)。 **4** [C] mark of honour; title; decoration; reward: 榮譽;榮銜;殊勳;獎賞: *academic ~s,* eg a doctor's degree; 學術上的榮譽(例如博士學位); *to win ~s for bravery.* 因英勇而獲殊勳。

dis·tinc·tive /dɪˈstɪŋktɪv ; dɪˈstɪŋktɪv/ *adj* serving to mark a difference or make distinct: 表示有別的;區別的;有特色的: *Soldiers wear a ~ uniform.* 軍人穿特殊的制服。 **~·ly** *adv*

dis·tin·guish /dɪˈstɪŋgwɪʃ ; dɪˈstɪŋgwɪʃ/ *vt, vi* **1** [VP14, 3A] ~ ***one thing from another; ~ between two things,*** see, hear, recognize, understand well, the difference: 辨別;區別: *People who cannot ~ between colours are said to be colour-blind.* 不能辨別顏色的人謂之色盲。 *The twins were so much alike that it was impossible to ~ (the) one from the other.* 這對孿生子像得使人無法分辨。 *It is not easy to ~ cultured pearls from genuine pearls.* 辨別眞珍珠與養珠不易。 **2** [VP6A] make out by looking, listening, etc: 辨識;認明: *A person with good eyesight can ~ distant objects.* 眼力好的人能看清遠處的物體。 **3** [VP14] ~ ***from,*** be a mark of character, difference: 作爲…的特性;使別於: *speech ~es man from the animals.* 言語使人與動物有別。 *What ~es the hare from the rabbit?* 野兎與家兎有何不同? **4** [VP6A] ~ ***oneself,*** behave so as to bring credit to oneself: 顯揚自己;使自己揚名: *to ~ oneself in an examination.* 考試成績出衆。 *He ~ed himself by his courage.* 他因英勇而揚名。 **~·able** /-əbl ; -əbḷ/ *adj* ***~able (from),*** able to be ~ed from sb/sth else: 可辨別的;可區別的: *Tom is hardly ~able from his twin brother.* 湯姆與他的孿生哥哥(弟弟)幾乎令人分辨不出。 *The coast was hardly ~able* (= could hardly be seen) *through the haze.* 從薄霧中幾乎無法看清海岸。 **~ed** *adj* famous; well known; remarkable; showing distinction(3): 著名的;卓越的;非凡的: *He is ~ed for his knowledge of economics/~ed as an economist.* 他在經濟學方面的知識是卓越的 (他是一位著名的經濟學家)。 *He has had a ~ed career in the diplomatic service.* 他在外交界具有不尋常的經歷。

dis·tort /dɪˈstɔːt ; dɪsˈtɔrt/ *vt* [VP6A] **1** pull, twist, out of the usual shape: 使變形;扭曲: *a face ~ed* *by pain.* 因痛苦而扭曲的面孔。*A curved mirror ~s the features.* 彎曲的鏡面使容貌變形。**2** give a false account of; twist out of the truth: 歪曲;曲解: *Newspaper accounts of international affairs are sometimes ~ed.* 報紙對國際事件的刊載有時是歪曲事實的。*You have ~ed my motives.* 你曲解了我的動機。**dis·tor·tion** /dɪˈstɔːʃn ; dɪsˈtɔrʃən/ *n* [U] ~ing or being ~ed; [C] instance of this; sth that is ~ed. 變形;扭曲;歪曲;曲解;被扭曲或曲解的事物。

dis·tract /dɪˈstrækt ; dɪˈstrækt/ *vt* [VP6A, 14] ~ ***from,*** draw away sb's attention from sth: 轉移注意力;使分心: *The noise in the street ~ed me from my reading.* 街上的嘈雜聲使我不能專心讀書。*What can we do to ~ her mind from the sorrow caused by her child's death?* 我們怎樣減輕她喪子的痛苦呢? **~ed** *adj* ***~ed (with/by),*** with the mind confused or bewildered: 心情紛亂的;困擾的;迷惑的: *to be ~ed with/by anxiety/grief.* 爲憂慮(悲傷)所煩擾。**~·ed·ly** *adv* in a ~ed manner. 心情紛亂地;困擾地;迷惑地。

dis·trac·tion /dɪˈstrækʃn ; dɪˈstrækʃən/ *n* **1** [U] distracting or being distracted. 轉移注意力;分心。**2** [C] sth that distracts, sth annoying and unwelcome: 分心的事物;使人煩擾的事物: *Noise is a ~ when you are trying to study.* 在你要讀書時,嘈雜聲是分散心神的。**3** [C] sth that holds the attention and gives pleasure: 吸引心神而令人快樂的事物;娛樂;消遣: *He complained that there were not enough ~s in the small village.* 他抱怨說在那小村子裏沒有足够的娛樂。*There are plenty of ~s* (= interesting and amusing things to see and do) *in a large city.* 大城市裏有許多有趣的事物。**4** [U] wildness or confusion of mind. 發狂;精神錯亂。***to ~***: *He loves her to ~,* loves her wildly, passionately. 他愛她愛得發狂。*You will drive me to ~ with your silly questions.* 你的傻問題將使我發狂。

dis·train /dɪˈstreɪn ; dɪˈstren/ *vi* [VP2A, 3A] ~ ***(upon),*** (legal) seize goods to compel a person to pay money due (esp rent): (法律)扣押物品强使一人付清到期的款項(尤指租金): *to ~ upon a person's furniture for rent.* 扣押一人的傢具以抵償租金。**dis·traint** *n* ~ing. (法律)扣押物品。

dis·trait /dɪˈstreɪ ; dɪˈstre/ *adj* (F) absent-minded; not paying attention. (法)心不在焉的;不注意的。

dis·traught /dɪˈstrɔːt ; dɪˈstrɔt/ *adj* distracted; violently upset in mind: 心情紛亂的;狂亂的: *~ with grief.* 悲痛得發狂。

dis·tress¹ /dɪˈstres ; dɪˈstrɛs/ *n* [U] **1** (cause of) great pain, discomfort or sorrow; (suffering caused by) want of money or other necessary things: 痛苦;痛苦的原因;窮困;貧苦: *At the end of the Marathon race several runners showed signs of ~.* 當馬拉松賽跑結束時,幾位參加賽跑的人顯示出痛苦的跡象。*His wild behaviour was a great ~ to his mother.* 他的放蕩的行爲使他的母親極爲苦惱。*He spent his fortune in relieving ~ among the poor.* 他以財產解除窮人的困苦。**2** serious danger or difficulty: 嚴重的危機或困難: *The lifeboat went out to a ship in ~.* 救生船去救一艘遇險的船隻。*The ship was flying a ~ signal.* 這船懸起遇險的信號。

dis·tress² /dɪˈstres ; dɪˈstrɛs/ *vt* [VP6A] cause distress(1) to: 使痛苦;使苦惱;使貧苦: *I am much ~ed to hear the news of your wife's death.* 聽到你妻子去世的消息我很難過。*What are you looking so ~ed about?* 什麼事情使你看來如此苦惱? *Don't ~ yourself,* Don't get worried. 不要擔憂。**ˌ~ed ˈarea,** part of a country where there is serious and continued unemployment. 一國之貧苦地區。**~·ful** /-fʊl ; -fəl/, **~·ing** *adjj* causing or experiencing ~. 使人痛苦的;苦惱的。**~·fully** /-fəlɪ ; -fəlɪ/, **~·ing·ly** *advv* in a manner that causes distress. 使人痛苦地;使人苦惱地。

dis·trib·ute /dɪˈstrɪbjuːt ; dɪˈstrɪbjʊt/ *vt* [VP6A, 14] ***~ (to/among),*** **1** put (parts of a set of things) in different places; give or send out: 分配;分給;分送;散置: *The firm ~d its profits among its workers.* 該公司將利潤分給工人。*The man had thirty parcels to be ~d at houses all over the town.* 這人有三十個包裹要分送全鎮各家。**2** spread out (over a larger area): 散佈(於廣大地區);分佈: *to ~ manure over a field.* 施肥於田地。**3** put into groups or classes. 分類;區分。**dis·tribu·tor** /-tə(r) ; -tɚ/ *n* person or thing that ~s. 分配者;分配機;散佈者;散佈機;分佈器。

dis·tri·bu·tion /ˌdɪstrɪˈbjuːʃn ; ˌdɪstrəˈbjuʃən/ *n* [U] distributing or being distributed; manner of being distributed; [C] instance or occasion of distributing: 分配;分佈;被分配或分佈的狀態;分配或分佈的實例: *They could not agree about the ~ of the profits.* 他們對於利潤的分配意見不一致。*Is the ~ of wealth uneven in your country?* 在你們的國家內財富分配得不均嗎? *The pine-tree has a very wide ~,* is found in many parts of the world. 松樹的分佈甚廣(見於世界許多地方)。

dis·tribu·tive /dɪˈstrɪbjʊtɪv ; dɪˈstrɪbjətɪv/ *adj* **1** of distribution: 分配的;分佈的: *the ~ trades,* eg railways, shop-keeping. 運銷業(例如鐵路,開店)。**2** (gram) referring to each individual, each member of a class: (文法)個別的: *'Each', 'every', 'either' and 'neither' are ~ pronouns.* Each, every, either 和 neither 是個別代名詞。**~·ly** *adv*

dis·trict /ˈdɪstrɪkt ; ˈdɪstrɪkt/ *n* **1** part of a country: 地區;區域: *a mountainous ~;* 山區; *purely agricultural ~s.* 純粹農業區域。**the Lake D~,** in north-west England. 英格蘭西北部的湖區。**2** part of a town or country marked out for a special purpose: 爲特殊目的而劃出的地區: *the London postal ~s,* eg NW5, EC4. 倫敦的郵政區(例如 NW5, EC4)。⇨ *postcode* at post³(4); *rural and urban ~s,* for purposes of local government. 鄉區和市區(爲地方行政目的所做之劃分)。**~ nurse,** one who visits people in their homes. 區域護士(至家裏訪視或看護病人者)。**the D~ of Columbia,** the city of Washington, the Federal government area of the US. 哥倫比亞特區(美國首都華盛頓的行政區,屬聯邦政府)。

dis·trust /dɪsˈtrʌst ; dɪsˈtrʌst/ *n* [U, C] ***(a) ~ (of),*** doubt or suspicion; want of trust or confidence: 懷疑;疑惑;不信任;不相信: *The child looked at the big stranger with ~.* 那小孩懷疑地望着那個高大的陌生人。*He has a ~ of foreigners.* 他不信任外國人。□ *vt* [VP6A] have no trust in; be doubtful about: 不信任;猜疑: *He would ~ his own friends.* 他不信任他自己的朋友。*He ~ed his own eyes.* 他不信任他自己的眼睛。**~·ful** /-fʊl ; -fəl/ *adj* unwilling to trust; suspicious: 不信任的;猜疑的: *I was ~ful of his motives.* 我懷疑他的動機。**~·fully** /-fəlɪ ; -fəlɪ/ *adv* **~·ful·ness** *n*

dis·turb /dɪˈstɜːb ; dɪˈstɝb/ *vt* [VP6A] break the quiet, calm, peace or order of; put out of the right or usual position; upset: 擾亂;驚動;攪亂;使騷動;使紊亂;使不安: *He put his oars in the water and ~ed the smooth surface of the lake.* 他把槳放入水中,攪亂了平靜的湖面。*She opened the door quietly so as not to ~ the sleeping child.* 她靜靜地開門以免驚擾了睡着的孩子。*Don't ~ the papers on my desk.* 不要亂動我桌上的文件。*He was ~ed to hear of your illness/was ~ed by the news of your illness.* 他聽到你生病的消息感到不安。***~ the peace,*** (legal) cause disorder, rioting, etc. (法律)擾亂治安。

dis·turb·ance /dɪˈstɜːbəns ; dɪsˈtɝbəns/ *n* [U] disturbing or being disturbed; [C] instance of this; sth that disturbs; disorder (esp social or political): 擾亂;動亂;不安;引起動亂或不安的事物;(尤指社會或政治上的)騷動: *Were there many political ~s in the country last year?* 這個國家去年有很多政治上的騷動嗎?

dis·union /dɪsˈjuːnɪən ; dɪsˈjunjən/ *n* [U] breaking of what unites; lack of union; dissension. 分裂;不統一;紛爭。

dis·unite /ˌdɪsjuːˈnaɪt ; ˌdɪsjʊˈnaɪt/ *vt, vi* [VP6A,

2A] (cause to) become separate. (使)分開;(使)分裂。

dis·unity /dɪsˈjuːnətɪ; dɪsˈjunɪtɪ/ *n* [U] lack of unity; dissension. 不統一;分裂;紛爭。

dis·use /dɪsˈjuːs; dɪsˈjus/ *n* [U] state of no longer being used: 不用: *rusty from ~;* 因不用而生銹; *words that have fallen into ~.* 廢而不用的字。 **~d** /dɪsˈjuːzd; dɪsˈjuzd/ *part adj* no longer used: 不用的: *a ~d well.* 廢井。

di·syl·labic (US = **dis·syl·labic**) /ˌdɪsɪˈlæbɪk; ˌdɪsɪˈlæbɪk/ *adj* of two syllables. 雙音節的。**di·syl·lable** (US = **dis·syl·lable**), /dɪˈsɪləbl; dɪˈsɪləbl/ *n* ~ word or metrical foot. 雙音節的字或音步。

ditch /dɪtʃ; dɪtʃ/ *n* narrow channel dug in or between fields, or at the sides of a road, etc to hold or carry off water. (田裡或路邊等用以儲水或排水的)溝。 ***dull as ˈ~ water,*** very dull(3) indeed. 極其乏味的。➪ die²(2). □ *vt, vi* **1** [VP6A, 2A] make, clean, repair or provide with ~es. 掘溝;清理溝;修溝;爲…開溝。 **2** [VP6A] send or throw into a ~ (or, sl, the sea); (fig, sl) abandon: 使墜入溝;丟入溝中; (俚)使墜入海; (喻,俚)拋棄: *The drunken man ~ed his car,* drove it into one. 那醉漢將車駛入溝中。*The pilot had to ~ his plane,* make a forced landing on the sea. 那飛行員被迫將飛機降落海上。*He's ~ed his girlfriend,* (sl) suddenly stopped seeing her. (俚)他突然拋棄了他的女友。

dither /ˈdɪðə(r); ˈdɪðɚ/ *vi* [VP2A, C] (old use) tremble; (colloq) hesitate about what to do; be unable to decide. (舊用法)顫抖;(俗)躊躇;猶豫。□ *n* trembling: 顫抖: *be all of/in a ~;* 渾身發抖; *have the ~s;* 發抖; (colloq) nervous, uncertain, indecisive state: (俗)緊張不安;猶豫不決: *be all of a ~;* 神經緊張; *have the ~s.* 緊張不安。

ditto /ˈdɪtəʊ; ˈdɪto/ *n* (abbr 略作 **d°, do**) the same thing (used in lists to avoid writing a word or words again): 同上(用於表格中以避免重複前面的字): *One hat at £2·25; ~ at £4·50.* 一頂帽 2·25 鎊;一頂帽 4·50 鎊。***say ~ to,*** (colloq) say the same thing as; agree with. (俗)說與…相同的話;同意…。

ditty /ˈdɪtɪ; ˈdɪtɪ/ *n* (*pl* -ties) short, simple song. 小曲;小調。

di·ur·nal /daɪˈɜːnl; daɪˈɝnl/ *adj* (formal) of the daytime; (astron) occupying one day. (正式用語)晝間的;(天文)一日的;周日的。

di·va·gate /ˈdaɪvəgeɪt; ˈdaɪvəˌget/ *vi* [VP2A, 3A] ~ ***(from),*** (formal) stray; wander from the point. (正式用語)入歧途;離題。**di·va·ga·tion** /ˌdaɪvəˈgeɪʃn; ˌdaɪvəˈgeʃən/ *n*

di·van /dɪˈvæn *US:* ˈdaɪvæn; ˈdaɪvæn/ *n* **1** long, low, soft, backless seat. 無靠背的長沙發椅。**ˈ~-bed** such a seat that can be converted into a bed. 可變爲床鋪的無靠背的長沙發椅。 **2** (in Muslim countries) public audience room; State council or council room. (回教國家)會議室;國務會議或會議室。

dive¹ /daɪv; daɪv/ *n* **1** the act of diving: 跳水;潛水: *a graceful ~.* 優美的跳水。 **2** (colloq) disreputable place for the sale of drink, or for gambling. (俗)下流的飲酒或賭博場所。

dive² /daɪv; daɪv/ *vi* (US alternative *pt* 美國用法之過去式亦作 dove /dəʊv; dov/) [VP2A, C] ~ ***(off/from/into),*** **1** go head first into water: 跳水: *He ~d from the bridge and rescued the drowning child.* 他從橋上跳到水中,救起那快要溺死的小孩。 **2** (of a submarine) go under water; (of divers) go under water in a special dress: (指潛艇)潛水;(指潛水者)着特種服裝潛水: *to ~ for pearls.* 潛水取珍珠。**ˈdiving-bell,** open-bottomed apparatus which can be lowered into water, supplied with air pumped through pipes, and used by underwater workers. 潛水鐘(底部敞開的一種潛水裝置,藉氣管供給空氣,可供水下工作人員使用)。**ˈdiving-board,** flexible board from which to ~ (eg into a swimming pool). 跳水踏板(如游泳池中所設者)。**ˈdiving-dress/-suit,** suit with weighted boots and an air-tight helmet into which air is pumped through tubes, used by divers. 潛水衣(一種附有重靴與不透氣頭盔的衣服,藉管將空氣通入盔內,供潛水者用)。 **3** go quickly to a lower level; move sth (eg the hand) quickly and suddenly downwards (into sth): 迅速向下去;(手等)突然向下插入: *The aircraft ~d steeply.* 那架飛機垂直俯衝。*The rabbit ~d into its hole.* 那兔子突然鑽入牠的洞內。*He ~d into his pocket and pulled out a handful of coins.* 他突然把手伸入口袋,掏出來一把錢幣。**ˈ~-bomb** *vt, vi* (of an aircraft, **a ˈ~-bomber**) drop bombs at the end of a steep dive. (指飛機,俯衝轟炸機)俯衝轟炸。**diver** *n* person who ~s, esp a person who works under water in a diving-suit. 跳水者;(尤指)潛水員(着潛水衣在水下工作者)。

di·verge /daɪˈvɜːdʒ; dəˈvɝdʒ/ *vi* [VP2A, 3A] ~ ***(from),*** (of lines, paths, opinions, etc) get farther apart from a point or from each other as they progress; turn or branch away from. (指線條,道路,意見等) 分歧; 離題; 逸出。**di·ver·gence** /-dʒəns; -dʒəns/, **-gency** /-dʒənsɪ; -dʒənsɪ/ *n* [U] diverging; [C] (*pl* -ces, -cies) instance of this: 分歧;離題;逸出: *divergencies from the normal.* 脫離正軌。**di·ver·gent** /-dʒənt; -dʒənt/ *adj*

di·vers /ˈdaɪvɜːz; ˈdaɪvɚz/ *adj* (old use) several; more than one. (舊用法)若干的;數個的。

di·verse /daɪˈvɜːs; dəˈvɝs/ *adj* of different kinds: 種類不同的: *The wild life in Africa is extremely ~.* 非洲野生動物的種類十分不同。**~·ly** *adv*

di·ver·sify /daɪˈvɜːsɪfaɪ; dəˈvɝsəˌfaɪ/ *vt* [VP6A] make diverse; give variety to: 使不同;使變化: *a landscape diversified by hills and woods.* 由於山林穿插而變化有致的景色。**di·ver·si·fi·ca·tion** /daɪˌvɜːsɪfɪˈkeɪʃn; dəˌvɝsəfəˈkeʃən/ *n*

di·ver·sion /daɪˈvɜːʃn *US:* -ʒn; dəˈvɝʒən/ *n* **1** [U] diverting; the act of turning sth aside or giving it a different direction: 轉向;改道: *the ~ of a stream;* 河流的改道; [C] instance of this: 轉向或改道的實例: *traffic ~s,* eg when traffic is directed by different routes because of road repairs. 交通改道(例如因修補馬路所致)。 **2** [C] sth which turns the attention from serious things; sth giving rest or amusement: 消遣;娛樂: *Chess and billiards are his favourite ~s.* 西洋棋和撞球是他最喜愛的消遣。 **3** [C] method used to turn the attention from sth that one does not wish to be noticed, as when, in war, the enemy's attention is drawn from one place by an unexpected attack at another place: 一種分散注意力的方法(例如在作戰時突襲乙地而轉移敵人對甲地之注意力);牽制(轉移);聲東擊西: *to create/make a ~.* 分散其注意力;聲東擊西。 **~ary** /daɪˈvɜːʃənərɪ *US:* -ˈʒənerɪ; dəˈvɝʒənˌɛrɪ/ *adj*: *a ~ary raid.* 牽制性的突襲。**~·ist** *n* person who engages in disruptive or subversive activities. 從事破壞活動者。

di·ver·sity /daɪˈvɜːsətɪ; dəˈvɝsətɪ/ *n* [U] the state of being diverse; variety. 異樣;不同;各式各樣。

di·vert /daɪˈvɜːt; dəˈvɝt/ *vt* [VP6A, 14] ~ ***(from),*** **1** turn in another direction: 使轉向;使改道: *to ~ the course of a river;* 使河改道; *to ~ a river from its course;* 使河改道; *to ~ water from a river into the fields.* 將河水導入田間。 **2** amuse; entertain; turn the attention away: 娛樂;消遣;使轉變注意力: *Some people are easily ~ed.* 有些人的注意力容易轉變。*How can we ~ her thoughts from her sad loss?* 我們如何使她不再想她的可悲的損失? **~·ing** *adj* amusing. 有趣的。**~·ing·ly** *adv*

Dives /ˈdaɪviːz; ˈdaɪviz/ *n* (typical name for a) rich man. 富翁;財主(代表有錢人的名稱)。➪ Luke 16: 19. 參看路加福音 16 章 19 節。

di·vest /daɪˈvest; dəˈvɛst/ *vt* [VP14] ~ ***sb of,*** **1** (formal) take off (clothes): (正式用語)脫去(衣服): *to ~ a king of his robes.* 脫去國王的王袍。 **2** take away from: 剝奪: *to ~ an official of power and authority.* 剝奪一官員的權柄。 **3** (reflex) get rid of; give up: (反身)去除; 放棄: *I cannot ~ myself of the idea,* It comes back to my mind.

我無法摒除這個念頭。

di·vide[1] /dɪˈvaɪd ; dəˈvaɪd/ *vt, vi* **1** [VP6A, 15B, 14, 2A, C] ***~ sth (up/out); ~ sth between/among sb; ~ sth from sth,*** separate; split or break up: 分開;劃分;分割: *We ~d (up/out) the money equally.* 我們將錢均分。*They ~d the money between/among themselves.* 他們分那筆錢。*The river ~s my land from his.* 這條河將我的地和他的地隔開。*The Nile ~s near its mouth and forms a delta.* 尼羅河於近河口處分岔,形成一三角洲。*He ~s his time between London and Cairo.* 他分配他在倫敦和開羅的時間。*How shall we ~ the work up/~ up the work?* 我們怎樣劃分這工作? **2** [VP14] ***~ into; ~ by,*** find out how often one number is contained in another: 除: *If you ~ 6 into 30/~ 30 by 6, the answer is 5.* 你如以6除30,答案爲5。(With passive force): (含被動意味): *12 ~s by 3,* can be ~d by 3. 12可被3除盡。 **3** [VP14] ***~ into,*** form into smaller parts: 分成若干較小部分: *The house was divided into flats.* 那房屋被隔成數套房間(公寓)。 **4** [VP6A] cause disagreement; cause to disagree: 使不和;使意見不合: *Please don't let such a small matter ~ us.* 請不要讓這小事使我們失和。*Opinions are ~d on the question,* There are opposed opinions. 對於這問題,意見不一致。 **5** [VP2A, 6A] (in Parliament, at debates, etc) part in order to vote; cause to part for this purpose: (在議會,辯論時等)分組以做正反之表決;使分組以做正反之表決: *After a long debate, the House ~d,* voted on the question. 經長時間辯論後,議院將該問題付諸表決。*The Opposition does not propose to ~ the House on this question,* does not insist upon the taking of a vote. 反對黨不主張議院表決這一問題。

di·vide[2] /dɪˈvaɪd ; dəˈvaɪd/ *n* sth that divides, esp a watershed (a line of high land that separates two different river systems). 使分開之物;(尤指)分水界(將兩條河分開的高地);分水嶺;分水線。

divi·dend /ˈdɪvɪdend ; ˈdɪvəˌdɛnd/ *n* **1** (maths) number to be divided by another. (數學)被除數。⇨ divisor **2** (comm) (usu periodical) payment of a share of profit, to shareholders in a business company, or of assets to creditors (eg of an insolvent company), or to a policy holder in a mutual insurance company: (商)(通常爲定期的)股息;紅利;破產債權人之償金: *to pay a ~ of 10 per cent.* 付一成股息。**ˈ~-warrant,** order on a bank to pay a ~. 股息支付券;股息單。

di·vid·ers /dɪˈvaɪdəz ; dəˈvaɪdəːz/ *n pl* ***(pair of) ~,*** pair of measuring compasses, used for dividing lines or angles, measuring or marking distances, etc. 兩脚規;分線規。

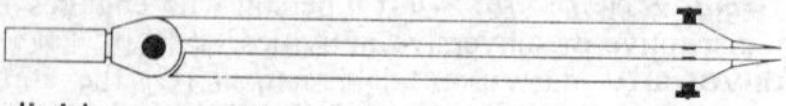

dividers

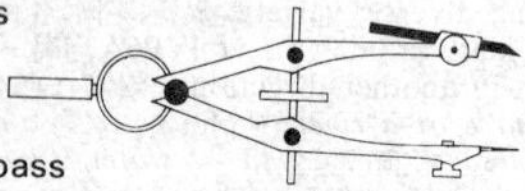

a compass

div·i·na·tion /ˌdɪvɪˈneɪʃn ; ˌdɪvəˈneʃən/ *n* [U] divining, ⇨ divine[3]; discovery of the unknown or the future by supernatural means; [C] clever guess or forecast. 占卜;(藉超自然的方法)發現或預知;巧妙的猜想或預測。

di·vine[1] /dɪˈvaɪn ; dəˈvaɪn/ *adj* **1** of, from, or like God or a god: 神的;神發出的;如神的: *King Charles I claimed to rule by ~ right,* right given to him by God. 查理王一世認爲他的王權是神授的。**D~ Service,** the public worship of God. 對於上帝之禮拜。 **2** (colloq) excellent; very beautiful: (俗)極好的;很美的: *~ weather;* 極好的天氣; *a ~ hat.* 一頂漂亮的帽子。*She looks ~ in that new dress.* 她穿起那件新衣服美極了。**~·ly** *adv*

di·vine[2] /dɪˈvaɪn ; dəˈvaɪn/ *n* person (usu a priest) learned in theology. 神學家;神學者(通常爲牧師)。

di·vine[3] /dɪˈvaɪn ; dəˈvaɪn/ *vt, vi* [VP6A, 10, 2A] discover or learn (sth) about future events, hidden things, etc by means not based on reason: (藉非根據理智的方法)預測;占卜: *to ~ sb's intentions;* 預測某人的意向; *to ~ what the future has in store.* 預卜未來。

di·viner /dɪˈvaɪnə(r) ; dəˈvaɪnə/ *n* person who divines, esp one who claims to have the power of learning the presence of subterranean water, metal, etc by using a Y-shaped stick or rod (called 稱作 a *diˈvining-rod*). 預測者;(尤指)用一丫形杖探測水源,金屬等者。⇨ dowsing.

di·vin·ity /dɪˈvɪnətɪ ; dəˈvɪnətɪ/ *n* **1** [U] the quality of being divine, ⇨ divine[1]: 神性: *the ~ of Christ;* 基督之神性; [C] (*pl* -ties) divine being. 神。 **2** [U] the study of theology: 神學: *the ~ school at Oxford;* 牛津大學神學院; *a doctor of ~* (abbr 略作 **DD**). 神學博士。

di·vis·ible /dɪˈvɪzəbl ; dəˈvɪzəbl/ *adj* (maths) that can be divided without remainder: (數學)可除盡的: *8 is ~ by 2.* 8可被2除盡。

di·vi·sion /dɪˈvɪʒn ; dəˈvɪʒən/ *n* **1** [U] dividing or being divided: 分開;劃分;除;除法: *the ~ of time into months, weeks and days;* 時間之劃分爲月,週,日; *a simple problem in ~* (eg 50÷5); 簡單的除法(例如50÷5); *the ~ of labour,* sharing work, giving different kinds of work to different people, according to their capabilities. 分工(按能力將各種工作分給不同的人)。 **2** [C] the effect of dividing; one of the parts into which sth is divided: 分開的結果;分成的一部分: *the export ~ of a business company.* 一商業公司的出口部門。*Is that a fair ~ of the money?* 那樣分款公平嗎? **3** [C] line that divides: 分界線: *A hedge forms the ~ between his land and mine.* 一道樹籬形成他的土地和我的土地之間的分界線。*The ~s between the various classes of society are not so sharply marked as they used to be.* 現在社會各階級的區分不如過去那樣顯明了。 **4** [C, U] disagreement; separation in thought, feeling, etc: 不和;思想,情感等分裂: *a nation in ~.* 分裂中的國家。 **5** [C] (army) unit of two or more brigades. (陸軍)師。 **6** [C] (Parliament, etc) separation into two groups for the counting of votes: (議會等)(爲便於計算正反票數而)分爲兩組表決: *The Bill was read for the second time without a ~.* 這議案無須分組卽進入二讀。**ˈ~ bell,** bell rung to warn members (who are outside the House) that there is to be a ~. 分組表決的通知鈴(提醒議院外的議員將舉行分組表決)。

di·vi·sive /dɪˈvaɪsɪv ; dəˈvaɪsɪv/ *adj* creating divisions or differences between people: 造成分裂的;造成不和的: *~ actions/ideas/policies.* 造成分裂的行爲(意見,政策)。**~·ly** *adv* **~·ness** *n.*

div·isor /dɪˈvaɪzə(r) ; dəˈvaɪzə/ *n* (maths) number by which another number is divided. (數學)除數。⇨ dividend(1).

di·vorce[1] /dɪˈvɔːs ; dəˈvɔrs/ *n* ***~ (from),*** **1** [U] legal ending of a marriage so that husband and wife are free to marry again; [C] instance of this: 離婚;離婚的實例: *to sue for a ~;* 請求離婚; *to take/start ~ proceedings;* 提出離婚訴訟; *to obtain a ~ (from...).* 獲准(與…)離婚。 **2** [C] ending of a connection or relationship: 斷絕關係;分裂: *the ~ between religion and science,* as when science claims or seems to show that religious beliefs have no foundation. 宗教與科學間的分裂(如科學主張或似乎表示宗教信仰缺乏根據的時候)。

di·vorce[2] /dɪˈvɔːs ; dəˈvɔrs/ *vt* [VP6A, 14] ***~ (from),*** **1** put an end to a marriage by law: 使離婚: *Did Mr Hill ~ his wife or did she ~ him?* 是希爾先生要和他太太離婚,還是他太太要和他離婚呢? **2** (fig) separate (things usually together): (喻)使(通常在一起的東西)分開: *What happens to the soul when it is ~d from the body?* 靈魂與肉體分開時,靈魂將如

何？**di·vor·cee** /dɪˌvɔːˈsiː; dəˌvɔrˈsi/ *n* ~d person. 離了婚的人。

divot /ˈdɪvət; ˈdɪvət/ *n* piece of turf sliced off by a golf club in making a bad stroke. (擊高爾夫球時,擊出不佳,球棒削起的)一塊草土。

di·vulge /daɪˈvʌldʒ; dəˈvʌldʒ/ *vt* [VP6A, 14] ~ *(to)*, make known (sth secret). 洩露(祕密)。**di·vul·gence** /-dʒəns; -dʒəns/ *n*

divvy /ˈdɪvɪ; ˈdɪvɪ/ *n* (*pl* -vies) (colloq abbr of) dividend(2), eg as formerly paid by a co-operative society. (俗, dividend 之略)股息;紅利。

dixie /ˈdɪksɪ; ˈdɪksɪ/ *n* large iron pot in which tea, stew, etc is made or carried (by soldiers, campers, etc). (士兵,露營者等用以煮茶,燉菜等的)大鐵鍋。

dizzy /ˈdɪzɪ; ˈdɪzɪ/ *adj* (-ier, -iest) **1** (of a person) feeling as if everything were turning round, as if unable to balance; mentally confused. (指人)暈眩的;昏亂的。 **2** (of places, conditions) causing such a feeling: (指地點,情況)使人暈眩的: *a ~ height*. 使人暈眩的高度。 □ *vt* make ~. 使暈眩。 **diz·zily** *adv* **diz·zi·ness** *n*

djinn /dʒɪn; dʒɪn/ *n* = genie.

do[1] /də; də; *strong form* duː; du/ *anom fin* (*1st and 2nd person sing pres t* neg don't /dəʊnt; dont/, *3rd person sing pres t* does /dəz; dəz; *strong form* dʌz; dʌz/, neg doesn't /ˈdʌznt; ˈdʌznt/, *pt* did /dɪd; dɪd/, neg didn't /ˈdɪdnt; ˈdɪdnt/, *pp* done /dʌn; dʌn/) (第一第二人稱、單數、現在式、否定爲 don't, 第三人稱、單數、現在式爲 does, 否定爲 doesn't, 過去式爲did, 否定爲 didn't, 過去分詞爲 done) **1** used with the *main verb* 與主要動詞連用 **(a)** for neg sentences with *not*: 與 not 一起用於否定句: *He didn't go.* 他沒有走。*Don't go yet.* 現在不要走。**(b)** for interr sentences: 用於疑問句: *Does/Did he want it?* 他需要它嗎？ **(c)** after a front-shifted *adverbial*, etc: 用於倒裝句中移置句前的副詞等之後: *So hard did they work that...;* 他們如此辛苦地工作,以致…; *Not only did they promise to help, but....* 他們不僅答應援助,而且…。**(d)** to emphasize the positive or negative nature of a sentence (declarative, interr or imper), always stressed: 用以加重一句(陳述句,疑問句或祈使句)的語氣(須重讀): *That's exactly what he 'did say.* 那正是他所說的話。*I tell you I 'don't like him.* 我告訴你我根本不喜歡他。*'Do stop that noise!* 不要吵！ **2** used alone, to refer to a *main verb* or *verb phrase*: 單獨使用,以代替 '動詞' 或 '動詞片語': **(a)** in comparisons: 用於比較句中: *She plays the piano better now than she did* (ie played) *last year*. 她現在彈鋼琴比去年(彈得)好。**(b)** in question phrases: 用於疑問片語中: *He lives in London, doesn't he?* 他住在倫敦,不是嗎？ *So you want to be a doctor, do you?* 所以你要做一個醫生,是嗎？ **(c)** in answers, comments, etc: 用於回答,評論等中: *'They work hard.'—'Oh, do they?'* '他們工作努力。'—'哦,眞的嗎？' *'Who broke the window?'—'I did!'* '誰打破了窗子？'—'是我！'

do[2] /duː; du/ *vt, vi* (For uses with *adverbial particles* and *preps* ⇨ 15 below.) (與副詞接語及介詞連用的用法參看下列第15義。) **1 (a)** [VP2A, 6A] perform, carry out (an action); busy oneself with: 做;做出(動作);忙於: *What are you doing now?* 你現在做些什麼？*What shall I do next?* 我下一步做什麼？*I will do what I can.* 我願盡我所能去做。*What does he do for a living,* What is his occupation? 他做何事謀生(他的職業是什麼)？ *I have nothing to do.* 我沒有事情做。*Are you doing anything tomorrow?* 明天你有什麼事情要做嗎？*There's nothing to do here,* ie no means of passing the time. 此地無事可做(無法消磨時間)。*What's done cannot be undone.* 做過的事無法挽回;覆水難收。*See what kindness will do,* Try the effect of kindness. 和氣一些試試看。***do it yourself*** (abbr 略作 **DIY**), (esp) do house decorating, furnishing, upkeep, etc oneself (instead of employing professional workers): 自己做(尤指家庭裝飾,維護保養等工作,自己動手,不請專業人員): (attrib) (形容用法) *do-it-yourself kits,* materials, etc for doing work of this kind. 自己做所需用的一套工具。***easier said than done,*** easier to talk about than to do. 說來容易做着難。***No sooner said than done,*** done at once. 說做就做。***Well begun is half done,*** A good start makes it easy to finish sth. 好的開始是成功的一半。**(b)** [VP2C] act; behave: 行動;行爲: *When in Rome do as the Romans do.* 入境從俗;入鄉問俗。*You would do well* (ie be wise) *to take your doctor's advice.* 你最好聽醫生的勸告。 **2** [VP6A, 12B, 13B] (combined with *nouns* in many senses) (與名詞相連用於許多意義) **(a)** produce; make: 產生;製作: *Patience and perseverance will do wonders,* produce remarkable results. 耐心和毅力可產生奇蹟(產生非凡的結果)。*I have done* (ie made) *six copies.* 我已複製了六份。*I will do* (ie make) *a translation for you/do you a translation.* 我願替你翻譯。**(b)** work at; be busy with: 工作;忙於: *She's doing her lessons/homework,* etc. 她正在做功課(作業等)。**(c)** perform: 實行;履行: *Do your duty.* 盡你的責任。*He still has to do his military service.* 他仍須服兵役。***do the*** + *gerund*: *Who'll do the cooking,* Who'll cook, who'll undertake the task of cooking? 誰來燒飯？also ⇨ *get sth done* at get(2). **(d)** study; learn: 攻讀;學習: *Are you doing science at school?* 你在學校裏學科學嗎？*He has been doing engineering at Sheffield University.* 他一直在雪非耳大學攻讀工程。**(e)** solve; find the answer to: 解決;求出…的答案: *I can't do this sum/this problem in algebra.* 我不會做這個算術(代數)題。 **(f)** put in order; arrange: 整理;佈置: *Please do the flowers,* arrange them in vases, etc. 請你插一下花。**(g)** make tidy: 使整潔: *Go and do your hair.* 去梳一梳你的頭髮。**(h)** clean, sweep, brush, etc: 清除、掃、刷等: *Have you done* (ie brushed) *your teeth?* 你刷過牙齒沒有？ **(i)** deal with, attend to: 處理;照料: *I will do you next, sir,* (eg at the barber's) I will attend to you next. 我下一個照料你,先生(例如在理髮店:我下一個給您理)。*I have a lot of correspondence to do.* 我有很多信件要處理。**(j)** use, exert: 用;運用: *do one's best/utmost;* 盡力做; *do all one can;* 盡己所能; *do everything in one's power.* 盡力做每一件事。*He did his best to help us.* 他盡最大能力幫助我們。 ⇨ also credit[1](7), favour[1](4), good[2], harm, homage, honour[1](1), injury, justice, *kindness* at kind[2], mischief, service, *a good/bad turn* at turn, wrong. **do-gooder** /ˌduːˈgʊdə(r); ˈduˈgʊdə/ *n* (colloq; often pej) person who is (over-)zealous to improve people, conditions, etc. (俗,常作蔑)(過份)熱心改良社會的人。 **3** (the *pp* and perfect tenses) bring to an end; finish: (用過去分詞和完成時態)結束;完成: [VP6A] *It's done.* 做完了。*I've done it.* 我已做完。*Will he ever have/be done?* 他有沒有完的時候呀？[VP3A] *Have you done* (ie finished) *with my pen yet?* 你用我的鋼筆用好了沒有？[VP6C] *I've done talking—I'm going to act.* 我話已說完—我要採取行動了。 **4** [VP3A, 6A] ***do (for),*** be good, satisfactory or convenient, enough (for a purpose, for sb): 可用;可以;方便;適用(與 for 連用,後接目的或人):*These shoes won't do* (ie are not strong enough) *for mountain-climbing.* 這些鞋子爬山不適用(不够牢)。*This log will do for a seat/do for us to sit on.* 這圓木材可以用作座位(可以供我們坐)。*This room will do me quite well,* will serve my needs. 這房間很適合我的需要。***make sth do/make do (with sth),*** make sth suffice, provide for a need: 使足以敷用;使適合需要: *Can you make £5 do,* make this sum cover your expenses? 你能設法使五鎊足敷你的費用嗎？ *Can't you make that shirt do* (ie wear it) *for another day?* 那件襯衫你不能再穿一天嗎？ *It isn't much but I will make it do/make do with it,* manage with it. 這不够多,但我

會設法應付過去。 ⇨ make¹(14). **5** [VP2A] be fitting, suitable, tolerable: 適合；行；可以: *This will never do,* cannot be accepted or allowed! 這事絕不可以！ *That will do!* You've said or done enough! 够了；行了！***be done,*** be considered polite; be the usual custom: 有禮貌；合乎風俗: *It's not done to talk with your mouth full.* 嘴裏滿含着食物時講話是不禮貌的。 **6** [VP2A] (with passive force; colloq) happen: (有被動意味；俗)發生: *He came to ask what was doing,* being done, happening. 他來問發生了什麼事。*'Can you lend me 50p?'—'Nothing doing!'* (sl) No! '你能借給我五十辨士嗎？'—(俚)'不行！' **7** [VP2C] **(a)** fare; get on well, badly, etc: 進行；發展(好，壞等): *Everything in the garden is doing* (= growing) *well.* 花園裏的每樣花木都長得好。*Roses do well in a clay soil.* 薔薇在黏土裏生長得很好。*He's doing well at school.* 他在學校裏成績很好。**(b)** (esp of health) make progress: (尤指健康)進步: *The patient is doing quite well.* 這病人大有起色。***How do you do?*** (formula used when people are formally introduced). 你好(人們經正式介紹後用的客套話)。 **8** [VP2B, 15A] complete (a journey); travel (a distance); go (at a certain speed): 完成(旅行)；走過(距離)；(以某種速度)行走: *How many miles a day did you do during your tour?* 你們旅行時每天走多少哩？ *We've done eighty miles since lunch.* 吃過午飯後我們已走了八十哩了。*We did the journey in six hours.* 我們於六小時內走完了這段旅程。*The car was doing sixty miles an hour.* 那汽車正以時速六十哩行駛。**9** [VP6A] play the part of: 扮演；充當…角色: *He does Hamlet well.* 他善演哈姆雷特一角。*He does the host admirably,* is an admirable host. 他是個令人讚賞的主人。*I suppose we must do the polite thing,* (colloq) be sociable, chat, etc. (俗)我認爲我們必須客氣。**10** [VP6A, 15B] ***do sb (out of sth),*** (colloq) cheat, swindle, get the better of: (俗)欺騙；勝過: *Please don't think I'm trying to do you.* 請不要以爲我想欺騙你。*I'm afraid you've been done.* 我恐怕你已受騙了。*She was done out of her money.* 她被人騙走了錢。*He once tried to do me out of my job,* supplant me. 他一度想攘奪我的職位。 **11** ***do sb/oneself well,*** (colloq) provide food, comforts, etc for: (俗)款待；招待: *They do you very well at the Bristol Hotel.* 布里斯托旅社招待得很好。*He does himself well,* provides well for his own comfort. 他的生活舒適(養尊處優)。**12** [VP6A] (colloq) visit as a sightseer; see the sights of: (俗)觀光；參觀: *Have you done the British Museum yet?* 你參觀過大英博物館嗎？ **13** [VP15A] cook in the right degree: 烹調至適當的程度: *Mind you do the beef well.* 記住將牛肉燒透。*How would you like your mutton chop done?* 你的羊排要煎到什麼程度？ ⇨ underdone, *overdone* at overdo. ***ˌdone to a ˈturn,*** extremely well cooked: 燒得恰到好處: *The steak was done to a turn,* cooked perfectly. 這牛排煎得恰到好處。 **14** [VP7B] (with *have*) ***have to do with,*** be connected with; result from: 與…有關；由…而產生: *I know he behaves badly—It all has to do with the way he was brought up.* 我知道他的行爲不端——這一切都與他所受的教養有關。***have sth/nothing/not much/a great deal, etc to do with,*** be/not be connected or concerned with; contribute to: 與…有(無，無多少，有很大等)關係；促成: *He had something to do with* (= was in some way connected with, perhaps was responsible for) *my decision to teach English.* 他與我決定教英文有關(我的決定多少或直接受他的影響)。*Hard work had a great deal to do with* (= contributed greatly to) *his success.* 工作努力與他的成功大有關係。 **15** [VP2C, 3A, 15B] (uses with *adverbial particles* and *preps*): (與副詞接語及介詞連用的用法):

do aˈway with, abolish, get rid of: 廢除；除去: *That department was done away with two years ago.* 那一部門於兩年前被廢除了。*That's a practice that should be done away with.* 那是個應該被戒除的習慣。*Our dog is getting so old and blind that we shall have to do away with him,* have him put to death. 我們的狗變得又老又瞎，我們不得不將牠弄死。

do well/badly by sb, treat, deal with, well/badly: 善待(對待不善): *A good employer always does well by good workmen.* 一個好的雇主總是善待好的工人。***(be) hard ˈdone by,*** (be) treated unfairly: 受不公平對待: *He complains that he has been hard done by.* 他抱怨說他受到不公平的對待。***ˌDo as you would be ˈdone by,*** (prov) Treat others as you would like to be treated. (諺)你願意旁人怎樣對待你，你就怎樣對待旁人(以己所欲施之於人)。

do sb down, (colloq) (俗) **(a)** get the better of sb (by outwitting or cheating him). (以計謀或欺騙)勝過某人。**(b)** speak ill of. 說某人壞話。⇨ *run sb down* at run¹(26).

do for sb/sth, (colloq) (俗) **(a)** act as housekeeper for; perform, esp domestic services, for: 爲…料理家務；做家事: *Old Mrs Green has been doing for me since my wife died.* 自從我的妻子死後，格林老太太一直爲我料理家務。*He won't employ a housekeeper; he prefers to do for himself.* 他不願意雇女管家，寧願自己料理家務。**(b)** manage: 設法: *What/How will you do for water* (= manage to have supplies of water) *while you're crossing the desert?* 穿過沙漠時，你將如何獲得水的供應？ **(c)** (usu passive) ruin; destroy; kill: (通常用被動語態)毀掉；破壞；殺死: *These shoes are done for,* worn out, useless. 這些鞋都破爛了。*Poor fellow, I'm afraid he's done for,* according to context, ruined in his career, likely to die, etc. 可憐的人，我恐怕他是完了(事業毀掉、可能死去等，視上下文而定)。*The country's done for,* ruined. 這國家毀滅了。

do sb in, (sl) kill him. (俚)殺死某人。***be done in,*** exhausted: 筋疲力竭: *The horse was done in after the race.* 那匹馬在競賽後已筋疲力竭了。

do sth out, sweep or clean out; put in order: 掃除；整理: *Tell Tom to do out the stables.* 叫湯姆打掃馬廐。*This room needs doing out.* 這房間需要清掃。***do sb out of sth,*** ⇨ 10 above. 參看上列第 10 義。

do sth over, redecorate: 再裝飾；重裝修: *The dining-room needs doing over.* 餐廳需要重裝修。***do sb over,*** (sl) assault sb. (俚)襲擊某人。

do sth up, **(a)** restore, repair, renovate: 修復；整修；刷新: *The house needs to be done up/needs doing up,* repainted, restored, etc. 這房屋需要重新裝修粉刷一番。**(b)** change the shape of, put new trimmings, etc on: 改變形式；重新裝飾: *She has been doing up her last summer's hat.* 她一直在重新裝飾她去年夏季的帽子。**(c)** tie or wrap up; make into a bundle or parcel: 捆好；包好；束起: *Please do up these books and post them to Mr Smith.* 請將這些書包紮好寄給史密斯先生。 **(d)** fasten (a dress or other garment) with buttons, hooks and eyes, etc: 用扣、領鈎等繫牢(衣服): *She asked me to do up her dress for her at the back.* 她要我把她衣服的背後扣好。**(e)** (of a dress, etc) fasten with buttons, etc: (指衣服等)用鈕扣等扣起: *This dress does up at the back.* 這衣服是從背後扣的。**(f)** (usu passive) tire out: (通常用被動語態)使極爲疲倦: *He/His horse was done up* (*done in* is more usu) *after the long ride.* 經長途乘騎後，他(他的馬)疲乏不堪了 (done in 較常用)。

do with sb/sth, **(a)** (meanings as in the examples): (含義見下列例句): *What did you do with my umbrella,* Where did you put it, leave it, etc? 你把我的傘放到哪裏去了？ *What are we to do with* (= How shall we deal with) *this naughty boy?* 我們怎樣處置這個頑皮的男孩？*She didn't know what to do with herself,* how to occupy her time. 她不知道做些什麼才好。*Tell me what you did with yourselves* (= how you passed the time) *on Sunday.* 告訴我你們星期天是怎樣度過的。*The children* *didn't know what to do with themselves for joy / excitement / impatience,* were so happy, excited, etc that they could not control their feelings. 孩子們高興（興奮，急躁）得無法控制自己。**(b)** tolerate: 忍受: *I can't do with him and his insolence.* 我無法忍受他和他的傲慢。**(c)** (with *can, could*) expressing a need or wish: (與 can, could 連用)表示需要或願望: *You look as if you could do with* (= as if you need) *a good night's sleep.* 你看來似乎需要好好睡上一夜。*That man could do with* (= would look better if he had) *a shave.* 那個人能够刮刮臉就好了。*I think we can do with* (= will need) *two extra loaves today.* 我認爲今天我們需要多加兩條麵包。*I could do with a cup of tea.* 我需要一杯茶。

do without sb / sth, dispense with; manage without: 不需要; 不用: *He can't do without the services of a secretary.* 他需要一位秘書的襄助。*We shall have to do without a holiday this summer.* 今年夏天我們不能有假日了。*The hens haven't laid any eggs; we shall have to do without.* 母鷄未生蛋，我們祇有不吃蛋了。

do³ /duː ; du/ *n* (*pl* dos or do's /duːz ; duz/) **1** (sl) swindle: (俚)欺詐: *The scheme was a do from the start.* 這方案從開始便是騙局。**2** (colloq) entertainment; party: (俗) 款待; 慶祝或娛樂性的集會: *We're going to a big do at the Fotherington's this evening.* 我們今晚要去參加佛林頓家的盛大宴會。**3** customs, rules: 風俗; 規則: *Some teachers have too many do's and don'ts.* 有些教師的規矩太多。**4** ***fair dos / do's,*** (GB sl) (as an exclamation) fair shares; let's be fair (eg in sharing something). (英俚) (作爲感嘆詞)公平分配;要公平(例如在分配東西時)。

do⁴ /ˈdɪtəʊ ; ˈdɪto/ (abbr of) ditto. 爲 ditto 之略。

do⁵, doh /dəʊ ; do/ *n* (music) first and eighth of the notes in the musical octave. (音樂)音階的第一音和第八音。

dob·bin /ˈdɒbɪn ; ˈdɑbɪn/ *n* (pet name for a) farm horse. (暱稱)農場用的馬。

doc·ile /ˈdəʊsaɪl *US:* ˈdɒsl ; ˈdɑsl/ *adj* easily trained or controlled: 易訓練或管制的;溫順的: *a ~ child / horse.* 溫順的小孩(馬)。**do·cil·ity** /dəʊˈsɪlətɪ ; doˈsɪlətɪ/ *n* [U] the quality of being ~. 馴良;溫順。

dock¹ /dɒk ; dɑk/ *n* **1** place in a harbour, river, etc with gates through which water may be let in and out, where ships are (un)loaded or repaired: 船塢(港口,河流等處供船隻裝卸貨物或修理船隻的地方,有門可將水放入和排出): *to go into / enter / leave ~;* 入(進,離)船塢; *to be in ~.* 在船塢。**ˈdry / ˈgraving ~,** one from which water may be pumped out. 乾船塢(塢中水可排除者)。**ˈfloating ~,** floating structure that may be used as a dry ~. 浮塢(一種漂浮的構造物,可做乾船塢使用)。 **ˈwet ~,** one in which the water may be kept at high-tide level. 船渠;濕塢(塢中水可保持高潮之高度者)。**ˈ~-dues,** money paid for the use of a ~. 使用船塢的費用。**2** (*pl*) number or row of ~s with the wharves, sheds, offices, etc round them. (複) (連帶碼頭,棚庫,辦公處等的)一排船塢。 **ˈ~·yard,** enclosure with ~s and facilities for building and repairing ships: 造船廠;修船所: *the naval ~yard at Chatham.* 占松的海軍造船廠。 **3** (US) wharf; ship's berth. (美)碼頭;碇泊處。**~er** *n* ~yard labourer. 船塢工人。

dock² /dɒk ; dɑk/ *vi, vt* **1** [VP2A] (of a ship) come or go into a dock. (指船)入塢。 **2** [VP6A] bring, take, (a ship) into a dock. 使(船)入塢。 **3** [VP6A] couple (two or more spacecraft) in space; [VP 2A] perform this manoeuvre. 在太空中連接(兩個或多個太空船);做此種演習。

dock³ /dɒk ; dɑk/ *n* enclosure in a criminal court for the prisoner: 法庭上的犯人席;被告席: *to be in the ~.* 在被告席;爲被告。

dock⁴ /dɒk ; dɑk/ *vt* [VP6A, 14] ~ ***(off),*** **1** cut short (an animal's tail). 剪短(動物的尾巴)。 **2** make wages, allowances, supplies, less: 減少(工資,津貼,供應物): *to ~ a workman's wages;* 減少一工人的工資; *to have one's salary ~ed;* 薪金被減少; *to ~ the soldiers off part of their rations.* 減少士兵一部分口糧。

dock⁵ /dɒk ; dɑk/ *n* common weed with large leaves and small green flowers. 酸模;羊蹄(生有大葉和小綠花的一種普通野草)。

docket /ˈdɒkɪt ; ˈdɑkɪt/ *n* **1** summary of the contents of a letter, document, etc. 信件,文件等的摘要。 **2** (comm) list of goods delivered, jobs done, etc; label on a package listing the contents, or giving information about use, method of assembly, etc. (商) 送貨單;工作程序表;載明內容,用途,裝配方法等的標籤。□ *vt* [VP6A] enter in or write on a ~; label. 摘記;加標籤。

doc·tor /ˈdɒktə(r) ; ˈdɑktɚ/ *n* **1** person who has been trained in medical science. 醫生。⇨ physician, surgeon. **2** person who has received the highest university degree: 博士: *D~ of Philosophy.* 哲學博士。□ *vt* [VP6A] **1** (colloq) give medical treatment to: (俗)醫治: *~ a cold / a child;* 醫治傷風(一小孩); *a ~ed tomcat,* one that has been neutered, ⇨ neuter(*v*). 閹割過的雄貓。 **2** make (esp food, drink) inferior by adding sth; add drugs to. 攙雜(尤指食物和飲料);攙混;加藥於。**3** (fig) falsify accounts, evidence. (喻)假造(帳目,證據)。 **~·ate** /ˈdɒktərət ; ˈdɑktərɪt/ *n* ~'s degree. 博士學位。

doc·tri·naire /ˌdɒktrɪˈneə(r) ; ˌdɑktrɪˈnɛr/ *n* person who wants his doctrines to be put into practice without allowing for circumstances, considering their suitability for particular cases, etc. 空論家(欲使其理論實現而不考慮環境及對於某些特殊狀況的適合性等的理論家)。□ *adj* theoretical; unpractical; dogmatic: 理論的;不合實際的;武斷的: *~ socialism.* 空論的社會主義。

doc·trinal /dɒkˈtraɪnl *US:* ˈdɒktrɪnl ; ˈdɑktrɪnl/ *adj* of doctrine(s). 教義的;主義的;學說的。

doc·trine /ˈdɒktrɪn ; ˈdɑktrɪn/ *n* [C, U] body of teaching; beliefs and teachings of a church, political party, school of scientists, etc: 教旨;教義;主義;學說: *a matter of ~;* 教旨問題; *the ~ that the Pope is infallible.* 教皇永不會錯的說法。

docu·ment /ˈdɒkjʊmənt ; ˈdɑkjəmənt/ *n* sth written or printed, to be used as a record or in evidence (eg birth, marriage and death certificates): 文件;公文;證件(例如出生,結婚,死亡證明書): *~ of title,* providing evidence of rights, ownership, etc; 契據;房地契; *a human ~,* number of facts or incidents that illustrate human nature. 人性記錄(說明人性的事實或事件)。□ /ˈdɒkjʊment ; ˈdɑkjəˌmɛnt/ *vt* [VP6A] prove by, supply with, ~s: 用文件證明;供以公文或證件: *to be well ~ed.* 有許多文件證明。 **docu·men·ta·tion** /ˌdɒkjʊmenˈteɪʃn ; ˌdɑkjəmɛnˈteʃən/ *n* [U].

docu·men·tary /ˌdɒkjʊˈmentrɪ ; ˌdɑkjəˈmɛntərɪ/ *adj* consisting of documents: 有文件的;有證件的: *~ proof / evidence.* 文書證據(證明文件)。 ˌ**~ (ˈfilm),** cinema or TV film showing some aspect of human or social activity (eg the work of the post-office, the lives of fishermen). 記錄影片(說明人類或社會活動的電影或電視影片,例如說明郵政工作,漁夫生活等)。

dod·der /ˈdɒdə(r) ; ˈdɑdɚ/ *vi* [VP2A, C] (colloq) walk, move, in a shaky way, as from weakness or old age: (俗) (因體弱或年邁)蹣跚;步履不穩;震顫: *to ~ along.* 蹣跚而行。 **~er** *n* person who ~s. 蹣跚而行者; 因體弱或年邁而震顫者。 **~·ing, ~y** *adjj* trembling; weak and uncertain in movement. 震顫的;行動不穩的。

dodge¹ /dɒdʒ ; dɑdʒ/ *n* **1** quick movement to evade sth. 閃避;躲閃。 **2** (colloq) trick; piece of deception: (俗)詭計;矇騙: *He's up to all the ~s,* knows them all. 他詭計多端。 **3** (colloq) plan;

method; ingenious way of doing sth. (俗)計畫;方法;巧妙的方法。

dodge² /dɒdʒ; dɑdʒ/ *vt, vi* [VP2A, 3A, 6A] **1** move quickly to one side, change position or direction, in order to escape or avoid sth: 閃避; 躲閃: *He ~d cleverly when I threw my shoe at him.* 我將我的鞋子擲向他時,他機敏地躲開了。*I ~d behind a tree so that he should not see me.* 我躲在樹後使他看不見我。*You need to be quick in order to ~ the traffic in London nowadays.* 要躲避今日倫敦的車輛,你需要機敏。**2** get round (difficulties), avoid (duties, etc) by cunning or trickery: 以巧計或詭計規避(困難),逃避(責任等): *to ~ military service.* 逃避兵役。**dodger** *n* person who ~s, esp an artful or cunning person. 狡猾的逃避者。

dod·gem /ˈdɒdʒəm; ˈdɑdʒəm/ *n* (colloq) (at fun fairs, etc) small car, electrically propelled, (to be) driven on a special platform where there are many others which have to be avoided or dodged. (俗)(遊樂園等中)電動小汽車(在一特設的平臺上行駛,而且必須閃避臺上許多其他車輛)。

dodgy /ˈdɒdʒɪ; ˈdɑdʒɪ/ *adj* (colloq) (俗) **1** artful. 狡猾的;詭計多端的。**2** involving risk or loss. 冒險性或有損失的。

dodo /ˈdəʊdəʊ; ˈdodo/ *n* (*pl* ~es, ~s /-dəʊz; -doz/) extinct, large, flightless bird of Mauritius. 渡渡鳥(產於模里西斯島的一種巨鳥,已絕種)。

doe /dəʊ; do/ *n* female fallow-deer, rabbit or hare. 母鹿;雌兎。ˈ**~ skin** *n* skin of a ~; [U] soft leather made from this skin. 母鹿皮;母鹿皮革。

doer /ˈdu:ə(r); ˈduɚ/ *n* person who does things (contrasted with persons who merely talk, etc): 實行者;做事者(以別於空談者等): *He's a ~, not a talker.* 他是個實行者,不是個空談者。(Also in compounds, as *evil-doer*). (亦用於複合字中,如 evil-doer)。

does /dʌz; dʌz/, **doesn't** /ˈdʌznt; ˈdʌznt/ ⇨ do¹.

doff /dɒf *US:* dɔ:f; dɑf/ *vt* [VP6A] (old use) take off one's hat, coat, etc. (舊用法)脫(衣帽等)。

dog¹ /dɒg *US:* dɔ:g; dɔg/ *n* **1** common domestic animal, a friend of man, of which there are many breeds; male of this animal and of the wolf and the fox. 犬;狗;雄狗;雄狼;雄狐。⇨ bitch. **2** (phrases): (片語): ***a case of dog eat dog,*** situation, eg in business, where ruthless methods are used. 互相殘害(例如商業上之使用無情手段)。***die like a dog; die a ˈdog's death,*** die in shame or misery. 潦倒而死。***a dog in the manger,*** person who prevents others from enjoying sth that is useless to himself. 狗佔馬槽;佔着茅坑不拉屎的人。***dressed like a dog's dinner,*** (colloq) in the height of fashion. (俗)穿着極講究。***give/throw sth to the dogs,*** throw it away as worthless, or as a sacrifice to save oneself. 丢棄某物;犧牲某物以自保。***give a dog a bad name (and hang him),*** (prov) give a person a bad reputation, slander him, and the bad reputation will remain. (諺)一旦加給某人一個壞名,他就永遠洗不清。***go to the dogs,*** be ruined. 墮落;敗壞。***help a lame dog over a stile,*** help a person in trouble. 助人於危難。***lead a ˈdog's life,*** be troubled all the time. 過困苦的生活。***lead sb a ˈdog's life,*** give him no peace; worry him all the time. 使不安寧;使某人經常苦惱。***let sleeping dogs lie,*** (prov) let well alone; not look for trouble. (諺)勿惹睡狗;勿惹事生非。***look like a dog's breakfast/dinner,*** (colloq) very untidy; messy. (俗)凌亂的;亂七八糟的。***love me, love my dog,*** (prov) if you want me as a friend, you must accept my friends as yours. (諺)愛屋及烏。***not stand (even) a ˈdog's chance,*** have no chance at all of beating a stronger enemy, surviving a disaster, etc. 毫無希望(擊敗强敵,度過災難等)。***be top dog,*** be in a position where one rules. 居於高位。***be (the) ˈunderdog,*** be in a position where one must always submit. 居於永遠聽命他人之位。**3** (colloq) (俗) **the dogs,** greyhound race-meetings. 賽狗;獵犬比賽。**4** (old use; of a man) worthless, wicked or surly person. (舊用法,指人)卑鄙的小人;乖戾的人。**5** (with *adjj*, colloq) person: (與形容詞連用,俗)人;傢伙: *He's a dirty/sly/lucky/gay dog.* 他是個骯髒(狡詐,幸運,快樂)的人。**6** (kinds of) mechanical device for gripping, etc. (各種)抓、扣等機械裝置;鐵鉤。**7** (*pl*, also 亦作 ˈ*fire-dogs*) metal supports for logs in a fireplace. (複)爐中鐵架;薪架。**8** (compounds) (複合字) ˈ**dog-biscuit,** hard, thick biscuit for feeding dogs. 飼狗餅乾(硬而厚者)。ˈ**dog-cart,** high, two-wheeled cart, pulled by a horse, with two seats back to back. (車身很高,有兩個背對背座位的)二輪單馬車。ˈ**dog-collar,** (colloq) clerical collar. (俗)(神父所戴的)硬白領。ˈ**dog-days,** period of very hot weather (July and August). 酷熱的暑天(七、八月);三伏天。ˈ**dog-eared,** (of a book) having the corners of the leaves turned down with use. (指書)書頁折角的。ˈ**dog-fish,** small kind of shark. 角鮫(一種小鯊)。⇨ the illus at sea. 參看 sea 之插圖。ˈ**dog·house,** (US) kennel. (美)

dogs

狗舍。*in the doghouse*, (colloq) in disgrace or disfavour. (俗)失體面;失寵。ˈ**dog paddle**, simple swimming stroke in which the arms and legs are moved in short, quick splashing movements. 狗扒式游泳(手臂和雙腿作短暫急促濺水動作的一種游泳)。ˈ**dogs·body**, drudge. 服賤役者;做苦工的人。ˌ**dog-ˈtired**, tired out, exhausted. 極疲倦的。ˈ**dog·tooth**, small pyramid-shaped ornament (in stonework, Norman and Early English architecture). (諾曼第和早期英國建築之石工上的) 角錐形裝飾。ˈ**dog's-tooth**, checked pattern (in cloth for men's suits, overcoats, etc). (男子西服,大衣等衣料上的)方格花樣。ˈ**dog·trot**, gentle, easy trot. (徐緩從容的)小跑。ˈ**dog-watch**, (on ships) one of the two-hour watches (4 to 6pm, 6 to 8pm). (船上)暮更(下午四至六時爲上暮更,六至八時爲下暮更)。ˈ**dog·wood**, tree with large white or pinkish flowers in spring. 山茱萸;水木(一種樹,春天開大而白或略帶粉紅色的花)。ˈ**dog-like** *adj* like or as of a dog, 如狗的, esp 尤用於 *dog-like devotion*, the kind of devotion given by a dog to its master. 如狗一般的忠實。**doggy, doggie** /ˈdɒgɪ *US:* ˈdɔːgɪ ; ˈdɔgɪ/ *n* (child's word for a) dog. (兒語)狗;狗狗。

dog[2] /dɒg *US:* dɔːg ; dɔg/ *vt* (-gg-) [VP6A] keep close behind, in the footsteps of: 追隨;尾隨: *dog a suspected thief;* 尾隨一有嫌疑的小偷; (fig) (喩) *dogged by misfortune*. 被災難緊隨着的。

doge /dəʊdʒ ; dodʒ/ *n* elected chief magistrate in the former republics of Venice and Genoa. (昔時威尼斯和熱那亞共和國之)總督。

dog·ged /ˈdɒgɪd *US:* ˈdɔːg- ; ˈdɔgɪd/ *adj* obstinate; stubborn. 頑强的;固執的。**~·ly** *adv* **~·ness** *n*

dog·gerel /ˈdɒgərəl *US:* ˈdɔːg- ; ˈdɔgərəl/ *n* [U] irregular, inexpert verse. 歪詩;打油詩。

doggo /ˈdɒgəʊ *US:* ˈdɔːg- ; ˈdɔgo/ *adv* **lie ~**, (sl) lie without making a movement or sound. (俚)一動也不動或一聲不響地靜臥着。

dogma /ˈdɒgmə *US:* ˈdɔːg- ; ˈdɔgmə/ *n* **1** [C] belief, system of beliefs, put forward by some authority (esp the Church) to be accepted as true without question. 教條;信條。**2** [U] such beliefs collectively. 教條或信條的總稱。

dog·matic /dɒgˈmætɪk *US:* dɔːg- ; dɔgˈmætɪk/ *adj* **1** put forward as dogmas: 做爲教條而提出的: *~ theology*. 教條神學。**2** (of a person) making purely personal statements as if they were dogmas; (of statements) put forward in this way without proof. (指人或言論)武斷的。**dog·mati·cally** /-klɪ ; -klɪ/ *adv*

dog·ma·tism /ˈdɒgmətɪzəm *US:* ˈdɔːg- ; ˈdɔgməˌtɪzəm/ *n* [U] the quality of being dogmatic; being dogmatic: 教條主義;武斷;獨斷: *His ~ aroused their opposition*. 他的武斷引起了他們的反對。

dog·ma·tize /ˈdɒgmətaɪz *US:* ˈdɔːg- ; ˈdɔgməˌtaɪz/ *vi, vt* [VP2A] make dogmatic statements; [VP6A] express (a principle, etc) as a dogma. 作武斷的主張;武斷地提出(主義等);當做教條提出。

doh ⇨ do[5].

doily /ˈdɔɪlɪ ; ˈdɔɪlɪ/ *n* (*pl* -lies) small, round piece of linen, lace, etc placed under a dish on a table or under an ornament on a shelf. (墊於盤碟或架上飾物下的)小圓布巾;小圓墊。

do·ings /ˈduːɪŋz ; ˈduɪŋz/ *n pl* (colloq) things done or being done: (俗)所做之事: *Tell me about all your ~ in London*. 告訴我你在倫敦所做的一切。

dol·drums /ˈdɒldrəmz ; ˈdɑldrəmz/ *n pl* **in the ~**, (colloq) in low spirits. (俗)精神沮喪。

dole /dəʊl ; dol/ *vt* [VP15B] **~ out**, distribute food, money, etc in small amounts. 布施;少量分配(食物,金錢等)。□ *n* **1** [C] sth ~d out. 布施之物;分與物。**2** [U] **the ~**, (colloq term for) weekly payment made under various Insurance Acts in GB (from contributions made by workers, employers and the State) to an unemployed worker. (俗) (依據英國各種保險法案,由工人、雇主及政府每週所給與失業人員的)失業救濟金。***be/go on the ~***, receive/begin to receive such payments. 因失業而(開始)接受救濟金。

dole·ful /ˈdəʊlfl ; ˈdolfəl/ *adj* mournful; dismal. 悲哀的;憂愁的。**~ly** /-fəlɪ ; -fəlɪ/ *adv*

doll[1] /dɒl ; dɑl/ *n* **1** model of a baby or person, usu for a child to play with. 玩偶;洋娃娃。**2** (sl) (pretty but silly) girl or woman. (俚)(美麗而無頭腦的)女人。

doll[2] /dɒl ; dɑl/ *vt, vi* [VP15B, 2C] **~ up**, (colloq) dress (oneself) up smartly: (俗) 漂亮地打扮(自己): *She was all ~ed up for the party*. 她打扮得漂漂亮亮的去參加那宴會。

dol·lar /ˈdɒlə(r) ; ˈdɑlɚ/ *n* unit of money (symbol $) in the US, Canada, Australia and other countries. 圓;元(美國,加拿大,澳洲等國家的貨幣單位,符號爲 $)。

dol·lop /ˈdɒləp ; ˈdɑləp/ *n* (colloq) shapeless quantity of food, etc: (俗)一團(食物等);一塊食物: *a ~ of cold rice pudding*. 一團冷的米布丁。

dolly /ˈdɒlɪ ; ˈdɑlɪ/ *n* (*pl* -lies) **1** (child's word for a) doll. (兒語)洋娃娃;玩偶。**2** small wheeled frame or platform for moving heavy objects; mobile platform for a heavy camera. 運送重物的小轆車;安放重攝影機的輪臺。**3** (sl) attractive, fashionably dressed but silly girl or young woman. (俚)漂亮而打扮入時的傻女郎。

dol·men /ˈdɒlmen ; ˈdɑlmɛn/ *n* = cromlech.

dol·our (US = **-lor**) /ˈdɒlə(r) *US:* ˈdəʊl- ; ˈdolɚ/ *n* (poet) grief; sorrow. (詩)悲傷;憂愁。**~·ous** /-rəs ; -rəs/ *adj* sorrowful; distressed; distressing. 悲哀的;憂愁的;令人煩惱的。

dol·phin /ˈdɒlfɪn ; ˈdɑlfɪn/ *n* sea animal like a porpoise. 海豚。⇨ the illus at sea. 參看 sea 之挿圖。

dolt /dəʊlt ; dolt/ *n* stupid fellow; blockhead. 愚蠢的人;傻瓜。**~·ish** *adj* stupid. 愚蠢的。

do·main /dəʊˈmeɪn ; doˈmen/ *n* lands under the rule of a government, ruler, etc; (fig) field or province of thought, knowledge, activity: 領土;版圖;領域;領地;(喩)(思想,知識,活動的)範圍: *in the ~ of science*. 在科學範圍中。

dome /dəʊm ; dom/ *n* rounded roof with a circular base; sth shaped like a ~: 圓屋頂;似圓屋頂之物: *the rounded ~ (= summit) of a hill*. 圓形山頂。**domed** *adj* rounded: 圓的;圓頂的: *a man with a ~d forehead*. 額頭隆起的人。

domes

Domes·day Book /ˈduːmzdeɪ bʊk ; ˈdumzˌde bʊk/ *n* record of the inquiry, made by King William I in 1086, into the ownership of all the lands in England. 英格蘭土地記錄書(威廉一世於 1086 年勘查英格蘭土地所有權後編成者)。

do·mes·tic /dəˈmestɪk ; dəˈmɛstɪk/ *adj* **1** of the home, family, household: 家庭的;家務的: *He has had a good many ~ troubles*. 他有許多家庭糾紛。*What a charming ~ scene!* eg of members of a family happy together at home. 這是多麼可愛的一個家庭情景啊!(例如一家人歡聚在家裏)。*She's a very ~ sort of woman*, prefers home life to social activities outside the home. 她是個十分喜歡家庭生活的女子。**2** not foreign; native; of one's own country: 非外國的;國內的;本國的: *The government could get neither foreign nor ~ loans*, could not borrow money either abroad or at home. 該政府

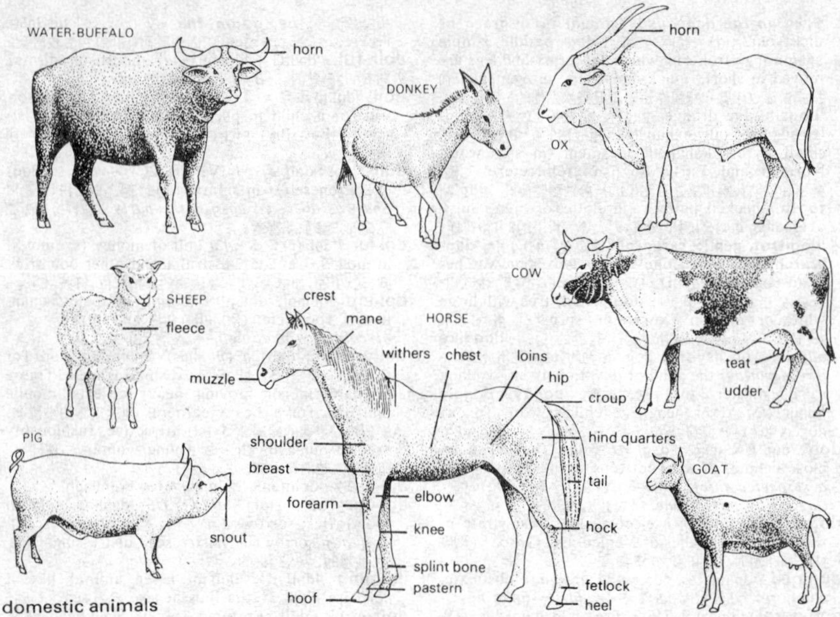

domestic animals

既無法借得外債，亦無法借到內債。*This newspaper provides more foreign news than ~ news.* 這家報紙刊登的國外消息多於國內消息。**3** (of animals, etc) kept by, living with, man: (指動物等) 由人飼養的; 與人生活在一起的: *Horses, cows and sheep are ~ animals.* 馬、牛和羊是家畜。⇨ wild. **domes·ti·cally** /-klɪ ; -klɪ/ *adv*

do·mes·ti·cate /dəˈmestɪkeɪt ; dəˈmɛstəˌket/ *vt* [VP6A] **1** (chiefly in *pp*) make fond of, interested in, household work and duties: (主要用過去分詞) 使喜歡家庭生活; 使喜歡家事: *She's not at all ~d,* is not fond of, skilled in, cooking, house-keeping, etc. 她絲毫不喜(不諳)家事。 **2** tame (animals). 馴服(動物)。 **do·mes·ti·ca·tion** /dəˌmestɪˈkeɪʃn ; dəˌmɛstəˈkeʃən/ *n*

do·mes·tic·ity /ˌdɒmesˈtɪsətɪ ; ˌdomɛsˈtɪsətɪ/ *n* [U] home or family life. 家庭生活。

domi·cile /ˈdɒmɪsaɪl ; ˈdɑməsḷ/ *n* (formal) dwelling-place; (legal) place where a person lives permanently. (正式用語) 住處; (法律) 永久居住地。

dom·i·cili·ary /ˌdɒmɪˈsɪlɪərɪ *US:* -lɪerɪ ; ˌdɑməˈsɪlɪˌɛrɪ/ *adj* (formal) of or to a dwelling-place: (正式用語) 住處的; 至住處的: *a ~ visit,* one made to a house, etc (eg by officials to search or inspect it, or by a doctor to a patient). 住宅訪查(例如官方的搜查或視察，或是醫生之探訪病人)。

domi·nant /ˈdɒmɪnənt ; ˈdɑmənənt/ *adj* **1** having control or authority; dominating; most important or influential: 有統治權的; 有支配力的; 最有勢力的; 佔優勢的: *the ~ partner in a business.* 商店中最有勢力的股東。 **2** (of heights) overlooking others: (指高處) 高於其他的: *a ~ cliff.* 聳立的絕壁。□ *n* (music) fifth note of a scale. (音樂) 音階的第五度音。 **~·ly** *adv* **domi·nance** /-nəns ; -nəns/ *n* being ~. 統治; 支配; 優勢。

domi·nate /ˈdɒmɪneɪt ; ˈdɑməˌnet/ *vt, vi* [VP6A, 2A, 3A] ~ ***(over)***, **1** have control, authority or influence: 統治; 支配; 控制: *A great man can ~ (over) others by force of character.* 偉人能以人格的力量支配他人。*The strong usually ~ (over) the weak.* 强者通常統治弱者。 **2** (of a place, esp a height) overlook: (地點，尤指高處) 俯臨: *The whole valley is ~d by this mountain.* 這座山俯臨着整個的山谷。 **domi·na·tion** /ˌdɒmɪˈneɪʃn ; ˌdɑməˈneʃən/ *n* [U] dominating or being ~d. 統治; 支配; 控制; 俯臨。

domi·neer /ˌdɒmɪˈnɪə(r) ; ˌdɑməˈnɪr/ *vi* [VP2A, 3A] ~ ***(over)***, act, speak, in a dominating manner; behave like a tyrant; be overbearing: 壓制; 跋扈; 擅權; 專横: *Big boys sometimes ~ over their small sisters.* 大的男孩們有時壓制他們的小妹妹。 **~·ing** *adj*: *He's a very ~ing sort of fellow,* likes to ~ over others. 他是個非常跋扈的人。 **~·ing·ly** *adv*

Dom·ini·can /dəˈmɪnɪkən ; dəˈmɪnɪkən/ *n, adj* (friar or nun) of the religious order founded in 1212 by St Dominic. (1212年聖多明尼克所創之) 聖多明尼克教派的; 聖多明尼克教派僧侶或修女。

domi·nie /ˈdɒmɪnɪ ; ˈdɑmənɪ/ *n* (Scot) schoolteacher. (蘇) 教師。

do·min·ion /dəˈmɪnɪən ; dəˈmɪnjən/ *n* **1** [U] ~ ***(over)***, authority to rule; control (over). 統治權; 主權; 支配。 **2** [C] territory of a sovereign government. 領土; 版圖。 **3** [C] (old use) one of the self-governing territories of the British Commonwealth of Nations. (舊用法) 大英國協的自治領。

dom·ino /ˈdɒmɪnəʊ ; ˈdɑməˌno/ *n* (*pl* ~es or ~s /-nəʊz ; -noz/) **1** small, flat, oblong piece of wood or bone, marked with spots. 骨牌 (小而扁的長方形木塊或骨塊，刻有黑點)。 **2** (*pl* with *sing v*) table game played with 28 of these. (複，與單數動詞連用) (用二十八枚骨牌玩的) 骨牌戲。 **3** loose cloak with a mask for the upper part of the face, worn at parties, fancy-dress balls, etc. (宴會、化裝舞會等所穿的) 帶有面罩可將面孔上部遮住的一種寬鬆外衣。

don[1] /dɒn ; dɑn/ *n* **1** (GB) teaching member of a university staff. (英) 大學教師。 **2** Spanish gentleman; Spanish title (used before a man's name): 西班牙紳士; 先生 (西班牙人的尊稱，冠於男子的名之前): *Don Juan.* 胡安先生; 唐璜。 **don·nish** /ˈdɒnɪʃ ; ˈdɑnɪʃ/ *adj* of or like a don(1). 大學教師的; 似大學教師的。

don[2] /dɒn ; dɑn/ *vt* (-nn-) [VP6A] (old use) put on clothing, etc. (舊用法) 穿(衣服等)。⇨ doff.

do·nate /dəʊˈneɪt *US:* ˈdəʊneɪt ; ˈdonet/ *vt* [VP6A, 14] ~ ***(to)***, give (eg money, to a charity, etc); contribute. 捐贈(例如捐錢給慈善機關等); 贈送。 **do-**

na·tion /dəʊˈneɪʃn ; doˈneʃən/ *n* [U] giving; [C] sth given: 捐贈；捐贈之物: *donations to the Red Cross/the refugee fund.* 對紅十字會(救濟難民基金)的捐款。

done /dʌn ; dʌn/ ⇨ do¹.

don·jon /ˈdɒndʒən ; ˈdʌndʒən/ *n* large, strongly fortified main tower of a castle. (城堡之)主樓；主塔。

don·key /ˈdɒŋkɪ ; ˈdɑŋkɪ/ *n* (*pl* ~s /-kɪz ; -kɪz/) (the common and usu word for an) ass. 驢(較ass 常用)。⇨ the illus at domestic. 參看 domestic之插圖。ˈ~ **engine,** small auxiliary steam-engine, esp one on a ship's deck. 小型蒸汽機(尤指用於甲板上者)；副機。 ˈ**~-jacket,** workman's thick, short coat. 工人穿的厚短外衣。ˈ**~-work** *n* drudgery. 辛苦而令人討厭的工作。

do·nor /ˈdəʊnə(r) ; ˈdonɚ/ *n* person who gives sth, eg property or money: 贈與者；捐贈者(如捐贈財產或金錢等者)：*blood* ~, person who gives his own blood for transfusion. 捐血者；供血者。

don't /dəʊnt ; dont/ **1** = *do not;* ⇨ do¹. **2** *do's and ~s,* ⇨ do³(3).

doodle /ˈduːdl ; ˈdudl̩/ *vi* [VP2A], *n* (colloq) (make) meaningless scrawls or scribbles (while one is or ought to be paying attention to sth else). (俗)胡寫；亂畫(當注意力正在或應該集中其他事物時)。

doodle·bug /ˈduːdlbʌg ; ˈdudl̩,bʌg/ *n* (colloq) flying bomb (a pilotless guided missile) used by the Nazis against London in 1944. (俗)飛彈(無人駕駛的導向飛彈，1944年納粹用以襲擊倫敦者)。

doom¹ /duːm ; dum/ *n* **1** (usu *sing*) ruin; death; sth evil that is to come: (通常用作單數)毀滅；死亡；惡運；劫數: *to go to one's ~;* 走向毀滅；*to send a man to his ~.* 將一人處死。 **2** (also 亦作 **Doomsday** /ˈduːmzdeɪ ; ˈdumz,de/) the Day of Judgement; the end of the world. 最後審判日；世界末日。*till D~sday,* for ever. 永遠。

doom² /duːm ; dum/ *vt* [VP6A, 14, 17] ~ *to,* (usu passive) condemn (sb to some fate/to do sth): (通常用被動語態)判定；註定: (esp in *pp*) (尤用過去分詞) *~ed to disappointment;* 註定失望的；*~ed to die;* 註定要死的；判定死罪的；*poems ~ed to oblivion,* certain to be forgotten. 註定湮沒無聞的詩。

door /dɔː(r) ; dɔr/ *n* **1** that which closes the entrance to a building, room, cupboard, safe, etc: 門；戶: *to open/close/lock, etc the ~;* 開(關，鎖)門；*hinged/sliding/revolving ~s.* 有鉸鏈的門(拉門；旋轉門)。*The ~ opened/was opened and a man came out.* 門開了，一個人走了出來。**back ~,** ~ at the back of the house (to the yard, garden, etc). 後門(通庭院、花園等者)。**front ~,** chief ~ from a house to the street or road. 前門；大門(通街道者)。***next ~,*** (in/to) the next house: (在，到)隔壁: *Who lives next ~ (to you)?* 誰住在(你的)隔壁？ *I'm just going next ~ to see Mrs Jones.* 我正要去隔壁探望瓊斯太太。***next ~ to,*** (fig) nearly, almost. (喻)幾乎。***two/three, etc ~s away/down/off,*** in the next house but one/two, etc: 過去第二(三等)家: *My brother lives three ~s away.* 我哥哥(弟弟)住在從這裏過去第三家。***from ~ to ~,*** **(a)** from the ~ of one building to the ~ of another: 沿門；從一家門口到另一家門口: *It was raining heavily, but the taxi took us from ~ to ~.* 雨下得很大，但計程車把我們送到每一家的門口。**(b)** from house to house: 逐家；挨戶: *He went from ~ to ~ delivering the milk/selling encyclopaedias.* 他挨戶送牛奶(推銷百科全書)。Hence, 由此產生, ***~-to-~*** *adj*: *a ~-to-~ salesman.* 挨戶推銷的售貨員。***out of ~s,*** in the open air: 在戶外: *It's cold out of ~s; put an overcoat on.* 戶外冷，穿上一件大衣罷。***within ~s,*** inside; in the house. 在戶內；在屋內。***at death's ~,*** near death. 垂死。***lay sth at sb's ~,*** say that he is responsible for it. 歸咎於某人。***show sb the ~,*** lead him out to it (esp when he is unwelcome). 將某人逐出門外。 **2** (fig) means of obtaining or approaching sth: (喻)門路；途徑: *a ~ to success;* 成功之道；*to close the ~ against an agreement upon disarmament,* make it impossible. 拒作裁軍的協定；使裁軍協議無實現之可能。 **3** (compounds) (複合字) ˈ**~·bell,** bell inside a building, operated by a button, etc outside. 門鈴。 ˈ**~-case / -frame,** framework into which a ~ fits. 門框。ˈ**~·handle,** one which releases the latch to open a ~. 門的把手。ˈ**~-keeper,** person on duty or on guard at a ~ or other entrance. 門房；守門人。ˈ**~-knob,** round knob turned to release the lock on a ~. 門的球形把手。ˈ**~-knocker,** ⇨ knocker. ˈ**~·man** /-mən ; -mən/ (*pl* -men) uniformed attendant at the entrance to a hotel, cinema, etc. (旅社，電影院等之穿着制服的)司門人。 ˈ**~-mat,** rough mat on which shoes may be wiped. 門前的擦鞋墊。ˈ**~-nail,** large-headed nail formerly used to decorate some ~s. 門釘(昔時用以裝飾門的大頭釘)。***dead as a ~-nail,*** certainly dead. 確實死了。 ˈ**~-plate,** plate (usu brass) fastened to a ~ and with the name of the person living or working in the building or room. 門上的名牌(通常是銅做的)。ˈ**~-post,** upright post, part of a frame. 門柱。***deaf as a ~-post,*** completely deaf. 完全聾的。 ˈ**~·step,** step up to (usu) an outer ~. 門階。ˈ**~·stopper,** heavy object placed in a ~way to prevent the ~ from closing. 制門物(置於門口以防門關閉的重物)。 ˈ**~·way,** opening into which a ~ fits: 門口: *standing in the ~way.* 站在門口。

dope /dəʊp ; dop/ *n* [U] **1** thick, heavy liquid used as varnish. 塗料；塗布液；塗布油。 **2** (colloq) harmful drug (eg opium); narcotic. (俗)有害的藥物(例如鴉片)；麻醉藥。 **3** (sl) information. (俚)情報。□ *vt* [VP6A] give ~(2) to; make unconscious with a drug or narcotic; stimulate (eg a race-horse) with a drug. 施以麻醉藥；用麻醉藥使失去知覺；用藥物刺激(競賽的馬等)。**~y** /ˈdəʊpɪ ; ˈdopɪ/ *adj* (sl) half asleep; (as if) drugged; stupid. (俚)半睡半醒的；(彷彿)用過麻醉藥的；迷迷糊糊的；魯鈍的。

Doric /ˈdɒrɪk *US:* ˈdɔːr- ; ˈdɔrɪk/ *adj* (archit) of the oldest and simplest of the three types of column(1) in ancient Greek architecture. (建築)多利斯式的(古希臘三種柱式中最古樸者)。⇨ the illus at column. 參看 column 之插圖。

dor·mant /ˈdɔːmənt ; ˈdɔrmənt/ *adj* in a state of inactivity but awaiting development or activity: 潛伏的；蟄伏的: *a ~ volcano;* 休火山；*~ facilities,* mental powers capable of being developed; 潛在的能力；*plants which are ~/lie ~ during the winter,* alive but not growing. 冬季停止生長的植物。

dor·mer /ˈdɔːmə(r) ; ˈdɔrmɚ/ *n* (usu 通常作 ˈ**~-window**) upright window built from a sloping roof. (屋頂斜坡上凸出的)天窗。⇨ the illus at window. 參看 window 之插圖。

dor·mi·tory /ˈdɔːmɪtrɪ *US:* -tɔːrɪ ; ˈdɔrmə,torɪ/ *n* (*pl* -ries) sleeping-room with several or many beds, esp in a school or institution. (有幾張牀或很多牀的)大寢室；(尤指學校或機關團體的)宿舍。

dor·mouse /ˈdɔːmaʊs ; ˈdɔr,maʊs/ *n* (*pl* dormice /ˈdɔːmaɪs ; ˈdɔr,maɪs/) small animal (like a mouse or squirrel) that sleeps during cold weather in winter. 睡鼠；冬眠鼠。

dor·sal /ˈdɔːsl ; ˈdɔrsl/ *adj* (anat) of, on, near, the back: (解剖)背部的；背上的；近背部的: *the ~ fin,* eg of a shark. (鯊等的)脊鰭。⇨ the illus at sea. 參看 sea 之插圖。

dory¹ /ˈdɔːrɪ ; ˈdɔrɪ/ *n* (*pl* -ries) ship's light, flat-bottomed rowing-boat (eg as used by cod-fishers in N America). 平底小船(如北美洲捕鱈漁人所用者)。

dory² /ˈdɔːrɪ ; ˈdɔrɪ/ *n* (also 亦作 ˌ**John ˈD~**) edible seafish. 魴(一種可食的海魚)。

dos·age /ˈdəʊsɪdʒ ; ˈdosɪdʒ/ *n* [U] giving of medicines in doses; quantity of a single dose. 下藥；劑量；服用的藥量。

dose /dəʊs ; dos/ *n* [C] **1** amount (of a medicine/drug) to be taken at one time: 劑量；一服；一劑:

The bottle contains six ~*s.* 這瓶內裝有六次的藥量。⇨ salt(4). **2** (fig, colloq) sth given or taken: (喻,俗)給與或接受的東西: *give sb a* ~ *of flattery.* 向某人灌迷湯。 **3** (sl) venereal disease: (俚)性病: *give sb a* ~. 使某人感染性病。□ *vt* [VP6A, 15B, 14] give ~(s) to: 使服藥: *to* ~ *oneself with quinine.* 服奎寧。

doss /dɒs ; dɑs/ *vi* (GB sl) [VP2C] ~ ***down,*** go to bed. (英俚)就寢;睡覺。 **'~-house** *n* cheap lodging-house. 下等旅館;小客棧。 **dos·ser** /-sə(r) ; -sɚ/ *n* tramp (*n,* 3). 飄泊者。

dos·sier /'dɒsɪeɪ *US:* 'dɔːs- ; 'dɑsɪˌe/ *n* set of papers giving information about a person or event, esp a person's record. 記錄文件(尤指有關個人的記錄)。

dost /dʌst ; dʌst/ *v* old form, used in *Thou* ~, You do. 古語中 do 的第二人稱單數,與 thou 連用。

dot /dɒt ; dɑt/ *n* **1** small round mark (as over the letters i and j); decimal points: 小點(如 i 和 j 上面者);小數點: *dots and dashes,* the marks (eg •— •——•• — •••) used for morse signals. 電報符號;摩爾斯電碼。 ***on the dot,*** (colloq) at the precise moment. (俗)準時。 **2** sth like a dot in appearance: 似小點之物: *We watched the ship until it was a mere dot on the horizon.* 我們望着那條船,一直到它在水平線上變成了一個小點。□ *vt* (-tt-) **1** mark with a dot. 加以小點。 ***dot one's/ the i's and cross one's/the t's,*** (fig) make (sth) clear and definite. (喻)使(某事)明確。 **2** make with, cover with, dots: 用點製成;覆以點: *dotted about,* scattered here and there; 散落在各處的;星散的; *a field dotted with sheep,* with sheep here and there; 遍處是羊的田野; *a dotted line,* eg on a document, for a signature. 虛線(例如文件上的簽名處)。 ***sign on the dotted line,*** (fig) agree without hesitation or protest. (喻)毫不遲疑地同意。

do·tage /'dəʊtɪdʒ ; 'dotɪdʒ/ *n* [U] weakness of mind caused by old age: 因年老而心力衰邁;老耄;老朽: *He is in his* ~, is growing foolish, is unable to remember things, fails to notice things, etc. 他年邁昏憒了。 **do·tard** /'dəʊtəd ; 'dotɚd/ *n* person in his ~. 年邁昏憒之人。

dote /dəʊt ; dot/ *vi* [VP3A] ~ ***on/upon,*** show much, or too much, fondness; centre one's affections (on): 溺愛;寵愛: *She* ~*s on her grandson.* 她溺愛她的孫子。 *He's a doting* (= very loving) *husband.* 他是個很疼太太的丈夫。

doth /dʌθ ; dʌθ/ old form used for *does.* does 的古時拼法。

dottle /'dɒtl ; 'dɑtl/ *n* small quantity of tobacco left unsmoked in a pipe. 煙斗中吸剩的少量殘煙。

dotty /'dɒtɪ ; 'dɑtɪ/ *adj* (-ier, -iest) (colloq) feeble-minded; idiotic; eccentric. (俗)智力不足的;愚魯的;古怪的。

double[1] /'dʌbl ; 'dʌbl/ *adj* **1** twice as (much, large, etc): 加倍的(多,大等);兩倍的: *His partner is ill and he has to do* ~ *work.* 他的夥伴病了,他必須做雙倍的工作。 *His income is* ~ *what it was five years ago.* 他的收入是五年前的兩倍。 *There was a* ~ *knock at the door,* two knocks in quick succession. 門口有連續兩次的敲門聲。 *Two* ~ *whiskies, please,* two glasses of whisky, each with twice the usual portion. 請倒兩杯照平時的量加倍的威士忌來。 **2** having two of the same things or parts: 成雙的;成對的: *a gun with a* ~ *barrel;* 雙管槍; *a railway with a* ~ *track;* 雙軌鐵路; ~ *doors;* 雙扇門; ~*-glazing/*~ *windows* (used in cold countries); 雙重窗(爲氣候寒冷國家所用); *a man with a* ~ *chin,* with a fold of loose flesh below the chin; 有雙下巴的人; *a ship/box/trunk with a* ~ *bottom;* 雙層底的船(盒,箱); *a sword with a* ~ *edge;* 雙刃劍; *a* ~ *exposure,* (photo) two exposures on the same plate or section of film. (攝影)雙重曝光。 ⇨ single. **3** made for two persons or things: 供二人或二物用的: *a* ~ *bed;* 雙人床; *a* ~ *harness,* for two horses. 雙馬馬具。 **4** combining two things, qualities, etc: 將兩種東西、性質等聯合在一起的;兩種的: *a* ~ *advantage;* 兩種利益;一舉兩得; *a piece of furniture that serves a* ~ *purpose,* eg one that is a settee and can be opened out to make a bed; 兩用傢具(例如可打開做床鋪用的長靠椅); *a man with a* ~ *character,* eg Jekyll and Hyde; 有雙重性格的人(例如 Jekyll 和 Hyde); *to engage in* ~ *dealing,* be dishonest and deceitful. 從事欺詐。 **5** (of flowers) having more than one set or circle of petals: (指花)重瓣的: ~ *daffodils.* 重瓣水仙花。

double[2] /'dʌbl ; 'dʌbl/ *adv* **1** twice (as much): 加倍地: *Many things now cost* ~ *what they did a few years ago.* 許多東西現在比數年前貴了一倍。 **2** in twos; in a pair; in pairs or couples: 成雙地;成對地: *to see* ~, to see two things when there is only one; 將一物看成兩物;眼花; *to sleep* ~, two to a bed. 雙宿;二人共一床。

double[3] /'dʌbl ; 'dʌbl/ *n* **1** twice the quantity: 加倍;兩倍: *Ten is the* ~ *of five.* 十爲五的兩倍。 ~ ***or quits,*** the decision by chance (eg by throwing dice) whether a person shall pay twice what he owes, or nothing at all. 靠運氣(如擲骰子)決定一人是否加倍清還欠債或一筆勾銷。 **2** person or thing that looks exactly, or almost exactly, like another: 極爲相似的人或物: *She is the* ~ *of her sister.* 她和她的妹妹像極了。 **3** (*pl*) (tennis) game with two pairs. (複)(網球)雙打。 ***mixed*** ~***s,*** a man and woman against another man and woman. 男女混合雙打。 **4** ***at the*** ~***,*** (colloq) quickly. (俗)很快地;迅速地。 **5** [C] (bridge) act of doubling. (橋牌)加倍;賭倍。 ⇨ double[4](6).

double[4] /'dʌbl ; 'dʌbl/ *vt, vi* **1** [VP6A, 2A] make or become twice as great: 使加倍;增加一倍: *to* ~ *one's income.* 使收入加倍。 *Money earning good interest will* ~ *itself in time.* 以優利放存的款到時候會增加一倍。 **2** [VP6A, 15B] ~ ***(up/over/across),*** bend or fold in two: 摺叠;對摺: *Let me* ~ *(over) the shawl and put it round you.* 讓我把這披巾摺起來圍在你身上。 *He* ~*d his fists,* clenched them as if ready to fight. 他捏緊了拳頭(似欲打架)。 **3** [VP2A, C] ~ ***(back),*** turn sharply back in flight (when running to escape pursuit): (逃避追逐時)急忙轉身而逃: *The fox* ~*d (back) on its tracks.* 這狐狸突然轉身循著原路急逃。 **4** [VP15B, 2C] ~ ***back,*** turn or fold (sth) back. 摺叠(某物)。 ~ ***up,*** **(a)** fold (sth) up: 摺叠(某物): *He* ~*d up his legs and kicked out,* eg when swimming. 他將腿彎起又伸開(如游泳時所作者)。 **(b)** be capable of folding up or rolling up: 可摺叠;可捲起: *This carpet is too thick to* ~ *up.* 這地毯太厚,無法摺起來。 **(c)** (of persons) (cause to) bend the body with pain or in helpless laughter: (指人)(使)痛或笑得彎下了身: *The stone struck him in the stomach and* ~*d him up.* 那石頭打在他的腹部,使他痛得彎下了身。 *He* ~*d up with the pain of the blow.* 他因受擊而痛得彎下了身。 **5** [VP2C, 6A] do two jobs at the same time; (of an actor) act two parts in the same play: 一身兼兩個工作;(指演員)在同一劇中扮演兩角: *doubling as/doubling the parts of king and slave.* 兼演國王和奴隸。 **6** (bridge) bid to cause the points, lost or won by the opponents on the hand (13c), to be twice as much as they would normally have been. (橋牌)加倍;賭倍。

double[5] /'dʌbl ; 'dʌbl/ *adj, adv* (in compounds) (用於複合字中) ˌ~-'**barrelled** *adj* (of a gun) having two barrels; (fig, of a compliment, etc) ambiguous; (of a surname) compound, hyphened (as *Smith-Jones*). (指槍)雙管的;(喻,指恭維語等)曖昧的;含糊的;(指姓氏)複合的(如 Smith-Jones)。 ˌ~-'**bass** *n* largest and lowest-pitched instrument in the violin family. 最低音的最大提琴;低音提琴。 ⇨ the illus at string. 參看 string 之插圖。 ˌ~-'**bedded** *adj* (of a room) with two beds or a ~ bed. (指房間)有兩張床的;有雙人床的。(Cf 參較 *single-/twin-bedded.*) ˌ~ '**bind** *n* dilemma. 進退

兩難之境。ˌ~-ˈ**breasted** *adj* (of a coat or waistcoat) made so as to overlap across the front of the body. (指上衣或大衣)對襟的;雙排扣的。ˌ~-ˈ**check** *vt* check¹(1), twice in order to be certain. 檢查兩次。ˌ~-ˈ**cross** *vt* [VP6A] (colloq) cheat or betray. (俗)欺騙或出賣。□ *n* act of this kind. 欺騙;出賣。ˌ~-ˈ**dealer** *n* person who says one thing and means another; deceiver. 口是心非之人;騙子。ˌ~-ˈ**dealing** *n, adj* deceit(ful) (esp in business). (尤指在商業上)詐欺(的)。ˌ~-ˈ**decker** *n* ship, tram, bus with two decks. 兩層甲板的船;雙層的電車或公共汽車。 ⇨ deck¹(2). ˌ~-ˈ**dutch** *n* (colloq) gibberish. (俗)無意義的聲音; 嘰哩咕嚕的談話。ˌ~-ˈ**dyed** *adj* (chiefly fig) having certain qualities to a very high degree: (主作喻)深重的;徹頭徹尾的: *a ~-dyed scoundrel,* deeply stained with guilt. 一個徹頭徹尾的惡漢。ˌ~-ˈ**edged** *adj* with two cutting edges; (fig, of an argument, compliment) that can be understood as being either for or against. 雙刃的;(喻,指論據或恭維)正反兩可的;雙關的。ˌ~-ˈ**entry** *n* system of book-keeping in which each transaction is entered (written) on the debit side of one account and the credit side of another. 複式簿記(每筆帳在借方與貸方均登記一次的簿記方法)。 ˌ~-ˈ**faced** *adj* (= *two-faced*) insincere. 口是心非的。 ˌ~-ˈ**first** *n* a first-class honours degree in two principal subjects gained at the same time. 雙重優等獎(同時獲得兩門主要科目的最高榮譽)。ˌ~-ˈ**jointed** *adj* having joints that allow the fingers (or arms, legs) to move or bend in unusual ways. 有可作不尋常活動或彎曲之關節的。ˌ~-ˈ**park** *vt, vi* park a car at the side of a car already parked at the side of a street. 將車停在街邊另一部車的旁邊。ˌ~-ˈ**quick** *adj, adv* very quick(ly): 極迅速的(地): *in ~-quick time.* 非常快。ˌ~ ˈ**take** *n* delayed reaction to a situation. 反應遲鈍。ˈ~-**talk** *n* kind of talk that really means the opposite of, or sth quite different from, what it seems to mean. 反話;所表示的意義與字面意義相反或相距甚遠的談話。ˈ~-**think** *n* ability to believe two contradictory things. 相信二種矛盾事物的能力;矛盾思想。

doub·let /ˈdʌblɪt ; ˈdʌblɪt/ *n* **1** close-fitting garment for the upper part of the body, worn by men (about 1400–1600). (十五、十七世紀男子穿的)一種緊身上衣。 **2** one of a pair, esp one of two words with the same origin but which have become different in form or meaning, eg *hospital/hostel.* 兩個異形或異義的同源字中的一個(例如 hospital 和 hostel)。

a doublet and hose

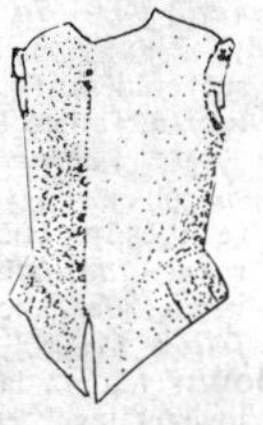

a jerkin

doub·loon /dʌbˈluːn ; dʌˈblun/ *n* (hist) Spanish gold coin. (史)西班牙的金幣名。

doubly /ˈdʌblɪ ; ˈdʌblɪ/ *adv* (used before *adjj*) to twice the extent or amount: (用於形容詞前) 加倍地: *to be ~ careful/sure.* 加倍小心(有信心)。

doubt¹ /daʊt ; daʊt/ *n* [U] uncertainty of mind; [C] feeling of uncertainty: 懷疑;疑問;疑慮: *I have no ~ that you will succeed/no ~ of your ability.* 我相信你會成功的(你的能力)。*There is not much ~ about his guilt,* He is almost certainly guilty. 他有罪是沒有多少問題的(是幾乎可以確定的)。*She had her ~s whether he would come.* 她拿不準他是否會來。*I have my ~s as to/about this being true.* 我懷疑這件事是否屬實。*There is no room for ~,* We can be quite certain about it. 沒有懷疑的餘地(我們可以確信)。*There is no ~ about it,* It is certain. 這是確實的。*It became a matter of ~* (= became uncertain) *whether....* 是否…尚未確定。***in ~,*** uncertain: 拿不準;不能確定: *When in ~ about the meaning of a word, consult a dictionary.* 你不能確定一個字的意義時,就去查一下字典。*He is in ~ (about) what to do.* 他尚未確定做些什麼。***beyond/past (all) ~; without (a) ~,*** certainly: 無疑地: *Don't worry; he'll come back without ~.* 不要擔心,他一定會回來。***no ~,*** very probably: 多半;十有八九: *He meant to help, no ~, but in fact he has been a hindrance.* 他原意是很想幫忙,但事實上他變成一個障礙了。***throw ~ upon sth,*** suggest that it is not to be regarded as certain or reliable. 懷疑。⇨ benefit.

doubt² /daʊt ; daʊt/ *vt* [VP6A, 9, 10] ~ ***(if/whether),*** feel doubt about; hesitate to believe; question the truth of: 懷疑;不相信;拿不準;不能確定: *You cannot ~ your own existence.* 你不能懷疑你的存在。*I ~ the truth of this report.* 我懷疑這項報告的眞實性。*Do you ~ my word,* think I am not telling the truth? 你不相信我的話嗎? *I don't ~ that he will come.* 我相信他會來。*Can you ~ that he will win?* 你能不相信他將得勝嗎? *I ~ whether he will come.* 我拿不準他是否會來。*I ~ if that was what he wanted.* 我不能確定那是否是他所要的。

doubt·ful /ˈdaʊtfl ; ˈdaʊtfəl/ *adj* ~ ***(about/of),*** feeling doubt; causing doubt; unreliable: 懷疑的;不能確定的;可疑的;不可靠的: *I am/feel ~ (about) what I ought to do.* 我不能確定應該做些什麼。*The future looks very ~.* 前途堪慮。*The weather looks very ~.* 天氣看來不可靠。*It's a ~ blessing,* may or may not be one. 這件事也許是福,也許不是。*Are you ~ of success?* 你懷疑是否能成功嗎? *He's a ~ character,* perhaps dishonest. 他是一個不可靠的人。*It is a ~ neighbourhood,* one with a bad reputation, one where ~ characters live. 這是一個名譽不佳的地區。~**ly** /-fəlɪ ; -fəlɪ/ *adv*

doubt·less /ˈdaʊtlɪs ; ˈdaʊtlɪs/ *adv* very probably. 很可能;十有八九。

douche /duːʃ ; duʃ/ *n* stream of water applied to a part of the body (outside or inside) for cleaning it or for medicinal purposes; instrument for forcing out such a stream of water. 灌洗身體(外部或內部)的水;灌洗器。

dough /dəʊ ; do/ *n* [U] mixture of flour, water, etc in a paste (for making bread, pastry, etc); (sl) money. (做麵包、點心等的)生麵團;(俚)金錢。ˈ~-**nut,** sweetened ~ cooked in deep fat, usu in the shape of a ring or a ball. 油炸圈餅。~**y** /ˈdəʊɪ ; ˈdoɪ/ *adj* of or like ~; soft; flabby. 生麵團的;似生麵團的;軟的;軟鬆的。

doughty /ˈdaʊtɪ ; ˈdaʊtɪ/ *adj* (old use, or joc) brave and strong; bold: (舊用法或謔)勇敢的;堅强的: *a ~ warrior;* 勇敢的戰士; *~ deeds.* 英勇的事蹟。

dour /dʊə(r) ; dur/ *adj* severe; stern; obstinate: 嚴厲的;冷峻的;執拗的: *~ looks;* 嚴厲的面容; *~ silence.* 冷寂。~**ly** *adv*

douse, dowse /daʊs ; daʊs/ *vt* [VP6A] put into water; throw water over; (colloq) extinguish (a light). 浸入水;潑以水;(俗)熄滅(燈)。

dove¹ /dʌv ; dʌv/ *n* **1** kind of pigeon; symbol of peace. 鴿;和平的象徵。ˈ~-**cote** /ˈdʌvkɒt ; ˈdʌvˌkot/ *n* small shelter or house with nesting-boxes for ~s. 鴿舍;鴿房。***flutter the ~-cotes,*** alarm quiet people. 驚擾安靜的人們。 **2** (colloq) member of a group promoting peace. (俗)提倡和平的人;鴿派人物。⇨ hawk¹(2).

dove² /dəʊv ; dov/ (US) alternative *pt* form of dive². (美) dive² 之另一過去式。

dove·tail /ˈdʌvteɪl ; ˈdʌvˌtel/ *n* joint for two pieces of wood. 楔形接榫;鳩尾榫。□ *vt, vi* [VP6A, 2A, 3A] ~ ***(with/into),*** join together by means of ~s; (fig) fit (together): 用鳩尾榫接合; (喻)吻合; 密合:

a dove

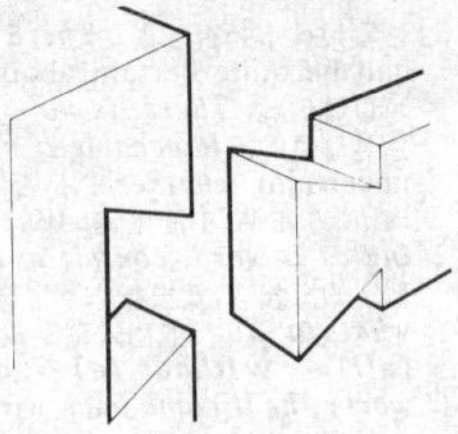

dove-tailing

My plans ~ed with his. 我的計畫和他的計畫吻合。

dow·ager /ˈdaʊədʒə(r) ; ˈdaʊədʒɚ/ *n* **1** woman with property or a title from her dead husband: 承受亡夫的遺產或爵位的寡婦: *the ~ duchess.* 公爵的未亡人。**2** (colloq) dignified elderly lady. (俗)年長的貴婦。

dowdy /ˈdaʊdɪ ; ˈdaʊdɪ/ *adj* (-ier, -iest) (of clothes, etc) shabby or unfashionable; (of a person) dressed in ~ clothes. (指衣服等)襤褸的; 不雅觀的; (指人)衣衫襤褸的;衣冠不整的。**dow·di·ly** *adv* **dow·di·ness** *n*

dowel /ˈdaʊəl ; ˈdaʊəl/ *n* headless pin or peg for keeping two pieces of wood, metal, stone, etc together. 綴縫釘;合釘;暗榫。

dower /ˈdaʊə(r) ; ˈdaʊɚ/ *n* **1** widow's share of her husband's property. 寡婦得自亡夫的財產。**2** dowry. 嫁妝; 妝奩; 陪嫁物。**3** gift of nature (eg beauty, intelligence). 天賦; 稟賦(例如美貌,智慧)。□ *vt* provide with a ~. 給與(寡婦)財產;給與嫁妝;賦與才貌。

down[1] /daʊn ; daʊn/ *n* [U] first, soft feathers of young birds; soft under-feathers of birds (as used for pillows and cushions); fine soft hair, eg the first hair that comes on a boy's face; the soft hair on some plants and seeds (eg the thistle). (雛鳥的)軟毛;柔羽毛 (如用以塡枕頭,褥墊者); (初生於男孩面孔上的)細軟鬍鬚; (某些植物和種子上的)茸毛(例如薊毛)。

down[2] /daʊn ; daʊn/ *adv part* **1** (with *vv* of motion) from a high(er) level to a low(er) level: (與表示動作之動詞連用)向下;自高至低: *The sun went ~.* 太陽下山了。*The flag was hauled ~ at sunset.* 日落時旗被降下。*If you can't jump ~, climb ~.* 如果你不能跳下來,就爬下來。*Some kinds of food go ~* (= can be swallowed) *more easily than others.* 有些食物比別的食物容易吞下。 **2** (with *vv* of motion) from an upright position to a horizontal position: (與表示動作的動詞連用) 倒下; 自直立的位置到橫躺的位置: *He was knocked ~ by a bus.* 他被公共汽車撞倒了。*If you're tired, go and lie ~.* 如果你累了,就去躺下。*He's ~* (= ill in bed) *with flu.* 他因患流行性感冒而臥在床上。 *Don't hit a man when he's ~,* (fig) attack him when he has suffered misfortune, etc. (喻) 不要落井下石; 不要打落水狗。 **3** (with *vv* indicating change of stance but not of position in space) to or in a lower position or direction: (與動詞連用表示姿態的變動, 而非位置的移動)至較低位置; 朝下: *Sit ~, please.* 請坐。*The tall man bent ~ to speak to me.* 那高個子彎下腰對我講話。 **4** (with *vv* indicating position or state): (與動詞連用表示位置或狀態): *Mary isn't ~ yet,* is not yet dressed and downstairs. 瑪莉還沒有穿好衣服下樓來。 *We can't use the telephone—the lines are all ~,* on the ground, eg after a storm. 我們不能打電話—電話線都掉在地上了(例如暴風雨後)。*The river is ~,* back to its normal height, eg after a flood. 河水退了(例如氾濫後退至正常水位)。 **5** from a more important place (eg the capital) to a less important place; from an inland place to the coast; from the university: 自重要地點(例如首都)至次要地點;自內陸至海岸;自大學: *We went ~ to Brighton* (eg from London) *for the weekend.* 我們去布來頓(例如從倫敦) 度週末。 *The Bill was sent ~* (from the House of Lords) *to the House of Commons.* 該項議案(自上議院)送往下議院。 **6** (used with *vv* to indicate reduction to a smaller volume, a lower degree, a state of less activity, etc): (與動詞連用,表示數量、程度、活動性等的減少): *The heels of my shoes have worn ~.* 我的鞋後跟磨壞了。 *Boil the fat ~.* 將脂肪熬一熬。*The wind died ~.* 風勢漸漸弱了。 *The sea is ~/has calmed ~,* is, has become, calm. 海浪已平靜了。 *The fire is burning ~,* getting low. 火勢減弱了。*One of the back tyres is ~,* is flat or getting flat. 有一個後胎跑氣了。*The clock has run ~,* needs to be wound up. 鐘停了。*The temperature has gone ~.* 溫度已降低。 *The price of fruit is ~.* 水果的價格跌了。**7** (used with reference to writing) on paper: (用以指書寫)於紙上: *to write sth ~;* 將某事記下; *to get sth ~,* write it. 寫下某事。 *Please take ~ this letter,* write it (eg in shorthand) as I dictate it. 請將這封信筆錄下來 (例如經我口授而用速記錄下)。 *Put me ~/Put my name ~ for 50p,* eg as willing to give this sum. 請把我的名字登記下來,我準備出五十辨士(例如願意繳此款項時)。*I see you're ~* (= your name appears in the programme) *for a speech at the next meeting.* 我知道下次開會你要演說(節目表上有你的名字)。 **8** from an earlier time (to a later time): 自較早時間 (至較晚時間): *the history of Europe ~ to 1914;* 自古以迄 1914 年的歐洲史; *looking ~ through the ages;* 縱觀古今; *coming ~ to modern times.* 以迄近代。 **9** including the lower limit in a series: (指一系列中)由上至下;由大至小: *from ocean liners ~ to rowing-boats.* 從班輪到划艇。 **10** (in various phrases) (用於各種片語中) ***D~ with,*** let us be rid of: 打倒: *D~ with the grammarians!* 打倒文法學者! ***~ under,*** (colloq) on the other side of the world from Europe (eg Australia). (俗)與歐洲對蹠之地(例如澳洲)。***up and ~,*** to and fro: 往返地: *walking up and ~.* 走來走去。***money/cash*** **ˈ~,** payment at the time of purchase (contrasted with credit): 付現金(與 credit 相對): *You must pay £10 ~.* 你必須付十鎊現金。Hence, 由此產生, **ˈ~ payment.** (分期付款的)首次款。***be ~ and out,*** (colloq) (俗) **(a)** (boxing) be knocked out, unable to resume the fight. (拳賽)被擊倒而不能繼續比賽。**(b)** (fig) be beaten in the struggle of life; be unemployed and without money. (喻)貧困潦倒; 落魄。Hence, 由此產生, **ˌ~-and-ˈout** *n* [C]. ***get ~ to work/business,*** start work in real earnest. 認眞開始工作。***be ~ on sb,*** feel ill-will towards him. 對某人不懷善意;仇視某人。***~ in the dumps,*** (colloq) dejected; in low spirits. (俗)沮喪; 心情不好。***~ in the mouth,*** (colloq) sad-looking. (俗)面容憂戚的。***~ on one's luck,*** (colloq) having suffered misfortune. (俗)倒霉的。***come ˈ~ in the world,*** fall to a lower social position. 社會地位降低;潦倒。***come ~ on sb,*** scold or rebuke him sharply. 嚴斥某人。**ˌ~-to-ˈearth** *adj* concerned with realities; practical (contrasted with *impractical, vague, idealistic*): 現實的; 實際的 (與 impractical, vague, idealistic 相對): *He's a ~-to-earth sort of fellow.* 他是個現實的人。

down[3] /daʊn ; daʊn/ *prep* **1** from a high(er) to a low(er) level: 自高處向下: *to run ~ a hill.* 自山上跑下。*The tears ran ~ her face.* 眼淚順着她的臉流下。*Her hair was hanging ~ her back.* 她的頭髮垂下來披在她的背上。 **2** at a lower part of: 在…之較低處: *Oxford is farther ~ the river.* 牛津在這條河的下游。 **3** along (not necessarily with reference to a lower level): 沿;循(不一定指較低處): *I was walking ~ the street.* 我沿着街道走。*He has gone ~ town,* from one of the outlying parts, eg a suburb, to the business or shopping quarters of the town. 他已進城去了 (例如自郊區至鬧區)。 ⇨ downtown. ***~ (the) wind,*** (of a boat) with the wind behind. (指船)順風的。**4** (of time) from a farther to a nearer period: (指時間)自較遠至較近的時期: *~ the ages.* 由古至今。

down[4] /daʊn; daʊn/ *vt* [VP6A] (colloq) bring, put, knock, down: (俗)打倒；擊倒: *to ~ a player with a tackle;* 以擒抱動作絆倒一球員; *to ~ a glass of beer,* empty the glass. 喝乾一杯啤酒。~ ***tools,*** (of workers) refuse to work, go on strike. (指工人)罷工。

down[5] /daʊn; daʊn/ *n* ***ups and ~s,*** changes in fortune, prosperity, etc: 時運等的變化: *have one's ups and ~s;* 有好運也有厄運; *the ups and ~s of life.* 人生的榮枯(浮沉)。***have a ~ on sb,*** feel ill-will towards him. 對某人不懷善意;仇視某人。

down·beat /ˈdaʊnbiːt; ˈdaʊnˌbit/ *n* (music) first beat of a bar (when the conductor's hand moves down). (音樂)下拍。

down·cast /ˈdaʊnkɑːst *US:* -kæst; ˈdaʊnˌkæst/ *adj* (of a person) depressed; discouraged; sad; (of eyes) looking downwards. (指人)沮喪的;氣餒的;悲哀的;(指眼睛)向下視的。

down·fall /ˈdaʊnfɔːl; ˈdaʊnˌfɔl/ *n* (usu *sing*) (通常作單數) **1** heavy fall (of rain, etc). (雨等的)大降。**2** (fig) ruin; fall from fortune or power: (喻)毀滅;敗落: *His ~ was caused by gambling and drink.* 他的身敗名裂是由賭博和酗酒造成的。

down·grade /ˌdaʊnˈgreɪd; ˈdaʊnˌgred/ *vt* [VP6A] reduce to a lower grade or rank. 使降級。

down·hearted /ˌdaʊnˈhɑːtɪd; ˈdaʊnˈhartɪd/ *adj* in low spirits; depressed. 鬱悶的;沮喪的。

down·hill /ˌdaʊnˈhɪl; ˈdaʊnˌhɪl/ *adv* in a downward sloping direction. 向下地。***go ~,*** (fig) get worse (in health, fortune, etc). (喻)(健康、運氣等)每況愈下。

Down·ing Street /ˈdaʊnɪŋ striːt; ˈdaʊnɪŋ strit/ *n* street in London with official residence of the Prime Minister; (hence) the British Government: 唐寧街(倫敦一街道名,有英國首相的官邸);(由此產生)英國政府: *What does ~ think of the matter?* 英國政府對此事作何想法?

down·pour /ˈdaʊnpɔː(r); ˈdaʊnˌpor/ *n* (usu *sing*) heavy fall (esp of rain): (常用單數)大降(尤指雨); 傾盆大雨: *to be caught in a ~.* 趕上傾盆大雨。

down·right /ˈdaʊnraɪt; ˈdaʊnˌraɪt/ *adj* **1** forth-right; honest; frank: 直爽的;誠實的;坦白的: *He has a ~ manner.* 他有坦白的態度。*He is a ~ sort of person.* 他是個直爽的人。**2** thorough; complete: 徹底的;完全的;純粹的: *It's a ~ lie.* 這完全是謊言。*It's ~ nonsense.* 這完全是一派胡言。□ *adv* thoroughly: 徹底地: *He was ~ rude.* 他眞是太粗魯了。**~·ness** *n*

downs /daʊnz; daʊnz/ *n* **1** expanse of open high land. 廣濶的高地。**the North/South D~,** the chalk uplands of S England. 北部(南部)高地(英格蘭南部含有石灰石的高地)。**2 the D~,** the sea off the coast of Kent (SE England): (英格蘭東南)肯特郡之外海: *anchor in the D~.* 在肯特郡外海拋錨。

down·stairs /ˌdaʊnˈsteəz; ˈdaʊnˈstɛrz/ *adv* to, at, on, of, a lower floor; down the stairs: 至樓下;在樓下;屬於樓下;下樓地: *He went ~ to breakfast.* 他下樓吃早餐。*Our neighbours ~* (= on the lower floor) *are very noisy.* 我們樓下的鄰居很吵鬧。*Your brother is waiting ~.* 你哥哥(弟弟)在樓下等着。□ **down·stair(s)** *adj: the ~(s) rooms.* 樓下的房間。

down·town /ˈdaʊntaʊn; ˈdaʊnˈtaʊn/ *adv* (esp US) to or in the lower part of a town; to or in the main or business part of a town: (尤美)至或在城市的較低地區;至或在鬧區;至或在商業區: (attrib) (形容用法) *~ New York;* 紐約市的商業區; *a ~ movie theatre.* 在鬧區的電影院。

down·trod·den /ˈdaʊntrɒdn; ˈdaʊnˈtradn̩/ *adj* oppressed; kept down and treated badly. 受壓迫的;被蹂躪的。

down·ward /ˈdaʊnwəd; ˈdaʊnwəd/ *adj* moving, leading, going, pointing, to what is lower: 向下的;下降的;下方的: *a ~ slope;* 一個下坡; *on the ~ path;* 在一向下傾斜的小路上; *prices with a ~ tendency.* 有下跌趨勢的物價。**down·ward(s)** *adv* towards what is lower: 向下地: *He laid the picture face ~s on the table.* 他將那幅畫反放在桌上。*The monkey was hanging head ~s from the branch.* 那猴子頭向下倒掛在樹枝上。

downy /ˈdaʊnɪ; ˈdaʊnɪ/ *adj* of, like, covered with, down. 軟毛的;似軟毛的;覆有軟毛的。⇨ down[1].

dowry /ˈdaʊərɪ; ˈdaʊrɪ/ *n* (*pl* -ries) [C] property, money, brought by a bride to her husband. 妝奩;嫁妝;陪嫁物。

dowse /daʊs; daʊs/ *vt* ⇨ douse.

dows·ing /ˈdaʊzɪŋ; ˈdaʊzɪŋ/ *n* [U] searching for underground water or metals by using a Y-shaped stick or rod. 用丫形桿探尋地下水或鑛藏;占杖測水。⇨ diviner. **dows·er** *n* person who does this. 用丫形桿探尋地下水或鑛藏者。

dox·ol·ogy /dɒkˈsɒlədʒɪ; dɑksˈɑlədʒɪ/ *n* (*pl* -gies) words of praise to God, used in church services (eg 'Glory be to God...'). (禮拜時)對上帝的讚頌(例如:'榮耀歸於上帝…')。

doyen /ˈdɔɪən; ˈdɔɪən/ *n* senior member of the diplomatic corps in a capital city, or a society, profession, etc. 外交使節團團長;(社團或某一行業等之)高級代表。

doy·ley, doyly *n* = doily.

doze /dəʊz; doz/ *vi* [VP2A, C] sleep lightly; be half asleep. 瞌睡;假寐。**~ *off,*** fall lightly asleep: 打瞌睡: *He ~d off during the sermon.* 他在做禮拜時打瞌睡。□ *n* [C] short, light sleep. 瞌睡;假寐。

dozen /ˈdʌzn; ˈdʌzn̩/ *n* (also used attrib, *pl* unchanged) (亦作形容用法,複數不變) **1** twelve: 十二個;一打: *Eggs are 35p a ~.* 鷄蛋三十五辨士一打。*I want three ~ of these.* 這些我要三打。*Pack them in ~s,* in sets or groups of twelve. 把它們一打一打地包裝起來。***talk nineteen to the ~,*** talk incessantly. 不停地談話;刺刺不休。**2** (*pl*) **~s of,** a large number of: (複)很多的: *I've been there ~s of times.* 我曾去過那裏很多次。

drab /dræb; dræb/ *adj* **1** (also as *n*) dull muddy brown. (亦做名詞用)土褐色(的)。**2** (fig) dull; uninteresting; monotonous: (喻)乏味的;單調的: *a ~ existence.* 單調的生活。**~·ly** *adv* **~·ness** *n*

drachm /dræm; dræm/ *n* **1** = dram(1). **2** (archaic) small quantity. (古)小量;微量。

drachma /ˈdrækmə; ˈdrækmə/ *n* ancient Greek silver coin; modern Greek unit of currency. 古希臘的銀幣名;近代希臘貨幣單位。

dra·co·nian /drəˈkəʊnɪən; dreˈkonɪən/ *adj* of a rigorous law or code of laws; harsh: 嚴峻法典的;嚴厲的: *~ measures.* 嚴厲的手段。

draft[1] /drɑːft *US:* dræft; dræft/ *n* [C] **1** outline (usu in the form of rough notes) of sth to be done: 草稿: *a ~ for a speech/letter;* 一篇演說(一封信)的草稿; preliminary version: 草案: *a ~ for a Parliamentary Bill;* 一項國會議案的草案; rough sketch: 草圖: *a ~ for a machine.* 一部機器的草圖。**2** written order for payment of money by a bank; drawing of money by means of such an order: 滙票;滙票的支付;提款: *a ~ for £500 upon London,* eg one written by a Paris bank upon its London branch. 在倫敦提取的五百鎊的一張滙票(例如由巴黎的銀行開出至倫敦分行者)。Hence, 由此產生, **ˈbank-~.** **3** group of men chosen from a larger group for a special purpose; (US) group of men conscripted for the armed forces. 特遣部隊;分遣隊;(美)徵召的兵員隊。**the ~,** conscription. 徵兵。**ˈ~ card,** card summoning a man to serve in the armed forces. 徵召令。**4** (US) (美) = draught.

draft[2] /drɑːft *US:* dræft; dræft/ *vt* [VP6A] **1** make a draft(1) of: 作…的草稿、草案、草圖;草擬: *to ~ a speech.* 草擬一演說稿。**2** choose men for a draft(3); (US) conscript (a man) for the armed forces: 選拔做爲特遣隊; (美)徵召服役: *to be ~ed into the Army.* 被徵召當兵。**~·ee** /ˌdrɑːfˈtiː *US:* ˌdræfˈtiː; dræfˈti/ *n* (US) man ~ed for military service. (美)被徵召的士兵。**~·ing** *n* the act of ~ing; way in which sth is ~ed(1): 起草;草擬;起草的方式: *a ~ing committee,* eg of a Parliamentary

Bill. (國會議案等的)起草委員會。*The ~ing of this section of the Bill is obscure.* 草案上的這一項含糊不清。

drafts·man /ˈdrɑːftsmən *US:* ˈdræfts-; ˈdræftsmən/ *n* (*pl* -men) man who prepares drafts(1), esp in engineering and architecture; person responsible for the careful and exact wording of a legal document, or a (clause in a) parliamentary bill. 作草圖者;作圖樣者;繪圖員;法案或議案的起草人。

drafty /ˈdrɑːftɪ *US:* ˈdræftɪ; ˈdræftɪ/ *adj* (-ier, -iest) (US) (美) = draughty.

drag[1] /dræg; dræg/ *n* **1** sth that is dragged, eg a net (ˈ**~-net**) pulled over the bottom of a river (eg to catch fish); a heavy harrow pulled over the ground to break up the soil. 被拖曳的東西(例如拖網,亦稱 drag-net);重耙(耕土用者)。 **2** (colloq) sth or sb that slows down progress because heavy, dull, etc: (俗)拖累之物;阻礙物: *His wife has been a ~ on him all his life*, has hindered him in his career. 他的妻子是他一生事業上的累贅。*Do we have to take your sister with us? She's such a ~.* 我們必須帶着你的妹妹嗎？她眞是個累贅。⇨ drag²(3). **3** [U] (sl) woman's clothes worn by a man: (俚)男扮女裝用的衣服: *'As You Like It' performed in ~*, with the women's parts acted by men dressed as women. 由男扮女裝演出的'如願'。 **4** (sl) puff at a cigarette or cigar. (俚)吸一口(香煙或雪茄)。

drag[2] /dræg; dræg/ *vt, vi* (-gg-) **1** [VP6A, 15B, 14] pull along (esp with effort and difficulty): 拖;曳;用力拉: *to ~ a heavy box out of a cupboard.* 把一個重箱子從櫥裏拖出來。*The escaped prisoner was ~ged from his hiding-place.* 那逃犯被人從他隱藏之處拖了出來。 **~ sb into doing sth**, involve him unwillingly in an undertaking: 使某人勉强做一事: *He hates parties; we had to ~ him into going.* 他不喜歡聚會;我們不得不勉强他參加。 **2** [VP6A, 15B, 2A, C] (allow to) move slowly and with effort; (allow to) trail: (使)緩慢而費力地行動;(使)拖曳而進: *to walk with ~ging feet.* 蹣跚而行。*He could scarcely ~ himself along.* 他幾乎走不動了。*The ship ~ged its anchor/The ship's anchor ~ged during the night*, it failed to hold, was drawn along the sea bottom. 這船的錨在夜裏拖動了(錨沒有鈎牢,沿着海底拖動)。 **~ one's feet**, go forward slowly, unwillingly (often fig): 拖曳前進;緩慢而勉强地前進(常作喻): *We suspect the Government of ~ging their feet.* 我們懷疑政府在拖延。 **~ up (a child)**, (colloq) (contrasted with bring up) educate, train, etc it badly. (俗)未能適當地管教(小孩)(與 bring up 相對)。 **3** [VP2A, C] **~ (on)**, (of time, work, an entertainment) go on slowly in a dull manner: (指時間、工作、娛樂)緩慢而單調地進行: *Classwork often ~s towards the end of term*, pupils lose interest. 學期近結束時,功課常是鬆懈而乏味地進行。*The performance ~ged on.* 表演緩慢而單調地進行著。*Time seemed to ~.* 時間好像過得很慢。 **~ out**, make longer (in time): 拖延(時間): *~ out a meeting/an argument/a performance.* 拖延會議(辯論、表演)的時間。 **4** [VP6A, 2A] use nets, tools, etc to search the bottom of a river, lake, etc (usu for sth lost or missing): (用網、工具等)在河底、湖底等撈取;打撈: *They ~ged the river for the missing child.* 他們打撈河底尋找這失踪的孩子。

drag·gled /ˈdrægld; ˈdrægl̩d/ *adj* (often 常作 **be·~**) wet, dirty or muddy (as if dragged through mud, etc). 潮濕而泥污的(如在泥漿等中拖行者)。

drago·man /ˈdrægəʊmən; ˈdrægəmən/ *n* (*pl* ~s) guide and interpreter (esp in Arabic-speaking countries). 通譯(尤指在說阿拉伯語的國家中者)。

dragon /ˈdrægən; ˈdrægən/ *n* fabulous creature like a crocodile or snake, often with wings and claws, able to breathe out fire, often guarding a treasure; (colloq) fierce person. 龍(神話中似鱷魚或蛇的一種動物,常生有翅及爪,能吐火,常守護一寶藏);(俗)兇狠的人。

drag·on·fly /ˈdrægənflaɪ; ˈdrægənˌflaɪ/ *n* (*pl* -flies) insect with a stick-like body and two pairs of large wings. 蜻蜓。⇨ the illus at insect. 參看 insect 之插圖。

dra·goon /drəˈguːn; drəˈgun/ *n* horse-soldier; cavalryman. 騎兵。□ *vt* [VP6A, 14] **~ sb (into doing sth)**, force him (to do sth), harass him. 逼迫某人(做某事)。

drain[1] /dreɪn; dren/ *n* **1** pipe, channel, trench, etc for carrying away water, sewage and other unwanted liquids; (*pl*) system of pipes and sewers for carrying away waste liquid, etc from buildings; (US) plug-hole: 水管;下水道;陰溝;(複)排水系統;排水裝置;(美)消防給水裝置: *There's a bad smell; something wrong with the ~s, I suppose.* 有難聞的氣味,我覺得排水道有毛病。 **go down the ~**, (fig) be wasted. (喻)被浪費;白費。 ˈ**~·pipe**, pipe used in a system of ~s. 排水管。 **2** (fig) sth that continually uses up force, time, wealth, etc; cause of weakening or loss: (喻)不斷消耗力量、時間、財富等之事物; 衰弱或損失的原因: *Military expenditure has been a great ~ on the country's resources.* 軍費消耗國家的財源甚大。*All this extra work was a ~ on his strength.* 所有這些額外的工作是耗損他體力的原因。 ˈ**brain ~**, movement of trained technical and scientific personnel from one country to another (because of better opportunities, etc). 人才外流(由於機會較好等，一國之技術和科學人才流向另一國)。 **3** (colloq) small drink; mouthful: (俗)小飲; 一口之量: *Don't drink it all; leave me a ~!* 不要把它喝光,給我留一口！

drain[2] /dreɪn; dren/ *vt, vi* **1** [VP15B, 2C] **~ away/off**, (of liquid) (cause to) run or flow away: (指液體)(使)排出;(使)流出: *Dig trenches to ~ the water away/off.* 挖溝以排水。*The water will soon ~ away/off.* 水不久便會流去了。 **2** [VP2A, C, 6A] (of land, etc) make, become, dry as water flows away: (指土地等)使乾涸; 因水流出而變乾: *to ~ swamps/marshes.* 排出沼澤的水。*Land must be well ~ed for some crops.* 土地必須做相當的排水以適合某些作物。*These fields ~ into the river.* 這些田地的水流入河中。*Leave the dishes on the board to ~.* 將盤碟放在水槽旁邊的板上晾乾。 ˈ**~·ing-board**, board at the side of a sink, on which washed dishes, etc are placed to ~. 滴乾板(在洗滌槽旁邊,可置放洗過的盤碟等使之晾乾)。 **3** [VP6A, 15B, 14, 2C] **~ (away/off); ~ (of)**, (fig) (cause to) lose (strength, wealth, etc) by degrees: (喻)(使)逐漸消耗(力量、財富等): *The country was ~ed of its manpower and wealth by war.* 這個國家因戰爭而逐漸耗盡了人力和財富。*His life was slowly ~ing away*, eg of a man bleeding to death. 他的生命逐漸枯竭了(例如指流血而死的人)。 **4** [VP6A, 22] drink; empty: 飲;飲乾: *to ~ a glass dry.* 飲乾一杯(酒等)。

drain·age /ˈdreɪnɪdʒ; ˈdrenɪdʒ/ *n* [U] **1** draining or being drained. 排水; 疏水。 ˈ**~-basin**, area drained by a river. 某一河流排水的區域; 流域。 **2** system of drains(1). 排水系統; 排水裝置。 **3** that which is drained away or off; sewage. 排出之物; 下水道中之汚物。

drake /dreɪk; drek/ *n* male duck. 公鴨。

dram /dræm; dræm/ *n* **1** unit of weight: (apothecaries' weight) 60 grains (8 drams = 1 oz or 31·1

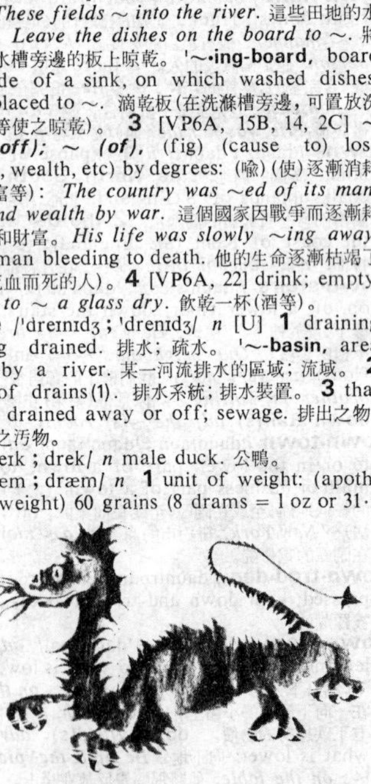

a dragon

grams); (avoirdupois weight) $27\frac{1}{3}$ grains (16 drams = 1 oz or 28·35 grams). 特拉姆(衡量單位,在藥量中等於 60 喱, 8 特拉姆等於 1 兩或 31·1 公克; 在常衡中等於 $27\frac{1}{3}$ 喱, 16 特拉姆等於 1 兩或 28·35 公克)。⇨ App 5. 參看附錄五。 **2** small drink of alcoholic spirits: 少量的酒: *He's fond of a ~*, eg of whisky. 他喜歡喝一點酒(例如飲威士忌)。

drama /ˈdrɑːmə ; ˈdrɑmə/ *n* **1** [C] play for the theatre, radio or TV; [U] **(the)** ~, composition, presentation and performance of such plays: 劇本;戲劇;戲劇的製作及演出: *a student of (the) ~;* 研究戲劇的人; *to be interested in (the) ~.* 對戲劇有興趣。 **2** [C, U] series of exciting events. 一連串緊張刺激的事件。

dra·matic /drəˈmætɪk ; drəˈmætɪk/ *adj* **1** of drama(1): 劇本的;戲劇的: *~ performances;* 戲劇的演出; *~ criticism.* 戲劇批評。 **2** sudden or exciting, like an event in a stage play: 如舞臺劇般緊張刺激的; 戲劇性的: *~ changes in the international situation.* 國際局勢之戲劇性的變化。 **3** (of a person, his speech, behaviour) showing the feelings or character in a lively or exaggerated way. (指人或人的言行)生動或誇張地表現情感或性格的。 **dra·mati·cally** /-klɪ ; -klɪ/ *adv* in a ~ manner. 緊張地;戲劇性地。 **dra·mat·ics** *n* (usu with *sing v*) (通常與單數動詞連用) **1** ~(1) works or performances by amateurs: 業餘者的戲劇作品或演出: *Are you interested in amateur ~s?* 你對於業餘演戲有興趣嗎? **2** ~(3) speech, behaviour, etc. 誇張情感的言詞、行爲等。

drama·tis per·sonae /ˌdræmətɪs pɜːˈsəʊnaɪ ; ˈdræmətɪspɚˈsoni/ *n pl* (Lat) (list of the) characters in a play. (拉)劇中人;登場人物。

drama·tist /ˈdræmətɪst ; ˈdræmətɪst/ *n* writer of plays. 劇作家;戲劇作者。

drama·tize /ˈdræmətaɪz ; ˈdræməˌtaɪz/ *vt* [VP6A] **1** put a story, novel, etc into the form of a drama. 改編(小說等)爲戲劇。 **2** treat (a situation, etc) as if it were a drama. 戲劇性地處理(事態等)。 **drama·tiz·ation** /ˌdræmətaɪˈzeɪʃn *US:* -tɪˈz ; ˌdræmətəˈzeʃən/ *n* [C, U].

drank /dræŋk ; dræŋk/ *pt* of drink.

drape /dreɪp ; drep/ *vt* [VP6A, 14] **1** ~ ***(round/over)***, hang curtains, cloth, a cloak or other garment in folds round or over sth: 用(窗簾、布、斗篷或其他有摺縐的衣物)覆蓋某物: *to ~ curtains over a window;* 用窗簾遮起窗子; *to ~ a cloak over one's shoulders/a flag over the coffin.* 將斗篷披在肩上(將旗覆於棺上)。 **2** ~ ***(with)***, cover or decorate: 覆蓋或裝飾: *walls ~d with flags;* 掛著旗子的牆壁; *a doorway ~d with a heavy curtain.* 懸有厚簾的門。 **3** ~ ***(round/over)***, allow to rest loosely: 使鬆弛地停靠於: *He ~d his legs over the arms of his chair.* 他將兩腿鬆弛地放在椅臂上。 □ *n* [C] (chiefly US) cloth hung in folds; curtain. (主美)摺縐而下垂的布;帘。

dra·per /ˈdreɪpə(r) ; ˈdrepɚ/ *n* (GB) shopkeeper who sells cloth, linen, clothing, etc. (英)布商。 **~y** *n* **1** [U] ~'s trade; goods sold by a ~: 布業;呢絨業;布商所售之貨: (attrib) (形容用法) *a ~y business/store.* 布業(店)。 **2** [C, U] (*pl* -ries) materials used for garments, hangings, curtains, etc; such materials arranged in folds. 用以製衣服、帳、幃、帘等的布料;摺縐的衣料、帳、帘等。

dras·tic /ˈdræstɪk ; ˈdræstɪk/ *adj* (of actions, methods, medicines) having a strong or violent effect: (指行動、方法、藥品)激烈的;猛烈的: *~ measures to cure inflation*, eg a steep increase in the bank rate; 抑制通貨膨脹之激烈的措施 (例如銀行貼現率之突增); *~ remedies to cure an illness.* 治療某一疾病的烈性藥物。 **dras·ti·cally** /-klɪ ; -klɪ/ *adv*

drat /dræt ; dræt/ *vt* (-tt-) (used chiefly in exclamations, dated, colloq) curse: (主要用於感嘆句;過時用語,俗)可惡;該死;討厭: *D~ that child!* 那個討厭的小鬼! *That ~ted* (= cursed) *boy!* 那個該死的男孩!

draught (US = **draft**) /drɑːft *US:* dræft ; dræft/ *n* **1** [C, U] current of air in a room, chimney or other enclosed place: 通風;氣流: *You'll catch cold if you sit in a ~.* 如果坐在風口上,你會傷風。 *Turn the electric fan on and make a ~.* 把電扇打開通一下風。 *There's not enough ~ up the chimney; that's why the fire doesn't burn well.* 煙囪上的通風不足;那便是火燒不旺的原因。 **2** [C] the pulling in of a net of fish(es). 拉網;一網。 **3** [U] depth of water needed to float a ship: 船底沒入水中的深度;船的吃水: *vessels of shallow ~;* 吃水淺的船隻; *a ship with a ~ of ten feet.* 吃水十呎的船。 ⇨ draw²(13). **4** [U] drawing of liquid from a container (eg a barrel): 自容器 (例如桶) 中汲取: *beer on ~; ~ beer.* 桶裝啤酒。Cf 參較 *bottled beer.* **5** [C] (amount drunk during) one continuous process of swallowing: 一飲(之量): *a ~ of water;* 一口氣飲下之水; *to drink half a pint of beer at a ~.* 一口氣飲下半品脫啤酒。 **6** (*pl*, with *sing v*) (US 美 = *checkers*) table game for two players using 24 round pieces (called 稱作 **ˈ~s(men)**) on a board with 32 black and 32 white squares. (複,用單數動詞)西洋象棋(供二人娛樂的一種桌上遊戲,用二十四個圓形棋子,在一有三十二黑方格與三十二白方格的棋盤上進行)。□ *vt* ⇨ draft². **ˈ~-horse**, one that pulls heavy loads. 拖馬。⇨ *packhorse* at pack¹(1). **draughts·man** /ˈdrɑːftsmən *US:* ˈdræ- ; ˈdræftsmən/ *n* (*pl* -men) **1** = draftsman. **2** piece used in ~s, ⇨ 6 above. 西洋象棋子(參看上列第 6 義)。

draughty (US = **drafty**) /ˈdrɑːftɪ *US:* ˈdræftɪ ; ˈdræftɪ/ *adj* (-ier, -iest) with draughts(1) blowing through: 通風的: *a ~ room.* 一個通風的房間。

draw¹ /drɔː ; drɔ/ *n* **1** the act of drawing (in various senses): 拉;牽;拖;曳;抽;拔;提取;吸引;吸入;使人吐露情感等;變長;移動;繪;寫;吃水;不分勝負;結束;吸取精華: *the ~ for the fourth round of the tennis tournament.* 網球賽第四局之平手。 *When does the ~ take place*, When will the winning numbers for the lottery, etc, be drawn? 何時開始抽獎? *The game ended in a ~*, neither side won. 比賽不分勝負。 *Our team has had five wins and two ~s this season.* 我們的隊本季贏了五次,打平二次。 **2** sb or sth that attracts attention, ⇨ draw²(5): 吸引注意力的人或物: *Mr A is always a great ~ at political meetings*, is a popular speaker. A 君在政治性的集會中是十分引人注意的人物。 *The new play is a great ~*, many people are going to the theatre to see it. 這齣新戲很賣座。 **3** ***be quick/slow on the ~***, quick/slow at pulling out a sword, revolver, etc; (fig) quick/slow to understand. 拔劍、槍等迅速(緩慢);(喻)思想敏捷(遲鈍)。

draw² /drɔː ; drɔ/ *vt, vi* (*pt* drew /druː ; dru/, *pp* drawn /drɔːn ; drɔn/) **1** [VP6A, 15B, 14] move by pulling: 拉; 牽: *to ~ a boat (up) out of the water/on to the beach;* 將一小船拉出水(至灘上); *to ~ one's chair up to the table;* 把椅子拉至桌旁; *to ~ sb aside*, eg to speak to him quietly; 將某人拉到一邊(例如與其悄悄說話); *to ~ on/off one's socks/gloves/tights;* 穿上(脫下)襪子(手套,緊身衣); *to ~ a curtain across a window;* 將窗帘拉上; *to ~ down the blinds* (of windows); 將百葉窗拉下; *to ~ one's belt tighter;* 拉緊褲帶; *to ~ one's pen through a word*, cross it out. 劃去一字。 *The fisherman drew in his net.* 那漁人將網拉起。 **2** [VP6A, 15B] (esp) move by pulling after or behind: (尤指)拖;曳: *a train ~n by two locomotives;* 由兩個機車拖行的火車; *tractor-~n ploughs.* 曳引機拖動的犁。 *The wagon was being ~n by two horses.* 這貨車由兩匹馬拖着。 **3** [VP6A, 15B, 14] ~ ***(out)***; ~ ***(from/out of)***, take or get out by pulling; extract: 抽出;拔出: *to ~ a cork*, out of a bottle; (自瓶上)拔出軟木塞; *to ~ nails from a plank;* 自厚板上拔出釘; *to have a tooth ~n;* 拔牙; *to ~ stumps*, (cricket) pull them out at the end of play; (板球戲)比賽終了時拔去標柱; *to ~ trumps*, (in card games such as bridge) cause them to be played; (牌戲,例如橋牌)吊王牌; *to ~ cards from a pack;* 自一副紙牌中抽取牌; *to ~ for partners,* eg when about to play a card game, allow this to decide the question; (玩牌等之前)抽牌以決定合夥人; *to ~ lots,* ⇨ lot²(1); 抽籤; *to ~ the winner,* get a ticket, etc at a lottery, on which there is a payment, prize, etc; 抽獎;抽彩; *to ~ a gun (on sb),* take it from its holster, ready for use. 拔槍(對着某人)。**~ a blank,** find nothing. 落空;未發現任何東西。**~ sb's teeth,** make him harmless. 使不能爲害。 **4** [VP6A, 14] **~ (from / out of),** obtain from a source: 自一來源獲取;提取: *to ~ water from a well;* 由井中汲水; *to ~ cider / beer from a cask / barrel;* 由桶中汲取蘋果酒(啤酒); *to ~ one's salary;* 領薪; *to ~ money from the bank / from one's account;* 自銀行(本人帳戶)中提款; *to ~ rations,* get, receive, supplies (of food, etc) from a store; 自店中取得糧食; *to ~ inspiration from nature.* 由自然獲得靈感。*What moral are we to ~ from this story?* 我們從這個故事裏體會到什麼教訓? **~ it mild,** (orig of beer; fig) be moderate; not exaggerate. (最初指啤酒,現爲比喩用法)適度; 不誇張。**~ tears / applause, etc,** be the cause of: 引起眼淚(鼓掌等): *Her singing drew long applause.* 她的歌聲引起歷時甚久的掌聲。 **5** [VP6A, 14, 15B, 2A] **~ (to),** attract: 吸引: *Street accidents always ~ crowds.* 街上發生的禍事總是吸引群衆。*The film drew large audiences.* 這影片吸引了許多觀衆。 *He drew* (= called) *my attention to a point I had overlooked.* 他提醒我注意我忽略了的一點。*She didn't feel ~n towards him,* There was nothing in his character, behaviour, etc that attracted her. 她對他沒有好感 (他的性格,擧止等不能吸引她)。 **6** [VP6A, 15B] take in: 吸入: *to ~ a deep breath;* 深深吸一口氣; *stop to ~ breath,* to rest after exertion. 歇息。**~ one's first / last breath,** be born / die. 降生(死亡)。 **7** [VP2A] (of a chimney, etc) allow a current of air to flow through; be built so that air and smoke pass up or through: (指煙囱等)通風;通氣: *This chimney ~s badly.* 這煙囱的通風情況不佳。*This cigar does not ~ well.* 這枝雪茄不太通氣。**8** [VP6A, 15B] **~ sb (out),** cause, persuade, (a person) to talk, show his feelings, etc: 使(一人)吐露其情感等: *He was not to be ~n,* He refused to say anything about the matter. 他不願吐露眞情。*He has many interesting stories of his travels if you can ~ him out.* 如果你能說動他,他有許多關於他的旅行的有趣的故事講給你聽。**9** [VP2C, D] move; come (in the direction indicated by the *adv*, etc): 移動;到來(移動方向按照其後之副詞等而定): *Christmas is ~ing near.* 聖誕節快到了。*The day drew to its close.* 這一天要過完了。*The two ships drew level.* 這兩條船並排行駛。*The favourite began to ~* (=gain) *on the other runners.* 那匹衆所認爲會獲勝的馬開始逼近其他的馬。 *The Queen's horse quickly drew away from the others,* went ahead of them. 女王的馬迅速地超越了其他的馬。*Everyone drew back in alarm.* 每個人都驚慌而後退。*When the enemy saw how strong our forces were, they drew off,* went back. 敵人發現我們的兵力是多麼强大時,他們就撤退了。 **10** [VP6A, 15B] cause to move or come (in the direction indicated by the *adv*, etc): 使移動(其方向按照後面的副詞等而定): *He drew himself up to his full height,* stood in an erect, stiff attitude. 他筆直地站着。**11** [VP6A, 2A] make with a pen, pencil, chalk, etc: 繪;畫: *to ~ a straight line / a circle;* 畫一直線(圓周); *to ~ a picture / plan / diagram;* 繪製圖畫(平面圖,圖表); *to ~ a horse.* 畫一匹馬。*She ~s well.* 她畫得好。(fig) describe in words: (喩)描寫: *The characters in Jane Austen's novels are well ~n.* 珍・奧斯汀的小說裏的人物描寫得很好。**~ a distinction (between),** point out differences; show the dividing line. 指出(…之)不同;指出界線。**~ a parallel / comparison / analogy (between),** show how two things are alike. 指出(…之)相似處。**~ the line (at),** set limits; declare what cannot be allowed; refuse to go as far as or beyond: 限制; 劃定界限; 宣佈不許做之事; 不肯做到或超越某種程度: *I don't mind lending him my razor, but I ~ the line at lending him my toothbrush.* 我不介意把剃刀借給他,但我不能把我的牙刷借給他。**12** [VP6A, 15B] write out: 寫: *to ~ a bill / a cheque / an order* (*on* a banker, etc, *for* a sum of money). 開票據(支票,滙票)(與 on 連用,後接銀行業者等;與 for 連用,後接開出的款數)。 **13** [VP6A] (of a ship) require (a certain depth of water) in order to float, ⇨ draught(3): (指船)吃(水): *The ship ~s 20 feet of water.* 這船吃水二十呎。 **14** [VP6A, 2A] end (a game, etc) without either winning or losing: 不分勝負地結束(比賽等): *to ~ a football or cricket match;* 不分勝負地結束一足球或板球賽; *a ~n game;* 不分勝負的比賽; *to ~ 2—2.* 二比二平手。*The teams drew.* 這些隊賽成平手。 **15** [VP6A, 2A, B] extract the essence of: 吸取…之精華: *to let the tea ~ for three minutes.* 讓茶泡三分鐘。 **16** (usu in *pp*) (of the features) pull out of shape: (通常用過去分詞)(指面貌)拉之使變形: *a face ~n with pain / anxiety;* 因痛苦(憂慮)而扭曲的面孔; *with ~n features.* 眉蹙嘴歪。 **17** [VP2C, 3A, 14, 15B] (special uses with *preps and adverbial particles*): (與介詞及副詞接語連用的特殊用法):

draw back, (fig) show unwillingness: (喩)表示不願意: *~ back from a proposal.* 不願接受建議。⇨ drawback(1).

draw in, (of a day) (指白晝) **(a)** reach its end. 結束。**(b)** become shorter: 變短: *The days begin to ~ in after midsummer.* 仲夏之後白晝開始變短了。

draw on, (of a period of time) approach: (指一段時間)接近: *Night drew on.* 夜卽來臨。**~ on sth / sb,** take or use as a source: 用做來源: *If newspapermen cannot get facts for their stories, they sometimes ~ on their imaginations.* 如果記者們採訪不到事實眞相來寫報導,他們有時就憑想像力去編造。*We mustn't ~ on our savings.* 我們不可挪用我們的積蓄。*You may ~ on me for any sum up to £500,* get sums up to this maximum from me or my agents. 五百鎊以內的款項我可以借給你。 **~ sb on,** attract, entice him. 吸引某人;誘惑某人。

draw out, (of a day) become longer: (指白晝)變長: *Christmas passed and the days began to ~ out.* 聖誕節過了,白晝開始變長。 **~ sth out,** stretch; cause to become longer: 伸展;使變長: *He heated the metal and drew it out into a long wire.* 他將那金屬燒熱,並將它拉成一條長的金屬線。*There was a long-~n-out discussion.* 有過長時間的討論。*He has ~n out the subject into three volumes.* 他將這題目加以引伸,寫了三卷。 **~ sb out,** ⇨ 8 above. 參看上列第 8 義。

draw (sth / sb) up, (a) (of a vehicle) (cause to) come to a stop: (指車輛)(使)停止: *The taxi drew up in front of the station.* 計程車駛至車站前面停下。**(b)** prepare; compose: 預備;草擬: *to ~ up a contract.* 草擬一合約。 **(c)** (usu passive) (of troops, etc) bring into regular order: (通常用被動語態)(指軍隊等)使排列整齊;列隊: *The troops were ~n up ready for the inspection.* 軍隊排列整齊準備接受檢閱。

draw·back /ˈdrɔːbæk ; ˈdrɔˌbæk/ *n* **1** [C] sth which lessens one's satisfaction, or makes progress less easy; disadvantage (*to*). 缺陷;障礙;不利(與 to 連用)。 **2** [U] amount of import duty paid back when goods are exported again. 退還之關稅。

draw·bridge /ˈdrɔːbrɪdʒ ; ˈdrɔˌbrɪdʒ/ *n* bridge that can be pulled up at the end(s) by chains (eg across the moat of a castle in ancient times to prevent passage, or across a river or canal to allow ships to pass). (可拉起或放下的) 活動橋; 曳起橋(例如古時設於防禦城堡之壕溝上以控制通行者,或設於河上可拉起讓船通行者)。

drawer /drɔ:(r) ; drɔr/ *n* **1** box-like container (with a handle or handles) which slides in and out of a piece of furniture, etc. 抽屜。ˌ**chest of** ˈ**~s**, piece of furniture consisting of a set of ~s. 帶抽屜的櫥櫃。 **2** (*pl*) old-fashioned two-legged undergarment for the lower part of the body; knickers. (複)舊式的內褲;燈籠短褲。 **3** /ˈdrɔ:ə(r) ; ˈdrɔɚ/ person who draws pictures; person who draws a cheque, etc. 繪製圖畫者;開支票等者。

draw·ing /ˈdrɔ:ɪŋ ; ˈdrɔ·ɪŋ/ *n* [U] the art of representing objects, scenes, etc by lines, with a pencil, chalk, etc; [C] sth made in this way; a sketch, plan, etc. 繪畫;製圖;圖畫;圖樣;圖案。***out of*** **~**, incorrectly drawn. 不合畫法;畫錯。ˈ**~-board**, flat board on which to fasten paper for ~, used eg by a draftsman; (fig) planning stage. 製圖板;(喻)計畫階段。ˈ**~-pin**, (US 美 = *thumb-tack*) flat-headed pin for fastening paper to a ~-board, notice-board, etc. 圖釘。

draw·ing-room /ˈdrɔ:ɪŋ rʊm *US:* ru:m ; ˈdrɔ·ɪŋˌrum/ *n* room in which guests are received. 客廳。

drawl /drɔ:l ; drɔl/ *vi, vt* [VP2A, C, 6A, 15B] speak so that the sounds of the vowels are longer than usual: 拖長語調地說;慢吞吞地說話: *The speaker ~ed on.* 那位發言者慢吞吞地繼續說。*Don't ~ (out) your words.* 不要慢吞吞地說話。□ *n* slow way of speaking. 慢吞吞的說話方式。

drawn /drɔ:n ; drɔn/ *pp* of draw²; ⇨ esp 2, 14, 16.

dray /dreɪ ; dre/ *n* low, flat, four-wheeled cart, without sides, for heavy loads, eg barrels from a brewery. 低平而無側板的四輪載貨馬車(例如自酒廠運桶裝酒者)。

dread /dred ; drɛd/ *n* [U] (also 亦作 ***a ~ of***) great fear and anxiety: 恐懼;憂懼: *to be in ~ of sb or sth;* 怕某人或某物; *to live in constant ~ of poverty.* 經常擔憂貧窮。*Cats have a ~ of water.* 貓怕水。□ *vt, vi* [VP6A, C, 7A] fear greatly: 畏懼: *to ~ a visit to/~ having to visit the dentist.* 害怕看牙醫。*I ~ to think of what may happen.* 我怕想可能發生的事。**~ed** *part adj* greatly feared. 非常可怕的。**~·ful** /-fl ; -fəl/ *adj* **1** causing ~: 可怕的: *a ~ful disaster.* 可怕的災難。*What a ~ful story!* 多麼可怕的故事啊! **2** (colloq) unpleasant: (俗)令人不愉快的: *What ~ful weather!* 多麼討厭的天氣! **~·fully** /-fʊlɪ ; -fəlɪ/ *adv* **~·ful·ness** *n*

dread·nought /ˈdrednɔ:t ; ˈdrɛdˌnɔt/ *n* type of battleship in the early years of the 20th century. 二十世紀初期一種戰艦;無畏戰艦。

dream¹ /dri:m ; drim/ *n* [C] **1** sth which one seems to see or experience during sleep: 夢: *to have a ~ (about sth);* 做夢(夢見某事物); *to awake from a ~.* 自夢中醒來。ˈ**~·land**; ˈ**~ world**, region outside the laws of nature, as experienced in sleep or in the imagination. 夢鄉;夢境。 **2** state of mind in which things going on around one seem unreal: 夢一般的感覺;幻然若夢: *to live/go about in a ~.* 夢一般地過日子(四處走動)。 **3** mental picture(s) of the future: 幻想;夢想: *to have ~s of wealth and happiness.* 夢想財富和幸福。 **4** (colloq) beautiful or pleasing person, thing, experience, etc: (俗)美麗或悅人的人,事物,經驗等: *His holiday by the sea was a ~.* 他在海濱的度假是一種快樂的經驗。**~·less** *adj* without ~s. 無夢的。**~·like** /ˈdri:mlaɪk ; ˈdrimˌlaɪk/ *adj* like a ~. 夢一般的。

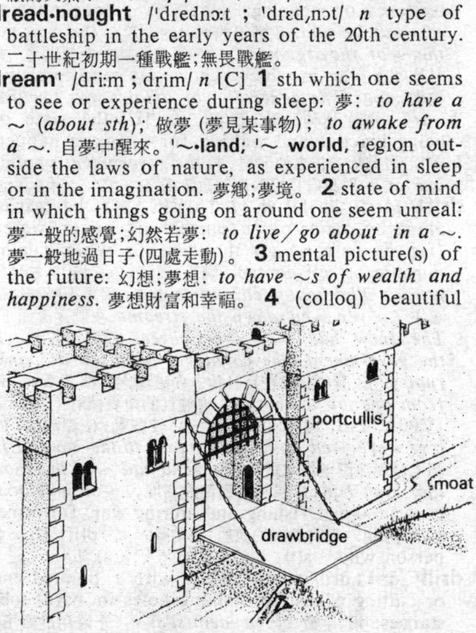

a drawbridge

dream² /dri:m ; drim/ *vi, vt* (*pt, pp* ~ed /dri:md ; drimd/ or dreamt /dremt ; drɛmt/) **1** [VP2A, 3A, 6A, 15B, 9, 8, 10] ~ ***(about/of)***, have ~s; see, experience, in a dream; imagine; suppose: 做夢;夢見;想像;假想: *He often ~s.* 他常做夢。*The soldier often ~t of/about home.* 這士兵常夢到家。*He ~t that he was at sea.* 他夢見他在航海。*I certainly didn't promise you £100; you must have ~t it.* 我的確未答應你一百鎊;一定是你在做夢。*I wouldn't ~ of doing such a thing,* The idea would never occur to me. 我絕不會想到做這件事。*He little ~ed that...,* did not imagine or suppose that.... 他做夢也想不到…。 **2** [VP15B] ~ ***away***, spend idly: 虛度: *~ away one's time/the hours.* 虛度光陰。 **3** [VP15B] ~ ***up***, (colloq) imagine, conceive (a plan, etc). (俗)構思(計畫等)。**~er** *n* person who ~s; person with impractical ideas, plans, etc. 做夢者;夢想家。

dreamy /ˈdri:mɪ ; ˈdrimɪ/ *adj* (-ier, -iest) **1** (of a person) with thoughts far away from his surroundings or work. (指人)心不在焉的。 **2** (of things, experiences) vague; unreal: (指事物,經歷)模糊的;不眞實的: *a ~ recollection of what happened;* 對往事的模糊回憶; (colloq) pleasing; soothing: (俗)悅人的;予人慰藉的: *~ music.* 輕柔而予人慰藉的音樂。**dream·ily** /-ɪlɪ ; -ɪlɪ/ *adv*

dreary /ˈdrɪərɪ ; ˈdrɪrɪ/ *adj* (-ier, -iest) (poet 詩 **drear** /drɪə(r) ; drɪr/) dull; gloomy; causing low spirits: 沉悶的; 陰沉的; 使人憂鬱的: *~ work/weather/people.* 沉悶的工作(陰沉的天氣;憂鬱的人們)。**drear·ily** /-əlɪ ; -əlɪ/ *adv*

dredge¹ /dredʒ ; drɛdʒ/ *n* apparatus for bringing up mud, oysters, specimens, etc from the bed of the sea, rivers, etc. 撈泥機;挖泥機;撈網(自水底撈泥,牡蠣,標本等所用者)。□ *vt, vi* [VP6A, 15B, 2A, 3A] ~ ***(up)***, bring up with a ~; clean with a ~: 用撈泥機撈取;用撈網撈取;用撈泥機清除: *to ~ (up) mud;* 挖泥; *to ~ (for) oysters;* 撈取牡蠣; *to ~ a channel/harbour.* 疏浚河床(港口)。**dredger** *n* boat carrying a ~. 撈泥船;疏浚船;採撈船。

dredge² /dredʒ ; drɛdʒ/ *vt* [VP6A, 14] sprinkle or scatter: 撒;撒佈: *to ~ meat with flour;* 將麵粉撒在肉上; *to ~ sugar over a cake.* 把糖撒在糕上。**dredger** *n* box with holes in the lid for sprinkling flour, sugar, etc on food. (蓋上有孔,可用以撒麵粉,糖等於食物上的)撒布盒。

dregs /dregz ; drɛgz/ *n pl* **1** bits of worthless matter which sink to the bottom of a glass, bottle, barrel, etc of liquid. 渣滓。***drink/drain to the*** **~**, drink and leave only the ~. 喝乾。 **2** (fig) worst and useless part: (喻)最劣和無用的部分: *the ~ of society/humanity.* 社會(人類)的渣滓。

drench /drentʃ ; drɛntʃ/ *vt* [VP6A] make wet all over, right through: 使濕透: *to be ~ed with rain/~ed to the skin.* 被雨淋濕(濕透)。*They were caught in a downpour and came back ~ed.* 他們遭逢大雨,回來時濕透了。**~·ing** *n* thorough wetting: 濕透: *We got a ~ing.* 我們濕透了。

dress¹ /dres ; drɛs/ *n* **1** [C] one-piece outer garment with a bodice and skirt worn by a woman or girl; gown or frock. 婦女的外衣;婦女的長服。 **2** [U] clothing in general (for both men and women), esp outer garments: 衣服(男女服裝的總稱,尤指外衣): *She doesn't care much about ~,* is not much interested in clothes. 她不太注意衣着。ˈ**~ circle**, lowest gallery in a theatre, in which evening ~ was formerly required. 戲院樓座中之最低座;樓座前排(昔時須着晚禮服始能入座)。ˈ**~ coat**, black, swallow-tailed coat worn by men for evening ~. 燕尾服。ˈ**~·maker**, woman who makes women's

~es. 製女服的女裁縫。'~ **rehearsal**, final rehearsal of a play, at which actors wear the costumes to be worn at actual performances. (演員着劇中人服裝之)最後排演;彩排。'**evening** ~, clothing worn at formal social occasions (eg dinners, evening parties). 晚禮服。ˌ**full** '~, kind of clothes worn on special occasions: 盛裝; 禮服: *ambassadors, naval and military officers, all in full* ~. 大使們,海陸軍軍官,均着禮服。

dress² /dres ; drɛs/ *vt, vi* **1** [VP6A, 2A] put on clothes: 給…穿衣服;穿衣: *Mary was ~ing her doll.* 瑪莉正爲她的洋娃娃穿衣服。*Jim isn't old enough to ~ himself.* 吉姆未到自己會穿衣服的年紀。*Have you finished ~ing?* 你衣服穿好了沒有? *How long does it take you to ~ (yourself)?* 你穿衣服需要多少時間? [VP15B, 2C] ~ **up**, put on special clothes, as for a play, a fancy dress ball, etc: (爲演戲,參加化裝舞會等)着特殊服裝: *The children ~ed (themselves) up as pirates.* 孩子們打扮成海盜。**2** [VP2A, C] put on evening dress: 着晚禮服: *We don't ~ for dinner nowadays.* 現今我們不着晚禮服赴宴了。*You've just time to ~* (= change into evening dress) *before we leave for the theatre.* 在我們赴劇院前,你剛好有時間換好晚禮服。**3** [VP2C] (of what is habitual) wear clothes: (指慣常的)穿衣: *He has to ~ well in his position.* 以他的地位他必須穿得很整齊。**4** **be ~ed in**, be wearing: 穿着: *She was ~ed in white.* 她穿着白色的衣服。*They were ~ed in the height of fashion,* wearing the most fashionable clothes. 他們穿着最時髦的衣服。**5** [VP6A] provide clothes for: 供以衣服: *How much does it cost them a year to ~ their children?* 他們一年花多少錢供給子女的衣服? **6** [VP6A] make ready to use; prepare: 處置妥當;準備;調製: *to ~ leather,* make it soft and smooth; 鞣革;製革(使軟而光滑); *to ~ a salad,* ⇨ dressing(3); 加調味油於生菜; *to ~ a chicken,* clean it ready for cooking. 剖洗一鷄。**7** [VP6A, 15B] brush and comb, arrange (one's hair): 梳理(頭髮);整刷(毛): *to ~ down a horse,* brush its coat well. 梳理馬毛。~ **sb down**, (fig) scold him severely; thrash him. (喻)嚴斥某人;笞打某人。Hence, 由此產生, ˌ~**ing-'down** *n* severe scolding. 嚴斥。**8** [VP6A] clean and bandage (a wound, etc). 包紮(傷處等)。**9** [VP6A] make cheerful and attractive: 使悅目動人;裝飾: *to ~ a shop-window,* eg with attractive goods; (以美觀的貨品等)裝飾商店櫥窗; *to ~ the streets,* eg with flags; (以旗幟等)裝飾街道; *to ~ a Christmas-tree.* 裝飾聖誕樹。**10** [VP6A, 2A] (mil) get or bring (soldiers) into a straight line: (軍)整列(士兵): ~ *the ranks.* 整列隊伍。

dress·age /'dresɑːʒ ; drɛ'sɑʒ/ *n* [U] (F) training of horses (for show-jumping, etc). (法)訓練馬(使表演跳躍等)。

dresser¹ /'dresə(r) ; 'drɛsɚ/ *n* person who dresses, 穿衣者,裝飾者,處理者, esp 尤指 **(a)** one who helps a surgeon to dress wounds in a hospital; (醫院中幫助外科醫生的)裹傷者; **(b)** person who helps actors and actresses to dress ready for the stage. (劇場中幫助演員着裝的)服裝師。

dresser² /'dresə(r) ; 'drɛsɚ/ *n* **1** piece of kitchen furniture with shelves for dishes, and cupboards below, often with drawers for cutlery, etc. 碗櫃。**2** (US) dressing-table. (美)梳粧臺。

dress·ing /'dresɪŋ ; 'drɛsɪŋ/ *n* **1** [U] process of dressing (putting on clothes, cleaning and bandaging a wound, etc). 穿衣;裹傷。'~-**case**, one for brushes, bottles and other articles of toilet, when travelling. 化粧箱(旅行時裝刷,瓶,及其他化粧用品者)。'~-**gown**, (US 美 = *bath-robe*) loose gown worn over pyjamas, etc before dressing, etc. 晨衣;睡袍。'~-**table**, one with a mirror, used in a bedroom. 化粧臺;梳粧臺。**2** [C, U] sth used for dressing wounds, eg an ointment, bandage, etc. 包傷用品(例如藥膏,綳帶等)。**3** [C, U] mixture of oil, vinegar, condiments, etc used as a sauce for salads and other dishes. 調味醬(油,醋,作料等調和後置於生菜等食物上者)。**4** [U] substance used to stiffen silk, cotton, etc during manufacture. 漿絲、棉等的材料。

dressy /'dresɪ ; 'drɛsɪ/ *adj* (-ier, -iest) (colloq) (of persons) fond of, looking smart in, fine clothes; (of clothes) stylish. (俗)(指人)講究穿的;衣着考究的;(指衣服)時髦的。

drew /druː ; dru/ *pt* of draw².

dribble /'drɪbl ; 'drɪbḷ/ *vt, vi* [VP6A, 2A] **1** (of liquids) flow, allow to flow, drop by drop or in a slow trickle (esp from the side of the mouth): (指液體)使滴下;滴下(尤指自口邊): *Babies often ~ on their bibs.* 嬰兒常流口水在圍嘴上。**2** (football) take (the ball) forward by means of quick, short kicks, either between the feet of one player, or by short passes from one player to another. (足球)盤(球);短傳(球)。**drib·bler** *n* person who ~s. 流口水者;盤球者。

drib·let /'drɪblɪt ; 'drɪblɪt/ *n* falling drop; small amount: 小滴;小量;微量: *in/by ~s,* a little at a time. 一點點地。

dribs and drabs /ˌdrɪbz n 'dræbz;'drɪbz ən 'dræbz/ *n pl* (colloq) small amounts. (俗)小量;微量。

dried /draɪd ; draɪd/ *pt, pp* of dry².

drier /'draɪə(r) ; 'draɪɚ/ *comp adj* ⇨ dry¹; *n* ⇨ dry².

drift¹ /drɪft ; drɪft/ *n* **1** [U] drifting movement; being carried along by currents: 漂流;飄動: *the ~ of the tide.* 潮汐的冲流。*The general ~ of the current was northerly.* 這水通常向北流。'~·**age** /-ɪdʒ ; -ɪdʒ/ *n* (of a ship) general movement off course due to currents, winds, tides, etc. (指船)(由於水流,風向,潮流等造成的)漂動;航差。'~-**net**, large net into which fish ~ with the tide. 漂網(捕魚的一種大網,魚可隨潮流入內)。**2** [C] sth caused by drifting: 由飄動或漂流造成之物;颳積而成之物;漂積而成之物: *Big ~s of snow/Big snow ~s made progress slow and difficult.* 大的雪堆使前進緩慢而困難。*It was buried in a ~ of dead leaves.* 它被埋在一堆枯葉中。'~-**ice**, broken ice carried along on the surface of the sea, a river, etc in masses by currents of water or air. 流冰。'~-**wood**, wood carried along by currents and washed up on beaches. 由水冲至岸邊的木頭;漂流木。**3** [U] general tendency or meaning: 大意;要旨: *I caught the ~ of what he said.* 我懂得他所說的大意。*Did you get the ~ of the argument?* 你懂得這論據的要旨嗎? **4** [U] the way in which events, etc tend to move: 趨勢;傾向: *The general ~ of affairs was towards war.* 一般的情勢是邁向戰爭。**5** [U] the state of being inactive and waiting for things to happen: 不採取行動;等待事情發展: *Is the government's policy one of ~?* 政府是採取觀望政策嗎?

drift² /drɪft ; drɪft/ *vi, vt* **1** [VP2A, C] be carried along by, or as by, a current of air or water; (fig, of persons) go through life without aim, purpose or self-control: 飄動;漂流;(喻,指人)無目的地生活: *The boat ~ed out to sea.* 那隻小船漂往海裏去了。*We ~ed down the stream.* 我們逐流而下。*The snow had ~ed everywhere.* 雪飄至各處。*Is the government/the country ~ing towards bankruptcy?* 政府(國家)在盲目地走向破產之路嗎? *She ~s from one job to another.* 她無目的地更換着工作。**2** [VP6A, 15B, 14] cause to ~: 使飄動;使漂流: *The logs were ~ed down the stream to the saw-mills.* 圓木料順流漂至鋸木廠。*The wind had ~ed the snow into high banks.* 風把雪飄積成高堆。~**er** *n* **1** boat used in ~-net fishing and, during war, for minesweeping. 帶有漂網的漁船;掃雷船。⇨ drift¹(1). **2** person who ~s(1). 生活無目的之人;流浪者。

drill¹ /drɪl ; drɪl/ *n* instrument with a pointed end or cutting edges for making holes in hard substances: 鑽;手鑽;錐: *a dentist's ~.* 牙醫用的鑽子。□ *vt, vi* [VP6A] make a hole with a ~: 用鑽孔機

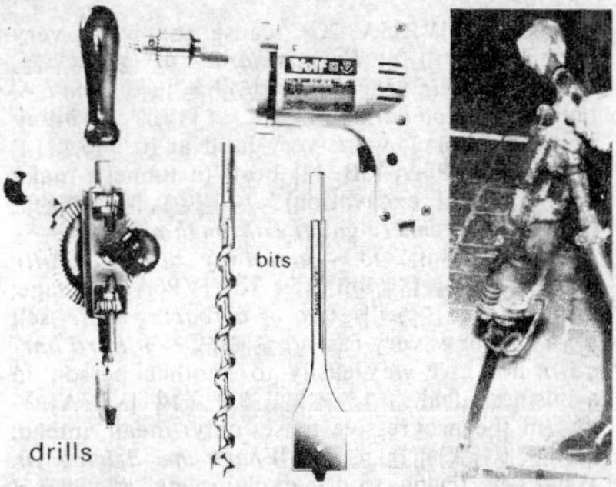

drills

鑽(孔): ~ *a hole in a stone wall;* 在一石牆上鑽孔。[VP2A] use a ~. 鑽孔。**'~·ing-rig,** ⇨ rig¹(2).

drill² /drɪl ; drɪl/ *n* [C, U] **1** army training in the handling of weapons; formal movements, eg marching, turning, to develop alertness: 軍事訓練; 操練: *'bayonet ~;* 劈刺操練; *'gun-~.* 砲操練。*The soldiers were at ~ in the barrack square.* 兵士們在營房的操場上操練。 **2** thorough training by practical experiences, usu with much repetition: 練習: *~s in the English vowel sounds.* 英語母音發音練習。 **3** routine procedure to be followed, eg in an emergency: (應付緊急情況等之)例行步驟: *'fire-~;* 救火演習;消防演習; *'lifeboat ~.* 救生艇演習。□ *vt, vi* [VP6A, 14, 2A] train, be trained, by means of ~s: 訓練;教練;操練;練習: *to ~ troops on a parade ground;* 在閱兵場訓練軍隊; *a well-~ed crew.* 訓練有素的船員。

drill³ /drɪl ; drɪl/ *n* furrow; machine for making furrows, sowing seeds in them, and covering the seeds; row of seeds sown in this way. 犂溝; 播種機; 用播種機播下的一排種子。□ *vt* [VP6A] sow (seeds) in ~s. 一排排地播(種子)。

drill⁴ /drɪl ; drɪl/ *n* [U] heavy, strong linen or cotton cloth. 堅實的斜紋布(一種厚而牢的麻布或棉布)。

drill⁵ /drɪl ; drɪl/ *n* kind of West African baboon. (西非產的一種)黑面狒狒。

drily /'draɪlɪ ; 'draɪlɪ/ *adv* ⇨ dry¹.

drink¹ /drɪŋk ; drɪŋk/ *n* [C, U] **1** liquid for drinking: 飲料: *We should die without food and ~.* 我們如果沒有飲食必死。*We have plenty of bottled ~s,* beer, lemonade, etc in bottles. 我們有很多瓶裝飲料(瓶裝啤酒,檸檬水等)。 **2** alcoholic liquor: 酒: *What about a ~?* 來杯酒如何? *I'll bring in the ~s,* eg the gin, whisky, sherry. 我去把酒拿來。*He's too fond of ~.* 他太愛飲酒。***be in ~/the worse for ~/under the influence of ~,*** intoxicated: 酒醉: *He's a good husband except when he's in ~.* 他在不醉酒的時候是一個好丈夫。 ***drive sb to ~,*** cause him to take to ~: 使某人嗜酒: *Mrs Bell's bad temper drove her husband to ~.* 貝爾太太的壞脾氣使得她丈夫耽於酒。***take to ~,*** acquire the habit of drinking regularly and too much. 嗜酒。 **3 the ~,** (sl) the sea. (俚)海。

drink² /drɪŋk ; drɪŋk/ *vt, vi* (*pt* drank/dræŋk ; dræŋk/, *pp* drunk/ drʌŋk ; drʌŋk/) **1** [VP6A, 15B, 2A] take (liquid) into the mouth and swallow: 飲;喝: *to ~ a pint of milk.* 飲一品脫牛奶。***~ sth down/off/up,*** ~ the whole of it (esp at once). 喝光(尤指一口氣喝乾)。 **2** [VP6A, 15B] ***~ (in/up),*** (of plants, the soil, etc) take in, absorb (liquid): (指植物,土壤等)吸收(水分): *The thirsty plants drank (up) the water I gave them.* 乾旱的植物把我澆的水都吸收了。*The parched soil drank (in) the rain.* 乾透了的土地吸收了雨水。 **3** [VP15B] ***~ sth in,*** (fig) take into the mind eagerly or with pleasure: (喻)欣賞: *The boy drank in every word of the sailor's story of his adventures.* 這男孩全神傾聽着那水手敍述他冒險故事的每一句話。 **4** [VP6A, 15B, 2A] take alcoholic liquors, beer, wine, etc, esp in excess: 飲(酒); (尤指) 縱飲: *He ~s far too much.* 他過度縱飲。*He ~s half his earnings,* spends it on alcoholic liquors. 他賺來的錢半數花在飲酒上。*He will ~ himself to death.* 他將因縱飲而致死。 **5** [VP6A, 3A] ***~ (to),*** wish good (to sb) while raising one's glass: 舉杯祝賀(某人): *to ~ a person's health;* 舉杯祝一人健康; *to ~ a toast to sb;* 舉杯祝賀(某人); *to ~ to sb's success;* 舉杯祝某人成功; *to ~ to sb's health.* 舉杯祝某人健康。 **~·able** /-əbl ; -əbl̩/ *adj* suitable or fit for ~ing. 可飲用的。**~·er** *n* (esp) person who ~s alcoholic liquor too often or too much: (尤指)縱飲者;酒徒: *He's a heavy ~er.* 他是個豪飲者。**~·ing** *n* process or habit of taking liquid(s), esp alcoholic liquor: 飲酒: *He's fond of ~ing.* 他喜歡飲酒。**'~·ing-bout,** long spell of ~ing. 酒宴。**'~·ing-fountain,** device for providing a supply of ~ing-water in a public place. (設於公共地方的)飲水器。**'~·ing-song,** one to be sung at a ~ing party; one celebrating the joys of ~ing. 飲酒歌。**'~·ing-water,** water fit for ~ing. 飲用水。

drip /drɪp ; drɪp/ *vi, vt* (-pp-) [VP2A, C, 6A] (of a liquid) fall, allow to fall, in drops: (指液體)滴落;滴下: *The rain was ~ping from the trees.* 雨從樹上滴下。*The tap was ~ping.* 龍頭在滴水。*Sweat was ~ping from his face.* 汗從他的臉上滴下。*He was ~ping sweat.* 他大汗淋漓。*Blood was ~ping from his hand.* 血從他的手滴下。*His hand was ~ping blood.* 他的手在滴血。***~ping wet,*** very wet. 很濕的;濕透的。**,~-'dry** *adj* (of a fabric) able to dry quickly, without previous squeezing or wringing out, when hung up to ~: (指織物)可用滴乾法(洗後不加扭絞,任其滴乾)的;快乾的: *~-dry shirts.* 可快速晾乾的襯衣。□ *vt* dry in this way. 滴乾。□ *n* **1** the drop-by-drop falling of a liquid: 滴;滴落: *the ~s from the trees/of the rain.* 自樹上滴下的水(雨滴)。 **2** (sl) a dull, insipid person. (俚)乏味的人;無風趣的人。

drip·ping /'drɪpɪŋ ; 'drɪpɪŋ/ *n* **1** [U] fat melted out of roasted meat, used for frying, or spread on bread: 烤肉時滴落之油滴(用以煎炸或敷於麵包上): *a slice of bread and ~.* 一片塗有烤肉油的麵包。**'~-pan,** pan in which ~ collects when meat is roasted. 烤肉時用以接油滴之鍋或盤。 **2** (*pl*) liquid that drips or has dripped from sth: (複)滴落之物: *the ~s from the roof.* 簷上滴落的雨水。

drive¹ /draɪv ; draɪv/ *n* **1** driving or being driven (in a car, etc, not in a public vehicle): 駕駛;乘坐(非公共車輛): *to go for a ~;* 駕車一遊; *to take sb for a ~.* 駕車載某人一遊。*The station is an hour's ~ away.* 從此地駕車到車站有一個小時的路程。 **2** (in US also 美亦作 **'~·way**) private road through a garden or park to a house. 穿過花園或邸園至一住宅的私人車路。 **3** (in games played with a ball, eg golf) [U] force given to a ball when it is struck; [C] stroke or hit: (球賽,如高爾夫) 擊球之力; 一擊: *a ~ to the boundary.* 擊往邊界。 **4** [U] energy; capacity to get things done: 精力; 魄力: *young men with brains, ~ and initiative.* 有頭腦,精力和進取精神的青年。*The new headmaster lacks ~/is lacking in ~.* 新校長缺乏魄力。 **5** organized effort or campaign: 有組織的努力或運動: *a 'sales ~,* one made to increase sales, eg by reducing prices; 推銷運動(例如藉減價); *the 'export ~,* to increase exports. 外銷運動。*The school made a great ~ to raise £5000 for a new sports ground.* 這學校發動籌募五千鎊以建築一新的運動場。 **6** tournament: 比賽;競賽: *a 'bridge-~.* 橋牌比賽。 **7** (mech) apparatus for driving: (機械)傳動裝置: *front/rear ~,* with power that operates the front/rear wheel(s); 前(後)輪傳動裝置; *a four-wheel ~,* with four wheels connected to the source of power; 四輪傳動; *right-/left-hand ~,* (of a motor vehicle) having the steering and other controls on the right/left side. (指汽車)駕駛控制在右(左)方的。

drive² /draɪv; draɪv/ *vt, vi* (*pt* drove /drəʊv; drov/, *pp* driven /ˈdrɪvn; ˈdrɪvən/) **1** [VP6A, 15B, 14] cause animals, people to move in some direction by using cries, blows, threats or other means: 驅;逐;趕;攆: *to ~ cattle to market;* 把牛趕向市場; *to ~ the enemy out of their positions.* 將敵人逐出陣地。***~ sb into a corner,*** (fig) force him (eg during an argument) into a position from which escape will be difficult. (喻)逼入死角;逼入絕境(例如在辯論時駁倒某人)。 **2** [VP6A, 2A] operate, direct the course of a railway engine, bus, motor-car or other vehicle; control, direct the course of an animal or animals drawing a cart, plough, etc: 駕駛;駕馭: *to ~ a taxi/cart;* 駕駛計程車(駕一輛二輪馬車); *to take driving lessons.* 上駕駛課。*D~ with caution.* 小心駕駛。**ˈdriving licence,** licence to ~ a motor vehicle. 駕駛執照。**ˈdriving school,** one for teaching persons to ~ a motor vehicle. 駕駛學校。**ˈdriving test,** test which must be passed to obtain a driving licence. 駕駛執照考試。 **3** [VP2A, C] travel in a car, etc which is at one's disposal (Cf *ride* in a bus, train or other public vehicle): 駕車旅行(乘公車,火車等公共交通工具用ride): *We drove right up to the front door.* 我們將車一直開到大門。*Shall we ~ home or walk?* 我們駕車回家還是步行? *We are merely driving through,* travelling through (the place) without intending to stay. 我們祇是開車從此經過。**ˈ~-in** *n* (and attrib) (亦作形容用法) restaurant, cinema, etc at which persons get service while in their cars: 駛車入內的餐館,電影院等(可在車內進餐或看電影等): *a ~-in cinema/bank.* 駛車入內的電影院(銀行)。**4** [VP15B, 14] carry, convey, (sb) in a car, etc (not a public vehicle): (非公共車輛)載送(某人): *He drove me to the station.* 他開車送我到車站。 **5** [VP6A] (usu passive) (of steam, electricity or other kind of power) set or keep going; be the power to operate: (通常用被動語態)(指蒸汽,電或其他動力)發動;推動: *The machinery is ~n by steam/water-power, etc.* 這些機器是由蒸汽(水力等)推動。 **ˈdriving-belt,** belt that carries motion from an engine, motor, etc to machinery. 傳動帶;掣帶。**ˈdriving-wheel,** one that communicates power to other parts of a machine. 傳動輪;主動輪。 **6** [VP15B, 14] (of wind, water) send, throw, (lifeless things) in some direction: (指風,水)推動(無生命之物): *The gale drove the ship on to the rocks.* 大風將這船吹至岩礁上。*The ship was ~n out of its course.* 這船被吹(冲)離了航線。*The wind was driving the rain against the window-panes.* 風吹雨點打在玻璃窗上。**7** [VP2C] go or move along fast or violently: 迅速行動;猛烈行動: *The ship drove on the rocks/was driving along before the wind.* 船觸礁(乘風而駛)。*The clouds drove across the sky.* 雲在天空疾馳。*The rain was driving in our faces.* 雨疾落在我們的臉上。 **8** [VP15B, 14] ***~ sth in; ~ sth into sth,*** force a nail, screw, stake, etc into sth: 釘入(釘子,螺絲,木樁等): *With one blow he drove the nail into the plank.* 他一錘便將釘子釘入木板。**9** [VP6A, 15B, 14, 2A] hit or strike with force: 擊: (cricket) (板球) *to ~ a ball to the boundary;* 把球擊至邊界; (tennis) (網球) *to ~ a ball out of the court.* 把球打出場外。(golf) (高爾夫球) *He ~s well.* 他打得好。***~ sth home,*** (fig) impress deeply on the mind. (喻)使印象深刻。 ***let ~ at,*** aim a blow at; send a missile at: 打擊;射擊: *He let ~ at me with his left,* aimed a blow at me with his left fist. 他用左拳打我。 **10** [VP15B, 17, 22] cause or compel (sb) to be (in a certain state); cause or compel (sb to do sth): (迫)使(某人)處於(某種狀態);(迫)使(某人做某事): *Failure drove him to despair/desperation.* 失敗使他絕望。*You'll ~ me mad/to my wits' end.* 你會把我氣瘋的(使我窮於應付的)。*He was ~n by hunger to steal.* 他爲饑餓所迫而偷竊。 **11** [VP15A, 2C] (cause to) work very hard: (使)努力工作: *He was hard ~n.* 他工作辛苦。*He ~s himself very hard.* 他努力地工作。*Don't ~ the workers too hard.* 不要使工人工作過度。***~ away at*** (one's work), work very hard at it. 努力做(工作)。 **12** [VP6A, 15B, 14] bore (a tunnel); make (a horizontal excavation): 挖(隧道);開鑿(橫的坑道): *to ~ a tunnel/gallery through a hill;* 掘一隧道(地道)通過小山; *to ~ a railway across a hilly district.* 築一鐵路通過山區。 **13** [VP6A] manage; bring about: 經營;引起: *to ~ a roaring trade,* sell a lot of things very fast. 生意興隆。***~ a hard bargain,*** not give way easily to another person in a business deal. 談生意不輕易讓步。 **14** [VP3A] ***~ at,*** (in the progressive tenses only) mean, intend: (祇用於進行式)用意;意欲: *What's he driving at,* What's he trying to do, explain, etc? 他的用意何在? **15** [VP14] postpone; defer: 延緩;展期: *Don't ~ it to the last minute.* 不要延至最後一分鐘。

drivel /ˈdrɪvl; ˈdrɪvl/ *vi* (-ll-, US -l-) [VP2A, C] talk nonsense; talk childishly: 胡說八道;談話幼稚: *What's he ~ling about?* 他胡說些什麼? *He's still ~ling on.* 他仍在胡說八道。□ *n* [U] silly nonsense; foolish talk. 胡說;亂說。**~·ler,** US **~er** /ˈdrɪvələ(r); ˈdrɪvl̩ɚ/ *n* person who ~s. 胡言亂語者。

driven /ˈdrɪvn; ˈdrɪvən/ *pp* of drive².

driver /ˈdraɪvə(r); ˈdraɪvɚ/ *n* **1** person who drives (vehicles): 駕駛人;司機: *a ˈtaxi-~;* 計程車司機; *a ˈbus-~.* 公共汽車司機。⇨ chauffeur. ***in the ~'s seat,*** in control. 居於控制地位。 **2** person who drives animals. 驅趕動物者。⇨ *drover* at drove², *slave-~* at slave. **3** (mech) part of a machine, etc that receives power directly, eg the driving-wheel of a locomotive. (機械)機器等直接接受動力部分(例如機車的主動輪)。 **4** (golf) wooden club for driving the ball long distances from the tee. (高爾夫球)長打棒。

drizzle /ˈdrɪzl; ˈdrɪzl̩/ *vi* [VP2A] rain (in many small fine drops): 下毛毛雨: *It ~d all day.* 下了一天的毛毛雨。□ *n* [U] fine rain. 毛毛雨。**driz·zly** /ˈdrɪzlɪ; ˈdrɪzlɪ/ *adj* drizzling: 下毛毛雨的: *drizzly weather.* 下毛毛雨的天氣。

drogue /drəʊg; drog/ *n* **1** sea anchor (sth like a bag, dragged in the sea to steady a boat's movement). 浮錨;海錨(一種袋狀物,拖在船後,以平衡船身者)。 **2** wind-sock, ⇨ wind¹(8). 風向指示袋。 **3** cone towed by one aircraft as a target for use by others in firing practice. 斗形拖靶(由一飛機拖曳供其他飛機練習射擊之用)。 **4** **ˈ~ parachute,** small parachute used to pull a large parachute from its pack. 小降落傘(用以將大降落傘拖出者)。

droll /drəʊl; drol/ *adj* causing amusement (because strange or peculiar). (因其怪異而)有趣的。**~·ery** /-ərɪ; -ərɪ/ *n* [U] jesting; [C] (*pl* -ries) sth peculiar and amusing; amusing trick. 滑稽;奇特而有趣之物;詼諧。

drom·edary /ˈdrɒmədərɪ *US:* -ˈderɪ; ˈdrʌmə,dɛrɪ/ *n* (*pl* -ries) fast, one-humped riding-camel. 單峯駱駝。

drone /drəʊn; dron/ *n* **1** male bee; person who does no work and lives on others. 雄蜂;不工作而依賴他人爲生者。 **2** [U] low humming sound (as) made by bees: 嗡嗡之聲(如蜜蜂所發出者): *the ~ of an aeroplane high in the sky/of distant motorway traffic.* 高空飛機(遠處高速公路車輛)的嗡嗡聲。 **3** [C] monotonous speech, sermon, speaker: 單調的演說,說教或演說者: *He's a boring old ~.* 他是個令人厭煩的講話單調的老人。□ *vi, vt* [VP15B, 2C] **1** make a ~(2). 發嗡嗡聲。 **2** talk or sing, say (sth) in a low, monotonous way: 單調而低沉地說或唱: *children droning through their lessons.* 以單調而低沈的聲音讀書的孩子們。*The parson ~d out the psalm.* 牧師以單調而低沉的聲音誦讀美詩。

drool /druːl; drul/ *vi* ***~ (over),*** drivel; slobber. 胡說;說傻話;流口水。

droop /druːp; drup/ *vi, vt* **1** [VP2A, C] bend or

hang downwards (through tiredness or weakness): (由於疲倦或衰弱而)低垂；下垂: *The flowers were ~ing for want of water.* 這些花因缺水而垂萎。*Her head ~ed sadly.* 她悲哀地垂着頭。*His spirits ~ed,* He became sad, low-spirited. 他的精神委頓。 **2** [VP6A] let (the head, face, eyes) move forward or down. 使(頭，面孔，眼睛)下垂或朝下。□ *n* ~ing attitude or position. 低垂；垂下。**~·ing·ly** *adv*

drop¹ /drɒp ; drap/ *n* **1 (a)** very small quantity of liquid, usu round- or pear-shaped: 滴；點滴: *'rain~s.* 雨點。*He emptied the glass to the last ~.* 他一滴不留地飲乾了那一杯。**(b)** (*pl*) liquid medicine taken in ~s: (複)論滴使用的藥水；滴劑: *ear/eye/nose ~s.* 滴耳(點眼，滴鼻)藥水。***in ~s; ~ by ~,*** slowly, one ~ at a time. 一滴一滴地。**2** very small quantity. 極少量。***only a ~ in the bucket/ocean,*** a negligible quantity. 滄海一粟；九牛一毛。 **3** (glass of) intoxicating liquor: (一杯)酒: *He has had a ~ too much,* is drunk. 他已喝醉了。 **4** sth like a ~ in shape or appearance: 滴狀物: *'acid ~s,* of boiled sugar; (熬糖做成的)一種圓形小糖果; *'ear~,* ⇨ ear¹(1). **5** movement from a higher to a lower level, esp distance of a fall: 下跌；(尤指) 落下之距離: *a sudden ~ in the temperature,* eg from 30°C to 20°C; 溫度之突降 (例如自攝氏三十度降至二十度); *a ~ in the price of wheat.* 小麥價格之下跌。*There was a ~ of 10 metres from the window to the ground.* 從窗子到地上的距離爲十公尺。***at the ~ of a hat,*** at once; readily or willingly. 立刻；自願地。 **6** thing that drops or is dropped(1): 滴落之物；落下之物: *a ~ in a gallows,* platform or trap-door which falls from under the feet of a person executed by hanging. 絞臺上犯人脚下陷落的踏板。**'~-curtain,** curtain lowered between the acts of a play in a theatre. 劇院中之垂幕。**'~-kick,** (Rugby football) one in which the ball is dropped and kicked as it rises. (橄欖球)落地踢(將球放落地面，趁彈起時踢出之動作)。 **'~-hammer; '~-press,** machine for shaping or stamping, eg metal sheets for motor-car bodies, using the power of a dropped weight. 落鎚 (一種用重力壓金屬的機器，例如壓造汽車車身的金屬板者)。

drop² /drɒp ; drap/ *vt, vi* (-pp-) (For uses with *adverbial particles* and *preps,* ⇨ 13 below.) (與副詞接語和介詞連用之用法，參看下列第 13 義。) **1** [VP2A, C, 6A] (of liquids) fall, cause to fall, in drops. (指液體)滴落；使滴下。⇨ drip. **2** [VP6A, 2A, C, 14, 15B] fall (by the force of gravity, by not being held, etc); allow to fall: (因地心引力，未能握住等)降落；使落下: *It was so quiet you could hear a pin ~.* 那時是如此的安靜，你可以聽到一根針落地的聲音。*The apple blossom is beginning to ~.* 蘋果樹上的花開始落了。*The teapot ~ped out of her hand.* 茶壺從她手上落下。 *She ~ped the teapot.* 她把茶壺掉落了。***~ anchor,*** lower the anchor; come to anchor. 下錨。 ***~ a brick,*** ⇨ brick. ***~ a stitch,*** (knitting) let it slip off the needle. (編織)使跳一針。 **3** [VP2A, C, 6A, 15A] (allow to) become weaker or lower; (allow to) fall in amount, degree, pitch, condition, etc: (使)變弱或降低；(使)減低；(使)減少: *The wind/temperature has ~ped.* 風勢已減(溫度已下降)。*His voice ~ped/He ~ped his voice to a whisper.* 他的聲音降低 (他的聲音降低成耳語)。 *Don't ~ your voice at the end of a sentence.* 不要在句尾時降低你的聲音。 *Our boat gently ~ped* (= moved with the current) *downstream.* 我們的小舟慢慢順流而行。 ⇨ drift²(1). **4** [VP2A, C, 6A, 15A] (cause to) fall or sink to the ground, etc: (使)跌落；(使)跌倒: *They were ready to ~ with fatigue,* were so tired that they could scarcely stand. 他們疲乏得隨時要倒下了。*She ~ped into a chair, utterly worn out.* 她一下子坐在椅子上，顯得精疲力竭。 *He ~ped (on) to his knees,* knelt down. 他跪下。*Supplies were ~ped by parachute.* 補給品由降落傘空投。Hence, 由此產生, **'~ping-zone,** area where men, supplies, etc are ~ped by parachute. (人員，補給等的)降落地區。*The enemy were still ~ping* (= firing) *shells into the town.* 敵人仍在砲轟這城市。*He ~ped a bird* (= hit one and caused it to fall) *with every shot.* 他每射一發便擊落一鳥。 *He ~ped* (= hit) *the ball to the back of the court.* 他把球打到球場後面去了。 **5** [VP 6A, 12A, 13A] utter or send casually: 偶然說出；偶然寄出: *to ~ sb a hint,* give him one; 偶然予某人一暗示; *to ~ a word in sb's ear;* 有意無意地將一話說給某人聽; *to ~ sb a postcard/a few lines, a note.* 寄給某人一張明信片(一封短信)。⇨ let¹(4) for *let ~.* **6** [VP6A] omit; fail to pronounce, write or insert: 略去；遺漏；未讀出，寫出或置入: *He ~s his h's,* eg by saying 'at for hat. 他略去 h 音 (例如將 hat 讀作 'at). *The relative pronoun is often ~ped if it is the object,* eg in 'the man (*whom*) we met yesterday'. 關係代名詞做受詞時常被省略(例如 the man whom we met yesterday 中之 whom). **7** [VP15A] set down; stop a car, etc to allow (sb) to get out: 使下車；停下汽車等讓(某人)下車: *Where shall I ~ you?* 你要我在什麼地方停下讓你下車? *Please ~ me at the Post Office.* 請讓我在郵局下車。 **8** [VP6A] cease to associate with (sb): 停止與(某人)交往: *He seems to have ~ped most of his friends,* no longer meets them. 他好像與大多數的朋友不再來往了。 **9** [VP6A] give up: 放棄: *to ~ a bad habit.* 革除一惡習。 **10** [VP6A, 2A] (cause to) come to an end; no longer deal with or discuss: (使)結束；不再討論: *The correspondence ~ped.* 通訊停止了。*We ~ped the subject.* 我們不再討論這問題。*The subject (was) ~ped.* 這問題不再討論了。*We couldn't agree about the matter, so we decided to let it ~.* 我們對此事意見不一致，所以我們決定不再討論它了。*Let's ~ it,* stop talking about it. 我們不要再談論此事了。 **11** [VP6A] (colloq) lose (money, esp in gambling or a risky enterprise): (俗)損失(金錢，尤指在賭博或投機事業方面): *He ~ped 1000 francs at the Casino last night.* 他昨夜在賭場輸了一千法郎。 **12** (Rugby football) (橄欖球) ***~ a goal,*** score one by a ~-kick, ⇨ drop¹(6). 用落地踢法踢進球門；反彈踢中。 **13** [VP2C, 3A, 15B] (special uses with *adverbial particles* and *preps*): (與副詞接語和介詞連用的特殊用法):

drop across sb/sth, (=*run across,* which is more usu) meet or find by chance. 偶然遇到或發現(某人或某事物，run across 較常用)。

drop away, = ~ off(a).

drop back; drop behind, come to a position behind: 落後: *The two lovers ~ped back.* 這對情侶落在後面。*They ~ped behind the rest of the party.* 他們落在他人的後面。

drop in on sb; drop by/in/over/round, pay a casual visit (to): 偶然拜訪: *I wish he wouldn't ~ in on me so often.* 我希望他不要時常來訪我。*Some friends ~ped in to tea/~ped by to see me.* 有幾位朋友偶然來喝茶(偶然來訪)。

drop off, **(a)** become fewer or less: 減少: *His friends ~ped off one by one.* 他的朋友一個個地棄他而去。*The doctor's practice has ~ped off,* He now has fewer patients. 這醫生的病人愈來愈少了。 **(b)** fall asleep; doze: 睡着；打瞌睡。*He ~ped off during the sermon.* 講道時他睡着了。 ***drop sth/sb off (at sth),*** deliver (to): 將某人(某物)送到(某處): *The bus will ~ you off at the station.* 這公共汽車送你到車站下車。⇨ drop(7) above. 參看上列第 7 義。

drop out, **(a)** (of persons taking part in a contest, etc) cease to compete: (指人參加比賽等)棄權: *Three of the runners ~ped out.* 三位賽跑者棄權。**(b)** (of persons engaged, or about to engage, in an activity, etc) not take part; give up the idea: (指從事或即將從事某項活動等之人)不參與；放棄: *Smith has ~ped out of the team.* 史密斯不參加那個隊了。 **(c)** (colloq) withdraw from conventional social activities, attitudes. (俗)脫離傳統的社會活動和觀念

等。Hence, 由此產生，'~-out *n* **(a)** person who ~s out, eg one who withdraws from a course of instruction: 放棄者(例如退學者): *University ~-outs*, who do not finish their courses. 大學退學者。**(b)** person who withdraws from conventional society. 退出傳統社會者。
drop through, (colloq) come to nothing; be no longer discussed: (俗)毫無結果；不再被討論: *The big scheme he was busy with seems to have ~ped through*. 他所忙着的那個大計畫似乎已成泡影。

dropsy /ˈdrɒpsɪ; ˈdrɑpsɪ/ *n* [U] disease in which watery fluid collects in some part of the body, eg the legs. 水腫；浮腫。**drop·si·cal** /ˈdrɒpsɪkl; ˈdrɑpsɪkḷ/ *adj* suffering from ~; of or like ~. 患水腫的；水腫的；似水腫的。

droshky /ˈdrɒʃkɪ; ˈdrɑʃkɪ/ *n* (*pl* -kies) light, four-wheeled, open horse-carriage, as formerly common in Russia. 一種輕便，四輪，敞篷馬車(如昔時俄國所用者)。

dross /drɒs *US:* drɔːs; drɔs/ *n* [U] waste material rising to the surface of melted metals; (fig) anything considered to be worthless, mixed with sth else. 浮渣(熔化金屬浮至表面的廢物)；(喻)任何與他物混在一起的無用之物。

drought /draʊt; draʊt/ *n* [C, U] continuous (period of) dry weather causing distress; want of rain. 久旱；乾旱時期；旱災。

drove[1] /drəʊv; drov/ *pt* of drive[2].

drove[2] /drəʊv; drov/ *n* large number of animals (a flock of sheep, a herd of cattle) being driven together; crowd of people moving together: 被驅趕的一群動物(牛羊等)；行動中的一群人: *~s of sightseers;* 一群群的遊覽者；*visitors in ~s*. 群群的訪客。**drover** *n* man who drives cattle, sheep, etc to market; cattle-dealer. 驅趕牛羊等至市場的人；牛羊商人。

drown /draʊn; draʊn/ *vt, vi* **1** [VP6A, 2A] (cause sb to) die in water because unable to breathe: (使某人)溺死；淹死: *a ~ing man*. 快要淹死的人。*He ~ed the kittens*. 他溺死了那些小貓。*Do cats ~ easily?* 貓容易淹死嗎？*He fell overboard and was ~ed*. 他從船上掉在水裏淹死了。**2** [VP6A, 15B] ~ ***(out)***, (of sound) be strong enough to prevent another sound from being heard: (指聲音)淹沒(另一聲音): *The noises in the street ~ed out the teacher's voice*. 街上的喧聲淹沒了老師的聲音。**3** (fig): (喻): *a face ~ed in tears*, wet with tears; 淚流滿面；*~ed in sleep*, in a deep sleep (eg caused by exhaustion); 酣睡(例如疲憊不堪以後)；*to ~ one's sorrows in drink*, to deaden them by getting drunk. 藉酒澆愁。

drowse /draʊz; draʊz/ *vi, vt* [VP15B, 2A, C] ~ ***(away)***, be half asleep; pass (time) half asleep: 假寐；打瞌睡；以假寐度過(時間): *to ~ away a hot afternoon*. 一個炎熱的下午都在打瞌睡。□ *n* half-asleep condition: 假寐；瞌睡: *in a ~*. 在瞌睡。

drowsy /ˈdraʊzɪ; ˈdraʊzɪ/ *adj* (-ier, -iest) feeling sleepy; half asleep; making one feel sleepy. 欲睡的；半睡的；使人昏昏欲睡的。**drows·ily** /-əlɪ; -ɪlɪ/ *adv* **drow·si·ness** *n*

drub /drʌb; drʌb/ *vt* (-bb-) [VP6A, 14] give repeated blows to; hit with a stick; (fig) beat an idea, a notion *into* or *out of* sb. 連續打擊；棒打；(喻)强使某人接受或放棄(觀念，與 into 或 out of 連用)。**~·bing** *n* beating: 毆打: *give sb a good/sound ~bing*, beat him well. 痛毆某人。

drudge /drʌdʒ; drʌdʒ/ *n* person who must work hard and long at unpleasant tasks. 做苦工的人。□ *vi* [VP2A, C, 3A] ~ ***(at)***, work as a ~ does: 做苦工；辛苦地工作: *to ~ at dictionary-making*. 辛苦地編字典。**drudg·ery** /-ərɪ; -ərɪ/ *n* [U] hard, unpleasant, uninteresting work. 辛苦而令人討厭的工作。

drug /drʌg; drʌg/ *n* [C] **1** substance used for medical purposes, either alone or in a mixture; substance that changes the state or function of cells, organs or organisms. 藥物；藥劑；藥材。'**~·store** *n* (US) place where a wide variety of articles is sold, where prescriptions can be made up, and where food and drink may be bought and eaten. (美)藥房(兼賣雜貨，並販賣食物，飲料)；雜貨店。**2** substance (often habit-forming) inducing sleep or producing stupor or insensibility, eg opium, cocaine: 麻醉藥(例如鴉片，古柯鹼): *the ~ habit*, the habit of taking harmful ~s; 服用麻醉品的習慣；*a '~ addict;* 有毒癮的人；*'~ addiction;* 耽溺於麻醉品；毒癮；藥癮；*a '~ pedlar*. 麻醉藥販子；毒販。**3** ***a ~ on the market***, an article that cannot be sold because there is no demand. 滯銷貨。□ *vt* [VP6A] (-gg-) **1** add harmful ~s to (food and drink): 下麻醉藥於(食物和飲料): *His wine had been ~ged, and they stole his money while he was sleeping heavily*. 他的酒中被人下了麻醉藥，乘他酣睡時他們偷走了他的錢。**2** give ~s to, esp in order to make unconscious: 用藥麻醉；用麻醉藥使昏迷: *They ~ged the caretaker and then robbed the bank*. 他們用藥將看守人麻醉，然後搶劫了這銀行。

drug·get /ˈdrʌgɪt; ˈdrʌgɪt/ *n* [C, U] (floor covering of) heavy coarse woollen material. 粗毛氈；粗毛呢；粗毛地毯。

drug·gist /ˈdrʌgɪst; ˈdrʌgɪst/ *n* **1** (GB) tradesman who sells drugs; pharmacist. (英)藥商；藥劑師。**2** (US) person who sells medicines, toilet articles and other goods, and usually food and drinks. (美)雜貨商。⇨ *drug-store* at drug(1).

Druid, druid /ˈdruːɪd; ˈdruɪd/ *n* member of the priesthood among the Celts of ancient Gaul, Britain and Ireland. (古高盧、不列顛及愛爾蘭之塞爾特族中)督伊德教之僧侶。

drum[1] /drʌm; drʌm/ *n* **1** (music) percussion instrument made of a hollow cylinder or hemisphere with parchment stretched over the open side(s), ⇨ the illus at percussion; sound of a ~ or ~s, or sound as of ~s. (音樂)鼓(參看 percussion 之插圖)；鼓聲；似鼓之聲。'**~·fire**, heavy continuous rapid fire from big guns. 猛烈的連珠砲火。**~·head court-martial**, one held while military operations are in progress, in order to try an offender without delay. 戰地臨時軍法審判。**~·head service**, open-air military church service in which ~s form an altar. (軍中之)野外禮拜式(用鼓形成祭壇)。ˌ**~-'major**, sergeant in charge of drummers, and leader of a regimental band on the march; (US) (also 亦作 ˌ**~-majo'rette** /ˌmeɪdʒəˈret; ˌmedʒəˈrɛt/) leader of any marching band. 領導鼓手和團樂隊的士官；(美)樂隊隊長。'**~·stick**, **(a)** stick for beating a ~. 鼓槌。**(b)** lower part of the leg of a cooked chicken, turkey, etc. 鷄腿(指煮熟的鷄，火鷄等的腿的下部)。**2** sth like a ~ in shape, eg a cylindrical container for oil, a cylinder or barrel on which thick wire or cable is wound. 鼓狀物(例如裝油的圓筒狀容器，纏繞粗鐵絲或纜的捲軸)。⇨ ear[1](1).

drum[2] /drʌm; drʌm/ *vt, vi* (-mm-) **1** [VP2A, C] play the drum. 擊鼓。**2** [VP6A, 14, 2C, 3A] ~ ***(on)***, make drum-like sounds; beat or tap continuously: 作似鼓之聲；連續敲擊: *to ~ on the table with one's fingers;* 用手指連續敲桌子；*to ~ the floor with one's feet;* 用脚連續敲踏地板；*~ming on the piano/at the door*. 連續彈奏鋼琴(咚咚敲門)。**3** [VP15B] ~ ***up***, summon by ~ming: 擊鼓召集: (fig) (喻) ~ *up* (=get, find) *support for a cause*. 爭取對一運動的支持。**4** [VP14] ~ ***sth into sb/into sb's head***, cause him to remember it by repeating it often. 反覆述說一事使某人記住。**~·mer** *n* person who plays a drum; (colloq, esp US) commercial traveller. 鼓手；(俗，尤美)旅行推銷員。

drunk /drʌŋk; drʌŋk/ *adj* (usu pred) (*pp* of drink[2]) intoxicated; overcome by drinking alcoholic liquor: (通常爲敍述用法)醉；酩酊: *He was dead/blind/half ~*. 他爛醉如泥(酩酊大醉；半醉)。*I've never seen anyone so ~*. 我從沒有看到過喝得這麼醉的人。***get ~***, become intoxicated: 醉: *It's easy* *to get ~ on brandy.* 喝白蘭地酒易醉。**~ with sth,** (fig) elated: (喻)陶醉: *He was ~ with joy/success.* 他陶醉於快樂(成功)中。□ *n* person who is ~; man charged (at a police-station) with drunkenness. 酒醉者;醉漢;酗酒者。**~·ard** /-əd; -ərd/ *n* man who is ~, or who often gets ~. 醉漢;酒徒。

drunken /ˈdrʌŋkən; ˈdrʌŋkən/ *adj* (usu attrib) (通常作形容用法) **1** intoxicated; in the habit of drinking; often drunk: 酒醉的;嗜酒的;常酒醉的: *a ~ and dissolute man.* 一個嗜酒而又放蕩的人。 **2** caused by drinking; showing the effects of drinking: 因飲酒而引起的;顯示酒力的: *a ~ frolic.* 酒後狂歡。**~·ly** *adv* **~·ness** *n*

drupe /druːp; drup/ *n* (bot) fruit with juicy flesh, usu with a hard stone enclosing a seed, eg an olive, a plum, a peach. (植)核果(例如橄欖,李子,桃子)。

dry[1] /draɪ; draɪ/ *adj* (drier, driest) **1** not wet; free from moisture: 乾的;乾燥的: *Is this wood dry enough to burn?* 這木柴是否乾到可以燃燒了? **ˌdry as a ˈbone; ˌbone-ˈdry,** quite dry. 十分乾的。 **2** not rainy: 無雨的: *dry weather;* 無雨的天氣; having a low annual rainfall: 年雨量少的;乾旱的: *a dry climate.* 乾旱的氣候。 **3** not supplying water: 缺水的: *a dry well;* 乾涸的井;枯井; not supplying milk: 無奶的: *The cows are dry.* 這些母牛無奶。 **4** solid, not liquid: 固體的;非液體的: *dry goods,* ⇨ 12 below. 參看下列第 12 義。 **5** without butter: 無奶油的: *dry bread/toast.* 無奶油的麵包(烤麵包片)。 **6** (of wine, etc) not sweet, not fruity in flavour: (指酒等)無甜味的;無水果味的: *dry wines;* 無甜味的酒; *a dry martini,* a kind of cocktail. 無甜味的馬丁尼酒(一種鷄尾酒)。 **7** (colloq) thirsty; causing thirst: (俗)口渴的;令人口渴的: *to feel dry;* 覺得口渴; *dry work.* 令人口渴的工作。 **8** uninteresting; dull: 無趣味的;枯燥的: *a dry lecture/book/subject.* 枯燥的演講(書,問題)。 **ˌdry as ˈdust,** very dull. 十分枯燥無味的。 **9** unemotional; undemonstrative: 感情不露於外的;不形於色的: *dry humour/sarcasm;* 一本正經地表達出來的幽默(諷刺); *a dry fellow.* 感情不形於色的人。 **10** plain; undisguised: 明白的;赤裸的: *dry facts.* 赤裸裸的事實。 **11** not connected with liquid: 與液體無關聯的: *a dry cough,* without phlegm; 乾咳; *a dry death,* not by drowning; 死於陸上; *a dry shampoo,* one in which water is not used. 不用水的洗髮劑;乾洗髮。 **12** (compounds) (複合字) **ˌdry ˈbattery,** electric battery with two or more dry cells. 乾電池組。**ˌdry-bulb therˈmometer,** one of two thermometers, one dry and the other kept wet, used for measuring the humidity of the atmosphere. 乾球溫度計(一對乾濕溫度計中之乾溫度計,用以測量大氣的濕度)。 **ˌdry ˈcell,** cell in which the chemicals are in a firm paste which does not spill. 乾電池。**ˌdry-ˈclean** *v* clean (clothes, etc) by using spirits (eg petrol) instead of water. (用汽油等)乾洗(衣服等)。 Hence, 由此產生, **ˌdry-ˈcleaner; ˌdry-ˈcleaning** *nn.* **ˈdry dock,** ⇨ dock[1](1). **ˌdry ˈgoods,** (also called 亦稱作 *soft goods*), (contrasted with *meat, groceries,* etc) (與 meat, groceries 等相對) corn; (esp US) textiles, drapery. 穀類;(尤用於美國)綢緞呢絨。**ˌdry ˈice,** solid carbon dioxide (used for refrigerating). 乾冰(固體的二氧化碳,用以冷却)。 **ˌdry ˈmeasure,** measure of capacity for dry goods such as corn. 乾量(量乾物如穀類等的容量單位)。 **ˈdry nurse,** not suckling the baby she is caring for. (不餵奶的)媬姆。**ˌdry ˈrot** *n* decay of wood (causing it to crumble to powder), occurring when there is no movement of air over its surface; (fig) hidden or unsuspected moral or social decay. 木之乾腐;(喻)隱伏或未料到的道德或社會之腐敗。 **ˈdry-shod** *adj, adv* without wetting the feet; with dry feet or shoes. 未濕脚的(地);脚或鞋未濕的(地)。 **ˌdry-ˈwalling,** building of stone walls (eg for a field) without mortar. 不塗灰泥而造石壁(例如圍於田地者)。 **drily** /ˈdraɪlɪ; ˈdraɪlɪ/ *adv* **dry·ness** *n*

dry[2] /draɪ; draɪ/ *vt, vi* (*pt, pp* dried) **1** [VP6A, 15B, 2A, C] **dry (out),** make or become dry: 使乾;變乾: *Dry your hands on this towel.* 用這毛巾擦乾你的手。*We were drying our clothes in front of the fire.* 我們正在火前烘乾我們的衣服。*Our clothes soon dried out.* 我們的衣服不久便乾了。**dry up,** make or become completely dry: 使完全乾;完全變乾: *The long drought dried up all the wells.* 長期的乾旱使所有的井乾涸了。*The stream dries up during the hot summer.* 河流在炎熱的夏季乾涸了。*His imagination seems to have dried up.* 他的想像力似乎已枯竭了。*Dry up!* (sl) Stop talking! Be quiet! (俚)停止談話!安靜! **2** [VP6A] (usu the *pp*) preserve by extracting moisture: (通常用過去分詞) 脫水以保藏: *dried eggs/milk.* 蛋(奶)粉。 **dryer, drier** /ˈdraɪə(r); ˈdraɪə/ *n* **1** substance mixed with oil-paints and varnish to quicken drying. 乾燥劑。 **2** (in compounds) thing that dries: (用於複合字中)乾燥器: *an electric ˈhair-dryer;* 電動吹髮器; thing on or in which clothes, etc are placed to dry: 使衣服等變乾之機器: *a ˈclothes-drier;* 烘乾機; *a ˈspin-drier.* 旋轉式脫水機。

dryad /ˈdraɪəd; ˈdraɪəd/ *n* (GK myth) tree nymph. (希神)森林女神。

dual /ˈdjuːəl *US:* ˈduːəl; ˈdjuəl/ *adj* of two; double; divided in two: 二的;雙重的;分爲二的: *~ control,* for or by two persons; 二人管轄;雙重管轄;雙操縱; *~ ownership;* 二人共有; *ˌ~ ˈcarriageway* (US 美 = *divided highway*); 雙車道公路; *ˌ~-ˈpurpose,* adapted so as to, intended to, serve two purposes. 兩用的。

dub /dʌb; dʌb/ *vt* (-bb-) **1** [VP22, 23] make (sb) a knight by touching him on the shoulder with a sword; give (sb) a nickname: 以劍輕擊(某人)肩膀以授與爵士位;給(某人)起綽號: *They dubbed him 'Shorty' because he was so tall.* 因爲他長得這麼高,他們給他起一個綽號叫'矮子'。 **2** [VP6A] replace or add to the sound-track of a film or magnetic tape, esp in a different language. (尤指用不同的語言)爲(影片或錄音帶)配音。

dub·bin /ˈdʌbɪn; ˈdʌbɪn/ *n* [U] kind of thick grease used to make leather soft and waterproof. 保護皮革油;皮革用防水油。

du·biety /djuːˈbaɪətɪ *US:* duː-; djuˈbaɪətɪ/ *n* [U] (formal) feeling of doubt; [C] (*pl* -ties) doubtful affair. (正式用語)懷疑;可疑之事。

du·bious /ˈdjuːbɪəs *US:* ˈduː-; ˈdjubɪəs/ *adj* **1** ~ *(of/about),* (of persons) feeling doubt: (指人)懷疑的: *I feel ~ of his honesty.* 我懷疑他的誠實。*I feel ~ about/as to what to do next.* 我不知下一步該怎麼辦。 **2** (of persons) causing doubt (because probably not very good or reliable): (指人)(由於可能不十分好或不大可靠而)可疑的: *He's a ~ character.* 他是個可疑的人物。**3** (of things, actions, etc) causing doubt; of which the value, truth, etc is doubtful: (指事物,動作等)可疑的;其價值,眞實性等有問題的;未定的: *a ~ compliment;* 含意不明的恭維; *a ~ blessing.* 不可確定的幸福。*The result is still ~.* 結果仍未定。**~·ly** *adv* **~·ness** *n*

du·cal /ˈdjuːkl *US:* ˈduːkl; ˈdjukl/ *adj* of or like a duke. 公爵的;似公爵的。

ducat /ˈdʌkət; ˈdʌkət/ *n* gold coin formerly used in many European countries. (昔時歐洲許多國家所用的)金幣名。

Duce /ˈduːtʃeɪ; ˈdutʃe/ *n* (I) leader (esp as used of Mussolini, Italian Fascist leader). (義)總裁;領袖(尤指義大利法西斯領袖墨索里尼)。

duch·ess /ˈdʌtʃɪs; ˈdʌtʃɪs/ *n* wife or widow of a duke; woman whose rank is equal to that of a duke. 公爵夫人;公爵未亡人;女公爵;公國之女君主。

duchy /ˈdʌtʃɪ; ˈdʌtʃɪ/ *n* (*pl* -chies) (also 亦作 *dukedom*) land ruled by a duke or duchess. 公爵之領地;公國。

duck[1] /dʌk; dʌk/ *n* (*pl* ~s, but often unchanged when collective) (用作集合稱時常無複數變化) **1** [C] common water-bird, both wild and domestic; female of this, ⇨ drake; ⇨ the illus at fowl; [U] its flesh as food. 鴨;母鴨(參看 fowl 之插圖);食用之鴨肉。ˌ*lame* ˈ*~,* disabled person or ship; business or commercial organization in financial difficulties. 行動失靈的人或船; 有財務困難的商業機構。***(take to sth) like a ~ to water,*** (begin doing, being etc it) naturally, without fear, hesitation or difficulty. (做某事)自然地;毫無疑懼或困難。***like water off a ~'s back,*** without producing any effect. 毫無效果或影響。***~s and drakes,*** game in which flat stones are made to skip along water. 擲出扁石使其在水上漂躍的遊戲;打水漂遊戲。***play ~s and drakes with*** (eg one's money), squander, waste. 揮霍(金錢等);浪費無度。 **2** (colloq, also 俗, 亦作 **~y**) (GB) darling; delightful person. (英)可愛的人。 **3** vehicle (also 亦作 **DUKW** /dʌk ; dʌk/) able to travel on land and water, used as a landing-craft by troops. 水陸兩用車輛; 兩棲載重車。 **4** (cricket, 板球, also sometimes 有時亦作 **ˈ~'s egg**) batsman's score of nought, 0: 零分: *to make a ~;* 獲零分; *be out for a ~.* 因零分而出局。 **5** (compounds) (複合字) **ˈ~·bill,** ˌ**~·billed ˈplatypus** ⇨ platypus. **ˈ~·boards,** boards with narrow slats fixed across, for use on soft or muddy ground. 鋪於泥濘地面上之木板道。**ˈ~·weed,** small flowering plant growing on the surface of shallow water (eg on ponds). (池塘等中所生的)水萍。**ˈ~·ling** /-lɪŋ ; -lɪŋ/ *n* young ~. 小鴨。ˌ***ugly ˈ~ling,*** plain or stupid child who grows up to be attractive or brilliant. 醜小鴨(指小時候不好看或愚笨,長大後變得漂亮或聰明的人)。

duck² /dʌk ; dʌk/ *vt, vi* [VP6A, 2A] **1** move quickly down (to avoid being seen or hit): 迅速俯下(以免被望見或閃避打擊): *to ~ one's head.* 迅速低下頭。 **2** go, push (sb), quickly under water for a short time: 短時沒入水中;將(某人)短時浸入水中: *The big boy ~ed all the small boys in the swimming-pool.* 那大男孩將游泳池中所有的小男孩都短時浸入水中。 □ *n* quick downward or sideways movement of the head or body; quick dip below water (when bathing in the sea, etc). 頭部或身體迅速俯下或側閃的動作;(海上游泳等時)突將頭浸入水中。**~·ing** *n* thorough wetting: 濕透: *to give sb a ~ing,* eg by pushing him into or under the water. 使某人全身濕透(例如將其推入水中)。*It rained heavily and we all got a ~ing.* 雨下得很大,我們都濕透了。**ˈ~ing-stool,** (hist) one (attached to a pole) on which a person was tied and ~ed into a pond, river, etc, as a punishment. (史)浸刑椅(將一人縛於其上,浸入水中,以作懲罰)。

duck³ /dʌk ; dʌk/ *n* [U] strong linen or cotton cloth used for outer clothing of sailors; (*pl*) trousers made of this. (用以製船員外衣的)一種堅牢的麻布或棉布;(複)此種布製成的褲子。

duct /dʌkt ; dʌkt/ *n* **1** tube or canal through which liquid is conveyed, esp in the body: (輸送液體之)導管;管(尤指身體內者): *ˈtear-~s.* 淚管。 **2** metal tube and outlet for air (to ventilate, eg an aircraft): 通氣的金屬管(例如飛機上者);通風管: *The air ~s above your seat may be adjusted to your convenience.* 你可任意調整你座位上方的通氣管。

duc·tile /ˈdʌktaɪl *US:* -tl ; ˈdʌktḷ/ *adj* **1** (of metals) that can be pressed, beaten or drawn into shape while cold, eg copper. (指金屬,不必加熱)可延展的;可拉長的(例如銅)。 **2** (fig of a person, his character) easily influenced, managed or directed; docile. (喻,指人或其性格)易指使的;馴良的。**duc·til·ity** /dʌkˈtɪlətɪ ; dʌkˈtɪlətɪ/ *n* [U] the quality of being ~(1). 延展性;韌性。

dud /dʌd ; dʌd/ *n, adj* (sl) (thing or person) of no use, eg a shell or bomb that fails to explode or a banknote or cheque of no value. (俚)無用的(人或物)(例如未能爆炸的砲彈或炸彈,失效的鈔票或支票)。

dude /djuːd *US:* duːd ; djud/ *n* (US) dandy. (美)紈袴子弟; 花花公子。 **ˈ~ ranch,** ranch organized for tourists. 供遊覽的農場。

dudg·eon /ˈdʌdʒən ; ˈdʌdʒən/ *n* ***in high ~,*** offended and feeling indignation, or sullen anger: 極爲憤怒: *He went off in high ~.* 他極爲憤怒地離去了。

duds /dʌdz ; dʌdz/ *n pl* (sl) clothes, esp old or ragged clothes. (俚)衣服(尤指破舊者)。

due¹ /djuː *US:* duː ; dju/ *adj* **1** ***due (to),*** to be paid: 當付的;應付給的: *When is the rent due?* 何時應付房租? *The wages due to him will be paid tomorrow.* 他應得的工資明天付給他。 **2** (attrib only) suitable; right; proper: (僅作形容用法) 適當的; 正當的;適宜的: *after due consideration;* 經過適當考慮後; *in due course,* at the right and proper time. 在適當時期;時機一至。 **3** (to be) expected; appointed or agreed (for a certain time or date): 預期的;應到的;預定的: *When is the steamer due?* 輪船預定何時到達? *The train is due (in) at 1.30.* 火車應於一點半到達。*Mr Hill is due to speak/lecture twice tomorrow.* 希爾先生預定明天演講兩次。 **4** ***due to,*** that may be ascribed or attributed to: 由於;起因於: *The accident was due to careless driving.* 這車禍起因於駕駛疏忽。(Cf 參較 owing to: *Owing to* (= Because of) *his careless driving, we had a bad accident.* 由於他駕駛疏忽,我們發生了一次大車禍)。 □ *adv* (of points of the compass) exactly, directly: (指羅盤方位)正向: *due east/north.* 向正東(北)。

due² /djuː *US:* duː ; dju/ *n* **1** (*sing* only) that which must be given to sb because it is right or owing: (僅用單數)應得之物: *give the man his due.* 給予那人應得之物。***give the devil his due,*** (prov) be fair to a person even though he is not a friend, or does not deserve much. (諺)對惡人亦公平相待;勿掩惡人之善(縱非其友,或無甚價值,亦予以應得之對待)。 **2** (*pl*) sums of money to be paid, eg for membership of a club, legal charges paid. (複)應付之款(例如會費,訴訟費等);應繳之費。

duel /ˈdjuːəl *US:* ˈduːəl ; ˈdjuəl/ *n* (hist) fight (usu with swords or pistols) agreed between two persons, esp to decide a point of honour, at a meeting arranged and conducted according to rules, in the presence of two other persons called seconds; any two-sided contest: (史)決鬥(通常用劍或手槍); 雙方的鬥爭: *a ~ of wits.* 二人鬥智。 □ *vi* (-ll-, US also -l-) fight a ~ or ~s. 決鬥。**~·list, ~·ist** /ˈdjuːəlɪst *US:* ˈduː- ; ˈdjuəlɪst/ *n* person who fights ~s. 決鬥者。

du·enna /djuːˈenə *US:* duː- ; djuˈɛnə/ *n* (esp in a Spanish or Portuguese family) elderly woman acting as governess and companion in charge of girls; chaperon. (尤指西班牙或葡萄牙家庭中)少女的媬姆;陪媼。

duet /djuːˈet *US:* duː- ; djuˈɛt/ *n* piece of music for two voices or for two players. 二部曲;二重唱;二重奏。

duf·fer /ˈdʌfə(r) ; ˈdʌfɚ/ *n* (colloq) slow-witted, unintelligent or incompetent person. (俗)笨拙無能之人。

duffle (also **duf·fel**) /ˈdʌfl ; ˈdʌfḷ/ *n* [U] coarse woollen cloth with a thick nap. 一種厚毛的粗呢。**ˈ~ bag,** a cylindrical kitbag (of cloth or canvas). (圓筒狀,布或帆布做的) 行囊;行李袋。 **ˈ~ coat,** one of this material, usu with toggles instead of buttons, and a hood. 此種粗呢製成的上衣(通常以套索代替鈕扣並有一兜帽)。

dug¹ /dʌg ; dʌg/ *pt, pp* of dig.

dug² /dʌg ; dʌg/ *n* udder or teat of a female mammal. (雌性哺乳動物之)乳房;乳頭。

du·gong /ˈduːgɒŋ ; ˈdugɑŋ/ *n* large sea mammal with flippers and a forked tail. 儒艮(一種大的海洋哺乳動物,生有鰭狀肢和叉形之尾)。⇨ manatee.

dug-out /ˈdʌg aʊt ; ˈdʌgˌaʊt/ *n* **1** rough covered shelter made by digging, esp by soldiers for protection in war. 掩蔽壕;(尤指)避彈壕。 **2** canoe made by hollowing a tree trunk. 獨木舟。

duke /djuːk *US:* duːk ; djuk/ *n* nobleman of high

rank (next below a prince); (in some parts of Europe) independent sovereign ruler of a small State. 公爵；歐洲某些公國之君主。**~·dom** /-dəm; -dəm/ *n* **1** position and duties, rank of a ~. 公爵的爵位；公國君主的地位。 **2** (= *duchy*) land ruled by a ~ who is a sovereign ruler. 公爵管轄地；公國。

dul·cet /ˈdʌlsɪt; ˈdʌlsɪt/ *adj* (usu of sounds) sweet; pleasing. (通常指聲音)美妙的；悅耳的。

dul·ci·mer /ˈdʌlsɪmə(r); ˈdʌlsəmɚ/ *n* (often portable) musical instrument like a zither with strings struck with two hammers. (常是可以携帶的)德西馬琴(類似齊特琴，用雙錘擊打)。

dull /dʌl; dʌl/ *adj* (-er, -est) **1** not clear or bright: 不清楚的；不鮮明的：*a ~ colour/sound/mirror/day/sky;* 暗晦的顏色(模糊的聲音；不明亮的鏡子；陰天；陰暗的天空)；*~ weather;* 陰沉的天氣；*~ of hearing,* unable to hear well. 聽覺不良。 **2** slow in understanding: 頭腦遲鈍的；愚笨的：*~ pupils;* 愚笨的學生；*a ~ mind.* 遲鈍的頭腦。 **3** monotonous; uninteresting; not exciting or appealing to the imagination: 單調的；無趣味的；枯燥的：*a ~ book/speech/sermon/play.* 枯燥無味的書(演說，說教，戲)。 **4** not sharp: 鈍的：*a ~ knife;* 鈍的刀子；*a knife with a ~ edge;* 口鈍的刀子；(of pain) not felt distinctly: (指痛)隱約感覺到的：*a ~ ache.* 隱約感到的痛。 **5** (of trade) not active; (of goods) not in demand. (指貿易)蕭條的；(指貨物)滯銷的。□ *vt, vi* [VP6A, 2A] make or become ~: (使)變鈍；使不清楚；(使)變遲鈍：*to ~ the edge of a razor;* 使剃刀口變鈍；*drugs that ~ pain.* 減輕痛苦的藥物。 **~y** /ˈdʌllɪ; ˈdʌllɪ/ *adv* **~·ness** *n*

dull·ard /ˈdʌləd; ˈdʌlɚd/ *n* mentally dull person. 愚笨的人。

duly /ˈdjuːlɪ *US:* ˈduː-; ˈdjulɪ/ *adv* in a right or suitable manner; at the right time. 適當地；及時地。

dumb /dʌm; dʌm/ *adj* (-er, -est) **1** unable to speak: 啞的：*~ from birth.* 生來即啞。 *We must be kind to ~ animals,* ie also to animals other than human beings. 我們必須善待不能言語的動物。 **2** temporarily silent: 暫時沉默的：*The class remained ~ when the teacher asked a difficult question.* 老師問一難題時，全班皆沉默無言。 ***strike ~,*** make speechless, unable to talk because of surprise, fear, etc: (因驚奇，恐懼等)說不出話；使嚇呆：*He was struck ~ with horror.* 他嚇得不能出聲。**~ ˈshow** *n* the communication of ideas by means of acting, etc but without words. 手勢；啞劇。 **3** (US colloq) stupid; dull. (美俗)笨的；愚蠢的。 **~·ly** *adv* **~·ness** *n*

dumb·bell /ˈdʌmbel; ˈdʌmˌbɛl/ *n* short bar of wood or iron with a metal ball at each end, used in pairs (one in each hand) for exercising the muscles of the arms and shoulders. 啞鈴(兩端有金屬球的短木棒或鐵棒，同時用一對，每手持一個，以鍛鍊臂肩之肌肉)。

dumb·found (US also **dum·found**) /dʌmˈfaʊnd; dʌmˈfaʊnd/ *vt* [VP6A] astonish; strike dumb with surprise. 使驚愕；使嚇呆。

dumb·waiter /ˌdʌmˈweɪtə(r); ˈdʌmˈwetɚ/ *n* **1** stand with (usu revolving) shelves for food, dishes, etc used at a dining-table. (廻轉式)食品枱。 **2** (US; in GB *food-lift*) box with shelves, pulled up and down a shaft, to carry food, etc from one floor to another, eg in a restaurant. (美)遞送食物的升降器；吊斗(英國稱 food-lift)。

dum·dum /ˈdʌmdʌm; ˈdʌmdʌm/ *n* **ˈ~ bullet,** soft-nosed bullet which expands on contact, causing a gaping wound. 達姆彈(一種軟頭子彈，擊中會擴散，造成嚴重傷害)。

dummy /ˈdʌmɪ; ˈdʌmɪ/ *n* **1** object made to look like and serve the purpose of the real person or thing: 模型：*a tailor's ~,* for fitting clothes; 服裝店之人像模型；*a baby's ~,* sucked like the nipple of a mother's breast. 橡皮奶頭。 **2** (attrib) sham, imitation: (形容用法)假的；仿造的：*a ~ gun.* 假槍。 **3** (in card games, esp bridge) player whose cards are placed upwards on the table and played by his partner; the cards so placed. (牌戲，尤指橋牌)夢家(將牌攤出者)；夢家之牌。 **4** person who is present at an event, etc, but who takes no real part, eg because he is a substitute for sb else. 名義代表(參與一事並不實際有所作爲，而係代表他人之人)；傀儡。 **5** (attrib) (形容用法) **ˌ~ ˈrun,** a trial or practice attack, shoot, performance, etc. 攻擊，射擊，演習等之試驗或練習。

dump /dʌmp; dʌmp/ *n* **1** place where rubbish, etc may be unloaded and left; heap of rubbish, etc. 垃圾場；垃圾堆。 **2** (place where there is a) temporary store of military supplies: 軍需品之臨時貯存(站)：*an ˌammuˈnition ~.* 軍火臨時堆積所。 **3** (sl; pej) poorly cared for, dirty or ugly place (eg a village or town): (俚；蔑)骯髒或醜陋的地方(例如一村鎮)：*I should hate to live in a ~ like this.* 我不願住在這樣骯髒的地方。□ *vt* [VP6A, 15A] **1** put on or into a ~(1); put or throw down carelessly; let fall with a bump or thud: 倒在垃圾場；隨便傾倒；砰然倒下：*Where can I ~ this rubbish?* 我將這垃圾倒在什麼地方？ *They ~ed the coal outside the shed instead of putting it inside.* 他們把煤倒在棚外，而不倒在棚內。 **2** (comm) sell abroad at low prices goods which are unwanted in the home market. (商)向國外廉價傾銷國內市場不需要的貨物。 **~er** *n* (also 亦作 **ˈ~ truck**) vehicle with a bin that can be tilted, for carrying and emptying soil, rubble, etc (eg for road building). (鋪路時)運土，碎石等的卡車。

dump·ling /ˈdʌmplɪŋ; ˈdʌmplɪŋ/ *n* **1** small round mass of dough steamed or boiled with meat and vegetables. 與肉和蔬菜蒸或煮的麵團。 **2** baked pudding made of dough with an apple or other fruit inside it. (將蘋果等放在麵團裡烘製而成之)蘋果布丁；水果布丁。

dumps /dʌmps; dʌmps/ *n pl* ***(down) in the ~,*** (colloq) in low spirits; feeling gloomy. (俗)沮喪的；憂鬱的。

dumpy /ˈdʌmpɪ; ˈdʌmpɪ/ *adj* (-ier, -iest) short and fat. 矮胖的。

dun¹ /dʌn; dʌn/ *adj, n* dull greyish-brown. 暗褐色的；暗褐色。

dun² /dʌn; dʌn/ *vt* (-nn-) (continue to) demand payment of a debt or debts: (連續)催討債款：*a dunning letter.* 討債的信。□ *n* person who duns; debt-collector; importunate demand for payment. 討債人；催債者；催付。

dunce /dʌns; dʌns/ *n* slow learner (esp a child at school); stupid person. 遲鈍的學習者(尤指學童)；笨人。 **ˈ~'s cap,** pointed paper cap which a ~ was formerly given to wear in class as a punishment. 昔時劣等生受罰所戴的圓錐形紙帽。

dun·der·head /ˈdʌndəhed; ˈdʌndɚˌhɛd/ *n* blockhead; stupid person. 蠢材；笨人。

dune /djuːn *US:* duːn; djun/ *n* mound of loose, dry sand formed by the wind, esp near the seashore. 沙丘(尤指海邊被風吹積成者)。

dung /dʌŋ; dʌŋ/ *n* [U] excrement dropped by animals (esp cattle), used on fields as manure: 家畜的糞便(尤指牛糞，可用作肥料)：*to cart and spread ~.* 用車裝送並施糞。 **ˈ~·hill,** heap of ~ in a farmyard. 糞堆。

dunga·rees /ˌdʌŋgəˈriːz; ˌdʌŋgəˈriz/ *n pl* overalls of (usu) coarse calico. 粗布製成的工作服。

dun·geon /ˈdʌndʒən; ˈdʌndʒən/ *n* (hist) dark underground cell used as a prison. (史)地牢。

dunk /dʌŋk; dʌŋk/ *vt* [VP6A, 14] dip (a piece of food) into a liquid: 浸泡(食物)：*~ a doughnut in one's coffee.* 把油炸圈餅在咖啡內浸一下。

duo·deci·mal /ˌdjuːəʊˈdesɪml *US:* ˌduːəˈd-; ˌdjuəˈdɛsəml̩/ *adj* of twelve or twelfths; proceeding by twelves: 十二的；十二分算的；十二進法的：*a ~ notation.* 十二進法。

duo·denum /ˌdjuːəˈdiːnəm *US:* ˌduːə-; ˌdjuəˈdinəm/

n (anat) first part of the small intestine immediately below the stomach. (解剖)十二指腸。⇨ the illus at alimentary. 參看 alimentary 之插圖。**duo·denal** /ˌdjuːəˈdiːnl *US:* ˌduːə- ; ˌdjuəˈdinl/ *adj* of the ~: 十二指腸的: *a duodenal ulcer.* 十二指腸潰瘍。

duo·logue /ˈdjuːəlɒg *US:* ˈduːəlɔːg ; ˈdjuəˌlɔg/ *n* conversation between two persons. 對話。

dupe /djuːp *US:* duːp ; djup/ *vt* [VP6A] cheat; make a fool of; deceive. 欺騙;欺瞞。□ *n* person who is ~d. 受騙者。

du·plex /ˈdjuːpleks *US:* ˈduː- ; ˈdjupleks/ *adj* double; twofold: 二倍的; 二重的: *a ~ (oil-)lamp,* one with two wicks; 雙燈心的(油)燈; *a ~ apartment,* (US) one with rooms on two floors with an inner staircase. (美)樓中樓的公寓。

du·pli·cate[1] /ˈdjuːplɪkət *US:* ˈduː- ; ˈdjupləkɪt/ *adj* **1** identical: 完全相同的: *~ keys for the front door of a house.* 開啓前門用的幾把相同的鑰匙。 **2** with two corresponding parts; doubled; twofold. 雙聯的;加倍的;雙重的。□ *n* [C] thing that is exactly like another. 完全相同之物。***in ~,*** (of documents, etc) with a ~ copy. (指文件等)一式兩份。

du·pli·cate[2] /ˈdjuːplɪkeɪt *US:* ˈduː- ; ˈdjupləˌket/ *vt* [VP6A] **1** make an exact copy of (a letter, etc); produce copies of. 複寫(信件等);複製。 **2** double. 加倍。**du·pli·ca·tor** /-tə(r) ; -tɚ/ *n* machine, etc that ~s sth written or typed. 複印機。**du·pli·ca·tion** /ˌdjuːplɪˈkeɪʃn *US:* ˌduː- ; ˌdjupləˈkeʃən/ *n* [U] duplicating or being ~d; [C] copy. 複寫;複製;加倍;複製物;副本。

du·plic·ity /djuːˈplɪsətɪ *US:* duː- ; djuˈplɪsətɪ/ *n* [U] deliberate deception. 欺騙。

dur·able /ˈdjʊərəbl *US:* ˈdʊə- ; ˈdjʊrəbl/ *adj* likely to last for a long time: 耐久的: *a ~ pair of shoes,* not soon worn out or needing repair. 一雙耐穿的鞋子。□ *n* (usu *pl*) (often 常作 **consumer ~s**) goods bought and expected to last a long time (eg vacuum cleaners). (通常作複數) 耐久的貨物 (例如吸塵器)。**dura·bil·ity** /ˌdjʊərəˈbɪlətɪ *US:* ˈdʊə- ; ˌdjʊrəˈbɪlətɪ/ *n* [U].

du·rance /ˈdjʊərəns *US:* ˈdʊə- ; ˈdjʊrəns/ *n* (old use) imprisonment. (舊用法)禁錮;監禁。

dur·ation /djʊˈreɪʃn *US:* dʊ- ; djʊˈreʃən/ *n* [U] time during which sth lasts or exists: 持續時間; 期間: *for the ~ of the war;* 戰爭進行的期間; *of short ~.* 短期的。

dur·bar /ˈdɜːbɑː(r) ; ˈdɝbɑr/ *n* (hist) Indian ruler's court; reception given by a ruler in India. (史)印度王的宮廷;印度王的接見。

dur·ess /djʊˈres *US:* dʊ- ; ˈdjʊrɪs/ *n* threats, imprisonment, or violence, used to compel sb to do sth: 强迫某人做某事所做的威脅、監禁或暴行: *under ~,* compelled by such means. 受脅迫。

dur·ing /ˈdjʊərɪŋ *US:* ˈdʊər- ; ˈdʊrɪŋ/ *prep* **1** throughout the duration of: 在…期間: *The sun gives us light ~ the day.* 太陽在白天給我們陽光。 **2** at some point of time in the duration of: 在…期間之某一時間: *He called to see me ~ my absence.* 我不在的時候他來看過我。

durst /dɜːst ; dɝst/ old *pt* form of dare. 舊時 dare 的過去式。

dusk /dʌsk ; dʌsk/ *n* [U] time just before it gets quite dark: 黃昏;薄暮: *scarcely visible in the ~.* 在黃昏時幾乎看不見的。

dusky /ˈdʌskɪ ; ˈdʌskɪ/ *adj* (-ier, -iest) rather dark; dark-coloured; dim. 頗暗的;黑暗的;暗淡的。

dust[1] /dʌst ; dʌst/ *n* **1** [U] dry earth or other matter in the form of fine powder, lying on the ground or the surface of objects, or blown about by the wind: 灰塵;塵土: *The ~ was blowing in the streets.* 街上塵土飛揚。 *When it rains ~ turns into mud.* 下雨時塵土變成了泥。***bite the ~,*** (sl) fall wounded or killed. (俚)受傷倒地或倒斃。***(humbled) in(to) the ~,*** humiliated (as if lying at the feet of an enemy). 受屈辱(如臥於敵人脚下者然)。***shake the ~ off one's feet,*** leave in anger or scorn. 憤然離去。***throw*** **ˈ~** ***in a person's eyes,*** mislead him; prevent him from seeing the truth. 蒙蔽一人;欺瞞一人。**ˈ~-bowl,** area that is denuded of vegetation by drought, unwise farming methods, etc. 因旱災，種植方法不良等而缺乏植物的地區。 **ˈ~-coat,** coat worn to keep ~ off or out. 禦灰塵的外衣;風衣。**ˈ~-jacket / -wrapper,** removable paper cover to protect the binding of a book. 書皮;包書紙。**ˈ~·pan,** pan into which ~ is swept from the floor. 畚箕;簸箕。**ˈ~-sheet** *n* one for covering furniture not in use. 遮蓋不用的傢具之防塵布。 **2 a ~,** cloud of ~: 雲狀塵埃;烟塵: *What a ~!* 灰塵漫天！(fig) commotion. (喻)騷動。***kick up / make / raise a ~,*** (sl, fig) cause a commotion. (俚,喻)引起騷動。 **3** (in compounds) (用於複合字中) (GB; Cf 參較 US 美 *refuse, trash, garbage*) household refuse. (英)垃圾。**ˈ~·bin,** rigid receptacle for this. 垃圾箱。(Cf 參較 US 美 *ash-can, garbage-box.*) **ˈ~-cart,** vehicle into which ~bins are emptied. 垃圾車。**ˈ~·man** /-mən ; -mən/ (*pl* -men) man employed (by municipal authorities, etc) to empty ~bins and cart away refuse. 清除垃圾的工人。 **4** (old use, poet or liter) remains of a dead human body: (舊用法,詩或文)遺骸: *buried with the ~ of* (= in the same grave as) *one's ancestors.* 與祖先遺骸葬在一起。

dust[2] /dʌst ; dʌst/ *vt* **1** [VP6A, 15B] ***dust sth (down / off),*** remove dust from, by wiping, brushing, flicking: 拭去灰塵;拂去灰塵: *~ the furniture;* 拭去傢具上的灰塵; *~ down / off the seat of a car.* 拭去汽車座位上的灰塵。 ***~ sb's jacket,*** (colloq) beat him. (俗)毆打某人。**ˈ~-up** *n* (colloq) fight; quarrel. (俗)打鬥;吵鬧。 **2** [VP15A] sprinkle with powder: 撒以粉: *to ~ a cake with sugar;* 撒糖於糕上; sprinkle (powder, etc): 撒(粉等): *to ~ sugar on to a cake.* 將糖撒在糕上。**~er** *n* cloth for removing dust from furniture, etc. 擦布;抹布;撣子。

dusty /ˈdʌstɪ ; ˈdʌstɪ/ *adj* (-ier, -iest) covered with dust; full of dust; like dust; dry as dust. 覆有灰塵的;滿是灰塵的;似灰塵的;灰塵般乾燥的。 ***~ answer,*** answer that is not pleasing or satisfactory (to the receiver). 不滿意的回答。

Dutch /dʌtʃ ; dʌtʃ/ *adj* **1** of or from the Netherlands (Holland), its people, their language: 荷蘭的;荷蘭人的;荷蘭語的: *~ cheese.* 荷蘭乳酪。 **2** (colloq uses) (俗語用法) ***~ auction,*** sale at which the price is reduced by the auctioneer until a buyer is found. 拍賣者自動落價直至有買主時的拍賣。 ***~ courage,*** that obtained by drinking (spirits, etc). 酒後之勇。 ***~ treat,*** meal, entertainment, etc at which each person pays for himself. 各自付費的聚餐、娛樂等;打平夥。***go ~ (with sb),*** share expenses. (與某人)各自付帳。***talk to sb like a ~ uncle,*** lecture him candidly but severely. 諄諄告誡;嚴厲斥責。□ *n* **1 the ~,** the people of Holland. 荷蘭人。 **2** their language. 荷蘭語。***double ~,*** unintelligible language. 無法了解的語言。**~·man** /-mən ; -mən/ *n* (*pl* -men) native of Holland. 荷蘭人。

du·teous /ˈdjuːtɪəs *US:* ˈduː- ; ˈdjutɪəs/ *adj* (formal) dutiful (the more usu word); obedient. (正式用語)盡職的 (dutiful 較常用);服從的。

duti·able /ˈdjuːtɪəbl *US:* ˈduː- ; ˈdjutɪəbl/ *adj* on which customs duties must be paid: 應納關稅的;應納稅的: *~ goods.* 應納關稅的貨物。 *Tobacco is ~ in most countries.* 在多數國家菸草須納稅。⇨ duty(3).

duti·ful /ˈdjuːtɪfl *US:* ˈduː- ; ˈdjutɪfəl/ *adj* ***~ (to),*** doing one's duty well; showing respect and obedience: 盡職的; 恭敬服從的; 孝順的: *a ~ son.* 孝順的兒子。**~ly** /-fəlɪ ; -fəlɪ/ *adv*

duty /ˈdjuːtɪ *US:* ˈduːtɪ ; ˈdjutɪ/ *n* (*pl* -ties) **1** [C, U] what one is obliged to do by morality, law, a trade, a calling, conscience, etc; inner voice urging one to behave in a certain way: 任務;義務;責任;本分;孝道;敬意: *When ~ calls, no man should disobey.*

當有義務需要履行時，任何人都義不容辭。*Do not forget your ~ to your parents.* 不要忘記對父母應盡的責任。*His sense of ~ is strong.* 他的責任感很强。*What are the duties of this post?* 這個工作的職務是什麼？ *The ~ of a postman is to deliver letters and parcels.* 郵差的職務是遞送信件和包裹。**on／off ~**, actually engaged／not engaged in one's regular work: 值(不值)班；上(下)班: *He goes on ~ at 9am and comes off ~ at 5pm.* 他上午九時上班，下午五時下班。***(as) in ~ bound***, as required by ~. 基於義務；有義務。 ***do ~ for***, be used instead of; serve for: 充作；當作…之用: *An old wooden box did ~ for a table.* 一個舊木箱充作桌子。 **2** (attrib) moral obligation. (形容用法)道德上的義務。 **'~ call**, visit one makes from a sense of ~, not because one expects to enjoy it. 出於義務感所作的拜訪。 **3** [C, U] **~ *(on)***, payment demanded by the government on certain goods exported or imported (*'customs duties*), or manufactured in the country (*'excise duties*), or when property, etc is transferred to a new owner by sale (*'stamp duties*) or death (*e'state ~*). 税: 關税 (customs duties)；消費税 (excise duties)；印花税 (stamp duties)；遺產税(estate duty)。**ˌ~-'free**, (of goods) allowed to enter a country without the payment of customs duties: (指貨物)免關税的: *~-free shops*, (eg at airports) selling ~-free goods. 免税商店(例如飛機場中者)。

duvet /'dju:veɪ *US:* du:'veɪ ; djʊ've/ *n* bed quilt (filled with feathers, eg swan's-down, or an artificial substitute) used in place of blankets. 絨毛(如天鵝毛或人造毛)製成的褥墊。

dwarf /dwɔ:f ; dwɔrf/ *n* (*pl* ~s) person, animal or plant much below the usual size; (in fairy tales) small being with magic powers; (attrib) undersized. 矮子；侏儒；較一般矮小的動物或植物；(神仙故事)小妖；(形容用法)矮小的。 **~ish** *adj* like a ~; undersized: 似侏儒的；矮小的: *~ish trees／fingers.* 矮小的樹(短小的手指)。 □ *vt* [VP6A] **1** prevent from growing to full size. 阻礙發育。 **2** cause to appear small by contrast or distance: 使相形之下顯得矮小或渺小: *The big yacht ~ed our little launch.* 這艘大遊艇使我們的小汽船相形之下顯得小了。

dwell /dwel ; dwɛl/ *vi* (*pt* dwelt /dwelt ; dwɛlt/) [VP3A] (liter) (文) **1** ~ ***in／at***, reside. 居住。 **2** ~ ***on／upon***, think, speak or write at length about: 細思；詳論；詳述: *She ~s too much upon her past.* 她過於詳細地敍述她的過去。 **~er** *n* (in compounds) inhabitant: (用於複合字中)居民: *'town-~ers;* 城市裏的人； *'cliff-~ers;* 崖洞的居民； *'cave-~ers.* 穴居者。 **~·ing** *n* place of residence (a house, flat, etc). 住處；住宅。 **'~ing-house**, one used for living in, not as an office, workshop, etc. 住宅。

dwindle /'dwɪndl ; 'dwɪndḷ/ *vi* [VP2A] become less or smaller by degrees. 減少；縮小。

dy·archy *n* = diarchy.

dye¹ /daɪ ; daɪ/ *vt, vi* (3rd pers *sing pres t*, dyes, *pt*, *pp* dyed, *pres part* dyeing) **1** [VP6A, 22] colour, usu by dipping in a liquid: 染: *to dye a white dress blue;* 將白色衣服染成藍色； *to have a dress dyed.* 把衣服送去染。 ***dye in the wool／in grain***, dye while the material is in the raw state, so that the process is thorough. 生染(未織前即染，故可染透)。 **ˌdyed-in-the-'wool** *adj* (fig) thorough; complete. (喻)徹底的；完全的。 **2** [VP6A] give colour to: 着色於: *Deep blushes dyed her cheeks.* 她的面頰發赤。 **3** [VP2A] take colour from dyeing: 染色: *This material does not dye well.* 這料子染不好。

dye² /daɪ ; daɪ/ *n* [C, U] substance used for dyeing cloth; colour given by dyeing. 染料；染色。 ***a villain／scoundrel of the blackest／deepest dye***, of the worst kind. 窮兇極惡的人；惡漢。 **'dye-stuff**, substance yielding a dye or used as a dye. 染料。 **'dye-works**, one where dyeing is done. 染廠。 **dyer** *n* one who dyes cloth. 染布工人；染匠。

dy·ing ⇨ die².

dyke *n* = dike.

dy·namic /daɪ'næmɪk ; daɪ'næmɪk/ *adj* **1** of physical power and forces producing motion. 動力的。 ⇨ static. **2** (of a person) having energy, force of character: (指人)精悍的；精力充沛的: *a ~ personality.* 精力充沛的人。 □ *n* **1** (*pl* with *sing v*) branch of physics dealing with matter in motion. (複數，與單數動詞連用)力學；動力學。 **2** moral force that produces activity or change: 引起活動或變化的道德力量: *driven by an inner ~.* 受內心道德力量的驅使。 **dy·nami·cally** /-klɪ ; -klɪ/ *adv* **dy·na·mism** /'daɪnəmɪzəm ; 'daɪnəˌmɪzəm/ *n* [U] (of a person or a thing) power, energy. (指人或物)活力；精力；動力。

dyna·mite /'daɪnəmaɪt ; 'daɪnəˌmaɪt/ *n* [U] powerful explosive (used in mining and quarrying). 炸藥。 □ *vt* [VP6A] blow up with ~. 用炸藥炸開或炸毀。

dy·namo /'daɪnəməʊ ; 'daɪnəˌmo/ *n* (*pl* ~s /-məʊz ; -moz/) machine for changing steam-power, water-power, etc into electrical energy. 發電機。

dyn·ast /'dɪnəst *US:* 'daɪnæst ; 'daɪnæst/ *n* lord; hereditary ruler. 君主；世襲的統治者。 **~y** /'dɪnəstɪ *US:* 'daɪ- ; 'daɪnəstɪ/ *n* (*pl* -ties) succession of rulers belonging to one family: 朝代；王朝: *the Tudor ~y* (in England). (英國)都鐸王朝。 **~tic** /dɪ'næstɪk *US:* daɪ- ; daɪ'næstɪk/ *adj* of a ~y. 朝代的；王朝的。

dyne /daɪn ; daɪn/ *n* unit of force in the metric system. 達因(公制中力的單位)。

dys·en·tery /'dɪsəntrɪ *US:* -terɪ ; 'dɪsnˌtɛrɪ/ *n* [U] painful disease of the bowels, with discharge of mucus and blood. 痢疾；赤痢。

dys·lexia /dɪs'leksɪə ; dɪs'lɛksɪə/ *n* [U] disturbance in the ability to read. 閱讀能力失常；讀字困難。 **dys·lexic** /-'leksɪk ; -'lɛksɪk/ *adj*

dys·pep·sia /dɪs'pepsɪə ; dɪ'spɛpʃə/ *n* [U] indigestion. 消化不良症。 **dys·pep·tic** /dɪs'peptɪk ; dɪ'spɛptɪk/ *adj* of ~. 消化不良的。 □ *n* person suffering from ~. 消化不良患者。

Ee

E, e /i: ; i/ (*pl* E's, e's /i:z ; iz/), fifth letter of the English alphabet. 英文字母之第五個字母。

each /i:tʃ ; itʃ/ *adj* (of two or more) every one, (thing, group, person, etc) taken separately or individually: (指二或二以上之物，群，人等)每一；各個: *He was sitting with a child on ~ side of him.* 他坐在那裏，兩邊各有一個小孩。 *On ~ occasion I just missed the target.* 我每次總是不能中的。 *He had words of encouragement for ~ one of us.* 他對我們每人都勉勵一番。 □ *pron* **1** ~ thing, person, group, etc: 各個(每物，每人，每組等): *E~ of them wants to try.* 他們每人都要試一試。 *E~ of the boys had a try.* 每個男孩子都試了一次。 *He had good advice for ~ of us.* 他對我們每人都贈以良言。 **2** used in apposition, like *all* and *both:* (用作同位字，類似 all 和 both)各自；各: *We ~ took a big risk.* 我們各自冒了一次大險。 *Tom, Dick and Harry ~ put forward a different scheme.* 湯姆，狄克和哈利各提出了一個不同的計畫。 **3** used *adverbially* meaning 'apiece': (用作副詞)每個；每件；每人: *He gave the* *boys 50p* ~. 他給男孩子們每人五十辨士。*The oranges are 6p* ~. 橙子賣六辨士一個。 **4** ~ ***other***, used as the object of a *v* or *prep*; both words usu unstressed; often replaced by *one another* when the reference is to a number more than two: 互相 (用做動詞或介系詞的受詞; 兩字通常都不重讀; 如多於兩個時，常用 one another 代替): *We see ~ other* (= ~ of us sees the other) *at the office every day.* 我們每天在辦公室見面。*They are afraid of ~ other.* 他們互相害怕。

eager /ˈiːgə(r) ; ˈigɚ/ *adj* ~ ***(for sth/to do sth)***, full of, showing, strong desire: 熱切的;渴望的: ~ *for success;* 渴望成功; ~ *to succeed.* 急欲成功。ˌ~ **ˈbeaver**, (colloq) hardworking and (over) enthusiastic person. (俗)工作努力並(過分)熱心之人。 ~**·ly** *adv* ~**·ness** *n*

eagle /ˈiːgl ; ˈigl̩/ *n* large, strong bird of prey of the falcon family with keen sight. 鷹。⇨ the illus at prey. 參看 prey 之挿圖。ˌ~-**ˈeyed** *adj* keen-sighted. 目光銳利的。 **eag·let** /ˈiːglɪt ; ˈiglɪt/ *n* young ~. 小鷹。

ear[1] /ɪə(r) ; ɪr/ *n* **1** organ of hearing. 耳;耳朵。⇨ illus here and the illus at head. 參看本條及 head 之挿圖。 ***be all ears***, be listening eagerly. 專心傾聽。***fall on deaf ears***, pass unnoticed. 未受注意。***feel one's ˈears burning***, imagine that one is being talked about. 覺得耳朵在發燒 (想像正被人談論)。 ***give one's ears (for sth/to do sth)***, make any sacrifice, pay any price. 不惜任何犧牲; 不惜任何代價。 ***go in (at) ˌone ear and out (at) the ˈother***, said of sth that, although heard, makes no impression. 左耳進右耳出; 當作耳邊風。 ***have an ear to the ground***, be alert for what may be happening in secret. 注意祕密中可能發生之事。***(have) a word in sb's ear***, (say) sth in confidence: 私下說出一事: *May I have a word in your ear?* 我可以和你私下談句話嗎? ***have/win sb's ear(s)***, his favourable attention. 獲得某人的好感;對某人講話有力。***over head and ears***, deeply (in debt, etc). 深陷(債務等中)。***prick up one's ears***, become suddenly attentive. 顯出突然注意或關切的神情。***set (persons) by the ears***, set them quarrelling. 挑撥離間。 ***turn a deaf ear (to)***, refuse to help. 拒絕幫助。***up to the/one's ˈears in (work, etc)***, overwhelmed by it. 工作等極繁忙。***wet behind the ears***, naïve. 天眞的。**ˈear-ache**, pain in the inner ear. 耳痛。**ˈear-drop**, ear-ring with a hanging ornament. 耳環;耳墜。**ˈear-drum**, thin membrane (in the inner ear) which vibrates when sound-waves strike it. 耳鼓;鼓膜。⇨ the illus here. 參看本條之挿圖。**ˈear·ful** /-fʊl ; -fʊl/, as much (usu abusive or unsolicited) talk as one can endure. 一個人聽對方(通常含有辱罵性或令人覺得多餘的)說話所能容忍的限度。**ˈear·mark** *n* mark on the ear of a sheep, etc, to mark ownership; (fig) special characteristic. 耳號(置於羊等之耳上，以示所有權); (喻)特徵。 □ *vt* [VP6A, 14] ***earmark sb/sth (for sth)***, put an earmark on (an animal); (fig) keep sb in mind for a special purpose, work, etc; set sth aside for a special purpose: 加耳號於(某動物); (喻)指定某人擔任特殊任務,工作等;指定某物做特殊用途: *earmark sb for an important post;* 指定某人擔任一件重要的工作; *earmark a sum of money for research.* 撥款做研究費用。**ˈear·piece**, earphone of a telephone receiver. (電話機之) 聽筒。 **ˈear·phone**, headphone. 耳機。**ˈear·ring**, ring worn in or on the lobe of the ear as an ornament. 耳環。 **ˈear·shot**, hearing distance: 聽力所及之距離: *out of/within earshot.* 在聽力所及之距離外(內)。 **ˈear-trumpet**, trumpet-shaped tube formerly used by partly deaf people. (昔時半聾之人用的喇叭狀)助聽器; 耳筒。⇨ *hearing-aid* at hearing. **ˈear·wax**, waxy substance secreted in the ear. 耳垢。 **2** sense of hearing. 聽覺。***have a good ear for music***, be able to discriminate sound. 音感好的;能辨音的。 ***(play sth) by ear***, (play) without printed music, or without having memorized it; (fig) (do it) unprepared. 憑聽過一次後不用樂譜演奏; (喻)無準備(而做某事)。 **3** ear-shaped thing, esp the handle of a pitcher. 耳狀物; (尤指)水壺耳。 **(-)eared**, used in compounds: 用於複合字中: ˌ*long-ˈeared*, having long ears. 長耳的。

ear[2] /ɪə(r) ; ɪr/ *n* seed-bearing part of a cereal (corn, barley, etc): (玉蜀黍,大麥等之)穗: *corn in the ear*, with ears developed. 正在長穗的玉蜀黍。⇨ the illus at cereal. 參看 cereal 之挿圖。

earl /ɜːl ; ɝl/ *n* (fem *countess*) title of a British nobleman. (英)伯爵(女伯爵爲 countess)。 ~**·dom** /-dəm ; -dəm/ *n* rank of an ~. 伯爵爵位。

early /ˈɜːlɪ ; ˈɝlɪ/ (-ier, -iest) *adj, adv* near to the beginning of a period of time, sooner than usual or than others: 早;初;初期的: *in the ~ part of this century;* 本世紀的初葉; *in ~ spring;* 在初春; *an ~ breakfast*, eg 5 am; 很早的早餐(例如早上五點鐘進食者); ~ *peaches*, ripening ~ in the season; 早熟的桃子; ˌ~-ˈ*closing day*, (GB) on which shops, etc are closed during the afternoon. (英)商店等早打烊(下午打烊)的日子。*He's an ~ riser*, gets up at an ~ hour. 他慣於早起。*Please come at your earliest convenience*, as soon as it is convenient for you to do so. 得便請儘可能早來。*He keeps ~ hours*, gets up, goes to bed, ~. 他早睡早起。 *It's better to be too ~ than too late.* 太早總比太遲好(不怕早只怕晚)。*Come as ~ as possible.* 儘早來。***The ~ bird gets/catches the worm***, (prov) The person who arrives, etc ~ will (probably) succeed. (諺)早起

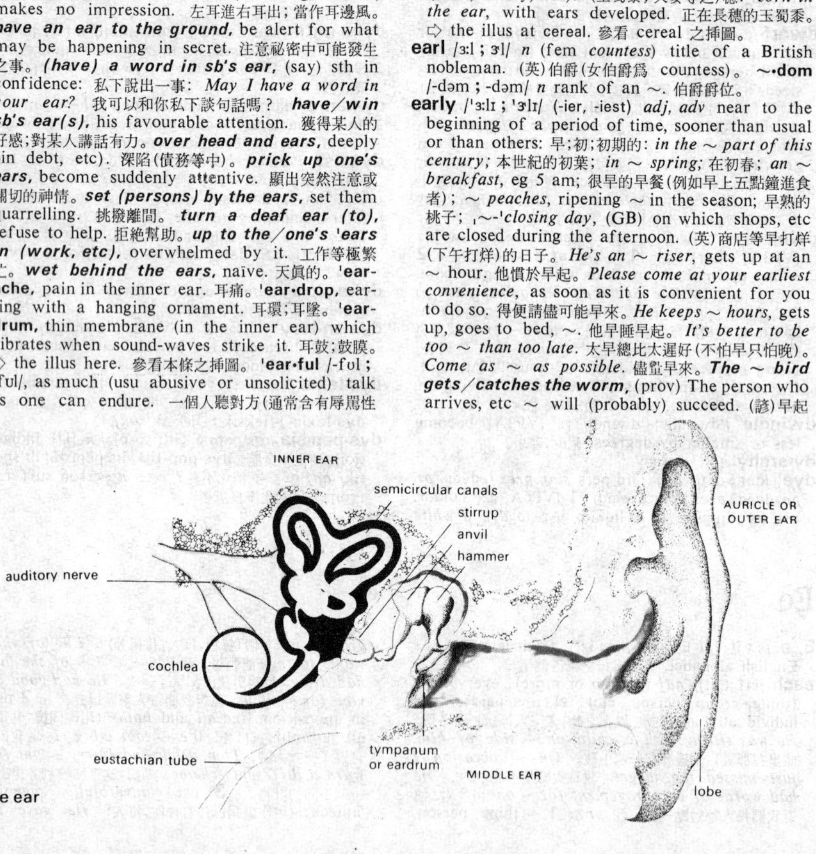

the ear

的鳥能捕到蟲(意謂早到等的人可能會成功)。 ~ ***days (yet),*** too soon to tell how sth will develop. 言之過早。***earlier on,*** at an earlier stage. 初時;在較早的階段。Cf 參較 *later on* at late² (1). ˌ~-ˈ**warning** *adj* (of radar) giving early indication of the approach of enemy aircraft, missiles, etc: (指雷達) 預先警報的 (可早期指示敵機,飛彈等之逼近的): *an ~-warning system.* 預先警報系統。

earn /ɜːn ; ɝn/ *vt* [VP6A, 12B, 13B] get in return for work, as a reward for one's qualities or in payment for a loan: 賺;挣得;博得: *to ~ £10000 a year;* 一年賺一萬鎊; *to ~ one's living/one's livelihood/one's daily bread.* 謀生。*The money ~s 7% interest.* 這筆錢得七厘利。*His achievements ~ed him respect and admiration.* 他的成就使他受到尊敬和欽佩。*His eccentricities had ~ed for him the nickname 'The Madman'.* 他的怪癖已爲他博得'瘋子'的綽號。*I had a well-~ed rest.* 我得到應得的休息了。**~·ings** *n pl* money ~ed: 賺得的錢: *He has spent all his ~ings.* 他把賺來的錢都花光了。ˈ**~ings yield,** (comm) ratio between annual profit and capital. (商)年利潤與資本間的比率。

ear·nest¹ /ˈɜːnɪst ; ˈɝnɪst/ *adj* serious; determined: 認眞的; 堅決的: *an ~ worker/pupil;* 認眞的工作者(學生); *a terribly ~ young man,* perhaps over-serious, over-conscientious. 過於認眞的青年。□ *n* ***in ~,*** in a determined manner; serious(ly): 鄭重; 認眞: *If you work in ~, you will succeed.* 如果你認眞工作,你會成功的。*I'm perfectly in ~,* am not joking. 我完全是正經的 (不是開玩笑)。*It is raining in real ~,* heavily, and likely to continue. 雨眞的下大了。**~·ly** *adv* in an ~ manner: 認眞地;堅決地: *We ~ly hope that....* 我們眞正希望…。**~·ness** *n*

ear·nest² /ˈɜːnɪst ; ˈɝnɪst/ *n* **1** (also 亦作 ˈ**~-money**) part payment made as a pledge that full payment will follow. 定金。 **2** sth coming in advance as a sign of what is to come after: 預兆: *As an ~ of my good intentions I will work overtime this week.* 本週我願加班以示我的善意。

earth /ɜːθ ; ɝθ/ *n* **1** **(the)** ~, this world; the planet on which we live: 地球;世界: *The moon goes round the ~ and the ~ goes round the sun.* 月亮繞地球運轉,而地球繞太陽運轉。*Who do you think was the greatest man on ~?* 你認爲誰是世界上最偉大的人?⇨ the illus at planet. 參看 planet 之挿圖。 **2** [U] land surface of the world; land contrasted with the sky: 陸地;大地: *The balloon burst and fell to ~.* 氣球爆了,落在地上。***come down/back to ~,*** stop daydreaming; return to practical realities. 返回現實。***move heaven and ~ (to do sth),*** make every possible effort. 用盡辦法;竭力。***how/why/where/who, etc on ~,*** how/why, etc ever.... (used for emphasis; ⇨ ever). 究竟如何(爲何,在何處,是誰等) (用以加强語氣)。 **3** [U] soil: 泥土: *to fill a pit with ~;* 用泥土塡坑; *to cover the roots of a plant with ~.* 將植物的根用泥土埋上。ˈ**~-closet,** latrine; substitute for a lavatory in places where there is no supply of water from mains, etc. (無抽水設備等的)廁所。ˈ**~-nut,** groundnut. 落花生。ˈ**~·work,** embankment of ~ used in fortifications as a defence. 泥土築成的防禦工事。ˈ**~-worm,** common kind of worm that lives in the soil. 蚯蚓。 **4** [C] hole of a fox, badger or other wild animal: (狐狸、獾或其他野獸之)洞; 獸穴: *to stop an ~,* block it up so that the animal cannot return to it. 塡塞獸洞(使其無法返洞)。***run/go to ~,*** (of a fox) go into its hole. (指狐) 入其洞穴。***run sth/sb to ~,*** hunt (a fox) to its burrow; (fig) discover (sth/sb) by searching. 追尋(狐)至洞; (喩)查明;追究到底。 **5** [C, U] (electr) (means of) contact with the ground at the completion of a circuit. (電)接地;接地的方法。 **6** [C] (chem) one of several metallic oxides. (化學)數種金屬氧化物之一。□ *vt* **1** [VP15B] ~ ***up,*** cover with ~: 覆以土: *to ~ up the roots of a newly-planted shrub.* 用土埋起新植灌木之根。 **2** [VP6A] (electr) connect (an apparatus, etc) with the ~. (電)接(裝置等)於地。⇨ 5 above. 參看上列第 5 義。**~y** *adj* **1** of or like ~ or soil: 泥土的;土狀的: *an ~y smell.* 土味;泥土氣息。 **2** (fig) grossly material; unaffected, unrefined: (喩)粗俗的;純樸的: *the ~y and robust men and women in the paintings of Rubens.* 魯賓斯畫中的純樸而壯健的男女。

earthen /ˈɜːθn ; ˈɝθən/ *adj* made of earth: 土製的: *~ floors;* 土鋪的地板; made of baked clay: 陶製的: *an ~ jar.* 陶瓶。ˈ**~·ware** /-weə(r) ; -ˌwɛr/ *n* [U] dishes, etc made of baked clay; 陶器; (attrib) (形容用法) *an ~ware casserole.* 陶製烤鍋。

earthly /ˈɜːθlɪ ; ˈɝθlɪ/ *adj* **1** of this world, not of heaven: 現世的;塵世的: *~ joys/possessions.* 塵世的享樂(財產)。 **2** (colloq) possible; conceivable: (俗)可能的; 可想像的: *You haven't an ~ (chance),* no chance at all. 你根本沒有機會。***no ~ use,*** quite useless. 完全無用。

earth·quake /ˈɜːθkweɪk ; ˈɝθˌkwek/ *n* [C] sudden, violent movement of the earth's surface. 地震。

ear·wig /ˈɪəwɪg ; ˈɪrˌwɪg/ *n* small harmless insect with pincers at the rear end of its abdomen. 蠼螋(無害的小蟲,腹部後端生有螯); 小蜈蚣。⇨ the illus at insect. 參看 insect 之挿圖。

ease¹ /iːz ; iz/ *n* [U] freedom from work, discomfort, trouble, difficulty, anxiety: 安逸;舒適;不費力;安心: *a life of ~;* 舒適的生活; *~ of body and mind.* 身心的舒適。 ***at ~,*** comfortable; comfortably: 舒適的(地);安逸的(地): *a mind at ~;* 心情安適; *sitting at ~.* 悠閒地坐着;安適地坐着。***ill at ~,*** anxious or embarrassed. 侷促不安。***stand at ~,*** (as a mil command) with the legs apart and the hands behind the back. (軍隊口令)稍息。(Cf 參較 *at attention, stand easy*). ***take one's ~,*** stop working or worrying. 悠閒。***with ~,*** without difficulty. 容易地;無困難地。

ease² /iːz ; iz/ *vt, vi* **1** [VP6A, 14] ~ ***(of),*** give relief to (the body or mind) from pain, discomfort, anxiety: 使(身心)舒適;使安心;減輕(身心之痛苦,不安,憂慮): *~ sb's anxiety;* 減輕某人的憂慮; *~ sb of his pain/trouble.* 減輕某人的痛苦(煩惱)。*Can I ~ you of your burden?* 我能減輕你的負擔嗎? **2** [VP6A, 15A, B, 2C] make looser, less tight; lessen speed, efforts: 放鬆;減低(速度或努力): *~ a coat under the armpits;* 將上衣的腋下部份放寬鬆; *~ a drawer,* eg one that sticks fast or opens with difficulty; 使一抽屜易於開關; *~ (down) the speed of a boat.* 減低船速。*E~ off a bit, we're going too fast.* 慢一點,我們走得太快了。 **3** [VP2A, C] ~ ***(off/up),*** become less tense or troublesome: 緩和;減少緊張或麻煩: *the easing of tension between the two countries.* 兩國間緊張局勢的緩和。*The situation has ~d off/up.* 局勢緩和了。

easel /ˈiːzl ; ˈizl/ *n* wooden frame to support a blackboard or a picture (while the artist is working at it). 黑板架;畫架。

east /iːst ; ist/ *n* **1** **the ~,** point of the horizon where the sun rises. 東; 東方。⇨ the illus at compass. 參看 compass 之挿圖。**the ˌFar ˈE~,** China, Japan, etc. 遠東(中國,日本等)。**the ˌMiddle ˈE~,** countries from Egypt to Iran. 中東(埃及伊朗間諸國)。**the ˌNear ˈE~,** Turkey, etc. 近東(土耳其等)。**the E~, (a)** the Orient. 東方諸國。**(b)** the eastern side of the USA ~ of the Allegheny Mountains and north of the Mason-Dixon line (the boundary between the states of Pennsylvania and Maryland). (美)東部各州(包括阿利根尼山脈以東,南北分界線以北諸州)。 **2** (attrib): (形容用法): *an ~ wind,* one blowing from the ~; 東風; towards, at, in the direction of the ~: 向東方的; 在東方的: *on the ~ coast.* 在東部海岸。**the ˌE~ ˈEnd,** the eastern part of London. 倫敦東區。□ *adv* towards the ~: 向東: *to travel ~;* 向東方旅行; *to face ~;* 朝東; *to sail due ~;* 向正東航行; *a town* *that lies ~ of the Rhine.* 萊因河東岸一城。**~·ward** /ˈiːstwəd ; ˈistwəd/ *adj* towards the ~: 向東方的: *in an ~ward direction.* 向東方。**~·ward(s)** *adv* towards the ~: 向東: *to travel ~wards.* 向東旅行。

Easter /ˈiːstə(r) ; ˈistə/ *n* anniversary of the Resurrection of Christ, observed on the first Sunday (*~ Day, ~ Sunday*) after a full moon on or after 21 Mar. (基督)復活節(在三月二十一日或該日後月圓以後第一個星期日,復活節日稱作 Easter Day 或 Easter Sunday)。Used attrib in 在下列各例中爲形容用法: ˈ*~-week* (beginning on ~ Sunday); 自復活節起的一週間; *the ~ holidays.* 復活節假期。**ˈ~ egg,** egg with a painted or dyed shell, or an egg made of chocolate. 復活節彩蛋(蛋殼塗有彩色,或由巧克力製成者)。

east·er·ly /ˈiːstəlɪ ; ˈistəlɪ/ *adj, adv* in an eastern direction or position; (of the wind) coming from the east. 在東方;(指風)來自東方的(地)。

east·ern /ˈiːstən ; ˈistən/ *adj* (attrib) of, from, living in, the east part of the world: (形容用法)東方的;自東方的; 居於東方的: *~ religions.* 東方的宗教。**the E~ Church,** the Greek Orthodox Church. 東方教會(希臘正教)。**the E~ Hemisphere,** Africa, Asia and Europe. 東半球(非洲,亞洲及歐洲)。**~-most** /-məʊst ; -ˌmost/ *adj* farthest east. 最東的; 極東的。

E

easy /ˈiːzɪ ; ˈizɪ/ (-ier, -iest) *adj* **1** not difficult: 容易的: *an ~ book.* 易讀的書。*The place is ~ to reach.* 那地方容易到達。*It is an ~ place to reach.* 那是個容易到達的地方。**2** free from pain, discomfort, anxiety, trouble, etc: 舒適的;安心的;暢快的; 輕鬆的: *to lead an ~ life;* 過舒適的生活; *in ~ circumstances,* having enough money to live comfortably; 生活優裕; *an ˈ~ chair,* one that is soft and restful; 安樂椅; 柔軟舒適的椅子; *~ manners,* not showing stiffness or embarrassment; 從容的態度; (*to buy furniture*) *on ~ terms,* trade term for hire-purchase; (購傢具)分期付款; *persons who are ~ to get on with,* people who are informal, not stiff. 容易相處的人(不拘謹的人)。**ˌ~-ˈgoing,** (of persons) placid and tolerant; casual; lazy and careless; lax. (指人)溫和寬容的; 隨便的; 懶惰並馬虎的;不嚴格的。**3** (comm) (of goods and money on loan) not much in demand. (商)(指貨物與貸款) 需求不殷的;鬆動的。⇨ tight. □ *adv* in an ~ manner: 安適地; 輕鬆地: *E~!* (as a command) Move (it) gently. (命令)輕輕地移動(它)! ***take it / things ~,*** don't work too hard or too energetically. 輕鬆一點;勿太緊張。***go ~ on / with,*** (colloq) be careful or moderate with: (俗)小心對待; 溫和對待: *Go ~ on the brandy—it's the last bottle!* 白蘭地要省著點喝——這是最後一瓶了! ***Easier said than done,*** It is easier to say one will do it than to do it. 說來容易做來難。***Stand ~!*** (as a mil command) Stand with more freedom of movement than when *at ease,* ⇨ ease¹. (軍隊口令)休息(比 stand at ease 有更多活動的自由)。**eas·ily** /ˈiːzəlɪ ; ˈizɪlɪ/ *adv* **1** with ease. 容易地;安適地。**2** without doubt: 無疑地: *easily the best TV programme.* 無疑爲最佳電視節目。**3** possibly: 可能地: *That may easily be the case.* 情況可能就是那樣。

eat /iːt ; it/ *vt, vi* (*pt* ate /et *US:* eɪt ; et/, *pp* eaten /ˈiːtn ; ˈitn̩/) **1** [VP6A, 15B, 2A, C, 4A] ***eat (up),*** take (solid food, also soup) into the mouth and swallow it: 吃;食: *to eat one's dinner;* 吃正餐; *to eat up* (= finish eating) *one's food.* 吃光食物。*Where shall we eat?* 我們到那兒吃飯? *He was too ill to eat.* 他病重得不能吃東西了。*We should eat to live, not live to eat,* not make eating the most important thing in life. 我們應爲生活而吃飯,不應爲吃飯而生活。***eat its head off,*** (of a horse) cost more to feed than it is worth. (指馬)飼養的費用較其本身價值高;吃得太多。***eat one's heart out,*** suffer in silence; be very sad. 默默忍受痛苦;極爲悲傷。***eat one's words,*** take a statement back, say in a humble way that one was wrong. 收回前言;低聲下氣地認錯。**2** [VP6A, 3A, 15B] destroy as if by eating: 侵蝕;嚙;蛀蝕: *Acids eat into metals.* 酸能腐蝕金屬。*He is eaten up with pride.* 他被驕傲冲昏了頭(他一味的驕傲)。*The river had eaten away the banks.* 河水侵蝕了兩岸。*The moths have eaten holes in my coat.* 蛀蟲將我的上衣蛀了一些小洞。**ˈeating-apple** *n* suitable for eating uncooked. 適於生吃的蘋果。**ˈeating-house,** restaurant. 餐館。**eats** *n pl* (sl) food: (俚)食物: *There were plenty of eats, but not enough drinks.* 有許多食物,但無足够的飲料。**eat·able** /-əbl ; -əbl̩/ *adj* fit to be eaten; good to eat: 可食的; 好吃的: *The prison food was scarcely eatable.* 獄中的伙食幾乎不能吃。□ *n* (usu *pl*) food. (通常用複數)食物。**~er** *n* **1** one that eats: 食者: *He's a big eater,* eats large quantities. 他的食量很大。**2** apple, pear, etc for dessert, good when eaten uncooked. 生吃的蘋果,梨等(做爲餐後水果)。

eau /əʊ ; o/ *n* **eau de Cologne** /ˌəʊ də kəˈləʊn ; ˌodəkəˈlon/ *n* (F) perfume made at Cologne. (法)德國科倫所產的香水。**eau-de-vie** /ˌəʊ də ˈviː ; ˌodəˈvi/ *n* (F) brandy. (法)白蘭地酒。

eaves /iːvz ; ivz/ *n pl* overhanging edges of a roof: 屋簷: *icicles hanging from the ~.* 屋簷上垂下的冰柱。

eaves·drop /ˈiːvzdrɒp ; ˈivzˌdrɑp/ *vi* (-pp-) [VP2A, 3A] ~ ***(on),*** listen secretly to private conversation: 竊聽: *~ on a discussion.* 竊聽一討論。**~·per** /-drɒpə(r) ; -ˌdrɑpə/ *n* person who does this. 竊聽者。

ebb /eb ; ɛb/ *vi* [VP2A, C] **1** (of the tide) flow back from the land to the sea. (指潮水)退;落。**2** (fig) grow less; become weak or faint: (喻)減少;衰落: *His fortune's beginning to ebb.* 他的財產開始減少了。*Daylight was ebbing away.* 白晝漸逝。□ *n* **1** the flowing out of the tide: 退潮;落潮: *the ebb and flow of the sea / the tide.* 海潮之漲落。*The tide is on the ebb,* is going out. 正在退潮。**2** (fig) low state; decline or decay: (喻)衰退;衰落: *His health is at a low ebb.* 他的健康在衰退中。**ˌebb-ˈtide** *n* =ebb.

eb·on·ite /ˈebənaɪt ; ˈɛbənˌaɪt/ *n* [U] (comm) hard black insulating material made by vulcanising rubber. (商)硬橡膠。

eb·ony /ˈebənɪ ; ˈɛbənɪ/ *n* [U] hard, black wood. 黑檀;烏木。□ *adj* made of, black as, ~: 烏木製的;烏木色的: *the ~ keys on a piano.* 鋼琴上烏木色的鍵。

ebul·lient /ɪˈbʌlɪənt ; ɪˈbʌljənt/ *adj* exuberant. 充溢的。**ebul·lience** /-əns ; -əns/ *n* exuberance; outburst (of feeling). 充溢;(感情的)奔放。

ec·cen·tric /ɪkˈsentrɪk ; ɛkˈsɛntrɪk/ *adj* **1** (of a person, his behaviour) peculiar; not normal or conventional. (指人或其舉動)怪癖的; 古怪的。**2** (of circles) not having the same centre, ⇨ the illus at concentric; (of orbits) not circular; (of planets, etc) moving in an ~ orbit. (指圓)不同中心的(參看 concentric 之插圖); (指軌道) 偏心的;離心的;(指行星等)在離心軌道運行的;呈偏心運動的。□ *n* **1** ~ person. 古怪的人。**2** (mech) device for changing circular motion into backward-and-forward motion. (機械)偏心器;偏心輪。

ec·cen·tric·ity /ˌeksenˈtrɪsətɪ ; ˌɛksənˈtrɪsɪtɪ/ *n* **1** [U] quality of being eccentric; strangeness of behaviour, etc: 怪癖;古怪: *~ in dress.* 衣着古怪。**2** [C] (*pl* -ties) instance of this; strange or unusual act or habit: 古怪的行動或習慣: *One of his eccentricities is sleeping under the bed instead of in it.* 他的怪癖之一是睡在床底下,而不睡在床上。

ec·clesi·as·tic /ɪˌkliːzɪˈæstɪk ; ɪˌklizɪˈæstɪk/ *n* clergyman. 傳教士;牧師。**ec·clesi·as·ti·cal** /-kl ; -kl̩/ *adj* of the Christian Church; of clergymen. 基督教會的;教士的;牧師的。**ec·clesi·as·ti·cally** /-klɪ ; -klɪ/ *adv*

eche·lon /ˈeʃəlɒn ; ˈɛʃəˌlɑn/ *n* step-like formation of troops, aircraft, ships, etc as shown in illus:

flying in echelon

(軍隊,飛機,船隻等的)梯隊(如圖): *flying in* ~. 成梯隊飛行。

echo[1] /ˈekəʊ ; ˈɛko/ *n* (*pl* ~es /-əʊz ; -oz/) **1** [C, U] sound reflected or sent back (eg from a wall of rock): 回聲;回音(例如由石壁返回者): *The speaker was cheered/applauded to the* ~, long and loudly. 這演說者受到了熱烈的喝采(掌聲)。ˈ~ **chamber,** natural or artificial space for producing ~es. 回聲室。ˈ~**-sounding,** method of ascertaining distances (eg of the ocean bed or underwater objects) by measuring the time taken for waves of sound, etc to be echoed back. 回音測深(利用回音的時間以測距離的方法,例如測海底或水底物體之距離)。Hence, 由此產生, ˈ~**-sounder** *n* instrument used for this. 回音測深器。 **2** [C] person who, statement etc which, is a copy or repetition of another. 附和者;應聲蟲;重複的陳述。

echo[2] /ˈekəʊ ; ˈɛko/ *vi, vt* [VP6A, 15B, 2A, C] ~ ***(back),*** **1** (of places) send back an echo: (指地方)發回聲: *The valley ~ed as he sang.* 他唱歌時山谷發出回聲。*The hills ~ed back the noise of the shot.* 山中發出槍聲的回音。 **2** (of sounds) be sent back as an echo: (指聲音)被傳回: *The shot ~ed through the woods.* 林中傳出槍聲的回音。 **3** be an echo of; repeat the words, etc of another: 隨聲附和;重複旁人的話等: *They ~ed every word of their leader.* 他們隨聲附和他們首領的每一句話。

éclair /eɪˈkleə(r) ; eˈklɛr/ *n* (F) small cylindrical pastry iced on top and filled with cream. (法)一種奶油餡,頂上有糖霜的長形小餅。

éclat /ˈeɪklɑː *US:* eɪˈklɑː ; ɪˈklɑ/ *n* [U] (F) brilliant, conspicuous success; applause from everyone:(法)顯赫的成功;大衆的喝采: *with great* ~. 極爲成功地;在大衆喝采聲中。

ec·lec·tic /ɪˈklektɪk ; ɪkˈlɛktɪk/ *adj* (of persons, methods, etc) choosing, accepting, freely from various sources. (指人,方法等)自各處隨意取材的。 **ec·lec·ti·cism** /-tɪsɪzəm ; -tɪˌsɪzəm/ *n*

eclipse /ɪˈklɪps ; ɪˈklɪps/ *n* [C] **1** total or partial cutting off of the light of the sun (when the moon is between it and the earth), or of the reflected light of the moon (when the earth's shadow falls on it). 日蝕;月蝕。 **2** (fig) loss of brilliance, power, reputation, etc: (喻)光亮,權力,聲望等的喪失;失色;晦暗: *After suffering an* ~ *he is now again famous.* 聲望一度跌落後,現在他已重振聲威。*An author's reputation is often in* ~ *for some years after his death.* 作家的名聲在其死後常有數載的晦暗時期。□ *vt* [VP6A] **1** (of the moon, a planet, etc) cause an ~; cut off the light from. (指月球,行星等)蝕;掩蔽…之光。 **2** (fig) make (sb or sth) appear dull by comparison; outshine: (喻)使(某人或某物)黯然失色;超越: *She was so beautiful that she ~d every other woman at the ball.* 她的美使舞會中其他婦女黯然失色。

eclip·tic /ɪˈklɪptɪk ; ɪˈklɪptɪk/ *n* the path of the sun in the sky. (天文)黄道。

ecol·ogy /iːˈkɒlədʒɪ ; iˈkɑlədʒɪ/ *n* [U] branch of biology that deals with the habits of living things, esp their relation to their environment. 生態學(研究生物之習慣,尤其是生物與環境的關係)。 **eco·logi·cal** /ˌiːkəˈlɒdʒɪkl ; ˌikəˈlɑdʒɪkl/ *adj* of ~: 生態學的: *the ecological effects of industry*, eg the pollution of the atmosphere, of rivers, etc. 工業對生物環境之影響(例如空氣,河流等之污染)。 **eco·logi·cally** /-klɪ ; -klɪ/ *adv* **ecol·ogist** /iːˈkɒlədʒɪst ; iˈkɑlədʒɪst/ *n* student of, expert in, ~. 生態學家。 **eco·system** /ˈiːkəʊˌsɪstəm ; ˈikoˌsɪstəm/ = ecological system. 生態系。

econ·omic /ˌiːkəˈnɒmɪk *US:* ˌek- ; ˌikəˈnɑmɪk/ *adj* **1** of economics (⇨ below): 經濟學的;國家經濟狀態的;經濟的(參看 economics): *the government's* ~ *policy.* 政府的經濟政策。 **2** designed to give a profit: 企圖給予利潤的;爲生利而設計的: *an* ~ *rent,* one that compensates the owner for the cost of the land, building, etc. 足以補償地主或房主土地,建築等費用的租金。 **3** connected with commerce and industry: 與工商業有關的: ~ *geography,* studied chiefly in connection with industry. 經濟地理(以研究與產業有關者爲主)。

econ·omi·cal /ˌiːkəˈnɒmɪkl *US:* ˌek- ; ˌikəˈnɑmɪkl/ *adj* careful in the spending of money, time, etc and in the use of goods; not wasteful: 經濟的;節儉的: *to be* ~ *of time and energy;* 節省時間和精力; *an* ~ *fire,* one that does not waste fuel. 省燃料的爐火。~**ly** /-klɪ ; -klɪ/ *adv*

econ·omics /ˌiːkəˈnɒmɪks *US:* ˌek- ; ˌikəˈnɑmɪks/ *n* (with *sing v*) [U] science of the production, distribution and consumption of goods; condition of a country as to material prosperity. (與單數動詞連用)經濟學;國家的經濟狀況。 **econ·om·ist** /ɪˈkɒnəmɪst ; ɪˈkɑnəmɪst/ *n* **1** expert in ~; person who writes or lectures on ~ or political economy. 經濟學家;經濟學專家。 **2** person who is economical or thrifty. 節儉的人。

econ·om·ize /ɪˈkɒnəmaɪz ; ɪˈkɑnəˌmaɪz/ *vt, vi* [VP6A, 2A, 3A] ~ ***(on sth),*** be economical; use or spend less than before, cut down expenses: 節儉;儉省;節約: *He ~d by using buses instead of taking taxis.* 他改乘公共汽車而不乘計程車以節省錢。*We must* ~ *on light and fuel.* 我們必須節省燈光和燃料。

econ·omy /ɪˈkɒnəmɪ ; ɪˈkɑnəmɪ/ *n* (*pl* -mies) **1** [C, U] (instance of) avoidance of waste of money, strength or anything else of value: 經濟;節儉;節省: *to practise* ~. 實行節約。*In the long run, it is an* ~ *to buy good quality goods, even though they cost more.* 購買質料好的貨物,雖然價格較貴,到頭來是經濟的。*By various little economies, she managed to save enough money for a holiday.* 在許多小地方節省,她設法儲够了度假的錢。 ˈ~ **class,** cheapest class of travel (esp by air). 經濟艙(尤指客機者)。 **2** [U] control and management of the money, goods and other resources of a community, society or household: 理財: *political* ~; 政治經濟學; *domestic* ~. 家庭經濟;家政。 **3** [C] system for the management and use of resources: 經濟制度: *the totalitarian economies of Germany*

a total eclipse of the sun

E

and Italy before the Second World War. 第二次世界大戰前德義兩國的極權經濟制度。

ec·stasy /ˈekstəsɪ ; ˈɛkstəsɪ/ *n* (*pl* -sies) [U, C] (feeling of) great joy and spiritual uplift: 狂喜; 心醉神迷: *in an ~ of delight;* 喜極; *to be in / go into / be thrown into ~ / ecstasies* (*over sth*). (對某物) 心醉神迷。**ec·static** /ɪkˈstætɪk ; ɪkˈstætɪk/ *adj* of, in, causing, ~. 狂喜的;心醉神迷的;使人狂喜的。**ec·stati·cally** /-klɪ ; -klɪ/ *adv*

ec·to·plasm /ˈektəplæzəm ; ˈɛktəˌplæzəm/ *n* [U] substance supposed to flow from a spiritualistic medium during a trance. 一種假想的,從恍惚狀態的靈媒體放射出的物質。

ecu·meni·cal /ˌiːkjuːˈmenɪkl ; ˌɛkjʊˈmɛnɪkl̩/ *adj* **1** of or representing the whole Christian world or universal Church: 全基督教會的: *an E~ Council,* eg of all the RC church as summoned by the Pope. 全基督教會會議(例如由教皇召集之全天主教會會議)。**2** seeking to restore the unity of the Christian churches: 促進基督教會團結的: *the ~ movement.* 促進基督教會團結的運動。

ec·zema /ˈeksɪmə ; ˈɛksəmə/ *n* [U] itching skin disease. 濕疹。

E

eddy /ˈedɪ ; ˈɛdɪ/ *n* (*pl* -dies) (of wind, smoke, fog, mist, dust, water) circular or spiral movement: (風、煙、霧、塵土、水之)漩流;渦流: *Eddies of mist rose from the valleys.* 捲捲霧氣自谷中升起。*The car went past in an ~ of dust.* 這汽車在一陣滾滾的塵土中駛過。□ *vi* [VP2A, C] move in small circles; move in or like eddies; whirl. 廻旋;旋轉。

edel·weiss /ˈeɪdlvaɪs ; ˈedl̩ˌvaɪs/ *n* small Alpine plant with white leaves and small flowers, growing among rocks. 火絨草(一種高山植物,有白色的葉及小花,生於岩石中)。

Eden /ˈiːdn ; ˈidn̩/ *n* (Bible) garden where Adam and Eve lived; place of delight. (聖經)(亞當與夏娃所居之)伊甸園;樂園。

edge[1] /edʒ ; ɛdʒ/ *n* **1** sharp, cutting part of a knife, sword or other tool or weapon: 刃;刀口: *a knife with a sharp ~;* 有利刃之刀; *to put an ~ on a knife,* sharpen it. 使刀口鋒利。***be on ~,*** be excited or irritable. 激動;急躁。***give sb the ~ of one's tongue,*** rebuke him sharply. 嚴斥某人。***have the ~ on sb,*** (colloq) have an advantage over him. (俗)較某人佔優勢;勝過某人。***set sb's ˈteeth on ~,*** upset his nerves (as when a scraping sound or a sharp, acid taste causes physical revulsion). 使某人牙齒發磣;刺激其神經(如聞刺耳聲或嚐酸物後引起身體上之急劇反應)。***take the ~ off sth,*** dull or soften; reduce, eg one's appetite. 使某物變鈍;挫其鋒鋩;減弱(胃口等)。**2** (line marking the) outer limit or boundary of a (flat) surface: 邊緣;邊線: *a cottage on the ~ of a forest;* 位於林邊的茅舍; *the ~ of a lake;* 湖邊; *trim the ~s of a lawn,* cut the grass there. 修剪草地之邊緣。*Don't put the glass on the ~ of the table; it may get knocked off.* 不要把杯子放在桌邊上,它可能被碰掉。*He fell off the ~ of the cliff.* 他自崖邊跌下。**edgy** /ˈedʒɪ ; ˈɛdʒɪ/ *adj* having one's nerves on ~. 激動的;急躁的。

edge[2] /edʒ ; ɛdʒ/ *vt, vi* **1** [VP6A, 14] ~ ***(with),*** supply with a border: 加以邊: *to ~ a handkerchief with lace / a garden path with plants;* 在手帕上加花邊(在花園小徑兩邊植花木); form a border to: 形成…之邊: *a road ~d with grass.* 兩邊種有草的道路。**2** [VP6A] sharpen (a tool, etc). 使(工具等)銳利。**3** [VP15A, B, 2C] (cause to) move slowly forward or along: (使)慢慢向前移動;漸移: *~ oneself / ~ one's way through a crowd;* 在人群中慢慢向前移動; *~ along a narrow ledge of rock;* 沿着突出的狹窄岩石慢慢移動; *~ a piano through a door;* 將鋼琴慢慢抬過門去; *~ one's chair nearer to the fire-place.* 將椅子移近壁爐。

edge·ways, edge·wise /ˈedʒweɪz, -waɪz ; ˈɛdʒˌwez, -ˌwaɪz/ *adv* with the edge outwards or forwards. 以刃向外或向前; 以邊緣向外或向前。***not get a word in ~,*** be unable to say anything when a very talkative person is speaking. 一極健談者談話時插不進嘴。

edg·ing /ˈedʒɪŋ ; ˈɛdʒɪŋ/ *n* narrow border: 窄邊: *an ~ of lace on a dress.* 一件衣服上的花邊。ˈ**~-shears,** tool for trimming grass on the edges of a lawn. 修剪草地邊緣的剪刀;修邊剪刀。

ed·ible /ˈedɪbl ; ˈɛdəbl̩/ *adj* fit to be eaten; not poisonous. 可食的;無毒的。□ *n* (usu *pl*) things fit to be eaten. (通常用複數)可食之物。**edi·bil·ity** /ˌedɪˈbɪlətɪ ; ˌɛdəˈbɪlətɪ/ *n*

edict /ˈiːdɪkt ; ˈidɪkt/ *n* order or proclamation issued by authority; decree. 敕令;詔書;法令;告示。

edi·fi·ca·tion /ˌedɪfɪˈkeɪʃn ; ˌɛdəfəˈkeʃən/ *n* [U] mental or moral improvement. 開導;啓發;薰陶。

edi·fice /ˈedɪfɪs ; ˈɛdəfɪs/ *n* [C] building (esp a large or imposing one); (fig) sth built up in the mind: 大廈;(喻)心中構思之物: *The whole ~ of his hopes was destroyed.* 他心中整個的希望都毀了。

edify /ˈedɪfaɪ ; ˈɛdəˌfaɪ/ *vt* (*pt, pp* -fied) [VP6A] improve in morals or mind: 開導;啓發;薰陶: *~ing books.* 陶冶人性的書籍。

edit /ˈedɪt ; ˈɛdɪt/ *vt* [VP6A] **1** prepare (another person's writing) for publication (as a book, or in a newspaper or other periodical): 編輯(他人之作品成書或發表於報紙或其他刊物); 刊行: *~ a newspaper;* 編輯一報紙; *~ a Shakespeare play for use in schools.* 編印莎士比亞的一個劇本供學校之用。**2** do the work of planning and directing the publication of a newspaper, magazine, book, encyclopaedia, etc. 主編(報紙,雜誌,書,百科全書等)。**3** prepare a cinema film, tape recording by putting together parts in a suitable sequence. 剪輯(影片,錄音)。**4** arrange data for computer processing. 編排資料供電腦處理。

edi·tion /ɪˈdɪʃn ; ɪˈdɪʃən/ *n* **1** form in which a book is published: 版本: *a cheap ~;* 廉價版; *a ˈpocket ~.* 袖珍版。**2** total number of copies (of a book, newspaper, etc) issued from the same types: (書籍,報紙等)一版所刊印的總數: *the first ~;* 初版; *a revised ~.* 修訂版。⇨ impression(3).

edi·tor /ˈedɪtə(r) ; ˈɛdɪtə/ *n* person who edits (esp a book, newspaper, periodical, radio news programme) or who is in charge of part of a newspaper: 編輯;主筆: *the ˈsports / fiˈnancial ~.* 體育(金融)新聞編輯。

edi·tor·ial /ˌedɪˈtɔːrɪəl ; ˌɛdəˈtɔrɪəl/ *adj* of an editor: 編輯的;主筆的: *the ~ office;* 編輯部; *~ work.* 編輯工作。□ *n* [C] special article or discussion of news in a newspaper, etc usu written by the editor. 社論。

edu·cate /ˈedʒʊkeɪt ; ˈɛdʒəˌket/ *vt* [VP6A, 15A, 16A] give intellectual and moral training to; train: 教育;訓練: *The boy had to ~ himself in the evening after finishing his work.* 這個男孩只能在工作做完後晚上自修。*I was ~d for the law.* 我是學法律的。*You should ~ your children to behave well.* 你應教導你的孩子們守規矩。**edu·ca·tor** /-tə(r) ; -tə/ *n* person who ~s. 從事教育者;教育家。

edu·ca·tion /ˌedʒʊˈkeɪʃn ; ˌɛdʒəˈkeʃən/ *n* [U] **1** systematic training and instruction (esp of the young, in school, college, etc): 教育 (尤指學校中對青年的教育): *No country can afford to neglect ~.* 任何國家都不容忽視教育。*Is ~ free and compulsory in your country?* 貴國是行免費的義務教育嗎? **2** knowledge and abilities, development of character and mental powers, resulting from such training. (學識、能力、品格、智力的)培養;教養。**~al** /-ʃənl ; -ʃnəl/ *adj* of, connected with, ~: 教育的;與教育有關的: *~al work;* 教育工作; *an ~al magazine.* 教育雜誌。**~ist** /-ʃənɪst ; -ʃənɪst/, **~·al·ist** /-ʃənəlɪst ; -ʃənl̩ɪst/ *nn* expert in ~. 教育家。

educe /ɪˈdjuːs *US:* ɪˈduːs ; ɪˈdjus/ *vt* [VP6A] (formal) bring out, develop (from what is latent or potential). (正式用語)引出;(自潛在物中)引發。

eel /iːl; il/ *n* long, snake-like fish. 鰻；鱔。⇨ the illus at sea. 參看 sea 之插圖。***as slippery as an eel***, very difficult to hold; (fig) (of a person) untrustworthy; difficult to manage. 似鱔魚般滑溜；難以握住；(喻)(指人)不可靠的；難以控制的。

e'en /iːn; in/ *adv* (poet) (詩) = even.

e'er /eə(r); ɛr/ *adv* (poet) (詩) = ever.

eerie, eery /ˈɪərɪ; ˈɪrɪ/ *adj* (-ier, -iest) causing a feeling of mystery and fear: 引起神祕而可怖感覺的: *an ~ shriek*. 悽慘的怪叫。**eer·ily** /ˈɪərəlɪ; ˈɪrɪlɪ/ *adv* **eeri·ness** *n*

eff /ef; ɛf/ *vi* (sl, euphem for ⚠ *fuck*): (俚，fuck 的委婉語): *I told him to eff off*. 我叫他滾開。*What an effing nuisance!* 眞令人討厭！

ef·face /ɪˈfeɪs; ɪˈfes/ *vt* [VP6A] **1** rub or wipe out; make indistinct; (fig) obliterate: 抹掉；塗抹；使不清楚；(喻)忘却: *~ an inscription;* 使銘刻不清楚；*~ unpleasant memories of the past*. 忘却過去不愉快的記憶。**2** *~ **oneself***, keep in the background in order to escape being noticed; make oneself appear to be unimportant. 隱於幕後以期不爲人所注意；埋沒自己。**~·ment** *n*

ef·fect /ɪˈfekt; ɛˈfɛkt/ *n* **1** [C, U] ([U] in phrases of degree or extent) result; outcome: (用作不可數名詞時指程度或限度)結果；效果: *the ~ of heat upon metals;* 熱對於金屬所發生的效應；*the ~s of the hot weather*. 炎熱天氣之苦。*Did the medicine have any ~/a good ~?* 這藥有效嗎？*Punishment had very little ~ on him*, did not reform him, frighten him, etc. 懲罰對他沒有什麼效果(不能使他改進，生畏等)。*Our arguments had no ~ on them*, did not influence them. 我們的議論對他們沒有影響。***of no ~***, useless, not doing what was intended or hoped for. 無用；無效。***in ~***, **(a)** in fact, really; for practical purposes. 事實上；實際上。**(b)** (of a rule, law, etc) in operation: (指規則，法律等)在實施中；有效: *The rule is still in ~*. 本規則仍在實施中。***bring/carry/put sth into ~***, cause it to operate: 實行(某事物)；實施: *The plans will soon be carried into ~*. 這些計畫不久便可實施。***come into ~***, reach the stage of being operative: 實行；實施: *The new tax regulations came into ~ last week*. 新稅法上週已開始實施。***give ~ to***, cause to become active or have a result. 使生效。***take ~***, **(a)** produce the result intended or required. 生效；奏效。**(b)** come into force; operate; become active. 實施；實行；起作用。**2** [C, U] impression produced on the mind of a spectator, hearer, reader, etc: 印象；感觸: *wonderful ˈcloud ~s*, impressions produced by light on clouds, eg at sunset; 陽光射在雲上形成的奇異景象(例如日落時)；*ˈsound ~s*, (in broadcasting, etc) sounds characteristic of a scene, or incidental to an event, eg the noise of a train. (廣播等)音響效果(表示某一情景或事件的聲音，例如火車的噪音)。*Everything he says and does is calculated for ~*, designed to impress spectators or hearers. 他的一言一行都是想給別人造成一個印象。**3** ***to this/that ~***, with this/that meaning: 大意是: *That is what he said, or words to that ~*, words with the same general meaning. 那便是他說的話，或者大意是如此。***to the ~ that...***, stating: 大意是說…: *I have received a cable to the ~ that...*, with the information that.... 我收到一封電報，大意是說…。***to the same ~***, giving the same information: 具有同樣意思；意思一樣: *I sent a telegram and wrote a letter to the same ~*. 我發出一份電報，並以同樣意思寫了一封信。**4** (*pl*) goods; property: (複)所有物；財產: *The hotel-keeper seized her personal ~s because she could not pay her bill*. 因爲她付不起帳，旅館主人扣留了她私人的所有物。***no ~s***, written (often 常略作 N/E) by bankers on a cheque which is dishonoured. 無存款(銀行職員書於空頭支票上者)。□ *vt* [VP6A] bring about; accomplish: 產生；引起；實現；完成: *~ one's purpose;* 達到目的；*~ a cure;* 完成治療；治癒；*~ (= take out) an insurance policy*. 取得保險單；加入保險。

ef·fec·tive /ɪˈfektɪv; əˈfɛktɪv/ *adj* **1** having an effect; able to bring about the result intended: 有效的；奏效的: *~ measures to cure unemployment*. 消除失業的有效措施。**2** making a striking impression: 予人深刻印象的: *an ~ scheme of decoration*. 引起深刻印象的裝飾法。**3** actual or existing: 實際的；實在的；現行的: *the ~ membership of the society;* 現在有效的會員資格；(of a military force, soldiers, sailors, etc) fit for service: (指軍隊，士兵，船員等)適於任務的；適於服役的: *the ~ strength of the army*. 軍隊的現有員額。**~·ly** *adv* **~·ness** *n*

ef·fec·tual /ɪˈfektʃʊəl; əˈfɛktʃʊəl/ *adj* (not used of persons) bringing about the result required; answering its purpose: (不用以指人)有效的；奏效的: *an ~ remedy/punishment;* 有效的治療(懲罰)；*to take ~ steps*. 採取有效步驟。**~·ly** /-lɪ; -lɪ/ *adv* **~·ness** *n*

ef·femi·nate /ɪˈfemɪnət; əˈfɛmənɪt/ *adj* (of a man, derog) feminine. (指男人，貶)女人氣的；無丈夫氣概的。**ef·femi·nacy** /ɪˈfemɪnəsɪ; əˈfɛmənəsɪ/ *n* [U].

ef·fendi /eˈfendɪ; ɛˈfɛndɪ/ *n* (old use, in Turkey) sir; (in Arab countries) educated or powerful person. 先生(土耳其昔時對男人之尊稱)；(阿拉伯國家)受過教育的人；有勢力的人。

ef·fer·vesce /ˌefəˈves; ˌɛfɚˈvɛs/ *vi* [VP2A] give off bubbles of gas; (of gas) issue in bubbles; (fig, of persons) be gay and excited. 起氣泡；(指氣)冒泡；(喻，指人)愉快而興奮。**ef·fer·ves·cence** /ˌefəˈvesns; ˌɛfɚˈvɛsn̩s/ *n* [U] **ef·fer·ves·cent** /-snt; -sn̩t/ *adj*

ef·fete /ɪˈfiːt; ɛˈfit/ *adj* exhausted; weak and worn out: 筋疲力竭的；衰弱不堪的: *~ civilizations/empires*. 衰落的文明(帝國)。**~·ness** *n*

ef·fi·ca·cious /ˌefɪˈkeɪʃəs; ˌɛfəˈkeʃəs/ *adj* (not used of persons) producing the desired result: (不用以指人)有效的: *an ~ cure for a disease*. 對一病之有效治療。**~·ly** *adv* **ef·fi·cacy** /ˈefɪkəsɪ; ˈɛfəkəsɪ/ *n* [U] state or quality of being ~. 有效；效能。

ef·fi·cient /ɪˈfɪʃnt; əˈfɪʃənt/ *adj* **1** (of persons) capable; able to perform duties well: (指人)有能力的；能勝任的: *an ~ secretary/staff of teachers*. 能幹的祕書(教師)。**2** producing a desired or satisfactory result: 有效力的: *~ methods of teaching*. 有效的教學方法。**~·ly** *adv* **ef·fi·ciency** /ɪˈfɪʃnsɪ; əˈfɪʃənsɪ/ *n* [U] state or quality of being ~. 有能力；能勝任；效力；效能；效率。

ef·figy /ˈefɪdʒɪ; ˈɛfədʒɪ/ *n* (*pl* -gies) [C] representation of a person (in wood, stone, etc). (木，石等製的)肖像；雕像。***in ~***, as an ~: 作爲肖像: *hang/burn a person in ~*, make an ~ of him and hang/burn it (as a sign of hatred, etc). 懸吊(焚毀)某人之肖像(以洩恨等)。

ef·flor·es·cence /ˌefləˈresns; ˌɛfloˈrɛsn̩s/ *n* [U] (formal) flowering; bursting out into flower. (正式用語)開花。**ef·flor·es·cent** /-snt; -sn̩t/ *adj*

ef·flu·ent /ˈeflʊənt; ˈɛflʊənt/ *n* **1** [C] stream flowing from a larger stream or from a lake. 自河，湖等流出之水道；支流。**2** [U] discharge of waste liquid matter, sewage, etc, eg from a factory. 廢水或污水(例如自工廠流出者)。

ef·flux /ˈeflʌks; ˈɛflʌks/ *n* [U] flowing out of liquid, gas, etc; [C] that which flows out. (液體，氣體等的)流出；流出之物。

ef·fort /ˈefət; ˈɛfɚt/ *n* **1** [U] trying hard; use of strength and energy (*to do* sth); [C] vigorous attempt: 努力；盡力(與不定詞連用)；努力的嘗試: *He lifted the big rock without ~*. 他不費力地舉起了那塊大石。*It doesn't need much ~*. 這事不需要費什麼力氣。*Please make an ~ to arrive early*. 請勞駕早到。*Does it require a great ~ of will to give up smoking?* 戒煙需要堅强的毅力嗎？*I will make every ~ (= do all I can) to help you*. 我願盡我的力量幫助你。*His ~s at clearing up the mystery failed*. 他企圖揭開此一奧祕之努力失敗了。**2** [C] (colloq)

E

result of ～; sth done with ～: (俗)努力的結果;精心之作: *That's a pretty good* ～, ie you have done well. 那是努力的良好成果(你做得不錯)。～**·less** *adj* making no ～; without ～; easy: 不盡力的;不費力的;容易的: *done with* ～*less skill*. 容易做成的。

ef·front·ery /ɪˈfrʌntərɪ ; əˈfrʌntərɪ/ *n* [U] shameless boldness; impudence; [C] (*pl* -ries) instance of this: 厚顏;無恥;厚顏無恥的行爲: *How can you have the* ～ *to ask for another loan?* 你怎能厚着臉皮再來借錢?

ef·ful·gent /ɪˈfʌldʒənt ; ɛˈfʌldʒənt/ *adj* (liter) radiant; resplendent. (文)光輝的;燦爛的。**ef·ful·gence** /-dʒəns ; -dʒəns/ *n* radiance. 光輝;燦爛。

ef·fu·sion /ɪˈfju:ʒn ; əˈfjuʒən/ *n* **1** [U] sending or pouring out (of liquid, eg blood); [C] quantity poured out. 流出(指液體,例如血液);傾注;流出之量。**2** [C] (esp unrestrained) outpouring of thought or feeling: (尤指未抑制的)思想或感情的流露: *poetical* ～*s;* 詩情奔放; ～*s in love letters*. 情書中感情的盈溢。

ef·fu·sive /ɪˈfju:sɪv ; ɛˈfjusɪv/ *adj* (of the feelings, signs of pleasure, gratitude, etc) pouring out too freely: (指感情,表露的快樂,感激等)洋溢的;充溢的;過份流露的: ～ *thanks;* 殷殷致謝; ～ *in one's gratitude*. 感激之情溢於言表。～**·ly** *adv* ～**·ness** *n*

eft /ɛft ; ɛft/ *n* newt. 水蜥。

egali·tar·ian /ɪˌgælɪˈteərɪən ; ɪˌgæləˈtɛrɪən/ *n, adj* (person) favouring the doctrine of equal rights, benefits and opportunities for all citizens. 主張人人平等的(人)。Cf 參較 elitist. ～**·ism** /-ɪzəm ; -ɪzəm/ *n*

egg[1] /eg ; ɛg/ *n* female reproducing cell; ovum, (esp an embryo enclosed in a shell, eg of a hen, used as food): 卵;蛋: *Birds, reptiles and insects come from eggs.* 鳥,爬蟲及昆蟲均係卵生。*Chickens are hatched from eggs.* 小鷄是由鷄蛋孵出的。*The hen laid an egg.* 這母鷄下了一個蛋。*Will you have your eggs boiled or fried?* 你的蛋是煮着吃還是煎着吃? [U] *You've got some egg* (ie a bit of a cooked egg) *on your chin.* 你的下巴上沾有一點蛋。⇨ the illus at amphibian, prey. 參看 amphibian, prey 之插圖。***a bad egg,*** (colloq) a worthless or dishonest person. (俗)壞蛋;壞人。***as sure as eggs is eggs,*** (colloq) undoubtedly. (俗)無疑地。***in the egg,*** at an early stage; undeveloped. 在初期;尚未發展的。***put all one's eggs in one basket,*** risk everything one has in a single venture, eg by investing all one's money in one business. 孤注一擲(例如將全部金錢投資於一項事業)。***teach one's grandmother to suck eggs,*** give advice to sb who has much more experience than oneself. 班門弄斧。**ˈegg-cup,** small cup for holding a boiled egg. 盛煮蛋的小杯。**ˈegg-head** *n* (colloq) intellectual person; theorist. (俗)知識份子;理論家。**ˈegg-plant,** plant with large, purple (rather egg-shaped) fruit (= aubergine), used as a vegetable. 茄子。⇨ the illus at vegetable. 參看 vegetable 之插圖。**ˈegg-shell,** shell of an egg: 蛋殼: *egg-shell china,* very thin kind; 薄瓷器; *egg-shell paint,* kind that gives a finish that is neither glossy nor matt. 蛋殼漆(一種光澤既不亮亦不暗的漆)。**ˈegg-whisk,** utensil for beating eggs. 攪蛋器。

egg[2] /eg ; ɛg/ *vt* [VP15B] ***egg sb on,*** urge him (*to do* sth). 慫恿某人(做某事,與不定詞連用)。

eg·lan·tine /ˈeglәntaɪn ; ˈɛglәnˌtaɪn/ *n* [U] kind of rose; sweet-briar. 野薔薇。

ego /ˈegəʊ *US:* ˈi:gəʊ ; ˈigo/ *n* **(the) ego,** (psych) individual's perception or experience of himself; individual's capacity to think, feel and act; self-esteem. (心理)自我; 個人的思想,感覺和行動的能力;自尊;自負。**ˈego·trip** *n* (colloq) self-centred or self-seeking act. (俗)以自我爲中心或自私自利的行爲。▭ *vi* act in this way. 行爲自私自利。

ego·cen·tric /ˌegəʊˈsentrɪk *US:* ˌi:g- ; ˌigoˈsɛntrɪk/ *adj* self-centred; egoistic. 以自我爲中心的;利己主義的。

ego·ism /ˈegəʊɪzəm *US:* ˈi:g- ; ˈigoˌɪzəm/ *n* [U] **1** (phil) theory that our actions are always caused by the desire to benefit ourselves. (哲)利己主義;自我主義。**2** systematic selfishness; state of mind in which one is always thinking of oneself. 自私;利己心。⇨ altruism. **ego·ist** /-ɪst ; -ɪst/ *n* believer in ～. 利己主義者;自我主義者。**ego·istic** /ˌegəʊˈɪstɪk *US:* ˌi:g- ; ˌigoˈɪstɪk/, **ego·isti·cal** /-kl ; -kəl/ *adj* of ～; of an egoist. 自我主義的;利己主義的;自私的;利己主義者的。

ego·tism /ˈegəʊtɪzəm *US:* ˈi:g- ; ˈigəˌtɪzəm/ *n* [U] practice of talking too often or too much about oneself; self-conceit; selfishness. 自我吹噓;自負;自私。**ego·tist** /-tɪst ; -tɪst/ *n* person who practises ～; selfish person. 自誇者;自負者;自私者。**ego·tis·tic** /ˌegəˈtɪstɪk *US:* ˌi:g- ; ˌigəˈtɪstɪk/ *adj* of ～; of or like an egotist. 自誇的;自負的;自私的;自誇者的;自負者的;自私者的。**ego·tis·ti·cally** /-klɪ ; -klɪ/ *adv*

egre·gious /ɪˈgri:dʒɪəs ; ɪˈgridʒəs/ *adj* (formal) outstanding, exceptional (used of sb or sth bad): (正式用語)顯著的; 異常的(用以指不良的人或事物): ～ *folly;* 驚人的愚蠢; *an* ～ *blunder.* 大錯。

egress /ˈi:gres ; ˈigrɛs/ *n* (formal) [U] (right of) going out; [C] way out; exit. (正式用語)出去;外出權;出路;出口。

egret /ˈi:gret ; ˈigrɪt/ *n* kind of heron with beautiful long feathers in the tail and on the back; bunch of these feathers as an ornament. 白鷺(尾部及背部生有美麗的長羽毛);裝飾用的白鷺羽毛。

Egyp·tian /ɪˈdʒɪpʃn ; ɪˈdʒɪpʃən/ *adj, n* (native) of Egypt. 埃及的;埃及人。

eh /eɪ ; e/ *int* used to express surprise or doubt, or to invite agreement. 呃!嗯!(表示驚奇,疑問,或徵求同意)。

eider·down /ˈaɪdədaʊn; ˈaɪdɚˌdaʊn/ *n* (bed-covering filled with) soft breast feathers of large, wild duck (called 稱作 ˈ*eider*). 棉鳧之絨毛;鴨絨(被)。

eight /eɪt ; et/ *adj, n* **1** the number 8. 八;八個。⇨ App 4. 參看附錄四。***have one over the*** ～, drink too much. 飲酒過量。**2** crew of ～ in a rowing-boat. 划艇之八人選手。⇨ bow[3](2), stroke[1](3). **eighth** /eɪtθ ; etθ/ *adj, n* **eighth·ly** *adv* ～**·pence** /ˈeɪtpəns *US:* -pens ; ˈetpɛns/ *n* ～**·penny** /ˈeɪtpənɪ *US:* -penɪ ; ˈetˌpɛnɪ/ *adj* ～**·een** /ˌeɪˈti:n ; eˈtin/ *adj, n* the number 18. 十八;十八個。～**·eenth** /eɪˈti:nθ ; eˈtinθ/ *adj, n* ～**y** /ˈeɪtɪ ; ˈetɪ/ *adj, n* the number 80. 八十;八十個。**the eighties,** 80–89. 80 至 89。～**·ieth** /ˈeɪtɪəθ ; ˈetɪɪθ/ *adj, n*

a rowing eight

eight·some /ˈeɪtsəm ; ˈetsəm/ *n* lively Scottish dance (a *reel*) for eight dancers. 一種活潑的蘇格蘭八人舞。

eis·tedd·fod /ˌaɪˈsteðvɒd ; eˈstɛðvɑd/ *n* (in Wales) annual gathering of poets and musicians for competitions. (威爾斯之)詩人與音樂家之競賽年會。

either /ˈaɪðə(r) *US:* ˈi:ðər ; ˈiðɚ, ˈaɪðɚ/ *adj, pron* **1** ～ ***(of),*** (Cf the use of *any*, or *any one of*, when the number is greater than two) one or the other (of two): 二者之一(如爲三者以上,參較 any 或 any one of 的用法): *Take* ～ *half; they're exactly the same.* 你任選一半;它們完全相同。*E*～ *of them*／*E*～ *one will be satisfactory.* 二者中任何一個都會令人滿意。*You must not favour* ～ *side in the dispute.* 你不可偏袒爭論中的任何一方。*In* ～ *event*／～ *of these* *events you will benefit.* 兩種情况均會對你有利。 **2** ~ ***(of),*** (Cf the use of *both* and *each*, which are more usu) one and the other (of two): 二者(參較 both和 each 的用法,此二字較爲常用): *There was an armchair at ~ end of the long table.* 在那長桌的兩端各有一張扶手椅。□ *adv, conj* **1** used in statements after *not;* 用於陳述句中 not 之後; (Cf the use of *neither*): (參較 neither 的用法): *I don't like the red one, and I don't like the pink one, ~,* ie I dislike both of them. 我不喜歡那個紅的,也不喜歡那個粉紅的。*A: 'I haven't been to Paris yet.' B: 'I haven't been there yet, ~.'* (= Neither have I). A: '我沒有到過巴黎'。 B: '我也沒有去過'。 **2** (used after a negative phrase) moreover; furthermore: (用於否定片語後)而且;再者: *There was a time, and not so long ago ~, when she could walk twenty miles a day.* 有一段時期,而且不是很久以前,她一天能够步行二十哩。 **3** ~... ***or,*** (used to introduce the first of two or more alternatives): (用以介紹兩個或多個可選擇的事物中之第一項): *He must be ~ mad or drunk.* 他不是瘋了,就是醉了。 *Please ~ come in or go out: don't stand there in the doorway.* 請你或是進來,或是出去:不要站在門口。*E~ the dog or the cat has eaten it.* 不是狗就是貓把它吃了。

ejacu·late /ɪ'dʒækjʊleɪt ; ɪ'dʒækjəˌlet/ *vt* [VP6A] **1** say suddenly and briefly. 突然而簡短地說出。 **2** eject (fluid, eg semen) from the body. 自體內射出(液體,例如精液)。**ejacu·la·tion** /ɪˌdʒækjʊ'leɪʃn ; ɪˌdʒækjə'leʃən/ *n* **1** [C] exclamation; sth said suddenly. 呼喊;突然說出的話。 **2** discharge or ejection of fluid (eg semen) (from the body). (自體內)射出液體(例如精液)。

eject /ɪ'dʒekt ; ɪ'dʒɛkt/ *vt, vi* [VP6A, 14] ~ ***(from),*** **1** compel (sb) to leave (a place); expel: 强迫(某人)離開(某地);逐出: *They were ~ed because they had not paid their rent for a year.* 他們因爲已經一年未付房租而被趕出去了。 **2** send out (liquid, etc): 噴出(液體等);射出: *lava ~ed from a volcano.* 自火山噴出的熔岩。 **3** [VP2A] make an emergency exit, with a parachute, from an aircraft. (自飛機)緊急跳傘。 **ejec·tion** /ɪ'dʒekʃn ; ɪ'dʒɛkʃən/ *n* **ejec·tor** /-tə(r) ; -tɚ/ *n* sth that ~s. 噴出物;射出物。 **e'jector-seat,** one in an aircraft for ~ing the pilot so that he may descend by parachute. (飛機上之)彈射座椅(可將駕駛員彈出,以便跳傘降落)。

eke /i:k ; ik/ *vt* [VP15B] ***eke sth out,*** make (small supplies of sth) enough for one's needs by adding sth; make (a living) by doing this: 補足;力求維持(生活): *eke out one's coal by saving the cinders for further use;* 留着煤渣再用,以彌補煤的不足; *eke out one's livelihood.* 力謀生計。

elab·or·ate /ɪ'læbərət ; ɪ'læbərɪt/ *adj* worked out with much care and in great detail; carefully prepared and finished; complicated: 精心做成的;細心完成的;複雜的: *~ plans;* 細心完成的計畫; *an ~ design;* 精心的設計; *an ~ dinner,* eg with many courses. 精緻的餐食(例如有許多道菜)。 □ *vt* /ɪ'læbəreɪt ; ɪ'læbəˌret/ [VP6A] work out, describe, in detail: 精心做成;詳盡描述: *Please ~ your proposals a little.* 請將你的建議詳細敘述一下。~**ly** *adv* ~**·ness** *n* **elab·or·ation** /ɪˌlæbə'reɪʃn ; ɪˌlæbə'reʃən/ *n* [U] elaborating or being ~d; [C] that which is added; detail that ~s. 精心做成;詳細描述;增加物;細節。

élan /eɪ'lɑ:n ; e'lɑ̃/ *n* [U] (F) vivacity; impetuosity; enthusiasm. (法)活力;衝勁;熱心。

eland /'i:lənd ; 'ilənd/ *n* kind of S African antelope. 南非洲產的一種羚羊。

elapse /ɪ'læps ; ɪ'læps/ *vi* [VP2A] (of time) pass. (指時間)經過;逝去。

elas·tic /ɪ'læstɪk ; ɪ'læstɪk/ *adj* **1** having the tendency to go back to the normal or previous size or shape after being pulled or pressed: 有彈性的: *~ bands.* 橡皮帶;鬆緊帶。*Rubber is ~.* 橡皮是有彈性的。*Sponges are ~.* 海綿有彈性。 **2** (fig) not firm, fixed or unalterable; able to be adapted: (喻)非固定或不可改變的;可以伸縮的: *~ rules;* 有伸縮性的規則; *an ~ temperament,* eg of a person who soon becomes cheerful again after being sad. 開朗的性情 (例如能迅速自悲傷的心情轉爲愉快)。□ *n* [U] cord or material made ~ by weaving rubber into it: 橡皮筋;鬆緊帶: *a piece of ~;* 一條鬆緊帶(橡皮筋); (attrib) (形容用法) *~ braces,* made of this material. 鬆緊吊袴帶。~**·ity** /ˌelæ'stɪsətɪ *US:* ɪˌlæ- ; ɪˌlæs'tɪsətɪ/ *n* [U] the quality of being ~: 彈性;伸縮性: *elasticity of demand,* (comm) change in demand because of price changes. (商)需求的彈性(因物價波動造成者)。

elate /ɪ'leɪt ; ɪ'let/ *vt* [VP6A] (usu passive) stimulate; make high-spirited: (通常用被動語態)鼓舞;使得意: *He was ~d at the news/by his success.* 這消息(他的成功)使他得意。**ela·tion** /ɪ'leɪʃn ; ɪ'leʃən/ *n* [U] high spirits: 得意揚揚;興高采烈: *filled with elation.* 得意揚揚。

el·bow /'elbəʊ ; 'ɛlˌbo/ *n* **1** (outer part of the) joint between the two parts of the arm, ⇨ the illus at arm; corresponding part of a sleeve (in a jacket, etc). 肘(參看 arm 之插圖);(衣服的)肘部。***at one's ~,*** close to; near by. 靠近;在近旁。***out at ~s,*** **(a)** (of a garment) worn-out. (指衣衫)襤褸的。**(b)** (of a person) in worn-out clothes. (指人)衣衫襤褸的。'~ **grease** *n* [U] vigorous polishing; hard work. 費力的擦;費力的工作。'~ **room** *n* [U] room to move freely. 可自由活動的餘地。 **2** ~-shaped bend, corner or joint (eg in a pipe or chimney). 彎管;肘管;彎頭(例如管子或烟囱之轉接處)。□ *vt* [VP6A, 15B, 14] push or force (one's way *through, forward,* etc): 擠進(與 through, forward 等連用): *to ~* (also *shoulder*) *one's way through a crowd.* 自人群中擠過 (shoulder 亦可用作此義)。

el·der[1] /'eldə(r) ; 'ɛldɚ/ *adj* (attrib only; 僅作形容用法; cf 參較 *older*) (of members of a family, esp closely related members, or of two indicated members) older; senior: (指家庭中的分子,尤指近親,或指兩個指明的分子)年紀較長的: *My ~ brother is in India.* 我的哥哥在印度。*The ~ sister is called Mary.* 姊姊名叫瑪莉。***the ~,*** (before or after a person's name to distinguish that person from another of the same name): (用於人名前後,以別於同姓名之人)老的;年長的: *Pliny the ~;* 老蒲林尼; *the ~ Pitt.* 老庇特。ˌ~ **'statesman** /-steɪtsmən ; -stetsmən/ (*pl* -men), person (usu retired from office) whose unofficial advice is sought and valued because of his long experience. 元老。□ *n* **1** (*pl*) persons of greater age: (複)年長者;長輩: *Should we always follow the advice of our ~s and betters?* 我們應當永遠聽從長輩和前輩的勸告嗎? **2** official in some Christian churches, member of a governing body (session) in Presbyterian churches. 某些教會中之職員;(長老會中之)長老。 **3** ***the/sb's ~,*** older of two persons: 二人中之較長者: *He is my ~ by several years.* 他比我大幾歲。

el·der[2] /'eldə(r) ; 'ɛldɚ/ *n* (kinds of) bush or small tree with clusters of white flowers and red or black berries. 接骨木(有白花和紅或黑果的一種矮樹)。ˌ~**·berry 'wine,** wine made from these berries. 接骨木果實製成的酒。

el·der·ly /'eldəlɪ ; 'ɛldɚlɪ/ *adj* getting old; rather old. 漸老的;年齡相當大的。

el·dest /'eldɪst ; 'ɛldɪst/ *adj* (attrib only; 僅作形容用法; cf 參較 *oldest*) first-born or oldest surviving (member of a family): (家族中)最年長的: *my ~ son/brother.* 我的長子(大哥)。

El Dorado /ˌel də'rɑ:dəʊ ; ˌɛldə'rado/ *n* (*pl* ~s /-dəʊz ; -doz/) fictitious country or city rich in precious metals. 假想中的黃金國。

elect[1] /ɪ'lekt ; ɪ'lɛkt/ *adj* **1** (after the *n*) chosen, selected: (用於名詞後)被選出的: *the bishop ~,* not yet in office. 被選出而尚未就職的主教。 **2** ***the ~,*** those persons specially chosen, or considered to be the best. 特別精選出來的人。

elect² /ɪ'lekt; ɪ'lɛkt/ *vt* **1** [VP6A, 25, 23, 14] ~ *(to)*, choose (sb) by vote: 選擧: *to ~ a president;* 選擧總統; *to ~ Smith (to be) chairman;* 選擧史密斯做主席; *to ~ Green to the Academy.* 推選格林爲研究院院士。**2** [VP7A] choose; decide: 選擇;決定: *He had ~ed to become a lawyer.* 他已決定做律師。

elec·tion /ɪ'lekʃn; ɪ'lɛkʃən/ *n* [U] choosing or selection (of candidates for an office, etc) by vote; [C] instance of this: 選擧: (attrib) (形容用法) ~ *results.* 選擧結果。ˌ**general** '~, of representatives, (GB members of the House of Commons), for the whole country. (議員等)普選;大選; (英)下議院議員選擧。ˌ**local** '~, of representatives, (GB 英 councillors), for a town／borough／district council. 市，郡等議員選擧; 地方議員選擧。'**by-~**, of one member, to fill a vacancy. 補選。**~·eer·ing** /ɪˌlekʃə'nɪərɪŋ; ɪˌlɛkʃən'ɪrɪŋ/ *n* [U] working in ~s, eg by canvassing, making speeches. 競選(如藉遊說,發表演講等)。

elec·tive /ɪ'lektɪv; ɪ'lɛktɪv/ *adj* **1** having the power to elect: 有選擧權的: *an ~ assembly.* 有選擧權的大會。**2** chosen or filled by election: 被選出的; 選任的: *an ~ office.* 選任的職位。**3** (US) not compulsory; that may be chosen: (美)非强迫的;可以選擇的: ~ *subjects in college.* 大學中的選修科目。⇨ *optional* at option.

elec·tor /ɪ'lektə(r); ɪ'lɛktɚ/ *n* person having the right to elect (esp by voting at a parliamentary election). 有選擧權者;選擧人(尤指選議員時有投票權者)。**~al** /ɪ'lektərəl; ɪ'lɛktərəl/ *adj* of an election; of ~s: 選擧的;選擧人的: *the ~al roll／register*, the list of ~s. 選擧人名單。*The E~al College in the USA elects the President.* 在美國選擧團選擧總統。**~·ate** /ɪ'lektərət; ɪ'lɛktərɪt/ *n* whole body of qualified ~s. 選擧團;選民。

elec·tric /ɪ'lektrɪk; ɪ'lɛktrɪk/ *adj* of, worked by, charged with, capable of developing, electricity: 電的;用電的;帶電的;發電的: *an ~ current／torch／iron／shock;* 電流(電筒;電熨斗;電震); ~ *light;* 電燈; ~ *flex／cord;* 花線;皮線; *the ~ chair*, used for electrocuting criminals; 電椅(用做刑具); ~ *blue*, steely blue; 鋼青色; *an ~ guitar*, one that has amplifiers for the sound; 電吉他; *an ~ eye*, a photo-electric cell. 光電管;光電儀。

elec·tri·cal /ɪ'lektrɪkl; ɪ'lɛktrɪkl̩/ *adj* **1** relating to electricity: 關於電的: ~ *engineering.* 電機工程學。**2** (fig) (eg of news) causing strong and sudden emotion. (喩)(指新聞等)震撼性的;刺激性的。**~ly** /-klɪ; -klɪ/ *adv*

elec·tri·cian /ɪˌlek'trɪʃn; ɪˌlɛk'trɪʃən/ *n* expert in setting up, repairing and operating electrical apparatus. 電機師;電器技師;電機匠。

elec·tric·ity /ɪˌlek'trɪsətɪ; ɪˌlɛk'trɪsətɪ/ *n* [U] **1** all the phenomena associated with electrons (negative charge) and protons (positive charge); the study of these phenomena. 電;電學。**2** supply of electric current: 電力供應: *When did ~ come to the village?* 這村莊何時開始有電力供應？

elec·trify /ɪ'lektrɪfaɪ; ɪ'lɛktrəˌfaɪ/ *vt* (*pt, pp* -fied) [VP6A] **1** charge (sth) with electricity. 使帶電; 充電。**2** equip (a railway, etc) for the use of electric power. 電氣化(鐵路等)。**3** (fig) excite, shock, as if by electricity: (喩)震撼;使驚駭: *to ~ an audience by an unexpected announcement.* 以意外的宣布使聽衆震驚。**elec·tri·fi·ca·tion** /ɪˌlektrɪfɪ'keɪʃn; ɪˌlɛktrəfə'keʃən/ *n* ~ing, eg the conversion of a steam railway to an electric railway. 充電;電氣化(例如將一使用蒸汽的鐵路電氣化)。

elec·tro- /ɪ'lektrəʊ; ɪ'lɛktro/ *pref* (in compounds) involving electricity: (用於複合字)電: ˌ**~-'cardio·gram** /-'kɑːdɪəʊgræm; -'kɑrdɪəˌgræm/ curve traced by an ~cardiograph, used in the diagnosis of heart disease. 心電圖(診斷心臟疾病所作者)。ˌ**~-'cardio·graph** /-'kɑːdɪəʊgrɑːf *US:* -græf; -'kɑrdɪəˌgræf/ apparatus which detects and records electric activity in the muscles of the heart. 心電圖描記器。ˌ**~-'chem·is·try**, electricity as applied to chemistry. 電化學。ˌ**~-'mag·net**, piece of soft iron that becomes magnetic when an electric current is passed through wire coiled round it. 電磁鐵;電磁體。ˌ**~·mag·'netic** *adj* having both electric and magnetic character. 有電磁性的; 電磁鐵的。Hence, 由此產生，ˌ**~-'mag·net·ism** *n* '**~·plate** *vt* coat with a thin layer of metal (eg silver) by electrolysis. 電鍍(例如鍍以銀面)。▭ *n* [U] articles plated with silver in this way. 銀面電鍍器。

elec·tro·cute /ɪ'lektrəkjuːt; ɪ'lɛktrəˌkjut/ *vt* [VP6A] kill accidentally, put to death, by means of an electrical current. 誤觸電而致死;處以電刑。**elec·tro·cu·tion** /ɪˌlektrə'kjuːʃn; ɪˌlɛktrə'kjuʃən/ *n*

elec·trode /ɪ'lektrəʊd; ɪ'lɛktrod/ *n* solid conductor by which an electric current enters or leaves a vacuum tube, etc. 電極;電極棒。⇨ anode, cathode.

elec·tro·ly·sis /ɪˌlek'trɒləsɪs; ɪˌlɛk'trɑləsɪs/ *n* [U] separation of a substance into its chemical parts by electric current. 電解。

elec·tron /ɪ'lektrɒn; ɪ'lɛktrɑn/ *n* [C] (phys) subatomic particle of matter having a negative electric charge. (物理)電子。~ **microscope**, using ~s instead of visible light. 電子顯微鏡。**~ic** /ˌɪlek'trɒnɪk; ɪˌlɛk'trɑnɪk/ *adj* of ~s; operated by, based on, ~s. 電子的;電子操作的;以電子爲基礎的。**~ic music**, produced by manipulating natural or artificial sounds by means of electric or ~ic equipment. 電子音樂(用電化或電子設備製作的)。ˌ**~ic** ˌ**data** '**processing**, (abbr 略作 EDP) use of ~ic computers to derive information or to achieve a required order of data. 電子資料處理。**~·ics** *n* (with *sing v*) the science and technology of ~ic phenomena, devices and systems, as in radio, TV, tape recorders, computers, etc. (與單數動詞連用)電子學。

elee·mosy·nary /ˌelɪiː'mɒsɪnərɪ *US:* -nerɪ; ˌɛlə'mɑsn̩ˌɛrɪ/ *adj* (formal) of, dependent upon, alms; charitable. (正式用語)依賴施捨的;施捨的;慈善的。

el·egant /'elɪgənt; 'ɛləgənt/ *adj* showing, having, good taste; graceful; done with care, skill and taste: 文雅的;優美的;優雅的;精美的: *an ~ young man;* 文雅的青年; ~ *manners;* 文雅的擧止; *leading a life of ~ ease.* 過着風雅的生活。**~·ly** *adv* **el·egance** /-əns; -əns/ *n* [U].

el·egiac /ˌelɪ'dʒaɪək; ɪ'lidʒɪˌæk/ *adj* **1** (of metre) suited to elegies: (指詩的韻律)適於輓歌的: ~ *couplets.* 輓歌對句。**2** mournful. 哀悼的。□ *n pl* ~ verses. 輓歌;哀歌。

el·egy /'elədʒɪ; 'ɛlədʒɪ/ *n* (*pl* -gies) poem or song of sorrow, esp for the dead. 輓歌;輓詩。

el·ement /'elɪmənt; 'ɛləmənt/ *n* **1** (science) substance which cannot be split up into a simpler form by ordinary chemical methods: (科學)元素: *Water is a compound containing the ~s hydrogen and oxygen.* 水是含有氫和氧元素的化合物。**2** (according to the ancient philosophers): (根據古代哲學家的說法): *the four ~s*, earth, air, fire and water (out of which the material universe was thought to be composed). 四行(卽土、風、火、水，認爲宇宙卽由此四行構成)。***in／out of one's ~***, in／not in suitable or satisfying surroundings: 在(不在)適當或滿意的環境中: *He's in his ~ when taking part in a political debate*, is doing sth that pleases and satisfies him. 他參加政治辯論時，眞是得其所哉(可以大展所長)。*I'm out of my ~ when people start talking about economics.* 當人們開始談論經濟學時,我就成了外行了。**3** (*pl*) (複) **the ~s**, the forces of nature, the weather, etc: 自然力;風雨等的力量: *exposed to the fury of the ~s*, to the winds, storms, etc. 暴露於風，暴風雨等中。**4** (*pl*) beginnings or outlines of a subject of study; parts that must be learnt first: (複)初步;大綱;基本原理: *the ~s of geometry*. 幾何學的初步。 **5** necessary or characteristic feature: 要素;特色: *Justice is an important ~ in good government*. 公正爲善治的要素。 **6** suggestion, indication, trace: 提示;表示;小量: *There's an ~ of truth in his account of what happened*. 他對所發生的事之敘述略有一些是眞實的。 ⇨ atom(2). **7** resistance wire in an electrical appliance (eg a heater). 電阻線(例如電熱器中者)。 **el·emen·tal** /ˌelɪˈmentl ; ˌɛləˈmɛntl̩/ *adj* of the four ~s(2); of the ~s(3): 四行的;自然力的: *the ~al fury of the storm*. 風雨的狂暴。

ele·men·tary /ˌelɪˈmentərɪ ; ˌɛləˈmɛntərɪ/ *adj* of or in the beginning stage(s); not developed; simple: 初步的;基本的;未發展的;簡單的: *the ~ rules of social conduct;* 社會行爲的基本守則; *~ arithmetic*. 初等算數。 **ele·men·tar·ily** /ˌelɪˈmentərəlɪ *US:* ˌelɪmənˈterəlɪ ; ˌɛləmənˈtɛrəlɪ/ *adv*

el·eph·ant /ˈelɪfənt ; ˈɛləfənt/ *n* largest four-footed animal now living, with curved ivory tusks and a long trunk (proboscis). 象。⇨ the illus at large. 參看 large 之挿圖。 ˌ**white** ˈ**~**, costly or troublesome possession useless to its owner. 昂貴而無用的東西;累贅。 **el·ephan·ti·asis** /ˌelɪfənˈtaɪəsɪs ; ˌɛləfənˈtaɪəsɪs/ *n* [U] skin disease causing great enlargement of limbs. 象皮病;結節癩。 **ele·phan·tine** /ˌelɪˈfæntaɪn ; ˌɛləˈfæntin/ *adj* of or like ~s; heavy; clumsy: 象的;似象的;重的;笨拙的: *an ~ine task;* 累贅的工作;*~ine humour;* 笨拙的幽默;*an ~ine memory*, extremely reliable one. 絶對可靠的記憶。

el·ev·ate /ˈelɪveɪt ; ˈɛləˌvet/ *vt* [VP6A, 14] *~ (to)*, (formal) lift up; raise; (fig) make (the mind, morals) higher and better: (正式用語)舉起;提高;(喩)使(思想,道德)高尙: *~ the voice*, speak louder; 提高講話聲音; *~ a man to the peerage*, make him a peer; 晋升一人爲貴族; *an elevating book/sermon;* 激勵人心的書(講道); *an ~d railway/railroad*, one built on piers (usu in a town) to run overhead. 高架鐵路。

el·ev·ation /ˌelɪˈveɪʃn ; ˌɛləˈveʃən/ *n* **1** [U] elevating or being elevated: 舉起;提高;激勵人心: *~ to the peerage;* 晉身爲貴族; [C] instance of this. 舉起或提高的實例。 **2** [U] grandeur or dignity: 高尙;莊嚴:*~ of thought/style/language*. 思想(風格,語言)的高尙。 **3** [C] height (esp above sea-level); hill or high place: 高度(尤指海拔);山;高地: *an ~ of 2000 metres*. 海拔二千公尺。 **4** [C] angle (eg of a gun) with the horizon. 仰角(例如砲之仰角)。 **5** [C] plan (drawn to scale) of one side of a building. (建築物之一面的)立視圖。 ⇨ plan. ⇨ the illus at perspective. 參看 perspective 之挿圖。

el·ev·ator /ˈelɪveɪtə(r) ; ˈɛləˌvetɚ/ *n* **1** machine like a continuous belt with buckets at intervals, used for raising grain, etc. (運送穀類等之)昇降機。 **2** store-house for grain. 穀倉。 **3** thing that elevates, eg part of an aircraft that is used to gain or lose altitude. 使升起之物(例如飛機之昇降舵)。 **4** (US) lift *n* (2). (美)電梯。

eleven /ɪˈlevn ; ɪˈlɛvən/ *adj, n* the number 11, ⇨ App 4; a team of eleven players for football, hockey or cricket. 十一;十一個(參看附錄四);由十一位球員組成的足球,曲棍球或板球隊。 **elev·enth** /ɪˈlevnθ ; ɪˈlɛvənθ/ *adj, n* ***at the ~th hour***, at the latest possible time. 在最後一刻;剛好來得及。 **elev·enses** /ɪˈlevnzɪz ; ɪˈlɛvənzɪz/ *n pl* (GB) snack and drink taken during the morning. (英)午前茶點(上午十一時左右進食的點心和飲料)。

elf /elf ; ɛlf/ *n* (*pl* elves /elvz ; ɛlvz/) small fairy; mischievous little creature. 小精靈;小妖精。 **elfin** /ˈelfɪn ; ˈɛlfɪn/ *adj* of elves: 小精靈的;小妖精的: *elfin dances/laughter*. 小妖精的舞蹈(歡笑)。**elf·ish** /ˈelfɪʃ ; ˈɛlfɪʃ/ *adj* mischievous. 惡作劇的。

eli·cit /ɪˈlɪsɪt ; ɪˈlɪsɪt/ *vt* [VP6A, 14] *~ sth (from sb)*, draw out; cause to come out: 引出;使發出: *to ~ the truth/a reply*. 使吐露眞情(回答)。**eli·ci·ta·tion** /ɪˌlɪsɪˈteɪʃn ; ɪˌlɪsəˈteʃən/ *n*

elide /ɪˈlaɪd ; ɪˈlaɪd/ *vt* [VP6A] leave out a vowel or syllable in pronunciation. 發音時省略(一母音或音節)。⇨ elision.

eli·gible /ˈelɪdʒəbl ; ˈɛlɪdʒəbl̩/ *adj ~ (for)*, fit, suitable, to be chosen; having the right qualifications: 適於被選的;合格的: *~ for promotion/a position/a pension/membership in a society;* 有資格升級(充任一職,領養老金,爲會員); *an ~ young man*, eg one who would be a satisfactory choice as a husband. 合格的青年(例如可做佳婿者)。 **el·igi·bil·ity** /ˌelɪdʒəˈbɪlətɪ ; ˌɛlɪdʒəˈbɪlətɪ/ *n* [U] the state of being ~. 合格;有資格。

elim·in·ate /ɪˈlɪmɪneɪt ; ɪˈlɪməˌnet/ *vt* [VP6A, 14] *~ (from)*, remove; take or put away, get rid of (because unnecessary or unwanted): 除去;剔除;淘汰: *~ slang words from an essay;* 將俚語自一篇文章中剔除; *~ a possibility*, set it aside and pay no consideration to it; 對一種可能性不予考慮; *~ waste products from the body*, excrete them. 自體內排泄廢物。 **elim·in·ation** /ɪˌlɪmɪˈneɪʃn ; ɪˌlɪməˈneʃən/ *n*

eli·sion /ɪˈlɪʒn ; ɪˈlɪʒən/ *n* (from 出自 elide) [U] leaving out of a vowel or syllable in pronunciation (as in *let's*); [C] instance of this. 省略;發音時一母音或一音節之省略(例如 let's)。

élite /eɪˈliːt ; ɪˈlit/ *n* group in society considered to be superior because of the power, talent, privileges, etc of its members: (因其權力,才能,特權等而被視爲)優秀的團體;傑出的人物;精華: *an educated ~*. 有教養的優秀人才。 ⇨ egalitarian. **élitism** /-tɪzəm ; -tɪzəm/ *n* [U] belief that the education system, etc should aim at developing ~s. 認爲教育目標應培植優秀人才的主張。**élitist** /-tɪst ; -tɪst/ *n*

elixir /ɪˈlɪksə(r) ; ɪˈlɪksɚ/ *n* [C] **1** preparation by which medieval scientists hoped to change metals into gold or (*~ of life*) to prolong life indefinitely. (中古時期科學家希望能變鐵成金的)鍊金藥;長生不老藥(亦作 elixir of life)。 **2** remedy that cures all ills. 萬靈藥。

Eliza·bethan /ɪˌlɪzəˈbiːθn ; ɪˌlɪzəˈbiθən/ *adj* of the time of Queen Elizabeth I of England: 英國伊利莎白女王一世時代的: *the ˈ~ age;* 伊利莎白一世時代; *~ drama*. 伊利莎白女王一世時代的戲劇。□ *n* person who lived during her reign, eg Shakespeare. 伊利莎白女王一世時代的人(例如莎士比亞)。

elk /elk ; ɛlk/ *n* one of the largest kinds of living deer, found in N Europe, N Asia, and (called a *moose*) N America. 麋鹿(產於北歐、北亞及北美,在北美此種鹿稱作 moose)。

el·lipse /ɪˈlɪps ; ɪˈlɪps/ *n* regular oval. 橢圓。 **el·lip·tic** /ɪˈlɪptɪk ; ɪˈlɪptɪk/, **el·lip·ti·cal** /-kl ; -kl̩/ *adj* shaped like an ~. 橢圓形的。

el·lip·sis /ɪˈlɪpsɪs ; ɪˈlɪpsɪs/ *n* (*pl* -pses /-psiːz ; -psiz/) [U] omission from a sentence of words needed to complete the construction or meaning; [C] instance of this. 一句中字的省略;省略法。**el·lip·ti·cal** /ɪˈlɪptɪkl ; ɪˈlɪptɪkl̩/ *adj* containing ~: 有省略之處的: *an elliptical sentence*. 含有省略之句子。

elm /elm ; ɛlm/ *n* [C] common deciduous tree that grows to a great size and height, ⇨ the illus at tree; [U] its hard, heavy wood. 榆樹(參看 tree 之挿圖);榆木。

elo·cu·tion /ˌeləˈkjuːʃn ; ˌɛləˈkjuʃən/ *n* [U] art or style of speaking well, esp in public. 演說術;雄辯術。**~·ary** /-ənərɪ *US:* -ənerɪ ; -ənɛrɪ/ *adj* of ~. 演說術的;雄辯術的。**~·ist** /-ʃənɪst ; -ʃənɪst/ *n* expert in ~. 演說家;雄辯家。

elon·gate /ˈiːlɒŋgeɪt *US:* ɪˈlɔːŋ- ; ɪˈlɔŋget/ *vt, vi* [VP6A, 2A] make or become long(er) in space. 伸長;延長。 **elon·ga·tion** /ˌiːlɒŋˈgeɪʃn *US:* -lɔːŋ- ; ɪˌlɔŋˈgeʃən/ *n* [U] making longer; [C] the part (of a line, etc) produced this way. 伸長;延長;(線等)延長部分。

elope /ɪˈləʊp ; ɪˈlop/ *vi* [VP2A, C, 3A] *~ (with)*,

(of a woman) run away from home or a husband (with a lover). (指女子)私奔。 ~**·ment** *n*

elo·quence /ˈeləkwəns ; ˈɛləkwəns/ *n* [U] skilful use of language to persuade or to appeal to the feelings; fluent speaking. 口才；雄辯；滔滔而言。 **elo·quent** /-ənt ; -ənt/ *adj* having or showing ~. 有口才的；善辯的。 **elo·quent·ly** *adv*

else /els ; ɛls/ *adv* **1** (with *indef* or *interr pron*) besides; in addition: (與不定或疑問代名詞連用)此外；別的: *Did you see anybody ~,* any other person(s)? 你還看到別的人沒有？ *Have you anything ~ to do?* 你有別的事情做沒有？ *Ask somebody ~ to help you.* 去請別人幫助你。 *That must be somebody ~'s* (= some other person's) *hat; it isn't mine.* 那一定是別人的帽子，不是我的。 *Nothing ~* (= Nothing more), *thank you.* 沒有別的事了，謝謝你。 *We went nowhere ~,* to no other place. 我們沒有去別的地方。 *What ~ should I do?* 我還應該做些什麼？ *Who ~ was there?* 還有誰在那裏？ *How ~* (= In what other way) *would you do it?* 你還有別的做法嗎？ ***little ~,*** not much more. 沒有多少了；沒有什麼了。 **2** otherwise; if not: 否則；不然的話: *Run (or) ~ you'll be late.* 快跑，否則你要遲到了。 *He must be joking, or ~ he's mad.* 他一定是開玩笑，不然他就是瘋了。

E

else·where /ˌelsˈweə(r) *US:* -ˈhweər ; ˈɛlsˌhwɛr/ *adv* somewhere else; in, at or to some other place. 在別處；至別處。

elu·ci·date /ɪˈlu:sɪdeɪt ; ɪˈlusəˌdet/ *vt* [VP6A] (formal) make clear; explain; throw light on (a problem, difficulty). (正式用語)闡明；說明(問題，困難)。 **elu·ci·da·tion** /ɪˌlu:sɪˈdeɪʃn ; ɪˌlusəˈdeʃən/ *n*

elude /ɪˈlu:d ; ɪˈlud/ *vt* [VP6A] escape capture by (esp by means of a trick); avoid: 逃避(尤指藉詭計)；躲避: *~ one's enemies;* 逃避敵人； *~ observation.* 躲避觀察。

elu·sive /ɪˈlu:sɪv ; ɪˈlusɪv/ *adj* tending to elude or escape: 逃避的；躲避的: *an ~ criminal;* 逃犯；tending to escape from the memory; not easy to recall: 難記憶的；不易記起的: *an ~ word.* 難記憶的字。

el·ver /ˈelvə(r) ; ˈɛlvə/ *n* young eel. 幼鰻。

elves /elvz ; ɛlvz/ *pl* of elf.

elv·ish /ˈelvɪʃ ; ˈɛlvɪʃ/ *adj* = elfish.

Ely·sium /ɪˈlɪzɪəm ; ɪˈlɪʒɪəm/ *n* (Gk myth) home of the blessed after death; place or state of perfect happiness. (希神)極樂世界；福地。 **Ely·sian** /ɪˈlɪzɪən ; ɪˈlɪʒən/ *adj* of ~; heavenly; blissful. 極樂世界的；福地的；天堂的；幸福的。

'em /əm ; əm/ *pron* (colloq) (俗) = them.

em·aci·ate /ɪˈmeɪʃɪeɪt ; ɪˈmeʃɪˌet/ *vt* [VP6A] make thin and weak (usu passive): 使瘦弱(通常用被動語態): *~d by long illness.* 由於長期生病而瘦弱了。 **emaci·ation** /ɪˌmeɪsɪˈeɪʃn ; ɪˌmeʃɪˈeʃən/ *n* [U].

ema·nate /ˈeməneɪt ; ˈɛməˌnet/ *vi* [VP3A] ***~ from,*** (formal) come, flow, proceed from. (正式用語)發出；流出；生出。 **ema·na·tion** /ˌeməˈneɪʃn ; ˌɛməˈneʃən/ *n* [U] emanating; [C] sth that ~s. 發出；流出；生出；發出物；流出物；生出物。

eman·ci·pate /ɪˈmænsɪpeɪt ; ɪˈmænsəˌpet/ *vt* [VP 6A, 14] ***~ (from),*** set free (esp from legal, political or moral restraint): 解放(尤指自法律，政治或道德的約束中解放): *~ slaves;* 解放奴隸； *an ~d young woman,* one who has freed herself from the conventions or restrictions of the community to which she belongs. 解放了的女青年。

eman·ci·pa·tion /ɪˌmænsɪˈpeɪʃn ; ɪˌmænsəˈpeʃən/ *n* [U] emancipating or being emancipated: 解放；被解放: *the ~ of women,* giving or obtaining all or some of the rights, opportunities, etc that men have; 婦女的解放； *~ from the authority of one's parents.* 擺脫父母的管束(獲得法定自立權)。

emas·cu·late /ɪˈmæskjʊleɪt ; ɪˈmæskjəˌlet/ *vt* [VP 6A] deprive of (masculine) vigour; weaken; impoverish. 使弱；使無丈夫氣。 **emas·cu·la·tion** /ɪˌmæskjʊˈleɪʃn ; ɪˌmæskjəˈleʃən/ *n*

em·balm /ɪmˈbɑ:m ; ɪmˈbɑm/ *vt* [VP6A] preserve (a dead body) from decay by using spices or chemicals; preserve from oblivion; fill with fragrance. 以香料或藥物防止(屍體)腐爛；使不被遺忘；使瀰漫香氣。 ~**·ment** *n*

em·bank·ment /ɪmˈbæŋkmənt ; ɪmˈbæŋkmənt/ *n* [C] wall or mound of earth, stone, etc to hold back water or support a raised road or railway; roadway supported by such a wall: 堤；(鐵路等的)路基；塡基；路堤；有路基的道路: *the Thames E~.* 泰晤士河河堤。

em·bargo /ɪmˈbɑ:gəʊ ; ɪmˈbɑrgo/ *n* (*pl* ~es /-gəʊz ; -goz/) order that forbids trade, movement of ships, etc; stoppage of commerce, or of a branch of commerce: 禁止貿易令；封港令；禁運；禁止通商: *a gold ~,* one that forbids or restricts the buying and selling of gold; 禁止買賣黃金； (fig) blocking; prohibition. (喻)阻止；禁止。 ***lift/raise/remove an ~ (from sb),*** start trading (with him) again. 解禁；重新開放貿易。 ***place/lay sb under (an) ~; put an ~ on sb,*** do no trade with him. 禁止貿易。 □ *vt* (*pt, pp* ~ed /-gəʊd ; -god/) [VP6A] lay under an ~; seize (ships or goods) by government authority, for the service of the State. 禁止貿易；禁止(船隻或貨物)出入；扣押(船隻或貨物)以供國家之用。

em·bark /ɪmˈbɑ:k ; ɪmˈbɑrk/ *vi, vt* **1** [VP2A, C, 6A] go, put or take on board a ship: 乘船；裝於船上；裝載: *The soldiers ~ed for Malta.* 士兵乘船往馬爾他。 *The ship ~ed passengers and cargo.* 這船裝載旅客和貨物。 **2** [VP3A] ***~ on/upon,*** start, take part in: 開始；從事: *~ upon a new business undertaking.* 從事一新的商業。 **em·bar·ka·tion** /ˌembɑ:ˈkeɪʃn ; ˌɛmbɑrˈkeʃən/ *n* [U] ~ing; [C] instance of this; that which is ~ed. 乘船；裝載；開始；從事；裝載物。

em·bar·rass /ɪmˈbærəs ; ɪmˈbærəs/ *vt* [VP6A] **1** make to feel awkward or ashamed; cause mental discomfort or anxiety to: 使困窘；使侷促不安；使焦急: *~ing questions;* 令人困窘的問題； *~ed by lack of money.* 因缺錢而窘迫。 **2** (old use) hinder the movement of: (舊用法)阻礙；妨礙: *He fell into the river and, because he was ~ed by his heavy overcoat, only just managed to swim to the bank.* 他跌入河中，因受其厚大衣的妨礙，很勉强地游至岸邊。 ~**·ing** *adj* ~**·ing·ly** *adv* ~**·ment** *n* [U] ~ing or being ~ed; [C] sth that ~es: 困窘；侷促不安；焦急；阻礙；令人困窘的事物: *financial ~ments;* 財務的困難； *an ~ment* (= an over-abundance) *of riches.* 財富過多的煩惱。

em·bassy /ˈembəsɪ ; ˈɛmbəsɪ/ *n* (*pl* -ssies) duty and mission of an ambassador; his official residence; ambassador and his staff: 大使之職務；大使館；大使館全體人員: *to go/come/send sb on an ~ (to sb);* 去(來，派某人)任大使； *the French ~ in London;* 倫敦的法國大使館； (attrib) (形容用法) *~ officials.* 大使館官員。

em·battled /ɪmˈbætld ; ɛmˈbætld/ *adj* (of an army, etc) drawn up ready for battle; (fig) in a condition of defence; (of a tower or building) having battlements. (指軍隊等)佈陣以待的；(喻)在防禦狀態中的；(指城樓或建築物)有城垛的。

em·bed /ɪmˈbed ; ɪmˈbɛd/ *vt* (-dd-) [VP6A, 14] (usu passive) ***~ (in),*** fix firmly (in a surrounding mass): (通常用被動語態)嵌入(周圍物體中): *stones ~ded in rock;* 嵌入岩石內的石頭； (fig) (喻) *facts ~ded in one's memory.* 深留記憶中的事實。

em·bel·lish /ɪmˈbelɪʃ ; ɪmˈbɛlɪʃ/ *vt* [VP6A, 14] ***~ (with),*** make beautiful; add ornaments or details to: 美化；裝飾；修飾: *~ a dress with lace and ribbons;* 用花邊及緞帶裝飾衣服； *~ a story,* eg by adding amusing but perhaps untrue details. 修飾一故事(例如加以有趣味而或許不眞實的細節) ~**·ment** *n* [U] ~ing or being ~ed; [C] that which ~es; artistic addition. 美化；裝飾；裝飾物；美化物。

em·ber /ˈembə(r)；ˈɛmbɚ/ *n* (usu *pl*) small piece of burning wood or coal in a dying fire; (*pl*) ashes of a dying fire. (通常用複數)燃屑；(複)餘燼。

em·bezzle /ɪmˈbezl；ɪmˈbɛzl̩/ *vt* [VP6A] use (money placed in one's care) in a wrong way for one's own benefit. 挪用(公款)；盜用。**~·ment** *n* [U] embezzling; [C] instance of this. 挪用公款；盜用公款。

em·bit·ter /ɪmˈbɪtə(r)；ɪmˈbɪtɚ/ *vt* [VP6A] arouse bitter feelings in: 使痛苦；使難過: *~ed by repeated failures.* 因連續失敗而難過。**~·ment** *n*

em·blazon /ɪmˈbleɪzn；ɛmˈblezn̩/ *vt* [VP6A, 14] *~ (with),* **1** adorn (eg a shield or banner) with heraldic devices: 以紋章裝飾(盾或旗)：*~ed with the coat of arms of the family.* 飾有家族盾徽的。**2** extol; exalt. 頌揚；讚揚。

em·blem /ˈembləm；ˈɛmbləm/ *n* symbol; device that represents sth: 象徵；標記: *an ~ of peace,* eg a dove; 和平的象徵(例如鴿子)；*an ~ of love,* eg a heart. 愛的象徵(例如一顆心)。**~·atic** /ˌembləˈmætɪk；ˌɛmbləˈmætɪk/ *adj ~ (of),* serving as an ~. 作爲象徵的；作爲標記的。

em·body /ɪmˈbɒdɪ；ɪmˈbɑdɪ/ *vt* (*pt, pp* -died) [VP6A, 14] *~ (in),* **1** give form to ideas／feelings, etc: 具體表現(思想，感情等)：*~ one's ideas in a speech.* 在一篇演說中具體表現個人的思想。**2** include; comprise: 包括；包含: *The latest locomotives ~ many new features.* 最新的火車頭含有許多新的特色。**3** clothe (a spirit) with a body: 賦(靈魂)以軀體: *an embodied spirit.* 有軀體的靈魂。**em·bodi·ment** /ɪmˈbɒdɪmənt；ɪmˈbɑdɪmənt/ *n* [C] that which embodies sth or is embodied: 能具體表現他物者；化身；被具體表現者: *She is the embodiment of kindness.* 她是仁慈的化身。

em·bolden /ɪmˈbəʊldən；ɪmˈboldn̩/ *vt* [VP6A, 17] give courage or confidence to: 給與勇氣或信心: *Their sympathy ~ed me to ask them for help.* 他們的同情使我有勇氣向他們求助。

em·bon·point /ˌɒmbɒnˈpwɑːŋ；ɑ̃bɔ̃ˈpwæ̃/ *n* (F) plumpness (used as a polite way of saying that sb, usu a woman, is very fat). (法)福泰(通常用以說女子肥胖的客氣話)。

em·boss /ɪmˈbɒs *US:* -ˈbɔːs；ɪmˈbɔs/ *vt* [VP6A, 14] *~ (with),* cause a pattern, figure, etc to stand out on (the surface of sth); raise the surface of sth into a pattern: 使(花樣，圖案等)浮凸於(某物之平面)上；使有浮雕花紋: *~ed notepaper,* with the address ~ed on it; 有浮凸的地址之信紙；*a silver vase ~ed with a design of flowers.* 飾有浮起花卉圖案的銀瓶。

em·brace /ɪmˈbreɪs；ɪmˈbres/ *vt, vi* **1** [VP6A, 2A] take (a person, etc) into one's arms, as a sign of affection: 擁抱: *~ a child.* 擁抱一小孩。*They ~d.* 他們互相擁抱。**2** [VP6A] accept; make use of: 接受；利用: *~ an offer／opportunity.* 接受提議(利用機會)。**3** [VP6A] (of things) include: (指事物)包括: *~ many examples in a single formula.* 將許多例子包括在一個公式內。□ *n* [C] act of embracing: 擁抱: *He held her to him in a warm ~.* 他熱情地擁抱她。

em·brasure /ɪmˈbreɪʒə(r)；ɛmˈbreʒɚ/ *n* [C] **1** bevelled opening in a parapet for a gun. (胸牆上之)射口；砲(槍)眼。**2** bevelled opening (esp interior side of a doorway or window), eg in an old stone castle. 四周內寬外窄的開口(尤指門窗之內側，如古老石堡中者)。

em·bro·ca·tion /ˌembrəˈkeɪʃn；ˌɛmbroˈkeʃən/ *n* [U] liquid (a liniment) for rubbing a bruised or aching part of the body. 擦劑(揉擦於傷處或痛處之液劑)。

em·broider /ɪmˈbrɔɪdə(r)；ɪmˈbrɔɪdɚ/ *vt, vi* **1** [VP6A, 2A] ornament (cloth) with needlework: 繡花於(布)；刺繡: *~ one's initials on a handkerchief;* 將姓名的起首字母繡在手帕上；*a design ~ed in gold thread.* 用金線繡成的圖樣。**2** [VP6A] (fig) add fanciful details to a story. (喻)添加想像的細節於故事中；修飾一故事。**~y** /-dərɪ；-dərɪ/ *n* [U] ~ed needlework. 刺繡；刺繡品。

em·broil /ɪmˈbrɔɪl；ɛmˈbrɔɪl/ *vt* [VP6A, 14] *~ sb／oneself (in),* cause (sb, oneself) to be mixed up in a quarrel: 使(某人或自己)捲入糾紛: *I don't want to become ~ed in their quarrels.* 我不願被捲入他們的爭端中。

em·bryo /ˈembrɪəʊ；ˈɛmbrɪˌo/ *n* (*pl* ~s /-əʊz；-oz/) [C] offspring of an animal in the early stage of its development before birth (or before coming out of an egg); (fig) sth in its rudimentary stage. 胚胎；(喻)在萌芽期的事物。*in ~,* (lit, fig) still undeveloped. (字面，喻)尚未發展的；在萌芽時期的。**em·bry·onic** /ˌembrɪˈɒnɪk；ˌɛmbrɪˈɑnɪk/ *adj* in ~: 胚胎期的；萌芽期的: *an ~nic plan.* 萌芽階段的計畫。

emeer /eˈmɪə(r)；əˈmɪr/ *n* = emir.

emend /ɪˈmend；ɪˈmɛnd/ *vt* [VP6A] take out errors from: 修正；訂正；修改: *~ a passage in a book.* 修正書中的一節。**emen·da·tion** /ˌiːmenˈdeɪʃn；ˌimɛnˈdeʃən/ *n* [U] ~ing; [C] sth that is ~ed. 修正；修改；被修正之處。

em·er·ald /ˈemərəld；ˈɛmərəld/ *n* bright green precious stone; colour of this. 祖母綠；純綠寶石；翠玉；翠綠色。

emerge /ɪˈmɜːdʒ；ɪˈmɝdʒ/ *vi* [VP2A, 3A] *~ (from),* **1** come into view; (esp) come out (from water, etc): 出現；(尤指從水中等)現出: *The moon ~d from behind the clouds.* 月亮自雲後現出。**2** (of facts, ideas) appear; become known: (指事實，意見)出現；顯出；暴露: *No new ideas ~d during the talks.* 談論中沒有新的意見出現。**emerg·ence** /-dʒəns；-dʒəns/ *n* [U] emerging. 出現；現出；顯露。**emerg·ent** /-dʒənt；-dʒənt/ *adj* emerging: 出現的；現出的: (*the recently ~d and*) *emergent countries of Africa,* those changing from dependence to independence, becoming modernized, etc. 非洲的新興國家。

emerg·ency /ɪˈmɜːdʒənsɪ；ɪˈmɝdʒənsɪ/ *n* (*pl* -cies) **1** [U, C] serious happening or situation needing prompt action: 緊急事件；緊急情況: *This fire extinguisher is to be used only in (an) ~.* 這滅火器祇在緊急時使用。**2** (attrib use): (形容用法): *an ˈ~ exit;* 太平門; *an ˈ~ fund,* one to be used in an ~. 應急基金。

emeri·tus /ɪˈmerɪtəs；ɪˈmɛrətəs/ *adj* (Lat) retired from service but retaining an honorary title: (拉)退休但仍保留榮譽頭銜的；名譽退休的: *~ professor.* 名譽退休教授。

em·ery /ˈemərɪ；ˈɛmərɪ/ *n* [U] hard metal used (esp in powdered form) for grinding and polishing: 鋼玉粉；剛石粉；金剛砂(磨擦用)：*ˈ~-cloth／-paper／-wheel,* with ~ on the surface. 砂布(砂紙，砂輪)。

em·etic /ɪˈmetɪk；ɪˈmɛtɪk/ *n* medicine causing a person to vomit, eg when suffering from food-poisoning. 催吐劑(例如食物中毒時所用者)。

emi·grate /ˈemɪgreɪt；ˈɛməˌgret/ *vi* [VP2A, 3A] *~ (to) (from),* go away (from one's own country to another to settle there). 自本國移居他國。⇨ immigrate. **emi·grant** /ˈemɪgrənt；ˈɛməgrənt/ *n* person who ~s: 自本國移居他國者: *emigrants to Canada;* 移居加拿大的人; (attrib) (形容用法) *emigrant labourers.* 移居他國的勞工。**emi·gra·tion** /ˌemɪˈgreɪʃn；ˌɛməˈgreʃən/ *n* [U] emigrating; [C] instance of this. 自本國移居他國；移民。

émi·gré /ˈemɪgreɪ *US:* ˌemɪˈgreɪ；ˈɛməˌgre/ *n* (F) person who has left his own country, usu for political reasons. (法)因政治原因而離國者。

emi·nence /ˈemɪnəns；ˈɛmənəns/ *n* **1** [U] state of being famous or distinguished; superiority of position: 著名；卓越；顯赫；顯要: *reach ~ as a doctor;* 成爲名醫; *win ~ as a scientist.* 成爲卓越的科學家。**2** [C] area of high or rising ground. 高地。**3** ***His／Your E~,*** title used of／to a cardinal. 對紅衣主教之尊稱。

emi·nent /ˈemɪnənt；ˈɛmənənt/ *adj* **1** (of a person) distinguished: (指人) 著名的；卓越的: *~ for her*

E

virtues; 以她的美德著名; ~ *as a sculptor*. 卓越的雕刻家。 **2** (of qualities) remarkable in degree: (指性質)優良的: *a man of ~ goodness*. 品德優良的人。 **~·ly** *adv*

emir /e'mɪə(r) ; ə'mɪr/ *n* (title of a) Muslim ruler. 回教統治者(的尊稱)。 **~·ate** /e'mɪəreɪt ; ə'mɪrɪt/ *n* rank, lands, etc of an ~: 回教統治者的地位,土地等: *the great ~ates of Northern Nigeria*. 北奈及利亞廣大的回族土地。

em·iss·ary /'emɪsərɪ ; 'ɛmə,sɛrɪ/ *n* (*pl* -ries) person sent to deliver a message (often of an unpleasant and secret kind). 使者;密使。

emission /ɪ'mɪʃn ; ɪ'mɪʃən/ *n* ~ ***(of)***, [U] sending out or giving off (of light, heat, smell, etc); [C] that which is sent out or given off. (光、熱、氣味等之)發出;發射;散發;發出之物;散發之物。

emit /ɪ'mɪt ; ɪ'mɪt/ *vt* (-tt-) [VP6A] give or send out: 發出;放射: *A volcano ~s smoke and ashes*. 火山噴出煙和灰。

emolu·ment /ɪ'mɒljʊmənt ; ɪ'mɑljəmənt/ *n* [C] (usu *pl*) (formal) profit from official employment; fee; salary. (通常用複數) (正式用語)報酬;酬金;薪金。

emo·tion /ɪ'məʊʃn ; ɪ'moʃən/ *n* **1** [U] stirring up, excitement, of the mind or (more usu) the feelings; excited state of the mind or feelings: (心情或感情的)激動: *He thought of his dead child with deep ~*. 他想起他死去的孩子就變得非常激動。 *He spoke in a voice touched with ~*. 他以激動的聲音說話。 **2** [C] strong feeling of any kind: 激情;情感;情緒: *Love, joy, hate, fear and grief are ~s*. 愛,喜,恨,懼和悲都是情感。 *He appealed to our ~s rather than to our reason*. 他訴諸我們的情感而非我們的理智。 **~·less** *adj* without ~. 無情感的。 **~al** /-ʃənl ; -ʃənl/ *adj* **1** of, directed to, the ~s: 情感的;情緒的;訴諸情感的: *an ~al appeal*; 訴諸情感的懇求; *~al music*. 抒情音樂。 **2** having ~s that are easily excited; capable of expressing ~s: 感情易激動的;能表達情感的: *an ~al woman/actor/nature*. 多情善感的女子(能表達情感的演員; 易激動的性情)。 **~·ally** /-ʃənəlɪ ; -ʃənlɪ/ *adv* **emot·ive** /ɪ'məʊtɪv ; ɪ'motɪv/ *adj* of, tending to excite, the ~s. 情感的;易激動情感的。

em·pale /ɪm'peɪl ; ɪm'pel/ *vt* = impale.

em·panel /ɪm'pænl ; ɪm'pænl/ *vt* (-ll-, US also -l-) [VP6A] enter (a person's name) on a panel; enrol (a jury). 將(人名)列入陪審員名簿;選任(陪審員)。

em·pa·thy /'empəθɪ ; 'ɛmpəθɪ/ *n* [U] (psych) (power of) projecting oneself into (and so fully understanding, and losing one's identity in) a work of art or other object of contemplation; (power of) sharing another person's feelings. (心理) 神入 (全神貫入一藝術品或其他引人沉思的事物以達忘我的境界); 神入的能力;移情(能體會到別人的情感);移情的能力。

em·peror /'empərə(r) ; 'ɛmpərɚ/ *n* ruler of an empire. 皇帝。 ⇨ empress.

em·pha·sis /'emfəsɪs ; 'ɛmfəsɪs/ *n* (*pl* -ases /-əsiːz ; -əsiz/) [C, U] force or stress laid on a word or words to make the significance clear, or to show importance; (the placing of) special value or importance: 加强語氣;强調;(賦予)特殊價值或重要性: *Some schools lay/put special ~ on language study*. 有些學校特別注重語言的學習。 *I insist, with all the ~ at my command, that....* 我全力堅持…。 **em·pha·size** /'emfəsaɪz ; 'ɛmfə,saɪz/ *vt* [VP6A] put ~ on; give ~ to: 强調;加强…的語氣: *He emphasized the importance of careful driving*. 他强調小心駕駛的重要。 **em·phatic** /ɪm'fætɪk ; ɪm'fætɪk/ *adj* having, showing, using, ~: 語氣强的;强調的;表示强調的: *an emphatic gesture/opinion*; 强調的手勢(意見); *an emphatic person*. 表示强調的人。 **em·phati·cally** /-klɪ ; -klɪ/ *adv*

em·pire /'empaɪə(r) ; 'ɛmpaɪr/ *n* **1** [C] group of countries under a single supreme authority: 帝國(在一個皇帝統治下的若干國家): *the Roman E~*. 羅馬帝國。 **2** [U] supreme political power: 至高的政治權力: *the responsibilities of ~*. 至高政治權力的責任。 **the First E~**, (in France) period of the reign of Napoleon I (1804—15); (**E~**, attrib) of the style of furniture or dress fashionable in this period. (法國) 第一帝國 (1804-15 年間拿破崙一世統治時期); (E~, 形容用法) 第一帝國流行的(指傢具或服裝式樣)。 **the Second E~**, the period of the reign of Napoleon III (1852—70). 第二帝國(1852-70年間拿破崙三世統治期)。

em·piric, em·piri·cal /ɪm'pɪrɪk, -kl ; ɛm'pɪrɪk, -kl/ *adj* relying on observation and experiment, not on theory. 全憑觀察和實驗的。 **em·piri·cally** /-klɪ ; -klɪ/ *adv* **em·piri·cism** /ɪm'pɪrɪsɪzəm ; ɛm'pɪrə,sɪzəm/ *n* ~ practice. 全憑觀察和實驗; 經驗主義。 **em·pir·i·cist** /-sɪst ; -sɪst/ *n* ~ person. 全憑觀察和實驗的人;經驗主義者。

em·place·ment /ɪm'pleɪsmənt ; ɪm'plesmənt/ *n* prepared position for a heavy gun or guns. 砲兵陣地。

em·plane /em'pleɪn ; ɛm'plen/ *vi, vt* [VP2A, 6A] go, put, on board an aircraft. 乘飛機;裝入飛機。

em·ploy /ɪm'plɔɪ ; ɪm'plɔɪ/ *vt* [VP6A, 16B, 14] **1** give work to, usu for payment: 雇用: *They ~ five waiters*. 他們雇用五個侍者。 *He is ~ed in a bank*. 他在一家銀行任職。 **2** make use of: 使用: *How do you ~ your spare time?* 你怎樣利用你的暇時? □ *n* ***in the ~ of***, ~ed by, working for. 爲…所雇用;替…工作。 **~·able** /-əbl ; -əbl/ *adj* that can be ~ed. 可雇用的; 可使用的。 **~er** /-ə(r) ; -ɚ/ *n* person who ~s others. 雇主。 **~ee** /,emplɔɪ'iː ; ɪm'plɔɪ·i/ *n* person ~ed for wages. 受雇者;雇工;雇員;職員。

em·ploy·ment /ɪm'plɔɪmənt ; ɪm'plɔɪmənt/ *n* [U] employing or being employed; one's regular work or occupation: 雇用;受雇;使用;工作;職業: *to find ~*; 找工作;求職; *to give ~ to sb*; 雇用某人; *the men in my ~*; 我所雇用的人員; *to be thrown out of ~*. 被解雇;失業。 ***be in/out of ~***, have/not have a job. 有工作(失業)。 **'~ agency**, business establishment which helps persons (for a fee) to find ~. 職業介紹所(收介紹費用者)。 **'~ exchange**, Government office which puts employers and unemployed persons in touch and where unemployment benefits are paid. 勞工介紹所(政府機構,並發放失業救濟金)。

em·por·ium /ɪm'pɔːrɪəm ; ɛm'pɔrɪəm/ *n* centre of commerce; market; large retail store. 商業中心;市場;大零售商店。

em·power /ɪm'paʊə(r) ; ɪm'paʊɚ/ *vt* [VP17] ***~ sb to do sth***, give power or authority to act. 授權給某人(做某事)。

em·press /'emprɪs ; 'ɛmprɪs/ *n* woman governing an empire; wife of or widow of an emperor. 女皇;皇后。

empty[1] /'emptɪ ; 'ɛmptɪ/ *adj* having nothing inside; containing nothing: 空的;內中無物的: *an ~ box*; 空匣; *~ promises*, not meaning anything, not giving satisfaction; 空的諾言; *feeling ~*, (colloq) hungry; (俗)感覺餓的; *words ~ of meaning*, meaningless words. 無意義的話。 *The house was ~*, unoccupied. 那房子是空着的。 **,~-'handed** *adj* bringing back nothing; carrying nothing away. 空手的;徒手的。 **,~-'headed** *adj* witless; lacking in common sense. 愚蠢的;無腦筋的。 □ *n* (usu *pl*) box, bottle, crate, etc that has been emptied: (通常用複數)空匣,空盒,空瓶,空箱等: *Empties* (eg ~ beer bottles) *are not taken back*, the brewery will not accept them and allow credit for them. 空瓶(例如啤酒瓶)不收回。 **emp·ti·ness** /'emptɪnɪs ; 'ɛmptɪnɪs/ *n*

empty[2] /'emptɪ ; 'ɛmptɪ/ *vt, vi* (*pt, pp* -tied) [VP6A, 15B, 2A, C, 3A] ~ ***(out)***, make or become empty, remove what is inside (sth): 使空;變空;騰空: *~ one's glass*, drink everything in it; 乾杯;喝乾; *~ (out) a drawer*; 騰空一抽屜; *~ a box of rubbish* *into a rubbish-cart;* 將一箱垃圾倒入垃圾車; ~ *one's pockets of their contents.* 將衣袋中之物全部取出。*The streets soon emptied/were soon emptied when the rain started.* 一開始下雨,街上立卽空無行人。*The Rhone empties* (= flows) *into the Mediterranean.* 隆河注入地中海。 *The water empties* (= flows out) *slowly.* 這水慢慢地流出。*The cistern empties* (= becomes empty) *in five minutes.* 這貯水池五分鐘流乾。

em·purpled /ɪm'pɜ:pld; ɛm'pɝpḷd/ *adj* made purple. 使成紫色的。

em·py·rean /ˌempaɪ'ri:ən; ˌɛmpə'riən/ *n* the highest heaven; the visible heavens. 最高空;天空。□ *adj* heavenly; celestial. 天空的;天上的。

emu /'i:mju:; 'imju/ *n* large flightless Australian bird that runs well. 食火鷄(澳洲產,不會飛,但跑得快);鷸鶓。⇨ the illus at rare. 參看 rare 之插圖。

emu·late /'emjʊleɪt; 'ɛmjə,let/ *vt* [VP6A] try to do as well as or better than. 欲趕上或超過;與…競爭。

emu·la·tion /ˌemjʊ'leɪʃn; ˌɛmjə'leʃən/ *n* [U] emulating: 競爭;爭勝: *in a spirit of* ~; 以競爭的精神; *in* ~ *of each other.* 互相爭勝。

emu·lous /'emjʊləs; 'ɛmjələs/ *adj* ~ *(of),* (formal) wishing or anxious to do as well as or better than: (正式用語)競爭心强的;求勝心切的: ~ *of all rivals;* 欲勝過所有的競爭者; imitating (others) in a jealous spirit, desiring to obtain: 出於嫉妬而倣傚(他人)的;急欲獲得的: ~ *of fame/honours.* 好名。 **~·ly** *adv*

emul·sion /ɪ'mʌlʃn; ɪ'mʌlʃən/ *n* [C, U] (kinds of) creamy liquid in which particles of oil or fat are suspended: 乳狀液;乳劑;乳膠: ~ *paint,* in which the colour is in an ~-like liquid. 乳狀漆。**emul·sify** /ɪ'mʌlsɪfaɪ; ɪ'mʌlsə,faɪ/ *vt* (*pt, pp* -fied) [VP6A] make an ~ of. 使成乳狀液;使成乳劑;乳漿化。

en·able /ɪ'neɪbl; ɪn'ebl/ *vt* [VP17] make able, give authority or means (*to do* sth): 使能够;使可以;授以權柄或方法(與不定詞連用): *The collapse of the strike ~d the company to resume normal bus services.* 罷工的失敗使公司恢復了正常的公共汽車營業。 **en·abling** /ɪ'neɪblɪŋ; ɪn'eblɪŋ/ *part adj* making possible: 使可能的: *enabling legislation.* 可行的法律。

en·act /ɪ'nækt; ɪn'ækt/ *vt* **1** [VP6A, 9] make (a law); decree; ordain: 制定(法律);頒令;規定: *as by law ~ed.* 如法律所規定。*Be it further ~ed that....* (legal style). 再進一步規定…(法律文體)。**2** [VP6A] perform on, or as though on, the stage of a theatre. 演出(戲);扮演(劇中或現實生活中的角色)。**~·ment** *n* [U] ~ing or being ~ed; [C] law. 制定;規定;頒令;法律。

en·amel /ɪ'næml; ɪ'næmḷ/ *n* [U] **1** glass-like substance used for coating metal, porcelain, etc, for decoration or as a protection: 瓷釉;搪瓷;珐瑯: '~ *ware,* manufactured goods with ~ surfaces; 搪瓷器; '~ *paint,* paint which dries to make a hard, glossy surface. 亮漆。**2** hard outer covering of teeth. (牙齒的)珐瑯質。□ *vt* (-ll-, US also -l-) cover, decorate, with ~ (esp with designs or decorations). 以瓷釉塗(尤指花樣)於;塗以搪瓷。

en·amour (US = **-amor**) /ɪ'næmə(r); ɪn'æmɚ/ *vt* [VP6A] (usu in passive) (通常用被動語態) ***be ~ed of,*** fond of, delighted with and inclined to use: 喜歡;戀慕;迷戀: *~ed of one's own voice.* 喜愛自己的聲音。

en·camp /ɪn'kæmp; ɪn'kæmp/ *vt, vi* [VP6A, 2A] settle in a camp; lodge in tents. 紮營;露營。**~·ment** *n* place where troops, etc are ~ed. 紮營地;露營地。

en·case /ɪn'keɪs; ɪn'kes/ *vt* [VP6A, 14] ~ *(in),* put into a case; surround or cover as with a case: 裝在箱內;納入套內;包圍;包裹: *a knight ~d in armour.* 披着甲胄的武士。

en·caus·tic /en'kɔ:stɪk; ɛn'kɔstɪk/ *adj* prepared by using heat: 以熱力製成的;上釉燒的: ~ *bricks/tiles,* inlaid with coloured clays that are burnt in. 琉璃磚(瓦)。

en·cepha·li·tis /ˌenkefə'laɪtɪs; ˌɛnsɛfə'laɪtɪs/ *n* [U] inflammation of the brain. 腦炎。

en·chain /ɪn'tʃeɪn; ɛn'tʃen/ *vt* [VP6A] fasten with chain(s); (fig) hold fast (the attention, etc). 用鎖鍊鎖住;(喻)抓牢(注意力等)。

en·chant /ɪn'tʃɑ:nt *US:* -'tʃænt; ɪn'tʃænt/ *vt* [VP6A] **1** charm; delight: 使心醉;使喜悅: *She was ~ed with/by the flowers you sent her.* 她極喜愛你送給她的花。 **2** use magic on; put under a magic spell: 施魔法於;蠱惑: *the ~ed palace,* eg in a fairy tale. 魔宮(例如神話中者)。**~er** /-ə(r); -ɚ/ *n* man who ~s. 施魔法的男人;妖人。**~·ress** /-trɪs; -trɪs/ *n* woman who ~s. 施魔法的女人;妖女。**~·ing·ly** *adv* **~·ment** *n* **1** [U] being ~ed. 心醉;銷魂;着迷。**2** [C] sth which ~s; magic spell. 蠱惑之物;法術。**3** [U] charm; delight: 誘惑力;樂趣: *the ~ment of moonlight.* 月光的媚力。

en·circle /ɪn'sɜ:kl; ɪn'sɝkḷ/ *vt* [VP6A] surround; form a circle round: 環繞;包圍: *a lake ~d by trees;* 被樹林環繞着的湖; *~d by enemy forces.* 被敵軍包圍。**~·ment** *n*

en clair /ˌɒn 'kleə(r); ɑ̃'klɛr/ *adv phrase* (F) (used in telegrams, official dispatches, etc) (= *in clear*) in ordinary language, not in code or cipher. (法)(指電報,官方發出的文件等)用普通文字(非電碼或密碼)。

en·clave /'enkleɪv; 'ɛnklev/ *n* [C] territory wholly within the boundaries of another. 被外國領地包圍的土地。

en·close /ɪn'kləʊz; ɪn'kloz/ *vt* [VP6A,14] ~ *(with),* **1** put a wall, fence, etc round; shut in on all sides: 圍以牆,籬等;包圍: ~ *a garden with a wall;* 用牆將花園圍起; ~ *common land,* put fences, etc round land which has been used by everyone. 用籬等將公地圍起。 **2** put (sth) in an envelope, parcel, etc: 將(某物)裝入(信封,包裹等)中;封入: *I'll ~ your letter with mine.* 我將你的信裝在我的信內寄出。*A cheque for £5 is ~d.* 附上五鎊支票一張。*E~d, please find...,* (comm style) You will find, ~d with this.... (商業文體)玆附上…。

en·clos·ure /ɪn'kləʊʒə(r); ɪn'kloʒɚ/ *n* **1** [U] enclosing: 圍以牆籬等;包圍: ~ *of common land;* 公地之用籬圍起; [C] instance of this. 圍以牆籬或包圍的實例。 **2** [C] sth that is enclosed (esp with a letter). 裝入物;(尤指)函中附件。

en·code /ɪn'kəʊd; ɛn'kod/ *vt* [VP6A] put in a code. 譯成密碼。⇨ code *v.*

en·co·mium /ɪn'kəʊmɪəm; ɛn'komɪəm/ *n* (usu *pl*) (formal) very high praise. (通常用複數)(正式用語)極高的頌讚或讚美。

en·compass /ɪn'kʌmpəs; ɪn'kʌmpəs/ *vt* [VP6A] encircle; surround; envelop; comprise. 圍繞;包圍;包含;包括。

en·core /'ɒŋkɔ:(r); 'ɑŋkor/ *int* Repeat! Again! 再來一個!再一次! □ *vt, n* [VP6A] (call for a) repetition (of a song, etc) or further performance by the same person(s): (要求)再唱或再演: *The violinist got an* ~. 這小提琴家被聽衆要求再演奏。*The singer gave three ~s.* 這歌唱家應聽衆之請而加唱三支歌。*The audience ~d the pianist.* 聽衆要求那鋼琴家再奏一曲。

en·coun·ter /ɪn'kaʊntə(r); ɪn'kaʊntɚ/ *vt* [VP6A] find oneself faced by (danger, difficulties, etc); meet (an enemy or enemies); meet (a friend, etc) unexpectedly. 遭遇(危險,困難等);遭逢(敵人);邂逅(友人等)。□ *n* [C] ~ *(with),* sudden or unexpected (esp hostile) meeting. 遭遇(尤指與敵人)。

en·cour·age /ɪn'kʌrɪdʒ; ɪn'kɝɪdʒ/ *vt* [VP6A, 14, 17] ~ ***sb in sth/to do sth,*** give hope, courage or confidence to; support: 鼓勵;激勵;支持;援助: ~ *a man to work harder;* 鼓勵一人更加努力工作; ~ *a boy in his studies;* 鼓勵孩子用功; *feel ~d by the progress one has made.* 由於自己的進步而感到鼓舞。*Don't* ~ *him in his idle ways.* 不要助長他的懶惰。**~·ment** *n* [U] encourag-

E

ing: 鼓勵;支持: *cries of ~ment;* 鼓勵的呼聲; [C] sth that ~s: 鼓勵之物;支持之物: *Praise acts as an ~ment to the young.* 稱讚對於青年是一種鼓勵。

en·croach /ɪnˈkrəutʃ ; ɪnˈkrotʃ/ *vi* [VP3A] **~ on/ upon,** go beyond what is right or natural or desirable: 超出正當範圍;侵入;侵害: ~ *(up)on sb's rights (time, land).* 侵害某人的權利(佔用某人的時間,土地)。*The sea is ~ing (up)on the land,* washing it away. 海水浸蝕了土地。**~·ment** *n* [U] ~ing; [C] sth gained by ~ing; advance beyond the original limits: 侵入;侵害;侵佔之物;超出範圍: *~ments made by the sea upon the land.* 海水對陸地的侵蝕。

en·crust /ɪnˈkrʌst ; ɪnˈkrʌst/ *vt, vi* **1** [VP6A, 14] **~ (with),** cover with a crust; overlay (a surface) with a crust of ornamental or costly material: 包以外殼;覆以裝飾性或貴重的外層: *a gold vase ~ed with precious stones.* 鑲有寶石的金瓶。 **2** [VP2A] form into a crust. 形成殼。

en·cum·ber/ ɪnˈkʌmbə(r) ; ɪnˈkʌmbɚ/ *vt* [VP6A, 14] **~ (with), 1** get in the way of, hamper, be a burden to: 阻礙;妨害;牽累: *be ~ed with a large family;* 爲一大家庭所累; *an estate ~ed with mortgages;* 被抵押的土地; *~ oneself with unnecessary luggage.* 使自己爲不必要的行李所累。 **2** crowd; fill up: 堆滿: *a room ~ed with old and useless furniture.* 堆滿了舊而無用的傢具的房間。**en·cum·brance** /ɪnˈkʌmbrəns ; ɪnˈkʌmbrəns/ *n* [C] thing that ~s; burden. 阻礙物;累贅;負擔。

en·cyc·li·cal /ɪnˈsɪklɪkl ; ɛnˈsɪklɪkl/ *adj, n* (letter written by the Pope) for wide circulation. 爲廣佈傳閱的;傳閱的教皇通諭。

en·cy·clo·pedia (also **-paedia**) /ɪnˌsaɪkləˈpiːdɪə ; ɪnˌsaɪkləˈpidɪə/ *n* book, or set of books, giving information about every branch of knowledge, or on one subject, with articles in ABC order. 百科全書。**en·cy·clo·pedic, -paedic** /ɪnˌsaɪkləˈpiːdɪk ; ɪnˌsaɪkləˈpidɪk/ *adj* dealing with, having knowledge of, a wide variety of subjects. 有關各種學科的;學識淵博的。

end[1] /end ; ɛnd/ *n* **1** farthest or last part: 端;終點;末梢: *the end of a road/stick/line, etc;* 路之終點(杖,線等之末端); *the house at the end of the street;* 在街道末端的房屋; (attrib) (形容用法) *the end house;* 最末尾的房屋;最後面的房屋; *the end carriage,* the last carriage in a train; 末節車(火車之末節車廂); *the west/east end of a town,* the parts in the west/east; 城之西(東)區; *the ends of the earth,* most remote parts, parts difficult of access. 最遙遠的地方;天涯海角。***begin/start at the wrong end,*** in the wrong way, at a wrong point. 開始即錯。***get hold of the wrong end of the stick,*** have a completely mistaken idea of what is intended or meant. 完全誤解。***keep one's ˈend up,*** (GB) continue cheerful, full of fighting spirit, in the face of difficulties, etc. (英)面對困難等時能保持愉快和戰鬪精神。***at a loose end,*** unoccupied, having nothing important or interesting to do. 無事可做。***on end,*** **(a)** upright: 豎起;直立着: *Place the barrel/box on (its) end.* 將這桶(箱子)豎起來放。*The ghost story set their hair on end.* 那個鬼故事使他們毛髮豎立。 **(b)** continuously: 繼續地: *two hours on end.* 一連兩小時。***end on,*** with the ends meeting: 兩端相遇: *The two ships collided end on,* The stern (or bows) of one struck the stern (or bows) of the other. 這兩條船的船尾(或船首)相碰。***end to end,*** in a line with the ends touching: 頭尾相接地成一行: *Arrange the tables end to end.* 把這些桌子銜接着擺起來。***go (in) off the ˈdeep end,*** express strong feeling without trying to control it. 情緒失去控制; 變得非常激動。 ***make (both) ends meet,*** live within one's income; balance one's income with one's expenditure. 量入爲出; 使收支相抵。***(reach) the end of the line/road,*** (fig) (reach) the point at which no more of what has happened before is possible or desirable. (喻)到此爲止。 **2** small piece that remains; remnant: 殘片;殘餘: *candle ends;* 蠟燭頭; *a cigarette end.* 香煙頭。**ˈend·papers,** (usu) blank pages pasted to the inside covers of a book. 襯頁(書籍卷首卷尾的空白頁)。 ⇨ odds(5). **3** finish; conclusion: 結束;結局: *at the end of the day/the century;* 在一日(世紀)之末; *the end of a story/adventure.* 故事(冒險)的結局。*We shall never hear the end of the matter,* It will be talked about for a long time to come. 我們將永遠聽不到這件事情的結尾(在未來的長時期中,此事將談論下去)。***(be) at an end; at the end (of):*** 結束;窮盡;到…之盡頭: *The war was at an end,* finished. 戰爭結束了。*She was at the end of her patience/tether,* had no patience left. 她已忍無可忍了。*He was at the end of his resources.* 他已智窮力竭(山窮水盡)了。***come to an end,*** finish: 結束; 完畢: *The meeting came to an end at last.* 會議終於結束了。***come to a bad end,*** be led by one's actions to ruin, disgrace, punishment, etc: 遭到惡報; 得到報應: *If you don't give up crime, you'll come to a bad end,* eg be sent to prison for life as a murderer. 如果你不停止犯罪,你會得到報應的(例如因行兇而被判處無期徒刑)。 ***draw to an end:*** *As the year drew to its end....* 當歲暮之時…。***make an end of sth; put an end to sth,*** finish it, get rid of it (according to context): 結束一事;消除一事物(根據上下文確定其意義): *We must put an end to these abuses.* 我們必須除去這些弊端。*Death put an end to his wicked career.* 死亡結束了他邪惡的一生。***in the end,*** finally, at last: 最後;終於: *He tried many ways of earning a living; in the end he became a farm labourer.* 他嘗試過許多謀生的方式,最後他做了農場工人。***no end of,*** (colloq) very many or much, very great, etc: (俗)很多;非常: *We met no end of interesting people.* 我們遇到很多有趣的人。*He thinks no end of himself,* has a high opinion of his abilities, etc. 他自命不凡。***without end,*** never reaching an end: 無盡的;無休止的: *We had trouble without end.* 我們有無盡的困難。 **4** death: 死亡: *He's nearing his end,* is dying. 他離死期不遠了。*She came to an untimely end,* died young. 她夭折了。 **5** purpose, aim: 目的; 目標: *gain/win/achieve one's end(s);* 達到目的; *With this end in view;* 以此爲目的; *for/to this end;* 爲達到此一目的; *to the end that,* in order that; 爲了;其目的在於; *to no end,* in vain. 無結果;徒勞。***The end justifies the means,*** (prov) for a good purpose even wrong or unfair methods may be allowed. (諺)祇要目的正當,可以不擇手段。

end[2] /end ; ɛnd/ *vi, vt* [VP2A, C, 3A, 6A, 15B] (cause to) come to an end; reach an end: 結束; 終止: *The road ends here,* goes no farther. 這條路到此爲止了。*How does the story end?* 這故事的結局如何? *Let's end our quarrel.* 我們不要再吵了。***end in sth,*** have as a result: 以…爲結果: *The scheme ended in failure.* 這計畫終於失敗了。*He ended his days in peace,* the last period of his life was peaceful. 他在平靜中度過了晚年。***end (sth) off,*** finish: 結束: *He ended off his speech with some amusing stories.* 他以一些有趣的故事結束了他的演說。***end (sth) up,*** finish: 結束: *If you continue to steal, you'll end up in prison,* will one day be sent to prison. 如果你繼續行竊,總有一天你要坐牢。*We started with soup, and had fruit to end up with.* 我們開始時喝湯,最後吃水果。 **end-all** ⇨ be[3](4). **end·ing** *n* [C] end, esp of a word or a story. 終止;末尾;(尤指)字尾;故事的結局。

en·dan·ger /ɪnˈdeɪndʒə(r) ; ɪnˈdendʒɚ/ *vt* [VP6A] put in danger; cause danger to: 使受危險;危及: *~ one's chances of success.* 危及成功的機會。

en·dear /ɪnˈdɪə(r) ; ɪnˈdɪr/ *vt* [VP14] ***~ sb/oneself to,*** make dear or liked: 使受喜愛;使爲人愛: *~ oneself to everyone;* 使自己爲大家所喜愛; *an ~ing smile.* 可愛的微笑。**~·ing·ly** *adv* **~·ment** *n* [C, U] act, word, expression, of affection: 表示親愛的行爲,言語或表情: *a term of ~ment*, eg *darling;* 表示親密的稱呼(例如: 親愛的); *the ~ments that a wife expects from her husband.* 妻子期望於丈夫的親愛的表示。

en·deav·our (US =-vor) /ɪn'devə(r); ɪn'dɛvɚ/ *n* [C] (formal) effort, attempt: (正式用語)努力;盡力;企圖: *Please make every ~ to be early.* 請盡量早點。*His ~s to persuade her to go with him failed.* 他盡力勸她同他一道去,但是失敗了。□ *vi* [VP 4A] (formal) try: (正式用語)試圖;努力: *~ to please one's wife.* 盡量使妻子快樂。

en·demic /en'demɪk; ɛn'dɛmɪk/ *n, adj* (disease) prevalent or often recurring in a country or area, or among a particular class of people, eg miners. 某一國家,地區或人群(例如礦工)經常有的(疾病);地方性的(病)。⇨ epidemic.

en·dive /'endɪv *US:* -daɪv; 'ɛndaɪv/ *n* [C] kind of curly-leaved chicory, used as salad. 菊萵苣(生菜食品)。

end·less /'endlɪs; 'ɛndlɪs/ *adj* having no end; never stopping: 無窮盡的; 永不停的: *a woman with ~ patience;* 有無限耐心的女子; *an ~ belt/chain/cable,* one with the ends joined, to pass continuously over wheels, etc to transmit power in a machine. 環帶(鏈,纜)(兩端相連接,繞於輪等之上,循環不息地轉動,以傳遞動力)。**~·ly** *adv*

en·dorse /ɪn'dɔ:s; ɪn'dɔrs/ *vt* [VP6A] **1** write one's name on the back of (a cheque); write comments, etc in, on the back of (a document): 簽名於(支票)的背面;背書;批註(文件): *His driving licence has been ~d,* a record of a motoring offence has been entered in it. 他的駕駛執照上曾有違規的記錄。 **2** approve, support a claim, statement, etc. 認可;贊同(要求,言論等)。**~·ment** *n* [U] endorsing; [C] instance of this; statement, etc that ~s. 簽名於支票背面;背書;簽註;認可;簽註或認可的記載。

en·dow /ɪn'daʊ; ɪn'daʊ/ *vt* [VP6A, 14] ~ ***(with),*** **1** give money, property, etc to provide a regular income for (eg a college): 捐贈(金錢,財產等,例如捐助基金興辦大學): *~ a bed in a hospital;* 在醫院中捐助一個病床(即經常資助一名住院病人的全部醫療費用); *~ a school.* 捐助基金辦一學校。 **2** (usu passive) (通常用被動語態) ***be ~ed with,*** possess naturally, be born with (qualities, etc): 賦有(資質等): *be ~ed by nature with great talents.* 賦有很大的才能。**~·ment** *n* **1** [U] ~ing. 捐贈;捐助。 **2** [C] money, property, etc given to provide an income: 捐贈的金錢,財產等: *The Oxford and Cambridge colleges have numerous ~ments.* 牛津和劍橋大學獲有許多的捐款。 **3** [C] talent: 禀賦;才能: *natural ~ments,* eg a good ear for music. 天資;天賦(例如辨音的能力)。

en·due /ɪn'dju: *US:* -'du:; ɪn'dju/ *vt* [VP14] (usu passive) (通常用被動語態) ***be ~d with,*** be furnished, supplied, with. 賦予;供以。

en·dur·ance /ɪn'djʊərəns *US:* -'dʊə-; ɪn'djʊrəns/ *n* [U] ability to endure: 忍耐力: *He showed remarkable powers of ~.* 他顯示了非凡的忍耐力。*He came to the end of his ~.* 他已忍無可忍了。***past/beyond ~,*** to an extent that can no longer be endured. 忍無可忍的。'**~ test,** test of how long sb or sth can endure sth. 耐力試驗;持久測驗。

en·dure /ɪn'djʊə(r) *US:* -'dʊər; ɪn'djʊr/ *vt, vi* **1** [VP6A, 2A, C] suffer, undergo pain, hardship, etc: 忍受;忍耐(痛苦,艱難等): *~ toothache.* 忍受牙痛。*If help does not come, we must ~ to the end,* suffer until death comes. 如無援助到來,我們必須忍耐到底(即到死爲止)。 **2** [VP6A, D, 17, esp in *neg*] bear; put up with: (尤用於否定句)容忍: *I can't ~ that woman.* 我無法容忍那個女人。*She can't ~ seeing/~ to see animals cruelly treated.* 她不能容忍看到動物受虐待。 **3** [VP2A] last; continue in existence: 持久;持續: *as long as life ~s;* 一直到死;有生之年; *fame that will ~ for ever.* 永垂不朽的聲名。**en·dur·able** /-rəbl; -rəbḷ/ *adj* that can be ~d; bearable. 可忍受的;可容忍的。**en·dur·ing** *adj* lasting: 持久的: *an enduring peace.* 持久的和平。**en·dur·ingly** *adv*

end·ways /'endweɪz; 'ɛnd,wez/, **end·wise** /-waɪz; -,waɪz/ *adv* with the end towards the spectator; end forward; end to end. 末端朝旁觀者;末端向前;兩端相接。

en·ema /'enɪmə; 'ɛnəmə/ *n* (syringe used for an) injection of liquid into the rectum. 灌腸;灌腸器。

en·emy /'enəmɪ; 'ɛnəmɪ/ *n* (*pl* -mies) ~ ***(of/to),*** **1** one who tries or wishes to harm or attack; one who has ill feeling or hatred towards sb or sth: 敵人;仇人;仇敵: *A successful man often has many enemies.* 一個成功的人往往有許多敵人。*Don't make an ~ of him,* Do nothing that will cause him to be your ~. 不要使他變成你的敵人。*He's an ~ of/to reform.* 他反對改革。 **2** ***the ~,*** armed forces of a nation with which one's country is at war: 敵軍: *~-occupied territory.* 敵軍佔領的土地。*The ~ were forced to retreat;* 敵軍被迫撤退了; (attrib) of the ~: (形容用法)敵人的;敵軍的: *~ aircraft/ships.* 敵軍的飛機(艦船)。 **3** member of such a hostile force. 敵軍中的一員。**4** anything that harms or injures: 爲害之事物: *Laziness is his chief ~.* 懶惰是他的主要敵人。*Idleness is an ~ to discipline,* weakens discipline. 閒散危害紀律。

en·ergy /'enədʒɪ; 'ɛnɚdʒɪ/ *n* **1** [U] force, vigour; capacity to do things and get things done: 精力;活力;能力: *He had so much ~ that he did the work of three men.* 他的精力旺盛,能做三個人的工作。*He's full of ~.* 他的精力充沛。 **2** (in *pl,* -gies) (person's) powers available for working, or as used in working: (複)(個人的)工作能力: *apply/devote all one's energies to a task.* 傾全力去做一工作。 **3** [U] (science) capacity for, power of, doing work: (科學)能量;能: *electrical ~;* 電能; *kinetic ~;* 動能; *potential ~.* 位能;勢能。**en·er·getic** /,enə'dʒetɪk; ,ɛnɚ'dʒɛtɪk/ *adj* full of, done with, ~(1). 精力充沛的;需要精力去做的;奮力完成的。**en·er·geti·cally** /-klɪ; -klɪ/ *adv*

en·er·vate /'enəveɪt; 'ɛnɚ,vet/ *vt* [VP6A] cause to lose physical (sometimes moral) strength: 使失去身體的,精神的力量; 使衰弱: *a country with an enervating climate.* 其氣候使人衰弱無力的國家。

en famille /,ɒn fæ'mi:; ,anfæ'mi/ *adv* (F) at home; among one's family. (法)在家;在家中。

en·fant ter·rible /,ɒnfɒn te'ri:bl; ,anfante'ribl/ *n* (F) young or new person whose behaviour, ideas, etc cause annoyance or embarrassment to those who hold conventional opinions. (法)其行爲,思想等使持有傳統思想的人厭惡或困窘的青年或新潮派的人;肆無忌憚的人。

en·feeble /ɪn'fi:bl; ɪn'fibl/ *vt* [VP6A] make feeble. 使衰弱。

en·fold /ɪn'fəʊld; ɪn'fold/ *vt* [VP6A, 14] ~ ***sb (in),*** enclose (esp in one's arms). 擁抱。

en·force /ɪn'fɔ:s; ɪn'fɔrs/ *vt* [VP6A, 14] **1** ~ ***(on/upon),*** compel obedience to; make effective; impose: 迫使服從;實施;厲行: *~ a law;* 實施法律; *~ discipline/silence;* 强制執行紀律(迫令安靜); *~ a course of action upon sb.* 以一項行動强行加諸某人。 **2** give force or strength to: 加强: *Have you any statistics that would ~ your argument?* 你有無任何統計資料可加强你的論點? **~·able** /-əbl; -əbl/ *adj* that can be ~d. 可强行的;可實施的。**~·ment** *n* [U] enforcing or being ~d: 强制;實施;加强: *strict ~ment of a new law.* 一項新法律的嚴格執行。

en·fran·chise /ɪn'fræntʃaɪz; ɛn'fræntʃaɪz/ *vt* [VP 6A] **1** give political rights to (esp, the right to vote at parliamentary elections): 給予政治上的權利(尤指選舉國會議員的投票權): *In Great Britain women were ~d in 1918.* 在英國婦女於1918年獲得選舉議員的投票權。 **2** set free (slaves). 解放(奴隸)。**~·ment**

E

/ɪnˈfræntʃɪzmənt ; ɛnˈfræntʃɪzmənt/ *n*

en·gage /ɪnˈgeɪdʒ ; ɪnˈgedʒ/ *vt, vi* **1** [VP6A, 16B] obtain the right to employ: 雇用: *~ a servant;* 雇用一僕人; *~ sb as a guide/as an interpreter;* 雇用一人做嚮導(通譯); get the right to use or occupy: 使用;佔用;預定: *~ a taxi* (*hire* is the preferred word). 租一計程車 (hire 較常用)。**2** [VP7A, 17, 9, 3A] promise; undertake; bind (oneself); guarantee: 允諾;答應;約束(自己);擔保: *I will ~ (myself) to manage the business if you will ~ (yourself) to provide the capital.* 如果你答應出資本,我答應經管這個事業。*Can you ~ that all his statements are trustworthy?* 你能擔保他的話都可靠嗎? *That is more than I can ~ for,* guarantee, take responsibility for. 那事我不能擔保。**3** [VP3A] *~ in,* take part in; busy oneself with: 從事;忙於: *~ in politics.* 從事於政治。**4** *be ~d to/to marry,* be bound by a promise to marry: 訂婚: *Tom and Anne are ~d.* 湯姆與安訂婚了。*Tom is ~d to Anne.* 湯姆已與安訂婚。 **5** *be ~d (in),* be busy, be occupied (with); take part in: 忙於;做着;參加: *be ~d in business/in writing a novel.* 忙着工作(寫小說)。*My time is fully ~d.* 我的時間完全被佔去了。*The line/number is ~d,* (telephoning) Someone else is using the line. (電話用語)電話線(號碼)被佔着(有人在講話)。 **6** [VP6A] (usu passive) attract: (通常用被動語態)吸引: *Nothing ~s his attention for long.* 沒有事物可長久吸引他的注意。*Her attention was ~d by the display of new sweaters in the shop window.* 她的注意力被商店櫥窗內展覽的新毛線衫吸引去了。 **7** [VP6A, 2A] attack; begin fighting with: 攻擊;與…交戰: *The general did not ~ the enemy.* 那將軍未與敵軍交戰。*Our orders are to ~ at once.* 我們的命令是卽刻進攻。 **8** [VP2A, 3A, 6A, 14] *~ (with),* (of parts of a machine) lock together; (cause to) fit into: (指機器各部)啣接;(使)嚙合: *The two cog-wheels ~.* 這兩個齒輪相嚙合。*The teeth of one wheel ~ with those of the other.* 一輪之齒與另一輪之齒相嚙合。(motoring) (駕車) *E~ the clutch/the first gear.* 使離合器嚙合(掛第一擋)。**en·gag·ing** *adj* likely to ~ the attention; charming: 引人注意的;美麗動人的: *an engaging smile/manner.* 迷人的一笑(姿態)。**en·gag·ingly** *adv*

en·gage·ment /ɪnˈgeɪdʒmənt ; ɪnˈgedʒmənt/ *n* [C] **1** (formal) promise or undertaking, esp one that is formal or made in writing: (正式用語)約定;契約: *He has only enough money to meet his ~s,* to make the payments he has undertaken to make. 他僅有約定要付的款。 **2** agreement to marry: 婚約: *Their ~ was announced in the papers.* 他們訂婚的消息登報了。**ˈ~ ring,** one given by a man to a woman when they agree to marry. 訂婚戒指。 **3** arrangement to go somewhere, meet someone or do sth, at a fixed time: 約會: *I have numerous ~s for next week.* 我在下週有很多約會。 **4** battle: 戰鬪;交戰: *The admiral tried to bring about an ~,* to make the enemy fight. 海軍上將設法迫敵人交戰。 **5** [C, U] engaging (of part of a machine, etc): (指機器之一部分等)嚙合: *~ of first gear.* 第一排擋的嚙合。

en·gen·der /ɪnˈdʒendə(r) ; ɪnˈdʒɛndɚ/ *vt* [VP6A] be the cause of (a situation or condition): 產生(某種局勢或情況);造成: *Crime is often ~ed by poverty.* 犯罪常因貧窮而產生。

en·gine /ˈendʒɪn ; ˈɛndʒən/ *n* **1** machine that converts energy into power or motion: 引擎;發動機;機車: *a ˈsteam-/ˈoil-~;* 蒸汽機(石油發動機); *a new ~ (petrol or diesel) for a motor-vehicle.* 機動車輛的新引擎(汽油或柴油者)。⇨ the illus at motor. 參看 motor 之挿圖。**ˈ~-driver** *n* (esp) man who drives a railway ~. (尤指)火車司機。 **2** (old use) machine or instrument: (舊用法)機器;器械: *~s of war,* eg cannons. 戰爭工具(例如大砲)。

en·gin·eer /ˌendʒɪˈnɪə(r) ; ˌɛndʒəˈnɪr/ *n* **1** person who works in a branch of engineering; person who designs engines, machines, bridges, railways, docks, etc: 工程師;設計引擎,機器,橋樑,鐵路,船塢等的人: *a civil/mining/electrical ~.* 土木(採礦,電機)工程師。 **2** skilled and trained person in control of an engine or engines: 機師;機工: *the chief ~ of a ship;* 船上的輪機長; (US) man who drives a locomotive. (美)火車司機。 **3** member of the branch of an army (called **the E~s**) that builds roads and bridges, controls communications, etc. 工兵。□ *vt, vi* [VP6A, 2A] **1** act as an ~; construct or control as an ~. 做工程師或機械師;建造;監督。 **2** (colloq) arrange or bring about skilfully: (俗)巧妙地安排或完成: *~ a scheme/plot;* 巧妙地擬定一項計畫(陰謀); *~ that....* 巧妙地安排…。

en·gin·eer·ing /ˌendʒɪˈnɪərɪŋ ; ˌɛndʒəˈnɪrɪŋ/ *n* [U] the application of science for the control and use of power, esp by the use of machines; the technology, work or profession of an engineer: 工程學; 工程; 工程業: *chemical/mechanical/electrical ~;* 化學工程(機械工程;電機工程); *a triumph of ~,* eg a magnificent bridge; 十分成功的工程(例如一座宏偉的橋樑); *an ~ works.* (電機等)工程廠。

Eng·lish /ˈɪŋglɪʃ ; ˈɪŋglɪʃ/ *n* [U] the ~ language. 英語;英文。***in plain ~,*** in language so simple that the meaning is quite clear. 用淺易明白的英語。**the ˌQueen's/ˌKing's ˈ~,** standard, educated English. 標準英語;純正英語。□ *adj* **1** of England. 英國的;英格蘭的。**the ~,** (*pl*) ~ people. (複)英國人。 **2** of, written in, spoken in, the ~ language. 英語的;用英文寫的;用英語說的。**~·man** /-mən ; -mən/ (*pl* -men) *n* **~·woman** /-wʊmən ; -ˌwʊmən/ (*pl* -women) *n*

en·graft /ɪnˈgrɑːft *US:* -ˈgræft ; ɛnˈgræft/ *vt* [VP6A, 14] *~ (into/on/upon),* insert (a shoot of one tree into another). 接(枝)。*~ (in),* (fig) implant (principles in the mind or character). (喻)灌輸(原則至心靈或性格中)。

en·grave /ɪnˈgreɪv ; ɪnˈgrev/ *vt* **1** [VP6A, 14] *~ on/upon,* cut or carve (lines, words, designs, on) a hard surface: 雕刻(線條,文字,圖案)於一硬面上: *~ a design on a metal plate* (for printing); 刻圖案於金屬板上(印刷用); *a name ~d on a tombstone.* 刻於墓碑上的姓名。 **2** [VP14] *~ with,* mark such surfaces with (an inscription, etc). 將(文字等)刻於硬面上。 **3** [VP14] *~ on/upon,* (fig) impress deeply (on the memory or mind). (喻)深印於(心上);使銘記。**en·graver** *n* person who ~s designs, etc on stone, metal, etc. 雕刻師。**en·grav·ing** /ɪnˈgreɪvɪŋ ; ɪnˈgrevɪŋ/ *n* [U] art of cutting or carving designs on metal, stone, etc; [C] copy of a picture, design, etc printed from an ~d plate. 雕刻術;雕板印成的圖畫,圖案等。

en·gross /ɪnˈgrəʊs ; ɪnˈgros/ *vt* **1** [VP6A] (usu passive) take up all the time or attention of: (通常用被動語態)佔去…所有的時間或注意力;使全神貫注: *~ed in his work;* 全神貫注於他的工作; *an ~ing story.* 引人入勝的故事。 **2** (legal) write (eg a legal document) in large letters or in formal legal style. (法律)用大字或正式的法律文體寫(法律文件等)。

en·gulf /ɪnˈgʌlf ; ɪnˈgʌlf/ *vt* [VP6A] swallow up (as in a gulf): 吞沒(如被漩渦吞噬): *a boat ~ed in/by the sea/waves.* 被海浪吞沒了的小舟。

en·hance /ɪnˈhɑːns *US:* -ˈhæns ; ɪnˈhæns/ *vt* [VP6A] add to (the value, attraction, powers, price, etc). 增加(價值,吸引力,力量,價格等)。

enigma /ɪˈnɪgmə ; ɪˈnɪgmə/ *n* [C] question, person, thing, circumstance, that is puzzling. 謎;令人迷惑的問題,人物或情況。 **enig·matic** /ˌenɪgˈmætɪk ; ˌɛnɪgˈmætɪk/ *adj* puzzling; mysterious. 令人迷惑的;神祕的。**enig·mati·cally** /-klɪ ; -klɪ/ *adv*

en·join /ɪnˈdʒɔɪn ; ɪnˈdʒɔɪn/ *vt* [VP6A, 17, 9, 14] *~ (on sb),* give an order for; urge; prescribe; command: 命令;催促;指示;吩咐: *~ silence/obedience;* 命令肅靜(服從); *~ on sb the necessity for economy;* 囑咐某人須節儉; *~ a duty on sb;* 交給某人一項責任; *~ sb to obey the rules;* 命令某人遵守

規則; ~ *that sth should be done.* 下令做某件事。

en·joy /ɪnˈdʒɔɪ ; ɪnˈdʒɔɪ/ *vt* [VP6A, C] **1** get pleasure from; take delight in: 享受…之樂趣;樂於: ~ *one's dinner.* 津津有味地吃飯。*I've ~ed talking to you about old times.* 我很高興曾經和你話舊。**2** have as an advantage or benefit: 享有: ~ *good health/a good income.* 享有健康之福(好的收入)。**3** ~ ***oneself***, experience pleasure; be happy. 感到快樂;玩得愉快。**~·able** /-əbl ; -əbl̩/ *adj* giving joy; pleasant. 令人快樂的;令人愉快的。**~·ably** /-əblɪ ; -əblɪ/ *adv*

en·joy·ment /ɪnˈdʒɔɪmənt ; ɪnˈdʒɔɪmənt/ *n* **1** [U] pleasure; joy; satisfaction: 享樂;快樂;滿意: *to think only of/live for ~.* 祇想到(生活祇爲了)享樂。**2** [U] possession and use: 享受;享有: *be in the ~ of the full possession of one's faculties,* be physically and mentally well. 享有身心健康。**3** [C] sth that gives joy and pleasure. 令人快樂的事物;樂事。

en·kindle /ɪnˈkɪndl ; ɛnˈkɪndl̩/ *vt* [VP6A] cause (flame, passion, etc) to flare up; inflame (with passion, etc). 使燃起(火焰,激情等);煽動;動之以激情。

en·large /ɪnˈlɑːdʒ ; ɪnˈlɑrdʒ/ *vt, vi* **1** [VP6A, 2A] make or become larger: 擴大; 增大: ~ *a photograph/one's house.* 放大相片(擴建房屋)。*Will this print ~ well,* Will it be good if it is reproduced on a larger scale? 這張照片可以放大得好嗎? **2** [VP3A] ~ ***on/upon***, say or write more about: 詳述: *I need not ~ upon this matter; you all know my views.* 我不需要詳述此事;你們都知道我的意見。**~·ment** *n* [U] enlarging or being ~d; [C] result of this, esp a photograph. 擴大;增大;擴大的結果(尤指放大的照片)。

en·lighten /ɪnˈlaɪtn ; ɪnˈlaɪtn̩/ *vt* [VP6A, 14] ~ ***(on)***, give more knowledge to; free from ignorance, misunderstanding or false beliefs: 教導;啓迪;開導: *Can you ~ me on this subject,* help me to understand it better? 你能幫助我明白這一問題嗎? **~ed** *part adj* free from ignorance, prejudice, superstition, etc: 文明的; 開明的; 不迷信的; 開通的: *in these ~ed days.* 値此文明的時代。**~·ment** *n* [U] ~ing or being ~ed: 教導; 啓迪; 開導; 開明; 開通: *living in an age of ~ment;* 生活於文明的時代; *work for the ~ment of mankind.* 爲啓迪人類而努力。**the E~ment,** the period (esp 18th c) when men believed that reason and science (and not religion) would advance human progress. 思想啓蒙時期(尤指十八世紀,人類相信理智和科學(而非宗教)爲推動人類進步的力量)。

en·list /ɪnˈlɪst ; ɪnˈlɪst/ *vt, vi* **1** [VP6A, 14, 16B, 2A, C] ~ ***(in)***, take into, enter, the armed forces: 使入伍;從軍: ~ *a recruit;* 徵募一新兵; ~ *as a volunteer;* 志願從軍; *~ed men,* soldiers, etc; 士兵; ~ *in the army.* 從軍。**2** [VP6A, 14] ~ ***(in/for)***, obtain; get the support of: 獲得;得到…的支持: ~ *sb's sympathy and help in a charitable cause/for the Red Cross.* 獲某人對一慈善運動(紅十字會)的同情與贊助。**~·ment** *n* [U] ~ing or being ~ed; [C] instance of this. 使入伍;從軍;被徵入伍;獲得。

en·liven /ɪnˈlaɪvn ; ɪnˈlaɪvən/ *vt* [VP6A] make lively: 使活潑;使有生氣: *How can we ~ the party?* 我們怎樣使這聚會熱鬧?

en masse /ˌɒn ˈmæs ; ɛnˈmæs/ *adv* (F) in a mass; all together. (法)全體;一齊。

en·mesh /ɪnˈmeʃ ; ɛnˈmɛʃ/ *vt* [VP6A, 14] ~ ***(in)***, take (as) in a net; entangle. 使陷入網;使陷入。

en·mity /ˈenmətɪ ; ˈɛnmətɪ/ *n* [U] condition of being an enemy; hatred: 仇恨;憎恨: *be at ~ with one's neighbours;* 與鄰人不睦; [C] (*pl* -ties) particular feeling of hostility or hatred. 某種仇恨心。

en·noble /ɪˈnəʊbl ; ɪˈnobl̩/ *vt* [VP6A] **1** make (sb) a member of the nobility. 使(某人)成爲貴族;授以爵位。**2** (fig) make morally noble; make dignified. (喻)使崇高;使高貴。**~·ment** *n*

en·nui /ɒnˈwiː ; ˈɑnwi/ *n* [U] (F) weariness of mind caused by lack of any interesting occupation; [C] instance of this. (法)(因缺乏有興趣的工作而)倦怠;無聊。

enor·mity /ɪˈnɔːmətɪ ; ɪˈnɔrmətɪ/ *n* **1** [U] great wickedness: 極惡;兇惡: *Does he realize the ~ of his offence?* 他知道他的罪惡深重嗎? **2** [C] (*pl* -ties) serious crime. 嚴重的罪行;大罪。**3** [U] immense size: 極大: *the ~ of the problem of feeding the world's population in* AD *2000.* 公元2000年供應全球人口糧食的大問題。

enor·mous /ɪˈnɔːməs ; ɪˈnɔrməs/ *adj* very great; immense: 極大的;巨大的;廣大的: *an ~ sum of money.* 巨額金錢。**~·ly** *adv* to an ~ extent: 極大地;巨大地: *The town has changed ~ly during recent years.* 近年來這城市大爲改變了。**~·ness** *n*

enough /ɪˈnʌf ; əˈnʌf/ *adj, n* (of a quantity) as great as is needed; as much or as many as necessary (數量)足够;充分 (as an *adj* ~ occurs in the pattern 做形容詞用時 enough 的句型爲 ~ + *noun* or *noun*+ ~): *There's ~ food/food ~ for everybody.* 有足够大家吃的食物。*Have you had ~ peanuts?* 你花生吃够了嗎? (as a *noun* ~ occurs in the pattern 做名詞用時 enough 的句型爲 ~ ***(of the/this/that/his etc + noun) (for sb/to do sth)***): *Will £5 be ~ for you/~ to cover the journey?* 五鎊够你用嗎/够你旅行嗎? *Have you had ~ of this TV programme yet?* 這電視節目你看够了嗎? *I've had ~ of your grumbling and groaning.* 我已聽够了你的抱怨和牢騷。***~ is as good as a feast,*** be glad that you have had as much as you needed. 吃得剛飽就等於吃一頓盛宴;足食猶如盛宴。***more than ~,*** too much. 過多;太多。□ *adv of degree* 表示程度的副詞 (placed after *adjj, advv* and *pp;* also after a *noun* used as an *adj,* as when *fool* means *foolish;* used in the pattern 置於形容詞,副詞和過去分詞之後;亦置於做形容詞用的名詞之後,如 fool 作 foolish 解時;用於下列句型 *adj* + ~ ***(for sb/to do sth)***) **1** to the right or necessary degree; sufficiently: 充分地;足够地: *The meat is not cooked ~.* 這肉火候不够。*Are you warm ~?* 你覺得够暖和嗎? *You know well ~* (= quite well) *what I mean.* 你很懂得我的意思。*I was fool* (= foolish) *~ to believe her.* 我相信了她,眞是够傻了。*He wasn't man* (= manly) *~ to admit his mistake.* 他沒有勇於認錯的丈夫氣概。*You're old ~ to know better.* 你已屆懂事的年齡了。*This book is easy ~ for a six-year-old child to read.* 這本書容易到六歲的孩子都可以讀得懂。**2** sometimes used in a disparaging way, suggesting that sth could be better, etc: 有時含有貶抑之意,暗示某事可以做得更好等: *It's interesting ~ in its way,* moderately interesting. 還有一點趣味。*She sings well ~,* indicating faint praise. 她唱得還可以(表示勉强的稱讚)。**3** ***oddly/curiously/strangely etc ~,*** in a way that is odd, etc. 很奇怪地。***sure ~,*** in a degree that satisfies doubt; as one expected. 確實地;正如所料。

en·plane /enˈpleɪn ; ɛnˈplen/ *vi, vt* ⇨ emplane.

en·quire, en·quiry /ɪnˈkwaɪə(r), ɪnˈkwaɪərɪ ; ɪnˈkwaɪr, ɪnˈkwaɪrɪ/ *v, n* = inquire, inquiry.

en·rage /ɪnˈreɪdʒ ; ɪnˈredʒ/ *vt* [VP6A] fill with rage: 激怒;觸怒: *~d at/by sb's stupidity.* 因某人的愚蠢而憤怒。

en·rap·ture /ɪnˈræptʃə(r) ; ɪnˈræptʃɚ/ *vt* [VP6A] fill with great delight or joy. 使狂喜。

en·rich /ɪnˈrɪtʃ ; ɪnˈrɪtʃ/ *vt* [VP6A, 14] ~ ***(with)***, make rich; improve in quality, flavour, etc: 使豐富;(在品質,味道等方面)改進: ~ *the mind (with knowledge);* (以知識)充實心智; *soil ~ed with manure.* 由於施肥料而肥沃的土壤。**~·ment** *n*

en·roll, en·rol /ɪnˈrəʊl ; ɪnˈrol/ *vt, vi* [VP6A, 14, 16B, 2A, C] ~ ***(in)***, (cause to) become a member (of): (使)成爲會員或社員; 登記; 註冊: *to ~ in evening classes;* 在夜間部註冊上課; *to ~ (sb) as a member of a society/club;* 登記(某人)爲會員; *to be ~ed in a register of electors;* 被登入選舉人名册; *to ~ new students.* 收新生。**~·ment** *n* [U] ~-

E

ing or being ～ed; [C] number ～ed: 登記爲會員；註册；登記或註册的人數: *a school with an ～ment of 800 pupils.* 有八百學生註册的學校。

en route /ˌɒn ˈruːt ; ɑnˈrut/ *adv* ～ ***(from／to),*** on the way (from／to): 在途中: *We stopped at Paris ～ from Rome to London.* 我們從羅馬至倫敦的途中曾在巴黎停留。

en·sconce /ɪnˈskɒns ; ɛnˈskɑns/ *vt* [VP14] ～ ***oneself in,*** establish oneself in (a safe, secret, comfortable, etc place). 安置(自己於一安全,隱祕,舒適等之地)。

en·semble /ɒnˈsɒmbl ; ɑnˈsɑmbl/ *n* [C] (F) **1** sth viewed as a whole; general effect. (法) 整體; 總效果。 **2** (music) passage of music in which all the performers unite; group of musicians who play together regularly (smaller than an orchestra). (音樂)重奏;合奏;合奏的一段;經常在一起演奏的樂隊(小於管絃樂隊)。 **3** (trade use) woman's matched clothing outfit (dress, coat, etc designed to be worn together). (商業用語)婦女之全套服裝(衣服,上衣等設計在一起者)。

en·shrine /ɪnˈʃraɪn ; ɪnˈʃraɪn/ *vt* [VP6A, 14] ～ ***(in),*** (formal) place or keep in, or as in, a shrine; serve as a shrine for: (正式用語) 置於神龕內;奉祀於神殿內;奉爲神聖;珍藏;作爲…的神龕或廟堂: *the casket that ～s the relics;* 珍藏遺物的小箱; *memories ～d in her heart;* 深藏在她內心的記憶; *basic human rights ～d in the constitution.* 憲法所孕藏的人類的基本權力。

en·shroud /ɪnˈʃraʊd ; ɛnˈʃraud/ *vt* [VP6A] cover completely: 遮蔽;掩蔽: *hills ～ed in mist.* 爲霧所遮蔽的群山。

en·sign /ˈensən ; ˈɛnsn̩/ *n* **1** (esp naval) flag or banner: (尤指海軍的) 旗幟: *white ～*, used by the Royal Navy; 英國皇家海軍旗(白色); *red ～*, used by British merchant ships; 英國商船旗(紅色); *blue ～*, used by the Royal Naval Reserve. 英國皇家海軍預備艦隊旗(藍色)。 **2** (US) lowest commissioned officer in the navy. (美)海軍少尉。 **3** /ˈensaɪn ; ˈɛnsaɪn/ (old uses) badge or symbol (showing office, authority, etc); infantry officer who carried the regimental colours. (舊用法) 徽章(表示職位,權威等);陸軍團中的掌旗官。

en·si·lage /ˈensɪlɪdʒ ; ˈɛnsḷɪdʒ/ *n* = silage.

en·slave /ɪnˈsleɪv ; ɪnˈslev/ *vt* [VP6A] make a slave of. 使成爲奴隸;奴役。 **～·ment** *n*

en·snare /ɪnˈsneə(r) ; ɛnˈsnɛr/ *vt* [VP6A, 14] ～ ***(in),*** catch in, or as in, a snare or trap. 使入羅網;使入陷阱。

en·sue /ɪnˈsjuː *US:* -ˈsuː ; ɛnˈsu/ *vi* [VP2A, 3A] ～ ***(from),*** happen later; follow, happen as a result: 隨着發生;續起;因而發生: *the trouble that ～d from this misunderstanding;* 由此誤會而產生的麻煩; *in the ensuing* (= next) *year.* 翌年。

en·sure (US = **in·sure**) /ɪnˈʃʊə(r) ; ɪnˈʃʊr/ *vt, vi* **1** [VP9] make sure; guarantee: 確定;使確實;保證: *I can't ～ that he will be there in time.* 我不能確定他會及時到那裏。 **2** [VP14, 3A] ～ ***(sb) against sth,*** make safe: 使安全: *We ～d (ourselves) against possible disappointment.* 我們避免可能產生的失望。 *You should ～ (yourself) against loss of heat by having double glazing.* 你應裝置雙重玻璃以免散熱。 **3** [VP12A, 13A] secure; assure: 獲得;保證得到: *These documents ～ to you the authority you need.* 這些文件使你獲得你需要的職權。 *I cannot ～ you a good post.* 我不能擔保你獲得一個好的職位。 **4** (formerly) (昔時) = insure.

en·tail /ɪnˈteɪl ; ɪnˈtel/ *vt* [VP6A, 14] ～ ***(on),*** **1** make necessary; impose (expense, etc *on* sb): 使必要;使負擔(花費等,與 on 連用,後接某人): *That will ～ an early start.* 那將使早些着手成爲必要。 *These plans ～ great expense on us.* 這些計畫需要花費我們很大的經費。 **2** (legal) leave, settle, (land) to a line of heirs so that none of them can give it away or sell it: (法律)限定(地產)繼承人: *～ an estate on sb.* 限定某人繼承地產。□ *n* [U] settlement of landed property in this way; [C] the property so settled. 限定繼承;限定繼承的地產。

en·tangle /ɪnˈtæŋgl ; ɪnˈtæŋgḷ/ *vt* [VP6A, 15A, 14] ～ ***(in),*** **1** catch in a snare or among obstacles: 使糾纏;纏住: *My fishing line got ～d in weeds.* 我的釣魚線與雜草纏在一起了。 *The duck flew into the nets and the more it struggled the more it ～d itself.* 那鴨子飛入網中,牠越掙扎,纏得越緊。 **2** (fig) put or get into difficulties, in unfavourable circumstances: (喻)使陷入困境;使陷入不利情況: *～ oneself with money-lenders.* 爲放債者所苦。 **～·ment** *n* **1** [U] entangling or being ～d; [C] situation that ～s: 糾纏; 陷入困境; 引起糾纏之情況; 糾紛: *～ments with rogues;* 與歹徒間的糾紛; *emotional ～ments.* 感情的糾纏。 **2** (*pl*) barrier of stakes and barbed wire to impede the enemy's advance. (複)鐵絲網(以阻敵人前進者)。

en·tente /ɒnˈtɒnt ; ɑnˈtɑnt/ *n* [C] (F) (group of States with a) friendly understanding. (法)國與國間之諒解;互相諒解的國家。 ˌ**～ cordiˈale** /ˌkɔːdɪˈɑːl ; kɔrˈdjɑl/ *n* ～, esp between two governments. 兩國間的諒解。

en·ter /ˈentə(r) ; ˈɛntə/ *vt, vi* **1** [VP6A, 2A] come or go into: 進入: *～ a room.* 進入室內。 *The train ～ed a tunnel.* 火車駛進隧道。 *Where did the bullet ～ the body?* 子彈是從哪裏進入身體的? (Stage direction in a printed play) (劇本中的舞臺說明) *E～ Hamlet,* Hamlet comes on to the stage. 哈姆雷特上場。 **2** [VP6A] become a member of; join: 加入;參加: *～ a school／college;* 進學校(大學); *～ the Army／Navy;* 投效陸軍(海軍); *～ the Church,* become a priest; 做教士;做牧師; *～ a profession.* 從事一職業。 **3** [VP3A] ～ ***into sth (with sb),*** begin, open: 開始: *～ into conversation with sb;* 與某人開始交談; *～ into negotiations with a business firm.* 與一公司商議。 ～ ***into sth,*** **(a)** begin to deal with: 開始處理: *～ into details／particulars.* 着手處理細節。 **(b)** sympathize with; be able to understand and appreciate: 同情;領略;體會: *～ into sb's feelings;* 同情某人的感受; *～ into the spirit of the occasion.* 領略某一場合的精神。 **(c)** form a part of: 成爲…之一部: *a possibility that had not ～ed into our calculations.* 我們未考慮到的一個可能性。 **4** [VP3A] ～ ***on／upon,*** **(a)** make a start on: 開始;着手: *～ upon a new career／one's duties／another term of office.* 開始一新事業(着手工作,開始另一任期)。 **(b)** take possession of; begin to enjoy: 獲得;開始享有: *～ upon one's inheritance.* 承受遺產。 **5** [VP6A, 14, 15B] ～ ***(in／up);*** ～ ***(in),*** unite, record names, details, etc in a book, etc: 登記姓名,細節等: *～ (in／up) an item in an account-book.* 將一筆帳記入帳簿。 **6** [VP3A, 14] ～ ***for;*** ～ ***sb for,*** give the name of sb for a competition, race, etc: (替…)報名參加(競賽等): *～ oneself for an examination;* 報名參加考試; *～ for the high jump;* 報名參加跳高賽; *～ a horse for the Derby.* 給一馬報名使參加英國大賽馬。

en·teric /enˈterɪk ; ɛnˈtɛrɪk/ *adj* of the intestines: 腸的: *～ fever,* typhoid. 腸熱病;傷寒。 **en·ter·itis** /ˌentəˈraɪtɪs ; ˌɛntəˈraɪtɪs/ *n* [U] inflammation of the intestines. 腸炎。

en·ter·prise /ˈentəpraɪz ; ˈɛntəˌpraɪz/ *n* **1** [C] undertaking, esp one that needs courage or that offers difficulty. 事業(尤指需要勇氣或難以進行者); 企業。 **2** [U] courage and willingness to engage in ～s(1): 企業心;事業心: *We need a spirit of ～ if we are to overcome our difficulties.* 如欲克服我們的困難,我們需要進取的精神。 *He is a man of great ～.* 他是個事業心很重的人。 **3** [U] carrying on of ～s(1): 從事企業或事業: *private ～ versus government control of commerce and industry.* 民營企業與工商業由政府控制的問題。 ⇨ free¹(3); private(1). **en·ter·pris·ing** *adj* having, showing, ～(2). 有或表現企業心的;具創業精神的。 **en·ter·pris·ing·ly** *adv*

en·ter·tain /ˌentəˈteɪn ; ˌɛntəˈten/ *vt* [VP6A, 14,

2A] **1** ~ ***(to)***, receive (people) as guests; give food and drink to: 款待;以食物飲料招待: ~ *friends to dinner.* 請朋友們吃飯。*The Smiths ~ a great deal/do a great deal of ~ing,* often give dinner parties, etc. 史密斯家常款待客人。 **2** ~ ***(with)***, amuse, interest: 使快樂;使感到興趣: ~ *the children with tricks.* 變戲法使孩子們快樂。*We were all ~ed by his tricks.* 我們都對他的戲法感到興趣。 **3** be ready to consider: 準備考慮: ~ *a proposal;* 準備考慮一建議; have in the mind: 持有;懷有: ~ *ideas/doubts, etc.* 持有意見(感到懷疑等)。**~·ing** *adj* pleasing; amusing. 令人愉快的;有趣的。 **~·ing·ly** *adv* **~·ment** *n* **1** [U] ~ing or being ~ed(2): (使)感到快樂或興趣: *He fell into the water, much to the ~ment of the onlookers.* 他掉進水中,使旁觀者大樂。 **2** [C] public performance (at a theatre, circus, etc). (戲院,馬戲團等之)娛樂;遊藝;技藝表演。 **~er** *n* person who ~s(2), esp professionally. 娛樂節目表演者;(尤指)職業性娛樂節目表演者。

en·thral (also, esp US **en·thrall**) /ɪnˈθrɔːl ; ɪnˈθrɔl/ *vt* (-ll-) [VP6A] **1** take the whole attention of; please greatly: 迷住;使極爲喜悅: *~ed by an exciting story.* 爲一動人的故事所迷。 **2** enslave (usu fig): 奴役(通常作喩): *~ed by a woman's beauty.* 爲一女子的美色迷住。

en·throne /ɪnˈθrəʊn ; ɪnˈθron/ *vt* [VP6A] place a king, bishop on a throne; (fig) give a high place to, in one's judgement or affection: 使(國王,主教)就位;(喩)崇拜;尊崇;愛戴: *a ruler ~d in the hearts of his subjects.* 爲臣民愛戴的君主。**~·ment** *n*

en·thuse /ɪnˈθjuːz *US:* -ˈθuːz ; ɪnˈθjuz/ *vi* [VP3A] ~ ***over***, (colloq) show enthusiasm for. (俗)熱心於。

en·thusi·asm /ɪnˈθjuːzɪæzəm *US:* -ˈθuː- ; ɪnˈθjuzɪˌæzəm/ *n* [U] ~ ***(for/about)***, strong feeling of admiration or interest: 渴慕;熱心;熱愛: *arouse ~ in sb;* 引起某人的熱愛; *a play that moved the audience to ~;* 使觀衆狂熱的戲劇; *feel no ~ for/about sth;* 對某事不熱心; *an outburst of ~.* 狂熱。

en·thusi·ast /ɪnˈθjuːzɪæst *US:* -ˈθuː- ; ɪnˈθjuzɪˌæst/ *n* ~ ***(for/about)***, person filled with enthusiasm: 熱心者;渴慕者: *a sports ~;* 酷愛運動者; *an ~ for/about politics.* 熱中於政治者。

en·thusi·astic /ɪnˌθjuːzɪˈæstɪk *US:* -ˈθuː- ; ɪnˌθjuzɪˈæstɪk/ *adj* ~ ***(about/over)***, full of enthusiasm: 熱心的;熱情洋溢的: ~ *admirers of a film star;* 熱烈仰慕某一電影明星者; *become ~ over sth.* 熱心於某事。**en·thusi·asti·cally** /-klɪ ; -klɪ/ *adv*

en·tice /ɪnˈtaɪs ; ɪnˈtaɪs/ *vt* [VP6A, 15A, 17] tempt or persuade: 誘惑;慫恿: ~ *a young girl away from home;* 誘騙一少女出走; ~ *sb into doing sth/to do sth wrong;* 慫恿某人做壞事; ~ *a man from his duty.* 引誘一人失職。**~·ment** *n* [U] enticing or being ~d; [C] sth that ~s. 誘惑;慫恿;誘惑物。

en·tire /ɪnˈtaɪə(r) ; ɪnˈtaɪr/ *adj* whole, complete; in one piece, unbroken: 整個的;完全的;完整的: *The ~ village was destroyed.* 整個村莊被毀掉了。 *Is your stamp collection still ~?* 你集的郵票還是那樣完整嗎? **~·ly** *adv* completely: 完全地;全然: *~ly unnecessary/different.* 完全不必要(不同)。*My life is ~ly given up to work.* 我的一生全部獻給了工作。 **~ty** /ɪnˈtaɪərətɪ ; ɪnˈtaɪrtɪ/ *n* [U] the state of being ~; completeness: 全部;完全: *We must examine the question in its ~ty,* as a whole, not in parts only. 我們必須將此問題整個研究一下。

en·title /ɪnˈtaɪtl ; ɪnˈtaɪtl/ *vt* **1** [VP23] ***be ~d***, have as a title: 稱作;以…爲名: *a book ~d 'Adam Bede'.* 稱作'亞當•比得'的一本書。 **2** [VP14, 17] ~ ***sb to sth/to do sth***, (usu in passive) (of conditions, circumstances, qualities, etc) give a right (to): (通常用被動語態)(指條件,情況,特性等)給予權利: *If you fail three times, you are not ~d to try any more.* 如果你失敗三次,你便無權再嘗試了。 **~·ment** *n* that which ~s(2). 給予權利之條件,情況等。

en·tity /ˈentətɪ ; ˈɛntətɪ/ *n* (*pl* -ties) **1** [C] sth that has real existence; a thing's existence (contrasted with its qualities, relations, etc). 實在物;實體(與性質,關係等相對)。 **2** [U] being; existence. 存在;實在。

en·tomb /ɪnˈtuːm ; ɪnˈtum/ *vt* [VP6A] place in a tomb; serve as a tomb for. 埋葬;作爲…之墓。

ento·mol·ogy /ˌentəˈmɒlədʒɪ ; ˌɛntəˈmɑlədʒɪ/ *n* [U] the study of insects. 昆虫學。 **en·to·mol·ogist** /-dʒɪst ; -dʒɪst/ *n* student of, expert in, ~. 昆虫學家。 **en·to·mo·logi·cal** /ˌentəməˈlɒdʒɪkl ; ˌɛntəməˈlɑdʒɪkl/ *adj*

en·tour·age /ˌɒntʊˈrɑːʒ ; ˌɑntuˈrɑʒ/ *n* all those accompanying and attending on an important or high-ranking person: 要人的所有隨員: *the President and his ~.* 總統及其隨員。

en·tr'acte /ˈɒntrækt ; ɑnˈtrækt/ *n* [C] (F) (performance in an) interval between acts in a play. (法)幕與幕間之休息;幕間休息之插演節目。

en·trails /ˈentreɪlz ; ˈɛntrəlz/ *n pl* bowels; intestines. 腸。

en·train /enˈtreɪn ; ɪnˈtren/ *vt, vi* [VP6A, 2A] get, put troops, etc into a train. 使(軍隊等)乘火車;乘火車。

en·trance[1] /ˈentrəns ; ˈɛntrəns/ *n* **1** [C] opening, gate, door, passage, etc by which one enters: 入口;大門;門;進入之道: *The ~ to the cave had been blocked up.* 那個洞的入口已被阻塞。 **2** [C, U] coming or going in; coming of an actor upon the stage; entering: 進入;(舞臺演員之)出場: *the university ~ examination.* 大學入學考試。*E~ into/upon ministerial office requires a visit to the Queen.* 就職閣員須覲見女王。 *Actors must learn their ~s and exits,* when to come upon and leave the stage. 演員必須知道何時出場和退場。 **3** [C, U] right of entering: 進入權: *to be refused ~.* 被拒絕進入。 **'~-fee, '~-money**, charge for admission. 入場費。

en·trance[2] /ɪnˈtrɑːns *US:* -ˈtræns ; ɪnˈtræns/ *vt* [VP6A] ~ ***(at/with)***, (usu in passive) fill with emotion and delight: (通常用被動語態)使狂喜;使出神: *~d with the music.* 聽音樂出神。*She stood ~d at the sight.* 她站在那裏望着那景色出神。

en·trant /ˈentrənt ; ˈɛntrənt/ *n* person who enters *to* a profession, *for* a competition, race, etc. 進入者;開始一種職業者(與to連用);參加比賽者(與for連用)。

en·trap /ɪnˈtræp ; ɪnˈtræp/ *vt* (-pp-) [VP6A] = trap (the usu word). (trap 一字較常用)。

en·treat /ɪnˈtriːt ; ɪnˈtrit/ *vt* [VP6A, 17, 14] ~ ***(of)***, (formal) ask (sb) earnestly: (正式用語)懇求;哀求: ~ *sb to show mercy;* 懇求某人憐憫; ~ *a favour of sb.* 求某人幫忙。**~·ing·ly** *adv*

en·treaty /ɪnˈtriːtɪ ; ɪnˈtritɪ/ *n* (*pl* -ies) [C, U] earnest request(ing): 懇求;哀求: *deaf to all entreaties;* 不理睬一切懇求; *with a look of ~.* 以哀求的眼光。

en·trée /ˈɒntreɪ ; ˈɑntre/ *n* (F) (法) **1** [U] right or privilege of admission. 進入權;入場權。 **2** [C] dish served between the fish and the meat course. 魚與大塊肉間的一道菜;旁碟。

en·trench /ɪnˈtrentʃ ; ɪnˈtrɛntʃ/ *vt* [VP6A] **1** surround or protect with a trench or trenches: 圍以壕溝;以壕溝防護: *The enemy were strongly ~ed on the other side of the river.* 敵軍在河的彼岸以堅固的壕溝防護自己。 **2** establish firmly: 確立: *customs ~ed by tradition;* 由傳統確立的風俗; *~ed clauses/provisions,* those (in a constitution(1)) which can be changed only by a special procedure. 確立的憲法條款(須經特殊程序始可更動者)。**~·ment** *n*

entre·pot /ˈɒntrəpəʊ ; ˈɑntrəˌpo/ *n* (F) storehouse; commercial centre for the import, export, collection and distribution of goods. (法)倉庫;貨物集散地。

entre·pre·neur /ˌɒntrəprəˈnɜː(r) ; ˌɑntrəprəˈnɝ/ *n* person who organizes and manages a commercial undertaking. 企業家。**~·ial** /-ˈnɜːrɪəl ; -ˈnɝɪəl/ *adj*

en·trust /ɪnˈtrʌst ; ɪnˈtrʌst/ *vt* [VP14] ~ ***sth to sb;*** ~ ***sb with sth***, trust sb to complete or safeguard sth: 委託某事給某人;信託某人做某事: *Can*

I ~ the task to you / ~ you with the task? 我可以將此事交給你辦嗎？ *Ought I to ~ to them / ~ them with such confidential and important plans?* 我應該將如此機密和重要的計畫交託他們嗎？

en·try /ˈentrɪ ; ˈɛntrɪ/ *n* [C] (*pl* -tries) **1** coming or going in: 進入: *the ~ of the USA into world politics.* 美國之參與世界政治。*The army made a triumphal ~ into the town.* 這批軍隊凱旋進入該城。*Thieves had forced an ~ into the building.* 竊賊强行進入那建築物。ˈ**~ visa**, ⇨ visa. **2** [C, U] (place of) entrance; right of entering: 入口;進入權: *The sign ⊖ means 'No ~'.* ⊖ 表示'不准入內'。**3** item in a list; item noted in an account book: (表中之)條目;項目;帳目: *dictionary entries;* 字典中列出之字目; *make an ~ of a transaction;* 記一筆交易; *book-keeping by double / single ~*, in which each item is entered twice / once in a ledger. 複(單)式簿記。**bill of ~**, ⇨ bill³(6). **4** list, number, of persons, etc entering for a competition: 參加比賽的名單,人數等: *a large ~ for the 5000 metres race;* 參加五千公尺賽跑的許多人; person or thing that is entered for a competition: 參加比賽的人或物: *nearly fifty entries for the Marathon race.* 幾乎有五十位參加馬拉松賽跑。

en·twine /ɪnˈtwaɪn ; ɪnˈtwaɪn/ *vt* [VP6A, 14] ~ ***(with / round)***, make by twining; curl (one thing) (*with* or *round* another). 編織;盤繞(一物於另一物,與 with 或 round 連用)。

enu·mer·ate /ɪˈnjuːməreɪt *US:* ɪˈnuː- ; ɪˈnjuməˌret/ *vt* [VP6A] count, go through (a list of articles) naming them one by one. 點查;數;列舉。**enu·mer·ation** /ɪˌnjuːməˈreɪʃn *US:* ɪˌnuː- ; ɪˌnjuməˈreʃən/ *n* [U] enumerating; [C] list. 數;列舉;目錄。

enun·ci·ate /ɪˈnʌnsɪeɪt ; ɪˈnʌnsɪˌet/ *vt, vi* **1** [VP6A, 2A] say, pronounce (words): 念(字);發音: *He ~s (his words) clearly.* 他發音(念字)清晰。**2** express a theory, etc clearly or definitely. 清楚或確切表明(理論等)。**enun·ci·ation** /ɪˌnʌnsɪˈeɪʃn; ɪˌnʌnsɪˈeʃən/ *n*

en·velop /ɪnˈveləp ; ɪnˈvɛləp/ *vt* [VP6A, 14] ~ ***(in)***, wrap up, cover, on all sides: 包圍;包住;掩蔽: *hills ~ed in mist;* 被霧遮蔽的群山; *a baby ~ed in a shawl;* 包在披肩內的嬰兒; *~ a subject in mystery.* 使一問題變得神秘。**~·ment** *n*

en·vel·ope /ˈenvələʊp ; ˈɛnvəˌlop/ *n* wrapper or covering, esp one made of paper for a letter; covering of a balloon or airship. 封皮;(尤指)信封;包袋;氣球或飛艇之氣囊。

en·venom /ɪnˈvenəm ; ɛnˈvɛnəm/ *vt* [VP6A] put poison on or in, eg a weapon; (fig) fill with bitter hate: 置毒藥於(例如武器); (喻)使痛恨: *~ed quarrels / tempers.* 充滿怨恨的爭吵(惡毒的脾氣)。

en·vi·able /ˈenvɪəbl ; ˈɛnvɪəbḷ/ *adj* causing envy; likely to excite envy (used both of the object and the person, etc, possessing it): 令人羨慕的;可羨慕的(用以指某物和擁有該物的人等): *an ~ school record,* one of great success, etc; 令人羨慕的在校成績; *an ~ woman,* eg one who has a kind, handsome and rich husband. 令人羨慕的女人(例如她丈夫和善,英俊而且富有)。

en·vi·ous /ˈenvɪəs ; ˈɛnvɪəs/ *adj* ~ ***(of)***, full of envy; feeling envy; showing or expressing envy: 嫉妒的;羡慕的;表示嫉妒或羡慕的: *~ of sb's success;* 羡慕某人的成功; *~ looks;* 嫉妒的神情; *looking at sth with ~ eyes.* 以羡慕的眼光望着某物。**~·ly** *adv*

en·viron /ɪnˈvaɪərən ; ɪnˈvaɪrən/ *vt* [VP6A] be in a position round; surround: 包圍;環繞: *a town ~ed by / with forests.* 爲森林所環繞的城鎮。

en·vi·ron·ment /ɪnˈvaɪərənmənt ; ɪnˈvaɪrənmənt/ *n* [U, C] surroundings, circumstances, influences: 環境: *a healthy ~.* 有益於健康的環境。*Students of social problems investigate the home, social and moral ~(s) of different classes of people.* 研究社會問題的學者調查各階層人民的家庭,社會和精神上的生活環境。**Department of the E~**, (GB) Government Department responsible for land planning, construction industries, transport, preservation of public amenities, control of air and water pollution, the protection of the coast and the countryside. (英)環境部(負責土地計畫,建築工業,運輸,公共休閒去處,管制空氣和水的污染,保護海岸與鄉間等)。**~al** /ɪnˌvaɪərənˈmentl ; ɪnˌvaɪrənˈmɛntl/ *adj* **~·ally** /-təlɪ ; -tḷɪ/ *adv*

en·virons /ɪnˈvaɪərənz ; ɪnˈvaɪrənz/ *n pl* districts surrounding a town, etc: 郊外;近郊: *Berlin and its ~.* 柏林及其近郊。

en·vis·age /ɪnˈvɪzɪdʒ ; ɛnˈvɪzɪdʒ/ *vt* [VP6A] picture in the mind (esp in a particular way): 想像;設想(尤指從某一方面): *He had not ~d the matter in that light.* 他沒有從那方面設想過此事。

en·voy¹ /ˈenvɔɪ ; ˈɛnvɔɪ/ *n* messenger, esp one sent on a special mission; diplomatic agent next in rank below an ambassador. 使者;特使;公使。

en·voy² (also **en·voi**) /ˈenvɔɪ ; ˈɛnvɔɪ/ *n* [C] concluding part of a poem, esp a short stanza at the end of some archaic forms of poetry. 一首詩的結尾;(尤指某些古詩的)結尾詩節。

envy¹ /ˈenvɪ ; ˈɛnvɪ/ *n* [U] **1** ~ ***at sth / of sb,*** feeling of disappointment and resentment (at another's better fortune): 嫉妒;羨慕: *He was filled with ~ of me / at my success.* 他十分羨慕我(我的成功)。*My success excited his ~.* 我的成功引起了他的羡慕。*They say such scandalous things about you out of ~.* 他們是由於嫉妒才這樣毀謗你。**2** object of such feeling: 羡慕的對象;嫉妒的對象: *His splendid new car was the ~ of all his friends / an object of ~ to all his friends.* 他那部豪華的新車是他所有的朋友羡慕的東西。

envy² /ˈenvɪ ; ˈɛnvɪ/ *vt* (*pt, pp* -vied) [VP6A, 12C] feel envy of: 羨慕;嫉妒: *I ~ you.* 我羡慕你。*I ~ your good fortune.* 我羡慕你的好運。*I don't ~ him his bad-tempered wife,* am glad I am not married to her. 我不羡慕他有個壞脾氣的妻子。

en·wrap /ɪnˈræp ; ɛnˈræp/ *vt* (-pp-) = wrap (the more usu word). (wrap 較常用)。

en·zyme /ˈenzaɪm ; ˈɛnzaɪm/ *n* [C] organic chemical substance (a catalyst) formed in living cells, able to cause changes in other substances without being changed itself. 酵素。

eon /ˈiːən ; ˈiən/ *n* = aeon.

ep·aulet (also **ep·aul·ette**) /ˈepəlet ; ˈɛpəˌlɛt/ *n* shoulder ornament on a naval or military officer's uniform. (海軍或陸軍軍官之)肩章。

épée /ˈeɪpeɪ ; ˈeˌpe/ *n* (F) sharp-pointed slender sword used in fencing. (法)(擊劍用的)一種狹長而且尖端鋒利的劍。

ephem·er·al /ɪˈfemərəl ; əˈfɛmərəl/ *adj* living, lasting for a very short time. 生命短促的;短暫的;瞬息的。

epic /ˈepɪk ; ˈɛpɪk/ *n, adj* (poetic account) of the deeds of one or more great heroes, or of a nation's past history, eg Homer's *Iliad*; (colloq) (subject) fit to be celebrated as heroic: 描寫英雄事蹟的詩(例如荷馬的'伊利亞德');史詩;敍事詩;寫英雄事蹟的; 史詩的; 敍事詩的;(俗)英勇值得頌揚的(事蹟): *an ~ achievement.* 值得頌揚的英勇成就。

epi·centre (US= **-center**) /ˈepɪsentə(r) ; ˈɛpɪˌsɛntɚ/ *n* point at which an earthquake reaches the earth's surface. 地震中心;震央;震源。

epi·cure /ˈepɪkjʊə(r) ; ˈɛpɪˌkjʊr/ *n* person who understands the pleasures to be had from delicate eating and drinking. 喜美食醇酒之人;會享受口福之人。

epi·cur·ean /ˌepɪkjʊˈriːən ; ˌɛpɪkjʊˈriən/ *n, adj* (person) devoted to pleasure (esp refined sensuous enjoyment): 享樂主義者;喜享樂(尤指感官上的享受)的: *an ~ feast.* 盛宴。

epi·demic /ˌepɪˈdemɪk ; ˌɛpəˈdɛmɪk/ *n, adj* (disease) spreading rapidly among many people in the same place for a time: 流行病;傳染病;流行性的: *an influenza ~.* 流行性感冒。⇨ endemic.

epi·der·mis /ˌepɪˈdɜːmɪs ; ˌɛpəˈdɝmɪs/ *n* [U] outer layer of the skin. 外皮;表皮。

epi·dia·scope /ˌepɪˈdaɪəskəʊp ; ˌɛpɪˈdaɪəˌskop/ *n* optical lantern which projects on a screen transparent objects (eg film-strip) and opaque objects (eg coins, pictures). 實物幻燈機(可映出透明物體如幻燈片,及不透明物體如硬幣和畫片)。

epi·glot·tis /ˌepɪˈglɒtɪs ; ˌɛpəˈglɑtɪs/ *n* structure of tissue at the root of the tongue, lowered during swallowing to prevent food, etc from entering the windpipe. 會厭軟骨(位於舌根,吞食時能降下以阻止食物等進入氣管)。⇨ the illus at head. 參看 head 之插圖。

epi·gram /ˈepɪgræm ; ˈɛpəˌgræm/ *n* short poem or saying expressing an idea in a clever and amusing way. 警句;雋語。 **~·matic** /ˌepɪgrəˈmætɪk ; ˌɛpəgrəˈmætɪk/ *adj* short and witty in expression; (of a person) fond of making ~s. 短而機智的;(指人)喜作雋語的。

epi·lepsy /ˈepɪlepsɪ ; ˈɛpəˌlɛpsɪ/ *n* [U] nervous disease causing a person to fall unconscious (often with violent involuntary movements). 癲癇症。 **epi·lep·tic** /ˌepɪˈleptɪk ; ˌɛpəˈlɛptɪk/ *adj* of ~: 癲癇症的: *an epileptic fit.* 癲癇症突發。 □ *n* person suffering from ~. 癲癇症患者。

epi·logue (US=**-log**) /ˈepɪlɒg *US:* -lɔːg ; ˈɛpəˌlɔg/ *n* last part of a literary work, esp a poem spoken by an actor at the end of a play; (radio, TV) religious programme at the end of the day's transmission. 文學作品之結尾;(尤指戲劇結尾由演員念出之)收場白;(廣播,電視)一日播送結束時之宗教節目。

Epiph·any /ɪˈpɪfənɪ ; ɪˈpɪfənɪ/ *n* commemoration (6 Jan) of the coming of the Magi /ˈmeɪdʒaɪ ; ˈmedʒaɪ/ (the *Three Wise Men*) to Jesus at Bethlehem. 主顯節(慶祝一月六日東方三博士至伯利恆禮拜耶穌)。Cf 參較 *Twelfth Night.*

epis·co·pal /ɪˈpɪskəpl ; ɪˈpɪskəpl/ *adj* of, governed by, bishops: 主教的;主教管轄的: *the E~ Church*, (esp) the Anglican Church in the US and Scotland. (尤指在美國和蘇格蘭的)英國國教;主教派教會;聖公會。 **epis·co·pa·lian** /ɪˌpɪskəˈpeɪlɪən ; ɪˌpɪskəˈpelɪən/ *n, adj* (member) of an ~ church. 主教派教友;聖公會教徒;主教派的;聖公會的。

epi·sode /ˈepɪsəʊd ; ˈɛpəˌsod/ *n* [C] (description of) one event in a chain of events. 一連串事件中的一個事件;插曲。 **epi·sodic** /ˌepɪˈsɒdɪk ; ˌɛpəˈsɑdɪk/ *adj* sporadic. 時有時無的;零星的。

epistle /ɪˈpɪsl ; ɪˈpɪsl/ *n* (old use, or joc) letter. (舊用法,或謔)書信。 **the E~s,** letters included in the New Testament, written by the Apostles. (新約)使徒書信。 **epis·tol·ary** /ɪˈpɪstələrɪ *US:* -lerɪ ; ɪˈpɪstəˌlɛrɪ/ *adj* of, carried on by, letters. 書信的;由書信傳遞的。

epi·taph /ˈepɪtɑːf *US:* -tæf ; ˈɛpəˌtæf/ *n* [C] words commemorating a dead person (eg as cut on his tombstone). 墓誌銘。

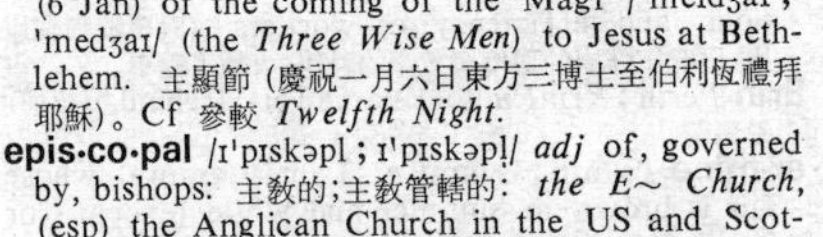
GOOD FREND FOR IESVS SAKE FORBEARE
TO DIGG THE DVST ENCLOASED HEARE
BLESE BE Y MAN Y SPARES THES STONES
AND CVRST BE HE Y MOVES MY BONES

the epitaph on Shakespeare's tombstone

epi·thet /ˈepɪθet ; ˈɛpəˌθɛt/ *n* adjective or descriptive phrase used to indicate the character of sb or sth, as in 'Alfred the *Great*'. 表性質的形容詞;附於人名後之描述詞(例如 Alfred the Great 中之 Great)。

epit·ome /ɪˈpɪtəmɪ ; ɪˈpɪtəmɪ/ *n* short summary of a book, speech, etc; sth which shows, on a small scale, the characteristics of sth much larger; sth or sb that perfectly displays a quality, type, etc: 摘要;縮影;完全顯示一性質,型態等的人或物;典型: *the ~ of a loving mother.* 慈母的典型。 **epit·om·ize** /ɪˈpɪtəmaɪz ; ɪˈpɪtəˌmaɪz/ *vt* [VP6A] make/be an ~ of: 摘要;為…之縮影;為…之典型: *She epitomizes a loving mother.* 她是慈母的典型。

ep·och /ˈiːpɒk *US:* ˈepək ; ˈɛpək/ *n* (beginning of a) period of time in history, life, etc marked by special events or characteristics: (新)紀元;(歷史,生活等中有特殊事件或特點的)時代: *Einstein's theory marked a new ~ in mathematics.* 愛因斯坦的學說在數學上開一新紀元。 **ˈ~-making,** beginning a new ~: 劃時代的;開新紀元的: *an ~-making discovery*, eg of America by Columbus. 劃時代的發現(例如哥倫布之發現美洲)。

Ep·som salts /ˌepsəm ˈsɔːlts ; ˈɛpsəm ˈsɔlts/ *n pl* hydrated magnesium sulphate (**$MgSO_4$**), used medically to empty the bowels. 瀉鹽。

equable /ˈekwəbl ; ˈɛkwəbl/ *adj* steady; regular; not changing much: 穩定的;固定的;變化甚小的: *an ~ climate/temper.* 穩定的氣候(平和的性情)。 **equably** /ˈekwəblɪ ; ˈɛkwəblɪ/ *adv*

equal /ˈiːkwəl ; ˈikwəl/ *adj* **1** the same in size, amount, number, degree, value, etc: (大小,數量,數目,程度,價值等)相等的;同樣的: *~ pay for ~ work;* 同工同酬; *~ opportunity;* 機會均等; *~ in ability;* 能力相等; *divide sth into two ~ parts;* 將某物二等分; *two boys of ~ height.* 一樣高的兩個男孩子。 *He speaks English and Arabic with ~ ease.* 他說英語和阿拉伯語同樣的流利。 *Things which are ~ to the same thing are ~ to one another.* 與同一物相同之各物彼此亦相同。 **2 ~ to sth/to doing sth,** having strength, courage, ability, etc for: 有…之力量,勇氣,能力等: *He was ~ to the occasion*, was able to deal with it. 他能應付這個局勢。 *She did not feel ~ to receiving visitors.* 她的身體不適,不能接見客人。 □ *n* person or thing ~ to another: 相等的人或物: *Is he your ~ in strength?* 他的力氣和你的一樣大嗎? *Let x be the ~ of y.* 設 x 與 y 相等。 □ *vt* (-ll-, US also -l-) [VP6A, 15A] be ~ to: 等於: *He ~s me in strength but not in intelligence.* 他在氣力方面和我相等,但在智力方面卻不如我。 *He is ~led by no one in strength.* 在氣力方面無人能比得過他。 **~ly** /ˈiːkwəlɪ ; ˈikwəlɪ/ *adv* in an ~ manner; in ~ shares: 同樣地;相等地: *~ly clever.* 同樣地聰明。 *Divide it ~ly.* 將它等分。 **~·ity** /ɪˈkwɒlətɪ ; ɪˈkwɑlətɪ/ *n* [U] the state of being ~: 相等;平等;同等: *on terms of ~ (with)*, on ~ terms (with). 與…平等相處。 **~i·tarian** /ɪˌkwɒlɪˈteərɪən ; ɪˌkwɑləˈtɛrɪən/ *n* = egalitarian. **~·ize** /ˈiːkwəlaɪz ; ˈikwəlˌaɪz/ *vt* [VP6A] make ~: 使相等;使平等: *~ize incomes.* 使收入均等。 **~·iz·ation** /ˌiːkwəlaɪˈzeɪʃn *US:* -lɪˈz- ; ˌikwələˈzeʃən/ *n*

equa·nim·ity /ˌekwəˈnɪmətɪ ; ˌikwəˈnɪmətɪ/ *n* [U] calmness of mind or temper: 平靜;鎮定: *bear misfortune with ~;* 對於不幸泰然處之; *disturb sb's ~.* 擾亂某人心中之平靜。

equate /ɪˈkweɪt ; ɪˈkwet/ *vt* [VP6A, 14] **~ (with),** consider, treat (one thing as being equal): 認為相等;視為相等: (maths) (數學) *~ two quantities.* 使二量相等。

equa·tion /ɪˈkweɪʒn ; ɪˈkweʒən/ *n* **1** [C] (maths) statement of equality between two expressions by the sign = as in: $2x+5=11$. (數學)等式;方程式(例如: $2x+5=11$)。 **2** [U] **~ (with),** making equal, balancing, eg of demand and supply. 使相等;平衡(例如需要和供給間之平衡)。

equa·tor /ɪˈkweɪtə(r) ; ɪˈkwetɚ/ *n* imaginary line round the earth; line drawn on maps to represent points at an equal distance from the north and south poles. 赤道。⇨ the illus at projection. 參看 projection 之插圖。 **~·ial** /ˌekwəˈtɔːrɪəl ; ˌikwəˈtɔrɪəl/ *adj* of or near the ~: 赤道的;近赤道的: *~ial Africa.* 非洲近赤道的地區。

equerry /ɪˈkwerɪ ; ˈɛkwərɪ/ *n* (*pl* -rries) officer in the court of a ruler; officer in attendance on a member of the royal family. 皇室武官;皇族侍衛官。

eques·trian /ɪˈkwestrɪən ; ɪˈkwɛstrɪən/ *adj* of horse-riding: 騎馬的: *~ skill;* 騎術; *an ~ statue*, of a person on horseback. 騎馬者的雕像。□ *n* person clever at horse-riding. 精通騎術者;善騎者。

equi·dis·tant /ˌiːkwɪˈdɪstənt ; ˌikwəˈdɪstənt/ *adj* ~ ***(from)***, separated by equal distances. 等距離的。

equi·lat·eral /ˌiːkwɪˈlætərəl ; ˌikwəˈlætərəl/ *adj* having all sides equal: 等邊的: *an ~ triangle.* 等邊三角形。

equi·lib·rium /ˌiːkwɪˈlɪbrɪəm ; ˌikwəˈlɪbrɪəm/ *n* [U] state of being balanced: 平衡;均勢: *maintain/lose one's ~;* 保持(失去)平衡; *scales* (on a balance) *in ~.* 平衡的天秤。

equine /ˈekwaɪn ; ˈikwaɪn/ *adj* (formal) of, like, a horse; of horses. (正式用語)馬的;似馬的。

equi·noc·tial /ˌiːkwɪˈnɒkʃl ; ˌikwəˈnɑkʃəl/ *adj* of, at or near, the equinox: 晝夜平分時的;近晝夜平分時的;春分的;秋分的: ~ *gales/tides.* 春(秋)分時的風(潮)。

equi·nox /ˈiːkwɪnɒks ; ˈikwəˌnɑks/ *n* time of the year at which the sun crosses the equator and when day and night are of equal length: 晝夜平分時;春分;秋分: *the spring* (= vernal) ~, around 20 Mar; 春分(約在三月二十日); *the autumnal* ~, around 22 Sept. 秋分(約在九月二十二日)。

equip /ɪˈkwɪp ; ɪˈkwɪp/ *vt* (-pp-) [VP6A, 14] ~ ***(with)***, supply (a person, oneself, a ship, etc) (with what is needed, for a purpose): 供給(某人,自己,船隻等)以所需的東西;裝備: ~ *oneself for a task;* 使自己準備好去做一工作; ~ *a ship for a voyage;* 裝備一船以便出航; ~ *soldiers with uniforms and weapons.* 以服裝和武器裝備軍隊。**~·ment** *n* [U] **1** ~ping or being ~ped: 裝備: *The ~ment of his laboratory took time and money.* 裝備他的實驗室花了很多時間和金錢。 **2** (collective *noun*) things needed for a purpose: (集合名詞)裝備品;設備品: *a factory with modern ~ment;* 有現代化設備的一家工廠; *ˈradar ~ment.* 雷達裝置。

equi·page /ˈekwɪpɪdʒ ; ˈɛkwəpɪdʒ/ *n* [C] equipment, outfit; carriage, horses and attendants (of a rich person in former times). 裝備;用具;(昔時富翁之)馬車,馬匹和隨從。

equi·poise /ˈekwɪpɔɪz ; ˈɛkwəˌpɔɪz/ *n* [U] equilibrium; [C] thing that counterbalances. 平衡;平衡物。

equi·table /ˈekwɪtəbl ; ˈɛkwɪtəbl̩/ *adj* fair; just; reasonable. 公平的;公正的;合理的。**equi·tably** /-blɪ ; -blɪ/ *adv*

equity /ˈekwətɪ ; ˈɛkwətɪ/ *n* **1** [U] fairness; right judgement; (esp, English law) principles of justice outside common law or Statute law, used to correct laws when these would apply unfairly in special circumstances. 公平;公正;(尤用於英國法律)平衡法(用以糾正在特殊情況下被誤用的法律)。 **2** (often *pl*) (-ties) ordinary stocks and shares not bearing fixed interest. (常用複數)無固定利息的股票。

equiv·al·ent /ɪˈkwɪvələnt ; ɪˈkwɪvələnt/ *adj* ~ ***(to)***, equal in value, amount, meaning: (價值,數量,意義)相等的: *What is $5 ~ to in French francs?* 五塊美金等於法國幾法郎?□ *n* sth that is ~: 相等物;等值;等量: *Is there a French word that is the exact ~ of the English word 'home'?* 法文中有沒有一個與英文中的'home'完全相等的字?**equiv·al·ence** /-əns ; -əns/ *n* [U] being ~; [C] sth that is ~. 相等;相等物。

equivo·cal /ɪˈkwɪvəkl ; ɪˈkwɪvəkl̩/ *adj* **1** having a double or doubtful meaning; open to doubt: 模稜兩可的;意義不明的;曖昧的: *an ~ reply.* 模稜兩可的答覆。 **2** questionable; suspicious: 不可靠的;可疑的: *an ~ success.* 可疑的成功。**equivo·ca·tion** /ɪˌkwɪvəˈkeɪʃn ; ɪˌkwɪvəˈkeʃən/ *n* **1** [U] the use of ~ statements to mislead people. 說模稜兩可的話。 **2** [C] ~ expression. 模稜兩可的話;曖昧語。

era /ˈɪərə ; ˈɪrə/ *n* [C] period in history, starting from a particular time or event: 紀元;時代;代: *the Christian era.* 耶穌紀元。

eradi·cate /ɪˈrædɪkeɪt ; ɪˈrædɪˌket/ *vt* [VP6A] pull up by the roots; put an end to, get rid of: 根除;消滅: ~ *crime/typhoid fever.* 根除罪惡(傷寒)。**eradi·ca·tion** /ɪˌrædɪˈkeɪʃn ; ɪˌrædɪˈkeʃən/ *n*

erase /ɪˈreɪz *US:* ɪˈreɪs ; ɪˈres/ *vt* [VP6A] rub or scrape out; remove all traces of: 擦掉;抹掉;抹去: ~ *pencil marks.* 擦去鉛筆的筆跡。**~r** /ɪˈreɪzə(r) *US:* -sər ; ɪˈresɚ/ *n* thing used to ~: 橡皮擦; 黑板擦: *a pencil ~r* (usu 通常= rubber¹(2)). 鉛筆擦。**eras·ure** /ɪˈreɪʒə(r) ; ɪˈreʒɚ/ *n* [U] erasing; [C] sth ~d; place where sth has been ~d. 擦去;被擦之物;被擦之處。

ere /eə(r) ; ɛr/ *adv, prep* (old use, or poet) before. (舊用法或詩)在前;在…以前。

erect¹ /ɪˈrekt ; ɪˈrɛkt/ *adj* upright; standing on end: 直立的;豎起的: *stand ~;* 直立; *hold a banner ~.* 掌着旗子使其直立。**~·ly** *adv* **~·ness** *n*

erect² /ɪˈrekt ; ɪˈrɛkt/ *vt* [VP6A] **1** build, set up, establish: 建築;建立;設立: ~ *a monument;* 立一紀念碑; ~ *a statue (to sb);* (給某人)立一雕像; ~ *a tent.* 搭帳篷。 **2** set upright: 使直立;豎起: ~ *a flagstaff.* 豎立一旗竿。**erec·tile** /ɪˈrektaɪl *US:* -tl ; ɪˈrɛktl̩/ *adj* (physiol) (capable of) becoming rigid from dilation of the blood-vessels: (生理)能勃起的;勃起性的: ~ *tissue.* 勃起性的組織。**erec·tion** /ɪˈrekʃn ; ɪˈrɛkʃən/ *n* **1** [U] act of ~ing; state of being ~ed; (physiol) hardening and swelling of the penis or clitoris. 建築;建立;豎立;(生理)陰莖或陰蒂之勃起。 **2** [C] sth ~ed; building or structure. 建築物。

ere·mite /ˈerɪmaɪt ; ˈɛrəˌmaɪt/ *n* = hermit.

erg /ɜːg ; ɝg/ *n* unit of energy in the metric system. 爾格(功之單位)。

ergo /ˈɜːgəʊ ; ˈɝgo/ *adv* (Lat) (usu hum) therefore. (拉)(通常用作詼諧語)所以。

ergo·nom·ics /ˌɜːgəˈnɒmɪks ; ˌɝgəˈnɑmɪks/ *n pl* (with *sing vb*) study of the environment, conditions and efficiency of workers. (與單數動詞連用)研究工作者的環境與效率的科學;人類工程學。

Erin /ˈerɪn ; ˈɛrɪn/ *n* (old name for) Ireland. (舊稱)愛爾蘭。

er·mine /ˈɜːmɪn ; ˈɝmɪn/ *n* **1** small animal whose fur is brown in summer and white (except for its black-pointed tail) in winter. 貂。 **2** [U] its fur; garment made of this fur: 貂皮;貂皮製的衣服: *dressed in ~;* 着貂皮衣服; *a gown trimmed with ~.* 飾有貂皮的長服。

erode /ɪˈrəʊd ; ɪˈrod/ *vt* [VP6A] (of acids, rain, etc) wear away; eat into: (指酸,雨等)侵蝕;腐蝕: *Metals are ~d by acids.* 金屬爲酸所侵蝕。**ero·sion** /ɪˈrəʊʒn ; ɪˈroʒən/ *n* [U] eroding or being ~d: 侵蝕;腐蝕: *soil erosion,* by wind and rain; (風雨所致之)土壤侵蝕; *coast erosion,* by the sea. (海洋所致之)海岸侵蝕。**ero·sive** /ɪˈrəʊsɪv ; ɪˈrosɪv/ *adj*

erogen·ous /ɪˈrɒdʒənəs ; ɪˈrɑdʒənəs/ *adj* (esp in): (尤用於): ,~ ˈ**zone**, area of the body particularly sensitive to sexual stimulation. (身體上對性刺激敏感之)動情區。

erotic /ɪˈrɒtɪk ; ɪˈrɑtɪk/ *adj* of sexual desire. 性慾的;色情的。**erot·ica** /ɪˈrɒtɪkə ; ɪˈrɑtɪkə/ *n pl* books, pictures, etc intended to arouse sexual desire. 黃色書刊;春宮畫片。**eroti·cism** /ɪˈrɒtɪsɪzəm ; ɪˈrɑtəˌsɪzəm/ *n* [U] sexual desire. 性慾。

err /ɜː(r) *US:* eər ; ɝ/ *vi* [VP2A, C] (formal) make mistakes; do or be wrong: (正式用語)犯錯;做錯: *It is better to err on the side of mercy,* be too merciful than too severe. 過於仁慈比過於嚴厲好。

er·rand /ˈerənd ; ˈɛrənd/ *n* **1** short journey to take or get sth, eg a message, goods from a shop: (短程)差使(例如送信,取貨等): *to go on ~s for sb;* 爲某人去辦事; *to run ~s.* 出差;跑腿。 **2** object or purpose of such a journey. 差使的目的;差事。 ˈ**fool's ~**, one with no real or useful purpose. 無目的之差事;無謂的奔走。

er·rant /ˈerənt ; ˈɛrənt/ *adj* erring; mistaken: 犯錯的;錯誤的: *an ~ husband,* one who is unfaithful to his wife. 對妻子不忠實的丈夫。

er·ratic /ɪˈrætɪk ; əˈrætɪk/ *adj* **1** (of a person or his behaviour) irregular in behaviour or opinion; likely to do unusual or unexpected things. (指人或其行爲)乖僻的;古怪的;言行反覆無常的。 **2** (of things, eg a clock) uncertain in movement; irregular. (指物,例如鐘)不穩定的;不規律的。**er·rati·cally** /-klɪ ; -klɪ/ *adv*

er·ratum /eˈrɑːtəm ; ɪˈretəm/ *n* (*pl* -ta /-tə ; -tə/) (Lat) error in printing or writing: (拉) 印刷或書寫錯誤: *an errata slip*, list of errors, misprints, etc in a printed book. 書中勘誤表。

er·ron·eous /ɪˈrəʊnɪəs ; əˈronɪəs/ *adj* incorrect; mistaken. 錯誤的。**~·ly** *adv*

er·ror /ˈerə(r) ; ˈɛrɚ/ *n* **1** [C] sth done wrong; mistake: 差錯;錯誤: *spelling ~s;* 拼字錯誤; *printer's ~s*, misprints; 印刷錯誤; *an ~ of judgement;* 判斷錯誤; *a clerical ~*, made in writing. 書寫錯誤;筆誤。**2** [U] condition of being wrong in belief or conduct: 謬見;行爲不正: *fall/lead sb into ~;* 誤(引某人)入歧途; *do sth in ~*, by mistake. 誤做一事。

er·satz /ˈeəzæts *US:* ˈeərzɑːts ; ɛrˈzɑts/ *adj* (G) imitation, substitute (esp inferior): (德)仿造的;人造的(尤指品質很差的): *~ coffee/whisky/silk.* 仿造的咖啡(威士忌,絲)。

Erse /ɜːs ; ɝs/ *n* Scottish Gaelic or Irish Gaelic. 蘇格蘭之蓋爾語;愛爾蘭之蓋爾語。

eruc·ta·tion /ˌiːrʌkˈteɪʃn ; ɪˌrʌkˈteʃən/ *n* [U, C] (formal) belching, esp of a volcano. (正式用語)(尤指火山之)噴出。

eru·dite /ˈeruːdaɪt ; ˈɛruˌdaɪt/ *adj* (formal) having, showing, great learning; scholarly. (正式用語)飽學的; 博學的。**~·ly** *adv* **eru·di·tion** /ˌeruːˈdɪʃn ; ˌɛruˈdɪʃən/ *n* [U] learning. 學問;學識。

erupt /ɪˈrʌpt ; ɪˈrʌpt/ *vi* [VP2A] (esp of a volcano) break out. (尤指火山)爆發。**erup·tion** /ɪˈrʌpʃn ; ɪˈrʌpʃən/ *n* [C, U] outbreak of a volcano; (fig) outbreak of war, disease, etc: 火山爆發;(喩)(戰爭,疾病等之)爆發;發作;發出: *~ions of ashes and lava;* 灰燼和熔岩的噴發; *in a state of ~ion.* 爆發。

ery·sip·elas /ˌerɪˈsɪpɪləs ; ˌɛrəˈsɪpḷəs/ *n* [U] skin disease that causes fever and produces deep red inflammation. 丹毒(一種皮膚病,會引起發燒,使皮膚發炎而且變成深紅色)。

es·ca·late /ˈeskəleɪt ; ˈɛskəˌlet/ *vt, vi* [VP2A, 6A] increase, develop, intensify by successive stages. 逐漸增加; 增强; 擴大。**es·ca·la·tion** /ˌeskəˈleɪʃn ; ˌɛskəˈleʃən/ *n*

es·ca·la·tor /ˈeskəleɪtə(r) ; ˈɛskəˌletɚ/ *n* moving stairway carrying people up or down between floors or different levels. 自動梯。

es·ca·lope /ˈeskələʊp ; ˈɛskəlop/ *n* slice of boneless meat, esp veal. 一片無骨的肉(尤指小牛肉)。

es·ca·pade /ˌeskəˈpeɪd ; ˈɛskəˌped/ *n* [C] daring, mischievous or adventurous act, often causing gossip or trouble. 大膽的,惡作劇的或冒險的行爲(常招致閒言或麻煩者)。

es·cape¹ /ɪˈskeɪp ; əˈskep/ *n* **1** [C, U] (act of) escaping; fact of having escaped: 逃走; 逃脫;漏出: *E~ from Dartmoor prison is difficult.* 從達特木監獄逃走是困難的。*There have been very few successful ~s from this prison.* 很少有人成功地自此獄中逃走。*I congratulate you on your ~ from the shipwreck.* 恭喜你自船難中生還。*Don't look for an ~ of gas with a lighted match.* 不要用燃着的火柴去尋找漏煤氣的地方。**ˈ~ velocity**, the speed at which a projectile or spacecraft must travel in order to leave a (eg the earth's) gravitational field. 發射體或太空船脫離地心吸力之速度;逃逸速度。**2** [C] means of escape: 逃脫之方法: *a ˈfire-~;* 太平梯;太平門; *an ˈ~-pipe/-valve*, for carrying off steam or water. 排氣管(活門);排水管(活門)。**3** (sth that provides) temporary distraction from reality or dull routine (eg through music, reading). 消遣(例如聽音樂,讀書等); 消遣物。**es·capee** /ɪˌskeɪˈpiː ; ˌɛskeˈpi/ *n* (esp) prisoner who has ~d. (尤指)越獄的逃犯。**es·cap·ism** /-ɪzəm ; -ɪzəm/ *n* [U] habit of escaping from unpleasant realities into a world of fancy. 逃避現實。**es·cap·ist** /-ɪst ; -ɪst/ *n* person whose conduct is characterized by escapism: 逃避現實者;逃避主義者: (attrib) (形容用法) *escapist literature.* 逃避現實的文學。

es·cape² /ɪˈskeɪp ; əˈskep/ *vi, vt* **1** [VP2A, 3A] ~ *(from)*, get free; get away; (of steam, fluids, etc) find a way out: 逃脫;逃走; (指蒸汽,液體等)漏出: *Two of the prisoners have ~d.* 有兩個囚犯逃走了。*The canary has ~d from its cage.* 金絲雀從籠中逃掉了。*Is the gas escaping somewhere?* 是不是有個地方漏煤氣? *Make a hole and let the water ~.* 弄一個洞讓水流出去。**2** [VP6A, C, 2A] avoid; keep free or safe from: 避免;免除: *You were lucky to ~ punishment/being punished.* 你逃過了受罰,眞幸運。*Where can we go to ~ the crowds?* 我們去何處才能躲開這些群衆? *How can we ~ observation/being seen?* 我們怎樣才不會讓人發現? **3** [VP6A] be forgotten or unnoticed by: 被…忘記;未被…注意: *His name ~s me for the moment*, I cannot recall it. 我一時想不起他的名字來。

es·cape·ment /ɪˈskeɪpmənt ; əˈskepmənt/ *n* [C] device in a clock or watch to regulate the movement. 鐘錶齒輪的擒縱器(控制速度的裝置)。

es·carp·ment /ɪˈskɑːpmənt ; ɛˈskɑrpmənt/ *n* long steep slope or cliff separating two areas of different levels. 陡坡;峭壁。

es·cha·tol·ogy /ˌeskəˈtɒlədʒɪ ; ˌɛskəˈtɑlədʒɪ/ *n* [U] branch of theology concerned with death, judgement, heaven and hell. (神學之一支)末世學(研究死亡,審判,天堂和地獄);終世論。

es·chew /ɪsˈtʃuː ; ɛsˈtʃu/ *vt* [VP6A] (formal) avoid (the more usu word); keep oneself away from, abstain from: (正式用語)避開 (avoid 一字較常用);戒除: *~ political debate.* 避開政治辯論。

es·cort¹ /ˈeskɔːt ; ˈɛskɔrt/ *n* [C] **1** one or more persons going with another or others, or with valuable goods, to protect them, or as an honour: 護送者;護送隊;儀(仗)隊: *an ~ of soldiers;* 一隊護衛的士兵; *under police ~.* 在警察護送下。**2** one or more ships, aircraft, etc giving protection or honour: 護航的艦隊或飛機等: *When the Queen sailed, her yacht had an ~ of ten destroyers and fifty aircraft.* 女王航海時,她的遊艇由十艘驅逐艦和五十架飛機擔任護航。**3** person or persons accompanying sb for courtesy's sake: 禮貌上的伴隨者: *Mary's ~ to the ball.* 伴隨瑪莉去舞會的人。

es·cort² /ɪˈskɔːt ; ɪˈskɔrt/ *vt* [VP6A, 15B] go with as an escort: 護送;護航: *a convoy of merchant ships ~ed by destroyers.* 由驅逐艦護航的商船隊。*Who will ~ this young lady home?* 誰願意護送這位小姐回家?

es·cri·toire /ˌeskrɪˈtwɑː(r) ; ˌɛskrɪˈtwɑr/ *n* writing-desk with drawers for stationery. 寫字檯。

es·cutcheon /ɪˈskʌtʃən ; ɪˈskʌtʃən/ *n* shield with a coat of arms on it. 飾有紋章的盾。⇨ the illus at armour. 參看 armour 之挿圖。***a blot on one's ~***, a stain on one's reputation. 名譽上的汚點。

Es·kimo /ˈeskɪməʊ ; ˈɛskəˌmo/ *n* (*pl* ~s or ~es /-məʊz ; -moz/), member of a people living in the Arctic regions of N America and E Siberia. 愛斯基摩人。

esopha·gus (also **oesopha·gus**) /iːˈsɒfəgəs ; iˈsɑfəgəs/ *n* passage from the pharynx to the stomach; gullet. 食道。⇨ the illus at alimentary, head. 參看 alimentary, head 之挿圖。

eso·teric /ˌesəʊˈterɪk ; ˌɛsəˈtɛrɪk/ *adj* intended only for those who are initiated, for a small circle of disciples or followers; abstruse. 祕密的;祕傳的。

es·palier /ɪˈspælɪə(r) ; ɛˈspæljɚ/ *n* (tree or shrub trained on a) trellis or a wire framework. 樹棚;樹架;樹架上的樹。

es·pecial /ɪˈspeʃl ; əˈspɛʃəl/ *adj* particular; exceptional: 特別的;特殊的: *a question of ~ importance;* 特別重要的問題; *for your ~ benefit.* 爲了你的特殊利益。***in ~***, above all. 尤其是。**~·ly** /-ʃəlɪ ; -ʃlɪ/ *adv* to an exceptional degree; in particular: 特別地;尤其: *She likes the country, ~ly in spring.* 她喜愛

鄉間,尤其在春天。

Es·per·anto /ˌespəˈræntəʊ; ˏɛspəˈrɑnto/ *n* [U] an artificial language designed for world use. (一種人造的)世界語。

espion·age /ˈespɪənɑːʒ; ˈɛspɪənɪdʒ/ *n* [U] practice of spying or using spies. 偵探;間諜活動。

es·pla·nade /ˌespləˈneɪd; ˏɛspləˈned/ *n* [C] level area of ground where people may walk or ride for pleasure, often by the sea. 遊逛的廣場(常指位於海濱者)。

es·pouse /ɪˈspaʊz; ɪˈspaʊz/ *vt* [VP6A] **1** give one's support to (a cause, theory, etc). 擁護(主義,學說等)。 **2** (old use; of a man) marry. (舊用法;指男子)娶。 **es·pousal** /ɪˈspaʊzl; ɪˈspaʊzl/ *n* **1** espousing (of a cause, etc). (主義等的)擁護;贊助。 **2** (old use; usu *pl*) marriage or betrothal. (舊用法;通常用複數)結婚;婚約。

es·presso /eˈspresəʊ; ɛsˈprɛso/ *n* ˌ~ ˈ**coffee**, coffee made by forcing boiling water under pressure through ground coffee. 一種使開水在壓力下沖過咖啡粉而煮成的咖啡。

esprit /eˈspriː; ɛˈspri/ *n* [U] (F) lively wit. (法)機智。 ~ **de corps** /eˌspriː də ˈkɔː(r); ɛˈspridəˈkɔr/ *n* spirit of loyalty and devotion which unites the members of a group or society. 團隊精神。

espy /ɪˈspaɪ; əˈspaɪ/ *vt* (*pt, pp* -pied) [VP6A] (usu joc) catch sight of. (通常爲謔)看見;發現。

Es·quire /ɪˈskwaɪə(r) *US:* ˈes-; əsˈkwaɪə/ *n* title of courtesy (used in GB and written **Esq**, esp in the address of a letter after a man's family name instead of *Mr* before it): 先生(用於英國,略作Esq,尤用作信件中男子姓氏後的尊稱,以代替用於姓氏前的Mr): *Edgar Broughton, Esq.* 愛德嘉·布勞頓先生。

es·say[1] /ˈeseɪ; ˈɛse/ *n* piece of writing, usu short and in prose, on any one subject. 文章;短論;隨筆;小品文。 ~**·ist** /-ɪst; -ɪst/ *n* writer of ~s. 散文家;隨筆作家;小品文作家。

es·say[2] /eˈseɪ; əˈse/ *vt, vi* [VP6A, 4A] try; attempt: 試驗;企圖: ~ *a task;* 試做一工作; ~ *to do sth.* 企圖做某事。□ *n* /ˈeseɪ; ɛˈse/ **1** testing or trial of the value or nature of sth. 對某物價值或性質的試驗。 **2** attempt. 企圖。

es·sence /ˈesns; ˈɛsn̩s/ *n* **1** [U] that which makes a thing what it is; the inner nature or most important quality of a thing: 本質;要素;精髓: *Is the ~ of morality right intention?* 道德的真髓在於心正嗎? *Caution is the ~ of that man's character.* 謹慎是那人性格的本質。 *The two things are the same in outward form but different in ~.* 那兩樣東西在外表上相同,但在本質上不同。 **2** [C, U] extract obtained from a substance by taking out as much of the mass as possible, leaving all its important qualities in concentrated form: 精;粹: *meat ~s;* 肉汁; *~ of peppermint.* 薄荷精。

es·sen·tial /ɪˈsenʃl; əˈsɛnʃəl/ *adj* **1** necessary; indispensable; most important: 必要的;不可缺少的;最重要的: *Is wealth ~ to happiness?* 財富對於幸福是必要的嗎? *Exercise, fresh air and sleep are ~ for the preservation of health.* 運動,新鮮空氣和睡眠對於保持健康是必要的。 *'Wanted, a good secretary: experience ~.'* '徵求優良祕書一名:須有經驗者。' **2** of an essence(2): 精的: ~ *oils.* 香精油。 **3** fundamental: 基本的: *Love of fair play is said to be an ~ part of the English character.* 喜愛公平據說是英國人的性格中的基本性質。 □ *n* [C] (usu *pl*) fundamental element: (通常用複數)要素;要點: *the ~s of English grammar.* 英文文法要義。 *We've time to pack only the basic ~s,* the minimum amount (of clothes, etc) that is necessary. 我們祇有將必要的東西(衣物等)包起來的時間。 ~**·ly** /ɪˈsenʃəlɪ; əˈsɛnʃəlɪ/ *adv* in an ~(3) manner: 基本上: *We are an ~ly peace-loving people.* 我們基本上是愛好和平的民族。

es·tab·lish /ɪˈstæblɪʃ; əˈstæblɪʃ/ *vt* [VP6A, 14, 16B] **1** set up, put on a firm foundation: 建立;設立: ~ *a new state/government/business.* 建立一新國家(政府,事業)。 **2** settle, place a person, oneself in a position, office, place, etc: 安置;使任職;使定居: *We are now comfortably ~ed in our new house.* 我們現在很舒適地住在我們的新居內了。 *Mr X was ~ed as governor of the province.* X 先生被任命爲省主席。 **3** cause people to accept a belief, claim, custom, etc: 使人民接受(信仰,要求,風俗等);確定: *He succeeded in ~ing a claim to the title.* 他成功地確立了對此權益或名份的要求權。 *Newton conclusively ~ed the law of gravity.* 牛頓確定了萬有引力的定律。 *E~ed customs are difficult to change.* 既有的風俗難以改變。 *His honesty is well ~ed.* 他的誠實是大家公認的。 **4** make (a church) national by law. 使(教會)成爲國教。

es·tab·lish·ment /ɪˈstæblɪʃmənt; əˈstæblɪʃmənt/ *n* **1** [U] establishing or being established: 建立;設立;確定: *the ~ of a new state.* 一新國家的建立。 **2** [C] that which is established, eg a large organized body of persons (eg the army or navy; a civil service; a business firm, with many employees; a hotel and the staff in it). 經建立的機構(例如陸軍,海軍,文職機關,有許多人員的公司行號,旅社及其服務人員等)。 **3 the E~,** (GB) those persons in positions of power and authority, exercising influence in the background of public life or other field of activity. (英)當權派。

es·tami·net /eˈstæmɪneɪ *US:* eˌstæmɪˈneɪ; ɛstamiˈnɛ/ *n* (F) small French café selling beer, wine, coffee, etc. (法)賣啤酒,葡萄酒,咖啡等的小店。

es·tate /ɪˈsteɪt; əˈstet/ *n* **1** [C] piece of property in the form of land, esp in the country: 地產(尤指在鄉間者): *He owns large ~s in Scotland.* 他在蘇格蘭有大批地產。 ˈ~ **agent,** (US 美 =*Realtor*) person who buys and sells buildings and land for others. 房地產經紀人。 ˈ**housing ~,** area of land on which many houses are built, either by private enterprise or (ˈ**council ~**) by a public authority. 住宅區(或由私人或由公家所建立的)。 **inˈdustrial ~,** area of land development for industrial use (factories, etc). 工業區。 **2** [U] (legal) a person's whole property. (法律)一人的全部財產。 ˈ**real ~,** land and buildings. 房地產;不動產。 ˈ**personal ~,** money and other kinds of property. 動產。 **3** [C] political or social group or class: 政治團體;社會階級: *the three ~s of the realm,* the Lords Spiritual (Bishops in the House of Lords), the Lords Temporal (other lords) and the House of Commons; 上議院主教議員,上議院貴族議員與下議院議員;貴族,僧侶和平民; *the fourth ~,* the press(3). 新聞界。 **4** (old use) condition; stage in life: (舊用法)狀況;生活階段: *reach man's ~;* 成年; *the holy ~ of matrimony.* 神聖的婚姻生活。 **5** ˈ~ **car,** (US 美 = *station-wagon*) saloon-type motor vehicle with removable or collapsible rear seats and door(s) at the back, for easy loading of luggage, etc. 旅行車(設有可以移動的座位和後門,以便易於裝行李等)。

es·teem /ɪˈstiːm; əˈstim/ *vt* **1** [VP6A] (formal) have a high opinion of; respect greatly: (正式用語)尊重;尊敬: *No one can ~ your father more than I do.* 沒有人比我更尊敬你的父親了。 **2** [VP25] (formal) consider; regard: (正式用語)認爲;以爲: *I shall ~ it a favour if....* 如果…我將深領厚意。 *I ~ it a privilege to address this audience.* 我認爲能向諸位演講是一種榮幸。□ *n* [U] high regard: 尊敬;尊重: *He lowered himself in our ~ by this foolish behaviour.* 由於此一愚行,他減低了我們對他的尊重。 *We all hold him in great ~.* 我們都十分尊敬他。

es·thetic /ˌiːsˈθetɪk; ɛsˈθɛtɪk/ = aesthetic.

es·ti·mable /ˈestɪməbl; ˈɛstəməbl/ *adj* worthy of esteem. 值得尊敬的。

es·ti·mate[1] /ˈestɪmət; ˈɛstəmɪt/ *n* [C] judgement; approximate calculation (of size, cost, etc): 判斷;(大小,價錢等之)估計: *I hope the builders don't exceed their ~.* 我希望營造商們不要超過他們的估計。 *I do not know enough about him to form an ~*

of his abilities. 我對他的了解不够,不能對他的能力作估計。*Can you give me a rough ~ of the cost?* 你能將費用大約地估計一下嗎? ⇨ rough¹(3); outside *adj* (2). **the E~s,** figures supplied each year by the Chancellor of the Exchequer showing the probable national expenditure, etc. 政府的歲費預算。

es·ti·mate² /ˈestɪmeɪt ; ˈɛstəˌmet/ *vt, vi* [VP 9, 14, 3A] ~ ***(at),*** form a judgement about; calculate the cost, value, size, etc of sth: 評定;估計(某物的價錢,價值,大小等): *The firm ~d the cost of the work at £8000.* 這公司估計這工作的費用爲八千鎊。*We ~ that it would take three months to finish the work.* 我們估計完成這工作需要三個月。*I ~ his income at/to be about £5000.* 我估計他的收入約爲五千鎊。*Ask a contractor to ~ for the repair of the building.* 請個包工估計一下修理這房屋需要多少錢。

es·ti·ma·tion /ˌestɪˈmeɪʃn; ˌɛstəˈmeʃən/ *n* [U] judgement; regard: 判斷;評價: *in my ~;* 據我的判斷; *in the ~ of most people.* 在大多數人的心目中。

es·trange /ɪˈstreɪndʒ ; əˈstrendʒ/ *vt* [VP6A, 14] ~ ***(from),*** bring about a separation in feeling and sympathy: 使疏遠: *foolish behaviour that ~d all his friends;* 使所有朋友們與之疏遠的愚行;*~ sb from his friends.* 使某人與其朋友們疏遠。*He is ~d from his wife,* living apart from her. 他和妻子分居。**~·ment** *n* [U] being ~d; [C] instance of this: 被疏遠;疏遠: *cause an ~ment between two old friends.* 導致兩位老朋友間之疏遠。

es·tu·ary /ˈestʃʊərɪ *US:* -uerɪ ; ˈɛstʃʊˌɛrɪ/ *n* (*pl* -ries) [C] river mouth into which the tide flows: (與海相連的)河口: *the Thames ~.* 泰晤士河河口。

et cet·era /ɪt ˈsetərə *US:* et ; ɛt ˈsɛtərə/ (Lat, 拉, usu shortened to 通常略作 **etc**) and other things; and so on. 及其他;等等。

etch /etʃ ; ɛtʃ/ *vt, vi* [VP6A, 2A] use a needle and acid to make a picture, etc on a metal plate from which copies may be printed; make (pictures, etc) in this way. (用針和酸類在金屬板上)蝕刻圖畫等;以蝕刻術作(圖畫等)。**~er** *n* person who ~es. 蝕刻師;用針和酸類在金屬板上蝕刻圖畫等者。**~·ing** *n* [U] the art of the ~er; [C] copy printed from an ~ed plate. 蝕刻術;用蝕刻版印出之圖畫。

eter·nal /ɪˈtɜːnl ; ɪˈtɝnl̩/ *adj* **1** without beginning or end; lasting for ever: 永恆的;永遠的: *the E~,* God; 上帝; *the E~ City,* Rome. 羅馬。*Does the Christian religion promise ~ life?* 基督教許諾永生嗎? **2** (colloq) unceasing; too frequent: (俗)不斷的;不停的: *Stop this ~ chatter.* 不要囉嗦個不停。***the ~ triangle,*** situation of conflict in which two men want the same woman or two women the same man. 三角戀愛。**~ly** /ɪˈtɜːnəlɪ ; ɪˈtɝnl̩ɪ/ *adv* throughout all time; for ever; (colloq) (too) frequently. 永恆地;永遠地;(俗)不停地。

eter·nity /ɪˈtɜːnətɪ ; ɪˈtɝnətɪ/ *n* (*pl* -ties) **1** [U] time without end; the future life: 永恆;來世: *send a man to ~,* to his death. 使某人死去。**2 an ~,** period of time that seems endless: 似乎無終止的一段時間: *It seemed an ~ before news of his safety reached her.* 他的平安的消息到達她那裏以前,那段時間似乎是漫長無限的。**3** (*pl*) eternal truths. (複)永久不變的眞理。

ether /ˈiːθə(r) ; ˈiθɚ/ *n* [U] **1** liquid made from alcohol, used in industry, and medically as an anaesthetic. 醚(由酒精製成的一種無色液體,用於工業,醫學上用作麻醉劑)。**2** medium(3) through which, it was once believed, light waves were transmitted through all space. 以太(一度被認爲充滿整個空間,可藉以傳送光波的一種物質)。**3** (poet) the pure, upper air above the clouds. (詩)上空;蒼天。

eth·ereal /ɪˈθɪərɪəl ; ɪˈθɪrɪəl/ *adj* **1** of unearthly delicacy; seeming too light or spiritual for this world: 輕妙的;靈妙的;超俗的: *~ beauty/music;* 輕妙的美(音樂); *the ~ figure of an angel.* 天使的飄然姿態。**2** (poet) of the pure, upper air above the clouds. (詩)天上的;蒼天的。

ethic /ˈeθɪk ; ˈɛθɪk/ *n* **an ~,** system of moral principles, rules of conduct: 道德原則及行爲準繩的體系: *Was Islam in Turkey a traditional social code or an ~ for living?* 在土耳其伊斯蘭教是一傳統的社會法典還是生活上的道德體系? **eth·ics** *n pl* **1** (with *sing v*) science of morals: (與單數動詞連用)倫理學: *E~s is a branch of philosophy.* 倫理學爲哲學之一支。**2** (with *pl v*) moral soundness: (與複數動詞連用)行爲的準繩;道德規範: *The ~s of his decision are doubtful.* 他的決定中的道德準繩令人懷疑。**ethi·cal** /-kl ; -kl̩/ *adj* of morals or moral questions: 道德的;倫理的;道德問題的: *an ~al basis for education.* 教育的道德基礎。**ethi·cally** /-klɪ ; -kl̩ɪ/ *adv*

eth·nic /ˈeθnɪk ; ˈɛθnɪk/ *adj* of race or the races of mankind; (colloq) of a particular cultural group: 人種的;種族的;(俗)某一特殊文化團體的;具有種族特色的: *~ clothes/food/music;* 具有種族特色的服裝(食物,音樂); *an ~ restaurant.* 具有種族特色的餐館。**eth·ni·cally** /-ɪklɪ ; -ɪkl̩ɪ/ *adv*

eth·no·gra·phy /eθˈnɒgrəfɪ ; ɛθˈnɑgrəfɪ/ *n* [U] scientific description of the races of mankind. 人種誌。**eth·no·gra·pher** /eθˈnɒgrəfə(r) ; ɛθˈnɑgrəfɚ/ *n* **eth·no·graphic** /ˌeθnəˈgræfɪk ; ˌɛθnəˈgræfɪk/ *adj*

eth·nol·ogy /eθˈnɒlədʒɪ ; ɛθˈnɑlədʒɪ/ *n* [U] science of the races of mankind, their relations to one another, etc. 人種學。**eth·nol·o·gist** /-dʒɪst ; -dʒɪst/ *n* student of, expert in, ~. 人種學家;人種學者。**eth·no·logi·cal** /ˌeθnəˈlɒdʒɪkl ; ˌɛθnəˈlɑdʒɪkl̩/ *adj* of ~. 人種學的。

ethos /ˈiːθɒs ; ˈiθɑs/ *n* characteristics of a community or of a culture; code of values by which a group or society lives. 社會的特質;文化精神;團體或社會的生活準則。

ethyl /ˈeθɪl ; ˈɛθəl/ *n* **~ alcohol,** the base of alcoholic drinks, also used as a fuel or solvent. 乙醇;普通酒精。

eti·ology /ˌiːtɪˈɒlədʒɪ ; ˌitɪˈɑlədʒɪ/ *n* assignment of a cause; (med) study of the causes of disease. 推究原因;(醫)病原學。

eti·quette /ˈetɪket ; ˈɛtɪkɛt/ *n* [U] rules for formal relations or polite social behaviour among people, in a class of society or a profession: 禮節;禮儀;規矩;成規: *medical/legal ~.* 醫(法)界的成規。

ety·mol·ogy /ˌetɪˈmɒlədʒɪ ; ˌɛtəˈmɑlədʒɪ/ *n* **1** [U] science of the origin and history of words. 語源學。**2** [C] account of the origin and history of a word. 語源之記述。**ety·mol·ogist** /-dʒɪst ; -dʒɪst/ *n* student of ~. 語源學者。**ety·mo·logi·cal** /ˌetɪməˈlɒdʒɪkl ; ˌɛtəməˈlɑdʒɪkl̩/ *adj* of ~. 語源學的。

euca·lyptus /ˌjuːkəˈlɪptəs ; ˌjukəˈlɪptəs/ *n* sorts of tall evergreen tree (including the Australian gum tree) from which an oil is obtained. 桉樹類;有加利樹(包括澳洲橡皮樹的數種長青樹,自其中可提取一種油)。

Eu·char·ist /ˈjuːkərɪst ; ˈjukərɪst/ *n* **the E~,** the Lord's Supper; the bread and wine taken at this. 聖餐;聖餐中食用的麵包和酒。⇨ lord(2).

Eu·clid·ean /juːˈklɪdɪən ; juˈklɪdɪən/ *adj* of the geometric principles of Euclid, the Greek mathematician. (希臘數學家)歐幾里德幾何學的。

eu·gen·ics /juːˈdʒenɪks ; juˈdʒɛnɪks/ *n pl* (with *sing v*) science of the production of healthy offspring with the aim of improving the human genetic stock. (與單數動詞連用)優生學;人種改良學。

eu·logize /ˈjuːlədʒaɪz ; ˈjuləˌdʒaɪz/ *vt* [VP6A] (formal) praise highly in speech or writing. (正式用語)頌揚。**eu·logist** /ˈjuːlədʒɪst ; ˈjulədʒɪst/ *n* person who does this. 頌揚者。**eu·logis·tic** /ˌjuːləˈdʒɪstɪk ; ˌjuləˈdʒɪstɪk/ *adj* giving or containing high praise. 頌揚的;歌頌的。**eu·logy** /ˈjuːlədʒɪ ; ˈjulədʒɪ/ *n* (*pl* -gies) [C, U] (speech or writing full of) high praise. 頌揚;頌詞;頌揚文。

eu·nuch /ˈjuːnək ; ˈjunək/ *n* castrated man, esp one formerly employed in some Oriental courts. 閹人;(尤指昔時東方宮廷的)太監;宦官。

eu·phem·ism /ˈjuːfəmɪzəm ; ˈjufəˌmɪzəm/ *n* [C, U]

(example of the) use of other (mild, vague and indirect) words or phrases in place of what is required by truth or accuracy: 委婉的說法;委婉的話: *'Pass away' is a ~ for 'die'*. pass away 爲 die 的委婉說法。*'Pass water' is a ~ for 'urinate'*. pass water 爲 urinate 的委婉說法。**eu·phem·is·tic** /ˌjuːfəˈmɪstɪk ; ˌjufəˈmɪstɪk/ *adj* of the nature of ~: 委婉的: *euphemistic language／expressions*. 委婉的言語(措辭)。**eu·phe·mis·ti·cally** /-klɪ ; -klɪ/ *adv*

eu·phony /ˈjuːfənɪ ; ˈjufənɪ/ *n* [U] pleasantness of sound; [C, U] (*pl* -nies) pleasant sound. 聲音的諧和;諧和的聲音。

eu·phoria /juːˈfɔːrɪə ; juˈfɔrɪə/ *n* [U] state of well-being and pleasant excitement; elation. 舒適;安樂;興高采烈。**eu·phoric** /juːˈfɒrɪk *US:* -ˈfɔːr- ; juˈfɔrɪk/ *adj*

eu·phu·ism /ˈjuːfjuːɪzəm ; ˈjufjʊˌɪzəm/ *n* [C] (instance of) elaborately artificial style of writing and speaking (as fashionable in England in the late 16th and early 17th cc). 誇飾的文體(如十六世紀末及十七世紀初英國所盛行者)。

Eur·asia /jʊəˈreɪʒə ; jʊˈreʒə/ *n* Europe and Asia. 歐亞大陸。**Eur·asian** /jʊəˈreɪʒn ; jʊˈreʒən/ *n, adj* (person) of mixed European and Asian parentage; of Europe and Asia. 歐亞混血的(人);歐亞大陸的。

eu·reka /jʊəˈriːkə ; jʊˈrikə/ *int* (Gk = 'I have found it!') cry of triumph at a discovery. (希)(發現時得意的歡呼)我找到了!

eu·rhyth·mics (also **eu·ryth-**) /juːˈrɪðmɪks ; jʊˈrɪðmɪks/ *n pl* (with *sing v*) harmony of bodily movement, esp as a system of physical training with music. (與單數動詞連用)身體動作的協調;(尤指)配合音樂的體操;韻律體操。

Euro·dollar /ˈjʊərəʊdɒlə(r) ; ˈjʊrəˌdɑlə/ *n* US dollar put in European bank to act as an international currency and help the financing of trade and commerce. 存於歐洲銀行的美元 (用作國際貨幣,以助貿易)。

Euro·pean /ˌjʊərəˈpɪən ; ˌjʊrəˈpiən/ *n, adj* (native) of Europe; happening in, extending over, Europe: 歐洲人;歐洲的;發生在歐洲的; 延伸至歐洲的: *~ countries;* 歐洲各國; *a ~ reputation*. 遍及全歐的名聲。

Euro·vision /ˈjʊərəvɪʒn ; ˈjʊrəvɪʒən/ *n* European TV network. 歐洲電視網。

Eu·sta·chian tube /juːˌsteɪʃn ˈtjuːb *US:* ˈtuːb ; juˈstekɪən ˈtjub/ *n* (anat) duct extending from the middle ear to the pharynx. (解剖)歐氏管;耳咽管。⇨ the illus at ear. 參看 ear 之揷圖。

eu·tha·nasia /ˌjuːθəˈneɪzɪə *US:* -ˈneɪʒə ; ˌjuθəˈneʒə/ *n* [U] (bringing about of a) mercifully easy and painless death (for persons suffering from an incurable and painful disease). (患不治而又痛苦的疾病者之)無痛苦的死亡;無痛苦致死術。

evacu·ate /ɪˈvækjʊeɪt ; ɪˈvækjʊˌet/ *vt* **1** [VP6A] (esp of soldiers) withdraw from; leave empty: (尤指軍隊)撤離;自…撤退: *~ a fort／town*. 撤離一堡壘(城鎮)。**2** [VP6A, 14] **~ sb (from) (to)**, remove him from a place or district, eg one considered to be dangerous in time of war: 自一地區(如戰時危險地區)遣走(某人);疏散: *The children were ~d to the country*. 孩子們被疏散至鄉下。**3** [VP6A] empty (*of* its contents); (esp) defecate. 排泄;(尤指)大便。**evacu·ation** /ɪˌvækjʊˈeɪʃn ; ɪˌvækjʊˈeʃən/ *n* [U] evacuating or being ~d; [C] instance of this. 撤離;疏散;除淸。**evacuee** /ɪˌvækjuːˈiː ; ɪˈvækjʊˌi/ *n* person who is ~d(2). 被疏散者。

evade /ɪˈveɪd ; ɪˈved/ *vt* [VP6A, C] **1** get, keep, out of the way of: 躲避;逃避: *~ a blow／one's enemies／an attack*. 躲避一擊(敵人,攻擊)。**2** find a way of not doing sth: 避免(做某事): *~ paying income tax;* 避付所得稅; *~ military service;* 逃避兵役; avoid answering (fully or honestly): 避免(充分或誠實地)回答: *~ a question*. 避免回答一問題。

evalu·ate /ɪˈvæljʊeɪt ; ɪˈvæljʊˌet/ *vt* [VP6A] find out, decide, the amount or value of. 求出…的數量或價值;決定…的數量或價值;評價; 估計。**evalu·ation** /ɪˌvæljʊˈeɪʃn ; ɪˌvæljʊˈeʃən/ *n*

evan·escent /ˌiːvəˈnesnt *US:* ˌev- ; ˌɛvəˈnɛsn̩t/ *adj* quickly fading; soon going from the memory: 迅速凋落的;不久便被遺忘的: *~ political triumphs*. 政治上曇花一現的勝利。**evan·escence** /-sns ; -sn̩s/ *n*

evan·geli·cal /ˌiːvænˈdʒelɪkl ; ˌivænˈdʒɛlɪkl̩/ *adj* **1** of, according to, the teachings of the Gospel: 福音的;根據福音的: *~ preaching*. 福音傳道。**2** of the beliefs and teachings of those Protestants who maintain that the soul can be saved only by faith in Jesus Christ. 福音派新教會(主張祇有相信耶穌,靈魂始能得救)的。**~·ism** /-ɪzəm ; -ɪzəm/ *n* [U] ~(2) beliefs or teachings. 福音派新教會之信仰或教義。

evan·gel·ist /ɪˈvændʒəlɪst ; ɪˈvændʒəlɪst/ *n* **1** one of the writers (Matthew, Mark, Luke or John) of the Gospels. 四福音書作者(馬太,馬可,路加,約翰)之一。**2** preacher of the Gospel, esp one who travels and holds religious meetings wherever he goes, preaching to any who are willing to listen. 福音傳道者(尤指旅行傳道者)。**evan·gel·is·tic** /ɪˌvændʒəˈlɪstɪk ; ɪˌvændʒəˈlɪstɪk/ *adj*

evap·or·ate /ɪˈvæpəreɪt ; ɪˈvæpəˌret/ *vt, vi* **1** [VP 6A, 2A] (cause to) change into vapour: (使)蒸發: *Heat ~s water*. 熱蒸發水。*The water soon ~d*. 水不久便蒸發了。**2** [VP6A] remove liquid from a substance, eg by heating: 除去(某物)之水分(例如用熱): *~d milk*. 煉乳。**3** [VP2A] disappear; die: 消失;死亡: *His hopes ~d*, He no longer felt any hope. 他的希望消失了。**evap·or·ation** /ɪˌvæpəˈreɪʃn ; ɪˌvæpəˈreʃən/ *n*

evas·ion /ɪˈveɪʒn ; ɪˈveʒən/ *n* **1** [U] evading: 躲避;逃避;避免: *~ of responsibility*. 逃避責任。**2** [C] statement, excuse, etc made to evade sth; act of evading: 遁詞;藉口;推託: *His answers to my questions were all ~s*. 他對我的問題的回答均爲遁詞。

evas·ive /ɪˈveɪsɪv ; ɪˈvesɪv/ *adj* tending, trying, to evade: 躲避的;逃避的;避免的: *an ~ answer;* 遁詞;推託; *take ~ action*, do sth in order to evade danger, etc. 採取某種行動以求躲避 (危險等)。**~·ly** *adv* **~·ness** *n*

Eve /iːv ; iv/ *n* (in the Bible story of the Creation) the first woman. (聖經創世紀中的)夏娃(世界第一個女人)。

eve /iːv ; iv/ *n* day or evening before a Church festival or any day or event; time just before anything: (宗教節日,任何日期或事件之) 前日或前夜;前夕: *Christmas Eve*, 24 Dec; 聖誕節前夕(十二月二十四日); *New Year's Eve*, 31 Dec; 除夕(十二月三十一日); *on the eve of great events*. 大事件之前夕。

even[1] /ˈiːvn ; ˈivən/ *adj* **1** level; smooth: 平坦的;平滑的: *A billiard-table must be perfectly ~*. 撞球檯必須十分平坦。**2** regular; steady; of unchanging quality: 有規律的;不變的;均匀的: *His ~ breathing showed that he had got over his excitement*. 他的均匀的呼吸顯示出他已由興奮轉爲平靜了。*His work is not very ~*, it is a mixture of good and bad. 他的作品時好時壞。**3** (of amounts, distances, values) equal: (指數量,距離,價值)相等的: *Our scores are now ~*. 我們的得分現在相等。*The two horses were ~ in the race*. 那兩匹馬競賽的成績相等。**be／get ~ with sb**, have／get one's revenge on him. 向某人報復。**~ odds**, chances which are the same for or against. 成敗或正反的機會相等。**break ~**, (colloq) make neither a profit nor a loss. (俗)不賺不賠; 得失相等。**4** (of numbers) that can be divided by two with no remainder: (指數目) 可被二除盡的; 偶數的: *The pages on the left side of a book have ~ numbers*. 一本書左面的頁碼是偶數。⇨ odd. **5** equally balanced: 公平的;均衡的: *an ~ chance;* 公平的機會; *~ money*, (in betting). (賭賽中)相等的錢。**~-handed** *adj* fair: 公正的: *~-handed justice*. 大公無私。**6** (of temper, etc) calm; not easily disturbed: (指性情等)平靜的;冷靜的: *an ~-tempered baby*. 性情平靜的嬰孩。□

vt [VP6A, 15B] ~ **(up)**, make ~ or equal: 使平坦;使平;使相等: *That will ~ things up*, make them equal. 這可以使事情得其平。**~·ly** *adv* **~·ness** *n*

even² /ˈiːvn ; ˈivən/ *adv* **1** (used to invite a comparison between what happened and what might have happened). 甚至;即使(用以就所發生者與可能發生者之間做一比較): *He never ~ ˈopened the letter* (so he certainly did not read it). 他甚至連那封信都未打開過(所以他一定沒有看過)。*He didn't answer ~ ˈmy letter* (not to mention letters from others). 他甚至連我的信都沒有回覆(不用說別人的信了)。*It was cold there ~ in Juˈly* (so you may imagine how cold it was in winter). 那地方即使在七月裏也是冷的(所以你可以想像在冬天是多麼寒冷)。*E~ a ˈchild can understand the book* (so adults can certainly do so). 即使小孩子也能看懂那本書 (所以大人一定也能看懂)。 **2 ~ if/though,** (used to call attention to the extreme nature of what follows): 縱然;即令(用以使人注意下文之極端性質): *I'll get there ~ if I have to pawn my watch to get the railway fare.* 縱然我必須將錶押當做爲火車旅費,我也要到那裏去。*She won't leave the TV set, ~ though her supper's on the table.* 縱使晚餐已擺在桌上,她也不願意離開電視機。 **3** (with comparatives) still, yet: (與比較級連用)更加;愈加: *You know ~ less about it than I do.* 關於此事你知道的比我更少。*You seem ~ more stupid than usual today.* 你今天好像比平時更加蠢笨。 **4 ~ as,** just at the time when: 正當;恰在…的時候: *E~ as I gave the warning the car skidded.* 正當我提出警告時,那車子滑到一邊去了。**~ now/then,** in spite of these or those circumstances, etc: 甚至此時(那時);雖然情況如此: *E~ now he won't believe me.* 甚至到現在他還不相信我。*E~ then he would not admit his mistake.* 甚至那時他還不承認錯誤。**~ so,** though that is the case: 雖然如此: *It has many omissions; ~ so, it is quite a useful reference book.* 那書有許多遺漏之處,雖然如此,尙不失爲一本有用的參考書。

even³ /ˈiːvn ; ˈivən/ *n* (poet) evening. (詩)日暮;晚間。**ˈ~·song** *n* Evening Prayer in the Church of England. 英國國教之晚禱。**ˈ~·tide** *n* (poet) evening. (詩)日暮;晚間。

even·ing /ˈiːvnɪŋ ; ˈivnɪŋ/ *n* **1** [C, U] that part of the day between sunset and bedtime: 晚間;傍晚;黃昏: *a cool ~;* 涼爽的晚間; *musical ~s*, evenings given to playing or listening to music; 演奏或欣賞音樂之夜; *two ~s ago;* 前天晚上; (no *prep*) *this/tomorrow/yesterday ~;* 今(明,昨)晚(前面不用介詞); *in the ~;* 在晚間; *on Sunday ~;* 在星期日晚間; *on the ~ of the 8th;* 在八日晚間; *one warm summer ~.* 一個暖和的夏夜。 **2** (attrib): (形容用法): **ˈ~ dress,** dress as worn for formal occasions in the ~. 晚禮服。**ˌ~ ˈpaper,** newspaper published after midday. 晚報。**ˌ~ ˈprayer,** church service; vespers. 晚禱。**the ˌ~ ˈstar,** planet, (Venus or Mercury), seen in the western sky after sunset. 晚星;金星;水星(日落後西天出現之星)。

even·song /ˈiːvnsɒŋ *US:* -sɔːŋ ; ˈivənˌsɔŋ/ ⇨ even³.

event /ɪˈvent ; ɪˈvɛnt/ *n* **1** happening, usu sth important: 事件;重要事件: *the chief ~s of 1789.* 1789年的大事。*It was quite an ~* (often used to suggest that what happened was on an unusual scale, memorable, etc). 那確是一件大事。**in the natural/normal/usual course of ~s,** in the order in which things naturally happen. 按照事情自然發生的程序;按照自然的趨勢。 **2** fact of a thing happening: 事情發生的事實: *in the ~ of his death,* if he dies. 如果他死去。 **3** outcome; result. 結果。**at ˈall ~s,** whatever is so. 無論如何。**in ˈany ~,** whatever is so. 無論如何。**in ˈeither ~,** whichever is so. 無論是這樣還是那樣;或此或彼。**in ˈthat ~,** if that is so. 如果是那樣的話。**in the ~,** as it in fact happens. 如事實所發生;結果。 **4** one of the races, competitions, etc in a sports programme: 運動節目表中之一項競賽: *Which ~s have you entered for?* 你參加了那幾項競賽? **~·ful** /-fl ; -fəl/ *adj* full of notable ~s: 多重要事件的;多事的: *He had had an ~ful life.* 他的一生多采多姿。*The past year has been ~ful.* 過去的一年是多事之秋。

even·tide /ˈiːvntaɪd ; ˈivənˌtaɪd/ *n* ⇨ even³.

event·ual /ɪˈventʃʊəl ; ɪˈvɛntʃʊəl/ *adj* coming at last as a result; ultimate: 結果的;最終的: *his foolish behaviour and ~ failure.* 他的愚行及最終的失敗。**~·ly** /-tʃʊəlɪ ; -tʃʊlɪ/ *adv* in the end: 最後;終於: *He fell ill and ~ly died.* 他得了病,最後去世了。**~·ity** /ɪˌventʃʊˈælətɪ ; ɪˌvɛntʃʊˈælətɪ/ *n* (*pl* -ties) [C] possible event. 可能發生的事件。

ever /ˈevə(r) ; ˈɛvɚ/ *adv* **1** (usu in neg and interr sentences, and in sentences expressing doubt or conditions; usu placed with the *v*) at any time: (通常用於否定句和疑問句,以及表示懷疑或條件的句子中;通常置於動詞旁)無論何時: *Nothing ~ happens in this village.* 這村子裏從未發生過什麼事情。*Do you ~ wish you were rich?* 你曾經希望過自己富有嗎? *She seldom, if ~, goes to the cinema.* 她很少看電影。*If you ~ visit London....* 你若是去倫敦…。 **2** (with the present perfect tense, in questions) at any time up to the present: (用於現在完成式疑問句中)曾經;曾: *Have you ~ been up in a balloon?* 你曾經乘過氣球嗎? (Note that *ever* is not used in the answer: either 'Yes, I have' or 'No, never', etc.) (注意: ever 不用於回答,回答時用 Yes, I have 或 No, never 等。) **3** (after a comparative or superlative): (用於比較級或最高級之後): *It is raining harder than ~,* than it has been doing so far. 雨比以前大了。*It is more necessary than ~* (= than it has been so far) *for all of us to win.* 我們大家比以往更須要獲勝。*This is the best work you have ~ done.* 這是你所做的最好的工作。 **4** (chiefly in phrases) at all times; continuously: (主要用於片語中)始終;老是: *~ afterwards;* 自此以後; *for ~ (and ~);* 永遠; *~ since I was a boy.* 從我孩提時代起。 **5** (colloq) (used as an intensifier): (俗)(用以加强程度): *Work as hard as ~ you can.* 儘量努力工作。*I'll tell her as soon as ~ she arrives.* 她一來到我就告訴她。**ˈ~ so; ˈ~ such (a),** (colloq) very: (俗)非常: *~ so rich;* 非常有錢; *~ such a rich man.* 非常有錢的人。 **6** (used after interrogatives as an intensifier): 究竟;到底(用於疑問句之後以增强語勢): *When/Where/How ~ did you lose it?* 你到底何時(何處,怎樣)將它遺失的? *What ~ do you mean?* 你究竟是什麼意思? **7 did you ~...!** used to express surprise, incredulity, etc: 用以表示驚訝,懷疑等: *Well, did you ~ hear such nonsense!* 啊,你們聽這一派胡言! **As if... ~,** used in a similar way: 用以表示驚訝,懷疑等: *As if he would ~ do such a thing!* He would certainly not do it! 就好像他一直做這種事情似的!(其實他决不會做出此事)。 **8** (old use) always: (舊用法)永遠: *You will find me ~ at your service.* 你會發現我永遠聽命於你。 **9 Yours ~,** used at the end of a letter, informal or familiar style. 你的永久的(朋友)(用於書信末尾簽名前的客套語,較不拘禮或親切的用法)。

ever·green /ˈevəgriːn ; ˈɛvɚˌgrin/ *n, adj* (tree, shrub) having green leaves throughout the year: 常綠樹;常綠的: *The pine, cedar and spruce are ~s.* 松,柏和針樅是常綠樹。⇨ deciduous.

ever·last·ing /ˌevəˈlɑːstɪŋ *US:* -ˈlæst- ; ˌɛvɚˈlæstɪŋ/ *adj* **1** going on for ever: 永久的;永恆的: *~ fame/glory.* 永久的聲譽(光榮)。**the E~,** God. 上帝。 **2** repeated too often: 重複太多次的: *I'm tired of his ~ complaints.* 我厭倦了他那不斷的抱怨。

ever·more /ˌevəˈmɔː(r) ; ˌɛvɚˈmɔr/ *adv* for ever. 永遠。

every /ˈevrɪ ; ˈɛvrɪ/ *adj* (used attrib with *sing* [C] *nouns;* cf the use of *all* with *pl nouns* and [U] *nouns*) (爲形容用法,與單數可數名詞連用;參較 all 與複數名詞以及與不可數名詞的用法) **1** (Cf *every* and *each.* When *every* is used, attention is directed to units comprising a whole; when *each* is used, attention is directed simply to the unit) all or each one of a whole: (參較 every 和 each。用 every 時,觀念着重於全體;用 each 時則着重於個別)所有的;每一: *E~ boy in the class* (= All the boys, The whole class) *passed the examination.* 班上所有的男生都考試及格了。(Cf 參較 *Each boy may have three tries.* 每個男孩可以試三次。) *I have read ~ book* (= all the books) *on that shelf.* 我讀遍了那書架上所有的書。*Not ~ horse* (= Not all horses) *can run fast.* 並非所有的馬都跑得快。**2** (not replaceable by *all* and the *plural noun*) each one of an indefinite number (the emphasis being on the unit, not on the total or whole): (不可被 all 和複數名詞代替) 每 (着重於單位而非整體): *He enjoyed ~ minute of his holiday.* 他享受他的假日的每一分鐘。*Such things do not happen ~ day.* 這種事情並非每天發生。*He spends ~ penny he earns.* 他賺來的每一分錢都花掉了。**3** (used with abstract *nouns*) all possible; complete: (與抽象名詞連用) 所有可能的; 完全的: *You have ~ reason to be satisfied.* 你有充分的理由應該滿意。*I have ~ reason/There is ~ reason to believe that....* 我有充分的理由相信…。*There is ~ prospect of success.* 有百分之百成功的希望。**4** (used with cardinal and ordinal numbers, and with *other* and *few*, to indicate recurrence, or intervals in time or space): (與基數,序數,other 和 few 連用,表示重現或時間空間的間隔): *Write on ~ other line,* on alternate lines. 隔行寫。*There are buses to the station ~ ten minutes.* 每隔十分鐘有公共汽車至車站。*I go there ~ other day/~ three days/~ third day/~ few days, etc.* 我每隔一日(每三日,每逢第三日,每隔數日等)到那裏去一次。*He was stopped ~ dozen yards by friends who wanted to congratulate him.* 他每走十幾碼便被欲向他祝賀的朋友們攔住。**~ now and then/again,** from time to time. 有時;間或;時常。**5** (used with, and placed after, possessives; replaceable by *all* + *pl*): (用於所有格形容詞後,此種用法可由 all + 複數名詞代替): *His ~ movement was watched,* All his movements.... 他的每一動作都受到注視。*He tries to meet her ~ wish,* all her wishes. 他試圖滿足她所有的願望。**6** (in phrases) (用於片語中) **~ bit,** quite: 完全: *This is ~ bit as good as that.* 這個和那個完全一樣好。**~ time, (a)** always: 總是: *Our football team wins ~ time.* 我們的足球隊總是得勝。**(b)** whenever: 無論何時;每當: *E~ time I meet him, he tries to borrow money from me.* 每當我遇到他,他便向我借錢。**~ 'one of them/us/you,** (placed at the end) without exception: (置於句後) 統統; 無例外: *You deserve to be hanged, ~ one of you.* 你們該受絞刑,統統都該。**in ~ way,** in all respects: 在各方面: *This is in ~ way better than that.* 這個在各方面都比那個好。**~·body** /ˈevrɪbɒdɪ; ˈɛvrɪ,bɑdɪ/, **~·one** /ˈevrɪwʌn; ˈɛvrɪ,wʌn/ *pron* ~ person: 每個人; 人人: *In a small village ~one knows ~one else.* 在一個小村子裏人人皆相識。**~·day** /ˈevrɪdeɪ; ˈɛvrɪˈde/ *adj* (attrib only) happening or used daily; common and familiar: (僅作形容用法) 每天發生的;每日所用的;日常的: *an ~day occurrence;* 日常之事; *in his ~day clothes.* 他穿着便服。**'~·place** (US colloq) ~where. (美俗)各處;到處。**~·thing** /ˈevrɪθɪŋ; ˈɛvrɪ,θɪŋ/ *pron* **(a)** all things: 一切事物; 每樣事物: *This shop sells ~thing needed for camping.* 這商店出售一切露營用具。*Tell me ~thing about it.* 告訴我這件事情的始末。**(b)** (pred) thing of the greatest importance: (敍述用法) 最重要的事物: *Money is ~thing to him.* 金錢對於他比什麼都重要。*She's beautiful, I agree, but beauty is not ~thing.* 我同意她是美麗的,但美並非最重要者。**~·where** /ˈevrɪweə(r) *US:* -hweər; ˈɛvrɪ,hwɛr/ *adv* in, at, to, ~ place: 各處;到處: *I've looked ~where for it.* 我曾到處尋找它。*E~where seemed to be quiet.* 各處似乎都很安靜。

evict /ɪˈvɪkt; ɪˈvɪkt/ *vt* [VP14] **~ (from),** expel (a tenant) (from a house or land) by authority of the law: 根據法律將(房客或佃戶)自房屋或土地逐出: *They were ~ed for not paying the rent.* 他們因欠房租而被逐出。**evic·tion** /ɪˈvɪkʃn; ɪˈvɪkʃən/ *n* [U] ~ing or being ~ed; [C] instance of this. (根據法律將房客或佃戶自房屋或土地)逐出;被逐出。

evi·dence /ˈevɪdəns; ˈɛvədəns/ *n* **1** [U] anything that gives reason for believing sth, that makes clear or proves sth: 證據; 根據: *There wasn't enough ~ to prove him guilty.* 沒有充分的證據證明他有罪。*Have you any ~ for this statement?* 你說這話有無根據? *We cannot condemn him on such slight ~.* 我們不能根據這樣少的證據而判他的罪。*The scientist must produce ~ in support of his theories.* 這科學家必須提出證據以支持其學說。***(be) in ~,*** (be) clearly or easily seen: 明白的;顯著的;易爲人所見的: *She's the sort of woman who likes to be very much in ~,* who likes to be seen and noticed. 她是那種喜歡出風頭的女子。*Smith was nowhere in ~,* could not be seen anywhere. 到處找不到史密斯。***bear/give/show ~ of,*** show signs of: 有…的跡象: *When the ship reached port, it bore abundant ~ of the severity of the storm,* ie signs of damage. 船抵港時,船上滿是受到暴風雨肆虐的痕跡。***turn Queen's/King's/*** (US) ***State's ~,*** (of a criminal) give ~ in court against accomplices. (指犯人)在庭上提出不利共犯的證據。**2** (used in *pl*) indication, mark, trace: (用複數)形跡;跡象;痕跡: *There were ~s of glacial action on the rocks.* 這些岩石上有冰河留下的痕跡。□ *vt* [VP6A] (rare) prove by ~; be ~ of: (罕)證明;作爲…的證據: *His answer ~d a guilty conscience.* 他的答覆證明他良心有愧。

evi·dent /ˈevɪdənt; ˈɛvədənt/ *adj* plain and clear (to the eyes or mind): 明顯的;顯然的: *It must be ~ to all of you that....* 你們顯然知道…。*He looked at his twelve children with ~ pride.* 他以明顯的得意態度望着他的十二個兒女。**~·ly** *adv*

evil /ˈiːvl; ˈivl/ *adj* **1** wicked, sinful, bad, harmful: 邪惡的;罪惡的;不良的;有害的: *~ men/thoughts;* 惡人(邪念); *live an ~ life;* 過着罪惡的生活; *the 'E~ One,* the Devil. 魔鬼;惡魔。**,~-'minded** *adj* having ~ thoughts and desires. 有邪惡之念頭及願望的;惡毒的;心毒的。**2** likely to cause trouble; bringing trouble or misfortune: 易引起麻煩的;不吉的;不幸的: *in an ~ hour;* 在不幸的時刻;不吉利; *fall on ~ days;* 遭逢厄運; *an ~* (= slanderous) *tongue.* 誹謗的嘴;惡毒的舌頭。**~ *eye,*** malicious look; supposed power to cause harm by a look or glance. 惡毒的眼光;兇狠的眼光;據說一瞥即可造成傷害的力量。□ *n* **1** [U] sin; wrong-doing: 罪惡;邪惡;犯罪: *return good for ~;* 以德報怨; *the spirit of ~.* 戾氣;惡魔。**'~-doer** *n* person who does ~. 作惡的人;犯罪者。**2** [C] ~ thing; disaster: 惡事;不幸;災禍: *War, famine and flood are terrible ~s.* 戰爭,饑荒和水災是可怕的災禍。***be/choose the lesser of two ~s,*** the less harmful of two bad choices. 兩害相權,擇其小者。**~·ly** /ˈiːvəlɪ; ˈivl̩ɪ/ *adv* in an ~ manner: 邪惡地;罪惡地;有害地: *He eyed her ~ly.* 他兇狠地瞪着她。

evince /ɪˈvɪns; ɪˈvɪns/ *vt* [VP6A, 9] (formal) show that one has (a feeling, quality, etc): (正式用語)表現(感情,性質等): *a child who ~s great intelligence.* 表現出極高智慧的兒童。

evis·cer·ate /ɪˈvɪsəreɪt; ɪˈvɪsə,ret/ *vt* [VP6A] disembowel. 取出…之腸。

evoca·tive /ɪˈvɒkətɪv; ɪˈvɑkətɪv/ *adj* that evokes, or is able to evoke: 召喚的;喚起的: *~ words,* that call up memories, emotions, in addition to their ordinary meanings. 勾起回憶或感情的言語。

evoke /ɪˈvəʊk; ɪˈvok/ *vt* [VP6A] call up, bring out: 召喚;引起: *~ a spirit from the other world;* 召來鬼魂; *~ admiration/surprise/a smile/memories of the past.* 引起羨慕(驚奇,微笑,過去的回憶)。**evo·ca·tion** /,iːvəʊˈkeɪʃn; ,ɛvoˈkeʃən/ *n*

evol·ution /ˌiːvəˈluːʃn *US:* ˌev-; ˌɛvəˈluʃən/ *n* **1** [U] evolving; process of opening out or developing: 開展;發育;發展: *the ~ of a plant from a seed.* 由種子發育成植物的過程。*In politics England has preferred ~* (= gradual development) *to revolution* (= sudden or violent change). 在政治上英國喜歡漸進,不喜歡革命。 **2** [U] (theory of the) development of more complicated forms of life (plants, animals) from earlier and simpler forms. 進化;進化論。 **3** [C] movement according to plan (of troops, warships, dancers, etc). (軍隊,軍艦,舞蹈者之) 按照計畫的行動。**~·ary** /ˌiːvəˈluːʃənrɪ *US:* ˌevəˈluːʃənerɪ; ˌɛvəˈluʃənˌɛrɪ/ *adj* of, being produced by, ~; developing. 開展的;進化的;發展的。

evolve /ɪˈvɒlv; ɪˈvɑlv/ *vi, vt* [VP2A, 6A] (cause to) unfold; develop; be developed, naturally and (usu) gradually: (使)開展;發展;自然而逐漸地進展: *The American constitution was planned; the British constitution ~d.* 美國的憲法是依計畫制定的,英國的憲法是自然演進的。*He has ~d a new plan/theory.* 他發展出一項新計畫(學說)。

ewe /juː; ju/ *n* female sheep. 牝羊;母羊。⇨ ram.

ewer /ˈjuːə(r); ˈjʊɚ/ *n* large wide-mouthed pitcher for holding water, eg as used with a basin on a wash-stand in a bedroom without a piped supply of water. 大口水罐(如寢室內無水管裝置時與面盆共置於臉盆架上者)。

ex- /eks; ɛks/ *pref* ⇨ App 3. 參看附錄三。

ex·acer·bate /ɪgˈzæsəbeɪt; ɪgˈzæsɚˌbet/ *vt* [VP 6A] (formal) irritate (a person); aggravate (= make worse) (pain, disease, a situation). (正式用語) 激怒(一人);加重(痛苦,疾病,局勢);使惡化。**ex·acer·ba·tion** /ɪgˌzæsəˈbeɪʃn; ɪgˌzæsɚˈbeʃən/ *n*

exact¹ /ɪgˈzækt; ɪgˈzækt/ *adj* **1** correct in every detail; free from error: 精確的;正確的: *Give me his ~ words.* 把他的話一字不差的告訴我。*What is the ~ size of the room?* 這房間的正確面積是多少? *I want ~ directions for finding your house.* 我需要如何能找到你住處的正確說明。**2** capable of being precise: 嚴謹的;精密的: *~ sciences;* 精密的(嚴謹的)科學; *an ~ memory;* 精確的記憶; *an ~ scholar.* 嚴謹的學者。 **~·ly** *adv* **1** correctly; quite: 正確地;完全地: *Your answer is ~ly right.* 你的答案完全對。*That's ~ly* (= just) *what I expected.* 那正是我所期待的。 **2** (as an answer or confirmation) quite so; just as you say. (作爲回答或認可)正是;不錯。**~·ness, ~·i·tude** /ɪgˈzæktɪtjuːd *US:* -tuːd; ɪgˈzæktəˌtjud/ *nn.*

exact² /ɪgˈzækt; ɪgˈzækt/ *vt* [VP6A, 14] **~ *(from)***, **1** demand and enforce payment of: 要求償付;强制要求付出: *~ taxes (from people);* (向人民)徵稅; *~ payment (from a debtor).* 强制(債務人)還債。**2** insist on: 堅持: *~ obedience.* 堅持要求服從。 **3** (of circumstances) require urgently; make necessary: (指情況)迫切需要;使必要: *work that ~s care and attention.* 需要小心和注意的工作。 **~·ing** *adj* making great demands; severe; strict: 苛求的;嚴厲的;嚴格的: *an ~ing piece of work;* 費力的工作; *an ~ing master.* 嚴厲的主人。**ex·action** /ɪgˈzækʃn; ɪgˈzækʃən/ *n* **1** [U] ~ing of money, etc. (對金錢等的)强求;强取。 **2** [C] that which is ~ed, esp a tax which is considered to be too high; a great demand (on one's time, strength, etc). 索取之物;(尤指)苛稅;(對時間,力量等之)大量需求。

exag·ger·ate /ɪgˈzædʒəreɪt; ɪgˈzædʒəˌret/ *vt, vi* [VP6A, 2A] stretch (a description) beyond the truth; make sth seem larger, better, worse, etc than it really is: 誇張;誇大: *You ~ the difficulties.* 你誇張那些困難。*If you always ~, people will no longer believe you.* 如果你老是誇張,人們便不會相信你了。*He has an ~d sense of his own importance,* thinks he is far more important than he really is. 他過於自大(自視過高)。**exag·ger·ation** /ɪgˌzædʒəˈreɪʃn; ɪgˌzædʒəˈreʃən/ *n* [U] exaggerating or being ~d; [C] ~d statement: 誇張;誇大;誇張的陳述: *a story full of exaggerations.* 充滿誇張的故事。

exalt /ɪgˈzɔːlt; ɪgˈzɔlt/ *vt* [VP6A] **1** make high(er) in rank, great(er) in power or dignity. 擢升;提高…之職位。 **2** praise highly. 讚揚。**~ed** *adj* dignified; ennobled: 崇高的;高貴的: *a person of ~ed rank.* 地位崇高之人。 **exal·ta·tion** /ˌegzɔːlˈteɪʃn; ˌɛgzɔlˈteʃən/ *n* [U] (fig) elation; state of spiritual delight. (喻)得意;意氣揚揚。

exam /ɪgˈzæm; ɪgˈzæm/ *n* (colloq abbr of) examination. (俗)爲 examination 之略。

exam·in·ation /ɪgˌzæmɪˈneɪʃn; ɪgˌzæməˈneʃən/ *n* **1** [U] examining or being examined: 檢查;訊問: *On ~, it was found that the signature was not genuine.* 檢查時發現此簽名不是眞的。*The prisoner is still under ~,* being examined. 這犯人仍在受審中。 **2** [C] instance of this, esp 檢查或訊問之實例,尤指 **(a)** a testing of knowledge or ability: 考試;測驗: *an ~ in mathematics;* 數學考試; *~ questions/papers;* 試題(試卷); *an oral ~.* 口試。**(b)** an inquiry into or inspection of sth: 調查;審查: *an ~ of a botanical specimen;* 審查一植物標本; *an ~ of business accounts;* 審查商業帳目; *an ~ of one's eyes.* 檢查眼睛。**(c)** questioning by a lawyer in a law court: 律師在法庭上的質詢: *an ~ of a witness.* 律師對證人的質詢。

exam·ine /ɪgˈzæmɪn; ɪgˈzæmɪn/ *vt* [VP6A, 14] **1** **~ *(for)***, look at carefully in order to learn about or from: 檢查;審查: *~ old records;* 檢查舊記錄; *have one's teeth/eyes ~d for decay/weakening;* 檢查牙齒是否有蛀牙(檢查視力是否衰退); *~ a new theory.* 審查一新學說。*She needs to have her head ~d,* (colloq) is foolish or impudent. (俗)她眞該去檢查一下她的腦袋了。 **2 ~ *(in)***, put questions to in order to test knowledge or get information: 考試;詢問: *~ pupils in Latin/on their knowledge of Latin;* 考學生的拉丁文; *~ a witness in a court of law.* 在法庭上質問一證人。 **exam·iner** *n* person who ~s. 檢查者;審查者;考試者;審問者。

example /ɪgˈzɑːmpl *US:* -ˈzæmpl; ɪgˈzæmpl/ *n* **1** fact, thing, etc which illustrates or represents a general rule: 實例;例證: *This dictionary has many ~s of how verbs are used.* 這部字典有許多說明動詞用法的實例。***for ~,*** (abbr 略作 **eg**) by way of illustration: 例如;譬如: *Many great men have risen from poverty—Lincoln and Edison, for ~.* 許多偉人由貧苦中崛起,例如林肯和愛迪生。**2** specimen showing the quality of others in the same group or of the same kind: 樣本;例子: *This is a good ~ of Shelley's lyric poetry.* 這是雪萊的抒情詩的一個良好的例子。**3** [C, U] thing or person, person's conduct, to be copied or imitated: 模範;榜樣: *follow sb's ~;* 模仿某人; *set an ~ to sb;* 給某人樹一楷模; *set sb a good ~;* 爲某人樹立好榜樣; *learn by ~.* 模仿;仿效。**4** warning: 警告: *Let this be an ~ to you.* 這便是給你的警告。 ***make an ~ of sb,*** punish him as a warning to others. 懲一儆百。

exas·per·ate /ɪgˈzæspəreɪt; ɪgˈzæspəˌret/ *vt* [VP 6A] irritate; produce ill feeling in; make ill feeling, anger, etc worse: 激怒;引起…之惡感;加深(惡感,憤怒等): *~d by/at sb's stupidity.* 因某人之愚笨而憤怒。*It is exasperating to lose a train by half a minute.* 因半分鐘之差而誤了火車是令人惱火的。 **exas·per·ation** /ɪgˌzæspəˈreɪʃn; ɪgˌzæspəˈreʃən/ *n* state of being ~d: 惱怒;憤怒: *'Stop that noise,' he cried out in exasperation.* '不要吵,' 他憤怒地大聲說。

ex·ca·vate /ˈekskəveɪt; ˈɛkskəˌvet/ *vt* [VP6A] make, uncover, by digging: 挖掘;發掘: *~ a trench/a buried city.* 挖壕(發掘一個埋在地下的城市)。**ex·ca·vator** /-tə(r); -tɚ/ *n* person engaged in, machine used for, excavating. 挖掘者;挖掘機。 **ex·ca·va·tion** /ˌekskəˈveɪʃn; ˌɛkskəˈveʃən/ *n* [U] excavating or being ~d; [C] place that is being or has been ~d. 挖掘;發掘;被挖掘之地。

ex·ceed /ɪkˈsiːd; ɪkˈsid/ *vt* [VP6A] **1** be greater

than: 比…大;駕乎…之上: *Their success ~ed all expectations.* 他們的成功出乎一切預料。*London ~s Glasgow in size and population.* 倫敦在面積和人口方面大於格拉斯哥。**2** go beyond what is allowed, necessary or advisable: 超出;超越: *~ the speed limit,* drive faster than is allowed; 駕車超速; *~ one's instructions,* do more than one has authority to do. 越權。**~·ing·ly** *adv* extremely; to an unusual degree: 非常;極度地: *an ~ingly difficult problem.* 一個非常困難的問題。

ex·cel /ɪk'sel ; ɪk'sɛl/ *vi, vt* (-ll-) ~ ***(in/at),*** **1** [VP2C, 3A] do better than others, be very good: 優於他人;勝過他人;優秀: *He ~s in courage/as an orator.* 他在勇氣(演說)方面勝過他人。*The firm ~s in/at producing cheap transistor radios.* 這家公司在生產價廉的晶體收音機方面勝過其他公司。**2** [VP6A, 15A] do better than; surpass (the more usu word): 優於;勝過 (surpass 一字較常用): *He ~s all of us in/at tennis.* 他的網球勝過我們所有的人。

ex·cel·lence /'eksələns ; 'ɛksḷəns/ *n* **1** [U] ~ ***(in/at),*** the quality of being excellent; great merit: 優越;卓越;優秀: *a prize for ~ in furniture design;* 傢具設計特優獎; *his ~ in/at all forms of sport.* 他在各項運動方面的優越。**2** [C] thing or quality in which a person excels: 優秀之處;長處;優點: *They do not recognize her many ~s.* 他們沒有發覺她的許多優點。

Ex·cel·lency /'eksələnsɪ ; 'ɛksḷənsɪ/ *n* (*pl* -cies) title of ambassadors, governors and their wives, and some other officers and officials: 閣下(對大使,省長,大使及省長夫人,以及若干其他官員的尊稱): *Your/His/Her ~.* 閣下。

ex·cel·lent /'eksələnt ; 'ɛksḷənt/ *adj* very good; of high quality. 極好的;優秀的。**~·ly** *adv*

ex·cel·sior /ek'selsɪɔ:(r) ; ɪk'sɛlsɪɚ/ *n* [U] (US) soft, fine wood shavings used for packing easily damaged goods, eg glassware. (美)細鉋花(包裝時用以填墊玻璃器皿等易損毀之貨物)。

ex·cept¹ /ɪk'sept ; ɪk'sɛpt/ *prep* not including; but not: 除…之外;但…不包括在內: *He gets up early every day ~ Sunday.* 除星期日外他每天早起。*Nobody was late ~ me.* 除我以外無人遲到。Cf 參較 Five others were late *besides* me. 在我之外尚有五人遲到。*My papers seem to be everywhere ~ where they ought to be.* 我的文件似乎完全不在它們應該放置的地方。**~ *for,*** (used when what is excluded is different from what is included): 除…外(用以說明除外者異於包括在內者);祇是: *Your essay is good ~ for the spelling.* 你的文章甚好,祇是拼字有誤。(The comparison is between the spelling, which is not good, and other things, eg ideas, grammar, which are satisfactory). (係就拼字與其他方面例如思想,文法等做一比較,拼字不佳,其他方面令人滿意)。Cf 參較 *All the essays are good ~ John's.* 除了約翰的以外,所有的文章都好。**~ *that,*** apart from the fact that: 除去…一點之外: *She knew nothing about his journey ~ that he was likely to be away for three months.* 關於他的旅行她不清楚,祇知道他大概要離開三個月。□ *conj* (old or liter use) unless: (舊用法或文學用語)除非: (biblical style) (聖經文體) *E~ ye be born again.* 除非你們重生。

ex·cept² /ɪk'sept ; ɪk'sɛpt/ *vt* [VP6A, 14] ~ ***(from),*** exclude (from); set apart (from a list, statement, etc): 將…除外;不包括…在名單,陳述等內: *I discovered that I had been ~ed from the list of those who were being sent to India.* 我發現我並沒有包括在派往印度去的人的名單上。*All those who took part in the plot, nobody ~ed, were punished.* 凡參與此一陰謀者,無人例外,均受到了處分。***present company ~ed,*** not including those here present. 在場者除外。**~·ing** *prep* (used after *not, always* and *without*) leaving out; excluding: (用於 not, always, without 之後)除…外: *the whole staff, not ~ing the heads of departments.* 全體人員,包括各部門首長。

ex·cep·tion /ɪk'sepʃn ; ɪk'sɛpʃən/ *n* **1** [U, C] excepting; sb or sth that is excepted (not included). 除外;(人或事物之)例外。***make an ~ (of sb/sth),*** treat (sb/sth) as an ~, a special case: 把…作爲例外: *You must all be here at 8am; I can make no ~s,* cannot excuse any of you. 你們都必須上午八點鐘到此,我不能特許任何人例外。***with the ~ of,*** except: 將…除外: *I enjoyed all his novels with the ~ of his last.* 我喜歡他所有的小說,最後一部例外。***without ~,*** excepting nobody/nothing: 無例外;一律: *All men between 18 and 45 without ~ are expected to serve in the army during a war.* 凡十八至四十五歲的男子一概應於戰時從軍。**2** [C] sth that does not follow the rule: 規則的例外: *~s to a rule of grammar.* 文法規則的例外。⇨ prove(1). **3** [U] objection. 反對。***take ~ (to sth),*** object to; protest against; be offended by: 反對;對…提出抗議;因…而不悅: *He took great ~ to what I said.* 他十分反對我的話。**~·able** /-əbl ; -əbḷ/ *adj* objectionable. 可反對的;可抗議的。**~·al** /-ʃənl ; -ʃənḷ/ *adj* unusual; out of the ordinary: 異常的;例外的;特別的: *weather that is ~al for June;* 六月裏異常的天氣; *~al advantages.* 特別好的利益。**~·ally** /-ʃənəlɪ ; -ʃənḷɪ/ *adv* unusually: 異常地;罕有地: *an ~ally beautiful boy.* 一個非常美麗的男孩。

ex·cerpt /'eksɜ:pt ; 'ɛksɝpt/ *n* [C] passage, extract, from a book etc, eg one printed separately. 摘錄;引述。

ex·cess¹ /ɪk'ses ; ɪk'sɛs/ *n* **1** ***an ~ of,*** fact of being, amount by which sth is, more than sth else, or more than is expected or proper: 超過;超越;過度;過剩;過分;過多之量: *an ~ of enthusiasm;* 過分熱心; *an ~ of imports over exports.* 輸入超過輸出;入超。***in ~ of,*** more than: 多於;超過: *Luggage in ~ of 100kg will be charged extra.* 超過一百公斤的行李要額外收費。***to ~,*** to an extreme degree: 過度: *Don't carry your grief to ~.* 不要過度悲傷。*She is generous to ~.* 她過度慷慨。**2** [U] immoderation; intemperance. 無節制。**3** (*pl*) personal acts which go beyond the limits of good behaviour, morality or humanity: (複)過分的行爲;超越道德或人性的行爲: *The ~es* (= acts of cruelty, etc) *committed by the troops when they occupied the capital will never be forgotten.* 那些軍隊佔領首都時所施的暴行將永遠不會使人忘記。**~·ive** /ɪk'sesɪv ; ɪk'sɛsɪv/ *adj* too much; too great; extreme: 過多的;過度的;極端的: *~ive charges.* 過高的索價。**~·ive·ly** *adv*

ex·cess² /'ekses ; 'ɛksɛs/ *adj* extra; additional: 額外的;附加的: *~ fare,* eg for travelling farther than is allowed by one's ticket; 額外票費;補票費; *~ luggage,* weight above what may be carried free; 超重的行李; *~ postage,* charged when a letter, etc is understamped: 欠資郵費; *~ profits duty,* extra tax on profits increased by, eg, war conditions. (戰時等)逾限利得稅;過分利得稅。

ex·change¹ /ɪks'tʃeɪndʒ ; ɪks'tʃendʒ/ *n* **1** [C, U] (act of) exchanging: 交換;互換: *Is five apples for five eggs a fair ~?* 用五個蘋果換五個蛋是一公平的交換嗎? *There have been numerous ~s of views between the two governments.* 兩國政府間曾多次交換意見。*E~ of prisoners during a war is unusual.* 戰時交換俘虜是少有的。*He is giving her French lessons in ~ for English lessons.* 他教她法文,她教他英文。**2** [U] the giving and receiving of the money of one country for that of another; relation in value between kinds of money used in different countries: 外幣兌換;兌換率: *the rate of ~* (between the dollar and the pound, etc). (美元與英鎊等之)兌換率。**'E~ Control,** system of protecting gold and reserves of foreign currency. (外幣之)滙兌管制。**3** [C] place where merchants or financiers meet for business: 交易所: *the 'Cotton E~;* 棉花交易所; *the 'Stock E~,* for the buying and selling of stocks, shares, bonds. 證券交易所。**4 *'labour ~,*** (GB) Government offices where unemployed workmen may be put in touch with prospective employers. (英)(政府所設)勞工介紹處。**'telephone ~,** control office where lines are connected. 電話局;電話交換所。

ex·change² /ɪks'tʃeɪndʒ ; ɪks'tʃendʒ/ *vt* [VP6A, 14] ***~ sth (for sth) (with sb),*** give, receive (one thing) in place of another: 交換;互換: *~ greetings/glances;* 互相問候(瞥視); *~ five apples for five eggs.* 用五個蘋果換五個蛋。*Mary ~d seats with Anne.* 瑪莉和安交換座位。***~ blows/words (with),*** fight/quarrel. 打架;爭吵。**~·able** /-əbl ; -əbl̩/ *adj* that may be ~d. 可交換的;可互換的。

ex·chequer /ɪks'tʃekə(r) ; ɪks'tʃɛkɚ/ *n* **1 the E~,** (GB) government department in charge of public money. (英) 財政部: ***Chancellor of the 'E~,*** minister at the head of this department (= Minister of Finance in other countries). 財政大臣(相當於其他國家之財政部長)。 **2** supply of money (public or private); treasury. (公共或私人的)財源;資金;國庫。

ex·cise¹ /'eksaɪz ; ɪk'saɪz/ *n* [U] government tax on certain goods manufactured, sold or used within a country: 國產稅;本國消費稅: *the ~ on beer/tobacco;* 啤酒(煙草)消費稅; *'~ duties;* 消費稅; *the Commissioners of Customs and E~.* 海關與國產稅務司官員。**'~·man** /-mən ; -mən/ (*pl* -men), **'E~ Officer,** officer collecting ~ and preventing breaking of ~ laws. 國產稅務官。

ex·cise² /ɪk'saɪz ; ɪk'saɪz/ *vt* [VP6A] (formal) remove by, or as if by, cutting (a part of the body, a passage from a book, etc). (正式用語)切除(身體之一部);刪去(書中之一段等)。**ex·cision** /ɪk'sɪʒn ; ɪk'sɪʒən/ *n* [U] excising or being ~d; [C] sth ~d. 切除;刪去;被切除或刪去的部分。

ex·cite /ɪk'saɪt ; ɪk'saɪt/ *vt* [VP6A, 14, 17] **1** ***~ (to),*** stir up the feelings of; cause (sb) to feel strongly: 激動;鼓舞;使興奮: *Don't ~ yourself!* Keep calm! 不要激動! *Everybody was ~d by the news of the victory.* 人人爲此勝利的消息而興奮。*It's nothing to get ~d about.* 這沒有什麼值得興奮的。*Agitators were exciting the people to rebellion/to rebel against their rulers.* 煽動者鼓動人民叛亂(反叛其統治者)。 **2** ***~ (in sb),*** get (a feeling) in motion; rouse; bring about: 引起(某種感情);激起;招惹: *~ admiration/envy/affection in an audience;* 引起觀衆的欽佩(羨慕,愛慕); *~ a riot.* 引起暴動。**3** cause (a bodily organ) to be active: 使(身體器官)活動;刺激: *drugs that ~ the nerves.* 刺激神經的藥物。**ex·cit·able** /ɪk'saɪtəbl ; ɪk'saɪtəbl̩/ *adj* easily ~d. 易興奮的;易激動的。**ex·cit·abil·ity** /ɪk,saɪtə'bɪlətɪ ; ɪk,saɪtə'bɪlətɪ/ *n* quality of being excitable. 易興奮;易激動。**ex·cit·ed·ly** *adv* in an ~d manner. 興奮地;激動地。

ex·cite·ment /ɪk'saɪtmənt ; ɪk'saɪtmənt/ *n* **1** [U] state of being excited: 興奮;激動;刺激;騷動: *news that caused great ~;* 令人極爲興奮的消息; *jumping about in ~.* 興奮地跳來跳去。 **2** [C] sth that excites; exciting incident, etc: 令人興奮的事物;使人激動的事件等: *He kept calm amid all these ~s.* 他在這些使人激動的事件中保持鎮靜。

ex·claim /ɪk'skleɪm ; ɪk'sklem/ *vt, vi* [VP9, 2A] cry out suddenly and loudly from pain, anger, surprise, etc: (因痛苦,憤怒,驚奇等)呼喊;驚叫: *'What!' he ~ed. 'Are you leaving without me?'* '什麼!'他喊道。'你要丢下我離去嗎?'

ex·cla·mation /,eksklə'meɪʃn ; ,ɛksklə'meʃən/ *n* **1** [U] exclaiming: 呼喊;驚叫: *'~ mark,* the mark (!). 感嘆號;驚嘆號(!)。 ⇨ App 9. 參看附錄九。 **2** [C] sudden short cry, expressing surprise, pain, etc: 感嘆詞;驚嘆語: *'Oh!' 'Look out!', and 'Hurrah!' are ~s.* '啊!''小心!'和'好哇!'是感嘆詞。

ex·clama·tory /ɪk'sklæmətrɪ *US:* -tɔːrɪ ; ɪk'sklæmə,torɪ/ *adj* using, containing, in the nature of, an exclamation: 驚嘆的;感嘆的: *an ~ sentence.* 驚嘆句。

ex·clude /ɪk'skluːd ; ɪk'sklud/ *vt* [VP6A, 14] ***~ (from),*** **1** prevent (sb from getting in somewhere): 拒絕(某人進入): *~ a person from membership of a society/immigrants from a country.* 拒絕一人入會(拒絕移民進入一國)。 **2** prevent (the chance of sth arising): 排除(某事發生的機會): *~ all possibility of doubt;* 排除一切疑慮; leave out of account, ignore as irrelevant: 不予考慮: *We can ~ (from the reckoning) the possibility that the money won't arrive.* 我們不必考慮(由於計算)該款項不會到達的可能性。**ex·clu·sion** /ɪk'skluːʒn ; ɪk'skluʒən/ *n* [U] ***~ (from),*** excluding or being ~d. 拒絕;排除。***to the exclusion of,*** so as to ~. 以便排除。

ex·clus·ive /ɪk'skluːsɪv ; ɪk'sklusɪv/ *adj* **1** (of a person) not willing to mix with others (esp those considered to be inferior in social position, education, etc). (指人)孤僻的;(尤指)孤傲的。 **2** (of a group or society) not readily admitting new members: (指社團)不願吸收新份子的: *He moves in ~ social circles and belongs to the most ~ clubs.* 他活動於限制甚嚴的社交圈內,而且屬於某些最不願吸收新份子的社團。 **3** (of a shop, goods sold in it, etc) of the sort not to be found elsewhere; uncommon. (指商店,售貨等)罕有的;不平常的;獨家的。**4** reserved to the person(s) concerned: 獨有的: *~ privileges;* 獨有的特權; *have ~ rights/an ~ agency for the sale of Ford cars in a town;* 享有福特汽車在一城市的專賣權(獨家代理權); *an ~ story/interview,* eg given to only one newspaper. (僅給一家報紙等的)獨家報導(訪問)。 **5** ***~ of,*** not including: 不包括…在內: *The ship had a crew of 57 ~ of officers.* 這船上有五十七位水手,高級船員除外。 **6** excluding all but what is mentioned: 唯一的: *Dictionary-making has not been his ~ employment.* 編字典一直都不是他唯一的工作。**~·ly** *adv*

ex·cogi·tate /eks'kɒdʒɪteɪt ; ɛks'kɑdʒə,tet/ *vt* [VP6A] (formal or hum) think out (a plan). (正式用語或詼諧語)想出(計畫)。**ex·cogi·ta·tion** /eks,kɒdʒɪ'teɪʃn ; ɛks,kɑdʒə'teʃən/ *n*

ex·com·muni·cate /,ekskə'mjuːnɪkeɪt ; ,ɛkskə'mjunə,ket/ *vt* [VP6A] exclude (as a punishment) from the privileges of a member of the Christian Church, eg marriage or burial in church, Holy Communion. 把…逐出教會(以作懲罰使不能享受教友特權,例如在教堂結婚,埋葬或參加聖餐等)。**ex·com·muni·ca·tion** /,ekskə,mjuːnɪ'keɪʃn ; ,ɛkskə,mjunə'keʃən/ *n* [U] excommunicating or being ~d; [C] instance of this; official statement announcing this. 逐出教會;逐出教會的公告。

ex·cori·ate /ɪk'skɔːrɪeɪt ; ɪk'skorɪ,et/ *vt* [VP6A] (formal) strip, peel off (skin); (fig) criticize severely. (正式用語)剝(皮);(喻)嚴厲批評;批評得體無完膚。**ex·cori·ation** /ɪk,skɔːrɪ'eɪʃn ; ɪk,skorɪ'eʃən/ *n*

excre·ment /'ekskrəmənt ; 'ɛkskrɪmənt/ *n* [U] solid waste matter discharged from the bowels. 糞便。

ex·cres·cence /ɪk'skresns ; ɪk'skrɛsn̩s/ *n* [C] abnormal (usu ugly and useless) outgrowth on an animal or vegetable body 瘤;贅疣。

ex·creta /ɪk'skriːtə ; ɛk'skritə/ *n pl* waste (excrement, urine, sweat) expelled from the body. 排泄物;糞便;尿;汗。

ex·crete /ɪk'skriːt ; ɪk'skrit/ *vt* [VP6A] (of an animal or plant) discharge from the system, eg waste matter, sweat. (指動植物)排泄;分泌。**ex·cre·tion** /ɪk'skriːʃn ; ɪk'skriʃən/ *n* [U] excreting; [C, U] that which is ~d. 排泄;分泌;排泄物;分泌物。

ex·cru·ciat·ing /ɪk'skruːʃɪeɪtɪŋ ; ɪk'skruʃɪ,etɪŋ/ *adj* (of pain, bodily or mental) acute. (指身心痛苦)劇烈的。**~·ly** *adv*

ex·cul·pate /'ekskʌlpeɪt ; 'ɛkskʌl,pet/ *vt* [VP6A, 14] ***~ (from),*** (formal) free from blame; say that (sb) is not guilty of wrongdoing: (正式用語)使無罪過;辯白(某人)無罪: *~ a person from a charge.* 申明某人無罪。

ex·cur·sion /ɪk'skɜːʃn *US:* -ʒn ; ɪk'skɝʒən/ *n* [C]

short journey, esp one made by a number of people together for pleasure: 短程旅行;遠足: *go on/make an ~ to the mountains;* 登山旅行; *an '~ train;* 遊覽火車; *an '~ ticket,* one issued at a reduced fare. (廉價的)遊覽票。**~·ist** *n* person who makes an ~. 作短程旅行者;遠足者。

ex·cuse¹ /ɪk'skju:s ; ɪk'skjus/ *n* **1** [C] reason given (true or invented) to explain or defend one's conduct; apology: 藉口;口實;託詞;辯解;解釋: *He's always making ~s for being late.* 他總是爲他的遲到找藉口。*He had numerous ~s to offer for being late.* 他對遲到有無數的藉口。*Please give them my ~s.* 請將我的解釋告訴他們。 **2** *in ~ of*: 爲…辯解: *Where the law is concerned, you cannot plead ignorance in ~ of your conduct.* 就法律而言,你無法以不知情來爲你的行爲辯白。***without*** ~: 無故: *Those who are absent without (good) ~ will be dismissed.* 無故缺席者將被開除。

ex·cuse² /ɪk'skju:z ; ɪk'skjuz/ *vt* **1** [VP6A, C, 14, 19C] ~ ***(for)***, give reasons showing, or intended to show, that a person or his action is not to be blamed; overlook a fault, etc: 爲…辯解;原諒;寬宥(過失等): *~ sb's conduct.* 原諒某人的行爲。*Nothing can ~ such rudeness.* 如此無禮絕不可寬恕。 *Please ~ my coming late/~ me for being late/~ my late arrival.* 請原諒我的遲到。 *E~ my interrupting you.* 原諒我打擾了你。 **2** [VP14, 6A] ~ ***(from)***, set (sb) free from a duty, requirement, punishment, etc: 使(某人)免除(責任,規定,處罰等): *He was ~d (from) attendance at the lecture.* 他獲准可不去聽講。*They may be ~d from complying with this regulation.* 他們可以不按照這規則行事。 **3** ***E~ me***, used as an apology when one interrupts, disagrees, has to behave impolitely or disapprove: 對不起(打攪他人,不同意,迫不得已而失禮或不贊成時的道歉語): *E~ me, but I don't think that statement is quite true.* 對不起,不過我認爲那話不十分眞實。⇨ pardon(2); sorry(2). **ex·cus·able** /ɪk'skju:zəbl ; ɪk'skjuzəbḷ/ *adj* that may be ~d: 可原諒的;可寬宥的;可免除的: *an excusable mistake.* 可原諒的錯誤。**ex·cus·ably** /-əblɪ ; -əblɪ/ *adv*

ex-di·rec·tory /ˌeksdɪ'rektərɪ ; ˌɛksdə'rɛktərɪ/ *adj* (of a telephone number) not listed in the telephone directory (for reasons of security, privacy, etc). (指電話號碼)(因安全,隱祕等理由而)未列入電話簿中的。

ex·ecrable /'eksɪkrəbl ; 'ɛksɪkrəbḷ/ *adj* very bad; deserving hate: 惡劣的;可惡的;可恨的: *~ manners/weather.* 惡劣的態度(天氣)。

ex·ecrate /'eksɪkreɪt ; 'ɛksɪˌkret/ *vt* [VP6A] express or feel hatred of. 憎恨;嫌惡。**ex·ecra·tion** /ˌeksɪ'kreɪʃn ; ˌɛksɪ'kreʃən/ *n*

ex·ecute /'eksɪkju:t ; 'ɛksɪˌkjut/ *vt* [VP6A] **1** carry out (what one is asked or told to do): 執行;實行;實現: *~ sb's commands;* 執行某人的命令; *~ a plan/a piece of work/a purpose.* 實現一計畫(完成一件工作;達到一目的)。 **2** (legal) give effect to: (法律)使生效;實施: *~ a will.* 使遺囑生效。 **3** (legal) make legally binding: (法律)使受法律約束: *~ a legal document,* by having it signed, witnessed, sealed and delivered. 簽發一法律文件。**4** carry out punishment by death on (sb): 處死(某人);處決: *~ a murderer.* 處死一兇手。 **5** perform on the stage, at a concert, etc: (在舞臺上或音樂會中等)演奏;表演: *The piano sonata was badly ~d.* 這鋼琴奏鳴曲演奏得不好。**execu·tant** /ɪg'zekjʊtənt ; ɛg'zɛkjʊtənt/ *n* person who ~s a design, etc; person who performs music, etc. 實行者;演奏者;表演者。

ex·ecu·tion /ˌeksɪ'kju:ʃn ; ˌɛksɪ'kjuʃən/ *n* **1** [U] the carrying out or performance of a piece of work, design, etc: (工作,計畫等的)實行;實現;完成: *His intention was good, but his ~ of the plan was unsatisfactory.* 他的用意甚佳,但對該計畫的實施不令人滿意。***put/carry sth into ~***, complete it, do what was planned. 完成一計畫。**2** [U] skill in performing, eg music: 演奏音樂等的技巧: *a pianist with marvellous ~.* 技高的鋼琴家。 **3** [U] (of weapons) destructive effect: (指武器)摧毀效果;威力;殺傷力: *The artillery did great ~,* killed and wounded many. 那些大砲的威力很大。 **4** [U] infliction of punishment by death; [C] instance of this: 處死刑;處死: *~ by hanging;* 以絞刑處死; *five ~s last year.* 去年的五次死刑執行。**~er** *n* public official who ~s criminals. 行刑者;死刑執行人。

execu·tive /ɪg'zekjʊtɪv ; ɪg'zɛkjʊtɪv/ *adj* **1** having to do with managing or executing(1): 執行的;實行的;實現的: *~ duties;* 執行的職責; *~ ability.* 執行的能力。 **2** having authority to carry out decisions, laws, decrees, etc: 有權執行決策、法律、命令等的;行政的: *the ~ branch of the government;* 政府的行政部門; *the ~ head of the State,* eg the President of the US. 一國之行政首長(例如美國的總統)。□ *n* **1** **the ~**, the ~ branch of a government. 政府的行政部門。⇨ administration, judiciary, legislature. **2** (in the Civil Service) person who carries out what has been planned or decided. (文職部門)執行計畫者;行政官;行政人員。 **3** person or group in a business or commercial organization with administrative or managerial powers. (大企業或商業機構中)決策人;負責釐定政策者;董事會。

execu·tor /ɪg'zekjʊtə(r) ; ig'zɛkjətə/ *n* person who is appointed by the maker of a will to carry out the terms of the will. (立遺囑者所委託之)遺囑執行人。 **execu·trix** /ɪg'zekjʊtrɪks ; ɪg'zɛkjətrɪks/ *n* woman ~. 女遺囑執行人。

exe·gesis /ˌeksɪ'dʒi:sɪs ; ˌɛksə'dʒisɪs/ *n* [U] explanation and interpretation (of a written work). (文字作品之)註釋。

exem·plary /ɪg'zemplərɪ ; ɪg'zɛmplərɪ/ *adj* serving as an example or a warning: 作爲模範的;作爲警戒的: *~ conduct/punishment.* 可作模範的行爲(作爲警戒的懲罰)。

exem·plify /ɪg'zemplɪfaɪ ; ɪg'zɛmpləˌfaɪ/ *vt* (*pt, pp* -fied) [VP6A] illustrate by example; be an example of. 例證;例示。 **exem·pli·fi·ca·tion** /ɪgˌzemplɪfɪ'keɪʃn ; ɪgˌzɛmpləfə'keʃən/ *n* [U] ~ing; [C] example. 例證;例子。

exempt /ɪg'zempt ; ɪg'zɛmpt/ *vt* [VP6A, 14] ~ ***(from)***, free (from an obligation): 使免除(義務): *Poor eyesight will ~ you from military service.* 視力不佳將使你免服兵役。□ *adj* ~ ***(from)***, not liable; free: 沒有義務的;免除的: *~ from tax.* 免稅。 **exemp·tion** /ɪg'zempʃn ; ɪg'zɛmpʃən/ *n* [U] ~***ion (from)***, ~ing or being ~ed; [C] instance of this. 免除;解除。

ex·er·cise¹ /'eksəsaɪz ; 'ɛksəˌsaɪz/ *n* **1** [U] employment or practice (of mental or physical powers, of rights): 智力運用;運動;權利運用: *Walking, running, rowing and horse-riding are all healthy forms of ~.* 散步,跑步,划船和騎馬都是有益健康的運動方式。*The doctor advised her to take more ~.* 醫生囑她多運動。*E~ of the mental faculties is as important as bodily ~.* 智能的鍛鍊與身體的運動同樣重要。*The ~ of patience is essential in diplomatic negotiations.* 忍耐力的運用在外交談判中是必要的。*His tales showed considerable ~ of the imagination.* 他的故事顯示他用過很多的想像力。 **2** [C] activity, drill, etc designed for bodily, mental or spiritual training: 身體,智力或精神訓練之活動;練習;操練: *vocal/gymnastic/deep-breathing, etc ~s;* 聲音練習(體操;深呼吸運動等); *~s for the harp/flute, etc;* 豎琴(橫笛等)練習; *five-finger ~s for the piano;* 彈鋼琴五指練習; *~s in logic/English composition;* 推理(英文作文)練習; *spiritual ~s,* eg prayer. 精神訓練之活動(例如祈禱)。 *An ~ in clear thinking would benefit many public speakers.* 思考清晰的訓練對許多在公共場合演說者有益。 **3** (*pl*) series of movements for training troops, crews of warships, etc: (複)(訓練軍隊,戰艦船員等之)演習: *military ~s;* 軍事演習; *The third cruiser squad-*

ron has left for ~s in the North Sea. 第三巡洋艦戰隊已去北海演習。 **4** (*pl*, US) ceremonies: (複,美)典禮;儀式: *graduation ~s;* 畢業典禮; *opening ~s,* eg speeches at the start of a conference. 開幕儀式。

ex·er·cise² /ˈeksəsaɪz ; ˈɛksɚ,saɪz/ *vt, vi* **1** [VP6A, 15A, 2A] take exercise; give exercise to, ⇨ exercise¹(1): 運動;鍛鍊: *Horses get fat and lazy if they are not ~d.* 馬如果不運動會肥胖和懶惰。 *He ~s himself in fencing.* 他練習劍術。 *You don't ~ enough.* 你的運動不够。 **2** [VP6A] employ; make use of: 運用;利用: *~ patience;* 運用耐力; *~ authority over sb;* 對某人使用權威; *~ one's rights.* 行使權利。 **3** [VP6A] (usu passive) perplex; trouble; worry the mind of: (通常用被動語態) 使迷惑; 使困擾; 使憂愁: *The problem that is exercising our minds....* 使我們困惱的問題是…。 *I am very much ~d about the future/about the education of my son.* 我對於未來(對於我兒子的教育)深爲擔憂。

exert /ɪgˈzɜːt ; ɪgˈzɝt/ *vt* [VP6A, 14, 16A] **1** *~ (on/upon),* put forth; bring into use: 發揮;運用: *~ all one's strength/influence, etc (to do sth);* 發揮個人所有的力量(影響力等) (去做某事); *~ pressure on sb.* 對某人施以壓力。 **2** *~ oneself,* make an effort: 努力: *~ oneself to arrive early;* 盡力早到; *~ yourself on my behalf.* 你盡量幫助我。

exer·tion /ɪgˈzɜːʃn ; ɪgˈzɝʃən/ *n* [U] exerting; [C] instance of this: 發揮;運用;努力: *E~ of authority is not always wise; persuasion may be better.* 運用權威並不永遠是明智的,用說服的方法可能較好。 *He failed to lift the rock in spite of all his ~s.* 他雖然費盡力氣,仍未能將那岩石抬起。 *Now that I am 90, I am unequal to the ~s of travelling.* 我因年屆九十,已無力旅行了。

ex·eunt /ˈeksɪənt ; ˈɛksɪənt/ (Lat) (as a stage direction) (拉) (舞臺說明) *~ Antony and Cleopatra,* they leave the stage. 安東尼及克利奧佩特拉退場。⇨ exit.

ex gratia /ˌeks ˈgreɪʃə ; ɛksˈgreʃə/ *n* (Lat) (拉) *~ pay·ment,* payment not legally binding but for which some moral obligation is felt. 基於道德上的義務而付的款。

ex·hale /eksˈheɪl ; ɛksˈhel/ *vt, vi* [VP6A, 2A] breathe out; give off gas, vapour; be given off (as gas or vapour): 呼出;發出(氣體,蒸氣);被發出(如氣體或蒸氣): *~ air from the lungs.* 自肺中呼出氣。 **ex·ha·la·tion** /ˌekshəˈleɪʃn ; ,ɛksəˈleʃən/ *n* **1** [C] act of exhaling. 呼出;發出。 **2** [U, C] sth ~d. 呼出之氣;發出之氣。

ex·haust¹ /ɪgˈzɔːst ; ɪgˈzɔst/ *n* [C, U] (outlet, in an engine or machine, for) steam, vapour, etc that has done its work. (機器等之)排氣口;排出之廢氣。 **ˈ~-pipe** *n* pipe for this. 排氣管。⇨ the illus at motor. 參看 motor 之挿圖。

ex·haust² /ɪgˈzɔːst ; ɪgˈzɔst/ *vt* [VP6A] **1** use up completely: 用盡; 耗盡: *~ one's patience/strength;* 失去耐心(用盡力氣); *~ oneself by hard work;* 因努力工作而疲憊不堪; *feeling ~ed,* tired out. 感覺筋疲力竭。 **2** make empty: 使空: *~ a well;* 汲乾一井; *~ a tube of air.* 抽盡管中空氣。 **3** say, find out, all there is to say about (sth): 詳論;詳盡闡述: *~ a subject.* 詳論一問題。

ex·haus·tion /ɪgˈzɔːstʃən ; ɪgˈzɔstʃən/ *n* [U] exhausting or being exhausted; total loss of strength: 用盡;竭盡;疲憊: *They were in a state of ~ after climbing the mountain.* 他們爬過山後筋疲力竭了。

ex·haus·tive /ɪgˈzɔːstɪv ; ɪgˈzɔstɪv/ *adj* thorough; complete: 徹底的; 完全的: *an ~ inquiry.* 徹查。 **~·ly** *adv*

ex·hibit¹ /ɪgˈzɪbɪt ; ɪgˈzɪbɪt/ *n* [C] **1** object or collection of objects, shown publicly, eg in a museum: 展覽品;陳列品 (例如博物館內者): *Do not touch the ~s.* 不要觸摸展覽品。 **2** document, object, etc produced in a law court and referred to in evidence, eg a weapon said to have been used by the accused person. (法庭上提出之)證件;證物;物證(例如指明被告所用的武器)。 **3** (US) exhibition(1). (美)商展;工展;動植物花卉等展覽。

ex·hibit² /ɪgˈzɪbɪt ; ɪgˈzɪbɪt/ *vt* [VP6A] **1** show publicly (for pleasure, for sale, in a competition, etc): (爲樂趣,售賣,競賽等而)陳列;展覽: *~ paintings in an art gallery/flowers at a flower show;* 在一美術館展覽畫(在花展陳列花); [VP2A, C]: *Mr X ~s in several galleries.* 某先生在數處畫廊展出作品。 **2** give clear evidence of (a quality): 顯示(一種性質): *The girls ~ed great powers of endurance during the climb.* 在攀登時,那些女孩子顯示出很大的耐力。 **ex·hibi·tor** /-tə(r) ; -tɚ/ *n* person who ~s at a show of pictures, a flower show, etc. (畫展、花展等之)展出者;參展者。

ex·hi·bi·tion /ˌeksɪˈbɪʃn ; ,ɛksəˈbɪʃən/ *n* **1** [C] collection of things shown publicly (eg of works of art); display of commercial or industrial goods for advertisement; public display of animals, plants, flowers, etc (often shown in competition, for prizes, and colloq called a *show*). 展覽品(例如藝術品);商展;工展;動植物花卉等展覽(常是競賽性的,俗稱 show)。 **2** (*sing* only) act of showing: (僅作單數)表現;顯示: *an ~ of bad manners;* 無禮貌之表現; *an opportunity for the ~ of one's knowledge.* 顯示個人知識的機會。 ***make an ~ of oneself,*** behave in public so that one receives contempt. 當衆出醜。 **3** (GB) money allowance to a student from school or college funds for a number of years. (英)獎學金。 **~er** *n* student to whom an ~(3) is granted. 獲得獎學金的學生。 **~·ism** /-ɪzəm ; -,ɪzəm/ *n* [U] tendency towards extravagant behaviour designed to attract attention to oneself. 表現主義;風頭主義。 **~·ist** /-ɪst ; -ɪst/ *n* person given to ~ism. 表現主義者;風頭主義者。

ex·hil·ar·ate /ɪgˈzɪləreɪt ; ɪgˈzɪlə,ret/ *vt* [VP6A] (usu passive) fill with high spirits; make lively or glad: (通常用被動語態)使高興;使興奮: *exhilarating news.* 令人興奮的消息。 **ex·hil·ar·ation** /ɪgˌzɪləˈreɪʃn ; ɪg,zɪləˈreʃən/ *n*

exhort /ɪgˈzɔːt ; ɪgˈzɔrt/ *vt* [VP6A, 14, 17] *~ sb to sth/to do sth,* (formal) urge, advise earnestly: (正式用語)力勸;勸告: *~ sb to do good/to work harder;* 勸告某人行善(更加努力); *~ one's listeners to action.* 勸聽衆採取行動。 **ex·hor·ta·tion** /ˌeksɔːˈteɪʃn ; ,ɛgzɔrˈteʃən/ *n* [U] ~ing; [C] earnest request, speech etc that ~s sb. 力勸;勸告;勸誡。

exhume /eksˈhjuːm *US:* ɪgˈzuːm ; ɪgˈzjum/ *vt* [VP 6A] take out (a dead body) from the earth (for examination). 掘出 (屍體以檢驗)。 **exhum·ation** /ˌekshjuːˈmeɪʃn ; ,ɛkshjuˈmeʃən/ *n* [U] exhuming or being ~d; [C] instance of this. 掘屍檢驗。

exi·gency /ˈeksɪdʒənsɪ ; ˈɛksədʒənsɪ/ *n* (*pl* -cies) [C] condition of great need; emergency: 急迫需要;緊急: *measures to meet the exigencies of this difficult period.* 爲應付此困難時期的急迫需要所採取的措施。 **exi·gent** /-dʒənt ; -dʒənt/ *adj* **1** urgent; pressing. 緊急的;急迫的。 **2** exacting. 嚴苛的。

exig·uous /egˈzɪgjuəs ; ɪgˈzɪgjuəs/ *adj* (formal) scanty: (正式用語)稀少的;不足的: *an ~ diet.* 少量的食物。

exile /ˈeksaɪl ; ˈɛgzaɪl/ *n* **1** [U] being sent away from one's country or home, esp as a punishment: 放逐;充軍;流放: *be/live in ~;* 過流亡生活;亡命他鄉; *go/be sent into ~;* 遭放逐; *a place of ~;* 流放之地; [C] instance of this: 放逐之實例: *after an ~ of ten years.* 經十年之放逐。 **2** [C] person who is sent away in this way. 被放逐者。 □ *vt* [VP6A, 15A] send (sb) into ~: 放逐;充軍: *~ sb from his country;* 將某人放逐國外; *~d for life.* 被終身放逐。

exist /ɪgˈzɪst ; ɪgˈzɪst/ *vi* **1** [VP2A, C] be; have being; be real: 存在;實在;實有: *The idea ~s only in the minds of poets.* 這觀念祇存在於詩人的心中。 *Do you believe that fairies ~,* that there really are fairies? 你相信眞有神仙嗎? *Does life ~ on*

Mars? 火星上有生物嗎？ **2** [VP2A, C, 3A] continue living: 生存: *We cannot ~ without food and water.* 沒有食物和水我們不能生存。*She ~s on very little.* 她的生活很艱苦。*How do they ~ in such wretched conditions?* 在這樣惡劣的環境中他們怎樣生存？ **~·ence** /-əns ; -əns/ *n* **1** [U] the state of ~ing: 存在;實在: *When did this world come into ~ence?* 這個世界是何時產生的？ *Do you believe in the ~ence of ghosts?* 你相信有鬼嗎？ *This is the oldest Hebrew manuscript in ~ence.* 這是現存最早的希伯來文手抄本。**2 an ~ence,** manner of living: 生存方式;生活: *lead a happy ~ence.* 過快樂的生活。**~·ent** /-ənt ; -ənt/ *adj* ~ing; actual. 存在的;現存的;實在的。

exis·ten·tial·ism /ˌegzɪˈstenʃəlɪzəm ; ˌɛgzɪsˈtɛnʃəlˌɪzəm/ *n* doctrine (deriving from Kierkegaard and popularized by Sartre) that man is a unique and isolated individual in an indifferent or hostile universe, responsible for his own actions and free to choose his destiny. 存在主義(爲齊克果所創,經沙特予以提倡,認爲人在冷漠或有敵意的宇宙中,是個獨特和孤立的份子,對自己的行爲負責,並可自由選擇其命運)。

exit /ˈeksɪt ; ˈɛgzɪt/ *n* **1** departure of an actor from the stage: (演員之)退場: *make one's ~,* go out or away. 離去。**2** way out, eg from a theatre or cinema. (戲院或電影院等之) 出口。□ (as a stage direction) (作爲舞臺說明) *E~ Macbeth,* Macbeth goes off the stage. 馬克白退場。⇨ exeunt.

ex·odus /ˈeksədəs ; ˈɛksədəs/ *n* [C] (*sing* only) (僅用單數) going out or away of many people: (許多人之)離開;(很多人之)離去: *the ~ of people to the sea and the mountains for the summer holidays.* 很多人到海濱和山間度暑假。 **the E~,** the ~ of the Israelites from Egypt, in about 1300 BC. (約在紀元前1300年)以色列人之離開埃及。

ex officio /ˌeks əˈfɪʃɪəʊ ; ˌɛksəˈfɪʃɪˌo/ *adv, adj* (Lat) because of one's office or position: (拉)由於職位;依照官職: *an ~ member of the committee;* (委員會中)由於職位而產生的當然委員; *present at the meeting ~.* 依照職權出席一會議。

exon·er·ate /ɪgˈzɒnəreɪt ; ɪgˈzɑnəˌret/ *vt* [VP6A, 14] **~ *sb (from),*** free, clear: 免除: *~ sb from blame/responsibility.* 免除某人之罪咎(責任)。**exon·er·ation** /ɪgˌzɒnəˈreɪʃn ; ɪgˌzɑnəˈreʃən/ *n*

exor·bi·tant /ɪgˈzɔːbɪtənt ; ɪgˈzɔrbətənt/ *adj* (of a price, charge or demand) much too high or great. (指價格,索價或要求)過高的;過份的。**~·ly** *adv* **exor·bi·tance** /-təns ; -təns/ *n*

ex·or·cize /ˈeksɔːsaɪz ; ˈɛksɔrˌsaɪz/ *vt* [VP6A, 14] **~ *(sth from)/(sb of),*** drive out (an evil spirit) by prayers or magic. 用祈禱或魔法驅除(妖魔)。

exotic /ɪgˈzɒtɪk ; ɪgˈzɑtɪk/ *adj* **1** (of plants, fashions, words, ideas) introduced from another country. (指植物,時樣,文字,觀念)來自外國的;外來的。**2** foreign or unusual in style; striking or pleasing because colourful, unusual: 樣式奇特的; 因富有色彩和奇特而引人注意或悅人的: *~ birds.* 奇特動人的鳥。

ex·pand /ɪkˈspænd ; ɪkˈspænd/ *vt, vi* [VP6A, 14, 2A, C] **~ *(in/into),*** **1** make or become larger: 使大;擴大;變大: *Metals ~ when they are heated.* 金屬遇熱則膨脹。⇨ contract³(1). *A tyre ~s when you pump air into it.* 當你打氣進去,輪胎會脹大。⇨ shrink. *The river ~s* (= broadens) *and forms a lake.* 該河擴大而成湖。*The small pocket dictionary was ~ed into a larger volume.* 該袖珍字典增訂爲較大的字典。 *Our foreign trade has ~ed during recent years.* 我們的對外貿易近年來已獲擴展。 **2** unfold or spread out: 展開: *His face ~ed in a smile of welcome.* 他的臉上綻開歡迎的笑容。*The petals of many flowers ~ in the sunshine.* 許多花的花瓣在陽光中綻放。 **3** (of a person) become good-humoured or genial. (指人)變爲愉快和藹。

ex·panse /ɪkˈspæns ; ɪkˈspæns/ *n* [C] wide and open area: 寬濶的區域: *the broad ~ of the Pacific;* 浩瀚的太平洋; *the blue ~ of the sky;* 廣袤的藍天; *a broad ~ of brow,* eg of a man with a high forehead and bald head. 寬濶的額頭。

ex·pan·sion /ɪkˈspænʃn ; ɪksˈpænʃən/ *n* [U] expanding or being expanded(1): 擴大;變大;膨脹: *~ of the currency,* by putting more banknotes into circulation; 通貨膨脹; *~ of territory,* eg by winning new territory; 領土的擴張; *the ~ of gases when heated.* 氣體受熱時之膨脹。

ex·pan·sive /ɪkˈspænsɪv ; ɪkˈspænsɪv/ *adj* **1** able, tending, to expand. 可擴大的;可擴展的。 **2** (of persons, speech) unreserved, effusive. (指人,言語)率直的;滔滔不絕的。 **~·ly** *adv* **~·ness** *n*

ex·patiate /ɪkˈspeɪʃɪeɪt ; ɪkˈspeʃɪˌet/ *vi* [VP3A] **~ *upon,*** (formal) write or speak at great length, in detail, about. (正式用語)詳述;細說。

ex·patri·ate /eksˈpætrɪət *US:* -ˈpeɪt- ; ɛksˈpetrɪɪt/ *n* person living outside his own country: 居於國外之人;僑民: *American ~s in Paris;* 居於巴黎的美國人; (attrib) (形容用法) *~ Americans.* 居於國外的美國人。□ *vt* /-rɪeɪt ; -rɪˌet/ [VP6A] **~ *oneself,*** leave one's own country to live abroad; renounce one's citizenship. 移居國外;脫離國籍。

ex·pect /ɪkˈspekt ; ɪkˈspɛkt/ *vt* [VP6A, 17, 7A, 9, 14] think or believe that sth will happen or come, that sb will come; wish for and feel confident that one will receive: 預期;盼望;期待;料想: *We ~ed you yesterday.* 我們昨天期待你來。*We were ~ing a letter from her.* 我們當時正期待着她的信。 *I ~ to be/~ that I shall be back on Sunday.* 我想在星期日回來。*You would ~ there to be/that there would be strong disagreement about this.* 你大概認爲關於此事將有激烈的爭論。*You can't learn a foreign language in a week; it's not to be ~ed.* 你無法在一週內學會一種外國語言，那是不可指望的事。 *You are ~ing too much of her.* 你對她的期望過高了。*'Will he be late?'—'I ~ so.'* '他會遲到嗎？'—'我想會的。' *'Will he need help?'—'No, I don't ~ so'* (or) *'No, I ~ not.'* '他需要幫助嗎？'—'不,我想他不需要。' *They ~* (= require) *me to work on Saturdays.* 他們要我在星期六工作。*I ~* (= require) *you to be punctual.* 我希望你守時。*'Who has eaten all the cake?'—'Oh, I ~* (colloq 俗 = suppose) *it was Tom.'* '誰把整個糕都吃掉了？'—'哦,我猜想是湯姆。' **~·ancy** /-ənsɪ ; -ənsɪ/ *n* the state of ~ing: 預期;期望;期待: *with a look/an air of ~ancy;* 以希冀的神情; *life ~ancy.* 平均壽命。**~·ant** /-ənt ; -ənt/ *adj* ~ing: 預期的;期望的;期待的: *an ~ant mother,* woman who is pregnant. 孕婦。**~·ant·ly** *adv* **~ed** *adj* that is ~ed: 所預期的;所預料的;所期望的: *an ~ed reply;* 預期的回覆; *~ed objections.* 預料中的反對。

ex·pec·ta·tion /ˌekspekˈteɪʃn ; ˌɛkspɛkˈteʃən/ *n* **1** [U] expecting; awaiting: 期望;期待: *He ate a light lunch in ~ of a good dinner.* 他草草用過午餐,期望吃一頓豐富的晚餐。 **2** (often *pl*) thing that is expected. (常用複數)期望的事物。 ***beyond ~,*** in a way greater or better than was expected. 出乎意料(較預期者大或好)。 ***contrary to ~(s),*** in a way different from what was expected. 與期望相違。 ***fall short of/not come up to one's ~s,*** be less good than what was expected. 未臻理想。 **3** (*pl*) future prospects, esp sth to be inherited: (複)期望之事物;前途;遠景;(尤指)有希望繼承之遺產: *a young man with great ~s,* eg one who has a millionaire uncle who has promised to leave him his wealth. 一位有希望繼承大筆遺產的青年。 **4 *~ of life,*** years a person is expected to live: 平均壽命;一個人可望活着的年數: *A life assurance company can tell you the ~ of life of a man who is 40 years old.* 人壽保險公司能告訴你一個四十歲的人的平均壽命。

ex·pec·tor·ate /ɪkˈspektəreɪt ; ɪkˈspɛktəˌret/ *vt, vi* [VP6A, 2A] (formal) spit; send out (phlegm from the throat, blood from the lungs) by coughing. (正式用語)吐;咳嗽而吐(痰,血)。 **ex·pec-**

tor·ant /-rənt ; -rənt/ *n* medicine promoting expectorating. 祛痰劑;助咳藥。

ex·pedi·ent /ɪk'spi:dɪənt ; ɪk'spidɪənt/ *adj* (usu pred) likely to be useful or helpful for a purpose; advantageous though contrary to principle: (通常爲敍述用法)有用的;有助益的;有利的(縱或不正當);權宜的: *In times of war governments do things because they are ~.* 戰時政府做一些事情,是因其有利。*Do what you think ~.* 做你認爲有利的事。□ *n* [C] ~ plan, action, device, etc. 有利的計畫或行動;權宜之計。**~·ly** *adv* **ex·pedi·ence** /-əns ; -əns/, **ex·pedi·ency** /-ənsɪ ; -ənsɪ/ *n* [U] suitability for a purpose; being ~; self-interest: 適宜;有利;利己: *act from expediency, not from principle.* 因有利而行事,而非根據原則。

ex·pedite /'ekspɪdaɪt ; 'ɛkspɪ,daɪt/ *vt* [VP6A] (formal) help the progress of; speed up (business, etc). (正式用語)幫助…之進展;加速發展(事業等)。

ex·pedi·tion /ˌekspɪ'dɪʃn ; ˌɛkspɪ'dɪʃən/ *n* **1** [C] (men, ships, etc making a) journey or voyage for a definite purpose: (爲一確定目的所做的)遠征;遠征隊: *a hunting ~;* 狩獵(隊); *go/send a party of men on an ~ to the Antarctic;* 至(派一隊人至)南極探險; *members of the Mount Everest ~.* 埃佛勒斯峯探險隊之隊員。**2** [U] (formal) promptness; speed. (正式用語)敏捷;迅速。**~·ary** /-ʃənərɪ *US:* -nerɪ ; -ʃən,ɛrɪ/ *adj* of, making up, an ~: 遠征(隊)的;組成遠征隊的: *an ~ary force,* eg an army sent to take part in a war abroad. 遠征軍。

ex·pedi·tious /ˌekspɪ'dɪʃəs ; ˌɛkspɪ'dɪʃəs/ *adj* (formal) acting quickly; prompt and efficient. (正式用語)迅速的;敏捷而有效的。**~·ly** *adv*

ex·pel /ɪk'spel ; ɪk'spɛl/ *vt* (-ll-) [VP6A, 14] ~ ***(from),*** send out or away by force: 驅逐;逐出: *~ the enemy from a town;* 將敵人逐出一城; *~ a boy from school,* as a punishment. 開除一男生。

ex·pend /ɪk'spend ; ɪk'spɛnd/ *vt* [VP6A, 14] ~ ***sth (on/upon sth/in doing sth),*** **1** spend: 花費;使用: *~ all one's capital on equipment;* 將所有的資本用於設備; *~ time and care in doing sth.* 費時間和精神去做某事。**2** use up: 耗盡;用光: *They had ~ed all their ammunition.* 他們的彈藥已盡。**~·able** /-əbl ; -əbl̩/ *adj* that may be ~ed, esp that may be sacrificed to achieve a purpose: 可消費的;(尤指)爲達成某一目的而可犧牲的: *The general considered that these troops were ~able.* 那將軍認爲這些部隊可以犧牲。

ex·pen·di·ture /ɪk'spendɪtʃə(r) ; ɪk'spɛndɪtʃɚ/ *n* **1** [U] spending or using: 花費;使用: *the ~ of money on armaments.* 軍費的開支。**2** [C, U] amount expended: 花費之量;開銷;經費: *an ~ of £500 on new furniture.* 花五百鎊購新傢具。*Limit your ~(s) to what is essential.* 將你的開銷限制在必要範圍內。

ex·pense /ɪk'spens ; ɪk'spɛns/ *n* **1** [U] spending of money; cost: 花費;代價: *Most children in Great Britain are educated at the public ~.* 英國大多數的兒童靠公家出錢受教育。*I want the best you can supply; you need spare no ~,* you need not try to economize. 我要你最好的貨,你不必爲我省錢。***at the ~ of,*** with the sacrifice of: 犧牲;以…作代價: *He became a brilliant scholar, but only at the ~ of his health.* 他成爲一個卓越的學者,但却犧牲了健康。***at his/her/my, etc ~,*** **(a)** with him, her, me, etc paying: 由他(她,我等)付錢: *We were all entertained at the director's ~.* 我們全由導演請客。**(b)** (fig) bringing discredit, ridicule or contempt on him, her, me, etc: (喩)嘲弄或輕視他(她,我等): *We had a good laugh at his ~,* We laughed at him because he had done sth ridiculous, been deceived, etc. 我們對他大加嘲笑一番。***go to/put sb to the ~ of,*** spend/cause him to spend money on: (使某人)花錢於: *It's foolish to go to the ~ of taking music lessons if you never practise.* 花錢上音樂課而永不練習是愚蠢的。*I don't want to put you to the ~ of providing my meals.* 我不想使你破費來爲我準備伙食。**'~ account,** record of expenses incurred and either paid out of money supplied by, or to be refunded by, the employer, eg of a business man for travel, entertainment, etc. 費用帳;支出帳(向雇主提出之報銷帳目)。**2** (usu *pl*) money used or needed for sth: (通常用複數)費用: *travelling ~s.* 旅費。*Illness, holidays and other ~s reduced his bank balance to almost nothing.* 患病,度假,以及其他費用使他在銀行內的存款所剩無幾了。

ex·pens·ive /ɪk'spensɪv ; ɪk'spɛnsɪv/ *adj* causing expense; high priced: 費用大的;昂貴的: *an ~ education;* 費用龐大的教育; *too ~ for me to buy.* 太貴而使我買不起。**~·ly** *adv*

ex·peri·ence /ɪk'spɪərɪəns ; ɪk'spɪrɪəns/ *n* **1** [U] process of gaining knowledge or skill by doing and seeing things; knowledge or skill so gained: 經驗;由經驗獲得的知識或技術: *We all learn by ~.* 我們都從經驗中學習。*Has he had much ~ in/of work of this sort?* 他對這種工作有很多經驗嗎? *He hasn't had enough ~ for the job.* 他沒有足够的經驗擔當這工作。**2** [C] event, activity, which has given one ~(1); event that affects one in some way: 經歷;閱歷: *an unpleasant/trying/unusual ~.* 一個令人不愉快的(難堪的,不平凡的)經歷。□ *vt* [VP6A] have ~ of; feel; meet with: 有…之經驗;經歷;感受;體驗: *~ pleasure/pain/difficulty/great hardships.* 經歷快樂(痛苦,困難,艱苦)。**ex·peri·enced** *adj* having ~; having knowledge or skill as the result of ~: 有經驗的;經驗豐富的;熟練的: *an ~d nurse/lover.* 有經驗的護士(愛人)。

ex·peri·ment /ɪk'sperɪmənt ; ɪk'spɛrəmənt/ *n* [C] test or trial carried out carefully in order to study what happens and gain new knowledge: 試驗;實驗: *perform/carry out an ~ in chemistry;* 做化學實驗; [U] *learn sth by ~.* 由實驗而學得某事。□ *vi* [VP2A, C, 3A] make ~s: 實驗;試驗: *~ with new methods;* 以新方法試驗; *~ upon dogs.* 以狗做試驗。**ex·peri·men·ta·tion** /ɪkˌsperɪmen'teɪʃn ; ɪk,spɛrəmɛn'teʃən/ *n* [U] ~ing. 實驗;試驗。

ex·peri·men·tal /ɪkˌsperɪ'mentl ; ɪk,spɛrə'mɛntl̩/ *adj* of, used for, based on, experiments: 實驗的;用做實驗的;根據實驗的: *~ methods;* 實驗方法; *an ~ farm.* 實驗農場。**~ly** /-təlɪ ; -tl̩ɪ/ *adv*

ex·pert /'ekspɜ:t ; 'ɛkspɝt/ *n* person with special knowledge, skill or training: 專家: *an agricultural ~;* 農業專家; *an ~ in economics;* 經濟學專家; *get the advice of the ~s.* 獲取專家們的意見。□ *adj* trained by practice; skilful: 熟練的;老練的: *according to ~ advice/opinions;* 根據專家的意見; *men who are ~ at driving racing cars.* 熟練於賽車的人。**~·ly** *adv* **~·ness** *n*

ex·pert·ise /ˌekspɜ:'ti:z ; ˌɛkspɚ'tiz/ *n* [U] **1** (comm) expert appraisal; valuation. (商)專門鑑定;評價。**2** expert's report. 專家的報告。**3** expert knowledge and skill. 專門知識和技術。⇨ *know-how* at know.

ex·pi·ate /'ekspɪeɪt ; 'ɛkspɪ,et/ *vt* [VP6A] make amends for, submit to punishment for (wrongdoing): 補償;贖(罪);爲(罪)而受懲罰: *~ sin/a crime.* 贖罪。**ex·pi·ation** /ˌekspɪ'eɪʃn ; ˌɛkspɪ'eʃən/ *n* [U].

ex·pir·ation /ˌekspɪ'reɪʃn ; ˌɛkspə'reʃən/ *n* [U] **1** ~ ***(of),*** expiring, ending, esp of a period of time: (尤指一段時期之)終止;滿期: *at the ~ of the lease.* 在租期屆滿時;於租約終止時。**2** (formal) breathing out (of air). (正式用語)(氣之)呼出。

ex·pire /ɪk'spaɪə(r) ; ɪk'spaɪr/ *vi* [VP2A] **1** (of a period of time) come to an end: (指一段時期)終止;滿期: *His term of office as President ~s next year.* 他當總統的任期明年屆滿。*When does your driving licence ~?* 你的駕駛執照何時滿期? **2** (liter) die. (文)死亡。

ex·piry /ɪk'spaɪərɪ ; ɪk'spaɪrɪ/ *n* (*pl* -ries) ~ ***(of),*** expiring, ending, esp of a period of time of a contract or agreement: (尤指一段時期,合約等之)終止;滿期: *the ~ of a driving licence.* 駕駛執照之滿期。

ex·plain /ɪk'spleɪn ; ɪk'splen/ *vt* **1** [VP6A, 9, 8, 10, 14] ~ ***sth (to sb),*** make plain or clear; show the meaning of: 解釋;講解;說明: *A dictionary tries to ~ the meanings of words.* 一部字典設法解釋字的意義。*Please ~ this problem to me.* 請將此問題解釋給我聽。*Please ~ to me what this means.* 請對我說明這是什麼意思。*He ~ed that he had been delayed by the weather.* 他解釋說他曾爲天氣而躭擱。*Please ~ yourself,* make your meaning clear. 請說明你的意思。⇨ 2 below. 參看下列第 2 義。**2** [VP6A, 15B] account for: 辯明;說明…的原因或理由: *Can you ~ his behaviour?* 你能辯明他的行爲嗎? *That ~s his absence.* 那就說明了他缺席的原因。*Please ~ yourself,* give reasons for your conduct. 請說明你這種行爲的理由。~ ***sth away,*** show why one should not be blamed for a fault, mistake, etc: 說明自己何以不應爲某項錯誤等而受責;辯護: *You will find it difficult to ~ away your use of such offensive language.* 你將發現你很難爲說過這種無禮的話辯護。

ex·pla·na·tion /ˌekspləˈneɪʃn ; ˌɛkspləˈneʃən/ *n* **1** [U] (process of) explaining: 解釋;說明;辯明: *Not much ~ will be needed.* 不需多做說明。*I had better say a few words by way of ~.* 我最好以解釋的方式說幾句話。*Had he anything to say in ~ of his conduct?* 他還有什麼話可以爲他的行爲辯白嗎? **2** [C] statement, fact, circumstances, etc that explains: 解釋的言語,事實,情形等: *an ~ of his conduct/of a mystery;* 爲他的行爲 (一神祕事件) 所作的解釋; *after repeated ~s.* 經反覆解釋後。

ex·plana·tory /ɪk'splænətrɪ *US:* -tɔ:rɪ ; ɪk'splænəˌtorɪ/ *adj* serving or intended to explain. 解釋的;說明的。

ex·ple·tive /ɪk'spli:tɪv *US:* 'eksplətɪv ; 'ɛksplɪtɪv/ *n* [C] violent (often meaningless) exclamation, eg 'My goodness', or an oath such as 'Damn'. 强烈的感嘆詞(常是無意義的,例如 'My goodness' 或咒語 'Damn' 等是)。

ex·plic·able /ek'splɪkəbl ; 'ɛksplɪkəbl̩/ *adj* (formal) that can be explained. (正式用語) 可解釋的;能說明的。

ex·pli·cate /'eksplɪkeɪt ; 'ɛksplɪˌket/ *vt* [VP6A] (formal) explain and analyse in detail. (正式用語)詳細解說和分析。

ex·plicit /ɪk'splɪsɪt ; ɪk'splɪsɪt/ *adj* (of a statement, etc) clearly and fully expressed; definite: (指陳述等)明白表示的;明確的: *He was quite ~ about the matter,* left no doubt about what he meant. 他對此事的態度表示得十分明白。**~·ly** *adv* **~·ness** *n*

ex·plode /ɪk'spləʊd ; ɪk'splod/ *vt, vi* **1** [VP6A,2A,C] (cause to) burst with a loud noise: (使)爆炸: *~ a charge of gunpowder/a bomb.* 使一個火藥包(一枚炸彈)爆炸。*When the boiler ~d many people were hurt by the steam.* 汽鍋爆炸時許多人爲蒸汽所傷。*The shell ~d in the barrel of the gun.* 砲彈在砲管內爆炸了。 **2** [VP2A, C] (of feelings) burst out; (of persons) show violent emotion: (指感情)激發;(指人)表示强烈感情: *At last his anger ~d.* 他的怒氣終於發作了。*He ~d with rage/jealousy.* 他勃然大怒(醋勁大發)。 **3** [VP6A] destroy, expose (an idea, a theory, etc); show the falsity of: 推翻 (觀念,學說等);破除;揭發其爲僞: *~ a superstition;* 破除一迷信; *an ~d idea.* 被推翻的一個觀念。

ex·ploit[1] /'eksplɔɪt ; 'ɛksplɔɪt/ *n* [C] bold or adventurous act; brilliant achievement. 英勇的行爲;輝煌的事蹟;勳業。

ex·ploit[2] /ɪk'splɔɪt ; ɪk'splɔɪt/ *vt* [VP6A] **1** use, work or develop (eg mines, waterpower, other natural resources of a country). 利用或開發(一國之礦藏,水利等天然資源)。 **2** use selfishly, or for one's own profit: 自私地利用;用以自肥;剝削: *~ child labour.* 剝削童工。**ex·ploi·ta·tion** /ˌeksplɔɪ'teɪʃn ; ˌɛksplɔɪ'teʃən/ *n* [U] ~ing or being ~ed (both senses): 利用;開發;自私的利用;剝削: *the ~ation of a new country.* 一個新國家的開發。

ex·plore /ɪk'splɔ:(r) ; ɪk'splɔr/ *vt* [VP6A] **1** travel into or through (a country, etc) for the purpose of learning about it: 探測;踏勘(一國家等): *~ the Arctic regions.* 探測北極地帶。*Columbus discovered America but did not ~ the new continent.* 哥倫布發現了美洲,但未對此新大陸加以探測。 **2** examine thoroughly in order to test, learn about: 探究;仔細探查: *~ possibilities/problems.* 仔細探查可能性(問題)。 **ex·plorer** /-rə(r) ; -rɚ/ *n* person who ~s. 探測者;探究者。**ex·plo·ra·tion** /ˌekspləˈreɪʃn ; ˌɛkspləˈreʃən/ *n* [U] exploring: 探測;探究;探查: *the exploration of the ocean depths;* 海深之探測; [C] instance of this. 探測的實例。**ex·plora·tory** /ɪk'splɒrətrɪ *US:* -tɔ:rɪ ; ɪk'splɔrəˌtorɪ/ *adj* for the purpose of exploring. 探測的;探查的。

ex·plosion /ɪk'spləʊʒn ; ɪk'sploʒən/ *n* [C] **1** exploding; (loud noise caused by) sudden and violent bursting: 爆炸;爆炸聲: *a bomb ~.* 炸彈的爆炸。*The ~ was heard a mile away.* 在一哩以外可聽到爆炸聲。 **2** ~ ***(of),*** outburst or outbreak (of anger, laughter, etc). (憤怒,大笑等之)爆發;發作。 **3** great and sudden increase: 大幅度突增;劇增: *the population ~ after the war.* 戰後人口之劇增。

ex·plos·ive /ɪk'spləʊsɪv ; ɪk'splosɪv/ *n, adj* (substance) tending to or likely to explode: 爆炸物;炸藥;易爆炸的;易發作的: *a shell filled with high ~.* 裝有强烈炸藥的砲彈。*Dynamite and gun-cotton are ~s.* 炸藥和火藥棉是易爆炸物。*The old man has an ~ temper,* often explodes with anger, etc. 這老人的脾氣暴躁。*That's an ~ issue,* one likely to inflame feeling. 那是個激動感情的問題。**~·ly** *adv*

expo /'ekspəʊ ; 'ɛkspo/ *n* international exposition (2). 世界商展;國際商展;世界博覽會。

ex·po·nent /ɪk'spəʊnənt ; ɪk'sponənt/ *n* ~ ***(of),*** **1** person or thing that explains or interprets, or is a representative or example: 解釋者;闡明者;代表;典型: *Huxley was an ~ of Darwin's theory of evolution.* 赫胥黎是達爾文進化論的解說者。**2** (alg) symbol that indicates what power of a factor is to be taken: (代數)指數;羃: *In a^3, the figure 3 is the ~; in x^n, the symbol ^{n} is the ~.* 在 a^3 中 3 是指數,在 x^n 中 n 是指數。

ex·port[1] /'ekspɔ:t ; 'ɛksport/ *n* **1** [U] (business of) exporting: 輸出;輸出業: *a ban on the ~ of gold;* 黃金出口之禁止; (attrib) (形容用法) *the '~ trade;* 出口貿易; *'~ duties.* 出口稅。 **2** [C] sth exported: 輸出品;出口貨: *Last year ~s exceeded imports in value.* 去年輸出品在價值上超過了輸入品。*What are the chief ~s of your country?* 你的國家有那些主要的輸出品?

ex·port[2] /ɪk'spɔ:t ; ɛks'port/ *vt* [VP6A] send (goods) to another country for purposes of trade: 輸出(貨物): *~ cotton goods.* 輸出棉織品。⇨ import. **~er** *n* trader who ~s goods. 出口商。**~·able** /-əbl ; -əbl̩/ *adj* that can be ~ed. 可輸出的。**ex·por·ta·tion** /ˌekspɔ:'teɪʃn ; ˌɛkspor'teʃən/ *n* [U] the ~ing of goods; goods ~ed. 輸出;出口貨。

ex·pose /ɪk'spəʊz ; ɪk'spoz/ *vt* [VP6A, 14, 15A] ~ ***(to),*** **1** uncover; leave uncovered or unprotected: 揭露;使暴露;棄置: *~ soldiers to unnecessary risks/to the enemy's gunfire;* 讓士兵們冒不必要的危險(受敵人砲火的射擊); *~d to the wind and rain;* 受風吹雨打; *be ~d to ridicule.* 遭受譏笑。**2** display: 展覽;陳列: *~ goods in a shop window.* 陳列貨物於商店櫥窗內。 **3** disclose, make known: 揭發;揭穿: *~ a plot/project/plan;* 揭發一陰謀(計畫); reveal the guilt or wrongdoing of; unmask: 揭穿…之罪惡;使暴露眞相: *~ a crime/criminal.* 揭穿一罪行(罪犯)。 **4** (photo) allow light to reach (camera film, etc): (攝影)使(軟片等)曝光;曝曬: *~ 30 metres of cinema film.* 曝曬三十公尺電影膠片。

ex·posé /ek'spəʊzeɪ *US:* ˌekspə'zeɪ ; ˌɛkspo'ze/ *n* **1** orderly setting out or précis of a body of facts or beliefs. (對事實或信仰的)有系統的陳述。 **2** making public of discreditable fact(s). 揭發不名譽之事。

ex·po·si·tion /ˌekspə'zɪʃn ; ˌɛkspə'zɪʃən/ *n* **1** [U] expounding or explaining; [C] instance of this; explanation or interpretation of a theory, plan, etc. 解釋;(原理,計畫等之)說明。 **2** [C] (abbr 略作 **expo** /ˈekspəʊ ; ˈɛkspo/) exhibition of goods, etc: 貨品等之展覽: *an industrial* ~. 工展。

ex·postu·late /ɪkˈspɒstʃʊleɪt ; ɪkˈspɑstʃə,let/ *vi* [VP2A, 3A] ~ ***(with sb) (on/about sth),*** make a friendly protest; reason or argue. 告戒;勸戒。 **ex·postu·la·tion** /ɪk,spɒstʃʊˈleɪʃn ; ɪk,spɑstʃəˈleʃən/ *n* [C, U] friendly protest(ing): 告戒;勸戒: *My expostulation(s) had no results.* 我的勸戒無效。

ex·po·sure /ɪkˈspəʊʒə(r) ; ɪkˈspoʒɚ/ *n* **1** [U] exposing or being exposed (all senses): 暴露;揭露;展覽;揭發;揭穿;曝曬: *The climbers lost their way on the mountain and died of* ~. 登山者在山間迷失了路而死於凍餒。 *E~ of the body to strong sunlight may be harmful.* 使身體受强烈的陽光所曬,可能有害。 *The ~ of the plot against the President probably saved his life.* 揭發危害總統的陰謀或許救了他的命。 **2** [C] instance of exposing or being exposed (all senses): 暴露,揭露,展覽,揭發,曝曬等的實例: *As a result of these ~s the government took strong measures against bribery and corruption.* 由於這些揭發,政府採取了强硬措施以懲治賄賂與舞弊。*How many ~s have you got left?* How many pictures remain on the (camera) film? 你還剩下多少張底片呀? *An ~ of one-hundredth of a second will be enough.* 百分之一秒的曝光就够了。 **'~ meter** *n* (photo) device to measure illumination and to indicate correct duration of ~. (攝影)曝光表。⇨ the illus at camera. 參看 camera 之挿圖。

ex·pound /ɪkˈspaʊnd ; ɪkˈspaʊnd/ *vt* [VP6A, 14] ~ ***(to),*** explain, make clear, by giving details: 詳加解釋;詳細說明: ~ *a theory/one's views (to sb).* (對某人)詳細說明一原理(自己的見解)。

ex·press[1] /ɪkˈspres ; ɪkˈsprɛs/ *adj* **1** clearly and definitely stated, not suggested or implied: 明白表示的;明確的: *You cannot ignore such an ~ command.* 你不能忽視如此明確的一項命令。 *It was his ~ wish that you should not wait for him.* 他明白表示不要你等他。 **2** going, sent, quickly; designed for high speed: 進行或發出迅速的;爲高速而設計的: *an '~ train;* 快車; ~ *delivery,* by special postal messenger; 快遞;限時專送; *an ~ letter/messenger.* 限時專送的信件(信差)。 **'~ way** *n* (US) major road for fast travel. (美)高速公路。⇨ (GB) (英) motorway. □ *adv* by ~ delivery; by ~ train: 用快遞;乘快車: *send a parcel ~;* 以快遞寄包裹; *travel ~.* 乘快車旅行。**~·ly** *adv* **1** plainly; definitely: 明白地;確定地: *You were ~ly forbidden to touch my papers.* 你絕不可碰我的文件。 **2** specially; on purpose: 特意地;故意地: *a dictionary ~ly compiled for foreign students of English.* 一部專爲學習英語的外國學生所編的字典。

ex·press[2] /ɪkˈspres ; ɪkˈsprɛs/ *n* **1** very fast train: 快車: *the 8.00am ~ to Edinburgh.* 上午八時去愛丁堡的快車。 **2** (US) company that undertakes to deliver goods fast and safely. (美)運送公司(送貨迅速安全)。 **3** [U] service rendered by the post office, railways, road services, etc for carrying goods quickly: 郵局,鐵路,公路局等之貨物迅速遞送: *send goods by ~.* (由鐵路等)運送貨物。

ex·press[3] /ɪkˈspres ; ɪkˈsprɛs/ *vt* **1** [VP6A, 10, 15A] make known, show by words, looks, actions: 表示;(由語言,表情,動作)表達: *I find it difficult to ~ my meaning.* 我發覺我難以表達我的意思。 *A smile ~ed her joy at the good news.* 微笑表示出她對這好消息的歡欣。 *I cannot easily ~ (to you) how grateful I am for your help.* 我難以向你表達我是多麼感激你的幫助。 ~ ***oneself,*** communicate one's thoughts or feelings through words, gestures, etc: 表達自己的意思: *He is still unable to ~ himself in English.* 他仍不能用英語表達他的意思。 *He ~ed himself strongly* (= spoke in a forceful way) *on the subject.* 他對此問題堅決表示他的意見。 **2** [VP6A] send a letter, goods, etc fast by special delivery. 快遞(郵件,貨物等)。 **3** [VP6A, 14] ~ ***(from/out of),*** (formal) press or squeeze out juices/oil: (正式用語)榨出(汁,油): *juice ~ed (pressed* is more usu) *from grapes.* 自葡萄榨出的汁 (pressed 較常用)。

ex·press·ion /ɪkˈspreʃn ; ɪkˈsprɛʃən/ *n* **1** [U] process of expressing (1): 表達;表示: *give ~ to one's gratitude,* say or show how grateful one is; 表示感激; *read* (aloud) *with ~,* in a way that shows feeling for the meaning; 帶有感情地朗讀; [C] instance of this (esp a look on sb's face): 表情: *There was an ~ of discontent on her face,* a discontented look. 她臉上有不滿的表情。 ***beyond/past ~,*** in a manner that cannot be expressed: 無法形容;無法表達: *The scenery was beautiful beyond ~,* indescribably beautiful. 那風景美麗的無法形容。 ***find ~ in,*** be expressed by means of: 由…表現出來: *Her feelings at last found ~ in tears.* 她的感情終於由眼淚發洩出來。 **2** [C] word or phrase: 辭句;措辭: *'Shut up'* (= Stop talking) *is not a polite ~.* '住嘴' 不是有禮貌的辭句。 *Slang ~s should be avoided in an essay.* 文章裏應避免用俚語。 **3** [C] (maths) group of symbols expressing a quantity, eg $3xy^2$. (數學)式(例如 $3xy^2$)。 **~·less** *adj* without ~(1): 無表情的: *in an ~less voice;* 以冷冰冰的聲音; *an ~less face.* 無表情的面孔。

ex·press·ion·ism /ɪkˈspreʃənɪzəm ; ɪkˈsprɛʃən,ɪzəm/ *n* [U] (in painting, music, etc) the symbolic or stylized expression of emotional experience. (繪畫,音樂等)表現主義 (以象徵的手法或特殊的風格表現內心的經驗)。 **ex·press·ion·ist** /-ɪst ; -ɪst/ *n*

ex·press·ive /ɪkˈspresɪv ; ɪkˈsprɛsɪv/ *adj* ~ ***(of),*** serving to express: 表示的;表現的: *looks ~ of despair;* 表示絶望的神情; *a cry ~ of pain;* 表示痛苦的哭叫; *an ~ smile.* 意味深長的微笑。 **~·ly** *adv*

ex·pro·pri·ate /eksˈprəʊprɪeɪt ; ɛksˈpropri,et/ *vt* [VP6A, 14] ~ ***(from),*** take away (property); dispossess (sb of an estate, etc). 徵用(私產);剝奪(某人之地產等)。**ex·pro·pri·ation** /,eks,prəʊprɪˈeɪʃn; ɛks,proprɪˈeʃən/ *n* [U].

ex·pul·sion /ɪkˈspʌlʃn ; ɪkˈspʌlʃən/ *n* [U] ~ ***(from),*** expelling or being expelled; [C] instance of this: 逐出;被逐;驅逐: *the ~ of a student from college;* 將一學生自大學開除; *an '~ order,* official order expelling a person from a country. 驅逐出境的命令。

ex·punge /ɪkˈspʌndʒ ; ɪkˈspʌndʒ/ *vt* [VP6A, 14] ~ ***(from),*** (formal) wipe or rub out words, names, etc from a book, etc. (正式用語)擦去;刪掉;劃掉(字,姓名等)。

ex·pur·gate /ˈekspəgeɪt ; ˈɛkspɚ,get/ *vt* [VP6A] take out from (a book, etc what are considered to be) improper or objectionable parts: 刪除 (書籍等)不妥之處: *an ~d edition of a novel.* 一小說的修訂版。 **ex·pur·ga·tion** /,ekspəˈgeɪʃn ; ,ɛkspɚˈgeʃən/ *n*

ex·quis·ite /ˈekskwɪzɪt *US:* ekˈskwɪzɪt ; ˈɛkskwɪzɪt/ *adj* **1** of great excellence; brought to a high state of perfection: 優美的;精緻的: ~ *workmanship;* 優美的技藝; ~ *designs;* 精緻的圖案; *a piece of ~ lace.* 一條精緻的花邊。 **2** (of pain, pleasure, etc) keenly felt. (指痛苦,快樂等)强烈地感受到的;極度的。 **3** (of power to feel) keen, delicate: (指感覺力)靈敏的;敏銳的: ~ *sensibility.* 靈敏的感覺能力。 **~·ly** *adv* **~·ness** *n*

ex-ser·vice /,eksˈsɜːvɪs ; ˈɛksˈsɝvɪs/ *adj* having formerly served in the armed forces. 退役的;退伍的。 **~·man** /-mən ; -mən/ *n* (*pl* -men) (GB): (英): *an ~men's organization.* 退伍軍人協會。

ex·tant /ekˈstænt *US:* ˈekstənt ; ɪkˈstænt/ *adj* still in existence (esp of documents, etc): 仍存在的;現存的(尤指文件等): *the earliest ~ manuscript of this poem.* 此詩現存的最早的原稿。

ex·tem·por·ary /ɪkˈstempərərɪ *US:* -pərerɪ ; ɪkˈstɛmpə,rɛrɪ/ *adj* = extempore. **ex·tem·por·ar·ily**

/-rərəlɪ *US:* -'rerəlɪ ; -ˌrɛrəlɪ/ *adv*

ex·tem·pore /ek'stempərɪ ; ɪk'stɛmpərɪ/ *adv, adj* (spoken or done) without previous thought or preparation: 臨時地(的)；無準備地(的)： *speak* ~, without notes; 臨時演說(未備草稿)； *an* ~ *address.* 即席演說。 **ex·tem·por·aneous(·ly)** /ekˌstempə'reɪnɪəs(lɪ) ; ɪkˌstɛmpə'renɪəs(lɪ)/ *adj, adv* = ~. 臨時的(地)；即席的(地)。

ex·tend /ɪk'stend ; ɪk'stɛnd/ *vt, vi* **1** [VP6A] make longer (in space or time); enlarge: 使(在空間或時間上)伸展；擴大；加長： ~ *a railway/a fence/a wall/the city boundaries.* 延長鐵路(圍牆，牆壁，市界)。 *Can't you* ~ *your visit for a few days,* stay a few days longer? 你不能多停留幾天嗎？ ~ ***credit,*** (fin) prolong the time for which credit is given. (財政)延長信用期限。 **2** [VP6A, 15A] lay or stretch out the body, a limb or limbs, at full length: 伸開；展開(身體或四肢)： ~ *one's arm horizontally;* 將臂平伸； ~ *one's hand to sb,* shake hands with him. 伸手與某人握手。 **3** [VP6A, 14] ~ ***sth (to sb),*** offer, grant, accord: 給與；施與： ~ *hospitality/an invitation/a greeting/a warm welcome to sb;* 款待(邀請，問候，熱烈歡迎)某人； ~ *help.* 給予幫助。 **4** [VP2B, C] (of space, land, etc) reach, stretch: (指空間，土地等)伸展；延展： *a road that* ~*s for miles and miles.* 伸展很多很多哩的道路。 *My garden* ~*s as far as the river.* 我的花園伸展到河邊。 **5** [VP6A, 15A] cause to reach or stretch: 使達到；延伸： ~ *a cable between two posts.* 在兩柱間拉一條鋼索。 **6** [VP6A] (usu passive) tax or use the powers of a person, horse, etc to the utmost: (通常用被動語態)使竭盡全力： *The horse was fully* ~*ed.* 那匹馬已竭盡全力。 ⇨ *flat out* at flat² *adv* (4).

ex·ten·sion /ɪk'stenʃn ; ɪk'stɛnʃən/ *n* **1** [U] extending or being extended: 伸展；延伸；擴大： *the* ~ *of useful knowledge;* 有用的知識之推廣； *University E*~, teaching for, examination of, part-time or extramural students; 大學附設的補習班；大學的附設部分； *the* ~ *of socialist influence in Africa.* 社會主義的勢力在非洲的擴張。 **2** [C] additional part; addition or continuance; enlargement: 附加部分；增加之物；延伸部分： *an* ~ *of one's summer holidays;* 暑假之延長期間； *build an* ~ *to a hospital;* 擴建一醫院； *get an* ~ *of time,* eg for paying a debt; 獲一延期(例如償債)； *an* ~ *to a sentence,* (gram) word or words amplifying the subject or predicate; (文法)擴大主詞或述詞之字； *telephone No 01-629-8494,* ~ *15,* ie a line extending from the switchboard to another room or office. 電話號碼 01-629-8494 轉 15 號分機。

ex·ten·sive /ɪk'stensɪv ; ɪk'stɛnsɪv/ *adj* extending far; far-reaching: 廣濶的；廣泛的；遠及的： *an* ~ *view;* 廣濶的視野； ~ *repairs/inquiries;* 廣泛的修理(調查)； *a scholar with an* ~ *knowledge of his subject.* 對其研究科目知識廣博的學者。 **~·ly** *adv*

ex·tent /ɪk'stent ; ɪk'stɛnt/ *n* [U] **1** ~ ***(of),*** length; area; range: 長度；區域；範圍： *From the roof we were able to see the full* ~ *of the park.* 從屋頂上我們能看到公園的全景。 *I was amazed at the* ~ *of his knowledge.* 我對他知識的淵博感到驚奇。 *They are building a new racing track, six miles in* ~. 他們正建築一條六哩長的新跑道。 **2** degree: 程度： *to a certain/to some* ~, partly, somewhat; 部分地；有些； *to such an* ~ *that...;* 達到此種程度以致…； *to what* ~*;* 達到什麼程度； *in debt to the* ~ *of £100.* 負債達一百鎊。

ex·tenu·ate /ɪk'stenjʊeɪt ; ɪk'stɛnjʊˌet/ *vt* [VP6A] make (wrongdoing) less serious (by finding an excuse): 掩飾(罪過)；(以藉口)使(罪過)減輕： *Nothing can* ~ *his base conduct.* 他的卑鄙的行爲無法掩飾。 *There are extenuating circumstances in this case.* 此案中有掩飾罪過的情形。 **ex·tenu·ation** /ɪkˌstenjʊ'eɪʃn ; ɪkˌstɛnjʊ'eʃən/ *n* **1** [U] extenuating or being ~d: 掩飾罪過；以藉口減輕罪過： *He pleaded poverty in extenuation of the theft.* 他以貧窮爲藉口請求減輕他的偷竊罪。 **2** [C] sth that ~s; partial excuse. 減輕罪過的藉口。

ex·terior /ɪk'stɪərɪə(r) ; ɪk'stɪrɪɚ/ *adj* outer; situated on or coming from outside: 外部的；在外部的；來自外部的： *the* ~ *surface of a hollow ball;* 空心球的表面； *the* ~ *features of a building.* 一建築物之外貌。 ⇨ interior. □ *n* outside; outward aspect or appearance: 外部；外面；外表： *a gentle man with a rough* ~. 一個外貌粗野而性情溫和的男人。 **~·ize** *vt* /-raɪz ; ˌraɪz/ = externalize.

ex·ter·mi·nate /ɪk'stɜːmɪneɪt ; ɪk'stɝməˌnet/ *vt* [VP6A] make an end of (disease, ideas, people's beliefs); destroy completely. 消除(疾病，觀念，信仰)；消滅。 **ex·ter·mi·na·tion** /ɪkˌstɜːmɪ'neɪʃn ; ɪksˌtɝmə'neʃən/ *n*

ex·ter·nal /ɪk'stɜːnl ; ɪk'stɝnl/ *adj* outside; situated on the outside; of or for the outside: 外部的；在外部的；外面的： ~ *evidence,* obtained from independent sources, not from what is being examined; 外證； *alcohol for* ~ *use,* for use on the skin, not to be drunk; 外用酒精(非飲用者)； ~ *examination,* one conducted by authorities outside the school, college, etc of the person(s) examined; 校外主持的考試； ~ *examiner,* person (not on the staff of those setting the examination) conducting such an examination. 校外主考人。 ⇨ internal. □ *n* (usu *pl*) ~ circumstances; outward features: (通常用複數)外部情況；外貌；外觀： *the* ~*s of religion,* acts and ceremonies (contrasted with inner and spiritual aspects); 宗教的外面形式(指其行爲和儀式，以別於內在的和精神方面的)； *judge people by* ~*s.* 以貌取人。 **~·ize** /-aɪz ; -aɪz/ *vt* [VP6A] make ~. 使在外部；使在外面。 **~ly** /ek'stɜːnəlɪ ; ɪk'stɝnḷɪ/ *adv*

ex·ter·ri·tor·ial /ˌeksˌterɪ'tɔːrɪəl ; ˌɛkstɛrə'torɪəl/ *adj* (eg of ambassadors, etc) free from the jurisdiction of the State in which one resides: (指大使等)享有治外法權的： ~ *privileges and rights.* 治外法權。

ex·tinct /ɪk'stɪŋkt ; ɪk'stɪŋkt/ *adj* **1** no longer burning; no longer active: 熄滅的；不再活動的： *an* ~ *volcano.* 死火山。 **2** (of feelings, passions) dead. (指感情)絕滅的。 **3** no longer in existence; having died out: 絕種的；死絕的： *an* ~ *species;* 已絶之種； *become* ~. 已絕種。

ex·tinc·tion /ɪk'stɪŋkʃn ; ɪk'stɪŋkʃən/ *n* [U] **1** making, being, becoming, extinct: 撲滅；消滅；毀滅；絕種： *a tribe threatened by* ~*;* 有絶種之虞的部落； *research that may lead to the* ~ *of a disease.* 可能導致滅絶某一疾病的研究工作。 **2** act of extinguishing: 熄滅： *the* ~ *of a fire/of sb's hopes.* 火之熄滅(某人希望之幻滅)。

ex·tin·guish /ɪk'stɪŋgwɪʃ ; ɪk'stɪŋgwɪʃ/ *vt* [VP6A] **1** put out (eg a light, fire). 熄滅(例如燈，火)。 **2** end the existence of (eg hope, love, passion, etc). 消滅(例如希望，愛情，情感等)。 **3** wipe out (a debt). 清償(債務)。 **~er** *n* (kinds of) apparatus for discharging a jet of liquid chemicals for ~ing a fire. 滅火器。

ex·tir·pate /'ekstəpeɪt ; 'ɛkstɚˌpet/ *vt* [VP6A] (formal) pull up by the roots; destroy utterly: (正式用語)連根拔起；根除；滅絶： ~ *social evils.* 根除社會弊端。 **ex·tir·pa·tion** /ˌekstə'peɪʃn ; ˌɛkstɚ'peʃən/ *n* [U].

ex·tol /ɪk'stəʊl ; ɪk'stɑl/ *vt* (-ll-) [VP6A, 15A] praise highly: 頌揚；極力稱讚： ~ *sb to the skies,* greatly; 把某人捧上天； ~ *sb's merits;* 頌揚某人的功德； ~ *sb as a hero.* 將某人當作英雄來頌揚。

ex·tort /ɪk'stɔːt ; ɪk'stɔrt/ *vt* [VP6A, 14] ~ ***(from),*** obtain by violence, threats, etc: 以暴力，威脅等獲得；强取；勒索： ~ *money from sb.* 向某人勒索錢財。 *The police used torture to* ~ *a confession from him.* 警方用刑逼他招供。 **ex·tor·tion** /ɪk'stɔːʃn ; ɪk'stɔrʃən/ *n* [U] ~ing; [C] instance of this. 强取；勒索；以暴力或威脅獲得。

ex·tor·tion·ate /ɪk'stɔːʃənət ; ɪk'stɔrʃənɪt/ *adj* (of *demands, prices*) much too great or high. (指要求，價格)過高的；太大的。 **~·ly** *adv*

extra /'ekstrə ; 'ɛkstrə/ *adj* additional; beyond what

is usual, expected or arranged for: 額外的;特別的;特加的: ～ *pay for ～ work;* 額外工作的額外報酬; *without ～ charge.* 不額外收費。*There were so many people that the company put on ～ buses.* 人數太多,公司加開了公共汽車。 □ *adv* **1** more than usually: 特別地;非常地: *an ～ strong box;* 特別堅牢的箱子; ～ *fine quality.* 特別好的質地。 **2** in addition: 除外: *price £1.30, packing and postage ～.* 價格爲1.30鎊,包裝與郵費除外。□ *n* **1** ～ thing; sth for which an ～ charge is made: 額外的事物;額外收費之物: *Her regular school fees are £50 a term; music and dancing are ～s.* 她的固定的學費是每學期五十鎊,音樂和舞蹈另行收費。 **2** (cricket) run not scored off the bat. (板球)未擊中球而跑得的分數。**3** (cinema, TV, etc) person employed and paid (usu by the day) for a minor part, eg in a crowd scene. (電影,電視等)臨時演員。

ex·tract /ɪk'strækt ; ɪk'strækt/ *vt* [VP6A, 14] ～ ***(from),*** **1** take or get out (usu with effort or by force): 拔取;拔出: ～ *a cork from a bottle;* 拔出一瓶塞; *have a tooth ～ed;* 拔掉一顆牙; ～ *a bullet from a wound;* 自傷口取出一子彈; (fig) (喻) ～ *money/information from sb,* who is unwilling to give it. 榨取某人的金錢(情報)。 **2** obtain (juices, etc) by pressing, crushing, boiling, etc: 榨出(汁等); 煎出: ～ *oil from cotton-seed/olives.* 自棉子(橄欖)中榨油。**3** select and present words, examples, passages, etc (from a book, speech, etc). (自書籍,演說等中)摘錄;選取(語句,例子,段落等)。 □ *n* /'ekstrækt ; 'ɛkstrækt/ **1** [U, C] that which has been ～ed(2) and concentrated: 榨出物;精;汁: *vanilla ～;* 香草精; *beef ～;* 牛肉汁; ～ *of malt.* 麥芽精。**2** [C] passage ～ed(3): (自書等中)摘錄的段落;選粹: ～*s from a long poem.* 一首長詩中摘錄下的精粹。 **ex·trac·tion** /ɪk'strækʃn ; ɪk'strækʃən/ *n* [U] **1** ～ing or being ～ed(1): 拔取;拔出: *the ～ion of a tooth.* 一顆牙齒之拔出。 **2** descent; lineage: 世系;家世: *Is Mr Mansion of French ～ion?* 曼遜先生有法國血統嗎?

extra·cur·ricu·lar /ˌekstrəkə'rɪkjʊlə(r) ; ˏɛkstrəkə'rɪkjələ/ *adj* outside the regular course of academic work or studies: 課外的;課程以外的: ～ *activities,* eg belonging to a dramatic society. 課外活動(例如參加戲劇社)。

ex·tra·dite /'ekstrədaɪt ; 'ɛkstrəˏdaɪt/ *vt* [VP6A] **1** give up, hand over (a person) from the State where he is a fugitive to the State where he is alleged to have committed, or has been convicted of, a crime. 引渡(逃犯)。 **2** obtain (such a person) for trial. 獲得(逃犯)的引渡。 **ex·tra·di·tion** /ˌekstrə'dɪʃn ; ˏɛkstrə'dɪʃən/ *n*

extra·ju·dicial /ˌekstrədʒuː'dɪʃl ; ˏɛkstrədʒu'dɪʃəl/ *adj* beyond the authority of a court; outside the (normal) authority of the law. 法院管轄以外的;法律(正常)權限以外的。

extra·mari·tal /ˌekstrə'mærɪtl ; ˏɛkstrə'mærətl/ *adj* outside marriage: 婚姻外的: ～ *relations,* adultery. 通姦。

extra·mural /ˌekstrə'mjʊərəl ; ˏɛkstrə'mjʊrəl/ *adj* **1** outside the boundaries (eg of a town). 在界線外的(例如在城市邊界以外的)。 **2** additional to the full-time activities of a university, etc: 大學等之活動範圍以外的;校外的: ～ *lectures/studies/students.* 校外演講(校外研究;大學推廣部的學生)。

ex·traneous /ɪk'streɪnɪəs ; ɪk'strenɪəs/ *adj* not related (to the object to which it is attached); not belonging (to what is being dealt with); coming from outside: 體外的;與本題無關的: ～ *interference.* 外來的干涉。

extra·ordi·nary /ɪk'strɔːdnrɪ *US:* -dənerɪ ; ɪk'strɔrdṇˏɛrɪ/ *adj* **1** beyond what is usual or ordinary; remarkable: 非常的;特別的;非凡的: *a man of ～ talents;* 有驚人才幹之人; ～ *weather.* 特別的天氣。 **2** (of officials) additional, specially employed: (指官員)特命的: *envoy ～.* 特使。 **ex·tra·ordi·nar·ily** /ɪk'strɔːdnrəlɪ *US:* -dənerəlɪ ; ɪk'strɔrdṇˏɛrəlɪ/ *adv*

extra·sen·sory /ˌekstrə'sensərɪ ; ˏɛkstrə'sɛnsərɪ/ *adj* (esp) (尤用於) ～ **perception** (abbr 略作 **ESP**), perception of external events without the use of any of the known senses. 超感覺力。

extra·terri·tor·ial /ˌekstrəˌterɪ'tɔːrɪəl ; ˏɛkstrəˏtɛrə'torɪəl/ *adj* = exterritorial.

ex·trava·gant /ɪk'strævəgənt ; ɪk'strævəgənt/ *adj* **1** wasteful; (in the habit of) wasting (money, etc): 浪費的;奢侈的;揮霍無度的: *an ～ man;* 奢侈的人; ～ *tastes and habits.* 奢侈的嗜好和習慣。 **2** (of ideas, speech, behaviour) going beyond what is reasonable, usual or conventional; not properly controlled: (指思想, 言論, 行爲)過分的; 過度的: ～ *praise/behaviour.* 過分的讚揚(行爲)。～**·ly** *adv* **ex·trava·gance** /-gəns ; -gəns/ *n* **1** [U] being ～: 奢侈;揮霍無度: *His extravagance explains why he is always in debt.* 他的揮霍無度說明他爲何總是負債。**2** [C] ～ statement, act, etc. 過分的言論,行爲等。

ex·trava·gan·za /ɪkˌstrævə'gænzə ; ɪkˏstrævə'gænzə/ *n* [C] (music, theatre, literature) irregular and fanciful composition; burlesque; spectacular entertainment. (音樂,戲劇,文學之)非正規的奇特的作品;諷刺性滑稽表演;壯觀的表演。

ex·treme /ɪk'striːm ; ɪk'strim/ *n* **1** either end of anything; (fig) highest degree: 末端; 盡頭; (喻)極端;極度: *annoying in the ～,* most annoying. 極爲討厭。 **2** (*pl*) qualities, etc as wide apart, as widely different, as possible: (複)極端不同的性質等: *the ～s of heat and cold.* 熱與冷之極端不同。*Love and hate are ～s.* 愛和恨是兩個極端。 ***go to/be driven to ～s,*** to ～ measures, to do more than is usu considered right or desirable. 走極端。□ *adj* **1** at the end(s); farthest possible: 在盡頭的;最遠的: *the ～ edge of a field;* 田地之邊界; *in ～ old age;* 在極老的時期; *The ～ penalty of the law* (in some countries) *is the death penalty.* 極刑(在某些國家)就是死刑。 **2** reaching the highest degree: 至最高限度的;極度的: ～ *patience/kindness;* 極度的耐心(仁慈); *in ～ pain.* 在極度痛苦中。 **3** (of persons, their ideas) far from moderate; going to great lengths in views or actions: (指人或其思想)極端的;偏激的: *hold ～ opinions;* 持偏激的意見; *the ～ left/right,* (in politics) those who support communism/fascism. (政治上)極左份子(擁護共產主義者); 極右份子(擁護法西斯主義者)。～**·ly** *adv* (used intensively with *adjj* and *advv*) to a very high degree. (與形容詞和副詞連用,表示強度)極端地;極度地。 **ex·trem·ist** /-ɪst ; -ɪst/ *n* person who holds ～ views (esp in politics). 極端主義者;意見偏激者(尤指在政治方面)。 **ex·trem·ity** /ɪk'stremətɪ ; ɪk'strɛmətɪ/ *n* (*pl* -ties) [C] **1** ～ point, end or limit; (*pl*) hands and feet. 極點;末端;極限;(複)手足。 **2** (*sing* only) ～ degree (of joy, misery, esp of misfortune): (僅用單數) (快樂,痛苦,尤指不幸之) 極度: *an extremity of pain.* 極度痛苦。*How can we help them in their extremity?* 我們怎樣幫助陷於極端不幸中的他們? **3** (usu *pl*) ～ measures, eg for punishing wrongdoers, taking revenge: (通常用複數)極端的措施;極端手段(例如懲罰犯人或報復者): *Both armies were guilty of extremities.* 兩軍皆犯有手段激烈之罪。

ex·tri·cate /'ekstrɪkeɪt ; 'ɛkstrɪˏket/ *vt* [VP6A, 14] ～ ***(from),*** free; disentangle: 使免除;解脫: ～ *oneself from a difficulty.* 使自己免除一困難。 **ex·tri·cable** /ek'strɪkəbl ; 'ɛkstrɪkəbl/ *adj* that can be ～d. 可免除的; 可解脫的。 **ex·tri·ca·tion** /ˌekstrɪ'keɪʃn ; ˏɛkstrɪ'keʃən/ *n* [U].

ex·trin·sic /ek'strɪnsɪk ; ɛk'strɪnsɪk/ *adj* ～ ***(to),*** (of qualities, values, etc) not a part of the real character; operating or originating from the outside; not essential. (指性質,價值等)非固有的;外來的;外在的。

ex·tro·vert /'ekstrəvɜːt ; 'ɛkstroˏvɝt/ *n* person more interested in what goes on around him than in his own thoughts and feelings; (colloq) lively, cheerful person; 性格外向的人; (俗) 活潑愉快的人; (attrib): (形容用法): ~ *behaviour*. 個性外向的行爲。 ⇨ introvert. **ex·tro·ver·sion** /ˌekstrəˈvɜːʃn *US:* -ʒn; ˌɛkstrəˈvɝʃən/ *n* [U] state of being ~ed. 外向性;外傾。

ex·trude /ɪkˈstruːd; ɪkˈstrud/ *vt* [VP6A, 14] ~ ***(from)***, force sb or sth out; shape (eg plastic or metal) by forcing through a die. 逐出;用印模壓製(例如塑膠或金屬)。 **ex·tru·sion** /ɪkˈstruːʒn; ɪkˈstruʒən/ *n*

ex·uber·ant /ɪgˈzjuːbərənt *US:* -ˈzuː-; ɪgˈzjubərənt/ *adj* **1** growing vigorously; luxuriant: 茂盛的;繁茂的: *plants with ~ foliage*. 枝葉茂盛的植物。 **2** full of life and vigour; high-spirited; overflowing: 活力充沛的;精神旺盛的; 充溢的; 豐富的: *children in ~ spirits;* 興高采烈的孩子們; *an ~ imagination*. 豐富的想像力。 **~·ly** *adv* **ex·uber·ance** /-rəns; -rəns/ *n* [U] state or quality of being ~: 茂盛;充溢;繁茂;豐富;活力充沛: *The speaker's exuberance won over an apathetic audience*. 那演說者以充沛的精神和感情說服了那些冷漠的聽衆。

ex·ude /ɪgˈzjuːd *US:* -ˈzuːd; ɪgˈzjud, -ˈzud/ *vt, vi* [VP2A, C, 6A] (of drops of liquid) come or pass out slowly; ooze out: (指水滴)慢慢流出;滲出: *Sweat ~s through the pores*. 汗從毛孔中滲出。

ex·ult /ɪgˈzʌlt; ɪgˈzʌlt/ *vi* [VP2A, 3A, 4C] rejoice greatly: 狂喜;非常高興: *~ at/in a success;* 因成功而狂喜; *~ to find that one has succeeded;* 發現自己成功後非常高興; ~ (= triumph) *over a defeated rival*. 將對手擊敗而得意。**~·ant** /-ənt; -n̩t/ *adj* ~ing; triumphant. 狂喜的;歡欣的;得意的。 **~·ant·ly** *adv* **ex·ul·ta·tion** /ˌegzʌlˈteɪʃn; ˌɛgzʌlˈteʃən/ *n* [U] great joy (*at*); triumph (*over*). 狂喜(與 at 連用); 歡欣;得意(與 over 連用)。

eye[1] /aɪ; aɪ/ *n* **1** organ of sight: 眼睛: *We see with our eyes*. 我們用眼睛看。 *He opened/closed his eyes*. 他睜開(閉上)了眼睛。*He is blind in one eye*. 他有一隻眼失明。 *He lost an eye in the war*. 他在戰爭中喪失一隻眼睛。⇨ the illus here and at head. 參看本條及 head 之插圖。 ***an eye for an eye***, punishment as severe as the injury suffered; retaliation. 以眼還眼;報復。 ***eyes right/left/front***, (mil command) Turn the head and look to the right, etc. (軍隊口令)向右(左,前)看。 ***if you had half an eye***, if you were not so dull, unobservant. 如果你稍加注意。 ***in the eyes of the law, etc***, from the point of view of the law, etc; as the law, etc sees it. 就法律等的觀點而言。 ***in the eyes of sb; in my/his, etc eyes***, in the judgement of: 在⋯的眼裏: *You're only a child in his eyes*. 你在他的眼裏祇是一個孩子。***under/before one's very eyes***, **(a)** in one's presence, in front of one. 在某人面前。 **(b)** with no attempt at concealment. 不欲隱瞞地;公開地。 ***up to the eyes in*** (work, etc), deeply engaged in. 埋頭於(工作等)。 ***with an eye to***, with a view to, hoping for. 爲了要;指望着。 ***be all eyes***, be watching intently. 極爲注意。 ***be in the public eye***, be often seen in public; be well known. 常公開出現;爲衆所周知。 ***close one's eyes to***, refuse to see or take notice of. 拒絕看;拒絕注意。 ***get one's eye in***, (cricket and other ball games) become able, through practice, to follow with one's eyes the movement of the ball. (板球及其他球戲)由於練習而能用眼跟上球的動向。 ***give sb a black eye; black sb's eye***, give him a blow so that there is a discoloured bruise round the eye. 將某人的眼圈打成瘀傷;把某人的眼眶打青。 ***have an eye for***, be a good judge of, have a proper sense of: 能判斷;能欣賞: *He has a good eye for beauty/the picturesque*. 他很會欣賞美(美的東西)。 ***have an eye to***, have as one's object: 着眼於: *He always has an eye to business*, looks for possibilities of doing business. 他總是着眼於商業。 ***keep an eye on***, (lit, fig) keep a watch on. (字面,喻)注意。 ***make eyes at***, look amorously at. 對⋯眉目傳情;向⋯送秋波。 ***make sb open his eyes***, make him take notice. 使某人注意。 ***Mind your eye***, (colloq) Take care, Look out. (俗)注意;當心。 ***open sb's eyes to***, cause him to realize. 使某人認清。***see eye to eye (with)***, agree entirely, have identical views. 完全同意;(與⋯)有相同的見解。 ***see sth with half an eye***, see it at a glance. 一目了然。 ***set/clap eyes on***, see: 看;看見: *I hope I shall never set eyes on her again*. 我希望我永遠不再看到她。***never take one's eyes off***, never stop watching. 永不停止注意。⇨ catch[1](7), dust[1](1). **2** thing like an eye: 似眼之物;眼狀物: *the eye of a needle*, the hole for the thread; 針眼; *a hook and eye*, fastening with a hook and loop for a dress, etc; (其作用相當於鈕釦的)領鈎;鈎釦;*the eye of a potato*, point from which a leaf-bud will grow. 馬鈴薯的芽眼。 **3** (compounds, etc) (複合字等) **ˈeye·ball** *n* the eye within the lids and socket. 眼球。***eyeball to eyeball***, (colloq) face to face. (俗)面對面。 **ˈeye-bath; ˈeye-cup** *nn* small glass for holding lotion, etc, in which to bathe the eye. 洗眼器;洗眼杯。 **ˈeye·brow** *n* arch of hair above the eye. 眉;眉毛。***raise one's eyebrows***, express surprise, doubt, etc. 揚揚眉毛(表示驚奇,懷疑等)。 **ˈeye·catching** *adj* easy to see and pleasant to look at; attractive. 顯明而悅目的;動人的。 **ˈeye·ful** /-fʊl; -ˌfʊl/ *n* as much as one is capable of viewing; as much as one can see at a glance. 一眼所能看到之物;一瞥之所見。 ***have/get an eyeful (of)***, have a good long look (at sth that has strongly attracted the attention because one is curious about it). 仔細看看(極使自己好奇之物)。 **ˈeye-glass** *n* lens (for one eye) to help defective sight. (一塊)眼鏡片;單眼鏡。 **ˈeye-glasses** *n pl* pair of lenses in a frame; spectacles or glasses (the usu words). 一副眼鏡(通常用 spectacles 或 glasses)。 **ˈeye·lash** *n* hair, row of hairs, on the edge of the eyelid. 睫毛。 **eye·less** *adj* without eyes. 無眼的。 **ˈeye·lid** *n* upper or lower covering of the eye. 眼皮;眼瞼。 ***hang on by the eyelids***, have a very slight, insecure hold. 一髮千鈞。 **ˈeye-opener** *n* circumstance, etc that brings enlightenment and surprise. 令人開眼界並感到驚奇的情形等。 **ˈeye·piece** *n* lens at the end of a telescope or microscope, to which the eye is applied. (望遠鏡或顯微鏡之)目鏡。 **ˈeye-shadow** *n* [U] cosmetic applied to the eyelids. 眼影(塗眼皮的化妝品)。 **ˈeye-shot** *n* [U] seeing distance: 視界;視野: *beyond/*

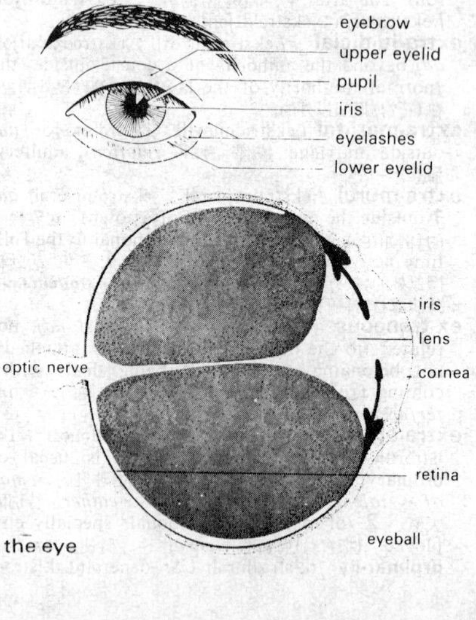

the eye

out of／in／within eyeshot. 在視界外(外,內,內)。 **'eye·sight** *n* [U] power, faculty, of seeing: 視力; 目力: *to have good／poor eyesight.* 目力佳(不佳)。 **'eye·sore** *n* ugly object; sth unpleasing to look at. 醜陋的東西;難看的東西。 **'eye-strain** *n* [U] tired condition of the eyes (as caused, for example, by reading very small print). 眼睛疲勞(例如由閱讀印刷字體太小的讀物所致)。 **'eye-tooth** *n* canine tooth. 犬齒。⇨ the illus at mouth. 參看 mouth 之挿圖。 **'eye·wash** *n* [U] **(a)** liquid for bathing the eyes. 洗眼藥水。 **(b)** (colloq) sth said or done to deceive; nonsense. (俗)騙人的言語或行動;胡言亂語。 **'eye-witness** *n* person who can bear witness from what he has himself seen: 目擊者;見證人: *an eye-witness account of a crime.* 見證人對於一項罪行的敍述。 **-eyed** *suff* (in compounds): (用於複合字中): *a blue-eyed girl*, girl having blue eyes; 藍眼睛的女郎; *a one-eyed man,* man having only one eye; 一個衹有一隻眼睛的人; *starry-eyed,* (colloq) idealistic. (俗)理想主義者的;幻想的;不實際的。

eye² /aɪ ; aɪ/ *vt* [VP6A, 15A] observe, watch: 觀看: *He eyed me with suspicion.* 他懷疑地望着我。 *They were ey(e)ing us jealously.* 他們嫉妬地看着我們。

eye·let /'aɪlɪt ; 'aɪlɪt/ *n* [C] small hole in cloth, in a sail, etc for a rope, etc to go through; metal ring round such a hole, to strengthen it. (布、帆等穿繩等之)小孔;嵌於上述小孔之金屬圈。

eyrie, eyry /'eərɪ ; 'ɛrɪ/ *n* ⇨ aerie.

Ff

F, f /ef ; ɛf/ (*pl* F's, f's /efs ; ɛfs/) the sixth letter of the English alphabet. 英文字母之第六個字母。

fa /fɑː ; fɑ/ *n* fourth note in the musical octave. 大音階之第四音。

fab /fæb ; fæb/ *adj* (dated sl) fabulous(3). (過時俚語)令人驚奇的;奇妙的。

Fabian /'feɪbɪən ; 'febɪən/ *n, adj* **1** (person) using cautious and slow strategy to wear out opposition: 使用謹慎和拖延策略以困敗敵手的(人): *a ~ policy.* 拖延的困敵政策。 **2** (GB) (person) aiming at gradual socialist change. (英)以緩進手段進行社會改變的(人)。

fable /'feɪbl ; 'febḷ/ *n* **1** [C] short tale, not based on fact, esp one with animals in it (eg **Aesop's** /'iːsɒps ; 'isɑps/ **~s**) and intended to give moral teaching. 寓言(例如伊索寓言)。 **2** [U] (collective *sing*) (集合單數) myths; legends: 神話;傳說: *sort out fact from ~.* 自傳說中選取事實。 **3** [C] false statement or account. 無稽之談。 **fabled** /'feɪbld ; 'febḷd/ *adj* celebrated in ~; legendary. 寓言中有名的;傳說的。

fab·ric /'fæbrɪk ; 'fæbrɪk/ *n* [C, U] **1** (kind of) textile material: 織物: *woollen／silk ~s;* 毛(絲)織物; *~ gloves,* made of woven material, not of leather. 織造的手套(非皮製的)。 **2** structure; sth put together: 結構;構造;構造物: *the ~ of society;* 社會的結構; *funds for the upkeep of the ~,* eg an ancient building. 保養建築物(如古老建築物)之專款。

fab·ri·cate /'fæbrɪkeɪt ; 'fæbrɪ,ket/ *vt* [VP6A] construct; put together; make up (sth false); forge (a document): 建造;裝配;捏造;僞造(文書): *~ an accusation／a will;* 捏造罪名(僞造遺囑); *a ~d account of adventures.* 虛構的冒險故事。 **fab·ri·ca·tion** /ˌfæbrɪ'keɪʃn ; ˌfæbrɪ'keʃən/ *n* [U] fabricating; [C] sth ~d, eg a forged document, a false story of events. 建造;裝配;捏造;僞造;僞造物(例如僞造的文書、虛構的故事)。

fabu·lous /'fæbjʊləs ; 'fæbjələs/ *adj* **1** celebrated in fable(2): 神話中有名的: *~ heroes.* 神話中有名的英雄。 **2** incredible or absurd: 令人難信的;荒謬的: *~ wealth.* 驚人的財富。 **3** (colloq) wonderful; marvellous. (俗)令人驚奇的;奇妙的。 **~·ly** *adv* incredibly: 難以置信地: *~ly rich.* 難以置信的富有。

fa·çade /fə'sɑːd ; fə'sɑd/ *n* [C] front or face of a building (towards a street or open place); (fig) false appearance: 建築物的正面;(喻)虛僞的外表: *a ~ of indifference.* 假裝冷漠。

face¹ /feɪs ; fes/ *n* **1** the front part of the head (forehead, eyes, nose, mouth, cheeks, chin): 面孔; 臉: *He fell on his ~.* 他臉朝下倒下去了。 *The stone struck him on the ~.* 石頭擊在他的臉上。 *Her ~ is her fortune,* (said of a woman who has beauty, but no dowry or talents). 她的面孔卽是她的財產(指一女子有姿色,但無嫁妝或才能)。 ***bring two persons／parties ~ to ~; bring sb ~ to ~ with sb,*** bring them together so that they confront one another: 使兩人面對面: *The two politicians were brought ~ to ~ in a TV interview.* 這兩位從政者曾在一次電視訪問中面對面。 ***come ~ to ~ with sb; meet sb ~ to ~,*** come into his presence, meet or confront him. 與某人碰面。 ***look sb in the ~,*** look at him steadily. 直視某人。 ***be unable to look sb in the ~,*** be unable to look at sb because of feeling ashamed, bashful, etc. (由於慚愧、害羞等)不敢正視某人。 ***set one's ~ against sb,*** oppose him. 反對某人。 ***show one's ~,*** appear, let oneself be seen: 露面;現身: *How can you show your ~ here after the way you behaved last night?* 在你昨夜那種表現之後,你怎能在此露面? ***in (the) ~ of,*** **(a)** confronted with: 在…面前;在…之前: *What could he do in the ~ of all these difficulties?* 面對着這一切困難,他能做些什麼? **(b)** in spite of: 不顧: *He succeeded in ~ of great danger.* 他不顧大的危險而成功了。 ***fly in the ~ of sth,*** openly defy, disregard (eg Providence／public disapproval／the facts): 甘冒大不韙(如悍然不顧天意、公衆非議、一切事實): *Your claim flies in the ~ of all the evidence.* 你的要求公然違背所有的證據。 ***in one's ~; in the ~,*** **(a)** straight against／at: 正對着: *The sun was shining in our ~s.* 太陽正對着我們照射。 **(b)** with no attempt at concealment: 公開地: *Death stared him in the ~.* 死神凝視着他(他命在旦夕)。 *She'll only laugh in your ~.* 她會當面笑你。 Cf 參較 *laugh up one's sleeve* at laugh(1). ***to one's ~,*** openly, in one's hearing. 當着某人的面。 *I'll tell him so to his ~,* ie I'm not afraid to tell him. 我要當面同他這樣說。 Cf 參較 *behind one's back* at back¹(1). **2** (compounds) (複合字) **'~-ache** *n* neuralgia. 面部神經痛。 **'~-card** *n* (playing-card) king, queen, or knave. (紙牌)老K,女王或傑克。 **'~-cloth,** (esp) small square towel for washing the ~. (尤指)洗臉毛巾;小方毛巾。 **'~-cream,** cosmetic cream for the skin on the ~. 面霜。 **'~-lift(ing)** *n* operation of tightening the skin to smooth out wrinkles and make the ~ look younger. 拉皮(使面部皮膚拉緊以消除皺紋的手術)。 **'~-pack** *n* paste applied to clean and freshen the skin of the ~. 擦面膏;面部潔霜。 **'~-powder** *n* cosmetic powder for the ~. 撲面粉。 **3** look; expression: 面容;表情: *a sad ~;* 悲傷的面容; *smiling ~s.* 微笑的面容。 *She is a good judge of ~s,* judges the character well from the expression of the ~. 她善於根據面部表情來判斷人的性格。 ***keep a straight ~,*** hide one's amusement (by not smiling or laughing). 不露笑容。 ***make／pull a ~／~s (at sb),*** pull the ~ out of shape; make grimaces (at him). (向某人)扮鬼臉。 ***put on／wear a (long) ~,*** look serious or dismal. 繃著臉;愁眉苦臉;拉長了臉。 **4** (in various senses) (用於各種意義) ***have the ~ (to do sth),*** (more usu *the cheek*) (cheek 較常用) be bold or impudent enough. 竟大膽或厚顏得;竟

有臉。***lose* ~,** be humiliated, suffer loss of credit or reputation. 丟臉;失面子。***put a good/bold/brave ~ on sth,*** make it look well; show courage in dealing with it. 使某物美觀;處置某事時顯出勇氣。***put a new ~ on sth,*** alter its aspect, make it look different. 使面目一新;使改觀。***save (one's) ~,*** refrain from, evade, shaming oneself openly; avoid losing one's dignity or suffering loss of credit or reputation. 保全面子;保持尊嚴。Hence, 由此產生, **'~-saver** *n* act or event that allows this. 保全面子的行動或事件。 **'~-saving** *n, part adj:* *~-saving moves.* 保全面子的行動。***on the ~ of it,*** judging by appearances, when first seen or heard: 就表面判斷: *On the ~ of it, his story seems unconvincing.* 就表面判斷,他的故事似乎不足以令人相信。**5** surface; façade (of a building); front: 表面;(建築物之)正面;前面: *the ~ of a clock.* 鐘面。*He laid the cards ~ down on the table.* 他將那些紙牌反放在桌上。*A dice has six ~s.* 骰子有六個面。*A diamond crystal has many ~s.* 鑽石有很多面。*The team climbed the north ~ of the mountain.* 該隊由山的北面攀登。*They disappeared from/off the ~ of the earth.* 他們從地面上消失了。*The miner worked at the coal~ for six hours.* 那礦工在煤礦的採掘面工作了六小時。*The value of a coin or banknote is shown on its ~.* 錢幣或鈔票的價值見於其表面。Hence, 由此產生, **~ value,** the nominal value of a coin or banknote; (fig) what sth or sb seems to be from appearances. 票面價值;票面額;(喻)某事物或某人的表面。***take sth at its ~ value,*** accept that it is what it seems to be. 相信某事物的表面價值。⇨ the illus at crystal; mountain. 參看 crystal, mountain 之挿圖。**6** size or style of the surface of a piece of type cast for printing: 印刷活字的大小或字體: *bold-~ type.* 粗體鉛字;黑體字。**~·less** *adj* (fig) anonymous; unknown to the general public: (喻)匿名的: *the ~less men who have power in commerce and industry.* 工商界有勢力的匿名人氏。

face² /feɪs ; fes/ *vt, vi* **1** [VP6A, C] have or turn the ~ to, or in a certain direction; be opposite to: 朝;向;面對: *Turn round and ~ me.* 轉過身來對着我。*Who's the man facing us?* 對着我們的那個人是誰?*The window ~s the street.* 那窗子面臨街道。*The picture ~s page 10.* 該圖在第十頁的對面。*'Which way does your house ~?'—'It ~s south.'* '你的房子朝那個方向?'—'它朝南。' ***About/Left/Right ~!*** (US mil commands) Turn right round/to the left/right. (美,軍隊口令)向後轉!向左(右)轉!Cf 參較 (GB) (英) *About/Left/Right turn!* **2** [VP6A, 15B, 2C] meet confidently or defiantly: 毅然相對;勇敢相對: *~ the enemy;* 毅然面對敵人; *~ dangers.* 勇敢地對付危險。***~ sth/it out,*** refuse to give way, carry it through with courage. 不讓步;堅持到底。***~ the music,*** show no fear at a time of trial, danger, difficulty. 毅然面對考驗、危險或難局;勇敢地承擔一切後果。***~ up to (sth),*** recognize and deal with, honestly and bravely: 誠實而又勇敢地承認和對付: *~ up to the fact that one is no longer young.* 勇敢地承認和面對不再年輕的事實。***let's ~ it,*** (colloq) it must be acknowledged. (俗)我們必須承認此事;我們必須面對事實。**3** [VP6A] recognize the existence of: 承認…的存在: *~ facts/altered circumstances.* 承認事實(改變了的情勢)。**4** [VP6A] present itself to: 呈現於…之前: *the problem that ~s us.* 擺在我們面前的問題。**5** [VP6A, 14] ***~ (with),*** cover with a layer of different material: 覆以一層不同的東西: *~ a wall with concrete;* 用混凝土塗牆壁; *a coat ~d with silk,* eg with silk on the lapels. 鑲有綢邊的上衣(如在翻領上鑲以綢邊)。**facer** *n* (GB dated colloq) serious difficulty by which one is suddenly or unexpectedly ~d. (英,過時俗語)突然遭遇的重大困難。

facet /'fæsɪt ; 'fæsɪt/ *n* one of the many sides of a cut stone or jewel; (fig) aspect, eg of a problem. 寶石等的小平面;刻面;(喻)(問題等的)一面。

fa·cetious /fə'siːʃəs ; fə'siʃəs/ *adj* humorously teasing or mocking; fond of, marked by, inappropriate or bitter joking: 詼諧的;戲謔的;(愛)亂開玩笑的;(愛)挖苦人的: *a ~ remark/young man.* 詼諧的話(愛亂開玩笑的青年)。**~·ly** *adv* **~·ness** *n*

facia /'feɪʃə ; 'feʃə/ *n* = fascia.

fa·cial /'feɪʃl ; 'feʃəl/ *adj* of or for the face: 面孔的;面部用的: *a ~ massage.* 面部按摩。□ *n* ~ massage. 面部按摩。

facile /'fæsaɪl *US:* -sl ; 'fæsḷ/ *adj* **1** easily done or obtained: 易做的;易得的: *a ~ victory.* 輕易獲得的勝利。**2** (of a person) able to do things easily; (of speech or writing) done easily but without attention to quality: (指人)能幹的;(指演說或寫作)流暢但不重內容的: *a ~ liar/remark;* 善於說謊的人(流暢而無內容的談話); *a man with a ~ pen/tongue.* 筆下(口頭)流暢的人。

fa·cili·tate /fə'sɪlɪteɪt ; fə'sɪlə,tet/ *vt* [VP6A] (of an object, process) make easy; lessen the difficulty of: (指物件、方式)使容易;使便利;減輕…的困難: *Modern inventions have ~d housework.* 現代的發明物使家事的操作便利了。(Note: ~ is never used when the subject is a person). (注意: ~ 不可用人做主詞)。

fa·cil·ity /fə'sɪlətɪ ; fə'sɪlətɪ/ *n* (*pl* -ties) **1** [U] quality which makes learning or doing things easy or simple: 靈巧;熟練: *have great ~ in learning languages;* 有學習語言的天才; *show ~ in performing a task;* 在一工作中表現熟練; *play the piano with ~.* 熟練地彈鋼琴。**2** (*pl*) aids, circumstances, which make it easy to do things: (複)使工作便利的工具或環境;設備: *facilities for travel,* eg buses, trains, air services; 便利旅行的工具(例如公共汽車、火車、航空設備); *facilities for study,* eg libraries, laboratories; 研究設備(例如圖書館、實驗室); *'sports facilities,* eg running tracks, swimming pools. 運動設備(例如跑道、游泳池)。

facing /'feɪsɪŋ ; 'fesɪŋ/ *n* **1** coating of different material, eg on a wall. 不同材料的覆飾;飾面(例如牆壁上者)。**2** (*pl*) material of a different colour on a garment, eg on the cuffs, collar: (複)衣服上不同顏色的飾物(例如袖口、衣領之飾邊): *a purple jacket with green ~s.* 一件有綠色飾邊的紫夾克。⇨ face²(5).

fac·sim·ile /fæk'sɪməlɪ ; fæk'sɪməlɪ/ *n* [C] exact copy or reproduction of writing, printing, a picture, etc: (寫作、印刷、畫片等)精確的複製;摹寫;傳眞: *reproduced in ~,* exactly. 精確複製的。

fact /fækt ; fækt/ *n* **1** [C] sth that has happened or been done. 已發生或所做之事;事件;行為。***accessary before the ~,*** (legal) accessary who is not present when a crime is committed. (法律)犯罪前的從犯(犯罪時未在場)。***accessary after the ~,*** (legal) who knowingly helps another who has committed a crime. (法律)犯罪後的從犯。**2** [C] sth known to be true or accepted as true: 事實: *No one can deny the ~ that fire burns.* 無人能否認火可燃燒的事實。*Poverty and crime are ~s.* 貧窮和犯罪是事實。*I know it for a ~,* I know that it is really true. 我知道這是眞的。***a ~ of life,*** sth that cannot be ignored, however unpleasant. 儘管不愉快而無法更改的事實。***the ~s of life,*** (colloq, euphem) details of human sexual reproduction (eg as told to children). (俗,委婉語)性知識(例如講給孩子們聽的)。**'~-finding** *adj: A ~-finding commission has been appointed,* one to inquire into ~s, to find out what is true and what is not true. 一個事實調查團已被派定。**3** [U] reality; what is true; what exists: 現實;眞實的事物;存在的事物: *The story is founded on ~.* 這故事係根據現實。*It is important to distinguish ~ from fiction.* 辨別現實與虛構是重要的。*The ~ of the matter is...,* The truth is.... 此事的眞相是…。***in ~; as a matter of ~; in point of ~,*** really: 事實上;實際上: *I think so; in ~, I'm quite sure.* 我想是如此,事實上我十分

相信是如此。

fac·tion /ˈfækʃn; ˈfækʃən/ *n* **1** [C] discontented, often unscrupulous and self-interested group of persons within a party (esp political): 派系;小派別(尤指政治上的): *The party split into petty ~s.* 該黨分裂成若干小派系。 **2** [U] quarrelling among such groups; party strife. 派系間之不和;傾軋;黨爭。 **fac·tious** /ˈfækʃəs; ˈfækʃəs/ *adj* of, caused by, ~; fond of ~: 黨派的;由派系間不和而造成的;喜傾軋的: *a factious spirit.* 喜傾軋的風氣。

fac·ti·tious /fækˈtɪʃəs; fækˈtɪʃəs/ *adj* (formal) unnatural; artificial; created or developed by design: (正式用語)不自然的;人爲的;設計而成的: *~ enthusiasm;* 虛假的熱心; *a ~ demand for goods,* eg as the result of extensive advertising. 對貨物之反常的需要(例如由大規模廣告宣傳造成者)。

fac·tor /ˈfæktə(r); ˈfæktɚ/ *n* **1** (arith) whole number (except 1) by which a larger number can be divided exactly: (算術)因數;因子: *2, 3, 4 and 6 are ~s of 12.* 2, 3, 4和6是12的因數。 **2** fact, circumstance, etc helping to bring about a result: 因素: *evolutionary ~s,* environmental influences, etc that have caused sth to evolve or develop; 進化的因素; *~s in the making of a nation;* 構成一個國家的因素; *an unknown ~,* sth unknown, likely to influence a result; 未知的因素; *the ~ of safety,* eg in engineering. (工程等中的)安全因素。 Hence, 由此產生, **ˈsafety-~** *n.* 安全因素。 **3** agent; person who buys and sells on commission; (in Scotland) land-agent, steward. 代理人;代理商;(蘇格蘭)土地經管人。 **~·ize** /ˈfæktəraɪz; ˈfæktəˌraɪz/ *vt* [VP6A] find the ~s of (a number). 分解(某數的)因子。

fac·tory /ˈfæktərɪ; ˈfæktərɪ/ *n* (*pl* -ries) **1** building(s) where goods are made (esp by machinery); workshop: 工廠;製造廠: (attrib) (形容用法) *~ workers.* 工廠工人。 **F~ Acts,** (in GB) laws dealing with safety regulations, working conditions of employees, etc. (英)工廠法案(規定工人的安全規章、工作環境等)。 **2** (hist) merchant company's trading station abroad. (史)駐外商店;代理店。

fac·to·tum /fækˈtəutəm; fækˈtotəm/ *n* **(general) ~,** (often hum) servant doing all kinds of work. (常作詼諧語)雜役。

fac·tual /ˈfæktʃuəl; ˈfæktʃuəl/ *adj* concerned with, full of, fact(s). 與事實有關的;充滿事實的。 **~·ly** *adv*

fac·ulty /ˈfækltɪ; ˈfækl̩tɪ/ *n* (*pl* -ties) [C] **1** power (of mind); ability (to do sth): 才能;能力: *the mental faculties,* the reason; 思想與理解等之能力;心智能力; *the ~ of making friends easily;* 善於交友的能力; *have a great ~ for learning languages;* 極富有學習語言的才能; *the ~ of speech;* 演說的才能;口才; *be in possession of all one's faculties,* be able to see, hear, speak, understand, etc. 有視、聽、說、理解等能力。 **2** (in a university) department or grouping of related departments: (大學的)系;學院: *the F~ of Law/Science;* 法(理)學院; all the teachers, lecturers, professors, etc in one of these: 學院或系科的全體教授: *a member of (the) ~;* 教授中的一員; *a ~ meeting;* 教授會; (US) the whole teaching staff of a university. (美)大學中之全體教授。

fad /fæd; fæd/ *n* [C] fanciful fashion, interest, preference, enthusiasm, unlikely to last: 新奇的時尙;一時流行的嗜好或狂熱: *Will Tom continue to collect foreign stamps or is it only a passing fad?* 湯姆將繼續搜集外國郵票呢,還是僅將它當作一時的嗜好? *She is full of fads and fancies,* has rather silly likes and dislikes. 她有許多怪誕的嗜好(在愛惡方面頗爲奇特)。 **faddy** /ˈfædɪ; ˈfædɪ/ *adj* having fads; having silly likes and dislikes, eg about food. 有新奇的時尙、嗜好或狂熱的;(對食物等)特別喜愛或特別厭惡的。 **fad·dily** /ˈfædɪlɪ; ˈfædəlɪ/ *adv*

fade /feɪd; fed/ *vt, vi* **~ (away), 1** [VP6A, 2A, C] (cause to) lose colour, freshness or vigour: (使)褪色;(使)凋落;(使)衰弱;凋謝: *The strong sunlight had ~d the curtains.* 强烈的陽光使窗簾褪了色。 *Flowers soon ~ when cut.* 花折下不久就會凋謝。 *Will the colour in this material ~?* 這塊料子會褪色嗎? *She is fading away,* losing strength. 她漸漸衰弱了。 **2** [VP2A, C] go slowly out of view, hearing or the memory: 自視界、聽界或記憶中漸漸消失: *Daylight ~d away.* 白晝漸漸消失了。 *As evening came the coastline ~d into darkness.* 夜晚降臨時,海岸線消失在黑暗中。 *The sound of the cheering ~d away in the distance.* 歡呼的聲音在遠處逐漸消失了。 *His hopes ~d.* 他的希望逐漸消逝了。 *All memory of her childhood ~d from her mind.* 所有她童年的記憶漸漸自她腦海中消逝了。 **3** [VP15B, 2C, 3A] (cinema, broadcasting) (cause to) decrease or increase in strength: (電影、廣播)(使)漸弱;(使)漸强;(使)淡出;(使)淡入;(使)漸隱;(使)漸顯: *~ one scene into another* (on a cinema screen); (銀幕上)使一畫面漸漸隱暗而融入另一畫面中; *~ a conversation out/in,* (in broadcasting) gradually reduce/increase the volume of sound to inaudibility/audibility. (廣播)使一音量漸弱(强)。

faeces (US = **feces**) /ˈfiːsiːz; ˈfisɪz/ *n pl* (med) waste matter excreted from the bowels. (醫)糞便。

faerie, faery /ˈfeərɪ; ˈfeərɪ/ *n* (old use) fairyland; (attrib) visionary; fancied. (舊用法)仙境;仙國;(形容用法)幻想的;想像的。

fag[1] /fæg; fæg/ *n* **1** [C, U] (*sing* only) (colloq) tiring job: (僅用單數)(俗)吃力的工作: *What a fag!* 多麼費力的工作! *It's too much (of a) fag.* 這工作眞使人吃不消。 **2** (formerly at public schools in England) junior pupil who performs certain duties for a senior pupil. (昔日英國公學)爲高年級生服務的低年級生。 **3** (GB sl) cigarette. (英俚)香煙。 **4** = faggot(3).

fag[2] /fæg; fæg/ *vi, vt* (-gg-) **1** [VP2C, 3A] **~ (at),** (colloq) do very tiring work: (俗)做極其令人疲倦的工作: *fag (away) at sth/at doing sth.* 辛苦地做某事。 **2** [VP6A, 15B] **~ (out),** (colloq) (of work) make very tired: (俗)(指工作)使極爲疲勞: *Doesn't that sort of work fag you (out)?* 那種工作不使你疲倦嗎? *He was almost fagged out,* exhausted. 他幾乎筋疲力盡了。 *Your horse looks fagged.* 你的馬看來疲倦了。 **3** [VP2A, 3A] **~ (for),** act as a fag(2). (英國公學)爲高年級生服務。

fag-end /ˈfæg end; ˈfægˌɛnd/ *n* (colloq) inferior or useless remnant; worthless part of anything; cigarette butt. (俗)低劣或無用的剩餘物;無用的部分;香煙頭。

fag·got (US also **fagot**) /ˈfægət; ˈfægət/ *n* **1** bundle of sticks or twigs tied together for burning as fuel. 束薪;柴綑。 **2** meat ball for frying. 供油煎的肉丸。 **3** ⚠ (US sl, derog) male homosexual. (諱)(美俚,蔑)男子同性戀者。

Fahr·en·heit /ˈfærənhaɪt; ˈfærənˌhaɪt/ *n* name of a thermometer scale with freezing-point at 32° and boiling-point at 212°. 華氏溫度計(冰點爲 32 度,沸點爲 212 度)。 ⇨ App 5. 參看附錄五。

fa·ience /feɪˈɑːns; faɪˈɑns/ *n* [U] (F) decorated and glazed earthenware or porcelain. (法)彩陶;彩色瓷器。

fail[1] /feɪl; fel/ *n* (only in) (僅用於) ***without ~,*** for certain, no matter what difficulties, etc there may be: 必定;不誤: *I'll be there at two o'clock without ~.* 我兩點鐘一定到那裏。

fail[2] /feɪl; fel/ *vi, vt* **1** [VP2A, 3A, 4A, 6A] **~ (in),** be unsuccessful: 失敗: *~ (in) an examination;* 考試不及格; *~ to pass an examination.* 考試失敗。 *All our plans/attempts ~ed.* 我們所有的計畫(企圖)都失敗了。 **2** [VP6A] (of examiners) reject (a candidate); decide that (a candidate) has ~ed: (主試者)給(應考者)不及格;不錄取(應考者): *The examiners ~ed half the candidates.* 主試者使半數應考者落榜。 **3** [VP2A, C] (often with an *indirect object*) (常接一間接受詞) be not enough; come to an end while still needed or expected: 不足;短少;缺乏: *The*

F

crops ~ed because of drought. 由於旱災,農作物歉收。Our water supply has ~ed. 我們的水供應不足。The wind ~ed (us), There was not enough wind for our sails. 風勢不足,吹不動我們的帆船。Words ~ me, I cannot find words (to describe my feelings, etc). 我找不到適當的言辭(來形容我的感情等)。His heart (= courage) ~ed him. 他失去了勇氣。'~-safe (attrib adj), (屬性形容詞), (of a mechanical device, etc) designed to compensate automatically for a failure (thus eliminating danger, etc). (指機械裝置等) 可自動補償失誤 (以免危險等)的。**4** [VP2A, C] (of health, eyesight, etc) become weak: (指健康、視力等) 衰退: *His eyesight is ~ing.* 他的視力漸漸衰退了。*He has suffered from ~ing health/has been ~ing in health for the last two years.* 近兩年來他的健康一直在衰退。 **5** [VP4A] omit; neglect (or, in many cases, simply making, with the *inf*, a neg of an affirm): 忽略;疏忽(或在許多情形下與不定詞連用形成否定意義): *He never ~s to write* (= always writes) *to his mother every week.* 他從未忘記每週寫信給他的母親。*His promises ~ed to* (= did not) *materialize.* 他的諾言未能實現。*He did not ~ to keep* (= he did keep) *his word.* 他未食言。 **6** [VP2A] become bankrupt: 破產;倒閉: *Several of the biggest banks ~ed during the depression.* 幾家最大的銀行在不景氣的時期倒閉了。 **7** [VP3A] ~ *in*, be insufficiently equipped with; be lacking in: 未充分具有;缺少: *He's a clever man, but ~s in perseverance.* 他是個聰明的人,但缺少毅力。

fail·ing¹ /'feɪlɪŋ; 'felɪŋ/ *n* [C] weakness or fault (of character); shortcoming: (品行的) 缺點;短處: *We all have our little ~s.* 我們都有小的缺點。

fail·ing² /'feɪlɪŋ; 'felɪŋ/ *prep* in default of; in the absence of: 若缺少…時;如果沒有: *~ this*, if this does not happen; 如果此事不發生; *~ an answer*, if no answer is received; 若無答覆; *~ Smith*, if Smith is not available. 如果沒有史密斯。

fail·ure /'feɪljə(r); 'feljɚ/ *n* **1** [U] failing; lack of success: 失敗;不成功: *F~ in an examination should not deter you from trying again.* 一次考試不及格不應妨礙你再次的嘗試。*All his efforts ended in ~*, were unsuccessful. 他所有的努力結果都失敗了。 **2** [C] instance of failing; person, attempt, or thing that fails: 失敗的實例;失敗的人、企圖或事物;失敗者: *Success came after many ~s.* 經多次失敗後,成功終於到來。*He was a ~ as a teacher.* 他不是個好教師。 **3** [U] state of not being adequate; non-performance of what is normal, expected or required; [C] instance of this: 不足;缺乏;未能達到正常、所期望或所要求的狀態;其實例: *'heart ~;* 心臟衰弱; *'engine ~s.* 發動機故障。*F~ of crops often results in famine.* 歉收常引起饑荒。*Crop ~s caused great hardship for the people.* 歉收造成了人民極大的痛苦。**4** [C] bankruptcy: 破產;倒閉: *numerous bank ~s.* 許多的銀行倒閉。 **5** [C, U] neglect, omission, inability (*to do* sth): 忽略;未做;無能爲力(與不定詞連用): *His ~ to help us was disappointing.* 他未能幫助我們令人失望。*His ~ to answer questions made the police suspicious.* 他不回答問題引起警方的懷疑。

fain /feɪn; fen/ *adv* (poet, or old use after *would*) willingly; with pleasure:(詩中或舊時用語,用於 would 之後)樂意;欣然: *I would ~ have stayed at home.* 我當時眞想留在家裏。

faint¹ /feɪnt; fent/ *adj* (-er, -est) **1** (of things perceived through the senses) weak; indistinct; not clear: (指覺察到的東西) 微弱的;模糊的;不清楚的: *The sounds of the music grew ~er in the distance.* 音樂的聲音在遠處漸漸模糊了。*She called for help in a ~ voice.* 她以微弱的聲音呼救。*Only ~ traces of the tiger's tracks could be seen.* 這老虎的踪跡祇有模糊的痕跡可循。**2** (of things in the mind) weak; vague: (指心中的事) 微弱的;模糊的: *There is a ~ hope that she may be cured.* 她痊癒的希望不大。*I haven't the ~est idea (of) what you mean.* 我一點也不懂你的意思。**3** (of the body's movements and functions) weak; failing: (指身體的動作和機能) 虛弱的;衰退的: *His breathing became ~.* 他的呼吸微弱了。*His strength grew ~.* 他的體力衰退了。**4** (*pred* only) (of persons) likely to lose consciousness; giddy: (僅作叙述用法) (指人) 昏暈的: *She looks/feels ~.* 她看來(感到) 快要昏倒似的。 **5** (*pred* only) (of persons) weak, exhausted: (僅作叙述用法) (指人) 委頓不堪的: *~ with hunger and cold.* 因饑寒而委頓不堪。**6** (of actions, etc) weak; unlikely to have much effect: (指動作等) 無力的; 似無效果的: *a ~ show of resistance;* 無力的抵抗; *make a ~ attempt to do sth.* 勉强嘗試做某事。 **7** ~ **heart**, timid spirit: 懦弱者;怯懦者: (pro) (諺) *F~ heart never won fair lady.* 懦弱的人永不會博得美人的歡心。,**~-'hearted** *adj* lacking in courage. 懦弱的;怯懦的。**~·ly** *adv* **~·ness** *n*

faint² /feɪnt; fent/ *vi* [VP2A, C] **1** lose consciousness (because of loss of blood, the heat, shock, etc): (因失血、受熱、受驚等) 昏厥;昏倒: *He ~ed from hunger.* 他餓昏了。 **2** become weak: 衰弱;委頓: *He was ~ing with hunger.* 他因饑餓而逐漸衰弱。**3** (= *fade*) become weak: 消失: *The sounds ~ed away.* 聲音漸漸消失了。□ *n* act, state, of ~ing(1). 昏厥;不省人事。***in a (dead) ~,*** (completely) unconscious. (完全) 不省人事。

fair¹ /feə(r); fɛr/ *adj* **1** not showing favour to either person, side, etc; acting in an honest and honourable manner; in accordance with what is deserved or with the rules (of a game, etc): 公平的;正直的;(遊戲等) 公正的: *Everyone must have a ~ share.* 每人須得其應得之份 (或負擔其應負擔之部分)。*It was a ~ fight*, eg the rules of boxing were observed. 那是一場公正的拳擊賽(例如遵守拳擊規則)。*We charge ~ prices and are content with ~* (= reasonable) *profits.* 我們索取公道的價錢,並滿足於公道的利潤。***give sb/get a ~ hearing,*** an opportunity to defend his conduct, etc, eg in a law court. (在法院等中)給予某人(獲得)爲其行爲辯護的機會。**~ *play*,** ⇨ play¹(2). ,**~-'minded,** not prejudiced. 公正的。 **2** average; quite good: 平常的;尚可的;相當好的;相當不錯的: *a ~ chance of success.* 相當好的成功機會。*His knowledge of French is ~, but ought to be better.* 他的法文還不錯,但應該還要好些。*The goods arrived in ~ condition.* 貨物運到,情況尚佳。*She has a ~ amount of sense.* 她有相當多的見識。 **3** (of the weather) good; dry and fine; (of winds) favourable: (指天氣) 美好的;晴朗的;(指風) 順暢的: *hoping for ~ weather.* 希望有好天氣。*They set sail with the first ~ wind.* 他們一有順風就起航。*The glass is at set ~*, The needle of the barometer is stationary (= set) at ~ (indicating a likelihood of good weather). 晴雨表預示有好天氣。,**~-weather 'friend,** person who ceases to be a friend when one is in trouble. 共安樂而不能共患難的朋友。**4** satisfactory; abundant: 令人滿意的;豐富的: *a ~ heritage;* 大量的遺產; promising: 有希望的: *be in a ~ way to succeed*, be at the stage where success seems assured; 頗有成功的希望; *in a ~ way of business*, quite prosperous. 生意興隆。**5** (of the skin, hair) pale; light in colour; blond: (指皮膚、頭髮) 淡色的;白皙的;金黃色的: *a '~-haired girl;* 金髮女郎; *a ~ complexion.* 白皙的膚色。 **6** (of speeches, promises, etc) carefully chosen to seem polite and gentle in order to please and persuade: (指演說、諾言等) 似乎可信的; 口惠的; 似乎動聽的: *put sb off with ~ words/promises;* 以虛與委蛇的言語(諾言)敷衍某人; *the ~ speeches of the politicians*, eg before an election. 政客們花言巧語的演說(例如在選舉前)。**7** clean; clear; without blemish: 整潔的;清楚的;無瑕疵的: *Please make a ~ copy of this letter*, a new one without the errors, corrections, etc. 請將這封信整潔地謄錄一遍。*Such behaviour will spoil your ~ name*, good reputation. 此種行爲將損毀你的令譽。 **8** (old use) beautiful: (舊用法) 美麗的: *a ~*

maiden. 美麗的少女。**the '~ sex,** women. 女性；婦女。**~·ish** /ˈfeərɪʃ ; ˈfɛrɪʃ/ *adj* of ~(2) size or quality. 大小或質料平常的；尚可的。

fair² /feə(r) ; fɛr/ *adv* **1** in a fair¹(1) manner: 公平地；正直地；公正地: *play* ~. 公正地比賽。**~ *enough*,** (colloq) used to indicate agreement or reasonable disagreement. (俗)還可以；還合理(用以表示同意或合理的不同意)。 **2** in a fair¹(7) manner: 整潔地；清楚地: *write/copy sth out* ~. 整潔地寫(謄錄)一文件。 **3** (old use) politely, courteously: (舊用法)有禮貌地: *speak sb* ~. 對人彬彬有禮地談話。

fair³ /feə(r) ; fɛr/ *n* **1** market (esp for cattle, sheep, farm products, etc) held periodically in a particular place, often with entertainments. 市集(尤指買賣牛羊、農產品等者，定期舉行，常伴有表演和娛樂)。***a day before/after the*** ~, too early/late. 太早；太晚。**'~·ground,** open space for ~s. 市集場地。 **2** large-scale exhibition of commercial and industrial goods: 博覽會；商展；工展: *a world* ~. 世界博覽會。 **3** bazaar(3). 義賣會。

fair·ly¹ /ˈfeəlɪ ; ˈfɛrlɪ/ *adv* **1** in a fair¹(1) manner; honestly: 公平地；公正地；誠實地: *treat sb* ~; 公平地對待某人; *come by* (= obtain) *sth* ~, by honest means. 光明正大地獲得某物。 **2** (colloq) utterly: completely: (俗)完全地: *We were ~ caught in the trap*, had no chance of escape. 我們完全落入陷阱中(無逃脫機會)。*He was ~ beside himself with rage*, as angry as he could possibly be. 他簡直氣得發瘋。*His suggestion ~ took my breath away*, left me quite breathless (with surprise, etc). 他的建議眞使我大吃一驚。

fair·ly² /ˈfeəlɪ ; ˈfɛrlɪ/ *adv of degree* (Cf *rather*, which may be used with *too* and comparatives; *fairly* cannot be used in this way 參較 rather, rather 可與 too 和比較級連用，fairly 則不可) moderately: 相當地；適度地: *This is a ~ easy book* (and is, therefore, perhaps suitable). 這是一本相當淺易的書(故或許適當)。(Cf 參較 *This is a rather easy book*, suggesting 'rather too easy', and, therefore, perhaps unsuitable. 這本書過於淺易(故或許不適當)。) *He wants a ~ large car*, not small, but not very large. 他要一部稍稍大一點的汽車。(Cf 參較 *That car is rather larger than he wants*. 那部汽車比他所需要的大了一點。)

fair·way /ˈfeəweɪ ; ˈfɛr,we/ *n* **1** navigable channel for ships. 航路；水路。 **2** (golf) part of a golf-links, between a tee and a green, free from hazards. (高爾夫球)無障礙的一部分球場。

fairy /ˈfeərɪ ; ˈfɛrɪ/ *n* (*pl* -ries) **1** small imaginary being with supernatural powers, able to help or harm human beings; (attrib) of or like fairies: 小仙；(形容用法)小仙的；似小仙的: *a ~ shape*, beautiful, small, delicate; 小巧可愛的形狀; ~ *voices/footsteps*. 嬌美的聲音(輕巧的脚步)。 **'~ lamps/lights,** small lamps of coloured glass used for decoration. 彩色小燈。**'~·land** *n* **(a)** home of fairies(1). 仙境；仙國。**(b)** enchanted region; beautiful place. 樂園；迷人之地。**'~·tale** *n* **(a)** tale about fairies. 神話；童話。**(b)** untrue account, esp by a child. 謊言(尤指小兒所說的)。**2** ⚠ (sl, derog) male homosexual. (諱)(俚，蔑)男子同性戀者。

fait accompli /ˌfeɪt əˈkɒmpliː *US:* əkɒmˈpliː ; fɛtakõˈpli/ *n* (F, 法= *accomplished fact*) sth done and, for this reason, not reversible. 既成事實。

faith /feɪθ ; feθ/ *n* **1** [U] ~ ***(in sb/sth)***, trust; strong belief; unquestioning confidence: 信任；信仰；信心: *have/put one's ~ in God*. 信仰上帝。*Have you any ~ in what he says?* 你相信他的話嗎？*I haven't much ~ in this medicine*. 我對於此藥沒有多大信心。*I've lost ~ in that fellow*, can no longer trust him. 我再也不信任那個傢伙了。**'~ cure,** one (alleged to be) made through religious ~. 信仰治療法。**'~-healing,** (belief in) healing (of disease, etc) by prayer, appealing to and strengthening a person's religious ~, apart from the use of medicines, etc. 信仰治療法(相信除了用藥物之外由祈禱或加强宗教信仰可以治病)。 **2** [C] belief in divine truth without proof; religion: 宗教信仰；宗教: *the Christian, Jewish and Muslim ~s*. 基督教、猶太教和回教。 **3** [U] promise; engagement. 諾言；約定。***give/pledge one's ~ to sb***, promise solemnly to support him. 保證擁護某人。***keep/break ~ with sb***, be loyal/disloyal to sb. 對某人守(不守)信用。 **4** [U] loyalty; sincerity. 忠實；誠實。***in bad*** ~, with the intention of deceiving. 存心欺詐地。***in good*** ~, honestly; sincerely. 誠實地；誠懇地。

faith·ful /ˈfeɪθfl ; ˈfeθfəl/ *adj* ~ ***(to)***, **1** keeping faith; loyal and true (*to* sb, *to* a cause, *to* a promise, etc): 守信的；忠實的(與 to 連用，後接人、主義、諾言等): *a ~ friend;* 忠實的朋友; ~ *to one's promise;* 守信; ~ *in* (= in respect of) *word and deed*. 言行忠實。 **2** true to the facts; accurate: 眞實的；翔實的；正確的: *a ~ copy/description/account*. 眞實的副本(描寫，報導)。 **3 the** ~ *n pl* the true believers, esp of Islam and Christianity. 忠實信徒(尤指回教徒和基督教徒)。**~·ly** /-fəlɪ ; -fəlɪ/ *adv* in a ~ manner. 忠實地。***Yours ~ly***, formula for closing a letter in formal or business style. 謹上(信尾之客套語，用於正式或商業書信中)。**~·ness** *n*

faith·less /ˈfeɪθlɪs ; ˈfeθlɪs/ *adj* not trustworthy. 不可信任的；不可靠的。**~·ly** *adv* **~·ness** *n*

fake /feɪk ; fek/ *n* [C] story, work of art, etc that seems genuine but is not; person who tries to deceive by claiming falsely to be or have sth: 杜撰的故事；僞造的藝術品等；贋品；冒充的人；騙子: (attrib) (形容用法) *a ~ picture*. 假畫。□ *vt* [VP6A, 15B] ~ ***(up)***, make (eg a work of art, a story) in order to deceive: 僞造(藝術品、故事等): ~ *an oil-painting*. 僞製一幅油畫。*There wasn't a word of truth in what he said; the whole story had been ~d (up)*, invented. 他說的話沒有一句是眞的，整個故事都是揑造的。

fakir /ˈfeɪkɪə(r) *US:* fəˈk- ; fəˈkɪr/ *n* Muslim or Hindu religious mendicant who is regarded as a holy man, a prophet, or a wonder-worker. (回教或印度教的)行者；托鉢僧(被視爲聖者，先知或異人)。

fal·con /ˈfɔːlkən *US:* ˈfælkən ; ˈfɔlkən/ *n* small bird of prey trained to hunt and kill other birds and small animals. 獵鷹。⇨ the illus at prey. 參看 prey 之插圖。**~·ry** /-rɪ ; -rɪ/ *n* [U] sport of hunting with ~s; art of training ~s. 放鷹捕獵；鷹獵；訓練獵鷹術。

fall¹ /fɔːl ; fɔl/ *n* [C] **1** act of falling: 落下；跌落；降落；墮落: *a ~ from a horse;* 從馬上跌下; *the ~ of an apple from a tree;* 蘋果自樹上落下; *a ~ in price/temperature;* 物價的下跌(溫度的下降); *the ~* (= collapse) *of the Roman Empire*. 羅馬帝國之滅亡。***the F~ (of man)***, Adam's sin and its results. 亞當之犯罪及其後果；人類之墮落。**'~ guy** *n* (colloq) (俗) **(a)** dupe; easy victim. 受騙者；易受害者。**(b)** scapegoat. 代罪羔羊。**2** amount of rain that falls; distance by which sth falls or comes down: 降雨量；降落的距離；落差: *The ~ of the river here is six feet*. 此地的河水降落六呎。 **3** (often *pl*) place where a river falls over cliffs, etc: (常用複數)瀑布: *Niagara F~s*. 尼加拉大瀑布。 **4** (US) autumn: (美)秋季: *in the ~ of 1970;* 1970年的秋天; (attrib) (形容用法) ~ *fashions*. 秋季式樣。

fall² /fɔːl ; fɔl/ *vi* (*pt* fell /fel ; fɛl/, *pp* ~en /ˈfɔːlən ; ˈfɔlən/) (For special uses with *adverbial particles* and *preps*, ⇨ 14 below.) (與副詞接語及介詞連用之特殊用法，參看下列第14義。) **1** [VP2A, B, C, 3A] ~ ***(down/over)***, come or go down freely (by force of weight, loss of balance, etc): 落下；降落；跌下: *The book fell from the table to the floor*. 那書從桌上掉落在地板上。*He fell over into the water*. 他掉在水裏了。*The rain was ~ing steadily*. 雨不停地下。*The leaves ~ in autumn*. 樹葉在秋天掉落。*He slipped and fell ten feet*. 他失足跌下十呎。*This basket is full of eggs—don't let it ~ down*.

F

這籃內盛滿了蛋,不要把它打翻了。*The lambs are beginning to* ~, be born. 小羊快要生下來了。⇨ drop[2] (2). ~ ***on one's feet,*** (fig) be fortunate; get out of a difficulty successfully: (喻)走好運;化險爲夷;避過危難: *Some people always seem to ~ on their feet,* be lucky and successful. 有些人似乎總是走好運。~ ***short,*** (of a missile) not go far enough: (指投射物)未達目標: *The arrow fell short.* 那箭未達目標。~ ***short of,*** fail to equal; be inferior to: 未達到;不及: *Your work ~s short of my expectations.* 你的工作未達到我的期望。ˌ~**ing 'star,** object (eg a meteor) seen as a bright streak in the sky as it burns up. 隕星;流星。 **2** [VP2A, C, 3A] ~ ***(down/over),*** no longer stand; come to the ground; collapse; be overthrown: 跌倒;跌下;倒塌;被推倒: *Many trees fell in the storm.* 許多樹在那場暴風雨中倒了。*Babies often ~ down when they are learning to walk.* 小兒學步時常會跌跤。*He fell over and broke his left leg.* 他跌倒並將左腿摔斷了。*He fell full length.* 他挺直地跌倒在地上。*He fell on/to his knees* (= knelt down) *and begged for mercy.* 他跪下來乞求憐憫。*He fell in battle,* was killed. 他陣亡了。*Six tigers fell to his rifle,* He shot six tigers. 他用步槍射倒了六隻虎。*Six wickets fell before lunch,* (cricket) Six batsmen were out. (板球)六位擊球員在中飯以前退場。~ ***flat,*** (fig) fail to have the intended effect: (喻)未產生預期的效果: *His best jokes all fell flat,* did not amuse his listeners. 他最拿手的笑話都失效了。*The scheme fell flat,* was unsuccessful. 這計畫失敗了。~ ***flat on one's face,*** ~ face down to the ground. 面朝下直挺挺地跌倒在地。~ ***to the ground,*** ⇨ ground[1] (1). ~ ***'over oneself,*** **(a)** ~ because one is awkward, clumsy, or in too much of a hurry. 由於笨拙或過於匆忙而跌倒。**(b)** (fig) be very eager: (喻)渴望;極想: *The big firms were ~ing over themselves/each other for the services of this brilliant young scientist.* 那些大公司競相爭取這位卓越的青年科學家爲他們服務。**the ~en,** those killed in war. 陣亡將士;戰死者。 **3** [VP2C] ~ ***(down),*** hang down: 垂下;低垂: *His beard fell to his chest.* 他的鬍鬚垂在胸前。*Her hair/cloak fell over her shoulders.* 她的頭髮(斗篷)披在肩上。 **4** [VP2A, B, C, 3A] come or go to a lower level or point; become lower or less: 降低;減退: *The temperature fell rapidly.* 溫度迅速下降。*His voice fell to a whisper.* 他的聲音降低成爲耳語。*Her spirits fell at the bad news,* She became low-spirited, sad. 她聽到這壞消息而精神沮喪。*His face/jaw fell,* He showed dismay. 他顯出沮喪的樣子。(Cf 參較 *put on a long face* at face[1](3)). *The wind fell during the night,* became less strong. 夜間風勢減弱了。**5** [VP2C, D, 3A] ~ ***(into),*** become; pass into (the state indicated by the *adj* or phrase): 成爲;變爲(其後形容詞或片語所表示的狀態): *His horse fell lame.* 他的馬跛了。*He fell silent.* 他變爲沉默。*The old man fell asleep.* 那老人睡着了。*He has ~en ill.* 他生病了。*When does the rent ~ due,* When must it be paid? 租金何時到期? *He fell into a doze,* began to doze. 他打瞌睡了。*Don't fall into bad habits!* Don't acquire or adopt them. 不要養成壞習慣! *They have ~en into poverty,* become poor. 他們已變爲貧窮。*She fell an easy prey to him.* 她輕易地被他控制了。~ ***in love (with),*** become filled with love (for): 喜愛;愛上: *He fell in love with an actress.* 他愛上一位女伶。*I've ~en in love with your beautiful house.* 我很喜歡你的漂亮的房子。~ ***out of love (with),*** cease to feel love (for). 不再喜愛。⇨ foul[1](6). **6** [VP2A, C, 3A] ~ ***(upon),*** descend (upon): 降臨: *Darkness fell upon the scene,* It became dark. 黑暗降臨這個地方。*A great stillness had ~en upon everything,* Everything had become quiet and motionless. 萬籟俱寂。*Fear fell upon them,* They became frightened. 他們均感恐懼。 **7** [PV2A, C] (old use) sin; give way to wrongdoing: (舊用法)犯罪;墮落: *Eve tempted Adam and he fell.* 夏娃誘惑亞當,於是他墮落了。ˌ~**en 'woman,** (old use) one who has lost her virginity before marriage. (舊用法)墮落的女人;婚前失貞的女人。 **8** [VP2A] (of a city, fort, etc) be captured: (指城市,要塞等)淪陷;失守: *Rome has ~en!* 羅馬已經淪陷了! be overcome or defeated: 被征服;被擊敗: *The Government has ~en again.* 政府又垮臺了。**9** [VP3A] ~ ***on,*** take the direction or position (indicated by the *adv* or phrase): 朝某一方向或佔據某一位置(由其後的副詞或片語表示): *A shadow fell on the wall.* 一個陰影投落在牆上。*His eye fell on* (= He suddenly saw) *a curious object.* 他突然看見一個奇怪的物體。*Strange sounds fell on our ears,* We heard strange sounds. 我們聽到了奇怪的聲音。*The lamplight fell on her face.* 燈光照射在她的臉上。*In 'formidable' the stress may ~ on either the first or the second syllable.* 在 formidable 一字中,重音在第一或第二音節上均可。 **10** [VP3A] ~ ***on/upon/to,*** come by chance, design, or right: 由於偶然,計畫或權利而來到: *All the expenses fell on me,* I had to pay them. 所有的開銷均由我付。*The responsibility/blame, etc fell upon me.* 這責任(過失等)落在我的身上。*It fell to my lot/to me to open the discussion,* I had to speak first. 我必須首先發言。*He has fallen on evil days,* is suffering misfortune. 他遭逢噩運。 **11** [VP2C] (of land) slope: (指土地)下斜: *The ground ~s towards the river.* 那土地向河邊傾斜。 **12** [VP2C] occur, have as date: (做爲日期)發生: *Easter ~s early next year.* 明年的復活節到得早。*Christmas Day ~s on a Monday this year.* 今年的聖誕節是星期一。 **13** [VP2A, C] be spoken: 被說出: *Not a word fell from his lips.* 他什麼話也沒有說。*I guessed what she was going to do from the few words that she let fall,* from what she said. 從她所說的幾句話中我猜得出她要做些什麼。**14** [VP2C, 3A] (special uses with *adverbial particles* and *preps*): (與副詞接語和介詞連用的特殊用法):

fall about (laughing/with laughter), (colloq) laugh uncontrollably: (俗)不禁大笑: *They fell about when Sir Harold slipped on the banana skin.* 當哈羅德爵士踏到香蕉皮而滑跤時,他們不禁大笑。

fall among sb, get mixed up with, come by chance among: 與某人結交;落入某人之手: *~ among thieves, evil companions.* 落入盜賊之手(交上壞人)。

fall away, **(a)** desert: 遺棄: *His supporters began to ~ away.* 支持他的人開始疏遠他了。**(b)** disappear, vanish: 消失: *In this crisis, prejudices fell away and all classes co-operated well.* 值此危急時期,各種偏見均已消除,各階層合作無間。

fall back, retreat; move or turn back: 撤退;後退: *Our attack was so vigorous that the enemy had to ~ back.* 我們的攻勢兇猛,敵人不得不撤退了。~ ***'back on sth,*** have recourse to; turn to for support: 求助於;依靠: *If you don't need the money now, bank it—it's always useful to have something to ~ back on.* 如果你目前不需要這筆錢,便將它存在銀行裏 —— 有點依靠的東西總是有用的。

fall behind (with sth), fail to keep level (with); lag: 落於…之後;落後: *He always ~s behind when we're going uphill.* 我們登山時他總是落在後面。*I've ~en behind with my correspondence,* have many unanswered letters. 我積壓了許多信尙未作覆。*Don't ~ behind with your rent, or you'll be evicted.* 不要逾期不繳房租,否則你將被逐出。

fall down (on sth), (colloq) fail (in a task, in expectation): (俗)(在…方面)失敗;未做到: *~ down on one's promises/obligations (to sb).* (對某人)未實踐諾言(未盡到責任)。

fall for sth/sb, (colloq) yield to the charms, attractions or merits of (esp when deceived): (俗)被…迷住(尤指受騙情況下);對…傾倒;受…的誘惑: *He ~s for every pretty face he sees.* 他見到美麗的面孔便爲之傾倒。*Did he ~ for your suggestion,*

Did he decide that it was good, and agree to it? 他喜歡你的建議嗎？

fall in, **(a)** collapse; give way: 塌陷；垮下: *The roof fell in.* 屋頂塌陷了。*The (sides of the) trench fell in.* 壕溝(壕溝的兩邊)塌陷了。**(b)** (mil) (cause to) go on parade: (軍)(使)站隊；集合: *The sergeant ordered the men to ~ in.* 士官命令兵士們集合。**(c)** (of a lease) expire. (指租約)期滿。**(d)** (of a debt) become due. (指債務)到期。***~ in with sb/sth,*** **(a)** happen to meet. 偶遇。**(b)** agree to: 同意: *He fell in with my views at once.* 他立刻同意了我的見解。

fall into sth, be naturally divisible into: 自然地分作: *The subject ~s into four divisions.* 這問題可自然地分作四部分。***~ into line (with sth/sb),*** agree (to what others are doing or wish to do); accept (a course of conduct, procedure, etc.) 同意(別人所做或欲做之事)；接受某種行動，方法等。

fall off, become smaller, fewer or less: 消減；減少: *The takings at the football stadium have ~en off,* Less money has been paid for admission. 足球運動場的收入減少了。*The daily number of passengers by this line shows a slight ~ing off.* 每日搭此航線的乘客數目略見減少。

fall on sth/sb, attack; assault (the enemy). 攻擊(敵人)。

fall out, **(a)** (mil) (cause to) go off parade. (軍)解散；離隊。**(b)** happen: 發生: *It (so) fell out that I could not get there in time.* 結果是我未能及時到那裏。*Everything fell out as we had hoped.* 一切均達到我們的願望。**(c)** discontinue; give up: 停止；放棄: *the '~-out rate,* eg of pupils who give up a course of study. 退出率(例如學生之退選一課程)；放棄率。⇨ *drop-out* at drop[2] (13). ***~ out (with sb),*** quarrel (with): (與某人)爭吵: *The two men fell out.* 那兩個人吵架了。*He has fallen out with the girl he was going to marry.* 他和要同他結婚的那位女郎吵架了。**'~-out** *n* [U] radio-active dust in the atmosphere, after a nuclear explosion. (核子爆炸後大氣中之)放射塵。

fall through, fail; miscarry; come to nothing: 失敗；成爲泡影: *His scheme fell through.* 他的計畫失敗了。

fall 'to, begin to do sth: 開始做某事: *They fell to with a good appetite.* 他們津津有味地開始大吃。***~ to 'doing sth:*** *I fell to wondering where to go for my holidays.* 我開始想去何處度假。

fall under sth, be classifiable under: 歸入…項下: *The results ~ under three heads.* 這些結果分在三個項目下。

fal·lacy /ˈfæləsɪ ; ˈfæləsɪ/ *n* (*pl* -cies) **1** [C] false or mistaken belief. 謬見；錯誤的信念。**2** [U] false reasoning or argument: 謬誤的推理；謬論: *a statement based on ~.* 基於謬誤推理之聲明。**fal·lacious** /fəˈleɪʃəs ; fəˈleʃəs/ *adj* misleading; based on error. 使人誤解的；謬誤的。

fallen *pp* of fall[2].

fal·lible /ˈfæləbl ; ˈfæləbḷ/ *adj* liable to error. 易犯錯誤的。**fal·li·bil·ity** /ˌfæləˈbɪlətɪ ; ˌfæləˈbɪlətɪ/ *n* (state of) being ~. 易犯錯誤。

Fallopian tube /fəˌləʊprən ˈtju:b *US:* ˈtu:b ; fəˈlopɪənˈtjub/ *n* (anat) (解剖) = oviduct. ⇨ the illus at reproduce. 參看 reproduce 之挿圖。

fal·low /ˈfæləʊ ; ˈfælo/ *adj, n* [U] (land) ploughed but not sown or planted: 犂過而未耕種的(土地)；休耕的(土地): *allow land to lie ~;* 讓土地休耕；*plough (up) ~ land.* 犂(起)休耕的田地。

fal·low-deer /ˈfæləʊ dɪə(r) ; ˈfælo dɪə(r)/ *n* (*pl* unchanged) small Eurasian deer with a reddish-yellow coat with, in the summer, white spots. (複數不變)梅花鹿(一種歐洲和亞洲產的小鹿，毛皮呈赤褐色，夏季有白斑)。

false /fɔ:ls ; fɔls/ *adj* **1** not right, true or real: 錯誤的；不對的；不眞實的: *a ~ alarm;* 虛假的警報；*~ ideas;* 錯誤的觀念；*~ weights,* eg one of 90 grammes marked as 100 grammes; 不足的砝碼(如將 90 克當作 100 克)；*take a ˌ~ 'step,* stumble; (fig) act wrongly; 絆跌；失足；(喩)行爲失檢；犯錯；*sing a ~ note;* 唱錯音符；*~ shame/pride,* based on wrong ideas, etc; 錯誤的羞耻(自負)；*make a ~ start,* (athletics) start before the signal has been given; (fig) start wrongly. (體育)起步太早(未發信號前卽開始)；(喩)錯誤地開始；不當地開始。**2** deceiving; lying: 欺騙的；不誠實的: *give a ~ impression;* 予人以不誠實的印象；*bear/give ~ witness,* tell lies or deceive (eg in a law court); 作僞證；*be ~ to one's word,* fail to keep a promise. 不守信。***act under ~ pretences,*** ⇨ pretence. ***put sb/be in a ~ position,*** in circumstances that cause misunderstanding or make it necessary for sb to act contrary to principles. (使某人)處於使人誤會的立場；(使某人)處於違背原則行事的地位。***sail under ~ colours,*** **(a)** (of a ship) with a flag which it has no right to use. (指船)掛其他國家的國旗航行。**(b)** (fig) pretend or appear to be different from what one really is. (喩)冒充。***a ~ bottom,*** a secret compartment in a container such as a suitcase. 假底；(箱底之)祕密夾層。**3** not genuine; sham; artificial: 不眞實的；假的；人造的: *~ hair/teeth;* 假髮(牙)；*~ coins.* 假錢幣。**4** improperly so called: 命名不當的: *the ~ acacia* (not really an acacia tree). 刺槐(非眞正的膠樹)。□ *adv* (only in) (僅用於) ***play sb ~,*** cheat or betray him. 欺騙或出賣某人。**~·ly** *adv* in a ~ manner: 錯誤地；欺騙地；不眞地: *~ly accused.* 被誣告的。**~·ness** *n*

false·hood /ˈfɔ:lshʊd ; ˈfɔls·hʊd/ *n* **1** [C] lie; untrue statement: 謊言；不實之言: *How can you utter such ~s?* 你怎能說出這種謊言？**2** [U] telling lies; lying: 說謊；撒謊: *guilty of ~.* 犯說謊罪。*Truth, if exaggerated, may become ~.* 眞相如加以渲染可能失眞。

fal·setto /fɔ:lˈsetəʊ ; fɔlˈsɛto/ *n* (*pl* ~s /-təʊz;-toz/) high voice in men; counter-tenor: (男子發出的尖銳的)假聲；上次中音: *to sing ~;* 唱上次中音；(attrib) of or in such a voice: (形容用法)(以)尖銳假聲的: *in a ~ tone.* 以尖銳的假音調。

fal·sies /ˈfɔ:lsɪz ; ˈfɔlsɪz/ *n pl* (colloq) brassieres filled with soft material to exaggerate the size of the breasts. (俗)假奶；義乳。

fals·ify /ˈfɔ:lsɪfaɪ ; ˈfɔlsəˌfaɪ/ *vt* (*pt, pp* -fied) [VP 6A] **1** make false: 使僞；僞造；竄改: *~ records/accounts;* 僞造記錄(帳目)；tell falsely: 僞稱: *~ a story.* 虛構一故事。**2** misrepresent: 錯誤表示；誤稱: *~ an issue.* 誤言一問題。**falsi·fi·ca·tion** /ˌfɔ:lsɪfɪˈkeɪʃn ; ˌfɔlsəfəˈkeʃən/ *n* [U] ~ing or being falsified; [C] change made in order to deceive. 使僞；僞造；竄改；僞稱；誤稱。

fals·ity /ˈfɔ:lsətɪ ; ˈfɔlsətɪ/ *n* **1** [U] falsehood; incorrectness; error. 錯誤；不正確；謬誤。**2** [C] (*pl* -ties) false or treacherous act, statement, etc. 虛僞或奸詐的行爲，言語等。

fal·ter /ˈfɔ:ltə(r) ; ˈfɔltɚ/ *vi, vt* **1** [VP2A, C] move, walk or act in an uncertain or hesitating manner, from either weakness or fear. (由於衰弱或恐懼)搖晃；蹣跚而行。**2** [VP2A] (of the voice) waver: (指聲音)顫抖: *His voice ~ed as he tried to speak.* 他要說話時聲音發顫了。[VP15B] ***~ (out),*** (of a person) speak in a hesitating way or with a broken voice: (指人)支吾地說出；結巴地說出: *He ~ed out a few words.* 他結結巴巴地說出幾個字。**~·ing·ly** /ˈfɔ:ltərɪŋlɪ ; ˈfɔltərɪŋlɪ/ *adv*

fame /feɪm ; fem/ *n* [U] (condition of) being known or talked about by all; what people say (esp good) about sb: 風聞；傳說；名聲；聲譽: *He was not anxious for ~.* 他不急於想成名。*His ~ as a poet did not come until after his death.* 他死後始獲得詩人之名。**famed** *adj* famous: 著名的: *~d for their courage.* 他們以勇敢聞名。

fam·il·iar /fəˈmɪlɪə(r) ; fəˈmɪljɚ/ *adj* **1** ***~ with,*** having a good knowledge of: 熟悉；熟諳: *facts with which every schoolboy is ~.* 每位學童所熟悉

的事實。*I am not very ~ with botanical names.* 我不太熟悉植物學方面的名稱。 **2** *~ to,* well known to: 爲…所熟知: *facts that are ~ to every schoolboy;* 每位學童所熟知的事實; *subjects that are ~ to you.* 你所熟知的科目。 **3** common; usual; often seen or heard: 日常的;通常的;常見的;常聽到的: *the ~ scenes of one's childhood;* 兒時常見的情景; *the ~ voices of one's friends.* 常聽到的朋友們的聲音。 **4** close; intimate; personal: 密切的;親密的;個人的: *Are you on ~ terms with Mr Green?* eg Do you address him as 'Tom'? 你和格林先生的交情好嗎?(譬如你稱他'湯姆'嗎?) *Don't be too ~ with him; he's a dishonest man.* 不要同他過分親密,他不是個誠實的人。 **5** claiming a greater degree of amorous friendship than is proper: 過分親密的: *He made himself much too ~ with my wife.* 他對我的妻子過分親密。 □ *n* intimate friend. 親密的朋友。 **~·ly** *adv* in a ~ manner; without ceremony. 親密地;不拘禮地。

fam·ili·ar·ity /fəˌmɪlɪˈærətɪ ; fəˌmɪlɪˈærətɪ/ *n* (*pl* -ties) **1** [U] *~ (with/to),* (the state of) being familiar: 熟悉;熟諳;親密: *His ~ with the languages used in Nigeria surprised me.* 他之精通奈及利亞的各種語言使我驚奇。 *You should not treat her with such ~.* 你不應該對她如此親密。 ***F~ breeds contempt,*** (prov) When we know sth or sb very well, we may lose respect, fear, etc. (諺)熟悉而生輕視之心;親暱生狎侮。 **2** (*pl*) acts that lack ceremony; instances of familiar behaviour: (複)不拘形式的行動;親密的舉動: *She dislikes such familiarities as the use of her first name by men she has only just met.* 她討厭這種不拘禮的行動,譬如剛見面的男子便呼喚她的名字。

fam·il·iar·ize /fəˈmɪlɪəraɪz ; fəˈmɪljəˌraɪz/ *vt* **1** [VP14] *~ **sb/oneself with,*** make well acquainted with: 使熟習: *~ oneself with a foreign language/the use of a new tool/the rules of a game.* 熟習一外國語(新工具的用法,比賽的規則)。 **2** [VP6A] make well known: 使周知: *The newspapers and radio have ~d the word 'automation'.* 報紙和無線電廣播使'工業自動化'一詞成爲家喻戶曉了。

fam·ily /ˈfæməlɪ ; ˈfæməlɪ/ *n* (*pl* -lies) **1** [C] (collective *n*) group of parents and children: (集合名詞)家庭: *Almost every ~ in the village has a man in the army* (Note here *sing v* after collective *n*). 這村子裏幾乎每一家都有一男子從軍(注意:此集合名詞後用單數動詞)。 *My ~ are early risers* (Note here *pl v* after *family* = members of my family.) 我全家都是早起的人(注意: family 在此指家裏的人,故其後動詞爲複數)。 **2** (collective *n*) (集合名詞) person's children: 子女: *He has a large ~.* 他的子女很多。 *Has he any ~?* 他有兒女嗎? *Tom is the eldest of the ~,* the eldest child. 湯姆是最大的孩子。 **3** [C] all those persons descended from a common ancestor: 家族: *families that have been in Surrey for hundreds of years.* 已在薩里居住數百年的各家族。 **4** [U] ancestry: 家世: *a man of distinguished ~.* 家世顯赫的人。 **5** [C] group of living things (plants, animals, etc) or of languages, with common characteristics and a common source: (動植物等的)族;科;系;語系: *animals of the cat ~,* eg lions and tigers; 貓科動物(如獅和虎); *the Germanic ~ of languages* (including German, Dutch, English). 日耳曼語系(包括德語、荷蘭語、英語)。 **6** (attrib) of or for a ~: (形容用法)家庭的;家族的;家庭用的: *the ~ estate/jewels, etc.* 家產(家中的珠寶等)。 ***in the ~ way,*** (sl; of a woman) pregnant. (俚,指女子)懷孕的。 **~ doctor,** a general practitioner. 家庭(特約)醫師。 **~ hotel,** one with lower rates for families. 家庭旅館(爲家庭設的經濟旅社)。 **~ likeness,** resemblance between members of a ~. 家族各份子間的相似。 **ˈ~ man,** one who is fond of home life with his ~. 喜好家庭生活的人。 **~ name,** surname. 姓;氏。 **~ planning,** (use of birth control, contraceptives, for) planning the number of children, intervals between births, etc in a ~. 家庭計畫;節育;生育控制。 **~ tree,** a genealogical tree or chart. 家譜。

fam·ine /ˈfæmɪn ; ˈfæmɪn/ *n* **1** [U] extreme scarcity of food in a region: (一地區之)饑荒: *Parts of India have often suffered from ~.* 印度有些地區常鬧饑荒。 **2** [C] particular occasion when there is such scarcity: 某一饑荒: *a ~ in Ethiopia.* 衣索比亞的一次饑荒。 **3** (attrib) caused by ~: (形容用法)因饑荒而造成的: *~ prices,* high prices. 因饑荒而造成的高價。

fam·ish /ˈfæmɪʃ ; ˈfæmɪʃ/ *vi, vt* **1** [VP2A, 3A] suffer from extreme hunger: 挨餓;饑餓: *They were ~ing for food.* 他們因缺食物而挨餓。 *I'm ~ing!* (colloq) very hungry. (俗)我很餓! **2** [VP6A] (usu passive) cause (sb) to suffer from hunger: (通常用被動語態)使挨餓;使受饑: *The child looked half ~ed.* 那孩子看來很餓了。 *I'm ~ed!* (colloq) very hungry. (俗)我餓死了!

fa·mous /ˈfeɪməs ; ˈfeməs/ *adj* **1** known widely; having fame; celebrated: 著名的;出名的;馳名的: *a ~ scientist.* 著名的科學家。 *The town is ~ for its gambling casino/~ as a gambling resort.* 該城以其賭場馳名(是個著名的賭博場所)。 **2** (dated colloq) excellent. (過時俗語)極好的;令人滿意的。 **~·ly** *adv* in a ~(2) manner: 極好;令人滿意地: *get on ~ly with sb;* 與某人相處極爲融洽; *do ~ly in/at sth.* 順利地進行某事。

fan¹ /fæn ; fæn/ *n* (flat, semi-circular, usu folding) object waved in the hand, or (with rotating blades) operated mechanically, for making a current of air (eg to cool a room, oneself or to blow dust, etc away); sth that is like a hand fan in shape, eg the tail of a peacock. 扇子;風扇;扇狀物(例如孔雀尾)。 **ˈfan belt** *n* rubber belt transferring circular motion to the cooling fan of an engine. 扇帶(傳送循環動作至發動機冷却扇的橡皮帶)。 **ˈfan·light** *n* fan-shaped window over a door. (門上的)扇形窗。 **ˌfan ˈvaulting** *n* (archit) style of vaulting in which ribs, like those of a folding fan, rise and spread from a single point. (建築)扇形圓屋頂。

fans

fan² /fæn ; fæn/ *vt, vi* (-nn-) **1** [VP6A] send a current of air on to: 搧;吹向: *fan oneself;* 搧自己;搧扇子; *fan a fire,* to make it burn up; 搧火; *fan the flame,* (fig) increase excitement or emotion. (喻)煽動情緒。 **2** [VP6A] (of a breeze) blow gently on: (指微風)徐徐吹在…上: *The breeze fanned our faces.* 微風輕輕吹在我們的臉上。 **3** [VP2C] *~ **out,*** open in fan-shaped formation: 作扇形散開: *The troops stormed the enemy's trenches and fanned out across the fields.* 軍隊猛襲敵人的戰壕並在戰場上呈扇形散開。 **4** [VP6A] spread out (eg playing cards) like a fan. 將(紙牌等)展成扇形。

fan³ /fæn ; fæn/ *n* (colloq) keen supporter of sth:

(俗)對某事物之狂熱者;迷: *'baseball fans;* 棒球迷; *'fan mail,* letters from fans, eg to a popular singer. 狂熱者寄來的信(例如歌迷寄給歌星者)。

fa·natic /fəˈnætɪk ; fəˈnætɪk/ *n* person filled with excessive (and often mistaken) enthusiasm, eg in religion: 狂熱者(常是盲目的,例如在宗教方面);盲信者: *food ~s,* willing to eat only certain kinds of food. 偏食者。□ *adj* (also亦作 **fa·nati·cal** /-kl ; -kl/) excessively enthusiastic; of or like a ~: 狂熱的; 狂熱者的: *~(al) beliefs.* 狂熱的信仰。**fa·nati·cally** /-klɪ ; -klɪ/ *adv* **fa·nati·cism** /-sɪzəm ; -ˌsɪzəm/ *n* [U] violent, unreasoning enthusiasm; [C] instance of this. 狂熱;盲信。

fan·cier /ˈfænsɪə(r) ; ˈfænsɪr/ *n* person with special knowledge of and love for some article, animal, etc (the name being prefixed): 對某物品、動物等有特殊知識或愛好之人;玩賞家(玩賞的對象名稱冠於前): *a 'dog ~;* 玩賞狗的人; *a 'rose ~.* 玩賞玫瑰的人。

fan·ci·ful /ˈfænsɪfl ; ˈfænsɪfəl/ *adj* **1** (of persons) full of fancies(2); led by imagination instead of reason and experience: (指人)富於幻想的;爲想像引導的: *a ~ writer.* 富於幻想的作家。 **2** unreal; curiously designed: 不眞實的;設計奇特的: *~ drawings.* 構想奇特的圖畫。**~·ly** /-fəlɪ ; -fəlɪ/ *adv*

fancy¹ /ˈfænsɪ ; ˈfænsɪ/ *n* (*pl* -cies) **1** [U] power of creating mental pictures (often a passive process). (⇨ imagination, in which the mind is more active): 想像力(常爲消極的過程)。(參看 imagination, 其思想過程較爲積極): *a world of mere ~.* 純想像的世界。 **2** [C] sth imagined; unfounded opinion or belief: 想像之物;空論;無根據的信念;幻想: *the fancies of a poet.* 詩人的幻想。*Did I really hear someone come in or was it only a ~?* 我是眞聽到有人來,或只是一種幻覺? *I have a ~* (= a vague idea) *that she will be late.* 我彷彿覺得她會遲到。**3** [C] ***a ~ (for),*** fondness, liking, desire: 愛好;喜愛: *I have a ~ for some wine with my dinner.* 我喜歡吃飯的時候喝點酒。***take a ~ to,*** become fond of: 喜愛: *The children have taken quite a ~ to their cousin.* 孩子們十分喜歡他們的表兄。***take/catch the ~ of,*** please or attract: 投合…的心意;吸引: *She saw the dress in a shop window and it caught her ~.* 她看到一家商店櫥窗內的衣服,而爲它所吸引。***a passing ~,*** sth that attracts one's attention and liking for a short period of time only. 一時爲人所愛好之物。**ˌ~-'free** *adj* not in love; not committed to anything; not taking things seriously. 未在戀愛中的; 無拘束的; 態度不嚴肅的。⇨ foot¹(8).

fancy² /ˈfænsɪ ; ˈfænsɪ/ *adj* (usu attrib; not in the comp or superl) (通常爲形容用法,不用於比較級或最高級) **1** (esp of small things) brightly coloured; made to please the eye: (尤指小東西)顏色鮮艷的;悅目的: *~ cakes;* 漂亮的蛋糕; *~ goods.* 精美小物品。**2** not plain or ordinary: 特別裝飾的: *~ bread.* 特製麵包。**~ dress,** unusual costume, often historical or exotic, as worn at balls, called **~-'dress balls.** 奇裝異服(如化裝舞會 fancy-dress balls 所穿者,常是有歷史或外國特色的)。**'~ work,** ornamental sewing. 用做裝飾的針織物;刺繡。 **3** bred for particular points of beauty: 因其珍奇而特別培育的: *~ dogs/pigeons;* 品種珍奇的狗(鴿子);*~ pansies,* having two or more colours. 珍品紫羅蘭(有兩種或多種顏色)。 **4** extravagant: 過度的;過分的: *~ ideas/prices.* 過分的思想(高昂的價格)。 **5** (US, of goods) superior in quality: (美,指貨物)品質優良的: *'F~ Crab'* (on a label, etc). '精選蟹' (見於標籤等)。 **6** imagined: 想像的;空想的: *a ~ portrait.* 想像的畫像。

fancy³ /ˈfænsɪ ; ˈfænsɪ/ *vt* (*pt, pp* -cied) **1** [VP6A, 16B, 19C] picture in the mind; imagine: 想像;假想: *Can you ~ me as a pirate?* 你能想像我是一個海盜嗎? *I can't ~ his doing such a thing.* 我不能想像他做這種事。**2** [VP25, 9] be under the impression that (without being certain, or without enough reason): (無把握或充份的理由而)以爲: *I rather ~ (that) he won't come.* 我認爲他不會來。*He fancied he heard footsteps behind him.* 他以爲他聽到身後有脚步聲。*Don't ~ that you can succeed without hard work.* 不要認爲你不努力工作而能成功。 *When she saw Tom, whom she had fancied (to be) dead,....* 當她看到她以爲已經死去的湯姆時,…。 **3** [VP6A] (colloq) have a fancy(3) for: (俗)喜愛: *What do you ~ for your dinner?* 你午(或晚)飯喜歡吃什麼? *I don't ~ this place at all.* 我一點也不喜歡這地方。*Do you ~ that girl,* find her attractive, likeable? 你喜歡那個女孩嗎? **4 *~ oneself,*** have an excessively high opinion of oneself; be rather conceited: 自負;自命不凡: *He fancies himself as an orator.* 他認爲自己是位了不起的演說家。 **5** [VP6A, C] exclamatory style, expressing surprise: 感嘆語氣,表示驚訝: *F~ her saying such unkind things about you!* 想想看,她竟然說出這些對你無情的話! *F~ that, now!* 噯呀! *Just ~!* How strange! How surprising! 多奇怪呀!眞想不到!

fan·dango /ˌfænˈdæŋgəʊ ; fænˈdæŋgo/ *n* (*pl* ~es /-gəʊz ; -goz/) (music for a) lively Spanish or S American dance. 方當果舞(一種輕快的西班牙或南美洲舞);方當果舞曲。

fan·fare /ˈfænfeə(r) ; ˈfænˌfɛr/ *n* [C] (music) flourish of trumpets or bugles. (音樂)喇叭或號角之高而急的吹奏;鼓號曲。

fang /fæŋ ; fæŋ/ *n* long, sharp tooth (esp of dogs and wolves); snake's poison-tooth. (犬、狼之)尖牙;(蛇的)毒牙。

fan·light ⇨ fan¹.

fan·ny /ˈfænɪ ; ˈfænɪ/ *n* (*pl* -nies) (US sl) buttocks. (美俚)屁股。

fan·tan /ˌfænˈtæn *US:* ˈfæntæn ; ˈfænˌtæn/ *n* Chinese gambling game. 番攤(中國的一種賭博)。

fan·tasia /fænˈteɪzɪə *US:* -ˈteɪʒə ; fænˈteʒɪə/ *n* artistic composition in which a fanciful style is more important than structure. 幻想曲。

fan·ta·size /ˈfæntəsaɪz ; ˈfæntəsaɪz/ *vi, vt* [VP2A, 3A, 6A] ***~ (about),*** have a fantasy(2) (of); imagine. 幻想;想像。**fan·ta·sist** *n* person who ~s. 幻想者;想像者。

fan·tas·tic /fænˈtæstɪk ; fænˈtæstɪk/ *adj* **1** wild and strange; grotesque: 奇異的;怪誕的: *~ dreams/shapes/fashions.* 怪異的夢(形狀,式樣)。 **2** (of ideas, plans) impossible to carry out; absurd. (指觀念、計畫)無法實現的;荒謬的。 **3** (sl) marvellous; wonderful: (俚)令人驚奇的;奇妙的: *Christina's a really ~ girl!* 克麗絲汀娜眞是個奇妙的女孩! **fan·tas·ti·cally** /-klɪ ; -klɪ/ *adv*

fan·tasy /ˈfæntəsɪ ; ˈfæntəsɪ/ *n* (*pl* -sies) **1** [U] fancy(1); imagination, esp when extravagant: 想像力;想像;(尤指過度的)幻想;狂想: *live in a world of ~;* 生活在幻想世界中; (attrib) (形容用法) *one's ~ life,* that part devoted to ~. 個人的幻想生活。 **2** [C] product of the imagination: 幻想出的東西: *sexual fantasies.* 性幻想。 **3** [C] = fantasia.

far¹ /fɑː(r) ; fɑr/ *adj* (⇨ farther, farthest, further, furthest) **1** (usu in liter style) distant: (通常用於文學的文體)遠的: *a far country.* 一個遙遠的國家。***a far cry from,*** a long way from; (fig) a very different thing from. 距離…很遠;(喻)與…大不相同之物。 **2 the Far East,** China, Korea, Japan, etc. 遠東(中、韓、日等)。**the Far West,** the Pacific coast area of the US. 美國西部太平洋沿岸地區。 **3** (= *farther*) more remote: 較遠的: *at the far end of the street;* 在街的那一頭; *on the far bank of the river.* 在河的彼岸。

far² /fɑː(r) ; fɑr/ *adv* (⇨ farther, farthest, further, furthest) **1** (indicating a great distance, commonly used in the interr and neg, but not usually, except as shown in 2 below, in the affirm): 遠;遙遠(通常用於疑問和否定句,除下列第 2 義所列之情形外,不常用於肯定句): *How far did you go?* 你走了多遠? *We didn't go far.* 我們沒有走遠。Cf 參較 (in the affirm): (在肯定句中): *We went*

F

a long way. 我們走了很長一段路。 *We went only a short way*. 我們僅走了短短的一段路。 **2** (with other *advv* and *preps*) (*indicating a great distance*): (與副詞和介詞連用)(表示很遠): *far away/off/out/back/in;* 遙遠(深遠); *far beyond the bridge;* 遠在橋那邊; *far above the clouds;* 遠在雲上; *not far from here;* 距此不遠; *far into the night;* 至深夜; *far back in history;* 很久以前; *as far back as 1902*. 遠在1902年。***far from,*** not at all: 毫不;一點也不;遠非: *Your work is far from (being)* (= is not at all) *satisfactory*. 你的工作一點也不令人滿意。*The newspaper accounts are far from (being) true,* are in many points false. 報紙的報導遠非事實(有許多地方不確)。*Far from* (= Instead of) *admiring his paintings, I dislike them intensely*. 我不但不欽佩反而十分討厭他的畫。***by far,*** (with comp or superl) by a large amount or degree: (與比較級或最高級連用)大量; 甚多: *by far the smallest/heaviest;* 顯然最小的(最重的); *better by far*. 好得多。***from far,*** from a great distance. 自遠處。***go far,*** **(a)** (of persons) be successful; do much: (指人)成功;有成就: *He's clever and intelligent, and will go far*. 他又伶俐又聰明,將來會成功的。**(b)** (of money) buy goods, services, etc: (指錢)買貨物、勞役等: *A pound does not go so far today as it did five years ago*. 今天的一鎊不如五年前那麼當用了。***go/carry sth too far,*** go beyond the limits of what is considered reasonable: 過分: *Don't carry the joke too far*. 不要把玩笑開得太過分。(Cf 參較 It's beyond a joke. 那不是開玩笑的事。) *Don't carry your modesty too far,* Don't be unnecessarily modest. 不要過分謙虛。***go far towards/to doing sth,*** help or contribute greatly to: 大有助於;對…大有貢獻: *The loan will go far towards clearing my debt*. 這筆貸款對於清償我的債務將大有幫助。***far and near/wide,*** everywhere: 到處: *They searched far and wide for the missing child*. 他們到處尋找那走失的孩子。*People come from far and near to hear the famous violinist*. 各處的人都來聆聽這位著名的小提琴家(演奏)。***far be it from me to do sth,*** I would/should/could never do it. 我決不會做某事。**'*so far,*** until now: 到目前爲止: *So far the work has been easy*. 到目前爲止,這工作是容易的。***ˌSo far, so 'good,*** Up to now everything has gone well. 到目前爲止,一切良好。***as/so far as,*** **(a)** to the place mentioned: 至某一指明的地點: *He walked as far as the post office*. 他步行到郵局。**(b)** the same distance: 同樣的距離: *We didn't go so far as the others (did)*. 我們不如其他的人走得那樣遠。**(c)** to the extent that (to indicate a limit of advance or progress): 就…之限度;在…範圍內: *So far as I know he will be away for three months*. 就我所知,他將離開三個月。*He will help you as far as he can/as far as (is) possible/as far as lies in his power*. 他會盡力幫助你。*We have gone so far as to collect some useful statistics*. 我們甚至收集了一些有用的統計資料。 **3** (with qualifying *adjj* and *advv*) (by) much; considerably; to a great extent: (與性質形容詞和副詞連用)很;甚;極: *This is far better*. 這個要好得多。*It fell far short of our expectations*. 此事遠未達到我們的期望。***far and away,*** (with comp or superl) by a large amount or degree: (與比較級或最高級連用)很;甚: *He's far and away the best actor I've seen*. 他是我所看到的最好的演員了。**'far-away** *adj* **(a)** distant, remote: 遙遠的;久遠的: *far-away places/times*. 遙遠的地方(很久以前的時代)。**(b)** (of a look in a person's eyes) dreamy; as if fixed on sth far away in space or time. (指人的眼睛)迷矇的;恍惚的。**ˌfar-'famed** *adj* (rhet) widely known. (修辭)馳名的;聞名的。**ˌfar-'fetched** *adj* (of a comparison) forced; unnatural. (指一比擬)牽强的;勉强的。**ˌfar-'flung** *adj* (rhet) widely extended. (修辭)廣汎的。**ˌfar 'gone,** deeply advanced (into eg illness, madness, drunkenness, debt). 病重;十分瘋狂;大醉;負債累累。**ˌfar-'off** *adj* = far-away. **ˌfar-'reaching** *adj* likely to have many consequences; having a wide application: 影響廣大的;遠及的: *far-reaching proposals*. 遠大的建議。**ˌfar-'seeing** *adj* seeing far into the future. 眼光遠大的。**ˌfar-'sighted** *adj* **(a)** able to see distant objects more clearly than near objects. 遠視的。**(b)** (fig) prudent; having a good judgement of future needs, etc. (喻)有智慮的;有先見之明的;有遠見的。

farce /fɑːs ; fɑrs/ *n* **1** [C] play for the theatre, full of ridiculous situations intended to make people laugh; [U] this style of drama. 笑劇;鬧劇。 **2** [C] series of actual events like a ~; absurd and useless proceedings: 似笑劇般的一連串事件;可笑和無謂的行動: *The prisoner's trial was a ~*. 那個囚犯的審訊簡直是胡鬧。**far·ci·cal** /'fɑːsɪkl ; 'fɑrsɪkl/ *adj* of or like a ~; absurd. 笑劇的;似笑劇的;可笑的。**far·ci·cally** /-klɪ ; -klɪ/ *adv*

fare¹ /feə(r) ; fɛr/ *n* [C] **1** money charged for a journey by bus, ship, taxi, etc: 車費;船費;乘客購票所付之費: *All ~s, please!* (cried by the conductor of a bus, etc). 請買票(公共汽車等收票員用語)! **2** passenger in a hired vehicle: (出租車輛的)乘客: *The taxi-driver had only six ~s all day*. 那計程車司機一天祇載了六位乘客。

fare² /feə(r) ; fɛr/ *n* [U] food provided at table: 伙食;飲食: *fine/simple/homely ~*. 美好的(簡單的,家常的)伙食。**ˌbill of '~,** list of dishes; menu. 菜單。

fare³ /feə(r) ; fɛr/ *vi* [VP2C] **1** progress; get on: 進展; 進步; 過日子: *How did you ~ during your journey,* What were your experiences? 你旅途好嗎? *It has ~d well with him,* He has done well, been fortunate. 他的情況如意。***You may go farther and ~ worse,*** (prov, used to suggest that one should be content with one's present conditions). (諺)走得更遠可能情形更壞(勸人安於現狀)。 **2** (old use) go, journey. (舊用法)行;旅行。***~ forth,*** start out. 動身。

fare·well /ˌfeə'wel ; 'fɛr'wɛl/ *int* goodbye. 再會;再見。***(bid/say) ~ to,*** (have) no more of. 不再(有)。□ *n* leave-taking: 告別;辭別: *make one's ~s,* say goodbye; 辭行; (attrib) (形容用法) *a ~ speech*. 告別演說。

fari·na·ceous /ˌfærɪ'neɪʃəs ; ˌfærə'neʃəs/ *adj* starchy; of flour or meal: 澱粉的;麵粉或穀粉的: *~ foods,* eg bread, potatoes. 含澱粉的食物(如麵包、馬鈴薯)。

farm¹ /fɑːm ; fɑrm/ *n* **1** area of land (usu divided into fields) and buildings (eg barns), under one management (either owned or rented) for growing crops, raising animals, etc: 農場;農田;飼養場: *working on the ~*. 在農場工作。Cf 參較 *in the fields*. **'~·hand** *n* (US) ~ worker; agricultural labourer. (美)農場工人; 農場勞動者。 **'~·yard** *n* space enclosed by ~ buildings (sheds, barns, etc). 農家的圍院。 **2** (also 亦作 **'~·house, '~·stead** /-sted ; -ˌstɛd/) farmer's house on a ~. 農舍。

farm² /fɑːm ; fɑrm/ *vt, vi* **1** [VP6A, 2A] use (land) for growing crops, raising animals, etc: 耕(田); 耕作;經營農場;飼養家畜: *He ~s 200 acres*. 他耕種二百英畝田。*He is ~ing in Africa*. 他在非洲務農。*He is engaged in 'sheep-~ing*. 他從事養羊。 **2** [VP15B] ***~ out (to),*** **(a)** send (work) out to be done by others. 招人承包工作。**(b)** arrange for (a child) to be cared for by others. 寄養(小孩)。**~er** *n* man who owns or manages a ~. 農人;農場主人。(Cf 參較 *peasant,* a word not used of a ~er or farm worker in GB or US. 在英國或美國農人不稱作 peasant)。

far·rago /fə'rɑːgəʊ ; fə'rego/ *n* (*pl* ~s, ~es /-gəʊz ; -goz/) medley, mixture: 混雜;混雜物: *a ~ of nonsense/useless knowledge*. 一派胡言(一套無用的知識)。

far·rier /'færɪə(r) ; 'færɪɚ/ *n* smith who shoes horses. 蹄鐵匠。

far·row /'færəʊ ; 'færo/ *vi* give birth to pigs: 產

F

小豬: *When will the sow ~?* 母豬何時產小豬? □ *n* litter of pigs; giving birth to pigs: 一窩小豬;產小豬: *15 at one ~.* 一胎十五隻小豬。

fart /fɑːt ; fɑrt/ *vi, n* ⚠ (not in polite use) (send out, sending out of) wind through the anus. (諱)(不禮貌的用語) 放屁;屁。

far·ther /ˈfɑːðə(r) ; ˈfɑrðɚ/ *adv* (comp of *far*) (far 的比較級) to/at a greater distance/depth: 較遠;更遠: *We can't go any ~ without a rest.* 我們如不休息便走不動了。*They went ~ into the forest.* 他們深入森林。□ *adj* more distant: 較遠的;更遠的: *on the ~ bank of the river;* 在河的彼岸; *at the ~ end of the street.* 在街道的另一端。

far·thest /ˈfɑːðɪst ; ˈfɑrðɪst/ *adv, adj* (superl of *far*) (far 的最高級) to/at the greatest distance/depth: 最遠(的);最久(的): *Which village in England is ~ from London?* 在英格蘭哪個村莊距離倫敦最遠? ***at (the) ~,*** **(a)** at the greatest distance: 最遠: *It's five miles away at the ~,* is not more than five miles away. 最遠不超過五哩。**(b)** (of time) at the latest. (指時間) 至遲。

far·thing /ˈfɑːðɪŋ ; ˈfɑrðɪŋ/ *n* (formerly) coin worth one-quarter of a penny. (昔時一錢幣名) 一辨士的四分之一。***It doesn't matter/He doesn't care a ~,*** not in the least. 這事毫無關係(他毫不在乎)。

fas·cia (also **facia**) /ˈfeɪʃə ; ˈfeʃə/ *n* dashboard or panel on a motor vehicle, etc (with gauges, dials, etc). (汽車等前部裝有計量表,針盤等之) 儀器板。⇨ the illus at motor. 參看 motor 之插圖。

fas·ci·nate /ˈfæsɪneɪt ; ˈfæsn̩ˌet/ *vt* [VP6A] **1** charm, attract or interest greatly: 使着迷;使神魂顛倒;使極感興趣: *The children were ~d by all the toys in the shop windows.* 孩子們被商店櫥窗內所有的玩具迷住了。**2** take away power of movement by a fixed look, as a snake does. 凝視而使之不能動(如蛇所爲者);蠱惑。**fas·ci·nat·ing** *adj* having strong charm or attraction: 迷人的;醉人的: *a fascinating voice/story/glimpse.* 迷人的聲音(故事,一瞥)。**fas·ci·nat·ing·ly** *adv* **fas·ci·na·tion** /ˌfæsɪˈneɪʃn ; ˌfæsn̩ˈeʃən/ *n* [U] fascinating or being ~d; power to ~; [C] thing that ~s: 迷惑;蠱惑;着迷;受蠱惑;魅力;魔力;迷人之物: *Girls have a fascination for Brian,* ie they ~ him. 女孩子使布萊恩着迷。*Brian has a fascination for girls,* ie he ~s them. 布萊恩使女孩子着迷。

fas·cism /ˈfæʃɪzəm ; ˈfæʃˌɪzəm/ *n* **F~,** philosophy, principles and organization of the aggressive nationalist and anti-communist dictatorship started in Italy in 1922 and dissolved in 1943; similar movement in other countries. 法西斯主義(爲侵略性國家主義和反共的獨裁政治,1922年始於義大利,1943年結束);其他國家中類似的運動。**fas·cist** /ˈfæʃɪst ; ˈfæʃɪst/ *n* supporter of ~. 法西斯主義者;法西斯黨員。□ *adj* of ~; extreme right-wing; reactionary. 法西斯主義的;極端右派的;反動的。

fashion /ˈfæʃn ; ˈfæʃən/ *n* **1** **a/the ~,** manner of doing or making sth: 樣子;方式: *He walks in a peculiar ~.* 他走路的樣子很奇特。***after/in a ~,*** somehow or other, but not satisfactorily: 略微地(但不令人滿意): *He can speak and write English, after a ~.* 他多少會說和寫英文,但不太好。***after the ~ of,*** like, in imitation of: 像…一樣;模倣: *a novel after the ~ of Graham Greene.* 模倣格雷安·格林的一部小說。**2** [C, U] (as shown in the examples) (用於下列例句中) (of clothes, behaviour, thought, custom, etc) prevailing custom; that which is considered most to be admired and imitated during a period or at a place: (指服裝,行爲,思想,風俗等) 風尚;時髦;時樣;風氣: *dressed in the latest ~.* 裝扮入時的。*F~s for men's clothes change less frequently than ~s for women's clothes.* 男裝的時樣不如女裝的時樣多變化。***be all the ~,*** (of dress, behaviour, etc) be very popular. (指服裝,行動等) 十分流行。***come into/go out of ~,*** become/no longer be popular: 流行(不流行): *When did that style of dress come into/go out of ~?* 那種衣服式樣什麼時候變爲流行(不流行)? ***follow/be in the ~,*** do what others do in matters of dress, behaviour, etc. (裝束,行動等) 迎合時尚。***set the ~,*** give the example by adopting new ~s. 開風氣;創新時樣。***a man/woman of ~,*** one belonging to fashionable society and conforming to its usages. 上流社會人物;時髦人物。**ˈ~ plate** *n* picture showing a style of dress. 時裝圖樣。□ *vt* [VP6A, 15A] give form or shape to; mould: 形成;做成…的形狀: *~ a canoe out of a tree-trunk/a whistle from a piece of wood/a lump of clay into a bowl.* 用樹幹做成獨木舟(用木塊製成一口笛;將黏土塑成一隻碗)。

fashion·able /ˈfæʃnəbl ; ˈfæʃənəbl̩/ *adj* following the fashion(2); used by, visited by, many people, esp the rich: 時新的;時髦的;流行的;有錢人所用的;有錢人常到的: *~ clothes;* 流行的服裝; *a ~ dressmaker/hotel/summer resort.* 有錢人所光顧的裁縫(常去的旅館,避暑勝地)。**fashion·ably** /-əblɪ ; -əblɪ/ *adv* in a ~ manner: 時髦地;流行地: *fashionably dressed.* 裝扮入時的。

fast¹ /fɑːst *US:* fæst ; fæst/ *adj* **1** firmly fixed; not easily moved: 牢固的;堅固的;堅牢的: *The post is ~ in the ground.* 那柱子牢牢地埋在地裏。*Make the boat ~,* Make it secure. 將船繫牢。*Take (a) ~ hold of the rope,* hold it tightly. 握緊繩子。***hard and ~ rules,*** rigid rules. 不容違犯的規則;嚴格的規則。**2** steady; steadfast; loyal; close: 可靠的;忠實的;親近的: *a ~ friend/friendship.* 忠實的朋友(友誼)。**3** (of colours) unfading. (指顏色) 不褪色的。□ *adv* firmly, securely, tightly: 牢固地;穩固地;緊緊地: *hold ~ to sth.* 緊握某物。*The ship was ~ aground,* could not be refloated. 那船擱淺了。*She was ~ asleep,* in a deep sleep. 她在酣睡。***stand ~,*** not move or retreat; refuse to give way. 立穩;堅定不移;不後退;不屈服。***stick ~,*** **(a)** = stand ~. **(b)** be unable to make progress. 不能前進。***F~ bind, ~ find,*** (prov) If you make things secure, eg by locking them up, you will not lose them. (諺) 鎖得牢,丢不了。***play ~ and loose with,*** repeatedly change one's attitude towards; trifle with: 不斷地改變對…的態度;對…反覆無常;玩弄: *play ~ and loose with a girl's affections.* 玩弄一個女孩子的感情。

fast² /fɑːst *US:* fæst ; fæst/ *adj* (-er, -est) **1** quick; rapid: 迅速的;快的: *a ~ train/horse;* 快車(馬); *a ~ trip;* 迅速之旅行; *a ~ draw,* of a gun from a holster. 拔槍迅速。**2** (dated) (of a person, his way of living) spending too much time and energy on pleasure and excitement; dissipated: (過時用語) (指人,人的生活方式) 耽於遊樂的; 放蕩的: *lead a ~ life;* 過放蕩的生活; *a ~ woman;* 浪漫的女子; *~ society.* 耽於逸樂的人們。**3** (of a watch or clock) showing time later than the true time: (指鐘錶) 走得快的: *My watch is five minutes ~,* eg showing 2.05 at 2.00. 我的錶快五分鐘。**4** (of a surface) promoting quick motion: (指表面) 促成迅速動作的: *a ~ cricket pitch/billiard-table.* 平滑的板球場(撞球檯)。**5** (of photographic film) suitable for very brief exposures. (指照像軟片) 適於拍快照的。

fast³ /fɑːst *US:* fæst ; fæst/ *adv* **1** quickly: 迅速地;快地: *Don't speak so ~.* 不要說得這樣快。*It was raining ~,* heavily. 雨下得很大。*Her tears fell ~.* 她的眼淚簌簌流下。**2** ***live ~,*** live in a dissipated way; use much energy in a short time. 生活放蕩;在短時間耗費很多精力。**3** (old use) close: (舊用法) 接近: *~ by/behind the church.* 在教堂旁邊(後面)。

fast⁴ /fɑːst *US:* fæst ; fæst/ *vi* [VP2A, B] go without food, or without certain kinds of food, esp as a religious duty: 禁食;齋戒: *days devoted to ~ing and penitence,* eg in Lent. 齋戒與懺悔期(例如四旬齋)。□ *n* **1** (period of) going without food: 禁食(期);齋戒(期): *a ~ of three days;* 禁食三日;齋戒三日; *break one's ~.* 開齋。**2** day (ˈ~-

F

day) or season of ~ing. 禁食日;齋日;齋期。

fas·ten /ˈfɑːsn *US:* ˈfæsn ; ˈfæsn̩/ *vt, vi* **1** [VP6A, 15A, B] ~ ***(up/down),*** make fast¹; fix firmly; tie or join together: 使牢固;使固定;繫住;綑在一起: *Have you ~ed all the doors and windows?* 你將所有的門窗關牢沒有？*He~ed the two sheets of paper together.* 他將那兩張紙釘在一起。*He ~ed up/down the box,* closed it and made it secure. 他將箱子關牢。 **2** [VP14] ~ ***on/upon,*** fix (a nickname, accusation, etc) upon sb; direct (one's looks, thoughts, attention, etc) upon sb: 把(綽號,罪名等)加在某人身上;使(目光,思想,注意力等)朝向某人: *He ~ed his eyes on me.* 他用眼睛盯着我。 **3** [VP2A, C] become fast¹ or secured: 變爲牢固;變緊: *The door won't ~.* 這門關不牢。*This dress ~s down the back,* has buttons, etc down the back. 這件衣服自背後扣鈕扣。 **4** [VP3A] ~ ***on/upon,*** lay hold of, seize upon; single (a person) out for attack: 握住;抓緊;選出(某人)作攻擊的對象: *He ~ed on the idea.* 他堅持這種想法。**~er** *n* thing that ~s things together: 將東西繫牢之物;繫結物: *a paper ~er;* 書釘;夾子;廻紋針; *a zip-~er.* 拉鍊。**~·ing** *n* thing that ~s, esp a slide or a bolt. 繫牢物(尤指髮夾或門閂)。

fas·tid·ious /fəˈstɪdɪəs *US:* fæ- ; fæsˈtɪdɪəs/ *adj* hard to please; quick to find fault: 難以取悅的;吹毛求疵的: *He is ~ about his food/clothes, etc.* 他對於食物(衣服等)很苛求。**~·ly** *adv* **~·ness** *n*

F

fast·ness /ˈfɑːstnɪs *US:* ˈfæs- ; ˈfæstnɪs/ *n* **1** [C] stronghold; fortress: 要塞;堡壘: *a mountain ~,* eg of bandits. 山寨(例如盜賊盤據者)。**2** [U] the quality of being fast¹(3): 不褪色: *We guarantee the ~ of these dyes.* 我們擔保這些顏料不褪色。

fat¹ /fæt ; fæt/ *adj* (fatter, fattest) **1** covered with, having much, fat: 肥的;胖的: *fat meat;* 肥肉; *a fat man;* 胖子; *fat cheeks;* 肥胖的面頰; *fat cattle,* made fat ready for slaughter. (備宰的)肥牛。**ˈfat-head** *n* dull, stupid person. 愚蠢的人。 **2** thick; well filled: 厚的;豐滿的: *a fat wallet,* one stuffed with banknotes. 裝滿鈔票的錢包。***a ˈfat lot,*** (sl) a great deal (ironic, = very little): (俚)很多(作反語用,表示很少): *A fat lot you care,* ie you don't care at all. 你介意得很(實指:你一點也不介意)。 **3** rich, fertile: 肥沃的: *fat lands.* 肥沃的土地。**fat·tish** *adj* rather fat. 稍肥的;略肥的。**fat·ness** *n*

fat² /fæt ; fæt/ *n* [C, U] (kinds of) white or yellow substance, oily or greasy, found in animal bodies; this substance purified for cooking purposes; oily substance obtained from certain seeds: 脂肪;肥肉;食用的動物油;植物油: *Give me red meat, please; I don't like fat.* 請給我瘦肉,我不喜歡肥肉。*Fried potatoes are cooked in deep fat.* 炸馬鈴薯是在很多油裏炸成的。*Vegetable cooking fats are sold in tins.* 烹飪用植物油是成罐賣的。***chew the fat,*** continue to grumble about sth. 不斷抱怨;不停地發牢騷。***live on/off the fat of the land,*** have the best of everything. 享受最好的東西;生活奢侈。***The fat's in the fire,*** What has been done (usu irrevocably) will cause a lot of trouble. 一旦做出無法挽回之事,將會引起許多麻煩;闖了大禍。**fat·less** *adj* ⇨ fatty.

fat³ /fæt ; fæt/ *vt* (-tt-) = fatten: *fatted cattle.* 養肥了的牛。***kill the fatted calf,*** (fig) welcome sb back with joy. (喻)熱烈歡迎(某人回來)。

fatal /ˈfeɪtl ; ˈfetl/ *adj* **1** ~ ***(to),*** causing, ending in, death or disaster: 致命的;悲慘的: *a ~ accident.* 慘禍。*The cyclist was knocked down by a lorry and received ~ injuries.* 那個騎脚踏車的人被卡車撞倒,受到了致命的傷。*His illness was ~ to our plans,* caused them to fail. 他的病使我們的計畫成爲泡影。 **2** like fate; of, appointed by, destiny: 注定的;命運的;命運決定的: *the ~ day.* 決定性的一日。 **~·ly** /ˈfeɪtəlɪ ; ˈfetl̩ɪ/ *adv* in a ~ manner: 致命地;悲慘地;注定地: *~ly injured/wounded.* 受到致命傷。

fatal·ism /ˈfeɪtəlɪzəm ; ˈfetl̩ˌɪzəm/ *n* [U] belief that events are decided by fate(1); submission to all that happens as inevitable. 宿命論;聽天由命。**fatal·ist** /ˈfeɪtəlɪst ; ˈfetl̩ɪst/ *n* believer in ~. 宿命論者。**fatal·is·tic** /ˌfeɪtəˈlɪstɪk ; ˌfetl̩ˈɪstɪk/ *adj* of ~: 宿命論的: *a fatalistic attitude.* 宿命論的態度。

fatal·ity /fəˈtælətɪ ; feˈtælətɪ/ *n* (*pl* -ties) **1** [C] misfortune, calamity, esp one that causes death and destruction: 災禍(尤指致命的和導致毀滅的): *floods, earthquakes and other fatalities.* 洪水,地震和其他的災禍。 **2** [C] death by accident, in war, etc: (意外,戰爭等造成的)死亡: *There have been numerous bathing fatalities this summer,* Many people have lost their lives while bathing. 今年夏季有許多人游泳慘遭滅頂。 **3** [U] state of being subject to fate(1) or destiny. 聽天由命;天數。 **4** [U] fatal influence; deadliness: 致命;致死: *the ~ of certain diseases,* eg cancer. 某些疾病(例如癌症)之致命。

fate /feɪt ; fet/ *n* **1** [U] power looked upon as controlling all events in a way that cannot be resisted; destiny: 命運;定數: *He had hoped to become President, but ~ decided otherwise.* 他本來希望做總統,但天意使他不能如願。***as sure as ~,*** quite certain(ly). 必定。**the F~s,** the three Greek goddesses of destiny. 希臘的命運三女神。 **2** [C] the future as decided by ~ for sth or sb; what is destined to happen: 未來的吉凶;命中注定之事: *They met their various ~s.* 他們遇到種種的禍福。*They left/abandoned the men to their ~.* 他們丢下那些人讓他們自生自滅。 **3** (*sing*) death; destruction; person's ultimate condition: (單)死亡;毀滅;人的結局: *go to one's ~;* 死; *decide a person's ~,* eg whether he shall be killed or allowed to live; 決定某人的生死; *meet one's ~,* be killed, die. 被殺;死。□ *vt* [VP17] (usu passive) destine: (通常用被動語態)命中注定;命該: *He was ~d to be hanged.* 他命該受絞刑。***It was ~d that...,*** F~ decided that...: 命中注定…: *It was ~d that we should fail.* 我們注定要失敗。

fate·ful /ˈfeɪtfl ; ˈfetfəl/ *adj* **1** controlled by, showing the power of, fate(1); important and decisive: 命中注定的;顯示命運之力量的;關係重大的;決定性的: *a ~ decision;* 關係重大的決定; *on this ~ day;* 在此決定性的一日; *these ~ events.* 這些重大事件。*When the judge pronounced the ~ words...,* eg sentence of death. 當法官宣佈決定命運的話時…(例如死刑宣判)。 **2** prophetic. 預言的。**~ly** /-fəlɪ ; -fəlɪ/ *adv*

fa·ther¹ /ˈfɑːðə(r) ; ˈfɑðɚ/ *n* **1** male parent: 父親: *You have been like a ~ to me.* 你一直像父親一般地對待我。*The property had been handed down from ~ to son for many generations.* 這財產父子相傳已經有很多代了。***The child is ~ to the man,*** (prov) One's childhood decides the way in which one will develop in later years. (諺)童年時代可決定一人之未來;從小看大。***The wish is ~ to the thought,*** (prov) We are likely to believe what we wish to be true. (諺) 願望爲思想之父(我們多半會把渴望之事信以爲眞)。**ˈ~-in-law** /ˈfɑːðər ɪn lɔː ; ˈfɑðərɪnˌlɔ/ *n* (*pl* ~s-in-law) ~ of one's wife or husband. 岳父;公公。**ˈ~ figure,** older man respected because of eg his concern for one's welfare. (因其關心一個人的幸福而)受人尊敬的長者。**2** (usu *pl*) ancestor(s): (通常用複數)祖先: *sleep with one's ~s,* be buried in the ancestral tomb or grave. 葬在祖墳。 **3** founder or first leader: 創始者;倡導者: *the F~s of the Church,* Christian writers of the first five centuries; 最初五世紀的基督教作家; *the Pilgrim F~s,* English Puritans who founded the colony of Plymouth, Massachusetts, USA in 1620; 美國的開國先驅(1620 年在美國麻薩諸塞州建立普里茅斯殖民地之英國清教徒); *the F~ of English poetry,* Chaucer. 英詩鼻祖(喬塞)。 **4** *Our (Heavenly) F~,* God. 我們的天父(上帝)。 **5** priest, esp one belonging to a religious order; head of a monastic house (⇨ brother for a monk): 神父;修道院長(修道士爲 brother): *the Holy F~,* the Pope. 教宗;羅馬教皇。 **6** title used in personifications:

用做擬人化名詞中之稱號: *F~ Christmas;* 聖誕老人; *F~ Time.* 時間老人。**'~·hood** /-hʊd ; -ˌhʊd/ *n* [U] state of being a ~. 做父親;父親的身份。**'~·land** /-lænd ; -ˌlænd/ *n* one's native country (*mother country* is the normal English usage). 祖國(mother country 是英語的標準用法)。**~·less** *adj* without a living ~ or a known ~. 喪父的;無父的。**~·ly** *adj* of or like a ~: 父親的;似父親的: *~ly love/smiles.* 父愛(慈愛如父的笑容)。

fa·ther² /'fɑːðə(r) ; 'fɑðɚ/ *vt* **1** [VP6A] be the originator of an idea, plan, etc. 創始(思想,計畫等); 創立。 **2** [VP6A] admit oneself to be the father or author of a child, book, etc. 承認是(某一孩子)的父親;承認是(某書等)的作者。 **3** [VP14] ***~ on/upon,*** fix the paternity of (a child), the authorship of or responsibility for (sth): 確定(一孩子)之父;確定…的作者或責任: *Please don't ~ this magazine article on me,* don't lead people to think that I wrote it. 請不要讓人認爲雜誌上這篇文章是我寫的。

fathom /'fæðəm ; 'fæðəm/ *n* measure (six feet or 1·8 metres) of depth of water: 噚(測水深之量度名,等於 6 呎或1.8公尺): *The ship sank in six ~s.* 該船沉下六噚。*The harbour is four ~(s) deep.* 港深四噚。□ *vt* [VP6A] find the depth of; get to the bottom of; comprehend: 測出…之深度;徹底了解;領悟: *I cannot ~ his meaning.* 我不能徹底了解他的意思。**~·less** *adj* too deep to ~. 深不可測的。

fa·tigue /fə'tiːg ; fə'tig/ *n* **1** [U] condition of being very tired: 疲勞;疲乏: *Several men dropped with ~ during the long march.* 有幾位士兵在長途行軍中因疲勞而倒下了。**2** [U] weakness in metals caused by prolonged stress. (金屬經長久應力後的)軟化;疲乏。 **3** [C] tiring task; non-military duty of soldiers, such as cleaning, cooking, etc. 令人勞累的工作;士兵所做的非軍事性勞動服務(如清掃,烹飪等)。**'~-party** *n* group of soldiers given such duties. 做勞動服務的一群士兵。□ *vt* [VP6A] cause ~ to: 使疲勞; 使勞累: *feeling ~d;* 感到疲勞; *fatiguing work.* 令人勞累的工作。

fat·ten /'fætn ; 'fætn/ *vt, vi* [VP6A, 15B, 2A, C] ***~ (up),*** make or become fat: 使肥;變肥: *~ cattle.* 將牛養肥。

fatty /'fætɪ ; 'fætɪ/ *adj* (-ier, -iest) like fat; consisting of fat: 像脂肪的;含脂肪的: *~ bacon.* 很肥的醃肉。

fatu·ous /'fætʃʊəs ; 'fætʃʊəs/ *adj* without purpose or sense; showing foolish self-satisfaction: 無謂的; 無意義的;愚昧而自滿的: *a ~ smile;* 傻笑; *a ~ young man.* 愚昧而自滿的年輕人。**~·ly** *adv* **fa·tu·ity** /fə'tjuːətɪ *US:* -'tuː- ; fə'tjuətɪ/ *n* [U] state of being ~; [C] (*pl* -ties) ~ remark, act, etc. 無意義;愚昧;自滿;昏庸;愚昧的言語,行動等。**~·ness** *n*

fau·cet /'fɔːsɪt ; 'fɔsɪt/ *n* (esp US) device (*tap* in GB) for controlling the outflow of liquid from a pipe or container. (尤美)(自來水管或容器之)龍頭(英國稱作 tap)。

faugh /fɔː ; fɔ (*spontaneously, as an explosive puffing sound*)/ *int* expression of disgust. 呸;嗤;啐(厭惡的表示)。

fault /fɔːlt ; fɔlt/ *n* **1** [C] sth that makes a person, thing, etc imperfect; defect; blemish; flaw: 缺點;缺陷;毛病;瑕疵: *She loves me in spite of all my ~s.* 雖然我有種種缺點,她仍然愛我。*Her only ~ is excessive shyness.* 她唯一的缺點是過份怕羞。*There is a ~ in the electrical system.* 電路系統有了毛病。***at ~,*** in the wrong, at a loss; in a puzzled or ignorant state: 出錯;茫然: *My memory was at ~.* 我記錯了;我忘記了。 ***to a ~,*** excessively: 過份地: *She is generous to a ~.* 她過份慷慨。***find ~ (with),*** complain (about): 抱怨;(對…)吹毛求疵;挑剔: *I have no ~ to find with your work.* 我對你的工作無可挑剔。*He's always finding ~.* 他總是吹毛求疵。Hence, 由此產生, **'~-finder; '~-finding.** **2** [U] responsibility for being wrong: 過失;過錯;咎: *Whose ~ is it that we are late?* 我們遲到是誰的過錯? *It's your own ~.* 這是你自已的錯。 *The ~ lies with you, not with me,* You are to blame. 錯在你,不在我。 **3** [C] thing wrongly done; (tennis, etc) ball wrongly served. 錯誤;謬誤;(網球等)發球失誤。 **4** [C] place where there is a break in the continuity of layers of rock, etc. 斷層。□ *vt* [VP6A] find ~ with: 挑剔;吹毛求疵: *No one could ~ his performance.* 沒有人能挑剔他的表演。 **~·less** *adj* **~·less·ly** *adv* **~y** *adj* having a ~ or ~s. 有缺點的;有過失的;有錯誤的。**~·ily** /-ɪlɪ ; -ɪlɪ/ *adv* in a ~y manner. 有缺點地;有過失地;有錯誤地。

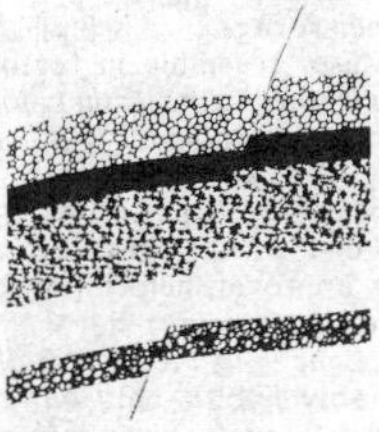

a fault in rock

a faun

faun /fɔːn ; fɔn/ *n* (Roman myth) one of a class of gods of the woods and fields, with a goat's horns and legs. (羅神)農牧神(生有山羊角和山羊腿)。

fauna /'fɔːnə ; 'fɔnə/ *n pl* all the animals of an area or an epoch: 某區域或時代的動物之總稱: *the ~ of E Africa.* 東非的動物。

faux pas /ˌfəʊ 'pɑː ; 'fo'pɑ/ *n* (F) (*pl* unchanged) indiscreet action, remark, etc esp a social blunder. (法)(複數不變)不謹愼的行爲,言語等(尤指觸犯社會習俗者);失禮;失言。

fa·vour¹ (US = **fa·vor**) /'feɪvə(r) ; 'fevɚ/ *n* **1** [U] friendly regard; willingness to help, protect, be kind to: 關切;愛護;恩寵: *win a person's ~;* 獲某人的好感或恩寵; *look on a plan with ~,* approve of it. 贊成一計畫。***be/stand high in sb's ~,*** be well regarded by him. 甚受某人的關切或尊重。***be in/out of ~ (with sb),*** have/not have his friendly regard, etc. 受(失去)某人的關切或尊重。***find/lose ~ with sb/in sb's eyes,*** win/lose sb's ~. 邀寵(失寵)於某人; 得到(失去) 某人的歡心。**2** [U] aid; support. 幫助;支持。***in ~ of,*** **(a)** in sympathy with; on the side of: 贊成;支持: *Was he in ~ of votes for women?* 他贊成婦女有選舉權嗎? **(b)** on behalf of; to the advantage or account of: 爲…的利益;有利於;支付給: *Cheques should be drawn in ~ of the Society, not in ~ of the Treasurer.* 支票應開給會社,不應開給會計員。***in sb's ~,*** to the advantage of: 對…有利: *The exchange rate is in our ~,* will benefit us when we change money. 兌換率對我們有利。 **3** [U] treatment that is too generous, lenient; partiality: 偏袒;偏愛: *He obtained his position more by ~ than by merit or ability.* 他靠別人的偏愛而非靠自己的長處或能力謀得那個職位。***without fear or ~,*** with impartial justice. 大公無私。 **4** [C] act of kindness: 善行;恩惠: *May I ask a ~ of you,* ask you to do sth for me? 我可以請你幫忙嗎? *I would consider it a ~ if you would answer promptly.* 若蒙早日賜覆則不勝感激。***do sb a ~; do a ~ for sb,*** do sth to help sb: 幫助某人: *Do me a ~—turn the radio down while I'm on the phone, will you?* 幫個忙 — 在我打電話時把收音機轉小聲一點好嗎? **5** [C] ornament or decoration, eg a badge, knot of ribbon, given or worn as a sign of favour. (贈與或佩戴以示愛護或支持的)裝飾物(例如徽章,花結等);紀念品;紀念章。

fa·vour² (US = **fa·vor**) /'feɪvə(r) ; 'fevɚ/ *vt* **1** [VP6A] show favour to; support: 關照;愛護;支持: *Fortune ~s the brave.* 命運愛護勇者。 **2** [VP6A] treat with partiality; show more favour to one person, group, etc than to another: 偏愛;偏袒: *A* *teacher should not ~ any of his pupils.* 教師不應偏愛任何學生。***most ~ed nation clause,*** clause (in a commercial treaty) agreeing that a nation shall be accorded the lowest scale of import duties. 最惠國條款(通商條約中,給予某一國家最低進口稅的商業條款)。 **3** [VP14] **~ *sb with sth,*** (old use, or formal) oblige; do something for: (舊用法或正式用語)賜助;爲某人做某事: *Will you ~ me with an interview?* 請准我謁見你好嗎? *Miss Sharp will now ~ us with a song,* will sing for us. 夏浦小姐現在願意爲我們唱一支歌。 **4** [VP6A] (of circumstances) make possible or easy: (指情況)便於;使順利: *The weather ~ed our voyage.* 天氣使我們的航行順利。 **5** [VP6A] (old use) resemble in features: (舊用法)容貌像;肖: *The child ~s its father,* looks more like its father than its mother. 這孩子的面貌像他父親。 **ˌill/ˌwell-'~ed** *adj* having an unpleasing/pleasing appearance. 容貌醜陋(漂亮)的。

fa·vour·able (US = **-vor-**) /ˈfeɪvərəbl ; ˈfevərəbl/ *adj* giving or showing approval; helpful: 贊成的;有幫助的: *a ~ report on one's work;* 贊許某人工作的報告; *~ winds.* 順風。*Is he ~ to the proposal?* 他贊成這建議嗎? **fa·vour·ably** /-əblɪ ; -əblɪ/ *adv* in a ~ manner: 贊成地;有助地: *speak favourably of a plan;* 贊成一計畫; *look favourably on sb.* 贊許地望着某人。

fa·vour·ite (US = **-vor-**) /ˈfeɪvərɪt ; ˈfevərɪt/ *n* **1** person or thing preferred above all others: 最受喜愛的人或物: *He is a ~ with his uncle/a ~ of his uncle's/his uncle's ~.* 他是他伯父最喜歡的人。*This book is a great ~ of mine.* 這本書是我最喜歡讀的。 **2 the ~,** (racing) the horse, etc generally expected to win: (競賽)咸認會獲勝的馬等;熱門馬;紅選手: *back the ~,* bet money on it. 下賭注於熱門馬。*The ~ came in third.* 咸認會獲勝的馬得到第三名。**3** person who receives too much favour, is given unfair advantages. 寵兒;得寵者。□ *attrib adj* best liked: 最受喜愛的: *He is his uncle's ~ nephew.* 他是他伯父最喜歡的姪兒。*What is your ~ colour?* 你最喜歡什麼顏色? **fa·vour·it·ism** (US = **-vor-**) /-ɪzəm ; -ˌɪzəm/ *n* [U] (practice of) having ~s(3). 偏愛;偏袒;循私。

fawn¹ /fɔːn ; fɔn/ *n* **1** young fallow deer less than one year old. 麑;未滿一歲的梅花鹿。 **2** light yellowish brown. 淺黃褐色(的)。

fawn² /fɔːn ; fɔn/ *vi* [VP2A, 3A] **~ *(on),*** **1** (of dogs) show pleasure and affection by jumping about, tail-wagging, etc. (指狗)(以跳來跳去,搖動尾巴的方式)表示快樂及感情。 **2** (of persons) try to win sb's favour by servile behaviour, flattery, etc: (指人)諂媚;奉承;巴結: *~ on a rich relative.* 巴結一富有的親戚。

fe·alty /ˈfiːəltɪ ; ˈfiəltɪ/ *n* (*pl* -ties) (in feudal times) tenant's or vassal's (acknowledgement of) fidelity to his lord: (封建時期家臣對領主之)效忠: *do/make/swear ~ (to* one's lord, *for* one's land); (對領主,爲領地)表示(宣誓)效忠; *take an oath of ~.* 宣誓效忠。

fear¹ /fɪə(r) ; fɪr/ *n* **1** [C, U] feeling caused by the nearness or possibility of danger or evil: 恐懼;懼怕: *They stood there in ~ and trembling,* frightened and shaking. 他們站在那裏嚇得發抖。*He was overcome with/by ~.* 他嚇壞了。*The thief passed the day in ~ of discovery.* 那賊在懼怕被人發覺的情況下度過了一天。*Grave ~s are felt for the safety of the missing climbers.* 對失踪的登山者的安全極爲擔心。*A sudden ~ came over him.* 他突然感到恐懼。*He obeyed from ~.* 他由於畏懼而服從。*He was unable to speak for ~.* 他嚇得說不出話來了。***for ~ of,*** because of anxiety about: 惟恐;生怕: *She asked us not to be noisy, for ~ of waking the baby.* 她請我們不要吵,因爲怕吵醒了嬰兒。***for ~ (that/lest). . . ,*** in order that. . . should not occur: 惟恐;以免: *I daren't tell you what he did, for ~ (that/lest) he should be angry with me.* 我不敢將他所做的事告訴你,因爲怕他對我發脾氣。 **2** [U] **~ *of,*** anxiety for the safety of: 擔憂;憂慮: *He is in ~ of his life.* 他爲他的生命擔憂。 **3** [U] likelihood: 可能性: *There's not much ~ of my losing the money.* 我失去這筆錢的可能性不大。*No ~!* (colloq) Certainly not! (俗)一定不會! **4** [U] dread and reverence: 敬畏: *the ~ of God.* 對上帝的敬畏。 **~·ful** /-fl ; -fəl/ *adj* **1** causing ~; terrible: 可怕的;可怖的: *a ~ful railway accident;* 火車慘禍; (colloq) annoying; very great: (俗)討厭的;非常的: *What a ~ful mess!* 簡直是一塌糊塗! **2** frightened; apprehensive: 受驚的;懼怕的: *~ful of wakening sb;* 怕吵醒某人; *~ful that/lest the baby should wake up.* 恐怕將嬰兒吵醒。 **~·fully** /-fəlɪ ; -fəlɪ/ *adv* **~·ful·ness** *n* **~·less** *adj* without ~: 無畏的;不怕的: *~less of the consequences.* 不計後果。 **~·less·ly** *adv* **~·less·ness** *n* **~·some** /ˈfɪəsəm ; ˈfɪrsəm/ *adj* (usu jokingly) frightening in appearance: (通常作戲謔語)外貌可怖的: *a ~some apparition.* 猙獰的幽靈。

fear² /fɪə(r) ; fɪr/ *vt, vi* **1** [VP6A, C] feel fear of, be afraid of: 懼怕;害怕: *~ death.* 怕死。*These men are not to be ~ed.* 這些人並不可怕。 **2** [VP2A, 4A] feel fear; be afraid; hesitate: 感到恐懼;猶豫: *Never ~!* Don't be afraid/Don't worry! 不要怕!放心罷! *She ~ed to speak in his presence.* 她怕在他的面前說話。*He did not ~ to die.* 他不怕死。 **3** [VP 3A] **~ *for,*** feel anxiety about: 擔心;憂慮: *We ~ed for his life/safety.* 我們擔心他的生死(安全)。 **4** [VP6A, 9] have an uneasy feeling or anticipation of: 擔憂: *~ the worst,* be afraid that the worst has happened or will happen. 擔心最壞的情況已經或會發生。*I ~ (that) he has failed.* 我擔心他已失敗了。*'Will he get well?'—'I ~ not.'* '他會痊癒嗎?'—'恐怕不會了。' *'Is he going to die?'—'I ~ so.'* '他會死去嗎?'—'恐怕會的。' **5** [VP6A] regard with awe and reverence: 敬畏: *F~ God and honour the Queen.* 敬畏上帝尊敬女王。

feas·ible /ˈfiːzəbl ; ˈfizəbl/ *adj* **1** that can be done: 可做的;可實行的;可能的: *The reconstruction of the destroyed town is ~,* We can, if we choose, do it. 重建這個毀壞的市鎮是可以做得到的。 **2** (colloq) that is convenient or plausible; that can be believed: (俗)方便的;似乎有理的;可信的: *His story sounds ~,* may be true. 他的故事可能是眞的。**feasi·bil·ity** /ˌfiːzəˈbɪlətɪ ; ˌfizəˈbɪlətɪ/ *n*

feast /fiːst ; fist/ *n* **1 '~(-day),** religious anniversary or festival, eg Christmas or Easter. 宗教節日或節期(例如聖誕節或復活節)。⇨ also movable. **2** splendid meal with many good things to eat and drink; (fig) sth that pleases the mind or senses: 宴會;盛宴;(喻)賞心悅目之事物: *a ~ of colours and sounds.* 賞心悅目的顏色和聲音。□ *vt, vi* **1** [VP6A,2A, B] take part in a ~; give a ~ to; pass (time) in ~ing: 宴樂;款宴;以宴樂消磨(時間): *~ one's friends;* 款宴朋友; *~ all evening.* 整晚宴樂。*He sat there ~ing (himself).* 他坐在那裏大吃大喝。 **2** [VP14] **~ *on,*** give sensuous pleasure to: 給予感官上的愉快;使享受: *~ one's eyes on beauty.* 飽覽美色。

feat /fiːt ; fit/ *n* sth difficult well done, esp sth showing skill, strength or daring: 技藝;武藝;英勇事績;偉績: *brilliant ~s of engineering;* 工程上的偉績; *perform ~s of valour.* 表演勇敢的技藝。

feather¹ /ˈfeðə(r) ; ˈfɛðə/ *n* one of the light coverings that grow from a bird's skin. 羽毛。⇨ the illus at bird, prey, rare, water. 參看 bird, prey, rare, water 之插圖。***a '~ in one's cap,*** sth one may justly be proud of. 的確值得驕傲的事物。***as light as a ~,*** very light indeed. 輕若羽毛。***in full/high ~,*** in high spirits. 意氣揚揚;精神抖擻;高興。***birds of a ~ (flock together),*** people of the same sort (will be found together). 同類的人(物以類聚);一丘之貉。***show the white ~,*** show fear. 示弱;膽怯。 **ˌ~-'bed** *n* mattress stuffed with ~s. 羽毛牀墊。□ *vt* (-dd-) pamper by giving generous help; make things easy for: 給予大量補助;使方便;

使順利: ~-*bed the farmers,* eg by subsidizing them. 給予農民補助。 ˌ~-ˈ**brained** *adj* empty-headed; flighty. 愚笨的;無頭腦的;輕浮的。ˈ~•**weight** *n* (esp) boxer weighing between 118 and 126 lb (or 53·5 to 57 kg). (尤指)羽量級拳擊手(體重在118至126磅或53·5至57公斤間者)。~**y** *adj* light and soft like ~s: 如羽毛的;輕而軟的: ~*y snow.* 羽毛似的雪片。

feather² /ˈfeðə(r) ; ˈfɛðɚ/ *vt* [VP6A] **1** supply with feathers: 裝以羽毛;飾以羽毛: ~ *an arrow.* 將羽毛裝在箭上。~ ***one's nest,*** make things comfortable for oneself; enrich oneself. 使自己生活舒適;飽私囊。 **2** ~ *one's oar,* (rowing) turn it so as to pass flat along the surface of the water. (划船)放平槳面。

fea•ture /ˈfiːtʃə(r) ; ˈfitʃɚ/ *n* [C] **1** one of the named parts of the face: 面貌的一部分(口,鼻等): *Her eyes are her best ~.* 她的面貌最好的一部分是眼睛。 **2** (*pl*) the face as a whole: (複)容貌;面貌;相貌: *a man of handsome ~s.* 相貌英俊的男子。 **3** characteristic or striking part: 特色;特徵: *the geographical ~s of a district,* eg mountains, lakes; 一地區地理上的特徵(例如山,湖); *unusual ~s in a political programme.* 政綱中不平常的特點。 **4** (often attrib) prominent article or subject in a newspaper; full-length film in a cinema programme, etc: (常作形容用法)(報紙上的)特寫;特別報導;(電影節目中之)正片;長片(等): *a newspaper that makes a ~ of* (= gives special prominence to) *sport;* 特別注重體育新聞的報紙; *a two-~ programme,* ie with two long films. 有兩部長片的節目。□ *vt* [VP6A] be a ~(3) of; make (sb or sth) a ~(3, 4) of; have a prominent part for: 爲…之特色;使(人或物)爲…之特色;特載;特登: *a film that ~s a new French actress.* 由法國新女星主演的一部影片。 ~•**less** *adj* uninteresting; with no obvious ~s(3). 無趣味的;平淡無奇的。

feb•rile /ˈfiːbraɪl ; ˈfibrəl/ *adj* of fever; feverish. 發燒的;熱病的。

Feb•ru•ary /ˈfebrʊərɪ *US:* -ʊerɪ ; ˈfɛbrʊˌɛrɪ/ *n* the second month of the year. 二月。

feces ⇨ faeces.

feck•less /ˈfeklɪs ; ˈfɛklɪs/ *adj* futile; inefficient; irresponsible. 無用的;無能力的;不負責任的。~•**ly** *adv* ~•**ness** *n*

fec•und /ˈfiːkənd *US* ˈfek-; ˈfikənd/ *adj* prolific, fertile. 多產的;豐饒的。~•**ity** /fɪˈkʌndətɪ ; fɪˈkʌndətɪ/ *n* [U] fertility; productiveness. 豐饒;多產。

fed *pt, pp* of feed.

fed•er•al /ˈfedərəl ; ˈfɛdərəl/ *adj* **1** of, based upon, federation: 聯邦制的;基於聯邦制的: *In the USA foreign policy is decided by the ~* (ie central) *government, and ~ laws are made by Congress.* 美國外交政策取決於聯邦政府,聯邦法律由國會制定。**F~ Bureau of Investigation** (abbr 略作 FBI), (US) department which is responsible for investigating violations of ~ law and safeguarding national security. (美)聯邦調查局。⇨ state¹(2). **2** relating to, supporting, central (as distinct from individual State) government. 關於聯邦政府的;擁護聯邦政府的。 ~•**ist** /ˈfedərəlɪst ; ˈfɛdərəlɪst/ *n* supporter of ~ union or power. 擁護聯邦主義者。 ~•**ism** /-ɪzəm ; -ˌɪzəm/ *n*

fed•er•ate /ˈfedəreɪt ; ˈfɛdəˌret/ *vt, vi* [VP6A, 2A] (of States, societies, organizations) combine, unite, into a federation. (指州,社會,團體)聯合;組成聯邦;聯盟。

fed•er•ation /ˌfedəˈreɪʃn ; ˌfɛdəˈreʃən/ *n* **1** [C] political system in which States control most of their internal affairs but leave foreign affairs, defence, etc to the central (Federal) government. 聯邦制(大部份內政由各州或邦自理,外交、國防等由聯邦政府處理的政治制度)。 **2** [C] such a union of States, eg the US; similar union of societies, trade unions, etc. 聯邦政府(例如美國者);(社團,工會等之)聯合會。 **3** [U] act of federating. 組成聯邦政府;聯盟。

fee /fiː ; fi/ *n* **1** [C] charge or payment for professional advice or services, eg private teachers, doctors, lawyers, surveyors; entrance money for an examination, club, etc. 費(例如私人教師,醫生,律師,測量員等所收的費用);報名費;會費(等)。 **2** [U] (legal) inherited estate: (法律)繼承的不動產: *land held in fee simple/fee tail,* with the right to pass it to any class of heirs/one particular class of heirs.不限定繼承人身份的土地(限定繼承人身份的土地)。⇨ entail. □ *vt* [VP6A] pay a fee to, engage for a fee: 繳費給;付費與: *fee a barrister.* 繳費給律師。

feeble /ˈfiːbl ; ˈfibl̩/ *adj* weak; faint; without energy: 衰弱的;虛弱的;無力的: *a ~ old man;* 衰弱的老人; *a ~ cry/argument.* 低弱的呼喊(無力的議論)。*His pulse was very ~.* 他的脈搏十分微弱。 ~•**minded** /-ˈmaɪndɪd ; -ˈmaɪndɪd/ *adj* subnormal in intelligence. 低能的。**feebly** /ˈfiːblɪ ; ˈfiblɪ/ *adv* ~•**ness** *n*

feed¹ /fiːd ; fid/ *n* **1** [C] (chiefly of animals and babies; jokingly of persons) meal: (主要指動物和嬰兒;指人,爲詼諧語)一頓;一餐: *We stopped to let the horses have a ~.* 我們停下來讓馬吃一頓。 **2** [U] food for animals: 飼料: *There isn't enough ~ left for the hens.* 母鷄的飼料不够了。 **3** [C] pipe, channel, etc through which material is carried to a machine; [U] material supplied. 輸送原料至機器的管子,溝槽等;進給管;進給槽;供給的原料。 ˈ~•**back** *n* [U] **1** return of part of the output of a system to its source (so as to modify it). 反饋(將部分產品送回原製作處,以作修正);回授。 **2** (colloq) information, etc (about a product) given by the user to the supplier, maker, etc; response: (俗)使用者供給供應者或製造者(有關某產品)的資料;反應: *interesting ~back via the market research department.* 經市場研究部門轉來的有趣的資料。

feed² /fiːd ; fid/ *vt, vi* (*pt, pp* fed /fed ; fɛd/) **1** [VP 6A, 14] ~ ***(on),*** give food to: 給予食物;餵: *Have the pigs been fed yet?* 猪餵過沒有? *Have you fed the chickens?* 你餵過鷄沒有? *What do you ~ your dog on,* What kind of food do you give it? 你用什麼餵你的狗? ~ ***oneself,*** put food into the mouth: 自己吃東西(不經他人餵): *The baby can't ~ itself yet.* 這嬰孩還不會自己吃東西。[VP15B] ~ ***up,*** give extra food to, give nourishing food to: 給與額外食物;給與有營養的食物: *There are hundreds of poor children there who need ~ing up.* 那裡有幾百個貧苦的孩子需要給與營養食物。 ***be fed up (with),*** (fig, sl) have had too much (of); be discontented (with): (喻,俚)因多而厭煩;不滿: *I'm fed up with your grumbling.* 我聽够了你的怨言。ˈ~•**ing-bottle** *n* bottle from which hand-fed infants are given milk, etc. 奶瓶。 **2** [VP14] ~ ***to,*** give to as food: 以…作爲食物餵養: ~ *oats to horses.* 以燕麥餵馬。*I wouldn't ~ that stinking meat to my dog.* 我不願用那臭肉餵我的狗。 **3** [VP2A, C] (chiefly of animals, colloq or hum of persons) eat: (主要指動物;指人,爲口語或詼諧語) 吃;食: *The cows were ~ing in the meadows.* 牛在草地上吃草。*Have you fed yet?* 你吃過飯沒有? **4** [VP3A] ~ ***on,*** take as food: 以…爲食: *Cattle ~ chiefly on grass.* 牛主要以草爲食。 **5** [VP6A, 15A] supply with material; supply (material) to: 供以原料;供(原料)給: *This moving belt ~s the machine with raw material/~s raw material into the machine.* 這轉動的皮帶輸送原料到機器裏。*The lake is fed by two rivers.* 這湖的水是由兩條河注入的。

feeder /ˈfiːdə(r) ; ˈfidɚ/ *n* [C] **1** (of plants and animals, with *adjj*) one that feeds: (指動植物,與形容詞連用)食者: *This plant is a gross ~,* needs much manure. 這植物需要大量肥料。 **2** child's feeding-bottle or bib. 奶瓶;圍嘴。 **3** (often attrib) branch railway line, airline, canal, etc linking outlying areas with the main line, etc. (常作形容用法)(鐵路,航空線,運河等之)支線。

feel¹ /fiːl ; fil/ *n* (*sing* only) (僅用單數) **1 the ~,** the sense of touch: 觸覺: *rough/smooth, etc to the ~,* when touched or felt. 摸起來粗糙(平滑等)。

2 the ~, the sensation characteristic of sth when touching or being touched: 觸摸或被觸摸時的感覺;觸覺: *You can tell it's silk by the ~.* 你摸一摸就知道是綢子。*The monk didn't like the ~ of the hair shirt they gave him.* 那修道士不喜歡他們送給他的那件毛布襯衫摸起來的感覺。 **3** act of feeling: 觸摸: *Let me have a ~.* 讓我摸摸看。

feel² /fi:l ; fil/ *vt, vi* (*pt, pp* felt /felt ; fɛlt/) **1** [VP6A, 10] (try to) learn about, explore, by touching, holding in the hands, etc: 觸試;摸摸看;由觸而得知: *Blind persons can often recognize objects by ~ing them.* 盲人常能憑觸摸辨識物體。*The doctor felt my pulse.* 醫生診我的脈。*Just ~ the weight of this box!* 試試看這箱子有多麼重! *F~ whether there are any bones broken.* 摸摸看有沒有骨頭斷了。**~ one's way, (a)** go forward carefully, as in the dark, or as a blind man does. 摸索着走。**(b)** be cautious in dealing with sth: 謹慎處事: *They were ~ing their way towards an agreement.* 他們正謹慎地試著達成一項協議。 **2** [VP2C, 3A] **~ (about) (for),** search with the hand(s) (or the feet, a stick, etc): (用手,足,杖等)摸索: *He was ~ing about in the dark for the electric-light switch.* 他在黑暗中摸索著找電燈開關。*He felt in his pocket for a penny.* 他在口袋裏摸索,找一個辨士。*He felt along the wall for the door.* 他沿着牆摸索著找門。 **3** [VP 6A, 18A, 19A] be aware of (through contact): (由接觸)感到: *I can ~ a nail in my shoe.* 我感到鞋裡有一根釘子。*I felt something crawl(ing) up my arm.* 我感到有東西在我臂上往上爬。 **4** [VP6A, 18A, 19A] be aware of, perceive (not through contact): (非由接觸)感到;覺得: *Did you ~ the earthquake?* 你感到地震了嗎? *He felt his heart beating wildly.* 他覺得他的心在猛跳。*She felt apprehension stealing over her.* 她感到恐懼襲上心頭。[VP15B] **~ sb out,** try cautiously to learn the opinion of him: 小心打聽某人的意見: *I'll ~ out the members of the committee.* 我會小心地把那些委員的意見打聽出來。 **5** [VP2D, C] be consciously; be in a certain physical, moral or emotional state: 感覺;覺得;處於身體,精神或情緒的某種狀態: *~ cold/hungry/comfortable/sad/happy, etc.* 感覺冷(餓,舒服,悲哀,快樂等)。*How are you ~ing today?* 你今天覺得怎麼樣? *You will ~ better after a night's sleep.* 經過一夜的睡眠你會覺得好些。*She doesn't ~ (quite) herself today,* is not as well, calm, self-possessed, etc as usual. 她今天感到不舒服(心慌,不安等)。*He ~s confident of success.* 他對成功感到有信心。*He felt cheated.* 他感到受騙了。*We don't ~ bound* (= obliged) *to accept this offer.* 我們並不覺得一定要接受這項提議。*Please ~ free* (= consider yourself welcome) *to call on us whenever you like.* 請隨時來玩。 **6** [VP2A] be capable of sensation: 能感覺;有知覺: *The dead cannot ~.* 死人不會有知覺。 **7** [VP3A] **~ for/with,** have sympathy (*with*), compassion (*for*): 同情(與 with 連用);憐憫(與 for 連用): *I ~ with you in your sorrow.* 我同情你的煩惱。*I ~ for you.* 我憐憫你。 **8 ~ as if/though,** have, give, the impression that: 彷彿覺得: *She felt as if her head were splitting.* 她彷彿覺得她的頭要裂開了。*Her head felt as if it were splitting.* 她的頭好像要裂開似的。 **9** [VP2D] give or produce the impression of being: 給與或產生…的印象: *Your hands ~ cold.* 你的手摸起來是冷的。*How does it ~ to be home again after twenty years abroad?* 出國二十年再回家園是一種什麼感覺? *This new shirt doesn't ~ right.* 這件新襯衫不太合身。 **10 '~ like,** (of persons) be in the mood for: (指人)欲;想要: *I don't ~ like (eating) a big meal now.* 我現在不想吃大餐。*We'll go for a walk if you ~ like it.* 如果你願意,我們去散散步。**~ equal to;** (colloq) (俗) **~ up to,** be well enough to, be capable of: 能擔任;有能力做: *I don't ~ equal to the task.* 我不能勝任這工作。*He doesn't ~ up to a long walk.* 他沒有走遠路的力氣了。 **11** [VP6A, C] be sensitive to; suffer because of: 對…敏感;由於…而受苦: *He doesn't ~ the heat at all,* is not troubled by it. 他一點也不怕熱。*He felt the insult keenly.* 那侮辱深深地傷害了他。*She will ~* (= be saddened by) *having to sell up her old home.* 必須賣掉她的老家會使她難過。 **12** [VP9, 25] have the idea; be of the opinion: 想到;以爲: *He felt the plan to be unwise/felt that the plan was unwise.* 他認爲這計畫是不智的。*We all felt that our luck was about to turn.* 我們都以爲我們的運氣就要轉變了。*He felt in his bones that he would succeed.* 他確信他會成功。 **13** [VP6A] appreciate; understand properly: 察知;認識清楚: *We all felt the force of his arguments.* 我們都覺得他的議論很有力。*Don't you ~ the beauty of this landscape?* 你不覺得這風景很美嗎?

feeler /'fi:lə(r) ; 'filə/ *n* [C] **1** organ, eg an antenna, in certain animals for testing things by touch. (某些動物的)觸鬚;觸毛;觸角。⇨ the illus at insect. 參看 insect 之插圖。 **2** proposal, suggestion, made to test the opinions or feelings of others, before one states one's own views. 試探性的建議。 ***put out ~s/a ~,*** test the views of others, by discreet inquiries. 提出試探性的建議。

feel·ing /'fi:lɪŋ ; 'filɪŋ/ *n* **1** [U] power and capacity to feel: 知覺: *He had lost all ~ in his legs.* 他的雙腿全失去了知覺。 **2** [C] physical or mental awareness; emotion: 感覺;感觸;情緒: *a ~ of hunger/well-being/discomfort/gratitude/joy;* 飢餓(幸福,不適,感激,快樂)的感覺; idea or belief not based wholly on reason: 預感: *a ~ of danger/that something dreadful was about to happen;* 感到危險(可怕的事即將發生); (usu *sing*) general opinion: (通常用單數)一般人的意見: *The ~ of the meeting* (= The opinion of the majority) *was against the proposal.* 與會的人大都反對此項提議。 **3** (*pl*) emotional side of a person's nature (contrasted with the intellect): (複)感情(與 intellect 相對): *Have I hurt your ~s,* offended you? 我傷了你的感情嗎? *The speaker appealed to the ~s of his audience rather than to their reason.* 那演說者訴諸聽衆的感情而非他們的理智。*No hard ~s, I hope!* ie no bitterness, no ill will. 希望沒有惡意(或怨恨)! **4** [U] sympathy; understanding: 同情;了解: *He doesn't show much ~ for the sufferings of others.* 他對於別人的痛苦不十分同情。*She's a woman of ~.* 她是個富有同情心的女子。 **good ~,** friendliness. 好感。 **ill/bad ~,** bitterness. 惡感。 **5** [C, U] excitement of mind, esp of enmity and resentment: 激動;(尤指)憤激;憤慨: *His speech aroused strong ~(s) on all sides.* 他的演說激起各方面强烈的憤慨。*F~ over the dismissal ran high,* There was much bitterness. 關於該一撤職事件,人們甚表憤慨。 **6** [U] taste and understanding; sensibility: 鑑賞力;感受力: *He hasn't much ~ for natural beauty.* 他對自然界的美缺少鑑賞力。*She plays the piano with ~.* 她奏鋼琴能表現出感受力。 □ *adj* sympathetic; showing emotion: 有同情心的;表現感情的: *a ~ remark.* 同情的話。 **~·ly** *adv* so as to express ~: 表現感情地: *speak ~ly on a subject.* 懇切地談論一個問題。

feet /fi:t ; fit/ *n pl* of foot.

feign /feɪn ; fen/ *vt* **1** [VP6A, 9] pretend: 假裝: *~ illness/indifference/death;* 裝病(佯作不關心;詐死); *~ that one is mad;* 裝瘋; *~ed modesty.* 假裝的謙恭。 **2** [VP6A] invent: 虛構;杜撰: *~ an excuse.* 捏造一藉口。

feint /feɪnt ; fent/ *n* **1** pretence (the more usu word): 假裝 (pretence 較常用): *make a ~ of doing sth.* 假裝做某事。 **2** sham attack (in war and boxing) in one place to draw attention away from the place where the real attack is made. (作戰或拳擊)聲東擊西。 □ *vi* [VP2A, 3A] make a *~ at/upon/against.* 假裝;聲東擊西(與 at, upon, against 連用)。

feld·spar, fel·spar /'feldspɑ:(r), 'felspɑ:(r) ; 'fɛld,spɑr, 'fɛl-/ *n* [U] (kinds of) crystalline mineral rock. 長石。

fel·ici·tate /fəˈlɪsɪteɪt ; fəˈlɪsəˌtet/ *vt* [VP6A, 14] ~ ***sb (on/upon sth),*** (formal) congratulate. (正式用語)祝賀;道賀。**fel·ici·ta·tion** /fəˌlɪsɪˈteɪʃn ; fəˌlɪsəˈteʃən/ *n*

fel·ici·tous /fəˈlɪsɪtəs ; fəˈlɪsətəs/ *adj* (formal) (of words, remarks) well chosen. (正式用語)(指措辭)精選的;適當的。**~·ly** *adv*

fel·ic·ity /fəˈlɪsətɪ ; fəˈlɪsətɪ/ *n* (formal) (正式用語) **1** [U] great happiness or contentment. 幸福;滿足。 **2** [U] pleasing manner of speaking or writing: 言辭的巧妙:*express oneself with ~;* 巧妙地表達自己的意思; [C] (*pl* -ties) well-chosen expression or phrase. 精選的措辭;貼切的措辭。

fe·line /ˈfiːlaɪn ; ˈfilaɪn/ *adj* of or like a cat: 貓的;似貓的: *walk with ~ grace.* 輕巧地行走。

fell[1] *pt* of fall[2].

fell[2] /fel ; fɛl/ *adj* (poet) fierce, ruthless, terrible: (詩)兇猛的;殘忍的;可怕的: *a ~ disease;* 可怕的疾病; *with one ~ blow.* 以狠狠的一擊。

fell[3] /fel ; fɛl/ *n* animal's hide or skin with the hair. 獸皮;毛皮。

fell[4] /fel ; fɛl/ *n* stretch of rocky, bare moorland or bare hilly land (esp in N England): 一片荒地(尤指英格蘭北部者): *the Derbyshire F~s.* 德貝夏的荒野。

fell[5] /fel ; fɛl/ *vt* [VP6A] cause to fall; strike down; cut down (a tree): 使倒下;打倒;砍伐(樹木): *He ~ed his enemy with a single blow.* 他一拳將他的敵人打倒了。

fel·lah /ˈfelə ; ˈfɛlə/ *n* (*pl* ~in, ~een /ˌfeləˈhiːn ; ˌfɛləˈhin/) peasant (in Arab countries). (阿拉伯國家的)農夫。

fel·low /ˈfeləʊ ; ˈfɛlo/ *n* **1** (colloq) man or boy: (俗)人;男人或男孩;傢伙: *He's a pleasant ~.* 他是個和氣的人。*Poor ~!* 可憐的人! *A ~ must have a holiday occasionally* (used here for 'one' or 'I'). 人總得偶爾度度假。**2** (usu *pl*) comrade, companion: (通常用複數)夥友;同伴: *ˈschool ~s;* 同學; *ˈbed-~s;* 同床者;友伴; *~s in good fortune/misery.* 共安樂(共患難)的夥伴。***be ˌhail-~-well-ˈmet with sb,*** be (superficially or falsely) on friendly terms with him. (表面或僞裝)與某人友善。 **ˌ~-ˈfeeling** *n* [U] sympathy. 同情心。 **3** (attrib) of the same class, kind, etc: (形容用法)同階級的;同類的: *ˌ~ ˈcreatures;* 同類動物;人類; *ˌ~-ˈcitizen;* 同胞;同市人; *ˌ~-ˈcountryman,* person from the same country or nation. 同胞。**ˌ~-ˈtraveller** *n* **(a)** person travelling with one. 旅伴;同路人;同行人。**(b)** one who sympathizes with the aims of a political party (esp the Communist Party) but is not a member. 同情某一政黨而非黨員之人;(尤指)共產黨的同路人。**4** member of a learned society: 學術團體之會員: *F~ of the British Academy;* 英國學會會員; member of the governing body of some university colleges; incorporated graduate member of a college. 某些大學之校務委員會委員;大學的特別研究員。 **5** one of a pair: 一對中之一: *Here's one of my shoes, but where's its ~?* 這裏有我一隻鞋子,另一隻在哪裏?

fel·low·ship /ˈfeləʊʃɪp ; ˈfɛloˌʃɪp/ *n* **1** [U] friendly association; companionship: 友誼; 交情: *offer sb the hand of ~;* 向某人伸出友誼之手; *enjoy ~ with people;* 享受人們的友情; *~ in misfortune.* 患難時之交情。 **2** [C] number of persons associated together; group or society; [U] membership in such a group: 團體;會;會員資格或地位: *admitted to ~.* 被准許入會。 **3** [C] position of a college fellow(4). 大學校務委員會委員的地位;大學特別研究員的地位。

fel·ony /ˈfelənɪ ; ˈfɛlənɪ/ *n* (*pl* -nies) [C, U] major serious crime, eg murder, armed robbery, arson. 重罪(例如謀殺,持械搶劫,縱火)。⇨ misdemeanour. **felon** /ˈfelən ; ˈfɛlən/ *n* person guilty of ~. 重罪犯。**fel·oni·ous** /fɪˈləʊnɪəs ; fəˈlonɪəs/ *adj* criminal. 犯重罪的。

fel·spar ⇨ feldspar.

felt[1] *pt, pp* of feel[2].

felt[2] /felt ; fɛlt/ *n* [U] wool, hair or fur, compressed and rolled flat into a kind of cloth: 毛氈: (attrib) (形容用法) *~ hats/slippers.* 氈帽(拖鞋)。

fe·lucca /feˈlʌkə ; fəˈlʌkə/ *n* narrow Mediterranean coasting vessel with oars or sails or both. (地中海沿岸之)小船(用槳或帆,或兩者皆用)。

fe·male /ˈfiːmeɪl ; ˈfimel/ *adj* **1** of the sex that produces offspring: 女性的;雌性的: *a ~ child/dog;* 女孩(母狗); (of plants or their parts) fruit-bearing. (指植物或其部分)結果實的; 雌的; 有雌蕊的。 **2** of women: 婦女的: *~ suffrage;* 婦女選舉權; *~ workers.* 女工。 **3** (mech) having a hollow part designed to receive an inserted part, eg a plug. (機械)凹的;陰的。□ *n* ~ animal; (derog) ~ person. 雌獸;(貶)女人。⇨ male.

femi·nine /ˈfemənɪn ; ˈfɛmənɪn/ *adj* **1** of, like, suitable for, women: 婦女的;似婦女的;適於婦女的: *a ~ voice.* 女人似的聲音。**2** (gram) of the gender proper to the names of females: (文法)陰性的: *~ nouns and pronouns,* eg actress, lioness, she, her. 陰性的名詞和代名詞(例如 actress, lioness, she, her)。**fem·i·nin·ity** /ˌfeməˈnɪnətɪ ; ˌfɛməˈnɪnətɪ/ *n* [U] quality of being ~. 婦女的氣質。⇨ masculine.

fem·in·ism /ˈfemɪnɪzəm ; ˈfɛməˌnɪzəm/ *n* [U] movement for recognition of the claims of women for rights (legal, political, etc) equal to those possessed by men. 女權運動;男女平等主義。 ⇨ lib. **fem·in·ist** /-ɪst ; -ɪst/ *n* supporter of ~. 女權運動者;男女平等主義者。

fe·mur /ˈfiːmə(r) ; ˈfimɚ/ *n* (anat) thigh-bone. (解剖)股骨。⇨ the illus at skeleton. 參看 skeleton 之插圖。

fen /fen ; fɛn/ *n* area of low marshy land. 沼澤;沼地。**the Fens,** lowlying districts in Cambridgeshire and Lincolnshire. 英國劍橋郡和林肯郡之低窪地區。

fence[1] /fens ; fɛns/ *n* [C] barrier made of wooden or metal stakes or rails, or wire, esp one put round a field, garden, etc to keep animals from straying or to keep out intruders. 柵欄;圍牆;籬笆。 ***come down on one side or the other of the ~,*** give one's support to one side or the other. 支持一方。***come down on the right side of the ~,*** join the winner. 附和勝利的一方。***mend one's ~s,*** make peace. 謀和;談和。***sit/be on the ~,*** not commit oneself; wait to see where one can win most advantage. 騎牆;觀望。Hence, 由此產生, **(a) ˈ~-sit·ter** *n* person who does this. 騎牆份子;持觀望態度者。 **(b) ˈ~-sit·ting** *n* □ *vt* [VP6A, 15B] surround, divide, provide with a ~ or ~s: 圍以柵欄;圍以籬笆: *Farmers ~ their fields.* 農人用柵籬將田地圍起。*His land is ~d with barbed wire.* 他的土地由鐵絲網圍着。*The land is ~d in/round.* 這土地是用柵欄圍着的。 **fenc·ing** /ˈfensɪŋ ; ˈfɛnsɪŋ/ *n* [U] material for making ~s. 圍牆材料。

fence[2] /fens ; fɛns/ *vi* [VP2A, C, 3A] practise the art of fighting with long slender swords or foils; (fig) avoid giving a direct answer to a question(er): 鬬劍;擊劍;(喻)不做正面答覆;搪塞: *~ with a question.* 搪塞一問題。**fencer** *n* person who ~s. 鬬劍者;擊劍者。 **fenc·ing** /ˈfensɪŋ ; ˈfɛnsɪŋ/ *n* [U] art of fighting with swords. 劍術;擊劍。

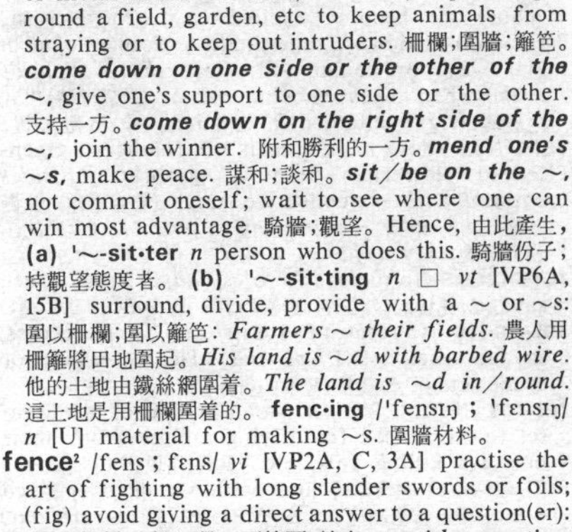

fencing

fence³ /fens ; fɛns/ *n* (sl) receiver of stolen goods; his place of business. (俚)收藏贓物者；買賣贓物者；買賣贓物之處。

fend /fend ; fɛnd/ *vt, vi* **1** [VP15B] ～ *off*, defend oneself from: 抵禦；抵擋：～ *off a blow*. 擋開一擊。**2** ～ *for oneself*, look after oneself: 照顧自己：*When his father died, Tom had to* ～ *for himslf.* 湯姆的父親死後，他必須自行謀生。*Most animals let their young* ～ *for themselves from an early age.* 大多數的動物讓牠們的幼仔從小就獨立生活。

fender /ˈfendə(r) ; ˈfɛndɚ/ *n* **1** metal frame bordering an open fireplace (to prevent burning coal, etc from rolling on to the floor). (防止爐炭滾落在地板上的)火爐欄杆。**2** (on the front of a vehicle, etc) strong bar, etc, used to lessen shock or damage in a collision. (車輛等前部之)擋板。**3** log of wood, heavy mass of rope, old rubber tyre etc hung on the side of a boat to prevent damage, eg when the boat comes alongside a wharf or another ship. 護舷材；碰墊(例如當船沿碼頭或另一船停靠時，爲避免碰損，繫於船側之木材或粗繩團)。**4** (US) (美) = *mudguard*, ⇨ mud.

fen·nel /ˈfenl ; ˈfɛnḷ/ *n* [U] yellow-flowered herb, used as a flavouring. 茴香(用來調味)。

feoff /fi:f ; fɛf/ *n* = fief.

fe·ral /ˈfɪərəl ; ˈfɪrəl/ *adj* wild; untamed; brutal. 野的；未馴的；野蠻的。

fer·ment¹ /ˈfɜ:ment ; ˈfɝmənt/ *n* **1** [C] substance, eg yeast, that causes other substances to ferment. 酵母；發酵劑。**2** *in a* ～, (fig) in a state of, eg social, political, excitement. (喩)在騷動中(例如在社會或政治方面)。

fer·ment² /fəˈment ; fɚˈmɛnt/ *vt, vi* [VP6A, 2A] **1** (cause to) undergo chemical changes through the action of organic bodies (esp yeast): (使)發酵：*Fruit juices* ～ *if they are kept a long time.* 果汁放置日久會發酵。*When wine is* ～*ed, it gives off bubbles of gas.* 酒發酵時發出氣泡。**2** (fig) (cause to) become excited. (喩)(使)激動；醞釀。**fer·men·ta·tion** /ˌfɜ:menˈteɪʃn ; ˌfɝmənˈteʃən/ *n* [U] ～ing or being ～ed: 發酵：*the* ～*ation of milk* (when cheese is being made); (做乳酪時)牛乳之發酵；(fig) excitement and unrest. (喩)激動；紛擾。

fern /fɜ:n ; fɝn/ *n* [C] sorts of feathery, green-leaved flowerless plant: 羊齒科植物：*hillsides covered with* ～ (collective *sing*) (集合單數)；長滿羊齒植物的山坡；～*s growing in pots.* 長在盆內的羊齒科植物。～**y** *adj*

fer·ocious /fəˈrəʊʃəs ; fəˈroʃəs/ *adj* fierce, cruel, savage. 兇猛的；殘忍的；野蠻的。～**·ly** *adv*

fer·oc·ity /fəˈrɒsətɪ ; fəˈrɑsətɪ/ *n* [U] fierceness; savage cruelty; [C] (*pl* -ties) fierce, savage or cruel act. 兇猛；殘暴；殘暴的行爲。

fer·ret /ˈferɪt ; ˈfɛrɪt/ *n* small animal of the weasel family, used for driving rabbits from their burrows, killing rats, etc. 雪貂(用以逐兎，捕鼠等)。□ *vt, vi* **1** [VP2A] hunt with ～s: 用雪貂行獵：*go* ～*ing*. 帶着雪貂出獵。**2** [VP15B, 2C] ～ *sth out;* ～ *about (for sth)*, discover by searching; search: 偵察；搜索：～ *out a secret;* 偵察一祕密；～ *about among old papers and books for sth lost.* 在舊報和書籍中搜尋(某物)。

fer·ro·con·crete /ˌferəʊˈkɒŋkri:t ; ˌfɛroˈkɑnkrit/ *n* [U] reinforced concrete. 鋼筋混凝土；鋼骨水泥。

fer·rous /ˈferəs ; ˈfɛrəs/ *adj* containing or relating to iron: 含有鐵的；關於鐵的：～ *chloride* (**$FeCl_2$**). 氯化亞鐵。

fer·rule /ˈferu:l *US:* ˈferəl ; ˈfɛrəl/ *n* metal ring or cap placed on the end of a stick (eg of an umbrella) or tube, to prevent splitting; band strengthening or forming a joint. (裝於傘把等長杖或管子上的)金屬箍或包頭；套圈；箍。

ferry /ˈferɪ ; ˈfɛrɪ/ *n* (*pl* -ries) [C] (place where there is a) boat, hovercraft or aircraft that carries people and goods across a river, channel, etc. 渡口；渡船；輸送人員貨物渡過河或海峽等的飛機。□ *vt, vi* [VP6A, 15A, B, 2A, C] take, go, across in a ～: 以船渡；用飛機輸送；乘船渡過；飛渡：～ *people／a boat across a river;* 渡人(小船)過河；*aircraft* ～*ing motor-cars between England and France.* 英法間輸送汽車的飛機。ˈ～**-boat** *n* ˈ～**-man** /-mən ; -mən/ (*pl* -men) *n*

fer·tile /ˈfɜ:taɪl *US:* ˈ-tl ; ˈfɝtḷ/ *adj* **1** (of land, plants, etc) producing much; (of a person, his mind, etc) full of ideas, plans, etc: (指土地，植物等)肥沃的；多產的；(指人，頭腦等)有才智的：～ *fields／soil;* 肥沃的土地(土壤)；*a* ～ *imagination.* 豐富的想像力。**2** able to produce fruit, young; capable of developing: 能結果實的；能生育的；能生長的：～ *seeds／eggs.* 能生長的種子(受精卵)。⇨ sterile. **fer·til·ity** /fəˈtɪlətɪ ; fɝˈtɪlətɪ/ *n* [U] state of being ～. 肥沃；多產；豐富；能結果實。

fer·til·ize /ˈfɜ:təlaɪz ; ˈfɝtḷˌaɪz/ *vt* [VP6A] make fertile or productive: 使肥沃；使多產：～ *the soil* (by using manure); 施肥於土壤；～ *flowers* (as bees do when they collect nectar). 使花受粉。**fer·ti·lizer** /-zə(r) ; -zɚ/ *n* [U] chemical plant food; artificial manure; [C] substance of this kind: 化學肥料；人造肥料；肥料：*Bonemeal and nitrates are common fertilizers.* 骨粉和硝酸塩是普通的肥料。**fer·ti·liz·ation** /ˌfɜ:təlaɪˈzeɪʃn *US:* -lɪˈz- ; ˌfɝtḷəˈzeʃən/ *n* [U] fertilizing or being ～d. 使肥沃；使多產；變爲肥沃；變爲多產。

fer·ule /ˈferu:l *US:* ˈferəl ; ˈfɛrəl/ *n* flat ruler for punishing children by striking them on the hand. (懲罰小孩的)戒尺。

fer·vent /ˈfɜ:vənt ; ˈfɝvənt/ *adj* **1** hot, glowing. 熱的；白熱的。**2** showing warmth of feeling; passionate: 熱烈的；熱情的：～ *love／hatred;* 熱烈的愛(强烈的恨)；*a* ～ *lover／admirer.* 熱情的愛人(景慕者)。～**·ly** *adv* **fer·vency** /ˈfɜ:vənsɪ ; ˈfɝvənsɪ/ *n*

fer·vid /ˈfɜ:vɪd ; ˈfɝvɪd/ *adj* fervent(2); spirited; showing earnest feeling: 熱烈的；熱心的；熱情的：*a* ～ *orator.* 激昂的演說者。～**·ly** *adv*

fer·vour (US = **-vor**) /ˈfɜ:və(r) ; ˈfɝvɚ/ *n* [U] strength or warmth of feeling; earnestness. 熱誠；熱心。

fes·tal /ˈfestl ; ˈfɛstḷ/ *adj* of a feast or festival; festive (the more usu word): 節日的；歡樂的(festive 較常用)：*a* ～ *occasion*, eg a wedding, a birthday party; 歡樂的場合(例如結婚，過生日)；～ *music.* 歡樂的音樂。

fes·ter /ˈfestə(r) ; ˈfɛstɚ/ *vi* [VP2A] **1** (of a cut or wound) fill with poisonous matter (pus): (指傷口)化膿；潰爛：*If the cut gets dirty, it will probably* ～. 如果傷口弄髒了，可能會化膿。**2** (fig) act like poison in the mind; become resentful, embittered: (喩)使人痛苦；使人氣憤；使人難過：*The insult* ～*ed in his mind.* 這侮辱使他心中痛苦。

fes·ti·val /ˈfestɪvl; ˈfɛstəvḷ/ *n* **1** (day or season for) rejoicing; public celebrations: 節日；節期；作樂；慶祝：*Christmas and Easter are Church* ～*s.* 聖誕節和復活節是教會的節日。**2** series of performances (of music, ballet, drama, etc) given periodically (usu once a year): (音樂，巴蕾舞，戲劇等之)節；季(通常每年一次)：*the Edinburgh F*～*;* 愛丁堡之戲劇季；*a jazz* ～. 爵士音樂節。**3** (attrib) festive; of a feast or feast-day. (形容用法)節日的；歡宴的。

fes·tive /ˈfestɪv ; ˈfɛstɪv/ *adj* of a feast or festival; joyous: 宴樂的；節日的；歡樂的：*a* ˈ～ *season*, eg Christmas; 歡樂的季節(例如聖誕節)；*the* ～ *board*, a table on which a feast is spread. 宴席。

fes·tiv·ity /feˈstɪvətɪ ; fɛsˈtɪvətɪ/ *n* (*pl* -ties) **1** [U] rejoicing; merry-making. 歡樂；宴樂。**2** (*pl*) festive, joyful events: (複)慶典；喜慶：*wedding festivities.* 結婚慶典。

fes·toon /feˈstu:n ; fɛsˈtun/ *n* [C] chain of flowers, leaves, ribbons, etc hanging in a curve or loop between two points, as a decoration. 花綵；垂花飾。□ *vt* [VP6A] make into, decorate with, ～s: 結成

花綵;飾以花綵: *a room ~ed with Christmas decorations.* 飾有聖誕花綵的房間。

fetch /fetʃ; fɛtʃ/ *vt, vi* **1** [VP6A, 15A, B, 13B, 12B] go for and bring back (sb or sth): 接來(人);取來(物): *F~ a doctor at once.* 立刻請位醫生來。*Please ~ the children from school.* 請到學校裏把孩子們接來。*The chair is in the garden; please ~ it in.* 椅子在花園裏,請將它搬進來。*Shall I ~ your coat for you/~ you your coat from the next room?* 要我去隔壁房間把你的外衣拿來嗎? ***~ and carry (for),*** be busy with small duties for; be a servant for: (替…)做雜事;(供…)差遣: *He expects his daughter to ~ and carry for him all day.* 他希望他的女兒終日供他差遣。 **2** [VP6A, 15A] cause to come out; draw forth: 使出來;使發出:*~ a deep sigh/a dreadful groan;* 發出深深的嘆息(可怕的呻吟); *~ tears to the eyes.* 使眼淚從眼中流出。 **3** [VP6A, 12B] (of goods) bring in; sell for (a price): (指貨物)售得(若干價錢): *These old books won't ~ (you) much.* 這些舊書賣不了多少錢。 **4** [VP12C] (colloq) deal, give (a blow) to: (俗)給予(打擊):*She ~ed me a slap across the face/a box on the ears.* 她打了我一耳光。**~·ing** *adj* (colloq) attractive, delightful: (俗)動人的;迷人的:*What a ~ing little hat!* 多麼漂亮的一頂小帽子!*What a ~ing smile!* 多麼迷人的一笑!

fête /feɪt; fet/ *n* (usu outdoor) festival or entertainment: (通常在戶外)慶祝會;遊樂會: *the village ~,* often one at which funds are raised. 村民遊樂會(常是募捐性質的)。**'~-day** *n* saint's-day. 聖徒紀念日;(天主教)祝名日;生日。⇨ saint(5). □ *vt* [VP6A] honour by entertaining; make a fuss of: 款待;熱烈歡迎: *The hero was ~d wherever he went.* 那英雄不論走到何處,均受到熱烈的款待。

fetid /'fetɪd; 'fɛtɪd/ *adj* stinking. 有惡臭的;臭的。

fet·ish /'fetɪʃ; 'fitɪʃ/ *n* **1** object worshipped by pagan people because they believe a spirit lives in it. 物神(認爲有神靈而受異教徒崇拜之物)。 **2** anything to which abnormal, excessive respect or attention is given; (colloq) obsession: 盲目崇拜物;過份受到注意之物;偶像;(俗)縈繞心頭之事物: *Some women make a ~ of clothes.* 有些婦女過於注意衣服。

fet·lock /'fetlɒk; 'fɛt,lɑk/ *n* (tuft of hair on a) horse's leg above and behind the hoof. 距毛(馬蹄上之叢毛);簇毛。⇨ the illus at domestic. 參看 domestic 之插圖。

fet·ter /'fetə(r); 'fɛtɚ/ *n* chain for the ankles of a prisoner or the leg of a horse; (fig, usu *pl*) sth that hinders progress. (犯人或馬之)足械; 脚鐐; (喻,通常用複數)障礙;羈絆。□ *vt* [VP6A] put in ~s or chains; (fig) restrain. 上以脚鐐;(喻)束縛;拘束。

fettle /'fetl; 'fɛtl̩/ *n* ***in fine/good ~,*** in good (physical) condition; in high spirits. 身體健壯; 精神奕奕。

fe·tus ⇨ foetus.

feud /fju:d; fjud/ *n* [C] bitter quarrel between two persons, families or groups, over a long period of time. (二人,家族或團體間之)長期不和;夙怨。

feu·dal /'fju:dl; 'fjudl̩/ *adj* of the method **(the '~ system)** of holding land (by giving services to the owner) during the Middle Ages in Europe: 封建制度的: *~ law;* 封建法; *the ~ barons.* 封建貴族;藩臣。⇨ vassal. **~·ism** /-ɪzəm; -,ɪzəm/ *n* [U] the ~ system. 封建制度。

feuda·tory /'fju:dətərɪ *US:* -tɔ:rɪ; 'fjudə,torɪ/ *adj* owing service to a lord: 臣事的: *~ obligations.* 爲臣的職責。□ *n* vassal. 家臣。

fe·ver /'fi:və(r); 'fivɚ/ *n* **1** [U, C] condition of the human body with temperature higher than usual, esp as a sign of illness: 發燒; 發熱: *She hasn't much ~.* 她發燒不太厲害。*He has a high ~.* 他發高燒。 **'~ heat,** high temperature of the human body in ~. 高燒。 **2** [U] one of a number of diseases in which there is high ~: 熱病: *yellow/typhoid/rheumatic ~.* 黃熱病 (腸熱病; 風濕病)。 **3** (usu 通常作 **a ~**) excited state; nervous agitation: 興奮; 激昂: *in a ~ of impatience.* 極度暴躁。***at/to '~ pitch,*** at/to a high level of excitement: 極爲激動: *The crowd was at ~ pitch.* 群衆極爲激昂。**~ed** *adj* affected by a ~: 發燒的;激動的: *a ~ed imagination,* highly excited. 狂熱的想像。**~·ish** /-rɪʃ; -rɪʃ/ *adj* having symptoms of ~; caused by ~; causing ~: 發燒的;害熱病的; 發燒引起的;引起發燒的: *in a ~ish condition;* 在發燒狀態中; *~ish dreams;* 發燒引起的夢; *~ish swamps.* 產生熱病的濕地。**~·ish·ly** *adv*

few /fju:; fju/ *adj* (-er, -est), *pron* (contrasted with *many*; 與 many 相對; ⇨ little, less, much) **1** (attrib, with a *pl n*) not many: (形容用法,與複數名詞連用)不多;很少: *Few people live to be 100 and fewer still live to be 110.* 很少人活到一百歲,活到一百一十歲的人則更少了。*Which of you made the fewest mistakes,* the smallest number of mistakes? 你們當中誰犯的錯誤最少? *He is a man of few words,* He says very little. 他是個沉默寡言的人。***no fewer than,*** as many as: 不下於;有…之多: *No fewer than twenty workers were absent through illness.* 因病而缺席的工人不下於二十位。 **2** (pred, rare in colloq style): (用於述語中,罕用於口語): *Such occasions are few.* 此種場合不多見。*We are very few, fewer than at the last meeting of the society.* 我們到會的人數不多,較上次開會的人數還少。**3 *a few,*** a small number (Note that *few* is neg and *a few* is positive): 少數;數個(注意: few 有否定意味, a few 則是肯定的): *We are going away for a few days.* 我們要離開幾天。*I'd like a few more red roses.* 我想再要幾朵紅玫瑰。***some few; a good few; quite a few; not a few,*** a considerable number, a fair number. 相當多;頗有幾個。**4 *every few minutes/days, etc.*** 每隔幾分鐘(天等)。⇨ every(5). **5 *the few,*** the minority. 少數。□ *pron* ***few of,*** (neg) not many of: (否定之義)不多的人或物;很少的人或物: *Few of those roses are worth buying.* 那些玫瑰花沒有幾朵值得買的。***a few of,*** (positive) a small number of: (肯定之義)少數的;數個: *I know a few of these people.* 這些人當中我認識幾個。**few·ness** *n*

fey /feɪ; fe/ *adj* **1** (Scot) having a feeling of approaching death. (蘇)感到死期近的。**2** clairvoyant. 有超人洞察力的。 **3** otherworldly. 來世的。

fez /fez; fɛz/ *n* red felt hat with a flat top and no brim, worn by some Muslim men. (某些回教徒戴的平頂無邊)紅氈帽。

fi·ancé (fem **fi·ancée**) /fɪ'ɒnseɪ *US:* ,fi:ɑ:n'seɪ; ,fiən'se/ *n* (F) man (woman) to whom one is engaged to be married. (法)未婚夫 (fiancé); 未婚妻 (fiancée)。

fi·asco /fɪ'æskəʊ; fɪ'æsko/ *n* (*pl* ~s, US also ~es /-kəʊz; -koz/) complete failure, breakdown, in sth attempted: 徹底失敗;慘敗: *The new play at the Ritz Theatre was a ~.* 在麗玆戲院演出的新劇完全失敗了。

fi·at /'faɪæt *US:* 'fi:ət; 'faɪət/ *n* [C] order or decree made by a ruler. 諭;命令。

fib /fɪb; fɪb/ *n* (colloq) untrue statement (esp about sth unimportant). (俗) 無關緊要的謊言;小謊。□ *vi* (-bb-) [VP2A] tell a fib. 撒小謊。**fib·ber** *n* person who tells fibs. 撒小謊的人。**fib·bing** *n* [U] telling fibs. 撒小謊。

fibre (US = **fiber**) /'faɪbə(r); 'faɪbɚ/ *n* **1** [C] one of the slender threads of which many animal and vegetable growths are formed, eg cotton, wood, nerves, muscles. (棉,木,神經,肌肉等之)纖維;纖維質。**2** [U] substance formed of a mass of ~s, for manufacture into various materials: (用以製成紗,線等材料之)纖維物質: *hemp ~,* for making rope; 大麻纖維(製繩用者); *cotton ~,* for spinning. 棉花纖維(紡績用者)。**'~·board** *n* [U] board made of compressed ~. 纖維板。**'~·glass** *n* [U] material of glass ~s in resin, used as an insulating material, and made into structural materials, eg for boatbuilding. 纖維玻璃; 玻璃棉(用作絕緣材料,並製成造船等建築材料)。 **3** [U] structure; texture: 構造;結

F

構;織地: *material of coarse ~;* 粗劣的料子; (fig) character: (喻)品格: *a person of strong moral ~.* 品德很好的人。 **fi·brous** /ˈfaɪbrəs ; ˈfaɪbrəs/ *adj* made of, like, ~s. 纖維製的;似纖維的;纖維狀的。

fib·ula /ˈfɪbjʊlə(r) ; ˈfɪbjələ/ *n* (anat) outer of the two bones between the knee and the foot. (解剖)腓骨。 ⇨ the illus at skeleton. 參看 skeleton 之插圖。

fickle /ˈfɪkl ; ˈfɪkl/ *adj* (of moods, the weather, etc) often changing; not constant: (指心情,天氣等)常變的;多變的: *~ fortune;* 變化無常的命運; *a ~ lover.* 情意不專的愛人。 **~·ness** *n*

fic·tion /ˈfɪkʃn ; ˈfɪkʃən/ *n* **1** [C] sth invented or imagined (contrasted with truth). 虛構之事;捏造的故事(與 truth 相對)。 *Truth is often stranger than ~.* 事實往往比想像的事物還奇怪。 ***a legal/polite ~,*** sth assumed to be true, although it may be false, for legal/social convenience. 法律上的假定(爲法律或社會上的方便,假定某事爲眞,雖然此事可能是假的)。 **2** [U] (branch of literature concerned with) stories, novels and romances: (作爲文學之一部門的)小說: *works of ~;* 小說作品; *prefer history to ~.* 喜歡歷史甚於小說。

fic·ti·tious /fɪkˈtɪʃəs ; fɪkˈtɪʃəs/ *adj* not real; imagined or invented: 假的;想像的;虛構的: *The account he gives of his movements is quite ~.* 他對他的行動之說明完全是虛構的。

fiddle /ˈfɪdl ; ˈfɪdl̩/ *n* **1** (colloq) violin; any instrument of the violin family, eg a cello or viola. (俗)小提琴;提琴類的樂器(例如大提琴或中音提琴)。 ***have a face as long as a ~,*** look dismal. 板着臉;顯得愁眉苦臉。 ***fit as a ~,*** very well; in good health. 精神健旺;身體健壯。 ***play second ~ (to),*** take a less important part (than). 居於(…的)次位。 **ˈ~-stick** *n* bow¹(2). 拉提琴的弓。 **ˈ~-sticks** *int* Nonsense! 胡說! **2** instance of fiddling; ⇨ 3 below. 虛報帳目等(參看下列第3義)。 □ *vt, vi* **1** [VP 6A, 2A] (colloq) play the ~; play a tune, etc on the ~. (俗)奏小提琴;以小提琴奏出(一曲調等)。 **2** [VP2A, C] ***~ (about) (with),*** make aimless movements; play aimlessly (*with* sth in one's fingers): 做無目的之動作;用手指無聊地撥弄(與 with 連用,後接某物): *Stop fiddling!* 不要虛耗光陰! *He was fiddling (about) with a piece of string.* 他在無聊地玩弄一條繩子。 **3** [VP6A] (sl) make or keep dishonestly inaccurate records of figures (in business accounts, etc): (俚)虛報帳目等: *~ an income-tax return,* prepare it so as to try to escape correct tax payments. 虛報所得稅申報書。 **fiddler** *n* person who plays the ~; person who ~s(3). 奏提琴者;虛報帳目等者。 **fid·dling** *adj* (colloq) trivial; futile: (俗)瑣細的;無益的: *fiddling little jobs.* 瑣細的工作。

fi·del·ity /fɪˈdelətɪ ; faɪˈdɛlətɪ/ *n* [U] ***~ (to),*** **1** loyalty, faithfulness: 忠貞;忠實: *~ to one's principles/religion/leader/wife.* 忠於主義(宗教,領袖,妻子)。 **2** accuracy; exactness: 正確;精確: *translate sth with the greatest ~;* 極爲確實地翻譯一篇東西; *high ~ equipment,* with high quality sound reproduction. 高度傳眞性音響設備。 ⇨ hi-fi.

fidget /ˈfɪdʒɪt ; ˈfɪdʒɪt/ *vi, vt* [VP2A, C, 6A] ***~ (about) (with),*** (cause sb to) move the body (or part of it) about restlessly; make (sb) nervous: (使某人)坐立不安;(使某人)煩躁不安: *Stop ~ing!* 不要坐立不安! *The boy was ~ing (about) with his knife and fork.* 那孩子不停地揮動他的刀叉。 *What's ~ing you,* making you nervous or uneasy? 何事使你煩躁不安? *Hurry up, your father's beginning to ~,* show signs of impatience. 趕快,你父親開始不耐煩了。 □ *n* **1** (usu 通常作 **the ~s**) ~ing movements: 坐立不安;煩躁不安: *Having to sit still for a long time often gives small children the ~s.* 必須靜坐很久,往往使小孩們煩躁不安。 **2** person who ~s: 坐立不安者;煩躁不安者: *What a ~ you are!* 你眞是個坐立不安的人! **~y** *adj* having the ~s; restless: 坐立不安的;煩躁不安的: *a ~y child.* 煩躁的小孩。

fie /faɪ ; faɪ/ *int* (usu hum) for shame: (通常爲詼諧語)呸! *Fie upon you,* You ought to be ashamed! 呸!眞不要臉!

fief /fiːf ; fif/ *n* [C] land held from a feudal lord. 封土;領地;采邑。

field¹ /fiːld ; fild/ *n* [C] **1** area of land, either grassland for cattle, etc or arable land for crops, usu enclosed by means of hedges, fences, etc (not normally used of unenclosed land or uncultivated land): 田野;田地(通常由籬笆等圍起,不用以指未被圍起或未開墾的土地): *working in the ~s* 在田地裏工作 (Cf 參較 *on the farm*). *What a fine ~ of wheat!* 多麼好的一片麥田! **2** (usu in compounds) wide area or expanse; open space: (通常用於複合字中)廣濶的區域;茫茫的一片;空地;場地: *an ˈice-~,* eg round the North Pole; 冰原(例如北極周圍者); *a ˈflying-~;* 飛機場; *a ˈlanding ~* (for aircraft); (飛機的)起落場; *a ˈbaseball/ˈcricket/ˈfootball ~.* 棒球(板球,足球)場。 **ˈ~ events** *n pl* athletic contests such as jumping and discus-throwing, but not races or other contests that take place on a track. 田賽(跳高,跳遠,擲鐵餅等項)。 **ˈ~ glasses** *n pl* long-distance binoculars for outdoor use. (戶外用)雙筒望遠鏡。 **ˈ~ sports** *n pl* hunting, shooting and fishing. 野外運動(狩獵,射擊,釣魚)。 **3** (usu in compounds) area of land from which minerals, etc are obtained: (通常用於複合字中)礦田;產地: *ˈgold-~s;* 金礦產地; *a new ˈoil-~;* 新油田; *ˈcoal-~s.* 煤田。 **4** province or department of study or activity: (學術或活動)範圍;領域;界: *the ~ of politics/art/science/medicine.* 政治(藝術,科學,醫學)界。 *That is outside my ~,* is not in the departments of knowledge that I have studied. 那不在我所學的範圍內。 **ˈ~ work** *n* [U] scientific, technical or social investigation made outside laboratories, etc eg by surveyors, geologists or by students of social science who visit and talk to people. 野外調查工作;實地調查工作(例如測量者,地質學家或社會科學學者所做的勘查工作)。 **5** range (of operation, activity, use); area or space in which forces can be felt: (動作,活動或作用之)範圍;力量可被感到的區域: *a magnetic ~,* round a magnet; 磁場; *a wide ~ of vision;* 廣濶的視野; *an object that fills the ~ of a telescope;* 由望遠鏡看到的一個物體; *the earth's gravitational ~,* the space in which the earth's gravity is exerted. 地心吸引力的範圍。 **6** place, area, where a battle or war is or was fought: 戰場: *the ~ of battle* (*ˈbattle-~*); 戰場; *take the ~,* go to war. 開戰;出陣。 **ˈ~ artillery; ˈ~ gun** *nn* light and mobile, for use in battle. 野戰砲。 **ˈ~ day** *n* day on which military operations are practised; (fig) great or special occasion. 野外演習日;(喻)重大事件。 ***have a ~ day,*** (fig) have a celebration or triumph. (喻)慶祝一番;喜氣洋洋;得意揚揚。 **ˈ~-hospital** *n* temporary hospital near the scene of fighting. 野戰醫院。 **ˈF~ ˈMarshal** *n* army officer of highest rank. 陸軍元帥。 **ˈ~-officer** *n* major or colonel. (陸軍)校級軍官。 **ˈ~-work** *n* temporary fortification made by troops in the ~. 戰地臨時築成的防禦工事。 **7** (sports and athletics) (in foxhunting) all those taking part in the hunt; (in a contest, esp a horse-race) all the competitors; (in cricket and baseball) team that is not batting; (cricket) the fielding side. (戶外活動及運動)(獵狐)全體獵者;參加比賽者的總稱;(賽馬)全體參加比賽的馬;(板球和棒球)守隊;(板球)守隊隊員;外場員。

field² /fiːld ; fild/ *vt, vi* **1** [VP6A, 2A] (cricket and baseball) (stand ready to) catch or stop (the ball): (板球和棒球)(準備)接或截(球);守(球);做外場員或守隊隊員: *He ~ed the ball smartly.* 他很巧妙地將球接住了。 *He ~s well.* 他截球技術很好。 *Well ~ed, sir!* 截得好!守得好! **2** [VP6A] (of football teams, etc) put into the ~: (指足球隊等)使入

場: *Brazil are ~ing a strong team for the World Cup.* 巴西派了一强大的球隊參加世界杯。**~er; fieldsman** /-mən; -mən/ *n* (*pl* -men) (cricket, etc) person who ~s: (板球等) 外場員; 守隊隊員: *He doesn't bat well, but he's an excellent ~er.* 他擊球的技術不好,但是他是個卓越的外場員。⇨ the illus at baseball. 參看 baseball 之揷圖。

fiend /fi:nd; find/ *n* devil; very wicked or cruel person; (colloq) person devoted to or addicted to sth (indicated by the word prefixed): 惡魔;窮兇極惡的人;(俗)耽於某一事物(由其前面一字指明)之人;…迷;酷愛…之人: *a drug ~;* 有毒癮的人; *a ˌfresh-ˈair ~.* 喜愛戶外生活之人。**~·ish** /-ɪʃ; -ɪʃ/ *adj* savage and cruel. 兇猛的;殘忍的。**~·ish·ly** *adv*

fierce /fɪəs; fɪrs/ *adj* (-r, -st) **1** violent and angry: 兇猛的;憤怒的: *~ dogs/winds;* 猛犬(强風); *look ~;* 樣子兇惡; *have a ~ look on one's face.* 面部有兇狠的表情。**2** (of heat, desire, etc) intense: (指熱,慾望等)强烈的: *~ hatred.* 痛恨。**~·ly** *adv* **~·ness** *n*

fiery /ˈfaɪərɪ; ˈfaɪrɪ/ *adj* **1** flaming; looking like, hot as, fire: 燃燒的;似火的;熾熱的: *a ~ sky;* 火紅的天空; *~ eyes,* angry and glaring. 冒着怒火的目光。**2** (of a person, his actions, etc) quickly or easily made angry; passionate: (指人,其行動等)易怒的;暴躁的;激烈的: *a ~ temper/speech.* 暴躁的脾氣(激昂的演說)。**fier·ily** /-əlɪ; -ɪlɪ/ *adv* **fieri·ness** *n*

fi·esta /fɪˈestə; fɪˈɛstə/ *n* (Sp) religious festival; saint's day; holiday, festival. (西)宗教節日;聖徒節;假日;節日。

fife /faɪf; faɪf/ *n* small musical wind instrument like a flute, used with drums in military music: 橫笛;短笛(與鼓伴奏,用於軍樂): *a drum and ~ band.* 鼓笛樂隊。

fif·teen /ˌfɪfˈti:n; ˈfɪfˈtin/ *n, adj* the number 15, ⇨ App 4; team of Rugby players. 十五;十五個(參看附錄四);橄欖球隊。**~th** /ˌfɪfˈti:nθ; ˈfɪfˈtinθ/ *n, adj* 第十五(個);十五分之一(的)。

fifth /fɪfθ; fɪfθ/ *n, adj* next after the 4th; one of five equal parts. 第五;第五個;五分之一(的)。⇨ App 4. 參看附錄四。**ˌ~ ˈcolumn,** organized body of persons sympathizing with and working for the enemy within a country at war. 第五縱隊(戰時同情敵人並在國內替敵人工作的組織)。**~·ly** *adv* in the ~ place. 第五。

fifty /ˈfɪftɪ; ˈfɪftɪ/ *n* (*pl* -ties), *adj* the number 50. 五十;五十個。⇨ App 4. 參看附錄四。**the fifties,** 50-59. 50 至 59。**go ˌ~-ˈ~ (with); be on a ~-~ basis (with),** have equal shares (with). 與…平分;均攤。**a ~-~ chance,** equal chance. 機會均等;各佔一半。**fif·ti·eth** /ˈfɪftɪəθ; ˈfɪftɪɪθ/ *n, adj* 第五十(個);五十分之一(的) ⇨ App 4. 參看附錄四。

fig /fɪg; fɪg/ *n* (broad-leaved tree having a) soft, sweet, pear-shaped fruit full of small seeds. 無花果;無花果樹。⇨ the illus at fruit. 參看 fruit 之揷圖。**not care/give a fig (for),** not care in the least; consider as valueless or unimportant. (對…)毫不介意;毫不重視。**ˈ~-leaf,** (with reference to the story of Adam and Eve) conventional device for concealing genital organs in old drawings, statues, etc. (源於亞當和夏娃的故事) 無花果之葉(古代的裸體畫像,彫像等常見之陰部覆蓋物)。

fight[1] /faɪt; faɪt/ *n* **1** [C] act of fighting: 打鬥;交戰;打架: *a ~ between two dogs;* 狗打架; *the ~ against poverty;* 對抗貧窮; *a prize-~* (boxing). 拳擊賽。**put up a good/poor ~,** fight with/without courage and determination. 奮勇(畏懼)地戰鬥。**a free ~,** ⇨ free[1](3). **a stand-up ~,** ⇨ stand[2](10). **2** [U] fighting spirit; desire or ability for fighting: 戰鬥精神;鬥志;戰鬥力: *In spite of numerous defeats, they still had plenty of ~ left in them.* 雖然屢遭敗績,他們仍甚有鬥志。*The news that their leader had surrendered took all the ~ out of them.* 他們首領投降的消息使他們失去了一切鬥志。**show ~,** show readiness to fight. 表示戰意。

fight[2] /faɪt; faɪt/ *vi, vt* (*pt, pp* fought /fɔ:t; fɔt/) **1** [VP2A, B, C, 3A, 4A, 6A] use the force of the body or of weapons (against); use physical force (as in war); use all resources available (against) to defeat: 與…格鬪;打架;戰鬪;作戰: *to ~ poverty/oppression.* 消滅貧窮(反抗壓迫)。*When dogs ~, they use their teeth.* 狗打架時用牙。*The dogs were ~ing over a bone/~ing for the possession of a bone.* 那些狗爲了爭一塊骨頭而打鬪。*Great Britain has often fought with* (= against) *her enemies.* 英國常和敵人作戰。*Great Britain fought with* (= on the side of) *France.* 英國與法國聯合作戰。*They were ~ing for* (= in order to secure or maintain) *their independence.* 他們在爲爭取(或維護)獨立而戰。*They were ~ing to preserve their freedom.* 他們爲維護自由而戰。**~ to a finish,** until there is a decision. 戰至分出勝負;決雌雄。**~ shy of,** keep away from, not get mixed up with. 避開;不與…接觸。**2** [VP6A] ~(1) in: 在…中作戰: *~ a battle/a duel/an election.* 打仗(決鬪;競選)。**3** [VP 15A, B] **~ sth down,** repress; overcome: 鎮壓;抑制: *~ down a feeling of repugnance.* 抑制厭惡感。**~ sb/sth off,** drive away; struggle against: 逐退;對抗: *~ off a cold,* eg by taking aspirin. 治好傷風(例如藉服阿斯匹靈)。**~ one's way forward/out (of),** advance, go forward, by ~ing. 向前(外)打開一條路。**~ it out,** ~ until a dispute is settled. 爭至爭論解決爲止。**4** [VP6A] manoeuvre (ships, etc) in battle: 調動(艦隊等)作戰: *The captain fought his ship well.* 該艦長善於指揮他的軍艦作戰。**~er** *n* person or thing that ~s, esp a fast aircraft designed for attacking bombers: 戰鬪者;(尤指)戰鬪機: *a ˌjet-ˈ~er;* 噴射戰鬪機; (attrib) (形容用法) *a ˈ~er pilot/squadron.* 戰鬪機駕駛員(中隊)。**~·ing** *n* [U]: *ˈstreet ~ing.* 街頭戰;巷戰。**a ~ing chance,** a possibility of success if great efforts are made. 特別努力或可成功的機會。

fig·ment /ˈfɪgmənt; ˈfɪgmənt/ *n* [C] sth invented or imagined: 虛構或想像之物: *~s of the imagination.* 想像中的事物。

figu·rat·ive /ˈfɪgjərətɪv; ˈfɪgjərətɪv/ *adj* (of words and language) used not in the literal sense but in an imaginative way (as when *fiery* is used of a man who is easily made angry). (指文字和語言)比喩的(如 fiery 一字指暴躁的人)。**~·ly** *adv*

fig·ure /ˈfɪgə(r) *US:* ˈfɪgjər; ˈfɪgjɚ/ *n* **1** symbol for a number, esp 0 to 9: 數字(尤指由 0 至 9): *He has an income of six figures,* £100 000 or more. 他有六位數字的收入(至少爲 100,000 鎊)。*We bought the house at a high/low ~,* for a high/low price. 我們以高(低)價買下那所房屋。**double ~s,** any number from 10 to 99 inclusive. 二位數字(自 10 至 99)。**2** (*pl*) arithmetic: (複)算術: *Are you good at ~s?* 你精於算術嗎? **3** diagram; drawing to illustrate sth: 圖形;圖解;圖表: *The blackboard was covered with geometrical ~s,* ie squares, triangles, etc. 黑板上畫滿了幾何圖形(正方形,三角形等)。**4** person's ~ drawn or painted, or cut in stone, etc; drawing, painting, image, of the body of a bird, animal, etc. (繪畫,彫刻等的)人像;肖像;鳥獸等的像。**ˈ~-head** *n* **(a)** carved image (either bust or full-length) placed for ornament at the prow of a ship. 艏像(船首所飾之彫像,半身或全身者)。**(b)** person in high position but with no real authority. 有名無實的首領;傀儡。**5** human form, esp the appearance and what it suggests: 人形;(尤指)體態;相貌;身材: *I saw a ~ approaching in the darkness.* 我看見黑暗中有個人影走近。*He has a good/poor/handsome, etc ~.* 他的體型很好(很差,很漂亮等)。*She's a fine ~ of a woman,* is well-shaped. 她的身材很美。*I'm dieting to keep my ~,* in order not to grow stout. 我在節食以保持我的身材(不使身體發胖)。*She was a ~ of distress,* Her attitude and appearance suggested distress. 她的樣子很窮苦。**cut a fine/poor/sorry, etc ~,** make a fine, etc, appearance. 嶄露頭角(出洋相;出

醜等)。 **6** person, esp his character or influence: 人物(尤指其性格或影響力): *dominating ~s like Napoleon.* 像拿破侖般的有領導力的人物。 **7 *~ of speech,*** expression, eg a simile or metaphor, that gives variety or force, using words out of their literal meaning. 比喻。□ *vt, vi* **1** [VP15A] imagine; picture mentally: 想像: *~ sth to oneself.* 想像某事物。 **2** [VP2C] ***~ (in),*** appear; have a part; be prominent: 出現;擔任一角色;露頭角: *~ in history/in a play.* 在歷史上留名(在一劇中扮演一角)。 *He ~s in all the books on the subject.* 所有關於此一問題的書籍中都提到了他。 **3** [VP15B] ***~ sth/sb out,*** calculate; think about until one understands: 演算出;想出;理解: *I can't ~ that man out,* He puzzles me. 我不了解那個人。 **4** [VP3A, 9, 25] ***~ (on),*** (US) reckon; estimate; conclude: (美)料想;指望;推斷: *They ~d on your arriving early.* 他們預料你會早到。 *I ~d (that) he was honest.* 我想他是誠實的。 *I ~ him (to be) honest.* 我認爲他是誠實的。 **fig·ured** *adj* ornamented; decorated: 有裝飾的;裝飾過的: *a ~d glass window,* with designs, eg in stained glass; 有圖案的玻璃窗(例如用彩色玻璃);花玻璃窗; *~d silk,* with patterns or designs on it. 紋織絹。

fila·ment /ˈfɪləmənt ; ˈfɪləmənt/ *n* [C] slender thread, eg of wire in an electric light bulb. 細線(例如電燈泡內之燈絲)。

fila·ture /ˈfɪlətʃə(r) ; ˈfɪlətʃɚ/ *n* workshop in which raw silk is reeled from cocoons. 繅絲廠。

fil·bert /ˈfɪlbət ; ˈfɪlbɚt/ *n* (nut of a) cultivated hazel. 榛樹;榛子。

filch /fɪltʃ ; fɪltʃ/ *vt* [VP6A] pilfer; steal (sth of small value). 竊取;偷(不貴重的東西)。

file[1] /faɪl ; faɪl/ *n* metal tool with rough surface(s) for cutting or smoothing hard substances. 銼刀;銼子。 ⇨ the illus at tool. 參看 tool 之插圖。□ *vt* [VP6A, 22, 15A] use a ~ on; make smooth with a ~; remove, cut through, with a ~: 用銼子銼;銼平;銼去;銼開: *~ one's fingernails;* 用銼修指甲; *~ sth smooth;* 銼光某物; *~ an iron rod in two.* 將一鐵棒銼爲二。 **fil·ings** /ˈfaɪlɪŋz ; ˈfaɪlɪŋz/ *n pl* bits ~d off or removed by a ~. 銼屑。

file[2] /faɪl ; faɪl/ *n* [C] holder, cover, case, box, drawer etc for keeping papers, etc together and in order for reference purposes, usu with wires, metal rods or other devices on which the papers, etc may be threaded: 公文箱(夾,匣);卷宗;文卷檔: *Where's the ~ of 'The Times'?* 泰晤士報的合訂本在哪裏? *We have placed the correspondence on our ~s.* 我們已將該信件歸檔了。 ***on ~,*** on or in a ~. 存卷;歸檔;彙存。□ *vt* [VP6A, 15B] place on or in a ~; place on record: 歸檔;存卷;彙存: *~ an application;* 將一申請書歸檔; *~ (away) letters;* 將信件歸檔; *a 'filing clerk,* one who ~s correspondence, etc. 管理檔案的職員。

file[3] /faɪl ; faɪl/ *n* line of persons or things one behind the other; (mil) man in the front rank and the man or men straight behind him. 行;(軍)縱隊。 ***(in) single ~; (in) Indian ~,*** (in) one line, one behind the other. (成)單行。 ***the rank and ~,*** soldiers who are not officers; (fig) ordinary, undistinguished persons. 士兵;行伍;(喻)普通人;常人。□ *vi* [VP2C] march in ~: 成單行或縱隊行進: *The men ~d in/out,* came or went in/out. 士兵們成單行進入(出去)。

fil·ial /ˈfɪlɪəl ; ˈfɪlɪəl/ *adj* of a son or daughter: 子女的: *~ duty/piety.* 孝道;孝心。

fili·bus·ter /ˈfɪlɪbʌstə(r) ; ˈfɪlə,bʌstɚ/ *n* **1** person who obstructs the making of decisions in meetings, parliament, etc by eg making long speeches. 以冗長的演說等阻礙會議,議會等做成決定之人。 **2** such a speech. 此種冗長的演說。□ *vi* act as a ~(1). 以冗長的演說等阻礙會議,議會等做成決定;阻撓議事。

fili·gree /ˈfɪlɪgriː ; ˈfɪlə,gri/ *n* [U] ornamental lace-like work of gold, silver or copper ware: 金,銀或銅絲製成的似花邊的細工: (attrib) (形容用法) *a ~ brooch;* 金(銀)絲胸針; *~ earrings.* 金(銀)絲耳環。

fil·ings /ˈfaɪlɪŋz ; ˈfaɪlɪŋz/ *n pl* ⇨ file[1].

fill[1] /fɪl ; fɪl/ *n* **1** [U] full supply; as much as is wanted: 充分的供應;所需之量: *eat/drink one's ~.* 盡量吃(喝)。 ***have one's ~ of sth,*** (colloq) have as much as one can bear. (俗)盡量用;盡性;受够了。 **2** [C] enough to fill sth: 填滿某物之量: *a ~ of tobacco,* enough to fill a pipe. 一斗煙;一煙斗的煙絲。 **~·ing** *n* [C] sth put in to ~ sth: 供填塞之物;充填物: *a ~ing in a tooth.* 補牙之物。

fill[2] /fɪl ; fɪl/ *vt, vi* **1** [VP6A, 14, 15B, 12B, 13B, 2A, C] ***~ (with),*** make or become full; occupy all the space in: 使滿;裝滿;充塞: *~ a hole with sand/a tank with petrol.* 用沙填滿一洞(將油箱裝滿汽油)。 *Tears ~ed her eyes.* 她眼中充滿了眼淚。 *I was ~ed with admiration.* 我內心充滿了景慕。 *The smoke ~ed the room.* 煙瀰漫了房間。 *Go and ~ this bucket with water for me/~ me* (less usu) *this bucket with water.* 去替我裝滿一桶水來。 (fill me…之句法較不常用)。 *The hall soon ~ed.* 那大廳不久便坐滿了。 *The wind ~ed the sails.* 風張滿了帆。 *The sails ~ed* (= swelled out) *with wind.* 帆被風所張滿。 ***~ in,*** add what is necessary to make complete: 填好: *~ in an application form,* write one's name, and other particulars required; 填申請表; *~ in an outline,* add details, etc. 加細節於大綱。 ***~ out,*** **(a)** make or become larger, rounded or fatter: 使膨脹;使擴張;膨脹;變胖;變圓: *Her cheeks began to ~ out.* 她的臉開始胖了。 **(b)** (esp US) (尤美) = ~ in. ***~ up,*** make or become quite full: 填滿;裝滿;充滿: *~ up with petrol;* 裝滿汽油; *~ up a tank.* 裝滿油箱。 *The channel of the river ~ed up with mud.* 河道爲泥所淤塞。 **'~·ing station,** place where petrol, oil, etc is sold to motorists. 加油站。 Cf 參較 *service station,* where motor repairs may be done. 附帶修理車輛等之加油站。 **2** [VP 6A] hold a position and do the necessary work; put (sb) in a position: 任職;使(某人)任某職: *The vacancy has already been ~ed.* 這空缺已遞補了。 *He ~s the post satisfactorily,* performs the duties well. 他很盡職。 ***~ the bill,*** (colloq) meet one's needs: (俗)適合需要;滿足需要: *These new machines really ~ the bill.* 這些新機器的確迎合需要。 **3** [VP 6A] execute, carry out an order, etc: 執行(命令等): *~ a doctor's prescription.* 配方。

fil·let /ˈfɪlɪt ; ˈfɪlɪt/ *n* **1** band (often ornamental) worn to keep the hair in place. 束髮帶(常爲裝飾用的)。 **2** slice of fish or meat without bones. (無骨的)魚片或肉片。□ *vt* [VP6A] cut (fish) into ~s: 切(魚)成片: *~ed plaice.* 鰈片。

fil·lip /ˈfɪlɪp ; ˈfɪləp/ *n* [C] quick, smart blow or stroke given with a finger; (fig) incentive or stimulus: 用指俐落的一彈;(喻)刺激: *an advertising campaign that gave a ~ to sales.* 刺激銷路的廣告活動。

filly /ˈfɪlɪ ; ˈfɪlɪ/ *n* (*pl* -lies) female foal. 牝駒。⇨ colt[1].

film[1] /fɪlm ; fɪlm/ *n* **1** [C] thin coating or covering: 薄的一層;薄膜: *a ~ of dust;* 一層灰塵; *a ~ of oil on water;* 浮於水面的一層油; *a ~ of mist.* 一層薄霧。 **2** [C, U] roll or sheet of thin flexible material for use in photography: 軟片;膠捲: *a roll* (US 美 = *spool*) *of ~;* 一捲軟片; *expose 50 feet of ~;* 使五十呎軟片曝光; *~ stock,* cinema ~ not yet exposed; 未曝光的電影膠片; *'~-strip,* length of ~ with a number of photographs (of scenes, diagrams, etc) to be shown on a screen separately (not as a motion picture). 幻燈式影片(攝有風景、圖表等,可分別放映,但非活動電影)。 **3** [C] motion picture. 電影。 **the ~s,** the cinema. 電影。 **'~ test,** photographic test of sb who wishes to act for the ~s. (希望演電影者之)試鏡。 **'~-star,** well-known cinema actor or actress. 電影明星。 **filmy** *adj* (-ier, -iest) like a ~(1): 似薄膜的: *~y clouds.* 薄雲。

film[2] /fɪlm ; fɪlm/ *vt, vi* **1** [VP2A, 6A] make a motion picture (of): (將…)拍電影: *~ a play.* 將一

劇拍成電影。*They've been filming for six months.* 他們已經拍了六個月的電影。 **2** [VP6A, 2A, C] ~ ***(over),*** cover, become covered, with a film (1): 覆以薄膜；起一層薄膜: *The mirror ~ed over.* 這鏡子變得朦朧了。 **3** [VP2A, C] be well, badly suited for reproduction in a motion picture: 適(不適)於拍電影: *She ~s well.* 她適於拍電影。 **~·able** /-əbl; -əbḷ/ *adj* (of a novel, etc) suitable for ~ing. (指小說等)適於拍成電影的。

fil·ter /ˈfɪltə(r); ˈfɪltɚ/ *n* apparatus (containing, eg sand, charcoal, paper, cloth) for holding back solid substances in an impure liquid passed through it; coloured glass (as used on a camera lens) which allows light only of certain wave-lengths to pass through; (radio) device which suppresses signals from unwanted frequencies. 過濾器 (含有沙,木炭,紙,布等)；濾光鏡；(無線電) 濾波器。 **ˈ~ tip,** cigarette end containing material that acts as a ~ for smoke. (香煙之)濾嘴。Hence, 由此產生, **ˈ~·tipped** *adj* □ *vt, vi* [VP6A, 14, 15B, 2A, C] **1** (cause to) flow through a ~; purify (a liquid) by using a ~. (使)過濾；濾清。**2** (fig, of a crowd, road traffic, news, ideas, etc) make a way; pass or flow: (喩,指群衆,車輛,新聞,思想等)通過；透出；滲入: *new ideas ~ing into people's minds.* 滲入人心的新思想。*The news of the defeat ~ed through.* 戰敗的消息傳出來了。**3** (of traffic in GB) be allowed to pass or turn to the left when traffic going straight ahead or to the right is held up by a red light. (指英國的車輛)亮紅燈禁止前行或右轉時准許通過或左轉。

filth /fɪlθ; fɪlθ/ *n* [U] disgusting dirt; obscenity. 骯髒；猥褻。**~y** *adj* (-ier, -iest) disgustingly dirty; vile; obscene; (colloq) very dirty. 骯髒的；邪惡的；猥褻的；(俗) 汚穢的。**~y rich,** (colloq) very rich. (俗)很有錢。**~·ily** /-ɪlɪ; -əlɪ/ *adv* **~i·ness** *n*

fil·trate /ˈfɪltreɪt; ˈfɪltret/ *vt, vi* = filter *v* (1). 過濾。 **fil·tra·tion** /-ˈtreɪʃn; -ˈtreʃən/ *n* [U] process of filtrating. 過濾；濾清。□ *n* /ˈfɪltreɪt; ˈfɪltret/ ~d liquid. 經過濾的液體。

fin /fɪn; fɪn/ *n* projecting part of a fish used in swimming; thing shaped like or used in the same way as a fin, eg the *ˈtail-fin* of an aircraft. 鰭；魚翅；鰭狀物(例如飛機的直尾翅)。⇨ the illus at fish, sea. 參看 fish, sea 之插圖。

fi·nal /ˈfaɪnl; ˈfaɪnḷ/ *adj* **1** coming at the end: 最後的；最終的: *the ~ chapter of a book.* 一本書最後的一章。 **2** putting an end to doubt or argument: 確定的；決定的: *a ~ decision/judgement.* 確定性的決定(判決)。□ *n* **1** (often *pl*) last of a series of examinations or contests: (常用複數)最後考試；決賽: *the law ~(s);* 律師業的最後考試； *take one's ~s;* 參加最後考試(決賽)；*the tennis ~s,* at the end of a tournament; 網球決賽；*the Cup F~,* last football match in a series. 足球杯決賽。 **2** (colloq) edition of a newspaper published latest in the day: (俗)報紙每日最後發行的一版: *'Late night ~'.* 夜晚最後版。**~·ist** /-nəlɪst; -nḷɪst/ *n* **1** player who takes part in the last of a series of contests. 決賽選手；獲決賽權者。 **2** undergraduate in his ~ year. 大學四年級學生。**~·ly** /-nəlɪ; -nḷɪ/ *adv* **1** lastly; in conclusion. 最後地；最後一點。 **2** once and for all: 祇此一次: *settle a matter ~ly.* 徹底解決一事。

fi·nale /fɪˈnɑːlɪ *US:* -ˈnælɪ; fɪˈnɑlɪ/ *n* (music) last movement of an instrumental composition, eg a symphony; closing scene of an opera; end. (音樂)(交響曲等的)最後樂章；終曲；(歌劇之)終場；結尾。

fi·nal·ity /faɪˈnælətɪ; faɪˈnælətɪ/ *n* [U] state or quality of being final: 最後；確定性；決定性: *speak with an air of ~,* giving the impression that there is nothing more to be said or done. 斬釘截鐵地說。

fi·nal·ize /ˈfaɪnəlaɪz; ˈfaɪnḷˌaɪz/ *vt* [VP6A] give a final form to. 予以最終形式；使定案。

fi·nance /ˈfaɪnæns *US:* fɪˈnæns; fəˈnæns/ *n* **1** [U] (science of) the management of (esp public) money: 財政；財政學: *an expert in ~;* 財政專家；*the Minister of F~* (in GB called 英稱作 *the Chancellor of the Exchequer*). 財政部長。**ˈ~ house/company,** one that provides ~ for hire-purchase sales. 金融機構；金融公司(貸款給分期付款購物者)。 **2** (*pl*) money (esp of a government or a business company): (複)(尤指政府或公司的)財源；資金: *Are the country's ~s sound?.* 這國家的財源殷實嗎？□ *vt* [VP6A] provide money for (a scheme, etc). 供(計畫等)以經費。

fi·nan·cial /faɪˈnænʃl *US:* fɪˈnæ-; fəˈnænʃəl/ *adj* of finance: 財政的；金融的: *in ~ difficulties,* short of money; 財政困難；*a ~ centre,* eg London or New York. 金融中心(例如倫敦或紐約)。***the ~ year,*** the annual period for which accounts are made up. 會計年度。**fi·nan·cially** /-ʃəlɪ; -ʃəlɪ/ *adv*

fin·an·cier /faɪˈnænsɪə(r) *US:* ˌfɪnənˈsɪər; ˌfɪnənˈsɪr/ *n* person skilled in finance; capitalist.財政家；資本家。

finch /fɪntʃ; fɪntʃ/ *n* kinds of small bird (usu with a distinctive epithet or prefix, as *ˈchaf~, ˈgreen~, ˈbull-~*). 雀類(通常與表示區別的形容詞或字首連用,如 ˈchaf~, ˈgreen~, ˈbull~)。

find[1] /faɪnd; faɪnd/ *n* [C] finding; sth found, esp sth valuable or pleasing: 發現物 (尤指貴重或悅人的): *I made a great ~ in a second-hand bookshop yesterday,* found a rare or valuable old book. 昨天我在一舊書店裏發現一本珍貴的舊書。

find[2] /faɪnd; faɪnd/ *vt* (*pt, pp* found /faʊnd; faʊnd/) **1** [VP6A, 12B, 13B] get back, after a search, (sth/sb lost, left behind, forgotten, etc): 尋得；找到；尋獲: *Did you ever ~ that pen you lost?* 你找到你遺失的那枝鋼筆沒有？ *Please help Mary to ~ her bag.* 請幫助瑪莉找她的提包。*Please ~ Mary her bag/~ Mary's bag for her.* 請替瑪莉找她的提包。*The missing child has not been found yet.* 那走失的孩子尚未找回。**~ one's place** (in a book, etc), turn to the page where one wishes to continue reading etc. 翻至(書等)要繼續讀下去的一頁。**~ one's voice/tongue,** be able to speak (after being silent because of shyness, etc). (因害羞等而沉默之後)說得出話來了。**2** [VP6A, 12A, B, 13A, B, 15A, B] get or discover (sth/sb not lost, forgotten, etc) after search, experience or effort: 發現；找到: *~ a cure/remedy (for sth);* 發現治療(補救)方法； *~ a solution/an answer (to a problem);* 發現(一問題的)解答(答案)； *~ (the) time to do sth.* 找到時間做事。*They dug five metres and then found water.* 他們掘了五公尺便發現了水。*I can ~ nothing new to say on this subject.* 關於此一問題我沒有什麼新的資料來討論。*Did you ~ him what he wanted?* 你找到他要的東西了嗎？ *They couldn't ~ the way in/out/back.* 他們找不到路進去(出去，回來)。 *Where will they ~ money for the journey?* 他們到哪裏去找這筆旅費？**~ favour with sb,** ⇨ favour[1] (1). **~ fault (with),** ⇨ fault. **~ one's feet, (a)** be able to stand and walk, eg as a baby does: 能站立和行走(例如嬰兒): *How old was the baby when it began to ~ its feet?* 這嬰兒開始站立和行走的時候有多大？ **(b)** become able to act independently, without the help and guidance of others. 能獨立行動。**~ oneself,** discover one's vocation; learn one's powers and abilities and how to use them. 發現自己適於某種職業；發現自己的能力並知如何去利用。⇨ also 5 below. 亦參看下列第 5 義。**~ it in one's heart/oneself to do sth,** (chiefly neg and interr with *can/could*) be so unkind or callous as to: (主要用於否定和疑問句，與 can 和 could 連用)忍心；無情: *How can you ~ it in your heart to drown these little kittens?* 你怎會忍心把這些小貓淹死？ **3** [VP 6A, 15A, B] arrive at naturally: 自然到達；自然成爲: *Rivers ~ their way to the sea.* 諸河皆流入海。*Water always ~s its own level.* 水總會自然成爲平面。 **4** [VP6A, 19B, 22, 15A] discover by chance; come across: 偶然發現；碰見；撞見: *He was found dying/dead/injured at the foot of a cliff.* 他被

人發現在一懸崖的脚下快要死(死去,受傷)了。*I found him in the cellar drinking my best brandy.* 我撞見他在地窖裏喝我最好的白蘭地。 **5** [VP9, 15A, 22, 25] become informed or aware of, by experience or trial: (由經驗或試驗)發覺;知道;覺得: *We found the beds quite comfortable.* 我們覺得那些床很舒服。*We found him (to be) dishonest/found he was dishonest.* 我們發覺他不誠實。*They found him (to be) the right man for the job.* 他們覺得他是最適合這工作的人。*Do you ~ that honesty pays/that it pays to be honest?* 你知道誠實不吃虧嗎? *I never ~ the best too good for me.* 我從不認爲我不能達到最高境界。*You must take us as you ~ us,* accept us as we are, not expect special treatment or ceremony. 我們就是這個樣子,你必須容忍遷就(不要指望受到特殊的待遇或禮遇)。*I ~ it difficult to understand him/~ him difficult to understand.* 我覺得難以了解他。*I called at Smith's this morning and found him still in bed.* 我今晨去史密斯家,發現他仍未起床。*I was disappointed to ~ her out* (ie not at home) *when I called.* 我去拜訪她時發覺她不在家,感到失望。**~ *oneself* + *adj/adv*,** discover, realize, that one is: 發覺自己在…;發覺自己是…: *When he regained consciousness, he found himself in hospital,* eg after a motor accident. 他恢復知覺後,發覺自己躺在醫院裏(例如在一車禍發生後)。*How do you ~ yourself this morning,* How are you feeling? 你今晨好嗎? *He found himself alone with a strange woman.* 他發覺自己跟一個陌生的女人單獨在一起。 **6** [VP6A, 15B, 8, 10] **~ *(out)*,** learn by study, calculation, inquiry: (由研究,計算,探詢)獲知;探知;得知: *What do you ~ the total?* 你得到的總數是多少? *Please ~ out when the train starts/whether there is an express train/how to get there.* 請查看一下火車何時開車(有無快車,如何到達該處)。**~ *sb out*,** detect sb in wrongdoing or error: 逮到某人做壞事或犯錯: *Do you think the police will ~ us out?* 你看警察會逮到我們嗎? **7** [VP15A] (equivalent to a construction with *there is/are*, etc with no suggestion of discovery or inquiry, the subject being *one* or *you*): 有(等於 there is/are 等,無發現或偵詢的含義;主詞爲 one 或 you): *One doesn't/You don't ~* (= There isn't) *much vegetation in this area.* 這一地區沒有什麼植物。*Pine-trees are found* (= There are pine-trees) *in most European countries.* 大多數歐洲國家內有松樹。 **8** [VP6A, 15A] supply; furnish; provide: 供給;供應: *Who will ~ the money for the expedition?* 誰負擔這探險的費用? **~ *sb/oneself in*,** provide with: 供應: *He pays his housekeeper £25 a week and she ~s herself in clothes,* buys them herself, from her wages. 他付給他管家的工資爲每週二十五鎊,服裝費由她自己出。***all found*,** everything provided: 一切都供給: *Wanted, a good cook, £100 a month and all found,* board, lodging, etc provided free in addition to wages. 兹徵求良厨一名:月薪一百鎊,供膳宿等。 **9** [VP22, 25, 9] (legal) determine and declare; give as a verdict: (法律)判定;判決: *How do you ~ the accused?* 你如何判決被告? *The jury found the accused man guilty.* 陪審團認定被告有罪。*They found* (= brought in) *a verdict of guilty.* 他們判定有罪。*They found it* (= the offence) *manslaughter.* 他們判定該項犯罪爲過失殺人。**~ *for*,** (elliptical use) decide in favour of: (省略用法)做有利於…之判決: *~ for the defendant/plaintiff.* 做有利於被告(原告)之判決。**~er** *n* **1** person who ~s sth: 尋得者;發現者: *Lost, a diamond ring: ~er will be rewarded.* 兹遺失鑽戒一枚:尋得者將獲重酬。 **2** device in a camera (*'view-~er*) or telescope used to ~ the object to be photographed, examined, etc. (照相機上的)取景器(亦作 view-finder);(望遠鏡上的)指導鏡;尋星鏡。 **~·ing** *n* (usu *pl*) (通常用複數) **1** what has been learnt as the result of inquiry: 調查的結果;發現物: *the ~ings of the Commission.* 調查團的調查結果。 **2** what is determined by a jury, etc. (陪審團等的)判決。

fine¹ /faɪn ; faɪn/ *n* [C] sum of money (to be) paid as a penalty for breaking a law or rule. 罰金;罰款。□ *vt* [VP6A, 14] **~ *(for)*,** punish by a ~: 處以罰金: *~ sb for an offence;* 爲一犯法行爲而處某人以罰金; *~sb £5.* 罰某人五鎊。**~·able** (also **finable**) /'faɪnəbl ; 'faɪnəbḷ/ *adj* liable to a ~. 應罰款的;可罰款的。

fine² /faɪn ; faɪn/ *n* (only in) (僅用於) ***in ~*,** (old use) in short, finally, to sum up. (舊用法)總之;最後。

fine³ /faɪn ; faɪn/ *adj* (-r, -st) **1** (of weather) bright; clear; not raining: (指天氣)晴朗的;無雲的;無雨的: *It rained all morning, but turned ~ later.* 一早上都在下雨,但後來轉晴了。***one ~ day*,** (in story-telling) one day past or future. (講故事時)有一天;某日。***one of these ~ days*,** at some (vague) time in the future. 改天;將來。 **2** enjoyable; pleasing; splendid: 可愛的;悅人的;美好的: *a ~ view;* 美麗的景色; *have a ~ time;* 有一段快樂的時間;玩得痛快; *~ clothes.* 漂亮的衣服。*She has grown up to be a ~ young lady.* 她已長成爲美麗的少女了。*That's a ~ excuse,* (ironic) a very poor excuse. (反語)那倒是個好藉口。*She thinks herself a ~ lady,* considers herself a lady of fashion, too superior to do housework, etc. 她自命爲上流社會婦女,不應該做家事等。 **3** delicate; carefully made and easily injured: 纖細的;精巧的: *~ workmanship;* 精巧的手工; *~ silk.* 細綢。 **4** of very small particles: 微小的: *~ dust.* 微塵。*Sand is ~r than gravel.* 沙比碎石微小。 **5** slender; thin; sharp: 細的;銳利的: *~ thread;* 細線; *a pencil with a ~ point.* 筆頭尖的鉛筆。***not to put too ~ a point on it*,** to express it plainly. 明白表達;直截了當地說。**~-tooth comb** ⇨ tooth(2). **6** (of metals) refined; pure: (指金屬)精製的;純的: *~ gold;* 純金; *gold 18 carats ~,* with 18 parts of pure gold and 6 of alloy. 十八開金。 **7** (to be) seen only with difficulty or effort: 難以辨識的;精微的: *a ~ distinction;* 精微的區別; capable of delicate perception, able to make delicate distinctions: 能作精微辨識的: *a ~ sense of humour;* 善於領會幽默; *a ~ taste in art.* 對藝術之精確鑑賞力。**the ~ arts; ~ art,** the visual arts that appeal to the sense of beauty, esp painting and sculpture. 美術(尤指繪畫和彫刻)。 **8** (of speech or writing) too ornate; insincerely complimentary. (指演說或寫作)過份虛飾的; 華而不實的。***call sth/sb by ~ names*,** **(a)** (of sth) use euphemisms about it. 委婉地敍述某事物。 **(b)** (of sb) flatter him. 奉承某人;恭維某人。 **9** in good health: 健康的: *I'm feeling ~.* 我很好。**~·ly** *adv* **1** splendidly: 美好地;華麗地: *~ly dressed.* 衣着華麗。 **2** into small particles or pieces: 微小地;細微地: *carrots ~ly chopped up.* 切碎的紅蘿蔔。 **~·ness** *n*

fine⁴ /faɪn ; faɪn/ *adv* **1** (colloq) very well: (俗)很好: *That will suit me ~.* 那很適合我。 **2** (in compounds) (用於複合字中) *ˌ~-'drawn,* subtle; 精細的; *ˌ~-'spoken,* insincerely complimentary; 假意奉承的; *ˌ~-'spun,* delicate. 纖細的。 **3** ***cut it ~*,** ⇨ cut¹(7).

fin·ery /'faɪnərɪ ; 'faɪnərɪ/ *n* [U] gay and elegant dress or appearance: 華麗的服裝;優雅的外表: *young men in their Saturday night ~,* smart clothes; 穿着漂亮衣服的年輕男士們; *the garden in its summer ~,* with its brightly coloured flowers, green lawns, etc. 妍麗的夏季花園。

fi·nesse /fɪ'nes ; fə'nɛs/ *n* [U] artful or delicate way of dealing with a situation: (應付某一情況的)技巧;手段: *show ~ in dealing with people;* 表現應付人的手腕; [C] (cards) attempt to win using ~. (紙牌戲)以技巧得分。

fin·ger /'fɪŋgə(r) ; 'fɪŋgɚ/ *n* one of the five members (*'little ~, 'ring ~, 'middle ~, 'index* or *'fore~, thumb*) at the end of the hand. 手指(小拇指稱 little finger, 無名指稱 ring finger, 中指稱 middle finger, 食指稱 index 或 forefinger, 大拇指稱 thumb)。⇨ the illus at arm. 參看 arm 之挿圖。

There are five ~s (or *four ~s and one thumb*) *on each hand.* 每隻手有五個手指(四個手指和一個大拇指)。***sb's ~s are all thumbs,*** he is very clumsy. 某人很笨拙。⇨ thumb. ***burn one's ~s,*** suffer because of incautious or meddlesome behaviour, etc. 因不謹愼或管閒事等而吃虧。***have a ~ in every/the pie,*** ⇨ pie. ***keep one's ~s crossed,*** ⇨ cross²(3). ***lay a ~ on,*** touch (however slightly): 觸(不論多麼輕微): *I forbid you to lay a ~ on the boy,* to punish him by hitting him, etc. 我不許你碰那孩子。***lay/put one's ~ on,*** point out precisely (where sth is wrong, the cause of a problem). 正確指出(錯處,癥結之所在)。***not lift a ~ (to help sb),*** do nothing to help when help is needed. 一點也不幫忙。***put the ~ on sb,*** (sl) inform against (a criminal). (俚)告發(犯人)。***slip through one's ~s,*** ⇨ slip²(3). ***twist sb round one's (little) ~,*** cajole him; dominate him. 籠絡某人;玩弄某人於股掌之上。**'~-alphabet** *n* method (using the ~s in various ways) for talking with the deaf. 指語法;手勢語(與聾人交談用者)。**'~•board,** wood (on a guitar, violin, etc) where the strings are held against the neck with the ~s. (吉他,小提琴等頸部之)指板。**'~-bowl** *n* one for rinsing the ~s at meals. (吃飯時用的)洗指缽。**'~-mark** *n* mark, eg on a wall, made by a dirty ~. 指痕。**'~-nail** *n* nail at the tip of the ~. 指甲。**'~-plate** *n* one fastened on a door near the handle or key-hole to prevent ~-marks. 門上把手或鎖眼附近防指污的板。**'~-post** *n* signpost giving directions with boards shaped like ~s. 指標;指路牌。**'~•print** *n* mark made by ~s when pressed on a surface, used for identifying criminals. 指紋。⇨ the illus at whorl. 參看 whorl 之插圖。**'~•stall** *n* protective cover (worn over an injured ~). (用以保護受傷手指的)指套。**'~•tip,** top of a ~. 指尖。***have sth at one's ~tips,*** be thoroughly familiar with it. 熟悉某事物。□ *vt* [VP6A] touch with the ~s: 以指觸摸: *~ a piece of cloth,* touch, feel, it (to test its quality). 用指摸一塊布(以試其質料)。

fini•cal /ˈfɪnɪkl; ˈfɪnɪkl/ *adj* too fussy or fastidious about food, clothing, etc. 過份講究飲食衣著等的;對衣食苛求的。

fin•icky /ˈfɪnɪkɪ; ˈfɪnɪkɪ/ *adj* = finical.

fi•nis /ˈfɪnɪs; ˈfaɪnɪs/ *n* (*sing* only) (Lat) (at the end of a book) the end. (僅用單數)(拉)(用於書尾)完;結束;終結。

fin•ish /ˈfɪnɪʃ; ˈfɪnɪʃ/ *vt, vi* **1** [VP6A, C, 2A, C, 15B, 3A] bring or come to an end; complete: 結束;完成: *~ one's work;* 結束工作; *~ reading a book.* 讀完一書。*Have you ~ed that book yet,* read it to the end? 你讀完那本書沒有? *Term ~es next week.* 學期下星期結束。*We have ~ed the pie,* eaten all of it. 我們已吃完水果餅。*That long climb almost ~ed me,* (colloq) almost caused my death. (俗)爬那麼久幾乎把我累死了。***~ sb off,*** (sl) kill, destroy, him. (俚)殺死某人;毀掉某人。*That fever nearly ~ed him off.* 那次發燒幾乎使他送命。***~ sth off/up,*** eat up completely: 吃光: *We ~ed up everything on the table.* 我們把桌上的東西全吃光了。***~ ('up) with sth,*** have at the end: 最後有: *We had an excellent dinner, and ~ed up with a glass of brandy.* 我們吃了一頓盛餐,最後喝了一杯白蘭地。***~ with sb/sth,*** no longer be engaged with sb or busy with sth: 與某人斷絕關係;不再忙於某事物: *I haven't ~ed with you yet,* still have sth to say. 我還有話要跟你說。*Have you ~ed with that dictionary?* 那部字典你用完了沒有? **2** [VP6A] make complete or perfect; polish: 使完美;潤飾: *The woodwork is beautifully ~ed,* smoothed and polished. 那件木器漆得很精美。*They gave a ~ed performance of the quartet.* 他們做了一次完美的四重奏表演。*He gave the picture a few ~ing touches.* 他將那幅畫潤飾了一番。**'~ing school,** private school preparing girls for social life. 女子精修學校(爲準備女子進入社會的私立學校)。□ *n* (*sing* only) (僅用單數) **1** [C] last part: 最終部分;終結;收場: *the ~ of a race.* 競賽的結尾。*It was a close ~,* The competitors were close together at the ~. 那是場結束時很緊張的競賽。***be in at the ~,*** be present when the fox is killed at the end of the hunt; (fig) be present during the last stage (of a struggle, etc). (狩獵時)狐狸最後被射死時在場;(喻)目覩(戰鬪等的)最後一幕。***a fight to the ~,*** until one side is defeated or exhausted. 打到底;拚出勝負。**2** [C, U] the state of being ~ed or perfect; the manner in which sth is ~ed: 完美;潤飾過的狀態: *woodwork with a smooth ~.* 漆得精美的木器。*His manners lack ~.* 他的儀態欠優雅。

fi•nite /ˈfaɪnaɪt; ˈfaɪnaɪt/ *adj* **1** limited; having bounds: 有限制的;有限度的: *Human understanding is ~,* There are things that man cannot understand. 人類的理解力是有限的。**2** (gram) agreeing with a subject in number and person: (文法)限定的(受數目和人稱限制的): *'Am', 'is', 'are', 'was', and 'were' are the ~ forms of 'be'; and 'be', 'being' and 'been' are the non-~ forms.* Am, is, are, was 和 were 是 be 的限定形式; be, being 和 been 是不限定形式。

Finn /fɪn; fɪn/ *n* native of Finland. 芬蘭人。**~•ish** *adj, n* (language) of the ~s. 芬蘭人的;芬蘭的;芬蘭語。

finnan /ˈfɪnən; ˈfɪnən/ *n* (also 亦作 ˌ~ **'haddock/haddie** /ˈhædɪ; ˈhædɪ/) (kind of) smoked haddock. 燻鱈魚。

fiord, fjord /fɪˈɔːd; fjord/ *n* long, narrow arm of the sea, between high cliffs (as in Norway). 峭壁間的狹長海灣;峽灣(例如在挪威者)。

fir /fɜː(r); fɝ/ *n* conifer with needle-like leaves, ⇨ the illus at tree; [U] wood of this tree. 冷杉(參看 tree 之插圖);樅木。**'fir-cone** *n*

fire¹ /ˈfaɪə(r); faɪr/ *n* **1** [U] condition of burning: 火: *F~ burns.* 火燃燒。***There is no smoke without ~,*** (prov) There is always some reason for a rumour. (諺)無火不起煙;無風不起浪。***on ~,*** burning: 着火;失火: *The house was on ~.* 這房屋失火了。***play with ~,*** take foolish risks. 玩火。***set sth on ~; set ~ to sth,*** cause it to begin burning: 放火;焚燒;縱火: *He set the haystack on ~.* 他將那乾草堆燃着了。***not (ever)/never set the 'Thames on ~,*** not do anything remarkable: 勿做驚人之擧: *Tom's not the sort of boy who will ever set the Thames on ~,* distinguish himself. 湯姆不是那種會做出驚人之擧的孩子。***take/catch ~,*** begin to burn: 着火;開始燃燒: *Paper catches ~ easily.* 紙易着火。***strike ~ from,*** get sparks from (by striking or rubbing): 由…打火;擦火: *strike ~ from flint.* 由燧石打火。**2** [U] destructive burning: 火災: *Have you insured your house against ~?* 你的房子保過火險沒有? ***~ and sword,*** burning and killing (in war). (戰時)殺人放火。**'~ risk(s),** possible or likely cause(s) of ~. 可能造成火災的原因。**3** [C] instance of destructive burning: 火災的實例: *forest ~s;* 森林火災; *a ~ in a coal-mine.* 煤礦火災。**4** [C] burning fuel in a grate, furnace, etc to heat a room, building, for cooking, etc: 爐火: *The weather is too warm for ~s.* 天氣很暖和,不需要生爐火。*There's a ~ in the next room.* 隔壁房間有爐火。***lay a ~,*** put paper, wood, coal, etc together ready for use. 堆起燃料以備生火。***make a ~,*** lay a ~ and light it. 生火。***make up a ~,*** add fuel as it burns low. 加燃料於火。**eˌlectric '~,** heater using an incandescent element(7). 電暖氣爐。**'gas ~,** heater using lighted gas(2). 瓦斯爐。**5** [U] shooting (from guns). 砲火。***between two ~s,*** shot at from two directions. 在兩面砲火夾攻下。***hang ~,*** ⇨ hang²(4). ***open/cease ~,*** start/stop shooting. 開(停)火。***under ~,*** being shot at. 在砲火下。**running ~,** **(a)** a succession of shots from a line of troops.

(一列士兵之)砲火連發。**(b)** (fig) succession of criticisms, hostile questions, etc. (喩)一連串的批評，責難等。 **6** [U] strong emotion; angry or excited feeling; enthusiasm: 熱情;憤怒;興奮;熱心: *a speech that lacks ~*, is uninspiring; 缺少熱情的演說; *eyes full of ~*. 充滿熱情(憤恨)的眼睛。 **7** (compounds) (複合字) **'~-alarm** *n* apparatus (bell, etc) for making known the outbreak of a ~. 火警警報器。 **'~•arm** *n* (usu *pl*) rifle, gun, pistol or revolver. (通常用複數)輕武器;槍砲。 **'~•ball** *n* (esp) centre of an exploding atomic bomb. 火球;(尤指)原子彈的爆炸中心。 **'~-bird** *n* N American bird with orange and black plumage. 金鵖鳥 (北美所產，有橙黃色和黑色羽毛)。 **'~-bomb** *n* one that burns fiercely and causes destruction by ~. 燒夷彈;燃燒彈。 ⇨ napalm. **'~•box** *n* fuel-chamber of a steam-engine. 蒸汽機之燃燒室; 火箱。 **'~•brand** *n* piece of burning wood; (fig) person who stirs up social or political strife. 燃燒的木柴; (喩) 煽動社會或政治變亂者。 **'~•break** *n* **(a)** (in a forest) wide strip of land without trees (to lessen the risk of a forest ~ spreading). 防火線(森林中一片無樹木的寬長地,以防火災蔓延)。 **(b)** wall or barrier of incombustible material in a warehouse, factory, etc. (倉庫,工廠等中之) 防火牆。 **'~•brick** *n* kind of brick, proof against ~, used in grates, furnaces, chimneys, etc. 耐火磚。 **'~-brigade** *n* organized team of men who put out ~s. 消防隊;救火隊。 **'~-bug** *n* (sl) person who commits arson. (俚)縱火犯。 **'~•clay** *n* [U] kind used for ~-bricks. 耐火黏土(製耐火磚用)。 **'~-control** *n* [U] system of regulating the firing of guns. 射擊控制(調整射擊之系統)。 **'~cracker** *n* small ~work that explodes with a cracking noise. 爆竹;鞭砲。 **'~•damp** *n* [U] gas in coal-mines, explosive when mixed in certain proportions with air. (煤礦坑內之)沼氣;甲烷。 **'~-dog** *n* andiron. (爐之)薪架。 **'~ drill** *n* practice of routine to be followed when ~ breaks out, eg on a ship. 消防演習;救火演習(例如船上擧行者)。 **'~-eater** *n* person who quickly gets angry and ready to fight. 性情暴躁而好鬪之人。 **'~-engine** *n* machine, manned by ~men, for throwing water on to a ~. 救火車。 **'~-escape** *n* outside staircase by means of which people may leave a burning building; apparatus, kind of extending ladder, used by ~men to save people from a burning building. 太平梯; 救火隊員所用的救火梯。 **'~-extinguisher** *n* portable metal cylinder with chemical substance, etc, inside, for putting out a small ~. 滅火器。 **'~-fighter** *n* = ~man(b); (esp) man who fights forest ~s. 消防隊員(尤指救森林火災者)。 **'~-fly** *n* (*pl* -flies) winged beetle that sends out phosphorescent light. 螢火蟲。 **'~•guard** *n* protective metal framework or grating round a ~ in a room. 爐欄。 **'~•hose** *n* hose-pipe used for extinguishing ~s. 水龍帶。 **'~-irons** *n pl* poker, tongs, shovel, etc (kept near a ~place). 火爐用具(撥火棒,火鉗,火鏟等)。 **'~•light** *n* light from the ~ in a ~place: 爐火之火光: *sitting in the ~light*. 圍爐而坐。 **'~•lighter** *n* piece or bundle of fuel for kindling a ~(4). 火種;引火物。 **'~•man** /-mən; -mæn/ *n* (*pl* -men) **(a)** man who looks after the ~ in a furnace or steam-engine. (管理爐火或蒸汽機的)火夫;司爐。 **(b)** member of a ~-brigade. 消防隊員;救火隊員。 **'~•place** *n* grate or hearth for a ~ in a room, usu of brick or stone in the wall. 壁爐。 **'~ plug** *n* connection in a water-main for a ~-hose. 消防栓。 **'~-power** *n* [U] capacity to fire(6), expressed as the total number and weight of shells fired per minute: 火力;火量(以每分鐘射出的砲彈總數和重量計算): *the ~-power of a cruiser*. 巡洋艦的火力。 **'~•proof** *adj* that does not burn; that does not crack or break when heated. 耐火的;防火的。 **'~-raising** *n* [U] arson. 縱火。 **'F~ Service,** (now the official term for) ~-brigade(s). 救火隊;消防隊(現爲正式名稱)。 **'~•side** *n* ***the ~side,*** part of a room round the ~place: 爐邊: *sitting at the ~side;* 坐在爐邊; (fig) home life; (喩)家庭生活; (attrib) (形容用法) *a ~side chair;* 爐邊之椅; *a homely ~side scene*. 家常的爐邊情景。 **'~ station** *n* building for a ~-brigade and its equipment. 消防隊駐所。 **'~•stone** *n* ~proof stone (in a ~place, etc). 爐石(壁爐之防火石)。 **'~-walking** *n* [U] ceremony of walking barefoot over stones heated by ~, or over white-hot wood-ash, etc. 渡火(赤足在灼熱的石上或炭灰等上行走的一種儀式)。 Hence, 由此產生， **'~-walker** *n* **'~-watcher** *n* (in World War II) person whose duty was to watch for ~s started by bombs dropped from the air. (二次世界大戰時)空襲火災警戒員。Hence, 由此產生， **'~-watching** *n* [U] **'~-water** *n* (colloq) spirits such as whisky, gin and rum. (俗)烈酒(如威士忌,杜松子酒和蘭酒)。 **'~•wood** *n* wood prepared for lighting ~s or as fuel. 柴;薪。 **'~•work** *n* [C] device containing gunpowder and chemicals, used for making a display at night, or as a signal; (*pl*) (fig) display of wit, anger, etc. 煙火; (複)(喩)機智,憤怒等的表現。

a firework display

fire² /ˈfaɪə(r); faɪr/ *vt, vi* **1** [VP6A] set fire to with the intention of destroying; cause to being burning: 縱火燒;使燃燒;點燃: *~ a haystack*. 點燃一乾草堆。 **2** [VP6A] use artificial heat on sth in order to change it in some way: 加熱使改變: ~ (= bake) *bricks/pottery in a kiln;* 於窰內燒磚(陶); ~ *tea*, cure it, make green leaves dry and dark. 焙茶。 **3** [VP6A] supply (a furnace) with fuel: 加燃料於(爐): *an oil-~d furnace*. 油爐。 **4** *~ up,* (of a person) (more usu *flare up*) become excited or angry: (指人, flare up 較常用)激動;光火;惱怒: *She ~s up at the least thing*. 她會爲了小事發怒。 **5** [VP6A] excite or stimulate. 刺激;激起。 ***~ sb with sth,*** fill with enthusiasm, zeal. 激發某人的熱忱。 **6** [VP6A] discharge (a gun, etc); send (a shell, etc) from a gun; explode (a charge of explosive): 放(槍砲等); 射出(砲彈, 子彈等); 使(炸藥)爆發: *~ a gun*. 開砲。*They ~d a salute*, discharged guns as a salute. 他們鳴放禮砲。[VP2A] shoot: 射擊;放槍或開砲: *The officer ordered his men to ~*. 那軍官下令他的士兵開槍。 ***~ at/ into/ on/ upon,*** [VP3A] direct fire towards: 對…射擊: *~ at a target;* 對目標射擊; *~ upon a fort/ship*. 對一堡壘(船隻)開砲。*The police ~d into the crowd*. 警察向群衆鳴槍。 ***~ away,*** [VP2C] **(a)** continue firing: 繼續開槍;繼續發砲: *They were firing away at the enemy*. 他們對敵人繼續開槍。 **(b)** (fig) go ahead; begin: (喩)繼續下去;開始: *I'm ready to answer questions; ~ away*. 我準備答覆問題，請問罷。 [VP15B] *They ~d away all their ammunition*, expended it all. 他們將所有的彈藥都打完了。 **'firing-line** *n* front line (of trenches) where soldiers ~ at the enemy. 火線;射擊線。 **'firing-party/-squad** *n* number of soldiers ordered to ~ volleys at a military funeral or to carry out a military execution. 鳴槍班 (喪禮時鳴放禮槍的一隊士兵); 行刑班(執行死刑之射擊隊)。 **7** [VP6A] (colloq) dismiss (an employee): (俗)辭退(僱員);解職: *~ the man-*

ager for being incompetent. 因經理無能而將之辭退。

fir·kin /ˈfɜːkɪn ; ˈfɝkɪn/ *n* small cask. 小桶。

firm¹ /fɜːm ; fɝm/ *adj* (-er, -est) **1** solid; hard; not yielding when pressed: 堅固的; 堅硬的; 堅實的: *~ flesh/muscles;* 堅實的肉; *~ ground;* 陸地; *as ~ as a rock.* 固若磐石。***be on ~ ground,*** be sure of one's facts. 立於穩固的基礎上。**2** not easily changed or influenced; showing strength of character and purpose: 不易改變或受影響的;堅定的;堅强的;堅決的: *a ~ faith;* 堅定的信心; *take ~ measures;* 採取堅決步驟; *be ~ with children,* insist upon obedience and discipline; 對孩子們嚴厲; *~ in/of purpose;* 意志堅定; *be ~ in one's beliefs.* 信仰堅定。**3** (of a person, his body, its movements, characteristics, etc) steady, stable: (指人,人的身體,動作,特點等)穩定的;穩固的;沉着的: *walk with ~ steps.* 以穩定的步伐行走。*The baby is not very ~ on its feet yet,* does not stand or walk confidently. 這嬰兒還站(走)不很穩。*He spoke in a ~ voice.* 他以沉着的聲音說話。*He gave me a ~ glance.* 他堅定地望了我一眼。□ *vt, vi* make or become ~. 使堅固;使堅定;使穩;變堅固;變堅定;變穩。□ *adv* in a ~ way: 穩固地;堅定地: *stand ~* (lit or fig); (字面或喻)站穩; *hold ~ to one's beliefs.* 堅守信仰。**~·ly** *adv* in a ~ way. 穩固地;堅定地。**~·ness** *n*

firm² /fɜːm ; fɝm/ *n* [C] (two or more) persons carrying on a business. 商號;公司;商行;廠商。

fir·ma·ment /ˈfɜːməmənt ; ˈfɝməmənt/ *n* **the ~,** the sky, thought of as containing the stars, planets, moon and sun. 蒼天;天空(包括日月星辰)。

first¹ /fɜːst ; fɝst/ *adj* **1** (abbr 略作 **1st**) coming before all others in time or order: 第一的;最早的;最先的: *January, the ~ month of the year;* 一月,一年的第一個月; *the ~ chapter* (or *Chapter One*); 第一章; *King Edward the F~* (often 常作 King Edward I); 英王愛德華一世; *a ~ edition copy of a book;* 一本書的初版; *the ~ man who arrived/the ~ man to arrive;* 最先到達的那人; *at the ~* (= earliest) *opportunity;* 一有機會; *~* (= basic) *principles.* 基本的原理。***at ~ sight,*** when seen or examined for the ~ time: 一見之下;乍看來: *fall in love at ~ sight.* 一見鍾情。*At ~ sight the problem seemed easy.* 這問題乍看起來很容易。***in the ˈ~ place,*** (in making a list) as a beginning; ~ly. 首先;第一。***~ thing,*** as a ~ action; before doing anything else: 第一件事;首先做的事: *~ thing tomorrow morning.* 明天早上首先要做的事。***~ things ~,*** the most important things before the others. 最重要的事優先;要事第一。***not to know the ~ thing about sth,*** to know nothing whatsoever about it. 對某事絲毫不知情。**2** (special uses, compounds): (特殊用法,複合字): ˌ**~ ˈaid** *n* [U] treatment given at once to a sick or injured person before a doctor comes. (醫生未來之前對傷患所做的)急救。ˌ**~ ˈbase** *n* (baseball) ~ base¹(6) on the field. (棒球)一壘。***get to ~ base,*** (fig) make a successful start. (喻)有一個成功的開始。ˌ**~ ˈclass** *n* [U] best accommodation in a train, ship, aircraft, etc. (火車的)頭等車;(輪船,飛機等的)頭等艙。⇨ class(1). ˌ**~-ˈclass** *adj* of the ~ class; excellent: 頭等的;頭等車的;頭等艙的;特優的: *~-class hotels/cabins/passengers;* 頭等旅館(艙,乘客); *a ~-class* (university) *degree;* 優等學位; *~-class food/entertainment.* 最好的食物(款待)。□ *adv* by the ~ class: 乘頭等車,船,機等: *travel ˌ~-ˈclass.* 乘頭等車或艙位旅行。ˌ**~ ˈcost** *n* (comm) cost not including profit. (商)最初成本。ˌ**~ deˈgree,** ⇨ degree. ˌ**~ ˈfloor** *n* (GB) floor immediately above the ground floor; (US) ground floor. (英)二樓;(美)一樓;底層。ˈ**~ form** *n* (GB) lowest class in secondary schools. (英)中學一年級。ˈ**~-fruits** *n pl* earliest produce (crops, etc) of the season; (fig) ~ results of one's work. 一季中最早的收成;(喻)初次的收益;最早的產品。ˌ**~ ˈgear,** lowest gear(1). 頭檔。ˌ**~-ˈhand** *adj, adv* (obtained) directly from the source: 直接得自來源的(地);第一手的(地): *~-hand information;* 直接得來的消息;第一手資料; *learn something ˌ~-ˈhand.* 直接獲知某事。***at ~ hand,*** directly. 直接地。ˌ**~ ˈlady** *n* (US) wife of a President or a Governor of a State. (美)總統夫人;州長夫人。ˈ**~ name** *n* given name (contrasted with family name): 教名;名(以別於姓): *be on ~ name terms with the boss* (suggesting informality). 可與老板互相直呼其名(表示不拘束)。ˌ**~ ˈnight** *n* evening on which a play or opera is presented for the ~ time. (戲劇或歌劇之)首演之夜。Hence, 由此產生, ˌ**~-ˈnighter,** person who regularly attends ~ nights. 經常觀戲劇首演的人。ˌ**~ ˈmate** *n* ⇨ mate¹(2). ˌ**~ ofˈfender,** one against whom no previous conviction has been recorded. 初犯。ˌ**~ ˈperson** (gram) the pronouns *I, me, we, us* (and the verb forms used with them). (文法)第一人稱(I, me, we, us 諸代名詞及其動詞形式)。ˌ**~-ˈrate** *adj* of the best class; excellent: 第一流的;最佳的: *~-rate acting.* 最佳的演出。□ *adv* (colloq) very well: (俗)很好: *getting on ˌ~-ˈrate.* 情形很好。**~·ly** *adv* (in making a list) as a beginning; in the ~ place. 首先;第一。

first² /fɜːst ; fɝst/ *adv* **1** before anyone or anything else (often, for emphasis, ***~ of all; ~ and foremost***): 第一;最初;最先(加强語氣時,常作 first of all, first and foremost): *Which horse came in ~,* won the race? 哪一匹馬跑得冠軍? *Women and children ~,* ie before men. 婦孺優先。***F~ come, ~ served,*** Those who come ~ will be served ~. 先到的先招待。***last in, ~ out,*** (esp) the last to be employed are the ~ to be dismissed when dismissals are necessary. (尤指)裁員時最後受僱者最先被裁掉。***~ and last,*** taking one thing with another; on the whole. 整個看來;就全體而論。ˈ**~·born** *n, adj* eldest (child). 最先出生的;長子;長女。**2** for the ~ time: 初次: *When did you ~ see him/see him ~?* 你第一次是在什麼時候看到他? **3** before some other (specified or implied) time: 首先(在另一特指或暗示的時間以前): *I must finish this work ~,* ie before starting sth else. 我必須先完成這件工作。**4** in preference: 寧願: *He said he would resign ~,* eg resign rather than do sth dishonest for his employers. 他說他寧願辭職(例如寧願辭職也不願爲雇主做欺詐之事)。

first³ /fɜːst ; fɝst/ *n* **1** ***at ~,*** at the beginning. 最初;當初。***from the ~,*** from the start. 從開始起。***from ~ to last,*** from beginning to end; throughout. 自始至終;始終;一直。**2** (in examinations, competitions) place in the first class; person who takes this: (考試或比賽的)第一名;冠軍: *He got a ~ in Modern Languages.* 他在近代語言一科得第一名。

firth /fɜːθ ; fɝθ/ *n* narrow arm of the sea; (esp in Scotland) river estuary. 狹窄的海灣;(尤指蘇格蘭之)河的入海口。

fis·cal /ˈfɪskl ; ˈfɪskl̩/ *adj* of public revenue. 國庫歲收的;財政的。⇨ year(4).

fish¹ /fɪʃ ; fɪʃ/ *n* (*pl* ~ or ~es) **1** [C] cold-blooded animal living wholly in water and breathing through gills, with fins for swimming: 魚: *catch a ~/two ~es/a lot of ~.* 捉到一(兩,許多)條魚。⇨ the illus here and at sea. 參看附圖及 sea 之插圖。***a ˈpretty kettle of ~,*** a state of confusion. 混亂。***have ˈother ~ to fry,*** more important business to attend to. 另有要事。***There's as good ~ in the sea as ever came out of it,*** (prov) Even if one chance, etc has not been seized, there will be plenty of others. (諺)海裏的好魚多的是(縱然失去一個機會等,尙有許多)。**2** [U] ~ as food: 魚肉: *boiled/fried/grilled ~;* 煮的(炸的,烤的)魚; *a ~ course* (as part of a meal). 一道魚。**3** (compounds) (複合字) ˈ**~·bone,** bone of a ~. 魚骨。ˈ**~·cake,** ~ rissole. 魚餅。ˌ**~ and ˈchips,** fried fish with fried chips of potato. 炸魚及炸馬鈴薯條。ˌ**~ ˈfinger** (US 美 ˌ**~ ˈstick**), small, long piece of ~, covered with breadcrumbs, eaten fried or grilled. 炸魚條;

fish

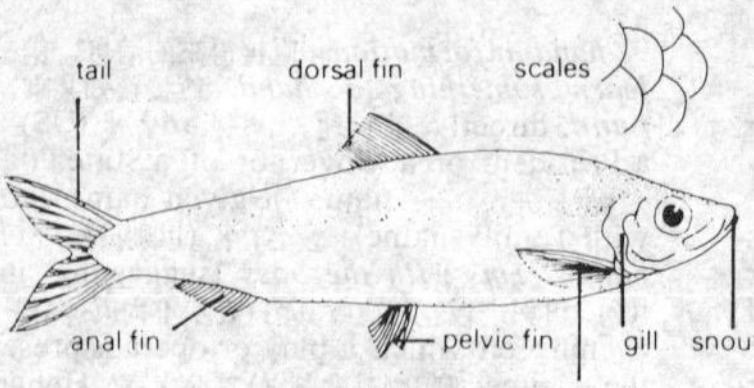

HERRING

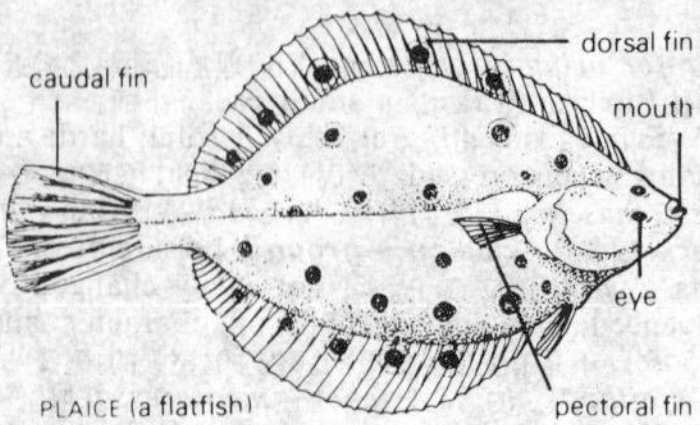

PLAICE (a flatfish)

烤魚條。 **'~-hook,** metal hook used for catching ~. 魚鉤。 **'~-knife,** knife with which ~ is eaten. (吃魚用之)魚刀。 **'~•monger,** tradesman who sells ~. 魚販。 **'~•paste,** paste of ~ or shellfish (spread on sandwiches, etc). 魚醬(魚或蝦蟹等之醬,塗於三明治等上)。 **'~-slice,** knife for carving and serving ~ at table.切魚刀;分魚刀。**'~•wife,** (colloq) crude, abusive woman. (俗)粗野的女人。 **~y** *adj* **1** smelling or tasting like ~: 魚腥味的;魚味的: *a ~y smell.* 魚腥味。 **2** (colloq) causing a feeling of doubt: (俗)可疑的;難以置信的: *a ~y story.* 難以置信的故事。

fish[2] /fɪʃ ; fɪʃ/ *vi, vt* **1** [VP2A, C] try to catch fish: 釣魚;捕魚: *go ~ing;* 去釣魚; *~ in the sea;* 在海上捕魚; (fig) try to get, by indirect methods: (喻)間接探聽;設法獲得讚賞: *~ for information/compliments.* 間接探聽消息(沽名釣譽)。 *~ **in troubled waters,*** try to win advantages for oneself from a disturbed state of affairs. 混水摸魚。 **2** [VP6A] try to catch ~ in: 在…中釣魚;在…中捕魚: *~ a river/a pool;* 在河(塘)中釣魚; try to catch by ~ing: 釣(魚);捕(魚): *~ trout.* 釣鱒魚。 **3** [VP15A, B] *~ **up (out of)/(from);** ~ **out (of/from),*** draw or pull (from): 拖出;拉出;掏出;撈出: *~ out a coin from/~ a coin out of one's pocket;* 從口袋裏掏出一枚硬幣; *~ up a dead cat out of a canal.* 自溝裏拖出一死貓。 **~•ing** *n* [U] catching fish for a living or for pleasure. 捕魚;釣魚。 **'~•ing-line** *n* line[1](1) with a ~-hook attached for ~ing. 釣絲;釣線。 **'~•ing-rod** *n* long tapered rod (often jointed) to which a ~ing-line is fastened. 釣竿。 **'~ing-tackle** *n* [U] equipment needed for ~ing. 釣具。

fisher /'fɪʃə(r) ; 'fɪʃɚ/ *n* (old use) fisherman. (舊用法)漁翁;漁人。 **~•man** /-mən ; -mən/ *n* (*pl* -men) man who earns a living by fishing. 漁人;漁夫。 ⇨ *angler* at angle[2].

fish•ery /'fɪʃərɪ ; 'fɪʃərɪ/ *n* (*pl* -ries) part of the sea where fishing is carried on: 漁場: *in-shore fisheries,* near the coast; 近海漁場; *deep-sea fisheries.* 遠洋漁場。

fish•plate /'fɪʃpleɪt ; 'fɪʃ,plet/ *n* one of two iron plates used to fasten rails to a sleeper (on a railway track). 接軌夾板(夾接鐵軌於枕木的鐵板);魚尾夾板。

fis•sile /'fɪsaɪl *US:* 'fɪsl ; 'fɪsḷ/ *adj* that tends to split: 易分裂的: *~ material,* eg that can be split up in a nuclear reactor. 可裂物質(例如可於核子反應器中分裂之物質)。

fis•sion /'fɪʃn ; 'fɪʃən/ *n* [U] splitting or division, eg of one cell into new cells, or of the nucleus of certain atoms, eg uranium, when an atomic bomb is exploded. 分裂(例如單細胞分裂成新細胞,原子彈爆炸時鈾的原子核分裂)。 **~•able** /-əbl ; -əbḷ/ *adj* that can be split by ~; capable of atomic ~. 可分裂的;可作原子分裂的。

fis•sipar•ous /fɪ'sɪpərəs ; fɪ'sɪpərəs/ *adj* (of cells) reproducing by fission. (指細胞)分裂繁殖的。

fis•sure /'fɪʃə(r) ; 'fɪʃɚ/ *n* [C] cleft made by splitting or separation of parts. 裂隙;裂縫。

fist /fɪst ; fɪst/ *n* hand when tightly closed (as in boxing): 拳;拳頭: *He struck me with his ~.* 他用拳頭打我。 *He shook his ~ at me.* 他向我揮拳。 ⇨ the illus at arm. 參看 arm 之插圖。 **~i•cuffs** /'fɪstɪkʌfs ; 'fɪstɪ,kʌfs/ *n pl* (usu hum) fighting with the ~s. (通常爲諧)鬥拳;互毆。

fis•tula /'fɪstjʊlə ; 'fɪstʃʊlə/ *n* long pipe-like ulcer with a narrow mouth. 瘻管。

fit[1] /fɪt ; fɪt/ *adj* (fitter, fittest) **1** ***fit (for),*** suitable or suited; well adapted; good enough: 合適的;切合的;適宜的;恰當的: *The food was not fit to eat,* was too bad to be eaten. 那食物不適宜吃。 *It was a dinner fit for a king.* 那是一適於王者的盛餐。 *That man is not fit for the position.* 那人不適合這職位。 *We must decide on a fit time and place for the meeting.* 我們必須決定適當的開會時間和地點。 **2** right and proper: 適當的;正當的: *It is not fit that you should mock your mother so.* 你如此嘲笑你母親是不應該的。 ***think/see fit (to do sth),*** decide to: 決定;決心: *He didn't see fit to adopt my suggestion.* 他不採納我的建議。 *Do as you think fit.* 你認爲怎麼做合適就怎麼做。 **3** ready; in a suitable condition; (also colloq, as an *adv*): 齊備的; 備妥的; (口語中亦用做副詞): *They went on working till they were fit to drop,* ready to drop from exhaustion. 他們繼續工作,直到快要累倒才停。 *He was laughing fit to burst himself,* so violently that he seemed ready to burst. 他笑得支持不住了。 **4** in good athletic condition; in good health: 强健的;健康的: *I hope you're keeping fit.* 我希望你能保持健康。 ⇨ keep[1](14). *He has been ill and is not fit for work/fit to travel yet.* 他一直在生病,尚不能工作(旅行)。 **fit•ly** *adv* **fit•ness** *n* [U] **1** suitability (*for*): 適當;合宜(與 for 連用): *the fitness of things,* what is right or suitable. 適當的事物;合宜之事。 **2** the state of being physically fit: 健康: *a national fitness campaign,* one for improving the nation's health. 國民健康運動。

fit[2] /fɪt ; fɪt/ *vt, vi* (-tt-) **1** [VP6A, 2A] be the right measure, shape and size for: 適合於;合適: *shoes that fit well;* 很合腳的鞋子; *a badly fitting door.* 不好關的門。 *This coat doesn't fit me.* 這件上衣不合我穿。 *The key doesn't fit the lock.* 這鑰匙不合這把鎖。 **2** [VP15A, B] ***fit (on),*** put on (esp clothing) to see that it is the right size, shape, etc: 試穿(尤指衣服)看是否合身: *have a new coat fitted.* 試穿一新上衣。 **3** [VP15A, B] ***fit (on),*** put into place: 安裝;裝置: *fit a new lock on a door.* 在門上裝一新鎖。 **4** [VP6A, 14, 16A] ***fit (for),*** make (sb, oneself) suitable or competent: 使(某人或自己)適應或勝任: *fit oneself for one's new duties.* 使自己能勝任新職責。 *Military training fits men for long marches/to make long marches.* 軍事訓練能使人適應長途行軍。 *Can we make the punishment fit the crime?* 我們能使懲罰與犯罪相稱嗎? **5** [VP 15B, 2C] ***fit in (with),*** (cause to) be in a suitable or harmonious relation (with); find, be in, the right or a suitable time or place for: (使)適合; 相合; 配合: *I must fit my holidays in with yours.* 我必須使我的假日與你的配合。 *My holiday arrangements must fit in with yours.* 我的假期計畫必須配合你的。 ***fit sb/sth out/up,*** supply with what is needed; equip: 供以必需品;裝備: *fit out a ship for a long voyage/a party for a polar expedition;* 裝備一船以作長期航行(一隊人以作極地探險); *a hotel fitted up with modern comforts and conveniences.* 有現代化設備的旅館。 □ *n* (usu ***a*** + *adj* + ~) (通常用於 a + adj + ~ 的句型) style, manner, in which sth, eg a garment, fits: (衣服等)適合的樣子: *The coat is a tight/good/excellent* *fit.* 這上衣很貼身(很合身,十分合身)。

fit³ /fɪt ; fɪt/ *n* **1** sudden (usu short) attack of illness: 疾病的突然發作(通常是短暫的): *a fit of coughing;* 一陣咳嗽; *a 'fainting fit.* 一陣昏厥。 **2** sudden attack of hysteria, apoplexy, paralysis, with loss of consciousness and violent movements: 歇斯底里症,中風,痲痺的突發(因而失去知覺或發出劇烈動作): *fall down in a fit.* (因中風等)突然昏倒。 ***give sb a fit,*** (colloq) do sth that greatly shocks or outrages him. (俗) 做某事而使某人大吃一驚或震怒。 ***have a fit,*** (colloq) be greatly surprised or outraged: (俗)大驚;大怒: *She almost had a fit when she saw the bill.* 她看到那帳單時幾乎大吃一驚。 **3** sudden onset lasting for a short time; outburst: 短時間的發作;突發: *a fit of energy/enthusiasm/anger.* 一股幹勁(一股熱忱,一陣憤怒)。 ***by/in fits and starts,*** in short periods, from time to time, not regularly. 一陣陣地;間或;不規則地。 **4** mood: 心情: *when the fit was on him,* when he felt in the right mood (*for* sth). 興之所至(與 for 連用,後接某事物)。 **fit·ful** /-fl ; -fəl/ *adj* occurring, coming and going, in short periods; irregular: 一陣陣的;不定的: *a fitful breeze;* 一陣陣的微風; *fitful bursts of energy.* 一陣陣的幹勁。 **fit·fully** /-fəlɪ ; -fəlɪ/ *adv*

fit·ment /'fɪtmənt ; 'fɪtmənt/ *n* piece of furniture or equipment: 傢具;設備: *kitchen ~s,* eg sinks, cupboards, working tables, esp when made as units in a series. 厨房設備(例如洗滌槽,碗橱,料理台,尤指成套者)。

fit·ter /'fɪtə(r) ; 'fɪtɚ/ *n* **1** (tailoring and dress-making) person who cuts out, fits and alters garments. (裁縫)剪裁和試樣的裁縫師。 **2** (eng) workman who fits together and adjusts the finished parts of an engine, machine, etc. (工程)裝配發動機,機器等之人;裝配匠。

fit·ting /'fɪtɪŋ ; 'fɪtɪŋ/ *adj* proper; right; suitable. 適當的;適合的。 □ *n* **1** act of fitting: 試衣;試穿: *go to the tailor's for a ~.* 去裁縫店試衣服。 **2** fixture in a building, esp (*pl*) things permanently fixed: 建築物中之裝置物;(複數尤指)固定裝置: *gas and electric light ~s.* 煤氣和電燈裝置。 **3** (*pl*) furnishings: (複)傢具;設備: *office ~s,* eg desks, chairs, filing cabinets. 辦公室的設備(例如桌,椅,檔案櫃)。

five /faɪv ; faɪv/ *n, adj* the number 5, ⇨ App 4, 5: 五;五個(參看附錄四,五): *a ~-day week,* one of ~ working days. 有五個工作天的一週。 **'~·fold** *adj* with ~ parts; ~ times as much. 有五部分的;五重的;五倍的。 **~·pence** /'faɪfpəns ; 'faɪvpəns/ *n* ~ pence. 五辨士。 **~·penny** /'faɪfpənɪ ; 'faɪv,pɛnɪ/ *adj* costing ~pence. 值五辨士的。 **fiver** /'faɪvə(r) ; 'faɪvɚ/ *n* (colloq) (GB) £5 note; (US) $5 bill. (俗)(英)五鎊鈔票;(美)五元鈔票。

fives /faɪvz ; faɪvz/ *n* (GB) ball game played with the hands or a bat in a walled court. (英)一種球戲(用手或球棒在有牆壁圍繞的庭院中進行)。

fix¹ /fɪks ; fɪks/ *vt, vi* **1** [VP6A, 15A, B] make firm or fast; fasten (sth) so that it cannot be moved: 使固定;縛緊;釘牢: *fix a post in the ground/a shelf to a wall;* 將一柱栽置地上(將一架釘在牆上); *fix facts/dates, etc in one's mind,* implant them deeply so that they will not be forgotten. 牢記事實(日期等)。 **2** [VP14] ***fix on,*** direct (the eyes, one's attention, etc) steadily on or to: 使(眼睛,注意力等)指向;注視;專心於: *fix one's attention on what one is doing.* 專心於正在從事的工作。 *He fixed his eyes on me.* 他注視着我。 **3** [VP6A] (of objects) attract and hold (the attention): (指物體)吸引(注意力): *This unusual sight fixed his attention/kept his attention fixed.* 這個不凡的景色吸引了他的注意力。 **4** [VP6A] determine or decide: 決定;確定: *fix the rent;* 決定租金; *fix a date for a meeting;* 決定開會日期; *sell goods only at fixed prices,* prices with no discount, with no possibility of bargaining; 以定價售賣貨物;售貨不二價; *a man with fixed* (= definite and decided) *principles.* 有定見之人。 ***fixed odds,*** ⇨ odds(3). **5** [VP6A] treat (photographic films, colours used in dyeing, etc) so that light does not affect them. 定(像);定(影);使(顏色等)固定不變。 **6** [VP15A] single out (sb) by looking steadily (at him): 凝視(某人): *fix a man with an angry stare.* 以憤怒的眼光瞪着一人。 **7** [VP15B] ***fix sb up (with sth); fix sth up (with sb),*** arrange; organize, provide for; put in order: 安排;解決;預備;整理: *fix sb up with a job;* 爲某人安排一工作; *fix up a friend for the night,* give him a bed; 替友人準備一過夜的住處; *fix up a meeting with sb;* 安排與某人相晤; *fix one's room/drawers/shelves up.* 整理房間(抽屜,架子)。 **8** [VP3A] ***fix on/upon,*** settle one's choice, decide to have: 選定: *They've fixed upon a little bungalow near Rye.* 他們已選定了瑞埃附近一所小平房。 **9** [VP6A] (sl) (俚) **(a)** use bribery or deception, improper influence: 賄賂;詐騙;作弊: *You can't fix a judge in Britain.* 在英國你不能賄賂法官。 **(b)** get even with sb: 報復: *I'll fix him.* 我要向他報復。 **10** [VP6A] (colloq) put in order; prepare: (俗)整頓;修理;準備: *fix one's hair,* brush and comb it; 梳理頭髮; *fix a watch,* repair it; 修理一錶; *fix a salad,* mix and dress it. 調製生菜食品。 **fixed** /fɪkst ; fɪkst/ *adj* unchanging: 不變的;固定的: *fixed costs,* overhead expenses. 固定費用;營業費用。 ⇨ overhead; *a fixed idea,* one in which a person persists and which tends to occupy his thoughts too much; 固定觀念; *a fixed star,* one that seems to keep the same position relative to others, not changing it as planets do. 恆星。 **fix·ed·ly** /'fɪksɪdlɪ ; 'fɪksɪdlɪ/ *adv* in a fixed manner (esp of looking): 固定地(尤指目光): *look/gaze fixedly at sb.* 注視某人。

fix² /fɪks ; fɪks/ *n* **1** ***be in/get oneself into a fix,*** a dilemma, an awkward situation. 處於進退兩難之境;陷入困境。 **2** finding of a position, position found, by taking bearings, observing the stars, etc. 確定方位;已確定的方位。 **3** (sl) hypodermic injection of a drug, eg heroin. (俚)注射痲醉藥(如海洛英)。

fix·ate /fɪk'seɪt ; 'fɪkset/ *vt* [VP6A] **1** stare at. 瞪視。 **2** (usu passive) cause a fixation(2). (通常用被動語態)引起病態的執着。 ***~ed (on),*** (colloq) obsessed (with). (俗)心神困擾。

fix·ation /fɪk'seɪʃn ; fɪks'eʃən/ *n* **1** [U] fixing or being fixed: 固定;決定;裝置;安排;定影;定色: *the ~ of a photographic film.* 照像軟片之定影。 **2** [C] ***~ (on),*** (psych) immature and abnormal emotional attachment to another person, with difficulty in forming other, normal, attachments; (colloq) obsession. (心理)執着(病態的眷戀某人);(俗)心神困擾;强迫觀念。

fixa·tive /'fɪksətɪv ; 'fɪksətɪv/ *n* substance that fixes(5) eg photographs, paintings; substance that preserves animal tissue for study under a microscope; substance for keeping hair or dentures in position. 定影劑;防止褪色劑;(顯微鏡下固定動物組織之)固定劑;固定頭髮或假牙之物。

fix·ture /'fɪkstʃə(r) ; 'fɪkstʃɚ/ *n* [C] **1** sth fixed in place, esp (*pl*) built-in cupboards, electric-light fittings, etc which are bought with a building: 固定之物;(複數尤指)建築物之附屬裝置(如壁橱,電燈裝置等): *The owner of the house charged us for ~s and fittings.* 房主要我們付使用附屬裝置物的費用。 **2** (day fixed or decided for a) sporting event: 運動項目;預定的運動項目舉行日: *football and racing ~s.* 足球與賽跑項目。 **3** (colloq) person or thing that appears unlikely to move from or leave a place: (俗)不會移動或離開的人或物: *Professor Gravity seems to be a ~ in the college.* 格萊維特教授似乎要在這個學院教一輩子。

fizz /fɪz ; fɪz/ *vi* [VP2A, C] make a hissing sound (as when gas escapes from a liquid). 發嘶嘶聲(如氣體自液體中漏出之聲)。 □ *n* [U] this sound; aer-ation by carbon dioxide: 嘶嘶聲；充以二氧化碳: *This soda-water has lost its ~*, has gone flat²(9). 這汽水跑氣了。**~y** *adj* (-ier, -iest).

fizzle /ˈfɪzl ; ˈfɪzl̩/ *vi* [VP2A, C] hiss or splutter feebly. 發微弱的嘶嘶聲。**~ out**, end feebly; come to a weak, unsatisfactory end. 虎頭蛇尾地結束；結果失敗。

fjord /fɪˈɔːd ; fjord/ = fiord.

flab·ber·gast /ˈflæbəɡɑːst *US:* -ɡæst ; ˈflæbɚˌɡæst/ *vt* [VP6A] (colloq) overwhelm with amazement. (俗)使驚愕。

flabby /ˈflæbɪ ; ˈflæbɪ/ *adj* (-ier, -iest) **1** (of the muscles, flesh) soft; not firm: (指肌肉)鬆軟的；鬆弛的: *A man who never takes exercise is likely to have ~ muscles.* 從來不運動的人肌肉會鬆軟。**2** (fig) weak; without moral force: (喻)軟弱的；無道德力的: *a ~ will/character.* 軟弱的意志(性格)。**flab·bily** /-ɪlɪ ; -əlɪ/ *adv* **flab·bi·ness** *n*

flac·cid /ˈflæksɪd ; ˈflæksɪd/ *adj* hanging loose and limp; flabby. 鬆軟的；軟弱的。**~·ity** /flækˈsɪdətɪ ; flækˈsɪdətɪ/ *n*

flag¹ /flæɡ ; flæɡ/ *n* (usu square or oblong) piece of cloth, attached by one edge to a rope, used as the distinctive symbol of a country, or as a signal: 國旗；旗幟(通常指方形或長方形者): *the national ~ of Great Britain*, the Union Jack, ⇨ illus here; 英國國旗(參看本條之插圖); *the Red Cross ~;* 紅十字會旗; *streets decorated with ~s.* 飾有旗幟的街道。**~ of convenience**, ~, eg of Panama, Liberia, used to obscure actual ownership of ships and so evade taxation. 爲逃稅而隱蔽船隻主權的旗(例如巴拿馬或賴比瑞亞旗)。***lower/strike one's ~***, take it down as a sign of surrender. 降旗表示投降。**ˈ~-captain** *n* captain of a ~ship. 旗艦艦長。**ˈ~-day (a)** day on which money is raised for a charitable cause by persons in public places, a small paper ~ being given to those who contribute. 售旗(小紙旗)募捐日。**(b)** (US) 14 June, anniversary of the day in 1777 when the Stars and Stripes became the national ~. (美)國旗紀念日(爲六月十四日，紀念1777年於該日採用星條旗爲美國國旗)。**ˈ~ officer**, admiral. 海軍將官。**ˈ~·pole**, pole on which a ~ is flown. 旗竿。**ˈ~·ship**, warship having an admiral on board. 旗艦(駐有海軍將官之戰艦)。**ˈ~·staff**, pole on which a ~ is flown. 旗竿。⇨ also black, white² and yellow. □ *vt* (-gg-) **1** [VP6A] place a ~ or ~s on; decorate with ~s: 懸旗於；飾以旗: *streets ~ged to celebrate a victory.* 懸旗慶祝勝利的街道。**2** [VP6A, 15B] ~ ***(down)***, signal to (sb), stop a train, car, etc by moving one's outstretched arm up and down or waving a ~. 對(某人)打旗語；揮臂或揮旗使(火車，汽車等)停止。⇨ semaphore.

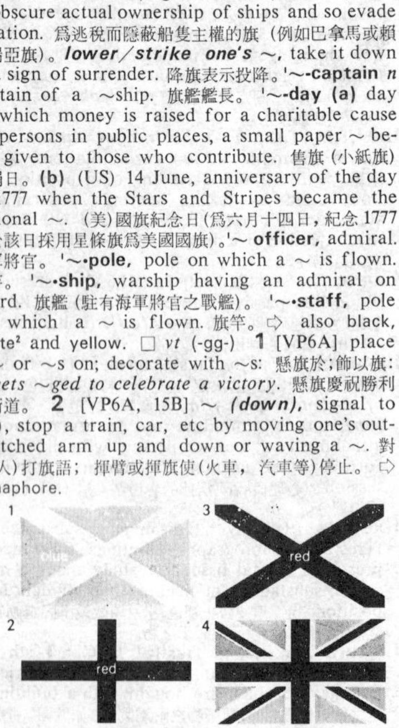

flags 1 St Andrew's 2 St George's 3 St Patrick's 4 the Union Jack

flag² /flæɡ ; flæɡ/ *vi* (-gg-) [VP2A] (of plants, etc) droop, hang down, become limp; (fig) become tired or weak: (指植物等)枯萎；(喻)疲倦；衰弱: *My strength/interest/enthusiasm is ~ging.* 我的體力(興趣，熱忱)減退了。

flag³ /flæɡ ; flæɡ/ *n* (also 亦作 **ˈ~·stone**) flat, square or oblong piece of stone for a floor, path or pavement. (鋪地或道路之)石板。

flag⁴ /flæɡ ; flæɡ/ *n* kinds of plant with blade-like leaves, growing in moist land, esp kinds of iris. 菖蒲；香蒲。

flagel·lant /ˈflædʒələnt ; ˈflædʒələnt/ *n* person who whips himself or another, eg as a religious penance. (作爲宗教贖罪等而)鞭笞自己或他人者。**flagel·late** /ˈflædʒəleɪt ; ˈflædʒəˌlet/ *vt* [VP6A] whip. 鞭笞；鞭打。**flagel·la·tion** /ˌflædʒəˈleɪʃn ; ˌflædʒəˈleʃən/ *n*

flageo·let /ˌflædʒəʊˈlet ; ˌflædʒəˈlɛt/ *n* small flute, like a whistle, with six stops. 六孔短笛；哨笛。

flagon /ˈflæɡən ; ˈflæɡən/ *n* **1** large, rounded bottle in which wine, cider, etc is sold, usu holding about twice as much as an ordinary bottle. 大肚酒瓶(通常可裝一般酒瓶兩倍之量)。**2** vessel with a handle, lip and lid for serving wine at table. (有把手，壺嘴和壺蓋的)酒壺。

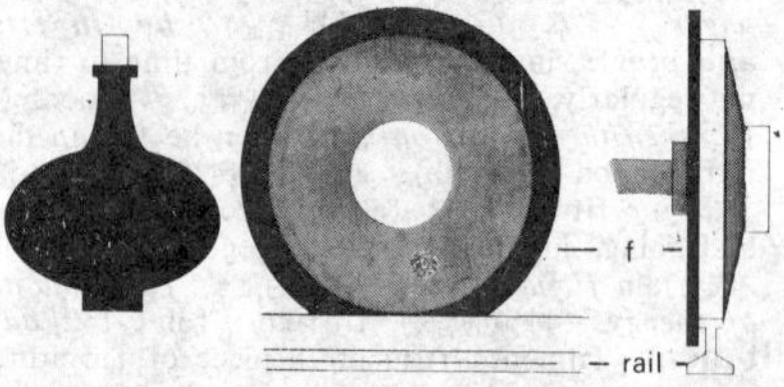

a flagon a flange

fla·grant /ˈfleɪɡrənt ; ˈfleɡrənt/ *adj* (of crime or a criminal, etc) openly and obviously wicked; glaring; scandalous: (指罪惡，罪犯等)罪惡昭彰的；昭然若揭的；聲名狼藉的: *~ offences/sinners.* 重罪(惡名昭著的罪人)。**~·ly** *adv*

flail /fleɪl ; flel/ *n* old-fashioned tool for threshing grain, consisting of a strong stick hinged on a long handle. 連枷(舊式打穀具)。□ *vt* [VP6A] beat with (or as with) a ~. 以連枷打；似以連枷打。

flair /fleə(r) ; flɛr/ *n* [U, C] natural or instinctive ability (to do sth well, to select or recognize what is best, most useful, etc): 天才；本領；鑑別眼光；敏銳的覺察力: *have a ~ for languages*, be quick at learning them; 有語言天才; *have a ~ for bargains*, be good at recognizing them. 有做買賣的眼光。

flak /flæk ; flæk/ *n* [U] anti-aircraft guns or gunfire; (fig) criticism: 高射砲；高射砲火；(喻)批評: *get/take a lot of ~.* 受到許多批評。**ˈ~ jacket**, protective jacket of heavy material, reinforced with metal. (用厚布料及金屬做成的)防彈背心；防彈衣。

flake /fleɪk ; flek/ *n* [C] small, light, leaf-like piece: 小薄片: *ˈsnow-~s;* 雪花；雪片; *~s of rust falling from old iron;* 自舊鐵上落下的一片片的銹; *ˈsoap-~s.* 皂片。□ *vi* [VP2A, C] ~ ***(off)***, fall off in ~s. 剝落。**flaky** *adj* (-ier, -iest) made up of ~s: 小薄片製成的: *flaky pastry.* 酥餅。**flaki·ness** *n*

flam·beau /ˈflæmbəʊ ; ˈflæmbo/ *n* (*pl* ~x or ~s /-bəʊz ; -boz/) flaming torch. 火炬；火把。

flam·boy·ant /flæmˈbɔɪənt ; flæmˈbɔɪənt/ *adj* brightly coloured and decorated; (of a person, his character) florid, showy. 燦爛的；(指人，性格)華而不實的；炫耀的。**~·ly** *adv* **flam·boy·ance** /-əns ; -əns/ *n*

flame¹ /fleɪm ; flem/ *n* **1** [C, U] (portion of) burning gas; visible part of a fire: 火焰: *The house was in ~s*, was on fire, burning. 這房子失火了。*He put a match to the papers and they burst into ~(s).* 他燃一根火柴在那些文件上，它們便燒着了。**ˈ~·thrower** *n* weapon which projects a steady stream of burning fuel. 火焰噴射器；噴火器(一種武器)。**2** [C] blaze of light; brilliant colour: 耀目的光輝；燦爛的顏色: *the ~s of sunset.* 夕陽的燦爛光輝。**3** [C] passion: 熱情；激情: *a ~ of anger/indignation/enthusiasm.* 怒火(憤激之火；熱情如火)。**4** [C] (colloq) sweetheart: (俗)愛人: *She's an old ~ of his*, a woman with whom he was once in love. 她是他的老情人。

flame² /fleɪm ; flem/ *vi* [VP2A,C] burn with, send out, flames; be or become like flames in colour:

焚燒;發火焰;變得紅如火焰: *make the fire ~ up;* 使爐火發火焰; *hillsides flaming with the colours of autumn*, eg of maple-trees. 紅如火焰的秋天的山坡(例如由楓樹造成者)。*His face ~d with anger.* 他氣得面紅耳赤。*His anger ~d out.* 他勃然大怒。*The boy's face ~d still redder,* became redder, with anger, embarrassment, etc. 這孩子的面孔紅得更厲害了(因憤怒,困窘等)。**flam·ing** *adj* burning; very hot: 燃燒的;灼熱的: *a flaming sun;* 灼熱的太陽; (colloq, vulg) bloody(3): (俗,鄙)非常的;很大的: *You flaming idiot!* 你這個大笨蛋!

fla·mingo /flə'mɪŋgəʊ ; flə'mɪŋgo/ *n* (*pl* ~s, ~es /-gəʊz ; -goz/) large, long-legged, long-necked wading bird with pink feathers. 紅鸛。⇨ the illus at water. 參看 water 之插圖。

flam·mable /'flæməbl ; 'flæməbḷ/ *adj* (= *inflammable*, but preferred in US and in technical contexts) having a tendency to burst into flames and to burn rapidly. 易燃燒的(在美國和專門術語中較 inflammable 常用)。

flan /flæn ; flæn/ *n* [C] tart containing fruit, etc, not covered with pastry. 含有水果等無硬皮的糕點。

flange /flændʒ ; flændʒ/ *n* projecting or outside rim or collar, eg of a wheel, to keep sth in position. 凸緣;輪緣。⇨ the illus at flagon. 參看 flagon 之插圖。

flank /flæŋk ; flæŋk/ *n* **1** fleshy part of the side of a human being or animal between the last rib and the hip. 脅腹;腰窩(人或動物之側邊在肋骨與臀部間的部分)。⇨ the illus at trunk. 參看 trunk 之插圖。**2** side of a building or mountain. 建築物或山之側面。**3** right or left side of an army or body of troops: (軍隊的)左翼或右翼;側翼: *attack the left ~;* 攻擊左翼; *make a ~ attack.* 側擊。□ *vt* [VP6A] **1** be situated at or on the ~ of. 在…之側。**2** go round the ~ of (the enemy). 側翼包圍(敵人)。

flan·nel /'flænl ; 'flænḷ/ *n* **1** [U] loosely woven woollen cloth: 法蘭絨: *a yard of ~;* 一碼法蘭絨; *~ trousers/shirts.* 法蘭絨褲(襯衫)。**2** (*pl*) ~ trousers used for summer sports and games, eg cricket. (複)夏季運動時所穿的法蘭絨褲(例如打板球時所穿的)。**3** [C] piece of ~ for cleaning, rubbing, etc: 抹擦用的法蘭絨布塊: *a 'face-~.* 擦面用的法蘭絨布塊。**4** [U] (sl) nonsense. (俚)胡說八道。**~·ette** /,flænə'let ; ,flænḷ'ɛt/ *n* [U] cotton material made to look like ~. 棉織法蘭絨;絨布。

flap¹ /flæp ; flæp/ *n* [C] **1** (sound of a) flapping blow or movement: 拍打(聲);輕動(聲): *A ~ from the tail of the whale upset the boat.* 鯨尾輕輕一拍便將那小船打翻了。**2** piece of material that hangs down or covers an opening: 垂下作爲覆蓋之物: *the ~ of a pocket;* 衣袋的口蓋;口袋蓋; *the gummed ~ of an envelope;* 塗有膠的信封口蓋; *the ~ of a table,* a hinged section that can hang down when not being used, as on a gate-legged table, ⇨ gate(1). 桌子的活邊(以鉸鏈與桌相連,不用時可垂下)。**3** part of the wing of an aircraft that can be lifted in flight to alter its upward direction and speed. (飛機的)襟翼(飛行中可抬起以改變向上的方向和速度)。⇨ the illus at aircraft. 參看 aircraft 之插圖。**4** *be in/get into a ~,* (sl) a state of nervous excitement or confusion (caused by fear of making errors, being incompetent, etc, eg while awaiting a visit from one's superiors). (俚)惴惴不安;神經緊張(例如在等待上司來臨時,由於擔心犯錯、不能勝任等而造成者)。

flap² /flæp ; flæp/ *vt, vi* (-pp-) **1** [VP2A, C, 6A] (cause to) move up and down or from side to side: (使)上下或左右移動: *The sails were ~ping against the mast.* 帆拍打着桅竿。*The wind ~ped the sails.* 風吹動著帆。*The curtains were ~ping at the open window.* 窗簾在敞開的窗前擺動。*The bird was ~ping its wings.* 那鳥拍動著翅膀。*The heron came ~ping over the water.* 那蒼鷺鼓動着翅膀從水面上飛來。**2** [VP6A, 15B] give a light blow to with sth soft and flat: (以軟而平之物)輕拍: *~ the flies off/away.* 將蒼蠅拍走。**3** [VP2A] (sl) get into a ~¹(4). (俚)惴惴不安;神經緊張。

flap·jack /'flæpdʒæk ; 'flæp,dʒæk/ *n* [C] sweet oatcake; (US) pancake. 甜燕麥餅;(美)薄煎餅。

flap·per /'flæpə(r) ; 'flæpɚ/ *n* **1** sth broad and flat (used to swat flies, etc). 拍子;蠅拍。**2** (fish's) broad fin. (魚的)寬濶的鰭。**3** (sl use in the 1920's) fashionable young woman. (1920年代之俚語)時髦的年輕女子。

flare¹ /fleə(r) ; flɛr/ *vi* **1** [VP2A] burn with a bright, unsteady flame: 火焰搖曳地燃燒: *flaring gas-jets.* 閃耀的煤氣口火焰。*The candle began to ~.* 燭光開始搖曳。**2** [VP2C] ~ *up,* burst into bright flame, (fig) into a rage; (of violence) suddenly break out: 閃耀;(喻)驟然震怒;(指暴亂)突然爆發: *When he was accused of lying, he ~d up.* 當他被控說謊時,他勃然大怒。*She ~s up at the least thing.* 她爲了小事情會突然發怒。*Rioting ~d up again later.* 暴動後來又突然爆發了。Hence, 由此產生, **'~-up** *n* sudden breaking into flame; short sudden outburst (of anger, etc). 突然發出火焰;(憤怒等)突然爆發。□ *n* **1** [U] flaring flame: 搖曳的火焰;閃爍的火光: *the ~ of torches;* 火把的搖曳的火焰; *the sudden ~ of a match in the darkness.* 黑暗中一根火柴之突然閃耀。**2** [C] device for producing a flaring light, used as a signal, etc: 閃光裝置(用以發出信號等): *The wrecked ship was using ~s to attract the attention of the coastguards.* 遇難的船正用閃光信號引起海岸巡邏隊的注意。**'~-path** *n* lit-up landing strip for aircraft. 飛機場之照明跑道。

flare² /fleə(r) ; flɛr/ *vi, vt* [VP2A, 6A] (of a skirt, a trouser-leg, the sides of a ship, etc) (cause to) spread gradually outwards; become, make, wider at the bottom. (指裙,褲腿,舷側等)(使)逐漸向外張開;(使)底部變濶。□ *n* gradual widening (eg of a skirt); upward bulge (eg in a ship's sides). (裙等之)逐漸張開;(舷側等之)向上擴展。

flash¹ /flæʃ ; flæʃ/ *n* **1** sudden burst of flame or light: 閃爍;閃光: *a ~ of lightning;* 閃電; *~es of light from a moving mirror;* 移動的鏡中的閃光; *~es from the guns during a battle;* 戰爭中砲火的閃光; (fig) (喻) *a ~ of wit/merriment/inspiration.* 機智(快樂,靈感)的閃現。***in a ~,*** instantly, at once. 瞬間;卽刻。***a ~ in the pan,*** an effort that at once ends in failure, or is quickly over and cannot be repeated or developed. 虎頭蛇尾;曇花一現。**'~·back** *n* (also 亦作 *cutback*) (cinema) part of a film that shows a scene earlier in time than the rest of the film (eg the childhood days of the hero). (電影)倒敍(例如對男主角童年往事的倒敍)。**'~-bulb** *n* (photo) bulb giving a momentary bright light. (攝影)閃光燈泡。**'~·gun** *n* (photo) device to synchronize the release of a ~bulb or electronic light source and a shutter in a camera. (攝影)閃光槍(一種能使閃光燈和快門同時操作的裝置)。**'~·light** *n* **(a)** light used for signals, in lighthouses, etc. (燈塔等處所用之)閃光信號燈。**(b)** (also 亦作 ~ or **'photo·~**) any device for producing a brilliant ~ of light for taking a photograph indoors or when natural light is too weak. (攝影用的)閃光燈。⇨ the illus at camera. 參看 camera 之插圖。**(c)** (US) electric hand-light (GB 英 = *torch*). (美)手電筒。**'~·point** *n* temperature at which vapour from oil may be ignited. 燃點;閃點;發光點。**2** coloured stripe worn as a distinguishing emblem on a military uniform, eg on the shoulder. (佩於軍服肩部等之)徽章。Cf 參較 *a badge of rank.* 表示階級的徽章。**3** (also 亦作 **'news·~**) brief item of news received by telephone, cable, teleprinter, etc. 簡短的新聞電報。**4** (attrib use; colloq) showy; smart: (形容用法;俗)過分裝飾的;漂亮的: *a ~ sports car.* 華麗的跑車。

flash² /flæʃ ; flæʃ/ *vi, vt* **1** [VP2A, C] send, give out, a sudden bright light: 閃光;閃爍: *The light-*

ning ~ed across the sky. 閃電自天空閃過。*A lighthouse was ~ing in the distance.* 一座燈塔在遠方閃出信號。 **2** [VP2C] come suddenly (into view; into the mind): 閃現;掠過(心頭): *The idea ~ed into／through his mind.* 這念頭掠過他的心頭。*The express train ~ed past.* 快車一閃而過。 **3** [VP6A, 15A, 12C] send suddenly or instantly: 突然發出;倏忽發出: *~ a light in sb's eyes;* 用光對着某人的眼睛突然一照; *~ a signal,* eg using a heliograph or torch; (用日光反射信號機或手電筒等)發出信號; *~ news across the world* (by radio or TV). (用無線電或電視)將一消息迅速傳遍世界。*She ~ed him a despairing glance.* 她向他投以絕望的眼光。 **4** [VP6A] send or reflect like a ~ or ~es: 似閃光般發出或射出: *Her eyes ~ed fire／defiance.* 她的眼睛閃現着熱情(反抗)。

flashy /ˈflæʃɪ ; ˈflæʃɪ/ *adj* (-ier, -iest) brilliant and attractive but not in good taste; given to (rather vulgar) display: 浮華的; 炫耀而庸俗的; 俗麗的: *~ clothes／jewellery;* 浮華的衣服(珠寶); *~ men.* 浮華的人。**flash·ily** /-ɪlɪ ; -əlɪ/ *adv* in a ~ manner: 浮華地: *a flashily-dressed girl.* 衣着浮華的女郎。

flask /flɑːsk *US:* flæsk ; flæsk/ *n* **1** narrow-necked bottle used in laboratories, etc. (實驗室等用的)細頸瓶;燒瓶。 **2** narrow-necked bottle for oil or wine. 細頸油瓶或酒瓶。 **3** (also 亦作 ˈ**hip-~**) flat-sided bottle of metal or (often leather-covered) glass for carrying spirits in the pocket. (可裝在口袋內盛酒用的)扁金屬瓶或(有皮套的)玻璃瓶。

flasks

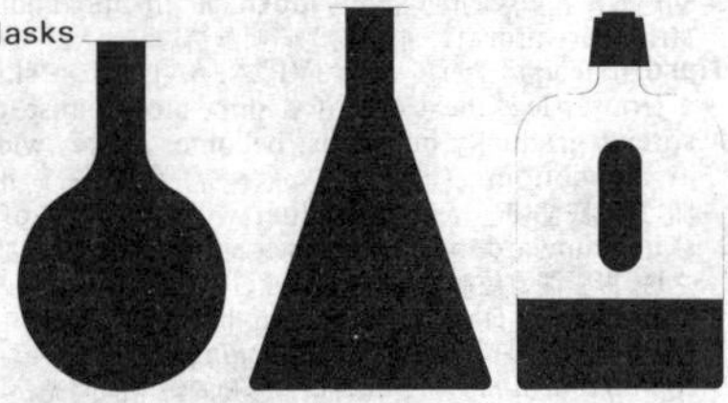

flat[1] /flæt ; flæt/ *n* (US 美 = *apartment*) suite of rooms (living-room, bedroom, kitchen, etc) on one floor of a building as a residence: 同一層建築上組成一個居住單位的數個房間;一套房間;公寓: *an old house divided into ~s;* 隔成數套房間的一座古宅; *a new block of ~s;* 新建的一排公寓; ˈ*~-dwellers,* people who live in ~s. 居於公寓中者。**~·let** /-lɪt ; -lɪt/ *n* tiny ~. 小公寓。

flat[2] /flæt ; flæt/ *adj* (-ter, -test) **1** smooth and level; even; having an unbroken surface: 平坦的; 平的: *A floor must be ~.* 地板必須平坦。*The top of a table is ~.* 桌面是平的。*People used to think that the world was ~; now we know that it is round.* 人們過去以爲地球是平的,現在我們知道它是圓的。*One of the tyres is ~,* has no or not enough air in it. 有一個輪胎漏氣了。ˌ**~-ˈbottomed** *adj* (of a boat) having a ~ bottom (for use in shallow water). (指船)平底的(行駛於淺水中)。ˈ**~-car** *n* (US) railway carriage without a roof or sides, for carrying freight. (美)平車(無頂篷或邊板的鐵路貨車)。ˈ**~·fish** *n* kinds of fish (including sole, plaice, turbot) having a ~ body and swimming on one side. 比目魚;鰈。⇨ the illus at fish. 參看 fish 之插圖。ˌ**~-ˈfooted** *adj* **(a)** having feet with flat soles. 脚掌扁平的。 **(b)** (colloq) downright; resolute. (俗)直截了當的;斷然的。ˈ**~-iron** *n* ⇨ iron[1](2). ˈ**~ racing; the F~,** (horse-racing) over level ground with no obstacles. (賽馬)平地比賽。⇨ *steeplechase* at steeple. ˈ**~·top** *n* (US colloq) aircraft-carrier. (美俗)航空母艦。 **2** with a broad level surface and little depth: 淺的: *~ plates／dishes／pans.* 淺盤(碟,鍋)。*The cake was ~,* had failed to rise while cooking. 這蛋糕沒有發起來。 **3** dull; uninteresting; monotonous: 枯燥的;平淡無味的; 單調的: *Life seemed ~ to him.* 他似乎覺得生活無味。*The party／conversation was rather ~.* 那聚會(談話)頗爲乏味。*The soup is ~,* lacks flavour. 這湯沒有味道。***fall ~,*** fail to win applause or appreciation: 未受到喝采或欣賞: *His best jokes fell ~.* 他最拿手的笑話未能引人發笑。 **4** (music) below the true pitch: (音樂)降半音的;變音的: *sing ~;* 降半音唱; *a ~ note;* 降半音的符號;變音號; *A ~* (= A♭), note half a tone lower than A. 降A調。⇨ sharp(10). **5** absolute; downright; unqualified: 斷然的;直截了當的;直率的: *give sb a ~ denial／refusal,* deny or refuse sth absolutely. 斷然拒絕某人。*And that's ~!* Let there be no doubt about that! 絕對是那樣! **6** (comm) ˈ**~ rate,** common price paid for each of different things or services bought in quantity. (商)一律的價格(對於大量購買的不同貨物或勞役所定的共同價格)。 **7** (of colours, coloured surfaces) uniform, without relief: (指顏色,有色的表面)無明暗之分的;無立體感的: *a ~ tint;* 無明暗之分的顏色; *~ paint,* without a gloss. 無光澤的漆。*His paintings all seem rather ~,* lack relief, shading, etc. 他的畫都似乎缺少立體感。 **8** (of a battery) run down; needing to be recharged. (指電池)變弱的;需再充電的。 **9** (of gaseous or aerated liquids) no longer containing gas: (指充有氣的液體)跑氣的: *This beer tastes／has gone ~.* 這啤酒喝起來無味(氣跑光了)。⇨ fizz. **10** ˌ**~ ˈspin, (a)** (often uncontrollable) fast descent of a horizontal, spinning aircraft. 飛機螺旋急降(常指失去控制者)。 **(b)** (colloq) (mental) state of great confusion: (俗)精神錯亂: *in a ~ spin.* 精神錯亂。□ *adv* **1** in a ~ manner: 平坦地;平直地;降半音地: *sing ~.* 降半音唱。 **2** (lying) spread out; (lying) at full length: 展開地;挺直地;平伸地: *He fell ~ on his back.* 他直挺挺地仰面跌倒了。*He knocked his opponent ~.* 他將對手擊倒了。*The earthquake laid the city ~,* caused all the buildings to fall. 地震震坍了全城的建築物。 **3** positively: 斷然地: *He told me ~ that....* 他斷然地告訴我說…。*He went ~ against orders.* 他斷然抗命。***~ broke,*** (colloq) with no money at all. (俗)一文不名。 **4** ***~ out,*** **(a)** (colloq) with all one's strength and resources: (俗)傾全力;拚命地: *He was working／running ~ out.* 他拚命工作(跑)。 **(b)** exhausted. 疲憊的。**~·ly** *adv* in a ~(6) manner: 斷然地;直截了當地: *The suggestions were ~ly opposed.* 那些建議受到斷然的反對。*He ~ly refused to join us.* 他斷然拒絕跟我們在一起。**~·ness** *n*

flat[3] /flæt ; flæt/ *n* **1** ***the ~ (of),*** flat part of anything: 平的部分: *the ~ of the hand;* 手掌; *with the ~ of his sword.* 以劍面。 **2** (usu *pl*) stretch of low flat land, esp near water: (通常用複數)窪地(尤指近水者): ˈ*mud ~s;* 泥沼; ˈ*salt ~s,* near the sea. 鹽田(近海者)。 **3** (music) flat note; the sign ♭: (音樂)降半音;降半音的符號(♭): *sharps and ~s,* the black notes on a piano keyboard. 鋼琴上的黑鍵。⇨ the illus at notation. 參看 notation 之插圖。 **4** (esp US) deflated tyre, eg after a puncture. (尤美)跑氣的輪胎。 **5** piece of stage scenery on a movable frame. (舞臺上的)佈景屛。

flat·ten /ˈflætn ; ˈflætn̩/ *vt, vi* [VP6A, 15A, B, 2A, C] ~ ***(out),*** make or become flat: 使平; 變平: *a field of wheat ~ed by storms;* 被暴風吹倒的一片麥田; *~ (out) a piece of metal by hammering it;* 將一塊金屬錘平; *~ oneself against a wall,* eg to avoid being struck by a lorry in a narrow street; (fig) humiliate. 使自己平貼在牆上(例如在狹窄的街道上避免被卡車撞上); (喻)屈辱。 ***~ out,*** (of an aircraft) fly horizontally again. (指飛機)恢復水平姿勢。

flat·ter /ˈflætə(r) ; ˈflætɚ/ *vt* **1** [VP6A] praise too much; praise insincerely (in order to please). 諂媚;奉承;阿諛。 **2** [VP6A] give a feeling of pleasure to: 予以愉快的感覺: *I feel greatly ~ed by your invitation to address the meeting.* 蒙你邀請在這會議中演說,我感到非常愉快。 **3** [VP6A] (of a picture, artist, etc) show (sb) as better looking than he is: (指像片,藝術家等)顯示(某人)較其本來面

目更漂亮: *This photograph ~s you.* 這照片比你本人漂亮。 **4 ~ *oneself that...*,** be pleased with one's belief that...: 自認爲;自以爲: *He ~ed himself that he spoke French with a perfect accent.* 他自以爲他說法文的腔調很完美。 **~er** *n* person who ~s. 諂媚者;奉承者。 **~y** *n* [U] ~ing; insincere praise; [C] (*pl* -ries) instance of this; ~ing remark: 諂媚;奉承;阿諛之詞: *Don't be deceived by her flatteries.* 勿爲她的阿諛之詞所騙。

flatu·lence /ˈflætjʊləns ; ˈflætʃələns/ *n* [U] gas in the alimentary canal; feeling of discomfort caused by an accumulation of this. 腸胃氣脹;因腸胃氣脹而引起的不舒服的感覺。

flaunt /flɔːnt ; flɔnt/ *vt, vi* **1** [VP6A] show off complacently; ostentatiously attract attention to: 誇示;炫耀: *~ oneself;* 炫耀自己; *~ one's new clothes/riches, etc.* 炫耀新衣服(財富等)。 **2** [VP 2A, C] wave proudly: 飄揚: *flags and banners ~ing in the breeze.* 在微風中飄揚的旗幟。

flau·tist /ˈflɔːtɪst ; ˈflɔtɪst/ *n* flute-player. 吹笛人。

fla·vour (US = **-vor**) /ˈfleɪvə(r) ; ˈflevɚ/ *n* **1** [U] sensation, when eating, of taste and smell: 味;滋味: *When you have a cold, your food sometimes has very little ~.* 你患傷風時,你的食物有時毫無滋味。 **2** [C] distinctive taste; special quality or characteristic: 特殊的味道;特點;特別風味: *a ~ of garlic;* 大蒜味; *various ~s in ice-cream;* 冰淇淋的種種味道; *a newspaper story with a ~ of romance.* 報紙上具有浪漫風味的故事。 □ *vt* [VP6A] give a ~ to: 調味;加味於;使有特殊風味: *~ a sauce with onions.* 加洋葱於調味汁以增其味。 **~·ing** *n* [C, U] sth used to give ~ to (food, etc): (加於食物等之)調味料;調味品: *too much vanilla ~ing in the cake.* 蛋糕中香草精太多。 *Many ~ings have little or no food value.* 許多調味品沒有什麼營養價值。**~·less** *adj* having no ~. 無味的;無滋味的;無特殊風味的。

flaw /flɔː ; flɔ/ *n* [C] crack (in an object); sth that lessens the value, beauty or perfection of sth: 裂紋;瑕疵;缺陷: *~s in a jewel/an argument/a person's character.* 珠寶(議論,人格)上的瑕疵。 **~·less** *adj* perfect. 完美的;無瑕的。 **~·less·ly** *adv*

flax /flæks ; flæks/ *n* [U] plant cultivated for the fibre obtained from its stem; this fibre (for making linen). 亞麻;亞麻纖維(織亞麻布用)。 **~en** /ˈflæksn ; ˈflæksn̩/ *adj* (of hair) pale yellow. (指毛髮)淡黃色的。

flay /fleɪ ; fle/ *vt* [VP6A] take the skin or hide off (an animal); (fig) criticize severely or pitilessly: 剝(動物)之皮;(喻)苛評;嚴責: *The tutor ~ed the idle students.* 導師嚴責那些懶惰的學生。

flea /fliː ; fli/ *n* small wingless jumping insect that feeds on the blood of human beings and some animals. 跳蚤。 ⇨ the illus at insect. 參看 insect 之插圖。 ***(go off/send sb off with a) ˈ~ in his ear,*** (with a) stinging rebuke. (被)譏誚話(氣走);(用)譏誚話(氣走某人)。 **ˈ~-bite** *n* (fig) small inconvenience, sth not very troublesome. (喻)微小之不便;不太傷腦筋的事。 **ˈ~-bitten** *adj* (fig) (of an animal's colouring) speckled. (喻)(指動物的顏色)有斑點的。 **ˈ~ market,** open-air market selling cheap and second-hand goods. (售賣價廉貨物和舊貨的)露天市場。 **ˈ~·pit** *n* (colloq) old and dirty place of entertainment, eg a cinema, theatre. (俗)又舊又髒的娛樂場所(例如電影院或戲院)。

fleck /flek ; flɛk/ *n* [C] **1** small spot or patch: 小點;斑點: *~s of colour on a bird's breast;* 一隻鳥胸部之彩色斑點; *~s of sunlight on the ground under a tree.* 樹蔭下的點點陽光。 **2** small particles (of dust, etc). (灰塵等的)微粒;小粒。 □ *vt* [VP6A] mark with ~s: 使有斑點;飾以斑點: *a sky ~ed with clouds.* 佈滿點點雲朵的天空。

fled *pt, pp* of flee.

fledged /fledʒd ; flɛdʒd/ *adj* (of birds) with fully grown wing feathers; able to fly. (指鳥)羽毛長成的;會飛的。 **ˌfully-ˈ~** (fig) *adj* trained and experienced: (喻)有訓練和經驗的: *a fully-~ engineer.* 有訓練和經驗的工程師。

fledg(e)·ling /ˈfledʒlɪŋ ; ˈflɛdʒlɪŋ/ *n* young bird just able to fly; (fig) young inexperienced person. 剛會飛的幼鳥;(喻)年輕而無經驗之人;初出茅廬之年輕人。

flee /fliː ; fli/ *vi, vt* (*pt, pp* fled /fled ; flɛd/) [VP 2A, C, 6A] run or hurry away (from): 逃跑;逃避;避開;逃離: *The enemy fled in disorder.* 敵人潰逃。 *The clouds fled before the wind.* 雲在風前飛馳。 *He killed his enemy and fled the country.* 他殺死了他的敵人,並逃離那個國家。

fleece /fliːs ; flis/ *n* [C, U] **1** woolly covering of a sheep or similar animal; quantity of wool cut from a sheep in one operation: 羊毛;自一隻羊身上一次所剪的毛量: *a coat lined with ~.* 羊毛襯裡的上衣。 ⇨ the illus at domestic. 參看 domestic 之插圖。 **2** ~-like head of hair. 似羊毛的頭髮;蓬鬆的捲髮。 □ *vt* [VP6A, 14] ***~ sb (of sth),*** (fig) rob (sb) by trickery: (喻)詐取(某人): *He was ~d of his money.* 他的錢被人騙走了。 **fleecy** *adj* (-ier, -iest) like ~: 似羊毛的: *fleecy clouds/hair/falls of snow.* 白雲(蓬鬆的捲髮;紛紛的落雪)。

fleet¹ /fliːt ; flit/ *n* [C] **1** number of warships under one commander; all the warships of a country. 艦隊;一國所擁有的全體戰艦。 **2** number of ships, aircraft, buses, etc moving or working under one command or ownership. 船隊;飛機隊;公共汽車隊等。

fleet² /fliːt ; flit/ *adj* (poet, liter) quick-moving: (詩,文)迅速的;輕捷的: *~ of foot, ~-footed.* 跑得快的。 **~·ly** *adv* **~·ness** *n*

fleet·ing /ˈfliːtɪŋ ; ˈflitɪŋ/ *adj* passing quickly: 飛逝的;疾馳的: *pay sb a ~ visit,* a short visit before one goes on to another place; 對某人做短暫的拜訪; *~ happiness,* lasting for a short time. 轉瞬卽逝的幸福。

Fleet Street /ˈfliːt striːt ; ˈflitˌstrit/ *n* (street in central London where there are many newspaper offices, hence) the press; London journalism. 艦隊街(倫敦一街道,爲許多報館所在地);(由此產生)新聞界;倫敦的報界。

flesh /fleʃ ; flɛʃ/ *n* [U] **1** soft substance, esp muscle, between the skin and bones of animal bodies: 肌肉;肉: *Tigers are ~-eating animals.* 虎是肉食動物。 ***~ and blood,*** human nature with its emotions, weaknesses, etc: 人性(包括其情感、弱點等): *more than ~ and blood can stand,* more than human nature can bear. 非人所能忍受者。 ***one's own ~ and blood,*** one's near relatives. 骨肉;親人。 ***in the ~,*** in life, in bodily form. 活生生的;本人。 ***go the way of all ~,*** die. 死。 ***have/demand one's pound of ~,*** insist cruelly on the exact repayment of what was borrowed. 無情地索債。 ⇨ Shakespeare's Mer of Ven IV, Sc I. 參看莎士比亞所著'威尼斯商人'第四幕,第一場。 ***make a person's ˈ~ creep,*** frighten or horrify him (esp with dread of sth supernatural). (尤指以神奇恐怖之事)使某人毛骨悚然。 ***put on/lose ~*** (more usu *weight*) (weight 較常用), become fat/thin. 長胖;發胖(變瘦;消瘦)。 **ˈ~-pots** *n pl* (places supplying) good food and material comforts. 美食及物質享受;供美食及物質享受的場所。 **ˈ~-wound** *n* one that does not reach the bone or vital organs. 皮肉之傷;輕傷。 **2 *the ~,*** physical or bodily desires; sensual appetites: 肉慾;色慾;情慾: *the sins of the ~.* 肉慾之罪惡。 **3** the body (contrasted with the *mind* and *soul*). 肉體(與 mind 及 soul 相對)。 ***The spirit is willing but ~ is weak,*** (of a person who is willing to do sth, but is physically or morally weak or lazy). 心有餘而力不足。 **4** pulpy part of fruits and vegetables. 果肉;蔬菜的柔嫩部分。 **~·ly** *adj* of the body; sensual. 肉體的;肉慾的。 **~y** *adj* fat; of ~. 肥胖的;肉的。

flesh·ings /ˈfleʃɪŋz ; ˈflɛʃɪŋz/ *n pl* flesh-coloured tights, eg as worn by ballet dancers. 肉色緊身衣

(例如芭蕾舞者所穿者)。

fleur-de-lis, -lys /ˌflɜː də ˈliː ; ˌflɝdəˈli/ *n* (*pl* fleurs-de-lis, -lys pronunciation unchanged) heraldic lily; royal arms of France. (紋章上的)鳶尾;法國之皇家紋章。⇨ the illus at armour. 參看 armour 之插圖。

flew /fluː ; flu/ *pt* of fly¹.

flex¹ /fleks ; flɛks/ *n* [C, U] (length of) flexible insulated cord for electric current. 花線;皮線;一段花線或皮線。

flex² /fleks ; flɛks/ *vt* [VP6A] bend, eg a limb, one's muscles. 彎曲(例如肢體或肌肉)。

flex·ible /ˈfleksəbl ; ˈflɛksəbl̩/ *adj* easily bent without breaking; (fig) easily changed to suit new conditions;(of persons) adaptable. 易彎曲的;柔韌的;(喻)可變通的;有彈性的;(指人)能適應環境的。**flexi·bil·ity** /ˌfleksəˈbɪlətɪ ; ˌflɛksəˈbɪlətɪ/ *n* [U].

flib·ber·ti·gib·bet /ˌflɪbətɪˈdʒɪbɪt ; ˈflɪbətɪˌdʒɪbɪt/ *n* frivolous person too fond of gossip. 輕浮饒舌之人。

flick /flɪk ; flɪk/ *n* [C] **1** quick light blow, eg with a whip or the tip of a finger. 輕擊;輕彈(例如用鞭或指尖)。**2** short sudden movement; jerk. 短暫而突然的動作;猛然一動。**ˈ~-knife** *n* knife with a blade (inside the handle) which can be brought into position with a ~ for use. 彈簧刀(刀刃藏於柄內,一振即可伸出)。**3** (sl) cinema film. (俚)影片。**the ~s,** the cinema. 電影。□ *vt* **1** [VP6A, 15A, 22] strike with a ~, give a ~ with (a whip, etc); touch lightly: 輕擊;以(鞭等)輕擊;輕彈: *He ~ed the horse with his whip/~ed his whip at the horse.* 他用鞭輕擊他的馬。*He ~ed the switch,* eg for electric light. 他輕按電燈開關。*He ~ed the knife open.* 他輕輕將刀刃彈出。**2** [VP15B] ~ *sth away/off,* remove with a ~: 彈去(某物): *She ~ed the crumbs off the table-cloth.* 她將桌布上的麵包屑彈掉。

flicker /ˈflɪkə(r) ; ˈflɪkɚ/ *vi* [VP2A, C] **1** (of a light; fig of hopes, etc) burn or shine unsteadily; flash and die away by turns: (指光;喻,指希望等)閃爍不定;搖曳;忽隱忽現: *The candle ~ed and then went out.* 那蠟燭閃爍不定,然後便熄了。*A faint hope still ~ed in her breast.* 她心中仍閃現着一線希望。**2** move back and forth, wave to and fro: 來回移動;擺動: *leaves ~ing in the wind;* 在風中擺動的樹葉; *~ing shadows;* 搖晃的影子; *the ~ing tongue of a snake.* 蛇的一吐一伸的舌頭。□ *n* (usu *sing*) ~ing movement: (通常用單數)閃爍不定;搖曳;閃動;擺動: *a weak ~ of hope.* 閃爍不定的一線希望。

flier /ˈflaɪə(r) ; ˈflaɪɚ/ = flyer.

flight¹ /flaɪt ; flaɪt/ *n* **1** [U] flying through the air: 飛行;飛翔: *the art of ~;* 飛行術; *study the ~ of birds,* how they fly. 研究鳥的飛翔。***in ~,*** while flying. 在飛行中。**2** [C] journey made by air; distance covered: 航空旅行;航程: *a non-stop ~ from Paris to New York;* 從巴黎至紐約的不着陸飛行; *~s in a balloon;* 乘氣球旅行; *the spring and autumn ~s* (= seasonal migrations) *of birds.* 鳥之春秋兩季的成群遷徙。**ˈ~ deck** *n* (on an aircraft-carrier) deck for taking off from and landing on; (in an airliner) compartment used by the pilot, navigator, engineer, etc. (航空母艦之)飛行甲板;(客機之)駕駛艙。**3** [U] movement (and path) through the air: 空中的行動(及路線): *the ~ of an arrow;* 箭的飛馳; (attrib) (形容用法) *the ~ path of an airliner.* 客機的航線。**4** [C] number of birds or objects moving together through the air: 飛行的鳥群或物體;飛行隊: *a ~ of arrows/swallows.* 連發的飛箭(一隊飛燕)。***in the first ~,*** taking or occupying a leading place. 領頭;佔首要地位。**5** [U] swift passing: 飛馳而過: *the ~ of time.* 光陰的疾馳。**6** [C] soaring; going up above the ordinary: 高聳;昇騰;飛躍: *a ~ of wit/fancy/ambition/the imagination.* 才智(幻想,志向,想像)之奔放。**7** [C] series (*of* stairs, etc without change of direction); stairs between two landings: (階梯等之)一段;一段樓梯: *My bedroom is two ~s up.* 向上走兩段樓梯便是我的臥室。*There was no lift and we had to climb six ~s of stairs.* 沒有電梯,我們不得不爬六段樓梯。**8** [C] group of aircraft in a country's Air Force. 一國空軍之飛行隊。**F~ Lieutenant,** rank in the Royal Air Force below Squadron Leader. 皇家空軍上尉。**F~ Sergeant,** rank in the Royal Air Force below Warrant Officer. 皇家空軍上士。□ *vt* [VP6A] (cricket) move (the ball) sideways when bowling it, so as to deceive the batsman. (板球)側投(球)以誘騙擊球員: *a well-~ed delivery.* 好的側投。**~·less** *adj* (of birds) unable to fly. (指鳥)不會飛的。

flight² /flaɪt ; flaɪt/ *n* **1** [U] (act of) fleeing or running away (from danger, etc): 逃走;逃亡: *seek safety in ~;* 逃走;溜之大吉; *put the enemy to ~,* defeat them and cause them to flee. 擊潰敵人。***take ~; take to ~,*** run away. 逃走。**2** [C] instance of this: 逃走的實例: *the ~ into Egypt* (of Mary with the infant Jesus); 逃亡至埃及(指馬利亞帶着嬰兒耶穌之逃亡); *a ~ of capital,* eg when capital is sent abroad during a financial crisis. 資金之外流(如財政危機時資金之被移往國外)。

flighty /ˈflaɪtɪ ; ˈflaɪtɪ/ *adj* (of behaviour, character) influenced by whims; unsteady; fickle. (指行徑,性格)好作奇想的;不穩定的;輕浮的。

flimsy /ˈflɪmzɪ ; ˈflɪmzɪ/ *adj* (-ier, -iest) (of material) light and thin; (of objects) easily injured and destroyed: (指原料)輕而薄的;(指物體)脆弱的;容易損壞的: *a ~ cardboard box;* 脆弱的紙板盒; (fig) (喻) *a ~ excuse/argument,* one that is not convincing. 薄弱的藉口(論據)。□ *n* [C] thin paper, eg as used when several carbon copies are made on a typewriter. 一種薄紙(例如打字複製時所用者)。**flim·sily** /-ɪlɪ ; -ɪlɪ/ *adv* **flim·si·ness** *n*

flinch /flɪntʃ ; flɪntʃ/ *vi* [VP2A, 3A] ~ *(from),* draw or move back; wince: 退縮;畏縮: *have a tooth pulled out without ~ing.* 毫不畏縮地去拔牙。*You mustn't ~ from an unpleasant duty.* 對你所厭惡的職責,你不可退縮。

fling /flɪŋ ; flɪŋ/ *vt, vi* (*pt, pp* flung /flʌŋ ; flʌŋ/) **1** [VP6A, 15A, B, 22, 12A, 13A] throw violently: 猛投;擲;拋: *~ one's hat up* (*in the air*); 將帽子拋向空中; *~ a stone at sb or sth;* 向某人或某物擲石頭; *~ one's clothes on,* dress hurriedly; 匆匆穿上衣服; *~ the doors and windows open,* open them quickly and forcibly; 將門窗猛然推開; *be flung into prison;* 被投入獄; *~ caution to the winds,* act recklessly; 行事魯莽; *~ off one's pursuers,* escape from them. 擺脫追趕的人。*She flung him a scornful look.* 她向他投以鄙夷的一瞥。**2** [VP6A, 15A, B] move oneself, one's arms, etc violently, hurriedly, impulsively or angrily: 猛烈移動(身體,手臂等);急動;暴躁地移動: *~ one's arms up/about;* 急伸(揮)手臂; *~ oneself into a chair.* 猛然坐於椅中;一屁股坐於椅中。**3** [VP2C] go angrily or violently; rush: 憤然而行;急行;衝: *She flung out of the room.* 她衝出房間。*He flung off without saying goodbye.* 他未經告辭卽憤然離去。□ *n* [C] **1** act of ~ing; ~ing movement. 擲;投;猛動;急動;急衝。***have a ~ at,*** (*shot* or *go* are the more usu words) make an attempt at. 試圖(shot 或 go 爲較常用之字)。**2** kind of energetic dance: 一種充滿活力的舞蹈: *the Highland ~,* as danced in Scotland. 一種充滿活力的蘇格蘭高地舞。***have one's ~,*** have a time of unrestricted pleasure. 盡情;恣意。

flint /flɪnt ; flɪnt/ *n* [U] hard kind of stone found in lumps like pebbles, steel-grey inside and white outside; [C] piece of this used with steel to produce sparks; [C] piece of hard alloy used in a cigarette-lighter to produce sparks. 燧石;火石;打火石。**ˈ~·stone** *n* [U] ~ pebbles used for building walls, etc. (築牆壁等所用之)燧石礫。**~y** *adj* (-ier, -iest) very hard, like ~. 極堅硬的;似燧石的。

flip /flɪp ; flɪp/ *vt, vi* (-pp-) [VP6A, 15A, B] put (sth) into motion by a snap of the finger and thumb; throw with a jerk: 以指捻擲;猝然一擲: *~ a coin (down) on the counter.* 將一硬幣擲在櫃臺上。□ *n* **1** quick, light blow. 迅速的輕擊。**2** (colloq) short flight in an aeroplane for pleasure. (俗)遊樂性的短程飛行。□ *adj* (colloq) flippant; glib. (俗)不客氣的;油腔滑調的。***the* '~ *side,*** (colloq) the reverse side (of a gramophone record). (俗)(唱片的)反面。

flip·pant /'flɪpənt ; 'flɪpənt/ *adj* not showing deserved respect or seriousness: 不客氣的;無禮的: *a ~ answer/remark.* 不客氣的回答(言語)。**~·ly** *adv* **flip·pancy** /-ənsɪ ; -ənsɪ/ *n* [U] being ~; [C] ~ remark, etc. 不客氣;不客氣的言語等。

flip·per /'flɪpə(r) ; 'flɪpə/ *n* **1** limb of certain sea animals (not fish) used in swimming: (某些海中動物的)鰭狀肢: *Seals, turtles and penguins have ~s.* 海豹,海龜和企鵝均有鰭形肢。⇨ the illus at sea. 參看 sea 之插圖。**2** device worn on the feet to increase the thrust of leg movements in swimming. 橡皮腳掌;蛙鞋(穿在脚上的鰭狀物,游泳時可增加腿部動作之衝力)。⇨ the illus at frogman. 參看 frogman 之插圖。

flirt /flɜːt ; flɝt/ *vi* [VP2A, 3A] ~ ***(with).*** **1** show affection for amusement, without serious intentions: 調情取樂: *She ~s with every handsome man she meets.* 她和她遇到的每個美男子調情。**2** pretend to be interested in; think about, but not seriously: 假裝對…有興趣; 非認眞地考慮到: *He's been ~ing with the idea of going to Moscow.* 他一直有去莫斯科的遐想。□ *n* sb who ~s with many people. 調情者;賣弄風情者。**flir·ta·tion** /flɜː'teɪʃn ; flɝ'teʃən/ *n* [U] ~ing; [C] instance of this: 調情: *carry on a ~ation.* 調情。**flir·ta·tious** /flɜː'teɪʃəs ; flɝ'teʃəs/ *adj* fond of ~ing; of ~ing. 喜調情的;調情的。

flit /flɪt ; flɪt/ *vi* (-tt-) **1** [VP2C] fly or move lightly and quickly: 輕快地飛;輕快地動: *bees ~ting from flower to flower;* 在花間飛來飛去的蜜蜂; *bats ~ting about in the dusk;* 黃昏時四處飛翔的蝙蝠; (fig) (喻) *fancies that ~ through one's mind.* 掠過心頭的幻想。**2** (colloq) remove from one house to another; change one's abode, eg secretly, to avoid paying debts. (俗)遷居;搬家(例如爲逃債而悄悄搬走)。□ *n* (colloq) act of ~ting(2): (俗)悄悄搬家: *do a (moonlight) ~.* 悄悄搬家逃債。

float¹ /fləʊt ; flot/ *n* [C] **1** piece of cork or other light material used on a fishing-line (to indicate when the bait has been taken) or to support the edge of a fishing-net. (釣魚線或魚網邊上的)浮標;浮子。**2** hollow ball or other air-filled container, eg to regulate the level of water in a cistern, or to support an aircraft on water. 浮球;浮筒(例如調節貯水池水位或支持水上飛機者)。**3** low platform on wheels, used for showing things in a procession; kind of wagon or cart with a low floor. 遊行車;一種底板低的車。

float² /fləʊt ; flot/ *vi, vt* **1** [VP2A, C] be held up in air, gas or (esp) on the surface of liquid; move with moving liquid or air: 飄浮; (尤指) 漂; 浮;漂行;漂動: *dust ~ing in the air.* 飄浮在空中的灰塵。*Wood ~s on water.* 木頭漂浮於水上。*A balloon ~ed across the sky.* 氣球飄過天空。*The boat ~ed down the river.* 那船順河漂行。**2** [VP6A, 15A, B] cause to ~; keep ~ing: 使漂; 使浮; 使漂動: *~ a raft of logs down a river.* 使一圓木筏順河漂下。*The ship was ~ed by the tide,* eg after sticking fast on a sand-bank. 那船被潮水冲動(例如在擱淺於沙洲上之後)。*There wasn't enough water to ~ the ship.* 沒有足够深的水使船漂浮起來。**3** [VP6A] (comm) get (esp financial) support for in order to start; launch: (商)獲經濟援助以創辦;開辦: *~ a new business company.* 創辦一公司。**4** [VP6A] (finance) allow the foreign exchange value (of a currency) to vary (usu within narrow limits): (財政)讓貨幣的國外兌換値浮動(通常是在有限制範圍內): *~ the pound/dollar.* 讓金鎊(金圓)的國外兌換値浮動。**5** circulate: 傳播: *~ a rumour/an idea.* 傳播一謠言(觀念)。**~·ing** *adj* **1** fluctuating; variable: 流動的;變動的: *the ~ing population,* that part which varies very much, eg sailors in a seaport; 流動性的人口(例如港口的海員); *the ~ing vote,* the votes of those persons who are not committed to a political party. 流動票(不一定投某一政黨的選票)。**2** **~ing debt,** one of which part must be paid on demand, or at a stated time. 流動債務;短期債務。**'~ing rib,** (anat) one of the two lower pairs of ribs not attached to the breastbone. (解剖)浮肋。

floa·ta·tion, flo·ta·tion /fləʊ'teɪʃn ; flo'teʃən/ *n* [C, U] floating(3) of a business company or enterprise. (公司企業之)創辦;設立。

flock¹ /flɒk ; flɑk/ *n* **1** number of birds or animals (usu sheep, goats) of one kind, either kept together or feeding and travelling together: 鳥群; 獸群;(通常指)羊群: *a ~ of wild geese;* 一群雁; *~s and herds,* sheep and cattle. 羊群和牛群。**2** crowd of people: 人群;群衆: *Visitors came in ~s to see the new bridge.* 成群的人來參觀這新橋。**3** Christian congregation; number of people together in sb's charge: 基督教會的會衆;受某人管理的一群人:*a priest and his ~.* 牧師和他的會衆。□ *vi* [VP2C, 4A] gather, come or go together in great numbers: 群集;成群結隊而行: *The children ~ed round their teacher.* 孩子們聚集在他們老師的周圍。*People ~ed to hear the new prophet.* 人們成群地去聽這新的先知演講。

flock² /flɒk ; flɑk/ *n* [C] tuft of wool or hair; (*pl*) wool or cotton waste for stuffing mattresses, etc. 羊毛叢;毛叢;(複)塡床墊等的羊毛或棉絮。

floe /fləʊ ; flo/ *n* [C] sheet of floating ice. 一片浮冰;浮冰塊。

flog /flɒg ; flɑg/ *vt* (-gg-) [VP6A] **1** beat severely with a rod or whip. 鞭撻;鞭笞。***~ a dead horse,*** waste one's efforts. 浪費精力;徒勞。***~ sth to death,*** be so persistent or repetitive about it (eg a joke, an idea) that people lose interest in it. 努力勸人接受某事物(例如一笑話或觀念)以致使人失去興趣。**2** (sl) sell or exchange (esp sth illicitly obtained, or sth secondhand):(俚)銷售或交換(尤指贓物或舊貨): *~ stolen goods/one's old car.* 銷售贓物(舊車)。**~·ging** *n* [U] beating or whipping; [C] instance of this. 笞打;鞭笞。

flood¹ /flʌd ; flʌd/ *n* [C] **1** (coming of a) great quantity of water in a place that is usually dry: 洪水;水災;氾濫: *The rainstorms caused ~s in the low-lying parts of the town.* 暴風雨在該城的低窪地區造成了水災。***in ~,*** (of a river) overflowing its banks. (指河)氾濫。**the F~; Noah's F~,** (biblical) that described in Genesis. (舊約創世紀中所敍述的)挪亞時代的大洪水。**2** great outpouring or outburst: 大量的流出或發出: *~s of rain/tears;* 豪雨(淚如泉湧); *a ~ of light/anger/words/letters.* 一片光明(大發雷霆;滔滔的言語;大量的信件)。**3** (also 亦作 **'~-tide**) the flowing in of the tide (form the sea to the land): 漲潮: *The tide is at the ~.* 潮水正在漲。⇨ ebb. **'~-gate** *n* gate opened and closed to admit or keep out water, esp the lower gate of a lock. 水門; 水閘。**'~·lights** *n pl* artificial lighting thrown in a bright and broad beam. 汎光燈;强力照明燈。**'~·light** *vt* (*pt, pp* -lighted, -lit /-lɪt ; -lɪt/) light up by this method: 以汎光燈照亮: *The cathedral was ~lit.* 那大教堂被汎光燈照耀着。

flood² /flʌd ; flʌd/ *vt, vi* **1** [VP6A, 14, 16A] ~ ***(with),*** cover or fill with a flood (lit, fig): 淹沒; 氾濫(字面,喻): *The meadows were ~ed.* 草地被洪水淹沒了。*The soldiers broke the dikes and ~ed the countryside to keep back the enemy.* 兵士們破堤將那一帶地方淹沒,以阻敵人。*We have been ~ed with requests for help.* 我們收到了大批求助的信函。*The stage of the theatre was ~ed with light.* 劇院的舞臺被大量的光線照耀着。**2** (of rain) fill (a river) to overflowing: (指雨)使(河)氾濫: *rivers ~ed by heavy rainstorms.* 因暴風雨而氾濫的河流。**3** [VP

15B] ~ ***out,*** compel to leave because of a ~; (fig) inundate: 被洪水迫使離開; (喻) 氾濫: *Thousands of people were ~ed out,* forced to leave their homes. 成千的人因洪水而被迫離家。 **4** [VP3A] ~ ***in,*** come in in great quantities or numbers: 湧進: *Applications ~ed in.* 申請書潮湧而來。

floor¹ /flɔ:(r); flɔr/ *n* [C] **1** lower surface of a room; part on which one walks: 地板; 室內之地: *sitting on the ~;* 坐在地板上; *a bare ~,* one with no carpet, rugs or other covering. 未鋪地毯的地板。 ***wipe the ~ with sb,*** utterly defeat him, eg in a fight or argument. 徹底擊敗某人(例如在打鬥或辯論中)。 **'~-board** *n* plank of a wooden floor. 一塊地板。 **'~ show,** cabaret, entertainment. (餐館等內的)歌舞表演。 **2** number of rooms, etc on the same level in a building. 樓層。 **'ground ~,** (GB) ~ level with the street. (英)底層樓; 一樓。 **'first ~,** (GB) ~ above the ground ~; (US) ground ~. (英)二樓; (美)一樓。 **'second/'third etc ~,** (GB) ~s above the first ~; (US) ~s above the ground ~. (英)三樓, 四樓等; (美)二樓, 三樓等。 ***get in on the ground ~,*** ⇨ ground¹(10). **'~-walker** *n* (US) (美) = shop-walker. **3** bottom of the sea, of a cave, etc. 海底; 洞底; 底部。 **4** part of an assembly hall, eg the Houses of Parliament, Congress, where members sit. 議員席(例如國會中者)。 ***take the ~,*** speak in a debate. 在辯論中發言。 **5** (opp of *ceiling*) lower limit (of prices). (價格的)最低標準(為 ceiling 之相反字)。 **~·ing** *n* [U] material, eg boards, used for making ~s. 地板材料。

floor² /flɔ:(r); flɔr/ *vt* [VP6A] **1** put (a floor) in a building. 鋪(地板)。 **2** knock down: 擊倒: *~ a man in a boxing match.* 賽拳時將一人擊倒。 **3** (of a problem, argument, etc) puzzle, defeat: (指問題, 議論等)使困惑; 難倒: *Tom was ~ed by two of the questions in the examination paper.* 湯姆被試題中的兩個題目難倒了。

floozy, floo·zie /'flu:zɪ; 'fluzɪ/ *n* (sl) slovenly woman, esp a prostitute. (俚)邋遢女人; (尤指)娼妓。

flop /flɒp; flɑp/ *vi, vt* (-pp-) **1** [VP2A, C] move, fall, clumsily or helplessly: 笨拙地移動或落下; 無可奈何地移動或落下: *The fish we had caught were ~ping about in the bottom of the boat.* 我們捉到的那些魚在船底無可奈何地跳動着。 *He ~ped down on his knees and begged for mercy.* 他叭塌一聲跪下來求饒。 **2** [VP15A, B] ~ ***down,*** put down or drop clumsily or roughly: 笨拙或粗野地拋下: *~ down a heavy bag.* 笨拙地拋下一重袋。 **3** [VP2A] (sl) (of a book, a play for the theatre, etc) fail. (俚)(指書, 戲劇等)失敗。 □ *n* act or sound of ~ping; (sl) failure of a book, play, etc. 笨拙的落下或拋下; 笨重的落下聲音; 撲通聲; (俚)(書, 戲劇等之)失敗。 □ *adv* with a ~: 撲通落下: *fall ~ into the water.* 撲通一聲掉進水裏。 **~py** *adj* (-ier, -iest) inclined to ~; hanging down loosely: 勢將撲通落下的; 鬆鬆下垂的: *a ~py hat.* 下垂的帽子。

flora /'flɔ:rə; 'flɔrə/ *n pl* all the plants of a particular area or period. (某地區或時代的)植物的總稱; 植物區系。

floral /'flɔ:rəl; 'flɔrəl/ *adj* of flowers: 花的: *~ designs.* 花的圖案。

flori·cul·ture /'flɔ:rɪkʌltʃə(r); 'flɔrɪˌkʌltʃɚ/ *n* [U] the cultivation of flowering plants. 養花; 花卉栽培。

florid /'flɒrɪd *US:* 'flɔ:r-; 'flɔrɪd/ *adj* **1** very much ornamented; (too) rich in ornament and colour: 大加裝飾的; 過於粉飾的; 華麗的; 絢爛的: *~ carving;* 過於粉飾的雕刻; *a ~ style,* eg of writing. 華麗的文體。 **2** (of a person's face) naturally red: (指人的面孔)紅潤的: *a ~ complexion.* 面色紅潤。 **~·ly** *adv*

florin /'flɒrɪn *US:* 'flɔ:r-; 'flɔrɪn/ *n* former name of a British coin worth one tenth of £1 (until 1971, two shillings; now ten pence). 英國昔時硬幣名(1971 年以前值二先令, 現值十辨士)。

flor·ist /'flɒrɪst *US:* 'flɔ:r-; 'flɔrɪst/ *n* person who grows or sells flowers. 花商; 經營花卉業者。

floss /flɒs *US:* flɔ:s; flɔs/ *n* [U] rough silk threads on the outside of a silkworm's cocoon; (also 亦作 **'~ silk**) silk spun from these for needlework. 蠶繭外層的粗絲; (此種粗絲紡成的)刺繡用的絲線。 **'candy-~,** soft, coloured mass of spun sugar, eaten off a stick. 棉花糖。

flo·ta·tion /fləʊ'teɪʃn; flo'teʃən/ = floatation.

flo·tilla /flə'tɪlə; flo'tɪlə/ *n* fleet of small warships, eg destroyers. 分遣艦隊(小型戰艦, 如驅逐艦, 組成的艦隊)。

flot·sam /'flɒtsəm; 'flɑtsəm/ *n* [U] (legal) parts of a wrecked ship or its cargo floating in the sea. (法律)遇難船隻漂浮在海上的殘骸或貨物。 ⇨ jetsam.

flounce¹ /flaʊns; flaʊns/ *vi* [VP2C] move with exaggerated or impatient movements: 誇張或不耐煩地走動: *~ out of/about the room.* 不耐煩地離開了屋子(在室內走來走去)。 □ *n* [C] fling; jerk; sudden impatient movement of the body. 急行; 急轉; 因不耐煩身體所作的突然扭動。

flounce² /flaʊns; flaʊns/ *n* [C] (often ornamental) strip of cloth or lace sewn by the upper edge to a woman's skirt. 衣裙上之荷葉邊裝飾。 □ *vt* [VP6A] trim with a ~ or ~s. 飾以荷葉邊。

floun·der¹ /'flaʊndə(r); 'flaʊndɚ/ *vi* [VP2A, C] make violent and usu vain efforts (as when trying to get out of deep snow, or when one is in deep water and unable to swim); (fig) hesitate, make mistakes, when trying to do sth: 掙扎(如陷入深雪中時或不會游泳而跌入深水中時所作的); (喻)躊躇或錯亂地做事: *~ through a speech,* eg in a foreign language. 錯亂地做完一次演說(例如用外國語)。

floun·der² /'flaʊndə(r); 'flaʊndɚ/ *n* small flatfish, used as food. 比目魚類(可食用)。

flour /'flaʊə(r); flaʊr/ *n* [U] fine meal, powder, made from grain, used for making bread, cakes, pastry, etc. 麵粉; 穀類之粉。 □ *vt* [VP6A] cover or sprinkle with ~. 覆以麵粉; 撒以粉末。 **~y** *adj* of, like, covered with, ~. 麵粉的; 似麵粉的; 粉狀的; 覆有粉末的。

flour·ish /'flʌrɪʃ; 'flɜɪʃ/ *vi, vt* **1** [VP2A] grow in a healthy manner; be well and active; prosper: 旺盛; 興隆; 茂盛: *His business is ~ing.* 他的生意興隆。 *I hope you are all ~ing,* keeping well. 我希望你們都安好。 **2** [VP6A] wave about and show: 揮舞並顯示: *~ a sword.* 舞劍。 **3** [VP2A] (of a famous person) be alive and active (at the time indicated): (指某一時代的名人) 享盛名; 生存並活躍: *When did the troubadours ~?* 吟遊詩人何時盛行? □ *n* [C] ~ing movement; curve or decoration, ornament in handwriting, eg to a signature; loud, exciting passage of music; fanfare: 揮舞; 花體字(如簽名用者); 響亮而令人興奮的一段音樂; 鼓號曲: *a ~ of trumpets,* eg to welcome a distinguished visitor. 一段響亮的喇叭樂曲(例如歡迎貴賓時所吹奏者)。

flout /flaʊt; flaʊt/ *vt* [VP6A] oppose; treat with contempt: 反對; 蔑視: *~ sb's wishes/advice.* 輕視某人的願望(勸告)。

flow /fləʊ; flo/ *vi* (*pt, pp* ~ed) [VP2A, C] **1** move along or over as a river does; move smoothly: 流; 流動: *Rivers ~ into the sea.* 諸河皆流入海。 *The tears ~ed from her eyes.* 淚水從她的眼中流出。 *The river ~ed over* (= overflowed) *its banks.* 那河氾濫了。 *Gold ~ed* (= was sent) *out of the country.* 黃金外流。 **2** (of hair, articles of dress, etc) hang down loosely: (指頭髮, 衣服等)飄垂: *~ing robes;* 飄垂的長袍; *a ~ing tie;* 飄懸的領帶; *hair ~ing down her back.* 飄垂在她背部的頭髮。 **3** come from; be the result of: 來自; 為…之結果: *Wealth ~s from industry and economy.* 財富由勤儉而來。 **4** (of the tide) come in; rise: (潮)漲: *The tide began to ~.* 開始漲潮了。 ⇨ ebb. □ *n* (*sing* only) ~ing movement; quantity that ~s: (僅用單數)流動; 飄垂; 漲潮; 流量: *a good ~ of water;* 大量流水; *a ~ of angry words;* 滔滔的怒言; *the ebb and ~ of the sea.* 海潮的漲落。 *The tide is on the ~,* coming in. 正在漲潮。

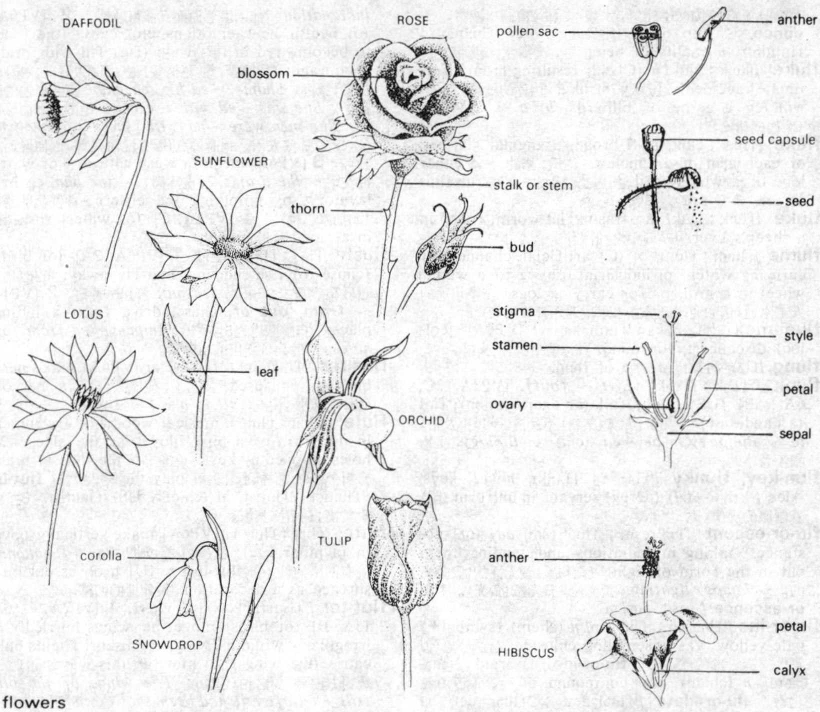

flowers

flower /ˈflaʊə(r) ; ˈflaʊə/ *n* **1** that part of a plant that produces seeds. 花。 ***in ~,*** with the ~s out. 開着花。 **ˈ~·bed** *n* plot of land in which ~s are grown. 花壇;花床。 **ˈ~ garden,** one with ~ing plants, not vegetables, etc. 花園。 **ˈ~-girl** *n* girl who sells ~s, eg in a market. 賣花女。 **ˈ~ children/people,** (colloq, in the 1960's) hippies favouring universal love and peace. (俗,1960年代之)嬉皮(主張博愛與和平)。 **ˈ~ power,** the ideals of these people. 上述嬉皮的理想。 **ˈ~·pot** *n* pot, eg of red earthenware or plastic, in which a plant may be grown. 花盆;花鉢。 **ˈ~ show** *n* exhibition at which ~s are shown (often in competition for prizes). 花展(常爲比賽性的)。 **2** ***the ~ of,*** the finest part of: 最佳部分;精華: *in the ~ of one's strength;* 年輕力壯之時; *the ~ of the nation's manhood.* the finest men. 一國中最優秀的男子。 **3** ***~s of speech,*** ornamental phrases. 華麗的詞藻。 □ *vi* [VP2A, C] produce ~s: 開花: *~ing bushes;* 開花的灌木; *late-~ing chrysanthemums.* 遲開的菊花。 **flow·ered** *adj* decorated with floral patterns: 飾有花的圖樣的: *~ed chintz.* 印花棉布。 **~y** *adj* (-ier, -iest) having many ~s: 多花的: *~y fields;* 多花的田野; (fig) full of ~s of speech: (喩)多華麗的詞藻的;絢麗的: *~y language.* 絢麗的文辭。 **~·less** *adj* not having, not producing, ~s: 無花的;不開花的: *~less plants.* 不開花的植物。

flown /fləʊn ; flon/ *pp* of fly.

flu /fluː ; flu/ *n* (colloq abbr of) influenza. (俗)流行性感冒(爲 influenza 之略)。

fluc·tu·ate /ˈflʌktʃʊeɪt ; ˈflʌktʃʊˌet/ *vi* [VP2A, C] (of levels, prices, etc) move up and down; be irregular: (指標準,價格等)波動;不規則: *fluctuating prices;* 波動的物價; *~ between hope and despair.* 徘徊於希望與失望之間。 **fluc·tu·ation** /ˌflʌktʃʊˈeɪʃn ; ˌflʌktʃʊˈeʃən/ *n* [U] fluctuating; [C] fluctuating movement: 變動;波動: *fluctuations of temperature;* 溫度的變動; *fluctuations in the exchange rates.* 兌換率的波動。

flue /fluː ; flu/ *n* [C] channel, pipe or tube for carrying heat, hot air or smoke to, from or through a boiler, oven, etc: 煙道;鍋爐通氣管;焰管: *clean the ~s of soot.* 清除煙道中的煤煙。

flu·ent /ˈfluːənt ; ˈfluənt/ *adj* (of a person) able to speak smoothly and readily: (指人)說話流利的: *a ~ speaker;* 口若懸河的演說者; (of speech) coming smoothly and readily: (指說話)流暢的;流利的: *speak ~ French.* 說流利的法語。 **~·ly** *adv* **flu·ency** /ˈfluːənsɪ ; ˈfluənsɪ/ *n* [U] the quality of being ~. 流利;流暢。

fluff /flʌf ; flʌf/ *n* **1** [U] soft, feathery stuff given off by blankets or other soft woolly material; soft fur or down¹. (毛毯或其他呢絨物之)絨毛;軟毛;柔毛。 **2** bungled attempt. 拙劣的嘗試;失誤。 ⇨ 2 below. 參看動詞第2義。 □ *vt* **1** [VP6A, 15B] ~ ***(out),*** shake, puff or spread out: 抖開;抖鬆: *~ out a pillow.* 抖鬆一枕頭。 *The bird ~ed (out) its feathers.* 這鳥抖開牠的羽毛。 **2** [VP6A] bungle (sth in games, in speaking one's lines in a play, etc): 拙劣地做(比賽失誤,背錯臺詞等): *~ a stroke,* eg in golf; 誤擊(例如在高爾夫球戲中); *~ a catch,* eg fail to catch the ball in cricket. 未接住球(例如在板球戲中)。 **~y** *adj* (-ier, -iest) of or like ~; covered with ~: 絨毛的;似絨毛的;覆有絨毛的: *Newly hatched chickens are like ~y balls.* 剛孵出的小鷄像絨毛球。

fluid /ˈfluːɪd ; ˈfluɪd/ *adj* able to flow (as gases and liquids do); (of ideas, etc) not fixed; capable of being changed: 流動的(如氣體和液體);(指思想等)不固定的;可改變的: *~ opinions/plans.* 不固定的意見(計畫)。 □ *n* [C, U] (chem) ~ substance, eg water, air, mercury; (colloq) liquid substance.

(化學)流質(例如水，空氣，水銀)；(俗)流體；液體。～ **ounce**, ⇨ App 5. 參看附錄五。~·**ity** /fluːˈɪdətɪ ; fluˈɪdətɪ/ *n* quality of being ～. 流動性;流動狀態。

fluke[1] /fluːk ; fluk/ *n* [C] sth resulting from a fortunate accident; lucky stroke: 僥倖的結果;僥倖: *win* (eg a game of billiards) *by a* ～. 僥倖得勝(例如撞球比賽)。

fluke[2] /fluːk ; fluk/ *n* **1** broad, triangular flat end of each arm of an anchor. 錨爪;錨鈎。 **2** either lobe of a whale's tail. 鯨尾二裂片之一。⇨ the illus at sea. 參看 sea 之插圖。

fluke[3] /fluːk ; fluk/ *n* parasite flat worm, found in a sheep's liver. (羊肝中之)肝蛭。

flume /fluːm ; flum/ *n* [C] artificial channel for carrying water for industrial use, eg to a water-wheel in a mill, or for carrying logs. 工業用途的人工水道(例如通往磨坊之水車或運送幹材用者)。

flum·mox /ˈflʌməks ; ˈflʌməks/ *vt* [VP6A] (colloq) disconcert; confound. (俗)使狼狽;使失措。

flung /flʌŋ ; flʌŋ/ *pt, pp* of fling.

flunk /flʌŋk ; flʌŋk/ *vi, vt* ～ ***(out)***, [VP2A, 2C, 6A, 15B] (US colloq) fail (an examination); fail (a candidate): (美俗)考試(某科)不及格;予以不及格: *to* ～ *Biology/to be* ～*ed (out) in Biology*. 生物學不及格。

flun·key, flunky /ˈflʌŋkɪ ; ˈflʌŋkɪ/ *n* (*pl* -keys, -kies /-kɪz ; -kɪz/) (derog) servant in uniform. (貶)着制服的男僕。

flu·or·escent /flʊəˈresnt ; ˌfluəˈrɛsn̩t/ *adj* (of substances) taking in radiations and sending them out in the form of light: (指物質)螢光性的;發螢光的: ～ *lamps/lighting*. 螢光燈,日光燈(螢光)。 **flu·or·escence** /-sns ; -sn̩s/ *n*

flu·or·ine /ˈflʊəriːn ; ˈfluəˌrin/ *n* (chem) (symbol F) pale-yellow gas resembling chlorine. (化學)氟(似氯之淡黃氣,符號爲 F)。 **flu·or·ide** /ˈflʊəraɪd ; ˈfluəˌraɪd/ *n* (chem) any compound of ～. (化學)氟化物。 **flu·ori·date** /ˈflʊərɪdeɪt ; ˈfluərəˌdet/ *vt* [VP6A] add a fluoride to (a water supply) to prevent dental decay. 加氟於(飲水)以防蛀齒。 **flu·ori·da·tion** /ˌflʊərɪˈdeɪʃn ; ˌflʊərəˈdeʃən/ *n* **flu·ori·dize** /ˈflʊərɪdaɪz ; ˈflʊərəˌdaɪz/ *vt* = fluoridate. **flu·ori·diz·ation** /ˌflʊərɪdaɪˈzeɪʃn *US:* -dɪˈz- ; ˌflʊrədɪˈzeʃən/ *n* = fluoridation.

flurry /ˈflʌrɪ ; ˈflɝɪ/ *n* (*pl* -ries) [C] short, sudden rush of wind or fall of rain or snow; (fig) nervous hurry: 一陣驟疾的風、雨或雪;(喻)慌張: *in a* ～ *of excitement/alarm*. 在突然一陣興奮(驚惶)中。 □ *vt* [VP6A] cause (sb) to be confused, in a nervous hurry, etc: 使(某人)迷亂,慌張等: *Keep calm! Don't get flurried*. 鎮靜些!不要慌。

flush[1] /flʌʃ ; flʌʃ/ *adj* ～ ***(with)***, **1** even; in the same plane; level: 平的;同平面的;齊平的: *doors* ～ *with the walls*. 與牆齊平的門戶。 **2** (pred) having plenty; well supplied: (敍述用法)很多的;豐富的;富裕的: ～ *with money*. 很多錢。

flush[2] /flʌʃ ; flʌʃ/ *n* **1** rush of water; rush of blood to the face; reddening caused by this; rush or emotion, excitement caused by this: 湧;激流;血液之衝上臉;暈紅;臉紅;激動;興奮: *in the first* ～ *of victory*. 初聞勝利之興奮。 **2** [U] ***(first)*** ～, fresh growth of vegetation, etc; high point or new access of strength: 草木之萌發;活力的充沛;旺盛: *the first* ～ *of spring*, the time when trees and plants send out new leaves; 春天草木的初茂; *in the first* ～ *of youth*. 青春活力的初現。

flush[3] /flʌʃ ; flʌʃ/ *n* (in card games) hand in which all the cards are of the same suit. (紙牌戲)同花的一手牌;清一色。 **ˈroyal** ～, (poker) hand with the five highest cards of one suit. (撲克牌)同花大順。

flush[4] /flʌʃ ; flʌʃ/ *vi, vt* **1** [VP2A, C, D] (of a person, his face) become red because of a rush of blood to the skin: (指人,面孔)變紅;發紅: *The girl* ～*ed (up) when the man spoke to her*. 當那男人對她講話時,那女孩的臉紅了。 *He* ～*ed crimson with indignation*. 他因憤怒而面孔漲得通紅。 **2** [VP6A] (of health, heat, emotions, etc) cause (the face) to become red in this way; (fig) fill with pride; encourage: (指健康,熱,感情等)使(面孔)發紅;(喻)使得意;激勵: *Shame* ～*ed his cheeks*. 羞愧使他的臉紅了。 *She was* ～*ed with exercise*. 她因運動而臉發紅。 *The men were* ～*ed with success/joy/insolence*. 那些人因勝利而得意(因喜悅而興奮,因侮辱而激動)。 **3** [VP6A] clean or wash with a ～ of water. 沖洗: ～ *the drains;* 沖洗陰溝; ～ *the pan*, eg in a lavatory, by emptying the cistern. 沖洗盆狀器皿(如抽水馬桶)。 **4** [VP2A, C] (of water) rush out in a flood. (指水)湧出。

flush[5] /flʌʃ ; flʌʃ/ *vt, vi* **1** [VP6A, 2A] (of birds) (cause to) rise suddenly and fly away: 驚起(鳥);(鳥)突然飛走: ～ *a pheasant*. 驚起一野鷄。 **2** [VP14] ～ ***from/out of***, chase, drive from a hiding-place: 自隱藏處趕出;逐出: *snipers* ～*ed from fox-holes*. 自散兵坑逐出的狙擊兵。

flus·ter /ˈflʌstə(r) ; ˈflʌstɚ/ *vt* [VP6A] make nervous or confused. 使緊張;使慌亂。 □ *n* nervous state: 緊張;慌亂: *all in a* ～. 狼狽不堪。

flute[1] /fluːt ; flut/ *n* musical woodwind instrument in the form of a pipe, blown at the side, with holes stopped by keys. 長笛。⇨ the illus at brass. 參看 brass 之插圖。 □ *vi* play the ～. 吹笛。 **flut·ist** /ˈfluːtɪst ; ˈflutɪst/ *n* (chiefly US) flautist. (主美)吹笛者;長笛演奏家。

flute[2] /fluːt ; flut/ *vt* [VP6A] make vertical grooves in (a pillar, etc): 在(柱上等)刻凹槽: ～*d columns*. 飾有凹槽的柱子。 **flut·ing** *n* [U] grooves cut on a surface as a decoration. 裝飾性的凹槽。

flut·ter /ˈflʌtə(r) ; ˈflʌtɚ/ *vt, vi* **1** [VP2A, C, 6A, 15A, B] (of birds) move the wings hurriedly or irregularly without flying, or in short flights only; cause (the wings) to move in this way: (指鳥)鼓翼;拍翅;鼓(翼);拍(翅膀): *The wings of the bird still* ～*ed after it had been shot down*. 那鳥被擊落後,翅膀仍在鼓動。 *The bird* ～*ed its wings in the cage*. 那鳥在籠中拍翅膀。 *The wounded bird* ～*ed to the ground*. 那受傷的鳥拍着翅膀落在地上。 **2** [VP2A, C, 6A] (cause to) move about in a quick, irregular way; (of the heart) beat irregularly: (使)迅速而無規律地亂動;(指心臟)撲動;無規律地跳: *curtains* ～*ing in the breeze;* 在微風中飄動的窗簾; *apple-blossom petals* ～*ing to the ground*. 飄落在地上的蘋果花瓣。 *She* ～*ed nervously about the room*. 她緊張地在室內走來走去。 □ *n* **1** (usu *sing*) ～ing movement: (通常用單數)鼓翼;無規律的急動: *the* ～ *of wings*. 鳥翼的拍動。 **2 a** ～, state of nervous excitement: 心緒不寧;不安;緊張: *in a* ～*;* 心緒不寧; *cause/make a* ～. 引起不安或緊張。 **3** [U] vibration: 顫動;擺動: *wing* ～, as a defect of an aircraft in flight; distortion in sound reproduced from a disc or tape caused by faulty recording or reproduction. (飛機飛行時的)機翼顫動;(唱片或錄音帶因錄音或播放不當而引起的)顫音。 **4** [C] (colloq) gambling venture; spree: (俗)孤注一擲;歡鬧: *go to the races and have a* ～, make a bet or bets. 去賭一賭賽馬。

flu·vial /ˈfluːvɪəl ; ˈfluvɪəl/ *adj* of, found in, rivers. 河的;河中的。

flux /flʌks ; flʌks/ *n* **1** [U] continuous succession of changes: 連續的改變: *in a state of* ～. 不斷改變中。 **2** [C] (*sing* only) flowing; flowing out. (僅用單數)流動;流出。 **3** [C] substance mixed with metal to promote fusion. 助鎔劑;鎔接劑;銲劑。

fly[1] /flaɪ ; flaɪ/ *n* (*pl* flies) two-winged insect, esp the common ˈ*housefly;* ⇨ the illus at insect. 蒼蠅(參看 insect 之插圖)。 ***a fly in the ointment***, (fig) a small circumstance that prevents pleasure from being perfect. (喻)美中不足之處;掃興的小事。 ***There are no flies on him***, (fig; sl) He is no fool, cannot be tricked, etc. (喻;俚)他很精(你騙不了他等)。 **ˈfly-blown** *adj* (of meat) (going bad because) containing flies' eggs; (fig) in bad condition; stale. (指肉)有蠅卵的;生蛆的;(喻)腐壞的。 **'fly·catcher** *n* kind of bird; trap for catching flies. 京燕;蠅虎類鳥;捕蠅器。 **'fly-fish** *vi* [VP2A] fish with artificial flies as bait. 以假蠅做餌釣魚。 Hence, 由此產生, **'fly-fishing** *n* [U]. **'fly-paper** *n* strip of sticky paper used for catching flies. 捕蠅紙。 **'fly-trap** *n* trap for catching flies. 捕蠅器。 **'fly·weight** *n* boxer weighing 112 lb (50·8kg) or less. 蠅量級拳擊手(體重不超過 112 磅或 50·8 公斤者)。

fly² /flaɪ; flaɪ/ *vi, vt* (*pt* flew /fluː; flu/, *pp* flown /fləʊn; flon/) **1** [VP2A, B, C, D, 4A] move through the air as a bird does, or in an aircraft: 飛;飛行;空中航行: *birds flying in the air;* 天上飛的鳥; *fly from London to Paris;* 自倫敦飛行至巴黎; *fly (across) the Atlantic.* 飛越大西洋。 ***fly high,*** be ambitious. 懷大志;野心很大。 ***The bird is/has flown,*** The person wanted has escaped. 要捕的人跑掉了。 **2** [VP6A, 15A, B] direct or control the flight of (aircraft); transport goods/passengers in aircraft: 駕駛(飛機,飛船等);以飛機運輸(貨物,乘客): *Five thousand passengers were flown to Paris during Easter weekend.* 復活節的週末有五千位乘客飛往巴黎。 **3** [VP2A, C, D, 4A] go or move quickly; rush along; pass quickly: 疾行;迅速地動: *He flew down the road.* 他沿着路飛奔。 *The children flew to meet their mother.* 孩子們跑着迎接他們的母親。 *It's getting late; we must fly.* 天色漸漸晚了,我們必須快跑。 *The door flew open.* 門突然敞開了。 *He paid us a flying visit,* a very short, fleeting visit. 他匆忙地拜訪我們。 ***fly at sb,*** rush angrily at sb. 憤怒地衝向某人。 ***let fly (at),*** ⇨ let¹(4). ***fly off the handle,*** ⇨ handle. ***fly in the face of,*** **(a)** defy openly: 公然反抗: *You're flying in the face of the law.* 你在公然犯法。 **(b)** be quite contrary to: 與…完全相反: *This version of what happened flies in the face of all the evidence.* 這個對事情發生的經過所作的叙述與證據完全相反。 ***fly into a rage/passion/temper,*** become suddenly angry. 勃然大怒。 ***fly to arms,*** take up arms eagerly. 急速武裝起來。 ***fly to bits/into pieces,*** break to bits and scatter. 成碎片而飛散。 ***make the 'feathers/'fur fly,*** cause quarrelling or fighting. 引起爭吵或爭鬥。 ***make the money fly,*** spend it quickly, recklessly. 揮霍。 ***send sb flying,*** strike him so that he falls over or backwards. 將某人擊倒或擊退。 ***send things flying,*** send or throw them violently in all directions. 將東西向四面八方投擲。 **4** [VP6A] cause (a *kite*) to rise and stay high in the air; raise (a *flag*) so that it waves in the air. 放(風箏);懸(旗)。 **5** flee from: 逃離;逃出: *fly the country.* 逃出國境。

fly³ /flaɪ; flaɪ/ *n* (*pl* flies) **1** (also, colloq, *pl* used with *sing* meaning) flap of cloth on a garment to contain or cover a zip fastener or buttonholes, eg down the front of a pair of trousers: (俗,複數形式單數意義)衣服上蓋拉鍊或鈕扣洞的遮蓋(例如褲子前面者): *John, your fly is/flies are undone!* 約翰,你褲子的拉鍊未拉上(鈕扣未扣好)。 **2** flap of canvas at the entrance to a tent or covered wagon. 帳篷或篷車的門簾。 **3** (old use) one-horse hackney carriage. (舊用法) 單馬的出租馬車。 **4** outer edge of a flag farthest from the flagpole. 旗的外端。

fly⁴ /flaɪ; flaɪ/ *adj* (sl) cunning; alert; not to be deceived or hoodwinked. (俚)狡猾的;機警的;不易受騙的。

flyer, flier /'flaɪə(r); 'flaɪɚ/ *n* **1** animal, vehicle, etc going with exceptional speed. 行走特快的動物,車輛等。 **2** airman. 飛行者。

fly·ing /'flaɪɪŋ; 'flaɪɪŋ/ *part adj, gerund* (in compounds): (用於複合字中): **'~ boat** *n* form of seaplane without floats and with a fuselage that floats on water. 水上飛機;飛艇。 **ˌ~-'bomb** *n* rocket filled with explosives that can be fired to a great distance. 自導飛彈。 **ˌ~ 'buttress** *n* (archit) one arching from a column up to a wall, ⇨ the illus at church. (建築)飛扶壁;拱柱 (參看 church 之揷圖)。 **'~ club,** club for those interested in ~ as a sport. 航空俱樂部。 **ˌ~ 'colours,** flags on display (as during a ceremony). 展示的旗幟 (如飄揚於慶典中者)。 ***come through/off with ~ colours,*** ⇨ colour¹(8). **ˌ~ 'column,** (mil) body of troops able to move rapidly and act independently. (軍)別動隊。 **'~ field,** airfield. 飛機場。 **'~-fish,** (kind of) tropical fish able to rise out of the water and move forward. 飛魚。 **ˌ~-'fox,** (kind of) large fruit-eating bat. 以水果爲食的大蝙蝠。 **'F~ Officer,** rank in the Royal Air Force below Flight Lieutenant. (英國皇家空軍之) 空軍中尉。 **ˌ~ 'jump,** one made with a running start. 急行跳高。 **ˌ~ 'saucer,** unidentified flying object seen, or thought to have been seen, moving across the sky, eg one said to have come from another planet. 飛碟。 **'~-squad,** part of a police force organized (with fast cars) for pursuit of (suspected) criminals. 機動警察隊(備有快速汽車,可迅速追捕犯人或嫌疑犯)。 **ˌ~ 'visit,** hasty visit made while passing. 匆匆拜訪;過訪。

fly·leaf /'flaɪliːf; 'flaɪˌlif/ *n* blank leaf at the beginning or end of a book. 蝴蝶頁(書籍前後的空白頁)。

fly·over /'flaɪəʊvə(r); 'flaɪˌovɚ/ *n* **1** (US 美 = *overpass*) roadway, bridge, etc which crosses above another roadway, etc (as on a motorway). 横跨另一道路之上的道路或天橋 (如高速公路上者)。 **2** (GB) (英) = flypast.

flyovers

fly·past /'flaɪpɑːst *US:* -pæst; 'flaɪˌpæst/ *n* flight of aircraft in formation, usu at a low altitude, as part of a military display. 空中分列式(閱兵之項目)。

fly·post /'flaɪpəʊst; 'flaɪpost/ *vt* [VP6A] post⁵(1) up rapidly (and often illegally). 迅速地(往往是非法地)張貼。 **~er** *n* sth ~ed; sb who ~s. 迅速(非法)張貼之物;迅速(非法)張貼之人。

fly·wheel /'flaɪwiːl *US:* -hwiːl; 'flaɪˌhwil/ *n* heavy wheel revolving on a shaft to regulate machinery. 飛輪;整速輪。

foal /fəʊl; fol/ *n* young horse (colt or filly). 小馬;幼馬;駒。 ⇨ the illus at domestic. 參看 domestic 之揷圖。 ***in/with ~,*** (of a mare) pregnant. (指母馬)懷孕。 □ *vi* [VP2A] give birth to a ~. 生小馬。

foam /fəʊm; fom/ *n* [U] **1** white mass of small air bubbles formed in or on a liquid by motion, or on an animal's lips, eg after exertion. 泡沫;涎沫;口角飛沫。 **2** (also 亦作 **ˌ~-'rubber**) spongy rubber used in upholstery (eg in seats, mattresses). 泡沫膠(例如座墊中者)。 □ *vi* [VP2A, C] form ~; break into ~; send out ~ (at the mouth): 起泡沫;變泡沫;(口)流泡沫: *waves ~ing along the beach;* 沿着海灘起泡沫的海浪; *a glass of ~ing beer,* beer with froth on it; 一杯起泡沫的啤酒; (fig) (喻) *~ing with rage,* looking angry. 生氣的。 **~y** *adj*

fob /fɒb; fɑb/ *vt* (-bb-) [VP15B] ***fob sth off on sb; fob sb off with sth,*** get a person to accept sth of little or no value by deceit or trickery. 以劣物混騙某人。

fo·cal /'fəʊkl; 'fokḷ/ *adj* of or at a focus: 焦點的;在焦點上的: *the ~ length/distance of a lens,* from the surface of a lens to its focus. 透鏡的焦距。

fo'c'sle /ˈfəʊksl ; ˈfoksl/ *n* = forecastle.

fo·cus /ˈfəʊkəs ; ˈfokəs/ *n* (*pl* ~es or foci /ˈfəʊsaɪ ; ˈfosaɪ/) **1** meeting-point of rays of light, heat, etc; point, distance, at which the sharpest outline is given (to the eye, through a telescope, through a lens on a camera plate, etc): 焦點; 焦距: *The image is in/out of* ~. 這影像在焦點上(外)。*Bring the object into* ~ *if you want a good photograph.* 你如果要照一張好像,就要把焦點對準物體。 **2** point at which interests, tendencies, etc meet: 興趣,趨勢等之中心: *the* ~ *of attention;* 注意力的中心; *the* ~ *of an earthquake/storm/disease, etc.* 震源(暴風圈的中心;疾病的主要患部等)。□ *vt, vi* (-s- or -ss-) **1** [VP2A, C, 6A, 14] ~ ***(on),*** (cause to) come together at a ~; adjust (an instrument, etc) so that it is in ~: (使)聚集於焦點; 調整(儀器等)使其在焦點上: ~ *the sun's rays on sth with a burning-glass;* 以取火鏡使太陽光線聚集於某物上; ~ *the lens of a microscope.* 調整顯微鏡的透鏡以定焦點。 **2** [VP14] ~ ***on,*** concentrate: 集中: ~ *one's attention/thoughts/efforts on a problem.* 集中注意力(思想,努力)於一問題。

fod·der /ˈfɒdə(r) ; ˈfɑdɚ/ *n* [U] dried food, hay, etc for farm animals, horses, etc. 牛馬等之飼料; 秣;草料。

foe /fəʊ ; fo/ *n* (poet) enemy. (詩)敵人。

foe·tus (US = **fe·tus**) /ˈfiːtəs ; ˈfitəs/ *n* fully developed embryo in the womb or in an egg. (發育完整的)胎兒;胚胎。➪ the illus at reproduce. 參看 reproduce 之挿圖。**foe·tal** (US = **fe·tal**) /ˈfiːtl ; ˈfitl/ *adj* of, like, a ~: 胎兒的;似胚胎的: *the foetal position* (in the womb). 胎兒(在子宮內)的位置。

fog /fɒg *US:* fɔːg ; fɑg/ *n* **1** [U] vapour suspended in the atmosphere at or near the earth's surface, thicker than mist and difficult to see through: 霧(比 mist 濃): *Fog is the sailor's worst enemy.* 霧是船員最大的敵人。***in a fog,*** (fig) puzzled; at a loss. (喻)迷惑;困惑;墜入五里霧中。**ˈfog·bank** *n* dense mass of fog on the sea. 海上的濃霧;霧堤。**ˈfog-bound** *adj* unable to proceed safely because of fog. 因霧而無法安全行進的。**ˈfog·horn** *n* instrument used for warning ships in fog. 霧角(用以警告霧中船隻的號角)。**ˈfog·lamp,** headlamp (on a motor vehicle) providing a strong beam of light for use in foggy weather. 霧燈(汽車在霧中行駛用的強光燈)。**ˈfog·signal,** device placed on railway lines in fog to explode when a train passes over it and so warn drivers. 霧中信號(置於有霧的鐵道上,火車經過時則爆炸以警告駕駛人員)。 **2** [C] period of fog; abnormal darkened state of the atmosphere: 有霧時期;大氣反常的昏暗狀態: *London used to have bad fogs in winter.* 過去倫敦在冬季有大霧。 **3** [C, U] (area of) cloudiness on a developed photographic plate or film. 照相底片或感光板上之模糊;底片或感光板上的模糊處。□ *vt* (-gg-) cover with, as with, fog; bewilder: 霧籠罩於;使朦朧;使迷惑: *I'm a bit fogged,* puzzled. 我有點糊塗了。**foggy** *adj* (-ier, -iest) **1** dense, not clear, because of fog: 有濃霧的;霧色朦朧的: *a foggy evening;* 有霧的晚上; *foggy weather.* 有霧的天氣。 **2** obscure, confused: 模糊的;迷惑的: *have only a foggy idea of what something means.* 對某事的意義僅有一模糊的觀念。*I haven't the foggiest idea,* I don't know. 我不知道。

fogey (US = **fogy**) /ˈfəʊgɪ ; ˈfogɪ/ *n* (*pl* ~s, US fogies) ***(old)*** ~, person with old-fashioned ideas which he is unwilling to change. 老頑固。

foible /ˈfɔɪbl ; ˈfɔɪbl/ *n* [C] slight peculiarity or defect of character, often one of which a person is wrongly proud. 性格上小的特色或缺點(常誤以自負者);瑕疵;沾沾自喜的性格特點。

foil[1] /fɔɪl ; fɔɪl/ *n* **1** [U] metal rolled or hammered into a thin, flexible sheet: 箔: *lead/tin/aluminium* ~, eg as wrapped round chocolate or cigarettes. 鉛(錫,鋁)箔(例如包裝巧克力或香煙者)。**2** [C] person or thing that contrasts with, and thus sets off, the qualities of another: 襯托的人或物: *A plain old woman serves as a* ~ *to a beautiful young woman.* 一面貌平庸的老婦可作爲一美麗的少婦的襯托。

foil[2] /fɔɪl ; fɔɪl/ *n* light sword without a sharp edge and with a button on the point, for fencing. 鈍頭劍;花梢劍。

foil[3] /fɔɪl ; fɔɪl/ *vt* [VP6A] baffle; prevent (sb) from carrying out his plans; make plans/designs ineffective: 挫敗;阻止(某人)實行其計畫; 阻撓(計畫): *We* ~*ed him/his plans.* 我們阻撓了他(他的計畫)。*He was* ~*ed in his attempt to deceive the girl.* 他企圖欺騙那女郎的計畫失敗了。

foist /fɔɪst ; fɔɪst/ *vt* [VP14, 15A] ~ ***sth (off) on sb,*** trick him into accepting (a useless article, etc). 混騙;騙某人接受(無用之物等)。

fold[1] /fəʊld ; fold/ *vt, vi* **1** [VP6A, 15B] bend one part of a thing back over on itself: 摺疊: ~ *a letter,* before putting it in an envelope; 摺疊一信; ~ *up a newspaper;* 將報紙摺起; ~ *back the bed-clothes.* 把被褥摺起來。**2** [VP2A, C] become ~ed; be able to be ~ed: 摺疊起來;可以折起: ~*ing doors,* having hinged parts; 摺門; *a* ~*ing boat/bed/chair,* made so as to occupy a smaller space when not in use. 可摺疊的舟(床,椅)。*The window shutters* ~ *back.* 百葉窗可以摺起來。~ ***(up),*** (fig; colloq) collapse; come to an end: (喻;俗)垮臺;失敗;結束: *The business finally* ~*ed up last week.* 生意終於在上週垮掉了。 **3** ~ ***one's arms,*** cross them over the chest. 交臂;抱臂。 ~ ***sb/sth in one's arms,*** hold him/it to the breast. 擁抱某人(抱着某物)。**4** [VP15A, B] cover, wrap up: 包起: ~ *sth (up) in paper;* 將某物用紙包起; ~ *sth round;* 將某物包起來; *hills* ~*ed in mist.* 爲霧所籠罩的群山。 **5** (cooking) mix an ingredient (eg beaten eggs) into another (eg flour) by turning them with a wooden spoon. (烹調)以木匙攪合(例如將麵粉和打散的蛋攪合)。□ *n* **1** part that is ~ed: 摺疊部分: *a dress hanging in loose* ~*s;* 有寬鬆摺子的衣服; line made by ~ing. 摺縫。 **2** hollow in mountains. 山坳;山谷;山窩。 ~**er** *n* **1** holder (made of ~ed cardboard or other stiff material) for loose papers. 硬紙夾。 **2** ~ing card or paper with advertisements, railway timetables, etc printed on it, or (US) as a container, eg for matches. (印有廣告,火車時間表等的) 摺疊式卡片;摺疊式小册子;(美)摺疊式火柴。

fold[2] /fəʊld ; fold/ *n* [C] enclosure for sheep; (fig) body of religious believers; members of a Church. 羊欄;(喻)教會團體;某一教會的教徒。***return to the*** ~, come or go back home (esp rejoin a body of believers). 回老家(尤指回教會)。□ *vt* [VP6A] enclose (sheep) in a ~. 關(羊)入欄。

fo·li·age /ˈfəʊlɪɪdʒ ; ˈfolɪɪdʒ/ *n* [U] all the leaves of a tree or plant. 樹或植物的葉子的總稱。

fo·lio /ˈfəʊlɪəʊ ; ˈfolɪˌo/ *n* (*pl* ~s) **1** sheet of paper numbered on one side only; page number of a printed book; (bookkeeping) two opposite pages of a ledger, used for both sides of an account. 單面記頁碼的一頁; (書籍之)頁碼; (簿記)總帳中左右對記的兩頁。 **2** large sheet of paper folded once to make two leaves or four pages (of a book); volume made of such sheets: (書本之)對摺紙;對開紙;對開本;對摺本: ~ *volumes;* 對開本的書卷; *in six volumes* ~. 分成六卷對開本。

folk /fəʊk ; fok/ *n* **1** (collective *n,* used with *pl v*) people in general: (集合名詞,與複數動詞連用)人們;人民: *Some* ~ *are never satisfied.* 有些人永遠不滿足。*Is there more honesty among country* ~ *than among towns*~*?* 鄉下人較城裏人誠實嗎? **2** (in compounds) of the common people of a country. (用於複合字中)民間的。 **ˈ~-dance** *n* (music for a) traditional popular dance. 民間舞(曲);土風舞(曲)。 **ˈ~-lore** *n* [U] (study of the) traditional beliefs, tales, etc of a community. 民俗;民間傳說;民俗學。 **ˈ~ music/song** *nn* popular music/song handed down from the past. 民間音樂;民謠;民歌。'~·tale *n* popular story handed down orally from past generations. 民間故事。**3** (*pl*) (colloq) relatives: (複) (俗) 親屬;家人: *the old ~s at home.* 家裏的老人家。

folksy /'fəʊksɪ; 'foksɪ/ *adj* (colloq) unpretentious in manners; simple; friendly and sociable. (俗) 平易的;樸實的;友善的。

fol·low /'fɒləʊ; 'fɑlo/ *vt, vi* **1** [VP2A, B, C, 6A] come, go, have a place, after (in space, time or order): 跟隨;跟着;繼起: *You go first and I will ~ (you).* 你先走,我就跟來。*Monday ~s Sunday.* 星期一在星期日之後。*They ~ed us for miles.* 他們跟着我們走了好幾哩路。*One misfortune ~ed (upon) another.* 災禍接踵而來。*His arguments were as ~s,* as now to be given. 他的意見如下。**~ on, (a)** ~ after a period of time. 經過一段時間後再繼續。**(b)** (cricket, of a side) bat again after failing to get the necessary number of runs. (板球,指一方)得分不足後繼續攻擊。Hence, 由此產生, **~-'on** *n* second innings following the first at once. 一局結束後緊接着舉行的第二局。**~ through, (a)** (tennis, golf, etc) complete a stroke by moving the racker, club, etc after hitting the ball. (網球,高爾夫球等)完成動作(球擊出後繼續揮動球拍或球棒以完成一擊)。Hence, 由此產生, **'~-through** *n* [C] such a stroke. (網球、高爾夫球等之)完成動作。**(b)** complete a task, carry out a promise. 完成工作;實踐諾言。**2** [VP6A] go along, keep to (a road, etc): 沿…而行;循(路等): *F~ this road until you get to the church; then turn left.* 順着這條路一直走到教堂,然後左轉彎。**3** [VP6A, 2A] understand (an argument, sth said, etc): 聽得懂(議論,說的話等): *Do you ~ my argument?* 你聽得懂我的意見嗎? *He spoke so fast that I couldn't ~ him/~ what he said.* 他說得太快,我聽不懂他的話。**4** [VP6A] engage in as a business, trade, etc: 從事;經營(商業等): *~ the law;* 做律師; *~ the trade of a builder.* 從事建築業;做營造商。**5** [VP6A] take or accept as a guide, an example, etc: 接受(做爲指導,例子等): *~ sb's advice;* 聽從某人的勸告; *~ the fashion.* 追隨時尚;講究時髦。**~ suit,** do what has just been done by sb else. 遵照先例;照樣做。**6** [VP2A] be necessarily true: 必然是眞實的;作爲必然的結果: *Because he is good, it does not ~ that he is wise.* 他人好,並不見得就聰明。*It ~s from what you say that....* 根據你的話來推斷,則…爲必然的結果。**7** [VP15B] **~ sth out,** keep to, carry out, to the end: 貫徹;徹底實行: *~ out an enterprise.* 貫徹一項事業。**~ sth up,** pursue, work at further: 追逐;追求: *~ up an advantage/a victory.* 乘機(乘勝追擊)。Hence, 由此產生, **'~-up** *n* (esp) second letter, circular, visit, referring to an earlier one. (尤指) 接連的信件,傳單,訪問。**~er** *n* **1** supporter; disciple: 擁護者;信徒;門徒: *Mahatma Gandhi and his ~ers.* 聖雄甘地及其信徒。**2** pursuer. 追捕者;追求者。**~·ing** *adj* **the ~ing,** the one or ones about to be mentioned. 下列的。□ *n* body of supporters: 一批追隨者或擁護者: *a political leader with a large ~ing.* 擁有大批追隨者的政治領袖。

folly /'fɒlɪ; 'fɑlɪ/ *n* (*pl* -lies) [U] foolishness; [C] foolish act, idea or practice; ridiculous thing. 愚蠢;愚蠢的行爲,思想或習慣;荒唐之事。

fo·ment /fəʊ'ment; fo'mɛnt/ *vt* [VP6A] **1** put warm water, clothes, lotions, etc on (a part of the body, to lessen pain, etc). (以溫水,熱布,洗滌劑等)熱敷;熱罨(身體之患部,以減輕痛苦等)。**2** (fig) cause or increase (disorder, discontent, ill feeling, etc). (喻)引起或增加(紊亂,不滿,惡意等)。**fo·men·ta·tion** /ˌfəʊmen'teɪʃn; ˌfomən'teʃən/ *n* [U] ~-ing; [C] that which is used for ~ing. 熱敷;熱敷物;熱罨劑。

fond /fɒnd; fɑnd/ *adj* (-er, -est) **1** (pred only) (僅作敍述用法) **be ~ of,** like, be full of love for, take pleasure in: 喜歡;愛好: *~ of music.* 愛好音樂。**2** loving and kind: 慈愛的: *a ~ mother;* 慈母; *~ looks.* 慈愛的樣子。**3** foolishly loving; doting: 癡愛的;溺愛的: *a young wife with a ~ husband.* 一少婦與溺愛她的丈夫。**4** (of hopes, ambitions) held, but unlikely to be realized. (指希望,抱負)不大能實現的。**~·ly** *adv* **1** lovingly: 親愛地;愛憐地: *look ~ly at sb.* 愛憐地望着某人。**2** in a foolishly optimistic manner: 以一種愚蠢的樂觀態度: *He ~ly imagined that he could learn French in six weeks.* 他天眞地想像他能在六個星期內學會法文。**~·ness** *n*

fon·dant /'fɒndənt; 'fɑndənt/ *n* [C] kind of soft sweet that melts in the mouth. 一種軟糖。

fondle /'fɒndl; 'fɑndḷ/ *vt* [VP6A] touch or stroke lovingly: 撫弄;撫愛: *~ a baby/a doll/a kitten.* 撫弄一嬰兒(洋娃娃,小貓)。

fon·due /'fɒndju:; 'fɑndu/ *n* dish of melted cheese, into which pieces of bread are dipped; dish of hot fat, into which pieces of raw meat are dipped; dish of hot chocolate, into which pieces of fruit are dipped. (蘸麵包片的)一碟融化的乾酪;(蘸生肉的)一碟熱油;(蘸水果片的)一碟熱巧克力。

font /fɒnt; fɑnt/ *n* **1** basin or vessel (often in carved stone) to hold water for baptism; basin for holy water. 洗禮盆(常爲一雕刻的石盆);聖水盆。**2** = fount(2).

food /fu:d; fud/ *n* **1** [U] that which can be eaten by people or animals, or used by plants, to keep them living and for growth: 食物;食料;食品;滋養品: *~ and water;* 食物和水; (attrib) (形容用法) *~ rationing;* 食物配給; (fig) (喻) *~ for thought/reflection,* sth to think/reflect about. 需要思考(考慮)之事。**2** [C] kind of ~: 某種食物: *breakfast/frozen/packaged ~s.* 早餐(冷凍,包裝)食品。**'~·stuff** *n* material used as ~. 食料;糧食。**~·less** *adj* without ~. 無食物的;無食料的。

fool[1] /fu:l; ful/ *n* **1** person without much sense; stupid or rash person; person whose conduct one considers silly: 愚人;獃子;傻瓜: *What ~s we were not to see the trap!* 我們沒有看出那個陷阱,多麼傻啊! *She was ~ enough* (= enough of a fool) *to believe him.* 她會相信他,眞是够傻了。**be a ~ for one's pains,** do sth for which one gets neither reward nor thanks. 做得不到報酬或感激之事。**be/live in a ~'s paradise,** be/live in a state of carefree happiness that cannot last. 生活在虛幻的樂境中。**be sent/go on a ~'s errand,** on an errand that is seen in the end to be useless. 做徒勞無功之奔走。**make a ~ of sb,** trick him; cause him to seem like a ~. 愚弄某人。**play the ~,** behave stupidly. 做傻樣;做傻事。**no ~ like an old ~,** (prov) said of an aged lover. (諺)沒有傻瓜像老傻瓜一樣傻(指老年戀愛之人)。**2** (in the Middle Ages) man employed by a ruler or noble as a clown or jester. (中世紀)帝王或貴族豢養的小丑;弄臣。**3** ˌ**April '~,** person deceived, or sent on a ~'s errand, on ˌ**All 'F~s' Day,** 1st April. 在萬愚節(All Fools' Day 四月一日)受愚弄之人。**4** (used attrib, colloq) foolish; silly: (形容用法,俗)愚蠢的;傻的: *a scheme devised by some ~ politician.* 某一愚蠢的政客想出的計策。□ *vi, vt* **1** [VP2A, C] **~ (about/around),** behave like a ~; trifle; be idle and silly: 做出似愚人般的行爲;玩弄;虛度光陰: *If you go on ~ing with that gun, there'll be an accident.* 如果你繼續玩弄那槍,就會發生意外。*Stop ~ing (about)!* 不要再做愚蠢無益之事!**2** [VP6A, 14, 15B] **~ sb (out of sth),** cheat; deceive: 欺騙: *He ~ed her out of her money.* 他騙走了她的錢。*You can't/don't ~ me!* 你騙不了(不要騙)我!

fool[2] /fu:l; ful/ *n* creamy liquid of stewed fruit (esp gooseberries), crushed and mixed with cream or custard. 果醬(尤指醋栗醬)與奶油或乳蛋糕製成的醬。

fool·ery /'fu:lərɪ; 'fulərɪ/ *n* [U] foolish behaviour; (*pl* -ries) foolish acts, ideas or utterances. 愚行;(複)愚蠢的行動,思想或言語。

fool·hardy /'fu:lhɑ:dɪ; 'fulˌhardɪ/ *adj* foolishly

bold; taking unnecessary risks. 有勇無謀的;蠻勇的。 **fool·hardi·ness** *n*

fool·ish /ˈfuːlɪʃ; ˈfulɪʃ/ *adj* without reason, sense or good judgement; silly: 愚蠢的;無頭腦的;傻的: *How ~ of you to consent!* 你竟會同意,多麼愚蠢啊! *It would be ~ for us to quarrel.* 我們爭吵是愚蠢的。**~·ly** *adv* **~·ness** *n*

fool·proof /ˈfuːlpruːf; ˈfulˈpruf/ *adj* incapable of failure, error or misinterpretation: 不會失敗的;不會有差錯的;不會有誤解的: *a ~ scheme/design/gadget.* 不會有差錯的計畫(設計,小器具)。

fools·cap /ˈfuːlskæp; ˈfulˌskæp/ *n* [U] size (17×13½ inches) of writing or printing paper. 大頁紙(大小爲 17×13½ 吋)。

foot[1] /fʊt; fʊt/ *n* (*pl* feet /fiːt; fit/) **1** part forming the lower end of the leg, beginning at the ankle; part of a sock, etc covering the ~: 足;脚;(襪子等的)脚部: *A dog has four feet.* 狗有四隻足。*A dog's feet are called paws.* 狗足稱作爪。*He rose to his feet,* stood up. 他站了起來。⇨ the illus at leg. 參看 leg 之插圖。***on ~,*** **(a)** walking, not riding. 徒步;步行。Cf 參較 *by bus/car/tram, etc.* 乘公共汽車(汽車,電車等)。**(b)** (fig) started: (喻)已經開始: *A project is on ~ to build a new tunnel here.* 在此建一新隧道的計畫已經開始。***be on one's feet,*** **(a)** be standing: 站着: *I've been on my feet all day.* 我站了一整天。**(b)** rise (to speak): 起立(以發言): *The Minister was on his feet at once to answer the charge.* 部長卽刻起立答覆那項指控。**(c)** (fig) be in good health after an illness: (喻)痊癒;復元: *It's nice to see you on your feet again.* 很高興看到你已復元了。***fall on one's feet,*** (colloq) be fortunate, have good luck. (俗)幸運;有好運。***find one's feet,*** ⇨ find[2](2). ***have feet of clay,*** be weak or cowardly. 衰弱;怯懦。***have one ~ in the grave,*** be near death, eg because of old age. 死期不遠;行將就木(例如因年邁)。***keep one's feet,*** not fall, eg when walking on ice. 不跌倒(如行走於冰上時)。***put one's ~ down,*** (colloq) object; protest; be firm. (俗)反對;抗議;堅持立場。***put one's ~ in it,*** (colloq) say or do sth wrong or stupid; blunder. (俗)說錯話或做錯事;犯錯誤。***put one's feet up,*** (colloq) rest with the legs in a horizontal position. (俗)將腿平放着休息。***put one's best ~ forward,*** walk (fig, get on with one's work) as fast as one can. 盡快往前走;(喻)全力以赴。***set sth/sb on its/his feet,*** make it/him self-supporting, no longer in need of help. 使某事物(或某人)自立。***set sth on ~,*** start it; get it going. 發動;開始。***sweep sb off his feet,*** fill him with strong enthusiasm. 使某人狂熱。***under ~,*** on the ground: 在地上: *wet under ~.* 地上濕。***wait on/bind sb hand and ~,*** ⇨ hand[1](1). **2** step, pace, tread: 脚步;步法;步態: *light/swift/fleet of ~,* stepping or walking lightly, swiftly, etc. 脚步輕快(疾速)的。**3** lowest part; bottom: 底部: *at the ~ of the page/ladder/wall/mountain.* 在頁底(梯脚,牆根,山脚)。**4** lower end of a bed or grave. (床鋪或墳墓之)尾端。⇨ head[1](10). **5** measure of length, = 12 inches: 呎(十二吋);英尺: (with *pl* unchanged) (複數不變) *George is very tall—he's six ~ two* (six feet two inches). 喬治很高,他有六呎二吋。**6** division or unit of verse, each with one strong stress and one or more weak stresses, as in: *for ˈmen/may ˈcome/and ˈmen/may ˈgo.* 音步(詩行的區分或單位,每一音步有一重音節和一個或多個非重音節,如: for ˈmen/may ˈcome/and ˈmen /may ˈgo)。**7** [U] (mil, old use) infantry: (軍,舊用法)步兵: *the Fourth Regiment of F~;* 第四步兵團; *~ and horse,* infantry and cavalry. 步兵和騎兵。**8** (compounds) (複合字) **ˌ~-and-ˈmouth disease,** disease of cattle and other cloven-hoofed animals. 口蹄病;蹄口瘡(牛羊等的一種病)。**ˈ~·ball** *n* [C] inflated leather ball used in games; [U] the game played with it. 足球;足球戲;足球運動。⇨ the illus below and at Rugby.

American football

參看附圖及 Rugby 之挿圖。**ˈ~-bath** *n* (small bath used for a) washing of the feet. 濯足;濯足具;洗脚盆。**ˈ~·board** *n* sloping board for the feet of the driver (in a carriage, etc). (馬車等駕駛者之)踏板。**ˈ~·bridge** *n* one for the use of persons on ~, not vehicles. 人行橋;天橋。**ˈ~·fall** *n* sound of a ~step. 脚步聲。**ˈ~·fault** *n* (tennis) service not allowed because the server's feet are wrongly placed. (網球)足部失誤(發球時足部踩線等);發球犯規。**ˈ~·hills** *n pl* hills lying at the ~ of a mountain or a range of mountains. (山或山脈之)山麓小丘。**ˈ~·hold** *n* support for the ~, eg when climbing on rocks or ice; (fig) secure position. 立足處(如攀登山岩或冰時);(喻)據點;立足點。**ˈ~·lights** *n pl* row of screened lights at the front of the stage of a theatre. (舞臺上的)脚燈。***the ~ lights,*** (fig) the profession of an actor. (喻)演員的職業。**ˈ~-loose** *adj* (also 亦作 ***~loose and fancy-free***) independent and without cares or responsibilities. 自由自在的;無拘束的。**ˈ~·man** /-mən; -mən/ *n* (*pl* -men) manservant who admits visitors, waits at table, etc. 男僕;閽者;侍者。**ˈ~·mark** *n* = ~print. **ˈ~·note** *n* note at the ~ of a page. 註脚(印於頁底者);附註。**ˈ~·path** *n* path for the use of persons on ~, esp one across fields or open country, or at the side of a country road. (田野中的)小徑;小路。Cf 參較 US 美 *trail.* ⇨ pavement, *sidewalk* at side[1](14). **ˈ~·plate** *n* platform in a locomotive for the driver and fireman: 火車機車上司機和火伕所立之平臺: *~plate workers,* drivers and firemen. 火車司機與火伕。**ˈ~-pound** *n* unit of work (done in lifting 1 lb through 1 ft). 呎磅(使一磅之物昇高一呎所做的功)。**ˈ~·print** *n* impression left on a soft surface by a ~. 足跡;脚印。**ˈ~-race** *n* running race between persons. 賽跑;競走。**ˈ~ rule** *n* ruler (strip of wood or metal) 12 inches long. 一呎長的尺。**ˈ~-slog** *vi* (colloq) walk, tramp, march far and with effort. (俗)長途費力地步行或行軍。Hence, 由此產生, **ˈ~-slogger** *n* (colloq) person who walks or marches long distances. (俗)長途步行或行軍者。**ˈ~·sore** *adj* having sore feet, esp from walking. 足痛的(尤指因走路過多而引起者)。**ˈ~·step** *n* (sound of a) step of sb walking; ~print. 脚步;脚步聲;足跡;脚印。***follow in one's father's ~steps,*** do as he did. 效法自己的父親。**ˈ~·stool** *n* low stool for resting the feet on. 脚凳。**ˈ~·sure** *adj* not stumbling; not making false steps. 脚步穩的;不會走錯步的。**ˈ~·wear** *n* [U] (tradesmen's term for) boots, shoes, etc. (商人用語)脚上穿用之物(如靴,鞋等)。**ˈ~·work** *n* [U] manner of using the feet, eg in boxing, dancing. (拳擊,跳舞等之)步法。

foot[2] /fʊt; fʊt/ *vt, vi* **1** [VP6A] knit the ~ of, eg a stocking. 織(襪子等)的足部。**2** ***~ it,*** (colloq) go on ~; walk: (俗)步行: *We've missed the last bus, so we'll have to ~ it.* 我們未趕上最後一班公共汽車,只好步行了。***~ the bill,*** (colloq) (agree to) pay it. (俗)(同意)付帳。**~ed,** (in compounds) having the kind of feet indicated: (用於複合字中)有…足的: *ˌwet-ˈ~ed;* 脚濕的; *ˌsure-ˈ~ed;* 脚步穩的;

GA goal area PA penalty area PS penalty spot
CC centre circle CS centre spot

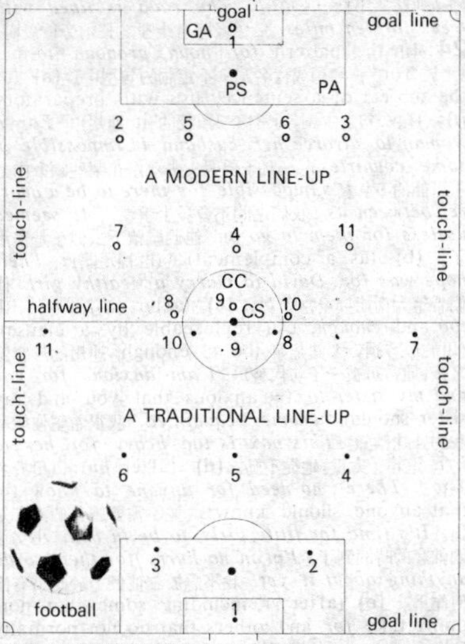

A TRADITIONAL LINE-UP 1 goalkeeper 2 right back 3 left back 4 right half (back) 5 centre half (back) 6 left half (back) 7 outside right or right winger 8 inside right 9 centre forward 10 inside left 11 outside left or left winger

A MODERN LINE-UP 1 goalkeeper 2 5 6 3 defenders or backs 7 4 11 midfield link men 8 9 10 strikers or forwards

Association football (soccer)

ˌ*flat-'~ed.* 腳掌扁平的。

foot·age /ˈfʊtɪdʒ; ˈfʊtɪdʒ/ *n* [U] length measured in feet, esp length of exposed cinema film. 以英尺計算的長度(尤用於曝曬的電影膠片)。

footer /ˈfʊtə(r); ˈfʊtɚ/ *n* **1** (colloq) the game of football. (俗)足球戲;足球運動。 **2** (compounds) (複合字) *a* ˌ*six-'footer*, a person six feet tall. 六呎高的人。

foot·ing /ˈfʊtɪŋ; ˈfʊtɪŋ/ *n* [C] (*sing* only) (僅用單數) **1** placing of the feet; surface for standing on: 立足;立足處: *He lost his* ~ (= stumbled, slipped) *and fell.* 他失足跌倒了。 **2** position (in society, a group): 社會地位;團體中的地位: *get a footing in musical circles;* 在音樂界取得地位; relationship (with sb); condition(s). (與人之)關係;狀態。 ***be/get on a... ~ (with),*** be/get in a ... relationship/state (with): 與…有某種關係: *be on a friendly ~ with Julie's family.* 與茱麗一家有友誼關係。 **3** conditions; state of the army, etc: 情況;(軍隊等之)編制: *on a peace/war ~,* in the state usual for peace/war. 按平時(戰時)編制。

footle /ˈfuːtl; ˈfutl/ *vi, vt* (colloq) trifle; play the fool: (俗)兒戲;做傻事: *~ about;* 做無聊的事; *~ away one's time.* 虛擲光陰。 **foot·ling** /ˈfuːtlɪŋ; ˈfutlɪŋ/ *adj* insignificant, trifling: 不關緊要的;微小的: *footling little jobs.* 無關緊要的工作。

fop /fɒp; fɑp/ *n* man who pays too much attention to his clothes and personal appearance. 過份注意衣着和外表的人;紈袴子。 **fop·pish** /-ɪʃ; -ɪʃ/ *adj* of or like a ~. 紈袴子的;似紈袴子的;浮華的。

for¹ /fə(r); fɚ; *strong form:* fɔː(r); fɔr/ *prep* **1** (indicating destination, or progress or endeavours towards) (表示目的地,向…進行或努力) **(a)** (after *vv*): (用於動詞後): *set out for home;* 動身回家; *make for home,* turn one's steps towards home; 朝家走; *a ship bound for the Baltic.* 駛往波羅的海的一艘船。*The ship was making for* (= sailing towards) *the open sea.* 那船正向大海行駛。*The swimmers struck out for the shore.* 那些游泳者用力向岸邊游去。**(b)** (after *nn*): (用於名詞後): *the train for Glasgow;* 開往格拉斯哥的火車; *letters for the provinces;* 寄往各省的信件; *passengers for Cairo.* 往開羅的乘客。 **2** (indicating what is aimed at, or the attaining of sth, shown by the *noun* after *for*): (表示目標或志向,欲達成之事,由 for 後面的名詞指出): *He was educated for the law/trained for the priesthood.* 他受教育準備做律師(接受訓練準備做牧師)。 *He felt that he was destined for something great.* 他覺得他注定要做偉大的事。 **3** (indicating eventual possession): (表示最終的所有權): *Here's a letter for you.* 這裏有你一封信。*Are all these for me?* 這些都是給我的嗎? *Save it for me.* 爲我留着。*She made some coffee for us.* 她爲我們煮了些咖啡。***be 'for it,*** (colloq) be likely to be punished, get into trouble; etc. (俗)大概要受罰;惹上麻煩等。 **4** (indicating preparation to deal with a situation): (表示準備應付一情況): *prepare/preparations for an examination;* 準備考試; *lay in supplies of coal for the winter;* 儲煤以備冬日之需; *dress for dinner;* 穿禮服赴宴; *get ready for school.* 準備上學。 **5** (indicating purpose) (表示目的) **(a)** (used in place of an *inf*) in order to be, have, obtain, etc; with a view to: (用以代替一不定詞)爲某種目的;爲了: *go for a walk/ride/swim, etc;* 去散步(騎一會兒馬,游泳等); *run for one's life;* 逃命; *work for one's living;* 爲生計而工作; *read for pleasure.* 讀書以求樂趣。 ***what . . . for,*** for what purpose: 爲何目的;爲什麼: *What's this tool for?* 這工具是做什麼用的? *What's this hole in the door for? It's for the cat to come in and out by.* 門上開此洞的目的何在?它是爲了貓的出入而設的。⇨ 24 (g) below. 參看下列 24 義 (g)。 *What did you do that for?* why did you do that? 你爲何做那事? **(b)** (followed by a gerund): (後接一動名詞): *a mill for* (= for the purpose of) *grinding coffee;* 研磨咖啡的機器; *a room for sleeping in.* 臥室。 **6** (introducing a complement): (引導一補足語): *They were sold for slaves.* 他們被賣爲奴。*They left him on the battlefield for dead.* 他們把他遺留在戰場,以爲他已經死了。*They chose him for* (= as, to be) *their leader.* 他們選他做首領。 ***take sb/sth for sb/sth,*** mistakenly conclude that he/it is sb/sth else: 將某人或某物誤作(他人或他物): *He took me for my brother.* 他把我誤作我哥哥(弟弟)。*What do you take me for?* You seem to have a mistaken or poor idea of my character, judging from what you say, etc. 你把我當作什麼呀? ***for certain,*** as being certain: 的確;確實: *I cannot say for certain that....* 我不確知…。 **7** (followed by an object of hope, wish, search, inquiry, etc): (後接所希望,願望,搜尋,調查等之人或事物): *hope for the best;* 盼望最好的情況; *pray for peace;* 祈求和平; *fish for trout;* 釣鱒; *ask for* (= to see) *the manager;* 求見經理; *go to sb for help;* 去某人處求援; *a cry for help;* 呼救; *fifty applicants for a post.* 一職位而有五十名申請者。 **8** (indicating liking, affection, etc): (表示喜好,情愛等): *have a liking for sb or sth;* 喜歡某人或某物; *a taste for art;* 愛好藝術; *no regret for the truth;* 不爲實情惋惜; *a weakness for fine clothes.* 特別喜愛漂亮衣服。 **9** (indicating aptitude): (表示才能): *an aptitude for foreign languages;* 學習外國語的才能; *a good ear for music;* 對音樂的高超鑑賞力; *an eye for the picturesque.* 審美眼光。 **10** (indicating suitability, fitness): (表示適合): *bad/good for your health;* 有損(益)於你的健康; *fit/unfit for food;* (不)適於做食物; *clothes proper for the occasion.* 適於某場合的衣服。*This is no place for a young, innocent girl.* 這地方不適合天真無邪的年輕女孩子。*You are the very man for the job.* 你是最適合這個工作的人。 **11** (with *adjj* not otherwise followed by *for*, in the patterns *too+adj+for*, or *adj+enough+for*): (與形容詞連用,用

於 too＋形容詞＋for, 或形容詞＋enough＋for 的句型中)：*too beautiful for words;* 美得無法形容；*quite risky enough for me.* 對我來說是够冒險了。**12** considering (the circumstances, etc); in view of: 就(情况等)而論;鑒於：*It's quite warm for January.* 就一月而言,天氣相當暖了。*Not bad for a beginner!* 就一位初學者而言,已經不錯了！*She is tall for her age.* 就她的年齡而論,她算是高的。*For all the good you're doing, you may as well stop trying to help.* 你做了這麼多善事,大可不必再幫忙了。***for 'all that,*** in spite of all that has been said, done, etc. 雖然如此；儘管如此。**13** representing; instead of; in place of: 代表;代替：*B for Benjamin;* B代表 Benjamin; *the member for Coventry*, the person representing Coventry in the House of Commons; 在下議院中代表科芬特里城的議員； *substitute one thing for another.* 以一物代替另一物。*Will you please act for me in the matter?* 請你替我處理這件事情好嗎？***stand for,*** represent: 代表：*The letters MP stand for Member of Parliament and the letters PM stand for Prime Minister.* MP 兩字母代表國會議員，PM 兩字母代表首相。**14** in defence or support of; in favour of: 支持;擁護;贊成：*Are you for or against the proposal?* 你是贊成這建議還是反對呢？*The rate of exchange is for us,* in our favour. 兌換率對我們有利。*Three cheers for the President!* 向總統歡呼三聲！*I'm all for an early start／for starting early.* 我十分贊成早些動身。**15** with regard to; so far as concerns: 關於;至於：*hard up for money;* 需款孔亟;缺錢;窮困；*anxious for sb's safety;* 擔心某人的安全；*for my part,* so far as it concerns me; 就我而言;至於我；*speaking for myself, and in the name of all my colleagues.* 爲我自己同時也代表我的全體同事發言。*You may take my word for it,* believe me so far as this is concerned. 關於此事你要相信我。**16** because of; on account of: 因爲;由於：*for this reason;* 爲此原因；*for my sake;* 爲了我的緣故；*for the sake of peace;* 爲了和平；*for fear of discovery;* 免得被發現；*noted／famous for its scenery;* 以風景著名；*dance／cry for joy;* 快樂得手舞足蹈(大聲喊叫)；*suffer for one's sins;* 因罪惡而受苦；*sent to prison for stealing;* 因偷竊而被關入獄；*win a medal for bravery.* 因英勇而獲勳章。*She couldn't speak for laughing,* because she was laughing so much. 她笑得說不出話來了。*We trembled for their safety.* 我們擔憂他們的安全。**17** (after a comparative) as the result of; because of:(用於比較級後)爲…之結果;由於：*My shoes are the worse for wear.* 我的鞋子穿破了。*Are you any the better for your long sleep?* 睡了一大覺以後你好些了嗎？**18** in spite of; notwithstanding: 雖然;儘管：*For* (＝In spite of) *all you say, I still like her.* 儘管你這樣說,我仍然喜歡她。*For all his wealth, he is unhappy.* 他雖然有錢,但不快樂。**19** to the amount or extent of: 達到…的數量或程度：*Put my name down for £5.* 請寫上我捐五鎊。*He drew on his bank for £40.* 他在銀行提款四十鎊。(cricket) (板球) *The score is 157 for 8 wickets.* 八位擊球員獲得一百五十七分。*They were all out for 80.* 他們在八十分時都被殺出場。**20** in exchange for: 交換：*I paid 60p for the book.* 我付了六十辨士買這本書。*He did the job for nothing.* 他做那工作沒有報酬。*Don't translate word for word.* 不要逐字翻譯。*Plant a new tree for every tree you cut down.* 你每砍倒一棵樹,便植一株新樹。**21** in contrast with: 與…對比：*For one enemy he has fifty friends.* 他的敵人和朋友爲一與五十之比。**22** (indicating extent in time): (表示經過多少時間)：*I'm going away for a few days.* 我要離開幾天。*He will be a cripple for life.* 他將終生是一個跛子。*That's enough for the present.* 在目前那是够了。***for good,*** ⇨ good²(2). **23** (indicating extent in space; *for* may be omitted if it occurs directly after the *v*): (表示經過若干距離; for 如直接在動詞後,可以省略)：*We walked (for) three miles.* 我們走了三哩路。*For miles and miles there's not a house to be seen.* 好多哩路望不見一座房屋。*The road is lined with trees for ten miles.* 沿這條路有十哩之長兩旁種着樹。**24** (in the pattern *for*＋*noun*／*pronoun*＋*to*-inf) (用於 for ＋名詞或代名詞＋不定詞的句型中) **(a)** (as the subject of a sentence, usu with preparatory *it*): (做一句之主詞,通常與一預設的 it 連用)：*For a woman to divorce her husband is impossible in some countries.* 一女子要與丈夫離婚在某些國家內是不可能的事。*It's impossible for there to be a quarrel between us.* 我們之間不會發生爭執。*It seemed useless for them to go on.* 他們繼續下去似乎是無用了。**(b)** (as a complement): (做補足語)：*Their hope was for David to marry a wealthy girl.* 他們希望大衞能娶一富家女。**(c)** (after *adjj*, esp with *too* and *enough*, usu replaceable by a clause): (用於形容詞，尤其是與 too 和 enough 連用的形容詞之後,通常可被一子句代替)：*I am anxious for you and my sister to* (＝ anxious that you and my sister should) *become acquainted.* 我很希望你能和我的妹妹結識。*This box is too heavy for her to lift.* 這箱子太重,她提不動。**(d)** (after *nn*): (用於名詞後)：*There's no need for anyone to know* (＝ that anyone should know). 並不需要讓每個人都知道。*It's time for little girls to be in bed.* 小女孩們就寢的時間到了。*I'm in no hurry for them to do anything about it yet.* 我不急於讓他們對於此事有任何作爲。**(e)** (after *vv*, including some that normally take *for* and others that do not normally take *for*): (用於動詞後,包括某些通常與 for 連用的動詞以及通常不與 for 連用者)：*We didn't wait for the others to join us.* 我們沒有等其餘的人參加我們的團體。*She couldn't bear for Tom and Mary not to be friends.* 湯姆與瑪莉不和睦使她難以忍受。**(f)** (after *than* and *as (if)*): (用於 than 和 as (if) 後)：*Is there anything more ridiculous than for a man of 80 to marry a girl of 18?* 還有比一位八十歲的老翁娶一位十八歲的少女更荒唐的事嗎？*She had her arms wide apart, as if for the child to run into them.* 她張開兩臂,像是去擁抱那個跑來的孩子。**(g)** (indicating purpose, design, determination, etc): (表示目的,計畫,決心等)：*I have brought the books for you to examine.* 我已將這些書帶來供你審閱。*The crowd made way for the procession to pass.* 群衆讓開路,使遊行的行列通過。*I'd have given anything for this not to have happened.* 我眞願付出一切使這件事不致發生。*It's for you to decide.* 此事由你決定。*For production to be increased we must have efficient organization.* 我們必須有有效的組織,才能使生產增加。

for² /fə(r); fɚ; *strong form:* fɔ:(r); fɔr/ *conj* (rare in spoken English; not used at the beginning of a sentence) seeing that; since, the reason, proof, explanation, being that: (罕用於口語中,不用於句首) 鑒於;因爲：*I asked her to stay to tea, for I had something to tell her.* 我請她留下來喝茶,因爲我有事要告訴她。

for·age /ˈfɒrɪdʒ *US:* ˈfɔ:r- ; ˈfɔrɪdʒ/ *n* [U] food for horses and cattle. 牛馬飼料。□ *vi* [VP2A, 3A] ～ ***(for),*** search (*for* food, etc). 搜尋(與 for 連用,後接食物等)。

for·as·much as /ˌfɔ:rəzˈmʌtʃ əz ; ˌfɔrəzˈmʌtʃ əz/ *conj* (legal) seeing that; since. (法律)鑒於;因爲。

foray /ˈfɒreɪ *US:* ˈfɔ:reɪ ; ˈfɔre/ *n* [C] raid; sudden attack (esp to get food, animals, etc): 侵襲;突襲(尤指爲了獲得食物,動物等)：*go on／make a* ～. 侵掠。□ *vi* [VP2A] make a ～. 侵掠。

for·bad, for·bade /fəˈbæd *US:* -ˈbeɪd ; fəˈbæd/ *pt* of forbid.

for·bear¹ /fɔ:ˈbeə(r) ; fɔrˈbɛr/ *vt, vi* (*pt* forbore /fɔ:ˈbɔ:(r) ; fɔrˈbor/, *pp* forborne /fɔ:ˈbɔ:n ; fɔrˈborn/) [VP6C, 7A, 2A, 3A] ～ ***(from),*** (formal) refrain (from); not use or mention; be patient: (正式用語)抑制；自制；不用；不提及；忍耐：*I* ～ *to go into details.* 我不欲詳述。*I cannot* ～ *from* *going into details.* 我不得不詳述。*We begged him to ~.* 我們懇求他忍耐。 **~·ance** /fɔːˈbeərəns ; fɔrˈbɛrəns/ *n* [U] patience; self-control: 耐性;自制: *show ~ance towards sb;* 對某人有耐性; *show ~ance in dealing with people.* 待人寬容。

for·bear² (US = **fore·bear**) /ˈfɔːbeə(r) ; ˈfɔr,bɛr/ *n* (usu *pl*) ancestor. (通常用複數)祖先。

for·bid /fəˈbɪd ; fəˈbɪd/ *vt* (*pt* forbade or forbad /fəˈbæd *US:* -ˈbeɪd ; fəˈbæd/, *pp* forbidden /fəˈbɪdn ; fəˈbɪdn̩/) [VP6A, 17, 12C] order (sb) not to do sth; order that sth shall not be done; not allow: 禁止;不許: *~ a girl to marry;* 不許一女孩結婚; *~ a marriage;* 禁止一婚事; *~ sb to leave;* 不許某人離開; *~ his departure.* 不許他離去。*Students are ~den the use of the office duplicator.* 學生們不許用辦公室的複印機。*I ~ you to use that word.* 我不許你用那個字。***God ~ that...,*** used to express a wish that something may not happen. 願上帝阻止…;但願…不會發生。 **ˌ~den ˈfruit,** sth desired because it is not allowed (with reference to Eve and the apple). 因禁止而更欲獲得之物;禁果(由夏娃之食禁果而來)。**~·ding** *adj* stern; repellent; threatening: 冷峻的;討厭的;險惡的: *a ~ding appearance/look;* 冷峻的面貌; *a ~ding coast,* one that looks dangerous. 形勢險惡的海岸。**~·ding·ly** *adv*

for·bore, for·borne ⇨ forbear¹.

force¹ /fɔːs ; fors/ *n* **1** [U] strength; power of body or mind; physical power: 力量;氣力;心智的力量;體力: *the ~ of a blow/an explosion/argument;* 一擊(爆炸,論據)之力; *~ of character;* 人格的力量; *overcome by the ~ of her emotion;* 被她的感情力量所征服; *by ~ of contrast.* 藉對照之力。*The enemy attacked in (great) ~.* 敵人猛烈攻擊。*He overcame his bad habits by sheer ~ of will.* 他全憑意志力克服了他的惡習。*Owing to ~ of circumstances the plans had to be postponed.* 由於情勢所迫,這些計畫不得不延期執行了。 ***in ~,*** (usu of people) in large numbers. (通常指人)衆多的。 **2** [C] person or thing that makes great changes: 引起重大改變的人或事物: *the ~s of nature,* eg storms, earthquakes. 大自然的力量(如暴風雨,地震等)。*Is religion a ~ for good in the lives of people?* 宗教在人們的生活當中是一種使人向善的力量嗎? *The Left and the Right have always been the principle political ~s.* 左派和右派一直是主要的政治力量。 **3** [C] organized body of armed or disciplined men: 有組織的武裝團體;有組織和經過嚴格訓練的團體: *the armed ~s of a country,* the Army, Navy, Air F~; 一國之武裝部隊(陸,海,空三軍); *join the F~s;* 從軍; (attrib) (形容用法) *a F~s newspaper,* one for members of the armed ~s; 軍中報紙; *the poˈlice ~.* 警察隊。 ***join ~s (with),*** unite (with) in order to use combined strength. (與…)聯合以求運用共同的力量。 **4** [C, U] (intensity of, measurement of) pressure or influence exerted at a point, tending to cause movement. 壓力;壓力的強度。 **5** [U] (legal) authority; power of binding(6). (法律) 權威; 拘束力。 ***in/into ~,*** in/into power: 實施: *put a law into ~,* make it binding. 實施一法律。*When does the new law come into ~?* 新法律何時生效? *The rule/regulation is no longer in ~.* 這規則已不再實行了。

force² /fɔːs ; fors/ *vt* **1** [VP6A, 15A, B, 17, 22] compel, oblige; use force to get or do sth, to make sb do sth; break open by using force: 强迫;迫使;强制;突破; *~ one's way through a crowd;* 在人群中擠過去; *~ a way in/out/through;* 衝入(出,過); *~ an entry into a building,* eg by breaking a door; 强行進入一建築物(如破門而入); *~ (open) a door;* 破門而入; *~ a confession from sb;* 强迫某人招供;逼供; *~ sb/oneself to work hard;* 强迫某人(自己)努力工作; *~ sb into doing sth.* 强迫某人做某事。*They said that the war had been ~d upon them,* that they had not wanted to make war, but had been compelled to do so. 他們說他們是被迫作戰。 **ˌ~d ˈlanding,** one that an aircraft is compelled to make, eg because of engine trouble. (飛機因引擎故障等)强迫降落。 Hence, 由此產生, **ˌ~-ˈland** *vt, vi* **ˌ~d ˈmarch,** eg by soldiers, one requiring special effort, made in an emergency. (軍隊等之)强行軍;兼程行軍。 ***~ sb's hand,*** make him do sth unwillingly, or earlier than he wished or intended to do it. 逼某人做事;逼某人提早行動。 **2** [VP6A] cause plants, etc to mature earlier than is normal, eg by giving them extra warmth: 使(植物等) 提早成熟 (如予以特別的溫暖以促成者): (fig) (喻) *~ a pupil,* hurry on his education by making him do extra study. 使一學童從事額外的學習以加速其教育之進行。 **3** [VP6A] produce under stress: 强作: *~ a smile,* eg when one is unhappy; 强作笑顏; *a ~d laugh,* one that is not the result of real amusement. 勉强的笑。*The singer had to ~ her top notes.* 那歌唱者必須勉强唱出最高音。

force-feed /ˈfɔːsfiːd ; ˈforsˈfid/ *vt* (*pt, pp* force-fed /ˈfɔːsfed ; ˈforsˈfɛd/) [VP6A] compel (an animal, a prisoner or a patient) to take food and drink. 强迫(動物,囚犯或病人)飲食。

force·ful /ˈfɔːsfl ; ˈforsfəl/ *adj* (of a person, his character, of an argument, etc) full of force: (指人,性格,辯論等)有力的: *a ~ speaker/style of writing.* 有力的演說者(文體)。**~ly** /-fəlɪ ; -fəlɪ/ *adv* **~·ness** *n*

force majeure /ˌfɔːs mæˈʒɜː(r) ; ˌfɔrs məˈʒɝ/ *n* [U] (F) (legal) compulsion; superior force. (法) (法律)不可抗力。

force·meat /ˈfɔːsmiːt ; ˈfɔrs,mit/ *n* [U] meat chopped up finely, mixed with herbs, etc used as stuffing, eg in a roast chicken. 加香料的碎肉(例如塡烤鷄等所用者)。

for·ceps /ˈfɔːseps ; ˈfɔrsəps/ *n* (*sing* or *pl*) small pincers or tongs used by dentists (when pulling out teeth) and by doctors for gripping things: (牙醫用的)齒鑷;牙鉗;(醫生用的)鑷子;鉗子: *a ~ delivery* (of a baby). (胎兒之)產鉗產。

forc·ible /ˈfɔːsəbl ; ˈforsəbl̩/ *adj* **1** done by, involving the use of, physical force: 强行的;用力的: *a ~ entry into a building;* 强行進入一建築物; *~ expulsion.* 强行驅逐。 **2** (of a person, his acts, words, etc) convincing; persuasive. (指人,行動,言語等)動聽的;有說服力的。 **forc·ibly** /-əblɪ ; -əblɪ/ *adj*

ford /fɔːd ; fɔrd/ *n* [C] shallow place in a river where it is possible to walk or drive across. 河流之可涉的淺處。□ *vt* [VP6A] cross (a river) by walking or driving through the water. 涉(河)。 **~·able** /-əbl ; -əbl̩/ *adj* that can be ~ed. 可涉的。

fore /fɔː(r) ; fɔr/ *adj* (attrib only) situated in the front (opp of *back, aft*): (僅作形容用法)在前部的(爲 back, aft 之相反字): *in the ~ part of the train;* 在火車的前部; *the ~ hatch,* (in a ship). (船)前艙口。□ *n* [U] ~ part (of a ship). (船之)前部。 ***to the ~,*** ready to hand; on the spot; prominent: 在手頭;隨時可資利用;當場;突出;顯著: *He has come to the ~ recently,* has become prominent. 他近來已出人頭地了。□ *adv* (naut) in front. (航海)在前。 ***~ and aft,*** at the bow and stern of a ship; lengthwise in a ship: 在船首和船尾;從船首至船尾: *~ and aft sails/rigged,* with sails set lengthwise. 縱帆(縱帆裝置的)。 ⇨ square-rigged. □ *int* (golf) warning (to people in front) that the player is about to drive the ball. (高爾夫)前面注意(擊球時警告前面的人以免被球所擊之呼聲)。

fore·arm¹ /ˈfɔːrɑːm ; ˈfor,ɑrm/ *n* arm from the elbow to the wrist or finger-tips. 前臂(肘至腕或指尖部分)。⇨ the illus at arm. 參看 arm 之挿圖。

fore·arm² /ˌfɔːrˈɑːm ; forˈɑrm/ *vt* [VP6A] (usu in passive) arm beforehand; prepare for trouble in advance: (通常用被動語態) 預先武裝;警備;預先準備: *To be forewarned is to be ~ed.* 預先獲得警告卽是預先有了準備。

fore·bear *n* = forbear².

fore·bode /fɔːˈbəʊd ; forˈbod/ *vt* (formal) (正式用語) **1** [VP6A] be a sign of warning of: 預示;預兆: *These black clouds ~ a storm.* 這些烏雲預示有暴風雨。 **2** [VP6A, 9] have a feeling of (usu sth evil); have a feeling (*that*): 預感(通常爲不祥之事;有時與 that 所引導的子句連用): *~ disaster.* 預感災禍。 **fore·bod·ing** *n* [C, U] feeling that trouble is coming. 凶兆;預兆。

fore·cast /ˈfɔːkɑːst *US:* -kæst ; forˈkæst/ *vt* (*pt, pp* ~ or ~ed) [VP6A] say in advance what is likely to happen. 預言;預測。 □ *n* statement that ~s sth: 預言; 預告: *inaccurate weather ~s.* 不正確的天氣預報。

fore·castle, fo'c'sle /ˈfəʊksl ; ˈfoksl/ *n* (in some merchant ships) part under the bows where the seamen have their living and sleeping accommodation. 艏艛(某些商船中船首甲板下之水手艙)。

fore·close /fɔːˈkləʊz ; forˈkloz/ *vt, vi* [VP2A, 3A, 6A] ~ ***(on),*** (legal) use the right (given by a mortgage) to take possession of property (when interest or capital has not been paid at the required time): (法律) (利息或資金未能按期繳付時)取消贖取抵押品之權利: *The Bank ~d (on) (the mortgage).* 銀行取消了此一贖取抵押品之權利。 **fore·clos·ure** /fɔːˈkləʊʒə(r) ; forˈkloʒɚ/ *n* [C, U] (act of) foreclosing a mortgage. 贖取抵押品權利之取消。

fore·court /ˈfɔːkɔːt ; ˈforˌkort/ *n* enclosed space in front of a building. 前院。

fore·doom /fɔːˈduːm ; forˈdum/ *vt* [VP6A, 14] (usu passive) ~ ***(to),*** destine (to): (通常用被動語態)預先注定: *an attempt that was ~ed to failure.* 注定失敗的一個嘗試。

fore·father /ˈfɔːfɑːðə(r) ; ˈforˌfɑðɚ/ *n* (usu *pl*) ancestor. (通常用複數)祖先。

fore·fin·ger /ˈfɔːfɪŋgə(r) ; ˈforˌfɪŋgɚ/ *n* first finger, next to the thumb; index finger. 食指。⇨ the illus at arm. 參看 arm 之插圖。

fore·foot /ˈfɔːfʊt ; ˈforˌfʊt/ *n* (*pl* forefeet /ˈfɔːfiːt ; ˈforˌfit/) one of the front feet of a four-legged animal. (四足動物之)前足。

fore·front /ˈfɔːfrʌnt ; ˈforˌfrʌnt/ *n* ***the ~,*** most forward part: 最前部: *in the ~ of the battle;* 在最前線; *in the ~ of my mind.* 在我心頭。

fore·gather ⇨ forgather.

forego[1] /fɔːˈgəʊ ; forˈgo/ *vt, vi* (*pt* forewent /fɔːˈwent ; forˈwɛnt/, *pp* foregone /fɔːˈgɒn *US:* -ˈgɔːn ; forˈgɔn/) precede (but rarely used except in) 在前(除下列形式外極爲少用) **fore·going** *adj* preceding, already mentioned. 前面的; 前述的。 **fore·gone** /ˈfɔːgɒn *US:* -gɔːn ; ˈforˌgɔn/ *adj* ***a foregone conclusion,*** ending that can be seen or could have been seen from the start. 自開始即可察知的結果;必然的結果。

forego[2] ⇨ forgo.

fore·ground /ˈfɔːgraʊnd ; ˈforˌgraʊnd/ *n* **1** part of a view (esp in a picture) nearest to the observer. 前景(尤指圖畫上最靠近觀賞者的部分)。 **2** (fig) most conspicuous position: (喻) 最引人注意的地位: *keep oneself in the ~,* where one is most easily seen or noticed. 使自己處於最引人注意的地位。

fore·hand /ˈfɔːhænd ; ˈforˌhænd/ *adj* (of a stroke at tennis, etc) made with the palm turned forward. (打網球等)正擊的;正手的。(Cf 參較 *backhand* = stroke made with the back of the hand turned forward and from the left side of the body, by a right-handed player 反手的打擊).

fore·head /ˈfɒrɪd *US:* ˈfɔːrɪd ; ˈfɔrɪd/ *n* part of the face above the eyes. 額。⇨ the illus at head. 參看 head 之插圖。

foreign /ˈfɒrən *US:* ˈfɔːr- ; ˈfɔrɪn/ *adj* **1** of, in, from, another country, not one's own: 外國的;在外國的;來自外國的: *~ languages/countries;* 外國語言(外國); *~ trade.* 對外貿易。 **the ˈF~ Office,** the department of state dealing with ~ affairs; its building in London. (倫敦之)英國外交部。 ˌ**F~ ˈSecretary,** head of the F~ Office. 外交部長。 **2** ~ ***to,*** not natural to, unconnected with: 非…所原有的;不適於;與…無關連: *Lying is ~ to his nature.* 說謊不是他的本性。 **3** coming or introduced from outside: 來自外部的;外來的: *a ~ body in the eye,* eg a bit of dirt blown into it by the wind. 眼中一異物 (如被風吹入的一粒灰塵)。 **~er** *n* person from, living in, or born in a ~ country. 外國人。

fore·knowl·edge /ˌfɔːˈnɒlɪdʒ ; ˌforˈnɑlɪdʒ/ *n* [U] knowledge of sth before its occurrence or existence. 預知;先知。

fore·land /ˈfɔːlənd ; ˈforlənd/ *n* cape; promontory. 岬;海角。

fore·leg /ˈfɔːleg ; ˈforˌlɛg/ *n* one of the front legs of a four-footed animal. (四足動物之)前腿。

fore·lock /ˈfɔːlɒk ; ˈforˌlɑk/ *n* lock of hair growing just above the forehead. 長在額頭上方的毛髮;額髮;額毛。 ***take time by the ~,*** not let an opportunity slip by; use an opportunity promptly. 把握時機;立即利用一個機會。

fore·man /ˈfɔːmən ; ˈformən/ *n* (*pl* -men /-mən ; -mən/) **1** workman in authority over others. 工頭;領班。 **2** chief member and spokesman of a jury. 陪審團之主席。

fore·mast /ˈfɔːmɑːst *US:* -mæst ; ˈforˌmæst/ *n* mast nearest the bow of a ship. 船之前桅。⇨ the illus at barque. 參看 barque 之挿圖。

fore·most /ˈfɔːməʊst ; ˈforˌmost/ *adj* first; most notable; chief: 第一的;首要的;主要的: *the ~ painter of his period.* 在他那個時期最重要的畫家。 □ *adv* first in position. 在最前面。 ***first and ~,*** before all else; in the first place. 第一;首先。

fore·name /ˈfɔːneɪm ; ˈforˌnem/ *n* (as used in official style, eg on forms) name preceding the family name. 名(用於表格等正式文體中)。

fore·noon /ˈfɔːnuːn ; forˈnun/ *n* (old use) part of the day between sunrise and noon. (舊用法)上午;午前。

for·en·sic /fəˈrensɪk ; fəˈrɛnsɪk/ *adj* of, used in, courts of law: 法庭的;用於法庭的: *~ skill,* skill as needed by barristers, etc; 律師等在法庭上的辯論才能; *~ medicine,* medical knowledge as needed in legal matters, eg a poisoning trial. 法醫學(法律事件,如用毒案件,所需要的醫學知識)。

fore·or·dain /ˌfɔːrɔːˈdeɪn ; ˌforɔrˈden/ *vt* [VP6A, 14, 17] determine or appoint beforehand: 預定;預先注定: *what God has ~ed.* 上帝所注定者。

fore·run·ner /ˈfɔːrʌnə(r) ; ˈforˌrʌnɚ/ *n* **1** sign of what is to follow: 預兆; 前兆: *swallows, the ~s of spring.* 燕子,春天的前兆。 **2** person who prepares for the coming of another. 先驅;先鋒。

fore·sail /ˈfɔːseɪl ; ˈforˌsel/ *n* principal sail on the foremast. 前桅帆。⇨ the illus at barque. 參看 barque 之挿圖。

fore·see /fɔːˈsiː ; forˈsi/ *vt* (*pt* foresaw /fɔːˈsɔː ; forˈsɔ/, *pp* foreseen /fɔːˈsiːn ; forˈsin/) [VP6A, 9, 10] know beforehand or in advance: 預知;預見: *~ trouble;* 預知困難; *~ what will happen/how things will turn out/that things will go well.* 預知將發生之事 (事情的結局，事情順利)。 **~·able** /-əbl ; -abl/ *adj* that can be known beforehand. 可預知的。 ***the ~able future,*** period from the present for which events can reasonably be predicted. 在可預見的將來。

fore·shadow /fɔːˈʃædəʊ ; forˈʃædo/ *vt* [VP6A] be a sign or warning of (sth to come). 預示(將來臨之某事物)。

fore·shore /ˈfɔːʃɔː(r) ; ˈforˌʃor/ *n* part of the shore between the sea and land that is cultivated, built on, etc. 前岸;前灘。

fore·shorten /fɔːˈʃɔːtn ; forˈʃortn̩/ *vt* [VP6A] (in drawing pictures) show (an object) by the use of perspective(1). (繪畫)用透視法顯示(物體)。

fore·sight /ˈfɔːsaɪt ; ˈforˌsaɪt/ *n* [U] ability to see future needs; care in preparing for these: 先見;

遠見;深謀遠慮: *If you had had more ~, you would have saved yourself a lot of trouble.* 如果那時你有更多的遠慮,你就會免除許多麻煩了。

fore·skin /ˈfɔːskɪn ; ˈforˌskɪn/ *n* fold of skin covering the end of the penis. (男性生殖器之)包皮。

for·est /ˈfɒrɪst *US:* ˈfɔːr- ; ˈfɔrɪst/ *n* **1** [C, U] (large area of) land covered with trees (and often undergrowth); the trees growing there: 森林地帶; 森林: *~s stretching for miles and miles;* 延伸無數哩的森林地帶; (attrib): (形容用法): *~ animals/fires.* 森林動物(森林火災)。 **2** (GB) area where game (eg deer) is or was hunted (and preserved), not necessarily wooded; (with proper name prefixed, as *Sherwood F~*) district that was formerly ~ but is now partly under cultivation: (英)狩獵場(並不一定樹木繁茂); (冠以專有名詞,如薛伍德林區)昔時的林區(現在已部份耕種): *the deer ~s in Scotland.* 蘇格蘭的獵鹿場。 **3** (fig) sth that suggests ~ trees: (喻)林立之物: *a ~ of masts,* eg in a harbour. (港內)林立之帆桅。 **~er** *n* officer in charge of a ~ (protecting wild animals, watching for fires, etc); man who works in a ~. 林務官;林務員;林中工作者。 **~ry** *n* [U] (science of) planting and caring for ~s. 森林學;造林與森林管理。

fore·stall /fɔːˈstɔːl ; forˈstɔl/ *vt* [VP6A] do sth first and so prevent another from doing it; upset (sb, his plans) by doing sth unexpectedly early: 先採取行動以阻止;先發制人: *~ a competitor.* 比一競爭者佔先。

fore·swear /fɔːˈsweə(r) ; forˈswɛr/ *vt* = forswear.

fore·taste /ˈfɔːteɪst ; ˈforˌtest/ *n* **~ *(of),*** partial experience (*of* sth) in advance: 預先得到的經驗: *a ~ of suffering/pleasure.* 預嘗到的苦(樂)。

fore·tell /fɔːˈtel ; forˈtɛl/ *vt* (*pt, pp* foretold /fɔːˈtəʊld ; forˈtold/) [VP6A, 9, 10, 12A, 13A] tell beforehand; predict: 預言;預測: *~ sb's future.* 預卜某人的未來。 *Is this the prophet whose coming was foretold (to) us?* 這便是預言要來的那位先知嗎?

fore·thought /ˈfɔːθɔːt ; ˈforˌθɔt/ *n* [U] careful thought or planning for the future. 先慮;預謀。

fore·told *pt, pp* of foretell.

fore·top /ˈfɔːtɒp ; ˈforˌtɑp/ *n* (naut) platform at the head of a foremast. (航海)前檣的平臺;前桅樓。 ⇨ the illus at barque. 參看 barque 之插圖。

for·ever /fəˈrevə(r) ; fəˈɛvɚ/ *adv* always; at all times; endlessly. 永遠地;無窮盡地。

fore·warn /fɔːˈwɔːn ; forˈwɔrn/ *vt* [VP6A] warn beforehand. 預先警告。

fore·woman /ˈfɔːwʊmən ; ˈforˌwʊmən/ *n* (*pl* -women /-wɪmɪn ; -ˌwɪmɪn/) woman in authority over other women workers. 女工頭;女工監督。

fore·word /ˈfɔːwɜːd ; ˈforˌwɝd/ *n* [C] introductory remarks to a book, printed in it, esp by someone not the author of the book. 前言;序;引言。

for·feit /ˈfɔːfɪt ; ˈfɔrfɪt/ *vt* [VP6A] (have to) suffer the loss of sth as a punishment or consequence, or because of rules: (作爲懲罰或結果,或由於規則等而)喪失;被沒收: *~ the good opinion of one's friends;* 失去朋友的好感; *~ one's health.* 喪失健康。 □ *n* [C] **1** sth (to be) ~ed: 喪失之物;沒收物: *His health was the ~ he paid for overworking.* 他的健康的喪失即是他工作過度所付的代價。 **2** (*pl*) game in which a player gives up various articles if he makes an error and can redeem them by doing sth ludicrous: (複)罰物遊戲(參加者如犯錯誤,必須放棄種種物品,如要贖回那些物品,須受罰做可笑的事): *Let's play ~s.* 讓我們來玩罰物遊戲。 **~·ure** /ˈfɔːfɪtʃə(r) ; ˈfɔrfɪtʃɚ/ *n* [U] ~ing; 喪失;沒收: *(the) ~ure of one's property.* 財產之被沒收。

for·gather, fore·gather /fɔːˈgæðə(r) ; fɔrˈgæðɚ/ *vi* [VP2A, C] come together. 聚會。

for·gave /fəˈgeɪv ; fɚˈgev/ *pt* of forgive.

forge[1] /fɔːdʒ ; fɔrdʒ/ *n* [C] **1** workshop with fire and anvil where metals are heated and shaped, esp one used by a smith for making shoes for horses, repairing agricultural machinery, etc. 鐵工廠;鐵匠店。 **2** (workshop with) furnace or hearth for melting or refining metal. 鍛爐;鍛鐵場。

forge[2] /fɔːdʒ ; fɔrdʒ/ *vt* [VP6A] **1** shape by heating and hammering: 錘鍊成;打製;鍛造: *~ an anchor;* 打製一錨; (fig) (喻) *Their friendship was ~d by shared adversity.* 他們的友誼是由於共患難而結成的。 **2** make a copy of sth, eg a signature, a banknote, a will, in order to deceive. 僞造(簽名,鈔票,遺囑等)。 **forger** *n* person who ~s(2). 僞造者。 **forg·ery** /ˈfɔːdʒərɪ ; ˈfɔrdʒərɪ/ *n* **1** [U] forging (2) of a document, signature, etc. (文件,簽名等的)僞造。 **2** [C] (*pl* -ries) ~d document, signature, etc. 僞造的文件、簽名等。 **forg·ing** *n* [C] piece of metal that has been ~d (1) or shaped under a press. 鍛造過的一塊金屬;鍛件。

forge[3] /fɔːdʒ ; fɔrdʒ/ *vi* [VP2C] **~ *ahead,*** make steady progress; take the lead (in a race, etc). 穩定而徐緩地前進;(競賽等)領先。

for·get /fəˈget ; fɚˈgɛt/ *vt, vi* (*pt* forgot /fəˈgɒt ; fɚˈgɑt/, *pp* forgotten /fəˈgɒtn ; fɚˈgɑtn̩/) **1** [VP6A, C, D, 8, 9, 10, 2A, 3A] **~ *(about),*** lose remembrance of; fail to keep in the memory; fail to recall: 忘記;忘却: *I ~/I've forgotten her name.* 我忘了她的名字。 *I shall never ~ your kindness to me.* 我永遠不會忘記你對我的厚意。 *Did you ~ (that) I was coming?* 你忘了我要來嗎? *I have forgotten how to do it/where he lives/whether he wants it.* 我忘記怎樣做(他住的地方,他是否需要它)了。 *I forgot all about it.* 我一點也記不得了。 *I shall never ~ hearing Chaliapin singing the part of Boris Godunov.* 我永不會忘記聽沙利亞賓唱波里・高德諾夫一角。 **forget-me-not** /fəˈget mɪ nɒt ; fɚˈgɛtmɪˌnɑt/ *n* small plant with blue flowers. 琉璃草;勿忘草。 **2** [VP7A] neglect or fail (to do sth): 疏忽;忘記(做某事): *Don't ~ to post the letters.* 不要忘了寄出這些信。 *He has forgotten to pay me.* 他忘了付錢給我。 **3** [VP6A, 2A] put out of the mind; stop thinking about: 不以…爲意;不再思念: *Let's ~ our quarrels.* 我們忘掉我們的爭執罷。 *Forgive and ~.* 不念舊惡。 **4** [VP6A] omit to pay attention to: 忽略: *Don't ~ the waiter,* Give him a tip. 別忘了給侍者小帳。 **5 ~ *oneself,*** **(a)** behave thoughtlessly in a way not suited to one's dignity, to the circumstances. 忘形;忘掉自己的身分。 **(b)** act unselfishly, thinking only of the interests of others. 爲他人而忘我。 **~·ful** /-fl ; -fəl/ *adj* in the habit of ~ting: 健忘的: *He's very ~ful of things.* 他十分健忘。 *Old people are sometimes ~ful.* 老年人有時很健忘。 **~·fully** /-fəlɪ ; -fəlɪ/ *adv* **~·ful·ness** *n*

for·give /fəˈgɪv ; fɚˈgɪv/ *vt, vi* (*pt* forgave /fəˈgeɪv ; fɚˈgev/, *pp* forgiven /fəˈgɪvn ; fɚˈgɪvən/) [VP6A, 14, 12C, 2A] **1 ~ *sb (sth/for doing sth),*** say that one no longer has the wish to punish sb; no longer have the wish to punish sb for an offence, a sin; pardon or show mercy to (sb); no longer have hard feelings towards (sb): 寬恕(某人);赦免;饒恕;原諒: *~ sb for being rude/~ his rudeness.* 寬恕某人的鹵莽。 *Am I ~n?* 我被饒恕了嗎? *F~ us our trespasses.* 赦免我們的罪。 *Your sins will be ~n you.* 你的罪將被赦免。 **2** not demand repayment of (a debt); not demand repayment of a debt from (sb): 不索取(債務);寬免(某人)之債: *He forgave the debt.* 他放棄了索債。 *Will you ~ me the debt?* 請寬免我的債好嗎? **for·giv·able** /-əbl ; -əbl̩/ *adj* that can be ~n. 可寬恕的;可原諒的。 **for·giv·ing** *adj* ready or willing to ~: 寬仁的;寬大的: *a forgiving nature.* 寬仁的天性。 **for·giv·ing·ly** *adv* **~·ness** *n* [U] forgiving or being ~n; willingness to ~: 寬恕;饒恕;寬仁: *ask for/receive ~ness;* 請求(受到)寬恕; *full of ~ness.* 富有寬仁之心。

forgo /fɔːˈgəʊ ; fɔrˈgo/ *vt* (*pt* forwent /fɔːˈwent ; fɔrˈwɛnt/, *pp* forgone /fɔːˈgɒn *US:* -ˈgɔːn ; fɔrˈgɔn/) do without; give up: 棄絕;放棄: *~ pleasures in order to study hard.* 爲了努力用功而放棄享樂。

for·got, for·got·ten ⇨ forget.

fork /fɔːk ; fɔrk/ *n* [C] **1** implement with two or more points (*prongs*), used for lifting food to the mouth, carving, etc. 叉(用以進食,切開食物等)。 **ˈ~ lunch/supper,** one (for more persons than can be seated at table) at which food is served as a buffet where guests serve themselves. 自助午餐(晚餐)(人數多於席位時而設)。 **2** farm or gardening tool for breaking up the ground, lifting hay, straw, etc. 草叉。⇨ the illus at tool. 參看 tool 之插圖。 **3** place where a road, tree-trunk, etc divides or branches; part of a bicycle to which a wheel is fixed. 路,樹等之分岔處;岔口;(腳踏車上固定輪子之)叉狀支架;前叉。⇨ also *tuning-~* at tune. **4** ˌ**~-lift ˈtruck,** powered truck or trolley with mechanical means of lifting and lowering goods (to or from storage space, or for loading and unloading). 叉式起重車;叉動車。□ *vt, vi* **1** [VP6A, 15A, B] lift, move, carry, with a ~: 以叉叉: *~ hay/straw;* 用叉叉乾草(稻草); *~ in manure,* dig it into the ground with a ~; 用叉將肥料埋入土中; *~ the ground over,* turn the soil over with a ~. 用叉翻土。 **2** [VP2A, C] (of a road, river, etc) divide into branches; (of persons) turn (left or right): (指道路,河流等)分岔;(指人)轉向(左或右): *We ~ed right at the church.* 我們自教堂向右走。 **3** [VP15B, 2C] **~ sth out, ~ up/out,** (colloq) hand over, pay: (俗)交出;支付: *I've got to ~ out a lot of money to the Collector of Taxes this year.* 今年我必須付許多錢給稅務徵收員。 **~ed** *adj* branching; dividing into two or more parts: 有叉的;分叉的: *a ~ed road;* 岔路; *the ~ed tongue of a snake;* 蛇的分叉的舌; *a bird with a ~ed tail;* 尾部分叉的鳥; *~ed lightning.* 叉狀閃電。

a fork-lift truck

for·lorn /fəˈlɔːn ; fəˈlɔrn/ *adj* (poet or liter) unhappy; uncared for; forsaken. (詩或文)不幸的;孤零的;被遺棄的。 **~ hope,** desperate enterprise; plan or enterprise which has very little likelihood of success. 希望甚微而不惜冒險的事業;絕少成功希望的計畫或事業。 **~·ly** *adv* **~·ness** *n*

form¹ /fɔːm ; fɔrm/ *n* **1** [U] shape; outward or visible appearance: 形狀;外形;外貌: *without shape or ~;* 不成形狀的; *take ~,* begin to have a (recognizable) shape; 成形; [C] person or animal as it can be seen or touched: 人形;形體: *A dark ~ could be seen in the distance.* 在遠處可看到一個黑影。 *Proteus was a Greek sea-god who could appear in the ~ of any creature he wished.* 普洛提由斯是一希臘海神,他能隨心所欲的以任何動物的形體出現。 *He has a well-proportioned ~,* a well-shaped body. 他有勻稱的體型。 **2** [U] general arrangement or structure; way in which parts are put together to make a whole or a group; style or manner of presentation: 形式;結構;表現的方式: *a piece of music in sonata ~;* 奏鳴曲式的樂章; *have a sense of ~ in painting* (~ being contrasted with colouring); 在繪畫中對形式之美具有靈敏的感覺('形式'爲'色彩'之對)。 *literary ~* (~ being contrasted with subject-matter). 文學形式(爲題材之對)。 **3** [C] particular kind of arrangement or structure; manner in which a thing exists; species, kind or variety: 特殊的形式;存在方式;種類: *~s of government;* 政治制度;政體; *~s of animal and vegetable life.* 動植物的生活方式。 *Ice, snow and steam are ~s of water.* 冰,雪和蒸汽是水的各種形態。 **4** [U] (gram) shape taken by a word (in sound or spelling): (文法)一字的讀音或拼寫形式;語形: *change ~;* 改變形式; *different in ~ but identical in meaning;* 形式不同但意義相同; [C] one of the shapes taken by a word (in sound or spelling): 一字(在發音或拼法上)的某種形式: *The word 'brother' has two plural ~s, 'brothers' and 'brethren'.* brother 一字有兩種複數形式,一爲 brothers, 一爲 brethren。 *The past tense ~ of 'run' is 'ran'.* run 的過去式是 ran. **5** [U] manner of behaving or speaking fixed, required or expected by custom or etiquette: 禮貌;禮節: *do sth for ~'s sake,* ie because it is usual, not because one wishes to do it or likes doing it; 爲了禮節而做某事(並非因爲喜愛而做); *say 'Good morning' as a mere matter of ~,* ie not because one is really pleased to see the person to whom the words are spoken. 祇是爲了禮貌問題而說'早安'(並非因眞喜歡見到對方而說)。 **good/bad ˈ~,** behaviour according to/not according to custom or etiquette. 有禮貌(失禮)。 **6** [C] particular way of behaving, etc; greeting, utterance, act, as required by custom or etiquette; established practice or ritual: 行爲等之特殊的方式;習慣或禮貌所要求的招呼,言語或動作;禮儀;儀式: *the ancient ~s observed at the coronation of a sovereign;* 國王加冕時所遵守的古代儀式; *pay too much attention to ~s;* 過於拘禮; *a ~ of prayer used at sea;* 航海時的祈禱式; *~s of worship.* 禮拜式。 **7** [C] printed paper with space to be filled in: 表格: *ˈtelegraph ~s;* 電報紙; *appliˈcation ~s;* 申請表格; printed or typewritten letter sent out in great numbers (also called 亦稱作 a **~ letter**). 大量發出的印刷或打字的信件。 **8** [U] condition of health and training (esp of horses and athletes): 健康和訓練情況(尤指馬和運動員者): *If a horse is not in good ~ it is unlikely to win a race.* 如果一匹馬的健康和訓練情況不佳,牠多半不會在賽馬中得勝。*On ~* (=Judging from recent performances as evidence of condition and training), *the Aga Khan's horse is likely to win the race.* 根據近況判斷,那位回教首領的馬可能獲勝。 ***in/out of ~; on/off ~,*** in good/bad condition: 情況良好(不好): *Smith is out of ~/is not on ~/is off ~ and is unlikely to run in the 100 metres race tomorrow.* 史密斯的情況失常,大概不會參加明天的百米賽跑。 **9** [U] spirits: 精神;心境: *Jack was in great ~ at the dinner party,* in high spirits, lively. 傑克在那宴會上十分愉快。 **10** [C] long wooden bench, usu without a back, for several persons to sit on. 長凳(通常無靠背,可以坐數人)。 **11** [C] class in GB schools, the youngest boys and girls being in the first ~ and the oldest in the sixth ~. (英國學校的)年級;級(自一年級至六年級)。 **~·less** *adj* without shape. 無形狀的;無形式的。 **~·less·ly** *adv*

form² /fɔːm ; fɔrm/ *vt, vi* **1** [VP6A, 15A] give shape or form to; make, produce: 形成;作成;製作: *~ words and sentences;* 形成字和句子; *~ the plural of a noun by adding -s or -es;* 加 s 或 es 以形成一名詞的複數式; *~ one's style* (in writing) *on good models.* 模倣良好的模範以形成自己的文體。 **2** [VP6A] develop, build up, conceive: 養成;培養;想出: *~ good habits;* 養成良好習慣; *~ a child's character/mind,* by training, discipline, etc; 陶冶一個孩子的品性(心性); *~ ideas/plans/judgements/opinions/conclusions.* 想出主意(計畫,意見,結論)。 **3** [VP6A, 15A] organize: 組織;編組: *~ a class for beginners in French.* 編組一法文初級班。 *They ~ed themselves into a committee.* 他們組織成一個委員會。 **4** [VP6A] be (the material of), be (one or part of): 作爲(…的材料);爲(…的一員或一部份): *What ~s the basis of this compound?* 這化合物的主要成分是什麼? *This series of lectures ~s part* *of a complete course on French history.* 這一系列的演講爲一門法國史課程的一部份。 **5** [VP14, 2C] ~ ***into,*** (mil) (cause to) move into a particular order: (軍)(使)排列;(使)成隊形: ~ *a regiment into columns;* 將一團排成縱隊; ~ *into line.* 排成行。*The company was ~ed into three ranks.* 該連排成三列。 **6** [VP2A, C] come into existence; become solid; take shape: 生出;形成;凝固;成形: *The idea ~ed in his mind.* 這觀念在他心中形成了。*The words would not ~ on her lips,* She could not bring herself to speak them. 她說不出那些話來。*Ice ~s at the temperature of 0°C.* 冰之形成是在攝氏零度時。

for·mal /ˈfɔːml ; ˈfɔrml̩/ *adj* **1** in accordance with rules, customs and convention: 正式的;合於習俗的;合於禮儀的: *pay a ~ call on the Ambassador;* 正式拜會大使; *~ dress,* as required by custom for certain occasions; 禮服; *make a ~* (= ceremonious) *bow to sb;* 對某人深深地鞠躬; *a ~ receipt,* according to commercial custom, regular and in good order. 正式收據。 **2** regular or geometric in design; symmetrical: 整齊的;井然有序的;勻稱的: ~ *gardens,* eg with flower beds, hedges, etc in geometrical patterns. 形式整齊的花園(例如有整齊而有系統之格式的花床,樹籬等)。 **3** of the outward shape or appearance (not the reality or substance): 形式上的;外表上的: *a ~ resemblance between two things.* 兩物在外表上的相似。 **4** ˌ~ ˈ**grammar,** of the forms of words, of rules (of syntax, etc). 形式文法(討論字的形式,句法規則等)。**~·ly** /-məlɪ ; -mlɪ/ *adv* **~·ism** /-ɪzəm ; -ˌɪzəm/ *n* [U] exact observance of forms and ceremonies, eg in religious duties, in behaviour. 形式主義;拘泥禮儀。

for·mal·de·hyde /fɔːˈmældɪhaɪd ; fɔrˈmældəˌhaɪd/ *n* [U] (chem) colourless gas **(HCHO)** used, dissolved in water, as a preservative and disinfectant. (化學) 甲醛(一種無色氣體,溶於水用作防腐劑和消毒劑)。 **for·malin** /ˈfɔːməlɪn ; ˈfɔrməlɪn/ *n* [U] (chem) solution of ~ used as a disinfectant. (化學)甲醛液(用作消毒劑);福馬林。

for·mal·ity /fɔːˈmælətɪ ; fɔrˈmælətɪ/ *n* (*pl* -ties) **1** [U] strict attention to rules, forms and convention: 嚴守禮節;拘泥形式: *There was too much ~ in the Duke's household.* 公爵的家裏過份拘泥形式。 **2** [C] formal act; sth required by custom or rules: 正式行動;禮節;儀式;手續: *legal formalities;* 法律上的正式手續; *comply with all the necessary formalities.* 遵守一切必要的禮儀。 ***a mere ~,*** sth one is required or expected to do, but which has little meaning or importance. 僅爲形式而已;祇是手續而已。

for·mat /ˈfɔːmæt ; ˈfɔrmæt/ *n* **1** shape and size of a book, including the type, paper and binding: (書籍的)版式: *reissue a book in a new ~.* 以新的版式重新出版一書。 **2** arrangement; procedure; style: 安排;程序;格式: *the ~ of a meeting/conference/interview.* 會議(討論會,訪問)的程序。

for·ma·tion /fɔːˈmeɪʃn ; fɔrˈmeʃən/ *n* **1** [U] forming or shaping: 形成: *the ~ of character/of ideas in the mind;* 性格(觀念)之形成; [C] that which is formed: 形成之物: *Clouds are ~s of condensed water vapour.* 雲乃凝聚的水蒸氣所形成者。 **2** [U] structure or arrangement: 構造;排列: *troops/warships in ˈbattle ~;* 成戰鬥隊形的軍隊(戰艦); *military aircraft flying in ~;* 編隊飛行的軍機; (attrib) (形容用法) *ˈ~ flying/dancing;* 編隊飛行(舞蹈); [C] particular arrangement or order: 特殊的排列: *rock ~s;* 岩層; [C] the arrangement of the players at the start of a (football, Rugby) match. (足球,橄欖球比賽開始時)在場球員之排列。

for·ma·tive /ˈfɔːmətɪv ; ˈfɔrmətɪv/ *adj* **1** giving, or tending to give, shape to: 使成形的;形成的: ~ *influences,* eg on a child's character. 形成力(如造成兒童性格的影響力)。 **2** pliable: 易受影響的: *the ~ years of a child's life,* the years during which its character is formed. 兒童性格的形成時期。

for·mer /ˈfɔːmə(r) ; ˈfɔrmɚ/ *adj* **1** of an earlier period: 早先的;以前的;從前的: *in ~ times;* 往昔;從前; *my ~ students;* 我從前的學生; *customs of ~ days.* 昔時的風俗。*She looks more like her ~ self,* eg looks well again after her illness. 她恢復她從前的樣子了(例如病後復元)。 **2** (also as *pron*) (亦作代名詞) ***the ~*** (contrasted with ***the latter***), the firstmentioned of two: 前者(與 the latter 相對): *I prefer the ~ alternative to the latter.* 我願選擇前者。*Of these alternatives I prefer the ~.* 就此兩者之間我願選擇前者。**~·ly** *adv* in ~ times. 從前;以前;往昔。

for·mic /ˈfɔːmɪk ; ˈfɔrmɪk/ *adj* ˌ~ ˈ**acid,** the acid (used to make insecticides, fumigants, etc) contained in the fluid emitted by ants but now usu produced synthetically. 蟻酸(用以製殺蟲藥,燻蒸消毒劑等,現在通常可由人工製造)。

For·mica /fɔːˈmaɪkə ; fɔrˈmaɪkə/ *n* [U] (P) heat-resistant plastic made in sheets (for covering surfaces). (商標)一種耐熱塑膠薄板(用以做餐桌等傢具之表面)。

for·mi·dable /ˈfɔːmɪdəbl ; ˈfɔrmɪdəbl/ *adj* **1** causing fear or dread: 可怕的;令人畏懼的: *a man with a ~ appearance.* 面目可怕的人。 **2** requiring great effort to deal with or overcome: 難以克服的;難纏的;艱難的: ~ *obstacles/opposition/enemies/debts.* 難以克服的障礙(難以平服的反抗;難以對付的敵人;難清償的債務)。**for·mi·dably** /-əblɪ ; -ablɪ/ *adv*

for·mula /ˈfɔːmjʊlə ; ˈfɔrmjələ/ *n* (*pl* ~s, or, in scientific usage, 在科學用語中作 ~e /-liː ; -li/) **1** form of words used regularly (as 'How d'you do?', 'Excuse me', 'Thank you'); phrase or sentence regularly used in legal documents, church services, etc: 客套語(如'你好','對不起','謝謝你');(法律文件,宗教儀式等之)慣用語: *the ~ used in baptism.* 受洗時的慣用語。 **2** statement of a rule, fact, etc esp one in signs or numbers, as in mathematics; (chem) expression in symbols of the constituent parts of a substance, eg H_2O (water). (數學)公式;(化學) 分子式(例如 水的分子式爲 H_2O)。 **3** set of directions, usu in symbols, for a medical preparation: 藥方;處方: *a ~ for a cough mixture.* 配咳嗽藥的藥方。

for·mu·late /ˈfɔːmjʊleɪt ; ˈfɔrmjəˌlet/ *vt* [VP6A] express clearly and exactly: 明確地表達: ~ *one's thoughts/a doctrine.* 明確地表達個人的思想(學說)。**for·mu·la·tion** /ˌfɔːmjʊˈleɪʃn ; ˌfɔrmjəˈleʃən/ *n* [U] formulating; [C] exact and clear statement. 明確的表達;確切的陳述。

for·ni·ca·tion /ˌfɔːnɪˈkeɪʃn ; ˌfɔrnɪˈkeʃən/ *n* [U] voluntary sexual intercourse between persons not married to one another, esp when both are unmarried.和姦;私通(未婚男女彼此間自願發生的性行爲)。 ⇨ adultery. **for·ni·cate** /ˈfɔːnɪkeɪt ; ˈfɔrnəˌket/ *vi* [VP2A] commit ~. (未婚男女與異性)和姦;私通。

for·ra·der /ˈfɒrədə(r) ; ˈfɑrədɚ/ *adv* (colloq) more forward: (俗)更向前: *can't get any ~,* can't make any progress. 毫無進展。

for·sake /fəˈseɪk ; fɚˈsek/ *vt* (*pt* forsook /fəˈsʊk ; fɚˈsʊk/, *pp* forsaken /fəˈseɪkən ; fɚˈsekən/) [VP6A] give up; break away from; desert: 放棄;棄絕;遺棄: ~ *one's wife and children;* 遺棄妻兒; ~ *bad habits.* 革除惡習。*His friends forsook him when he became poor.* 當他窮困時,他的朋友們背棄了他。

for·sooth /fəˈsuːθ ; fɚˈsuθ/ *adv* (used in irony) no doubt; in truth. (用作反語)的確;確實。

for·swear /fɔːˈsweə(r) ; fɔrˈswer/ *vt* (*pt* forswore /fɔːˈswɔː(r) ; fɔrˈswor/, *pp* forsworn /fɔːˈswɔːn ; fɔrˈsworn/) [VP6A] **1** give up doing or using (sth): 放棄;戒絕: ~ *bad habits/smoking.* 戒除惡習(戒煙)。 **2** ~ ***oneself,*** perjure oneself. 作僞誓;背誓。

for·sythia /fɔːˈsaɪθɪə *US:* fɚˈsɪθɪə ; fɚˈsɪθɪə/ *n* [U] shrub with bright yellow flowers in spring. 連翹(春季開鮮黃色花朵的灌木)。

fort /fɔːt ; fort/ *n* building or group of buildings

specially erected or strengthened for military defence. 要塞;堡壘;碉堡;城堡。

forte[1] /ˈfɔːteɪ US: fɔːrt ; fort/ *n* person's special talent; sth a person does particularly well: (人的)長處;特長: *Singing is not my ~*, I do not sing well. 我不擅長唱歌。

forte[2] /ˈfɔːteɪ ; ˈfɔrtɪ/ *adj, adv* (I; music) (abbr 略作 **f**) loud(ly). (義;音樂)強音的;用強音。

forth /fɔːθ ; forθ/ *adv* **1** (archaic) out. (古)向外。 **2** (formal) onwards; forwards: (正式用語) 向前: *from this day ~*. 自今日起。 ***and so ~***, and so on. 等等。 ***back and ~***, to and fro (which is more usu). 前後;來回(to and fro 較常用)。 **3** ***hold ~***, ⇨ hold[1](14).

forth·com·ing /ˌfɔːθˈkʌmɪŋ ; ˈforθˈkʌmɪŋ/ *adj* **1** about to come out: 即將出現的: *a list of ~ books*, books about to be published. 即將出版的書籍的目錄。 **2** (pred) ready for use when needed: (敘述用法) 需要時即可供給的;隨要隨有的;現成的: *The money/help we hoped for was not ~*, We did not receive it. 我們所期待的那筆款(那項幫助)沒有來到。 **3** ready to be helpful, give information, etc: 熱心的;肯幫忙的;樂意提供消息的: *The girl at the reception desk was not very ~*. 接待處那位小姐服務不太熱心。

forth·right /ˈfɔːθraɪt ; forθˈraɪt/ *adj* outspoken; straightforward. 坦白的;直率的。

forth·with /ˌfɔːθˈwɪθ US: -ˈwɪð ; forθˈwɪθ/ *adv* at once; without losing time. 立刻;卽刻。

for·ti·eth /ˈfɔːtɪəθ ; ˈfɔrtɪɪθ/ ⇨ forty.

for·tify /ˈfɔːtɪfaɪ ; ˈfɔrtəˌfaɪ/ *vt* (*pt, pp* -fied) [VP6A, 14] ~ ***(against)***, strengthen (a place) against attack (with walls, trenches, guns, etc); support or strengthen oneself, one's courage, etc: 加強防衛(地方);加強(自己,勇氣等): *~ a town against the enemy;* 加強防衛一城以對付敵人; *a fortified city/zone;* 設防的城市(地帶); *~ oneself against the cold*, eg by wearing a fur coat; 加強自己(例如穿一皮外衣)以禦寒冷; *fortified with the rites of the Church*, prepared, by having received the Sacraments, for death. 臨終前領有聖體 (對死已有準備)。 **fortified wine**, wine, eg sherry, strengthened by the addition of grape brandy. 加有葡萄白蘭地的酒(例如雪利酒)。 **for·ti·fi·ca·tion** /ˌfɔːtɪfɪˈkeɪʃn ; ˌfɔrtəfəˈkeʃən/ *n* [U] ~ing; [C] (often *pl*) defensive wall(s), tower(s), earthwork(s), etc. 加強防衛;(常用複數)防禦工事。

for·tis·simo /fɔːˈtɪsɪməʊ ; fɔrˈtɪsəˌmo/ *adj, adv* (I; music) (abbr 略作 **ff**) very loud(ly). (義;音樂)最強音的;用最強音。

for·ti·tude /ˈfɔːtɪtjuːd US: -tuːd ; ˈfɔrtəˌtjud/ *n* [U] calm courage, self-control, in the face of pain, danger or difficulty. 不屈不撓的精神;堅忍不拔;剛毅。

fort·night /ˈfɔːtnaɪt ; ˈfɔrtnaɪt/ *n* period of two weeks: 兩星期;兩禮拜: *a ~'s holiday;* 兩禮拜的假期; *go away for a ~;* 離開兩星期; *a ~* (=a ~ from) *today/tomorrow/next Monday;* 從今天(明天,下星期一) 算起兩星期以後(或以前); *a ~ ago yesterday*. 從昨天算起兩星期前。 **~·ly** *adj, adv* happening or occurring every ~: 每兩星期的;隔週: *~ly sailings to Bombay;* 每兩週駛往孟買一次; *go ~ly*. 隔週行駛;隔週去一次。

for·tress /ˈfɔːtrɪs ; ˈfɔrtrɪs/ *n* fortified building or town. 堡壘;要塞;城堡。

for·tu·itous /fɔːˈtjuːɪtəs US: -ˈtuː- ; fɔrˈtjuətəs/ *adj* (formal) happening by chance: (正式用語) 偶然發生的: *a ~ meeting*. 偶遇。 **~·ly** *adv*

for·tu·nate /ˈfɔːtʃənət ; ˈfɔrtʃənɪt/ *adj* favoured by fortune; lucky; prosperous; having, bringing, brought by, good fortune: 幸運的;運氣好的;吉利的;帶來好運的;好運帶來的: *be ~ in life*. 一生幸運。 *You were ~ to escape being injured*. 你沒有受傷眞是幸運。 *He was ~ enough to have a good income*. 他很幸運,有一筆好收入。 *That was ~ for you*. 你的運氣眞好。 *You were ~ in your choice/in winning his sympathy*. 你作這樣的選擇(能獲得他的同情)很幸運。 **~·ly** *adv* in a ~ manner: 幸運地: *~ly for everybody*. 爲每人帶來幸運。

for·tune /ˈfɔːtʃuːn ; ˈfɔrtʃən/ *n* **1** [C, U] chance; chance looked upon as a power deciding or influencing sb or sth; fate; good or bad luck coming to a person or undertaking: 機會;運氣;命運;好運或壞運: *have ~ on one's side*, be lucky. 走好運。 ***the ~(s) of war***, what may happen in war. 戰爭中可能發生之事;戰爭中的運氣。 ***try one's ~***, take a risky step. 碰運氣。 ***tell sb his ~***, say, eg as gypsies do, from a reading of playing cards, or the lines on his palm, what will happen to him. (用紙牌或根據掌紋等)爲某人算命;爲某人看相。 **ˈ~ teller** *n* person who claims to be able to do this. 算命者;看相者。 **2** [C, U] prosperity; success; great sum of money: 興隆;成功;鉅富;鉅資: *a man of ~;* 富人; *seek one's ~ in a new country*. 至一新國家淘金(尋出路)。 ***come into a ~***, inherit a lot of money. 繼承大筆遺產。 ***make a ~***, make a lot of money. 發財;致富。 ***marry a ~***, marry sb who is or will be rich, eg an heiress. 娶一有錢或將來會有錢(例如女繼承人)的女人。 ***a small ~***, a lot of money: 許多錢: *spend a small ~ on clothes*. 花許多錢買衣服。 **ˈ~ hunter** *n* man seeking a rich woman to marry. 欲娶富有女子爲妻者;欲發妻財者。

forty /ˈfɔːtɪ ; ˈfɔrtɪ/ *adj, n* the number 40: 四十;四十個: *a man of ~*, aged 40; 四十歲的人; *under/over ~*. 四十以下(上)。 ⇨ App 4. 參看附錄四。 **the forties**, 40-49. 四十至四十九。 ***have ~ winks***, ⇨ wink. **for·ti·eth** /ˈfɔːtɪəθ ; ˈfɔrtɪɪθ/ *adj, n* ⇨ App 4. 參看附錄四。

fo·rum /ˈfɔːrəm ; ˈforəm/ *n* (in ancient Rome) public place for meetings; any place for public discussion: (古羅馬)集會的廣場;公共集會地點: *TV is an accepted ~ for the discussion of public affairs*. 電視爲一般公認的討論公共事務的場所。

for·ward[1] /ˈfɔːwəd ; ˈfɔrwəd/ *adj* (⇨ backward) **1** directed towards the front; situated in front; moving on, advancing: 向前的;在前的;向前進行的: *a ~ march/movement;* 前進(向前移動); *the ~ ranks of a column of troops;* 一縱隊軍隊的前幾排; *~ planning*, for future needs, etc; 預先的謀畫; *be well ~ with one's work*. 工作進度很快。 **2** (of plants, crops, seasons, children) well advanced; making progress towards maturity: (指植物,農作物,季節,兒童)早的;早熟的: *a ~ spring*. 早臨的春天。 **3** eager or impatient; ready and willing: 急切的;熱心的: *~ to help others;* 熱心助人; too eager; rather presumptuous: 過於急切的;孟浪的: *a ~ young girl*. 孟浪的少女。 **4** advanced or extreme: 前進的;急進的: *~ opinions*. 急進的意見。 **5** (comm) relating to future produce: (商)有關將來出品的: *~ prices*, for goods to be delivered later; 預約價目; *a ~ contract*. 期貨契約。 □ *n* one of the first-line players in football (now often called 現在常稱作 a *striker*), hockey, etc. (足球,曲棍球等之)前鋒。 ⇨ the illus at football. 參看 football 之插圖。 **~·ness** *n* [U] the state of being ~(2): 早;早熟: *the ~ness of the season*. 季節之早臨。

for·ward[2] /ˈfɔːwəd ; ˈfɔrwəd/ *vt* [VP6A, 12A, 13A, 15A] **1** help or send forward; help to advance: 協助;促進: *~ sb's plans*. 協助某人的計畫。 **2** send, dispatch: 發送;遞送: *~ goods to sb*. 送貨給某人。 *We have today ~ed you our new catalogue*. 我們今天已將我們的新目錄寄給你了。 **ˈ~ing agent** *n* person or business company that ~s goods. 運輸業者;運輸行。 **ˈ~ing instructions**, instructions concerning the destination, etc of goods. (有關貨物之目的地等之)運送指示。 **3** send a letter, parcel, etc after a person to a new address: 轉遞 (信件,包裹等): *Please ~ my letters to this address*. 請將我的信件轉到這個地址。

for·ward(s) /ˈfɔːwəd(z) ; ˈfɔrwəd(z)/ *adv* (Note: ~s is not much used except as in 4 below.) (注意: 除下列第 4 義外, ~s 的形式極少用。) **1** onward so as to make progress: 向前；前進: *rush/step* ～, 衝(跨步)向前; *go* ～. 走向前；進步。⇨ carriage(3); forrader. **2** towards the future; onwards in time: 至未來；至將來: *from this time* ～; 從此以後; *look* ～, think ahead, think about the future. 前瞻；考慮將來。***look*** **～** ***to sth,*** ⇨ look¹(7). **3** to the front; into prominence: 至前面；至顯着處: *bring* ～ (=call attention to) *new evidence;* 提出新證據; *come* ～, offer oneself for a task, a post, etc. 自願做一工作或擔任一職務。**4** ***backward(s) and*** **～*****(s),*** to and fro. 來回；前後。

fosse /fɒs ; fɔs/ *n* [C] long, narrow ditch or trench, eg a moat, or as a fortification. 壕(例如防禦城堡或防禦工事者)。

fos·sil /ˈfɒsl ; ˈfɑsl̩/ *n* [C] **1** recognizable (part, trace or imprint of a) prehistoric animal or plant once buried in earth, now hardened like rock: 化石: *hunt for* ～*s;* 尋覓化石; (attrib) (形容用法) ～ *bones/shells;* 成化石的骨頭(貝殼); ～ *ferns in coal.* 煤層中成化石的羊齒植物。**2** (colloq) person who is out of date and unable to accept new ideas: (俗)守舊的人；落伍的人: *Isn't Professor Baboon an old* ～*!* 巴布恩教授眞是個落伍的人！ **～·ize** /ˈfɒsəlaɪz ; ˈfɑsl̩ˌaɪz/ *vt, vi* [VP6A, 2A] change or turn into stone; (fig) make or become out of date or antiquated. 使成化石；變爲化石；(喩)使古舊；變爲古舊。**～·iz·ation** /ˌfɒsəlaɪˈzeɪʃn *US:* -əlɪˈz- ; ˌfɑsləˈzeʃən/ *n*

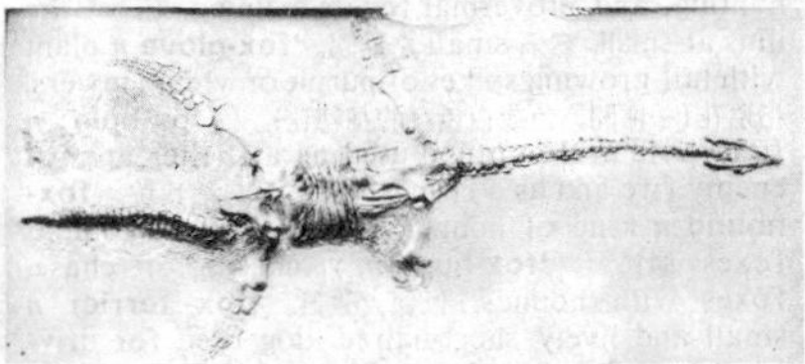

a fossil

fos·ter /ˈfɒstə(r) *US:* ˈfɔː- ; ˈfɔstɚ/ *vt* [VP6A] care for; help the growth and development of; nurture: 照顧；撫育；養育；培養: ～ *a child,* bring it up as one's own without legally adopting it; 養育一小孩(作爲家庭之一員，但未合法收養爲養子或養女); ～ *the sick;* 照顧病人; ～ *musical ability;* 培養音樂才能; ～ *evil thoughts/a desire for revenge.* 心懷惡念(復仇的慾望)。**ˈ～-brother/-sister** *nn* one ～ed by one's parent(s). 義兄弟(姐妹)。**ˈ～-child** *n* one brought up by ～-parents. 義子；螟蛉子。**ˈ～-parent/-mother/-father** *nn* one who acts as a parent in place of a natural parent, but without legal guardianship. 義母；義父。⇨ adopt.

fought /fɔːt ; fɔt/ *pt, pp* of fight.

foul¹ /faʊl ; faʊl/ *adj* **1** causing disgust; having a bad smell or taste; filthy: 令人厭惡的；有惡臭的；味惡的；汚穢的: *a* ～ *prison cell;* 汚濁的小牢房; *medicine with a* ～ *taste;* 味惡的藥; ～*-smelling drains;* 有惡臭的陰溝; *a* ～ *meal,* (sl) a poor meal. (俚)令人發嘔的飯。**2** wicked; evil; (of language) full of oaths; obscene; (of the weather) stormy, rough. 邪惡的；(指言語)粗鄙的；猥褻的；(指天氣)暴風雨的；惡劣的。**ˌ～-ˈspoken/-ˈmouthed** *adj* using ～ language. 言語粗鄙的。***by ˌfair means or ˈ***～***,*** somehow or other, whether by good or evil methods. 用正當或不正當的手段；用種種手段；不擇手段。**3** **ˌ～ ˈplay, (a)** (in sport) sth contrary to the rules. (運動)犯規。**(b)** violent crime, esp murder: 兇暴罪；(尤指)謀殺: *Is* ～ *play suspected,* Do the police think this is a case of murder? 警方猜疑到這是一件謀殺案嗎？ **4** entangled: 糾纏的: *a* ～ *rope.* 糾纏着的繩子。**5** (of a flue, pipe, gun-barrel, etc) clogged up, not clear: (指通煙道，水管，槍管等)塡塞住的；阻塞的: *The fire won't burn; perhaps the chimney is* ～, needs sweeping. 火生不着，或許是煙囱塞住了。**6** ***fall*** **～** ***of,*** **(a)** (of a ship) run against, collide with, become entangled with. (指船)與…相撞；與…糾纏在一起。**(b)** (fig) get into trouble with: (喩)招致…的困難；陷入困境: *fall* ～ *of the law.* 招致法律上的困難。□ *n* **1** [C] (sport) sth contrary to the rules; irregular stroke or piece of play. (運動)犯規。**2** [U] ***through fair and*** **～*****,*** through good and bad fortune; through everything. 不論遭遇好運或惡運；在任何情形下。**～·ly** /ˈfaʊllɪ ; ˈfaʊllɪ/ *adv* in a ～ manner: 汚穢地；發惡臭地；味惡地；邪惡地；粗鄙地: *He was* ～*ly murdered.* 他被人以殘暴的手段殺害了。**～·ness** *n*

foul² /faʊl ; faʊl/ *vt, vi* [VP6A, 2A, 2C] ～ ***(up),*** **1** make or become foul: 使汚穢；使臭；變汚穢；變臭；阻塞: *factory chimneys that* ～ *up the air with smoke;* 冒煙使空氣汚濁的工廠煙囱; ～ *one's name/reputation;* 玷汚名聲; ～ *a drain/gun-barrel.* 阻塞陰溝(槍管)。**2** collide; collide with; make or become entangled: 碰撞；與…相撞；(使)糾纏；糾結: *The rope* ～*ed the anchor chain.* 繩與錨鏈纏在一起了。*His fishing-line got* ～*ed up in the weeds.* 他的釣絲和雜草纏在一起了。**3** (sport) commit a ～(1) against: (運動)對…犯規: ～ *an opponent.* 向對手犯規。

found¹ /faʊnd ; faʊnd/ *pt, pp* of find.

found² /faʊnd ; faʊnd/ *vt* **1** [VP6A] start the building of; lay the base of; establish: 建立；立…的基礎；設立: ～ *a new city/a colony in a new country.* 建一新城市(在一新的國家建立殖民地)。**2** [VP6A] get sth started by providing money (esp endowments): 出資(尤指捐款)興辦: ～ *a new school.* 捐款興辦一新學校。**3** [VP14] ～ ***sth on/upon,*** base on: 根據: *a novel* ～*ed on fact;* 根據事實寫成的一部小說; *arguments* ～*ed on facts.* 基於事實的論據。

foun·da·tion /faʊnˈdeɪʃn ; faʊnˈdeʃən/ *n* **1** [U] founding or establishing (of a town, school, church or other institution). (城市，學校，教堂或其他機關之)建立；創立；建設。**2** [C] sth that is founded, eg a college, monastery, hospital; fund of money for charity, research, etc: 建立物(例如學院，寺院，醫院)；(慈善、研究等)基金: *the Ford F*～. 福特基金。**3** [C] (often *pl*) strong base of a building, usu below ground-level, on which it is built up: (常用複數)地基；屋基: *the* ～*(s) of a block of flats.* 一排公寓的地基。*The huge lorries shook the house to its* ～*s.* 大卡車駛過連屋基都震動了。**ˈ～-stone** *n* stone laid at a ceremony to celebrate the founding of a building. 基石。**4** [C, U] that on which an idea, belief, etc rests; underlying principle; basis; starting-point: (思想，信仰等之)基礎；根據；根本；出發點: *the* ～*s of religious beliefs;* 宗教信仰的基礎; *lay the* ～*(s) of one's career;* 爲事業奠立基礎; *a story that has no* ～ *in fact/is without* ～. 無事實根據的故事。**5** **ˈ～ garment,** (trade use) woman's corset or other garment to shape and support the body (often with a bra attached); (商業用語)女用緊身胸衣(常連奶罩一起); **ˈ～ cream,** (cosmetics) cream used on the skin before other cosmetics are applied. (化粧品)粉底霜。

foun·der¹ /ˈfaʊndə(r) ; ˈfaʊndɚ/ *n* person who founds or establishes a school, etc. (學校等之)創立人；建立者。**found·ress** /ˈfaʊndrɪs ; ˈfaʊndrɪs/ *n* woman ～. 女創立人；女建立者。

foun·der² /ˈfaʊndə(r) ; ˈfaʊndɚ/ *vi, vt* [VP2A, 6A] **1** (of a ship) (cause to) fill with water and sink. (指船)(使)進水而沉沒。**2** (of a horse) fall or stumble (esp in mud or from overwork); cause (a horse) to break down from overwork. (指馬)跌倒在泥中；因過度疲勞而跌倒；使(馬)工作過度而衰弱。**3** (of a plan, etc) fail. (計畫等)失敗。

found·ling /ˈfaʊndlɪŋ ; ˈfaʊndlɪŋ/ *n* deserted or abandoned child of unknown parents. 棄兒。**ˈ～ hospital,** (formerly) institution where ～s are taken in and cared for. (昔時)棄兒養育院。

foun·dry /ˈfaʊndrɪ ; ˈfaʊndrɪ/ *n* (*pl* -dries) place where metal or glass is melted and moulded: 鑄造廠；玻璃廠: *a ˈtype* ～, where type for printing is made. 鑄字工廠。

fount /faʊnt ; faʊnt/ *n* **1** (poet) spring of water. (詩)泉;噴泉。 **2** (also 亦作 *font*) set of printer's type of the same size and face. 一套活字。 **3** (poet or rhet) source. (詩或修辭)來源;根源。

foun·tain /ˈfaʊntɪn *US:* -tn ; ˈfaʊntn̩/ *n* **1** spring of water, esp one made artificially with water forced through holes in a pipe or pipes for ornamental purposes. 噴泉(尤指人造的裝飾用者);噴水池。 **ˈdrinking-~** *n* one that supplies drinking-water in a public place. (設於公共場所之)飲用噴泉。 **ˈ~-pen** *n* pen with a supply of ink inside the holder. 自來水筆。 **ˈsoda-~,** ⇨ soda. **2** (fig) source or origin: (喻)源泉;源流: *the ~ of justice.* 正義的源泉。 **ˈ~-head** *n* original source. 根源;本源。

four /fɔ:(r) ; for/ *n, adj* the number 4: 四;四個: *a child of ~,* ~ years old; 四歲的小孩; *a coach and ~,* with ~ horses; 四匹馬拉的馬車; *the ~ corners of the earth,* the farthest parts; 天涯海角; *scatter sth to the ~ winds,* in all directions. 使某物向四面八方飛散。⇨ App 4. 參看附錄四。 **ˌ~-letter ˈword,** word of ~ letters, eg *shit,* which is regarded as obscene. 四個字母的字(指某些四個字母的下流語,例如shit)。 ***on all ~s,*** (crawling) on the hands and knees. 匍匐;爬着。 ***be on all ~s (with),*** be quite the same (as). (與…)完全相同。 ***a ~,*** a rowing-boat with a crew of ~; 四人划行之船; (cricket) hit for ~ runs. (板球)得四分的一擊。 **ˌ~-in-ˈhand** *n* vehicle (coach or carriage) pulled by ~ horses and with no outrider. 無騎馬侍從的四馬馬車。 **ˈ~-part** *adj* (music) arranged for ~ voices to sing. (音樂)四部合唱的。 **~·pence** /ˈfɔ:pəns ; ˈforpəns/ *n* the sum of 4p: 四辨士: *apples, ~pence each.* 蘋果,四辨士一個。 **~·penny** /ˈfɔ:pnɪ *US:* -penɪ ; ˈforˌpenɪ/ *adj* costing 4p: 值四辨士的: *a ~penny loaf.* 四辨士一條的麵包。 **ˈ~-ply** *adj* (of wool, wood, etc) having ~ strands or thicknesses. (指毛線,木材等)四股的;四層的。 **ˌ~-ˈposter** *n* bed with ~ posts to support a canopy or curtains. 有四柱和帳帷的床。 **ˌ~-ˈpounder** *n* gun throwing a 4 lb shot. 發射四磅重砲彈的砲。 **ˈ~·score** *adj, n* 80. 八十。 **ˈ~·square** *adj* square-shaped; (fig) steady; solidly based. 方形的;四方的;(喻)穩固的;鞏固的。 **ˌ~-ˈwheeler** *n* hackney carriage with ~ wheels (not a hansom cab). 四輪出租馬車。 **~·fold** /ˈfɔ:fəʊld ; ˈforˈfold/ *adj, adv* repeated ~ times; having ~ parts; ~ times as much or as many. 重複四次的;四重的;有四部分的;四倍的(地)。 **~·some** /ˈfɔ:səm ; ˈforsəm/ *n* game (esp of golf) between two pairs: 四人分爲兩組的比賽(尤指高爾夫球);雙打: *a mixed ~some,* with one man and one woman in each pair. 每邊一男一女的對賽;男女混合雙打。 **~·teen** /ˌfɔ:ˈti:n ; forˈtin/ *n, adj* the number 14; ⇨ App 4. 十四;十四個(參看附錄四)。 **~·teenth** /ˌfɔ:ˈti:nθ ; forˈtinθ/ *n, adj* ⇨ App 4. 參看附錄四。 **fourth** /fɔ:θ ; forθ/ *n, adj* ⇨ App 4. 參看附錄四。 **Fourth of July,** (US) anniversary of the Declaration of Independence (1776). 美國獨立紀念日。 **fourth·ly** *adv*

fowl /faʊl ; faul/ *n* **1** (old use) any bird: (舊用法)鳥;禽: *the ~s of the air.* 飛禽。 **2** (with a *pref*) one of the larger birds: (冠以字首)較大的鳥: *ˈwild~,* 獵鳥, *ˈwater~.* 水鳥。 **3** domestic cock or hen: 家禽;鷄: *keep ~s.* 養家禽。 **ˈ~-pest** *n* infectious disease of ~s. 家禽疫病;鷄瘟。 **ˈ~-run** *n* piece of (usu enclosed) land where ~s are kept. 養鷄場。 **4** [U] flesh of ~s as food: 禽肉;鷄肉: *roast ~ for dinner.* 烤禽供餐食。 □ *vi* (usu as gerund) catch, hunt, snare, wild~: (通常用作動名詞)捕鳥;獵鳥: *go ~ing.* 去獵鳥。 **ˈ~ing-piece** *n* light shotgun used in ~ing. 鳥槍。 **~er** *n* person who shoots or traps wild birds for food. 獵野禽者;捕鳥者。

fox[1] /fɒks ; fɑks/ *n* (fem **vixen** /ˈvɪksn ; ˈvɪksn̩/) wild animal of the dog family, with (usu) red fur and a bushy tail, preserved in Britain for hunting, and proverbial for its cunning. 狐。⇨ the illus at small. 參看 small 之挿圖。 **ˈfox·glove** *n* plant with tall-growing spikes of purple or white flowers. 指頂花(一種開紫色或白色花的長穗花)。 **ˈfox·hole** *n* (mil) hole in the ground used as a shelter against enemy fire and as a firing-point. (軍)散兵坑。 **ˈfox-hound** *n* kind of hound bred and trained to hunt foxes. 獵狐犬。 **ˈfox·hunt** *n, vi* chasing of, chase, foxes with hounds. 以獵犬獵狐。 **ˌfox-ˈterrier** *n* small and lively short-haired dog used for driving foxes from earths, or kept as a pet. 一種獵狐小犬(活潑的短毛小犬,用以自狐穴中逐狐,或養作寵物)。 **ˈfox·trot** *n* (music for a) ballroom dance with slow and quick steps. 狐步舞;狐步舞曲。 **foxy** *adj* crafty; crafty-looking. 狡猾的;樣子狡猾的。

fox[2] /fɒks ; fɑks/ *vt* [VP6A] (colloq) deceive by cunning; confuse; puzzle: (俗)用狡計欺騙;使迷惑;使困惑: *He was completely foxed.* 他完全受騙了。

foyer /ˈfɔɪeɪ *US:* ˈfɔɪər ; ˈfɔɪɚ/ *n* large space in a theatre for the use of the audience during in-

fowl

tervals; entrance hall of a cinema or hotel. 戲院中觀衆休息處;電影院或旅社入口廳堂。

fra·cas /ˈfrækɑː US: ˈfreɪkəs ; ˈfrekəs/ *n* (*pl* GB ~ /-kɑːz ; -kɑz/; *US* ~es /-kəsəz ; -kəsɪz/) noisy quarrel. 吵鬧。

frac·tion /ˈfrækʃn ; ˈfrækʃən/ *n* **1** small part or bit. 小塊;碎片。 **2** number that is not a whole number 分數;小數 (eg 如 $\frac{1}{3}$, 5/8, 0·76). **~al** /-ʃənl ; -ʃənl/ *adj* of or in ~s: 小塊的;斷片的;分數的: **~al distillation,** partial separation of liquids, eg petroleum, having different boilingpoints by gradual heating. 分餾法。

frac·tious /ˈfrækʃəs ; ˈfrækʃəs/ *adj* irritable; peevish; bad-tempered. 易怒的;乖張的;脾氣壞的。**~·ly** *adv* **~·ness** *n*

frac·ture /ˈfræktʃə(r) ; ˈfræktʃɚ/ *n* [U] breaking or being broken, eg of a bone, a pipe-line; [C] instance of this: 折斷;斷裂(例如骨或管線);破碎: *compound/simple ~s,* with/without skin wounds. 複合骨折(單純骨折)。 □ *vt, vi* [VP6A, 2A] break; crack: 折斷;破碎: *~ one's leg;* 折斷腿; *bones that ~ easily.* 易斷的骨。

frag·ile /ˈfrædʒaɪl US: -dʒəl ; ˈfrædʒəl/ *adj* easily injured, broken or destroyed: 易受傷害的;易碎的;易毀壞的: *~ china/health/happiness.* 易碎的瓷器(虛弱的體質;易逝去的幸福)。**fra·gil·ity** /frəˈdʒɪlətɪ ; fræˈdʒɪlətɪ/ *n* [U].

frag·ment /ˈfrægmənt ; ˈfrægmənt/ *n* [C] part broken off; separate or incomplete part: 斷片;碎片;破片: *try to put the ~s of a broken vase together;* 試將一破花瓶的碎片拼起來; *overhear ~s of conversation.* 無意中聽到談話的片斷。□ /frægˈment ; ˈfræg,mɛnt/ *vi* [VP2A] break into ~s: 破碎;成爲碎片: *The shell ~s on impact.* 貝殼受撞擊會破碎。**frag·men·tary** /ˈfrægməntrɪ US: -terɪ ; ˈfrægmən,tɛrɪ/ *adj* incomplete: 不完整的;片斷的: *a ~ary report of an event.* 關於一事件之不完整的報導。**frag·men·ta·tion** /ˌfrægmenˈteɪʃn ; ˌfrægmənˈteʃən/ *n* **ˈ~ation bomb,** one that breaks up into small ~s. 殺傷炸彈;爆炸時裂成碎片的炸彈。

fra·grant /ˈfreɪgrənt ; ˈfregrənt/ *adj* sweet-smelling: 芳香的;馥郁的: *~ flowers;* 芳香的花; (fig) pleasant: (喩)愉快的;甜蜜的: *~ memories.* 甜蜜的回憶。**fra·grance** /-əns ; -əns/ *n* [U, C] sweet or pleasing smell. 香味;香氣。

frail /freɪl ; frel/ *adj* weak; fragile: 虛弱的;薄弱的;脆弱的: *a ~ child,* one with a weak constitution; 體質虛弱的孩子; *a ~ support;* 不堅實的支柱; *~ happiness.* 不穩固的幸福。**~ty** /ˈfreɪltɪ ; ˈfreltɪ/ *n* [U] the quality of being ~: 虛弱;薄弱;脆弱: *the ~ty of human life;* 人的生命之脆弱; [C] (*pl* -ties) fault; moral weakness: 過失;品德上的弱點: *He loved her in spite of her little frailties.* 雖然她在品德上有些小缺點,他依然愛她。

frame¹ /freɪm ; frem/ *n* [C] **1** skeleton or main structure, eg steel girders, brick walls, wooden struts, of a ship, building, aircraft, etc which makes its shape, esp in the process of building. (船、建築物、飛機等之)骨架。 **ˈ~ aerial** *n* one in which the wire is round a ~ (instead of being stretched out between two poles, etc). 框形天線。**ˈ~ house** *n* one with a wooden skeleton covered with wooden boards or shingles. 木架屋;木屋。 **2** border of wood or other material in which a picture, photograph, window or door is enclosed or set; structure that holds the lenses of a pair of spectacles. 框架;畫框;相框;窗框;門框;眼鏡框。⇨ the illus at window. 參看window之插圖。 **3** human or animal body: 身體: *a girl of slender ~.* 身體細長的女孩子。*Sobs shook her ~.* 她哭得身體發抖。 **4** box-like structure of wood and glass for protecting plants from the cold: 保護植物的玻璃溫室: *a cold/heated ~.* 冷(熱)室。 **5 ~ of mind,** temporary condition of mind; temper: 心境;心情: *in a cheerful ~ of mind;* 心情愉快; *in the ~ of mind to welcome any diversion.* 有娛樂的心情。 **6** (more usu 較常用 ˈ*~work*) established order or system: 組織;體制: *the ~ of society.* 社會組織。 **7** single exposure on a roll of photographic film. 一捲照片軟片中的一個畫面。 **ˈ~·work** *n* that part of a structure that gives shape and support: 構架;結構;組織: *a bridge with a steel ~work;* 鋼架橋; *the ~work of a policy.* 政策的大綱。

frame² /freɪm ; frem/ *vt, vi* **1** [VP6A] put together; shape; build up: 構造;組織;建築: *~ a plan/theory/sentence;* 擬訂計畫(建立學說;造句); *a man not ~d for severe hardships,* unable to endure them well. 不能吃苦的人。 **2** [VP6A] put a frame(2) round; enclose in a frame: 加以框;裝框於: *~ a photograph;* 給照片裝框; *have an oil-painting ~d;* 爲油畫裝框; serve as a frame: 作爲框架: *a landscape ~d in an archway.* 經由拱門所看到的風景。 **3** [VP2A, C] develop; give promise of developing: 發展;有發展的希望: *plans that ~ well/badly.* 發展順利(不順利)的計畫。 **4** [VP6A] (sl) form a plan to make (sb) appear guilty of sth; put together a false charge against (sb): (俚)陷害(某人);誣告(某人): *The accused man said he had been ~d.* 被告說他是被人陷害了。**ˈ~-up** *n* (sl) scheme or conspiracy to make an innocent person appear guilty. (俚)誣陷之計;陰謀。

franc /fræŋk ; fræŋk/ *n* standard unit of a decimal currency in eg Belgium, France, Switzerland. 法郎(如比利時、法國、瑞士通用的貨幣名)。

fran·chise /ˈfræntʃaɪz ; ˈfræntʃaɪz/ *n* **1** [U] **the ~,** full rights of citizenship given by a country or town, esp the right to vote at elections. 公民權; (尤指) 選舉權;投票權。 **2** [C] (chiefly US) special right given by public authorities to a person or company: (主美)政府給予個人或團體的特權: *a ~ for a bus service.* 設公共汽車之特權。□ *vt* [VP6A] (US) grant a ~(2) to. (美)給予特權。

Fran·cis·can /frænˈsɪskən ; frænˈsɪskən/ *n, adj* (friar or nun) of the religious order founded in 1209 by St Francis /ˈfrɑːnsɪs ; ˈfrænsɪs/ of Assisi /əˈsiːsɪ ; əˈsizɪ/. 聖芳濟會(1209年聖芳濟所建立之教會)的;聖芳濟會修道士或修女。

Franco- /ˈfræŋkəʊ ; ˈfræŋko/ *pref* (used in compounds) French: (用於複合字中)法國的: *the ˌ~-German ˈWar of 1870-71;* 1870 至 1871年間的法德戰爭; *ˈ~phile,* (one who is) friendly towards France; 親法的(人); *ˈ~phobe,* (one who is) hostile towards France. 反法的(人)。

Frank /fræŋk ; fræŋk/ *n* member of the Germanic tribes that conquered Gaul (= France) in the 6th c AD. (日耳曼民族中之)法蘭克人(於六世紀征服了高盧)。

frank¹ /fræŋk ; fræŋk/ *adj* showing clearly the thoughts and feelings; open: 坦白的;率直的: *a ~ look/smile/face;* 率直的神色(微笑,面孔); *make a ~ confession of one's guilt;* 坦白認罪; *be quite ~ with sb (about sth).* 對某人(某事)十分坦白。**~·ly** *adv* **~·ness** *n*

frank² /fræŋk ; fræŋk/ *vt* [VP6A] put a stamp or a mark on (a letter, etc) to show that postage has been paid. 加印記於(信件等)表示郵資已付。 **ˈ~ing-machine** *n* machine that automatically stamps letters etc passed through it, with a counting mechanism to show the total charge. 自動郵資蓋印機(附有計算裝置,可表明郵資總額)。

frank·furter /ˈfræŋkfɜːtə(r) ; ˈfræŋkfɚtɚ/ *n* seasoned and smoked sausage made of beef and pork. 牛肉和豬肉製的臘腸。

frank·in·cense /ˈfræŋkɪnsens ; ˈfræŋkɪn,sɛns/ *n* [U] kind of resin from trees, giving a sweet smell when burnt. 乳香(一種樹脂,燃時發出香氣)。

frank·lin /ˈfræŋklɪn ; ˈfræŋklɪn/ *n* (in GB, 14th and 15th cc) landowner not of noble birth, higher in rank than a yeoman. (英國十四和十五世紀之)非貴族出身的地主(地位高於自耕農)。

fran·tic /ˈfræntɪk ; ˈfræntɪk/ *adj* wildly excited

with joy, pain, anxiety, etc: (因喜悅、痛苦、焦慮等而)狂亂的: ~ *cries for help;* 狂呼求救; *drive sb* ~. 使某人狂亂。**fran·ti·cally** /-klɪ; -kl̩ɪ/ *adv*

fra·ter·nal /frəˈtɜːnl; frəˈtɝnl̩/ *adj* brotherly: 兄弟般的: ~ *love.* 手足之情。**~ly** /-nəlɪ; -nl̩ɪ/ *adv*

fra·ter·nity /frəˈtɜːnətɪ; frəˈtɝnətɪ/ *n* (*pl* -ties) **1** [U] brotherly feeling. 手足之情;友愛;博愛。**2** [C] society of men, eg monks, who treat each other as equals; men who are joined together by common interests: 彼此平等相待的團體(如修道團體);爲共同利益而結合的團體: *the ~ of the Press,* newspaper writers. 報界同人。 **3** [C] (US) society of students, with branches in various colleges, usu with names made up of Greek letters. (美)大學中的兄弟會(通常以希臘字母爲名)。⇨ sorority.

frat·er·nize /ˈfrætənaɪz; ˈfrætɚˌnaɪz/ *vi* [VP2A, C, 3A] ~ ***(with),*** become friendly (with): 變爲友善;與…友善: *Men from the two armies stopped fighting and ~d on Christmas Day.* 兩軍的士兵於聖誕節停止交戰並友善地交往。 **frat·er·niz·ation** /ˌfrætənaɪˈzeɪʃn *US:* -nɪˈz-; ˌfrætɚnɪˈzeʃən/ *n*

frat·ri·cide /ˈfrætrɪsaɪd; ˈfrætrəˌsaɪd/ *n* [C, U] (person guilty of) wilful killing of one's brother or sister. 殺害兄弟或姊妹;殺害兄弟或姊妹者。

Frau /fraʊ; fraʊ/ *n* (*pl* Frauen /ˈfraʊən; ˈfraʊən/) (G) (of a German wife or widow) Mrs; German woman. (德)(指德國婦人或寡婦)太太(冠於姓名前);德國婦人。

fraud /frɔːd; frɔd/ *n* **1** [U] criminal deception; [C] act of this kind: 詐欺;詐欺的行爲: *get money by ~.* 騙得錢。 **2** [C] person or thing that deceives: 詐欺者;行騙的人;騙人的事物: *This hair-restorer is a ~; I'm as bald as ever.* 這生髮劑是騙人的玩意,我還是和從前一樣的禿頂。**~u·lent** /ˈfrɔːdjʊlənt *US:* -dʒʊ-; ˈfrɔdʒələnt/ *adj* acting with ~; deceitful; obtained by ~: 詐欺的;詐騙的;騙得的: *~ulent gains.* 騙得的財物。**~u·lent·ly** *adv*

fraught /frɔːt; frɔt/ *pred adj* **1** involving; attended by; threatening (unpleasant consequences): 牽涉…的;伴隨…的;預示…之惡兆的: *an expedition ~ with danger.* 充滿危險的探險。 **2** filled with: 充滿…的: ~ *with meaning.* 充滿意義的。

Fräu·lein /ˈfrɔɪlaɪn; ˈfrɔɪlaɪn/ *n* (G) (of an unmarried German woman) Miss; German spinster. (德)(指未婚德國女子)小姐(冠於姓名前);德國未婚女子。

fray[1] /freɪ; fre/ *n* (lit, fig) fight; contest: (字面,喻)打鬥;爭吵;爭辯: *eager for the ~.* 急欲爭鬪。

fray[2] /freɪ; fre/ *vt, vi* [VP6A, 2A, C] (of cloth, rope, etc) become worn, make worn, by rubbing so that there are loose threads: (指布、繩等)磨破;磨損: *~ed cuffs,* eg on a coat sleeve; 磨破了的袖口; (fig) become strained; become exasperated: (喻)變得緊張;變得惱怒: *~ed nerves/tempers.* 神經緊張(脾氣急躁)。

frazzle /ˈfræzl; ˈfræzl̩/ *n* exhausted state: 疲憊不堪: *worn to a ~.* 身心疲憊的。

freak /friːk; frik/ *n* **1** abnormal or unusual idea, act or occurrence: 怪誕的思想、行動或事件: (attrib) (形容用法) *a ~ storm.* 極其反常的暴風。 **2** (also 亦作 ˌ**~ of ˈnature**) person, animal or plant that is abnormal in form, eg a five-legged sheep. 畸形的人、動物或植物(例如五隻腿的羊)。□ *vi, vt* [VP2C, 15B] ~ ***out,*** (sl) (cause to) have an intense emotional experience as from hallucinatory drugs. (俚)(使)感到非常興奮(如服用迷幻藥後)。Hence, 由此產生, ˈ**~-out** *n* **~·ish** /-ɪʃ; -ɪʃ/ *adj* abnormal: 不正常的: *~ish behaviour.* 怪異的行爲。 **~·ish·ly** *adv* **~·ish·ness** *n* **~y** *adj* = ~ish.

freckle /ˈfrekl; ˈfrɛkl̩/ *n* one of the small light-brown spots on the human skin; (*pl*) such spots on the face and hands caused by sunburn. 雀斑; (複)面部和手因日曬而生的斑點。□ *vt, vi* [VP6A, 2A] (cause to) become covered with ~s: (使)生雀斑或斑點: *a ~d forehead.* 生有雀斑的額頭。*Some people ~ more easily than others.* 有些人較他人易生斑點。

free[1] /friː; fri/ *adj* (freer /ˈfriːə(r); ˈfriɚ/, freest /ˈfriːɪst; ˈfriɪst/) **1** (of a person) not a slave; not in the power of another person or other persons; not in prison; having personal rights and social and political liberty: (指人)自由的;不受別人控制的;不在獄中的;有個人權利及社交和政治自由的: *The prisoners were pardoned and set ~.* 那些囚犯獲赦並被釋放。*Were the Pyramids built by slave labour or by ~ labour?* 金字塔是由奴隸的勞工還是自由勞工築成的? ⇨ also ~ labour below. 亦參看下列之 ~ labour. ˈ**~·born** *adj* inheriting liberty and rights of citizenship. 生而自由的。ˈ**~·man** /-mən; -mən/ *n* (*pl* -men) person who is not a slave or a serf. 自由人;自由民。⇨ also ~man at (9) below. 亦參看下列第9義之 freeman。 **2** (of a State, its citizens, and institutions) not controlled by a foreign government; having representative government in which private rights are respected: (指國家、國民、機關)非由外國政府管轄的;自主的: *~ democracies;* 自由民主國家; *Ruritania, the land of the ~.* 理想國,自由人民的國家。 **3** not fixed or held back; able to move about without hindrance; unrestricted; not controlled by rules, regulations or conventions: 鬆的;可不受阻礙而移動的;不受約束的;無拘束的;隨便的: *leave one end of the rope ~,* loose; 放鬆繩子的一端; ~ *hydrogen,* not combined with another element. 游離氫。*You are ~ to go or stay as you please.* 去或留隨你的便。*Please feel ~ to ask questions.* 請隨便發問。*She is not ~ to marry,* cannot do so, eg because she has to look after her parents. 她不能結婚(例如因爲必須照顧雙親)。*One of the parts has worked ~,* become loose, out of position. 有一部分鬆脫了。***allow sb/give sb/have a ~ hand,*** permission or discretion to do what seems best without consulting others. 給予某人(有)處理的自由。ˌ**~ ˈagent** *n* person who is ~ to act without restrictions. 行動不受限制者。ˌ**~-and-ˈeasy** *adj* unceremonious. 不拘禮的。ˌ**F~ ˈChurch,** *n* **(a)** nonconformist Church. 非國教派教會。**(b)** Church not under State control. 獨立教會。ˌ**~ ˈenterprise** *n* the conduct of trade and industry with the minimum of State control. 自由企業(工商業之經營不受國家控制)。ˌ**~ ˈfall** *n* fall from an aircraft at a great height without use of a parachute (until this is needed): 自由降落(高空跳傘時跳傘者最初不將傘打開,至必要時始打開): *a ~-fall parachutist.* 自由降落的跳傘者。 ˌ**~ˈfight,** one in which anyone present may join; one without rules. 在場的任何人皆可參加的打鬪;混戰。ˈ**~-for-all** *n* dispute, quarrel, etc in which all are allowed to express their views, fight for their own points of view, etc. 可自由參加的爭辯等。ˈ**~·hand** *adj* (of drawings) done by hand with easy movements, no rules, compasses or other instrument being used: (指繪畫)憑手畫的(不藉儀器的): *a ~hand sketch.* 手畫的略圖。 ˌ**~-ˈhanded** *adj* generous; giving and spending money generously. 慷慨的;出手大方的。ˈ**~·hold** *n* (legal) (holding of) land in absolute ownership. (法律)完全保有的土地;土地之完全保有。⇨ *leasehold* at lease. ˈ**~·holder** *n* person who possesses ~hold estate. 地產之完全保有人。ˈ**~ house** *n* (GB) public-house not controlled by a brewery, and able, for this reason, to stock and sell all brands of beer, etc. (英)售賣各種酒的酒店(未受某家酒廠特約,可售賣各種牌子的酒)。⇨ *tied house* at tie[2]. ˌ**~ ˈkick** *n* (football) kick allowed for a penalty without opposition from any other player. (足球)罰自由球。ˌ**~ ˈlabour** *n* workers not belonging to trade unions. 不屬於工會的工人。⇨ 1 above. 參看上列第1義。ˈ**~·lance** /-lɑːns *US:* -læns; -ˈlæns/ *n* **(a)** (in the Middle Ages) soldier ready to serve anyone for pay. (中世紀之)傭兵。**(b)** independent journalist, writer, etc earning his living by selling his services, wherever he can. 藉到處出賣文稿等爲生的自由記者、

作者等。□ *vi* work in this way: 做自由寫作者: *He gave up his regular job in order to ~lance.* 他放棄了他固定的工作以便做自由投稿的寫作者。 ˌ**~-ˈliver** *n* person who indulges ~ly in (esp) food and drink; 縱情享受(尤指吃喝)的人; hence, 由此產生, ˌ**~-ˈliving** *adj, n* [U]. ˌ**~-ˈload** *vi* [VP2A] (sl) (俚) = sponge(3); hence, 由此產生, ˌ**~-ˈloader** *n.* ˌ**~ ˈlove** *n* [U] (old use) agreed sexual relations without marriage. (舊用法)自由性愛(同意無須結婚而發生性關係)。ˈ**~ port** *n* port open to all traders alike, with no trade restrictions, taxes, import duties, etc. 自由港。ˌ**~-ˈrange** *adj* (of poultry) allowed to range freely (contrasted with *battery* birds). (指家禽) 自由散居的 (以別於飼養於固定房舍內者)。ˌ**~ ˈspeech** *n* [U] right to speak in public without interference from the authorities. 言論自由。ˌ**~-ˈspoken** *adj* not concealing one's opinions; speaking or spoken frankly. 坦白的;直言的。ˌ**~-ˈstanding** *adj* not supported; standing independently so that it may be viewed from all sides. 不需要支持物的;獨立的(故自四方皆可觀賞)。ˈ**~·stone** *n* [U] easily sawn sandstone and limestone. 易鋸斷的砂石或石灰石;軟石。ˈ**~·style** *n* [U] (swimming) race where the competitors choose their own stroke, usually the crawl. (游泳)自由選擇方式的比賽(通常爲自由式)。ˌ**~-ˈthinker** *n* person not accepting traditional religious teaching, but basing his ideas on reason. 不接受傳統宗教信仰而根據理智思考的人;自由思想者。 Hence, 由此產生, ˌ**~-ˈthinking** *adj,* ˌ**~-ˈthought** *n* [U]. ˌ**~-ˈtrade** *n* [U] trade not hindered by customs duties to restrict imports or protect home industries; 自由貿易 (不以關稅限制進口貨或保護國內工業之貿易); hence, 由此產生, ˌ**~-ˈtrader** *n* supporter of this principle. 贊成自由貿易者。ˌ**~ transˈlation** *n* not word for word, but giving the general meaning. 意譯。ˌ**~ ˈverse** *n* [U] without regular metre and rhyme. 自由體詩。ˈ**~-way** *n* (US) highway with several lanes; expressway. (美) 高速公路。 ˌ**~-ˈwheel** *vi* [VP2A, C] move along on a bicycle with the pedals at rest (as when going downhill); (fig) act or live without effort or constraint. 不踩踏板任脚踏車滑行(如下坡時); (喻) 不費力或無約束地行動或生活。 ˌ**~ ˈwill** *n* [U] individual's power of guiding and choosing his actions (subject to limitations of the physical world, social environment, and inherited characteristics): 自由意志: *do sth of one's own ~ will,* without being required or compelled. 自願做某事。ˈ**~·will** *adj* voluntary: 自願的: *a ~will offering.* 自願的奉獻。 **4** ***~ from,*** without: 無…的: *~ from blame/error/anxiety;* 不會受責難(無錯誤, 無憂慮)的; released or exempt from: 免去…的: *~ from the ordinary regulations.* 免去通常規則的。***~ of,*** **(a)** outside: 在…之外: *as soon as the ship was ~ of the harbour.* 當船剛剛出港後。**(b)** without: 無…的: *a harbour ~ of ice.* 不凍港。*At last I am ~ of her,* have got away from her. 我終於離開了她。 **5** without payment; costing nothing: 免費的: *~ tickets for the theatre;* 免費戲票; *give sth away ~;* 免費贈送某物; *50p post ~,* 50p including cost of postage; 五十辨士, 郵費在內; *admission ~;* 免費入場; *~ of income tax,* on which income tax need not be paid, or has been paid in advance (eg dividends on shares). 免所得稅(不需付所得稅, 或已預付過所得稅, 例如股息)。 ***(get sth) for ~,*** (colloq) without charge or payment. (俗)不要錢; 免費(獲得某物)。 ˈ**~-list** *n* **(a)** list of persons (to be) admitted ~, eg to a theatre or concert-hall. 准許免費入場者(例如戲院或音樂廳的優待者)之名單。**(b)** list of goods (to be) admitted ~ of customs duties. 免稅貨物表。ˌ**~ ˈpass** *n* authority to travel etc without paying. (旅行等的)免費乘車證;免票證。ˌ**~ on ˈboard,** (abbr 略作 **fob**) (comm) where the exporter pays all the charges for putting the goods onto the ship. (商)船上交貨;出口港離岸交貨(出口商負擔貨物上船費用)。 **6** (of place or time) not occupied or engaged; not being used; (of persons) not having time occupied; not doing anything: (指地點或時間)未被佔用的; 空着的;(指人)有空的; 閒着的: *There will be no rooms ~ in the hotel until after the holidays.* 旅館的房間要在假期過後才有空。*Her afternoons are usually ~.* 她下午通常有空。*She is usually ~ in the afternoon(s).* 她通常下午閒着。***have one's hands ~,*** **(a)** have them empty, not being used. 手空着。**(b)** be in a position to do as one likes; have no work or duties that demand attention. 可以自由行動; 沒有需要料理的工作或職務。⇨ *be tied up* at tie². **7** coming or given readily; lavish; profuse: 隨時有的;慷慨的;豐富的: *a ~ flow of water;* 水的暢流; *~ with his money;* 他用錢豪爽; *~ bloomers,* plants that have a large number of blooms. 多花的植物。*He is very ~ with his advice,* willingly gives plenty of advice. 他很喜歡勸告別人。 **8** without restraint: 無拘束的: *He is somewhat ~ in his conversation,* not quite as proper or decent as he ought to be. 他講話有點隨便(講話有些放肆)。 ***make ~ with sth/sb,*** use property, persons as if they were one's own: 隨意使用他人之物;對某人隨便: *He seems to have made ~ with my whisky while I was away.* 在我離開時, 他好像隨便飲用了我的威士忌。 *He is/makes rather too ~ with the waitresses/the wives of his friends,* is too familiar or impudent in his behaviour. 他對女侍(朋友之妻)有些放肆。 **9** ***make sb ~ of,*** give him the right to share in the privileges *of* a company, citizenship *of* a city; give him the unrestricted use *of* one's library, etc. 給予某人分享公司特權或市民資格之權利; 讓某人任意利用書房等。**~·man** /-mən ; -mən/ *n* (*pl* -men) one who has been given the privileges of a city, usu a distinguished person. 享有市民特權的人;市民;榮譽市民。⇨ 1 above. 參看上列第 1 義。**~·ly** *adv* in a ~ manner; readily. 自由地;直率地;隨意地;爽快地。

free² /friː ; fri/ *vt* (*pt, pp* freed /friːd ; frid/) [VP6A, 14] ***~ (from/of),*** make free (*from*); rid (*of*); set at liberty: 使自由;免除;釋放: *~ an animal from a trap;* 自一陷阱釋放一動物; *~ a country of cholera;* 使一國家免受霍亂之災; *~ oneself from debt.* 還淸債務。**freed·man** /ˈfriːdmən ; ˈfridmən/ *n* (*pl* -men) slave set free. 被解脫奴隸身份的人。

free·booter /ˈfriːbuːtə(r) ; ˈfriˌbutɚ/ *n* pirate; buccaneer. 海盜。

free·dom /ˈfriːdəm ; ˈfridəm/ *n* [U] condition of being free (all senses); [C] particular kind of ~: 自由;自主;無拘束;免除;率直;隨便;特權;出入權;使用權: *the four ~s,* ~ of speech, ~ of religion, ~ from fear, ~ from want; 四大自由(言論自由、信仰自由、免於恐懼的自由、不虞匱乏的自由); *give slaves their ~;* 還給奴隸以自由; *give sb ~ to do what he thinks best;* 給某人隨意處理事務的自由; *speak with ~,* without constraint, fearing nothing; 侃侃而言;直言; *the ~ of the seas,* (in international law) the right of ships of neutral countries to sail the seas without interference from warships of countries at war;(國際公法)戰時中立國船隻之自由航海權; *give a friend the ~ of one's house/library,* allow him to use it freely. 讓朋友隨便使用自己的房屋(書房)。***give sb/receive the ~ of a town/city,*** full rights of citizenship (as an honour for distinguished services). 給某人(接受)市民權(作爲卓越貢獻的榮譽)。

Free·mason /ˈfriːmeɪsn ; ˈfriˌmesn̩/ *n* member of a secret society (with branches in many parts of Europe and America) for mutual help and fellowship. 互助會(在歐美有許多地方有分會的一種互濟的祕密結社)會員。**~ry** *n* [U] system and institutions of the ~s; **(f~ry)** instinctive sympathy between people of similar interests, the same sex: 互助會之制度;(旨趣相同或同性別的人之間的)本然的同情共鳴;默契: *the f~ry of the Press.* 報界的默契。

free·sia /ˈfriːzɪə *US:* ˈfriːʒə ; ˈfriʒə/ *n* kinds of

flowering bulbous plant. 鳶尾科植物。

freeze /friːz ; friz/ *vt, vi* (*pt* froze /frəʊz ; froz/, *pp* frozen /ˈfrəʊzn ; ˈfrozn̩/) **1** [VP2A, C] (impers) be so cold that water turns into ice: (無人稱用法)冷至結冰;酷寒: *It was freezing last night.* 昨夜天氣酷寒。*What freezing weather!* 多麼冷的天氣啊! *It froze hard yesterday.* 昨天的天氣眞冷。 **ˈ~ing-point** *n* temperature at which a liquid (esp water) turns solid. (液體的)凝固點;(尤指水的)冰點。 **2** [VP2A, C] ~ ***(over/up)***, (of water) become ice; (of other liquids) become solid; (of other substances) become hard or stiff from cold: (指水)結冰;(指其他物質)凍結: *Water ~s when the temperature falls below 0°C (32°F).* 當溫度降至攝氏零度(華氏32度)以下時,水會結冰。*The lake froze over,* became covered with ice. 湖面全結了冰。 ***make one's ˈblood ~***, fill one with terror. 令人戰慄。 **3** [VP2A, C] be or feel very cold: 冰冷;感覺很冷: *I'm freezing.* 我覺得很冷。*Two of the men froze to death,* died of cold. 有兩個人凍死了。 **4** [VP6A, 15B] ~ ***(over/up)***, make cold; make hard; cover with ice: 使冷;使凍結;使結冰;覆以冰: *frozen food,* preserved by being kept very cold, 冰凍的食物;冷藏的食物, ⇨ *refrigeration* at refrigerate; *frozen roads,* with the surface of mud, snow, etc hardened by frost. 結凍的道路。*The lake was frozen over.* 湖面全結了冰。*If this frost lasts the ships in the harbour will be frozen in,* be fast in the ice. 如果這種嚴寒的天氣繼續下去,港內的船隻將被冰封住。 ~ ***one's blood***, fill one with terror. 使人戰慄。 **ˈfreezing-mixture** *n* one of salt, snow, etc used to ~ liquids. 冷凍劑(鹽、雪等之混合物,以冷凍液體者)。 **5** [VP6A] (fin) make assets, credits, etc temporarily or permanently unable to be exchanged for money; stabilize prices, wages: (財政)封存;凍結(財產、存款等);穩定(價格、工資): *ˈprice-ˌfreezing* and *ˈwage-ˌfreezing* (as methods to cure inflation). 平定物價與穩定工資(作爲防止通貨膨脹的方法)。 **6** [VP 15B] ~ ***sb out***, (colloq) exclude him from business, society, etc by competition, cold behaviour, etc. (俗)(以競爭、冷淡態度等)逼走某人。 **7** [VP2C] ~ ***on to sth***, (colloq) take or keep a very tight hold of it. (俗)緊握;緊執某物。 **8** [VP2A, C] become motionless, eg of an animal that stands quite still to avoid attracting attention. 不動(例如動物爲避免引起注意而靜立)。[VP2C] ~ ***up***, (of an actor) be unable to speak, move, etc on the stage. (指演員)在舞臺上說不出話或做不出動作;穿梆。□ *n* **1** period of freezing weather. 冰凍期;嚴寒期。 **2** (fin) severe control, stabilization, of incomes, wages, dividends, etc: (財政)穩定(收入、工資、股息等): *a ˈwage-~.* 穩定工資。 **3** ˌ**deep-ˈ~**, (part of a) refrigerator where a very low temperature is used. 冰箱;冰箱之冷凍庫。⇨ also *deep-freeze* at deep².

freezer /ˈfriːzə(r) ; ˈfrizɚ/ *n* (part of a) refrigerator or room for storing food etc at a very low temperature for a long time. 冰箱;冰庫;冷凍庫。

freight /freɪt ; fret/ *n* [U] (money charged for) the carriage of goods from place to place by water (in US also by land); the goods carried. 貨物之水上運輸 (美國亦指陸上運輸); 運費; 運輸的貨物。 **ˈ~-liner** *n* liner-train, ⇨ liner(2). 長途快速貨運火車。 **ˈ~-train** *n* (US) goods train, ⇨ goods(2). (美)貨運火車。□ *vt* [VP6A, 14] ~ ***(with)***, load (a ship) with cargo; send or carry (goods): 裝貨於(船);運輸(貨物): *a ship ~ed with wheat;* 載小麥的船;~ *a boat with fruit.* 將水果裝在船上。 **~er** *n* ship or aircraft that carries mainly ~ (cargo). 貨船;運貨機。

French /frentʃ ; frɛntʃ/ *adj* of France or the people of France. 法國的;法國人的。 ***take ~ leave***, do sth, go away, without asking permission or giving notice. 未經許可而貿然做某事;不辭而別。 ˌ~ **ˈbread/ˈloaf** *n* long, thin, crisp, light, white bread/loaf. 法國麵包。ˌ~ **ˈdressing** *n* [U, C] salad dressing of oil and vinegar. 法國式生菜調味品(有油和醋)。ˌ~ **ˈfries** *n pl* (US) potato chips. (美)炸馬鈴薯條。ˌ~ **ˈhorn** *n* brass wind instrument. 法國號;圓喇叭(一種銅管樂器)。⇨ the illus at brass. 參看 brass 之挿圖。ˌ~ **ˈletter** *n* (GB colloq) protective sheath. (英俗)保險套。⇨ sheath(2). ˌ~ **ˈwindow** *n* one that is both a window and a door, opening on to a garden or balcony. 落地窗。⇨ the illus at window. 參看 window 之挿圖。□ *n* the ~ language. 法語;法文。 **ˈ~·man** /-mən ; -mən/ **ˈ~·woman** *nn* man/woman of ~ birth or nationality. 法國男人;法國女人。

fren·etic /frəˈnetɪk ; frəˈnɛtɪk/ *adj* frenzied; frantic. 狂亂的;發狂的。

frenzy /ˈfrenzɪ ; ˈfrɛnzɪ/ *n* [U] violent excitement: 狂亂;極爲激動: *in a ~ of despair/enthusiasm;* 在一陣絕望(熱情)的狂亂中; *rouse an audience to absolute ~.* 使聽衆極爲激動。 **fren·zied** /ˈfrenzɪd ; ˈfrɛnzɪd/ *adj* driven to ~; wildly excited. 狂亂的;狂暴的。 **fren·zied·ly** *adv*

fre·quency /ˈfriːkwənsɪ ; ˈfrikwənsɪ/ *n* **1** [U] frequent occurrence: 時常發生;頻繁: *the ~ of earthquakes in Japan.* 日本地震之頻繁。 **2** [C] (*pl* -cies) rate of occurrence; number of repetitions (in a given time): 頻率;週率;發生次數(在某一時間內): *a ~ of 25 per second,* eg of an alternating electric current. (如交流電之)每秒 25 頻率。

fre·quent¹ /frɪˈkwent ; frɪˈkwɛnt/ *vt* [VP6A] go often to (a place); be often found in or at: 常去(一地點);常在…見到: *Frogs ~ wet places.* 青蛙常在濕地見到。*He no longer ~s bars.* 他不再常去酒吧了。

fre·quent² /ˈfriːkwənt ; ˈfrikwənt/ *adj* often happening; habitual: 時常發生的;慣常的: *Hurricanes are ~ here in autumn.* 在秋天此地時常有颶風。*He's a ~ visitor.* 他是常來的客人。 **~·ly** *adv* often: 時常地: *~ly occurring hurricanes.* 時常發生的颶風。

fresco /ˈfreskəʊ ; ˈfrɛsko/ *n* (*pl* ~s, ~es /-kəʊz ; -koz/) **1** [U] pigment applied to moist plaster surfaces and allowed to dry; method of painting with this pigment: 壁畫顏料;壁畫法: *painting in ~.* 作壁畫。 **2** [C] picture painted in this way: 壁畫; 用壁畫法作成之畫: *the ~(e)s in the Sistine Chapel, Rome.* 羅馬西斯汀教堂中的壁畫。□ *vt* paint (a wall, etc) in ~. 用壁畫法作畫於(牆壁等)。

fresh /freʃ ; frɛʃ/ *adj* (-er, -est) **1** newly made, produced, gathered, grown, arrived, etc: 新做的;新鮮的;新到的: ~ *flowers/fruit/eggs/milk;* 新鮮的花(水果,蛋,牛奶); ~ *paint* (= still wet); 剛刷上的漆; *a man ~ from the country;* 剛從鄉間來的人; *a boy ~ from school,* who has only recently finished his school course. 剛從學校畢業的男孩子。⇨ stale; ⇨ *faded* at fade. **ˈ~·man** /-mən ; -mən/ *n* (*pl* -men) student in his first year at a college or university. 大學一年級學生。 **2** (of food) not salted, tinned or frozen: (指食物)未加鹽的;未保存在罐頭中的;未冰凍的: ~ *butter/meat;* 淡牛油(鮮肉); (of water) not salt; not sea-water. (指水)淡的。 **ˈ~·water** *adj* of ~ water, not of the sea: 淡水的: *~water fish;* 淡水魚; *~water fishermen.* 在淡水捕魚的人。 **3** new or different: 新奇的;不同的: *Is there any ~ news?* 有什麼新的消息嗎? *Take a ~ sheet of paper and start again.* 另外拿一張紙重新開始。 *He didn't throw much ~ light* (= give much new information) *on the subject.* 關於這問題他沒有提供很多新的見解或資料。 ***break ~ ground***, (fig) start sth new, find new facts. (喻)開新園地;着手新事業;尋求新事實。 **4** (of the air, wind, weather) cool; refreshing: (指空氣、風、天氣)涼爽的;清新的: *go out for some ~ air;* 出外呼吸新鮮空氣; *in the ~ air,* out of doors. 在戶外。 ~ ***breeze/wind***, blowing rather strongly. 涼爽的風;清風。 **5** bright and pure: 鮮艷的: ~ *colours;* 鮮艷的顏色; bright and pure in colour: 氣色好的: *a ~ complexion.* 氣色好的面容。 **6** (US colloq) presumptuous, impudent (esp towards sb of the opposite sex): (美俗)鹵莽的；無禮的(尤指對於異性): *Tell that young man not to get/be so ~ with your sister.* 告訴那個年輕人不要對你的姊妹(妹妹)如此無禮。□ *adv* (in hyphened compounds) ~ly, newly: (用於加有連字號的複合字中)新近地: *~-caught fish;* 方才捕到的魚; *~-killed meat;* 新鮮肉; *~-painted doors.* 新漆的門。**~·ly** *adv* (only with *pp*, without hyphen) recently: (僅與過去分詞連用，無連字號)新近地: *~ly picked peaches.* 新採下來的桃子。**~er** *n* = ~man. **~·ness** *n*

freshen /ˈfreʃn ; ˈfrɛʃən/ *vi, vt* [VP2A, C, 6A, 15B] **~ (up),** become or make fresh; revive: 使新鮮；變為新鮮；(使)復活: *feel ~ed up after a shower;* 淋浴後感到舒暢; *~ a drink,* add more to it; 加添飲料; *the breeze ~ed,* grew stronger. 風力增强。

fret[1] /fret ; frɛt/ *vi, vt* (-tt-) **1** [VP2A, C, 3A, 15A] worry; (cause to) be discontented or bad-tempered: 煩惱；(使)不滿或煩躁: *What are you ~ting about?* 你為何煩躁不安? *Don't ~ over trifles.* 勿為瑣事煩惱。*She ~s at even the slightest delays.* 稍微晚一點她都要發脾氣(着急)。*Small babies often ~ in hot weather.* 天熱時嬰兒常煩躁。*She'll ~ herself to death one of these days.* 不久她會急死。**2** [VP6A] wear away by rubbing or biting at: 磨損；侵蝕: *a horse ~ting its bit;* 咬著口銜的馬; *~ted rope;* 磨損了的繩子; *a channel ~ted through the rock by a stream.* 溪流侵蝕岩石而成的水道。□ *n* state of irritation or querulousness: 急躁；煩躁；牢騷滿腹: *in a ~.* 焦急地；煩躁地。**~·ful** /-fl ; -fəl/ *adj* discontented; irritable: 不滿的；煩躁的: *a ~ful baby.* 煩躁的嬰兒。**~·fully** /-fəlɪ ; -fəlɪ/ *adv*

fret[2] /fret ; frɛt/ *vt* (-tt-) [VP6A] decorate (wood) with patterns made by cutting or sawing. 以格子細工裝飾(木)。**ˈ~·saw** *n* very narrow saw, fixed in a frame, for cutting designs in thin sheets of wood. 細工鋸；鋼絲鋸。**ˈ~·work** *n* [U] work in decorative patterns; wood cut with such patterns by using a ~saw. 格子細工；凸花細工；飾有格子細工之木。

fret[3] /fret ; frɛt/ *n* one of the metal ridges set at intervals across the fingerboard of a guitar, banjo, etc to act as a guide for the fingers to press the strings at the correct place. (吉他、班究琴等指板上的)柱；馬；品。

Freud·ian /ˈfrɔɪdɪən ; ˈfrɔɪdɪən/ *adj* of the psychoanalytic theories of Sigmund Freud. 佛洛伊德之精神分析學說的。ˌ**~ ˈslip,** (colloq) instance when a speaker accidentally says something contrary to what was intended and which seems to reveal his true thoughts. (俗)偶然說出心中不欲講的話。

fri·able /ˈfraɪəbl ; ˈfraɪəbḷ/ *adj* easily crumbled. 易碎的。**fria·bil·ity** /ˌfraɪəˈbɪlətɪ ; ˌfraɪəˈbɪlətɪ/ *n*

friar /ˈfraɪə(r) ; ˈfraɪɚ/ *n* man who is a member of one of certain religious orders. 修道士。

fric·assee /ˈfrɪkəsiː ; ˌfrɪkəˈsi/ *n* [C, U] (dish of) meat or poultry cut up, fried or stewed, and served with sauce. 一種由細切之肉或雞煎成或燉成後加以醬汁的食品。□ *vt* /ˌfrɪkəˈsiː ; ˌfrɪkəˈsi/ make a ~ of. 將…製成上述之食品。

frica·tive /ˈfrɪkətɪv ; ˈfrɪkətɪv/ *adj, n* (phon) (consonant) produced with audible friction when the air is expelled through a narrowing of the air passage: (語音)由摩擦而產生的；摩擦子音: *The sounds /f, v, θ/ are ~s.* /f, v, θ/ 是摩擦子音。

fric·tion /ˈfrɪkʃn ; ˈfrɪkʃən/ *n* **1** [U] the rubbing of one thing against another, esp when this wastes energy. 摩擦。**2** [C, U] (instance of a) difference of opinion leading to argument and quarrelling: 不和；衝突: *political ~ between two countries;* 兩國間政治上的不和; *~(s) between parents and children.* 父母與子女間之衝突。

Fri·day /ˈfraɪdɪ ; ˈfraɪdɪ/ *n* sixth day of the week. 星期五；禮拜五。ˌ**Good ˈ~,** the ~ before Easter; the anniversary of the crucifixion of Jesus. 耶穌受難日(復活節前的星期五)。ˌ**man ˈ~,** (from the story of Robinson Crusoe) faithful servant. 忠僕(源自魯賓遜漂流記)。

fridge /frɪdʒ ; frɪdʒ/ *n* (abbr of) refrigerator. 冰箱 (refrigerator 之略)。

fried /fraɪd ; fraɪd/ *pt, pp* of fry.

friend /frend ; frɛnd/ *n* **1** person, not a relation, whom one knows and likes well: 朋友；友人: *We are great/good ~s.* 我們是好朋友。*He has been a good ~ to me.* 他一向是我的好朋友。***be ~s with,*** be a ~ of. 是…的朋友。***make ~s,*** become mutual ~s. 交上朋友；成為朋友。***make ˈ~s again,*** become ~s again after a disagreement, etc. 言歸於好。***make ˈ~s with; make a ˈ~ of,*** become the ~ of. 與…交朋友。**2** helpful thing or quality: 有幫助的東西或性質: *Among these wild young people, her shyness was her best ~.* 置身在這些放蕩的青年當中，她的羞怯給予她最大的幫助。**3** helper or sympathizer: 贊助者；同情者: *a good ~ of the poor.* 十分幫助貧民的人。**4 F~,** member of the Society of F~s; Quaker. 基督教教友派教徒。**~·less** *adj* having no ~s. 沒有朋友的。**~·less·ness** *n*

friend·ly /ˈfrendlɪ ; ˈfrɛndlɪ/ *adj* (-ier, -iest) acting, or ready to act, as a friend; showing or expressing kindness: 作為朋友而做出的；友善的；親切的: *be ~ with sb;* 對某人友善; *be ~ to a cause;* 贊助一主義; *a ~ smile;* 親切的微笑; *be on ~ terms with sb;* 與某人友好; *a ~ match/game,* one not played in competition for a prize, etc. 友誼賽。**ˈF~ Society,** one for the mutual benefit of its members, eg during illness, unemployment, old age. 互助會。**friend·li·ness** *n* [U] ~ feeling and behaviour. 友善；友好；親切。

friend·ship /ˈfrendʃɪp ; ˈfrɛndʃɪp/ *n* **1** [U] being friends; the feeling or relationship that exists between friends: 友愛；友情；友誼: *live together in ~;* 友善地生活在一起; *my ~ for her.* 我對她的友誼。**2** [C] instance or period of this feeling: 友情的實例；友誼期間: *a ~ of twenty years;* 二十年的友誼; *never to forget old ~s.* 永不忘記舊時的友情。

frieze /friːz ; friz/ *n* [C] ornamental band or strip along a wall (usu at the top), eg a horizontal band of sculpture on the outside of a building, or a strip of wallpaper with a special design just below the ceiling of a room. 壁緣(沿牆的飾帶，通常在牆的上端，例如建築物外部之雕刻的橫飾帶，或緊接天花板下，牆頭上印有圖案的一條壁紙)。⇨ the illus at column. 參看 column 之插圖。

frig·ate /ˈfrɪgət ; ˈfrɪgɪt/ *n* fast sailing-ship formerly used in war; (modern use) (GB) fast escort vessel; (US) medium sized warship. 舊時掛帆的快速戰艦；(近代用法)(英) 快速護航艦；巡防艦；(美)中型戰艦。

fright /fraɪt ; fraɪt/ *n* **1** [U] great and sudden fear: 驚駭: *die of ~;* 驚駭致死; *take ~ (at sth);* (因某事物)吃驚; [C] instance of this. 驚駭的實例。***give sb/get/have a ~.*** 使某人吃驚(感到吃驚)。**2** [C] (colloq) ridiculous-looking person or thing: (俗)怪樣子的人或物: *What a ~ you look in that old hat!* 你戴着那頂舊帽子樣子多麼可笑啊! □ *vt* (poet) frighten. (詩)使吃驚；使驚駭。

frighten /ˈfraɪtn ; ˈfraɪtṇ/ *vt* [VP6A, 15B, 14] fill with fright or terror; alarm suddenly: 使吃驚；使驚駭；使害怕: *Did the noise ~ you?* 那聲音使你吃驚嗎? *The barking of the dog ~ed the burglar away.* 狗吠聲將那竊賊嚇跑了。*She was nearly ~ed out of her life.* 她幾乎嚇死。***~ sb into/out of doing sth,*** cause him to do/not to do sth by ~ing him. 恐嚇某人做(不做)某事。**fright·ened** *adj* (colloq) afraid: (俗)害怕的: *be ~ed of sb or sth;* 害怕某人或某物; alarmed: 受驚的: *~ed at the idea of sth happening.* 想到某事之發生而驚恐。**~·ing** *adj* causing fright or terror: 可怕的；令人恐怖的: *a ~ing experience.* 可怕的經驗。

fright·ful /ˈfraɪtfl ; ˈfraɪtfəl/ *adj* **1** causing fear; dreadful: 可怕的；令人恐怖的: *a ~ accident.* 可怕的事故。**2** (colloq) very great; unpleasant: (俗)極

大的;討厭的: *a ~ mess;* 亂七八糟; *a ~ journey,* a very uncomfortable one. 一次極不舒服的旅行。**~ly** /-fəlɪ ; -fəlɪ/ *adv* **1** in a ~ way. 可怕地;令人恐怖地。**2** (colloq) very. (俗)非常地。**~·ness** *n*

frigid /ˈfrɪdʒɪd ; ˈfrɪdʒɪd/ *adj* **1** cold: 寒冷的: *a ~ climate;* 寒冷的氣候; *the ~ zones,* those within the polar circles. 寒帶。**2** unfriendly; without ardour or sympathy; apathetic: 無情的;冷淡的;缺乏情感的: *a ~ welcome;* 冷淡的歡迎; *a ~ manner;* 冷淡的態度;*~ conversation;* 冷淡的談話;*a ~ woman,* lacking in sexual desire. 性冷感的女人。**~·ly** *adv* **frigid·ity** /frɪˈdʒɪdətɪ ; frɪˈdʒɪdətɪ/ *n* [U].

frill /frɪl ; frɪl/ *n* **1** ornamental border on a dress, etc. (衣服等的)飾邊。**2** (*pl*) unnecessary adornments, eg to speech or writing; airs¹(6b), affectations. (複)矯飾(例如言語或寫作中者);裝腔作勢;虛飾。**frilled** *adj* having ~s(1): 有飾邊的: *a ~ed skirt.* 有飾邊的裙子。**frilly** *adj* having ~s; (colloq) too much ornamented. 有飾邊的;(俗)過份裝飾的。

fringe /frɪndʒ ; frɪndʒ/ *n* **1** ornamental border of loose threads, eg on a rug or shawl. (地毯或圍巾等之)鬚邊;縫;流蘇。**2** edge (of a crowd, forest, etc): (人群,森林等之)邊緣: *on the ~(s) of the forest.* 在森林之邊緣。ˈ**~ area,** area on the border of a district etc; (fig) less important area. 邊界地區;(喻)不太重要的地區。ˈ**~ benefits,** eg a rent-free house, the use of a car, additional to wages or salary. 額外的福利(例如除正式薪資外,尙有不收租金的房屋,可使用汽車等)。ˈ**~ group,** group of persons loosely attached to a larger group or party (but who may be rebellious or nonconformist in some respects); 邊緣團體;外圍團體(不太密切地隸屬於一較大團體或政黨,但在某些方面可能不一致行動); hence, 由此產生, ˌ~ ˈ*medicine/*ˈ*theatre,* etc. 輔藥(外圍戲院等)。**3** part of hair cut short and allowed to hang over the forehead. 額頭之垂髮;劉海。□ *vt* [VP6A] put a ~ on; be a ~ to: 加以縫;飾以邊;作爲…之邊緣: *a roadside ~d with trees.* 植有樹的路邊。

frip·pery /ˈfrɪpərɪ ; ˈfrɪpərɪ/ *n* [U] needless ornament, esp on dress; [C] (*pl* -ries) cheap ornament or useless trifle. 不需要的裝飾(尤指衣服上者);賤價的裝飾品;瑣屑無用之物。

Fris·bee /ˈfrɪzbiː ; ˈfrɪzbi/ *n* (P) piece of light plastic, shaped like a plate, thrown between players in a game. (商標)飛盤(一種擲著玩的塑膠盤)。

frisk /frɪsk ; frɪsk/ *vi, vt* **1** [VP2A, C] jump and run about playfully. 歡躍;雀躍。**2** [VP6A] pass the hands over (sb) to search for concealed weapons. 搜查(某人)有無私藏武器。**~y** *adj* lively; ready to ~: 活潑的;好歡躍的: *as ~y as a kitten.* 像小貓一樣活潑。ˈ**~·ily** /-ɪlɪ ; -ɪlɪ/ *adv*

fris·son /ˈfriːsɒn *US:* friːˈsɒn ; friˈsɑn/ *n* (F) emotional thrill: (法)震顫;戰慄: *a ~ of delight/horror.* 高興(害怕)得發抖。

frit·ter¹ /ˈfrɪtə(r) ; ˈfrɪtɚ/ *vt* [VP15B] ~ ***sth away,*** waste it on divided aims: 零碎地消耗: *~ away one's time/energy/money.* 零碎地消耗時間(精力,金錢)。

frit·ter² /ˈfrɪtə(r) ; ˈfrɪtɚ/ *n* [C] piece of fried batter, usu with sliced fruit in it. 油炸餅(通常以水果爲餡)。

frivol /ˈfrɪvl ; ˈfrɪvl̩/ *vi, vt* (-ll-) **1** [VP2A] behave in a silly, time-wasting way. 作無聊和浪費時間的行動。**2** [VP15B] ~ ***away,*** waste time, money, etc, foolishly. 浪費(時間,金錢等)。

friv·ol·ous /ˈfrɪvələs ; ˈfrɪvələs/ *adj* **1** not serious or important: 不莊重的;不重要的: *~ remarks/behaviour.* 不莊重的言語(舉動)。**2** (of persons) not serious; pleasure-loving. (指人)輕浮的;喜享樂的。**~·ly** *adv* **friv·ol·ity** /frɪˈvɒlətɪ ; frɪˈvɑlətɪ/ *n* **1** [U] ~ behaviour; lightness of character. 行爲不莊重;輕浮。**2** [C] (*pl* -ties) ~ act or utterance. 不莊重的行動或言語。

frizz /frɪz ; frɪz/ *vt* [VP6A] (of hair) form into masses of small curls. (指毛髮)使鬈曲。**~y** *adj* (of hair) ~ed. (指毛髮)鬈曲的。

frizzle¹ /ˈfrɪzl ; ˈfrɪzl̩/ *vt, vi* [VP6A, 2A] cook, be cooked, with a spluttering noise: 烹煎時發噝噝聲: *bacon frizzling in the pan.* 在鍋內煎至發噝噝聲的醃肉。

frizzle² /ˈfrɪzl ; ˈfrɪzl̩/ *vt, vi* [VP2C, 15B] ~ ***up,*** (of hair) twist in small, crisp curls. (指毛髮)鬈曲;使鬈曲。

fro /frəʊ ; fro/ *adv* ***to and fro,*** backwards and forwards: 往返地;來回地: *walking to and fro;* 來回地走; *journeys to and fro between London and Paris.* 倫敦與巴黎間往返的旅行。

frock /frɒk ; frɑk/ *n* **1** woman's or girl's dress. (女子的)洋裝。**2** monk's long gown with loose sleeves. 僧袍。**3** ˌ**~-ˈcoat** *n* long coat, usu with square corners, formerly worn by men in the 19th c (now replaced by the *morning-coat*). 十九世紀男子所穿的一種方領角的長外衣(現已被晨禮服所代替)。

frog /frɒg *US:* frɔːg ; frɑg/ *n* **1** small, cold-blooded, tailless jumping animal living in water and on land. 蛙。⇨ the illus at amphibian. 參看 amphibian 之插圖。ˈ**~·man** /-mən ; -mən/ *n* (*pl* -men) person skilled in swimming under water with the aid of flippers on the feet and breathing apparatus. 蛙人。ˈ**~·march** *vt* [VP6A] carry (a prisoner) away, face downwards, by four men holding his arms and legs. 蛙式抬運(令囚犯面向下,由四人執其四肢而抬運之)。**2** long button and loop for fastening to it, used to fasten cloaks, etc. (外衣等的)長扣;花扣。

a frogman

frolic /ˈfrɒlɪk ; ˈfrɑlɪk/ *vi* (*pt, pp* -ked) [VP2A, C] play about in a gay, lively way. 嬉戲。□ *n* [C] outburst of gaiety or merrymaking; wild or merry prank. 嬉戲;作樂。**~·some** /-səm ; -səm/ *adj* inclined to ~; playful and merry. 愛嬉戲的;歡樂的。

from /frəm ; frəm; *strong form:* frɒm ; frɑm/ *prep* **1** (used to introduce the place, point, person, etc that is the starting-point): 自;從(表示起點): *jump (down) ~ a wall;* 從牆上跳下; *travel ~ London to Rome;* 自倫敦旅行至羅馬; *bees going ~ flower to flower.* 逐花飛行的蜜蜂。**2** (used to indicate the starting of a period of time): 自;從(表示時期的起始): *~ the first of May;* 從五月一日起; *~ childhood;* 自童年起; *~ day to day;* 日復一日; *~ beginning to end.* 自始至終。**3** (used to indicate the place, object, etc whose distance, absence, etc is stated): 距;離: *ten miles ~ the coast;* 距海岸十哩; *stay away ~ school;* 缺課; *be/go away ~ home;* 離家; *far ~ blaming you,* not in any way doing so. 絕不責備你。**4** (showing the giver, sender, etc): 由…發出: *a letter ~ my brother;* 我哥哥(弟弟)的來信; *a present ~ his father.* 他父親給他的一件禮物。*Tell him ~ me that....* 替我轉告他…。**5** (art, showing the model, etc): (藝術,表示模倣的題材等): *painted ~ nature/life,* with the actual scene, object, etc in front of the artist. 寫生。**6** (showing the lower limit): (表示較低的限度): *We have good Italian wine ~ £1·50 a bottle,* at this price and at higher prices. 我們有好的義大利酒,售價自1·50鎊起。*There were ~ ten to fifteen boys absent.* 有十至十五個男孩子缺席。**7** (used to indicate the source from which sth is taken): 由(表示來源): *quotations ~ Shakespeare;* 由莎士比亞作品中引來的文句; *draw water ~ a well;* 由井中汲水; *draw* *conclusions ~ the evidence;* 由證據獲得結論; *judge ~ appearances;* 以貌取人;由外表看來; *~ this point of view.* 由此觀點。 **8** (showing the material, etc used in a process, the material being changed as a result): (表示原料等在製造過程中有所改變): *Wine is made ~ grapes.* 葡萄酒是用葡萄釀製的。*Steel is made ~ iron.* 鋼是鐵鍊成的。Cf 參較 *That bridge is made of steel.* 那座橋是用鋼建造的。 **9** (used to indicate separation, removal, prevention, escape, avoidance, deprivation, etc. ⇨ *v/n + ~*, in *v* and *n* entries): (表示分離,除去,阻止,逃避,避免,剝奪等;參看動詞及名詞各條中之*v/n*+~): *Take that knife (away) ~ the baby.* 將那刀子從那嬰兒身旁拿走。*When were you released ~ prison?* 你是什麼時候出獄的? *What prevented/stopped/hindered you ~ coming?* 何事阻止你前來? **10** (used to indicate change): (表示變化): *Things are going ~ bad to worse.* 事情愈來愈糟了。*The price has been increased ~ 20p to 25p.* 價格已由二十辨士增至二十五辨士。 **11** showing reason, cause or motive: 由於;因爲: *collapse ~ fatigue;* 累倒; *suffer ~ starvation and disease;* 因飢餓和疾病而受苦; *do sth ~ necessity, not ~ a sense of duty.* 因需要而做某事,並非由於責任感。*F~ his looks you might think him stupid.* 由外表看來你可能認爲他是愚蠢的。*F~ what I heard, the driver was to blame.* 就我所聽到的,駕駛人應受指責。 **12** (showing distinction or difference): (表示區別): *distinct/different ~ others;* 與其他者不同的; *to differ ~ others.* 與其他的不同。*How would you know an Englishman ~ an American?* 你怎樣分辨英國人和美國人? **13** (governing *advv* and *prep* phrases): (限制副詞和介詞片語): *seen ~ above/below;* 由上(下)而看; *looking at me ~ above/under her spectacles.* 她從眼鏡上面(下面)看我。

frond /frɒnd; frɑnd/ *n* leaf-like part of a fern or palm-tree. 羊齒植物或棕櫚等的複葉。

front /frʌnt; frʌnt/ *n* **1** ***the ~***, foremost or most important side: 正面;前面: *the ~ of a building,* that with the main entrance; 建築物的正面; *the east/west ~ of the Palace;* 宮殿之東(西)面; *sitting in the ~ of the class,* in one of the foremost rows facing the teacher 坐在班上前排 (cf 參較 *standing in ~ of the class,* facing the pupils 站在全班學生面前); (attrib): (形容用法): *a ~ seat;* 前排座; *the ~ garden;* 前花園; *a ~ room,* one in the ~ of a house; 前面的房間; *the ~ page of a newspaper,* page 1; 報紙的第一版; *~-page news,* news important enough for the ~ page; 登在第一版的重要新聞; *a seat in the ~ part of the train.* 火車前部的座位。***(be) in the ~ rank,*** (fig) (be) well known or important. (喻)著名;顯要。***come to the ~,*** (fig) become conspicuous, well known, etc. (喻)出名。***in ~*** *(adv)*, 在前面, ***in ~ of*** *(prep)*: 在…的前面: *Please go in ~.* 請在前面走。*There are some trees in ~ of the house.* 那房屋前有幾棵樹。 ˌ**~ 'runner** *n* (in an election, etc) person likely to win. (選舉等中) 可能獲勝者; 領先者。⇨ also bench, door. **2** [C] (war) part where the fighting is taking place: 前線;前方: *go/be sent to the ~;* 上前線; *a ~ of 500 miles;* 長達五百哩的前線; (fig) organized body or department of activity: (喻)有組織的團體或活動部門: *How are things on the domestic ~,* (colloq) at home? (俗)國內的情形如何? **3** road, promenade bordering the part of a town facing the sea; road or path bordering a lake: 城邊海濱之步道; 環湖的道路: *have a walk along the ('sea) ~;* 在海濱散步; *drive along the lake ~;* 駛車於湖濱; *a house on the ~,* facing the sea. 位於海濱的一所房屋。 **4** [U] ***have the ~ (to do sth),*** be impudent enough. 厚顏(做某事)。 ***put on/show/present a bold ~,*** face a situation with (apparent) boldness. (表面上)勇敢地面對某情況。 **5** **('shirt) ~,** breast of a shirt (esp the starched ~ part of a man's (dress) shirt). 襯衫的胸部(尤指男子襯衫漿硬的胸部)。 **6** (theatre) auditorium; part where the audience sits. (戲院)大廳。 **7** (met) boundary between masses of cold and warm air: (氣象)鋒(冷熱氣團間的交界面): *a cold/warm ~.* 冷(熱)鋒。 **8** (poet, rhet) forehead; face. (詩,修辭)額;面孔。 **9** apparent leader (**'~ man**) or group of persons (**'~ organization**) serving as a cover for the secret or illegal activities of an anonymous person or group. 秘密或不法活動份子的掩護人; 掩護機構; 幌子(亦稱 '~ man 或 '~ organization)。 □ *vt, vi* **1** [VP6A, 2A, C] face: 面向;朝: *hotels that ~ the sea;* 朝海的旅社; *windows ~ing the street;* 朝街的窗子; *a house ~ing north, ~ing upon/towards the lake.* 朝北(湖)的房子。 **2** [VP6A] (old use) confront; oppose: (舊用法)面對;對抗: *~ danger.* 面對危險。

front·age /'frʌntɪdʒ; 'frʌntɪdʒ/ *n* [C] extent of a piece of land or a building along its front, esp bordering a road or river: 土地或建築物之正面長度; 土地或建築物之前沿(尤指臨道路或河川者); 臨街面: *For sale, office buildings with ~s on two streets;* 面臨兩街之辦公大樓出售; *factory premises with a good river ~;* 廠房連同一片良好的面河的空地; *a building site with a road ~ of 500 metres.* 一塊建築用地,五百碼臨路。

frontal /'frʌntl; 'frʌntl/ *adj* of, on or to, the front: 正面的;在正面的;至正面的: *a ~ attack;* 正面攻擊; *full ~ nudity,* of the whole of the front of the body. 正面全部裸體。⇨ flank; rear.

fron·tier /'frʌntɪə(r) *US:* frʌn'tɪər; frʌn'tɪr/ *n* [C] **1** part of a country bordering on another country; (land on each side of a) boundary: 國境;邊疆;邊界: *a town on the ~;* 位於邊區的城市; (attrib) (形容用法) *~ disputes/incidents;* 邊疆的爭端(事件); (esp US, in the past) farthest part of a country to which settlement has spread, beyond which there is wild or unsettled land. (尤指昔時美國之)新開闢地。 **~s·man** /-zmən; -zmən/ *n* (*pl* -men) man who lives on a ~; pioneer in a newly settled district near the ~. 邊疆居民; 拓荒者。 **2** (fig) extreme limit: (喻)極限: *the ~s of knowledge;* 知識的極限; underdeveloped area (eg of scientific research). 未開發的領域(如科學研究方面者)。

front·is·piece /'frʌntɪspi:s; 'frʌntɪsˌpis/ *n* illustration placed opposite the title-page of a book. (書籍之)與書名頁相對的插畫;卷頭插畫。

frost /frɒst *US:* frɔ:st; frɔst/ *n* **1** [U] weather condition with temperature below the freezing-point of water; [C] occasion or period of such weather: 嚴寒的天氣; 溫度在冰點以下的天氣; 嚴寒期: *plants killed by ~;* 爲寒天所摧毀的植物; *ten degrees of ~;* 冰點下十度(華氏二十二度); *early ~s,* ie in autumn; 早寒(在秋季者); *late ~s,* ie in spring. 春寒。ˌ**Jack 'F~,** ~ personified. (擬人語)嚴寒。 **'~-bite** *n* [U] injury to tissue in the body from freezing. 凍瘡;凍傷。 **'~-bitten** *adj* having, suffering from, ~-bite. 被凍傷的;受凍傷的。 **'~-bound** *adj* (of the ground) made hard by ~. (指地)凍硬的。 **2** [U] white powder-like coating of frozen vapour on the ground, roofs, plants, etc: 霜: *'white/'hoar ~,* with this coating; 白霜; *'black ~,* without it. 無霜的酷寒;嚴寒。 **3** [C] (colloq) event which fails to come up to expectations or to arouse interest: (俗)未達期望或引不起興趣的事: *The party was a ~,* no one enjoyed it. 那聚會使人不感興趣。 □ *vt, vi* **1** [VP6A] cover with ~(2): 覆以霜: *~ed window-panes;* 覆有霜的窗玻璃; cover (a cake, etc) with finely powdered sugar. 以糖粉覆於(蛋糕等)之上。 **2** [VP6A] injure or kill (plants, etc) with ~(1). 凍壞或凍死(植物等)。 **3** [VP6A] give a roughened surface to (glass) to make it opaque: 給與(玻璃)不透明之面: *~ed glass.* 不透明的玻璃;磨砂玻璃;毛玻璃。 **4** [VP2A, C] *~ (over/up),* become covered with ~(2): 覆有霜; 結霜: *The windscreen of my car ~ed over during the* *night.* 我車子上的擋風玻璃夜裏結了霜。**~·ing** *n* [U] icing(1). 糖霜(覆於蛋糕上之糖與蛋白等的混合物)。

frosty /ˈfrɒstɪ *US:* ˈfrɔːstɪ ; ˈfrɔstɪ/ *adj* **1** cold with frost: 下霜的;嚴寒的: *~ weather;* 下霜的天氣; *a ~ morning.* 寒冷的早晨。 **2** (fig) unfriendly; without warmth of feeling: (喻)冷淡的;無情的: *~ smiles/looks;* 冷淡的笑(表情); *a ~ welcome.* 冷淡的歡迎。 **frost·ily** *adv* **frosti·ness** *n*

froth /frɒθ ; frɔθ/ *n* [U] **1** creamy mass of small bubbles; foam: 泡沫: *a glass of beer with a lot of ~ on it.* 有許多泡沫的一杯啤酒。 **2** light, worthless talk or ideas. 膚淺的談話或觀念。□ *vi* [VP2A, C] have, give off, ~: 起泡沫: *A rabid dog may ~ at the mouth.* 瘋狗可能嘴流泡沫。**~y** *adj* (-ier, -iest) of, like, covered with, ~: 泡沫的;似泡沫的;起泡沫的: *~y beer/conversation.* 起泡沫的啤酒(膚淺的談話)。 **~·ily** /-ɪlɪ ; -əlɪ/ *adv* **~i·ness** *n*

fro·ward /ˈfrəʊəd ; ˈfroəd/ *adj* (old use) perverse; not easily controlled. (舊用法)剛愎的;頑强的。

frown /fraʊn ; fraʊn/ *vi* [VP2A, 3A] draw the eyebrows together, causing lines on the forehead (to express displeasure, puzzlement, deep thought, etc): 顰眉;皺眉頭;蹙額(表示不悅,迷惑,沉思等): *~ at sb.* 對某人顰眉。 *~* ***on/upon,*** disapprove of: 不贊成: *Gambling is very much ~ed upon here.* 此地十分反對賭博。□ *n* [C] ~ing look; drawing together of the eyebrows: 顰眉;皺眉頭;蹙額: *a ~ of disapproval.* 皺眉頭表示不贊成。*There was a deep ~ on his forehead.* 他深深皺着額頭。**~·ing·ly** *adv*

frowsty /ˈfraʊstɪ ; ˈfraʊstɪ/ *adj* (of the atmosphere of a room) warm and musty; fuggy. (指房間內的空氣)悶熱而有霉味的;污濁的。

frowzy /ˈfraʊzɪ ; ˈfraʊzɪ/ *adj* **1** ill-smelling; stuffy (like an overheated room). 臭的;悶氣的(如一過於悶熱的房間)。 **2** untidy; uncared for. 不整潔的;無人照管的。

froze, frozen ⇨ freeze.

fruc·tify /ˈfrʌktɪfaɪ ; ˈfrʌktəˌfaɪ/ *vt, vi* (*pt, pp* -fied) [VP6A, 2A] (formal) make or become fruitful or fertile. (正式用語)(使)結果實;(使)多產。 **fruc·ti·fi·ca·tion** /ˌfrʌktɪfɪˈkeɪʃn ; ˌfrʌktəfəˈkeʃən/ *n*

fru·gal /ˈfruːgl ; ˈfrugl/ *adj* ~ ***(of),*** careful, economical (esp *of* food, expenditure); costing little: 節儉的(尤指食物和開銷方面,可與 of 連用);儉省的;節約的: *a ~ meal;* 儉省的餐食; *a ~ housekeeper;* 節儉的女管家; *be ~ of one's time and money.* 儉省時間與金錢。 **~·ly** /-gəlɪ ; -glɪ/ *adv* **~·ity** /fruːˈgælətɪ ; fruˈgælətɪ/ *n* [U] being ~; [C] (*pl* -ties) instance of this. 節儉;儉省;節約。

fruit /fruːt ; frut/ *n* **1** [U] (collective *n*) that part of a plant or tree that contains the seeds and is used as food, eg apples, bananas; [C] kind of ~: (集合名詞)水果;一種水果: *People are eating more ~ than they used to.* 人們現在吃水果較以往爲多了。*F~ is expensive these days.* 水果近來很貴。*Is a tomato a ~?* 蕃茄是水果嗎? **ˈ~-cake** *n* rich cake containing dried currants, peel, etc. 含有葡萄乾,果皮等的餅糕;水果蛋糕。**ˈ~-fly** *n* (*pl* -flies) small fly that feeds on decaying ~. 果蠅(以腐爛果實爲食)。**ˈ~-knife** *n* one with an acid-proof blade, for cutting ~ at meals. 水果刀。**ˌ~ ˈsalad** *n* [U, C] (GB) various kinds of ~, cut up and mixed in a bowl, often served with cream; (US) jelly(2) prepared with pieces of fruit in it. (英)水果沙拉(各種水果混合一起食用);水果盅;(美)水果凍。 **2** [C] (bot) that part of any plant in which the seed is formed. (植物)果實。 **3** ***the ~s of the earth,*** those plant or vegetable products that may be used for food, including grain, etc. 可用作食物的植物或蔬菜產物(包括穀類等)。 **4** (fig, often *pl*) profit, result or reward (of labour, industry, study, etc): (喻,常用複數)收穫;成果: *the ~s of industry.* 勤苦的收穫。*I hope your hard work will bear ~.* 我希望你的辛苦工作會有收穫。*His knowledge is the ~ of long study.* 他的知識是長期求學的成果。 **5** **ˈ~-machine** *n* (GB colloq) coin-operated gambling machine. (英俗)吃角子老虎;由硬幣操縱的賭具。□ *vi* (of trees, bushes, etc) bear ~: (指樹木等)結果實: *These trees ~ well.* 這些樹結的果實很多。**~·erer** /ˈfruːtərə(r) ; ˈfrutərə/ *n* person who sells ~. 水果商。**~·ful** /-fl ; -fəl/ *adj* producing ~ or (fig) good results; productive: 結果實的;(喻)有良好結果的;多產的: *a ~ful career.* 成功的事業。*The last session of Parliament was particularly ~ful,* much useful work was accomplished. 上次國會開會特別成功(完成甚多有用的工作)。 **~·fully** /-fəlɪ ; -fəlɪ/ *adv* **~·ful·ness** *n* **~·less** *adj* without ~ or (fig) results or success; profitless: 不結果實的;無果實的;(喻)無結果的;失敗的;無收穫的: *~less efforts.* 徒勞。**~·less·ly** *adv* **~·less·ness** *n* **~y** *adj* **1** of or like ~ in smell or taste. 水果的;有水果香味的;有水果滋味的。 **2** (colloq) full of rough (often suggestive) humour: (俗)充滿不雅(常爲猥褻的)之戲謔的: *a ~y novel.* 充滿不雅之戲謔的小說。 **3** (colloq) rich; mellow; florid: (俗)豐腴的;圓潤的;華麗的: *a ~y voice.* 圓潤的聲音。

fru·ition /fruːˈɪʃn ; fruˈɪʃən/ *n* [U] realization of hopes; getting what was wanted: 希望之實現;達到願望: *aims brought to ~;* 實現了的目的; *plans that come to ~.* 完成的計畫。

frump /frʌmp ; frʌmp/ *n* person dressed in old-fashioned and dowdy clothes. 衣着舊式而邋遢的人。**~·ish** /-ɪʃ ; -ɪʃ/, **~y** *adjj*

frus·trate /frʌˈstreɪt *US:* ˈfrʌstreɪt ; ˈfrʌstret/ *vt* [VP6A, 15A] prevent (sb) from doing sth; prevent (sb's plans) from being carried out: 阻止(某人)做某事;破壞(某人的計畫): *~ an enemy in his plans/the plans of an enemy;* 破壞敵人的計畫; *be ~d in an attempt to do sth.* 欲做某事而遭受挫折。**frus·tra·tion** /frʌˈstreɪʃn ; frʌsˈtreʃən/ *n* [U] frustrating or being ~d; [C] instance of this; defeat or disappointment: 阻止;破壞;挫折;頓挫: *embittered by numerous frustrations.* 受許多挫折之苦。

fry[1] /fraɪ ; fraɪ/ *vt, vi* (*pt, pp* fried /fraɪd ; fraɪd/) [VP6A, 2A] cook, be cooked, in boiling fat: 油煎;油炸: *fried chicken.* 炸雞。*The sausages are frying/being fried.* 香腸正在煎着。**ˈfry·ing-pan,** (US also 美亦作 **ˈfry-pan**) *n* shallow pan with a long handle used for frying. 煎鍋(有長柄的淺鍋)。***out of the frying-pan into the fire,*** from a bad situation to one that is worse. 每況愈下。**fryer; frier** /ˈfraɪə(r) ; ˈfraɪə/ *n* small young chicken for frying. 炸食用的小雞。

fry[2] /fraɪ ; fraɪ/ *n pl* newly hatched fishes. 魚苗;魚秧。**ˈsmall fry,** young or insignificant creatures; persons of no importance. 幼小或不重要的生物;不重要的人物。

fuchsia /ˈfjuːʃə ; ˈfjuʃə/ *n* shrub with bell-like drooping flowers, pink, red or purple. 晚櫻科植物。

fuck /fʌk ; fʌk/ *vt, vi* ⚠ (sl) [VP6A, 2A] have sexual intercourse (with). (諱;俚)(與…)性交。***~ (it)!*** (int, used to express irritation, anger, etc.) 混帳! 滾開! (用以表示惱怒,憤怒等。) ***~ off,*** (esp imper) go away. (尤用於祈使法)走開。 ***~ sth up,*** spoil, ruin it. 把某事物弄糟。Hence, 由此產生, ***~ed (up),*** spoilt, ruined. 弄糟了。**ˈ~-all** *n* nothing. 沒什麼。**~er** *n* fool. 傻瓜;笨蛋。**~·ing** *adj* (used to express irritation, etc, but often meaningless.) 該死的;討厭的(用以表示惱怒等,但常常沒有意義)。 ***~ing well,*** surely(1). 當然;一定。

fuddle /ˈfʌdl ; ˈfʌdl/ *vt* [VP6A, 15A] confuse, stupefy, (esp with alcoholic drink): 使迷糊;使爛醉: *~ oneself/one's brain with gin;* 喝杜松子酒喝得爛醉; *in a ~d state.* 爛醉如泥。

fuddy-duddy /ˈfʌdɪ dʌdɪ ; ˈfʌdɪˌdʌdɪ/ *n* (*pl* -duddies) (colloq) fussy and old-fashioned person. (俗)嘮叨而守舊的人。

fudge /fʌdʒ ; fʌdʒ/ *n* [U] sort of soft sweet made with milk, sugar, chocolate, etc. 一種由牛奶、糖、巧克力等製成的軟糖。□ *int* (dated) Nonsense! (過時

fruit

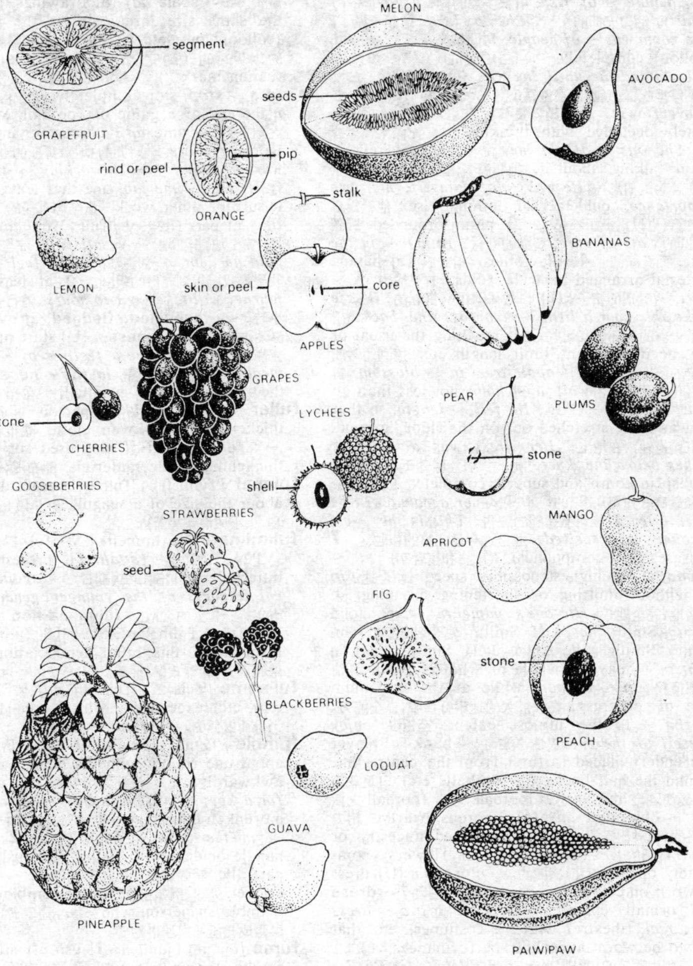

用語)胡説！

fuel /ˈfjuːəl ; ˈfjuəl/ *n* [U] material for producing heat or other forms of energy, eg wood, coal, oil, uranium; [C] kind of ~; (fig) sth that inflames the passions. 燃料(例如木、煤、油、鈾)；(喻)刺激感情之物。***add ~ to the flames,*** make passions stronger. 火上加油；使情緒更爲激烈。□ *vt, vi* (-ll-, US also -l-) [VP6A, 2A] supply with or obtain ~: 供以燃料；加以燃料；加燃料: *a power station ~led by uranium;* 以鈾做燃料的發電所；*~ a ship;* 給船加燃料；*a '~ling station,* one where oil, coal, etc may be obtained. 加油站；燃料供應站。

fug /fʌg ; fʌg/ *n* (colloq) stuffy atmosphere (as in an overcrowded or badly ventilated room, etc): (俗) 汚濁難聞的空氣 (如一人數過多或通風不良的房間內的情形): *What a fug!* 空氣多麼汚濁！**fuggy** *adj*

fugi·tive /ˈfjuːdʒətɪv ; ˈfjudʒətɪv/ *n* ~ ***(from),*** person running away from justice, danger, etc: 逃亡者；逃犯；亡命徒: *~s from an invaded country;* 自受侵國家逃出的難民；*~s from justice;* 逃犯；(attrib) (形容用法) *a ~ prisoner.* 逃跑的犯人。□ *adj* (attrib) of temporary interest or value; lasting a short time only: (形容用法)祇有暫時的興趣或價值的；短暫的: *~ verses.* 即興的詩。

fugue /fjuːg ; fjug/ *n* [C] musical composition in which one or more themes are introduced by the different parts or voices in turn and then repeated in a complex design. 遁走曲(有一個或多個主題，經不同部分或聲音輪流引出，然後予以重複的複音樂曲)。

ful·crum /ˈfʊlkrəm ; ˈfʌlkrəm/ *n* (*pl* ~s or fulcra /ˈfʊlkrə ; ˈfʌlkrə/) point on which a lever turns. 槓桿的支點。⇨ the illus at lever. 參看 lever 之插圖。

ful·fil (US also **ful·fill**) /fʊlˈfɪl ; fʊlˈfɪl/ *vt* (-ll-) [VP 6A] perform or complete a task, duty, etc; do what is required (by conditions, etc): 履行(工作，任務等)；做(根據條件等需要做的事): *~ one's duties/a command/an obligation/sb's expectations or hopes.* 盡職(執行命令；盡義務；滿足某人的期望)。**~·ment** *n* ~ling or being ~led. 履行；完成；實踐。

full /fʊl ; fʊl/ *adj* (-er, -est) **1** ~ ***(of),*** holding or having plenty (*of*), holding or having as much or as many (*of*) as possible; completely filled:

滿的;裝滿的;充滿的: *pockets ~ of money;* 裝滿錢的口袋;*a lake ~ of fish;* 有很多魚的湖; *a girl ~ of vitality.* 活力充沛的女孩。*The box is ~.* 這箱子滿了。*The room was ~ of people.* 房間裏充滿了人。**~ up,** (colloq) completely ~: (俗)全滿的: *The greedy girl ate and ate until she was ~ up.* 那個貪心的女孩不停地吃,直到吃得很飽爲止。*The drawers were ~ to overflowing.* 抽屜滿得裝不下了。 **2 ~ of,** completely occupied with thinking of: 充滿某種思想的: *She was ~ of the news,* could not refrain from talking about it. 她腦海裏盡想着這個消息(禁不住談論這消息)。*He was ~ of himself/his own importance,* could talk of nothing else. 他祇爲自己打算(自以爲很了不起)。 **3** plump; rounded: 豐滿的;圓的: *a ~ figure;* 豐滿的身材; *rather ~ in the face.* 面孔頗圓。**4** (of clothes) (指衣服) **(a)** having material arranged in wide folds: 有寬摺的: *a ~ skirt.* 有寬摺的裙子。**(b)** easy fitting:寬鬆的: *Please make this coat a little ~er across the back.* 請將這上衣的背部做寬鬆些。 **5** reaching the usual or the specified extent, limit, length, etc: 達到通常或指定的限度、長度等的: *apple-trees in ~ blossom;* 盛開着花的蘋果樹; *wait a ~ hour,* not less than an hour. 等了足足一個鐘頭。*He fell ~ length,* so that he was lying stretched out on the floor/ground. 他直挺挺地跌在地上。 *Her dress was a ~ three inches below the knee.* 她的衣服達膝蓋下足有三吋。 **6** (esp in comp and superl) complete: (尤與比較級和最高級連用)完全的: *A ~/~er account will be given later.* 以後將有完整的報告。*This is the ~est account yet received.* 這是迄今最完整的報告。 **7** (phrases and compounds) (片語和複合字) ***at ~ speed,*** at the highest possible speed. 傾全速。***in ~,*** without omitting or shortening anything: 未省略地;完全地: *write one's name in ~,* eg John Henry Smith, *not* J H Smith; 寫全名(例如 John Henry Smith 卽是,不寫作 J H Smith); *pay a debt in ~,* pay the whole of what is owed. 還清全部債務。***in ~ career,*** while at the maximum rate of progress. 在以最大的速率行進中;以全速力。***to the ~,*** to the utmost extent: 至極限: *enjoy oneself to the ~.* 盡情享樂。**'~-back** *n* player (defender) placed farthest from the centre line, behind the half-backs (in football, etc). (足球等的)後衞。⇨ the illus at football. 參看 football 之插圖。**ˌ~-'blooded** *adj* **(a)** vigorous; hearty. 精力旺盛的;精神飽滿的。**(b)** of unmixed ancestry or race. 純種的。**ˌ~-'blown** *adj* (of flowers) completely open. (指花)盛開的。**ˌ~ 'dress** *n* [U] dress as worn on ceremonial occasions. 盛裝。**ˌ~-'dress** *adj* formally complete: 正式的;全副的: *a ~-dress rehearsal,* (theatre) with the costumes, etc that are to be worn at public performances; (戲劇)(穿着劇中服裝的)彩排; *a ~-dress debate (in Parliament) on an important question.* (國會) 對一重要問題的正式辯論。 **ˌ~ 'face** *n* with the face turned to the viewer(s): 正面的臉: *a ~-face portrait.* 正面肖像。 ⇨ profile. **ˌ~-'fashioned** *adj* (trade use, of garments) made to fit the shape of the body: (商業用語,指衣服)完全合身的: *~-fashioned stockings/sweaters.* 完全合乎腿形的長襪(合身的毛線衫)。**ˌ~-'fledged** *adj* (of a bird) having all its flight feathers; able to fly; (fig) having completed training, etc: (指鳥)毛長全的;能飛的;(喻)完成訓練等的: *a ~-fledged barrister.* 有充份資格的律師。 **ˌ~-'grown** *adj* having reached maturity. 成熟的;長成的。**ˌ~ 'house** *n* (theatre) with no unoccupied seats. (戲院)客滿。**ˌ~-'length** *adj* **(a)** (of a portrait) showing the whole figure. (指肖像)全身的。**(b)** of standard or usual length: 標準長度的;通常長度的: *a ~-length novel.* 通常字數的小說。**ˌ~ 'marks** *n pl* highest marks¹(5) possible. 滿分。**ˌ~ 'moon** *n* seen as a complete disc. 滿月;圓月;望月。⇨ the illus at phase. 參看 phase 之插圖。**ˌ~-'page** *adj* filling a whole page: 全頁的: *a ~-page advertisement in a newspaper.* 報紙上全頁的廣告。 **ˌ~-'scale** *adj* (of drawings, plans, etc) of the same size, area, etc as the object itself; (colloq) complete. (指繪圖,設計圖等)與原物大小相等的;原尺寸的;(俗)完全的;全部的。**ˌ~ 'stop,** the punctuation mark (.) ⇨ App 9. 句點(參看附錄九)。***come to a ~ stop,*** stop completely. 完全停止。**ˌ~ 'time** *n* the end of a game of football, etc. 足球等比賽之結束。**ˌ~-'time** *adj, adv* occupying all normal working hours: 全時間的(地);專任的(地): *a ~-time worker;* 專任的工作者; *working ~-time;* 全時間工作; *It's a ~-time job,* one that leaves no time for leisure or other work. 這是個專任的工作。⇨ *part-time* at part¹(1). **~y** /ˈfʊlɪ ; ˈfʊlɪ/ *adv* **1** completely: 完全地;全部地: *~y satisfied;* 完全滿意的; *a ~y paid up debt.* 全部還清的債。*I feel ~y rewarded.* 我覺得我已得到充份的報酬。 **2** at least: 至少: *The journey will take ~y two hours.* 這行程至少要花費兩小時。**~y-fashioned/fledged/grown** ⇨ 7 above. 參看上列第7義。**~·ness** *n* [U] state of being ~: 滿;充滿;完全;豐滿: *have a feeling of ~ness after a meal.* 飯後有飽脹之感。***in the ~ness of time,*** at the appointed time; eventually. 在預定的時候;終於。

fuller /ˈfʊlə(r) ; ˈfʊlɚ/ *n* person who cleans and thickens freshly woven cloth. 漂布者;漿洗布疋者。**ˌ~'s 'earth,** kind of clay used for cleaning and thickening textile materials. 漂布泥;漂土。

ful·mar /ˈfʊlmə(r) ; ˈfʊlmɚ/ *n* seabird like a petrel, about the size of a seagull. 管鼻鸌(一種似海燕的海鳥,大小與海鷗相若)。

ful·mi·nate /ˈfʌlmɪneɪt *US:* ˈfʊl- ; ˈfʌlmə,net/ *vi* [VP2A, 3A] **~ *(against),*** protest loudly and bitterly: 猛烈抗議;嚴詞譴責: *~ against the apparent idleness of the younger generation.* 嚴詞譴責年輕一代人的懶散。 **ful·mi·na·tion** /ˌfʌlmɪˈneɪʃn *US:* ˌfʊl- ; ˌfʌlməˈneʃən/ *n* [U] fulminating; [C] instance of this; bitter denunciation or protest. 嚴詞譴責;猛烈攻擊;抨擊。

ful·some /ˈfʊlsəm ; ˈfʊlsəm/ *adj* (of praise, flattery, etc) excessive and insincere. (指稱讚,諂媚等)過份而虛僞的。**~·ly** *adv* **~·ness** *n*

fumble /ˈfʌmbl ; ˈfʌmbḷ/ *vi, vt* **1** [VP2A, C] feel about uncertainly with the hands; use the hands awkwardly: 摸索;笨拙地用手: *~ in one's pockets for a key;* 在口袋裏摸索鑰匙; *~ at a lock,* eg, as a drunken man might; 亂摸弄一鎖(如一醉漢所爲者); *~ in the dark.* 在黑暗中摸索。 **2** [VP6A, 2A] handle or deal with (sth) nervously or incompetently: 緊張或無能地處理(事物): *~ a ball,* eg in cricket. 失球(例如在板球戲中)。**fumbler** /ˈfʌmblə(r); ˈfʌmblɚ/ *n* person who ~s. 摸索者;笨手笨脚的人;緊張或無能地處理事物者。

fume /fjuːm ; fjum/ *n* **1** (usu *pl*) strong-smelling smoke, gas or vapour: (通常用複數)氣味强烈的煙,氣或汽: *air thick with the ~s of cigars;* 充滿雪茄煙味的空氣; *petrol ~s;* 强烈的汽油味; *~s of incense.* 濃郁的香的煙味。**2** (liter) excited state of mind: (文)激動的心境: *in a ~ of anxiety.* 一陣焦慮。□ *vi, vt* **1** [VP2A, C, 3A] **~ *(at),*** give off ~s; pass away in ~s; (fig) betray repressed anger or irritation: 發散出强烈的煙氣;以濃烈的氣味蒸發;(喻)發怒: *~ because one is kept waiting;* 因久等而生氣; *~ at sb's incompetence.* 爲某人的無能而生氣。 **2** [VP6A] treat (wood, etc) with ~s (to darken the surface, etc): 燻: *~d oak.* 燻橡木。

fu·mi·gate /ˈfjuːmɪgeɪt ; ˈfjumə,get/ *vt* [VP6A] disinfect by means of fumes: 以煙燻消毒: *~ a room used by someone with an infectious disease;* 以煙燻消毒一傳染病患者住過的房間; *~ rose-bushes,* to kill insect pests. 燻玫瑰樹(以除害蟲)。**fu·mi·ga·tion** /ˌfjuːmɪˈgeɪʃn ; ˌfjuməˈgeʃən/ *n*

fun /fʌn ; fʌn/ *n* [U] **1** amusement; enjoyment; playfulness: 娛樂;快樂;嬉戲: *What fun the children had at the seaside,* How they enjoyed themselves! 孩子們在海邊玩得眞開心! *He's full of fun.* 他很風

趣。*I don't see the fun of doing that,* do not think it is amusing. 我不覺得做那事有什麼趣味。 **'fun·fair** *n* amusement park. 兒童樂園;遊樂場。 ⇨ amuse. ***fun and games,*** (colloq) lively merry-making; pranks. (俗)歡樂;開玩笑。 ***make fun of; poke fun at,*** ridicule; cause people to laugh at: 嘲弄;取笑: *It is cruel to make fun of a cripple.* 取笑一跛者是殘忍的。***for/in fun,*** as a joke, for amusement; not seriously: 開玩笑地;鬧着玩地;非認眞地: *He said it only in fun.* 他祇是說着玩的。 **2** that which causes merriment or amusement: 有趣的人或物: *Your new friend is great fun,* is very amusing. 你的新朋友很有趣。 **3** (attrib, colloq): (形容用法,俗): *a 'fun car/hat/fur,* used, worn, for amusement. 娛樂用的汽車(帽子,毛皮衣)。

func·tion /'fʌŋkʃn ; 'fʌŋkʃən/ *n* [C] **1** special activity or purpose of a person or thing: 職責;作用;功能: *the ~s of a judge/an officer of state;* 法官(部長)的職責; *the ~ of the heart,* ie to pump blood through the body; 心臟的功能(即司血液循環); *the ~s of the nerves;* 神經的機能; *the ~ of education.* 教育的功能。 **2** public ceremony or event; social gathering of an important and formal kind: 祝典;正式集會: *the numerous ~s that the Queen must attend.* 女王必須參加的無數集會。 **3** (maths) variable quantity, dependent in value on another. (數學)函數。□ *vi* [VP2A, C] fulfill a ~(1); operate; act: 盡職責;起作用;有效用: *The telephone was not ~ing,* was out of order. 電話壞了。 *Some English adverbs ~ as adjectives.* 有些英語的副詞有形容詞的作用。**~al** /-ʃənl ; -ʃənḷ/ *adj* of a ~; having, designed to have, ~s(1): 職責的;功能的;機能的;有作用的;有功能的: *a ~al disorder,* an illness caused by the failure of an organ of the body to perform its ~; 官能病; *~al architecture,* designed to serve practical purposes, beauty of appearance being secondary; 實用的建築(以功用爲主,美觀其次); *schools designed according to ~al principles.* 根據實用的原則而設計的學校。 **~·al·ism** /-ʃənəlɪzəm ; -ʃənḷ,ɪzəm/ *n* principle that the ~ of objects, etc should determine their design, the materials used, etc. (生產,建築等)實用主義;效用主義。**~·al·ist** /-ʃənəlɪst ; -ʃənḷɪst/ *n* adherent of ~-alism. 實用主義者。

func·tion·ary /'fʌŋkʃənərɪ *US:* -nerɪ ; 'fʌŋkʃən,ɛrɪ/ *n* (*pl* -ries) (often derog) person with official functions. (常含貶抑意味)公務員;官員。

fund /fʌnd ; fʌnd/ *n* [C] **1** store or supply (of non-material things): 貯藏物(指非物質的東西): *a ~ of common sense/humour/amusing stories.* 大量的常識(幽默,有趣的故事)。 **2** (often *pl*) sum of money available for a purpose: (常用複數)專款;基金: *a re'lief ~,* eg to help sufferers from a flood or other disaster; 救濟基金; *'school ~s,* to finance schools. 學校基金(經費)。**the (public) ~s,** the stock of the national debt as a form of investment: 公債: *have £5000 in the ~s.* 有五千鎊的公債。***no ~s,*** notice (given by a bank) that the person who has drawn a cheque on it has no money in his account. 無存款(銀行通知開空頭支票者之用語)。□ *vt* [VP6A] **1** provide with money: 供以款項: *a project ~ed by the government.* 經費由政府補助的一項計畫。 **2** (fin) convert (a short-term debt) into a long-term debt at fixed interest. (財政)將(短期債)改爲長期債。

fun·da·men·tal /,fʌndə'mentl ; ,fʌndə'mɛntḷ/ *adj* ***~ (to),*** of or forming a foundation; of great importance; serving as a starting-point: 基本的;基礎的;十分重要的;作爲起點的: *the ~ rules of arithmetic,* those which must be learnt first and on which everything that follows depends. 算術的基本規則。□ *n* essential part. 根本。**the ~s,** ~ rules or principles: 基本規則;基本原理: *the ~s of mathematics.* 數學的基本原理。 **~·ly** /-təlɪ ; -tḷɪ/ *adv* **~·ism** /-ɪzəm ; -,ɪzəm/ *n* [U] maintenance of the literal interpretation of the traditional beliefs of the Christian religion (such as the accuracy of everything in the Bible), in opposition to more modern teachings. 原教旨主義(相信聖經所記載的傳統的基督教信仰,反對較爲近代的教義)。**~·ist** /-ɪst ; -ɪst/ *n* supporter of ~ism. 原教旨主義信徒。

fu·neral /'fju:nərəl ; 'fjunərəl/ *n* [C] **1** burial or cremation of a dead person with the usual ceremonies. 葬禮。 **2** (attrib use) of or for a ~: (形容用法)葬禮的;送殯的;出殯用的: *a '~ procession;* 送葬的行列; *a '~ march,* sad and solemn piece of music; 送葬曲; *a '~ pile/pyre,* pile of wood, etc on which a corpse is burnt; 火葬柴堆; *a '~ parlor,* (US) undertaker's offices. (美)殯儀館。***it's/that's 'my/'your etc ~,*** (colloq) it's/that's my/your etc concern, worry etc. (俗)這是我(你等)所關心的事(煩惱等)。 **fu·ner·eal** /fju:'nɪərɪəl ; fju'nɪrɪəl/ *adj* of or like a ~; gloomy; dismal; dark: 葬禮的;似葬禮的;憂鬱的;陰森的;陰沉的: *a funereal expression.* 憂鬱的表情。

fun·gus /'fʌŋgəs ; 'fʌŋgəs/ *n* (*pl* -gi /-gaɪ ; -dʒaɪ/ or ~es /-gəsɪz ; -gəsɪz/) plant without leaves, flowers or green colouring matter, growing on other plants or on decaying matter, eg old wood: 眞菌類: *Mushrooms, toadstools and mildew are all fungi.* 蘑菇、蕈與黴都是眞菌類。**fun·gi·cide** /'fʌndʒɪsaɪd ; 'fʌndʒə,saɪd/ *n* [U, C] substance that destroys fungi. 殺眞菌類劑。 **fun·goid** /'fʌŋgɔɪd ; 'fʌŋgɔɪd/ *adj* of or like fungi. (似)眞菌類的。 **fun·gous** /'fʌŋgəs ; 'fʌŋgəs/ *adj* of or like, caused by, fungi. (似)眞菌類的;眞菌類引起的。

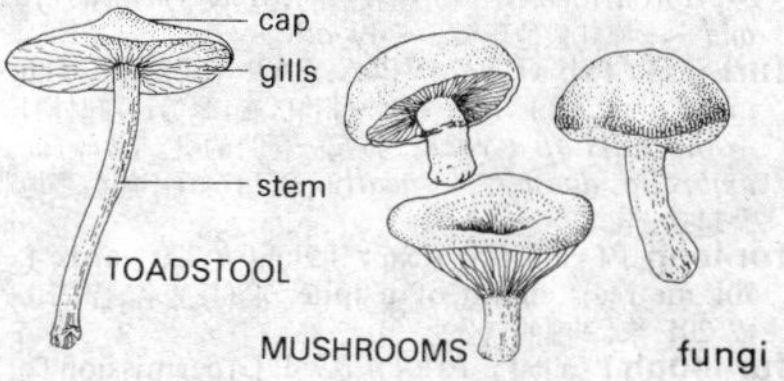

fungi

fu·nicu·lar /fju:'nɪkjʊlə(r) ; fju'nɪkjələ/ *n* **~ (rail-way),** railway on a slope, worked by a cable and a stationary engine. 纜索鐵路。

funk /fʌŋk ; fʌŋk/ *n* (colloq) (俗) **1** great fear: 驚惶;恐懼: *be in a ~.* 大爲恐懼。 **2** coward. 怯懦者。□ *vi, vt* [VP6A, 2A] show fear; (try to) escape (doing sth) because of fear. 畏懼;畏縮;因畏懼而(試圖)避免(做某事)。 **~y** *adj* (US sl) (of music) emotional and rhythmic. (美俚)(指音樂)有感情和韻律的。

funnel /'fʌnl ; 'fʌnḷ/ *n* **1** tube or pipe wide at the top and narrowing at the bottom, for pouring liquids or powders into a small opening. 漏斗。 **2** outlet for smoke (ie smoke-stack, metal chimney) of a steamship, locomotive etc. (輪船,火車等的)煙囪。⇨ the illus at ship. 參看 ship 之插圖。 **,two-/,three-'~led** *adj* having two/three ~s. 有兩(三)個煙囪的。□ *vt, vi* (-ll-, US -l-) [VP6A, 2A] (cause to) move through, or as if through, a ~. (使)通過漏斗或煙囪;(使)彷彿通過漏斗或煙囪。

funny /'fʌnɪ ; 'fʌnɪ/ *adj* (-ier, -iest) **1** causing fun or amusement: 有趣的;好玩的: *~ stories.* 有趣的故事。 **2** strange; queer; causing surprise: 奇特的;古怪的;令人驚奇的: *There's something ~ about the affair,* sth strange, perhaps not quite honest or straight-forward. 這件事有點奇怪(或許其中有不誠實或不坦白之處)。 **'~-bone** *n* part of the elbow over which a very sensitive nerve passes. (肘的)尺骨端。 **the funnies,** *n pl* (colloq) comic strips. (俗)連環圖畫。 **fun·nily** /-ɪlɪ ; -ɪlɪ/ *adv* in a ~ way: 有趣地;奇特地: *funnily* (= strangely) ***enough.*** 十分古怪。 **fun·ni·ness** *n*

fur /fɜ:(r) ; fɝ/ *n* **1** [U] soft thick hair covering certain animals, eg cats, rabbits. (貓,兎等動物之)軟毛。***make the 'fur fly,*** cause a disturbance. 引起騷動。***fur and feather,*** furred animals and birds. 鳥獸。 **2** [C] animal skin with the fur on it, esp when made into garments: 獸類的毛皮;(尤指)毛皮衣: *a fine fox fur;* 上等狐皮; *wearing expensive furs;* 穿着昂貴的皮衣; (attrib) (形容用法) *a fur coat,* one made of furs. 皮上衣。 **3** [U] rough coating on a person's tongue when ill; crust forming on the inside of a kettle, boiler, etc when the water heated in it contains lime. 舌苔;壺,鍋等的水銹。□ *vt, vi* (-rr-) [VP6A, 2A, C] ~ ***(up),*** cover, be or become covered, with fur: 覆以毛皮;覆有舌苔;生有水銹: *a furred animal/tongue/kettle.* 有毛皮的動物(有舌苔的舌;生水銹的壺)。**furry** /ˈfɜːrɪ ; ˈfɝɪ/ *adj* (-ier, -iest) of or like fur; covered with fur. 毛皮的;似毛皮的;覆有毛皮的。

fur·be·low /ˈfɜːbɪləʊ ; ˈfɝblˌo/ *n* (often used in 常用於 ***frills and ~s***) (old-fashioned) piece of elaborate or unnecessary trimming (on a dress, etc). (衣服等上)(舊式的)精巧或不必要的裝飾。

fur·bish /ˈfɜːbɪʃ ; ˈfɝbɪʃ/ *vt* [VP6A] polish, eg by removing rust from; make like new (esp sth that has not been used for a long time): 擦亮;刷新: *~ a sword;* 擦亮一劍; *newly ~ed skills.* 最近溫習過的技能。

furi·ous /ˈfjʊərɪəs ; ˈfjʊrɪəs/ *adj* violent; uncontrolled; full of fury: 猛烈的;狂暴的;狂怒的: *a ~ struggle/storm/quarrel;* 猛烈的鬪爭(暴風雨,爭吵); *running at a ~ pace;* 急奔; *be ~ with sb/at what sb has done.* 對某人(某人所做之事)發狂怒。***fast and ~,*** uproarious, wild: 瘋狂般的: *The fun was fast and ~.* 瘋狂般地玩樂。**~·ly** *adv*

furl /fɜːl ; fɝl/ *vt, vi* [VP6A, 2A] (of sails, flags, umbrellas, etc) roll up: (指帆,旗,傘等)捲起;摺起: *~ the sails of a yacht.* 捲起一輕舟的帆。*This fan/umbrella doesn't ~ neatly.* 這扇(傘)不能整齊地收疊起來。

fur·long /ˈfɜːlɒŋ *US:* -lɔːŋ ; ˈfɝlɔŋ/ *n* 220 yards (= 201 metres); eighth of a mile. 浪(長度名,合 220 碼或 201 米;一哩的八分之一)。

fur·lough /ˈfɜːləʊ ; ˈfɝlo/ *n* [C, U] (permission for) absence from duty (esp civil officials, members of the armed forces, working abroad): 休假(尤指在國外的公務員,軍人);休假之許可: *going home on ~;* 返鄉度假; *six months' ~;* 六個月的休假; *have a ~ every three years.* 每三年休假一次。⇨ leave².

fur·nace /ˈfɜːnɪs ; ˈfɝnɪs/ *n* **1** enclosed fireplace for heating buildings with hot water or steam in pipes. 火爐。 **2** enclosed space for heating metals, making glass, etc. 鎔爐。

fur·nish /ˈfɜːnɪʃ ; ˈfɝnɪʃ/ *vt* [VP6A, 14] ***~ sth (to sb); ~ sb/sth with sth,*** supply or provide; put furniture in: 供給;佈置傢具於: *~ a library with books;* 供給一圖書館書籍; *~ an army with supplies/~ supplies to an army;* 供給軍隊補給品; *~ a room/an office;* 以傢具佈置一房間(辦公室); *a ~ed house/flat,* one rented with the furniture. 備有傢具的出租房屋(公寓)。**~·ings** *n pl* furniture and equipment. 傢具與陳設品。

fur·ni·ture /ˈfɜːnɪtʃə(r) ; ˈfɝnɪtʃɚ/ *n* [U] all those (usu) movable things such as chairs, beds, desks, etc needed in a house, room, office, etc. 傢具。

fu·rore (US = **fu·ror**) /fjʊˈrɔːrɪ *US:* ˈfjuːrɔːr ; ˈfjurɔr/ *n* general uproar: 轟動;騷動: *The new play at the National Theatre created a ~,* was received with general excitement. 在國家劇院演出的新劇轟動一時。

fur·rier /ˈfʌrɪə(r) ; ˈfɝɪɚ/ *n* person who prepares, or who deals in, furs. 修整毛皮之人;毛皮衣商。

fur·row /ˈfʌrəʊ ; ˈfɝo/ *n* [C] **1** long cut in the ground made by a plough: 犂溝;畦: *newly turned ~s.* 新犂的犂溝。 **2** wrinkle; line in the skin of the face, esp the forehead. (額上的)皺紋。□ *vt* [VP6A] make ~s in: 犂;使起皺紋: *a forehead ~ed by old age/anxiety, etc.* 因年邁(焦慮等)而起皺紋的額頭。

furry /ˈfɜːrɪ ; ˈfɝɪ/ ⇨ fur.

fur·ther /ˈfɜːðə(r) ; ˈfɝðɚ/ *adv, adj* **1** (often used for *farther*) more far: (常用作 farther 之義)較遠的(地);更遠的(地): *It's not safe to go any ~.* 再走遠些就不安全了。 **2** (not interchangeable in this sense with *farther*) more; in addition; additional: (用作此義不可與 farther 互用)更多的;添加的;另外的;更進一步的(地): *We must get ~ information.* 我們必須獲得更多的消息。*The Museum will be closed until ~ notice.* 該博物館將關閉,開放時另行通知。*We need go no ~ into the matter,* need make no more inquiries. 我們不需要進一步調查此事。*I'll offer you £50 but I can't go any ~,* offer more. 我願出價五十鎊,但不能再多了。 **3** (also 亦作 *~more,* ⇨ below 參看下面) moreover; also; besides: 而且;此外;並且: *He said that the key was lost and, ~, that there was no hope of its being found.* 他說那鑰匙遺失了,而且也沒有希望找回來。□ *vt* [VP6A] help forward; promote: 增進;促進: *~ sb's interests;* 提高某人的興趣; *~ the cause of peace.* 促進和平。**~·ance** /-rəns ; -rəns/ *n* [U] ~ing; advancement: 增進;促進: *for the ~ance of public welfare;* 爲促進大衆的福利; *in ~ance of your aims.* 爲促成你的目的。**~·more** /ˌfɜːðəˈmɔː(r) ; ˈfɝðɚˌmor/ *adv* moreover; in addition. 而且;此外。**'~·most** /-məʊst ; -ˌmost/ *adj* most distant; furthest. 最遠的。

fur·thest /ˈfɜːðɪst ; ˈfɝðɪst/ *adj, adv* = farthest.

fur·tive /ˈfɜːtɪv ; ˈfɝtɪv/ *adj* done secretly so as not to attract attention; having or suggesting a wish to escape notice: 偷偷摸摸的;鬼鬼祟祟的: *a ~ glance/manner;* 偷瞧(鬼鬼祟祟的樣子); *~ behaviour;* 偷偷摸摸的行爲; *be ~ in one's movements.* 行動鬼祟。**~·ly** *adv* **~·ness** *n*

fury /ˈfjʊərɪ ; ˈfjʊrɪ/ *n* (*pl* -ries) **1** [U] violent excitement, esp anger: 狂暴;(尤指)憤怒: *filled with ~;* 氣憤塡胸; *the ~ of the elements,* wild storms, winds; 狂風暴雨; *in the ~ of battle.* 在激戰中。 **2** [C] outburst of wild feelings: 憤怒之爆發: *She was in one of her furies.* 她在憤怒中。*He flew into a ~ when I refused to lend him the money.* 當我拒絕借錢給他時,他勃然大怒。 **3** [C] violently furious woman or girl: 憤怒的女子;潑婦: *What a little ~ she is!* 她眞是個小潑婦! **4 the Furies,** snake-haired goddesses in Greek mythology sent from the underworld to punish crime. (希臘神話中生有蛇髮的)復仇女神。

furze /fɜːz ; fɝz/ *n* [U] = gorse.

fuse¹ /fjuːz ; fjuz/ *n* [C] tube, cord, etc for carrying a spark to explode powder, etc, eg in a firecracker, bomb or blasting charge; (US 美 = *fuze*) part of a shell or mine that detonates the explosive charge. 導火線;引信;信管。**'time-~** *n* one that does this after a pre-arranged interval of time. 定時信管。

fuse² /fjuːz ; fjuz/ *vt, vi* **1** [VP6A, 15A, B, 2A] make or become liquid as the result of great heat; join, become joined, as the result of melting: 鎔化;鎔合: *~ two pieces of wire together.* 將兩條金屬線鎔合起來。**2** [VP2A] (of an electric circuit, or part of it) be broken through melting of the fuse²: (指電路,或其部分)因保險絲燒斷而中斷: *The light has ~d.* 保險絲燒斷,燈不亮了。**3** [VP6A, 15A, B] (fig) make into one whole. (喩)使成爲一體;合併。□ *n* [C] (in an electric circuit) short piece of wire which melts and breaks the circuit if the circuit is overloaded. (電路中的)保險絲。**'~ wire** *n* [U] kinds of wire used for this purpose. 保險絲。

fu·sel·age /ˈfjuːzəlɑːʒ ; ˈfjuzḷɪdʒ/ *n* body of an aircraft (to which the engine(s), wings and tail are fitted). (飛機之)機身。⇨ the illus at air. 參看 air 之插圖。

fu·sil·ier /ˌfjuːzəˈlɪə(r) ; ˌfjuzḷˈɪr/ *n* soldier (of certain British regiments) formerly armed with a light musket. (英軍某些團中) 昔時持有輕滑膛槍的槍手。

fus·il·lade /ˌfjuːzɪˈleɪd *US:* -səˈlɑːd ; ˌfjuzḷˈed/ *n* [C] continuous discharge of firearms. 槍砲的連發。

fusion /ˈfjuːʒn ; ˈfjuʒən/ *n* [C, U] mixing or uniting of different things into one: 融合;熔合;聯合: *the ~ of copper and tin;* 銅與錫之熔合; *a ~ of races/political parties.* 種族之融合 (政黨之合併)。 ˈ**~ bomb** *n* hydrogen bomb; ⇨ atomic. 氫彈。

fuss /fʌs ; fʌs/ *n* [U] unnecessary nervous agitation, esp about unimportant things; [C] nervous state: 小題大做;大驚小怪;無謂紛擾;緊張;急躁: *Don't make so much ~/get into such a ~ about trifles.* 不要因細故而大事紛擾 (如此急躁)。 ***make a ~,*** **(a)** be nervously agitated. 激動;紛擾。 **(b)** be ostentatiously active. 誇張地活動。 **(c)** complain vigorously. 猛烈地抱怨。 ***make a ~ of,*** pay ostentatious attention to: 過於注意: *Don't make so much ~ of the children.* 不要過份注意孩子們。 ˈ**~·pot** *n* (colloq) very ~y person. (俗) 很愛小題大做之人。 □ *vt, vi* [VP6A, 2A, C] get into a ~; cause (sb) to be in a ~: 小題大做;急躁;使(某人)爲瑣事煩擾: *Stop ~ing.* 不要大驚小怪。 *She ~ed about, unable to hide her impatience.* 她無謂煩擾,無法掩飾她的急躁。 *Don't ~ over the children so much.* 不要爲孩子們過於操心。 *Don't ~ me,* make me nervous. 不要以瑣事煩擾我。 **~y** *adj* (-ier, -iest) **1** nervously active or agitated. 緊張的;大驚小怪的。 **2** full of, showing, close attention to detail: 多紛擾的;爲瑣事擔憂的: *be too ~y about one's clothes/food.* 過於挑剔衣服(食物)。 **3** (of dress, style, etc) over-ornamented; having too many unimportant details, etc. (指衣服,文體等) 裝飾過份的;有太多不重要的細節的。 **~·ily** /-ɪlɪ ; -əlɪ/ *adv* **~i·ness** *n*

fus·tian /ˈfʌstɪən *US:* -tʃən ; ˈfʌstʃən/ *n* [U] **1** thick, strong, coarse cotton cloth; (attrib) made of this cloth. 一種粗而牢的棉布;(形容用法) 此種棉布所製的。 **2** (fig) high-sounding but empty talk; (attrib) worthless; bombastic. (喻) 浮誇而空洞的話;(形容用法) 無價值的;誇大的。

fusty /ˈfʌstɪ ; ˈfʌstɪ/ *adj* stale-smelling; smelling of mould and damp; (fig) old-fashioned in ideas, etc: 腐臭的;有霉濕味的;(喻) 思想等陳腐的: *a ~ old professor,* eg one who has much book knowledge, but is out of touch with modern ideas, real life. 思想陳腐的老教授。

fu·tile /ˈfjuːtaɪl *US:* -tl ; ˈfjutḷ/ *adj* **1** (of actions) of no use; without result: (指行動) 無用的;無效果的: *a ~ attempt.* 無效果的嘗試。 **2** (of persons) unlikely to accomplish much; vain or frivolous. (指人) 無成就的;輕浮的;不足取的。 **fu·til·ity** /fjuːˈtɪlətɪ ; fjuˈtɪlətɪ/ *n* (*pl* -ties) [U] the state of being ~; [C] ~ action or utterance. 無用;無效;無用的行動或言語。

fu·ture /ˈfjuːtʃə(r) ; ˈfjutʃɚ/ *n, adj* **1** [U, C] (time, events) coming after the present: 將來的時間或事件;將來;未來;將來的;未來的: *The ~ must always be uncertain.* 未來的一切難以預卜。 *I hope you have a happy ~ before you.* 我希望你有一個幸福的將來。 *I've given up my job; there was no ~ in it/it didn't have a ~,* no prospects of higher salary, advancement, etc. 我已放棄了我的工作;那工作沒有前途。 ***for the ~,*** with ~ time in mind: 在將來: *Have you provided for the ~,* saved money, taken out an insurance policy, etc? 你爲將來作準備沒有(儲蓄,保險等)? ***in ~,*** from this time onwards: 從今以後: *Try to live a better life in ~.* 今後要努力過更好的生活。 **2** (*adj,* or attrib use of the *n*) of or in the ~: (形容詞或以名詞做形容用法) 屬於未來的;在將來的: *the ~ life,* after death of the body; 來世; *his ~ wife,* the woman he will marry. 他將與之結婚的女子。 **3** (*pl*) (comm) (orders for) goods and stocks bought at prices agreed upon at the time of purchase, but to be paid for and delivered later. (複)(商) 期貨;期貨定單。 **~·less** *adj* having no (successful) ~. 無前途的;前途無望的。

fu·tur·ism /ˈfjuːtʃərɪzəm ; ˈfjutʃɚˌɪzəm/ *n* [U] (early 20th c) movement in art and literature marked by a complete abandonment of tradition in favour of expressing the energy of contemporary life as influenced by modern machinery. 未來派 (二十世紀初期,因受現代機械的影響,文藝界欲徹底打破傳統,主張表達當代生活精力的一種運動)。 **fu·tur·ist** /-ɪst ; -ɪst/ *n* supporter of ~. 未來派文藝家。

fu·tur·ity /fjuːˈtjʊərətɪ *US:* -ˈtʊər- ; fjuˈtʊrətɪ/ *n* (*pl* -ties) [U] future; [U, C] future events. 未來;將來;未來的事件。

fuze /fjuːz ; fjuz/ *n* (US) = fuse[1].

fuzz /fʌz ; fʌz/ *n* [U] fluff; fluffy or frizzed hair. 絨毛;細毛。 ***the ~,*** (US sl) the police. (美俚) 警察。

fuzzy /ˈfʌzɪ ; ˈfʌzɪ/ *adj* (-ier, -iest) like fuzz; blurred, indistinct (in shape or outline); frayed or fluffy. 似絨毛的;模糊的;(形狀或輪廓) 不清楚的;有絨毛的。

G

Gg

G, g /dʒiː ; dʒi/ (*pl* G's, g's /dʒiːz ; dʒiz/) the seventh letter of the English alphabet; (US sl) one thousand dollars. 英文字母之第七個字母;(美俚) 一千元。

gab /gæb ; gæb/ *n* [U] (colloq) talk(ing): (俗) 談話: *Stop your gab,* (sl) be quiet. (俚) 住嘴。 ***have the gift of the gab,*** be good at speaking eloquently. 有口才。

gab·ar·dine, gab·er·dine /ˌgæbəˈdiːn ; ˈgæbɚˌdin/ *n* [U] strong, smooth twill-woven cloth. 軋別丁 (堅牢平滑的斜紋布料)。

gabble /ˈgæbl ; ˈgæbḷ/ *vt, vi* [VP6A, 15B, 2A, C] speak, say things, quickly and indistinctly: 急促而不清楚地說話: *The little girl ~d her prayers and jumped into bed.* 那小女孩急急說過祈禱詞,就跳上了床。 *Listen to those children gabbling away.* 聽那些孩子嘰哩咕嚕地說個沒完。 □ *n* [U] fast, confused, unintelligible talk. 急促而不清楚的談話。

gable /ˈgeɪbl ; ˈgebḷ/ *n* [C] three-cornered part of an outside wall, under sloping roofs. (雙斜面屋頂形成的) 山(形)牆。 **gabled** /ˈgeɪbld ; ˈgebḷd/ *adj* having a ~ or ~s: 有山形牆的: *a ~d house.* 有山形牆的房屋。 ⇨ the illus at window. 參看 window 之插圖。

gad[1] /gæd ; gæd/ *vi* (-dd-) [VP2C] ***gad about,*** (colloq) go from place to place for excitement or pleasure. (俗) 閒遊;遊蕩。 ˈ**gad·about** *n* person who does this. 閒遊者;遊蕩者。

gad[2] /gæd ; gæd/ *int* (also 亦作 ***By*** ˈ***gad!***) (old-fashioned) used to express surprise, etc. (舊式用語) (表示驚訝等) 噯呀!天哪!

gad·fly /ˈgædflaɪ ; ˈgædˌflaɪ/ *n* (*pl* -flies) fly that stings horses and cattle. 牛蠅;牛虻。

gadget /ˈgædʒɪt ; ˈgædʒɪt/ *n* (colloq) small (usu mechanical) contrivance or device: (俗) 小器具;小機械: *a new ~ for opening tin cans.* 開罐頭用的新器具。 **~ry** *n* [U] ~s collectively. (集合稱) 小器具;小機械。

Gael /geɪl ; gel/ *n* Scottish or Irish Celt. 蓋爾人 (蘇格蘭或愛爾蘭的塞爾特人)。 **~ic** /ˈgeɪlɪk ; ˈgelɪk/ *adj, n* (language) of the Scottish or Irish Celts. 蓋爾人的;蓋爾語;蘇格蘭或愛爾蘭之塞爾特人的。

gaff[1] /gæf ; gæf/ *n* stick with an iron hook for landing fish caught with rod and line. 魚叉;魚鉤 (將釣得之魚鉤至岸上所用者)。

gaff[2] /gæf ; gæf/ *n* ***blow the ~,*** (sl) let out a secret; disclose the plot. (俚)洩露祕密;洩露計畫。

gaffe /gæf ; gæf/ *n* [C] blunder; indiscreet act or remark. 過失;出醜;言行的失態。

gaffer /'gæfə(r) ; 'gæfɚ/ *n* (colloq) elderly man, esp a countryman; foreman (of a gang of workmen). (俗)年長者(尤指鄉下老漢);工頭。⇨ boss¹, guvnor.

gag /gæg ; gæg/ *n* [C] **1** sth put in a person's mouth to keep it open (eg by a dentist), or into or over it to prevent him from speaking or crying out. 置於口中使口撐開之物(例如牙醫所用之張口器);塞入口中或覆於口上使不能講話或哭喊之物。 **2** words or action added to his part by an actor in a play. 演員臨時插入的臺詞或動作。 **3** joke, funny story, esp as part of a comedian's act (in the theatre, on radio or TV). (劇院,廣播或電視)插科打諢。□ *vt, vi* (-gg-) **1** [VP6A] put a gag (1) into or over the mouth of; silence; (fig) deprive (sb) of free speech. 塞物於…之口中;覆物於…之口上;使閉口無言;(喻)禁止發言;剝奪(某人)言論自由。 **2** [VP2A] (of an actor, etc) use gags (2, 3). (指演員等)插科打諢。 **3** [VP2A] (colloq) retch. (俗)作嘔。

gaga /'gɑ:gɑ: ; 'gɑgɑ/ *adj* (sl) in senile dotage; crazy. (俚)老朽的;瘋狂的。

gage¹ /geɪdʒ ; gedʒ/ *n* **1** (old use) sth given as security or a guarantee; pledge. (舊用法)抵押物;擔保物。 **2** (= *gauntlet*) glove thrown down (by knights in the Middle Ages) as a challenge to a fight. 中古武士拋於地上表示挑戰的手套。□ *vt* [VP6A] (old use) give or offer as a ~; pledge as a guarantee. (舊用法)以…做抵押;以…爲擔保。

gage² /geɪdʒ ; gedʒ/ ⇨ gauge.

gaggle /'gægl ; 'gægl̩/ *n* flock (of geese); (hum) group (of talkative girls or women). 鵝群;(諧)一群(饒舌婦女)。

gai·ety /'geɪətɪ ; 'geətɪ/ *n* **1** [U] being gay; cheerfulness; bright appearance: 歡樂;愉快;歡樂的氣象: *flags and bunting that added to the ~ of the scene.* 爲那場面增加歡樂氣氛的旗幟。 **2** (*pl* -ties) merrymaking; joyful, festive occasions: (複)作樂;歡樂的場合: *the gaieties of the Christmas season.* 聖誕節期間的歡樂場合。

gaily /'geɪlɪ ; 'gelɪ/ *adv* ⇨ gay.

gain¹ /geɪn ; gen/ *n* **1** [U] increase of possessions; acquiring of wealth: 財物的增加;財富的獲取: *the love of ~;* 愛財; *interested only in ~.* 祇想發財。 **2** (*pl*) (複) **capital ~s,** ⇨ capital. **ill-gotten ~s,** dishonestly obtained profits, etc. 以不正當手段獲得的錢財等。 **3** [C] increase in amount or power: 數量或力量的增加;增進: *a ~ in weight/health;* 體重增加(健康之增進); *a ~ to knowledge.* 知識的增進。**~·ful** /-fl ; -fəl/ *adj* yielding money: 有報酬的;賺錢的: *~ful occupations.* 有報酬的職業。**~·fully** /-fəlɪ ; -fəlɪ/ *adv* in a ~ful manner: 有報酬地: *~fully employed.* 受僱有酬。

gain² /geɪn ; gen/ *vt, vi* **1** [VP6A, 14, 12B, 13B] obtain (sth wanted or needed); increase, add: 獲得(需要之物);增加: *~ experience/momentum/weight;* 得到經驗(增加動量;增加重量); *~ an advantage over a competitor;* 勝過對手;佔上風; *~ strength,* eg become strong again after an illness. 恢復體力(例如病後)。 **~ *ground,*** make progress. 進步。 **~ *time,*** improve one's chances by delaying sth, making pretexts, etc. 拖延時間。 **~ *the upper hand,*** be victorious. 得勝;佔上風。 **2** [VP2A, B, C] **~ *(from),*** make progress; be improved; benefit: 進步;改進;獲益: *~ from an experience.* 從經驗中獲益。*She is ~ing in* (more usu 較常用 *putting on*) *weight.* 她的體重在增加。 **3** [VP2A, B] (of a watch or clock) become fast, ahead of the correct time: (指鐘錶)快於正確的時間: *This watch neither ~s nor loses.* 這錶不快也不慢。*The clock ~s three minutes a day.* 這鐘每天快三分鐘。 **4** [VP3A] **~ *on/upon,*** **(a)** get closer to (the person or thing pursued): 逼近(被追的人或物);趕上: *~ on the other runners in a race.* 在賽跑中趕上其他的選手。 **(b)** go faster than, get farther in advance of: 跑得較…快;超過: *~ on one's pursuers.* 跑得比追趕者快。 **(c)** (of the sea) advance gradually and eat away (the land). (指海)逐漸侵蝕(陸地)。 **5** [VP6A] reach, arrive at (a desired place, esp with effort): 抵達(心中想去的地方,尤指經過一番努力): *~ the top of a mountain.* 到達山頂。*The swimmer ~ed the shore.* 那游泳者抵達岸上。**~·ings** *n pl* earnings; profits; winnings. 收入;收益;贏得之物。

gain·say /,geɪn'seɪ ; ,gen'se/ *vt* (*pt, pp* -said /-'sed ; -'sed/) [VP6A] (liter) (chiefly in neg and interr) deny; contradict: (文)(主要用於否定和疑問句)否認;反駁: *There is no ~ing his honesty,* We cannot deny that he is honest. 我們不能否認他的誠實。

gait /geɪt ; get/ *n* manner of walking or running: 步態;步法: *an awkward/slouching ~.* 難看(垂頭喪氣)的步態。

gai·ter /'geɪtə(r) ; 'getɚ/ *n* cloth or leather covering for the leg from knee to ankle, or for the ankle: 綁腿;皮腿套: *a pair of ~s.* 一副綁腿。

gal /gæl ; gæl/ *n* (dated colloq) girl. (過時俗語)女郎。

gala /'gɑ:lə *US:* 'geɪlə ; 'gelə/ *n* festive occasion; 節日; (attrib): (形容用法): *a ~ night,* eg at a theatre, with special features. 歡樂之夜(例如劇院中有特殊節目之夜)。

ga·lac·tic /gə'læktɪk ; gə'læktɪk/ *adj* of a galaxy or the Galaxy: 太空星群的;銀河系的;天河的: *extra-~ systems,* systems outside the Galaxy. 銀河外面的星系。

gal·an·tine /'gælənti:n ; 'gælən,tin/ *n* white meat, boned, spiced, cooked in the form of a roll, and served cold. 去骨,加香料製成的冷食的肉捲。

gal·axy /'gæləksɪ ; 'gæləksɪ/ *n* (*pl* -xies) **1** any of the large-scale clusters of stars in outer space. 太空中任何大規模的星群;星系。 **the G~,** that which includes our solar system, visible as a luminous band known as 'the Milky Way'. 銀河系;天河。 **2** brilliant company of persons: 一群顯赫的人: *a ~ of talent/beautiful women.* 一群才子(美女)。

gale /geɪl ; gel/ *n* **1** strong and violent wind: 强風;大風: *The ship lost her masts in the ~.* 這船的桅檣被强風吹斷了。*It was blowing a ~.* 刮着大風。 **2** noisy outburst: 一陣喧鬧: *~s of laughter.* 陣陣笑聲。

gall¹ /gɔ:l ; gɔl/ *n* [U] **1** bitter liquid (bile) secreted by the liver. 膽汁。 **'~ bladder** *n* (anat) vessel attached to the liver containing and discharging ~. (解剖)膽囊。⇨ the illus at alimentary. 參看 alimentary 之插圖。 **'~·stone** *n* hard mass that forms in the ~ bladder. 膽石。 **2** bitter feeling: 惡毒;怨恨;痛苦: *with a pen dipped in ~,* used of a writer who makes bitter attacks. 以惡毒的筆調。 **3** (colloq) impudence: (俗)厚顏;鹵莽: *Of all the ~!* 臉皮眞厚!

gall² /gɔ:l ; gɔl/ *n* [C] painful swelling on an animal, esp a horse, caused by rubbing (of harness, etc); place rubbed bare. 擦傷(尤指馬的);擦傷之處。□ *vt* **1** [VP6A] rub sore. 磨傷;擦破。 **2** (fig) hurt the feelings of; humiliate: (喻)傷害…之感情;侮辱: *~ sb with one's remarks.* 用言語傷害某人的感情。*It was ~ing to him to have to ask for a loan.* 必須向人求貸使他感到屈辱。

gall³ /gɔ:l ; gɔl/ *n* unnatural growth produced on a tree by insects, eg on the oak. 蟲癭(例如橡樹上者);沒食子;五倍子。

gal·lant /'gælənt ; 'gælənt/ *adj* **1** (archaic) brave: (古)勇敢的;英勇的: *a ~ knight;* 勇敢的騎士; *~ deeds.* 英勇的事蹟。 **2** fine; grand; stately: 華麗的;堂皇的;壯麗的;雄偉的: *a ~-looking ship;* 華麗的船隻; *a ~ display.* 華麗的展覽。 **3** (also 亦作 /gə'lænt ; gə'lænt/) showing special respect and courtesy to women: 對婦女特別慇懃的: *He was very ~ at the ball.* 他在舞會中對婦女大獻慇懃。□ (also 亦作 /gə'lænt ; gə'lænt/) *n* young man of fashion, esp one who is fond of and attentive to women. 時髦的青年(尤指喜歡女人並對女人獻慇懃者)。**~·ly** *adv* **~ry** *n* **1** [U] bravery. 勇敢;英勇。**2** [U] devotion, chivalrous attention, to women. 尊崇婦女;扶助婦女。**3** [C] (*pl* -ries) elaborately polite or amorous act or speech to a woman. 對婦女慇懃的言行。

gal·leon /ˈgæliən ; ˈgæliən/ *n* Spanish sailing-ship (15th to 17th cc) with a high stern. (十五至十七世紀的)西班牙大帆船(船尾很高)。

galleons

gal·lery /ˈgæləri ; ˈgæləri/ *n* (*pl* -ries) **1** room or building for the display of works of art. 美術品陳列室;美術陳列館;畫廊。**2** (people in the) highest and cheapest seats in a theatre. (戲院中)票價最便宜的最高樓座;樓座觀衆。***play to the ~***, try to win approval or popularity by appealing to the taste of the masses. 設法迎合大衆趣味。**3** raised floor or platform extending from an inner wall of a hall, church, etc: (大廳,教堂等中自內壁伸展出去的)廊臺: *the ˈpress ~ of the House of Commons*, used by newspaper reporters. 下議院的記者席。**4** covered walk or corridor, partly open at one side; colonnade. 走廊;柱廊。**5** long, narrow room: 狹長的房間: *a ˈshooting-~*, for indoor target practice. 室內靶場。**6** horizontal underground passage in a mine. (橫)坑道。⇨ shaft.

gal·ley /ˈgæli ; ˈgæli/ *n* (*pl* ~s) **1** (hist) low, flat single-decked ship, using sails and oars, rowed by slaves or criminals; ancient Greek or Roman warship. (史)(昔時奴隸或犯人划行的用帆與槳的)單甲板平底船;古希臘或羅馬的戰艦。**ˈ~-slave** *n* person condemned to row in a ~. 被罰划船的奴隸;船役囚犯。**2** ship's kitchen. 船上厨房。**3** oblong metal tray in which type is assembled by compositors. 長方形活字盤;檢字盤。**ˈ~-proof** *n* proof(4) on a long slip of paper, before division into pages. 尚未分成頁的校樣;長條校樣。

Gal·lic /ˈgælik ; ˈgælik/ *adj* of Gaul or the Gauls; (often hum) French. 高盧的;高盧人的;(常爲諧語)法國的。**gal·li·cism** /ˈgælisizəm ; ˈgæləˌsizəm/ *n* [C] French way of saying sth, used in another language. 外語中的法國語風。

gal·li·vant /ˌgæliˈvænt ; ˈgæləˌvænt/ *vi* [VP2C] **~ *about／off***, (not used in the simple tenses) (不用於簡單時態) = gad about, ⇨ gad¹: *Where are you ~ing off to now?* 你現在要到哪裏去遊逛?

gal·lon /ˈgælən ; ˈgælən/ *n* measure for liquids, four quarts (4.5 litres). 加侖(液量名,合四夸爾或4.5公升)。⇨ App 5. 參看附錄五。

gal·lop /ˈgæləp ; ˈgæləp/ *n* (of a horse, etc) fastest pace with all four feet off the ground at each stride; period of riding at such a pace: (馬等四蹄同時離地之)飛奔;疾馳;騎馬飛奔之期間: *He rode away at a ~／at full ~*. 他騎着馬疾馳而去。*Shall we go for a ~?* 我們去騎一陣快馬如何?□ *vi, vt* **1** [VP2A, B,C, 6A] (cause to) go at a ~: 疾馳;使飛奔: *He ~ed across the field.* 他騎馬馳過田野。**2** [VP2A, B, C] hurry: 匆匆地做: *~ through one's work／lecture;* 匆匆趕完工作(演說); progress rapidly: 迅速進行: *in a ~ing consumption,* ill with tuberculosis which is rapidly getting worse. 患奔馬癆(卽急劇惡化的肺結核病)。

gal·lows /ˈgæləuz ; ˈgæloz/ *n pl* (usu with *sing v*) wooden framework on which to put criminals to death by hanging: (通常用單數動詞)絞架: *send a man to the ~*, condemn him to be hanged. 處某人以絞刑。*He'll end up on the ~*, will end by being hanged. 他總有一天要受絞刑的。**ˈ~-bird** *n* person who is thought by some to deserve hanging. 應受絞刑的人。

Gal·lup poll /ˈgæləp pəul ; ˈgæləpˈpol/ *n* questioning of a representative sample of people to assess general public opinion about sth, eg how they will vote at a general election, esp as a means of making a forecast. (蓋洛普)民意測驗。

ga·lore /gəˈlɔː(r) ; gəˈlor/ *adv* in plenty: 豐富地: *a meal with beef and beer ~*. 有牛肉和啤酒的豐盛的一餐。

ga·loshes /gəˈlɒʃiz ; gəˈlɑʃiz/ *n pl* **(pair of) ~**, rubber overshoes worn in wet weather. (雨天用)膠套鞋。

ga·lumph /gəˈlʌmf ; gəˈlʌmf/ *vi* (made from *gallop* and *triumph*) prance clumsily or noisily in triumph. (由 gallop 和 triumph 二字轉成)得意揚揚而行;昂首濶步。

gal·van·ism /ˈgælvənizəm ; ˈgælvəˌnizəm/ *n* [U] (science of, medical use of) electricity produced by chemical action from a battery. 由化學作用自電池產生的電;流電;流電學;電療。**gal·vanic** /gælˈvænik ; gælˈvænik/ *adj* **1** of ~. 化學電池之電流的;流電的;用流電的;流電學的;電療的。**2** (fig) (of smiles, movements, etc) sudden and forced (as if produced by an electric shock). (喩)(指微笑,動作等)突然而勉强的(如被電擊般)。

gal·van·ize /ˈgælvənaiz ; ˈgælvəˌnaiz/ *vt* **1** [VP6A] coat (sheet iron, etc) with metal, eg zinc: 電鍍(鐵片等);鍍鋅於: *~d iron.* 鍍鋅鐵;白鐵。**2** [VP 6A, 14] ***~ sb (into doing sth)***, shock or rouse. 驚起或激勵(某人做某事)。

gam·bit /ˈgæmbit ; ˈgæmbit/ *n* kinds of opening move in chess (in which a player sacrifices a pawn or other piece to secure certain ends); (fig) any initial move: 西洋棋開局時犧牲一子以達到目的之一着棋;(喩)任何開始的行動: *His opening ~ at the debate was a direct attack on Government policy.* 他在辯論開始的演說乃直接抨擊政府的政策。

gamble /ˈgæmbl ; ˈgæmbl/ *vi, vt* **1** [VP2A, B, C] play games of chance for money; take great risks for the chance of winning sth or making a profit: 賭博;爲贏取某物或牟利而冒大險;投機: *He lost his money gambling at cards／gambling on the Stock Exchange／gambling in oil shares, etc.* 他賭紙牌(買賣股票,投資油股等)輸(損失)了錢。**2** [VP15B] ***~ sth away***, lose by gambling: 賭輸: *He has ~d away half his fortune.* 他賭博輸去了一半的財產。□ *n* [C] undertaking or attempt with risk of loss and chance of profit or advantage. 冒險的事業;賭博;投機。***take a ~ (on sth)***, risk (it). 冒險。**gam·bler** *n* person who ~s. 賭徒;賭博者;爲利益而冒險者。**gam·bling** *n* [U] playing games for money; taking risks for possible advantage: 賭博;爲可能利益而冒險: *fond of gambling.* 嗜賭。**ˈgambling-den／-house** *n* (old use) place where gambling is carried on. (舊用法)賭窟。⇨ game³.

gam·boge /gæmˈbuːʒ *US:* -ˈbəuʒ ; gæmˈbuʒ/ *n* [U] deep yellow colouring matter used by artists. 藤黃;雌黃(畫家所用深黃色顏料)。

gam·bol /ˈgæmbl ; ˈgæmbl/ *n* (usu *pl*) quick, playful, jumping or skipping movements, eg of lambs, children. (通常用複數)(小羊,小孩等)雀躍;嬉戲。□ *vi* (-ll-, US also -l-) [VP2A, C] make such movements. 雀躍;嬉戲。

game¹ /geim ; gem/ *n* **1** [C] form of play, esp with rules, eg tennis, football, cards: (有規則的)遊戲(例如網球,足球,紙牌): *play ~s;* 做遊戲; *have a ~ of whist.* 玩惠斯特牌。*He plays a good ~ of snooker*, is a good player. 他撞球打得很好。***be off one's ~***, be out of form, not playing well. 健康與訓練情形不佳,玩得不好。***have the ~ in one's***

hands, be sure to win it, be able to direct it. 有把握獲勝。***play the ～,*** keep the rules; (fig) be straightforward and honest. 遵守規則；(喻)正直誠實。**'～s-master／-mistress,** teacher in charge of ～s at a school. 教遊戲的男(女)老師。**～s·manship** /'geɪmzmənʃɪp ; 'gemzmən,ʃɪp/ *n* (colloq) the art of winning ～s by upsetting the confidence of one's opponents. (俗)擾亂對手信心而獲勝之道。**2** [C] apparatus, etc needed for a ～, eg one played by children with a board and dice and counters, such as ludo and draughts. 遊戲器具(例如骰子和西洋棋遊戲的器具)。**3** (*pl*) (international) athletic contests: (複)(國際)運動會: *the Olympic／Commonwealth／Highland G～s;* 奧林匹克(大英國協,蘇格蘭高地)運動會; (in Greece and Rome, ancient times) athletic and dramatic contests. (古希臘和羅馬)運動和戲劇競賽會。 **4** [C] single round in some contests, eg tennis: (網球等比賽之)一次；一盤；一場；一局: *win four ～s in the first set;* 在第一盤中贏四局; score needed to win; state of the ～: 比賽的積分；比賽狀況: *the ～ is four all;* 雙方各得四分； *～ all,* equal score; 各贏一次；平手；打平； *～, set and match.* 一局、一盤、一場比賽。 **5** [C] scheme, plan or undertaking; dodge or trick: 計畫；策略；詭計: *He was playing a deep ～,* engaged in a secret scheme of some sort. 他在從事一祕密計畫。*I wish I knew what his ～ is,* what he is trying to do. 但願我能知道他想做些什麼。*That's a ～ two people can play,* said when two people use the same scheme against each other. 那是一場兩個人都會玩的把戲(意謂兩個人彼此向對方玩同一把戲)。*So that's your little ～,* said when one discovers what sb is scheming to do. 原來那就是你的鬼把戲。*The ～ is up,* The scheme is discovered and thwarted. 計謀被拆穿而成功無望了。*You're playing Smith's ～,* You are, unintentionally, helping to advance Smith's scheme. 你無意中幫助了史密斯的計謀。*None of your little ～s!* Don't try to play tricks on me! 我不會上你的當！不要要你那套把戲！ *You're having a ～ with me,* trying to trick me, deceive me, etc. 你在欺騙我。***ˌgive the '～ away,*** reveal a secret trick, scheme, etc. 洩露祕密計謀等。***make ～ of sb,*** ridicule him. 嘲弄某人。 **6** [U] (collective) (flesh of) wild animals and birds hunted for sport or food. (集合用法)獵物；野獸或野禽之肉。**big ～** *n* [U] the larger animals (elephants, lions, tigers). 大獵物(象,獅,虎)。**fair ～,** *n* [U] what may be lawfully hunted or shot; (fig) person or institution that may with reason be attacked or criticized. 不禁獵的鳥獸；(喻)可據理加以攻擊或批評的人或制度。**'～-bag,** bag for holding ～ killed by sportsmen. (盛裝獵物之)獵袋。**'～-bird,** wild bird (eg grouse, pheasant) hunted for sport or food. 獵鳥；獵禽(例如松鷄,雉等)。⇨ illus at fowl. 參看 fowl 之插圖。**'～-cock,** of the kind bred for cock-fighting. 鬪鷄。**'～-keeper,** man employed to breed and protect ～, eg pheasants, grouse, on a country estate. 獵物看守人。**'～ laws,** laws regulating the killing and preservation of ～. 狩獵規則；狩獵法。**'～-licence,** one to kill and deal in ～. 狩獵許可證；狩獵執照。 **gamy** /'geɪmɪ ; 'gemɪ/ *adj* having the flavour and odour of ～(6), esp when high[1](8). 有獵物氣味的(尤指略有臭味時)。

game[2] /geɪm ; gem/ *adj* **1** brave; ready to go on fighting; spirited. 勇敢的；奮勇的；精神抖擻的。**2** ***～ for／to do sth,*** spirited enough, willing: 高興做…的；願意…的: *Are you ～ for a 10-mile walk?* 你有興趣走十哩路嗎？ *He's ～ to do anything you may suggest.* 不論你做何建議,他都願接受。**～·ly** *adv*

game[3] /geɪm ; gem/ *vi, vt* [VP2A, C, 15B] gamble. 賭博。**'gaming-house／-rooms／-table,** house etc (usu licensed) for gambling. 賭場(通常有許可執照)。

game[4] /geɪm ; gem/ *adj* (of a leg, arm, etc) lame; crippled. (指腿,臂等)跛的；殘廢的。

gamma /'gæmə ; 'gæmə/ *n* third letter of the Greek alphabet. 希臘字母之第三個字母。⇨ App 4. 參看附錄四。**'～-rays** *n pl* rays of very short wave-length emitted by radio-active substances. *r* 射線；加馬射線(放射性元素所放出的極短波射線)。

gam·mon /'gæmən ; 'gæmən/ *n* [C] piece of bacon from the side of a pig, including the hind leg; [U] smoked or cured ham. 醃豬後腿；臘腿；燻腿。

gammy /'gæmɪ ; 'gæmɪ/ *adj* (colloq) (俗) ＝game[4]: *a ～ leg.* 跛的腿。

gamp /gæmp ; gæmp/ *n* (hum; dated) umbrella (esp a large, untidy one). (諧；過時用語)傘(尤指大而不整潔者)。

gamut /'gæmət ; 'gæmət/ *n* **the ～,** complete extent or scope of sth: 全部；整個範圍: *the whole ～ of feeling,* eg from the greatest joy to the depths of despair or misery. 全部感情歷程(例如從極端喜悅至絕望或痛苦)。***run the ～ (of sth),*** experience the whole range (of it). 經驗全部歷程。

gan·der /'gændə(r) ; 'gændɚ/ *n* male goose. 雄鵝。

gang /gæŋ ; gæŋ/ *n* **1** group of persons going about or working together, esp for criminal purposes. 幫；一夥(尤指有犯罪企圖者)。⇨ gangster. **2** (colloq) group of persons going about together, disapproved of by the speaker: (俗)一幫(爲說話者所不滿者): *Don't get mixed up with that ～; they spend too much time drinking and gambling.* 不要同那一幫人混在一起,他們終日飲酒賭博。□ *vi* [VP2C] ***～ up,*** act together as a ～: 聯合起來；結成一夥: *They ～ed up on／against me.* 他們聯合起來對付我。**～er** /'gæŋə(r) ; 'gæŋɚ/ *n* foreman of a ～(1). 工頭。

gan·gling /'gæŋglɪŋ ; 'gæŋglɪŋ/ *adj* (of a person) lanky; tall, thin and awkward-looking. (指人)瘦長的；瘦長而難看的。

gan·glion /'gæŋglɪən ; 'gæŋglɪən/ *n* (*pl* ～s or -lia /-lɪə ; -lɪə/) group of nerve-cells from which nerve-fibres radiate; (fig) centre of force, activity or interest. 神經節；神經中樞；(喻)(力量,活動或興趣的)中心。

gang·plank /'gæŋplæŋk ; 'gæŋ,plæŋk/ *n* movable plank placed between a ship or boat and the land, or between two boats or ships. (上下船的)跳板。

gan·grene /'gæŋgriːn ; 'gæŋgrin/ *n* [U] death and decay of a part of the body, eg because the supply of blood to it has been stopped: 壞疽: *G～ set in and his leg had to be amputated.* 他的腿生了壞疽,必須切掉。□ *vt, vi* [VP6A, 2A] affect, become affected, with ～. 使生疽；生疽。**gan·gren·ous** /'gæŋgrɪnəs ; 'gæŋgrənəs/ *adj*

gang·ster /'gæŋstə(r) ; 'gæŋstɚ/ *n* member of a gang of armed criminals: 歹徒；匪徒: (attrib) (形容用法) *'～ films.* 警匪片。

gang·way /'gæŋweɪ ; 'gæŋ,we/ *n* **1** opening in a ship's side; movable bridge from this to the land. (船邊之)梯口；(由梯口至岸上的)舷梯。 **2** (US 美＝*aisle*) passage between rows of seats, eg in the House of Commons, in a theatre or concert-hall, or between rows of people. 兩排座位或人之間的通道(例如下議院,劇院或音樂廳中者)。□ *int* Make way, please! 請讓路！請閃開！

gan·net /'gænɪt ; 'gænɪt/ *n* kind of large sea-bird. 塘鵝。

gan·try /'gæntrɪ ; 'gæntrɪ/ *n* (*pl* -ries) structure of steel bars to support a travelling crane, railway signals over several tracks, etc. (支撐移動起重機,鐵路信號裝置等的)橋形臺架。

gaol, jail /dʒeɪl ; dʒel/ *n* (usu *jail* in US) [C] public prison; [U] confinement in prison: (美國通常用 jail) 監牢；牢獄；監禁: *three years in ～;* 坐監三年; *be sent to ～.* 被下獄。**'～-bird** *n* prisoner, esp one who has often been in prison; rogue. 囚犯；(尤指)慣犯；惡棍。 **'～-break** *n* [C] escape from ～. 越獄。□ *vt* [VP6A] put in ～. 下牢；監禁。 **gaoler, jailer, jailor** /'dʒeɪlə(r) ; 'dʒelɚ/ *nn* man in charge of a ～ or the prisoners in it. 看守監獄者；獄卒；獄吏。

gap /gæp ; gæp/ *n* **1** break or opening in a wall,

hedge, etc: (牆壁,樹籬等之)裂縫;缺口: *The sheep got out of the field through a gap in the hedge.* 羊從樹籬的間隙跑出牧場。*We must see that there is no gap in our defences.* 我們必須注意不要使我們的防線有漏洞。 **2** unfilled space; interval; wide separation (of ideas, etc): 空白;間隔;(思想,意見等之)懸隔;歧異: *a gap in a conversation,* interval of silence; 談話的間斷; *fill in the gaps in one's education,* study what one failed to learn while at school, etc; 補充一個人的教育; *a wide gap between the views of the two statesmen.* 兩位政治家意見之歧異。***bridge/fill/stop a gap,*** supply sth lacking. 補充所缺之物。 ⇨ *stopgap* at stop¹(8). **credi'bility gap,** failure of one person, group, etc to convince another that he or it is telling the truth. 信用的差距(無法使對方相信所說的話)。**gene'ration gap,** failure or inability of the younger and older generations to communicate, understand one another. 代溝(年輕一代與年長一代間之不能溝通思想或彼此了解)。 **ˌgap'-toothed** /'tu:θt ; 'tuθt/ *adj* having teeth which are wide apart. 牙齒間縫隙很大的。**3** gorge or pass between mountains. 山峽;山間狹路;隘口。

gape /geɪp ; gep/ *vi* [VP2A, C] **1** ~ ***(at sb/sth)*** open the mouth wide; yawn; stare open-mouthed and in surprise: 張口;打哈欠;目瞪口呆地注視;張口驚視: *country visitors gaping at the neon lights.* 張口驚視霓虹燈的鄉下人。**2** be or become open wide: 裂開: *a gaping chasm.* 裂罅。□ *n* yawn; open-mouthed stare. 打哈欠;目瞪口呆;張口凝視。**the ~s, (a)** disease of poultry causing them to gape until they die (with the beak wide open). 家禽之一種張嘴病。**(b)** (joc) fit of yawning. (謔)一陣哈欠。

gar·age /'gærɑ:ʒ *US:* gə'rɑ:ʒ ; gə'rɑʒ/ *n* **1** building in which to keep a car or cars. 汽車間;汽車房。**2** (US 美 = *service station*) roadside petrol and service station. 路邊加油站;修車廠。□ *vt* [VP6A] put (a motor-vehicle) in a ~. 將(汽車)送入車房。

garb /gɑ:b ; gɑrb/ *n* [U] (style of) dress (esp as worn by a particular kind of person): 服裝(尤指某一種人所穿者);裝束: *a man in clerical ~.* 穿着牧師服裝的人。□ *vt* [VP6A] (usu passive) dress: (通常用被動語態)裝扮: *~ed in motley.* 穿着雜色衣服。

gar·bage /'gɑ:bɪdʒ ; 'gɑrbɪdʒ/ *n* [U] **1** waste food put out as worthless, or for pigs, etc; (US) rubbish, refuse (of any kind). (丟棄或餵豬等之)剩飯殘羹;(美)垃圾。**'~-can** *n* (US) dustbin. (美)垃圾箱。**2** (colloq) worthless material; meaningless or irrelevant data in a storage device of a computer. (俗)無價值的資料;無意義或不相關的電腦資料。

garble /'gɑ:bl ; 'gɑrbl̩/ *vt* [VP6A] make an incomplete or unfair selection from statements, facts, etc, esp in order to give false ideas: 斷章取義: *a ~d report of a speech.* 曲解一演說的報導。

gar·den /'gɑ:dn ; 'gɑrdn̩/ *n* **1** [C, U] (piece of) ground used for growing flowers, fruit, vegetables, etc: 花園;果園;菜園: *a kitchen ~,* for vegetables; 菜園; *a market ~,* for vegetables, fruit and flowers for sale in public markets; 供應市場蔬菜,水果和花的農圃; (attrib) (形容用法) *a ~ wall;* 花園之牆; *~ flowers/plants.* 園中的花(植物)。*We have not much ~/only a small ~.* 我們的花園不大。***lead sb up the ~ path,*** (colloq) mislead him. (俗)使入歧途;使迷惑。**ˌ~ 'city/'suburb** *n* one laid out with many open spaces, and planted with numerous trees. (多空地,種有大量樹木之)花園城市(市郊)。**'~ party** *n* social gathering held out of doors on a lawn, in a ~ or park, etc. 園遊會。 **2** (usu *pl*) public park: (通常用複數)公園: *Kensington G~s,* in London; (倫敦之)肯星頓公園; *botanical/zoological ~s.* 植物(動物)園。□ *vi* [VP2A] cultivate a ~: 從事園藝;種植花木: *He's been ~ing all day.* 他已做了一整天的園藝工作。**~er** *n* person who works in a ~, either for pay or as a hobby. 園丁;花匠;園藝家。**~·ing** *n* [U] cultivating of ~s: 園藝: *fond of ~ing;* 愛好園藝; (attrib) (形容用法) *~ing gloves/tools.* 園藝用手套(工具)。

gar·denia /gɑ:'di:nɪə ; gɑr'dinɪə/ *n* (kind of) tree or shrub with large white or yellow flowers, usu sweetsmelling. 梔子;梔子屬(開白花或黃花的樹或灌木,其花通常有香味)。

gar·gan·tuan /gɑ:'gæntjʊən ; gɑr'gæntʃʊən/ *adj* enormous; gigantic. 龐大的;巨大的。

gargle /'gɑ:gl ; 'gɑrgl̩/ *vt, vi* [VP6A, 2A] wash the throat with liquid kept in motion by a stream of breath. 漱喉。□ *n* liquid used for this purpose; act of gargling. 含漱劑;漱口劑;漱喉。

gar·goyle /'gɑ:gɔɪl ; 'gɑrgɔɪl/ *n* stone or metal spout, usu in the form of a grotesque human or animal creature, to carry off rain-water from the roof of a building (esp Gothic-style churches). 承霤口;滴水;筧嘴(通常作古怪之人形或動物形狀,尤指哥德式建築之教堂上者)。⇨ the illus at church. 參看 church 之挿圖。

gar·ish /'geərɪʃ ; 'gɛrɪʃ/ *adj* unpleasantly bright; over-coloured or over-decorated: 炫耀的;過於艷麗的;過份裝飾的: *~ clothes.* 過於艷麗的衣服。**~·ly** *adv*

gar·land /'gɑ:lənd ; 'gɑrlənd/ *n* circle of flowers or leaves as an ornament or decoration; this as a prize for victory, etc. (作爲裝飾或勝利獎品等之)花圈;花環;花冠。□ *vt* [VP6A] decorate, crown, with a ~ or ~s. 飾以花圈;戴以花冠。

gar·lic /'gɑ:lɪk ; 'gɑrlɪk/ *n* [U] onion-like plant with strong taste and smell, used in cooking: 蒜;蒜頭;大蒜: *a clove of ~,* one of the small bulbs making up the compound bulb of a ~ plant; 一瓣蒜; *too much ~ in the food;* 食物中放太多的蒜; *smelling of ~.* 有大蒜氣味。

gar·ment /'gɑ:mənt ; 'gɑrmənt/ *n* [C] article of clothing: 衣服: (US, attrib) (美,形容用法) *the '~ industry;* 製衣工業; *'~ workers.* 製衣工人。

gar·ner /'gɑ:nə(r) ; 'gɑrnɚ/ *n* (poet, rhet) storehouse for grain, etc (also fig). (詩,修辭)穀倉;倉庫(亦作喻)。□ *vt* [VP6A, 15B] ~ ***(in/up),*** store, gather. 儲藏;收藏。

gar·net /'gɑ:nɪt ; 'gɑrnɪt/ *n* semi-precious gem of deep transparent red. 柘榴石。

gar·nish /'gɑ:nɪʃ ; 'gɑrnɪʃ/ *vt* [VP6A, 14] ~ ***(with),*** decorate, esp food for the table: 裝飾(尤指食物): *fish ~ed with slices of lemon.* 用檸檬片裝飾的魚。□ *n* sth used to decorate a dish of food for the table. 食物上的裝飾物。

gar·ret /'gærət ; 'gærɪt/ *n* room (often small, dark, etc) on the top floor of a house, esp in the roof. 閣樓;屋頂室(常是小而暗的)。

gar·ri·son /'gærɪsn ; 'gærəsn̩/ *n* [C] military force stationed in a town or fort: 衞戍部隊;要塞駐軍;駐軍: (attrib) (形容用法) *a ~ town,* one in which a ~ is permanently stationed. 有部隊駐防之城市。□ *vt* [VP6A] supply a town, etc with a ~; place troops, etc on ~ duty. 以衞戍部隊駐守(城市等);派(軍隊等)駐守。

gar·rotte, ga·rotte /gə'rɒt ; gə'rot/ *vt* [VP6A] execute (a person condemned to death) by strangling or throttling (a stick being twisted to tighten a cord over the windpipe); murder (sb) in this way. 執行絞刑(扭動一棒,拉緊繩索,勒咽喉以絞殺);絞殺(某人)。□ *n* this method of capital punishment; apparatus used for it. 以上述方法所作的絞刑;上述絞刑所用的刑具。

gar·ru·lous/ 'gærələs ; 'gærələs/ *adj* talkative; talking too much about unimportant things. 愛說話的;絮聒的。**gar·ru·lity** /gə'ru:lətɪ ; gə'rulətɪ/ *n* [U].

gar·ter /'gɑ:tə(r);'gɑrtɚ/ *n* (elastic) band worn round the leg to keep a stocking in place. (彈性)襪帶。**the G~,** (badge of) the highest order of English knighthood. 嘉德勳位(英國爵士之最高勳位);嘉德勳章。

gas /gæs ; gæs/ *n* (*pl* gases /'gæsɪz ; 'gæsɪz/ **1** [C] kind of air-like substance (used chiefly of those that do not become liquid or solid at or-

G

dinary temperatures): 氣體(主要用以指在通常溫度下不會變爲液體或固體者): *Air is a mixture of gases.* 空氣是各種氣體的混合物。*Hydrogen and oxygen are gases.* 氫和氧是氣體。 **2** [U] pure gas or mixture of gases used for lighting and heating, eg natural gas or the kind manufactured from coal; gas manufactured for use in war (*poison gas*), or occurring naturally, eg in a coal mine: 天然氣;煤氣;瓦斯;毒氣: *put the kettle on the gas*, ie on the gas-ring or cooker. 將壺放在煤氣爐上。 **'gas-bag** *n* **(a)** bag for holding gas, eg in an airship. 蓄氣囊(例如飛艇中者)。 **(b)** (colloq) person who talks too much without saying anything useful or interesting. (俗)廢話連篇的人。 **'gas-bracket** *n* pipe with one or more burners projecting from a wall. 牆上伸出的有噴嘴的煤氣管。 **'gas chamber** *n* room filled with gas for lethal purposes. 毒氣室。 **'gas-cooker** *n* stove (with gas-rings and an oven) for cooking by gas. 煤氣爐。 **'gas fire** *n* one for heating a room by gas. 煤氣暖爐。 **'gas-fitter** *n* workman who provides a building with gas-fittings. 安裝煤氣裝置的工人。 **'gas-fittings** *n pl* apparatus, eg pipes, burners, etc for heating or lighting with gas. 煤氣裝置(如用煤氣加熱或點燈之管道、燈頭、爐心等)。 **'gas-helmet** *n* = gas-mask. **'gas-holder** *n* = gasometer. **'gas·light** *n* [U] light produced by burning coal-gas. 煤氣燈光。 **'gas-mask** *n* breathing apparatus to protect the wearer against harmful gases. 防毒面罩;防毒面具。 **'gas-meter** *n* meter for registering the amount of gas that passes through it. 煤氣表(記錄煤氣之用量)。 **'gas-oven** *n* **(a)** one heated by gas. 煤氣爐。 **(b)** = gas chamber. **'gas poker** *n* metal rod with holes in one end, connected to a supply of gas, used to light fires in a fireplace. 煤氣火棒(一端有孔之金屬棒,與煤氣源相接,用以在火爐中燃火者)。 **'gas-ring** *n* metal ring with numerous small holes and supplied with gas for cooking, etc. (有環形噴火孔的輕便)煤氣爐。 **'gas-stove** = gas-cooker. **'gas tar** *n* [U] coal-tar produced during the manufacture of coal-gas. (製煤氣時產生的)煤焦油。 **'gas-works** *n pl* (*sing v*) place where coal-gas is manufactured. (後接單數動詞)煤氣廠。 **3** (also 亦作 *'laughing-gas*) nitrous oxide (N_2O), used by dentists as an anaesthetic. 笑氣(牙醫用作麻醉劑的氧化亞氮)。 **4** (US colloq) (abbr of *gasoline*) petrol. (美俗)汽油(爲 gasoline 之略)。 ***step on the gas***, press down the accelerator pedal; increase speed. 踩加速器;加速。 **'gas-engine** *n* one from which power is obtained by the regular explosion of gas in a closed cylinder. 燃氣(發動)機。 **'gas-station**, (US) = petrol station. (美)加油站。 **5** (fig, colloq) empty talk; boasting. (喻,俗)空談;吹牛。 □ *vt, vi* (-ss-) **1** [VP6A] poison or overcome by gas. 以毒氣毒害;以毒氣克服。 **2** [VP2A, C] (colloq) talk for a long time without saying much that is useful. (俗)空談;瞎扯。

gas·eous /ˈgæsɪəs ; ˈgæsɪəs/ *adj* of or like gas: 氣體的;似氣體的: *a ~ mixture*. 氣體混合物。

gash /gæʃ ; gæʃ/ *n* [C] long deep cut or wound. 長而深的切痕或傷口。 □ *vt* [VP6A] make a ~ in. 長而深地切傷。

gas·ify /ˈgæsɪfaɪ ; ˈgæsə,faɪ/ *vt, vi* [VP6A, 2A] (cause to) change into gas. (使)變成氣體;氣化。 **gasi·fi·ca·tion** /ˌgæsɪfɪˈkeɪʃn ; ˌgæsəfɪˈkeʃən/ *n*

gas·ket /ˈgæskɪt ; ˈgæskɪt/ *n* **1** strip or soft, flat piece of material used for packing a joint, piston, etc to prevent steam, gas, etc from escaping. 墊圈;墊板;密合墊;接合墊料(裝於接頭處,活塞周圍,以免漏氣等的帶形或軟扁的填塞物)。 **2** (usu *pl*) (naut) small cords used for tying a furled sail to a yard. (通常用複數)(航海)束帆索。

gaso·line (also **-lene**) /ˈgæsəliːn ; ˈgæsḷˌin/ *n* [U] (US) petrol; motor spirit. (美)汽油。

gas·ometer /gəˈsɒmɪtə(r) ; gæsˈɑmətɚ/ *n* large round tank in which gas is stored and measured (usu at a gas-works) and from which it is distributed through pipes. 氣櫃;煤氣貯存計量器(通常設於煤氣廠中,裝有管子輸送煤氣)。

gasp /gɑːsp *US:* gæsp ; gæsp/ *vi, vt* **1** [VP2A, C] struggle for breath; take short, quick breaths as a fish does out of water: 喘氣;喘息: *~ing for breath;* 喘息; *~ing* (= breathless) *with rage／surprise.* 氣(驚奇)得喘不過氣來。 **2** [VP6A, 15B] *~ (out)*, utter in a breathless way: 喘着氣說出: *He ~ed out a few words.* 他喘着氣說出了幾個字。 □ *n* [C] catching of the breath through pain, surprise, etc: (因痛苦,驚奇等)喘氣;屏息: *at one's last ~*, exhausted; at the point of death. 奄奄一息;卽將斷氣。

gassy /ˈgæsɪ ; ˈgæsɪ/ *adj* of or like gas; full of gas; (of talk, etc) empty; vain and boastful. 氣體的;氣狀的;充滿氣體的;(指談話等)空洞的;誇張的。

gas·tric /ˈgæstrɪk ; ˈgæstrɪk/ *adj* of the stomach: 胃的: *a ~ ulcer;* 胃潰瘍; *~ fever;* 胃熱; *~ juices.* 胃液。 **gas·tri·tis** /gæˈstraɪtɪs ; gæsˈtraɪtɪs/ *n* [U] inflammation of the stomach. 胃炎。

gas·tron·omy /gæˈstrɒnəmɪ ; gæsˈtrɑnəmɪ/ *n* [U] art and science of choosing, preparing and eating good food. 美食術;美食學。 **gas·tron·omic**/ ˌgæstrəˈnɒmɪk ; ˌgæstrəˈnɑmɪk/ *adj* of ~. 美食術的;美食學的。

gate /geɪt ; get/ *n* **1** opening in the wall of a city, hedge, fence or other enclosure, capable of being closed by means of a barrier; barrier that closes such an opening, either of solid wood or of iron gratings or bars, usu on hinges; barrier used to control the passage of water, eg into or out of a lock on a canal: 城門;籬笆門;圍牆門;大門;門扇;扉;閘門: *He opened the garden ~ and went into the street.* 他打開花園的門走到街上去。 *He jumped over the ~ into the field.* 他跳過柵門進入田野。 **'~-crash** *vt* [VP6A] enter (a building at which there is a private social occasion of some sort) without invitation or payment. 未被邀請或付費而參加(私人社交場合); 擅行入場。 Hence, 由此產生, **'~-crasher** *n.* **'~-house** *n* house built at the side of, or over, a ~, eg at the entrance to a park, the house being used by a *'~-keeper*. 門房(例如公園入口處供守門人所用者)。 **,~-legged 'table**, table with legs that can be moved out to support a folding top. (桌腳可拉開以支撐摺疊式桌面的)摺疊式桌子。 **'~ money** *n* total sum paid for admission to a public spectacle in a stadium, etc. 入場費。 **'~-post** *n* post on which a ~ is hung or against which it is closed. 門柱。 ***between you (and) me and the ~-post***, in strict confidence. 極祕密的;嚴守祕密的。 **'~·way** *n* way in or out that can be closed by a ~ or ~s; (fig) means of approach: 門口;通路;(喻)接近的手段: *a ~way to fame／knowledge.* 求得名譽(知識)之門徑。 **2** = ~ money, ⇨ 1 above. 參看上列第 1 義。 **3** **'starting ~**, barrier (either of horizontal ropes that are lifted or of rows of stalls with barriers) at the start of a horse or greyhound race. (賽馬或賽狗時的)起跑門;起賽柵門。 □ *vt.* [VP6A] confine (a student) to college or school (as a penalty). (大學或中學)禁止

a gate-legged table

G

(學生)外出(作爲懲罰)。

gâ·teau /'gætəu *US:* gæ'təu; gɑ'to/ *n* (*pl* ~x /-təuz; -toz/ or ~s) (F) rich fancy cake, often served in slices. (法)一種味濃特製的糕餅(常切成片食用)。

gather /'gæðə(r); 'gæðɚ/ *vt, vi* **1** [VP6A, 15A, B, 2A, C] get, come or bring together: 集合;聚集: *He soon ~ed a crowd round him.* 他不久便聚合了一群人在他周圍。*A crowd soon ~ed round him.* 一群人不久便聚集在他的周圍。*The clouds are ~ing; it's going to rain.* 雲在集結,天要下雨了。***be ~ed to one's fathers,*** (liter or rhet) die. (文或修辭)死。**2** [VP6A, 12B, 13B] pick (flowers, etc); collect: 採集(花等);收集: *~ one's papers and books together.* 將文件和書籍收集起來。*Please ~ me some flowers/~ some flowers for me.* 請爲我採一些花。**3** [VP6A] obtain gradually; gain little by little: 逐漸獲得;漸增: *~ information/impressions/experience.* 逐漸獲得消息(印象,經驗)。*The train ~ed speed as it left the station.* 火車離站時速度漸增。**4** [VP6A, 9] understand; conclude: 瞭解;推斷: *What did you ~ from his statement?* 你推想他的聲明是什麼意思? *I ~, from what you say, that....* 從你的話中,我得到的結論是…。**5** [VP6A, 15A, B] (in sewing) pull together into small folds by putting a thread through; draw parts of material, a garment closer together: (縫紉)縫衣摺;打摺: *a skirt ~ed at the waist.* 腰部打摺的裙子。**6** [VP2A] (of an abscess or boil) form pus and swell up; come to a head. (指膿腫或瘡)化濃;出頭。**~·ing** *n* [C] **1** coming together of people; meeting. 聚集;集合。**2** swelling with pus in it. 膿腫。

gauche /gəuʃ; goʃ/ *adj* socially awkward; tactless. 不善交際的;不圓滑的;無手腕的。**gauch·erie** /'gəuʃərɪ *US:* ˌgəuʃə'riː; ˌgoʃə'ri/ *n* [U] ~ behaviour; [C] ~ act, movement, etc. 不善交際;無手腕;笨拙的行動。

gaucho /'gautʃəu; 'gautʃo/ *n* (*pl* ~s) cowboy of mixed European and American Indian descent. 有歐洲與美洲印第安人混合血統的牧人。

gaud /gɔːd; gɔd/ *n* [C] showy ornament. 華麗的裝飾物。

gaudy[1] /'gɔːdɪ; 'gɔdɪ/ *adj* (-ier, -iest) too bright and showy; gay or bright in a tasteless way: 炫麗的;俗麗的: *~ decorations;* 俗麗的裝飾品; *cheap and ~ jewels.* 價廉而炫麗的珠寶。**gaud·ily** /-ɪlɪ; -əlɪ/ *adv*

gaudy[2] /'gɔːdɪ; 'gɔdɪ/ *n* annual college dinner, given to former members. 大學每年爲校友舉行的宴會。

gauge (US also **gage**) /geɪdʒ; gedʒ/ *n* **1** [U] standard measure; extent: 標準度量;程度;範圍: *take the ~ of* (*eg sb's character*), estimate, judge. 估計;判斷(某人的品行等)。**2** [U, C] distance between rails (or between opposite wheels on a vehicle that runs on rails): 鐵道兩軌間的距離; 軌距; 軌幅: *standard ~;* 標準軌距; *broad ~*, more than 4 ft 8½ in; 寬軌(寬於4呎8·5吋); *narrow ~*, less than 3 ft 8½in.窄軌(不足3呎8·5吋)。**3** [U] thickness of wire, sheet-metal, etc; diameter of a bullet, etc. 金屬線的直徑; 金屬板的厚度; 子彈等的直徑。**4** [C] instrument for measuring, eg rainfall, strength of wind, size, diameter, etc of tools, wire, etc. 計量器(例如雨量計,風力計,量度工具、金屬線等的大小、直徑等的儀器)。□ *vt* [VP6A] measure accurately: 精確計量: *~ the diameter of wire/the contents of a barrel/the rainfall/the strength of the wind;* 計量金屬線的直徑(桶之容積,雨量,風力); (fig) make an estimate, form a judgement, of: (喻)估計;判斷: *~ a person's character.* 估量一人的品格。

Gaul /gɔːl; gɔl/ *n* Celt of ancient ~ (the area now known as France and Belgium). 高盧人(古代高盧地區之克爾特人,所居地區卽現今之法國和比利時)。

gaunt /gɔːnt; gɔnt/ *adj* (of a person) lean, haggard, as from hunger, ill-health or suffering; (of a place) grim or desolate: (指人)憔悴的;形容枯槁的; 枯瘦的(如因飢餓,不健康或受苦而形成); (指地方)荒涼的: *a ~ hillside.* 荒涼的山坡。**~·ness** *n*

gaunt·let[1] /'gɔːntlɪt; 'gɔntlɪt/ *n* **1** glove with metal plates worn by soldiers in the Middle Ages. (中古士兵所戴的)鐵手套。⇨ the illus at armour. 參看 armour 之挿圖。***throw down/pick up/take up the ~,*** give/accept a challenge to a fight. 挑(應)戰。**2** strong glove with a wide cuff covering the wrist, used for driving, fencing, etc. (駕駛,擊劍等所戴的)寬口大手套。

gaunt·let[2] /'gɔːntlɪt; 'gɔntlɪt/ *n* (only in) (僅用於) ***run the ~,*** run between two rows of men who strike the victim as he passes; (fig) be exposed to continuous severe criticism, risk, danger: 在兩排人中跑過並受衆人夾笞; (喻)受嚴厲批評;冒大險: *He ran the ~ of their criticism/scorn.* 他受到他們嚴厲的批評(尖刻的嘲笑)。

gauze /gɔːz; gɔz/ *n* [U] thin, transparent net-like material of silk, cotton, etc (for medical use) or of wire (for screening windows against insects, etc). 薄紗;紗布 (醫用); 鐵紗; 紗網 (做紗窗等用者)。**gauzy** *adj*

gave /geɪv; gev/ *pt* of give.

gavel /'gævl; 'gævḷ/ *n* hammer used by an auctioneer or a chairman as a signal for order or attention. 拍賣者或主席所用的槌。

ga·votte /gə'vɒt; gə'vɑt/ *n* [C] (music for an) old French dance like the minuet but more lively. 嘉禾舞 (昔時法國一種似小步舞而更爲活潑的一種舞蹈); 嘉禾舞曲。

gawk /gɔːk; gɔk/ *n* awkward or bashful person. 笨拙或害羞的人。**~y** *adj* (-ier, -iest) (of persons) awkward, bashful, ungainly. (指人)笨拙的;害羞的;愚蠢的。**~i·ness** *n*

gawp /gɔːp; gɔp/ *vi* [VP2A, 3A] ***~ (at),*** look at in an intense, foolish way: 呆呆地看: *What are they all ~ing at?* 他們都在呆呆地看什麼?

gay /geɪ; ge/ *adj* (-er, -est) **1** light-hearted; cheerful; happy and full of fun: 快樂的;愉快的;歡欣的: *the gay voices of young children;* 小孩們歡樂的聲音; *gay looks/laughter.* 快樂的表情(笑聲)。**2** suggesting happiness and joy: 表示快樂的: *gay music;* 輕快的音樂; *gay colours;* 繽紛的色彩; *streets that were gay with flags.* 旗幟飄揚的街道。**3** (colloq) homosexual. (俗) 同性戀愛的。□ *n* [C] (colloq) homosexual. (俗)同性戀者。**gaily** /'geɪlɪ; 'gelɪ/ *adv* in a gay manner. 快樂地;歡欣地。**gay·ness** *n*

gaze /geɪz; gez/ *n* (*sing* only) long, steady look: (僅用單數)凝視;注視: *with a bewildered ~.* 以茫然的凝視。□ *vi* [VP2A, C, 3A] ***~ (at),*** look long and steadily: 凝視;注視: *What are you gazing at?* 你在凝視什麼? *Stop gazing round.* 不要左顧右盼。***~ on/upon,*** (formal) set eyes on: (正式用語)看: *She was the most beautiful woman he had ever ~d upon.* 她是他所見過的最美麗的女子。

ga·zelle /gə'zel; gə'zɛl/ *n* small, graceful kind of antelope. 小羚羊;瞪羚。

ga·zette /gə'zet; gə'zɛt/ *n* **1** official periodical with legal notices, news of appointments, promotions, etc of officers and officials. 政府的公報。**2** (as part of a title) newspaper: 報紙(作爲報紙名稱之一部分): *the Marlowe G~.* 馬婁報。□ *vt* (usu passive) (通常用被動語態) ***be ~d,*** be published in the official ~: 刋載於公報上: (of an army officer) *be ~d to a regiment.* (指軍官)刋載於公報上被調派至某團任職。

ga·zet·teer /ˌgæzə'tɪə(r); ˌgæzə'tɪr/ *n* index of geographical names, eg at the end of an atlas. 地名索引(例如附於地圖集之後者)。

ga·zump /gə'zʌmp; gə'zʌmp/ *vi, vt* [VP2A, 6A] (colloq) cheat by increasing the price demanded for property between the date of acceptance of an offer and the date for signing the contract. (俗)出售房地產價格議成後於簽約前提高價錢。

gear /gɪə(r); gɪr/ *n* **1** [C] set of toothed wheels working together in a machine, esp such a set to connect the engine of a motor-vehicle with the

G

road wheels: 齒輪組 (尤指聯繫汽車引擎與車輪者)；汽車之排檔: *change* ~; 換排檔; particular state of adjustment of such a set: 排檔之排列: *a car with five ~s, first, second, third, fourth and reverse.* 一輛有五檔的汽車，卽頭檔，二檔，三檔，四檔和倒檔。⇨ the illus at bicycle, motor. 參看 bicycle, motor 之挿圖。***high／low*** ~, mechanism causing the driven part to move relatively fast／slowly, low ~ being used when starting, or when driving on a steep hill. 高(低)速齒輪；高(低)速排檔。***in／out of*** ~, engaged／disengaged from the mechanism. 搭上(脫下)齒輪；齒輪與引擎聯繫(脫開)。***top／bottom*** ~, highest／lowest ~. 最高(低)速齒輪。'**~-box／-case**, case that encloses the ~ mechanism. (汽車等之)齒輪箱。'**~ shift／lever／stick**, device for engaging or disengaging ~s. 操縱桿(變速桿)。**2** [C] apparatus, appliance, mechanism, arrangement, of wheels, levers, etc for a special purpose: 輪與槓桿等裝置: *the 'steering-~ of a ship;* 船隻的操舵機; *the 'landing-~ of an aircraft.* 飛機的起落架。**3** [U] equipment in general: 裝備；用具: *'hunting-~;* 狩獵用具; (modern colloq) clothes: (現代俗語)衣服: *party* ~. 宴(舞)會穿的衣服。□ *vt, vi* [VP15A, 14, 2A, C, 3A] ~ ***up／down***, (= change up／down) put into a higher／lower ~. 使與高(低)速齒輪相連；開快(慢)車。~ ***to***, adjust one thing to the working of another, make dependent on: 使一物的作用與另一物搭配: *The country's economics must be ~ed to wartime requirements.* 這國家的經濟必須配合戰時的需要。

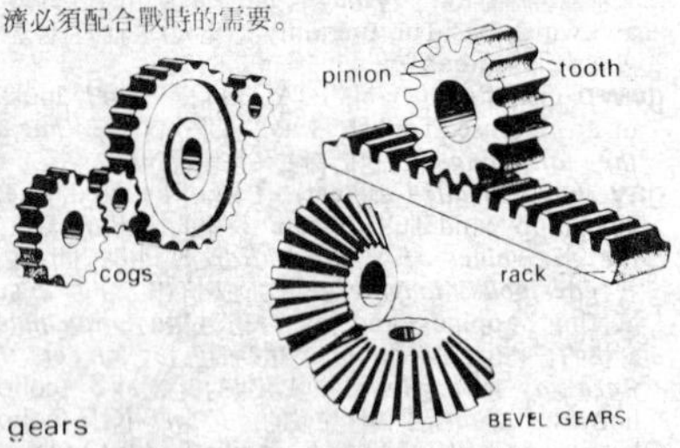

gears

gecko /'gekəʊ ; 'gɛko/ *n* (*pl* ~s, ~es /-kəʊz ; -koz/) kind of small house lizard, found in warm countries. (熱帶國家房屋中所見到的)壁虎類。

gee¹ (also **gee-up**) /ˌdʒiː('ʌp) ; ˌdʒi('ʌp)/ *int* (command to a horse) go on; go faster. (馭馬用語)前進！加快！ **gee-gee** /'dʒiː dʒiː ; 'dʒiˌdʒi/ *n* (child's word for a) horse. (小兒語)馬。

gee² (also **gee whiz**) /ˌdʒiː ('wɪz) ; ˌdʒi ('wɪz)/ *int* (US) mild exclamation indicating surprise, admiration, etc: (美)唧(表示驚奇，讚賞等的感嘆語): *Gee, I like your new hat!* 唧！我喜歡你的新帽子！

geese /giːs ; gis/ *n pl* of goose.

geezer /'giːzə(r) ; 'gizɚ/ *n* (sl) (old) person, esp if eccentric. (俚)(老)人(尤指古怪的)。

Geiger /'gaɪgə(r) ; 'gaɪgɚ/ *n* (esp 尤用於 '**~ counter**) metal tube containing an electrode, used for detecting and measuring radio-activity. 蓋氏計算器(爲含有電極的金屬管，用以測量放射作用)。

geisha /'geɪʃə ; 'geʃə/ *n* Japanese girl or woman trained to entertain men by singing and dancing at parties, etc. (日本的)藝妓。

gel /dʒel ; dʒɛl/ *n* semisolid like a jelly. 凝膠；膠滯體。□ *vi* (-ll-) **1** set into a jelly. 成爲凝膠狀；膠化。**2** = jell.

gela·tine /ˌdʒelə'tiːn *US:* 'dʒelətn ; 'dʒɛlətn̩/ (also 亦作 **gela·tin** /'dʒelətɪn ; 'dʒɛlətn̩/) *n* [U] clear, tasteless substance, made by boiling bones and waste parts of animals, dissolved in water to make jelly. 明膠；骨膠；動物膠。**gel·ati·nous** /dʒɪ'lætɪnəs ; dʒə'lætənəs/ *adj* of or like ~; jelly-like in consistency, etc. 骨膠的；似骨膠的；膠質的；膠狀的。

geld /geld ; gɛld/ *vt* [VP6A] castrate. 閹割；去勢。**~·ing** *n* ~ed animal, esp a horse. 被閹割的動物(尤指馬)。

gel·ig·nite /'dʒelɪgnaɪt ; 'dʒɛlɪgˌnaɪt/ *n* [U] explosive made from nitric acid and glycerine. 爆炸膠(一種含有硝酸和甘油的炸藥)。

gem /dʒem ; dʒɛm/ *n* **1** precious stone or jewel, esp cut or polished. 寶石；珠寶。**2** sth valued because of great beauty; sth much prized: 珍愛的美麗之物；珍貴之物: *the gem of the collection,* the most valued item in it. 所蒐集物品中之逸品。**gemmed** *part adj* adorned with, or as with, gems: 飾以寶石的；似飾有寶石的: *the night sky, gemmed with stars.* 點綴着晶瑩的星星的夜空。

Gem·ini /'dʒemɪnɪ ; 'dʒɛməˌnaɪ/ *n* third sign of the zodiac. 雙子星座；雙子宮。⇨ the illus at zodiac. 參看 zodiac 之挿圖。

gen /dʒen ; dʒɛn/ *n* (sl) **(the) gen**, information. (俚)情報。□ *vt* [VP15B] ***gen up***, provide with information. 供以情報。

gen·darme /'ʒɒndɑːm ; 'ʒandarm/ *n* (in France and some other countries, but not GB or US) member of a military force employed in police duties. (在法國或其他國家，但非英美的)憲兵。**~·rie** /ʒɒn'dɑːmərɪ ; ʒan'darmərɪ/ *n* (collective sing) force of ~s. (集合單數)憲兵隊。

gen·der /'dʒendə(r) ; 'dʒɛndɚ/ *n* **1** grammatical grouping of words (nouns and pronouns) into classes (masculine, feminine and neuter). (文法)性(名詞及代名詞分作陽性，陰性與中性)。**2** sex (1). 性別。

gene /dʒiːn ; dʒin/ *n* [C] (biol) unit in chromosome controlling heredity. (生物)遺傳因子；基因。

gen·eal·ogy /ˌdʒiːnɪ'ælədʒɪ ; ˌdʒinɪ'ælədʒɪ/ *n* **1** [U] science of the development of plants and animals from earlier forms. 系譜學；系圖學。**2** [C] (*pl* -gies) (diagram illustrating the) descent or line of development of a plant or animal from earlier forms; person's pedigree. 家系；血統；宗譜；系譜；家譜。**gen·eal·ogist** /ˌdʒiːnɪ'ælədʒɪst ; ˌdʒinɪ'ælədʒɪst/ *n* student of ~. 系譜學者。**genea·logi·cal** /ˌdʒiːnɪə'lɒdʒɪkl ; ˌdʒinɪə'lɑdʒɪkl/ *adj* of ~: 系譜的；宗譜的；家系的: *a genealogical tree,* a diagram (a table like a tree with branches showing the descent of a family or species. 家譜；系譜圖。**genea·logi·cally** /-klɪ ; -kl̩ɪ/ *adv*

gen·era /'dʒenərə ; 'dʒɛnərə/ *n pl* of genus.

gen·eral /'dʒenrəl ; 'dʒɛnərəl/ *adj* **1** of, affecting, all or nearly all; not special, local or particular: 普遍的；全面的；非特殊或地方性的；一般人的: *a matter of ~ interest,* one in which all or most people are likely to be interested; 引起大衆興趣的事; *a ~ meeting,* one to which all members (of a society, etc) are invited; 全體大會; *a ~ strike,* one by workmen of all, or nearly all, the trade unions; 集體罷工；總罷工; *a good ~ education,* in all the chief subjects; 良好的普通教育; *a word that is in ~ use,* used by all people; 一般人普遍使用的一個字; *the ~ opinion on this subject,* what most people think about it. 大多數人對此問題的意見。*The cold weather has been ~,* has been experienced in all or most parts of the country. 這些時全國大部分地區天氣寒冷。***as a ~ rule; in ~***, in most cases; usually. 概言之；一般說來；通常。'**~ degree**, non-specialist university degree involving a course in two or more subjects. 普通學位(含兩個或多個科目修得的非專才的大學學位)。ˌ**~ 'election**, one for representatives in Parliament from the whole country. 大選。Cf 參較 *by-election, local election.* ˌ**~ 'knowledge**, of a wide variety of subjects. 一般知識；各方面的知識。Cf 參較 *common knowledge,* knowledge (of a particular fact, etc) possessed by every member of a class or community of people. 常識。ˌ**~ 'practice**, work of a ˌ**~ prac'titioner** (abbr 略作 **GP**), (GB) doctor who is not a specialist or consultant. (英)全科醫師(非專科醫生)的業務。**2** not in detail; not definite: 概括的；大概的: *a ~*

outline of a scheme; 一個計畫的大綱; *have a ~ idea of what a book is about;* 對一本書的內容有一概括的觀念; *explain something in ~ terms.* 概括地說明某事物。 **3** (after an official title) chief: (用於官銜後)首要的: *ˌpostmaster-ˈ~;* 郵務部長; 郵政總長; *inˌspector-ˈ~.* 首席監察官;督察署署長。 □ *n* army officer with the highest rank below Field Marshal (and also, by courtesy, of *Lieuˌtenant-ˈ~* and *ˌMajor-ˈ~*). 陸軍上將;將軍;將官 (禮貌上亦指中將及少將)。

gen·er·al·is·simo /ˌdʒenrəˈlɪsɪməʊ ; ˌdʒɛnərəlˈɪsəˌmo/ *n* (*pl* ~s) commander of combined military and naval and air forces, or of combined armies. 大元帥;總司令;最高統帥。

gen·er·al·ity /ˌdʒenəˈrælətɪ ; ˌdʒɛnəˈrælətɪ/ *n* (*pl* -ties) **1** [C] general rule or statement; vague or indefinite remark, etc: 通則;概論;概說: *I wish you would come down from generalities to particularities.* 希望你不要談一般性的,談談特殊的。 **2** [U] ***the ~ (of),*** majority or greater part: 大多數;大部份: *The ~ of Swedes are blonde.* 大多數瑞典人都是頭髮金黃皮膚白皙的。 **3** [U] quality of being general: 普遍性;一般性: *a rule of great ~,* one with few exceptions. 普遍性的法則。

gen·er·al·iz·ation /ˌdʒenrəlaɪˈzeɪʃn *US:* -lɪˈz- ; ˌdʒɛnərələˈzeʃən/ *n* **1** [U] generalizing: 一般化;歸納;概論: *It is unwise to be hasty in ~.* 急於歸納是不智的。 **2** [C] statement or proposition obtained by generalizing, esp one based on too few examples. 概括的敘述或命題(尤指根據很少的例子而作的)。

gen·er·al·ize /ˈdʒenrəlaɪz ; ˈdʒɛnərəlˌaɪz/ *vi, vt* **1** [VP2A, 3A] ***~ (from),*** draw a general conclusion; make a general statement. 歸納; 泛論。 **2** [VP6A, 14] ***~ (from),*** state (sth) in general terms or principles: 概括地說: *~ a conclusion from a collection of instances or facts.* 從一些事例中做出結論。 **3** [VP6A] bring into general use: 推廣;普及: *~ the use of a new invention.* 推廣一新發明物的使用。

gen·erally /ˈdʒenrəlɪ ; ˈdʒɛnərəlɪ/ *adv* (usu with the finite *v*) (通常與限定動詞連用) **1** usually; as a general rule: 通常: *I ~ get up at six o'clock.* 我通常六時起床。 **2** widely; for the most part: 廣泛地; 普遍地: *The new plan was ~ welcomed,* was welcomed by most people. 新計畫受到普遍的歡迎。 **3** in a general sense; without paying attention to details: 一般地;概括地: *~ speaking.* 一般言之。

gen·er·ate /ˈdʒenəreɪt ; ˈdʒɛnəˌret/ *vt* [VP6A] cause to exist or occur; produce: 使發生;產生: *~ heat/electricity;* 生熱(發電); *hatred ~d by racial prejudices.* 因種族偏見而產生的仇恨。

gen·er·ation /ˌdʒenəˈreɪʃn ; ˌdʒɛnəˈreʃən/ *n* **1** [U] generating; bringing into existence: 產生; 發生: *the ~ of electricity by steam or water-power;* 用蒸汽或水力發電; *the ~ of heat by friction.* 摩擦生熱。 **2** [C] single stage or step in family descent: 家族中的一代;一世: *three ~s,* children, parents, grandparents. 三代 (兒女, 父母, 祖父母)。 **3** [C] average period (regarded as 30 years) in which children grow up, marry, and have children: 一代 (自子女長成, 結婚再生子女, 通常爲三十年): *a ~ ago.* 一代以前。 **ˈ~ gap,** ⇨ gap(2). **4** [C] all persons born about the same time, and, therefore, of about the same age: 同時代的人: *the present/past/coming ~;* 現在 (過去, 未來) 的一代人; *the rising ~,* the young ~. 青年。

gen·er·at·ive /ˈdʒenərətɪv ; ˈdʒɛnəˌretɪv/ *adj* able to produce; productive. 能生產的;有生產力的。

gen·er·ator /ˈdʒenəreɪtə(r) ; ˈdʒɛnəˌretɚ/ *n* [C] machine or apparatus that generates (electricity, steam, gas, vapour, etc) (US美 = *dynamo*). 發電機;蒸汽發生器;發生器。

gen·eric /dʒɪˈnerɪk ; dʒəˈnɛrɪk/ *adj* of a genus; common to a whole group or class, not special. 屬的;類的;一般的。 **gen·eri·cally** /-klɪ ; -kḷɪ/ *adv*

gen·er·os·ity /ˌdʒenəˈrɒsətɪ ; ˌdʒɛnəˈrɑsətɪ/ *n* **1** [U] the quality of being generous; nobility of mind; greatness of heart: 慷慨;大度;寬大: *show ~ in dealing with a defeated enemy.* 對一戰敗敵人表示寬大。 **2** [C] (*pl* -ties) generous act, etc. 慷慨的行爲;寬大的行爲。

gen·er·ous /ˈdʒenərəs ; ˈdʒɛnərəs/ *adj* **1** giving, ready to give, freely; given freely; noble-minded: 慷慨的;大方的;寬大的;思想高尚的: *He is ~ with his money/~ in giving help.* 他用錢大方(慨於助人)。 *It was ~ of them to share their house with the refugees.* 他們眞慷慨,讓難民住在他們家裡。 *What a ~ gift!* 多麼大方的禮物啊! *He has a ~ nature.* 他的稟性寬大。 **2** plentiful: 豐富的: *a ~ helping of meat and vegetables;* 一份豐富的肉和蔬菜; *a ~ harvest.* 豐收。 **~·ly** *adv*

gen·esis /ˈdʒenəsɪs ; ˈdʒɛnəsɪs/ *n* **1** beginning; starting-point: 開始;起源: *the ~ of civilization.* 文明的起源。 **2** **G~,** the first book of the Old Testament. (舊約)創世紀。

gen·etic /dʒɪˈnetɪk ; dʒəˈnɛtɪk/ *adj* of genes; of ~s. 遺傳因子的;遺傳學的。 **gen·etics** *n pl* (with *sing v*) science (branch of biology) dealing with heredity, the ways in which characteristics are passed on from parents to offspring. (與單數動詞連用) 遺傳學;發生學(生物學之一支)。 **gen·eti·cist** /dʒɪˈnetɪsɪst ; dʒəˈnɛtəsɪst/ *n* specialist in ~s. 遺傳學家。

ge·nial /ˈdʒiːnɪəl ; ˈdʒinjəl/ *adj* **1** kindly, sympathetic; sociable: 親切的;和藹的;友善的: *a ~ old man;* 一位和藹的老人; *~ smiles;* 親切的微笑; *under the ~ influence of good wine.* 在好酒暖意之下。 **2** favourable to growth; mild; warm: 利於生長的;溫和的;溫暖的: *a ~ climate;* 溫和的氣候; *~ sunshine.* 和煦的陽光。 **~·ly** *adv* **~·ity** /ˌdʒiːnɪˈælətɪ ; ˌdʒinɪˈælətɪ/ *n* [U] quality of being ~; [C] (*pl* -ties) ~ look, act, utterance, etc. 親切;和藹;溫和;親切的表情,行動,言語等。

ge·nie /ˈdʒiːnɪ ; ˈdʒinɪ/ *n* (*pl* ~s or genii /ˈdʒiːnɪaɪ ; ˈdʒinɪˌaɪ/) (in Arabic stories) spirit or goblin with strange powers. (阿拉伯故事中的)神怪;妖怪。

geni·tal /ˈdʒenɪtl ; ˈdʒɛnətḷ/ *adj* of generation(1) or of animal reproductive organs. 生產的;生殖的;生殖器的。 **~s** *n pl* external sex organs. 外陰部;生殖器。

geni·tive /ˈdʒenətɪv;ˈdʒɛnətɪv/ *adj* **~ (case),** (gram) showing source or possession. (文法)所有格;屬格。

gen·ius /ˈdʒiːnɪəs ; ˈdʒinjəs/ *n* (*pl* ~es, but ⇨ 5 below 參看下列第5義) **1** [U] great and exceptional capacity of the mind or imagination; creative or inventive capacity: 天才;創造能力: *men of ~.* 有天才的人。 **2** [C] person having this capacity: 天才;才子: *Einstein was a mathematical ~.* 愛因斯坦是一位數學天才。 **3** ***a ~ for,*** natural ability for: 天資;天賦: *have a ~ for languages/acting/making friends.* 有語言(表演,交友)的才能。 **4** ***the ~ (of),*** guardian spirit of a person, place or institution, (hence, by extension) special and inborn character, spirit or principles of a language, a period of time, an institution, etc; prevalent feeling, opinions, taste, etc of a race of people: 守護神;保佑的神靈;(由此引申)語言,時代,制度等的特點或精神;民族的特徵: *the French ~;* 法國人的特徵; *the ~ of the British Constitution/the Renaissance period in Italy.* 英國憲法(義大利的文藝復興時期)的精神。 **ˌ~ ˈloci** /ˈləʊsaɪ ; ˈlosaɪ/ *n* (*sing* only) (Lat) associations, atmosphere, etc of a place. (僅用單數)(拉)一地方的風氣。 **5** (*pl* **genii** /ˈdʒiːnɪaɪ ; ˈdʒinɪˌaɪ/) supernatural being. 神靈;精靈。 ***one's good/evil ~,*** spirit or angel working for one's salvation/damnation; person who has a strong influence upon one for good/ill. 使人得救的神(使人毀滅的魔鬼);予人以好(壞)影響的人。

geno·cide /ˈdʒenəsaɪd ; ˈdʒɛnəˌsaɪd/ *n* [U] extermination of a race or community by mass murder, or by imposing conditions that make survival im-

G

possible. 種族滅絕;種族大屠殺。

genre /ˈʒɑːnrə ; ˈʒɑnrə/ *n* **1** (F) kind; style; category (esp of literary form, eg poetry, drama, the novel). (法)種類;式樣;類型(尤指詩歌,戲劇,小說等文學上的形式)。 **2** (also 亦作 **ˈ～-painting**) portrayal of scenes, etc, from ordinary life. 浮世繪;以日常生活爲題材的繪畫;世態畫。

gent /dʒent ; dʒɛnt/ *n* (colloq abbr of) gentleman. (俗)紳士(爲 gentleman 之略)。**the／a G～s** *n* (GB colloq) public toilet for men. (英俗)公共男厠。

gen·teel /dʒenˈtiːl ; dʒɛnˈtil/ *adj* (usu ironic in modern use, but serious in former use) polite and well-bred; elegant; characteristic of, suitable for, the upper classes of society: (近代用法通常爲反語,但昔時爲認眞的用語)有教養的; 文雅的; 有上流社會之特點的;適於上流社會的: *living in ～ poverty,* trying to maintain the style of the upper classes, although too poor to do so. 過着窮而擺濶的生活;打腫臉充胖子。**～·ly** *adv*

gen·tian /ˈdʒenʃn ; ˈdʒɛnʃən/ *n* (kind of usu) blue-flowered plant growing in mountainous districts. 龍膽屬植物(生於山區,通常開藍花);龍膽;陵游。

gen·tile /ˈdʒentaɪl ; ˈdʒɛntaɪl/ *n, adj* (person) not Jewish. 非猶太人;非猶太人的。

gen·til·ity /dʒenˈtɪlətɪ ; dʒɛnˈtɪlətɪ/ *n* [U] state of being genteel: 有教養;文雅: *living in shabby ～,* trying, without real success, to keep up an appearance of being genteel. 硬充上流。

gentle /ˈdʒentl ; ˈdʒɛntḷ/ *adj* (-r, -st) **1** mild, quiet, careful; not rough, violent, severe: 和善的;友善的;溫柔的;溫和的;文雅的;輕輕的: *a ～ nature／heart／look／voice／call／touch;* 溫和的性情(仁慈的心腸;和善的面貌; 柔和的聲音; 低聲的呼喚; 輕輕的觸摸); *～ manners;* 溫和的態度; *a ～ breeze;* 和風; *a ～ heat,* ie not too hot; 暖和; *a ～ slope,* ie not steep. 不太陡的斜坡。**2** (of a family) with good social position: (指家庭)有社會地位的: *a person of ～ birth.* 出身名門的人。**ˈ～·folk** *n pl* persons of ～ birth. 出身名門的人;有身分的人;上流人士。**～·ness** *n*

gentle·man /ˈdʒentlmən ; ˈdʒɛntḷmən/ *n* (*pl* -men /-mən ; -mən/) **1** man who shows consideration for the feelings of others, who is honourable and courteous. 紳士;君子。**～'s agreement,** one that is binding in honour, but cannot be enforced at law. 君子協定。**2** (hist) man of good family attached to a court or the household of a great noble: (史) 國王或貴族的侍從: *one of the king's gentlemen.* 國王的一位侍從。**ˌ～-at-ˈarms,** one of the sovereign's bodyguard. 國王的侍衞。**3** (hist) man entitled to bear arms but not a member of the nobility. (史)有資格從軍的平民。**4** (dated use) man of wealth and social position, esp one who does not work for a living: (過時用語)有錢和社會地位的人(尤指無需工作以謀生者): *'What does he do for a living?'—'Nothing; he's a ～.'* '他做什麼謀生?'—'什麼也不做, 他是個有錢不需工作的人。' **ˌ～ ˈfarmer,** ～ who has a farm, but does no manual work himself. (擁有農場,但不從事勞力工作之)鄉紳。**5** polite form of address to men (eg in an audience): 諸位先生(對男性聽衆的禮稱): *Gentlemen!* 諸位先生! *Ladies and Gentlemen!* 諸位女士和先生! Also used instead of *Sirs* or *Dear Sirs* when writing to a business firm, etc. (在商業信件中亦代替 Sirs 或 Dear Sirs)。**～·ly** *adj* feeling, behaving, or looking like a ～(1); suitable or right for a ～(1): 紳士風度的;似紳士的;合乎紳士的: *a ～ly apology.* 紳士似的道歉。

gentle·woman /ˈdʒentlwʊmən ; ˈdʒɛntḷˌwʊmən/ *n* (*pl* -women /-wɪmɪn ; -ˌwɪmɪn/) lady.女士;淑女;貴婦。

gen·tly /ˈdʒentlɪ ; ˈdʒɛntlɪ/ *adv* in a gentle manner: 和善地;溫和地;溫柔地;文雅地;輕輕地: *Hold it ～,* carefully. 小心地拿着它。*Speak ～* (= softly, kindly) *to the child.* 對孩子溫和地談話。*The road slopes ～* (= gradually) *to the sea.* 那條路逐漸向海邊傾斜下去。

gen·try /ˈdʒentrɪ ; ˈdʒɛntrɪ/ *n pl* **(the) ～,** people of good social position next below the nobility. 紳士; 上等人。**gen·tri·fy** /ˈdʒentrɪfaɪ ; ˈdʒɛntrɪˌfaɪ/ *vt* [VP6A] (colloq) modernize, smarten, restore (a house, area, etc) to make suitable for middle-class occupiers: (俗)將(一房屋、地區等)現代化,翻新,改建(俾適於中產階級之人居住): *the gentrifying of inner city working-class districts.* 市中心勞工住宅區的現代化。

genu·flect /ˈdʒenjʊflekt ; ˈdʒɛnjʊˌflɛkt/ *vi* [VP2A] bend the knee, esp in worship. 屈膝(尤指禮拜);跪拜。**genu·flec·tion, genu·flex·ion** /ˌdʒenjʊˈflekʃn ; ˌdʒɛnjʊˈflɛkʃən/ *nn*

genu·ine /ˈdʒenjʊɪn ; ˈdʒɛnjʊɪn/ *adj* true; really what it is said to be: 眞正的;眞實的: *a ～ picture by Rubens;* 魯賓斯的眞蹟(畫); *～ pearls;* 眞珍珠; *～ sorrow;* 眞正的傷感; *a ～ signature.* 親筆簽名。**～·ly** *adv* **～·ness** *n*

ge·nus /ˈdʒiːnəs ; ˈdʒinəs/ *n* (*pl* genera /ˈdʒenərə ; ˈdʒɛnərə/) **1** (biol) division of animals or plants within a family: (生物)(動植物的)類;屬: ˌ～ *'Homo* /ˈhəʊməʊ ; ˈhomo/, mankind. 人類。 **2** sort; kind; class. 種類。

geo- /ˌdʒiːəʊ ; ˌdʒio/ *pref* (form of Greek word for 'earth', used in combinations): (希臘語形,表示'地'或'地球' 之義, 用於複合字中): **geo·cen·tric** /ˌdʒiːəʊˈsentrɪk ; ˌdʒioˈsɛntrɪk/ *adj* having or representing the earth as centre. 以地球爲中心的。**geo·phys·ics** /ˌdʒiːəʊˈfɪzɪks ; ˌdʒioˈfɪzɪks/ *n pl* (*sing v*) study of the earth's magnetism, meteorology, etc. (接單數動詞)地球物理學。 **geo·physi·cal** /-ˈfɪzɪkl ; -ˈfɪzɪkḷ/ *adj* **geo·poli·tics** /ˌdʒiːəʊˈpɒlətɪks ; ˌdʒioˈpɑlətɪks/ *n pl* (*sing v*) country's politics as determined by its geographical position. (接單數動詞)地緣政治學。

ge·ogra·phy /dʒɪˈɒgrəfɪ ; dʒiˈɑgrəfɪ/ *n* [U] science of the earth's surface, physical features, divisions, climate, products, population, etc. 地理學。 **ge·ogra·pher** /dʒɪˈɒgrəfə(r) ; dʒiˈɑgrəfɚ/ *n* authority on ～. 地理學家。**geo·graphi·cal** /ˌdʒɪəˈgræfɪkl ; ˌdʒiəˈgræfɪkḷ/ *adj* of ～. 地理學的。**geo·graphi·cally** /-klɪ ; -klɪ/ *adv*

ge·ol·ogy /dʒɪˈɒlədʒɪ ; dʒiˈɑlədʒɪ/ *n* [U] science of the earth's history as shown by its crust, rocks, etc. 地質學。 **ge·ol·ogist** /dʒɪˈɒlədʒɪst ; dʒiˈɑlədʒɪst/ *n* authority on ～. 地質學家。**geo·logi·cal** /ˌdʒɪəˈlɒdʒɪkl ; ˌdʒiəˈlɑdʒɪkḷ/ *adj* of ～. 地質學的。**geo·logi·cally** /-klɪ ; -klɪ/ *adv*

ge·ometry /dʒɪˈɒmətrɪ ; dʒiˈɑmətrɪ/ *n* [U] science of the properties and relations of lines, angles, surfaces and solids. 幾何學。**geo·met·ric, -metri·cal** /ˌdʒɪəˈmetrɪk(l) ; ˌdʒiəˈmɛtrɪk(ḷ)/ *adj* of ～; of or like the lines, figures, etc used in ～: 幾何學的;幾何學中所用的線條,圖形等的;似幾何線條圖形等的: *geometrical patterns.* 幾何圖案。**geoˌmetrical proˈgression,** series of numbers with a constant ratio between successive quantities, the numbers either increasing by a common multiplier, or decreasing by a common divisor, as 1:3:9:27:81. 幾何級數;等比級數(如 1:3:9:27:81)。 **geo·met·ri·cally** /-klɪ ; -klɪ/ *adv*

George /dʒɔːdʒ ; dʒɔrdʒ/ *n* **1 St ～,** patron saint of England; 聖喬治(英國的守護神); *St ˈ～'s day,* 23 Apr; 守護神日(四月二十三日); *St ˌ～'s ˈCross,* vertical and horizontal red bars crossing in the centre. 聖喬治十字(在中心交叉之紅色十字形)。⇨ the illus at flag. 參看 flag 之插圖。 **2** (sl) automatic pilot of aircraft.(俚)飛機的自動駕駛儀。□ *int* **by ～!** (dated) exclamation of surprise, determination, etc. (過時用語)(表示驚訝、決心的感嘆詞)的確!

geor·gette /dʒɔːˈdʒet ; dʒɔrˈdʒɛt/ *n* [U] thin silk dress material. 喬治紗(一種做衣料的薄縐紗)。

Geor·gian /ˈdʒɔːdʒən ; ˈdʒɔrdʒən/ *adj* **1** of the time (1714–1811) of any of the Kings George I, II and III of Britain: (1714–1811)英王喬治一世至三世時期的: (esp) (尤指) *～ architecture.* 英王喬治一世至三

世時期的建築。 **2** of **Geor·gia** /ˈdʒɔːdʒə ; ˈdʒɔrdʒə/ (republic in USSR, of state in US). (蘇聯之)喬治亞共和國的;(美國之)喬治亞州的。

ger·anium /dʒəˈreɪnɪəm ; dʒəˈrenɪəm/ *n* kind of garden plant with red, pink or white flowers. 天竺葵(長紅色,粉紅色或白色的花)。

geri·atrics /ˌdʒerɪˈætrɪks ; ˌdʒerɪˈætrɪks/ *n pl* (*sing v*) medical care of old people. (接單數動詞) 老人醫學;老年衛生學。 **geri·atric** *adj* of ~: 老人醫學的; 老年衛生學的: *the geriatric ward*, of a hospital. 老人病房。 **geria·tri·cian** /ˌdʒerɪəˈtrɪʃn ; ˌdʒerɪəˈtrɪʃən/ *n* expert in ~. 老人醫學專家;老人病科醫師。

germ /dʒɜːm ; dʒɝm/ *n* [C] **1** portion of a living organism capable of becoming a new organism; (fig) beginning or starting-point (of an idea, etc). 芽胞;胚芽;幼芽;(喻)(觀念等的) 起源; 根源。 **2** microbe or bacillus, esp one causing disease: 細菌;病菌: ~ *warfare*, use of bacteria as a weapon in war. 細菌戰。

Ger·man /ˈdʒɜːmən ; ˈdʒɝmən/ *adj* of Germany and its people. 德國的;德國人的。 ˌ~ **ˈshepherd** *n* (US) (美) = Alsatian (dog). □ *n* native of Germany; language of the ~ people. 德國人;德文;德語。 **~ic** /dʒəˈmænɪk ; dʒɝˈmænɪk/ *adj* of the group of languages now including German, English and Dutch. 日耳曼語(現包括德,英,荷語)的。

ger·mane /dʒəˈmeɪn ; dʒɝˈmen/ *adj* ~ *(to)*, relevant, pertinent (to). 適切的。

ger·mi·cide /ˈdʒɜːmɪsaɪd ; ˈdʒɝməˌsaɪd/ *n* substance used to destroy germs (esp bacteria). 殺菌劑。

ger·mi·nate /ˈdʒɜːmɪneɪt ; ˈdʒɝməˌnet/ *vi, vt* [VP2A, 6A] (of seeds) (cause to) start growth. (指種子) (使)發芽;萌芽。 **ger·mi·na·tion** /ˌdʒɜːmɪˈneɪʃn ; ˌdʒɝməˈneʃən/ *n* [U] germinating; sprouting. 發芽;萌芽。

ger·on·tol·ogy /ˌdʒerɒnˈtɒlədʒɪ ; ˌdʒerənˈtɑlədʒɪ/ *n* [U] branch of science concerned with the processes of growing old, esp in human beings. (尤指人類) 衰老學。

gerry·man·der /ˌdʒerɪˈmændə(r) ; ˈgɛrɪˌmændɚ/ *vt* [VP6A] manipulate (a constituency, etc by division into voting areas) so as to give unfair advantages to one party or class in elections; practise trickery. 操縱(選舉區,如藉劃分)而爲己黨圖利;欺詐。 □ *n* such a falsification. 藉劃分操縱選舉區而爲己黨圖利;欺詐。

ger·und /ˈdʒerənd ; ˈdʒɛrənd/ *n* **1** form of a verb when used as a noun. 動名詞(動詞用做名詞的形式)。 **2** the *-ing* form of an English verb when used as a noun (as in 'fond of *swimming*'). (英語) 動名詞(由動詞加 ing 形成,如 fond of swimming 中之 swimming)。

Ges·tapo /geˈstɑːpəʊ ; gəˈstɑpo/ *n* German secret State police of the Nazi regime. 蓋世太保(德國納粹掌權時期的祕密警察)。

ges·ta·tion /dʒeˈsteɪʃn ; dʒɛsˈteʃən/ *n* carrying or being carried in the womb between conception and birth; this period. 懷孕;懷孕期。

ges·ticu·late /dʒeˈstɪkjʊleɪt ; dʒɛsˈtɪkjəˌlet/ *vi* [VP 2A] use movements of the hands, arms or head instead of, or to accompany, speaking. 做表達情意的動作或姿態;做手勢等。 **ges·ticu·la·tion** /dʒeˌstɪkjʊˈleɪʃn ; ˌdʒɛstɪkjəˈleʃən/ *n* [U] gesticulating; [C] movement used in this. 做表達情意的動作;做手勢;表達情意的動作。

ges·ture /ˈdʒestʃə(r) ; ˈdʒɛstʃɚ/ *n* **1** [C] movement of the hand or head to indicate or illustrate an idea, feeling, etc; sth done to convey a friendly intention: 手勢; 姿勢; 友善的表示: *a ~ of refusal;* 拒絕的手勢; *make a friendly ~ to sb.* 向某人做友善的表示。 **2** [U] use of expressive movements: 表情的運用: *an actor who is a master of the art of ~.* 一個精於表情的演員。□ *vi* [VP2A] gesticulate. 做表達情意的動作或姿態;做手勢等。

get /get ; gɛt/ *vt, vi* (*pt* got /gɒt ; gɑt/, *pp* got, (US), gotten /ˈgɒtn ; ˈgɑtn̩/) (For uses with *adverbial particles* and *preps* ⇨ 15, 16, 17, below.) (與副詞接語和介詞連用的用法,參看下列第 15, 16, 17 義。) **1** [VP2D] (cause oneself to) become; pass from one state to another: (使自己)變成;變得: *get dressed/excited/lost/married/tired/wet.* 穿好衣服(變得興奮;迷路;結婚;感到疲倦;變得潮溼)。*He went out and got drunk.* 他到外面去喝醉了。*She'll soon get well/better again.* 她不久就會康復的。*You'll soon get used to the climate here.* 你不久卽可適應此地的氣候了。*It's time you got married.* 你該結婚了。*Get lost!* (sl) Go away! (俚)走開! ***get even with sb,*** ⇨ even¹(3). ⇨ also wise¹. **2** [VP22, 24C] bring to a certain condition; cause to be or become: 使成爲某種狀態; 使變成某種情況或結果: *She soon got the children ready for shool.* 她很快就把孩子們準備好讓他們去上學。*I must get the breakfast ready/cooked.* 我必須準備好早餐。*Did you get the sum right,* produce the correct answer? 你算對了嗎? *He got his wrist broken,* broke it by accident. 他折斷了手腕。 ***get sth done,*** complete it: 完成某事; 做好某事: *The farmer got his planting done before the rains came.* 那農人在雨季前完成了他的種植。 **3** [VP2E] reach the stage where one is doing something: 達到(做某事)的階段: *Get going!* Start! 開始! *It's time we got going,* made a start. 我們該開始了。*Things haven't really got going yet,* are not yet at the stage of full activity. 事情尚未展開(一切尚未充分活動)。*When these women get talking, they go on for hours.* 這些女人一談便是幾小時。 **4** [VP 19B] bring sb/sth to the point where he/it is doing sth: 使(人或物)達到動作之某一點: *Can you really get that old car going again,* restart or repair it? 你眞的能發動(修好)那部舊車嗎? *It's not hard to get the children talking; the problem is to stop them.* 讓孩子們談話不難,停止他們談話却有問題。*We'll soon get things going.* 我們不久便要展開活動。 **5** [VP4A] reach the stage where one knows, feels, etc sth: 達到認識,感覺等之階段: *When you get to know him you'll like him.* 等你了解他的時候,你就會喜歡他。 *They soon got to be* (= became) *friends.* 他們不久便成了朋友。 *After a time you get to realize that....* 過一段時期你就會了解…。*One soon gets to like it here.* 一個人不久便會喜歡此地。*How did you get to know* (= learn) *that I was here?* 你怎麼知道我在此地? **6** [VP17, 24C] bring, persuade, cause (sb/sth) to do sth or act in a certain way: 使(人或物)以某種方式做某事或行動: *You'll never get him to understand.* 你永遠不會使他了解。*I can't get this old radio to work.* 我無法使這架舊收音機播音。*I can't get her to talk.* 我無法使她說話。 *I can't get anyone to do the work/can't get the work done by anybody.* 我找不到人做這工作。(Cf 參較 *I must get my hair cut/get somebody to cut my hair.* 我必須去理髮。) **7** [VP6A, 14] ***get sth (of),*** receive; have; obtain; procure; acquire: 收到;獲得; 得到; 取得: *get news/knowledge/possession of sth.* 獲得消息(知識,某物)。*I've got* (= now have) *your telegram.* 我已經收到你的電報。*This room gets* (= receives, admits) *very little sunshine.* 這房間幾乎晒不到太陽。*I'll come as soon as I get time.* 我一有時間便會來。*The soldier got leave* (= permission) *to go home.* 這士兵請假返鄉。*He got* (= received) *a nasty blow on the head.* 他的頭部受到兇險的一擊。*The bullet got him/The soldier got it in the leg,* He was injured there. 子彈打中了他 (這士兵腿部中彈)。 *Where did you get that hat?* 你那頂帽子在哪裏買的? *How does he get* (= earn) *his living?* 他怎樣謀生? *If we divide 12 by 4, we get 3.* 我們如以 4 除 12, 便得 3。*Can you get* (= receive) *distant stations on your transistor?* 你的電晶體收音機能收到遠處的電臺嗎? *Go and get* (= take, eat) *your breakfast.* 去吃你的早餐。 [VP12B, 13B] *Get me a ticket, please.* 請給我準備一張票。*Get yourself a haircut!* 快去理個髮吧! *Get some more food for the guests.* 再給客人拿些

G

食物來。**'get one,** = *get one's goat,* ⇨ goat. **get the better/best of,** ⇨ better[3] and best[3]. **get the boot,** ⇨ boot[1](1). **get a glimpse of,** ⇨ glimpse. **get hold of sth,** ⇨ hold[2](1). **get the sack,** ⇨ sack[2]. **get (a) sight of,** ⇨ sight[1](2). **get the upper hand (of),** ⇨ upper. **get one's own way,** ⇨ way. **get wind of,** ⇨ wind[1](4). **get the wind up,** ⇨ wind[1](1). **get the worst of,** ⇨ worst. **8** [VP6A] catch (an illness): 生(病); 得(病); 患(病): *get the measles;* 得痲疹; *get religion,* (colloq) be converted (from disbelief or indifference). (俗)信仰宗教。 **9** [VP6A] receive as a penalty: 受罰: *get six months,* be sentenced to six months' imprisonment. 被判六個月的徒刑。**get told off,** (colloq) be admonished: (俗)受訓誡: *I daren't be late home again or I'll get told off.* 我再也不敢晚回家了,否則會挨罵的。 **10** [VP6A] (colloq) understand: (俗)瞭解: *I don't get you/your meaning.* 我不明白你的意思。 *She didn't get the joke.* 她沒有聽懂那個笑話。*Get it?* Do you understand? 懂嗎?(明白了嗎?) *You've got it wrong,* have misunderstood it. 你誤會了。*I didn't get* (= hear) *your name.* 我沒有聽清楚你的姓名。 **11** [VP6A] (esp in the perfect tenses) puzzle; catch in an argument; bring an accusation against sb to which he cannot supply a good answer: (尤用於完成式)使迷惑;難住;問倒: *Ah! I've got you there!* 啊!我可將你難住了! *That's got him!* 那問題難住了他! **12** [VP6A] **have got,** have, eg as a possession or characteristic: 有(擁有或具有): *We've got a new car.* 我們有一輛新車。 *What ugly teeth he's got!* 他的牙齒眞難看! **13** [VP7B] **have got to,** must, be compelled or obliged: 必須: *It has got to* (= must) *be done today.* 此事今天必須做好。 *She's got to work hard for her living.* 爲了生活她必須辛苦地工作。 *You haven't got to* (= needn't) *go to the office today, have you?* 你今天不須要上班,對不對? ⇨ have[3](1). **14** [VP7A] (US) succeed: (美)能够: *Do you ever get to see him,* have opportunities of seeing him? 你有機會見到他嗎? **15** [VP2C, 3A] (non-idiomatic intransitive uses with *adverbial particles* and *preps;* for idiomatic uses, ⇨ 17 below) move to or from a specified point or in a particular direction: (下列例句中與副詞接語及介詞連用係非成語不及物用法,至於成語用法,參看下列第 17 義)至;到;去到;移動;移向: *He gets about a good deal.* 他常旅行。 *A car makes it easier to get about.* 汽車使行動容易多了。*The bridge was destroyed so we couldn't get across,* couldn't cross the river. 橋被毀壞,所以我們無法過河。 *Did you manage to get away* (= have a holiday) *this Easter?* 這次復活節你有沒有去度假呀? *Get back!* (imper) Move backwards, eg away from danger. (祈使)退後!(例如離開危險)。*When did you get back* (= return) *from the country?* 你何時從鄉下回來的? *She got back into bed.* 她回到床上。*Please let me get by,* pass. 請讓我過去。 *He got down from the bus.* 他下公共汽車。 *I can't get in/out,* I can't enter/leave. 我進不去(出不來)。*I'm getting off* (= leaving the train) *at the next station.* 我下一站下火車。 *When did you get here/there,* arrive here/there? 你何時到此地(那裡)的? *Dust got into his eyes.* 灰塵進入他的眼睛。*Get off the grass/my toes!* 不要踐踏草地(我的脚趾)! *Get a move on!* Hurry up! 快點! *Can you get over that wall?* 你能爬過那牆嗎? *We didn't get to bed until 2 am.* 我們直到凌晨二時始就寢。 *Where have they got to?* 他們到那裏去了? *Where can it have got to?* Where can it be? 它到那裏去了? **get (sb) under one's skin,** ⇨ skin(1). **get somewhere/anywhere/nowhere,** obtain some/any/no result; make some/any/no progress. 有(有任何,無)結果; 有(有任何,無)進展。 **'get there,** (colloq) succeed; accomplish sth. (俗)成功;有成就。 **16** [VP15A, B] (non-idiomatic transitive uses with *adverbial particles* and *preps;* for idiomatic uses, ⇨ 17 below) cause to move to or from a point, or in a particular direction: (下列例句中與副詞接語及介詞連用係非成語及物用法,至於成語用法,參看下列第 17 義)使移動;使移向: *The general had to get his troops across the river.* 將軍必須使他的部隊過河。 *He never lends books; he says it's too difficult to get them back.* 他從來不借書給別人;他說書借出去以後很難收回來。*If you'll come and help me, I promise to get you back* (= see that you reach home again) *before dark.* 如果你願意來幫助我,我擔保在天黑以前送你回去。*He's drunk again—we'd better call a taxi and get him home.* 他又喝醉了──我們最好叫輛計程車送他回家。*It was nailed to the wall and I couldn't get it off.* 它被釘在牆上,我無法將它取下。 *Get* (= Put) *your hat and coat on.* 戴上你的帽子,穿上你的上衣。*I can't get the lid on/off.* 我蓋不上(打不開)這蓋子。*We couldn't get the piano through the door.* 我們無法將鋼琴從此門搬進去。 **17** [VP2C, 15B, 3A, 14] (idiomatic uses with *adverbial particles* and *preps*):(與副詞接語及介詞連用之成語用法):

get about, **(a)** (of sb who has been ill) be no longer confined to bed, to the house: (指病人)可以走動: *He's getting about again after his accident.* 經此意外事件後,他又可以走動了。**(b)** (of news, rumours, stories) spread from person to person, usu by gossip: (指新聞,謠言,故事)傳開(通常係由口傳): *The news of his resignation soon got about.* 他辭職的消息很快就傳開了。

get a'bove oneself, have a feeling of self-satisfaction not in strict proportion to one's merits; have too high an opinion of oneself. 自傲;自視過高。⇨ *swollen-headed* at swell.

get sth across (to sb), (cause sth to) be understood: 使(某事物)被人了解: *I spoke slowly, but my meaning didn't get across.* 我慢慢地講,但我的意思仍不被人了解。 *I failed to get my joke across to the crowd.* 我未能使群衆了解我的笑話。

get ahead (of sb), go forward and pass sb; make progress: 前進並越過(某人); 有進展: *Tom has got ahead of all the other boys in the class.* 湯姆勝過了班上其他的男孩子。

get along, **(a)** manage: 過活;生活: *We can't get along without money.* 沒有錢我們無法生活。 **(b)** make progress: 進展: *How are you getting along?* 你好嗎? *How is he getting along with his French?* 他的法文學習的情況如何? **get along (with sb),** be friendly and in harmony: (與某人)和好相處;相處和諧: *He gets along well with his boss.* 他和他的上司相處甚好。*He and his boss get along well.* 他同他的上司相處甚好。 **Get a'long with you!** (colloq imper) Go away! (or) Don't expect me to believe that! (俗,祈使)走開!去你的!胡說!

get at sb/sth, reach; gain access to: 到達;得到;接近: *The books are locked up and I can't get at them.* 書被鎖起來了,我無法拿到它們。 Hence, 由此產生, **get-'at-able** /ˌgetˈætəbl; ˌgɛtˈætəbl/ *adj* accessible. 可達到的;可進入的。**get at sb,** **(a)** bribe, corrupt: 賄賂;行賄: *One of the witnesses had been got at.* 一位證人曾受賄賂。**(b)** taunt: 責罵;辱罵: *He's always getting at his wife.* 他總是罵他的妻子。**get at sth,** discover; lay bare: 發現: *get at the truth/the facts.* 發現眞情(事實)。**be getting at,** (colloq) be implying; be trying to say or suggest: (俗)意指: *What are you getting at?* 你的意思是什麼?

get away, manage to leave; escape: 設法離開;逃脫: *Two of the prisoners got away.* 兩位犯人逃走了。 Hence, 由此產生, **'get-away** *n: make one's get-away,* escape; 逃走; (attrib) (形容用法) *The get-away car had been stolen.* 那部用來逃走的汽車是偸來的。 **get away with sth,** pursue successfully a course of action which might usually be expected to result in blame, punishment or misfortune: 避開責備,懲罰或災難而能順利行事: *The thieves got away with the contents of the safe.* 這些賊順

利地將保險櫃內之物竊走。*If I cheat in the examination, do you think I might get away with it?* 如果我考試作弊,你想我能避開懲罰嗎? ***Get a'way with you!*** Get along with you! 走開! ⇨ get along above. 參看上列之 get along。

get back, return to power or prominence after losing it for a time: (一度失去後)恢復力量;東山再起: *The Democrats hope to get back at the next election.* 民主黨員希望在下次選擧中重振威勢。 ***get 'back at sb/get one's 'own back (on sb),*** have one's revenge: 報復: *He tricked me this time but I'll get my own back one day.* 這次他騙了我,可是我有一天要向他報復。

get by, **(a)** pass; be accepted, without comment or criticism: 通過;未受批評而被接受: *I have no formal clothes for this occasion; perhaps I can get by in a dark suit.* 我沒有參加這個場合的禮服,或許我穿深色服裝可以應付過去。 **(b)** manage; survive: 設法;繼續存在: *How can he get by on such low wages?* 以如此低微的工資他如何能度日? *She can't get by without him.* 沒有他她無法生活。

get down, leave the table, after a meal. 飯後離開餐桌。***get sb down,*** (colloq) depress: (俗)使沮喪: *Don't let this cold weather get you down.* 不要讓這寒冷的天氣使你沮喪。***get sth down,*** **(a)** swallow: 呑下: *The medicine was bitter, and she couldn't get it down.* 藥很苦,她嚥不下去。**(b)** write down: 記下: *Did you get that telephone message down?* 你將電話裏所留的話記下來沒有? ***get down to sth,*** deal seriously with; tackle: 認眞應付;處理: *get down to one's work after the holidays;* 假期過後靜心工作; *get down to the facts,* deal with them, ignoring speculations, etc. 認眞研究事實。 ***get down to brass tacks,*** ⇨ brass.

get home (to) sb, be fully understood (by): 被充份瞭解: *That remark of yours about Sally got home,* She understood (and reacted). 莎麗聽懂了你針對她所說的話(而且有所反應)。

get in, **(a)** arrive: 到達: *The train got in five minutes early.* 那班火車早到了五分鐘。**(b)** be elected: 當選: *He got in* (= was elected MP) *for Islington.* 他當選爲伊斯靈頓的國會議員。 ***get sb in,*** call sb to one's house, etc to perform a service: 使某人到家中等做事: *We must get someone in to repair the TV.* 我們必須請個人來修理電視機。 ***get sth in,*** **(a)** collect; gather: 收集;收割: *get in the crops/the harvest;* 收割莊稼; *get in debts/taxes.* 收回借款(收稅)。**(b)** obtain a supply of sth: 獲某物之供應: *get coal in for the winter;* 貯煤以備冬日之需; *get in more wine for Christmas.* 多備酒以供聖誕節之用。 ***get one's hand/eye in, not get a word in edgeways, get a blow in,*** ⇨ hand[1](5), eye[1](1), edgeways, and blow[3](1).

get into sth, **(a)** put on: 穿上: *I can't get into these shoes—they're two sizes too small!* 這雙鞋我穿不進—它們小了二號。 **(b)** pass into a particular condition: 進入特殊狀態: *get into trouble/a rage/a temper;* 惹上麻煩(發怒;發脾氣); *get into debt.* 負債。 ***get a girl into trouble,*** (colloq) make her pregnant. (俗)使一女子懷孕。⇨ also get with below. 亦參看下列之 get with。**(c)** acquire: 得到: *get into bad habits.* 養成惡習。**(d)** associate with: 結交: *get into undesirable company.* 結交不良的朋友。**(e)** learn by experience or experiment: 由經驗或實驗而學得: *get into the way/habit/routine of doing something.* 學會做某事的方法(養成做某事的習慣;學得做某事之常規)。 ***get it into one's head that...; get 'this into your head that...,*** become convinced, understand, that.... 相信…;了解…。

get off, start: 出發: *We got off immediately after breakfast.* 我們於早餐後卽刻出發。***get off lightly/cheaply,*** escape severe punishment or suffering. 未受重罰或痛苦。 ***tell sb where to get off/where he gets off,*** (colloq) tell him how far his misbehaviour, impudence, etc will be tolerated, or that it will no longer be tolerated (= put sb in his place). (俗)告訴某人其行爲、無禮等將被容忍到什麼地步。 ***get sb/sth off,*** send: 送;傳遞: *get letters/parcels off in good time;* 按時寄出信件(包裹); *get the children off to school.* 送孩子們去上學。***get sth off one's chest/hands,*** ⇨ chest(2), hand[1](1). ***get sb off,*** save from punishment or a penalty: 使某人免於受罰: *His youth and inexperience got him off.* 他的年輕和無經驗使他免於受罰。*A clever barrister may be able to get you off.* 一位聰明的律師可能爲你脫罪。 ***get sb off to sleep,*** help him to fall asleep: 助某人入睡: *She got the baby off to sleep,* eg by rocking it. 她幫助嬰兒入睡(例如搖動嬰兒)。***get sth off,*** remove: 脫下;除下: *get a ring off one's finger;* 脫下指環; *get off one's gloves.* 脫下手套。***get sth off (by heart),*** learn it until the words can be repeated mechanically. 能機械般地背誦出來。***get off with sb,*** (colloq) have a romantic or sexual encounter with him: (俗)釣上某人(與某人發生戀情或性關係): *The nurse got off with a young doctor at the dance.* 那護士在舞會中釣上一位年輕的醫生。***get off with sth,*** escape more severe punishment or misfortune: 逃脫較嚴重的懲罰或災禍: *He got off with only a fine,* eg instead of possible imprisonment. 他僅受到罰款(例如代替監禁)。

get on, **(a)** become older. 年事漸高。 **(b)** make progress; advance: 進步;進展: *How's Jim getting on at school?* 吉姆的學業有進步嗎? *He is getting on well.* 他頗有進步。*Time is getting on,* is passing. 時光流逝。***get on sth,*** mount: 登上;騎上: *He got on his bike/horse/the train.* 他騎上脚踏車(騎上馬,登上火車)。***get on one's feet,*** stand; (fig) recover after a set-back: 站立;(喻)經挫折後而復元: *The industry will need time to get on its feet again.* 工業需要一段時期才能恢復舊觀。 ***get on one's nerves,*** ⇨ nerve(2). ***be getting 'on for,*** (of age or time) be approaching: (指年齡或時間) 接近: *He's getting on for seventy,* will soon be 70 years old. 他快七十歲了。*It's getting on for midnight.* 快到半夜了。 ***get 'on to sb,*** **(a)** get in touch with, eg by telephone; make contact with: 與某人聯絡(例如以電話): *If you're not satisfied with the firm's service, get on to the manager.* 如果你對公司的服務不滿意,請和經理聯絡。**(b)** (colloq) succeed in recognizing, eg dishonesty, deceit: (俗)認清某人之虛僞,欺騙等: *He has tricked many of us but people are beginning to get on to him at last.* 他騙過我們當中許多人,但是人們終於開始認清了他的面目。 ***get on (with sb),*** work or live in a sociable way: (與某人)相處: *The new manager is easy to get on with.* 新經理易於相處。*They don't get on at all well (together).* 他們相處得一點也不好。***get on (with sth),*** continue: 繼續: *Please get on with your work.* 請繼續你的工作。

get out, become known: 被人知道;洩露: *The secret got out.* 秘密洩露了。 *If the news gets out there'll be trouble.* 如果這消息洩露出去,將會引起麻煩。 ***get sth out,*** **(a)** utter: 說出: *He managed to get out a few words of thanks.* 他勉强說出幾句感謝的話。**(b)** produce; publish; distribute: 生產;出版;分配: *Will we get the new dictionary out by the end of the year?* 我們在年底可將新字典出版嗎? ***get out of (doing) sth,*** **(a)** (fig) avoid; escape (from): (喻)避免;逃避: *I wish I could get out of (going to) that wedding.* 我希望我能不參加那婚禮。 **(b)** (fig) abandon gradually: (喻)逐漸放棄: *get out of bad habits.* 逐漸棄絕惡習。***get sth out of sb,*** extract: 設法取得: *The police have got a confession out of him,* have made him confess. 警方已使他招供。*Just try getting money out of him!* 設法從他那裏弄點錢看看!

get over sb, (colloq) forget: (俗)忘記: *He never got over Jane, you know,* She stayed in his memory. 你知道,他永遠忘不掉珍。 ***get over sth,*** **(a)** recover from, eg illness, surprise, a loss: (自疾病,驚訝,損失等情況中)恢復;痊癒;復元: *I can't get over* *his rudeness.* 我無法忘懷他的無禮。*Fred didn't remarry; he never got over the shock of losing Jane.* 富萊德沒有再婚,他永遠忘不掉失去珍時所受的震驚。**(b)** overcome: 克服: *She can't get over her shyness.* 她不能克服她的羞怯。***get sth over (with),*** reach the end of sth unpleasant or troublesome: 結束不愉快的事: *I have to see my dentist today; I'll be glad to get it over with.* 今天我得去看牙齒,希望能就此結束這件惱人的事。***get sth over (to sb),*** cause (him) to understand it. 使(某人)了解某事。

get round sb, persuade sb into some action to which he was at first opposed or indifferent; influence sb in one's favour; coax: 說服某人去做其最初反對或不熱心的事;籠絡某人;哄誘: *Alice knows how to get round her father.* 愛麗絲知道如何說服她的父親。***get round sth,*** evade, eg a law or regulation, but without committing a legal offence; circumvent: 逃避某事物(例如法律或規則)但不違法;鑽(法律)漏洞: *A clever lawyer might find ways of getting round that clause.* 聰明的律師可能有辦法逃避那條法律。***get round to (doing) sth,*** deal with it (when more important matters have been dealt with): (較重要之事處理完畢後)處理某事: *I'm very busy this week but I hope to get round to (answering) your request next week.* 我本週內很忙,但是我希望下週能處理(答覆)你的請求。

get through (to sb), arrive; reach (sb); make contact (with sb): 到達某人處;(與某人)接觸: *I left as soon as your message got through (to me).* 一接到你的信我就離開了。*I rang you several times yesterday but couldn't get through.* 我昨天打了幾次電話給你,但是都找不到你。***get through (sth),*** pass, eg an examination: 通過(例如考試): *Tom failed but his sister got through.* 湯姆不及格,但他的妹妹及格了。***get through (with) sth,*** reach the end of: 結束;完成: *I've got through a lot of correspondence today.* 今天我寫了許多信。*He has got through* (= spent) *all his money.* 他已將他所有的錢花光了。*As soon as I get through (with) my work, I'll join you.* 我一做完我的工作,就去找你們。***get through to sb that...,*** communicate to him that...: 通知某人說…: *Try to get through to him that he's ruining his own life.* 設法告訴他他正在摧毀他的一生。***get sb through (sth),*** help to pass an examination: 助某人考試及格: *get pupils through (an examination).* 讓學生們考試及格。***get sth through,*** ensure that it is done; make it law: 使完成;使通過爲法律: *get the proposal through the committee,* have it discussed and accepted; 使提議爲委員會所接受; *get a Bill through Parliament.* 使一法案在國會通過。

get to sth/sb, reach (a place, state, person, etc): 到達(某地,某種狀態,某人等): *When she got to the station, the train had already left.* 她到達車站時,火車已經開走了。*He got to thinking* (= began to think) *that she wouldn't come after all.* 他開始覺得她畢竟不會來了。***get to work,*** ⇨ work¹(1).

get together (with sb), come or meet together, eg for discussion or for social purposes: (與某人)聚會(例如爲討論或爲社交活動): *get together for a friendly chat;* 聚在一起閒話家常; *get together with sb to discuss a problem.* 與某人聚在一起討論問題。Hence, 由此產生, **'get-together** *n* [C]. 聚會;敘舊。***get it/sth together,*** (colloq) organize or manage it; put it in order. (俗)組織;管理;整頓。***get oneself together,*** (colloq) get control of oneself, one's feelings, etc. (俗)控制自己、自己的感情等。***get people/things together,*** collect them: 聚集: *The rebel leader couldn't get an army together.* 叛軍首領無法召集一支軍隊。

get sth under control, ⇨ control. ***get sth under way,*** ⇨ way(8).

get up, **(a)** rise: 起床;起立: *When do you get up,* ie from bed? 你早上幾點鐘起床? *He got up* (= stood up) *to sing.* 他站起來唱歌。Hence, 由此產生, **,get-up-and-'go** *n* [U] (colloq) energy. (俗)精力;活力。**(b)** mount (a horse). 登上;乘;騎。**(c)** begin to be violent: 開始强烈;變劇烈: *The wind/sea is getting up.* 風勢開始增强(海浪開始洶湧)。***get sb/sth up,*** **(a)** cause to rise, be out of bed: 使起立;使起床: *Get the children up and dressed for school.* 讓孩子們起床,穿好衣服去上學。**(b)** arrange sb's/sth's appearance: 裝扮某人之外表;整理某物之外表: *got up to look like an Arab princess.* 裝扮成阿拉伯公主的樣子。*The book is well got up,* well printed and bound. 這本書印刷和裝訂得很好。Hence, 由此產生, **'get-up** *n* (colloq) (俗) **(a)** style or arrangement, eg of a book, periodical. (書籍刋物等的)裝訂形式。**(b)** style of dress, esp if unusual: 衣服式樣(尤指特別的): *I wouldn't be seen dead with you in that get-up!* 你穿着那種怪衣服,我說什麼也不願意同你在一起! ***get sth up,*** organize: 組織;籌畫: *We're getting up a party for his birthday.* 我們正在籌畫爲他的生日舉行一個慶祝會。***get up steam,*** ⇨ steam. ***get up to sth,*** **(a)** reach: 到達: *We got up to page seventy-two last lesson.* 我們上一課上到第七十二頁。*We soon got up to the others,* caught up with them. 我們不久便趕上其他的人了。**(b)** become involved in (sth unusual): 專心於(不平常之事): *What will they get up to next?* 他們下一步計畫做些什麼?

get sb with child, (archaic) make her pregnant. (古)使一女子懷孕。***get with it,*** (colloq) (俗) ⇨ with(12).

geum /ˈdʒiːəm ; ˈdʒiəm/ *n* [C] kind of small garden plant. 水楊梅屬。

gey·ser /ˈgiːzə(r) *US:* ˈgaɪzər ; ˈgaɪzɚ/ *n* **1** natural spring sending up at intervals a column of hot water or steam. 天然噴泉(間歇地噴出一股溫水或熱氣)。**2** (GB) apparatus for heating water, eg by gas, in a kitchen, bathroom, etc. (英)(厨房,洗澡間等的)熱水器;熱水鍋爐。

a geyser

gharry /ˈgærɪ ; ˈgærɪ/ *n* (*pl* -ries) (in India, etc) (horse-drawn) carriage. (印度等地之)馬車。

ghast·ly /ˈgɑːstlɪ *US:* ˈgæs- ; ˈgæstlɪ/ *adj* (-ier, -iest) **1** death-like; pale and ill: 死一般的;慘白的: *looking ~;* 面色慘白的; (also as *adv*): (亦作副詞): *~ pale.* 慘白。**2** causing horror or fear: 可怖的;可怕的: *a ~ accident.* 可怕的意外。**3** (colloq) very unsatisfactory or unpleasant: (俗)十分令人不滿或不快的: *a ~ dinner.* 糟糕的一頓飯。

ghat /gɔːt ; gɔt/ *n* [C] (in India) flight of steps leading to a landing-place on a river bank. (印度)河岸上下之階梯。**'burning ~,** level area at the top of a ~ on which Hindus cremate their dead. 河旁的火葬場。

ghee /giː ; gi/ *n* [U] clarified Indian buffalo-milk butter. (印度)酥油(將水牛乳煮沸澄清而成)。

gher·kin /ˈgɜːkɪn ; ˈgɝkɪn/ *n* small, green cucumber for pickling. (供醃泡用的)小黃瓜。

ghetto /ˈgetəʊ ; ˈgɛto/ *n* (*pl* ~s /-təʊz ; -toz/) **1** (formerly, in some countries) Jewish quarter of a town. (昔時某些國家中)城市中猶太人的居留區。**2** section of a town, lived in by underprivileged classes, or people who are discriminated against, eg because of race or religion. 城市中未享受正當權利階級或遭受歧視的人民居住的地區。

ghost /gəʊst ; gost/ *n* **1** spirit of a dead person appearing to sb still living: 鬼;幽靈: *He looked as if he had seen a ~,* looked frightened. 他的樣子好像碰見了鬼。*I don't believe in ~s.* 我不相信有鬼。 **2** (old use) spirit of life. (舊用法) 靈魂。***give up the ~,*** die. 死。 **3** Spirit of God: 上帝之靈: (only in) (僅用於) **the Holy G~,** the Third Person of the Trinity. 聖靈(三位一體之第三位)。 **4** sth shadowy or without substance. 幻影;一絲;一點;些微。'**~ town,** one now deserted, eg an area where gold was once mined, but is now abandoned. 鬼城(例如昔時曾有金礦而現被遺棄的城鎮)。***not have the '~ of a chance,*** no chance at all. 一點機會也沒有。 **5** (also 亦作 '**~-writer**), person who does literary or artistic work for which his employer takes the credit. 爲人代筆的作家;捉刀人。 **6** duplicated image on a television screen. 電視幕上重複的影像。□ *vt, vi* act as a ~-writer (for): 爲人代筆;爲人捉刀: *~ed memoirs,* compiled by a ~-writer. 由他人代筆撰寫的回憶錄。

ghost·ly /'gəustlɪ; 'gostlɪ/ *adj* **1** of, like, suggesting, a ghost: 鬼的; 似鬼的; 鬼狀的: *vague shapes, looking ~ in the darkness.* 黑暗中看來似鬼魂的模糊的影子。 **2** (archaic) spiritual; from a priest: (古) 精神上的;來自敎士的: *~ comfort/counsel.* 精神上的安慰(敎士的勸誡)。**ghost·li·ness** *n*

ghoul /gu:l; gul/ *n* **1** (in stories) spirit that robs graves and feeds on the corpses in them. (故事中)食屍鬼。 **2** person with gruesome and unnatural tastes and habits. 嗜好和習慣古怪可怕的人。**~·ish** /-ɪʃ; -ɪʃ/ *adj* gruesome; revolting. 可怕的;使人嫌惡的。

GI /ˌdʒi: 'aɪ; 'dʒi'aɪ/ *n* enlisted soldier of the US army: 美國兵: *a GI bride,* bride, (in or from a country other than the US) of such a soldier. 美國兵的(外國)新娘。

gi·ant /'dʒaɪənt; 'dʒaɪənt/ *n* **1** (in fairy tales) man of very great height and size. (童話中)巨人。 **2** man, animal or plant much larger than normal; (fig) person of extraordinary ability or genius. 特別大的人,動物或植物; (喩)偉人;天才。 **3** (attrib) of great size or force: (形容用法)巨大的: *~ strength;* 巨大的力量; *a ~ cabbage.* 一顆特大的捲心菜。 **~·ess** /'dʒaɪəntes; 'dʒaɪəntɪs/ *n* female ~. 女巨人。

gib·ber /'dʒɪbə(r); 'dʒɪbɚ/ *vi* [VP2A, C] talk fast or make meaningless sounds (like an ape, or as when the teeth knock together through cold or fear). 嘰哩咕嚕地談話;作無意義的聲音(如猿,或因寒冷恐懼等牙齒震顫時者然)。 **~·ish** /'dʒɪbərɪʃ; 'dʒɪbərɪʃ/ *n* [U] meaningless sounds; unintelligible talk. 無意義的聲音;嘰哩咕嚕的談話。

gib·bet /'dʒɪbɪt; 'dʒɪbɪt/ *n* **1** (hist) gallows. (史)絞架。 **2** wooden post with an arm, on which corpses of executed criminals were formerly exposed as a warning. 示衆架(昔時將已處死的犯人的屍體陳列其上,以儆他人)。 **3** death by hanging. 絞死。□ *vt* put to death by hanging; expose on a ~; (fig) hold up to contempt or ridicule. 絞死;陳列於示衆架; (喩)當衆侮辱或嘲弄;使人出醜或丟人。

gib·bon /'gɪbən; 'gɪbən/ *n* kinds of long-armed ape. 長臂猿。⇨ the illus at ape. 參看 ape 之挿圖。

gib·bous /'dʒɪbəs; 'gɪbəs/ *adj* **1** (of the moon) having the bright part greater than a semicircle and less than a circle. (指月亮) 凸圓的 (大於半月小於滿月的)。⇨ the illus at phase. 參看 phase 之挿圖。 **2** humped; hunchbacked. 隆起的;駝背的。

gibe, jibe /dʒaɪb; dʒaɪb/ *vi* [VP2A, 3A] ***~ (at),*** jeer or mock; make fun of: 譏笑或嘲弄;捉弄: *~ at a boy's mistakes.* 譏笑一孩子的錯誤。□ *n* taunt; cruel joke: 笑罵;嘲弄: *cheap ~s,* easy but unnecessary mockery. 輕易的但是不必要的嘲笑。 **gib·ing·ly** /'dʒaɪbɪŋlɪ; 'dʒaɪbɪŋlɪ/ *adv*

gib·lets /'dʒɪblɪts; 'dʒɪblɪts/ *n pl* heart, liver, gizzard, etc of a goose, hen, etc taken out before the bird is cooked: 鵝,鷄等的雜碎: *giblet soup,* soup made from these parts. 鷄(鵝等)雜湯。

giddy /'gɪdɪ; 'gɪdɪ/ *adj* (-ier, -iest) **1** causing, having, the feeling that everything is turning round; feeling that one cannot stand firm: 令人眩暈的;頭暈的: *look down from a ~ height.* 從一令人眩暈的高處向下望。*If you turn round quickly fifty times, you will feel ~.* 如果你很快地轉五十次,你會感到頭暈。 **2** too fond of pleasure; not serious; without steady principles: 過於喜歡享樂的;輕佻的;輕浮的: *a ~ young girl;* 一位輕佻的少女; *a ~ life of pleasure.* 放蕩的生活。***play the ~ goat,*** ⇨ goat. **gid·dily** *adv* **gid·di·ness** *n*

gift /gɪft; gɪft/ *n* **1** [C] sth given: 禮物; 贈品: *~s to charities;* 捐贈給慈善事業的東西; *'~ vouchers/coupons.* 禮劵。Cf 參較 *birthday and Christmas presents.* **2** [C] natural ability or talent: 天賦;天才: *have a ~ for art/languages;* 有藝術 (語言) 天才; *a woman of many ~s,* talented by nature. 多才多藝的女子。***look a ~-horse in the mouth,*** ⇨ mouth[1](1). **3** [U] right or power to give: 贈與權: *The post is in the ~ of the Prime Minister,* He has the right to bestow it. 該職位的委派權在首相手中。□ *vt* [VP6A] bestow, eg land, as a ~ to sb. 贈與(例如土地)。**~ed** *adj* having great natural ability: 有天才的: *~ed with rare talents;* 有罕見的天才; *a ~ed pianist.* 天才鋼琴家。

gig /gɪg; gɪg/ *n* **1** (hist) small, light two-wheeled carriage pulled by one horse. (史)小型輕便的二輪單馬車。 **2** (naut) ship's small boat for oars or sails, eg for the captain's use. (航海) (大船上的)小艇; (艦長)座艇。 **3** (colloq) (pop or jazz music) engagement to play. (俗) (流行或爵士音樂)預訂表演期間。

gi·gan·tic /dʒaɪ'gæntɪk; dʒaɪ'gæntɪk/ *adj* of immense size: 巨大的;龐大的: *He has a ~ appetite, and eats ~ meals.* 他的食量很大,能吃很多食物。

giggle /'gɪgl; 'gɪgl/ *vi, vt* [VP2A] laugh lightly in a nervous or silly way; [VP6A] express by giggling: 咯咯地笑;傻笑;咯咯地笑著表示: *She ~d her appreciation of my silly joke.* 她咯咯地笑著表示欣賞我愚蠢的笑話。□ *n* laugh of this kind. 咯咯的笑;傻笑。

gig·olo /'ʒɪgələu; 'dʒɪgəˌlo/ *n* (*pl* ~s /-ləuz; -loz/) professional male dancing-partner who may be hired by wealthy women; paid male companion of a wealthy older woman. 職業性的男舞伴(可受有錢婦女所僱用者);有錢而較年長的婦女僱用的男伴。

Gilbertian /gɪl'bɜ:tɪən; gɪl'bɝtɪən/ *adj* ***a ~ situation,*** humorously ridiculous or paradoxical situation as in Gilbert and Sullivan operas. 可笑或荒謬的詼諧場面(如吉柏特和蘇利文喜歌劇中者)。

gild[1] /gɪld; gɪld/ *vt* (*pp* usu ~ed, sometimes gilt /gɪlt; gɪlt/, ⇨ gilt below) (過去分詞通常用 ~ed, 有時用 gilt, 參看下列之 gilt) [VP6A] cover with gold leaf or gold-coloured paint; make bright as if with gold: 鍍金於;覆以金箔; 塗或漆以金色; 使有金子般的光彩: *~ a picture-frame.* 給畫框鍍金。***~ the lily,*** spoil the beauty of sth by unnecessary embellishment. 過份裝飾而破壞某物之美;畫蛇添足。***~ the pill,*** make an unpleasant necessity seem attractive. 使討厭之必需品顯得可愛;虛飾外觀。**~ed youth,** young people of fashion and wealth. 紈袴子弟。 **~er** *n* person who ~s (picture-frames, etc). 鍍金工;鍍金者。**~·ing** *n* [U] material with which things are ~ed. 鍍金用的材料。

gild[2] ⇨ guild.

gill[1] /gɪl; gɪl/ *n* (usu *pl*) (通常用複數) **1** organ (one on each side) with which a fish breathes. 鰓。⇨ the illus at fish. 參看 fish 之挿圖。 **2** one of the many thin vertical sheets on the under side of a mushroom. 菌褶。⇨ the illus at fungus. 參看 fungus 之挿圖。 **3** (*pl*) person's flesh under the ears and jaw. (複) (人之)腮。***be green/white about the ~s,*** be sick/afraid. 有病(害怕)。

gill[2] /dʒɪl; dʒɪl/ *n* one-quarter of a pint liquid measure. 吉爾(液量單位,合四分之一品脫)。⇨ App 5. 參看附錄五。

gil·lie /'gɪlɪ; 'gɪlɪ/ *n* man or boy attending a sportsman in Scotland while fishing or shooting. 蘇格

G

蘭釣魚或遊獵者的從僕。

gilt /gɪlt ; gɪlt/ *n* [U] gilding. 鍍金材料。⇨ gild. ***take the ~ off the gingerbread,*** (prov) take away the most attractive feature. (諺)除去最誘人的外貌。 **ˌ~-edged ˈstocks/seˈcurities,** investments that are considered safe. 優良股票(證券);金邊股票(證券)(卽可靠的股票或證券)。

gim·bals /ˈdʒɪmblz ; ˈdʒɪmbl̩z/ *n* (usu *pl*) contrivance (of rings and pivots) for keeping instruments, eg a compass, horizontal on a ship at sea. (通常用複數)(羅盤等的)平衡環;水平環。

gim·crack /ˈgɪmkræk ; ˈdʒɪmˌkræk/ *adj* worthless, flimsy and badly made: 製造粗劣而無價值的: *~ ornaments.* 做得粗劣而無價值的裝飾品。

gim·let /ˈgɪmlɪt ; ˈgɪmlɪt/ *n* small tool, with a handle usu fixed crosswise, used for boring holes in wood, etc. 螺絲錐;木鑽;手錐。⇨ the illus at tool. 參看 tool 之插圖。 **~ eye,** searching glance. 銳利的眼光。

gim·mick /ˈgɪmɪk ; ˈgɪmɪk/ *n* [C] (colloq) trick, device, catchword, mannerism, article of wear, etc used for publicity purposes, to identify sth or sb. (俗)爲宣傳某物或某人所用的花樣,策略,妙句,怪樣,衣著等;噱頭。

gin¹ /dʒɪn ; dʒɪn/ *n* **1** trap or snare for catching animals, etc. 陷阱。 **2 (cotton) ~,** machine for separating raw cotton from its seeds. 軋棉機。 □ *vt* (-nn-) [VP6A] **1** catch (animals, etc) in a trap or snare. 以陷阱誘捕(動物等)。 **2** treat (cotton) in a gin. 以軋棉機除去(棉花)之子。

gin² /dʒɪn ; dʒɪn/ *n* [U] colourless alcoholic drink distilled from grain or malt and flavoured with juniper berries, often drunk with tonic water, and used in many kinds of cocktail. 杜松子酒。

gin·ger /ˈdʒɪndʒə(r) ; ˈdʒɪndʒɚ/ *n* [U] **1** (plant with) hot-tasting root used in cooking, as a flavouring and for making a kind of wine. 生薑;薑。 **2** liveliness; spirit; energy: 活潑;元氣;精力: *a ˈ~ group,* (in Parliament) group of MP's that urges the Government to be more active. (國會中)督促政府更加積極行事的一群議員。 **3** (also as *adj*) light reddish-yellow colour: (亦用作形容詞)淡赤黃色(的): *~ hair.* 淡赤黃色的頭髮。 **4 ˌ~ ˈbeer/ˈale,** kinds of non-alcoholic aerated drink flavoured with ~. 薑啤酒。 **ˈ~·bread** *n* dark-coloured cake or biscuit flavoured with ~. 薑餅;薑汁餅乾。⇨ gilt. **ˈ~ nut,** biscuit flavoured with ~. 薑汁餅乾。□ *vt* [VP6A, 15B] ***~ (up),*** make more vigorous or lively. 使更有生氣;使更爲活潑。

gin·ger·ly /ˈdʒɪndʒəlɪ ; ˈdʒɪndʒɚlɪ/ *adv* with great care and caution to avoid harming, making a noise, etc: 極爲小心地(以避免傷害或弄出聲音): *set about sth ~.* 極爲小心地開始做。□ *adj* cautious: 小心的;謹愼的: *in a ~ fashion.* 小心翼翼。

ging·ham /ˈgɪŋəm ; ˈgɪŋəm/ *n* [U] printed cotton or linen cloth, usu with designs in stripes or checks. 印花棉布;印花麻布(通常有條紋或方格圖案)。

gingko /ˈgɪŋkəʊ ; ˈgɪŋko/ *n* (*pl* ~s, ~es /-kəʊz ; -koz/) tree native to China and Japan with fan-shaped leaves. 白果樹;銀杏。

gin·seng /ˈdʒɪnseŋ ; ˈdʒɪnsɛŋ/ *n* [U] plant of which the aromatic root is used in medicine. 人參。

gipsy, Gypsy /ˈdʒɪpsɪ ; ˈdʒɪpsɪ/ *n* (*pl* -sies) **1** **gipsy,** (playfully) attractive or mischievous person, esp one with black, sparkling eyes. (戲謔語)漂亮或頑皮的人(尤指有黑色明亮的眼睛者)。 **2 Gypsy,** member of a wandering, originally Asiatic people, who move about in caravans and make camps from time to time, and earn a living by collecting scrap material, horse-dealing, fortune-telling, basket-making, etc: 吉普賽人(亞洲一流浪民族,現居於歐洲各地,乘馬拉的篷車流浪,隨時露營,以收廢料、販馬、算命、製籃等謀生): (attrib)(形容用法) *a ~ girl/camp/orchestra.* 吉普賽女郎(營地,管絃樂隊)。

gi·raffe /dʒɪˈrɑːf *US:* -ˈræf ; dʒəˈræf/ *n* African animal with a very long neck and legs and dark patches on its coat. 長頸鹿。⇨ the illus at large. 參看 large 之插圖。

gird /gɜːd ; gɝd/ *vt* (*pt, pp* girded or girt /gɜːt ; gɝt/) (poet or rhet) (詩或修辭) **1** [VP15B] ***~ on,*** fasten, attach: 繫結;佩帶: *~ on a sword.* 佩帶劍。 **2** [VP15B] ***~ up,*** raise and fasten, eg with a belt or sash: 以帶等繫緊;束以帶: *~ up one's clothes.* 束緊衣服。 ***~ up one's loins,*** prepare for action. 準備行動。 **3** encircle: 圍起;圍繞: *a sea-girt isle,* surrounded by the sea. 四面環海的小島。

girder /ˈgɜːdə(r) ; ˈgɝdɚ/ *n* wood, iron or steel beam to support the joists of a floor; compound structure of steel forming the span of a bridge, roof, etc. 大梁;桁;樑。

girdle¹ /ˈgɜːdl ; ˈgɝdl̩/ *n* **1** cord or belt fastened round the waist to keep clothes in position. 腰帶。 **2** corset. 女人的緊身褡。 **3** sth that encircles like a ~: 似腰帶狀的圍繞物: *a ~ of green fields round a town.* 圍繞在城市四周的一片綠野。□ *vt* [VP15A, B] ***~ about/around/with,*** encircle: 圍繞: *a lake ~d with trees.* 四周植有樹的湖。

girdle² /ˈgɜːdl ; ˈgɝdl̩/ *n* (Scot) (蘇) = griddle.

girl /gɜːl ; gɝl/ *n* female child; daughter; young woman; woman working in a shop, office, etc. 女孩;女兒;少女;女店員;女職員。 **ˈ~·(friend)** regular companion with whom one may or may not be in love. 愛人;女友。(GB)(英) **ˌG~ ˈGuide,** (US)(美) **ˌG~ ˈScout,** member of an organization for ~s, with principles and aims similar to those of the Scout Association. 女童子軍。 **ˈ~·hood** /-hʊd ; -hʊd/ *n* [U] state or time of being a ~. 少女時代。 **~·ish** /-ɪʃ ; -ɪʃ/ *adj* of, for, like a ~: 女孩的;少女的;似女孩的: *~ish games/behaviour/laughter.* 女孩子們的遊戲(行爲,大笑)。 **~·ish·ly** *adv* **~·ish·ness** *n*

giro /ˈdʒaɪrəʊ ; ˈdʒaɪro/ *n* [U] (comm) system of credit transfer between banks. (商)若干合資銀行集體淸算帳目的一種制度。 **National G~,** (GB) similar system operated by the Post Office. (英)郵局採用的類似上述的制度。

girt /gɜːt ; gɝt/ ⇨ gird.

girth /gɜːθ ; gɝθ/ *n* **1** leather or cloth band tightened round the body of a horse to keep the saddle in place. (馬的)肚帶。⇨ the illus at harness. 參看 harness 之插圖。 **2** measurement round anything that is roughly like a cylinder in shape: 周圍的長度: *a tree 10 metres in ~,* in circumference; 周長十公尺的樹; *my ~,* my waist measurement. 我的腰圍。

gist /dʒɪst ; dʒɪst/ *n* **the ~,** main points or substance; general sense: 要點;要旨;要義: *Tell me the ~ of what he said.* 告訴我他所說的要點。

give¹ /gɪv ; gɪv/ *vt, vi* (*pt* gave /geɪv ; gev/, *pp* given /ˈgɪvn ; ˈgɪvən/) (For uses with *adverbial particles* and *preps,* ⇨ 13 below.) (與副詞接語和介詞連用的用法,參看下列第 13 義。) **1** [VP12A, 13A, 2A] ***~ (to),*** hand over (to sb) without payment or exchange, eg as a present or gift: 給予;贈給: *I gave David a book.* 我給了大衛一本書。 *I gave a book to each of the boys.* 我給每個孩子一本書。 *Each of the boys was ~n a book.* 每個孩子得到一本書。 *A book was ~n to each of them.* 他們每人獲一本書。 *I gave it him* (= to him). 我把它給了他。 *G~ me one.* 給我一個。 *G~ one to me.* 拿一個給我。 *He ~s generously,* is generous in giving money, etc. 他很慷慨。 **2** [VP12B, 16A] ***~ for sth; ~ to do sth,*** cause (sb) to have (sth) in exchange for sth else, for payment, as compensation, etc: 付給;報償: *How much will you ~ me for my old car?* 你願意出多少錢買我的舊車? *I would ~ anything to know what happened.* 我願付出一切以探聽究竟發生了什麼事。 **3** [VP12A, 13A] ***~ (to),*** allow (sb or sth) to pass into the care or safekeeping or custody of; entrust (to): 交付;委託: *G~ the porter your bags.* 把你的提包交給搬運行李的人。 *G~ your money* *to the hotel manager to be looked after.* 把你的錢交給旅館經理保管。 **4** [VP12A] allow (sb) to have, eg time; cause (sb) to have, eg trouble; concede; grant: 使(某人)有時間等; 使 (某人) 遭受麻煩等; 讓與; 容許: *You'd better ~ yourself half an hour for the journey.* 你最好打算以半小時走完這段路程。*G~ me five minutes and I'll change the wheel.* 給我五分鐘的時間,我來換輪子。*They gave me a week to make up my mind.* 他們給我一週的時間作決定。*'The car has a good engine' 'OK, I'll ~ you that* (= concede that you're right on that point) *but the body's very rusty'.* '這部汽車的引擎很好''不錯,你說得很對,但是車身很銹了'。**~ sb (some/no/any, etc) trouble,** cause or make trouble to: 使有(有些,沒有,任何等)麻煩: *Did you ~ your parents much trouble when you were young?* 你小的時候給你父母許多麻煩嗎? **5** [VP6A, 12A, 13A] furnish; supply; provide: 供給;供應: *The sun ~s us warmth and light.* 太陽供給我們溫暖和光。*You should ~* (more usu *set*) (set 較常用) *them a good example.* 你應當給他們做個好榜樣。*You should ~ a good example to your young brothers and sisters.* 你應當給你的弟弟妹妹們做個好榜樣。 **6** [VP12A, 13A] be the source or origin of: 爲…的來源;爲…的起因: *You've ~n me your cold,* I've caught a cold from you. 你把感冒傳染給我了。**7** [VP6A, 13A Note that 12A is not used 注意不用於 12A 型] devote; dedicate: 致力;獻身: *He gave his life to the cause of peace.* 他終生獻身於和平。**8** [VP12A] (used in the *imper* to show preference): (用於祈使句表示偏愛或選擇): *G~ me liberty or ~ me death,* If I cannot have liberty, I prefer to die. 不自由毋寧死。*G~ me Bach and Beethoven, not these modern crash-bang-tinkle composers.* 我喜歡巴哈與貝多芬,不喜歡這些近代的喧囂的作曲家。 **9** [VP6A, 12A, 13A] (used with a *n* in a pattern that may be replaced by one in which the *n* is used as a *v*): (與一名詞連用,此種語型可由將該名詞換作動詞之語型代替): *~ a groan/laugh/sigh/yell,* groan, laugh, sigh, yell; 呻吟(大笑;嘆氣;號叫); *~ a shrug of the shoulders,* shrug the shoulders; 聳肩; *~ three cheers,* cheer three times; 歡呼三次; *~ sb a kick/push/shove,* kick/push/shove him; 踢(推,撞)某人; *~ sb a ring,* phone him. 給某人打電話。 **10** (in fixed phrases) (用於固定片語中) **~ *birth (to),*** ⇨ birth. **~ *chase (to),*** ⇨ chase[1]. **~ *currency (to),*** ⇨ currency. **~ *one's ears,*** ⇨ ear[1](1). **~ *evidence of,*** ⇨ evidence. **~ *ground,*** ⇨ ground[1](2). **~ *place to,*** ⇨ place[1](10). **~ *rise to,*** ⇨ rise[1](5). **~ *or take...,*** plus or minus: 加或減: *She'll be here at 4 o'clock, ~ or take a few minutes.* 她大概四點鐘到此地,或早或遲幾分鐘。*He's six feet tall, ~ or take an inch or two.* 他身高大約六呎,不會超過一兩吋的差別。Cf 參較 *give and take* at give[2]. **~ *sb best,*** (old use) admit his superiority. (舊用法)承認某人的優越。 **~ *sb to understand that...,*** inform, assure him, that...: 使某人了解;告知某人;使某人相信: *I was ~n to understand that you might help me to find employment.* 我聽說你可能幫我找工作。**~ *it to sb,*** (colloq) punish or reprimand him. (俗)懲罰或嚴斥某人。 **~ *sb sth to cry for,*** ⇨ cry[1](2). **~ *sb what 'for/a piece of one's mind,*** (colloq) punish or scold him. (俗)懲罰或責罵某人。 **~ *way,*** **(a)** retire, retreat: 退後; 撤退: *Our troops had to ~ way.* 我們的部隊不得不撤退了。**(b)** fail to support: 不能支持: *The ice gave way and we all went through into the water.* 冰裂了,我們都掉進水中。*I felt the foundations giving way.* 我覺得地基在下陷。*The rope gave way,* broke, snapped. 繩子斷了。**~ *way (to sth/sb),*** **(a)** yield; allow priority to: 順從;讓…優先: *G~ way to traffic coming in from the right.* 讓從右面來的車輛先走。**(b)** be replaced by: 被代替: *Tears gave way to smiles.* 破涕爲笑。 **(c)** abandon oneself to: 耽於; 放縱自己: *Don't ~ way to despair/grief/tears.* 不要絕望(悲痛,哭泣)。 **(d)** make concessions (to): 讓步: *We mustn't ~ way to these unreasonable demands.* 我們不可對這些不合理的要求讓步。 **11** [VP2A] lose firmness; bend; yield to pressure: 垮下; 彎曲;凹下: *The branch gave* (eg swung downwards) *but did not break.* 這樹枝彎下來了,但並未折斷。*His knees seemed to ~,* to feel weak (so that he fell down). 他的膝蓋弱得像是直不起來。 *This chair ~s comfortably,* is soft and springy. 這椅子很有彈性。*The frost is beginning to ~,* is less severe. 嚴寒減退了。 **12 g~n** *pp* **(a)** (in formal documents) delivered: (在正式文件中) 發出的;簽訂的: *~n under my hand and seal in this fifth day of May, 1705.* 簽訂於 1705 年 5 月 5日。**(b)** granting or assuming that one has, eg as a basis for reasoning: 假定;倘若: *G~n good health, I hope to finish the work this year.* 假若健康情況良好,我希望今年完成這工作。**(c)** agreed upon; assigned: 約定的;指定的: *under the ~n conditions.* 在約定的條件下。*They were to meet at a ~n time and place.* 他們將在一約定的時間和地點相會。 **(d) '~n name,** name ~n to a child in addition to its family name, eg *David* in *David Hume.* 名(例如 David Hume 中之 David)。**(e) *be ~n to sth/doing sth,*** have as a habit: 習慣於;沈溺於;深愛: *He's ~n to boasting.* 他喜歡自誇。*I'm not much ~n to wild forecasts.* 我不大喜歡作輕率的預言。**13** [VP2C, 15B, 3A] (uses with *adverbial particles* and *preps*): (與副詞接語和介詞連用的用法):

give sb away, (esp) hand over (the bride) to the bridegroom at a wedding: (尤指)在婚禮中將(新娘)交付新郎: *The bride was ~n away by her father.* 新娘由她父親將她交給了新郎。**~ *sth away,*** **(a)** allow sb else to have; sacrifice: 讓別人得去;犧牲: *You've ~n away a good chance of winning the match.* 你已失掉一個比賽得勝的良好機會。**(b)** distribute: 分配; 分送: *The Mayor gave away the prizes at the sports meeting.* 市長頒發運動會的獎品。 **(c)** ~ freely, not expecting anything in return: 贈送: *He gave away all his money.* 他把所有的錢都送給別人了。**(d)** reveal, intentionally or unintentionally: (有意或無意地)洩露: *Don't ~ away my secret.* 不要洩露我的祕密。*His accent gave him away,* made known who or what he was. 他的口音暴露了他的身分。Hence, 由此產生, **'~-away** *n* (colloq) (俗) **(a)** sth given without charge: 贈品: *airlines which present ~-aways* (= gifts) *to their passengers.* 給乘客贈品的航空公司。*The last question on the exam paper was a ~-away,* so easy that it needed no effort, etc. 考試的最後一題等於贈送分數。**(b)** sth revealed, intentionally or unintentionally: (有意或無意)洩露的事: *The expression on the thief's face was a ~-away,* showed his guilt. 那竊賊面部的表情顯示他有罪。 **,~ *the 'game away,*** ⇨ game[1](5).

give sth back (to sb); ~ sb back sth, restore; return: 恢復;歸還;送還: *~ a thing back to its rightful owner;* 將一物歸還原主; *~ a man back his liberty;* 恢復一人的自由; *a wall of rock that ~s back loud echoes.* 產生響亮回音的一塊岩壁。

give sth forth, (old use or liter) give sth off. (舊用法或文)放出。

give in (to sb), surrender; yield; submit: 投降;屈服;歸順: *The rebels were forced to ~ in.* 叛軍被迫投降。*He has ~n in to my views,* has accepted them. 他已接受了我的觀點。*Mary usually has to ~ in to her big brother,* accept his plans, etc and abandon her own. 瑪莉通常必須聽從她大哥的話。 **~ *sth in,*** hand over (papers, etc) to the proper authorities: 呈交(文件等): *Please ~ in your examination papers now.* 現在請將試卷交來。 **~ *one's name in (to sb),*** make known one's willingness or readiness for sth, eg a duty, as a candidate, etc. (向某人)公開宣佈願做某事(如擔任某一職務,做候選人等)。

give sth off, emit, send out, eg smoke, smell, etc. 放出(煙,氣味等)。

give on to, look out on; overlook: 面對；俯視；俯瞰：*The bedroom windows ~ on to a courtyard.* 臥室的窗子面對着庭院。
give out, come to an end; be exhausted: 用盡；耗盡：*Our food supplies began to ~ out.* 我們存的食物要吃完了。*Her patience/strength gave out.* 她失去了耐心(她力竭了)。***~ sb out/not out,*** (cricket, of the umpire) say that the batsman has been/has not been defeated. (板球，指裁判員)判一擊球員出局(未出局)。***~ sth out,*** distribute; send out: 分配；分發：*~ out books/handbills.* 分發書籍(傳單)。***~ sb out to be; ~ it out that sb is,*** announce: 宣佈；公佈：*It was ~n out that Mr Hall would be the chief speaker.* 據宣佈，霍爾先生將爲主要的演說者。
give over, (sl) stop: (俚)停止：*Please ~ over crying.* 請不要再哭了。*Do ~ over!* 停止！***~ sb/sth over (to sb),*** hand (the usu word) over; deliver: 交與(通常用 hand over)：*~ sb over to the police.* 將某人交與警察。***be ~n over to sth,*** **(a)** be abandoned to (an undesirable state): 沉溺於(不良的狀態)：*be ~n over to despair.* 陷於絕望。**(b)** be devoted to: 專供…之用：*The period after supper was ~n over to games.* 晚飯後的時間用來做遊戲。
give up, abandon the attempt (to do sth, to find the answer to sth): 放棄(做某事，尋求答案等)：*I can do nothing more; I ~ up.* 我無能爲力，我放棄。*I can't answer that puzzle; I ~ up.* 我猜不出那個謎，我放棄。***~ sb up,*** **(a)** say that one regards sb, or his estate, as hopeless: 宣稱某人或其財產已無希望：*Even his teachers have ~n him up,* have decided that he cannot be reformed. 甚至他的老師們也認爲他無可救藥。*The doctors have ~n him up,* say that they cannot cure him. 醫生們說他的病已不能治了。**(b)** (colloq) stop keeping company with him: (俗)與(某人)斷絕往來：*She was tired of Tom's nagging so she gave him up.* 她厭倦了湯姆嘮嘮叨叨的責罵，所以她不同他往來了。**(c)** no longer expect sb: 不再期待某人：*She was so late that we had ~n her up.* 她到得太遲，我們以爲她不會來了。***~ sb up for lost,*** no longer expect him to be found or saved. 認爲某人不會被發現或得救。***~ sb/oneself/sth up (to sb),*** surrender; part with: 投降；自首；把…交給；放棄；讓與：*~ up a fortress;* 放棄一要塞；*~ up one's seat to sb,* eg in a crowded bus. 將座位讓給別人(例如在一擁擠的公共汽車上)。*Shall we let the thief go or ~ him up* (= deliver him) *to the police?* 我們是將這竊賊放走呢，還是將他交給警察？*The escaped prisoner gave himself up.* 那逃犯投案了。***~ sth up,*** stop (doing) it: 停止(做某事)：*I wish I could ~ up smoking.* 我希望我能戒煙。***~ up the ghost,*** die. 死。
give upon, = ~ on to.

give² /gɪv ; gɪv/ *n* [U] quality of being elastic, of yielding to pressure: 彈性；彈力：*A good dance floor should have a certain amount of ~ in it.* 好的跳舞用的地板應有相當的彈力。*A stone floor has no ~ in it;* 石頭地面沒有彈性；(fig) (of a person) quality of yielding: (喻)(指人)屈服性；讓步：*There's no ~ in him,* He does not concede anything, eg in negotiations, argument. 他絲毫不讓步(例如在談判或爭論中)。⇨ give¹(11)。***~ and take,*** compromise; mutual concession; willingness on both sides to give way: 妥協；互相讓步；雙方遷就：*There must be ~ and take if the negotiations to settle an industrial dispute are to succeed.* 解決工業糾紛的磋商如欲成功，必須雙方讓步。(attrib) (形容用法) *Is marriage a ~-and-take affair?* 婚姻是一件互相讓步的事嗎？

given /ˈgɪvn ; ˈgɪvən/ *pp* of give¹.

giver /ˈgɪvə(r) ; ˈgɪvɚ/ *n* one who gives: 給與者；施贈者：*a generous/cheerful ~.* 慷慨(樂意)的給與者。

giz·zard /ˈgɪzəd ; ˈgɪzɚd/ *n* bird's second stomach for grinding food; (fig, colloq) throat: 砂囊(鳥的第二胃，用以將食物磨碎)；(喻，俗)喉嚨：*It sticks in my ~,* is a proposal, etc that I dislike intensely. 這事我十分厭惡(不合我的胃口)。

glacé /ˈglæseɪ *US:* glæˈseɪ ; glæˈse/ *adj* (of fruits) iced, sugared; (of leather, cloth) smooth, polished. (指水果)覆有糖霜的；加糖的；(指皮革，布疋)光滑的。

gla·cial /ˈgleɪsɪəl *US:* ˈgleɪʃl ; ˈgleʃəl/ *adj* of ice or the ice age: 冰的；冰河時代的：*the ~ era/epoch,* the time when large areas of the northern hemisphere were covered with ice; 冰河時代；(fig) (喻) *a ~* (= icy) *manner/smile.* 冷冰冰的態度(笑)。

gla·cier /ˈglæsɪə(r) *US:* ˈgleɪʃər ; ˈgleʃɚ/ *n* [C] mass of ice, formed by snow on mountains, moving slowly along a valley. 冰河。⇨ the illus at mountain. 參看 mountain 之插圖。

glad /glæd ; glæd/ *adj* (-der, -dest) **1** (*pred* only) pleased: (僅作敍述用法)高興的；歡喜的：*be/look/feel ~ about something;* 對某事感到高興；*~ to see someone.* 看見某人而高興。*I am ~ of your success/that you have succeeded.* 你的成功使我高興。**2** causing or bringing joy; joyful: 使人快樂的；令人愉快的：*Have you heard the ~ news/tidings?* 你聽到那喜訊沒有？*All nature seemed ~,* was bright and beautiful, as if rejoicing. 萬物欣欣向榮(燦爛而美麗，像是高興的樣子)。***give sb the ˈ~ eye,*** (sl) give an amorous, inviting look. (俚)向某人拋媚眼。***give sb the ~ hand,*** (sl) offer the hand of welcome. (俚)向某人伸出歡迎的手。**ˈ~ rags,** (sl) clothes for a festive occasion. (俚)慶祝場合所穿的衣服。**~·den** /ˈglædn ; ˈglædn̩/ *vt* [VP6A] make ~. 使高興；使快樂。**~·ly** *adv* **~·ness** *n* **~·some** /-səm ; -səm/ *adj* (liter) cheerful; joyful. (文)愉快的；可喜的。

glade /gleɪd ; gled/ *n* clear, open space in a forest. 森林中的空地。

gladi·ator /ˈglædɪeɪtə(r) ; ˈglædɪˌetɚ/ *n* (in ancient Rome) man trained to fight with weapons at public shows in an arena. (古羅馬)(在鬪技場公開作打鬥表演的)鬪士。**gladia·tor·ial** /ˌglædɪəˈtɔːrɪəl ; ˌglædɪəˈtorɪəl/ *adj* of ~s: 鬪士的：*~ial combats.* 鬪技。

gladi·olus /ˌglædɪˈəʊləs ; ˌglædɪˈoləs/ *n* (*pl* -li /-laɪ ; -laɪ/ or ~es) plant with sword-shaped leaves and spikes of brightly coloured flowers. 劍蘭；唐菖蒲。

glam·our (US also **glamor**) /ˈglæmə(r) ; ˈglæmɚ/ *n* [U] **1** charm or enchantment; power of beauty or romance to move the feelings: 魅力；魔力；迷人的力量：*the ~ of moonlight on the sea.* 海上迷人的月色。**2** alluring beauty or charm, often with sex-appeal. 誘惑力(常是性感的)。**glamor·ous** /-əs ; -əs/ *adj* full of ~: 富有魅力的：*glamorous film stars.* 富有魅力的電影明星。**glamor·ize** /-aɪz ; -aɪz/ *vt* [VP6A] make glamorous: 使有魅力：*newspapers that glamorize the lives of film stars.* 把影星的生活描寫得十分動人的報紙。**glamor·iz·ation** /ˌglæməraɪˈzeɪʃn *US:* -rɪˈz- ; ˌglæmərɪˈzeʃən/ *n*

glance /glɑːns *US:* glæns ; glæns/ *vi, vt* **1** [VP2C, 3A] ***~ at/over/through/round,*** take a quick look: 瞥視；匆匆一看：*~ at the clock;* 匆匆看一下鐘；*~ over/through a letter;* 匆匆閱讀一信；*~ round a room.* 略略環視一房間。*She ~d shyly at him from behind her fan.* 她羞怯地從她的扇子後面看了他一眼。[VP15A] *He ~d his eye down the classified advertisements.* 他瀏覽分類廣告欄。**2** [VP3A] ***~ off,*** (of a weapon or a blow) quickly slip or slide: (指武器或一擊)擦過：*The arrow ~d off his armour.* 箭擦過他的甲胄。**3** [VP2C] (of bright objects, light) flash: (指明亮的物體，光)閃耀；閃光：*Their helmets ~d in the sunlight.* 他們的鋼盔在陽光下閃耀着。□ *n* **1** quick look: 一瞥；匆匆一看：*take a ~ at the newspaper headlines;* 瀏覽報上的標題；*loving ~s.* 脈脈含情的眼神。***at a ~,*** immediately on looking. 一瞥之下。***at first ~,*** = at first sight, ⇨ sight¹(2). **2** (sudden movement producing a) flash of light: 閃耀；閃爍；發閃光的突然動作：*a ~ of spears in the sunlight.* 矛在陽光下的閃爍。

gland /glænd ; glænd/ *n* simple or complex organ that separates from the blood substances that are to be used by or expelled from the body: 腺：

a snake's poison ~s; 蛇的毒腺；*milk-producing ~s in a female;* 雌性動物的乳腺；*sweat ~s.* 汗腺。**~u·lar** /ˈglændjʊlə(r) *US:* -dʒʊ-；ˈglændʒələ/ *adj* of, like, or involving a gland. 腺的；似腺的。

glan·ders /ˈglændəz；ˈglændəz/ *n* [U] contagious disease of horses with swellings below the jaw, and sores in the nose and throat. 馬的鼻疽病。

glare[1] /gleə(r)；glɛr/ *n* **1** [U] strong, fierce, unpleasant light: 强烈刺目的光：*the ~ of the sun on the water;* 水面上刺目的陽光；(fig) (喻) *in the full ~ of publicity,* with public attention directed towards one. 衆目睽睽之下。**2** [C] angry or fierce look; fixed look: 怒目而視；瞪視：*look at someone with a ~.* 怒視某人。

glare[2] /gleə(r)；glɛr/ *vi, vt* **1** [VP2A, C] shine in a dazzling or disagreeable way: 發强烈的光；發眩光：*The tropical sun ~d down on us all the day.* 熱帶的太陽整日灼照着我們。**2** [VP2A, C, 3A] **~ *(at),*** stare angrily or fiercely: 怒目而視：*They stood glaring at each other.* 他們站著互相怒目而視。[VP6A, 14] **~ *(at),*** *They ~d defiance/hate at me.* 他們以輕蔑(仇恨)的眼神瞪着我。**glar·ing** *adj* **1** dazzling: 耀目的；刺目的：*a car with glaring headlights;* 有刺目的前燈的汽車；*glaring neon signs.* 耀目的霓虹燈廣告。**2** angry; fierce: 憤怒的；兇惡的：*glaring eyes.* 憤怒的眼光。**3** gross; conspicuous: 顯著的；易見的：*a glaring error/blunder;* 顯著的謬誤；*glaring injustice.* 昭彰的不公。**4** (of colours) crude; gaudy. (指顏色)粗俗的；俗麗的。

glass /glɑːs *US:* glæs；glæs/ *n* **1** [U] hard, brittle substance (as used in windows), usu transparent: 玻璃：*bottles made of ~;* 玻璃瓶；*a man with a ~ eye.* 鑲有假眼的人。**2** [C] article made of this substance. 玻璃製品。**(a)** ~ drinking vessel or its contents: 玻璃杯；酒杯；一杯之量；杯內之飲料：*drink a ~ of milk;* 喝一杯牛奶；*have a ~ too much,* drink too much alcoholic liquor, be rather drunk. 酒喝得過多。**(b)** (also 亦作 **ˈlooking-~**) mirror made of ~. 鏡子。**(c)** telescope: 望遠鏡：*The sailor looked through his ~.* 那船員由望遠鏡瞭望。**(d)** barometer: 晴雨表：*The ~ is falling.* 晴雨表在下降。**(e)** (*pl*) (rarely 罕 **ˈeye-~es**) spectacles: (複)眼鏡：*She can't read without ~es.* 不戴眼鏡她無法看書。**(f)** (*pl*) binoculars. (複)雙筒望遠鏡。**(g)** *ˈmagnifying ~,* ~ lens on a handle for making writing, etc appear larger. 放大鏡。⇨ the illus at magnet. 參看 magnet 之插圖。**3** [U] vessels and articles made of ~: 玻璃器皿：*There's plenty of ~ in the house,* plenty of drinking ~es, wine ~es, ~ bowls and dishes, etc. 這房屋內有許多玻璃器皿。*There are many acres of ~ in Jersey,* acres covered with ~houses (for growing plants). 在澤西有許多畝的溫室。**4** (compounds) (複合字) **ˈ~-blower** *n* workman who blows molten ~ to shape it into bottles, etc. 吹製玻璃器者。**ˈ~-cutter** *n* workman who cuts designs on ~; tool for cutting ~. 玻璃雕切匠；割切玻璃之器具；割玻璃刀。**ˈ~·house** *n* building with ~ sides and roof (for growing plants); (sl) military prison. 溫室；暖房；(俚)軍人監獄。***People who live in ~houses shouldn't throw stones,*** (prov) People with faults shouldn't criticize those of others. (諺)人居溫室不可投石(自己有毛病不可批評他人)。**ˈ~·ware** /-weə(r)；-wɛr/ *n* [U] articles made of ~. 玻璃器皿。**ˌ~-ˈwool** *n* [U] fine ~ fibres used for filtering and in man-made fibres. 玻璃絨；玻璃纖維。**ˈ~-works** *n pl* (with *sing v*) factory where ~ is manufactured. (接單數動詞)玻璃工廠。□ *vt* [VP6A, 15B] **~ *(in),*** fit with ~; glaze: 裝以玻璃；鑲以玻璃：*a ~ed-in veranda.* 裝有玻璃的走廊。**~·ful** /-fʊl；-ˌfʊl/ *n* as much as a drinking ~ will hold. 一杯之量。**~y** *adj* (-ier, -iest) like ~ in appearance: 外表像玻璃的：*a ~y calm;* 平靜如鏡；(of the sea, etc) smooth and shiny; (指海洋等) 平穩如鏡的；*a ~y stare/look/eye,* lifeless, expressionless, fixed. 呆滯的凝視(目光，眼神)。

glau·coma /glɔːˈkəʊmə；glɔˈkomə/ *n* [U] eye disease involving gradual loss of sight. 綠內障；青光眼(使眼睛逐漸失明的疾病)。

glau·cous /ˈglɔːkəs；ˈglɔkəs/ *adj* **1** dull greyish green or blue. 淡灰綠色的；淡灰藍色的。**2** (of leaves, grapes, etc) covered with bloom(3). (指葉、葡萄等)有粉衣的；有霜粉的。

glaze /gleɪz；glez/ *vt, vi* **1** [VP6A, 15B] **~ *(in),*** fit glass into: 裝以玻璃：*~ a window/house;* 給窗子(房屋)裝玻璃；*~ in a porch/veranda,* enclose it with glass. 給走廊裝上玻璃。**2** [VP6A, 15B] **~ *(over),*** cover with a glass-like surface: 覆以玻璃狀的表面；上釉：*~ pottery/porcelain/bricks.* 給陶器(瓷器，磚)上釉。**3** [VP2A, C] **~ *(over),*** (of the eyes) become glassy: (指眼神) 變爲呆滯：*His eyes ~d over.* 他的目光呆滯。*His eyes were ~d in death.* 他死時目光呆滯。□ *n* [C, U] (substance used for, surface obtained by giving, a) thin glassy coating: 釉；上釉的表面；光滑的薄面：*a Satsuma vase with a fine crackle ~.* 飾有上等紋釉的薩摩瓷花瓶。

glaz·ier /ˈgleɪzɪə(r) *US:* -ʒə(r)；ˈgleʒə/ *n* workman who fits glass into the frames of windows, etc. 裝玻璃的工人。

gleam /gliːm；glim/ *n* [C] **1** beam or ray of soft light, esp one that comes and goes: 一絲光線；微弱的閃光：*the ~ of a distant lighthouse;* 遠處燈塔的閃光；*the first ~s of the morning sun.* 曙光。**2** (fig) brief show of some quality or emotion: (喻)某種性質或感情的閃現：*a novel with an occasional ~ of humour/intelligence;* 偶爾閃現着幽默(智慧)的一部小說；*a ~ of hope;* 一線希望。*a man with a dangerous ~ in his eye,* with a threatening look. 眼中閃現兇光的一個人。□ *vi* [VP2A, C] send out ~s: 發閃光；閃爍：*a cat's eyes ~ing in the darkness;* 在黑暗中閃爍的貓眼；*glass reflector studs ~ing in the roadway.* 在車道上閃爍的玻璃反光釘。

glean /gliːn；glin/ *vi, vt* [VP2A, 6A] pick up grain left in a harvest field by the workers; (fig) gather news, facts in small quantities: 拾(穗)；(喻)一點點地搜集(消息，事實)：*~ a field;* 在田中拾落穗；*~ corn.* 拾餘穀。**~er** *n* person who ~s. 拾落穗者；搜集消息或事實者。**~·ings** *n pl* (usu fig) small items of knowledge ~ed from various sources. (通常作喻)自各處蒐集的零碎知識。

glebe /gliːb；glib/ *n* **1** (poet) earth; field. (詩)大地；土地。**2** portion of land that forms part of a clergyman's benefice. 作爲牧師俸給之一部分的土地。

glee /gliː；gli/ *n* **1** [U] feeling of joy caused by success or triumph: (由於成功或勝利而產生的)歡欣；高興：*shout with ~.* 歡呼。*She was in high ~ when she learnt the news.* 她得悉此消息高興之至。**2** [C] song for three or four voices singing different parts in harmony. 格里(三部或四部重唱曲)。**~·ful** /-fl；-fəl/ *adj* full of ~; joyous. 高興的；愉快的。**~·fully** /-fəlɪ；-fəlɪ/ *adv*

glen /glen；glɛn/ *n* narrow valley. 狹谷；幽谷。

Glen·garry /ˌglenˈgærɪ；glɛnˈgærɪ/ *n* (*pl* -ries) kind of cap worn in the Highlands of Scotland. 蘇格蘭高地人所戴的一種帽子。

glib /glɪb；glɪb/ *adj* (-bber, -bbest) (of a person, what he says or how he says it) ready and smooth, but not sincere: (指人，言語，說話方式)口齒伶俐但不眞誠的；油腔滑調的：*a ~ talker;* 口齒伶俐的談話者；*~ excuses;* 流利但不眞實的託詞；*~ in finding excuses;* 找藉口時口齒伶俐；*have a ~ tongue.* 有伶俐的口舌。**~·ly** *adv* **~·ness** *n*

glide /glaɪd；glaɪd/ *vi* [VP2A, C] move along smoothly and continuously: 滑行；滑動；滑翔：*The skier ~d skilfully down the snow-covered slope.* 那滑雪者熟練地自覆着雪的斜坡上滑下。*The skaters ~d across the ice.* 那些溜冰者滑過冰面。*A boat ~d past.* 一隻小船滑過。□ *n* gliding movement or sound. 滑動；滑行；滑音。**~r** /ˈglaɪdə(r)；ˈglaɪdə/ *n*

G

aircraft without an engine. 滑翔機。**glid·ing** *n* sport of flying in ~rs. 滑翔運動。

glim·mer /ˈglɪmə(r) ; ˈglɪmɚ/ *vi* [VP2A, C] send out a weak, uncertain light: 發出閃爍的微光: *lights ~ing in the distance.* 遠處忽隱忽現的燈光。□ *n* weak, faint, unsteady light: 微弱的閃光: *a ~ of light through the curtains;* 透過窗簾的一線微弱的閃光; (fig) (喻) *a ~ of hope;* 一線希望; *not the least ~ of intelligence.* 毫無智力(情報)。

glimpse /glɪmps ; glɪmps/ *n* short look (*at* sth or sb). 一瞥(與 at 連用,後接人或物)。***get/catch a ~ of sb/sth,*** have a quick, imperfect view: 一瞥; 瞥見: *get/catch a ~ of something from the window of a train.* 自火車的窗中瞥見某物。□ *vt* [VP6A, 19A] catch a ~ of. 瞥見。

glint /glɪnt ; glɪnt/ *vi* gleam. 閃爍。□ *n* gleam or flash: 閃爍;閃光: *~s of gold in her hair.* 她頭髮中的金黃色閃光。

glis·sade /glɪˈseɪd *US:* -ˈsɑːd ; glɪˈsɑd/ *vi* (mountaineering) slide on the feet down a steep slope of ice or snow (usu with the support of an ice-axe); (ballet) make a sliding step. (登山)(通常以破冰斧支撐自覆有冰雪之陡坡)滑下; (芭蕾舞)滑步。□ *n* such a slide or step. 下滑;滑步。

glissando /glɪˈsændəʊ ; glɪˈsɑndo/ *adv, adj* (music) passing quickly up or down the scale. (音樂)滑奏。

glis·ten /ˈglɪsn ; ˈglɪsn̩/ *vi* [VP2A, C] (esp of wet or polished surfaces, tear-filled eyes) shine brightly; sparkle: (尤指潮濕或光澤的表面,充滿眼淚的眼睛) 閃耀;閃爍: *~ing dew-drops;* 晶瑩的露珠; *eyes ~ing with tears.* 淚光閃閃的眼睛。

glis·ter /ˈglɪstə(r) ; ˈglɪstɚ/ *vi, n* (poet) glitter. (詩)閃爍。

glit·ter /ˈglɪtə(r) ; ˈglɪtɚ/ *vi* [VP2A, C] shine brightly with flashes of light; sparkle: 閃爍: *stars ~ing in the frosty sky;* 閃爍在寒空的星斗; *~ing with jewels.* 珠光燦爛。□ *n* [U] brilliant, sparkling light: 燦爛的光輝: *the ~ of the Christmas tree decorations.* 聖誕樹上裝飾品的燦爛。**~·ing** *adj* brilliant; attractive: 燦爛的;動人的: *~ing prizes.* 燦爛的獎品。

gloam·ing /ˈgləʊmɪŋ ; ˈglomɪŋ/ *n* **the ~,** (poet) evening twilight. (詩)薄暮;黃昏。

gloat /gləʊt ; glot/ *vi* [VP2A, 3A] ***~ (over sth),*** look at with selfish delight: 懷着自私心理的喜悅去看;幸災樂禍地看;貪婪地看: *~ over one's wealth/the ruin of a rival;* 心滿意足地看自已的財富(幸災樂禍地看着敵對者的敗落); *a miser ~ing over his gold.* 心滿意足地望着他的金子的守財奴。**~·ing·ly** *adv*

glo·bal /ˈgləʊbl ; ˈglobl̩/ *adj* world-wide; embracing the whole of a group of items, etc. 全球性的;包括一切的。

globe /gləʊb ; glob/ *n* **1** object shaped like a ball; model of the earth; spherical chart of the earth or the constellations. 球形體;球體;地球儀;天體儀。**the ~,** the earth. 地球。 **2** spherical glass vessel, esp a lampshade or a fishbowl. 球狀玻璃器(尤指燈罩或金魚缸)。 **3** **ˈ~ fish** *n* fish able to inflate itself into the shape of a ~. 河豚。**ˈ~-trot** *vi* [VP2A] travel hurriedly through many foreign countries. 匆匆遊歷世界。 **ˈ~-trotter** *n* person who does this. 匆匆遊歷世界者。

glob·ule /ˈglɒbjuːl ; ˈglɑbjʊl/ *n* tiny drop, esp of liquid. 小球狀物;(尤指)水珠;點滴。**globu·lar** /ˈglɒbjʊlə(r) ; ˈglɑbjəlɚ/ *adj* globe-shaped; made of ~s. 球狀的;由點滴集成的。

glock·en·spiel /ˈglɒkənspiːl ; ˈglɑkənˌspil/ *n* musical instrument consisting of metal bars which are struck with two light hammers. 鐘琴(由金屬棒構成之一種樂器,以二小錘擊之);鐵琴。⇨ the illus at percussion. 參看 percussion 之插圖。

gloom /gluːm ; glum/ *n* [C, U] **1** semi-darkness; obscurity. 陰暗;幽暗;朦朧。 **2** feeling of sadness and hopelessness: 憂鬱;愁悶: *The future seems to be filled with ~.* 前途似乎充滿了黯淡。*The news cast a ~ over the village.* 這消息給整個村子罩上了一層憂鬱。

gloomy /ˈgluːmɪ ; ˈglumɪ/ *adj* (-ier, -iest) **1** dark, unlighted. 黑暗的;幽暗的。**2** depressed; depressing: 陰鬱的;令人沮喪的: *a ~ outlook over roofs and chimneys;* 籠罩在屋頂和煙囱上的一片陰沉的景色; *feeling ~ about the future.* 感到前途黯淡。**gloom·ily** /-ɪlɪ ; -ɪlɪ/ *adv*

glor·ify /ˈglɔːrɪfaɪ ; ˈglorəˌfaɪ/ *vt* (*pt, pp* -fied) [VP6A] **1** give adoration and thanksgiving to (God); worship; give honour and glory to (a hero). 讚美(上帝);禮拜;褒揚(英雄)。 **2** invest (sth common or simple) with splendour; make (sth or sb) seem more imposing: (使普通或樸素之物)增色;美化: *His weekend cottage is only a glorified barn.* 他的週末別墅祇是一個美化了的穀倉。**glori·fi·ca·tion** /ˌglɔːrɪfɪˈkeɪʃn ; ˌglorəfəˈkeʃən/ *n* [U] ~ing or being glorified. 讚美;禮拜;褒揚。

glori·ous /ˈglɔːrɪəs ; ˈglorɪəs/ *adj* **1** splendid; magnificent: 輝煌的;燦爛的;壯麗的: *a ~ sunset/view.* 光輝燦爛的落日(景色)。 **2** illustrious; honourable; possessing or conferring glory: 顯赫的;光榮的;輝煌的: *a ~ victory;* 光榮的勝利; *the ~ reign of Queen Elizabeth I.* 英國女王伊利莎白一世的輝煌朝代。 **3** (colloq) enjoyable: (俗)愉快的: *have a ~ time;* 過一段愉快的時間; *~ fun.* 愉快的情趣。 **4** (ironic) dreadful: (反語)可怕的: *What a ~ mess!* 眞是亂七八糟! **~·ly** *adv*

glory /ˈglɔːrɪ ; ˈglorɪ/ *n* [U] **1** high fame and honour won by great achievements. 光榮;榮譽。**2** adoration and thanksgiving offered to God: (對上帝的)讚美;讚頌: *'G~ to God in the highest.'* '榮耀歸於至高的上帝。' **3** quality of being beautiful or magnificent: 壯麗;燦爛;輝煌: *the ~ of a sunset.* 落日的燦麗。 **4** (sometimes [C] *pl* -ries) reason for pride; subject for boasting; sth deserving respect and honour: (有時用作可數的名詞)誇耀的原因;誇耀的事物;榮耀的事: *the glories of ancient Rome.* 古羅馬的光榮事蹟。**5** heavenly splendour: 天國的榮耀: *the saints in ~.* 天國的聖徒。 **6** (colloq uses) (俗語用法) *go to ~,* die; 死; *send sb to ~,* kill him. 殺死某人。**ˈ~-hole** *n* room, drawer, filled untidily with miscellaneous articles. 裝滿雜亂物件的房間或抽屜。□ *vi* [VP3A] ***~ in,*** rejoice in, take great pride in: 爲…而得意;以…而自豪: *~ in one's strength/in working for a good cause.* 因强壯(從事有益人群的工作)而自豪。

gloss¹ /glɒs ; glɔs/ *n* **1** [U] smooth, bright surface: 光滑的表面: *the ~ of silk and satin;* 綢緞之光滑的表面; *material with a good ~.* 表面光滑的料子。**ˌ~ ˈpaint** *n* paint which, when dry, leaves a ~ (usu washable) surface. 亮光漆。 **2** (usu 常作 **a ~**) deceptive appearance: 欺人的表面;虛飾: *a ~ of respectability,* eg over a life of secret wrong-doing. 金玉其外的聲望(例如掩飾暗中犯罪生活者)。□ *vt* [VP15A] ***~ over,*** give a ~(2) to; cover up or explain away (an error, etc): 予以光滑的表面; 掩飾(錯誤等): *~ over sb's faults.* 掩飾某人的過失。**~y** *adj* (-ier, -iest) smooth and shiny: 光滑的;有光澤的: *a ~y photographic print;* 光面的相片; *~y hair;* 光滑的頭髮; *~y periodicals,* those printed on high quality ~y paper, with photographs, coloured illustrations, etc, esp those periodicals dealing with clothes, fashions, etc. 由光滑的上等紙印成的有照片,彩色插圖等的刊物(尤指介紹服裝,時尙等者)。**~·ily** /-ɪlɪ ; -ɪlɪ/ *adv* **~i·ness** *n*

gloss² /glɒs ; glɔs/ *n* [C] explanation (in a footnote, or in a list at the end of an article, a book, etc) of a word in the text; comment; interpretation. 註釋;評註;解釋。□ *vt* [VP6A] add a ~ or ~es to (a text); write ~es on; make comments on. 註釋(本文);註解;評註。

gloss·ary /ˈglɒsərɪ ; ˈglɑsərɪ/ *n* (*pl* -ries) [C] collection of glosses; list and explanations of special, eg technical, obsolete, words. 字彙;語彙;術語彙編。

glot·tis /ˈglɒtɪs ; ˈglɑtɪs/ *n* opening between the

vocal cords at the upper part of the windpipe. 聲門。➪ the illus at head. 參看 head 之挿圖。**glottal** /ˈglɒtl; ˈglɑtl̩/ *adj* of the ~. 聲門的。**glottal stop,** speech sound produced by a complete closure of the ~, followed by an explosive release of breath. 喉塞音;聲門閉鎖音。

glove /glʌv; glʌv/ *n* covering of leather, knitted wool, etc for the hand, usu with separated fingers. 手套。➪ the illus at base. 參看 base 之挿圖。***fit like a ~,*** fit perfectly. 十分相合。***be hand in ~ (with),*** be in close relations (with). (與…)關係密切。***take off the ~s to sb; handle sb without ~s,*** argue or contend in earnest, without mercy. 認眞地或不留情地與某人爭辯或爭鬪。**'~-compartment** *n* compartment in the dashboard of a car, for small articles. 汽車儀器板上放零星物件的隔間。

glow /gləʊ; glo/ *vi* [VP2A, C] **1** send out brightness or warmth without flame: 發熾熱;發光輝;無焰地燃燒: *~ing embers/charcoal;* 熾燃的餘燼(木炭); *~ing metal from the furnace.* 自鎔爐中取出的熾熱的金屬。 **2** (fig) be, look, feel, warm or flushed (as after exercise or when excited): (喩)身體發熱或面孔發紅(如運動後或興奮時): *~ing with enthusiasm/health/pride.* 熱情洋溢(容光煥發;得意揚揚)。 **3** show strong or warm colours: 顯示鮮艷的顏色: *woods and forests ~ing with autumn tints.* 帶有鮮艷秋色的樹林。□ *n* (*sing* only, with *def* or *indef art*) ~ing state; warm or flushed look; warm feeling: (僅用單數,與定冠詞或不定冠詞連用)熾熱;容光煥發;熱情: *in a ~ of enthusiasm;* 熱情洋溢地; *cheeks with the ~ of health on them;* 紅潤的面頰; (*all*) *in a ~ after a hot bath;* 洗過熱水澡後渾身通紅; *the ~ of the sky at sunset.* 落日餘暉。**'~-worm** *n* insect of which the wingless female gives out a green light at its tail. 螢火蟲。**~·ing** *adj* showing warm colour or (fig) enthusiasm: 顏色鮮明的;(喩)熱心的;熱烈的: *give a ~ing account of what happened;* 熱烈地敍述所發生之事; *describe an event in ~ing colours.* 生動地描述一事件。**~·ing·ly** *adv*

glower /ˈglaʊə(r); ˈglaʊɚ/ *vi* [VP2A, 3A] ~ ***(at),*** look in an angry or threatening way. 怒目而視;兇狠地瞪着。**~·ing·ly** *adv*

glu·cose /ˈgluːkəʊs; ˈglukos/ *n* [U] grape sugar. 葡萄糖。

glue /gluː; glu/ *n* [U] thick, sticky liquid used for joining things, eg broken wood, crockery. 膠(黏接斷木、陶器等者)。□ *vt* (*pt, pp* glued; *pres p* gluing) [VP6A, 15A, B] ~ ***(to),*** **1** stick, make fast, with ~: 用膠黏合: *~ two pieces of wood together;* 將兩塊木頭黏在一起; *~ a piece of wood on to something.* 將一塊木頭黏在某物上。 **2** put tightly or closely: 使密結;使固着: *His eyes were/His ear was ~d to the keyhole.* 他的眼睛(他的耳朶)緊貼在鑰匙孔上。*Why must you always remain ~d to your mother,* Why can you never be separated from your mother? 你爲何總是離不開你的母親?**~y** /ˈgluːɪ; ˈgluɪ/ *adj* sticky, like ~. 黏的;似膠的。

glum /glʌm; glʌm/ *adj* (-mmer, -mmest) gloomy; sad. 陰鬱的;憂愁的。**~·ly** *adv* **~·ness** *n*

glut /glʌt; glʌt/ *vt* (-tt-) [VP6A, 14] ~ ***(with),*** **1** supply too much to: 過多地供應;過度供給;充斥: *~ the market* (*with fruit, etc*). (水果等)充斥市場。 **2** overeat; satisfy to the full; fill to excess: 過量地食用;使飽;使過量: *~ one's appetite;* 吃得過飽; *~ oneself with rich food;* 吃太多油膩的食物; *~ted with pleasure.* 縱情享樂。□ *n* [C] supply in excess of demand: 過量供應: *a ~ of pears in the market.* 市場上梨子的充斥。

glu·ten /ˈgluːtən; ˈglutn̩/ *n* [U] sticky substance (protein) that is left when starch is washed out of flour. 麵筋;麩質。**glu·ti·nous** /ˈgluːtɪnəs *US:* -tənəs; ˈglutənəs/ *adj* of or like ~; sticky. 麵筋的;似麵筋的;黏的。

glut·ton /ˈglʌtn; ˈglʌtn̩/ *n* person who eats too much: 貪食者;食用過量者: *You've eaten the whole pie, you ~!* 你把整個餡餅都吃掉了,你這個好吃鬼! *He's a ~ for work,* (fig) is always willing and ready to work. (喩)他是個愛工作的人。 **~·ous** /ˈglʌtənəs; ˈglʌtn̩əs/ *adj* very greedy (for food). 貪吃的。**~·ous·ly** *adv* **~y** /-tənɪ; -tn̩ɪ/ *n* [U] habit or practice of eating too much. 吃過量的習慣;貪食;暴食。

gly·cer·ine (US = **gly·cer·in**) /ˈglɪsəriːn *US:* -rɪn; ˈglɪsrɪn/ *n* [U] thick, sweet, colourless liquid made from fats and oils, used in medical and toilet preparations and explosives. 甘油;丙三醇。

G-man /ˈdʒiːmæn; ˈdʒiˌmæn/ *n* (US colloq) federal criminal investigation officer. (美俗)聯邦調查局的探員。

gnarled /nɑːld; nɑrld/ *adj* (of tree trunks) twisted and rough; covered with knobs: (指樹幹)歪扭而粗糙的;多瘤節的: *a ~ old oak;* 多瘤節的老橡樹; ~ (= knotty, deformed) *hands/fingers.* 粗糙的手(手指)。

gnash /næʃ; næʃ/ *vi, vt* **1** [VP2A] (of the teeth) strike together, eg in rage. (指牙齒)切齒;咬牙(例如憤怒時)。 **2** [VP6A] (of a person) cause (the teeth) to do this: (指人)咬(牙);切(齒): *wailing and ~ing of teeth.* 大聲吼叫並咬牙切齒。

gnat /næt; næt/ *n* small two-winged fly that stings; (fig) insignificant annoyance. 蚋;蠓蟲;(喩)小煩擾。***strain at a ~,*** hesitate over a trifle. 爲瑣碎事而遲疑。

gnaw /nɔː; nɔ/ *vt, vi* **1** [VP6A,15B,3A] ~ ***(at),*** bite steadily at (sth hard): 咬;啃;囓;噬(硬物): *The dog was ~ing (at) a bone.* 那狗在啃一根骨頭。*The rats had ~ed away some of the woodwork.* 老鼠將一些木器咬壞了。*He was ~ing his finger-nails with impatience.* 他焦灼地咬着他的指甲。 **2** [VP6A, 3A] ~ ***(at),*** torment; waste away: 使苦惱;折磨;消耗;侵蝕: *fear and anxiety ~ing (at) the heart;* 磨噬內心的恐懼和焦慮; *the ~ing pains of hunger.* 飢餓的痛苦。

gnome /nəʊm; nom/ *n* (in tales) small goblin living under the ground (often guarding treasures of gold and silver). (故事中)地下的小妖魔;地精(常常保護金銀珍藏)。

gnu /nuː; nu/ *n* wildebeest. 非洲產的一種大羚羊。➪ the illus at large. 參看 large 之挿圖。

go[1] /gəʊ; go/ *vi* (*3rd pers pres t* goes /gəʊz; goz/, *pt* went /went; wɛnt/, *pp* gone /gɒn *US:* gɔːn; gɔn/) (For idiomatic uses with *adverbial particles* and *preps,* ➪ 29 below.) (與副詞接語和介詞連用的習慣用法,參看下列第 29 義。) **1** [VP2A, C, 3A, 4A] (with a *prep* or *adv* of place or direction, present or implied; ➪ come) (與表示地點或方向的介詞或副詞連用) ***go (from/to),*** move, pass, *from* one point *to* another and away from the speaker, etc (cf 參較 *come from/to*): 走動;走過;行走;離去: *Shall we go (there) by train or by plane?* 我們乘火車還是飛機去(那裏)? *He has gone to China,* is now in, or on his way to, China. 他到中國去了。*He has gone to see his sister.* 他探望他的姐姐(妹妹)去了。*Go and get your hat.* 去拿你的帽子。*Let's go to the cinema.* 我們去看電影吧。*Let's go,* Let's leave. 我們走吧。*They came at six and went* (= left) *at nine.* 他們六時來到,九時離去。*I must be going now,* must leave now. 我現在必須走了。*I wish this pain would go (away).* 我希望這疼痛會消失。*All hope is gone* (more usu today, *has gone*). 一切希望都沒有了(現較常用 has gone)。*Be gone! Go away!* (the more usu expression today). 走開!(現較常用 go away)。*Who goes there?* (challenge from a sentry = Say who you are). 誰?(哨兵盤問時用語)。 **2** [VP2C] **(a)** be placed; have as a usual or proper position: 被安置;以…爲通常或適當的位置: *Where do you want your piano to go?* Where shall we put it? 你要我們把你的鋼琴放在哪裏? *'Where does this teapot go?' 'In that cupboard.'* '這茶壺放在何處?'

'放在那個食櫥內。' *This dictionary goes on the top shelf.* 這部字典是放在頂層書架上的。**(b)** be fitted or contained in: 納入;被包容: *My clothes won't go into this small suitcase.* 我的衣服裝不進這小提箱。*7 into 15 won't go,* 15 does not contain exact multiples of 7. 七除十五除不盡。**3** [VP2A, B, C, 3A] ***go (from/to),*** reach, extend; last; (of a person's behaviour, remarks, achievements, etc) reach certain limits: 到達;延及;持續;(指人的行爲,言論,成就等)達到某種限度: *This road goes to London.* 這條路通倫敦。*I want a rope that will go from the top window to the ground.* 我要一條能從頂上的窗戶伸到地上的繩子。*Differences between employers and workers go deep,* Their views are far apart. 雇主與工人間意見上的衝突甚大。***go a long way,*** **(a)** last: 持續: *She makes a little money go a long way,* buys many things, etc by careful spending. 她能用很少的錢買很多的東西。*A little of this paint goes a long way,* covers a large area. 這種漆一點點便可漆一大塊面積。**(b)** (colloq) be as much as one can bear: (俗)所能忍受的限度: *A little of his company goes a long way,* One can endure his company for a short time only. 同他在一起祇要短時間就够受了。***go a long way/go far towards doing sth,*** make a considerable contribution towards: 對…有相當的貢獻: *The Prime Minister's statement went a long way towards reassuring the nation.* 首相的話,在使國民恢復信心方面,甚爲收效。***go (very) far,*** **(a)** last: 維持: *A pound doesn't go far nowadays,* doesn't last, doesn't buy much. 現今一英鎊不當用了。**(b)** (of a person, future tense) succeed: (指人,用於未來式)成功: *He will go far in the diplomatic service,* will win promotion, etc. 他將來在外交界會有所成就。***go too far,*** go beyond acceptable limits: 過份: *That's going too far,* saying or doing more than is right. 那太過份了。*You must apologize at once—you've gone too far,* exceeded the limits of accepted behaviour, etc. 你必須立刻道歉——你太過份了。***go (any) further,*** go beyond a certain point: 進一步: *I'll give you £50, but I can't go any further.* 我願意給你五十鎊,但我不再多給了。*Need I go any further,* do or say anything more? 還有需要我做(說)的嗎? ***go as/so far as to do sth,*** do or say sth to a certain limit: 做事或說話至某種限度: *I won't go as far as to say he's dishonest,* won't accuse him of this, even though I may suspect him of it. 我不願意說他是不誠實(縱然我懷疑他,我不願意這樣指控他)。*I would go so far as to suggest that the House of Lords should be abolished.* 我甚至想建議廢除上議院。***as far as it goes,*** to a limited extent: 至一限度: *That's all very well as far as it goes,* The limitations of the statement, explanation, etc must be realised. 就目前情形而言,一切良好。*What he says is true as far as it goes,* suggesting that further information, knowledge, etc is needed or desirable. 就某種程度而言,他的話是對的。***go to great lengths/trouble/pains (to do sth),*** take care to do sth well: 費心將某事做好: *He went to great trouble to make his guests comfortable.* 他盡力讓他的客人感到舒服。***go to one's head,*** ⇨ head¹(19). ***go as low/high as,*** (of a price) reach a certain level: (指價格)達到某一標準: *I'll go as high as £250,* will offer this sum, eg at an auction. 我願意出二百五十鎊(例如在拍賣中)。***go one better (than sb),*** improve on what he has done: 較某人所做更佳: *I hit the target 17 times out of 20, but Tom went one better and scored 18.* 我在二十次中擊中了目標十七次,但湯姆勝我一籌,擊中了十八次。*It all/just goes to show/prove that,* tends or helps to show/prove that. 一切顯示出(證明了)…。**4** ***go on a journey/trip/outing,*** make a journey, take a trip, have an outing, etc. 去旅行(旅行,遠足)。***go for a walk/swim, etc,*** go out in order to walk, swim, etc. 去散步(游泳等)。***go walking/swimming, etc,*** take part in the activity of walking, swimming, etc: 散步(游泳等)(指參與散步,游泳等活動): *Do they often go sailing?* Is sailing sth they often do? 他們時常去駕船嗎? (Cf 參較 *Let's go for a walk,* referring to a specified occasion. 指特殊場合。) *Bill has gone (out) shopping,* has gone to buy things in the shops. 比爾買東西去了。**5** (in the pattern, ***go*** + *prep* + *n*) (用於 go + 介詞+名詞語型中) **(a)** pass into/from the state indicated by the *n*. 變成某種狀態。***go into abeyance,*** ⇨ abeyance. ***go from bad to worse,*** ⇨ bad¹(4). ***go into a coma/trance,*** ⇨ coma, trance. ***go out of fashion,*** ⇨ fashion. ***go into liquidation,*** ⇨ *liquidation* at liquidate. ***go to pieces,*** ⇨ piece¹(1). ***go to pot,*** ⇨ pot¹(2). ***go to rack and ruin,*** ⇨ rack⁴. ***go into retirement,*** ⇨ *retirement* at retire. ***go to seed,*** ⇨ seed. ***go to sleep,*** ⇨ sleep¹(3). ***go out of use,*** ⇨ use¹(1). ***go to war,*** ⇨ war. **(b)** go to the place, etc indicated for the purpose associated with it. 到一指明的地點等做與其有關之事。***go to the block/stake,*** ⇨ block¹(3), stake. ***go to church,*** attend a church service. 做禮拜。***go to hospital,*** ⇨ hospital. ***go to market,*** ⇨ market. ***go to school/college/university,*** attend school, etc in order to learn or study. 上學(大學)。***go to sea,*** become a sailor. 做海員。***go on the stage,*** ⇨ stage. ***go on the streets,*** ⇨ street. **(c)** have recourse to. 求助於;訴諸。***go to the country,*** ⇨ country. ***go to law,*** ⇨ law(6). **6** [VP3A] ***go to sb,*** pass into sb's possession; be allotted to: 歸某人所有;歸某人所得: *Who did the property go to when the old man died,* Who inherited it? 那老人死後,財產歸誰所有? *Honours do not always go to those who merit them.* 榮譽並不總是歸於應得之人。*The first prize went to Mr Hill.* 第一獎爲希爾先生所得。**7** [VP2D] become; pass into a specific condition: 變成;進入某種特殊的情況: *go blind/mad, etc.* 變瞎(瘋等)。*He went purple with anger/grey with worry.* 他氣得臉色發紫(憂愁得頭髮灰白了)。*Fish soon goes bad* (= rotten) *in hot weather.* 魚在熱天不久便變壞了。*The children went wild with excitement.* 孩子們興奮得發狂。*This material has gone a nasty colour.* 這料子變成髒兮兮的顏色。*Kensington went Labour at the by-election,* changed politically by returning the Labour candidate to Parliament. 肯辛頓於補選國會議員時改投工黨候選人的票。*Will the country go Democrat next year?* 該國明年會變成民主黨的天下嗎? ***go berserk,*** ⇨ berserk. ***go broke,*** become penniless. 破產。***go dry,*** ⇨ dry¹(12). ***go flat,*** (of liquid) lose its gas content: (指液體)跑氣: *This beer has gone flat.* 這啤酒跑氣了。***go haywire,*** ⇨ hay. ***go native,*** adopt the mode of life of the natives of the country in which one is living. 過當地人的生活。***go phut,*** (colloq) (of machines) collapse: (俗)(指機器)垮了;不靈光了: *The old car went phut half way up the hill;* 那部老爺車在爬山的半途拋錨了; (fig): (喻): *His plan/scheme/project has gone phut.* 他的計畫泡湯了。***go scot-free/unchallenged/unpunished,*** be free from penalty or punishment; escape being challenged. 未受罪;未受詰難。**8** [VP2A, C] be moving, working, etc: 正在活動,工作等: *This clock doesn't go.* 這鐘不走了。*Is your watch going?* 你的錶在走嗎? *Her tongue was going nineteen to the dozen,* ⇨ dozen. 她刺刺不休(話講個沒完)。*The play went (down) like a bomb,* (colloq) was very favourably received. (俗)那齣戲非常叫座。⇨ go down in 28 below. 參看下列第28義之 go down。***a going concern,*** a business in working order, operating well. 營業情況良好的商行。**9** [VP2C, D] be or live habitually in a specific state or manner: 習慣於某種狀態;過慣某種生活: *Refugees often go hungry.* 難民時常挨餓。*The men of this tribe used to go naked.* 這個部落裏的男子過去常是裸體的。*He went in fear of his life.* 他經常恐懼會喪失生命。*You'd better go armed*

(= carry a weapon) *while in the jungle.* 你在叢林中最好携帶武器。*She is six months gone,* six months pregnant. 她已懷孕六個月了。 **10** [VP2C, D, E] (after *How*) progress: (用於 'How' 之後) 進展: *How's everything going.* 事情發展情形如何? *How's work going? How goes work?* 工作進展情況如何? *How goes it?* (colloq) How are you? (俗)你好嗎? (with an *adv* or *adv* equivalent, eg *adjj* such as *slow, easy,* indicating manner of progress): (與副詞或相當於副詞如 slow, easy 等形容詞連用,表示進行的狀態): **go badly/well,** (of work, events) proceed (un)satisfactorily: (指工作,事件)進行(不)滿意: *All has gone well with our plans,* they've succeeded. 我們的計畫順利進行。*Things went better than had been expected.* 事情的進行較預期者令人滿意。 **go easy (on/with sb/sth),** be less strenuous, less severe; handle gently or carefully: 輕鬆一些;不要緊張;不要太嚴厲;小心處理: *Go easy with/on the butter, that's all we have,* don't be wasteful. 不要浪費牛油,我們祇有那麼多了。*Go easy with her, she's too young to realize her mistake.* 對她不要太嚴厲,她太年輕而不知道她犯了錯誤。 **go slow, (a)** (of traffic) move forward slowly. (指交通)慢行。**(b)** (of workers in factories, etc) work slowly, esp to reduce output, as a protest against sth or to draw attention to demands. (指工廠等的工人) 怠工以示抗議。Hence, 由此產生, **'go-slow** *n* [C] such slow work. 表示抗議的怠工。 **be going strong,** be proceeding vigorously; be still flourishing: 有力地進行;仍然旺盛: *He's ninety and/but still going strong.* 他九十歲了,但仍然健壯。 **11** [VP2A, C] work; operate: 工作;運轉: *This machine goes by electricity.* 這機器由電推動。*I've been going hard (at it) all day and I'm exhausted.* 我一整天辛苦地工作,我感到疲憊了。 **12** [VP2A, C] (in progressive tenses only) be available, be offered: (僅用於進行式) 可獲得;被提供: *Are there any jobs going?* 有什麼工作機會嗎? **13** [VP2C, 3A] **go (to sb) for,** be sold (to sb) for: (以…的價錢)被賣出(被售與某人): *The house went cheap.* 這房子賣得很便宜。*I shan't let mine go* (= sell it) *for less than £8000.* 少於八千鎊我的就不賣。 **go for a song,** ⇨ song. **Going! Going! Gone!** (used at an auction to announce the closing of the bidding). (拍賣時用語) 要賣掉了!要賣掉了!賣掉了! **14** [VP3A] **go on/in,** (of money) be spent on: (指金錢)用於;花在…上: *How much of your money goes on food and clothes/in rent?* 你的錢有多少花費在食物和衣服(房租)上? *Half the money he inherited went in gambling debts.* 他所繼承的金錢一半付了賭債。 **15** [VP2A, C] be given up, abandoned, lost: 被放棄,廢除或失去: *I'm afraid the car must go,* We can no longer afford to run it, so must sell it. 我恐怕這車子必須賣掉了。 *My sight is going,* I'm losing my ability to see. 我的視力正在減退。 **16** [VP2A, C] be current or accepted; be commonly thought of or believed: 流通;流傳: *The story goes that ....* It is said that .... 據說…。 **17** [VP2A] **as people/things go,** considering the average person/thing: 照一般人,東西等而論: *They're good cars as cars go nowadays,* judging them from the average or usual type today. 就目前一般汽車而論,他們是好汽車。*Five pounds for a pair of shoes is not bad as things go today,* in view of how much things cost today. 照如今一般物價而言,一雙鞋賣五鎊不算貴。 **18** [VP2A] fail; collapse; give way; break off: 失敗;坍塌;折裂;中斷: *First the sails and then the mast went in the storm.* 在那暴風雨中先是帆壞了,其次桅也斷了。*The bank may go* (= fail) *any day.* 這家銀行隨時可能倒閉。*He's far gone,* is critically ill or (colloq) is mad. 他的病況甚爲嚴重;(俗)他瘋狂了。**let oneself go,** relax, enjoy oneself, etc. 放鬆自己;享樂。 **19** die: 死: *He is going/has gone, poor fellow!* 他要死了(已死了),可憐的人! **dead and gone,** dead and buried. 死去並已埋葬了。 **20** [VP2A, C] be decided: 被決定: *The case* (ie in a law court) *went against him,* he lost. 他官司打輸了。*The case went in his favour,* he won. 他官司打贏了。*How did the election go at Hull,* Who was elected? 赫爾城的選舉結果如何? *Does promotion go by favour in your firm?* 你們公司中的升遷是憑主管的偏愛嗎? **21** (various phrases) (各種片語) **go bail (for sb),** ⇨ bail[1]. **go Dutch (with sb),** ⇨ Dutch. **go shares/halves (in sth with sb),** ⇨ share[1] (1), half. **go sick,** ⇨ sick[1] (2). **'go it,** (colloq) act vigorously, indulge in wild spending, etc. (俗)使勁幹;浪費金錢等。**go it alone,** act by oneself, without support. 自己幹。 **22** [VP2A, C] **(a)** have a certain wording or tune: 有某種語法或調子: *I'm not quite sure how the words go/tune goes.* 我不太確定那些話是怎麼說的(那個曲調是怎麼唱的)。**(b)** (of a verse or song) be adaptable (to a certain tune): (指詩歌)可適合(某曲調): *It goes to the tune of 'Three Blind Mice'.* 它可適合 'Three Blind Mice' 的調子。 **23** (colloq) (followed by *and* and another *v*) proceed to do sth: (俗)(後接 and 及另一動詞)去做某事: *Go and shut the door, would you?* (as an informal request). 去把門關上好嗎?(作爲非正式的請求)。*Go and ask that policeman the way.* 去向那個警察問路。*Now you've gone and done it,* (sl) have made a mistake, blundered. (俚)如今你犯了一個大錯。 **24** [VP2A, C] make a specific sound: 發某種聲音: *The clock goes 'tick-tock, tick-tock'.* 時鐘發出 '滴答滴答' 的聲音。*'Bang!' went the gun.* '砰!'槍聲響了。 **25** (in bridge[2]) [VP6A] bid; declare: (橋牌)叫牌: *go two spades/three no trumps.* 叫二黑桃(三無王)。 **26** [VP2A] begin an activity: 開始動作: *One, two, three, go!* or *Ready, steady, go!* (eg as a signal for competitors in a race to start). 一,二,三,開始!(競賽開始的口令)。*Well, here goes!* (used to call attention to the fact that one is about to start to do sth). 喂,開始了!(用以使人注意將要開始做某事)。 **27** (used to express the future) (用以表示未來) **be going to do sth, (a)** indicating what is intended, determined or planned: 表示打算,決定或計畫做某事: *We're going to spend our holidays in Wales this year.* 今年我們要在威爾斯度假。*I'm going to have my own way.* 我要照自己的意思去做。*We're going to buy a house when we've saved enough money.* 我們存夠了錢的時候,打算買一棟房子。 **(b)** indicating what is considered likely or probable: 表示可能會發生…事: *Look at those black clouds—we're going to have/there's going to be a storm.* 看那些烏雲——暴風雨要來了。 **(c)** expressing the immediate or near future (= about to): 表示卽將發生: *I'm going to tell you a story.* 我要給你們講一個故事。*I'm going to be twenty next month.* 我下個月就二十歲了。 **28** (compounds) (複合字) **'go-ahead** *n* ⇨ go ahead in 29 below. 參看下列 29 義中之 go ahead。**ˌgo-as-you-'please,** *attrib adj* untroubled by regulations. 無拘束的;自由行動的。 **'go-by,** ⇨ go by in 29 below. 參看下列 29 義中之 go by。**go-'slow,** ⇨ 10 above. 參看上列第 10 義。 **ˌgo-to-'meeting,** *attrib adj* (dated colloq of hats, clothes, etc) worn on special occasions, eg for church: (過時俗語,指衣帽等) 爲某種場合 (例如赴教堂) 而穿戴的: *wearing their Sunday go-to-meeting clothes.* 穿着他們星期日做禮拜的衣服(體面衣服,最好的衣服)。 **29** [VP2C, 15B, 3A] (idiomatic uses with *adverbial particles* and *preps*): (與副詞接語及介詞連用的習慣用法):

go about, (a) move from place to place; pay visits: 走來走去;四處走動: *I don't go about much anymore.* 我不再經常四處走動了。**(b)** (of rumours, stories, etc) pass from person to person, usu verbally; be current: (指謠言,故事等)流傳(通常爲口頭上地): *A story/rumour is going about that ....* 據傳說(謠傳)…。**(c)** (of a ship) change course or tack(3). (指船)改變航行方向。***go about sth,*** set to work at: 着手於: *You're not going about that job in the right way.* 你做那事的方法不對。*We'll have to go about it more carefully.* 我們必須細心去做此事。***go about one's business,*** deal with one's own affairs (rather than with sb else's). 處理自己的事(勿管他人之事)。***go about with sb,*** spend time (in public) regularly with him: 經常(公開地)與某人在一起: *go about with a bunch of thugs.* 跟一群惡棍鬼混。

go after sb/sth, try to win or obtain: 設法追求某人(獲得某物): *He's going after that pretty Swedish girl,* is trying to win her interest or affection. 他正在追求那位美麗的瑞典女郎。*He's gone after a job in the City.* 他去倫敦老城求職。

go against sb, **(a)** oppose: 反對: *Don't go against your father.* 不要反對你的父親。**(b)** have an unsatisfactory outcome: 結果不令人滿意: *The war is going against them,* They seem likely to be defeated. 戰爭似乎對他們不利。⇨ also 20 above. 亦參看上列第 20 義。***go against sth,*** be contrary to: 與…相反: *It goes against my principles/interests.* 這與我的主張(利益)相反。***go against the grain,*** ⇨ grain.

go ahead, **(a)** make progress: 進步: *He's going ahead fast.* 他進步很快。*The Joneses are very go-ahead* (= progressive) *people; it's difficult to keep up with them.* 瓊斯一家人很前進,令人難以趕上。**(b)** proceed without hesitation: 不猶豫地進行: *'May I start now?' 'Yes, go ahead.'* '我可以動身嗎?' '是的,動身罷。' Hence, 由此產生, **'go-ahead** *n* permission to proceed: 准許進行: *give them the go-ahead.* 准許他們進行。

go along, proceed: 進行: *You may have some difficulty first but you'll find it easier as you go along.* 最初你或許有些困難,但過些時你會覺得較爲容易。***go along with sb,*** **(a)** accompany: 陪伴: *I'll go along with you as far as the main road.* 我將陪你走到大路。**(b)** agree with: 同意: *I can't go along with you on that point.* 我不同意你的那一點。

go at sb/sth, **(a)** rush at; attack: 衝向;攻擊: *They went at each other furiously.* 他們猛烈地互相撲打。*They went at it tooth and nail/hammer and tongs,* fought furiously. 他們猛烈地攻擊。**(b)** take sth in hand, deal with it energetically: 努力去做;努力對付: *They were going at the job for all they were worth,* making the utmost possible effort to do the work. 他們在盡最大努力做此事。

go away, leave. 離去。***go away with sb/sth,*** take with, abscond with: 帶走;捲逃: *He has gone away with my razor,* has taken it with him. 他把我的剃刀帶走了。

go back, **(a)** return. 回來。**(b)** extend backwards in space or time: 回溯: *His family goes back to the time of the Norman Conquest,* can be traced back to then. 他的家族可追溯至諾曼第人征服英國的時代。***go back on/upon,*** fail to keep; break or withdraw from, eg a promise: 違背;背棄 (例如諾言): *He's not the sort of man who would go/to go back on his word.* 他不是那種背信的人。

go before (sth), precede: 居前: *Pride goes before a fall.* 驕者必敗。

go behind sth, search for sth: 尋求某物: *go behind a person's words,* look for a hidden meaning in what he says. 探求一人言語中的含義。***go behind sb's back,*** do or say sth without his knowledge. 瞞着某人做或說某事。

go beyond sth, exceed: 超過: *You've gone beyond your instructions.* 你已逾越你所受到的指示。*That's going beyond a joke,* is too serious to be amusing. 那樣開玩笑是太過火了。

go by, pass: 經過: *Time went by slowly.* 時間慢慢逝去。*We waited for the procession to go by.* 我們等着那行列走過。***'go by sth,*** **(a)** be guided or directed by: 受…之指導: *I shall go entirely by what my solicitor says,* shall follow his advice. 我將完全遵照律師的指示。*That's a good rule to go by,* to be guided by. 那是個可以遵守的好規則。**(b)** form an opinion or judgement from: 憑…而判斷: *Have we enough evidence to go by?* 我們有足够的證據以資判斷嗎？ *It's not always wise to go by appearances.* 憑外表判斷不一定是明智的。*I go by what I hear.* 我根據我聽到的而判斷。***ˌgo by the 'book,*** follow the rules closely. 按照規則行事。***go by/under the name of,*** use the name of; be called. 稱爲;叫做。**'go-by** *n.* ***give sb/sth the go-by,*** (colloq) ignore; disregard; slight or snub: (俗)忽視;不理;輕視;冷落: *He gave me the go-by in the street yesterday,* ignored me completely. 他昨天在街上視我爲路人。

go down, **(a)** (of a ship, etc) sink. (指船隻等)沉沒。**(b)** (of the sun, moon, etc) set. (指日,月等)下落。**(c)** (of food and drink) be swallowed: (指食物與飲料)被吞下: *This pill won't go down,* I can't swallow it. 這藥丸吞不下去。**(d)** leave a university for the vacation, having graduated, etc. 離開大學去度假;已畢業。**(e)** (of the sea, wind, etc) become calm: (指海,風等)平靜;平息: *The wind has gone down a little,* is less strong. 風勢減弱了。**(f)** (of prices) go lower: (指物價)跌落: *The price of eggs/The cost of living has gone down.* 鷄蛋的價格(生活費用)下跌了。**(g)** ***go down to the sea/country etc,*** pay a visit to the seaside, countryside, etc. 去海濱(鄉村等)。***go down before sb,*** be defeated or overthrown: 被擊敗;被推翻: *Rome went down before the barbarians.* 羅馬被野蠻人征服。***go down (in sth),*** be written in; be recorded or remembered in: 被記錄下來;被記得: *It all goes down in his notebook.* 他將它都記在筆記簿裏了。*He'll go down in history as a great statesman.* 他將成爲歷史上偉大的政治家。***go down to,*** be continued or extended as far as: 繼續至;延續至: *This 'History of Europe' goes down to 1970.* 這部 '歐洲史' 記述至 1970 年止。***go down (with sb),*** (of an explanation or excuse; of a story, play, etc) be accepted or approved (by the listener, reader, audience, etc): (指解釋或藉口,故事,戲劇等)爲聽者,讀者,聽衆等接受或讚許: *The new play went down well/like a bomb* (= extremely well) *with provincial audiences.* 這新戲甚爲(深爲)地方觀衆讚賞。*That explanation won't go down well with me.* 我不相信那種解釋。*The new teacher doesn't go down well with his pupils.* 新教師不受學生們的歡迎。***go down (with sth),*** fall ill (with an illness): 染病: *Poor Peter—he's gone down with flu.* 可憐的彼得——他染上了流行性感冒。

go for sb, **(a)** go to fetch: 去取來或接來: *Shall I go for a doctor?* 要我去請一位醫生嗎？**(b)** attack: 攻擊: *The dog went for the postman as soon as he opened the garden gate.* 郵差一打開花園的門,那狗便向他撲了過去。*Go for him!* (said to a dog to urge him to attack). 去咬他！(對狗說的話)。*They went for me in the correspondence columns of the papers.* 他們在報上通信欄內攻擊我。**(c)** be applicable to: 可以應用於: *What I have said about Smith goes for you, too.* 我所說的有關史密斯的話也可以用在你的身上。***go for nothing/little,*** be considered of no/little value: 被認爲無價值: *All his work went for nothing.* 他的一切工作都歸於零(被認爲無何價值)。

go forth, (formal) be published or issued: (正式用語)公佈;發表: *The order went forth that ....* 命令宣佈說…。

go forward, **(a)** advance: 前進: *A patrol went forward to investigate.* 一支巡邏隊前去調查。**(b)** make progress: 進步: *The work is going forward well.* 工作進展良好。

go in, **(a)** enter: 進入: *The key won't go in (the lock).* 這鑰匙塞不進(鎖裏)去。*This cork's too big; it won't go in.* 這軟木塞太大了,塞不進去。*She went in to cook the dinner.* 她進去燒飯。**(b)** (of the sun, moon, etc) be obscured by clouds: (指日,月等)被雲遮蔽: *The sun went in and it grew rather cold.* 太陽被雲遮蔽,天氣變得有些冷了。**(c)** (cricket, etc) begin an innings: (板球等) 開始一局比賽: *Who goes in next?* 下一局該誰了? **(d)** enter as a competitor: 參加比賽: *Go in and win!* (used as a form of encouragement). 去好好比賽一場!(用以鼓勵參加比賽者)。***go in for sth,*** **(a)** take, enter (an examination or competition). 參加(考試或比賽)。**(b)** have an interest in, have as a hobby, etc: 以…爲興趣,嗜好等;愛好: *go in for golf/stamp-collecting/growing orchids.* 愛好高爾夫球(集郵,種蘭)。

go into sth, **(a)** enter: 進入;加入: *go into business;* 從商; *go into the Army/the Church/Parliament.* 從軍(做傳教士;當國會議員)。*When did Britain go into Europe,* join the EEC? 英國在何時加入了歐洲共同市場? ***go into details,*** ⇨ detail[1](2). **(b)** investigate; examine carefully: 調查;審查: *go into the evidence;* 調查證據; *go deeply into a question.* 深究一問題。*This problem will need a lot of going into,* will need thorough investigation. 這問題需要徹底調查。**(c)** (allow oneself to) pass into (a certain state): (使自己)進入(某種狀態): *go into fits of laughter/hysterical fits.* 發出陣陣笑聲(歇斯底里症發作)。***go into mourning,*** wear black clothes as a symbol of mourning. 着喪服。

go off, **(a)** explode; be fired: 爆炸;發射: *The gun went off by accident.* 這槍走火了。**(b)** lose good quality; deteriorate: 變質;變壞: *The cooking in the hotel has started to go off.* 旅館內的烹調已開始變壞了。 *This milk has gone off,* turned sour. 這牛奶變酸了。*Meat and fish go off quickly in hot weather.* 肉和魚在熱天很快會變壞。**(c)** become unconscious, either in sleep or in a faint: (睡眠或暈倒時) 失去知覺: *Hasn't the baby gone off yet?* 這嬰兒還沒有睡着嗎? *She went off into a faint.* 她暈倒昏迷過去了。**(d)** (of goods) be got rid of by sale: (指貨物)賣掉;售出: *The goods went off quickly.* 那些貨物很快地賣掉了。**(e)** (of events) proceed well, etc: (指事件)進行良好等: *The performance/concert went off well.* 表演(音樂會)進行甚佳。*How did the sports meeting go off?* 運動會進行的情況如何? **(f)** (as a stage direction in a printed play) leave the stage; exit/exeunt: (劇本中的演出說明)下場: *Hamlet goes off.* 哈姆雷特下。***go off sb/sth,*** lose interest in or one's taste for: 對某人(某物)失去興趣;不再喜歡: *Jane seems to have gone off Peter.* 珍好像已不再喜歡彼得了。*I've gone off beer.* 我不喜歡啤酒了。***go off the beaten track,*** ⇨ beaten. ***go off the deep enp,*** ⇨end[1](1). ***go off one's head,*** ⇨ head[1](19). ***go off with sb/sth,*** go away with, esp abscond with or steal: 帶走;(尤指)拐帶(某人或某物): *He's gone off to Edinburgh with his neighbour's wife.* 他已與鄰居的妻子私奔至愛丁堡。*The butler went off with some of the duke's treasured possessions.* 那管事席捲公爵的一些珍藏而逃。

go on, **(a)** (of time) pass: (指時間)過去: *As the months went on, he became impatient.* 一月月地過去,他變得不耐煩了。 **(b)** conduct oneself; behave, esp in a wrong, shameful or excited way: 舉動(尤指錯誤、可恥或激動地行動): *If you go on like this you'll be thrown out.* 如果你繼續此種行爲,你將被開除。 **(c)** happen; take place; be in progress: 發生;進行: *What's going on there?* 那裏發生了什麼事? *There's nothing interesting going on here at present.* 這裏目前沒有有趣的事情發生。 *Harvesting was going on in the south.* 南部在收割。*Things are going on much as usual.* 一切如常。 **(d)** (theatre) appear on the stage: (戲劇)出場: *She doesn't go on until Act Two.* 她要到第二幕才出場。**(e)** take one's turn at doing sth; (eg cricket) begin bowling: 輪到做某事;(例如板球) 投球: *The captain told Snow to go on next.* 隊長叫斯諾下一個投球。'***go on sth,*** take or accept, eg as evidence: 接受(作爲證據等): *What evidence have we got to go on,* to be guided by in reaching a decision, etc? 我們必須接受什麼證據? ***go on the dole/social security/*** (US) (美) ***welfare,*** obtain, eg when unemployed, payments under various government schemes. 接受失業津貼。***go on the pill,*** start using contraceptive pills. 服用避孕藥丸。***go on about sth,*** talk persistently and often irritatingly about: 不斷地(常是令人氣憤地)談論: *I wish you'd stop going on about my smoking.* 請不要再談論我抽煙的事。***go on (at sb),*** rail; nag; scold: 責罵;埋怨;挑剔: *She goes on at her husband continually.* 她不停地埋怨她的丈夫。*Oh, you do go on!* 哎喲,你眞在罵人! ***be going on (for),*** (of age or time) be approaching: (指年齡或時間)接近: *He's going on (for) seventy.* 他快七十歲了。***be gone on,*** (sl) be infatuated with: (俚)迷戀: *It's a pity Peter's so gone on Jane.* 彼得如此迷戀着珍眞是遺憾。***go on to sth/to do sth,*** do or say it next; proceed to it: 接着做;接着說: *Let's now go on to the next item on the agenda.* 現在讓我們接着討論議程的下一項。*He went on to say that...,* He next said that.... 他接着說…。*I shall now go on to deal with our finances.* 現在我要接着處理我們的財務。***go on (with sth/doing sth),*** continue, persevere, with: 繼續;保持: *Go on with your work.* 繼續你的工作。*How much longer will this hot weather go on?* 這種熱天氣還要繼續多久? *That's enough to go on with/to be going on with,* enough for our immediate needs. 那足够目前的需要了。*Go on trying.* 繼續嘗試。*I hope it won't go on raining all day.* 我希望不會整天下雨。***Go on (with you)!*** (colloq) Don't expect me to believe that! Don't be so silly! etc, according to context. (俗)不要胡說!我才不信呢!別傻! ˌ**goings-'on** *n pl* (colloq) (often with *such strange/queer*) happenings; behaviour: (俗) (常與 such strange, such queer 連用)發生的事情;舉動: *I've never seen such queer goings-on!* 我從未見過這種怪事! **'on-going** *adj* continuing; progressing; evolving. 繼續的;進行的;發展的。

go out, **(a)** leave the room, building, etc: 離開房間、建築物等: *She was (all) dressed to go out,* wearing outdoor clothes. 她打扮好準備外出。*Out you go!* 滾出去! *Do you often go out riding* (ie on a horse)? 你常出外騎馬嗎? **(b)** attend social functions, go to parties, dances, etc: 參加社交活動;參加聚會、舞會等: *She still goes out a great deal, even at seventy-five.* 她雖然已七十五歲,仍時常參加社交活動。***go out on a spree/on the town,*** ⇨ spree, town. **(c)** be extinguished: 熄滅: *The fire* (eg the fire burning in the grate) *has gone out.* 火已熄滅。*There was a power cut and all the lights went out.* 停電了,所有的燈都熄了。**(d)** become unfashionable: 不再流行;過時: *Has the fashion for boots/Have boots gone out?* 長靴已過時了嗎? **(e)** (of a government) retire from power. (指政府)下臺。**(f)** (as used by workers of themselves) strike: (工人們用語)罷工: *Are we likely to gain anything by going out?* 我們罷工能得到什麼好處嗎? ⇨ *come out*(d) in come(16). **(g)** (of a year, etc) end: (指歲月)結束: *The year went out gloomily.* 那一年悲慘地結束了。***go out on a limb,*** ⇨ limb(2). ***go out to,*** leave, eg one's own country, and go to: 離開(例如本國)而去: *He couldn't get work at home* (eg in England) *so went out to Australia.* 他在國內(例如英國)找不到工作,所以去了澳洲。***go out to sb,*** (of the heart, feelings) be extended to: (指心、感情)給與;施與: *Our hearts/sympathies go out to those poor children orphaned by war.* 我們同情那些因戰爭而變成孤兒的可憐的孩子。 ***go out with sb,*** (colloq) be regularly in sb's company: (俗)經常陪伴某人;與異性交往: *How long has Jane been going out with David? How long have Jane and David been going out together?* 珍和大衛交往有多久了?

go over, (colloq) make an impression: (俗)予人

以印象: *I wonder whether this new play will go over,* whether it will impress the public, be favourably received. 我不知道這新劇是否給予觀衆良好印象。*David didn't go over well with Jane's parents at the weekend.* 大衞在週末給珍的父母的印象不太好。**go over sth,** **(a)** examine the details of: 仔細檢查: *We must go over the accounts carefully before we settle them.* 在結帳以前,我們必須將這帳目仔細核對一番。**(b)** look at; inspect: 看;視察: *We should like to go over the house before deciding whether we want to buy it.* 我們要將這房屋查看一遍,然後再決定是否要買。**(c)** rehearse; study or review carefully: 演習;溫習: *Let's go over this chapter/lesson/the main facts/Scene 2 again.* 我們將這一章(一課,主要事實,第二場)再溫習一遍。Hence, 由此產生, **ˌgoing-ˈover** *n* (*pl* goings-over) **(a)** (colloq) process of examining or putting in good working order: (俗)檢查;核對: *The document will need a careful going-over before we can make a decision.* 在我們作決定以前,需要將這文件仔細看一下。*The patient was given a thorough going-over by/from the doctor.* 那病人由醫師徹底檢查了一下。**(b)** (sl) beating: (俚)毆打: *The thugs gave him a thorough going-over,* beat him repeatedly. 流氓們將他毒打一頓。**go over to sb/sth,** change one's political party, side, a preference, etc: 變黨;倒戈;投向;改用: *He has gone over to the Democrats.* 他已投入民主黨。*I'm going over to a milder brand of cigarettes.* 我現在改抽一種較淡的香煙。

go round, **(a)** be enough, in number or amount, for everyone to have a share: (在數量上)足够分配: *There aren't enough apples/isn't enough whisky to go round.* 蘋果(威士忌)不够分配了。**(b)** reach one's destination by using a route other than the usual or nearest way: 繞道: *The main road to Worcester was flooded and we had to go (a/the long way) round.* 至烏斯特的要道被洪水淹沒,我們必須繞道(繞很遠)。**go round (to a place/to do sth),** visit: 拜訪: *We're going round to my mother's/to see my mother at the weekend.* 我們打算在週末去拜望我的母親。**go round the bend,** (colloq) become hysterical, enraged, mad, etc. (俗)變爲歇斯底里、激怒、瘋狂等。

go through, **(a)** (= get through) be passed or approved: 被通過: *The Bill* (ie in Parliament) *did not go through.* 這議案未被通過。**(b)** be concluded: 被訂立;被締結: *The deal did not go through.* 這項交易未談成。**go through sth,** **(a)** discuss in detail: 詳細討論: *Let's go through the arguments again.* 我們將這些論據再詳細討論一遍。**(b)** search: 搜查: *The police went through the pockets of the suspected thief.* 警員搜查那個竊盜疑犯的口袋。**(c)** perform; take part in: 履行;參加: *She made him go through both a civil and religious wedding.* 她使他擧行了照俗約和宗教儀式的婚禮。*How long will it take to go through* (= complete) *the programme?* 整個節目要多久結束? **(d)** undergo; suffer: 經歷;遭受: *go through hardships.* 經歷艱難。*If you only knew what she has to go through with that husband of hers!* 你要是知道她得跟着她那位丈夫受什麼樣的苦,就好啦! **(e)** (of a book) be sold: (指書)被售出: *The book went through ten editions,* Ten editions were sold out. 這本書賣完了十版。**(f)** reach the end of; spend: 至…之盡頭;花費: *go through a fortune/all one's money.* 耗盡財產(所有的金錢)。**go through with sth,** complete; not leave unfinished: 完成;做完: *He's determined to go through with the marriage in spite of his parents' opposition.* 他不顧父母的反對,決心要完成這婚事。

go to/towards sth, contribute to, be contributed to: 有助於;促成: *What qualities go to the making of a statesman?* 有何條件才能做一個政治家? *This money can go towards the motor-bike you're saving up for.* 你可以用這筆錢加上你的存款買部你所需要的摩托車。

go together, **(a)** (of two or more things) be a normal accompaniment (of one another): (指兩件以上的事物)經常(互相)伴隨: *Crime and poverty often go together.* 罪惡與貧窮常常互相伴隨。**(b)** match; be suitable together: 相配;調和: *Do my green shirt and my blue jeans go together?* 我的綠襯衫與藍牛仔褲相配嗎? ⇨ go with (c) below. 參看下列之 go with (c).

go under, **(a)** sink. 沉沒。**(b)** (fig) fail; succumb; become bankrupt: (喩)失敗;屈從;破產: *The firm will go under unless business improves.* 這家公司如不改進業務將會倒閉。

go up, **(a)** rise: 上升: *The barometer/temperature/thermometer is going up.* 氣壓計(溫度,寒暑表)上升。*Everything went up* (ie in price) *in the budget except pensions.* 預算中樣樣都增加了,祇有養老金例外。**(b)** be erected: 被建立: *New office blocks are going up everywhere.* 新辦公大樓到處建立起來。**(c)** be blown up; be destroyed by explosion or fire: 被炸壞;被焚毁: *The bridge went up with a roar when the mine exploded.* 地雷爆炸時,那橋樑轟然一聲被炸毁了。*The whole building went up in flames.* 整個建築物爲火所焚毁。**(d)** enter a university or travel to a town, esp the capital: 進大學;進城(尤指首都): *go up to London/to town.* 去倫敦(進城)。*When will you go up* (eg to Cambridge)? 你何時進大學(例如進劍橋大學)? **go up sth,** climb: 攀登: *go up a tree/ladder/wall/hill.* 爬樹(登梯;攀牆;爬山)。**go up the wall,** ⇨ wall.

go with sb/sth, **(a)** accompany: 陪伴: *I'll go with you.* 我陪你一道去。*We must go with the times/tide,* do as others do nowadays. 我們必須跟上時代(潮流)。*He always goes with his party,* votes, etc as the party does. 他總是追隨他的政黨行事。**(b)** take the same view as: 與…有相同的觀點: *I can't go with you on that,* can't agree with you. 關於那一點我不同意你的看法。**(c)** be a normal accompaniment of: 通常伴隨;附帶;連同: *Five acres of land go with the house,* become the property of the buyers or are for the use of the tenant. 這所房子附帶有五畝空地。*Disease often goes with squalor, but it is wrong to say that crime always goes with poverty.* 疾病通常因不潔而起,但如果說罪惡永遠因貧窮而生則是不正確的。**(d)** match; be fitting and suitable with: 配合;適合: *These new curtains don't go well with your carpet,* don't suit them. 這些新窗簾與你的地毯不太調合。*I want some shoes to go with these trousers.* 我要一些配這些長褲的鞋子。**(e)** (colloq) (of a young man or girl) be often in the company of a person of the opposite sex possibly with a view to marriage: (俗)(指青年男女)常與…在一起(希望能結婚): *go with a girl,* ⇨ go out with sb above. 常和一女孩子在一起,(參看上列之 go out with sb)。

go without (sth), endure the lack of: 忍受沒有…之苦: *The poor boy often has to go without supper.* 這可憐的男孩時常沒有晚飯吃。*There's no money for a holiday this year; we'll just have to go without.* 今年無錢度假,我們祇好不度假了。**go without saying,** be understood without actually being stated: 不用說;不待言: *It goes without saying that she's a good cook.* 她是個好厨子,自不待言。

go² /gəʊ ; go/ *n* (*pl* goes /gəʊz ; goz/) (all uses colloq) (俗) **all systems go,** (of launching or operating eg a spacecraft) all is ready to proceed. (指太空船等之發射或操作)一切就緒,等着開始。**all the go,** very popular, fashionable: 流行的; 時髦的: *Leather pyjamas were all the go last year.* 寬鬆的皮褲去年很流行。**at one go,** at one attempt: 一擧;一氣;一次: *He blew out all the candles on his birthday cake at one go.* 他一口氣把生日蛋糕上的蠟燭都吹滅了。**be full of go; have plenty of go,** be full of energy, enthusiasm. 精力充沛;熱心。**be on the go,** be busy, active: 忙碌;活躍: *She's been on the go all day,* has had no rest. 她終日忙碌。

have a go (at sth), make an attempt: 企圖;嘗試(做某事): *He had several goes at the high jump before he succeeded in clearing it.* 他嘗試跳高數次,最後才跳了過去。*The police warned the public not to have a go because the bank raiders were armed*, not to try to intercept, catch them. 警方警告群衆不要嘗試攔截,因爲那些搶劫銀行的暴徒帶着武器。***near go***, narrow escape. 驚險的逃脫。***no go***, **(a)** false start. 錯誤的開始;不適當的開始。**(b)** impossible or hopeless situation: 不可能;不行: *It'll be no go to ask/asking for a rise when you arrive so late.* 你到得這樣晚而要求加薪是不可能的。 **ˌno-'go area**, one to which access is prohibited to those who do not live there. 禁止外地人進入之地區。

goad /gəʊd ; god/ *n* pointed stick for urging cattle on; (fig) sth urging a person to action. 驅畜之刺棒;(喻)激勵物;刺激物。□ *vt* [VP6A, 15B, 14, 17] ~ ***sb (on); ~ sb into doing sth***, urge, drive forward: 驅策;激勵: ~ *sb into a fury;* 激怒某人; *be ~ed by hunger into stealing.* 爲飢餓所迫而行竊。

goal /gəʊl ; gol/ *n* **1** point marking the end of a race; (football) posts between which the ball is to be driven in order to score; point(s) made by doing this: (賽跑之)終點;(足球)球門;踢進球門所得之分: *score/kick a ~;* 得(踢得)一分; *win by three ~s to one;* 以三比一之分數獲勝; *keep ~*, protect the ~. 守球門。 **'~·keeper**, (colloq) (俗) **~ie** /ˈgəʊlɪ ; ˈgolɪ/ *n* player whose duty is to keep the ball out of the ~. (足球)守門員。**'~-kick** *n* (Association football) kick by the defending side after the attacking side sends the ball over the ~-line; (Rugby football) attempt to kick a ~. (英式足球)球門球;(橄欖球)射門。**'~-line** *n* (football) line behind the ~ posts, reaching to the touch-lines. (足球)球門線。⇨ *touch-line* at touch¹(7); ⇨ the illus at football, Rugby. 參看 football, Rugby 之插圖。 **2** (fig) object of efforts or ambition: (喻)目標: *one's ~ in life;* 生活的目標; *the ~ of his desires.* 他的欲望的目標。

goat /gəʊt ; got/ *n* small, active horned animal, ⇨ the illus at domestic. 山羊(參看 domestic 之插圖)。**'she-~** (or *'nanny-~*), female goat, kept for its milk. 牝山羊。**'he-~** (or *'billy-~*), male goat. 雄山羊。⇨ kid¹(1). ***get one's ~***, (sl) irritate or annoy one. (俚)激怒某人;令某人煩躁。***play/act the giddy ~***, play the fool; behave in a foolish and excited way. 行爲如小丑。***separate the sheep from the ~s***, the good from the bad. 將好的與壞的分開。**'~-herd** *n* person who looks after a flock of ~s. 照看山羊者。**'~·skin** *n* [C, U] (garment made of) skin of a goat. 山羊皮;山羊皮衣。**~·ee** /gəʊˈtiː ; goˈti/ *n* small tuft of hair on the chin like a ~'s beard. 山羊鬍子(似山羊之鬚者)。

gob¹ /gɒb ; gɑb/ *n* (vulg) clot or lump of slimy substance. (鄙)黏物塊。

gob² /gɒb ; gɑb/ *n* (derog sl) mouth. (貶俚)嘴。

gob³ /gɒb ; gɑb/ *n* (US sl) sailor. (美俚)水兵。

gob·bet /ˈgɒbɪt ; ˈgɑbɪt/ *n* [C] lump or chunk, esp of meat. 一塊(尤指肉);一厚塊。

gobble¹ /ˈgɒbl ; ˈgɑbḷ/ *vt, vi* [VP6A, 15B, 2A] ~ ***(up)***, eat fast, noisily and greedily. 狼吞虎嚥。

gobble² /ˈgɒbl ; ˈgɑbḷ/ *vi* [VP2A, C] (of a turkeycock) make the characteristic sound in the throat; (of a person) make such a sound when speaking, because of rage, etc. (指火鷄)作咯咯聲;(指人)因憤怒等而發出咯咯聲。□ *n* characteristic sound made by a turkeycock. (火鷄的)咯咯聲。

gobble·dy·gook /ˈgɒbldɪguːk ; ˈgɑbḷdɪˌguk/ *n* [U] incomprehensible or pompous specialist's jargon. 不能理解的或浮誇的專門術語。

gob·bler /ˈgɒblə(r) ; ˈgɑblɚ/ *n* (US) male turkey. (美)雄火鷄。

go-between /ˈgəʊ bɪtwiːn ; ˈgobəˌtwin/ *n* messenger or negotiator for two persons or groups who do not or cannot meet: 居間人;中人;媒人: *In some countries marriages are arranged by ~s.* 有些國家中婚姻係由媒人撮合的。

gob·let /ˈgɒblɪt ; ˈgɑblɪt/ *n* glass or pottery drinking-vessel with a stem and base and no handle. (無把手之)高脚玻璃杯或瓷杯。

gob·lin /ˈgɒblɪn ; ˈgɑblɪn/ *n* mischievous demon; ugly-looking evil spirit. 惡鬼;醜妖怪。

go-cart /ˈgəʊ kɑːt ; ˈgoˌkɑrt/ *n* light handcart. 輕便手推車。

god /gɒd ; gɑd/ *n* **1** being regarded or worshipped as having power over nature and control over human affairs; image in wood, stone, etc to represent such a being: 神;神像: *the blind god* (or *god of love*), Cupid; 愛神; *the god of the sea,* Neptune; 海神; *a feast/sight for the gods,* something extraordinary, exquisite, etc. 不尋常的事物;精美的事物。 **2 God**, the Supreme Being, creator and ruler of the universe. (大寫)上帝。***God (almighty)! Good God!*** *int* (colloq) exclamations of surprise, shock etc. (俗)(表示驚異、震驚等)上帝啊!老天啊! ***God willing***, if circumstances permit. 如情況許可。***God knows***, = *goodness knows*, ⇨ goodness(3). **3** person greatly adored or admired; very influential person; sth to which excessive attention is paid: 受尊崇之人;極有影響力的人;極受注意之事物: *make a god of one's belly*, think excessively about food and drink. 尊崇自己的肚子;非常重視飲食。*He thinks he's a (little) tin god*, used eg of an official who expects undeserved and excessive respect. 他認爲他自己是個很了不起而且極受尊崇的人物 (用以指希望受到不應得的過分尊崇的官員等)。 **4** (theatre) **the gods**, (persons in the) gallery seats. (戲院)最高樓座(之觀衆)。 **5** (compounds) (複合字) **'god·child, 'god·daughter, 'god·son** *nn* person for whom a godparent acts as sponsor at baptism. 教子;教女(受洗時由教父或教母擔保其宗教教育的孩子)。**'god-damn(ed)**; (US) **'god·dam** /ˈgɒdæm ; ˈgɑdˈdæm/ *adj, adv* ⚠ (sl; intensive) very; very great. (諱;俚;增强語氣之字)很;很大。**'god·father, 'god·mother, 'god·parent** *nn* person who undertakes, when a child is baptized, to take an active interest in its welfare. 教父;教母(孩子受洗時,擔保其宗教教育之人)。 **'god-fearing** *adj* reverent; living a good life and sincerely religious. 虔誠的;虔敬的。**'god·for·saken** *adj* (of places) dismal; wretched. (指地方)陰森的;荒涼的。**God's 'acre** *n* (old use) churchyard. (舊用法)教堂墓地。**'god·send** /-send ; -ˌsɛnd/ *n* piece of good fortune coming unexpectedly; sth welcome because it is a great help in time of need. 意外的好運;緊急時大有幫助因而受歡迎之物;天賜之物。**god·'speed** *n* ***bid/wish sb godspeed***, wish him success on a journey, etc. 祝某人一帆風順;祝某人一路平安。

god·dess /ˈgɒdɪs ; ˈgɑdɪs/ *n* female god, esp in Greek and Latin mythology: 女神(尤指希臘羅馬神話中者): *Diana, the ~ of hunting.* 戴安娜,狩獵之女神。

god·head /ˈgɒdhed ; ˈgɑdhɛd/ *n* [U] being God or a god; divine nature. 爲神;神性。**the G~**, God. 上帝。

god·less /ˈgɒdlɪs ; ˈgɑdlɪs/ *adj* wicked; not having belief in God; not recognizing God. 邪惡的;不信上帝的;不承認上帝存在的。**~·ness** *n*

god·like /ˈgɒdlaɪk ; ˈgɑdˌlaɪk/ *adj* like God or a god in some quality. 似神的;如神的。

god·ly /ˈgɒdlɪ ; ˈgɑdlɪ/ *adj* (-ier, -iest) loving and obeying God; deeply religious. 敬愛神的;虔誠的。 **god·li·ness** *n*

go·down /ˈgəʊdaʊn ; goˈdaʊn/ *n* (in the East) warehouse. (東方之)倉庫。

go-get·ter /ˌgəʊ ˈgetə(r) ; ˈgoˈgɛtɚ/ *n* (colloq) pushing, enterprising person. (俗)積極而進取之人。

goggle /ˈgɒgl ; ˈgɑgḷ/ *vi* [VP2A, 3A] ~ ***(at)***, roll the eyes about (or *at* sth); stare at with bulging eyes: 轉動眼睛望着;睁視: *He ~d at her in surprise.* 他驚奇地瞪着她。*The frog's eyes seemed to be goggling out of its head.* 青蛙的眼睛從頭上凸出,像

是要掉下來似的。'**~-box** *n* (sl) TV set. (俚)電視機。'**~-eyed** *adj* having staring, prominent, or rolling eyes. 睜視的;眼睛凸出的;眼睛轉動的。

goggles /'gɒglz ; 'gagl̩z/ *n pl* large round spectacles with hoods to protect the eyes from the wind, dust, water etc (worn by racing motorists, frogmen etc). (賽車駕駛人、蛙人等所戴的)護目鏡;遮灰鏡;風鏡。⇨ the illus at frog. 參看 frog 之插圖。

go·ing /'gəʊɪŋ ; 'goɪŋ/ *n* (⇨ also go[1]) **1** [U] condition of the ground, a road, a race-course, etc, for walking, riding, etc: 地面、道路、跑道等供行走或駕駛等的狀況: *The ~ is hard over this mountain road.* 在這山路上行走甚爲吃力。**2** [U] method or speed of working or travelling: 工作或行駛的方法或速度: *For a steam train, 70 miles an hour is good ~.* 以蒸汽火車而論，每小時行駛七十哩是快的速度。 **3** (usu *pl*) (通常作複數) ***comings and ~s,*** (lit or fig) arrivals and departures: (字面或喻)到達和離去;來往: *the comings and ~s in the corridors of power.* 來往於權力的走廊上。□ *adj* ***a ~ concern,*** ⇨ go[1](8).

goitre (US = **goi·ter**) /'gɔɪtə(r) ; 'gɔɪtə/ *n* morbid swelling of the thyroid gland (in the neck). (頸部之)甲狀腺腫。

go-kart /'gəʊ kɑːt ; 'go ˌkart/ *n* small low racing car with open framework. 一種車身低的小賽車。

gold /gəʊld ; gold/ *n* [U] **1** precious yellow metal used for making coins, ornaments, jewellery, etc: 黃金;金子: *currencies backed by ~;* 以黃金爲準備金的通貨; *£500 in ~,* in ~ coins; 五百鎊金幣; (attrib) (形容用法) *a ~ watch/bracelet.* 金錶(手鐲)。 ***worth one's weight in ~,*** invaluable; indispensable. 無價的;不可缺少的。 **2** money in large sums; wealth. 大量金錢;財富。 **3** (fig) brilliant or precious things or qualities: (喻)華麗或貴重之物;華貴的性質: *a heart of ~;* 高貴的心; *a voice of ~.* 甜美的聲音。**4** colour of the metal: 金黃色: *the red and ~ of the woods in autumn;* 秋季樹林中的紅色和金黃色; *old ~,* a dull, brownish-golden yellow. 古金色;暗黃褐色。**5** (compounds) (複合字) '**~-beater** *n* person whose trade is to beat ~ into ~-leaf. 金箔工人。'**~-digger** *n* person who digs for ~; (sl) girl or woman who uses her attractions to extract money from men. 掘金者;(俚)以美色騙取男人金錢的女人。'**~-dust** *n* ~ in the form of dust, as often found in ~fields. 砂金。'**~·field** *n* district in which ~ is found. 金田;採金區。 '**~·finch** *n* bright-coloured song-bird with yellow feathers in the wings. 金翅雀。 '**~·fish** *n* small red carp kept in bowls or ponds. 金魚。ˌ**~-'foil,** ˌ**~-'leaf** *n* [U] ~ beaten into thin sheets. 金箔;金葉。 '**~·mine** *n* place where ~ is mined; (fig) source of wealth, eg a shop that is very successful in making money. 金礦;(喻)富源(例如非常賺錢的商店)。ˌ**~-'plate** *n* [U] articles (spoons, dishes and other vessels) made of ~. 金器;金製匙、盤等容器。'**~-rush** *n* rush to a newly discovered ~field. 湧向新金礦之熱潮;淘金潮。'**~·smith** *n* smith who makes articles of ~. 金匠。'**~ standard,** ⇨ standard(4).

golden /'gəʊldən ; 'goldn̩/ *adj* **1** of gold or like gold in value or colour: 黃金的;價值似金的;金黃色的: *~ hair.* 金黃色的頭髮。**2** precious; excellent; important: 可貴的;極好的;重要的: *a ~ opportunity.* 絕好的機會。**the** ˌ**~ 'age,** (in Gk stories) the earliest and happiest period in history; period in a nation's history when art or literature was most flourishing. (希臘故事)黃金時代;一國歷史上的黃金時代(文學或藝術最興盛的時代)。ˌ**~ 'handshake,** (usu large) sum of money given to a high-ranking member of a company when he retires (in recognition of good work and loss of continuation of salary). (高級職員退休時公司給與之)大筆退休金(以酬謝其過去的服務並彌補其停薪後之損失)。**the** ˌ**~ 'mean,** the principle of moderation. 中庸之道。 **the** ˌ**~ 'rule,** any important rule of conduct (esp **Matt** 7: 12, *Treat others as you would like them to treat you*). 金科玉律; 金箴(尤指馬太福音第7章第12節者,例如:以期待別人對你之心對待他人)。ˌ**~ 'wedding,** fiftieth wedding anniversary. 金婚紀念(結婚五十週年紀念)。

golf /gɒlf ; galf/ *n* [U] game played by two or four persons, each with a small, hard '**~-ball,** driven with a '**~-club,** into a series of 9 or 18 holes on smooth greens(4) over a stretch of land (a '**~-course/links**). 高爾夫球(由二或四人比賽,用球棒將小球打入場中九或十八個洞中,其球場稱作 golf-course 或 links)。□ *vi* play ~. 打高爾夫球。**~er** *n* person who plays ~. 打高爾夫球者。

Gol·iath /gə'laɪəθ ; gə'laɪəθ/ *n* giant. 巨人。⇨ 1 Sam 17. 參看舊約聖經撒母耳記上第 17 章。

gol·li·wog /'gɒlɪwɒg ; 'galɪˌwag/ *n* black-faced doll with thick stiff hair. 黑面豎髮之木偶。

golly /'gɒlɪ ; 'galɪ/ *int* (sl) used to express surprise. (俚)表驚異之聲;天哪。

go·losh *n* ⇨ galosh.

gon·dola /'gɒndələ ; 'gandələ/ *n* long, flat-bottomed boat with high peaks at each end, used on canals in Venice. (威尼斯運河中航行之)長形平底輕舟。**gon·do·lier** /ˌgɒndə'lɪə(r) ; ˌgandə'lɪr/ *n* man who propels a ~. 威尼斯運河中駕長形平底輕舟者。

a gondola

gone /gɒn *US:* gɔːn ; gɔn/ *pp* of go.

goner /'gɒnə(r) *US:* 'gɔːn- ; 'gɑnə/ *n* (sl) person or thing in desperate straits, ruined or doomed. (俚)即將滅亡之人或物;無可救藥者。

gong /gɒŋ ; gɔŋ/ *n* metal disc with a turned rim giving a resonant note when struck with a stick, esp as a signal, eg for meals. 鑼(尤指擊之以作爲信號,如通知用膳等者)。□ *vt* (of traffic police) direct (a motorist) to stop by striking a ~. (指交通警察)敲鑼使(駕駛汽車者)停車。

gonna /'gɒnə ; 'gɑnə/ (US sl) (美俚) = going to. ⇨ go[1](27).

gon·or·rhea (also **-rhoea**) /ˌgɒnə'rɪə ; ˌgɑnə'riə/ *n* [U] contagious venereal disease which causes an inflammatory discharge from the genital organs. 淋病。

goo /guː ; gu/ *n* [U] (sl) sticky wet material; sentimentality. (俚)黏而濕的東西;傷感。**gooey** /'guːɪ ; 'guɪ/ *adj* sticky. 黏的。

good[1] /gʊd ; gʊd/ *adj* (better, best) **1** having the right or desired qualities; giving satisfaction: 美好的;良好的;令人滿意的: *a ~* (eg sharp) *knife;* 一把好刀; *a ~ fire,* one that is bright and cheerful, giving warmth; 明亮旺盛的爐火; ~ (= fertile) *soil.* 肥沃的土壤。*Is raw herring ~ eating,* Is it enjoyable to eat it? 生鯡好吃嗎? **2** beneficial; wholesome: 有益的;對健康有益的: *Is this water ~ to drink,* Is it clean and pure? 這水適於喝嗎? *Milk is ~ for children.* 牛奶對小孩有益。*Exercise is ~ for the health.* 運動有益於健康。**3** efficient; competent; able to do satisfactorily what is required: 能勝任的;有能力的;能幹的: *a ~ teacher/driver/worker;* 好教師(駕駛,工作者); *a ~ man for the position;* 對某一職位之適當人選; *~ at mathematics/languages/describing scenery.* 擅長數學(語言,描寫風景)。*She has been a ~ wife to him.* 她一直是他的好妻子。 **4** pleasing; agreeable; advantageous: 令人快樂的;悅人的;有利的: *~ news.* 好消息。*It's ~ to be home again.* 重回家園是令人快樂的。***have a ~ time,*** enjoy oneself. 過得很快樂。Hence, 由此

產生，ˈ~-time girl, (colloq) one whose chief aim is enjoyment. (俗)以享樂爲目的之女子。*(all) in ~ time*, at a suitable or advantageous time. 在適當或有利的時刻。*be a ~ thing*, be sth that one approves of: 爲人所贊成之事: *Do you think lower taxes are a ~ thing?* 你贊成降低納稅嗎？*be a ~ thing that...*, be fortunate that.... 幸好…;好在…。*have a good/bad night*, sleep well/badly. 睡得好(不好)。*put in/say a ~ word for sb*, say sth in his favour. 爲某人說幾句好話。*start/arrive/leave in ~ time*, early. 及早動身(到達,離去)。 **5** kind; benevolent; willing to help others: 和善的;仁慈的;樂於助人的: *It was ~ of you to help them.* 你眞好,幫了他們的忙。*Will you be ~ enough to/be so ~ as to come early?* 請早些來好嗎？*How ~ of you!* 你眞好！Cf 參較 *do sb a ~ turn*, ⇨ turn¹(5); (in exclamations of surprise, shock, etc.) (在驚嘆句中) ˌ*G~* ˈ*God!* 天啊！ ˌ*G~* ˈ*Gracious!* 天啊！ ˌ*G~* ˈ*Heavens!* 天啊！ **6** thorough; sound; complete: 徹底的;痛快的;完全的: *give sb a ~ beating/scolding;* 痛毆(責)某人; *have a ~ drink;* 喝個痛快; *find a ~ excuse;* 找一充分的藉口; *go for a ~ long walk.* 作一次痛快而遙遠的漫步。*have a ~ mind (to do sth)*, feel a strong desire to: 很想做;極有意: *I've a ~ mind to report you to the police.* 我很想將你報警。 **7** strong; vigorous: 强健的;有力的: *His eyesight is still ~.* 他的目力仍然很强。*The children were in ~ spirits.* 孩子們都興高采烈。⇨ *low spirits* at low¹(6). **8** amusing: 有趣的: *a ~ story/joke;* 有趣的故事(笑話); *as ~ as a play.* 像戲劇般有趣;十分有趣。 **9** fresh; eatable; untainted: 新鮮的;可食的;未腐敗的: *Fish does not keep ~ in hot weather.* 魚在熱天不能保持新鮮。*This meat doesn't smell quite ~.* 這肉的氣味不太新鮮。 **10** reliable; safe; sure: 可靠的;安全的;確實的: *a car with ~ brakes;* 煞車可靠的汽車; *~ debts*, debts that will certainly be paid. 確可償還的債。⇨ *bad debts* at bad¹(4). *He's a ~ life*, is healthy and is, therefore, likely to be acceptable for life assurance. 他是保險公司樂意承保的健康的人。*~ for*, **(a)** safely to be trusted for (the amount stated): 可信賴或託付(列明的款數): *His credit is ~ for £5000.* 他的信用可以週轉五千鎊。**(b)** (of a draft, etc) drawn for (the amount stated): (指滙票等)可支付(列明的款數): *~ for £5.* 可支付五鎊。**(c)** having the necessary energy, inclination, etc: 有必需的精力、意願等: *He's ~ for several years' more service.* 他還有精力再服務幾年。*My car is ~ for another five years.* 我的汽車還可以再用五年。*Are you ~ for a five-mile walk?* 你有氣力走五哩路嗎？**(d)** valid: 有效: *The return half of the ticket is ~ for three months.* 回程票有效期爲三個月。 ˈ**~-for-nothing**, ˈ**~-for-naught** *adjj, nn* worthless (person). 無用的;無用之人。 **11** (esp of a child) well behaved; not giving trouble: (尤指兒童)守規矩的;聽話的: *Try to be a ~ boy.* 儘量做個乖孩子。*as ~ as gold*, giving no trouble. 不惹麻煩。 **12** morally excellent; virtuous: 品行優良的;有品德的: *a ~ and holy man;* 有品德的人; *live a ~ life.* 過高尚的生活。ˌ~ ˈ**works**, charitable deeds, helping the poor, the sick, etc. 慈善事業。 **13** right; proper; expedient: 正當的;適合的;權宜的: *He thought it ~ to offer his help.* 他認爲他應該提供幫助。(As an *int*, expressing approval): (用做感嘆詞,表示贊同): *'You will come with us?' 'G~!'* '你和我們一道去嗎？''好的！' **14** in forms of greeting and farewell: 用於問候和告別詞句中: *G~ morning/afternoon/evening/night.* 早(午,晚,晚)安。 **15** as a polite (but often ironical, patronizing or indignant) form of address: 作爲客氣(但常是譏諷、傲慢或憤慨)的稱呼: *my ~ sir/man/friend;* 我的好先生(人,朋友); or as a polite (but often condescending) description: 或作爲客氣(但常含上對下關懷)的描述: *How's your ~ man* (ie your husband)? 你的先生好嗎？*How's the ~ lady* (ie your wife)? 你的太太好嗎？*the* ˈ*~ people*, the fairies. 小神仙。 **16** as a form of commendation: 作爲讚揚之詞: *~ men and true.* 善良誠實的君子;溫厚篤實之士。*G~ old Smith!* 厚道的老史密斯！*That's a ~ 'un!* /ˈgʊdn; ˈgʊdn̩/ (colloq) an amusing lie or story. (俗)那是個有趣的謊言或故事！ **17** considerable in number, quantity, etc: 相當多的: *a ~ deal of money;* 很多金錢; *a ~ many people;* 很多人; *a ~ few*, a considerable number. 相當多的數目。*We've come a ~ way*, quite a long way. 我們已走了相當遠了。 **18** not less than; rather more than: 不少於…的;頗多於…的: *We waited for a ~ hour.* 我們等了整整一小時。*It's a ~ three miles to the station.* 到車站足足有三哩路。*He ate a ~ half of the duck.* 他至少吃掉了半隻鴨子。 **19** *as ~ as*, practically, almost: 實際上;幾乎: *He as ~ as said I was a liar*, suggested that I was a liar without actually using the word 'liar'. 他實際上等於說我是個說謊者。*My car is as ~ as new, even though I've had it a year.* 我的汽車雖然用了一年,幾乎還是新的。*The matter is as ~ as settled*, We may look upon it as being settled. 這事等於解決了。 **20** *make ~*, accomplish what one attempts; prosper: 有成就;成功: *He went to Canada, where he soon made ~.* 他去到加拿大,在那裏不久便很有成就了。[VP 22] *make sth ~*, **(a)** compensate for; pay for (sth lost or damaged): 補償;賠償(損失): *make ~ a loss or theft.* 賠償損失或失竊。**(b)** effect (a purpose): 實現(目的): *make ~ one's escape.* 順利逃脫。**(c)** prove the truth of an accusation, a statement, etc. 證實(控告之罪、言論等)。**(d)** restore to sound condition: 修復: *The plaster will have to be made ~ before you paint it.* 在你粉刷前,灰泥必須修補好。 **21** (phrases and compounds) (片語與複合字) ˌ**~-ˈfellowship** *n* sociability. 友善;親睦。ˌ**~ ˈhumour** *n* cheerful mood; happy state of mind. 愉快;高興。ˌ**~-ˈhumoured** *adj* cheerful, amiable. 愉快的;親切的。ˌ**~ ˈlooks** *n pl* personal beauty. 美貌。ˌ**~-ˈlooking** *adj* (usu of persons) handsome. (通常指人)貌美的;漂亮的。ˌ**~ ˈmoney**, **(a)** genuine money. 眞正的錢。**(b)** (colloq) high wages. (俗)高的工資。*throw ~ money after bad*, lose money in trying to regain money lost. 賠了夫人又折兵;一虧再虧。ˌ**~-ˈnatured** *adj* kind; ready and willing to help others, even by sacrificing one's own interests. 和藹的;不計自身利益樂於幫助他人的。ˌ**~-ˈneighbourliness** *n* friendly conduct and relations. 親睦;交情。ˌ**~ ˈsense** *n* [U] soundness of judgement; practical wisdom. 判斷正確;見識。ˌ**~-ˈtempered** *adj* not easily irritated or made angry. 好脾氣的。

good² /gʊd; gʊd/ *n* [U] **1** that which is ~; what is morally right, beneficial, advantageous, profitable, etc; what has use, worth, value. 良好的事物;善良;善行; 利益; 好處(等)。*do ~*, help: 行善: *Social workers do a lot of ~.* 社會工作者做了許多善事。⇨ *do-gooder* at do²(2). *(do sth) for the ~ of*, in order to benefit: (做某事)爲…之利益: *He works for the ~ of the country.* 他爲國家謀福利。*I'm giving you this advice for your ~.* 我這樣勸你是爲了你好。*Is it right to deceive people, even if it's for their own ~?* 卽使爲了人們好而去欺騙他們是正當的嗎？*do sb ~*, benefit him: 對某人有益: *Eat more fruit: it will do you ~.* 多吃些水果,那會對你有益。*Smoking does you more harm than ~.* 吸煙對你有害無益。*Much ~ may it do you*, (usu ironic, meaning) You won't get much benefit from it. 但願這對你有很大的好處(通常作反語,意謂:這對你不會有多大好處)。*be up to no ~*, be engaged in sth wrong, mischievous, etc. 做壞事;惡作劇。*be no/not much/any/some ~ (doing sth)*, be no, not much, etc use, of no, little, etc value: (做某事)沒有(有些)用;沒有(有些)價值: *It's no ~ (my) talking to him.* (我)同他談沒有用。*Was his advice ever any ~?* 他的勸告有用嗎？*What ~ was it?* 有什麼用處？*This gadget isn't much ~.* 這小器具沒有

什麼價值。 **2** ***for ~ (and all),*** permanently; finally: 永久地;決定性地: *He says that he's leaving the country for ~*, intending never to return to it. 他說他出國後便不再回來了。**3** ***to the ~,*** as balance on the right side, as net profit: 作爲盈餘;作爲純益: *We were £5 to the ~.* 我們淨賺了五鎊。 **4** (*adj* as *pl n*) good or virtuous persons: (形容詞用作複數名詞)好人: *G~ and bad alike respected him.* 不分好人與壞人都尊敬他。

good·bye /ˌgʊdˈbaɪ ; gʊdˈbaɪ; *fast or informal:* gʊˈbaɪ; gʊˈbaɪ/ *int, n* (saying of) farewell: 再見;再會: *'I must say ~ now'*, It is time for me to leave. 我必須告辭了。*Have you said all your ~s?* 你同大家告別了沒有?

good·ish /ˈgʊdɪʃ ; ˈgʊdɪʃ/ *attrib adj* rather large, extensive, etc: 頗大的;相當的: *It's a ~ step from here*, quite a long way. 距此頗遠。

good·ly /ˈgʊdlɪ ; ˈgʊdlɪ/ *adj* (-ier, -iest) (liter) (文) **1** handsome; pleasant-looking. 漂亮的;美觀的。 **2** of considerable size: 相當大的: *a ~ sum of money*, 相當大的一筆錢; *a ~ heritage.* 相當可觀的遺產。

good·ness /ˈgʊdnɪs ; ˈgʊdnɪs/ *n* [U] **1** quality of being good; virtue: 善良;美德: *~ of heart.* 心地之善良。***have the ~ to,*** be kind enough to: 有…之善意;懇請: *Have the ~ to come this way, please.* 請從這邊走。**2** strength or essence: 眞髓;精華: *meat with the ~ boiled out.* 將精華煮去的肉。 **3** (in exclamations) used instead of *God!*: (在感嘆句中)用以代替 God: *G~ Gracious!* 啊呀! *G~ me!* 啊呀!天啊! *For ~' sake!* 看在老天爺的面上!務請! *Thank ~!* 謝天謝地! *I wish to ~ that...*, wish very strongly that.... 務祈…。***G~ knows,*** **(a)** I do not know. 天曉得;我不知道。**(b)** I appeal to Heaven to witness: 上天作證: *G~ knows I've tried hard.* 上天作證,我確實努力嘗試過。

goods /gʊdz ; gʊdz/ *n pl* **1** movable property; merchandise: 動產;貨物: *He buys and sells leather ~.* 他買賣皮貨。*Half his ~ were stolen.* 他半數的財產(貨物)被人偸走了。**ˌ~ and ˈchattels,** (legal) personal belongings. (法律)有體動產。 **2** things carried by rail, etc (contrasted with passengers): 火車等所運之貨物(與 passengers 相對): *a ˈ~ agent／station.* 貨運代理行(站)。**ˈ~ train,** ie not a passenger train (US 美 = *freight train*). (火車)貨車。***piece of ~,*** (colloq) person: (俗)人: *She's a sexy little piece of ~*, a sexy young girl. 她是個性感的女郎。

good·will /ˌgʊdˈwɪl ; ˈgʊdˈwɪl/ *n* [U] **1** friendly feeling: 親善;友善: *a policy of ~ in international relations.* 國際關係上的親善政策。 **2** privilege of trading as the successor to a well-established business: 一個老店鋪所享有的信譽;商譽: *The ~ is to be sold with the business.* 這商行將連同其商譽一併售出。

goody /ˈgʊdɪ; ˈgʊdɪ/ *n* (colloq) sweetmeat; desirable thing. (俗)糖果;蜜餞;想要的東西。

goody-goody /ˈgʊdɪ gʊdɪ ; ˈgʊdɪˈgʊdɪ/ *adj, n* (person who is) primly or pretentiously virtuous. 道學的;道學先生。

gooey /ˈgu:ɪ ; ˈguɪ/ *adj* ⇨ goo.

goof /gu:f ; guf/ (sl) (俚) *n* silly or stupid person. 愚蠢的人。□ *vi, vt* [VP2A, 6A] make a mess (of). 弄亂;弄糟。**~y** *adj* silly, stupid, crazy. 愚蠢的;蠢笨的。

goog·ly /ˈgu:glɪ ; ˈguglɪ/ *n* (*pl* -lies) (cricket) ball bowled as if to break in one way that actually breaks in the opposite way. (板球)曲球(先向一方,繼而轉向相反方向的球)。

goon /gu:n ; gun/ *n* (sl) stupid or awkward person (俚)愚笨之人;笨拙之人。

goose /gu:s ; gus/ *n* (*pl* geese /gi:s ; gis/) **1** water bird larger than a duck; female of this, ⇨ gander; ⇨ the illus at fowl; [U] its flesh as food. 鵝;雌鵝(參看 fowl 之插圖);鵝肉。***cook sb's ~,*** put an end to his hopes; prevent him from being a nuisance, etc. 使某人絕望;阻止某人做一討厭的人等。***kill the ~ that lays the golden eggs,*** (prov) sacrifice future gains to satisfy present needs. (諺)殺雞取卵(爲滿足目前需要而犧牲將來的財源)。 ***be unable to say 'boo' to a ~,*** be very timid. 非常膽小。 ***All one's geese are swans,*** One overestimates or exaggerates the good qualities of persons and things. (某人)喜歡誇大。 **ˈ~-flesh** *n* [U] rough bristling skin caused by cold or fear. (因寒冷或恐懼皮膚上所生的)鷄皮疙瘩。**ˈ~-step** *n* way of marching without bending the knees. 正步。 **2** simpleton: 傻瓜;笨蛋: *You silly ~!* 你這個笨蛋!

goose·berry /ˈgʊzbərɪ *US:* ˈgu:sberɪ ; ˈgusˌbɛrɪ/ *n* (*pl* -ries) [C] (bush with) green, smooth berry (used for jam, tarts, etc). 醋栗(綠色光滑的漿果,用做果醬,果餡糕點等)。⇨ the illus at fruit. 參看 fruit 之插圖。***play ~,*** be present with two persons, eg lovers, who prefer to be alone. 陪伴兩個想單獨在一起的人(例如情侶);當電燈泡。

go·pher /ˈgəʊfə(r) ; ˈgofɚ/ *n* burrowing rat-like animal in N America. 北美產的一種地鼠。

Gor·dian /ˈgɔ:dɪən ; ˈgɔrdɪən/ *adj* (only in) (僅用於) **~ knot,** knot difficult or impossible to untie; difficult problem or task. 難解的結;難題。***cut the ~ knot,*** solve a problem by force or by disregarding the conditions. 用强硬手段解決難題;以快刀斬亂麻的手段解決問題。

gore[1] /gɔ:(r) ; gor/ *n* [U] (liter, chiefly in descriptions of fighting) thickened blood from a cut or wound. (文,主要用於描寫戰鬥)傷口的凝血。

gore[2] /gɔ:(r) ; gor/ *vt* [VP6A] pierce, wound, with the horns or tusks: 用角或長牙牴: *~d to death by an infuriated bull.* 被一發狂的公牛用角牴死。

gorge[1] /gɔ:dʒ ; gɔrdʒ/ *n* **1** narrow opening, usu with a stream, between hills or mountains. 峽。**2** gullet; contents of the stomach: 食道;嚥下之物;胃內之物: *His ~ rose at the sight／It made his ~ rise*, He was sickened or disgusted. 他看到那景象就作嘔。

gorge[2] /gɔ:dʒ ; gɔrdʒ/ *vi, vt* [VP6A, 14, 2A, C] ***~ (oneself) (on／with sth),*** eat greedily; fill oneself: 狼吞虎嚥;塞飽: *~ on rich food;* 貪婪地吃着油膩的食物; *~ oneself with meat.* 肚子裏塞滿了肉。□ *n* act of gorging; surfeit. 狼吞虎嚥;塞飽。

gorg·eous /ˈgɔ:dʒəs ; ˈgɔrdʒəs/ *adj* **1** richly coloured; magnificent: 華麗的;燦爛的: *a ~ sunset.* 光輝燦爛的落日。 **2** (colloq) giving pleasure and satisfaction: (俗)宜人的;令人滿意的: *~ weather;* 宜人的天氣; *a ~ dinner.* 盛餐。**~·ly** *adv*

Gor·gon /ˈgɔ:gən ; ˈgɔrgən/ *n* (Gk myth) one of three snake-haired sisters whose looks turned to stone anyone who saw them. (希神)三蛇髮女怪之一(人見其貌則化爲石)。

Gor·gon·zola /ˌgɔ:gənˈzəʊlə ; ˌgɔrgənˈzolə/ *n* [U] rich creamy blue-veined cheese (from ~ in Italy). 一種味濃,含多量乳脂,有藍色紋理的乾酪(因產於義大利哥根索拉市而得名)。

gor·illa /gəˈrɪlə ; gəˈrɪlə/ *n* man-sized, tree-climbing African ape. (非洲)大猩猩。⇨ the illus at ape. 參看 ape 之插圖。

gor·man·dize /ˈgɔ:məndaɪz ; ˈgɔrmənˌdaɪz/ *vi* eat, devour, greedily for pleasure. 狼吞虎嚥。

gorse /gɔ:s ; gɔrs/ *n* [U] yellow-flowered evergreen shrub with sharp thorns, growing on waste land (also called *furze* or *whin*). 金雀花(生黃花之長青灌木,有尖刺,生長於荒地,亦稱 furze 或 whin)。

gory /ˈgɔ:rɪ ; ˈgorɪ/ *adj* (-ier, -iest) covered with blood; of bloody physical violence: 血汚的;染滿血的;流血暴亂的: *~ details／incidents.* 血汚的詳情(流血暴亂的事件)。

gosh /gɒʃ ; gaʃ/ *int* (sl) (also 亦作 ***by ~***) by God. (俚)哎呀!

gos·ling /ˈgɒzlɪŋ ; ˈgazlɪŋ/ *n* young goose. 小鵝。

gos·pel /ˈgɒspl ; ˈgaspl/ *n* **the G~** [U] (the life and teachings of Jesus as recorded in the) first four books of the New Testament; [C] any one of these; set of principles that one acts upon or believes in: (大寫)新約聖經四福音書;四福音書中所

記載之耶穌生平與教訓;四福音書之一;(小寫)信條;主義: *the ~ of health;* 健康之道; *the ~ of soap and water,* (hum for) firm belief in the value of cleanliness. (諧)淸潔主義。

gos·sa·mer /ˈgɒsəmə(r) ; ˈgɑsəmɚ/ *n* **1** [C, U] (thread of the) fine silky substance of webs made by small spiders, floating in calm air or spread on grass, etc. 蛛絲;遊絲。 **2** [U] soft, light, delicate material: 薄紗: *as light as ~;* 輕如薄紗的; (attrib) (形容用法) *a ~ veil.* 薄面紗。

gos·sip /ˈgɒsɪp ; ˈgɑsəp/ *n* **1** [U] idle, often ill-natured, talk about the affairs of other people: 閒話: *Don't believe all the ~ you hear.* 不要相信你聽到的一切閒話。*She's too fond of ~.* 她太喜歡說閒話。 **2** [C] instance of this; friendly chat: 閒談;聊天: *have a good ~ with a neighbour over the garden fence.* 隔着花園籬笆同一隣居愉快地聊天。 **3** [U] informal writing about persons and social happenings, eg in letters or in newspapers: 隨筆;漫談: (attrib) (形容用法) *the ˈ~ column,* of a newspaper; (報上的)隨筆欄; *a ˈ~ writer/columnist.* 隨筆作家(專欄作家)。 **4** [C] person who is fond of ~: 喜閒談之人: *She's an old ~.* 她是個老長舌婦。 □ *vi* (-p- or -pp-; US -p-) [VP2A, C] talk or write ~. 閒談;漫談。

got *pt, pp* of get.

Goth /gɒθ ; gɑθ/ *n* member of a Germanic tribe that invaded the Roman Empire in the 3rd and 4th cc; rough, uncivilized person. 哥德人(於三、四世紀侵略羅馬帝國的日耳曼人之一支);野蠻人。⇨ Vandal.

Gothic /ˈgɒθɪk ; ˈgɑθɪk/ *adj* **1** of the Goths or their language. 哥德人的;哥德語的。 **2** of the style of architecture common in Western Europe in the 12th to 16th cc, characterized by pointed arches, clusters of columns, etc. 哥德式建築的(哥德式爲十二至十六世紀常見於西歐之建築風格,以尖拱、簇柱等爲特色)。⇨ the illus at church. 參看 church 之挿圖。 **3** of an 18th c style of fantastic, romantic literature: 哥德式文學的(十八世紀一種怪異幻想文學風格的): *~ novels.* 哥德式小說。 **4** (of printing type) thick or heavy, as formerly used for German. (指活字)哥德體的;粗黑體的。□ *n* ~ language; ~ architecture; ~ type. 哥德語;哥德式建築;粗黑體活字。

gotta /ˈgɒtə ; ˈgɑtə/ (US sl) (美俚) = *have got to.* ⇨ get(13).

got·ten *pp* (in US) of get. (美) get 的過去分詞。

gouache /gʊˈɑːʃ ; gʊˈɑʃ/ *n* [U] opaque water-colour paint; method of painting using this material. 樹膠水彩;樹膠水彩畫法。

gouge /gaʊdʒ ; gaʊdʒ/ *n* tool with a sharp semi-circular edge for cutting grooves in wood. 半圓鑿。 □ *vt* [VP6A, 15B] **~ *(out),*** cut with a ~; shape with a ~; force out with, or as with, a ~: (用半圓鑿)鑿;挖;鑿成;挖成;挖出: *~ out the stone from a horseshoe.* 自馬蹄鐵中將石頭挖出。

gou·lash /ˈguːlæʃ ; ˈgulæʃ/ *n* [C, U] (dish of) stew of steak and vegetables, seasoned with paprika. 菜燉牛肉(肉片與蔬菜煮成並加辣椒調味);一道菜燉牛肉。

gourd /gʊəd ; gord/ *n* (large, hard-skinned fleshy fruit of) kind of climbing or trailing plant; bottle or bowl consisting of the dried skin of this fruit. 葫蘆;結葫蘆的攀緣植物;葫蘆製的瓶;葫蘆瓢。

gour·mand /ˈgʊəmənd ; ˈgʊrmənd/ *n* lover of food. 饕餮;喜美食者。

gour·met /ˈgʊəmeɪ ; ˈgʊrme/ *n* person who enjoys, and is expert in the choice of, delicate food, wines, etc. 講究美食,美酒等者。

gout /gaʊt ; gaʊt/ *n* [U] disease causing painful swellings in joints, esp toes, knees and fingers. 痛風 (使足趾,膝蓋,手指關節腫痛的一種病)。 **~y** *adj* suffering from ~. 患痛風病的。

gov·ern /ˈgʌvn ; ˈgʌvɚn/ *vt, vi* **1** [VP6A, 2A] rule (a country, etc); control or direct the public affairs of (a city, country, etc): 統治(國家等);治理(城市,國家等): *In Great Britain the sovereign reigns but does not ~.* 在英國,君主臨國但不治理。 **2** [VP6A] control: 控制: *~ one's temper.* 控制自己的脾氣。 **3** [VP6A] (usu passive) determine; influence: (通常爲被動語態)支配;影響: *be ~ed by the opinions of others.* 受他人意見的影響。*Don't be ~ed by what other people say.* 不要被別人的話所左右。 **4** (gram, esp of a *v* or *prep*) require, make necessary (a certain case or form of another word). (文法,尤指動詞或介詞)需用 (某一字之某種格或形式)。 **~·ing** *adj* having the power or right to ~: 有統治權的: *the ~ing body of a school/college, etc.* 學校(學院等)的行政部門。

gov·ern·ance /ˈgʌvənəns ; ˈgʌvɚnəns/ *n* [U] (formal) act, fact, manner, of governing; sway, control. (正式用語)統治;統治之法;權勢;支配。

gov·ern·ess /ˈgʌvənɪs ; ˈgʌvɚnɪs/ *n* woman who is employed to teach young children in a private family. 女家庭教師。

gov·ern·ment /ˈgʌvənmənt ; ˈgʌvɚnmənt/ *n* **1** [U] governing; power to govern: 統治;統治權: *What the country needs is strong ~.* 這國家所需要的是有力的統治。 **2** [U] method or system of governing: 統治方法;政體: *We prefer democratic ~.* 我們比較喜歡民主政體。 **3** [C] body of persons governing a State: 內閣;政府: *The Prime Minister has formed a G~,* has chosen his colleagues, selected Ministers for the Cabinet. 首相已組閣。*The G~* (collectively 集合用法) *has welcomed the proposal.* 政府接受了這項建議。*The G~* (its members 政府成員) *are discussing the proposal.* 政府當局正在討論這項建議。 **G~ House,** official residence of the Governor (of a province, etc). 州長(總督,省長等)的官邸。 **G~ securities,** bonds, exchequer bills, etc, issued by the state. 政府證券,公債券等。 **~al** /ˌgʌvnˈmentl ; ˌgʌvɚnˈmɛntḷ/ *adj* connected with ~. 統治的;政府的。

gov·ernor /ˈgʌvənə(r) ; ˈgʌvənɚ/ *n* **1** G~, person who governs a province or colony or (US) a State: 省主席;省長;總督;(美)州長: *the G~ of New York State.* 紐約州州長。Cf 參較 *the Mayor of New York City.* 紐約市市長。 **ˌG~-ˈGeneral** *n* (in the British Commonwealth) representative of the Crown, having no special powers: (大英國協中代表王室的)總督: *the G~-General of Canada.* 加拿大總督。 **2** member of the governing body of an institution (eg a school in England, a college, a hospital). (英國學校,學院,醫院等內之)主管人員;管理者;理事。 **3** (colloq) chief; employer; father. (俗)首長;雇主;父親。 **4** regulator in a machine, automatically controlling speed or the intake of gas, steam, etc. (機械)調速器;調節器。

gown /gaʊn ; gaʊn/ *n* **1** woman's dress, esp one for special occasions: 女人穿的長服(尤指爲特殊場合所穿者): *a ˈball-/ˈnight-~.* 舞會長服(睡袍)。 **2** loose, flowing robe worn by members of a university, judges, etc. 大學學人、法官等所穿的長服。⇨ the illus at judge. 參看 judge 之挿圖。 □ *vt* (chiefly *pp*) dress in a ~: (主要用過去分詞)使穿着長服: *beautifully ~ed women.* 穿着美麗長袍的婦女。

decorated gourds

grab /græb; græb/ *vt, vi* (-bb-) [VP6A, 3A] ~ ***(at),*** take roughly; selfishly or eagerly snatch: 搶奪;攫取: *The dog ~bed the bone and ran off with it.* 那狗搶了骨頭就跑。*Don't ~!* 不要搶！*He ~bed at the opportunity of going abroad.* 他急急抓住出國的機會。□ *n* [C] **1** sudden snatch: 攫取;突攫: *make a ~ at something.* 攫取某物。**2** mechanical device for taking up and holding sth to be lifted or moved. 攫取機;抓斗;抓子。**~·ber** *n* person who ~s; greedy person whose chief aim in life appears to be making money. 搶奪者;以賺錢爲人生目的之貪取者。

grace /greɪs; gres/ *n* **1** [U, C] quality of being pleasing, attractive or beautiful, esp in structure or movement: 優美;優雅(尤指在結構或動作上): *She danced with ~/with a ~ that surprised us.* 她的舞姿優美(優雅得使我們驚奇)。**2** [C] (usu *pl*) pleasing accomplishment; elegance of manner. (通常用複數)文雅;溫雅。***airs and ~s,*** ways of speaking and behaving that are intended to impress and attract people. (說話與舉止之)做作態度;裝模作樣。**3** [U] favour; goodwill. 恩賜;善意。***an act of ~,*** sth freely given, not taken as a right. 恩典;仁慈的行爲。***days of ~,*** time allowed by the law or custom after the day on which a payment, eg of a bill of exchange, an insurance premium, is due. 付款(如付滙票,保險費)之法定或習慣的寬限日期。***give sb a day's/week's, etc ~,*** allow him an extra day, etc before requiring him to fulfil an obligation. 給與某人一日(一週等)的寬限。***be in sb's good ~s,*** enjoy his favour and approval. 受某人之寵愛。**4** [U] ***have the ~ to do sth,*** realize that it is right and proper, and do it: 明理地做某事: *He had the ~ to say that he was sorry.* 他明理地道歉。***do sth with a good/bad ~,*** do it willingly/reluctantly. 樂意地(勉强地)做某事。**5** [U, C] short prayer of thanks before or after a meal: 飯前或飯後簡短的謝恩禱告: *say (a) ~.* 作謝恩禱告。**6** [U] God's mercy and favour towards mankind; influence and result of this. 上帝對人類的慈悲;天恩的影響與結果。***in the year of ~ 19...,*** in the 19...th year after the birth of Jesus. 在紀元19...年。***in a state of ~,*** being influenced by the strength and inspiring power of God, having been pardoned; having received the Sacraments. 受天惠;受上帝的恩寵;受聖禮。***fall from ~,*** fall to a lower moral state after being in a state of ~. 失上帝恩寵;墮落。**7** as a title, used when speaking of or to an archbishop, duke or duchess: 對大主教、公爵或公爵夫人之尊稱;閣下;夫人: *His/Her/Your G~.* 閣下;夫人。**8 the G~s,** (Gk myth) three beautiful sister goddesses who gave beauty, charm and happiness. (希神)賜人美麗、魅力與快樂的三位美麗的姐妹女神。□ *vt* [VP6A] add ~ to; confer honour or dignity on; be an ornament to: 使優美;使增光;爲…之裝飾: *The occasion was ~d by the presence of the Queen.* 女王之駕臨使場面爲之增色。*Her character is ~d with every virtue.* 她的品格因具有一切美德而顯得高尚。

grace·ful /ˈgreɪsfl; ˈgresfəl/ *adj* having or showing grace (1, 4): 優雅的;優美的;得體的: *a ~ dancer;* 優美的舞者; *a ~ letter of thanks.* 得體的謝函。**~ly** /-fəlɪ; -fəlɪ/ *adv*

grace·less /ˈgreɪslɪs; ˈgreslɪs/ *adj* without grace (4); without a sense of what is right and proper: 不知禮的;不明理的: *~ behaviour.* 粗野的行爲。**~·ly** *adv*

gra·cious /ˈgreɪʃəs; ˈgreʃəs/ *adj* **1** (of persons and their behaviour) kind; generous; courteous: (指人及其行爲)親切的;和善的;大方的;有禮的: *her ~ Majesty the Queen.* 女王陛下。*It was ~ of her to come.* 蒙她駕臨,不勝感激。**2** (of God) merciful. (指上帝)仁慈的。**3** (in exclamations) expressing surprise: (在感嘆句中)表示驚奇: *Good(ness) G~! G~ me!* 天啊！噯呀！**~·ly** *adv* **~·ness** *n*

gra·da·tion /grəˈdeɪʃn *US:* greɪ-; greˈdeʃən/ *n* [C, U] step, stage, degree in development; gradual change from one thing to another or from one state to another: 進展的過程,階段,程度;漸變: *the ~s of colour in the rainbow.* 彩虹中顏色的漸變。

grade[1] /greɪd; gred/ *n* [C] **1** step, stage or degree in rank, quality, value, etc; number or class of things of the same kind: 階級;品位;等級;同類或同等級的事物: *The rank of major is one ~ higher than that of captain.* 少校的階級較上尉者高一級。*Potatoes are sold in ~s, and G~ A potatoes are of the best quality.* 馬鈴薯分等售出,甲等馬鈴薯品質最好。*This pupil has a high ~ of intelligence.* 這個學生的智力很高。**2** (US) division of the school course; one year's work; pupils in such a division: (美)班級;年級;同一班或年級的全體學生: *An elementary school in the US has eight ~s and is called a '~ school'. Its teachers are called '~ teachers'.* 美國的小學分爲八個年級,因而稱作 'grade school'。小學教師稱作 'grade teachers'。**3** the mark, eg 80%, or rating, eg 'Excellent' or 'Fair', given to a pupil for his work in school. (學校中給學生的)分數(例如80分);等級(例如優或尙佳);成績。***make the ~,*** (colloq) reach a good standard; do as well as is required. (俗)達到良好標準;合乎要求。**4** (US) slope of a road, railways, etc (GB 英 = *gradient*). (美)道路,鐵路等的坡度。***on the 'up/'down ~,*** rising/falling: 上升(下降);興盛(衰敗): *Business is on the up ~,* is improving. 商業興隆。**~ crossing,** (US) level crossing. (美)平交道。

grade[2] /greɪd; gred/ *vt* [VP6A] **1** arrange in order in grades or classes: 分等;分類;分級: *~ potatoes;* 將馬鈴薯分成等級; *~d by size.* 按大小分類。**2** make land (esp for roads) more nearly level by reducing the slope. 減少土地(尤指道路用地)之斜度使較近於水平。**3** [VP6A, 15B] ~ ***(up),*** cross (cattle) with a better breed. 使(牲畜)與優良種交配。

gradi·ent /ˈgreɪdɪənt; ˈgredɪənt/ *n* degree of slope: 坡度;傾斜度;斜率;梯度: *a ~ of one in nine;* 九比一的傾斜度(約合仰角6·34度); *a steep ~.* 陡峭的坡度。

grad·ual /ˈgrædʒʊəl; ˈgrædʒʊəl/ *adj* taking place by degrees; (of a slope) not steep: 逐漸的;(指斜坡)不陡峭的: *a ~ increase in the cost of living.* 生活費的逐漸增高。**~·ly** /-dʒʊlɪ; -dʒəlɪ/ *adv* by degrees. 逐漸。**~·ness** *n*

grad·uate[1] /ˈgrædʒʊət; ˈgrædʒʊɪt/ *n* **1** (GB) person who holds a university degree, esp the first, or Bachelor's, degree: (英)獲大學學位(尤指學士學位)者;大學畢業生: *Oxbridge ~s;* 牛津或劍橋大學畢業生; *a ~ student;* 研究生; *post-~ studies.* 研究所的課程。**2** (US) one who has completed a course at an educational institution: (美)畢業生: *high school ~s;* 高中畢業生; *a ~ nurse,* one from a College or School of Nursing. 護理學校畢業的護士。(Cf 參較 *trained nurse* in GB 英國稱 trained nurse).

grad·uate[2] /ˈgrædʒʊeɪt; ˈgrædʒʊˌet/ *vt, vi* **1** [VP6A] mark with degrees for measuring: 刻度數於: *a ruler ~d in both inches and centimetres;* 刻有英寸及公分的尺; *a ~d glass,* for measuring quantities of liquid. 量杯(上有刻度,量液體用)。**2** [VP6A] arrange according to grade. 分等級;定以等級。**3** [VP2A, C] take an academic degree: (自大學)畢業;獲學位: *He ~d from Oxford/~d in law.* 他畢業於牛津大學(獲得法學學位)。(US, of other institutions): (在美國亦指自其他學校畢業): *~ from the Boston School of Cookery.* 畢業於波士頓烹飪學校。**4** [VP6A] (chiefly US) give a degree or diploma to: (主美)授以學位;准予畢業: *The university ~d 350 students last year.* 該大學去年有350位學生畢業。*He had been ~d from Maryland College in the Class of 1868.* 他畢業於馬里蘭學院1868年級。**gradu·ation** /ˌgrædʒʊˈeɪʃn; ˌgrædʒʊˈeʃən/ *n* graduating or being ~d; (US) ceremony at which degrees are conferred. 刻度;分等級;畢業;授學位;獲學位;(美)畢業典禮;授學位典禮。

graf·fito /grəˈfiːtəʊ; grəˈfito/ *n* (*pl* -ti /-tiː; -ti/)

(usu *pl*) (I) drawing, words, scratched on a hard surface, esp a wall. (通常用複數)(義)亂刻於牆上等的畫或文字。

graft[1] /grɑːft *US:* græft ; græft/ *n* **1** shoot from a branch or twig of a living tree, fixed in a cut made in another tree, to form a new growth. 接枝;接木。 **2** (surgery) piece of skin, bone, etc from a living person or animal, transplanted on another body or another part of the same body. (外科)移植物;移植的皮膚、骨骼等。□ *vt, vi* [VP6A, 15A, B, 2A] put a ~ in or on: 接木於;接枝;移植: *~ one variety on/upon/in/into another;* 將一品種接到另一品種上; *~ on briar roots;* 接枝於石南根上; *~ new skin.* 移植新皮膚。

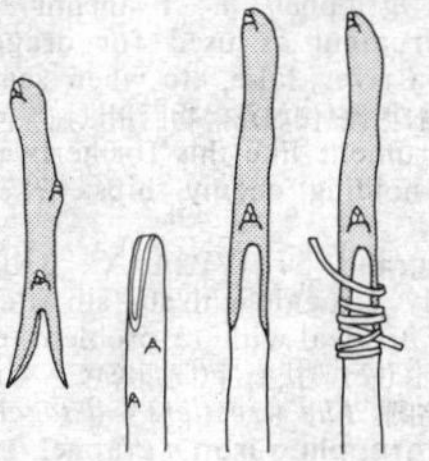

grafting

wood grain

graft[2] /grɑːft *US:* græft ; græft/ *n* [C, U] (instance of) getting business advantages, profit-making, etc through illegal or unethical means, eg by taking wrong advantage of connections in politics, by bribery etc. 貪污;受賄;瀆職。□ *vi* practise ~. 貪污;受賄;瀆職。

grail /greɪl ; grel/ *n* (usu 通常作 **the Holy G~**) platter or cup used by Jesus at the Last Supper and in which one of his followers is said to have received drops of his blood at the Crucifixion. 聖盤;聖杯 (耶穌在最後晚餐時所用,據說耶穌被釘於十字架上時,其門徒之一曾用以盛裝耶穌的血)。

grain /greɪn ; gren/ *n* **1** [U] (collective *sing*) small, hard seed of food plants such as wheat and rice: (集合單數)穀類: *~ imports;* 穀類輸入; *a cargo of ~.* 一船穀類; *'~ elevator,* storehouse for ~, with devices for lifting ~. 穀倉。⇨ the illus at cereal. 參看 cereal 之插圖。 **2** [C] single seed of such a plant: 穀粒: *give a beggar a few ~s of rice;* 給一乞丐少許的米飯; *eat up every ~ of rice in one's bowl.* 將碗中的米飯吃得一粒也不剩。 **3** [C] tiny, hard bit: 小硬粒: *~s of sand/salt/gold;* 沙(鹽,金)粒; (fig) small amount: (喻)少許: *a boy without a ~ of sense;* 沒有一點頭腦的男孩; *receive a few ~s of comfort.* 得到些許安慰。 **4** smallest unit of weight, 1/7000 lb or 0·065 gm. 喱(最小的重量單位,等於1/7000磅或0·065克)。⇨ App 5. 參看附錄五。 **5** [U] natural arrangement or pattern of the lines of fibre in wood, etc as seen on a surface that has been sawn or cut: 木等之紋;紋理: *woods of fine/coarse ~.* 細(粗)紋木。 ***be/go against the ~,*** (fig) contrary to one's nature or inclination. (喻)不合自己的性情或意願。

gram græm ; græm/ *n* metric unit of weight. 克。⇨ App 5. 參看附錄五。

gram·mar /ˈgræmə(r) ; ˈgræmɚ/ *n* **1** [U] study or science of, rules for, the combination of words into sentences (*syntax*), and the forms of words (*morphology*). 文法;文法規則。 **2** [C] book containing the rules of ~ of a language. 文法書。 **'~ school,** (in GB) type of secondary school which provides academic (contrasted with technical) courses. (英國之)文法學校(一種中等學校,設有文學或古典作品的課程,以別於工藝或技術學校)。 **~·ian** /grəˈmeərɪən ; grəˈmɛrɪən/ *n* expert in ~. 文法學者;文法家。

gram·mati·cal /grəˈmætɪkl ; grəˈmætɪkl/ *adj* of, conforming to, the rules of grammar: 文法的;合乎文法規則的: *a ~ error/explanation/sentence.* 文法上的錯誤(文法的解釋;合文法的句子)。 **~ly** /-klɪ ; -klɪ/ *adv*

gramme /græm ; græm/ *n* = gram.

gramo·phone /ˈgræməfəʊn ; ˈgræməˌfon/ *n* (US 美 = *phonograph*) machine for reproducing music and speech recorded on flat discs (*record-player* is now the usu word). 留聲機;唱機(現較常用 record-player)。

gram·pus /ˈgræmpəs ; ˈgræmpəs/ *n* large dolphin-like sea animal; person who breathes loudly. 逆戟鯨;鯱(一種大海豚);呼吸粗沉之人。

gran·ary /ˈgrænərɪ ; ˈgrænərɪ/ *n* (*pl* -ries) storehouse for grain. 穀倉。

grand /grænd ; grænd/ *adj* **1** (in official titles) chief; most important: (用於官銜中)主要的;最高級的: *G~ Master,* eg of some orders of knighthood; 騎士團的首領; *a ~ master,* chess champion; 西洋棋王(西洋棋冠軍); *G~ Vizier,* (former title of) chief minister of Turkey. 昔時土耳其的首相。 **2** of most or greatest importance: 最重要的: *the ~ finale;* 大結局;大終曲; *the ~ question;* 最重要的問題; *the ~ staircase/entrance,* of a large building. 主要的樓梯(入口)。 **3** magnificent; splendid: 壯麗的;堂皇的: *a ~ view;* 壯麗的景色; *living in ~ style;* 過豪華生活; *~ clothes.* 華麗的服裝。 **4** self-important; proud: 自大的;驕傲的: *He puts on a very ~ manner/air.* 他的態度驕傲。 **5** (colloq) very fine or enjoyable: (俗)極好的;快樂的: *We had a ~ time.* 我們玩得很痛快。 *What ~ weather!* 天氣眞好! **6** full; complete: 完全的;全部的: *a ~ orchestra,* one with all kinds of instruments (not strings only); 大管絃樂隊 (配有各種樂器,不限於絃樂器); *the ~ total,* including everything; 總計; *the ~ result of our efforts.* 我們努力的總結果。 **7** impressive because of high moral or mental qualities: 崇高的;高貴的: *Lincoln had a ~ character.* 林肯有崇高的人格。 *Gladstone was called the G~ Old Man.* 格萊斯頓被稱作偉大的長者。 **8** (phrases) (片語) **the ˌG~ 'National,** annual steeplechase at Liverpool. 利物浦每年舉行的越野障礙大賽馬。 **ˌ~ 'opera,** in which there are no spoken parts, everything being sung. 大歌劇(無對白,全部爲歌唱者)。 **ˌ~ pi'ano,** large piano with horizontal strings. 平臺鋼琴。⇨ the illus at keyboard. 參看 keyboard 之插圖。 **ˌbaby '~,** small-size ~ piano. 小型平臺鋼琴。 **G~ Prix** /ˌgrɑːn ˈpriː ; ˌgrɑnˈpri/, (F) (motor-racing) one of several international races. (法)國際大賽車。 **'~·stand,** rows of roofed seats for spectators at races, sports-meetings, etc. (賽馬場,運動場等之)大看臺。 **the ˌG~ 'Tour,** (formerly) tour of the chief towns, etc of Europe, completing the education of a wealthy young person. (昔時)教育旅行(富家子弟至歐洲各大都市之旅行,做爲教育之最後一個階段)。 **~·ly** *adv*

grand- /grænd ; grænd/ *pref* **'~·child, '~·daughter, '~·son** *nn* daughter or son of one's son or daughter. 孫(外孫);孫女(外孫女);孫子(外孫)。 **'~·parent, '~·father, '~·mother** *nn* father or mother of one's father or mother. (外)祖父或(外)祖母;(外)祖父;(外)祖母。 **'~·nephew, '~·niece** *nn* son or daughter or one's nephew or niece. 姪孫(姪外孫);姪孫女(姪外孫女)。 **'~·uncle, '~·aunt** *nn* uncle or aunt of either of one's parents. 伯祖(叔祖,姑公,姨公,舅公);伯祖母(叔婆,姑婆,姨婆,舅婆)。 **'~·father clock** *n* clock worked by weights in a tall wooden case. 裝於高木匣中有擺的大鐘。

grand-dad, gran·dad /ˈgrændæd ; ˈgrænˌdæd/ *n* (colloq for) grandfather. (俗)爺爺;外公。

gran·dee /grænˈdiː ; grænˈdi/ *n* (hist) Spanish or Portuguese nobleman of high rank. (史)大公(西班牙或葡萄牙之貴族)。

gran·deur /ˈgrændʒə(r) ; ˈgrændʒɚ/ *n* [U] greatness; magnificence: 偉大;壯麗;華麗: *the ~ of the*

Swiss Alps. 瑞士境內阿爾卑斯山之壯麗。

gran·dilo·quent /græn'dɪləkwənt ; græn'dɪləkwənt/ *adj* using, full of, pompous words: 誇張的;誇大的: *a ~ speaker;* 說話誇大的人; *written in a ~ style.* 文體浮華的。**gran·dilo·quence** /-əns ; -əns/ *n* [U].

gran·di·ose /'grændɪəʊs ; 'grændɪ,os/ *adj* planned on a large scale; imposing. 宏偉的;堂皇的。

grand·ma /'grænmɑː ; 'grænmɑ/ *n* (colloq for) grandmother. (俗)奶奶;外婆。

grand·pa /'grænpɑː ; 'grænpɑ/ *n* (colloq for) grandfather. (俗)爺爺;外公。

grange /greɪndʒ ; grendʒ/ *n* country house with farm buildings attached. 農莊。

gran·ite /'grænɪt ; 'grænɪt/ *n* [U] hard, usu grey, stone used for building. 花崗岩;花崗石。

granny, gran·nie /'grænɪ ; 'grænɪ/ *n* (colloq for) grandmother. (俗)奶奶;外婆。'~ **knot,** reef-knot crossed the wrong way and therefore insecure. 祖母結(交叉錯誤的方結,故而不牢)。⇨ the illus at knot. 參看 knot 之插圖。

grant /grɑːnt *US:* grænt ; grænt/ *vt* **1** [VP6A, 12A, 13A] consent to give or allow (what is asked for): 允許;准許;答應給與: *~ a favour/request;* 答應一項幫助(請求); *~ sb permission/a request to do sth.* 准許某人做某事。*He was ~ed a pension.* 他獲得年金。 **2** [VP6A, 9, 25] agree (that sth is true): 承認(某事爲眞): *~ the truth of what someone says;* 承認某人的話是眞的; *~ing this to be true/that this is true.* 姑認此係眞情。*I ~ his honesty/~ that he is honest.* 我承認他是誠實的。*He's an honest man, I ~ you.* 我保證他是個誠實的人。***take sth for ~ed,*** regard it as true or as certain to happen. 認爲眞實;視爲當然。***take sb for ~ed,*** treat his presence and actions as a due rather than a favour. 認爲某人之到場和行動是應該的(而非恩惠)。□ *n* sth ~ed, eg money or land from a government: 賜與之物(例如由政府授與的金錢或土地): *~s towards the cost of a university education;* 給與大學生的助學金; *~-aided schools/students.* 獲有補助金的學校(學生)。

granu·lar /'grænjʊlə(r) ; 'grænjələ/ *adj* of or like grains. 小粒的;粒狀的。

granu·late /'grænjʊleɪt ; 'grænjə,let/ *vt, vi* [VP6A, 2A] form into grains; roughen the surface of: (使)成粒;粒化;使…之表面粗糙: *~d sugar,* sugar in the form of small crystals. 砂糖。

gran·ule /'grænjuːl;'grænjʊl/ *n* [C] small grain. 小粒。

grape /greɪp ; grep/ *n* green or purple berry growing in clusters on vines, used for making wine: 葡萄: *a bunch of ~s.* 一串葡萄。⇨ the illus at fruit. 參看 fruit 之插圖。***sour ~s; the ~s are sour,*** said when sb says that sth he wants but cannot get has little or no value. 酸葡萄(得不到某種東西便說那種東西不好)。'~**-shot** *n* [U] (hist) cluster of small iron balls fired together from a cannon to make a hail of shot. (史)同時發出的一群小彈丸;葡萄彈。⇨ shrapnel. '~**-sugar** *n* dextrose or glucose, a kind of sugar found in ripe ~s and other kinds of fruit. 葡萄糖。'~**-vine** *n* **(a)** kind of vine on which ~s grow. 葡萄藤。**(b)** (fig) means by which news gets about, eg in an office, school or a group of friends: (喻)(辦公處,學校或朋友間等)傳達消息的方法: *I heard on the ~-vine that Jill is to be promoted.* 我聽別人說吉爾要升級了。

grape·fruit /'greɪpfruːt ; 'grep,frut/ *n* (*pl* ~ or ~s) [C] fruit like a large orange but with an acid taste. 葡萄柚。⇨ the illus at fruit. 參看 fruit 之插圖。

graph /grɑːf *US:* græf ; græf/ *n* [C] diagram consisting of a line or lines (often curved) showing the variation of two quantities, eg the temperature at each hour. 圖;圖表;曲線圖(例如表明每小時之溫度變化者)。'~ **paper,** paper with small squares of equal size. 方格紙;坐標紙。

graphic /'græfɪk ; 'græfɪk/ *adj* **1** of visual symbols (eg lettering, diagrams, drawings): 文字的;書寫的;圖表的;繪畫的: *a ~ artist;* 書畫雕刻藝術家; *~ displays;* 圖表展示; *the ~ arts.* 書畫雕刻藝術;平面藝術。**2** (of descriptions) causing one to have a clear picture in the mind: (指描寫)生動的: *a ~ account of the battle.* 對該戰役生動的敍述。□ *n pl* **~s,** lettering, drawings, etc. 文字,圖樣等。**graphi·cally** /-klɪ ; -kl̩ɪ/ *adv* by writing or diagrams; (fig) vividly. 用書寫或圖表;(喻)生動地。

graph·ite /'græfaɪt ; 'græfaɪt/ *n* [U] soft, black substance (a form of carbon) used in lubrication, as a moderator in atomic piles, and in making lead pencils. 石墨。

grap·nel /'græpnl ; 'græpnəl/ *n* **1** anchor with many flukes²; instrument as used for dragging along the bed of a river, lake, etc when searching for sth. 多爪錨;抓機(例如爲尋物而用以拖抓河床,湖床等者)。**2** instrument like this formerly used in sea battles for holding enemy ships. 昔時海戰中用以鈎住敵船的戰具。

grapple /'græpl ; 'græpl̩/ *vi* [VP2A, C, 3A] ~ ***(with),*** seize firmly; struggle with sb/sth at close quarters; (fig) try to deal with (a problem, etc): 捉牢;抓住;互揪;格鬪;(喻)設法對付(問題等): *~ with an enemy.* 與敵人格鬪。*The wrestlers ~d together.* 摔角選手揪在一起。'**grappling-iron** *n* grapnel. 抓機;多爪錨。

grasp /grɑːsp *US:* græsp ; græsp/ *vt, vi* **1** [VP6A] seize firmly with the hand(s) or arm(s); understand with the mind: 抓住;緊握;抱住;領悟: *~ sb's hand/a rope;* 抓住某人的手(一根繩); *~ an argument/sb's meaning.* 領會一論點(某人的意思)。**2** [VP3A] ~ **at,** try to seize; accept eagerly: 欲抓住;急欲接受: *~ at an opportunity.* 欲抓住一機會。*A man who ~s at too much may lose everything.* 貪得無厭的人可能毫無所得。□ *n* (usu *sing*) firm hold or grip; (power of) grasping: (通常用單數)緊握;把握;抓緊;把握力;領悟力: *in the ~ of a wicked enemy;* 在一邪惡的敵人的掌握中; *have a thorough ~ of the problem;* 徹底理解一問題; *a problem within/beyond my ~,* that I can/cannot understand. 我所能(不能)瞭解的一個問題。**~·ing** *adj* eager to ~; greedy (for money, etc): 急欲抓住的;貪婪的: *a ~ing rascal.* 貪婪的惡漢。

grass¹ /grɑːs *US:* græs ; græs/ *n* **1** [U] kinds of common, wild, low-growing plant of which the green blades and stalks are eaten by cattle, horses, sheep, etc. 青草;草。***not let the ~ grow under one's feet,*** (fig) waste no time in doing sth. (喻)及時行動。**2** [C] (*pl* ~es) any species of this plant (including, in botanical use, cereals, reeds and bamboos). 禾本科植物(在植物學上的用法,包括穀類、蘆葦和竹)。**3** [U] grazing land; pasture: 牧地;草原;草地: (of animals) (指動物) *at ~,* grazing. 在吃青草。***put/send/turn animals out to ~,*** put them to graze. 放動物出去吃草。**~·land** /-lænd ; -,lænd/ *n* area of land covered with ~ where there are few trees. 草原。,~·'**roots** *n pl* (often attrib) ordinary people remote from political decisions, but who are affected by these decisions: (常作形容用法)(不參與政治決策但受其影響的)一般人民: *a ~roots movement/rebellion.* 一般民衆的運動(叛亂)。*We must not neglect the ~roots.* 我們不可忽視一般民衆。,~ '**widow** *n* wife whose husband is temporarily not living with her. 獨守空閨的妻子。**~y** *adj* (-ier, -iest) covered with ~. 長滿草的;多草的。

grass² /grɑːs *US:* græs ; græs/ *vt, vi* **1** [VP6A, 15B] ~ ***(over),*** cover with turf; [VP6A] (US) feed with grass. 以草覆蓋;鋪以草皮;(美)飼以青草;放牧。**2** [VP2A, 3A] ~ ***(on sb),*** (GB sl) inform (on); betray. (英俚)向警方告發;告密;出賣。

grass·hopper /'grɑːshɒpə(r) *US:* 'græs- ; 'græs,hɑpə/ *n* jumping insect which makes a shrill, chirping noise. 蚱蜢。⇨ the illus at insect. 參看 insect 之插圖。

grate[1] /greɪt ; gret/ *n* (metal frame for holding coal, etc, in a) fireplace. 壁爐;爐條;爐格子;爐柵。

grate[2] /greɪt ; gret/ *vt, vi* **1** [VP6A, 15A] rub into small pieces, usu against a rough surface; rub small bits off: 磨碎;擦碎;磨損: ~ *cheese into beaten eggs*, eg when making a cheese omelette. 磨碎乾酪置入攪過的蛋中(例如做乾酪煎蛋捲時)。 **2** [VP6A, 2A, 3A] ~ ***(on)***, make a harsh noise by rubbing; (fig) have an irritating effect (*on* a person, his nerves): 因磨擦而發刺耳聲;(喻) 刺激; 激怒 (人或其神經): *His bad manners ~d on everyone.* 他的無禮使大家都不愉快。*Out-of-date slang ~s.* 過時的俚語聽來刺耳。*The gate ~s on its hinges.* 那大門開關時鉸鏈吱吱作響。**grat·ing·ly** *adv* **~r** *n* device with a rough surface for grating food, etc: (將食物等磨成碎塊的)擦子: *a 'nutmeg ~r.* 磨荳蔻的擦子。

grate·ful /'greɪtfl ; 'gretfəl/ *adj* **1** ~ ***(to sb) (for sth)***, feeling or showing thanks: 感激的;感謝的: *We are ~ to you for your help.* 我們感激你對我們的幫助。**2** (liter) pleasant; agreeable; comforting: (文)令人愉快的;悅人的;使人舒適的: *trees that afford a ~ shade.* 有樹蔭可供人乘涼的樹木。**~ly** /-fəlɪ ; -fəlɪ/ *adv*

grat·ify /'grætɪfaɪ ; 'grætə,faɪ/ *vt* (*pt, pp* -fied) [VP6A] **1** give pleasure or satisfaction to: 使高興;使滿意: *We were all gratified with/at the result.* 我們都對此結果感到欣慰。*It gratified me to learn that you had been successful.* 獲悉你成功了,我很高興。**2** indulge; give what is desired to: 使滿足;給與所欲望者: ~ *a person's whims/his fancies for something;* 滿足一人的奇想 (滿足他想要某物的願望); ~ *a child's thirst for knowledge.* 滿足一兒童的求知欲。**~·ing** *adj*: *It is always ~ing to have one's efforts rewarded.* 努力而有收穫,總是令人高興的。**grati·fi·ca·tion** /ˌgrætɪfɪ'keɪʃn; ˌgrætəfə'keʃən/ *n* **1** [U] ~ing or being gratified; state of being pleased or satisfied: 喜悅;滿意;滿足: *I have the gratification of knowing that I have done my duty.* 得悉我已盡到職責,我很高興。 **2** [C] that which causes one to feel gratified. 令人滿意的事物。

grat·ing /'greɪtɪŋ ; 'gretɪŋ/ *n* [C] framework of wooden or metal bars, either parallel or crossing one another, placed across an opening, eg a window, to keep out burglars or to allow air to flow through. 格子;格簾;柵欄(例如裝於窗上以防盜賊所用者)。

gra·tis /'greɪtɪs ; 'gretɪs/ *adv, adj* free of charge: 免費的(地): *be admitted ~.* 受免費招待。

grati·tude /'grætɪtju:d *US:* -tu:d ; 'grætə,tjud/ *n* [U] ~ ***(to sb) (for sth)***, thankfulness, being grateful. 感謝;感激。

gra·tu·itous /grə'tju:ɪtəs *US:* -'tu:- ; grə'tjuətəs/ *adj* **1** given, obtained or done, without payment: 不收費的; 免費的: ~ *service/information / help/advice.* 免費的服務(消息,幫助,忠告)。 **2** done or given, acting, without good reason: 無故的;無理由的: *a ~ insult;* 無故的侮辱; *a ~ lie/liar.* 無故的謊言(無故扯謊者)。**~·ly** *adv*

gra·tu·ity /grə'tju:ətɪ *US:* -'tu:- ; grə'tjuətɪ/ *n* (*pl* -ties) **1** gift (of money in addition to pay) to a retiring employee for services. 退休雇員的獎金。 **2** tip (for service). 小帳。

grave[1] /greɪv ; grev/ *adj* (-r, -st) serious; requiring careful consideration: 嚴肅的;嚴重的: ~ *news;* 重大的新聞; *make a ~ mistake;* 犯一嚴重的錯誤; *as ~ as a judge.* 像法官一樣嚴肅。*The situation is more ~/is ~r than it has been since the end of the war.* 戰爭結束以來,目前局勢爲最嚴重的時期。**~·ly** *adv*

grave[2] /greɪv ; grev/ *n* hole dug in the ground for a corpse; the mound of earth or the monument over it. 墓穴;墳墓;墓上建築物。***have one foot in the ~,*** be nearing death, be very old. 行將就木;十分年邁。**'~-clothes** *n pl* wrappings in which a corpse is buried. 死人所穿的衣服;壽衣。**'~·stone** *n* stone over a ~, with the name, etc of the person buried there. 墓碑。⇨ the illus at church. 參看 church 之插圖。**'~·yard** *n* burial ground. 墓地。

grave[3] /grɑ:v ; grɑv/ *n* (also 亦作 ~ **accent**) mark ` placed over a vowel to indicate how it is to be sounded (as in French *mère*). 抑音符(例如法文 mère 中之 `)。

grave[4] /greɪv ; grev/ *vt* (*pp* graven /'greɪvn;'grevən/) (archaic or liter) carve: (古或文)雕刻: ~*n on my memory*, indelibly fixed. 銘記心頭。ˌ**~n 'image,** an idol. 雕像;偶像。

gravel /'grævl ; 'grævḷ/ *n* [U] small stones with coarse sand, as used for roads and paths: (鋪路用的)砂礫;礫石;碎石和粗砂: *a load of ~;* 一車(擔等)碎石; (attrib) (形容用法) *a ~ path/pit.* 碎石路(坑)。**grav·elly** /'grævəlɪ ; 'grævḷɪ/ *adj* (of a voice) deep and rough. (指聲音)低沈而沙啞的。□ *vt* (-ll-, US also -l-) [VP6A] **1** cover with ~: 鋪碎石於: ~ *a road;* 鋪碎石於道路; ~*led paths.* 碎石路。**2** (colloq) perplex; puzzle. (俗)使困窘;使困惑。

grav·ing dock /'greɪvɪŋ dɒk ; 'grevɪŋ dɑk/ *n* dry dock in which the outside of a ship's hull may be cleaned. 乾船塢。

gravi·tate /'grævɪteɪt ; 'grævə,tet/ *vi* [VP3A] ~ ***to/towards,*** move or be attracted: 移動;被吸引: *Young people in the country districts seem to ~ towards the cities.* 鄉村的青年有向都市移動的趨勢。**gravi·tation** /ˌgrævɪ'teɪʃn ; ˌgrævə'teʃən/ *n* [U] process of gravitating; gravity(1). 吸引作用;萬有引力;地心吸力。

grav·ity /'grævətɪ ; 'grævətɪ/ *n*[U] **1** (phys) force of attraction between any two objects, esp that force which attracts objects towards the centre of the earth. (物理)萬有引力;(尤指)地心吸力;重力。**2** (phys) weight:(物理)重量: *centre of ~.* (物體的)重心。**speˌcific '~,** relation between the weight of a substance and that of the same volume of a standard substance (usu water for liquids and solids, and air for gases). 比重。 **3** quality of being serious or solemn: 嚴重;嚴肅: *the ~ of the international situation;* 國際局勢的嚴重; *the ~ of his appearance.* 他外表的嚴肅。*He could hardly keep his ~*, could with difficulty refrain from smiling or laughing. 他幾乎保持不住他莊重的態度(禁不住要笑)。

gra·vure /grə'vjʊə(r) ; 'grevjər/ *n* = photogravure.

gravy /'greɪvɪ ; 'grevɪ/ *n* [U] **1** juice which comes from meat while it is cooking; sauce made from this. 肉汁;調味肉汁。**'~-boat** *n* vessel in which ~ is served at table. 盛調味肉汁的器皿。**2** (sl) money or profit easily or unexpectedly acquired. (俚)輕易或意外獲得之錢財。**'~ train** *n* source of much and easy money, etc: 可輕易賺大錢的機會: *get on the ~ train*, get a job where such money, etc is easily acquired. 獲一可輕易賺大錢的工作。

gray /greɪ ; gre/ *adj, n* = grey.

graze[1] /greɪz ; grez/ *vi, vt* **1** [VP2A, C] (of cattle, sheep, etc) eat growing grass: (指牛羊等)吃青草: *cattle grazing in the fields.* 在田野中吃青草的牛群。**2** [VP6A] put (cattle, etc) in fields to ~: 放牧(牛羊等): ~ *sheep;* 放羊; use grassland for cattle: 用做牧地: ~ *a field.* 用一田野做牧地。**'grazing-land** *n* land used for grazing cattle. 放牧(牛羊之)草地。**graz·ier** /'greɪzɪə(r) *US:* 'greɪʒə(r) ; 'greʒɚ/ *n* person who feeds cattle for market. 畜牧業者。

graze[2] /greɪz ; grez/ *vt, vi* **1** [VP6A] touch or scrape lightly in passing; rub the skin from: 輕擦;擦去…之皮: *The bullet ~d his cheek.* 子彈擦傷了他面頰上的皮膚。 **2** [VP2C] pass and touch while going *against/along/by/past.* 經過時觸及;擦過。□ *n* place where the skin is ~d. 皮膚擦傷之處。

grease /gri:s ; gris/ *n* [U] **1** animal fat melted soft. 熔化之軟獸脂。 **2** any thick, semi-solid oily substance:油脂;滑脂:*'axle* ~, used to lubricate axles. 滑潤輪軸之油;車軸脂。**'~-gun** *n* device for forcing ~ into the parts of an engine, machine, etc. 滑脂槍(將油擠入引擎,機器等之一種裝置)。**'~-paint** *n* [U] mixture of ~ and paint used by actors to make up their faces. 演員化裝用之油彩。□ *vt* put or rub ~ on or in (esp parts of a machine). 塗以油;搽以油(尤指機器之各部分)。~ ***sb's palm,*** bribe him. 賄賂某人。**~r** *n* man who ~s machinery, eg a ship's engines. 搽油工人(例如爲船隻引擎搽油者)。

greasy /ˈgriːsɪ ; ˈgrisɪ/ *adj* (-ier, -iest) covered with grease; slippery: 塗有油脂的;油污的;油膩的;滑的: *~ fingers;* 油污的手指; *a ~ road.* 滑溜的道路。**greas·ily** /-ɪlɪ ; -əlɪ/ *adv* **greasi·ness** *n*

great /greɪt ; gret/ *adj* (-er, -est) **1** well above the average in size, quantity or degree: (體積,數量,程度)超過一般標準的;巨大的;很多的;非常的: *take ~ care of sth;* 對某物特別用心照顧(對某事特別審慎); *an essay that shows ~ ignorance of grammar;* 顯示出文法十分不通的一篇文章; *a ~ friend of mine,* one for whom I feel more than ordinary friendship. 我的一位親密的朋友。~ ***with child,*** (old use) pregnant. (舊用法)懷孕的。**'~-coat** *n* heavy overcoat. 厚大衣。**2** of remarkable ability or quality: 偉大的: *~ men;* 偉人; *a ~ painter / painting / musician.* 偉大的畫家(畫,音樂家)。**3** important; noted; of high rank or position: 重要的;著名的;地位高的: *a ~ occasion;* 重大的場合; *the G~ Powers of Europe;* 歐洲列强; *a ~ lady;* 貴婦人; *Alexander the G~.* 亞歷山大大帝。**4** (colloq, preceding another *adj* which is often weakly stressed; implying surprise, indignation, contempt, etc according to context): (俗)(用在另一個常輕讀的形容詞前;表示驚異,憤怒,輕蔑等,視上下文而定): *See what a ~ big fish I've caught!* 看我捉到多麼大的一條魚啊! *Take your ~ big head out of my light!* 把你的大頭移開,不要遮住我的光線! *What a ~ thick stick!* 多麼粗的一根棍子啊! **5** (also 亦作 **G~er**) used as a distinctive epithet of the larger of two. 用做區別性質的形容詞,指兩者中之較大者。**the G~ Bear,** ⇨ bear¹ (3). **G~ Britain,** (abbr 略作 **GB**) England, Wales and Scotland, excluding Northern Ireland. 英國;大不列顛(包括英格蘭,威爾斯與蘇格蘭,北愛爾蘭除外)。**the G~ Lakes,** series of five large lakes in N America along the boundary between Canada and the US. 大湖(加拿大與美國之間的五個大湖)。**G~er London,** an administrative area of local government that includes inner London and the outer suburbs. 大倫敦(包括倫敦市及其郊區)。**the G~ War,** that of 1914—18. 第一次世界大戰。**6** (attrib only) (僅作形容用法) fully deserving the name of: 應得…之名的: *He's a ~ liar.* 他是個名副其實的說謊者。*They are ~ friends.* 他們是眞正的朋友。**7** (with agent *nouns;* attrib only) doing or being sth to a high degree: (與表示動作者的名詞連用;僅作形容用法)非常的: *He's a ~ reader / eater,* reads / eats very much. 他書讀得很多(食量很大)。*He's a ~ landowner,* owns a large area of land. 他是個大地主。**8** combined with words indicating quantity, etc: 與表示數量等的字連用: *a ~ deal,* very much; 很多; *a ~ number;* 很多; *a ~ while ago;* 許久以前; *the ~ majority,* much the larger part. 大多數。**9** (colloq) splendid; satisfactory: (俗)絕妙的;快活的;令人滿意的: *We had a ~ time in Paris.* 我們在巴黎的那段時期很快樂。*Wouldn't it be ~ if we could go there again!* 如果我們能够再去那裏該多好啊! **10** (colloq; pred only) (俗;僅作敍述用法) ~ ***at,*** clever or skilful at. 擅長;精於。~ ***on,*** having a good knowledge of. 精通。**11** prefixed to a kinship words in *grand-* to show a further stage in relationship: 冠於以grand起首表示親屬之字前,以示更高或低一輩的親屬關係: ˌ~-ˈ*grandfather,* one's father's or mother's grandfather; 曾祖;外曾祖。ˌ~-ˈ*grandson,* grandson of one's son or daughter. 曾孫;外曾孫。**~·ly** *adv* much; by much: 很;非常: *~ly amused.* 很高興。**~·ness** *n*

greaves /griːvz ; grivz/ *n pl* pieces of armour to protect the shins. 護脛;脛甲。⇨ the illus at armour. 參看 armour 之插圖。

grebe /griːb ; grib/ *n* kind of short-bodied diving bird. 鸊鷉。⇨ the illus at water. 參看 water 之插圖。

Gre·cian /ˈgriːʃn ; ˈgriʃən/ *adj* (eg of architecture, pottery, culture and features of the face) Greek. (指建築,陶器,文化,面貌等)希臘的。

greed /griːd ; grid/ *n* [U] strong desire for more food, wealth, etc, esp for more than is right or reasonable. (對食物,財富等之)貪心;貪婪。

greedy /ˈgriːdɪ ; ˈgridɪ/ *adj* (-ier, -iest) **1** ~ ***(for sth / to have sth),*** filled with greed: 貪心的;貪婪的: *not hungry, just ~;* 不餓,祗是貪食而已; *looking at the cakes with ~ eyes;* 以貪婪的目光望着蛋糕; *~ for gain / honours.* 貪財(名)。**2** ~ ***(to do sth),*** intensely desirous. 渴望(做某事)的;急欲(做某事)的。**greed·ily** /-ɪlɪ ; -əlɪ/ *adv* **greedi·ness** *n*

Greek /griːk ; grik/ *n* [C] member of the Greek people, either of ancient Greece or modern Greece; [U] the Greek language. 希臘人;希臘語。***be ~ to one,*** be beyond one's understanding. 不能了解;完全不懂。□ *adj* of Greece, its people, or the Greek language. 希臘的;希臘人的;希臘語的。

green¹ /griːn ; grin/ *adj* (-er, -est) **1** of the colour between blue and yellow in the spectrum, the colour of growing grass, and the leaves of most plants and trees: 綠色的: *a ~ Christmas,* Christmas season when the weather is mild and there is no snow. 綠色的聖誕節(天氣溫暖,沒有下雪的聖誕節)。ˌ~ **ˈbelt,** wide area of land round a town, where building is controlled (by town-planning) so that there are ~ fields, woods, etc. 都市四周之綠化地帶(按都市計畫控制建築,故有綠野、樹林等)。***give sb / get the ~ light,*** (colloq, from the ~ of traffic lights) permission to go ahead with a project, etc. (俗,源於交通燈之綠燈) 准許某人(得到許可)照計畫等行事。**2** (of fruit) not yet ripe: (指水果)未成熟的: *~ apples;* 未熟的蘋果; *~ figs,* young and tender figs; 嫩無花果; (of wood) not yet dry enough for use: (指木材) 未乾燥的: *G~ wood does not burn well.* 未乾燥的木柴不易燃燒。**3** inexperienced; undeveloped; gullible; untrained: 無經驗的;未發展的;易受騙的;無訓練的: *a boy who is still ~ at his job.* 對其工作尙無經驗的青年。*I'm not so ~ as to believe that.* 我不會無知至相信那事。**4** (fig) flourishing; full of vigour: (喩)旺盛的;精力充沛的: *live to a ~ old age;* 老當益壯; *keep a person's memory ~,* not allow it to fade. 使記憶不忘。**5** (of the complexion) pale; sickly looking. (指臉色)蒼白的;有病容的。ˌ~-ˈ**eyed** *adj* jealous. 嫉妒的。**the** ˌ**~-eyed ˈmonster,** jealousy. 嫉妒。~ ***with envy,*** very envious. 非常嫉妒的。**6** (special uses and compounds): (特殊用法與複合字): **'~·back** *n* US banknote, the back printed in ~. 美鈔(背面印成綠色)。ˌ~ **ˈfingers** *n* (colloq) skill in gardening. (俗)園藝才能。**'~·fly** *n* (collective *pl;* [U]) kinds of aphis. (集合複數)綠蚜蟲;蚊鉤之一種。**'~-gage** /-geɪdʒ;-ˈgedʒ/ *n* kind of plum with greenish-yellow skin and flesh and fine flavour. 青梅。**'~·grocer** *n* shopkeeper selling vegetables and fruit. 賣蔬菜及水果的商人;果菜商。**'~·grocery** *n* (*pl* -ries) business of, things sold by, a ~grocer. 果菜業;蔬菜水果店;蔬菜水果類。**'~·horn** *n* inexperienced and easily deceived person. 無經驗易受騙的人。**'~-house** *n* building with sides and roof of glass, used for growing plants that need protection from the weather. 溫室;花房。**'~ room** *n* room in a theatre for actors and actresses when they are not on the stage. 演員休息室。**'~-stuffs, ~s** *n pl* ~ vegetables. 綠色蔬菜。**'~·sward** *n* [U] turf. 草皮。ˌ~ **ˈtea** *n* tea made from steam-dried leaves. 綠茶。**'~·wood** *n* woodlands, esp in summer; forest in full leaf, esp as the home of outlaws in olden times. 林地(尤指夏季者);青鬱的森林;綠林(尤指古時不法之徒落草之地)。

green² /griːn; grin/ *n* **1** [U, C] green colour; what is green: 綠色;綠色的東西: *a girl dressed in ~;* 著綠衣的女郎; *a picture in ~s and blues,* with various shades of ~ and blue. 以各種綠色和藍色繪成之圖畫。**2** (*pl*) green leaf vegetables, eg cabbage, spinach, before or after cooking; vegetation: (複)青菜(如未煮或煮過的甘藍,菠菜);植物: (US) (美) *Christmas ~s,* eg branches of fir and holly for decoration. 聖誕節結綵用的樹枝(例如樅樹和多青之樹枝)。**3** [C] area of land with growing grass. 草原;草地。**(a)** public or common land: 公有草地: *the village ~.* 村中公有草地。**(b)** for the game of bowls: 滾球戲所用的草地: *a 'bowling-~.* 滾球場。**(c)** surrounding a hole on a golf course: 高爾夫球場上球洞四周之草地: *a 'putting ~.* 穴周之輕打區域。

greenery /'griːnərɪ; 'grinərɪ/ *n* [U] green foliage; verdure: 綠葉;綠色草木;葱翠: *the ~ of the woods in spring.* 春天樹林的青葱。

greenish /'griːnɪʃ; 'grinɪʃ/ *adj* somewhat green: 淺綠色的;帶有綠色的: (in compounds) (用於複合字中) *,~-'yellow;* 黃綠色; *,~-'brown.* 褐綠色。**~·ness** *n*

Greenwich /'grenɪtʃ; 'grɪnɪdʒ/ *n* suburb of London, east and west of whose meridian longitude is measured. 格林尼治(倫敦一郊區,經度由該地作起點,向東西計算)。~ **'mean time** (abbr 略作 GMT), mean² time for the meridian of ~, used as a basis for calculating time in most parts of the world (now called 現稱作 *Universal time*). 格林尼治時間;世界標準時間。

greet /griːt; grit/ *vt* [VP6A, 14] ~ ***(with).*** **1** say words of welcome to; express one's feelings on receiving (news, etc); write (in a letter) words expressing respect, friendship, etc: 向某人致歡迎之詞;致候;獲悉(消息等)時而表現某種感情;(以書信)致敬: *~ a friend by saying 'Good morning!';* 向一友人道'早安'致候; *~ someone with a smile.* 含笑歡迎某人。*The news was ~ed with dismay.* 那消息令人驚慌。*They ~ed me with a shower of stones.* 他們紛紛向我投擲石頭。**2** (of sights and sounds) meet the eyes and ears: (指景象和聲音)映入眼簾;入耳: *the view that ~ed us at the hill-top.* 在山頂上收入我們眼底的景色。**~·ing** *n* first words used on seeing sb or in writing to sb; expression or act with which sb or sth is ~ed: 與人見面(寫信)時最初所說的話(所寫出的字);問候之詞;致候;致候之動作: *'Good morning' and 'Dear Sir' are ~ings;* '早安'與'敬啓者'爲問候和致敬之詞; *a '~ings telegram,* one sent with, eg birthday, ~ings. 賀電(例如祝賀生日者)。

greg·ari·ous /grɪ'geərɪəs; grɪ'gɛrɪəs/ *adj* living in groups or societies; liking the company of others. 群居的;合群的。**~·ly** *adv* **~·ness** *n*

Greg·or·ian /grɪ'gɔːrɪən; grɛ'gorɪən/ *adj* **1** ~ **chant,** the kind of church music (*plainsong*) named after Pope Gregory I (540–604). 格列高里聖歌(以教皇格列高里一世爲名之聖歌)。**2** ~ **calendar,** the calendar introduced by Pope Gregory XIII (1502–85), with the days and months arranged as now. 格列高里曆(教皇格列高里十三世所倡用,卽今之陽曆)。⇨ Julian.

grem·lin /'gremlɪn; 'grɛmlɪn/ *n* goblin said to cause mechanical trouble. (傳說可使機械發生故障的)小妖怪。

gre·nade /grɪ'neɪd; grɪ'ned/ *n* small bomb thrown by hand (*'hand-~*) or fired from a rifle (*'rifle-~*). 手榴彈;槍榴彈。

grena·dier /,grenə'dɪə(r); ,grɛnə'dɪr/ *n* (formerly) soldier who threw grenades; (昔時)手榴彈兵; (now) soldier in *the G~s, the G~ Guards,* British infantry regiment. (現今)英國近衞步兵團之士兵。

grew /gruː; gru/ *pt* of grow.

grey, gray /greɪ; gre/ *adj* between black and white, coloured like ashes, or the sky on a dull, cloudy day: 灰色的: *His hair has turned ~.* 他的頭髮已灰白。**'~·beard** *n* old man. 老人。**,~-'headed** *adj* old; of long service. 老的;服務久的。**'~ matter,** material of the brain: (腦的)灰白質: *a boy without much ~ matter,* a not very intelligent boy. 智力低的男孩。□ *n* [U, C] ~ colour; ~ clothes: 灰色;灰色衣服: *dressed in ~.* 着灰色衣服。□ *vt, vi* [VP 6A, 2A] make or become ~. 使成灰色;變爲灰色。

grey·hound /'greɪhaʊnd; 'gre,haʊnd/ *n* slender, long-legged, keen-sighted dog, able to run fast, used in chasing live hares and, as a modern sport (*~ racing*), mechanical hares moved along a rail. 靈猩(一種軀瘦,腿長,眼光銳利的獵犬,奔跑迅速,用以追野兔或在現代遊戲中用以追趕沿一軌道移動之機械假兔)。

grey·ish /'greɪɪʃ; 'greɪʃ/ *adj* somewhat grey. 帶灰色的;略灰的。

grid /grɪd; grɪd/ *n* [C] **1** system of overhead cables carried on pylons, for distributing electric current over a large area. (架設於鐵塔上,將電流輸送至廣大地區之)高壓輸電線路網。**2** network of squares on maps, numbered for reference. 地圖上的方格(標有號碼備參考)。**3** grating: 格子;柵欄: *a 'cattle ~,* one placed at a gate, etc designed to prevent cattle from straying on to a road, etc. 牛柵欄(裝於大門口等,以防牛走失者)。**4** frame of spaced parallel spirals or networks of wires in a radio valve. 眞空管中之柵極。**5** gridiron. 鐵格架子;烤架。

griddle /'grɪdl; 'grɪdl/ *n* circular iron plate used for baking cakes. (烤餅用的)淺鐵鍋。

grid·iron /'grɪdaɪən; 'grɪd,aɪəːn/ *n* **1** framework of metal bars used for cooking meat or fish over a clear fire. (架在明火上烤肉或魚用的)鐵格架子;烤架。**2** field for American football (marked with numerous parallel lines). 橄欖球場(標有許多平行線)。

grief /griːf; grif/ *n* **1** [U] deep or violent sorrow: 悲傷;憂傷: *driven almost insane by ~;* 因憂傷而幾乎瘋狂; *die of ~.* 憂傷而死。**2** [C] sth causing ~: 傷心事;令人悲傷之事物: *His taking to drugs was a great ~ to his parents.* 他的吸毒成癮是他父母的一大傷心事。**3** ***bring sb/come to ~,*** (cause sb to) meet with misfortune, injury or ruin. (使某人)遭受不幸,傷害或災難。

griev·ance /'griːvns; 'grivəns/ *n* [C] ~ ***(against),*** real or imagined cause for complaint or protest: 寃情;委屈;不滿: *The trade union leader spoke about the ~s of the workers.* 工會的領袖述說工人們的苦情。

grieve /griːv; griv/ *vt, vi* **1** [VP6A] cause grief to: 使悲傷: *~ one's parents.* 使父母傷心。**2** [VP2A, C] feel grief: 悲傷;傷心: *~ for the dead/over sb's death;* 爲死者(某人之死)感到悲傷; *~ about one's misfortunes/at bad news.* 因不幸(噩耗)而悲傷。

griev·ous /'griːvəs; 'grivəs/ *adj* **1** causing grief or suffering: 令人悲傷或痛苦的: *a ~ railway accident;* 悲慘的火車車禍; *~ wrongs.* 令人痛心的過失。**2** severe: 嚴重的: *~ pain;* 劇痛; *~ bodily harm.* (法律)嚴重的人身傷害。**~·ly** *adv*

grif·fin /'grɪfɪn; 'grɪfɪn/ (also 亦作 **grif·fon, gry·phon** /'grɪfən; 'grɪfən/) *n* (Gk myth) fabulous creature with the head and wings of an eagle and a lion's body. (希神)傳說中頭翼似鷹,軀體似獅之怪獸。⇨ the illus at armour. 參看 armour 之挿圖。

grill /grɪl; grɪl/ *n* [C] **1** grating; grille; gridiron. 鐵格子;鐵格窗;烤架。**2** dish of meat, etc cooked directly over or under great heat: 燒烤食品: *a mixed ~,* steak, liver, bacon, etc. 什錦烤肉(牛排,肝,鹹肉等)。**3** (also 亦作 **'~-room**) room (in a hotel or restaurant) where ~s are cooked and served. (飯店或餐館中之)烤肉間。□ *vt, vi* **1** [VP6A, 2A, C] cook, be cooked, on a gridiron, or over great heat; expose oneself to great heat: 烤;受烤;炙;使自己受酷熱之苦: *lie ~ing in the hot sun.* 臥於酷熱的陽光下。**2** [VP6A] (eg of the police) question closely and severely. (指警察等)嚴加盤問。

grille /grɪl ; grɪl/ *n* screen of parallel bars used to close an open space, eg in a convent; similar screen over a counter, eg in a post office or bank as a protection. 鐵柵(例如裝於修女院門上者); (郵局或銀行等)櫃臺前之格柵。

grim /grɪm ; grɪm/ *adj* (-mmer, -mmest) stern; severe; forbidding; without mercy: 嚴厲的;嚴格的;險惡的;冷酷的: *a ~ struggle;* 生死之鬭; *a ~ smile/expression;* 獰笑(冷酷的表情); *looking ~;* 表情冷酷; *a ~ joke/story,* one with an element of cruelty in it. 內容有殘忍成分的笑話(故事)。**hold on like ~ death,** very firmly. 堅持。**~·ly** *adv* **~·ness** *n*

gri·mace /grɪˈmeɪs *US:* ˈgrɪmɪs ; grɪˈmes/ *n* [C] ugly, twisted expression (on the face), expressing pain, disgust, etc or intended to cause laughter. (表示痛苦,厭惡等,或欲使人發笑之)面部的歪扭;苦相;鬼臉。□ *vi* [VP2A] make ~s. 扮鬼臉。

grime /graɪm ; graɪm/ *n* [U] dirt, esp a coating on the surface of sth or on the body: 汚穢物(尤指東西或身體表面之一層汚穢物): *the soot and ~ of a big manufacturing town;* 大工業城市的煤煙與塵垢; *a face covered with ~ and sweat.* 滿是汚垢與汗水的面孔。□ *vt* [VP6A] make dirty with ~: 使覆有汚穢物;使髒: *~d with dust.* 被灰塵弄髒。**grimy** /ˈgraɪmɪ ; ˈgraɪmɪ/ *adj* (-ier, -iest) covered with ~: 覆有汚穢物的;骯髒的: *grimy faces/roofs/windows.* 骯髒的面孔(屋頂,窗戶)。

grin /grɪn ; grɪn/ *vi, vt* (-nn-) **1** [VP2A, C] smile broadly so as to show the teeth, expressing amusement, foolish satisfaction, contempt, etc: 露齒而笑(表示高興,愚蠢的滿足,輕蔑等): *~ning with delight;* 高興得露齒而笑; *~ from ear to ear.* 咧着嘴笑。**~ and bear it,** endure pain, disappointment, etc, uncomplainingly. 不抱怨地忍受痛苦,失望等;逆來順受。**2** [VP6A] express by ~ning: 露齒笑着表示: *He ~ned his approval.* 他露齒一笑表示贊許。□ *n* [C] act of ~ning: 露齒笑: *the tigerish ~ on the murderer's face;* 那兇手之露齒獰笑; *~s of derision.* 露齒嘲笑。

grind /graɪnd ; graɪnd/ *vt, vi* (*pt, pp* ground /graʊnd ; graund/) **1** [VP6A, 15A, B] **~ (down) (to/into),** crush to grains or powder between millstones, the teeth, etc: (用磨,牙齒等)磨碎;磨成粉狀;嚼碎: *~ sth to pieces;* 將某物磨碎; *~ sth down;* 碾碎某物; *~ coffee beans;* 磨碎咖啡豆; *~ wheat in a mill;* 用磨粉機磨小麥; *~ corn into flour.* 將穀磨成粉。**2** [VP2A, C] be capable of ~ing: 可被磨碎;可磨成粉狀: *This wheat ~s well.* 這種小麥易磨成粉。*This wheat will not ~ fine,* cannot be ground fine. 這種小麥沒法子磨細。**3** [VP6A] produce in this way: 磨成;碾成: *~ flour.* 磨成麵粉。**4** [VP6A, 15A, B] **~ (down),** (usu passive) (fig) oppress or crush: (通常用被動語態) (喻) 壓迫;折磨: *people who were ground (down) by poverty/taxation/tyranny;* 受窮困(苛稅,暴政)折磨的人民; *tyrants who grind down the poor.* 壓搾貧民的暴君。**5** [VP6A] polish or sharpen by rubbing on or with a rough, hard surface: 磨光;磨尖銳: *~ a knife/lens.* 磨刀(鏡片)。**have an axe to ~,** ⇨ axe. **6** [VP6A, 15A, B] rub harshly together, esp with a circular motion: 摩擦(尤指旋轉摩擦): *~ one's teeth (together);* 切齒;磨牙齒; *a ship ~ing on the rocks;* 觸礁的船; *~ one's heel into the ground.* 用脚跟碾地。**~ to a halt,** (of a vehicle) stop noisily (with brakes that ~); (fig) (of a process) stop slowly: (指車輛)嘎的一聲煞住; (喻) (指過程) 慢慢停止: *The strikes brought industry ~ing to a halt.* 罷工使工業逐漸停頓。**7** [VP6A,15A] work by turning; produce by turning: 轉動;旋轉而生: *~ a hand-mill/coffee-mill/barrel-organ;* 轉動手磨機(咖啡磨,筒風琴); *~ out a tune on an organ;* 用筒風琴奏出一曲; (fig) (喻) *~ out some verses,* produce them slowly and with effort. 搜索枯腸作成幾句詩。**8** [VP2C, 15B] **~ (away)(at),** (cause to) work or study hard and long: (使)刻苦用功: *~ away at one's studies;* 用功讀書; *~ for an exam.* 刻苦用功準備考試。□ *n* (colloq) long, monotonous task: (俗)長期而枯燥的工作: *the examination ~,* the task of preparing for an examination. 長期辛苦的準備考試。*Do you find learning English a ~?* 你覺得學習英文是件苦事嗎?

grinder /ˈgraɪndə(r) ; ˈgraɪndɚ/ *n* **1** thing that grinds, eg a molar tooth, apparatus for grinding coffee: 研磨之物; 研磨機(例如臼齒,磨咖啡機): *a ˈcoffee-~.* 磨咖啡機。**2** (in compounds) person who grinds: (用於複合字中)研磨者;磨光者;轉動者: *a ˈknife-~;* 磨刀人; *an ˈorgan-~,* person who produces tunes by turning the handle of a barrel-organ. 搖動筒風琴奏曲者。

grind·stone /ˈgraɪndstəʊn ; ˈgraɪndˌston/ *n* stone shaped like a wheel, turned on an axle, used for sharpening tools. 磨石。**keep sb's nose to the ~,** force him to work hard without rest. 使某人不停地勞動。

grip /grɪp ; grɪp/ *vt, vi* (-pp-) [VP6A, 2A] take and keep a firm hold of; seize firmly: 緊握;抓緊: *The frightened child ~ped its mother's hand.* 那受驚的孩子緊抓住他母親的手。*The brakes failed to ~ and the car ran into a wall.* 煞車失靈,汽車撞在一堵牆上。*The speaker ~ped the attention of his audience.* 演說者吸引住聽衆的注意力。*The film is a ~ping story of love and hate.* 這電影是一個扣人心弦的愛與恨的故事。□ *n* **1** (*sing* only except as shown) act, manner, or power of ~ping: (除見於下列句中之外,僅作單數)緊握;抓緊;緊握的方式;緊握力: *let go one's ~ of sth;* 鬆開所握之物; *take a ~ on a rope;* 抓緊一繩索; *have a good ~* (fig, = understanding) *of a problem;* (喻)深入了解一問題; *have a good ~ on an audience,* hold their attention and interest. 能吸引聽衆的注意力和興趣。**be at ~s with; come/get to ~s with,** be attacking, begin to attack, in earnest; be in close combat: 猛攻;(與…)肉搏: *get to ~s with a problem.* 認眞處理一難題。**take a ˈ~ on oneself,** (colloq) stop being idle and inattentive. (俗)不再懶散;集中注意力。**2** [C] (in a machine, etc) part that ~s or clips; clutch; part that is to be ~ped. (機器等之)把手;柄;夾。**3** [C] (also 亦作 **ˈ~·sack**) (US) traveller's handbag: (美)旅行袋;手提包: *a leather ~.* 皮製旅行袋。

gripes /graɪps ; graɪps/ *n pl* **(the) ~,** (colloq) violent pains in the abdomen. (俗)肚子痛;腹絞痛。

grippe /griːp ; grɪp/ *n* **the ~,** influenza. 流行性感冒。

gris·ly /ˈgrɪzlɪ ; ˈgrɪzlɪ/ *adj* causing horror or terror; ghastly. 恐怖的;可怕的。

grist /grɪst ; grɪst/ *n* [U] grain to be ground (chiefly in fig phrases). 準備磨成粉的穀物(主要用於比喻的詞句中)。**It's all ~ to the mill; All is ~ that comes to his mill,** (prov) He makes use of everything. (諺)他善於利用每件事物。

gristle /ˈgrɪsl ; ˈgrɪsl/ *n* [U] tough, elastic tissue in animal bodies, esp in meat: 軟骨;脆骨(尤指食用肉中者): *I can't eat this meat—it's all ~.* 我不能吃這肉 — 它全是軟骨。

grit /grɪt ; grɪt/ *n* [U] **1** (collective *sing*) tiny, hard bits of stone, sand, etc: (集合單數)砂礫: *spread ~ on icy roads.* 撒砂礫於覆有冰的道路。*I've got some ~ in my shoe.* 我鞋子裏進去了一些砂子。**2** quality of courage and endurance: 勇氣和耐力: *The soldiers showed that they had plenty of ~.* 那些兵士表現得很有勇氣和耐力。□ *vt* (-tt-) **~ one's teeth,** keep one's jaws tight together; (fig) show courage and endurance. 咬緊牙關;(喻)勇敢堅忍。**~ty** *adj* (-ier, -iest) of or like ~(1): 砂礫的;似砂礫的: *The sandstorm made the food ~ty.* 大風砂使這食物盡是砂子。

grits /grɪts ; grɪts/ *n pl* husked but unground oats; coarse oatmeal. 去殼而未碾細的燕麥;粗燕麥片。

grizzle /ˈgrɪzl; ˈgrɪzl̩/ *vi* (colloq) (esp of children) cry fretfully. (俗) (尤指兒童) 號哭。

griz·zled /ˈgrɪzld; ˈgrɪzl̩d/ *adj* grey; grey-haired. 灰色的;灰色頭髮的。

griz·zly /ˈgrɪzlɪ; ˈgrɪzlɪ/ *n* (also 亦作 ~ **bear**) large, fierce grey bear of N America. 北美的兇猛的大灰熊。⇨ the illus at bear. 參看 bear 之插圖。

groan /grəʊn; gron/ *vi, vt* **1** [VP2A, C] make a deep sound forced out by pain, or expressing despair or distress: 呻吟: *The wounded men lay there ~ing, with no one to help them.* 受傷的人們躺在那裏呻吟,而無人去救助他們。*The teacher ~ed with dismay.* 那老師因驚慌而呻吟。*The people ~ed under injustice.* 人民受盡了不公正的壓迫。 **2** [VP 2A, C] (of things) make a noise like that of ~ing: (指東西)作似呻吟之聲: *The ship's timbers ~ed during the storm.* 船骨在暴風雨中發出響聲。*The table ~ed with food,* (fig) was weighed down with large quantities of food. (喻)桌上擺滿大量食物,快把桌子壓垮了。 **3** [VP6A, 15B] ~ ***(out)***, express with ~ing: 呻吟着表示: *He ~ed out a sad story.* 他呻吟着說出一個悲慘的故事。 **4** [VP15B] ~ ***down***, silence by ~ing: 以似呻吟之聲使停止作聲: *The speaker was ~ed down by his audience,* They prevented him from being heard. 那演說者的聲音被聽衆起鬨的聲音壓倒了。□ *n* [C] deep sound made in ~ing: 呻吟;似呻吟之深沉聲: *the ~s of the injured men;* 傷者的呻吟; *give a ~ of dismay;* 發出驚慌的呻吟; *a speech interrupted by ~s of disapproval.* 被起鬨聲打斷的演說。

groat /grəʊt; grot/ *n* (hist) (14th to 17th cc) English silver coin worth fourpence. (史) (14至17世紀間)英國的銀幣(值四辨士)。

groats /grəʊts; grots/ *n pl* (crushed) grain, esp oats, that has been hulled. 去殼的穀(尤指燕麥);(去殼而壓碎的)燕麥片。

grocer /ˈgrəʊsə(r); ˈgrosɚ/ *n* shopkeeper who sells food in packets, tins, or bottles, and general small household requirements. 雜貨商(販賣包裝,罐裝及瓶裝食品,以及一般零星家庭必需品)。**~y** *n* **1** [U] ~'s trade: 雜貨業: *a ˈ~y business.* 雜貨店。 **2** (*pl*) **~ies**, things sold by a ~. (複)雜貨。

grog /grɒg; grɑg/ *n* [U] (a word used by sailors) drink of spirits mixed with water. (船員用語)酒(烈酒與水的混合飲料)。

groggy /ˈgrɒgɪ; ˈgrɑgɪ/ *adj* (-ier, -iest) **1** unsteady; likely to collapse or fall: 不穩的;搖搖欲墜的: *The legs of that chair look rather ~.* 那椅子的腿看來很不穩。 **2** weak and unsteady as the result of illness, shock, lack of sleep, etc: (因生病,震驚,缺少睡眠等而顯得)軟弱的: *That last attack of flu left me rather ~.* 上次患流行性感冒使我頗爲軟弱無力。

groin /grɔɪn; grɔɪn/ *n* **1** depression between the stomach and the thigh. 鼠蹊(腹與股間之凹處)。⇨ the illus at trunk. 參看 trunk 之挿圖。**2** (archit) curved edge where two vaults meet (in a roof). (建築)弧稜;穹稜;穹窿交接線。⇨ the illus at church. 參看 church 之挿圖。 **3** (US) = groyne. □ *vt* build with ~s. 使成弧稜。

groom /gru:m; grum/ *n* **1** person in charge of horses. 馬夫。 **2** bridegroom. 新郎。□ *vt* [VP6A] **1** feed, brush and in other ways look after (horses); (of apes, monkeys) clean the fur and skin of: 餵(馬);刷(馬);照看(馬);(指猿、猴)清理…之毛皮: *a female ape ~ing her mate.* 清理其伴侶毛皮之母猿。 **2** (usu in the *pp*, of persons): (通常用過去分詞,指人): *well/badly ~ed,* well/badly dressed (esp of the hair, beard and clothes). 修飾得好(不好)(尤指髮,鬍鬚與衣服)。 **3** (colloq) prepare (sb for a career, etc). (俗)準備(讓某人從事某一事業等);推薦;培植。

groove /gru:v; gruv/ *n* **1** long, hollow channel in the surface of hard material, esp one made to guide the motion of sth that slides along it, eg a sliding door or window; spiral cut on a gramophone disc (in which the needle or stylus moves). 溝; 凹槽 (尤指可使物體在上面滑動者,如使門窗滑動的槽);唱片上的紋路。 **2** way of living that has become a habit. 生活習慣。***get into/be stuck in a ~***, become set in one's ways, one's style of living. 養成一種習慣。 ***in the ~***, (dated sl) in the right mood (for sth); exhilarated. (過時俚語)有心情(做某事);興高采烈。□ *vt* make ~s in: 作槽於: *a ~d shelf.* 有槽的架子。**~r** *n* (sl) up-to-date person. (俚)時髦的人。**groovy** *adj* (sl) up-to-date; in the latest fashion (esp of young people): (俚)新式的;時髦的(尤指年輕人): *a groovy restaurant;* 新式的餐館; *groovy clothes/people.* 時髦的衣服(人)。

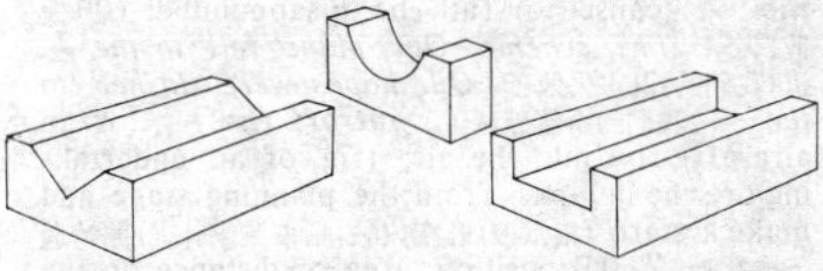

grooves

grope /grəʊp; grop/ *vi, vt* [VP2A, C, 3A, 15A] ~ ***(about) (for/after)***, (lit or fig) feel or search about as one does in the dark: (字面或喻)摸索;搜尋: *~ for the door-handle/the light switch/an answer.* 摸索着找門柄(電燈開關,搜尋答案)。 *We ~d our way along the dark corridor.* 我們在黑暗的走廊上摸索着走。 **grop·ing·ly** *adv* in the manner of one who ~s. 摸索着。

gross[1] /grəʊs; gros/ *n* (*pl* unchanged) twelve dozen; 144. (複數不變)十二打;籮。⇨ App 4. 參看附錄四。

gross[2] /grəʊs; gros/ *adj* **1** vulgar; not refined; coarse in mind or morals: 粗鄙的;不雅的;粗野的: *~ language/jokes/morals.* 粗鄙的言語(笑話,品行)。 **2** (of food) coarse, greasy; liking such food: (指食物) 粗糙而油膩的;喜歡粗糙而油膩之食物的: *a ~ eater.* 喜歡粗糙而油膩之食物者。 **3** (of the senses) heavy and dull. (指感覺)遲鈍的。 **4** flagrant; glaring; clearly seen: 罪惡昭彰的;顯著的;易見的: *~ injustice/negligence;* 顯著的不公(疏忽); *a ~ error/overcharge.* 顯然的錯誤(索價過高)。 **5** (of vegetation) luxuriant: (指草木)茂密的: *the ~ vegetation of the tropical rain forest.* 熱帶雨林中茂密的植物。 **6** (of persons) repulsively fat. (指人)過於肥胖的。 **7** (opposite of *net*) total, whole: (爲 net 之相反字) 全部的;整個的;總的;毛的: *the ~ amount;* 總額; *his ~ income.* 他的全部收入。~ **national product** (abbr 略作 **GNP**), annual total value of goods produced, and services provided, in a country. 國民生產毛額。 **8** ***in (the) ~***, wholesale; in bulk; in a general way. 批發;大體上;一般地。□ *vt* [VP6A] make as a total amount: 總共賺得: *His last film ~ed five million pounds.* 他最後製的影片總共獲利五百萬鎊。 **~·ly** *adv* extremely: 極度地;十分地: *~ly unfair/fat.* 極不公平(十分肥胖)。**~·ness** *n*

grot /grɒt; grɑt/ *n* (poet) grotto. (詩)洞穴;洞室。

gro·tesque /grəʊˈtesk; groˈtɛsk/ *adj* **1** absurd; fantastic; laughable because strange and incongruous: 可笑的;怪誕的;因古怪與不協調而可笑的: *a ~ appearance;* 可笑的外表; *~ manners.* 古怪的樣子。 **2** (in art) combining human, animal and plant forms in a fantastic way; made up of comically distorted figures and designs. (藝術)奇形怪狀的;滑稽奇異的。□ *n* **1** ~ person, animal, figure or design. 奇形怪狀的人,動物,圖形或圖案。 **2** ***the ~***, painting, carving, etc in which the ~ style appears. 怪異的圖畫,雕刻等。**~·ly** *adv* **~·ness** *n*

grotto /ˈgrɒtəʊ; ˈgrɑto/ *n* (*pl* ~es, ~s /-təʊz; -toz/) cave, esp one made artificially as a garden shelter. 洞穴;(尤指)花園中的人造洞室。

grotty /ˈgrɒtɪ; ˈgrɑtɪ/ *adj* (sl) unpleasant; ugly. (俚)令人不悅的;難看的。

grouch /graʊtʃ; graʊtʃ/ *vi* (colloq) complain. (俗)

抱怨。□ *n* fit of ill temper; sulky, discontented person.愠怒;愠怒的人;愛發牢騷的人。~**y** *adj* sullenly discontented. 愠怒的;不滿的。

ground[1] /graʊnd ; graʊnd/ *n* **1 the ~,** solid surface of the earth: 地面: *lie on/sit on/fall to the ~;* 躺在(坐在,落在)地上; (in compounds): (用於複合字中): *~-to-air missiles,* fired from the ~ (at aircraft). (自地面向天空射擊飛機的)地對空飛彈。*The airliner made a ~-controlled approach,* approached the runway directed by the control tower. 該客機作由地面控制的降落 (由人在塔台引導飛機降於跑道)。**above ~,** alive. 活着。**below ~,** dead and buried. 死掉被埋葬。**fall/be dashed to the ~,** (cause to) fail, be disappointed: (使)失敗;失望: *The scheme/Our plans fell to the ~.* 這(我們的)計畫失敗了。*Our hopes were dashed to the ~.* 我們的希望破滅了。**get off the ~,** (of an aircraft) rise into the air; (fig, of an undertaking or scheme) pass from the planning stage and make a start. (指飛機)升空;(喻,指事業或計畫)開始進行或行動。**2** [U] position, area or distance on the earth's surface. 在地面上的位置,區域或距離。**cut the ~ from under sb's feet,** anticipate his plans, arguments, defences, etc and in this way embarrass him. 先發制人;使某人之計畫、論據、答辯等失去憑藉;使站不住腳。**cover (much, etc) ~, (a)** travel: 旅行: *We've covered a great deal of ~ today,* have come a long way. 我們今天走了很長一段路。**(b)** (fig, of a lecture, report, inquiry, etc) deal with a variety of subjects; be far-reaching: (喻,指演說,報告,詢問等)牽涉許多問題;範圍很廣: *The committee's report covers much new ~,* deals with many new matters. 委員會的報告涉及許多新問題。**gain ~,** make progress; win a success or an advantage. 進步;前進;獲勝;獲利。**give/lose ~,** retreat; fail to keep one's position or advantage. 撤退;讓步。**hold/stand/keep one's ~,** stand firm; not yield; maintain one's claim, intention, argument, etc. 堅守;不讓步;堅持立場。**shift one's ~,** change one's argument, etc. 改變立場。**suit sb down to the ~,** suit him thoroughly: 十分適合某人: *Her new hairstyle/job suits her down to the ~.* 她的新髮型(工作)很適合她。**common ~,** subject on which two or more persons or parties are in agreement or on which they have similar views. (兩個以上的人或團體之間的) 一致之處; 共同的立場。**forbidden ~,** subject that must be avoided. 必須避免的問題;犯忌諱的論題。**3** [U] soil; earth: 泥土;土地: *till the ~.* 耕地。*The frost has made the ~ hard.* 嚴寒使土地凍硬了。**break fresh/new ~, (a)** cultivate land that has not been cultivated before. 開墾處女地。**(b)** (fig) do sth new; deal with a subject for the first time. (喻) 着手一新事業;初次處理一問題。**4** [C] area or piece of land for a special purpose or a particular use: 場地(供特殊用途的一塊地): *a 'football/'cricket/'sports ~;* 足球(板球,運動)場; *a pa'rade/ˌrecre'ation ~;* 校閱場(娛樂場); *a 'play~;* 運動場;遊戲場; *'hunting/'fishing-~s,* areas used for hunting/fishing. 狩獵場(漁場)。**5** (always *pl*) land, gardens, round a building, often enclosed with walls, hedges or fences: (經常用複數) 房屋四周的土地和花園 (常用牆或籬圍起);庭園: *the ~s of Buckingham Palace.* 白金漢宮的庭園。*The mansion has extensive ~s.* 這大廈四周的庭園廣闊。**6** [U] bottom of the sea or of any other body of water: 海底;水底: (chiefly in) (主要用於) **touch ~,** (of a ship) strike the bottom. (指船)達水底;擱淺。⇨ aground. **7** (*pl*) particles of solid matter that sink to the bottom of a liquid: (複)渣滓;沉澱物: (esp) (尤用於) *'coffee-~s.* 咖啡渣滓。**8** (*pl* 複 or [U]) reason(s) for saying, doing or believing sth. 理由;根據。**be/give/have ~s for,** be/give/have a cause or reason for: 有…之理由: *There are no ~s for anxiety.* 沒有理由憂慮。*I have good ~s for believing his version of events.* 我有相當理由相信他對事件的說明。*They don't give me much ~/many ~s for complaint.* 我沒有理由抱怨他們。*What are the ~s for divorce in this country,* What is recognized as a basis for an action of divorce? 在這個國家那些理由可離婚? **on the ~s of,** because of: 因為: *excused on the ~s of youth;* 因其年輕而被原諒; *reject a man on 'medical ~s.* 拒絕一個身體不合格的人。*On what ~s do you suspect him?* 你根據什麼懷疑他? **9** [C] surface on which a design is painted, printed, cut, etc; undecorated part: (圖案之繪製,印刷,雕刻等的)底子;板面: *a design of pink roses on a white ~.* 白底粉紅玫瑰的花樣。**10** (compounds) (複合字) **'~-bait** *n* [U] food thrown to the bottom of a fishing-~ to attract fish. 投入水底誘魚之餌。**'~-fish** *n* fish living at or near the bottom. 生活於水底之魚。ˌ**~ 'floor** *n* the floor of a building level with the ~. 建築物平地面的一層;地面層;一樓。**be/get in on the ~ floor,** (colloq) join an enterprise at its beginning. (俗)從某企業開始創立時卽已加入。**'~·nut** *n* kind of pea with pods ripening under the ~ (also called *earthnut* and *peanut*). 落花生(亦稱作 earthnut 和 peanut)。**'~-plan** *n* plan of a building at ~ level. 房屋的底層平面圖。**'~-rent** *n* rent paid for the use of land leased for building. (租用土地蓋房屋的)地租。**~s·man** /-mən ; -mən/ *n* (*pl* -men) man employed to look after a cricket ~. 板球場管理員。**'~·sheet** *n* waterproof sheet spread on the ~, eg under bedding in a tent. 鋪於地面之防水布(例如帳篷內鋪在被褥下面者)。**'~ speed** *n* aircraft's speed on the ~ (contrasted with *air speed*). (航空器之)地面速度(與 air speed 相對)。**'~ staff/crew** *n* mechanics who service aircraft on the ~; non-flying members of the staff of an airfield, etc. (修護飛機等的)地勤人員。**'~ swell** *n* [U] heavy, slow-moving waves caused by a distant or recent storm. 由遠處或剛過去的暴風引起的移動緩慢的巨浪;長浪。**'~-work** *n* [U] (usu fig) foundation; basis. (通常作喻)基礎;根基。

ground[2] /graʊnd ; graʊnd/ *vt, vi* **1** [VP6A, 2A] (of a ship) (cause to) touch the sea bottom; (of aircraft, airmen) compel to stay on the ground: (指船)(使)觸海底;擱淺; (指飛機,飛行員) 强迫停留在地面;停飛: *Our ship ~ed in shallow water.* 我們的船在淺水中擱淺了。*All aircraft at London Airport were ~ed by fog yesterday.* 倫敦機場的所有飛機在昨天因霧而被迫停飛。**2** [VP6A] ~ **arms,** (mil) lay (esp rifles) on the ground. (軍)將(尤指步槍)放在地上。**3** [VP14] ~ **sth on sth,** base (the more usu word) (a belief, etc) on: 建立(信仰等)於(…之)基礎上 (較常用 base): ~ *one's arguments on facts;* 根據事實以立論: *a well-~ed theory.* 基礎穩固的學說。**4** [VP14] ~ **sb in sth,** give (sb) good teaching or basic training in: 給(某人)良好的教導或基本訓練: *The teacher ~ed his pupils in arithmetic.* 該教師給他的學生打下了良好的算術基礎。**5** [VP6A] connect (a piece of electrical apparatus) with the ~ as conductor, as a safety precaution (*earth* is the usu word). 使(電器)接地(以地面作爲導體,以策安全,通常用 earth);接地;通地。**~·ing** *n* thorough teaching of the elements of a subject: 對一科目在基礎上徹底的教授;基礎;底子: *a good ~ing in grammar.* 對於基本文法的良好的教授;良好的文法基礎。

ground[3] /graʊnd ; graʊnd/ *pt, pp* of grind: ~ *rice,* reduced to fine powder. 用米磨成的粉。**~ glass,** made non-transparent by grinding. 毛玻璃。

ground·less /'graʊndlɪs ; 'graʊndˌlɪs/ *adj* without foundation or good reason: 無根據的;無理由的: ~ *fears/anxieties/rumours.* 無理由的恐懼(無理由的焦慮;無根據的謠言)。⇨ ground[1](8).

ground·sel /'graʊnsl ; 'graʊnsl̩/ *n* [U] kinds of weed, the commonest kind of which is used as food for some cage-birds. 禀吾屬之雜草 (最普通者常用以飼鳥)。

group /gruːp ; grup/ *n* [C] number of persons or things gathered or placed together, or naturally associated; number of jointly-controlled business companies, eg as the result of a merger: 群;團體;組;類;公司的聯合組織(例如由於合併之結果): *a ~ of girls/trees/houses;* 一群女孩子(一片樹;一片房屋); *people standing about in small ~s;* 三五成群散立着的人們; *the Germanic ~ of languages.* 日耳曼語系。ˈ**G~ captain,** Air Force officer. (英國)空軍上校。□ *vt, vi* [VP6A, 15A, B, 2C] form into, gather in, a ~ or ~s: 使成群;集合;類集: *The police ~ed (themselves) round the demonstrators.* 警察圍聚在示威者的四周。*G~ the roses together.* 將薔薇集在一起。

grouse[1] /graʊs ; graʊs/ *n* (*pl* unchanged) (複數不變) bird with feathered feet, shot for sport and food: 松鷄;松鷄類: ˈ*~ shooting,* the shooting of red ~ on the moors of Scotland and northern England. (在蘇格蘭與英格蘭北部之松鷄獵場上)獵紅松鷄。⇨ the illus at fowl. 參看 fowl 之插圖。

grouse[2] /graʊs ; graʊs/ *vi* [VP2A, C] (colloq) grumble; complain. (俗)抱怨;發牢騷。□ *n* complaint. 抱怨。

grove /grəʊv ; grov/ *n* group of trees; small wood. 樹叢;小樹林。

grovel /ˈgrɒvl ; ˈgrɑvl/ *vi* (-ll-; US also -l-) [VP 2A, C] lie down on one's face, crawl, in front of sb whom one fears, (as if) begging for mercy; (fig) humble oneself; behave in a way that shows one has no self-respect: 匍匐(作乞憐狀);(喻)奴顏婢膝;卑躬屈節: *~ at the feet of a conqueror.* 向征服者屈膝。**~·ler** *n* person who ~s. 奴顏婢膝者。

grow /grəʊ ; gro/ *vi, vt* (*pt* grew /gruː ; gru/, *pp* grown /grəʊn ; gron/) **1** [VP2A, C, D] develop; increase in size, height, length, etc: 發育;生長;長大;增長: *Rice ~s in warm climates.* 稻生長在溫暖的地區。*How quickly you are ~ing!* 你長得眞快啊! *How tall you've ~n!* 你長得好高啊! *She has decided to let her hair ~,* not have it cut short. 她已決定留頭髮。*A full-~n elephant is very large.* 長成了的象很大。*He has ~n into a fine young man.* 他已長成爲英俊的年輕小伙子。*Plants ~ from seeds.* 植物由種子長成。*She has ~n in stature but not in wisdom.* 她的身材長高了,但智慧沒有增加。*~ **out of,*** **(a)** become too big for: 長得太高大而不能: *~ out of one's clothes.* 長得高大而衣服穿不上了。**(b)** become too old for; cease to practise; abandon: 年齡增長而革除;停止做;戒絕: *He has ~n out of the bad habits of his boyhood days.* 他已長大,戒掉兒時的壞習慣了。**(c)** have as a source: 由…而生: *His troubles grew out of his bad temper.* 他的煩惱是由於他的壞脾氣所引起的。*~ **up,*** **(a)** (of persons, animals) reach the stage of full development; become adult or mature: (指人,動物)長大;成年;成熟: *When the boys ~ up....* 當孩子們長大時…。*He has a ~n-up son.* 他有一個成年的兒子。**(b)** develop: 發展: *A warm friendship grew up between the two men.* 溫暖的友誼在他們兩人之間滋長。ˈ**~·ing-pains** *n pl* **(a)** pains in the limbs of young children, popularly believed to be caused by rapid growth. 兒童或少年時期的一種關節痛(一般認爲係因發育迅速所導致)。**(b)** (fig) problems arising while a new enterprise is developing: (喻)新事業發展過程中所產生的問題: *The business is still suffering from ~ing pains.* 這事業仍面臨許多難題。ˈ**~n-up** /ˈgrəʊnʌp ; ˈgronˌʌp/ *n* [C] adult person (contrasted with a child). 成年人(與 child 相對)。□ *adj* adult; mature. 成年的;成熟的。**2** [VP2D] become: 變成;逐漸: *~ older;* 漸老; *~ smaller.* 漸小。*It began to ~ dark.* 天漸漸暗了。**3** [VP4A] *~ **to be/like, etc,*** reach the point or stage where one is/likes, etc: 達到某一點或階段;達到喜歡的程度: *One ~s to like what one is accustomed to.* 人漸漸會喜歡所習慣的事物。*My friendship with them grew to be* (= by degrees became) *considerable.* 我與他們間的友誼漸增。**4** [VP6A, 12B, 13B] cause or allow to ~: 使生長;種植;蓄;留: *~ roses.* 種玫瑰。*He's ~ing a beard.* 他留鬍鬚。*Will you ~ some herbs for me/~ me some herbs this year?* 你今年爲我種些香草好嗎? **5** [VP3A] *~ **on/upon,*** **(a)** become more deeply rooted: 變爲更根深蒂固: *a habit that ~s on you.* 在你身上日益根深蒂固的習慣。**(b)** come to have a greater attraction for; win the liking of: 更加吸引;受…的喜愛: *a book/a piece of music that ~s on you.* 你所喜愛的一本書(一支曲)。**~er** *n* **1** person who ~s things: 種植者: *a* ˈ*fruit-~er;* 種果木者; ˈ*rose-~ers.* 種薔薇者。**2** plant, etc that ~s in a certain way: 在某種方式下生長的植物等: *a free/rapid ~er.* 自由生長(生長快)的植物。

growl /graʊl ; graʊl/ *vi, vt* **1** [VP2A, C] (of animals, men, thunder) make a low, threatening sound: (指動物,人,雷)作低沉的怒吼聲;作隆隆聲: *The dog ~ed at me.* 那狗向我咆哮。*We heard thunder ~ing in the distance.* 我們聽見遠處隆隆的雷聲。**2** [VP6A, 15B] *~ **(out),*** say in a ~ing manner: 咆哮着說: *He ~ed (out) his answer.* 他咆哮着回答。□ *n* [C] low threatening sound; angry complaint. 低沉的怒吼;咆哮;忿忿不平。**~·ing·ly** *adv*

growler /ˈgraʊlə(r) ; ˈgraʊlɚ/ *n* (old colloq use) four-wheeled horse-drawn cab. (昔時口語用法)四輪馬車。

grown /grəʊn ; gron/ *pp* of grow: *a ~ man,* a mature man. 成人。

growth /grəʊθ ; groθ/ *n* **1** [U] growing; development; process of growing: 生長;發展;生長過程: *the rapid ~ of our economy.* 我們的經濟之迅速成長。*At what age does an elephant reach full ~,* its greatest size? 象到了幾歲才達到發育完成的階段? **2** [U] increase: 增加: ˈ*~ shares,* thought likely to increase in value. 有希望增值之股票。**3** [U] cultivation: 種植;栽培: *apples of foreign ~,* grown abroad. 外國產的蘋果。**4** [C] sth that grows or has grown: 生長物;長成物: *a thick ~ of weeds;* 濃密的野草; *a three-days' ~ of beard.* 長了三天的鬍鬚。**5** [C] diseased formation in the body, eg a cancer. 身體內部的腫瘤(例如癌)。

groyne (US=**groin**) /grɔɪn ; grɔɪn/ *n* [C] structure of wood, etc, or a low, broad wall of stone, concrete, etc built to prevent sand and pebbles from being washed away by the sea, the current of a river, etc. (木或石與三合土等作成的)丁堤;丁壩。

grub[1] /grʌb ; grʌb/ *n* **1** [C] larva of insect. 蠐螬;蛆。**2** [U] (sl) food. (俚)食物。

grub[2] /grʌb ; grʌb/ *vt, vi* (-bb-) [VP6A, 15B, 2C] turn over the soil, esp in order to get sth up or out: 挖土;掘(尤指爲掘出某物): *~bing up weeds.* 掘除雜草。*The pigs were ~bing about among the bushes.* 那些豬在樹叢中到處亂挖。

grubby /ˈgrʌbɪ ; ˈgrʌbɪ/ *adj* (-ier, -iest) **1** dirty; unwashed. 骯髒的;不潔的。**2** having grubs in it. 有蠐螬的。

grudge /grʌdʒ ; grʌdʒ/ *vt* [VP12A, 13A, 6C] be unwilling to give or allow: 不願給;吝惜: *I don't ~ him his success,* I admit that he deserves it. 我認爲他的成功是應該的。*His cruel master ~d him even the food he ate,* gave him his food unwillingly. 他那殘忍的主人甚至連他吃的食物也不大願意給他。*I ~ paying £2 for a bottle of wine that is not worth 50p.* 我不願爲一瓶不值五十辨士的酒付出二英鎊。□ *n* [C] feeling of ill-will, resentment, envy or spite: 惡意;怨恨;嫉妒;遺恨: *I bear him no ~.* 我對他沒有怨恨。*He has a ~ against me.* 他對我懷恨。*I owe that man a ~,* think I have good reason to feel ill-will towards him. 我有充分理由對那人懷恨。**grudg·ing·ly** *adv* in a grudging manner: 不情願地;吝惜地;勉强地: *His employer grudgingly raised his salary.* 他的雇主很勉强地替他加了薪。

gruel /ˈgruːəl ; ˈgruəl/ *n* [U] liquid food of oatmeal, etc boiled in milk or water. (用燕麥等煮於牛奶或

水中的)粥。

gruel·ling (US = **gruel·ing**) /ˈgruːəlɪŋ ; ˈgruəlɪŋ/ *adj* severe; exhausting: 嚴厲的;使人筋疲力竭的: *a ~ling race.* 令人筋疲力竭的競賽。

grue·some /ˈgruːsəm ; ˈgrusəm/ *adj* filling one with horror or disgust; frightful. 使人毛骨悚然的;討厭的;可怕的。**~·ly** *adv* **~·ness** *n*

gruff /grʌf ; grʌf/ *adj* (of a person, his voice, behaviour) rough; surly. (指人,聲音,行爲)粗野的;粗暴的。**~·ly** *adv* **~·ness** *n*

grumble /ˈgrʌmbl ; ˈgrʌmbḷ/ *vi, vt* **1** [VP2A, C, 3A] ~ ***(at/about/over sth),*** complain or protest in a bad-tempered way: 發怨言;鳴不平: *He's always grumbling.* 他老是發牢騷。*He ~d at the low pay offered to him.* 他抱怨給他的待遇低微。**2** [VP6A, 15B] ~ ***(out),*** say in a sullen, dissatisfied way: 抱怨地說出: ~ *(out) a reply.* 抱怨地回答。**3** [VP2A, C] make a low, growling sound: 作隆隆聲: *thunder grumbling in the distance.* 遠處隆隆的雷聲。□ *n* [C] (usu bad-tempered) complaint or protest: (通常爲壞脾氣的)怨言;不平: *That fellow is full of ~s.* 那傢伙滿腹牢騷。**grum·bler** /ˈgrʌmblə(r) ; ˈgrʌmblɚ/ *n* person who ~s. 埋怨者;發牢騷的人。

grumpy /ˈgrʌmpɪ ; ˈgrʌmpɪ/ *adj* (-ier, -iest) bad-tempered; surly. 脾氣壞的;脾氣暴躁的。**grump·ily** /-ɪlɪ ; -ɪlɪ/ *adv* **grumpi·ness** *n*

Grundy·ism /ˈgrʌndɪɪzm ; ˈgrʌndɪɪzm/ *n* [U] conventional propriety; prudery. 拘泥習俗;過分守禮。

grunt /grʌnt ; grʌnt/ *vi, vt* **1** [VP2A] (of animals, esp pigs) make a low, rough sound; (of persons) make a similar sound expressing disagreement, boredom, irritation, etc. (指動物,尤指豬)作咕嚕聲;(指人)發類似的哼聲(表示不滿,厭煩,激怒等)。**2** [VP 6A, 15B] ~ ***(out),*** utter in a ~ing way: 咕嚕地說出: ~ *(out) an answer.* 咕嚕着回答。□ *n* [C] low, rough sound. 咕嚕聲。

gry·phon /ˈgrɪfən ; ˈgrɪfən/ *n* = griffin.

guano /ˈgwɑːnəʊ ; ˈgwɑno/ *n* (*pl* -nos /-nəʊz ; -noz/) [C] dung dropped by sea-birds, used as fertilizer. 海鳥糞(用作肥料)。

guar·an·tee[1] /ˌgærənˈtiː ; ˌgærənˈti/ *n* [C] **1** (in law, **guaranty**) promise or undertaking (usu in writing or print) that certain conditions agreed to in a transaction will be fulfilled: (法律上用 guaranty) (交易中某些同意的條件將會實現的)保證;保證書: *a year's ~ with a watch,* a promise to keep it in good repair, etc. 手錶使用一年的保證。**2** (in law, **guaranty**) undertaking given by one person to another that he will be responsible for sth to be done, eg payment of a debt, by a third person. (法律上用 guaranty) 擔保;保證(某人將做某事,例如償還債務)。**3** (in law, **guarantor**) person who gives such an undertaking: (法律上用 guarantor)保證人;擔保人: *be ~ for a friend's good behaviour.* 保證一位朋友品行良好。*If I try to borrow £1000 from the bank, will you be my ~?* 如果我從銀行設法借一千鎊,你願做我的保證人嗎?**4** (in law, **guaranty**) sth offered, eg the deeds of a house or other document of ownership of property, as security for the fulfilling of conditions in a ~(1, 2): (法律上用 guaranty) 抵押品;作爲保證之物(例如房契或其他所有權狀): *'What ~ can you offer?' 'I can offer my house and land as a ~.'* '你能以什麼做抵押?' '我能以我的房屋和地產做抵押品。' **5** (colloq) sth that seems to make an occurrence likely: (俗)似乎使一事件可能發生的事物: *Blue skies are not always a ~ of fine weather.* 蔚藍的天空並不永遠保證晴朗的天氣。

guar·an·tee[2] /ˌgærənˈtiː ; ˌgærənˈti/ *vt* [VP6A, 7A, 25, 9, 12A, 13A] **1** give a guarantee (1, 2, 3) for (sth or sb): 保證;擔保: ~ *a man's debts;* 擔保一人的債務; ~ *to pay a man's debts;* 保證爲一人還債; ~ *that the debts will be paid;* 保證債會付清; ~ *the payment of the debts.* 保證償還債務。*We cannot ~ the punctual arrival of trains in foggy weather.* 霧天我們不能擔保火車準時到達。*This clock is ~d for one year.* 此鐘保用一年。*We can't ~ our workers regular employment.* 我們不能保證我們的工人經常受僱。**2** (colloq) promise (without legal obligation): (俗)約定;許諾(無法律上的義務): *Many shopkeepers ~ satisfaction to customers.* 許多商店老闆對顧客保證滿意。

guar·an·tor /ˌgærənˈtɔː(r) ; ˈgærəntɚ/ *n* (legal word for) guarantee(3). (法律名詞)保證人;擔保人。

guar·an·ty /ˈgærəntɪ ; ˈgærəntɪ/ *n* (legal word for) guarantee(1, 2, 4). (法律名詞)保證書;擔保;保證;抵押品;作爲保證之物。

guard[1] /gɑːd ; gɑrd/ *n* **1** [U] state of watchfulness against attack, danger or surprise: 警戒;戒守;守望: *The sentry/soldier is on ~,* at his post, on duty. 那哨兵(士兵)在擔任警戒。*The soldier was ordered to keep ~.* 那士兵奉命守望。**2** [U] attitude of readiness to defend oneself, eg in fencing, boxing, bayonet-drill. (劍術,拳擊,劈刺等)防禦的姿勢;防備。***be on/off one's ~,*** be prepared/unprepared against an attack or surprise: (未)戒備着: *Be on your ~ against pickpockets.* 謹防扒手。*He struck me while I was off my ~.* 他在我不提防時襲擊我。**3** [C] soldier or party of soldiers keeping ~; sentry. 衞兵;警衞隊;哨兵。***change ~,*** (mil) replace one ~ by another. (軍)換哨;換崗。Hence, 由此產生, ***the changing of the ~,*** eg at Buckingham Palace. 換崗(例如白金漢宮之更換警衞)。***mount ~,*** take up one's post as a sentry. 放哨;去站崗。***relieve ~,*** take the place of a sentry who has finished his period of duty. 接班(擔任警戒);換哨。***stand ~,*** act as a sentry. 當哨。**4** man (also called *warder*) or group of men in charge of a prison. 監獄之看守;典獄官(亦稱 warder)。**5** (GB) official in charge of a railway train (US 美 =*brakeman*). (英)(火車之)列車長。**6** (*pl*) **G~s,** (in GB and some other countries) troops employed originally to protect the sovereign: (複)(英國及某些國家之)禁衞軍;警衞部隊: *the G~s;* 禁衞隊; *the Royal Horse G~s;* 禁衞騎兵隊; *a G~s officer.* 禁衞隊軍官。**ˈ~s·man** /-mən ; -mən/ *n* (*pl* -men) soldier of the G~s. 禁衞隊之士兵。**7** [C] body of soldiers with the duty of protecting, honouring or escorting a person: 衞士隊;儀隊: *The Duke, on his arrival, inspected the ~ of honour at the station.* 公爵蒞臨時,在車站檢閱儀隊。⇨ also *rear~* at rear[1](4), *Home G~* at home[1](7). **8** (esp in compounds) (part of) an article or apparatus designed to prevent injury or loss: (尤用於複合字中)保護器;防護罩;防衞物: *a ˈfire-~,* in front of a fireplace; 圍護火爐的鐵絲網; *a ˈmud~* (over the wheel of a bicycle, etc); (腳踏車等的)擋泥板; *the ~ of a sword,* the part of the hilt that protects the hand. 劍的護手。**9** (compounds) (複合字) **ˈ~-boat** *n* one sent round a fleet of warships in harbour. 警戒艇;巡邏艇。**ˈ~·house** *n* (mil) building for a military ~ or one in which prisoners are kept. (軍)衞兵室;哨房;禁閉室。**ˈ~-rail** *n* rail, eg on a staircase, to prevent falling or (elsewhere) to prevent persons from danger, eg from traffic. (樓梯等處之)護欄。**ˈ~·room** *n* room for soldiers on ~ or for soldiers under ~. 衞兵室;禁閉室。**ˈ~-ship** *n* ship protecting a harbour. (保護港口之)警戒艦。

guard[2] /gɑːd ; gɑrd/ *vt, vi* **1** [VP6A, 15A] protect; keep from danger: 保護;保衞: ~ *a camp;* 守營; ~ *one's life/one's reputation;* 保護一人的生命(名譽); ~ *prisoners,* prevent them from escaping. 看守囚犯。**2** [VP3A] ~ ***against,*** use care and caution to prevent: 預防: ~ *against disease/bad habits/suspicion.* 預防疾病(杜絕惡習;避免嫌疑)。**~ed** *adj* (of statements, etc) cautious: (指言論等)謹慎的: *a ~ed answer;* 愼重的回答; *be ~ed in what one says.* 言語謹愼。**~·ed·ly** *adv* cautiously. 謹愼地。

guard·ian /ˈgɑːdɪən ; ˈgɑrdɪən/ *n* (official or private) person who guards, esp (legal use) one who is responsible for the care of a young or incapable person and his property. (官方或私人的)保護人;(尤指)(法律)監護人。ˌ~ **ˈangel**, spirit watching over a person or place. 守護神。**ˈ~·ship** /-ʃɪp; -ʃɪp/ *n* position or office of a ~. 監護人的職責。

guava /ˈgwɑːvə; ˈgwɑvə/ *n* (tropical tree with) pink edible fruit surrounded by a light yellow outer skin. (產於熱帶之)蕃石榴樹;蕃石榴(粉紅色果實,可食,有淺黃色外皮);芭樂。⇨ the illus at fruit. 參看 fruit 之插圖。

gu·ber·na·torial /ˌguːbənəˈtɔːrɪəl; ˌgjubɚnəˈtorɪəl/ *adj* (US, Nigeria, etc) of a (state) Governor. (美,奈及利亞等)州長的。

gudg·eon /ˈgʌdʒən; ˈgʌdʒən/ *n* small freshwater fish used as bait. 白楊魚(用以作餌的一種小淡水魚)。

guel·der rose /ˈgeldə rəʊz; ˈgɛldɚˌroz/ *n* plant with round bunches of white flowers; snowball tree. 雪球(生有一束束白花的一種植物)。

guer·rilla, guer·illa /gəˈrɪlə; gəˈrɪlə/ *n* person, not a member of a regular army, engaged in fighting in small, secret groups. 游擊隊員。~ **warfare** *n* [U] such fighting. 游擊戰。~ **war** *n* [C] war fought by ~s on one side or both sides. 游擊戰。**urban** ~ *n* ~ who operates in towns only. 都市游擊隊員。

guess /ges; gɛs/ *vt, vi* [VP6A, 25, 9, 8, 10, 2A, C, 3A] ~ ***(at)***, form an opinion, give an answer, make a statement, based on supposition, not on careful thought, calculation or definite knowledge: 猜想;臆測;推測: *Can you ~ my weight/what my weight is/how much I weigh?* 你能猜出我的體重嗎? *I should ~ his age at 50/~ him to be 50/~ that he is 50.* 我猜想他有五十歲了。*Can't you even ~ at her age?* 你甚至連她的年齡也猜不出嗎? *G~ what I'm thinking.* 你猜我在想些什麼。*You've ~ed right/wrong.* 你猜對(錯)了。*I ~* (US colloq 美俗= *suppose*) *you're right.* 我想你是對的。□ *n* [C] opinion formed by ~ing: 猜測: *make/have a ~ (at sth).* 猜想。*One man's ~ is as good as another's.* 無論誰的猜測都是一樣 (猜測終歸是猜測)。***it's anybody's ~***, no one can be sure about it. 此事無人能確定。***at a ~***, making a ~: 依猜測: *At a ~ I should say there were 50 people present.* 憑猜測我認為有五十人在場。***by ~***, by the use of ~ing: 憑推測: *Don't answer by ~; work the problem out.* 不要憑推測作答,把這個問題解出來。**ˈ~·timate** /ˈgestɪmət; ˈgɛstəmɪt/ *n* (modern colloq) estimate made by combining ~ing with reasoning. (現代俗語)(憑猜測的)估計。**ˈ~-work** *n* [U] ~ing; result of ~ing. 猜測;臆斷。

guest /gest; gɛst/ *n* person staying at or paying a visit to another's house or being entertained at a meal: 賓客;客人: *We're expecting ~s to dinner.* 我們在等候着客人進餐。**ˈ~·room** *n* bedroom kept for the use of ~s. 供賓客留宿的寢室。**ˈ~·house** *n* boarding-house. 上等寄宿舍;賓館。**ˈ~-night** *n* evening on which members of a club, college, mess², etc may bring in and entertain their friends as ~s. (俱樂部,學院等)招待來賓之夜晚。**ˌpaying ˈ~** *n* boarder in sb's house. 寄宿客。⇨ board¹(8), board²(2).

guf·faw /gəˈfɔː; gʌˈfɔ/ *vi, n* (give a) noisy laugh. 哄笑。

guid·ance /ˈgaɪdns; ˈgaɪdn̩s/ *n* [U] guiding or being guided; leadership. 引導;指導;領導。

guide /gaɪd; gaɪd/ *n* **1** person who shows others the way, esp a person employed to point out interesting sights on a journey or visit. 嚮導。**ˌGirl ˈG~**, ⇨ girl. **2** sth that directs or influences (conduct, etc): 指導或影響(品行等)之物: *Instinct is not always a good ~.* 本能並不永遠是一良好的指導者。**ˈ~-line** *n* (usu *pl*) advice (usu from sb in authority) on policy, etc: (通常用複數)(政策等的)指導方針;指標: *~-lines on prices and incomes.* 物價和收入方面之指標。**3** (also 亦作 **ˈ~·book**) book for travellers, tourists, etc with information about a place: 指南: *a ~ to the British Museum;* 大英博物館指南; *a ~ to Italy.* 義大利旅行指南。**4** book of information; manual: 入門書;手册: *a G~ to Poultry Keeping.* 家禽飼養手册。**5** bar, rod or part of a machine or apparatus that keeps other parts, etc, moving as desired. 導桿;導體;導機。□ *vt* [VP6A, 15A, B] act as ~ to: 引導;指導;領導: *~ sb to a place;* 引導某人至一地; *~ sb in/out/up, etc.* 引導某人進入(出去,上去等)。*You must be ~d by your sense of what is right and just.* 你必須受正義感的引導。**ˌ~d ˈmissile**, rocket (for use in war) which can be ~d to its destination while in flight by electronic devices. 電導飛彈;導向飛彈。

guild /gɪld; gɪld/ *n* (older spelling 昔時拼作 **gild**) society of persons for helping one another, forwarding common interests, eg trade, social welfare. 互助會;協會;行會;同業工會。**ˌG~-ˈhall** *n* hall in which members of a ~ met in the Middle Ages. (中古時公會的)會館。**the ˈG~·hall**, hall of the Corporation of the City of London, used for banquets, receptions, etc. 倫敦市政廳之會堂(供舉行宴會,招待會等者)。~ **socialism**, system by which an industry is to be controlled by a council of its members. 公會制社會主義。

guilder /ˈgɪldə(r); ˈgɪldɚ/ *n* unit of currency of the Netherlands. 基爾德(荷蘭之貨幣單位)。

guile /gaɪl; gaɪl/ *n* [U] deceit; cunning: 詐欺;狡猾: *a man full of ~;* 奸詐之人; *get sth by ~.* 詐取某物。**~·less** *adj* **~·ful** /-fl; -fəl/ *adj*

guille·mot /ˈgɪlɪmɒt; ˈgɪləˌmɑt/ *n* kinds of arctic sea-bird. 海鳩。⇨ the illus at water. 參看 water 之插圖。

guillo·tine /ˈgɪlətiːn; ˈgɪləˌtin/ *n* **1** machine for beheading (criminals in France) with a heavy blade sliding in grooves dropped from a height. (法國處決犯人之)斷頭臺。**2** kind of machine for cutting the edges of books during manufacture, trimming sheets of paper, etc. 切紙機。**3** (in Parliament) method of stopping obstruction of a bill (by excessive debate) by fixing times for taking votes. (國會中)決定投票時間以防止(藉過多辯論)阻礙議案的措施。□ *vt* [VP6A] use the ~ on. 處以斬刑;切(紙);規定(議案之)投票時間。

guilt /gɪlt; gɪlt/ *n* [U] condition of having done wrong; responsibility for wrong-doing: 犯罪;罪狀;有罪: *The ~ of the accused man was in doubt.* 被告之罪有疑問。**~·less** *adj* ***~less (of)***, innocent; without ~: 無辜的;無罪的: *~less of the offence;* 無罪; not having knowledge or possession. 不知;沒有。**~y** *adj* (-ier, -iest) ***~y (of)***, **1** having done wrong: 有罪的;犯罪的: *plead ~y to a crime;* 服罪;認罪; *be ~y of a crime.* 有罪。**2** showing or feeling guilt: 表示有罪的;感覺有罪的: *look ~y;* 像有罪的樣子;心虛; *~y looks;* 感到有罪的表情; *a ~y conscience.* 內疚。**~·ily** /-ɪlɪ; -əlɪ/ *adv* **~·iness** *n*

guinea /ˈgɪnɪ; ˈgɪnɪ/ *n* (*pl* ~s abbr 複數略作 **gns**) (called 稱作 *money of account,* ⇨ account¹(2)) formerly the sum of twenty-one shillings (now £1.05, or 105p), for which there was neither coin nor banknote, used in stating prices of goods, professional fees, charges, subscriptions, etc: 基尼(昔時值 21 先令,現值 1·05 鎊或 105 辨士,非硬幣亦非紙幣,用以計算貨物價格、專業人員之收費、費用、訂費等): *the 2000 Gns race,* horse-race with a prize of 2000 ~s. 二千基尼獎金的賽馬。

guinea-fowl /ˈgɪnɪ faʊl; ˈgɪnɪ faʊl/ *n* (*pl* unchanged) domestic fowl of the pheasant family, with dark grey feathers spotted with white. (複數不變)珠鷄(一種屬於雉類的家禽,生有帶白點的深灰色羽毛)。

guinea-pig /ˈgɪnɪ pɪg; ˈgɪnɪ pɪg/ *n* short-eared animal like a big rat, often used in scientific experiments; sb allowing himself to be used in medical or other experiments. 天竺鼠;豚鼠(常供科

學實驗用)；供醫學或其他實驗的人。➪ the illus at small. 參看 small 之插圖。

Guin·ness /ˈgɪnɪs ; ˈgɪnɪs/ *n* (P) kind of bitter stout; bottle or glass of this: (商標)一種黑啤酒;一瓶或一杯此種黑啤酒: *A pint of draught ~, please.* 請來一品脫桶裝黑啤酒。

guise /gaɪz ; gaɪz/ *n* [C] **1** (old use) style of dress: (舊用法)裝束: *in the ~ of a monk.* 作和尚的裝束。**2** ***in／under the ~ of,*** assuming a particular manner or appearance: 僞裝;假裝: *under the ~ of friendship.* 假裝友善。

guitar /gɪˈtɑː(r) ; gɪˈtɑr/ *n* (usu) six-stringed musical instrument, plucked with the fingers or a plectrum. 吉他;六絃琴(一種通常爲六絃的樂器,用手指或琴撥彈奏)。➪ the illus at string. 參看 string 之插圖。

gulch /gʌltʃ ; gʌltʃ/ *n* (US) deep, narrow, rocky valley. (美)峽谷。

gul·den /ˈgʊldən ; ˈgʊldən/ *n* = guilder.

gulf /gʌlf ; gʌlf/ *n* **1** part of the sea almost surrounded by land: 海灣: *the G~ of Mexico.* 墨西哥海灣。**the ˈG~ Stream,** warm ocean current flowing north from the G~ of Mexico to Europe. 墨西哥灣流(自墨西哥海灣向北流向歐洲的暖流)。**2** deep hollow; chasm; abyss; (fig) dividing line, division (*between* opinions, etc). 深坑;深淵;(喻)懸隔;鴻溝(與 between 連用,後接意見等)。

gull[1] /gʌl ; gʌl/ *n* large, long-winged sea-bird. 鷗。➪ the illus at water. 參看 water 之插圖。

gull[2] /gʌl ; gʌl/ *vt* [VP6A, 15A] cheat; deceive: 欺騙;詐欺: *~ a fool out of his money.* 騙取傻子的錢。□ *n* person who is easily ~ed. 易受欺騙的人。**~·ible** /-əbl ; -əbḷ/ *adj* easily ~ed. 易受欺騙的。**~i·bil·ity** /ˌgʌləˈbɪlətɪ ; ˌgʌləˈbɪlətɪ/ *n*

gul·let /ˈgʌlɪt ; ˈgʌlɪt/ *n* food passage from the mouth to the stomach; throat. 食道;咽喉。➪ the illus at head. 參看 head 之插圖。

gully /ˈgʌlɪ ; ˈgʌlɪ/ *n* (*pl* -lies) narrow channel cut or formed by rainwater, eg on a hillside, or made for carrying water away from a building. (山腰等地之)水沖溝;壑;溪谷;溝渠。

gulp /gʌlp ; gʌlp/ *vt, vi* [VP2A, 6A, 15B] ***~ (down),*** swallow (food or drink) quickly or greedily: 吞食;吞飲;狼吞虎嚥: *~ down a cup of tea;* 一口氣喝下一杯茶; hold back or suppress (as if swallowing sth); make a ~ing motion. 抑制(若吞下去一般);吞。□ *n* [C] act of ~ing: 吞食;吞飲: *empty a glass at one ~;* 一口氣喝完一杯; amount that is ~ed; mouthful, esp of sth liquid: 吞食或吞飲之量;一大口(尤指液體): *a ~ of cold tea.* 一大口冷茶。

gum[1] /gʌm ; gʌm/ *n* (usu *pl*) firm, pink flesh round the teeth: (通常用複數)齒齦: *The dog bared its gums at me.* 那狗對着我露齒而吠。➪ the illus at mouth. 參看 mouth 之插圖。**gum·boil** /ˈgʌmbɔɪl ; ˈgʌmˌbɔɪl/ *n* boil or abscess on the gums. 齦潰瘍;齦膿腫。

gum[2] /gʌm ; gʌm/ *n* **1** [U] sticky substance exuded from some trees, used for sticking things together. 樹膠;樹脂。**2** [U] gum that has been specially prepared in some way: 經過特殊方法處理的樹膠: *chewing-gum;* 口香糖; [C] (also 亦作 *ˈgum-drop*) hard, transparent sweet made of gelatine, etc. 橡皮糖。**3** (also 亦作 *ˈgum-tree*) eucalyptus tree. 橡皮樹;橡膠樹。***up a gum-tree,*** (sl) in difficulties. (俚)有困難;在困境。**ˈgum·boot,** high rubber boot. 長統橡皮靴。**ˈgum·shoe,** (US) (美) **(a)** rubber shoe or overshoe. 橡膠鞋或套鞋。**(b)** (sl) detective. (俚)偵探。□ *vt* (-mm-) [VP6A, 15A, B] stick together with gum; spread gum on the surface of: 以樹膠黏合;塗以樹膠: *gum sth down;* 用膠黏住某物; *gum two things together.* 將兩物用膠黏起。**gummy** *adj* (-ier, -iest) sticky. 黏的。

gum[3] /gʌm ; gʌm/ *n* (esp N England) (in oaths, etc) God: (尤用於北英格蘭)(誓語等中)上帝: *By gum!* 憑上帝發誓！

gum·bo /ˈgʌmbəʊ ; ˈgʌmbo/ *n* (US) thick okra soup. (美)加秋葵莢之濃湯。

gump·tion /ˈgʌmpʃn ; ˈgʌmpʃən/ *n* [U] (colloq) common sense and initiative; qualities likely to bring success: (俗)常識與進取精神;可以使人成功的性質: *The lad lacks ~.* 這孩子缺乏進取精神。

gun /gʌn ; gʌn/ *n* **1** general name for any kind of firearm that sends shells or bullets from a metal tube: 砲;槍: *a warship with 16-inch guns;* 裝有十六吋口徑大砲的戰艦; *machine-guns.* 機關槍。➪ cannon, carbine, musket, pistol, revolver, rifle[1]. ***be going great guns,*** be proceeding vigorously and successfully. 正在努力而且順利地進行。***blow great guns,*** (of the wind) blow violently. (指風)狂吹。***stick to one's guns,*** maintain one's position against attack or argument. 堅守陣地;堅守立場。**ˈgun·boat** *n* small warship carrying heavy guns, or long-range missiles. 砲艇。***gunboat diplomacy,*** (fig) diplomacy backed by the threat of force. (喻)砲艇外交(以武力威脅作後盾之外交政策)。**ˈgun-carriage** *n* wheeled support of a big gun, or part on which a gun slides when it recoils. 砲架。**ˈgun-cotton** *n* [U] explosive of acid-soaked cotton. 强棉藥;硝化棉。**ˈgun·fire** *n* [U] firing of gun(s). 砲火。**ˈgun·man** /-mən ; -mæn/ *n* (*pl* -men) man who uses a gun to rob or kill people. 持槍搶刼或殺人的歹徒。**ˈgun-metal** *n* alloy of copper and tin or zinc; dull blue-grey colour. 砲銅;青銅(銅與錫或鋅的合金);鐵灰色。**ˈgun·powder** *n* explosive powder used in guns, fireworks, blasting, etc. 火藥。**the ˈGunpowder Plot,** plot to blow up the Houses of Parliament, 5 Nov 1605. 火藥陰謀(1605年11月5日陰謀炸毀英國國會的事件)。**ˈgun·room** *n* (in a warship) room for junior officers. (戰艦中)下級軍官室。**ˈgun-running** *n* [U] introduction of firearms, secretly and illegally, into a country, eg to help a revolt. 私運軍火(以幫助叛亂等)。**ˈgun-runner** *n* person engaged in this. 私運軍火者。**ˈgun·shot** *n* **(a)** [C] shot fired by a gun. (射出之)砲彈。**(b)** [U] range of a gun: 砲的射程: *be out of／within gunshot.* 在大砲射程以外(內)。**ˈgun·smith** *n* person who makes and repairs small firearms. 造槍工人;修槍匠。**2** person using a sporting gun, as a member of a shooting party. 狩獵隊員。**3** **big gun,** (colloq) important or powerful person. (俗)重要或有權勢的人物。□ *vt* [VP6A, 15B] ***gun sb (down),*** shoot with a gun. 用槍將某人射倒。

gun·ner /ˈgʌnə(r) ; ˈgʌnɚ/ *n* (in the army) soldier in the artillery; (in the navy) warrant officer in charge of a battery of guns. (陸軍)砲兵;(海軍)槍砲士官長。**~y** *n* [U] construction and management of large guns. 射擊學;槍砲學;砲術。

gunny /ˈgʌnɪ ; ˈgʌnɪ/ *n* [U] strong, coarse material used for making sacks, bales, bags, etc. (製袋,包,囊等的)粗麻布。

gun·wale /ˈgʌnl ; ˈgʌnḷ/ *n* (naut) upper edge of the side of a boat or a small ship. (航海)舷緣(小船船舷的上緣)。➪ the illus at row. 參看 row 之插圖。

gurgle /ˈgɜːgl ; ˈgɝgḷ/ *n* [C, U] bubbling sound as of water flowing from a narrow-necked bottle: 汩汩聲(如水自一窄頸瓶內倒出的聲音): *~s of delight.* 咯咯的笑聲。□ *vi* make this sound: 作汩汩聲: *The baby was gurgling happily.* 那嬰兒高興得咯咯作聲。

Gur·kha /ˈgɜːkə ; ˈgʊrkə/ *n* member of a ruling group in Nepal who became famous as soldiers in the British Indian army. 廓爾喀人(尼泊爾的主要種族,在英印軍中爲著名的軍人)。

guru /ˈgʊruː ; ˈguru/ *n* Hindu spiritual teacher; (colloq) respected and influential teacher or authority. 印度之宗教師;(俗)受人尊敬和具有影響力的教師或權威。

gush /gʌʃ ; gʌʃ/ *vi* [VP2A, C, 3A] **1** burst, flow, out suddenly: 湧出;迸出: *oil ~ing from a new well;* 從新油井中湧出的油; *blood ~ing from a wound.* 傷口湧出的血。**2** talk with excessive enthusiasm:

滔滔不絕地說;過分熱心地說: *young mothers ~ing over their babies;* 滔滔不絕地談論她們嬰兒的年輕母親; *girls who ~ over handsome film stars.* 過分熱心談論漂亮電影明星的女孩子。□ *n* sudden outburst or outflow: 湧出;迸發: *a ~ of oil/anger/enthusiasm.* 油的湧出(一陣憤怒;熱情的奔放)。**~er** *n* oil-well with a strong natural flow (so that pumping is not needed). 噴油井(自動流出的油井)。**~·ing** *adj*: *~ing compliments.* 滔滔不絕的問候。⇨ 2 above. 參看上列第2義。**~·ing·ly** *adv*

gus·set /ˈgʌsɪt ; ˈgʌsɪt/ *n* [C] (usu triangular or diamond-shaped) piece of cloth inserted in a garment to strengthen or enlarge it. 爲加强或加大衣服而插接於衣服中的一塊布(通常爲三角形或菱形);衽;襠。

gust /gʌst ; gʌst/ *n* [C] sudden, violent rush of wind; burst of rain, hail, fire or smoke; (fig) outburst of feeling: 突然一陣狂風;雨,雹,火或煙之突然的一陣;(喻)感情的爆發: *The wind was blowing in ~s.* 狂風陣陣吹來。**~y** *adj* (-ier, -iest) stormy; with wind blowing in ~s. 有風暴的;有陣陣狂風的。

gus·ta·tion /gʌˈsteɪʃn ; gʌsˈteʃən/ *n* [U] (formal) tasting. (正式用語)嘗味。

gusto /ˈgʌstəʊ ; ˈgʌsto/ *n* [U] enjoyment in doing sth. 趣味;興趣。

gut /gʌt ; gʌt/ *n* **1** (*pl*) (colloq) intestines; bowels: (複)(俗)內臟;腸: *stick a bayonet into a man's guts.* 將刺刀戳入一人的內臟。***hate sb's guts,*** (sl) hate him intensely. (俚)恨死某人;恨之入骨。**2** (*pl*) (colloq) contents of anything: (複)(俗)內容: *His speech had no guts in it,* no real arguments, force, etc. 他的演說沒有內容。*The real guts* (= The essence) *of his speech is....*他的演說之要義爲…。**3** (*pl*) (colloq) courage and determination: (複)(俗)勇氣與決心;膽量;魄力: *a man with plenty of guts.* 很有魄力的人。**4** [U] strong cord made from the intestines of animals, used for the strings of violins, etc. (用做提琴絃等的)腸線。⇨ *catgut.* □ *vt* (-tt-) [VP6A] **1** take the guts(1) out of (a fish, etc). 取出(魚等的)內臟。**2** destroy the inside of or the contents of: 毀壞…的內部或內容: *a building gutted by fire.* 內部爲火焚毀的房屋。**gut·less** *adj* lacking in guts(3). 缺少勇氣和決心的;沒有膽量的。

gutta-per·cha /ˌgʌtə ˈpɜːtʃə ; ˈgʌtəˈpɝtʃə/ *n* [U] rubber-like substance made from the juice of various Malayan trees. 馬來樹膠;古塔波膠。

gut·ter[1] /ˈgʌtə(r) ; ˈgʌtɚ/ *n* [C] **1** channel or trough (usu metal) fixed under the edge of a roof to carry away rainwater; channel at the side of a road for the same purpose. (簷下之)承霤;天溝;屋頂邊溝;(道旁之)陰溝;排水溝。**2 the ~,** (fig) poor or debased state of life: (喻)貧苦低級的生活: *the language of the ~,* low and vulgar language. 下流粗鄙的言語。***take a child out of the ~,*** remove it from poor and wretched conditions. 使孩子離開貧困環境。***the ˈgutter press,*** newspapers giving much space to salacious stories, scandals, etc. 低級趣味的報紙(以大量篇幅刊登淫穢故事,醜行等者)。**ˈ~·snipe** /-snaɪp ; -ˌsnaɪp/ *n* poor, badly-dressed child who plays in slum streets. 街頭流浪兒。

gut·ter[2] /ˈgʌtə(r) ; ˈgʌtɚ/ *vi* [VP2A] (of a candle) burn unsteadily so that the melted wax flows down the sides. (指蠟燭)燃燒不穩而融化流下;淌蠟。

gut·tural /ˈgʌtərəl ; ˈgʌtərəl/ *n, adj* (sound that seems to be) produced in the throat: (似)喉間發出的;(似)喉間發出的聲音: *~ consonants.* 喉間發出的子音。**~·ly** *adv*

guv·nor /ˈgʌvnə(r) ; ˈgʌvnɚ/ *n* (GB sl) boss. (英俚)老板;工頭。

guy[1] /gaɪ ; gaɪ/ *n* [C] rope or chain used to keep sth steady or secured, eg to hold a tent in place. (支帳篷等的)支索;牽索;拉索。

guy[2] /gaɪ ; gaɪ/ *n* **1** figure in the form of a man, dressed in old clothes (eg as burned on 5 Nov in memory of Guy Fawkes's Gunpowder Plot). 着舊時衣服的偶像(例如爲紀念發覺 Guy Fawkes 之火藥陰謀於每年11月5日所焚者)。**2** person dressed in a strange or queer-looking way. 衣着古怪的人。**3** (sl) man. (俚)人。⇨ *fall-guy* at fall[1](1). □ *vt* (*pt, pp* guyed) [VP6A] ridicule; exhibit (sb) in effigy. 嘲弄;以肖像展示(某人)。

Guy's /gaɪz ; gaɪz/ *n* (used for) Guy's Hospital (in London). (用於指倫敦之)蓋氏醫院。

guzzle /ˈgʌzl ; ˈgʌzl/ *vi, vt* [VP2A, 6A, 15B] (colloq) eat or drink greedily: (俗)狼吞虎嚥;狂飲: *be always guzzling;* 老是狼吞虎嚥; *~ beer.* 狂飲啤酒。**guz·zler** /-zlə(r) ; -zlɚ/ *n* person who ~s. 狼吞虎嚥者;狂飲者。

gybe (US **jibe**) /dʒaɪb ; dʒaɪb/ *vi, vt* [VP2A, 6A] (naut) (of a sail or boom) swing from one side of the ship to the other; (of a ship or a ship's crew) cause this to happen. (航海)(指帆或其下桁)自船之一側轉向另一側;(指船或船員)使帆自一側轉向另一側;(使)改變航道。⇨ the illus at barque. 參看 barque 之插圖。

gym /dʒɪm ; dʒɪm/ *n* (sl) (short for) gymnasium, gymnastics: (俚)體育館;健身房;體操(爲 gymnasium 及 gymnastics 之略): *ˈgym-shoes;* 運動鞋; *the ˈgym mistress.* 女體育教師。**ˈgym-slip** *n* sleeveless tunic worn in GB by some girls as part of school uniform. 無袖的束腰外衣(英國某些女學生做爲制服)。

gym·khana /dʒɪmˈkɑːnə ; dʒɪmˈkɑnə/ *n* public display of athletics, horse-riding or vehicle-driving competitions. 運動會;賽馬會;賽車會。

gym·nasium /dʒɪmˈneɪzɪəm ; dʒɪmˈnezɪəm/ *n* (*pl* ~s) room or hall with apparatus for physical training. 體育館;健身房。

gym·nas·tic /dʒɪmˈnæstɪk ; dʒɪmˈnæstɪk/ *adj* of physical training. 體操的;體育的。**~s** *n pl* (forms of) exercises for physical training. 體操。**gym·nast** /ˈdʒɪmnæst ; ˈdʒɪmnæst/ *n* expert in ~s. 體操家。

gynae·col·ogy (US = **gyne-**) /ˌgaɪnɪˈkɒlədʒɪ ; ˌdʒaɪnɪˈkɑlədʒɪ/ *n* [U] science of the diseases of women and pregnancies. 婦科(醫)學。**gynae·colo·gist** (US = **gyne-**) *n* expert in ~. 婦科醫生。**gynae·co·logi·cal** (US = **gyne-**) /ˌgaɪnɪkəˈlɒdʒɪkl ; ˌdʒaɪnɪkəˈlɑdʒɪkl/ *adj*

gyp[1] /dʒɪp ; dʒɪp/ *vt* [VP6A] (sl) cheat. (俚)欺騙。

gyp[2] /dʒɪp ; dʒɪp/ *n* ***give sb gyp,*** (sl) scold or punish him without mercy. (俚)嚴斥或嚴懲某人。

gyp·sum /ˈdʒɪpsəm ; ˈdʒɪpsəm/ *n* [U] mineral (calcium sulphate, $CaSO_4$) from which plaster of Paris is made; also used as a fertilizer. 石膏(亦可用做肥料)。

Gypsy /ˈdʒɪpsɪ ; ˈdʒɪpsɪ/ *n* ⇨ gipsy.

gy·rate /ˌdʒaɪˈreɪt *US:* ˈdʒaɪreɪt ; ˈdʒaɪret/ *vi* move round in circles or spirals; revolve. 旋轉;迴旋。**gy·ra·tion** /ˌdʒaɪˈreɪʃn ; dʒaɪˈreʃən/ *n* [C, U] revolving; revolution. 旋轉;迴旋。

gyro /ˈdʒaɪərəʊ ; ˈdʒaɪro/ *n* (colloq abbr of) gyroscope. (俗)爲 gyroscope 之略。

gyro·scope /ˈdʒaɪrəskəʊp ; ˈdʒaɪrəˌskop/ *n* wheel which, when spinning fast, keeps steady the object in which it is fixed. 迴轉儀;環動儀(快速旋轉時可使裝有此器之物體保持穩定)。**gyro·scopic** /ˌdʒaɪrəˈskɒpɪk ; ˌdʒaɪrəˈskɑpɪk/ *adj*

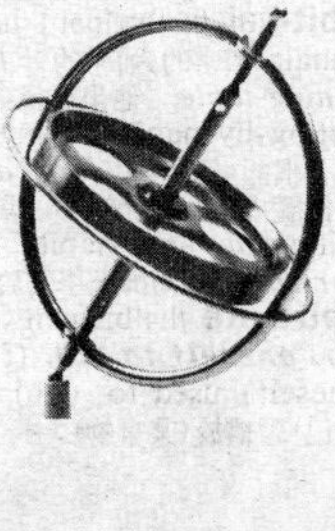

a gyroscope

Hh

H, h /eɪtʃ ; etʃ/ (*pl* H's, h's /ˈeɪtʃɪz ; ˈetʃɪz/), the eighth letter of the English alphabet. 英文字母的第八個字母。***drop one's h's,*** omit the sound /h ; h/, eg by saying, *'ot* for *hot.* 略去h之音(如讀hot爲'ot)。
ha /hɑː ; hɑ/ *int* used to express surprise, joy, triumph, suspicion, etc. When repeated in print ('*Ha! Ha! Ha!*') it indicates laughter. 哈！(表示驚異、快樂、得意、懷疑等,如連續寫出或印出則表示大笑聲)。
ha·beas cor·pus /ˌheɪbɪəs ˈkɔːpəs ; ˈhebɪəs ˈkɔrpəs/ *n* (Lat; legal) (拉;法律) ***(writ of) ~,*** order requiring a person to be brought before a judge or into court, esp to investigate the right of the law to keep him in prison. 人身保護令(要求將人移送法院處理之令狀,特別爲調查應否受拘留者)。
hab·er·dasher /ˈhæbədæʃə(r) ; ˈhæbɚˌdæʃɚ/ *n* shopkeeper who sells clothing, small articles of dress, pins, cotton, etc. 賣零星服飾、針線等的商人。**~y** *n* [U] ~'s goods or business. 服飾雜貨;服飾雜貨業。
ha·bili·ments /həˈbɪlɪmənts ; həˈbɪləmənts/ *n pl* (liter or hum) clothing. (文或諧)衣服。
habit /ˈhæbɪt ; ˈhæbɪt/ *n* **1** [C] sb's settled practice, esp sth that cannot easily be given up: 習慣: *the ~ of smoking;* 吸煙的習慣; *~-forming drugs.* 易於上癮的麻醉藥物。***be in/fall into/get into the ~ of,*** have, acquire, the ~ of. 有…的習慣;養成…習慣。***fall/get into bad ~s,*** acquire them: 養成壞習慣: *Don't let yourself get into bad ~s.* 不要讓你自己養成壞習慣。***get sb into the ~ of/into bad ~s,*** cause him to have the ~ of/bad ~s: 使養成(壞)習慣: *Don't let him get you into the ~ of taking drugs.* 不要讓他使你養成吸毒的習慣。***fall/get out of the ~ of,*** abandon the ~ of. 革除…的習慣。***make a ~ of sth,*** do it regularly. 經常做某事。 **2** [U] usual behaviour: 脾性;習性;慣常的行爲: *H~ is second nature.* 習慣成自然。***creature of ~,*** sb whose life is marked by many ~s(1). 受習性驅使的人。***do sth/act from force of ~,*** because it is one's ~. 習慣使然而做某事。***do sth out of ~,*** because it is one's ~. 因習慣而做某事。 **3** [C] (old use) condition, general quality (of mind or body): (舊用法)心境;體質: *a cheerful ~ of mind.* 心情愉快。 **4** [C] dress worn by members of a religious order: 某一宗教會派所著之服裝: *a monk's ~.* 僧袍。 **ˈriding ~,** woman's coat and skirt for horse-riding. 女子騎馬裝。
hab·it·able /ˈhæbɪtəbl ; ˈhæbɪtəbl̩/ *adj* fit to be lived in: 適於居住的: *The old house is no longer ~.* 這古老的房屋已不適於居住了。
habi·tat /ˈhæbɪtæt ; ˈhæbəˌtæt/ *n* (of plants, animals) usual natural place and conditions of growth; home. (指動植物)產地;棲息地。
habi·ta·tion /ˌhæbɪˈteɪʃn ; ˌhæbəˈteʃən/ *n* **1** [U] living in: 居住: *houses that were not fit for ~.* 不適於居住的房屋。 **2** [C] (liter) place to live in: (文)住所: *On these plains there was not a single human ~.* 在這些平原上沒有一處人的住所。
ha·bit·ual /həˈbɪtʃʊəl ; həˈbɪtʃʊəl/ *adj* **1** regular, usual: 慣常的;通常的: *He took his ~ seat at the dining-table.* 他坐於餐桌旁他慣常所坐的座位上。 **2** acting by habit; having a regular habit: 慣常做的;有習慣的: *a ~ liar/drunkard/cinema-goer.* 慣於說謊者(經常喝醉的人;常看電影者)。**~ly** /-tʃʊəlɪ ; -tʃʊlɪ/ *adv* as a habit: 習慣性地: *Tom is ~ly late for school.* 湯姆上學慣於遲到。
ha·bitu·ate /həˈbɪtʃʊeɪt ; həˈbɪtʃʊˌet/ *vt* [VP14] ***~ sb/oneself to sth,*** (formal) accustom; get (sb/oneself) used to (sth): (正式用語)使熟習;使(某人,自己)習慣於(某事物): *~ oneself to hard work/getting up early/a cold climate;* 使自己慣於艱苦的工作(早起,寒冷的氣候); *~ a horse to the sound of gunfire.* 使一馬習慣於砲火聲。
habi·tude /ˈhæbɪtjuːd *US:* -tuːd ; ˈhæbəˌtjud/ *n* [U] (formal) custom; tendency; habitual way of acting or doing things. (正式用語)習慣;癖性;習性。
ha·bitué /həˈbɪtʃʊeɪ ; həˈbɪtʃʊˌe/ *n* person who regularly goes to a place: 常至某一地方的人;常客: *a ~ of the orchestral concerts/of the Café Royal.* 常聽管絃樂隊演奏會者(皇家飯店的常客)。
haci·enda /ˌhæsɪˈendə ; ˌhɑsɪˈɛndə/ *n* (*pl* ~s) (in Latin American countries) large landed estate with a house. (拉丁美洲國家的)莊園;大田莊。
hack¹ /hæk ; hæk/ *vt, vi* [VP6A, 15A, B, 2A, C, 3A] ***~ (at),*** cut roughly or clumsily; chop: 亂砍;劈;砍: *After the murderer had killed his victim, he ~ed the body to pieces.* 兇手殺死受害者後,將其屍體砍碎。*He ~ed at the branch* (ie struck heavy blows at it) *until it fell to the ground.* 他砍那樹枝,直到它落在地上。**~ing cough,** short, dry cough. 短促的乾咳。**ˈ~·saw** *n* one with a replaceable blade in a frame, for cutting through metal. 弓形鋼鋸(鋸金屬用者)。⇨ the illus at tool. 參看 tool之挿圖。
hack² /hæk ; hæk/ *n* **1** horse that may be hired. 出租之馬。 **2** person paid to do hard and uninteresting work as a writer: (受雇從事辛苦而又乏味之寫作的)文丐: *publisher's ~s.* 出版商雇用的文人。□ *vi* ride on horseback on roads, at an ordinary pace: 以普通速度在路上騎馬: *go ~ing.* 以普通速度騎馬。
hackles /ˈhæklz ; ˈhækl̩z/ *n pl* long feathers on the neck of the domestic cock: 雄鷄頸上的長羽毛: *with his ~ up,* (of a cock, dog or man) angry; ready to fight. (指雄鷄,狗或人)發怒;準備打鬥。***have one's/get sb's ~ up,*** be, make sb angry, ready to fight. (使某人)憤怒欲戰。
hack·ney /ˈhæknɪ ; ˈhæknɪ/ *n* ordinary kind of horse for riding or driving. 普通騎乘或駕車之馬。**ˈ~ carriage,** one that may be hired. 出租馬車。**~ed** /ˈhæknɪd ; ˈhæknɪd/ *adj* (esp of sayings) too common; repeated too often. (尤指格言)陳舊的;陳腐的。
had /hæd ; hæd/ ⇨ have¹.
had·dock /ˈhædək ; ˈhædək/ *n* (*pl* unchanged) sea-fish much used for food, esp *smoked ~.* (複數不變)黑線鱈(食用甚廣,尤用於製成燻魚)。
Hades /ˈheɪdiːz ; ˈhediz/ *n* (Gk myth) the underworld; place where the spirits of the dead go. (希神)冥府;黃泉。
Hadji /ˈhædʒɪ ; ˈhædʒi/ *n* (title of a) Muslim pilgrim who has been to Mecca. 至聖地麥加朝拜過的回教徒(之頭銜)。
haem- ⇨ hem-.
haft /hɑːft *US:* hæft ; hæft/ *n* handle of an axe, knife, dagger, etc. (斧、刀、匕首等之)柄。
hag /hæg ; hæg/ *n* witch; ugly old woman, esp one who does, or is thought to do, evil. 女巫;老醜婦(尤指做或被認爲會做壞事者)。**ˈhag-ridden,** afflicted by nightmares; harassed. 受夢魘侵擾的;被困擾的。
hag·gard /ˈhægəd ; ˈhægɚd/ *adj* (of a person, his face) looking tired and lined, esp from worry, lack of sleep. (指人,人的面孔)憔悴的;枯槁的(尤指由於憂愁或缺少睡眠所致)。
hag·gis /ˈhægɪs ; ˈhægɪs/ *n* Scottish dish of various parts of a sheep, cut up, mixed with oatmeal, and cooked in a sheep's stomach. (蘇格蘭)將羊雜切碎加麥片納入羊胃中煮成的食物。
haggle /ˈhægl ; ˈhægl̩/ *vi* [VP2A, 3A] ***~ (with sb) (about/over sth),*** argue, dispute, esp the price of sth or the terms of a bargain. 爭論;(尤指)討價

H

還價。

hagi·ol·ogy /ˌhægɪˈɒlədʒɪ ; ˌhægɪˈɑlədʒɪ/ *n* literature of the lives and legends of saints. 聖徒傳；聖徒言行錄。

haha /ˈhɑːhɑː ; ˈhɑˌhɑ/ *n* wall or fence bounding a park or garden, sunk in a hollow so as not to interfere with the view. (築於公園或花園四周之溝中以免妨礙視線之)矮牆；矮籬。

hail[1] /heɪl ; hel/ *n* **1** [U] frozen raindrops falling from the sky. 雹。ˈ**~·stone** *n* [C] small ball of ~: 冰雹: *~stones as big as peas.* 像豌豆般大小的雹粒。ˈ**~·storm** *n* storm with fall of ~. 雹暴。 **2** (usu 常作 ***a ~ of***) sth coming in great numbers and force: 大量和猛烈到來的事物: *a ~ of blows／curses.* 一陣打擊(咒罵)。□ *vi, vt* **1** (impers) (of ~) come down: (無人稱)(指雹)下降: *It ~ed in the late afternoon.* 傍晚時下了雹。 **2** [VP2C, 15B] ***~ (sth) down (on sb),*** (of blows, etc) come, send down, hard and fast (on): (指打擊等)猛烈迅速地落下: *Blows ~ed down on his back.* 打擊猛烈迅速地落在他的背上。*They ~ed curses down on us.* 他們猛烈地咒罵我們。

hail[2] /heɪl ; hel/ *vt, vi* **1** [VP6A, 16B, 23] greet; give a welcoming cry to; call out to (so as to attract attention): 歡迎；向…歡呼；向…招呼 (以引其注意): *Cheerful voices ~ed us as we entered the hall.* 我們進入會堂時，向我們歡呼之聲四起。*They ~ed him (as) king.* 他們高呼擁他爲王。*He was ~ed as a hero.* 他受到了英雄式的歡迎。 *Let's ~ a taxi, shall we?* 我們叫一輛計程車好嗎？ **2** [VP3A] ***~ from,*** come from: 來自: *Where does the ship ~ from,* Which is her home port? 這隻船來自何處 (原屬何港)？(colloq, of persons) (俗，指人) *They ~ from all parts of the country.* 他們來自全國各地。□ *n* greeting; ~ing cry. 歡迎；歡呼；招呼。***within ~,*** (esp of ships) near enough to be ~ed. (尤指船)在可以招呼的距離內。 ***be ˌ~-fellow-well-ˈmet (with sb),*** be very familiar and friendly. 極親密；很要好。

hair /heə(r) ; hɛr/ *n* **1** [U] (collective *sing*) all the thread-like growths on the skin of animals, esp on the human head, ⇨ the illus at head; thread-like growth on the stems and leaves of some plants; ~-like thing: (集合單數)毛髮；(尤指)頭髮(參看 head 之插圖)；植物的茸毛；毛狀物: *brush one's ~;* 梳頭髮; *have one's ˈ~ cut;* 理髮; *a cat with a fine coat of ~;* 長有一身好毛的貓; [C] single thread of ~: 一根毛；一根髮: *find a ~ in the soup;* 在湯內發現了一根毛(髮); *two blonde ~s on his coat collar;* 他上衣領上的兩根金黃色頭髮; (archaic) (*pl*, in collective sense): (古)(複數，作集合之義)一人的全部頭髮: *It will bring down my grey ~s in sorrow to the grave,* cause me, who am old, to die of sorrow. 這將使我在老年憂心至死。***get sb by the ˈshort ~s,*** (sl) have him at one's mercy; get complete control of him. (俚)支配某人；完全操縱某人。***keep your ˈ~ on,*** (sl) keep cool; don't lose your temper. (俚)保持鎮靜；勿發脾氣。***let one's ˈ~ down,*** (of a woman) remove the pins and allow the ~ to fall over the shoulders; (fig) relax after a period of being formal. (指女子)拿下髮針使髮垂落肩頭; (喻) 經過一段拘謹後使身心放鬆一下。***lose one's ~,*** **(a)** become bald. 禿頭。**(b)** lose one's temper. 發脾氣。***make one's ˈ~ stand on end,*** fill one with fright or horror. 使之毛髮悚然。***put one's ˈ~ up,*** arrange it so that it is rolled up on one's head. 束髮；結髻。***split ~s,*** make or pretend to see differences of meaning, distinctions, etc, so small as to be unimportant. 作無謂的細微的分析。Hence, 由此產生，ˈ**~-splitting** *n* [U] acting in this way. 作無謂的細微的分析。***tear one's ~,*** show great sorrow or vexation. 表示極度悲傷或煩惱。***not turn a ~,*** give no sign of being troubled. 毫不受干擾；絲毫不爲所動。***to a ~,*** (of describing sth) exactly. (描寫事物)精確地。 **2** (compounds) (複合字) ˈ**~('s)-breadth** *n* very small distance: 極短的距離；一髮之距: *escape by a ~'s-breadth; have a ~-breadth escape,* a very narrow one. 間不容髮；倖免於難。ˈ**~·brush** *n* toilet brush for the ~. 髮刷。⇨ the illus at brush. 參看 brush 之插圖。ˈ**~·cloth** *n* cloth made of a mixture of fabric and animal's ~ for various purposes. 毛織成之布(做各種用途)。ˈ**~·cut** *n* act or style of cutting the ~ (by a barber or ~dresser). 理髮；做頭髮；髮型；髮式。 ˈ**~-do** *n* (colloq) haircut. (俗)理髮；做頭髮；髮型；髮式。ˈ**~-dresser** *n* person who dresses and cuts ~. 理髮師；美容師。⇨ barber. ˈ**~-dye** *n* dye for the ~. 染髮劑。ˈ**~·line** *n* area where the roots of ~ join the forehead; width of a ~; (attrib) very narrow: 額部生髮部分之輪廓；一髮之距；(形容用法)極窄的: *a ~line space／fracture.* 極窄的空間(細微的裂縫)。ˈ**~·net** *n* net for keeping the ~ in place. 髮網。ˈ**~-oil** *n* oil for dressing the ~. 髮油。ˈ**~·piece** *n* tress of false ~. 假髮。ˈ**~·pin** *n* (woman's) pin for keeping the ~ in place. (女子的)髮夾。 ˌ**~pin ˈbend** *n* sharp bend on a road, esp on a steep road, so that the road doubles back. 道路(尤指陡路)之U字形急彎。ˈ**~-raising** *adj* terrifying. 恐怖的；令人毛髮悚然的。ˌ**~-ˈshirt** *n* shirt made of ~cloth, uncomfortable to wear, for ascetics. 毛布做的襯衣(穿在身上不舒適，爲苦行者所用)。ˈ**~-slide** *n* metal clip for keeping ~ tidily in place. 髮夾。ˈ**~·spring** *n* very delicate spring in a watch, controlling the balance-wheel. 錶內的游絲(控制平衡輪之極細的彈簧)。 ˈ**~·style** *n* style of haircut. 髮型。ˈ**~·stylist** *n* ~dresser. 理髮師；美容師。ˈ**~-trigger,** one that fires a gun, etc at the slightest pressure. (槍之)微力扳機。 **~·less** *adj* without ~; bald. 無毛的；無髮的；禿頭的。ˈ**~·like** *adj* **~y** *adj* (-ier, -iest) of or like ~; covered with ~: 毛的；毛狀的；長有毛的: *a ~y chest.* 長有毛的胸部。**~i·ness** *n*

hairpin bends

hake /heɪk ; hek/ *n* (*pl* unchanged) fish of the cod family, used as food. (複數不變)鱈魚類(用作食物)。

hal·berd /ˈhælbəd ; ˈhælbəd/ *n* weapon used in the Middle Ages, a combined spear and battle-axe on a long handle. 戟(中古一種槍鉞兩用的長柄武器)。

hal·ber·dier /ˌhælbəˈdɪə(r) ; ˌhælbəˈdɪr/ *n* soldier armed with a ~. 戟兵。

hal·cyon /ˈhælsɪən ; ˈhælsɪən/ *adj* calm and peaceful: 平靜的；太平的: *~ days／weather.* 太平的日子(平靜的天氣)。

hale /heɪl ; hel/ *adj* (usu of old persons) (通常指老年人) (rare except in) (除下列用法外極爲少用) ***~ and hearty,*** strong and healthy. 矍鑠的；健壯的。

half /hɑːf *US:* hæf ; hæf/ *n* (*pl* halves /hɑːvz *US:* hævz ; hævz/) *adj, adv* **1** one of two equal or corresponding parts into which a thing is divided: 一半；半個: *The ~ of 6 is 3／H~ of 6 is 3.* 六的一半是三。*Two halves make a whole.* 兩個一半成爲整個。*Two pounds and a ~／Two and a ~ pounds.* 兩磅半。*H~ of the fruit is bad.* 水果的一半壞了。*H~ (of) the plums are bad.* 半數的李子壞了。*I want ~ as much again,* one and a ~ the amount. 我要一倍半。*Cut it in ~／into halves.* 把它切成兩半。***(do sth) by halves,*** incompletely, imperfectly. (做某事)不完全地；不完善地。***go halves (with sb) (in sth),*** share equally. (與人)平分(某事物)。***too clever, etc by ~,*** far too clever, etc. 過於聰明等。***one's better ~,*** (colloq) one's wife, husband, etc. (俗)妻子，丈夫等。 **2** (as *adv*) (作副詞)

to the extent of a ~; to a considerable degree; nearly: 一半地；相當程度地；幾乎: *meat that is only ~ cooked;* 半熟的肉; *~-cooked cabbage;* 半熟的包心菜; *not ~* (= not nearly) *long enough;* 根本就不够長; *~ dead,* (colloq) tired out, exhausted; (俗) 筋疲力竭的; *not ~ bad,* (sl) not at all bad; quite good. (俚) 相當好。***not ~,*** (sl) to the greatest possible extent: (俚) 極端地: *He didn't ~ swear,* He swore very violently. 他破口大罵。'*Was she annoyed?*' '*Not ~!*' (ie she was intensely annoyed). '她受到煩擾嗎？' '被煩擾得很厲害！' **3** (in compounds) (用於複合字中) **ˌ~ a ˈcrown, a ˌ~-ˈcrown** *nn* (before 1971) coin or amount of $2\frac{1}{2}$ *shillings* ($12\frac{1}{2}$*p*). (1971 年以前) $2\frac{1}{2}$ 先令 ($12\frac{1}{2}$ 辨士)。**ˌ~ a ˈdozen** *n* six. 半打；六個。**ˌ~ and ˈ~** *n* what is ~ one thing and ~ the other, eg a mixture of beer and lemonade. 兩者各半混成之物(例如啤酒與檸檬水混成之飲料)。**ˈ~-back** *n* (in football／hockey, etc) (position of) player (defender) between the forwards and the backs. (足球，曲棍球等) 中衞(的位置)。**ˌ~-ˈbaked** *adj* (colloq) dull-witted; crude and inexperienced: (俗) 愚笨的；粗魯而又無經驗的: *a ~-baked young man;* 粗魯而又缺乏經驗的青年; foolish; of poor quality: 愚蠢的；質劣的: *~-baked ideas.* 愚蠢的思想。**ˈ~-blood** *n* (relationship of a) person having one parent in common with another. 同父異母或同母異父的兄弟或姊妹；此種血統關係。**ˈ~-breed** *n* **(a)** person with parents of different races. 混血兒。**(b)** offspring of two animals or plants of different species. 動植物的雜種；混合種。**ˈ~-brother** *n* brother by one parent only. 同父異母或同母異父的兄弟。**ˈ~-caste** *n* ~-breed person. 混血兒。**ˌ~ ˈcock** *n* position of the hammer of a gun when pulled ~-way back. 槍機半擊發之位置。***go off at ~ cock,*** (fig) act too soon and fail. (喻) 行動過早而失敗。**ˌ~-ˈhardy** *adj* (of plants) requiring protection from frost but otherwise suitable for growing in the open. (指植物) 適於戶外生長但不耐霜雪的。**ˌ~-ˈhearted** *adj* done with, showing, little interest or enthusiasm: 無興趣的；不熱心的: *a ~-hearted attempt.* 不熱心的嘗試。Hence, 由此產生，**ˌ~-ˈheartedly** *adv* **ˌ~-ˈholiday** *n* day of which ~ (usu the afternoon) is free from work or duty. 半日(通常是下午) 休假。**ˌ~ an ˈhour, a ˌ~-ˈhour** *nn* period of 30 minutes. 半小時；三十分鐘。**ˌ~-ˈhourly** *adj, adv* done, occurring every 30 minutes: 每半小時(做成或發生)的；每半小時地: *a ~-hourly bus service.* 每半小時一班的公共汽車。**ˌ~-ˈlength** *adj* (of a portrait) of the upper ~ of a person. (指畫像) 上半身的。***at ˌ~-ˈmast,*** (of a flag) at the position, near the middle of a mast, to indicate mourning: (指旗) 下半旗(在旗桿中部的位置以表示哀悼): *Flags were at ~-mast everywhere on the day of the President's funeral.* 總統安葬之日一律下半旗。**ˌ~-ˈpay** *n* [U] reduced pay given to sb when not fully employed but not yet retired: 半薪 (半退休者所領的核減過的薪水): *placed on ~-pay.* 領半薪。**~penny** /ˈheɪpnɪ *US:* ˈhæfpenɪ ; ˈhepnɪ/ *n* British coin worth ~ a penny ($\frac{1}{2}$d before 1971, $\frac{1}{2}$p now). 英國半辨士銅幣。**~-penny·worth** /ˈheɪpnɪwɜːθ *US:* hæfˈpenɪwɜːθ ; ˈhepənɪˌwɝθ/, **ha'p'orth** /ˈheɪpəθ ; ˈhepɚθ/ *n* as much as $\frac{1}{2}$d would buy before 1971; now chiefly fig. 值半辨士之物(現在主要用做比喻)。⇨ App 5. 參看附錄五。**ˌ~-ˈprice** *adv* at ~ the usual price: 以半價: *Children admitted ~-price.* 兒童入場半價優待。**ˌ~-seas-ˈover** *pred adj* (colloq) ~ drunk. (俗) 半醉的。**ˈ~-sister** *n* sister by one parent only. 同父異母或同母異父的姊妹。**ˌ~-ˈsize** *adj* ~ the usual or regular size. 爲通常大小之一半的。**ˌ~-ˈtimbered** *adj* (of a building) having walls of a wooden framework filled in with brick, stone or plaster. (指建築物) 半露木的(牆壁爲木架加磚、石或灰泥築成的)。**ˌ~-ˈtime** *n* [U] **(a)** work and pay for ~ the usual time: 半工半薪: *Owing to the business depression the workers are on ~-time this month.* 由於商業蕭條，工人們本月半工半薪。**(b)** the interval between the two halves of a game of football, etc: (足球等比賽中) 上半場與下半場間的休息時間: *The score at ~-time was 2-2.* 上半場結束時的比數爲二比二。**ˈ~-tone** *n* black and white photograph reproduced on paper, eg as an illustration in a book. (印在紙上做書中挿圖等的) 黑白圖片。**ˈ~-track** *n* troop-carrying vehicle with tracks(5) on both sides at the rear and wheels at the front. 半履帶軍車。Hence, 由此產生，**ˌ~-ˈtracked** *adj* **ˈ~-truth** *n* statement that conveys only a part of the truth. 部份眞實的陳述。**ˌ~-ˈway** *adj* **(a)** situated at an equal distance from two places. 位於兩地中途的。**(b)** going ~ the way; not thorough: 至中途的；不徹底的: *In an emergency ~-way measures are usually unsatisfactory.* 在緊急時，不徹底的措施通常是不能令人滿意的。□ *adv* to or at ~ the distance: 至半途；中途地: *meet a person ~-way,* be ready to make a compromise. 願意跟某人妥協；遷就某人。**ˌ~-ˈwitted** *adj* weak-minded. 魯鈍的。Hence, 由此產生，**ˈ~-wit** *n* ~-witted person. 魯鈍的人。**ˌ~-ˈyearly** *adj, adv* (done, occurring) every ~ year. 每半年(完成或發生)的；每半年地。

hali·but /ˈhælɪbət ; ˈhæləbət/ *n* (*pl* unchanged) large, flat sea-fish used as food. (複數不變) 大比目魚。

hali·tosis /ˌhælɪˈtəʊsɪs ; ˌhæləˈtosɪs/ *n* [U] bad-smelling breath. 口臭。

hall /hɔːl ; hɔl/ *n* **1** (building with) large room for meetings, concerts, public business, etc: 廳；堂；會堂；禮堂: *the Town／City H~;* 市政廳; *the County H~;* 州會堂; *the H~ of Justice;* 審判廳; *the Festival H~,* for concerts, in London; (倫敦之) 音樂廳; *ˈdance-~s.* 舞廳。**2** [U] (in colleges at English universities) large room for meals: (英國大學各學院之) 餐廳: *dine in ~.* 在餐廳進餐。**3** building for university students: 供大學生使用之建築物: *a ~ of residence.* 大學的宿舍。**4** (in England) large country house, usu one that belongs to the chief landowner in the district. (英國) 大地主的府第。**5** passage, space, into which the main entrance or front door of a building opens: 正門廳廊；門廳；穿堂: *Leave your hat and coat in the ~.* 把你的帽子和大衣放在門廳裏。**ˈ~-stand** *n* piece of furniture for hats, coats, umbrellas, etc. 衣帽架(掛衣帽、傘等的傢具)。**6** building of a guild: 公會會館: *Saddlers' H~.* 馬具公會會館。

hal·le·lu·jah /ˌhælɪˈluːjə ; ˌhæləˈlujə/ *n, int* praise to God. 哈利路亞(讚美上帝之語)。

hal·liard /ˈhæljəd ; ˈhæljɚd/ *n* = halyard.

hall·mark /ˈhɔːlmɑːk ; ˈhɔlˌmɑrk/ *n* mark used for marking the standard of gold and silver in articles (as a guarantee of quality); (fig) distinguishing characteristic (usu of excellence). 證明金銀器純度的印記；(喻) 特性(通常指特優之性質)。□ *vt* stamp a ~ on. 在…上壓印純度證明印記。

hallo /həˈləʊ ; həˈlo/ *int* = hullo.

hal·loo /həˈluː ; həˈlu/ *int, n* cry to urge on hounds; shout to attract attention. 嗾使獵犬的呼聲；引人注意的喊叫。□ *vi* shout 'H~!', esp to hounds. 呼叫(尤指對獵犬)。

hal·low[1] /ˈhæləʊ ; ˈhælo/ *vt* [VP6A] (usu passive) make holy; regard as holy: (通常用被動語態) 使神聖；視爲神聖: *ground ~ed by sacred memories.* 因宗教上之紀念而視爲神聖的土地。

hal·low[2] /ˈhæləʊ ; ˈhælo/ *n* (only in) (僅用於) **All H~'s Day,** ⇨ all[1](6).

Hal·low·e'en /ˌhæləʊˈiːn ; ˌhæloˈin/ *n* 31 Oct, eve of All Saints' Day or All Hallows' Day. 萬聖節之前夕(十月三十一日)。

hal·luci·na·tion /həˌluːsɪˈneɪʃn ; həˌlusn̩ˈeʃən/ *n* [C, U] (instance of) seeming to see sth not present, sth imagined: 幻覺；幻覺中的事物: *Drunken men are sometimes subject to ~s.* 酒醉者有時易生幻覺。**hal·luci·na·tory** /həˈluːsɪnətrɪ *US:* -tɔːrɪ ; həˈlusn̩əˌtorɪ/, **hal·luci·no·genic** /həˌluːsɪnəˈdʒenɪk ; həˌlusɪnə-

ˈdʒɛnɪk/ *adjj* (of drugs) inducing ~. (指藥物)產生幻覺的。

halma /ˈhælmə; ˈhælmə/ *n* [U] game played on a board of 256 squares where pieces are moved from one corner to the other. 一種跳棋(棋盤有256格)。

halo /ˈheɪləʊ; ˈhelo/ *n* (*pl* ~es, ~s /-ləʊz; -loz/) circle of light round the sun or moon or (in paintings) round or above the heads of Christ or sacred figures. 暈(環繞着日月的光輪);光圈;(繪於耶穌或神像頭上之)光環。

halt[1] /hɔːlt; hɔlt/ *n* **1** (chiefly mil, of soldiers) (主要爲軍語,指士兵) ***call a ~ (to),*** make a short stop on a march or journey: (行進中)下令停止前進;下令短暫休息: *The officer called a ~.* 軍官下令停止前進。*It's time to call a ~ to vandalism,* (fig) end it. (喻)故意破壞天然環境的行爲應該予以制止了。**2** (more general use) ***come to a ~,*** make a stop or pause: (較普通用法)停止: *The train came to a ~.* 火車停了。⇨ grind(6). **3** stopping-place (smaller than a station) on a railway-line, where trains stop for a short time only. 火車短暫停留的小站。□ *vi, vt* **1** [VP2A] (as a mil command) stop marching; come to a ~. (軍隊口令)立定;停止行進。**2** [VP6A] bring to a ~: 使停止行進: *The officer ~ed his troops for a rest.* 軍官令軍隊停止行進,休息一下。

halt[2] /hɔːlt; hɔlt/ *vi* [VP2A, C] hesitate; walk in a hesitating way: 猶豫;躊躇: *~ between two opinions;* 躊躇於兩個意見之間; *in a ~ing voice.* 囁嚅地。□ *adj* (archaic) lame: (古)跛的: *the ~ and the blind.* 跛者與盲者。**~·ing·ly** *adv* in a ~ing way. 猶豫地;躊躇地。

hal·ter /ˈhɔːltə(r); ˈhɔltɚ/ *n* **1** rope or leather strap put round a horse's head (for leading or fastening the horse). 韁繩;馬韁。**2** rope used for hanging a person. 絞刑用之繩索。

halve /hɑːv *US:* hæv; hæv/ *vt* [VP6A] **1** divide into two equal parts: 二等分;分成兩半: *~ an apple.* 將一蘋果分成兩半。**2** lessen by one half: 減半: *The newest planes have ~d the time needed for crossing the Atlantic.* 最新式的飛機使横越大西洋所需的時間減少了一半。

halves /hɑːvz *US:* hævz; hævz/ *pl* of half.

hal·yard /ˈhæljəd; ˈhæljɚd/ *n* rope for raising or lowering a sail or flag. 帆或旗的升降索。

ham /hæm; hæm/ *n* **1** [C] upper part of a pig's leg, salted and dried or smoked: 火腿: *hams hanging on hooks;* 掛在鈎上的火腿; [U] this as meat: 火腿肉: *a slice of ham;* 一片火腿; *a ham sandwich.* 火腿三明治。**2** [C] (chiefly used of animals) back of the thigh, thigh and buttock. (主要指動物)大腿的後部;大腿及臀部。**3** (sl) poor actor or performer; amateur who sends and receives radio messages: (俚)拙劣的演員;無線電收發報業餘愛好者: *a radio ham;* 無線電收發報業餘愛好者; (attrib) (形容用法) *ham actors/acting/radio.* 拙劣的演員(拙劣的演出;業餘愛好者所用的無線電收發報機)。**ˌham-ˈhanded/-ˈfisted** *adj* clumsy in using the hands. 手笨的。□ *vt, vi* (-mm-) [VP2A, 6A, 15B] ***ham (up),*** (colloq) act in a deliberately artificial, exaggerated way. (俗)作過火之表演。

hama·dryad /ˌhæməˈdraɪəd; ˌhæməˈdraɪəd/ *n* nymph living and dying with the tree she inhabited; poisonous Indian snake. 樹神(與其所棲守的樹共存亡的女神);印度的一種毒蛇。

ham·burger /ˈhæmbɜːgə(r); ˈhæmbɝgɚ/ *n* **1** ground or chopped beef made into round flat cakes and fried. 漢堡牛排;牛肉餅(牛肉絞碎煎成的圓餅)。**2** sandwich or bread roll filled with this. 漢堡牛排三明治;牛肉餅三明治。

ham·let /ˈhæmlɪt; ˈhæmlɪt/ *n* group of houses in the country; small village, esp one without a church. 鄉間的一片房屋;小村(尤指無教堂者)。

ham·mer /ˈhæmə(r); ˈhæmɚ/ *n* **1** tool with a heavy metal head used for breaking things, driving in nails, etc. 鎚;榔頭。⇨ the illus at tool. 參看 tool 之插圖。***be/go at it ~ and tongs,*** fight, argue, with great energy and noise. 猛烈喧騰地打鬥或爭論。***throwing the ~,*** athletic competition in which a heavy long-handled ~ is thrown as far as possible. 擲鏈球(一種運動比賽,擲一長柄重鎚,遠者爲勝)。**2** (in a piano, etc) one of the ~-like parts that strike the strings. (鋼琴等之)琴槌。**3** part of the firing device of a gun that strikes and explodes the charge. (槍之)擊鐵。**4** wooden mallet used by an auctioneer. (拍賣者所用的)木槌。***be/come under the ~,*** be sold by auction. 被拍賣。**5** (anat) bone in the ear. (解剖)(耳之)鎚骨。⇨ the illus at ear. 參看 ear 之插圖。□ *vt, vi* **1** [VP6A, 22, 15B, 2A, C, 3A] ***~ (in/out/down); ~ (at),*** strike or beat with a ~, or as if with a ~: 鎚打;似用鎚般敲打: *~ nails into wood;* 將釘子鎚進木頭; *~ down the lid of a box,* fasten it down by ~ing; 用鎚將盒蓋釘上; *~ in a nail/~ a nail in;* 用鎚敲進一釘; *~ a piece of metal flat;* 將一片金屬鎚平; *~ sth out,* make it flat or smooth by ~ing; 鎚平某物; *~ at the door,* eg with a stick, one's fists; 敲打門(例如用杖或拳); *~ at the keys,* play the piano loudly, without feeling. (無感情地)猛彈鋼琴。**2** (fig) (喻) [VP15B] ***~ out,*** produce by hard work: 辛苦做成: *~ out a scheme;* 苦心想出一計畫; [VP3A] ***~ at,*** work hard at: 辛苦工作: *~ away at a problem/a solution/a compromise;* 苦研一問題(解答,折衷之道); [VP6A] force: 强迫: *~ an idea into sb's head.* 將一觀念灌入某人的頭腦中。**3** (colloq) inflict heavy defeats on (sb) in war or in games. (俗)使(某人)在戰爭或比賽中慘敗。

ham·mock /ˈhæmək; ˈhæmək/ *n* hanging bed of canvas or rope network, eg as used by sailors, or in gardens. 吊床(例如船員或花園中所用者)。

ham·per[1] /ˈhæmpə(r); ˈhæmpɚ/ *n* packing-case or basket with a lid, esp one used for sending food: 有蓋的盒或籃(尤指送食物所用者): *a Christmas ~,* one sent as a present, with food, wine, etc. 裝有食物、酒等做爲聖誕禮物的盒或籃。

ham·per[2] /ˈhæmpə(r); ˈhæmpɚ/ *vt* [VP6A] hinder; prevent free movement or activity: 阻礙;使不能任意行動: *~ed by a heavy overcoat.* 受一件厚大衣的妨礙。

ham·ster /ˈhæmstə(r); ˈhæmstɚ/ *n* rodent like a large rat, kept by children as a pet. 鼴鼠(一種似大鼠的齧齒動物,兒童養做玩物)。

ham·string /ˈhæmstrɪŋ; ˈhæmˌstrɪŋ/ *vt* (*pt, pp* ~ed or hamstrung /ˈhæmstrʌŋ; ˈhæmˌstrʌŋ/) [VP6A] cripple (a person or animal) by cutting the tendon(s) at the back of the knee(s); (fig) destroy the power or efficiency of. 割斷腿筋使(人或動物)殘廢;(喻)摧毀…之力量或效能。

hand[1] /hænd; hænd/ *n* **1** part of the human arm beyond the wrist: 手: *with his ~s in his pockets.* 他的手放在口袋中。⇨ the illus at arm. 參看 arm 之插圖。***at ~,*** near; within reach: 在近處;在手邊;卽將到來: *He lives close at ~,* quite near. 他住在近處。*The examinations are at ~.* 考試卽將舉行了。***at sb's ~s,*** from sb: 出自某人之手: *I did not expect such unkind treatment at your ~s.* 我未料到你會如此無情。***bind sb ~ and foot,*** (lit, fig) make him completely helpless. (字面,喻)把某人的手脚全綁起來;使某人完全無助。***serve/wait on sb ~ and foot,*** attend to his every wish; perform every sort of service for him. 竭力侍候;忠心侍候。***by ~,*** **(a)** without the use of machinery: 手工做的: *Are your socks knitted by ~/~-knitted or machine-made?* 你的襪子是手工織的還是機器織的? **(b)** without the use of the post office: 專人送的: *The note was delivered by ~,* by a messenger. 這短簡是專人送來的。***bring up a baby/a calf, etc by ~,*** rear it by feeding from a bottle: 以奶瓶餵養嬰兒、小牛等: *The lamb had to be brought up by ~.* 這小羊必須以奶瓶餵養。***eat/feed out of one's ~,*** **(a)** (eg of a bird) be quite tame. (指鳥等)十分馴服。**(b)** (fig) be ready to obey without question. (喻)十分順從。***from ~ to ~,*** directly, from one person to another: 用手傳遞;自甲手到乙手: *Buckets of water were passed from ~ to ~ to put the fire out.* 一桶桶的水用手傳遞着去救火。***fight ~ to ~,*** at close quarters. 肉搏;短兵相接。Hence, 由此產生, *~-to-~ fighting.* 肉搏戰。***give/lend (sb) a ~ (with sth),*** help with, take a part in, doing sth: 幫助;參與: *Give (me) a ~ with the washing-up, please.* 請幫我洗餐具。***give one's ~ on a bargain,*** take sb's ~ and clasp it to seal the bargain. 與某人握手表示成交。***be ~ in glove (with sb),*** ⇨ glove. ***have one's '~s full,*** have all the work one can do; be fully occupied. 忙碌。***have/get the upper ~ (of sb),*** ⇨ upper. ***have a free ~; give/allow sb a free ~,*** ⇨ free[1](3). ***~ in ~,*** holding ~s; together: 手牽手;一起: *They walked away ~ in ~.* 他們攜手離去。(fig) (喻) *War and misery go ~ in ~.* 戰爭與苦難永不分開。***H~s off!*** Don't touch or interfere! 不許摸(干涉)! ***H~s up!*** Put your ~s up! Surrender! 舉起手來!投降! ***~ over ~,*** with each ~ used alternately (as when climbing, etc); (fig) rapidly and steadily. 雙手交互地(如攀登時);(喻)迅速而穩定地。***in ~,*** **(a)** in reserve, available for use: 保有;可用: *I still have some money in ~.* 我手頭還有些錢。*Cash in ~, £27.25.* 手頭現金,二十七鎊二十五辨士。**(b)** receiving attention; in course of completion: 在處理或從事中;在進行中: *The work is in ~ and will be finished by the end of the month.* 這工作在進行中,本月底將完成。*We have the situation well in ~,* are dealing with it satisfactorily. 我們充分掌握了局勢。***in the ~s of,*** being looked after or managed by. 在…的照顧中;由…管理。***in good ~s,*** being well cared for. 在妥爲照顧中。***lay (one's) ~s on sth/sb,*** ⇨ lay[1](2). ***lend a ~,*** ⇨ *give a ~,* above. 參看上列之 give a ~。***not lift a ~; not do a ~'s turn,*** make not the least attempt to help. 毫不幫助。***lift/raise a ~/one's ~ against sb,*** threaten, attack him. 威脅某人;打擊某人。***live from ~ to mouth,*** precariously, spending money as soon as it is received. 賺一個用一個; 生活不穩定。Hence, 由此產生, *a ~-to-mouth existence.* 做一日吃一日的生活。***(get sth) off one's ~s,*** taken from one's responsibility: 卸除責任: *I'd be glad to get it off my ~s,* to rid myself of responsibility for it. 我願意擺脫對此事的責任。***on ~,*** available: 可用;握有: *We have some new woollen goods on ~,* in our shop, warehouse, etc. 我們現有一些新的毛貨(在商店,倉庫等中)。***on one's ~s,*** resting on one as a responsibility: 做爲一項責任而仰賴着某人;由某人負責: *I have an empty house on my ~s,* one for which I want to find a buyer or tenant. 我有一所空房屋待賣或出租。*Time hangs heavy on his ~s,* seems burdensome, passes slowly. 時間慢得使他難以度過。***out of ~,*** **(a)** out of control; undisciplined: 難控制;無紀律;無法約束: *The football fans have got quite out of ~.* 足球迷們變得難以控制了。**(b)** at once, without hesitation: 卽刻;無猶豫地: *The situation needs to be dealt with out of ~.* 這情勢須要卽刻處理。***shake ~s with sb; shake sb's ~,*** grasp his ~ as a greeting, or to express agreement, etc. 與某人握手。***take a ~ (in),*** help; play a part (in sth). 幫助;參與。***take sth/sb in ~,*** take charge of; undertake to control or manage. 負責照料;管理。***be to ~,*** (comm style for) be received: (商業文體) 收到: *Your letter is to ~,* has reached me and is receiving attention. 大函敬悉。***wash one's ~s of,*** say that one will no longer be responsible for. 聲稱不再對某事負責;洗手不幹。***win ~s down,*** win easily. 輕易地贏得。***(rule) with a heavy ~,*** oppressively; severely. 壓制地;嚴格地(統治)。***win a lady's ~,*** win her consent to marriage. 獲某女子同意結婚。 **2** (*pl*) power; possession; responsibility. (複)掌握;擁有;責任。***in sb's hands:*** *The property is no longer in my ~s,* It is no longer mine, or my responsibility. 這財產已非我所有(我所管)。*The matter is in your ~s,* You must decide how to deal with it. 這事你必須處理。*He's still in the ~s of the money-lenders.* 他仍受高利貸者的剝削。***change ~s,*** pass to another owner: 易手;易主: *The property has changed ~s recently,* has been sold. 這財產最近已易主。 **3** (*sing* only) influence or agency: (僅用單數) 勢力;作用: *The ~ of an enemy has been at work here.* 敵人已在此處活動。 **4** (*sing* only) person from whom news, etc comes. (僅用單數) 提供消息等的人。(only in) (僅用於) ***at first ~,*** directly, without an intermediary: 直接地: *I heard/learnt the news at first ~.* 我直接聽到(得悉)這消息。***at second ~,*** indirectly. 間接地。 **5** (*sing* only) skill in using one's ~s: (僅用單數)技巧: *She has a light ~ at pastry,* makes it with skill. 她很會做點心。*Why don't you try your ~ at editing the staff magazine,* see whether you have the skill needed? 你爲何不去嘗試一下編輯職員刊物呢? ***get one's '~ in,*** acquire or return to one's usual degree of skill by practice. 經練習而獲得或恢復平時的技術。***keep one's '~ in,*** practise a skill, in order to retain it: 藉練習保持技術: *practise the piano every day to keep one's ~ in.* 每天練鋼琴以保持熟練。 **6** [C] person who does what is indicated by the context; performer: 做某事的人(所做之事由上下文表示): *a good ~ at fencing,* a good fencer. 劍術家。*He's an old ~ at this sort of work,* has long experience of it. 他做這種工作很有經驗。*He's an old parliamentary ~,* a person with long experience of parliamentary duties. 他是精通議會事物的人。 **7** workman, eg in a factory or dockyard; member of a ship's crew: (工廠或船塢等之)工人;船員: *The factory has taken on 200 extra ~s.* 工廠額外雇用了二百名工人。*All ~s on deck!* All seamen are needed on deck! 所有船員都到甲板上來! **8** turn; share in an activity. 輪值;活動中的一份。***have a ~ (in sth),*** have a share: 參與(某事): *Let me have a ~ now.* 讓我參加一份。*Do you think he had a ~ in it,* was involved? 你認爲他參與了此事嗎? **9** [C] pointer or indicator on the dial of a watch, clock or other instrument: 鐘面或錶面等上之針: *the 'hour/'minute/'second ~ of a watch.* 錶的時(分,秒)針。 **10** position or direction (to right or left). 方面;方向。***on every/either ~; on all ~s,*** to or from all quarters. 向四面八方;從四面八方。***on the one ~ ... on the other ~,*** used to indicate contrasted points of view, arguments, etc. 一方面…,另一方面…。 **11** (*sing* only) handwriting: (僅用單數)筆跡;書法: *He writes a good/legible ~.* 他的書法很好(寫得很清楚)。 **12** (formal) signature: (正式用語)簽名: *set one's ~ to a document.* 在一文件上簽名。*Given under my ~ and seal,* authenticated by my signature and seal. 由我的簽名及印鑑證明。 **13** (card games, eg bridge) (橋牌等牌戲) **(a)** (number of) cards dealt to, held by, a player at one time. 一手牌;手中牌。***have a good/bad/poor ~,*** good/bad, etc cards. 拿到一手好(壞)牌。***play a good/bad ~,*** play well/badly. 玩得好(差)。***take a ~ at sth,*** join in and play it. 參加打牌。***play into sb's ~s,*** do sth that is to his advantage. 上某人的當;讓某人佔便宜。**(b)** player at cards: 牌手;玩牌者: *We have only three players—we need a fourth ~.* 我們祇有三個牌手,我們需要第四位。 **(c)** one round in a game of cards: 牌戲中之一局: *Let's play one more ~, shall we?* 我們再來一局如何? **14** [C] unit of measurement, about four inches (10·16 cm), the breadth of the ~, used for the height of a horse (from the ground to the top of the shoulder). 一手之寬(約爲四吋或10·16公分,用以量馬從地面到肩頭的高度)。 **15** (colloq) applause by clapping. (俗)拍手喝采。***give sb/get a good ~,*** a lot of applause. 對某人(獲得)熱烈拍手喝采。 **16** (compounds) (複合字) **'~-bag** *n* woman's bag for money, keys, handkerchief, etc. (US 美 = *purse.*) 女用手提包。ˈ~-**barrow** *n* light two-wheeled barrow. 輕便雙輪手推車。ˈ~-**bill** *n* printed advertisement or announcement distributed by ~. 傳單。ˈ~•**book** *n* small book giving useful facts; guide-book. 手册；指南。ˈ~•**brake** *n* auxiliary brake in a motor-vehicle, used when the vehicle is stationary. 手煞車。ˈ~-**cart** *n* small cart pushed or pulled by ~. 手車；手推車。ˈ~•**clap** *n* clapping: 拍手: *a slow ~clap,* slow rhythmical clapping to show impatience. 緩慢而有節奏的拍手(喝倒采)。ˈ~•**cuff** *n* (usu *pl*) one of a pair of metal rings joined by a chain, fastened round a prisoner's wrists. (通常用複數)手銬。□ *vt* put ~cuffs on. 加手銬於。~•**ful** /-fʊl; -ˌfʊl/ *n* (*pl* ~fuls) **1** as much or as many as can be held in one ~. 一握之量;一把。 **2** small number: 少數: *Only a ~ful of people came to the meeting.* 祇有少數人到會。 **3** (colloq) person or animal difficult to control: (俗)難控制的人或動物: *That young boy of hers is quite a ~ful,* is lively and unruly. 她那個小兒子極難管束。ˈ~-**grenade** *n* grenade thrown by hand. 手榴彈。ˈ~-**hold** *n* (esp) anything a climber may grip, eg on a rock face. (尤指)攀登者可抓緊之物(如岩石表面上者)。ˈ~-**luggage** *n* luggage light enough to be carried by hand. 手提的輕便行李。ˌ~-ˈ**made** *adj* made by ~ (contrasted with *machine-made*). 手工製的(與 machine-made 相對)。ˈ~•**maid** *n* (archaic) woman servant or attendant. (古)女僕; 侍女。 ˈ~-**me-down** *n* sth passed on (esp sth used and discarded, eg clothes) to another. 給予別人的舊東西(例如舊衣服)。ˈ~-**organ** *n* portable barrel-organ with a crank turned by ~. 手搖風琴。ˌ~-ˈ**picked** *adj* carefully selected. 精選的;仔細挑選的。ˈ~•**rail** *n* railing along the edge of a staircase, etc. 欄杆;扶手。ˈ~•**saw** *n* saw used with one hand only. 手鋸。ˈ~•**shake** *n* greeting given by grasping a person's ~ with one's own. 握手。ˈ~•**stand** *n* acrobatic feat of supporting oneself in an upright position on the ~s: 以手着地倒立;竪蜻蜓: *do a ~stand.* 竪蜻蜓。ˈ~•**work** *n* [U] work done by ~, not by machinery. 手工。ˈ~•**writing** *n* [U] (person's style of) writing by ~: 筆跡;書法: *Whose ~writing is this?* 這是誰的筆跡？ˌ**off**-ˈ~ *adj* ⇨ off-hand.

hand² /hænd; hænd/ *vt* [VP12A, 13A, 15A, B] give or pass (to sb); help with the ~(s): 交給;傳遞;用手幫助: *Please ~ me that book.* 請把那本書遞給我。 *He ~ed the book to the man at his side.* 他把書遞給他旁邊的那個人。 *He ~ed* (= helped) *his wife out of the railway carriage.* 他扶他的太太下火車。 ***~ sth down (to sb),*** pass by tradition, inheritance, etc: 傳遞: *We cannot always observe the traditions ~ed down to us from the past.* 我們不能永遠遵守過去傳下來的傳統。 ***~ sth on (to sb),*** send, give, to another: 傳給: *Please ~ on the magazine to your friends.* 請將這雜誌傳給你的朋友們看。***~ sth out (to sb),*** distribute; (colloq) give as alms. 分配;(俗)施捨。Hence, 由此產生, ˈ~-**out** *n* **(a)** prepared statement given, eg by a politician, to newspaper men; leaflet, etc, distributed free of charge. (政治人物等)交給記者的備妥的聲明; (免費的)印刷品,傳單等。 **(b)** sth given as alms, eg food or money to a beggar at the door. 施捨的東西(例如給予門口乞丐的食物或金錢)。***~ sb over (to sb),*** deliver a person to authority: 將某人交給當局: *~ sb over to the police.* 將某人交給警局。***~ sth over (to sb),*** transfer: 交給他人: *You can't play with my gun—hand it over at once.* 你不能玩弄我的槍,把它立刻交給我。*I've ~ed over my place on the committee.* 我已將我在委員會中的職位移交他人。***~ it to sb,*** (colloq) give him the credit that is his due: (俗)給予某人應得之榮譽;歸功於某人: *He's done well! You've got to ~ it to him.* 他做得好！你必須歸功於他。

handi•cap /ˈhændɪkæp; ˈhændɪˌkæp/ *n* [C] **1** (competition, race, in which there is a) disadvantage imposed on a competitor to make the chances of success more nearly equal for all, eg a weight to be carried by a horse. (競賽時爲使得勝機會近乎相等)給與優者的不利條件(例如賽馬時使一馬負一重物與他馬比賽)；使用此種障礙的比賽；讓分比賽。 **2** anything likely to lessen one's chance of success: 障礙;阻礙: *Poor eyesight is a ~ to a student.* 視力不良是學生的障礙。□ *vt* (-pp-) [VP6A] give or be a ~ to: 加障礙於;爲…之障礙: *~ped by ill health;* 受健康不良的障礙; *~ped children,* suffering from some disability. 殘障兒童。

handi•craft /ˈhændɪkrɑːft *US:* -kræft ; ˈhændɪˌkræft/ *n* [C] art or craft needing skill with the hands, eg needlework, pottery, woodwork, weaving. 手工;手工藝(例如縫級,製陶,木工,紡織)。

handi•work /ˈhændɪwɜːk ; ˈhændɪˌwɝk/ *n* [U] work done, [C] thing made, by the hands; sth done by a named person: 手工;手工製品;某人所做之事物: *That's some of Smith's ~.* 那是史密斯所做的一些手工品。

hand•ker•chief /ˈhæŋkətʃɪf ; ˈhæŋkɚtʃɪf/ *n* square piece of cotton, silk, linen, etc carried in the pocket or handbag, for blowing the nose into or wiping the face; similar square worn for ornament, eg round the neck. 手帕;手絹;裝飾用的方巾(例如圍巾)。

handle /ˈhændl ; ˈhændl/ *n* **1** part of a tool, cup, bucket, door, drawer, etc by which it may be held in the hand. (工具,杯,桶,門,抽屜等之)柄;把手;提手。ˈ~•**bar** *n* (usu *pl*) bar with a ~ at each end, for steering a bicycle, etc. (通常作複數)脚踏車等的把手。⇨ the illus at bicycle. 參看 bicycle 之插圖。***fly off the ~,*** (colloq) get into a rage and lose self-control. (俗)十分激怒;大怒。***give a ~ (to sb) (against sb),*** provide an excuse or pretext that may be taken advantage of and used: 予以可乘之隙;予以把柄: *Your indiscreet behaviour may give your enemies a ~ against you.* 你的不審愼的行爲會給你的敵人可乘的機會。 **2** (sl) title: (俚)頭銜: *have a ~ to one's name,* have, eg 'Sir' or 'Lord' as part of it. 姓名前有一頭銜(例如 Sir, Lord 等)。□ *vt* [VP6A] **1** touch with, take up in, the hands: 用手觸摸;用手拿起: *Gelignite is dangerous stuff to ~.* 爆炸膠是不可隨便觸摸的危險之物。*Wash your hands before you ~ my books, please.* 在你拿我的書之前,請你先洗手。 **2** manage; deal with; control (men): 管理;處理;控制(人): *An officer must know how to ~ men.* 一個軍官必須知道如何統御士兵。 *Can you ~ the situation,* deal with it? 你能處理這情況嗎？ **3** treat; behave towards: 對待;對付: *The speaker was roughly ~d by the crowd.* 那演說者受到了群衆的侮辱。 **4** (comm) buy and sell: (商)買賣;經銷: *This shop does not ~ imported goods.* 這家商店不經銷進口貨。**han•dler** /ˈhændlə(r) ; ˈhændlɚ/ *n* person who trains and controls an animal, eg a police dog. 訓練動物(例如警犬)者。

hand•some /ˈhænsəm ; ˈhænsəm/ *adj* **1** of fine appearance; (of men) good-looking, having virile beauty; (of women) having a fine figure, vigour and dignity: 美觀的;(指男子)漂亮的;英俊的;(指女子)身材秀麗,充滿活力而儀態高貴的: *What a ~ horse you have!* 你的這匹馬眞漂亮！*What a ~ old building it is!* 多麼美觀的一座古老的建築啊！ *Would you describe that woman as ~ or beautiful?* 你覺得那女子是俊俏還是美麗？ **2** (of gifts, behaviour) generous: (指禮物,行爲)慷慨的; 大方的: *He said some very ~ things about you.* 他說了一些稱讚你的話。*£500 is quite a ~ birthday present.* 五百鎊是相當大方的生日禮物。***H~ is as／that ~ does,*** (prov) A fine person is one who acts generously. (諺)行爲善者始爲美;唯善爲美。 ~•**ly** *adv* in a ~(2) manner: 慷慨地;大方地: *He came down ~ly,* made a generous gift. 他出手大方。

H

handy /ˈhændɪ ; ˈhændɪ/ *adj* (-ier, -iest) **1** (of persons) clever with the hands. (指人)手巧的。**~·man** /-mæn ; -mæn/ *n* (*pl* -men) person clever at doing odd jobs of various kinds. 做雜事靈巧的人。**2** (of things, places) convenient; useful: (指東西,地方)方便的;便利的: *A good toolbox is a ~ thing to have in the house.* 家庭裡如果預備一個好的工具箱就方便多了。***come in ~,*** be useful some time or other: 遲早有用: *Don't throw that plastic bag away; it may come in ~.* 不要把那塑膠袋丟掉,它遲早會有用的。 **3** not far away; available for use: 近便的;可利用的: *Always keep a first-aid kit ~.* 手邊要經常保有一個急救箱。**hand·ily** /-ɪlɪ ; -ɪlɪ/ *adv* **handi·ness** *n*

hang[1] /hæŋ ; hæŋ/ *n* (*sing* only) (僅用單數) **1** way in which a thing hangs: 懸,掛,吊,垂的狀態: *the ~ of a coat / skirt.* 上衣(裙子)下垂的樣子。**2** ***get the ~ of sth,*** (colloq) (俗) **(a)** see how sth, eg a machine, works or is managed: 查看某物(如機器)工作或被管理情形: *I've been trying to get the ~ of this new electric typewriter.* 我一直想知道這部新的電動打字機的用法。**(b)** see the meaning or significance of sth said or written: 了解言語或文字的意義: *I don't quite get the ~ of your argument.* 我不十分了解你的論據的意義。 **3** ***not give / care a ~,*** (colloq) (euphem for *damn*) not care at all. (俗) (damn 之委婉語)毫不在乎。

hang[2] /hæŋ ; hæŋ/ *vt, vi* (*pt, pp* hung /hʌŋ ; hʌŋ/ or, for 2 and 3 below, 下列第 2 義和第 3 義用, ~ed) (For uses with *adverbial particles* and *preps,* ⇨ 7 below.) (與副詞接語和介詞連用之用法,參看下列第7義。) **1** [VP 6A, 15A, B, 2A, C] support, be supported, from above so that the lower end is free: 懸;掛;垂;吊: *~ a lamp from the ceiling;* 將一燈吊在天花板上; *curtains ~ing over the window;* 掛在窗上的窗簾; *windows hung with curtains;* 掛着窗簾的窗子; *pictures ~ing on the wall.* 掛在牆上的圖畫。*She hung the washing out in the garden.* 她把洗好的衣服晾在花園裡。*H~ your coat on that hook.* 把你的外套掛在那個鉤上。*A dog's tongue ~s out when it runs fast.* 狗快跑時舌頭伸在外面。 **2** (*pt, pp* ~ed) put, be put, to death by ~ing with a rope around the neck: 施以絞刑;絞死;被絞死: *He was ~ed for murder* 他因殺人而被絞死。 *He said he would ~ himself,* commit suicide by ~ing. 他說他要自縊。**3** (dated sl; mild equivalent of *damn.*) (過時俚語;相當於 damn 但較溫和之用語)。 **4** (various uses) (各種用法) ~ *wallpaper,* attach it to a wall with paste; 貼壁紙; ~ *bells,* fit them (eg in a belfry); 懸鐘(例如懸於鐘樓中); ~ *a door,* fasten it on hinges so that it swings freely to and fro. 將門安裝在絞鏈上。***~ by a hair / a single thread,*** (of a person's fate etc) be in a delicate state, depend upon sth small. (指人的命運等)千鈞一髮。***~ one's head,*** let it fall forward (eg when ashamed). 低下頭(例如羞愧時)。***~ fire,*** **(a)** (of a gun) be slow in going off. (指槍砲)發火慢。**(b)** (of events) be slow in developing. (指事件)發展緩慢。***let things go ~,*** (colloq) be indifferent to them; take no interest in or care of them. (俗)對事情不關心。***~ in the balance,*** (of a result, decision, etc) not be certain. (指結果,決定等)尚未確定;仍舊是個未知數。 **5** [VP6A, 2B] leave, eg meat, ~ing until in the right condition for eating: 懸掛(肉等)至可食用的狀態: *Hares and pheasants need to be well hung.* 野兔和野鷄需要掛起來吹晾許久方可食用。*How long has this meat hung for?* 這肉已晾了多久了? **6** (compounds) (複合字) **ˈ~·dog** *attrib adj* (of sb's look) sly and ashamed. (指人的外表)狡猾而畏縮的。**~·man** /-mən ; -mən/ *n* (*pl* -men) executioner who ~s criminals. 執行絞刑者;絞刑吏。**ˈ~·over** *n* **(a)** unpleasant after-effects of excessive drinking. 過度飲酒後令人不爽的後作用;宿醒。**(b)** (fig) survival of out-of-date news, rules, etc. (喻)殘存的過時新聞,規則等。 **7** [VP2C, 15B, 3A] (with *adverbial particles* and *preps*): (與副詞接語和介詞連用):

hang about / (a)round, be standing or loitering about, doing nothing definite: 無所事事地待著;閒蕩: *men ~ing about at street corners, waiting for the pubs to open.* 閒待在街道拐角上等着酒店開門的人們。*There's thunder ~ing about,* Thunder seems likely at any time. 隨時可聞雷聲。

hang back, hesitate; show unwillingness to act or advance: 猶豫;躊躇不前: *When volunteers were asked for, not one man hung back.* 當徵求志願者時,沒有一人退縮。

hang on, **(a)** hold tight: 緊握: *He hung on until the rope broke.* 他緊握着繩子,直到繩斷爲止。 **(b)** persevere: 堅忍: *It's hard work, but if you ~ on long enough you'll succeed.* 這是艱苦的工作,但如果你堅持下去,你會成功的。***H~ on (a minute)!*** (colloq) Wait (a minute)! (俗)等一下! ***~ on / upon sb's words,*** listen attentively to them. 仔細聽某人的話。***~ on to sth,*** hold it tightly. 緊握某物。

hang out, (sl) live; lodge: (俚)居住: *Where are you ~ing out now?* 你現在住在哪裡? ***~ sth out,*** **(a)** hang (wet clothes, etc) out to dry: 晾(濕衣等): *She's in the yard, ~ing out the washing.* 她在院子裡晾洗好的衣服。 **(b)** display: 展示: *~ out flags for the Queen's visit.* 懸旗以迎接女王的蒞臨。

hang together, **(a)** (of persons) support one another; act in unison: (指人)團結一致;行動一致: *If we all ~ together, our plan will succeed.* 如果我們大家團結一致,我們的計畫會成功。 **(b)** fit well together: 和諧一致: *Their accounts of what happened don't ~ together,* are inconsistent, contradictory. 他們對於發生之事報導不一致(有矛盾之處)。

hang up, replace the receiver at the end of a telephone conversation: 掛斷電話: *She hung up on me,* (colloq) hung up the receiver before I had said all I wanted to say. (俗)她未等我把話說完便將電話掛斷了。***be hung up,*** (colloq) (俗) **(a)** be delayed or frustrated. 被拖延;受挫折。**(b)** be emotionally inhibited or disturbed. 情緒受抑制或騷擾。Hence, 由此產生, **ˈ~-up** *n* **(a)** difficulty. 困難。**(b)** inhibition; obsession; neurosis. 抑制;强迫觀念;神經官能病。

hang·ar /ˈhæŋə(r) ; ˈhæŋɚ/ *n* building in which aircraft are housed. (停放飛機的)棚廠;飛機庫。

hang·er /ˈhæŋə(r) ; ˈhæŋɚ/ *n* device, loop, etc to, on or by which sth is hung; 掛物之環,鉤,架等; (in compounds): (用於複合字中): **ˈdress- / ˈclothes- / ˈcoat-~,** device on which dresses, etc are hung. 掛衣架。**~-on** /ˌhæŋər ˈɒn ; ˈhæŋɚˈɑn/ (*pl* ~s-on) *n* person who forces his company upon another or others in the hope of profit or advantage. 希望獲得利益而纏依他人者。**ˈpaper-~,** person who hangs (= pastes) wallpaper on to walls. 裱貼壁紙者;裱糊匠。

hang·ing /ˈhæŋɪŋ ; ˈhæŋɪŋ/ *n* **1** [U, C] death by hanging: 絞刑;絞死: *There were three ~s here last month.* 上月此地有三起絞刑。 **2** (usu *pl*) curtains, drapery, etc with which walls are hung. (通常用複數)窗簾,幃幕等。

hang·nail /ˈhæŋneɪl ; ˈhæŋˌnel/ *n* loose skin near the root of a finger-nail. 逆剝(指甲根上的肉刺)。

hank /hæŋk ; hæŋk/ *n* (twisted) coil of wool, silk, etc thread: (扭絞的)一束毛線,絲等;一仔線: *wind a ~ of wool into balls.* 將一束毛線纏成線球。

han·ker /ˈhæŋkə(r) ; ˈhæŋkɚ/ *vi* [VP3A] ***~ after / for sth,*** have a strong desire: 渴望: *~ for sympathy;* 渴望着同情; *~ after wealth.* 渴望得到財富。**~·ing** *n* strong desire: 渴望: *have a ~ing for / after fame.* 渴望成名。

hanky /ˈhæŋkɪ ; ˈhæŋkɪ/ *n* (*pl* -kies) (child's word for) handkerchief. (小兒語)手帕。

hanky-panky /ˌhæŋkɪ ˈpæŋkɪ; ˈhæŋkɪˈpæŋkɪ/ *n* [U] (colloq) underhand dealing; trickery. (俗)欺詐;騙術。

Han·sard /ˈhænsɑːd ; ˈhænsɚd/ *n* official report of proceedings in Parliament. 英國國會議事錄。

han·som /ˈhænsəm ; ˈhænsəm/ *n* (also 亦作 ˌ~ ˈ**cab**) (hist) two-wheeled horse-drawn cab for two passengers, with the driver's seat high at the back and reins going over the roof. (史)漢孫式馬車(爲一種雙輪供二人乘坐的馬車，御者座位高踞車後，轡繩自車頂越過)。

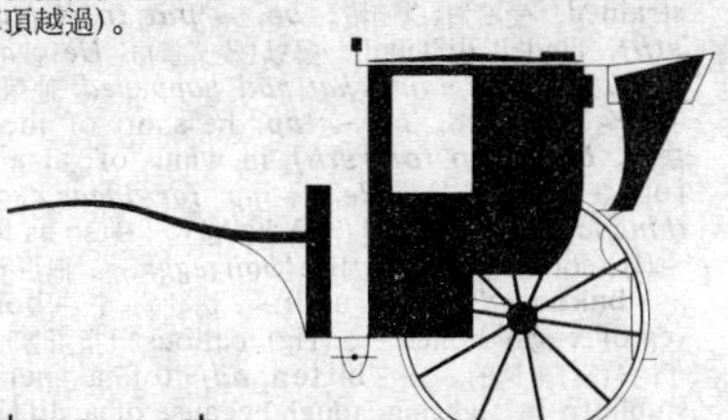

a hansom cab

hap /hæp ; hæp/ *n* (archaic) chance; luck. (古)機會;幸運。□ *vi* (-pp-) come about by chance; happen. 偶然發生;發生。

hap·haz·ard /hæpˈhæzəd ; ˌhæpˈhæzɚd/ *adj, adv* without order or plan; (at) random. 隨便的(地)；偶然的(地)。**~·ly** *adv*

hap·less /ˈhæplɪs ; ˈhæplɪs/ *adj* (archaic) unlucky. (古)不幸的。

hap·ly /ˈhæplɪ ; ˈhæplɪ/ *adv* (archaic) by chance; perhaps. (古)偶然;或許。

ha'p'orth /ˈheɪpəθ ; ˈhepɚθ/ *n* (colloq) halfpennyworth. (俗)值半辨士之物。⇨ half(3).

hap·pen /ˈhæpən ; ˈhæpən/ *vi* **1** [VP2A, 3A] ~ ***(to)***, take place; come about: 發生: *How did the accident ~?* 這意外是怎樣發生的？ *What ~ed next?* 以後怎麼樣了？ *Accidents will ~*, They are to be expected. 意外事件總會發生。*If anything ~s to him* (= If he meets with an accident), *let me know*. 如果他發生什麼意外,請通知我。**2** [VP2A, 4E] chance; have the fortune: 偶然發生;碰巧: *I ~ed to be out when he called.* 他來訪時碰巧我出去了。*It so ~ed that I had no money with me.* 恰巧我身上沒有錢。***as it ~s***, by chance: 偶然: *As it ~s, I have my cheque-book with me.* 碰巧我帶着支票簿。**3** [VP3A] ~ ***on／upon***, find by chance: 偶然發現: *I ~ed on just the thing I'd been looking for.* 我偶然發現我一直在尋找的東西。 **~·ing** /ˈhæpənɪŋ ; ˈhæpənɪŋ/ *n* (often *pl*) event: (常用複數)事件: *There have been strange ~ings here lately.* 此地近來發生了一些奇怪的事件。

happy /ˈhæpɪ ; ˈhæpɪ/ *adj* (-ier, -iest) **1** fortunate; lucky; feeling or expressing pleasure, contentment, satisfaction, etc: 幸運的;幸福的;快樂的;滿足的: *Their marriage has been a ~ one.* 他們的婚姻一直很幸福。*He is ~ in having congenial work.* 他很幸運,有一份適合他的工作。***as ~ as the day is long***, very ~. 非常快樂。**2** (in polite formulas) pleased: (客套語)高興的;愉快的: *We shall be ~ to accept your kind invitation.* 我們樂於接受你的邀請。**3** (of language, conduct, suggestions) well suited to the situation: (指言語,行爲,建議)很適當的: *a ~ thought／idea, etc.* 一個很適當的想法(觀念等)。**~-go-lucky** /ˌhæpɪ gəʊ ˈlʌkɪ ; ˈhæpɪˌgoˈlʌkɪ/ *adj* taking what fortune brings; carefree: 樂天知命的;無憂無慮的: *She goes through life in a ~-go-lucky fashion.* 她過着無憂無慮的日子。**hap·pily** /-ɪlɪ ; -ɪlɪ/ *adv* **hap·pi·ness** *n*

hara-kiri /ˌhærə ˈkɪrɪ ; ˈhɑrəˈkɪrɪ/ *n* [U] suicide by disembowelment as practised in the past by Japanese samurai when they believed they had failed in their duty. (過去日本武士或軍官之)切腹自殺;剖腹。

har·angue /həˈræŋ ; həˈræŋ/ *n* long, loud (often scolding) talk or speech. 長篇而高聲的(常是斥責性的)講話或演說。□ *vt, vi* [VP6A, 2A] make a ~ (to). (對…)作長篇而高聲的講話或演說。

har·ass /ˈhærəs *US:* həˈræs ; ˈhærəs/ *vt* [VP6A] **1** trouble; worry: 使煩惱;使憂愁: *~ed by the cares of a large family;* 爲照顧一大家庭所苦; *~ed-looking housewives.* 愁容滿面的家庭主婦。**2** make repeated attacks on: 一再襲擊: *In olden days the coasts of England were ~ed by the Vikings.* 古時英國沿海一帶一再受到北歐海盜的侵擾。**~·ment** *n* [U] ~ing or being ~ed. 煩惱;困苦;侵擾。

har·bin·ger /ˈhɑːbɪndʒə(r) ; ˈhɑrbɪndʒɚ/ *n* sb or sth that foretells the coming of sb or sth: 先驅;前兆: *The crowing of the cock is a ~ of dawn.* 鷄啼爲黎明之前兆。*The cuckoo is a ~ of spring.* 杜鵑鳥是春的前兆。

har·bour (US = **-bor**) /ˈhɑːbə(r) ; ˈhɑrbɚ/ *n* **1** place of shelter for ships: 港: *a natural ~*, eg an inlet of the sea; 天然港(例如海灣)；*an artificial ~*, one made with sea-walls, breakwaters. (以海堤,防波堤造成之)人工港。ˈ**~ dues** *n pl* money (to be) paid for anchoring or mooring a ship in a ~. 船停在港中之碇泊費;入港稅。**2** (fig) any place of safety or shelter. (喻)安全地方;避難所。□ *vt, vi* **1** [VP6A] give lodging or shelter to; protect; conceal: 庇護;保護;藏匿: *~ an escaped criminal.* 藏匿一逃犯。*My dog has long, thick hair that ~s fleas.* 我的狗生有長而厚的毛,易藏跳蚤。**2** [VP6A] hold in the mind: 心懷: *~ thoughts of revenge.* 心懷報復之念頭。**3** [VP2A] come to anchor (in a ~). 停泊(於港內)。**~·age** /ˈhɑːbərɪdʒ ; ˈhɑrbərɪdʒ/ *n* (place of) shelter. 庇護;庇護所;避難所。

hard[1] /hɑːd ; hɑrd/ *adj* (-er, -est) **1** (contrasted with *soft*) (與 soft 相對) firm; not yielding to the touch; not easily cut; solid: 堅硬的;堅固的: *as ~ as rock;* 堅硬如岩石; *ground made ~ by frost.* 凍硬的土地。*Teak is a ~ kind of wood.* 柚木是一種堅硬的木材。***a ~ nut to crack***, (fig) a difficult problem; person difficult to deal with or influence. (喻)難題;難以對付或接受影響的人。**2** (contrasted with *easy*) (與 easy 相對) difficult (to understand or explain); needing mental or moral effort: 難以了解或解釋的;困難的: *~ words*, difficult for learners, (also ⇨ 4 below); 難解釋的字;難字(參看下列第4義)；*a ~ problem／book／language;* 困難的問題(書,語言)；*a subject that is ~ to understand.* 難了解的課題。*She found it ~ to make up her mind.* 她發覺她難以下決心。*That man is ~ to please／He is a ~ man to please.* 那人(他)是個難以取悅的人。*It's ~ to say which is better.* 很難說那一個較好。*It's ~ for an old man to change his way of living.* 老年人難以變更他的生活方式。**3** causing unhappiness, discomfort, or pain; difficult to endure: 引起不快,不適或痛苦的;難以忍受的: *have／be given a ~ time*, experience difficulties, misfortunes, etc; 經歷一段困苦的日子; *in these ~ times*, in these times of money shortage, unemployment, etc when life is difficult. 値此困苦時期(缺錢,失業等生活困苦時期)。***(find sth) ~ going***, (find progress) difficult. (覺得某事)很難進行。***(find sb) ~ going***, (find him) difficult (to understand), or boring (to listen to) (覺得某人)很難了解, 言談乏味。***learn (sth) the ~ way***, with perseverance and hardship. 艱苦地學習。**4** severe; harsh: 嚴厲的;苛刻的: *a ~ father*, one who treats his children severely; 嚴父; *~ words*, harsh, showing lack of sympathy. 嚴厲的言語。***be ~ on sb***, treat him severely. 對某人嚴厲。***drive a ~ bargain***, ⇨ bargain. ***take a ~ line***, be uncompromising. 不妥協。Hence, 由此產生, ˌ**~-ˈliner** *n* person who is uncompromising. 不妥協的人。⇨ line[1](21). **5** (of the body) having ~ muscles and not much fat: (指身體)結實的: *Regular physical exercises soon made the boys ~.* 經常的運動不久便使那些男孩的身體結實了。***as ~ as nails***, **(a)** strong and muscular. 强健的。**(b)** (fig) without sentiment, or sympathy; ~-hearted. (喻)沒有感情的;硬心腸的。**6** done, doing (sth), with much effort or force; strenuous: 辛苦的;費力的;猛烈的: *a ~ blow;* 重擊; *go for a ~ gallop;* 去騎一

H

陣快馬; *a ~ worker.* 辛苦的工作者。 **7** (of the weather) severe: (指天氣)酷烈的: *a ~ winter／frost.* 嚴冬(寒)。 **8** (of sounds) (指聲音) *The letter 'c' is hard in 'cat' and soft in 'city'.* 字母 'c' 在 'cat' 一字中是硬音,在 'city' 一字中是軟音。 *The letter 'g' is ~ in 'gun' and soft in 'gin'.* 字母 'g' 在 'gun'一字中是硬音,在 'gin' 一字中是軟音。 **9** (various uses) (各種用法) ***~ and fast (rules, etc),*** that cannot be altered to fit special cases. 不許變更的;嚴格的(規則等)。 ***~ of hearing,*** rather deaf. 重聽;聽力不好。 **ˈ~·back／·cover** *n* book bound in a ~ (= stiff) cover (contrasted with paper-backed books): 精裝書(硬書皮裝訂,與平裝書相對): *The book has just appeared in ~back.* 這書剛有精裝本出版。 Hence, 由此產生, **ˈ~·backed／·covered／·bound** *adj.* **ˈ~·board** /-bɔːd ; -bord/ *n* [U] kind of material like plywood in appearance and use, made by compressing waste wood that has been ground up finely. 高壓板(由木屑壓成,外觀與用途都很像夾板)。 **ˌ~ ˈcash** *n* [U] coins and notes, not a cheque or a promise to pay. 現金;現款。 **ˈ~ core** *n* **(a)** broken brick, rubble, etc (as used for foundations, roadmaking). (作爲地基,路基用的)碎磚、碎石等。 **(b)** solid central, basic or underlying part; nucleus: 堅實的中心,基底或底層;核心: *the ~ core of the opposition／rebellion.* 反對黨(叛黨)的中堅分子。 **ˈ~ court** *n* (tennis) court with a ~ surface, not of grass. (網球)硬地球場(非草地)。 **ˌ~ ˈcurrency** *n* one that is reliable and stable. 可靠穩定之貨幣。 **ˌ~ ˈdrug** *n* one likely to lead to addiction, eg *heroin.* 麻醉藥(例如海洛英)。 **ˌ~-ˈheaded** /ˈhedɪd ; ˈhɛdɪd/ *adj* practical; not sentimental; business-like. 講求實際的;不感情用事的;實事求是的。 **ˌ~-ˈhearted** /ˈhɑːtɪd ; ˈhɑrtɪd/ *adj* unfeeling; lacking in sympathy or the gentler emotions. 無情的;硬心腸的。 **ˌ~ ˈlabour** *n* [U] imprisonment with ~ physical labour as a punishment. 勞役;苦役。 **ˌ~ ˈliquor／ˈdrink** *n* [U] with high alcoholic content eg *whisky.* 烈酒(酒精成分多的,例如威士忌)。 **ˌ~ ˈluck／ˈlines** *n* [U] worse fortune than is deserved. 倒霉。 Hence, 由此產生, **ˌ~-ˈluck story,** one seeking pity, sympathy (for oneself). (用以取得憐憫、同情等的)倒霉事。 **ˌ~ ˈshoulder** *n* ~ surface at the side of a motorway, to be used in an emergency: 高速公路之路側(緊急情況時使用): *The lorry driver pulled over to the ~ shoulder when one of the tyres burst.* 有一個輪胎爆裂,卡車司機連忙把車開到高速公路的路側。 **ˌ~ ˈstanding** *n* [U] area of ~ surface, eg, concrete, for the parking of vehicles. 硬地面(例如由混凝土鋪成可停放車輛者)。 **ˈ~·top** *n* car with a steel top and no sliding roof. 有固定金屬頂篷(非活動頂篷)之汽車。 **ˈ~·ware** *n* [U] **(a)** ironmongery; metal goods for domestic use, eg *pans, nails, locks.* 鐵器類;五金類(如鍋,釘,鎖等)。 **(b)** *military ~ware,* weapons and equipment, eg armoured vehicles. 武器和裝備(例如裝甲車輛)。 **(c)** *computer ~ware,* mechanical equipment (contrasted with information and programmes, called *software*). 計算機硬體(與稱作 software 之資訊及程式相對)。 **ˌ~ ˈwater** *n* [U] containing mineral salts that interfere with the lathering of soap. 硬水(含有干擾肥皂起泡之礦鹽)。 **ˈ~·wood** *n* [U] ~ heavy wood, eg *oak, ebony, teak,* contrasted with soft wood, eg *pine, fir:* 硬材(例如橡木,烏木,柚木,與松木,樅木等軟木相對): (attrib) (形容用法) *~wood floors.* 硬木地板。 **~·ness** *n*

hard² /hɑːd ; hɑrd/ *adv* **1** with great energy; strenuously; with all one's force: 努力地;費力地;費盡全力地: *work／study／think／pull／push ~;* 努力工作(讀書,思考,拉,推); *try ~ to succeed;* 努力以期成功; *drink／swear ~.* 拚命喝(咒詛)。 **ˌ~-ˈhitting** *adj* vigorous, direct: 猛烈的;直接的: *a ~-hitting speech.* 猛烈的演說。 **ˌ~-ˈworking** *adj* working with care and energy. 努力工作的。 **2** severely; heavily: 劇烈地;猛烈地: *freezing／raining ~.* 酷寒(下大雨)。 **3** with difficulty; with a struggle; painfully: 困難地;勞苦地;辛苦地: *my ~-earned money* 我辛辛苦苦賺來的錢 ⇨ hardly(5). ***be ~ hit,*** be suffering severely, eg by financial losses, the death of sb much loved. 受嚴重打擊(例如財務受損失,深愛之人去世等)。 ***be ~ pressed (for sth),*** be under pressure, strained. 受壓迫;處困境。 ***be ~ ˈput to it (to do sth),*** find it difficult: 難以(做某事): *He was ~ put to it to explain what had happened.* 他難以說明發生了些什麼事。 ***be ~ ˈup,*** be short of money. 缺錢。 ***be ~ ˈup for (sth),*** in want of; at a loss for: 缺少;不知所措: *He's ~ up for ideas／something to do.* 他缺少主見(沒有事情做)。 **4** so as to be ~(1), solid: 堅硬地;堅固地: *boil eggs ~.* 把蛋煮老。 **ˌ~-ˈbaked** *adj* baked until ~. 烤硬的。 **ˌ~-ˈboiled,** (eg of eggs) boiled ~; (fig) callous. (指蛋等)煮老了的;(喻)無情的。 **ˌ~-ˈbitten** *adj* (of a person) stubborn in fighting; tough because of a difficult life, etc. (指人)不屈服的;頑强的;堅忍的。 **5** closely; immediately: 接近地;緊隨地: *follow ~ after／upon／behind someone.* 緊隨某人。 ***~ by,*** close by; not far away. 在近旁;在近處;附近。 ***run sb ~,*** pursue him closely. 緊追某人。

harden /ˈhɑːdn ; ˈhɑrdn̩/ *vt, vi* [VP6A, 2A] make or become hard, strong, hardy, etc: 使硬;使堅强;使堅固;變硬;變堅强;變堅固: *~ steel;* 硬化鋼; *~ the heart;* 硬起心腸; *a ~ed criminal,* one who is callous, who shows no signs of shame or repentance; 怙惡不悛的罪犯; *~ the body,* eg by taking exercise. 鍛鍊身體(例如藉運動)。 ***be ~ed to,*** made insensitive to. 對…麻木;對…無動於衷。 [VP15B, 2C] ***~ off,*** (of young plants, esp seedlings) make or become hardy, ready for planting outside. (指植物幼苗)(使)變耐寒(以備露天種植)。

hardi·hood /ˈhɑːdɪhʊd ; ˈhɑrdɪˌhʊd/ *n* [U] boldness; audacity. 大膽;膽識。

hard·ly /ˈhɑːdlɪ ; ˈhɑrdlɪ/ *adv* **1** only just; not quite; scarcely: 剛剛;不十分;簡直沒有: *I ~ know her,* have only a very slight acquaintance with her. 我跟她不熟。 *We had ~ got／H~ had we got into the country when it began to rain.* 我們剛到鄉間就下雨了。 (Cf 參較 No sooner... than). *I'm so tired I can ~ walk.* 我太累,簡直走不動了。 **2** (used to suggest that sth is improbable, unlikely or unreasonable): (用以表示某事大概不會發生或不合理): *He can ~ have arrived yet.* 他大概還沒有到。 *You can ~ expect me to lend you money again.* 你別希望我再借錢給你。 **3** (neg in meaning) almost no; almost not: (否定意義) 幾乎沒有; 幾乎不: *He ~ ever* (= very seldom) *goes to bed before midnight.* 他很少在午夜以前就寢。 Cf 參較 His wife *almost always* goes to bed before midnight. 他的妻子幾乎總是在午夜以前就寢。 *I need ~ say* (= It is almost unnecessary for me to say) *that I am innocent.* 我幾乎用不著說我是無罪的。 *There's ~ any coal left.* 幾乎沒有煤剩下了。 *H~ anybody* (= Very few people) *came to the meeting.* 幾乎沒有人到會。 **4** (from hard¹(4)) severely: (由 hard¹ 第 4 義而來)嚴厲地: *~ treated.* 受嚴苛對待。 **5** (from hard¹ (6)) with effort or difficulty. (由 hard¹ 第 6 義而來)辛苦地。 For this sense the *adv* 'hard' is usu preferred. 指此義時,通常多用副詞 'hard'。 (Cf 參較 *hard-earned money* 辛苦賺來的錢 and *salary that was ~* (ie only just, barely) *earned.* 僅僅能够賺到的薪水;勉强賺到的薪水)。

hard·ship /ˈhɑːdʃɪp ; ˈhɑrdʃɪp/ *n* **1** [C] circumstance that causes discomfort or suffering: 困苦的情況;艱辛的情形: *the ~s borne by soldiers during a war.* 戰爭時士兵所忍受的艱辛。 **2** [U] severe suffering: 痛苦;苦難: *bear ~ without complaining.* 毫無怨言地忍受困苦。

hardy /ˈhɑːdɪ ; ˈhɑrdɪ/ *adj* (-ier, -iest) **1** strong; able to endure suffering or hardship: 强壯的;能吃苦的: *A few ~ men broke the ice on the lake and had a swim.* 幾個健壯的人打破湖上的冰游泳。 **2** (of plants) able to endure frost without being injured: (指植物)耐寒的: ~ *annuals.* 耐寒的一年生植物。 **3** bold; ready to face danger. 勇敢的;勇於面對危險的。 **hardi·ness** *n*

hare /heə(r) ; hɛr/ *n* fast-running field animal with long ears and a divided upper lip, like but larger than a rabbit. 野兔。**~ *and hounds,*** paper-chase, a game in which two persons called 'hares' run across country dropping torn-up bits of paper and are followed by others, called 'hounds', who try to catch them. 追紙戲(由二人做'兔',在田野中一面跑一面撒下碎紙,由其他稱作'獵犬'的人在後追逐)。 ***run with the ~ and hunt with the hounds,*** try to keep the favour of both sides in a dispute; play a double game. 在爭論中欲兩面討好;騎牆。***mad as a March ~,*** very mad or wild 十分瘋狂的;野性大發的。***start a ~,*** raise a topic, argument, etc unrelated to the main issue. 提出一個與主題無關的話題,議論等。 **'~·bell** *n* round-leaved plant with blue bell-like flowers 藍鈴花 (in Scotland called 蘇格蘭稱作 *bluebell*). **'~-brained** *adj* rash; foolish: 輕率的;鹵莽的;愚蠢的: *~-brained schemes.* 愚蠢的計畫。**,~·'lip** *n* person's upper lip divided (from birth) like that of a ~. 兔唇;唇裂;豁嘴;缺唇。□ *vi* [VP2C] run fast or away: 快跑;逃走: *They ~d off.* 他們跑掉了。

harem /'hɑːriːm ; 'hɛrəm/ *n* women's part of a traditional Muslim household; women living in it. 回教徒之閨房;回教徒之女眷。

hari·cot /'hærɪkəʊ ; 'hærɪ,ko/ *n* (also 亦作 **~ bean**) kidney bean; French bean. 扁豆。

hark /hɑːk ; hɑrk/ *vi* **1** (chiefly imper) (主作祈使) **~ *at,*** (colloq, teasing) listen to: (俗,揶揄語)聽: *Just ~ at him!* 聽聽他! **2 ~ *back (to),*** refer back to sth done or said earlier. 言歸(正傳)。

har·le·quin /'hɑːlɪkwɪn ; 'hɑrləkwɪn/ *n* character in Italian comedy; mute character in English pantomime, full of tricks and very lively, wearing a mask and multi-coloured costume; (hence) person fond of practical jokes; buffoon. 義大利喜劇中一角色;英國啞劇中一諧角(戴面具,着彩衣);(由此產生) 喜開玩笑的人;丑角。 **~·ade** /,hɑːlɪkwɪ'neɪd ; ,hɑrləkwɪn'ed/ *n* part of a pantomime in which a ~ plays the chief part. 啞劇中丑角主演的部分。

Har·ley Street /'hɑːlɪ striːt ; 'hɑrlɪ strit/ *n* London street where many fashionable doctors and surgeons live. 哈萊街(倫敦一街道,有許多名醫居於此)。

har·lot /'hɑːlət ; 'hɑrlət/ *n* (archaic, or as a term of abuse) prostitute. (古,或辱罵語)娼妓。

harm /hɑːm ; hɑrm/ *n* [U] damage; injury: 損害;傷害: *He probably meant no ~,* did not intend to hurt anyone or anyone's feelings. 他大概沒有惡意。 *There's no ~ in your staying up late occasionally,* no reason why you should not do so. 你偶爾遲睡並無害處。***do sb ~,*** cause injury to him: 傷害某人: *A few drinks will do you no ~.* 稍微喝幾杯對你不會有害。***out of ~'s way,*** in a place of safety. 在安全的地方。□ *vt* [VP6A] cause ~ to: 傷害;損害: *It hasn't ~ed you, has it?* 那沒有傷害你吧,對嗎? **~·ful** /-fl ; -fəl/ *adj* causing ~ (*to*). (對…)有害的(與 to 連用)。**~·fully** /-fəlɪ ; -fəlɪ/ *adv* **~·less** *adj* **1** not doing ~ (*to*): (對…)無害的(與 to 連用): *~less snakes.* 無毒的蛇。 **2** innocent; inoffensive: 無辜的;無惡意的: *Several ~less spectators were wounded during the rioting.* 在騷亂中有幾個無辜的旁觀者受傷了。 **~·less·ly** *adv*

har·mat·tan /,hɑːmə'tæn ; ,hɑrmə'tæn/ *n* cold, dry wind from the north that blows in W Africa from December to March. 非洲西部十二月至三月所吹的寒冷乾燥北風。

har·monic /hɑː'mɒnɪk ; hɑr'mɑnɪk/ *n* (music) higher note produced (by vibration of strings) with a note that is played, and having a fixed relation to it. (音樂)泛音;和音(由絃之顫動而產生的音高於基音,並與基音有固定的關係)。

har·mon·ica /hɑː'mɒnɪkə ; hɑr'mɑnɪkə/ *n* mouth-organ. 口琴。

har·moni·ous /hɑː'məʊnɪəs ; hɑr'monɪəs/ *adj* **1** pleasingly or satisfactorily arranged: 調和的;協調的;排列悅目的: *a ~ group of buildings.* 一片調和的建築物。 **2** in agreement; free from ill feeling: 和諧的;和睦的: *~ families/neighbours.* 和睦的家庭(鄰居)。 **3** sweet-sounding; tuneful. 音調和諧的;悅耳的。 **~·ly** *adv*

har·mo·nium /hɑː'məʊnɪəm ; hɑr'monɪəm/ *n* small musical keyboard instrument (like an organ), with the notes produced by air blown through metal reeds. 簧風琴(類似風琴的小鍵盤樂器,藉空氣振動金屬簧片而發音)。

har·mon·ize /'hɑːmənaɪz ; 'hɑrmə,naɪz/ *vt, vi* **1** [VP6A, 14] **~ *(with),*** bring (one thing) into harmony (with another); (music) add notes (to a melody) to make chords. 使調和;(音樂)加音(於樂曲)使成和絃。 **2** [VP2A, C] **~ *(with),*** be in harmony or agreement: 調和;和諧: *colours that ~ well (with the decorations/with each other).* (與裝飾物,彼此之間) 很調和的色彩。 **har·mon·iz·ation** /,hɑːmənaɪ'zeɪʃn *US:* -nɪ'z- ; ,hɑrmənaɪ'zeʃən/ *n*

har·mony /'hɑːmənɪ ; 'hɑrmənɪ/ *n* (*pl* -nies) **1** [U] agreement (of feeling, interests, opinions, etc): (感情,興趣,意見等的)和睦;一致: *There was not much ~ in international affairs during those years.* 那些年國際間的事務不太和諧。***be in ~ (with),*** match; agree (with): 相配;(與…)一致: *His tastes are in ~ with mine.* 他的愛好與我的相同。 **2** [C, U] (instance or example of) pleasing combination of related things: 調和;協調: *the ~ of colour in nature,* eg the greens, browns, etc of trees in autumn. 自然界色彩的協調(例如秋季樹木之綠色,褐色等)。 **3** [C, U] (music) pleasing combination of notes sounded together to make chords. (音樂)和聲學;和聲。

har·ness /'hɑːnɪs ; 'hɑrnɪs/ *n* (collective *sing*) all the leather-work and metal-work by which a horse is controlled and fastened to the cart, waggon, plough, etc, that it pulls. (集合單數) 馬具 (將馬繫於車或犂上,及御馬用的所有皮製與金屬用具);軛具。 ⇨ yoke. ***in ~,*** (fig) doing one's regular work. (喻)在做經常所做的工作。***die in ~,*** die while engaged in one's regular work, not after retiring.

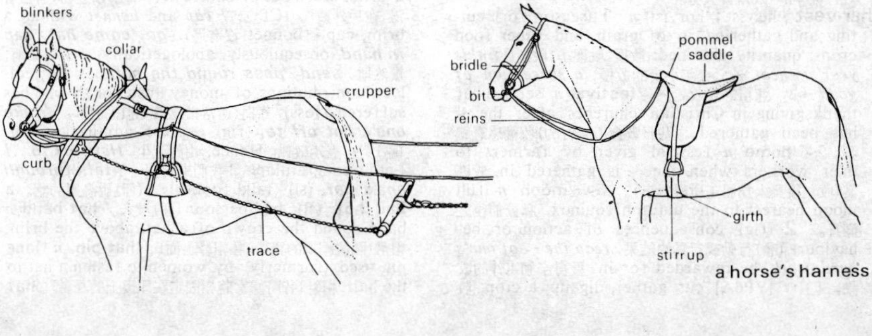

a horse's harness

殉職;在工作中死去。***work / run in double ~,*** work with a partner, or with a husband or wife. 與夥伴共同工作;夫妻雙雙工作。□ *vt* [VP6A] **1** put a ~ on (a horse). 套馬具於(馬)。 **2** use (eg a river, waterfall, etc) to produce (esp electric) power. 利用(河,瀑布等)產生動力(尤指電力)。

harp /hɑːp ; hɑrp/ *n* freestanding musical instrument with vertical strings played with the fingers. 豎琴。⇨ the illus at string. 參看 string 之插圖。□ *vi* **1** play the ~. 彈豎琴。 **2** *~ on sth,* (fig) talk repeatedly or tiresomely about: (喻)反覆地或令人厭倦地談論: *She is always ~ing on my faults.* 她老是反覆述說我的缺點。 **~er, ~·ist** /-ɪst ; -ɪst/ *nn* player on the ~. 彈豎琴者。

har·poon /hɑːˈpuːn ; hɑrˈpun/ *n* spear on a rope, thrown by hand or fired from a gun, for catching whales and other large sea animals. 魚叉(繫於繩上,由手擲出,或用砲射出,用以捕鯨及其他大的海生動物)。□ *vt* strike with a ~. 用魚叉叉。

harp·si·chord /ˈhɑːpsɪkɔːd ; ˈhɑrpsɪˌkɔrd/ *n* piano-like instrument used from the 16th to the 18th cc (and today for music of these centuries). 大鍵琴(一種似鋼琴的樂器,風行於十六至十八世紀,今日用以奏該世紀的音樂)。⇨ the illus at keyboard. 參看 keyboard 之插圖。

harpy /ˈhɑːpɪ ; ˈhɑrpɪ/ *n* (*pl* -pies) **1** (Gk myth) cruel creature with a woman's face and a bird's wings and claws. (希神)生有女人面孔及鳥翅與爪的殘酷怪物。 **2** cruel, greedy, hard-hearted woman. 殘酷、貪婪、無情的女人。

har·ri·dan /ˈhærɪdən ; ˈhærədən/ *n* worn-out, bad-tempered old woman. 面容枯槁,脾氣暴躁的老婦。

har·rier /ˈhærɪə(r) ; ˈhærɪə/ *n* **1** hound used for hunting hares; (*pl*) pack of these with huntsmen. 獵兔犬;(複)一群獵兔犬及獵人。 **2** cross-country runner. 越野賽跑者。

har·row /ˈhærəʊ ; ˈhæro/ *n* heavy frame with metal teeth or discs for breaking up ground after ploughing. 耙。□ *vt* [VP6A] pull a ~ over (a field, etc); (fig) distress (the feelings): 耙(地等); (喻)使(感情)痛苦;使傷心: *a ~ing tale of misfortunes.* 一個令人傷心的不幸的故事。

H

harry /ˈhærɪ ; ˈhærɪ/ *vt* (*pt, pp* -rried) [VP6A] **1** lay waste and plunder; attack frequently: 蹂躪;時常侵襲: *The Vikings used to ~ the English coast.* 北歐海盜昔時常常侵襲英國沿海地方。 **2** annoy or worry: 使苦惱: *money-lenders ~ing their debtors.* 苦逼債務人的放利者。

harsh /hɑːʃ ; hɑrʃ/ *adj* (-er, -est) **1** rough and disagreeable, esp to the senses: 粗糙而令人不快的(尤指在感官上): *a ~ texture / voice / contrast;* 粗糙的織物(刺耳的聲音;刺目的對比); *~ to the ear.* 刺耳。 **2** stern, cruel, severe: 苛刻的;殘酷的;嚴厲的: *a ~ judge / judgement / punishment.* 嚴厲的法官(判決,懲罰)。 **~·ly** *adv* **~·ness** *n*

hart /hɑːt ; hɑrt/ *n* adult male of (esp red) deer; stag. 牡鹿(尤指紅鹿)。

harum-scarum /ˌheərəm ˈskeərəm ; ˈhɛrəmˈskɛrəm/ *adj, n* (colloq) reckless, impulsive (person). (俗)輕率的(人);冒失鬼。

har·vest /ˈhɑːvɪst ; ˈhɑrvɪst/ *n* **1** (season for) cutting and gathering in of grain and other food crops; quantity obtained: 收穫;收穫季;收穫量: *this year's wheat ~;* 今年小麥的收穫; *a succession of good ~s.* 連續的豐收。 **ˌ~ ˈfestival** *n* service of thanksgiving in Christian churches after the ~ has been gathered. (基督教會所舉行的)收穫感恩禮拜。 **~ ˈhome** *n* festival given by farmers to their workers when the ~ is gathered in. 收穫宴(收割後農人爲雇工所舉行者)。 **ˌ~ ˈmoon** *n* full moon nearest to the autumn equinox. 秋分前後之滿月。 **2** (fig) consequences of action or behaviour: (喻)行動或行爲的結果: *reap the ~ of one's hard work,* be rewarded for it. 獲得辛勤工作的成果。□ *vt* [VP6A] cut, gather, dig up, a crop: 收割;收穫: *~ rice / potatoes.* 收割稻穀(馬鈴薯)。 **~er** *n* **1** person who ~s; reaper. 收割者。 **2** machine for cutting and gathering grain, esp the kind that also binds the grain into sheaves or (**ˌcombine-ˈ~er**) threshes the grain. 收割機(尤指連帶捆穀與打穀者)。

has ⇨ have¹.

has-been /ˈhæz biːn ; ˈhæzˌbɪn/ *n* (colloq) person who, or thing which, has lost a quality, skill, etc formerly possessed; sb or sth now out of date. (俗)曾具有某種性質,技術等的人或物;過時的人或物。

hash /hæʃ ; hæʃ/ *vt* [VP6A, 15B] *~ (up),* chop or cut up (meat) into small pieces. 把(肉)切丁或切碎。□ *n* **1** [U] (dish of) cooked meat, ~ed and re-cooked. 回鍋肉丁(將熟肉切丁再行烹製的菜肴)。 **2** ***make a ~ of sth,*** (fig) do it very badly, make a mess of it. (喻)弄糟某事物。***settle sb's ~,*** deal with him in such a way that he gives no more trouble. 使某人不再找麻煩。 **3** (colloq) hashish. (俗)印度大麻。

hash·ish /ˈhæʃiːʃ ; ˈhæʃiʃ/ *n* [U] dried hemp leaves made into a drug for smoking or chewing; cannabis. 由乾大麻葉製成的吸食或嚼用的藥物;印度大麻。

hasn't /ˈhæznt ; ˈhæznt/ = has not. ⇨ have¹.

hasp /hɑːsp *US:* hæsp ; hæsp/ *n* metal fastening for a door, window, etc used with a staple. 門窗等之搭鈕(與U形釘連用)。⇨ the illus at padlock. 參看 padlock 之插圖。

has·sle /ˈhæsl ; ˈhæsl/ *n* (colloq) (俗) **1** difficulty; struggle: 困難;掙扎: *a real ~ to get on the train.* 上火車時的爭先恐後。 **2** argument; quarrel. 爭辯;爭吵。□ *vi, vt* **1** [VP2A, 3A] *~ (with sb),* argue; quarrel. 爭辯;爭吵。 **2** [VP6A] bother; annoy: 打擾;煩擾: *Don't keep hassling me!* 不要老煩我!

has·sock /ˈhæsək ; ˈhæsək/ *n* cushion for kneeling on, eg in church. 膝墊(例如教堂內所用者)。

hast /hæst ; hæst/ (archaic): (古): *thou ~,* = you have.

haste /heɪst ; hest/ *n* [U] quickness of movement; hurry: 急速;匆忙: *Why all this ~?* Why are you in such a hurry? 爲何如此匆忙? *He went off in great ~.* 他匆匆離去。***Make ~!*** Hurry! 趕快! ***More ~, less speed,*** (prov) The more you hurry, the less real progress you will make. (諺) 欲速則不達。

hasten /ˈheɪsn ; ˈhesn̩/ *vi, vt* **1** [VP2A, C, 4A] move or act with speed: 急忙;趕快: *~ away / home / to the office;* 急忙離去(回家,到辦公室); *~ to tell sb the good news.* 急忙把好消息告訴某人。 **2** [VP6A] cause (sb) to hurry; cause (sth) to be done or to happen quickly or earlier: 催促(某人);促進(某事物): *Artificial heating ~s the growth of plants.* 人工加熱法加速植物的生長。

hasty /ˈheɪstɪ ; ˈhestɪ/ *adj* (-ier, -iest) said, made or done (too) quickly: 急忙的;匆匆的;過於匆忙的;輕率的: *~ preparations for flight;* 急忙準備逃走; *a ~ departure;* 匆匆離去; *~ words that are regretted afterwards.* 事後懊悔的輕率言詞。 **hast·ily** /-ɪlɪ ; -l̩ɪ/ *adv* **hasti·ness** *n*

hat /hæt ; hæt/ *n* covering for the head, usu with a brim, worn out of doors. 帽(一種蓋頭之物,通常有邊,在戶外戴)。(Cf 參較 *cap* and *bonnet* without a brim, cap 和 bonnet 沒有邊). ***go / come hat / cap in hand,*** obsequiously, apologetically. 卑躬屈節地;歉然地。***send / pass round the hat,*** ask for, collect, contributions of money (usu for sb who has suffered a loss). 募捐(通常指爲遭受損失者募款)。***take one's hat off to,*** (fig) express admiration for. (喻)對…表示敬佩。Hence, 由此產生, ***Hats off to...!*** Let us congratulate...! 我們來祝賀…! ***talk through one's hat,*** (sl) talk foolishly. (俚)說愚蠢的話。 **a bad hat,** (sl) bad person. (俚)壞人。 **ˈhat-band** *n* band round the crown of a hat, above the brim. 帽帶(圍繞帽頂的寬帶,在帽緣上面)。 **ˈhat-pin** *n* long pin used (formerly) by women to fasten a hat to the hair. 帽針(昔時婦女將帽固定在頭髮上的長針)。**ˈhat**

trick *n* (cricket) taking of three wickets with successive balls; similar success in other sports or activities. (板球)連續使三個擊球員退場;其他運動或活動中類似的成就。**hat·ful** /-fʊl; -fʊl/ *n* as much as a hat holds. 一帽所容之量。**hat·less** *adj* not wearing a hat. 未戴帽的。**hat·ter** *n* man who makes or sells hats. 製帽人;帽商。***as mad as a hatter,*** very mad. 極爲瘋狂。

hatch[1] /hætʃ; hætʃ/ *n* **1** (movable covering over an) opening in a door or floor, esp **('~·way)** one in a ship's deck through which cargo is lowered and raised; opening in a wall between two rooms, esp a kitchen and a dining room, through which dishes, etc, are passed. 門上或地板上之開口;(尤指甲板上裝卸貨物之)艙口(亦稱 hatchway);門或地板上之開口可移動的蓋;艙口蓋;兩室間牆壁上的開口(尤指厨房與餐廳間用以傳遞菜肴者)。***under ~es,*** below deck. 在甲板下。**2** lower half of a divided door. 上下開合門之下半扇門。

hatch[2] /hætʃ; hætʃ/ *vt, vi* **1** [VP6A, 2A] (cause to) break out (of an egg): 孵(卵);孵(雞);使(自卵中)孵出: *~ an egg;* 孵卵; *~ chickens.* 孵小雞。*When will the eggs ~?* 這些蛋何時孵出小雞? *Three chickens ~ed today.* 今天有三隻小雞孵出來了。***Don't count one's chickens before they're ~ed,*** (prov) Don't rely too much upon sth which is uncertain. (諺)不要在蛋尚未孵出時先數雞 (勿過份指望沒有把握之事)。**2** [VP6A] think out and produce (a plot, etc). 策畫(計謀等)。**~·ery** /ˈhætʃərɪ; ˈhætʃərɪ/ *n* (*pl* -ries) place for ~ing (esp fish): 孵卵處(尤指魚卵孵化處): *a 'trout-~ery.* 鱒魚孵化處。Cf 參較 *incubator,* for chicks. 孵雞器。

hatch[3] /hætʃ; hætʃ/ *vt* [VP6A] draw on or engrave (a surface) with parallel lines. 在(一平面)繪製或雕刻影線。**~·ing** *n* [U] such lines. 影線。

hatchet /ˈhætʃɪt; ˈhætʃɪt/ *n* light, short-handled axe. 手斧;斧頭。⇨ the illus at tool. 參看 tool 之插圖。***bury the ~,*** stop quarrelling or fighting and be friendly. 媾和;言歸於好。

hatch·way /ˈhætʃweɪ; ˈhætʃ,we/ *n* ⇨ hatch[1].

hate /heɪt; het/ *vt* [VP6A, D, 7A, 17, 19] have a strong dislike of or for; (colloq) regret: 憎恨;憎惡;(俗)抱歉;遺憾: *My cat ~s dogs.* 我的貓恨狗。*I ~ to trouble you.* 我不願麻煩你。*I ~ you to be troubled.* 我不願你受到麻煩。*She ~s getting to the theatre late.* 她不喜歡到戲院時遲到。*She ~s anyone listening while she's telephoning.* 她打電話時討厭別人聽。□ *n* [U] strong dislike or ill-will: 憎惡;憎恨: *He was filled with ~ for his opponent.* 他對他的對手滿懷憎恨。

hate·ful /ˈheɪtfl; ˈhetfəl/ *adj* exciting hatred or strong dislike: 可恨的;可惡的;討厭的: *The sight of food was ~ to the seasick girl.* 那暈船的女孩看到食物就感到厭惡。**~ly** /-fəlɪ; -fəlɪ/ *adv*

hath /hæθ; hæθ/ (archaic) 3rd pers sing pres t of *have.* (古) have 的第三人稱,單數,現在式。

hatred /ˈheɪtrɪd; ˈhetrɪd/ *n* ***~ of/for,*** hate; strong dislike: 憎恨;憎惡: *He looked at me with ~.* 他以憎恨的眼光望着我。

hat·ter /ˈhætə(r); ˈhætɚ/ *n* ⇨ hat.

hau·berk /ˈhɔːbɜːk; ˈhɔbɝk/ *n* coat of chain mail (as worn by soldiers in the Middle Ages); ⇨ the illus at armour. (中古時武士所著之)鎖子鎧(參看 armour 之插圖)。

haughty /ˈhɔːtɪ; ˈhɔtɪ/ *adj* (-ier, -iest) arrogant; having or showing a high opinion of oneself: 傲慢的;驕傲的: *The nobles used to treat the common people with ~ contempt.* 貴族在過去慣於傲慢和輕蔑地對待平民。**haught·ily** /-ɪlɪ; -ḷɪ/ *adv* **haugh·ti·ness** *n*

haul /hɔːl; hɔl/ *vt, vi* [VP6A, 15A, B, 2C, 3A] pull (with effort or force): 拖;拉;牽;曳: *elephants ~ing logs;* 拖木材的象; *~ timber to a saw-mill;* 將木材拖到鋸木廠; *~ at/upon a rope.* 拖繩子。*They ~ed the boat up the beach.* 他們把船拖到岸上。***~ down one's flag/colours,*** surrender. 投降。***~ sb over the coals,*** scold him severely (for wrongdoing). (因其過失)嚴責某人。□ *n* [C] **1** act of ~ing; distance along which sth is ~ed: 拖;拉;拖曳的距離: *long ~s on the railways.* 鐵路上長距離的拖運。**2** amount gained as the result of effort, esp of fish ~ed up in a net: 努力所獲致的結果;(尤指)一網打起之魚量: *a good ~ of fish.* 滿滿一網魚。*The thief made a good ~,* What he stole was valuable. 那賊偷了不少值錢的東西。

haul·age /ˈhɔːlɪdʒ; ˈhɔlɪdʒ/ *n* [U] transport (of goods): (貨物之)運輸: *the road ~ industry,* concerned with carriage of goods by road in lorries, etc; 公路貨運業; *a ~ contractor.* 貨運承辦者。

haul·ier /ˈhɔːlɪə(r); ˈhɔljɚ/ *n* person or firm that owns lorries, and contracts to carry goods by road; haulage contractor. 承辦陸路貨運者。

haulm /hɔːm; hɔm/ *n* (collective *sing*) stems and stalks of peas, beans, potatoes, etc, esp after the crop is gathered. (集合單數)豆,馬鈴薯等之莖(尤指收穫後者);豆稭。

haunch /hɔːntʃ; hɔntʃ/ *n* (in man and animals) part of the body round the hips, or between the ribs and the thighs: (人與動物之)腰臀部分: *a ~ of venison.* 腰臀部鹿肉。*The dog was sitting on its ~es.* 那狗蹲着。

haunt /hɔːnt; hɔnt/ *vt* [VP6A] **1** visit, be with, habitually or repeatedly; (esp of ghosts and spirits) appear repeatedly in: 常至;常去;(尤指鬼和幽靈)常出沒於: *The old castle is said to be ~ed.* 那座古堡據說鬧鬼。**2** return to the mind repeatedly: 縈繞心頭: *a ~ing melody/face.* 縈繞心頭的曲子(面孔)。*A wrongdoer is constantly ~ed by fear of discovery.* 做惡者經常提心吊膽,怕被別人發覺。□ *n* place frequently visited by the person(s) named: (某人)常去的地方: *a ~ of criminals;* 罪犯常去的地方; *revisit the ~s of one's schooldays,* the places where one spent one's time then. 重遊學生時代常去的地方。

haut·boy /ˈhəʊbɔɪ; ˈhobɔɪ/ *n* = oboe.

hau·teur /əʊˈtɜː(r); hoˈtɝ/ *n* [U] hautiness of manner. 傲慢。

Ha·vana /həˈvænə; həˈvænə/ *n* cigar made at ~ or elsewhere in Cuba. 哈瓦那或古巴其他地方所製的雪茄煙。

have[1] /*usu form after 'I, we, you, they'*: v; v; *usu form after a pause*: həv; həv; *usu form elsewhere*: əv; əv; *strong form*: hæv; hæv/ *aux v* (*3rd pers sing* has /*usu form*: z; z; *after* p, t, k, f, θ *only*: s; s; *after* s, z, ʃ, ʒ, tʃ, dʒ *only*: əz; əz; *after a pause*: həz; həz; *strong form*: hæz; hæz/, *pt* had /*usu form after 'I, we, you, they'*: d; d; *usu form after a pause*: həd; həd; *usu form elsewhere*: əd; əd; *strong form*: hæd; hæd/; *neg forms*: haven't /ˈhævnt; ˈhævṇt/, hasn't /ˈhæznt; ˈhæzṇt/, hadn't /ˈhædnt; ˈhædṇt/) **1** used in forming the perfect tenses and the perfect inf: 用以形成完成時態與不定詞的完成式: *I ~/I've finished.* 我已做完了。*He has/He's gone.* 他走了。*H~ you done it?* 你做了嗎? *Yes, I ~.* 是的,我做了。*No, I ~n't.* 不,我沒有。*I shall ~ done it by next week.* 我將於下週前做完(它)。*You ought to ~ done it.* 你應該做了這事。**2** (By inverting the finite *had* with the subject, the equivalent of an *if*-clause is obtained): (以其限定形式 had 與主詞倒置,成爲一表示條件的子句): *Had I* (= If I had) *known, ...* 如果我那時知道的話,…。⇨ if(1).

have[2] /hæv; hæv/ *anom v* (*3rd pers sing* has /hæz; hæz/; *pt, pp* had /hæd; hæd/; neg forms haven't /ˈhævnt; ˈhævṇt/, hasn't /ˈhæznt; ˈhæzṇt/, hadn't /ˈhædnt; ˈhædṇt/) (conjugated (for the neg and interr forms) without the *aux v* 'do' in GB usage, but not always in US usage; in GB colloq style often replaced by *have*[1] *got,* eg *I've got* for *I ~*) (其否定和疑問形式變化,在英國不需要助

H

動詞 do, 但在美國的用法則不盡然。在英國口語中常與 got 連用,例如 I've got 以代替 I have) **1** (in sentences that can be recomposed with the *v* 'be'): (在可以用 be 重組成的句中): [VP6B] *I ~ no doubt* (= There is no doubt in my mind) *that....* 我確信…。*Has the house* (= Is there with the house) *a good garden?* 那房子有一個好花園嗎? **2** [VP6B] possess; own (sth concrete): 擁有;有(具體之物): *He's (got) a house in the country.* 他在鄉間有一棟房子。*How many books ~ you/do you ~?* 你有多少本書? **3** [VP6B] possess or show as a mental or physical characteristic (often equivalent to a construction with *be*): 據有;有(指精神或身體上的特點,常相當於某種含 be 的結構): *Has she blue eyes or brown eyes?* Are her eyes blue or brown? 她的眼睛是藍色的還是棕色的? *He hasn't a good memory,* His memory isn't good. 他的記憶力不好。(Notes: In US usage aux *do* is common: 注意:在美國通常用助動詞 do: *Does she ~ blue eyes?* 她的眼睛是藍色的嗎? *Do you ~ a good memory?* 你的記憶力好嗎?In GB colloq styles, the *pp got* is common: 在英國口語中常用過去分詞 got: *Has she got blue eyes?* 她的眼睛是藍色的嗎?) **4** [VP6B] used to indicate various connections: 用以表示各種關係: *How many children ~ they?* 他們有多少孩子? *He hasn't many friends here.* 他在此地沒有多少朋友。(The notes above on GB and US usage apply here, too.) (上述英美用法上的不同亦適用於此)。 **5** (followed by an abstract *n* + *to*-inf, in a construction equivalent to *be* + *adj* + *to*-inf): (後接抽象名詞及不定詞,相當於 be 加形容詞及不定詞): *Will you ~ the kindness/goodness, etc* (= Please be kind or good enough) *to hand me that book?* 請將那本書遞給我好嗎? *How dare you ~ the impudence* (= be so impudent as) *to say that!* 你竟敢如此無禮,說出那種話來! *Had she/Did she ~ the cheek* (= Was she cheeky enough) *to ask for more money?* 她還有臉要更多的錢嗎? **6** (in colloq style usu with *got*) hold or keep in the mind; exercise some quality of the mind; experience (some emotion): (在口語中通常與 got 連用)心中有;心存;經歷(某種情感): *H~ you (got)/Do you ~ any idea where he lives?*你知道他住在哪裏嗎? *What reason ~ you (got) for thinking that he's dishonest?* 你憑什麼認爲他不誠實? *What kind of holiday ~ you in mind?* 你打算怎樣度假? **7** [VP6A, 18C, 19B] (in the inf only and always stressed) allow; endure: (僅用其不定詞形式,並須重讀)允許; 忍受: *I won't '~ such conduct.* 我不容許此種行爲。*I won't '~ you saying such things.* 我不容許你講這種話。

have³ (for pronunciations ⇨ have²) *vt* (Used in the neg and interr with or without the *aux v* 'do'. The distinction is not always clear and there can be recommendations only, not rules. When the reference is to sth regular or habitual, the use of *do* for neg and interr is to be preferred. When the reference is to a particular occasion, constructions without *do*, and, in colloq style, with *got*, are to be preferred.) (用於否定和疑問句時,用助動詞 do 或不用皆可。用 do 與不用 do 的區別不太明確,並無規則可循,僅有下列的提示可供參考: 指通常或習慣上的事情時,在否定和疑問句中多用 do; 指一特殊事例時,多不用 do,並且在口語中多與 got 連用。) **1** [VP7B] **~ to do sth,** (*have to* = /ˈhæf tə ; ˈhæftə/; *has to* = /ˈhæs tə ; ˈhæstə/; *had to* = /ˈhæt tə ; ˈhædtə/) expressing obligation or necessity: (表示義務或必要)必須(做某事): *Do you often ~ to go to the dentist's?* 你必須常常去看牙嗎? *H~ you (got) to go to the dentist's today?* 你今天必須去看牙嗎? *The children don't ~ to go to school on Sundays, do they?* 孩子們星期日不須上學,是嗎? *You ~n't (got) to go to school today, ~ you?* 你今天不須去上學,是嗎? *I ~ to be getting along* (= must leave) *now.* 現在我必須走了。*He's so rich that he doesn't ~ to work.* 他很富有,不須工作。*We had to leave early.* 我們必須早些離去。*Had you/Did you ~ to leave early?* 你必須早些離去嗎? *These shoes will ~ to be repaired.* 這些鞋子必須修補了。 ⇨ must², need². **2** [VP6A] (in various senses as shown in these examples): (用於下列例句中的各種用法): *Do you often ~* (= suffer from) *colds?* 你時常感冒嗎? *H~ you (got)* (= Are you suffering from) *a cold now?* 你感冒了嗎? *Do you ~* (ie as a rule, generally) *much time for reading?* 你平常有很多時間讀書嗎? *H~ you (got)* (ie now, or on the occasion specified) *time to come with me?* 你有時間(指現在或特定的時間)同我去嗎? *Has your dog (got) any puppies now?* 你的狗生小狗了嗎? *How often does your dog ~* (ie give birth to) *puppies?* 你的狗多久生一次小狗? *Can you ~* (= take and look after) *the children for a few days?* 你能把孩子們帶去照顧幾天嗎?

have⁴ (for pronunciations ⇨ have²) *non-anom v* (neg and interr always with the *aux v* 'do') (在否定和疑問句中經常與助動詞 do 連用) **1** [VP6A] take; receive; accept; obtain: 吃; 飲;接受; 得到: *There was nothing to be had,* obtained. 一點東西也得不到。*Do you ~ tea or coffee for breakfast?* 你早餐時飲茶還是喝咖啡? *What shall we ~ for dinner?* 我們晚餐吃什麼? **2** [VP6A] (with a *n*, so that *have* and the *n* are equivalent to a *v* identical with the *n*): (與一名詞連用,等於與該名詞相當的動詞的意義): *~ a swim/walk/wash/rest.* 去游泳(散步,盥洗,休息)。*Let me ~ a try/look.* 讓我試一試(看一看)。*Go and ~ a lie down.* 去躺下休息一會兒。*Do you ever ~ dreams?* 你做過夢嗎? **3** [VP6A] experience; undergo: 經歷;遭受: *We didn't ~ much difficulty.* 我們沒有遭受什麼困難。*Did you ~ a good holiday?* 你過了一個快樂的假日嗎? *You've never had it so good,* never had so much, or such good quality, of it before. 你從未得到這樣多(過得這樣好)。***let him/them ~ it,*** (sl) shoot, punish sb, etc according to the situation. (俚)射殺或懲罰某人。 ***~ had it,*** (sl) not be going to receive or enjoy sth: (俚)得不到某物;不能享受某物: *Here come the police—I'm afraid we've had it!* 警察來了 — 我恐怕我們得不到了! **4** [VP24C] ***~ sth done,*** cause (sb to do sth): 使(某人做某事): *You'd better ~ that bad tooth pulled out.* 你最好把那顆蛀牙拔掉。 *I must ~ these shoes repaired.* 我必須把這些鞋子拿去修。*When did you last ~ your hair cut?* 你上一次理髮是什麼時候? ⇨ get(2). ⇨ also 6 below. 亦參看下列第 6 義。 **5** [VP18C] ***~ sb do sth,*** want him to do it: 要(某人做某事): *I would ~ you know that...,* I want you to know that.... 我要讓你知道…。*What would you ~ me do?* 你要我做什麼? *I wouldn't ~ you do that,* should prefer you not to do it. 我不願你做那事。***~ to do with,*** ⇨ do²(14). **6** [VP24B] ***~ sth done,*** experience or suffer it: 蒙受: *He had his pocket picked,* sth stolen from his pocket. 他遭受到扒竊。*Charles I had his head cut off.* 查理一世遭到斷頭之禍。**7** [VP6A] (colloq) (俗) **(a)** trick; deceive: 欺騙: *I'm afraid you've been had.* 我恐怕你受騙了。*Mind he doesn't ~ you.* 當心勿使他騙你。**(b)** beat; win an advantage over: 擊敗;勝過: *He had me in that argument.* 他在那次辯論中戰勝了我。*You had me there!* 你擊敗我了! **8** (with *it* and a clause) express; maintain: (與 it 及一子句連用)表示;堅持: *Rumour has it* (= There is a rumour) *that the Prime Minister is going to resign.* 傳聞首相將要辭職。*He will ~ it* (= He insists) *that our plan is impracticable.* 他會堅持說我們的計畫行不通。 *...as Plato has it* (used when giving a quotation, etc). 如柏拉圖所說…(用於引用文句等時)。 **9** [VP15B] (uses with *adverbial particles* and *preps*): (與副詞接語及介詞連用的用法):

have sth back: *You shall ~ it back* (= It will be returned to you) *next month.* 下月把它還給你。*Let me ~ it back soon.* 快些把它還給我。

have sb down, entertain sb as a visitor or guest: 請某人做客;款待某人: *We're having the Greens down* (eg from London) *for a few days.* 我們將請格林一家人來住幾天(例如從倫敦來)。
have sb in, receive him in the room, house, etc: 請某人到房屋等內: *We shall be having the decorators in next month,* The men will be decorating the house. 我們下月將請人來裝飾房屋。~ ***sth in,*** possess in the house, etc: 置備某物於房屋等內: *Do we ~ enough coal in for winter?* 我們貯備的煤夠冬季用嗎?
have it off/away (with sb), ⚠ (sl) ~ sexual intercourse (with). (諱)(俚)(與某人)發生性關係。
have sb on, (colloq) play a trick on him, deceive him. (俗)欺騙某人。⇨ 7 above. 參看上列第7義。~ ***sth on,*** **(a)** be wearing: 穿着;戴着: *He had nothing on,* was naked. 他赤裸着。**(b)** ~ an engagement: 有約會: *I ~ nothing on tomorrow evening,* I am free. 我明天晚間沒有約會。
have sth out, cause sth to be taken out: 使某物在外;將某物去除: ~ *a tooth out.* 拔掉一牙。~ ***one's sleep out,*** continue sleeping until one wakes naturally: 繼續睡到自己醒來: *Let her ~ her sleep out.* 讓她繼續睡夠。~ ***it out with sb,*** reach an understanding about sth by frank discussion. 坦白地與某人討論某事以達成諒解。
have sb over/round, be visited at home by him: 請某人到家來: *We had Sue and Steve round for dinner last night.* 昨晚我們請蘇和史提夫來家中晚餐。
have sb up, **(a)** receive sb as a visitor (up to one's room, up from the country, etc). 請某人來做客(至室內或由鄉下來等)。**(b)** (usu passive) (colloq) cause sb to appear before a magistrate, in a court of law, etc: (通常用被動語態)(俗)使某人受控訴,出庭等: *He was had up* (= was prosecuted) *for exceeding the speed limit.* 他因超速而受控訴。

have[5] /hæv; hæv/ *n pl* ***the* ˌ*~s and the* ˈ*~-nots,*** the rich and the poor (of people and countries). 富人與窮人;富國與窮國。

ha·ven /ˈheɪvn; ˈhevən/ *n* harbour; (fig) place of safety or rest. 港;(喻)安全地方;避難所;休息處。

hav·er·sack /ˈhævəsæk; ˈhævɚˌsæk/ *n* canvas bag, esp as used by soldiers, hikers and others, for carrying food, etc. 帆布袋(尤指士兵,遠足者等用以攜帶食物等者);乾糧袋。

havoc /ˈhævək; ˈhævək/ *n* [U] widespread damage; destruction: 廣佈的損害;毀壞: *The floods caused terrible ~.* 那洪水造成了可怕的災害。***play ~ with/among; make ~ of,*** destroy or injure. 破壞;傷害。

haw[1] /hɔː; hɔ/ *n* fruit (a red berry) of the hawthorn bush. 山楂實(一種紅漿果)。

haw[2] /hɔː; hɔ/ *vi, n* ⇨ hum(4).

haw-haw /ˈhɔːhɔː; ˈhɔˈhɔ/ *n, int* boisterous laugh. 哈哈大笑。

hawk[1] /hɔːk; hɔk/ *n* **1** strong, swift, keen-sighted bird of prey. 鷹。⇨ the illus at prey. 參看 prey之插圖。ˌ**~-ˈeyed** *adj* having keen sight. 眼光銳敏的。**2** person who favours the use of military force in foreign policy. 鷹派分子(外交政策上主戰者)。⇨ dove.

hawk[2] /hɔːk; hɔk/ *vt* [VP6A, 15B] ~ ***(about/around),*** offer (goods) for sale, by going from house to house, street to street, etc; (fig) spread: 沿街叫賣;(喻)散播: ~ *news/gossip about.* 散播消息(謠言)。**~er** *n* person who ~s goods (usu from a barrow or cart). 沿街叫賣之小販(通常推一小車)。⇨ pedlar.

haw·ser /ˈhɔːzə(r); ˈhɔzɚ/ *n* thick, heavy rope; thin steel cable (used on ships). 大索;小鋼纜(用於船上)。

haw·thorn /ˈhɔːθɔːn; ˈhɔˌθɔrn/ *n* thorny shrub or tree with white, red or pink blossom and small red berries (called *haws*), often used for hedges in GB. 山楂(一種有刺的灌木或樹,開白色,紅色或粉紅色花,結小紅漿果,稱作山楂子,在英國常被用來做圍籬)。

hay /heɪ; he/ *n* [U] grass cut and dried for use as animal food. 秣;乾草(用作牲口食料)。***make hay,*** turn it over for exposure to the sun; 翻草讓日晒以製乾草; (hence) (由此產生) ˈ**hay-maker,** ˈ**hay-making** *nn* ***make hay of,*** throw into confusion. 使混亂;弄亂。***make* ˌ*hay while the* ˈ*sun shines,*** (prov) make the earliest use of one's opportunities. (諺)把握時機。ˈ**hay·cock** *n* cone-shaped pile of hay in a field, to be carted away when dry. 圓錐形之乾草堆(乾後以備用車運走)。ˈ**hay fever** *n* [U] disease affecting the nose and throat, caused by pollen or dust. 花粉熱(由植物花粉或塵埃引起感染鼻與喉的病)。ˈ**hay-fork** *n* long-handled two-pronged fork for turning and lifting hay. 乾草叉。ˈ**hay-rick,** ˈ**hay·stack** *nn* large pile of hay firmly packed for storing, with a pointed or ridged top. 大乾草堆(頂端呈尖形或拱起,貯以備用)。ˈ**hay·wire** *n* [U] wire for tying up bales of hay. 綑乾草束用的金屬線。□ *pred adj* (colloq) out of order; excited or distracted. (俗)紊亂的;狂亂的。***go haywire,*** (of persons) become distraught; (of sth, eg a plan) become badly disorganised. (指人)狂亂;(指事物,例如一計畫)紊亂。

haz·ard /ˈhæzəd; ˈhæzɚd/ *n* **1** [C] risk; danger: 冒險;危險: ˈ*health ~s,* eg smoking cigarettes; 健康上的冒險(例如抽煙); *a life full of ~s.* 充滿冒險的一生。***at all ~s,*** whatever the risks may be. 不顧任何危險。**2** [U] game at dice, with complicated chances. 一種機會複雜的擲骰子戲。□ *vt* [VP6A] **1** take the risk of; expose to danger: 冒…之險;使遭受危險: *Rock-climbers sometimes ~ their lives.* 攀岩石者有時冒着生命的危險。**2** venture to make: 冒險而作: ~ *a guess/remark.* 冒險試作猜測(評論)。**~·ous** /-əs; -əs/ *adj* risky: 冒險的;危險的: *a ~ous climb.* 危險的攀登。

haze[1] /heɪz; hez/ *n* [C, U] thin mist; (fig) mental confusion or uncertainty. 薄霧;靄;(喻)疑惑;心中不定。

haze[2] /heɪz; hez/ *vt* (US) harass (sb) by making him perform humiliating jobs; bully or persecute. (美)使做丟臉之事而折磨(某人);欺侮。

hazel /ˈheɪzl; ˈhezl̩/ *n* [C] bush with edible nuts; [U] (esp of eyes) colour of the shell of the nut, reddish brown. 榛(一種小樹,結可食之堅果);榛果殼的顏色;紅褐色(尤指眼睛的顏色)。

hazy /ˈheɪzɪ; ˈhezɪ/ *adj* (-ier, -iest) misty: 有薄霧的: ~ *weather;* 有薄霧的天氣; (fig) vague; slightly confused; uncertain: (喻)模糊的;有些困惑的;不定的: ~ *about what to do next.* 不知下一步該做什麼。**haz·ily** /-ɪlɪ; -lɪ/ *adv* **hazi·ness** *n*

H-bomb /ˈeɪtʃ bɒm; ˈetʃˌbɑm/ *n* hydrogen bomb. 氫彈。

he /*strong or initial form:* hiː; hi; *medial weak form:* iː; i/ *pron* **1** male person or animal previously referred to: 他(代表前面所提及的男子或雄性動物): *Where's your brother? He's in Paris.* 你哥哥(弟弟)在哪裏?他在巴黎。**2** (as *pref*) male: (作爲字首)雄性;男性: ˈ*he-goat.* 雄山羊。ˈ**he-man** /-mæn; -mæn/ *n* (*pl* -men) (facet) strong man. (玩笑語)雄壯的男人。**3** (liter style) ***he who,*** the one who, anyone who. (文學用語)凡…者。

head[1] /hed; hɛd/ *n* **1** that part of the body which contains the eyes, nose, mouth and brain: 頭;頭部;首: *They cut his ~ off.* 他們割下他的頭。*Hit him on the ~* (note: *the ~,* not *his ~*). 打他的頭(注意: on 後用 the 而不用 his)。*It cost him his ~,* his life. 那使他喪失了生命。*Many nobles lost their ~s during the French Revolution.* 法國大革命期間許多貴族斷送了性命。⇨ the illus here and at insect. 參看本條及 insect 之插圖。**2** (as a measure) ~'s length: (量度單位)一頭之長: *The Queen's horse won by a ~.* 女王的馬以一頭之先獲勝。*Tom is taller than Harry by a ~.* 湯姆比哈利高一個頭。***be ~ and* ˈ*shoulders above sb,*** (fig) be considerably superior in intelligence or ability. (喻)在智慧或能力上超越他人很多。**3 ~(s),** that side of a coin on which the ~ of a person appears, the other side being *tails* or *the tail.* (硬幣之)正面(即有人像的一

H

面，另一面稱做背面）。 ***H~s or tails?*** (said when spinning a coin to decide sth by chance): 要正面還是背面？(擲錢以憑機會決定某事物): *H~s—I win!* 正面 — 我贏了！ ***be unable to make ~ or tail of sth,*** be unable to understand it in the least. 一點也不明白。 **4** person: 人: *50 dinners at £1.50 a ~.* 每人一鎊半一餐的飯五十份。 **5** (*pl* unchanged) unit of a flock or herd: (複數不變)牲畜之頭數: *50 ~ of cattle;* 五十頭牛; *a large ~* (= number) *of game.* 很多獵物。 **6** intellect; imagination; power to reason: 智力；想像力；理解力: *He made the story up out of his own ~,* It was an original story, not one that he had heard or read. 這故事是他自己想出來的。 **7** natural aptitude or talent: 天資；天才: *He has a good ~ for business.* 他很有經商的天才。 **8** sth like a ~ in form or position, eg the part that is pressed (*the ~ of a pin*), struck (*the ~ of a nail*), used for striking (*the ~ of a hammer*) or for cutting (*the ~ of an axe*); *a tape-recorder ~,* attachment that holds or contains an electronic device to record, read or erase material on magnetic tape, disc, etc. 形狀或位置似頭的東西(例如針頭，釘頭，鎚頭或斧的頭)；(錄音機上的)錄音頭。 **9** top: 頂端: *at the ~ of the page;* 在該頁之頂端; *standing at the ~ of the staircase;* 站在樓梯的頂端; *at the ~ of the poll,* having received most votes at an election. 獲最多的選票。 **10** upper end: 上端: *the ~ of a lake,* the end at which a river enters it; 湖的源頭; *the ~-waters of the Nile,* its sources and upper streams; 尼羅河的上游; *the ~ of a bed,* where a person's ~ rests. 床頭(放頭的部分)。 **11** (of plants) mass of leaves or flowers at the top of a stem or stalk: (指植物)莖頂端的一團葉或花: *a fine ~ of cabbage;* 一顆好的包心菜; *a ~ of lettuce;* 一個萵苣頭; *a 'clover ~;* 苜蓿花; *a 'flower ~.* 花頭；頭狀花。 **12** (often attrib) ruler; chief; position of command: (常作形容用法)統治者；領袖；首長地位: *~s of government,* eg the President of the US, the Prime Minister of GB; 政府首長(例如美國總統，英國首相)； *the crowned ~s of Europe,* the kings and queens; 歐洲的國王和女王們; *the ~ of the family;* 家長; *the ~ office,* the chief or most important office (contrasted with *branch* offices); 總店；總局；總公司 (與 branch offices 相對)； *the ~ waiter.* 侍者領班；茶房頭。 **ˌH~ of 'State** *n* (*pl* H~s of State) the chief public representative of a country, who may also be the head of government. 國家之元首。 **13** front; front part: 前面；前部: *at the ~ of the procession;* 在遊行行列的前排; *marching at the ~ of the regiment.* 行軍時在團的前排。 *The ship was down by the ~,* with the bows deeper in the water than the stern. 船首吃水較深。 **14** (chiefly in proper names) cape or promontory: (主要用於專有名詞)岬；海角: *Beachy H~.* 俾赤岬。 ⇨ *headland* in 20 below. 參看下列第 20 義中之 headland。 **15** body of water kept at a certain height (eg for a water-mill or a hydro-electric power station); pressure or force (per unit of area) of a confined body of steam, etc: 水頭 (保持某種高度的水源，例如水車或水力發電廠所用)；水位差；蒸汽等的壓力；水壓: *They kept up a good ~ of steam.* 他們保持良好的蒸汽壓。 **16** main division in a discourse, essay, etc: 演講，文章等之要項: *a speech arranged under five ~s;* 分爲五項的一篇演說; *treat a question under several ~s.* 分幾點討論一問題。 ⇨ heading. **17** foam of liquid (esp liquor) that has been poured out: 傾出後的液體(尤指酒)所生的泡沫: *the ~ on a glass of beer.* 一杯啤酒上的泡沫。 **18** point rising from a boil or other swelling on the flesh, esp when the boil is ripening and about to burst: 癤等之膿包(尤指成熟而要出頭者): *The boil came to a ~.* 這癤快要出頭了。 ***come to a ~,*** (fig) reach a crisis, culminate: (喻)至嚴重關頭；達於頂點: *Discontent has come to a ~.* 不滿之情緒達於頂點。 **19** (various phrases) (各種片語) ***above/over one's ~,*** (in a way that is) too difficult for one to understand: 難以理解的: *be/talk above one's ~;* 難以理解; *go above one's ~,* be too difficult for one. 太難。 ***an old ~ on young shoulders,*** wisdom in a young person. 年輕而有見識；少年老成。 ***bite sb's '~ off,*** scold them angrily. 怒責某人。 ***eat one's '~ off,*** (of a horse) eat a great deal and do little work. (指馬)食量大而工作少。 ***give sb his ~,*** allow him to act freely, unchecked. 任其隨意而爲。 ***go to one's ~,*** **(a)** (of liquor) intoxicate: (指酒)上頭；使人醉: *The whisky went to his ~.* 他喝那威士忌酒喝醉了。 **(b)** excite: 使激動: *His successes have gone to his ~,* made him over-confident, conceited, etc. 成功使他變得自負了(成功冲昏了他的頭)。 ***have a ˌgood '~ on one's shoulders,*** have practical ability, common sense, etc. 有實際才能，常識等。 ***~ over heels,*** topsy-turvey; (fig) deeply or completely: 頭朝下；顚倒地；(喻)深深

the head and the neck

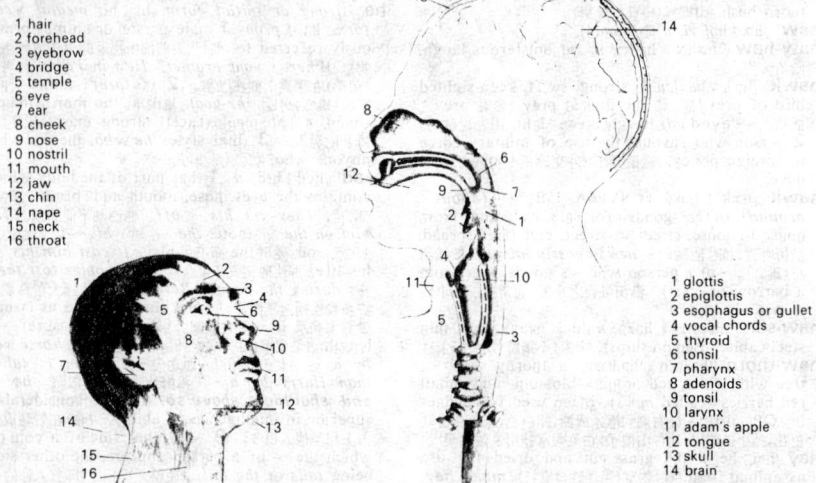

1 hair
2 forehead
3 eyebrow
4 bridge
5 temple
6 eye
7 ear
8 cheek
9 nose
10 nostril
11 mouth
12 jaw
13 chin
14 nape
15 neck
16 throat

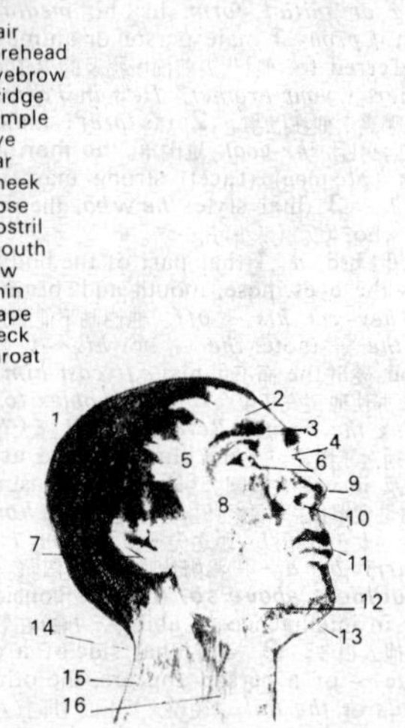

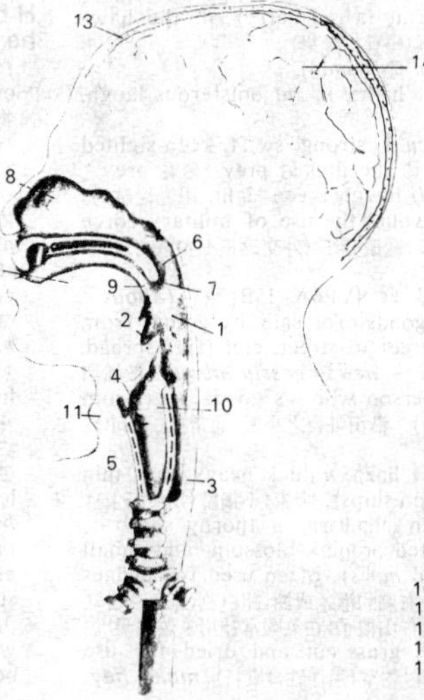

1 glottis
2 epiglottis
3 esophagus or gullet
4 vocal chords
5 thyroid
6 tonsil
7 pharynx
8 adenoids
9 tonsil
10 larynx
11 adam's apple
12 tongue
13 skull
14 brain

地或完全地: ～ *over heels in debt/in love*. 負債累累(深深墜入情網)。***keep one's ～***, keep calm. 保持鎭靜。***keep one's ～ above water***, (fig) stay out of debt, difficulty, etc. (喩)未欠債;未遭受困難。***keep one's '～ down***, avoid danger or distraction. 避免危險或分心。***laugh/scream one's '～ off***, laugh/scream loudly, with great energy. 大笑(大叫)。***lose one's ～***, become confused or over-excited. 衝動;失去理智。***(go) off one's ～***, (become) crazy. (變得)精神錯亂。***(stand, etc) on one's ～***, with feet in the air: 倒立: *I could do it (standing) on my* ～, (colloq) It is very easy. (俗)我做這事輕而易擧。***on one's own ～ be it***, the consequences will rest on one. 某人應負責。***over one's ～***, = *above one's* ～. ***(be promoted) over another's ～/over the ～s of others***, before another or others with prior or stronger claims. (被晉升)至他人之上;升遷比别人快。***'put our/your/their '～s together***, consult together. 聚議;在一起商量。***put sth into a person's ～***, suggest it to him. 將某事提示給某人。***put sth out of one's ～***, stop thinking about it; give up the idea: 不再想某事;放棄一念頭: *You'd better put the idea of marriage out of your* ～. 你最好放棄結婚的念頭。***put sth out of sb's ～***, make him forget it: 使某人忘記某事: *An interruption put it out of my* ～. 一打岔我就把這事忘了。***take sth into one's ～***, come to believe it: 相信某事: *He took it into his ～ that I was secretly opposing him*. 他相信我在祕密地反對他。***talk one's '～ off***, talk too much. 說得太多。***talk sb's '～ off***, weary him with talk. 談得使某人厭倦。***turn sb's ～***, make him conceited. 使自負。***Two ～s are better than one***, (prov) The opinions, advice, etc of a second person are valuable. (諺)集思勝過獨斷。***(be) weak in the ～***, (be) not very intelligent. 智慧很低。**20** (compounds) (複合字) **'～·ache** *n* [C, U] **(a)** continuous pain in the ～: 頭痛: *suffer from ～ache(s)*; 患頭痛; *have a bad ～ache*. 頭痛得很厲害。**(b)** (sl) troublesome problem: (俚)頭痛的問題: *more ～aches for the Department of the Environment*. 更多使環境衞生部頭痛的問題。**'～·band** *n* band worn round the ～. 束髮帶。**'～·dress** *n* covering for the ～, esp woman's ornamental kind. 頭巾(尤指婦女做裝飾用者)。**'～·gear** *n* hat, cap, ～dress. 帽子;頭巾。**'～-hunter** *n* savage who cuts off and keeps as trophies the ～s of his enemies; (fig) ruthless recruiter. 割取敵人之頭以作戰利品的野蠻人;(喩)無情的徵募人員者。**'～·lamp** *n* = headlight. **'～·land** /-lənd; -ˌlænd/ *n* promontory, cape. 岬;海角。**'～-light** *n* large lamp on the front of a locomotive, motor-car, etc. (火車,汽車等的)前燈。⇨ the illus at bicycle, motor. 參看 bicycle, motor 之插圖。**'～·line** *n* newspaper heading; line at the top of a page containing title, etc; (*pl*) summary of broadcast news: 報紙的標題;頁頭標題;(複)新聞廣播提要: *'Here are the news ～lines.'* '現在報告新聞提要。' **'～·man** /-mæn; -mən/ *n* (*pl* -men) chief men of a village, tribe, etc. 村長;酋長(等)。**ˌ～·'master/·'mistress** *nn* principal master/mistress of a school. 校長(女校長)。**ˌ～-'on** *adj, adv* (of collisions) with the front parts (of vehicles) meeting: (指相撞)(車輛)正面的(地): *a ～-on collision*; 正面相撞; *meet/strike ～-on*. 正面互撞。**'～·phones** *n pl* receivers fitting over the ～ (for radio, etc); earphones. (收聽無線電等之)耳機。**'～·piece** *n* **(a)** helmet. 盔。**(b)** (colloq) intelligence; brains. (俗)智力;頭腦。**ˌ～-'quarters** *n* (*sing* or *pl*) place from which (eg police, army) operations are controlled. (單或複)(警察,軍隊等之)總局;總部;司令部。**'～-rest** *n* sth that supports the ～. 墊頭之物;靠頭之物。**'～·room** *n* = clearance(2). **'～·set** *n* ～phones. 耳機。**'～·ship** /-ʃɪp; -ʃɪp/ *n* position of a ～master or ～mistress: 校長的職位: *apply for a ～ship*. 申請做校長。**'～-stall** *n* part of a bridle or halter that fits round the ～. (馬之)絡頭;籠頭。**'～·stone** *n* stone set up at the ～ of a grave. 墓碑。**'～-waters** *n pl* ⇨ 10 above. 參看上列第 10 義。**'～·way** *n* [U] progress. 前進;進步。***make some/no ～way***, (not) make progress. (無)有進展。**'～-wind** *n* one that blows directly into one's face, or against the course of a ship, etc. 頂頭風;逆風。**'～·word** *n* word used as a heading, eg the first word, in heavy type, of a dictionary entry. 作爲標題的字(例如字典中用粗體字所列的一個項目);首字。**～ed** *adj* (in compounds) (用於複合字) *ˌthree-'～ed*, having three ～s; 有三個頭的; *ˌlong-'～ed*, having a long skull. 長腦殼的。**～·less** *adj* having no ～. 無頭的。

head² /hed; hɛd/ *vt, vi* **1** [VP6A] be at the head or top of: 在…前頭;爲…之首;在…之頂部: ～ *a procession*; 在遊行行列之前排; ～ *a revolt/rebellion*, act as the leader. 領導叛亂。*Smith's name ～ed the list*. 史密斯的名字在表上的最上端。**2** [VP6A] strike, touch, with the head (eg the ball in football). 用頭撞,頂,觸(例如足球中之用頭頂球)。**3** [VP 15B] ～ ***sth/sb off***, get in front of, so as to turn back or aside: 至…的前面使其回轉或轉向;攔截: ～ *off a flock of sheep* (to prevent them from going the wrong way); 至羊群前攔阻以免其走錯方向; (fig) prevent: (喩)防止: ～ *off a quarrel*. 防止口角發生。**4** [VP2C] move in the direction indicated: 朝某方向前進: ～ *south*; 向南行進; ～ *straight for home*; 直向家走去; (fig) (喩) *be ～ing for disaster*. 走向災禍。*Where are you ～ed (for)?* 你朝哪個方向去?

header /'hedə(r); 'hɛdə/ *n* **1** fall, dive or jump with the head first: 倒栽着跌落,跳水或跳: *take a ～ into a swimming pool*. 倒栽着跳入游泳池。**2** (football) act of striking the ball with the head. (足球)以頭頂球。

head·ing /'hedɪŋ; 'hɛdɪŋ/ *n* word or words at the top of a section of printed matter (to show the subject of what follows). 標題。

head·long /'hedlɒŋ *US:* -lɔːŋ; 'hɛdˌlɔŋ/ *adv, adj* **1** with the head first: 頭在先的(地): *fall* ～. 頭向下跌落。**2** thoughtless(ly) and hurried(ly): 輕率的(地);匆促的(地): *rush ～ into danger*; 輕率地奔赴險境; *a ～ decision*. 輕率的決定。

head·strong /'hedstrɒŋ *US:* -strɔːŋ; 'hɛdˌstrɔŋ/ *adj* self-willed; obstinate. 任性的;頑固的。

heady /'hedɪ; 'hɛdɪ/ *adj* (-ier, -iest) **1** acting, done, on impulse; headstrong. 鹵莽的;任性的;頑固的。**2** (of alcoholic drink) having a quick effect on the senses; quickly causing intoxication: (指酒)易使人醉的;上頭的: *a ～ wine*; 易使人醉的酒; (fig) (eg of sudden success) having an exciting effect. (喩)(例如指突然獲得的成功)令人興奮的。

heal /hiːl; hil/ *vt, vi* **1** [VP6A, 2A, C] (esp of wounds) (cause to) become healthy and sound: (尤指傷口)治愈;痊愈: *The wound is not yet ～ed*, the new skin has not yet covered it. 這傷口尙未痊愈(尙未生出新皮)。*The wound ～ed slowly*. 這傷口痊愈得很慢。*It soon ～ed up/over*. 不久卽告痊愈。**2** [VP6A] (archaic or biblical) restore (a person) to health; cure (a disease): (古或聖經文體) 恢復(某人)之健康;醫治(疾病): ～ *sb of a disease* (*cure* is now the usu word). 醫治某人的病(現在常用 cure)。⇨ also *faith-～ing* at faith. **3** [VP6A] end: 結束: ～ *a quarrel*. 平息一口角。*Time ～s all sorrows*. 時間可醫治一切憂傷。**～er** *n* person or thing that ～s: 治療的人或物: *Time is a great ～er*. 時間是很有效的治療物。**～·ing** *adj* having the power to ～: 有治療功能的;能治愈的: *～ing ointments*. 藥膏。

health /helθ; hɛlθ/ *n* **1** [U] condition of the body or the mind: 人體或心智的狀況: *be in/enjoy/have good/poor ～*. 身體好(不好)。*Fresh air and exercise are good for the ～* (more colloq *good for you*). 新鮮空氣和運動有益於健康(用 good for you 較通俗)。**'～ food** *n* [U] food that is nutritious and free of artificial substances: (未加人工物質之)營養食品: (attrib) (形容用法) *a ～ food restaurant/*

shop. 營養食品餐館(商店)。 **2** (in names of organizations, etc): (用於機關等名稱中): *the ˌWorld ˈH~ Organization* (abbr 略作 **WHO**); 世界衞生組織; *the Department of H~ and Social Security* (in GB, 英, abbr 略作 **DHSS**); 衞生及社會安全部; *the ˌNational ˈH~ Service* (in GB, 英, abbr 略作 **NHS**). 國民衞生局。 **3** [U] state of being well and free from illness: 健康: *restored to ~.* 恢復健康。 **4** ***drink sb's ~; drink a ~ (to sb),*** (as a social custom) raise one's glass and wish good ~ to him. (按照社交習慣)舉杯祝(某人)健康。 **~·ful** /-fl; -fəl/ *adj* ~-giving; good for the ~. 衞生的;有益於健康的。

healthy /ˈhelθɪ; ˈhɛlθɪ/ *adj* (-ier, -iest) **1** having good health; well, strong and able to resist disease: 健康的;健壯的: *The children look very ~.* 孩子們看來很健康。*The children are quite ~, although they have slight colds at present.* 孩子們雖然目前患輕微的傷風,但他們十分健康。(Note that *well* is the usu word when the reference is to a specific occasion: eg *I hope you're quite well*). (注意:指特殊的健康情形時通常用 well, 例如: I hope you're quite well. 我希望你身體很好。) **2** likely to produce good health: 有益於健康的; 衞生的: *a ~ climate;* 有益於健康的氣候; *a ~ way of living.* 衞生的生活方式。 **3** showing good health: 表示健康的: *a ~ appetite.* 健康的胃口。**health·ily** /-ɪlɪ; -əlɪ/ *adv* in a ~ way. 健康地。

heap /hiːp; hip/ *n* [C] **1** number of things, mass of material, piled up: 堆: *a big ~ of books;* 一大堆書; *a ~ of sand;* 一堆沙; *building material lying about in ~s.* 一堆堆的建築材料。***be struck/knocked all of a ~,*** (colloq) be overwhelmed; be thrown into a state of bewilderment or confusion. (俗) 嚇成一團; 陷入困惑或慌亂的狀態中。 **2** ***~s (of),*** (colloq) large number; plenty: (俗)大量;許多: *We have ~s of books/time.* 我們有很多書(時間)。*She has been there ~s of times,* very often. 她曾經去過那裏好多次。 *There is ~s more I could say on this question.* 關於此問題我尚有許多話可說。 **3** **~s,** (as *adv;* colloq) much: (作副詞;俗) 很: *feeling ~s better.* 覺得好得多。□ *vt* **1** [VP6A, 15A, B] ~ ***(up),*** put in a ~: 堆積: *~ (up) stones;* 堆積石頭; *~ up riches.* 積財富。 **2** [VP14] ***~ sth on/upon sb/sth; ~ sb/sth with sth,*** fill; load: 裝滿;裝載: *~ a plate with food;* 將一盤子裝滿食物; *~ favours upon a person;* 施種種恩惠於某人; *~ a person with favours;* 給與某人種種恩惠; *a ~ed spoonful,* more than a level spoonful. 滿滿的一匙。

hear /hɪə(r); hɪr/ *vt, vi* (*pt, pp* heard /hɜːd; hɝd/) **1** [VP2A, 6A, 18A, 19A, 24A] perceive (sound, etc) with the ears: 聽見(聲音等): *Deaf people cannot ~.* 聾子聽不見。*I ~d someone laughing.* 我聽見有人笑。*He was ~d to groan.* 有人聽見他呻吟。*Did you ~ him go out?* 你聽見他走出去嗎? *Have you ever ~d that song sung in Italian?* 你聽過那支歌用義大利文演唱嗎? *We listened but could ~ nothing.* 我們注意聽,但什麼也聽不見。 *She doesn't/can't ~ very well.* 她的聽力不大好。(Note the frequent use of *can-could* when an effort of perception is implied.) (注意:如含有費力聽之義,用 can 或could。) **2** [VP6A, 9, 3A] be told or informed: 聽說;聞知: *Have you ~d the news?* 你聽到那消息沒有? *I ~d that he was ill.* 我聽說他病了。*I've ~d (say) that your country is beautiful.* 我聽說你的國家很美麗。 ***~ about sth,*** be given information about; learn about: 聽說;得悉: *I've just ~d about his dismissal/illness.* 我剛聽說他被解雇(生病)了。 *You will ~ about this later,* sometimes implying that there will be a rebuke, etc. 你過些時便會知道這事(有時暗示將有指責等之義)。 ***~ from sb,*** receive a letter, news, etc: 收到某人的信件、消息等: *How often do you ~ from your sister?* 你多久接到你姊姊(妹妹)一次信? ***~ of sb/sth,*** have knowledge of: 知道某人(某事物): *I've never ~d of her/the place,* know nothing of her/the place. 我從來沒有聽說過她(那地方)。 ***~ tell of,*** ~ people talking about: 聽人談起: *I've often ~d tell of such happenings.* 我常聽人談起這類事情(的發生)。 **3** [VP6A, 10, 15A, 3A] listen to; pay attention to; (of a judge in a law court) try (a case): 傾聽;注意;(指法官)審問(案件): *You'd better ~ what they have to say.* 你最好聽他們要說些什麼。*The court ~d the evidence.* 法官們聽取證言。*Which judge will ~ the case?* 哪位法官將審問這案件? ***~ sb out,*** listen to the end: 聽某人說完: *Don't judge me before I've finished my explanation: ~ me out, please.* 在我未解釋完以前不要批評我,請聽我說完。 ***not ~ of,*** (usu with *will, would*) refuse to consider or allow: (通常與 will, would 連用) 不予考慮;不允許: *I won't ~ of such a thing!* 我不同意此事! *She wouldn't ~ of it.* 她拒絕考慮。 **4** ***ˌH~! ˈH~!*** used as a form of cheering to express approval or agreement, but also ironically. 好哇!好哇!(用以喝采,表示贊同,但有時亦有譏諷之意)。~**er** *n* person who hears, eg in an audience. 聽者;聽衆。

hear·ing /ˈhɪərɪŋ; ˈhɪrɪŋ/ *n* **1** [U] perception by sound: 聽覺: *Her ~ is poor,* she is rather deaf. 她的聽覺不好。***hard of ~,*** rather deaf. 有點聾;重聽。 **ˈ~-aid** *n* electronic device for helping deaf people to hear. 助聽器。**2** [U] distance within which one can hear: 聽力所及的距離: *In some countries it is unwise to talk about politics in the ~ of strangers,* where strangers may hear. 在某些國家內,在陌生人聽得見的範圍內談論政治是不智的。 ***within/out of ~,*** near enough/not near enough to hear or be heard: 在聽得見(聽不見)的距離內: *Please keep within ~.* 請保持在聽得見的距離內。 **3** [C] opportunity of being heard (esp in self-defence). 發言的機會;(尤指)申訴。***gain a ~,*** an opportunity to be heard. 獲得申訴的機會。***give sb/get a fair ~,*** an opportunity of being listened to impartially. 公平地聽某人申訴(獲得申訴機會)。**4** (legal) trial of a case at law, esp before a judge without a jury. (法律)聽訟;審問(尤指無陪審團在場者)。

hearken /ˈhɑːkən; ˈhɑrkən/ *vi* (archaic) listen (*to*). (古)傾聽(與 to 連用)。

hear·say /ˈhɪəseɪ; ˈhɪrˌse/ *n* [U] common talk; rumour; what one has heard another person or other persons say: 道聽途說; 謠言: *I don't believe it; it's merely ~.* 我不相信,這僅是謠傳罷了。*H~ evidence is not accepted in law courts.* 風聞的證據在法庭上是不予接受的。

hearse /hɜːs; hɝs/ *n* carriage, car, for carrying a coffin at a funeral. 柩車;靈車。

heart /hɑːt; hɑrt/ *n* **1** that part of the body which pumps blood through the system: 心;心臟: *When a man's ~ stops beating, he dies.* 一個人的心臟停止跳動時,他便死了。*He had a ˈ~ attack,* a sudden illness with irregular and violent beating of the ~. 他的心臟病發作了。⇨ the illus at respiratory. 參看 respiratory 之插圖。 **2** centre of the emotions, esp love; deepest part of one's nature: 內心;愛心;衷情;衷心;心地;心腸;心情;心境: *a man with a kind ~;* 心腸仁慈的人; *a kind-~ed man.* 好心腸的人。***sb after one's own ~,*** of the sort one very much likes or approves of. 正合己意之人。***at ~,*** deep down; basically. 在內心;基本上。***have sth at ~,*** be deeply interested in it, anxious to support or encourage it. 對某事甚爲關心;急於贊助某事。***from (the bottom of) one's ~,*** sincerely. 眞誠地。***in one's ~ of ~s,*** in one's inmost feelings. 在內心深處。***to one's ~'s content,*** as much as, for as long as, etc one wishes. 心滿意足;盡情;盡歡。***with all one's ~,*** completely and willingly: 全心地;欣然: *I love you with all my ~.* 我全心全意地愛你。***~ and soul,*** completely: 完全地: *I'm yours ~ and soul.* 我是完全屬於你的。***break a person's ~,*** make him very sad. 使人傷心;令人斷腸。 Hence, 由此產生, **ˌbroken-ˈ~ed, ˈ~-broken** *adjj.* ***cry***

one's **'~ *out,*** pine or brood over sth, esp in secret. 痛哭欲絕;(尤指)爲某事暗自憂傷。 ***do one's*** **'~ *good,*** cause one to feel encouraged, cheerful, etc. 使人歡欣鼓舞。***(get/learn/know sth) by ~,*** from memory. 熟記;能背出。 ***have a ~,*** show sympathy, understanding. 同情;諒解。 ***(have) a change of ~,*** (experience) a change of opinion. 改變主意。 ***have the ~ to,*** (usu *neg*, or *interr* with *can-could*) be hard-~ed or unsympathetic enough to: (通常用於否定或疑問句,與 can 或 could 連用)硬心腸;忍心: *How can you have the ~ to drown the kittens?* 你怎能忍心把這些小貓淹死? ***have one's ~ in sth,*** be interested in it and fond of it. 對某事物有興趣;喜歡某事物。 ***have one's ~ in one's boots,*** be greatly discouraged, feel hopeless. 深爲沮喪;絕望。 ***have one's ~ in one's mouth,*** be badly frightened. 深爲驚恐。***have one's ~ in the right place,*** have true or kind feelings. 有熱誠;懷善意。 ***have one's ~ set on sth,*** desire greatly. 渴望;極想。***lose ~,*** be discouraged. 灰心。 ***lose one's ~ to sb/sth,*** become very fond of; fall in love with. 十分喜愛某人或某物;傾心於。 ***set one's ~ on sth/having sth/doing sth, etc,*** be very anxious (to have, to do, etc). 渴望(某事物或做某事)。 ***take (fresh) ~ (at sth),*** be confident. (對…)有信心;振起精神。***take sth to ~,*** be much affected by it; grieve over it. 深爲某事所感動;爲某事物感到悲傷。 ***wear one's ~ on/upon one's sleeve,*** show one's feelings quite openly. 表露自己的感情。 **3** central part: 中心部分: *in the ~ of the forest;* 在森林的中心; *the ~ of the matter,* the essence; 事情的要點; *get to the ~ of a subject/mystery;* 抓住一問題(謎團)的中心; *a cabbage with a good solid ~.* 一棵捲得很好的包心菜。**4** [U] (of land) fertility: (土地之)生產力;肥沃程度: *in good ~,* in good condition; 肥沃的; *out of ~,* in poor condition. 不肥沃。**5** ~-shaped thing, esp the design used on playing-cards: 心形物(尤指紙牌上的紅心): *the ten/queen/etc of ~s.* 紅心十點(女王等)。*H~s are trumps.* 紅心是王牌。⇨ the illus at card. 參看 card 之插圖。 **6** (as a term of endearment to a person) (作爲對某人表示親愛之詞) *dear ~;* 親愛的; *'sweet~.* 情人;愛人。 **7** (compounds) (複合字) **'~·ache** *n* [U] deep sorrow. 悲痛;傷心。**'~-beat** *n* [C] movement of the ~ (about 70 beats a minute). 心搏;心跳(每分鐘約七十次)。**'~·break** *n* [U] overwhelming sorrow. 心碎;傷心。**'~·breaking** *adj* causing ~break. 令人傷心的;令人心碎的。**'~·broken** *adj* crushed by ~break. 傷心的;心碎的。**'~·burn** *n* [U] burning sensation in the lower part of the chest, caused by indigestion. (由於消化不良引起的)胃灼熱。**'~·burning** *n* [U] (and also in *pl*) envious, discontented feeling(s), usu caused by disappointment. (亦用複數)(通常由失望引起的)嫉妒;不滿。**'~-disease** *n* [U] disease of the ~. 心臟病。**'~-failure** *n* [U] failure of the ~ to function. 心臟衰竭;心臟麻痺。**'~·felt** *adj* sincere: 誠意的;至誠的: *~felt emotion/thanks.* 衷誠(衷心感激)。**'~-rending** *adj* causing deep grief. 使人深爲悲痛的;使人傷心的。 **'~'s-ease** *n* [U] (old name for) pansy. (舊稱)三色堇。**'~·sick** *adj* low-spirited. 鬱悶的;垂頭喪氣的。**'~·strings** *n pl* deepest feelings of love: 最深摯的愛情;心弦: *play upon sb's ~strings,* touch his feelings. 打動某人的心弦。 **~ed** *adj* in compounds: 用於複合字中: *hard-~ed;* 硬心腸的; *sad-~ed;* 悲傷的; *faint-~ed,* lacking in courage. 儒弱的。**~·less** *adj* unkind; without pity. 無情的;殘酷的。**~·less·ly** *adv* **~·less·ness** *n*

hearten /'hɑ:tn; 'hɑrtn̩/ *vt* [VP6A] give courage to; cheer: 鼓勵;使振奮: *~ing news.* 使人振奮的消息。

hearth /hɑ:θ; hɑrθ/ *n* floor of a fireplace; (fig) fireside as representing the home: 爐床; (喻)爐邊(代表家庭): *fight for ~ and altar,* (rhet) in defence of one's home and religion. (修辭)爲保衞家庭與宗教而戰。**'~-rug** *n* rug spread out in front of the ~. 爐前地毯。

heart·ily /'hɑ:tɪlɪ; 'hɑrtɪlɪ/ *adv* **1** with goodwill, courage or appetite: 熱忱地;奮勇地;有好胃口地: *set to work ~;* 熱忱地着手工作; *eat ~.* 痛快地吃。 **2** very: 十分;很: *~ glad that...;* 十分高興…; *~ sick of this wet weather.* 十分厭惡這雨天。

hearty /'hɑ:tɪ; 'hɑrtɪ/ *adj* (-ier, -iest) **1** (of feelings) sincere: (指感情)誠懇的: *give sb a ~ welcome;* 竭誠歡迎某人; *give one's ~ approval/support to a plan.* 衷心贊同(支持)一項計畫。 **2** strong; in good health: 强健的;健康的: *still hale and ~ at eighty-five.* 八十五歲仍很健壯。 **3** big: 大的: *a ~ meal/appetite.* 豐盛的一餐(很好的食慾)。

heat[1] /hi:t; hit/ *n* **1** [U] **(the) ~,** high temperature: 熱;高溫: *the ~ of the sun's rays.* 陽光的熱力。*Cold is the absence of ~.* 冷卽熱的不存在。 *She's suffering from the ~,* from the hot weather. 她深受炎熱天氣之苦。 **ˌprickly '~,** ⇨ prickle. **2** [U] **(the) ~,** (fig) intense feeling: (喻)熱烈;激烈: *speak with considerable ~;* 講話頗爲激昂; *in the ~ of the debate/argument.* 在激烈辯論期間。 **3** [C] competition the winners of which take part in (the further competitions leading to) the finals: 預賽(得勝者可參加複賽或決賽): *trial/preliminary ~s.* 預賽;初賽。⇨ also *dead ~,* at dead(6). **4** [U] (of female mammals) period or condition of sexual excitement. (指雌性哺乳動物) 性慾衝動期;交尾期性慾之衝動。***be in/on/at ~.*** 性慾衝動。 **5** (compounds) (複合字) **'~ barrier** *n* = thermal barrier, ⇨ thermal. **'~-flash** *n* intense ~, eg as released from the explosion of an atomic bomb. 强熱(例如原子彈爆炸所發出者)。**'~ pump** *n* machine that transfers ~ from a substance at a relatively low temperature to one at a higher temperature, eg for ~ing a building. 變熱機(將低溫變爲高溫之機器,如供一建築物暖氣所用者)。**'~ shield** *n* device (esp on the nose-cone of a spacecraft) that gives protection against excessive ~. 熱屏(尤指用於太空船之鼻錐體者,以抗拒高溫)。 **'~·spot** *n* mark or point on the skin caused by or sensitive to ~. 熱覺點;痱子(皮膚上感覺發熱處)。**'~-stroke** *n* sudden illness, prostration, caused by excessive ~. 中暑。**'~·wave** *n* unbroken period of unusually hot weather. 一段非常炎熱的期間;熱浪。

heat[2] /hi:t; hit/ *vt, vi* [VP6A, 15B, 2C] **~ *(up),*** make or become hot: 使熱;變熱: *~ (up) some water;* 燒熱一些水; *~ up the cold meat for supper;* 將冷肉熱一熱以備晚餐食用。 **~ed** *adj* excited; passionate: 熱烈的;激烈的: *a ~ed discussion,* one during which feelings are roused; 激昂的討論; *get ~ed with wine.* 因喝酒而興奮。 **~·ed·ly** *adv* in a ~ed manner. 熱烈地;激烈地。 **~er** *n* device for supplying warmth to a room, or for ~ing water, etc: 暖氣設備;火爐;熱水器: *a 'gas-~er;* 煤氣爐; *an 'oil-~er.* 煤油爐。**~·ing** *n* [U] means of creating ~: 暖氣裝置: *electric/gas/oil ~ing.* 電(煤氣,煤油)暖氣裝置。⇨ central.

heath /hi:θ; hiθ/ *n* **1** [C] area of flat unused land, esp if covered with ~. 荒地;(尤指)石南荒地。 **2** [C, U] (kind of) low evergreen shrub with small purple, pink or white bell-shaped flowers, eg *ling* and *heather.* 石南屬常青灌木(生有紫色、粉紅色或白色鐘形小花,如 ling 及 heather 等石南)。

hea·then /'hi:ðn; 'hiðən/ *n* **1** [C] (*pl* ~s or, collectively, **the** ~) believer in a religion other than the chief world religions: 所相信之宗教非世界上主要的宗教者;異教徒: *The Saxons who invaded England were ~s.* 侵略英格蘭的撒克遜人是異教徒。*He went abroad to preach Christianity to the ~.* 他去國外向異教徒宣傳基督教。**2** [C] (colloq) person whose morals, etc are disapproved of: (俗)道德敗壞的人: *They've allowed their daughter to grow up as a young ~,* wild, ill-mannered, without moral training. 他們聽任他們的女兒長大成爲道德敗壞的年輕人。 **3** (attrib): (形容用法): *a ~ land;* 信異教的地

方；～ *customs.* 異教社會的風俗。 **～·ish** /-ɪʃ; -ɪʃ/ *adj* of or like ～s; barbarous. 異教徒的；似異教徒的；野蠻的。

heather /'heðə(r); 'hɛðɚ/ *n* [U] variety of heath(2), with small light-purple or white flowers, common in Scotland. 石南屬植物。 ***take to the ～,*** (in olden times) become an outlaw. (古時)做歹徒；做亡命之徒。 **'～-mixture** *n* cloth of mixed colours supposed to be like ～. 雜色呢。

heave /hi:v; hiv/ *vt, vi* (*pt, pp* ～d or (6 and 7 below), nautical use, (下列第6義及第7義)航海用語作, hove /həʊv; hov/) **1** [VP6A] raise, lift up (sth heavy): 舉起(重物)： ～ *the anchor.* 起錨。 **2** [VP6A] utter: 發出： ～ *a sigh / groan.* 發出一聲嘆息(呻吟)。 **3** [VP6A, 15A, B] (colloq) lift and throw: (俗)投擲；扔；拋： ～ *sth overboard;* 將某物擲出船外； ～ *a brick through a window.* 把一塊磚自窗中拋出。 **4** [VP2A, C, 3A] ～ ***(at / on sth),*** pull (*at* a rope, etc): 拖；拉(繩等)： ～ (*away*) *at the capstan.* 起錨。 *H～ away!* 用力拉！ *H～ ho!* (sailors' cries when pulling at ropes or cables). 用力拉呀！(水手拖繩或纜時的呼聲)。 **5** [VP2A] rise and fall vigorously and regularly: 猛烈而又規律地升降；起伏： *a heaving chest;* 起伏的胸部； *the heaving billows,* ie waves. 洶湧的波濤。 **6** [VP2C, 15B] ～ ***to,*** (of a sailing-ship) (cause to) come to a standstill (without anchoring or mooring). (帆船未拋錨或碇泊而)停止；使停止。 **7** ～ ***in sight,*** become visible. 可以看得見；進入視線範圍。 □ *n* act of heaving: 舉；拋；拖；起伏： *with a mighty* ～, a strong pull or throw. 用力拉或拋。

heaven /'hevn; 'hɛvən/ *n* **1** home of God and the saints: 天堂；天國： *die and go to* ～. 死後進天堂。 **2** **H～,** God, Providence: 上帝： *It was the will of H～.* 這是天意。 *H～ forbid!* 上帝不容許！ *Thank H～ you were not killed.* 感謝蒼天，你未被殺死。 Also in exclamations: 亦用於感嘆句中： *For H～'s sake!* 看在老天爺的份上！ *Good H～s!* 天啊！ **,～-'sent** *adj* providential: 由神而來的；天賜的： *a ～sent opportunity.* 天賜良機。 **3** place, state, of supreme happiness. 極樂之地；至福。 **4** (often 常作 **the ～s**) the firmament: 天空；蒼天： *the broad expanse of ～ / the ～s.* 一望無際的蒼天。 ***move ～ and earth,*** do one's utmost. 竭盡全力。 **～·ward(s)** /-wəd(z); -wɚd(z)/ *adj, adv* towards ～. 向天空的(地)；向天國的(地)。

heav·en·ly /'hevnlɪ; 'hɛvənlɪ/ *adj* **1** of, from, like, heaven: 天國的；自天國的；似天堂的；天空的；自天空的： *a ～ angel / vision.* 天使 (天國的幻景)。 **the ～ bodies,** ie the sun, moon, planets, etc. 天體(日，月，星辰)。 **the ～ city,** Paradise. 天堂。 **2** of more than earthly excellence. 超絕的。 **3** (colloq) very pleasing: (俗)極爲可愛的： *What ～ peaches!* 多麼可愛的桃子啊！

Heavi·side layer /'hevɪsaɪd leɪə(r); 'hɛvɪ,saɪd 'leɚ/ ⇨ ionosphere.

heavy /'hevɪ; 'hɛvɪ/ *adj* (-ier, -iest) **1** having weight (esp great weight); difficult to lift, carry or move: 重的；難以舉起、携帶或移動的： *It's too ～ for me to lift.* 它太重了，我舉不起來。 *Lead is a ～ metal.* 鉛是重金屬。 **'～-weight** *n* boxer weighing 175 lb (79·3kg) or more. 重量級拳手(體重在175磅或79·3公斤以上)。 **2** of more than usual size, amount, force, etc: 超出一般大小，數量，力量等的： ～ *guns / artillery,* of the largest class; 重砲(砲兵)； ～ (= abundant) *crops;* 豐收； ～ *rain;* 大雨； ～ *work;* 繁重的工作； *a ～ blow,* one with great force behind it; 重擊； *a ～ fall,* one likely to cause shock; 重重的跌倒； *a ～ heart,* made sad; 沉重的心情； ～ *tidings,* bad news; 壞消息； ～ *soil,* difficult to cultivate; 難耕種的土地； ～ *roads,* muddy and sticky, difficult to travel over; 泥濘的道路； *a ～ sky,* dark with clouds; 陰沉的天空； *a ～ sea,* rough, with big waves; 洶湧的大海； ～ *food,* rich, difficult to digest; 油膩而難消化的食物； ～ *bread,* dense, sticky, like dough; 沒有發起來的麵包； *a ～ day,* full of difficult work; 工作艱苦的一天； *a ～ sleep / sleeper,* a deep sleep / a person who is difficult to wake up; 熟睡(睡得很熟的人)； *a ～ drinker / smoker,* sb who drinks (alcoholic drink) / smokes much; 酒鬼(老煙槍)； ～ *reading,* difficult to read. 難讀的讀物。 **,～ 'hydrogen,** isotope of hydrogen with atoms twice the normal weight. 重氫(氫的同位素，其原子量大一倍)。 **,～ 'water,** water whose molecules consist of two ～ hydrogen atoms and one ordinary oxygen atom. 重水(其分子含有兩個重氫原子和一個普通的氧原子)。 **3** (of persons) slow in speech or thought; (of writing or painting) dull, tedious; (of parts in a play for the theatre) serious or solemn: (指人)談話或思想遲緩的；(指寫作或繪畫)沉悶的；乏味的；(指劇中角色)嚴肅的；莊重的： *play the part of the ～ father;* 扮演嚴肅的父親； (of bodily states) inactive: (指身體狀況)不活動的；遲鈍的： ～ *with sleep / wine.* 因睡眠(飲酒)而呆滯。 ***(find sth) ～ going,*** (find progress) difficult. (覺得某事)很難。 ***(find sb) ～ going,*** (find him) difficult (to understand), or boring (to listen to). (覺得某人)很難了解；(覺得某人)所說的話很乏味。 ***make ～ weather of sth,*** ⇨ weather(1). **4** (US sl) dangerous; troublesome. (美俚)危險的；麻煩的。 **5** (compounds) (複合字) **,～-'handed** *adj* awkward, clumsy. 笨拙的。 **,～-'hearted** *adj* melancholy. 憂鬱的。 □ *adv* heavily: 沉重地： *The crime lies ～ on his conscience.* 那罪行沉重地壓在他心上。 *Do you ever find time hangs ～ on your hands,* Does it ever pass too slowly? 你曾經發現時間不易度過嗎？ **,～-'laden** *adj* carrying a ～ load; (fig) having a ～ (= sad) heart. 負重的；載重的；(喻)心情沉重的。 **heav·ily** /'hevɪlɪ; 'hɛvlɪ/ *adv* in a ～ manner: 沉重地： *a heavily loaded lorry.* 裝載很重的卡車。 **heavi·ness** *n*

heb·doma·dal /heb'dɒmədl; hɛb'dɑməd!/ *adj* weekly: 一週的；每週一次的： *H～ Council,* one that meets weekly. 每週召開一次的會。

He·braic /hi:'breɪɪk; hi'bre·ɪk/ *adj* Hebrew. 希伯來人的；希伯來語的。

He·brew /'hi:bru:; 'hibru/ *n* **1** [C] Jew; Israeli. 希伯來人；猶太人；以色列人。 **2** [U] language used by the ancient ～s (as in the Old Testament); language now spoken by the people of Israel. 古希伯來語(如舊約聖經中所用者)；現代希伯來語(即現今以色列人的語言)。 □ *adj* of the ～ language or people. 希伯來語的；希伯來人的。

heca·tomb /'hekətu:m; 'hɛkə,tom/ *n* (in ancient Greece) great public sacrifice; blood-offering (esp of 100 oxen). (古希臘)大祭；百牲祭(尤指一次祭一百頭牛者)。

heck /hek; hɛk/ *n* (sl, euphem) hell (used in exclamations): (俚，婉)地獄(用於感嘆句中)： *Oh! What the ～!* 嗬！去他的！什麼東西！我才不在乎呢！

heckle /'hekl; 'hɛkl/ *vt* [VP6A] interrupt and ask many troublesome questions at a public meeting: (在公開會議中)詰問；質問： ～ *the Socialist candidate.* 詰問社會黨候選人。 **heck·ler** /'heklə(r); 'hɛklɚ/ *n*

hec·tare /'hekteə(r); 'hɛktɛr/ *n* measure of area in the metric system, 10000 sq metres (= 2·471 acres). 公頃(合10000平方公尺或 2.471 英畝)。 ⇨ App 5. 參看附錄五。

hec·tic /'hektɪk; 'hɛktɪk/ *adj* **1** unnaturally red; feverish; consumptive: 紅得不自然的；患熱病的；患肺癆病的： ～ *cheeks;* 潮紅的雙頰； *a ～ colouring.* 不自然的紅色。 **2** (colloq) full of excitement and without rest: (俗)極爲興奮的；緊張忙碌的： *have a ～ time;* 興高采烈； *lead a ～ life;* 過着緊張忙碌的生活； *for one ～* (= exciting) *moment.* 一段興奮的時刻。

hecto- /'hektəʊ; 'hɛktə/ *pref* (in comb) hundred: (用於複合字中)一百： *'～gram(me),* 100 grammes. 百公分；瓸 ⇨ App 5. 參看附錄五。

hec·tor /'hektə(r); 'hɛktɚ/ *vt, vi* bully; bluster. 威嚇；欺凌。

he'd /*strong or initial form:* hi:d; hid; *medial weak* *form:* iːd ; id/ = he had; he would.

hedge /hedʒ ; hɛdʒ/ *n* **1** row of bushes, shrubs or tall plants, etc usu cut level at the top, forming a boundary for a field, garden, etc: (圍於田地,花園等周圍之)樹籬: *a* ˈ*beech-*~. 山毛櫸樹籬。 *Will this* ~ *keep the sheep in the field?* 這樹籬可將羊群圍在這田地中嗎? **ˈ~-hop** *vi* fly (an aircraft) not much above ground level, eg when spraying crops. (駕飛機)超低空飛行(例如噴射殺蟲劑時)。 **ˈ~-row** *n* row of bushes forming a ~. 一排樹籬。 **ˈ~-sparrow** *n* common GB and US bird. 籬雀(常見於英國和美國的一種鳥)。 **2** (fig) means of defence against possible loss: (喻)防備損失的對策: *buy gold/diamonds as a* ~ *against inflation.* 購買黃金(鑽石)以防通貨膨脹。□ *vt, vi* **1** [VP6A, 15A, B] put a ~ or (fig) barrier round: 圍以樹籬; (喻) 妨礙: ~ *a field;* 用樹籬圍起田地; ~ *a person in/round with rules and regulations,* restrict his freedom of action. 以種種規則限制一人使其不能自由行動。 **2** [VP2A] refuse to commit oneself; avoid giving a direct answer to a question: 不答應負責; 避免作正面答覆; 閃爍其詞: *Answer 'yes' or 'no'—don't* ~*!* 回答'是'或'否'—勿閃避問題! **3** [VP2A, 6A] (colloq) secure oneself against loss, esp when betting, by compensating transactions: (俗)作兩面買賣以防損失; (尤指)(賭博爲防損失而)兩面下注; 兩面下注以防…之損失: ~ *one's bets.* 兩面下注。 **4** [VP2A] make or trim ~s. 圍樹籬; 修樹籬。

hedge·hog /ˈhedʒhɒg *US:* -hɔːg ; ˈhɛdʒˌhag/ *n* insect-eating animal covered with spines, that rolls itself up into a ball to defend itself. 猬。⇨ the illus at small. 參看 small 之挿圖。

he·don·ism /ˈhiːdənɪzəm ; ˈhidn̩ˌɪzəm/ *n* [U] belief that pleasure is the chief good. 享樂主義。 **he·don·ist** /-ɪst ; -ɪst/ *n* believer in ~. 享樂主義者。 **he·don·is·tic** /ˌhiːdəˈnɪstɪk ; ˌhidəˈnɪstɪk/ *adj*

heed /hiːd ; ˈhid/ *vt* [VP6A] (formal) pay attention to: (正式用語)注意: ~ *a warning;* 注意一項警告; ~ *what a person says.* 注意某人說的話。□ *n* [U] ***pay/give ~ (to); take ~ (of),*** give attention, notice: 注意: *pay no* ~ *to a warning.* 不注意一項警告。 **~·ful** /-fl ; -ˌfʊl/ *adj* ***~ful (of),*** attentive: 注意的: *be more ~ful of advice.* 多留心忠告。 **~·less** *adj* ***~less (of),*** inattentive: 不注意的: *~less of danger.* 不注意危險。

hee·haw /ˈhiːhɔː ; ˈhiˌhɔ/ *n* ass's bray; loud laugh. 驢叫; 大笑。

heel[1] /hiːl ; hil/ *n* **1** back part of the human foot; part of a sock, stocking, etc covering this; part of a shoe, boot, etc supporting this. 足跟; 踵; 襪等的踵部; 鞋、靴等的後跟。⇨ the illus at leg. 參看 leg 之挿圖。 ***at/on the ~s of sth; at/on sb's ~s,*** close behind it/him: 緊跟在某物(某人)之後: *Famine often follows on the ~s of war.* 饑荒常緊隨戰爭之後。 *The thief ran off with an angry crowd at his ~s.* 那小偷在前面跑, 一群憤怒的人緊隨後面追。 ***bring/come to ~,*** (of a dog) bring/come close behind its master, under control; (fig) submit to discipline and control. (指狗)(使)緊隨主人之後; (喻)(使)服從訓練和管治。 ***down at ~,*** (of shoes) with the ~s badly worn down; (of a person) wearing such shoes, or untidy and slovenly in appearance. (指鞋)後跟穿破的; (指人)穿着後跟破了的鞋的; 邋遢的; 潦倒的。 ***head over ~s,*** upside down, in a somersault; (fig) completely. 倒轉; 顛倒; (喻)完全地; 徹底地。 ***kick/cool one's ~s,*** be kept waiting. 等候; 久等。 ***kick up one's ~s,*** behave excitedly (esp to show joy at freedom). 狂歡; 手舞足蹈; (尤指)盡情享樂。 ***lay sb by the ~s,*** confine or imprison him. 監禁某人。 ***show a clean pair of ~s,*** escape in a great hurry. 匆匆逃脫。 ***take to one's ~s,*** run away. 逃走。 ***turn on one's ~,*** turn sharply round. 急轉身。 ***under the ~ of,*** (fig) dominated by. (喻)在…支配之下。 **2** (US sl) cad; low-down person. (美俚)鄙漢; 下流人。□ *vt* [VP6A] put a ~ on: 裝鞋跟於: *sole and* ~ *a pair of shoes.* 上一雙鞋的鞋底及鞋跟。 **ˌwell-ˈ~ed** *adj* (sl) very rich. (俚)很富有的。

heel[2] /hiːl ; hil/ *vi, vt* [VP2A, C, 15B] ***~ (over),*** (of a ship) (cause to) lean over to one side. (指船)(使)傾向一邊。

hef·ty /ˈheftɪ ; ˈhɛftɪ/ *adj* (-ier, -iest) (colloq) big and strong: (俗)大而壯的: *a* ~ *farm worker.* 粗大體壯的農工。

he·gem·ony /hɪˈgemənɪ *US:* ˈhedʒəməʊnɪ ; hiˈdʒɛmənɪ/ *n* (*pl* -nies) [U, C] (formal) leadership, authority, influence, esp of one state in a group of states. (正式用語)領導權; 覇權(尤指數國中之盟主權); 權威; 勢力。

He·gira, He·jira /ˈhedʒɪrə *US:* hɪˈdʒaɪərə ; hiˈdʒaɪrə/ *n* **the** ~, Muhammad's flight from Mecca to Medina; Muslim era reckoned from this (AD 622). 穆罕默德從麥加到麥地那之逃亡; 回教紀元(公元 622 年)。

heifer /ˈhefə(r) ; ˈhɛfɚ/ *n* young cow that has not yet had a calf. 小牝牛。

heigh·ho /ˌheɪˈhəʊ ; ˈheˈho/ *int* used to express disappointment, boredom, etc. 嗨嗬! (用以表示失望, 厭煩等)。

height /haɪt ; haɪt/ *n* **1** [U, C] measurement from bottom to top; distance to the top of sth from a level, esp sea-level: 高度; 海拔: *the* ~ *of a mountain.* 一山之高度。 *What is your* ~, How tall are you? 你有多高? *He is six feet in* ~. 他有六呎高。 **2** [C] high place: 高地: *on the mountain ~s.* 在山岡上。 **3** [U] utmost degree: 頂點; 極度: *the* ~ *of his ambition;* 他的最高志願; *dressed in the* ~ *of fashion.* 打扮得最爲時髦。 *The storm was at its* ~. 風暴達到最猛烈的程度。

heighten /ˈhaɪtn ; ˈhaɪtn̩/ *vt, vi* [VP6A, 2A] make or become high(er); make greater in degree: 提高; 加高; 變高; 增强; 增加; 增大: ~ *a person's anger;* 增加一人之怒氣; ~ *an effect;* 提高效果; *her ~ed colour,* the increased colour in her face, eg caused by emotion. 她逐漸變紅的面孔(例如因感情的激動所致)。

hei·nous /ˈheɪnəs ; ˈhenəs/ *adj* (of crime) odious; atrocious. (指罪行)極惡的; 兇暴的。 **~·ly** *adv* **~·ness** *n*

heir /eə(r) ; ɛr/ *n* person with the legal right to receive a title, property, etc when the owner dies: 繼承人: *The eldest son is usually the* ~. 長子通常爲繼承人。 *He is* ~ *to a large fortune.* 他是一大筆財產的繼承者。 *Who is* ~ *to the throne?* 誰是王位繼承人? **ˌ~ apˈparent** *n* (*pl* ~s apparent) ~ whose right cannot be superseded by the birth of a nearer ~. 指定繼承人(其繼承權不因較近親屬的誕生而受影響)。 **ˌ~ preˈsumptive** *n* whose right of inheritance may be lost by the birth of a nearer ~. 假定繼承人(其繼承權可能因較近親屬的誕生而失去)。 **~·ess** /ˈeərɪs ; ˈɛrɪs/ *n* female ~. 女繼承人。

heir·loom /ˈeəluːm ; ˈɛrˌlum/ *n* sth handed down in a family for several generations. 祖傳物; 傳家寶。

He·jira /ˈhedʒɪrə *US:* hɪˈdʒaɪərə ; hiˈdʒaɪrə/ *n*=Hegira.

held /held ; hɛld/ *pt, pp* of hold.

heli·cop·ter /ˈhelɪkɒptə(r) ; ˈhɛlɪˌkɑptɚ/ *n* kind of aircraft with horizontal revolving blades or rotors, able to take off and land in a very small space and remain stationary in the air. 直升飛機。

a helicopter

he·lio·graph /ˈhiːlɪəgrɑːf *US:* -græf ; ˈhilɪəˌgræf/ *n* apparatus formerly used for sending signals by reflecting flashes of sunlight. 日光反射信號機。□ *vt* send (a message) by ~. 以日光反射信號機發出(消息)。

he·lio·trope /ˈhiːlɪətrəʊp ; ˈhiljəˌtrop/ *n* plant with small, sweet-smelling purple flowers; colour of these. 天芥菜屬植物(生有芳香的小紫花);淡紫色。

heli·port /ˈhelɪpɔːt ; ˈhɛlɪˌpɔrt/ *n* airport for helicopters. 直升飛機站。

he·lium /ˈhiːlɪəm ; ˈhilɪəm/ *n* [U] light, colourless gas (symbol **He**) that does not burn, used in balloons and airships.氦(無色,不燃的輕氣體,符號爲He)。

hell /hel ; hɛl/ *n* **1** (in some religions) home of devils and of damned souls after death. (某些宗教)地獄;冥府。 **2** place, condition, of great suffering or misery: 痛苦的地方;苦境: *suffer ~ on earth;* 受人間之苦; *make sb's life a ~.* 使某人的生活像地獄般的苦。*We gave the enemy ~.* 我們讓敵人吃盡苦頭。 **3** (colloq, in exclamations, to express anger, or to intensify a meaning) (俗,在感嘆句中表示憤怒或加强意義) *H~!* 混蛋! *What the ~ do you want?* 你到底要什麼? *He ran like ~,* very fast. 他跑得極快。*I like him a ~ of a lot.* 我非常喜歡他。*What a ~ of a noise!* 眞是吵死人了! ***for the ~ of it,*** for no particular reason. 無特別理由地。***ride ~ for leather,*** as quickly as possible. 盡快地騎。**'~-cat** *n* spiteful or furious person. 惡人;潑辣的人。**~·ish** /-ɪʃ ; -ɪʃ/ *adj* horrible; devilish. 可怕的;如惡魔的。***be ˌ~-'bent on sth,*** (sl) be recklessly determined to do it. (俚)不顧一切地做某事。

he'll /*strong or initial form:* hiːl ; hil; *medial weak form often:* iːl ; il/ = he will; he shall.

Hel·lene /ˈheliːn ; ˈhɛlin/ *n* subject of modern Greece; person of genuine Greek race in ancient times. 近代希臘國民;古希臘人。**Hel·lenic** /heˈliːnɪk *US:* heˈlenɪk ; hɛˈlɛnɪk/ *adj* of the Greeks, their arts, culture, etc. 希臘人的;希臘之藝術、文化等的。

hello /həˈləʊ ; həˈlo/ *int* = hullo.

helm¹ /helm ; hɛlm/ *n* handle (also called 亦稱作 *tiller*) or wheel for moving the rudder of a boat or ship: 舵柄;舵輪;駕駛盤: *the man at the ~,* the steersman, (fig) leader; 舵手;(喩)領袖; *the ~ of state,* (fig) the government of the nation. (喩)國家的政府。**~s·man** /-zmən ; -zmən/ *n* (*pl* -men) man at the ~. 舵手。

helm² /helm ; hɛlm/ *n* (archaic) helmet. (古)盔。

hel·met /ˈhelmɪt;ˈhɛlmɪt/ *n* protective head-covering worn by soldiers, firemen, miners, motorbike riders, divers (as part of a diving-suit), and some policemen. (士兵,救火人員,礦工,摩托車騎士,潛水者,以及某些警察所戴的)頭盔;鋼盔。 ⇨ the illus at armour. 參看 armour 之插圖。⇨ also *sun-~* at sun. **~ed** *adj* wearing, provided with, a ~. 戴盔的。

helot /ˈhelət ; ˈhɛlət/ *n* one of a class of slaves in ancient Sparta; (fig) member of any social class that is despised and kept in subjection. 古斯巴達的奴隸階級之一員; (喩) 任何受鄙視與奴役的社會階級之一員。

help¹ /help ; hɛlp/ *n* **1** [U] act of ~ing: 幫助;救助: *Thank you for your kind ~.* 謝謝你的惠助。***be of ~ (to sb); be (of) any/much/no/some ~ (to sb),*** be ~ful: 有助於;對…有(很有,沒有,有一些)幫助: *Can I be of any ~ to you?* 我能幫助你嗎? *It wasn't much ~,* didn't ~ much. 它沒有多大幫助。**2** **a ~,** sb or sth that ~s: 幫助者;幫助的人或事物: *Your advice was a great ~.* 你的勸告是一很大的幫助。*Far from being a ~ to me, you're a hindrance.* 你不但對我沒有幫助,反而是個障礙。**3** [U] remedy: 補救方法: *There's no ~ for it,* it can't be ~ed. 沒有辦法了。⇨ help²(3). **4** [C] (usu non-resident) person who ~s with the housework: (通常是不住宿的)僕人;佣人: *a home ~,* ⇨ home¹(3). *The ~ hasn't come this morning.* 佣人今早還沒有來。 **~·ful** /-fl ; -fəl/ *adj* giving ~: 有幫助的;有益的: *be ~ful to one's friends.* 對朋友有幫助。**~·fully** /-fəlɪ ; -fəlɪ/ *adv* **~·ful·ness** *n* **~·less** *adj* **1** without ~; not receiving ~. 無助的;未受幫助的。**2** unable to act; dependent upon others: 不能行動的; 不能自立的; 依賴他人的: *a ~less invalid;* 依賴他人的病人; *as ~less as a baby.* 像嬰兒般依賴他人。 **~·less·ly** *adv* **~·less·ness** *n* **~er** *n* person who ~s. 幫助者。**~·ing** *n* (esp) portion of food served at a meal: (尤指)一份食物;一客: *three ~ings of pie;* 三份水果餅; *a generous ~ing of pudding.* 豐富的一客布丁。

help² /help ; hɛlp/ *vt, vi* **1** [VP6A, 17, 18B, 15A, B, 2A, C] do part of the work of another person; make it easier for (sb) to do sth or for (sth) to happen; do sth for the benefit of (sb in need): 幫助;幫忙;援助;資助: *I can't lift this box alone, please ~ me.* 我一個人提不起這箱子,請幫助我。*I ~ed him (to) find his things.* 我幫他找到他的東西。(The omission of *to* is more usual in US than in GB usage.) (help 之後的不定詞省去 to,在美國用法中較在英國習見。) *Please ~ me up/down/out, etc with this heavy trunk,* ~ me to carry it up, etc. 請幫我把這重箱子抬起來(放下去, 抬出去等)。*Will you ~ me on with my overcoat, please,* ~ me to put it on? 請你幫我把大衣穿上好嗎? *We ~ed the injured man off with his clothes,* ~ed him to get them off. 我們幫助那傷者,將他的衣服脫下。*Tom has to ~ his father, who is too old to work.* 湯姆必須幫助他父親,他父親太老了不能工作。*Would it ~ you to know that...,* if I told you that...? 如果我告訴你…對你會有幫助嗎? **~ out,** give ~ (esp in a crisis). 幫助(尤指在危機時)。 **2** [VP6A, 14] ***~ sb/oneself (to sth),*** serve with food, drink, etc: 替某人(自己)取(食物,飲料等): *May I ~ you to some more meat?* 再來一點肉好嗎? *H~ yourself to the fruit/cigarettes.* 請隨便用水果(香煙)。 **3** [VP6A, C] ***can ~ sth/doing sth,*** avoid; refrain; prevent: 避免;抑制;阻止: *Don't tell him more than you can ~,* more than you must. 不要把不應該告訴他的話告訴他(不要告訴他太多了)。*I can't ~ thinking he's still alive.* 我不能不認爲他還活着。*She burst out crying; she couldn't ~ it.* 她放聲大哭,無法抑制自己。*I can't ~ my husband having so many dull relations.* 我丈夫有這麼多呆笨的親戚,我也沒有法子。 *It can't be ~ed,* is inevitable. 這是不可避免的。 **4** ***So ~ me God,*** (in an oath) (as I speak the truth, etc) may God ~ me. (用於誓言)(由於我在說實話等)願上帝幫助我。

help·mate /ˈhelpmeɪt;ˈhɛlpˌmet/, **help·meet** /ˈhelpmiːt ; ˈhɛlpˌmit/ *nn* helpful partner, esp a wife or husband. 良伴 (尤指妻子或丈夫)。

hel·ter-skel·ter /ˌheltə ˈskeltə(r) ; ˈhɛltɚˈskɛltɚ/ *adv* in disorderly haste. 手忙脚亂地。□ *n* tall spiral slide¹(2) in a fairground, etc. (露天市場等供兒童遊樂之)高螺旋滑梯。

helve /helv ; hɛlv/ *n* handle of a tool, esp an axe. 工具的柄(尤指斧柄)。

hem¹ /hem ; hɛm/ *n* border or edge of cloth, esp one on an article of clothing, when turned and sewn down. 布的邊緣;(尤指)衣服的邊緣。**ˈhemming-stitch** *n* style of sewing hems on dresses, skirts, etc by joining the turned edge to the length of material using diagonal stitches. 縫衣邊之對角針法。 **ˈhem·line** *n* (esp) lower edge of a skirt or dress: (尤指)裙子或衣服的下擺: *lower/raise the hemline,* make a skirt, etc longer/shorter. 將下擺放低(提高);使裙子等變長(短)。 □ *vt* (-mm-) **1** [VP6A] make a hem on: 縫…之邊: *hem a handkerchief.* 縫一條手帕的邊。 **2** [VP15B] ***~ about/around/in,*** enclose; confine; surround: 包圍;關閉: *hemmed in by the enemy.* 被敵人包圍。

hem² (also **h'm**) /hem, hm ; hɛm, hm/ *int* sound used to indicate doubt or sarcasm, or to call attention. (表示疑惑或譏諷,或促使人注意的聲音)哼! □ *vi* (-mm-) make this sound; hesitate in speech. 發哼聲;結結巴巴地說話。***hem and haw/ha,*** = *hum and haw/ha,* ⇨ hum.

he·ma·tite (also **hae-**) /ˈhemətaɪt ; ˈhɛməˌtaɪt/ *n* iron oxide **(Fe_2O_3)** the main ore of iron. 赤鐵鑛 (Fe_2O_3)。

hemi·sphere /ˈhemɪsfɪə(r) ; ˈhɛməsˌfɪr/ *n* half a sphere; half the earth. 半球;地球的一半。**the Northern/Southern ~,** north / south of the equator. 北(南)半球(赤道以北或以南)。**the Eastern ~,** Europe, Asia, Africa and Australia. 東半球(指歐,亞,非,澳四洲)。**the Western ~,** N and S America. 西半球(指南北美洲)。

hem·lock /ˈhemlɒk; ˈhɛmlɑk/ *n* plant with finely divided leaves and small, white flowers, from which a poison is made. 毒人參(生有羽狀分裂的葉和小白花,可製毒藥)。**ˈ~ spruce** *n* evergreen tree, common in America and Asia, valuable for its timber. 一種松柏科栂屬的常綠樹(常見於美洲及亞洲,其木料甚有價值);加州鐵杉。

he·mo·glo·bin (also **hae-**) /ˌhiːməˈgləʊbɪn; ˌhiməˈglobɪn/ *n* [U] substance present in the red corpuscles of the blood. 血紅蛋白;血紅素。

he·mo·philia (also **hae-**) /ˌhiːməˈfɪlɪə; ˌhiməˈfɪlɪə/ *n* [U] (usu hereditary) tendency of blood (from a wound, etc) not to clot, so that bleeding continues. (通常是遺傳的)出血不止症;血友症。**he·mo·phil·iac** (also **hae-**) /ˌhiːməˈfɪlɪæk; ˌhiməˈfɪlɪæk/ *n* person having ~. 患出血不止症者;血友病者。

hem·or·rhage (also **hae-**) /ˈhemərɪdʒ; ˈhɛmərɪdʒ/ *n* [U] bleeding; [C] escape of blood. 出血;溢血。

hem·or·rhoids (also **hae-**) /ˈhemərɔɪdz; ˈhɛməˌrɔɪdz/ *n pl* swelling of a vein or veins, esp at or near the anus; piles. 痔;痔瘡。

hemp /hemp; hɛmp/ *n* [U] (kinds of) plant from which coarse fibres are obtained for the manufacture of rope and cloth. 大麻。**(Indian) ~,** narcotic from the flowering tops, seed and resin of such plants, 大麻製的麻醉劑, also called 亦稱作 *bhang, cannabis, hashish, marijuana.* **~en** /ˈhempən; ˈhɛmpən/ *adj* made of ~; like ~: 大麻製的;似大麻的: *a ~en rope.* 大麻製的繩。

hem·stitch /ˈhemstɪtʃ; ˈhɛmˌstɪtʃ/ *vt, n* (ornament the hem of a handkerchief, dress, skirt, towel, etc with a) decorative stitch made by pulling out some of the threads and tying the cross-threads in groups. 垂縫;抽絲結縫;結縫於布、手帕、衣服、裙子、毛巾等邊緣以作裝飾。

hen /hen; hɛn/ *n* **1** female of the common domestic fowl. 母鷄。⇨ cock[1](1). ⇨ the illus at fowl. 參看 fowl 之插圖。**ˈhen-bane** *n* (narcotic obtained from a) poisonous plant. 莨菪;菲沃斯(一種毒草);由莨菪提取的麻醉劑。**ˈhen-coop** *n* coop for keeping poultry in. 鷄窩;鷄棚。**ˈhen-house** *n* (usu wooden) building for poultry. (通常是木造的)鷄舍。**ˈhen-party** *n* (colloq) party for woman only. (俗)女人的聚會。⇨ *stag party* at stag. **ˈhen-pecked** *adj* (of a man) ruled by his wife. (指男子)受妻子管治的;懼內的。**ˈhen-roost** *n* place where fowls roost at night. 鷄窩。**2** female (of the bird named): (某種鳥的) 雌性: *ˈguinea-hen,* 雌珠鷄, *ˈpea-hen.* 雌孔雀。

hence /hens; hɛns/ *adv* (formal) (正式用語) **1** from here; from now: 從此處;從此時: *a week ~,* in a week's time. 從現在起一星期的時間;今後一星期。**2** for this reason. 因此;由是。**ˌ~ˈforth, ˌ~ˈforward** *advv* from this time on; in future. 從今以後;今後。

hench·man /ˈhentʃmən; ˈhɛntʃmən/ *n* (*pl* -men /-mən; -mən/) faithful supporter, esp a political supporter who obeys without question the orders of his leader: 忠實的支持者(尤指在政治上無條件服從其領袖的支持者): *the Dictator and his henchmen.* 獨裁者及其親信。

henna /ˈhenə; ˈhɛnə/ *n* [U] (plant, kind of Egyptian privet, producing) reddish-brown dye stuff for colouring leather, the finger-nails, the hair, etc. 指甲花(埃及產的一種水蠟樹類植物);指甲花所產的一種紅褐色的染料(可染皮革,指甲,頭髮等)。**hen·naed** /ˈhenəd; ˈhɛnəd/ *adj* dyed with ~. 以指甲花染料染過的。

hep /hep; hɛp/ *adj* ⇨ hip[4].

hepa·ti·tis /ˌhepəˈtaɪtɪs; ˌhɛpəˈtaɪtɪs/ *n* [U] inflammation of the liver. 肝炎。

hep·ta·gon /ˈheptəgən *US:* -gɒn; ˈhɛptəˌgɑn/ *n* plane figure with 7 (esp equal) sides. 七邊形;(尤指)等邊七角形。

her /*strong or initial form:* hɜː(r); hɝ; *medial weak form:* ɜː(r); ɚ/ *pers pron* (as an object, corresponding to *she*): 她(爲 she 的受格): *She's in the garden; I can see her.* 她在花園裡,我看得見她。*Give her the book.* 把這本書給她。□ *poss adj* belonging to her: 她的: *Mary's mother is dead but her father is alive.* 瑪莉的母親死了,但她的父親還健在。*That's her hat, not yours.* 那是她的帽子,不是你的。**hers** /hɜːz; hɝz/ *poss pron* belonging to her: 她的: *Is that his or hers?* 那是他的還是她的? *I've borrowed a book of hers,* one of her books. 我借了她的一本書。

her·ald /ˈherəld; ˈhɛrəld/ *n* **1** (hist) person making public announcements for, and carrying messages from, a ruler. (史)傳令官;使者。**2** person or thing foretelling the coming of sb or sth: 先驅;預兆: *In England the cuckoo is a ~ of spring.* 在英國杜鵑鳥預示春天的來臨。**3** official who keeps records of families that have coats of arms. 司宗譜紋章的官。**H~s' College,** corporation that records pedigrees and grants coats of arms. 宗譜紋章院。□ *vt* [VP6A] proclaim the approach of. 宣佈…之將臨。**her·al·dic** /heˈrældɪk; hɛˈrældɪk/ *adj* of ~s or ~ry. 使者的;司宗譜紋章之官的;紋章學的。**~ry** *n* [U] science dealing with the coats of arms, descent, and history of old families. 紋章學。

herb /hɜːb *US:* ɜːrb; ɝb/ *n* low-growing, soft-stemmed plant which dies down at the end of the growing season; plant of this kind whose leaves or seeds, because of their scent or flavour, are used in medicine or for flavouring food, eg sage, mint, dill. 草本植物;藥草;香草(因其葉或種子的氣味,故可製藥或香料,例如鼠尾草、薄荷、蒔蘿)。**~ beer** *n* drink made from ~s. 藥草製的飲料。**~·age** /-ɪdʒ; -ɪdʒ/ *n* [U] ~s collectively; grass and other field plants. 草本植物的總稱;草類。**~al** /ˈhɜːbl *US:* ˈɜːrbl; ˈɝbl̩/ *adj* of (esp) medicinal ~s: (尤指)藥草的: *~al remedies.* 藥草治療法。**~·al·ist** /ˈhɜːbəlɪst *US:* ˈɜːrb-; ˈɝbl̩ɪst/ *n* person who grows or sells ~s for medical use. 種植或售賣藥草者。**her·bivor·ous** /hɜːˈbɪvərəs *US:* ɜː-; hɝˈbɪvərəs/ *adj* (of animals) feeding on ~age. (指動物)食草的。⇨ *carnivorous* at carnivore.

her·ba·ceous /hɜːˈbeɪʃəs *US:* ɜː-; hɝˈbeʃəs/ *adj* (of plants) having stems that are not woody: (指植物)草本的: *a ~ border,* (in a garden) border with plants which come up and flower year after year (not shrubs, annuals, etc). (庭園中)種有多年生花草的邊緣(非種有灌木及一年生的植物等者)。

her·cu·lean /ˌhɜːkjʊˈliːən; hɝˈkjulɪən/ *adj* having, needing, great powers of body or mind: 有大體力或智力的;需要大的體力或智力的: *a ~ task.* 艱鉅的任務。

herd /hɜːd; hɝd/ *n* **1** number or company of animals, esp cattle, feeding or going about together: 獸群(尤指牛群): *a ~ of cattle/deer/elephants.* 一群牛(鹿,象)。**2** (chiefly in compounds) keeper of a ~: (主要用於複合字中)牧人: *ˈcow~;* 牧牛人; *ˈgoat~.* 牧羊人。**3** (derog) (貶) *the common/vulgar ~,* the mass of common people; 群衆; *the ~ instinct,* the instinct to act, feel, think, etc like the mass of people, and to be with the mass. 群衆本能(行動、感覺、思想等與群衆相似並且想跟群衆在一起的本能)。□ *vi, vt* [VP2C, 15A, B] (cause to) gather into a ~ or as in a ~; look after a ~: (使)成群;放牧: *people who ~ed/were ~ed together like cattle.* 像牛一般群集的人們。**~s·man** /-mən; -mən/ *n* (*pl* -men) keeper of a ~. 牧人。

here /hɪə(r); hɪr/ *adv* **1** in, at, to this point of place: 在這裡;向這裡: *Come ~.* 到這裡來。*I live ~.* 我住在這裡。*Put the box ~.* 把盒子放在這裡。*Look ~.* 看這裡。**2** (with front position, and inversion of the subject and finite *v* if the subject is a *n,* but not if the subject is a *pers pron*): (位於句

首,如主詞爲一名詞,則主詞與定動詞倒置,如主詞爲一人稱代名詞,則不倒置): *H~ comes the bus!* 公共汽車來了! *H~ it comes!* 它來了! *H~ are the others!* 其餘的在這裡! *H~ they/we are!* 他們(我們)終於到了! *H~'s something interesting.* 這裡有個有趣的東西。*H~ you are/it is!* H~ is what you asked for, are looking for, etc according to context. 你所要的東西在這裡!你要找的東西在這裡!(視上下文之意義而定)。 **3** at this point (in a series of events, in a process, etc): (在一連串事件、某一過程等中)此時;這時: *H~ he stopped reading and looked up.* 這時他停止看書,抬起頭來往上看。 *H~ the speaker paused to have a drink.* 這時那說話的人停下來喝了一口水。***H~ goes!*** Now I'm going to make a start, have a go. 現在我要開始了! **4** (after *preps*): (在介詞後): *Come over ~*, near to where I am. 到我這裡來。*Do you live near ~*, near this place? 你住在這附近嗎? **5** *~ **and there,*** in various places. 各處;在不同的地方。*~, **there and everywhere,*** in all parts; all round. 到處;處處。***neither ~ nor there,*** (colloq) irrelevant. (俗)不切題;不相干。 **6** (used after a *n* to call attention, or for emphasis): (用於名詞後以引人注意或加强語氣): *My friend ~ was a witness of the accident.* 我的朋友就是這意外事件的見證。 **7** (used when drinking to sb's health, wishing success to an enterprise, etc): (用於敬酒時祝某人健康,事業成功等): *H~'s to the bride and bridegroom!* 敬新娘新郎一杯! **~·abouts** /ˌhɪərəˈbaʊts ; ˌhɪrəˈbaʊts/ *adv* near or about ~. 在附近;在這一帶。 **~·after** /hɪərˈɑːftə(r) *US:* -ˈæf- ; hɪrˈæftə˞/ *adv, n* (in the) future; the life to come. (在)將來;來世。**~·by** /hɪəˈbaɪ ; hɪrˈbaɪ/ *adv* (legal) by means or by reason of this. (法律)藉此;由此。**~·in** /ˌhɪərˈɪn ; hɪrˈɪn/ *adv* (legal) in this. (法律)在這當中;於此處。**~·of** /hɪərˈɒv ; hɪrˈɑv/ *adv* (legal) of or about this. (法律)於此;關於此點。**~·to** /hɪəˈtuː ; hɪrˈtu/ *adv* (legal) to this. (法律)至此。**~·to·fore** /ˌhɪətuːˈfɔː(r) ; ˌhɪrtəˈfor/ *adv* (legal) until now; formerly. (法律)直到此時;以前。 **~·upon** /ˌhɪərəˈpɒn ; ˌhɪrəˈpɑn/ *adv* (formal) at this point; in consequence of this. (正式用語)於此;於是。**~·with** /ˌhɪəˈwɪð *US:* -ˈwɪθ ; hɪrˈwɪθ/ *adv* (comm) with this. (商)同此;並此;附此。

her·edita·ment /ˌherɪˈdɪtəmənt ; ˌhɛrəˈdɪtəmənt/ *n* (legal) property that can be inherited. (法律)可繼承的財產;世襲財產。

her·ed·itary /hɪˈredɪtrɪ *US:* -terɪ ; həˈrɛdəˌtɛrɪ/ *adj* passed on from parent to child, from one generation to following generations: 世襲的;代代相傳的;遺傳的: *~ rulers/beliefs/diseases.* 世襲的統治者(代代相傳的信仰;遺傳病)。

her·ed·ity /hɪˈredətɪ ; həˈrɛdətɪ/ *n* [U] tendency of living things to pass their characteristics on to offspring, etc; characteristics, qualities, etc so passed on: 遺傳性; 遺傳; 遺傳的特徵、性質等: *~ factors/genes.* 遺傳因素(因子)。

her·esy /ˈherəsɪ ; ˈhɛrəsɪ/ *n* (*pl* -sies) [C, U] (holding of a) belief or opinion contrary to what is generally accepted, esp in religion: 異端邪說(尤指宗教方面的);信奉異端邪說: *fall into ~;* 陷入旁門左道中; *be guilty of ~;* 犯了異端邪說罪; *the heresies of the Protestants.* 新教徒的異說。**her·etic** /ˈherətɪk ; ˈhɛrətɪk/ *n* person guilty of ~ or supporting a ~; person who holds an unorthodox opinion. 持異端邪說者;異教徒。**her·eti·cal** /hɪˈretɪkl ; həˈrɛtɪkl̩/ *adj* of ~ or heretics: 異端邪說的;持異端邪說的: *heretical beliefs.* 異端邪說。

heri·table /ˈherɪtəbl ; ˈhɛrətəbl̩/ *adj* (legal) capable of inheriting or being inherited. (法律)可繼承的;可傳讓的。

heri·tage /ˈherɪtɪdʒ ; ˈhɛrətɪdʒ/ *n* that which has been or may be inherited. 遺產;繼承物。

her·maph·ro·dite /hɜːˈmæfrədaɪt ; hɝˈmæfrəˌdaɪt/ *n* [C] animal or other creature, eg an earthworm, which has both male and female sexual organs or characteristics. 具有雌雄兩性的動物(例如蚯蚓);雌雄同體。

her·metic /hɜːˈmetɪk ; hɝˈmɛtɪk/ *adj* completely air-tight: 不透氣的;密封的: *a ~ seal.* 密封。**her·meti·cally** /-klɪ ; -klɪ/ *adv*: *~ally sealed,* sealed so as to keep all the air in or out. 密封的。

her·mit /ˈhɜːmɪt ; ˈhɝmɪt/ *n* person (esp man in early Christian times) living alone. 隱士(尤指基督教早期者)。**~·age** /-ɪdʒ ; -ɪdʒ/ *n* cell or living-place of a ~ or groups of ~s. 隱士隱居之處。

her·nia /ˈhɜːnɪə ; ˈhɝnɪə/ *n* [U, C] rupture, esp one caused by a part of the bowel being pushed through a weak point of the muscle wall of the abdomen. 脫腸;疝氣。

hero /ˈhɪərəʊ ; ˈhɪro/ *n* (*pl* ~es /-rəʊz ; -roz/) **1** person respected for bravery or noble qualities. 英雄;豪傑。**2** chief person in a poem, story, play, etc. (詩,小說,戲劇等中之)男主角。**ˈ~·ine** /ˈherəʊɪn ; ˈhɛro·ɪn/ *n* female ~. 女英雄;(詩,小說,戲劇等中之)女主角。 **~·ism** /ˈherəʊɪzəm ; ˈhɛroˌɪzəm/ *n* [U] quality of being a ~; courage. 英雄氣慨;英勇。

her·oic /hɪˈrəʊɪk ; hɪˈro·ɪk/ *adj* **1** of, like, fit for, a hero: 英雄的;英雄般的;適於英雄的;英勇的: *~ deeds/tasks;* 英勇的事蹟(工作); *use ~ remedies,* hazardous remedies but worth trying. 採取冒險但值得一試的補救法。 **2** of a size larger than life: 大於眞人或實物的: *a statue of ~ size/on a ~ scale.* 大於眞人的彫像。**3** of poetry dealing with heroes. 敍述英雄故事之詩篇的;史詩的。**ˌ~ ˈverse,** lines of ten syllables and five stresses, rhyming in pairs. 英雄詩體(每行有十個音節,五個重音,每兩行押韻)。 **4** (of language) grand; attempting great things; (指語言)堂皇的;誇大的; (hence) (由此產生) **~s** *n pl* high-flown or high-sounding talk or sentiments. 誇大的言談或意見。**he·roi·cally** /-klɪ ; -klɪ/ *adv*

her·oin /ˈherəʊɪn ; ˈhɛro·ɪn/ *n* [U] narcotic drug prepared from morphine, used medically to cause sleep or relieve pain, or used by drug addicts. 海洛英;嗎啡精。

heron /ˈherən ; ˈhɛrən/ *n* long-legged water-bird living in marshy places. 蒼鷺。⇨ the illus at water. 參看 water 之插圖。**~ry** *n* (*pl* -ries) place where ~s breed. 蒼鷺繁殖之處。

Herr /heə(r) ; hɛr/ *n* (*pl* Herren /ˈherən ; ˈhɛrən/) German equivalent of *Mr;* German gentleman. (德)先生(相當於 Mr);德國紳士。

her·ring /ˈherɪŋ ; ˈhɛrɪŋ/ *n* (*pl* often unchanged) sea-fish, usu swimming in immense shoals, valued as food (fresh, salted, or dried). (複數常不變)鯡;青魚。 ⇨ the illus at fish. 參看 fish 之插圖。**ˈ~-bone** *n* [U] pattern (like the spine and bones of a ~) used for stitching, designs on cloth, etc. 魚脊型(鯡魚骨狀形,用做縫級的式樣、布的圖案等)。**ˌred ˈ~,** ⇨ red(3).

hers /hɜːz ; hɝz/ ⇨ her.

her·self /hɜːˈself ; həˈsɛlf; *weak form:* ɜːˈs- ; ɚˈs-/ *reflex, emph pron* **1** (reflex) (反身) *She hurt ~.* 她傷了自己。*She ought to be ashamed of ~.* 她應當自感羞愧。***(all) by ~,*** **(a)** alone. 孤獨;單獨。**(b)** without help: 獨力: *Can she do it by ~ or does she need help?* 她能自己做還是需要幫助? **2** (emph) (强勢語) *She ~ told me the news.* 她親自將這消息告訴我的。 *She told me the news ~.* 她親自將這消息告訴我的。*I saw Mrs Smith ~,* ie not one of her family, one of her staff, etc. 我看見史密斯太太本人了。 **3** *She's not quite ~ today,* not in her normal state of health or mind. 她今天不大舒服;她今天有些失常。 *She has come to ~,* is now in her normal mental state. 她的心理狀態恢復正常了。(Cf 參較 *She has come to,* has regained consciousness. 她清醒過來了。)

hertz /hɜːts ; hɛrts/ *n* (symbol **Hz**) unit of frequency equal to one cycle per second. 赫(每秒周波數,符號爲 Hz)。

Hertz·ian /ˈhɜːtsɪən ; ˈhɛrtsɪən/ *adj* **~ waves,** electromagnetic waves as used in radio. 赫芝電波;電磁波(如無線電中者)。

he's /*strong or initial form:* hi:z ; hiz; *medial weak form:* i:z ; iz/ = he is; he has.

hesi·tant /ˈhezɪtənt ; ˈhɛzətənt/ *adj* tending or inclined to hesitate. 猶豫的;躊躇的。**~·ly** *adv* **hesi·tance** /-əns ; -əns/, **hesi·tancy** /-ənsɪ ; -ənsɪ/ *nn* [U] (formal) state or quality of being ~. (正式用語)猶豫;躊躇。

hesi·tate /ˈhezɪteɪt ; ˈhɛzə͵tet/ *vi* [VP2A, 3A, B, 4C] show signs of uncertainty or unwillingness in speech or action: 猶豫; 躊躇; 不願: *He's still hesitating about joining/over whether to join the expedition.* 他對於是否參加這探險隊仍在猶豫。*He ~s at nothing.* 他對什麼都毫不遲疑。*I ~ to spend so much money on clothes.* 我不願花這麼多錢做衣服。*He ~d (about) what to do next.* 他對於下一步做什麼猶豫不定。**hesi·tat·ing·ly** *adv*

hesi·ta·tion /͵hezɪˈteɪʃn ; ͵hɛzəˈteʃən/ *n* [U] state of hesitating; [C] instance of hesitating: 猶豫;躊躇: *She agreed without the slightest ~.* 她毫不猶豫地同意了。*I have no ~ in stating that....* 我願意說出…。*There's no room for ~.* 沒有躊躇的餘地。*His doubts and ~s were tiresome.* 他的疑慮和猶豫令人厭煩。

hes·sian /ˈhesɪən *US:* ˈheʃn ; ˈhɛʃən/ *n* [U] strong, coarse cloth of hemp or jute; sack-cloth. 一種結實的粗麻布;麻袋布。

het·ero·dox /ˈhetərədɒks ; ˈhɛtərə͵dɑks/ *adj* not orthodox. 非正統的。**~y** /-sɪ ; -sɪ/ *n* [U] opposite of orthodoxy. 反正統;異端。

het·ero·gen·eous /͵hetərəˈdʒi:nɪəs ; ͵hɛtərəˈdʒinɪəs/ *adj* made up of different kinds: 由不同種類組成的: *the ~ population of the USA,* of many different races. 由不同種族形成的美國人口。⇨ homogeneous.

het·ero·sex·ual /͵hetərəˈsekʃʊəl ; ͵hɛtərəˈsɛkʃʊəl/ *adj* sexually attracted to persons of the opposite sex. 異性愛的;異性戀的。□ *n* ~ person. 異性戀者。**~·ity** /͵hetərə͵sekʃʊˈælətɪ ; ͵hɛtərə͵sɛkʃʊˈælətɪ/ *n* [U] the condition of being ~. 異性戀。

het-up /͵het ˈʌp ; ͵hɛtˈʌp/ *adj* excited; over-wrought. 激動的;過度興奮的。

heu·ris·tic /hjʊəˈrɪstɪk ; hjʊəˈrɪstɪk/ *adj* of the theory in education that a learner should discover things for himself. 啓發式教學法的。**~s** *n* method of solving problems by inductive reasoning, by evaluating past experience and moving by trial and error to a solution. 藉歸納檢討等解決問題的方法。

hew /hju: ; hju/ *vt, vi* (*pt* hewed, *pp* hewed or hewn /hju:n ; hjun/) [VP6A, 15A, B, 2A, C] **1** cut (by striking or chopping); aim cutting blows (*at, among*): 砍; 伐; 劈; 砍向(與 at, among 連用): *hew down a branch.* 砍下一樹枝。*He hewed his enemy to pieces,* eg with his sword. 他將敵人劈成數段(例如用劍)。**2** shape by chopping: 砍成某種形狀: *hewn timber,* roughly shaped by hewing. 粗劈的木材。**3** make by hard work: 辛苦做成: *hew one's way through dense jungle,* cut out and beat a path; 在濃密的森林裡開闢一條路; *hew out a career for oneself.* 艱苦地創一番事業。**hewer** *n* person who hews, esp a man who cuts out coal in a mine: 砍伐者;(尤指)採煤夫: *hewers of wood and drawers of water,* persons doing hard menial work. 劈柴挑水的人。(⇨ Josh 9:21.) (參看聖經約書亞記第9章第21節。)

hexa·gon /ˈheksəgən *US:* -gɒn ; ˈhɛksə͵gɑn/ *n* plane figure with 6 (esp equal) sides. 六邊形;(尤指)等邊六角形。**hex·ag·onal** /heksˈægənl ; hɛksˈægənl/ *adj* six-sided. 六邊的。

hex·am·eter /heksˈæmɪtə(r) ; hɛksˈæmətɚ/ *n* (kind of) line of verse (esp Gk or Lat) with six feet. 六音步的詩或詩行(尤指希臘或拉丁文者)。

hey /heɪ ; he/ *int* used to call attention, or to express surprise or interrogation. (用以促使注意,表示驚異或詢問的聲音)嘿!喂! **͵Hey ˈpresto!** conjuror's phrase used to announce the completion of a trick. (魔術師宣佈戲法已完成的用語)說變就變!

hey·day /ˈheɪdeɪ ; ˈhe͵de/ *n* (*sing* only) time of greatest prosperity or power: (僅用單數)全盛時期: *in the ~ of youth.* 在年輕力壯的時候。*The 19th century was the ~ of steam railways.* 十九世紀爲蒸汽火車最盛時期。

hi /haɪ ; haɪ/ *int* **1** = hey. **2** (esp US) (尤美) = hullo.

hi·atus /haɪˈeɪtəs ; haɪˈetəs/ *n* (*pl* ~es /-sɪz ; -sɪz/) gap in a series, making it incomplete; break in continuity. 脫漏之處;中斷。

hi·ber·nate /ˈhaɪbəneɪt ; ˈhaɪbɚ͵net/ *vi* [VP2A] (of some animals) pass the whole of the winter in a torpid state. (指某些動物) 冬眠; 蟄伏。**hi·ber·na·tion** /͵haɪbəˈneɪʃn ; ͵haɪbɚˈneʃən/ *n* [U].

hi·bis·cus /hɪˈbɪskəs *US:* haɪ- ; haɪˈbɪskəs/ *n* [U] cultivated plant or shrub with brightly coloured flowers (chiefly in the tropics). 木槿(屬)。⇨ the illus at flower. 參看 flower 之插圖。

hic·cup, hic·cough /ˈhɪkʌp ; ˈhɪkʌp/ *vi, n* (have a) sudden stopping of the breath with a cough-like sound. 打嗝;打呃。**(the) ~s,** an attack of ~s: 打嗝: *have the ~s.* 打嗝。

hick /hɪk ; hɪk/ *n, adj* (sl; derog) (of a) countryman, yokel. (俚;貶)鄉巴佬(的)。

hick·ory /ˈhɪkərɪ ; ˈhɪkrɪ/ *n* (*pl* -ries) (hard wood of a) N American tree with edible nuts. (北美所產之)山胡桃樹;山胡桃木。

hid, hidden ⇨ hide¹.

hide¹ /haɪd ; haɪd/ *vt, vi* (*pt* hid /hɪd ; hɪd/, *pp* hidden /ˈhɪdn ; ˈhɪdn̩/ or (archaic) hid) **1** [VP6A, 14] **~ *(from),*** put or keep (sb, sth, oneself) out of sight; prevent from being seen, found or known: 隱藏;藏起;遮掩;隱瞞: *Quick, ~ yourself!* 快點,躲起來! *The sun was hidden by the clouds.* 太陽爲雲遮掩。*The future is hidden from us.* 未來是我們難以預卜的。*She tried to ~ her feelings.* 她設法掩藏她的感情。*His words had a hidden meaning.* 他的話裡有話。**2** [VP2A] be or become hidden: 被隱藏;躲藏起來: *You had better ~.* 你最好躲起來。*Where is he hiding?* 他躲在哪裡? **~-and-seek** /͵haɪd n ˈsi:k ; ˈhaɪdn̩ˈsik/ *n* [U] children's game in which one child ~s and others try to find him. 捉迷藏。□ *n* (US 美 = *blind*) place where wild animals, birds, etc may be observed, eg by photographers, without alarming them. (攝影者等觀察野生動物和鳥類之)隱藏處。**ˈ~-out/-away** *nn* (colloq) hiding-place: (俗)隱匿之處: *a guerrilla ~-out in the mountains.* 游擊隊在山中的隱匿處。**hid·ing** *n* [U] (used of persons) (用以指人) ***be in/go into hiding,*** be hidden/~ oneself. 躲藏起來。***come out of hiding,*** show oneself. 出現;現身。**ˈhiding-place** *n* place where sb or sth is or could be hidden. 藏匿處;隱藏處。

hide² /haɪd ; haɪd/ *n* **1** [C] animal's skin, esp as an article of commerce and manufacture. 獸皮;(尤指作爲商業和製造業貨品的)皮革。**2** [U] (colloq) human skin. (俗)人皮。***save one's ~,*** save oneself from a beating, from punishment. 避免挨打;避免受罰。***tan sb's ~,*** give him a beating. 打某人一頓。

hide·bound /ˈhaɪdbaʊnd ; ˈhaɪd͵baʊnd/ *adj* narrow-minded; having, showing, too much respect for rules and traditions. 心地狹窄的; 過份重視規則和傳統的;墨守成規的。

hid·eous /ˈhɪdɪəs ; ˈhɪdɪəs/ *adj* very ugly; filling the mind with horror; frightful: 十分醜惡的;恐怖的;可怕的: *a ~ face/crime/noise.* 醜惡的面孔(極惡的罪行;可怕的聲音)。**~·ly** *adv*

hid·ing /ˈhaɪdɪŋ ; ˈhaɪdɪŋ/ *n* [C] beating; thrashing: 打;鞭笞: *give sb/get a good ~.* 把某人痛打一頓(挨一頓痛打)。

hie /haɪ ; haɪ/ *vi* (archaic, or joc) go quickly (*to*). (古或謔)快走;疾行(與 to 連用)。

hi·er·archy /ˈhaɪərɑ:kɪ ; ˈhaɪə͵rarkɪ/ *n* (*pl* -chies)

[C] organization with grades of authority from lowest to highest: 階級組織;等級制度: *the ~ of the Civil Service;* group of persons in authority; 文官階級組織; group of bishops of a country. (一個國家之)主教團。**hi·er·archi·c(al)** /ˌhaɪəˈrɑːkɪk(l); ˌhaɪəˈrɑrkɪk(l̩)/ *adj*

hi·ero·glyph /ˈhaɪərəglɪf; ˈhaɪərəˌglɪf/ *n* picture or figure of an object, representing a word, syllable or sound, as used in the writing of the ancient Egyptians and Mexicans; other secret or unintelligible written symbol. 象形文字(如古埃及與墨西哥人所用者);秘密的或難解的符號。**~ic** /ˌhaɪərəˈglɪfɪk; ˌhaɪərəˈglɪfɪk/ *adj* of, written in, ~s. 象形文字的;用象形文字寫成的。**~·ics** *n pl* = ~s.

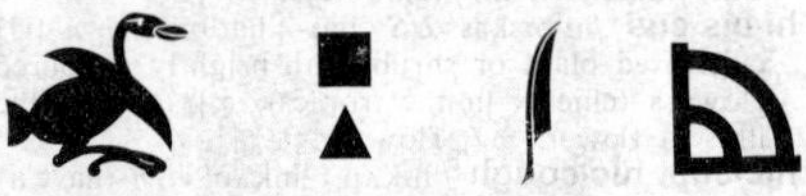

hieroglyphics

hi-fi /ˌhaɪ ˈfaɪ; ˌhaɪˈfaɪ/ *n, adj* (colloq abbr of) high fidelity; apparatus producing this: (俗)高度傳眞的(爲 high fidelity 之略);高度傳眞音響設備: *a ~ (set).* 一套高度傳眞音響設備。⇨ high(12).

hig·gledy-pig·gledy /ˌhɪgldɪ ˈpɪgldɪ; ˈhɪgl̩dɪˈpɪgl̩dɪ/ *adj, adv* (colloq) mixed up; without order. (俗)混雜的(地);雜亂無章的(地)。

high¹ /haɪ; haɪ/ *adj* (-er, -est) (For combinations of ~ and *nn, participles*, etc with meanings not at once to be identified from the meanings in the definitions, ⇨ 12 below.) (與名詞、分詞等構成之複合字,其意義不能自各定義中卽刻辨出者,參看下列第12義。) **1** extending far upwards; measuring (the distance given) from the base to the top. 高的;有若干高度的。(Note that *tall* is used for human beings and for a few things which have great height in relation to breadth, eg *a tall building/tower*): (注意: tall 指人或某些就寬高關係而言高度特別突出的物體,例如 a tall building/tower 一座高建築物(塔)): *There was an aeroplane ~ in the sky.* 有一架飛機高高在天空。*How ~ is Mt Everest?* 埃佛勒斯峯有多高? *~ and dry,* **(a)** (of a ship) stranded; aground; out of the water. (指船)出水;擱淺。**(b)** (fig) abandoned; isolated; out of the current of events. (喻)被棄的;孤立的;脫離社會潮流的。***be/get on one's ~ horse,*** ⇨ horse(1). ***(do sth) with a ~ hand,*** arrogantly (~-ˈ*handed(ly)* is preferred). (做事)專橫地;傲慢地(high-handed(ly) 較常用)。 **2** chief; important: 高級的;重要的: *a ~ official;* 高級官員; *a ~ caste;* 高的社會階級; *the ~ altar,* in a church; 主祭壇; *the Most H~,* (in the Bible) God; (聖經)上帝; *~ society,* the upper classes. 上流社會。 ***~ and low,*** all classes of society. 社會各階層。 **3** (of sounds) at or near the top of the scale; shrill; sharp: (指聲音)尖銳的: *speak in a ~ tone/key.* 以尖銳的嗓音說話。 **4** extreme; intense; great: 極度的;强烈的;大的: *~ prices/temperatures;* 高價(高溫); *bought at a ~ cost;* 以鉅資購買; *a ~ wind;* 勁風;大風; *in ~ favour;* 極爲得寵; *have a ~ opinion of sb;* 極器重某人; *in ~ spirits;* 興致勃勃;高興; *~ (= angry) words;* 憤怒之言; *in ~ latitudes,* near the Poles; 在高緯度地區(近南北極); *have a ~ (= enjoyable) time;* 過一段愉快的時間; *~ (= luxurious) living;* 奢侈的生活; *~ noon/summer,* at or near its peak. 正午(盛夏)。 **5** ***~ time,*** time when sth should be done at once: 應該卽刻做某事的時間: *It's ~ time you started,* You should start at once. 你該動身了。*It's ~ time to go,* We must go at once. 我們應該馬上就走。 **6** noble; virtuous: 高尙的;良好的: *a woman of ~ character;* 品格高尙的女子; *~ aims/ideals;* 高尙的目標(理想); *a ~ calling,* eg that of a priest, doctor or nurse. 高尙的職業(例如做牧師,醫生或護士)。 **7** **H~ Church,** that section of the C of E that gives an important place to the authority of bishops and priests, to ritual and the sacraments. (英國)高派敎會(英國國敎中注重主敎和牧師權勢,以及儀式及聖事的敎派)。Hence, 由此產生, **H~ Churchman.** **8** (of food, esp meat and game) slightly tainted. (食物,尤指肉和獵物)略微腐壞的。 **9** (colloq) drunk. (俗)酒醉的。 **10** (colloq) under the influence of hallucinatory drugs: (俗)受迷幻藥影響的: *~ on marijuana.* 沉醉於大麻煙中。 **11** (as *n*) (作爲名詞) ~ level: 高水準;高峰;高處: *from (on) ~,* from Heaven. 自天空;自上蒼。*Shares* (ie on the Stock Excnange) *reached a new ~* (= the ~est recorded level) *last month.* 股票在上月達到了一個新的最高點。 **12** (compounds) (複合字) **ˈ~-ball** *n* (US) spirits with soda water, ginger ale, etc, served with ice in a tall glass. (美)加汽水或薑汁啤酒等的烈酒(加冰並用高杯盛裝)。**ˈ~·born** *adj* of noble birth. 出身高貴的;出身名門的。**ˈ~·boy** *n* (US) tallboy. (美)高衣櫃。**ˈ~·brow** *n, adj* (person) with tastes and interests considered to be superior (often used contemptuously for *intellectual*): 嗜好和興趣高雅的(人)(常用做 intellectual 之輕蔑語): *~brow drama/music.* 適合嗜好和興趣高雅的人們的戲劇(音樂)。**ˌ~ ˈchair** *n* one on ~ legs for an infant at table, or a baby's chair with a hinged tray attached to it. (嬰兒用餐時坐的)高腿椅。**ˌH~ ˈChurch** *n* ⇨ 7 above. 參看上列第7義。**ˌ~-ˈclass** *adj* first-class. 高級的;第一流的。**ˌ~ ˈcolour** *n* reddish complexion. 微紅的面色。**ˌH~ Comˈmissioner** *n* representative of one Commonwealth country in another, equivalent to an ambassador. 不列顚國協會員國家間互派之代表(相當於大使)。**ˈH~ Court** *n* supreme court of justice. 最高法院。**ˈ~ day** *n* festival 節日 (only in) (僅用於): *~ days and holidays.* 節日和假日。**ˈ~er-ups** *n pl* (colloq) persons ~er in rank or status. (俗)階級或地位較高的人。**ˌ~ exˈplosive** *n* very powerful explosive, eg TNT. 高爆炸藥(例如 TNT)。**ˌ~-faˈlutin** /fəˈluːtn; fəˈlutn̩/ *adj* (colloq) ridiculously pompous, bombastic or pretentious: (俗)過份誇張的;虛飾的: *~-falutin ideas/language.* 誇張的思想(語言)。**ˌ~-fiˈdelity** *n, adj* (abbr 略作 **hi-fi**) (of radios, records, tapes and equipment for reproducing sound) (quality of) giving faithful reproduction by the use of a wide range of sound waves. (指收音機、唱片、錄音帶及唱機、錄音機等)高度傳眞(的)。**ˌ~-ˈflier/-ˈflyer** *n* ambitious person who goes to great extremes to get what he aims at. 野心勃勃不擇手段的人。**ˌ~-ˈflown** *adj* exalted; bombastic and pretentious: 崇高的;誇大的;虛飾的: *a ~flown style,* eg of writing. 誇張的風格(例如寫作)。**ˌ~-ˈflying** *adj* (fig) (of persons) ambitious. (喻)(指人)充滿野心的。**ˌ~-ˈfrequency** *n* (abbr 略作 **hf**) radio frequency between 3 and 30 megacycles per second. 高頻率;高週率(每秒3至30百萬週)。**H~ German** *n* literary German; standard spoken German. 德文的文言文;標準德語。**ˌ~-ˈgrade** *adj* of ~ or superior quality. 品質高級的。**ˌ~-ˈhanded** *adj* domineering; using power or authority without consideration for the feelings of others. 專橫的;高壓的。**ˌ~-ˈhanded·ly** *adv* **ˌ~ ˈhat** *adj, n* snobbish (person). 勢利的(人)。□ *vt* treat (sb) in a snobbish or condescending way. 勢利地對待(某人);盛氣凌人地對待(某人)。**ˈ~·jack** *vt* (variant spelling of) hijack. 爲 hijack 之不同拼法。**ˌ~ ˈjinks,** ⇨ jinks. **the ˈ~ jump** *n* athletic contest for jumping over an adjustable horizontal bar: 跳高: *enter for/win the ~ jump.* 參加跳高(跳高得勝)。***be for the ~ jump,*** (sl) due for severe punishment. (俚)應受嚴刑。**ˌ~-ˈkeyed** *adj* (⇨ 3 above) (參看上列第3義) having a ~ pitch; (fig) easily excited or made nervous. 調子高的;(喻)易興奮或緊張的。**ˈ~·land** /-lənd; -lənd/ *n* mountainous region; (*pl*) mountainous parts of a country (esp **The H~-**

lands, those of N W Scotland). 高地;丘陵地;(複)一國之丘陵地區(大寫時尤指蘇格蘭西北高地)。ˌ**H~land ˈfling** *n* Scottish reel³. 蘇格蘭利爾舞。ˈ**H~·lander** *n* one who lives in The H~lands; soldier in a (Scottish) H~land regiment. 蘇格蘭高地人;蘇格蘭高地兵團之士兵。ˌ**~-ˈlevel** *adj* (attrib only) (of conferences, etc) conducted by persons in ~ position, eg in government, commerce. (僅作形容用法)(指會議等)高階層的。ˈ**~ life** *n* [U] **(a)** fashionable and luxurious style of living. 奢侈的生活。**(b)** (in W Africa) popular kind of music and dance. (非洲西部) 一種流行的音樂和舞蹈。ˈ**~·light** *n* (usu *pl*) luminous area on a photograph, picture, etc which shows reflected light; reflection of light on a shiny object; (fig) most conspicuous or prominent part: (通常用複數) 像片、圖畫等光亮的部分;閃光體上光的反射;(喻)最顯著部分;最精采部分: *the ~lights of the week's events.* 一週事件中之最重要者。□ *vt* give prominence or emphasis to. 使顯著;使精采;加强。ˌ**H~ ˈMass** *n* (RC Church) (天主教) ⇨ Mass. ˌ**~-ˈminded** /ˈmaɪndɪd ; ˈmaɪndɪd/ *adj* of morally ~ character; having ~ ideals or principles. 品格高尙的;有崇高理想或原則的。Hence, 由此產生, ˌ**~-ˈminded·ly** *adv* ˌ**~-ˈminded·ness** *n* ˌ**~-ˈnecked** *adj* (of a dress) with the neckline cut ~. (指女服)領口高的。ˌ**~-ˈoctane** *adj* having a ~ octane number. 高辛烷的。⇨ octane. ˌ**~-ˈpitched** *adj* **(a)** (of sounds) shrill. (指聲音) 尖銳的。**(b)** (of roofs) having a steep slope. (指屋頂)坡度陡的。ˌ**~-ˈpowered** *adj* having, using, great power: 很有能力的;强有力的: *a ~-powered salesman*, aggressive in selling his goods. 很有衝勁的推銷員。ˌ**~-ˈpressure** *n* [U] pressure ~er than normal, esp ~er than atmospheric pressure; (fig) aggressive and persistent: 高壓;(尤指)高氣壓;(喻)有衝勁而且堅持的: *~-pressure salesmanship*. 强迫推銷術。ˌ**~-ˈpriced** *adj* expensive. 高價的;昂貴的。ˌ**~ ˈpriest** *n* chief priest. 主教;大祭司。ˌ**~-ˈprincipled** *adj* honourable. 光明正大的。ˈ**~-ranking** *adj* (of officers, etc) having ~ rank. (指軍官等)高階級的。ˌ**~ reˈlief** *n* ⇨ relief²(1). ˈ**~-rise** *adj* (attrib only) used of tall buildings with many storeys or levels, reached by lifts (elevators): (僅作形容用法)(指有電梯的建築物)有很多層的;高聳的: *~-rise flats.* 有很多層的公寓。⇨ *tower-block* at tower. ˈ**~·road** *n* main road; (fig) most direct way: 大道;(喻)捷徑: *Is there a ~road to happiness?* 有達到幸福的捷徑嗎? ˈ**H~ School** *n* secondary school giving more advanced education than primary or elementary schools. 中學。**the** ˌ**~ ˈseas** *n pl* all parts of the seas and oceans beyond territorial waters. 外洋; 外海; 公海。ˈ**~-sounding** *adj* (of style) impressively pretentious. (指文體)誇飾的。ˌ**~-ˈspeed** *adj* (able to be) operated at very fast speeds. 高速度的。ˌ**~-ˈspirited** *adj* lively; (of a horse) frisky. 有生氣的;(指馬)亂蹦亂跳的。ˈ**~ spot** *n* outstanding feature, memory, event, etc. 特色;顯著的記憶、事件等。ˈ**~ street** *n* (esp in proper names) main street of a town: (尤用於專有名詞中)大街: *There are three banks in the ~ street.* 大街上有三家銀行。ˌ**~ ˈtable** *n* table (on a dais) where senior members of a college dine. 大學餐廳中教師用的餐桌。ˌ**~ ˈtea** *n* (GB) early evening meal (or late tea) in homes where dinner is not eaten in the evening, usu with meat or fish. (英)黄昏茶點(不在黄昏進晚餐的家庭所食用,通常有肉或魚)。ˌ**~-ˈtension** *adj* (electr) (of wires) having a ~ voltage. (電)(指電線)高壓的。ˌ**~ ˈtide** *n* (time at which the) tide is at its ~est level. 高潮;高潮時期。ˌ**~ ˈtime** *n* ⇨ 5 above. 參看上列第 5 義。ˌ**~-ˈtoned** *adj* socially or intellectually superior: 高尙的;時髦的;優秀的: *a ~-toned finishing school for girls.* 高尙的女子精修學校。ˌ**~ ˈtreason** *n* [U] treason against the State or a sovereign. 叛國;叛逆。ˈ**~-up** *n* (colloq) person of ~ rank or great importance. (俗)社會地位高的人;要人。ˌ**~ ˈwater** *n* [U] ~ tide. 高潮。ˌ**~-ˈwater mark** *n* mark showing the ~est point reached by the tide (or any body of water); (fig) ~est point of achievement. 高潮線;高水標;高水位線;(喻)成就的最高峯。ˈ**~·way** *n* main public road; main route (by air, sea or land); (fig) easiest or most direct way. 公路;大道;主要航路;(喻)捷徑。ˌ**H~·way ˈCode** *n* official guide-book for users of public roads. 公路旅行指南。ˈ**~·way·man** /-mən ; -mən/ *n* (*pl* -men) (formerly) man (usu on horseback) who robbed travellers on ~ways by using, or threatening to use, violence. (昔時)攔路的强盜(通常騎着馬)。

high² /haɪ ; haɪ/ *adv* in or to a ~ degree: 高; 高度地: *climb ~;* 向高處攀登; *aim ~;* 向高處瞄準;懸着高的目標;懷大志;(lit, fig) (字面,喻) *pay ~*, pay a ~ price; 付高價; *play ~*, play a card of ~ value, eg an ace; 出大牌(例如么點); *live ~*, on rich, luxurious food and drink. 過奢侈的生活。***fly ~,*** (fig) have great ambitions. (喻) 有雄心。***hold one's head ~,*** be proud. 驕傲。***run ~,*** **(a)** (of the sea) have a strong current with a ~ tide. (指海)起大風浪;波濤洶湧。**(b)** (of the feelings) be excited: (指感情)激動: *Popular feelings/passions ran ~,* were strong. 群情激昂。***search/hunt/look ~ and low (for sth),*** look everywhere (for it). 到處尋找(某物)。

high·ly /ˈhaɪlɪ ; ˈhaɪlɪ/ *adv* in or to a high degree: 高;高度地;非常地: *a ~ paid official;* 薪俸優厚的官員; *a ~ amusing film;* 非常有趣的影片; *think ~ of sb*, have a high opinion of him; 器重某人; *speak ~ of sb*, praise him. 稱讚某人。

high·ness /ˈhaɪnɪs ; ˈhaɪnɪs/ *n* **1** [U] (opposite of *lowness*) state or quality of being high:(爲 lowness 之相反字)高;高貴;高尙: *the ~ of his character/aims.* 他的品格(志向)之高尙。**2** title used of and to British and various foreign princes: 殿下;閣下(對英國和其他國家皇族的尊稱): *His/Her/Your Royal/Imperial H~.* 殿下;閣下。

hi·jack (also **high·jack**) /ˈhaɪdʒæk ; ˈhaɪˌdʒæk/ *vt* [VP6A] **1** steal goods from (an aircraft or vehicle) by stopping it in transit. 劫取(飛機或車輛之)貨物。**2** use force, or the threat of force, against those in control of an aircraft or vehicle, in order to achieve certain aims or to reach a desired destination. 劫持(飛機或車輛)。□ *n* [C] instance of ~ing. 劫持。**~er** *n* person taking part in a ~. 劫持飛機或車輛者。

hike /haɪk ; haɪk/ *vi, n* (colloq) (go for a) long walk in the country, taken for pleasure or exercise. (俗)遠足;健行;徒步旅行。**~r** *n* person who ~s. 遠足者;健行者;徒步旅行者。⇨ hitchhike.

hil·ari·ous /hɪˈleərɪəs ; həˈlɛrɪəs/ *adj* noisily merry. 熱鬧的。**~·ly** *adv* **hil·ar·ity** /hɪˈlærətɪ ; həˈlærətɪ/ *n* [U] noisy merriment; loud laughter. 熱鬧;歡笑。

hill /hɪl ; hɪl/ *n* **1** natural elevation on the earth's surface, lower than a mountain. 丘陵;小山。ˈ**~-side** *n* side of a ~. 山坡。ˈ**~·top** *n* top of a ~. 山頂。**2** slope, eg on a road: (道路等之)斜坡: *push a bicycle up a steep ~.* 把脚踏車推上陡坡。**3** heap of earth: 土堆: *ˈant-~s;* 蟻丘; *ˈmole-~s.* 鼹鼠窩;鼹鼠丘。**~y** *adj* (-ier, -iest) having many ~s: 多丘陵的;多小山的;多斜坡的: *~y country;* 丘陵地帶; *a ~y road.* 多斜坡的路。

hill-billy /ˈhɪl bɪlɪ ; ˈhɪlˌbɪlɪ/ *n* (*pl* -lies) (colloq, often used derog) farmer, farm-worker, etc from the mountains in the S E of the US; (attrib) of these people: (俗,常用作貶抑語) 美國東南部山區的農人;(形容用法) 美國東南部山地農人的: *~ music.* 美國東南部山地音樂。

hill·ock /ˈhɪlək ; ˈhɪlək/ *n* small hill(1). 小丘。

hilt /hɪlt ; hɪlt/ *n* handle of a sword or dagger. 刀柄;劍柄。⇨ the illus at sword. 參看 sword 之插圖。***(up) to the ~,*** completely: 完全地: *His guilt was proved to the ~.* 他的罪完全證實了。

him /*strong form:* hɪm ; hɪm; *medial weak form:*

ɪm ; ɪm/ *pers pron* used as object form of *he*: 他(he 的受格): *Mr Smith is in town; I saw him yesterday.* 史密斯先生在城裡,我昨天見過他。*Give him the money.* 把錢給他。*That's him*, (colloq) That's he. (俗)就是他。

him·self /hɪm'self ; hɪm'sɛlf; *weak form:* ɪm's- ; ɪm's-/ *reflex, emph pron* **1** (reflex) (反身) *He cut ~.* 他割傷了自己。*He ought to be ashamed of ~.* 他應該爲自己感到羞愧。***(all) by ~,*** **(a)** alone. 孤獨;單獨。**(b)** without help. 獨力。 **2** (emph) (强勢語) *He ~ says so.* 他親口這樣說的。*He says so ~.* 他親口這樣說的。*Did you see the manager ~?* 你看見經理本人了嗎? **3** *He's not quite ~ today*, not in his normal state of health or mind. 他今天不大舒服;他今天有些失常。

hind[1] /haɪnd ; haɪnd/ *adj* (of things in pairs, front and back; cf *fore*) at the back: (指前後成對的東西;參較 fore) 在後的;後面的: *the ~ legs of a horse.* 馬的後腿。 ˌ**~ 'quarters** *n pl* ~ legs and loin of the carcass of lamb, mutton, beef, etc. (羊,牛等屠宰後的)後腿肉。 **'~·most** /-məʊst ; -most/ *adj* farthest behind or back. 最後面的;最後方的。 **'~·sight** /-saɪt ; -saɪt/ *n* [U] perception of an event after its occurrence. 事後的領悟;事後聰明。

hind[2] /haɪnd ; haɪnd/ *n* female of (esp the red) deer. 雌鹿;(尤指)紅雌鹿。

hin·der /'hɪndə(r) ; 'hɪndɚ/ *vt* [VP6A, C, 15A] obstruct; delay; get in the way of: 阻礙;妨害;妨礙: *Don't ~ me in my work.* 不要妨礙我的工作。*I was ~ed from getting here earlier.* 我受阻不能早些到此。*I have much business that has ~ed my answering your letter.* 我有很多事,使我不能早日回覆你的信。

Hindi /'hɪndiː ; 'hɪndi/ *n, adj* (of) one of the official languages of N India. 印地語(的)(爲印度北部官方語言之一)。

hin·drance /'hɪndrəns ; 'hɪndrəns/ *n* [C] sth or sb that hinders: 妨礙的人或物;阻礙者: *You are more of a ~ than a help.* 你與其說是助手,不如說是障礙。

Hin·du /ˌhɪn'duː *US:* 'hɪnduː ; 'hɪndu/ *n* person, esp of N India, whose religion is ~ism. 信奉印度教者;印度人;(尤指)信奉印度教之北印度人。 □ *adj* of the ~s. 印度人的; 北印度人的; 印度教徒的。 **~ism** /'hɪnduːɪzəm ; 'hɪndʊˌɪzəm/ *n* religion of most of the ~s. 印度教。

Hin·du·stani /ˌhɪndʊ'stɑːnɪ ; ˏhɪndʊ'stænɪ/ *n, adj* (of) a form of Hindi. 興都斯坦語(的)(爲印地語的一種形式)。

hinge /hɪndʒ ; hɪndʒ/ *n* joint on which a lid, door or gate turns or swings; (fig) central principle on which sth depends: 鉸鏈;(喻)重點;主旨;關鍵: *Take the door off its ~s and rehang it.* 把這門自鉸鏈拿下來重裝。□ *vt, vi* **1** [VP6A] support, attach with, a ~ or ~s. 裝以鉸鏈。 **2** [VP3A] ***~ on/upon,*** turn or depend on: 以…而定: *Everything ~s upon what happens next.* 一切以下一步發展而定。

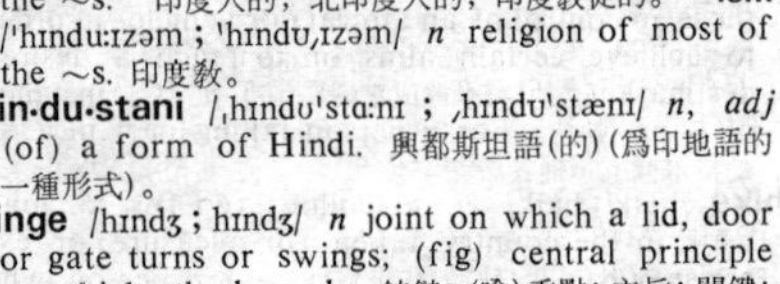

hinges

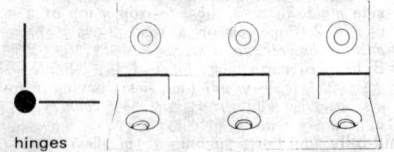

hint /hɪnt ; hɪnt/ *n* [C] slight or indirect indication or suggestion: 提示;暗示: *She gave him a ~ that she would like him to leave.* 她向他暗示希望他離開。 ***drop (sb) a ~,*** indicate or suggest sth indirectly (to sb). 暗示(某人)。 ***take a ~,*** realise and do what is suggested. 接受暗示。□ *vt, vi* **1** [VP9, 6A] ***~ (to sb),*** suggest indirectly; give a ~: 暗示;示意: *I ~ed that he ought to work harder.* 我暗示他應該更努力工作。 *He ~ed to me nothing of his intentions.* 他沒有向我暗示他的心意。 **2** [VP3A] ***~ at,*** refer indirectly to: 間接提及: *He ~ed at my extravagance.* 他間接提到我的奢侈。

hin·ter·land /'hɪntəlænd ; 'hɪntɚˌlænd/ *n* parts of a country behind the coast or a river's banks. 海岸或河岸的後方地區;內地;腹地。

hip[1] /hɪp ; hɪp/ *n* part on either side of the body where the bone of a person's leg is joined to the trunk: 臀部;髖部: *He stood there with his hands on his hips.* 他兩手叉腰站在那裡。 ⇨ the illus at trunk. 參看 trunk 之插圖。 **'hip-bath** *n* small tub in which one can sit immersed up to the hips. 小浴盆(坐入可將下半身浸入水中)。 **'hip-flask** *n* small flask (for brandy, etc) to be carried in the hip-pocket. 一種裝白蘭地等的小酒瓶,可放在臀部口袋裡携帶。 ˌ**hip-'pocket** *n* pocket (in a pair of trousers) on the hip. 臀部口袋。

hip[2] /hɪp ; hɪp/ *n* fruit (red when ripe) of the wild rose. 野薔薇的子(熟時爲紅色)。

hip[3] /hɪp ; hɪp/ *int* (only in) (僅用於) ***ˌHip, hip, hur'rah!*** cry, cheer, of satisfaction or approval. 表示滿意或贊同的呼聲。

hip[4] /hɪp ; hɪp/ *adj* (also 亦作 *hep*) (sl) aware of, in keeping with, advanced trends. (俚)知道最新發展的;內行的;跟上發展趨勢的。

hip·pie /'hɪpɪ ; 'hɪpɪ/ *n* ⇨ hippy.

hippo /'hɪpəʊ ; 'hɪpo/ *n* (*pl* ~s /-pəʊz ; -poz/) (colloq abbr of) hippopotamus. (俗)河馬(爲 hippopotamus 之略)。

Hip·po·cratic /ˌhɪpə'krætɪk ; ˏhɪpə'krætɪk/ *adj* ˌ**~ 'oath,** oath to observe the medical code of ethical and professional behaviour, sworn by entrants to the profession. 新開業醫生所立之誓言。

hip·po·drome /'hɪpədrəʊm ; 'hɪpəˌdrom/ *n* place for horse- or chariot-races in ancient Greece and Rome. (古希臘,羅馬之)賽馬或戰車競賽場。

hip·po·pota·mus /ˌhɪpə'pɒtəməs ; ˏhɪpə'pɑtəməs/ *n* (*pl* ~es /-sɪz ; -sɪz/ or -mi /-maɪ ; -maɪ/) large, thick-skinned African river animal. 河馬。⇨ the illus at large. 參看 large 之插圖。

hippy, hip·pie /'hɪpɪ ; 'hɪpɪ/ *n* (*pl* -pies) (late 1960's) person who rejects established social conventions and institutions and expresses his personality by unusual styles of dress, living habits, etc. 嬉痞。

hire /'haɪə(r) ; haɪr/ *vt* [VP6A, 15B] ***~ (out),*** obtain or allow the use or services of in return for fixed payment: 租;雇用: *~ a horse/a concert-hall;* 租一匹馬(一音樂廳); *~ out boats.* 出租小船。(Cf 參較 *rent a house.* 租房屋用 rent。) □ *n* [U] (money paid for) hiring: 租用;雇用;租金;工資: *bicycles on ~, 50p an hour;* 脚踏車出租,每小時五十辨士; *pay for the ~ of a hall;* 付會堂租金; *work for ~.* 做雇工。***(pay for/buy sth) on ~ purchase,*** (abbr 略作 **HP**) (buy by a) contract to pay by instalments, and the right to use it after the first payment. 以分期付款方式(購買某物)。 **~·ling** /'haɪəlɪŋ ; 'haɪrlɪŋ/ *n* (derog) person whose services may be ~d. (貶)可被人雇用者。

hir·sute /'hɜːsjuːt *US:* -suːt ; 'hɝsut/ *adj* (formal) hairy; rough; shaggy (eg of a man with untidy long hair and beard). (正式用語)多毛的;蓬亂的;毛髮蓬鬆的(例如指生有蓬亂的長髮和鬍鬚的人)。

his /*strong or initial form:* hɪz ; hɪz; *medial weak form:* ɪz ; ɪz/ *adj, pron* belonging to him: 他的: *He hurt his hand.* 他弄傷了自己的手。*That book is his, not yours.* 那本書是他的,不是你的。*I'm a friend of his.* 我是他的朋友。

hiss /hɪs ; hɪs/ *vi, vt* **1** [VP2A] make the sound /s/, or the noise heard when water falls on a very hot surface: 發 /s/ 聲;發嘶嘶聲: *The snake raised its head and ~ed.* 那蛇抬起了頭並發出嘶嘶聲。*The steam escaped with a ~ing sound.* 蒸汽嘶嘶地漏出。 **2** [VP6A, 15A, 3A] ***~ (off); ~ (at),*** show disapproval by making this sound: 發噓聲表示反對: *~ an actor off the stage;* 將一演員噓下臺; *~ (at) a new play.* 噓一新劇。□ *n* [C] ~ing sound: 嘶嘶聲;噓聲: *The speaker was received with a mixture of applause and ~es.* 那演說者同時獲得了喝采聲與噓聲。

his·tor·ian /hɪˈstɔːrɪən ; hɪsˈtorɪən/ *n* writer of history. 歷史學家。

his·toric /hɪˈstɒrɪk *US:* -ˈstɔːr- ; hɪsˈtɔrɪk/ *adj* **1** notable or memorable in history; associated with past times: 歷史上著名的;與過去時代有關的: *a ~ spot/event/speech.* 歷史上著名的地點(事件,演說)。***~ times,*** of which the history is known and recorded (contrasted with *prehistoric times*). 有歷史記載的時期(與 prehistoric times 相對)。**2** ***the ~present,*** (gram) simple present tense used for events in the past (to make the description more vivid). (文法)歷史的現在式(爲求描述較爲生動,用簡單現在時態敍述過去事件的方法)。

his·tori·cal /hɪˈstɒrɪkl *US:* -ˈstɔːr- ; hɪsˈtɔrɪkl/ *adj* **1** belonging or pertaining to history (as contrasted with legend and fiction): 歷史上的(以別於傳說或虛構的): *~ events and people,* real, not imaginary; 歷史上的事件和人物(眞實的,非想像的); *a ~ novel/play/film/painting, etc,* one dealing with real events in history. 歷史小說(戲劇,影片,繪畫等)。**2** having to do with history: 有關歷史的: *~ studies;* 對歷史之研究; *the ~ method of investigation.* 依據歷史的研究方法。**~ly** /-klɪ ; -klɪ/ *adv*

his·tory /ˈhɪstrɪ ; ˈhɪstrɪ/ *n* (*pl* -ries) **1** [U] branch of knowledge dealing with past events, political, social, economic, of a country, continent or the world: 歷史學;歷史: *a student of ~.* 史學者。***make ~,*** do sth which will be recorded in ~. 創造歷史。**ancient ~,** to AD 476, when the Western Roman Empire was destroyed. 古代史(至紀元後 476 年西羅馬帝國滅亡)。**medieval ~,** to 1453, when Constantinople was taken by the Turks. 中古史(至 1453 年君士坦丁堡被土耳其人佔領)。**modern ~,** since 1453. 近代史(1453年至今)。**2** [C] orderly description of past events: 對過去事件按照順序的描述: *a new ~ of Europe.* 新著歐洲大事記。**3** [C] train of events connected with a person or thing; interesting or eventful past career: 有關某人或某事物的連續事件; 沿革; 有趣的或重要的經歷: *a house with a strange ~;* 有一段奇怪來歷的房屋; *the inner ~ of the papal conclave.* 羅馬天主教會秘密會議的內幕。**4** **natural ˈ~,** systematic account of natural phenomena. 博物學。

his·tri·onic /ˌhɪstrɪˈɒnɪk ; ˌhɪstrɪˈɑnɪk/ *adj* **1** of drama, the theatre, acting: 戲劇的;劇場的;演劇的: *~ ability.* 演劇的能力。**2** theatrical; insincere. 做戲的;不誠懇的。**his·tri·on·ics** *n pl* **1** theatrical performances. 戲劇的演出。**2** dramatic or theatrical manners, behaviour, etc, esp when exaggerated to create an effect. 戲劇化的擧止,行動等(尤指爲求效果而誇張時所做)。

hit /hɪt ; hɪt/ *vt, vi* (-tt-; *pt, pp* hit) **1** [VP6A, 15A, 12C] give a blow or stroke to; strike (a target, an object aimed at); come against (sth) with force: 擊;打;擊中;碰;撞: *hit a man on the head;* 打一人的頭; *be hit by a falling stone;* 被落石擊中; *hit sb a hard blow;* 痛擊某人; *hit the mark/target;* 中的(擊中目標); *hit a ball over the fence.* 將一球打過圍牆。*He hit his forehead against the kerb when he fell.* 當他跌倒時,他的額頭撞在街道的邊石上。***hit a man when he's down; hit a man below the belt,*** act contrary to the rules of boxing; (fig) take an unfair advantage. 違犯拳擊規則;(喻)用不正當的手段。***hit it; hit the nail on the head,*** guess right; say or do exactly the right thing. 猜對了; 一語說中; 完全做對了。***hit it off (with sb/together),*** agree, get on well: 相投;相處得好: *They hit it off well.* 他們相處得很好。**ˌhit-and-ˈrun** *attrib adj* (of a road accident) in which a pedestrian or vehicle is hit by a vehicle which does not stop. (指車禍) 肇事後卽逃逸的。**2** ***hit sb hard,*** cause him to suffer: 使某人痛苦: *The slump hit his business hard.* 物價暴跌使他的生意大受打擊。*He was hard hit by his financial losses.* 他深受財務損失的打擊。*He has fallen in love and is hard hit.* 他已墜入情網,甚爲痛苦。**3** [VP6A] go to; find; reach: 至;發現;到達: *hit the right path,* find it during a journey. 找到正確的道路。***hit the headlines,*** (colloq, of news) be printed prominently in the headlines (because sensational, etc). (俗,指新聞,由於轟動等) 以顯著標題登出。***hit the road,*** (colloq) set out on the road. (俗)出發;上路。**4** [VP2C] strike: 打擊: *Hit hard!* 用力打! ***hit out (against),*** strike vigorously; (fig) attack strongly: 用力打;(喻)猛烈攻擊: *The Minister hit out against trade union leaders.* 部長猛烈攻擊工會領袖們。**5** [VP3A] ***hit on/upon sth,*** find by chance or unexpectedly: 偶然發現;無意中遇見: *hit upon an idea/the right answer/a plan for making money.* 偶然想起一個主意(正確的答案,賺錢的計畫)。**6** [VP 15B] ***hit sth/sb off,*** (colloq) describe briefly and accurately (in words); make a quick sketch of. (俗) (用文字) 簡明正確地描寫;略述。**7** [VP6A] (cricket) score: (板球) 得分: *He quickly hit 60 runs.* 他很快得到六十分。□ *n* **1** blow; stroke: 打;擊: *three hits and five misses;* 三次擊中五次未中; *a clever hit.* 巧妙的一擊。**ˈhit man** *n* (sl) person who is paid to kill sb.(俚)(受雇的)殺手。**2** successful attempt or performance: 成功的嘗試或表演: *hit songs, ˈsong hits,* songs that win wide popularity; 流行歌曲; *a lucky hit.* 僥倖成功。*The new play is quite a hit,* has been welcomed by the public. 這新戲十分成功。***make a hit (with sb),*** (colloq) make a very favourable impression (with him). (俗)予(某人)良好印象。**ˈhit parade** *n* list of top selling popular records. 暢銷唱片排行榜。**3** stroke of sarcasm, etc: 諷刺;抨擊: *That was a hit at me,* the words were directed against me. 那是抨擊我的。

hitch /hɪtʃ ; hɪtʃ/ *vt, vi* **1** [VP6A, 15B] ***~ sth up,*** pull up with a quick movement: 迅速拉上;急拉: *~ up one's trousers.* 迅速穿起褲子。**2** [VP15A, 2C] fasten, become fastened, on or to a hook, etc, or with a loop of rope, etc: 繫於鉤等上;用繩套住;被鉤住;被套住: *~ a horse to a fence;* 將馬栓於柵欄上; *~ a rope round a bough of a tree.* 將繩繞繫於樹枝上。*Her dress ~ed on a nail.* 她的衣服被釘子鉤住了。**3** [VP2A, 6A] ***~ (a ride/lift),*** (colloq) ask the driver of a vehicle for a ride. (俗)搭便車。⇨ hitchhike. □ *n* **1** sudden pull or push. 急拉;急推。**2** kind of noose or knot used by sailors. 船員用的一種繩套或索結。⇨ the illus at knot. 參看 knot 之挿圖。**3** temporary stoppage or impediment: 暫時的阻礙: *Everything went off without a ~,* quite smoothly, without difficulty. 一切進行順利。*The blast-off was delayed by a technical ~.* 由於技術上臨時的障礙,火箭的發射受到延誤。

hitch·hike /ˈhɪtʃhaɪk ; ˈhɪtʃˌhaɪk/ *vi* [VP2A] (colloq abbr 俗語略作 *hitch*) get a free ride by signalling for one (from a passing car, lorry, etc). 搭乘他人便車。**hitch·hiker** *n*

hither /ˈhɪðə(r) ; ˈhɪðɚ/ *adv* (old use) to this place. (舊用法) 向此處;到此處。**~·to** /ˌhɪðəˈtuː ; ˌhɪðɚˈtu/ *adv* until now. 迄今;至今。

hive /haɪv ; haɪv/ *n* **1** (also 亦作 **ˈbee·~**) box (of wood, straw, etc) for bees to live in; the bees living in a ~. (木,草等製成的) 蜂房;蜂箱;居於蜂房內之蜂群。**2** place full of busy people: 喧鬧的地區;鬧市: *What a ~ of industry!* 多麼擾攘的工業區! □ *vt, vi* **1** [VP6A] cause (bees) to go into a ~: 使(蜂)進入蜂房: *~ a swarm;* 使蜂群進蜂房; (of bees) store (honey) in a ~. (指蜂)儲(蜜)於蜂房。**2** [VP 2C] enter a ~; live close together as bees do. 進入蜂房;如蜂般集居。***~ off (from),*** (fig) become a separate (and perhaps self-governing) body (as when a colony of bees leaves a ~ and forms a new ~); separate and make independent (a part of an organization): (喻) 變成單獨的 (或爲自治的)

團體(如一群脫離蜂房另建蜂巢者然);使脫離組織而獨立: ~*off parts of the nationalized steel industry*. 開放部分國營鋼鐵工業(爲民營)。

hives /haɪvz ; haɪvz/ *n pl* skin disease with red patches and itching. 蕁麻疹。

h'm /hm ; hm/ ⇨ hem².

ho /həʊ ; ho/ *int* expressing surprise, admiration, etc. (表示驚愕,羨慕等之聲)嗬!

hoar /hɔː(r) ; hor/ *adj* (liter) (of hair) grey or white with age; (of a person) having such hair. (文)(指頭髮)灰白的;斑白的;(指人)有白髮的。'~-**frost** *n* [U] white frost; frozen dew on grass, the surface of leaves, roofs, etc. 白霜;(草,葉,屋頂等上的)霜。

hoard /hɔːd ; hord/ *n* carefully saved and guarded store of money, food or other treasured objects; collection of coins, valuable objects, etc dug up, eg one dating from Saxon times in GB: 節省下來並妥爲貯藏的金錢,食物或其他寶物;密藏物;窖藏;挖掘出來的一批金幣,貴重物件等(例如英國薩克遜時代的古物): *a miser's ~; a squirrel's ~ of nuts*. 守財奴的窖藏;松鼠貯藏的堅果。□ *vt, vi* [VP6A, 15B] ~ ***(up)***, save and store: 貯藏: ~ *gold;* 貯藏黃金; ~ *up treasure*. 聚藏財寶。~**er** *n* person who ~s. 貯藏者。

hoard·ing /'hɔːdɪŋ ; 'hordɪŋ/ *n* (US 美 = *billboard*) (often temporary) fence of boards round waste land, building work, etc, frequently used for posting advertisements. (圍於荒地,建築工程等,常被用以張貼廣告的)柵牆(常爲臨時性的)。

hoarse /hɔːs ; hors/ *adj* (of the voice) rough and harsh; (of a person) having a ~ voice: (指聲音)粗啞的;嘶啞的;(指人)聲音嘶啞的: *He shouted himself ~*. 他的嗓子都喊啞了。~·**ly** *adv* ~·**ness** *n*

hoary /'hɔːrɪ ; 'horɪ/ *adj* (-ier, -iest) grey or white with age; very old: 因年邁而灰白的;古老的: *the ~ ruins of English abbeys*. 古老英國寺院的遺蹟。 **hoari·ness** *n*

hoax /həʊks ; hoks/ *n* [C] mischievous trick played on sb for a joke. 惡作劇;戲弄。□ *vt* [VP6A, 14] deceive (sb) in this way: 欺騙; 戲弄(某人): ~ *sb into believing or doing sth foolish*. 騙某人相信或做愚蠢之事。~**er** *n*

hob /hɒb ; hab/ *n* flat metal shelf at the side of a fireplace (with a surface level with the top of the grate) where pots and pans can be kept warm or a kettle boiled. 壁爐旁邊的金屬平架(其面與爐架頂平),置鍋於上可以保溫,或置以開水壺保持沸騰。

hobble /'hɒbl ; 'habḷ/ *vi, vt* **1** [VP2A, C] walk as when lame, or as when the feet or legs are impeded: 跛行;蹣跚: *The old man ~d along with the aid of his stick*. 那老人藉手杖之助蹣跚而行。 **2** [VP6A] tie two legs of a horse or donkey to prevent it from going far away. 綑縛馬或驢之雙腿,以阻其遠離。□ *n* stumbling or limping way of walking. 蹣跚;跛行。'~-**skirt** *n* very narrow skirt which caused the wearer to walk with short steps. 一種很窄之裙,穿者須碎步行走。

hobble·de·hoy /'hɒbldɪhɔɪ ; 'habḷdɪ,hɔɪ/ *n* awkward overgrown youth. 笨拙而且過於高大的青年。

hobby /'hɒbɪ ; 'habɪ/ *n* (*pl* -bies) [C] occupation, not one's regular business, for one's leisure time, eg stamp-collecting, growing roses. 嗜好(例如集郵,種植薔薇)。

hobby·horse /'hɒbɪhɔːs ; 'habɪ,hɔrs/ *n* [C] wooden horse on rockers as a child's toy, or on a merry-go-round; long stick with a horse's head; figure of a horse (in wickerwork) fastened to a dancer (in the morris-dance); (fig) favourite topic (of conversation, etc): 木馬(裝於搖軸上作兒童玩具,或裝置於旋轉遊樂臺上);裝有馬頭形物之長棒;(鄉村化裝舞會中)繫於跳舞者身上的柳條編成的馬;(喩)(指談話等的)喜愛的話題: *Now he's started on his ~*, begun to talk on his favourite subject. 現在他開始談論他最喜愛的話題。

hob·gob·lin /,hɒb'gɒblɪn ; 'hab,gablɪn/ *n* [C] mischievous imp; ugly and evil spirit. 小妖魔;惡鬼。

hob·nail /'hɒbneɪl ; 'hab,nel/ *n* short nail with a heavy head used for the soles of heavy shoes and boots, eg for mountain-climbing. (釘於爬山等所用笨重鞋靴底上的)粗頭短釘。~**ed** *adj* (of boots, etc) set with ~s. (指靴等)裝有粗頭短釘的。

hob·nob /'hɒbnɒb ; 'hab,nab/ *vi* (-bb-) [VP2A, C, 3A] ~ ***(together)/(with sb)***, have friendly social relations: 親切地與人交往: *I used to ~ with the rich and famous*. 我過去常與富有而又著名的人交往。

hobo /'həʊbəʊ ; 'hobo/ *n* (*pl* ~s, ~es /-bəʊz ; -boz/) (US, sl) unemployed worker who wanders from place to place; vagrant. (美俚)無業游民;流浪漢。

Hob·son's choice /,hɒbsnz'tʃɔɪs ; 'habsṇz'tʃɔɪs/ *n* ⇨ choice.

hock¹ /hɒk ; hak/ *n* middle joint of an animal's hind leg. 飛節(動物後腿中間的關節)。⇨ the illus at dog, domestic. 參看 dog, domestic 之挿圖。

hock² /hɒk ; hak/ *n* [U] (kind of) German white wine. (一種)德國產的白葡萄酒。

hock³ /hɒk ; hak/ *vt* (sl) [VP6A] pawn²(1). (俚)典當;抵押。□ *n* ***in*** ~, pawned. 當掉。

hockey /'hɒkɪ ; 'hakɪ/ *n* [U] '**field** ~, game played with sticks on a field by two teams of eleven players each and a ball. 曲棍球;陸上曲棍球(由各有十一人之兩隊,在運動場上用一球及曲棍所進行的球戲)。 '**ice** ~, game played on ice by two teams of six players each wearing skates and with sticks and a rubber disc (a *puck*). 冰上曲棍球(由各有六人之兩隊,穿冰鞋在冰上用曲棍及一橡皮圓盤 (puck) 所進行的球戲)。'~ **stick**, long curved or angled stick used to hit the ball or puck. 曲棍球棒。

ho·cus-po·cus /,həʊkəs 'pəʊkəs ; 'hokəs'pokəs/ *n* [U] talk, behaviour, designed to draw one's attention away from sth; deception. 故意使人轉移注意力的言談或行動;欺騙。

hod /hɒd ; had/ *n* light open box with a long handle used by workmen for carrying bricks, etc on the shoulder. 磚斗(輕便無蓋之箱狀工具,有長柄,工人用以肩負搬運磚瓦等)。

hodge·podge /'hɒdʒpɒdʒ ; 'hadʒ,padʒ/ *n* [U] = hotchpotch.

hoe /həʊ ; ho/ *n* tool for loosening the soil, uprooting weeds among growing crops, etc. 鋤頭。⇨ the illus at tool. 參看 tool 之挿圖。 **Dutch hoe**, the kind pushed forward by the user. 鍬。□ *vt*,

field hockey

ice hockey

vi (*pt, pp* hoed) [VP6A, 15B, 2A] work with a hoe: 鋤: *hoeing up weeds.* 鋤草。

hog /hɒg *US:* hɔ:g ; hɑg/ *n* castrated male pig reared for meat, ⇨ boar(2), sow¹; (fig) greedy, dirty, selfish person. (閹過的供食用的)公豬; (喻)貪婪、骯髒、自私的人。 ***go the whole hog,*** do sth thoroughly. 徹底做某事。 **'hog·wash** *n* swill(2); (fig) nonsense; rubbish (esp of sth said or written). (餵豬之)潲水;(喻)胡說;廢話。 □ *vt* [VP6A] take more than one's fair share of; take greedily and selfishly. 取用超出應得的一份;貪婪而自私地取用。 **hog·gish** /-ɪʃ ; -ɪʃ/ *adj* greedy and selfish. 貪婪而且自私的。

Hog·ma·nay /'hɒgmənei ; ˌhɑgmə'ne/ *n* (Scotland) New Year's Eve (and its festivities). (蘇格蘭)除夕(及其慶祝活動)。

hogs·head /'hɒgzhed *US:* 'hɔ:g- ; 'hɑgzˌhɛd/ *n* large barrel for beer; liquid measure ($52\frac{1}{2}$ gallons in GB or about 238·5 litres, 62 gallons in US or about 234·5 litres). 大啤酒桶; 豪格海(液量名,在英國合 $52\frac{1}{2}$ 加侖或約 238·5 公升,在美國合 62 加侖或約 234.5 公升)。

hoi pol·loi /ˌhɔɪ pə'lɔɪ ; 'hɔɪpə'lɔɪ/ *n* **the ~,** (pej) the masses; the rabble. (蔑)民衆;賤民。

hoist /hɔɪst ; hɔɪst/ *vt* [VP6A, 15B] lift with an apparatus of ropes and pulleys or a kind of elevator: (用繩索及滑輪裝置或一種升降機) 升起; 舉起: *~ a flag/sail;* 升旗(帆); *~ casks and crates aboard;* 將桶和簍裝上船; *~ in the boats,* raise them from the water up to the deck. 將小船從水面吊至甲板上。□ *n* apparatus for ~ing: 吊機; 起重機; 升起裝置: *an ammunition ~* (on a warship); (軍艦上)彈藥起卸機; (colloq) pull or push: (俗) 拉;推: *give sb a ~,* eg when he is climbing a wall. 將某人向上推一下(例如當其爬牆時)。

hoity-toity /ˌhɔɪtɪ 'tɔɪtɪ ; 'hɔɪtɪ'tɔɪtɪ/ *adj* (colloq) supercilious and haughty. (俗)傲慢的。□ *int* used to a ~ person to express disapproval of him or her. 對一傲慢的人所用的感歎詞,表示對其不滿。

hold¹ /həuld ; hold/ *vt, vi* (*pt, pp* held /held ; hɛld/) (For uses with *adverbial particles* and *preps,* ⇨ 14 below.) (與副詞接語及介詞連用的用法,參看下列第 14 義。) **1** [VP6A, 15A, B] have or keep in one's possession, keep fast or steady, in or with the hand(s), arm(s) or other part of the body, eg the teeth, or with a tool: 執住;握住;抓緊;拿住: *The girl was ~ing her father's hand.* 那女孩握住她父親的手。*They held hands/held each other's hands.* 他們互相握住手。*She held me by the sleeve.* 她抓住我的袖子。*She was ~ing up an umbrella.* 她打着雨傘。*He held the knife in his teeth as he climbed the tree.* 他爬樹時用牙齒叼着刀子。 ***~ the line,*** keep a telephone connection (eg while the person at the other end goes away to find sth or sb). 不把電話掛斷;繼續維持通話。 ⇨ also baby, brief²(1), pistol. **2** [VP6A, 15A, B] restrain; keep back; control: 壓抑;阻止;抑制;控制: *The police held back the crowd.* 警察阻止了群衆。*It took three of us to ~ the madman.* 我們三個人合力制住那個瘋子。*Try to ~ the thief until the police arrive.* 設法制住那小偷,等警察到來。*He held his attacker at arm's length.* 他把攻擊者阻止在一臂之外。*The dam gave way; it was not strong enough to ~ the flood waters.* 水壩坍塌了;它不夠堅固,擋不住洪水。 ***~ one's breath,*** eg from excitement or fear: (例如因興奮或恐懼而)屏息: *The watchers held their breath as the acrobat crossed the tightrope.* 當賣藝者走過綱索時,觀衆都屏息。 ***~ (one's) fire,*** stop shooting for a time. 停火。 ***~ one's tongue/peace,*** be quiet. 緘默;住嘴。 ***There is no ~ing sb/sth,*** It is impossible to restrain or control him/it: 無法約束或控制某人(某事物): *There was no ~ing her,* eg because she was so determined or high-spirited. 沒有辦法阻止她(例如因爲她太堅決或太高興)。 **3** [VP15A, B, 2C] keep or maintain sb/sth in a specified position, manner, attitude or relationship: 使某人或某物保持特定位置,態度,姿勢或關係: *H~ your head up.* 把你的頭抬起來。*H~ your arms up/out.* 把你的手臂舉起來(伸出來)。*H~ yourself still for a moment while I take your photograph.* 我給你拍照的那一刹那,你不要動。 ***~ oneself in readiness (for),*** be prepared (for sth, an emergency). 準備好(做某事,應付緊急事件)。 ***~ one's sides with laughter,*** laugh heartily. 捧腹大笑。 **4** [VP6A] maintain a grip of: 抓緊;握牢: *This new car ~s the road well/has good road-~ing qualities,* is stable, eg when cornering at speed. 這部新汽車很穩(例如在快速轉彎時)。 **5** [VP6A] support; bear the weight of: 支持;承受重量: *This nail won't ~ such a heavy mirror.* 這釘子支持不住這樣重的鏡子。*Come down—that branch won't ~ you!* 下來 — 那樹枝承受不了你的重量! **6** [VP6A] be filled by; have the capacity to contain or accommodate: 裝;盛;能夠容納: *Will this suitcase ~ all your clothes?* 這衣箱能裝得下你所有的衣服嗎? *This barrel ~s 25 litres.* 這桶能裝 25 公升。*What does the future ~ for us?* 我們將來的命運如何? *He ~s* (= has) *strange views on religion.* 他對宗教持有奇怪的看法。 ***~ sth in one's head,*** retain, not forget, eg a mass of details, statistics. 牢記; 記得(細節,統計數字等)。 ***(not) ~ water,*** (not) be sound, valid, logical: 站得住(站不住);(不)正確;(不)合乎邏輯: *Your argument doesn't ~ water.* 你的論點站不住。 **7** [VP6A, 22] keep the interest or attention of: 維持…興趣或注意力: *The speaker held his audience spellbound.* 演說者使聽衆聽得入迷。 **8** [VP9, 15A, B, 22, 25] consider; regard; believe; affirm: 認爲; 視爲;相信; 確定: *~ a man to be a fool/~ that he is foolish;* 認爲某人是傻子; *~ the view that a plan is/~ a plan to be impracticable.* 認爲某計畫不切實際。*The President is not held in great respect.* 那位總統並不十分受人尊敬。*He does not ~ himself responsible for his wife's debts.* 他並不認爲他應該對妻子的債務負責。 ***~ sb in high/low esteem,*** have a high/low regard for him. 非常(不很)尊敬某人。 ***~ sth dear/cheap,*** place a high/low value on it: 重視(不重視)某事物: *He ~s his reputation dear.* 他重視他的名譽。 **9** [VP 6A] defend; keep possession of: 保衞;保持: *They held the fort against all attacks.* 他們堅守那堡壘,抵抗所有的進攻。 ***~ the fort,*** (fig) be in charge during sb's absence: (喻)當某人不在時,代理職掌: *Jane had to ~ the fort* (be in charge of the house) *while her mother was in hospital.* 在她母親住醫院期間,珍只好代理持家。 ***~ one's ground,*** stand firm, not retreat: 堅守陣地;不撤退: *Our soldiers held their ground bravely.* 我們兵士英勇地堅守陣地。 ***~ one's own,*** not give way: 堅持立場;不讓步: *The patient is still ~ing his own,* maintaining his strength. 那病人仍然在支撑着。*Mr Green held his own,* eg in a debate, maintained his position (by arguing well). 格林先生堅持自己立場(例如在辯論中,立論精闢)。 **10** [VP6A] be the legal owner or possessor of: 保有;擁有: *~ shares/stock.* 保有股份(股票)。⇨ *land~er* at land¹(6), *share~er* at share¹(3), *stock~er* at stock¹(5). **11** [VP6A] occupy; have the position of: 佔有;在位: *The Social Democrats held office then,* were the government. 當時是社會民主黨執政。 Hence, 由此產生, **'office-~er. 12** [VP6A] have; conduct; cause to take place: 舉行: *~ a meeting/debate/examination.* 舉行會議(辯論,考試)。 *We ~ a General Election every four or five years.* 我們每四年或五年舉行大選。*The Motor Show is usually held in October.* 汽車展覽會通常在十月舉行。 ***~ court,*** (fig) entertain, welcome, admirers: (喻)接待敬慕者: *a film-star ~ing court at London Airport.* 一位電影明星在倫敦機場接待影迷。 ⇨ court¹(2). **13** [VP2A, D] remain unbroken, unchanged, secure, under strain, pressure, etc. (在緊張,壓力等下)不破;不變;安全。 ⇨ 5 above. 參看上列第 5 義。 *How long will the anchor*

~, stay fast in the sea bed? 這錨會固定在海底多久？*How long will this fine weather ~,* continue? 這好天氣將繼續多久？⇨ break¹(5). *The argument still ~s (good/true),* is still valid. 這論據仍舊有效。**14** [VP15B, 3A, 2C, 14] (uses with *adverbial particles* and *preps;* for non-idiomatic uses ⇨ 1, 2, 3 above): (與副詞接語及介詞連用的用法；非習慣語用法參看上列第 1, 2, 3 義)：

hold sth against sb, allow sth to influence one's opinions adversely: 由於受某事的影響而對某人持不好的看法: *Don't ~ his criminal convictions against him.* 不要因爲他判過刑而對他存偏見。

hold (oneself) aloof, ⇨ aloof.

hold back, hesitate; show unwillingness: 躊躇；退縮: *Buyers are ~ing back,* making few or no offers. 買主們不願出價。*When danger came, no one held back.* 危險來到時，無人退縮。***~ sb/sth back,*** **(a)** ⇨ 2 above. 參看上列第 2 義。**(b)** hinder the progress of: 阻礙；阻止: *His poor education is ~ing him back.* 他的教育程度差阻碍了他的發展。**(c)** keep secret or to oneself: 隱而不宣；不公開: *~ back information.* 隱藏着消息不宣佈。

hold sb/sth down, **(a)** ⇨ 3 above. 參看上列第 3 義。**(b)** oppress; keep down or under: 控制；壓制: *rulers who ~ the people down,* oppress them. 壓迫人民的統治者。*We must ~ (= keep) prices down.* 我們必須抑低物價。***~ a job down,*** (colloq) keep it by proving one's capabilities. (俗)表現才能而保持住職位。

hold forth, speak rather pompously, as if in public. 高談闊論。***~ sth forth,*** (*~ sth out,* below is preferred) offer; propose. 提供；提議 (hold sth out 較常用)。

hold sth in, check; restrain: 抑制；壓抑: *~ in one's temper;* 抑制自己的脾氣; *~ oneself in,* control one's feelings, eg of indignation. 壓抑自己的感情(例如憤慨)。

hold off, **(a)** remain at a distance: 保持距離: *The storm held off.* 風暴滯留在遠處。*Will the rain ~ off until after the picnic?* 雨會延緩到野餐之後下嗎？**(b)** delay action: 延擱行動: *H~ off for a minute.* 延緩一分鐘。***~ sb/sth off,*** keep at a distance: 使保持距離: *H~ your dog off!* 趕開你的狗！*His cold manner ~s* (better *keeps*) *people off,* deters them from trying to be friendly. 他的冷淡態度使人不敢親近 (用 keeps 較佳)。

hold on, **(a)** stand firm when there is danger, difficulty, etc: 堅定: *How much longer do they think we can ~ on?* 他們以爲我們還能支持多久？**(b)** (usu imper) stop: (通常作祈使用法)停止: *H~ on a minute!* Not so fast! Don't go further in what you're doing. 停一停！***~ on to,*** **(a)** keep one's grip on; not let go of: 抓住；不放手: *~ on to one's hat on a windy day.* 在大風的日子抓住自己的帽子。*The boy held on to the bush until someone climbed down the cliff to rescue him.* 這男孩抓住那矮樹，直到有人爬下懸崖去救他。**(b)** not give up the ownership of: 不放棄擁有；不出讓: *You should ~ on to your oil shares.* 你應該掌握你的石油股份。***~ sth on,*** keep in position: 使固定: *These bolts and nuts ~ the wheels on.* 這些螺栓及螺帽使輪子固定。

hold out, **(a)** maintain resistance; not give way: 抵抗；不退讓: *How long can we ~ out against these attacks?* 我們對這些攻擊能抵抗多久？**(b)** last: 維持；繼續: *How long will our food supplies ~ out?* 我們的貯糧還能維持多久？*I can't ~ out* (= retain my urine) *much longer—I must find a toilet.* 我內急不能再久等了——我必須找個厠所。***~ out for,*** continue to demand: 繼續要求；堅持: *The workers are still ~ing out for higher wages,* insisting on being granted their demands. 工人們仍舊堅持更高工資。***~ out on,*** refuse to deal with: 拒絕與…來往: *He's still ~ing out on me,* still opposing my wishes, refusing my request. 他仍然拒絕跟我來往。***~ sb/sth out,*** **(a)** ⇨ 3 above. 參看上列第 3 義。**(b)** offer: 給予: *The doctors ~ out little hope of recovery.* 醫生們認爲痊癒的希望甚微。

hold sth over, defer; postpone; adjourn: 延擱；延期；休會: *The matter was held over until the next meeting.* 此事被延至下次會議解決。***~ sth over sb,*** use it as a threat: 以某事要脅某人: *He's ~ing my past record over me.* 他用我過去的記錄威脅我。

hold to sth, **(a)** remain loyal or steadfast to: 忠實；堅定: *He held to his convictions/choice/course of action.* 他忠於他的信仰(抉擇，行動方針)。**(b)** keep to: 遵行: *The ship held to a Southerly course.* 那艘船遵行南方航線。***~ sb to sth,*** make sb keep, eg a promise: 使某人遵守(諾言等): *We must ~ the contractors to their estimates,* not allow them to exceed them. 我們一定要承包商遵守他們的估價。***~ sb (up) to ransom,*** demand money by threatening penalties, etc; blackmail: 以處罰等作威脅而索取金錢；勒索；敲詐: *Those strikers were not ~ing the country (up) to ransom.* 那些罷工者並不是在向全國敲詐。⇨ ransom.

hold together, **(a)** be and continue whole: 在一起；成一整體: *The bodywork of this old car hardly ~s together,* is falling apart, eg from rust. 這部舊汽車的車身由於生銹等幾乎要脫落開了。**(b)** remain united: 團結一起: *We Tories always ~ together in times of crisis.* 我們保守黨黨員在危急時期永遠團結在一起。***~ sb/sth together,*** cause to remain together; unite: 使結合在一起；使團結: *The country needs a leader who will ~ the nation together.* 那國家需要一個能使全國團結的領袖。

hold sb/sth up, **(a)** ⇨ 1, 2 above. 參看上列第 1, 2 義。**(b)** delay: 延擱；阻滯: *They were held up by fog/the immigration authorities.* 他們爲霧(移民當局)所延擱。**(c)** stop by the use or threat of force, for the purpose of robbery: 攔路搶刼: *The travellers were held up by bandits.* 旅客遭强盜攔刼。Hence, 由此產生，**'~-up** *n*: *a ~up on the Underground,* eg by a power failure; 地下火車運輸因爲停電等的延擱; *a bank ~up,* eg one by armed robbers. 銀行被持械强盜等搶刼。**(d)** put forward as an example: 舉出作爲例證: *Don't ~ me up as a model husband.* 不要拿我作爲模範丈夫的例子。***~ sb up to derision/scorn/ridicule,*** expose him to derision, etc. 嘲笑某人。

hold with sth, approve of: 贊成某事: *Do you ~ with nudity on the stage?* 你贊成演員在舞臺上裸體麼？

hold² /həʊld; hold/ *n* **1** [C, U] act, manner, power of holding: 抓；握；把握；把持力: *catch/get/take/lay/seize ~ of sth;* 抓住某物; *let go/lose (one's) ~ of sth.* 鬆手；對某物失去把持力。*He has a great ~ (= influence) over his younger brother.* 他對他弟弟很有影響力。*How long can the Government keep its ~ over the district,* keep the district under control? 政府在該地區的統治權能維持多久？**2** [C] sth that may be used for holding on to: 可抓握之物；可踏腳之處: *The rock face afforded few ~s to climbers.* 該岩石的正面很少有攀登者可以踏腳之處。⇨ *foothold* at foot¹(8). **3** (boxing and wrestling) (kinds of) grip: (拳擊與摔角)抓緊；擒拿法: *all-in wrestling, with no ~s barred.* 自由式的摔角，不禁擒拿。

hold³ /həʊld; hold/ *n* part of a ship below deck, where cargo is stored. 貨艙。

hold-all /ˈhəʊld ɔːl; ˈholdˌɔl/ *n* portable bag or case large enough to hold clothes, etc when travelling. 裝衣物用的輕便旅行袋。⇨ hold¹(6).

holder /ˈhəʊldə(r); ˈholdɚ/ *n* person or thing that holds: 支持之人或物；持有者；保持者: *a 'share~;* 股東; *a ciga'rette-~;* 香煙嘴; *an 'office-~;* 公務員；職員; *a 'kettle-~,* cloth for handling a hot kettle. 用來拿熱水壺的布。

hold·ing /ˈhəʊldɪŋ; ˈholdɪŋ/ *n* sth (esp land) held or owned; tenure or ownership (esp of land). 所有物(尤指土地)；(尤指土地之)使用權或所有權。**'small-~** *n* small area of land farmed by the tenant himself. 佃農自己耕作的小塊土地。**a '~ company,** one formed to hold the shares of subsidiary companies. 股權公司(控制附屬公司股份的公司)。

hold-up /ˈhəʊld ʌp; ˈhold,ʌp/ *n* ⇨ hold¹(14).

hole /həʊl; hol/ *n* **1** opening or hollow place in a solid body: 洞;孔;坑: *a ～ in a tooth;* 牙齒上的空洞; *roads full of ～s;* 滿是坑窪的道路; *～s in the walls and roof of a building, caused by shell fire;* 一建築物牆壁及屋頂上被砲彈擊成的洞孔; *wear one's socks into ～s,* wear them until there are ～s. 把襪子穿破。 ***make a ～ in,*** use a large amount of: 用去一大筆錢: *The hospital bills made a large ～ in his savings.* 住院費花掉他儲蓄的一大半。 ***pick ～s in,*** find fault with, eg an argument. 找(論據等)的漏洞;吹毛求疵。 ***a square peg in a round ～,*** person not fitted for the position he occupies. 不適於其職位的人。 **2** (colloq) awkward situation: (俗)窘境: *You've put me in a bad ～.* 你使我十分困窘。 **3** animal's burrow: 獸穴: *a mouse's ～/ˈmouse-～;* 鼠穴; *the ～ of a fox;* 狐穴; (fig) small, dark, wretched place; den; hiding-place: (喻)狭小,陰暗,卑陋的地方;巢穴;隱匿處: *What a wretched little ～ he lives in!* 他住的房子多麽狹小簡陋啊! **ˌ～-and-ˈcorner** *adj* (colloq, attrib) secret; underhand: (俗,形容用法)祕密的;偷偷摸摸的: *We don't like these ～-and-corner methods.* 我們不喜歡這些不光明正大的方法。 **4** (golf) hollow into which the ball must be hit; point scored by a player who gets his ball from one ～ to another with the fewest strokes: (高爾夫)球洞;自一高爾夫球洞至另一洞間,球員以最少桿數進球所得的分數: *a ˈnine-～ golf course;* 一個九洞的高爾夫球場; *win the first ～.* 在第一洞時領先。□ *vt, vi* **1** [VP6A] make a ～ or ～s in or through: 鑿洞於;穿孔於: *～ a ship,* eg by striking a rock. 將船撞破(例如由於碰撞到岩石)。 **2** [VP6A, 15B, 2C] ***～ (out),*** get (a ball) into a ～ (in golf, etc): (高爾夫球等)打(球)入洞: *～ out in one,* get the ball from the tee into the ～ with only one stroke. 一擊而使球入洞。 **3** [VP2C] ***～ up,*** (sl) hide. (俚)藏;躲避。

holi·day /ˈhɒlədeɪ; ˈhɑlə,de/ *n* **1** day of rest from work: 假日: *Sunday is a ～ in Christian countries; Friday is a ～ in Muslim countries.* 星期天在基督教國家中是假日;星期五在回教國家中是假日。 ⇨ also *bank ～* at bank³(1). **2** (often *pl*) (US 美 = *vacation*) period of rest from work: (常用複數)假期: *the school ～s;* 學校的假期; *the Christmas ～s;* 聖誕節假期; *take a month's ～ in summer;* 度一個月的暑假; (attrib) (形容用法) *ˈ～ camps.* 度假營。 ***on ～,*** having a ～: 在度假;休假: *Our typist is away on ～ this week.* 我們的打字員本週休假。 **ˈ～-maker** *n* person on ～. 度假者。

holi·ness /ˈhəʊlɪnɪs; ˈholɪnɪs/ *n* **1** [U] being holy or sacred. 神聖。 **2 His／Your H～,** title used of／to the Pope. 教皇陛下(對教皇的尊稱)。

hol·ler /ˈhɒlə(r); ˈhɑlɚ/ *vi, vt* (sl) yell (to indicate excitement, etc): (俚)喊叫(表示興奮等): *Stop ～ing —nobody's going to hurt you!* 别叫了—沒有人要傷害你!

hol·loa /ˈhɒləʊ; ˈhɑlo/ *n, vi, int* shout, esp to hounds (during a fox-hunt). 呼喊(尤指獵狐時對獵犬的吆喝)。

hol·low /ˈhɒləʊ; ˈhɑlo/ *adj* **1** not solid; with a hole or empty space inside: 空的;中空的: *a ～ tree;* 中空的樹; *a ～ ball.* 中空的球。 **2** (of sounds) as if coming from sth ～: (指聲音)空洞的;重濁的: *a ～ voice／groan.* 沉重的聲音(呻吟)。 **3** (fig) unreal; false; insincere: (喻)不眞實的;虛僞的;虛假的: *～ sympathy／words／promises;* 虛僞的同情(言語,允諾); *a ～ laugh;* 虛僞的笑聲; *～ joys and pleasures,* not giving true happiness; 空幻的歡樂; *a ～ victory,* one without real value. 空虛的勝利。 **4** sunken: 凹陷的: *～ cheeks;* 凹陷的雙頰; *ˌ～-ˈeyed.* 雙眼凹陷的。 **5** (colloq, as *adv*) (俗,用作副詞) ***beat sb ～,*** completely. 徹底擊敗某人。□ *n* hole; ～ place: 洞;穴;坑;凹地: *a ～ in the ground;* 地上的坑; small valley: 小山谷: *a wooded ～,* small valley with trees. 有樹林的小山谷。□ *vt* [VP6A, 15A, B] ***～ (out),*** make a ～ or ～s in; bend into a ～ shape: 挖空;使成空洞;彎曲成凹形: *river banks ～ed out by rushing water.* 爲急流沖刷而凹了進去的河岸。

holly /ˈhɒlɪ; ˈhɑlɪ/ *n* [U] evergreen shrub with hard, shiny, dark-green sharp-pointed leaves and, in winter, red berries. 冬青屬灌木(生有堅硬、有光澤、深綠色的尖葉,冬季結紅色漿果)。

holly

holly·hock /ˈhɒlɪhɒk; ˈhɑlɪ,hɑk/ *n* [C] tall garden plant with brightly coloured flowers. 蜀葵(一種高的園藝植物,生有鮮艷的花)。

Holly·wood /ˈhɒlɪwʊd; ˈhɑlɪ,wʊd/ *n* centre of the US film industry: 好萊塢(美國電影工業中心): *～ films／stars.* 好萊塢影片(明星)。

holm-oak /ˈhəʊm əʊk; ˈhom ok/ *n* [C] evergreen oak, ilex. 冬青檞。

holo·caust /ˈhɒləkɔːst; ˈhɑlə,kɔst/ *n* [C] large-scale destruction, esp of human lives by fire, etc: 大規模的毀滅(尤指人命毀於火災等): *a nuclear ～.* 大規模的核子毀滅。

holo·graph /ˈhɒləgrɑːf *US:* -græf; ˈhɑlə,græf/ *n* document written wholly by the person in whose name it appears. 親筆文書。

hol·ster /ˈhəʊlstə(r); ˈholstɚ/ *n* leather case for a pistol or revolver. 手槍皮套。

holy /ˈhəʊlɪ; ˈholɪ/ *adj* (-ier -iest) **1** of God; associated with God or with religion: 上帝的;神聖的;與上帝或宗教有關的: *the H～ Bible;* 聖經; *H～ Writ,* the Bible; 聖經; *the ˈH～ Land,* where Jesus lived; 聖地(耶穌居住之地); *the H～ City,* Jerusalem; 聖城(耶路撒冷); *ˈH～ Week,* the week before Easter Sunday; 復活節前一週; *H～ Communion;* 聖餐; *the H～ Father,* the Pope; 教皇; *the H～ Office,* the Inquisition; 宗教法庭; *the H～ Ghost／Spirit,* the Third Person of the Trinity; 聖靈; *～ ground,* land held in religious awe; 神聖的土地; *～ water,* water blessed by a priest; 聖水;淨水; *a ～ war,* one (said to be) fought in defence of sth sacred. 聖戰(據稱爲保衛神聖事物的戰爭)。 **2** devoted to religion: 獻身於宗教的: *a ～ man;* 獻身於宗教的人; *live a ～ life.* 過聖潔的生活。 **3** ***a ～ terror,*** (sl) formidable person; mischievous, embarrassing child. (俚)可怕的人;淘氣的孩子。□ *n* **the ˌH～ of ˈHolies, (a)** most sacred inner chamber in a Jewish temple, entered by the High Priest once a year. 猶太教堂中之至聖所(祭司長每年進入一次)。 **(b)** (fig) any sacred place. (喻)任何神聖之地。

holy·stone /ˈhəʊlɪstəʊn; ˈholɪ,ston/ *n* [U] soft sandstone used for scrubbing the wooden deck of a ship. (磨木甲板用的)磨石。□ *vt* scrub with ～. 以磨石摩擦。

hom·age /ˈhɒmɪdʒ; ˈhɑmɪdʒ/ *n* [U] **1** expression of respect; tribute paid (*to* sb, his merits). 尊敬;敬意;尊崇(與 to 連用,後接某人或其功績)。 ***do／pay ～ (to sb),*** express respect for: (向某人)表示敬意: *Many came to do the dead man ～.* 很多人前來向死者致敬。 *We pay ～ to the genius of Shakespeare.* 我們對莎士比亞的天才表示敬意。 **2** (in feudal times) formal and public acknowledgement of loyalty to a lord or ruler. (封建時期對君主或統治者正式公開表示的)效忠;臣服。

home¹ /həʊm; hom/ *n* **1** place where one lives, esp with one's family: 家;家庭: *He left ～ at the age of 16,* left his parents and began an independent life. 他十六歲離開了家(離開父母過獨立生活)。 *He looks forward to seeing the old ～ again,* eg his birthplace. 他盼望能再看到老家。 *He was born* *in England, but he now looks on Paris as his* ~. 他生在英國,但現在將巴黎當作他的家鄉。*When I retire I shall make my* ~ *in the country.* 我退休後將在鄉間安家。*He left India for* ~, for his own country. 他離開印度回國去了。**at** ~, **(a)** in the house: 在家裏: *I've left my books at* ~. 我把我的書留在家裏了。*Is there anybody at* ~? 有人在家嗎? **(b)** (football, etc) in the town, etc to which the team belongs: (足球賽等)在球隊所屬的城市等: *Is our next match at* ~ *or away?* 我們下次比賽是在本地還是在他處舉行? Hence, 由此產生, **the** ˈ~ **team,** the team playing at ~. 地主隊。**(c)** expecting and ready to receive visitors at an appointed time: 在一指定的時間會客: *'Mrs Carr will be at* ~, *Monday, 1 May, 5pm.'* '卡爾太太將於五月一日,星期一,下午五時會客。' **at-ˈ~** *n* social function at which guests are expected at a time announced. 約定時日之接待賓客。***not at* ~ *(to),*** not receiving visitors: 不會客: *Mrs Hill is not at* ~ *to anyone except relatives.* 奚爾太太不會客,但親屬除外。***make oneself/be/feel at* ~,** as if in one's own house; at one's ease: 感覺如在自己家中;無拘束: *The boy did not feel at* ~ *in such a splendid house.* 那男孩子在這樣堂皇的房子內感到拘束。***at* ~ *in,*** familiar with, accustomed to: 熟悉;習慣: *Is it difficult to feel at* ~ *in a foreign language,* to feel easy and confident while using one? 精通一種外國語言困難嗎? ***be* ~ *and dry,*** (colloq) succeed. (俗)成功。***a* ~ *from* ~,** a place where one is as happy, comfortable, etc as in one's own ~: 像家一樣安適的處所: *Prison is not usually a* ~ *from* ~. 監獄通常不是像家一樣安適的處所。***nothing to write* ~ *about,*** (colloq) nothing remarkable. (俗)乏善可陳;平淡無奇。 **2** institution or place (for the care of children, old or sick people, etc): (照顧兒童,老弱,殘疾等之)機構或處所: *an ˈorphans'* ~; 孤兒院; *a ˈnursing* ~; 療養院; *maˈternity* ~*s.* 婦女收容所。 **3** (often attrib) family or domestic life: (常作形容用法)家庭生活: *the pleasures of* ~; 天倫之樂;家庭生活之樂; ~ *comforts/joys;* 家庭生活的舒適(歡樂); ~ *life.* 家庭生活。ˌ~ **ecoˈnomics** = housecraft. ˌ~ ˈ**help** *n* (GB) person employed to help the elderly, infirm or ill (and who are without the help of relatives or friends). (英) 幫做家事的人(僱用以協助年長,體弱或生病,而無親友協助之人們)。 **4** (= habitat) place where an animal or plant is native or most common: 動植物的棲息地或生長地: *the* ~ *of the tiger and the elephant,* eg the jungle; 虎及象之棲息地(例如叢林地帶); *the* ~ *of the fur-seal.* 海狗的生長地。 **5** (in sport and in various games) goal; place where a player is safe and cannot be caught, put out, etc. (運動及多種遊戲中) 終點; 安全之處; 不能被捉住、逐出等之處。**the** ˈ~ **plate,** (baseball) base at which the batsman stands to bat. (棒球)本壘。ˌ~ ˈ**run,** (baseball) one made after a hit which enables the batsman to go round all the bases without stopping. (棒球)本壘打; 全壘打(打出一球後,可安全跑完一圈,經過各壘,不必停留)。**the** ˌ~ ˈ**straight**/ˈ**stretch,** last part of a track, near the winning-post. 終點直道; 接近終點的一段跑道。 **6** (attrib) of the ~; of one's own country (= *domestic, inland,* contrasted with *foreign*): (形容用法)家庭的;本國的 (與 foreign 相對): ~ *industries/products;* 國內工業(產品); *the* ~ *trade/market.* 國內貿易(市場)。**one's** ˌ~ ˈ**town,** town (not necessarily one's birthplace) in which one lives permanently. 永久居留地(並不一定是出生地)。**the** ˌ**H**~ ˈ**Counties,** those round London. 倫敦附近各郡。**the** ˈ**H**~ **Office,** department controlling local government, police, etc in England and Wales, under the minister called the *H~ Secretary,* or *Secretary of State for H~ Affairs* (US 美 = *Department of the Interior*). 內政部(在英國內政部長稱作 Home Secretary 或 Secretary of State for Home Affairs)。 **7** (compounds) (複合字) ˌ~-ˈ**baked** *adj* (of bread, etc) baked at ~, not bought from a shop. (指麪包等)家裏烘製的,不是從商店買來的。ˌ~-ˈ**brewed** *adj* (of beer, etc) brewed at ~ (contrasted with beer from a brewery). (指啤酒等)家裏釀製的(以別於釀造廠釀製的)。ˈ~-**coming** *n* arrival at ~, coming to one's ~: 到家;回家; 回國: ~*coming weekend,* (US) when alumni or alumnae return to their school, etc. (美) 校友返回母校之週末。ˌ~-ˈ**cured** *adj* (of food, esp bacon) treated (by smoking, salting, etc) at ~ (contrasted with food cured in factories). (食物,尤指鹹肉)在家裏(用煙燻、鹽醃等)處理的 (以別於在工廠中處理的)。ˈ~-**farm** *n* farm that supplies the needs of a large estate or establishment (contrasted with farmland that is rented out). 供應一大家庭或產業的農場(以別於租給佃戶的農場);家庭農場。**the** ˌ~ ˈ**front,** the civilians (in a country at war). (戰時一個國家的)後方民衆;所有平民。ˌ~-ˈ**grown** *adj* (of food, etc) produced in the country (contrasted with what is imported). (指食物等)國產的(以別於進口的)。ˌ**H**~ ˈ**Guard** *n* (member of the) British citizen army (1940-57). 1940-57 年間的英國國民軍(隊員)。ˈ~•**land** /-lænd ; -ˌlænd/ *n* native land; country from which one's ancestors came. 故鄉;祖國。ˌ~-ˈ**made** *adj* (of bread, cakes, etc) made at ~ (contrasted with what is bought from shops). (指麪包、糕餅等) 家庭製的; 自製的(以別於商店中買來的)。ˌ**H**~ ˈ**Rule,** government of a country by its own citizens. 地方自治;獨立自主。ˈ~•**sick** *adj* sad because away from ~; 想家的;懷鄉的; Hence, 由此產生, ˈ~•**sick•ness** *n* ˈ~•**spun** *adj, n* (cloth made of yarn) spun at ~; 手織的(布); (fig) (anything) plain and homely. (喻) 樸素的 (任何東西)。ˈ~•**stead** /-sted ; -ˌstɛd/ *n* house with the land and outbuildings round it; farmhouse; (US) land given to sb by the state on condition that he lives on it and cultivates it. 家園;農舍; (美) 分給人民開墾的土地。ˈ~ **thrust** *n* attack (with a weapon or in words) that is effective. (以武器或言語)命中要害的一擊。ˌ~ ˈ**truth** *n* unpleasant fact that one is made aware of. 明瞭後令人不愉快的事實。ˈ~•**work** *n* [U] **(a)** work which a pupil is required to do at ~ in the evening and take to his teacher(s) at school. (在晚間作好,再帶去學校交給老師的) 課外作業。**(b)** (colloq) preparatory work, eg for a report or discussion. (俗) (報告或討論等之) 準備工作。⇨ *housework* at house¹(7). ~•**less** *adj* having no ~. 無家可歸的。~•**like** *adj* like ~. 如在家般的。~•**ward** /-wəd ; -wərd/ *adj* going towards ~. 向家的。~•**ward(s)** /-wəd(z) ; -wərd(z)/ *adv* towards ~. 向家地。

home² /həʊm ; hom/ *adv* **1** at, in or to one's ~ or country: 在家; 到家; 向家; 在國內; 向國內: *Is he* ~ *yet?* 他到家了嗎? *I saw him on his way* ~. 我看見他在回家的路上。*He went* ~. 他回家去了。*Send the children* ~. 把孩子們送回家去。*We ought to turn back and get* ~, ie to the starting-point, whether this is or is not one's usual place of residence. 我們應當返回原地(即原出發點,不論其是否爲平常居所)。**2** to the point aimed at; so as to be in the right place: 中的地;適切地;徹底地: *drive a nail* ~, strike it so that it is completely in. 將釘完全打進。***bring sth/come* ~ *to sb,*** (cause sb to) realize fully: (使某人)徹底瞭解: *The stupidity of his behaviour was brought/came* ~ *to him.* 他徹底明白了他行爲的愚蠢。***drive a point/an argument* ~,** cause its full force to be understood. 使一論點爲人徹底明白。

home•ly /ˈhəʊmlɪ ; ˈhomlɪ/ *adj* (-ier, -iest) **1** simple and plain; of the sort used every day: 樸素的;家常的: *a* ~*-looking old lady,* not trying to seem important or dignified; 容貌樸素的老婦人(不欲作顯貴之態者); *a* ~ *meal.* 家常便飯。 **2** causing one to think of home or feel at home: 令人思家的; 令人有在家之感的: *a* ~ *atmosphere.* 如在家中般的氣氛。

3 (US) (of people, their features) not attractive or good-looking. (美,指人或其容貌)不吸引人的;不漂亮的。**home·li·ness** *n*

ho·meo·path *n* = homoeopath.

Ho·meric /həʊˈmerɪk ; hoˈmɛrɪk/ *adj* of, in the style of, Homer or his epics. 荷馬的;荷馬風格的;荷馬之史詩的。 ~ **laughter,** loud, boisterous laughter like that of the gods in Homer's epics. 縱聲大笑(如荷馬史詩中諸神所作者)。

homey /ˈhəʊmɪ ; ˈhomɪ/ *adj* (US colloq) like home; cosy. (美俗)似家的;舒適的。

homi·cide /ˈhɒmɪsaɪd ; ˈhɑməˌsaɪd/ *n* [U] killing of a human being; [C] person who kills a human being: 殺人; 殺人者: *H~ is not criminal when committed in self-defence.* 爲自衞而殺人無罪。 ˈ~ **squad,** (US) group of police officers who investigate ~s. (美)調查殺人案件之警察小組。 ⇨ murder. **homi·cidal** /ˌhɒmɪˈsaɪdl ; ˌhɑməˈsaɪdl/ *adj* of ~: 殺人的; 殺人者的: *a homicidal lunatic;* 殺人狂者; *homicidal tendencies.* 殺人的癖性。

hom·ily /ˈhɒmɪlɪ ; ˈhɑmlɪ/ *n* (*pl* -lies) [C] sermon; long and tedious moralizing talk. 講道;冗長而令人厭倦的說教。**homi·letic** /ˌhɒmɪˈletɪk ; ˌhɑməˈlɛtɪk/ *adj* of homilies. 講道的;說教的。**homi·let·ics** *n pl* art of preaching. 講道術。

hom·ing /ˈhəʊmɪŋ ; ˈhomɪŋ/ *adj* (of pigeons) having the instinct to fly home (when released a long way from home); (of torpedoes, missiles) fitted with electronic devices that enable them to reach a predetermined target: (指鴿子)(在離巢很遠處被釋放)有歸家本能的; (指魚雷,飛彈)裝有電子裝置能使其擊中預定目標的;追踪的: ˈ*~ devices;* 追踪裝置(能使魚雷等擊中預定目標); *a* ˌ*~* ˈ*guidance system.* 追踪導向系統。

hom·iny /ˈhɒmɪnɪ ; ˈhɑmənɪ/ *n* [U] ground maize boiled in water or milk: 碎玉米粥 (用水或牛奶煮成者): ~ *grits,* biscuits made from ground maize. 用碾碎之玉米做成的餅乾。

homo /ˈhəʊməʊ ; ˈhomo/ *n* (Lat) man. (拉)人。ˌ~ ˈ**sapiens** /ˈsæpɪenz ; ˈsepɪˌɛnz/, modern man regarded as a species. 近代人類。

ho·moe·opathy (US = **ho·me·o-**) /ˌhəʊmɪˈɒpəθɪ ; ˌhomɪˈɑpəθɪ/ *n* [U] treatment of disease by drugs (usu in small doses) that, if given to a healthy person, would produce symptoms like those of the disease. 以毒攻毒療法;類似療法; 順勢醫療(予患者以微量藥物,此種藥物如施予健康之人,將產生與患者類似的症狀)。**ho·moeo·path** (US = **ho·meo-**) /ˈhəʊmɪəpæθ ; ˈhomɪəˌpæθ/ *n* person who practises ~. 使用類似療法之醫師。

ho·mo·gene·ous /ˌhɒməˈdʒiːnɪəs ; ˌhoməˈdʒinɪəs/ *adj* (formed of parts) of the same kind. 同類的;同性質的;由同類之部份組成的。 ⇨ heterogeneous. **ho·mo·gene·ity** /ˌhɒmədʒɪˈniːətɪ ; ˌhomədʒəˈniətɪ/ *n* quality of being ~. 同類;同質。**hom·ogen·ize** /həˈmɒdʒɪnaɪz ; hoˈmɑdʒəˌnaɪz/ *vt* [VP6A] make ~; (esp) make milk more uniform in consistency by breaking down and blending the particles of fat. 使性質相同;(尤指)(將脂肪粒攪碎並加以混合)使(牛奶)成分均勻。

homo·graph /ˈhɒməgrɑːf *US:* -græf ; ˈhɑməˌgræf/ *n* word spelt like another but with a different meaning or pronunciation, eg *bow*[1] /baʊ ; bo/; *bow*[2] /baʊ ; baʊ/. 同形異義字(例如 bow[1], bow[2])。

homo·nym /ˈhɒmənɪm ; ˈhɑməˌnɪm/ *n* homograph or homophone; word that is the same in form and sound as another but different in meaning, eg *see*[1]; *see*[2]. 同形異義字;同音異義字(例如 see[1], see[2])。

homo·phone /ˈhɒməfəʊn ; ˈhɑməˌfon/ *n* word pronounced like another but different in meaning, spelling or origin, eg *some/sum* /sʌm ; sʌm/; *knew/new* /njuː ; nju/. 同音字(同音但意義,拼法或字源不同的字,例如 some 和 sum, knew 和 new)。

homo·sex·ual /ˌhɒməˈsekʃʊəl ; ˌhoməˈsɛkʃʊəl/ *adj* sexually attracted to persons of one's own sex. 同性戀的。□ *n* ~ person. 同性戀者。**~·ity** /ˌhɒməsekʃʊˈælətɪ ; ˌhoməˌsɛkʃʊˈælətɪ/ *n* [U] the condition of being ~. 同性戀。

hone /həʊn ; hon/ *n* [C] stone used for sharpening tools (eg old-style razors). 磨刀石(例如用以磨舊式剃刀者)。□ *vt* [VP6A] sharpen on a ~. 在磨刀石上磨。

hon·est /ˈɒnɪst ; ˈɑnɪst/ *adj* **1** not telling lies; not cheating or stealing; straightforward: 誠實的;忠實的;坦白的: *an ~ man;* 誠實的人; *~ in business;* 在商業方面誠實; *give an ~ opinion.* 提出坦誠的意見。***to be quite ~ about it,*** phrase used before a statement that one wishes to be believed. 說老實話; 老實說 (用於希望別人相信之陳述的前面)。***earn an ~ penny,*** earn money fairly. 以正當手段賺錢。**2** showing, resulting from, an ~ mind: 顯示出心地誠實的;由誠意產生的: *an ~ face;* 一副誠實的面孔; *look ~;* 看來誠實; *an ~ piece of work,* done conscientiously; 一件盡責做成的工作; *~ weight,* not short weight. 够稱頭;斤兩不少。***make an ~ woman of sb,*** (dated use) marry her after seducing her. (過時用語)誘姦某女子後再娶她。**~·ly** *adv* in an ~ manner; really: 誠實地;實在地: *Honestly, that's all the money I have.* 說實在地,我所有的錢就是這些。**hon·esty** *n* [U] the quality of being ~; freedom from deceit, cheating, etc. 誠實;老實。

honey /ˈhʌnɪ ; ˈhʌnɪ/ *n* **1** [U] sweet, sticky yellowish substance made by bees from nectar; (fig) sweetness. 蜂蜜;(喩)甜蜜。ˈ**~·bee** *n* ordinary kind of bee that lives in hives. 蜜蜂。ˈ**~·dew** *n* [U] **(a)** sweet, sticky substance found on the leaves and stems of plants in hot weather. 樹蜜(植物的葉和莖在熱天所分泌的甜而黏的東西)。**(b)** tobacco sweetened with molasses. 加有糖蜜的煙草。**~·suckle** /ˈhʌnɪsʌkl ; ˈhʌnɪˌsʌkl/ *n* [U] climbing shrub with sweet-smelling tube-shaped yellow or reddish flowers. 忍冬; 金銀花(攀緣灌木,生有黃色或淡紅色的管狀有香味的花)。**2** [C] (*pl* ~s) (colloq) sweetheart; darling: (俗)愛人;親愛的人: *Come here, my ~s,* eg a mother to her children. 到這兒來,親愛的(例如母親召喚孩子們)。**~ed** /ˈhʌnɪd ; ˈhʌnɪd/ *adj* sweet as ~: 甜如蜜的: *~ed words.* 甜言蜜語。

honey·comb /ˈhʌnɪkəʊm ; ˈhʌnɪˌkom/ *n* [C, U] wax structure of six-sided cells made by bees for honey and eggs; (piece of) ornamental work in a ~ pattern. 蜂房; 蜂巢; 蜂巢圖案裝飾物。□ *vt* [VP6A] fill with holes, tunnels, etc: 使有許多孔洞: *The rock at Gibraltar is ~ed with galleries.* 直布羅陀的岩石有很多孔道。

honeycomb

honey·moon /ˈhʌnɪmuːn ; ˈhʌnɪˌmun/ *n* holiday taken by a newly married couple; (fig) period of harmony at the start of an undertaking, etc. 蜜月;(喩)事業等開始時的和諧期間。□ *vi* spend a ~: 度蜜月: *They will ~ in Paris.* 他們將在巴黎度蜜月。

honk /hɒŋk ; hɔŋk/ *n* cry of the wild goose; sound made by (the old style of) motor horn. 野鵝叫聲;(舊式之)汽車喇叭聲。□ *vi* make a ~. (野鵝)叫;(舊式汽車喇叭)響。

hon·or·ar·ium /ˌɒnəˈreərɪəm ; ˌɑnəˈrɛrɪəm/ *n* fee offered (but not claimed) for professional services. 酬勞金;謝禮。

hon·or·ary /ˈɒnərərɪ *US:* ˈɒnərerɪ ; ˈɑnəˌrɛrɪ/ *adj* **1** (shortened in writing to 縮寫爲 **Hon**) (of a position) unpaid: (指職位) 無薪給的; 無報酬的; 義務的:

the ~ secretary. 做事而不支薪的秘書；義務秘書。 **2** (of a degree, rank) conferred as an honour, without the usual requirements: (指學位,階級)作爲一種榮譽而授與的;名譽的: *an ~ degree / doctorate;* 名譽學位(博士學位); holding an ~ title or position: 擁有名譽頭銜或職位的: *an ~ vice-president.* 名譽副會長。

ho·nor·ific /ˌɒnəˈrɪfɪk ; ˌɑnəˈrɪfɪk/ *n, adj* (expression) implying respect: 尊敬的言語;含有敬意的: *the ~s so frequently used in oriental languages.* 東方語言中十分常用的敬語。

hon·our[1] (US = **honor**) /ˈɒnə(r) ; ˈɑnə/ *n* **1** [U] great respect; high public regard: 尊敬; 大衆的敬重: *win ~ in war;* 立戰功; *a ceremony in ~ of those killed in battle;* 紀念陣亡將士的儀式; *show ~ to one's parents.* 尊敬父母。***do sb ~; do ~ to sb,*** show courtesy to, esteem of: 向某人致敬: *Twenty heads of state attended the Queen's coronation to do her ~.* 二十位國家元首參加女王加冕典禮以向她致敬。ˌ**maid of** ˈ**~**, lady in attendance upon a queen, princess, etc. 宮女。ˌ**guard of** ˈ**~**, number of soldiers chosen to escort or welcome a distinguished person as a mark of respect. 儀(仗)隊。 **2** [U] good personal character; reputation for good behaviour, loyalty, truthfulness, etc. 人格;名譽;榮譽;信譽。***on one's ~,*** on one's reputation for telling the truth. 以人格擔保。***an affair of ~,*** (hist) duel fought to settle a question of ~. (史)決鬥。***be / feel in ~ bound to do sth,*** required to do it as a moral duty, but not by law. 道義上(覺得)應做某事。***one's word of ~,*** guarantee to fulfil an obligation, keep a promise, etc. 名譽擔保。***pay / incur a debt of ~,*** one that need not be paid legally, but which one's good name requires one to pay. 償還(欠負)(法律上不能追索的)信用借款。***put sb on his ~,*** trust him, his ~ being lost if he fails to do what is required, breaks a promise, etc. 使某人以人格擔保。 **3** (in polite formulas) (用於客套語中) giving of ~. 榮幸。***do sb the ~ of; have the ~ of / to:*** 給某人…之榮幸; 有…之榮幸: *May I have the ~ of your company at dinner?* 敬備菲酌,恭請光臨。*Will you do me the ~ of dining with me this evening?* 今晚備有便餐,敬請賞光。(formal style) (正式文體) *I have the ~ to inform you that....* 敬啓者…。 **4 Your / His H~,** title of respect used to / of some judges. 閣下(對某些法官之尊稱)。 **5 an ~,** person or thing bringing credit: 帶來光榮的人或物: *He is an ~ to his school / family.* 他是他的學校(家庭)引以爲榮的人。 **6** (*pl*) marks of respect, distinction, etc; titles; civilities. (複)榮譽的標識; 官銜; 爵位; 禮儀。**birthday ~s,** (in GB) list of titles, decorations, etc conferred by the Sovereign on her or his birthday. (在英國)國君誕辰授予的勳爵,勳章等。**New Year H~s,** similar list awarded on 1 Jan. 元旦所授予的勳爵,勳章等。**full military ~s,** ceremonies, marks of respect, paid by soldiers at the burial of a soldier, to distinguished visitors, eg Presidents. 軍葬禮;(向總統等貴賓致敬之)軍禮。***do the ~s,*** (colloq) (of the table, house, etc) act as host(ess), guide, etc and do what politeness requires; perform some small ceremony, eg propose a toast. (俗)(席間、房屋等內)盡主人、嚮導等之誼;執行某種小禮儀(例如提議舉杯祝頌健康)。 **7** (*pl*) (in universities) (place in) top division of marks in degree examinations; special distinction for extra proficiency. (複)(大學)學位考試的優等;特優之榮譽。 **~s degree,** one requiring some specialization. 優等學位(需要專修某科目而獲得者)。⇨ general, pass[1](1). **8** (in card games, whist and bridge) card of highest value, eg 10, knave, queen, king, ace of trumps. (惠斯特及橋牌等牌戲中)價值最高的牌(王牌之10, J, Q, K, A)。

hon·our[2] (US = **honor**) /ˈɒnə(r) ; ˈɑnə/ *vt* [VP6A] **1** respect highly, feel honour for; confer honour on: 尊敬;以…爲榮; 給與榮譽: *Fear God and ~ the Queen.* 敬畏上帝,尊敬女王。*I feel highly ~ed by the kind things you say about me.* 你恭維我的話使我感到十分榮幸。*Will you ~ me with a visit?* 如蒙造訪,十分榮幸。 **2** (comm) accept and pay when due: (商)承認並如期支付;承兌: *~ a bill / cheque / draft, etc;* 承兌票據(支票,匯票等); *~ one's signature,* agree that one has signed a bill, note, etc and pay the money. 承認自己的簽名並付款。

hon·our·able (US = **hon·or-**) /ˈɒnərəbl ; ˈɑnərəbḷ/ *adj* **1** possessing or showing the principles of honour; consistent with honour (1, 2): 可敬的;高尙的;光明正大的;光榮的: *~ conduct;* 高尙的行爲; *conclude an ~ peace;* 締結光榮的和約; *~ burial.* 光榮的葬禮。 **2 H~** (abbr 略作 **Hon**) title given eg to judges, to the children of peers below the rank of Marquis, and (during debates) to members of the House of Commons: 對法官、低於侯爵的貴族子弟,以及(辯論時)對下議院議員之尊稱: *my H~ friend the member for Chester.* 吾友赤斯特城議員。**Right H~,** (abbr 略作 **Rt Hon**) title given eg to cabinet ministers, privy councillors and peers below the rank of Marquis. 對閣員、樞密顧問官、以及低於侯爵的貴族之尊稱。**hon·our·ably** /-əblɪ ; -əblɪ/ *adv*

hooch /huːtʃ ; hutʃ/ *n* [U] (US sl) alcoholic liquor. (美俚)烈酒。

hood[1] /hʊd ; hʊd/ *n* **1** bag-like covering for the head and neck, often fastened to a cloak so that it can hang down at the back when not in use; (in universities) fold of cloth worn over an academic gown showing by its colour the degree gained by the wearer and the university by which it was conferred. 兜帽;頭巾(呈口袋狀,常連在外衣上,不用時可垂在背後);(大學)垂布(加在學位服外,以其顏色表示學位及授予學校)。 **2** anything like a ~ in shape or use; folding roof over a carriage (for protection against rain or sun), or over an open motor-car; (US) hinged cover over the engine of a motor-car (GB 英 = *bonnet*). 任何形狀或作用似兜帽或頭巾之物;馬車或敞篷汽車上可折合的車篷;(美)汽車引擎蓋(覆蓋引擎,裝有鉸鏈之蓋)。 ⇨ the illus at motor. 參看 motor 之插圖。□ *vt* (chiefly in *pp*) cover with, or as with, a ~: (主要用過去分詞)覆以頭巾;加以車篷;覆蓋: *a ~ed falcon.* 戴着頭罩的鷹。

hood[2] /hʊd ; hʊd/ *n* (US sl) (abbr of) hoodlum. (美俚) hoodlum 之略。

hood·lum /ˈhuːdləm ; ˈhudləm/ *n* (sl) gangster; dangerous criminal. (俚)盜匪;歹徒;暴徒。

hoo·doo /ˈhuːduː ; ˈhudu/ *n* (chiefly US) (person or thing regarded as bringing) bad luck. (主美)惡運;帶來惡運的人或物;不祥之人或物。□ *vt* render unlucky. 使不幸;使倒霉。

hood·wink /ˈhʊdwɪŋk ; ˈhʊdˌwɪŋk/ *vt* [VP6A, 14] ~ ***sb (into),*** deceive; trick; mislead. 欺騙;欺瞞;矇騙。

hooey /ˈhuːɪ ; ˈhuɪ/ *n* [U] (sl) humbug; nonsense. (俚)騙人的鬼話;廢話;胡說八道。

hoof /huːf ; hʊf/ *n* (*pl* ~s or hooves /huːvz ; hʊvz/) horny part of the foot of a horse, ox or deer: (馬、牛或鹿之)蹄: *buy cattle on the ~,* alive. 買活牛。⇨ the illus at domestic. 參看 domestic 之插圖。

hook[1] /hʊk ; hʊk/ *n* **1** curved or bent piece of metal or other material, for catching hold of sth, or for hanging sth on: 鈎: *a* ˈ*fish-~;* 釣魚鈎; *a* ˈ*crochet-~;* 鈎針; *a* ˈ*clothes-~;* 掛衣鈎; *~s and eyes,* for fastening a dress. 領鈎和鈎釦。***~, line and sinker,*** (from fishing) (fig) entirely; completely. (出自釣魚)(喻)整個地;完全地。***be on the ~,*** (colloq) in a position where one has problems, difficult or distressing decisions to make. (俗)處於困難或難以作決定的境地。***be / get off the ~,*** no longer in such a position. 脫離困境。***sling one's ~,*** ⇨ sling[1](1). ˈ**~-nosed** *adj* having a nose shaped like a ~ (or like the nose of an eagle). 鈎鼻的;鷹鈎鼻的。ˈ**~·worm** *n* worm that infests the intestines of men and animals, the male of which has ~-like spines. 鈎蟲;十二指腸蟲。 **2** curved tool for cutting (grain, etc) or for chopping (branches, etc): 鐮刀;彎刀: *a 'reaping-~;* (收割用的)鐮刀; *a 'bill-~.* 砍樹枝用的彎刀。 ***by ~ or by crook,*** by one means or another. 用種種方法。 **3** (cricket, golf) kind of stroke; (boxing) short blow with the elbow bent: (板球,高爾夫球)一種擊法;左曲球;(拳擊)鈎擊: *a left ~.* 左鈎拳。

hook[2] /hʊk ; hʊk/ *vt, vi* **1** [VP6A, 15A, B, 2C] fasten, be fastened, catch, with a ~ or ~s: 用鈎鈎住;被鈎鈎住: *a dress that ~s/is ~ed at the back;* 背後用鈎扣住的女服; *~ something on/up;* 將某物掛於鈎上(鈎住某物); *~ a fish;* 用鈎釣魚; *~ a husband,* (fig) catch a man and marry him. (喩)釣個丈夫;釣個金龜婿。 **2** make into the form of a ~: 使成鈎形: *~ one's finger.* 彎曲手指。 **3** *~ it,* (sl) run away. (俚)逃跑。 **4** '~-up *n* network of broadcasting stations connected to transmit the same programme: 廣播電臺聯播網: *speak over an international ~-up.* 經聯播網向國外廣播。 **~ed** *adj* **1** ~-shaped: 鈎形的: *a ~ed nose;* 鷹鈎鼻; furnished with hooks. 有鈎的。 **2** ***~ed (on),*** (sl) addicted to; completely committed to: (俚)上癮;耽溺於;着迷於;完全受擺佈: *be/get ~ed on heroin.* 吸海洛英成癮。 *My aunt is ~ed on package holidays in Spain.* 我的姑母着迷於旅行社包辦的西班牙度假。

hookah /'hʊkə ; 'hʊkə/ *n* tobacco pipe (also called 亦稱作 a *hubble-bubble*) with a long flexible tube through which smoke is drawn through water in a vase and so cooled. 水煙袋。

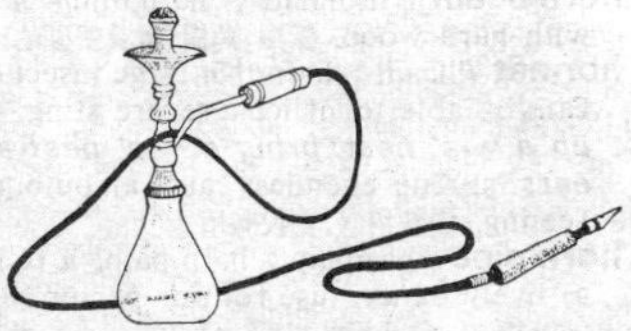

a hookah

hooky /'hʊkɪ ; 'hʊkɪ/ *n* ***play ~,*** (US sl) play truant. (美俚)逃學。

hoo·li·gan /'hu:lɪgən ; 'hulɪgən/ *n* one of a gang of disorderly persons making disturbances in the streets or other public places. 流氓;阿飛;不良少年。 **~·ism** /-ɪzəm ; -,ɪzəm/ *n*

hoop[1] /hu:p ; hʊp/ *n* **1** circular band of wood, metal etc. 箍;鐵環。 **2** small iron arch fixed in the ground, through which balls are hit in the game of croquet. 槌球戲中的弓形鐵門。 **3** large ring with paper stretched over it through which circus riders and animals jump. 馬戲團用的大鐵環(用紙覆蓋,由騎師或動物自中間跳過)。 ***put sb/go through the ~(s),*** (fig) undergo an ordeal. (喩)(使某人)受磨鍊。 □ *vt* bind (a cask, etc) with ~s. 加箍於(桶等)。

hoop[2] /hu:p ; hʊp/ *vt* = whoop.

hoop-la /'hu:p lɑ: ; 'hup,lɑ/ *n* [U] game in which rings are thrown at small objects which are won if the rings encircle them. 投環套物遊戲(如套中,則得該物)。

hoo·ray /hu:'reɪ ; hu're/ *int* = hurrah.

hoot /hu:t ; hut/ *n* **1** cry of an owl. 梟叫聲。 **2** sound made by a motor-car horn, steam-whistle, fog-horn, etc. 汽車喇叭,汽笛,霧笛等發出的聲音。 **3** shout or cry expressing disapproval or scorn. 表示不滿或輕蔑的叫囂。 ***not care a ~/two ~s,*** (sl) not care at all. (俚)毫不在乎。 □ *vi, vt* **1** [VP2A, C] make a ~ or ~s: 梟叫;(汽車喇叭,汽笛等)鳴叫;(表示不滿或輕蔑而)叫囂: *an owl ~ing in the garden.* 在花園裏叫的貓頭鷹。 *The crowd ~ed and jeered at the speaker.* 群衆向那演說者叫囂嘲弄。 **2** [VP6A, 15A, B] make ~s at, drive away by doing this: 向…叫囂;以叫囂驅逐: *~ an actor;* 向一演員叫囂; *~ a speaker down/off/away.* 藉叫囂把演說者轟下台(轟走)。 **~er** *n* siren or steam-whistle, esp as a signal for work to start or stop; similar device in a motor-vehicle to attract attention from other motorists, pedestrians, etc. 汽笛(尤指表示上下班者);警笛;汽車喇叭。

Hoover /'hu:və(r) ; 'huvə/ *n* (P) kind of vacuum cleaner. (商標)一種眞空吸塵器;胡佛眞空吸塵器。□ *vt* [VP6A] (colloq) clean (carpets, etc) with a vacuum cleaner. (俗)用眞空吸塵器清潔(地毯等)。

hooves /hu:vz ; hʊvz/ *pl* of hoof.

hop[1] /hɒp ; hɑp/ *n* [C] tall climbing plant with flowers growing in clusters; (*pl*) ripe cones (seed-vessels) of this plant, dried and used for giving a bitter flavour to beer, etc. 蛇麻草(一種高的攀緣植物,開花成叢);(複)蛇麻子(此種植物所結之毬果,乾後用以使啤酒等帶苦味)。 **'hop-garden/-field** *nn* field for the cultivation of hops. 蛇麻草園。 **'hop·pole** *n* tall pole to support wires on which hop plant is trained. 支撐蛇麻草蔓的桿子。 **'hop-picker, hopper** *nn* worker, machine, employed to pick hops. 摘蛇麻子的人或機器。□ *vi* (-pp-) gather hops: 摘蛇麻子: *go hopping in Kent.* 去肯特採蛇麻子。

hop[2] /hɒp ; hɑp/ *vi, vt* (-pp-) **1** [VP2A, C] (of persons) jump on one foot; (of other living creatures, eg birds, frogs, grasshoppers) jump with both or all feet together: (指人)單足跳躍;(指鳥,青蛙,蚱蜢等)雙足或齊足跳躍: *Sparrows were hopping about on the lawn.* 麻雀在草地上跳來跳去。 *He had hurt his left foot and had to hop along.* 他的左脚受傷,不得不單足跳行。 ***hop off; hop it,*** (sl) go away. (俚)走開。 ***hopping mad,*** (colloq) very angry. (俗)極怒;氣得跳起來。 **2** [VP6A] cross (a ditch, etc) by hopping. 躍過(溝等)。□ *n* **1** the action of hopping. (單足或齊足)跳躍。 ***on the hop,*** active, restless. 活動的;不安靜的。 ***catch sb on the hop,*** when he is unprepared, off guard. 乘某人疏忽或不注意時抓住他。 ***keep sb on the hop,*** keep him active, alert. 使某人活躍,機敏。 **2** short jump. 短跳。 ***hop, skip/step and jump,*** athletic exercise consisting of these three movements one after the other. (運動)三級跳遠。 **3** (colloq) informal party and dance, with popular music. (俗)放流行音樂之非正式舞會。 **4** (flying) one stage in a long-distance flight: (飛行)長途飛行中的一段: *from Berlin to Tokyo in three hops.* 分三段從柏林飛行至東京。 **hop·scotch** /'hɒpskɒtʃ ; 'hɑp,skɑtʃ/ *n* [U] children's game of throwing a stone into numbered squares, etc marked on the ground, and hopping from square to square to collect it. 跳房子(兒童遊戲)。

hope[1] /həʊp ; hop/ *n* **1** [C, U] feeling of expectation and desire; feeling of trust and confidence: 希望;信心: *There is not much ~ that they are/of their being still alive.* 他們仍然活著的希望不大。 ***hold out some/no/little/not much ~ (of sth),*** give some, etc encouragement or expectation: (對某事)抱一些希望(不抱希望,抱很少希望,不大抱希望): *The doctors could hold out no ~ of recovery.* 醫生們不抱痊癒的希望。 ***be past/beyond ~; not have a ~,*** be without possibility of success, recovery, etc. (成功,痊癒等)無望。 ***in the ~ of doing sth,*** hoping to do it: 希望做某事: *I called in the ~ of finding her at home.* 我希望她會在家而去看她。 ***live in ~(s) (of sth),*** have ~(s) (of): 對某事物抱着希望: *I haven't much money now but live in ~.* 我現在錢不多,但是抱着希望。 *We live in ~s of better times.* 我們希望情況會好轉。 ***raise sb's ~s,*** give him encouragement of better fortune, etc: 給予某人希望: *Don't raise his ~s too much.* 不要給他太多希望。 **2** [C] person, thing, circumstance, etc on which ~ is based: 屬望的人,事情,情況等: *He was the ~ of the school.* 他是全校所屬望的人。 *You are my last ~; if you can't help, I'm ruined.* 你是我最後的指望,如果你不能幫助我,我就完了。 **'~ chest** *n* (US) chest or drawer used by a young woman for storing linen, articles for household use, etc in anticipation of marriage (GB 英 = *bottom drawer*). (美)嫁妝箱(未出嫁少女收藏家庭用品,牀單等,以備結婚使用之箱或抽斗)。

hope² /həʊp; hop/ *vt, vi* [VP7A, 9, 2A, 3A] expect and desire: 希望;期望: *We ~ to see you soon.* 我們希望不久能見到你。*I ~ you haven't hurt yourself.* 我希望你沒有受傷。*'Will it be fine tomorrow?'—'I ~ so.'* '明天是晴天嗎?'—'我希望是。' *'Will it rain tomorrow?'—'I ~ not.'* '明天會下雨嗎?'—'我希望不會下。' *Let us ~ for the best.* 我們抱樂觀態度(往最好處想)吧。*We've had no news from him but we're still hoping.* 我們沒有他的消息,但仍舊希望能有他的消息。**~ against ~,** ~ even though there is only a mere possibility. 抱一線希望。

hope·ful /'həʊpfl; 'hopfəl/ *adj* **1** having hope: 抱有希望的: *be/feel ~ about the future;* 對前途感到樂觀; *feel ~ of success/that he will succeed.* 對成功(他的成功)抱着希望。**2** giving hope; promising: 有希望的;有前途的: *The future does not seem very ~.* 前途似不太樂觀。*He seems quite a ~ pupil,* likely to do well. 他似乎是個相當有前途的學生。**3** (as *n*) (作名詞) **(young) ~,** boy or girl who seems likely to succeed. 有希望的青年。**~ly** /-fəlɪ; -fəlɪ/ *adv* **1** in a ~ way. 抱有希望地。**2** = 'I hope' or 'it is to be hoped'. 希望;可望。**~·ness** *n*

hope·less /'həʊplɪs; 'hoplɪs/ *adj* **1** feeling no hope; giving or promising no hope: 不抱希望的; 絕望的; 無希望的: *give way to ~ grief;* 陷入絕望的悲哀中; *a ~ case;* 無希望的情況; *a ~ illness.* 絕症。**2** incurable: 不可救藥的: *a ~ idiot.* 不可救藥的呆子。**~·ly** *adv* **~·ness** *n*

hopped-up /hɒpt 'ʌp; hɑpt 'ʌp/ *adj* (US sl) souped up, supercharged: (美俚)增加過馬力的: *a ~ engine.* 增加過馬力的引擎。

hop·per¹ /'hɒpə(r); 'hɑpɚ/ *n* hop-picker. 採蛇麻子的人或機器。⇨ hop¹.

hop·per² /'hɒpə(r); 'hɑpɚ/ *n* **1** structure like an inverted cone or pyramid through which grain passes to a mill, coal or coke to a furnace, etc; any similar contrivance for feeding materials into a machine, etc. (碾磨機,煤爐等的) 漏斗; 將原料注入機器等的任何漏斗狀裝置;給料漏斗。**2** any hopping insect, eg a flea, a young locust; (in Australia) kangaroo. 任何跳躍的昆蟲(例如跳蚤,小蝗蟲);(澳洲)袋鼠。

horde /hɔːd; hord/ *n* **1** wandering tribe (of nomads): 游牧部落: *a Gypsy ~;* 吉卜賽人部落; *~s of Tartars.* 韃靼人各部落。**2** (usu contemptuous) crowd; great number: (通常為輕蔑語)群衆;大群: *~s of people.* 大群的人。**3** multitude: 大批;衆多: *a ~ of locusts.* 大批蝗蟲。

hor·izon /hə'raɪzn; hə'raɪzn̩/ *n* **1** **the ~,** line at which the earth or sea and sky seem to meet: 地平線;海平線: *The sun sank below the ~.* 太陽沉落在地平線以下了。**2** (fig) limit of one's knowledge, experience, thinking, etc. (喻)一個人的知識,經驗,思想等的限度或範圍;眼界;見識。**hori·zon·tal** /ˌhɒrɪ'zɒntl *US:* ˌhɔːr-; ˌhɔrə'zɑntl̩/ *adj* parallel to the ~; flat or level: 與地平線平行的;平的;水平的: *a ~tal line;* 水平線; *~tal bars,* above the floor for gymnastic exercises. 單槓。⇨ vertical. □ *n* ~tal line, bar, etc. 水平線,單槓等。**~·tally** /-təlɪ; -tl̩ɪ/ *adv*

hor·mone /'hɔːməʊn; 'hɔrmon/ *n* (kinds of) internal secretion that passes into the blood and stimulates the bodily organs; medical preparation made from a secretion of this kind. 荷爾蒙(人體之內分泌,進入血液可刺激器官功能);荷爾蒙製劑。

horn /hɔːn; hɔrn/ *n* **1** [C] one of the hard, pointed, usu curved, outgrowths on the heads of cattle, deer, and some other animals. (牛,鹿等動物的)角。⇨ the illus at domestic, large. 參看 domestic, large 之插圖。⇨ bull¹(1). **2** [U] substance of these outgrowths: 角質: *a knife with a handle of ~/a ~ handle;* 角柄小刀; *a ~ spoon.* 角質匙。**'~-rimmed** *adj* (of spectacles) with the frame made of material that resembles ~. (指眼鏡)鏡框由似角質材料製成的。**3** article made from this substance (or a modern substitute): 角製品;似角質製品: *a 'shoe-~.* (用角質等製成的)鞋拔。**a ~ of plenty,** = cornucopia. **4** (music) wind instrument: (音樂)管樂器;吹奏樂器;號角;喇叭: *a 'hunting ~.* 獵號。**(French) ~,** brass orchestral instrument. 法國號;圓喇叭。⇨ the illus at brass. 參看 brass 之插圖。**English ~,** (also, 亦作, esp GB 尤英 **cor anglais** /ˌkɔːr'ɒŋgleɪ *US:* ɒŋ'gleɪ; ˌkɔr ɑŋ'gle/) woodwind instrument like, but larger than, an oboe, and lower in pitch. 英國管(一種雙簧木管樂器)。**5** device for making warning sounds: 示警裝置: *a 'fog-~;* 霧笛; *a 'motor-~.* 汽車喇叭。**6** ~like part, eg on the head of a snail. 角狀部份(例如蝸牛的觸角)。**'~·bill** *n* bird with a ~like growth on its beak. 犀鳥。***draw in one's ~s,*** (fig) draw back, show less zeal for an undertaking. (喻)退縮;對一事不再熱心。**7** either of the ends of the crescent moon. 新月的鈎尖。⇨ the illus at phase. 參看 phase 之插圖。***on the ~s of a dilemma,*** faced with a choice between things that are equally undesirable, etc. 進退維谷。□ *vi* (sl, only in) (俚,僅用於) **~ in (on),** intrude; join in without being invited. 闖入;侵入;打岔;干涉。**~ed** *adj* having ~s(1): 有角的: *~ed cattle;* 有角的牛; *the ~ed owl,* with tufts like ~s. 鵰鴞(猫頭鷹,其頭上毛簇似角)。**~·less** *adj* without ~s: 無角的: *~less cattle.* 無角的牛。**'~·like** *adj* **~y** *adj* (-ier, -iest) made of ~; hard like ~: 角製的;堅硬似角的: *hands ~y from hard work.* 由於辛苦工作而粗硬的手。

horn·beam /'hɔːnbiːm; 'hɔrnˌbim/ *n* small tree with hard wood. 榛類;角樹(木質堅硬的小樹)。

hor·net /'hɔːnɪt; 'hɔrnɪt/ *n* large insect of the wasp family, able to inflict a severe sting. 大黃蜂。***stir up a '~s' nest; bring a '~s' nest about one's ears,*** stir up enemies; cause an outburst of angry feeling. 樹敵招怨;自找麻煩。

horn·pipe /'hɔːnpaɪp; 'hɔrnˌpaɪp/ *n* [C] (music for a) lively dance (usu for one person, esp a sailor). 號管舞 (一種活潑的舞蹈,通常由一人,尤其是一水手來跳);號管舞曲。

hor·ol·ogy /hɒ'rɒlədʒɪ; hə'rɑlədʒɪ/ *n* [U] art of designing and constructing clocks. 鐘錶製造術。

horo·scope /'hɒrəskəʊp *US:* 'hɔːr-; 'hɔrəˌskop/ *n* diagram of, observation of, positions of planets at a certain time, eg a person's birth, for the purpose of forecasting future events; such a forecast. (算命用的)天宮圖;占星;占星術;依天宮圖算命。

hor·rible /'hɒrəbl *US:* 'hɔːr-; 'hɔrəbl̩/ *adj* **1** exciting horror: 可怕的; 令人恐怖的: *~ cruelty/crimes.* 可怕的殘忍(罪行)。**2** (colloq) unpleasant: (俗)令人不愉快的: *~ weather.* 討厭的天氣。**hor·ribly** /-əblɪ; -əblɪ/ *adv*

hor·rid /'hɒrɪd *US:* 'hɔːrɪd; 'hɔrɪd/ *adj* **1** frightful; terrible. 可怕的;可怖的。**2** (colloq) disagreeable: (俗)討厭的: *~ weather.* 討厭的天氣。**~·ly** *adv* **~·ness** *n*

hor·rific /hə'rɪfɪk; hɔ'rɪfɪk/ *adj* (colloq) horrifying. (俗)可怕的。

hor·rify /'hɒrɪfaɪ *US:* 'hɔːr-; 'hɔrəˌfaɪ/ *vt* (*pt, pp* -fied) [VP6A] fill with horror; shock: 使恐怖;使驚駭: *We were horrified by what we saw.* 我們看到那情景感到恐怖。*Don't let the children see such ~ing scenes.* 不要讓孩子們看到如此駭人的景象。

hor·ror /'hɒrə(r) *US:* 'hɔːr-; 'hɔrɚ/ *n* [C, U] (sth that causes a) feeling of extreme fear or dislike: 恐怖;極端厭惡;令人恐怖或極端厭惡的事物: *She recoiled in ~ from the snake.* 她看見那條蛇而嚇得退縮。*She expressed her ~ of cruelty.* 她表示她對殘忍的憎惡。*To her ~ she saw her husband knocked down by a bus.* 她看見她丈夫被公共汽車撞倒時嚇壞了。*We have all read about the ~s of modern warfare.* 我們都曾讀到有關現代戰爭的慘狀。**chamber of '~s,** collection of objects, representations, etc, connected with crime, cruelty, etc. 恐怖之室

(與犯罪,殘忍有關之一批物件、模型等)。 '~ **fiction／comics／films,** in which the subject matter and treatment are intended to arouse feelings of ~. 恐怖小說 (連環圖畫，影片)。 '**~-struck／-stricken** *adj* overcome with ~. 驚恐的;受驚嚇的。

hors de com·bat /ˌɔ: də 'kɒmbɑ:;'ɔrdə'kɑmbɑ/ *pred adj* (F) unable to take further part in fighting because wounded or disabled. (法)因受傷或殘廢而失去戰鬥力的。

hors d'oeuvres /ˌɔ: 'dɜ:vrə *US:* 'dɜ:v ; ɔr'dœvrə/ *n pl* dishes of food served at the beginning of a meal as a relish. 主菜前所上的開胃小菜。

horse /hɔ:s ; hɔrs/ *n* **1** four-legged solid-hoofed animal with flowing mane and tail, used from early times to carry loads, for riding, etc. 馬。⇨ the illus at domestic. 參看 domestic 之挿圖。⇨ colt¹, filly, foal, mare, stallion. ***a dark ~,*** person whose chances of success are not yet known, or have been overlooked. 黑馬; 獲勝之成算尙未得知之人;爆出冷門的獲勝者。 ***a ~ of another colour,*** quite a different matter. 完全是另一回事。 ***back the wrong ~,*** support the loser in a contest. 支持競爭中的失敗者。 ***be／get on one's high ~,*** insist on being treated with proper respect. 擺架子;趾高氣揚;倨傲作態;盛氣凌人。 ***eat／work like a ~,*** eat a lot／work hard. 大吃(努力工作)。 ***flog a dead ~,*** ⇨ flog. ***hold one's ~s,*** hesitate; show restraint. 猶豫;自制。 ***look a gift ~ in the mouth,*** accept sth ungratefully esp by examining it critically for faults (because a ~'s teeth indicate its age). 接受禮物不知感激反而挑剔、批評(因馬齒可表示其年齡)。 ***put the cart before the ~,*** ⇨ cart. ***(straight) from the ~'s mouth,*** (of tips, advice, information) from a first-hand source. (指祕密消息,勸告,情報) 直接得來的。 **2** (collective *sing*) cavalry; (集合單數)騎兵: *~ and foot,* cavalry and infantry; 騎兵和步兵; *light ~,* lightly armed mounted soldiers; 輕騎兵; *~ artillery,* light artillery with mounted gunners; 騎砲兵; *the 'H~ Guards,* ⇨ guard¹(6). **3** framework, often with legs, on which sth is supported: 支架(常帶有腿的): *a 'clothes-~,* on which clothes may be dried in front of a fire; 烘衣架; *a 'vaulting-~,* block used in a gymnasium for vaulting over. (體操用的)木馬。 **4** (compounds) (複合字) '**~·back** *n* (only in) (僅用於) ***on ~back,*** on a ~. 在馬上;騎着馬。'**~·box** *n* closed vehicle for taking a ~ by rail, or towing behind a car, etc. (鐵路上或拖於汽車後面之)運馬用的有篷貨車。ˌ**~-'chestnut** *n* large tree with spreading branches and clusters of white or pink blossom; shiny reddish-brown nut of this tree. 七葉樹(一種樹枝展開,開白色或粉紅色花簇的大樹); 七葉樹之明亮的紅褐色堅果。'**~·flesh** *n* [U] **(a)** flesh of ~s as food. 馬肉(用作食物)。 **(b)** ~s collectively: 馬(集合稱): *He's a good judge of ~flesh.* 他是個鑑別馬匹的行家。 '**~·fly** *n* (*pl* -flies) large insect troublesome to ~s and cattle. 虻;馬蠅。'**~·hair** *n* [U] hair from the mane or tail of ~s, formerly used for stuffing sofas, etc. 馬鬃;馬尾(昔時用做沙發塡塞料等)。'**~-laugh** *n* loud, coarse laugh. 呵呵大笑。'**~·man** /-mən ; -mən/ *n* (*pl* -men) rider on ~back, esp one who is skilled. 騎馬者(尤指善騎者)。'**~·man·ship** /-ʃɪp ; -ˌʃɪp/ *n* [U] art of riding, skill in riding, on ~back. 馬術。'**~-meat** *n* = ~flesh. '**~-play** *n* [U] rough, noisy fun or play. 喧鬧的娛樂。'**~-pond** *n* pond for watering and washing ~s. 飲馬池;洗馬池。'**~·power** *n* [U] (shortened to 略作 **hp**) unit for measuring the power of an engine, etc (550 foot-pounds per second). 馬力(測量引擎等動力的單位,一匹馬力爲每秒 550 呎磅)。'**~·race** *n* race between ~s with riders. 賽馬。'**~·racing** *n* [U]. '**~-radish** *n* [U] (plant with a) hot-tasting root which is ground or scraped to make a sauce (eaten with beef). 蔊菜;蔊菜根(有辣味,磨碎或刮碎可製成一種調味品,與牛肉共食。) '**~-sense** *n* ordinary wisdom. 常識。'**~-shoe** /'hɔ:ʃʃu: ; 'hɔrʃˌʃu/ *n* U-shaped metal shoe for a ~; sth of this shape, eg ***a ~-shoe table.*** 馬蹄鐵;馬掌;馬蹄鐵形物(例如馬蹄形桌)。'**~·whip** *n, vt* (-pp-) (thrash with a) whip for ~s. 馬鞭;用馬鞭鞭打。'**~·woman** *n* woman who rides on ~back. 女乘馬者;女騎師。

horsy /'hɔ:sɪ ; 'hɔrsɪ/ *adj* concerned with, fond of, horses or horse-racing; showing by dress, conversation, manners, etc familiarity with horses, horse-racing, grooms, jockeys, etc. 關於馬的;關於賽馬的;愛馬的; 愛賽馬的; 衣着、談吐、態度等表現出熟悉馬、賽馬、馬夫、賽馬騎師等的。

hor·ta·tive /'hɔ:tətɪv;'hɔrtətɪv/ *adj* (formal) exhorting; serving to encourage. (正式用語)勸告的;鼓勵的。

hor·ti·cul·ture /'hɔ:tɪkʌltʃə(r) ; 'hɔrtɪˌkʌltʃɚ/ *n* [U] (art of) growing flowers, fruit and vegetables. 園藝; 園藝學。 **hor·ti·cul·tural** /ˌhɔ:tɪ'kʌltʃərəl ; ˌhɔrtɪ'kʌltʃərəl/ *adj* of ~: 園藝的;園藝學的: *a horticultural show／society.* 園藝展覽 (協會)。 **hor·ti·cul·tur·ist** /ˌhɔ:tɪ'kʌltʃərɪst ; ˌhɔrtɪ'kʌltʃərɪst/ *n* person who practises ~. 園藝家;園藝學家。

ho·sanna /həʊ'zænə ; ho'zænə/ *n, int* cry of praise and adoration (to God). 和散那(讚美上帝之語)。

hose¹ /həʊz ; hoz/ *n* [C, U] (length of) flexible tubing (of rubber, canvas or plastic) for directing water on to fires, watering gardens, cleaning streets, etc: 軟管 (橡皮、帆布或塑膠製成,用以輸水救火、澆花、清除街道等);一段軟管: *60 feet of plastic ~;* 六十呎塑膠管; *plenty of fire ~s in the building.* 建築物中的許多消防水管。'**~·pipe** *n* length of ~. (一段)軟管。 □ *vt* [VP6A, 15B] ~ ***(down),*** water (a garden, etc) with a ~; wash (a motorcar, etc) by using a ~: 用軟管輸水澆(花園等);用軟管輸水洗(汽車等): ~ *(down) the car.* 用軟管輸水洗汽車。

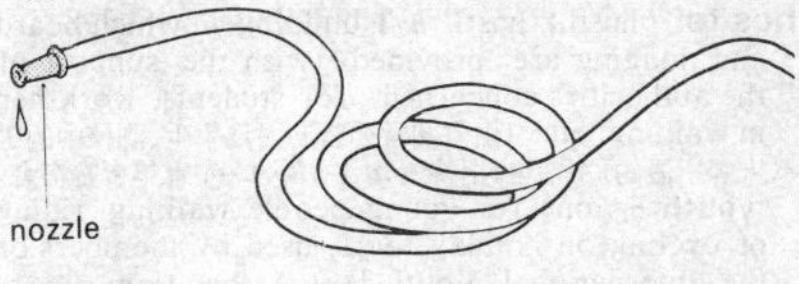

a hosepipe

hose² /həʊz ; hoz/ *n* **1** (collective, as *pl*) (trade name for) stockings and socks: (集合稱,作複數用)(商品名稱)長統襪及短襪: *six pair of ~.* 六雙長統襪(短襪)。 **2** (hist) garment from the waist to the knees or feet worn by men in former times; tights: (史)昔時男子穿的緊身褲(由腰部至膝部或脚部); 緊身衣: *dressed in doublet and ~.* 穿着緊身上衣和緊身褲。⇨ the illus at doublet. 參看 doublet 之插圖。

ho·sier /'həʊzɪə(r) *US:* -ʒə(r) ; 'hoʒɚ/ *n* tradesman who sells hose²(1) and knitted underwear. 售賣長襪、短襪、針織內衣之商人。 **ho·siery** /'həʊzɪərɪ *US:* 'həʊʒərɪ ; 'hoʒərɪ/ *n* [U] goods sold by a ~. 長襪、短襪、內衣等貨品。

hos·pice /'hɒspɪs ; 'hɑspɪs/ *n* **1** house of rest for travellers.供旅客休息的招待所。**2** hospital for dying people. 爲垂死者而設立之醫院。

hos·pit·able /hɒ'spɪtəbl ; 'hɑspɪtəbl/ *adj* giving, liking to give, hospitality: 招待慇懃的; 好客的: *a ~ man／household.* 好客的人(家庭)。 **hos·pit·ably** /-əblɪ ; -əblɪ/ *adv*

hos·pi·tal /'hɒspɪtl ; 'hɑspɪtl/ *n* place where people are treated for, nursed through, their illness or injuries: 醫院: *He's still in ~.* 他仍在住院。*I'm going to the ~ to see my brother.* 我要去醫院看望我的哥哥(弟弟)。*His sister is a ~ nurse.* 他姊姊(妹妹)是個醫院護士。***go to ~,*** enter a ~ as a patient. 入醫院。**~·ize** *vt* send to, admit into, ~. 送入醫院;允許住院。 **~·iz·ation** /ˌhɒspɪtlaɪ'zeɪʃn *US:* -lɪ'z- ; ˌhɑspɪtəlɪ'zeʃən/ *n* state of being ~ized. 入院;住院治療。

hos·pi·tal·ity /ˌhɒspɪˈtælətɪ ; ˌhɑspɪˈtælətɪ/ *n* [U] friendly and generous reception and entertainment of guests, esp in one's own home. 對客人的慇懃款待(尤指在自己家中);好客。

host¹ /həʊst ; host/ *n* **1** great number (*of*): 多數;許多(與 of 連用): *He has ~s of friends.* 他有很多朋友。*We are faced with a ~ of difficulties.* 我們面臨許多困難。 **2** (archaic) army: (古)軍隊: *Lord of H~s*, Jehovah, God of the Hebrews. 萬軍之主(耶和華,希伯來人的上帝)。

host² /həʊst ; host/ *n* **1** person who entertains guests: (款待客人的)主人: *As Mr Hill was away, Tom, the eldest son, acted as ~ at the dinner party*, welcomed the guests, etc. 希爾先生不在家,由長子湯姆做宴會的主人。(In the *pl* this word may be common gender.) (複數時此字可指通性。) *The Parnwells are such good ~s.* 巴威爾一家眞是善於款待客人的主人。 **2** inn-keeper; hotel-keeper. 旅館老闆。 ***reckon without one's ~***, make calculations, plans, etc without consulting the chief person(s) concerned; overlook possible opposition. 作計畫、考慮等時未與有關的主要人士磋商;忽略可能的反對。 **3** (biol) organism which harbours a parasite. (生物)寄生動植物之宿主;寄主。 □ *vt* [VP6A] (US colloq) act as ~ to or at. (美俗)作東;款待。

Host /həʊst ; host/ *n* **the ~**, bread eaten at Holy Communion. (聖餐禮中之)聖餅。

hos·tage /ˈhɒstɪdʒ ; ˈhɑstɪdʒ/ *n* person (less often, a thing) given or left as a pledge that demands will be satisfied: 人質;作抵押的人或物(多指人): *take sb ~.* 把某人做爲人質。*The bandits demanded that one of the travellers should stay with them as a ~.* 匪徒要一位旅客留下來做人質。 ***give ~s to fortune***, by an unwise step, take the risk of being harmed in future. 由於不智的步驟,冒將來受到傷害之險。

hos·tel /ˈhɒstl ; ˈhɑstl/ *n* **1** building in which board and lodging are provided (with the support of the authorities concerned) for students, workmen in training, etc: (由有關當局贊助而爲學生、訓練中的工人等所設的)寄宿舍;招待所: *a YMCA ~.* 青年會寄宿舍。 **ˈyouth ~**, one for young people walking, riding or cycling on holiday tours, used by members of the International Youth H~ Association. 青年招待所(招待國際青年招待所協會徒步、騎馬或騎脚踏車作假期旅行之會員)。 **2** (archaic) inn. (古)旅館。 **~ry** *n* (archaic) inn. (古)旅館。 **~·ler** /ˈhɒstələ(r) ; ˈhɑstl̩ɚ/ *n* person travelling from ~ to ~, esp youth ~lers. 沿途投宿招待所(尤指青年招待所)之旅客。

host·ess /ˈhəʊstɪs ; ˈhostɪs/ *n* **1** woman who entertains guests; wife of one's host. (款待客人的)女主人。 **2** woman inn-keeper. 旅館女老闆。 **3 ˈair ~**, ⇨ air¹(7).

hos·tile /ˈhɒstaɪl *US:* -tl ; ˈhɑstl̩/ *adj* **1** of an enemy: 敵人的: *a ~ army.* 敵軍。 **2** feeling or showing enmity (*to*); unfriendly: 懷敵意的;表示敵意的(與 to 連用);敵對的: *a ~ crowd;* 懷有敵意的羣衆; *~ looks;* 顯示敵意的神色; *~ to reform.* 反對改革。 **~·ly** /-llɪ ; -llɪ/ *adv*

hos·til·ity /hɒˈstɪlətɪ ; hɑsˈtɪlətɪ/ *n* **1** [U] enmity; ill will: 敵視;敵意: *feelings of ~;* 敵視的情緒;敵意; *feel no ~ towards anyone;* 對任何人無敵意; *show ~ to sb.* 對某人表示敵意。 **2** (*pl;* -ties) (acts of) war: (複)戰爭;戰鬥: *at the outbreak of hostilities;* 戰爭爆發時; *open/suspend hostilities*, begin/stop fighting. 開(停)戰。

hot /hɒt ; hɑt/ *adj* (-ter, -test) **1** having a high temperature: 熱的: *hot weather;* 熱天氣; *a hot day;* 熱天; *feel hot.* 感覺熱。 *I like my food hot.* 我喜歡吃熱食。 *This coffee is too hot to drink.* 這咖啡太熱了,不能喝。 ***be in/get into hot water***, in trouble or disgrace (because of foolish behaviour, etc). (因愚蠢的行爲等)惹來麻煩或羞辱。 ***be/get hot under the collar***, angry, excited, indignant. 發怒;興奮;憤慨。 ***make a place/make it too hot for sb***, (fig) compel him to leave by rousing hostility against him. (喻)以敵視態度强迫某人離開一地方;排擠某人。 **2** producing a burning sensation to the taste: 辛辣的: *This curry is too hot.* 這咖哩太辣了。*Pepper and mustard are hot.* 胡椒和芥末是辣的。 **3** fiery; eager; intense; violent; impetuous: 激情的;熱烈的;强烈的;激烈的;猛烈的: *get hot over an argument;* 辯論時十分激動; *a man with a hot temper;* 一個脾氣暴躁的人; *in the hottest part of the election campaign.* 在競選活動最激烈的部份。 ***be hot on the trail of sb/on sb's tracks***, near to what is being pursued; close behind. 逼近追求物;緊追不捨。 **4** (in hunting, of the scent) fresh and strong. (指狩獵時野獸的氣味)新鮮而强烈的。 **5** (of music, esp jazz) strongly rhythmical and emotional. (指音樂,尤指爵士音樂)富有節奏和情感的。 **6** (sl) (of stolen goods) difficult to dispose of (because of determined efforts made by the police to trace them): (俚)(指贓物)不易脫手的(由於警察決心努力追踪該項物品): *These articles are too hot to handle/hold.* 這些贓物太不容易脫手,所以不便買賣(持有)。 **7** (as *adv*) (作爲副詞) **(a)** recently: 最近地: *hot off the press.* 最新出版的。 ⇨ hot news below. 參看下列之 hot news。 **(b)** ***blow hot and cold***, (fig) be by turns favourable and unfavourable. (喻)無定見;反覆不定。 **(c)** ***give it sb hot***, punish or scold severely. 嚴懲或嚴斥某人。 **8** (special uses with *nn* and *participles*) (與名詞及分詞連用之特殊用法) **ˌhot ˈair** *n* [U] meaningless talk, promises, etc. 無意義的話、許諾等;空話。 **hot-air balloon** *n* ⇨ balloon. **ˈhot·bed** *n* bed of earth heated by rotting manure to promote growth of plants; (fig) place favourable to growth, esp of sth evil: (培養植物之)溫床;(喻)(尤指邪惡事物)便於滋長的地方: *a hotbed of vice/crime.* 罪惡(犯罪)之溫床。 **ˌhot-ˈblooded** *adj* passionate. 熱情的。 **ˌhot cross ˈbun** *n* one with a cross marked on it, eaten on Good Friday. 上有十字架形花飾的圓形小麪包,於耶穌受難節食用。 **ˌhot ˈdog** *n* hot sausage served with onions and mustard in a sandwich or bread roll. 熱狗(三明治或圓形麪包中,夾熱香腸配以碎洋葱及芥末之食品)。 **ˌhot·ˈfoot** *adv* eagerly; in great haste: 急忙;火急: *run hotfoot after the pickpocket.* 急追扒手。 □ *vi* go hastily: 急走;趕急: *hotfoot it down to the swimming-pool.* 急忙趕到游泳池。 **ˌhot ˈgospeller** *n* (colloq) fervent evangelist preacher. (俗)熱情的福音傳道者。 **ˈhot·head** *n* impetuous person. 性急的人。 **ˌhot-ˈheaded** *adj* impetuous. 性急的。 **ˈhot-house** *n* heated building, usu made of glass, for growing delicate plants. 溫室;暖房。 **ˈhot line** *n* direct line of communication (telephone or teleprinter) between heads of governments, eg between Moscow and Washington. 熱線(兩國政府首領之間,例如莫斯科與華盛頓之間,直接聯絡的電話或打字電報機專線)。 **ˌhot ˈmoney** *n* [U] short-term funds moved from one financial centre to another by speculators seeking high interest rates and security. 流動的國際短期資金(投機者爲謀高利及不受貶值損失,由一金融中心轉移至另一金融中心者)。⇨ also 6 above. 亦參看上列第6義。 **ˌhot ˈnews** *n* [U] recent (esp sensational) news. 最近(尤指轟動的)消息。 **ˈhot·plate** *n* flat surface of a cooking-stove; similar surface (not part of a stove) that can be heated, eg electrically, for cooking, boiling water, etc. 火爐上之平頂炊具;可加熱的平面炊具(非火爐之一部份,例如用電者,供烹飪、燒水等用)。 **ˌhot poˈtato** *n* (fig, colloq) sth difficult or unpleasant to deal with: (喻,俗)棘手之事;使人厭惡之事: *The issue is a political hot potato.* 這問題是政治上棘手之事。 **ˈhot rod** *n* (US sl) supercharged car. (美俚)馬力强大之汽車。 **the ˈhot seat** *n* electric chair (for the electrocution of murderers); (fig) position of sb who has to make difficult, often agonizing, decisions, eg of a head of state. 電椅(對謀殺者施電刑之用);(喻)(國家元首等必須作困難而且往往痛苦的決定時所處之)困境。 **ˌhot ˈspring** *n* naturally heated spring¹(2). 溫泉。 ˌ**hot** ˈ**stuff** *n* [U] (sl) sb/sth of first-rate quality. (俚)第一流的人或物。 ˌ**hot-**ˈ**tempered** *adj* easily angered. 性急的;脾氣暴躁的。 ˌ**hot-**ˈ**water-bottle** *n* container (often of rubber) to be filled with hot water for warmth in bed. (往往是橡皮製的,使床鋪溫暖的)熱水袋。□ *vt, vi* (-tt-) [VP2C, 15B] ***hot (sth) up,*** (colloq) make or become hotter or (fig) more exciting: (俗)使或成爲更熱;(喻)使或成爲更令人興奮: *Things are hotting up.* 事情熱鬧起來了。 **hot·ly** *adv* passionately; excitedly: 激烈地;熱烈地: *He replied hotly that...;* 他怒氣冲冲地回答…; *It was a hotly contested match.* 那是一場競爭激烈的比賽。

hotch·potch /ˈhɒtʃpɒtʃ ; ˈhɑtʃˌpɑtʃ/ *n* jumble; number of things mixed together without order: 雜亂的一堆東西; 雜混在一起的東西: *His essay was a ~ of other people's ideas.* 他的文章係將別人的思想湊合而成。

ho·tel /həʊˈtel ; hoˈtɛl/ *n* (either *a* ~ or *an* ~) (可用冠詞 a 或 an) building where meals and rooms are provided for travellers. 旅社;飯店。**~·ier** /həʊˈtelɪeɪ *US:* ˌhəʊtelˈjeɪ ; ˌhotɛlˈje/ *n* a ~-keeper. 旅館老闆。

hound /haʊnd ; haund/ *n* **1** (kinds of) dog used for hunting and racing: 獵犬;猩: *ˈfox~;* 獵狐犬; *ˈblood~;* 血猩; *ˈgrey~.* 靈猩。 (When not in a compound, ~ usu means *fox~*.) (不用於複合字時, hound 通常指獵狐犬。) ***follow the ~s; ride to ~s,*** hunt with a pack of ~s. 帶一群獵犬狩獵。**Master of H~s,** the master of a hunt(2). 獵狐會會長。 **2** (dated colloq) mean, wretched, contemptible fellow. (過時俗語)可鄙的人;卑鄙之徒。□ *vt* [VP6A] chase or hunt with, or as with, ~s; harass: 用獵犬追逐或狩獵; 追逼: *be ~ed by one's creditors,* worried by requests for payment of money owing. 爲債主所追逼。

hour /aʊə(r) ; aʊr/ *n* **1** twenty-fourth part of a day; 60 minutes: 小時;鐘頭: *hire a horse by the ~;* 按鐘頭租用一匹馬; *walk for ~s (and ~s);* 走好幾個鐘頭; *a three ~s' journey;* 三小時的旅程; *the happiest ~s* (= period) *of my life;* 我一生中最快樂的時期; *work a forty-~ week;* 每週工作四十小時; *18.00 ~s,* time calculated on a 24-~ basis, = 6.00 pm, 十八點(按每天廿四小時推算),卽下午六點, ➩ App 4. 參看附錄四。 ***at the eleventh ~,*** when almost too late. 在最後時刻;在危急之時。***the ˈsmall ~s,*** the three or four ~s after midnight. 午夜後的三或四個小時。 **ˈ~·glass** *n* sand-glass which runs out in one ~. 沙漏;更漏(所盛之沙於一小時後漏盡)。 **ˈ~ hand** *n* small hand on a clock or watch, pointing to the ~. 時針。 **2** time of day; point or period of time: 時刻;鐘點: *The church clock was striking the ~ as we got home.* 我們到家時,教堂的鐘正在報時。 *This clock strikes the ~s and the half-~s, but not the quarters.* 這鐘每到一小時及半小時均報時,但每刻鐘不報時。 *Please come at an early ~.* 請早些來。 *They disturb me at all ~s of the day and night,* constantly. 他們日夜不斷地打擾我。 **3** (*pl*) fixed periods of time, esp for work: (複)固定的時間 (尤指工作時間): *ˈschool ~s.* 上課時間。 *ˈOffice ~s, 9 am to 5 pm.* 辦公時間,上午九點至下午五點。 ***after ~s,*** after the period of regular business, etc. 下班後。 ***out of ~s,*** outside (before or after) regular ~s (of duty, etc). 非上班時間; 非辦公時間。 ***keep good/bad/early/late/regular, etc ~s,*** get up, go to bed, start/stop work, leave/arrive home, etc, early/late, etc. 按(不按)時作息;早(晚)起;早(晚)睡;早(晚)開始工作;早(晚)停止工作;早(晚)離家;早(晚)到家等。 **4** a particular, or the present, point in time: 某一時刻;現時: *questions of the ~,* now being discussed; 目前所談的問題; *in the ~ of danger/temptation;* 在危險(誘惑)之時; *in a good/evil ~,* at a lucky/unlucky time. 在幸運(不幸)之時。

houri /ˈhʊərɪ ; ˈhʊrɪ/ *n* young and beautiful woman of the Muslim Paradise. 回教天堂之美女。

hour·ly /ˈaʊəlɪ ; ˈaʊrlɪ/ *adv* **1** every hour; once every hour: 每小時;每小時一次: *This medicine is to be taken ~.* 這藥每小時服一次。 **2** at any hour: 時時;隨時: *We're expecting news ~.* 我們時時期待着消息。□ *adj* **1** done or occurring every hour: 每小時一次的: *an ~ service of trains;* 每小時一班的火車; *an ~ bus service.* 每小時一班的公共汽車。 **2** continual: 不斷的: *live in ~ dread of discovery.* 時時刻刻怕被人發覺。

house¹ /haʊs ; haus/ *n* (*pl* ~s /ˈhaʊzɪz ; ˈhauzɪz/) **1** building made for people to live in, usu for one family (or a family and lodgers, etc): 房屋; 住宅: *New ~s are going up everywhere.* 到處在建築新房屋。 *I've bought a ~.* 我買了一幢房子。 ➩ home¹(1). ***get on like a ˈ~ on fire,*** (of people) quickly become friendly and jolly together. (指人)很快地成爲好友。***under ~ arrest,*** forbidden by law to leave one's ~ or receive visitors. (依法)軟禁在家中。 **2** (usu with a *pref*) building made or used for some particular purpose or occupation: (通常加一字首)作特殊用途的建築物: *ˈhen~;* 雞舍; *ˈcow~;* 牛欄; *ˈstore~;* 倉庫; *ˈware~;* 倉庫; *ˈalms-~;* 貧民院;養老院; *ˈbake~;* 麵包廠; *ˈcustom-~,* 海關, etc, ➩ these entries. 參看各項。 **the H~ of God,** church or chapel. 教堂。 ***~ of cards,*** one built by a child out of playing cards; (fig) scheme likely to collapse. 兒童用紙牌做的房屋;(喻)不可靠的計畫。 ***~ of ill fame,*** (old use) brothel. (舊用法)妓院。 ***on the ~,*** at the expense of the inn, firm, etc. 由鄉村旅館、商號等負擔費用的。 **3** (building used by an) assembly: 議會; 議會所用的建築物: *the H~ of Commons/Lords.* (英國)下(上)議院。*the H~s of Parliament.* (英國)國會兩院。 **the H~,** (colloq, GB) (俗,英) **(a)** the Stock Exchange. 證券交易所。**(b)** the H~ of Commons or Lords: 下(上)議院: *enter the H~,* become an MP. 成爲國會議員。 **(c)** (US) the H~ of Representatives. (美)衆議院。**(d)** business firm. 商號;公司。 **4** [U] ***keep ~,*** manage the affairs of a ~hold. 料理家務;管家。***keep a good ~,*** provide good food and plenty of comfort. 使家庭豐衣足食。***keep open ~,*** be ready to welcome guests at any time. 隨時歡迎客人;開門揖客。 ***set/put one's ˈ~ in order,*** put one's affairs straight. 整頓本身事務;清理自己事務。 **5** household; family line; dynasty: 家族;家系;朝代: *the H~ of Windsor,* the British Royal family; 英國王室;英國皇族; *an ancient ~;* 古老的家族; *an old trading ~,* business firm. 歷史悠久的貿易商行。 **6** spectators, audience, in a theatre: 觀衆;聽衆: *make oneself heard in every part of the ~;* 使自己的聲音能讓戲院中所有的聽衆聽到; *a full ~,* every seat occupied. (戲院)客滿。 *The second ~* (= performance) *starts at 9 o'clock.* 第二場戲九點開始。 *Is there a doctor in the ~?* 觀衆中有醫生嗎? ***bring down the ~; bring the ˈ~ down,*** win very great applause and approval. 博得滿堂喝采。 **7** (compounds) (複合字) **ˈ~ agent** *n* (GB) person who sells or lets ~s for others. (英) 房屋經紀人。 ➩ (US) (美) realtor. **ˈ~·boat** *n* boat fitted up as a place to live in, eg on a river or estuary. 船宅;船屋(河上或河口等處可居住的船隻)。 **ˈ~·bound** *adj* confined to the ~, eg through ill-health: 不能離家外出的(例如因健康不佳): *Should wives with children be ~bound?* 有小孩的太太們應該留在家裏嗎? **ˈ~·breaker** *n* **1** person who enters another's ~ by day to steal. 白日侵入家宅行竊者。 ➩ burglar. **2** (US 美 = **ˈ~-wrecker**) workman employed to pull down old buildings. 拆屋工人。**ˈ~·coat** *n* usu cotton or silk coat worn by women in the house during the day. 婦女日常家居所著之外衣 (通常爲棉或絲質)。 **ˈ~-craft** *n* [U] theory and practice of running a home¹(1). 家政(學)。 **ˈ~·dog** *n* dog trained to guard a ~. 守門犬;看門狗。 **ˈ~·father** *n* man in charge of children in an institution. 男舍監。ˈ~

flag *n* flag flown by a firm's ships. 商船公司旗號;桅頂公司旗。 ⇨ 5 above. 參看上列第5義。 '~-fly *n* (*pl* -flies) ⇨ fly¹. ~·ful /-ful; -ˌfʊl/ *n* as much as a ~ can contain or accommodate. 滿屋。 '~·hold *n* all persons (family, lodgers, etc) living in a ~: 同居在一家的人(家人及房客); 全家的人: *~hold cavalry/troops,* employed to guard the Sovereign; (護衛國王的)禁衛騎兵隊;御林軍; *~hold duties/expenses.* 家務(家庭開銷)。 ˌ~-hold 'word, commonly used word or name. 家喻戶曉的字或名字。 '~·holder *n* person leasing or owning and occupying a ~, not sb living in a hotel, lodgings, etc. 住家的人(非指住在旅舍,寄宿舍等的人)。 '~·keeper *n* person employed to manage the affairs of a ~hold. 管家。 '~·lights *n pl* lights in the auditorium of a theatre, cinema, etc. 戲院、電影院等觀衆席之燈光。 '~·maid *n* female servant in a ~, esp one who cleans rooms, etc. 女僕(尤指清潔房間等者)。 ˌ~maid's 'knee, inflammation of the kneecap due to kneeling. (因跪下工作而引起的) 膝蓋黏液囊腫。 '~·man /-mən; -mən/ *n* (*pl* -men) (GB) doctor who is an assistant to a physician or surgeon in a hospital (US 美 = *intern*). (英)住在醫院中之見習醫生。 '~ martin *n* common bird which nests in the walls of ~s and cliffs. 築巢於牆壁或絶壁上的燕子。 '~·master *n* teacher in charge of a school boarding-~. 男舍監。 '~·mother *n* woman in charge of children in an institution. 女舍監。 '~-party *n* party of guests being entertained for several days at a country ~, etc. 連續數日在鄉間府第等地接受招待之全體賓客。 '~ physician *n* one who resides in a hospital. 住院內科醫師。 '~·proud *adj* very much concerned with the care of the ~, with the appearance of the furnishings, etc. 十分關心家事,傢俱陳列等的。 '~·room *n* space: 空間: *I wouldn't give that table ~room,* would not have it in my ~, would not accept it even as a gift. 我不要那桌子(即使送給我我也不要)。 '~ sparrow *n* common grey and brown bird. 家雀。 '~ surgeon *n* one who resides in a hospital. 住院外科醫師。 '~·top *n* (chiefly in) (主用於) *cry/publish/proclaim sth from the ~tops,* make known to all; declare publicly. 宣佈;公開宣揚某事物。 '~·trained *adj* (of domestic pets) trained not to defecate and urinate inside buildings. (指家庭寵物)受過訓練而知道不在室內便溺的。 '~-warming *n* party given to friends by a person who moves into a new ~. 遷入新居之慶宴。 '~·wife *n* **1** woman head of a family, who runs the home, brings up the family, etc. 主婦。 **2** /'hʌzɪf; 'hʌzɪf/ (dated) case for needles and thread. (過時用語)針線盒。 '~·wife·ly *adj* of a ~wife(1). 主婦的。 '~·wifery /-wɪfərɪ; -ˌwaɪfrɪ/ *n* [U] work of a ~wife. 家事;家務。 '~·work *n* [U] work done in a ~, cleaning, cooking, etc. 家務。 ⇨ *homework* at home¹(7).

house² /haʊz; haʊz/ *vt* [VP6A] **1** provide a house or shelter for; find room for: 供以房屋: *We can ~ you and your friends if the hotels are full.* 如果旅館已住滿,我們可供給你和你的朋友們住處。 **2** store (goods, etc): 貯藏(貨物等): *~ one's old books in the attic.* 將舊書藏置頂樓。

hous·ing /'haʊzɪŋ; 'haʊzɪŋ/ *n* [U] accommodation in houses, etc: 供給房屋;住宅;房屋: *More ~ is needed for old people.* 需要更多的老年人住宅。 *The ~ in this part of the town is sub-standard.* 城裏這一部分的住宅低於標準。 '~ association *n* non-profitmaking society for the construction and provision of ~ing. 住宅協會(建築及供應住宅之非營利組織)。 '~ estate *n* area of houses planned and built either by a local authority or other organization, to be let or sold. 住宅區;社區(由當地政府或其他機構計畫及興建,供出租或出售者)。

hove /həʊv; hov/ *pt, pp* of heave.

hovel /'hɒvl *US:* 'hʌvl; 'hʌvḷ/ *n* small house or cottage that is unfit to live in; open-sided shed or outhouse. 不適於居住的小屋;棚;外屋。

hover /'hɒvə(r) *US:* 'hʌvər; 'hʌvɚ/ *vi* [VP2A, C] **1** (of birds) remain in the air at one place: (指鳥) 翺翔;盤旋: *a hawk ~ing overhead/~ing over its prey;* 在頭上盤旋(在獵物頭頂盤旋)的一隻鷹; *a helicopter ~ing over the house.* 盤旋於房屋上空的一架直升飛機。 '~·craft *n* craft capable of moving over land or water while supported on a cushion of air made by jet engines. 噴射飛車(由噴射引擎造成的氣墊所支持,可在地面及水面上方移動)。 **2** (of persons) wait about; remain at or near: (指人)守在附近;留在一地或附近: (fig) (喻) *~ between life and death.* 處於生死關頭。

a hovercraft

how /haʊ; haʊ/ *adv* **1** in what way or manner; by what means: 怎樣;用何方法: *How is the word spelt?* 這字怎樣拼法? *Tell me how to spell the word.* 告訴我如何拼這字。 *How did you escape?* 你怎樣脫逃的? *Tell me how you escaped.* 告訴我你如何脫逃的。 **2** (in questions and exclamations) to what extent; in what degree: (用於疑問句及驚嘆句中) 多麼;何等: *How old is he?* 他有多大年紀了? *How often do you go there?* 你多久去那裏一次? *How many are there?* 有多少? *How much do you want?* 你要多少? *How dirty the house is!* 這房屋多麼髒啊! *How kind you are!* 你多麼客氣啊! *How he snores!* ie he snores very loudly. 他的鼾聲多麼大啊! *How well you look!* 你看來多麼健康啊! ***And how!*** (emphatic) Yes! (强勢語) 是的! 當然! **3** in what state of health: 健康情形如何: *How are you?* 你好嗎? *How's your father?* 你父親好嗎? *How do you do?* (formula used as a conventional greeting, esp when persons are formally introduced; used only with the *pron* 'you'.) 你好(用於一般的問候,尤其是初次見面經人正式介紹後的客套語;祇可用於代名詞 you。) **how-d'ye-do** /ˌhaʊ djə du:; ˌhaʊdjə'du/ *n* (colloq) awkward state of affairs: (俗)令人困窘的情況: *Well, here's a pretty how-d'ye-do!* 啊,這眞令人爲難! **4** (introducing an indirect statement) that: (引導一間接敍述) 等於 that: *He told me how* (= that) *he had read about it in the newspapers.* 他告訴我他在報上獲悉此事。 **5** used in asking for an opinion, decision, explanation, etc: 如何(用以詢人之意見、決定、解釋等): *How about going* (=What do you think about going) *for a walk?* 去散散步怎麼樣? *How do you find your new job?* Do you like it, etc? 你對你的新工作覺得怎樣? ***How come. . . ,*** (colloq) Why is it that...: (俗)爲何…: *How come we don't see you more often?* 爲什麼我們不常看到你? ***How's that?*** **(a)** What's the explanation of that? 那是怎麼回事? **(b)** What's your opinion of that? eg an object pointed to. 你對那個的意見如何(例如指着一物問)? **(c)** (in cricket, to the umpire) Is the batsman out or not out? (板球賽中詢問裁判)那擊球員怎麼樣(他是否出局)? ***How so?*** Can you prove that it is so? 爲什麼是這樣? **how·beit** /haʊ'bi:ɪt; haʊ'biɪt/ *conj* (archaic) nevertheless. (古)然而;雖然如此。 **how·ever** /haʊ'evə(r); haʊ'ɛvɚ/ *adv* **1** in whatever way or degree: 無論如何: *He will never succeed, however hard he tries.* 無論他如何努力嘗試,他都不會成功。 *We must do something, on however humble a scale.* 我們必須做點事,不論多麼微不足道。 **2** (also *conj*) although that is/may be/was, etc so: 然而；依然: *Later, however, he decided to go.* 後來，他仍然決定去了。*He was mistaken, however.* 可是他錯了。

how·dah /ˈhaʊdə ; ˈhaʊdə/ *n* seat (usu with a canopy) on an elephant's back. 象輿(象背上的座位，通常有篷蓋)。

how·it·zer /ˈhaʊɪtsə(r) ; ˈhaʊɪtsɚ/ *n* short gun for firing shells at a high angle at short range. 榴彈砲。

howl /haʊl ; haʊl/ *n* [C] long, loud cry, eg of a wolf; long cry of a person in pain, or of sb expressing scorn, amusement, etc: 號叫(例如狼嗥)；(人於痛苦時的) 哀號；(表示輕蔑、高興等的) 高聲叫嚣: *~s of derision.* 表示嘲笑的吼叫。□ *vi, vt* **1** [VP2A, C] utter such cries: 號叫；哀號；高聲叫嚣: *wolves ~ing in the forest.* 在森林中嗥叫的狼。*The wind ~ed through the trees.* 風在林間怒號。*The boys ~ed with laughter.* 男孩子們高聲大笑。**2** [VP6A, 15A, B] ~ ***(down),*** utter ~s at; utter with ~s: 對…吼叫；吼叫着說出: *~ defiance at the enemy;* 吼叫着對敵人挑戰； *~ down a speaker,* prevent him from being heard. 用吼叫聲掩蓋演說者的聲音。**~er** *n* (colloq) foolish and laughable mistake. (俗)愚蠢可笑的錯誤。 **~·ing** *adj* (sl) extreme; glaring: (俚)極端的；顯而易見的: *a ~ing shame.* 奇恥大辱。

hoy·den /ˈhɔɪdn ; ˈhɔɪdn̩/ *n* boisterous girl. 頑皮喜喧鬧的女孩。**~·ish** /-ɪʃ ; -ɪʃ/ *adj* of or like a ~. (似)頑皮女孩的。

hub /hʌb ; hʌb/ *n* central part of a wheel from which the spokes radiate, ⇨ the illus at bicycle; (fig) central point of activity or importance: 輪轂；輪軸 (參看 bicycle 之挿圖)；(喻)中心；中樞: *a hub of industry/commerce.* 工業(商業)中心。*He thinks that Boston is the hub of the universe.* 他認爲波士頓是世界的中心。

hubble-bubble /ˈhʌbl bʌbl ; ˈhʌbl̩ˌbʌbl̩/ *n* = hookah.

hub·bub /ˈhʌbʌb ; ˈhʌbʌb/ *n* [U] confused noise, eg of many voices; uproar. 嘈雜；喧嚣。

hubby /ˈhʌbɪ ; ˈhʌbɪ/ *n* (GB) (colloq) husband. (英)(俗)丈夫。

hu·bris /ˈhju:brɪs ; ˈhjubrɪs/ *n* [U] (Gk) arrogant pride. (希)傲慢。

hucka·back /ˈhʌkəbæk ; ˈhʌkəˌbæk/ *n* strong, rough, cotton or linen material used for towels, etc. (做毛巾等用的)一種堅固的粗棉布或麻布。

huckle·berry /ˈhʌklbərɪ *US:* -berɪ ; ˈhʌkl̩ˌbɛrɪ/ *n* (*pl* -ries) (small, dark-blue berry of a) low shrub common in N America. 越橘樹(北美之一種矮灌木)；越橘(越橘樹產的一種深藍色的小漿果)。

huck·ster /ˈhʌkstə(r) ; ˈhʌkstɚ/ *n* hawker. 沿街叫賣之小販。

huddle /ˈhʌdl ; ˈhʌdl̩/ *vt, vi* **1** [VP2C] crowd together: 擠在一起: *sheep huddling together for warmth.* 擠成一團以取暖的羊。 **2** [VP2C] ~ ***up (against),*** curl or coil up against: 縮成一團(緊靠)；蜷起身體(緊靠): *Tom was cold, so he ~d up against his brother in bed.* 湯姆感覺冷，所以他在床上縮成一團，緊靠著他哥哥(弟弟)。**3** [VP15A, B] heap up in a confused mass: 雜亂地堆起: *~ things together/up/into sth.* 把東西堆在一起(堆起來，塞入某物)。□ *n* number of things or persons close together without order or arrangement: 雜亂無章的一堆東西或一羣人: ***be in/go into a ~,*** (colloq, of persons) be/get together to confer. (俗，指人)在一起商議。

hue[1] /hju: ; hju/ *n* [C] (shade of) colour: 顏色；色度: *the hues of the rainbow;* 虹之色彩； *the dark hue of the ocean.* 海洋之暗色。**hued** /hju:d ; hjud/ (in compounds) having the hue(s) indicated: (用於複合字中)有…顏色的: *ˈdark-hued;* 暗色的； *ˈmany-hued.* 有許多顏色的。

hue[2] /hju: ; hju/ *n* (only in) (僅用於) ***hue and cry,*** /ˌhju: ən ˈkraɪ ; ˈhju ən ˈkraɪ/ general outcry of alarm (as when a criminal is being pursued, or when there is opposition to sth): (追捕犯人或表示反對之)喊叫: *raise a hue and cry against new tax proposals.* 叫嚣反對新稅的提議。

huff[1] /hʌf ; hʌf/ *n* fit of ill temper. 發怒。***be in/get into a ~.*** 發怒。**~ish** /-ɪʃ ; -ɪʃ/, **~y** *adjj* in a ~; taking offence easily. 發怒的；易生氣的。**~·ily** /-ɪlɪ ; -əlɪ/ *adv*

huff[2] /hʌf ; hʌf/ *vi* puff; blow. 吹氣；噴氣。

hug /hʌg ; hʌg/ *vt* (-gg-) [VP6A] **1** put the arms round tightly, esp to show love: 緊抱(尤指表示愛)；摟抱: *The child was hugging her doll.* 那小孩緊抱着她的洋娃娃。**2** cling to: 固持；堅持: *hug cherished beliefs.* 堅持所抱的信念。 **3** ***hug the shore,*** (of a ship) keep close to it. (指船)緊靠海岸。 **4** ***hug oneself (with pleasure/delight) over sth,*** be very pleased with oneself, congratulate oneself. 竊喜；深自慶幸。□ *n* [C] tight embrace: 緊抱: *She gave her mother a big hug.* 她緊緊地抱着她母親。

huge /hju:dʒ ; hjudʒ/ *adj* very great. 巨大的。**~·ly** *adv* enormously; very much. 極大地；十分地。

hug·ger-mug·ger /ˈhʌgə mʌgə(r) ; ˈhʌgɚˌmʌgɚ/ *n, adj, adv* secrecy; secret(ly); confusion; confused(ly). 秘密；混亂；秘密的(地)；混亂的(地)。

Hu·gue·not /ˈhju:gənəʊ ; ˈhjugəˌnɑt/ *n* (16th and 17th cc) French Protestant. (十六、十七世紀) 法國新教徒。

hula /ˈhu:lə ; ˈhulə/ *n* native Hawaiian dance. 夏威夷土風舞；草裙舞。

hulk /hʌlk ; hʌlk/ *n* **1** old ship no longer in use or used only as a storehouse; (formerly) old ship used as a prison. 廢船；用作倉庫之舊船；(昔時)囚船。**2** big, clumsy ship, thing or person. 笨大之船、物或人。 **~·ing** *adj* clumsy; awkward: 笨大的；笨拙的: *Get out of my way, you ~ing great idiot!* 給我滾開，你這個大笨蛋！

hull[1] /hʌl ; hʌl/ *n* outer covering of some fruits and seeds, esp the pods of peas and beans. (某些水果和種子的)殼；(尤指)豆莢。□ *vt* remove the ~s of. 去…之殼；去莢。

hull[2] /hʌl ; hʌl/ *n* body or frame of a ship. 船殼。⇨ the illus at barque. 參看 barque 之挿圖。***~ down*** **(a)** (of a ship almost below the horizon) with only the mast(s), funnel(s), etc, visible. (指幾乎隱於水平線下之船)不見船身，只露出桅、烟囱等。 **(b)** (of a tank) with only the turret showing. (指坦克車)只露出砲塔。

hul·la·ba·loo /ˌhʌləbəˈlu: ; ˈhʌləbəˌlu/ *n* uproar; disturbance: 喧嚣；騷擾: *What a ~!* 多吵鬧啊！*What's all this ~ about?* 吵些什麼？

hullo (also **hallo, hello**) /həˈləʊ ; həˈlo/ *int* used as a greeting, to call attention, to express surprise, and to answer a call, eg on the telephone. (打招呼，引人注意，表示驚訝及回答之呼聲，例如打電話招呼聲)喂！

hum /hʌm ; hʌm/ *vi, vt* (-mm-) [VP6A, 2A, C] **1** make a continuous sound like that made by bees; sing with closed lips: 作嗡嗡聲；哼唱: *She was humming a song to herself.* 她自己在哼唱着。*The bees were humming in the garden.* 蜜蜂在花園裏嗡嗡叫着。**ˈhum·ming·bird** *n* name used of several species, usu small and brightly coloured, that make a humming sound by vibration of the wings. 蜂鳥(通常體小而毛色鮮豔，鼓動翅膀發嗡嗡聲)。**ˈhumming-top** *n* top that hums when it spins. 響簧陀螺。 **2** be in a state of activity: 活躍: *make things hum;* 使事情活躍起來； *a factory humming with activity.* 忙碌的工廠。**3** (sl) smellu npleasantly: (俚)發臭味: *This ham is beginning to hum.* 這火腿開始發臭了。 **4** usu 通常作 ***hum and haw/ha,*** (colloq) make sounds expressing hesitation or doubt. (俗)發咕噥聲(表示遲疑)。□ *n* humming noise: 嗡嗡聲: *the hum of bees/of distant traffic;* 蜜蜂(遠處往來之車輛)之嗡嗡聲； *a hum of voices/conversation from the next room.* 鄰室之嗡嗡的談話聲。

hu·man /ˈhju:mən ; ˈhjumən/ *adj* **1** of man or mankind (contrasted with animals, God): 人的；人類的(以別於動物的或上帝的): *a ~ being;* 人； *~ nature;*

人性；～ *affairs.* 人事。‘*To err is ～, to forgive divine.*’ ‘犯錯是人之常情，寬恕是超凡入聖的。’ **2** having, showing, the qualities that distinguish man: 有人情味的；有人性的：*His cruelty suggests that he is less than ～.* 他的殘忍表示他沒有人性。**～·ly** *adv* (esp) by ～ means; without divine help: (尤指)用人力：*The doctors have done all that is ～ly possible.* 醫生們已盡了所有的人事。**ˌ～·'kind** *n* [U] mankind. 人類。

hu·mane /hjuːˈmeɪn; hjuˈmen/ *adj* **1** tender; kind-hearted: 仁慈的；好心腸的：*a man of ～ character;* 厚道的人；仁者；*a ～ officer.* 有惻隱之心的軍官。**～ killer,** instrument for the painless killing of animals. 無痛屠宰機(無痛苦的屠宰動物的工具)。**2** (of branches of study) tending to refinement; polished. (指學科)高尚的；文雅的。⇨ humanity(4). **～·ly** *adv.*

hu·man·ism /ˈhjuːmənɪzəm; ˈhjumənˌɪzəm/ *n* [U] **1** devotion to human interests; system that is concerned with ethical standards (but not with theology), and with the study of mankind. 人性；人道；人文主義；人本主義。**2** literary culture (of about the 14th to 16th cc) based on Greek and Roman learning. 人文學；古典文化之研究；(約自十四至十六世紀基於希臘及羅馬學術思想的)古典文學。

hu·man·ist /ˈhjuːmənɪst; ˈhjumənɪst/ *n* **1** student of human nature or human affairs (as opposed to theological subjects). 人性學者；人本學者；人文學者。**2** supporter of humanism. 人本主義者；人文主義者。**3** (esp in the 14th to 16th cc) student of Greek and Roman literature and antiquities. (尤指十四至十六世紀)研究希臘羅馬之古典文化學者。

hu·mani·tar·ian /hjuːˌmænɪˈteərɪən; hjuˌmænəˈtɛrɪən/ *adj, n* (of, holding the views of, a) person who works for the welfare of all human beings by reducing suffering, reforming laws about punishment, etc. 人道主義者；人道主義者的；持人道主義者之觀點的。**～·ism** /-ɪzəm; -ˌɪzəm/ *n*

hu·man·ity /hjuːˈmænətɪ; hjuˈmænətɪ/ *n* [U] **1** the human race; mankind: 人類：*crimes against ～.* 對人類有害的罪惡。**2** human nature. 人性。**3** quality of being humane(1): 仁愛；仁慈：*treat people and animals with ～.* 以仁慈對待人和動物。**4** (*pl*) **the humanities,** the branches of learning concerned with ancient Greek and Latin culture; the Arts subjects, esp literature, history and philosophy. (複)古典文學(與古希臘及拉丁文化有關的學科)；人文學(尤指文學、歷史和哲學)。

hu·man·ize /ˈhjuːmənaɪz; ˈhjuməˌnaɪz/ *vt, vi* [VP 6A, 2A] make or become human or humane. 使成爲人；賦與人性；變爲有人性。

humble /ˈhʌmbl; ˈhʌmbl/ *adj* (-r, -st) **1** having or showing a modest opinion of oneself, one's position, etc: 謙恭的；謙遜的：*He is very ～ in the company of his superiors.* 他跟上級在一起時非常謙恭。***eat ～ pie,*** make an abject apology, humiliate oneself. 低聲下氣地道歉；丟臉。**2** (of persons) low in rank or position; obscure and unimportant; (of things) poor; mean: (指人)微賤的；(指物)卑下的：*men of ～ birth;* 出身微賤的人；*a ～ home;* 簡陋的家；*a ～ occupation.* 卑下的職業。□ *vt* [VP6A] make ～; make lower in rank or self-opinion: 使卑下；貶抑：*～ one's enemies;* 挫敵人的銳氣；*～ sb's pride;* 挫某人的氣焰；*～ oneself before God.* 在上帝面前表示卑下。**hum·bly** *adv* in a ～ way: 謙恭地；微賤地：*beg most humbly for forgiveness;* 極謙恭地懇求饒恕；*humbly born,* of ～ parents. 出身微賤的。

hum·bug /ˈhʌmbʌg; ˈhʌmˌbʌg/ *n* **1** [C, U] (instance of) dishonest and deceiving behaviour or talk; [C] dishonest, deceitful person. 欺詐的言行；騙子。**2** (GB) hard boiled sweet flavoured with peppermint. (英)一種熬成的薄荷糖。□ *vt* (-gg-) [VP 6A, 14] deceive or trick (sb *into* or *out of* sth): 欺騙(騙某人做某事與 into 連用，騙去某人之物與 out of 連用)：*Don't try to ～ me!* 不要想騙我！□ *int* Nonsense! 胡說！

hum·dinger /ˌhʌmˈdɪŋə(r); ˌhʌmˈdɪŋɚ/ *n* (US sl) sth marvellous or extraordinary. (美俚)奇妙的或特殊的事物。

hum·drum /ˈhʌmdrʌm; ˈhʌmˌdrʌm/ *adj* dull; commonplace; monotonous: 乏味的；平凡的；單調的：*live a ～ life;* 過單調的生活；*engaged in ～ tasks.* 從事乏味的工作。

hu·merus /ˈhjuːmərəs; ˈhjumərəs/ *n* (anat) bone of the upper arm in man. (解剖)上膊骨；肱骨。⇨ the illus at skeleton. 參看 skeleton 之插圖。

hu·mid /ˈhjuːmɪd; ˈhjumɪd/ *adj* (esp of air, climate) damp. (尤指空氣或氣候)潮濕的。**～·ify** /hjuːˈmɪdɪfaɪ; hjuˈmɪdəˌfaɪ/ *vt* (*pt, pp* -fied) make ～. 使潮濕。**～·ity** /hjuːˈmɪdətɪ; hjuˈmɪdətɪ/ *n* [U] (degree of) moisture (in the air). 潮濕；濕氣；(空氣的)濕度。

hu·mili·ate /hjuːˈmɪlɪeɪt; hjuˈmɪlɪˌet/ *vt* [VP6A] cause to feel ashamed; put to shame; lower the dignity or self-respect of: 使蒙羞；使丟臉；屈辱；使失面子：*a country that was ～d by defeat;* 因戰敗而受屈辱的國家；*humiliating peace terms.* 屈辱的和平條款。**hu·mili·ation** /hjuːˌmɪlɪˈeɪʃn; hjuˌmɪlɪˈeʃən/ *n* [U] humiliating or being ～d; [C] instance of this: 蒙羞；丟臉；屈辱：*the humiliation of having to surrender.* 被迫投降之恥辱。

hu·mil·ity /hjuːˈmɪlətɪ; hjuˈmɪlətɪ/ *n* [U] humble condition or state of mind. 謙恭；謙讓；謙卑。

hum·ming·bird /ˈhʌmɪŋbɜːd; ˈhʌmɪŋˌbɝd/ *n* ⇨ hum(1).

hum·mock /ˈhʌmək; ˈhʌmək/ *n* hillock; rising ground in a marsh; hump in an ice-field. 小丘；沼澤中之小高地；冰丘。

hu·mor·ist /ˈhjuːmərɪst; ˈhjumərɪst/ *n* humorous talker or writer; facetious person. 談話幽默者；幽默作家；詼諧的人。

hu·mor·ous /ˈhjuːmərəs; ˈhjumərəs/ *adj* having or showing a sense of humour; funny: 有幽默感的；詼諧的：*a ～ writer,* eg Mark Twain; 幽默作家(例如馬克吐溫)；*～ remarks.* 幽默語。**～·ly** *adv*

hu·mour (US = **hu·mor**) /ˈhjuːmə(r); ˈhjumɚ/ *n* **1** [U] (capacity to cause or feel) amusement: 幽默；詼諧；幽默感：*a story full of ～;* 富於幽默的故事；*have no/not much/a good sense of ～.* 無(不大有，很有)幽默感。**2** [U] person's state of mind (esp at a particular time); temper: 心情(尤指某一時間的)；心境：*in a good/bad ～;* 高興(心情不佳)；*not in the ～ for work,* not feeling inclined to work; 無心工作；*in no ～ to trifle;* 無心嬉玩；*when the ～ takes him,* when he feels so inclined. 在他高興的時候。***out of ～,*** displeased; in a bad mood. 不高興；心情不好。**3** [C] (old use) one of four liquids (blood, phlegm, choler, melancholy) in the body, said to determine a person's mental and physical qualities. (舊用法)(血液，黏液，膽汁，憂鬱液四種)體液之一(據說能決定人之精神與身體情況)。□ *vt* [VP6A] give way to, gratify: 遷就；使滿足：*When a person is ill he may have to be ～ed,* his wishes may have to be granted, even if they are senseless. 一個人生病時，別人都得遷就他。*Is it wise to always ～ a child,* give it everything it wants? 老是縱容小孩是明智的嗎？

hump /hʌmp; hʌmp/ *n* **1** round lump, eg on a camel's back or (as a deformity) on a person's back. 圓形隆起物；駝峯；人背上之畸形隆肉。⇨ the illus at large. 參看 large 之插圖。**ˈ～·back** *n* (person having a) back with a ～. 駝背；駝背之人。**ˈ～-backed** *adj* having such a back. 駝背的；傴僂的。**2** ***have/give sb the ～,*** (sl) fit of depression or irritation. (俚)感覺(令某人)心情抑鬱或煩燥。□ *vt* [VP6A, 15B] ～ ***(up),*** make ～-shaped; gather the shoulders into a ～: 使隆起成圓形；弓起(背)：*The cat ～ed (up) her back when she saw the dog.* 這貓看見那狗時便弓起她的背。

humph /hʌmf; hʌmf *or spontaneously as a grunt*

with lips closed and then puffed open/ int used to show doubt or dissatisfaction. (表示懷疑或不滿)哼！

hu·mus /'hjuːməs ; 'hjuməs/ *n* [U] earth formed by the decay of vegetable matter (dead leaves, plants). 腐植土；腐植質。

Hun /hʌn ; hʌn/ *n* member of an Asiatic race which ravaged Europe in the 4th and 5th cc. 匈奴人(亞洲一種族之一員，曾於第四、五世紀蹂躪歐洲)。

hunch /hʌntʃ ; hʌntʃ/ *n* **1** thick piece; hunk; hump. 厚塊；厚片；圓形隆起物。**'~-back(ed),** = humpback(ed). **2** ***have a ~ that...,*** (colloq) think it likely that.... (俗)預感到…。□ *vt* [VP6A, 15B] **~ *(up),*** arch to form a hump: 彎曲而使之隆起；弓起: *sitting at the table with his shoulders ~ed up.* 聳着肩坐在桌旁。

hun·dred /'hʌndrəd ; 'hʌndrəd/ *n, adj* the number 100: 百；百個: *two ~ and five,* 205; 二百零五; *a few ~ people;* 數百人; *~s of people.* 數以百計的人。⇨ App 4. 參看附錄四。**'~·weight** *n* (often written 常寫爲 **cwt**) $\frac{1}{20}$ of one ton, 112 lb (in US 100 lb). 一噸之 $\frac{1}{20}$; 112 磅(在美國爲 100 磅)。⇨ App 5. 參看附錄五。**'~·fold,** (US) **ˌ~·'fold** *adv* one ~ times as much or as many. 百倍地。**~th** /'hʌndrədθ ; 'hʌndrədθ/ *n, adj* next after the 99th; one of a ~ equal parts. 第一百(的)；百分之一。

hung /hʌŋ ; hʌŋ/ *pt, pp* of hang.

hun·ger /'hʌŋgə(r) ; 'hʌŋgɚ/ *n* **1** [U] need, desire for food: 飢餓: *die of ~;* 餓死; *satisfy one's ~.* 充飢。***be/go on (a) '~-strike,*** (eg of a prisoner) refuse to take food as a protest, in order to win release, etc. (指囚犯等)絕食抗議(以求獲釋等)。**'~-march** *n* one undertaken, eg by unemployed workers, to call attention to sufferings, etc. 飢餓遊行(例如失業者所作的)。Hence, 由此產生, **'~-marcher** *n.* **2** (fig) any strong desire: (喻)慾望；渴望: *a ~ for excitement/adventure.* 尋求刺激(冒險)的慾望。□ *vi* [VP2A, 3A, 4C] **~ *(for/to do sth),*** feel, suffer from, ~; have a strong desire: 饑餓；渴望: *~ for news.* 渴望消息。

hun·gry /'hʌŋgrɪ ; 'hʌŋgrɪ/ *adj* (-ier, -iest) feeling, showing signs of, causing, hunger: 感到餓的；顯示飢餓的；引起飢餓的: *be/go ~.* 餓；挨餓。*The boy had a ~ look.* 那男孩顯出飢餓的樣子。*Hay-making is ~ work.* 晒乾草是易使人感到肚子餓的工作。*The orphan child was ~ for affection.* 這孤兒渴望著愛。**hun·grily** /'hʌŋgrəlɪ ; 'hʌŋgrɪlɪ/ *adv*

hunk /hʌŋk ; hʌŋk/ *n* thick piece cut off: (切下的)厚片；厚塊: *a ~ of bread/cheese/meat.* 厚厚的一塊麵包(乾酪，肉)。

hun·kers /'hʌŋkəz ; 'hʌŋkɚz/ *n pl* (colloq) haunches, (俗)臀部, esp 尤用於 ***on one's ~,*** in a squatting position. 蹲著。

hunt[1] /hʌnt ; hʌnt/ *n* **a/the ~, 1** act of ~ing: 狩獵；搜尋: *have a good ~;* 做一次滿意的狩獵; *find sth after a long ~,* search. 經長期搜尋後發現某物。**2** (esp in GB) group of persons who regularly ~ foxes and stags with horses and hounds; the area in which they do this: (尤用於英國)經常騎馬帶著獵狗狩獵狐及鹿之狩獵隊；其狩獵地區: *The Quorn H~;* 庫恩獵狐隊; *a member of the ~.* 獵隊中之一員；獵狐隊隊員。**ˌ~ 'ball,** ball organized by members of a ~. 獵人舞會。

hunt[2] /hʌnt ; hʌnt/ *vi, vt* **1** [VP6A, 2A, C] go after (wild animals) for food or sport: 狩獵: *~ big game;* 獵大獵物; *go out ~ing.* 去打獵。*Wolves ~ in packs.* 狼成羣獵食。⇨ *shooting at* shoot. **2** [VP 2A, 3A, 15B] search for. 搜索；尋找。**~ *down,*** pursue and find; bring to bay: 追尋而且捕獲；窮追: *~ down a criminal/an escaped prisoner.* 捕獲一罪犯(逃犯)。**~ *for,*** search for; try to find: 尋找；尋求: *~ for a lost book.* 尋找一本遺失的書。**~ *out,*** (try to) find by searching (sth that has been put away and forgotten): 尋出(放置起來而被遺忘之物): *~ out an old diary/a black tie that hasn't been needed for years.* 尋出一舊日記(數年未用的黑領帶)。**~ *up,*** search for (sth hidden or difficult to find): 尋找(隱藏或難發現之物): *~ up old records/references/quotations.* 搜尋舊記錄(參考資料，引用之文句)。**3** [VP6A, 15A] drive or chase away: 驅逐: *~ the neighbour's cats out of the garden.* 將鄰家的貓逐出花園。**4** [VP6A] (special uses in GB; foxhunting) follow the hounds through or in (a district): (英國之特殊用法；指獵狐)在(一地區)狩獵: *~ the county;* 在此郡中狩獵; employ (a horse) in ~ing: 騎(馬)狩獵: *~ one's horse all winter;* 整個冬季騎馬狩獵; act as master or huntsman of (a pack of hounds): 帶領(一隊獵犬)狩獵: *~ the hounds.* 帶着獵犬狩獵。**~er** *n* **1** person who ~s: 狩獵的人；獵人；搜尋者: *~ers of big game in Africa.* 狩獵非洲大獵物之獵人。(Note that in GB a person who ~s foxes, etc on horseback or shoots grouse, pheasants, etc is not called a ~er. 'Do you hunt/shoot?' is preferred to 'Are you a ~er?') (注意: 在英國騎馬獵狐等或以槍打獵松鷄、雉等之人，不稱爲 hunter。Do you hunt/shoot? 較 Are you a hunter? 爲佳。) **2** horse used in fox-hunting. 獵馬(獵狐用者)。**3** pocket watch with a metal cover protecting the glass face. 獵人錶(有金屬蓋保護錶面之懷錶)。**~·ing** *n* [U] **1** the act of ~ing; (esp in GB) fox-~ing: 狩獵；(尤用於英國)獵狐: *He's fond of ~ing.* 他喜歡打獵。**2** (attrib) (形容用法) *a '~ing-man;* 獵人; *a '~ing-horn.* 獵人用的號角。**'~ing ground,** (fig) place where one may search for sth with hope of success. 獵場；(喻)可尋獲某物之處。**ˌ~ing 'pink,** shade of red worn by huntsmen. 一種獵人裝常採用的紅色。**~·ress** /'hʌntrɪs ; 'hʌntrɪs/ *n* (liter) woman who ~s, eg the goddess Diana. (文)女獵人；狩獵女神(月神)。

hunts·man /'hʌntsmən ; 'hʌntsmən/ *n* (*pl* -men) **1** hunter(1). 狩獵之人；獵人。**2** man in charge of the hounds during a hunt(2). 獵狐時管理獵犬者。

hurdle /'hɜːdl ; 'hɝdl/ *n* **1** (GB) movable upright oblong frame of wood, etc used for making temporary fences, eg for sheep pens. (英)作臨時柵欄(如羊圈)用的長方形木架等；臨時圍欄。**2** light upright frame to be jumped over in a *'~-race.* 跳欄賽跑用的欄架。**3** (fig) difficulty to be overcome. (喻)障礙。□ *vt, vi* **1** [VP15B] **~ *off,*** fence with ~s. 圍以臨時圍欄。**2** [VP2A] jump over a ~; run in a ~-race. 跳欄；跳欄賽跑。**hur·dler** *n* person who makes ~s(1); person who runs in ~-races. 製臨時圍欄者；跳欄賽跑者。

hurdling

hurdy-gurdy /'hɜːdɪ gɜːdɪ ; 'hɝdɪˌgɝdɪ/ *n* street piano or barrel organ, usu mounted on wheels, played by turning a handle. 搖絃琴(街頭鋼琴或筒風琴，通常裝於輪上，演奏時旋轉一柄)。

hurl /hɜːl ; hɝl/ *vt* [VP6A, 15A, B] throw violently: 用力投擲；猛投: *~ a spear at a tiger.* 向一虎投擲矛。*They ~ed themselves at/upon the enemy and attacked them violently.* 他們撲向敵人並猛烈攻擊他們。□ *n* violent throw. 用力的投擲。

hurl·ing /'hɜːlɪŋ ; 'hɝlɪŋ/ *n* [U] Irish ball game resembling hockey. 類似曲棍球的愛爾蘭球戲。

hurly-burly /'hɜːlɪ bɜːlɪ ; 'hɝlɪˌbɝlɪ/ *n* [U] noisy commotion; uproar. 喧囂；騷動。

hur·rah /hʊˈrɑː; həˈrɔ/ (also **hur·ray** /hʊˈreɪ; həˈre/) *int* expressing joy, welcome, approval, etc: 歡呼聲(表示欣喜,歡迎,贊成等): *H~ for the Queen!* 女王萬歲! *Hip, hip, ~!* 歡呼之聲! □ *vi* shout ~; cheer. 歡呼。

hur·ri·cane /ˈhʌrɪkən *US:* ˈ-keɪn; ˈhɝɪˌken/ *n* [C] violent windstorm, esp a W Indian cyclone. 颶風(尤指西印度羣島之旋風)。 **ˈ~ lamp/lantern** *nn* kind with the light protected from the wind. 防風燈。

hurry /ˈhʌrɪ; ˈhɝɪ/ *n* [U, C] eager haste; wish to get sth done quickly; (with neg, or in the interr) need for haste: 急忙;匆忙;(用於否定或疑問句中)匆忙的必要: *Everything was ~ and excitement.* 一切都是匆忙與興奮。*Why all this ~?* 爲什麼這樣匆忙? *Is there any/a ~*, need for ~? 有急忙的必要嗎? *Don't start yet—there's no ~*, there's plenty of time. 還不要動身──時間還早。*in a ~,* **(a)** impatient; acting, anxious to act, quickly: 急忙的;匆忙的;慌忙的: *He was in a ~ to leave.* 他急着要離去。*In his ~ to catch the train, he left his luggage in the taxi.* 他慌忙地去趕火車的時候,把行李忘在計程車中了。**(b)** (colloq) soon, willingly: (俗)不久;願意地: *I shan't ask that rude man to dinner again in a ~.* 我不願再請那個粗魯的人吃飯了。**(c)** (colloq) easily: (俗)容易地: *You won't find a better specimen than that in a ~.* 你不容易找到比那更好的樣品。□ *vt, vi* (*pt, pp* -ried) [VP6A, 15A, B, 2A, C] (cause to) move or do sth quickly or too quickly: (使)匆忙;趕快;慌張;催促;急趕: *Don't ~; there's plenty of time.* 不要忙,時間還多哩。*It's no use ~ing her/trying to make her ~.* 催她是無用的。*If we ~ the work, it may be spoiled.* 要是我們趕工,可能將工作弄糟。*He picked up his bag and hurried off.* 他拿起提包匆匆離去。*More soldiers were hurried to the front line.* 更多的軍隊被急急調往前線。*H~ up!* Make haste. 趕快! *H~ him up!* Make him ~. 催他趕快! **hur·ried** *adj* done, etc in a ~; showing haste: 匆忙的;急促的;慌忙的: *a hurried meal;* 匆忙的一頓飯; *write a few hurried lines.* 草草寫幾行。**hur·ried·ly** *adv*

hurt /hɜːt; hɝt/ *vt, vi* (*pt, pp* hurt) **1** [VP6A, B, 2A] cause bodily injury or pain (to); damage: (使)受傷;(使)疼痛;傷害: *He ~ his back when he fell.* 他跌倒時傷了背部。*He was more frightened than ~.* 他受驚較受傷更重。*Did you ~ yourself?* 你弄傷自己了嗎? *These shoes are too tight; they ~ (me).* 這雙鞋太緊,使我的脚痛。**2** [VP6A] pain a person, his feelings: 傷害(某人,其感情);使傷心: *Their criticisms have ~ him deeply.* 他們的批評使他非常傷心。*She was ~ to find that no one admired her performance.* 她發現無人讚賞她的表演而感到傷心。 **3** [VP2A] suffer injury; come to harm; have a bad effect: 受損傷;有害;有不良影響: *It won't ~ to postpone the matter for a few days.* 將此事擱置幾天並無妨礙。□ *n* [U] (or with *indef art*) harm; injury: (或與不定冠詞連用)傷害;損害; *I intended no ~ to his feelings.* 我無意傷害他的感情。*It was a severe ~ to his pride.* 那對他的自尊心是個嚴重的創傷。 **~·ful** /-fl; -fəl/ *adj* causing ~: 造成傷害的;有害的: *~ful to the health.* 有害於健康。

hurtle /ˈhɜːtl; ˈhɝtl̩/ *vi* [VP2C] rush or fly violently: 猛衝;急飛: *During the gale chimney-pots and roof-tiles came hurtling down.* 狂風期間,煙囱頂管和屋頂瓦急遽地落下。

hus·band /ˈhʌzbənd; ˈhʌzbənd/ *n* man to whom a woman is married. 丈夫。□ *vt* [VP6A] use sparingly: 節省;節用: *~ one's resources/strength.* 節用資金(體力)。

hus·band·man /ˈhʌzbəndmən; ˈhʌzbəndmən/ *n* (*pl* -men /-mən; -mən/) (old use) farmer. (舊用法)農夫。 **hus·bandry** /ˈhʌzbəndrɪ; ˈhʌzbəndrɪ/ *n* [U] farming; management: 耕作;飼養;管理: *animal husbandry;* 畜牧;畜牧學; *good/bad husbandry.* 管理(不)得法。

hush /hʌʃ; hʌʃ/ *vt, vi* [VP2A, 15A, B] make or become silent or quiet: 使肅靜;使安靜;變爲安靜: *H~!* Be silent! 肅靜! *She ~ed the baby to sleep.* 她使嬰兒安靜入睡。 **~ sth up,** prevent it from becoming public knowledge: 秘而不宣: *She tried unsuccessfully to ~ up the fact that her husband was an ex-convict.* 她企圖隱瞞她丈夫以前犯過案的事實,但未成功。□ *n* **a/the ~,** silence; stillness: 肅靜;安靜: *in the ~ of night.* 在夜的寂靜中。*There was a sudden ~.* 突然肅靜下來。**ˈ~-money** *n* money paid to ~ sth up (usu sth scandalous or discreditable). (爲防止某人洩露醜聞或不名譽之事等而予以賄賂之)緘口錢;遮羞費。**ˌ~-ˈ~** *adj* (colloq) (to be) kept very secret: (俗)極秘密的;需要高度保密的: *a ~-~ affair.* 極秘密的事。

husk /hʌsk; hʌsk/ *n* (usu *pl*) dry outer covering of seeds, esp of grain: (通常用複數)外殼;外皮(尤指穀類者): *rice in the ~*, with the ~s not removed; 稻穀; (fig) worthless outside part of anything. (喻)無價值的外部。⇨ the illus at cereal. 參看cereal 之插圖。□ *vt* remove ~s from. 去…之殼。

husky /ˈhʌskɪ; ˈhʌskɪ/ *adj* (-ier, -iest) **1** (dry) like husks. 似穀殼的;似穀殼般乾燥的。 **2** (of a person, his voice) hoarse; with a dry and almost whispering voice: (指人及人聲)嘶啞的;嗄聲的: *a ~ voice/cough.* 嘶啞之聲(乾咳)。*You sound ~ this morning.* 今早你的聲音有些啞。 **3** (colloq) big and strong: (俗)高大强壯的: *a fine ~ woman, excellent as a farmer's wife.* 高大强壯的好女子,農人理想的妻子。□ *n* **1** thick-coated dog of N American Eskimos. 北美洲愛斯基摩人的厚毛狗。 **2** ~(3) person. 高大强壯的人。**husk·ily** /-ɪlɪ; -əlɪ/ *adv* **huski·ness** *n*

hus·sar /hʊˈzɑː(r); hʊˈzɑr/ *n* soldier of a light cavalry regiment. 輕騎兵。

hussy /ˈhʌsɪ; ˈhʌsɪ/ *n* (*pl* -sies) worthless woman; ill-mannered girl. 賤婦;粗野的女子。

hus·tings /ˈhʌstɪŋz; ˈhʌstɪŋz/ *n pl* **the ~,** proceedings (canvassing, speech-making, etc) leading up to a parliamentary election. 國會議員之競選程序(遊說;講演等)。

hustle /ˈhʌsl; ˈhʌsl̩/ *vt, vi* [VP6A, 15A, B, 2A, C] **1** push or jostle roughly; (force sb to) hurry: 粗野地推;匆忙;催促: *The police ~d the thief into their van.* 警察將那竊賊粗野地推進囚車中。*I don't want to ~ you into a decision.* 我不想催促你作決定。 **2** (esp US) (colloq) sell or obtain sth by energetic (esp deceitful) activity. (尤美)(俗)以積極的(尤指欺詐的)行動賣出或得到某物。 **3** (US sl) engage in prostitution. (美俚)做娼妓。□ *n* (*sing* only) quick and energetic activity: (僅用單數)迅速而有力的活動: *The railway station was a scene of ~ and bustle.* 火車站是喧囂擾攘的場所。**hus·tler** *n* person who ~s; (US sl) prostitute. 猛推者;催促者;(美俚)妓女。

hut /hʌt; hʌt/ *n* **1** small, roughly made house or shelter: 簡陋的小屋: *Alpine huts*, for the use of mountain climbers. 阿爾卑斯山上的小屋(爲爬山者所設)。 **2** temporary wooden building for soldiers. 臨時的木造營房。**ˈhut·ment** *n* encampment of huts. 臨時營區;臨時營房。 **hut·ted** *adj*: *hutted camps*, with huts, not tents (for troops, etc) 臨時營房(有木造營房,而非帳篷,供軍隊等使用)。

hutch /hʌtʃ; hʌtʃ/ *n* box or cage with a front of wire netting, esp one used for rabbits. 正面用鐵絲網網起的箱或籠;(尤指)兔籠。

hya·cinth /ˈhaɪəsɪnθ; ˈhaɪəˌsɪnθ/ *n* plant growing from a bulb; its sweet-smelling flowers. 風信子;風信子之花。 **ˈwater ~,** wild plant that grows in floating masses on rivers, lakes, etc and may hinder navigation. 一種大批漂浮於河流、湖泊等上並可能妨礙航行之野生植物。

hy·aena /haɪˈiːnə; haɪˈinə/ ⇨ hyena.

hy·brid /ˈhaɪbrɪd; ˈhaɪbrɪd/ *n, adj* (animal, plant, etc) from parents of different species or varieties: 雜種的(動植物等);雜種;混合之物;混合的: *A mule is a ~ animal.* 騾是雜種動物。*'Cablegram' is a ~; half* *the word is Latin and half is Greek.* cablegram —字是混合語,半爲拉丁語,半爲希臘語。**~·ize**/-aɪz ; -ˌaɪz/ *vt, vi* [VP6A, 2A] (cause to) produce ~s; interbreed. (使)產生雜種;雜交繁殖。

hy·dra /ˈhaɪdrə ; ˈhaɪdrə/ *n* (GK myth) great sea serpent with many heads that grew again if cut off. (希神)海蛇怪(生有許多頭,斬去後仍會生出)。

hy·drangea /haɪˈdreɪndʒə ; haɪˈdrendʒə/ *n* shrub with large round heads of white, blue or pink flowers. 八仙花屬;紫陽花(有白、藍或粉紅色大花球)。

hy·drant /ˈhaɪdrənt ; ˈhaɪdrənt/ *n* pipe from a water-main (esp in a street) with a nozzle to which a hose can be attached for street-cleaning, putting out fires, etc. (尤指街上的)給水栓;消防栓。

hy·drate /ˈhaɪdreɪt ; ˈhaɪdret/ *n* chemical compound of water with another substance. 水合物;水化物。□ *vt, vi* combine with water to make a ~; become a ~. 使與水結合而成水化物;成爲水化物。

hy·drau·lic /haɪˈdrɔːlɪk ; haɪˈdrɔlɪk/ *adj* of water moving through pipes; worked by the pressure of a fluid, esp water: 通過水管流動之水的;用液體(特指水)的壓力控制的; 水力的; 水壓的; 用水發動的: *a ~ lift;* 水力昇降機; *~ brakes*, in which the braking force is transmitted by compressed fluid; 水力制動器(制動之力量由壓縮之液體傳送); hardening under water: 在水中變硬的;水硬的: *~ cement.* 水硬水泥。**hy·drau·lics** *n pl* science of using water to produce power. 水力學。

hy·dro·car·bon /ˌhaɪdrəˈkɑːbən ; ˌhaɪdroˈkɑrbən/ *n* [C] substance formed of hydrogen and carbon, eg benzene, paraffin, coal-gas. 烴,碳化氫(例如苯,石蠟,煤氣)。

hy·dro·chloric /ˌhaɪdrəˈklɒrɪk *US:* -ˈklɔːr- ; ˌhaɪdrəˈklorɪk/ *adj*: *~ acid,* acid **(HCl)** containing hydrogen and chlorine. 氫氯酸;鹽酸(HCl)。

hy·dro·elec·tric /ˌhaɪdrəʊɪˈlektrɪk ; ˌhaɪdro·ɪˈlɛktrɪk/ *adj* of electricity produced by water-power. 水力發電的。

hy·dro·foil /ˈhaɪdrəfɔɪl ; ˈhaɪdroˌfɔɪl/ *n* boat equipped with plates or fins which, when the boat is in motion, raise the hull out of the water. 水翼船。

hy·dro·gen /ˈhaɪdrədʒən ; ˈhaɪdrədʒən/ *n* gas (symbol **H**) without colour, taste or smell, that combines with oxygen to form water. 氫(無色,無味,無臭的氣體,符號爲H,與氧化合變成水)。**ˈ~ bomb** (also 亦作 *fusion bomb*) variety of *atomic bomb*, ⇨ atomic. 氫彈。**ˌ~ peˈroxide** *n* solution of peroxide of ~, **(H_2O_2)**, used as an antiseptic and bleaching agent. 過氧化氫;雙氧水(H_2O_2, 用作防腐劑或殺菌劑以及漂白劑)。

hy·drop·athy /haɪˈdrɒpəθɪ ; haɪˈdrɑpəθɪ/ *n* [U] use of water (internally and externally) in the treatment of disease. 水療法。**hy·dro·pathic** /ˌhaɪdrəˈpæθɪk ; ˌhaɪdrəˈpæθɪk/ *adj* of ~. 水療法的。

hy·dro·pho·bia /ˌhaɪdrəˈfəʊbɪə ; ˌhaɪdrəˈfobɪə/ *n* [U] rabies; disease marked by strong contractions of the muscles of the throat and consequent inability to drink water. 狂犬病;恐水症。

hy·dro·plane /ˈhaɪdrəpleɪn ; ˈhaɪdrəˌplen/ *n* hydrofoil; motor-boat with a flat bottom, able to skim very fast over the surface; (old name for) seaplane. 水翼船;水上滑行艇;(舊稱)水上飛機。

hy·dro·pon·ics /ˌhaɪdrəˈpɒnɪks ; ˌhaɪdrəˈpɑnɪks/ *n pl* art of growing plants without soil, in water to which necessary chemical food is supplied. 水栽法(不用土壤,而用水加以化學養料培植植物的方法)。

hy·ena, hy·aena /haɪˈiːnə ; haɪˈinə/ *n* flesh-eating wild animal, like a wolf, with a laughing cry. 鬣狗;土狼。⇨ the illus at large. 參看 large 之插圖。

hy·giene /ˈhaɪdʒiːn ; ˈhaɪdʒin/ *n* [U] science of, rules for, healthy living; cleanliness. 衞生學;衞生。**hy·gienic** /haɪˈdʒiːnɪk *US:* ˌhaɪdʒɪˈenɪk ; ˌhaɪdʒɪˈɛnɪk/ *adj* of ~; likely to promote health; free from disease germs: 衞生學的;保健的;衞生的: *hygienic conditions.* 衞生環境。**hy·gieni·cally** /-klɪ ; -klɪ/ *adv*

hy·men /ˈhaɪmən ; ˈhaɪmən/ *n* **1 H~**, Greek god of marriage. 海門(希臘神話中司婚姻之神)。**2** (anat) fold of tissue partly closing the vagina of a virgin girl or woman. (解剖)處女膜。

hymn /hɪm ; hɪm/ *n* song of praise to God, esp one for use in a religious service. 讚美詩;聖歌。□ *vt* praise (God) in ~s; express (praise) in ~s. 唱聖歌讚美(上帝); 以聖歌表示(讚美)。**hym·nal** /ˈhɪmnəl ; ˈhɪmnəl/ *n* book of ~s. 讚美詩集。

hy·per·bola /haɪˈpɜːbələ ; haɪˈpɝbələ/ *n* curve produced when a cone is cut by a plane passing anywhere except through its point. 雙曲線。

hy·per·bole /haɪˈpɜːbəlɪ ; haɪˈpɝbəˌli/ *n* [U] (use of) exaggerated statement(s) made for effect and not intended to be taken literally; [C] instance of this, eg *waves as high as Everest.* 誇張法;誇張的敍述(例如:像埃佛勒斯峯一般高的海浪)。

hy·per·criti·cal /ˌhaɪpəˈkrɪtɪkl ; ˌhaɪpəˈkrɪtɪkl/ *adj* too critical, esp of small faults. 吹毛求疵的;苛評的。

hy·per·market /ˈhaɪpəmɑːkɪt ; ˈhaɪpəˌmɑrkɪt/ *n* immense supermarket occupying an extensive area, outside a town, with a large car park, selling all varieties of goods. 巨型超級市場(在市鎮之外,佔地甚廣,有大停車場,銷售各種貨品)。

hy·phen /ˈhaɪfn ; ˈhaɪfən/ *n* the mark (-) used to join two words together (as in *Anglo-French*), or to show that a word has been divided between the end of one line and the beginning of another. 連字號;短橫;短劃(用以連接一複合字,如Anglo-French,或在轉行時用以劃分一字的音節)。⇨ App 9. 參看附錄九。□ *vt* join (words) with a ~; write (a compound word) with a ~. 以連字號連接(字);用連字號連接(複合字)。**~·ate** /-eɪt ; -ˌet/ *vt* = ~.

hyp·no·sis /hɪpˈnəʊsɪs ; hɪpˈnosɪs/ *n* (*pl* -ses /-siːz ; -siz/) [U, C] state like deep sleep in which a person's acts may be controlled by another person. 催眠狀態。**hyp·notic** /hɪpˈnɒtɪk ; hɪpˈnɑtɪk/ *adj* of ~: 催眠的: *in a hypnotic state.* 在催眠狀態中。**hyp·not·ism** /ˈhɪpnətɪzəm ; ˈhɪpnəˌtɪzəm/ *n* [U] artificial production of ~. 催眠;催眠術。**hyp·not·ize** /ˈhɪpnətaɪz ; ˈhɪpnəˌtaɪz/ *vt* [VP6A] produce ~ in (sb). 施催眠術於(某人)。**hyp·not·ist** /ˈhɪpnətɪst ; ˈhɪpnətɪst/ *n* person able to produce ~. 能施催眠術者。

hypo /ˈhaɪpəʊ ; ˈhaɪpo/ *n* (colloq abbr of) sodium thiosulphate **$(Na_2S_2O_2)$**, used in photography as a fixing agent. (俗, sodium thiosulphate之略)低亞硫酸鈉($Na_2S_2O_2$, 在攝影中用作定影劑)。

hy·po·chon·dria /ˌhaɪpəˈkɒndrɪə ; ˌhaɪpəˈkɑndrɪə/ *n* [U] state of mental depression either without apparent cause or due to unnecessary anxiety about one's health. 疑病(症);憂鬱症。**hy·po·chon·driac** /ˌhaɪpəˈkɒndrɪæk ; ˌhaɪpəˈkɑndrɪˌæk/ *adj* of, affected by, ~. 疑病症的;患疑病症的。▭ *n* person who suffers from ~. 疑病症患者。

hy·poc·risy /hɪˈpɒkrəsɪ ; hɪˈpɑkrəsɪ/ *n* (*pl* -sies) [C, U] (instance of) falsely making oneself appear to be virtuous or good. 僞善;虛僞。**hyp·ocrite** /ˈhɪpəkrɪt ; ˈhɪpəˌkrɪt/ *n* person guilty of ~. 僞君子;僞善者。**hy·po·criti·cal** /ˌhɪpəˈkrɪtɪkl ; ˌhɪpəˈkrɪtɪkl/ *adj* of ~ or a hypocrite. 僞善的;僞君子的;虛僞的。**hy·po·criti·cally** /-klɪ ; -klɪ/ *adv*

hy·po·der·mic /ˌhaɪpəˈdɜːmɪk ; ˌhaɪpəˈdɝmɪk/ *adj* (of drugs, etc) injected beneath the skin: (指藥物等)皮下注射的: *~ injections;* 皮下注射; *a ~ needle/syringe,* used for giving such injections. 皮下注射針(器)。⇨ the illus at syringe. 參看 syringe 之插圖。□ *n* ~ injection or syringe. 皮下注射;皮下注射器。

hy·pot·en·use /haɪˈpɒtənjuːz *US:* -tnuːs ; haɪˈpɑtn̩ˌus/ *n* side of a right-angled triangle opposite the right angle. (直角三角形之)斜邊;弦。

hy·poth·ecate /haɪˈpɒθɪkeɪt ; haɪˈpɑθəˌket/ *vt* (legal) pledge; mortgage. (法律)抵押;質押。

hy·poth·esis /haɪˈpɒθəsɪs ; haɪˈpɑθəsɪs/ *n* (*pl* -ses /-siːz ; -ˌsiz/) idea, suggestion, put forward as a starting-point for reasoning or explanation. 假設；假說。**hy·po·theti·cal** /ˌhaɪpəˈθetɪkl ; ˌhaɪpəˈθɛtɪkḷ/ *adj* of, based on, a ～; not based on certain knowledge. 假設的；假定的；臆說的。

hys·sop /ˈhɪsəp ; ˈhɪsəp/ *n* strong-smelling plant formerly used in medicine. 牛膝草(一種氣味濃烈的植物，昔時用作藥品)。

hys·teria /hɪˈstɪərɪə ; hɪsˈtɪrɪə/ *n* [U] **1** disturbance of the nervous system, with outbursts of emotion, often uncontrollable. 癔病；歇斯底里症(一種精神神經病，患者情緒無常，常不能自制)。 **2** senseless, uncontrolled excitement, eg in a crowd at a football match. 無意義的不可抑制的興奮(例如群衆觀看足球賽時)。 **hys·teri·cal** /hɪˈsterɪkl ; hɪsˈtɛrɪkḷ/ *adj* caused by, suffering from, ～: 歇斯底里症引起的；患歇斯底里症的: *hysterical laughter;* 狂笑; *an hysterical outburst of fury.* 勃然大怒。**hys·teri·cally** /-klɪ ; -klɪ/ *adv* **hys·ter·ics** /hɪˈsterɪks ; hɪsˈtɛrɪks/ *n pl* attack of ～: 歇斯底里症的發作: *go into hysterics,* become hysterical. 發歇斯底里症。

Ii

I¹ i /aɪ ; aɪ/ (*pl* I's i's /aɪz ; aɪz/), the ninth letter of the English alphabet; symbol for Roman numeral 1, ⇨ App 4. 英文字母之第九個字母；羅馬數字的1(參看附錄四)。

I² /aɪ ; aɪ/ *pers pron* used by a speaker or writer to refer to himself. 我(說話者或作者指自己)。 Cf 參較 *me,* object form, and *we, us,* plural forms. 受格爲 me, 複數爲 we 及 us。

iamb /ˈaɪæm ; ˈaɪæmb/ *n* = iambus.

iam·bus /aɪˈæmbəs ; aɪˈæmbəs/ *n* (*pl* ～es or -bi /-baɪ ; -baɪ/) (prosody) metrical foot of one unaccented and one accented syllable eg *a'lone.* (韻律)抑揚格(卽一輕音節及一重音節構成的音步，例如 a'lone)。 **iam·bic** /aɪˈæmbɪk ; aɪˈæmbɪk/ *adj* of, containing, ～es: 抑揚格的；含有抑揚格的: *iambic feet,* 抑揚格音步, eg 例如 I ˈcome/from ˈhaunts/of ˈcoot/and ˈfern. □ *n pl* **iam·bics** iambic verse. 抑揚格的詩。

ibex /ˈaɪbeks ; ˈaɪbɛks/ *n* wild goat (of the Alps and Pyrenees) with large curved horns. (阿爾卑斯山和庇里牛斯山之)生有大彎角的野山羊。

ibi·dem /ˈɪbɪdem ; ɪˈbaɪdɛm/ *adv* (abbr 略作 *ibid*) (Lat) in the same book, chapter, etc (previously quoted). (拉)在(前所引用之)同一書、章等中；出處同上。

ibis /ˈaɪbɪs ; ˈaɪbɪs/ *n* large wading bird (like a stork or heron) found in lakes and swamps in warm climates. 朱鷺(大的涉禽，似鸛或蒼鷺，見於溫帶之湖泊與沼澤中)。

ice¹ /aɪs ; aɪs/ *n* **1** [U] frozen water; water made solid by cold: 冰: *Is the ice thick enough for skating?* 這冰的厚度可以溜冰嗎？ ***break the ice,*** (fig) get people on friendly terms; overcome formality or reserve; take the first steps in a delicate matter. (喻)使人們融洽；打破拘束或矜持；着手做一須愼重處理之事。 ***cut no ice (with sb),*** have little or no effect or influence (on him). 對(某人)無作用，無影響力。 ***keep sth on ice,*** in a refrigerator; (fig) reserve for later use. 貯藏於電冰箱中；(喻)保留供日後使用。 ***be skating on thin ice,*** (fig) in a dangerous or delicate situation. (喻)如履薄冰；在危險或須愼重將事的境況中。 **dry ice,** ⇨dry¹(12). **2** [C] frozen sweet of various kinds: 冰凍的各種甜食: *water-ice;* 冰糕；果汁棒; *cream ices;* 冰淇淋; *two strawberry ices.* 兩份草莓冰。⇨ ice-cream below. 參看下列之 ice-cream. **3** (compounds) (複合字) **ˈIce Age** *n* time when much of the N hemisphere was covered with glaciers; glacial period. 冰河時代。 **ˈice-axe** *n* axe used by mountain climbers for cutting steps in ice. (爬山者所用之)破冰斧。 **ˈice·berg** *n* mass of ice (broken off a glacier) moving in the sea; (fig) unemotional person: 冰山(漂浮於海上之大塊冰層，爲冰河的斷離部份)；(喻)冷淡的人: *his iceberg of a wife.* 他那冷淡的妻子。 **ˈice·boat** *n* boat fitted with runners and sails for travelling on a frozen lake or sea. 冰上滑行的船。 **ˈice·bound** *adj* (of harbours, etc) obstructed by ice. (指港口等)冰封的。 **ˈice·box** *n* box in which ice is used to keep food cool; (US) refrigerator. 冰箱；(美)電冰箱。 **ˈice·breaker** *n* ship with strong curved bows used for breaking a passage through ice. 破冰船。 **ˈice·cap** *n* permanent covering of ice sloping down on all sides from a high centre. 冰帽；冰臺(永積的冰層，自中心向各方傾斜)。 **ˌice-ˈcream** *n* [C, U] (portion of) cream or custard (or various modern substitutes), sweetened, and flavoured and frozen. (一份)冰淇淋。 **ˈice·cube** *n* cube of ice made in an icetray in a refrigerator. (冰箱內結冰盤中製成的)冰塊。 **ˈice·fall** *n* steep part of a glacier, like a frozen waterfall. 冰布(冰河之陡峭部份，似結冰之瀑布)。 **ˈice·field** *n* large expanse of (esp marine) ice in the Polar regions. 兩極地區之(尤指海上)冰原。 **ˈice·floe** /-fləʊ ; -ˌflo/ *n* large sheet of floating ice. 大浮冰。 **ˈice-free** *adj* (of a port or harbour) free from ice. (指港口)不凍的。⇨ icebound above. 參看上列之 icebound。 **ˈice hockey,** ⇨ hockey. **ˈice·house** *n* building often partly or wholly underground for storing ice in winter for use in summer. 儲冰庫(常是部份或整個建於地下，在多季貯冰以備夏季之用)。 **ˌice-ˈlolly** *n* flavoured ice on a stick. 冰棒。 **ˈice-man** /-mæn ; -ˌmæn/ *n* (*pl* -men) (US) man who retails and delivers ice (for use in iceboxes, etc). (美)冰商；送冰人。 **ˈice·pack** *n* **(a)** stretch of sea covered with broken ice that has drifted into masses. (海中的)冰積塊。 **(b)** bag of broken ice used as an application, eg to the head, for fever. 冰袋(作爲敷用物，例如發燒時置於頭上者)。 **ˈice·pick** *n* tool for breaking ice. (將冰擊碎之)冰鋤。 **ˈice·rink** *n* indoor skating-rink with a floor of artificial ice. 用人造冰作冰池之室內溜冰場。 **ˈice-show** *n* variety entertainment in which the performers are on ice-skates (on a floor of artificial ice). (在人造冰上之)溜冰綜藝表演。 **ˈice-skate** *n* thin metal runner or blade on a boot for skating on ice. 溜冰鞋底之滑刀或冰刀。□ *vi* skate on ice. 溜冰。⇨ the illus at skate. 參看 skate 之插圖。 **ˈice-tray** *n* one kept in the deep-freeze compartment of a refrigerator, for making cubes of ice. 冰箱內製冰塊的盤。

an iceberg

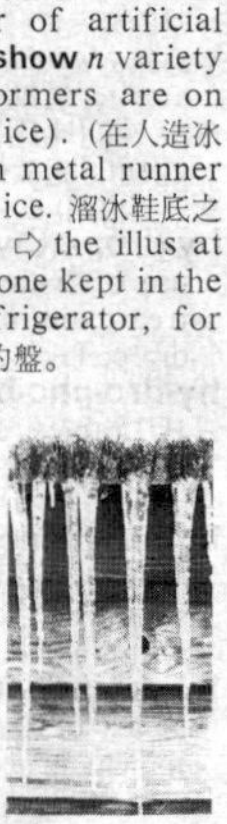

icicles

ice² /aɪs ; aɪs/ *vt, vi* **1** [VP6A] make very cold: 使冰冷: *ice a bottle of beer;* 冰一瓶啤酒; *iced water.* 冰水。 **2** [VP2C, 15B] ～ ***over/up,*** cover, become covered, with a coating of ice: 用冰層覆蓋；覆有冰層: *The pond (was) iced over.* 池水表面結了冰。*The wings of the aircraft had iced up.* 飛機

的兩翼覆有冰。 **3** [VP6A] cover (a cake) with sugar icing. 加糖霜於(糕)上。⇨ icing.

ich·neu·mon /ɪkˈnjuːmən *US:* -ˈnuː- ; ɪkˈnjumən/ *n* **1** small brown weasel-like animal noted for destroying crocodiles' eggs. 貓鼬(棕色似鼬小動物,善於破壞鱷卵)。 **2** (also 亦作 ˈ~-**fly**) insect which lays its eggs in or on the larva of another insect. 姬蜂(產卵於其他昆蟲之幼蟲體上或體內的一種昆蟲)。

icicle /ˈaɪsɪkl ; ˈaɪsɪkl̩/ *n* pointed piece of ice formed by the freezing of dripping water. 冰柱。

icing /ˈaɪsɪŋ ; ˈaɪsɪŋ/ *n* [U] **1** mixture of sugar, white of egg, flavouring, etc for covering cake(s). (糖,蛋白,香料等混合覆於糕點上的)糖衣;糖霜。 **2** formation of ice on the wings of aircraft. 積冰(機翼上的結冰現象)。

icon /ˈaɪkɒn ; ˈaɪkɑn/ *n* (in the Eastern Church) painting, carving or mosaic of a sacred person, itself regarded as sacred. (東方正教中被視爲神聖物的)聖像。

icons

icono·clast /aɪˈkɒnəklæst ; aɪˈkɑnəˌklæst/ *n* person who took part in the movement against the use of images in religious worship in the churches of Eastern Europe in the 8th and 9th cc (also applied to Puritans in England, 17th c); (fig) person who attacks popular beliefs or established customs which he thinks mistaken or unwise. (第八、九世紀東歐教會中)反對崇拜偶像者(亦指十七世紀英國的淸教徒);(喻)抨擊一般信仰與既定習俗者。

icy /ˈaɪsɪ ; ˈaɪsɪ/ *adj* (-ier, -iest) very cold, like ice: 極冷的;冰冷的: *icy winds;* 寒風; covered with ice: 覆蓋着冰的: *icy roads;* 覆蓋着冰的道路; (fig) (喩) *an icy welcome/manner.* 冷淡的歡迎(態度)。 **icily** /ˈaɪsɪlɪ ; ˈaɪslɪ/ *adv* (lit, fig) in an icy manner. (字面,喩)冰冷地;冷冰冰地。

id /ɪd ; ɪd/ *n* (psych) **(the)** ~, person's unconscious instincts and impulses. (心理)本我(人類不知覺的本能與衝動)。

I'd /aɪd ; aɪd/ = I had; I would.

idea /aɪˈdɪə ; aɪˈdiə/ *n* **1** thought; picture in the mind: 思想;槪念: *This book gives you a good ~ of life in ancient Greece.* 這本書使你對於古希臘的生活得到清楚的槪念。 **2** plan; scheme; design; purpose: 計畫;主意;計策;目的: *That man is full of new ~s.* 那人有很多新主意。 **3** opinion: 意見: *You shouldn't force your ~s on other people.* 你不應該强迫別人聽從你的意見。 **4** vague belief; fancy; feeling that sth is probable: 模糊的想法;想像;認爲某事可能發生的感覺: *I have an ~ that she will be late.* 我認爲她會遲到。 **5** conception: 觀念: *What ~ can a man who is blind from birth have of colour?* 生來卽盲的人對顏色會有何觀念? *Picnicking is not my ~ of pleasure.* 我覺得野餐沒有什麼樂趣。 *You can have no ~ (of) how anxious we have been.* 你不知道我們有多麼着急。 ***put ˈ~s into sb's head,*** give him expectations that are not likely to be realized. 使存幻想;使抱空想。 **6** (in exclamations): (用於感嘆句): *The ~ of such a thing! What an ~!* (used to suggest that what has been suggested is unrealistic, outrageous, etc). (用以表示所建議者不切實際,駭人聽聞等)竟然有這樣的念頭!多麼奇怪的念頭啊! **7** way of thinking: 想法: *the young ~,* the child's mind. 孩子的想法。

ideal /aɪˈdɪəl ; aɪˈdiəl/ *adj* **1** satisfying one's idea of what is perfect: 理想的;完美的: *~ weather for a holiday.* 理想的假日天氣。 **2** (contrasted with *real*) existing only in the imagination or as an idea; not likely to be achieved: (與 real 相對)想像中的;理想中的: *~ happiness;* 想像中的快樂; *~ plans for reforming the world.* 改造世界的理想中的計畫。 □ *n* [C] idea, example, looked upon as perfect: 理想;理想的東西: *the high ~s of the Christian religion.* 基督教的崇高的理想。 *She's looking for a husband but hasn't found her ~ yet.* 她正在找丈夫,但尙未找到一位理想的。 **~ly** /aɪˈdɪəlɪ ; aɪˈdiəlɪ/ *adv*

ideal·ism /aɪˈdɪəlɪzəm ; aɪˈdiəlˌɪzəm/ *n* [U] **1** living according to, being guided by, one's ideals. 根據個人理想的生活。 **2** (in art) (opposite of *realism*) imaginative treatment, showing beauty and perfection even if this means being untrue to facts. (藝術)(爲 realism 之相反字)理想主義;想像的創作手法(表現完美的境界而不問是否與事實相符)。 **3** (in philosophy) system of thought in which ideas are believed to be the only real things or the only things of which we can know anything. (哲學)觀念論;唯心論。 **ideal·ist** /-ɪst ; -ɪst/ *n* person who believes in ~. 理想主義者;唯心論者。 **ideal·istic** /aɪˌdɪəˈlɪstɪk ; aɪˌdiəlˈɪstɪk/ *adj* of idealists and ~. 理想主義(者)的;唯心論(者)的。

ideal·ize /aɪˈdɪəlaɪz ; aɪˈdiəlˌaɪz/ *vt* [VP6A] see, think of, as perfect: 使合於理想;視爲理想;理想化: *Some biographers ~ their subjects.* 有些傳記作家將他們的寫作對象理想化了。 **ideal·iz·ation** /aɪˌdɪəlaɪˈzeɪʃn *US:* -lɪˈz- ; aɪˌdiələˈzeʃən/ *n*

idem /ˈaɪdem ; ˈaɪdɛm/ *n, adj* (Lat) (by) the same author, etc; the same word, book, authority, etc (already mentioned). (拉)同作者;同一字、書、根據等;同上;同前。

ident·ical /aɪˈdentɪkl ; aɪˈdɛntɪkl/ *adj* **~ (to/with), 1** the same: 同一的: *This knife is ~ to the one with which the murder was committed.* 這便是謀殺時所用的那把刀子。 **2** exactly alike; agreeing in every way: 完全相同的;完全一樣的: *The fingerprints of no two persons are ~.* 沒有兩個人的指紋是完全相同的。 *Our views of what should be done are ~.* 我們對於應該採取的行動持完全相同的看法。 *40 inches is ~ with 3 feet 4 inches.* 四十吋和三呎四吋是相等的。 **3** ˌ**~ ˈtwins,** twins from one single fertilized ovum. 同卵孿生;同卵雙胎。**~ly** /-klɪ ; -klɪ/ *adv*

ident·ify /aɪˈdentɪfaɪ ; aɪˈdɛntəˌfaɪ/ *vt, vi* (*pt, pp* -fied) [VP6A, 14, 3A] **1** say, show, prove, who or what sb or sth is; establish the identity of: 認出;認明;鑑定: *Could you ~ your umbrella among a hundred others?* 你能在一百把傘中認出你的傘嗎? *His accent was difficult to ~.* 他的口音甚難認出是什麼地方的。 **2** ***~ sth with sth,*** treat (sth) as identical (with); equate (one thing with another). 認爲同一;視(甲與乙)爲相等。 **3** ***~ (oneself) with sb/sth,*** give support to, be associated with; feel close to: 支持;與…認同;覺得與…接近: *He refused to ~ himself/become identified with the new political party.* 他拒絕支持該一新政黨。 **identi·fi·ca·tion** /aɪˌdentɪfɪˈkeɪʃn ; aɪˌdɛntəfəˈkeʃən/ *n* [U] ~ing or being identified: 認出;認明;鑑定;視爲同一: *the identification of persons killed in a road accident,* finding out who they are. 查明路上車禍死者的姓名和身份。

iden·ti·kit /aɪˈdentɪkɪt ; aɪˈdɛntɪkɪt/ *n* composite drawing of the face of an unidentified person (esp a suspected criminal), from features recalled by those who saw him. 根據目擊者所憶及的面部特徵對身分不明之人(尤指嫌疑犯)所作之面部畫像。

ident·ity /aɪˈdentətɪ ; aɪˈdɛntətɪ/ *n* (*pl* -ties) **1** [U] state of being identical; absolute sameness; exact likeness. 同一;絕對相同;完全相同。 **2** [C, U] who sb is; what sth is: 身份;本身;本體: *There is no clue to the ~ of the thief,* nothing to show who he is. 沒有線索查明這竊賊是誰。 *The cheque will be cashed upon proof of ~.* 這支票於驗明取款人身份後

卽兌現。*He was arrested because of mistaken ~.* 他因身份被誤認而被捕。'~ **card/disc/certificate,** card, etc that gives proof of one's ~. 身份證。

ideo·gram /ˈɪdɪəgræm ; ˈɪdɪəˌgræm/, **ideo·graph** /ˈɪdɪəgrɑːf *US:* -græf ; ˈɪdɪəˌgræf/ *nn* written or printed character, used in making up words, that symbolizes the idea of a thing without indicating the sounds that make up the word, eg as used in Chinese writing. 表意文字(如中文)。**ideo·graphic** /ˌɪdɪəˈgræfɪk ; ˌɪdɪəˈgræfɪk/ *adj*

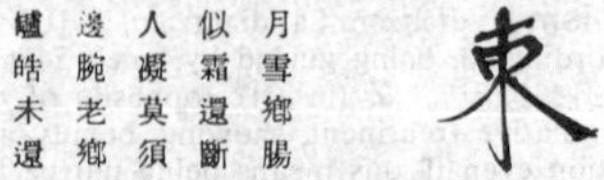

ideograms

ideol·ogy /ˌaɪdɪˈɒlədʒɪ ; ˌaɪdɪˈɑlədʒɪ/ *n* (*pl* -gies) **1** [C] manner of thinking, ideas, characteristic of a person, group, etc, esp as forming the basis of an economic or political system: (代表個人,團體等,尤指形成一經濟或政治制度基礎的)思想方式; 意識形態: *bourgeois, Marxist and totalitarian ideologies.* 中產階級,馬克思主義者及極權主義者的意識形態。**2** [U] unproductive thought. 無效果的思想;空想。**ideo·logi·cal** /ˌaɪdɪəˈlɒdʒɪkl ; ˌaɪdɪəˈlɑdʒɪkəl/ *adj* **ideo·logi·cally** /-klɪ ; -klɪ/ *adv*

ides /aɪdz ; aɪdz/ *n pl* (in the calendar of ancient Rome) the 15th of March, May, July, Oct or the 13th of other months. (古羅馬曆)三月,五月,七月,十月的十五日;其他月份的十三日。

id est /ˌɪd ˈest ; ˌɪdˈɛst/ (abbr 略作 **ie**) (Lat) that is to say. (拉)卽。

idi·ocy /ˈɪdɪəsɪ ; ˈɪdɪəsɪ/ *n* **1** [U] state of being an idiot; extreme stupidity. 白癡;極愚蠢。**2** [C] (*pl* -cies) extremely stupid act, remark, etc. 極愚蠢的行爲,言語等。

idio·lect /ˈɪdɪəlekt ; ˈɪdɪəˌlɛkt/ *n* the total of a person's language that he knows and uses at any stage of his language development: 一個人在其語言發展過程的任何階段所知曉及使用的語言的總稱; 個人習語;個人語彙: *Is the word 'psychosis' part of your ~?* 你知道 psychosis 這個字嗎?

I

id·iom /ˈɪdɪəm ; ˈɪdɪəm/ *n* **1** language of a people or country; specific character of this, eg one peculiar to a country, district, group of people, or to one individual: 一民族或國家的語言; (國家,地區,團體或個人的)特殊語法: *the French ~;* 法國人的語法; *the ~ of the New England countryside,* ie the kind of English used by country people there; 新英格蘭鄉間的方言; *Shakespeare's ~,* the method of expression peculiar to him. 莎士比亞的語法。**2** [C] phrase or sentence whose meaning is not obvious through knowledge of the individual meanings of the constituent words but must be learnt as a whole, 成語; 慣用語, eg 例如 *give way, in order to, be hard put to it.* **idio·matic** /ˌɪdɪəˈmætɪk ; ˌɪdɪəˈmætɪk/ *adj* **1** in accordance with the ~s(2) of a language, dialect, etc: 合於某一語言,方言等之語法的: *speak ~atic English.* 說合乎習慣用法的英語。**2** full of ~s(2): 多成語的: *an ~atic language.* 多成語的語言。**idi·om·ati·cally** /ˌɪdɪəˈmætɪklɪ ; ˌɪdɪəˈmætɪklɪ/ *adv*

idio·syn·crasy /ˌɪdɪəˈsɪŋkrəsɪ ; ˌɪdɪəˈsɪnkrəsɪ/ *n* (*pl* -sies) [C] way of thinking or behaving that is peculiar to a person; personal mannerism. 個人的癖性; 個人的習性。 **idio·syn·cratic** /ˌɪdɪəsɪŋˈkrætɪk ; ˌɪdɪosɪnˈkrætɪk/ *adj*

id·iot /ˈɪdɪət ; ˈɪdɪət/ *n* **1** person so weak-minded that he is incapable of rational conduct. 白癡;下愚者。**2** (colloq) fool: (俗)愚蠢之人: *'I've left my suitcase in the train. What an ~ I am!'* '我把提箱忘在火車上了,我眞是個糊塗蟲!' **idi·otic** /ˌɪdɪˈɒtɪk ; ˌɪdɪˈɑtɪk/ *adj* stupid. 愚蠢的。**~i·cally** /-klɪ ; -klɪ/ *adv*

idle /ˈaɪdl ; ˈaɪdḷ/ *adj* (-r, -st) **1** doing no work; not employed; not active or in use; (of time) not spent in doing something: 不做事的; 無工作的; 停頓的;未用的;(指時間)空閒的: *When men cannot find employment they are ~* (though not necessarily lazy). 當人們找不到工作時,他們是閒着的(並不一定是懶惰的)。*During the business depression half the machines in the factory were ~.* 在商業蕭條的期間,這工廠裡的機器半數是停頓的。*We spent many ~ hours during the holidays.* 假期內我們過了許多優閒的時刻。**2** (of persons) not willing to work; lazy (which is the commoner word for this sense): (指人)不願工作的; 懶惰的 (lazy 一字較常用): *an ~, worthless girl.* 懶惰無用的女孩。**3** useless; worthless: 無用的;無價值的: *Don't listen to ~ gossip/tales.* 不要聽無益的閒言。*It's ~ to expect help from that man.* 指望那人幫忙是無用的。□ *vi, vt* **1** [VP2A, C] be ~: 不做事;懶散;遊手好閒: *Don't ~ (about).* 不要閒混。**2** [VP15B] **~ away,** spend in an ~ manner: 虛度: *Don't ~ away your time.* 不要虛度光陰。**3** (of a car engine) run slowly in neutral gear. (指汽車引擎)放空檔;空轉。**idler** /ˈaɪdlə(r) ; ˈaɪdlə/ *n* person who ~s. 閒散者;懶人。**idly** /ˈaɪdlɪ ; ˈaɪdlɪ/ *adv* **~·ness** *n* state of being ~: 無工作;閒散;懶惰: *live in ~ness.* 遊手好閒。

idol /ˈaɪdl ; ˈaɪdḷ/ *n* **1** image in wood, stone, etc of a god; such an image used as an object of worship; false god. (木,石等製的)神像;偶像;假神。**2** sb or sth greatly loved or admired: 極被寵愛或崇拜的人或物: *He was an only child, and the ~ of his parents.* 他是個獨子,是他父母的寵兒。*Don't make an ~ of wealth.* 不要崇拜財富。**~·ater** /aɪˈdɒlətə(r) ; aɪˈdɑlətə/ *n* **1** worshipper of ~s. 偶像崇拜者。**2** devoted admirer (*of...*). 崇拜…者(與 of 連用)。**~·atress** /aɪˈdɒlətrɪs ; aɪˈdɑlətrɪs/ *n* woman ~ater. 崇拜偶像的女人;女崇拜者。**~·atrous** /aɪˈdɒlətrəs ; aɪˈdɑlətrəs/ *adj* (of a person) worshipping ~s; of the worship of ~s. (指人) 崇拜偶像的; 偶像崇拜的。**~·atrous·ly** *adv.* **~·atry** /aɪˈdɒlətrɪ ; aɪˈdɑlətrɪ/ *n* **1** [U] the worship of ~s; excessive devotion to or admiration of (sb or sth). 偶像崇拜;(對某人或某事物的)過份崇拜。**2** [C] (*pl* -ries) instance of this. 偶像崇拜的實例;過份崇拜的實例。**~·ize** /ˈaɪdəlaɪz ; ˈaɪdḷˌaɪz/ *vt* [VP6A] make an ~ of; love or admire to excess. 偶像化; 過份崇拜。**~·iz·ation** /ˌaɪdəlaɪˈzeɪʃn *US:* -lɪˈz- ; ˌaɪdḷəˈzeʃən/ *n* ~izing or being ~ized. 偶像化;過份崇拜。

idyll /ˈɪdɪl *US:* ˈaɪdl ; ˈaɪdḷ/ *n* short description, usu in verse, of a simple scene or event, esp of country life; period of great peace and happiness. 田園詩 (尤指對鄉村生活純樸的情景作簡短描述的詩歌); 安詳快樂的一段時間。**idyl·lic** /ɪˈdɪlɪk *US:* aɪˈd- ; aɪˈdɪlɪk/ *adj* suitable for, like, an ~; simple, peaceful and pleasant. 適於田園詩的;似田園詩的;純樸安詳而宜人的。

if /ɪf ; ɪf/ *conj* **1** on the condition that; supposing that: 假使;如果: **(a)** (Present or Present Perfect Tense in the *if*-clause, indicating that sth is possible, probable, or likely): (if 子句中用現在式或現在完成式,表示某事之可能發生): *If you ask him, he will help you.* 如果你向他請求,他會幫助你。*If (it is) necessary, I can come at six.* 必要時我可以六點鐘來。*If you have finished with that book, take it back to the library.* 假使你已看完那本書,便將它還回圖書館。**(b)** (with *should* in the *if*-clause, to indicate that an event is unlikely or improbable): (if 子句中用 should 表示不大可能發生之事): *If anyone should call, please let me know.* 萬一有人來訪,請通知我。*If it should be necessary, I could come at six.* 若有必要我可以六點鐘來。**(c)** (with *will* in an *if*-clause, not to show future time, but as part of the polite formula 'Will you, please'): (if 子句中如用 will, 並非指將來,而是客套語 Will you, please 的一部份): *If you will wait a moment* (= Please wait a moment and) *I'll go and tell the manager* *that you are here.* 請等一下,我去告訴經理你已經來了。**(d)** (Past Tense in the *if*-clause, indicating a condition that cannot be, or is unlikely to be realized, or is one put forward for consideration): (if 子句中用過去式,表示不可能實現,大概不會實現,或提出作爲考慮的假定條件): *If you were a bird, you could fly.* 假使你是隻鳥,你便會飛了。 *If I asked him/If I were to ask him for a loan, would he agree?* 如果我向他借錢,他會答應嗎? *If you would lend me £5 until Monday, I should be grateful.* 如果你願意借給我五鎊,到下星期一償還,我將感謝你。**(e)** (Past Perfect Tense in the *if*-clause, indicating that the condition was not fulfilled, eg because it was an impossible one, or through sb's failure to act): (if 子句中用過去完成式,表示過去未實現的條件,例如由於不可能實現或某人之未能實行): *If they'd started earlier, they would have arrived in time.* 要是他們早些動身,他們便可及時到達了。 *If they had not started when they did, they wouldn't be here now.* 如果他們那時不動身,現在他們就不會在此地了。(After some *vv*, eg *think, remember, ask*, the main clause depending upon the condition is usu omitted): (在某些動詞,例如 think, remember, ask 之後,依條件而生的主要子句通常省略): *If you think about it,* (you realize that) *there were many bright boys in that class.* 如果你想一想,(你就知道)那一班級中有許多聰明男孩。 *If you ask me,* (I will tell you) *he's a fool.* 如果你問我,(我會告訴你)他是個笨蛋。 **2** (In literary style *if* may be omitted, and an inversion of subject and *aux v*, esp *were/had/should*, used instead): (在文學體式中, if 有時可省略,然後將主詞與所用的助動詞,尤其是 were, had, should 倒置): *Should it* (= If it should) *be necessary...;* 倘若必定要⋯; *Were I* (= If I were) *in your place...;* 如果我處於你的地位⋯; *Had I* (= If I had) *known earlier....* 如果我早一些知道⋯。**3** (When *if* is used meaning 'when' or 'whenever', so that there is no condition, tenses in the main clause and the *if*-clause may be the same): (if 做'當⋯時'或'無論何時'解而不含條件之義時, if 子句中的時態可與主句中者相同): *If you mix yellow and blue you get green.* 你將黃色與藍色混合,便會得到綠色。 *If she wants the steward she rings the bell.* 每當她需要僕人時,她便按鈴。 **4** ***(even) if,*** granting or admitting that: 就算: *If I'm mistaken, you're mistaken, too.* 就算我錯了,你也錯了。*Even if he did say that, I'm sure he didn't intend to hurt your feelings.* 就算他眞的那樣說,我相信他並無意傷你的感情。 **5** ***(even) if,*** although: 卽使;縱然: *I'll do it, even if it takes me all the afternoon.* 卽使花費我一下午的時間,我還是要做這事。 **6** (colloq) (*if* replacing *whether*, to introduce an interrogative clause): (俗) (if 可代替 whether, 引導一疑問子句): *Do you know if Mr Smith is at home?* 你知道史密斯先生是否在家嗎? *She asked if that was enough.* 她問那是否够了。(Note: *if* should not replace *whether* in cases where there may be ambiguity: 注意:如果意義含糊時, if 不可代替 whether: cf 參較 *Let me know whether you are coming,* (information wanted in either case). 告訴我你是否要來(不管來與不來均須回覆)。*Let me know if* (= only if) *you are coming,* (information wanted only in the one case). 如果你要來,就請通知我(決定要來時始回覆)。) **7** ***as if,*** as it would be if (*it isn't as if...* suggests that the contrary of what follows is true): 彷彿;好像 (It isn't as if... 表示與其下列所述相反者爲事實): *It isn't as if we were rich,* ie We are *not* rich. 我們不像富有的樣子(卽我們不富有)。*It isn't as if he doesn't know the rules,* ie He *does* know the rules. 他不像不懂得規則的樣子(卽他懂得規則)。(*As if* often introduces an exclamation): (As if 常引導一感嘆句): *As if I would allow it!* ie I would certainly *not* allow it! 好像我會答應似的!(卽我才不答應哩!) ⇨ as²(11). **8** ***if only,*** (often introduces a wish, or indicates an unfulfilled condition, esp in exclamations): (常表示願望或未實現的條件,尤用於感嘆句): *If only he arrives in time!* 他若能及時到達就好了! *If only she would marry me!* 但願她能嫁給我! *If only she had known about it* (but she did not know)! 她那時要是知道(但她不知道)這事就好了! *If only you could/If you could only have seen it.* 我眞希望你當時能看到它! **9** (*if*, followed by a *v* in the neg, is used in exclamations to indicate dismay, surprise, etc): (if 後接否定動詞,用於感嘆句中,表示沮喪、驚奇等): *Well, if I haven't left my umbrella in the train!* 眞倒霉,我把雨傘丢在火車上了! *And if he didn't try to knock me down!* What do you think he did? He tried to knock me down! 你猜他想做什麼?他竟然想把我擊倒!

ig·loo /ˈɪgluː; ˈɪglu/ *n* (*pl* ~s) dome-shaped hut made of blocks of hard snow, used by the Eskimos. 愛斯基摩人所居住的用硬雪塊砌成的圓頂小屋。

ig·neous /ˈɪgnɪəs; ˈɪgnɪəs/ *adj* (of rocks) formed by volcanic action. (指岩石)火成的。

ig·nis fatuus /ˌɪgnɪs ˈfætjʊəs; ˈɪgnɪsˈfætʃʊəs/ *n* (*pl* ignes fatui /ˌɪgniːz ˈfætjʊaɪ; ˈɪgnizˈfætʃuˌaɪ/) **1** = will-o'-the-wisp. **2** (colloq) sth misleading. (俗)使人發生錯誤或引人入歧途的事物。

ig·nite /ɪgˈnaɪt; ɪgˈnaɪt/ *vt, vi* [VP6A, 2A] set on fire; take fire. 點燃;發火。 **ig·ni·tion** /ɪgˈnɪʃn; ɪgˈnɪʃən/ *n* igniting or being ~d; (in a petrol engine) electrical mechanism for igniting the mixture of explosive gases: 點燃;發火;着火;(汽油引擎的)點火電門(俗稱:電門開關): *switch on the ignition.* 開開(汽車的)點火電門。 ⇨ the illus at motor. 參看 motor 之挿圖。

ig·noble /ɪgˈnəʊbl; ɪgˈnobl̩/ *adj* **1** dishonourable; shameful: 不名譽的;可恥的: *an ~ man/action;* 可恥的人(行爲); *an ~ peace.* 不光榮的和平。 **2** (old use) of low birth. (舊用法)出身微賤的。 **ig·nobly** /-ˈnəʊblɪ; -ˈnoblɪ/ *adv*

ig·nom·ini·ous /ˌɪgnəˈmɪnɪəs; ˌɪgnəˈmɪnɪəs/ *adj* bringing contempt, disgrace, shame; dishonourable: 可鄙的;可恥的;不光榮的: *~ behaviour;* 可鄙的行爲; *an ~ defeat.* 不光榮的失敗。 **~·ly** *adv*

ig·nom·iny /ˈɪgnəmɪnɪ; ˈɪgnəˌmɪnɪ/ *n* **1** [U] public dishonour or shame. 不名譽;恥辱。 **2** [C] (*pl* -nies) dishonourable or disgraceful act; [U] dishonourable behaviour. 可恥的行動;不名譽的行爲。

ig·nor·amus /ˌɪgnəˈreɪməs; ˌɪgnəˈreməs/ *n* (*pl* ~es /-sɪz; -sɪz/) ignorant person. 無知的人。

ig·nor·ance /ˈɪgnərəns; ˈɪgnərəns/ *n* [U] ***~ (of),*** the state of being ignorant; want of knowledge: 不知;無知: *We are in complete ~ of his plans.* 我們完全不知道他的計畫。 *If he did wrong, it was from/through ~.* 要是他做錯了,那是由於無知。

ig·nor·ant /ˈɪgnərənt; ˈɪgnərənt/ *adj* **1** ***~ (of),*** (of persons) knowing little or nothing; not aware: (指人)無知識的;不知道的: *He's not stupid, merely ~.* 他不是愚蠢,祇是無知。 *You are not ~ of the reasons for her behaviour.* 你不是不知道她的行爲的原因。 *What his plans are I am quite ~ of.* 我一點也不知道他的計畫是什麼。 **2** showing ignorance; resulting from ignorance: 顯示無知的;因無知而產生的: *an ~ reply;* 無知的回答; *~ conduct.* 無知的行爲。 **~·ly** *adv*

ig·nore /ɪgˈnɔː(r); ɪgˈnor/ *vt* [VP6A] take no notice of; refuse to take notice of: 不理;不顧;忽視: *~ rude remarks;* 不理無禮的談話; *be ~d by one's superiors.* 被上級忽視。

iguana /ɪˈgwɑːnə; ɪˈgwanə/ *n* large tree-climbing lizard of tropical America. 鬣蜥蜴(美洲熱帶所產之善爬樹大蜥蜴)。

ikon /ˈaɪkɒn; ˈaɪkɑn/ *n* = icon.

ilex /ˈaɪleks; ˈaɪlɛks/ *n* holm-oak; (bot) genus of trees including the common holly. 多青樹;(植物)多青屬。

ilk /ɪlk; ɪlk/ *n* ***of that/his etc ilk,*** (colloq, hum) of that/his etc family, set, type. (俗,諧)屬於那個(他那個等)家族,種類等的。

I'll /aɪl ; aɪl/ = I will; I shall.

ill /ɪl ; ɪl/ *adj* **1** (usu pred) in bad health; sick: (通常作敍述用法)健康不佳的;生病的: *She was ill with anxiety.* 她因憂慮而病了。***fall/be taken ill,*** become ill. 生病。⇨ worse, worst. **2** (attrib) bad: (形容用法)惡劣的;壞的: *ill health;* 不健康; *in an ill temper/humour;* 心情不好; *ill repute;* 聲名狼藉; *do sb an ill turn;* 危害某人; *have ill luck;* 遭惡運; *a bird of ill omen.* 兇兆之鳥;帶來惡運的人。***It's an ill wind that blows 'nobody any good,*** (prov) An affair must be very bad indeed if it does not benefit somebody. (諺) 任何人都得不到好處的事,可眞是一件壞事 (意謂: 世上沒有對人人皆不利的事)。***Ill weeds grow apace,*** (prov) Harmful things grow or spread rapidly. (諺)莠草易滋;有害之事蔓延迅速。**ˌill-'breeding** *n* bad manners. 無敎養; 粗魯無禮。**ˌill-'favoured** *adj* (of a person) unpleasant to look at; ugly. (指人) 難看的; 醜的。 **ˌill-'mannered** *adj* having bad manners; rude. 無禮貌的;粗野的。**ˌill-'natured** *adj* bad-tempered. 脾氣壞的。**ˌill-'omened** *adj* destined to misfortune. 不吉祥的; 惡兆的。 **ˌill-'starred** *adj* born under an evil star; unlucky. 星宿不利的;命運壞的。 **ˌill-'treatment/-'usage** *n* [U] cruelty; harsh treatment. 虐待。**ˌill 'will** *n* enmity; unkind feeling. 敵意;惡意。□ *n* **1** [U] evil; injury: 罪惡;傷害: *do ill.* 作惡;爲害。 **2** [C] misfortune; trouble: 不幸;災難: *the various ills of life.* 人生的種種不幸。 □ *adv* badly; imperfectly; unfavourably: 惡劣地;不完美地;不利地: *They were ill* (= insufficiently) *provided with ammunition.* 他們的軍火供應不足。*We could ill* (= not well, not easily) *afford the time and money.* 我們無力負擔所需的時間與金錢。*It ill becomes you to criticize him,* It is not right or proper for you to do so. 你不宜批評他。***be/feel ill at ease,*** uncomfortable, embarrassed. 覺得不自在;覺得困窘。***speak ill of sb,*** in an unkind or unfavourable way. 說某人的壞話。**ˌill-ad'vised** *adj* unwise; imprudent. 不智的;鹵莽的。 **ˌill-af'fected (towards)** *adj* not well-disposed; not feeling favour. 不懷好意的;沒有好感的。**ˌill-'bred** *adj* badly brought up; rude. 無敎養的;粗野的。**ˌill-dis'posed (towards)** *adj* **(a)** wishing to do harm (to). 懷惡意的。**(b)** unfavourable (towards a plan, etc). 不贊成(計畫等)的。**ˌill-'fated** *adj* destined to misfortune; bringing misfortune. 苦命的;不吉的;招致不幸的。**ˌill-gotten 'gains** *n pl* money gained by evil or unlawful methods. 以卑鄙或不法手段得到的錢財;不義之財。 **ˌill-'judged** *adj* done at an unsuitable time; showing poor judgement: 不合時宜的;缺乏判斷力的;判斷失當的: *an ill-judged attempt.* 不合時宜之舉。**ˌill-'timed** *adj* badly timed; done at a wrong or unsuitable time. 不合時宜的;失時機的。**ˌill-'treat/-'use** *vt* treat badly or cruelly. 虐待。

il·legal /ɪ'li:gl ; ɪ'ligḷ/ *adj* not legal; contrary to law. 不合法的;違法的。**~ly** /-gəlɪ ; -glɪ/ *adv* **~·ity** /ˌɪlɪ'gælətɪ ; ˌɪli'gælətɪ/ *n* [U] being ~; [C] (*pl* -ties) ~ act. 不合法;違法;違法的行爲。

il·leg·ible /ɪ'ledʒəbl ; ɪ'lɛdʒəbḷ/ *adj* difficult or impossible to read. 難讀的;無法辨認的; 不清楚的。 **il·leg·ibly** /-əblɪ ; -əblɪ/ *adv* **il·leg·ibil·ity** /ɪˌledʒə'bɪlətɪ ; ɪˌlɛdʒə'bɪlətɪ/ *n* [U].

il·legit·imate /ˌɪlɪ'dʒɪtɪmət ; ˌɪlɪ'dʒɪtəmɪt/ *adj* **1** not authorized by law; contrary to law. 未經法律允許的;不合法的;違法的。 **2** born of parents who were not married to each other: 私生的: *an ~ child;* 私生子; *of ~ descent.* 私生的。 **3** (of a conclusion in an argument, etc) not logical; wrongly inferred. (指辯論的結論等)不合邏輯的;推理錯誤的。□ *n* an ~ person. 沒有合法身分的人;私生子。**~·ly** *adv* **il·legit·imacy** /ˌɪlɪ'dʒɪtɪməsɪ ; ˌɪlɪ'dʒɪtəməsɪ/ *n* [U].

il·lib·eral /ɪ'lɪbərəl ; ɪ'lɪbərəl/ *adj* not befitting a free man; narrow-minded; intolerant; ungenerous; mean. 無敎養的;氣量狹小的;不容異己的;吝嗇的;卑鄙的。**~ly** /-rəlɪ ; -rəlɪ/ *adv* **~·ity** /ɪˌlɪbə'rælətɪ ; ɪˌlɪbə'rælətɪ/ *n*

il·licit /ɪ'lɪsɪt ; ɪ'lɪsɪt/ *adj* unlawful; forbidden: 非法的;被禁止的: *the ~ sale of opium.* 非法販賣鴉片。**~·ly** *adv*

il·limit·able /ɪ'lɪmɪtəbl ; ɪ'lɪmɪtəbḷ/ *adj* boundless; without limits: 無邊際的;無限的: *~ space/ambition.* 無限的空間(雄心)。

il·lit·er·ate /ɪ'lɪtərət ; ɪ'lɪtərɪt/ *adj* with little or no education; unable to read or write; showing such ignorance: 未受教育的;目不識丁的;文字不通的: *an ~ letter,* one full of spelling and grammatical errors. 一封錯字連篇、文句不通的信。□ *n* ~ person. 目不識丁者;文盲。 **il·lit·er·acy** /ɪ'lɪtərəsɪ ; ɪ'lɪtərəsɪ/ *n* [U, C] (instance of) being ~. 未受教育;目不識丁。

ill·ness /'ɪlnɪs ; 'ɪlnɪs/ *n* **1** [U] state of being ill (contrasted with *health*): 不健康;疾病(與 health 相對): *There has been no/not much/a great deal of ~ in the village this winter.* 今年冬季這村裡沒有(沒有什麼,有許多)疾病。 **2** [C] specific kind of, occasion of, ~: 某種疾病;生病: *~es of children;* 兒童所患的各種疾病; *a serious ~;* 重病; *one ~ after another.* 一次又一次的生病。

il·logi·cal /ɪ'lɒdʒɪkl ; ɪ'lɑdʒɪkḷ/ *adj* without logic; contrary to logic. 不合邏輯的;不合理的。**~ly** /-klɪ ; -klɪ/ *adv* **~·ity** /ɪˌlɒdʒɪ'kælətɪ ; ɪˌlɑdʒɪ'kælətɪ/, **~·ness** *nn* [U, C] (instance of) being ~. 不合邏輯;不合理。

il·lume /ɪ'lu:m ; ɪ'lum/ *vt* (poet) illuminate. (詩)使明亮;照亮。

il·lumi·nate /ɪ'lu:mɪneɪt ; ɪ'luməˌnet/ *vt* [VP6A] **1** give light to; throw light on: 使明亮;照亮: *a street ~d by oil lamps;* 油燈照明的街道; *poorly ~d rooms.* 燈光不够亮的房間。 **2** decorate (streets, etc) with bright lights as a sign of rejoicing. 以明燈裝飾(街道等)以示歡欣。 **3** decorate (initial letters in a manuscript) with gold, silver and bright colours (as was the custom in the Middle Ages). (在中古的習俗中)以金、銀、鮮艷顏色裝飾(稿件上的起首字母)。 **4** make clear; help to explain: 說明;闡明: *~ a difficult passage in a book.* 闡明書中一難解的段落。 **il·lumi·na·tion** /ɪˌlu:mɪ'neɪʃn ; ɪˌlumə'neʃən/ *n* **1** [U] illuminating or being ~d. 照明;明亮;說明。 **2** (usu *pl*) lights, etc, used to ~(2) a town for a special occasion. (通常用複數)爲特殊節慶裝飾一城市所用的明燈等;燈綵裝飾。 **3** (*pl*) decorations on a manuscript. (複)文稿上的裝飾物;加有裝飾的起首字母。

il·lu·mine /ɪ'lu:mɪn ; ɪ'lumɪn/ *vt* [VP6A] (liter) enlighten spiritually; make bright. (文)啓發;使明亮。

il·lu·sion /ɪ'lu:ʒn ; ɪ'luʒən/ *n* **1** [C] (the seeing of) sth that does not really exist, or of sth as different from the reality; false idea or belief: 幻象;幻影;錯視;錯誤的觀點或信念: *an optical ~.* 視錯覺。***be under an ~,*** be deceived by one. 產生錯覺;搞錯。***cherish an ~/the ~ that...,*** like to believe.... 誤以爲…。***have no ~s about sb/sth,*** have no false beliefs about him/it. 對某人(某事)不存幻想。 **2** [U] state of mind in which one is deceived in this way. 錯覺。**~·ist** /-ɪst ; -ɪst/ *n* person who produces optical ~s on the stage; conjurer. 幻術師;魔術師。

il·lu·sive /ɪ'lu:sɪv ; ɪ'lusɪv/, **il·lu·sory** /ɪ'lu:sərɪ ; ɪ'lusərɪ/ *adjj* deceptive; based on illusion. 欺騙的;虛幻的。

il·lus·trate /'ɪləstreɪt ; 'ɪləstret/ *vt* [VP6A] **1** explain by examples, pictures, etc. 舉例或以圖畫等說明。 **2** supply a book, article, lecture, etc with pictures, diagrams, etc: 以圖畫、圖表等挿入(書籍,文章,演講等): *a well-~d textbook.* 一本挿圖豐富的教科書。 **il·lus·tra·tor** /-tə(r) ; -tə/ *n* person who ~s books, etc. 爲書籍等作挿圖的人。 **il·lus·tra·tion** /ˌɪlə'streɪʃn ; ˌɪləs'treʃən/ *n* **1** [U] illustrating or being ~d: 舉例或以圖表等說明; 例證: *cite instances in illustration of a theory.* 舉例說明一理論。*Illustration is often more useful than definition for giving the meanings of words.* 就賦予單字之意義而言,舉例說明

常較下定義有用。 **2** [C] sth that ~s; picture, diagram, etc. 例證；挿圖；圖解等。**il·lus·tra·tive** /ˈɪləstrətɪv *US:* ɪˈlʌs- ; ɪˈlʌstrətɪv/ *adj* serving to ~, as an explanation or example (*of* sth). 說明的；作爲(某事物之)例證的(與of連用)。

il·lus·tri·ous /ɪˈlʌstrɪəs ; ɪˈlʌstrɪəs/ *adj* greatly distinguished; celebrated. 極爲傑出的；著名的。**~·ly** *adv*

I'm /aɪm ; aɪm/ = I am. ⇨ be¹.

im·age /ˈɪmɪdʒ ; ˈɪmɪdʒ/ *n* [C] **1** likeness or copy of the shape of sb or sth, esp one made in wood, stone, etc: 像；肖像(尤指以木，石等製成者)：*an ~ of the Virgin Mary;* 聖母馬利亞像； *graven ~s,* ~s carved in wood, etc and regarded as gods. 雕刻的神像。 **2** close likeness; counterpart: 極爲相像；與另一個極爲相像的人或物： *Did man create God in his own ~?* 人是照他自己的形像創造上帝的嗎？ ***be the (very／spitting) ~ (of sth／sb),*** be exactly like it／him. 酷似某物或某人。 **3** mental picture or idea; concept of sth or sb, eg a politician, political party, commercial firm, product, held by the public: 心像；意像；形象；觀念；公衆對某事物或某人(例如政界人士，政黨，商行，製品)之觀念： *How can we improve our ~?* 我們如何纔能增進公衆對我們的好感？ **4** simile; metaphor: 直喩；隱喩： *speak in ~s,* use figures of speech that bring pictures to the mind. 用比喩說。**5** reflection seen in a mirror or through the lens of a camera. 映像；影像。⇨ the illus at camera. 參看 camera 之挿圖。□ *vt* [VP6A] **1** make an ~ of, portray. 作…之像；作…之肖像；描繪。 **2** reflect; mirror. 反映；映照。**~ry** /ˈɪmɪdʒərɪ ; ˈɪmɪdʒrɪ/ *n* [U] the use of ~s(4), or figures of speech, in writing; ~s(1) collectively. 寫作中直喩或比喩的使用；像或肖像的總稱。

im·agin·able /ɪˈmædʒɪnəbl ; ɪˈmædʒɪnəbl/ *adj* that can be imagined: 可想像的： *We had the greatest difficulty ~ getting here in time.* 我們爲了及時趕到這裡，而經歷了所能想得到的最大困難。

im·agin·ary /ɪˈmædʒɪnərɪ *US:* -ənerɪ ; ɪˈmædʒəˌnɛrɪ/ *adj* existing only in the mind; unreal. 想像中的；不眞實的。

im·agin·ation /ɪˌmædʒɪˈneɪʃn ; ɪˌmædʒəˈneʃən/ *n* **1** [C, U] power of the mind to imagine: 想像力： *He hasn't much ~.* 他缺乏想像力。 *Novelists use their ~.* 小說家善用他們的想像力。*Children are encouraged to use their ~s.* 兒童受到鼓勵去運用他們的想像力。 **2** what is imagined: 想像的事物： *You didn't really see a ghost—it was only ~.* 你並沒有眞正看到鬼——那祇是你想像中的東西。 **im·agin·ative** /ɪˈmædʒɪnətɪv *US:* -əneɪtɪv ; ɪˈmædʒəˌnetɪv/ *adj* of, having, using, ~: 想像的；有想像力的；運用想像力的： *imaginative writers.* 富有想像力的作者。

im·ag·ine /ɪˈmædʒɪn ; ɪˈmædʒɪn/ *vt* [VP6A, C, 9, 10, 16B, 19A, C, 25] form a picture of in the mind; think of (sth) as probable: 想像；認爲(某事物)可能發生或存在： *wild imaginings.* 妄想的事物。*Can you ~ life without electricity and other modern conveniences?* 你能想像出沒有電和其他現代化設備時的生活情形嗎？ *I~ yourself (to be) on a desert island.* 想像你自己在一個荒島上的情景。 *I~ you've been shipwrecked.* 想像你遭受了船難。 *I ~ him as a big, tall man.* 我以爲他是個高大的人。*Can you ~ him／yourself becoming famous as an actor?* 你能想像他(你自己)成爲一個名演員時候的情形嗎？ *I can't ~ (my) marrying a girl of that sort.* 我難於想像(我)與那種女子結婚後的情形。 *Don't ~* (= get the idea) *that I can lend you money every time you need it!* 不要認爲每當你需要錢的時候，我便會借給你。

imam /ɪˈmɑːm ; ɪˈmɑm/ *n* prayer leader in a mosque. 回教寺院中祈禱時之領導人。 **I~**, title of various Muslim leaders. 回教首領之尊稱。

im·bal·ance /ˌɪmˈbæləns ; ɪmˈbæləns/ *n* absence of balance between two totals, eg payments; lack of proportion: 兩總數的不相等(例如支付)；不均衡: *the country's ~ in world payments,* the state that exists when the total sum paid for imports, etc, is unequal to the total received for exports, services, etc; 該國在國際貿易收支上的不均衡(進口等付出之款與出口、勞務等收入不相等)； *the increasing ~ between rich and poor countries,* the increasing wealth of some and the increasing poverty of others. 富有國家與貧窮國家間日益增加的不均衡。

im·be·cile /ˈɪmbəsiːl *US:* -sl ; ˈɪmbəsl/ *adj* weak-minded; stupid: 低能的；魯鈍的：*~ remarks／conduct.* 愚蠢的言語(行爲)。□ *n* ~ person; fool. 低能者；愚蠢之人。 **im·be·cil·ity** /ˌɪmbəˈsɪlətɪ ; ˌɪmbəˈsɪlətɪ/ *n* [U] stupidity; [C] (*pl* -ties) stupid act, remark, etc. 愚蠢；愚蠢的行動，言語等。

im·bed /ɪmˈbed ; ɪmˈbɛd/ *vt* (-dd-) = embed.

im·bibe /ɪmˈbaɪb ; ɪmˈbaɪb/ *vt* (formal) drink; take in: (正式用語)飲；吸收： *~ ideas／knowledge.* 吸收思想(知識)。

im·bro·glio /ɪmˈbrəʊlɪəʊ ; ɪmˈbroljo/ *n* (*pl* ~s /-z ; -z/) complicated, confused or embarrassing (esp political or emotional) situation. 複雜錯綜的情勢(尤指政治或情緒上者)。

im·bue /ɪmˈbjuː ; ɪmˈbju/ *vt* (*pt, pp* -bued) [VP14] ***~ with,*** (formal) fill, inspire: (正式用語)使充滿；激起： *~d with patriotism／hatred, etc;* 充滿愛國心(仇恨等)； *politicians ~d with a sense of their own importance.* 自大的政客。

imi·tate /ˈɪmɪteɪt ; ˈɪməˌtet/ *vt* [VP6A] **1** copy the behaviour of; take as an example: 傚效…的行爲；模倣： *You should ~ great and good men.* 你應傚效偉大善良的人。 **2** mimic (consciously or not): (自覺或不自覺地)模擬： *Parrots ~ human speech.* 鸚鵡學人語。 **3** be like; make a likeness of: 看似；倣造： *wood painted to ~ marble.* 漆成大理石樣子的木材。**imi·ta·tor** /-tə(r) ; -tə/ *n*

imi·ta·tion /ˌɪmɪˈteɪʃn ; ˌɪməˈteʃən/ *n* **1** [U] imitating: 倣效；模倣；模擬： *I~ is the sincerest form of flattery.* 倣效是最眞誠的恭維。 *He sets us a good example for ~.* 他爲我們樹立一個可效法的楷模。*She was pirouetting in ~ of her teacher.* 她在學着老師踮趾尖旋轉舞。**2** (attrib) not real: (形容用法)假的： *~ leather／jewellery.* 人造的皮革(珠寶)。**3** [C] sth made or done in ~: 仿造物；模擬之物： *~s of the cries of birds and animals.* 模擬鳥獸的鳴叫聲。 *Beware of ~s.* 謹防假冒。

imi·tat·ive /ˈɪmɪtətɪv *US:* -teɪtɪv ; ˈɪməˌtetɪv/ *adj* following the model or example of: 模倣的；倣效的；模擬的： *the ~ arts,* painting and sculpture; 模倣藝術(指繪畫與雕刻)； *~ words,* eg *buzz, plop,* the sound of the word being considered similar to the sound it represents; 形聲字；擬聲字(例如 buzz, plop 等)； *as ~ as a monkey.* 像猴子般喜模倣。

im·macu·late /ɪˈmækjʊlət ; ɪˈmækjəlɪt/ *adj* **1** pure; faultless: 純潔的；無瑕疵的： *~ conduct.* 純潔的行爲。 **the I~ Conception,** (RC church) teaching that the Virgin Mary was free of Original Sin. (天主教)聖母馬利亞生來純潔而無原罪之教義。 **2** perfectly clean; without a flaw; right in every detail: 潔淨的；完美的；處處都對的： *an ~ suit／record.* 一套潔淨的衣服(完美的紀錄)。**~·ly** *adv:* *~ly dressed.* 衣着整潔。

im·ma·nent /ˈɪmənənt ; ˈɪmənənt/ *adj* ***~ (in),*** (of qualities) present; inherent; (of God) permanently pervading the universe. (指性質)存在的；固有的；(指上帝)無所不在的。 **im·ma·nence** /-əns ; -əns/ *n*

im·ma·terial /ˌɪməˈtɪərɪəl ; ˌɪməˈtɪrɪəl/ *adj* ***~ (to),*** **1** unimportant: (對…)不重要的： *~ objections.* 不重要的反對意見。 *That's quite ~ to me.* 那對我無關緊要。 **2** not having physical substance: 無實質的： *as ~ as a ghost.* 像鬼魂般的虛幻。

im·ma·ture /ˌɪməˈtjʊə(r) *US:* -ˈtʊər ; ˌɪməˈtjʊr/ *adj* not yet fully developed: 未發育完全的；未成熟的： *an ~ girl;* 一個未成熟的女孩； *the ~ minds of young children.* 孩子們未成熟的心理。**im·ma·tur·ity** /ˌɪməˈtjʊərətɪ *US:* -ˈtʊər- ; ˌɪməˈtjʊrətɪ/ *n* [U].

im·measur·able /ɪˈmeʒərəbl ; ɪˈmɛʒərəbl/ *adj* that cannot be measured. 不能衡量的。

I

im·medi·ate /ɪ'mi:dɪət ; ɪ'midɪɪt/ *adj* (of time or space) (指時間或空間) **1** without anything coming between; nearest: 直接的;最接近的: *two objects in ~ contact;* 直接接觸的兩個物體; *the ~ heir to the throne,* the next in succession, not a remote heir; 王位的直接繼承人; *my ~ neighbours;* 我的緊隣; *~ information,* first-hand or direct, not second-hand. 直接的消息。 **2** occurring, done, at once: 卽刻的;立卽的: *an ~ answer;* 卽刻的答覆; *take ~ action.* 立刻採取行動。 **im·medi·acy** /-əsɪ ; -əsɪ/ *n* [U] being ~. 直接;卽刻。 **~·ly** *adv* **1** at once; without delay. 立刻;立卽。 **2** directly or closely. 直接地;緊接地。 ▭ *conj* as soon as: 一等…立卽: *You may leave ~ly he comes.* 他一來到,你可立卽離開。

im·mem·or·ial /ˌɪmə'mɔ:rɪəl ; ˌɪmə'morɪəl/ *adj* going back beyond the reach of memory: 人所不能記憶之往昔的;久到難以追憶的: *the ~ privileges of the House of Commons.* 由來已久的(英國)下議院特權。 ***from time ~,*** for a very long time back. 自古以來。

im·mense /ɪ'mens ; ɪ'mɛns/ *adj* very large. 極大的。 **~·ly** *adv* in an ~ degree; (colloq) very much: 極度;(俗)非常: *They enjoyed themselves ~ly.* 他們極爲高興。 **im·men·sity** /ɪ'mensətɪ ; ɪ'mɛnsətɪ/ *n* [U] great size; (*pl* -ties) things that are ~. 巨大;巨大之物。

im·merse /ɪ'mɜ:s ; ɪ'mɝs/ *vt* [VP6A, 14] ~ ***(in),*** **1** put under the surface of (water or other liquid): 浸入(水或其他液體): *~ one's head in the water.* 將頭浸入水中。 **2** absorb, involve deeply: 使專心;使陷入: *be ~d in a book/thought/work/one's business.* 專心閱讀一本書(陷入沉思;專心工作;專心於自已的事業)。 **im·mer·sion** /ɪ'mɜ:ʃn *US:* -ʒn ; ɪ'mɝʃən/ *n* immersing or being ~d; (esp) baptism by putting the whole body into water. 浸入;沉溺;(尤指)浸禮(將全身浸入水中的洗禮)。 **im'mersion heater,** electric water-heater (usu one that is fixed in a hot-water tank). 浸入式電熱水器(通常指裝置於熱水箱中者)。

im·mi·grate /'ɪmɪgreɪt ; 'ɪməˌgret/ *vi* [VP2A, 3A] ~ ***(to/into),*** come as a settler (to/into another country), not as a tourist or visitor. 移居(另一國家);移民。 **im·mi·grant** /'ɪmɪgrənt ; 'ɪməgrənt/ *n* person who ~s: 移民;移居另一國者: *European immigrants in Australia.* 在澳洲的歐洲移民。 **im·mi·gra·tion** /ˌɪmɪ'greɪʃn ; ˌɪmə'greʃən/ *n* [U] immigrating; [C] instance of this: 移民別國;移民之實例: *the numerous immigrations into the US.* 移入美國的大批移民。

im·mi·nent /'ɪmɪnənt ; 'ɪmənənt/ *adj* (of events, esp dangers) likely to come or happen soon: (指事件,尤指危險)逼近的;卽將發生的: *A storm is ~.* 暴風雨卽將來臨。 *He was faced with ~ death.* 他面臨逼近的死亡。 **~·ly** *adv* **im·mi·nence** /-əns ; -əns/ *n* [U] being ~. 逼近;卽至。

im·mo·bile /ɪ'məʊbaɪl *US:* -bl ; ɪ'mobḷ/ *adj* not able to move or be moved; motionless. 不能移動的;不動的。 **im·mo·bi·lize** /ɪ'məʊbəlaɪz ; ɪ'mobḷˌaɪz/ *vt* [VP6A] make ~; render armed forces, vehicles, etc incapable of being moved; take capital, specie out of circulation. 使不動;使(軍隊、車輛等)不能行動;停止(資金、硬幣)之流通。 **im·mo·bil·iz·ation** /ɪˌməʊbəlaɪ'zeɪʃn *US:* -lɪ'z- ; ɪˌmobḷə'zeʃən/ *n* **im·mo·bil·ity** /ˌɪmə'bɪlətɪ ; ˌɪmo'bɪlətɪ/ *n* [U] being ~. 不動;不能移動。

im·mod·er·ate /ɪ'mɒdərət ; ɪ'mɑdərɪt/ *adj* excessive; extreme: 無節制的;極端的: *~ eating and drinking.* 暴食暴飲。 **~·ly** *adv*

im·mod·est /ɪ'mɒdɪst ; ɪ'mɑdɪst/ *adj* **1** lacking in modesty; indecent or indelicate: 不謙虛的;不莊重的;不禮貌的;粗野的: *an ~ dress;* 不莊重的衣著; *~ behaviour.* 粗魯的行爲。 **2** impudent: 厚顏的;無恥的: *~ boasts.* 厚顏的自誇。 **~·ly** *adv* **~y** *n* [U] ~ behaviour; boldness; [C] (*pl* -ties) ~ act or remark. 不適當的行爲;厚顏;粗野的行動或言語。

im·mo·late /'ɪməleɪt ; 'ɪməˌlet/ *vt* [VP6A, 14] ~ ***(to),*** (formal) kill as an offering; sacrifice (one thing *to* another). (正式用語)爲祭神而殺;殺…作爲祭品;犧牲。 **im·mo·la·tion** /ˌɪmə'leɪʃn ; ˌɪmə'leʃən/ *n* [U] immolating or being ~d; [C] instance of this. 爲祭神而殺;殺之以作祭品;犧牲;殉死。

im·moral /ɪ'mɒrəl *US:* ɪ'mɔ:rəl ; ɪ'mɔrəl/ *adj* contrary to morality; wicked and evil: 不道德的;邪惡的: *~ conduct.* 不道德的行爲。 *You ~ swindler!* 你這個邪惡的騙子! **~ly** /-rəlɪ ; -rəlɪ/ *adv* **~·ity** /ˌɪmə'rælətɪ ; ˌɪmə'rælətɪ/ *n* [U] ~ conduct: 不道德的行爲: *a life of ~ity;* 不道德(淫邪)的生活; [C] (*pl* -ties) ~ act. 不道德的行爲。

im·mor·tal /ɪ'mɔ:tl ; ɪ'mɔrtḷ/ *adj* living for ever: 不朽的;永遠生存的: *the ~ gods/soul;* 永生不死的神祇(靈魂); never forgotten: 永不爲人遺忘的;永垂不朽的: *~ poetry/music;* 不朽的詩歌(音樂); *~ fame.* 不朽的名譽。 ▭ *n* ~ being. 不朽的人物;永生不死者。 **the ~s,** the gods of ancient Greece and Rome. 古希臘羅馬的神祇。 **~·ity** /ˌɪmɔ:'tælətɪ ; ˌɪmɔr'tælətɪ/ *n* [U] endless life or fame. 不朽;不朽的生命或聲名。 **~·ize** /ɪ'mɔ:təlaɪz ; ɪ'mɔrtḷˌaɪz/ *vt* [VP6A] give endless life or fame to. 使不朽;賦與不朽的生命或聲名。

im·mov·able /ɪ'mu:vəbl ; ɪ'muvəbḷ/ *adj* **1** that cannot be moved: 不能移動的: *~ property,* eg buildings, land. 不動產 (例如建築物,土地)。 **2** steadfast: 堅定不移的: *~ in purpose.* 目的堅定不移。 **im·mov·ably** /-əblɪ ; -əblɪ/ *adv*

im·mune /ɪ'mju:n;ɪ'mjun/ *adj* ~ ***(from/against/to),*** free, secure: 免除的;安全的: *~ from smallpox as the result of vaccination;* 由於種痘的結果而不會感染天花; *~ to/against poison/disease/infection/criticism/attack.* 免受中毒 (疾病,傳染,批評,攻擊)。 **im·mun·ity** /ɪ'mju:nətɪ ; ɪ'mjunətɪ/ *n* [U] safety, security (*from* disease, etc); exemption (*from* taxation, etc): 免除;免疫(與 from 連用);(捐稅等的)免除(與 from 連用): *diplomatic immunity.* 外交豁免權。 **im·mu·nize** /'ɪmjʊnaɪz ; 'ɪmjəˌnaɪz/ *vt* [VP6A, 14] ~ ***(against),*** make ~ (*against*). 使免除。 **im·mu·niz·ation** /ˌɪmjʊnaɪ'zeɪʃn *US:* -nɪ'z- ; ˌɪmjʊnə'zeʃən/ *n* [U]. **im·mu·nology** /ˌɪmjʊ'nɒlədʒɪ ; ˌɪmjə'nɑlədʒɪ/ *n* [U] study of resistance to infection. 免疫學。

im·mure /ɪ'mjʊə(r) ; ɪ'mjʊr/ *vt* [VP6A] (formal) imprison; shut (oneself) up: (正式用語) 監禁; 幽禁(自己): *~d in a windowless prison cell;* 被監禁在沒有窗戶的小牢房裡; *~ oneself in one's study to work undisturbed.* 將自己關在書房內讀書以免受干擾。

im·mut·able /ɪ'mju:təbl ; ɪ'mjutəbḷ/ *adj* (formal) that cannot be changed. (正式用語)不可改變的。 **im·mut·ably** /-əblɪ ; -əblɪ/ *adv* **im·muta·bil·ity** /ɪˌmju:tə'bɪlətɪ ; ɪˌmjutə'bɪlətɪ/ *n*

imp /ɪmp ; ɪmp/ *n* child of the devil; little devil; (playfully) mischievous child. 魔鬼之子; 小魔鬼; 頑童;小淘氣。

im·pact /'ɪmpækt ; 'ɪmpækt/ *n* ~ ***(on),*** **1** [C] collision. 碰撞;撞擊。 **2** [U] force exerted by one object when striking against another: 撞擊力: *The car body collapses on ~,* when it collides with sth. 汽車的車身在碰撞時塌陷。 **3** strong impression or effect: 強烈印象或影響: *the ~ of new ideas on discontented students.* 新觀念對情緒不滿之學生的巨大影響。 ▭ *vt* /ɪm'pækt ; ɪm'pækt/ pack, drive or wedge firmly together: 裝緊;緊壓;揷緊: *an ~ed tooth,* not able to grow out of the jawbone. (緊壓在顎骨中長不出來的)箝閉齒;阻生牙。

im·pair /ɪm'peə(r) ; ɪm'pɛr/ *vt* [VP6A] weaken; damage: 使弱;損害: *~ one's health by overwork.* 因工作過度而損及健康。 **~·ment** *n*

im·pala /ɪm'pɑ:lə ; ɪm'pɑlə/ *n* (kind of) African antelope. (一種)非洲羚羊。

im·pale /ɪm'peɪl ; ɪm'pel/ *vt* [VP6A, 15A] pierce through, pin down, with a sharp-pointed stake, spear, etc. (以尖樁,矛等)刺穿,刺住。 **~·ment** *n*

im·pal·pable /ɪm'pælpəbl ; ɪm'pælpəbḷ/ *adj* that cannot be touched or felt; not easily grasped by the mind. 摸不到的;感覺不到的;難以理解的。

im·panel /ɪm'pænl ; ɪm'pænl̩/ = empanel.

im·part /ɪm'pɑːt ; ɪm'pɑrt/ *vt* [VP6A, 14] ~ ***(to),*** (formal) give, pass on, a share of sth, a quality, a secret, news, etc: (正式用語)(把一份物品,性質等)給予;傳予;(把祕密,新聞等)通知;告知: *I have nothing of interest to ~ to you.* 我沒有有趣的事情告訴你。

im·par·tial /ɪm'pɑːʃl ; ɪm'pɑrʃəl/ *adj* fair (in giving judgements, etc); not favouring one more than another. (作判斷等時)公平的;不偏袒的;無私的。**~·ly** *adv* **im·par·tial·ity** /ˌɪmˌpɑːʃɪ'ælətɪ ; ˌɪmpɑr'ʃælətɪ/ *n* [U] the quality of being ~. 公平;無私。

im·pass·able /ɪm'pɑːsəbl *US:* -'pæs- ; ɪm'pæsəbl̩/ *adj* impossible to travel through or on: 不可通行的: *country roads/Alpine passes ~ in winter.* 在冬季無法通行的鄉村道路(阿爾卑斯山道)。

im·passe /'æmpɑːs *US:* 'ɪmpæs ; ɪm'pæs/ *n* blind alley; place, position, from which there is no way out; deadlock. 死巷;死路;絕境;僵局。

im·pas·sioned /ɪm'pæʃnd ; ɪm'pæʃənd/ *adj* full of, showing, deep feeling: 充滿熱情的;顯示熱情的: *an ~ speech.* 一篇熱情的演說。

im·pass·ive /ɪm'pæsɪv ; ɪm'pæsɪv/ *adj* showing no sign of feeling; unmoved. 冷淡的;無感覺的;不動感情的。**~·ly** *adv* **~·ness, im·pass·iv·ity** /ˌɪmpæ'sɪvətɪ ; ˌɪmpæ'sɪvətɪ/ *nn*

im·pa·tient /ɪm'peɪʃnt ; ɪm'peʃənt/ *adj* **1** ~ ***(at sth/with sb),*** not patient: 不耐煩的;急躁的: *~ at the delay;* 對延誤感到不耐煩; *~ with a tired child.* 對疲倦的孩子感到不耐煩。**~ *of sth,*** (formal) intolerant of it. (正式用語)無法容忍某事物。**2** ~ ***(for sth/to do sth),*** eager: 急切的;渴望的: *~ for a journey to start; ~ to start a journey.* 急著動身去旅行。*The audience are growing ~.* 觀衆漸漸急躁不安。**~·ly** *adv* **im·pa·tience** /ɪm'peɪʃns ; ɪm'peʃəns/ *n* [U].

im·peach /ɪm'piːtʃ ; ɪm'pitʃ/ *vt* **1** [VP6A] (formal) question, raise doubts about (sb's character, etc): (正式用語) 指摘; 責問; 表示懷疑 (某人的品行等): *Do you ~ my motives,* suggest that they are dishonourable? 你對我的動機表示懷疑嗎? **2** [VP14] **~ *sb for/of/with sth; ~ sb for doing sth,*** (legal) accuse sb of wrongdoing; (esp) accuse (sb) of a crime against the State: (法律)控告(某人);(尤指)檢擧;彈劾(某人)叛國或瀆職: *~ a judge for taking bribes;* 檢擧一法官受賄; *~ sb of a crime.* 控告某人犯罪。**~·ment** *n* [U] ~ing or being ~ed; [C] instance of this. 指摘;責問;控告;彈劾。

im·pec·cable /ɪm'pekəbl ; ɪm'pɛkəbl̩/ *adj* (formal) faultless; incapable of doing wrong: (正式用語)無瑕疵的;不會作錯的;完美的: *an ~ character/record.* 完善的品行(紀錄)。

im·pe·cuni·ous /ˌɪmpɪ'kjuːnɪəs ; ˌɪmpɪ'kjunɪəs/ *adj* (formal) having little or no money. (正式用語)無錢的;貧困的。

im·pede /ɪm'piːd ; ɪm'pid/ *vt* [VP6A] get in the way of; hinder: 阻礙;妨礙: *What ~s your making an early start?* 何事妨礙你早些動身?

im·pedi·ment /ɪm'pedɪmənt ; ɪm'pɛdəmənt/ *n* [C] sth that hinders, esp a defect in speech, eg a stammer. 妨礙物;障礙 (尤指說話方面的缺點,例如口吃)。**im·pedi·menta** /ɪmˌpedɪ'mentə ; ˌɪmpɛdə'mɛntə/ *n pl* baggage (esp of an army). 行李;(尤指)軍隊之輜重。

im·pel /ɪm'pel ; ɪm'pɛl/ *vt* (-ll-) [VP17, 14] ~ ***(to),*** drive, force, urge: 推進;驅使;驅策: *He said he had been ~led to crime by poverty.* 他說他是爲窮困所逼而犯罪。*The President's speech ~led the nation to greater efforts.* 總統的演說激勵全國更加努力。**~·ler** *n* rotor or rotor blade (of a jet engine). 轉輪;(噴射引擎之)旋轉翼。

im·pend /ɪm'pend ; ɪm'pɛnd/ *vi* (chiefly in *pres part*) (formal) be imminent; be about to come or happen: (主要用現在分詞) (正式用語) 逼近; 卽將來到或發生: *her ~ing arrival;* 她的卽將來臨; *the ~ing storm;* 迫近的暴風雨; *the danger ~ing over us.* 逼近我們的危險。

im·pen·etrable /ɪm'penɪtrəbl ; ɪm'pɛnətrəbl̩/ *adj* ~ ***(to),*** that cannot be penetrated: 不能穿過的;不能透過的;不能刺入的: *~ forests and swamps;* 無法通過的森林與沼澤; *dig down to ~ rock;* 挖掘至堅不可破的岩石; *~ darkness;* 漆黑。*men who are ~ to reason.* 不可理喻的人。

im·peni·tent /ɪm'penɪtənt ; ɪm'pɛnətənt/ *adj* (formal) not penitent. (正式用語)不悔悟的。**~·ly** *adv* **im·peni·tence** /-əns ; -əns/ *n*

im·pera·tive /ɪm'perətɪv ; ɪm'pɛrətɪv/ *adj* **1** urgent; essential; needing immediate attention: 緊急的;必要的;急切的: *Is it really ~ for them to have such a large army?* 他們眞的迫切需要如此龐大的一支軍隊嗎? *Is it ~ that they should have/for them to have six cars?* 他們必須要六部汽車嗎? **2** not to be disobeyed; done, given with, authority: 必須服從的;强制的: *The duke's orders were ~.* 公爵的命令必須服從。*'Go at once!', he said, with an ~ gesture.* '立刻去!'他說,並作了個强制的手勢。**3** (gram) (also *n*) (of the) form of a verb or a sentence expressing a command: (文法)(亦作名詞用)祈使的;祈使動詞;祈使句: *the ~ mood.* 祈使語氣。**~·ly** *adv*

im·per·cep·tible /ˌɪmpə'septəbl ; ˌɪmpə'sɛptəbl̩/ *adj* that cannot be perceived; very slight or gradual. 覺察不到的;不可覺的;極輕微或逐漸的。**im·per·cep·tibly** /-əblɪ ; -əblɪ/ *adv*

im·per·fect /ɪm'pɜːfɪkt ; ɪm'pɝfɪkt/ *adj* **1** not perfect or complete. 不完善的;不完全的。**2** ~ **tense,** (gram) that denotes action in progress but not completed (also called 亦稱作 *progressive* or *continuous* tenses), (文法)未完時態(指尙在進行中的動作) as in eg 例如: 'I am/was/have been/will be speaking.' □ *n* ~ tense. 未完時態。**~·ly** *adv* **im·per·fec·tion** /ˌɪmpə'fekʃn ; ˌɪmpə'fɛkʃən/ *n* [U] state of being ~; [C] fault. 不完善;不完全;缺點。

im·perial /ɪm'pɪərɪəl ; ɪm'pɪrɪəl/ *adj* **1** of an empire or its ruler(s): 帝國的;皇帝的: *~ trade;* 帝國的貿易; *His I~ Majesty.* 皇帝陛下;皇上。**2** majestic; august; magnificent: 威嚴的;崇高的;堂皇的: *with ~ generosity.* 以寬宏的精神。**3** (of weights and measures) used by law in the United kingdom: (指度量衡)英國法定的: *an ~ pint/gallon.* 英國法定一品脫(加侖)。□ *n* small, pointed beard grown beneath the lower lip. 留在下唇下面的尖形小鬍;皇帝鬍。**~·ly** /-rɪəlɪ ; -rɪəlɪ/ *adv*

im·peri·al·ism /ɪm'pɪərɪəlɪzəm ; ɪm'pɪrɪəlˌɪzəm/ *n* belief in the value of colonies; policy of extending a country's empire and influence. 帝國主義;擴大一國版圖及勢力的政策。**im·per·ial·ist** /-ɪst ; -ɪst/ *n* supporter of, believer in, ~. 帝國主義者。**im·per·ial·is·tic** /ɪmˌpɪərɪə'lɪstɪk ; ɪmˌpɪrɪəl'ɪstɪk/ *adj* of ~: 帝國主義的: *imperialistic views.* 帝國主義的觀點。

im·peril /ɪm'perəl ; ɪm'pɛrəl/ *vt* (-ll-, US also -l-) [VP6A] (liter) put or bring into danger. (文)使陷於危險;危及。

im·peri·ous /ɪm'pɪərɪəs ; ɪm'pɪrɪəs/ *adj* (formal) (正式用語) **1** commanding; haughty; arrogant: 專橫的;傲慢的;自大的: *~ gestures/looks.* 專橫的姿態(樣子)。**2** urgent; imperative. 急切的;緊急的。**~·ly** *adv* **~·ness** *n*

im·per·ish·able /ɪm'perɪʃəbl ; ɪm'pɛrɪʃəbl̩/ *adj* (formal) that cannot perish; that will never pass away: (正式用語) 不滅的;不朽的: *~ fame/glory.* 不朽的聲名(光榮)。

im·per·ma·nent /ɪm'pɜːmənənt ; ɪm'pɝmənənt/ *adj* (formal) not permanent. (正式用語)非永久的。**im·per·ma·nence** /-əns ; -əns/ *n*

im·per·me·able /ɪm'pɜːmɪəbl ; ɪm'pɝmɪəbl̩/ *adj* ~ ***(to),*** (formal) that cannot be permeated (esp by fluids); impervious. (正式用語)不被(尤指液體)滲透的;不透水的。

im·per·sonal /ˌɪm'pɜːsənl ; ɪm'pɝsn̩l/ *adj* **1** not influenced by personal feeling; not referring to any particular person: 不受個人感情影響的;非特指

某人的;和個人無關的: ~ *remarks;* 非特指某人的評論; *an ~ discussion.* 和個人無關的討論。~ **pronoun,** the pronouns one⁴ and you(2). 非特指某人的代名詞(卽 one⁴ 及 you(2)); 泛指的代名詞。 **2** having no existence as a person: 不具人格的: ~ *forces,* eg those of nature. 非人的力量(例如自然力)。 **3** (of *verbs*) used after 'it' to make general statements such as '*It is raining/freezing*'. (指動詞)非人稱的;無主的(用於 it 之後作一般陳述,例如: It is raining/freezing 中的動詞)。 **~·ly** /-ənəlɪ ; -n̩lɪ/ *adv*

im·per·son·ate /ɪm'pɜːsəneɪt ; ɪm'pɝsn̩,et/ *vt* [VP6A] **1** act the part of (in a play, etc); pretend to be (another person). (在劇中等)扮演…的角色;假扮(另一人)。 **2** personify. 擬人化;賦與人格。 **im·per·son·ation** /ɪm,pɜːsə'neɪʃn ; ˌɪmpɝsn̩'eʃən/ *n* **1** [U] impersonating or being ~d. 扮演;假扮;被扮演或假扮;人格化;被人格化。 **2** [C] instance of this: 上述者的實例: *He gave some clever impersonations of well-known men.* 他巧妙地扮演了幾位名人。 **im·per·son·ator** /-neɪtə(r) ; -ˌnetɚ/ *n* person who ~s. 扮演某角色的人;假扮他人之人。

im·per·ti·nent /ɪm'pɜːtɪnənt ; ɪm'pɝtn̩ənt/ *adj* **1** not showing proper respect; impudent; saucy: 無禮的;失禮的;厚顏的;莽撞的: ~ *remarks;* 鹵莽的言詞; *an ~ boy.* 失禮的男孩。 **2** not pertinent; not pertaining to the matter in hand. 不切題的;不相干的。 **~·ly** *adv* **im·per·ti·nence** /-əns ; -əns/ *n* [U] being ~; [C] ~ act or remark. 無禮;粗魯;不切題;無禮的行爲或言語;不適當的行動或言詞。

im·per·turb·able /ˌɪmpə'tɜːbəbl ; ˌɪmpɚ'tɝbəbl̩/ *adj* (formal) not capable of being excited; calm. (正式用語)不會激動的;鎭靜的。 **im·per·turb·abil·ity** /ˌɪmpəˌtɜːbə'bɪlətɪ ; ˌɪmpɚˌtɝbə'bɪlətɪ/ *n* [U].

im·per·vi·ous /ɪm'pɜːvɪəs ; ɪm'pɝvɪəs/ *adj* ~ ***(to),*** **1** (of materials) not allowing (water, etc) to pass through: (指材料)不爲水等滲透的: *Rubber boots are ~ to water.* 橡膠靴是不透水的。 **2** (fig) not moved or influenced by: (喩)不爲所動的;不受影響的。 *~ to criticism/argument.* 不爲批評(爭論)所動的。

im·pe·tigo /ˌɪmpɪ'taɪgəʊ ; ˌɪmpɪ'taɪgo/ *n* [U] contagious skin disease. 膿疱病(一種接觸傳染性皮膚病)。

im·petu·ous /ɪm'petʃʊəs ; ɪm'pɛtʃʊəs/ *adj* moving quickly or violently; acting, inclined to act, on impulse, energetically but with insufficient thought or care; done or said hastily: 急促或猛烈的;衝動的;鹵莽的;輕擧妄動的: *Children are usually more ~ than old people.* 孩童們通常較老年人衝動。 *Your ~ remarks will get you into trouble.* 你輕率的言談會給你帶來麻煩。 **~·ly** *adv* **im·petu·os·ity** /ɪmˌpetʃʊ'ɒsətɪ ; ˌɪmpɛtʃʊ'ɑsətɪ/ *n* [U] quality of being ~; [C] (*pl* -ties) ~ act, remark, etc. 急促;猛烈;衝動;鹵莽;衝動的言語、行動等。

im·pe·tus /'ɪmpɪtəs ; 'ɪmpətəs/ *n* (*pl* ~es /-sɪz ; -sɪz/) **1** [U] force with which a body moves. 動力;原動力。 **2** [C] impulse; driving force: 刺激;推動力。 *The treaty will give an ~ to trade between the two countries.* 這條約將促進兩國間的貿易。

im·pi·ety /ɪm'paɪətɪ ; ɪm'paɪətɪ/ *n* (formal) (正式用語) **1** [U] lack of reverence or dutifulness. 不尊敬;不恭。 **2** [C] (*pl* -ties) act, remark, etc that shows lack of reverence or dutifulness. 不恭敬的行爲,言語等。

im·pinge /ɪm'pɪndʒ ; ɪm'pɪndʒ/ *vi* [VP3A] ~ ***on/upon,*** (formal) make an impact. (正式用語)撞擊;衝擊。 **~·ment** *n*

im·pi·ous /'ɪmpɪəs ; 'ɪmpɪəs/ *adj* (formal) not pious. (正式用語)不虔敬的。 **~·ly** *adv*

imp·ish /'ɪmpɪʃ ; 'ɪmpɪʃ/ *adj* of or like an imp; mischievous. 小魔鬼的;似小魔鬼的;頑皮的。 **~·ly** *adv* **~·ness** *n*

im·plac·able /ɪm'plækəbl ; ɪm'plekəbl̩/ *adj* (formal) that cannot be appeased; relentless: (正式用語)不能平息的;無情的: *an ~ enemy;* 殘酷的敵人; *~ hatred/love.* 深仇(深愛)。

im·plant /ɪm'plɑːnt *US:* -'plænt ; ɪm'plænt/ *vt* [VP 6A, 14] ~ ***in,*** fix or put ideas, feelings, etc in: 灌輸,注入(思想、感情等): *deeply ~ed hatred;* 深植內心的仇恨; *~ sound principles in the minds of children.* 將健全的原則灌輸在兒童心中。

im·ple·ment¹ /'ɪmplɪmənt ; 'ɪmpləmənt/ *n* tool or instrument for working with: 工具: *farm ~s;* 農具; *stone and bronze ~s made by primitive man.* 原始人所製的石器和青銅器。 ⇨ the illus at tool. 參看 tool 之挿圖。

primitive stone implements

im·ple·ment² /'ɪmplɪment ; 'ɪmpləˌmɛnt/ *vt* [VP6A] carry an undertaking, agreement, promise into effect: 實現;完成(任務等);履行(協定;諾言): ~ *a scheme.* 實現一計畫。 **im·ple·men·ta·tion** /ˌɪmplɪmen'teɪʃn ; ˌɪmpləmən'teʃən/ *n*

im·pli·cate /'ɪmplɪkeɪt ; 'ɪmplɪˌket/ *vt* [VP6A, 14] ~ ***(in),*** (formal) show that (sb) has a share (*in* a crime, etc): (正式用語)使(某人)牽連於(罪行等中);顯示(某人)和(罪行等)有連帶關係: ~ *officials in a bribery scandal.* 顯示一些官員與受賄醜聞有所牽連。 ⇨ involve.

im·pli·ca·tion /ˌɪmplɪ'keɪʃn ; ˌɪmplɪ'keʃən/ *n* (formal) (正式用語) **1** [U] implicating or being implicated (in a crime, etc). 牽連(於罪行等中)。 **2** [C] what is implied; sth hinted at or suggested, but not expressed: 含意;暗示: *What are the ~s of this statement?* What is implied by it? 這一聲明的含意是什麼?

im·pli·cit /ɪm'plɪsɪt ; ɪm'plɪsɪt/ *adj* (formal) (正式用語) **1** ~ ***(in),*** implied though not plainly expressed: 暗示的;含蓄的: *an ~ threat;* 暗示的恐嚇; *~ in the contract.* 在契約中暗示的。 ⇨ explicit. **2** unquestioning: 不置疑的: ~ *belief.* 絕對相信;盲信。 **~·ly** *adv*

im·plore /ɪm'plɔː(r) ; ɪm'plor/ *vt* [VP6A, 17, 14] ~ ***(for),*** request earnestly: 懇求;哀求: ~ *a judge for mercy;* 懇求法官給予憐憫; *~ a friend to help one;* 懇求一位友人幫助; *an imploring glance.* 哀求的眼光。 **im·plor·ing·ly** *adv*

im·plo·sion /ɪm'pləʊʒn ; ɪm'ploʒən/ *n* [U, C] bursting inward, collapse, of a vessel, eg an electric light bulb, from external pressure. (由外界壓力引起的)向內破裂或陷入(例如電燈泡)。 ⇨ explosion.

im·ply /ɪm'plaɪ ; ɪm'plaɪ/ *vt* (*pt, pp* -plied) [VP6A, 9] give or make a suggestion (*that*); involve the truth (of sth not definitely stated): 暗示;含有…的意思: *an implied rebuke.* 暗示的指責。 *Silence sometimes implies consent,* Failure to say 'No' may be taken to mean 'Yes'. 沉默有時含有同意的意思。 *Are you ~ing that I am not telling the truth?* 你的意思是說我沒講實話嗎?

im·po·lite /ˌɪmpə'laɪt ; ˌɪmpə'laɪt/ *adj* not polite. 不禮貌的。 **~·ly** *adv* **~·ness** *n*

im·poli·tic /ɪm'pɒlətɪk ; ɪm'pɑlətɪk/ *adj* (formal) not politic; not expedient. (正式用語)失策的;不利的。

im·pon·der·able /ɪm'pɒndərəbl ; ɪm'pɑndərəbl̩/ *adj* **1** (phys) that cannot be weighed or measured. (物理)不可稱量的。 **2** of which the effect cannot be estimated. 其結果無法估計的。 □ *n* ~ thing; (esp *pl*) qualities, emotions, etc of which the effect cannot be estimated. 不可稱量之物;(尤用複數)其結果無法估計的性質,感情等。

im·port /ɪm'pɔ:t ; ɪm'port/ *vt* **1** [VP6A, 14] ~ ***(from) (into),*** bring in, introduce, esp goods from a foreign country: 輸入;進口: ~ *wool from Australia.* 自澳洲輸入羊毛。 **2** [VP6A, 9] (formal) mean; signify; make known (that): (正式用語)含有…之意;表示;說明: *What does this ~?* What is its significance? 這事的意義是什麼? □ *n* /'ɪmpɔ:t ; 'ɪmport/ **1** (usu *pl*) goods ~ed: (通常用複數)輸入品;進口貨: ~*s of raw cotton;* 輸入的原棉; *food ~s.* 進口的食品。 **2** [U] act of ~ing goods. 輸入;進口。 **3** [U] what is implied; meaning: 含義;意義: *What is the ~ of his statement?* 他的聲明的意義是什麼? **4** [U] (formal) importance: (正式用語)重要: *questions of great ~.* 極爲重要的問題。 **~er** *n* person (usu a merchant) who ~s goods. 進口商人。 **im·port·ation** /ˌɪmpɔ:'teɪʃn ; ˌɪmpor'teʃən/ *n* [U] act of ~ing (goods); [C] sth ~ed. 輸入;進口;輸入品;進口貨。

im·port·ant /ɪm'pɔ:tnt ; ɪm'pɔrtn̩t/ *adj* **1** of great influence; to be treated seriously; having a great effect: 重要的;嚴重的;重大的: ~ *decisions/statements, etc.* 重大的決定(重要的聲明等)。 **2** (of a person) having a position of authority. (指人)顯要的;位尊的。 **~·ly** *adv* **im·port·ance** /-tns ; -tn̩s/ *n* [U] being ~: 重要;重大;顯要: *The matter is of great/no/not much/little importance to us.* 這事對我們極爲(不,不太)重要。 *He spoke with an air of importance.* 他神氣十足地說話。

im·por·tu·nate /ɪm'pɔ:tʃʊnət ; ɪm'pɔrtʃənɪt/ *adj* (formal) (正式用語) **1** (of persons) making repeated and inconvenient requests: (指人)不斷作予人不便之要求的;纏擾不休的: *an ~ beggar.* 纏擾不休的乞丐。 **2** (of affairs, etc) urgent: (指事務等)急切的: ~ *demands/claims.* 急切的要求。 **~·ly** *adv* **im·por·tun·ity** /ˌɪmpə'tju:nətɪ *US:* -'tu:- ; ˌɪmpɚ'tjunətɪ/ *n* [U] being ~(1); (*pl* -ties) instance of this. 不斷作予人不便的要求;纏擾不休;(複)上述的實例。

im·por·tune /ˌɪmpə'tju:n ; ˌɪmpɚ'tjun/ *vt* [VP6A, 9, 14, 17] ~ ***(for),*** (formal) (正式用語) **1** beg urgently and repeatedly: 再三要求;不斷請求: *She ~d her husband for more money/with requests for money/to give her more money.* 她不斷請求她丈夫多給她些錢。 **2** (of a prostitute) solicit(2). (指娼妓)拉客。

im·pose /ɪm'pəʊz ; ɪm'poz/ *vt, vi* **1** [VP14] ~ ***on,*** lay or place a tax, duty, etc on: 加(稅,義務等)於: *New taxes were ~d on wines and spirits.* 酒類加徵新稅。 *I must perform the task that has been ~d upon me.* 我必須要做已加在我身上的工作。 **2** [VP14] ~ ***on sb,*** force (sth, oneself, one's company) on sb: 强使(某人接受某事物,自己);硬纏著某人: *Don't ~ yourself/your company on people who don't want you.* 不要纏着不願和你在一起的人。 **3** [VP3A] ~ ***upon sth,*** take advantage of: 利用: ~ *upon sb's good nature.* 利用某人的好心腸。 **im·pos·ing** *adj* making a strong impression because of size, character, appearance: 因體積,性格,外貌而予人强烈印象的;壯麗的;堂皇的: *an imposing old lady;* 儀態雍容的老婦人; *an imposing display of knowledge.* 在學識方面令人讚賞的表現。 **im·pos·ing·ly** *adv*

im·po·si·tion /ˌɪmpə'zɪʃn ; ˌɪmpə'zɪʃən/ *n* **1** [U] the act of imposing(1): 徵稅;課稅: *Everyone grumbled at the ~ of new taxes.* 每個人都對新課的稅不滿。 **2** [C] sth imposed, eg a tax, burden, punishment, unwanted guest. 强加之事物(例如稅,負擔,懲罰,不速之客)。

im·poss·ible /ɪm'pɒsəbl ; ɪm'pɑsəbl̩/ *adj* **1** not possible: 不可能的: *an ~ scheme/story.* 不可能的計畫(故事)。 ***the ~,*** that which is ~: 不可能的事: *Don't ask me to do the ~.* 別要求我作不可能的事。 **2** that cannot be endured: 無法忍受的: *It's an ~ situation!* 這種局勢令人無法忍受! *He's an ~ person.* 他是個令人無法忍受的人。 **im·poss·ibly** /-əblɪ ; -əblɪ/ *adv* **im·possi·bil·ity** /ɪmˌpɒsə'bɪlətɪ ; ˌɪmpɑsə'bɪlətɪ/ *n* [U] state of being ~; [C] (*pl* -ties) sth that is ~. 不可能;不可能的事。

im·pos·tor /ɪm'pɒstə(r) ; ɪm'pɑstɚ/ *n* person pretending to be sb he is not. 冒充者;騙子。

im·pos·ture /ɪm'pɒstʃə(r) ; ɪm'pɑstʃɚ/ *n* [C] act of deception by an impostor; [U] fraudulent deception: 冒充;矇騙: *make a living by lying and ~.* 以說謊及矇騙爲生。

im·po·tent /'ɪmpətənt ; 'ɪmpətənt/ *adj* lacking sufficient strength (to do sth); unable to act; (of males) wholly lacking in sexual power. 無力(做某事)的;無行動能力的;(指男子)陽萎的;無性交能力的。 **~·ly** *adv* **im·po·tence** /-əns ; -əns/ *n* [U] state of being ~: 無力;無行動能力;陽萎: *We have reduced the enemy to impotence,* made them quite powerless. 我們已徹底消滅敵人的戰鬥力。

im·pound /ɪm'paʊnd ; ɪm'paʊnd/ *vt* [VP6A] **1** take possession of by law or by authority. 收押;扣押;沒收;充公。 **2** (in former times) shut up (cattle that had strayed) in a pound. (昔時)將(迷途的牛隻)關入欄中。 ⇨ pound².

im·pov·er·ish /ɪm'pɒvərɪʃ ; ɪm'pɑvərɪʃ/ *vt* [VP6A] (formal) cause to become poor; take away good qualities: (正式用語)使窮困;除去優點: ~*ed by doctors' bills;* 因付醫藥費而窮困; ~*ed soil,* eg when crops are grown year after year without the use of fertilizers; 貧瘠的土壤(例如年復一年種植作物而不使用肥料); ~*ed rubber,* rubber that has lost its elasticity. 失去彈性的橡皮。 **~·ment** *n*

im·prac·ti·cable /ɪm'præktɪkəbl ; ɪm'præktɪkəbl̩/ *adj* **1** that cannot be put into practice: 不能實行的: *an ~ scheme.* 不能實行的計畫。 **2** (of routes) impassable; that cannot be used. (指道路或航線)不能通行的;不能使用的。 **im·prac·ti·cably** /-əblɪ ; -əblɪ/ *adv* **im·prac·ti·ca·bil·ity** /ɪmˌpræktɪkə'bɪlətɪ ; ˌɪmpræktɪkə'bɪlətɪ/, **~·ness** *nn*

im·prac·ti·cal /ɪm'præktɪkl ; ɪm'præktɪkl̩/ *adj* not practical. 不切實際的;不能實行的。

im·pre·cate /'ɪmprɪkeɪt ; 'ɪmprɪˌket/ *vt* [VP14] ~ ***on/upon sb,*** (formal) invoke, call down (evil on sb). (正式用語)求天降(禍於某人);詛咒。 **im·pre·ca·tion** /ˌɪmprɪ'keɪʃn ; ˌɪmprɪ'keʃən/ *n* [C] curse. 咒語。

im·preg·nable /ɪm'pregnəbl ; ɪm'prɛgnəbl̩/ *adj* that cannot be overcome or taken by force; able to resist all attacks: 不能克服的;不能以暴力取得的;攻不破的: *an ~ fortress;* 鞏固的堡壘; ~ *defences/arguments.* 攻不破的防禦工事(駁不倒的論點)。 **im·preg·nably** /-əblɪ ; -əblɪ/ *adv* **im·preg·na·bil·ity** /ɪmˌpregnə'bɪlətɪ ; ˌɪmprɛgnə'bɪlətɪ/ *n*

im·preg·nate /'ɪmpregneɪt *US:* ɪm'preg- ; ɪm'prɛgnet/ *vt* [VP6A, 14] ~ ***(with),*** **1** make pregnant; fertilize, eg an ovum. 使懷孕;授胎;使(卵子等)受精。 **2** fill, saturate: 灌滿;浸透;使飽和: *water ~d with salt.* 飽含食鹽的水。 **3** imbue, fill with feelings, moral qualities, etc. 使充滿(感情,美德等);灌輸。

im·pre·sario /ˌɪmprɪ'sɑ:rɪəʊ ; ˌɪmprɪ'sɑrɪˌo/ *n* (*pl* -s /-z ; -z/) manager of an operatic or concert company; sponsor of commercial public entertainment. 歌劇團或音樂團的經理人;商業性娛樂節目的贊助人。

im·press /ɪm'pres ; ɪm'prɛs/ *vt* [VP6A, 14] ~ ***(on/upon)/(with),*** **1** press (one thing on or with another); make (a mark, etc) by doing this: 以一物壓(另一物);蓋(印);壓印(記號等): ~ *wax with a seal;* 用印蓋在火漆上; ~ *a seal on wax;* 蓋印於火漆上; ~ *a figure/design on sth.* 將一圖形(圖案)印於某物上。 **2** have a strong influence on; fix deeply (on the mind, memory): 給予强烈影響;使留深刻印象;使銘記: *His words are strongly ~ed on my memory.* 他的話深深銘記在我心頭。 *The book did not ~ me at all,* I did not think it good, useful, etc. 這書沒有給我任何印象。 *I ~ed on him the importance of his work.* 我使他知曉他工作的重要性。 *He ~ed me unfavourably,* I formed an unfavourable opinion of him. 我對他的印象不好。 □ *n* /'ɪmpres ; 'ɪmprɛs/ mark made by stamping a seal, etc on sth. 印記。

im·pression /ɪm'preʃn ; ɪm'prɛʃən/ *n* [C] **1** mark made by pressing: 印記: *the ~ of a seal on wax.* 蓋於火漆上的印記。 **2** print (of an engraving, etc). (彫版等的)版圖;版畫;印出的圖畫。 **3** (product of) any one printing operation: 一版;一次印刷;一次印行之書刊: *a first ~ of 5000 copies.* 第一次印刷的五千册。*Forty ~s* (= reprints without resetting; ⇨ edition) *of this book have been sold so far.* 此書迄今已銷了四十版(指原版第四十次印刷)。 **4** effect produced on the mind or feelings: 印象: *It's my ~ that...;* 我的印象是…; *The speech made a strong ~ on the House.* 這演說給下議院議員們留下深刻的印象。*I'm surprised you got an unfavourable ~ of him.* 我很驚訝你對他印象不佳。*What were your first ~s of London?* 你對倫敦的最初印象如何? *First ~s are often misleading.* 第一印象時常使人發生錯覺。 **5** (vague or uncertain) idea, belief: (模糊或不確定的)觀念;意念: *It's my ~ that he doesn't want to come.* 我覺得他好像不想來。**be under the ~ that...,** have a vague idea, think, that.... 以爲;認爲。 **~·ism** /-ɪzəm ; -ˌɪzəm/ *n* [U] method of painting or writing so as to give the general effect without elaborate detail. (繪畫或寫作之)印象派;印象主義。 **~·ist** /-ɪst ; -ɪst/ *n* person who uses this method. 印象主義者。 **~·is·tic** /ɪmˌpreʃə'nɪstɪk ; ɪmˌprɛʃən'ɪstɪk/ *adj* **1** of, characteristic of, ~ism or ~ists. 印象主義(者)的。 **2** giving only a general ~. 僅給予一般印象的。

im·pression·able /ɪm'preʃənəbl ; ɪm'prɛʃənəbḷ/ *adj* easily influenced: 易受影響的; 易受感動的: *children who are at the ~ age,* adolescent; 處於感受性强烈的年齡的孩子; 青春期的孩子; *an ~ young lady,* eg one who easily falls in love. 容易動感情的少女(例如易墜入情網者)。

im·press·ive /ɪm'presɪv ; ɪm'prɛsɪv/ *adj* making a deep impression on the mind and feelings: 給人深刻印象的: *an ~ ceremony.* 予人以深刻印象的典禮。 **~·ly** *adv* **~·ness** *n*

im·pri·ma·tur /ˌɪmprɪ'meɪtə(r);ˌɪmprɪ'metɚ/ *n* (RC Church) official permission to print; (fig) sanction, approval. (天主教)印書許可證;(喻)許可;准許。

im·print /ɪm'prɪnt ; ɪm'prɪnt/ *vt* [VP14] **~ with/on,** print; stamp: 印;蓋印於: *~ a letter with a postmark/a postmark on a letter;* 蓋郵戳於信件上; *ideas ~ed on the mind.* 銘記於心中的觀念。□ *n* /'ɪmprɪnt ; 'ɪmprɪnt/ [C] that which is ~ed: 印象;印跡;印記: *the ~ of a foot* (= footprint); 脚印;足跡; *the ~ of suffering on a person's face;* 苦難在人臉上留下的痕跡; *a publisher's/printer's ~,* his name, address, etc on the title-page or at the end of the book. 書籍內書名頁或封底所印的出版者或印刷者的姓名、地址等資料。

im·prison /ɪm'prɪzn ; ɪm'prɪzṇ/ *vt* [VP6A] put or keep in prison. 監禁;下獄。 **~·ment** *n* [U] ~ing or being ~ed: 監禁;坐牢: *sentenced to one year's ~ment.* 被判有期徒刑一年。

im·prob·able /ɪm'prɒbəbl ; ɪm'prɑbəbḷ/ *adj* not likely to be true or to happen: 似不可信的;不大可能發生的: *an ~ story/result.* 似不可信的故事(不大可能的結果)。*Rain is ~.* 不像要下雨的樣子。 **im·prob·ably** /-əblɪ ; -əblɪ/ *adv* **im·prob·abil·ity** /ɪmˌprɒbə'bɪlətɪ ; ɪmˌprɑbə'bɪlətɪ/ *n* [U] being ~; [C] (*pl* -ties) sth which is or seems ~: 似不確實;不大可能;不大可能發生的事: *Don't worry about such improbabilities as floods and earthquakes.* 不要爲像洪水和地震等不大可能發生的事而憂慮。

im·promptu /ɪm'prɒmptjuː *US:* -tuː ; ɪm'prɑmptu/ *adj, adv* without preparation: 未事先準備的(地): *an ~ speech;* 即席的演說; *speak ~.* 作即席演講。□ *n* musical composition that seems to have been improvised. 似是演奏中臨時作成的樂曲;即興曲。

im·proper /ɪm'prɒpə(r) ; ɪm'prɑpɚ/ *adj* **1** not suited for the purpose, situation, circumstances, etc: 不適當的;不合式的: *Laughing and joking are ~ at a funeral.* 在葬禮時大笑和開玩笑是不適合的。 **2** incorrect: 不正確的;錯誤的: *~ diagnosis of disease.* 對疾病的錯誤診斷。 **3** indecent: 不道德的;下流的: *~ stories.* 低級故事。 **~·ly** *adv*

im·pro·pri·ety /ˌɪmprə'praɪətɪ ; ˌɪmprə'praɪətɪ/ *n* (formal) [U] incorrectness; unsuitability; [C] (*pl* -ties) improper act, remark, etc. (正式用語)不正確;不適當;不適當的行動、言語等。

im·prove /ɪm'pruːv ; ɪm'pruv/ *vt, vi* **1** [VP6A, 2A] make or become better: 改良;改善: *This is not good enough; I want to ~ it.* 這還不够好,我要加以改進。*He came back from his holiday with greatly ~d health.* 他度假回來,健康大爲增進。*He is improving in health.* 他的健康正增進中。 *His health is improving.* 他的健康正在增進。 [VP3A] **~ on/upon,** produce sth better than: 改良;改進: *Your complexion is wonderful; don't try to ~ upon nature.* 你的膚色好得很;不要企圖改良天生的膚色。 **2** [VP6A] make good use of; turn to account: 善用;利用: *~ the occasion.* 善用時機。 **~·ment** *n* **1** [U] improving or being ~d: 改良;進步: *There is need for ~ment in your handwriting.* 你的書法需要改進。 *Little/no/not much ~ment seemed possible.* 似乎很少有(沒有,不太有)改善的可能了。 **2** [C] sth which ~s, which adds to beauty, usefulness, value, etc: 改良的事物;增加美,用途,價值等的事物: *I have noticed a number of ~ments in the town since I was here six years ago.* 我發現這城鎮,自從我六年前來過後,有許多改進之處。*We all hope for an ~ment in the weather.* 我們都希望天氣好轉。*This is an ~ment upon your first attempt.* 這比你第一次所做的進步了。

im·provi·dent /ɪm'prɒvɪdənt ; ɪm'prɑvədənt/ *adj* (formal) wasteful; not looking to future needs. (正式用語)浪費的;不顧將來需要的。 **~·ly** *adv* **im·provi·dence** /-əns ; -əns/ *n*

im·pro·vise /'ɪmprəvaɪz ; 'ɪmprəˌvaɪz/ *vt, vi* [VP6A, 2A]. **1** compose music while playing, compose verse while reciting, etc: 演奏時臨時作曲;朗誦時臨時作詩;即席作曲或詩: *If an actor forgets his words, he has to ~.* 如果一個演員忘記了臺詞,他必須臨時編作。*The pianist ~d an accompaniment to the song.* 那鋼琴家爲那首歌作了即興伴奏。 **2** provide, make or do sth quickly, in time of need, using whatever happens to be available: (爲配合需要利用任何可用材料)臨時湊成;臨時準備: *an ~d meal for unexpected guests;* 爲不速之客臨時準備的一餐飯; *an ~d bed,* eg one made up on a couch. 臨時作成的床鋪 (例如在長沙發椅上所作的)。 **im·pro·vis·ation** /ˌɪmprəvaɪ'zeɪʃn *US:* -vɪ'z- ; ˌɪmprəvaɪ'zeʃən/ *n* [U, C].

im·prud·ent /ɪm'pruːdnt ; ɪm'prudṇt/ *adj* rash; indiscreet: 輕率的;不謹愼的: *Isn't it ~ of you to marry while your salary is so low?* 在你薪水這樣低之際結婚,不是欠考慮嗎? **~·ly** *adv* **im·prud·ence** /-ns ; -ṇs/ *n* [U] being ~; [C] ~ act, remark, etc. 輕率;不謹愼;輕率的行動,言語等。

im·pu·dent /'ɪmpjʊdənt ; 'ɪmpjədənt/ *adj* shamelessly rude; rudely disrespectful: 厚顏的;鹵莽的;冒昧的: *He was ~ enough to call me a fool.* 他無禮之極,竟敢把我稱作傻瓜。 **~·ly** *adv* **im·pu·dence** /-əns ; -əns/ *n* [U] being ~; ~ words and actions: 厚顏;鹵莽;厚顏的言語和行動: *None of your impudence!* 不要如此鹵莽! *He had the impudence to thumb his nose at me.* 他竟然厚着臉皮嘲弄我。

im·pugn /ɪm'pjuːn ; ɪm'pjun/ *vt* [VP6A] (formal) challenge, express doubt about (a statement, act, quality, etc). (正式用語)指摘(一聲明,行爲,性質等);責難;抨擊。

im·pulse /'ɪmpʌls ; 'ɪmpʌls/ *n* **1** [C] push or thrust; impetus: 推動;推進力: *give an ~ to trade/education.* 促進貿易(教育)。 **2** [C] sudden inclination to act without thought about the consequences: 衝動: *seized with an ~ to do sth;* 情不自禁地欲做某事; *feel an irresistible ~ to jump out* *of a window*, eg during a fit of insanity. 感覺到無法抵抗的衝動，欲跳出窗外（例如當瘋狂發作時）。 **3** [U] state of mind in which such inclinations occur; tendency to act without reflection: 衝動的心理狀態；不加思索而行事的傾向：*a man of* ～. 易衝動的人。***on (an)*** **～,** without reflection or planning: 憑衝動地；未經思考或計畫地：*phone sb on* ～. 一時衝動打電話給某人。**'～-buy** *vt, vi* buy on ～. 未經考慮或計畫而購買。**4** (science) sudden, brief force. (科學) 脈衝；衝量。

im·pul·sion /ɪm'pʌlʃn ; ɪm'pʌlʃən/ *n* [U] impelling; driving or being driven forward; [C] impetus; mental impulse. 驅使；推進；推動力；衝動。

im·pul·sive /ɪm'pʌlsɪv ; ɪm'pʌlsɪv/ *adj* **1** (of persons, their conduct) acting on impulse; resulting from impulse: (指人，人的行爲) 憑衝動行事的；由衝動造成的：*a girl with an* ～ *nature.* 天性易衝動的女郎。 **2** (of a force) tending to impel. (指力量) 推進的。**～·ly** *adv* **～·ness** *n*

im·pun·ity /ɪm'pju:nətɪ ; ɪm'pjunətɪ/ *n* [U] freedom from punishment. 免受懲罰。***with*** **～,** without risk of injury or punishment. 不受損害或懲罰地。

im·pure /ɪm'pjʊə(r) ; ɪm'pjʊr/ *adj* not pure: 不純的；不純潔的：*the* ～ *air of towns;* 城市中不潔的空氣；～ *milk;* 不純的牛奶；～ *motives.* 不純潔的動機。**im·pur·ity** /-ətɪ ; -ətɪ/ *n* [U] state of being ～; [C] (*pl* -ties) ～ thing: 不純；不純潔；不純潔之物；雜質：*impurities in food.* 食物中的雜質。

im·pute /ɪm'pju:t ; ɪm'pjut/ *vt* [VP14] ～ ***to,*** (formal) consider as the act, quality, or outcome of: (正式用語) 認係…之行爲，性質或結果；歸於；歸咎於；諉於：*They* ～*d the accident to the driver's carelessness.* 他們將這次車禍歸咎於駕駛的疏忽。*He was innocent of the crime* ～*d to him.* 對於所加之於他的罪，他是無辜的。**im·pu·ta·tion** /ˌɪmpjʊ'teɪʃn ; ˌɪmpjʊ'teʃən/ *n* [U] act of imputing; [C] accusation or suggestion of wrongdoing, etc: 歸咎；歸罪；非難：*imputations on a person's character.* 對一人品格的種種責難。

in[1] /ɪn ; ɪn/ *adv part* (contrasted with *out*) (與 out 相對) **1** (used with many *vv*, in obvious meanings, as *come in* (= enter) and meanings that are not obvious, as *give in* (= surrender); ⇨ the *v* entries for these). (與許多動詞連用，有時意義明顯，如 come in 中之 in, 有時意義不明顯，如 give in 中之 in; 參看動詞各項)。 **2** ***be in,*** **(a)** at home: 在家；未外出：*Is there anyone in?* 有人在家嗎？*My husband won't be in until six o'clock.* 我先生要到六點才在家。**(b)** arrive: 到達：*Is the train in yet,* Has it arrived? 火車到了嗎？**(c)** (of crops) harvested; brought in from the fields: (指農作物) 收割了的；已收穫的：*The wheat crop／the harvest is safely in.* 小麥 (收穫物) 安全地收割完了。**(d)** in season; obtainable: 正當時令；可獲得的：*Strawberries are in now.* 草莓正當時令。*When will oysters be in?* 蠔什麼時候上市？**(e)** in fashion: 流行：*Long skirts are in again.* 長裙子又流行了。**(f)** elected; in power; in office: 當選；掌握政權；執政：*The Democrats are in.* 民主黨在執政。*The Liberal candidate is in,* has been elected. 自由黨候選人當選了。**(g)** burning: 燃燒着：*Is the fire still in?* 火仍在燃燒嗎？**(h)** (cricket, baseball) batting: (板球，棒球) 擊球：*Which side is in?* 那一邊在擊球？*He was bowled before he had been in* (= at the wicket) *five minutes.* 他擊球尙未到五分鐘便被迫退場了。**3** ***be in for sth,*** **(a)** likely to have or experience (esp sth unpleasant): 可能嘗受或經驗 (尤指不愉快的事)：*I'm afraid we're in for a storm.* 我恐怕我們要遭受暴風雨了。*You're in for an unpleasant surprise.* 你可能遇到不愉快的意外之事。**(b)** committed to; having agreed to take part in: 答應；同意參加：*I'm in for the competition,* shall be a competitor. 我將參加比賽。*Are you in for the 1000 metres race?* 你參加一千米賽跑嗎？***have it in for sb,*** be wanting to take revenge on him. 欲懲罰某人。***be in on sth,*** (colloq) participate in; have a share in: (俗) 參加；加入：*I'd like to be in on this scheme.* 我想參與這個計畫。***day in, day out; week in, week out; year in, year out,*** day after day, week after week, etc in a monotonous way. 一天又一天；一週又一週；年復一年。***in and out,*** now in and now out: 時進時出：*He's always in and out of hospital,* is frequently ill and in hospital. 他時常生病住院。***be (well) in with sb,*** be on good terms with him (and likely to benefit from his friendship). 與某人相處甚好 (並可能因其友誼而獲益)。 **4** (preceding a *n*): (用於名詞前)：*an 'in-patient,* one who lives in a hospital while receiving treatment (contrasted with *'out-patient*). 住院病人 (與 out-patient 相對)。

in[2] /ɪn ; ɪn/ *prep* (For the use of *in* with many *nn* and *vv*, ⇨ the *n* and *v* entries, 與許多名詞和動詞連用的用法，請參看名詞和動詞各項，eg 例如 *in print, in memory of, fail in an examination*). **1** (of place; ⇨ at): (指地點)：*the highest mountain in the world;* 世界上最高的山；*in Africa;* 在非洲；*in the east of Asia;* 在亞洲東部；*in Denmark;* 在丹麥；*in the provinces;* 在各省；*in Kent;* 在肯特郡；*in London;* 在倫敦；*the village in which he was born;* 他出生的那個村子；*the only shop in the village;* 這村中唯一的商店；*islands in the Pacific Ocean;* 太平洋的島嶼；*sailing in British waters,* ie on the seas round Britain; 在英國近海航行；*in every quarter of the town;* 在這城中每一地區；*children playing in the street;* 在街上遊玩的孩子們；*not a cloud in the sky;* 天空中沒有一片雲；*swimming in the lake;* 在湖中游泳；*standing in the corner of the room.* 站在該房間的角落裏。Cf 參較 the house *at* the corner; *working in the fields／in coal-mines;* 在田野 (煤礦) 工作；*a picnic in the woods;* 林中的野餐；*a holiday in the country／in the mountains.* 在鄉間 (山間) 所度的一個假日。Cf 參較 *at* the seaside; *a light in the distance;* 在遠處的燈；*in the background／foreground;* 在暗中 (在顯著地方)；*lying in bed.* 躺在床上。Cf 參較 sitting *on* the bed; *sitting in an armchair.* 坐在有扶手的椅上。Cf 參較 *on* a chair without arms; *in school／church／prison;* 在學校 (在教堂；在獄中)；*a ride in a motor-car.* 乘汽車兜風。*He was wounded in the leg.* 他的腿部受傷。*The key is in the lock.* 鑰匙在鎖中。*There were plants in the window,* ie *on* the window-sill, framed by the window. 窗檻上有花木。*What would you do in my place,* if you were situated as I am situated? 你如果處在我的地位將怎樣做？*I read about it in the newspapers.* 我在報上看到有關此事的報導。*He had a stick in his hand and a cigar in his mouth.* 他手上拿着一根手杖，嘴裏啣着一枝雪茄。*You will find the verse in the second chapter of Genesis.* 你在創世紀第二章會找到這一節。 **2** (of direction): (指方向)：*in this／that direction;* 朝此 (那) 方向；*in all directions.* 四面八方；各處。 **3** (indicating direction of motion or activity) into: (指運動或動作的方向) 進入：*He dipped his pen in the ink.* 他將他的筆尖浸入墨水中。*He put his hands in his pockets.* 他把手放進口袋裏。*Cut the apple in two,* into halves. 把這蘋果切成兩半。*Cut／break it in two.* 把它切 (破) 成兩半。*Throw it in the fire.* 把它丟到火中。*They fell in love.* 他們在戀愛。 **4** (of time when): (指時間)：*in the 20th c;* 在二十世紀裏；*in 1970;* 在 1970 年；*in the reign of Queen Anne;* 在安女王統治時期；*in spring／summer, etc;* 在春季 (夏季等)；*in my absence;* 在我不在的時間；*in his youth;* 在他年輕時；*in old age;* 在晚年；*still in her teens;* 在她還是十幾歲時；*in these／those days;* 近來 (在那些日子裏)；*in the morning／afternoon／evening.* 在早晨 (下午，晚間)。Cf 參較 *on* Monday morning; *in the daytime;* 在白晝；*at ten o'clock in the night.* 在晚上十點鐘。Cf 參較 *at* night; *in (the) future;* 今後 (在將來)；*in the past;* 在過去；*in the end,* finally; 最後；*in time of war;* 在戰時；*in the hour of victory／death, etc.* 在勝利 (死亡等) 的時刻。*He has met many famous men in his time,* during his lifetime. 他一生中遇到過許多名人。 *She was a famous beauty in her day*, during her best years. 她年輕時是一位著名的美人。*The school was quite small in my time*, when I was there. 我在那裏的時候這學校還很小。 **5** (of time) in the course of; within the space of: (指時間)過(若干時間);在(若干時間)內: *I shall be back in a short time/in a few days/in a week's time, etc.* 我過一會兒(幾天,一星期等)回來。*Can you finish the work in an hour?* 你能在一小時內完成這工作嗎？*I'll be ready in a moment.* 過一會兒我便準備好了。Cf also 亦參較 *in time.* **6** (indicating inclusion): (表示包含之義): *seven days in a week;* 一星期有七天; *four quarts in a gallon;* 一加侖有四夸脫; *a man in his thirties*, ie between 30 and 39 years of age; 一個三十多歲(自 30 至 39 歲)的男子; *in the early thirties of this century*, ie between 1930 and 1934 or 1935. 在本世紀三十年代的初期(在 1930 與 1934 或 1935 年之間)。*There is 10 per cent for service in the (hotel) bill.* 這(旅館)帳單內有百分之十的服務費。*He has nothing of the hero in him*, Heroism is not among his characteristics. 他沒有英雄氣概。*He has in him the makings of a good soldier*, has qualities, abilities, etc that will help him to become a good soldier. 他具有成為一個優秀軍人的資質。 **7** (indicating ratio): (表示比率): *a slope/gradient of one in five.* 五分之一的斜坡(坡度)(約合仰角$11\frac{1}{3}$度)。*He paid his creditors 25p in the pound.* 他向他的債權人按每鎊廿五辨士(即原值的四分之一)償還。*Not one in ten of the boys could spell well.* 這些男孩中拼字正確的不到十分之一。**8** (of dress, etc): (指衣服等)穿着; 戴着: *dressed/clothed in rags;* 衣衫襤褸; *the man in the top hat;* 那個戴着高頂禮帽的男子; *a prince in disguise;* 喬裝的王子; *the woman in white*, wearing white clothes; 那個穿白衣服的女子; *in uniform;* 穿着制服; *in mourning;* 穿着喪服; *in brown shoes;* 穿着棕色皮鞋; *in his shirt sleeves*, not wearing a jacket or coat; 僅穿着襯衫(未穿外套); *a prisoner in irons.* 戴着鐐銬的囚犯。 **9** (indicating physical surroundings, circumstances, etc): (表示環境或境遇等)在…環境下: *go out in the rain;* 冒雨出去; *sitting in the sun(shine);* 坐在陽光下; *standing outside in the cold;* 站在外面受寒冷; *sleep in the open;* 在露天睡眠; *a temperature of 95°F in the shade;* 在蔭涼處華氏 95 度的氣溫; *lose one's way in the dark;* 在黑暗中迷了路; *unable to work in this heat;* 在這種炎熱的天氣無法工作; *go for a walk in the moonlight.* 在月光下散步。 **10** (indicating state or condition): (表示情況或狀態): *in a troubled state;* 在煩惱中; *in good order;* 整齊;情況良好; *in poor health;* 健康不佳; *in good repair;* 情況良好; *in a good humour;* 心情好; *in a fever of excitement;* 極為興奮; *in despair;* 在絕望中; *in a rage;* 在憤怒中; *in tears;* 在哭泣; *in a hurry;* 匆忙中; *living in luxury;* 生活奢侈; *in poverty;* 在貧困中; *in ruins;* 在頹廢狀態中; *not in the mood for work;* 沒有心情工作; *in debt;* 負債; *in love;* 戀愛中; *in doubt;* 懷疑; *in wonder;* 驚奇; *in public;* 公開地; *in secret;* 祕密地; *in fun/jest/joke;* 玩笑地; *in earnest.* 認眞地;熱心地。 **11** (indicating form, shape, arrangement): (表示形式,形狀,排列): *a novel in three parts;* 分作三部份的一本小說; *books packed in bundles of ten;* 每十本一包的書籍; *men standing about in groups;* 成羣地站在各處的人們; *children sitting in rows;* 排排坐的孩子們; *wolves hunting in packs;* 成群獵食的狼; *words in alphabetical order;* 按字母順序排列的字; *with her hair in curls/in ringlets;* 她的頭髮捲曲着; *dancing in a ring;* 圍成一圓圈跳舞; *cloth hanging in folds.* 摺著懸掛的布。 **12** (indicating the method of *in* expression, the medium, means, material, etc): (表示表達的方法,媒介,工具,材料等): *speaking/writing in English;* 用英語說(寫); *a message in code;* 以密碼發出的消息; *written in ink/pencil;* 用墨水(鉛筆)寫的; *(printed) in italic type;* 以斜體(印刷的); *in two colours;* 以二種顏色; *in writing;* 書寫地; *in a few words;* 簡言之; *in round numbers*, eg 200 000 for 197 563; 以約略數字言之(例如以 200 000 代替 197 563); *talking in a loud voice;* 大聲談話; *bound in leather;* 皮面裝訂的; *painted in oils;* 油彩畫的; *carved in oak;* 橡木雕刻的; *cast in bronze;* 青銅鑄的; *a statue in marble;* 大理石雕像; *payment in cash/in kind.* 現金(實物)給付。 **13** (indicating degree or extent): (表示程度或限度): *in large/small quantities;* 大(少)量的; *in great numbers;* 許多; *in some measure;* 有幾分; *in part.* 一部份;有幾分。*The enemy appeared in great strength.* 敵人的兵力似乎很强。***in all***, as the total: 合計: *We were fifteen in all.* 我們共有十五位。 **14** (indicating identity): (表示同一人或物): *You will always have a good friend in me*, I shall always befriend you. 我永遠是你的朋友。*We have lost a first-rate teacher in Jim*, Jim, who has left us, was a first-rate teacher. 我們失去了第一流的教師吉姆。*The enemy lost 200 in killed and wounded*, 200 of them were killed or wounded. 敵人傷亡二百名。 **15** (indicating relation, reference, respect): (表示關係,方面): *in some/all respects;* 在某些(各)方面; *in every way;* 各方面; *inferior in physique but superior in intellect;* 體格較差但智力較高; *young in years but old in wisdom;* 年紀雖輕但智慧甚高; *weak in the head*, not intelligent; 智力低的; *deficient in courage;* 缺少勇氣; *a country rich/poor in minerals;* 鑛物豐富(缺乏)的國家; *blind in the left eye;* 左眼失明; *my equal in strength;* 力量與我相等之人; *ten feet in length/depth/diameter, etc;* 長度(深度,直徑等)為十呎; *wanting/lacking in judgement.* 缺乏判斷力。 **16** (indicating occupation, activity, etc): (表示職業,活動等): *He's in the army/in insurance/in the motor business/in the Cabinet/in the Air Ministry.* 他在陸軍(保險業,汽車業,內閣,空軍部)服務。*He's in politics*, is a politician. 他在從政。*He was killed in action*, while fighting in war. 他於作戰時陣亡。*How much time do you spend in reading?* 你花費多少時間閱讀？ **17** (used in numerous prepositional phrases of the pattern ***in + n + prep***, ⇨ the *n* entries, eg): (用於許多介詞片語中,其後跟一名詞,名詞後再接一介詞,參看各該名詞,例如): *in defence of;* 保衞; *in exchange for;* 交換; *in justice to;* 對…公平; *in memory of;* 紀念; *in touch with.* 接觸。 **18** ***in camera***, (legal) in private, in the judge's private room, not in open court; (colloq) secretly. (法律)不公開審訊; 閉庭審訊; (俗)祕密地。***in that***, since, because; 由於;因為: *The higher income tax is harmful in that it may discourage people from trying to earn more.* 所得稅增高是有害的,因為它可能使人不願多賺錢。***in as/so far as***, in such measure as; to the extent that: 就…之限度;至於…的程度;就…而論: *He is a Russian in so far as he was born in Russia, but he became a French citizen in 1920.* 就他出生在蘇俄而言,他是個俄國人,但他在 1920 年入了法國籍。***in itself***, in its own nature; absolutely; considered apart from other things: 在本質上;完全地;就其本身言: *Card playing is not harmful in itself; it is only when combined with wild gambling that it may be harmful.* 玩牌本身並無害處,但若加上狂賭,則有害處。

in³ /ɪn; ɪn/ *n* (only in) (僅用於) ***the ins and (the) outs***, **(a)** political party in office and political party out of office. 執政黨與在野黨。**(b)** the different parts; the details and complexities: 詳情; 細節: *know all the ins and outs of a problem.* 熟悉一問題之詳情。

-in /ɪn; ɪn/ *suff* added to another word (usu a *v*) to indicate participation in a group activity, etc. 附加於另一字 (通常為一動詞) 後,表示參與集體活動等。⇨ the *v* entries, 參看動詞各項, eg 例如 *sit-in, teach-in.*

in·abil·ity /ˌɪnəˈbɪlətɪ; ˌɪnəˈbɪlətɪ/ *n* [U] ~ ***(to do sth)***, being unable; lack of power or means. 無能力;無力量;無方法。

in·ac·cess·ible /ˌɪnæk'sesəbl ; ˌɪnək'sɛsəbl̩/ *adj* ~ ***(to),*** (formal) not accessible. (正式用語)不能接近的; 不能進入的; 不能達到的。 **in·ac·cessi·bil·ity** /ˌɪnækˌsesə'bɪlətɪ ; ˌɪnəkˌsɛsə'bɪlətɪ/ *n* [U].

in·ac·cur·ate /ɪn'ækjʊrət ; ɪn'ækjərɪt/ *adj* not accurate. 不準確的。 **~·ly** *adv* **in·ac·cur·acy** /-əsɪ ; -əsɪ/ *n* [U] being ~; [C] (*pl* -cies) ~ statement, etc. 不準確;不正確的陳述等。

in·ac·tion /ɪn'ækʃn ; ɪn'ækʃən/ *n* [U] doing nothing; lack of activity. 不做事;不活動。

in·ac·tive /ɪn'æktɪv ; ɪn'æktɪv/ *adj* not active. 不活動的;不活躍的。**in·ac·ti·vate** /ˌɪn'æktɪveɪt ; ɪn'æktəˌvet/ *vt* make ~: 使不活動: *inactivate a virus.* 使濾過性病原體停止活動。 **in·ac·tiv·ity** /ˌɪnæk'tɪvətɪ ; ˌɪnæk'tɪvətɪ/ *n* [U].

in·ad·equate /ɪn'ædɪkwət ; ɪn'ædəkwɪt/ *adj* ~ ***(for sth/to do sth),*** not adequate; insufficient. 不適當的;不充分的。**~·ly** *adv* **in·ad·equacy** /ɪn'ædɪkwəsɪ ; ɪn'ædəkwəsɪ/ *n* [U].

in·ad·miss·ible /ˌɪnəd'mɪsəbl ; ˌɪnəd'mɪsəbl̩/ *adj* that cannot be admitted or allowed: 不能承認的; 不可允許的: ~ *evidence;* 不能承認的證據; ~ *in evidence.* 不能作爲證據的。

in·ad·ver·tent /ˌɪnəd'vɜːtənt ; ˌɪnəd'vɝtn̩t/ *adj* (formal) not paying or showing proper attention; (of actions) done thoughtlessly or not on purpose. (正式用語)不注意的;不當心的;(指行動)疏忽或無意中所做的。 **~·ly** *adv* **in·ad·ver·tence** /-təns ; -tn̩s/ *n* [U] the quality of being ~; [C] oversight or error which is the result of being ~. 不注意;粗心;疏忽。

in·alien·able /ˌɪn'eɪlɪənəbl ; ɪn'eljənəbl̩/ *adj* (formal) (of rights, etc) that cannot be given away or taken away. (正式用語)(指權利等)不能讓與的;不可剝奪的。

in·ane /ɪ'neɪn ; ɪn'en/ *adj* silly; senseless: 愚蠢的;無意義的: *an* ~ *remark.* 無意義的話。 **~·ly** *adv* **in·an·ity** /ɪ'nænətɪ ; ɪn'ænətɪ/ *n* [U] being ~; [C] (*pl* -ties) ~ remark, act, etc. 愚蠢;無意義;愚蠢或無意義的言語,行動等。

in·ani·mate /ɪn'ænɪmət ; ɪn'ænəmɪt/ *adj* **1** lifeless: 無生命的: ~ *rocks and stones.* 無生命的岩石。 **2** without animal life: 非動物的: ~ *nature,* outside the animal world. 非動物界。 **3** spiritless; dull: 無生氣的;單調的: ~ *conversation.* 枯燥的談話。

in·ani·tion /ˌɪnə'nɪʃn ; ˌɪnə'nɪʃən/ *n* [U] (formal) (正式用語) **1** emptiness. 空虛。 **2** extreme weakness from lack of food. 因飢餓而極端虛弱;營養不足。

in·ap·pli·cable /ɪn'æplɪkəbl ; ɪn'æplɪkəbl̩/ *adj* ~ ***(to),*** not applicable. 不適用的。

in·ap·preci·able /ˌɪnə'priːʃəbl ; ˌɪnə'priʃɪəbl̩/ *adj* not worth reckoning; too small or slight to be perceived: 不值得計算或估價的; 細微不可辨的; 微不足道的: *an* ~ *difference.* 細微不可辨的差異。

in·ap·pro·pri·ate /ˌɪnə'prəʊprɪət ; ˌɪnə'proprɪɪt/ *adj* ~ ***to,*** not appropriate or suitable. 不適當的;不合宜的。

in·apt /ɪn'æpt ; ɪn'æpt/ *adj* unskilful; not bearing on the subject: 拙劣的;不適切的: ~ *remarks.* 不適切的言語。 **in·ap·ti·tude** /ɪn'æptɪtjuːd *US:* -tuːd ; ɪn'æptəˌtjud/ *n* [U] being ~. 拙劣;不適切。

in·ar·ticu·late /ˌɪnɑː'tɪkjʊlət ; ˌɪnɑr'tɪkjəlɪt/ *adj* **1** (of speech) not clear or distinct; not well joined together; (of a person) not speaking distinctly; not able to express himself clearly and fluently; not of the nature of speech: (指說話)不清楚的;不連貫的;(指人)說話不清楚的;不能清楚和流利地表達的;不似說話的: ~ *rage/sounds/letters.* 氣得說不出話(不清楚的聲音;不知所云的信件)。 **2** not jointed: 無關節的: *an* ~ *body,* eg a jelly-fish. 無關節的身體(例如水母)。

in·as·much as /ˌɪnəz'mʌtʃ əz ; ˌɪnəz'mʌtʃ əz/ *conj* since; because. 由於;因爲。

in·at·ten·tion /ˌɪnə'tenʃn ; ˌɪnə'tɛnʃən/ *n* [U] lack of, failure to pay, attention. 缺少注意力;不注意。 **in·at·ten·tive** /ˌɪnə'tentɪv ; ˌɪnə'tɛntɪv/ *adj* not attentive. 不注意的。

in·aud·ible /ɪn'ɔːdəbl ; ɪn'ɔdəbl̩/ *adj* that cannot be heard. 聽不見的;不可聞的。 **in·audi·bil·ity** /ɪnˌɔːdə'bɪlətɪ ; ˌɪnɔdə'bɪlətɪ/ *n* [U].

in·aug·ural /ɪ'nɔːgjʊrəl ; ɪn'ɔgjərəl/ *adj* of or for an inauguration: 就職的;就職典禮的: *an* ~ *lecture.* 就職演說。□ *n* ~ address. 就職演說。

in·au·gur·ate /ɪ'nɔːgjʊreɪt ; ɪn'ɔgjəˌret/ *vt* [VP6A] **1** introduce (a new official, professor, etc) at a special ceremony: 爲(一新的官員,教授等)舉行就職典禮: ~ *a president.* 舉行總統就職典禮。 **2** enter, with public formalities, upon (an undertaking); open an exhibition/a new public building with formalities. 以公開儀式開始(某一事業);爲展覽會(新公共建築物)舉行開幕式或落成典禮。 **3** be the beginning of: 爲…之始: *The invention of the internal combustion engine ~d a new era in travel.* 內燃機之發明爲旅行開一新紀元。**in·aug·ur·ation** /ɪˌnɔːgjʊ'reɪʃn ; ɪnˌɔgjə'reʃən/ *n* [U, C] inaugurating or being ~d: 就職典禮;開創;舉行開幕式;落成: *the inauguration of the President of the US* (20 Jan). 美國總統的就職典禮(一月二十日)。

in·aus·pi·cious /ˌɪnɔː'spɪʃəs ; ˌɪnɔ'spɪʃəs/ *adj* not auspicious; not of good omen. 不吉祥的。 **~·ly** *adv*

in·board /'ɪnbɔːd ; 'ɪnˌbord/ *adj* within the hull of a ship: 在船內的: *an* ~ *motor.* 船內馬達。 ⇨ outboard.

in·born /ˌɪn'bɔːn ; ɪn'bɔrn/ *adj* (of a quality) possessed (by a person or animal) at birth; implanted by nature: (指人或動物的性質)天生的;天賦的: *a boy with an* ~ *love of mischief;* 生來喜歡惡作劇的男孩子; *an* ~ *talent for art.* 天賦的藝術才能。

in·bound /'ɪnbaʊnd ; 'ɪn'baʊnd/ *adj* (of a ship) inward or homeward bound. (指船)歸航的;開向本國的。

in·bred /ˌɪn'bred ; ɪn'brɛd/ *adj* **1** inborn; innate: 天生的;與生俱來的: ~ *courtesy.* 天生的謙恭有禮。 **2** bred for several or many generations from ancestors closely related. 近親繁殖的。 **in·breed·ing** /ˌɪn'briːdɪŋ ; 'ɪnˌbridɪŋ/ *n* [U] breeding from closely related ancestors, stocks, etc. 近親繁殖;血族交配。

in·built /ˌɪn'bɪlt ; 'ɪn'bɪlt/ *adj* = *built-in,* ⇨ build¹(3).

in·cal·cu·lable /ɪn'kælkjʊləbl ; ɪn'kælkjələbl̩/ *adj* **1** too great to be calculated: 不可勝數的;極大的: *This has done* ~ *harm to our reputation.* 這已經對我們的名譽造成極大的傷害。 **2** that cannot be reckoned beforehand. 不能預計的。 **3** (of a person, his character, etc) uncertain: (指人,性情等)捉摸不定的;善變的: *a lady of* ~ *moods.* 情緒捉摸不定的婦人。

in·can·descent /ˌɪnkæn'desnt ; ˌɪnkən'dɛsn̩t/ *adj* giving out, able to give out, light when heated: 遇熱發光的;白熱的;白熾的: *an* ~ *filament,* eg in an electric-light bulb. 白熾燈絲(例如電燈絲)。 **in·can·descence** /-sns ; -sn̩s/ *n* [U] being or becoming ~. 遇熱發光;白熱;白熾。

in·can·ta·tion /ˌɪnkæn'teɪʃn ; ˌɪnkæn'teʃən/ *n* [C, U] (the use of) (a form of) words used in magic; charm or spell. 咒語;魔法;咒符;念咒。

in·capable /ɪn'keɪpəbl ; ɪn'kepəbl̩/ *adj* ~ ***(of),*** not capable: 無能力的;不能的: ~ *of telling a lie,* too honest to do so. (因太誠實)不會說謊。 ***drunk and ~,*** helplessly drunk. 爛醉如泥。 **in·capa·bil·ity** /ɪnˌkeɪpə'bɪlətɪ ; ˌɪnkepə'bɪlətɪ/ *n* [U].

in·ca·paci·tate /ˌɪnkə'pæsɪteɪt ; ˌɪnkə'pæsəˌtet/ *vt* [VP6A, 14] ~ ***sb (for/from),*** **1** make incapable or unfit: 使不能或不適合: *His poor health ~d him for work/from working.* 他的健康不佳使他不能工作。 **2** disqualify. 使失去資格。

in·ca·pac·ity /ˌɪnkə'pæsətɪ ; ˌɪnkə'pæsətɪ/ *n* [U] ~ ***(for sth/for doing sth/to do sth),*** inability; powerlessness. 無能力;無力。

in·car·cer·ate /ɪn'kɑːsəreɪt ; ɪn'kɑrsəˌret/ *vt* [VP6A] (formal) imprison. (正式用語)監禁。 **in·car·cer·ation** /ɪnˌkɑːsə'reɪʃn ; ɪnˌkɑrsə'reʃən/ *n*

in·car·nate /ɪn'kɑːneɪt ; ɪn'kɑrnɪt/ *adj* **1** having a body; (esp) in human form: 具有肉體的;(尤指)成爲人形的: *That prison officer is a devil ~/an ~ fiend.* 那獄吏是惡魔的化身。 **2** (of an idea, ideal, etc) appearing in human form: (指思想,理想等)以人形顯現的;具體化的: *Liberty ~.* 自由的化身。 □ *vt* /ɪn'kɑːneɪt ; ɪn'kɑrnet/ [VP6A] **1** make ~. 使具有肉體;使成爲人形。 **2** put (an idea, etc) into a real or material form. 使(思想等)具體化;實現。 **3** (of a person) be a living form of (a quality): (指人)爲(某性質)之化身: *a wife who ~s all the virtues.* 具有所有美德之妻子。

in·car·na·tion /ˌɪnkɑː'neɪʃn ; ˌɪnkɑr'neʃən/ *n* **1** the **I~**, the taking of bodily form by God in Jesus. 上帝之化身爲耶穌基督。 **2** [C] person looked upon as a type of a quality: 被視爲某性質之典型的人;化身: *She looked the ~ of every desirable quality.* 她看來像是各種美德的化身。

in·cau·tious /ɪn'kɔːʃəs ; ɪn'kɔʃəs/ *adj* not cautious; rash. 不謹愼的;鹵莽的。 **~·ly** *adv*

in·cen·di·ary /ɪn'sendɪərɪ *US:* -dɪerɪ ; ɪn'sɛndɪˌɛrɪ/ *n* (*pl* -ries), *adj* **1** (person) setting fire to property unlawfully and with an evil purpose; (person) tending to stir up violence: 縱火的;縱火者;煽動的;煽動者: *an ~ speech/newspaper article.* 煽動的演說(報紙文章)。 **2** (bomb) causing fire. 引起燃燒的;燃燒彈。 **in·cen·di·ar·ism** /ɪn'sendɪərɪzəm ; ɪn'sɛndɪəˌrɪzəm/ *n* [U].

in·cense[1] /'ɪnsens ; 'ɪnsɛns/ *n* [U] (smoke of a) substance producing a sweet smell when burning (焚燒時可產生香氣的)香;香發出的煙。

in·cense[2] /ɪn'sens ; ɪn'sɛns/ *vt* [VP6A] make angry: 激怒: *~d by sb's conduct;* 被某人的行爲激怒; *~d at sb's remarks.* 被某人的言語激怒。

in·cen·tive /ɪn'sentɪv ; ɪn'sɛntɪv/ *n* ~ ***(to sth/to do sth/to doing sth)***, [C,U] that which incites, rouses or encourages a person: 刺激;動機;鼓勵;誘因: *He hasn't much ~/many ~s to work hard/to hard work.* 他並沒有努力工作的强烈動機。

in·cep·tion /ɪn'sepʃn ; ɪn'sɛpʃən/ *n* (formal) start. (正式用語)開始。

in·cer·ti·tude /ɪn'sɜːtɪtjuːd *US:* -tuːd ; ɪn'sɝtəˌtjud/ *n* [U] (formal) uncertainty. (正式用語)不確定。

in·cess·ant /ɪn'sesnt ; ɪn'sɛsn̩t/ *adj* continual; often repeated: 不斷的;不停的: *a week of ~ rain.* 連續下了一星期的雨。 **~·ly** *adv*

in·cest /'ɪnsest ; 'ɪnsɛst/ *n* [U] sexual intercourse between near relations, eg brother and sister. 亂倫(例如兄妹相姦)。 **in·ces·tuous** /ɪn'sestjʊəs ; ɪn'sɛstʃʊəs/ *adj* of ~; guilty of, involving, ~. 亂倫的;犯亂倫罪的;涉及亂倫的。

inch /ɪntʃ ; ɪntʃ/ *n* **1** measure of length, one-twelfth of a foot: 吋(一呎的十二分之一): *six ~es of rain in one day.* 一天的雨量達六吋。 ➪ App 5. 參看附錄五。 **2** small amount. 少量。 **~ *by* ~**, by degrees. 逐漸地。 ***by ~es***, **(a)** only just: 剛剛: *The car missed me by ~es.* 那部汽車差一點撞上我。 **(b)** bit by bit; gradually. 一點一點地;逐漸地。 ***every ~***, entirely, completely: 完全地: *He's every ~ a soldier.* 他是個十足的軍人。 ***within an ~ of***, very near, almost: 距離很近;幾乎: *He came within an ~ of being struck by a falling tile.* 他差一點被落下的瓦打着。 ***not yield an ~***, not give way at all. 絲毫不讓步。 □ *vt, vi* [VP15A, B, 2C] move by ~es; edge one's way: 慢慢移動;漸進: *~ one's way forward;* 慢慢前進; *~ along a ledge on a cliff.* 沿懸崖之突出部分蠕動而進。

in·cho·ate /ɪn'kəʊɪt ; ɪn'ko·ɪt/ *adj* (formal) just begun; in an underdeveloped, half-formed state. (正式用語)剛開始的;未開展的;未形成的。 **in·choa·tive** /ɪn'kəʊətɪv ; ɪn'koətɪv/ *adj* expressing the beginning of an action or state: 表示一動作或狀態之開始的: (gram) (文法) *inchoative verbs,* eg *get* in *get dark, fall* in *fall ill.* 表始動詞(例如 get dark 中之 get, fall ill 中之 fall)。

in·ci·dence /'ɪnsɪdəns ; 'ɪnsədəns/ *n* way in which sth affects things: 發生的方式;影響事物的方式: *the ~ of a disease,* the range or extent of its effect, the number and kind of people who catch it; 發病率(某疾病蔓延的範圍,病患的數目及種類); *the ~ of a tax,* the way it falls to certain people to pay it. 徵稅的方式;賦稅歸宿。

in·ci·dent[1] /'ɪnsɪdənt ; 'ɪnsədənt/ *adj* **~ *to***, (formal) forming a natural or expected part of; naturally connected with: (正式用語)形成…的自然的或預料中的一部分;自然與…相關連的;隨帶的: *the risks ~ to the life of a test pilot;* 飛機試飛員生活中易遭遇的危險; *the social obligations ~ to life in the diplomatic service.* 與外交界生活相關的社交義務。

in·ci·dent[2] /'ɪnsɪdənt ; 'ɪnsədənt/ *n* **1** event, esp one of less importance than others: 事件(尤指比較不重要的小事件): *frontier ~s,* eg disputes between forces on a frontier. 邊境糾紛(例如邊境上兩方部隊間的爭執)。 **2** happening which attracts general attention. 引起公衆注意的事件。 **3** (modern use) happening, eg rebellion, bomb explosion, war, which for various reasons persons in authority do not wish to describe precisely. (現代用法)事變(例如叛亂,爆炸,戰爭等,當局人士因各種原因不願說明的事件)。 **4** separate piece of action in a play or poem. (戲劇或詩中的)挿曲;枝節。

in·ci·den·tal /ˌɪnsɪ'dentl ; ˌɪnsə'dɛntl/ *adj* ~ ***(to)***, **1** accompanying but not forming a necessary part: 附屬的;隨帶的: *~ music to a play.* 戲劇的配樂;劇樂。 **2** small and comparatively unimportant: 微小而較不重要的: *~ expenses,* additional to the main expenses. 雜費。 **3** liable to happen or occur: 易發生的: *discomforts ~ to exploration in a wild country.* 蠻荒探險易遭遇到的艱苦。 **~·ly** /-tlɪ ; -tl̩ɪ/ *adv* in an ~ manner; by chance. 附帶地;偶然地。

in·cin·er·ate /ɪn'sɪnəreɪt ; ɪn'sɪnəˌret/ *vt* [VP6A] burn to ashes. 燒成灰。 **in·cin·er·ator** /-tə(r) ; -tɚ/ *n* furnace, enclosed fireplace, for burning rubbish, etc. (垃圾等之)焚化爐。 **in·cin·er·ation** /ɪnˌsɪnə'reɪʃn ; ˌɪnsɪnə'reʃən/ *n* [U] burning up: 燒盡;焚化: *Household and industrial waste disposal—the choice is between tipping and incineration.* 家庭及工業廢物處理——其方式是丢棄或焚化。

in·cipi·ent /ɪn'sɪpɪənt ; ɪn'sɪpɪənt/ *adj* beginning; in an early stage: 開始的;初期的;初發的: *~ decay of the teeth.* 牙齒的初期蛀壞。

in·cise /ɪn'saɪz ; ɪn'saɪz/ *vt* [VP6A] make a cut in; engrave. 切割;雕刻。 **in·ci·sion** /ɪn'sɪʒn ; ɪn'sɪʒən/ *n* [U] cutting (into sth); [C] cut, eg one made in a surgical operation. 割切;切開;切口(例如外科手術中所作者)。

in·cis·ive /ɪn'saɪsɪv ; ɪn'saɪsɪv/ *adj* sharp and cutting; (of a person's mind, remarks) acute; clear-cut: 鋒利的;(指人的思想)敏銳的;(指言論)清晰中肯的。 *~ criticism.* 清晰中肯的批評。 **~·ly** *adv*

in·cisor /ɪn'saɪzə(r) ; ɪn'saɪzɚ/ *n* (in human beings) any one of the eight sharp-edged front cutting teeth, four in the upper and four in the lower jaw. (人之)前齒;門牙。 ➪ the illus at mouth. 參看 mouth 之挿圖。

in·cite /ɪn'saɪt ; ɪn'saɪt/ *vt* [VP6A, 14, 17] **~ *sb (to sth/to do sth)***, stir up, rouse: 激勵;煽動: *Insults ~ resentment.* 侮辱激起憤恨。 *The soldier was shot for inciting his comrades to rise against their officers.* 那士兵因煽動同志反叛其長官而被槍決。 **~·ment** *n* [U] inciting or being ~d; [C] instance of this; sth that ~s. (被)激勵;(被)煽動;(被)煽動或激勵之實例;煽動物;激勵物。

in·civ·il·ity /ˌɪnsɪ'vɪlətɪ ; ˌɪnsə'vɪlətɪ/ *n* (formal) [U] impoliteness; [C] (*pl* -ties) impolite act, remark, etc. (正式用語)無禮;無禮的行動,言語等。

in·clem·ent /ɪn'klemənt ; ɪn'klɛmənt/ *adj* (formal) (of weather or climate) severe; cold and stormy. (正式用語)(指天氣或氣候)酷寒的;寒冷而有狂風暴雨的。 **in·clem·ency** /-ənsɪ ; -ənsɪ/ *n* [U] being ~. 酷寒;寒冷而有暴風雨。

in·cli·na·tion /ˌɪnklɪˈneɪʃn ; ˏɪnkləˈneʃən/ *n* **1** [C] bending; bowing; slope; slant: 傾斜;彎曲;斜度;傾度: *an ~ of the head*, a nod; 點頭; *an ~ of the body*, a bow; 鞠躬; *the ~ of a roof*, its degree of slope. 屋頂的斜度。 **2** [C, U] ***~ (to sth/to do sth)***, mental leaning; liking or desire; disposition: 意向;癖性;愛好;性向: *Are you usually ready to sacrifice ~ to duty*, put on one side what you like doing in order to do your duty? 你通常願意爲了盡忠職守而犧牲個人的愛好嗎? *He showed no ~ to leave.* 他沒有表示離去的意思。*She is not free to follow her own ~s, even in the matter of marriage.* 她無法照自己的意願行事,甚至在婚姻方面也是如此。*He has an ~*(= tendency) *to stoutness/to grow fat.* 他有發胖的趨勢。

in·cline[1] /ɪnˈklaɪn ; ɪnˈklaɪn/ *vt, vi* **1** [VP6A, 15A, 2A] (cause to) lean, slope or slant; bend (the head, body, oneself) forward or downward: 傾斜;使傾斜;俯(首);彎(身): *~ the head in prayer.* 低下頭祈禱。**2** [VP17] (liter) dispose; direct: (文)使傾向;指令: *'I~ our hearts to keep this law.'* '讓我們傾心遵守此戒律。' **3** [VP17] (usu passive) direct the mind in a certain direction; cause (sb) to have a tendency or wish (*to do* sth): (通常用被動語態)使心向;使(某人)有意 (作某事,與不定詞連用): *The news ~s me/I am ~d to start at once.* 這消息使我想(我想)立刻動身。*His letter ~s me to believe that he doesn't want to come.* 他的來信使我相信他不要來。*I am ~d to think* (= I have a feeling or idea) *that he is opposed to the plan.* 我覺得他反對這計畫。*He's ~d to be lazy.* 他性懶散。*We can go for a walk if you feel so ~d.* 假如你願意的話,我們可以去散步。**4** [VP4C] tend; be disposed: 傾向;願意: *I ~ to believe in his innocence.* 我願意相信他的無辜。 **5** [VP3A] ***~ to/towards sth***, have a physical or mental tendency: 身心的傾向;有某種體質: *He ~s to leanness.* 他體質屬瘦型。*She ~s towards melancholia.* 她有憂鬱症的傾向。

in·cline[2] /ˈɪnklaɪn ; ˈɪnklaɪn/ *n* slope; sloping surface: 斜坡;斜面: *run down a steep ~*; 跑下一陡坡; *an ~ of 1 in 5.* 斜度爲五分之一的斜坡。⇨ gradient.

in·close, in·clos·ure /ɪnˈkləʊz, ɪnˈkləʊʒə(r) ; ɪnˈkloz, ɪnˈkloʒə/ = enclose, enclosure.

in·clude /ɪnˈkluːd ; ɪnˈklud/ *vt* [VP6A, C] bring in, reckon, as part of the whole: 包括;包含: *This atlas contains fifty maps, including six of North America.* 這部地圖集含有五十幅地圖,包括北美地圖六幅。*Price £2·75, postage ~d.* 價格 2.75 鎊,郵費包括在內。*Your duties will ~ putting the children to bed.* 你的職責包括照顧孩子們就寢。**in·clu·sion** /ɪnˈkluːʒn ; ɪnˈkluʒən/ *n* [U] including or being ~d. 包括;包含。

in·clus·ive /ɪnˈkluːsɪv ; ɪnˈklusɪv/ *adj* ***~ (of)***, **1** including: 包括的;包含的: *£10, ~ of interest;* 十鎊,包括利息在內; *from 1 May to 3 June ~*, 1 May and 3 June being included. 從五月一日至六月三日,首尾兩日包括在內。 ⇨ (US) (美) through[2](4). **2** including much or all: 包括許多或一切的: *~ terms,* (at a hotel, etc) without any extra charges. (旅館等)包括一切費用的價目。**~·ly** *adv*

in·cog·nito /ˌɪnkɒgˈniːtəʊ ; ɪnˈkɑgnɪˏto/ *adj* concealed under a disguised identity; with an assumed name: 隱藏原來身份的;使用化名的: *a king ~.* 微服而行的國王。□ *adv* with one's name, identity, etc concealed: 隱姓埋名地;隱藏身份的: *The millionaire called himself Dick Brown and travelled ~.* 那富豪自稱狄克·布朗而化名旅行。

in·co·her·ent /ˌɪnkəʊˈhɪərənt ; ˏɪnkoˈhɪrənt/ *adj* not coherent: 思想不連貫的;語無倫次的: *so drunk as to be quite ~.* 醉得語無倫次。**~·ly** *adv* **in·co·her·ence** /-əns ; -əns/ *n*

in·com·bus·tible /ˌɪnkəmˈbʌstəbl ; ˏɪnkəmˈbʌstəbḷ/ *adj* (formal) that cannot be consumed by fire. (正式用語)不能燃燒的。

in·come /ˈɪŋkʌm ; ˈɪnˏkʌm/ *n* money received during a given period (as salary, receipts from trade, interest from investments, etc): 收入;所得(指某一段時間中所得而言,如薪金,商業收益,投資所獲利潤等): *live within one's ~*, spend less than one receives. 量入爲出。*Tax was payable on ~ over £2000.* 收入在二千鎊以上者應該繳稅。 **~-tax** /ˈɪŋkəm tæks ; ˈɪnkəm tæks/ *n* tax levied on ~ above a certain level. 所得稅(所得超過某一標準所抽之稅)。

in·com·ing /ˈɪnˌkʌmɪŋ ; ˈɪnˏkʌmɪŋ/ *adj* coming in: 進來的;來到的: *the ~ tide/tenant.* 漲潮(住進來的房客)。

in·com·men·sur·ate /ˌɪnkəˈmenʃərət ; ˏɪnkəˈmɛnʃərɪt/ *adj* ***~ (to/with)***, **1** not comparable (*to*) in respect of size; not worthy to be measured (*with*): 大小不成比例的;不值得計量的: *His abilities are ~ to the task he has been given.* 他的能力與給予他的工作不相稱。 **2** that cannot be compared; having no common measure. 不能相比較的;無共同單位可計量的。

in·com·mode /ˌɪnkəˈməʊd ; ˏɪnkəˈmod/ *vt* [VP6A] (formal) cause trouble or inconvenience to: (正式用語)使爲難;使不方便: *Will it ~ you if I don't pay what I owe you until next year?* 如果我明年才償還所欠你的錢,你會感到不方便嗎?

in·com·muni·cado /ˌɪnkəˌmjuːnɪˈkɑːdəʊ ; ˏɪnkəˏmjunɪˈkɑdo/ *adj* (of sb in confinement) not permitted to communicate with persons outside. (指被監禁者)不准與外面的人接觸的。

in·com·par·able /ɪnˈkɒmprəbl ; ɪnˈkɑmpərəbḷ/ *adj* ***~ (to/with)***, not to be compared; without equal: 不能比較的;無匹的: *her ~ beauty.* 她那舉世無雙的美。**in·com·par·ably** /-əblɪ ; -əblɪ/ *adv*

in·com·pat·ible /ˌɪnkəmˈpætəbl ; ˏɪnkəmˈpætəbḷ/ *adj* ***~ (with)***, opposed in character; unable to exist in harmony; inconsistent: 性質相反的;不能和諧並存的;矛盾的: *Excessive drinking is ~ with good health.* 縱酒與健康是不能並存的。 *They are sexually ~.* 他們二人性生活不合諧。**in·com·pati·bil·ity** /ˌɪnkəmˌpætəˈbɪlətɪ ; ˏɪnkəmˏpætəˈbɪlətɪ/ *n* [U] being ~: 性質相反;無法合諧並存;矛盾: *Incompatibility of temper may cause friction between husband and wife.* 性情不合可能造成夫妻間的摩擦。

in·com·pe·tent /ɪnˈkɒmpɪtənt ; ɪnˈkɑmpətənt/ *adj* not qualified or able: 不合格的;不能勝任的: *~ to teach science/for teaching science/as a teacher of science.* 無資格擔任科學教職。**~·ly** *adv* **in·com·pe·tence** /-əns ; -əns/, **in·com·pe·tency** /-ənsɪ ; -ənsɪ/ *nn* [U] being ~. 不合格;不能勝任。

in·com·plete /ˌɪnkəmˈpliːt ; ˏɪnkəmˈplit/ *adj* not complete. 不完全的。**~·ly** *adv*

in·com·pre·hen·sible /ˌɪnˌkɒmprɪˈhensəbl ; ˏɪnkɑmprɪˈhɛnsəbḷ/ *adj* (formal) that cannot be understood. (正式用語)不能理解的。**in·com·pre·hen·si·bil·ity** /ɪnˌkɒmprɪˌhensəˈbɪlətɪ ; ˏɪnkɑmprɪˏhɛnsəˈbɪlətɪ/ *n* [U].

in·com·pre·hen·sion /ɪnˌkɒmprɪˈhenʃn ; ˏɪnkɑmprɪˈhɛnʃən/ *n* [U] failure to understand. 不能理解。

in·com·press·ible /ˌɪnkəmˈpresəbl ; ˏɪnkəmˈprɛsəbḷ/ *adj* (formal) that cannot be compressed; hard and unyielding. (正式用語)不能壓縮的;堅硬的。

in·con·ceiv·able /ˌɪnkənˈsiːvəbl ; ˏɪnkənˈsivəbḷ/ *adj* that cannot be imagined; (colloq) hard to believe; very remarkable. 無法想像的;(俗)難以相信的;非凡的。

in·con·clus·ive /ˌɪnkənˈkluːsɪv ; ˏɪnkənˈklusɪv/ *adj* (of evidence, arguments, discussions, actions) not decisive or convincing; not bringing a definite result. (指證據,論據,討論,行動)非決定性的;不能使人信服的;不能產生明確效果的。**~·ly** *adv*

in·con·gru·ous /ɪnˈkɒŋgruəs ; ɪnˈkɑŋgruəs/ *adj* ***~ (with)***, not in harmony or agreement; out of place. 不和諧的;不一致的;不適宜的;不調和的。 **~·ly** *adv* **in·con·gru·ity** /ˌɪnkɒŋˈgruːətɪ ; ˏɪnkɑŋˈgruətɪ/ *n* [U] the quality of being ~; [C] (*pl* -ties) sth ~. 不合諧;不適宜;不調合;不和諧或不調合之事物。

in·con·sequent /ɪn'kɒnsɪkwənt ; ɪn'kɑnsə,kwɛnt/ *adj* not following naturally what has been said or done before: 前後不符的；先後不連貫的：*an ~ remark;* 前後不符的話； (of a person) saying or doing ~ things. （指人）言行前後不符的。 **~·ly** *adv* **in·con·sequen·tial** /ɪn,kɒnsɪ'kwenʃl ; ,ɪnkɑnsə'kwɛnʃəl/ *adj* = ~; unimportant. 前後不符的；先後不連貫的；不重要的。

in·con·sid·er·able /,ɪnkən'sɪdrəbl ; ,ɪnkən'sɪdərəbḷ/ *adj* not worth considering; of small size, value, etc. 不值得考慮的；微不足道的。

in·con·sid·er·ate /,ɪnkən'sɪdərət ; ,ɪnkən'sɪdərɪt/ *adj* (of a person, his actions) thoughtless; lacking in regard for the feelings of others: （指人或其行動）鹵莽的；輕率的；不顧及別人感情的：*~ children;* 鹵莽的孩子； *~ remarks.* 輕率的言語。 **~·ly** *adv*

in·con·sist·ent /,ɪnkən'sɪstənt ; ,ɪnkən'sɪstənt/ *adj* **~ (with).** **1** not in harmony: 不一致的：*actions that are ~ with one's principles.* 與自己的原則不一致的行動。 **2** contradictory; having parts that do not agree: 矛盾的；各部分不協調的：*His account of what happened was ~.* 他對於所發生事情的敍述前後矛盾。 **~·ly** *adv* **in·con·sist·ency** /-ənsɪ ; -ənsɪ/ *n* [U] the quality of being ~; [C] (*pl* -cies) instance of this. 不一致；矛盾；不協調；此種事例。

in·con·sol·able /,ɪnkən'səʊləbl ; ,ɪnkən'soləbḷ/ *adj* that cannot be consoled: 不能安慰的；無法慰藉的：*~ grief.* 無法安慰的憂傷。*The widow was ~.* 那寡婦悲傷不已。

in·con·spicu·ous /,ɪnkən'spɪkjʊəs ; ,ɪnkən'spɪkjʊəs/ *adj* not conspicuous: 不顯著的；不引人注目的：*The shy girl tried to make herself as ~ as possible,* tried to avoid attention. 那個怕羞的女孩盡量使自己不被人注意。*She always dresses in ~ colours,* colours that are not striking or obvious. 她總是穿顏色不顯眼的衣服。 **~·ly** *adv*

in·con·stant /ɪn'kɒnstənt ; ɪn'kɑnstənt/ *adj* (formal) (of persons) changeable in feelings, intentions, purpose, etc: （正式用語）（指人，在感情，用意，目的等方面）多變的；無常的；不專的：*an ~ lover.* 用情不專的愛人。 **in·con·stancy** /-ənsɪ ; -ənsɪ/ *n* [U] being ~; [C] instance of this. （感情、用意、目的等）善變；無常；不專。

in·con·test·able /,ɪnkən'testəbl ; ,ɪnkən'tɛstəbḷ/ *adj* that cannot be disputed. 無法爭辯的；不容置疑的。

in·con·ti·nent /ɪn'kɒntɪnənt *US:* -tənənt ; ɪn'kɑntənənt/ *adj* lacking in self-control or self-restraint; (med) unable to control excretion or urination. 不能自制的；（醫）排泄或小便失禁的。 **in·con·ti·nence** /-əns ; -əns/ *n* [U].

in·con·tro·vert·ible /ɪn,kɒntrə'vɜːtəbl ; ,ɪnkɑntrə'vɝtəbḷ/ *adj* (formal) that cannot be disputed. （正式用語）無爭辯餘地的；不容置疑的。

in·con·ven·ience /,ɪnkən'viːnɪəns ; ,ɪnkən'vinjəns/ *n* [C, U] (cause or instance of) discomfort or trouble: 不便；麻煩；困難；不便或困難的原因；不便或困難之處：*I was put to / I suffered great ~.* 我感到極不方便。*They have been at great ~ in order to help us.* 爲了幫助我們，他們遭遇了極大的困難。*Think of the ~s of living in such a small house with a large family.* 想想一大家人住在這樣小的房子內的不便之處。□ *vt* [VP6A] cause ~ to. 使感不便；使感困難。

in·con·ven·ient /,ɪnkən'viːnɪənt ; ,ɪnkən'vinjənt/ *adj* causing discomfort, trouble or annoyance. 使人不便的；引起困擾的。 **~·ly** *adv*

in·con·vert·ible /,ɪnkən'vɜːtəbl ; ,ɪnkən'vɝtəbḷ/ *adj* that cannot be converted, eg paper money that cannot be exchanged for gold. 不能變換的（例如不能兌換成黃金的紙幣）。 **in·con·ver·ti·bil·ity** /,ɪnkən,vɜːtə'bɪlətɪ ; ,ɪnkən,vɝtə'bɪlətɪ/ *n*

in·cor·por·ate[1] /ɪn'kɔːpərət ; ɪn'kɔrpərɪt/ *adj* incorporated; formed into, united in, a corporation. 合併的；組成或聯合成爲法人組織或公司的。

in·cor·por·ate[2] /ɪn'kɔːpəreɪt ; ɪn'kɔrpə,ret/ *vt, vi* [VP6A, 14, 23, 2A, 3A] **~ (in/into/with),** make, become, united in one body or group; (legal) form into, become, a corporation(2): 使結合；使合併；結合；合併；（法律）使組成或成爲法人組織或公司：*Hanover was ~d into Prussia in 1886.* 漢諾威於 1886 年被併入普魯士。*He was ~d a member of the college.* 他成爲該學院的一員。*Your suggestions will be ~d in the plan.* 你的建議將併入這計畫中。*The firm ~d with others.* 這公司與別家合併了。 **in·cor·por·ation** /ɪn,kɔːpə'reɪʃn ; ɪn,kɔrpə'reʃən/ *n* incorporating or being ~d. 結合；合併；形成法人或公司組織。

in·cor·por·eal /,ɪnkɔː'pɔːrɪəl ; ,ɪnkɔr'porɪəl/ *adj* (formal) not composed of matter; having no bodily form. （正式用語）無實體的；無形體的。

in·cor·rect /,ɪnkə'rekt ; ,ɪnkə'rɛkt/ *adj* not correct. 不正確的。 **~·ly** *adv* **~·ness** *n*

in·cor·ri·gible /ɪn'kɒrɪdʒəbl *US:* -'kɔːr- ; ɪn'kɔrɪdʒəbḷ/ *adj* (of a person, his faults, etc) that cannot be cured or corrected: （指人，其缺點等）無藥可救的；難以矯正的：*an ~ liar;* 無藥可救的說謊者；*~ bad habits.* 難以矯正的惡習。

in·cor·rupt·ible /,ɪnkə'rʌptəbl ; ,ɪnkə'rʌptəbḷ/ *adj* that cannot decay or be destroyed; that cannot be corrupted, esp by being bribed: 不腐朽的；不能毁壞的；不貪汚受賄的：*as ~ as an English judge.* 像英國法官一樣廉正。 **in·cor·rupti·bil·ity** /,ɪnkə,rʌptə'bɪlətɪ ; ,ɪnkə,rʌptə'bɪlətɪ/ *n*

in·crease[1] /'ɪŋkriːs ; 'ɪnkris/ *n* [U] **~ (in),** increasing; growth; [C] amount by which sth ~s: 增加；增大；增多；繁殖；增加量：*I~ in population made emigration necessary.* 人口的增加使向外移民成爲必要。*There was a steady ~ in population.* 人口一直在增加。 ***on the ~,*** growing: 在增加中：*Is the consumption of beer still on the ~?* 啤酒的消耗量仍在增加中嗎？

in·crease[2] /ɪn'kriːs ; ɪn'kris/ *vt, vi* [VP6A, 2A] make or become greater in size, number, degree, etc: 增加；增大；增多：*The population has ~d by 200 000 to 50 000 000.* 人口已增加了二十萬，達到五千萬的總數。*The driver ~d speed.* 司機加速行駛。*Our difficulties are increasing.* 我們的困難正在增多中。 **in·creas·ing·ly** /ɪn'kriːsɪŋlɪ ; ɪn'krisɪŋlɪ/ *adv* more and more. 逐漸地；漸增地。

in·cred·ible /ɪn'kredəbl ; ɪn'krɛdəbḷ/ *adj* that cannot be believed; (colloq) difficult to believe; surprising. 不能相信的；（俗）難以置信的；可驚的。 **in·cred·ibly** /-əblɪ ; -əblɪ/ *adv* **in·credi·bil·ity** /ɪn,kredə'bɪlətɪ ; ,ɪnkrɛdə'bɪlətɪ/ *n*

in·credu·lous /ɪn'kredjʊləs *US:* -dʒʊ- ; ɪn'krɛdʒələs/ *adj* unbelieving; showing disbelief: 不相信的；表示懷疑的：*~ looks/smiles.* 懷疑的表情（微笑）。 **~·ly** *adv* **in·cred·ul·ity** /,ɪnkrɪ'djuːlətɪ *US:* -'duː- ; ,ɪnkrə'dulətɪ/ *n*

in·crement /'ɪnkrəmənt ; 'ɪnkrəmənt/ *n* **1** [U] profits; increase: 利潤；增加：*unearned ~,* increased value of sth, eg land, due not to the owner's labour but to other causes, eg a big demand for land. （土地等之）不勞增值（非因所有者的勞力，而由於其他因素，例如土地之大量需求等，而產生的增值。） **2** [C] amount of increase: 增加量：*'Salary £4000 per annum, with yearly ~s of £250 to a maximum of £5500.'* '年薪四千鎊，每年增加二百五十鎊，直到最高薪額五千五百鎊。'

in·crimi·nate /ɪn'krɪmɪneɪt ; ɪn'krɪmə,net/ *vt* [VP6A] say, be a sign, that (sb) is guilty of wrongdoing: 控告；顯示（某人）有罪：*Don't say anything that may ~ your friends.* 不要說任何可能牽連你朋友入罪的話。

in·crus·ta·tion /,ɪnkrʌ'steɪʃn ; ,ɪnkrʌs'teʃən/ *n* [U] encrusting; [C] crust; hard coating. 覆以硬殼；外皮；硬殼。

in·cu·bate /'ɪnkjʊbeɪt ; 'ɪnkjə,bet/ *vt, vi* [VP6A, 2A] **1** hatch (eggs) by sitting on them or by artificial warmth; sit on eggs. 孵（卵）；人工孵（卵）；孵卵。 **2** (of bacteria, etc) develop under favourable conditions. （指細菌等）在有利情況下培養。

in·cu·ba·tion /ˌɪnkjuˈbeɪʃn ; ˌɪnkjəˈbeʃən/ *n* **1** hatching (of eggs): 孵卵;孵化: *artificial incubation,* hatching by artificial warmth. 人工孵卵。**2 incubation (period),** (path) (of a disease) period between infection and the appearance of the first symptoms. (病理)(指疾病)潛伏期。**in·cu·ba·tor** /-tə(r) ; -tɚ/ *n* apparatus for hatching eggs by artificial warmth or for rearing small, weak babies (esp those born prematurely). 人工孵卵器;育嬰箱(培育身體弱小之嬰兒,特指早產兒)。

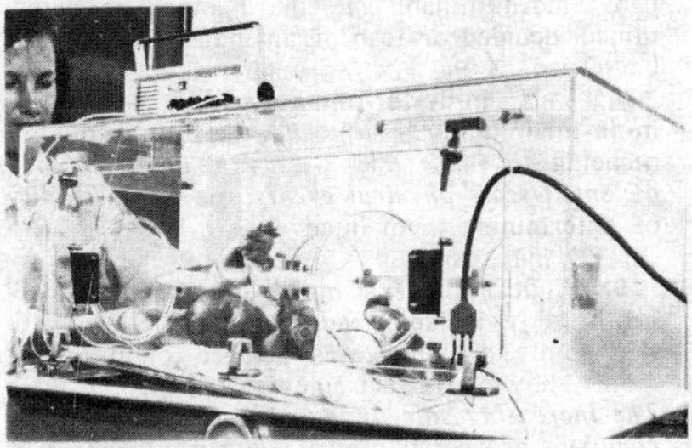

an incubator

in·cu·bus /ˈɪŋkjubəs ; ˈɪnkjəbəs/ *n* (*pl* ~es /-sɪz ; -sɪz/, or -bi /-baɪ ; -ˌbaɪ/) nightmare; evil spirit supposed to lie on a sleeping person and weigh him down; sb or sth, eg a debt, an approaching examination, that oppresses one like a nightmare. 夢魘;夢魔;傳說中壓在熟睡者身上的魔鬼;如夢魘般壓迫人的人或事物(例如債務,即將來臨的考試等)。

in·cul·cate /ˈɪnkʌlkeɪt *US:* ɪnˈkʌl- ; ɪnˈkʌlket/ *vt* [VP6A, 14] ~ ***sth (in sb),*** (formal) fix (ideas, etc) firmly by repetition: (正式用語)反覆灌輸(思想等);諄諄教誨: ~ *in young people the duty of loyalty.* 以忠貞之道諄諄教誨年輕人。

in·cul·pate /ˈɪnkʌlpeɪt *US:* ɪnˈkʌl- ; ɪnˈkʌlpet/ *vt* [VP6A] (formal) involve (sb) in a charge or wrongdoing; blame. (正式用語)連累(某人)受控;責難。

in·cum·bent /ɪnˈkʌmbənt ; ɪnˈkʌmbənt/ *adj* ***be ~ on/upon sb (to do sth),*** (formal) be his duty: (正式用語)負有義務;負某種責任: *It is ~ upon you to warn the boy of the danger of smoking.* 你有責任去警告那男孩吸烟的危險。□ *n* person holding an official position. 在職者;有正式職位者。**in·cum·bency** /-ənsɪ ; -ənsɪ/ *n* (*pl* -cies) position of an ~. 職位。

in·cur /ɪnˈkɜː(r) ; ɪnˈkɝ/ *vt* (-rr-) [VP6A] bring upon oneself: 招致;蒙受: ~ *debts;* 負債; ~ *hatred;* 招致仇恨; ~ *great expense.* 引起很大的花費。

in·cur·able /ɪnˈkjʊərəbl ; ɪnˈkjʊrəbl/ *adj* that cannot be cured: 不能治療的; 不可救藥的: ~ *diseases/habits.* 不治之症(無法矯正的習慣)。□ *n* person who is ~: 患不治之症者: *a home for ~s.* 患不治之症者的收容所。**in·cur·ably** /-əblɪ ; -əblɪ/ *adv*

in·curi·ous /ɪnˈkjʊərɪəs ; ɪnˈkjʊrɪəs/ *adj* (formal) having no curiosity; not inquisitive; inattentive. (正式用語)無好奇心的;不追根究底的;不注意的。

in·cur·sion /ɪnˈkɜːʃn *US:* -ʒn ; ɪnˈkɝʒən/ *n* ~ ***on/upon,*** sudden attack or invasion (not usu made for the purpose of permanent occupation): 侵入;侵犯(通常爲不欲作永久佔領者): *the Danish ~s on our coasts in early times;* 古時丹麥人對我國(指英國)沿岸的侵犯; (fig) (喻) *~s upon my leisure time.* 我閒暇時間之受打擾。

in·curved /ˌɪnˈkɜːvd ; ɪnˈkɝvd/ *adj* curved inwards; bent into a curve. 內曲的;變成曲線的。

in·debted /ɪnˈdetɪd ; ɪnˈdɛtɪd/ *adj* ~ ***to sb,*** owing money or gratitude: 負債的;欠情的;感恩的: *I am greatly ~ to you for your help.* 我非常感激你對我的幫助。**~·ness** *n*

in·de·cent /ɪnˈdiːsnt ; ɪnˈdisn̩t/ *adj* **1** (of behaviour, talk, etc) not decent(2); obscene. (指行爲、言語等)下流的;粗鄙的;猥褻的。 **2** (colloq) improper: (俗)不合適的: *leave a party in ~ haste,* eg as if to suggest that one is glad to escape from boredom. 匆忙而欠妥地離開一社交集會(彷彿暗示樂於逃避其枯燥等)。**~·ly** *adv* **in·de·cency** /-nsɪ ; -n̩sɪ/ *n* [U] being ~; [C] (*pl* -cies) act, gesture, expression, etc that is ~. 粗鄙;下流;猥褻;粗鄙的行動、姿態、言語等。

in·de·cipher·able /ˌɪndɪˈsaɪfrəbl ; ˌɪndɪˈsaɪfrəbl/ *adj* that cannot be deciphered. 無法解釋的;無法闡明的。

in·de·ci·sion /ˌɪndɪˈsɪʒn ; ˌɪndɪˈsɪʒən/ *n* the state of being unable to decide; hesitation. 無決斷力;猶豫。

in·de·cis·ive /ˌɪndɪˈsaɪsɪv ; ˌɪndɪˈsaɪsɪv/ *adj* not decisive: 非決定性的: *an ~ battle/answer;* 非決定性的戰役(答覆); ~ *evidence;* 非決定性的證據; hesitating; uncertain: 猶豫不決的;不定的: *a man with an ~ manner.* 一個樣子優柔寡斷的人。**~·ly** *adv*

in·dec·or·ous /ɪnˈdekərəs ; ɪnˈdɛkərəs/ *adj* (formal) in bad taste; not in accordance with good manners. (正式用語)不雅的;不合禮節的。**~·ly** *adv*

in·de·cor·um /ˌɪndɪˈkɔːrəm ; ˌɪndɪˈkorəm/ *n* [U] lack of decorum; improper behaviour. 沒有禮貌;不適當的行爲;不雅的舉止。

in·deed /ɪnˈdiːd ; ɪnˈdid/ *adv* **1** really; as you say; as you may imagine: 實在地;的確;眞地: *I was ~ very glad to hear the news.* 我聽到了這消息,的確很高興。*'Are you pleased at your son's success?'—'Yes, ~'* (or) *'I~, yes.'* '你對於你兒子的成功感到高興嗎?' '是的,實在高興。' **2** (to intensify) (加强語氣) *Thank you very much ~.* 實在感激你。*It was very kind ~ of you to help.* 承蒙協助,至爲感謝。**3** used as a comment to show interest, surprise, irony, etc: 用作批評語,表示興趣、驚奇、譏刺等: *'He spoke to me about you.'—'Oh, ~!'* 'Oh, did he?' '他對我談起了你。'—'噢,眞的!' *'Who is this woman?'—'Who is she, ~?'* 'That's what we all want to know!' '這位女士是誰?'—'她到底是誰?'(我們都想知道她是誰。)

in·de·fati·gable /ˌɪndɪˈfætɪgəbl ; ˌɪndɪˈfætɪgəbl/ *adj* (formal) untiring; that cannot be tired out: (正式用語)不疲倦的;不屈不撓的: ~ *workers.* 不倦的工作者。

in·de·feas·ible /ˌɪndɪˈfiːzəbl ; ˌɪndɪˈfizəbl/ *adj* (formal) that cannot be forfeited or done away with: (正式用語)不能取消的;不能廢除的: ~ *rights/claims.* 不能取消的權利(要求權)。

in·de·fens·ible /ˌɪndɪˈfensəbl ; ˌɪndɪˈfɛnsəbl/ *adj* that cannot be defended, justified or excused. 不能防守的;無法辯護的;不可原諒的。

in·de·fin·able /ˌɪndɪˈfaɪnəbl ; ˌɪndɪˈfaɪnəbl/ *adj* that cannot be defined. 不能下定義的;難以描述的。

in·defi·nite /ɪnˈdefɪnət ; ɪnˈdɛfənɪt/ *adj* vague; not clearly defined or stated: 不確定的;模糊的: *He has rather ~ views on the question.* 他對此問題的觀念相當模糊。*He gave me an ~ answer,* neither 'Yes' nor 'No'. 他給我一個含糊的答覆(不置可否)。 **the ˌ~ ˈarticle,** *a* or *an.* 不定冠詞(a 或 an)。**~·ly** *adv*

in·del·ible /ɪnˈdeləbl ; ɪnˈdɛləbl/ *adj* (of marks, stains, ink or (fig) of disgrace) that cannot be rubbed out or removed: (指記號、污跡、墨跡或比喻用法指恥辱)不能擦掉的;不能洗雪的: *an ~ pencil;* 筆跡難擦掉的鉛筆; ~ *shame.* 洗雪不掉的恥辱。**in·del·ibly** /-əblɪ ; -əblɪ/ *adv*

in·deli·cate /ɪnˈdelɪkət ; ɪnˈdɛləkət/ *adj* (of a person, his speech, behaviour, etc) lacking in refinement; immodest: (指人、其言行等)不雅的;粗鄙的: ~ *remarks.* 粗鄙的言語。**in·deli·cacy** /-kəsɪ ; -kəsɪ/ *n* [U] being ~; [C] (*pl* -cies) ~ act, utterance, etc. 不雅;粗鄙;粗鄙的言行等。

in·dem·nify /ɪnˈdemnɪfaɪ ; ɪnˈdɛmnəˌfaɪ/ *vt* (*pt, pp* -fied) **1** [VP6A, 14] ~ ***sb (from/against),*** (legal, comm) make (sb, oneself) safe: (法律,商)使(某人、自己)安全;保障;保護: ~ *a person against harm/loss.* 使某人不受傷害(損失)。 **2** [VP6A, 14] ~ ***sb (for sth),*** pay sb back: 償付(某人): *I will ~ you for any expenses you may incur on my behalf.* 我會償付你爲了我而負擔的任何花費。**in·dem-**

ni·fi·ca·tion /ɪnˌdemnɪfɪˈkeɪʃn ; ɪnˏdɛmnəfəˈkeʃən/ *n* [U] ~ing or being indemnified; [C] sth given or received as compensation or repayment. 使安全;保障;免受傷害或損失;賠償;賠償物。

in·dem·nity /ɪnˈdemnətɪ ; ɪnˈdɛmnətɪ/ *n* (*pl* -ties) **1** [U] security against damage or loss; compensation for loss. 保證;保障;賠償;補償。 **2** [C] sth that gives security against damage or loss; sth given or received as compensation, esp a sum of money, or goods, demanded from a country defeated in war. 保證物;賠償物;(尤指向戰敗國索取的)賠款;作爲賠償的貨物。

in·dent /ɪnˈdent ; ɪnˈdɛnt/ *vt, vi* **1** [VP6A] break into the edge or surface of (as if with teeth): 使成鋸齒狀;使成犬牙狀: *an ~ed* (= very irregular) *coastline.* 犬牙交錯的海岸線。 **2** [VP6A] start (a line of print or writing) farther from the margin than the others: 縮進 (一行印刷或書寫文字): *You must ~ the first line of each paragraph.* 你必須將每段的第一行縮進書寫(或排印)。 **3** [VP3A] ~ ***(on sb) for sth,*** (comm) order goods by means of an ~: (商)用訂貨單訂貨: *The firm ~ed for new machinery.* 這家公司以訂貨單購新機器。 □ *n* /ˈɪndent ; ˈɪndɛnt/ (comm) trade order placed in the United Kingdom for goods to be exported; official requisition for stores. (商)在英國訂購出口貨物的訂貨單;徵用物資命令。 **in·den·ta·tion** /ˌɪndenˈteɪʃn ; ˏɪndɛnˈteʃən/ *n* **1** [U] ~ing or being ~ed. (使)成鋸齒狀;(使)成犬牙交錯。 **2** [C] deep recess in a coastline; notch; space left at the beginning of a line of print or writing. 海岸線凹入之處;缺口;印刷或書寫文字一行開始處所留的空格。

in·den·ture /ɪnˈdentʃə(r) ; ɪnˈdɛntʃɚ/ *n* agreement of which two copies are made, esp one binding an apprentice to his master. 契約(一式兩份,尤指約束學徒對師傅盡義務者)。***take up one's ~s,*** receive them back at the end of the period of training. 做學徒期滿領回學徒契約。□ *vt* [VP6A] bind (a person) by ~s (as an apprentice). 以契約束縛(某人,使作學徒)。

in·de·pen·dence /ˌɪndɪˈpendəns ; ˏɪndɪˈpɛndəns/ *n* [U] ~ ***(from),*** the state of being independent: 獨立;自立;自主: *When a boy leaves college and begins to earn money he can live a life of ~.* 男孩子大學畢業開始賺錢時,便可獨立生活了。 *Several of these colonies have claimed and have been given ~ from the mother country.* 這些殖民地中有幾個曾經向它們的母國要求獨立並已獲得獨立。 **ˈI~ Day,** 4 July, celebrated in the US as the anniversary of the day, in 1776, on which the Declaration of I~ (that the American colonies were free and independent of GB) was made. 美國獨立紀念日(爲七月四日,紀念 1776 年是日發表獨立宣言)。

in·de·pen·dent /ˌɪndɪˈpendənt ; ˏɪndɪˈpɛndənt/ *adj* **1** ~ ***(of),*** not dependent on or controlled by (other persons or things); not relying on others; not needing to work for a living: 獨立的;不依賴他人或他物的;不受他人控制的;不勞而能生活的: *If you have a car you are ~ of trains and buses.* 如果你有汽車,你就不需乘火車和公共汽車了。*They went camping, so as to be ~ of hotels.* 他們去露營,免得住旅館。 ~ ***means,*** private means. 私人財力。 **2** self-governing: 自治的: *when the colony became ~.* 當該殖民地獨立時。 **3** acting or thinking upon one's own lines; free from control; not influenced by others: 行動或思想自主的;不受控制的;不受他人影響的: *an ~ thinker;* 獨立的思想家; *an ~ witness;* 不受人左右的證人; *~ proof / research,* resulting from ~ work, not related to the work of others. 獨立的證據(研究)(由獨立的工作達成,與他人的工作無關聯者)。□ *n* (esp) MP, candidate, etc who does not belong to a political party: (尤指)無黨派的國會議員、候選人等: *Vote for the ~s!* 請投無黨派人士一票! **~·ly** *adv*

in·de·scrib·able /ˌɪndɪˈskraɪbəbl ; ˏɪndɪˈskraɪbəbl̩/ *adj* that cannot be described. 難以描述的。**in·de·scrib·ably** /-əblɪ ; -əblɪ/ *adv*

in·de·struct·ible /ˌɪndɪˈstrʌktəbl ; ˏɪndɪˈstrʌktəbl̩/ *adj* that cannot be destroyed: 不能毀滅的: *~ plastics.* 不能毀滅的塑膠。 **in·de·struct·ibil·ity** /ˌɪndɪˌstrʌktəˈbɪlətɪ ; ˏɪndɪˏstrʌktəˈbɪlətɪ/ *n* [U].

in·de·ter·mi·nate /ˌɪndɪˈtɜːmɪnət ; ˏɪndɪˈtɝmənɪt/ *adj* not fixed; vague or indefinite: 不固定的;模糊的或不確定的: (maths) (數學) *an ~ quantity,* with no fixed value. 不定數。**in·de·ter·min·able** /ˌɪndɪˈtɜːmɪnəbl ; ˏɪndɪˈtɝmɪnəbl̩/ *adj* that cannot be determined, decided or (esp of an industrial dispute) be settled. 不能確定的;不能決定的;(尤指工業界爭端)不能解決的。 **in·de·ter·min·ably** /-əblɪ ; -əblɪ/ *adv* **in·de·ter·min·acy** /-əsɪ ; -əsɪ/ *n* the state or quality of being ~: 不固定;模糊;不確定: *the indeterminacy of small-scale physical events,* the impossibility of determining them in advance. 小規模的自然界變化之難以預測。

in·dex /ˈɪndeks ; ˈɪndɛks/ *n* (*pl* ~es or, in science, 科學用語亦作 indices /ˈɪndɪsiːz ; ˈɪndəˏsiz/) **1** sth that points to or indicates; pointer (on an instrument) showing measurements: 指示物;指標;指針: *The increasing sale of luxuries was an ~ of the country's prosperity.* 奢侈品銷售之增加顯示出這個國家的繁榮。**the ˈ~ finger,** the finger next to the thumb, used for pointing. 食指。⇨ the illus at arm. 參看 arm 之插圖。 **2** list of names, subjects, references, etc in ABC order, at the end of a book, or on cards (a **ˈcard ~**) in a library, etc. 索引(名稱、科目、參考書等之名單,按照字母順序排列,附於書後或載於圖書館等之索引卡上)。**the I~,** (hist) list of books not to be read by members of the RC Church without permission. (史)天主教徒未經准許不得閱讀之書目單。 **3** **ˈ~ number / figure,** one that indicates the relative level of prices or wages at a particular date compared with the figure 100 (for an earlier period) as a standard: (物價、工資等之)指數: *the cost of living ~;* 生活費指數; (of wages, pensions) (指薪資,退休金) ~ *linked / related,* adjusted accordingly. 按照指數調整的。 **4** (alg) exponent: (代數)指數: *In* $b^3 + x^n$, *3 and n are indices.* 在$b^3 + x^n$中, 3 和 n 是指數。□ *vt* [VP6A] make an ~ for a book, collection of books, etc; put a word, reference, etc in an ~: 爲(書籍等)編索引;將(一字、參考指示等)編入索引中: *The book is not well ~ed.* 這本書的索引編得不好。 **~er** *n* person who prepares an ~(2). 索引編者。

In·dia /ˈɪndɪə ; ˈɪndɪə/ *n* **ˈ~ paper** *n* very thin paper, eg for airmail editions of newspapers. 印度紙;聖經紙(一種很薄的紙,例如報紙的航空版所採用者)。**ˈ~·man** /-mən ; -mən/ *n* (*pl* -men) (formerly) sailing-ship engaged in the trade with India. (昔時)從事對印度貿易的帆船。 **ˌ~-ˈrubber** *n* [C] piece of rubber for rubbing out pencil or ink marks. (擦鉛筆字或墨水跡用的)橡皮。

In·dian /ˈɪndɪən ; ˈɪndɪən/ *adj, n* **1** (native) of the Republic of India. 印度的;印度人。 **2** **Aˌmerican ˈ~,** (one) of the original inhabitants of America. 美洲印第安人的;印第安人。**ˌWest ˈ~,** (native) of the West Indies. 西印度群島的;西印度群島人。 **3** (various uses) (各種用法) **ˈ~ club,** bottle-shaped club, for use in gymnastic exercises. 瓶狀棒;棍棒(體操用具)。 **ˈ~ corn,** [U] maize. 玉蜀黍;玉米。***in ~ file,*** in single file, one behind the other. 成一路縱隊。 **ˌ~ ˈhemp,** ⇨ hemp. **ˌ~ ˈink,** black ink made in China and Japan (used when writing ideographs with a brush). (中國及日本製造,寫毛筆字所用)墨;墨汁。 **ˌ~ ˈred,** (soil of a) yellowish-red colour. 淺黃紅色;淺黃紅色土壤。 **ˌ~ ˈsummer,** period of calm, dry hazy weather in late autumn, esp in the northern part of the US; (fig) revival of the feelings of youth in old age. 小陽春;秋老虎(尤指美國北部深秋時之無風、乾燥、有薄霧的天氣);

(喻)回春期。

in·di·cate /ˈɪndɪkeɪt ; ˈɪndəˌket/ *vt* [VP6A, 9, 14] point to; point out; make known; be a sign of; show the need of; state briefly: 指示;指出;表示;象徵;表示需要;簡單地陳述: *A sign-post ~d the right road for us to follow.* 路標指示我們應走的路。*He ~d that the interview was over.* 他簡短地說接見結束了。*The sudden rise in temperature was indicating the use of penicillin.* 體溫突然上升表示需要使用盤尼西林。*A fresh approach to industrial relations is ~d,* is necessary or advisable. 勞資關係需要採取新的步驟。**in·di·ca·tion** /ˌɪndɪˈkeɪʃn ; ˌɪndəˈkeʃən/ *n* **1** [U] indicating or being ~d. 指示;指出;表示。**2** [C, U] sign or suggestion; that which ~s: 象徵;暗示;指示之物: *Did he give you any indication of his feelings?* 他向你表示過他的感情嗎? *There was not much indication/were not many indications that the next few years would be peaceful.* 沒有多少跡象顯示以後數年將會太平。

in·dica·tive /ɪnˈdɪkətɪv ; ɪnˈdɪkətɪv/ *adj* **1** (gram) stating a fact or asking questions of fact: (文法)直述的;直陳的;直陳問句的: *the ~ mood.* 直述語氣;直說法。**2** ~ ***of/that,*** giving indications (of): 指示的;表示的: *Is a high forehead ~ of great mental power?* 前額高表示智慧高嗎?

in·di·ca·tor /ˈɪndɪkeɪtə(r) ; ˈɪndəˌketɚ/ *n* person, thing, that points out or gives information, eg a pointer, needle, recording apparatus, on a machine, etc showing speed, pressure, etc: 指示者;指示物;指示劑;指示器(例如機器上表示速度、壓力等的指針或記錄器): *Litmus paper can be used as an ~ of the presence or not of acid in a solution;* 石蕊試紙可用於指示溶液中是否含有酸; (ˈ*traffic-~*) (on a motor vehicle) flashing light or other device to indicate a change of direction; (ˈ*train ~*) one in a railway station showing times of arrivals and departures of trains, their platform numbers, etc. (汽車等的)方向指示器;方向燈;(火車站內表示火車來往時刻,其月臺號碼等的)火車指示牌。

in·di·ces /ˈɪndɪsiːz ; ˈɪndəˌsiz/ *pl* of index.

in·dict /ɪnˈdaɪt ; ɪnˈdaɪt/ *vt* [VP6A, 14, 16B] (legal) accuse (sb): (法律)控訴;控告: *~ sb for riot/as a rioter/on a charge of rioting.* 以暴亂罪控告某人。**in·dict·able** /-əbl ; -əbl/ *adj* liable to be ~ed; for which one may be ~ed: 可提起告訴的;可控告的: *~able offences,* that may be tried by jury. 刑事罪。**~·ment** *n* [C] written statement that ~s sb: 起訴書;訴狀: *bring in an ~ment against sb.* 控告某人。*This is a clear ~ment of government mismanagement.* 這顯然是對政府管理不善的指控。[U] ~ing or being ~ed. 控訴;被控。

in·dif·fer·ence /ɪnˈdɪfrəns ; ɪnˈdɪfrəns/ *n* [U] ~ ***(to),*** the state of being indifferent; absence of interest or feeling: 不關心;不重視;無興趣;冷淡: *He treated my request with ~.* 他不重視我的請求。*Success or failure cannot be a matter of ~ to you.* 成敗對你不可能是件無足輕重的事。*His ~ to future needs is unfortunate.* 他對未來的需要漠不關心眞令人遺憾。

in·dif·fer·ent /ɪnˈdɪfrənt ; ɪnˈdɪfrənt/ *adj* **1** ~ ***(to),*** having no interest in; neither for nor against; not caring for: 對…不感興趣的; 漠不關心的; 不重視的: *How can you be so ~ to the sufferings of these children?* 對於這些孩子的苦難你怎能如此漠不關心? *The explorers were ~ to the discomforts and dangers of the expedition.* 那些探險家對於那次探險的艱苦與危險不以爲意。*We cannot remain ~* (= neutral) *in this dispute.* 在這場爭辯中,我們不能保持中立。*It is quite ~ to me whether you go or stay,* I don't care which you do. 你的去留對我都無所謂。**2** commonplace; not of good quality or ability: 平常的;品質或能力欠佳的: *an ~ book;* 一本平凡的書; *a very ~ footballer.* 技術甚差的足球員。**~·ly** *adv*

in·digen·ous /ɪnˈdɪdʒɪnəs ; ɪnˈdɪdʒənəs/ *adj* ~ ***(to),*** native, belonging naturally (to): 土生的;天生的: *~ language,* that of the people regarded as the original inhabitants of an area. 某一地區之土著所用之語言;土語。*Kangaroos are ~ to Australia.* 袋鼠原產於澳洲。

in·di·gent /ˈɪndɪdʒənt ; ˈɪndədʒənt/ *adj* (formal) poor. (正式用語)貧窮的。**in·di·gence** /-əns ; -əns/ *n* [U] poverty. 貧窮。

in·di·gest·ible /ˌɪndɪˈdʒestəbl ; ˌɪndəˈdʒɛstəbl/ *adj* difficult or impossible to digest. 難消化的;不能消化的。

in·di·ges·tion /ˌɪndɪˈdʒestʃən ; ˌɪndəˈdʒɛstʃən/ *n* [U] (pain from) difficulty in digesting food: 消化困難;不消化;消化不良症: *suffer from ~;* 患消化不良症; *have an attack of ~.* 患消化不良。

in·dig·nant /ɪnˈdɪɡnənt ; ɪnˈdɪɡnənt/ *adj* angry and scornful, esp at injustice or because of undeserved blame, etc: (尤指對不平或受冤屈等而)憤慨的;憤怒的: *~ at a false accusation;* 對誣告憤憤不平; *~ with a cruel man.* 對一殘忍的人感到憤慨。**~·ly** *adv*

in·dig·na·tion /ˌɪndɪɡˈneɪʃn ; ˌɪndɪɡˈneʃən/ *n* [U] anger caused by injustice, misconduct, etc: 憤慨;義憤: *arouse the ~ of the people;* 引起公憤; *to the ~ of all decent people.* 激起所有正直人士的義憤。*They felt strong ~ against their teachers.* 他們對他們的教師們感到强烈憤慨。

in·dig·nity /ɪnˈdɪɡnətɪ ; ɪnˈdɪɡnətɪ/ *n* [U] rude or unworthy treatment causing shame or loss of respect; [C] (*pl* -ties) sth said or done that humiliates a person: 侮辱;輕蔑;侮辱的言行: *The hijackers subjected us to all sorts of indignities.* 刦持者對我們施以各種侮辱。

in·digo /ˈɪndɪɡəʊ ; ˈɪndɪˌɡo/ *n* [U] deep blue dye (obtained from plants). (自植物中提取的)靛;靛青;藍靛。**~ (blue),** blue-violet. 紫藍色。⇨ the illus at spectrum. 參看 spectrum 之插圖。

in·direct /ˌɪndɪˈrekt ; ˌɪndəˈrɛkt/ *adj* **1** not straight or direct; not going straight to the point: 非直接的;間接的;迂迴的: *an ~ road;* 迂迴的道路; *make an ~ reference to sb,* not mentioning his name although making clear who is referred to; 間接提到某人(暗指某人); *an ~ answer to a question;* 對一問題的間接答覆; *~ lighting,* by reflected light. 間接照明(以反射光照明)。**2** (of taxes) not paid direct to a tax-collector, but in the form of higher prices for taxed goods: (指稅)間接的(非直接交給收稅員,而是以對課稅貨物付出較高價格的方式): *the ~ taxes on tobacco, wines, etc.* 菸草、酒等的間接稅。**3** ˌ**~ ˈobject,** person etc secondarily affected by the *v*, and replaceable by *to/for* + object, eg *him* (= *to him*) in *Give him the money.* 間接受詞(間接受到動詞動作影響者,可以 to 或 for 加受詞代替,例如 Give him the money 或 Give the money to him 中之 him 卽是)。ˌ**~ ˈquestion,** question in ~ speech. 間接問句(以間接敍述法表達的疑問句)。ˌ**~ ˈspeech,** speech as it is reported with the necessary changes of pronouns, tenses, etc, eg *He said he would come* for *He said 'I will come'.* 間接敍述法(例如以 He said he would come 代替 He said 'I will come')。**4** not directly aimed at: 非直接作爲目標的: *an ~ result.* 間接的結果。**~·ly** *adv* **~·ness** *n*

in·dis·cern·ible /ˌɪndɪˈsɜːnəbl ; ˌɪndɪˈzɝnəbl/ *adj* that cannot be discerned. 無法辨認的;看不清楚的。

in·dis·ci·pline /ɪnˈdɪsɪplɪn ; ɪnˈdɪsəplɪn/ *n* [U] absence of discipline. 缺少訓練;無紀律。

in·dis·creet /ˌɪndɪˈskriːt ; ˌɪndɪˈskrit/ *adj* not wary, cautious or careful. 不穩重的;不慎重的;輕率的。**~·ly** *adv* **in·dis·cre·tion** /ˌɪndɪˈskreʃn ; ˌɪndɪˈskrɛʃən/ *n* [U] ~ conduct; lack of discretion; [C] ~ remark or act; offence against social conventions. 不穩重;不謹慎;輕率的言行;不檢點的行爲。

in·dis·crete /ˌɪndɪˈskriːt ; ˌɪndɪˈskrit/ *adj* not formed of distinct or separate parts. 密合不分的。

in·dis·crimi·nate /ˌɪndɪˈskrɪmɪnət ; ˌɪndɪˈskrɪmənɪt/

adj acting, given, without care or taste: 不分皂白的;不加選擇的;不加鑑別的: ~ *in making friends;* 交友不加選擇; *give* ~ *praise;* 不加鑑別,一味讚揚; *deal out* ~ *blows*, hit out at anyone, whether an enemy or not. 不分敵我地亂打。~·ly *adv*

in·dis·pens·able /ˌɪndɪˈspensəbl ; ˌɪndɪˈspɛnsəbḷ/ *adj* ~ **to,** that cannot be dispensed with; absolutely essential: 不可缺少的; 絕對必要的: *Air, food and water are* ~ *to life.* 空氣,食物與水都是維持生命所不可缺的。**in·dis·pen·sa·bil·ity** /ˌɪndɪˌspensəˈbɪlətɪ ; ˌɪndɪˌspɛnsəˈbɪlətɪ/ *n* [U].

in·dis·posed /ˌɪndɪˈspəʊzd ; ˌɪndɪˈspozd/ *adj* **1** unwell: 身體不適的: *She has a headache and is* ~. 她頭痛,感到不適。**2** ~ **for/to do sth,** not inclined: 不願意的: *He seems* ~ *to help us.* 他似乎不願意幫助我們。

in·dis·po·si·tion /ˌɪndɪspəˈzɪʃn ; ˌɪndɪspəˈzɪʃən/ *n* [C, U] **1** ill health; slight illness. 身體不適;微恙。**2** ~ **for/to do sth,** feeling of unwillingness or disinclination; feeling of aversion. 不願;嫌惡。

in·dis·put·able /ˌɪndɪˈspjuːtəbl ; ˌɪndɪˈspjutəbḷ/ *adj* that cannot be disputed. 不容置辯的。

in·dis·sol·uble /ˌɪndɪˈsɒljʊbl ; ˌɪndɪˈsɑljəbḷ/ *adj* (formal) that cannot be dissolved or broken up; firm and lasting: (正式用語)不能溶解的;不能分解的;堅固不變的: *the* ~ *bonds of friendship between my country and yours.* 貴國和我國間不渝的友誼。*The Roman Catholic Church regards marriage as* ~. 天主教會視婚姻爲不可分拆的。

in·dis·tinct /ˌɪndɪˈstɪŋkt ; ˌɪndɪˈstɪŋkt/ *adj* not distinct: 不清楚的;模糊的: ~ *speech;* 含糊不清的言語; ~ *sounds/memories.* 模糊的聲音(記憶)。~·ly *adv* ~·ness *n*

in·dis·tin·guish·able /ˌɪndɪˈstɪŋgwɪʃəbl ; ˌɪndɪˈstɪŋgwɪʃəbḷ/ *adj* that cannot be distinguished. 不能分辨的。

in·dite /ɪnˈdaɪt ; ɪnˈdaɪt/ *vt* [VP6A] (archaic) put into words; compose. (古)撰寫;著作。

in·di·vid·ual /ˌɪndɪˈvɪdʒʊəl ; ˌɪndəˈvɪdʒʊəl/ *adj* **1** (opp of *general*) specially for one person or thing: (爲 general 之相反字) 個別的: *A teacher cannot give* ~ *attention to his pupils if his class is very large.* 如果班上的人數很多,教師便不能對他的學生個別注意了。 **2** characteristic of a single person, animal, plant or thing: 獨特的: *an* ~ *style of speaking/dressing.* 獨特的談話(衣著)風格。□ *n* **1** any one human being (contrasted with *society*): 個人(與 society 相對): *Are the rights of the/an* ~ *more important or less important than the rights of society as a whole?* 個人的權利與整個社會的權利孰輕孰重? **2** (colloq) person: (俗)人: *What a scruffy* ~ *he is!* 他是多麼骯髒的一個人啊! ~**ly** /-dʒʊəlɪ ; -dʒʊəlɪ/ *adv* (opp of *collectively*) separately; one by one: (爲 collectively 之相反字) 個別地;逐一地: *speak to each member of a group* ~*ly.* 對一團體中每個成員個別談話。

in·di·vid·ual·ism /ˌɪndɪˈvɪdʒʊəlɪzəm ; ˌɪndəˈvɪdʒʊəlˌɪzəm/ *n* [U] **1** social theory that favours the free action and complete liberty of belief of individuals (contrasted with the theory favouring the supremacy of the state). 個人主義(一種社會學理論,主張個人行動及信仰完全自由,與國家主義相對)。**2** feeling or behaviour of a person who puts his own private interests first; egoism. 利己的想法或行爲;利己主義。**in·di·vid·ual·ist** /-ɪst ; -ɪst/ *n* supporter of ~. 個人主義者;利己主義者。**in·di·vid·ual·is·tic** /ˌɪndɪˌvɪdʒʊəˈlɪstɪk ; ˌɪndəˌvɪdʒʊəlˈɪstɪk/ *adj* of ~ or its principles. 個人主義的;利己主義的。

in·di·vidu·al·ity /ˌɪndɪˌvɪdʒʊˈælətɪ ; ˌɪndəˌvɪdʒʊˈælətɪ/ *n* (*pl* -ties) **1** [U] all the characteristics that belong to an individual and that mark him out from others: 個性;個人的特性: *a man of marked* ~. 個性特別的人。**2** state of separate existence. 獨立存在狀態;個別存在狀態。 **3** (usu *pl*) individual tastes, etc. (通常用複數)個人的嗜好等。

in·di·vid·ual·ize /ˌɪndɪˈvɪdʒʊəlaɪz ; ˌɪndəˈvɪdʒʊəlˌaɪz/ *vt* [VP6A] **1** give an individual or distinct character to: 使有個性;使有特性: *Does your style of writing* ~ *your work?* 你的寫作風格使你的作品具有個性嗎? **2** specify; treat separately and in detail. 指明;個別詳述。

in·di·vis·ible /ˌɪndɪˈvɪzəbl ; ˌɪndəˈvɪzəbḷ/ *adj* that cannot be divided. 不能分割的;除不盡的。

Indo- /ˌɪndəʊ ; ˌɪndo/ *pref* (in compounds 用於複合字中) = Indian. ˌ~-ˌ**Euroˈpean,** of the family of languages spoken in Europe and parts of western Asia, esp Iran, Pakistan and India. 印歐語系(歐洲及西亞尤其伊朗、巴基斯坦及印度等地所使用之語言系統)的。

in·doc·tri·nate /ɪnˈdɒktrɪneɪt ; ɪnˈdɑktrɪnˌet/ *vt* [VP6A, 14] ~ **sb with,** fill the mind of (sb) (with particular ideas or beliefs). (以某種思想或信仰)灌輸(某人)。**in·doc·tri·na·tion** /ɪnˌdɒktrɪˈneɪʃn ; ɪnˌdɑktrɪˈneʃən/ *n* [U].

in·do·lent /ˈɪndələnt ; ˈɪndələnt/ *adj* lazy; inactive. 懶惰的;怠惰的。~·ly *adv* **in·do·lence** /-əns ; -əns/ *n* [U].

in·domi·table /ɪnˈdɒmɪtəbl ; ɪnˈdɑmətəbḷ/ *adj* that cannot be subdued or conquered; unyielding: 不可征服的;不屈的: ~ *courage;* 不屈不撓的勇氣; *an* ~ *will.* 不屈的意志。

in·door /ˈɪndɔː(r) ; ˈɪnˌdor/ *adj* (attrib only) belonging to, carried on, situated, inside a building: (僅作形容用法)戶內的;室內的: ~ *games/photography;* 室內遊戲(室內攝影); *an* ~ *swimming-bath.* 室內游泳池。

in·doors /ˌɪnˈdɔːz ; ˈɪnˈdorz/ *adv* in or into a building: 在戶內;入戶內: *go/stay* ~*;* 進入室內(留在室內); *kept* ~ *all week by bad weather.* 因天氣不好而整週留在戶內。

in·dorse /ɪnˈdɔːs ; ɪnˈdɔrs/ = endorse.

in·drawn /ˌɪnˈdrɔːn ; ˈɪnˈdrɔn/ *adj* drawn in: 吸入的: *an* ~ *breath.* 吸入的一口氣。

in·dubi·table /ɪnˈdjuːbɪtəbl *US:* -ˈduː- ; ɪnˈdjubɪtəbḷ/ *adj* (formal) that cannot be doubted. (正式用語)不容置疑的。

in·duce /ɪnˈdjuːs *US:* -ˈduːs ; ɪnˈdjus/ *vt* **1** [VP17] ~ **sb to do sth,** persuade or influence; lead or cause: 勸誘;誘導;促使(某人做某事): *What* ~*d you to do such a thing?* 什麼促使你作這種事的? *We couldn't* ~ *the old lady to travel by air.* 我們無法勸服那老太太乘飛機旅行。 **2** [VP6A, 14] bring about: 導致;招惹: *illness* ~*d by overwork;* 工作過度而引起的病; ~ *labour,* (in childbirth) by artificial means; 人工分娩; ~ *magnetism in a piece of iron,* by holding it near a magnet. (將鐵置於磁鐵旁)使一塊鐵產生磁性。~·**ment** *n* [C, U] that which ~s; incentive: 誘因;引誘物;動機: *He hasn't much* ~*ment/many* ~*ments to study English.* 他沒有什麼學習英語的動機。

in·duct /ɪnˈdʌkt ; ɪnˈdʌkt/ *vt* [VP6A, 14, 16B] ~ **sb (to/into/as),** install formally or with ceremony in position or office; admit as a member of. 使正式就職;使入會。

in·duc·tion /ɪnˈdʌkʃn ; ɪnˈdʌkʃən/ *n* **1** inducting or being inducted: 正式就職;入會: *an* ~ *course,* one designed to provide general knowledge of future activities, requirements, etc. 就職課程(使就職者對將來工作上的活動、需求等有通盤了解)。 **2** method of reasoning which obtains or discovers general laws from particular facts or examples; production of facts to prove a general statement. 歸納(法);歸納推理。⇨ deduction. **3** the bringing about of an electric or magnetic state in a body by proximity (without actual contact) of an electrified or magnetized body: (電或磁之)感應: ~ *coils/motors.* 感應線圈(電動機)。⇨ induce(2).

in·duc·tive /ɪnˈdʌktɪv ; ɪnˈdʌktɪv/ *adj* **1** (of reasoning) based on induction(2). (指推理)歸納的。 **2** of magnetic or electrical induction. (磁或電之)感應的。

in·due /ɪnˈdjuː *US:* -ˈduː ; ɪnˈdju/ = endue.

in·dulge /ɪn'dʌldʒ; ɪn'dʌldʒ/ *vt, vi* **1** [VP6A] gratify; give way to and satisfy (desires, etc); overlook the faults of: 使滿足;放縱(慾望等);縱容;放任: *It is sometimes necessary to ~ a sick child/the fancies of a sick child.* 遷就一個生病的小孩(滿足一個生病小孩的喜好)有時是必要的。 **2** [VP3A] **~ in,** allow oneself the pleasure of: 耽溺於;縱情於;盡情享受: *He occasionally ~s in the luxury of a good cigar.* 他偶而享受一枝好雪茄。 **in·dul·gent** /-ənt; -ənt/ *adj* inclined to ~: 縱容的;放縱的: *indulgent parents,* parents who ~ their children. 溺愛子女的父母。 **in·dul·gent·ly** *adv*

in·dul·gence /ɪn'dʌldʒəns; ɪn'dʌldʒəns/ *n* **1** [U] indulging(1); the state of being indulged(1). 縱容;受到縱容。 **2** [U] **~ (in),** (the habit of) gratifying one's own desires, etc: 耽溺;縱情: *Constant ~ in bad habits brought about his ruin.* 經常耽溺於惡習導致了他的毀滅。 **3** [C] sth in which a person indulges(2): 耽溺的事物;嗜好: *One pint of beer a day and an occasional game of billiards are his only ~s.* 每天一品脫啤酒及偶爾打打撞球是他僅有的嗜好。 **4** [U] (in the RC Church) granting of freedom from punishment still due for sin after sacramental absolution; [C] instance of this. (天主教)赦免;免罪。

in·dus·trial /ɪn'dʌstrɪəl; ɪn'dʌstrɪəl/ *adj* of industries: 工業的;產業的: *the ~ areas of England* (contrasted with *agricultural,* etc). 英國之工業地區(與農業地區等相對)。 **~ action,** striking²(5). 罷工。 ***take ~ action,*** strike²(5). 罷工。 **~ alcohol,** for ~ use (unfit for drinking). 工業用酒精(不可飲用)。 **~ dispute,** one between workers and management. 工業糾紛;勞資糾紛。 **~ estate,** area of land planned and used for the building of factories (to be rented to manufacturers). 工業用地;工業區(分租於廠家作修建廠房之用)。 **the ~ revolution,** the changes brought about by mechanical inventions in the 18th and early 19th cc. 工業革命(由於機器的發明所導致之改革,發生於十八世紀及十九世紀初期)。 **~·ism** /-ɪzəm; -,ɪzəm/ *n* social system in which large-scale industries have an important part. 工業社會制度;工業主義。 **~·ist** /-ɪst; -ɪst/ *n* owner of a large-scale ~ undertaking; supporter of ~ism. 工業家;工業主義者。

in·dus·tri·ous /ɪn'dʌstrɪəs; ɪn'dʌstrɪəs/ *adj* hard-working; diligent. 勤勉的;刻苦的。 ⇨ industry(1). **~·ly** *adv*

in·dus·try /'ɪndəstrɪ; 'ɪndəstrɪ/ *n* (*pl* -tries) **1** [U] quality of being hard-working; being always employed usefully: 勤勉;工作努力: *His success was due to ~ and thrift.* 他的成功是由於勤勉和節儉。 **2** [C, U] (branch of) trade or manufacture (contrasted with distribution and commerce): 工業;產業;生產(或其分支)(與分配及商業相對): *the cotton and woollen industries.* 棉毛工業。

in·dwell·ing /,ɪn'dwelɪŋ; ,ɪn'dwɛlɪŋ/ *adj* (formal) living, always present, in the mind or soul. (正式用語)在心中的;經常在心中的。

in·ebri·ate /ɪ'ni:brɪeɪt; ɪn'ibrɪ,et/ *vt* [VP6A] (formal or joc) make drunk; intoxicate. (正式用語或謔)使醉;使大醉。 □ *n, adj* /ɪ'ni:brɪət; ɪn'ibrɪɪt/ (person who is habitually) drunk: 醉漢;酒徒;酒醉的: *an institution for ~s.* 酗酒者收容所。 **in·ebri·ation** /ɪ,ni:brɪ'eɪʃn; ɪn,ibrɪ'eʃən/, **in·ebri·ety** /,ɪnɪ'braɪətɪ; ,ɪnɪ'braɪətɪ/ *nn* [U] drunkenness. 酒醉。

in·ed·ible /ɪn'edɪbl; ɪn'ɛdəbl̩/ *adj* (formal) (of a kind) not suitable to be eaten. (正式用語)(指某類東西)不可食的。

in·ef·fable /ɪn'efəbl; ɪn'ɛfəbl̩/ *adj* (formal) too great to be described in words: (正式用語)難以言語形容的;不可名狀的;說不出的: *~ joy/beauty.* 說不出的高興(美) **in·ef·fably** /-əblɪ; -əblɪ/ *adv*

in·ef·fec·tive /,ɪnɪ'fektɪv; ,ɪnə'fɛktɪv/ *adj* not producing the effect(s) desired; (of a person) inefficient. 無效力的;(指人)無效率的。 **~·ly** *adv* **~·ness** *n*

in·ef·fec·tual /,ɪnɪ'fektʃʊəl; ,ɪnə'fɛktʃʊəl/ *adj* without effect; unsuccessful; lacking confidence and unable to get things done: 無效的;不成功的;缺乏信心而不能成事的;不稱職的: *an ~ teacher/leader.* 不稱職的教師(領袖)。 **~·ly** /-tʃʊəlɪ; -tʃʊəlɪ/ *adv*

in·ef·fic·ient /,ɪnɪ'fɪʃnt; ,ɪnə'fɪʃənt/ *adj* (of persons) wasting time, energy, etc in their work or duties: (指人)無效率的: *an ~ management/administration;* 無效率的經理人員(行政當局); (of machines, processes, etc) wasteful; not producing adequate results. (指機器、程序等)浪費的;不能產生適當成果的;效率低的。 **~·ly** *adv* **in·ef·fic·iency** /-nsɪ; -ənsɪ/ *n* [U].

in·elas·tic /,ɪnɪ'læstɪk; ,ɪnɪ'læstɪk/ *adj* not flexible or adaptable; unyielding: 無彈性的;無適應性的;不彎曲的: *an ~ programme/timetable.* 毫無彈性的計畫(時間表)。

in·el·egant /,ɪn'elɪgənt; ɪn'ɛləgənt/ *adj* not graceful or refined. 不雅的。 **~·ly** *adv* **in·el·egance** /-əns; -əns/ *n*

in·eli·gible /ɪn'elɪdʒəbl; ɪn'ɛlɪdʒəbl̩/ *adj* **~ (for),** not eligible; not suitable or qualified: 不合格的;無資格的: *~ for the position.* 無資格任該職。 **in·eli·gi·bil·ity** /ɪn,elɪdʒə'bɪlətɪ; ɪn,ɛlɪdʒə'bɪlətɪ/ *n* [U].

in·eluc·table /,ɪnɪ'lʌktəbl; ,ɪnɪ'lʌktəbl̩/ *adj* (formal) that cannot be escaped from: (正式用語)不能避免的: *the victim of ~ fate.* 無法逃過命運之犧牲者。

in·ept /ɪ'nept; ɪn'ɛpt/ *adj* unskilful; said or done at the wrong time: 笨拙的;不適當的;非其時的: *~ remarks.* 不適當的談話。 **~·ly** *adv* **in·ep·ti·tude** /ɪ'neptɪtju:d *US:* -tu:d; ɪn'ɛptə,tjud/ *n* [U] quality of being ~; [C] ~ action, remark, etc. 笨拙;不適當;笨拙或不當的言行等。

in·equal·ity /,ɪnɪ'kwɒlətɪ; ,ɪnɪ'kwɑlətɪ/ *n* (*pl* -ties) **1** [U] want of, absence of, equality in size, degree, circumstances, etc; difference in size, rank, wealth, etc; [C] instance of this: (大小、程度、情況等)不相等;不平均;不平等;(大小、地位、財富等的)差別: *Great inequalities in wealth cause social unrest.* 貧富過於懸殊會引起社會不安。 **2** (*pl*) (of a surface) irregularity: (複)(指表面)不平坦: *the inequalities of the landscape,* the rise and fall of the ground, etc. 地形的起伏不平。

in·equi·table /ɪn'ekwɪtəbl; ɪn'ɛkwɪtəbl̩/ *adj* (formal) unjust; unfair: (正式用語)不公正的;不公平的: *an ~ division of the profits.* 利潤的分配不公平。

in·equity /ɪn'ekwətɪ; ɪn'ɛkwɪtɪ/ *n* (*pl* -ties) [C, U] (instance of) injustice or unfairness. 不公正;不公平。

in·eradi·cable /,ɪnɪ'rædɪkəbl; ,ɪnɪ'rædɪkəbl̩/ *adj* that cannot be rooted out; firmly and deeply rooted: 不能根除的;根深蒂固的: *an ~ fault/failing.* 根深蒂固的缺點。

in·ert /ɪ'nɜ:t; ɪn'ɝt/ *adj* **1** without power to move or act: 無活動力的: *~ matter.* 無活動力的物質。 **2** without active chemical properties: 不起化學作用的: *~ gases.* 不生化學作用的氣體;惰性氣體。 **3** heavy and slow in (mind or body). (身或心)遲鈍的;呆滯的。 **in·er·tia** /ɪ'nɜ:ʃə; ɪn'ɝʃə/ *n* [U] **1** state of being ~(3). 遲鈍;呆滯。 **2** property of matter by which it remains in a state of rest or, if it is in motion, continues in the same direction and in a straight line unless it is acted upon by an external force. 惰性;慣性。

in·es·cap·able /,ɪnɪ'skeɪpəbl; ,ɪnə'skepəbl̩/ *adj* not to be escaped from: 不可逃避的: *We were forced to the ~ conclusion that he was an embezzler.* 我們無法避免的結論是,他盜用了公款。

in·es·ti·mable /ɪn'estɪməbl; ɪn'ɛstəməbl̩/ *adj* too great, precious, etc to be estimated. (因過大,過於貴重等)不能估計的;難評價的。

in·evi·table /ɪn'evɪtəbl; ɪn'ɛvətəbl̩/ *adj* **1** that cannot be avoided, that is sure to happen. 不可避免的;必然發生的。 **2** (colloq) so frequently seen, heard, etc that it is familiar and expected: (俗)

因時常看到或聽到等而熟悉及預料中的；照例的；慣常的：*a tourist with his ~ camera.* 一個慣常帶著照像機的觀光客。**in·evi·ta·bil·ity** /ɪnˌevɪtəˈbɪlətɪ ; ˌɪnɛvətəˈbɪlətɪ/ *n*

in·ex·act /ˌɪnɪɡˈzækt ; ˌɪnɪɡˈzækt/ *adj* not exact. 不正確的；不精確的。**in·ex·acti·tude** /ˌɪnɪɡˈzæktɪtjuːd *US:* -tuːd ; ˌɪnɪɡˈzæktəˌtjud/ *n* [U] being ~; [C] instance of this: 不正確；不精確：*terminological ~itudes,* (joc euphem for) lies. (戲謔性委婉語)謊言。

in·ex·cus·able /ˌɪnɪkˈskjuːzəbl ; ˌɪnɪkˈskjuzəbl̩/ *adj* that cannot be excused: 不可原諒的；不可辯解的：~ *conduct/delays.* 不可原諒的行爲(耽擱)。

in·ex·haust·ible /ˌɪnɪɡˈzɔːstəbl ; ˌɪnɪɡˈzɔstəbl̩/ *adj* that cannot be exhausted: 取之不竭的；無窮盡的：*My patience is not ~.* 我的忍耐是有限度的。

in·exor·able /ˌɪnˈeksərəbl ; ɪnˈɛksərəbl̩/ *adj* relentless; unyielding: 無情的；堅決不變的：~ *demands/pressures.* 堅決的要求(無情的壓力)。**in·exor·ably** /-əblɪ ; -əblɪ/ *adv*

in·ex·pedi·ent /ˌɪnɪkˈspiːdɪənt ; ˌɪnɪkˈspidɪənt/ *adj* not expedient. 不得當的；不合權宜的。**in·ex·pedi·en·cy** /-ənsɪ ; -ənsɪ/ *n* [U] quality of being ~. 不得當；不合權宜。

in·ex·pen·sive /ˌɪnɪkˈspensɪv ; ˌɪnɪkˈspɛnsɪv/ *adj* not expensive; low-priced. 不貴的；廉價的。**~·ly** *adv*

in·ex·pe·ri·ence /ˌɪnɪkˈspɪərɪəns ; ˌɪnɪkˈspɪrɪəns/ *n* [U] lack of experience: 無經驗；缺乏經驗：*He didn't get the job because of his ~.* 他由於無經驗而未獲得該職。**in·ex·pe·ri·enced** *adj* lacking experience. 無經驗的；缺乏經驗的。

in·ex·pert /ɪnˈekspɜːt ; ˌɪnɪksˈpɝt/ *adj* unskilled: 缺乏技巧的；不熟練的：~ *advice/guidance.* 無技巧的勸告(指導)。**~·ly** *adv*

in·ex·pi·able /ɪnˈekspɪəbl ; ɪnˈɛkspɪəbl̩/ *adj* (formal) (of an offence) that cannot be expiated; (of resentment, hatred, etc) that cannot be appeased. (正式用語)(指罪過)不可贖的；(指憎恨等)不能化解的；不能平息的。

in·ex·plic·able /ˌɪnɪkˈsplɪkəbl ; ɪnˈɛksplɪkəbl̩/ *adj* that cannot be explained. 無法解釋的。

in·ex·press·ible /ˌɪnɪkˈspresəbl ; ˌɪnɪkˈsprɛsəbl̩/ *adj* that cannot be expressed in words: 言語無法表達的：~ *sorrow/anguish.* 無法以言語表達的憂傷(痛苦)。

in·ex·tin·guish·able /ˌɪnɪkˈstɪŋɡwɪʃəbl ; ˌɪnɪkˈstɪŋɡwɪʃəbl̩/ *adj* that cannot be extinguished or quenched: 不能撲滅的；不能消除的：~ *hatred.* 無法化解的仇恨。

in·ex·tri·cable /ˌɪnɪkˈstrɪkəbl ; ɪnˈɛkstrɪkəbl̩/ *adj* that cannot be reduced to order, solved, untied, or escaped from: 無法整理的；不能解決的；解不開的；不能避免的：~ *confusion/difficulties.* 無法整理的紊亂(無法解決的困難)。

in·fal·lible /ɪnˈfæləbl ; ɪnˈfæləbl̩/ *adj* **1** incapable of making mistakes or doing wrong: 不會犯錯的；不會做錯事的：*None of us is ~.* 我們當中沒有人不會犯錯的。**2** never failing: 絕對可靠的：~ *remedies/cures/methods/tests.* 萬無一失的藥(治療法，方法，測驗)。**in·fal·li·bil·ity** /ɪnˌfæləˈbɪlətɪ ; ɪnˌfæləˈbɪlətɪ/ *n* complete freedom from the possibility of being in error: 絕無錯誤：*the infallibility of the Pope.* 天主教教宗之絕無謬誤。

in·fa·mous /ˈɪnfəməs ; ˈɪnfəməs/ *adj* wicked; shameful; disgraceful: 邪惡的；可恥的；不名譽的：~ *behaviour;* 可恥的行爲；*an ~ plot/traitor.* 邪惡的陰謀(無恥的賣國賊)。**in·famy** /ˈɪnfəmɪ ; ˈɪnfəmɪ/ *n* **1** [U] being ~; public dishonour: 邪惡；無恥；不名譽：*hold a person up to infamy.* 使某人名譽掃地。**2** [U] ~ behaviour; [C] (*pl* -mies) ~ act. 無恥的行爲；不名譽的行動。

in·fancy /ˈɪnfənsɪ ; ˈɪnfənsɪ/ *n* [U] **1** state of being, period when one is, an infant; early childhood; (legal, in GB) minority(1), period before one reaches 18. 幼稚狀態；幼兒期；(英國法律)未成年(未滿十八歲)。⇨ minority. **2** early stage of development or growth: 發展或成長的初期：*the ~ of a nation;* 一國家立國之初期；*when aviation was still in its ~.* 當航空仍在萌芽階段。

in·fant /ˈɪnfənt ; ˈɪnfənt/ *n* **1** child during the first few years of its life; (legal) minor. 幼兒；嬰兒；(法律)未成年者。**2** (attrib) (形容用法) ~ *voices;* 童音；~ *food;* 嬰兒食品；*an* ˈ~-*school,* part of a primary school for children under 7; 幼稚園(小學之一部，爲七歲以下之兒童而設)；~ *industries,* new, in an early stage. 幼稚工業(新創並在初期之工業)。

in·fan·ti·cide /ɪnˈfæntɪsaɪd ; ɪnˈfæntəˌsaɪd/ *n* [U] crime of killing an infant; the custom, among some peoples in the past, of killing unwanted new-born children. 殺害嬰兒罪；昔日某些民族殺害其不要的新生兒之風俗。

in·fan·tile /ˈɪnfəntaɪl ; ˈɪnfənˌtaɪl/ *adj* characteristic of infants: 嬰兒的；幼兒的；幼稚的：~ *diseases/pastimes;* 小兒病(幼兒的娛樂)；~ *paralysis,* name formerly used for poliomyelitis. 小兒痲痺症(脊髓灰白質炎之舊名)。**in·fan·til·ism** /ɪnˈfæntɪlɪzəm ; ɪnˈfæntəlɪzm̩/ *n* [U] mentally and physically underdeveloped or arrested state. 幼稚病(心智及身體發育不足或停止之狀態)；幼稚狀態。

in·fan·try /ˈɪnfəntrɪ ; ˈɪnfəntrɪ/ *n* (collective *sing*) [U] soldiers who fight on foot: (集合單數)步兵：*two regiments of ~;* 兩團步兵；*an ~ regiment.* 一個步兵團。**ˈ~·man** /-mən ; -mən/ *n* (*pl* -men) soldier in an ~ regiment. 步兵。⇨ cavalry.

in·fatu·ate /ɪnˈfætʃʊeɪt ; ɪnˈfætʃʊˌet/ *vt* ***be ~d with/by sb,*** be filled with a wild and foolish love for: 瘋狂迷戀：*He's ~d with that girl.* 他瘋狂地愛戀着那個女郎。**in·fatu·ation** /ɪnˌfætʃʊˈeɪʃn ; ɪnˌfætʃʊˈeʃən/ *n* [U] infatuating or being ~d; [C] ***~ (for),*** instance of this; unreasoning love or passion. 瘋狂迷戀；痴迷。

in·fect /ɪnˈfekt ; ɪnˈfɛkt/ *vt* [VP6A, 14] ***~ (with),*** contaminate; give disease, (fig) feelings, ideas, to a person, his body or mind: 汚染；傳染疾病；(喻)使某人、其身或心受情感或思想的感染：~ *a wound;* 使一傷口受到感染；*~ed with cholera.* 染上了霍亂。*Mary's high spirits ~ed all the girls in the class.* 瑪莉的高興感染了班上所有的女孩。

in·fec·tion /ɪnˈfekʃn ; ɪnˈfɛkʃən/ *n* **1** [U] infecting or being infected; communication of disease, esp by agency of the atmosphere or water, ⇨ contagion. 汚染；被汚染；傳染疾病(尤指藉空氣或水)。**2** [C] disease, (fig) influence, that infects. 傳染病；(喻)影響力。

in·fec·tious /ɪnˈfekʃəs ; ɪnˈfɛkʃəs/ *adj* **1** infecting with disease; (of disease) that can be spread by means of bacteria carried in the atmosphere or in water. 傳染疾病的；(指疾病)可藉空氣或水中細菌傳染的。⇨ contagious. **2** (fig) quickly influencing others; likely to spread to others: (喻)迅速影響他人的；易傳播的：~ *humour.* 易使他人感受的幽默。

in·fer /ɪnˈfɜː(r) ; ɪnˈfɝ/ *vt* (-rr-) [VP6A, 9, 14] ***~ (from sth) (that...),*** conclude; reach an opinion (from facts or reasoning): 推斷；(由事實或推理)推知：*Am I to ~ from your remarks that you think I am a liar?* 你的話是否表示你認爲我說謊呢？**~·ence** /ˈɪnfərəns ; ˈɪnfərəns/ *n* **1** [U] process of ~ring: 推斷；推論；推知：*by ~ence,* as the result of drawing a conclusion. 根據推斷。**2** [C] that which is ~red; conclusion: 推斷的結果；結論：*Is that a fair ~ence from his statement?* 對於他的聲明那樣推斷公平嗎？**~·en·tial** /ˌɪnfəˈrenʃl ; ˌɪnfəˈrɛnʃəl/ *adj* that may be ~red. 可以推斷的；可以推知的。

in·ferior /ɪnˈfɪərɪə(r) ; ɪnˈfɪrɪɚ/ *adj* low(er) in rank, social position, importance, quality, etc: 階級低的；社會地位低的；次要的；劣勢的；質劣的；次等的；較低劣的：~ *goods/workmanship;* 低劣的貨物(手藝)；*an ~ officer/court of law;* 下級軍官(低等法院)；*make sb feel ~.* 使人感到自卑。□ *n* person who is ~ (in rank, ability, etc). (階級，能力等)較低之人。**~·ity** /ɪnˌfɪərɪˈɒrətɪ *US:* -ˈɔːr- ; ɪnˌfɪrɪˈɔrətɪ/ *n* [U] state of being ~. 較低；較不重要；低劣。**ˈ~ity**

complex, state of mind in which a person who has a morbid feeling of being ~ to others may try to win recognition for himself by boasting and being aggressive. 自卑感(一種病態心理,自覺不如他人,欲藉吹噓和出鋒頭以獲取他人的讚譽)。

in·fer·nal /ɪn'fɜːnl ; ɪn'fɝnl̩/ *adj* of hell; devilish; abominable: 地獄的; 惡魔般的; 可憎的: *the ~ regions;* 地獄; ~ *cruelty.* 惡魔般的殘忍。**~ly** /-nəlɪ ; -nlɪ/ *adv*

in·ferno /ɪn'fɜːnəʊ ; ɪn'fɝno/ *n* (*pl* ~s /-nəʊz ; -noz/) hell; scene of horror, eg a blazing building in which people are trapped. 地獄;恐怖的景象(例如有人困於熊熊大火的建築物中)。

in·fer·tile /ɪn'fɜːtaɪl *US:* -tl ; ɪn'fɝtl̩/ *adj* not fertile; barren.不肥沃的;不結果實的;不能生育的。**in·fer·til·ity** /ˌɪnfə'tɪlətɪ ; ˌɪnfɚ'tɪlətɪ/ *n*

in·fest /ɪn'fest ; ɪn'fɛst/ *vt* [VP6A] (of rats, insects, etc) be present in large numbers: (指老鼠,蟲類等)大批出動;成群出現: *warehouses ~ed with rats;* 老鼠橫行的倉庫; *clothes ~ed with vermin/lice.* 生滿跳蚤(蝨子)的衣服。 **in·fes·ta·tion** /ˌɪnfe'steɪʃn ; ˌɪnfɛs'teʃən/ *n* [U, C] (instance of) ~ing or being ~ed. (老鼠,蟲類等)大批出現。

in·fi·del /'ɪnfɪdəl ; 'ɪnfədl̩/ *n* **1** (hist) person with no belief in a religion, esp in what is considered to be the true religion. (史)不信仰宗教(尤指正統宗教)者;無宗教信仰者。**2** (attrib) unbelieving; of unbelievers: (形容用法)不信教的;異教徒的: *He showed an ~ contempt for sacred places.* 他對聖地表示一種異教徒的輕蔑。

in·fi·del·ity /ˌɪnfɪ'delətɪ ; ˌɪnfə'dɛlətɪ/ *n* (*pl* -ties) [C, U] (formal) (act of) disloyalty or unfaithfulness; adultery: (正式用語)不忠實; 不貞;不貞的行爲;通姦: *conjugal ~,* ~ to one's husband or wife. 對配偶的不忠。

in·field /'ɪnfiːld ; 'ɪnˌfild/ *n* (cricket) (opp of *outfield*) part of the ground near the wicket; fieldsmen stationed there; baseball diamond. (板球)(爲 outfield 之相反字)內場;內場全部球員;(棒球)內場;內野。

in·fight·ing /'ɪn faɪtɪŋ ; 'ɪnˌfaɪtɪŋ/ *n* [U] boxing at rather close quarters; (colloq) often ruthless competition between colleagues or rivals (esp in commerce and industry). (拳擊)接近戰;短打;(俗)(特指工商業界)同事或對手間時常無情的競爭。

in·fil·trate /'ɪnfɪltreɪt ; ɪn'fɪltret/ *vt, vi* [VP6A, 14, 2A, 3A] ~ ***sth (into sth);*** ~ ***(into/through),*** (cause to) pass through or into by filtering; (of troops) pass through defences without attracting notice; (of ideas) pass into people's minds. (使)滲透;(指軍隊) 悄悄越過對方防線;滲透;(指思想) 滲入人的心中。 **in·fil·tra·tion** /ˌɪnfɪl'treɪʃn ; ˌɪnfɪl'treʃən/ *n* [U] infiltrating or being ~d; (esp) gradual and unnoticed occupation of land by small groups, eg of soldiers or settlers. 滲透;被滲透;(尤指)滲透運動;滲透侵佔(例如小股軍隊或殖民者的不爲人注意之逐漸佔領或侵佔土地)。

in·fi·nite /'ɪnfɪnət ; 'ɪnfənɪt/ *adj* endless; without limits; that cannot be measured, calculated, or imagined: 無窮的;無限的;無法計量或想像的: ~ *space;* 無窮的太空; *the ~ goodness of God;* 上帝的無限恩典; *Such ideas may do ~ harm.* 這種思想可能會造成極大的害處。**the I~,** God. 上帝。**~·ly** *adv* in an ~ degree: 無窮地;無限地;無法計量或想像地: *Atoms and molecules are ~ly small.* 原子與分子極小。 **in·fini·tesi·mal** /ˌɪnfɪnɪ'tesɪml ; ˌɪnfɪnə'tɛsəml̩/ *adj* ~ly small. 極微小的。

in·fini·tive /ɪn'fɪnətɪv ; ɪn'fɪnətɪv/ *adj, n* (gram) (in English) non-finite form of a *v* used with or without *to,* eg let him *go;* allow him *to go.* (文法)不定詞的; 不定詞(英文中一動詞的不限定形式,可與 to 或不與 to 連用,例如 let him go 中的 go,及 allow him to go 中的 to go)。

in·fini·tude /ɪn'fɪnɪtjuːd *US:* -tuːd ; ɪn'fɪnəˌtjud/ *n* [U] (formal) the state of being endless or boundless; boundless number or extent (*of*): (正式用語)無限;無限的數目或範圍(與 of 連用): *the ~ of God's mercy;* 上帝慈悲的無限; [C] infinite number, quantity, or extent: 無數;無限量;無限範圍: *an ~ of small particles.* 無數的微小粒子。

in·fin·ity /ɪn'fɪnətɪ ; ɪn'fɪnətɪ/ *n* [U] the state of being endless or boundless; (maths) infinite quantity (expressed by the symbol ∞). 無限;(數學)無限大(符號爲∞)。

in·firm /ɪn'fɜːm ; ɪn'fɝm/ *adj* **1** physically weak (esp through age): 體弱的 (尤指由於年邁): *walk with ~ steps.* 以虛弱的步子行走。 **2** mentally or morally weak. 懦弱的;意志薄弱的。~ ***of purpose,*** not purposeful; undecided. 意志薄弱的;猶豫不決的。 **in·firm·ity** /ɪn'fɜːmətɪ ; ɪn'fɝmətɪ/ *n* (*pl* -ties) [C, U] (particular form of) weakness: 體弱;虛弱: *I~ity often comes with old age.* 虛弱常與老年俱來。*Deafness and failing eyesight are among the ~ities of old age.* 耳聾與眼花是年老體衰的現象。

in·firm·ary /ɪn'fɜːmərɪ ; ɪn'fɝmərɪ/ *n* (*pl* -ries) **1** hospital. 醫院。 **2** (in a school, institution, etc) room used for people who are ill or injured. (學校,機關等的)醫務室。

in·flame /ɪn'fleɪm ; ɪn'flem/ *vt, vi* [VP2A, 6A] (cause to) become red, angry, overheated: 使紅;使怒;使紅腫;使發炎;使熾熱;變紅;發炎;被激怒;變熱: *~d eyes;* 紅腫的眼睛; *an ~d boil,* red and angry looking; 紅腫的癤子; *speeches that ~d popular feeling,* roused people to anger, indignation, etc; 煽動群情的演說; *~d with passion.* 情緒激動。

in·flam·mable /ɪn'flæməbl ; ɪn'flæməbl̩/ *adj* easily set on fire or (fig) excited: 易燃的; (喻) 易激動的: *Petroleum — Highly I~!* 汽油 — 極易燃燒! ⇨ flammable.

in·flam·ma·tion /ˌɪnflə'meɪʃn ; ˌɪnflə'meʃən/ *n* [U] inflamed condition (esp of some part of the body): 激怒;熾熱;(尤指)發炎: ~ *of the lungs/liver;* 肺部(肝部)發炎; [C] instance of this; place on or in the body where there is redness, swelling and pain. 發炎症;發炎部位。

in·flam·ma·tory /ɪn'flæmətrɪ *US:* -tɔːrɪ ; ɪn'flæməˌtorɪ/ *adj* **1** tending to inflame: 易使人憤怒的;煽動性的: ~ *speeches.* 煽動性的演說。 **2** of, tending to produce, inflammation: 發炎的;引起發炎的;炎性的: *an ~ condition of the lungs,* eg as a symptom of pneumonia. 肺部發炎的狀況 (例如爲肺炎的症候)。

in·flate /ɪn'fleɪt ; ɪn'flet/ *vt, vi* [VP6A, 14, 2A, C] ~ ***sth (with),*** **1** fill a tyre, balloon, etc with air or gas; (cause to) swell: 灌氣於(輪胎,氣球等);使膨脹;膨脹: (fig) (喻) *~d with pride;* 傲氣十足; *~d language,* full of high-sounding words but containing little substance. 浮誇的言詞。 **2** take action to increase the amount of money in circulation so that prices rise. 使(通貨)膨脹而引起物價上漲。⇨ deflate. **in·flat·able** /-əbl ; -əbl̩/ *adj* that can be ~d: 可充氣的;可使之膨脹的: *an inflatable rubber dinghy.* 一條可充氣的橡皮艇。 **in·fla·tion** /ɪn'fleɪʃn ; ɪn'fleʃən/ *n* [U] act of inflating; state of being ~d; (esp) (rise in prices brought about by the) expansion of the supply of bank money, credit, etc. 灌氣;膨脹;(尤指)通貨膨脹; 信用膨脹; 因通貨或信用膨脹而引起的物價上漲。**in·fla·tion·ary** /ɪn'fleɪʃnrɪ *US:* -nerɪ ; ɪn'fleʃənˌɛrɪ/ *adj* of, caused by, inflation: 膨脹的;通貨膨脹的;由膨脹或通貨膨脹而引起的: *the inflationary spiral,* economic situation in which prices and wages rise in turn as the supply of money is increased. 螺旋性通貨膨脹(因通貨膨脹而引起物價及工資上漲的經濟狀況)。

in·flect /ɪn'flekt ; ɪn'flɛkt/ *vt* [VP6A] **1** (gram) change the ending or form of (a word) to show its relationship to other words in a sentence. (文法)變化(一字)之字尾或形式(以表示該字與句中其他字間的關係)。 **2** modulate (the voice); bend inwards; curve. 改變(聲音)的聲調;使向內彎折;彎曲。

in·flec·tion /ɪnˈflekʃn ; ɪnˈflɛkʃən/ *n* **1** [U] inflecting. 字尾變化;字形變化;改變聲調;彎曲。 **2** [C] inflected form of a word, eg *am, are, is;* suffix used to inflect, eg *-ed, -ing.* 一字變化的形式(例如 am, are, is);表示變化的字尾(例如 -ed, -ing)。 **3** [U] rise and fall of the voice in speaking. 講話音調的抑揚變化。 **~al** /-ʃənl ; -ʃənḷ/ *adj* of ~: 字形變化的;字尾變化的;音調變化的: *~al endings/forms,* eg *-ed.* 變化字形的字尾(形式)(例如 -ed)。

in·flex·ible /ɪnˈfleksəbl ; ɪnˈflɛksəbḷ/ *adj* that cannot be bent or turned; (fig) rigid; unbending; not to be turned aside: 不能彎曲的;(喻)不可改變的;不屈的;堅定的: *~ courage;* 不屈不撓的勇氣; *an ~ will.* 堅定的意志。 **in·flex·ibly** /-əblɪ ; -əblɪ/ *adv* **in·flexi·bil·ity** /ɪnˌfleksəˈbɪlətɪ ; ɪnˌflɛksəˈbɪlətɪ/ *n* [U].

in·flexion /ɪnˈflekʃn ; ɪnˈflɛkʃən/ *n* = inflection.

in·flict /ɪnˈflɪkt ; ɪnˈflɪkt/ *vt* [VP6A, 14] **~ *sth (on/upon),*** give (a blow, etc); cause to suffer; impose: 予以(打擊等);使受痛苦;强加之於: *~ a blow/a severe wound upon sb.* 予某人以打擊(嚴重傷害)。 *The judge ~ed the death penalty upon the murderer.* 法官處該殺人犯以死刑。 *I'm sorry to have to ~ myself/my company upon you,* force my company upon you. 我很抱歉不得不打攪你。 **in·flic·tion** /ɪnˈflɪkʃn ; ɪnˈflɪkʃən/ *n* [U] ~ing or being ~ed: 打擊;傷害;强加;施加痛苦;受苦: *the unnecessary ~ion of pain and suffering;* 不必要的施予痛苦; [C] sth ~ed; painful or troublesome experience. 所受的痛苦或處罰;痛苦的經驗。

in·flor·escence /ˌɪnflɔːˈresns ; ˌɪnfloˈrɛsṇs/ *n* [U] arrangement of a plant's flowers on the stem; collective flower of a plant; (lit or fig) flowering. 花序;花(一植物上花的總稱);(字面或喻)開花。 ⇨ the illus at flower. 參看 flower 之插圖。

in·flow /ˈɪnfləʊ ; ˈɪnˌflo/ *n* [U] flowing in; [C, U] that which flows in: 流入;流入物: *an ~ of capital/investment;* 資本(投資)的流入; *an ~ of 25 litres an hour;* 每小時流入 25 公升; (attrib) (形容用法) *an ~ pipe.* 流入管道。

in·flu·ence /ˈɪnfluəns ; ˈɪnfluəns/ *n* **~ *on/upon,*** **1** [U] power to affect sb's character, beliefs or actions through example, fear, admiration, etc; [C] person, fact, etc that exercises such power; [U] the exercise of such power: 影響力;感化力;有影響力的人,事實等;影響;感化: *Many a woman has had a civilizing ~ upon her husband.* 許多婦女對其丈夫有感化力。 *He's an ~ for good in the town.* 他在本市具有使人向善的影響力。 *Heredity and environment are ~s on character.* 遺傳和環境是影響性格的因素。 *He was under the ~ of alcohol,* had had too much to drink. 他喝醉了。 **2** [U] action of natural forces: 自然力的作用: *the ~ of the moon (on the tides);* 月亮(對於潮汐)的影響; *the ~ of climate (on vegetation).* 氣候(對於植物)的影響。 **3** [U] power due to wealth, position, etc: 勢力;權力: *Will you please use your ~ with the manager on my behalf?* 請你對經理運用你的權力,幫忙我好嗎? *Will you use your ~ to get me a job?* 你願意運用你的影響力替我找一份工作嗎? □ *vt* [VP6A] exert an ~ on; have an effect on: 影響;對…有作用: *Can the planets ~ human character, as astrologers claim?* 行星能像占星家所宣稱那樣對人的性格有所影響嗎? *Don't be ~d by bad examples.* 勿受壞榜樣的影響。

in·flu·en·tial /ˌɪnfluˈenʃl ; ˌɪnfluˈɛnʃəl/ *adj* having influence: 有影響力的;有勢力的: *~ politicians;* 有影響力的政界人士; *considerations which are ~ in reaching a decision.* 對於作決定有影響的因素。 **~ly** /-ʃəlɪ ; -ʃəlɪ/ *adv*

in·flu·enza /ˌɪnfluˈenzə ; ˌɪnfluˈɛnzə/ *n* [U] (colloq abbr 俗語略作 **flu**) infectious disease with fever, muscular pain and catarrh. 流行性感冒。

in·flux /ˈɪnflʌks ; ˈɪnˌflʌks/ *n* [U] flowing in; [C] (*pl* ~es) constant inflow of large numbers or quantities: 流入;注入;巨大數目或量的經常流入: *repeated ~es of visitors;* 訪客的川流不息; *an ~ of wealth.* 財富的湧入。

in·form /ɪnˈfɔːm ; ɪnˈfɔrm/ *vt, vi* **1** [VP6A, 11, 14, 21] **~ *sb (of sth)/(that...),*** give knowledge to: 通知;報告;告訴: *We were ~ed that two prisoners had escaped.* 我們聽說有兩個囚犯逃跑了。 *Keep me ~ed of fresh developments.* 隨時告訴我新的發展。 *He's a well-~ed man.* 他是個消息靈通的人。 *Have you ~ed them of your intended departure?* 你通知了他們你想離去嗎? **2** [VP3A] **~ *against/on sb,*** (legal) bring evidence or an accusation against him (to the police). (法律)(向警方)告發某人。 **~·ant** /-ənt ; -ənt/ *n* person who gives information; (ling) native speaker of a language who helps a foreign scholar who is making an analysis of it. 提供消息的人;通知者;(語言學)(協助外國學者分析研究本國語之)講說本國語者。 **~er** *n* person who ~s(2), esp against a criminal or fugitive. 告發者(特指告發罪犯或逃犯)。

in·for·mal /ɪnˈfɔːml ; ɪnˈfɔrmḷ/ *adj* not formal (1, 2); irregular; without ceremony or formality: 非正式的;非正規的;不規則的;不拘禮儀的: *an ~ visit;* 非正式的訪問; *~ dress;* 便服; *~ conversations between the statesmen of two countries,* no official records being kept. 兩國政治家之間非正式的談話(不列入官方紀錄者)。 **~ly** /-məlɪ ; -mḷɪ/ *adv* **~·ity** /ˌɪnfɔːˈmælətɪ ; ˌɪnfɔrˈmælətɪ/ *n* [U] being ~; [C] (*pl* -ties) ~ act, etc. 不正式;不拘禮儀;非正式的行動等。

in·for·ma·tion /ˌɪnfəˈmeɪʃn ; ˌɪnfəˈmeʃən/ *n* [U] **~ *on/about,*** **1** informing or being informed. 通知;報告;接到通知。 **2** sth told; news or knowledge given: 消息;情報;知識: *That's a useful piece/bit of ~.* 那是一項重要的情報(知識)。 *Can you give me any ~ on/about this matter?* 關於此事你能供給我任何消息嗎? *The ˈ~ bureau may be able to help you.* 新聞局可能對你有所幫助。

in·forma·tive /ɪnˈfɔːmətɪv ; ɪnˈfɔrmətɪv/ *adj* giving information; instructive: 供給消息的;給予知識的: *~ books;* 增益知識的書; *an ~ talk.* 有助益的談話。 **~·ly** *adv*

in·fra /ˈɪnfrə ; ˈɪnfrə/ *adv* (Lat, formal) below; farther or later on (in a book, etc): (拉,正式用語)在下;(書中等)以下: *See ~, p 21,* See p 21 farther on in this book. 參看以下第 21 頁。 **ˌ~ ˈdig** /dɪg ; dɪg/ *pred adj* beneath one's dignity. 有失身份的。 □ *pref* **ˌ~-ˈred** *adj* of those invisible rays below the red in the spectrum. 紅外線的。 **ˈ~·structure** *n* the parts of a system that compose the whole; (esp) permanent military installations forming a basis for defence. 形成整體的一個系統之各部分;(尤指)永久性軍事防衛設施。 ⇨ supra.

in·frac·tion /ɪnˈfrækʃn ; ɪnˈfrækʃən/ *n* [U] breaking of a rule, law, etc; [C] instance of this. 犯規;違法。

in·fre·quent /ɪnˈfriːkwənt ; ɪnˈfrikwənt/ *adj* not frequent; rare. 罕見的;少有的。 **~·ly** *adv* **in·fre·quency** /-kwənsɪ ; -kwənsɪ/ *n* [U].

in·fringe /ɪnˈfrɪndʒ ; ɪnˈfrɪndʒ/ *vt, vi* **1** [VP6A] break (a rule, etc); transgress; violate: 違背(規章等);觸犯;侵犯: *~ a rule/an oath/copyright/a patent.* 違犯規章(違背誓言;侵犯版權;侵害專利權)。 **2** [VP3A] **~ *upon,*** encroach: 侵佔;侵害: *Be careful not to ~ upon the rights of other people.* 當心不要侵害別人的權利。 **~·ment** *n* [U] infringing; [C] ***~ment of,*** instance of this, eg the unlawful use of a trade name or of copyright material. 違背;侵犯;侵佔;(如冒用商標或侵害版權)。

in·furi·ate /ɪnˈfjʊərɪeɪt ; ɪnˈfjʊrɪˌet/ *vt* [VP6A] fill with fury or rage: 使狂怒;激怒: *infuriating delays.* 令人非常憤怒的耽擱。

in·fuse /ɪnˈfjuːz ; ɪnˈfjuz/ *vt, vi* (formal) (正式用語) **1** [VP14] **~ *into/with,*** put, pour (a quality, etc *into*); fill (sb *with*): 灌輸(性質等);向(某人)灌輸: *~ fresh courage/new life into soldiers;* 給士兵們灌輸新勇氣(新生命); *~ soldiers with fresh courage.*

灌輸士兵們以新勇氣。**2** [VP6A] pour (hot) liquid on (leaves, herbs, etc) to flavour it or to extract its constituents: 沏或泡(葉子、草藥等,使液體加味或提出其成分): ~ *herbs.* 浸泡草藥。**3** [VP2A] undergo infusion: 經過泡製: *Let the herbs ~ for three minutes.* 將草藥泡三分鐘。

in·fu·sion /ɪn'fjuːʒn; ɪn'fjuʒən/ *n* **1** [U] infusing or being infused. 灌輸;泡製。**2** [C] liquid made by infusing. 泡浸製成的液體;浸劑;泡劑。**3** [U] pouring in; mixing: 注入;混合: *the ~ of new blood into old stock,* the use of new breeds to improve old breeds. 注入新血以改良舊種。

in·gath·er·ing /'ɪngæðərɪŋ; 'ɪn,gæðrɪŋ/ *n* [C] (formal) gathering in; harvest. (正式用語)採集;收穫。

in·geni·ous /ɪn'dʒiːnɪəs; ɪn'dʒinjəs/ *adj* **1** (of a person) clever and skilful (at making or inventing); showing skill, etc: (指人)有發明天才的;機敏的;靈巧的: *an ~ mind.* 靈巧的心智。**2** (of things) skilfully made: (指物)製作精巧的: *an ~ toy/tool.* 精巧的玩具(工具)。**~·ly** *adv* **in·gen·uity** /,ɪndʒɪ'njuːətɪ *US:* -'nuː-; ,ɪndʒə'nuətɪ/ *n* [U] cleverness and skill; originality in design. 靈巧;機敏;設計之創新;創造力。

in·gé·nue /'ænʒeɪnjuː *US:* 'ændʒənuː; æ̃ʒe'ny/ *n* (F) (formal) simple, innocent girl, esp as a type in dramas; actress playing such a part. (法)(正式用語)天眞無邪的女郎(尤指戲劇中此種角色);扮演此種角色之女演員。

in·genu·ous /ɪn'dʒenjʊəs; ɪn'dʒenjuəs/ *adj* (formal) frank; open; innocent; natural: (正式用語)坦白的;直率的;天眞的;自然的: *an ~ smile.* 坦率的微笑。**~·ly** *adv* **~·ness** *n*

in·gest /ɪn'dʒest; ɪn'dʒɛst/ *vt* [VP6A] (formal) (lit or fig) take in (food, etc) by, or as if by, swallowing. (正式用語)(字面或喩)吞嚥(食物等);吸收。

ingle-nook /'ɪŋgl nʊk; 'ɪŋgl̩,nuk/ *n* chimney-corner (in a wide old-fashioned fireplace) where the fire burns on an open hearth. (舊式廣濶的壁爐之)爐邊;爐隅;爐角。

in·glori·ous /ɪn'glɔːrɪəs; ɪn'glorɪəs/ *adj* **1** shameful; ignominious. 可恥的;不名譽的。**2** obscure. 默默無聞的。**~·ly** *adv*

in·go·ing /'ɪngəʊɪŋ; 'ɪn,goɪŋ/ *adj* going in: 進來的: *the ~* (= new) *tenant of a house/flat.* 一所房屋(公寓)的新來房客。

in·got /'ɪŋgət; 'ɪŋgət/ *n* [C] (usu brick-shaped) lump of metal (esp gold and silver), cast in a mould. (尤指金、銀之)鑄塊(通常爲磚形);錠。

in·graft /ɪn'grɑːft *US:* -'græft; ɪn'græft/ *v* = engraft.

in·grained /,ɪn'greɪnd; ɪn'grend/ *adj* **1** (of habits, tendencies, etc) deeply fixed; thorough: (指習慣、傾向等)深染的;根深蒂固的;徹底的: ~ *prejudices/honesty.* 根深蒂固的偏見(絕對的誠實)。**2** going deep: 變深的: ~ *dirt.* 深陷的泥土。

in·grati·ate /ɪn'greɪʃɪeɪt; ɪn'greʃɪ,et/ *vt* [VP14] ~ ***oneself with sb,*** bring oneself into favour, esp in order to gain an advantage: 討好;逢迎(某人)(尤指以利益爲目的者): *with an ingratiating smile.* 帶着討好的微笑。**in·grati·at·ing·ly** *adv*

in·grati·tude /ɪn'grætɪtjuːd *US:* -tuːd; ɪn'grætə,tjud/ *n* [U] want of gratitude. 忘恩負義。

in·gredi·ent /ɪn'griːdɪənt; ɪn'gridɪənt/ *n* [C] one of the parts of a mixture: (混合物的)成分: *the ~s of a cake;* 糕餅的各種成分; *the ~s of a man's character,* all those qualities, etc that together form it. 形成一個人的性格的種種因素。

in·gress /'ɪngres; 'ɪngrɛs/ *n* [U] (formal) going in; (right of) entrance: (正式用語)進入;進入權;入場權: *a means of ~.* 進入的方法。⇨ egress.

in·grow·ing /'ɪngrəʊɪŋ; 'ɪn,groɪŋ/ *adj* growing inwards: 向內生的: *an ~ toe-nail,* one growing into the flesh. (向肉裡生長的)嵌趾甲。

in·habit /ɪn'hæbɪt; ɪn'hæbɪt/ *vt* [VP6A] live in; occupy. 居住於。**in·hab·it·able** /-əbl; -əbl̩/ *adj* that can be lived in. 可居住的。**in·hab·it·ant** /-ənt; -ənt/ *n* person living in a place. 居住者;居民。

in·hale /ɪn'heɪl; ɪn'hel/ *vt, vi* [VP6A, 2A] draw into the lungs: 吸入肺部: ~ *air/gas/tobacco smoke.* 吸入空氣(氣體,煙草之煙氣)。*I~! Exhale!* Breathe in! Breathe out! 吸入!呼出!**in·haler** *n* device for producing a chemical vapour to make breathing easier. 產生化學氣體以協助呼吸困難者之裝置;吸入器。

in·har·moni·ous /,ɪnhɑː'məʊnɪəs; ,ɪnhɑr'monɪəs/ *adj* not harmonious. 不和諧的;不協調的。

in·herent /ɪn'hɪərənt; ɪn'hɪrənt/ *adj* ~ ***(in),*** existing as a natural and permanent part or quality of: 固有的;生來的;天生的: *Weight is an ~ quality of matter.* 重量是物質固有的特性。*He has an ~ love of beauty.* 他天生愛美。*The power ~ in the office of President must not be abused.* 總統一職所具有的權力不得濫用。

in·herit /ɪn'herɪt; ɪn'hɛrɪt/ *vt, vi* [VP6A, 2A] **1** receive property, a title, etc as heir: 繼承(財產,爵位等): *The eldest son will ~ the title.* 長子將繼承爵位。**2** derive (qualities, etc) from ancestors: 由遺傳而得(特質等): *She ~ed her mother's good looks and her father's bad temper.* 她繼承了母親的美貌和父親的壞脾氣。**in·herit·ance** /-əns; -əns/ *n* [U] ~ing: 繼承;遺傳: *receive sth by ~ance;* 由繼承而獲得; [C] (lit, fig) what is ~ed: (字面,喩)繼承或遺傳之物;遺產;天稟: *an ~ance of ill-feeling.* 遺留下來的怨恨。

in·hibit /ɪn'hɪbɪt; ɪn'hɪbɪt/ *vt* [VP6A, 14] ~ ***sb (from sth/doing sth),*** hinder, restrain: 阻止;禁止;抑制: ~ *wrong desires and impulses;* 抑制不正當的慾望和衝動; *an ~ed person,* one who is unable or unwilling to express his feelings. 無能力或不願表示情感的人;抑制感情者。**in·hi·bi·tion** /,ɪnɪ'bɪʃn; ,ɪnɪ'bɪʃən/ *n* [U] (psych) restraint on, habitual shrinking from, an action for which there is an impulse or desire; [C] instance of this: (心理)抑制;抑制的實例: *Wine weakens a person's ~ions.* 酒能減弱人的抑制力。**in·hibi·tory** /ɪn'hɪbɪtrɪ *US:* -tɔːrɪ; ɪn'hɪbə,torɪ/ *adj* tending to ~; of an inhibition. 有抑制傾向的;抑制的。

in·hos·pi·table /,ɪnhɒ'spɪtəbl; ɪn'hɑspɪtəbl̩/ *adj* not hospitable; (of a place, coast, etc) not affording shelter: 待客不親切的;冷淡的;(指地點,海岸等)無遮蔽處的;荒涼的: *an ~ coast.* 荒涼的海岸。

in·hu·man /ɪn'hjuːmən; ɪn'hjumən/ *adj* cruel; unfeeling: 殘忍的;無情的: ~ *treatment.* 虐待。**~·ity** /,ɪnhjuː'mænətɪ; ,ɪnhju'mænətɪ/ *n* [U] ~ conduct or behaviour: 殘忍;殘忍的行爲: *man's ~ity to man;* 人類的自相殘殺; [C] (*pl* -ties) ~ act. 殘忍的舉動。

in·hu·mane /,ɪnhjuː'meɪn; ,ɪnhju'men/ *adj* not humane; cruel; without pity. 不人道的;殘忍的;無憐憫心的。**~·ly** *adv*

in·imi·cal /ɪ'nɪmɪkl; ɪn'ɪmɪkl̩/ *adj* ~ ***(to),*** (formal) unfriendly or harmful: (正式用語)不友善的;有害的: *actions ~ to friendly relations between countries.* 對兩國友善關係有害的行動。

in·imi·table /ɪ'nɪmɪtəbl; ɪn'ɪmətəbl̩/ *adj* (formal) too good, clever, etc to be imitated. (正式用語)(太好,太聰明等而)無法模仿的。**in·imi·tably** /-əblɪ; -əblɪ/ *adv*

in·iqui·tous /ɪ'nɪkwɪtəs; ɪ'nɪkwətəs/ *adj* (formal) very wicked or unjust: (正式用語)極邪惡的;極不公正的: *an ~ system/regime.* 極邪惡的體系(政權)。**~·ly** *adv* **in·iquity** /ɪ'nɪkwətɪ; ɪ'nɪkwətɪ/ *n* [U] being ~; [C] (*pl* -ties) ~ act. 極邪惡;極不公正;極邪惡或極不公正的行爲。

in·itial /ɪ'nɪʃl; ɪ'nɪʃəl/ *adj* of or at the beginning: 開始的;起初的: *the ~ letter of a word;* 一字起首的字母; *the ~ stages of an undertaking.* 一事業最初的階段。□ *n* ~ letter, esp (*pl*) first letters of a person's names, as *GBS* (for *George Bernard Shaw*). 起首的字母;(尤指)(複)姓名起首的各字母(例如GBS 代表 George Bernard Shaw)。□ *vt* (-ll-, US also -l-) [VP6A] mark, sign, with one's ~s: 標注或簽自己姓名的起首各字母於: ~ *a note or document.*

在一短簡或文件上簽上自己姓名的起首各字母。**~ly** /-ʃə-lɪ; -ʃəlɪ/ *adv* at the beginning. 在起初;在開始。

in·iti·ate /ɪˈnɪʃɪeɪt; ɪˈnɪʃɪˌet/ *vt* **1** [VP6A] set (a scheme, etc) working: 開始;着手(一計畫等): *~ a plan.* 推動一計畫。**2** [VP14] *~ sb into sth,* admit or introduce sb to membership of (a group, etc). 准許或介紹某人參加(某一團體等)。**3** [VP14] *~ sb into sth,* give sb elementary instruction, or secret knowledge of: 傳授(某人)入門知識或祕密知識: *~ students into the mysteries of interstellar communication.* 將星際通訊的奧祕教給學生。□ *n, adj* /ɪˈnɪʃɪət; ɪˈnɪʃɪɪt/ (person) who has been ~d (2,3): 被准許或介紹加入的(人); 被傳授知識的(人): *an ~ member of a secret society.* 一祕密會社的新社員。**in·iti·ation** /ɪˌnɪʃɪˈeɪʃn; ɪˌnɪʃɪˈeʃən/ *n* [U] initiating or being ~d; being made acquainted with the rules of a society, etc: 開始;着手;加入會社;傳授知識;熟悉一會社等的規章: (attrib) (形容用法) *initiation ceremonies.* 入會儀式。

in·iti·at·ive /ɪˈnɪʃətɪv; ɪˈnɪʃɪˌetɪv/ *n* **1** [U, C] first or introductory step or move: 初步的階段或行動: *peace ~s.* 和平的初步。***act / do sth on one's own ~,*** without an order or suggestion from others. 主動地作某事。***have the ~,*** be in the position to make the first move, eg in war. 處於主動的地位(例如在戰爭中)。***take the ~ (in doing sth),*** make the first move towards it. 採取(作某事之)初步行動。**2** [U] capacity to see what needs to be done and enterprise enough to do it: 創始力;進取心: *A statesman must have / show / display ~.* 政治家必須有(表示,表現)開創精神。**3** [C] power or right of citizens outside the legislature to put forward proposals for legislation (as in Switzerland). 創制權(如瑞士所實行者)。

in·ject /ɪnˈdʒekt; ɪnˈdʒɛkt/ *vt* [VP6A, 14] ***~ sth (into sb / sth); ~ sb / sth (with sth),*** drive or force a liquid, drug, etc into sth with, or as with, a syringe; fill (sth with a liquid, etc) by ~ing: 注射(液劑、藥物等);(以液劑等)注入: *~ penicillin into the blood-stream;* 將盤尼西林注射入血液; *~ sb's arm with morphia;* 給某人的臂注射嗎啡; (fig, colloq) (喻,俗) *His appointment may ~ some new life into the committee.* 他的任命可能給這委員會注入新生命。**in·jec·tion** /ɪnˈdʒekʃn; ɪnˈdʒɛkʃən/ *n* [U] ~ing; [C] instance of this: 注射;注入: *five ~ions of glucose;* 注射了五針葡萄糖; *an ~ion in the left buttock;* 在左臀注射的一針; [C] liquid, etc that is ~ed. 注射劑;針藥。ˈ**fuel injection,** method by which liquid fuel is converted to vapour and sprayed into the cylinders of an internal combustion engine. 燃料注射(將液體燃料變爲氣體並噴入一內燃引擎的汽缸之方法)。

in·ju·di·cious /ˌɪndʒuːˈdɪʃəs; ˌɪndʒuˈdɪʃəs/ *adj* (formal) not well-judged: (正式用語)欠考慮的;不智的: *~ remarks.* 不智的言詞。**~·ly** *adv*

in·junc·tion /ɪnˈdʒʌŋkʃn; ɪnˈdʒʌŋkʃən/ *n* [C] authoritative order, esp a written order from a law court, demanding that sth shall or shall not be done (called an *interdict* in Scotland). 必須服從的命令; (尤指法院發布之書面)强制令; 禁止令(在蘇格蘭稱爲 interdict)。

in·jure /ˈɪndʒə(r); ˈɪndʒɚ/ *vt* [VP6A] hurt; damage. 傷害;損害。**in·jured** *adj* wounded; hurt; wronged; offended: 受傷的;被傷害的;受寃屈的;感情受傷害的: *~d looks;* 受寃屈的樣子;感情受到傷害的樣子; *in an ~d voice;* 以不高興的聲音; *the dead and the ~d,* those people killed and hurt (in an accident, etc). (意外事件等中)死者及傷者。

in·juri·ous /ɪnˈdʒʊərɪəs; ɪnˈdʒʊrɪəs/ *adj ~ (to),* (formal) causing, likely to cause, injury; hurtful: (正式用語)引起傷害的;可能引起傷害的;有害的: *behaviour that is ~ to social order;* 妨害社會治安的行爲; *habits that are ~ to health.* 有害健康的習慣。

in·jury /ˈɪndʒərɪ; ˈɪndʒərɪ/ *n* (*pl* -ries) **1** [U] harm; damage; wrongful treatment: 傷害;損害;不公平的待遇: *If you knock a man down with your car, and then call him a fool, you are adding insult to ~.* 如果你開汽車撞倒一人,然後說他是個傻瓜,你是在傷害以外又加上了侮辱。***do sb an ~,*** cause sb harm. 傷害某人。**2** [C] place (in the body) that is hurt or wounded; act that hurts; insult: (身體的)受傷之處;傷害的行動;侮辱: *The cyclist suffered severe injuries.* 那騎脚踏車的人受了嚴重的傷。*This attack was a severe ~ to his reputation.* 這項攻擊對他的名譽是嚴重的傷害。

in·jus·tice /ɪnˈdʒʌstɪs; ɪnˈdʒʌstɪs/ *n* [U] lack of justice; [C] unjust act, etc. 不公正;不講道義;不公正的行動等。***do sb an ~,*** judge him unfairly. 寃枉某人。

ink /ɪŋk; ɪŋk/ *n* [U] (kinds of) coloured liquid used for writing and printing; black liquid ejected by cuttlefish, etc: 墨水;墨汁;油墨;(烏賊等噴出的)墨汁: *written in ink;* 用墨水寫的;鋼筆寫的; *a pen and ink drawing.* 鋼筆畫。ˈ**ink-bottle / -pot** *nn* for holding ink. 墨水瓶。ˈ**ink-pad** *n* pad for ink used on rubber stamps. 印墨;打印臺。ˈ**ink·stand** *n* stand for one or more ink-bottles, with grooves or a tray for pens, etc. 墨水瓶架(旁有凹槽或盤可置筆)。ˈ**ink-well** *n* ink-pot that fits into a hole in a desk. 墨水池(鑲於桌上凹洞中之墨水瓶)。□ *vt* [VP6A, 15B] ***~ (in),*** mark with ink: 塗以墨汁;塗以油墨: *ink one's fingers;* 以墨水染污手指; *ink in a drawing,* mark with ink lines previously drawn in pencil. (將鉛筆畫的線條)用墨水描過。**inky** *adj* (-ier, -iest) marked with ink: 塗有墨水的;塗有油墨的: *inky fingers;* 染有墨水(或油墨)的手指; black like ink: 墨黑的;深黑的: *inky darkness.* 漆黑。

ink·ling /ˈɪŋklɪŋ; ˈɪŋklɪŋ/ *n* [C] ***give sb / have / get an / some / no ~ (of sth),*** give sb / have / get a hint, slight understanding of it. (使某人)對(某事)略有(一無)所知。

in·laid /ˌɪnˈleɪd; ɪnˈled/ *pt, pp* of inlay.

in·land /ˈɪnlənd; ˈɪnlənd/ *adj* **1** situated in the interior of a country, far from the sea or border: 內陸的;內地的: *~ towns;* 內陸城市; *the I~ Sea of Japan,* area of sea almost enclosed by large islands. 日本瀨戶內海。**2** carried on, obtained, within the limits of a country: 國內的: *~ (= domestic) trade.* 國內貿易。**the ˌI~ ˈRevenue,** (GB) money obtained by taxation within the country (excluding taxes on imported goods); (colloq) department responsible for collecting these taxes. (英國)國內稅收(輸入貨物之稅除外);(俗)負責徵收國內稅款之部門。□ *adv* /ɪnˈlænd; ˈɪnˌlænd/ in or towards the interior. 在內陸地;向內陸地。

in-laws /ˈɪn lɔːz; ˈɪnˌlɔz/ *n pl* (colloq) relatives by marriage: (俗)姻親: *All my ~ will be visiting us this summer.* 我所有的姻親今年夏天都要來探望我們。

in·lay /ˌɪnˈleɪ; ɪnˈle/ *vt* (*pt, pp* inlaid /-leɪd; -led/) [VP6A, 14] ***~ (in / into / with),*** set pieces of (designs in) wood, metal, etc in the surface of another kind of wood, metal, etc so that the resulting surface is smooth and even: 鑲;嵌: *gold inlaid into ivory;* 嵌入象牙的黃金; *ivory inlaid with gold.* 嵌金的象牙。□ *n* /ˈɪnleɪ; ˈɪnˌle/ **1** [U] inlaid work; materials used for this; [C] design, pattern, made by ~ing. 鑲嵌細工;鑲嵌所用材料;鑲嵌圖案。**2** [C, U] (dentistry) (method of making a) solid filling of gold, plastic, etc for a cavity in a tooth. (牙科)(用以鑲填牙洞之金質、塑膠等)鑲體;此種鑲填牙齒之方法。

in·let /ˈɪnlet; ˈɪnˌlɛt/ *n* **1** strip of water extending into the land from a larger body of water (the sea, a lake), or between islands. 灣;(海、湖之)汊。**2** sth let in or inserted, eg a piece of material inserted into a garment. 插入物;鑲入物(例如鑲入衣服中的一塊衣料)。**3** (attrib) way in: (形容用法)進入的通路: *~ and outlet channels,* eg in a reservoir. 入水和出水的通道(例如水庫中者)。

in loco par·en·tis /ɪn ˌləʊkəʊ pəˈrentɪs; ɪnˈlokopəˈrɛntɪs/ (Lat) in the place or position of a parent:

(拉)代替父或母；以父或母之地位：*I stood towards him* ~. 我以父母的立場對待他。

in·mate /ˈɪnmeɪt ; ˈɪnmet/ *n* one of a number of persons living together, esp in a hospital, prison or other institution. 許多同居人中之一(尤指醫院，監獄或其他機構中者)。

in mem·oriam /ˌɪn məˈmɔːrɪəm ; ˌɪnməˈmorɪˌæm/ (Lat) (used in epitaphs, on gravestones) in memory of; as a memorial to. (拉)(用於墓誌銘中或墓碑上)紀念；悼念。

in·most /ˈɪnməʊst ; ˈɪnˌmost/ *adj* most inward; farthest from the surface; (fig) most private or secret: 最內部的；最內裏的；(喻)最祕密的；祕藏心中的：*my* ~ *feelings.* 祕藏我心底的感情。

inn /ɪn ; ɪn/ *n* **1** public house where lodgings, drink and meals may be had, usu (today) in the country. 酒館兼供宿，酒及餐食者；兼營旅館之酒館(目前通常在鄉間)。⇨ hotel. **ˈinn-keeper** *n* person who keeps an inn. 此種旅館主人。 **2** **ˌInn of ˈCourt,** (building of) one of four law societies in London having the exclusive right of admitting persons to the bar. (倫敦之)四律師學校之一(獨享檢定律師之權。名爲 law societies, 實爲學校)；四律師學校之校址。⇨ bar¹(12).

in·nards /ˈɪnədz ; ˈɪnɚdz/ *n pl* (colloq) (俗) **1** stomach and bowels; entrails. 胃腸；內臟。 **2** any inner parts. 內部；內在部份。

in·nate /ɪˈneɪt ; ɪˈnet/ *adj* (of a quality, etc) in one's nature; possessed from birth: (指性質等)天生的；與生俱來的；先天的：~ *aggression.* 天生的好攻擊。**~·ly** *adv*

in·ner /ˈɪnə(r) ; ˈɪnɚ/ *adj* (of the) inside: 在內的；內部的：*an* ~ *room.* 內室。**ˌ~ ˈcity,** the oldest parts of a city, at or near its centre: 內城；舊市區：~ *city decay.* 內城的衰敗。**ˈ~ tube,** circular tube, filled with air, in a pneumatic tyre. (輪胎之)內胎。***the* ~ *man,*** **(a)** sb's soul or mind (contrasted with *body*). 靈魂；心(與 body 相對)。**(b)** (joc) the stomach: (謔)肚子：*satisfy the* ~ *man.* 填飽肚子。**~·most** /-məʊst ; -ˌmost/ *adj* = inmost.

in·ning /ˈɪnɪŋ ; ˈɪnɪŋ/ *n* **1** (baseball) division of a game in which each team bats. (棒球)一局。 **2** **~s,** (with *sing v*) (cricket) time during which a player or team is batting: (用單數動詞)(板球)一局：*Our team made 307 runs in its first* ~*s.* 我們球隊在第一局獲307分。*The first batsman had a short* ~*s.* 第一位擊球員的一局甚短。(fig) period of power, eg of a political party, or of opportunity to show one's ability, period of active life: (喻)(例如一政黨之)當權時期；表現能力的機會；活躍時期：*have a good* ~*s,* (colloq) have a long and happy life. (俗)長壽而且幸福。

in·no·cent /ˈɪnəsnt ; ˈɪnəsn̩t/ *adj* **1** ~ ***(of),*** not guilty: 清白的；無罪的；無辜的：~ *of the charge/accusation.* 無罪(無所控的罪行)。 **2** harmless: 無害的：~ *amusements.* 無害的娛樂。 **3** knowing nothing of evil or wrong: 天眞無邪的：*as* ~ *as a new-born babe.* 如新生嬰兒一般的天眞無邪。 **4** foolishly simple: 無知的；頭腦簡單的：*Don't be so* ~ *as to believe everything the politicians say.* 不要太天眞，竟至相信政客們說的每一句話。□ *n* ~ person, esp a young child. 無罪的人；天眞無邪的人(尤指小孩)。**~·ly** *adv* **in·no·cence** /-sns ; -sn̩s/ *n* [C] quality or state of being ~. 清白；無罪；無害；天眞無邪；無知。

in·nocu·ous /ɪˈnɒkjʊəs ; ɪˈnɑkjʊəs/ *adj* causing no harm: 無害的：~ *snakes/drugs.* 無害的蛇(良性的藥物)。

in·no·vate /ˈɪnəveɪt ; ˈɪnəˌvet/ *vi* [VP2A] make changes; introduce new things. 改革；革新；創新。**in·no·va·tor** /-tə(r) ; -tɚ/ *n* person who ~s. 改革者；革新者；創新者。**in·no·va·tion** /ˌɪnəˈveɪʃn ; ˌɪnəˈveʃən/ *n* [U] innovating; [C] instance of this; sth new that is introduced: 改革；革新；創新；革新之處：*technical innovations in industry.* 工業技術上的創新。

in·nu·endo /ˌɪnjuːˈendəʊ ; ˌɪnjʊˈɛndo/ *n* (*pl* ~es /-dəʊz ; -doz/) indirect reference (usu sth unfavourable to a person's reputation): 間接涉及；影射(通常指間接的誹謗)：*If you throw out such* ~*es against the Minister, you'll be sued for libel.* 如果你這樣間接誹謗部長，你將被控誹謗罪。

in·numer·able /ɪˈnjuːmərəbl *US:* ɪˈnuː- ; ɪˈnjumərəbl̩/ *adj* too many to be counted. 數不清的；無數的。

in·ocu·late /ɪˈnɒkjʊleɪt ; ɪnˈɑkjəˌlet/ *vt* [VP6A, 14] ~ ***sb (with sth) (against sth),*** inject a serum or vaccine into him to give him a mild form of the disease to safeguard him against it: 接種；注射血清或疫苗於(人或動物使其預防該疾病)：~ *sb against cholera;* 給某人注射以預防霍亂；(fig) fill the mind with opinions, etc: (喻)向…灌輸(思想等)：~*d with evil doctrines.* 被灌輸以邪惡的主義。**in·ocu·la·tion** /ɪˌnɒkjʊˈleɪʃn ; ɪnˌɑkjəˈleʃən/ *n* [U] inoculating or being ~d; [C] instance of this: 接種；注射疫苗而預防；灌輸；上述之實例：*have inoculations against cholera and yellow fever.* 接受預防霍亂和黃熱病的注射。⇨ vaccinate.

in·of·fen·sive /ˌɪnəˈfensɪv ; ˌɪnəˈfɛnsɪv/ *adj* not giving offence; not objectionable: 無礙的；不令人討厭的：*an* ~ *remark/person.* 不令人討厭的言語(人)。

in·op·er·able /ˌɪnˈɒpərəbl ; ɪnˈɑpərəbl̩/ *adj* (of tumours, etc) that cannot be cured by a surgical operation. (指瘤等)無法以手術治癒的。

in·op·er·at·ive /ˌɪnˈɒpərətɪv ; ɪnˈɑpəˌretɪv/ *adj* (of laws, rules, etc) not working or taking effect; invalid. (指法律，規章等)無效果的；不生效果的。

in·op·por·tune /ˌɪnˈɒpətjuːn *US:* -tuːn ; ˌɪnɑpɚˈtjun/ *adj* (esp of time) not appropriate: (尤指時間)不適當的；不合時宜的：*at an* ~ *moment.* 於不適當的時機。**~·ly** *adv*

in·or·di·nate /ɪˈnɔːdɪnət ; ɪnˈɔrdn̩ɪt/ *adj* (formal) not properly restrained or controlled; excessive: (正式用語)無節制的；過度的：~ *passions;* 奔放的熱情；*the* ~ *demands of the Tax Collector.* 收稅員過度的需索。**~·ly** *adv*

in·or·ganic /ˌɪnɔːˈgænɪk ; ˌɪnɔrˈgænɪk/ *adj* **1** not having an organized physical structure, esp as plants and animals have; not forming part of the substance of living bodies: 無機的(無動植物之有機體組織的)；不形成生物體質之一部的：~ *chemistry.* 無機化學。*Rocks and metals are* ~ *substances.* 岩石及金屬是無機物。 **2** not the result of natural growth: 非自然生長而形成的：*an* ~ *form of society.* 一種非由自然發展而形成的社會形式。**in·or·gani·cally** /-klɪ ; -klɪ/ *adv*

in·pa·tient /ˈɪnpeɪʃnt ; ˈɪnˌpeʃənt/ *n* person who lives in hospital while receiving treatment. 住院病人。⇨ out-patient.

in·pour·ing /ˈɪnpɔːrɪŋ ; ˈɪnˌporɪŋ/ *n, adj* (formal) pouring in: (正式用語)傾入；傾入的：*an* ~ *of spiritual comfort.* 大量的精神安慰。

in·put /ˈɪnpʊt ; ˈɪnˌpʊt/ *n* [U] ~ ***(to),*** what is put in or supplied, eg data for processing in a computer, power supplied to a machine. 置入或供應之物(例如供電子計算機處理的資料，供機器所用的動力)；輸入。

in·quest /ˈɪnkwest ; ˈɪnkwɛst/ *n* ~ ***(on),*** official inquiry to learn facts, esp concerning a death which may not be the result of natural causes. 偵訊；審訊(尤指調查非自然死亡者)；驗屍。

in·quie·tude /ɪnˈkwaɪətjuːd *US:* -tuːd ; ɪnˈkwaɪəˌtjud/ *n* [U] (formal) uneasiness of mind; anxiety. (正式用語)不安心；焦慮。

in·quire /ɪnˈkwaɪə(r) ; ɪnˈkwaɪr/ *vt, vi* **1** [VP6A, 8, 10, 14, 2A] ~ ***sth (of sb),*** ask to be told: 詢問：~ *a person's name;* 詢問某人的姓名；~ *what a person wants/where to stay/how to do sth/at the railway station;* 問某人需要什麼(問那裏可以住宿；問如何作某事；在火車站詢問)；~ *of sb the reason for sth.* 問某人某事的原因。 **2** [VP3A] ~ ***about/concerning/upon,*** ask for information about:

查問;查明: ~ *about trains to London.* 查詢去倫敦的火車。*I~ within upon everything,* eg as the title of a small encyclopaedia. 本書解答一切疑難(例如一小型百科全書的標題)。**~ after,** ask about (sb's health, welfare). 問候。**~ for,** ask for (goods in a shop), ask to see (sb): 查詢(商店中之貨物);求見(某人): ~ *for a book in a shop;* 在一店中查詢一書; ~ *for the manager.* 求見經理。**~ into,** try to learn the facts about; investigate: 查究;調查: *We must ~ into the matter.* 我們必須調查此事。**in·quirer** *n* person who ~s. 詢問者;調查者。**in·quir·ing** *adj* in the habit of asking for information: 愛詢問的;喜探究的: *an inquiring mind;* 喜愛探究的精神; showing a desire to learn: 顯示好奇的: *inquiring looks.* 好奇的神情。**in·quir·ing·ly** *adv*

in·quiry /ɪn'kwaɪərɪ *US:* 'ɪnkwərɪ ; ɪn'kwaɪrɪ/ *n* (*pl* -ries) **1** [U] asking; inquiring: 詢問;探問: *learn sth by ~.* 詢問得知某事。**on ~,** when one has asked. 有人詢問時。**court of ~,** (mil) one to investigate charges brought against sb. (軍)調查庭。**2** [C] question; investigation: 質詢;調查: *make inquiries about sb or sth;* 調查某人或某事物; *hold an official ~ into sth.* 正式調查某事物。

in·qui·si·tion /ˌɪnkwɪ'zɪʃn ; ˌɪnkwə'zɪʃən/ *n* **1** [U] thorough search or investigation; [C] instance of this, esp a judicial or official inquiry. 徹底調查;(尤指法院或官方的)調查或審訊。**2 the I~,** (also called 亦稱作 *the Holy Office*) court appointed by the Church of Rome to suppress heresy (esp active in 15th and 16th cc) and to compile the Index(2). (尤指十五及十六世紀之)天主教宗教法庭(以鎮壓邪說並編撰天主教禁書目錄)。

in·quisi·tive /ɪn'kwɪzətɪv ; ɪn'kwɪzətɪv/ *adj* fond of, showing a fondness for, inquiring into other people's affairs. 喜歡打聽別人的事情的;好管閒事的; **~·ly** *adv* **~·ness** *n*

in·quisi·tor /ɪn'kwɪzɪtə(r) ; ɪn'kwɪzətɚ/ *n* investigator, esp an officer of the Inquisition(2); person appointed by law to make an inquiry. 調查者;(尤指)天主教宗教法庭調查官;司法機關任命之調查者或審訊者。**in·quisi·tor·ial** /ɪnˌkwɪzɪ'tɔ:rɪəl ; ɪnˌkwɪzə'torɪəl/ *adj* of or like an ~. 天主教宗教法庭調查官的;審訊者的;似調查官的。

in·road /'ɪnrəʊd ; 'ɪnˌrod/ *n* sudden attack (into a country, etc), esp one made for the purpose of plunder. 襲擊;突襲(與 into 連用,後接地區等,尤指目的爲劫掠者)。***make ~s on/upon,*** encroach: 侵佔: *make ~s upon one's leisure time/one's savings.* 侵佔一人的空閒時間(積蓄)。

in·rush /'ɪnrʌʃ ; 'ɪnˌrʌʃ/ *n* rushing in: 湧入;闖入: *an ~ of water/tourists.* 水(遊客)之湧入。

in·sane /ɪn'seɪn ; ɪn'sen/ *adj* mad; senseless: 瘋狂的;愚蠢的: *an ~ person;* 瘋子; *an ~ asylum,* place where ~ people are cared for, now called a mental hospital or home. 瘋人院(現在通常稱作精神病院)。**~·ly** *adv* **in·san·ity** /ɪn'sænətɪ ; ɪn'sænətɪ/ *n* [U] madness. 瘋狂;癲狂。

in·sani·tary /ɪn'sænɪtrɪ *US:* -terɪ ; ɪn'sænəˌtɛrɪ/ *adj* not sanitary: 不衞生的: *living under ~ conditions.* 生活在不衞生的環境中。

in·sa·tiable /ɪn'seɪʃəbl ; ɪn'seʃɪəbḷ/ *adj* **~ *(of/for),*** (formal) that cannot be satisfied; very greedy: (正式用語)不能滿足的;極貪心的: ~ *appetites;* 無饜的食慾; *politicians who are ~ of power.* 貪權的政客。**in·sa·tiably** /-ʃəblɪ ; -ʃəblɪ/ *adv*

in·sa·tiate /ɪn'seɪʃɪət ; ɪn'seʃɪɪt/ *adj* (formal) never satisfied. (正式用語)永不滿足的。

in·scribe /ɪn'skraɪb ; ɪn'skraɪb/ *vt* [VP6A, 15A] ~ ***(on/in/with),*** write (words, one's name, etc in or on); mark (sth with words, etc): 題寫(文字,姓名等);(以文字等)銘刻(某物): ~ *names on a war memorial/one's name in a book;* 銘刻姓名於陣亡將士紀念碑上(題記姓名於書中); ~ *a tomb with a name.* 銘刻姓名於墓碑上。**~d stock,** (comm) stock of which the names of the holders are recorded in lists or registers. (商)記名股票。**in·scrip·tion** /ɪn'skrɪpʃn ; ɪn'skrɪpʃən/ *n* [C] sth ~d, esp words cut on a stone, eg a monument, or stamped on a coin or medal. 題名;題字;刻勒文字;銘文(尤指刻於紀念碑石上,或壓印於硬幣或獎章等上者)。⇨ the illus at epitaph. 參看 epitaph 之挿圖。

in·scru·table /ɪn'skru:təbl ; ɪn'skrutəbḷ/ *adj* that cannot be understood or known; mysterious: 不可了解的;神祕的: *the ~ ways of Providence;* 難解之天道; *the ~ face of the Sphinx.* 獅身人面怪的神秘的面部。

in·sect /'ɪnsekt ; 'ɪnsɛkt/ *n* sort of small animal, eg ant, fly, wasp, having six legs and no backbone and a body divided into three parts (head, thorax, abdomen); (incorrect but pop usage) similar tiny, crawling creature, eg spider. 昆蟲(例如螞蟻,蒼蠅,黃蜂等);(不正確但普遍的用法)小蟲(例如蜘蛛)。**'~-powder** *n* powder for killing or driving away ~s. 殺蟲粉;驅蟲粉。**in·sec·ti·cide** /ɪn'sektɪsaɪd ; ɪn'sɛktəˌsaɪd/ *n* preparation used for killing ~s, eg DDT. 殺蟲劑 (例如 DDT)。**in·sec·tivor·ous** /ˌɪnsek'tɪvərəs ; ˌɪnsɛk'tɪvərəs/ *adj* eating ~s as food: 以昆蟲爲食的: *Swallows are ~ivorous.* 燕子以蟲爲食。

in·se·cure /ˌɪnsɪ'kjʊə(r) ; ˌɪnsɪ'kjʊr/ *adj* **1** not safe; not providing good support; not to be relied on: 不安全的;不堅固的;不可靠的: *have an ~ hold on sth,* eg when rock-climbing. 未抓牢某物(例如攀登岩壁時)。**2** feeling unsafe; without protection; lacking confidence. 感覺不安全的;沒有保護的;缺乏自信心的。**~·ly** *adv* **in·se·cur·ity** /ˌɪnsɪ'kjʊərətɪ ; ˌɪnsɪ'kjʊrətɪ/ *n* [U]: *suffer from feelings of insecurity.* 因爲沒有安全感而覺得痛苦。

in·semi·nate /ɪn'semɪneɪt ; ɪn'sɛməˌnet/ *vt* [VP6A] sow seed into; introduce semen into. 播種於;栽植;使受胎;授精於。**in·semi·na·tion** /ɪnˌsemɪ'neɪʃn ; ɪnˌsɛmə'neʃən/ *n* [U] inseminating. 播種;使受胎;授精。**ˌartificial inˌsemi'nation,** the introduction of semen taken, eg from a pedigree animal, into the generative organs of a female animal so that offspring may be produced without sexual union. 人工授精。

in·sen·sate /ɪn'senseɪt ; ɪn'sɛnset/ *adj* (formal) (正式用語) **1** without the power to feel or experience: 無感覺力的;無知覺的: ~ *rocks.* 頑石。**2** unfeeling; without sensibility; foolish: 無情的;遲鈍的;愚蠢的: ~ *rage/cruelty.* 無理的憤怒(殘忍)。

in·sen·si·bil·ity /ɪnˌsensə'bɪlətɪ ; ˌɪnsɛnsə'bɪlətɪ/ *n* [U] (formal) lack of mental feeling or emotion; state of being unable to know, recognize, understand or appreciate: (正式用語)無感情;無知覺;不了解;不會欣賞: ~ *to pain/beauty/art;* 對痛苦無感覺(不會欣賞美;不會欣賞藝術); *in a state of ~,* unconscious. 無知覺;失去知覺。

in·sen·sible /ɪn'sensəbl ; ɪn'sɛnsəbḷ/ *adj* **1** unconscious as the result of injury, illness, etc: (因受傷,生病等)昏迷的;不省人事的: *The rock struck her on the head and she was ~ for nearly an hour.* 石塊打在她頭上,使她昏迷了將近一小時。**2** ~ ***(of),*** unaware (of): 不知道的: *He seemed to be ~ of his danger.* 他似乎不知道他的危險。*I'm not ~ how much I owe to your help.* 我並非不知道你曾予我甚多幫助。**3** ~ ***(to),*** without feeling: 無感覺的: *When your hands are frozen they become ~,* numb. 當你的手凍僵時,它們就麻木了。**4** unsympathetic; emotionless; callous. 無同情心的;無感情的;硬心腸的。**5** (of changes) too small or gradual to be perceived: (指變化)太小或太慢而難以覺察的: *by ~ degrees.* 極緩慢地。**in·sen·sibly** /-əblɪ ; -əblɪ/ *adv*

in·sen·si·tive /ɪn'sensətɪv ; ɪn'sɛnsətɪv/ *adj* ~ ***(to),*** not sensitive (to touch, light, the feelings of other people). (對接觸,光,他人的感情等)感覺遲鈍的。**~·ly** *adv* **in·sen·si·tiv·ity** /ɪnˌsensə'tɪvətɪ ; ˌɪnsɛnsə'tɪvətɪ/ *n* [U].

in·sen·tient /ɪn'senʃnt ; ɪn'sɛnʃɪənt/ *adj* (formal)

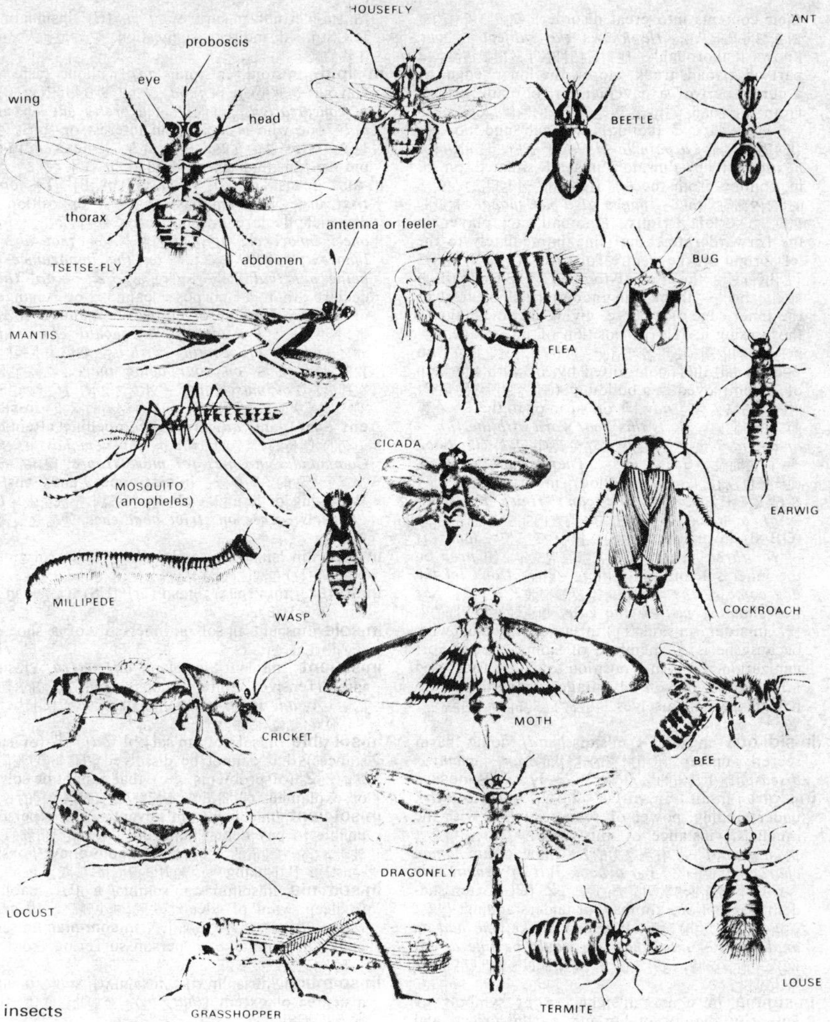

insects

inanimate; without feeling or awareness. (正式用語)無生命的;無感覺的;無知覺的。

in·sep·ar·able /ɪn'seprəbl ; ɪn'sɛpərəbl/ *adj* ~ *(from),* that cannot be separated: 不能分離的: ~ *friends.* 不能分開的朋友。

in·sert /ɪn'sɜːt ; ɪn'sɝt/ *vt* [VP6A, 15A] put, fit, place (sth *in, into, between,* etc): 插入;嵌進(某物,後接 in, into, between 等): ~ *a key in a lock/an advertisement in a newspaper/a new paragraph in an essay.* 插鑰匙於鎖中(將廣告插刊於報紙;將一新段落加入一文章中)。□ *n* /'ɪnsɜːt ; 'ɪnsɝt/ sth ~ed, eg in a book. 插入部份;插入之物 (例如在一書中)。 **in·ser·tion** /ɪn'sɜːʃn ; ɪn'sɝʃən/ *n* [U] ~ing or being ~ed; [C] sth ~ed, eg an announcement or advertisement in a newspaper, a piece of lace, etc ~ed in a dress. 插入;被插入;被插入之物(例如報紙上的啓事或廣告;衣裙上的花邊等)。

in·ser·vice /'ɪn sɜːvɪs ; 'ɪn'sɝvɪs/ *attrib adj* while in service (contrasted with *pre*-service training, etc): 在職中的(與 pre-service training 相對): *the* ~ *training of teachers.* 教師的在職訓練。Cf 參較 *refresher course.*

in·set /'ɪnset ; 'ɪn,sɛt/ *n* [C] extra page(s) inserted in a book, etc; small map, diagram, etc within the border of a printed page or of a larger map; piece of material, eg lace, let into a dress. (書等中的)插頁;(一頁印刷品或大地圖中嵌入的)小地圖,圖解,插圖等;(衣裙上的)鑲料(如花邊)。□ *vt* /,ɪn'set ; ɪn'sɛt/ (*pt, pp* inset) put in; insert. 嵌入;插入。

in·shore /,ɪn'ʃɔː(r) ; 'ɪn,ʃor/ *adj, adv* close to the shore: 近海岸的(地): *an* ~ *current;* 近海流; ~ *fisheries.* 近海漁場。

in·side /ɪn'saɪd ; 'ɪn'saɪd/ *n* **1** inner side or surface; part(s) within: 內側;內面;內部: *the* ~ *of a box;* 盒的內部; *a door bolted on the* ~. 自裏面閂住的門。~ /'ɪnsaɪd ; 'ɪn'saɪd/ ***out,*** with the inner side out: 內部翻到外面地;翻轉地: *He put his socks on* ~ *out.* 他的襪子穿反了。*The wind blew her umbrella* ~ *out.* 風把她的傘吹反過來了。*The burglars turned everything* ~ *out,* put drawers, boxes, etc and their contents into great disorder. 竊賊將所有的東西都翻得亂七八糟。*He knows the subject ~ out*, knows it thoroughly. 他對這個科目了解得很透徹。**2** part of a road, track, etc on the inner edge of a curve; part of a pavement or footpath farthest from the road. 道路、跑道等轉彎處的內側;人行道或步行小徑的內側。 **3** (colloq) stomach and bowels: (俗)內臟;腸胃: *a pain in his ~*. 肚子痛。□ *adj* (or *n* used attrib) /ˈɪnsaɪd ; ˈɪnˈsaɪd/ situated on or in, coming from the ~: (或名詞的形容用法)在內部的;自內部的: *the ~ pages of a newspaper*. 報紙的裏頁。 ˌ**~ ˈleft/ˈright,** (football, etc) player in the forward (attacking) line immediately to the left/right of the centre-forward. (足球等)左內鋒(右內鋒)。⇨ the illus at football. 參看 football 之插圖。**the ˈ~ track,** (in racing) track nearest to the inner edge of a curve, giving an advantage to those using it; (fig) a position of advantage. (賽跑)跑道的內圈 (使用者可佔便宜);(喻) 有利之地位。**an ˈ~ job,** (sl) theft committed by, or with the help of, sb employed in a building. (俚)內賊所作的竊案;有內應的竊案。□ *adv* **1** on or in or to the ~: 在裏面;在內部;向裡面: *Is this coat worn with the fur ~ or outside?* 這件上衣的毛皮穿在裏面還是外面? *Look ~*. 向裏面看。*Go ~*. 進去。*There's nothing ~*. 裏面什麼也沒有。**~ of,** (colloq) in less than: (俗)在(某數額)以內;不到: *We can't finish the work ~ of a week*. 我們無法在一週之內完成這工作。 **2** (GB sl) in prison: (英俚)在獄中;受監禁: *Jones is ~ for three years*. 瓊斯入獄服刑三年。□ *prep* on the inner side of: 在…之內;在…裏面: *Don't let the dog come ~ the house*. 不要讓狗進入房子裏。 *She was standing just ~ the gate*. 她正好站在大門的內側。**in·sider** /ɪnˈsaɪdə(r) ; ɪnˈsaɪdɚ/ *n* person who, because he is a member of some society, organization, etc is in a position to obtain facts and information, or win advantages, that others cannot get for themselves. 內部的人;局內人;熟悉內幕者。⇨ outsider.

in·sidi·ous /ɪnˈsɪdɪəs ; ɪnˈsɪdɪəs/ *adj* doing harm secretly, unseen: 暗中爲害的;隱伏的: *an ~ enemy/disease*. 暗中爲害的敵人(暗疾)。**~·ly** *adv* **~·ness** *n*

in·sight /ˈɪnsaɪt ; ˈɪnˌsaɪt/ *n* **1** [U] **~ *(into sth)*,** understanding; power of seeing into sth with the mind; [C] instance of this: 瞭解;洞察力;此種之實例: *a man of ~;* 有洞察力的人; *show ~ into human character;* 能洞察人性; *a book full of remarkable ~s*. 一本充滿不尋常洞察力的書。 **2** [C] (often sudden) perception, glimpse, or understanding: 覺察;領悟;瞭解;(常指)頓悟: *When he spoke, she had an unpleasant ~ into what life would be like as his wife*. 他說話時,她突然領悟到嫁給他以後的生活將多麼令人不快。

in·sig·nia /ɪnˈsɪgnɪə ; ɪnˈsɪgnɪə/ *n pl* symbols of authority, dignity, or honour, eg the crown and sceptre of a king; (mil) identifying badge of a regiment, etc. 權威,尊嚴或榮譽的象徵或標幟(例如國王的王冠及權杖);(軍)(代表一團等的)徽章;領章;肩章;臂章。

in·sig·nifi·cant /ˌɪnsɪgˈnɪfɪkənt ; ˌɪnsɪgˈnɪfəkənt/ *adj* having little or no value, use, meaning or importance: 無價值的;無用的;無意義的;不重要的: *~ talk;* 無意義的談話; *an ~-looking little man*. 一個看起來無足輕重的矮小的人。**~·ly** *adv* **in·sig·nifi·cance** /-əns ; -əns/ *n* [U].

in·sin·cere /ˌɪnsɪnˈsɪə(r) ; ˌɪnsɪnˈsɪr/ *adj* not sincere. 不眞誠的;不誠懇的。**~·ly** *adv* **in·sin·cer·ity** /ˌɪnsɪnˈserətɪ ; ˌɪnsɪnˈsɛrətɪ/ *n* [U].

in·sinu·ate /ɪnˈsɪnjʊeɪt ; ɪnˈsɪnjʊˌet/ *vt* **1** [VP6A, 14] **~ *sth/oneself (into)*,** make a way for (oneself/sth) gently and craftily: 使(某事物或自己)巧妙地進入;巴結: *~ oneself into a person's favour*. 巴結某人;向某人紆曲求寵。 ⇨ worm. **2** [VP9] **~ *(to sb) that*,** suggest unpleasantly and indirectly: (向某人)暗示(不愉快之事);暗諷: *~ (to sb) that a man is a liar*. (向某人)暗示某人說謊。**in·sinu·ation** /ɪnˌsɪnjʊˈeɪʃn ; ɪnˌsɪnjʊˈeʃən/ *n* [U] insinuating; [C] sth ~d; indirect suggestion. 巧妙地進入;令人不快的暗示;暗諷。

in·sipid /ɪnˈsɪpɪd ; ɪnˈsɪpɪd/ *adj* without taste or flavour: 無味道的: *~ food;* 無味道的食物; (fig) (喻) *~ conversation;* 乏味的言談; *a pretty but ~ young lady*, one who is lacking in interest or spirit. 一貌美但枯燥乏味的女郎。**~·ly** *adv* **~·ness** *n* **in·si·pid·ity** /ˌɪnsɪˈpɪdətɪ ; ˌɪnsɪˈpɪdətɪ/ *n* [U].

in·sist /ɪnˈsɪst ; ɪnˈsɪst/ *vi, vt* [VP3A, B] **1 ~ *on/that,*** urge with emphasis, against opposition or disbelief; declare emphatically: 堅持;强調: *~ on one's innocence;* 力言某人的無辜; *~ that one is innocent;* 堅稱某人無辜; *~ on the importance of being punctual*. 强調守時的重要。 **2 ~ *on/that,*** declare that a purpose cannot be changed; urge in a forcible or emphatic manner: 堅決主張;堅決要求: *I ~ed that he should come with us/~ed on his coming with us*. 我堅決主張他與我們同行。*I ~ on your being there*. 我堅持要你在那裏。*'You must come'—'All right, if you ~.'* '你一定要來啊' — '好吧,如果你堅持的話。' **in·sist·ent** /-ənt ; -ənt/ *adj* urgent; compelling attention: 迫切的;堅持的;緊急的: *the ~ent demands of the Commander-in-Chief for more troops*. 總司令對增加軍隊所做的迫切要求。**in·sist·ence** /-əns ; -əns/ *n* [U] ~ing or being ~ed: 堅持;强調;堅決主張: *the officer's ~ence on strict obedience*. 軍官之强調絕對服從。

in situ /ˌɪn ˈsɪtjuː ; ɪnˈsaɪtju/ (Lat) in its (original) place. (拉)在其位置;在原處。

in·so·far /ˌɪnsəˈfɑː(r) ; ˌɪnsoˈfɑr/ (US) (美) = in so far. ⇨ in²(18).

in·sole /ˈɪnsəʊl ; ˈɪnˌsol/ *n* inner sole of a shoe. 鞋子的內底;鞋墊。

in·so·lent /ˈɪnsələnt ; ˈɪnsələnt/ *adj* **~ *(to)*,** insulting; offensive; contemptuous. 侮辱的;無禮的;傲慢的。**~·ly** *adv* **in·so·lence** /-əns ; -əns/ *n* [U] being ~. 侮辱;無禮;傲慢。

in·sol·uble /ɪnˈsɒljʊbl ; ɪnˈsɑljəbl/ *adj* **1** (of substances) that cannot be dissolved. (指物質)不能溶解的。 **2** (of problems, etc) that cannot be solved or explained. (指問題等)不能解決的;難以解釋的。

in·sol·vent /ɪnˈsɒlvənt ; ɪnˈsɑlvənt/ *n, adj* (person) unable to pay debts; bankrupt. 無力償付債務的人;破產者;無力還債的;破產的。**in·sol·vency** /-ənsɪ ; -ənsɪ/ *n* [U] being ~. 無力償還債務;破產。

in·som·nia /ɪnˈsɒmnɪə ; ɪnˈsɑmnɪə/ *n* [U] inability to sleep; want of sleep: 失眠;缺少睡眠: *ill after weeks of ~*. 經數週失眠而生病。**in·som·niac** /ɪnˈsɒmnɪæk ; ɪnˈsɑmnɪæk/ *n* person suffering from ~. 失眠者;患失眠症者。

in·so·much /ˌɪnsəʊˈmʌtʃ ; ˌɪnsəˈmʌtʃ/ *adv* to such a degree or extent (*that/as*). 至如此程度(與 that 或 as 連用)。

in·souci·ance /ɪnˈsuːsɪəns ; ɪnˈsusɪəns/ *n* [U] freedom from care; state of being unconcerned. 無憂無慮; 無牽掛; 漠不關心; 漫不經心。 **in·souci·ant** /-ənt ; -ənt/ *adj*

in·span /ɪnˈspæn ; ɪnˈspæn/ *vt* (S African) (-nn-) yoke or harness (oxen, etc) to a vehicle. (南非) 套(牛等)於車。

in·spect /ɪnˈspekt ; ɪnˈspɛkt/ *vt* [VP6A] examine carefully; visit officially to see that rules are obeyed, that work is done properly, etc. 檢查;視察。**in·spec·tion** /ɪnˈspekʃn ; ɪnˈspɛkʃən/ *n* **1** [U] ~ing or being ~ed: 檢查;視察: *On ~ion the notes proved to be forgeries*. 經過檢查,那些鈔票證明是僞造的。 **2** [C] instance of this: 檢查或視察的實例: *carry out ten ~ions a week*. 每週視察十次。

in·spec·tor /ɪnˈspektə(r) ; ɪnˈspɛktɚ/ *n* **1** official who inspects, eg schools, factories, mines: (檢查學校、工廠、礦場等的)檢查員;督察;督學;視察者;檢閱官: ˌ*I~ of ˈTaxes*, official who examines returns of income and assesses the tax to be paid. 稅務審核

員；稅務稽察員（審查所得稅申報表及估定稅額者）。 **2** (GB) police officer who is, in rank, below a superintendent and above a sergeant. (英)(警察)巡官。 **~·ate** /ɪn'spektərət ; ɪn'spɛktərɪt/ *n* body of ~s: 檢查(視察)人員之團體: *the Ministry of Education ~ate.* 教育部督學團。

in·spi·ra·tion /ˌɪnspə'reɪʃn ; ˌɪnspə'reʃən/ *n* **1** [U] influence(s) arousing creative activity in literature, music, art, etc: 靈感: *Many poets and artists have drawn their ~ from nature.* 許多詩人和藝術家從大自然獲得他們的靈感。 **2** [C] **~ (to/for),** person or thing that inspires: 激勵或鼓勵的人或物: *His wife was a constant ~ to him.* 他的妻子經常鼓勵他。 **3** [C] (colloq) good thought or idea that comes to the mind: (俗)妙想;好主意: *have a sudden ~.* 忽得一妙計。 **4** [U] divine guidance held to have been given to those who wrote the Bible. 神靈之啓示(上帝給予撰寫聖經者的啓示)。

in·spire /ɪn'spaɪə(r) ; ɪn'spaɪr/ *vt* [VP6A, 14, 17] **~ *sth (in sb)*; ~ *sb (with sth/to do sth)*,** **1** put uplifting thoughts, feelings or aims into: 激勵;鼓勵: *~ sb with hope/enthusiasm/confidence;* 激起某人的希望(熱情,信心); *~ confidence in sb.* 激起某人的信心。*What ~d him to give such a brilliant performance?* 什麼鼓勵了他因而作出如此精采的表演? **2** fill with creative power: 使充滿創造力;予以靈感: *~d poets/artists;* 具有靈感的詩人(藝術家); *in an ~d moment.* 在有靈感的時刻。**3** (*pp*) **~d,** (of sth written or spoken) one secretly suggested by an influential person who has special information. (指文章或談話)(由擁有特殊消息之有勢力人士)授意的。

in·sta·bil·ity /ˌɪnstə'bɪlətɪ ; ˌɪnstə'bɪlətɪ/ *n* [U] lack of stability (usu of character, moral qualities). (通常指性格或精神方面)不穩定;無常。

in·stall (US also **in·stal**) /ɪn'stɔːl ; ɪn'stɔl/ *vt* [VP6A, 14] **~ *sb/sth (in sth)*,** **1** place (sb) in a new position of authority with the usual ceremony: (以例行儀式)使(某人)就新職: *~ a priest.* 使一教士就職。 **2** place, fix (apparatus) in position for use: 裝設(器械): *~ a heating or lighting system.* 裝置暖氣或照明設備。**3** settle (sb/oneself) in a place: 安置(某人或自己)於某處: *be comfortably ~ed in a new home.* 舒適地安居於新家之內。*She ~ed herself in her father's favourite chair.* 她坐在她父親最心愛的椅子上。**in·stal·la·tion** /ˌɪnstə'leɪʃn ; ˌɪnstə'leʃən/ *n* [U] ~ing or being ~ed; [C] sth that is ~ed, esp apparatus: 使就職;就職;裝設;安置;裝置物(尤指器械): *a heating ~ation.* 暖氣裝置。

in·stal·ment (US also **in·stall·ment**) /ɪn'stɔːlmənt ; ɪn'stɔlmənt/ *n* [C] **1** any one of the parts in which sth is presented over a period of time: 一段時期中所供應之物的任一部分；一期；一批；一段: *a story that will appear in ~s*, eg in a periodical. 將分段連載的故事(例如在定期刊物中)。 **2** any one of the parts of a payment spread over a period of time: 分期付款: *We're paying for the television by monthly ~s.* 我們按月分期付款以償付電視機價款。 **'~ plan,** (chiefly US) this method of paying for goods (also called, chiefly GB, 英亦稱作 *hire purchase*). (主美)分期付款購物法。

in·stance /'ɪnstəns ; 'ɪnstəns/ *n* [C] **1** example; fact, etc supporting a general truth: 例;實例: *This is only one ~ out of many.* 這不過是許多例子中的一個。***for ~,*** by way of example. 例如。***in the first ~,*** firstly. 首先;第一。 **2** ***at the ~ of,*** at the request of. 應…之請求。□ *vt* [VP6A] give as an example. 引以爲例。

in·stant[1] /'ɪnstənt ; 'ɪnstənt/ *adj* **1** coming or happening at once: 即刻的;立刻的: *feel ~ relief after taking a dose of medicine.* 服用一劑藥後立即感覺病況減輕。 *The novel was an ~ success.* 這本小說立即獲得成功。**2** urgent: 緊急的: *in ~ need of help.* 急需幫助。**3** (abbr 略作 **inst**) (comm; dated style) of the present month: (商;過時文體)本月的: *in reply to your letter of the 9th inst.* 爲答覆本月九日的貴函。 **4** (of food preparations) that can be made ready for use quickly and easily: (指食品)可迅速備好供食用的;速食的;即溶的: *~ coffee,* prepared by adding boiling water or milk to a powder. 即溶咖啡(加沸水或牛乳於咖啡粉就可以飲用)。 **~·ly** *adv* at once. 立即;即刻。□ *conj* as soon as. 一…就。

in·stant[2] /'ɪnstənt ; 'ɪnstənt/ *n* **1** precise point of time: 即時;即刻: *Come here this ~!* at once! 即刻到這裡來！*He left that ~/on the ~,* immediately. 他立即離開了。*I sent you the news the ~ (that) I heard it,* as soon as I heard it. 我一聽到這消息，便立刻通知你了。**2** moment: 瞬間;刹那;時刻: *I shall be back in an ~.* 我馬上就回來。*Help arrived not an ~ too soon.* 幫助及時來到了(來得恰是時候)。

in·stan·taneous /ˌɪnstən'teɪnɪəs ; ˌɪnstən'tenɪəs/ *adj* happening, done, in an instant: 即時的;瞬間的: *Death was ~*, eg in an accident. 瞬間就死了(例如在意外事件中)。**~·ly** *adv*

in·stead /ɪn'sted ; ɪn'stɛd/ *adv* as an alternative or substitute: 代替;更換: *If Harry is not well enough to go with you, take me ~.* 如果哈利不舒服不能跟你去,那就帶我去好了。*The water here is not good, so I'm drinking beer ~.* 此地的水不好,所以我改喝啤酒。**~ of,** *prep phrase* in place of; as an alternative to or substitute for (followed by a *n, pron, gerund,* or *prep phr*): 代替(後接名詞,代名詞,動名詞或介詞片語): *Shall we have fish ~ of meat today?* 我們今天不吃肉改吃魚如何？ *I will go ~ of you.* 我代替你去。*He has been playing all afternoon ~ of getting on with his work.* 他整個下午一直在遊玩,而不繼續工作。*We'll have tea in the garden ~ of in the house.* 我們將在花園裡用茶,而不在室內用。

in·step /'ɪnstep ; 'ɪnˌstɛp/ *n* upper surface of the human foot between the toes and the ankle; part of a shoe, etc covering this. 足背;跗;鞋等之足背部份;鞋面。⇨ the illus at leg. 參看 leg 之挿圖。

in·sti·gate /'ɪnstɪgeɪt ; 'ɪnstəˌget/ *vt* [VP6A, 17] **~ *sth/sb to do sth*,** incite; goad (sb to do sth); cause (sth) by doing this: 鼓動;教唆(某人作某事);煽動(某事): *~ workers to down tools;* 鼓動工人罷工; *~ a strike.* 煽動罷工。**in·sti·ga·tor** /-tə(r) ; -tɚ/ *n* **in·sti·ga·tion** /ˌɪnstɪ'geɪʃn ; ˌɪnstə'geʃən/ *n* instigating or being ~d. 鼓動;被煽動。

in·stil (US = **in·still**) /ɪn'stɪl ; ɪn'stɪl/ *vt* (-ll-) [VP 6A, 14] **~ *sth into sb*,** introduce (ideas, etc) gradually. 逐漸灌輸(思想等)。**in·stil·la·tion** /ˌɪnstɪ'leɪʃn ; ˌɪnstɪ'leʃən/ *n*

in·stinct /'ɪnstɪŋkt ; 'ɪnstɪŋkt/ *n* **1** [U] natural tendency to behave in a certain way without reasoning or training: 本能: *Birds learn to fly by ~.* 鳥學飛係出於本能。 **2** [C] innate impulse or intuition; instance of ~(1): 本性的衝動;直覺;憑本能行事的實例: *He seems to have an ~ for always doing and saying the right thing.* 他好像有做事說話永不出錯的本能。□ *pred adj* /ˌɪn'stɪŋkt ; ɪn'stɪŋkt/ **~ *with*,** filled with, animated by: 充滿;受…的鼓舞: *a picture ~ with life;* 充滿生氣的一幅畫; *a poem ~ with passion.* 充滿熱情的一首詩。**in·stinc·tive** /ɪn'stɪŋktɪv ; ɪn'stɪŋktɪv/ *adj* based on ~, not coming from training or teaching: 憑本能的;天生的: *Animals have an ~ive dread of fire.* 動物天生怕火。**in·stinc·tive·ly** *adv*

in·sti·tute[1] /'ɪnstɪtjuːt *US:* -tuːt ; 'ɪnstəˌtjut/ *n* [C] society or organization for a special (usu a social or educational) purpose; its office(s) or building(s). (社會或教育等方面之)會,社,協會,學會;會館;會址;社址。

in·sti·tute[2] /'ɪnstɪtjuːt *US:* -tuːt ; 'ɪnstəˌtjut/ *vt* **1** [VP6A] establish, start, an inquiry, custom, rule, etc: 設立;制定(風俗,規則等);着手(調查等): *~ legal proceedings against sb;* 對某人提起訴訟; *~ an action at law;* 提起訴訟;採取法律行動; *~ restrictions on the use of pesticides.* 對殺蟲藥的使用予以限制。 **2** [VP6A, 14] **~ *sb (to)*,** appoint him (to an official position). 任命(某人充任一職)。

in·sti·tu·tion /ˌɪnstɪˈtjuːʃn *US:* -ˈtuːʃn ; ˌɪnstəˈtjuʃən/ *n* **1** [U] instituting or being instituted: 設立;制定;任命: *the ~ of customs/rules, etc;* 風俗(規則等)的創立: *~ as a bishop.* 任命爲主教。 **2** [C] long-established law, custom, or group (eg a club or society); familiar object or person. 由來已久的法律,風俗習慣或團體(如會、社、協會等);熟悉的人或物。 **3** (building of) organization for social welfare, eg an orphanage, a home for old people. 慈善機關;社會福利機構(例如孤兒院,養老院)。 **~al** /-ʃənl ; -ʃənl̩/ *adj* of or connected with an ~(3): 慈善機關的: *old people in need of ~al care.* 需要慈善機關照顧的老年人。 **~al·ize** /-ʃənəlaɪz ; -ʃənl̩ˌaɪz/ *vt* [VP6A] make into an ~(2). 使制度化;使成爲習俗。

in·struct /ɪnˈstrʌkt ; ɪnˈstrʌkt/ *vt* **1** [VP6A, 15A] teach a school subject, a skill: 教;教授: *~ a class in history;* 教授一班級歷史; *~ recruits/a class of apprentices.* 教授新兵(一班學徒)。 **2** [VP17, 20, 21] give orders or directions to: 命令;指導: *~ sb to start early;* 命令某人早動身; *~ sb how to do his work.* 指導某人如何工作。 **3** [VP11, 20, 21] inform: 通知: *I have been ~ed by my agent that you still owe me £50.* 我的代理人通知我,你尙欠我五十鎊。 **in·struc·tor** /-tə(r) ; -tɚ/ *n* person who ~s; trainer. 教師;教練。 **in·struc·tress** /-trɪs ; -trɪs/ *n* woman who ~s. 女教師;女教練。

in·struc·tion /ɪnˈstrʌkʃn ; ɪnˈstrʌkʃən/ *n* **1** [U] instructing or being instructed: 教授;教導;被教導: *~ in chemistry;* 教授化學; *give/receive ~.* 教授(受教)。 **2** (*pl*) directions; orders: (複)指令;命令: *give sb ~s to arrive early;* 命令某人早到達; *~s* (= coded commands) *to a computer.* 給予電子計算機之指示(代號指令)。 **~al** /-ʃənl ; -ʃənl̩/ *adj* educational: 教育的: *~al films,* eg of industrial processes. 教育影片(例如介紹工業過程者)。

in·struc·tive /ɪnˈstrʌktɪv ; ɪnˈstrʌktɪv/ *adj* giving or containing instruction: 教導的;教訓的: *~ books.* 教育性的書籍。 **~·ly** *adv*

in·stru·ment /ˈɪnstrʊmənt ; ˈɪnstrəmənt/ *n* [C] **1** implement, apparatus, used in performing an action, esp for delicate or scientific work: 器具;工具;器械;儀器(尤指精細工作或科學上所用者): *optical ~s,* eg a microscope; 光學儀器(例如顯微鏡); *surgical ~s,* eg a scalpel. 外科器械(例如解剖刀)。 Cf 參較 *tools* used by labourers and craftsmen. tools 指工人和工匠用的工具。 **2** apparatus for producing musical sounds, eg a piano, violin, flute or drum. 樂器(例如鋼琴,小提琴,笛或鼓)。⇨ the illus at brass, percussion, string. 參看 brass, percussion, string 各項之插圖。 **3** person used by another for his own purposes: 被人利用的人;傀儡: *be made the ~ of another's crime.* 被利用作他人犯罪的工具。 **4** formal (esp legal) document: 正式文件(尤指法律上的): *The King signed the ~ of abdication.* 國王簽署了退位的正式文件。 **in·stru·men·ta·tion** /ˌɪnstrʊmenˈteɪʃn ; ˌɪnstrəmɛnˈteʃən/ *n* [U] arrangement of music for ~s; the development and manufacture of ~s for scientific use. 器樂的譜曲;樂器法;樂器學;科學儀器之發展及製造。

in·stru·men·tal /ˌɪnstrʊˈmentl ; ˌɪnstrəˈmɛntl̩/ *adj* **1** serving as an instrument or means: 作爲工具或手段的;有幫助的: *be ~ in finding well-paid work for a friend.* 有助於一友人獲得待遇優厚的工作。 **2** of or for musical instruments: 樂器的;供樂器用的: *~ music.* 器樂。 **~·ist** /-təlɪst ; -tl̩ɪst/ *n* player of a musical instrument. 樂器演奏者;器樂家。 **~·ity** /ˌɪnstrʊmenˈtælətɪ ; ˌɪnstrəmɛnˈtælətɪ/ *n* [U] agency: 工具;媒介: *by the ~ity of,* by means of. 憑藉;以…爲工具或方法。

in·sub·or·di·nate /ˌɪnsəˈbɔːdɪnət ; ˌɪnsəˈbɔrdn̩ɪt/ *adj* disobedient; rebellious. 不服從的;犯上的。 **in·sub·or·di·na·tion** /ˌɪnsəˌbɔːdɪˈneɪʃn *US:* -dnˈeɪʃn ; ˌɪnsəˌbɔrdn̩ˈeʃən/ *n* [U] being ~; [C] instance of this. 不服從;犯上;此等之實例。

in·sub·stan·tial /ˌɪnsəbˈstænʃl ; ˌɪnsəbˈstænʃəl/ *adj* **1** not solid or real; lacking substance: 非實在的;無實體的: *an ~ vision.* 幻像。 **2** without good foundation: 無根據的: *an ~ accusation.* 無稽的指控。

in·suf·fer·able /ɪnˈsʌfrəbl ; ɪnˈsʌfrəbl̩/ *adj* overproud; unbearably conceited; unbearable: 過度驕傲的;非常自負的;令人難以忍受的: *~ insolence.* 令人難以忍受的侮慢。

in·suf·fi·cient /ˌɪnsəˈfɪʃnt ; ˌɪnsəˈfɪʃənt/ *adj* not sufficient: 不充足的;不够的: *~ evidence/grounds.* 證據(理由)不充分。 **~·ly** *adv* **in·suf·fi·ciency** /-ʃnsɪ ; -ʃənsɪ/ *n*

in·su·lar /ˈɪnsjʊlə(r) *US:* -sələr ; ˈɪnsəlɚ/ *adj* **1** of an island: 島嶼的: *an ~ climate.* 海島氣候。 **2** of or like islanders; (esp) narrow-minded: 島民的;似島民的;(尤指)心胸褊狹的: *~ habits and prejudices.* 褊狹的習慣與偏見。 **~·ism** /-ɪzəm ; -ɪzm̩/, **in·su·lar·ity** /ˌɪnsjʊˈlærətɪ *US:* -səˈl- ; ˌɪnsəˈlærətɪ/ *nn* [U] state of being ~ (esp 2). 島民心理;(尤指)心胸褊狹。

in·su·late /ˈɪnsjʊleɪt *US:* -səl- ; ˈɪnsəˌlet/ *vt* [VP6A, 14] *~ (from).* **1** cover or separate (sth) with nonconducting materials to prevent loss of heat, prevent passage of electricity, etc: 使絕熱;使絕緣: *~ a cooking-stove with asbestos;* 以石綿使一烹調用的爐灶絕熱; *ˈinsulating tape,* as used for covering joins in flex for electric current. 絕緣膠帶(如包於電線接頭處者)。 **2** separate (sb or sth) (from): 使(某人或某物)隔離: *children carefully ~d from harmful experiences;* 被人小心隔離,以免接觸有害經驗的孩子們; isolate. 使孤立。 **in·su·la·tor** /-tə(r) ; -tɚ/ *n* [C] substance, device, for insulating, esp a device of porcelain used for supporting bare electric wires and cables. 絕緣體;絕熱器;絕緣器(尤指架設裸電線用的瓷絕緣器)。 **in·su·la·tion** /ˌɪnsjʊˈleɪʃn *US:* -səˈl- ; ˌɪnsəˈleʃən/ *n* [U] insulating or being ~d; materials used for this. 絕熱;絕緣;隔離;絕緣材料。

in·su·lin /ˈɪnsjʊlɪn *US:* -səl- ; ˈɪnsəlɪn/ *n* [U] substance (a hormone) prepared from the pancreas of sheep, used in the medical treatment of sufferers from diabetes. 胰島素(一種荷爾蒙,由羊的胰臟提煉而得,用於治療糖尿病患者)。

in·sult /ɪnˈsʌlt ; ɪnˈsʌlt/ *vt* [VP6A] speak or act in a way that hurts or is intended to hurt a person's feelings or dignity. 侮辱;侮慢。□ *n* /ˈɪnsʌlt ; ˈɪnsʌlt/ [C, U] remark or action that ~s. 侮辱;侮辱的言行。 **~·ing** *adj* **~·ing·ly** *adv*

in·super·able /ɪnˈsjuːprəbl *US:* -ˈsuː- ; ɪnˈsupərəbl̩/ *adj* (of difficulties, etc) that cannot be overcome: (指困難等)不能克服的: *~ barriers.* 不能克服的障礙。

in·sup·port·able /ˌɪnsəˈpɔːtəbl ; ˌɪnsəˈportəbl̩/ *adj* unbearable; that cannot be endured. 不堪的;不能忍受的。

in·sur·ance /ɪnˈʃʊərəns ; ɪnˈʃurəns/ *n* **1** [U] (undertaking, by a company, society, or the State, to provide) safeguard against loss, provision against sickness, death, etc in return for regular payments. 保險;保險業。 **2** [U] payment made to or by such a company, etc: 保險費;保險金額: *When her husband died, she received £20000 ~.* 她丈夫去世後,她得到二萬鎊的保險金。 *He pays out £110 in ~/in ~ premiums every year.* 他每年付保險費一百一十鎊。 **ˈ~ policy** *n* contract made about ~. 保險單。 **3** [C] ~ policy: 保險單: *How many ~s have you?* 你保了多少種險? **4** any measure taken as a safeguard against loss, failure, etc: 保險;預防損失、失敗等之措施: *He's sitting an entrance exam at Leeds University as an ~ against failure at York.* 他正參加里玆大學的入學考試以備約克大學考不取。

in·sure /ɪnˈʃʊə(r); ɪnˈʃur/ *vt* [VP6A, 14] *~ (against),* make a contract that promises to pay, secures payment of, a sum of money in case of accident, damage, loss, injury, death, etc: 保險;投保: *~ one's house against fire;* 將自己房屋保火險; ~

oneself/one's life for £50000. 自己保壽險五萬鎊。*Insurance companies will ~ ships and their cargoes against loss at sea.* 保險公司會給船隻及其貨物作海上保險。**the ~d**, the person to whom payment will be made. 被保險人;保險戶。**the ~r**, the person or company undertaking to make payment in case of loss, etc. 承保人;保險公司。**the insurant** /ɪnˈʃʊərənt ; ɪnˈʃurənt/, (legal) the person who pays the premiums. (法律)付保險費者;被保險者;投保人。

in·sur·gent /ɪnˈsɜːdʒənt ; ɪnˈsɝdʒənt/ *adj* (rarely *pred*) rebellious; in revolt: (罕作敍述用法)叛亂的;暴動的: *~ troops.* 叛軍。□ *n* rebel soldier. 叛亂的士兵。

in·sur·mount·able /ˌɪnsəˈmaʊntəbl ; ˌɪnsɚˈmaʊntəbl/ *adj* (of obstacles, etc) that cannot be surmounted or overcome. (指障礙等)無法超越的;不能克服的。

in·sur·rec·tion /ˌɪnsəˈrekʃn ; ˌɪnsəˈrɛkʃən/ *n* [U] rising of people in open resistance to the government; [C] instance of this. 起義;叛亂;此種實例。

in·tact /ɪnˈtækt ; ɪnˈtækt/ *adj* untouched; undamaged; complete: 未觸動的;未損傷的;完整的: *He lived on the interest and kept his capital ~.* 他靠利息生活,本金不動。

in·taglio /ɪnˈtɑːlɪəʊ ; ɪnˈtæljo/ *n* (*pl* ~s /-z ; -z/) [U] (I) (process of) carving in depth; [C] (gem with) figure or design made by cutting into the surface of metal or stone. (義)凹刻;凹刻術;凹刻之花紋或刻有此種花紋之寶石。⇨ cameo.

in·take /ˈɪnteɪk ; ˈɪnˌtek/ *n* **1** [C] place where water, gas, etc is taken into a pipe, channel, etc. (水、氣體等流入管、溝等之)入口;進入口;進氣口。**2** [C, U] quantity, number, etc entering or taken in (during a given period): (一定時期內)引入之量: *an annual ~ of 100000 men,* eg for military service. 每年徵召十萬人(如徵兵)。 **3** (area of) land reclaimed from a moor, marsh or the sea. 開發荒野、塡充沼澤或海而成之地。

in·tan·gible /ɪnˈtændʒəbl ; ɪnˈtændʒəbl/ *adj* that cannot be touched or grasped; (esp) that cannot be grasped by the mind: 不可觸摸的;無形的;(尤指)捉摸不定的;難以明瞭的: *~ ideas;* 難以明瞭的觀念; *~ assets,* assets (of a business) which cannot be measured, eg a good reputation. (一商業機構之)無形資產(例如其良好商譽)。**in·tan·gi·bil·ity** /ɪnˌtændʒəˈbɪlətɪ ; ɪnˌtændʒəˈbɪlətɪ/ *n*

in·te·ger /ˈɪntɪdʒə(r) ; ˈɪntədʒɚ/ *n* whole number (contrasted with *fraction*): 整數(與 fraction 相對): *1, 3 and −3 are ~s, ¾ is not an ~.* 1, 3 及 −3 是整數, ¾ 不是整數。

in·te·gral /ˈɪntɪgrəl ; ˈɪntəgrəl/ *adj* **1** necessary for completeness: 構成整體所需要的: *The arms and legs are ~ parts of a human being.* 臂和腿是構成完整的人體所需要的。 **2** whole; having or containing all parts that are necessary for completeness. 完整的;整個的。**3** (maths) of, denoted by, an integer; made up of integers. (數學)整數的;由整數表示的;整數組成的;積分的。⇨ calculus. **~ly** /-grəlɪ ; -grəlɪ/ *adv*

in·te·grate /ˈɪntɪgreɪt ; ˈɪntəˌgret/ *vt, vi* [VP6A, 2A] **1** combine (parts) into a whole; complete (sth that is imperfect or incomplete) by adding parts: 連接(各部)使成一整體; 使完全; 使成完整之物;結合成一體: *an ~d personality,* person whose physical, mental and emotional components fit together well. 完整人格(身體、心理及情緒各方面配合良好的人)。**ˌ~d ˈcircuit** *n* very small circuit(4) made of a single chip of eg silicon. 積體電路。**2** bring or come into equality by the mixing of groups or races. 使打成一片;種族融合。**in·te·gra·tion** /ˌɪntɪˈgreɪʃn ; ˌɪntəˈgreʃən/ *n* [U] integrating or being ~d: 使完整;合而爲一;整合;融合: *the integration of black children into the school system in the Southern States of America.* 美國南部各州的(白人)學校之准許黑人子弟入學。

in·teg·rity /ɪnˈtegrətɪ ; ɪnˈtɛgrətɪ/ *n* [U] **1** quality of being honest and upright in character: 廉正;誠實: *a man of ~;* 正直的人; *commercial ~.* 商業上的誠實。**2** state or condition of being complete: 完整: *The old Roman walls may still be seen, but not in their ~.* 古代羅馬人築的城牆仍然可見,但已殘缺不全了。*Wasn't this Treaty supposed to guarantee our territorial ~?* 這一條約不是認爲可以保證我們領土的完整嗎?

in·tegu·ment /ɪnˈtegjʊmənt ; ɪnˈtɛgjəmənt/ *n* (formal) (usu natural) outer covering, eg skin, a husk, rind or shell. (正式用語)覆蓋物(通常爲天然者,例如皮膚,外皮,硬皮或外殼)。

in·tel·lect /ˈɪntəlekt ; ˈɪntḷˌɛkt/ *n* **1** [U] power of the mind to reason (contrasted with feeling and instinct): 理解力;推理力;悟力; 智力(與感情及本能相對): *I~ distinguishes man from the animals.* 智力使人異於禽獸。*He's a man of ~.* 他是有思辨力的人。 **2** (collective *sing,* or in *pl*) person(s) of good understanding, reasoning power, etc: (集合單數,或用複數)知識分子;有推理力者;智者: *the ~(s) of the age.* 當代的知識分子。

in·tel·lec·tual /ˌɪntəˈlektʃʊəl ; ˌɪntḷˈɛktʃʊəl/ *adj* **1** of the intellect: 智力的: *the ~ faculties.* 智能。**2** having or showing good reasoning power; interested in things of the mind (the arts, ideas for their own sake): 有理解力的; 有智力的; 顯示智力的; 對需要用智力之事(如藝術,思想等)有興趣的: *~ people;* 有智力的人; *~ interests/pursuits.* 需用智力的愛好(消遣)。□ *n* [C] ~ person: 有智力者;知識份子: *a play/book for the ~s.* 爲知識份子所寫的劇本(書)。**~ly** /-tʃʊəlɪ ; -tʃʊəlɪ/ *adv*

in·tel·li·gence /ɪnˈtelɪdʒəns ; ɪnˈtɛlədʒəns/ *n* [U] **1** the power of perceiving, learning, understanding and knowing; mental ability: 智力;才智: *a boy who shows little ~.* 智力不高的男孩。*The children were given an ~ test.* 那些孩子們接受了智力測驗。*When the water-pipe burst, she had the ~ to turn the water off at the main.* 當水管裂開時,她很有頭腦,連忙把總水管關起來。 **2** news; information, esp with reference to important events: 消息;情報(尤指與重要事件有關者): *have secret ~ of the enemy's plans;* 獲得有關敵方計畫之秘密情報; *the I~ Department/Service,* eg of an army or navy, collecting and studying information useful in war. 情報部門(例如陸軍或海軍中搜集及研判戰時有用之情報資料者)。**in·tel·li·gent** /-ənt ; -ənt/ *adj* having, showing, ~: 有智力的;有才智的; 聰明的: *intelligent questions/answers;* 聰明的問題(答覆); *an intelligent child;* 聰明的孩子; *an intelligent expression on sb's face.* 某人臉上聰明的表情。**in·tel·li·gent·ly** *adv*

in·tel·li·gent·sia /ɪnˌtelɪˈdʒentsɪə ; ɪnˌtɛləˈdʒɛntsɪə/ *n* (usu collective *sing* 通常爲集合單數 **the ~**) that part of a community which can be regarded (or which regards itself) as intellectual and capable of serious independent thinking. 知識份子;知識階級。

in·tel·li·gible /ɪnˈtelɪdʒəbl ; ɪnˈtɛlɪdʒəbl/ *adj* that can be easily understood; clear to the mind: 易了解的;易領悟的: *~ speech;* 清晰的言語; *an ~ explanation.* 明白的解釋。**in·tel·li·gibly** /-əblɪ ; -əblɪ/ *adv* **in·tel·li·gi·bil·ity** /ɪnˌtelɪdʒəˈbɪlətɪ ; ɪnˌtɛlɪdʒəˈbɪlətɪ/ *n* the quality of being ~. 易了解;易領悟。

in·tem·per·ate /ɪnˈtempərət ; ɪnˈtɛmpərɪt/ *adj* (formal) (of a person or his behaviour) not moderate; showing lack of self-control: (正式用語)(指人或其行爲)放縱的;無節制的: *~ habits,* (esp) habits of excessive drinking. 無節制的習慣(尤指無節制的飲酒)。**~·ly** *adv* **in·tem·per·ance** /-pərəns ; -pərəns/ *n* [U].

in·tend /ɪnˈtend ; ɪnˈtɛnd/ *vt* [VP6A, D, 7A, 9, 14, 17] **1 ~ (for),** have in mind as a purpose or plan: 意欲;打算: *What do you ~ to do/~ doing today?* 你今天打算做些什麼? *They ~ that this reform shall be carried through this year.* 他們計畫今年完成此一改革。 *We ~ them to do it/that they shall do it.* 我們打算讓他們做那事。*His son is ~ed for the medical profession.* 他計畫讓他的兒子

習醫。*This book is ~ed for you,* is to be given to you. 這本書是要給你的。*Is this sketch ~ed to be me,* Is it a sketch of me? 這張素描畫的是我嗎？*Does he ~ marriage or is he only flirting with her?* 他打算跟她結婚,還是僅僅跟她調情？ *Let me introduce you to my ~ed,* (sl 俚 for 'my future wife'). 讓我向你介紹我未來的妻子。 **2 ~ *(by),*** (old use) mean: (舊用法)意指;意謂: *What do you ~ by this word?* 你說這話是什麼意思？

in·tense /ɪn'tens ; ɪn'tɛns/ *adj* **1** (of qualities) high in degree: (指性質)强烈的;劇烈的;高度的: *~ heat.* 酷熱。 **2** (of feelings, etc) ardent; violent; (of persons) highly emotional: (指感情等)熱烈的;激烈的;(指人)熱情的: *~ political convictions.* 熱烈的政治信仰。 **~·ly** *adv*

in·ten·sify /ɪn'tensɪfaɪ ; ɪn'tɛnsə,faɪ/ *vt, vi* (*pt, pp* -fied) [VP6A, 2A] make or become more intense. 使更劇烈;使更强烈;加强;變得更劇烈;變得更强烈。 **in·ten·si·fi·ca·tion** /ɪn,tensɪfɪ'keɪʃn ; ɪn,tɛnsəfə'keʃən/ *n* [U, C].

in·ten·sity /ɪn'tensətɪ ; ɪn'tɛnsətɪ/ *n* [U] state or quality of being intense; strength or depth (of feeling, etc); [C] instance of these. 强烈;劇烈;緊張;(感情等之)强度;深度。

in·ten·sive /ɪn'tensɪv ; ɪn'tɛnsɪv/ *adj* **1** characterized by, relating to, intensity (as opposed to extent); deep and thorough: 强烈的;關於深度(與廣度相反)的;精深的;密集的: *make an ~ study of a subject;* 就一題目作精深的研究; *~ methods of horticulture,* producing large quantities by concentrating labour and care on small areas of land; 精耕園藝術; 密集園藝法(集中勞力照料小塊土地,使之大量生產的方法); *an ~ bombardment.* 密集砲擊。 **~ care** *n* medical treatment with constant observation etc of the patient. 重症治療;加意護理(給予病人密切觀察等之醫療方法)。 **~ 'care unit,** part of a hospital where this is given. (醫院中之)重症病房;加護病房。 **2** (gram) giving force and emphasis: (文法)加强語氣的: *In 'a bloody difficult book' and 'a terribly hot day', 'bloody' and 'terribly' are used colloquially as ~ words.* 在 a bloody difficult book 和 a terribly hot day 中, bloody 及 terribly 用作口語中加强語氣的字。 **~·ly** *adv*

in·tent[1] /ɪn'tent ; ɪn'tɛnt/ *adj* **1** (of looks) eager; earnest: (指樣子)急切的;熱心的: *There was an ~ look on her face as she watched the game.* 她看比賽時臉上顯出急切的樣子。 **2 ~ *on/upon sth/doing sth,*** (of persons) with the desires or attentions directed towards: (指人)專心的;熱中的: *He was ~ on his work/on getting to the office in time.* 他專心於他的工作(一心一意要及時趕到辦公室)。 **~·ly** *adv* **~·ness** *n*

intent[2] /ɪn'tent ; ɪn'tɛnt/ *n* **1** [U] (chiefly legal) purpose; intention: (主要爲法律用語)目的;意向: *shoot with ~ to kill;* 存心開槍殺人; *with good/evil/malicious ~.* 好(惡)意地。 **2** (*pl*) (複) ***to all ~s and purposes,*** in all essential points. 就各要點看來;實際上。

in·ten·tion /ɪn'tenʃn ; ɪn'tɛnʃən/ *n* [C, U] intending; thing intended; aim; purpose: 意圖;意向;目的;意旨: *If I've hurt your feelings, it was quite without ~.* 如果我傷害了你的感情,那完全是無意的。 *He went to Paris with the ~ of learning French.* 他去巴黎目的在學法語。 *His ~s are good, but he seldom carries them out.* 他的目的很好,但很少實現。 *Has he made known his ~s,* said what he intends to do? 他表示過他的意向沒有？ **(-)in·ten·tioned** *adj*: *,well-'~ed,* having good ~s; 好意的; *,ill-'~ed,* having bad, wrong, etc ~s. 惡意的。

in·ten·tional /ɪn'tenʃnəl ; ɪn'tɛnʃənḷ/ *adj* intended; done with purpose: 有意的;故意的: *If I hurt your feelings, it was not ~.* 如果我傷害了你的情感,那並不是有意的。 **~·ly** /-ʃənəlɪ ; -ʃnəlɪ/ *adv* with purpose. 故意地;有意地。

in·ter /ɪn'tɜː(r) ; ɪn'tɝ/ *vt* (-rr-) (formal) place (a corpse) in a grave or tomb; bury. (正式用語)埋葬(屍體)。

in·ter·act /,ɪntər'ækt ; ,ɪntɚ'ækt/ *vi* act on each other. 相互作用;相互影響。 **in·ter·ac·tion** /-'ækʃn ; -'ækʃən/ *n* **in·ter·ac·tive** /-'æktɪv ; -'æktɪv/ *adj*

in·ter alia /,ɪntər 'eɪlɪə ; 'ɪntɚ'elɪə/ (Lat) among other things. (拉)除了其他事物以外。

in·ter·breed /,ɪntə'briːd ; ,ɪntɚ'brid/ *vt, vi* (*pt, pp* -bred /-'bred ; -'brɛd/) [VP6A, 2A] crossbreed; produce hybrids. (使)雜交繁殖;生育雜種。

in·ter·ca·lary /ɪn'tɜːkələrɪ *US:* -lerɪ ; ɪn'tɝkə,lɛrɪ/ *adj* (of a day or month) added to make the calendar year correspond to the solar year; (of a year) having such an addition. (指月或日)閏的;(指年)閏的(即有閏月或閏日的)。

in·ter·cede /,ɪntə'siːd ; ,ɪntɚ'sid/ *vi* [VP3A] **~ *(with sb) (for sb),*** plead (as a peacemaker, or to obtain a favour): (作爲調停者或爲獲得贊助而)(向某人,爲某人)說項;求情: *~ with the father for/on behalf of the daughter.* 替女兒向父親求情。 **in·ter·ces·sion** /,ɪntə'seʃn ; ,ɪntɚ'sɛʃən/ *n* [U] interceding; [C] prayer or entreaty for another. 說項;求情;代禱;代爲求情。

in·ter·cept /,ɪntə'sept ; ,ɪntɚ'sɛpt/ *vt* [VP6A] stop, catch (sb or sth) between starting-point and destination: 中途阻止或攔截(某人或某物): *~ a letter/a messenger.* 中途截取一信(攔阻一信差)。 *Can our fighter-planes ~ the enemy's bombers?* 我們的戰鬥機能攔截敵人的轟炸機嗎？ **in·ter·cep·tion** /,ɪntə'sepʃn; ,ɪntɚ'sɛpʃən/ *n* [U, C]. **in·ter·cep·tor** /-tə(r); -tɚ/ *n* sb or sth that ~s, eg a fast fighter-plane. 中途阻止或攔截的人或物(例如一架快速的戰鬥機)。

in·ter·change /,ɪntə'tʃeɪndʒ ; ,ɪntɚ'tʃendʒ/ *vt, vi* **1** [VP6A] (of two persons, etc) give and receive; make an exchange of: (指二人等)交換: *~ views/gifts/letters.* 交換意見(交換禮物;互通書信)。 **2** [VP 6A, 2A] put (each of two things) in the other's place. 使(二物)互換;輪換。 **~·able** /-əbl ; -əbḷ/ *adj* that can be ~d: 可交換的;可輪換的: *True synonyms are ~able.* 眞正的同義字是可以交替互用的。 *This machine has ~able parts.* 這部機器有互換零件。 □ *n* /'ɪntətʃeɪndʒ ; 'ɪntɚ,tʃendʒ/ [U, C] interchanging: 交換;互換;輪換: *an ~ of views.* 意見的交換。

in·ter·col·legi·ate /,ɪntəkə'liːdʒɪət ; ,ɪntɚkə'lidʒɪɪt/ *adj* carried on, etc between colleges: 大學間的;學院間的: *~ games/debates.* 學院間的運動(辯論)比賽。

in·ter·com /'ɪntəkɒm ; 'ɪntɚ,kɑm/ *n* (colloq) system of (inter)communication, eg in aircraft: (俗)內部通話裝置(例如飛機內的對講裝置): *receive a message on/over the ~.* 接到對講機傳話。

in·ter·com·mu·ni·cate /,ɪntəkə'mjuːnɪkeɪt ; ,ɪntɚkə'mjunə,ket/ *vi* communicate with one another: 互通;互通消息;互相連絡: *The prisoners ~ by using the Morse code.* 囚犯們用摩爾斯電碼互通消息。 **in·ter·com·mu·ni·ca·tion** /,ɪntəkə,mjuːnɪ'keɪʃn ; ,ɪntɚkə,mjunə'keʃən/ *n* [U].

in·ter·com·mu·nion /,ɪntəkə'mjuːnɪən ; ,ɪntɚkə'mjunjən/ *n* mutual communion, esp between different Churches, eg Catholic and Orthodox. 互相交往;特指不同教會間的互相交往(例如天主教與希臘正教間的互相交往)。

in·ter·con·ti·nen·tal /,ɪntə,kɒntɪ'nentl ; ,ɪntɚ,kɑntə'nɛntəl/ *adj* between continents: 洲際的;洲與洲間的: *~ ballistic missiles,* that can be fired from one continent to another. 洲際彈道飛彈。

in·ter·course /'ɪntəkɔːs ; 'ɪntɚ,kors/ *n* [U] **1** social dealings between individuals; exchanges of trade, ideas, etc between persons, societies, nations, etc: 交際;交往;(貿易,思想等的)交流: *our commercial ~ with S America.* 我們與南美洲的通商。 **2 (sexual) ~,** = coitus.

in·ter·de·nomi·na·tional /,ɪntədɪ,nɒmɪ'neɪʃənl ; ,ɪntɚdɪ,nɑmə'neʃənḷ/ *adj* common to, shared by, different religious denominations, eg Methodist, Baptists, Catholic. 各不同宗教派別(例如美以美會,浸

信會,天主教)間所共有的。

in·ter·de·pen·dent /ˌɪntədɪˈpendənt; ˌɪntəˈdɪˈpɛndənt/ *adj* depending on each other. 互相依賴的;相依的。**in·ter·de·pen·dence** /-əns; -əns/ *n*

in·ter·dict /ˌɪntəˈdɪkt; ˌɪntəˈdɪkt/ *vt* [VP6A] (formal) prohibit (an action); forbid (the use of sth); (RC Church) exclude from sacraments and church services. (正式用語)禁止(行動);禁止(某物的使用);(天主教)禁止參加各種聖禮及彌撒;停止…的教權。□ *n* /ˈɪntədɪkt; ˈɪntəˌdɪkt/ [C] formal or authoritative prohibition, esp (RC Church) an order debarring a person or place from sacraments and church services: 正式禁止;(尤指天主教之)停止職權令;停止宗教活動之命令: *lay a priest/a town under an* ~. 停止一神父的職權(停止一城市的宗教活動)。**in·ter·dic·tion** /ˌɪntəˈdɪkʃn; ˌɪntəˈdɪkʃən/ *n* [U, C] ~ing; ~(*n*). 禁止;禁止參加各種聖禮及彌撒;停止教權。

in·ter·dis·ci·plin·ary /ˌɪntəˌdɪsɪˈplɪnərɪ; ˌɪntəˌdɪsəˈplɪnərɪ/ *adj* of more than one branch of learning: 各學科間的;科際的;跨越學科的: ~ *studies/degrees.* 各學科間的研究(學位)。

in·ter·est[1] /ˈɪntrəst; ˈɪntərɪst/ *n* **1** [U] condition of wanting to know or learn about sth or sb: 興趣;關心: *feel/take no/not much/a great* ~ *in politics;* 對政治不感(不太感,很感)興趣; *events that arouse great* ~. 引起很多人關心的事件。⇨ lose. **2** [U] quality that arouses concern or curiosity, that holds one's attention: 引起關心或好奇心的性質;趣味: *a matter of considerable/not much* ~. 一件相當(不太)令人感興趣的事。*Suspense adds* ~ *to a story.* 懸疑增加一個故事的趣味。 **3** [C] sth with which one concerns oneself: 愛好的事物;嗜好: *Her chief* ~ *seems to be horse-racing.* 她主要的嗜好似乎是賽馬。*His two great* ~*s in life are music and painting.* 他生活中的兩大愛好是音樂及繪畫。 **4** [C] (often *pl*) advantage; profit; well-being: (常用複數)利益;裨益;福利: *look after one's own* ~*s;* 照顧自己的利益; *work in the* ~(*s*) *of humanity;* 爲人類謀福利; *travel in Asia in the* ~*s of a business firm.* 爲一商行的利益而旅行於亞洲。*It is to your* ~ *to go.* 去對你有利。 **5** [C] legal right to a share in sth, esp in its profits: 股份;權益: *have an* ~ *in a brewery,* eg by owning shares; 在一釀啤酒廠有股份; *have an* ~ *in an estate,* a legal claim to part of it; 在一地產中有部分產權; *American* ~*s in the Caribbean,* eg capital invested in the countries of that area; 美國在加勒比海地區的權益(例如在該地區國家中的投資金額); *He has sold his* ~ *in the company.* 他已售出他在那公司中的股份。 **6** [U] money charged or paid for the use of money: 利息: *rate of* ~/$\frac{1}{4}$ ~ *rate,* payment made by a borrower for a loan, expressed as a percentage, eg 5%; 利率(四分之一利率)(以百分比表示,例如利率5%); *pay 6 per cent* ~ *on a loan.* 借款付六厘息。***with*** ~, (fig) with increased force: (喻)加强地;加重地: *return a blow/sb's kindness with* ~, give back more than one received. 加重回擊(加重報答某人的善意)。 **7** (often *pl*) group of persons engaged in the same trade, etc or having sth in common: (常用複數)同業;同行;同道: *the landed* ~, landowners collectively; 地主們; *the business* ~*s,* large business firms collectively; 公司業者; *the brewing* ~, brewers collectively. 釀啤酒業者。

in·ter·est[2] /ˈɪntrəst; ˈɪntərɪst/ *vt* [VP6A, 14] ~ ***sb (in sth),*** cause (sb) to give his attention to: 使注意;使關心;使感興趣: *Can I* ~ *you in this question?* 我可以請你注意這個問題嗎? *He is* ~*ed in shipping,* **(a)** likes to know and learn about ships. 他對船舶感興趣。 **(b)** has money invested in the shipping industry. 他投資於航運業。~**ed** *adj* ~***ed (in),*** **1** having an interest(5) in; not impartial: 有利害關係的;有權益的;偏私的: *When manufacturers demand higher tariffs, we may suspect them of having* ~*ed motives.* 廠商要求提高關稅時,我們會懷疑他們有自私的動機。 **2** showing interest(1): 表現出興趣的: *an* ~*ed look.* 一付有興趣的樣子。 **3** taking an interest(1) in: 感興趣的: ~*ed spectators;* 感興趣的觀覽者。*not* ~*ed in botany/his work.* 對植物學(他的工作)不感興趣。*I shall be* ~*ed to know what happens.* 我很想知道將要發生什麼事。~**·ing** *adj* holding the attention; arousing interest(1): 有趣味的;令人發生興趣的: ~*ing men/books/conversation.* 有趣的人(書籍,談話)。~**·ing·ly** *adv*

in·ter·face /ˈɪntəfeɪs; ˈɪntəˌfes/ *n* **1** surface common to two areas. 界面;分界面。 **2** (fig) area common to two or more systems, processes, etc: (喻)(兩個或多個系統、程序等之)共同範圍: *at the* ~ *of creative art and experimental science.* 創作藝術與實驗科學之共同範圍。

in·ter·fere /ˌɪntəˈfɪə(r); ˌɪntəˈfɪr/ *vi* **1** [VP2A, 3A] ~ ***(in sth),*** (of persons) break in upon (other person's affairs) without right or invitation: (指人)干預(他人之事): *Please don't* ~ *in my business.* 請不要干涉我的事。*Isn't she an interfering old lady!* 她眞是個愛管閒事的老太婆! *It's unwise to* ~ *between husband and wife.* 干預別人夫妻間的事是不智的。 **2** [VP2A, 3A] ~ ***(with),*** (of persons) meddle; tamper (with): (指人)干涉;亂弄: *Do not* ~ *with this machine.* 不要亂動這部機器。 **3** [VP3A] ~ ***with,*** (of events, circumstances, etc) come into opposition; hinder or prevent: (指事件、環境等)妨害;妨礙;干擾: *Do you ever allow pleasure to* ~ *with duty?* 你曾爲了玩樂而妨礙了你的職責嗎? **in·ter·fer·ence** /ˌɪntəˈfɪərəns; ˌɪntəˈfɪrəns/ *n* [U] interfering: 干涉;妨礙;干擾: *interference from foreign broadcasting stations,* eg when these have a wavelength close to that of the station one wishes to receive; 外來廣播電臺的干擾(例如當外來廣播電台的波長與某人欲收聽的電臺波長接近時); (computers) existence of unwanted signals in a communications circuit. (電子計算機)通訊電路中的干擾。

in·terim /ˈɪntərɪm; ˈɪntərɪm/ *n* **1** *in the* ~, meanwhile; during the time that comes between. 在其時;在其間。 **2** (attrib) as an instalment: (形容用法)作爲一段時間所供應物之一部;期間的: ~ *dividends,* paid between annual dividends as advance payments; 期中股利; provisional or temporary: 臨時的;暫時的: *an* ~ *report,* one that precedes the final report. 暫時的報告(在最終報告前所作者)。

in·terior /ɪnˈtɪərɪə(r); ɪnˈtɪrɪə/ *adj* **1** situated inside; of the inside. 在內的;內部的。 **2** inland; away from the coast. 內地的;內陸的。 **3** home or domestic (contrasted with *foreign*). 國內的(與 foreign 相對)。□ *n* **the** ~, **1** the inside: 內部: (used attrib) (形容用法) ~ *decorators,* those who decorate the inside of a building (with paint, wall-paper, etc). 室內裝潢設計師;室內裝飾工匠。 **2** inland areas. 內地。 **3** (department dealing with the) domestic affairs of a country: 內政;內政部門: (US) (美) *the Department of the I*~. 內政部。(Cf 參較 *Home Office* in GB. 英國稱 Home Office。)

in·ter·ject /ˌɪntəˈdʒekt; ˌɪntəˈdʒɛkt/ *vt* [VP6A] put in suddenly (a remark, etc) between statements, etc made by another. (他人講話時)突然插入(評語等)。**in·ter·jec·tion** /ˌɪntəˈdʒekʃn; ˌɪntəˈdʒɛkʃən/ *n* word or phrase used as an exclamation, eg *Oh! For goodness sake!* 感歎詞(例如:啊!看在老天爺的面上!)。

in·ter·lace /ˌɪntəˈleɪs; ˌɪntəˈles/ *vt, vi* [VP6A, 2A, 14] ~ ***(with),*** join, be joined, by weaving or lacing together, one with another; cross as if woven: (使)交織;(使)交錯: *interlacing branches.* 交錯的樹枝。

in·ter·lard /ˌɪntəˈlɑːd; ˌɪntəˈlɑrd/ *vt* [VP14] ~ ***with,*** (formal) mix writing, speech, etc with foreign phrases, etc: (正式用語)使(寫作,演說等)雜有(外國詞句等): *essays* ~*ed with quotations from the poets.* 混有引用詩人文句的文章。

in·ter·leave /ˌɪntəˈliːv; ˌɪntəˈliv/ *vt* [VP6A, 14] ~ ***(with),*** insert (usu blank leaves) between the leaves of (a book, etc): 在(書等)之各頁中插以(空白紙等): *a diary ~ed with blotting-paper.* 插有吸墨紙的日記簿。

in·ter·link /ˌɪntəˈlɪŋk ; ˌɪntɚˈlɪŋk/ *vt, vi* [VP6A, 2A] link together. 使連鎖;連環;環結。

in·ter·lock /ˌɪntəˈlɒk ; ˌɪntɚˈlɑk/ *vt, vi* [VP6A, 2A] lock or join together; clasp firmly together. 連結;結合;連鎖;互鎖。

in·ter·locu·tor /ˌɪntəˈlɒkjʊtə(r) ; ˌɪntɚˈlɑkjətɚ/ *n* person taking part in a discussion or dialogue. 討論者;對話者。

in·ter·lo·per /ˈɪntələʊpə(r) ; ˌɪntɚˈlopɚ/ *n* person who, esp for profit or personal advantage, pushes himself in where he has no right. 闖入者(尤指爲個人利益而妨害他人者)。

in·ter·lude /ˈɪntəluːd ; ˈɪntɚˌlud/ *n* **1** interval of different character between two events or two periods of time: 二事件間不同性質的穿插事件; 兩段時期中間的時間;間隔的時間: *~s of bright weather.* 間隔的晴朗天氣。 **2** interval between two acts of a play, two scenes of an opera or between parts of a psalm, hymn etc; music played during such an interval. 戲劇兩幕間,歌劇兩場間,聖詩、讚美詩等兩段間之間歇;上述間歇時的插曲;間奏。

in·ter·marry /ˌɪntəˈmærɪ ; ˌɪntɚˈmærɪ/ *vi* (*pt, pp* -married) [VP2A, 3A] ~ ***(with),*** (of tribes, races, etc) become connected by marriage with other tribes, etc. (指不同部落,種族等)通婚。 **in·ter·mar·riage** /ˌɪntəˈmærɪdʒ ; ˌɪntɚˈmærɪdʒ/ *n* [U] marriage between members of different families, tribes, castes, etc. (不同家族,部落,階級等間的)通婚。

in·ter·medi·ary /ˌɪntəˈmiːdɪərɪ *US:* -dɪerɪ ; ˌɪntɚˈmidɪˌɛrɪ/ *n* (*pl* -ries), *adj* **1** ~ ***(between),*** (sb or sth) acting as a link between (persons and groups); go-between; mediator. 居間的(人或物);斡旋的;中人;調解人。 **2** (sth) intermediate. 中間物;中間;中間的。

in·ter·medi·ate /ˌɪntəˈmiːdɪət ; ˌɪntɚˈmidɪɪt/ *adj* situated or coming between in time, space, degree, etc: (時間,空間,程度等)中間的: *at an ~ stage,* eg the cocoon stage of development of a butterfly; 在中間的階段(像如蝴蝶的作繭期); *~ courses,* between elementary and advanced; 中級課程; *~-range ballistic missiles.* 中程彈道飛彈。□ *n* sth that is ~. 中間物。**~·ly** *adv*

in·ter·ment /ɪnˈtɜːmənt ; ɪnˈtɝmənt/ *n* [U] being buried; [C] instance of this; burial. 被埋葬;埋葬;葬禮。

in·ter·mezzo /ˌɪntəˈmetsəʊ ; ˌɪntɚˈmɛtso/ *n* (*pl* ~s /-tsəʊz ; -tsoz/ or -zzi /-tsɪ ; -tsɪ/) short musical composition to be played between the acts of a drama or an opera, or one that connects the main divisions of a large musical work such as a symphony. 幕間插曲;間奏曲。

in·ter·mi·nable /ɪnˈtɜːmɪnəbl ; ɪnˈtɝmɪnəbḷ/ *adj* endless; tedious because too long: 無終止的;冗長的: *an ~ debate/sermon.* 冗長的辯論(講道)。 **in·ter·mi·nably** /-əblɪ ; -əblɪ/ *adv*

in·ter·mingle /ˌɪntəˈmɪŋgl ; ˌɪntɚˈmɪŋgḷ/ *vt, vi* [VP 6A, 14, 2A, 3A] ~ ***(with),*** mix together (two things, one with the other); mingle: 互相混合;混合: *The conference delegates ~d over coffee.* 會議代表們一面喝咖啡一面互相交談。

in·ter·mission /ˌɪntəˈmɪʃn ; ˌɪntɚˈmɪʃən/ *n* pause; interval: 暫停;間歇: *The film lasted for three hours without ~/with a short ~ half-way through.* 那電影演出三小時沒有休息(中間有片刻的休息)。

in·ter·mit·tent /ˌɪntəˈmɪtnt ; ˌɪntɚˈmɪtn̩t/ *adj* pausing or stopping at intervals; stopping and starting again: 間歇的;斷續的: *~ fever.* 間歇熱。**~·ly** *adv*

in·ter·mix /ˌɪntəˈmɪks ; ˌɪntɚˈmɪks/ *vt, vi* = mix (the usu word). (mix 較常用)。 **~·ture** /-tʃə(r) ; -tʃɚ/ *n*

in·tern[1] /ɪnˈtɜːn ; ɪnˈtɝn/ *vt* [VP6A] compel (a person, esp an enemy alien during a war) to live within certain limits or in a special building, camp, etc. 拘留(尤指戰時敵國之人)於某地。 **~·ment** *n* [U] ~ing or being ~ed: 拘留;被拘留: **'~ment** *camp.* 拘留營。**~ee** /ˌɪntɜːˈniː ; ˌɪntɝˈni/ *n* person who is ~ed. 被拘留者。

in·tern[2] (US also **in·terne**) /ˈɪntɜːn ; ˈɪntɝn/ *n* (US) young doctor who is completing his training by residing in a hospital and acting as an assistant physician or surgeon there. (美)住院實習醫生;住院助理醫師。(GB 英 = *houseman.*)

in·ter·nal /ɪnˈtɜːnl ; ɪnˈtɝnḷ/ *adj* **1** of or in the inside: 內部的;在內部的: *suffer ~ injuries in an accident;* 在一意外事件中受內傷; *~ bleeding,* eg in the bowels. 內出血(例如在腸中)。 **~ combustion,** the process by which power is produced by the explosion of gases or vapours inside a cylinder (as in the engine of a car). 內燃(由氣缸內氣體的爆發而產生動力的方法,如汽車的內燃機)。 **2** domestic; of the home affairs of a country: 國內的;內政的: *~ trade/revenue,* (also 亦作 *Inland Revenue*). 國內貿易(稅收)。 **3** derived from within the thing itself: 由本身得來的: *~ evidence,* eg of when an old book was written, or of the date of an old manuscript. 內證據(例如在考證一古書或稿件的日期時,由該書或稿件本身獲得證據)。 **~·ly** /-nəlɪ ; -nḷɪ/ *adv*

in·ter·na·tional /ˌɪntəˈnæʃənl ; ˌɪntɚˈnæʃənḷ/ *adj* existing, carried on, between nations: 國際的: *~ trade/law/agreements/conferences.* 國際貿易(法,協定,會議)。 **ˌ~ 'money order,** one which may be cashed in a country other than the country of origin. 國際滙票(可在他國兌現者)。□ *n* **the 1st/2nd/3rd I~,** three socialist or communist associations for workers of all countries, formed in 1864, 1889 and 1919. 第一(二,三)國際(先後成立於1864, 1889, 1919 年的三個國際社會主義或共產主義組織)。 **~·ism** /-nəlɪzəm ; -nḷˌɪzəm/ *n* the doctrine that the common interests of nations are greater and more important than their differences. 國際主義(認爲各國的共同利益較其歧見更重要的學說)。 **~·ist** /-ɪst ; -ɪst/ *n* person who supports and advocates ~ism. 國際主義者。 **~·ize** /-ʃənəlaɪz ; -ʃənḷˌaɪz/ *vt* [VP6A] make ~; bring under the combined control or protection of all or many nations: 使國際化;使歸國際共管: *Should the Suez and Panama Canals be ~ized?* 蘇伊士運河和巴拿馬運河應歸國際共管嗎? **~·iz·ation** /ˌɪntəˌnæʃənəlaɪˈzeɪʃn *US:* -lɪˈz- ; ˌɪntɚˌnæʃənḷəˈzeʃən/ *n* [U]. **~·ly** *adv*

in·ter·na·tio·nale /ˌɪntənæʃəˈnɑːl ; ˌɪntɚnæʃəˈnɑl/ *n* **The I~,** (revolutionary) socialist song. 共產國際歌。

in·terne /ˈɪntɜːn ; ˈɪntɝn/ *n* ⇨ intern[2].

in·ter·necine /ˌɪntəˈniːsaɪn ; ˌɪntɚˈnisɪn/ *adj* (usu of war) causing destruction to both sides. (通常指戰爭)互相毀滅的;兩敗俱傷的。

in·ternee /ˌɪntɜːˈniː ; ˌɪntɝˈni/ *n* ⇨ intern[1].

in·ter·pel·late /ɪnˈtɜːpəleɪt *US:* ˌɪntərˈpeleɪt ; ˌɪntɚˈpɛlet/ *vt* [VP6A] (in some Parliaments, eg the French and Japanese) interrupt the proceedings and demand a statement or explanation from (a Minister). (某些國會中,例如在法國和日本)議員於會中阻撓議程並要求(部長)加以說明;質詢。 **in·ter·pel·la·tion** /ɪnˌtɜːpəˈleɪʃn *US:* ˌɪntər- ; ˌɪntɚpɛˈleʃən/ *n* [U] interpellating or being ~d; [C] instance of this. 質詢;被質詢。

in·ter·phone /ˈɪntəfəʊn ; ˈɪntɚˌfon/ *n* (US) (美) = intercom.

in·ter·plan·etary /ˌɪntəˈplænɪtrɪ *US:* -terɪ ; ˌɪntɚˈplænəˌtɛrɪ/ *adj* between planets: 行星間的: *an ~ journey in a spacecraft.* 乘太空船作行星間的旅行。

in·ter·play /ˈɪntəpleɪ ; ˈɪntɚˌple/ *n* [U] operation of two or more things on each other: 相互作用: *the ~ of colours,* their combined effect. 顏色的相互作用。

in·ter·pol /ˈɪntəpɒl ; ˈɪntɚˌpol/ *n* International Police Commission. 國際刑警委員會。

in·ter·po·late /ɪnˈtɜːpəleɪt ; ɪnˈtɝpəˌlet/ *vt* [VP6A] make (sometimes misleading) additions to a book, etc. 加添(有時會引起誤解的)字句於一書等。 **in-**

ter·po·la·tion /ɪnˌtɜːpəˈleɪʃn ; ɪnˌtɝpəˈleʃən/ *n* [U] interpolating; [C] sth ~d. 加添字句;加添的字句。

in·ter·pose /ˌɪntəˈpəʊz ; ˌɪntɚˈpoz/ *vt, vi* **1** [VP6A] put forward an objection, a veto, etc as an interference: 提出(異議,否決等): *Will they ~ their veto yet again?* 他們又將提出否決嗎? **2** [VP6A, 2A] say (sth) as an interruption; make an interruption. 插入(言語)打斷談話;插嘴。 **3** [VP2A, 3A, 14] ***~ (oneself) between; ~ in,*** place oneself, be, between others: 介入二者之間: *~ between two persons who are quarrelling;* 介入兩個吵架的人的中間; mediate (in a dispute). 調停(爭端)。**in·ter·po·si·tion** /ˌɪntəpəˈzɪʃn ; ˌɪntɚpəˈzɪʃən/ *n* [U] interposing; [C] sth ~d. 提出異議,否決等;插嘴;介入;調停;插入物。

in·ter·pret /ɪnˈtɜːprɪt ; ɪnˈtɝprɪt/ *vt, vi* **1** [VP6A] show, make clear, the meaning of (either in words or by artistic performance): (用言語或表演)解釋;說明: *~ a difficult passage in a book;* 解釋書中一段困難文字; (of an actor) (指演員) *~ a role;* 演出一角色; (of a conductor) (指樂隊指揮) *~ a symphony.* 指揮一交響樂。*Poetry helps to ~ life.* 詩有助於闡釋人生的意義。 **2** [VP6A, 16B] consider to be the meaning of: 認爲是…的意思: *We ~ed his silence as a refusal.* 我們認爲他的沉默是拒絕的表示。 **3** [VP2A] act as ~er: 口譯;通譯: *Will you please ~ for me,* translate what is (to be) said? 請你爲我翻譯一下好嗎? **~er** *n* person who gives an immediate oral translation of words spoken in another language. 口譯者;通譯者;譯員。**in·ter·pre·ta·tion** /ɪnˌtɜːprɪˈteɪʃn ; ɪnˌtɝprɪˈteʃən/ *n* [U] interpreting; [C] result of this; explanation or meaning: 解釋;解釋的結果;說明;翻譯;含意: *The announcement may be given several ~ations.* 這段聲明可能有幾種不同的解釋。

in·ter·racial /ˌɪntəˈreɪʃl ; ˌɪntɚˈreʃəl/ *adj* between, involving, different races. 各種族間的。

in·ter·reg·num /ˌɪntəˈregnəm ; ˌɪntɚˈrɛgnəm/ *n* (*pl* ~s, -na /-nə ; -nə/) period during which a State has no normal or legitimate ruler, esp between the end of a Sovereign's reign and the beginning of his successor's reign; pause or interval. 國家無正常統治者的時期 (尤指一君主的統治權結束而繼任者尙未執政的一段時間);休止時間;空位期。

in·ter·re·late /ˌɪntərɪˈleɪt ; ˌɪntərɪˈlet/ *vt, vi* [VP6A, 2A] come or bring together in reciprocal relationship: (使)相互關連: *~d studies,* of separate but related subjects as a united group, eg politics, philosophy and economics. 相關的學科(例如政治學,哲學和經濟學)。

in·ter·re·la·tion /ˌɪntərɪˈleɪʃn ; ˌɪntɚrɪˈleʃən/ *n* ~ ***of/between,*** mutual relation. 相互關係。**~·ship** /-ʃɪp ; -ʃɪp/ *n* mutual relationship. 相互關係。

in·ter·ro·gate /ɪnˈterəgeɪt ; ɪnˈtɛrəˌget/ *vt* [VP6A] put questions to, esp closely or formally: 詢問(尤指嚴密地或正式地): *~ a prisoner.* 審問一犯人。**in·ter·ro·ga·tor** /-tə(r) ; -tɚ/ *n* person who ~s. 詢問者;審問者;質問者。**in·ter·ro·ga·tion** /ɪnˌterəˈgeɪʃn ; ɪnˌtɛrəˈgeʃən/ *n* **1** [U] asking questions. 訊問;發問。**interrogation point,** question mark; the mark (?). 問號(?)。 **2** [C, U] oral examination; inquiry: 審問;偵訊: *long and tiring interrogations by police officers.* 受警官長期和令人疲倦的審問。

in·ter·roga·tive /ˌɪntəˈrɒgətɪv ; ˌɪntəˈrɑgətɪv/ *adj* **1** showing or having the form of a question; of inquiry: 表示疑問的;疑惑的;質問的: *an ~ look/glance;* 疑惑的樣子(目光); *in an ~ tone.* 以疑問的聲調。 **2** (gram) used in questions: (文法)用於疑問句的: *~ pronouns/adverbs,* eg who, why. 疑問代名詞(副詞)(例如 who, why)。□ *n* ~ word, esp a pronoun. 表示疑問的字(尤指疑問代名詞)。**~·ly** *adv*

in·ter·roga·tory /ˌɪntəˈrɒgətrɪ *US:* -tɔːrɪ ; ˌɪntəˈrɑgəˌtorɪ/ *adj* of inquiry: 疑問的;質問的: *in an ~ tone.* 以疑問的口氣。

in·ter·rupt /ˌɪntəˈrʌpt ; ˌɪntəˈrʌpt/ *vt, vi* [VP6A, 2A] **1** break the continuity of: 使中斷;阻斷: *The war ~ed the flow of commerce between the two countries.* 戰爭使該兩國間的通商中斷了。*Traffic was ~ed by floods.* 交通被洪水阻斷。*Those trees are growing so high that they ~* (= obstruct) *the view.* 那些樹長得過高而遮住了視線。 **2** break in upon (a person's action, speech, etc): 打斷(某人的行動,言語等);打岔;插嘴;打擾: *Don't ~ (me) while I'm busy.* 在我忙的時候不要打攪我。 *Don't ~ the speaker; ask your questions afterwards.* 不要打斷那演說者的演說,等他講完後再問問題。**~er** *n* person or thing that ~s. 使中斷者;打斷者;打岔者。**in·ter·rup·tion** /ˌɪntəˈrʌpʃn ; ˌɪntəˈrʌpʃən/ *n* [U] ~ing or being ~ed; [C] instance of this; sth that ~s: 阻斷;打斷;打岔;打攪;使中斷的事物: *Numerous ~ions have prevented me from finishing the work.* 無數的打岔的事使我未能完成此工作。

in·ter·sect /ˌɪntəˈsekt ; ˌɪntɚˈsɛkt/ *vt, vi* **1** [VP6A] divide by cutting, passing or lying across. 橫斷;橫切;貫穿。 **2** [VP6A, 2A] (of lines) cut or cross each other: (指線條)相交;交叉: *The lines AB and CD ~ at E.* 直線 AB 與直線 CD 相交於 E 點。*The line AB ~s the line CD at E.* 直線 AB 和直線 CD 於 E 點相交。**in·ter·sec·tion** /ˌɪntəˈsekʃn ; ˌɪntɚˈsɛkʃən/ *n* [U] ~ing or being ~ed; [C] point where two lines, etc ~. 橫斷;橫切;相交;交叉;交叉點。

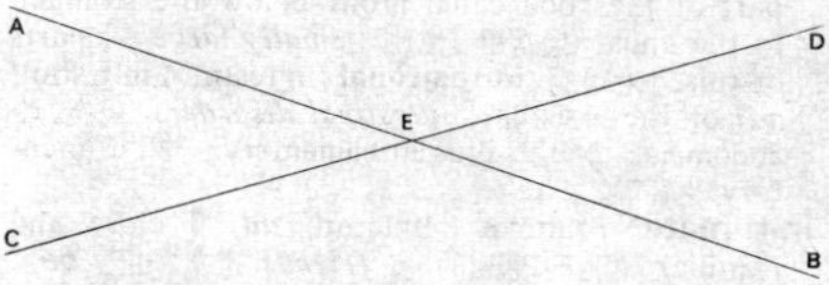

intersecting lines

in·ter·sperse /ˌɪntəˈspɜːs ; ˌɪntɚˈspɝs/ *vt* [VP14] ~ ***among/between,*** place here and there. 散置。~ ***with,*** diversify: 使有變化;穿插;點綴: *a speech ~d with witty remarks.* 穿插著妙語的一篇演說。

in·ter·state /ˌɪntəˈsteɪt ; ˌɪntɚˈstet/ *adj* (US) between States: (美)州與州間的;州際的: *~ commerce.* 州際貿易。

in·ter·stel·lar /ˌɪntəˈstelə(r) ; ˌɪntɚˈstɛlɚ/ *adj* between the stars: 星與星間的;星際的: *~ matter,* eg the masses of gas between stars; 星際的物質(例如氣團); *~ communications.* 星際通訊系統。

in·ter·stice /ɪnˈtɜːstɪs ; ɪnˈtɝstɪs/ *n* crack; chink; crevice: 罅隙;空隙;裂縫: *~s* (= very small spaces) *between stones in a heap.* 一堆石頭間狹小的空隙。

in·ter·tribal /ˌɪntəˈtraɪbl ; ˌɪntɚˈtraɪbl/ *adj* between tribes: 種族間的;部族間的: *~ wars.* 部族間的戰爭。

in·ter·twine /ˌɪntəˈtwaɪn ; ˌɪntɚˈtwaɪn/ *vt, vi* [VP6A, 2A] twine or twist together; become twined or twisted together: 糾纏;纏繞在一起: *a lattice ~d with vines.* 攀附著藤蔓的格子窗。

in·ter·val /ˈɪntəvl ; ˈɪntɚvl/ *n* **1** time (between two events or two parts of an action); (esp) time between two acts of a play, two parts of a concert, etc: (兩件事或兩部分動作)間隔的時間;間歇;(尤指)戲劇兩幕間或音樂會上下半場間的間歇: *buses leaving at short ~s,* ie very frequently. 開出班次頻繁的公共汽車。 **2** space between (two objects or points): 間隔: *arranged at ~s of ten feet.* 以十呎的間隔排列。 **3** (music) difference of pitch between two notes on a given scale. (音樂)音程。

in·ter·vene /ˌɪntəˈviːn ; ˌɪntɚˈvin/ *vi* **1** [VP2A] (of events, circumstances) come between (others) in time: (指事件或情況)插入(其他的事件或情況);在其間發生: *I shall leave on Sunday if nothing ~s.* 如果沒有別的事,我星期天動身。 **2** [VP2A, 3A] ~ ***(in),*** (of persons) interfere so as to prevent sth or change the result: (指人)干涉;阻撓;調停: *~ in a* *dispute;* 調停爭端; ~ *between people who are disputing.* 調停他人間的爭端。 **3** [VP2A] (of time) come or be between: (指時間) 介於其間: *during the years that ~d.* 在其間的幾年中。 **in·ter·ven·tion** /ˌɪntəˈvenʃn ; ˌɪntɚˈvɛnʃən/ *n* [U] intervening (esp 2 above): 插入; 介於其間; (尤指) 干涉; 阻撓; 調停: *armed intervention by one country in the affairs of other countries;* 一國對他國內政之武力干涉; [C] instance of this. 干涉或調停的實例。

in·ter·view /ˈɪntəvjuː ; ˈɪntɚˌvju/ *n* [C] meeting with sb for formal consultation or examination, eg between employers and applicants for posts; meeting (of a reporter, etc) with sb whose views are requested: 接見; 會見 (例如僱主與求職者間者); 新聞記者的訪問: *The Ambassador refused to give any ~s to journalists or TV men.* 該大使拒絕任何新聞或電視記者的訪問。□ *vt* [VP6A] (of a reporter, etc) have or obtain an ~ with. (指記者等) 訪問; 會見; 接見。

in·ter·weave /ˌɪntəˈwiːv ; ˌɪntɚˈwiv/ *vt* (*pt* -wove /-ˈwəʊv ; -ˈwov/, *pp* -woven /-ˈwəʊvn ; -ˈwovən/) [VP6A, 14] ~ ***(with),*** weave together (one with another). 交織。

in·tes·tate /ɪnˈtesteɪt ; ɪnˈtɛstet/ *adj* not having made a will before death occurs: 未留遺囑的: *die ~.* 未留遺囑而死。

in·tes·tine /ɪnˈtestɪn ; ɪnˈtɛstɪn/ *n* (usu *pl*) lower part of the food canal from below the stomach to the anus: (通常用複數) 腸: *small/large ~,* parts of this. 小(大)腸。 **in·tes·ti·nal** /ɪnˈtestɪnl ; ɪnˈtɛstɪnl̩/ *adj* of the ~s: 腸的: *intestinal disorders.* 腸疾。⇨ abdominal; ⇨ the illus at alimentary. 參看 alimentary 之插圖。

in·ti·mate[1] /ˈɪntɪmət ; ˈɪntəmɪt/ *adj* **1** close and familiar: 親近的; 親密的: ~ *friends.* 密友; 知己。 ***be/get on ~ terms (with),*** eg when one calls a man 'Jack' instead of 'Mr Hill'. 與某人很親近 (例如對希爾先生直呼其名傑克)。 **2** innermost; private and personal: 最內部的; 私人的; 秘密的: *tell a friend the ~ details of one's life;* 將一生中個人的瑣碎私事告訴一友人; *an ~ diary,* one in which one records experiences, thoughts, emotions, etc usu kept secret. 私人日記。 **3** resulting from close study or great familiarity: 精湛的; 仔細研究而得的; 熟悉的: *an ~ knowledge of Greek philosophy.* 對希臘哲學的精湛的知識。□ *n* ~ friend. 知己; 密友。 **~·ly** *adv* **in·ti·macy** /ˈɪntɪməsɪ ; ˈɪntəməsɪ/ *n* (*pl* -cies) **1** [U] the state of being ~; close friendship or relationship; (euphem) sexual relations. 親密; 親近; (委婉語) 性關係。 **2** (*pl*) ~ actions, eg caresses or kisses. (複) 親密的行爲 (例如撫摸或接吻)。

in·ti·mate[2] /ˈɪntɪmeɪt ; ˈɪntəˌmet/ *vt* [VP6A, 9, 14] ~ ***sth (to sb); ~ (to sb) that...,*** make known; show clearly: 宣佈; 明白表示: ~ *one's approval of a plan/that one approves of a plan.* 表示贊成一計畫。 *He ~d to me his intention of leaving early/that he intended to leave early.* 他告訴我他有意早些離去。 **in·ti·ma·tion** /ˌɪntɪˈmeɪʃn ; ˌɪntəˈmeʃən/ *n* [U] intimating; [C] sth ~d; notification; suggestion. 宣佈; 明白表示; 明白表示的事物; 通知; 暗示。

in·timi·date /ɪnˈtɪmɪdeɪt ; ɪnˈtɪməˌdet/ *vt* [VP6A, 14] ~ ***(into),*** frighten, esp in order to force (sb into doing sth): 脅迫; 威迫 (某人做某事): ~ *a witness,* eg by threatening him. 恐嚇一證人。 **in·timi·da·tion** /ɪnˌtɪmɪˈdeɪʃn ; ɪnˌtɪməˈdeʃən/ *n* [U] intimidating or being ~d: 脅迫; 威迫: *surrender to intimidation.* 屈服於脅迫。

into /ˈɪntə ; ˈɪntə; *strong form:* ˈɪntuː ; ˈɪntu/ *prep* **1** (indicating motion or direction to a point within): (表示向內的動作或方向) 進入…之內; 向內: *Come ~ the house/garden.* 到房屋(花園)裏來。 *Throw it ~ the fire.* 把它丟到火中。 *He worked late ~ the night.* 他工作至深夜。 **2** (indicating change of condition, result): (表示狀況的變化或結果) 變成…之狀況: *She burst ~ tears.* 她突然號啕大哭。 *Don't get ~ trouble.* 不要惹麻煩。 *The rain changed ~ snow.* 雨變成了雪。 *He poked the fire ~ a blaze,* poked it so that it blazed up. 他將火撥大了。 *Collect them ~ heaps.* 將它們聚成堆。 *He frightened her ~ submission.* 他恐嚇她使她順從。 ***be ~ sth,*** (mod use, colloq) be involved in, concerned with, it: (現代用法, 俗) 牽扯; 與…有關: *She's heavily ~ vegetarianism.* 她十分主張素食。 **3** (maths): (數學) 除: *5 ~ 25* (= 25 divided by 5) *goes 5.* 5 除 25 得 5。

in·tol·er·able /ɪnˈtɒlərəbl ; ɪnˈtɑlərəbl̩/ *adj* that cannot be tolerated or endured: 無法忍受的; 不能忍耐的: ~ *heat/insolence.* 無法忍受的熱(侮辱)。 *Is the world becoming an ~ place to live in?* 這世界逐漸變成一個無法居住的地方了嗎? **in·tol·er·ably** /-əblɪ ; -əblɪ/ *adv*

in·tol·er·ant /ɪnˈtɒlərənt ; ɪnˈtɑlərənt/ *adj* ~ ***(of),*** not tolerant: 不能容納異己的; 不寬容的: *a man who is ~ of opposition.* 不能容忍反對的人。 **~·ly** *adv* **in·tol·er·ance** /-əns ; -əns/ *n*

in·ton·ation /ˌɪntəˈneɪʃn ; ˌɪntoˈneʃən/ *n* [U] the rise and fall of the pitch of the voice in speaking; this as an element of meaning in language. 說話時聲音的升降; 語調; 音調。

in·tone /ɪnˈtəʊn ; ɪnˈton/ *vt, vi* [VP6A, 2A] recite a prayer, psalm, etc in a singing tone; speak with a particular tone. 吟誦(祈禱文, 讚美詩等); 以特殊音調說話。

in toto /ɪn ˈtəʊtəʊ ; ɪnˈtoto/ (Lat) totally; altogether. (拉) 整個地; 全部。

in·toxi·cant /ɪnˈtɒksɪkənt ; ɪnˈtɑksəkənt/ *adj, n* intoxicating (liquor). 醉人的; 酒類飲料。

in·toxi·cate /ɪnˈtɒksɪkeɪt ; ɪnˈtɑksəˌket/ *vt* [VP6A] **1** make stupid with, cause to lose self-control as the result of taking, alcoholic drink: 使醉: *If a man drinks too much whisky, he becomes ~d.* 如果一人飲過多的威士忌, 他會醉。 **2** excite greatly, beyond self-control: 使極度興奮; 使陶醉: *be ~d by success;* 因成功而極度興奮; *~d with joy.* 高興極了。 **in·toxi·ca·tion** /ɪnˌtɒksɪˈkeɪʃn ; ɪnˌtɑksəˈkeʃən/ *n* [U] being ~d; alcoholic poisoning. 醉; 極度興奮; 酒精中毒。

in·trac·table /ˌɪnˈtræktəbl ; ɪnˈtræktəbl̩/ *adj* not easily controlled or dealt with; hard to manage: 難控制的; 難對付的; 難處理的: ~ *children;* 難管教的孩子們; *an ~ temper.* 頑強的脾氣。 **in·trac·ta·bil·ity** /ɪnˌtræktəˈbɪlətɪ ; ˌɪntræktəˈbɪlətɪ/ *n*

in·tra·mural /ˌɪntrəˈmjʊərəl ; ˌɪntrəˈmjʊrəl/ *adj* **1** existing, done, within the walls of a town, building, etc: 在城市內的; 在一建築物內的: ~ *burial,* inside a church instead of in the churchyard. 教堂內的埋葬 (而非葬於毗連教堂的墓地中)。 **2** intended for full-time, residential students. 爲住校正式生而設的; 校內的。⇨ extramural.

in·tran·si·gent /ɪnˈtrænsɪdʒənt ; ɪnˈtrænsədʒənt/ *adj* (formal) uncompromising, esp in politics. (正式用語) 不妥協的; 不讓步的 (尤指在政治上)。 **in·tran·si·gence** /-əns ; -əns/ *n*

in·tran·si·tive /ɪnˈtrænsətɪv ; ɪnˈtrænsətɪv/ *adj* (of verbs) used without a direct object. (指動詞) 不及物的。 **~·ly** *adv* ⇨ transitive.

in·tra-uter·ine /ˌɪntrə ˈjuːtəraɪn ; ˌɪntrəˈjutərɪn/ *adj* (med) within the uterus. (醫) 子宮內的。 ~ **device,** (abbr 略作 **IUD**), loop or spiral inserted in the uterus as a contraceptive. 子宮環 (一種避孕器)。

in·tra·venous /ˌɪntrəˈviːnəs ; ˌɪntrəˈvinəs/ *adj* within a vein or veins: 靜脈內的: ~ *injections,* and so into the blood stream. 靜脈注射。

in·trench /ɪnˈtrentʃ ; ɪnˈtrɛntʃ/ = entrench.

in·trepid /ɪnˈtrepɪd ; ɪnˈtrɛpɪd/ *adj* fearless. 無畏的。 **~·ly** *adv* **in·trep·id·ity** /ˌɪntrɪˈpɪdətɪ ; ˌɪntrəˈpɪdətɪ/ *n* [U] fearlessness; [C] (*pl* -ties) fearless act. 無畏; 無畏的行動。

in·tri·cate /ˈɪntrɪkət ; ˈɪntrəkɪt/ *adj* complicated; puzzling; difficult to follow or understand: 複雜的; 使人迷惑的; 難了解的: *a novel with an ~ plot;*

情節複雜的一部小說; *an ~ piece of machinery.* 一部複雜的機器。 **~·ly** *adv* **in·tri·cacy** /ˈɪntrɪkəsɪ; ˈɪntrəkəsɪ/ *n* (*pl* -cies) [U] the quality of being ~; (*pl*) ~ things, events, etc. 複雜;難了解;(複)複雜的事物,事件等。

in·trigue /ɪnˈtri:g; ɪnˈtrig/ *vi, vt* **1** [VP2A, 3A] ~ ***(with sb) (against sb),*** make and carry out secret plans or plots: 設陰謀;密謀: *~ with Smith against Robinson.* 與史密斯密謀對付魯賓遜。 **2** [VP6A] arouse the interest or curiosity of: 激起…的興趣或好奇心: *The news ~d all of us.* 這消息引起我們大家的興趣。 □ *n* **1** [U] secret plotting. 密謀;設陰謀。 **2** [C] plot; secret plan; secret love affair. 陰謀;祕密計畫;私通。

in·trin·sic /ɪnˈtrɪnsɪk *US:* -zɪk; ɪnˈtrɪnsɪk/ *adj* (of value, quality) belonging naturally; existing within, not coming from outside: (指價值或性質)固有的;內在的: *a man's ~ worth,* eg such qualities as honour and courage, contrasted with *extrinsic* qualities, eg family connections; 一個人內在的優點(例如榮譽、勇敢等,與家世關係等外在的優點相對); *the ~ value of a coin,* the value of the metal in it, usu less than its face value. 一錢幣的內在價值(指其所含金屬的價值,通常低於面值)。 **in·trin·si·cally** /-klɪ; -klɪ/ *adv*

in·tro·duce /ˌɪntrəˈdju:s *US:* -ˈdu:s; ˌɪntrəˈdjus/ *vt* [VP6A, 15A] **1** bring in; bring forward: 提出: *~ a Bill before Parliament.* 向國會提出一法案。 **2** [VP14] ~ ***into/to,*** bring (sth) into use or into operation for the first time; cause (sb) to be acquainted with (sth): 採用;引進;提倡;使(某人)認識某事物: *~ new ideas into a business.* 引進新觀念於一事業。*Tobacco was ~d into Europe from America.* 煙草係由美洲傳入歐洲。 *The teacher ~d his young pupils to the intricacies of geometry.* 那教師把幾何的複雜的原理傳授給他年輕的學生。 **3** [VP6A, 14] ***~ sb (to sb),*** make (persons) known by name (to one another), esp in the usual formal way: 介紹相識(尤指正式介紹): *~ two friends.* 介紹兩位朋友相識。*He ~d me to his parents.* 他把我介紹給他的父母。 *The chairman ~d the lecturer to the audience.* 主席將演說者介紹給聽衆。 **4** [VP6A, 14] ***~ (into),*** insert: 插入: *~ a tube into a wound;* 將一管插入傷口; *~ a subject into a conversation.* 將一題目引入談話中。

in·tro·duc·tion /ˌɪntrəˈdʌkʃn; ˌɪntrəˈdʌkʃən/ *n* **1** [U] introducing or being introduced: 提倡;採用;介紹: *a letter of ~,* one that introduces the bearer to friends of the writer; 介紹信; *foreign words of recent ~,* recently introduced into the language. 最近採用的外來語。 **2** [C] introducing of persons to one another: 介紹人們相識: *It was necessary to make ~s all round,* to introduce many people to one another. 需要將大家一一互爲介紹。 **3** [C] sth that leads up to sth else; the opening paragraph of a letter, essay, speech, etc; explanatory article at or before the beginning of a book. 導引之事物;引言;序言;序論。 **4** [C] elementary textbook: 入門;初學書: *'An I~ to Greek Grammar'.* '希臘文法入門'。

in·tro·duc·tory /ˌɪntrəˈdʌktərɪ *US:* -tɔ:rɪ; ˌɪntrəˈdʌktərɪ/ *adj* serving to introduce: 介紹的;導引的: *an ~ chapter;* 序篇; *a few ~ remarks by the chairman.* 主席的簡短的介紹詞。

in·tro·spect /ˌɪntrəˈspekt; ˌɪntrəˈspɛkt/ *vi* [VP2A] (formal) examine one's own thoughts and feelings. (正式用語)內省;反省。 **in·tro·spec·tion** /ˌɪntrəˈspekʃn; ˌɪntrəˈspɛkʃən/ *n* [U] ~ing. 內省;反省。 **in·tro·spec·tive** /-tɪv; -tɪv/ *adj* inclined towards, based on, ~ion. 好內省的;根據內省的。

in·tro·vert /ˌɪntrəˈvɜ:t; ˌɪntrəˈvɜt/ *vt* [VP6A] turn (the mind, thought) inward upon itself. 使(心性,思想)內向。 □ *n* /ˈɪntrəvɜ:t; ˈɪntrəˌvɜt/ person who habitually does this; one who is more interested in his own thoughts and feelings than in things outside himself. 慣於內省之人;內向性格的人。 **in·tro·ver·sion** *n* [U] state of being ~ed. 內向。 ⇨ extrovert.

in·trude /ɪnˈtru:d; ɪnˈtrud/ *vt, vi* [VP14, 2A, 3A] ~ ***(oneself) on/upon sb; ~ (oneself/sth) into sth,*** force (sth, oneself, upon sb, into a place); enter without invitation: 强使(某人)接受(某事物,自己);强行進入(某地);闖入; 侵入; 侵擾: *the thought/suspicion that ~d itself into my mind;* 侵入我心中的念頭(懷疑); *~ oneself into a meeting;* 闖入一會議; *~ upon a person's time/privacy.* 侵擾一人的時間(靜居)。 *I hope I'm not intruding.* 我希望沒有打擾你。 **in·truder** *n* person or thing that ~s: 闖入者;侵入者: (attrib) (形容用法) *~r aircraft;* 突襲飛機; *~r patrols,* ie intruding into the enemy's country. 闖入敵國的巡邏隊。

in·tru·sion /ɪnˈtru:ʒn; ɪnˈtruʒən/ *n* ~ ***(on/upon/into),*** [U] intruding: 闖入;侵擾: *guilty of unpardonable ~ upon sb's privacy;* 犯不可原諒的侵擾某人靜居罪; [C] instance of this: 闖入或侵擾的實例: *angry at numerous ~s on one's privacy by rude journalists.* 因無禮的記者屢次侵擾其清靜生活而發怒。 **in·tru·sive** /ɪnˈtru:sɪv; ɪnˈtrusɪv/ *adj* intruding: 闖入的;侵擾的;挿入的: *the intrusive 'r',* eg the r-sound often heard in eg 'awe and wonder'. 挿入的 r 音 (例如 awe and wonder 讀音中者)。

in·trust /ɪnˈtrʌst; ɪnˈtrʌst/ = entrust.

in·tuit /ɪnˈtju:ɪt *US:* -ˈtu:-; ˈɪntjuɪt/ *vt, vi* [VP2A, 6A] sense by intuition. 直覺。

in·tu·ition /ˌɪntju:ˈɪʃn *US:* -tu:-; ˌɪntjuˈɪʃən/ *n* **1** [U] (power of) the immediate understanding of something without conscious reasoning or study. 直覺;直覺力。 **2** [C] piece of knowledge gained by this power. 直覺的知識。 **in·tu·itive** /ɪnˈtju:ɪtɪv *US:* -ˈtu:-; ɪnˈtjuɪtɪv/ *adj* of ~: 直覺的: *intuitive knowledge;* 直覺的知識; possessing ~: 有直覺力的: *Are women more intuitive than men?* 女子較男子更具有直覺力嗎? **in·tu·itive·ly** *adv*

in·tu·mescence /ˌɪntju:ˈmesns *US:* -tu:-; ˌɪntjuˈmɛsns/ *n* (med) process or condition of swelling or expanding. (醫)腫大;膨脹。

in·un·date /ˈɪnʌndeɪt; ˈɪnənˌdet/ *vt* [VP6A, 14] ~ ***(with),*** flood; cover (with water) by overflowing; (fig, esp passive) overwhelm: 氾濫;淹沒;(喻,尤用於被動語態)壓倒: *be ~d with requests for help/applications for a post.* 因請求援助(求職信)過多而不勝其擾。 **in·un·da·tion** /ˌɪnʌnˈdeɪʃn; ˌɪnənˈdeʃən/ *n* [U] flooding; [C] instance of this; flood. 氾濫;淹沒;洪水。

in·ure /ɪˈnjʊə(r); ɪnˈjʊr/ *vt* [VP14] ~ ***oneself/sb to,*** (usu passive) accustom: (通常用被動語態)使慣於: *Living in the far North had ~d him to cold.* 居於極北部使他慣於寒冷。*He had become ~d to ridicule.* 他已受慣了他人的譏笑。

in·vade /ɪnˈveɪd; ɪnˈved/ *vt* [VP6A] **1** enter (a country) with armed forces in order to attack; (fig) crowd into; enter: 侵略(一國);侵犯;(喻)蜂擁而至;進入: *a city ~d by tourists;* 遊客蜂擁而至的城市; *a mind ~d by worry and anxiety.* 充滿憂傷和焦慮的心境。 **2** violate; interfere with: 侵害;干犯: *~ sb's rights.* 侵害某人的權利。 **in·vader** *n* person or thing that ~s. 侵略者;侵犯者;侵入物。

in·valid[1] /ɪnˈvælɪd; ɪnˈvælɪd/ *adj* not valid: 無效的;作廢的: *~ excuses/claims/arguments;* 無效的辯解(要求,論據); *an ~ will/cheque,* eg one without a signature; 無效的(例如未簽字的)遺囑(支票); *declare a marriage ~.* 宣告一婚姻無效。 **in·vali·date** /ɪnˈvælɪdeɪt; ɪnˈvælədet/ *vt* [VP6A] make ~. 使無效;使作廢。 **in·vali·da·tion** /ɪnˌvælɪˈdeɪʃn; ɪnˌvæləˈdeʃən/ *n* [U] state of being ~; [C, U] (act of) rendering sth ~: 無效;作廢;使某事物無效(之行動): *the invalidation of a passport.* 一護照之無效。 **in·val·id·ity** /ˌɪnvəˈlɪdətɪ; ˌɪnvəˈlɪdətɪ/ *n* [U] state of being ~. 無效。

in·va·lid[2] /ˈɪnvəlid; ˈɪnvəlɪd/ *adj* **1** weak or disabled through illness or injury: 因生病或受傷而虛弱或殘廢的;病弱的;傷殘的: *a home of rest for ~ soldiers.* 傷患士兵之休養所。 **2** suitable for ~ persons: 適於傷患的: *an ~ chair,* one with wheels; 適於傷患坐的輪椅; *an ~ diet.* 傷患的飲食。 □ *n* ~ person. 傷殘者;病人。 □ *vt* [VP15A] (esp of members of the armed forces) remove from active service as an ~; send (*home*) as an ~: 因殘病而使(尤指軍中人員)退役;因殘病而遣返家鄉: *be ~ed home;* 因殘病而退役回鄉; *~ed out of the army.* 因殘病而退役。 **~·ism** /-ɪzəm ; -ˌɪzəm/ *n* chronic ill health. 久病衰弱;慢性虛弱病。

in·valu·able /ɪn'væljʊəbl ; ɪn'væljəbl̩/ *adj* ~ ***(to),*** of value too high to be measured: 價值高到無法估量的;無價的: *Her services are ~ to me.* 她的服務對我是非常珍貴的。

in·vari·able /ɪn'veərɪəbl ; ɪn'vɛrɪəbl̩/ *adj* never changing; unchangeable; constant: 永不變的;無變化的;恆久的: *an ~ pressure/temperature.* 不變的壓力(氣溫)。 **in·vari·ably** /-əblɪ ; -əblɪ/ *adv*

in·va·sion /ɪn'veɪʒn ; ɪn'veʒən/ *n* [U] invading or being invaded; [C] instance of this: 侵略;侵犯;被侵襲;侵害: *an ~ of privacy.* 侵擾清居。

in·vas·ive /ɪn'veɪsɪv ; ɪn'vesɪv/ *adj* making invasion; tending to spread. 侵略的;侵入的;蔓延性的。

in·vec·tive /ɪn'vektɪv ; ɪn'vɛktɪv/ *n* [U] abusive language: 抨擊的言語;謾罵: *speeches filled with ~;* 充滿抨擊的演說; (*pl*) curses; violent expressions: (複)咒語;罵人的話: *a stream of coarse ~s.* 一連串下流的罵人話。

in·veigh /ɪn'veɪ ; ɪn've/ *vi* [VP3A] ~ ***against sb/sth,*** speak bitterly; attack violently in words. 痛罵;用言語猛烈抨擊。

in·veigle /ɪn'veɪgl ; ɪn'vigl̩/ *vt* [VP14] ~ ***sb into (doing) sth,*** trick by using flattery, deception, etc: 誘騙: *~ sb into investing his money unwisely.* 誘騙某人將錢亂投資。

in·vent /ɪn'vent ; ɪn'vɛnt/ *vt* [VP6A] **1** create or design (sth not existing before): 發明;創造: *When was the steam engine ~ed?* 蒸汽機是何時發明的? Cf 參較 *discover,* find sth existing before, but unknown. 指發現早已存在,但不爲人們所知的東西。 **2** make up, think of: 虛構;杜撰: *~ a story/an excuse.* 虛構一故事(藉口)。 **in·ven·tive** /ɪn'ventɪv ; ɪn'vɛntɪv/ *adj* able to ~: 有發明力的;有創造力的;有發明才智的: *an ~ive mind;* 有創造力的頭腦; *~ive powers.* 發明力。 **in·ven·tor** /-tə(r) ; -tɚ/ *n* person who ~s things. 發明者。

in·ven·tion /ɪn'venʃn ; ɪn'vɛnʃən/ *n* **1** [U] inventing: 發明;創造;虛構: *the ~ of the telephone;* 電話的發明; capacity for inventing: 發明之才能;杜撰之才: *Necessity is the mother of ~.* 需要爲發明之母。 **2** [C] sth invented: 發明物;虛構的事物: *the numerous ~s of Edison;* 愛迪生發明的許多東西; *newspapers that are full of ~s,* invented, untrue stories. 充滿不實報導的報紙。

in·ven·tory /'ɪnvəntrɪ *US:* -tɔːrɪ ; 'ɪnvənˌtorɪ/ *n* (*pl* -ries) detailed list, eg of household goods, furniture, etc. 詳細目錄(例如動產,傢具等的清單);財產清冊;存貨;盤存。

in·verse /ɪn'vɜːs ; ɪn'vɝs/ *adj* inverted; reversed in position, direction or relations: 倒轉的;(位置,方向或關係)顛倒的: *~ ratio/proportion,* that between two quantities one of which increases proportionately as the other decreases. 反比(反比例)。 □ *n* /'ɪnvɜːs ; ɪn'vɝs/ [U] inverted state. 倒轉;顛倒。 **~·ly** *adv*

in·vert /ɪn'vɜːt ; ɪn'vɝt/ *vt* [VP6A] put upside down or in the opposite order, position or arrangement: 倒轉;上下倒置;前後顛倒: *~ a glass,* so that it is bottom upwards. 倒放杯子。 **ˌ~ed 'commas,** quotation marks (" " or ' '). 引號(" " 或 ' ')。 ⇨ App 9. 參看附錄九。 **in·ver·sion** /ɪn'vɜːʃn *US:* -ʒn ; ɪn'vɝʃən/ *n* [U] ~ing or being ~ed; [C] instance of this; sth ~ed. 倒轉;倒置;倒轉物;倒置物。

in·vert·ebrate /ɪn'vɜːtɪbreɪt ; ɪn'vɝtəbrɪt/ *adj* not having a backbone or spinal column, eg molluscs, insects, worms; (fig) weak-willed. 無脊椎的(例如軟體動物,昆蟲,蠕蟲);(喻)意志薄弱的。 □ *n* ~ animal. 無脊椎動物。

in·vest /ɪn'vest ; ɪn'vɛst/ *vt, vi* **1** [VP6A, 14] ~ ***(in),*** put (money in): 投資;投資於: *~ £1000 in government stock;* 投資一千鎊於公債; *~ one's savings in a business enterprise.* 將儲金投資於一企業。 **2** [VP3A] ~ ***in,*** (colloq) buy (sth considered useful): (俗)購買(認爲有用之物): *~ in a new kettle.* 買一把新的開水壺。 **3** [VP14] ~ ***with,*** clothe; endow; decorate; surround (with qualities): 包覆;授與;授以勳章;使籠罩(某種性質): *The military governor has been ~ed with full authority.* 該軍政長官被授以全權。 *The old ruins were ~ed with romance.* 那古廢墟富有傳奇色彩。 **4** [VP6A] surround a fort, town, etc with armed forces; lay siege to. 包圍(要塞,城鎮等);圍攻。 **~or** /-tə(r) ; -tɚ/ *n* person who ~s money. 投資者。 **~·ment** *n* **1** [U] ~ing money: 投資: *By careful ~ment of his capital, he obtained a good income.* 由於愼重的投資,他獲得很好的收入。 **2** [C] sum of money that is ~ed; that in which money is ~ed: 投入的資本;投資額;投資的對象: *an ~ment of £500 in oil shares;* 投資五百鎊於石油股票; *wise and profitable ~ments.* 明智而有利的投資。 **3** [U] act of ~ing a town, fort, etc; blockade. 包圍(城,要塞等);封鎖。 **4** = investiture.

in·ves·ti·gate /ɪn'vestɪgeɪt ; ɪn'vɛstəˌget/ *vt* [VP6A] examine, inquire into; make a careful study of: 調查;審查: *~ a crime/the causes of a railway accident;* 調查一犯罪案(火車失事原因); *~ the market for sales of a product.* 爲一產品的銷路調查市場。 **in·ves·ti·ga·tor** /-tə(r) ; -tɚ/ *n* person who ~s. 調查者;審查者。 **in·ves·ti·ga·tion** /ɪnˌvestɪ'geɪʃn ; ɪnˌvɛstə'geʃən/ *n* [U] careful and thorough inquiry; [C] instance of this: 調查;審查: *The matter is under investigation.* 此事在調查中。

in·ves·ti·ture /ɪn'vestɪtʃə(r) *US:* -tʃʊər ; ɪn'vɛstətʃɚ/ *n* (from invest(3)) ceremony of investing sb *with* an office, rank, power or dignity. (由 invest 第 3 義而來)授職,授爵,授權等之儀式(與 with 連用)。

in·vest·ment ⇨ invest.

in·vet·er·ate /ɪn'vetərət ; ɪn'vɛtərɪt/ *adj* (esp of habits, feelings) deep-rooted; long-established: (尤指習慣,感情)根深蒂固的;由來已久的: *an ~ smoker;* 積習已久的抽煙者; *~ prejudices.* 根深蒂固的偏見。

in·vidi·ous /ɪn'vɪdɪəs ; ɪn'vɪdɪəs/ *adj* likely to cause ill-feeling (because of real or apparent injustice): (由於眞正的或表面上的不公)易引起反感的;易招怨恨的: *make ~ distinctions.* 造成易引起反感的差別。**~·ly** *adv*

in·vigi·late /ɪn'vɪdʒɪleɪt ; ɪn'vɪdʒəˌlet/ *vi, vt* [VP 2A, 6A] watch over (eg students during examinations.) 監考。 **in·vigi·la·tor** /-tə(r) ; -tɚ/ *n* person who ~s. 監考員。 **in·vigi·la·tion** /ɪnˌvɪdʒɪ'leɪʃn ; ɪnˌvɪdʒɪ'leʃən/ *n* [U, C].

in·vig·or·ate /ɪn'vɪgəreɪt ; ɪn'vɪgəˌret/ *vt* [VP6A] make vigorous; give strength or courage to: 使有生氣;鼓舞: *an invigorating climate/speech.* 令人奮發的氣候(演說)。

in·vin·cible /ɪn'vɪnsəbl ; ɪn'vɪnsəbl̩/ *adj* too strong to be overcome or defeated: 不能克服的;不能征服的: *an ~ will.* 堅强的意志。 **in·vin·cibly** /-əblɪ ; -əblɪ/ *adv* **in·vin·ci·bil·ity** /ɪnˌvɪnsə'bɪlətɪ ; ɪnˌvɪnsə'bɪlətɪ/ *n* [U].

in·viol·able /ɪn'vaɪələbl ; ɪn'vaɪələbl̩/ *adj* (formal) not to be violated, dishonoured or profaned: (正式用語)不可侵犯的;不可違背的;不容褻瀆的: *an ~ oath/law.* 不容違背的誓言(法律)。

in·viol·ate /ˌɪn'vaɪələt ; ɪn'vaɪəlɪt/ *adj* (formal) kept sacred; held in respect; not violated: (正式用語)神聖的;受敬重的;不可侵犯的: *keep an oath/a promise/rule ~;* 堅守一誓約(諾言,規則); *remain ~.* 保持不可侵犯。

in·vis·ible /ɪn'vɪzəbl ; ɪn'vɪzəbl̩/ *adj* that cannot be seen: 看不見的: *stars that are ~ to the naked eye.* 肉眼看不見的星星。 ~ **exports/imports,** money that goes out of/comes into a country as interest on capital, payments for shipping services, tourist expenditure, etc. 無形輸出(入)(如投資的利息,運費,觀光費等收支)。 ~ **ink,** ink which, when used for writing, can be seen only after treatment by heat, etc. 隱形墨水(經加熱等始顯出的一種墨水)。~ **mending,** repair of woven materials, silk stockings, etc by interweaving threads so that the repair is hardly noticeable. 看不出的修補 (編織物,絲襪等幾乎看不出的修補);織補。 **in·vis·ibly** /-əblɪ; -əblɪ/ *adv* **in·visi·bil·ity** /ɪnˌvɪzəˈbɪlətɪ; ˌɪnvɪzəˈbɪlətɪ/ *n* [U].

in·vite /ɪnˈvaɪt; ɪnˈvaɪt/ *vt* **1** [VP15A, B, 17] ask (sb to do sth, come somewhere, etc): 懇請;邀請: *~ a friend to dinner/to one's house.* 請一朋友吃飯(到家裏來)。*He didn't ~ me in.* 他未請我入內。*We are old now, and seldom get ~d out.* 我們現在老了,很少受邀外出。 **2** [VP6A] ask for: 要求;請求: *~ questions/opinions/confidences.* 請人提出問題(發表意見,說出心裡的秘密)。 **3** [VP6A, 17] encourage: 鼓勵;引誘: *The cool water of the lake ~d us to swim.* 清涼的湖水使我們想游泳。*Don't leave the windows open—it's inviting thieves to enter.* 不要讓窗子開著──那會引誘竊賊進入。□ *n* /ˈɪnvaɪt; ˈɪnvaɪt/ (sl) = invitation(2). **in·vit·ing** *adj* tempting; attractive. 誘惑的;動人的。**in·vit·ing·ly** *adv* in an inviting way: 誘惑地;動人地: *The doors were invitingly open,* open in a way that ~d people to enter. 門開着像是邀人入內。**in·vi·ta·tion**/ ˌɪnvɪˈteɪʃn; ˌɪnvəˈteʃən/ *n* **1** [U] inviting or being ~d: 邀請;被邀請: *a letter of invitation;* 邀請函; *admission by invitation only.* 非請勿入。 **2** [C] request to come or go somewhere, or do sth: 邀請的表示;請帖;招待券: *send out invitations to a party.* 發出宴客請帖。

in·vo·ca·tion /ˌɪnvəˈkeɪʃn; ˌɪnvəˈkeʃən/ *n* ⇨ invoke.

in·voice /ˈɪnvɔɪs; ˈɪnvɔɪs/ *vt, n* [VP6A] (make a) list of goods sold with the price(s) charged: (開)發票;(開)發貨單: *~ sb for goods.* 給某人開貨物發貨單。

in·voke /ɪnˈvəʊk; ɪnˈvok/ *vt* **1** [VP6A] call upon God, the power of the law, etc for help or protection. 祈求(上帝,法律的力量等)幫助或保護。**2** [VP 6A, 14] ~ ***sth on/upon,*** request earnestly; call down from heaven: 懇求;迫切地要求;祈求天降…: *~ vengeance on one's enemies.* 祈求天神向敵人報仇。 **3** [VP6A] summon up (by magic): (以法術)召喚: *~ evil spirits.* 召喚惡鬼。**in·vo·ca·tion** /ˌɪnvəˈkeɪʃn; ˌɪnvəˈkeʃən/ *n* [U] invoking or being ~d; [C] prayer or appeal that ~s. 祈求;祈禱;懇求;以法術召喚;召鬼或降神唸的咒語。

in·vol·un·tary /ɪnˈvɒləntrɪ *US:* -terɪ; ɪnˈvɑlənˌtɛrɪ/ *adj* done without intention; done unconsciously: 非本意的;不隨意的;不知不覺的: *an ~ movement of fear.* 由於恐懼所引起的不隨意的動作。**in·vol·un·tar·ily** /ɪnˈvɒləntrəlɪ *US:* ɪnˌvɒlənˈterəlɪ; ɪnˈvɑlənˌtɛrəlɪ/ *adv*

in·vo·lute /ˈɪnvəluːt; ˈɪnvəˌljut/ *adj* complex; intricate; (bot) curled spirally. 複雜的;錯雜的;(植物)內旋的;捲成螺狀的。**in·vo·lu·tion** /ˌɪnvəˈluːʃn; ˌɪnvəˈluʃən/ *n* anything internally complex or intricate. 任何內部複雜錯綜之物。

in·volve /ɪnˈvɒlv; ɪnˈvɑlv/ *vt* **1** [VP6A, 14] ***~ (in),*** cause (sb or sth) to be caught or mixed up (in trouble, etc); get (sb or sth) into a complicated or difficult condition: 使陷於(麻煩等中);使捲入複雜或困難的情況: *They are deeply ~d in debt.* 他們債臺高築。*Don't ~ yourself in unnecessary expense.* 勿做不必要的花費。 **2** [VP6A, B, 19C] have as a necessary consequence: 產生某種必然結果;牽涉;包含: *To accept the position you offer would ~ my living in London.* 若接受你提出的職位,我必然得住在倫敦了。*The war ~d a great increase in the national debt.* 那戰爭使國債大爲增加。 **~d** *adj* **1** complex: 複雜的: *an ~d sentence/explanation;* 複雜的句子(說明); *Henry James's ~d style of writing.* 亨利・詹姆士之複雜文體。 **2** ***be/become/get ~d in sth/with sb,*** be, etc concerned with sth/connected with sb: 與某事(某人)有關連: *become ~d in criminal activities;* 與犯罪活動有關連; *get emotionally ~d with sb.* 與某人相愛。**~·ment** *n*

in·vul·ner·able /ɪnˈvʌlnərəbl; ɪnˈvʌlnərəbḷ/ *adj* that cannot be wounded or hurt: 不能傷害的: (fig) (喻) *in an ~ position.* 處於無懈可擊的地位。

in·ward /ˈɪnwəd; ˈɪnwəd/ *adj* **1** situated within; inner: 在內的;內部的: *~ happiness,* ie of the spirit; 內在的快樂(即精神的快樂); *one's ~* (ie mental or spiritual) *nature.* 一個人內在的性情(或心性)。 **2** turned towards the inside: 向內的: *an ~ curve.* 向內的弧線。**~·ly** *adv* in mind or spirit: 內心或精神方面: *grieve ~ly,* ie so as not to show one's grief. 苦在心裏(不將痛苦表現出來)。 **~·ness** *n* (person's) inner nature; spiritual quality: (人之)心性;本性;本質: *the true ~ness of Christ's teaching.* 基督教義眞正的本質。 **~(s)** *adv* towards the inside; into or towards the mind or soul. 向內;入內心;向心靈。

in·wrought /ˌɪnˈrɔːt; ɪnˈrɔt/ *adj* (of a fabric) decorated (*with* a pattern, etc); (of a pattern or design) worked or woven (*in* or *on*). (指織物)繡有(花型等)的(與 with 連用);(指花型或圖案)繡入的;織入的(與 in 或 on 連用)。

iod·ine /ˈaɪədiːn *US:* -daɪn; ˈaɪəˌdaɪn/ *n* [U] non-metallic element (symbol **I**) found in seawater and seaweed, widely used as an antiseptic (in the form *tincture of ~*) and in photography. 碘(存於海水和海藻中的非金屬元素,符號爲I,製成碘酒普遍用做消毒劑,亦用於攝影)。

ion /ˈaɪən; ˈaɪən/ *n* electrically charged particle formed by losing or gaining electrons. Such particles make a solution of certain chemicals a conductor of electricity. 離子;游子。 **ion·ize** /ˈaɪənaɪz; ˈaɪənˌaɪz/ *vi, vt* [VP2A, 6A] be converted or convert into ions. (使)變成離子;電離。 **ion·iz·ation** /ˌaɪənaɪˈzeɪʃn *US:* -nɪˈz-; ˌaɪənəˈzeʃən/ *n* [U]. **iono·sphere** /aɪˈɒnəsfɪə(r); aɪˈɑnəˌsfɪr/ *n* (also known as 亦稱作 the *Heaviside Layer*) set of layers of the earth's atmosphere, which reflect radio waves and cause them to follow the earth's contour. 電離層(大氣之一層,反射電波並傳送至地球各處)。

Ionic /aɪˈɒnɪk; aɪˈɑnɪk/ *adj* (archit) of the type of column(1) in ancient Greek architecture having scrolls on the capital(4). (建築)愛奧尼亞式的(古希臘之一種建築式,其柱頭有渦卷形裝飾)。⇨ the illus at column. 參看 column 之插圖。

iota /aɪˈəʊtə; aɪˈotə/ *n* the Greek letter ι; (fig) smallest amount: 希臘字母(ι);(喻)極小量: *not an ~ of truth in the story,* no truth at all. 故事中絲毫沒有眞實性。

IOU /ˌaɪ əʊ ˈjuː; ˈaɪˌoˈju/ *n* (= *I owe you*) signed paper acknowledging that one owes the sum of money stated. 借據;欠條 (本義爲'我欠你'或'玆借到')。

ipse dixit /ˌɪpsɪ ˈdɪksɪt; ˈɪpsɪˈdɪksɪt/ (Lat) (= *he himself said it*) dogmatic statement made on sb's unsupported word. (拉)武斷的陳述;武斷的言辭。

ipso facto /ˌɪpsəʊ ˈfæktəʊ; ˈɪpsoˈfækto/ *adv phrase* (Lat) by that very fact. (拉)就該事實而論。

iras·cible /ɪˈræsəbl; aɪˈræsəbḷ/ *adj* (formal) easily made angry. (正式用語)易怒的;性情暴躁的。**iras·ci·bil·ity** /ɪˌræsəˈbɪlətɪ; aɪˌræsəˈbɪlətɪ/ *n* tendency to anger; angry behaviour. 易怒;性情暴躁。

irate /aɪˈreɪt; ˈaɪret/ *adj* (formal) angry. (正式用語)發怒的;憤怒的。 **~·ly** *adv*

ire /ˈaɪə(r); aɪr/ *n* (poet or formal) anger. (詩中或正式用語)發怒;憤怒。**ire·ful** /-fl; -fəl/ *adj* angry. 憤怒的。

iri·des·cent /ˌɪrɪˈdesnt; ˌɪrəˈdɛsṇt/ *adj* (formal) showing colours like those of the rainbow; changing colour as light falls from different directions. (正式用語)呈虹彩的;現暈光的。**iri·des·cence** /-ˈdesns; -ˈdɛsṇs/ *n* [U].

irid·ium /ɪˈrɪdɪəm; aɪˈrɪdɪəm/ *n* [U] hard white

metal (symbol **Ir**). 銥(一種堅硬的白色金屬,符號爲Ir)。

iris /ˈaɪərɪs ; ˈaɪrɪs/ *n* **1** coloured part round the pupil of the eye. 眼球之虹彩;虹膜。⇨ the illus at eye. 參看 eye 之插圖。 **2** kinds of flowering plant with sword-shaped leaves. 鳶尾屬植物。

Irish /ˈaɪərɪʃ ; ˈaɪrɪʃ/ *adj* of Ireland: 愛爾蘭的: *the ~ Free State/the ~ Republic* (also 亦作 *Eire* /ˈeərə ; ˈerə/), part of Ireland that became independent in 1922. 愛爾蘭自由邦;愛爾蘭共和國(愛爾蘭之一部,於1922年獨立)。ˌ~ ˈ**stew**, one of mutton, boiled with onions and other vegetables. (加洋葱和其他蔬菜煮成的)燉羊肉。□ *n* the ~ language (= ~ *Gaelic*, ⇨ Gael). 愛爾蘭語。 **the** ~, ~ people. 愛爾蘭人。 **~·man** /-mən ; -mən/ *n* (*pl* -men) **~·woman** /-wʊmən ; -ˌwʊmən/ *n* (*pl* -women) native of Ireland. 愛爾蘭人;愛爾蘭女人。

irk /ɜːk ; ɝk/ *vt* trouble; annoy 使厭煩;使苦惱 (chiefly in 主要用於): *It irks me to* (*do sth*). 我討厭(做某事)。**irk·some** /-səm ; -səm/ *adj* tiresome. 令人厭煩的。

iron[1] /ˈaɪən *US:* ˈaɪərn ; ˈaɪɚn/ *n* **1** [U] commonest of all metallic elements (symbol **Fe**), used in various forms (⇨ *cast* ~ at cast[1](3), *wrought* ~ at wrought): 鐵(符號爲 Fe): *~ ore;* 鐵礦; *as hard as ~;* 鐵一般堅硬; (fig) (喻) *an ~ will.* 堅强的意志。 ***rule with a rod of ~/with an ~ hand,*** with extreme severity. 壓制;施高壓政策統治。***a man of ~,*** a hard, unyielding or merciless man. 鐵漢;意志堅强之人;鐵石心腸之人。 ***an ~ fist in a velvet glove,*** an appearance of gentleness concealing severity, determination. 外柔內剛。 ***Strike while the ~ is hot,*** act while the opportunity is good. 打鐵趁熱;把握良機。 **the ˈI~ Age,** prehistoric period, following the Bronze Age, when ~ came into use for tools and weapons. 鐵器時代。~ **curtain,** (fig) frontier between countries, considered as a barrier to information and trade. (喻) 鐵幕 (使一國與其他國家在消息和貿易上隔絕的界線)。~ **lung,** apparatus fitted over the whole body, except the head, to provide a person with artificial respiration by the use of mechanical pumps. 鐵肺(裝於身體四周,頭部除外,藉機械氣筒造成人工呼吸的裝置)。~ **rations,** store of food for use in an emergency as for troops/explorers. 鐵糧;携帶口糧(應急之用,例如軍隊或探測者所用者)。 **2** [C] (esp in compounds) tool, etc made of ~: (尤用於複合字中) 鐵器: (ˈ*flat-*)~, flat-bottomed household implement, heated (usu electrically) and used for smoothing clothes, etc; 熨斗; ˈ*fire-~s*, poker, tongs, etc used at a fireplace or stove; 火爐用具(撥火棒,火鉗等); golf-club with an ~ head; branding tool; 鐵頭高爾夫球棒;烙鐵; (*pl*) fetters: (複)鐐銬: *put sb in ~s*, fasten his wrists and ankles in chains. 給某人加以鐐銬。 ***have too many ~s in the fire,*** too many undertakings needing attention at the same time. 同時要辦的事太多。**3** (compounds) (複合字) ˈ**~·clad** *adj* protected by ~. 裝甲的。ˈ**~-foundry** *n* foundry where cast~ is produced. 鑄鐵廠。ˌ**~-ˈgrey** *adj, n* (of) the colour of freshly broken cast~. 鐵灰色(的)。ˈ**~·monger** /-mʌŋgə(r); -ˌmʌŋgɚ/ *n* dealer in metal goods. 五金商。ˈ**~-mongery** /-mʌŋgərɪ ; -ˌmʌŋgərɪ/ *n* business of an ~monger. 五金業。ˈ**~·mould** *n* discolouration caused by ~ rust or ink. 銹痕;墨水痕。 ˈ**~·side** *n* one of Oliver Cromwell's cavalry troopers (17th c); (fig) tough, obstinate man. 十七世紀克倫威爾所率騎兵隊之隊員;(喻)剛毅固執之人。ˈ**~·ware** /-weə(r) ; -ˌwɛr/ *n* [U] goods made of ~; hardware. 鐵器;五金。 ˈ**~·work** *n* anything made of ~, eg gratings, rails, railings. 鐵製之物(例如柵欄,鐵軌等)。ˈ**~-works** *n* (usu with *sing v*) place where ~ is smelted or where heavy ~ goods are made. (通常用單數動詞)鍊鐵廠;鐵工廠。

iron[2] /ˈaɪən *US:* ˈaɪərn ; ˈaɪɚn/ *vt, vi* [VP6A, 15A, B, 2A, C] smooth cloth/clothes with an ~ (a ˈflat-~): (以熨斗)熨平(衣物): ~ *a shirt.* 熨一襯衫。 *Do clothes ~ more easily when they are damp?* 衣服潮濕時是否易於熨平? *She's been ~ing all afternoon.* 她一下午都在熨衣服。~ **out,** remove by ~ing: 藉熨燙而除去: ~ *out wrinkles;* 將皺摺熨平; (fig) remove: (喻)消除: ~ *out misunderstandings/points of disagreement.* 消除誤會(歧見)。 ˈ**~ing-board** *n* padded board on which to ~ clothes, etc. 熨衣板。

ironic /aɪˈrɒnɪk ; aɪˈrɑnɪk/, **ironi·cal** /aɪˈrɒnɪkl ; aɪˈrɑnɪkl/ *adjj* of, using, expressing, irony: 反語的;用反語的;諷刺的: *an ~ smile/remark/person.* 譏諷的笑(諷刺之言; 喜歡譏諷別人的人)。 **ironi·cally** /-klɪ ; -klɪ/ *adv*

irony /ˈaɪərənɪ ; ˈaɪrənɪ/ *n* **1** [U] the expression of one's meaning by saying sth which is the direct opposite of one's thoughts, in order to make one's remarks forceful. 反語; 反語法 (說出與自己思想恰恰相反的話以增强講話力量之表現法)。 **2** [C] (*pl* -nies) event, situation, etc which is itself desirable, but which, because of the circumstances, is of little or no value, thus appearing to be directed by evil fate: 命運的嘲弄; 諷刺性的事件,情況等(本來是一件適意之事,但由於環境演變,而失去價值,故而像是受了命運的捉弄): *the ~ of fate/circumstances.* 命運(環境)的嘲弄。*If a poor man inherits a large fortune and dies a month later, one might call it one of life's ironies.* 如果一個窮人繼承一大筆財產後一個月便死了,我們可稱之爲人生的一大嘲弄。

ir·ra·di·ate /ɪˈreɪdɪeɪt ; ɪˈredɪˌet/ *vt* [VP6A] (formal) (正式用語) **1** send rays of light upon; subject to sunlight, ultraviolet rays, or radioactivity; (fig) throw light on (a subject). 照耀;用陽光,紫外線或放射線照射;(喻)闡釋(一問題);啓發。 **2** light up: 使生輝: *faces ~d with joy.* 因高興而煥發的面孔。

ir·ra·tional /ɪˈræʃənl ; ɪˈræʃənl̩/ *adj* **1** not endowed with reason: 無理性的: *behave like an ~ animal.* 舉止像一無理性的野獸。 **2** not guided by reason: 荒謬的;不合理的: *~ fears/behaviour.* 荒唐無稽的恐懼(行爲)。**~ly** /-ʃnəlɪ ; -ʃənl̩ɪ/ *adv*

ir·rec·on·cil·able /ɪˌrekənˈsaɪləbl ; ɪˈrɛkənˌsaɪləbl̩/ *adj* (formal) (of persons) that cannot be reconciled; (of ideas, actions) that cannot be brought into harmony. (正式用語) (指人)不能和解的;(指思想,行動)不能調和的。

ir·re·cover·able /ˌɪrɪˈkʌvərəbl ; ˌɪrɪˈkʌvərəbl̩/ *adj* (formal) that cannot be recovered or remedied: (正式用語)不能挽回的;不能治療的;不能補救的: *~ losses.* 不可挽回的損失。

ir·re·deem·able /ˌɪrɪˈdiːməbl ; ˌɪrɪˈdiməbl̩/ *adj* **1** (of paper currency) that cannot be exchanged for coin; (of government annuities) that cannot be terminated by repayment. (指紙幣)不能兌換的;(指政府年金)不能藉償還而終止的。**2** that cannot be restored, reclaimed, saved: 不能恢復的;不可救藥的;不能挽救的: *an ~ loss/misfortune.* 不能挽救的損失(不幸)。

ir·re·den·tist /ˌɪrɪˈdentɪst ; ˌɪrɪˈdɛntɪst/ *n* person who advocates the reunion to his own country of territory which has been lost to a foreign government, or which is culturally related to his own country, eg to Italy of Italian-speaking districts. 主張國土統一者(主張收復喪失之領土或將與本國文化相關之地區併入國土之人,例如將說義大利語的地區併入義大利)。**ir·ri·den·tism** /-ɪzəm ; -ɪzm̩/ *n*

ir·re·duc·ible /ˌɪrɪˈdjuːsəbl *US:* -ˈduːs- ; ˌɪrɪˈdjusəbl̩/ *adj* ~ ***(to),*** (formal) (正式用語) **1** that cannot be reduced or made smaller: 不能減低的; 不能縮小的: *£250 is the ~ minimum for repairs to the house.* 二百五十鎊是修理這房子所需要的最低額了。 **2** that cannot be brought (*to* a desired condition). 不能歸復(所期望之狀態)的。

ir·re·fut·able /ˌɪrɪˈfjuːtəbl ; ɪˈrɛfjʊtəbl̩/ *adj* that cannot be proved false: 不能駁倒的: *an ~ argument/case.* 無法反駁的論點(供詞)。

ir·regu·lar /ɪˈregjʊlə(r) ; ɪˈrɛgjəlɚ/ *adj* **1** contrary to rules, to what is normal and established: 不合

常規的；不規則的；非正規的：*an ~ proceeding／marriage;* 非按正規的處置(非正式的婚姻)；*be ~ in church attendance*, be absent frequently; 做禮拜的次數不規則(常常不到)；*~ troops*, not trained for, or not forming part of, the regular army. 非正規軍。**2** uneven; not regular in shape, arrangement, etc: 不平坦的；不整齊的：*~ lines and figures;* 零亂的線條和圖形；*a coast with an ~ outline*, with many bays, inlets, etc. 曲折的海岸線。**3** (gram) not inflected in the usual way: (文法)變化不規則的：*'Child' has an ~ plural.* Child一字之複數變化不規則。□ *n* (usu *pl*) member of an ~ military force. (通常用複數)非正規軍。**~·ly** *adv* **~·ity** /ɪˌregjʊ'lærətɪ；ˌɪrɛgjə'lærətɪ/ *n* (*pl* -ties) [U] state or quality of being ~; [C] sth ~: 不合常規；不規則；不平坦；不整齊；不規則的事物；不平坦的東西：*~ities in behaviour;* 行爲反常之處；*the ~ities of the earth's surface.* 地球表面之凹凸不平。

ir·rel·evant /ɪ'reləvənt；ɪ'rɛləvənt/ *adj* **~ (to)**, not relevant (to); not connected (with): 不切題的；不相關的：*~ remarks／evidence.* 不相關的話(證據)。*What you say is ~ to the subject.* 你說的話不切題。**ir·rel·evance** /-əns；-əns/, **ir·rel·evancy** /-ənsɪ；-ənsɪ/ *nn* (*pl* ~s, -cies) [U] state of being ~; [C] ~ remark, question, etc: 不切題；不相關；不相關的言論，問題等：*Let us ignore these irrelevancies.* 我們不要管這些不相干的事。

ir·re·li·gious /ˌɪrɪ'lɪdʒəs；ˌɪrɪ'lɪdʒəs/ *adj* opposed to, showing no interest in, religion: 反宗教的；對宗教無興趣的：*~ acts／persons.* 反宗教的行爲(人)。

ir·re·medi·able /ˌɪrɪ'mi:dɪəbl；ˌɪrɪ'midɪəbl̩/ *adj* that cannot be remedied: 無可救藥的；不能補救的：*~ acts／faults.* 不能補救的行爲(過失)。

ir·re·mov·able /ˌɪrɪ'mu:vəbl；ˌɪrɪ'muvəbl̩/ *adj* that cannot be removed (esp from office). 不能移動的；(尤指)不能撤免其職務的。

ir·rep·ar·able /ɪ'repərəbl；ɪ'rɛpərəbl̩/ *adj* (of a loss, injury, etc) that cannot be put right or restored: (指損失，傷害等)不能彌補的；無可挽救的：*~ harm.* 無可挽救的傷害。

ir·re·place·able /ˌɪrɪ'pleɪsəbl；ˌɪrɪ'plesəbl̩/ *adj* of which the loss cannot be supplied. 不能替換的。

ir·re·press·ible /ˌɪrɪ'presəbl；ˌɪrɪ'prɛsəbl̩/ *adj* that cannot be held back or controlled: 不能抑制的；不能控制的：*a girl with ~ high spirits.* 抑制不住高興的女孩。

ir·re·proach·able /ˌɪrɪ'prəʊtʃəbl；ˌɪrɪ'protʃəbl̩/ *adj* free from blame or fault: 無可責難的；無過失的：*~ conduct.* 無可非難的行爲。

ir·re·sist·ible /ˌɪrɪ'zɪstəbl；ˌɪrɪ'zɪstəbl̩/ *adj* too strong, convincing, delightful, etc to be resisted: (過於堅强，有說服力，令人快樂等而)不可抵抗的；不能壓制的；禁不住的：*~ desires／temptations.* 不能抗拒的慾望(誘惑)。*On this hot day the sea was ~*, We couldn't resist the desire to go to or into the sea. 在這種熱天，我們不禁想到海邊去玩。

ir·res·ol·ute /ɪ'rezəlu:t；ɪ'rɛzəˌlut/ *adj* undecided; hesitating. 無決斷的；猶豫不決的。**ir·res·ol·ution** /ɪˌrezə'lu:ʃn；ˌɪrɛzə'luʃən/ *n* [U].

ir·re·spec·tive /ˌɪrɪ'spektɪv；ˌɪrɪ'spɛktɪv/ *adj* **~ of**, not paying consideration to; not taking into account: 不考慮；不顧：*He rushed forward to help, ~ of the consequences.* 他不顧後果，衝上前去救助。

ir·re·spon·sible /ˌɪrɪ'spɒnsəbl；ˌɪrɪ'spɑnsəbl̩/ *adj* **1** not responsible for conduct, etc; not to be blamed or punished: (對行爲等)不須負責任的；不受指責或懲罰的：*an ~ child.* 不須負責的孩子。**2** (doing things, done) without a proper sense of responsibility; not trustworthy: (做事)無責任感的；不可靠的：*~ teenagers;* 無責任感的青少年；*~ behaviour.* 不可靠的行爲。**ir·re·spon·si·bil·ity** /ˌɪrɪˌspɒnsə'bɪlətɪ；ˌɪrɪˌspɑnsə'bɪlətɪ/ *n* [U].

ir·re·triev·able /ˌɪrɪ'tri:vəbl；ˌɪrɪ'trivəbl̩/ *adj* that cannot be retrieved or remedied: 不可挽回的；不能補救的：*an ~ loss.* 不能補救的損失。

ir·rev·er·ent /ɪ'revərənt；ɪ'rɛvərənt/ *adj* feeling or showing no respect for sacred things. 不虔敬的；不恭敬的。**~·ly** *adv* **ir·rev·er·ence** /-əns；-əns/ *n* [U].

ir·re·vers·ible /ˌɪrɪ'vɜ:səbl；ˌɪrɪ'vɝsəbl̩/ *adj* that cannot be reversed or revoked: 不能反轉的；不能撤銷的：*an ~ decision.* 不能取消的決定。

ir·revo·cable /ɪ'revəkəbl；ɪ'rɛvəkəbl̩/ *adj* final and unalterable; that cannot be revoked: 已確定而不能改變的；最後的；不能取消的：*an ~ decision／judgement;* 最後的決定(判決)；*an ~ letter of credit.* 不能取消的信用狀。

ir·ri·gate /'ɪrɪgeɪt；'ɪrəˌget/ *vt* [VP6A] **1** supply (land, crops) with water (by means of rivers, water-channels, overhead pipes, etc): 灌溉(田地，作物)：*~ desert areas and make them fertile.* 灌溉荒蕪地區使之變爲肥沃良田。**2** construct reservoirs, canals, etc for the distribution of water (to fields). 築水庫，溝渠等以分配水(至農田)。**3** wash out (a wound, etc) with a constant flow of liquid. 冲洗(傷口等)。**ir·ri·ga·tion** /ˌɪrɪ'geɪʃn；ˌɪrə'geʃən/ [U] irrigating: 灌溉；冲洗：(attrib) (形容用法) *an irrigation project;* 灌溉計畫；*irrigation canals.* 灌溉用的溝渠。

ir·ri·table /'ɪrɪtəbl；'ɪrətəbl̩/ *adj* easily annoyed or made angry. 急躁的；易怒的。**ir·ri·tably** /-əblɪ；-əblɪ/ *adv* **ir·ri·ta·bil·ity** /ˌɪrɪtə'bɪlətɪ；ˌɪrətə'bɪlətɪ/ *n* [U].

ir·ri·tant /'ɪrɪtənt；'ɪrətənt/ *adj* causing irritation. 有刺激性的。□ *n* ~ substance, eg dust or pepper in the nose; sth that irritates the mind. 刺激物(例如鼻孔中之灰塵或胡椒)；使精神受刺激的事物。

ir·ri·tate /'ɪrɪteɪt；'ɪrəˌtet/ *vt* [VP6A] **1** make angry or annoyed; excite the temper of: 激怒；使急躁：*~d by the delay.* 被躭擱所激怒。**2** cause discomfort to (part of the body); make sore or inflamed: 使(身體某部)感到不適；刺激；使痛或發炎：*The smoke ~d her eyes.* 煙熏得她眼睛不舒服。**ir·ri·ta·tion** /ˌɪrɪ'teɪʃn；ˌɪrə'teʃən/ *n* [U] irritating or being ~d; [C] instance of this. (被)激怒；憤怒；刺激；感到痛或發炎。

ir·rup·tion /ɪ'rʌpʃn；ɪ'rʌpʃən/ *n* sudden and violent entry; bursting in. 突然衝入；闖入。

is ⇨ be¹.

isin·glass /'aɪzɪŋglɑ:s *US:* -glæs；'aɪzɪŋˌglæs/ *n* [U] clear white jelly made from the air bladders of some freshwater fish, used for making glue. 魚膠(由某些淡水魚之鰾製成，用以製膠)。

Is·lam /ɪz'lɑ:m *US:* 'ɪslɑ:m；'ɪsləm/ *n* faith, religion, proclaimed by the Prophet Muhammad; all Muslims; all the Muslim world. 回教信仰；伊斯蘭教；回教；回教徒(總稱)；回教世界。**~ic** /ɪz'læmɪk *US:* ɪs'lɑ:mɪk；ɪs'læmɪk/ *adj*

is·land /'aɪlənd；'aɪlənd/ *n* piece of land surrounded by water; sth resembling an ~ because it is detached or isolated: 島；島嶼；孤立似島之物：*a 'traffic ~*, a raised place in a busy street where people may be safe from traffic. (馬路上之)安全島。**~er** *n* person born on or living on an ~. 島人；島民。

isle /aɪl；aɪl/ *n* island (not much used in prose, except in proper names): 島；嶼(除用於專有名詞外，罕用於散文中)：*the I~ of Wight;* 威特島(在英國)；*the British I~s.* 不列顛諸島。**is·let** /'aɪlɪt；'aɪlɪt/ *n* small island. 小島；小島嶼。

ism /'ɪzəm；'ɪzəm/ *n* distinctive doctrine or practice: 主義；學說；制度：*behaviourism and all the other isms of the twentieth century.* 二十世紀之行爲主義及所有其他的學說。

isn't ⇨ be¹.

iso·bar /'aɪsəbɑ:(r)；'aɪsəˌbɑr/ *n* line on a map, esp a weather chart, joining places with the same atmospheric pressure at a particular time. 等壓線(地圖上，尤指氣象圖上，連接在某一時間氣壓相等之各地點的線)。

iso·late /'aɪsəleɪt；'aɪsl̩ˌet/ *vt* [VP6A, 14] **~ (from)**, **1** separate, put or keep apart from others: 使隔離；使孤立；使隔絕：*feel ~d from one's* *fellows.* 在同伴中感到孤立。*When a person has an infectious disease, he is usually ～d.* 當一人患傳染病時，他通常是被隔離起來。*Several villages in the north have been ～d by heavy snowfalls.* 北部有幾個村莊因大雪而與外界隔絕了。**2** (chem) separate a substance, germ, etc from its combinations. (化學)分解(物質等)；使游離；使(細菌)分離。

iso·la·tion /ˌaɪsəˈleɪʃn ; ˌaɪslˈeʃən/ *n* [U] ～ ***(from),*** isolating or being isolated. 隔離；孤立；隔絕；分解；游離；分離。***in*** ～, alone; separated: 單獨的；隔離的：*consider facts in ～ from others.* 單獨考慮某些事實。**ˈ～ hospital／ward,** one for persons with infectious diseases. 隔離醫院(病房)。**～·ism** /-ɪzm ; -ɪzm/ *n* (in international affairs) policy of non-participation in the affairs of other countries. (國際事務中的)孤立主義。**～·ist** /-ɪst ; -ɪst/ *n* supporter of ～ism. 孤立主義者。

isos·celes /aɪˈsɒsəliːz ; aɪˈsɑslˌiz/ *adj* (of a triangle) having two sides equal. (指三角形)二等邊的；等腰的。

iso·therm /ˈaɪsəθɜːm ; ˈaɪsəˌθɝm/ *n* line on a map joining places having the same mean temperature. 等溫線(地圖上連接平均溫度相等之地點的線)。

iso·tope /ˈaɪsətəʊp ; ˈaɪsəˌtop/ *n* atom of an element, eg heavy hydrogen, having a nuclear mass different from that of other atoms of the same element although chemically identical: 同位素(同一元素中之原子，其核質量與其他原子不同而化學性質完全相同者，如氫中之重氫)：*radio-active ～s,* unstable forms used in medicine and industry. 放射同位素。

issue /ˈɪʃuː ; ˈɪʃu/ *vi, vt* **1** [VP2A, 3A] ～ ***(out／forth) (from),*** come, go, flow, out: 出來；發出；流出：*smoke issuing from chimneys;* 煙囱冒出的煙；*blood issuing from a wound.* 自傷口流出的血。**2** [VP6A, 14] ～ ***(sth to sb),*** ～ ***(sb with sth),*** distribute for use or consumption: 分發；發給：～ *warm clothing to the troops;* 發暖和的衣服給軍隊；～ *them with warm clothing.* 發給他們暖和的衣服。**3** [VP6A, 14] ～ ***(to),*** publish (books, etc); put stamps, banknotes, shares¹(3), etc into circulation. 出版(書等)；發行(郵票，鈔票，股票等)。□ *n* **1** [U] outgoing; outflowing: 發出；流出：*the point or place of ～;* 發出點；[C] the act of flowing out; that which flows out: 流出；流出物：*an ～ of blood from the nose.* 鼻子流血。**2** [U] putting forth; sending out; publication: 發行；出版；印行：*the ～ of a newspaper／a new coinage;* 報紙(新幣)之發行；*buy new stamps on the day of ～;* 於發行日購買新郵票；[C] that which is sent out, etc: 發行等之物：*new ～s of banknotes;* 新發行的鈔票；*the most recent ～s of a periodical;* 一定期刊物最近的發行本；*an ～ of winter clothing to the troops.* 發給軍隊冬衣。**3** [C] question that arises for discussion: 引起討論的問題：*debate an ～;* 爲一問題辯論；*raise a new ～;* 提出一新問題；*argue political ～s.* 爭論政治問題。***join／take ～ with sb (on／about sth),*** proceed to argue with him (about it). 與某人爭辯(某事)。***the point／matter at ～,*** the point being discussed. 爭論點；正在討論的問題。**4** [C] result; outcome; consequence: 結果；後果：*bring a campaign to a successful ～;* 使一活動獲致良好結果；*await the ～.* 等待結果。**5** [U] (legal) offspring: (法律)子孫：*die without ～,* ie childless. 死時無子嗣。

isth·mus /ˈɪsməs ; ˈɪsməs/ *n* (*pl* ～es /-sɪz ; -sɪz/) neck of land joining two larger bodies of land: 地峽：*the I～ of Panama.* 巴拿馬地峽。

it /ɪt ; ɪt/ *pron* (*pl* they /ðeɪ ; ðe/, them /ðəm ; ðəm; *strong form* ðem ; ðɛm/) **1** (used of lifeless things, of animals (when sex is unknown or unimportant), and of a baby or small child when the sex is unknown or a matter of indifference): 它；牠(指無生命的東西，性別不明或不重要的動物，亦指性別不明或無關緊要的嬰兒或小孩)：*This is my watch; it's a Swiss one.* 這是我的錶，它是瑞士製的。*Where's my book?— Have you seen it?* 我的書在那裏？——你看見它沒有？*'Where's the cat?'—'It's in the garden.'* '貓在那裏？'——'牠在花園裏。' *She's expecting another baby and hopes it will be a boy.* 她又有孕了，她希望生個男孩。**2** (used to refer to a group of words which follows, this being the grammatical subject. This may be) (用以指其後的一組字，該組字可能爲) **(a)** an infinitive phrase: 不定詞片語：Is *it* difficult *to learn written Chinese?* 學習中國文字很難嗎？**(b)** a construction with *for,* a *noun／pronoun,* and a *to*-infinitive: 接 for＋名詞或代名詞＋不定詞：*It* was hard *for him to live on his small pension.* 依靠菲薄的養老金生活使他感到甚爲艱苦。**(c)** a gerundial phrase: 動名詞片語：*It* doesn't seem much use *going on.* 繼續下去似乎沒有什麼用處。*It*'s no use *your trying to do that.* 你試圖那樣做是無用的。**(d)** a clause: 一子句：*It* seems unlikely *that he will catch the train.* 他大概趕不上火車了。I think *it* a pity *that you didn't try harder.* 我認爲你未曾更加努力嘗試是一憾事。*It* doesn't matter *whether we start now or later.* 我們現在開始還是以後開始都沒有關係。Does *it* matter *what you do next?* 你下一步所做的事關係重大嗎？**3** (used to refer backwards or forwards to identify sb or sth. Note that if the identity of a person is already known, *it* is not used): (用以指明前述或後述的人或物。注意：若已知爲某人時，則不用 it)：*'Who's that at the door?'—'It's the postman.'* '誰在門口？'——'是郵差。' (Cf 參較 *Mr Smith is at the door. He wants to see you.* 史密斯先生在門口，他想要見你。) *'What was that noise?'—'It was a mouse.'* '那是什麼聲音？'——'那是一隻老鼠。' **4** (used as a formal or meaningless word to supply a subject) (用做形式上的或無意義的主詞) **(a)** dealing with the weather, atmospheric conditions, etc: 指天氣，大氣狀況等：*It is raining／snowing, etc.* 正在下雨(下雪等)。*It's warm／cold／windy, etc.* 天氣溫暖(寒冷，有風等)。*Isn't it a nice day!* 天氣眞好！*How dark it is!* 天好黑呀！**(b)** for time: 指時間：*It's six o'clock.* 六點鐘了。*It is past midnight.* 已過半夜了。*It's Monday, the 1st of May.* 今天是五月一日，星期一。*It is three years since I last met you.* 自從我上次遇見你到現在有三年了。*It's a month to Christmas.* 距聖誕節還有一個月。**(c)** for distance: 指距離：*It's ten miles to Oxford.* 到牛津有十哩。*It's only a short way now.* 現在沒有多遠了。**(d)** vaguely for the general situation, or for sth that is to be understood from the context: 模糊地指一般情形，或指由上下文可以了解的事物：*So it seems.* 好像是如此。*It can't be helped.* 沒有辦法了。*Whose turn is it next?* 下一個輪到誰了？*That's the best／worst of it!* 那最好(糟)了！*Keep at it,* ie at whatever you are doing. 繼續下去！不要放棄！*You've got what it takes,* have the qualities, etc needed for this job, situation, etc. 你有資格擔任此一工作(有辦法應付此一情況等)。*You've had it,* there's nothing more to be had from this situation, experience, etc. 你已够了(從這個情況，經驗等中再也得不到什麼了)。*Go it!* Go o[n] with your efforts, etc. 繼續努力！*Now you'[ve] done it!* ie You've done sth wrong or foolish. 現在可糟了(你做了錯事或傻事了)！*Now you'll catc[h] it!* You'll be reprimanded, punished, etc! 現在你可倒霉了(你將受責罰等)！*As it happened,...;* 碰巧…；*If it hadn't been for your help,....* 倘若沒有你的幫助…。**5** (used to bring into prominence one part of a sentence) (用以加强句中某一部分) **(a)** the subject: 主詞：*It was his work during the weekend that exhausted him.* 使他疲憊不堪的是他週末的工作。**(b)** the object of a *v:* 動詞的受詞：*It's the red book that I want, not the green one.* 我要的是那本紅書，不是綠書。**(c)** the object of a *prep:* 介詞的受詞：*It was John I gave the book to, not Harry.* 我把書交給約翰的，不是交給哈利的。**(d)** an adverbial adjunct: 副詞修飾語：*It was on Sunday that I saw him, not on Saturday.* 我看見他的那天是星期天，不是星期六。**its** /ɪts ; ɪts/ *poss adj* of it:

它的；牠的：*The dog wagged its tail.* 那狗搖著尾巴。*The child fell and hurt its knee.* 那小孩跌傷了膝蓋。*I don't like this hat—its shape is wrong.* 我不喜歡這帽子—它的式樣不對勁。**itself** /ɪt'self ; ɪt'sɛlf/ *reflex pron*: 反身代名詞：*The dog got up and stretched itself.* 那狗站起來伸展一下身子。□ *emph pron*: 加强語氣的代名詞：*The thing itself is not valuable, but I want it as a keepsake.* 這東西的本身並無價值，但我要把它留做紀念品。**by itself, (a)** automatically: 自動地：*The machine works by itself.* 這機器是自動的。**(b)** alone: 單獨地：*The farmhouse stands by itself in the fields.* 那農舍孤零零地座落在農田中。

italic /ɪ'tælɪk ; ɪ'tælɪk/ *adj* (of printed letters) sloping: (指印刷字母)斜體的：*This is ~ type.* 這是斜體。□ *n pl* ~ letters: 斜體字母：*in ~s.* 用斜體。**italicize** /ɪ'tælɪsaɪz ; ɪ'tælə,saɪz/ *vt* print in ~s. 用斜體印刷。⇨ Roman(1).

itch /ɪtʃ ; ɪtʃ/ *n* **1** (with *def* or *indef art*, but rarely *pl*) feeling of irritation on the skin, causing a desire to scratch: (與定冠詞或不定冠詞連用，但罕用複數)癢：*have／suffer from the ~／an ~.* 覺得癢。**2** (usu with the *indef art* or a *poss adj*) restless desire or longing: (通常與不定冠詞或所有格形容詞連用)熱望；渴望：*have an ~ for money;* 渴望發財；*his ~ to go to the South Seas.* 他之渴望去南太平洋。□ *vi* **1** [VP2A, 4A] have an ~: 發癢：*scratch where it ~es.* 搔癢處。*Scratch yourself if you ~.* 如果你覺得癢，就搔好了。*Are your mosquito bites still ~ing?* 你被蚊子咬的地方還在癢嗎？ **2** [VP3A] ~ **for,** (colloq) long for: (俗)渴望：*The boys were ~ing for the lesson to end.* 那些男孩子渴望快點下課。***have an ~ing palm,*** be ~ing for money. 貪財。~**y** *adj* (-ier, -iest): *an ~y scalp.* 發癢的頭皮。

item /'aɪtəm ; 'aɪtəm/ *n* **1** single article or unit in a list, etc: (目錄等的)條款；項目：*the first ~ on the programme;* 節目中的第一項；*number the ~s in a catalogue.* 把目錄中的項目加以編號。**2** detail or paragraph (of news): (新聞之)一條；一則：*Are there any interesting 'news ~s／~s of news in the paper this morning?* 今晨報上有什麼有趣的新聞沒有？□ *adv* also (used to introduce successive articles in a list): 又；亦(用以介紹目錄中連續的項目)：*I~, one chair; ~, two carpets.* 椅子一把，又地毯兩張。~**·ize** /-aɪz ; -aɪz/ *vt* [VP6A] give, write, every ~ of: 分項列舉；分條列記：*an ~ized account;* 細帳；*~ize a bill.* 詳列一帳單。

it·er·ate /'ɪtəreɪt ; 'ɪtə,ret/ *vt* [VP6A] say again and again; make (an accusation, etc) repeatedly. 重複地說；反覆予以(控訴等)。**it·er·ation** /,ɪtə'reɪʃn ; ,ɪtə'reʃən/ *n* [U] iterating; [C] sth ~d. 重述；反覆說的話。

i·tin·er·ant /aɪ'tɪnərənt ; aɪ'tɪnərənt/ *adj* travelling from place to place: 巡迴的：*~ musicians.* 巡迴的樂師們。

i·tin·er·ary /aɪ'tɪnərərɪ *US:* -rerɪ ; aɪ'tɪnə,rɛrɪ/ *n* (*pl* -ries) [C] plan for, details or records of, a journey; route. 旅行計畫；旅行日誌；旅行路線。

it'll /'ɪtl ; 'ɪtl/ = it will.

it's /ɪts ; ɪts/ = it is; it has.

its, it·self /ɪts, ɪt'self ; ɪts, ɪt'sɛlf/ ⇨ it.

I've /aɪv ; aɪv/ = I have.

ivory /'aɪvərɪ ; 'aɪvərɪ/ *n* [U] white, bone-like substance forming the tusks of elephants, used for ornaments, piano-keys, etc; (attrib) the colour of ~: 象牙(質)(用做裝飾品、鋼琴鍵等)；(形容用法)象牙色的；乳白色的：*an ~ skin／complexion.* 乳白色的皮膚(面色)。~ **tower,** place of seclusion or retreat from the realities of life. 象牙塔(與世隔絶之境界)。

ivy

ivy /'aɪvɪ ; 'aɪvɪ/ *n* [U] climbing, clinging, evergreen plant with dark, shiny (often five-pointed) leaves. 常春藤(一種攀附性長青植物，葉子深色發亮，通常有五個尖)。**ivied** /'aɪvɪd ; 'aɪvɪd/ *adj* covered with ivy: 長滿常春藤的：*ivied walls.* 長滿常春藤的牆壁。

Jj

J, j /dʒeɪ ; dʒe/ (*pl* J's, j's /dʒeɪz ; dʒez/) the tenth letter of the English alphabet. 英文字母之第十個字母。

jab /dʒæb ; dʒæb/ *vt, vi* (-bb-) **1** [VP3A] ***jab at,*** poke or push at sb／sth with force: 猛戳；猛推：*jab at sb／sth with a knife.* 用刀猛戳某人(某物)。*He jabbed at his opponent,* (boxing) aimed a quick blow at him. (拳擊)他猛擊他的對手。 **2** [VP14] ***jab sth into sth／sb,*** force sth into sth／sb: 以…猛戳：*He jabbed his elbow into my side.* 他用肘猛戳我的腰部。 **3** [VP15B] ***jab sth out,*** force or push out by jabbing: 戳出：*Be careful! Don't jab my eye out with your umbrella!* 當心你的傘不要戳到我的眼睛！□ *n* sudden, rough blow or thrust: 猛戳；猛擊；猛刺：*a jab in the arm,* (colloq) an injection or inoculation. (俗)臂上打針或接種。*Have you had your cholera jabs yet?* 你打過霍亂預防針了嗎？

jabber /'dʒæbə(r) ; 'dʒæbə/ *vi, vt* **1** [VP2A, C] talk excitedly; talk in what seems to be a rapid and confused manner: 興奮地說；似是急促而含糊地講：*Listen to those children ~ing away!* 聽那些孩子們嘰哩咕嚕地說個不停！ **2** [VP6A, 15B] utter (words, etc) rapidly and indistinctly: 急促而模糊地說出(話等)：~ *(out) one's prayers.* 喃喃地祈禱。□ *n* [U] ~ing; chatter: 急促而含糊的說；嘰哩咕嚕的說；喋喋不休：*Listen to the ~ of those monkeys.* 聽那些猴子吱吱喳喳的叫。~**er** *n* person who ~s. 說話急促含糊的人。

jabot /'ʒæbəʊ ; ʒæ'bo/ *n* [C] ornamental frill on the front of a woman's blouse or a man's shirt. 男女襯衫胸部的裝飾縐褶。

jack[1] /dʒæk ; dʒæk/ *n* **1 J~,** familiar form of the name *John.* John 的暱稱。**J~ Frost,** frost personified. (擬人語)霜。**'J~ in office,** self-important official who fusses over details. 擺架子的官吏。**,J~ of 'all trades,** person who can turn his hand to anything; workman knowing something of many trades. 萬能先生；對許多事都懂一點的人；博藝而不精的工人。 ***before one can say J~ Robinson,*** very quickly or suddenly. 迅速地；突然地。***J~ is as good as his master,*** the workman is the equal of his employer. 夥計不比老闆差。 **2** (colloq) man. (俗)人。***every man ~,*** everybody. 每個人；人人。 **3** (usu portable) device for raising heavy weights off the ground, esp one for raising the axle of a car so that a wheel may be changed. (通常可用手提的)頂重器；(尤指)(支起汽車輪軸的)千斤頂。 **4** (in the game of bowls) small white ball towards which bowls are rolled. (滾木球戲中)小白球(木球即向該球滾去)。 **5** ship's flag to show nationality. 船艦上表示國籍的旗。 **the Union J~,** flag of the United Kingdom. 英國國旗。⇨ the illus at flag. 參看 flag 之挿圖。'~ **staff** *n* staff on

J

which a ship's flag is flown to show nationality. 艏旗桿(船艦上用以懸掛國旗者)。 **6** (in a pack of playing-cards) knave. (紙牌中之)傑克。 **7** (compounds) (複合字) '**~-in-the-box** *n* toy in the form of a box with sth inside which springs up when the lid is opened. 玩偶盒(一種盒狀玩具,蓋啓開時,有一玩偶跳出)。 ,**~-o'-'lantern** *n* will-o'-the-wisp; pumpkin cut to look like a face and used as a lantern (by placing a candle inside) in fun. 鬼火;南瓜製成的人面形燈籠。 '**~ rabbit** *n* large hare of Western N America. 北美西部所產之一種大野兎。**~tar** *n* (old name for a) naval rating; ordinary seaman in the Navy, wearing a jumper and wide-bottomed trousers. 海軍兵類之舊稱;普通水兵(穿套頭上衣及喇叭褲)。

jack² /dʒæk ; dʒæk/ *vt* [VP15B] ~ ***sth in,*** (sl) abandon (the work, attempt, etc). (俚)放棄(工作,企圖等)。~ ***sth up,*** lift with a jack(3): 用頂重器或千斤頂抬起: *J~ up the car and change the wheel with the punctured tyre.* 用千斤頂將汽車抬起,把跑氣的輪胎換掉。

jackal /'dʒækɔːl *US:* -kl ; 'dʒækɔl/ *n* wild dog-like animal. 胡狼。

jack·a·napes /'dʒækəneɪps ; 'dʒækə,neps/ *n* **1** conceited person. 自負的人。 **2** (often playfully of a child) impudent or mischievous person. 無禮或喜惡作劇的人;(常戲指)頑童。

jack·ass /'dʒækæs ; 'dʒæk,æs/ *n* male ass; foolish person. 公驢;牡驢;愚人;笨伯。 **laughing ~,** (in Australia) giant kingfisher. (澳洲產的)笑鴗;大魚狗。

jack-boot /'dʒæk buːt ; 'dʒæk,but/ *n* large boot coming above the knee (as formerly worn by cavalrymen). 過膝之長靴(如昔時騎兵所穿者)。

jack·daw /'dʒækdɔː ; 'dʒæk,dɔ/ *n* bird of the crow family (noted for flying off with small bright objects). 穴烏(一種小烏鴉,因其愛啣走明亮之小東西而著名)。

jacket /'dʒækɪt ; 'dʒækɪt/ *n* **1** short, sleeved coat. 短上衣;夾克。 ***dust a person's ~,*** beat him. 打某人。 **2** outer covering round a boiler, tank, pipe, etc to lessen loss of heat, or (*a water ~*) to cool an engine. (鍋爐,槽,管等之)護套(有保溫或冷却作用)。 **3** skin (of a potato): (馬鈴薯的)皮: *baked in their ~s.* (指馬鈴薯)連皮烘的。 **4** (also 亦作 '*dust-~*) loose paper cover in which a hardback book is issued. (精裝書的)封面套紙。

jack-knife /'dʒæk naɪf ; 'dʒæk,naɪf/ *n* large pocket-knife with a folding blade. 大摺刀。□ *vi* [VP2A] (esp of an articulated truck) fold and double back like the blade and handle of a ~. (尤指掛接拖車的貨車)(如刀刃與刀柄般)回轉摺合。

jack-plane /'dʒæk pleɪn ; 'dʒæk,plen/ *n* plane² for rough smoothing of wood. 粗鉋。

jack·pot /'dʒækpɒt ; 'dʒæk,pɑt/ *n* accumulated stakes in various games (esp poker), increasing in value until won. (尤指撲克牌賭博中)累積的賭注(逐漸增加直到被贏去)。 ***hit the ~,*** have great success or good fortune. 大獲成功;發大財。

Jaco·bean /,dʒækə'bɪən ; ,dʒækə'biən/ *adj* of the reign of James I (1603-25) of England: 英王詹姆士一世時代 (1603-25)的: ~ *literature/architecture/furniture.* 英王詹姆士一世時代的文學(建築,傢具)。

Jac·obin /'dʒækəbɪn ; 'dʒækəbɪn/ *n* member of a group of revolutionaries organized in 1789 during the French Revolution. 雅各賓派(1789年法國大革命時之一革命黨派)之黨徒。□ *adj* violent; extremely radical. 激烈的;極端激進的。**~·ism** /-ɪzəm ; -ɪzm/ *n* (politics) extreme radicalism. (政治)激進主義。

Jac·obite /'dʒækəbaɪt ; 'dʒækəbaɪt/ *n* supporter of James II (reigned 1685-1688) of England after his overthrow or of his descendants who claimed the English throne. 英王詹姆士二世(在位於1685-1688年)被推翻後或其爭取王位之子孫的擁護者。

jade¹ /dʒeɪd ; dʒed/ *n* [U] hard, usu green stone, carved into ornaments, etc. 碧玉;玉;翡翠。

jade² /dʒeɪd ; dʒed/ *n* **1** tired out or worn-out horse. 疲憊之馬;老馬。 **2** (either contemptuous or playful) woman: (輕蔑或戲謔語)女人: *You saucy little ~!* 你這個無禮的女孩子! **~d** /'dʒeɪdɪd ; 'dʒedɪd/ *adj* worn out; overworked; dulled; 疲倦的;工作過度的;變得遲鈍的: *He looks ~d.* 他看來疲憊不堪。*He has a ~d appetite.* 他的食慾不振。

jag¹ /dʒæg ; dʒæg/ *n* sharp projection, eg of rock. 尖銳的突出物(例如尖銳的岩石)。 **jaggy** *adj* having ~s. 有尖銳突出部分的;鋸齒狀的;凹凸不平的。

jag² /dʒæg ; dʒæg/ *vt* (-gg-) [VP6A] cut or tear in an uneven manner; give an edge like that of a saw to. 不整齊地切或撕;使成鋸齒狀。**jag·ged** /'dʒægɪd ; 'dʒægɪd/ *adj* notched; with rough, uneven edges: 有V字形凹痕的;邊緣不整齊的: *jagged rocks.* 巉岩。

jag·uar /'dʒægjʊə(r) ; 'dʒægwɑr/ *n* large, fierce, cat-like meat-eating animal of Central and South America. 美洲虎(中美及南美產的一種貓科食肉的兇猛大野獸)。 ⇨ the illus at cat. 參看 cat 之插圖。

jail /dʒeɪl ; dʒel/ ⇨ gaol.

jakes /dʒeɪks ; dʒeks/ *n* (sl) water-closet. (俚)(有抽水設備的)厠所。

ja·lopy /dʒə'lɒpɪ ; dʒə'lɑpɪ/ *n* (*pl* -pies) (colloq) old, rickety or battered automobile or aircraft. (俗)破舊的汽車或飛機。

jam¹ /dʒæm ; dʒæm/ *n* [U] fruit boiled with sugar until it is thick, and preserved in jars, pots, tins, etc. 果醬。 ***money for jam,*** (sl) something for nothing; something coming by good luck. (俚)白撿的財物;幸運得來的財物。 '**jam-jar/-pot** *nn* one for containing jam. 果醬瓶(罐)。 '**jam session** *n* impromptu performance by jazz musicians. 爵士樂師的即興演奏。

jam² /dʒæm ; dʒæm/ *vt, vi* (-mm-) **1** [VP6A,15A,B, 14, 2A, C] ~ ***(in/under/between, etc),*** crush, be crushed, between two surfaces or masses; squeeze, be squeezed: 壓緊;擠緊;夾住;被夾住: *a ship jammed in the ice.* 被夾在冰中的船。 *The logs jammed in the river,* become tightly packed. 圓木材擠塞在河裡。 **2** [VP15B, 2A, C] ~ ***(on),*** (of parts of a machine, etc) (cause to) become fixed so that movement or action is prevented: (指機器零件等)卡住不動;(使)發生故障: *jam the brakes on/jam on the brakes.* 猛然刹車。*The brakes jammed and the car skidded badly.* 刹車故障,汽車向一側滑衝。 **3** [VP6A, 15A, B] push (things) together tightly: 把(東西)擠塞在一起: *jam one's clothes into a small suitcase.* 把衣服塞入一小箱內。 *The corridors were jammed by/with hordes of schoolchildren.* 走廊上擠滿了一群群的小學生。 **4** [VP6A] make the reception of a broadcast programme impossible or difficult by broadcasting a signal that deliberately interferes: (無線電)干擾: *jam the enemy's stations during a war.* 戰爭期間干擾敵人的電臺。□ *n* [C] **1** number of things or peopl[e] crowded together so that movement is difficult [or] impossible: 擁塞之物;擁擠的人群: *'traffic-jams [in] our big towns;* 我們大城市中交通的擁塞; *a 'log-jam* on a river, etc. (河上等)圓木材擁塞。 **2** stoppage of a machine due to jamming(2). 機器之因故障而停頓。 **3** (sl) awkward position; difficult situation: (俚)窘境;困難的處境: *be in/get into a jam.* 陷入困難的處境。

jamb /dʒæm ; dʒæm/ *n* vertical side post of a doorway, window frame, etc; (*pl*) stone sides of a fireplace. 門,窗等之側柱;楹子;(複)壁爐兩旁的石壁。

jam·boree /,dʒæmbə'riː ; ,dʒæmbə'ri/ *n* **1** merry meeting. 快樂的聚會。 **2** large rally or gathering, esp of Scouts or Guides. 大集會;(尤指)童子軍大會。

jam·pack /,dʒæm'pæk ; 'dʒæm'pæk/ *vt* [VP6A] (colloq) crowd to capacity: (俗)擠滿;塞滿: *a stadium ~ed with spectators.* 擠滿觀衆的運動場。

jangle /'dʒæŋgl ; 'dʒæŋgl/ *vt, vi* [VP6A, 2A] (cause to) give out a harsh metallic noise; argue noisily.

(使)發出刺耳的金屬碰擊聲;喧鬧地爭論。□ *n* [U] harsh noise. 刺耳的聲音。

jani·tor /ˈdʒænɪtə(r) ; ˈdʒænətɚ/ *n* **1** doorkeeper. 看門者;管門者。**2** (US) person hired to take care of a building, offices, etc, eg by cleaning, stoking the furnaces. (美)照顧一建築物,辦公室等(例如打掃房間,照料火爐)者;工友。

Jan·uary /ˈdʒænjʊərɪ *US:* -jʊerɪ ; ˈdʒænjʊˌɛrɪ/ *n* the first month of the year. 一月;正月。

Ja·nus /ˈdʒeɪnəs ; ˈdʒenəs/ *n* ancient Roman god, guardian of gates and doors, beginnings and ends, represented with two faces, one on the front and the other on the back of his head. 古羅馬之門神(司管門戶,開始與結束,有兩個面孔,一在頭的前面,一在頭的後面)。

ja·pan /dʒəˈpæn ; dʒəˈpæn/ *vt* (-nn-), *n* (cover with) hard, shiny black enamel. 漆;亮漆;假漆;塗以假漆。

jape /dʒeɪp ; dʒep/ *n* (old use) joke. (舊用法)玩笑;笑話。

ja·pon·ica /dʒəˈpɒnɪkə ; dʒəˈpɑnɪkə/ *n* [U] (sorts of) ornamental variety of pear or quince. 裝飾用的梨樹或榅桲類植物。

jar¹ /dʒɑː(r) ; dʒɑr/ *n* [C] **1** (usu harsh) sound or vibration: (通常指刺耳的)聲音或震動;軋音: *We felt a jar when the engine was coupled to the train.* 當機車連接到火車上時,我們感到了震動。**2** shock; thrill of the nerves; discord: 震盪;震驚;神經的刺激;不和;爭吵: *The fall from his horse gave him a nasty jar.* 他自馬上跌下受到劇烈的震盪。*It was an unpleasant jar to my nerves.* 那使我神經不安。

jar² /dʒɑː(r) ; dʒɑr/ *n* tall vessel, usu round, with a wide mouth, with or without handle(s), of glass, stone or earthenware; its contents: 罈子;罇;廣口瓶;一廣口瓶內所裝之物或量: *a jar of strawberry jam.* 一瓶草莓醬。**jar·ful** /-fʊl ; -fəl/ *n*

jar³ /dʒɑː(r) ; dʒɑr/ *vi, vt* (-rr-) **1** [VP3A] ***jar against／on,*** strike with a harsh unpleasant sound. 以刺耳的聲音撞擊。**2** [VP3A] ***jar on,*** have an unpleasant effect (on): 使有不愉快的感覺: *The way he laughs jars on me／on my ears／on my nerves.* 他大笑的樣子使我有不愉快的感覺(刺激我的耳朵,刺激我的神經)。**3** [VP6A] send a shock through (the nerves): 震動(神經): *He was badly jarred by the blow.* 那打擊使他的神經震動得很厲害。*She was jarred by this sad news.* 她爲此不幸的消息而受了刺激。**4** [VP2A, 3A] ***jar (with),*** be out of harmony: 不和諧;不一致: *His opinions jar with mine.* 他的意見與我的不一致。*Try to avoid colours that jar when choosing curtains and rugs.* 選擇窗簾和地毯時,設法避免顏色不調和。**jar·ring** *adj* causing disharmony; harsh: 引起不調和的;刺耳的: *a jarring note.* 刺耳的音調。**jar·ring·ly** *adv*

jar·gon /ˈdʒɑːgən ; ˈdʒɑrgən/ *n* [U] **1** language difficult to understand, because it is badly formed or spoken badly: 因形式不好或說得不好而使人難懂的話;怪異難懂的話語: *Only a mother can understand her baby's ～.* 祇有母親能了解她的嬰兒說的那種難懂的話。**2** language full of technical or special words: 多專門術語的話;行話;切口: *the ～ of radio technicians／linguists.* 無線電技術人員(語言學家)用的行話。

jas·mine /ˈdʒæsmɪn ; ˈdʒæsmɪn/ *n* [U] shrub with white or yellow sweet-smelling flowers. 茉莉;素馨。

jas·per /ˈdʒæspə(r) ; ˈdʒæspɚ/ *n* [U] semi-precious stone, red, yellow or brown. 碧石(紅,黃或褐色的次等寶石)。

jaun·dice /ˈdʒɔːndɪs ; ˈdʒɔndɪs/ *n* [U] disease, caused by stoppage of the flow of bile, marked by yellowness of the skin and the whites of the eyes; (fig) state of mind in which one is jealous, spiteful, envious and suspicious. 黃疸病;(喻)嫉妒,怨恨,猜忌的心情。□ *vt* (usu passive) affect with ～: (通常用被動語態) 使患黃疸病;使懷嫉妒,怨恨,猜忌的心情: *take a ～d view,* one influenced by jealousy, spite, etc. (因嫉妒、怨恨等而)持有偏見。

jaunt /dʒɔːnt ; dʒɔnt/ *n* short journey for pleasure. 短程遊覽。□ *vi* [VP2A, C] make such a journey. 作短程遊覽。ˈ**～·ing-car** *n* light, two-wheeled horse-drawn vehicle with seats back to back, used in Ireland. 愛爾蘭的一種有背靠背座位的雙輪輕便馬車。

jaunty /ˈdʒɔːntɪ ; ˈdʒɔntɪ/ *adj* (-ier, -iest) feeling or showing self-confidence and self-satisfaction: 感到自信和自滿的;揚揚得意的: *He wore his hat at a ～ angle,* tipped to one side as a sign of high spirits, etc. 他歪戴着帽子,顯得揚揚得意。**jaunt·ily** /-ɪlɪ ; -əlɪ/ *adv* **jaunti·ness** *n* [U].

javelin /ˈdʒævlɪn ; ˈdʒævlɪn/ *n* light spear for throwing (usu in sport). (運動用之)標槍。

throwing the javelin

jaw /dʒɔː ; dʒɔ/ *n* **1** **(lower／upper) jaw,** either of the bone structures containing the teeth: (下,上)顎: *Which jaw moves up and down when you talk?* 你談話時哪個顎上下活動？ ⇨ the illus at head. 參看 head 之挿圖。ˈ**jaw-bone** *n* one of the bones in which the teeth are set. 顎骨;牙床骨。ˈ**jaw-breaker** *n* (colloq) word hard to pronounce. (俗)難發音的字。**2** (*pl*) framework of the mouth, including the teeth; (*sing*) lower part of the face: (複)頜;(單)下巴: *a man with a strong jaw.* 下巴大的人。**3** (*pl*) narrow mouth of a valley, channel, etc: (複)山谷、水道等之狹窄入口: (fig) (喻) *into／out of the jaws of death,* into／out of great danger. 進入(脫離)險境。**4** (*pl*) parts of a tool, machine, etc, eg a vice, between which things are gripped or crushed. (複)工具,機器等(例如虎頭鉗)之鉗夾部分;叉鉗。**5** (colloq) talkativeness: (俗)嘮叨;多嘴: *None of your jaw!* 不要囉嗦！**6** (colloq) long, dull talk giving moral advice. (俗) 冗長枯燥的教訓。□ *vi* [VP2A, C, 3A] ***jaw (at),*** (colloq) talk, esp at tedious length; give a moral talk to: (俗)閒談(尤指喋喋不休);教訓: *Stop jawing at me!* 不要向我嘮叨！

jay /dʒeɪ ; dʒe/ *n* noisy European bird with brightly coloured feathers; (fig) impertinent person who chatters too much. 樫鳥(一種愛叫的歐洲鳥,有顏色鮮艷的羽毛);(喻)愛嘮叨的無禮之人。ˈ**jay-walker** *n* person who walks erratically across or along streets without paying attention to traffic. 不遵守交通規則而穿越馬路者。ˈ**jay-walk** *vi* walk in this way. 不遵守交通規則而穿越馬路。

jazz /dʒæz ; dʒæz/ *n* [U] popular music first played by Negro groups in Southern USA in the early 20th c, characterized by improvisation and strong rhythms, called *traditional* ～; similar music played by large bands for dancing; a later variation much influenced by the *blues* to produce an unhurried unemotive style, called *modern* ～: 爵士樂(二十世紀初期美國南部黑人倡導的流行音樂,以即席演奏和明快的節奏爲特點,稱之爲傳統的爵士樂,後來受布魯斯爵士樂之影響,變爲緩慢而不表現感情的風格,稱之爲現代爵士樂);爵士舞樂: *the* ˈ*～ age;* 爵士樂的時代; (attrib) (形容用法) *～ music;* 爵士音樂; *a* ˈ*～ band.* 爵士樂隊。□ *vt, vi* **1** [VP6A, 2A] play or arrange in the style of ～: 奏爵士樂;改寫成爵士樂: *～ a song／tune;* 將一歌曲奏成爵士樂; dance to ～ music. 跳爵士舞。**2** [VP15B] ***～ sth up,*** (fig, colloq) liven up; put more energy into: (喻,俗)使快樂活潑;使有活力: *～ up a party;* 使一聚會愉快; *～ things up*

J

a bit. 使事情有點生氣。**jazzy** *adj* (-ier, -iest) (colloq) of or like ～; flashy, showy: (俗)爵士樂的;似爵士樂的;浮華的;炫麗的: *～y cushions;* 顏色刺眼的墊子; *a ～y sports car.* 炫麗的跑車。

jeal·ous /ˈdʒeləs ; ˈdʒɛləs/ *adj* **1** feeling or showing fear or ill will because of possible or actual loss of rights or love: 嫉妒的;妒忌的: *a ～ husband;* 嫉妒的丈夫; *～ looks.* 妒忌的樣子。 **2** *～ (of sb／sth),* feeling or showing unhappiness because of the better fortune, etc of others: 妒羨的: *～ of sb else's success.* 妒羨別人的成功。 **3** *～ (of sb／sth),* taking watchful care (*of*): 注意的(與 of 連用): *～ of one's rights;* 注意自己的權利; *keep a ～ eye on sb.* 注意看守某人。**4** (in the Bible, of God) requiring exclusive loyalty and whole-hearted worship and service. (聖經中指上帝)要求絕對忠實和崇敬的。**～·ly** *adv* **jeal·ousy** /ˈdʒeləsɪ ; ˈdʒɛləsɪ/ *n* (*pl* -sies) **1** [U] being ～: 嫉妒;妒羨: *a lover's ～y.* 愛人的嫉妒。 **2** [C] instance of this; act or utterance that shows ～y: 嫉妒或妒羨的實例;嫉妒或妒羨的行爲或言語: *I'm tired of all these jealousies and quarrels.* 我已厭倦這些嫉妒和爭吵的事情了。

jean /dʒiːn ; dʒin/ *n* **1** [U] heavy, strong cotton cloth: 斜紋布: (attrib) (形容用法) *～ overalls.* 斜紋布的工裝褲。 **2** **～s,** tough (usu denim) trousers worn informally by men, women and children. (男子,女子及兒童穿的)斜紋布褲;牛仔褲。

jeep /dʒiːp ; dʒip/ *n* small, light utility motor vehicle with great freedom of movement, useful on rough ground. 吉普車(一種小型,輕便,活動範圍大,可在崎嶇地面行駛的汽車)。

jeer /dʒɪə(r) ; dʒɪr/ *vi, vt* [VP2A, 3A, 6A] *～ (at sb),* mock, laugh rudely: 嘲弄;譏笑: *～ at a defeated enemy;* 嘲弄一戰敗的敵人; *～ (at) the speaker;* 譏笑演說者; *a ～ing crowd.* 譏笑的群衆。□ *n* [C] ～ing remark; taunt. 譏笑的言語;嘲罵。**～·ing·ly** *adv*

Je·ho·vah /dʒɪˈhəʊvə ; dʒɪˈhovə/ *n* name of God used in the Old Testament. 耶和華(舊約聖經中對上帝的稱呼)。

je·june /dʒɪˈdʒuːn ; dʒɪˈdʒun/ *adj* (formal) (of writings) dry; uninteresting; unsatisfying to the mind. (正式用語)(指寫作)枯燥的;無趣味的;令人不滿意的。**～·ly** *adv* **～·ness** *n* [U].

Jekyll and Hyde /ˌdʒekl ən ˈhaɪd ; ˌdʒikl̩ ən ˈhaɪd/ *n* single person with two personalities, one good (*Jekyll*) and one bad (*Hyde*). 有善惡雙重人格者。

jell /dʒel ; dʒɛl/ *vi, vt* [VP2A, 6A] (colloq) (cause to) become like jelly; take shape: (俗)(使)成凍子狀;(使)結凍;(使)凝結;成形;具體化;明確化: *My ideas are beginning to ～.* 我的思想逐漸明確。

jel·laba /ˈdʒeləbə ; ˈdʒɛləbə/ *n* loose hooded cloak worn by Arab men. 阿拉伯男子所穿有頭巾的披風。

jelly /ˈdʒelɪ ; ˈdʒɛlɪ/ *n* (*pl* -lies) **1** [U] soft, semi-solid food substance made from gelatin; similar substance made of fruit juice and sugar. 凍子(一種由膠質製成的軟的半固體食品);果子凍。 **2** [C, U] (portion of) this substance prepared in a mould, flavoured and coloured, as a sweet dish. 果凍甜食;一份果凍甜食。 **3** [C, U] ～-like substance. 凍狀物質。**ˈ～-fish** *n* ～-like sea animal. 水母;海蜇。⇨ the illus at sea. 參看 sea 之插圖。□ *vt, vi* [VP6A, 2A] (cause to) become like ～. 使成凍狀;變成凍子。**jel·lied** *adj* set in ～; prepared in ～; like ～: 成凍的;製成凍的;凍狀的: *jellied eels.* 鰻凍。

jemmy /ˈdʒemɪ ; ˈdʒɛmɪ/ *n* (*pl* -mies) (US 美 = *jimmy*) crowbar, esp as used by burglars for forcing open doors, windows and drawers. 鐵撬(尤指竊盜用以撬門,窗,抽屜等者)。

jenny /ˈdʒenɪ ; ˈdʒɛnɪ/ *n* ⇨ *spinning ～* at spin.

jeop·ard·ize /ˈdʒepədaɪz ; ˈdʒɛpɚdˌaɪz/ *vt* [VP6A] put in danger. 使受危險;使陷險境。**jeop·ardy** /ˈdʒepədɪ ; ˈdʒɛpɚdɪ/ *n* [U] danger of harm or loss, usu in the phrase: 危險(指傷害或損失,通常用於下列片語中): ***be／place／put in jeopardy,*** (使)陷入危險。

jer·boa /dʒɜːˈbəʊə ; dʒɚˈboə/ *n* small rat-like animal of Asia and the N African deserts with long hind legs and the ability to jump well. 跳鼠(產於亞洲及非洲北部沙漠,後腿長,善跳躍)。

jere·miad /ˌdʒerɪˈmaɪæd ; ˌdʒɛrəˈmaɪæd/ *n* long, sad and complaining story of troubles, misfortunes, etc. 苦難不幸等之漫長的哀訴;哀史。

jerk¹ /dʒɜːk ; dʒɝk/ *n* [C] **1** sudden push, pull, start, stop, twist, lift or throw: 急推;急拉;急動;急停;急扭;急抬;急投: *The train stopped with a ～／a series of ～s.* 火車顛了一下(顛了幾下)才停住。 **2** sudden involuntary twitch of a muscle or muscles. (肌肉的)痙攣;反射。 **3 physical ～s,** (colloq) gymnastic exercises. (俗)體操;運動。**4** (sl) foolish person. (俚)愚笨的人。□ *vt, vi* [VP6A, 15A, B, 2C] give a ～ to; move with a ～ or ～s: 猛然一推(拉,動,停,扭,抬,擲等);顛簸而行: *He ～ed the fish out of the water.* 他猛地一拉把魚從水中釣起。*The train ～ed along／～ed to a stop.* 火車顛簸而行(猛然停住)。*Don't ～ out your words; try to recite more smoothly.* 不要斷斷續續地背誦字句,要背得更流利些。**～y** *adj* (-ier, -iest) with ～s; not smooth: 急動的;不平穩的: *a ～y ride in an old bus.* 乘破舊公共汽車顛簸行進。**～·ily** /-ɪlɪ ; -əlɪ/ *adv* **～i·ness** *n* [U].

jerk² /dʒɜːk ; dʒɝk/ *vt* [VP6A] cure (esp beef) by cutting it into long slices and drying it in the sun. 將(尤指牛肉)切成長片曬乾;乾製(牛肉)。

jer·kin /ˈdʒɜːkɪn ; ˈdʒɝkɪn/ *n* short, close-fitting jacket, usu of leather (as worn by men in olden times). (昔時男子所穿之)皮製緊身短上衣。⇨ the illus at doublet. 參看 doublet 之插圖。

jerry /ˈdʒerɪ ; ˈdʒɛrɪ/ *n* (*pl* -ries) **1 ˈ～-builder／-building,** builder／building of houses of poor quality with bad materials. 偷工減料的營造商(建築工程)。Hence, 由此產生, **ˈ～-built** *adj.* **2 ˈ～-can,** army-style metal container used for carrying extra supplies of water or petrol on long journeys. (仿軍中樣式供長途運輸貯備水或汽油用的)金屬製液體容器。 **3 J～,** (army sl) German soldier. (軍中俚語)德國兵。 **4** (sl) chamber-pot. (俚)尿罐;便壺。

jer·sey /ˈdʒɜːzɪ ; ˈdʒɝzɪ/ *n* (*pl* -seys) **1** [U] (*ˈ～-wool*) soft, fine knitted fabric used for clothes; [C] close-fitting knitted woollen garment with sleeves. 毛織緊身上衣; 毛織運動衫。 ⇨ jumper, pullover, sweater. **2 J～,** cow of the breed that originally came from J～, one of the Channel Islands (near the French coast). 喬西乳牛(原產於英國海峽群島之喬西島)。

jest /dʒest ; dʒɛst/ *n* [C] **1** joke; sth said or done to cause amusement. 玩笑;笑話;戲謔。***in ～,*** as a joke, not in earnest. 開玩笑地;不認眞地。 **2** object of ridicule: 笑柄;嘲笑對象: *a standing ～,* sth or sb always laughed at. 經常被人嘲笑的對象。□ *vi* [VP2A, 3A] *～ (with),* make ～s; act or speak lightly: 開玩笑;取笑;講笑話: *Don't ～ about serious things.* 對於重要的事不能兒戲。*He's not a man to ～ with.* 他是個不能開玩笑的人。**～·ing** *adj* spoken in ～: 說着玩的;打趣的: *～ing remarks;* 開玩笑的話; fond of ～s: 愛開玩笑的: *a ～ing fellow.* 喜歡開玩笑的人。**～·ing·ly** *adv*

jest·er /ˈdʒestə(r) ; ˈdʒɛstɚ/ *n* person who jests, esp (in olden times) a man whose duty it was to make jokes to amuse the court or noble household in which he was employed. 開玩笑者;(尤指古時宮庭或貴族豢養的)弄臣。

Jesuit /ˈdʒezjʊɪt *US:* ˈdʒeʒʊɪt ; ˈdʒɛʒʊɪt/ *n* member of the Society of Jesus, a RC order founded in 1534 by Ignatius Loyola, Spanish priest, taking vows of obedience, poverty and chastity; (as used by opponents of the Society) person who thinks that it may be right to dissemble or prevaricate if this helps to obtain good results. 耶穌會會員(耶穌會爲天主教之一派,1534年由西班牙教士伊格那修·羅耀拉所創,宣誓順從、刻苦及堅貞);(反對該會者用語)認爲只要能達到良好結果就可以虛僞的人。**～i·cal** /ˌdʒezjʊˈɪtɪkl *US:* ˌdʒeʒʊ- ; ˌdʒɛʒʊˈɪtɪkl̩/ *adj* of or

J

like the ~s. 耶穌會會員的;似耶穌會會員的;虛僞的。

Jesus /ˈdʒiːzəs ; ˈdʒizəs/ *n* the founder of the Christian religion. 耶穌(基督教的創始者)。

jet[1] /dʒet ; dʒɛt/ *n* [C] **1** fast, strong stream of gas, liquid, steam or flame, forced out of a small opening: (氣體,液體或火焰之)噴射: *The pipe burst and a jet of water shot across the kitchen.* 管子破了,一股水由厨房這邊噴到那邊。**ˌjet-proˈpulsion (engine)**, propulsion of aircraft and spacecraft by engines that suck in air at the front, mix the air with gases, and send out the hot, burnt gases in jets at the back. (飛機和太空船之)噴射推進(引擎)。Hence, 由此產生, **ˌjet (ˈaircraft / ˈairliner / ˈfighter)** *nn* **ˌjet-proˈpelled** *adj.* ➪ the illus at air. 參看 air 之揷圖。**the ˈjet set**, wealthy persons who often travel by jet aircraft for holidays. 常乘噴射客機旅行度假的有錢人。**2** (*pl*) (often a brief but repeated) stream of liquid, gas, etc: (複)液體,氣體等之陣陣的湧出: *He cut his wrist so badly that jets of blood spurted out.* 他的手腕割傷得很厲害,血陣陣地湧出。**3** narrow opening from which a jet comes out: 噴射口;噴嘴: *a ˈgas-jet.* 煤氣噴嘴;煤氣噴燈。□ *vi, vt* (-tt-) **1** come, send out, in a jet or jets. 噴出;噴射。**2** (colloq) travel by jet airliner. (俗)乘噴射客機旅行。

jet[2] /dʒet ; dʒɛt/ *n* [U] hard, black mineral that takes a brilliant polish, used for buttons, ornaments, etc; the colour of this mineral; (attrib) made of jet; (also 亦作 **ˌjet-ˈblack**) deep, glossy black. 貝褐炭;黑玉;黑玉色;(形容用法)黑玉製的;黑玉色的;黑黝黝的。

jet·sam /ˈdʒetsəm ; ˈdʒɛtsəm/ *n* [U] goods thrown overboard from a ship at sea to lighten it, eg in a storm; such goods washed up on the seashore. 投棄貨物(船舶爲減輕負擔而抛棄的貨物,例如遇有暴風雨時);冲至岸上的投棄貨物。**flotsam and ~**, (fig use) persons whose lives have been wrecked: (比喻用法)流離失所的人: *Sick and starving refugees are the flotsam and ~ of war.* 生病挨餓的難民乃戰爭中流離失所的人。

jet·ti·son /ˈdʒetɪsn ; ˈdʒɛtəsn̩/ *vt* [VP6A] throw (goods) overboard in order to lighten a ship, eg during a storm; abandon, discard (what is unwanted): 爲減輕船上負擔而抛棄(貨物)(例如遇暴風雨時);投棄;抛棄(不要的東西): *~ an unpleasant passenger / an unworkable plan.* 放棄一使人厭惡的乘客(難實行的計畫)。

jetty /ˈdʒetɪ ; ˈdʒɛtɪ/ *n* (*pl* -ties) structure built out into a body of water as a breakwater or as a landing-place for ships and boats. 突堤;防波堤;碼頭。

Jew /dʒuː ; dʒu/ *n* person of the Hebrew people or religion. 猶太人;猶太教徒。**Jew·ess** /ˈdʒuːɪs ; ˈdʒuɪs/ *n* female Jew. 猶太女人。**Jew·ish** /ˈdʒuːɪʃ ; ˈdʒuɪʃ/ *adj* of the Jews. 猶太人的。

jewel /ˈdʒuːəl ; ˈdʒuəl/ *n* **1** precious stone, eg a diamond or a ruby; ornament with a ~ or ~s set in it. 寶石(例如鑽石或紅寶石);鑲有寶石的裝飾品;珠寶。**2** artificial diamond: 人造鑽石: *This watch has 15 ~s.* 這隻錶有十五個人造鑽石。**3** (fig) sth or sb highly valued: (喩)被珍視的東西或人;寶貝: *His wife is a ~.* 他的妻子是他的寶貝。□ *vt* (-ll-, US -l-) adorn with ~s: 飾以珠寶: (usu in *pp*) (通常用過去分詞) *a ~led ring;* 鑲有珠寶的戒指; *a ~led watch*, with industrial, not gem diamonds, in the movement. 裝有寶石軸承的錶。**~·ler**, (US = **~er**) /ˈdʒuːələ(r) ; ˈdʒuələ˞/ *n* trader in ~s; person who sells ~s. 寶石業者;珠寶商。**~ry**, **~·lery** /ˈdʒuːəlrɪ ; ˈdʒuəlrɪ/ *n* [U] ~s collectively, ie precious stones, ornaments set with ~s, etc. 珠寶(集合稱);珠寶類。

Jeze·bel /ˈdʒezəbl *US:* -bel ; ˈdʒɛzəbl̩/ *n* (as a term of abuse) shameless, immoral woman. (辱罵之詞)耶洗別;無恥而放蕩的女人。➪ 1 Kings 16: 31. 參看舊約聖經列王記上第16章第31節。

jib[1] /dʒɪb ; dʒɪb/ *n* **1** small triangular sail (in front of the mainsail). 艄帆;船首三角帆(在主帆之前)。**ˌjib-ˈboom** *n* spar to which the lower part of a jib is fastened. 艄帆斜桅(繫船首三角帆之下端的圓木)。➪ the illus at barque, sail. 參看 barque 和 sail 之揷圖。***the cut of his jib***, his personal appearance. 某人的風采。**2** projecting arm of a crane or derrick. 起重機之臂;突梁。➪ the illus at crane. 參看 crane 之揷圖。

jib[2] /dʒɪb ; dʒɪb/ *vi* (-bb-) [VP2A] (of a horse, etc) stop suddenly; refuse to go forwards; (fig) refuse to proceed: (指馬等)突然停止;不肯前進;(喩)躊躇不前: *On seeing the gate the horse jibbed.* 那馬看到了門,便不肯前進了。[VP3A] ***jib at***, (fig) show unwillingness or dislike: (喩)表示不願或厭惡: *He jibbed at working overtime every day.* 他不願意每天都加班工作。*My small car sometimes jibs at a steep hill.* 我的小汽車有時遇到陡坡便爬不上去了。

jibe /dʒaɪb ; dʒaɪb/ *vi* (US) (美) **1** = gibe. **2** = gybe.

jiffy /ˈdʒɪfɪ ; ˈdʒɪfɪ/ *n* (colloq) moment. (俗)瞬間。***in a ~***, very soon. 卽刻;片刻。

jig /dʒɪg ; dʒɪg/ *n* [C] **1** (music for a) quick, lively dance. 基格舞(一種急速輕快的舞);基格舞曲。**2** appliance that holds a piece of work and guides the tools that are used on it. 可將製品承住並引導工具工作的機械裝置;鑽模;裝架。□ *vi, vt* (-gg-) **1** [VP2A, C] dance a jig. 跳基格舞。**2** [VP15B, 2C] move up and down in a quick, jerky way: 活潑地急跳;蹦跳;使上下急動: *jigging up and down in excitement;* 興奮得直蹦直跳; *jig a baby (up and down) on one's knees.* 將一嬰兒放在膝上(上下)顚動。

jig·ger /ˈdʒɪgə(r) ; ˈdʒɪgə˞/ *n* **1** flea or other parasite that burrows under the skin; (in England) harvest mite. 跳蚤或其他皮膚寄生蟲;(英國)秋蟎。**2** small measure for liquor (esp spirits), as fitted to bottles in bars. 量酒之小杯(尤指量烈酒者。)

jig·gered /ˈdʒɪgəd ; ˈdʒɪgə˞d/ *adj* (*pred* only, colloq) (僅用於述語,俗) **1** amazed: 驚奇的: *Well, I'm ~!* 哪有這種事(眞叫人驚奇)! **2** exhausted. 筋疲力竭的。

jig·gery-po·kery /ˌdʒɪgərɪ ˈpəʊkərɪ ; ˈdʒɪgərɪˈpokərɪ/ *n* [U] (colloq) hocus-pocus; humbug. (俗)欺騙;詐騙。

jig·gle /ˈdʒɪgl ; ˈdʒɪgl̩/ *vt, vi, n* joggle. 搖擺;搖動。

jig·saw /ˈdʒɪgsɔː ; ˈdʒɪgˌsɔ/ *n* **1** machine fretsaw. 鋸曲線機。**2** **ˈ~ (puzzle)**, picture, map, etc pasted on thin board or wood and cut in irregularly shaped pieces which are to be fitted together again. 拼圖玩具。

ji·had /dʒɪˈhɑːd ; dʒɪˈhɑd/ *n* religious war by Muslims against unbelievers; (fig) campaign for or against a teaching, practice, etc. 回教徒對異教徒之戰爭;(喩)維護或反對教義、教規等之運動。

jilt /dʒɪlt ; dʒɪlt/ *vt* [VP6A] give up, send away, (sb) after giving him encouragement or a promise to marry: 遺棄(情人): *When he lost his job, she ~ed him.* 他失業以後,她便遺棄了他。□ *n* person who jilts sb. 負心之人。

Jim Crow /ˌdʒɪm ˈkrəʊ ; ˈdʒɪmˈkro/ *n* ⚠ (U contemptuous name for a Negro. (諱)(美)對黑 之蔑稱。

ji·miny /ˈdʒɪmənɪ ; ˈdʒɪmənɪ/ *int* (colloq) exclamation of surprise. (俗)表示驚奇的感嘆詞。

jim-jams /ˈdʒɪmdʒæmz ; ˈdʒɪmˌdʒæmz/ *n pl* (sl) **the ~**, the jitters. (俚)神經緊張。

jimmy /ˈdʒɪmɪ ; ˈdʒɪmɪ/ *n* (US) (美) = jemmy.

jingle /ˈdʒɪŋgl ; ˈdʒɪŋgl̩/ *n* [C] **1** metallic clinking or ringing sound (as of coins, keys or small bells). 叮噹聲(如錢幣,鑰匙,小鈴發出的聲音)。**2** series of the same or similar sounds in words, esp when designed to attract the attention; jingling verse. 一連串同音或類似音反覆的文字(尤指欲引人注意者);叠韻的詩句。□ *vt, vi* **1** [VP6A, 15B, 2A, C] (cause to) make a light, ringing sound: (使)作叮噹聲: *He ~d his keys.* 他把鑰匙弄得叮噹地響。*The money in his pocket ~d.* 他口袋裏的錢叮噹作響。**2** [VP2A] (of verse) be full of alliterations and

J

rhymes that make it easy to learn and remember. (指詩)充滿頭韻和韻脚而易學易記;押韻。

jingo /ˈdʒɪŋgəʊ ; ˈdʒɪŋgo/ *n* (*pl* ~es /-gəʊz ; -goz/) person who combines excessive patriotism with contempt for other countries, esp one who supports a warlike policy. (蔑視他國之)極端愛國主義者;(尤指)支持好戰政策者。***By ~!*** (dated sl) exclamation expressing surprise, pleasure, etc or giving emphasis to a statement. (過時俚語)(表示驚異、快樂等,或加强語勢)嗳呀!一定!**~·ism** /-ɪzəm ; -ɪzəm/ *n* attitude of mind, principles, of ~es. 極端的愛國主義;侵略主義;好戰主義。**~·ist** /-ɪst ; -ɪst/ *n* **~·is·tic** /ˌdʒɪŋgəʊˈɪstɪk ; ˌdʒɪŋgoˈɪstɪk/ *adj* characteristic of ~es. 極端愛國的;侵略主義的;好戰的。

jinks /dʒɪŋks ; dʒɪŋks/ *n* [U] (only in) (僅用於) ***high ~,*** noisy merrymaking; uncontrolled fun. 狂歡作樂。

jinn /dʒɪn ; dʒɪn/ *n* = genie.

jinx /dʒɪŋks ; dʒɪŋks/ *n* (colloq) person or thing that brings bad luck. (俗)不祥的人或物。***put a ~ on sb,*** do sth to bring him bad luck. 做某事使某人倒霉。

jit·ney /ˈdʒɪtnɪ ; ˈdʒɪtnɪ/ *n* (US colloq) (美俗) **1** (old use) nickel. (舊用法)五分錢;五分鎳幣。**2** small motor-bus. 小型公共汽車。

jit·ters /ˈdʒɪtəz ; ˈdʒɪtɚz/ *n pl* **the ~,** (sl) extreme nervousness: (俚)極度緊張;極爲神經過敏: *have / get / give sb the ~.* 覺得極爲緊張(使某人極爲緊張)。**jit·ter·bug** /ˈdʒɪtə bʌg ; ˈdʒɪtɚˌbʌg/ *n* **1** (person who participated in a) lively, popular dance of the 1940's to swing music. 吉特巴舞(1940–49年間流行的一種活潑的伴隨搖擺音樂的舞蹈);跳吉特巴舞的人。**2** (old use) flustered person. (舊用法)緊張的人。**jit·tery** /ˈdʒɪtərɪ ; ˈdʒɪtərɪ/ *adj* nervous; frightened. 神經緊張的;害怕的。

jive /dʒaɪv ; dʒaɪv/ *n* style of popular music with a strong beat; dancing to this. 搖擺樂(一種節拍强烈的爵士樂);搖擺舞。□ *vi* dance to ~ music. 跳搖擺舞。

job[1] /dʒɒb ; dʒɑb/ *n* **1** piece of work, either to be done, or completed: 一件工作(將要做或已完成者);成果;成品: *Your new Bentley car is a lovely job,* is magnificent. 你的新本特利車很漂亮。***on the job,*** (colloq) at work; busy. (俗)工作中;忙碌的。***be paid by the job,*** separately for each job. 按件計酬。***make a good / fine job of sth,*** do it well. 做得好。***odd jobs,*** bits of work not connected with one another. 零碎工作;散工。**ˌodd-ˈjob man,** one who makes a living by doing any bits of work he is asked to do. 做零工者;做短工者。**2** ***a good job,*** (colloq) a fortunate state of affairs: (俗)幸運之事: *He lost his seat in Parliament, and a good job, too!* 他失去了國會中的席位,這倒也是件好事! ***give sb / sth up as a bad job,*** (colloq) decide that sb / sth is hopeless. (俗)因無希望等而放棄某人(某事物)。***make the best of a bad job,*** do what one can to remedy an unfortunate state of affairs. (爲補救不幸事件而)盡力爲之。**3** ***be / have a (hard) job doing / to do sth,*** be / have a difficult task: 爲(有)困難的工作: *It's a (hard) job for a poor man to keep his wife and children clothed and fed.* 一個窮人使他的妻子兒女有衣穿有飯吃不是件容易的事。*You'll have a job convincing your wife that you were really detained at the office.* 讓你的妻子相信你是眞的被阻留在辦公室裏不是件容易的事。**4** employment: 職業;工作: *to have / lose a job;* 獲得工作(失業); (attrib) (形容用法) *job safety / satisfaction.* 職業保障(補償)。***out of a job,*** unemployed. 失業的。***jobs for the boys,*** (colloq) positions for one's supporters, friends, etc. (俗)做爲政治酬庸等之職位。**ˈjob centre,** employment exchange, ⇨ employment. 勞工介紹所。**5** ***job lot,*** mixed collection of articles, bought together. 整批買進的各種貨物。**6** ***just the job,*** (colloq) exactly what is wanted. (俗)恰爲所需。**7** (sl) sth done by intrigue or dishonesty for private profit or advantage: (俚)以陰謀或欺騙手段爲私人利益所做之事: *a put-up job.* 意圖蒙混之事。⇨ *put-up* at put[1](11). **8** (sl) criminal act, esp theft: (俚)罪行(尤指竊盜): *He got three years for a job he did in Leeds.* 他因在里玆犯竊盜罪行而被判三年徒刑。

job[2] /dʒɒb ; dʒɑb/ *vt, vi* **1** [VP2A] ⇨ 1 above; do odd jobs: 做零工;做散工(參看 job[1] 第1義): *a jobbing gardener,* one who works for several employers and is paid by the hour / day; 做零工的園丁; *a jobbing printer,* one who prints leaflets, posters, etc. 印刷散頁印刷品之商人。**2** [VP6A] (on the Stock Exchange) act as a broker; buy, sell (stocks and shares) for others. 做股票經紀;代客買賣(公債,股票)。**3** [VP2A, 14] (colloq) use a position of trust for private advantage or for the benefit of one's friends: (俗)假公濟私;利用公職爲己或爲友人謀利;以假公濟私的手段牟利: *He jobbed his brother into a well-paid post.* 他假公濟私爲他哥哥(弟弟)找到一個待遇很好的工作。**job·ber** *n* **1** dealer in Stock Exchange securities. 股票經紀人。⇨ broker. **2** person who jobs(1). 做散工者。**3** person who jobs(3). 假公濟私的人。**job·bery** /ˈdʒɒbərɪ ; ˈdʒɑbərɪ/ *n* [U] jobbing; (esp) use of unfair means to gain private advantage. 徇私舞弊;假公濟私。

Job /dʒəʊb ; dʒob/ *n* (from Job in the Book of Job in the Old Testament) person of great patience. (由舊約聖經約伯記中的約伯而來)非常有耐心之人。***try the patience of Job,*** be very difficult to endure, very vexatious. 令人十分難以忍受;十分使人煩惱。***a Job's comforter,*** one who aggravates the distress of the person he is supposed to be comforting. 增加對方痛苦的安慰者。

jockey /ˈdʒɒkɪ ; ˈdʒɑkɪ/ (*pl* ~s) professional rider in horse-races. 賽馬的職業騎師。⇨ also disc. **ˈJ~ Club,** club that controls horse-racing in England. (在英國主持賽馬的)賽馬俱樂部。□ *vt, vi* [VP15A, 3A] trick; cheat: 欺騙: *He ~ed Green out of his job.* 他欺騙格林,使他失業。***~ for position,*** **(a)** (in racing) jostle other riders in order to get a more favourable position. (賽馬)擠其他的騎師以圖佔取有利的位置。**(b)** (fig) try by skilful management, by tricky manoeuvring, to gain an advantage. (喻)運用(欺詐)手段圖獲利益。

jo·cose /dʒəʊˈkəʊs ; dʒoˈkos/ *adj* (formal) humorous; playful. (正式用語)詼諧的;開玩笑的。**~·ly** *adv* **~·ness, jo·cos·ity** /dʒəʊˈkɒsətɪ;dʒoˈkɑsətɪ/ *nn* [U].

jocu·lar /ˈdʒɒkjʊlə(r) ; ˈdʒɑkjəlɚ/ *adj* meant as a joke; given to joking. 滑稽的;喜開玩笑的。**~·ly** *adv* **~·ity** /ˌdʒɒkjʊˈlærətɪ ; ˌdʒɑkjəˈlærətɪ/ *n* (*pl* -ties) [U] being ~; [C] ~ act or utterance. 滑稽;詼諧;滑稽的言行。

joc·und /ˈdʒɒkənd ; ˈdʒɑkənd/ *adj* (liter) merry; cheerful. (文)歡樂的;愉快的。**~·ity** /dʒəʊˈkʌndətɪ ; dʒoˈkʌndətɪ/ *n* (*pl* -ties) [U] being ~; [C] ~ act or utterance. 歡樂;愉快;愉快的言行。

jodh·purs /ˈdʒɒdpəz ; ˈdʒɑdpɚz/ *n pl* long breeches for horse-riding, close-fitting from knee to ankle. 騎馬褲(膝至踝部分爲緊身的長褲)。

jog /dʒɒg ; dʒɑg/ *vt, vi* (-gg-) **1** [VP6A, 15B] give a slight knock or push to; shake with a push or jerk: 輕撞;輕推;搖動: *The horse jogged its rider up and down.* 那馬上下顚動着牠的主人。*He jogged my elbow,* touched it, eg to attract my attention, to warn me, etc. 他輕輕撞我的肘(例如引起我的注意,警告我等)。***jog sb's memory,*** try to make him remember or recall sth. 喚起某人的記憶;提醒某人。**2** [VP15B] cause to move unsteadily, in a shaking manner: 使顚簸行進: *The old bus jogged us up and down on the rough mountain road.* 那輛舊公共汽車載着我們在崎嶇的山路上顚簸着行駛。**3** [VP 2C] ***jog along / on,*** make slow, patient progress: 緩緩地前進或進行: *We jogged along the bad roads.* 我們沿着那些壞路緩緩前進。*Matters jog along.* 事情在緩緩進行中。*We must jog on somehow until business conditions improve.* 我們必須慢慢熬到商業

情況改進爲止。 **4** [VP2A] (mod colloq) run slowly and steadily for a time, for physical exercise. (現代俗語)慢跑(作爲運動)。 **jog·ger** /ˈdʒɒgə(r) ; ˈdʒɑgɚ/ *n* person who jogs(4). 慢跑者。 **jog·ging** /ˈdʒɒgɪŋ ; ˈdʒɑgɪŋ/ *n* [U] the physical exercise of jogging(4). 慢跑。 □ *n* [C] **1** slight push, shake or nudge. 輕推;輕搖;輕撞。 **2** (also 亦作 **ˈjog-trot**) slow walk or trot. 漫步;緩行。

joggle /ˈdʒɒgl ; ˈdʒɑgl̩/ *vt, vi* [VP6A, 2A] shake, move, by or as if by repeated jerks. 搖;搖擺;搖動。□ *n* slight shake. 輕搖。

john /dʒɒn ; dʒɑn/ *n* (sl) water-closet. (俚)(有抽水設備的)廁所。

John Bull /ˌdʒɒn ˈbʊl ; ˈdʒɑn ˈbʊl/ *n* the English nation; typical Englishman. 英國;典型的英國人;約翰牛。

John Doe /ˌdʒɒnˈdəʊ ; ˌdʒɑnˈdo/ *n* (esp US) (尤美) **1** (legal) invented name for an unknown person. (法律)某甲。 **2** ordinary, typical man. 普通人。

joie de vivre /ˌʒwɑː də ˈviːvrə ; ʒwadəˈvivr/ *n* (F) carefree enjoyment of life. (法)無憂無慮的享受生活。

join /dʒɔɪn ; dʒɔɪn/ *vt, vi* **1** [VP6A, 14, 15A, B] *~ sth to sth; ~ things together / up*, put together; unite; connect (two points, things) with a line, rope, bridge, etc: 連結;結合;聯合: *~ one thing to another;* 將一物與另一物連接起來; *~ two things together;* 將二物連接在一起; *~ the pieces together;* 將片段接合起來; *~ an island to the mainland (with a bridge);* (以橋樑)將一島與大陸連接; *~ two persons in marriage*, make them man and wife. 使二人結爲夫妻。*Where does this stream ~ the Danube?* 這條河在何處與多瑙河會合? *~ battle*, begin fighting. 交戰。*~ hands*, clasp each other's hands; (fig) combine in an enterprise, etc. 握手; (喩)携手共事。*~ forces (with...)*, unite in action; work together. (與…)聯合行動;合作。 **2** [VP2A, C] come together; unite: 交會;連合;相連: *Parallel lines are, by definition, lines that never ~.* 按照定義,平行線卽永不相交的線。*Which two rivers ~ at Lyons?* 那兩條河在里昂相會合? **3** [VP6A] become a member of: 參加;加入: *~ the army / a club.* 從軍(加入會社)。 [VP2C] *join up*, (colloq) join the army. (俗)從軍。 **4** [VP6A, 15A, 3A] *~ (sb) in sth*, come into the company of; associate with (sb in sth): 與…在一起;伴隨(某人做某事): *I'll ~ you in a few minutes.* 我過幾分鐘將和你們會合。 *Will you ~ us in a walk*, come with us? 你願意和我們一塊去散步嗎? *Why doesn't Tom ~ in the conversation*, Why is he silent? 湯姆爲什麼不講話? *May I ~ in (the game)?* 我可以參加(這遊戲)嗎? □ *n* place or line where two things are ~ed: 相交點;連接處: *The two pieces were put together so cleverly that the ~ could not be seen.* 這兩塊接合得很巧妙,故而看不出相接之處。

joiner /ˈdʒɔɪnə(r) ; ˈdʒɔɪnɚ/ *n* skilled workman who makes the inside woodwork of buildings, etc. 細工木匠。 ⇨ carpenter, *cabinet-maker* at cabinet. **join·ery** *n* [U] work of a ~: 細木工;細木作: *learn ~y;* 學習細木工; *lessons in ~y.* 細木工課程。

joint[1] /dʒɔɪnt ; dʒɔɪnt/ *adj* (attrib only) held or done by, belonging to, two or more persons together: (僅作形容用法) 共同的; 共有的; 共享的: *~ efforts / ownership / responsibility;* 共同的努力(所有權,責任); *~ heirs to a legacy;* 一遺產之共同繼承人; *a ~ account*, bank account in the name of more than one person, eg a husband and wife; 二人以上(例如夫婦)共有之銀行戶頭; *a ~-ˈstock company*, a number of persons who carry on a business with capital contributed by all; 股份公司; *during their ~ lives*, (legal) while they are both (or all) living; (法律)當他們都活着的時候; *settle a trade dispute by ~ consultation*, eg workers and management. 共同磋商 (例如工人與資方) 解決一勞資爭議。 **~·ly** *adv*

joint[2] /dʒɔɪnt ; dʒɔɪnt/ *n* **1** place, line or surface at which two or more things are joined: 連接處;接合點;接縫;接合面: *the ~s in a jigsaw puzzle.* 拼圖玩具的接縫。 **2** device or structure by which things, eg lengths of pipe, bones, are joined together: 接頭;關節: *ˈfinger ~s.* 指關節。 *out of ~*, (of bones) dislocated; pushed out of position: (指骨)脫臼;脫節: *He fell and put his knee out of ~.* 他跌倒了,並且把膝蓋摔脫了臼。 *put sb's ˈnose out of ~*, (fig) take his place in another's affections or favour; upset or humble sb who is a nuisance. (喩)奪某人之寵;騷擾或貶抑一討厭之人。 **3** limb (shoulder, leg) or other division of an ox, a sheep, etc which a butcher supplies to customers: 牛羊等的腿肉或肩膀肉;大片肉: *a slice off the ~*, eg of roast beef. 一大片肉(例如烤牛肉)。 **4** (sl) place visited by people for gambling, drinking or drug-taking. (俚)下流場所 (賭窟,酒館或煙館)。 *ˈclip ~*, bar, night-club, etc at which extortionate charges are made (often for services not rendered). 敲竹槓的酒吧,夜總會等。 **5** (sl) cigarette containing a drug. (俚)含有麻醉劑的香煙。

joint[3] /dʒɔɪnt ; dʒɔɪnt/ *vt* [VP6A] **1** provide with a joint or joints(2): 裝以接頭或關節: *a ~ed fishing-rod / doll.* 有接頭的魚竿(有活動關節的洋娃娃)。 **2** divide at a ~ or into ~s(3). 在牛羊等之腿部或肩膀關節處切開;將(牛羊等之腿或肩膀)切成大片肉。

join·ture /ˈdʒɔɪntʃə(r) ; ˈdʒɔɪntʃɚ/ *n* [C] (legal) property settled on a woman during her marriage, to be used by her after her husband's death. (法律)(夫生前指定的)由妻繼承的遺產;寡婦所得產。

joist /dʒɔɪst ; dʒɔɪst/ *n* one of the parallel pieces of timber (from wall to wall) to which floorboards are fastened; steel beam supporting a floor or ceiling. 地板的托梁;擱柵。

joke /dʒəʊk ; dʒok/ *n* sth said (eg a story with a funny ending) or done to cause amusement, laughter, etc: 笑話;玩笑: *tell / make a joke;* 說笑話; sth that causes amusement. 笑柄;笑料。 *have a ~ with sb*, share one with him. 與某人說笑話。 *make a ~ about sb or sth*, speak lightly or amusingly about. 拿某人或某事開玩笑。 *play a ~ on sb*, cause him to be the victim of a practical ~. 戲弄某人。 *a practical ~*, a trick played on sb in order to make him appear ridiculous. 惡作劇。 *It's no ~*, It's a serious matter. 這可不是鬧着玩的事。 *the ~ of the village / town, etc*, the laughing-stock; person, event, etc which causes great amusement. 村(鎭等)內的笑柄;取笑的對象。□ *vi* [VP2A, C] make ~s: 開玩笑: *He's always joking.* 他老愛開玩笑。 *I was only joking.* 我祇是在開玩笑。 **jok·ing·ly** *adv* in a joking manner. 開玩笑地;戲謔地。

joker /ˈdʒəʊkə(r) ; ˈdʒokɚ/ *n* **1** person who is fond of making jokes. 詼諧者;喜開玩笑的人。 **2** (sl) fellow. (俚)人;傢伙。 **3** extra playing card (the 53rd) which is used in some games as the highest trump or as a wild(10) card. 紙牌中的百搭(在某些牌戲中可做最大的王牌或飛牌)。

jolly /ˈdʒɒlɪ ; ˈdʒɑlɪ/ *adj* (-ier, -iest) joyful; gay; merry; slightly drunk. 高興的;愉快的;歡樂的;微醉的。 *ˈJ~ Roger*, pirate's black flag (with skull and crossbones). 海盜的黑旗(骷髏旗)。□ *adv* (GB colloq) very: (英俗)非常;很: *I'll take ~ good care not to lend him money again.* 我將特別當心不再借錢給他了。□ *vt* [VP6A, 15A, B] (colloq) keep (sb) in a good humour (esp in order to win his cooperation): (俗)使(某人)高興 (尤指欲獲彼之合作時); 奉承: *They jollied me along until I agreed to help them.* 他們一直奉承我,直到我答應幫助他們。 **jol·li·fi·ca·tion** /ˌdʒɒlɪfɪˈkeɪʃn ; ˌdʒɑləfəˈkeʃən/ *n* [U] merry-making; festivity; [C] instance of this. 作樂;歡樂;歡宴。 **jol·lity** /ˈdʒɒlətɪ ; ˈdʒɑlətɪ/ *n* [U] state of being ~. 高興;愉快;歡樂。

jolly·boat /ˈdʒɒlɪbəʊt ; ˈdʒɑlɪbot/ *n* kind of ship's boat. 大船所携帶的一種小艇。

jolt /dʒəʊlt ; dʒolt/ *vt, vi* [VP6A, 15A, B, 2A, C]

give a jerk or jerks to; shake up; (of a vehicle) move along by jerks: 使顛簸;搖動;(指車輛)顛簸而行: *The old bus ~ed us as it went over the stony road.* 舊公共汽車駛過碎石路時顛簸着我們。 *The bus ~ed along.* 那公共汽車顛簸而行。□ *n* jerk; sudden bump or shake; (fig) surprise, shock. 顛簸;震搖;(喻)驚奇;震驚。 **~y** *adj* ~ing. 顛簸的;搖動的。

Jo·nah /ˈdʒəʊnə ; ˈdʒonə/ *n* person whose presence seems to bring ill luck; person who is sacrificed lest he should bring ill luck. 不祥之人;因恐其不祥而被犧牲之人。

jon·quil /ˈdʒɒŋkwɪl ; ˈdʒɑŋkwɪl/ *n* kind of narcissus. 長壽花;黃水仙。

joss /dʒɒs ; dʒɑs/ *n* (in China) carving in stone, etc, of a god. 中國的神像;菩薩。 **ˈ~-house** *n* temple. 廟。 **ˈ~-stick** *n* stick of incense. 香。

jostle /ˈdʒɒsl ; ˈdʒɑsl̩/ *vt, vi* [VP6A, 2C] push roughly (against); push: 撞;擠(與 against 連用);推: *We were ~d by the crowd.* 我們被人群擠來擠去。 *The pickpocket ~d against me in the crowd.* 那扒手在人群中撞我。

jot[1] /dʒɒt ; dʒɑt/ *n* **a jot**, (usu with neg) small amount: (通常與否定語連用)少量;些許: *There's not a jot of truth in a story*, no truth at all. 故事中一點眞實性都沒有。

jot[2] /dʒɒt ; dʒɑt/ *vt* (-tt-) [VP15B] ***jot sth down***, make a quick written note of: 匆匆摘記下來: *The policeman jotted down my name and address.* 那警察把我的姓名和住址匆匆記下。 **jot·ter** *n* notebook or pad for rough notes. 筆記簿;拍紙簿。 **jot·tings** *n pl* notes jotted down. 匆匆記下的東西。

joule /dʒuːl ; dʒaʊl/ *n* (electr) (abbr **J**) unit of energy or work. (電)焦耳(能量或功的單位,略作 J)。

jour·nal /ˈdʒɜːnl ; ˈdʒɝnl̩/ *n* **1** daily newspaper; other periodical: 日報;雜誌;定期刊物: *the Ladies' Home J~;* 婦女家庭雜誌; *the Economic J~.* 經濟雜誌。 **2** daily record of news, events, business accounts, etc. 日記;日誌;流水帳。 **~·ese** /ˌdʒɜːnəˈliːz ; ˌdʒɝnl̩ˈiz/ *n* [U] style of language full of clichés, common in some ~s, eg the use of 'prior to interment' for 'before burial'. (常見於某些報紙之多陳辭的)新聞文體(例如不用 before burial 而用 prior to interment)。 **~·ism** /-ɪzəm ; -ɪzəm/ *n* [U] work of writing for, editing, or publishing ~s. 新聞業;新聞工作;新聞寫作;新聞編輯;新聞出版。 **~·ist** /-ɪst ; -ɪst/ *n* person engaged in ~ism. 從事新聞業者;報人;新聞記者;爲報紙雜誌撰稿者。 **~·is·tic** /ˌdʒɜːnəˈlɪstɪk ; ˌdʒɝnl̩ˈɪstɪk/ *adj* of ~ism; characteristic of ~ism. 新聞事業的;新聞事業特有的。

jour·ney /ˈdʒɜːnɪ ; ˈdʒɝnɪ/ *n* (*pl* ~s) (distance travelled (esp on land) in) going to a place, esp a distant place: 旅行(尤指至遙遠地方之旅行);旅程;路程: *reach one's ~'s end;* 到達旅行目的地; *go／come／send sb on a ~;* 去旅行(旅行前來;遣某人旅行); *make a ~ half-way round the world.* 旅行半個地球。⇨ flight[1](2), voyage. □ *vi* [VP2A, C] travel; make a ~. 旅行。

jour·ney·man /ˈdʒɜːnɪmən ; ˈdʒɝnɪmən/ *n* (*pl* -men /-mən ; -mən/) skilled workman who works for a master (contrasted with an *apprentice*). 熟練的工人(與 apprentice 相對)。

joust /dʒaʊst ; dʒʌst/ *vi, n* (hist) (engage in a) fight on horseback with lances (as between knights in the Middle Ages). (史)騎着馬用長矛打鬪(如中古時代之武士)。

Jove /dʒəʊv ; dʒov/ *n* Jupiter, 古羅馬之主神, esp (尤用於) ***By ~!*** (as an exclamation of surprise, etc). (表示驚異等的感嘆詞)啊!

jov·ial /ˈdʒəʊvɪəl ; ˈdʒovɪəl/ *adj* full of fun and good humour; merry: 快活的;愉快的;快樂的: *a ~ fellow;* 快活的人; *in a ~ mood.* 心情愉快。 **~ly** /-ɪəlɪ ; -ɪəlɪ/ *adv* **~·ity** /ˌdʒəʊvɪˈælətɪ ; ˌdʒovɪˈælətɪ/ *n* [U] being ~; good humoured behaviour; [C] (*pl* -ties) ~ acts or utterances. 快活;高興的行爲;快樂的行動或言語。

jowl /dʒaʊl ; dʒaʊl/ *n* jaw; lower part of the face: 顎;下顎: *a man with a heavy ~／a heavy-jowled man*, one with heavy jaws, a fold or folds of flesh hanging from the chin. 一個有雙下巴的人。 ***cheek by ~***, ⇨ cheek(1). **~y** *adj* with a heavy ~. 下顎寬厚的;雙下巴的。

joy /dʒɔɪ ; dʒɔɪ/ *n* **1** [U] deep pleasure; great gladness: 快樂;欣喜;極爲高興: *I wish you joy.* 祝你快樂。 *We heard with joy that she had escaped injury.* 我們聽說她未曾受傷感到很高興。 *He has been a good friend to me, both in joy and in sorrow.* 他是與我同甘共苦的好朋友。 *They danced／jumped for joy*, because they were full of joy. 他們高興得舞(跳)起來了。 **ˈjoy-bells** *n pl* bells rung to celebrate a happy occasion. 賀喜鐘;祝賀鐘。 **ˈjoy-ride** *n* (sl) ride in a vehicle for fun and thrills. (俚)開車兜風。 **ˈjoy-stick** *n* (sl) control lever on an aircraft. (俚)飛機之操縱桿。 **2** [C] sth that gives joy; occasion of great happiness: 令人高興的事物;樂事: *the joys and sorrows of life.* 人生的悲歡。□ *vi* (poet) rejoice: (詩)欣喜: *joy in a friend's success.* 因友人的成功而欣喜。 **joy·ful** /-fl ; -fəl/ *adj* filled with, showing, causing, joy. 充滿快樂的;表示快樂的;令人高興的。 **joy·fully** /-fəlɪ ; -fəlɪ/ *adv* **joy·less** *adj* without joy; gloomy; sad. 不快樂的;憂鬱的;悲傷的。 **joy·less·ly** *adv* **joy·ful·ness, joy·less·ness** *nn* **joy·ous** /ˈdʒɔɪəs ; ˈdʒɔɪəs/ *adj* full of joy. 充滿快樂的。 **joy·ous·ly** *adv* **joy·ous·ness** *n*

ju·bi·lant /ˈdʒuːbɪlənt ; ˈdʒubl̩ənt/ *adj* (formal) triumphant; showing joy. (正式用語)歡欣的;喜悅的;喜氣洋洋的。 **~·ly** *adv* **ju·bi·la·tion** /ˌdʒuːbɪˈleɪʃn ; ˌdʒubl̩ˈeʃən/ *n* [U] rejoicing; [C] occasion of this. 欣喜;歡欣慶祝;樂事。

ju·bi·lee /ˈdʒuːbɪliː ; ˈdʒubl̩ˌi/ *n* [C] (celebration of) a special anniversary of some event, eg a wedding. 週年紀念(例如結婚);週年紀念的慶祝。 **ˈdiamond ~**, 60th anniversary. 鑽石婚紀念;六十週年紀念。 **golden ~**, 50th anniversary. 金婚紀念;五十週年紀念。 **silver ~**, 25th anniversary. 銀婚紀念;二十五週年紀念。

Ju·da·ism /ˈdʒuːdeɪɪzəm *US:* -dɪɪzəm ; ˈdʒudɪˌɪzəm/ *n* the religion of the Jewish people; their culture and social way of life. 猶太教;猶太人的文化及社會生活方式。 **Ju·daic** /dʒuːˈdeɪɪk ; dʒuˈde·ɪk/ *adj* of Jews and ~. 猶太人的;猶太教的。

Judas /ˈdʒuːdəs ; ˈdʒudəs/ *n* (from ~ who betrayed Jesus Christ; ⇨ Mark 3: 19) betrayer; traitor. (由聖經中出賣耶穌的猶大而來;參看馬可福音第 3 章第19節)出賣朋友的人;叛徒。

jud·der /ˈdʒʌdə(r) ; ˈdʒʌdɚ/ *vi* shudder violently. 顫抖。

judge[1] /dʒʌdʒ ; dʒʌdʒ/ *n* **1** (of God) supreme arbiter; public officer with authority to hear and decide cases in a law court: 最高審判者(指上帝);審判官;法官: *~-made law*, principles based on ~s' decisions, not statute law; (法官之)判例;解釋例; *as grave as a ~.* 像法官般的嚴肅。⇨ justice (3, 4), magistrate. **2** person who decides in a contest, competition, dispute, etc: 裁判;仲裁人;評判員: *the ~s at a flower show.* 花卉展覽會的評判員。 **3** person qualified and able to give opinions on merits and values: 鑑識家;鑑定家: *a good ~ of horses.* 善於鑑定馬的人。 *He says the diamonds are not genuine; but then, he's no ~*, does not know much about diamonds. 他說這些鑽石非眞貨,但他並非識貨者。 **4** (in Hebrew history) officer given temporary authority as ruler in the period between Joshua and the Kings. (希伯來史)士師(約書亞與列王之間暫時的統治者)。 **J~s**, the book of the Old Testament recording this period. (舊約)士師記。

judge[2] /dʒʌdʒ ; dʒʌdʒ/ *vt, vi* (*pres p* judging) **1** [VP6A, 2A] act as a judge(1); hear and try (cases) in a law court: 審判;審理(案件): *God will ~ all men.* 上帝將審判所有的人。 **2** [VP6A, 2A] give a decision (in a competition, etc): (在競賽等中)評判;裁判: *Who is going to ~ the roses at the Flower Show?* 誰將評判花卉展覽中的薔薇？*Will you ~ at the Baby Show next week?* 你願意在下週嬰兒健康比賽會中擔任評審嗎？ **3** [VP6A, 9, 10, 22, 25, 2A, 3A] estimate; consider; form an opinion about: 斷定;認爲;判斷: *I ~d him to be about 50.* 我判斷他大約五十歲。*I can't ~ whether he was right or wrong.* 我不能斷定他是對還是錯。*I ~d, from his manner, that he was guilty.* 從他的態度上,我判斷他有罪。*The committee ~d it better to postpone the meeting.* 委員會認爲最好延期開會。*Don't ~ (of) a man by his looks.* 勿以外貌取人。*Judging from what you say, he ought to succeed.* 照你的話看來,他應該會成功。

judge·ment (US, and in GB legal use 美國拼法及英國法律用語作 **judg·ment**) /ˈdʒʌdʒmənt ; ˈdʒʌdʒmənt/ *n* **1** [U] judging or being judged: 審判;被審判: *sit in ~ on a case,* (in a law court); 開庭審案; *pass ~ on a prisoner,* give a decision after trial. 判決一犯人。**the Day of J~,** (also 亦作 **ˈJ~ Day, the Last ˈJ~**) the day when God will judge all men. 最後審判日;世界末日。 **2** [C] decision of a judge or court: (法官或法庭的)判決: *The ~ was in his favour.* 該判決對他有利。 **3** [U] process of judging: 評判;判斷: *an error of ~.* 判斷的錯誤。*His ~ was at fault.* 他的判斷有誤。 **4** [U] good sense; ability to judge (2, 3): 見識;判斷力: *a man of ~.* 有見識的人。*He showed excellent ~ in choosing the wine.* 他在擇酒方面顯示出卓越的判斷力。 **5** [C] misfortune considered to be a punishment from God: 報應;天譴: *Your failure is a ~ on you for being so lazy.* 你的失敗即是你懶惰的報應。 **6** [C, U] opinion: 意見: *in my ~;* 就我看來; *in the ~ of most people.* 據大多數人的意見。

ju·di·ca·ture /ˈdʒuːdɪkətʃə(r) ; ˈdʒudɪkətʃɚ/ *n* **1** [U] administration of justice: 司法行政: *the Supreme Court of J~,* full title of the English Courts of Justice. 英國最高法院的全銜。 **2** [C] body of judges. 法官之總稱。

ju·di·cial /dʒuːˈdɪʃl ; dʒuˈdɪʃəl/ *adj* **1** of or by a court of justice; of a judge or of judgement: 法庭的;法官的;審判的: *the ~ bench,* the judges; 法官之總稱; *take／bring ~ proceedings against sb,* bring a law case against him; 提起訴訟控告某人; *a ~ separation,* the right to separate from a husband or wife, granted by a judge, usu with arrangements favourable to the wronged person concerning money or children; 判決分居(指夫婦的分居,通常在金錢或兒女方面對受委屈的一方作有利的安排); *~ murder,* legal but unjust sentence of death. 寃死(合法但不公平的死刑判決)。 **2** critical; impartial: 有判斷力的;明斷的;公正的: *a man with a ~ mind.* 心地公正的人。**~ly** /-ʃəlɪ ; -ʃəlɪ/ *adv*

ju·dici·ary /dʒuːˈdɪʃərɪ *US:* -ʃɪerɪ ; dʒuˈdɪʃɪˌɛrɪ/ *n* (*pl* -ries) **1** the judges of a country collectively. 一國司法官之總稱。 **2** the system of law courts in a country. 司法制度。

ju·di·cious /dʒuːˈdɪʃəs ; dʒuˈdɪʃəs/ *adj* (formal) showing or having good sense. (正式用語)有見識的;明智的。**~·ly** *adv* **~·ness** *n*

judo /ˈdʒuːdəʊ ; ˈdʒudo/ *n* [U] Japanese art of wrestling and self-defence in which an opponent's

judges

own weight and strength are used against him. 柔道。

jug¹ /dʒʌg ; dʒʌg/ *n* **1** deep vessel with a handle and lip; the contents of such a vessel: 壺;帶柄水罐;壺中物: *a ˈmilk-jug;* 牛奶罐; *drink a jug of milk.* 飲一罐牛奶。 **2** (sl) prison. (俚)監牢。**jug·ful** /-fʊl ; -fʊl/ *n* (*pl* jugfuls) amount a jug will hold. 一壺(之量)。

jug² /dʒʌg ; dʒʌg/ *vt* (-gg-) [VP6A] **1** (usu in *pp*) stew or boil (hare, etc) in a jug or jar: (通常用過去分詞)在壺或罐中煨燉(野兔等): *jugged hare.* 用罐煨燒的野兔。 **2** (colloq) imprison. (俗)監禁。

jug·ger·naut /ˈdʒʌgənɔːt ; ˈdʒʌgɚˌnɔt/ *n* **1** cause or belief to which persons are sacrificed or to which they sacrifice themselves: 使人爲之犧牲的主義或信仰: *the ~ of war.* 使人爲之犧牲的戰爭。 **2** (colloq) huge long-distance transport vehicle. (俗)巨型長途運輸車輛。

juggle /ˈdʒʌgl ; ˈdʒʌgl/ *vi, vt* **1** [VP2A, 3A] ~ *(with),* do tricks, perform (with balls, plates, etc) to amuse people; play tricks (with facts, figures, etc) to deceive people. (用球,盤等)耍把戲;變戲法;玩弄事實,數字等以騙人。 **2** [VP6A, 16A] play tricks with; deceive: 以…耍把戲;誆騙;欺騙: *The manager ~d his figures to make it seem that the company was prosperous.* 那經理玩弄數字,以使他的公司顯得興隆。**jug·gler** *n* person who ~s. 耍把戲者;變戲法者;騙子。

jugu·lar /ˈdʒʌgjʊlə(r) ; ˈdʒʌgjəlɚ/ *adj* of the neck or throat: 頸部的;喉部的: *~ veins,* the large veins of the neck, returning blood from the head to the heart. 頸靜脈。

juice /dʒuːs ; dʒus/ *n* [C, U] **1** fluid part of fruits, vegetables and meat: 果汁;菜汁;肉汁: *a glass of ˈorange ~;* 一杯柑汁; *a mixture of ˈfruit ~s.* 綜合果汁。 **2** fluid in organs of the body: 體內分泌液;體液: *gastric／digestive ~s,* those that help to digest food. 胃(消化)液。 **3** [U] (colloq) electricity, petrol or other source of power. (俗)電,汽油,或其他動力的來源。

juicy /ˈdʒuːsɪ ; ˈdʒusɪ/ *adj* (-ier, -iest) **1** containing much juice: 多汁液的: *~ oranges.* 多汁的柑。 **2** (colloq) interesting (esp because scandalous, etc). (俗)有趣味的(尤指由於誹謗等)。**juici·ness** *n*

ju-jitsu /ˌdʒuː ˈdʒɪtsuː ; dʒuˈdʒɪtsu/ *n* Japanese art of self-defence from which judo was developed. 柔術(柔道係由此發展而來)。

juju /ˈdʒuːdʒuː ; ˈdʒudʒu/ *n* West African charm or fetish; its magic power. 非洲西部的符咒或神物;其魔力。

ju·jube /ˈdʒuːdʒuːb ; ˈdʒudʒub/ *n* [C] lozenge of gelatin, flavoured and sweetened. (含藥物之)膠糖。

juke-box /ˈdʒuːk bɒks ; ˈdʒukˌbɑks/ *n* [C] coin-operated record-player. 用錢幣操縱的電唱機;自動點唱機。

ju·lep /ˈdʒuːlɪp ; ˈdʒulɪp/ *n* (US) spirit (eg whisky), mint and ice: (美)加薄荷和冰的酒(例如威士忌): *mint ~.* 薄荷酒。

Jul·ian /ˈdʒuːlɪən ; ˈdʒuljən/ *adj* of Julius Caesar. 凱撒的。**~ calendar,** the calendar introduced by him in Rome in 46 BC. 凱撒曆(紀元前46年凱撒倡用者);儒略曆。⇨ Gregorian.

July /dʒuːˈlaɪ ; dʒuˈlaɪ/ *n* seventh month of the year. 七月。

jumble /ˈdʒʌmbl ; ˈdʒʌmbl/ *vi, vt* [VP15B, 2C] ~ *(up),* mix, be mixed, in a confused way: 混雜: *The untidy girl's toys, books, shoes and clothes were all ~d up together in the cupboard.* 那不整潔的女孩子的玩具,書籍,鞋子和衣服都亂堆在櫥裏。□ *n* confused mixture; muddle. 雜亂的一堆;一團糟。ˈ**~-sale** *n* sale of a mixed collection of old or second-hand articles. 舊雜貨拍賣。

jumbo /ˈdʒʌmbəʊ ; ˈdʒʌmbo/ *adj* unusually large: 巨大的: *~ jets;* 巨無霸噴射客機; *~-sized.* 巨大型的。

jump¹ /dʒʌmp ; dʒʌmp/ *n* **1** act of jumping; sudden spring from the ground. 跳；躍。**the ˈlong／ˈhigh ～**, athletic competitions in which competitors jump a distance／height. 跳遠(高)。**2** sudden movement caused by fear. 驚跳。***give sb a ～***, frighten him. 使某人嚇一跳。**the ～s**, (colloq) form of nervous excitement with uncontrollable bodily movements. (俗)神經性抽動；舞蹈病；震顫譫妄。**3** sudden rise in amount, price, value, etc: (數額，價格，價值等之)突增；突升；暴漲：*a ～ in car exports.* 汽車出口之突增。**jumpy** *adj* (-ier, -iest) excited and nervous. 激動而緊張的。**～i·ness** *n*

jump² /dʒʌmp ; dʒʌmp/ *vi, vt* **1** [VP2A, C] move quickly by the sudden use of the muscles of the legs or (of fish) the tail; rise suddenly (from a seat, etc); move quickly (*into* sth): 跳；躍；(自座位等)突然起來；迅速進入(與 into 連用)：*～ to one's feet;* 突然站起來；*～ over a fence;* 跳過籬笆；*～ up out of one's chair;* 突然從椅子上站起來；*～ into a taxi*, enter one quickly; 跳上一部計程車；(fig) (喻) *～ from one subject to another in a speech.* 演說中自一問題突然轉入另一問題。***～ down sb's throat***, answer, interrupt, him violently. 粗暴地回答或打斷某人的談話。**ˌ～ing-ˈoff place**, starting point. 起點；出發點。**ˈ～ed-up** *adj* (colloq) upstart. (俗)暴富的；驟貴的。 **2** [VP6A] pass over by moving in this way: 跳過；躍過：*～ a ditch;* 躍過一溝；cause (a horse, etc) to move in this way: 使(馬等)跳過：*～ a horse over a fence.* 騎馬跳過籬笆。**～ *the rails／track***, (of a train, tram, etc) leave the rails suddenly. (指火車，電車等)出軌。 **3** [VP2A,C] move with a jerk or jerks from excitement, joy, etc; start suddenly: (因興奮，喜悅等)跳動；驚跳：*～ for joy;* 高興得跳起來；*～ up and down in excitement.* 興奮得跳來跳去。*Her heart ～ed when she heard the news.* 她聽到那消息時心跳了起來。**4** [VP2A, C] rise suddenly in price: 價格突升；暴漲：*Gold shares ～ed on the Stock Exchange yesterday.* 昨天證券交易所中金子的股票暴漲。 **5 ～ *at***, accept eagerly: 迫不及待地接受；欣然接受：*～ at an offer.* 迫不及待地接受一提議。**～ *to conclusions***, reach them hastily. 匆匆做結論。**ˌ～ ˈ*to it***, act quickly or promptly. 行動迅速。**～ *on／upon***, attack, reprove severely; scold. 攻擊；譴責；責罵。**6 ～ *(one's) bail***, fail to appear for trial, ⇨ bail¹. 未能按時到庭應訊；棄保潛逃。**～ *a claim***, (colloq) take possession of land or mining rights, eg in a new goldfield, to which another person has already established a claim. (俗)霸佔土地或採礦權。**～ *the gun***, start too soon (as from the use of a shot to start a race). 起動過早(由鳴槍起跑而來)。***(go and) ～ in the lake***, (colloq, imper) go away (said dismissively or angrily). (俗，祈使)走開；滾開(說時含不屑或憤怒)。**～ *the queue***, (lit or fig) obtain sth without waiting for one's proper turn. (字面或喻)在未輪到前搶先獲得某物；插隊。**～ *a train***, travel illegally by goods train, eg by riding in or under a closed wagon. 違規搭乘運貨火車。

jumper /ˈdʒʌmpə(r) ; ˈdʒʌmpɚ/ *n* **1** outer knitted garment, with or without sleeves, pulled on over the head and coming down to the hips, ⇨ jersey, pullover, sweater; (US) pinafore. 一種帶袖或無袖針織外衣(自頭部套下，下面齊臀部)；(美)(小孩的)圍兜。**2** person, animal or insect, that jumps. 跳躍的人，動物或昆蟲。

junc·tion /ˈdʒʌŋkʃn ; ˈdʒʌŋkʃən/ *n* **1** [U] joining or being joined; [C] instance of this: 連接；會合：*The allied armies hope to effect a ～*, meet and unite. 聯軍希望能會師。 **2** [C] place where roads, railway lines or sections of an electrical circuit meet or diverge. 道路交叉點；鐵路交叉站；樞紐站；聯軌站；(電路之)中繼線。

junc·ture /ˈdʒʌŋktʃə(r) ; ˈdʒʌŋktʃɚ/ *n* [C] (formal) (正式用語) **1** junction(1). 接合處；接合點。**2** state of affairs, esp in the phrase: 事情的狀況(尤用於下列片語中)：***at this ～***, at this time, when affairs are／were in this state. 在此時；值此際。

June /dʒu:n ; dʒun/ *n* sixth month of the year. 六月。

jungle /ˈdʒʌŋgl ; ˈdʒʌŋgḷ/ *n* **1** (usu 通常作 **the ～**, *sing* or *pl* 單數或複數) (land covered with) thickly growing underwood and tangled vegetation: 叢林；叢林地帶：*cut a path through the ～;* 自叢林中開一條路；*～ warfare;* 叢林戰；*～ birds and animals;* 叢林地帶的鳥獸；ˈ*～ fever*, malarial fever. 叢林熱(瘧疾)。***the law of the ～***, (fig) ruthless competition or exploitation. (喻)無情的競爭或利用；優勝劣敗；弱肉强食。**2** (in compounds) (用於複合字) ˈ*～-cat*, 林貓，ˈ*～-fowl*. 原鷄；林鷄。**jun·gly** /ˈdʒʌŋglɪ ; ˈdʒʌŋglɪ/ *adj* of, like, from the ～ or its inhabitants. 叢林的；叢林地帶的；似叢林的；叢林地帶居民的。

jun·ior /ˈdʒu:nɪə(r) ; ˈdʒunjɚ/ *n, adj* **1** (person) younger, lower in rank, than another: 較年幼的；地位較低的；較幼者；地位較低者：*a ～ high school;* 初中；初級中學；*～ dress sizes.* 年幼者穿的衣服尺碼。*He is my ～ by two years.* 他比我小兩歲。*He is the ～ partner in the firm.* 他是這公司地位較低的股東。*Tom Brown, Junior* (or abbr 略作 **Jun, Jnr, Jr**), used of a son having the same first name as his father, or the younger of two boys of the same surname in a school, etc. 小湯姆·布朗(父子同名時，用於兒子姓名後，或同一學校之二男生同姓時，用於年幼者之名後)。**2** (US schools and colleges) student in his third year (of four). (美)(四年制的中學或大學)三年級生。

ju·ni·per /ˈdʒu:nɪpə(r) ; ˈdʒunəpɚ/ *n* evergreen shrub with dark berries from which an oil (*oil of ～*) is obtained, used in medicine, etc. 杜松(生有黑色漿果，可以製杜松子油 oil of juniper, 用於藥品等中)。

junk¹ /dʒʌŋk ; dʒʌŋk/ *n* [U] old, discarded things of little or no value: 廢棄的舊物；破爛物：*an attic full of ～;* 裝滿廢棄物的頂樓；*a ～ dealer.* 買賣廢棄舊物的商人；舊貨商。**ˈ～-shop**, one selling cheap second-hand goods. 舊貨店。

junk² /dʒʌŋk ; dʒʌŋk/ *n* [C] flat-bottomed Chinese sailing-vessel. (平底的)中國帆船。

a junk

junket /ˈdʒʌŋkɪt ; ˈdʒʌŋkɪt/ *n* **1** [C, U] (dish of) milk curdled by the addition of acid, often sweetened and flavoured. (一份)凝乳食品(由牛奶加酸製成，常調有糖和香料)。**2** social gathering for a feast; picnic. 宴會；野宴。□ *vi* take part in a ～(2). 參加宴會；參加野宴。Hence, 由此產生，**～ing** *n* [U] feasting; merrymaking. 宴樂；作樂。

junkie, junky /ˈdʒʌŋkɪ ; ˈdʒʌŋkɪ/ *n* (sl) drug (esp heroin) addict. (俚)有毒癮者；煙毒犯。

Juno·esque /ˌdʒu:nəʊˈesk ; ˌdʒunoˈɛsk/ *adj* (of a woman) having a stately beauty (like the goddess Juno). (指女子)有高貴美的；端莊的(似女神 Juno 的)。

junta /ˈdʒʌntə *US:* ˈhʊntə ; ˈhʊntə/ *n* (in Spain and Italy) deliberative or administrative council; group of army officers who have seized power by a coup d'état. (西班牙和義大利)評議或行政會議；以武力奪得政權的軍官團。

Jupi·ter /ˈdʒu:pɪtə(r) ; ˈdʒupətɚ/ *n* (ancient Rome) ruler of gods and men; largest planet of the solar system. (古羅馬)主神；木星(太陽系中最大之行星)。⇨ the illus at planet. 參看 planet 之插圖。

ju·ridi·cal /dʒʊəˈrɪdɪkl ; dʒʊˈrɪdɪkḷ/ *adj* of law or legal proceedings. 法律的；訴訟程序的。

ju·ris·dic·tion /ˌdʒʊərɪsˈdɪkʃn ; ˌdʒʊrɪsˈdɪkʃən/ *n* [U] administration of justice; legal authority; right to exercise this; extent of this: 法律的執行;司法;司法權;裁判權;審判的權限;管轄權;管轄區域: *The courts have ~ not only over our own citizens but over foreigners living here.* 法庭的裁判權不僅及於我們的國民,而且及於僑居此地的外國人。*This matter does not come/fall within our ~*, We have no authority to deal with it. 我們無權過問此事。

ju·ris·pru·dence /ˌdʒʊərɪsˈpruːdns ; ˌdʒʊrɪsˈprudn̩s/ *n* [U] science and philosophy of human law. 法學;法理學。

jur·ist /ˈdʒʊərɪst ; ˈdʒʊrɪst/ *n* expert in law. 法學家;法理學家。

juror /ˈdʒʊərə(r) ; ˈdʒʊrɚ/ *n* member of a jury. 陪審團之一員;陪審員;評判員。

jury /ˈdʒʊərɪ ; ˈdʒʊrɪ/ *n* (*pl* -ries) [C] **1** body of persons (in US and GB twelve) who swear to give a decision (*verdict*) on issues of fact in a case in a court of justice: 陪審團(英美皆由十二人組成): *trial by ~*. 陪審。*The ~ found the prisoner not guilty.* 陪審團認爲該囚犯無罪。**ˈ~-box** *n* enclosure for a ~ in court. 陪審團席。 **2 grand ~,** specially chosen body of 12 to 23 persons who (GB until 1933) inquire into a charge in order to decide whether there is enough evidence to justify a trial or whether the case should be abandoned. 大陪審團(由十二至二十三人組成,在英國於1933年前,可調查一項指控,俾決定是否有充份證據應使被告受審,或對該案不予受理)。**coroner's ~,** one that decides the cause of a death (if unnatural death, eg suicide or murder, is suspected). 驗屍陪審團(於有自殺或謀殺等非自然死亡之嫌疑時鑑定死因者)。 **3** body of persons chosen to give a decision or make an award in a competition; (比賽等之)評判委員會; (fig) (喻) *the ~ of public opinion*, the public, thought of as a ~, deciding a question. 輿論。**ˈ~·man** /-mən ; -mən/ (*pl* -men) *n* member of a jury; juror. 陪審員。

jury-mast /ˈdʒʊərɪ mɑːst *US*: mæst ; ˈdʒʊrɪˌmæst/ *n* temporary mast put up in place of one that is broken or lost overboard. 應急桅杆。

just¹ /dʒʌst ; dʒʌst/ *adj* **1** in accordance with what is right: 公平的;公正的;正直的: *a ~ man;* 正直的人; *a ~ sentence;* 公平的判決; *be ~ to a person.* 對某人公正。 **2** well deserved; fairly earned: 應得的;應該有的: *get/receive one's ~ deserts*, be rewarded or punished as one deserves. 得到應得的賞罰。 **3** reasonable; based on reasonable grounds: 合理的;有理的: *a ~ opinion;* 合理的意見; *~ suspicions.* 有根據的懷疑。 **~·ly** *adv*: *to feel ~ly ashamed.* 應感到慚愧。**~·ness** *n*

just² /dʒʌst ; dʒʌst/ *adv* **1** used (GB) in the perfect tenses and (US often) with the simple past tense, placed with the *v*, to indicate an immediate past: 剛才;方才 (在英國用於完成時態,在美國常用於簡單過去時態,置於動詞之前): (GB) (英) *I've ~ had dinner.* 我剛才吃完晚飯。(US) (美) *I ~ had dinner.* 我剛才吃完晚飯。 Cf 參較 *I had dinner an hour ago.* 我在一小時前吃完了晚飯。*My son had ~ left school.* 我兒子剛剛離開學校(畢業)。 **2** (followed by *nn, n phrases* and *clauses*) exactly; precisely: 正好;恰好(後接名詞,名詞片語和子句): *It's ~ two o'clock.* 現在的時間是兩點鐘正。*This is ~ what I wanted.* 這正是我所要的。*That's ~ what I was going to say.* 那恰好是我正要說的。*J~ my luck!* 我的運氣就是這麼壞! *J~ the thing!* 就是這個東西(意思)! **3 ~ as** (*+adj+ as*), **(a)** exactly as: 恰如: *Leave everything ~ as (tidy as) you find it.* 讓每件東西都保持原樣(像原來一樣整齊)。*Come ~ as you are,* Do not make any special preparations. 你就這樣來 (勿做特別準備)。 *This is ~* (= quite) *as good as the other.* 這個同另外一個簡直一樣的好。 **(b)** (introducing adverbials of time) when: (引導表示時間的副詞片語或子句)當…之時;其時: *He arrived ~ as I was about to go out/~ as I was shaving.* 他來到時我正要出去(正在刮臉)。**(c)** (introducing clauses of comparison) in the same way as: (引導表示比較的子句)如同…一樣: *J~ as you find it difficult to like Mr Green, so I find it easy to like his wife.* 如同你覺得格林先生難以討人喜歡一樣,我覺得他的太太容易討人喜歡。 **4** (with *advv*) exactly: (與副詞連用)正確地: *~ here/there.* 就在這裏(那裏)。 **5** (used to indicate approximation) more or less: (用以表示近似)大約: *I've had ~ about enough of your impudence,* almost more than I can endure. 你的無禮幾乎使我無法容忍了。*Put it ~ over there,* near that place. 把它放在那附近。 *It's ~ about tall enough,* will be satisfactory. 差不多够高了。 **6** at this/that very moment: 此時;現在;那時: *We're ~ off/~ about to start.* 我們現在正要出去(動身)。*His new book is ~ out/~ published.* 他的新書剛出版。 **~ now, (a)** at this moment: 此刻;現在: *I'm busy ~ now.* 我現在很忙。**(b)** a short time ago: 剛才;方才: *Tom came in ~ now—he's probably upstairs.* 湯姆剛剛進來 — 他大概在樓上。 **7 (only) ~,** almost not; with a very little time/space/margin etc to spare: 幾乎不;僅僅地: *We (only) ~ caught the train,* almost missed it. 我們剛好趕上火車。*Jane ~ managed to pass the exam.* 珍考試剛好及格。 Cf 參較 She *almost* failed. 她幾乎不及格。 *I've ~ enough money to last me till pay-day.* 我的錢剛好够我維持到發薪。 **8** (used in familiar, colloquial style, esp with imperatives, to call attention to sth, sometimes to soften what follows): (用於日常的口語中,尤用於祈使句,以引起對某事物的注意,有時可使語氣婉轉): *J~ listen to him!* and note how clever/silly/amusing, etc he is! 聽他說說看!(看他多麼聰明,愚蠢,有趣等)! *J~ taste this!* (so that you may judge its quality, say whether it is right, etc). 嚐嚐看!(以便評定它的品質,看看是否滿意等)。*J~ feel it!* and note how hard, soft, smooth, etc it is! 摸摸看!(看它多麼硬,軟,光滑等)。 *J~* (= Please) *come here a moment.* 請過來一下。*J~ a moment, please,* Please wait a moment. 請稍等片刻。 **9** only; merely: 僅;祇: *He's ~ an ordinary man.* 他祇是個普通人。 *I've come here ~* (= on purpose) *to see you.* 我專程來此看望你。*Would you walk five miles ~ to see a film?* 你願意只是爲了看一場電影而走五哩路嗎? **10** (colloq) very; very much: (俗)很;十分: *The concert was ~ splendid.* 那音樂會很不錯。 *'Did you enjoy yourselves?'—'I should ~ say we did!'* or *'Didn't we ~!'* (emph) We had a most enjoyable time. '你們玩得痛快嗎?'—(强勢語)'我們玩得實在痛快極了!'

jus·tice /ˈdʒʌstɪs ; ˈdʒʌstɪs/ *n* **1** [U] just conduct; the quality of being right and fair: 公平;公正;合理;公道;公理;正義: *treat all men with ~.* 公平對待所有的人。**in ~ to,** in order to be just to. 爲對…公平起見。**do ~ to,** treat fairly; show that one has a just opinion of, that one realizes the value of: 公平對待;公平評判;賞識: *To do him ~, we must admit that his intentions were good.* 公平而論,我們必須承認他的用意是好的。 *He did ~ to the dinner,* showed by eating heartily that the food was good. 他津津有味地吃那頓飯。**do oneself ~,** behave in a way that is worthy of one's abilities: 發揮自己的能力: *You're not doing yourself ~,* You could do much better if you tried. 你尙未發揮你的能力。 **2** [U] the law and its administration: 法律制裁;司法;審判: *a court of ~.* 法庭。 **bring sb to ~,** arrest, try and sentence (a criminal). 使(犯人)歸案受審。 **3** [C] judge of the Supreme Courts: (英)高等法院法官;(美)最高法院法官: *the Lord Chief J~;* 高等法院的庭長或首席法官; *the Lords J~s;* 高等法院法官們; *the Chief J~ of England;* 英國高等法院的庭長或首席法官; *Mr J~ Smith.* 法官史密斯先生。 **4 ˌJ~ of the ˈPeace,** (abbr 略作 **JP**) magistrate. 保安官;治安法官。 **Department of J~,** (US) executive department, headed by the Attorney General, supervising internal security, naturalization, immigration, etc. (美)司法部。

jus·tici·ary /dʒʌˈstɪʃərɪ *US:* -ʃɪerɪ ; dʒʌsˈtɪʃɪˌɛrɪ/ *n* (*pl* -ries) (jurisdiction of a) judge or chief justice: 司法官;法院推事;裁判權: (in Scotland) (蘇格蘭) *the High Court of J~*. 高等法院。

jus·tify /ˈdʒʌstɪfaɪ ; ˈdʒʌstəˌfaɪ/ *vt* (*pt, pp* -fied) [VP6A, 19C] **1** show that (a person, statement, act, etc) is right, reasonable or proper: 證明(人,言論,行動等)爲正當: *The Prime Minister justified the action of the Government.* 首相證明政府的該一行動是正當的。*You can hardly ~ such conduct.* 你幾乎無法證明此種行爲是正當的。*You'd be hard put to it to ~ your behaviour.* 你難以證明你的行爲是正當的。**2** be a good reason for: 爲…之好的理由;爲…辯護;辯明: *Your wish to go for a walk does not ~ your leaving the baby alone in the house.* 你想出去散步並不構成將嬰兒獨自丟在屋中的理由。 **3** adjust (a line of type) to fill a space neatly. 調整(一行鉛字)使排滿一空間。 **jus·ti·fi·able** /ˌdʒʌstɪˈfaɪəbl ; ˈdʒʌstəˌfaɪəbl/ *adj* that can be justified: 可證明爲正當的;有理由的: *justifiable homicide.* 正當殺人。 **jus·ti·fi·ably** /-əblɪ ; -əblɪ/ *adv* **jus·ti·fi·ca·tion** /ˌdʒʌstɪfɪˈkeɪʃn ; ˌdʒʌstəfəˈkeʃən/ *n* [U] **1** sth that justifies: 理由: *His justification for stealing was that his children were starving.* 他偸竊的理由是他的兒女快要餓死了。 ***in justification (for/of sth/sb)***, ~ing it/him: 作爲某事物之理由;爲某人辯護: *It can be said in justification for what he had done that....* 他所以這樣做的理由是…。 **2** the act of ~ing sth. 證明爲正當;辯明。 **3** the state of being free from blame. 無咎。

jut /dʒʌt ; dʒʌt/ *vi* (-tt-) [VP2C] ***jut out***, stand out from; be out of line (from what is around): 突出;伸出: *The soldier saw a gun jutting out from a bush.* 那兵士看見一枝槍自矮樹叢伸出來。*The balcony juts out over the garden.* 陽臺在花園上方突出來。

jute /dʒuːt ; dʒut/ *n* [U] fibre from the outer skin of certain plants, used for making canvas, rope, etc: 黃麻的纖維: *the ~ mills of Bangladesh.* 孟加拉共和國的黃麻纖維製造廠。

ju·ven·ile /ˈdʒuːvənaɪl ; ˈdʒuvənl̩/ *n* young person. 少年。 □ *adj* of, characteristic of, suitable for, ~s: 少年的;少年特有的;適於少年的: *~ books;* 少年讀物; *a ~ appearance;* 少年的外貌; *a ~ court,* where children are tried; 少年法庭; *~ delinquency,* law-breaking by young people; 少年犯罪; *~ delinquent,* young offender; 少年犯; *a ~ sense of humour,* eg in an adult. 少年人的幽默感(例如用以形容某成年人)。

jux·ta·pose /ˌdʒʌkstəˈpəʊz ; ˌdʒʌkstəˈpoz/ *vt* [VP 6A] place side by side. 並列;並置。 **jux·ta·po·si·tion** /ˌdʒʌkstəpəˈzɪʃn ; ˌdʒʌkstəpəˈzɪʃən/ *n* [U] placing side by side; the state of being placed side by side. 並列;並置。

Kk

K, k /keɪ ; ke/ (*pl* K's, k's /keɪz ; kez/) the 11th letter of the English alphabet. 英文字母之第十一個字母。

Kaf·fir /ˈkæfə(r) ; ˈkæfɚ/ *n* ⚠ (offensive word for) black African person. (諱)(蔑)非洲黑人。

Kaiser /ˈkaɪzə(r) ; ˈkaɪzɚ/ *n* Emperor (esp of Germany before 1918). 皇帝(尤指1918年前之德國皇帝)。

kake·mono /ˌkækɪˈməʊnəʊ ; ˈkɑkeˈmono/ *n* Japanese painting in a hanging scroll of silk or paper. 日本人掛於牆上的畫;條幅。

kale, kail /keɪl ; kel/ *n* kind of curly-leaved cabbage. 一種甘藍。

ka·leido·scope /kəˈlaɪdəskəʊp ; kəˈlaɪdəˌskop/ *n* [C] **1** tube containing mirrors and small, loose pieces of coloured glass. When the tube is turned, constantly changing patterns are seen through the eye-piece. 萬花筒。**2** (fig) frequently changing pattern of bright scenes: (喩)時時變化之鮮明景色: *Sunlight and shadow made the landscape a ~ of colour.* 陽光與陰影使那風景的顏色千變萬化。 **ka·leido·scopic** /kəˌlaɪdəˈskɒpɪk ; kəˌlaɪdəˈskɑpɪk/ *adj* quickly changing. 迅速變化的;千變萬化的。

kal·ends /ˈkælendz ; ˈkælɪndz/ *n pl* ⇨ calends.

kam·pong /ˈkæmpɒŋ ; ˈkæmpɑŋ/ *n* (in Malaysia) enclosed space; village. (馬來西亞之)房屋四周等圍起來的空地;村莊。

kan·ga·roo /ˌkæŋgəˈruː ; ˌkæŋgəˈru/ *n* Australian marsupial that jumps along on its strong hind legs. The female has a pouch in which its young are carried. (產於澳洲之)袋鼠。⇨ the illus at large. 參看 large 之挿圖。**~ court,** one set up without authority by workers, prisoners, etc to try someone whom they consider to have acted against their interests. 工人,犯人等私設之法庭。

kao·lin /ˈkeɪəlɪn ; ˈkeəlɪn/ *n* [U] fine white clay used in making porcelain, etc. (製瓷器等之)白陶土;高嶺土。

ka·pok /ˈkeɪpɒk ; ˈkepɑk/ *n* [U] soft cotton-like material (from seeds of a tropical tree) used for filling cushions, life-belts, mattresses, etc. 木棉。

ka·put /kəˈpʊt ; kəˈpʊt/ *adj* (*pred* only) (G) (sl) done for; ruined; smashed. (僅作述語)(德)(俚)不行了;完了;壞了。

karat /ˈkærət ; ˈkærət/ *n* (US) = carat(2).

ka·rate /kəˈrɑːtɪ ; kəˈrɑtɪ/ *n* [U] Japanese method of unarmed combat using blows made with the hand, foot, head or elbow. (日本之)空手道。

karma /ˈkɑːmə ; ˈkɑrmə/ *n* (in Buddhism) person's acts in one of his successive existences, looked upon as deciding his fate in his next existence. (佛教)羯磨;業;因果報應(個人在其輪廻生命中之行爲,被視爲可決定其來生之命運)。

kava /ˈkɑːvə ; ˈkɑvə/ *n* [U] (intoxicating drink made from the roots of a) Polynesian shrub. 卡法樹(太平洋波里尼西亞群島所產之一種灌木);卡法酒(此種灌木根製成的酒)。

kayak /ˈkaɪæk ; ˈkaɪæk/ *n* Eskimo canoe of light wood covered with sealskins; any small, covered canoe. 愛斯基摩人用的覆有海豹皮的獨木舟;任何有覆蓋的小獨木舟。⇨ the illus at canoe. 參看 canoe 之挿圖。

ke·bab /kəˈbæb ; kəˈbæb/ *n* dish of small pieces of meat, seasoned and roasted on skewers. 以小木棒或叉串起的烤肉;沙嗲。

ked·ger·ee /ˈkedʒəriː ; ˈkɛdʒəˌri/ *n* [U] rice cooked with fish, eggs, etc. 以米、魚、蛋等燒成的食品。

keel /kiːl ; kil/ *n* timber or steel structure on which the framework of a ship is built up: 龍骨;船脊骨: *lay down a ~*, start the building of a ship. 安龍骨(起工造船)。***(keep) on an even ~***, **(a)** (of a ship) without movement to one side or the other. (指船)平穩的。**(b)** (fig) steady; steadily; calm(ly). (喩)穩定的(地);安靜的(地)。□ *vt, vi* **1** [VP6A] turn (a ship) over on one side to repair it, clean the ~, etc. 將(船)翻至一側(以修理,洗刷龍骨等)。 **2** [VP15B, 2C] ~ ***over***, capsize; upset. (船)傾覆;使(船)傾覆。

keen[1] /kiːn ; kin/ *adj* (-er, -est) **1** (of points and edges) sharp: (指尖和刃)鋒利的;銳利的: *a knife with a ~ edge;* 刀刃鋒利的小刀; (fig) (喩) *a ~ (=cutting) wind;* 刺骨的風; *~ sarcasm.* 尖刻的諷刺。 **2** (of interest, the feelings) strong; deep: (指興趣,情感)強烈的;深刻的: *He has a ~ interest in his*

K

work. 他對他的工作極感興趣。 **3** (of the mind, the senses) active; sensitive; sharp: (指心智,感官)敏捷的;敏銳的: ~ *sight;* 敏銳的視力; ˌ~-ˈ*sighted;* 視力敏銳的; *a ~ intelligence*. 敏捷的智力。 **4** (of persons, their character, etc) eager; anxious to do things: (指人,性格等)切望的;熱心的:*a ~ sportsman*. 熱心運動者。*He's very ~ to see his birthplace again*. 他非常渴望能再見他的故鄉。 **~ on,** (colloq) interested in, fond of, eager to/for: (俗)對…有興趣;喜歡;渴望: *~ on going abroad*. 渴望着出國。*Mrs Hill is ~ on Tom('s) marrying Stella/~ that Tom should marry Stella*. 希爾太太很希望湯姆和斯戴拉結婚。*Tom is not very ~ on Stella*, does not like her much. 湯姆不太喜歡斯戴拉。*I'm not very ~ on jazz*. 我對爵士樂不太感興趣。 **~·ly** *adv* **~·ness** *n*

keen² /kiːn ; kin/ *n* Irish funeral song accompanied by wailing. 愛爾蘭的伴有慟哭的輓歌。□ *vi, vt* utter this song; lament (a person) in this way. 以哀哭唱出輓歌;以哀哭唱出輓歌追悼(某人)。

keep¹ /kiːp ; kip/ *vt, vi* (*pt, pp* kept /kept ; kɛpt/) (For idiomatic uses with *adverbial particles* and *preps*, ⇨ 18 below. For *keep* and *nn* not given here, ⇨ the *n* entries, eg *~ pace/step, ~ time, ~ watch, ~ good/early hours.*) (與副詞接語和介詞連用之習慣用法參看下列第 18 義。keep 與名詞連用如未列於本字項下者,則參看於各該名詞。) **1** [VP22, 15A] cause sb/sth to remain in a specified state or position: 使(人或物)保持某種狀態: *~ the children quiet/happy*. 使孩子們安靜 (快樂)。 *The cold weather kept us indoors*. 寒冷的天氣使我們待在家裡。 *If your hands are cold, ~ them in your pockets*. 如果你的手覺得冷,就把它們放在口袋裡。*Will they ~ me in prison/custody?* 他們會監禁(拘留)我嗎? *Extra work kept* (= detained) *me at the office*. 額外的工作使我留在辦公室裡。*Will you ~ these things safe for me?* 你願意爲我保管這些東西嗎? **~ an eye on,** (colloq) watch over closely: (俗)注意看守: *Please ~ an eye on the baby while I'm in the garden*. 我去花園裡的時候,請照看着這嬰兒。**~ sth in mind,** remember it: 記住(某事物): *Do ~ it in mind that we expect a report next week*. 千萬記住下週提出報告。**~ track of/tabs on/a tab on,** ⇨ track(1), tab(2). **2** [VP19B] cause a process or state to continue: 使一過程或狀態繼續: *Please ~ the fire burning*. 請使火保持燃燒。*I'm sorry I've kept you waiting*. 我很抱歉使你久等了。 **~ sb going,** help him to continue in some way: 幫助某人繼續某種活動方式: *Will £10 ~ you going until payday*, cover your expenses? 十鎊可使你維持到發薪日嗎? *The doctors manage to ~ me going*, help me to remain active. 醫生們設法助我活下去。**~ the ball rolling,** ⇨ ball¹. **~ the pot boiling,** ⇨ pot¹(2). **3** [VP14] **~ sb/sth from doing sth,** prevent, hold back, refrain: 阻止;防止;阻礙: *What kept you from joining me?* Often shortened to 常略作 '*What kept you?*'. 什麼事情使你躭擱了? *We must ~ them from getting to know our plans*. 我們必須防止他們知道我們的計畫。*We must do something to ~ the roof from falling in*. 我們必須設法防止屋頂塌下來。[VP3A] **~ from doing sth,** refrain: 抑制: *I couldn't ~ from laughing*. 我不禁大笑起來。 **4** [VP15B, 14] **~ sth (back) (from),** **(a)** not let others know about it: 不讓他人知道: *She can ~ nothing (back) from her friends*. 她在她的朋友面前沒有秘密。 **(b)** hold back; withhold: 留下;保留: *They ~ back £20 a month from my salary for National Insurance*. 他們從我的薪金中每月扣下二十鎊付國民保險費。**~ sth to oneself,** **(a)** (often *imper*) not express, eg comments, views, etc: (常爲祈使用法)不表示意見等: *K~/You may ~ your remarks to yourself*, I don't want to hear them. 我不要聽你的評論。**(b)** refuse to share: 不讓他人分享: *He kept the good news to himself*. 他沒有把這好消息告訴別人。**~ one's own counsel,** ⇨ counsel¹. **~ a secret,** ⇨ secret. **5** [VP6A] (with an implied complement, eg *inviolate*) pay proper respect to; be faithful to; observe; fulfil: (含有暗示的補足詞,例如 inviolate) 遵守;忠於;履行: *~ a promise/a treaty/an appointment/the law*. 遵守諾言(條約,約定,法律)。**~ faith with sb,** ⇨ faith. **6** [VP6A] celebrate: 慶祝;過(節,生日等): *~ the Sabbath*, ie ~ it sacred; 守安息日; *~ Christmas/one's birthday*. 過聖誕節(生日)。 **7** [VP6A] guard; protect: 保衛;保護: *~ goal*, ⇨ goalkeeper; 守球門; *~ wicket*, (cricket) stand behind the wicket to stop or catch the ball, ⇨ wicket-keeper. (板球)守三柱門。*May God/the Lord bless and ~ you*, ie keep you safe. 願上帝保祐你。 **8** [VP6A] continue to have; have in one's possession and not give away; not lose; preserve, eg for future use or reference: 保有;保管;保存;保留: *You may ~ this—I don't want it back*. 你可以把這個留下來,我不要了。*K~ the change*, ie from money offered in payment. 零錢不要找了。*Please ~ these things for me while I'm away*. 我離開期間請你替我保管這些東西。*We'll ~ these for another day*. 我們還要將這些再保留一天。**~ hold of; ~ a firm/tight hold on,** not let go: 握住;緊緊握住: *K~ a tight hold on the horse's reins*. 緊緊握住馬韁。 **9** [VP6A, 15A, 22] support; take care of; provide what is needed for; maintain: 贍養;照顧;供給所需之物;養護: *Does he earn enough to ~ himself and his family?* 他的收入够維持自己和家人的生活嗎? *He has a wife and ten children to ~, poor fellow!* 他要養活妻子和十個孩子,眞是個可憐的人! *She lives with her parents but earns enough to ~ herself in clothes*, to buy her own clothes. 她和父母住在一起,但她賺的錢够添置衣服。 *He ~s sheep in the Highlands*. 他在蘇格蘭高地養羊。*He ~s a mistress in Chelsea* 他在契爾西養了一個情婦(hence, 由此產生, now dated, 現爲過時用語, **kept woman**, one whose needs are provided by a man whose mistress she is 受贍養的情婦)。 **10** [VP6A] have habitually on sale or in stock: 經售: *'Do you sell batteries for transistor sets?'—'Sorry, but we don't ~ them.'* '你們經售電晶體收音機的電池嗎?'—'對不起,我們不賣那種電池。' **11 ~ house,** be responsible for the housework, cooking, shopping, etc: 管家; 料理家務: *His sister ~s house for him*. 他姐姐(妹妹)爲他管家。⇨ *housekeeper* at house¹. **~ open house,** be ready to entertain friends, etc at any time. 隨時歡迎客人來臨。 **12** [VP6A] own or manage, esp for profit: 經營(尤指爲了牟利): *~ hens/bees/pigs;* 養母鷄(蜜蜂,豬); *~ a shop/an inn*. 經營一商店(旅館)。Hence, 由此產生, **ˈshop·~er, ˈinn·~er.** **13** [VP6A] make entries in, records of: 記入;記錄: *~ a diary*. 記日記。**~ accounts,** records of money paid out and received. 記帳。 **~ books,** = ~ accounts. Hence, 由此產生, **ˈbook·~er.** **14** [VP2C, D] continue to be, remain, in a specified condition: 保持(某種狀態): *If you've got the 'flu, you'd better go to bed and ~ warm*. 你如已患流行性感冒,最好躺在床上蓋暖和些。 *Please ~ quiet!* 請保持安靜! *I hope you're ~ing well*. 我希望你保持健康。*K~ cool!* (fig) Don't get excited! (喩)保持冷靜(勿激動)! **~ fit,** (do physical exercise to) remain in good health: (做運動)保持健康: (attrib) (形容用法) *~-fit classes*. 體育課。 **15** [VP6A, 2C, 3A] **~ on/to,** continue in a particular direction; remain in a particular relationship to a place, etc: 繼續朝某方向;繼續循…而行;保持某種方向;留在(某地);保持在(某位置上): *We kept (on) our way/course all morning*. 我們整個早上繼續前行。*While that big lorry ~s (to) the middle of the road, we can't possibly overtake it*. 只要那輛大卡車一直沿着路中央行駛,我們就無法超越它。*K~ straight on until you get to the church*. 一直向前走,便可到達教堂。*Traffic in Britain ~s (to the) left*. 英國往來的車輛行人等

是靠左邊走的。*K~ left*, as a traffic sign. 靠左邊走(指示交通向左的標誌)。*He was ill and had to ~ to his bed/the house for weeks.* 他病了,不得不躺在床上(留在房屋內)好幾個禮拜。*She couldn't ~ her seat*, ie on her horse. 她無法安穩地騎在馬上。**16** [VP2E, 3A] ~ ***(on) doing sth***, continue doing sth; do sth frequently or repeatedly: 繼續做某事;不斷或反覆做某事: *K~ smiling!* 保持笑容! *Why does she ~ (on) giggling?* 她爲什麼不斷吃吃地笑? *My shoe lace ~s (on) coming undone.* 我的鞋帶老是鬆開。~ ***going***, not stop; not give up; continue to function: 不停止;不放棄;繼續起作用: *This is exhausting work, but I manage to ~ going.* 這是件累人的工作,但我設法做下去。*I'm not sure that the company can ~ going*, continue in business. 我不能確定這家公司能否繼續營業。**17** [VP2A] (of food) remain in good condition: (指食物)保持良好狀態: *Will this meat ~ till tomorrow?* 這肉能放到明天嗎? Cf 參較 ~ *fresh*, ⇨ 14 above. 參看上列第14義。*This news will ~*, (fig) need not be told now, can be told later. (喻)這消息以後再宣佈吧。**18** [VP2C, 3A, 14, 15B] (uses with *adverbial particles* and *preps*): (與副詞接語及介詞連用之用法):

keep 'at sth, work at it: 不息地做: *K~ at it*, don't give up! 不要放棄!堅持下去! ~ ***sb 'at sth***, make him work: 使某人做事: *K~ them at it!* Don't let them get lazy! 讓他們做事(不要讓他們偷懶)!

keep away (from sth), avoid coming/going near (to): 遠離;不接近: *K~ away from the water's edge.* 遠離水邊。~ ***sb/sth away (from)***, prevent from going/coming near: 阻止某人或某物前去或接近: *K~ the child away from the water's edge.* 讓孩子離水邊遠一點。

keep back (from sth), remain in the rear, at the back. 留在後面。~ ***sb back***, restrain sb; prevent sb from advancing. 阻止某人向前。~ ***sth back***, ⇨ 4 above. 參看上列第4義。

keep sb down, hold in subjection; oppress: 壓服: ~ *down subject nations.* 壓服臣屬的國家。~ ***sth down***, **(a)** control: 控制: *He couldn't ~ down his anger.* 他無法控制他的憤怒。*This chemical will ~ the weeds down.* 這化學藥品能消除野草。**(b)** limit: 限制: *We must ~ down expenses.* 我們必須限制開銷。**(c)** retain: 保留: *He couldn't ~ his food down*, had to vomit. 他將食物吐了出來。

keep in, eg of a coal fire in a grate, continue burning: (例如煤火等)繼續燒着;不熄: *Will the fire ~ in until we get back?* 這火能燒到我們回來嗎? Cf 參較 *go out.* ~ ***in with sb***, remain on good terms with, continue to be friendly with: 與某人保持友誼: *You must ~ in with your customers*, retain their goodwill. 你必須對顧客友善。~ ***sb in***, (esp) detain (a child in school) as a punishment. (尤指)使(學童)留校作爲處罰。~ ***sth in***, **(a)** see that (a fire) continues to burn; ⇨ ~ in, above: 讓(火)燃着: *Shall we ~ the fire in or let it out?* 我們讓火燒着還是將它熄滅? **(b)** restrain: 抑制: *He couldn't ~ in his indignation.* 他抑制不住他的憤慨。Cf 參較 *burst out.*

keep off, remain at a distance; not come: 遠離;不來: *if the rain ~s off*, if it doesn't start to rain. 如果不下雨。~ ***off sth***, refrain from: 制止;抑制: *Please ~ off that subject*, say nothing about it. 請不要談那問題。*Do please ~ off drugs*, Don't use them. 千萬請不要服用麻醉藥。~ ***sb/sth off***, hold, cause to remain, at a distance: 使避開;不讓接近: *They made a big fire to ~ wild animals off.* 他們生起大火不讓野獸接近。*K~ your hands off*, Don't touch it, me, etc. 把手拿開(不要碰它,我等)。

keep on (doing sth), continue; persist: 繼續(做某事): ~ *on (working) although one is tired.* 雖疲倦仍繼續(工作)。*Don't ~ on asking silly questions.* 不要老是問些可笑的問題。*Why do the dogs ~ on barking?* 這些狗爲什麼不停地叫? ⇨ also 16 above. 亦參看上列第16義。~ ***sth on***, continue to wear: 繼續穿戴: ~ *one's hat on.* 一直戴着帽子。~ ***your hair on***, ⇨ hair. ~ ***one's shirt on***, ⇨ shirt(1). ~ ***sb on***, continue to employ: 繼續雇用: ~ *an old employee on*, not dismiss her/him. 繼續雇用着一年老的職員。~ ***on at sb***, worry with repeated complaints, questions, etc. 以不斷的抱怨,發問等困擾某人。

keep out (of sth), remain outside: 留在外面;置身於(某事物)之外: *Danger! K~ out!* 危險!不要入內! *K~ out of their quarrels*, Don't get involved in them. 不要捲入他們的糾紛。~ ***sb/sth out (of sth)***, prevent from entering: 不讓入內: *Shut the window and ~ the cold out.* 把窗子關上,免得冷風吹進來。*K~ that dog out of my study.* 不要讓那狗進入我的書房。

keep to sth, **(a)** do what one has agreed to do: 履行;遵守: *He always ~s to his promises/an agreement/his word.* 他是個守信(約)的人。**(b)** limit oneself to: 限制自己: *keep to the subject/the point at issue.* 把握討論的主題(要點)。~ ***(oneself) to oneself***, avoid meeting people. 獨居;不交際。

keep sb/sth under, control; repress: 控制;壓制: *The firemen managed to ~ the fire under*, prevented it from spreading. 救火人員控制了火勢。*That boy needs ~ing under*, needs discipline. 那孩子需要嚴格管教。~ ***sb under observation***, ⇨ observation(1).

keep up (with sb/sth), progress at the same rate (as sb/sth): 趕上;不落後: *I can't ~ up with you*, eg walk as fast as you. 我趕不上你(例如走得沒有你那樣快)。*Dave couldn't ~ up with the rest of the class*, eg learn as quickly as his fellow pupils. 德夫跟不上班上的同學。*Is your salary ~ing up with inflation*, growing as fast? 你的薪水趕得上通貨膨脹嗎? ***keep up with sb/sth***, stay in contact with: 保持連繫: *try to ~ up with old friends far away;* 設法與遠方的老友保持連繫; stay informed about: 經常有…的消息: *Alexander is careful to ~ up with the latest fashions in clothes.* 亞歷山大特別留心最新的服裝式樣。~ ***up with the Joneses***, compete with one's neighbours, etc (in the purchase of articles, eg clothes, a car, indicating social status). 和瓊斯一家人比(在購買物品如衣物、汽車等方面與鄰人等相比以示社會地位)。~ ***sb up***, delay sb from going to bed: 使遲睡: *It's wrong to ~ the children up so late*, They should go to bed. 這麼晚還不讓孩子們去睡覺是不對的。*I don't want to ~ you up; you look sleepy and ready for bed.* 我不想讓你熬夜,你像是睏倦欲睡了。~ ***sth up***, **(a)** prevent from sinking or getting low: 振起;使不低落: *K~ up your courage/spirits.* 鼓起你的勇氣(振作精神)。*K~ your chin up!* Cheer up, have courage, etc. 振作精神! **(b)** observe: 遵守: ~ *up old customs.* 遵守古老的風俗。**(c)** continue: 繼續: *They kept up the attack all day.* 他們一整天不斷地攻擊。**(d)** maintain in proper condition: 使保持適當的狀態;維護: *How much does it cost you to ~ up your large house and garden?* 維護你的大房子和花園需要多少花費? ⇨ upkeep. ~ ***up appearances***, ⇨ appearance. **(e)** continue; carry on: 使繼續進行: ~ *up a correspondence with an old friend.* 與一老朋友保持通信。~ ***one's end up***, ⇨ end[1]. *Do you still ~ up your Greek*, still read the Greek classics? 你仍在研讀古希臘文學嗎? ~ ***it up***, continue without slackening: 繼續下去而不鬆弛: *He works far too hard; he'll never be able to ~ it up.* 他工作過於努力,他絕對無法繼續這樣工作下去的。

keep[2] /kiːp; kip/ *n* **1** [U] (food needed for) support: 生計;生活所需之食糧: *The dog doesn't earn his ~*, is not useful enough to be worth the cost of keeping him. 這條狗不值得養。**2** [C] tower of a fortress, etc (in olden times): (昔時)要塞、城堡等的高樓: *the castle ~.* 城堡的高樓。**3** ***for ~s***, (colloq) permanently: (俗)永久地: *Is this mine for ~s?* 這個是永久屬於我的嗎?

keeper /ˈkiːpə(r) ; ˈkipɚ/ *n* **1** guard, eg a person who looks after animals in a zoo. 看守者(例如動物園中的照顧動物者)。 **2** (in compounds) person with special duties: (用於複合字)有特殊職務的人: *ˈpark-~;* 公園(停車場等)看守人; *ˈlighthouse-~;* 燈塔看守人; *game~,* ⇨ game¹(6); *ˈgoal~,* ⇨ goal; person who manages a shop, inn, etc: 經營商店、旅館等之人: *ˈshop~;* 店主; *ˈinn~.* 旅館老闆。⇨ keep¹(11, 12, 13).

keep·ing /ˈkiːpɪŋ ; ˈkipɪŋ/ *n* [U] **1** care. 保管;照看。***in safe ~,*** being kept carefully: 安全地保管着: *The valuables are in safe ~.* 貴重物品都安全地保管着。 **2** (in verbal senses): (由動詞變來各義): *the ~ of bees;* 蜂之飼養; *ˈbee-~.* 養蜂。***in／out of ~ (with),*** in／out of harmony (with): (與…)一致(不一致): *His actions are not in ~ with his promises.* 他的言行不一致。

keep·sake /ˈkiːpseɪk ; ˈkipˌsek/ *n* sth kept in memory of the giver: 紀念物: *Please have this ring for a ~.* 請收下這個戒指作爲紀念。

keg /keg ; kɛg/ *n* small barrel, usu of less than 10 gallons: 小桶(通常容量在十加侖以下): *a ~ of brandy.* 一小桶白蘭地。

kelp /kelp ; kɛlp/ *n* [U] large kinds of seaweed. 大海藻。

Kelt /kelt ; kɛlt/ *n* = Celt.

ken¹ /ken ; kɛn/ *n* [U] (only in)(僅用於) ***beyond／outside my ~,*** (colloq) not within one's range of knowledge. (俗)在我的知識範圍以外。

ken² /ken ; kɛn/ *vt* (-nn-) [VP6A, 9] (Scot) know. (蘇)知道。

ken·nel /ˈkenl ; ˈkɛnl̩/ *n* **1** hut to shelter a dog. 狗舍;狗房。 **2** (establishment for a) pack of hounds; place where dogs are cared for (eg during quarantine). 一群獵犬;飼養獵犬場;狗房(例如檢疫隔離時期者)。□ *vt, vi* (-ll-, US also -l-) put, keep, in a ~; live in a ~. 置於狗舍;養於狗舍;居於狗舍。

kepi /ˈkeɪpɪ ; ˈkɛpɪ/ *n* French military cap with a horizontal peak. 法國軍人戴的平頂帽。

kept /kept ; kɛpt/ ⇨ keep¹.

kerb (also **curb**) /kɜːb ; kɝb/ *n* stone edging to a raised path or pavement. 突起於道路或行人道的石邊;緣石;邊欄。 **ˈ~·stone** *n* stone forming a part of this. 街道的邊石。

ker·chief /ˈkɜːtʃɪf ; ˈkɝtʃɪf/ *n* [C] (old use) square piece of cloth or lace used by women as a head covering. (舊用法)頭巾。

ker·nel /ˈkɜːnl ; ˈkɝnl̩/ *n* [C] **1** softer, inner (usu edible) part of a nut or fruit-stone. 堅果或核果的仁(通常是可食的)。 **2** part of a seed, eg a grain of wheat, within the husk; (fig) central or important part of a subject, problem, etc. (麥粒等的)粒;(喻)(問題等的)要點;中心。

kero·sene /ˈkerəsiːn ; ˈkɛrəˌsin/ *n* [U] paraffin oil: 煤油;火油: (attrib) (形容用法) *a ~ lamp.* 煤油燈。

kes·trel /ˈkestrəl ; ˈkɛstrəl/ *n* kind of small hawk. 茶隼(一種小鷹)。

ketch /ketʃ ; kɛtʃ/ *n* small two-masted sailing vessel used in coastal trading. 雙桅小帆船(用於沿岸貿易)。

ketch·up /ˈketʃəp ; ˈkɛtʃəp/ *n* [U] highly-flavoured sauce made from tomato juice, vinegar etc. 蕃茄醬(蕃茄、醋等製成的醬)。

kettle /ˈketl ; ˈkɛtl̩/ *n* metal vessel with lid, spout and handle, for boiling water. (燒開水用的)壺。***a ˈpretty ~ of fish,*** ⇨ fish¹(1).

kettle·drum /ˈketldrʌm ; ˈkɛtl̩ˌdrʌm/ *n* drum shaped like a hemisphere, made of brass or copper, with parchment stretched over the edge. 釜狀銅鼓; 定音鼓。⇨ the illus at percussion. 參看 percussion 之插圖。⇨ timpani.

key¹ /kiː ; ki/ *n* **1** metal instrument for moving the bolt of a lock: 鑰匙: *put the key in the lock;* 把鑰匙放入鎖中; *turn the key.* 轉動鑰匙。⇨ the illus at bunch. 參看 bunch 之插圖。**ˈmaster／ˈskeleton key,** one that will open several locks. 萬能鑰匙。**ˈkey·hole** *n* hole in a lock, door, etc, into which a key fits. 鑰匙孔。**ˈkey money** *n* [U] extra payment (requested by some house agents, now illegal in GB) before completion of an agreement about renting a house, flat, etc. 房屋代理人於房屋租約完成前所索取的額外費用 (在英國現認爲不合法)。**ˈkey-ring** *n* (usu split) ring on which to keep keys. 鑰匙環(通常可裂開,將鑰匙裝上)。 **2** instrument for winding a clock or a watch by tightening the spring. (上鐘錶發條的)鑰匙。**3** ***~ (to),*** (fig) sth that provides an answer (to a problem or mystery). (喻)(問題或神祕事物之)解答;關鍵。**4** set of answers to exercises or problems; translation of sth from a foreign language: 題解;翻譯: *a key for the use of teachers only,* eg to a book of problems in algebra. 專供教師用的題解(例如代數題解)。 **5** (also attrib) place which, from its position, gives control of a route or area: (亦作形容用法)在地勢上可控制一路線或地區的地方;要衝: *a key position.* 險要的位置。*Gibraltar has been called the key to the Mediterranean.* 直布羅陀一向被稱作地中海的門戶。 **6** (attrib) essential: (形容用法) 基本的: *key industry,* one (eg coal-mining) that is essential to the carrying on of others; 基本工業(例如煤礦工業); *a key man／a man in a key position,* one whose work is essential to the work of others. 重要人物;中心人物。**ˈkey·stone** *n* (archit) stone at the top of an arch locking the others into position; (fig) central principle on which everything depends. (建築)拱頂石;楔石;冠石;(喻)根本原理;主旨。⇨ the illus at window. 參看 window 之插圖。 **7** operating part (lever or button) of a typewriter, piano, organ, flute, etc pressed down by a finger. (打字機、鋼琴、風琴、笛等之)鍵。⇨ the illus here and at brass. 參看本字及 brass 之插圖。**ˈkey·board** *n* row of such keys (on a piano, organ, typewriter). (鋼琴、風琴、打字機之)鍵盤。 **8** (bot) usu one-seeded winged fruit of some trees, eg the ash and elm. (植物)(秦皮樹和榆樹等之)翅果。 **9** (music) scale of notes definitely related to each other and based on a particular note called the *ˈkeynote*: (音樂)調: *the key of C major;* C大調; (fig) tone or style of thought or expression: (喻)思想或表達的格調: *in a minor key,* sadly; 憂鬱地; *all in the same key,* monotonously, without expression; 單調地;無表情地; *speak in a high／low key,* urgently／not urgently. 用急切(緩和)的聲調說話。**ˈkey·note** *n* **(a)** (music) note on which a key is based. (音樂)主音。**(b)** (fig) prevailing tone or idea: (喻)主旨;要旨: *The keynote of the Minister's speech was the need for higher productivity.* 該部長演說的要旨是更高生產力的需要。**key·less** *adj* not having or needing a key. 無鑰匙的;無鍵的;不需要鑰匙的;不需要鍵的;(指鐘錶)不需用鑰匙上發條的。

key² /kiː ; ki/ *vt* [VP6A] tune (the strings of a musical instrument by tightening or loosening). 調整(樂器之絃);調音。***key sth ˈin,*** bring it into harmony. 使和諧。***key sth to sth,*** bring sth into harmony with sth; make connections between (the two things). 使一物與另一物相和;連合(兩事物)。***key sb up,*** stimulate or raise the standard of (a person, his activity, etc): 激勵;鼓舞(人、其行爲等): *The thought of the coming adventure keyed him up to a state of great excitement.* 他一想到即將來臨的冒險就感到非常興奮。*The crowd was keyed up for the football match.* 群衆爲該足球比賽所鼓舞。

key³ /kiː ; ki/ *n* low island or reef, esp off the coasts of Florida, W Indies. 低島;暗礁(尤指美國佛羅里達州和西印度群島岸外者)。

khaki /ˈkɑːkɪ ; ˈkɑkɪ/ *n, adj* (cloth, military uniform, of a) dull yellowish-brown. 黃卡其布;黃卡其布軍服;黃褐色;黃褐色的。

K

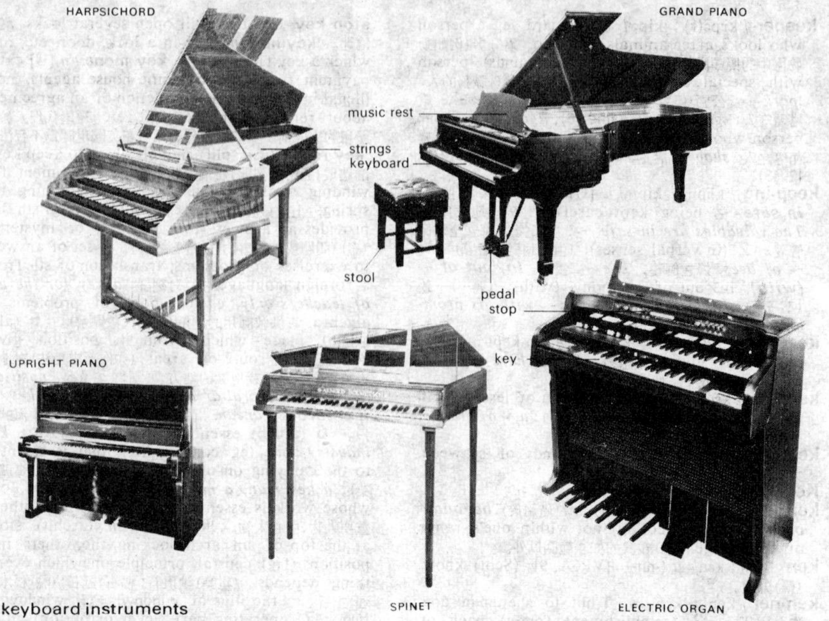

keyboard instruments

khan[1] /kɑːn ; kɑn/ *n* title used by some rulers and officials in Central Asia, Afghanistan, etc; (in olden times) title used by supreme rulers of Turkish, Tartar and Mongol tribes. 中亞細亞，阿富汗等地對某些統治者或官員的尊稱；(古時)可汗(土耳其、韃靼及蒙古對至高統治者的稱呼)。

khan[2] /kɑːn ; kɑn/ *n* (in the East) inn built round a court-yard where caravans may rest. (東方)供旅行隊停宿的旅館。

kib·butz /kɪˈbʊts ; kɪˈbʊts/ *n* (*pl* ~im /kɪbʊˈtsiːm ; kɪbʊˈtsim/) communal farm or settlement in Israel. 以色列之集體農場。**~nik** /-nɪk ; -nɪk/ *n* member of a ~. 以色列集體農場之農人。

kick[1] /kɪk ; kɪk/ *n* **1** act of kicking: 踢: *give a ~ at the door;* 踢門; *give sb a ~ in the arse.* 踢某人的屁股。*The bruise was caused by a ~.* 這瘀傷是脚踢的。***more ~s than halfpence,*** more harsh treatment than reward (for what one does). 所受虐待多於優遇；得不償失。**ˈ~-back** *n* (US sl) percentage payment made to sb who has enabled one to make money. (美俚)佣金；回扣。⇨ *rake-off* at rake[1]. **ˌ~-ˈstart(er)** *n* lever on a motorcycle or lawn-mower which is ~ed to start the engine. 摩托車或除草機之發動桿(藉踢此桿，始可發動)。**2** (colloq) thrill; excitement: (俗)快感；興奮: *He gets a good deal of ~/a big ~ out of motor-racing.* 他自賽車中得到很大的樂趣。*He gets his ~s by playing football.* 他自踢足球中獲得樂趣。***do sth/live for ~s,*** for thrills; for excitement: 爲刺激或興奮而做某事(生活): *I don't expect to win when I bet—I do it for ~s.* 我打賭時並不指望贏——我是爲了刺激。***be on a ~,*** (sl) be deeply absorbed in a new activity: (俚)全神貫注一新活動: *She's on a health-food ~ at the moment.* 她此刻正全神貫注在有益健康的食物上。**3** [U] (colloq) resilience; strength: (俗)彈力；力氣: *He has no ~ left in him,* is exhausted. 他筋疲力盡了。*This beer has a lot of ~ in it,* is strong. 這啤酒有點烈。

kick[2] /kɪk ; kɪk/ *vt, vi* **1** [VP6A, 15A, B, 2A, C] hit with the foot; move the foot; move sth by doing this; move the foot or feet jerkily: 踢；蹴: *~ a ball;* 踢一球; *~ a man on the shin;* 踢某人的脛部; *~ a hole in sth,* make one by ~ing. 將某物踢穿一洞。*The baby was ~ing and screaming.* 那嬰兒又踢又叫。*This horse ~s,* has the habit of ~ing. 此馬有好踢的習慣。***~ the bucket,*** (sl) die. (俚)死。***~ a goal,*** (Rugby football) score a penalty; convert a try. (橄欖球)罰得一分。Cf 參較 *score a goal* in Association football. (足球)踢得一分。***~ one's heels,*** be idle (as when forced to waste time when waiting for sth/sb). 閒著；苦等；久候。***~ sb upstairs,*** (fig) get sb out of the way, eg from the House of Commons, by giving him a higher position, eg a peerage, so that he sits in the House of Lords. (喻)使某人明升暗降(例如授以爵位使某人離開下議院去做上議院議員)。**2** [VP2A] (of a gun) recoil when fired: (指槍發射時)反衝；後坐: *The old rifle ~s badly.* 這枝老式步槍後坐得厲害。**3** [VP2A, C, 3A, 15B] (special uses with *adverbial particles* and *preps*): (與副詞接語及介詞連用之特殊用法):

kick against/at, show annoyance; protest: 抱怨；反對；抗議: *He ~ed at/against the treatment he was receiving.* 他對他受到的對待表示抗議。

kick off, (football) start the game; resume after half-time, by making the first ~. (足球)開賽；開球。Hence, 由此產生，**ˈ~-off** *n*: *~-off at 2.30.* 下午兩點半開賽。***~ sth off,*** remove by ~ing: 踢掉: *He ~ed off his slippers.* 他踢脫拖鞋。

kick sb out, expel him: 逐出某人: *The drunken man was ~ed out of the bar.* 那醉漢被人從酒吧中逐出。

kick over the traces, ⇨ trace[3].

kick sth up, raise by ~ing: 踢起某物: *~ up the carpet,* turn up the edge by striking it with the foot. 踢起一地毯。***~ up a fuss/shindy/row/stink,*** (colloq) cause a disturbance, eg by protesting vigorously. (俗)引起騷擾(例如由於激烈地抗議)。***~ up one's heels,*** (of a horse) make lively jumps, showing enjoyment of freedom after a period of work; (fig) enjoy oneself. (指馬)踢跳嬉戲(表示經一段時期的工作後享受自由)；(喻)享樂。

kid[1] /kɪd ; kɪd/ *n* **1** [C] young goat. 小山羊。**2** [U] leather made from skin of this: 小山羊皮革: *a book bound in kid.* 小山羊皮裝的書。**kid gloves**

K

n pl gloves made of kid. 小山羊皮製的手套。***handle sb with kid gloves,*** deal with him gently, avoiding severe methods. 以溫和手段對付某人。Hence, 由此產生, (attrib): (形容用法): *kid-glove methods.* 溫和方法。**3** (sl) child; (US sl) young person: (俚)小孩; (美俚)年輕人: *college kids.* 大學生。**kiddy** *n* (*pl* -dies) (sl) (young) child. (俚)小孩。

kid² /kɪd ; kɪd/ *vt, vi* (-dd-) (sl) tease by telling a lie; hoax: (俚)欺騙;哄騙: *You're kidding (me)!* 你在騙我！Cf 參較 *You're pulling my leg!*

kid·nap /ˈkɪdnæp ; ˈkɪdnæp/ *vt* (GB -pp-, US -p-) steal (a child); carry away (sb) by force and unlawfully (esp in order to obtain a ransom). 誘拐(小孩);綁架;勒贖。**~·per** *n* person who ~s. 誘拐小孩者;綁匪。

kid·ney /ˈkɪdnɪ ; ˈkɪdnɪ/ *n* (*pl* ~s) one of a pair of organs in the abdomen that separate waste liquid (urine) from the blood; ~ of sheep, cattle, etc as food. 腎;(牛羊等的)腰子(可用作食物)。ˌ**~-ˈbean** *n* (plant with pod containing) reddish-brown ~-shaped bean (either the dwarf French bean or the runner bean). 腎形豆;菜豆。ˈ**~ machine** *n* one which does the work of diseased ~s by washing the blood and removing waste materials. 洗腎機。

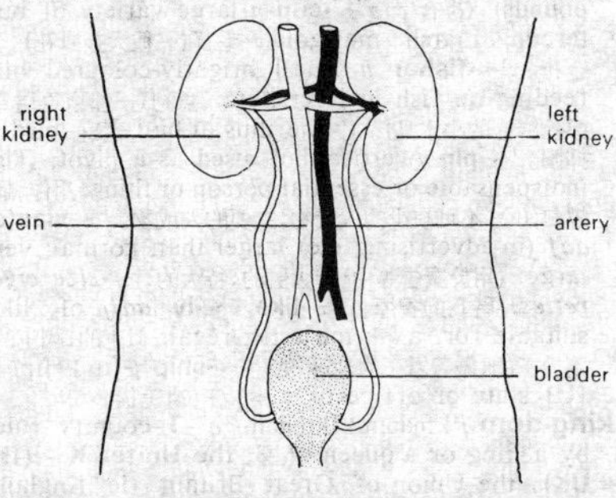

the kidneys and the bladder

kill /kɪl ; kɪl/ *vt, vi* **1** [VP6A, 2A] put to death; cause the death of: 殺死;使死: *~ animals for food.* 宰殺動物爲食。*Thou shalt not ~,* (biblical, one of the Ten Commandments). 汝不可殺人(聖經十誡之一)。*The troops were shooting to ~,* eg in a riot, shooting with the intention of ~ing, not merely to warn or wound the rioters. 軍隊開槍射殺(例如平定暴動時開槍不僅爲示警或傷害,而欲擊斃暴動者)。*The frost ~ed the flowers.* 嚴寒使花枯死了。***~ sb/sth off,*** [VP15B] get rid of: 除去;殺掉: *The frost ~ed off most of the insect pests.* 嚴寒殺掉了大半的蟲害。***~ time,*** find ways of passing the time without being bored, eg when compelled to wait for sb/sth. 消遣;消磨時間。***~ two birds with one stone,*** ⇨ bird. **2** [VP6A] neutralize, make ineffective, by contrast: 中和;抵消: *The scarlet carpet ~s* (= deadens) *your curtains.* 這猩紅色的地毯中和了你的窗簾的顏色。**3** [VP6A] cause the failure or defeat of; veto: 使失敗;否決: *~ a proposal/a Bill in Parliament.* 否決一建議(國會議案)。ˈ**~·joy** *n* person who throws gloom over those who are enjoying themselves. 掃興之人;敗興的人。**4** [VP6A, 2A] overwhelm; impress deeply. 令人不勝羨慕;予人深刻印象。***~ sb with kindness,*** harm him by being excessively or mistakenly kind. 盛意對待某人使感不安;寵壞某人。***(be) dressed/got up to ~,*** dressed elaborately, so as to impress people. 打扮得十分迷人。□ *n* (*sing* only) (僅用單數) **1** act of ~ing, esp in hunting. 殺(尤指狩獵中)。***be in at the ~,*** be present when sth, eg a fox, is ~ed. 某物(例如狐)被殺時在場。**2** (in hunting) number of animals ~ed: (狩獵)獵獲物的數目: *There was a plentiful ~,* many animals were ~ed. 獵獲的動物甚多。**~·ing** *adj* (colloq, dated) amusing: (俗,過時用語)有趣的: *a ~ing joke;* 有趣的笑話; exhausting: 令人筋疲力竭的: *a ~ing experience.* 令人筋疲力竭的經驗。□ *n* ***make a ~ing,*** be extraordinarily successful. 非常成功。**~·ing·ly** *adv* **~er** *n* one who, that which, ~s; (journalese) murderer. 殺人者;(二流新聞文體)兇手。

kiln /kɪln ; kɪl/ *n* furnace or oven for burning, baking or drying, esp ˈ*brick-~,* for baking bricks; ˈ*hop-~,* for drying hops; ˈ*lime-~,* for burning lime. 火爐;窰(尤指磚窰 brick-kiln, 烘乾蛇麻草的窰 hop-kiln, 以及石灰窰 lime-kiln)。

kilo /ˈkiːləʊ ; ˈkɪlo/ *n* (pl ~s) (abbr of) kilogram. 爲 kilogram 之略。

kilo- /ˈkɪlə- ; ˈkɪlə-/ *pref* 1000, 一千 esp in 尤用於 **kilo·cycle** /ˈkɪləsaɪkl ; ˈkɪləˌsaɪkl/ *n* unit of frequency of vibration, used of wireless waves. (無線電波)千週;千週率;千赫。**kilo·gram** /ˈkɪləgræm ; ˈkɪləˌgræm/ *n* 1000 grams. 公斤;兛。**kilo·litre** *n* 1000 litres. 千公升。**kilo·metre** (US = **-meter**) /ˈkɪləmiːtə(r) *US:* kɪˈlɒmɪtər ; ˈkɪləˌmitɚ/ *n* 1000 metres. 公里;千公尺。**kilo·watt** /ˈkɪləwɒt ; ˈkɪləˌwɑt/ *n* 1000 watts. 千瓦;瓩。⇨ App 5. 參看附錄五。

kilt /kɪlt ; kɪlt/ *n* pleated skirt, usu of tartan cloth, from waist to knee, worn as part of male dress in the Scottish Highlands; similar skirt worn by women and children. (蘇格蘭高地男子穿的)褶裙(通常是格子呢做的); (婦女和兒童穿的)類似的裙子。**~ed regiments,** regiments of Scottish soldiers wearing ~s. 穿褶裙的蘇格蘭兵團。

kilts

kim·ono /kɪˈməʊnəʊ *US:* -nə ; kəˈmonə/ *n* (*pl* ~s) **1** wide-sleeved long flowing gown, characteristic of Japanese traditional costume. (日本的)和服。⇨ the illus at sarong. 參看 sarong 之挿圖。**2** style of loose garment worn as a dressing-gown. 一種寬鬆的晨衣。

kin /kɪn ; kɪn/ *n* (collective *pl*) family; relations: (集合複數)家族;親戚: *We are near kin,* are closely related. 我們是近親。***next of kin,*** nearest relation(s). 最近的親戚。

kind¹ /kaɪnd ; kaɪnd/ *adj* (-er, -est) having, showing, thoughtfulness, sympathy or love for others: 親切的;和藹的;仁慈的;慈愛的: *be ~ to animals.* 愛護動物。*Will you be ~ enough/so ~ as to close the door?* 請把門關上。*It was ~ of you to help us.* 承蒙惠助,不勝感激。ˌ**~-ˈhearted** *adj* having a ~ nature; sympathetic. 好心腸的;仁慈的。**~·ly** *adv* **1** in a ~ manner: 親切地;和善地;仁慈地: *speak ~ly to sb;* 溫和地對某人說話; *treat sb ~ly.* 和善地對待某人。**2** (in polite formulas) (用於客套) *Will you ~ly tell me the time?* 請告訴我幾點鐘了？**3** naturally; easily: 自然地;容易地: *He took ~ly to his new duties.* 他很喜歡他的新職務。*He doesn't take ~ly to being treated as an inferior.* 他不喜歡被當作地位低的人看待。**~·ness** *n* **1** [U] ~ nature; being ~. 親切;和藹;仁慈;慈愛。***out of ~ness (to sb),*** because of feeling ~ (towards): (對某人)出於仁慈之心: *He did it all out of ~ness,* not in the hope of reward. 他做此事完全是出於仁慈之心(不希望受報酬)。**2** [C] ***do/show sb a ~ness,*** perform a ~ act: 幫助某人: *He has done/shown me many ~nesses.* 他幫過我很多忙。

kind² /kaɪnd ; kaɪnd/ *n* **1** race, natural group, of

animals, plants, etc: (動植物等的)類;屬: ˌ*man*ˈ~; 人類; ˌ*human*ˈ~. 人類。 **2** class, sort or variety: 種類: *apples of several ~s／several ~s of apples;* 幾種蘋果; *people of this ~.* 此類人。*What ~ of tree is this?* 這是哪一種樹?*She's the ~ of woman who likes to help other people.* 她是那種喜歡幫助別人的女子。*She's not the ~ (of person) to talk scandal.* 她不是那種誹謗他人的人。***nothing of the ~,*** not at all like it. 毫不相似;決非如此。***something of the ~,*** sth like the thing in question. 類似之事物。***of a ~,*** **(a)** of the same ~: 同類的: *two of a ~.* 同類的兩個。**(b)** (implying contempt) scarcely deserving the name: (含有輕蔑之意)徒有其名的: *They gave us coffee of a ~.* 他們給我們品質極劣的咖啡。***a ~ of...,*** used when there is uncertainty: 用以表示不太確定: *I had a ~ of suspicion* (= I vaguely suspected) *that he was cheating.* 我有點懷疑他在欺騙。***~ of,*** (sl, sometimes spelt 俚,有時拼作 **~a** /ˈkaɪndə ; ˈkaɪndə/) *adv* to some extent: 有幾分;有點: *I ~ of thought this would happen.* 我當時就有預感,這事將會發生。 **3** [U] nature; character: 性質;本質: *They differ in degree but not in ~.* 他們的程度不同,並非性質不同。 **4** ***in ~,*** (of payment) in goods or natural produce, not in money: (指償付)以貨物; 以產品; 以實物: *benefits in ~,* benefits other than wages or salary received by employees, eg the right to buy articles at cost price; (薪資以外之)福利(例如給予員工以成本價格購物之權利); (of repayment, fig) with what was received: (指回報,喻)以所受者: *repay insolence in ~,* be insolent in return. 以無禮報無禮。

kin·der·gar·ten /ˈkɪndəgɑːtn ; ˈkɪndɚˌgɑrtn̩/ *n* school for children too young to begin formal education. 幼稚園。

kindle /ˈkɪndl ; ˈkɪndl/ *vt, vi* [VP6A, 2A] **1** (cause to) catch fire or burst into flames or flaming colour: (使)燃燒;(使)發火焰般的顏色: *The sparks ~d the dry wood.* 火星燃着了乾木。*This wood is too wet to ~.* 此木柴太濕,不易燃燒。*The setting sun ~d the sky.* 落日照紅了天空。 **2** rouse, be roused, to a state of strong feeling, interest, etc: 激起或被激起强烈的情感,興趣等: *~ the interest of an audience.* 引起聽衆的興趣。*Her eyes ~d with excitement.* 她的眼睛顯出興奮的神色。**kind·ling** /ˈkɪndlɪŋ ; ˈkɪndlɪŋ/ *n* [U] material for lighting a fire, esp light, dry sticks of wood. 引火物(尤指輕的乾木柴)。

kind·ly[1] /ˈkaɪndlɪ ; ˈkaɪndlɪ/ *adj* (-ier, -iest) friendly: 友善的;親切的: *speak in a ~ tone;* 以親切的音調說話; *give sb ~ advice.* 給予某人友善的勸告。

kind·ly[2] /ˈkaɪndlɪ ; ˈkaɪndlɪ/ *adv* ➪ kind[1].

kin·dred /ˈkɪndrɪd ; ˈkɪndrɪd/ *n* **1** [U] relationship by birth between persons: 血親關係: *claim ~ with sb.* 聲稱與某人有血親關係。 **2** (collective *pl*) family; relations: (集合複數)家族;親戚: *Most of his ~ are still living in Ireland.* 他的大部分親戚現仍住在愛爾蘭。□ *adj* (attrib only) (僅作形容用法) **1** related; having a common source: 有親戚關係的;同宗的;同源的: *~ languages,* eg English and Dutch; 同源的語言(例如英語和荷蘭語); *dew, frost and ~ phenomena;* 露、霜及其同類的現象; *~ tribes／races.* 同族的部落(同類的種族)。 **2** similar: 相似的: *~ natures;* 相似的性質; *a ~ spirit,* sb whom one feels to be congenial, sympathetic. 性情相投之人。

kine /kaɪn ; kaɪn/ *n pl* (old form) cows. (古)母牛。

kin·etic /kɪˈnetɪk ; kɪˈnɛtɪk/ *adj* of, relating to, produced by, motion. 運動的;由運動引起的。ˌ~ ˈ**art,** sculptural objects parts of which may be in motion, eg from air currents. 動態彫刻藝術(例如由於氣流而使彫刻品某部分可運動者)。ˌ~ ˈ**energy,** energy of a moving body because of its motion. 動能。 **~s** *n pl* (with *sing v*) science of the relations between the motions of bodies and the forces acting on them. (用單數動詞)動力學。

king /kɪŋ ; kɪŋ/ *n* **1** male sovereign ruler (esp one whose position is hereditary) of an independent state: 國王;君主: *the K~ of Denmark.* 丹麥國王。➪ queen. **K~'s／Queen's Bench,** ➪ bench. **K~'s／Queen's Counsel,** ➪ counsel[1](3). ***turn K~'s／Queen's evidence,*** (of one who has shared in a crime) give evidence against accomplices (often in order to escape punishment). (指參與犯罪者)提出對共犯不利的證據(常是自己欲逃脫處罰而爲之)。 **~'s evil,** scrofula, formerly thought to be curable by the touch of a ~. 瘰癧(昔時認爲經君王觸摸即可痊癒的一種疾病)。 **K~s,** either of two books in the Old Testament, giving the history of the ~s of Israel and Judah. (舊約聖經之)列王紀。 **2** person of great influence: 極有勢力之人: *an ˈoil ~.* 石油大王。 **3** principal piece in the game of chess, ➪ the illus at chess; (playing cards) court-card with a picture of a ~: (西洋棋中的)王;將(參看 chess 之挿圖); (紙牌中的)老K: *the ~ of spades.* 黑桃老K。 **4** largest variety of a species; most prominent member of a group, category, etc: 某一種類中之最大者;某一群、類等中之最顯著者: *the ~ of beasts,* the lion; 獸中之王(即獅子); *the ~ of the forest,* the oak; 橡樹; *the ~ of terrors,* death; 死亡; *~ cobra／crab／penguin.* 一種大眼鏡蛇(蟹;大企鵝)。 **5** (compounds) (複合字) ˈ**~·cup** *n* large variety of buttercup; marsh marigold. 毛茛(一種大金鳳花);立金花。 ˈ**~·fisher** *n* small brightly-coloured bird feeding on fish in rivers, etc. 魚狗(一種啄魚爲食,顏色鮮亮的小水鳥)。➪ the illus at bird. 參看 bird 之挿圖。 ˈ**~·pin** *n* vertical bolt used as a pivot; (fig) indispensable or essential person or thing. 用作軸的螺釘;(喻)不可缺少的人或物;主要的人或物。 ˈ**~-size(d)** *adj* (in advertising, etc) larger than normal; very large: (用於廣告等中)特大號的;特大的: *~-size cigarettes.* 特長的香煙。 ˈ**~·like, ~·ly** *adjj* of, like, suitable for, a ~; majestic; regal. 似王的;國王的;適於王的;儼若君王的;威嚴的。 **~·ship** /-ʃɪp ; -ʃɪp/ *n* [U] state or office of a ~. 王位;王權。

king·dom /ˈkɪŋdəm ; ˈkɪŋdəm/ *n* **1** country ruled by a king or a queen. 王國。**the United K~ (the UK),** the Union of Great Britain (ie England, Scotland and Wales) and Northern Ireland. 聯合王國(包括英格蘭、蘇格蘭、威爾斯及北愛爾蘭,卽英國)。 **2** the spiritual reign of God: 上帝在精神上的統治;神政: *Thy ~ come,* May the rule of God be established. 願你的國降臨。***gone to k~ come,*** (colloq) dead, gone to the next world. (俗)死。 **3** any one of the three divisions of the natural world: 自然三界之一: *the animal, vegetable and mineral ~s.* 動物、植物與礦物界。 **4** realm or province: 領域: *the ~ of thought,* the mind. 思想的領域。

kink /kɪŋk ; kɪŋk/ *n* **1** irregular back-twist in a length of wire, pipe, cord, etc such as may cause a break or obstruction. (金屬絲、軟管、繩索等之)紐結;纏絡。 **2** (fig) mental twist; sth abnormal in a person's way of thinking. (喻)奇想;怪念頭。□ *vt, vi* make a ~ in; form a ~ or ~s: 使糾結;打結;糾纏: *This hosepipe ~s easily.* 這橡皮軟管容易糾結。 **~y** *adj* (colloq) eccentric; perverted. (俗)古怪的;乖僻的。

kins·folk /ˈkɪnzfəʊk ; ˈkɪnzˌfok/ *n pl* relations by blood. 親戚;血親。 **kins·man** /-mən ; -mən/ *n* (*pl* -men) male relative. 男親戚。 **kins·woman** *n* (*pl* -women) female relative. 女親戚。

kin·ship /ˈkɪnʃɪp ; ˈkɪnʃɪp/ *n* [U] relationship by blood; similarity in character. 親戚關係;血族關係;性質之相似。

kiosk /ˈkiːɒsk ; kɪˈɑsk/ *n* **1** small open-fronted structure, esp a round one, for the sale of newspapers, sweets, cigarettes, etc, eg in a park. 小亭(尤指圓形的,如公園等內販賣報紙、糖果、香煙等者)。 **2** small booth for a public telephone. 電話亭;公共電話間。

kip /kɪp ; kɪp/ *n* (GB sl) (room or bed in a) house where beds may be rented; sleep. (英俚)寄宿舍;客棧;客棧的房間或床;睡眠。□ *vi* [VP2A, C] go to

K

bed; sleep: 睡眠: *time to kip down.* 該睡覺的時間。

kip·per /ˈkɪpə(r); ˈkɪpɚ/ *n* kind of salted herring, dried or smoked. 晾乾或燻的鹹鯡。➪ bloater.

kirk /kɜːk; kɝk/ *n* (Scot) church. (蘇)教堂。

kirsch /kɪəʃ; kɪrʃ/ *n* [U] colourless liqueur made from the juice of wild cherries. 櫻桃酒(野櫻桃製的無色烈酒)。

kirtle /ˈkɜːtl; ˈkɝtl̩/ *n* (archaic) woman's gown or outer petticoat; man's tunic. (古)女子的長袍或外裙;男子的上衣。

kis·met /ˈkɪzmet; ˈkɪzmɛt/ *n* [U] destiny; the will of Allah. 命運;(回教)阿拉的旨意;天命。

kiss /kɪs; kɪs/ *vt, vi* [VP6A, 2A,15A,B] touch with the lips to show affection or as a greeting: 吻;接吻(以表示親密或致意): *~ the children goodnight.* 向孩子們接吻道晚安。*He ~ed her (on the) cheek.* 他吻她的面頰。*She ~ed the child goodbye.* 她同那孩子吻別。*She ~ed away the child's tears.* 她吻去那孩子的眼淚。**~ *the book,*** ~ the Bible on taking an oath. 吻聖經宣誓。**~ *the dust/ground,*** **(a)** give abject submission to a conqueror. 向征服者屈服。**(b)** be killed. 被殺死。**~ *hands/the Queen's hand,*** ~ the sovereign's hand on being appointed to an office (eg as a member of the Cabinet). 吻君王或女王之手(例如內閣閣員被授任時)。**~ *the rod,*** accept punishment meekly. 溫順地接受處罰。□ *n* touch, caress, given with the lips. 吻;接吻。**~ *of life,*** method of mouth-to-mouth resuscitation, eg for sb rescued from drowning. 口對口的人工呼吸(例如救溺水者)。**~er** *n* (sl) mouth. (俚)嘴。

kit /kɪt; kɪt/ *n* **1** (collective *sing*) all the equipment (esp clothing) of a soldier, sailor or traveller: (集合單數)(兵士、海員或旅行者)所有的裝備(尤指衣服): *ˈkit inspection,* examination of kit by an officer to see that it is complete, etc. (軍官對士兵之)裝備檢查。**ˈkit-bag** *n* long canvas bag in which kit is carried. 背包;背袋;行李袋。**2** [C] equipment needed by a workman for his trade: 工人的一套工具: *a plumber's kit.* 水管工人的工具。**3** [C, U] outfit or equipment needed for sport or some other special purpose: 運動等的用具: *ˈshooting/ˈgolfing/ˈskiing kit;* 射擊(高爾夫,滑雪)用具; *a surˈvival kit,* articles to be used by a person in distress, eg an airman who has come down in a desert or jungle. (遇難時用之)求生用品(例如飛行人員降落在沙漠地區或森林中所需要者)。**4** [C] ***ˌdo-it-yourˈself kit,*** collection of parts, eg for a piece of furniture, or a set, to be assembled by the purchaser. 由買主自己裝配的一套零件(例如傢具或收音機者)。□ *vt* (-tt-) [VP15B] ***kit sb out/up (with sth),*** equip. 裝備。

kit·chen /ˈkɪtʃɪn; ˈkɪtʃɪn/ *n* room in which meals are cooked or prepared, and for other forms of housework; (in many homes in GB) general purpose rooms, eg where meals are eaten. 廚房;(英國許多家庭中)廚房;起居室兼餐廳。**ˌ~ ˈgarden** *n* one for fruit and vegetables. 菜圃;菜園。**~ sink,** ➪ sink¹. **ˌ~-sink ˈdrama,** drama in GB (late 1950's, early 1960's) portraying working-class family life, showing political, social and educational awareness. (1950 年代末期與 1960 年代初期在英國)描寫工人階級之家庭生活,顯示政治、社會及教育意識的戲劇。**ˈ~ unit,** unit combining two or more articles of ~ equipment, eg a sink and a storage cabinet. 一套廚具(包括兩件或多件用具,例如一洗滌槽及一餐具櫃)。**~·ette** /ˌkɪtʃɪˈnet; ˌkɪtʃɪnˈɛt/ *n* tiny room or alcove used as a ~ (esp in a small flat). 小廚房(尤指小公寓中者)。

kite /kaɪt; kaɪt/ *n* **1** bird of prey of the hawk family. 鳶。**2** framework of wood, etc covered with paper or cloth, made to fly in the wind at the end of a long string or wire. 風箏;紙鳶。***fly a ~,*** (fig) test possible public reactions by means of hints, rumours, etc. (喻)藉暗示、謠言等試探大衆的反應。Cf 參較 *see which way the wind blows.* **ˈ~-balloon,** sausage-shaped captive balloon for military observation. (軍事觀察用的)繫留氣球;風箏氣球。

kith /kɪθ; kɪθ/ *n* (only in) (僅用於) **~ *and kin,*** friends and relations. 親友。

kitsch /kɪtʃ; kɪtʃ/ *adj* (in the arts, design, etc) pretentious; superficial; showy. (藝術、設計等)矯飾的;膚淺的;炫耀的。

kit·ten /ˈkɪtn; ˈkɪtn̩/ *n* young cat. 小貓。**~·ish** /-ɪʃ; -ɪʃ/ *adj* like a ~; playful. 似小貓的;頑皮的。

kitty /ˈkɪtɪ; ˈkɪtɪ/ *n* **1** (in some card games) pool of stakes to be played for; (colloq) any joint pool or fund, eg of savings. (某些紙牌戲中)賭注;(俗)共同的資金(例如儲金)。**2** (bowls) jack¹(4). (滾木球戲中)小白球。**3** child's name for a cat. (兒語)貓咪。

kiwi /ˈkiːwiː; ˈkiwɪ/ *n* New Zealand bird with undeveloped wings; (sl) New Zealander. 幾維;鷸鴕(產於紐西蘭的一種無翼鳥);(俚)紐西蘭人。➪ the illus at rare. 參看 rare 之插圖。

klaxon /ˈklæksn; ˈklæksən/ *n* (P) powerful electric warning horn(5). (商標)一種聲音大的示警用電動喇叭。

kleenex /ˈkliːneks; ˈkliˌnɛks/ *n* (P) [U, C] tissue paper. (商標)一種衞生紙。➪ tissue(3).

klep·to·mania /ˌkleptəˈmeɪnɪə; ˌklɛptəˈmenɪə/ *n* obsessive wish to steal, not necessarily from poverty. 偷竊狂;盜癖。**klep·to·maniac** /-nɪæk; -nɪæk/ *n* person with ~. 有偷竊狂的人。

knack /næk; næk/ *n* (rarely *pl*) cleverness (intuitive or acquired through practice) enabling one to do sth skilfully: (罕用複數)(直覺的或由練習而得的)技巧;訣竅: *There's a ~ in it,* You have to learn by doing it. 這裏面有技巧(你必須做方能學會)。*It's quite easy to drive a car when you have/get the ~ of it.* 你要是知道竅門駕駛汽車就容易了。

knacker /ˈnækə(r); ˈnækɚ/ *n* **1** person who buys and slaughters useless horses (to sell the meat and hides). 購買並屠殺廢馬之人(爲賣馬肉和皮)。**2** person who buys and breaks up old houses, ships, etc for the materials in them. 收買廢屋、廢船等者(買來拆掉取其材料)。**~'s yard,** place where old metal goods, etc are broken up for scrap. 拆舊金屬物品等之場所。

knap /næp; næp/ *vt* (-pp-) break (flints for roads) with a hammer. 以鎚敲碎(燧石用以鋪路)。

knap·sack /ˈnæpsæk; ˈnæpˌsæk/ *n* [C] canvas or leather bag, strapped to the back and used (by soldiers, travellers) for carrying clothing, food, etc. (兵士、旅行者用的帆布或皮製的)背囊。

knave /neɪv; nev/ *n* **1** (old use) dishonest man; man without honour. (舊用法)不誠實的人;不名譽的人。**2** (playing cards) court-card between 10 and Queen in value: (紙牌)介於十點與王后間的一張牌;傑克: *the ~ of hearts.* 紅心 J。➪ Jack. **knav·ery** /ˈneɪvərɪ; ˈnevərɪ/ *n* [U] dishonesty; [C] (*pl* -ries) dishonest act. 不誠實;不誠實的行爲。**knav·ish** /ˈneɪvɪʃ; ˈnevɪʃ/ *adj* deceitful: 欺詐的: *knavish tricks.* 欺詐的手段。**knav·ish·ly** *adv*

knead /niːd; nid/ *vt* [VP6A] **1** make (flour and water) into a firm paste (dough) by working with the hands; do this with wet clay; make (bread, pots) in this way. 揉(麵粉和水)成團;揉(濕的黏土)成團;捏製(麵包、陶器)。**2** massage; apply

kites

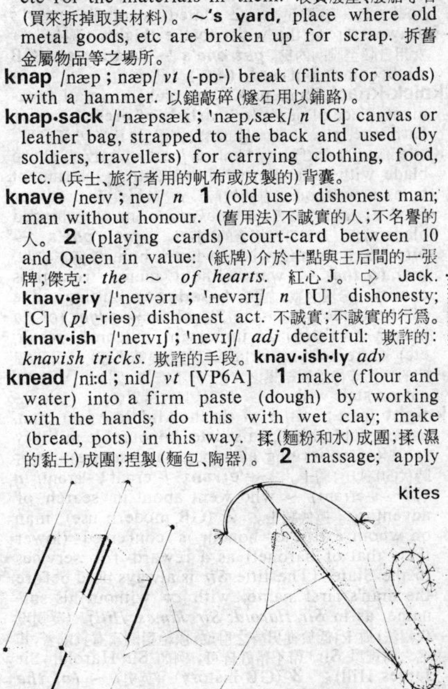

hands to (muscles, etc) as if making dough. 按摩;揉捏(肌肉等)。

knee /ni: ; ni/ *n* **1** joint between the thigh and the lower part of the leg in man, ⇨ the illus at leg; corresponding part in animals. (人或動物之)膝;膝蓋(參看 leg 之挿圖): ***be on/go (down) on one's ~s,*** be kneeling/kneel down (to pray, or in submission). 跪着(祈禱或屈服);跪下。***bring sb to his ~s,*** force him to submit. 迫使某人屈服。**2** part of a garment covering the ~s: 服裝之膝部: *the ~s of a pair of trousers.* 褲之膝部。**3** (compounds) (複合字) '**~-breeches** /-brɪtʃɪz ; -brɪtʃɪz/ *n pl* breeches reaching down to or just below the ~s. (長及膝部的)短褲。'**~·cap** *n* **(a)** flat, movable bone forming the front part of the ~-joint. 膝蓋骨。⇨ the illus at skeleton. 參看 skeleton 之挿圖。**(b)** protective covering for the ~. 護膝之物。ˌ**~-'deep** *adj, adv* so deep as to reach the ~s: 深及膝的(地): *The water was ~-deep.* 水深及膝。ˌ**~-'high** *adj, adv* so high as to reach the ~s: 高及膝的(地): *The grass was ~-high.* 草高及膝。

kneel /ni:l ; nil/ *vi* (*pt, pp* knelt /nelt ; nɛlt/) [VP2A, C] ~ ***(down),*** go down on the knees; rest on the knees: 跪下;跪倒: *He knelt down to look for a coin he had dropped.* 他跪下找他掉了的一個錢幣。*Everyone knelt in prayer.* 每個人都跪下來祈禱。

knell /nel ; nɛl/ *n* (*sing* with *a* or *the*) sound of a bell, esp for a death or at a funeral; (fig) sign of the end or death of sth: (單數,與 a 或 the 連用)鐘聲;(尤指)喪鐘聲;(喻)結束或死亡之徵兆: *toll the ~;* 敲喪鐘; *the ~ of her hopes.* 她的希望破滅的徵兆。

knelt /nelt ; nɛlt/ ⇨ kneel.

Knes·set /'kneset ; 'knɛsɛt/ *n* Israeli parliament. 以色列國會。

knew /nju: *US:* nu: ; nju/ ⇨ know.

knicker·bock·ers /'nɪkəbɒkəz ; 'nɪkɚˌbɑkɚz/ *n pl* loose wide breeches gathered in below the knees. 燈籠褲。

knickers /'nɪkəz ; 'nɪkɚz/ *n pl* **1** (US) knickerbockers. (美)燈籠褲。**2** (dated) woman's or girl's drawers from the waist to the thighs. (過時用語)女用自腰至股的內褲。***get one's '~ in a twist,*** (GB sl) become confused. (英俚)混亂;糊塗。

knick-knack /'nɪk næk ; 'nɪkˌnæk/ *n* small ornament, piece of jewellery, article of dress, piece of furniture, etc. 小裝飾品、珠寶、衣服、傢具等;小玩意兒。

knife /naɪf ; naɪf/ *n* (*pl* knives /naɪvz ; naɪvz/) sharp blade with a handle, used as a cutting instrument or as a weapon: (有柄的)刀: *a 'table ~,* used for food at table; 餐刀; *a 'pocket ~,* one with hinged blade(s). (刀刃可以摺合的)小刀。***get one's ~ into sb,*** have the wish to harm him. 欲傷害某人。***war to the ~,*** war without mercy; relentless enmity. 慘烈之戰;血戰。'**~-edge** *n* cutting edge of the blade of a ~. 刀刃。***on a ~-edge,*** (of (a person awaiting) an important outcome, result, etc) extremely uncertain. (指重要結果等) 十分不確定的;(指等待重要結果之人)十分不安的。□ *vt* [VP6A] cut or stab with a ~. 用刀切割;用刀刺。

knight /naɪt ; naɪt/ *n* **1** (in the Middle Ages) man, usu of noble birth, raised to honourable military rank (after serving as a page and squire). (中古時代的)武士;騎士。ˌ**~-'errant** /-'erənt ; -'ɛrənt/ *n* (*pl* ~s-errant) ~ who went about in search of adventure. 遊俠騎士。**2** (GB modern use) man on whom a title or honour is conferred (lower than that of baronet) as a reward for services to the State. (The title *Sir* is always used before the man's first name, with or without his surname, as in *Sir Harold; Sir James Hill*). (英國現代用法)爵士(低於從男爵之爵位,頒給對國家有貢獻者,其名之前冠以 Sir, 帶不帶姓皆可,例如 Sir Harold; Sir James Hill)。**3** (GB history) (英史) ~ ***(of the shire),*** person who represented a shire or county in Parliament. 郡選議員。**4** piece in the game of chess, usu made with a horse's head. (西洋棋)馬(有馬頭的棋子)。⇨ the illus at chess. 參看 chess 之挿圖。□ *vt* [VP6A] make (sb) a ~. 授以爵士位。**~·hood** /-hʊd ; -hʊd/ *n* **1** [U] rank, character or dignity of a ~; [C] a particular ~hood: 騎士或爵士的地位,身份或尊嚴;某一爵士地位: *The Queen conferred ~hoods on two magicians.* 女王授與兩位魔術師爵士之位。**2** [U] ~s collectively: 騎士;爵士(總稱): *the ~hood of the Commonwealth.* 大英國協所有的騎士。**~·ly** *adj* chivalrous; brave and gentle; like a ~: 俠義的;勇敢而文雅的;似騎士的: *~ly qualities.* 武士氣概。

knit /nɪt ; nɪt/ *vt, vi* (*pt, pp* ~ted or (old use) (舊用法) knit; -tt-) [VP6A, 15A, B, 2A, C] **1** ~ ***sth (up) (from/into),*** make (an article of clothing, etc) by looping wool, silk, etc yarn on long needles: 編織(衣物等): *~ stockings out of wool;* 用毛線織長襪; *~ wool into stockings;* 織毛線長襪; *~ sth up,* repair it by ~ting. 織補某物。*She often ~s while reading.* 她常常在看書時織東西。**2** unite firmly or closely: 堅固或密切地結合: *~ broken bones;* 接合碎骨; *a closely ~ argument.* 緊湊的論據。*Mortar is used to ~ bricks together.* 灰泥是用來黏合磚的。*The two families are ~ together by common interests.* 這兩家族因共同的利益而結合在一起。**3** draw together. 皺起。~ ***one's/the brows,*** frown. 皺眉頭。**~·ter** *n* person who ~s. 編織者。**~·ting** *n* [U] **1** action of one who ~s. 編織。**2** material that is being ~ted: 編織物: *Her ~ting fell from her lap to the floor.* 她織的東西從她膝上掉在地板上。'**~·ting-machine** *n* machine that ~s. 針織機。'**~·ting-needle** *n* long slender rod of steel, wood, etc two or more of which are used together in ~ting. 織針。**~·wear** /-weə(r) ; -ˌwɛr/ *n* [U] (trade use) ~ted garments. (商業用法)編織之衣物。

knives /naɪvz ; naɪvz/ ⇨ knife.

knob /nɒb ; nɑb/ *n* [C] **1** round-shaped handle of a door, drawer, walking-stick, etc; control, eg of a radio or television set: (門、抽屜、手杖等的)圓形把手;旋鈕;捻頭(例如收音機或電視機者): *turn the ~ clockwise to switch the set on.* 將旋鈕順時針方向轉打開收音機(電視機)。**2** round-shaped swelling or mass on the surface of sth, eg a tree trunk. 圓形突出物;節(如樹幹上者);球塊;瘤;疙瘩。**3** small lump (eg of coal). 小塊(例如煤塊)。'**~·ker·rie** /'nɒbkerɪ ; 'nɑbˌkɛrɪ/ *n* short stick with a ~ at one end of it, formerly used as a weapon (by S African tribes). 圓頭棒(南非土人昔時用作武器)。

knob·ble /'nɒbl ; 'nɑbl/ *n* small knob. 小節;小瘤;小球塊。**knob·bly** /'nɒblɪ ; 'nɑblɪ/ *adj* (-ier, -iest) having ~s: 有圓形突出物的;有節的;有疙瘩的;有球塊的: *~bly knees.* 有疙瘩的膝蓋。

knock[1] /nɒk ; nɑk/ *n* [C] **1** (short, sharp sound of a) blow: 擊;打;敲;短促的敲擊聲: *He got a nasty ~ on the head when he fell.* 他跌倒時頭部受到嚴重的碰撞。*I heard a ~ at the door.* 我聽到了敲門聲。*I knew him by his ~,* because of the way he ~ed (at the door). 從他的敲門聲我知道是他。~ ***for ~,*** situation in a motoring accident when insurance companies agree to pay only for the damage to the vehicle for which they are liable. 車禍發生後保險公司僅賠償車輛之損壞。**2** sound of ~ing in a petrol engine. 汽油發動機因故障而發出的爆聲。⇨ knock[2](3), and anti~. **3** (cricket) innings: (板球)一局: *have a good ~.* 好好地打一局球。**4** (sl) criticism; insult; financial loss: (俚)批評;侮辱;財務損失: *He's taken a bad ~,* suffered a financial reverse. 他損失不少錢財。**~er** *n* person or thing that ~s; (esp) hinged metal device on a door for ~ing on it (now often replaced by an electric bell). 敲擊之人或物;(尤指)門環(現多以電鈴取代之)。

knock[2] /nɒk ; nɑk/ *vt, vi* **1** [VP6A, 15A, B, 14, 22, 2A, C] hit; strike; cause to be (in a certain state) by hitting; make by hitting: 擊;打;敲;擊成(某種狀態): *Someone is ~ing at the door/on the window.* 有人敲門(窗子)。*Come in—don't ~.* 進來,不要敲門。*He ~ed the bottom out of the box.* 他把箱底打掉了。*Let's ~ a hole in the wall.* 我們就在牆上打個洞罷。*He ~ed* (= struck by accident) *his head on/against the wall.* 他的頭撞在牆上了。*The blow ~ed me flat/senseless.* 那一擊把我擊倒在地上(使我失去了知覺)。**~ one's head against a brick wall,** (fig) achieve nothing. (喻)無成就;失敗。**~ sb/sth into a cocked hat,** ⇨ cock³(1). **~ the bottom out of an argument,** ⇨ bottom(7). **~ spots off sth/sb,** ⇨ spot. **2** [VP6A] (sl) surprise; shock: (俚)使驚訝;使震驚: *What ~s me is his impudence.* 使我大爲驚訝的是他的厚顏無恥。**3** [VP2A] (of a petrol engine) make a tapping or thumping noise (because of a defect that prevents the engine from running smoothly): (指用汽油的發動機)發爆聲 (因有毛病故機器不能暢動): *The engine of this old car is ~ing badly.* 這部老汽車的引擎發爆聲響得厲害。⇨ antiknock. **4** [VP6A] (sl) criticize unfavourably: (俚)批評;攻擊: *Why must you always ~ my driving?* 你爲何總是批評我的駕駛技術? **5** (compounds) (also ⇨ (6) below) (複合字) (亦參看下列第6義) **'~-about** *adj* (of a comic performance) = *slapstick,* ⇨ slap; (of clothes) suitable for rough wear. (指滑稽演出)喧囂的;(指衣服)粗牢的。**'~-down** *adj* **(a)** (of prices, eg at an auction) lowest at which goods are to be sold; reserve price. (指價格,例如拍賣時)最低的;起碼的;最低價的。**(b)** (fig) overwhelming; stunning. (喻)壓倒的;銳不可當的。**,~-'kneed** *adj* having legs curved so that the knees touch when walking. 膝內翻的(兩腿向內彎曲,故行走時兩膝互撞)。**'~-out** *adj, n* **(a)** (abbr 略作 **KO**) (blow) that ~s a boxer out. (拳擊)打倒對手的(一擊);獲勝的一擊。**(b)** (of a) tournament or competition for eliminating weaker competitors. 淘汰賽(的)。**(c)** (colloq) (person, thing) impressive or attractive: (俗)予人印象深刻的;動人的(人或物): *Isn't she a ~-out!* 她多麼動人啊! **(d)** (sl) drug, etc which induces sleep or unconsciousness: (俚)迷藥: *~-out pills.* 迷藥丸。**6** [VP2C, 15B] (uses with *adverbial particles* and *preps*): (與副詞接語和介詞連用之用法):

knock about, (colloq) lead an unsettled life, travelling and living in various places: (俗)過漂泊不定的生活: *He has ~ed about all over Asia.* 他曾在亞洲到處漂泊。**~ about (with sb),** (sl) have a (casual) (sexual) relationship with sb: (俚)與某人發生(隨便的)(性) 關係: *She's ~ing about with a married man.* 她正同一位已婚的男人有染。**~ sb/sth about,** hit repeatedly, treat roughly: 接連敲打;粗魯地對待: *The ship had been ~ed about by storms.* 那船曾飽受風暴的摧殘。

knock sth back, (sl) drink: (俚)飲: *~ back a pint of beer.* 飲一品脫啤酒。

knock sb down, strike to the ground or floor: 擊倒;打倒: *He was ~ed down by a bus.* 他被公共汽車撞倒了。*He ~ed his opponent down.* 他將他的對手擊倒。***You could have ~ed me down with a feather,*** I was very surprised. 我甚爲吃驚。**~ sth down,** **(a)** demolish: 拆除: *These old houses are to be ~ed down.* 這些舊房屋將被拆除。**(b)** take to pieces to save cost and space in transport: 拆散以節省運費和空間: *The machines will be ~ed down before being packed for shipment to Singapore.* 這些機器在包裝運往新加坡之前將被拆卸。Hence, 由此產生, *'~-down furniture, etc,* which can be taken to pieces. 可拆卸的傢具。**~ sth down to sb,** (at an auction sale) sell (to a bidder): (拍賣時)賣(給出價者): *The painting was ~ed down to Mr Smith for £50.* 那幅畫以五十鎊拍賣給史密斯先生了。**~ sth/sb down (to sth),** (compel sb to) lower a price: (强迫某人)減價: *He asked £500 for his car but I managed to ~ him down 10 per cent/~ed his price down to £450.* 他的汽車要賣五百鎊,但我總算使他減價百分之十(使其價格減低爲四百五十鎊)。Hence, 由此產生, *~-down prices.* 減低的價格。also ⇨ *knock-down* at (5) above. 亦參看上列第5義中之 knock-down。

knock sth in, strike so that sth goes/stays in: 打入;敲進: *~ in a nail;* 敲進一釘; *~ in the top of a barrel.* 將桶頂敲進。

knock off (work), stop work: 停止(工作): *It's time to ~ off for tea.* 該停工喝茶了。**~ sb off,** (sl) quickly seduce and then abandon. (俚)迅速誘姦然後遺棄。**~ sth off,** **(a)** deduct: 減除: *I'll ~ 50p off the price.* 我願減價五十辨士。**(b)** compose or finish rapidly: 迅速做成: *~ off an article/some verses for a magazine.* 爲一雜誌匆匆寫一文章(幾節詩)。**(c)** (cricket) score quickly: (板球)迅速得分: *~ off the runs needed to win a match.* 迅速獲得贏得比賽所需要的分數。**(d)** (sl) break into, rob: (俚)搶劫: *~ off a bank.* 搶劫銀行。***K~ it off!*** (sl) Stop it! (俚)停止!住手!不要吵!

knock on, (Rugby) ~ the ball forward when trying to catch it (a foul). (橄欖球)欲接球時將球擊向前(爲犯規動作)。Hence, 由此產生, **'~-on** *n.* **'~-on effect** *n* (colloq) (usu unpleasant) consequence. (俗)結果;(通常指)不愉快的結果。

knock sb out, **(a)** (boxing) strike (an opponent) so that he cannot rise to his feet for the count. (拳擊)擊倒(對手,使無法於規定時間內站起)。**(b)** (fig) overwhelm; stun: (喻)使震驚: *She was ~ed out by the news.* 這消息使她異常吃驚。**(c) ~ sb out (of),** eliminate him (from a competition) (by defeating him). (擊敗某人)使退出(比賽)。**~ sth out,** empty by ~ing: 敲空: *~ out one's pipe,* ie of ash, etc. 磕烟斗。

knock (things) together, make roughly or hastily: 匆匆湊成: *~ boards together for a camp table.* 用木板匆匆湊成一露營用的桌子。*The bookshelves had obviously been ~ed together,* not made with care. 那些書架顯然是匆匆拼成的。**~ your/their heads together,** use force to prevent you/them from quarrelling, being foolish or stubborn. 迫使你們(他們)停止爭吵,不再愚蠢或固執。

knock up, (tennis) practise shots before the start of a match. (網球)賽前練球。**~ sb up,** **(a)** (GB colloq) waken or rouse sb by ~ing at his door, etc: (英俗)敲門等以喚醒: *Please could you ~ me up at seven o'clock.* 請在七點鐘敲門叫醒我。**(b)** (GB colloq) make tired; exhaust: (英俗)使疲倦;使筋疲力竭: *He was ~ed up after the long steep climb.* 經長時間險峻的攀登後,他已疲憊不堪了。**(c)** (US sl) attack; beat up. (美俚)攻擊;痛打。**(d)** ⚠ (US vulg sl) (of a man) have sexual intercourse with; make pregnant. (諱) (美鄙俚) (指男人) 與某女子有性關係;使懷孕。**~ sth up,** **(a)** drive upwards with a blow: 向上擊: *K~ his arm up!* 向上打他的胳臂! **(b)** arrange, put together quickly: 迅速安排;匆匆湊成: *~ up a meal from whatever there is in the larder;* 用食櫥中所有的東西匆匆做好一餐飯。*~ up a shelter for mountain-climbers.* 爲登山者草草搭成一棚。**(c)** score (runs) at cricket. (板球)得(分)。**~ up copy,** prepare material for printing (in a newspaper, etc). (爲報紙等)預備排印資料。

knoll /nəʊl ; nol/ *n* small hill; mound. 小山;小丘。

knot /nɒt ; nɑt/ *n* [C] **1** parts of one or more pieces of string, rope, etc, twisted together, usu to make a fastening: (繩索等之)結: *tie a ~ in a rope;* 在繩上打一結; *tie a rope in a firm ~;* 將繩打一牢結; *make a ~;* 打一結; (fig) sth that ties together: (喻)結合物: *the 'marriage-~.* 婚姻結合。**2** piece of ribbon, etc twisted and tied as an ornament. (絲帶等打成的裝飾用的)花結。**3** difficulty; hard problem. 困難;難題。***tie oneself in/up in/into ~s,*** get badly confused about sth. 對某事深感困惑。⇨ Gordian. **4** hard lump in wood where a branch grew out from a bough or trunk;

round cross-grained piece caused by this in a board. (樹木或木板上的) 節;節瘤;木節。 **'~-hole** *n* hole (in a board) from which such a piece has come out. 木板上的節疤孔。 **5** group of persons or things: 一群人或物: *People were standing about in ~s, anxiously waiting for news.* 人們成群佇立，急切等候消息。 **6** measure of speed for ships: 節(測船速的單位);浬: *a vessel of 20 ~s,* able to sail 20 nautical miles an hour. 時速二十浬之船。⇨ App 5. 參看附錄五。□ *vt, vi* (-tt-) [VP6A, 15B, 2A] make a ~ or ~s in; tie sth with ~s; form ~s: 打結於;包紮;成結: *~ two ropes together;* 將兩繩打一結連起來; *~ a parcel firmly;* 將一包裹紮緊; *string that ~s easily.* 容易打結的繩子。**~ty** *adj* (-ier, -iest) full of ~s: 多結的;多節的;多困難的: *a ~ty board.* 多節的木板。**~ty problem,** one that is difficult to solve. 難題。

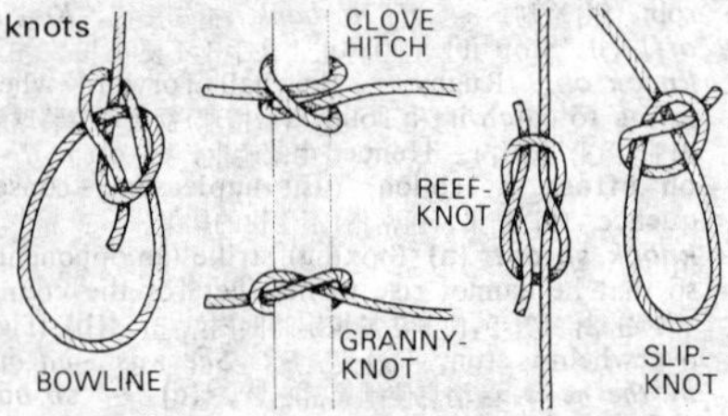

know /nəʊ; no/ *vt, vi* (*pt* knew /nju: *US:* nu:; nju/, *pp* known /nəʊn; non/) **1** [VP6A, 8, 9, 10, 17, 25, 2A] have in the mind as the result of experience or of being informed, or because one has learned: 知道;曉得;懂得: *Every child ~s that two and two make four.* 每個孩子都知道二加二等於四。 *He ~s a lot of English.* 他懂得許多英文。*Do you ~ how to play chess?* 你會下西洋棋嗎？*I don't ~ whether he is here or not.* 我不知道他是否在此地。*I ~ (that) he's an honest man.* 我知道他是個誠實的人。*I ~ him to be honest.* 我知道他是誠實的。*I'm not guessing—I really ~.* 我不是在猜想──我眞的知道。*Oh, yes, I ~ all about that.* 哦，是的，我對那事全知道。*There's no ~ing (= It is impossible to ~) when we shall meet again.* 不知道何時我們再相見。 [VP17, 18B] (past and perfect tenses only): (僅用於過去和完成時態): *I have never ~n a man (to) die of love, but I have ~n a disappointed lover (to) lose weight.* 我從未看到有人因戀愛而死，但我曾看到失戀的人消瘦。**~ one's business / what's 'what / the ropes / a 'thing or two,** have common sense, good judgement, practical experience. 明事理;有頭腦;精明能幹。**~ better than to do sth,** be wise enough not to...: 明白事理而不至於…: *You ought to ~ better than to go swimming on such a cold day.* 你應該知道在這樣冷的天去游泳是不對的。**2** [VP 6A] be acquainted with (a person); be able to distinguish (sb) from others: 認識(一人);認出: *Do you ~ Mr Hill?* Have you met him, talked with him, etc? 你認識希爾先生嗎？(Cf 參較 *Do you ~(1) who Napoleon was?* 你知道拿破崙是誰嗎？) *I ~ Mr White by sight but have never spoken to him.* 我認識懷特先生，但從未同他說過話。*I've ~n Mrs Grey since I was a child.* 我從小便認識格雷太太。*I was introduced to Miss Wood last week, but I've a bad memory for faces and might not ~ (= recognize) her again.* 上星期我經介紹結識了伍德小姐，但我對面孔的記憶力很壞，再見面時可能認不出她來了。**make oneself ~n to sb,** introduce oneself: 自我介紹: *There's your host; you'd better make yourself ~n to him.* 那邊就是(你的)主人，你最好向他做一番自我介紹。**be ~n to:** 爲…所熟知: *He's ~n to the police,* The police have his name in their records, eg because he has been a criminal. 警方認識他 (例如因其曾犯過案，在他們的記錄中有他的名字)。**be ~n as:** 以…著稱;通稱爲: *He's ~n as (= has the reputation of being) a successful architect.* 他以成功的建築師聞名。**~ sb from sb,** distinguish from: 辨識: *They're twins and it's almost impossible to ~ one from the other.* 他們是雙生，旁人幾乎無從辨別。**not ~ sb from Adam / from a bar of soap,** (colloq) have no idea who he is. (俗)不曉得某人是誰。 **3** [VP6A] have personal experience of: 經歷;遭受: *He knew poverty and sorrow in his early life.* 他早年經歷過窮困與憂患。*He's ~n better days,* has not always been so poor, unfortunate, etc, as he is now. 他曾享受過好日子(並不總是像現在這樣窮愁潦倒等)。 **4** [VP6A] be able to recognize: 能辨識: *He ~s a good singing voice when he hears one.* 他有辨識好的歌聲的能力。*She doesn't ~ a swallow from a house-martin.* 她分別不出移居的燕和牆上築巢的燕。 **5** [VP3A] **~ about / of,** have information concerning; be aware of: 聽說關於…的事情;知道: *I knew about that last week.* 我上星期聽說過那事。*I didn't ~ about that,* was in ignorance. 我不知道那事。*I ~ of an excellent little restaurant near here.* 我聽說附近有一家非常好的小餐館。*'Has Smith been ill?' — 'Not that I ~ of.'* I am not aware of his having been ill. '史密斯病了嗎？'—'我沒聽說。' *I don't actually ~(2) the man you mention, but of course I ~ 'of him,* I'm aware of his existence. 我不認識你提到的這個人，不過我的確聽說過他。**6** (compounds) (複合字) **,don't-'~** *n* (colloq) person who is unable to give an answer in a *poll*¹(2). (俗)民意調查中不能回答問題之人。**'~-all** *n* person who ~s, or claims to ~, everything. 無所不知之人;自稱無所不知之人。 **'~-how** *n* [U] faculty of ~ing how (to do sth); knowledge of methods; ingenuity (contrasted with theoretical knowledge). 技能;方法上的知識;技巧(以別於理論上的知識)。□ *n* (only in) (僅用於) **in the ~,** (colloq) having information not shared by all or not available to all. (俗)知道實情的;熟識內幕的。

know·ing /'nəʊɪŋ; 'noɪŋ/ *adj* cunning; wide-awake; having, showing that one has, intelligence, sharp wits, etc: 狡黠的;機警的;聰穎的;伶俐的: *a ~ fellow;* 機警的人; *~ looks.* 狡黠的樣子。**~·ly** *adv* **1** consciously; intentionally: 有意地;故意地: *He would never ~ly do anything to hurt your interests.* 他絕不會故意做出任何損害你利益的事。 **2** in a ~ manner: 狡黠地;機警地: *look ~ly at someone.* 狡黠地瞧着某人。

knowl·edge /'nɒlɪdʒ; 'nɑlɪdʒ/ *n* [U] **1** understanding: 瞭解;理解: *A baby has no ~ of good and evil.* 嬰兒不瞭解善惡。 **2** familiarity gained by experience; range of information: 通曉;知識;見聞;消息: *My ~ of French is poor.* 我的法文不太好。*K~ of the defeat soon spread.* 戰敗的消息不久便傳播開來。*It has come to my ~ (= I have been informed) that you have been spreading gossip about me.* 我聽說你一直在說我的閒話。 *To the best of my ~ (= As far as I know) he is honest and reliable.* 據我所知，他是誠實可靠的。*She married without the ~ of her parents.* 她結婚連她的父母都不知道。**~·able** /-əbl; -əbl̩/ *adj* well-informed; having much ~. 博識的;有知識的。

knuckle /'nʌkl; 'nʌkl̩/ *n* **1** bone at a finger-joint: 指節;指關節: *give a boy a rap over / on the ~s.* 責備一男孩。⇨ the illus at arm. 參看 arm 之插圖。 **2** (in animals) knee-joint, or part joining leg to foot (esp as food). 動物的膝關節或足踝(尤指可做食物用者);肘;蹄。□ *vi* **~ down to,** (of a task, etc) apply oneself earnestly. 專心於(工作等)。**~ under,** submit, yield. 屈服;投降。

ko·ala /kəʊ'ɑ:lə; kə'ɑlə/ *n* Australian tree-climbing tailless mammal, like a small bear. 科拉熊(一種澳洲產會攀樹的無尾哺乳動物，似小熊)。⇨ the illus at small. 參看 small 之插圖。

kobo /ˈkɒbəʊ; ˈkobo/ *n* (Nigeria) 100th part of a naira; coin of this value. (奈及利亞之)科博(値百分之一奈拉);價值一科博之硬幣。

kohl /kəʊl; kol/ *n* [U] cosmetic preparation used in the East to darken the eyelids. 東方婦女用以把眼皮塗黑的一種化粧品。

kohl·rabi /ˌkəʊlˈrɑːbɪ; ˈkolˌrɑbɪ/ *n* [C, U] cabbage with turnip-shaped stem. 一種球莖甘藍。

kola /ˈkəʊlə; ˈkolə/ *n* W African tree. 可拉樹(產於非洲西部)。 **ˈ~-nut** *n* the white or pink bitter edible seed of the ~ tree, used in cooking or to chew. 可拉果(可拉樹之白色或粉紅色種子,有苦味,用於烹飪或嚼食)。

kooka·burra /ˈkʊkəbʌrə; ˈkʊkəˌbʌrə/ *n* large Australian kingfisher (also called 亦稱 *laughing jackass*). (澳洲產的一種)大魚狗。

ko·peck /ˈkəʊpek; ˈkopɛk/ *n* = copeck.

kopje, kop·pie /ˈkɒpɪ; ˈkɑpɪ/ *n* (in S Africa) small hill. (南非)小山。

Ko·ran /kəˈrɑːn *US:* ˈræn; koˈrɑn/ *n* sacred book containing the Prophet Muhammad's oral revelations, written in Arabic. 可蘭經(載有穆罕默德口述的啓示,用阿拉伯文寫成的回教經典)。 **~ic** *adj*

ko·sher /ˈkəʊʃə(r); ˈkoʃɚ/ *n, adj* (food, foodshop) fulfilling the requirements of Jewish dietary law. 合於猶太飲食戒律的;合於猶太戒律的食物或飲食店。

kou·miss /ˈkuːmɪs; ˈkumɪs/ *n* = kumis.

kow·tow, ko·tow /ˌkaʊˈtaʊ; kaʊˈtaʊ/ *n* (former Chinese custom) touching of the ground with the forehead (as a sign of respect, submission, etc). 叩頭;磕頭(昔時中國的風俗,以示尊敬、屈服等)。 □ *vi* **~ *(to),*** make a ~; act obsequiously (to). 叩頭;(向…)磕頭;(向…)卑躬屈節。

kraal /krɑːl *US:* krɔːl; krɑl/ *n* (in S Africa) fenced-in village of huts; enclosure for domestic animals. (南非)用柵欄圍起來的茅舍村莊;家畜欄。

krem·lin /ˈkremlɪn; ˈkrɛmlɪn/ *n* citadel of a Russian town, esp that of Moscow. (蘇俄的,尤指莫斯科的)城堡。 **the K~,** the Government of the USSR. 克里姆林宮;蘇俄政府。

krona /ˈkrəʊnə; ˈkronə/ *n* (*pl* -nor /-nə; -nɔr/) unit of currency in Sweden. 克隆納(瑞典之一種貨幣單位)。

krone /ˈkrəʊnə; ˈkronɛ/ *n* (*pl* -ner /-nə; -nɛr/) unit of currency in Denmark and Norway. 克隆納(丹麥及挪威之一種貨幣單位)。

ku·dos /ˈkjuːdɒs; ˈkjudɑs/ *n* [U] (colloq) honour and glory; credit. (俗)光榮;榮譽。

kumis, kou·miss /ˈkuːmɪs; ˈkumɪs/ *n* [U] fermented liquor of Central Asia made from mare's milk. (亞洲中部之)馬乳酒。

küm·mel /ˈkʊməl; ˈkɪml̩/ *n* [U] herb-flavoured liqueur. 一種用香草調味的酒。

kung fu /ˌkʊŋˈfuː; ˌkʊŋˈfu/ *n* [U] Chinese form of karate. 中國功夫。

kvass /kvæs; kvæs/ *n* [U] kind of Russian beer. 蘇俄製的一種啤酒。

kwela /ˈkweɪlə; ˈkwelə/ *n* [U] kind of S African jazz music. 一種爵士樂(流行於南非)。

Ll

L, l /el; ɛl/ (*pl* L's l's /elz; ɛlz/) the 12th letter of the English alphabet; symbol for the Roman numeral 50, ⇨ App 4. 英文字母之第十二個字母;羅馬數字的 50 (參看附錄四)。

la /lɑː; lɑ/ *n* sixth note of the musical octave. 大音階的第六音。

laa·ger /ˈlɑːgə(r); ˈlɑgɚ/ *n* camp, defensive encampment, esp inside a circle of carts or wagons; (mil) park for armoured vehicles. 紮營(尤指四周以車輛圍成一圓陣者);(軍)裝甲車停車處。

lab /læb; læb/ *n* (colloq abbr of) laboratory. (俗)實驗室(爲 laboratory 之略)。

label /ˈleɪbl; ˈlebl̩/ *n* piece of paper, cloth, metal, wood or other material used for describing what sth is, where it is to go, etc: 標籤;籤條: *plant ~s;* 植物標籤; *put ~s on one's luggage.* 在行李上貼標籤。 □ *vt* (-ll-, US -l-) [VP6A] put a ~ or ~s on: 貼標籤於: *properly ~led luggage;* 標籤貼得妥當的行李; (fig) (喩) ~ *sb as a demagogue*, assign him to this class of persons. 指某人爲煽動家。

la·bial /ˈleɪbɪəl; ˈlebɪəl/ *adj* of the lips; made with the lips: 唇的: ~ *sounds*, eg /m, p, v/. 唇音(例如 m, p, v/)。

labor /ˈleɪbə(r); ˈlebɚ/ *n* (US) = labour.

lab·ora·tory /ləˈbɒrətrɪ *US:* ˈlæbrətɔːrɪ; ˈlæbrəˌtorɪ/ *n* (*pl* -ries) room or building used for scientific experiments, research, testing, etc esp in chemistry. 實驗室(尤指化學方面者)。⇨ language.

la·bori·ous /ləˈbɔːrɪəs; ləˈborɪəs/ *adj* **1** (of work, etc) requiring great effort: (指工作等)艱苦的;費力的: *a ~ task.* 艱苦的工作。 **2** showing signs of great effort; not fluent or easy: 具見苦心的;艱澀的;不流暢的: *a ~ style of writing.* 艱澀的文體。 **~·ly** *adv*

la·bour (US = **la·bor**) /ˈleɪbə(r); ˈlebɚ/ *n* **1** [U] bodily or mental work: (身或心之)勞作;勞動: *The majority of men earn their living by manual ~.* 大多數的人靠雙手勞動以謀生。 **hard ~** *n* [U] work done by criminals (sentenced to penal servitude) as a punishment. (判處勞役監禁之罪犯所服之)勞役。 **ˈ~-saving** *adj* that reduces the amount of ~ needed: 減輕勞動的;節省勞力的;省工的: *~-saving devices*, eg washing-machines, vacuum cleaners. 省工用具(例如洗衣機、吸塵器)。 **2** [C] task; piece of work. 工作;一件工作。 ***a ~ of love,*** task gladly undertaken (eg one for the good of sb one loves). 出於愛心的工作。 **3** [U] workers as a class (contrasted with the owners of capital, etc): 勞動階級;勞工(與資方等相對): *skilled and unskilled ~;* 技術工與非技術工; *~ relations,* between workers and employers. 勞工與雇主間的關係。 **ˈL~ Exchange,** Government agency used by employers for finding workers and by workers for finding jobs. 勞工介紹所。 **the ˈL~ Party,** one of the two large political parties in Britain, representing socialist opinion. 工黨(英國二大政黨之一,代表社會主義思想)。 **L~ leaders,** leaders of this party; trade union officials. 工黨領袖;工會高級職員。 **the L~ vote,** of those who support the L~ Party. 工黨票數。 **ˈLabor Day,** (US) first Monday in September, a legal holiday in honour of the working class. (美) 勞工節 (九月的第一個禮拜一)。 **ˈlabor union,** (US) (美) = trade union. **4** [U] process of childbirth: 分娩過程: *a woman in ~.* 分娩中的女人;產婦。 □ *vi, vt* **1** [VP2A, C, 4A] work; try hard: 工作;勞動;努力: ~ *for the happiness of mankind;* 爲人類的幸福而努力; ~ *at a task;* 努力做一工作; ~ *to complete a task;* 努力完成一工作; ~ *in the cause of peace.* 爲謀和平而努力。 **2** [VP2A, C] move, breathe, slowly and with difficulty: 緩慢吃力地行動或呼吸: *The ship ~ed through the heavy seas.* 船在巨浪洶湧的海上緩慢費力地航行。 *The old man ~ed up the hillside.* 那老人緩慢吃力地走上山坡。 **3** [VP3A] **~ *under sb/sth,*** be the victim of, suffer because of: 受害於;苦於: ~ *under a delusion/difficulty/disadvantage.* 爲幻想(困難,不利條件)所苦。 **4** [VP6A] work out in detail; treat at great length: 詳細地做;詳細說明或討論: *There's no need to ~ the point/argument.* 該論點(論據)無需詳細說明或討論。**~ed** *adj* **1** slow and troublesome:

L

緩慢而困難的: *~ed breathing.* 緩慢困難的呼吸。**2** not easy or natural; showing too much effort: 不流暢的;艱澀的;具見苦心的: *a ~ed style of writing.* 艱澀的文體。**~er** *n* man who performs heavy unskilled work: 勞工;苦力: *agricultural ~ers,* farm workers. 農場工人。**L~·ite** /-aɪt ; -aɪt/ *n* member or supporter of the L~ Party. 英國工黨黨員;擁護工黨者。

la·bur·num /lə'bɜːnəm ; lə'bɝnəm/ *n* small tree with yellow flowers that hang down gracefully and with seeds in long pods. 金鏈花(一種小樹,開美麗下垂的黃花,並生有長莢,內含種子)。

lab·y·rinth /'læbərɪnθ ; 'læbə,rɪnθ/ *n* network of winding paths, roads, etc through which it is difficult to find one's way without help; (fig) entangled state of affairs. 迷宮;迷津;(喻)事情之錯綜複雜。**laby·rin·thine** /ˌlæbə'rɪnθaɪn *US:* -θɪn ; ˌlæbə'rɪnθɪn/ *adj*

lace /leɪs ; les/ *n* **1** [U] delicate, ornamental openwork fabric of threads: 花邊;飾帶: *a dress trimmed with ~;* 飾有花邊的服裝; *a ~ collar.* 鑲着花邊的衣領。**gold／silver ~,** braid used for trimming uniforms, eg of diplomats, army officers. (外交官和軍官等服裝所飾的)金(銀)邊。**2** [C] string or cord put through small holes in shoes, etc to draw edges together: 鞋帶;帶: *a pair of* '*shoe-~s.* 一雙鞋帶。□ *vt, vi* **1** [VP6A, 15A, B, 2A, C] ~ ***(up),*** fasten or tighten with ~s(2): 用鞋帶繫牢;用帶繫緊: *~ (up) one's shoes;* 結好鞋帶; *a corset that ~s (up) at the side.* 自側面用帶繫緊的女用束腹。**2** [VP3A] ~ ***into sb,*** lash him, beat him. 打某人。**3** [VP14] ~ ***with,*** flavour or strengthen (a liquid) (with some kind of spirit): 攙酒於(飲料): *a glass of milk ~d with rum.* 一杯攙有蘭酒的牛奶。

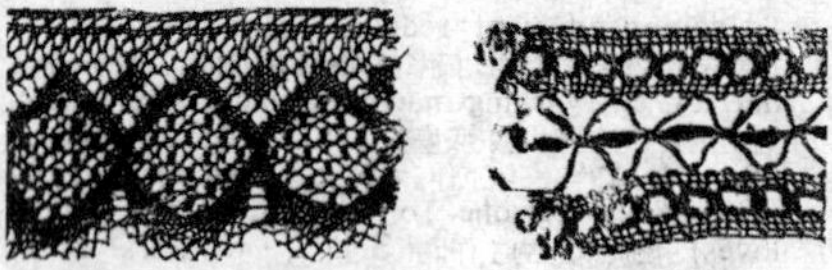

lace

lac·er·ate /'læsəreɪt ; 'læsə,ret/ *vt* [VP6A] tear (the flesh); (fig) the feelings). 劃破(肉);(喻)傷害(感情)。**lac·er·ation** /ˌlæsə'reɪʃn ; ˌlæsə'reʃən/ *n* [U] tearing; [C] tear or injury. 劃破;撕裂;裂傷;破口。

lach·ry·mal /'lækrɪml ; 'lækrəml/ *adj* of tears: 眼淚的: (esp) (尤用於) *~ glands.* 淚腺。**lach·ry·mose** /'lækrɪməʊs ; 'lækrə,mos/ *adj* tearful; in the habit of weeping. 含淚的;愛哭的。

lack /læk ; læk/ *vt, vi* **1** [VP6B, 3A] ~ ***(in),*** be without; not have; have less than enough of: 缺乏;沒有;缺少: *~ wisdom.* 缺乏智慧。*I ~ words with which to express my thanks.* 我無法以言語來表示我的感激。*What I ~ in experience I make up in curiosity.* 我以求知慾彌補我經驗的缺乏。***be ~ing in sth,*** not have enough of it: 缺乏: *He's ~ing in* (= He ~s) *courage.* 他缺乏勇氣。**2** ***be ~ing,*** be in short supply, not be available: 缺乏;沒有: *Money was ~ing* (= There was no money) *for the plan.* 此一計畫尚缺錢。**3** [VP3A] ~ ***for,*** (formal) need: (正式用語)需要: *They ~ed for nothing,* had everything they wanted. 他們什麼也不缺少(需要的東西都有了)。□ *n* [U] want, need, shortage: 缺乏;缺少;不足: *The plants died for ~ of water.* 那些植物因缺水而枯死了。'**~-lustre** *adj* (of eyes) dull. (指眼睛)無光澤的。

lacka·daisi·cal /ˌlækə'deɪzɪkl ; ˌlækə'dezɪkl/ *adj* appearing tired, uninterested, unenthusiastic. 無精打采的;冷漠的。**~ly** /-klɪ ; -klɪ/ *adv*

lackey /'lækɪ ; 'lækɪ/ *n* (*pl* ~s) manservant (usu in livery); (fig) person who is too obsequious, who obeys orders without question, etc. 男僕(通常着制服);(喻)卑躬屈膝之人。

la·conic /lə'kɒnɪk ; lə'kɑnɪk/ *adj* using, expressed in, few words: 簡潔的;簡明的: *a ~ person／reply.* 說話簡潔之人(簡明的回答)。**la·coni·cally** /-klɪ ; -klɪ/ *adv* **la·coni·cism** /-nɪsɪzəm ; -nɪsɪzəm/, **lac·on·ism** /'lækənɪzəm ; 'lækənɪzəm/ *nn* [U] being ~; [C] instance of this; short, pithy saying. 簡潔;簡明;簡潔之語句;警句。

lac·quer /'lækə(r) ; 'lækɚ/ *n* [U] varnish used to give a hard, bright coating to metal (esp brass); varnish used for wooden articles (esp **Japanese** ~); liquid sprayed on the hair to keep it in place. 假漆(用以漆金屬,尤其是黃銅);亮漆(漆木器者,尤指日本漆);(噴在頭髮上用以固定髮型之)膠水。□ *vt* [VP6A] coat with ~. 塗假漆於;塗以亮漆;噴以膠水。

la·crosse /lə'krɒs *US:* -'krɔːs ; lə'krɔs/ *n* [U] outdoor game, popular in N America, played with a ball which is caught in, carried in, and thrown from, a racket with a net (called a *crosse*). 長曲棍球(盛行於北美之一種戶外球戲,進行時以一帶網的曲棍球棒捕球、持球和擲球)。

lac·tic /'læktɪk ; 'læktɪk/ *adj* of milk. 乳的。ˌ~ '**acid,** the acid in sour milk. 乳酸。

la·cuna /lə'kjuːnə ; lə'kjunə/ *n* (*pl* ~s or ~e /-niː ; -ni/) blank; empty part; missing portion, esp in writing, or in an argument. 空白;空隙;脫漏部分(尤指寫作或議論中者);漏洞。

lacy /'leɪsɪ ; 'lesɪ/ *adj* (-ier, -iest) of or like lace. 花邊的;似花邊的。

lad /læd ; læd/ *n* boy; young man. 少年;青年。

lad·der /'lædə(r) ; 'lædɚ/ *n* **1** two lengths of wood, metal or rope, with crosspieces (called *rungs*), used in climbing up and down walls, a ship's side, etc. 梯(梯級稱作 rung)。⇨ '*step-~* at step²(5). **2** (US 美 = *run*) fault in a stocking caused by stitches becoming undone, so that there is a vertical ~-like flaw. 襪子因脫線而成的梯形裂縫;抽絲。'**~-proof** *adj* proof against such flaws. 防抽絲的;不抽絲的。□ *vi* (of stockings, etc) develop ~s: (指襪子等)抽絲: *Have you any tights that won't ~?* 你有不會抽絲的緊身衣嗎?

lad·die /'lædɪ ; 'lædɪ/ *n* = lad.

lade /leɪd ; led/ *vt* (*pp* laden /'leɪdn ; 'ledn̩/) [VP6A] load (which is the usu word). 裝載(load 爲常用字)。

laden /'leɪdn ; 'ledn̩/ *adj* ~ ***with,*** weighted or burdened with: 載滿;裝着: *trees ~ with apples;* 結滿蘋果的樹; *a mind ~ with grief.* 充滿憂傷的心。

la-di-da /ˌlɑː dɪ 'dɑː ; ˌlɑdɪ'dɑ/ *adj* (colloq) pretentious; genteel; affected (esp in pronunciation). (俗)裝模作樣的;裝作有教養的;做作的(尤指發音方面)。

lad·ing /'leɪdɪŋ ; 'ledɪŋ/ *n* [U] (naut) cargo; freight. (航海)船貨;裝載的貨物。ˌ**bill of** '**~,** list with details of a ship's cargo. (船貨之)提貨單。

ladle /'leɪdl ; 'ledl̩/ *n* large, deep, cup-shaped spoon for dipping out liquids: 長柄杓;杓子: *a* '*soup ~.* 湯杓。□ *vt* [VP6A, 15B] ~ ***(out),*** serve with or as from a ~: 以杓舀取;似以杓給與: *~ out soup;* 用杓舀湯; (fig) (喻) *~ out honours.* 給與榮譽。

lady /'leɪdɪ ; 'ledɪ/ *n* (*pl* -dies) **1** (corresponding to *gentleman*) woman belonging to the upper classes; woman who has good manners and some claim to social position. (與紳士相對)貴婦;淑女;有教養和社會地位的婦女。ˌ**~-in-**'**waiting,** ˌ**~ of the** '**bed-chamber,** ~ attending upon a queen. 宮女。**2** (used courteously for any) woman of any kind or class, with or without good manners and refinement. 女士(對所有婦女的客氣稱呼,不論其身份或是否有教養)。**3** (*pl* only) form of address, (僅用複數)稱呼的套語, esp (尤用於) *'Ladies and Gentlemen'.* '諸位先生和女士'。**4** (attrib) female: (形容用法)女性的: *~ doctor／clerk,* (*woman* being preferable). 女醫生(職員)(woman 較普通)。**5 Ladies** (as a *sing n*), women's public lavatory: (作單數名詞)女廁所;女盥洗室: *Is there a Ladies near here?* 這附近有女廁所嗎? **6 L~,** (title in GB) used of and to the wives of some nobles; (prefixed to Christian names) titles used of and to the daughters of some nobles. (英)夫人(對某些貴族之妻子之尊稱);(冠於教名前) 小姐 (對某些貴族之女兒的尊稱)。 **7** ***My L~,*** formal term of address used to holders of the title *Lady* (as in 6 above). 夫人;小姐(對貴族的妻女的尊稱)。 **8** (compounds) (複合字) **ˈ~·bird** *n* reddish-brown or yellow insect (a small flying beetle) with black spots. 瓢蟲(一種紅褐色或黃色會飛的小甲蟲,身上有黑點)。 **ˌOur ˈL~,** the Virgin Mary. 聖母馬利亞。 **ˈL~-chapel,** chapel (in a large church) dedicated to the Virgin Mary. (大教堂中之)聖母堂。 **ˈL~ Day,** the feast of the Annunciation, 25th March. 報喜節(三月二十五日)。 **ˈ~-killer** *n* man with the reputation of being very successful with women. 很會吸引婦女的男人。 **ˈ~'s-maid** *n* ~'s personal servant, esp in charge of her toilet. 侍女;(尤指)專管女主人化粧的女僕。 **ˈ~'s/ˈladies' man,** man fond of the society of women. 喜歡與婦女交際的男人。 **ˈ~·like** *adj* behaving as a ~; befitting a ~; genteel. 行爲似貴婦的;淑雅的。 **ˈ~·ship** /-ʃɪp ; -ʃɪp/ *n* ***Your/Her L~ship,*** used in speaking to or of a titled ~. 夫人; 小姐 (對有 Lady 頭銜之婦女的尊稱,當面稱 Your Ladyship, 談話中提及稱 Her Ladyship).

lag¹ /læg ; læg/ *vi* (-gg-) [VP2A, C] go too slow, not keep up with: 走得太慢;落後: *The lame child lagged behind.* 那跛足的孩子落在後面。□ *n* **(ˈtime) lag,** period of time by which sth is slower or later. 遲延的時間;時滯。

lag² /læg ; læg/ *n* (sl) person convicted of crime; (俚)犯人; (esp) (尤用於) ***old lag,*** one who has served several sentences of imprisonment. 常坐牢的犯人;慣犯。

lag³ /læg ; læg/ *vt* (-gg-) [VP6A, 14] ***lag (with),*** encase (waterpipes, cisterns, etc) with material that will not conduct heat or cold, esp to prevent freezing of water in pipes, waste of heat, etc. 以隔熱或隔冷的材料保護 (水管, 貯水器等,以防止管中的水結冰或散熱等)。 **lag·ging** *n* [U] material used for this. 隔熱或隔冷的材料。

la·ger /ˈlɑ:gə(r) ; ˈlɑgɚ/ *n* [U] sort of light beer; [C] bottle or glass of this. 一種淡啤酒;一瓶或一杯淡啤酒。

lag·gard /ˈlægəd ; ˈlægɚd/ *n* person who lags behind; person who is lacking in energy, etc. 落後者;缺乏精力等者。

la·goon /ləˈgu:n ; ləˈgun/ *n* (usu shallow) salt-water lake separated from the sea by sandbank(s) or coral reef(s); water enclosed by an atoll. 由沙洲或珊瑚礁與海相隔之鹹水湖(通常是淺的);礁湖。⇨ the illus at atoll. 參看 atoll 之插圖。

laic /ˈleɪɪk ; ˈle·ɪk/ *adj* of the laity; secular. 常人的;俗人的;世俗的。 **lai·cize** /ˈleɪɪsaɪz ; ˈleəˌsaɪz/ *vt* [VP6A] free from ecclesiastic control; make, eg priest, a layman. 使不受教會管制;使還俗。

laid /leɪd ; led/ *pt, pp* of lay¹.

lain /leɪn ; len/ *pp* of lie².

lair /leə(r) ; lɛr/ *n* wild animal's resting-place or den. 野獸的窩穴。

laird /leəd ; lɛrd/ *n* (Scot) landowner. (蘇)地主。

laissez-faire /ˌleɪseɪ ˈfeə(r) ; ˌlɛseˈfɛr/ *n* [U] (F) (policy of) allowing individual activities (esp in commerce) to be conducted without government control. (法)自由競爭(尤指商業上者);放任政策。

laity /ˈleɪətɪ ; ˈleətɪ/ *n* (usu **the ~,** and a *pl v*) (通常作 the ~, 與複數動詞連用) **1** all laymen (ie all those persons not in Holy Orders, those who are not clergy). 俗人(以別於僧侶或教士)。 **2** all those persons outside a particular learned profession (thus, used by a doctor, the word may mean all those not trained for the medical profession). 外行人(以別於專家,例如醫生用此字,則指未受過醫學訓練的人)。

lake¹ /leɪk ; lek/ *n* large area of water enclosed by land. 湖。 **the ˈL~ District, the L~s,** part of N W England with many ~s. 英格蘭西北部之湖泊區。 **ˈL~ Poets,** poets who lived in this area, esp Coleridge and Wordsworth. 湖畔詩人(居住在這個湖泊區之詩人,尤指柯爾雷基與華茨華斯)。 **the Great L~s,** ⇨ great. **ˈ~ dwelling,** ⇨ *pile-dwelling* at pile¹.

lake² /leɪk ; lek/ *n* (often 常作 *crimson* ~) dark red colouring material. 深紅色的顏料。

lakh /lɑ:k ; lɑk/ *n* (India and Pakistan) 100000. (印度和巴基斯坦)十萬。⇨ crore.

lam /læm ; læm/ *vt, vi* (-mm-) (sl) (俚) [VP6A] thrash. 鞭打。[VP3A] ***lam into sb,*** attack him, physically or verbally. 鞭打某人;攻擊某人;抨擊某人。

lama /ˈlɑ:mə ; ˈlɑmə/ *n* Buddhist monk in Tibet or Mongolia. 喇嘛 (西藏或蒙古的佛教僧人)。 **~·sery** /ˈlɑ:məsərɪ *US:* -serɪ ; ˈlɑməˌsɛrɪ/ *n* (*pl* -ries) monastery of ~s. 喇嘛寺院。

lamb /læm ; læm/ *n* [C] **1** young of the sheep, ⇨ the illus at domestic; [U] its flesh as food: 小羊;羔羊(參看 domestic 之插圖);羔羊肉(作爲食物): *a leg of ~;* 羔羊腿肉; *roast ~.* 烤羊肉。 **2** innocent, mild-mannered person; dear person. 天眞溫和之人;可愛的人。 ***like a ~,*** without resistance or protest. 無抵抗或抗議的。□ *vi* bring forth ~s: 生小羊: *the ˈ~ing season,* when ~s are born. 生小羊的季節。 **ˈ~·kin** /-kɪn ; -kɪn/ *n* very young ~. 很小的羊;小羔羊。 **ˈ~·skin** *n* [C] skin of a ~ with the wool on it (as used for coats, gloves, etc); [U] leather made from ~skin. 帶毛的羔皮(用做上衣,手套等);羔羊皮革。

lam·baste /ˌlæmˈbeɪst ; læmˈbest/ *vt* (sl) thrash; beat; scold violently. (俚)笞打;打;嚴厲責罵。

lam·bent /ˈlæmbənt ; ˈlæmbənt/ *adj* (liter) (of a flame or light) moving over the surface with soft radiance; (of the eyes, sky) shining softly; (of humour, wit) gently brilliant. (文) (指火或光) 輕輕搖曳的;(指眼睛或天空)微微發亮的;(指幽默,機智)巧妙的。 **lam·bency** /-ənsɪ ; -ənsɪ/ *n*

lame /leɪm ; lem/ *adj* **1** not able to walk normally because of an injury or defect: 跛的: *~ in the left leg.* 左腿跛。 ***~ duck,*** ⇨ duck¹(1). **2** (of an excuse, argument, etc) unconvincing; unsatisfactory. (指辯解,論據等)不能說服人的;令人不滿意的。 **3** (of metre) halting. (指詩的韻律)不合詩韻的。□ *vt* make ~. 使跛。 **~·ly** *adv* **~·ness** *n*

lamé /ˈlɑ:meɪ *US:* lɑ:ˈmeɪ ; lɑˈme/ *n* [U] fabric with metal threads interwoven. 金屬絲織物。

la·ment /ləˈment ; ləˈmɛnt/ *vt, vi* [VP6A, 3A, 2A] ***~ (for/over),*** show, feel, express, great sorrow or regret: 悲傷;哀悼;惋惜: *~ the death of a friend;* 哀悼朋友的死; *~ for a friend;* 爲朋友哀傷; *~ (over) one's misfortunes.* 爲自己的不幸而悲傷。□ *n* [C] expression of grief; (music) song or poem expressing grief: 悲傷;哀悼;輓詩;(音樂)悲歌;哀樂: *a funeral ~.* 送葬的哀樂。 **lam·en·table** /ˈlæməntəbl ; ˈlæməntəbḷ/ *adj* regrettable; to be deplored: 令人惋惜的;可悲的: *a ~able* (= poor, unsatisfying) *performance of an opera.* 一歌劇之令人惋惜的演出(卽演出失敗)。 **ˈlam·en·tably** /-əblɪ ; -əblɪ/ *adv* **lam·en·ta·tion** /ˌlæmenˈteɪʃn ; ˌlæmənˈteʃən/ *n* [U] ~ing; [C] ~; expression of grief. 悲傷;哀悼;哀傷。

lami·nate /ˈlæmɪneɪt ; ˈlæməˌnet/ *vt, vi* [VP6A, 2A] beat or roll (metal) into thin plates; split into layers; manufacture by placing layer on layer; cover with metal plates: 鎚打或輾壓(金屬)成薄片; 破開使成薄片; 用疊片製造; 覆以金屬片: *~d wood/plastics,* of layers one over the other. 層板(疊合塑膠板)。

Lam·mas /ˈlæməs ; ˈlæməs/ *n* (hist) 1st August, formerly a harvest festival in England. (史)(昔時英國之)收穫節(八月一日)。

lamp /læmp ; læmp/ *n* container with oil and wick, used to give light; (in modern times) any apparatus for giving light (from gas, electricity, etc).

油燈;(近代用法)燈(指任何發光之燈,如煤氣燈,電燈等)。 '~-**black** *n* [U] black colouring matter made from the soot of burning oil, formerly used in making paint and printing-ink. 燈黑;燈烟;油烟(昔時用以製顏料和油墨)。 '~•**light** *n* [U] light from a ~: 燈光: *read by ~light.* 藉燈光看書。 '~•**lighter** *n* (hist) man who went round the streets to light public ~s (when gas was used). (史)(用煤氣燈時代)點燃路燈之燈夫。 '~-**post** *n* (usu metal) post for a street ~. 街燈柱(通常是金屬的)。 '~•**shade** *n* globe of glass, screen of silk, parchment, etc placed round or over a lamp. 燈罩。

lam•poon /læm'puːn ; læm'pun/ *n* [C] piece of satirical writing attacking and ridiculing sb. 攻擊和譏諷的文章。□ *vt* [VP6A] write a ~ against. 寫文章攻擊和諷刺。

lam•prey /'læmprɪ ; 'læmprɪ/ *n* (*pl* ~s) eel-like water animal. 八目鰻(一種似黃鱔的水生動物)。

lance¹ /lɑːns *US:* læns ; læns/ *n* (hist) weapon with a long wooden shaft and a pointed steel head used by a horseman; similar instrument used for spearing fish. (史)騎兵用的長矛;魚叉。,~-'**corporal** *n* grade of non-commissioned officer in the army. (英)陸軍代理下士(領上等兵薪水)。 **~r** *n* soldier of a cavalry regiment originally armed with ~s. 槍騎兵。**~rs** *n pl* (with *sing v*) (music for a) dance for four or more couples. (與單數動詞連用)由四對或多於四對所跳的一種舞;此種舞曲。

lance² /lɑːns *US:* læns ; læns/ *vt* [VP6A] cut open, prick, with a lancet: 以刺血針切開或刺破: *~ an abscess.* 以刺血針刺破一膿瘡。

lan•cet /'lɑːnsɪt *US:* 'læn- ; 'lænsɪt/ *n* **1** pointed, two-edged knife used by surgeons. 刺血針;柳葉刀(外科醫生用的雙刃小尖刀)。**2** (archit) high, narrow, pointed arch or window. (建築)尖頂拱門或窗戶。

land¹ /lænd ; lænd/ *n* **1** [U] solid part of the earth's surface (contrasted with *sea, water*): 陸地(與 sea, water 相對): *travel over ~ and sea;* 在陸上和海上旅行; *come in sight of ~;* 看見陸地; *glad to be on ~/to reach ~/to come to ~ again;* 很高興重登陸地; *a ~ breeze,* one blowing from the land towards the sea (after sunset); 陸風(日落後由陸上吹向海上的微風); *~-based aircraft,* using bases on ~ (contrasted with aircraft based on carriers). 陸上基地的飛機(以別於航空母艦上者)。*Are you going by ~ or by sea,* by train, car, etc, or by boat? 你將由陸路還是海路去? ***make ~,*** see, reach the shore. 見到岸;抵岸。***see/find out how the '~ lies,*** ⇨ lie²(4). **2** [U] ground, earth, as used for farming, etc: 土地;田地: *working on the ~;* 在農田工作; *'~-workers;* 農田工人; *rough and stony ~.* 崎嶇多石的土地。 '~ **army,** (GB) body of women farm workers in World War II. (英)二次大戰期間的農田女工。**3** [U] property in the form of ~: 地產: *How far does your ~ extend?* 你的地產伸展多遠? *Do you own much ~ here?* 你在此地有很多地產嗎? '~-**agent,** (chiefly GB) person employed to manage an estate; person who buys and sells estates (US 美 = *real estate agent*). (主英)地產管理人;地產經紀人。**4** (*pl*) estate; area of ~ with the trees, etc on it: (複)地產;(含樹木等在內的)所有地: *own houses and ~s.* 擁有房地產。**5** country and its people (liter or emotive in this sense, *country* being the ordinary word): 國土;國家(爲文學上或含有感情的用語, country 一字是普通用語): *my native ~;* 我的祖國; *visit distant ~s.* 遊歷遙遠的國家。 ***the ~ of the living,*** this present existence. 現世。**the Promised L~, the L~ of Promise,** Canaan /'keɪnən ; 'kenən/, promised by God to the Israelites. 迦南地(上帝應許賜予以色列人的土地)。**6** (compounds, etc) (複合字等) '~•**fall** *n* approach to ~, esp for the first time during a voyage: 接近陸地(尤指航行中初次發現陸地): *a good ~fall,* one that corresponds well to the calculations made by the ship's officers. 如期見到陸地。 '~ **forces** *n pl* military forces (not naval). 陸軍。 '~•**holder** *n* owner or (more usu) tenant of ~. 地主;(較常指)租地人。 '~•**lady** *n* (*pl* -ladies) woman who owns a house which she leases to a tenant, or who rents a house, rooms of which she sublets to tenants: 女房東: *owe one's ~lady a month's rent.* 欠女房東一個月房租。 '~-**locked** *adj* (of a bay, harbour, etc) almost or entirely surrounded by ~. (指海灣,港口等)幾乎全爲陸地包圍的。 '~•**lord** *n* **(a)** person from whom another rents ~ or building(s). 地主;房東。**(b)** keeper of an inn, a public house, a boarding-house or lodging-house. 旅社、酒館或寄宿舍之主人。 '~-**lubber** /lʌbə(r) ; ˌlʌbɚ/ *n* (used by sailors to describe a) person not accustomed to the sea and ships. (船員用語)不習慣海上生活及船上事物者。 '~•**mark** *n* [C] **(a)** object that marks the boundary of a piece of ~. 界標。**(b)** object, etc easily seen from a distance and helpful to travellers (eg navigating officers of a ship). 易自遠處看見並對旅行者(例如船上的航行人員)有幫助的目標;陸標。**(c)** (fig) event, discovery, change, etc that marks a stage or turning-point: (喻)劃時代的大事、發現、變化等; 里程碑: *~marks in the history of mankind.* 人類歷史上劃時代的事件。 '~•**mine** *n* [C] explosive charge laid in or on the ground or dropped by parachute and exploded by vehicles passing over it. (埋於地下,置於地上或由飛機用降落傘投下的)地雷。 '~•**owner** *n* owner of ~. 地主。 '**L~•rover** *n* (P) strongly-built motor vehicle for use over rough ground. (商標)用以行駛崎嶇陸地的堅固車輛。 '~•**slide** *n* [C] **(a)** sliding down of a mass of earth, rock, etc from the side of a cliff, hillside, railway cutting, etc. 山崩;土崩;坍方。 **(b)** sudden change in political opinion resulting in an overwhelming majority of votes for one side in an election: 選舉中獲壓倒性多數票: *a Democratic ~slide,* a great victory for the Democratic party. 民主黨的大勝利。 '~•**slip** *n* = ~slide(a). '~**s•man** /-mən ; -mən/ *n* (*pl* -men) person who is not a sailor. 陸居者(以別於海員)。

land² /lænd ; lænd/ *vt, vi* **1** [VP6A, 2A, C] go, come, put, on ~ (from a ship, aircraft, etc): (自船,飛機等)(使)登岸;(使)登陸;(使)着陸: *The passengers ~ed/were ~ed as soon as the ship reached harbour.* 船剛一抵港,乘客們卽迅速地登岸。*We ~ed at Bombay.* 我們在孟買登陸。*The airliner ~ed safely.* 該客機安全降落了。*The pilot ~ed the airliner safely.* 駕駛員使那客機安全降落。⇨ also *crash-~* at crash¹ and *soft~* at soft. ***~ on one's feet,*** (fig) be lucky; escape injury. (喻)幸運;逃脫傷害。**2** ***~ sb/oneself in sth,*** get into (trouble, difficulties, etc): 使處於(麻煩、困難等中): *What a mess you've ~ed us all in!* 你看你爲我們大家惹來多少麻煩! ***~ up,*** (colloq) arrive; find oneself: (俗)到達;處於: *If you go on behaving in this way, you'll ~ up in prison one day.* 你如果繼續這種行爲,有一天你會坐牢。*Tom has been away for months, but he'll ~ up one of these days.* 湯姆已離開數月,但這幾天他會回來。*She ~ed up in a strange city without any money or friends.* 她到達一個陌生的城市,沒有錢或朋友。 **3** [VP6A] (colloq) obtain: (俗)得到: *~ a good job/a contract for building a factory.* 獲得一良好工作(建一工廠之合同)。**4** [VP12C] (sl) strike (a blow): (俚)擊;打: *She ~ed him one in the eye.* 她在他眼睛上打了一拳。**~ed** *adj* **1** consisting of ~: 含有土地的: *~ed property.* 地產。**2** owning ~: 擁有土地的: *the ~ed classes/gentry.* 地主階級(擁有土地的縉紳)。 **~•less** *adj* without ~; not owning ~. 無土地的;無陸地的;無地產的。

lan•dau /'lændɔː ; 'lændɔ/ *n* (hist) four-wheeled horse-carriage with a folding roof in two sections. (史)分頂式四輪馬車(其折疊式頂篷可分作兩半)。

land•grave /'lændgreɪv ; 'lændˌgrev/ *n* (hist) title of some German princes. (史)德國某些王子的稱號。

land•ing /'lændɪŋ ; 'lændɪŋ/ *n* **1** act of coming or

bringing to land: 登陸;着陸: *the ~ of the Pilgrim Fathers in America.* 1620 年英國清教徒之在美國登陸。*The pilot made an emergency ~.* 該駕駛員作緊急降落。'**~-craft** *n* ship whose bows can be opened up to allow (usu military) vehicles to get ashore without being lifted out. 登陸艇。'**~-field/-strip** *n* area of land for aircraft to take off from and land on. 飛機起落場(起落地帶)。 '**~-gear** *n* undercarriage and wheels of an aircraft. 飛機起落架(包括起落輪)。'**~-net** *n* bag-shaped net on a long handle for landing fish caught with a rod and line. (用以抄取釣上之魚的長柄)袋網。'**~-party** *n* party of armed men who are landed (eg to keep order). (武裝之)登陸隊(例如維持治安者)。 **2** (also 亦作 '**~-place**) place where people and goods may be landed from a boat, etc. (船等)卸貨處;登陸處。'**~-stage** *n* platform (usu floating) on which passengers and goods are landed. 棧橋(通常浮於水上,供人貨登陸者);浮動碼頭。 **3** area at the top of a flight of stairs on to which doors may open. 樓梯平台(一段樓梯頂端之駐脚處,樓上門戶可朝此裝設)。

land·scape /'lændskeɪp ; 'lænskep/ *n* [C] (picture of) inland scenery; [U] branch of art dealing with this. 陸上風景;風景畫;(繪畫之一支)山水畫。ˌ**~ 'gardening/'architecture** *n* [U] the laying out of grounds and gardens in imitation of natural scenery. (模仿天然景色的)庭園佈置。

lane /leɪn ; len/ *n* **1** narrow country road, usu between hedges or banks. 鄉村小道(通常在籬或坡間);小徑。 **2** (usu as part of a proper name) narrow street or alley between buildings: (通常爲專有名稱之一部)巷;衖: *Drury L~.* 杜里巷。 **3** passage made or left between lines of persons. 兩列人間的通路。 **4** route regularly used by ships or aircraft. (船或飛機之定期)航線;航路。 **5** marked division of a wide road for the guidance of motorists; line of vehicles within such a division: (寬大馬路上用白線畫出的)車道;在車道內行駛的一列車輛: *the inside/nearside ~;* 內車道(外車道); *the outside/offside ~;* 外車道(內車道); *four-~ traffic.* 四線交通。 **6** marked course for a competitor in a race (eg on a running track or a swimming pool). 競賽中爲比賽者畫出之道(例如賽跑之跑道或游泳之水道)。

lang·syne /ˌlæŋ'saɪn ; 'læŋ'saɪn/ *adv, n* (Scot) (in) the old days; (in) past time. (蘇)昔日;往時;往昔。

lan·guage /'læŋgwɪdʒ ; 'læŋgwɪdʒ/ *n* **1** [U] human and non-instinctive method of communicating ideas, feelings and desires by means of a system of sounds and sound symbols. 語言。 **2** [C] form of ~ used by a group: 一群人所用的語言: *the ~s of Asia;* 亞洲的各種語言; *foreign ~s.* 外國語。 ***dead ~***, one no longer in spoken use (eg classical Greek). 死的語文 (不再被使用者,例如古希臘文)。 '**~ laboratory**, classroom(s) where ~s are taught using tape-recorders, etc. 語言教室;語言實驗室。 **3** [U] manner of using words: 用語文的方式: *a person with a good command of ~*, person who is fluent or eloquent. 善於詞令之人。 **4** [U] words, phrases, etc used by a profession or class: 專門語;術語: *technical/legal ~;* 專門(法律)術語; *the ~ of diplomacy.* 外交界的術語。 **5** [U] **bad ~; strong ~**, language full of oaths, violent words, etc. 粗野的話語。 **6** [U, C] system of signs used as ~: 用做語言的一套符號: *com'puter ~*, ordered system for giving instructions to a computer; 電腦語言 (指示電腦作業的一套方法); '*finger ~*, as used by deaf and dumb persons; 手語(聾啞之人所用者); *the ~ of flowers;* 以花表示情感的方法; *the ~ of algebra.* 代數語。

lan·guid /'læŋgwɪd ; 'læŋgwɪd/ *adj* lacking in energy; slow-moving. 無精神的;不活潑的;行動遲緩的。 **~·ly** *adv*

lan·guish /'læŋgwɪʃ ; 'læŋgwɪʃ/ *vi* [VP2A, C] be or become languid; lose health and strength; be unhappy because of a desire (*for* sth): 無生氣;變得衰弱無力;因渴望而煩惱(與 for 連用,後接某事物): *~ in prison;* 在獄中變得衰弱無力; *~ for love and sympathy.* 因渴望愛情和同情而煩惱。 *She gave the young man a ~ing look,* one that suggested a desire for love or sympathy. 她向那青年作渴望愛情或同情的一瞥。

lan·guor /'læŋgə(r) ; 'læŋgɚ/ *n* **1** [U] weakness of body (as produced by hard work) or of spirit (as produced by sorrow or an unhappy love affair); lack of life or movement; stillness or heaviness: (辛苦工作引起的)身體衰弱;(悲傷或失戀引起的)精神消沉;無精打采;沉悶;低沉: *the ~ of a summer day.* 夏日的沉悶。 **2** (often *pl*) soft or tender mood. (常用複數)柔情。 **~·ous** /-əs ; -əs/ *adj* **~·ous·ly** *adv*

lan·gur /lʌŋ'gʊə(r) ; lʌŋ'gʊr/ *n* (kind of) long-tailed monkey. 一種長尾猴。

lank /læŋk ; læŋk/ *adj* **1** (of hair) straight and lying limp or flat. (指髮)平直的。 **2** tall and lean. 瘦長的。

lanky /'læŋkɪ ; 'læŋkɪ/ *adj* (-ier, -iest) (of a person, his arms or legs) long and lean in an ungraceful way: (指人,四肢)瘦長的;細長而難看的: *a ~, overgrown girl.* 一個長得太高的瘦長女孩。

lano·lin /'lænəlɪn ; 'lænəlɪn/ *n* [U] fat extracted from sheep's wool used as the basis of ointments for the skin. 羊毛脂(供製潤膚膏)。

lan·tern /'læntən ; 'læntɚn/ *n* case (usu metal and glass) protecting a light from the wind, etc, outdoors. 燈籠;提燈。 ⇨ dark²(1), magic. '**~-jawed** *adj* having long and thin jaws so that the face has a hollow look. 下巴長而瘦削的。

lan·yard /'lænjəd ; 'lænjɚd/ *n* **1** cord (worn by sailors and soldiers) for a whistle or knife. (水手或士兵用以)懸哨子或小刀的繩索。 **2** short rope used on a ship for fastening or moving sth. 船上繫物或搬動東西之短索;小索。

lap¹ /læp ; læp/ *n* front part of a person's legs from the waist to the knees, when sitting, as the place on which a child is nursed or sth held: 人坐着時自腰至膝之部分;大腿前部(可放置嬰兒或東西之處): *The mother had the baby on her lap.* 母親把嬰兒放在腿上。 ***be/live in the lap of luxury,*** in fortunate and luxurious circumstances. 生活在幸福奢侈的環境中。 ***in the lap of the gods,*** (of future events) uncertain. (指未來事件) 不確定的。 '**lap-dog** *n* small pet dog. 寵愛的小狗。

lap² /læp ; læp/ *vt, vi* (-pp-) **1** [VP15B] wrap or fold (cloth, etc) *round* or *in.* 包裹;纏繞(布等)於(後接 round 或 in)。 **2** [VP6A, 2A, C] (cause to) overlap: (使)重疊: *Put the slates on the roof so that they lap over.* 將石板瓦鱗比地安放於屋頂上。⇨ overlap. □ *n* **1** amount by which one thing laps over. 重疊部分。 **2** one circuit round a track or race-course: (競賽跑道之)一圈: *Smith overtook the other runners/riders/drivers on the last lap.* 史密斯於最後一圈追上了其他的賽跑者(騎馬者,駕駛者)。

lap³ /læp ; læp/ *vi, vt* (-pp-) **1** [VP15B] ***lap up,*** drink by taking up with the tongue, as a cat does: 舐;舔食: *The cat quickly lapped up all the milk.* 那貓很快地將所有的牛奶舐光了。 **2** (colloq) (of human beings) take quickly or eagerly: (俗)(指人)迅速或急切地接受: *lap up compliments.* 愛聽恭維的話。 **3** [VP2A, C] (of water) move with a sound like the lapping up of liquid: (指水)輕拍;冲拍: *waves lapping on the beach;* 輕拍海灘的波浪; *water lapping against the sides of a canoe.* 輕拍着小舟兩側的水。 **4** [VP6A] (in a race) become ahead of by a lap²(2). (競賽)以一圈領先。□ *n* **1** act of lapping: 舐;舔食: *The dog emptied the plate with three laps of the tongue.* 那狗舐了三次便將盤中的食物舐乾淨了。 **2** [U] sound of lapping: 水的輕拍聲: *the lap of the waves against the side of the boat.* 波浪沖擊船側的輕拍聲。

la·pel /lə'pel ; lə'pɛl/ *n* part of the breast of a coat or jacket folded back and forming a continuation of the collar. 西服上衣的翻領。

lapi·dary /'læpɪdərɪ *US:* -derɪ ; 'læpə,dɛrɪ/ *adj* cut on stone; (fig) neat; precise: 刻於石上的;(喻)整齊的;精確的: *a ~ inscription/speech.* 刻在石上的題銘(精確的演說)。□ *n* person who cuts, polishes or engraves, gems. 寶石匠。

lap·is la·zuli /,læpɪs 'læzjʊlɪ *US:* 'læʒəlɪ ; 'læpɪs'læzjə,laɪ/ *n* [U, C] bright blue semi-precious stone; its colour. 青金石;璧琉璃;金精;天藍色。

lapse /læps ; læps/ *n* [C] **1** slight error in speech or behaviour; slip of the memory, tongue or pen. 言行上些微的差錯;記錯;失言;筆誤。**2** *~ (from) (into),* falling away from what is right: 過失;錯誤: *a ~ from virtue;* 道德上的過失(墮落); *a ~ from true belief into heresy.* 背棄眞正信仰,相信異端邪說。 **3** (of time) passing away; interval: (指時間)流逝;間歇: *the ~ of time;* 時間的流逝; *a long ~ of time.* 一段長時間。 **4** (legal) ending of a right, etc from failure to use it or ask for its renewal. (法律)權利等的終止或喪失(因未加使用或未要求賡續所致)。□ *vi* **1** [VP2A, 3A] *~ (from) (into),* fail to keep one's position; fall (from good ways into bad ways): 失足;墮落: *~ from virtue into vice;* 墮落; *~ into bad habits;* 養成惡習; *a ~d Catholic.* 叛教的天主教徒。 **2** [VP2A] (legal) (of rights and privileges) be lost because not used, claimed or renewed. (法律)(指權利及特權因未使用,未要求或未賡續而)終止;失效。

lap·wing /'læpwɪŋ ; 'læp,wɪŋ/ *n* bird of the plover family; pewit. 田鳧(千鳥之類);京燕。

lar·board /'lɑ:bəd ; 'lɑrbɚd/ *n, adj* left side of a ship when looking forward (now always called 現常稱作 the *port* side). 左舷(的)。⇨ starboard.

lar·ceny /'lɑ:sənɪ ; 'lɑrsn̩ɪ/ *n* (*pl* -nies) [U] (legal) stealing; theft; [C] instance of this. (法律)竊盜罪;偷竊。

larch /lɑ:tʃ ; lɑrtʃ/ *n* [C] deciduous tree with small cones and light-green leaves; [U] its wood. 落葉松;落葉松木。

lard /lɑ:d ; lɑrd/ *n* [U] fat of pigs prepared for use in cooking. 豬油。□ *vt* [VP6A] put ~ on; put pieces of bacon into or on (meat, etc) before cooking, in order to add to the flavour. 塗豬油於;於烹調前塞塡或加添鹹肉於(肉等)以增其味。 ***~ with,*** (fig, often derog) enrich: (喻,常爲貶抑語)以…充實;潤飾: *a speech ~ed with boring quotations.* 充滿令人厭惡的引用文句的一篇演說。

lar·der /'lɑ:də(r) ; 'lɑrdɚ/ *n* room or cupboard where meat and other kinds of food are stored. 肉及其他食物的貯藏室;伙食房;食橱。

large /lɑ:dʒ ; lɑrdʒ/ *adj* (-r, -st) **1** of considerable size; taking up much space; able to contain much: 大的;巨大的;容量大的: *A man with a ~ family needs a ~ house.* 有一大家庭的人需要一所大房子。 *She inherited a ~ fortune.* 她繼承了一大筆財產。 ***as ~ as life,*** ⇨ life(10). (Note that *large* is less colloq than *big* and not so emotive as *great*. 'A great city' is large, but the use of 'great' suggests that it is also important or famous. *Large* is seldom used of persons, but note ***~ of limb,*** having ~ limbs.) (注意: large 一字不如 big 通俗,亦不如 great 帶有感情。'a great city' 不僅指一城市的面積大,而且含有 '重要' 或 '著名' 的意思。large 很少用以形容人,但可形容四肢,如 ~ of limb, 四肢粗大。) **'~-scale** *adj* **(a)** extensive: 大規模的: *~-scale operations.* 大規模的軍事行動。 **(b)** made or drawn to a ~ scale: 大比例尺繪製的: *a ~-scale map.* 大比例尺繪製的地圖。 **2** liberal; generous; unprejudiced (chiefly in the following): 寬大的;慷慨的;大公無私的(主要用於下列文詞): *a ~ heart,* 寬大的心胸, hence, 由此產生, *,~-'hearted;* 寬大爲懷的; *,~-'minded,* 寬宏大量的, hence, 由此產生, *,~-'mindedness.* 寬宏大量。 **3** of wide range; not confined or restricted: 廣濶的;廣泛的;無限制的: *give an official ~ powers/discretion;* 給予一官員廣泛的權力(自由處理權); *a man with ~ ideas;* 思想廣濶的人; *~ and small farmers,* men farming on a ~ and a small scale. 大農場主人和小規模自耕農。□ *n* (only in) (僅用於) ***at ~,*** **(a)** at liberty; free: 自由的;自由行動的: *The escaped prisoner is still at ~.* 該逃犯仍逍遙法外。 **(b)** at full length; with details: 詳細地;仔細地: *to talk/write at ~.* 詳細地說(寫)。 **(c)** in general: 一般的: *Did the people at ~ approve of the government's policy?* 一般老百姓贊成政府的政策嗎? **(d)** at random; without definite aim: 隨便地;無目標地: *scatter accusations at ~.* 隨便指控。□ *adv* **1** (only in) (僅用於) ***bulk/loom/writ ~,*** ⇨ bulk, loom², write(6). ***by and ~,*** ⇨ by¹(4). **2** boastfully: 誇大地: *talk ~.* 誇其詞;說大話。**~·ish** /-ɪʃ ; -ɪʃ/ *adj* rather ~. 頗大的。 **~·ly** *adv* **1** to a great extent: 大部分;大半: *His success was ~ly due to luck.* 他的成功大都由於幸運。 **2** generously; freely: 慷慨地;大方地: *He gives ~ly to charity.* 他慷慨捐助慈善事業。**~·ness** *n*

lar·gesse (US also **lar·gess**) /lɑ:'dʒes ; 'lɑrdʒɪs/ *n* [U] generous or excessive giving; money or other things generously or excessively given. 慷慨的贈與;慷慨的贈金或贈物。

largo /'lɑ:gəʊ ; 'lɑrgo/ *n* (*pl* ~s /-gəʊz ; -goz/), *adv* (piece of music, movement) in very slow and solemn time. 緩慢地;緩慢的音樂或樂章;最緩板。

lar·iat /'lærɪət ; 'lærɪət/ *n* rope for tethering a horse; long rope with a noose; lasso. 繫馬於樁上之繩;一端有活結之長繩;套索。

lark¹ /lɑ:k ; lɑrk/ *n* small songbird, esp the skylark. 小鳴禽;(尤指)鷚;雲雀;百靈鳥。⇨ the illus at bird. 參看 bird 之插圖。

lark² /lɑ:k ; lɑrk/ *n* [C] bit of fun; frolic: 歡樂;嬉戲;樂趣: *Boys are fond of having a ~.* 男孩子喜歡嬉戲。 *He did it for a ~,* in fun. 他是爲了好玩而做的。 *What a ~!* How amusing! 眞有趣! □ *vi* [VP2A, C] play pranks: 戲謔;玩樂: *Stop ~ing about and get on with your work.* 不要玩樂,去做你的工作。

lark·spur /'lɑ:kspɜ:(r) ; 'lɑrk,spɝ/ *n* tall garden plant with blue, white or pink flowers. 飛燕草(一種高的園藝植物,開藍、白或粉紅色花)。

larn /lɑ:n ; lɑrn/ *vt, vi* (dial) learn. (方)學習。

larva /'lɑ:və ; 'lɑrvə/ *n* (*pl* ~e /-vi: ; -vi/) insect in the first stage of its life-history, after coming out of the egg. 昆蟲的幼蟲。⇨ the illus at butterfly. 參看 butterfly 之插圖。 **lar·val** /'lɑ:vl ; 'lɑrvl̩/ *adj* of or in the form of a ~. 幼蟲的;幼蟲狀的。

lar·ynx /'lærɪŋks ; 'lærɪŋks/ *n* (anat) upper part of the windpipe where the vocal cords are. (解剖)喉。⇨ the illus at head. 參看 head 之插圖。 **lar·yn·gi·tis** /,lærɪn'dʒaɪtɪs ; ,lærɪn'dʒaɪtɪs/ *n* [U] inflammation of the ~. 喉炎。

las·car /'læskə(r) ; 'læskɚ/ *n* seaman from the East Indies. 東印度水手。

las·civ·ious /lə'sɪvɪəs ; lə'sɪvɪəs/ *adj* feeling, causing, expressing, lust. 淫蕩的; 挑動春情的; 猥褻的。 **~·ly** *adv* **~·ness** *n*

laser /'leɪzə(r) ; 'lezɚ/ *n* device for generating, amplifying and concentrating light waves into an intense beam in one specific direction: 雷射(產生和擴大光波,並將其聚成强烈光柱之裝置): (attrib) (形容用法) *~ beams.* 雷射光柱。

lash¹ /læʃ ; læʃ/ *n* **1** part of a whip with which strokes are given; (usu leather) thong; blow or stroke given with a ~: 鞭之抽打或皮條部分;細縛用的(皮)帶;鞭撻: *He was given twenty ~es.* 他挨了二十鞭。 **the ~,** punishment of flogging: 鞭打(刑罰): *mutinous sailors sentenced to the ~;* 被判鞭打的叛變的水手; (fig) (喩) *the ~ of criticism;* 嚴酷的批評;譏刺; *the ~ of an angry woman's tongue.* 一憤怒女子的漫罵。 **2** = eyelash.

lash² /læʃ ; læʃ/ *vt, vi* **1** [VP6A, 14, 2C] strike violently; make a sudden movement of (a limb,

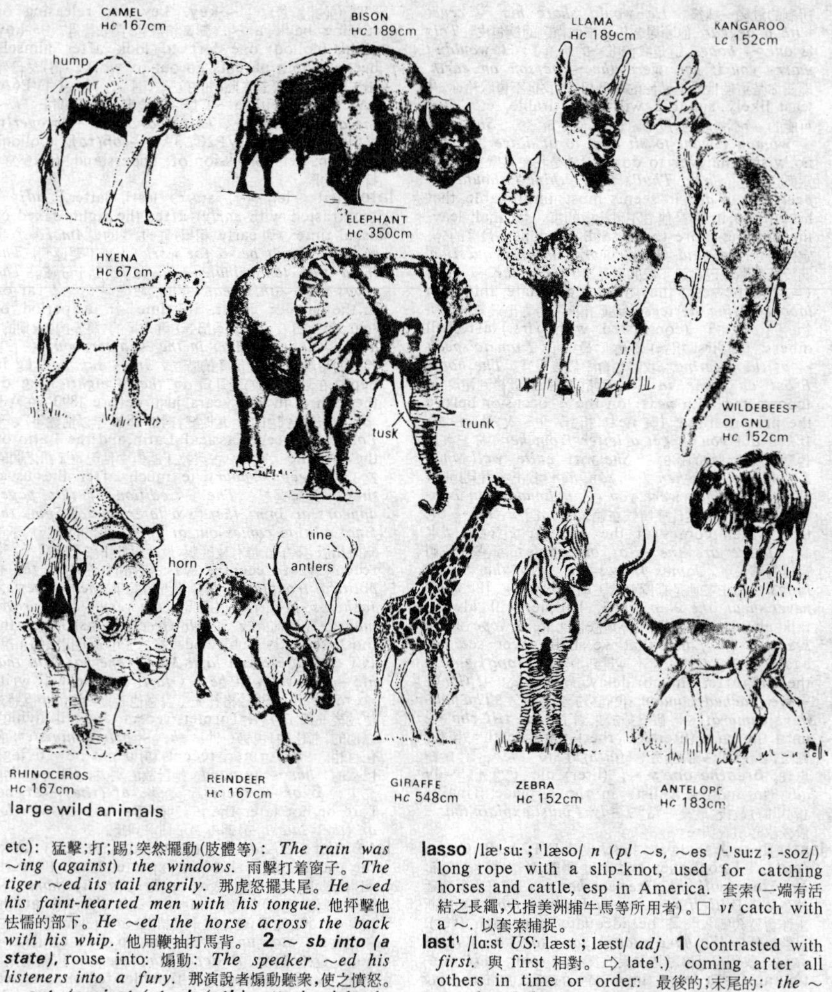

large wild animals

etc): 猛擊;打;踢;突然擺動(肢體等): *The rain was ~ing (against) the windows.* 雨擊打着窗子。*The tiger ~ed its tail angrily.* 那虎怒擺其尾。*He ~ed his faint-hearted men with his tongue.* 他抨擊他怯懦的部下。*He ~ed the horse across the back with his whip.* 他用鞭抽打馬背。 **2** *~ **sb into (a state),*** rouse into: 煽動: *The speaker ~ed his listeners into a fury.* 那演說者煽動聽衆,使之憤怒。 ***~ out (against/at sb/sth),*** attack violently (with blows or words): 攻擊;抨擊: *The horse ~ed out at me,* kicked or tried to kick, me 那馬(想)踢我。*The speaker ~ed out against the government.* 那演說者抨擊政府。 **3** [VP15A, B] ***~ one thing to another; ~ things together,*** fasten tightly together (with rope, etc). (用繩等)將一物與另一物牢繫在一起。***~ sth down,*** make it secure with rope, etc. 綑緊某物。 '**~-up** *n* improvised or roughly constructed piece of apparatus. 臨時拼湊的器具。

lash·ing /ˈlæʃɪŋ; ˈlæʃɪŋ/ *n* **1** [C] cord or rope used for binding or fastening. 綑縛用的繩子。 **2** [C] whipping or beating. 鞭打。 **3** (*pl*, colloq) plenty: (複,俗)許多: *strawberries with ~s of cream;* 拌有許多奶油的草莓; *~s of drink/~s to drink.* 大量飲料。

lass /læs; læs/ *n* girl; sweetheart. 少女;愛人。

las·sie /ˈlæsɪ; ˈlæsɪ/ *n* = lass.

lassi·tude /ˈlæsɪtjuːd *US:* -tuːd; ˈlæsəˌtjud/ *n* [U] tiredness; state of being uninterested in things. 倦怠;對事物缺乏興趣;厭倦。

lasso /læˈsuː; ˈlæso/ *n* (*pl* ~s, ~es /-ˈsuːz; -soz/) long rope with a slip-knot, used for catching horses and cattle, esp in America. 套索(一端有活結之長繩,尤指美洲捕牛馬等所用者)。□ *vt* catch with a ~. 以套索捕捉。

last[1] /lɑːst *US:* læst; læst/ *adj* **1** (contrasted with *first.* 與 first 相對。 ⇨ late[1].) coming after all others in time or order: 最後的;末尾的: *the ~ month of the year;* 一年的最後一月; *the ~ Sunday in June;* 六月的最後一個星期日; *the ~ time I saw you;* 上次我見到你的時候; *the ~ letters of the alphabet,* ie XYZ; 英文字母中最後的幾個字母(即 X Y Z); *the two ~/the ~ two persons to arrive;* 將最後到達的二位; *a ~-minute appeal,* one made just before sth is to be done, decided, etc. 最後一分鐘的懇求。***~ but not least,*** coming at the end, but not least in importance. 最後的但非最不重要的。 ***be on one's ~ legs,*** ⇨ leg(1). ***the L~ Day,*** ⇨ *Doomsday* at doom[1]. ***the ~ post,*** ⇨ post[2]. ***the ~ straw,*** ⇨ straw. ***have the ~ word,*** ⇨ word. **2** (contrasted with *next*) coming immediately before the present: (與 next 相對) 就在現在以前的; 剛過去的: *~ night/week/month/summer/year;* 昨夜(上週;上月;去夏;去年); *on Tuesday ~;* 剛過去的(上或本)星期二; *~ May;* 剛過去的(去年或今年)五月; *in May ~;* 在去年(或今年)五月; *in/for/during the ~ few days/weeks, etc;* 在過去數日(週等)中; *this day ~ week,* a week ago. 上禮拜的今天;一週前。 **3** only remaining: 僅餘的;留在最後的: *He had spent his ~ dollar.* 他已用去他

所剩的最後一塊錢。*He would share his ~ crust with a beggar.* 他願與乞丐分享他僅剩的麵包皮。*This is our ~ hope.* 這是我們唯一的希望了。*I wouldn't marry you if you were the ~ person on earth.* 即使你是這個世界上僅餘的一個男人,我也不會嫁給你。**4** least likely, suitable, willing, desirable, etc: 最不可能的;最不適合的;最不願意的;最不希望的: *She's the ~ woman I want to sit next to at dinner*, I have no wish whatever to do so. 她是我在宴席上最不願意與之隣座的女人。*That's the ~ thing I should expect him to do*, it seems most improbable that he will do it. 那是他最不可能做的事。**5** final; leaving nothing more to be said or done: 最終的;決定性的: *I've said my ~ word on this question.* 關於此問題我已盡述了我的意見。*This is the ~ thing* (= the newest, the most up-to-date, thing) *in labour-saving devices.* 這是在節省勞力上最新的發明物。□ *adv* **1** (contrasted with *first*) after all others: (與 first 相對)最後地;最末了: *I am to speak ~ at the meeting.* 我將在會中最後發言。*The horse I bet on came in ~.* 我賭的那匹馬最後到達。**2** (contrasted with *next*) on the ~ occasion before the present time: (與 next 相對) 上一次;最近一次: *When did you ~ get a letter from her?* 你上次是什麼時候接到她的信的? *She was quite well when I saw her ~/when I ~ saw her.* 我上次看見她時,她很健康。*When were you ~ in London/in London ~?* 你上次是什麼時候在倫敦的? □ *n* ***the ~ of,*** that which comes at the end of: 最後的人或事物: *These are the ~ of our apples.* 這些是我們最後的蘋果了。*James II was the ~ of the Stuart kings.* 詹姆士二世是斯圖亞特王朝最後的一王。*We shall never hear the ~ of this,* People will always talk about it. 人們將不停地談論此事。*I hope we've seen the ~ of her,* that we shall never see her again. 我希望我們永遠不再見到她。***at (long) ~,*** in the end; after (much) delay: 最後;終於: *At (long) ~ we reached London.* 我們終於到達倫敦。*The holidays came at ~.* 假日終於來到了。***to/till the ~,*** until the end; (liter or rhet) until death: 至終;到底;(文學或修辭)至死: *faithful to the ~.* 始終忠實。***breathe one's ~,*** (liter) die. (文)死。**~·ly** *adv* (in making a list) in the ~ place; finally: (列舉時)最後;最後一點: *L~ly I must explain that....* 最後我必須說明…。

last[2] /lɑːst *US:* læst ; læst/ *vi* [VP2A, B, C] ~ ***(out),*** **1** continue; endure: 繼續;延續;持久;維持: *How long will the fine weather ~?* 這好天氣會延續多久? *Will Jim ~ out in his new job?* 吉姆的新工作會持久嗎? **2** be adequate or enough (for): 足够維持: *We have enough food to ~ (us) three days.* 我們有足够維持三天的食糧。**~·ing** *adj* continuing for a long time: 持久的;恆久的: *a ~ing peace.* 持久的和平。

last[3] /lɑːst *US:* læst ; læst/ *n* block of wood shaped like a foot for making shoes on. 鞋楦(製鞋用的模型)。***stick to one's ~,*** not try to do things one cannot do well. 守本分;做不好的事情不做。

L

latch /lætʃ ; lætʃ/ *n* **1** simple fastening for a door or gate, the bar falling into a catch and being lifted by a small lever. 門閂。**2** small spring lock for a door opened from outside with a ~key. (自外面用門鎖鑰匙啓開的)小彈簧鎖;門鎖。***on the ~,*** fastened with a ~, but not locked. 栓着門閂(並非鎖着)。**'~·key,** key for releasing or turning back a ~. 彈簧鎖鑰匙;門鎖鑰匙。**'~key child,** (colloq) one left to look after himself because both parents go out to work. (俗)父母外出工作留在家裏乏人照顧的孩子。□ *vt, vi* **1** [VP6A, 2A] fasten with a ~: 以門閂栓牢;以門閂關上: *L~ the doors.* 把門栓上。*This door won't ~ properly.* 這門閂不牢。**2** [VP2C, 3A] ~ ***on(to),*** (colloq) cling to; get possession of; understand. (俗)堅守;持有;了解。

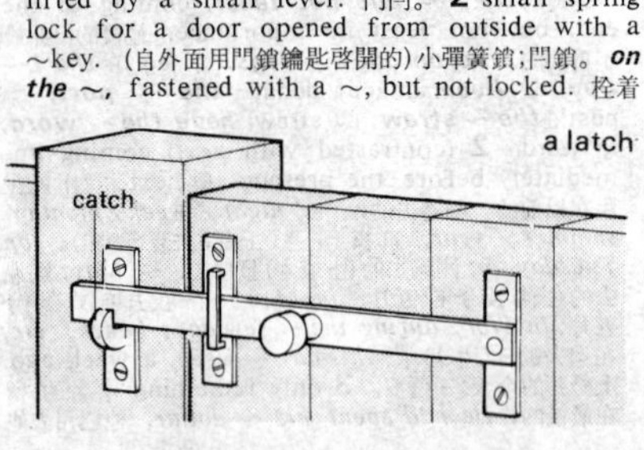

late[1] /leɪt ; let/ (-r, -st. ⇨ last[1], latter.) *adj* **1** (contrasted with *early*) after the right, fixed or usual time: (與 early 相對)遲的;晚的: *Am I ~?* 我晚了嗎? *Don't be ~ for work.* 上班不要遲到。*The train was ten minutes ~.* 火車誤點十分鐘。*The crops are ~ this year.* 今年的收穫遲了。**2** far on in the day or night, in time, in a period or season: (日夜,時間,季節等) 近末尾的;將盡的;末期的: *at a ~ hour;* 在深夜; *in the ~ afternoon;* 在下午將盡的時候;在接近傍晚的時候; *in ~ summer*, eg in Sept; 在夏末(例如九月); *in the ~ eighties*, eg of the 19th c, in the years just before 1890; 在八十年代的末期(例如在十九世紀,則指 1890 年以前數年); *~ Latin,* between classical Latin and the Latin of the Middle Ages; 古典拉丁語與中世紀拉丁語之間的拉丁語; *keep ~ hours,* ie much after the usual times. 遲睡遲起。*The ~ edition of this paper appears at 3pm; there's a later one at 5pm; the final edition comes out at 7pm.* 此報的晚版於下午三時出版,下午五時有較晚版,最晚版於下午七時發行。**3** recent; that recently was: 近時的;近來的: *the ~ political troubles;* 近來政治上的紛爭; *the ~st news/fashions;* 最近的消息(風尚); *the very ~st improvements;* 不久前的改善; *Mr Greene's ~st novel,* the most recently published. 格林先生新近出版的小說。(Cf 參較 *latest* and *last: Mr Greene has said that his ~st novel will be his last,* that he will write no more novels. 格林先生說過他新近出版的小說將是他最後一部了。) **4** former, recent (and still living): 以前的;前任的(現仍在世): *the ~ prime minister.* 前任首相。**5** former, recent (and not now living): 已故的: *her ~ husband;* 她已故的丈夫; *the ~ King.* 先王。**6** ***of ~,*** recently. 近來。***at (the) ~st,*** before or not later than: 最遲: *Be here on Monday at (the) latest.* 最遲不過星期一到此。

late[2] /leɪt ; let/ *adv* **1** (contrasted with *early*) after the usual, right, fixed or expected time: (與 early 相對)遲;晚: *get up/go to bed/arrive home ~;* 起床(睡覺,到家)很晚; *marry ~ in life,* eg at the age of 50; 晚婚(例如五十歲結婚); *two years ~r;* 二年後; *sit/stay up ~,* not go to bed until a ~ hour. 遲睡;熬夜。*Better ~ than never.* 遲做總比不做好。***~ in the day,*** ~r than desired or expected. 較期望者爲晚。***~r on,*** at a ~r time; afterwards: 後來;以後: *a few days ~r on;* 數日後; *as we shall see ~r on.* 正如我們以後將要看到的。***early and ~,*** at all hours: 從早到晚: *He's at his desk early and ~.* 他一天到晚在桌前工作。***sooner or ~r,*** some time or other. 遲早;總有一天。**2** recently: 近來;新近: *I saw him as ~ as/no ~r than yesterday.* 我昨天還看見過他。**lat·ish** /ˈleɪtɪʃ ; ˈletɪʃ/ *adj* rather ~. 稍遲的;稍晚的。

la·teen /ləˈtiːn ; læˈtin/ *adj* (naut) (航海) (only in) (僅用於) ~ ***sail,*** triangular sail on a long yard at an angle of 45° to the mast. 大三角帆(在與桅成 45 度角的長帆桁上)。

late·ly /ˈleɪtlɪ ; ˈletlɪ/ *adv* (usu in neg and interr sentences, or with *only*, or in *as ~ as*) in recent times; recently: (通常用於否定和疑問句,或與 only 連用,或用於片語 as lately as 中)近來;最近: *Have you seen Sam ~?* 你近來看見過山姆嗎? *I haven't been home ~.* 我最近沒有回過家。(Cf 參較 in the affirm: 在肯定句中: *I saw Sam a few days ago.* 我於數日前看見山姆。*I was home not long ago.* 我不久前在家裏。) *I saw her as ~ as last Sunday.* 我上星期

天還看見她。*It is only ～ that she has been well enough to go out.* 她身體復元能够外出還是最近的事。

latent /ˈleɪtnt ; ˈletn̩t/ *adj* present but not yet active, developed or visible: 隱藏的;潛伏的: *～ bacteria;* 潛伏的病菌; *～ energy;* 潛能; *the ～ image on a photographic film,* not visible until the film is developed; 照相軟片上的潛像; *～ abilities.* 潛在的才能。

lat·eral /ˈlætərəl ; ˈlætərəl/ *adj* of, at, from, to, the side(s): 側面的; 從旁邊的;至側面的: *Pinch out the ～ buds to get large chrysanthemum blooms.* 將側生的蕾剪除,使菊花開大。

lat·erite /ˈlætəraɪt ; ˈlætəˌraɪt/ *n* [U] kind of red soil much used for road-making in the tropics. 紅土;紅泥(熱帶地方用以鋪路)。

latex /ˈleɪteks ; ˈletɛks/ *n* [U] milk-white liquid of (esp rubber) plants; emulsion of rubber globules used in paints, etc. 植物之乳汁;(尤指)橡膠乳汁;(用於油漆等中之)乳膠。

lath /lɑːθ *US:* læθ ; læθ/ *n* (*pl* ～s /lɑːðz *US:* læðz ; læðz/) long, thin strip of wood, esp as used in plaster walls and ceilings, and for making trellises, Venetian blinds. 板條(尤指用以做塗灰泥之牆壁和天花板之骨架,與做格子棚,百葉窗者)。

lathe /leɪð ; leð/ *n* machine for holding and turning pieces of wood or metal while they are being shaped, etc. 車床;鏇床。

a lathe

lather /ˈlɑːðə(r) *US:* ˈlæð- ; ˈlæðɚ/ *n* [U] **1** soft mass of white froth from soap and water (as made on a man's face before shaving). 肥皂泡沫(如刮臉前塗於臉上者)。 **2** frothy sweat on a horse. 馬的汗沫。□ *vt, vi* **1** [VP6A] make ～ on: 塗以肥皂泡沫;使生汗沫: *～ one's chin before shaving.* 刮臉前在下巴上塗肥皂泡沫。*The horse was badly ～ed.* 那匹馬滿身是汗。 **2** [VP2A] form ～: (肥皂)起泡沫;(馬)冒汗沫: *Soap does not ～ in sea-water.* 肥皂在海水中不起泡沫。 **3** [VP6A] (colloq) whip or beat. (俗)鞭打;打。

lathi /ˈlɑːtɪ ; ˈlætɪ/ *n* long, iron-bound stick used as a weapon (by the police) in India. 包鐵長杖(印度警察的武器)。

Latin /ˈlætɪn *US:* ˈlætn ; ˈlætn̩/ *n* language of ancient Rome. 拉丁文。□ *adj* of the ～ language; of peoples speaking languages descended from ～ (in Italy, France, Spain, Portugal, etc). 拉丁文的;(義大利,法蘭西,西班牙,葡萄牙等)拉丁語系民族的。 **～ America,** countries of S and Central America in which Spanish and Portuguese are spoken. 拉丁美洲(南美洲及中美洲說西班牙和葡萄牙語諸國)。 **the ～ Church,** the RC Church. 天主教。 **～ cross,** ⇨ the illus at cross. 參看 cross 之插圖。 **the ˈ～ Quarter,** (in Paris) area on the south bank of the Seine, a centre for students and artists for many centuries. 拉丁區(巴黎塞納河南岸一地區,幾百年來爲學生及藝術家薈集之處)。 **～·ist** /-ɪst ; -ɪst/ *n* ～ scholar. 拉丁語文學者。 **～·ize** /-aɪz ; -aɪz/ *vt* give a ～ form to (a word); put (sth) into ～. 使 (一字) 具有拉丁文形式;譯成拉丁文。

lati·tude /ˈlætɪtjuːd *US:* -tuːd ; ˈlætəˌtjud/ *n* **1** [U] distance north or south of the equator measured in degrees. 緯度。⇨ the illus at projection. 參看 projection 之插圖。 **2** (*pl*) regions or districts: (複)地區: *high／low ～s,* places a long way from／near to the equator; 高(低)緯度地區;距赤道遠(近)的地區; *warm ～s.* 熱帶地區。 **3** [U] (measure of) freedom in action or opinion: (行動或言論的)自由;自由的範圍: *Does your government allow much ～ in political belief,* allow people to hold widely different political beliefs? 貴國政府在政治信仰上給予人民很多自由嗎? **4** (photo) time limits within which a film may safely be under- or over-exposed. (攝影)底片安全曝光的時限。 **lati·tudi·nal** /ˌlætɪˈtjuːdɪnl *US:* -ˈtuːdənl ; ˌlætəˈtjudn̩l/ *adj* **lati·tudi·nar·ian** /ˌlætɪtjuːdɪˈneərɪən *US:* -ˌtuːdnˈeər- ; ˌlætəˌtjudn̩ˈɛrɪən/ *adj, n* (person who is) tolerant, broad-minded (esp in religious beliefs and dogmas). (尤指在宗教信仰和教條方面)寬容的;放任的;(對宗教信仰等)放任的人。

la·trine /ləˈtriːn ; ləˈtrin/ *n* (in places where there are no sewers, eg camps) pit or trench to receive human urine and excrement. (營地等無下水道地方之)厠所;便所;茅坑。

lat·ter /ˈlætə(r) ; ˈlætɚ/ *adj* **1** recent; belonging to the end (of a period): 近來的;(一段時期之)末尾的;較後的: *the ～ half of the year.* 下半年。 **ˌ～-ˈday** *adj* modern. 近代的。 **2** (also as 亦用作 *pron*) **the ～,** (contrasted with ***the former***) the second of two things or persons already mentioned: (與 the former 相對)後者: *Of these two men the former is dead, but the ～ is still alive.* 此二人中前者已死,但後者仍活着。 **～·ly** *adv* of late; nowadays. 近來;現今。

lat·tice /ˈlætɪs ; ˈlætɪs/ *n* framework of crossed laths or metal strips as a screen, fence or door, or for climbing plants to grow over: 板條製成的格子架(作爲屛障,籬,門或供植物攀緣);格構: (attrib) (形容用法) *a ～ frame／girder／pylon,* made with iron or steel ～-work. 格構框架(梁,塔)。 **～ window,** one with small square- or diamond-shaped pieces of glass in a framework of lead. 格子窗。⇨ the illus at window. 參看 window 之插圖。 **～d** /ˈlætɪst ; ˈlætɪst/ *adj* made in the form of a ～; provided with a ～. 格子狀的;有格子的。

laud /lɔːd ; lɔd/ *vt* [VP6A] (formal) praise; glorify. (正式用語)稱讚;讚美。 **～·able** /-əbl ; -əbl/ *adj* deserving praise. 值得稱讚的。 **～·ably** /-əblɪ ; -əblɪ/ *adv*

lauda·num /ˈlɔːdənəm ; ˈlɔdənəm/ *n* [U] opium prepared for use as a sedative. 鴉片劑;鴉片酊(用作鎭靜劑)。

lauda·tory /ˈlɔːdətərɪ *US:* -tɔːrɪ ; ˈlɔdəˌtorɪ/ *adj* (formal) expressing or giving praise. (正式用語)表示稱讚的;讚賞的。

laugh /lɑːf *US:* læf ; læf/ *vi, vt* **1** [VP2A, B, C, 3A] make sounds and movements of the face and body, showing amusement, joy, contempt, etc: 笑;發笑: *The jokes made everyone ～.* 那些笑話使人人都笑了。 **～ at, (a)** be amused by: 因…有趣而發笑: *～ at a joke／a funny story.* 聽到笑話(有趣的故事)而笑。 **(b)** make fun of; ridicule: 嘲笑;譏笑: *It's unkind to ～ at a person who is in trouble.* 嘲笑一個陷入困境的人是不仁慈的。 **(c)** disregard; treat with indifference: 不顧;漠視;對…一笑置之: *～ at difficulties.* 對困難一笑置之。 ***～ in sb's face,*** defy openly, show contempt for. 公然反抗某人;當面嘲笑某人。 ***～ one's ˈhead off,*** ～ heartily. 痛快地笑。 ***～ on the other side of one's face,*** change from joy or triumph to sorrow or regret. 轉喜爲憂。 ***～ over,*** ～ while discussing, examining, etc: 笑着討論,審查等: *～ over a letter.* 一面看信一面笑。 ***～ up one's sleeve,*** be secretly amused. 竊喜;偸笑。 ***He ～s best who ～s last; He who ～s last ～s longest,*** (prov) warning against expressing triumph too soon. (諺)勿高興過早。 **2** [VP15B] ***～ away,*** dismiss (a subject) by ～ing: 藉笑以驅走: *～ away sb's fears or doubts,* suggest, by ～ing, that they are without real cause. 藉笑以驅走某人的恐懼或疑慮。 ***～ down,*** silence by ～ing scornfully; reject by ～ing: 以輕蔑的笑使沉默;藉笑以拒絕: *They*

~*ed the speaker/the proposal down.* 他們以笑使那講演者中止(拒絕那建議)。**~ off,** escape from, get rid of, by ~ing: 藉笑以逃避或消除: ~ *off an embarrassing situation.* 對尷尬的處境一笑置之。**3** [VP22, 15A] arrive at a state, obtain a result, by ~ing: 笑至某種狀態或結果: ~ *oneself silly/helpless;* 笑傻了(笑得不能停止); ~ *oneself into convulsions;* 笑得前仰後合; ~ *a person out of his depression/out of a foolish belief.* 笑得別人不再沮喪(笑得別人放棄一愚昧的信仰)。 **~ sb/sth out of court,** dismiss him/it completely by ridicule. 對…一笑置之。 **4** [VP6B] express with or by means of a ~: 以笑表示: *He ~ed his denial.* 他以笑表示否認。□ *n* [C] sound made in ~ing; act of ~ing: 笑聲;笑: *We've had a good many ~s over his foolishness.* 他的愚蠢讓我們笑了個够。 *They all joined in the ~.* 他們都笑了起來。*'Oh, yes,' she answered with a ~.* '哦,是的,'她笑着回答道。**have/get the ~ of sb,** score off him. 羞辱某人;駁倒某人。 ⇨ score² (4). **have the last ~,** get one's satisfaction. 獲得最後勝利。**'belly-~,** ⇨ belly¹ (1). **~·able** /-əbl ; -əbl/ *adj* amusing; causing persons to ~: 有趣的;可笑的: *a ~able mistake.* 可笑的錯誤。**~·ably** /-əblɪ ; -əblɪ/ *adv* **~·ing** *adj* showing happiness, amusement, etc: 笑的;帶笑的: ~*ing faces.* 帶笑的面孔。**'~ing-gas** *n* nitrous oxide (N_2O) used in dental surgery. 笑氣(氧化亞氮,牙科手術時用之)。**'~ing-stock** *n* ⇨ stock¹ (7). **~·ing·ly** *adv*

laugh·ter /'lɑːftə(r) *US:* 'læf- ; 'læftɚ/ *n* [U] laughing: 笑: *burst into ~;* 失聲大笑; *roar with ~;* 哄然大笑; *an outburst of ~.* 一陣大笑。

launch¹ /lɔːntʃ ; lɔntʃ/ *vt, vi* **1** [VP6A] set (a ship, esp one newly built) afloat: 使(船,尤指新船)下水: ~ *a new passenger liner.* 使一新的定期客輪下水。 **2** [VP6A, 15A] **~ sth (against/at),** set in motion; send; aim: 發動;發出;發射: ~ *an attack;* 發動攻擊; ~ *threats at an opponent;* 威脅對手; ~ *a missile/spacecraft into outer space.* 發射飛彈(太空船)至太空。**'~ing-pad** *n* base or platform from which spacecraft, etc are ~ed. (太空船等的)發射臺。 **'~ing-site** *n* place for ~ing-pads. (太空船等的)發射場。 ⇨ the illus at rocket. 參看 rocket 之挿圖。 **3** [VP6A, 15A] (fig) get started; set going: (喻)使開始;開辦: ~ *a new business enterprise;* 創辦一新企業; ~ *a man into business.* 使一人入商業界。 **4** [VP2C, 3A] **~ out; ~ (out) into,** make or start (on): 開始: ~ *out into a new argument/debate;* 開始新的辯論; ~ *into a new subject;* 開始一新題目; ~ *out into extravagance.* 開始揮霍。□ *n* act of ~ing (a ship or spacecraft). (船之)下水;(太空船之)發射。

launch² /lɔːntʃ ; lɔntʃ/ *n* mechanically propelled passenger-carrying boat (on rivers and lakes, in harbours). (在河湖及海港上載客,由機器操縱的)小艇。

launder /'lɔːndə(r) ; 'lɔndɚ/ *vt, vi* [VP6A, 2A] wash and press (clothes): 洗熨(衣服): *Send these sheets to be ~ed.* 把這些被單送去洗熨。 *Will these shirts ~ well?* 這些襯衫禁洗嗎?

laun·der·ette /lɔːn'dret ; lɔn'drɛt/ *n* laundry at which members of the public may launder their clothes, etc in coin-operated automatic washing-machines and dryers. (設有丟進錢幣就能自動操作的自動洗衣機和烘乾機的)自助洗衣店。

L

laun·dress /'lɔːndrɪs ; 'lɔndrɪs/ *n* woman who earns money by washing and ironing clothes. 洗衣婦。

laun·dry /'lɔːndrɪ ; 'lɔndrɪ/ *n* (*pl* -dries) **1** [C] laundering business; place where clothes, sheets, etc, are sent to be laundered. 洗衣業;洗衣店。 **2 the ~,** clothes (to be) laundered: 所洗的衣服;待洗的衣服: *Has the ~ come back yet?* 洗的衣服送回來了嗎? **'~·man** /-mæn ; -mən/ *n* (*pl* -men) man who collects and delivers ~. (洗衣店所雇的)取送衣服之男工。

laur·eate /'lɒrɪət *US:* 'lɔːr- ; 'lɔrɪɪt/ *adj* crowned with a laurel wreath. 戴桂冠的。*n* **the (ˌPoet) 'L~,** poet officially appointed to the Royal Household in GB. The holder may write poems on great national occasions. 桂冠詩人(英國國王所任命者,視為王室之一員,獲此榮譽者於國家大典時可能寫詩慶祝)。

laurel /'lɒrəl *US:* 'lɔːrəl ; 'lɔrəl/ *n* evergreen shrub with smooth, shiny leaves, used by ancient Romans and Greeks as an emblem of victory, success and distinction. 月桂樹(生有平滑發亮的樹葉的常青灌木,古羅馬人及希臘人用以作勝利、成功及榮譽的象徵)。**look to one's ~s,** beware of losing one's reputation; be on the look-out for possible successes among rivals. 愛惜名聲;小心保持紀錄。**rest on one's ~s,** be content with one's successes and rest. 對既得之成功心滿意足。**win/gain one's ~s,** win reputation, honour. 博得榮譽。**~led** *adj* crowned with ~. 戴桂冠的。

lav /læv ; læv/ *n* (colloq abbr of) lavatory. (俗)為 lavatory 之略。

lava /'lɑːvə ; 'lɑvə/ *n* [U] hot liquid material flowing from a volcano: (火山流出之)熔岩: *a stream of ~;* 熔岩流; this material when it has cooled and hardened: 火山岩(由熔岩凝結而成): *'~ beds.* 火山岩床。 ⇨ pumice.

lava·tory /'lævətrɪ *US:* -tɔːrɪ ; 'lævəˌtorɪ/ *n* (*pl* -ries) [C] room for washing the hands and face in; water-closet. 盥洗室;厠所。

lave /leɪv ; lev/ *vt* (poet) wash; bathe; (of a stream) flow gently past or against. (詩)洗;沐浴;(指河流)緩慢流過;冲洗。

lav·en·der /'lævəndə(r) ; 'lævəndɚ/ *n* [U] plant with pale purple sweet-scented flowers; the dried flowers and stalks (sewn up in bags and placed among linen sheets, etc); the colour of ~. 歐薄荷;薰衣草(開淡紫香花的一種植物);歐薄荷的乾花及乾莖(裝於縫好的袋內,置於床單等內);淡紫色。 **'~ water** *n* [U] perfume distilled from ~. 歐薄荷香水。

lav·ish /'lævɪʃ ; 'lævɪʃ/ *adj* **1 ~ (of sth/in doing sth),** giving or producing freely, liberally or generously: 慷慨的;大方的: *He is never ~ of praise/in giving money to charity.* 他吝於稱讚他人(捐助慈善事業)。 **2** (of what is given) given abundantly; excessive: (指給予之物)過多的;過度的: ~ *praise/expenditure on luxuries.* 過多的稱讚(奢侈品過度的開銷)。□ *vt* [VP14] **~ on,** give abundantly and generously to: 慷慨給與;不吝惜地給與: ~ *care on an only child.* 對獨生子過度溺愛。**~·ly** *adv*

law /lɔː ; lɔ/ *n* **1** [C] rule made by authority for the proper regulation of a community or society or for correct conduct in life: 法律;法令: *When a Bill is passed by Parliament and signed by the Sovereign, it becomes a law.* 當一法案由國會通過再經國王簽署,即成為法律。 **'law-giver** *n* man who gives a code of laws (eg Moses in Hebrew history, Solon in Greek history). 立法者(例如希伯來歷史上的摩西,希臘歷史上的梭倫)。 **'law-officer** *n* (esp) Attorney or Solicitor-General. (尤指)檢察長或副檢察長。 ⇨ regulation, statute. **2** [U] **the law,** the whole body of laws considered collectively: 法律(集合用法): *If a man fails to observe the law he can be punished.* 一個人如果犯法將受懲罰。*Does the law allow me to do this?* 法律允許我這樣做嗎? **break the law,** fail to observe it. 違法;犯法。**lay down the law,** talk authoritatively, as if one were certain of being right. 獨斷地說;命令似地說。**'law-abiding** *adj* obeying the law. 守法的。**'law-breaker** *n* person who disobeys the law. 犯法者。 **3** [U] controlling influence of the laws: 法治: *maintain law and order,* see that the laws are respected. 維持法治和秩序。*Necessity knows no law,* When sth cannot be avoided, ordinary laws and rules will be ignored or broken. 需要不知法律(迫不得已時將鋌而走險)。**4** [U] the laws as a system or science; the legal profession: 法律系統;法律學;法學;法律業: *study law;* 研

讀法學；*law students;* 法科學生；法律學者；*read law,* study in order to become a lawyer. 學習法律以期做律師。⇨ jurisprudence. **5** [U] (with a defining word) one of the branches of the study of law: (與一說明的字連用)法律學之一支；法律學之一部門：*commercial law;* 商法；*the law of nations;* 國際法；*international law.* 國際法。 **6** [U] operation of the law (as providing a remedy for wrongs). 法律的實施(如對損害等之補償)。***go to law (against sb); have the law on sb,*** (colloq) appeal to the law courts. (俗)控告某人。***take the law into one's own hands,*** use force to redress a wrong. 私行治罪。**'law court** *n* court of justice. 法庭。**'law suit** *n* prosecution of a claim in a law court. 訴訟。 **7** [C] rule of action or procedure, esp in the arts or a game: 規則(尤指藝術或遊戲中者)；原則；原理：*the laws of perspective／harmony;* 透視(和聲)原則；*the laws of cricket.* 板球規則。***be a law unto oneself,*** disregard rules and conventions; do what one thinks right. 忽視慣例；照自己的意思行事。**8** [U, C] (also 亦作 ***law of nature*** or ***natural law***) factual statement of what always happens in certain circumstances; regularity in nature, eg the order of the seasons: 自然的法則；自然律(例如四季的循環)；定律：*Newton's law;* 牛頓定律；*the laws of motion;* 運動定律；*the law of supply and demand;* 供求律；*the law of self-preservation,* the instinct of men and animals to behave in a way that will save them from danger. 自衛的本能。 **law·ful** /-fl; -fəl/ *adj* **1** allowed by law; according to law: 合法的；法定的；依法的：*lawful acts;* 合法的行爲；*the lawful ruler.* 合法的統治者。 **2** (of offspring) legitimate: (指子孫)合法的：*the lawful heir.* 合法的繼承人。**law·fully** /-fəlɪ; -fəlɪ/ *adv* **law·less** *adj* not in accordance with the law; not conforming to the law; not restrained by law; unruly: 不法的；不遵守法律的；不受法律控制的；違法的：*lawless acts;* 不法的行爲；*lawless tribes.* 法律所不能及的部落。**law·less·ly** *adv* **law·less·ness** *n* [U].

lawn[1] /lɔːn; lɔn/ *n* [C] area of grass (turf) kept closely cut and smooth, eg in a private garden or a public park; such an area of grass used for a game: (經過修剪而平坦的)草地(例如私人花園或公園中者)；草場(供運動用)：*a 'croquet ～;* 槌球場；*a 'tennis ～.* 草地網球場。**'～-mower** *n* machine for cutting grass on ～s. 刈草機；剪草機。**,～ 'tennis** *n* [U] the game of tennis played on an unwalled court, either hard surfaced or turfed. 草地網球。⇨ the illus at tennis. 參看 tennis 之揷圖。

lawn[2] /lɔːn; lɔn/ *n* [U] kind of fine linen used for dresses, blouses and esp for a bishop's sleeves. 細竹布；軟洋紗(一種細麻布，用以製女服和罩衫，特別用以製主教法衣之袖)。

law·yer /'lɔːjə(r); 'lɔjə/ *n* person who practises law, esp a barrister or solicitor. 律師。

lax /læks; læks/ *adj* **1** negligent; inattentive; not strict or severe: 疏忽的；不小心的；不嚴格的：*lax discipline／behaviour;* 不嚴格的紀律(疏忽的行爲)；*lax in morals.* 品行不檢。 **2** (of the bowels) free in action. (指腸)鬆弛的；腹瀉的。**lax·ity** /'læksətɪ; 'læksətɪ/ *n* [U] being lax; [C] (*pl* -ties) instance of being lax. 疏忽；不嚴格；腹瀉。**lax·ly** *adv*

laxa·tive /'læksətɪv; 'læksətɪv/ *n, adj* (medicine, drug) causing the bowels to empty. 通便的；通便劑；輕瀉劑。

lay[1] /leɪ; le/ *vt, vi* (*pt, pp* laid /leɪd; led/) For uses with *adverbial particles* and *preps* ⇨ 12 below. 與副詞接語和介詞連用之用法，參看下列第 12 義。 **1** [VP6A, 15A] put on a surface; put in a certain position, in the proper place for a purpose: 置放；鋪設；裝於適當位置：*Who will lay the carpet,* spread it out, fasten it down, etc? 誰將鋪設地毯？*He laid his hand on my shoulder.* 他把他的手放在我的肩上。*A new submarine cable was laid between England and Holland.* 英國至荷蘭間鋪設了新的海底電纜。*The woodcutter laid his axe to the tree,* began to chop. 那砍柴者舉斧砍樹。*A bricklayer is a man who lays bricks.* 磚瓦匠即砌磚之人。***lay a snare／trap／an ambush (for sb／sth),*** prepare one. (爲…)設陷阱(埋伏)。 **2** [VP6A, 15B] (of non-material things, and fig uses) place; put. (指非物質事物及比喩用法)安放。***lay (one's) hands on sth／sb,*** **(a)** seize; get possession of: 攫取；佔有：*He keeps everything he can lay (his) hands on.* 他佔有每一樣能得到手的東西。 **(b)** do violence to: 對…行兇；傷害：*How dare you lay hands on me?* 你怎敢向我動手？*He laid violent hands on himself,* (dated) tried to commit suicide. (過時用語)他企圖自殺。**(c)** find: 尋獲：*I have the book somewhere, but can't lay my hands on it just now.* 我是有那本書，不知擺在什麼地方，現在就是找不到。 **(d)** (eccles) confirm; ordain; consecrate. (教會)施堅信禮；行按手禮(立爲牧師、神父或其他神職人員)。Hence, 由此產生，***laying-on of hands,*** confirmation; ordination; consecration. 堅信禮；按手禮。***lay the blame (for sth) on sb,*** say that he is responsible for what is wrong, etc. 歸咎於某人。***lay a (heavy) burden on sb,*** cause sb to be responsible for sth likely to be difficult, to cause suffering, etc. 使負(艱苦)重責。***lay one's hopes on,*** = pin (the more usu word) one's hopes on. ***lay a strict injunction on sb (to do sth),*** give him strict orders (to do it). 予以嚴格命令；强制。***lay great／little store by／on sth,*** value very much／little. (不)重視。***lay stress／emphasis／weight on sth,*** treat it as important; emphasize it. 認爲重要；强調某事之重要。***lay a tax on sth,*** impose one. 加稅於。**3** [VP15A] cause to be in a certain state, condition, or situation. 使處於某種狀態，狀況或情勢。***lay sb to rest,*** (esp) bury sb: (尤指)埋葬某人：*He was laid to rest in the churchyard.* 他被葬於教堂之墓地。***lay sb under a／the necessity／obligation,*** make it necessary or obligatory for him (to do sth): 使某人(對某事物)有義務：*Your conduct lays me under the necessity of dismissing you.* 你的行爲使我必須解除你的職務。*He was laid under an obligation to support the wife he had deserted.* 他必須贍養被他遺棄的妻子。***lay sb under contribution,*** compel him to contribute money, etc. 强迫某人捐獻金錢等。***lay sth to sb's charge,*** hold him responsible. 委過於某人。***lay claim to sth,*** ⇨ claim. ***lay sth at sb's door,*** ⇨ door. ***lay one's finger on,*** ⇨ finger. ***lay siege to,*** ⇨ siege. **4** [VP22] (*lay + n, adj* or *adv phrases*) cause to be in a specified condition. (與名詞，形容詞或副詞片語連用)使處於某指明的狀態。***lay sth bare,*** show; reveal: 顯示；表露：*lay bare one's heart,* reveal one's inmost feelings, etc. 表明心曲。***lay sth flat,*** cause to be flat: 使倒下：*crops laid flat by heavy rainstorms.* 被暴雨擊倒的作物。***lay sth open,*** **(a)** expose, reveal: 顯示；揭露：*lay open a plot.* 揭露一陰謀。**(b)** cut, gash: 刺傷；割傷：*lay open one's cheek,* eg by falling and striking it against a rock. 使面頰受傷(例如跌倒撞在一岩石上)。***lay oneself open to sth,*** render oneself liable to criticism, calumny, etc. 使自己易受(批評，毀謗等)。***lay sth waste,*** ravage, destroy: 蹂躪；破壞：*a countryside laid waste by invading armies.* 被入侵敵軍夷爲平地的鄉間一地區。 **5** [VP6A] cause to be down, settle: 使倒下；使降落：*sprinkle water on the roads to lay the dust.* 灑水在路上不使塵土飛揚。***lay sb's doubts,*** get rid of them, ⇨ allay, the more usu word. 消除某人的疑惑 (allay 較常用)。 ***lay a ghost／spirit,*** expel or exorcize it; cause it to stop appearing to people. 驅除鬼魂。 **6** [VP6A, 2A] (of birds and insects) produce (eggs): (指鳥與昆蟲)產(卵)：*Are your hens laying yet?* 你那些母鷄下蛋了嗎？*How many eggs does this hen lay each week?* 這隻母鷄一星期下多少個蛋？*New laid eggs, 5p* *each.* 新鮮鷄蛋,五辨士一個。 **7** [VP15A] (usu passive) set (a story, etc) in time and place: (通常用被動語態)爲(故事等)安排時間和地點: *The scene is laid in Athens, in the third century BC.* 背景是紀元前三世紀的雅典。 **8** [VP6A] place or arrange by laying (ready for use, etc): 佈置(以備使用): *lay the table (for breakfast),* put out plates, knives, etc; 擺設餐具(準備吃早餐); *lay the cloth,* spread it on the table ready for a meal; 鋪餐桌布; *lay a fire,* put wood, coal, etc in a fireplace, ready for lighting. 準備生火。 **9** [VP6A, 12C, 14] put down (a sum of money) as a wager or stake (on sth of which the result is uncertain); offer as a bet: 下(若干錢)作爲賭注;打賭: *They laid a wager on the result of the race.* 他們以競賽的結果打賭。*I'll lay you £5 that he won't come.* 我願和你賭五鎊,他不會來。*I'll lay* (= make) *you a bet that....* 我和你打賭…。**10** [VP6A, 15A] cover; coat: 覆蓋;覆以一層: *lay carpet on the floor/lay the floor with carpet;* 將地毯鋪於地板上; *lay straw over the yard/lay the yard with straw;* 將稻草鋪在院中; *lay colours on canvas.* 塗顏料於畫布上。⇨ *lay on* at 12 below. 參看下列第12義之 lay on。**11** [VP6A] (sl) have sexual intercourse with. (俚)和…發生肉體關係。 **12** [VP2C, 3A, 15B] (uses with *adverbial particles* and *preps*): (與副詞接語及介詞連用的用法):

lay about one (with sth), hit out in all directions: 向四周揮打: *When they rushed at him, Harry laid about him with his big stick.* 當他們向他衝去時,哈利用他的大手杖向四周揮打。

lay sth aside, **(a)** save; keep for future use: 儲蓄(以備將來之用): *lay aside money for one's old age.* 儲蓄金錢以備老年之需。**(b)** put down: 放下: *He laid his book aside to listen to me.* 他放下書聽我說話。**(c)** abandon; give up: 拋棄;放棄: *lay aside bad habits.* 革除惡習。

lay sth back, turn back: 使向後: *The horse laid back its ears.* 那馬將耳朵伸向後面。

lay sth by, = lay sth aside(a).

lay sb/oneself down, place in a lying or recumbent position: 使躺下: *Lay the baby down gently.* 將嬰兒輕輕放下。*She laid herself down.* 她躺下。***lay sth down,*** **(a)** pay or wager: 付(款); 下(賭注): *How much are you ready to lay down?* 你準備賭(付)多少? **(b)** (begin to) build: (開始)建築: *lay down a new ship.* 開始造新船。**(c)** convert (land) to pasture: 使(土地)變爲牧場: *lay down land in/to/with/under grass.* 使土地變爲草地。**(d)** store (wine) in a cellar: 貯藏(酒)於酒窖: *lay down claret and port.* 貯藏紅葡萄酒和紫葡萄酒。***lay sth down; lay it down that...,*** establish: 設立;制定: *You can't lay down hard and fast rules.* 你不能制定嚴格的規則。 *It was laid down that all applicants should sit a written examination.* 根據規定,所有申請人均應參加筆試。*These prices have been laid down by the manufacturers.* 這些價格都是廠商規定的。***lay down one's arms,*** put one's weapons down as a sign of surrender. 放下武器投降。***lay down the law,*** say with (or as if with) authority what must be done. 獨斷地說;命令似地說。***lay down one's life,*** sacrifice it: 犧牲生命: *He laid down his life for his country.* 他爲國捐軀。 ***lay down office,*** resign a position of authority. 罷官;辭職。

lay sth in, provide oneself with a stock of: 貯備: *lay in provisions/stores.* 貯備糧食(貨物)。

lay off, (colloq) (俗) **(a)** discontinue work or activity; rest: 停止工作或活動; 休息: *The doctor told me to lay off for a week.* 醫生要我休息一星期。 **(b)** stop doing sth which irritates or annoys: 停止做惹人生氣或煩惱之事: *I hear you've been pestering my sister again—Well, you can just lay off.* 我聽說你又去糾纏我妹妹了——哼,你不可再去纏她了。***lay sb off,*** dismiss temporarily: 暫時解雇: *lay off workmen,* eg because of a shortage of materials. 將工人暫時解雇(例如由於原料之缺乏)。Hence, 由此產生, **'lay-off** *n* period during which men are temporarily dismissed. 工人被暫時解雇期間。

lay sth on, **(a)** supply gas, water, electricity to a building: 爲建築物接煤氣、自來水、電: *We can't occupy the new house until gas and water are laid on.* 我們要等煤氣和水接好始能移居新屋。 **(b)** (colloq) provide: (俗)準備: *Sightseeing tours were laid on for the distinguished visitors from Poland.* 爲波蘭來的貴賓安排了觀光旅行。***lay it on (thick/with a trowel),*** use exaggerated praise, flattery, etc: 過份稱讚;過度奉承: *To call him a genius is laying it on a bit too thick!* 稱他是天才是有點過份稱讚了!

lay sth out, **(a)** spread out ready for use or so as to be seen easily: 展開以便使用或易見: *lay out one's evening clothes;* 取出晚禮服以待穿; *the magnificent scene that was laid out before the climbers when they reached the summit.* 當爬山者到達山頂時呈現在他們眼前的壯麗的風景。**(b)** prepare for burial: 準備埋葬: *lay out a corpse.* 準備一屍體以備埋葬。**(c)** spend (money): 用(錢): *lay out one's money carefully.* 謹慎用錢。**(d)** make a plan for; arrange: 計畫;設計: *well laid-out streets and avenues;* 設計良好的街道和馬路; *lay out a printed page.* 設計一印刷版面。Hence, 由此產生, **'lay-out** *n* arrangement, plan, design of a printed page, an advertisement, a book, a group of buildings. 佈置;圖樣;(書,廣告,房屋等之)設計。***lay oneself out (to do sth),*** exert oneself, take pains: 盡力(做某事): *She laid herself out to make her guests comfortable.* 她煞費苦心地款待她的客人。

lay over, (US) (GB 英 = *stop over*) stop at a place during a journey because of a requirement in a schedule. (美)(因行程之需要)中途停留於某地。**'lay-over** *n* such a stop. 中途停留。

lay sth up, **(a)** save; store: 貯藏: *lay up provisions.* 貯糧。 **(b)** ensure by what one does or fails to do that one will have trouble, etc in future: (所做所爲)必將招惹麻煩等: *You're only laying up trouble for yourself.* 你簡直是在爲自已找麻煩嘛。**(c)** put (a ship) out of commission: 使(船)不被使用: *lay a ship up for repairs.* 將船拖入船塢修理。***lay sb up,*** (usu passive) force sb to stay in bed: (通常用被動語態)迫使某人臥床: *He's laid up with a broken leg.* 他因一腿折斷而臥床。 *The flu has laid him up for a few days.* 流行性感冒使他臥床數日。

lay[2] /leɪ; le/ *n* (chiefly in) (主要用於) ***the lay of the land*** (*lie* is more usu), the nature or formation of an area of land. 地形;地勢(lie 較常用)。

lay[3] /leɪ; le/ *n* (sl) partner in sexual intercourse. (俚)發生肉體關係之對方;姘頭。⇨ lay[1](11).

lay[4] /leɪ; le/ *n* (liter) minstrel's song; ballad. (文)歌謠;民歌。

lay[5] /leɪ; le/ *pt* of lie[2].

lay[6] /leɪ; le/ *adj* (attrib only) (僅作形容用法) **1** of, for, done by, persons who are not priests: 凡俗的(與神職人員相對而言);普通人的: *a lay brother/sister,* one who wears the dress and has taken the vows of a religious order, but who does manual work and is excused other duties. 凡人修士(修女)(穿修士或修女服,並發誓修道,但從事勞力之工作,不擔任其他職務者)。⇨ laity. **2** non-professional; not expert (esp with reference to the law and medicine): 非屬於專門職業的;外行的(尤指對法律和醫學方面而言): *lay opinion,* what non-professional people think. 外行人的意見。*To the lay mind the language of a lawyer seems to be full of jargon.* 對外行人而言,律師所用的語言中似乎充滿了術語。 **'layman** /-mən; -mən/ *n* (*pl* -men) lay(2) person: 外行人;門外漢: *Where the law is concerned I am only a layman,* I have no expert knowledge. 談到法律,我不過是個外行人。

lay·about /'leɪəbaʊt; 'leəˌbaʊt/ *n* (GB sl) loafer:

person who avoids working for a living. (英俚)遊蕩之人；不務正業者。

lay·by /ˈleɪbaɪ ; ˈleˌbaɪ/ *n* (GB) area at the side of a road where vehicles may park without hindering the flow of traffic. (英)馬路旁邊可停車之處。

layer /ˈleɪə(r) ; ˈleɚ/ *n* [C] **1** thickness of material (esp one of several) laid or lying on or spread over a surface, or forming one horizontal division: 層(尤指數層中之一)：*a ~ of clay.* 一層泥土。**ˈ~-cake,** one with horizontal divisions separated by cream, jam, etc. 夾心蛋糕。**2** (gardening) shoot of a plant fastened down to take root while still growing from the parent plant. (園藝)壓枝；壓條。**3** (of hens) (指母鷄) *good/bad ~s,* hens that lay eggs in large/small numbers. 生蛋多(少)的母鷄。□ *vt* [VP6A] fasten down (a shoot of a plant): 壓植(植物的枝條)：~ *carnations.* 用壓條法培植康乃馨。

lay·ette /leɪˈet ; leˈɛt/ *n* garments, blankets, etc for a new-born baby. 新生嬰兒所需的衣物。

lay fig·ure /ˌleɪ ˈfɪgə(r) ; ˌleˈfɪgɚ/ *n* jointed wooden figure of the human body (used by artists for arranging drapery, etc); (fig) dummy. (藝術家用以陳列裝飾用織物等的)人體模型；(喩)傀儡。

lay·man ⇨ lay[6].

lazar /ˈlæzə(r) ; ˈlæzɚ/ *n* (archaic) poor and diseased person, esp a leper. (古)貧病交迫者(尤指痲瘋患者)。

laza·retto /ˌlæzəˈretəʊ ; ˌlæzəˈrɛto/ (*pl* ~s /-təʊz ; -toz/) (also 亦作 **laza·ret, laza·rette** /ˌlæzəˈret ; ˌlæzəˈrɛt/) *nn* quarantine station; ship's storeroom. 檢疫所；(船上的)貯藏室。

Laz·arus /ˈlæzərəs ; ˈlæzərəs/ *n* beggar; (in contrasts) very poor man: 乞丐；(用於對比)極窮的人：~ *and Dives.* 拉撒路和財主(窮人和富人)。⇨ Luke 16: 20. 參看路加福音第 16 章第 20 節。

laze /leɪz ; lez/ *vi, vt* [VP2A, C, 15B] ~ ***(away),*** be lazy; pass (time) in idleness: 懶散；混(時光)：~ *all day;* 終日懶散；*lazing away the afternoon.* 混過一下午。

lazy /ˈleɪzɪ ; ˈlezɪ/ *adj* (-ier, -iest) unwilling to work; doing little work; suitable for, causing, inducing, inactivity: 懶惰的；怠惰的；適於閒散的；令人閒散的：*a ~ fellow;* 懶人；*a ~ afternoon.* 令人懶散的下午。⇨ idle. **ˈ~-bones** *n* ~ person. 懶人；懶骨頭。**lazi·ly** *adv* **lazi·ness** *n*

lea /liː ; li/ *n* (poet) stretch of open grass land. (詩)草地；草原。

leach /liːtʃ ; litʃ/ *vt* **1** [VP6A] cause (a liquid) to percolate through some material. 使(液體)過濾。**2** [VP15B] ~ ***out/away,*** purge (a soluble matter) away or out by the action of a percolating fluid: 濾除(可溶性物質)：*the ~ing of the soil,* the washing away, eg by heavy rainfall, of elements in it necessary for plant growth. 土壤中植物成長所需成分之淋溶(例如被大雨沖掉)。

lead[1] /led ; lɛd/ *n* **1** [U] soft, heavy, easily melted metal (symbol **Pb**) of a dull bluish-grey colour used for water- and gas-pipes, as a roofing material, and in numerous alloys. 鉛(符號爲 Pb)。**ˈ~-ore** *n* [U] rock containing ~. 鉛礦。**ˌ~ ˈpoisoning** *n* diseased condition caused by taking ~ into the system. 鉛中毒。~ **shot,** ⇨ shot[1](4). **ˈ~ works** *n sing* place where ~-ore is smelted. (單數)鉛礦熔鍊所。**2** [U] (also 亦作 **ˈblack ~**) graphite; stick of graphite as used in a ~-pencil. 石墨；黑鉛(如用做鉛筆心者)。**3** [C] lump of ~ fastened to a line marked in fathoms for measuring the depth of the sea from ships. (自船上測海水深度的)鉛錘；測錘。***cast/heave the ~,*** take soundings. 投測錘以測水深。***swing the ~,*** (sl) evade one's proper share of work by pretending to be ill, using tricks, etc. (俚)裝病或以其他欺騙方法逃避份內的工作。**4** (*pl*) strips of ~ used to cover a roof; area of (esp horizontal) ~-covered roof; ~ frames for glass, eg in a lattice window. (複)鋪屋頂的長條鉛板；鉛板鋪的屋頂面積(尤指水平之鉛板屋頂面積)；裝玻璃的鉛框(例如格子窗上者)。**~ed** /ˈledɪd ; ˈlɛdɪd/ *adj* secured with strips of ~: 以長條鉛板固定的：*~ed windows.* 鉛框窗子。**~ed light,** ⇨ light[3](9). **~en** /ˈledn ; ˈlɛdn̩/ *adj* **1** made of ~: 鉛製的：*a ~en coffin.* 鉛製的棺材。**2** having the colour or appearance of ~: 鉛色的；鉛灰色的；似鉛的：*~en clouds.* 鉛灰色的雲。**3** dull and heavy like ~: 沉悶的；沉重的：*~en sleep;* 沉睡；*a ~en heart.* 沉重的心。**~·ing** /ˈledɪŋ ; ˈlɛdɪŋ/ *n* [U] space between lines of print. 印刷行間之空間。

lead[2] /liːd ; lid/ *n* **1** [U, C] (*sing* only) action of guiding or giving an example; direction given by going in front; sth that helps or hints. (僅用單數)領導；帶頭；率先；榜樣；提示。***follow sb's ~,*** follow his example. 效法某人。***give sb a ~,*** encourage him by doing sth first, or by giving a hint towards the solution of a problem. 帶領某人；提示某人。***take the ~,*** take the leading place, give an example. 領導；帶頭；做榜樣。**2 the ~,** first place or position: 首位；最先之地位；領先：*have/gain the ~ in a race;* 在賽跑中領先；(attrib) (形容用法) *the ~ story,* (journalism, news broadcasting) item of news given the greatest prominence. (新聞，新聞廣播)頭條新聞。**a ~,** distance by which one leads: 領先的距離：*have a ~ of ten feet.* 領先十呎。***take over/lose the ~,*** move to the front/fall behind in a race, in business, etc. (競賽，商業等)領先(落後)。**3** [C] cord, leather strap, for leading a dog: 牽狗的繩或皮帶：*Keep your dog on the ~ in these busy streets.* 在這些熱鬧的街道上要好好牽着你的狗。**4** [C] principal part in a play; actor or actress who plays such a part: 劇中的主角；扮演主角的演員：*the juvenile ~,* eg the actor who plays the part of the handsome young hero. 扮演英俊年輕男主角的演員。**5** [C] artificial watercourse leading to a mill; channel of open water in an ice-field. 通往磨粉廠的人工水道；冰間水路。**6** [C] (electr) conductor conveying current from a source to the place where it is used. (電)導線；引線。**7** [C] (in card games) act or right of playing first: (牌戲)首先出牌；首先出牌權：*Whose ~ is it?* 誰先出牌？

lead[3] /liːd ; lid/ *vt, vi* (*pt, pp* led /led ; lɛd/) **1** [VP6A, 15A, B] guide or take, esp by going in front: 引導：*Our guide led us through a series of caves.* 我們的嚮導引導我們穿過一連串的洞穴。*The servant led the visitors in/out/back.* 那僕人引導客人入內(出去，回去)。~ ***the way (to),*** go first; show the way. 帶路；引路。**ˈ~-in** *n* **(a)** preliminary remarks, introduction (to). 引語；介紹辭。**(b)** wire joining an aerial to a wireless receiver or television set. 引入線(自天線接至收音機或電視機的電線)。**2** [VP6A, 15A, B] conduct (sb) by the hand, by touching him, or by a rope, etc: 牽引：~ *a blind man;* 牽引一盲人；~ *a horse,* by holding the halter and walking at its head. 牽馬。~ ***sb astray,*** (fig) tempt him to do sth wrong. (喩)將某人引入歧途。~ ***sb by the nose,*** control him completely; make him do everything one wishes him to do. 完全控制某人；牽着某人的鼻子走。~ ***sb on,*** (fig) entice sb to do more than he intended. (喩)慫恿某人做非其心願之事。~ ***a woman to the altar,*** (joc) marry her. (諧)與一女子結婚。**3** [VP6A, 2A] act as chief; direct by example or persuasion; direct the movements of: 領導；率領；指揮：~ *an army/an expedition/a mutiny;* 指揮軍隊(率領探險隊；領頭叛變)；~ *the Conservative Party;* 領導保守黨；~ *the fashion;* 開風氣；創時尚；~ *the choir/the singing.* 領導唱詩班(歌唱)。*Who's going to ~?* 誰將領導？**4** [VP6A, 2A, C] have the first place in; go first: 居於…之首位；領先：*A brass band led the regiment.* 該團由一銅管樂隊引導。*Which horse is ~ing,* eg in a race? 哪一匹馬領先(例如賽馬時)？~ ***off,*** start: 開始：*Who's going to ~ off?* 誰先開始？

He led off by saying that.... 他開始時說…。 **5** [VP6A, 17, 14] ~ ***(to)***, guide the actions and opinions of; influence; persuade: 領導…的行動和意見;影響;勸誘: *What led you to this conclusion?* 什麼使你下此結論? *He is easier led than driven.* 他適於誘導而不適於驅使。*I am led to believe* (= Certain facts, etc cause me to believe) *that he is disloyal to us.* 某些事實使我相信他對我們不忠。*What led you to think so?* 什麼使你這樣想? **6** [VP2C] be a path, way or road to; (fig) have as a result: 通;達;(喻)導致某種結果: *Where does this road ~?* 這條路通到哪裏? *Your work seems to be ~ing nowhere,* getting no result. 你的工作似乎沒有什麼效果。*This led to great confusion.* 此事導致大的混亂。~ ***up to,*** be a preparation for or an introduction to; direct the conversation towards: 作爲…的準備或前導;使話題(漸漸)轉向: *That's just what I was ~ing up to.* 那正是我要說的。*Chapter One describes the events that led up to the war.* 第一章描寫引起戰爭的一些事件。***All roads ~ to Rome,*** (fig) There are many ways of reaching the same result. (喻)條條道路通羅馬;殊途同歸。**7** [VP6A, 12C] (cause sb to) pass, go through, spend (life, etc): 過(生活等);使某人過(生活等): ~ *a miserable existence;* 生活困苦; ~ *a double life/a Jekyll and Hyde existence.* 過雙重人格的生活。~ ***sb a (pretty) dance,*** ⇨ dance¹(1). ~ ***sb a 'dog's life,*** make his life wretched. 使某人過困苦的日子。**8** [VP6A, 2A] (in card games) put down, as first player (a certain card or kind of card): (牌戲)首先出(某張或某種牌): ~ *the two of clubs;* 首先出梅花2; ~ *trumps.* 首先出王牌。 **9** [VP3A] ~ ***with,*** (journalism) have as the main article or news story: (新聞)使成爲頭條新聞或特別報導: *We'll ~ with the dock strike.* 我們將以船塢罷工作頭條新聞。

leader /ˈli:də(r); ˈlidɚ/ *n* **1** person who leads: 領導者;率領者;領袖;指揮者: *the ~ of an army/an expedition/the Labour Party;* 軍隊之指揮(探險隊之領隊;工黨領袖); *the ~ of the choir;* 唱詩班的指揮; *the ~ of an orchestra* (usu the first violinist). 管絃樂隊的首席(通常爲第一小提琴手)。 **2** principal counsel in a law court case: 首席法律顧問;主要辯護人: *the ~ for the defence.* 被告之主要辯護人。**3** (GB) leading article (in a newspaper). (英)(報紙的)社論。⇨ leading below. 參看下列之 leading。**4** shoot growing at the end of a stem or principal branch. 自莖或大枝頂端發出的嫩枝。 **5** tendon or sinew. 腱。~**·less** *adj* **ˈ~·ship** /-ʃɪp; -ʃɪp/ *n* [U] being a ~; power of leading; the qualities of a ~. 作爲領導者;領導權;領導地位;領導能力。

lead·ing /ˈli:dɪŋ; ˈlidɪŋ/ *adj* chief; most important: 主要的;最重要的: *the ~ men of the day;* 今日之領導人物; *the ~ topics of the hour,* those now being discussed; 當前主要的論題; *the ~ lady,* the actress with the chief part in a play; (劇中的)女主角; *L~ Aircraftman,* non-commissioned rank in the RAF. 英國皇家空軍上等兵。ˌ~ **ˈarticle,** (in a newspaper) one giving editorial opinions on events, policies, etc. (報紙的)社論。ˌ~ **ˈcase,** (legal) one that establishes a precedent. (法律)成爲判例之案件。ˌ~ **ˈlight,** (colloq) prominent person. (俗)重要人物。ˌ~ **ˈquestion,** one that suggests the answer that is hoped for. 誘導詢問。□ *n* act of leading. 領導;率領;領先。**ˈ~-rein** *n* for ~ a horse. 轡。**ˈ~-strings** *n pl* straps, etc with which babies were formerly taught to walk: 昔時教幼兒學步用的引帶: *in ~-strings,* (fig) guided and controlled like a young child. (喻)似幼兒般受管束。

leaf /li:f; lif/ *n* (*pl* leaves /li:vz; livz/) **1** one of the parts (usu green and flat) growing from the side of a stem or branch or direct from the root of a tree, bush, plant, etc (collectively called *foliage*): 葉(集合用法作 foliage): *sweep up dead leaves in autumn;* 掃掉秋季的枯葉; (colloq) petal (as in *rose-leaves*) (俗)花瓣(如薔薇花瓣)。⇨ the illus at flower, tree. 參看 flower, tree 之插圖。***in ~,*** with the leaves grown: 長葉子: *The trees will soon be in ~.* 這些樹不久就會長葉子。***come into ~,*** grow leaves: 長葉子: *The trees come into ~ in spring.* 樹木在春季長葉子。**ˈ~-bud** *n* one from which leaves, not flowers, develop. 葉芽。**ˈ~-mould** *n* [U] soil composed chiefly of decaying leaves. 腐葉土。**2** single sheet of paper forming two pages of a book. (書籍的)一張(即兩頁)。***take a ~ out of sb's book,*** take him as a model. 模倣某人。***turn over a new ~,*** make a new and better start. 過新生活;改過自新;重新開始。**3** hinged or loose part of an extending table (used to make the table larger). 桌子的活邊(支起可使桌子加大)。**4** [U] very thin sheet of metal, esp of gold or silver: (金、銀)箔: *gold ~.* 金箔。□ *vi* ~ ***through (a book, etc),*** turn over the pages quickly; glance through. 迅速翻閱(書頁等);瀏覽。~**·less** *adj* having no leaves. 無葉的。~**y** *adj* (-ier, -iest) covered with leaves; having leaves; made by leaves: 覆有葉的;生葉的;葉做成的: *a ~y shade.* 樹蔭。

leaf·let /ˈli:flɪt; ˈliflɪt/ *n* **1** young leaf. 小葉;嫩葉。**2** printed sheet (unbound but sometimes folded) with announcements, etc esp one for free distribution. 散頁的印刷品(有時是摺疊的,尤指免費分送者);傳單。

league¹ /li:g; lig/ *n* (old) measure of distance (about three miles or 4·8 kms). (舊)里格(長度名,約等於三哩或4·8公里)。

league² /li:g; lig/ *n* [C] **1** agreement made between persons, groups or nations for their common welfare, eg to work for peace; the parties that make such an agreement. 盟約(例如爲謀和平者);聯盟;同盟;參加盟約的會員。**the L~ of Nations,** that formed in 1919 after the First World War, with headquarters at Geneva, dissolved in 1946. 國際聯盟(成立於1919年第一次世界大戰後,總部設於日內瓦,1946年解散)。⇨ United Nations. ***in ~ with,*** allied with; having made an agreement with. 與…聯盟。**2** group of sports clubs or teams playing matches among themselves: (運動競賽之)聯盟: ~ *football matches.* 足球聯賽。□ *vt, vi* [VP6A, 15A, B, 2C] form into, become, a ~: 組成聯盟;成爲同盟: *countries that are ~d together.* 聯盟國家。

leak /li:k; lik/ *n* **1** hole, crack, etc caused by wear, injury, etc through which a liquid, gas, etc may wrongly get in or out: 漏洞;漏隙: *a ~ in the roof,* allowing rain to enter; 屋頂的漏隙; *a ~ in the gas-pipe,* allowing gas to escape; 瓦斯管上的漏氣處; (fig) (喻) *a ~ of information;* 情報的洩漏; *an inspired ~,* of news that is deliberately disclosed. 消息之故意洩漏。***spring a leak,*** ⇨ spring³(6). **2** the liquid, gas, etc that gets out or in. 漏出或漏進的液體、氣體等。□ *vi, vt* **1** [VP2A, C] (allow to) pass out or in through a ~: 漏: *The rain is ~ing in.* 漏雨了。*The ship was ~ing badly.* 那船漏得厲害。**2** [VP2A, 6A, 14] ~ ***(out) (to),*** (of news, secrets, etc) (cause to) become known by chance or with authority: (指消息、祕密等)(使)洩漏: *The news has ~ed out.* 消息已洩漏出去了。*Who ~ed the news to the press?* 誰將消息洩漏給新聞界的? **ˈ~·age** /-ɪdʒ; -ɪdʒ/ *n* **1** [U] the process of ~ing: 漏;洩漏: *~age of military secrets.* 軍事祕密的洩漏。**2** [C] instance of this; that which ~s in or out; amount that ~s in or out. 漏的實例;漏入物;漏出物;漏泄量。~**y** *adj* having a ~: 有漏隙的;漏的: *a ~y kettle.* 一把會漏水的壺。

leal /li:l; lil/ *adj* (Scot or liter) loyal. (蘇或文)忠實的。

lean¹ /li:n; lin/ *adj* (-er, -est) **1** (of persons and animals) having less than the usual proportion of fat; (of meat) containing little or no fat. (指人和動物)瘦的;(指肉)脂肪很少的;無脂肪的。 **2** not productive; of poor quality: 無生產力的;質劣的: *a ~ harvest;* 歉收; *~ years,* years of scarcity. 歉收之年;荒年。□ *n* [U] meat with little or no fat.

L

瘦肉。~•ness *n*

lean² /liːn; lin/ *vi, vt* (*pt, pp* ~t /lent; lɛnt/ or leaned /liːnd; lind/) **1** [VP2A, C] be or put in a sloping position: 傾斜: ~ *backwards;* 向後傾; ~ *out of a window;* 斜伸出窗外; *trees that* ~ *over in the wind;* 被風吹斜的樹; *the L~ing Tower of Pisa.* 比薩斜塔。 ~ ***over backward(s) (to do sth),*** (colloq) make a great effort (to please sb, get a result, etc). (俗)(爲取悅某人,獲一結果等)過份努力;矯枉過正。 **2** [VP2C, 3A] ~ ***(on/upon),*** rest in a sloping position for support: 倚;靠: ~ *on a table;* 靠在桌上; ~ *upon one's elbows;* 倚於兩肘上; ~ *on sb's arm.* 靠在某人的臂上。 **3** [VP15A] cause to rest against and be supported by: 使倚靠: ~ *a ladder against a wall/one's elbows on a table.* 將一梯靠於牆上(把兩肘倚於桌上)。 **4** [VP3A] ~ ***towards,*** have a tendency: 傾向: *Do some oriental philosophies* ~ *towards fatalism?* 有些東方的哲學傾向於宿命論嗎? **5** [VP3A] ~ ***on/upon,*** depend: 依靠;依賴: ~ *on a friend's advice;* 依賴朋友的忠告; ~ *upon others for guidance.* 依靠别人的指導。 ~•ing *n* [C] tendency (of mind *towards* sth): 傾向(指思想等,與 towards 連用): *He has pacifist ~ings/~ings towards pacificism.* 他有和平主義者的傾向(傾向於和平主義)。 ˈ~-to *n* building with the rafters of its roof resting against the side of another building: 披屋(單斜面屋頂之屋,其屋頂之椽緊靠於另一房屋之牆壁上): (attrib) (形容用法) *a* ~*-to greenhouse.* 單斜面屋頂之溫室。

leap /liːp; lip/ *vi, vt* (*pt, pp* leapt /lept; lɛpt/ or leaped /liːpt; lipt/) **1** [VP2A, C, 3A] jump (*jump* is the usu word; *leap* is used in liter and rhet style): 跳;躍 (jump 是普通用語, leap 是文學和修辭用語): *He* ~*t at the opportunity,* seized it eagerly. 他即刻抓住了這機會。 ***Look before you ~,*** ⇨ look¹(1). **2** [VP6A, 15A] (cause to) jump over: (使)跳過;躍過: ~ *a wall;* 跳過牆; ~ *a horse over a fence.* 縱馬躍過柵欄。 □ *n* [C] jump; sudden upward or forward movement: 跳;躍: *a great* ~ *forward,* (fig) a great advance. (喻)一大進步。 ***a ~ in the dark,*** an attempt to do sth the result of which cannot be foreseen. 後果不可預料的行動;冒險的行動。 ***by ~s and bounds,*** very rapidly. 極迅速地。 ˈ~-frog *n* [U] game in which players jump with parted legs over others who stand with bent backs. 跳蛙遊戲;跳背遊戲(部分人彎背而立,供其他參加者將兩腿分開自上躍過之遊戲)。 □ *vt* (-gg-) jump over in this way. 跳蛙般地躍過。 ˈ~-year *n* in which February has 29 days. 閏年。

learn /lɜːn; lɝn/ *vt, vi* (*pt, pp* ~t /lɜːnt; lɝnt/, ~ed /lɜːnd; lɝnd/) [VP2A, 3A, 6A, 7A, 8, 9, 10, 15A, B] **1** gain knowledge of or skill in, by study, practice or being taught: 學習;學;學會: ~ *a foreign language;* 學習一外國語文; ~ *to swim/how to ride a horse.* 學游泳(騎馬)。 *Has he* ~*t his lessons?* 他的功課都學會了嗎? *Some boys* ~ *slowly.* 有些男孩子學習得慢。 ~ ***sth by heart,*** memorize it. 諳記;能背出。 **2** be told or informed: 聞知;獲悉;聽說: *I'm sorry to* ~ *of his illness/that he's ill.* 我聽說他生病,甚爲難過。 *We have not yet* ~*ed whether he arrived safely.* 我們尚未獲悉他是否已安全抵達。 **3** (vulg or dialect, sometimes *larn* /lɑːn; lɑrn/) teach: (鄙或方,有時作 larn) 教: *I'll* ~ *you* (= punish you and so teach you how unwise it is) *to come into my orchard and steal apples.* 我要叫你知道進入我的果園偷蘋果會得到什麼教訓。 ~ed /ˈlɜːnɪd; ˈlɝnɪd/ *adj* having or showing much knowledge, esp of the humanities: 有學問的(尤指在人文科學方面): *the ~ed professions,* those needing much knowledge; 需要學問的職業; *~ed men;* 有學問的人; *~ed books/periodicals/societies;* 學術性的書籍(刊物,社團); *to look ~ed.* 看起來有學問。 ~ed•ly *adv* ~er *n* person who is ~ing; beginner: 學習者;初學者: *He hasn't passed his driving test yet; he's only a* ~*er.* 他尚未通過駕駛考試,他不過剛開始學駕駛。 ~•ing *n* [U] wide knowledge gained by careful study: 學問;學識: *a man of great* ~*ing.* 學識豐富的人。

lease /liːs; lis/ *n* [C] contract by which the owner of land or a building (*the lessor*) agrees to let another (*the lessee*) have the use of it for a certain time for a fixed money payment (called *rent*); the rights given under such a contract: (土地或房屋之)租約(出租人稱作 lessor, 承租人稱作 lessee, 租金稱作 rent); 租借權: *take a farm on a* ~ *of several years.* 以若干年爲期租一農田。 *When does the* ~ *expire?* 租約何時期滿? ***by/on ~:*** 以租借的方式: *We took the land on* ~. 我們租用那塊地。 ***give sb/get a new ~ of life,*** a better chance of living longer, or of being happier, more active. (使某人)得以長壽或過更快樂和更有活力的生活。 □ *vt* [VP6A] give, take possession of (land, etc), by ~. 租出,租得,租借(土地等)。 ˌ~-ˈlend *n* [U] arrangement (1941) by which the President of the US could supply war materials to countries whose defence he considered important. 租借法案(1941年美國所定,授權美國總統可以戰爭物質援助在防衛上認爲重要的同盟國家)。 ˈ~•hold *n, adj* (land) (to be) held for a term of years on ~. 租借地;租借的。 ⇨ *freehold* at free¹(3). ˈ~•holder *n* person who holds a ~; lessee. 租借人;承租人;租賃人。

leash /liːʃ; liʃ/ *n* [C] leather strap or thong for holding or controlling an animal (esp a hound): 拴動物(尤指獵犬)的皮帶: *hold in* ~, (fig) control. (喻)控制。 ***strain at the ~,*** (fig) show eagerness to be free, to have an opportunity to do sth. (喻)渴望獲得自由或有機會做某事。

least /liːst; list/ *adj, n* (contrasted with *most;* ⇨ less, little) (與 most 相對;參看 less, little) **1 (the)** ~, smallest in size, amount, extent, etc: 最小的;最少的;最小;最少: *A has little, B has less, and C has (the)* ~. A所有的不多,B所有的更少,C所有的最少。 *There isn't the* ~ *wind today,* no wind at all. 今天一點風也沒有。 *That's the* ~ *of my anxieties.* 那是我最不擔心的。 ***The ~ said the better,*** The best thing is silence. 說得愈少愈好(最好不說)。 ***L~ said soonest mended,*** (prov) Talking will only make things worse. (諺)話越少越好;話說多了反而糟糕。 **2** (phrases) (片語) ***at ~:*** 至少: *It will cost at* ~ *five pounds,* five pounds and perhaps more. 它至少值五鎊。 *He is at* ~ *as tall as you.* 他至少和你一樣高。 *You should at* ~ *have warned her.* 你至少也應該警告她。 *You can at* ~ *try.* 你至少可以試試看。 ***(not) in the ~:*** 一點(也不);毫不: *It doesn't matter in the* ~. 一點也沒有關係。 *I don't understand in the* ~ *what this author is trying to say.* 我絲毫不明白這位作者在說些什麼。 *'Would you mind holding this box?' 'Not in the* ~.*'* I do not mind at all. '請你拿着這個箱子好嗎?' '好的。' ***to say the ~ (of it),*** without saying more; without exaggeration: 至少可以這樣說;不誇張地說: *It wasn't a very good dinner, to say the* ~ *of it.* 至少可以這樣說,那宴會不太好。 □ *adv* **(the)** ~, to the smallest extent: 最少: *He works hardest and is being paid* ~. 他工作最辛苦,待遇卻最低。 *This is the* ~ *useful of the four books.* 這是四本書中用處最少的。 ~ ***of all:*** 最不: *None of you can complain, Charles* ~ *of all,* Charles has the ~ reason for complaining. 你們誰都不應抱怨,查理尤不應該。 *L~ of all would I want to hurt your feelings,* That is sth I would never do. 我絕對沒有意思要傷害你的感情。 ˈ~•wise /-waɪz; -ˌwaɪz/ ˈ~•ways /-weɪz; -ˌwez/ *advv* or at least, or rather. 至少;無論如何。

leather /ˈleðə(r); ˈlɛðɚ/ *n* [U] material made by curing animal skins, used for making shoes, gloves, bags, etc: 皮革: ~ *upholstery,* eg for the seats of a car. 皮椅套(例如汽車座位上者)。 ˈ~-jacket *n* grub of the crane-fly. 長脚蠅的蛆。 ˈ~•neck *n* (US, sl) marine. (美,俚)海軍陸戰隊員。 ~y *adj* like ~: 似革的: *~y meat,* hard, tough. 堅韌的肉。 ˌ~-

L

'ette /-'ret ; -'rɛt/ *n* imitation ~. 假皮;人造皮。

leave¹ /liːv ; liv/ *vt, vi* (*pt, pp* left /left ; lɛft/) **1** [VP6A, 2A, 3A] go away from: 離開: *When did you ~ London?* 你什麼時候離開倫敦的? *It's time for us to ~/time we left.* 我們現在該走了。**~ for,** go away to: 到…地方去;去某地: *We're leaving for Rome next week.* 我們下星期要到羅馬去。**2** [VP6A, 15A, 2A] go away finally or permanently; no longer live (in a place); cease to belong to a school, society, etc; give up working for (an employer, etc): 永久離開;不再居於(某地);退出(學校、社團等);不再爲(某雇主等)工作: *When did you ~ school?* 你是什麼時候離開學校的? *The secretary has threatened to ~.* 那秘書曾威脅說要辭職。*The boy left home and went to sea.* 那男孩離開家去做船員。*He left medicine for the law,* changed from the medical to the legal profession. 他離開醫界而轉入法界。*My typist has left me,* has resigned. 我的打字員已辭職了。***be/get nicely left,*** (colloq) be tricked, deceived or deserted. (俗)上當;受騙;被遺棄。**3** [VP15A, B] neglect or fail to take, bring or do sth: 忽略或忘記拿、帶或做;遺忘: *I've left my umbrella in the train.* 我把傘忘在火車上了。*I left my books on the table.* 我把書忘在桌上了。*He left half his work until the next day.* 他留下一半的工作到第二天才做。**~ sb/sth behind,** neglect or forget to bring or take: 留下;遺落;忘記携帶: *The luggage has been left behind!* 行李忘記帶了! *Don't ~ me behind!* 不要把我忘了! **4** [VP 15A, B, 22, 19B, 2C, 24A, 25] allow or cause to remain in a certain place or condition: 聽任其在某處;使保持某一狀態: *L~ your hat and coat in the hall.* 把你的帽子和上衣放在門廳裏好了。*Always ~ things where you can find them again.* 永遠把東西放在你能再找到的地方。*Did you ~ the doors and windows firmly fastened?* 你把門窗關牢了嗎? *Who left that window open?* 誰讓窗開着? *His illness has left him weak.* 他的病使他身體衰弱了。*Don't ~ her waiting outside in the rain.* 不要讓她在外面雨中等待。**~ sb/sth alone,** not touch, spoil or interfere with: 不要干涉某人或某事: *L~ the cat alone,* Don't tease it. 不要逗那貓。**~ well alone,** (prov) Don't try to improve what is already satisfactory. (諺)事情已經够好了,不要再去管它;不要畫蛇添足。**~ off,** stop: 停止: *Has the rain left off yet?* 雨停了嗎? *We left off at the end of Chapter Five.* 我們在第五章末尾停止。**~ sth off, (a)** stop: 停止: *It's time to ~ off work.* 該停工了。*Do ~ off biting your nails, Jane!* 珍,千萬不要再咬妳的指甲了! **(b)** no longer wear: 不再穿. *They left off their woollen underwear when the weather got warm.* 天氣轉暖的時候,他們不再穿羊毛內衣。**~ sth/sb out,** omit; fail to consider: 忽略;遺漏: *~ out a possibility;* 忽略一個可能性; *~ out a letter,* eg spell *embarrass* with one r instead of two r's. 遺漏一個字母(例如拼 embarrass 時遺漏了一個 r)。*Don't ~ me out, please!* Don't forget me—I want a share, a place, etc. 請不要把我忘了(不要忘記我,我也要一份等)。**~ sth over,** postpone: 延後: *That matter can be left over until the committee meets next week.* 此事可延至下週委員會開會時再行處理。**~ it at that,** do or say nothing more: 不再做或說什麼;就那樣好了: *There's nothing we can do; we must ~ it at that.* 我們無能爲力,我們必須聽其自然。**~ sb to himself/to his own devices,** not try to control or direct his activities: 不要管某人;任其自由行動: *The children were left very much to themselves during the holidays,* were allowed to do what they liked, without guidance or help. 孩子們在假期中的行動未受管束。**~ sth unsaid,** not say it: 不要說出來: *Some things are better left unsaid,* It is better to remain silent about them. 有些事情最好不要說出來。**~ much/a lot/sth/nothing to be desired,** be (un)satisfactory: 不令人滿意(令人滿意): *His behaviour ~s a lot/nothing to be desired,* is very unsatisfactory/is quite satisfactory. 他的行爲不令人滿意(令人十分滿意)。**~ go/hold (of sth),** (more usu *let go*) cease holding: 放掉;放手 (let go 較常用): *L~ go of my hair, you brute!* 放開我的頭髮,你這個可惡的人! **5** [VP6A, 12B, 13B, 14] (cause to) remain; allow to remain: (使)留下;剩餘;剩下: *Three from seven ~s four* (7 − 3 = 4). 七減三餘四。*When I've paid all my debts, there'll be nothing left/I'll have nothing left.* 等我把所有的債還清,便什麼也不剩了。*Have you left anything for me/left me anything?* 你有沒有留下什麼東西給我呀? ***To be left until called for,*** used as a direction for a letter, package, etc which is to be collected. 留待來取(如書信、包裹等)。**6** [VP6A, 14, 12B, 13B] hand over before going away: (離開之前)交給;遺留: *Did the postman ~ anything for me?* 郵差給我留下什麼信件嗎? **~ word (with sb) (for sb),** give a message etc: 留信;留言: *Please ~ word (for me) with your secretary if you get news of what happened.* 如果你對發生之事有了消息,請留話給你的秘書。**7** [VP16A, 14] entrust; commit; hand over: 委託;託付;交給: *I'll ~ the matter in your hands/~ it to you/~ you to attend to the matter.* 我將這事交給你辦(我委託你辦此事)。*He left his assistant in charge of the shop/left the shop in his assistant's charge.* 他讓他的助手管理店鋪(將店鋪交給他的助手管理)。**8** [VP6A, 12A, 13A, 15A, 22] **~ sth (to sb); ~ sb sth,** bequeath by will; have at the time of one's death: 遺贈(給某人);死後留下: *She left all her money to charity.* 她將所有的錢遺留給慈善團體。*He left me £500.* 他遺留給我五百鎊。*He died leaving nothing but debts.* 他死後只留下一身債。*He ~s a widow and two sons.* 他遺下寡妻和兩個兒子。*He left her poor.* 他死後使她受窮。**9** [VP15A] pass beyond (a place, etc) so that it is in the direction or relation indicated: 經過(某個地方等): *L~ the church on your left and go on up the hill.* 經過左手邊的教堂,然後上那座山。

leave² /liːv ; liv/ *n* **1** [U] permission; consent; authority, esp to be absent from duty or work: 許可;(尤指職務或工作之)請假許可;准假: *You have my ~ to stay away from the office tomorrow.* 我准許你明天不上班。**~ of absence,** permission to be absent: 請假許可: *The soldier asked for ~ of absence.* 那士兵請假。**on ~,** absent with permission: 告假中: *He went home on ~.* 他請假回家了。**by/with your ~,** with your permission. 如果你允許的話。***(take) French ~,*** absence without permission. 未獲許可而離開;擅離職守;不辭而別。**2** [C] period of such absence; occasion of being absent from duty, etc: 假期;請假;休假: *have only two ~s in six years;* 六年中僅有兩次假; *a six months' ~.* 六個月的假。**3** [U] departure. 離開;離去。***take (one's) ~ (of sb),*** say goodbye. (向某人)告別;辭別。Hence, 由此產生, **'~-taking** *n* ***take ~ of one's senses,*** behave as if mad. 舉止若狂。

leaven /'levn ; 'lɛvən/ *n* [U] substance, eg yeast, used to make dough rise before it is baked to make bread; (fig) quality or influence spreading in and changing sth. 酵母;酵素;(喻)散佈其間而具有改變力量的性質或影響力。□ *vt* [VP6A] add ~ to; act like ~ upon. 加以酵母;使發酵;影響。

leaves /liːvz ; livz/ *pl* of leaf.

leav·ings /'liːvɪŋz ; 'livɪŋz/ *n pl* what is left, esp sth unwanted or of little value: 剩餘物(尤指不需要或無價值者): *Give the ~* (eg unwanted food) *to the dog.* 把殘餘的食物給狗吃。

lech·er·ous /'letʃərəs ; 'lɛtʃərəs/ *adj* lustful; having, giving way to, strong sexual desires. 淫蕩的;好色的。**lecher** /'letʃə(r) ; 'lɛtʃɚ/ *n* ~ person. 淫蕩的人;好色之徒。**lech·ery** /'letʃərɪ ; 'lɛtʃərɪ/ *n* [U] lust; [C] (*pl* -ries) lustful or lascivious act. 淫蕩;淫亂的行爲。

lec·tern /'lektən ; 'lɛktɚn/ *n* sloping reading-desk

L

as for a Bible in church. 教堂中的讀經枱；講桌。

lec·ture /ˈlektʃə(r)；ˈlɛktʃɚ/ *n* [C] **1** talk (to an audience or class) for the purpose of teaching: 教導性的演講；講課: *give／read a ～;* 演講(講學)；*a course of ～s on Greek philosophy;* 關於希臘哲學的一系列的演講；*go on a ～ tour.* 作講學旅行。**2** reproof: 譴責；訓誡: *give sb a ～,* scold or reprove him. 訓誡某人。□ *vi, vt* **1** [VP2A, 3A] **～ *(on),*** give a ～ or course of ～s: 演講；講課: *～ on modern drama.* 講授現代戲劇。**2** [VP6A, 14] **～ *sb (for),*** scold, reprove: 責罵；譴責: *The teacher ～d the boys for being lazy.* 教師責罵那些男孩子懶惰。**～r** /ˈlektʃərə(r)；ˈlɛktʃərɚ/ *n* person, lower in rank than a professor, who gives ～s, esp at a college or university. (大學之)講師。**～·ship** /-ʃɪp；-ˏʃɪp/ *n* post as a ～r at a university, etc. 大學講師之職位。

led /led；lɛd/ *pt, pp* of lead³.

ledge /ledʒ；lɛdʒ/ *n* **1** narrow horizontal shelf coming out from a wall, cliff or other upright surface: (牆壁、懸崖或其他直面上)突出的狹長部分: *a ˈwindow ～;* 窗枱；*a ～ for chalk at the bottom of a blackboard.* 黑板底邊的粉筆槽。**2** ridge of rocks under water, esp near the shore. 暗礁(尤指近岸者)。

ledger /ˈledʒə(r)；ˈlɛdʒɚ/ *n* **1** book in which a business firm's accounts are kept. 分類帳。**2** (music) ˈ～ (or ˈ*leger*) *line,* short line added above or below the stave for outside notes. (音樂)加線。⇨ the illus at notation. 參看 notation 之插圖。

lee /liː；li/ *n* [U] (place giving) protection against wind. 下風；背風處。**lee (side),** the side away from the wind (contrasted with the *windward* or *weather* side): 下風面；背風面 (與 windward side 或 weather side 相對): *the lee side of a ship;* 船的背風面；*a ˈlee shore,* on the lee side of one's ship; 下風岸；*a ˈlee tide,* one flowing in the same direction as the wind. 下風潮。

leech /liːtʃ；litʃ/ *n* **1** small blood-sucking worm living in wet places of which one kind was formerly used by doctors for bleeding patients: 水蛭(有一種水蛭昔時被醫生用以吸取病人之血)：***stick like a ～,*** (fig) be very persistent, be difficult to get rid of. (喻)糾纏不休。**2** (fig) person who sucks profit out of others. (喻)榨取他人利益者；吸血鬼。**3** (old use) doctor. (舊用法)醫生。

leek /liːk；lik/ *n* onion-like vegetable with a long, slender white bulb. 青葱的一種；韮。⇨ the illus at vegetable. 參看 vegetable 之插圖。

leer /lɪə(r)；lɪr/ *n* [C] sly, unpleasant look that suggests evil desire or ill will. 含惡意的一瞥；不懷好意的一瞥。□ *vi* [VP2A, 3A] **～ *(at sb),*** look with a ～: 不懷好意地瞥視: *～ing at his neighbour's pretty young wife.* 色迷迷地瞥視隣居漂亮的年輕太太。

lees /liːz；liz/ *n pl* dregs; sediments (of wine, etc); basest part; refuse (as at the bottom of a cask, etc). 渣滓；(酒等的)沉渣；沉澱部分；糟粕；(桶等底部之)廢物。***drink／drain to the ～,*** (fig) experience the last extremes of suffering, passion, etc. (喻)嘗盡辛酸。

lee·ward /ˈliːwəd；ˈliwɚd/ (among sailors: 海員讀作: /ˈluːəd；ˈluɚd/) *adj, adv* on or to the sheltered side (contrasted with *windward*). 在下風；向下風(與 windward 相對)。□ *n* [U] lee side; sheltered side: 下風面；背風面: *on the ～;* 在下風方向；*steer to ～.* 向下風行駛。

lee·way /ˈliːweɪ；ˈliˏwe/ *n* [U] sideways drift (of a ship) in the direction towards which the wind is blowing; (fig) freedom to vary (while still being tolerated or safe). 風壓差；偏航(船隻因風之作用向下風方向之偏航)；(喻)變化之餘地；改變之餘地。***make up ～,*** make up for lost time; get back into position. 趕上；回到原來的位置。

left¹ *pt, pp* of leave.

left² /left；lɛft/ *adj, n, adv* (opposite of *right*) (of, in, on, the) side of a person's body which is towards the west when he faces north: (爲 right 之相反字) 左邊的；左方的；左方；左側；在左邊；在左側: *Not many people write with the ～ hand.* 沒有多少人用左手寫字。*The ～ bank of a river is on your ～ as you face the direction in which it flows.* 當你面向河水所流的方向時，河的左岸卽在你的左方。*Come and sit on my ～,* ie at my ～ side. 來坐在我的左邊。*Turn (to the) ～ at the pub.* 在酒館那裏向左轉。**the L～ (Wing),** more radical group(s), party or parties, eg socialists, communists: 左翼(激進的黨派，例如社會黨員、共產黨員)：(attrib) (形容用法) *～-wing militants.* 左翼的好戰份子。**ˈ～-hand** *adj* of, situated on, the ～ side: 左方的；左邊的: *a house on the ～-hand side of the street;* 在街道左側的一所房屋；*a ～-hand blow／stroke.* 用左手的一擊。**ˌ～-ˈhanded** *adj* (of a person) using the ～ hand more easily or with more skill than the right. (指人) 慣用左手的。***a ～-handed compliment,*** one that is ambiguous, of doubtful sincerity. 曖昧的恭維；無誠意的恭維。**ˈ～·ist** /-ɪst；-ɪst/ *n* supporter of socialism or radicalism. 左翼份子；激進份子。

leg /leg；lɛg/ *n* **1** one of the parts of an animal's or a person's body used for walking, esp (of a human body) the part above the foot: 腿；腿部: *have a leg of mutton for dinner.* 以一隻羊腿佐餐。*He lost his right leg in the war.* 他在戰爭中失去了右腿。***be all legs,*** (of a person) be overgrown, lanky and thin. (指人) 個子過高而細瘦。***be off one's legs,*** resting: 休息: *Poor woman! She's never off her legs,* is always working. 可憐的女人！她永遠得不到休息。***be on one's legs (*** or joc, 或謔, ***on one's hind legs),*** **(a)** be standing, esp to make a speech. 站立着(尤指演說)。**(b)** (after an illness) be well enough to walk about again. (病後)開始能走路。***be on one's last legs,*** **(a)** fatigued, exhausted. 疲倦；疲憊。**(b)** near one's death or end. 將死。***feel／find one's legs,*** (*feet* is more usu) (feet 較常用) **(a)** (of a baby) get the power of standing or walking. (指嬰兒)會站立；會走。**(b)** (fig) begin to realize one's powers, abilities, etc; become self-confident. (喻)開始認識自己的能力；有了自信。***find one's ˈsea-legs,*** ⇨ sea(7). ***give sb a leg up,*** (lit) help him to mount a horse or to climb up sth; (fig) help him in time of need. (字面)扶人上馬；助某人攀登；(喻)助某人一臂之力。***pull sb's leg,*** try, for a joke, to make him believe sth that is untrue. 愚弄某人以作爲玩笑。Hence, 由此產生，**ˈleg-pull** [C] and **ˈleg-pulling** [U] *nn.* ***run sb off his legs,*** tire him by keeping him constantly busy. 使某人疲於工作。***shake a leg,*** (colloq) dance; (imper) start. (俗)跳舞；(祈使)開始。***show a leg,*** (colloq) get out of bed; (imper) do sth with more effort. (俗)起床；下床；(祈使)加勁做事。***not have a ˌleg to ˈstand on,*** have nothing to support one's opinion, defence, etc. 沒有立論根據；站不住脚。***stretch one's legs,*** go for a walk (esp to take exercise after sitting for a long time). 出外散步(尤指久坐後作爲運動者)。***take to one's legs,*** (*heels* is more usu) run away. (heels 較常用)逃走。***walk one's ˈlegs off; walk sb off his legs,*** tire oneself／him out with walking. 使自己(某人)走累。**2** that part of a garment that closely covers a leg: 衣物的腿部: *the leg of a stocking;* 襪筒；*the legs of a pair of trousers.* 褲腿。**3** support of a chair, table, etc: (桌椅等之)腿；脚: *a stool with three legs;* 三脚凳；*the legs of a bed.* 床腿。***be on its last legs,*** weak and likely to collapse. 不穩而欲倒塌。**4** [U] (cricket) part of the field to the left rear of a right-handed batsman in position (or vice versa): (板球)右手擊球員之左後方場地；左手擊球員之右後方場地: *leg-stump,* stump nearest to this; 擊球員後方三柱門之柱；*hit a ball to leg.* 擊球至後方場地。⇨ the illus at cricket. 參看 cricket 之插圖。**5**

one section of a journey, esp by air: 旅行(尤指空中者)的一段路程: *the first leg of a round-the-world flight;* 環球飛行之第一段路程; one of a series of games in a competition. (競賽中一連串比賽之)一場;一局;一項;一段賽程。 **-legged** /legd; lɛgd/ *adj* (in compounds) (用於複合字) ˌ*long-'legged,* having long legs; 長腿的; ˌ*three-'legged,* having three legs, eg a stool; 三條腿的(例如凳);三脚的; ˌ*bare-'legged,* having bare legs. 赤着腿的。ˌ**three-'legged** /'legɪd; 'lɛgɪd/ **race** *n* race for pairs with two legs tied together. 三足賽跑(每二人爲一組,將其相靠之二足捆在一起)。

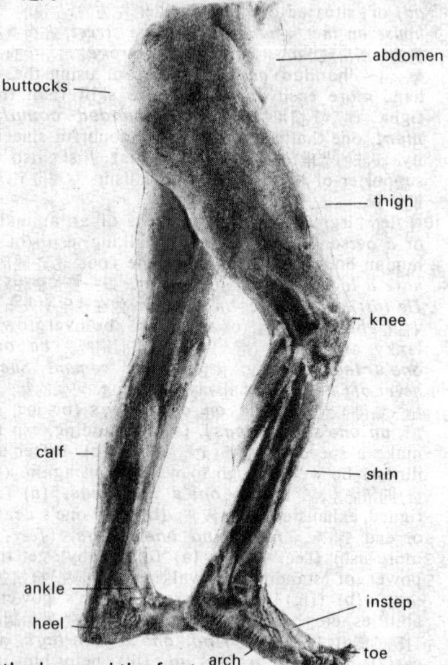

the leg and the foot

leg·acy /'legəsɪ; 'lɛgəsɪ/ *n* (*pl* -cies) [C] **1** money, etc (to be) received by a person under the will of and at the death of another person. 遺產;遺贈(物)。 **2** (fig) sth handed down from ancestors or predecessors: (喩) 祖先或先輩傳留下來的東西: *a ~ of ill will.* 宿恨;世仇。

legal /'li:gl; 'ligḷ/ *adj* connected with, in accordance with, authorized or required by, the law: 法律上的; 合法的; 法律承認的; 法律要求的; 法定的: *~ affairs;* 法律事務; *my ~ adviser/representative,* eg a solicitor; 我的法律顧問(代表)(例如律師); *take ~ action (against sb);* 提起訴訟(控告某人); *the ~ fare;* 訴訟費; *~ tender,* form of money which must be accepted if offered in payment; 法幣;法償; *a ~ offence,* one against the law, contrasted with an offence against convention; 違法(以別於違反習俗); *free ~ aid,* help (from lawyers paid by the State) given to persons unable to pay the usual charges. (由政府花錢聘請律師給予無錢請辯護律師者)免費的法律上的援助。 **~ly** /'li:gəlɪ; 'ligḷɪ/ *adv* **'~-ism** /-ɪzəm; -ˌɪzəm/ *n* [U] strict adherence to, undue respect for, the law and ~ forms. 絕對遵守法律;墨守法規;條文主義。

legal·ity /li:'gælətɪ; lɪ'gælətɪ/ *n* [U] the state or quality of being legal: 合法: *the ~ of an act.* 一行動之合法。

legal·ize /'li:gəlaɪz; 'ligḷˌaɪz/ *vt* [VP6A] make legal: 使合法;使成爲法定: *~ the sale of alcoholic drinks.* 使販賣酒類合法。 **legal·iz·ation** /ˌli:gəlaɪ'zeɪʃn *US:* -lɪ'z-; ˌligḷə'zeʃən/ *n* [U].

leg·ate /'legɪt; 'lɛgət/ *n* the Pope's ambassador to a country. 羅馬教皇的使節。

lega·tee /ˌlegə'ti:; ˌlɛgə'ti/ *n* [C] (legal) person who receives a legacy. (法律)遺產繼承人。

leg·ation /lɪ'geɪʃn; lɪ'geʃən/ *n* [C] (house, offices, etc, of a) diplomatic minister below the rank of ambassador, with those under him, representing his government in a foreign country. 公使館全體人員;公使館;公使職權。

le·gato /lɪ'gɑ:təʊ; lɪ'gɑto/ *adj, adv* (musical direction) (to be played) smoothly, without breaks. (樂譜說明)滑暢而無中斷的(地)(演奏);圓滑的(地)。

leg·end /'ledʒənd; 'lɛdʒənd/ *n* **1** [C] old story handed down from the past, esp one of doubtful truth: 傳奇;稗史: *the ~s of King Arthur.* 亞瑟王的稗史。 **2** [U] literature of such stories: 傳奇文學: *heroes who are famous in ~.* 傳奇文學中著名的英雄。 **3** [C] inscription on a coin or medal; explanatory words on a map, a picture, etc. 錢幣或獎章上的刻字;(地圖、圖畫等之)說明;圖例;題詞。 **~-ary** /'ledʒəndrɪ *US:* -derɪ; 'lɛdʒəndˌɛrɪ/ *adj* famous, known only, in ~s: 傳奇中著名的;只有稗史中記載的: *~ary heroes.* 傳奇故事中著名的英雄。

leger /'ledʒə(r); 'lɛdʒɚ/ ⇨ ledger(2).

leger·de·main /ˌledʒədə'meɪn; ˌlɛdʒɚdɪ'men/ *n* [U] juggling; quick and clever performance of tricks with the hands; (fig) deceitful argument. 戲法;魔術的明快的手法;(喩)詭辯。

leg·ging /'legɪŋ; 'lɛgɪŋ/ *n* (usu *pl*) outer covering, of leather or strong cloth, for the leg up to the knee, or (for small children) for the whole of the leg: (通常用複數)(皮或堅牢之布製成的)護脛;綁腿;(小孩之)脛衣: *a pair of ~s.* 一雙護脛。

leggy /'legɪ; 'lɛgɪ/ *adj* having long legs (esp of young children, puppies and colts). (尤指小孩、小狗和小馬)腿長的。

leg·horn /le'gɔ:n *US:* 'legən; 'lɛgɚn/ *n* **1** kind of domestic fowl. 來亨鷄。 **2** hat made of the kind of straw imported from Leghorn (also called 亦稱作 Livorno), a town in NW Italy. (用義大利西北部來亨城所產的一種草所製成的)來亨草帽。

leg·ible /'ledʒəbl; 'lɛdʒəbḷ/ *adj* (of handwriting, print) that can be read easily. (指字跡、印刷物)易讀的;清楚的。 **leg·ibly** /-əblɪ; -əblɪ/ *adv* **legi·bil·ity** /ˌledʒə'bɪlətɪ; ˌlɛdʒə'bɪlətɪ/ *n*

legion /'li:dʒən; 'lidʒən/ *n* **1** division of several thousand men in the armies of ancient Rome; (fig) great number: 古羅馬的軍團(由數千人組成);(喩)衆多: *Their numbers are ~.* 他們的數目衆多。 **2 British L~,** national association of ex-service men formed in 1921. 英國退伍軍人協會(創立於 1921 年)。**(French) Foreign L~,** body of non-French volunteers who serve in the French army, usu overseas. 法國軍隊中之外籍志願兵團(通常駐在海外)。 **L~ of Honour,** high French decoration (civilian and military). 法國高級勳章(授與文武官員)。 **3** (in liter or rhet style) vast host or number. (文學或修辭用語)衆多。 **legion·ary** /'li:dʒənərɪ *US:* -nerɪ; 'lidʒənˌɛrɪ/ *n* (*pl* -ries), *adj* (member) of a ~, esp the (French) Foreign L~. 古羅馬之軍團的(士兵);英國退伍軍人協會的(會員);(尤指)(法國)外籍兵團的(士兵)。

legis·late /'ledʒɪsleɪt; 'lɛdʒɪsˌlet/ *vi* [VP2A, 3A] make laws: 立法;制定法律: *~ against gambling.* 立法以禁止賭博。 **legis·la·tion** /ˌledʒɪs'leɪʃn; ˌlɛdʒɪs'leʃən/ *n* [U] making laws; the laws made. 立法;法律。

legis·lat·ive /'ledʒɪslətɪv *US:* -leɪtɪv; 'lɛdʒɪsˌletɪv/ *adj* (of) law-making: (關於)立法的: *~ assemblies;* 立法會議; *~ reforms.* 關於立法上的改革。

legis·la·tor /'ledʒɪsleɪtə(r); 'lɛdʒɪsˌletɚ/ *n* member of a law-making body. 立法委員;國會議員。

legis·la·ture /'ledʒɪsleɪtʃə(r); 'lɛdʒɪsˌletʃɚ/ *n* law-making body, eg Parliament in GB. 立法機關(例如英國的國會)。

le·git·imate /lɪ'dʒɪtɪmət; lɪ'dʒɪtəmɪt/ *adj* **1** lawful, regular: 合法的;正規的: *the ~ king;* 正統的國王; *use public money only for ~ purposes.* 公款只能用於合法的用途上。 **2** reasonable; that can be justified: 合理的;可說明爲正當的: *a ~ reason for being absent from one's work.* 未上班工作之正當的理由。 **3** born of persons married to one another; the result of lawful marriage: 婚生的; 嫡出的: *a ~ child;* 嫡子;婚生子; *of ~ birth.* 嫡出。 **4** ***the ~ theatre,*** drama, not revue or musical comedy etc. 正統的戲劇(非時事諷刺劇或音樂喜劇等)。**~·ly** *adv* **le·git·imacy** /lɪˈdʒɪtɪməsɪ ; lɪˈdʒɪtəməsɪ/ *n* [U] being ~. 合法; 合理; 嫡出。 **le·git·ima·tize** /lɪˈdʒɪtɪmətaɪz ; lɪˈdʒɪtəmə,taɪz/ *vt* make ~. 使合法;使合理;立爲嫡嗣。

leg·umin·ous /lɪˈgjuːmɪnəs ; lɪˈgjumənəs/ *adj* of, like, the botanical family that includes peas and beans (and other seeds in pods). 荳科的;似荳科的。

lei /ˈleɪiː ; ˈle·ɪ/ *n* garland of flowers worn round the neck (as in Polynesian islands). (玻里尼西亞群島等之人戴於頸上的)花環。

lei·sure /ˈleʒə(r) *US:* ˈliːʒər ; ˈliʒɚ/ *n* [U] **1** spare time; time free from work: 閒暇;空閒: *have no ~ for sport.* 沒有空閒做戶外活動。 ***at ~,*** (when) not occupied: 空閒的;閒暇中的: *I am seldom at ~.* 我很少有空閒。 ***at one's ~,*** when one has free time: 在空閒之時: *Please look through these papers at your ~.* 請你在閒暇時翻閱這些報紙。 **2** (attrib) (形容用法) *~ time/hours/clothes.* 空閒時間(空閒時刻;閒暇時穿的衣服)。 **~·ly** *adv* without haste or hurry: 不匆忙地;從容地: *work ~ly.* 從容地工作。 □ *adj* unhurried; deliberate: 不匆忙的;從容的: *~ly movements.* 從容的動作。 **~d** /ˈleʒəd *US:* ˈliːʒərd ; ˈliʒɚd/ *adj* having plenty of ~: 有許多空暇的: *the ~d classes.* 有閒階級。

lem·ming /ˈlemɪŋ ; ˈlɛmɪŋ/ *n* small arctic migratory rodent like a field-mouse. 旅鼠(產於北極,似田鼠)。

lemon /ˈlemən ; ˈlɛmən/ *n* **1** (tree with) pale yellow fruit with acid juice used for drinks and flavouring. 檸檬;檸檬樹。⇨ the illus at fruit. 參看 fruit 之插圖。 **ˈ~ drop** *n* piece of boiled sugar flavoured with ~. 檸檬糖。 **ˌ~ ˈsquash** *n* drink of ~-juice and water or soda-water. 檸檬水;檸檬汽水。 **ˈ~ squeezer** *n* device for pressing juice out of a ~. 檸檬榨汁器。 **ˌ~ ˈsole** *n* kind of edible flatfish, like a plaice. 一種鰈。 **2** (GB sl) silly and plain-looking person. (英俚)帶有傻氣而不漂亮的人。 **~·ade** /ˌleməˈneɪd ; ˌlɛmənˈed/ *n* [U] drink made from ~-juice, sugar and water. 檸檬水。

lemur /ˈliːmə(r) ; ˈlimɚ/ *n* nocturnal animal of Madagascar, similar to a monkey but with a fox-like face. 狐猴(馬達加斯加島所產之夜間活動的動物,狀似猴但面孔似狐)。

lend /lend ; lɛnd/ *vt* (*pt, pp* lent /lent ; lɛnt/) **1** [VP6A, 12A, 13A, 14] ***~ sth to sb; ~ sb sth,*** give (sb) the use of (sth) for a period of time on the understanding that it or its equivalent will be returned: 借出;借與;把(某物)借給(某人)使用: *I will ~ you £100, but I can't ~ money to everyone.* 我願意借給你一百鎊,但我不能借錢給每一個人。 ***~ a hand (with sth),*** help. 幫助。 **ˈ~·ing-library,** one from which books may be borrowed. 書可借出的圖書館。 **2** [VP14] ***~ sth to sth,*** contribute: 貢獻: *facts that ~ probability to a theory.* 使一理論可能成立的事實。 **3** [VP14] ***~ oneself to sth,*** give; accomodate: 協助;參與;適於: *Don't ~ yourself to such dishonest schemes.* 你不要參與此種欺詐的計畫。 *This peaceful garden ~s itself to* (= is favourable for) *meditation.* 這個恬靜的花園適合冥想。 **~er** *n* person who ~s. 借出者;貸款人。

length /leŋθ ; lɛŋθ/ *n* **1** [U] measurement from end to end (in space or time): (空間的)長;長度;(時間的)長短;期間: *the ~ of a road/field/stick;* 道路(田地,手杖)的長度; *a river 300 miles in ~;* 長達三百哩的一條河; *a room 8 metres in ~ and 6 in breadth;* 長八公尺寬六公尺的一間屋子; *a river navigable for most of its ~;* 大部分河道均可航行的一條河; *make a stay in Rome for some ~,* for a considerable period of time; 在羅馬停留一段時期; *the ~ of time needed for the work.* 完成該工作所需之時間。 ***at ~,*** **(a)** at last; finally. 終於;最後。 **(b)** for a long time: 長時間地: *speak at (great) ~.* (極)長時間地演說。 **(c)** in detail; thoroughly: 詳細地;徹底地: *treat a subject at ~.* 詳細處理一問題。 ***(at) full ~,*** with the body stretched out and flat: 全身平伸地: *lying at full ~ on the grass.* 全身平伸地躺在草地上。 ***keep sb at arm's ~,*** avoid being friendly with him. 避免與某人親近。 **2** [C] measurement of a particular thing from end to end: 某一物體之長度: *The car can turn in its own ~.* 這汽車能在相當於其本身長度的空間內轉彎。 *The horse/boat won by a ~,* by its own ~, this being used as a unit of measurement. 那馬(艇)以一身之距獲勝。 **3** [U, C] extent; extreme. 程度;極度。 ***go to any ~(s),*** do anything necessary to get what one wants. 盡一切力量達到目的。 **4** [C] piece of cloth, etc, long enough for a purpose: (其長度足以供作某用途之)一段(布料等): *a ˈdress ~;* 一塊衣料; *a ~ of tubing/pipe.* 一段管子。 **~en** /ˈleŋθən ; ˈlɛŋθən/ *vt, vi* [VP6A, 2A] make or become longer: 使長;加長;變長: *~en a skirt.* 將一裙放長。 *The days ~en in March.* 三月裏的白晝變長。 **ˈ~·wise** /-waɪz ; -ˌwaɪz/, **ˈ~·ways** /-weɪz ; -ˌwez/ *adv, adj* in the direction from end to end. 縱長地(的)。 **~y** *adj* (of speech, writing) very long; too long. (指演說,寫作)冗長的;過長的。

leni·ent /ˈliːnɪənt ; ˈlinɪənt/ *adj* not severe (esp in punishing people): 不嚴厲的(尤指在懲罰上);寬大的: *~ parents/judges.* 寬大的父母(法官)。 **leni·ence** /-əns ; -əns/, **leni·ency** /-ənsɪ ; -ənsɪ/ *nn* [U] being ~. 不嚴厲;寬大。 **~·ly** *adv*

len·ity /ˈlenətɪ ; ˈlɛnətɪ/ *n* [U] (formal) mercifulness; mercy shown. (正式用語)慈悲;寬厚。

lens /lenz ; lɛnz/ *n* (*pl* lenses) **1** piece of glass or glasslike substance with one or both sides curved, for use in spectacles, cameras, telescopes and other optical instruments. 透鏡(用於眼鏡,照相機,望遠鏡及其他光學儀器);鏡頭。⇨ the illus at camera, convex. 參看 camera, convex 之插圖。 **2** (anat) transparent part of the eye, behind the pupil, through which light is refracted. (解剖)眼睛中之水晶體。⇨ the illus at eye. 參看 eye 之插圖。

lent /lent ; lɛnt/ *pt, pp* of lend.

Lent /lent ; lɛnt/ *n* (in Christian Churches) period of forty days before Easter, the weekdays of this period being observed by devout persons as a period of fasting and penitence. (基督教)四旬齋(復活節前四十日,在此期內非星期日時需齋戒和懺悔);封齋期。 **~ lily,** daffodil. 水仙。 **~en** /ˈlentən ; ˈlɛntən/ *adj* of ~: 四旬齋的;封齋期的: *~en services* (in church); (教會中)四旬齋期的禮拜; sparse: 稀少的: *~en fare.* 稀少的飲食。

len·til /ˈlentl ; ˈlɛntl/ *n* [C] kind of bean plant; edible seed of this: 扁豆: *~ soup.* 扁豆湯。

lento /ˈlentəʊ ; ˈlɛnto/ *adj, adv* (musical direction) slow(ly). (樂譜說明)緩慢的(地)。

Leo /ˈliːəʊ ; ˈlio/ *n* the fifth sign of the zodiac. 獅子宮(黃道帶之第五宮)。⇨ the illus at zodiac. 參看 zodiac 之插圖。

leo·nine /ˈlɪənaɪn ; ˈliə,naɪn/ *adj* of or like a lion. 獅的;似獅的。

leop·ard /ˈlepəd ; ˈlɛpɚd/ *n* large African and South Asian flesh-eating animal with a yellowish coat and dark spots. 豹。⇨ the illus at cat. 參看 cat 之插圖。 **~·ess** /ˌlepəˈdes ; ˈlɛpɚdɪs/ *n* female ~. 母豹。

leper /ˈlepə(r) ; ˈlɛpɚ/ *n* person suffering from leprosy. 痲瘋患者。

lep·re·chaun /ˈleprəkɔːn ; ˈlɛprə,kɔn/ *n* (in Irish folklore) fairy or sprite. (愛爾蘭民間傳說中之)妖精。

lep·rosy /ˈleprəsɪ ; ˈlɛprəsɪ/ *n* [U] skin disease that forms silvery scales on the skin, causes local

L

insensibility to pain, etc and the loss of fingers and toes. 痲瘋病。 **lep·rous** /ˈleprəs ; ˈlɛprəs/ *adj* of, having, ~. 痲瘋病的;患痲瘋病的。

les·bian /ˈlezbɪən ; ˈlɛzbɪən/ *n* homosexual woman. 同性戀愛之女子。 **~·ism** /-ɪzəm ; -ɪzm̩/ *n*

lese maj·esty /ˌleɪz ˈmædʒɪstɪ *US:* ˌliːz- ; ˈliz ˈmædʒɪstɪ/ *n* [U] treason; (joc) presumptuous conduct on the part of inferiors. 叛逆; (謔) 地位低者的僭越行爲。

lesion /ˈliːʒn ; ˈliʒən/ *n* [C] harmful change in the tissues of a bodily organ, caused by injury or disease. (因受傷或疾病而引起的)身體上的損害。

less /les ; lɛs/ *adj* (~ is contrasted with *more.* It is an independent comparative, with no real corresponding positive. ⇨ little, least.) (與 more 相對,乃一獨立的比較級,無眞正相當的原級。) **1** (used with a *n* that stands for what is measured by amount or quantity or degree; *fewer* is used before a *pl n*) not so much; a smaller quantity of: 少量的; 較少的(與可用數量或程度量度的名詞連用; 在複數名詞前用 fewer) : *~ butter.* 較少的奶油。Cf 參較 *fewer eggs; ~ food.* 較少的食物。Cf 參較 *fewer meals; ~ manpower.* 較少的人力。Cf 參較 *fewer workers; ~ shipping.* 較少的船舶。Cf 參較 *fewer ships; pay ~ money for the house.* 付較少的房租。Cf 參較 *pay a lower rent; have ~ difficulty with one's work.* 工作較少困難。Cf 參較 *meet with fewer difficulties; ~ size means ~ weight;* 較小卽較輕; *of ~ value/importance.* 價值較少(較不重要)的。**2** (followed by *than*): (其後與 than 連用): *I have ~ money than you.* 我的錢比你的少。□ *adv* **1** (modifying *vv*) to a smaller extent; not so much: (修飾動詞)較少;少: *Eat ~, drink ~, and sleep more.* 少吃,少飲酒,多睡眠。**2** (with *adjj, participles* and *advv*) not so: (與形容詞,分詞,副詞連用)不如; 不及;不如此: *Tom is ~ clever than his brother.* 湯姆不及他的哥哥(弟弟)聰明。*Please behave ~ foolishly.* 請不要這樣愚蠢。Note that *less...than* may be replaced by *not so...as,* 注意: less...than 可由 not so...as 代替, eg 例如 *He was ~ hurt than frightened.* 他受的傷不重,但是被嚇得厲害。Cf 參較 *He was not so hurt as frightened. Try to be ~ impatient.* 不要這樣急躁。Cf 參較 *Try not to be so impatient.* **3** ***the ~:*** *I was the ~ surprised as I had been warned,* My surprise was ~ because.... 因爲我事先受到警告,故不十分吃驚。*The ~ you worry about it the better it will be.* 你越不爲此事擔心越好。⇨ the. ***any the ~,*** in a lower degree: 程度較少: *I don't think any the ~ of him* (= My opinion of him is not lower) *because of this one failure.* 我並不因爲此一失敗而輕視他。 ***even/still ~,*** and certainly not: 而且當然不會: *I don't suspect him of robbery, still ~ of robbery with violence.* 我不懷疑他會搶劫,更不用說用暴力打劫了。***no less(...) than...,*** not a smaller amount (of sth) than...: 不少於;不減於: *He won no ~ than £50 in the lottery/He won £50, no ~, in the lottery* (expressing surprise at the amount). 他居然中了五十鎊的獎券(表示對此數額的驚奇)。 *Our soldiers fought with no ~ daring than skill,* Their daring equalled their skill. 我們的士兵作戰的英勇不亞於他們的戰技。 ***none the ~,*** but for all that; all the same: 仍舊;依然: *Though he cannot leave the house, he is none the ~* (= he is, in spite of that) *busy and active.* 雖然他不能離開房屋,但他依舊是忙碌和活躍的。 □ *n* [U] smaller amount, quantity, time, etc: 較少的數額,數量,時間等: *in ~ than an hour.* 不到一小時。*I won't sell it for ~ than £50.* 少於五十鎊我不賣。*I want ~ of this and more of that.* 我少要點這個,多要點那個。Cf 參較 *fewer of these and more of those. I expect to see ~ of her* (= to see her ~ often) *in future.* 我希望今後少同她見面。□ *prep* minus; with the deduction of: 減除: *£30 a week ~ £2 for National Insurance contribution.* 每週三十鎊,扣除二鎊國民保險費。

L

les·see /leˈsiː ; lɛsˈi/ *n* person who holds land, a building, etc on a lease. 租地人;租屋人;承租者。

les·sen /ˈlesn ; ˈlɛsn̩/ *vt, vi* **1** [VP6A, 2A] make or become less: 減少;變少: *to ~ the impact/effect of sth.* 減少某事物之衝擊力(影響)。**2** [VP6A] cause (sth) to appear smaller, less important; belittle: 使變小;使較不重要;貶抑: *~ a person's importance.* 貶抑某人的重要性。

les·ser /ˈlesə(r) ; ˈlɛsɚ/ *adj* (attrib only) not so great as the other: (僅作形容用法) 較小的; 次要的: *choose the ~ evil.* (兩禍害中)選擇較輕的禍害。***in/to a ~ degree,*** not so much as the other. 程度較輕。

les·son /ˈlesn ; ˈlɛsn̩/ *n* **1** sth to be learnt or taught; period of time given to learning or teaching: 課; 一節課; 課程: *ˈEnglish ~s;* 英文課; *a ~ in music.* 音樂課。**2** (*pl*) children's education in general: (複)兒童的功課;課業: *Tom is very fond of his ~s.* 湯姆很喜歡他的課業。**3** sth experienced, esp sth serving as an example or a warning: 經驗(尤指作爲警誡者);教訓: *Let his fate be a ~ to all of you!* 讓他的下場給你們大家一個教訓! **4** passage from the Bible read aloud during a church service. 禮拜儀式中誦讀的一段聖經。

les·sor /ˈlesɔː(r) ; ˈlɛsɔr/ *n* (legal) person who grants a lease. (法律)出租土地,房屋等者;出租人。

lest /lest ; lɛst/ *conj* **1** for fear that; in order that... not: 因恐;以免: *He ran away ~ he should be seen.* 他因爲怕被人看見而逃跑了。 **2** (after *fear, be afraid/anxious etc*) that: (用於 fear, be afraid/anxious 等之後,等於) that: *We were afraid ~ he should get here too late.* 我們恐怕他會來得太遲。

let[1] /let ; lɛt/ *vt, vi* (*pt, pp* let) (-tt-) (For uses with *adverbial particles* and *preps* ⇨ 8 below.) (與副詞接語和介詞連用之用法,參看下列第8義。) **1** [VP18B] (followed by a *noun/pronoun* and an *infinitive* without *to;* rarely used in the passive in this sense) allow to: 允許;讓(其後跟一名詞或代名詞,再接一沒有 to 的不定詞,用於此義罕作被動): *Her father will not let her go to the dance.* 她父親不會讓她去參加舞會。*She wants to go to the party but her father won't let her* (ie let her *go.* The omission of the *infinitive* is frequent when it may be inferred from the context). 她要去參加那聚會,但她父親不允許她去(her 之後省略了 go,當有上下文可以推知時,此種不定詞常省略)。*Please let me know* (ie inform me) *what happens.* 請告訴我發生了什麼事情。*Don't let the fire go out.* 不要讓火熄滅。 **2** [VP18B] (used with first and third person *pronouns* to supply an indirect imperative): (與第一人稱和第三人稱的代名詞連用,形成間接的祈使句):*Let's start at once, shall we?* 我們卽刻動身吧,好嗎? *Don't let's start yet!* 還不要開始! *Let me see—where did I leave my hat?* 讓我想一想 —— 我的帽子放到哪兒去了呢? *Let us both have a try!* 讓我們兩人都試試看! *Let her do it at once.* 讓她馬上做此事。*Let there be no mistake about it,* Don't make any mistake, don't misunderstand me, etc. 此事不要弄錯了。***Live and let live,*** ⇨ live[2](2). **3** [VP18B] (*let,* in the imperative, may also indicate an assumption. It may also indicate permission, with a suggestion of defiance): (let 在祈使句中亦可指假設,有時亦指許可,但含有挑戰的意味): *Let AB be equal to CD.* 假設 AB 等於 CD。*Let ABC be an angle of ninety degrees.* 假設 ABC 爲一九十度角。*Let them do their worst!* I defy them to do their worst! 讓他們蠻幹好啦(我不相信他們敢蠻幹)! *Let them all come!* 讓他們都來吧! **4** [VP 18B] (The pattern *let + noun + infinitive,* as in *let the waitress go,* is sometimes replaced by the pattern *let + infinitive + noun,* as in *let drop a hint.* In some cases, eg in *let fly,* the object of *let* is omitted). (let+名詞+不定詞之句型,例如: let the waitress go, 有時可改作 let + 不定詞+名詞,例如: let drop a hint。有時 let 的受詞可以省略,例如: let fly)。Note the following: 注意下列者:

let sb/sth be, allow to be quiet or unworried: 不攪擾某人或某物: *Let me be,* Don't worry me. 不要打擾我。*Let the poor dog be,* Don't tease it. 不要捉弄那隻可憐的狗。***let drive (at sb/sth),*** aim a blow (at); throw sth (at): 瞄擊;向…投擲: *He let drive with his left fist.* 他用左拳擊出。*He let drive at me with a stone.* 他拿一石頭對我擲來。***let sb/sth drop,*** allow to drop; (fig) utter (on purpose or by chance). 使跌下;丢下;(喻)(故意或偶然)說出。***let sth fall,*** allow to fall; (fig) allow to be heard: 使跌倒;丢下;(喻)說出;吐露出: *He let fall a hint of his intentions.* 他吐露出一點他的意向。***let fly (at sb/sth),*** discharge; send out violently; shoot; strike out (at): 發出;猛烈地發出;射出;擊出: *He aimed carefully and then let fly* (ie fired) *at the ducks.* 他仔細地瞄準,然後射向那些鴨子。*The angry man let fly a volley of oaths.* 那憤怒的人發出一連串的咒語。***let sb/sth go; let go of sb/sth,*** release one's hold of him/it: 放手;鬆手;放開: *Don't let the rope go/let go of the rope.* 不要鬆開那繩子。*Let me go!* Take your hands off me; don't hold or keep me. 放開你的手!不要拉我!讓我走! ***let oneself go,*** give way to, no longer hold back, one's feelings, desires, impulses, etc: 儘量發洩情感、慾望、衝動等: *He let himself go on the subject.* 他暢談此一問題。***let it go at that,*** say no more about it; dismiss the subject: 不再談論某事;停止討論一問題: *I don't agree with all you say but we'll let it go at that.* 我並不全同意你說的話,但我們不要再談此事了。***let sth pass,*** overlook; disregard: 忽略;忽視: *It's not a serious error; we can let it pass, I think.* 這不是個嚴重的錯誤,我想我們可以不必重視它。***let sth slip,*** **(a)** miss (an opportunity, etc). 錯過(機會等)。**(b)** = let sth drop/fall, (see above). **5** [VP22] (combined with *adjj*) (與形容詞連用) ***let sb/sth alone,*** allow (sb) to do sth unaided; not interfere with: 不管;不要干涉: *Let it alone!* 不要管它! ***Let well alone,*** (prov) Don't try to improve sth that is already satisfactory. (諺) 對已感滿意之事不要再求改善;不要畫蛇添足。***let alone,*** (colloq) to say nothing of; not to mention: (俗)遑論;至於…更不必說了: *There were seven people in the car, let alone a pile of luggage and three dogs.* 那部汽車載了七個人,更不必說還有一堆行李和三隻狗了。***let sb/sth loose (on sb/sth),*** allow to be free (somewhere); (fig) release (one's anger, etc on sb): 釋放;放掉;(喻)發洩(憤怒等): *Don't let that dog loose.* 不要放開那條狗。**6** [VP6A, 14, 22, 24A] ~ ***sth (to),*** give the use of (buildings, land) in return for regular money payments: 出租(房屋,土地): *This house is to be let.* 此屋出租。*The house would let* (= could be let) *easily.* 這房子容易出租。*She has let her house furnished.* 她已將她備有傢具的房屋租出。***to let,*** offered for renting. 出租。***let out,*** put out to hire: 出租: *He used to let out horses by the day.* 他以前常按日出租馬。**7** [VP6A] (surgery) ~ ***blood,*** cause it to flow. (外科)放血。Hence, 由此產生, **'blood-letting** *n* [U]. **8** [VP15A, B, 2C, 14] (uses with *adverbial particles* and *preps*): (與副詞接語和介詞連用之用法):

let sth down, lower; put or take down: 放低;放下: *Please let the window down.* 請放下窗子。*This skirt needs letting down,* lengthening by lowering the hemline. 這條裙子需要放長。*She let down her hair.* 她鬆下她的頭髮。*That chair has a broken leg, it might let you down,* might not support you. 那椅子有一條腿斷了,它可能會使你跌倒。***let sb down,*** (fig) disappoint; fail to help: (喻)使某人失望;不幫助: *Harry will never let you down,* You can rely upon him to help you always. 哈利永不會置你於不顧(你永遠可以依賴他的幫助)。*I've been badly let down,* placed in a difficult or awkward situation through the failure of others to support me. 我非常失望(由於別人不支持我而陷入困境)。Hence, 由此產生, **'let-down** *n* feeling of having been let down; disappointment. 失望。***let the side down,*** ⇨ side[1](10).

let sb/sth in/into sth, allow to enter: 允許進入;放入: *Windows let in light and air.* 窗子使光線和空氣進入。*These shoes let in water.* 這些鞋子會進水。*He let himself in/into the flat with a latch-key,* opened the door using the key. 他用鑰匙打開彈簧鎖而進入公寓。*Who let you into the building?* 誰讓你進入那房屋的?

let sth in, make (a garment, etc) narrower: 將(衣物等)改窄: *This skirt needs letting in at the waist.* 這裙子的腰部需要改窄。***let sb in for sth,*** involve in loss, difficulty, hard work, etc: 使陷入(損失,困難,辛苦工作等): *He didn't know what a lot of unpaid work he was letting himself in for when he agreed to become secretary of the society.* 當他同意擔任該社的秘書時,他不知道他將做許多無報酬的工作。

let sb into sth, allow to share (a secret): 使知道(秘密): *She has been let into* (= told) *the secret.* 她已知道這秘密了。***let sth into sth,*** put into the surface of: 嵌進: *We must let another window into this wall.* 我們必須在這牆上再裝一個窗戶。

let sb off, excuse; not compel; not punish; not punish severely: 原諒;不强迫;不懲罰;使免受重罰: *He was let off with a fine instead of being sent to prison.* 他沒有坐牢,而祇是受罰款了事。*You have let him off lightly,* eg by excusing him from too much work, by punishing him lightly, etc. 你輕易地放過了他(例如免除他過多的工作,減輕懲罰等)。***let sth off,*** fire off: 放(槍砲,烟火等): *The boys were letting off fireworks.* 男孩子們在放烟火。

let on (that...), (colloq) reveal a secret: (俗)洩露秘密: *He knew where the boy was hiding but he didn't let on,* didn't tell anyone. 他知道那男孩藏在哪裡,但他不洩露給別人。

let sb/sth out, allow to go (flow, etc) out: 使出去;使流出;放出: *He let the air out of the tyres.* 他將輪胎的氣放掉。*Let the water out of the bath-tub.* 把浴盆中的水放掉。***let sth out,*** make (a garment, etc) looser, larger, etc: 放寬(衣服等);放大: *He's getting so fat that his trousers need to be let out round the waist.* 他愈來愈胖,故而他的褲腰需要放寬。⇨ also 6 above. 亦參看上列第6義。***let out at sb,*** aim a violent blow, kick, etc, at him; (fig) use violent language to him. 向某人猛擊,猛踢等;(喻)猛烈地攻訐某人: *Be careful! That mule has a habit of letting out at people.* 當心!那匹騾子有踢人的習慣。

let sb/sth through (sth), allow to pass (an examination, etc): 使通過(考試等): *He got only 40%, so the examiners couldn't possibly let him through.* 他祇得到四十分,所以主試者不可能讓他通過。

let up, become less strong, etc: 減弱: *Will the rain never let up?* 雨勢永不會減弱嗎? **'let-up** *n* (colloq) cessation; diminution: (俗)停止;中止;減小: *There has been no let-up in the rain yet.* 雨一直沒有停過。*I've been working ten hours without a let-up.* 我已工作了十小時未曾中斷。***let up on sb,*** (colloq) treat more leniently. (俗)對待某人比較寬大。

let[2] /let; lɛt/ *n* (from let[1](6)) letting; lease: (出自動詞 let 第6義)出租;租出: *I can't get a let for my house,* can find no one willing to rent it from me. 我的房子租不出去。**let·ting** *n* [C] property that is let: 出租的房屋等: *a furnished letting,* a furnished house or flat that is let. 備有傢具的出租的房屋或公寓。

let[3] /let; lɛt/ *vt* (archaic) hinder; obstruct. (古)妨礙;阻礙。□ *n* **1** hindrance, esp in the legal phrase: 阻礙(特別作法律上用語): *without let or hindrance.* 毫無阻礙。**2** (tennis) ball which when served, strikes the net before dropping into the opponent's court. (網球)(發球時)球觸網。

lethal /'li:θl; 'liθəl/ *adj* causing, designed to cause, death: 致命的: *a ~ dose of poison;* 一劑致命的毒藥; *~ weapons;* 兇器; *a ~ chamber,* eg in which sick animals may be put to death painlessly. 致命室(例如可使有病動物無痛苦地死去者)。

leth·argy /ˈleθədʒɪ; ˈlɛθədʒɪ/ *n* [U] (state of) being tired, uninterested; want of energy. 倦怠;無興趣;無生氣。 **leth·ar·gic** /lɪˈθɑːdʒɪk; lɪˈθɑrdʒɪk/ *adj* sleepy; lacking in energy; caused by, likely to cause, ~. 睏倦的;無力氣的;倦怠所引起的;易引起倦怠的。 **leth·ar·gi·cally** /-klɪ; -klɪ/ *adv*

Lethe /ˈliːθɪ; ˈliθɪ/ *n* (Gk myth) (river in Hades, the Greek underworld, producing) forgetfulness of the past. (希神)冥府的遺忘河(飲其水令人遺忘過去);忘却往事。

let's /lets; lɛts/ = let us. ⇨ let¹(2).

let·ter /ˈletə(r); ˈlɛtɚ/ *n* **1** character or sign representing a sound, of which words in writing are formed: 字母: *the 26 ~s of the English alphabet;* 英文的二十六個字母; *capital ~s* (A, B, C, etc) *and small ~s* (a, b, c, etc). 大寫字母(A, B, C 等)和小寫字母(a, b, c 等)。Cf 參較 phonetic *symbol.* **2** written message, request, account of events, etc sent by one person to another: 書信;函件: *I have some ~s to write.* 我有幾封信要寫。*Inform me by ~ of your plans.* 寫信告訴我你的計畫。ˌ**~ of ˈcredit,** ⇨ credit¹(1). ˈ**~-box** *n* (US 美 = *mail box*) **(a)** box (in the street, at a post office) in which ~s are posted; pillar-box. (街道上或郵局之)郵箱;郵筒。**(b)** box (in a building) for receiving ~s from the post. (房屋等內之)信箱。ˈ**~-card** *n* folded card with a gummed edge for use instead of notepaper and an envelope. 郵簡;封緘信片。ˈ**~-case** *n* pocket-book for holding ~s. 夾信件的小夾。ˈ**~·head** *n* (sheet of paper with a) printed name and address, eg of a business firm. 印於信紙上的信頭(例如公司行號的名稱和地址);有信頭的信紙。ˈ**~·press** *n* [U] contents of an illustrated book other than the pictures; printing from type. 有插圖的印刷物中的文字部分;本文(以別於插圖);活字印刷;凸板印刷。**3** (phrases) (片語) ***keep (to) the ~ of the law/an agreement,*** carry out the stated conditions without regard to its spirit or true purpose. 拘泥於法律(協約)的條文而忽略其精神或宗旨。***to the ~,*** paying strict attention to every detail: 嚴密周詳地: *carry out an order to the ~.* 徹底執行命令。**4** (*pl*) literature and learning: (複)文學;文學修養: *the profession of ~s;* 文人的職業;著作業; *a man of ~s.* 文學家;文人。**~ed** /ˈletəd; ˈlɛtɚd/ *adj* having a good knowledge of books: 有學問的: *a ~ed young man.* 有學問的青年。**~·ing** /ˈletərɪŋ; ˈlɛtərɪŋ/ *n* [U] ~s, words, esp with reference to their style and size: 文字(尤指就其字體和大小而言): *the ~ing on a book cover;* 一書封面上所印的文字; *poor ~ing on a gravestone.* 墓碑上拙劣的彫刻文字。

let·tuce /ˈletɪs; ˈlɛtɪs/ *n* [C] garden plant with crisp green leaves used in salads; [U] these leaves as food. 萵苣;萵苣葉;生菜。⇨ the illus at vegetable. 參看 vegetable 之插圖。

leu·co·cyte (US = **leu·ko·cyte**) /ˈluːkəsaɪt; ˈlukəˌsaɪt/ *n* [C] white blood-cell. 白血球。

leu·kae·mia (US = **leu·ke·mia**) /luːˈkiːmɪə; luˈkimɪə/ *n* [U] disease in which there is an excess of leucocytes, with changes in the lymph glands. 白血球過多症;血癌。

Lev·ant /lɪˈvænt; ləˈvænt/ *n* **the ~,** Eastern part of the Mediterranean, its countries and islands. 地中海東部諸國家和島嶼。**~·ine** /-aɪn; -aɪn/ *n, adj* (native) of the ~. 地中海東部諸國家和島嶼的(人)。

lev·ant /lɪˈvænt; ləˈvænt/ *vi* abscond; leave (esp without paying gambling losses). 潛逃;離去(尤指未付賭債而走掉)。

levee¹ /ˈlevɪ; ləˈvi/ *n* (hist) formal reception; (GB) assembly held by a king or his representative at which men only were received. (史)正式接見;(英)君王或其代表爲男士們所舉行的接見會。

levee² /ˈlevɪ; ˈlɛvɪ/ *n* (US) embankment built to protect land from a river in flood: (美)防洪堤;河堤: *the ~s along the Mississippi.* 密西西比河沿岸的防洪堤。

level¹ /ˈlevl; ˈlɛvl̩/ *adj* **1** having a horizontal surface: 平的;水平的: *~ ground;* 平地; *make a surface ~.* 使一表面變平。**~ crossing,** (US 美 = *grade crossing*) place where a road and a railway cross on the same ~. 平交道。**2** on an equality: 同等的;相等的: *a ~ race,* one in which the competitors keep close together; 勢均力敵的賽跑; *draw ~ with the other runners.* 與其他賽跑者相齊。**3 *have a ~ head,*** be steady and well-balanced, able to judge well. 有穩健清晰的頭腦。Hence, 由此產生, ˌ**~-ˈheaded** *adj.* ***do one's ~ best,*** do all that one can do, do everything possible. 盡最大的努力。

level² /ˈlevl; ˈlɛvl̩/ *n* **1** [C] line or surface parallel with the horizon; such a surface with reference to its height: 水平線;水平面;就其高度而論的平面: *1000 metres above sea ~.* 海拔一千公尺。*The water rose until it was on a ~ with the river banks.* 河水漲至與河岸相平的高度。*Water always finds its own ~.* 水總會找到它的水平面(水往低處流直到形成水平面)。**2** natural or right position, stage, social standing, etc: 自然或適當的位置,階段,社會地位等: *He has found his own ~,* (fig) has found the kind of people with whom he is morally, socially or intellectually equal. (喻)他已找到與他相稱的人(指在品行、身分或智力方面相當者)。*They'll rise to higher ~s* (= advance in civilization, etc) *very quickly.* 他們在文明方面將會很迅速地提高。**3** [U] (group of persons having) equal position or rank: 相等的地位或階級;同等地位的人: *consultations at cabinet ~,* among members of the cabinet; 內閣閣員間的磋商; *top-level talks,* talks between persons in the highest positions (in government, etc). (政府等中的)高階層會議。(Cf 參較 *summit talks.*) ˈ**O-/ˈA-~ (examination)** *n* [C] ~ of achievement (Ordinary/Advanced) in the school-leaving examination in England and Wales: (英格蘭和威爾斯)普通(高級)畢業標準考試: *a girl with five O-~s and three A-~s.* 通過五次普通考試和三次高級考試的女孩。**4 *on the ~,*** (colloq) honest(ly); straightforward(ly): (俗)誠實的(地);坦率的(地): *Is he on the ~?* 他誠實嗎? ⇨ crooked(2). **5 ˈ*spirit ~,*** ⇨ spirit(11).

level³ /ˈlevl; ˈlɛvl̩/ *vt, vi* (-ll-, US -l-) **1** [VP6A, 15A, B] make or become ~ or flat: 使平;使平坦;變平: *~ a building with the ground.* 拆除一建築物。*Death ~s all men,* makes them equal by ending social distinctions, etc. 死使一切人皆平等(死使社會地位等無差別)。***~ sth down/up,*** make (incomes, marks, standards, surfaces, etc) equal by lowering the higher or raising the lower. (藉降低高者或提高低者)使(收入,分數,標準,表面等)相等。**2** [VP6A, 14, 2C, 3A] bring or come into a horizontal plane: 使成平面;變成平面: *~ a gun at a tiger,* raise it and aim. 舉槍瞄準一虎。***~ sth against sb,*** put forward (a charge, an accusation, etc). 控訴某人。***~ off/out,*** **(a)** cause an aircraft to fly parallel to the earth's surface: 使飛機平飛: *On reaching 1000 metres, the pilot ~led off.* 到達一千公尺高時,那駕駛員便作水平飛行。**(b)** (fig) reach a point in one's career beyond which no further progress is likely: (喻)事業到達不大可能再有發展的階段: *You're unlikely to get further promotion—we all have to ~ off some time.* 你大概不會得到擢升 ── 我們的事業必定會到達不再有發展的時候。**~·ler,** US **~er** /ˈlevələ(r); ˈlɛvl̩ɚ/ *n* (esp) person who wishes to abolish social distinctions. (尤指)主張社會地位平等者。

lever /ˈliːvə(r) *US:* ˈlevər; ˈlɛvɚ/ *n* bar or other tool turned on a fulcrum to lift sth or to force sth open, eg a window or drawer; (fig) means by which moral force may be exerted. 槓桿；(喩)激發道德力量的方法。□ *vt* [VP6A, 15B] move (sth *up, along, into／out of position*, etc) with a ～. 用槓桿移動(與 up, along, into position, out of position 等連用)。 **～·age** /-ɪdʒ ; -ɪdʒ/ *n* [U] action of, power or advantage gained by, using, a ～. 槓桿作用；由槓桿獲得的力量或利益；槓桿利率。

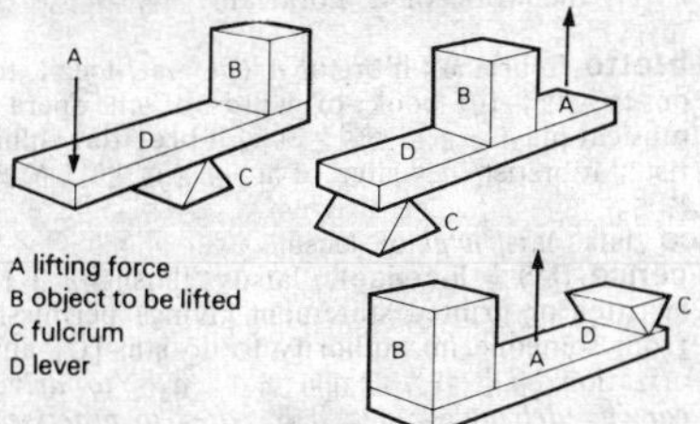

leverage

lev·eret /ˈlevərɪt ; ˈlɛvərɪt/ *n* young (esp first-year) hare. 小野兎(尤指未滿一歲者)。

lev·ia·than /lɪˈvaɪəθən ; ləˈvaɪəθən/ *n* **1** (in the Bible) sea animal of enormous size. (聖經中)巨大海獸；鱷魚。 **2** anything of very great size and power. 任何巨大有力的東西。

levis /ˈliːvaɪz ; ˈlivaɪz/ *n pl* (P) jeans. (商標)牛仔褲。

levi·tate /ˈlevɪteɪt ; ˈlɛvəˌtet/ *vt, vi* [VP6A, 2A] (with reference to powers claimed by spiritualists) (cause to) rise and float in the air in defiance of gravity. (關涉招魂論者所聲稱的力量)(使)飄浮在空中。 **levi·ta·tion** /ˌlevɪˈteɪʃn ; ˌlɛvəˈteʃən/ *n*

lev·ity /ˈlevətɪ ; ˈlɛvətɪ/ *n* [U] (formal) tendency to treat serious matters without respect; lack of seriousness; [C] (*pl* -ties) instance of this. (正式用語)輕率；輕浮。

levy /ˈlevɪ ; ˈlɛvɪ/ *vt, vi* (*pt, pp* levied) **1** [VP6A, 14] **～(on),** impose; collect by authority or force: 徵收；徵集；强迫收集: *～ a tax／a fine／a ransom on sb;* 向某人徵收稅(罰金，索取贖金)； *～ing an army／troops*, using compulsion to get men as soldiers. 徵集軍隊。 **2** **～ war upon／against,** declare, make, war on after ～ing men and supplies. 向…開戰。 **3** [VP3A] **～ on,** seize by law: 扣押: *～ on a person's property／estate*, seize this in order to get money for an unpaid debt. (爲未付欠債)扣押某人的財產。□ *n* (*pl* levies) [C] act of ～ing; amount of men, number of men, so obtained. 徵收；徵集；徵集的員額。 **capital ～,** ⇨ capital².

lewd /ljuːd *US:* luːd ; lud/ *adj* indecent; lustful. 猥褻的；淫蕩的。 **～·ly** *adv* **～·ness** *n*

lexi·cal /ˈleksɪkl ; ˈlɛksɪkḷ/ *adj* (contrasted with *grammatical*) of the vocabulary of a language. (與grammatical相對)語彙的；語詞的。 **～ly** /-klɪ ; -klɪ/ *adv* **lexis** /ˈleksɪs ; ˈlɛksɪs/ *n* [U] vocabulary. 字彙。

lexi·cogra·phy /ˌleksɪˈkɒɡrəfɪ ; ˌlɛksəˈkɑɡrəfɪ/ *n* [U] dictionary compiling. 字典編纂。 **lexi·cogra·pher** /ˌleksɪˈkɒɡrəfə(r) ; ˌlɛksəˈkɑɡrəfɚ/ *n* person who compiles a dictionary. 字典編輯人。

lexi·con /ˈleksɪkən *US:* -kɒn ; ˈlɛksɪkən/ *n* dictionary (esp of Greek, Latin or Hebrew). 字典(尤指希臘，拉丁或希伯來語者)。

ley /leɪ ; le/ *n* [C] area of land temporarily under grass: 暫時長滿草之可耕地；休耕地: *new-sown leys.* 剛播過種的休耕地。

lia·bil·ity /ˌlaɪəˈbɪlətɪ ; ˌlaɪəˈbɪlətɪ/ *n* (*pl* -ties) **1** [U] the state of being liable: 應負責；有義務；易遭受；有某種傾向: *～ to pay taxes;* 納稅的義務； *～ for military service*, in a country where there is conscription; (在行徵兵制度的國內)服兵役的義務； *～ to disease.* 易患疾病。 *Don't admit ～ for the accident*, eg because of car insurance claims. 不要承認對此意外事件負責(例如由於汽車保險之要求)。 **ˌlimited ˈ～ company,** ⇨ limit². **2** (*pl*) debts; sums of money that must be paid (contrasted with *assets*). (複)債務；負債(與 assets 相對)。 **3** (colloq) handicap: (俗)阻礙；不利: *His wife is more of a ～ at a party than an asset.* 在宴會中他的妻子不是得力助手，反而是個礙事的人。

li·able /ˈlaɪəbl ; ˈlaɪəbḷ/ *adj* (usu *pred*) (通常作敍述用法) **1** **～ for,** responsible according to law: 應負責任: *Is a man ～ for his wife's debts in your country?* 在你的國家裏丈夫應爲其妻之債務負責嗎？ **2** **be ～ to sth,** be subject to: 易遭受: *If you drive a car to the danger of the public, you make yourself ～ to a heavy fine, or even to imprisonment.* 如果你開汽車危及公衆的安全，你可能受到重的罰款，甚或坐牢。 *He is ～ to seasickness.* 他易暈船。 **3** **be ～ to do sth,** have a tendency to, be likely to: 有做…的傾向；易爲: *We are all ～ to make mistakes occasionally.* 我們有時都會犯錯。

li·aise /lɪˈeɪz ; lɪˈez/ *vi* [VP2A, 3A] **～ (with／between),** (colloq) act as a link. (俗)做連絡人；連絡。

li·aison /lɪˈeɪzn *US:* ˈlɪəzɒn ; ˌlieˈzɔ̃/ *n* **1** [U] connection; linkage between two separate groups. 連絡；團體間的連繫。 **ˈ～ officer,** one who keeps two such groups in touch with each other; member of a committee, etc acting as a link between the committee and other people. 連絡員；委員會之連絡人。 **2** [C] illicit (eg sexual) relationship. (男女間的)私通；通姦。

li·ana /lɪˈɑːnə *US:* -ˈænə ; lɪˈænə/ *n* climbing and twining tropical plant. (熱帶的)攀繞植物；葛藤類。

liar /ˈlaɪə(r) ; ˈlaɪɚ/ *n* person who tells an untruth or who has told an untruth; person who habitually tells lies. 說謊者；慣於說謊者。

lib /lɪb ; lɪb/ *n* (colloq abbr for) liberation. (俗)爲 liberation 之略。 **gay／women's lib,** movement (early 1970's) for the liberation of homosexuals／women from legal, social, economic and self oppression. (1970 年代早期)同性戀(婦女)解放運動。

li·ba·tion /laɪˈbeɪʃn ; laɪˈbeʃən/ *n* [C] (pouring out of an) offering of wine, etc to a god: 奠酒；灌奠(傾酒於地以祭神): *make a ～ to Jupiter.* 向羅馬主神祭酒。

li·bel /ˈlaɪbl ; ˈlaɪbḷ/ *n* **1** [U, C] (the publishing of a) written or printed statement that damages sb's reputation: 誹謗人的文字；出版或刋登誹謗性文字: *sue a newspaper for ～;* 控告某報刋登誹謗性文字； *utter／publish a ～ against sb.* 誹謗某人(發表文字誹謗某人)。 **2** [C] **～ on,** (colloq) anything that brings discredit upon or fails to do justice to: (俗)有損名譽或對人不公平的東西: *The portrait is a ～ on me.* 這畫像把我畫得太難看。□ *vt* (-ll-, US -l-) [VP6A] publish a ～ against; fail to do full justice to. 發表誹謗…的文字；對…不公平。 **～·lous,** US **～·ous** /ˈlaɪbələs ; ˈlaɪbḷəs/ *adj* containing a ～; in the nature of a ～: 含有誹謗文字的；誹謗性的: *～lous reports;* 誹謗性的報導； in the habit of uttering ～s: 有誹謗習慣的；愛誹謗的: *a ～lous person／periodical.* 愛誹謗的人(定期刋物)。

lib·eral /ˈlɪbərəl ; ˈlɪbərəl/ *adj* **1** giving or given freely; generous: 慷慨的；大方的；豐富的；充足的；不吝嗇的: *a ～ giver to charities;* 對慈善事業慷慨的施捨者； *a ～ supply of food and drink;* 食物和飲料的充分供給； *a ～ table*, one with plenty of food and drink. 豐盛的一餐。 *He is ～ of promises but not ～ of money*, gives plenty of promises but not much money. 他在承諾上慷慨，但給錢時吝嗇(口惠而實不至)。 **2** open-minded; having, showing, a broad mind, free from prejudice. 大度的；磊落的；無偏見的。 **3** (of education) directed chiefly towards the broadening of the mind, not specially to professional or technical needs. (指教育)着重於智力的開闊和通才的。 **the ～ arts,** eg philosophy, history, languages. 文(理)科(例如哲學，歷史，語言)。 **4** (politics in GB) of the party (dominant until the 1920's), favouring moderate democratic reforms. (英國政治)自由黨的(自由黨於 1920 年代前很有

勢力,主張緩和性的民主改革)。□ *n* person in favour of progress and reform and opposed to privilege. 自由主義者。**L~,** member of the L~ party in GB. 英國自由黨員。**~·ism** /-ɪzəm ; -ɪzəm/ *n* [U] ~ views, opinions and principles. 自由主義。**~·ize** /ˈlɪbrəlaɪz ; ˈlɪbərəlˌaɪz/ *vt* make ~; free from narrow-mindedness. 使磊落;使心胸寬大。**~·iz·ation** /ˌlɪbrəlaɪˈzeɪʃn *US:* -lɪˈz- ; ˌlɪbərəlɪˈzeʃən/ *n*

lib·er·al·ity /ˌlɪbəˈrælətɪ ; ˌlɪbəˈrælətɪ/ *n* (*pl* -ties) **1** [U] generosity; free giving; quality of being broad-minded; freedom from prejudice. 慷慨;大方;胸襟開濶;無偏見。**2** (*pl*) instances of generosity: (複)慷慨好施的實例: *He has made himself poor by his liberalities.* 他由於慷慨好施而變窮了。

lib·er·ate /ˈlɪbəreɪt ; ˈlɪbəˌret/ *vt* [VP6A, 14] ~ ***(from),*** set free: 解放;使獲自由: ~ *slaves;* 解放奴隸; ~ *the mind from prejudice.* 解除心中的偏見。**lib·er·ator** /-tə(r) ; -tə/ *n* **lib·er·ation** /ˌlɪbəˈreɪʃn ; ˌlɪbəˈreʃən/ *n* [U] liberating or being ~d. 解放;獲自由。⇨ lib.

lib·er·tine /ˈlɪbətiːn ; ˈlɪbəˌtin/ *n* licentious person. 淫佚放蕩之人;浪子。**chartered ~,** person whose irregularities and eccentricities of behaviour are tolerated. 被寬容的浪子。

lib·erty /ˈlɪbətɪ ; ˈlɪbətɪ/ *n* (*pl* -ties) **1** [U] state of being free (from captivity, slavery, imprisonment, despotic control, government by others); right or power to decide for oneself what to do, how to live, etc: 自由;自由權: *They fought to defend their* ~. 他們爲保衞自由而戰。***at ~,*** (of a person) free; not imprisoned: (指人)自由的;未被監禁的: *You are now at ~ to leave any time,* may do so. 你現在隨時可以離去。***set sb at ~,*** release: 釋放: *set prisoners/slaves at* ~. 釋放囚犯(奴隸)。***~ of conscience,*** freedom to have one's own (esp religious) beliefs without interference. 信仰(尤指宗教上的)自由。***~ of speech,*** freedom to say openly, in public, what one thinks, eg on social and political questions. 言論自由。***~ of the press,*** freedom to write and print in periodicals, books, etc whatever one wishes without interference. 出版自由。**2** [U] ungranted and sometimes improper familiarity; setting aside of convention. 冒昧;失禮。***take the ~ of doing sth/to do sth:*** 冒昧地做某事: *I took the ~ of borrowing your lawn-mower while you were away on holiday.* 當你外出度假時我借用你的刈草機,甚爲冒昧。***take liberties with:*** 對…太隨便: *You must stop taking liberties with the young woman,* stop treating her with too much familiarity. 你不能對那年輕女子太隨便。**3** (*pl*) privileges or rights granted by authority: (複)當局給予之特權或權利: *the liberties of the City of London.* 倫敦市的特權。

li·bid·in·ous /lɪˈbɪdɪnəs ; lɪˈbɪdṇəs/ *adj* lustful. 淫蕩的;好色的。

li·bido /lɪˈbiːdəʊ ; lɪˈbaɪdo/ *n* [U, C] (psych) sexual desire; emotional energy or cravings. (心理)性慾;情慾。

Libra /ˈliːbrə ; ˈlaɪbrə/ *n* the seventh sign of the zodiac (also called 亦稱作 'the scales' or 'the balance'). 天秤宮(黃道之第七宮)。⇨ the illus at zodiac. 參看 zodiac 之挿圖。

li·brary /ˈlaɪbrərɪ *US:* -brerɪ ; ˈlaɪˌbrerɪ/ *n* (*pl* -ries) **1** room or building for a collection of books kept there for reading; the books in such a room or building: 圖書室;圖書館;圖書館或圖書室的藏書: *the public* ~, maintained by a town or city council, etc; 公立圖書館; *a ˈcirculating* ~, one that lends books for profit, members paying a subscription fee; 流通圖書館(借書以牟利者,借書者須付訂閱費); *ˈreference* ~, one in which books may be consulted but not taken away. 參考圖書室(書籍祇供參考,不可借出者)。**2** (attrib) (形容用法) *a ˈ~ book;* 圖書館的書; *a ˈ~ edition,* book usu of large size and print and with a strong binding. 圖書館版(通常爲大字本,裝訂牢固者)。**3** writing and reading room in a private house. 書房。**4** series of books issued by a publisher in uniform binding and connected in some way: 叢書;文庫: *the Home University L~.* 家庭大學叢書。**li·brar·ian** /laɪˈbreərɪən ; laɪˈbrɛrɪən/ *n* person in charge of a ~. 圖書館長;圖書館員;圖書管理員。**li·brar·ian·ship** *n* [U] the work of a librarian. 圖書館長或館員的工作。

li·bretto /lɪˈbretəʊ ; lɪˈbrɛto/ *n* (*pl* ~s /-təʊz ; -toz/ or -tti/ -tiː ; -ti/) book of words of an opera or musical play. 歌劇或樂劇之脚本。**li·bret·tist** /lɪˈbretɪst ; lɪˈbrɛtɪst/ *n* writer of a ~. 歌劇或樂劇的脚本作者。

lice /laɪs ; laɪs/ *n pl* of louse.

li·cence (US = **li·cense**) /ˈlaɪsns ; ˈlaɪsṇs/ *n* **1** [C] (written or printed statement giving) permission from someone in authority to do sth; [U] authorization: 執照;特許證;許可;特許: *a ~ to drive a car/a ˈdriving ~;* 駕駛執照; *a ~ to practise as a doctor;* 醫師開業執照; *marry by* (*special*) ~ (contrasted with *banns*); 獲得特許而結婚(與 banns 相對); *a ~ for the sale of alcoholic drinks.* 賣酒特許證。**ˈ~-plate** *n* (US) *number-plate,* ⇨ number(2). (美)(汽車等之)號碼牌。**ˈon-~** *n* [C] (GB) licence for the sale of alcoholic drinks to be consumed on the premises. (英)販賣的酒只准許在酒店內飲用之許可證。**ˈoff-~** *n* [C] (GB) licence for the sale of liquor to be taken away; shop where liquor is sold and taken away. (英)販賣的酒准許帶走的許可證;販賣的酒可帶走的酒店。**2** [U] wrong use of freedom; disregard of laws, customs, etc; licentious behaviour: 放肆;不顧法律,風俗等;放縱: *The ~ shown by the troops when they entered enemy territory disgusted everyone.* 那些部隊進入敵人領土所表現的放肆使人厭惡。**poetic ~,** freedom from the ordinary rules of language, eg of word order, allowed in verse. 詩的破格(寫詩所特許的可打破語言之一般規格的自由,例如文字順序上的破格)。

li·cense (also **li·cence**) /ˈlaɪsns ; ˈlaɪsṇs/ *vt* [VP6A, 17] give a licence to: 許可;特許;給予執照或特許證: *shops ~d to sell tobacco;* 被特許賣煙之商店; *~ a doctor to practise medicine;* 許可醫師行醫; *a ~d house/~d premises,* where the sale of alcoholic drinks is allowed, eg hotels, restaurants; 特許的賣酒處(例如旅館,飯店); *a ~d victualler;* 有販賣酒類許可證的酒店店主; *the ~d quarters,* (in some countries) part of a town where there are ~d brothels. (某些國家中)公娼區。**li·cen·see** /ˌlaɪsənˈsiː ; ˌlaɪsṇˈsi/ *n* person holding a licence (esp to sell alcohol). 領有執照者;(尤指)持有賣酒特許證者。

li·cen·tiate /laɪˈsenʃɪət ; laɪˈsɛnʃɪɪt/ *n* person who has a licence or certificate showing that he is competent to practice a profession. 持有證件證明其在某一專門職業有相當資格之人。

li·cen·tious /laɪˈsenʃəs ; laɪˈsɛnʃəs/ *adj* immoral (esp in sexual matters); not held back by morality. 淫蕩的;淫佚的;放縱的。**~·ly** *adv* **~·ness** *n*

li·chee, li·chi /ˈlaɪtʃiː ; ˈlitʃi/ = lychee.

li·chen /ˈlaɪkən ; ˈlaɪkɪn/ *n* [U] dry-looking plant that grows on rocks, walls, tree-trunks, etc, usu green, yellow or grey. 石耳;地衣。

lich·gate, lych·gate /ˈlɪtʃgeɪt ; ˈlɪtʃˌget/ *n* roofed gateway of a churchyard, where, at a funeral, the coffin used to await the arrival of the clergyman. 教堂墓園之有頂蓋的門口(葬禮時停棺該處等候牧師來臨)。

licit /ˈlɪsɪt ; ˈlɪsɪt/ *adj* lawful; permitted. 合法的;許可的。

lick /lɪk ; lɪk/ *vt, vi* **1** [VP6A, 15A, B, 22] pass the tongue over or under: 舐: *The cat was ~ing its paws.* 貓在舐爪。*He ~ed the spoon clean.* 他將那調羹舐乾淨了。***~ sb's boots,*** cringe before sb; be abject, servile. 在某人面前卑躬屈膝;拍人馬屁。***~ one's lips,*** show eagerness or satisfaction. 表示

垂涎或滿足。～ ***one's wounds,*** try to recover after a defeat. 失敗後求復元;重整旗鼓。～ ***sth off,*** remove by ～ing: 舐掉某物: *The boy ～ed the jam off his lips.* 那男孩舐掉他唇上的果醬。～ ***sth up,*** take it up by ～ing: 舐盡: *The cat ～ed up the milk.* 那貓舐光了牛奶。～ ***into shape,*** (fig) make presentable, efficient, properly trained: (喻)使像樣;整頓: *The recruits were soon ～ed into shape by the drill sergeants.* 新兵不久便被教育班長訓練得像樣了。～ ***the dust,*** (rhet) fall to the ground, defeated or killed. (修辭)被擊倒;被打敗;被殺死。 **2** [VP6A] (esp of waves, flames) touch lightly: (尤指波浪和火焰)冲洗;捲繞: *The flames ～ed the sides of the fireplace.* 火焰捲繞壁爐邊。 **3** [VP6A] (colloq) overcome; triumph over; give a whipping to: (俗)克服;征服;打擊: *Well, that ～s everything!* That is more surprising than anything I've ever seen or heard! 嗯,那眞是聞所未聞、見所未見的事! **4** [VP2A] (sl) go; hurry: (俚)走;匆忙: *He went off as hard as he could ～.* 他飛快地跑走了。 □ *n* **1** act of ～ing with the tongue. 舐。 ***give sth a ～ and a promise,*** a feeble attempt to clean, polish, etc (with a promise of sth more thorough later). 馬馬虎虎地洗擦某物(準備以後再好好洗擦)。 **2** (also 亦作 **'salt-～**) place to which animals go for salt. 動物舐鹽之處。 **3** (sl) ***at a great ～; at full ～,*** at a great pace. (俚)極速地;急忙。 **～·ing** *n* (colloq) beating; defeat: (俗)打敗;擊敗: *Our football team got a ～ing yesterday.* 我們的足球隊昨天敗了。

licor·ice /ˈlɪkərɪs ; ˈlɪkərɪs/ *n* ⇨ liquorice.

lid /lɪd ; lɪd/ *n* **1** movable cover (hinged or detachable) for an opening, esp at the top of a container: 蓋(尤指容器上者): *the lid of a kettle/box;* 壺(箱)蓋; *the ˈteapot lid.* 茶壺蓋。 **2** eyelid. 眼瞼。 **～·less** *adj*

lido /ˈliːdəʊ ; ˈlido/ *n* (*pl* ～s /-dəʊz ; -doz/) public open-air swimming pool or bathing beach. 公共露天游泳池;海濱浴場。

lie[1] /laɪ ; laɪ/ *vi* (*pt, pp* lied, *pres p* lying) [VP2A] make a statement that one knows to be untrue: 說謊: *He lied to me.* 他對我說謊。 *He's lying.* 他在撒謊。□ *n* such a statement: 謊言: *He's telling lies.* 他在說謊。 *What a pack of lies!* What a lot of untrue statements! 眞是一派謊言! *He lived a lie,* deceived without using words. 他以行爲欺騙。 **white lie,** ⇨ white[1](2). ***give sb the lie,*** accuse him of lying. 責某人說謊。 **ˈlie-detector** *n* device which records physiological changes, eg heart beats, rate of breathing, caused by emotional stresses while a person is being questioned. 測謊器(人受質詢時,由於情緒緊張而引起生理上的變化,如心臟跳動、呼吸的速率等,根據此種變化記錄以測是否說謊)。

lie[2] /laɪ ; laɪ/ *vi* (*pt* lay /leɪ ; le/, *pp* lain /leɪn ; len/, *pres p* lying) [VP2A, C, D, 3A] **1** be, put oneself, flat on a horizontal surface or in a resting position; be at rest: 臥;躺: *lie on one's back/side;* 仰臥(側臥); *lie face downwards.* 俯臥。 *Don't lie in bed all morning!* 不要整個早上都躺在床上! *His body lies* (= He is buried) *in the churchyard.* 他被葬於教堂的墓地裏。 *He lay on the grass enjoying the sunshine.* 他躺在草地上享受陽光。 ***lie back,*** get into, be in a resting position: 向後靠: *lie back in an armchair.* 向後靠着坐在扶手椅上。 ***take sth lying down,*** submit to a challenge, an insult without protest. 甘受挑戰或侮辱。 ***lie down under (an insult, etc),*** fail to protest, resist, etc. 未抗議或抵抗(侮辱等)。 ***lie in,*** **(a)** stay in bed after one's usual time for getting up. 睡懶覺。 Hence, 由此產生, **ˌlie-ˈin** *n*: *have a nice lie-in on Sunday morning.* 星期天早上好好睡個懶覺。 **(b)** remain in bed to give birth to a child: 分娩;待產: *The time had come for her to lie in.* 她生產的時間到了。 **ˌlying-ˈin hospital,** (old use) maternity hospital. (舊用法)產科醫院。 ***lie in ambush,*** ⇨ ambush. ***lie low,*** (colloq) ⇨ low[1](12). ***lie up,*** stay in bed or in one's room (from illness, etc). (因病等)臥床不起;不能離室。 ***lie with,*** (old use, biblical, now usu *sleep with*) have sexual intercourse with. (舊用法,聖經文體,現在通常用 sleep with) 與…性交。 ***Let sleeping dogs lie,*** (prov) Avoid discussing problems that are likely to cause trouble. (諺)莫惹事生非;不要討論麻煩問題。 **ˈlie-abed** /-əbed ; -əbɛd/ *n* lazy person who lies in bed instead of getting up. 睡懶覺的人。 **2** (of things) be resting flat on sth: (指物)平放在某物之上;在某處: *The book lay open on the table.* 那書在桌上打開着。 *How long has your bicycle been lying out on the wet grass?* 你的脚踏車放在外面潮濕的草地上有多久了? **3** be kept, remain, in a certain state or position: 保持在某種狀態或位置: *money lying idle in the bank;* 閒存在銀行內的錢; *towns lying in ruins;* 成廢墟狀態的城市; *men who lay* (= were) *in prison for years.* 坐牢數載的人。 *The snow lay thick on the ground.* 雪厚厚的堆積在地上。 *The fields lay thickly covered with snow.* 田野積著厚厚的雪。 ***lie heavy on sth,*** cause discomfort, trouble, distress to it: 使不舒服,煩惱,痛苦: *The lobster lay heavy on his stomach.* 那龍蝦使他的肚子難受。 *The theft lay heavy on his conscience.* 那次偷竊使他良心不安。 ***lie over,*** be left for action at a future time: 延期處理;擱延: *Let the matter lie over until the next committee meeting.* 將此事擱延至委員會下次會議。 **4** be spread out to view; extend: 展現;展開: *The valley lay before us.* 那山谷展現在我們的眼前。 *The coast was undefended and lay open to attack.* 該海岸未設防,易受攻擊。 *If you are young, life still lies before you.* 如果你年輕,你仍然有遠大的前途。 ***find out/see how the ˈland lies,*** (fig) learn how matters stand, what the state of affairs is. (喻)探知事情的眞相。 **5** be situated: 位於: *ships lying at anchor.* 停泊着的船隻。 *The ship is lying at No 5 berth.* 該船停於五號碇泊處。 *The fleet lay off the headland.* 艦隊停在岬外。 ***lie ˈto,*** (of a ship) come almost to a stop, facing the wind. (指船)因逆風而幾乎不能前進。 **6** (of abstract things) exist; be in a certain position or manner: (指抽象事物)存在;在某種情況: *The trouble lies* (= is) *in the engine.* 毛病發生在引擎。 *The answer to this difficulty lies in not putting too much pressure on the engine.* 解決這毛病的方法是不要給引擎加太大的壓力。 *He knows where his interest lies,* where he may win an advantage, make a profit. 他知道他的利益之所在。 *I will do everything that lies in* (= that is within) *my power.* 我願就我能力範圍儘量去做。 ***lie at sb's door,*** be attributable to: 歸於: *At whose door should the blame/fault/responsibility lie,* Who should we attribute it to? 我們應該歸咎於誰? (Cf 參較 *lay sth at sb's door,* ⇨ door(1).) ***lie with sb,*** be sb's duty or responsibility: 爲某人的責任: *The solution/The burden of proof lies with you.* 解決問題的辦法(舉證的責任)落在你身上。 *It lies with you* (= It is your duty) *to accept or reject the proposal.* 接受或拒絕此提議全由你做主。 ***as far as in me lies,*** to the best of my power. 盡我的力量。 **7** (legal) be admissible: (法律)可承認;成立: *The appeal will not lie,* is not according to law, cannot be admitted. 該上訴不能成立。□ *n* (*sing* only) the way sth lies; (golf) the position of a ball when it comes to a stop. (僅用單數)位置;形勢;(高爾夫球)球停下來的位置。 ***the lie of the land,*** the natural features (esp the contours) of an area; (fig) the state of affairs. 地勢;(喻)情勢;情況。

lied /liːt ; lit/ *n* (*pl* ～er /ˈliːdə(r) ; ˈlidɚ/) (G) German song or lyric. (德)德國歌曲或抒情曲。 **ˈ～er-singer,** person who sings ～er. 唱德國歌曲或抒情曲者。

lief /liːf ; lif/ *adv* (archaic or liter) willingly: (古或文)欣然: *I would/had as ～ join the Crusade as* *anything,* would do this more willingly than anything else. 參加十字軍是我最樂意的事。

liege /liːdʒ ; lidʒ/ *adj* (only in) (僅用於) **ˈ~ lord/sovereign,** (feudal times) ruler, landowner, entitled to receive service and homage. (封建時代之)君主;王侯。**ˈ~·man** /-mən ; -mən/ *n* (*pl* -men) feudal vassal; faithful follower. 封建時代的家臣;忠實的部下。□ *n* ~ lord; ~man. 君主;王侯;家臣。

lien /lɪən ; lin/ *n* (legal) legal claim (*upon* property) until a debt on it is repaid: (法律)留置權(扣押財產以待償還借款的權利,後接 upon): *A shipping company has a ~ upon cargo until the freight is paid.* 航運公司對於運貨有留置到運費付清始可提貨的權利。

lieu /luː ; lu/ *n* (only in) (僅用於) ***in ~ (of),*** instead (of). 代替。

lieu·ten·ant /lefˈtenənt *US:* luːˈt- ; luˈtɛnənt/ *n* **1** army officer below a captain; (/ləˈtenənt ; luˈtɛnənt/) junior officer in the Navy. 陸軍中尉;海軍上尉。 **2** (in compounds) (用於複合字) officer with the highest rank under: 僅次於複合字中後面一字所示官職的官員: ˌ*~-ˈgeneral;* 陸軍中將;空軍中將; ˌ*~-ˈcolonel;* 陸軍中校;空軍中校; ˌ*~-comˈmander;* 海軍少校; ˌ*~-ˈgovernor,* official under a governor-general. 副總督。 **3** deputy or substitute; one who acts for a superior. 副主官;代理上級官者。**Lord L~ (of the County),** the Queen's representative in a county. 女王駐郡代表。**L~ of the Tower,** (ie the Tower of London). 倫敦塔的副主官。**lieu·ten·ancy** /-ənsɪ ; -ənsɪ/ *n* rank, position, of a ~. 陸軍中尉,海軍上尉,代理上級官者的階級或職位。

life /laɪf ; laɪf/ *n* (*pl* lives /laɪvz ; laɪvz/) **1** [U] condition that distinguishes animals and plants from earth, rock, etc: 生命: *How did ~ begin?* 生命是怎樣開始的？ *Where did ~ come from?* 生命是從哪裏來的？ **life force,** vital energy thought of as working for the survival of the human race and the individual. 生命力。 **2** [U] living things collectively, in general; plants, animals, people: 生物(集合用法);動植物和人: *Is there any ~ on the planet Mars?* 火星上有生物嗎？*A naturalist studies animal and plant ~.* 博物學者研究動植物。 **3** [U] state of existence as a human being: 人生;人的生存: *L~ is sweet.* 人生是甜美的。 *The battle was won, but only with great loss of ~,* many were killed. 那一戰雖然勝了,但傷亡慘重。 ***bring to ~,*** cause to live; cause to recover from a faint, an illness thought to be fatal, etc. 使復活;使蘇醒;使康復。***come to ~,*** recover consciousness, recover from a faint, etc: 甦醒: *We all thought he was drowned, but after an hour's artificial respiration he came* (*back*) *to ~.* 我們都認爲他淹死了,但經過一小時的人工呼吸後,他又甦醒了。***run for one's ~/for dear ~,*** in order to, or as if to, save oneself from death. 逃命。***a matter of ~ and/or death,*** one on which sb's continued existence depends. 生死關頭;生死攸關之事。***kiss of ~,*** ⇨ kiss. ***this ~,*** ~ on earth. 此生;現世。***the ˈother ~; future/eternal/everlasting ~,*** conscious existence, the state of existence, after bodily death. 來世;永生。***with all the pleasure in ~,*** with the greatest possible pleasure. 極高興地。 **4** [C] state of existence, as an individual living being: 性命: *How many lives were lost in the disaster?* 在那災禍中喪失了多少性命？ ***take sb's ~,*** kill him. 殺死某人。***take one's own ~,*** kill oneself; commit suicide. 自殺。***a ~ for a ~,*** phrase used to express the view that murder must be revenged by the killing or execution of the murderer or (in a vendetta) by the killing of a member of his family. 一命抵一命(此片語用以表示兇手必須被殺或處死,以爲死者報仇,若爲兩家族間之血仇,必須殺死對方家族一份子以償命)。***cannot for the ˈ~ of one,*** cannot, however hard one tries: 怎麼也不能;要了命也不能: *For the ~ of me I couldn't recall her name.* 我怎麼樣也想不起她的名字來了。 ***Not on your ~!*** (colloq *int*) Quite definitely not. (俗,感嘆詞)絶對不。 **5** [C] period between birth and death, or between birth and the present, or between the present and death: 一生;一輩子;終身: *He lived all his ~ in London.* 他一生都住在倫敦。*I have lived here all my ~.* 我自出生卽住在此地。*The murderer received a ~ sentence/was sentenced to imprisonment for ~.* 該殺人犯被判無期徒刑。*The murderer is doing ~/was given ~,* (sl) imprisonment for ~.(俚)那殺人犯在服無期徒刑(被判無期徒刑)。**~ annuity,** one that will be paid for the rest of a person's ~. 終身年金;終身俸。**ˈ~ cycle,** progression through different stages of development: 生命環;生命周期(經過不同發育階段之過程): *the ~ cycle of a frog,* from the egg to the tadpole to the final stage. 青蛙之生命環(自卵至蝌蚪至最後階段)。 **~ interest,** (legal) benefit valid (from property, etc) during a person's ~.(法律)終身權益。**~ peer,** member of the House of Lords, whose title is not inherited by his heirs. 英國國會中其頭銜不爲子孫所承襲的上議院議員。***early/late in ~,*** during the early/late part of one's ~: 一生中之早(晚)期;早年(晚年): *marry early/late in ~.* 早(晚)婚。***have the time of one's ~,*** (colloq) enjoy oneself immensely, as never before. (俗)享受從未有過的快樂。 **6** [U] human relations; the business, pleasures, social activities, etc, of the world: 社交關係;社交生活;世事;人世繁華: *Sailors don't earn much money, but they do see ~,* see how people everywhere live. 船員的收入雖不多,但他們的閱歷極廣。*There is not much ~* (eg social activity) *in our small village.* 我們的小村子裏沒有多少社交活動。 ***true to ~,*** (of a story, drama, etc) giving a true description of how people live. (指故事,戲劇等) 描寫眞實;與實際生活相同。 **7** [C, U] (way of) living; career: 生活;生活方式;生涯: *Some people have easy lives.* 有些人生活舒適。 *Which do you prefer, town ~ or country ~?* 你比較喜歡都市生活還是鄉村生活？*That's the ~ for me!* That's how I should like to live. 那才是我嚮往的生活。**ˈhigh ~,** ⇨ high¹(12). **8** [C] written account of sb's ~; biography: 言行錄;傳記: *Do you enjoy reading the lives of great men?* 你喜歡讀偉人的傳記嗎？*He has written a new ~ of Newton.* 他寫了一部新的牛頓傳。**ˈ~ story,** biography. 傳記。**9** [U] activity, liveliness, interest: 活力;生氣;興趣: *The children are full of ~,* are active and cheerful. 孩子們生氣勃勃。*Put more ~ into your work.* 你工作時要提起精神。***the ~ (and soul) of the party,*** person who is the most lively and amusing member of a social gathering. 社交場合的靈魂人物(最活潑而又風趣之人)。 **10** [U] living form or model: 活人;實物;模特兒: *a portrait/picture taken from* (*the*) *~;* 以活人做模特兒的畫像; *a ˈ~ drawing;* 實物圖畫; *a ˈ~ class,* (in an art school) one in which students draw or paint from living models. (美術學校中之)人體寫生課。 ***to the ~,*** with great fidelity or exactness: 逼眞: *draw/portray/imitate sb to the ~.* 將某人畫得栩栩如生 (模倣某人很逼眞)。 ⇨ lifelike below. 參看下列之 lifelike。***as large as ~,*** **(a)** of natural or ordinary size: 與眞人或原物一樣大的: *a statue as large as ~.* 與眞人一樣大的影像。 **(b)** (colloq and in joke) in person; without possibility of doubt or error. (俗,謔) 親自;無容置疑。 **11** [C] fresh start or opportunity after a narrow escape from death, disaster, etc: (死裏逃生後之)新生命;新機會: *The batsman was given a ~,* eg when the fielders missed an easy catch. 那擊球員獲一新機會(例如當外場員未能接住一易接的球時)。 *They say a cat has nine lives.* 據說貓有九條命。 **12** [C] period during which sth is active or useful: 一物之活動或有用的時期;壽命: *the ~ of a steamship/a government.* 輪船(政府)的壽命。 **13** **ˈ~ assurance/insurance,** ⇨ these words. 參看 assurance, insurance。***expectation of ~; ˈ~ expectancy,*** (insurance) statistically determined number of years that a person at a particular age may expect to live. (保險業) (某一年齡者所能活的) 平均壽命。 ***a good/bad ~,*** person who is likely to pass/not to reach this average. 可能活過(不到)平均壽命者。 **14** (compounds) (複合字) **'~·belt** *n* belt of cork or other buoyant material to keep a person afloat in water. 救生帶;浮帶。 **'~·blood** *n* [U] blood necessary to ~; (fig) vitalizing influence; sth that gives strength and energy. 保持生命的血液;(喻)元氣;活力的來源。 **'~·boat** *n* **(a)** boat specially built for going to the help of persons in danger at sea along the coast. (岸邊的) 救生艇。 **(b)** boat carried on a ship for use in case the ship is in danger of sinking, is on fire, etc. (大船上的) 救生艇。 **'~·buoy** *n* ~belt in the form of a ring, through which a person puts his head, shoulders and arms. 救生圈。 **'~ cycle** *n* ⇨ 5 above. 參看上列第5義。 **'~ estate** *n* property that a person enjoys for ~, but cannot dispose of further. (僅限於一代的) 終身財產。 **'~-giving** *adj* that strengthens or restores physical or spiritual ~. 賦與生命的;給與生氣的。 **'~·guard** *n* **(a)** expert swimmer on duty at dangerous places where people swim. (游泳場的) 救生員。 **(b)** bodyguard of soldiers. 侍衞;衞隊。 **'L~ Guards** *n pl* cavalry regiment in the British army. (英國陸軍中的) 禁衞騎兵團。 **,~ 'history** *n* (biol) record of the ~ cycle of an organism. (生物) (生物體之) 生活史。 **'~-jacket** *n* one of cork or other buoyant material or one that can be inflated. 救生衣。 **~·less** *adj* **1** never having had ~: 無生命的: *~less stones.* 無生命的石頭。 **2** having lost ~; dead. 失去生命的;死的。 **3** dull; not lively: 枯燥無味的;無生氣的: *answer in a ~less manner.* 要死不活地回答。 **~·less·ly** *adv* **'~-like** *adj* **1** resembling real ~; looking like the person represented: 栩栩如生的;維妙維肖的: *a ~like portrait.* 栩栩如生的畫像。 **2** like a living thing: 似生物的: *a ~like cloud.* 一片似生物的雲。 **'~·line** *n* rope used for saving ~, eg one attached to a ~buoy, or one fastened along the deck of a ship during a storm, for persons to cling to; 救生索(例如繫於救生圈或暴風雨中繫於船甲板上供人攀附之繩索); diver's line for signalling to the ship from which he is working; 自船上繫於潛水人員以作信號之繩索; (fig) anything on which one's ~ depends; (喻) 生命寄託之物; (palmistry) line across the palm of the hand, alleged to show one's length of ~, major events in one's ~, etc. (手相) 生命線。 **'~·long** *adj* continuing for a long time; lasting throughout ~. 長期的;終身的。 **'~-office** *n* life assurance office or business. 人壽保險公司辦事處;人壽保險業。 **~ peer** *n* ⇨ 5 above. 參看上列第5義。 **'~-preserver** *n* **(a)** (GB) short stick with a heavy, weighted end, used as a weapon of defence. (英) 護身棒(用作防禦武器之一端重的短棒)。 **(b)** (US) (美) = ~-jacket. **lifer** /'laɪfə(r); 'laɪfɚ/ *n* **1** (with *adj* prefixed) person who lives a certain kind of ~: (前面冠以形容詞) 過某種生活者: *a simplelifer.* 生活簡樸的人。 **2** (sl) (one who serves a) sentence of ~ imprisonment. (俚) 無期徒刑;被判無期徒刑者。 **'~-saver** *n* (esp in Australia) ~guard(a). (尤用於澳洲) 救生員。 **'~-size(d)** *adj* (of pictures, statues, etc) having the same size, proportions, etc, as the person represented. (指圖畫,彫像等) 與眞人一般大小的。 **'~-span** *n* (biol) longest period of ~ of an organism known from the study of it. (生物) 壽命(某生物體的最長生命期)。 **,~-sup'port system,** equipment in a spacecraft which provides an environment in which astronauts may live. 太空生活裝備(太空船中供太空人生活之裝置)。 **'~-time** *n* duration of a person's ~. 一生;終身。 ***the chance of a ~time,*** an opportunity that comes only once. 一生祇有一次的機會。 **,~-'work** *n* task that occupies one's whole ~ or to which one

a life-buoy

a life-jacket

devotes all one's ~. 畢生的工作;終身的事業。

lift /lɪft; lɪft/ *vt, vi* **1** [VP6A, 15A, B] raise to a higher level or position: 舉起;抬起: *~ (up) a table;* 抬起一桌子; *~ sth out of a box/a child out of his cot.* 從箱中將某物抬出(把小孩從小兒床中抱出)。 *This box is too heavy for me to ~ (it).* 這箱子太重,我搬不動。 *This piece of good luck ~ed her spirits.* 這次幸運使她非常高興。 ***~ up one's eyes (to...),*** look up (at). 向上看。 ***have one's face ~ed,*** have a face-lift; ⇨ face¹(2). 做面部拉皮(使面部皮膚拉緊以消除皺紋)。 ***not ~ a finger,*** ⇨ finger. ***~ up one's voice,*** raise it, cry out. 高呼。 **2** [VP2C] ***~ off,*** (of a rocket, spacecraft) rise from the launching site. (指火箭、太空船)升空;發射。Hence, 由此產生, **'~-off** *n*: *We have ~-off.* 我們的火箭(太空船)升空了。 **3** [VP2A] yield to an attempt to ~: 被舉起;被抬起: *This window won't ~,* won't go up. 這窗子推不上去。 **4** [VP2A] (of clouds, fog, etc) rise; pass away: (指雲霧等) 消散: *The mist began to ~.* 霧開始消散。 **5** [VP6A] dig up (root crops); remove (plants, shrubs, etc) from the ground: 掘出 (塊根作物); 掘除(植物、灌木等): *~ potatoes.* 掘馬鈴薯。 **6** [VP6A] steal: 偷竊: *~ articles in a supermarket.* 在一超級市場偷竊物件。 **'shop-~,** ⇨ shop(1). take without permission or proper acknowledgement: 偷取;剽竊: *Long passages in that textbook have been ~ed from other authors.* 那教科書中幾段長的文字係剽竊自其他作者。 **7** [VP6A] end a ban, prohibition, blockade, siege. 解除(禁令,封鎖,包圍)。 □ *n* [C] **1** act of ~ing. 舉起;抬起。 ***give sb/get a ~,*** **(a)** offer sb/be offered a ride in a car or other vehicle: 讓某人搭自己的車(獲得准許搭別人的車): *Can you give me a ~ to the station?* 你能讓我搭你的車到車站嗎? ⇨ also *air ~* at air¹(7). **(b)** (of a person's spirits) become/make more cheerful, contented: (指人的心情)變爲(使)更愉快、滿足: *The big increase in her salary gave her a tremendous ~.* 她的薪水大幅度增加使她極爲振奮。 **2** (US 美 = *elevator*) box-like apparatus in a building for taking people up or down to another floor: 電梯: *take the ~ to the tenth floor.* 乘電梯至十樓。 **'~·man** /-mæn; -mən/ *n* one who operates a ~. 電梯管理員。

liga·ment /'lɪgəmənt; 'lɪgəmənt/ *n* [C] band of tough, strong tissues that holds two or more bones together in the body. (連接體內骨骼之) 靭帶。

liga·ture /'lɪgətʃə(r); 'lɪgə,tʃʊr/ *n* [C] **1** bandage, piece of thread, etc used in tying, esp cord used to tie up a bleeding artery. 綁縛用的綳帶。 **2** (printing) two or more letters joined, eg *f* and *l* joined as fl. (印刷) 連字(例如 f 和 l 連成 fl)。

light¹ /laɪt; laɪt/ *adj* (-er, -est) (opposite of *dark*) (爲 dark 之相反字) **1** (of a place) well provided with light³(1): (指地方) 光線充足的;明亮的: *a ~ room.* 光線充足的房間。 *It's beginning to get ~.* 天開始亮了。 **2** pale-coloured: 淡色的;淺色的: *~ hair;* 淡色的頭髮; *a ~ complexion;* 白皙的膚色; *~ blue/green/brown.* 淡藍(綠,褐)色。 **'~-coloured** *adj* having a ~ colour: 淡色的;淺色的: *a ~-coloured dress.* 淺色的女裝。

light[2] /laɪt ; laɪt/ *adj* (-er, -est) (opposite of *heavy*) (爲 heavy 之相反字) **1** not heavy; not having much weight (for its size): 不重的;輕的;沒有多少重量的(與體積相較): *as ~ as air/as a feather;* 像空氣(羽毛)一樣輕; *a ~ fall of snow;* 雪花輕飄: *a pair of ~ shoes;* 一雙輕便的鞋; *a ~ cart or van,* one made for ~ loads and quick movement; 輕快的馬車或貨車; *~ clothing,* for summer; 輕便的衣服(夏季穿用); *a ~ building/bridge;* 輕巧的建築物(橋樑); *a ~ railway,* for ~ traffic; 輕便鐵道(供交通不擁擠的地區使用); *a ~ cruiser,* with ~ armour and guns. 輕巡洋艦。**~ horse,** light-armed cavalry: 輕騎兵: *a '~ (horse) brigade,* with ~ equipment and weapons. 輕裝備(騎兵)旅。Hence, 由此產生, **ˌ~-'armed** *adj* **2** gentle; delicate: 輕輕的;輕巧的: *give sb a ~ touch on the shoulder;* 輕輕一拍某人的肩頭; *walk with ~ footsteps/movements;* 輕輕地走; *have a ~ hand for pastry,* have delicacy of touch that gives good results. 在做麵點方面手很巧。Hence, 由此產生, **ˌ~-'handed** *adj* having a ~ hand. 手靈巧的。**ˌ~-'handedly** *adv* **ˌ~-'fingered** *adj* skilful in using the fingers; clever at stealing, eg as a pick-pocket. 手指靈巧的; 偷竊技術高明的(例如扒手)。 **3** below the correct weight, amount, etc: 不够重的;分量不够的: *a ~ coin;* 分量不够的錢幣; *give ~ weight.* 未給足够分量。*We're about 50p ~ on the petty cash,* 50p short. 我們短少五十辨士的零用金。**4** (of beer, wines) not very strong; (of food) easily digested; (of meals) small in quantity: (指啤酒或葡萄酒)味淡的; (指食物)易消化的; (指餐食)少量的: *a ~ supper,* 少量的晚餐, (hence) (由此產生) *a ~ eater;* 飯量小的人; (of sleep) not deep; easily disturbed; (of sleepers) easily waked; (of books, plays, music) primarily for amusement, not for serious entertainment or study: (指睡眠)不深的;易受騷擾的; (指睡眠者) 容易驚醒的; (指書籍,戲劇,音樂)娛樂性的;輕鬆的: *~ reading/music/comedy;* 輕鬆的讀物(音樂,喜劇); *a ~ comedian;* 輕鬆的喜劇演員; (of soil) easily broken up; (of work) easily done; (of taxes, punishment) not difficult to bear; (of a syllable) not stressed, unemphatic. (指土壤)鬆的; (指工作)容易做的; (指稅,懲罰)輕微的; (指音節)非重音的;弱音的;輕讀的。***make ~ work of sth,*** do it without much effort. 輕易地做某事。**5** not serious or important: 不嚴重的: *a ~ attack of illness.* 不嚴重的疾病發作。***make ~ of,*** treat as of no or little importance: 輕視;不把…當一回事: *He makes ~ of his illness.* 他不把他的病當一回事。**6** thoughtless; frivolous; jesting: 輕率的;輕浮的;開玩笑的: *~ conduct;* 輕浮的行爲; *a man of ~ character,* not troubling much about moral questions. 性格輕率的人。**ˌ~-'minded** *adj* frivolous. 輕浮的。Hence, 由此產生, **ˌ~-'mindedness** *n* **7** cheerful; free from sorrow: 愉快的;無憂無慮的: *a ~ heart.* 愉快的心情。Hence, 由此產生, **ˌ~-'hearted** *adj* **ˌ~-'heartedly** *adv* **ˌ~-'heartedness** *n* **8** without moral discipline; wanton: 放蕩的;不貞潔的: *a ~ woman.* 水性楊花的女人。 **9** dizzy, delirious: 暈眩的;昏迷的: (chiefly in) (主要用於) **ˌ~-'headed** *adj* **ˌ~-'headedly** *adv* and **ˌ~-'headedness** *n* **10** (compounds) (複合字) **~-'heavyweight** *n* (esp) boxer weighing between 160 and 175 lb (or 72·5 to 79·3 kg). (尤指)重乙級(體重在 160 至 175 磅或 72·5 至 79·3 公斤間之拳擊家)。**ˌ~-o'-'love** *n* fickle woman; harlot. 蕩婦; 娼妓。**'~·weight** *n, adj* (man or animal) below average weight; (esp, boxing) boxer weighing between 126 and 135 lb (or 57 to 61 kg); (fig) (person) not important or serious. 平均重量以下的; 平均重量以下的人或動物; (尤指,拳擊)體重在 126 磅至 135 磅(57 至 61公斤)間的拳擊家;輕量級(拳擊家); (喩)不重要的(人);不認眞的(人)。□ *adv* in a ~ manner: 輕: *tread/sleep ~;* 輕輕走(小睡); *travel ~,* with little luggage; 帶很少的行李旅行; *get off ~(ly),* (colloq) escape without heavy punishment. (俗)逃過嚴厲的懲罰。**~·ly** *adv* **~·ness** *n*

light[3] /laɪt ; laɪt/ *n* (opposite of *dark*[1] or *darkness*) (爲 dark[1] 或 darkness 之相反字) **1** [U] (and with *indef art* and *adjj*) that which makes things visible: (亦可與不定冠詞及形容詞連用)光;光線: *the ~ of the sun/a lamp/the fire;* 陽光(燈光;火光); *read by the ~ of a candle;* 藉燭光讀書; *a bright/dim ~;* 明亮(朦朧)的光線; *go for a walk by 'moon~;* 月光下散步; *bathed in 'sun~.* 接受日光浴;晒太陽。*We need more ~.* 我們需要更多的光線。*The ~* (ie daylight) *began to fail,* It began to get dark. 天開始黑了。***in a good/bad ~,*** **(a)** so as to be seen well/badly: 在亮處(在暗處): *The picture has been hung in a bad ~.* 那幅畫被掛在光線不好的地方。**(b)** (fig) so as to make a good/bad impression: (喩)予人以良好(不好)的印象: *Press reports always make him appear in a bad ~.* 新聞報導總是使他予人不良的印象。***see the ~,*** **(a)** (liter or rhet) be born. (文學或修辭)降生。**(b)** be made public. 被公開。**(c)** realize the truth of sth that one has been obstinate about. 認清自己所固執的事情之眞相。**(d)** undergo religious conversion. 改信某一宗教。***be/stand in sb's ~,*** **(a)** obscure what he is looking at. 遮住某人的光線。**(b)** (fig) hamper, hinder (sb's chances of success, progress). (喩)妨礙某人成功,進步等的機會。***stand in one's own ~,*** **(a)** so as to obscure one's work, etc. 遮住自己的光線;背光。**(b)** (fig) act against one's own interests. (喩)損害自己的利益;使自己受損。**'~ year,** (astron) unit of measurement for distances between stars; distance travelled by ~ in one year (about 6 million million miles). (天文)光年; 光一年所行的距離 (約爲 6,000,000,000,000 哩)。 **2** [C] source of ~; sth that gives ~, eg a candle or lamp: 光源;發光物(例如蠟燭或燈): *'traffic ~s;* 交通燈;紅綠燈; *ˌnavi'gation ~s.* 航行燈。*L~s were burning in every room.* 每個房間裏都點着燈。*Turn/Switch the ~s on/off.* 把燈打開(關掉)。*Put that ~ out!* 把那燈熄掉! *All the ~s went out—there was a power failure.* 所有的燈都熄了 — 停電了。***L~s out,*** (bugle call signalling) the time when ~s are to be turned out. 熄燈時間;熄燈號。**northern/southern ~s,** ⇨ aurora. **3** [C] flame; spark; sth used for producing a spark or flame: 火焰;火花;引火物: *Can you give me a ~, please?* eg for a cigarette or pipe. 請借個火好嗎?(例如用以抽香煙或煙斗)。Note that *fire* is not used in this sense. 注意: fire 不可用作此義。***Strike a ~,*** make a ~ by striking a match. 擦火柴。**4** [U] expression of brightness or liveliness in a person's face (esp in the eyes), suggesting happiness or other emotion: 表示快樂等的面部光彩(尤指眼睛發出者): *The ~ died out of her eyes,* Her looks changed from happiness to sadness, from liveliness to lack of interest. 她眼中的光彩消失了(她的表情由快樂轉爲悲傷,由活潑轉爲冷淡)。***the ~ of sb's countenance,*** (biblical) his favour, approval. (聖經)恩惠;贊許。**5** [U] knowledge or information that helps understanding; [C] fact or discovery that explains. 見解;見識;幫助說明的事實或發現。***come/bring sth to ~,*** become/cause sth to be visible or known: 顯露;揭露: *Much new evidence has come to ~/has been brought to ~ in recent years.* 近年來許多新證據已紛紛出現。***shed/throw ~/(a) new ~ on sth,*** make sth clearer, provide new information: 幫助說明某事物; 供給新知識: *These facts shed (a) new ~ on the matter.* 這些事實幫助說明此事。***by the ~ of nature,*** without the help of revelation or teaching. 本能地;自然而然地。***in the ~ of,*** with the help given by or gained from. 借助;徵諸;按照;根據。 **6** [C] aspect; way in which sth appears: 觀點;外觀: *I cannot view your conduct in a favourable ~,* cannot approve of it. 我不能贊成你的行爲。*I have never looked upon the matter in that ~.* 我從未就該觀點看此事。*In the ~ of the new evidence, it was decided to take the manufacturers to court.* 根據新的證據,

a lighthouse

決定向法院控告那些製造商。 **7** (*pl*) (natural or acquired) abilities; mental powers. (複) (先天或後天的) 能力;智力。***according to one's ~s,*** to the best of one's abilities. 盡個人之所能。**8** [C] famous person; person (to be) regarded as an example or model: 名人;被視作模範的人: *one of the leading/shining ~s of our age.* 我們這個時代的領導 (顯赫) 人物之一。**9** [C] window or opening in a wall or roof for the admission of ~ (esp in a roof): 進光的窗戶; (尤指) 天窗: *a 'sky~;* 天窗; compartment of glass in the side or roof of a greenhouse or frame (used for ventilation). (溫室側牆或屋頂上所開之) 通風玻璃窗。**leaded ~,** small pane or panel of glass, secured in strips of lead, often coloured, forming part of a larger window. 鉛框小玻璃窗 (常是彩色的,形成大窗戶之一部分)。⇨ also *quarter-~* at quarter(16). **10** [C] (painting) part of a picture shown as lighted up: (繪畫) 圖畫的明亮部分: *'high ~s,* the brightest parts; 最明亮的部分; *~ and shade.* 明與暗。 **11** (compounds) (複合字) **'~-house** *n* tower or other tall structure containing beacon ~s for warning or guiding ships at sea. 燈塔。**'~•ship** *n* ship moored or anchored and provided with beacon ~s for the same purpose as those in a ~house. 燈船;信號船。

light[4] /laɪt ; laɪt/ *vt, vi* (*pt, pp* lit /lɪt ; lɪt/ or ~ed) (*~ed* is more usu as an *attrib adj*, as in *a ~ed candle*). (lighted 較常用做置於名詞前的形容詞,例如: a lighted candle)。 **1** [VP6A] cause to begin burning or to give out ~: 點燃;使發光: *~ a lamp/candle/cigarette;* 點燃一燈 (蠟燭,香煙); *~ a fire,* put a burning match to the material in a fireplace, etc. 點火。**2** [VP6A] provide lights[3](2) to or for: 供以光源;供以燈: *Is your flat ~ed/lit by gas or by electricity?* 你們的公寓用煤氣燈還是電燈? *Our streets are ~ed/lit by electricity.* 我們的街道用電照明。**3** [VP15B] *~ **sth up,*** cause to become bright: 使明亮: *The shops were brilliantly lit up.* 那些商店燈光明亮。*The burning building lit up the whole district.* 那燃燒的建築物照亮了整個的地區。 **4** [VP2C] *~ **up,*** **(a)** switch on (electric) ~s; turn on gas-lamps, etc: 開(電)燈; 點亮煤氣燈等: *It's getting dark—time to ~ up.* 天漸漸黑了—該點燈了。Hence, 由此產生, **,~ing-'up time** *n* time at which, according to regulations, lamps in the roads and on vehicles must be lit. (法令規定之) 街道和行車開燈時間。**(b)** (colloq) begin to smoke a pipe or cigarette: (俗) 開始抽煙斗或香煙: *He struck a match and lit up.* 他擦燃一根火柴,點上煙斗(香煙)。 **5** [VP2C, 15B] *~ **up (with),*** (of a person's face or expression) (cause to) become bright: (指人的面孔或表情) 使容光煥發;春風滿面: *Her face lit up with pleasure.* 她的臉上煥發着喜色。*A smile lit up her face.* 微笑使她容光煥發。**6** [VP15A] guide with or by a light: 以燈引導: *~ a person on his way.* 用燈替某人引路。

light[5] /laɪt ; laɪt/ *vi* (*pt, pp* lit /lɪt ; lɪt/ or ~ed) [VP3A] *~ **on/upon,*** come upon a find by chance: 偶遇;偶然發現: *~ upon a rare book in a secondhand bookshop.* 在一舊書店裏偶然發現一珍本書。

lighten[1] /'laɪtn ; 'laɪtn̩/ *vt, vi* [VP6A, 2A] make or become less heavy; reduce the weight of: 使輕;變輕;減輕: *~ a ship's cargo;* 減輕船上的載貨; *~ a ship of her cargo;* 減輕一船的負載; *~ taxes.* 減輕稅收。 *Her heart ~ed when she heard the news.* 她聽到這消息心情輕鬆了。

lighten[2] /'laɪtn ; 'laɪtn̩/ *vt, vi* **1** [VP6A] make light or bright: 使亮;使光明: *A solitary candle ~ed the darkness of the cellar.* 一枝孤燭照耀着黑暗的地窖。**2** [VP2A] become light or bright: 變亮;變光明: *The eastern sky ~ed.* 東方的天空亮了。 **3** [VP2A] send out lightning: 閃電: *It's thundering and ~ing.* 雷電交作。

lighter[1] /'laɪtə(r) ; 'laɪtɚ/ *n* [C] **1** device for lighting cigarettes or cigars. 打火機。 **2** (chiefly in compounds) person or thing that lights: (主要用於複合字) 點火的人或物: *'lamp-~,* man who went round the streets with a ladder to light gas-lamps. 點街燈者。

lighter[2] /'laɪtə(r) ; 'laɪtɚ/ *n* boat, usu flat-bottomed, used for loading and unloading ships not brought to a wharf, and for carrying goods in a harbour or river: 駁船;平底船: *a tug with a string of ~s behind it.* 拖着一些駁船的拖船。□ *vt* remove (goods) in a ~. 以駁船運(貨)。**'~•age** /-ɪdʒ ; -ɪdʒ/ *n* fees charged for carrying goods in ~s. 駁船運貨費。

light•ning /'laɪtnɪŋ ; 'laɪtnɪŋ/ *n* [U] flash of bright light produced by natural electricity between clouds in the sky or clouds and the ground, with thunder: 閃電: *struck/killed by ~;* 爲閃電所擊(遭閃電擊死); ***like ~; with ~ speed,*** very fast. 閃電似地迅速;風馳電掣地。**~ bug,** (US) firefly. (美) 螢火蟲。**'~-rod/-conductor** *nn* metal rod fixed on the top of a high building, etc and connected with the earth, to prevent damage by ~. 避雷針。**~ strike** *n* strike, of workers, started without warning. 工人的突然罷工。

lightning

lights /laɪts ; laɪts/ *n pl* lungs of sheep, pigs, bullocks, etc used as food. (羊、豬、閹牛等之) 肺臟 (用做食物)。

light•some /'laɪtsəm ; 'laɪtsəm/ *adj* **1** graceful. 優雅的。 **2** merry; light-hearted; frivolous. 快活的; 愉快的;輕浮的。**~•ly** *adv* **~•ness** *n*

lig•neous /'lɪgnɪəs ; 'lɪgnɪəs/ *adj* (of plants) woody. (指植物) 木質的;木本的。⇨ herbaceous.

lig•nite /'lɪgnaɪt ; 'lɪgnaɪt/ *n* [U] soft, brownish-black coal. 褐煤。

lik•able, like•able /'laɪkəbl ; 'laɪkəbl̩/ *adj* of a kind that is, or deserves to be, liked; pleasing: 可愛的; 悅人的;討人喜歡的: *a ~ man/tune.* 可愛的人(曲子)。

like[1] /laɪk ; laɪk/ *adj* ⇨ alike. (used attrib and pred) similar; having the same or similar qualities, etc; having a resemblance: (可做形容用法和敍述用法) 相似的;同樣的: *The two girls are very ~.* 這兩個女孩子很相似。*L~* (ie similar) *causes produce ~* (ie similar) *results.* 相似的原因產生相似的結果。*He writes well on this and ~ subjects.* 他對於這個和類似的題目寫得很好。*They are as ~ as two peas.* 他們一模一樣。*L~ father, ~ son; ~ master, ~ man,* (prov) As the one is, so the other will be. (諺) 有其父必有其子;有其主必有其僕。**,~-'minded** /'maɪndɪd ; 'maɪndɪd/ *adj* having the same tastes, aims, etc. 志趣相投的。□ *adv* **1** *~ **as,*** (archaic) in the same manner as. (古) 如同。 **2** probably: 大概: (only in) (僅用於) *~ **enough;***

most/very* ~; *as* ~ *as not*,** very probably (*likely* is more usu, ⇨ likely(2)). 大概;很可能 (likely 較常用,參看 likely 第2義)。□ *conj* **1** as (common use among those who have not been taught to avoid it; considered incorrect, but found in many good writers): (用作 as) 像;如(爲不知避免此種用法的人所常用,此用法被認爲不正確,但許多好的作者也這樣用): *She can't cook ~ her mother does.* 她烹飪的技術不如她的母親。*Don't think you can learn grammatical rules ~ you learn the multiplication tables.* 不要以爲你學習文法規則就像背乘法表一樣。 **2** (non-standard use) as if: (不標準的用法,用作 as if) 彷彿: *It rained ~ the skies were falling.* 雨下得就像天要塌下來的樣子。□ *n* **1** ~ person or thing; that which is equal or similar to sth else: 相似的人或事物; 與他物相等或相似之物: *That was acting, the ~ of which we shall not see again*, We shall not see acting equally good. 我們再也看不到那樣好的演技了。*Music, painting and the ~*, and similar branches of the arts. 音樂、繪畫等等。*I never heard the ~ (of it)*, anything so strange, etc according to context. 我從未聽說過這種事(這樣奇怪的事等,視上下文而定)。**2** ***the ~s of, (colloq) person(s), thing(s), similar to: (俗) 類似的人、物等: *the ~s of us/them.* 與我們 (他們) 類似的人。*Have you ever seen the ~s of this?* 你看到過和這個相同的嗎? □ *prep* **1** (Often governing a *pron*, *n*, or *gerund*; originally ~ *to/unto*, this being now archaic or poet) such as; resembling: (常用於代名詞、名詞或動名詞之前;最初 like 後接 to 或 unto 的用法,現已作廢或僅用於詩中)像;如;似: *What is he ~?* What sort of person is he—in looks, behaviour, etc, according to the situation? 他是個什麼樣的人? *He was wearing a hat rather ~ this one.* 他戴着一頂很像這一頂的帽子。*It looks ~ gold*, has the appearance of gold. 它看來像是金子。*This is nothing ~ as good*, not nearly so good. 這個差多了。***nothing* ~,** nothing to equal; nothing to be compared with: 無物能及;無物能與之相比: *There's nothing ~* (= nothing as good as) *leather.* 沒有比皮革更好的了。*There's nothing ~ walking as a means of keeping fit.* 做爲保持健康的方法,沒有比散步更好的了。***something* ~,** nearly; about: 幾乎;大約;有點像: *The cost will be something ~ five pounds.* 費用約爲五鎊。*This is something ˈ~ a dinner!* This is a remarkably good or satisfactory dinner! 這才像是一頓盛餐! **2** **ˈ*feel* ~,** be in a state or mood right or suitable for: 適於;心情適合;想要: *Do you feel ~ having a rest?* 你想休息嗎? *She felt ~ crying.* 她想哭。*We'll go for a walk if you feel ~ it.* 如果你想散步,我們就去吧。**ˈ*look* ~,** look as if sb/it might be (used to show probability or likelihood): 好像;似乎: *He looks ~ winning*, It seems likely that he will win. 他好像要勝了。*It looks ~ being a fine day*, Appearances suggest that the day will be fine. 天氣好像不錯。*It looks ~ rain.* 好像要下雨。 **3** characteristic of: 表現出…之特點的: *That's just ~ him!* He has behaved, spoken, etc just as one would expect! 那正像他那個人! *It's (just) ~ her to think of others before thinking of herself.* 先想到別人再想到自己,這正像她的爲人。 **4** in the manner of; to the same degree as: 像;像…一樣: *Don't talk ~ that*, in that way. 不要那樣說話。*If I were to behave ~ you...*, in the way you behave.... 如果我的行爲像你一樣,…。 *If everyone worked ~ me,....* 如果每一個人都像我一樣的工作,…。*It fits him ~ a glove*, closely, tightly. 它恰好適合於他。*He drinks ~ a fish.* 他喝酒喝得很兇。**5** (colloq, sl) (俗,俚) ~ ***anything*,** as hard, etc as can be expected or imagined: 極其努力等;非常: *She works ~ anything when she's interested.* 她有興趣時工作非常努力。~ ***mad/crazy*,** as if crazy: 像瘋狂一般地;猛烈地: *He complains ~ mad when things go wrong.* 事情不對勁的時候,他猛烈地抱怨。~ ***hell/blazes*,** **(a)** furiously; energetically: 猛烈地;奮力地: *He moans ~ hell when he loses a bet.* 他賭輸了便猛烈地抱怨。 **(b)** (as an *int*) of course (not)!: (作爲感嘆詞)當然不!: *'But you were there, weren't you?' 'L~ hell, I was!'* I certainly wasn't! '但是你在那裏,是不是?' '我當然沒有在那裏!'

like[2] /laɪk; laɪk/ *vt* **1** [VP6A, D, 7A] be fond of; have a taste for; find satisfactory or agreeable: 喜歡;喜愛;愛好;中意: *Do you ~ fish?* 你喜歡魚嗎? *I ~ to read in bed but I don't ~ having meals in bed.* 我喜歡躺在床上看書,但我不喜歡在床上吃飯。*She ~s him but she doesn't love him.* 她喜歡他但並不愛他。*I ~ his impudence!* (ironic, meaning that his impudence is preposterous or amusing). (反語)他眞不怕難爲情! *Well, I ~ that!* (ironic, meaning that what has been said or done is surprising, unexpected, etc). (反語)哎呀,虧你說得出口!眞出乎意料! **2** [VP6D, 7A] (in *neg* sentences) be unwilling or reluctant: (用於否定句)不願意: *I didn't ~ to disturb you.* 我不願打攪你。*I don't ~ troubling her.* 我不願麻煩她。 **3** [VP6A, 7A] (with *should, would*) used to indicate a wish: (與 should, would 連用)表示願望: *I should ~ to go there*, if it were possible, if I were invited, etc. 我想去那裏(如果可能、如我受邀請的話)。 *I shouldn't ~ to do that*, have no wish to do it. 我不願意做那事。*She would ~ a cup of tea, I think.* 我覺得她想喝一杯茶。*I should ~ to know/to see...*, often ironic, meaning that it would be difficult to explain, show, etc. (常作反語)我倒想了解一下(看一看)…。*They would have ~ed to come....* 他們本來想來…。 **4** [VP6A, 7A, 17, 19B, C, 22] prefer; choose; wish: 比較喜歡;寧擇;希望: *I ~ people to tell the truth.* 我喜歡人講實話。*How do you ~ your tea?* 你喜歡喝什麼樣的茶? *I ~* (= prefer) *it rather weak.* 我比較喜歡淡一點的。*I ~ this more* (or, colloq *better*) *than that.* 我比較喜歡這個,不太喜歡那個(口語中用 better 代替 more)。*You wouldn't ~ there to be another war, would you?* 你不會希望再有一次戰爭的,對嗎? *I don't ~ you to smoke/you smoking/your smoking.* 我不喜歡你抽煙。***if you* ~,** used to express consent to a request or suggestion: 如果你高興的話(用以表示同意一請求或建議): *I will come if you ~.* 如果你高興的話,我願意來。 **5** [VP6A] suit the health of: 適合…的健康: *I ~ lobster but it doesn't ~ me*, ie it gives me indigestion. 我喜歡吃龍蝦,但它不宜於我的健康(使我消化不良)。□ *n* (*pl*, only in) (複,僅用於) **ˌ~s and ˈdis~s**, ⇨ dislike.

like·ly /ˈlaɪklɪ; ˈlaɪklɪ/ *adj* (-ier, -iest) **1** that is expected: 很可能發生的;有希望的: *the ~ winner of the contest.* 很可能在比賽中獲勝的人。*Is he ~ to win?* 他有希望獲勝嗎? **2** that seems reasonable, suitable, or right for a purpose: 似乎合理的;似乎合適的; 好像適當的: *That's a ~ story/excuse* (often used ironically). 那似乎是合理的故事(藉口)(常用作反語)。*This looks a ~ field for mushrooms.* 這地看來適合於長蘑菇。*What do you think is the likeliest/the most ~ time to find him at home?* 你認爲什麼時候最可能在他家裏找到他? *Which are the most ~ candidates*, those with the best chance of success? 哪些是最有希望當選的人? **3** ~ + *to*-inf; ~ ***that...***, to be expected: 很可能的: *He is not ~ to succeed.* 他大概不會成功。*It's highly* (= very) *~ that he will succeed.* 他成功的可能性很大。 *An incident ~ to lead to war is reported from X.* 某方面報導出一可能導致戰爭的事件。*That is not ~ to happen.* 那事不大可能發生。□ *adv* ***most/very* ~,** probably. 或許;大概;很可能。 *I shall very ~ be here again next month.* 我下個月很可能再來此地。***as* ~ *as not*,** with greater probability: 多半: *He will succeed as ~ as not.* 他多半會成功。*He'll forget all about it as ~ as not.* 他多半會將此事忘了。**like·li·hood** /-hʊd; -hʊd/ *n* [U] probability: 可能性: *In all likelihood* (= Very probably), *we shall be away for a week.* 我們很可能離開一個星期。

liken /ˈlaɪkən; ˈlaɪkən/ *vt* [VP14] ~ ***sth to sth***, point out the likeness of one thing (to another): 指出一物與另一物之相像；將…比喻作：～ *the heart to a pump.* 將心臟比作唧筒。

like·ness /ˈlaɪknɪs ; ˈlaɪknɪs/ *n* **1** [U] resemblance; being like: 相似；相像：*I can't see much ~ between the two boys.* 我看不出這兩個男孩子有多少相似。***in the ~ of,*** in the form, shape or external appearance of. 狀似；貌似。**2** [C] point of resemblance; instance of being like: 相似點；相似的實例：*There's a family ~ in all of them.* 他們之間有一種家族的相似之處。**3** [C] representation (in a portrait, picture, photograph, etc): 肖像；畫像；像片：*The portrait is a good ~.* 這畫像很像本人。

like·wise /ˈlaɪkwaɪz ; ˈlaɪkˌwaɪz/ *adv* in the same or a similar way: 同樣地；照樣地：*Watch him and do ~.* 注意看著他並且照樣做。□ *conj* also; moreover. 亦；而且。

lik·ing /ˈlaɪkɪŋ ; ˈlaɪkɪŋ/ *n* **(a) ~,** fondness. 愛好；喜愛。***have a ~ for,*** be fond of. 喜歡。***to one's ~,*** as one likes it; satisfactory: 投某人之所好；合某人之意：*Is everything to your ~?* 一切都合你的意嗎？

li·lac /ˈlaɪlək ; ˈlaɪlək/ *n* **1** shrub with sweet-smelling pale purple or white blossom: 紫丁香：*an avenue of ~s, ~* shrubs; 兩旁種着紫丁香的道路；*a bunch of ~* (*sing* for the blossom). 一束紫丁香花（單數指花）。**2** pale purple or pinkish-purple: 淡紫色；淡紫紅色：*a ~ dress.* 淡紫色女裝。

Lil·li·pu·tian /ˌlɪlɪˈpjuːʃn ; ˌlɪləˈpjuʃən/ *n* native of Lilliput /ˈlɪlɪpʌt ; ˈlɪləˌpʌt/ (the country described in Swift's *Gulliver's Travels*). (史威夫特所著格利佛遊記中的)小人國的人。□ *adj* very small. 很小的。

lilt /lɪlt ; lɪlt/ *n* [C] (lively song or tune with a) well-marked rhythm or swing. 明顯的韻律或旋律；節拍顯明而又活潑的歌曲。□ *vt, vi* go, sing with a ~: 活潑輕快地走動或唱出：*a ~ing waltz.* 活潑輕快的華爾玆。

lily /ˈlɪlɪ ; ˈlɪlɪ/ *n* (*pl* -lies) (kinds of) plant growing from a bulb, of many sizes, shapes and colours: 百合；百合花：*ˌ~ of the ˈvalley;* 鈴蘭；*ˈwater lilies;* 睡蓮；*ˈEaster lilies;* 白百合；*ˈcalla lilies.* 茨菇花；白星海芋。**~-livered** /ˈlɪlɪ lɪvəd ; ˈlɪlɪˈlɪvɚd/ *adj* cowardly. 怯懦的；膽小的。**ˌ~-ˈwhite** *adj* as white as a ~; pure white. 如百合般白的；純白的。

limb /lɪm ; lɪm/ *n* **1** leg, arm or wing (the more usu words): 肢；臂；手足；翼 (leg, arm 或 wing 較常用)：*rest one's tired ~s;* 讓疲倦的四肢休息；*be torn ~ from ~ by wolves;* 被狼群肢解；*escape with life and ~,* without serious injury. 逃出而未受嚴重傷害。**2** bough (of a tree). (樹之)大枝。***leave sb/be/go out on a ~,*** (colloq) leave sb/be/put oneself in a vulnerable position, eg because separated from supporters. (俗)(使)處於易受傷害或攻擊的地位(例如因脫離擁護者而孤立)。**3** (colloq) (俗) ***~ of the devil/of Satan,*** mischievous child. 惡作劇的小孩；頑童。**-limbed** /lɪmd ; lɪmd/ *suff* (in compounds) (用於複合字) *ˌlong-/ˌstrong-ˈ~ed,* having long/strong ~s. 四肢長(強健)的。

lim·ber /ˈlɪmbə(r) ; ˈlɪmbɚ/ *adj* flexible, pliable. 柔軟的；易曲折的。□ *vt, vi* [VP15B, 2C] ***~ (oneself) up,*** make oneself (one's muscles) pliant, flexible. 使(自己或肌肉)柔軟。

limbo /ˈlɪmbəʊ ; ˈlɪmbo/ *n* (*pl* ~s /-bəʊz ; -boz/) **1** [U] ***in ~,*** in a condition of being forgotten and unwanted: 被遺忘；被遺棄：(colloq) (俗) *The idea of forming a staff association is in ~* (= has been put to one side) *until the new Manager is appointed.* 成立職員協會的計畫被擱置了，要等到新的經理上任後才能再提出。**2** [C] place for forgotten and unwanted things. 丟棄廢物的地方。**3** (usu 通常作 L~) region for souls of unbaptized infants and pre-Christian righteous persons. 未受洗禮的嬰兒與基督誕生前的善人死後所去的地方。

lime[1] /laɪm ; laɪm/ *n* [U] **1** white substance (calcium oxide, **CaO**) obtained by burning limestone, used in making cement and mortar. 石灰。**ˈquick-~,** ~ before water is added. 生石灰(未加水的石灰)。**ˌslaked ˈ~,** ~ after being acted upon by water. 熟石灰(加水者)。⇨ calcium. **ˈ~·kiln** *n* kiln in which ~stone is burnt. 石灰窰。**ˈ~·light** *n* [U] intense white light produced by heating ~ in a very hot flame, formerly used for lighting the stage in theatres. 石灰光(在極熱的火焰中燒石灰棒所產生的强烈白光，昔時爲舞臺照明所用)。***the ~-light,*** publicity: 受注目；出風頭：*fond of the ~-light.* 喜引人注目；愛出風頭。***in the ~light,*** receiving publicity. 受注目；出風頭。**ˈ~·stone** *n* [U] (kinds of) rock containing much ~, quarried for industrial use. 石灰石。**2** [U] **(ˈbird-)~,** sticky substance made from holly bark for catching small birds. 黏鳥膠(多青屬灌木皮製成，用以捕捉小鳥)。□ *vt* [VP6A] put ~ on (fields, etc) (to control acidity). 撒石灰於(田地等中)(以控制酸度)。

lime[2] /laɪm ; laɪm/ *n* (also 亦作 **ˈ~-tree**) tree with smooth heart-shaped leaves and sweet-smelling yellow blossoms. 菩提樹。

lime[3] /laɪm ; laɪm/ *n* (tree with) round juicy fruit like, but more acid than, a lemon. 宜母子(一種似檸檬但較檸檬更酸的果物)；宜母子樹。**ˈ~·juice** *n* juice of this fruit used for flavouring, as a drink, and medicinally. 宜母子汁(用作調味、飲料和醫藥用途)。

lim·er·ick /ˈlɪmərɪk ; ˈlɪmərɪk/ *n* humorous or nonsense poem of five lines. 五行打油詩。

limey /ˈlaɪmɪ ; ˈlaɪmɪ/ *n* (*pl* ~s) (US sl) British person. (美俚)英國人。

limit[1] /ˈlɪmɪt ; ˈlɪmɪt/ *n* [C] line or point that may not or cannot be passed; greatest or smallest amount, degree, etc of what is possible: 界線；邊界；界限；(最大或最小的)極限；限度：*within the city ~s,* boundaries; 在該城界線內；*within a ~ of five miles/a five-mile ~.* 在五哩內。*We must set a ~ to the expense of the trip,* fix a sum not to be exceeded. 我們必須對這次旅行的費用定一個限度。*As we grow older we learn the ~s of our abilities,* learn what we can do and what we cannot do. 當我們的年齡漸長時，我們就會知道自己能力的限度。*His greed knows no ~s.* 他的貪心是無止境的。*There is a ~ to my patience.* 我的耐心是有限度的。*She reached the ~ of her patience.* 她已達到忍耐的極限。***within ~s,*** in moderation: 適度地；有限度地：*I'm willing to help you, within ~s.* 我願意有限度地幫助你。***without ~,*** to any extent or degree: 無限地；無限制地：*If only the banks would lend money without ~!* 但願銀行能無限制地貸款！***off ~s,*** (US) (美) = out of bounds. ⇨ bound[1]. ***That's the ~,*** (colloq) that is as much as (or more than) can be tolerated. (俗)無法再忍耐了。**ˈage ~** *n* age[1](1) given as a ~ for participation in an activity, etc. 年齡限制。

limit[2] /ˈlɪmɪt ; ˈlɪmɪt/ *vt* [VP6A, 14] ***~ sb/sth (to sth),*** put a limit or limits to; be the limit of: 限制；限定；作爲…的界限：*We must ~ the expense to what we can afford.* 我們必須限制開銷不超出我們經濟能力的範圍。*I shall ~ myself to three aspects of the subject.* 我將限制自己就三方面討論此問題。**~ed** *pp* small; restricted; narrow: 少的；有限制的；有限的；狹小的：*a ~ed edition,* one ~ed to a specified number of copies. 發行有限的版本。*Our accommodation is very ~ed.* 我們住宿的地方極爲有限。*He seems to have only a ~ed intelligence.* 他的智力似乎有限。**ˌ~ed liaˈbility company,** (abbr 略作 **Ltd**, placed after the name 置於名稱之後) business company whose members are liable for its debts only to the extent of the capital sum they have provided. 股份有限公司。**ˌ~ed ˈmonarchy,** one that is restricted by the constitution. 君主立憲政體。⇨ absolute(2). **~·less** *adj* without ~: 無界限的；無限制的：*the ~less ocean;* 茫茫大海；*a dictator whose ambitions were ~less.* 有無限野心的獨裁者。

limi·ta·tion /ˌlɪmɪˈteɪʃn ; ˌlɪməˈteʃən/ *n* **1** [U] limiting; condition of being limited. 限制;受限制。 **2** [C] condition, fact or circumstance that limits; disability or inability: 限制的條件、事實或環境;無能力;能力上的缺陷: *He knows his ~s,* knows well that in some respects his abilities are limited. 他知道他在能力上的缺陷(他的能力有限)。

limn /lɪm ; lɪm/ *vt* (old use) paint (a picture); portray (in drawing or in words). (舊用法)繪(畫); (用圖畫或文字)描寫。

limou·sine /ˈlɪməziːn ; ˈlɪmə,zin/ *n* large, luxurious motor-car with an enclosed body, the front seats being separated by means of a partition (as in a London taxi). 大型豪華轎車(駕駛人座位被玻璃板隔開者,如倫敦之計程車)。(Cf 參較 *saloon-car,* with no partition behind the driver. 駕駛人背後未用玻璃板隔開之大轎車。)

limp¹ /lɪmp ; lɪmp/ *adj* not stiff or firm; lacking strength: 柔軟的;軟弱的;無力的: *The book is bound in ~ cloth;* 這本書是用軟布裝訂的; *a ~ edition of a book.* 一書之軟訂本。 *The flowers looked ~ in the heat.* 花在熱天顯得軟弱無力。 **~·ly** *adv* **~·ness** *n*

limp² /lɪmp ; lɪmp/ *vi* [VP2A, C] walk lamely or unevenly as when one leg or foot is hurt or stiff: 跛行;一瘸一瘸地走: *The wounded soldier ~ed off the battlefield.* 那負傷的兵士一瘸一瘸地離開了戰場。 *The damaged ship ~ed* (= managed with difficulty to get) *back to port.* 那受損壞的船費力地駛回港口。 □ *n* (usu 通常作 **a ~**) lame walk: 跛行: *walk with/have a bad ~.* 跛得厲害。

lim·pet /ˈlɪmpɪt ; ˈlɪmpɪt/ *n* small shellfish that fastens itself tightly to rocks, ⇨ the illus at mollusc; (fig) person who sticks tightly to an office, a position or another person. 蝛(一種緊貼在礁上的貝,參看 mollusc 之插圖); (喻)堅守職位者;緊隨他人者。 **ˈ~ mine,** explosive mine (to be) placed in position against the hull of a ship, eg by frogmen. 蝛雷(蛙人等附置於敵艦艦體上的水雷)。

lim·pid /ˈlɪmpɪd ; ˈlɪmpɪd/ *adj* (lit, fig, rhet) (of liquids, the atmosphere, the eyes) clear; transparent. (字面,喻,修辭)(指液體、大氣、眼睛)清澈的;清澄的;明晰的;清晰的。 **~·ly** *adv* **~·ity** /lɪmˈpɪdətɪ ; lɪmˈpɪdətɪ/ *n* [U] quality or state of being ~. 清澈;清澄;明晰;清晰。

linch·pin /ˈlɪntʃpɪn ; ˈlɪntʃ,pɪn/ *n* iron pin passed through the end of an axle to keep the wheel in position; (fig) vital part; person who, because of his work, etc, keeps an organization, etc together. (軸端之)輪轄;制輪楔;(喻)重要部分;關鍵;樞紐人物。

Lin·coln green /,lɪŋkən ˈgriːn ; ˈlɪŋkənˈgrin/ *n* bright green cloth as made at Lincoln: 英國林肯城所產的鮮綠色的布: *Robin Hood and his men, dressed in ~.* 着鮮綠色服裝的羅賓漢及其一夥人。

lin·den /ˈlɪndən ; ˈlɪndən/ *n* (also 亦作 **ˈ~-tree**) = lime².

line¹ /laɪn ; laɪn/ *n* **1** piece or length of thread, string, rope or wire for various purposes: 線;索;繩: *ˈfishing ~s;* 釣魚線; *ˈtelephone ~s.* 電話線。 *Hang (out) the clothes on the ~,* (ie *the ˈclothes-~*). 把這些衣服掛在晒衣繩上。 *L~ fishing is quite different from net-fishing.* 用線釣魚和用網捕魚完全不同。 *He's clever with rod and ~,* is a good angler. 他很會釣魚。 *The ~s* (ie telephone, etc ~s) *are all down as a result of the blizzard.* 暴風雪將電線通通吹落了。 *Give me a ~, please,* (to the operator of a telephone switchboard) Connect me to the Exchange, please (so that I can dial direct). (對接線生用語) 請接電話局 (以便直接撥號)。 *L~ engaged!* (US 美 *L~ busy*) used of a telephone ~ already in use. (指電話線路)有人講話! **crossed ~,** ⇨ cross²(5). **ˈhot ~,** ⇨ hot(8). **ˈparty/shared ~,** telephone ~ serving two or more subscribers. 數家共用的電話線路。 **2** long, narrow mark made on a surface: 線;線條: *L~s may be straight, crooked or curved.* 線條可能是直的,扭曲的或彎曲的。 *Draw a ~ from A to B.* 從 A 到 B 畫一條線。 *In mathematics a ~ is defined as having length but not breadth or thickness.* 數學上線的定義是有長度但無寬度或厚度。 **3** [U] the use of ~s(2) in art, etc: 藝術等中線條之使用: *a ˈ~ drawing,* eg with a pen or pencil; 線條畫(例如用鋼筆或鉛筆畫); *ˈ~-engraving,* done with ~s cut on a surface; 線彫(以線條刻於平面顯示形像者); *the beauty of ~ in the work of Botticelli;* 包提柴里作品中線條的美; *translate life into ~ and colour,* represent living things by means of ~s and colour. 以線條和色彩表現生命。 **4** (in games) mark made to limit a court or ground, or special parts of them: (競技)運動場的界線;場線: *Did the ball cross the ~?* 那球過線了嗎? ⇨ lineman. **5** mark like a ~ on the skin of the face; furrow or wrinkle; one of the marks on the palm of the hand: (面部等的皮膚上的)皺紋;掌紋: *There were deep ~s on her face.* 她的臉上有很深的皺紋。 **6** (*pl*) contour; outline: (複)輪廓;外形: *a ship of fine ~s,* with a graceful outline; 外貌美觀的船; *the delicate ~s of Gothic architecture;* 哥德式建築之精緻的外貌; (in shipbuilding) plans, esp of horizontal, vertical and oblique sections. (造船)船體線圖。 **7** row of persons or things: (人或物之)排; 列: *a ~ of trees/chairs/people waiting to go into a cinema;* 一排樹(椅子,等待進入電影院的人); *manufactured goods on the assembly ~;* 在裝配線上的成品; *a long ~ of low hills.* 一長列小山。 ***in (a) ~,*** forming a ~: 成行;排隊: *The boys were standing in (a) ~.* 男孩子們排成隊站着。 ***in ~ for,*** next in order for: 卽將輪到;下一個卽輪到: *He's in ~ for promotion.* 他卽將晉升。 ***on the ~,*** (of objects exhibited, esp paintings) with the centre about level with the eyes of the viewer. (指展覽的物件,尤指圖畫) 中心與參觀者的眼睛平行的。 **8** edge, boundary, that divides: 邊界: *cross the ~ into Canada* (ie from US); (自美國) 越過邊界至加拿大; equator: 赤道: *cross the ~.* 越過赤道。 ***draw the ~ (at),*** ⇨ draw²(11). **9** railway; single track of railway ~s: 鐵路;鐵軌: *the ˈup/ˈdown ~,* to/from the chief terminus; 上(下)行鐵路線; *the main ~;* 鐵路幹線; *a ˈbranch ~.* 鐵路支線。 *Cross the ~ by the bridge.* 自此(天)橋越過鐵道。 ***reach the end of the ~,*** (fig, eg of a relationship) reach the point where it breaks down, ends. (喻,指關係等)破裂。 **10** organized system of transport under one management and giving a regular service: 運輸路線; 運輸系統; 運輸公司: *an ˈair~;* 航空公司; *a new ˈbus ~;* 一條新闢的公共汽車路線; *a ˈsteamship ~.* 輪船公司。 **11** direction; course; track; way of behaviour, dealing with a situation, etc: 方向;路線;行程;行爲的方式;處理情況等的方法: *the ~ of march of an army;* 軍隊行軍的路線; *,communiˈcation ~s.* 交通路線。 *Don't stand in the ~ of fire! You'll get shot!* 不要站在發射方向!你會被射到! *You should keep to your own ~,* be independent of others. 你應該單獨行動。 ***choose/follow/take the ~ of least resistance,*** the easiest way of doing things. 採取最簡便的方法。 ***take a strong/firm ~ (over sth),*** deal with a problem, etc resolutely: 斷然處理一問題等: *Should the government take a stronger ~ over inflation?* 政府應以較堅決的態度處理通貨膨脹的問題嗎? *What ~ do you intend to take,* How will you approach the problem? 你準備如何處理此問題? ***do sth along/on sound/correct, etc ~s,*** use good, etc methods: 用良好或正確的方法處理事務: *He is studying the subject on sound ~s/on the wrong ~s.* 他正以正確的 (錯誤的) 方法研究此問題。 *I shall proceed along/on these ~s until further notice.* 在未獲進一步的通知前,我將以如此方式進行。 ***(be) in/out of ~ (with),*** in agreement/disagreement (with). 與…一致(不一致)。 ***bring sth into ~,*** cause sth to conform. 使某事物一致;使某事物符合。 ***come/fall into ~ (with),*** accept views, conform, agree.

服從;遵守;同意。 ***toe the ~,*** (fig) submit to discipline, accept the ideas, programme, etc of a (political, etc) party. (喻)服從紀律;接受團體(政黨等)的思想、計畫等。 **the party ~,** the agreed or established policy of a political party: 政黨的路線;黨的政策: *follow the party ~*, vote, speak, write, etc in accordance with this policy. 遵守黨的政策。 **12** connected series of persons following one another in time, esp of the same ancestry: 一連串接續有關的人(尤指同世系者);家系: *a long ~ of great kings;* 一長系列偉大的君主; *the last of his ~;* 他的家系中的最後一人; *trace back one's family ~*, one's ancestry; 追溯自己的家世; *a descendant of King David in a direct ~/in the male ~.* 大衛王的直系(男系)子孫。 **13** row of words on a page of writing or in print: (文字的)一行: *page 5, ~ 10.* 第5頁第10行。 '*L~s to a friend on her birthday*', eg as the title of a poem. '友人華誕祝詞' (例如作爲一首詩的題目)。 ***drop sb a ~,*** (colloq) write to sb: (俗)給某人寫信: *Drop me a ~ to say how you're getting on.* 來封信告訴我你的生活情形。 ***read between the ~s,*** (fig) find more meaning than the words appear to express. (喻)領會言外之意。 **'marriage ~s,** (GB colloq) certificate of marriage. (英俗)結婚證書。 **~s, (a)** words of an actor's part: (演員之)臺詞: *The leading actor was not sure of his ~s.* 那男主角記不清臺詞。 **(b)** form of punishment by which a schoolchild is required to write out a specified number of ~s. 罰寫(處罰小學生的一種方法)。 **14** series of connected military defence posts, trenches, etc: (碉堡、戰壕等連成的)防線: *go into the front ~(s)*, the area nearest to the enemy's ~s; 至前線; *high-ranking officers well behind the ~s.* 離防線很遠的高級軍官。 ***all along the ~,*** at every point; in every way. 在每一點;在每一方面。 ***go up the ~,*** leave base for the front ~(s). 離開基地至前線。 **15** (mil) row of tents, huts, etc in a camp: (軍)營地中的一排帳篷、臨時木造營房等: *inspect the ~s;* 視察營帳; *the 'horse ~s.* 馬棚。 **16 the ~,** (GB army) regular infantry regiments (excluding the Guards and Rifles): (英軍)戰列步兵(禁衞軍及步槍隊除外的正規兵)。 *regiments of the ~;* 戰列步兵團; *a ~ regiment;* 一團戰列步兵; *infantry of the ~;* 戰列步兵; (US army) regular fighting forces of all classes. (美軍)戰鬥兵;戰列部隊(包括各兵種)。 **17** [U] (mil) double row (front and rear ranks) of men standing side by side (contrasted with *file* and *column*): (軍)二列横隊(與 file 和 column 相對): *The troops attacked in extended ~.* 那些軍隊以展開的二列横隊攻擊。 *The men formed into ~.* 兵士們成二列横隊。 **18** (naval) ***~ abreast,*** (number of parallel ships) abreast of each other. (海軍)横陣;艦隊並列。 ***~ astern,*** (number of ships) in a ~ one behind the other. 縱陣;艦隊縱列。 **ship of the ~; ~-of-battle ship,** (in former times) ship of 74 or more guns; largest type of warship. (昔時之)主力艦(配有七十四門以上的砲)。 **19** department of activity; business; occupation: 活動的範圍;行業;事業;職業: *He's in the 'drapery ~.* 他從事綢布業。 *His ~ is stockbroking/banking.* 他從事證券經紀(銀行業)。 *That's not much in my ~*, I don't know much about it, am not much interested in it. 那不是我的本行(我對此行業不大清楚,沒有什麼興趣)。 **20** (trade use) class of commercial goods: (貿易用語)商品的一種: *a cheap ~ in felt hats;* 一種便宜的氈帽; *the best-selling ~ in woollen underwear.* 最暢銷的一種羊毛內衣。 **21 *Hard ~s!*** Bad luck! 你眞倒霉!你的運氣實在太壞了! **22** (sl) (俚) ***shoot a ~,*** brag, boast. 吹噓;吹牛。 Hence, 由此產生, **'~-shooting, '~-shooter** *nn* **23** (colloq) (俗) ***give sb/get/have a ~ on sth,*** give etc information about it. 給予某人(獲得,有)有關…的消息。

line² /laɪn; laɪn/ *vt, vi* **1** [VP6A, 15B] mark (sth) with lines: 畫線於: *~d paper*, with lines printed on it. 有橫線格的紙。 *~ in a contour*, on a blank map; 畫地圖區分線; *~ sth out on paper*, mark it out with ~s. 用線條在紙上標出某物。 **2** [VP6A] cover with lines: 使起皺紋: *a ~d face;* 生皺紋的面孔; *a face ~d with anxiety.* 因憂慮而起皺紋的面孔。 *Pain had ~d her forehead.* 痛苦使她的額上生了皺紋。 **3** [VP2C, 15B] **~ up,** (cause to) be in a line, get into a line: 排成行列;使成行: *The general ~d up his troops.* 將軍整列他的隊伍。 *The soldiers quickly ~d up.* 士兵們迅速地排好了隊。 ⇨ line-up. ***~ up (for sth),*** (US) queue (for it). (美)排隊(做某事)。 **4** [VP6A] form, be placed, in a line or lines along: 沿着…形成行列: *a road ~d with trees;* 旁邊種著一排排樹的道路; *a road ~d with police.* 排列着警察的道路。 *Crowds of people ~d the kerb to see the funeral procession.* 成群的人排列在人行道的邊上看那送葬的隊伍。

line³ /laɪn; laɪn/ *vt* [VP6A, 14] ***~ sth (with sth),*** **1** provide with an inside covering; add a layer of (usu different) material to the inside of (bags, boxes, articles of clothing): 加以襯裡;襯裡於(袋、箱、衣物): *fur-~d gloves;* 毛皮裡的手套; *an overcoat ~d with silk.* 襯有綢裡的大衣。 ⇨ lining. **2** (fig) fill (one's purse, pocket, stomach, etc): (喻)填裝(錢袋、口袋、胃等): *He has ~d his purse well*, made a lot of money. 他賺了很多錢。

lin·eage /'lɪnɪɪdʒ; 'lɪnɪɪdʒ/ *n* [U] family line; ancestry; line of descent. 家系;世系;血統。

lin·eal /'lɪnɪəl; 'lɪnɪəl/ *adj* in the direct line of descent (from father to son, etc): 直系的;嫡系的: *a ~ descendant/heir.* 嫡系後裔(繼承人)。 **~·ly** /-ɪəlɪ; -ɪəlɪ/ *adv*

lin·ea·ment /'lɪnɪəmənt; 'lɪnɪəmənt/ *n* (formal) (usu *pl* except after *each* and *every*) line, detail, distinctive feature or characteristic (of the face): (正式用語)(除在 each 和 every 後,通常用複數)(面部之)輪廓;外貌;特徵: *the ~s of a Mongol face.* 蒙古人面孔的特徵。

lin·ear /'lɪnɪə(r); 'lɪnɪɚ/ *adj* **1** of or in lines: 線的;線狀的: *a ~ design.* 線構成的圖案。 **2** of length: 長的;長度的: *~ measure*, eg feet and inches or metres. 長度(例如呎、吋或公尺)。⇨ App 5. 參看附錄五。

line·man /'laɪnmən; 'laɪnmən/ *n* **1** man who puts up and maintains telegraph and telephone lines. 架設和保養電報線和電話線的工人;線工。 **2** (US) (美) = linesman.

linen /'lɪnɪn; 'lɪnɪn/ *n* [U] cloth made of flax; articles made from this cloth, esp shirts and collars, bedsheets, tablecloths and table napkins: 亞麻布;亞麻布製成之物(尤指襯衫、衣領、床單、桌布和餐巾): (attrib) (形容用法) *~ handkerchiefs.* 亞麻布製的手帕。 **'~-draper** *n* person who sells ~ and cotton goods. 賣亞麻布及棉布製品的布商。 ***wash one's dirty ~ in public,*** discuss family quarrels, unpleasant personal affairs, etc in the presence of other people. 宣揚家醜。

liner /'laɪnə(r); 'laɪnɚ/ *n* **1** ship or aircraft of a line(10) of ships or aircraft: (輪船公司的)郵輪;班輪;(航空公司的)班機: *a fast 'air~;* 迅速的班機; *a trans-Atlantic ~.* 航行大西洋的班輪。⇨ the illus at ship. 參看 ship 之插圖。 **2 '~ (-train)** (also 亦作 *'freight ~*), long distance express goods train between industrial centres and seaports, with facilities for fast (un)loading of goods. 長途貨運快車(行駛於工業中心和海港間之快速貨運火車,有快速裝卸貨物之設備)。

lines·man /'laɪnzmən; 'laɪnzmən/ *n* (sport) person who helps the umpire or referee by saying whether or where the ball touches or crosses one of the lines. (運動)(球賽等中協助裁判認定球是否或在何處觸線或越界之)巡邊員;司線員。

line-up /'laɪn ʌp; 'laɪn,ʌp/ *n* **1** way in which persons, states, etc are arranged or allied; alignment: (人民、國家等聯合的)陣容;聯盟: *a new ~ of Afro-Asian powers;* 亞非國家之新陣容; *a ~ of men in* *an identification parade.* 一列供證人指認的人。**2** formation of players ready for action (in a game such as baseball or football). (棒球、足球等)在場運動員之排列;配置。**3** programme of items (esp for radio or TV): 節目(尤指廣播電臺或電視臺者): *This evening's ~ includes an interview with the Chairman of British Rail.* 今晚的節目包括訪問英國鐵路工會主席。

ling[1] /lɪŋ; lɪŋ/ *n* [U] (kinds of) heather. 石南。

ling[2] /lɪŋ; lɪŋ/ *n* long, slender N European seafish (usu salted) for food. 北歐產的一種長身鱈魚(通常用鹽醃後食用)。

lin·gam /ˈlɪŋgəm; ˈlɪŋgəm/ *n* phallic emblem (as a symbol of the Hindu god Siva /ˈʃiːvə; ˈsivə/). 男性生殖器像(印度神 Siva 之象徵)。

lin·ger /ˈlɪŋgə(r); ˈlɪŋgə/ *vi* [VP2A, C] be late or slow in going away; stay at or near a place: 逗留;徘徊: *~ on after everyone else has left;* 於他人皆離去後逗留; *~ about/around.* 徘徊。*The custom ~s on,* is still observed but is now weak. 該風俗歷久猶存(但不若往昔之盛行)。**~·ing** *adj* long; protracted: 拖久的;延長的: *a ~ing illness;* 纏綿的疾病; *a ~ing look,* one showing regret, unwillingness to leave or give up sth; 戀戀不捨的表情; *a few ~ing* (remaining) *doubts.* 幾個縈繞於心的疑問。**~·ing·ly** *adv* **~er** *n* person who ~s. 逗留者;徘徊者。

linge·rie /ˈlænʒəriː *US:* ˌlɑːndʒeˈreɪ; ˈlænʒəˌri/ *n* [U] (F) (trade name for) women's underclothing. (法)(商品名)女內衣。

lingo /ˈlɪŋgəʊ; ˈlɪŋgo/ *n* (*pl* ~es /-gəʊz; -goz/) (hum or derog) language, esp one that one does not know; way of talking, vocabulary, of a special subject or class of people: (諧或貶)語言(尤指某人所不懂者); 專門術語; 某一階級的人所用的語彙: *the strange ~ used by experts in radio and television.* 廣播和電視專家用的奇怪術語。

lin·gua franca /ˌlɪŋgwə ˈfræŋkə; ˈlɪŋgwəˈfræŋkə/ *n* language adopted for local communication over an area in which several languages are spoken, eg Swahili in E Africa. (使用數種語言的地區內所採用的)共同的語言(例如東非的斯瓦西里語)。

lin·gual /ˈlɪŋgwəl; ˈlɪŋgwəl/ *adj* of the tongue, speech or languages, esp in compounds, 舌頭的;說話的;語言的(尤用於複合字), as 例如 **ˌaudio-ˈ~,** (of methods, devices, etc) requiring one to listen and speak: (指方法器材等)聽和說的: *audio-~ aids,* eg a tape-recorder. 聽和說的教具(例如錄音機)。**ˌbiˈ~,** speaking two languages. 說兩種語言的。**ˌmulti-ˈ~,** speaking many languages. 說多種語言的。

lin·guist /ˈlɪŋgwɪst; ˈlɪŋgwɪst/ *n* **1** person skilled in foreign languages: 精通數種外國語文者: *She's a good ~.* 她精通數國語文。*I'm no ~,* am poor at foreign languages. 我不懂外國語。**2** one who makes a scientific study of language(s). 語言學家。

lin·guis·tic /lɪŋˈgwɪstɪk; lɪŋˈgwɪstɪk/ *adj* of (the scientific study of) languages: 語言的;語言學的;語言研究的: *the ~ study of literature,* centred on the language. 對文學作品中之語文研究。**~s** *n pl* (with *sing v*) the science of language, eg of its structure, acquisition, relationship to other forms of communication. (與單數動詞連用) 語言學。**apˌplied ˈ~s,** this study put to practical uses, esp in the teaching of languages. 應用語言學(尤指語言教學研究)。

lini·ment /ˈlɪnɪmənt; ˈlɪnəmənt/ *n* [C, U] (kind of) liquid usu made with oil for rubbing on stiff or aching parts of the body. (一種)擦劑(通常爲油質液體,擦於身體的疼痛部位)。

lin·ing /ˈlaɪnɪŋ; ˈlaɪnɪŋ/ *n* **1** [C] layer of material added to the inside of sth: 襯裡;裡子: *an overcoat with a fur ~;* 毛皮裡的大衣; *a jewel-box with a velvet ~.* 用天鵝絨做襯裡的珠寶盒。***Every cloud has a silver ~,*** (prov) There is sth good in every evil. (諺)禍中有福。**2** [U] material used for this purpose. 襯料。

link[1] /lɪŋk; lɪŋk/ *n* **1** one ring or loop of a chain. 鏈環;環。**2** (usu *pl*) one of a pair of fasteners for the sleeves of a shirt: (通常用複數)(襯衫的)鴛鴦袖扣之一;鏈扣: *ˈcuff-~s.* (襯衫袖口的)鏈扣。**3** person or thing that unites or connects two others: 連接的人或物;連鎖物: *a ~ in a chain of evidence;* 一串證據中之一環; *the ~ between the past and the future.* 過去與未來間的橋樑;承先啓後者。**missing ~,** that which is needed to complete a series; animal supposed to have existed, of a type between the apes and man. 缺少的一環; 被認爲曾存在過的一種介於猿與人之間的動物。**ˈ~·man** /-mæn; -mən/ *n* (*pl* -men) person who provides the connecting ~ between two groups. 兩團體間的連絡人。**4** measure of length, one hundredth of a chain; 7·92 inches or about 20 centimetres. 令(長度名,爲 chain 的百分之一,合 7·92 吋或 20 公分左右)。⇨ App 5. 參看附錄五。□ *vt, vi* [VP6A, 15A, B, 2A, C] ~ ***(up),*** join, be joined, with, or as with, a ~ or ~s: 連接;接合: *~ things together;* 將諸物連接起來; *~ one's arm in/through another person's arm;* 挽着他人的臂; *two towns ~ed by a canal;* 由一運河連接的兩個城鎮; *~ing verbs,* eg *be.* 連繫動詞(例如be)。*How do religion and philosophy ~ up?* 宗教與哲學如何連接? Hence, 由此產生, **ˈ~-up** *n* act or result of ~ing. 連接;接合。

link[2] /lɪŋk; lɪŋk/ *n* (hist) torch formerly used for lighting people along streets. (史) 昔時街上行人用以照明的火把。**ˈ~·boy, ˈ~·man** /-mæn; -mən/ *nn* one formerly employed to carry ~s and guide people through badly lighted streets. 火把僮(昔時受雇持火把引導行人走過晦暗街道之男孩或男子)。

links /lɪŋks; lɪŋks/ *n* **1** (with *pl v*) grassy land, esp sand-hills, near the sea. (用複數動詞)近海岸的草地(尤指沙丘)。**2** (often **a ~,** with *sing v*) golf-course. (常作 a ~, 與單數動詞連用)高爾夫球場。

lin·net /ˈlɪnɪt; ˈlɪnɪt/ *n* small brown songbird, common in Europe. 紅雀(常見於歐洲之一種小的褐色鳴禽)。

lino /ˈlaɪnəʊ; ˈlaɪno/ *n* [U] (abbr for) linoleum. 爲 linoleum 之略。**ˈ~-cut** *n* [C] design cut in relief on a block of linoleum; print made from this. 油氈浮彫;油氈浮彫版;油氈浮彫的印刷圖樣。

lin·oleum /lɪˈnəʊlɪəm; lɪˈnolɪəm/ *n* [U] strong floor-covering of canvas treated with powdered cork and oil. 油地氈(一種堅牢的地板布,由帆布塗以軟木屑及油製成)。

lino·type /ˈlaɪnəʊtaɪp; ˈlaɪnəˌtaɪp/ *n* (P) machine (with a keyboard like that of a typewriter) used for setting type, each line of type being cast in the form of a complete bar of metal. (商標)長條活字鑄造機(有一似打字機般的鍵盤,可將一行活字成條鑄出)。

lin·seed /ˈlɪnsiːd; ˈlɪnˌsid/ *n* [U] seed of flax. 亞麻子。**~ oil** *n* [U] oil pressed from ~, used in making printing-ink, linoleum, etc. 亞麻子油(用以製造油墨,油地氈等)。

lin·sey-wool·sey /ˌlɪnzɪ ˈwʊlzɪ; ˈlɪnzɪˈwulzɪ/ *n* [U] strong, coarse material made from inferior wool woven with cotton. 棉毛織品。

lint /lɪnt; lɪnt/ *n* [U] linen, with one side scraped so as to be fluffy, used for dressing wounds: 裹傷用的亞麻布: (attrib) (形容用法) *a ~ bandage.* 亞麻布繃帶。

lin·tel /ˈlɪntl; ˈlɪntl/ *n* horizontal piece of wood or stone forming the top of the frame of a door or window. 楣;(門窗上面的)過梁。⇨ the illus at window. 參看 window 之插圖。

lion /ˈlaɪən; ˈlaɪən/ *n* **1** large, strong, flesh-eating animal found in Africa and S Asia, called 'the King of Beasts' because of its fine appearance and courage. 獅。⇨ the illus at cat. 參看 cat 之插圖。***the ~'s share,*** the larger or largest part. 較大或最大部分。**ˈ~-hearted** *adj* brave. 勇敢的。**2** person whose company is very much desired at social gatherings, eg a famous author or musician. 社交場合的寵兒;名人(例如著名的作家或音樂家)。'~•hunter *n* person who tries to get ~s as guests at dinner parties, etc. 巴結名人者。~•**ess** /-es ; -ɪs/ *n* female ~. 母獅。⇨ the illus at cat. 參看 cat 之挿圖。'~•**ize** /-aɪz ; -aɪz/ *vt* [VP6A] treat as a ~(2): 奉爲社交場合的寵兒;奉爲名士: *The famous explorer was ~ized when he returned home.* 那著名的探險家返鄉後被奉爲社交場合的寵兒。

lip /lɪp ; lɪp/ *n* **1** one or other of the fleshy edges of the opening of the mouth: 唇: *the lower/upper lip;* 下(上)唇; *a man with a cigar between his lips.* 口裏銜着一枝雪茄的人。*She refused to open her lips,* wouldn't say anything. 她拒絕開口。⇨ the illus at mouth. 參看 mouth 之挿圖。***bite one's lip,*** show vexation. 咬唇(表示煩惱)。***curl one's lip,*** show scorn. 撇嘴(表示輕蔑)。***give/pay 'lip-service to sth,*** make promises, express regret, admiration etc about it, not sincerely felt. 口惠而實不至。***hang on/upon sb's lips,*** listen eagerly to every word he says. 急切地傾聽某人說的每一個字。***keep a stiff upper lip,*** show no emotion, sign of fear, anxiety, etc. 不顯示激動,恐懼,憂慮等。***lick/smack one's lips,*** show (anticipation of) enjoyment. 舐(咂)嘴唇(表示享受或垂涎)。'**lip-reading** *n* [U] method (taught to deaf people) of understanding speech from lip movements. 讀唇法(敎導耳聾者由嘴唇的動作瞭解說話的方法)。Hence, 由此產生, '**lip-read** *vt.* '**lip•stick** *n* [C, U] (stick of) cosmetic material for reddening the lips: (一支)口紅;唇膏: *buy three lipsticks;* 買三支口紅; *use too much lipstick.* 搽太多的口紅。 **2** edge of a hollow vessel or opening: 凹陷的器皿的邊;洞邊: *the lip of a saucer/crater.* 碟(火山口)邊。 **3** [U] (sl) impudence: (俚)冒昧;無禮: *None of your lip!* Don't be impudent! 不要冒失地說話! **-lipped,** in compounds: (在複合字中): *ˌthick-/ˌdry-'lipped,* having thick/dry lips. 嘴唇厚(乾)的。

liquefy /'lɪkwɪfaɪ ; 'lɪkwəˌfaɪ/ *vt, vi* (*pt, pp* -fied) [VP6A, 2A] make or become liquid. 使成液體;液化。**lique•fac•tion** /ˌlɪkwɪ'fækʃn ; ˌlɪkwɪ'fækʃən/ *n* [U] making or becoming liquid; being liquified. 液化。

li•ques•cent /lɪ'kwesnt ; lɪ'kwɛsn̩t/ *adj* becoming, apt to become, liquid. 液化的;易液化的。

li•queur /lɪ'kjʊə(r) *US:* -'kɜːr ; lɪ'kɝ/ *n* strong usu sweet alcoholic drink for taking in small quantities: 味甜性烈的酒(適於少量飲用): ~ *brandy,* of special quality for drinking as a ~; 適於少量飲用的特種白蘭地; '~ *glass,* very small for ~s. 小酒杯。

liquid /'lɪkwɪd ; 'lɪkwɪd/ *n* **1** [C, U] substance like water or oil that flows freely and is neither a solid nor a gas: 液體: *Air is a fluid but not a ~; water is both a fluid and a ~.* 空氣是流體不是液體,水是流體也是液體。*You have added too much ~ to the mixture.* 這混合物中你加了過多的液體。 **2** (phon) the consonants /r/ or /l/. (語音)流音(卽 /r/ 或 /l/)。□ *adj* **1** in the form of a ~; not solid or gaseous: 液態的;液體的: ~ *food,* soft, easily swallowed, suitable for sick people; 液體食物(適合病人的易吞嚥的流質食物); ~ *mud,* so soft that it can be poured. 稀泥。~ **gas,** gas reduced to a ~ state by intense cold. 液態氣體。 **2** clear, bright and moist-looking: 清澄的;明亮的;水汪汪的: ~ *eyes,* bright and shining; 明亮的眼睛; *a ~ sky.* 清澄的天空。 **3** (of sounds) clear; pure; not guttural: (指聲音)淸脆的;純正的;流暢的: *the ~ notes of a blackbird.* 山鳥的淸脆的鳴聲。 **4** not fixed; easily changed: 不定的;易變的: ~ *opinions.* 不定的意見。**5** (in finance) easily sold or changed into cash: (財務)易變賣的: ~ *assets.* 易變賣的資產;流動資產。

liqui•date /'lɪkwɪdeɪt ; 'lɪkwɪˌdet/ *vt, vi* **1** [VP6A] pay or settle (a debt). 償付(債務)。 **2** [VP6A] bring (esp an unsuccessful business company) to an end by dividing up its property to pay debts; [VP2A] (of a company) go through this process. 清理(尤指商業失敗的公司)債務以作結束;(指公司)清理;清算;結束。**3** [VP6A] (colloq or newspaper style) get rid of, put an end to; kill: (俗或新聞用語)清除;肅清;殺掉: *gangsters who ~ their rivals.* 將對手殺掉的匪徒。**liqui•da•tion** /ˌlɪkwɪ'deɪʃn ; ˌlɪkwɪ'deʃən/ *n* [U] liquidating or being ~ed. 清償;清理債務以作結束;清算;清除。***go into liquidation,*** become bankrupt. 破產。**liq•ui•da•tor** /-tə(r); -tɚ/ *n* official who ~s(2). 清理公司債務之官員;破產管理人;淸盤人。

li•quid•ity /lɪ'kwɪdətɪ ; lɪ'kwɪdətɪ/ *n* [U] state of being liquid(5); state of being able to raise funds easily by selling assets. 資產之易變賣;資產流動性。

liquid•ize /'lɪkwɪdaɪz ; 'lɪkwəˌdaɪz/ *vt* [VP6A] crush, eg fruit, vegetables, to a liquid pulp. 搾(水果,蔬菜)成汁。 ~**r** *n* device (usu with an electric motor) for liquidizing fruit, etc. 果汁機(通常爲電動)。

liquor /'lɪkə(r) ; 'lɪkɚ/ *n* [C, U] **1** (GB) any alcoholic drink: (英)酒;酒類: *under the influence of ~,* partly drunk; 有些醉; *the worse for ~,* drunk; 喝醉; *malt ~,* beer; 啤酒; *brandy and other spirituous ~s.* 白蘭地和其他烈酒。 **2** (US) any distilled alcoholic drink: (美)蒸餾法製造的酒類: ~ *store.* 酒店。 **3** liquid produced by boiling or fermenting a food substance. 煮出的汁;發酵而成的汁液。

liquor•ice (US = **licor•ice**) /'lɪkərɪs ; 'lɪkərɪs/ *n* [U] (plant from whose root is obtained a) black substance used in medicine and in sweets. 甘草。

lira /'lɪərə ; 'lɪrə/ *n* (*pl* lire /'lɪəreɪ, 'lɪərə ; 'lɪre/ or ~s) unit of money in Italy. 里拉(義大利貨幣單位)。

lisle /laɪl ; laɪl/ *n* [U] fine, hard-twisted cotton fabric, used for stockings, gloves, etc. 一種光滑堅韌的棉線(用以製襪,手套等)。

lisp /lɪsp ; lɪsp/ *vi, vt* [VP2A, 6A, 15B] fail to use the sounds /s/ and /z/ correctly, eg by saying /θɪk'θiːn ; θɪk'θin/ for *sixteen;* say in a ~ing manner: 發不正確 /s/ 和 /z/ 的音(例如將 sixteen 讀作 /θɪk'θiːn ; θɪk'θin/); 口齒不清地說話: *She ~s.* 她發不清楚 /s/ 和 /z/ 的音。*He ~ed (out) his words.* 他口齒不清地說出他的話。□ *n* lisping way of speaking: 口齒不清: *The child has a bad ~.* 這孩子的口齒十分不清。~•**ing•ly** *adv*

lis•som, lis•some /'lɪsəm ; 'lɪsəm/ *adj* lithe; quick and graceful in movement. 柔軟的;輕快而優雅的。~•**ness** *n*

list[1] /lɪst ; lɪst/ *n* number of names (of persons, items, things, etc) written or printed: 名單;目錄;一覽表;名册: *a 'shopping ~;* 購物單; *make a ~ of things one must do;* 將必須做的事情列一表; *put sb's name on/take his name off the list.* 將某人的姓名列入名單(自名單中除掉)。~ **price,** (comm) published or advertised price. (商)價目表所列之價格;標價。**the active ~,** ~ of officers in the armed forces who may be called upon for service. 現役軍官名册。**the free ~, (a)** those goods admitted into a country free of duty. 海關免稅品目錄。**(b)** those persons who are admitted to a cinema, theatre, concert hall, etc without payment. 免費入場觀衆名單。□ *vt* [VP6A] make a ~ of; put on a ~: 造表;造册;編目錄;列於表上: ~ *all one's engagements;* 將所有的約會列一表; ~ *sb's name.* 將某人的姓名列於表上。

list[2] /lɪst ; lɪst/ *vi* [VP2A, C] (esp of a ship) lean over to one side, eg because the cargo has shifted: (尤指船)橫傾側(例如因貨物之移動引起者): *The ship ~s to starboard.* 這船向右舷傾側。□ *n* ~ing of a ship: 船之傾側: *a bad ~ to port.* 向左舷傾側得厲害。

list[3] /lɪst ; lɪst/ *vt, vi* (old use) listen (*to*). (舊用法)傾聽(與 to 連用)。

list[4] /lɪst ; lɪst/ *vi* (old use) please; choose: (舊用法)高興;願意: *'The wind bloweth where it ~eth.'* '風任意地吹。'

lis•ten /'lɪsn ; 'lɪsn/ *vi* [VP2A, C, 3A] **~ *(to),* 1** try to hear; pay attention: 傾聽;留心聽: *We ~ed but heard nothing.* 我們留心聽,但沒有聽見什麼。*The boys heard their father's voice but were not ~ing* *to what he was saying.* 男孩們聽見了他們父親的聲音,但並沒有留心聽他所說的話。*Please ~ carefully for the telephone while I'm upstairs.* 我在樓上時請你注意聽着電話。**~ *in (to),*** **(a)** listen to a broadcast programme: 聽廣播節目: *Did you ~ in to the Prime Minister yesterday evening?* 你昨晚收聽首相的廣播沒有? **(b)** ~ in to a conversation, eg by tapping telephone lines or using an extension telephone receiver. 用搭線或分機聽他人在電話中的談話。**2** agree to a suggestion, request, etc: 同意一建議,請求等: *Don't ~ to him; he wants to get you into trouble.* 不要聽他的話,他想使你陷入困境。**~er** *n* one who ~s. 傾聽者。

list·less /ˈlɪstlɪs ; ˈlɪstlɪs/ *adj* too tired to show interest or do anything. 倦怠的;無精打采的。**~·ly** *adv* **~·ness** *n*

lists /lɪsts ; lɪsts/ *n pl* (hist) (palisades enclosing an) area of ground for fights between men on horseback wearing armour and using lances. (史)比武場。***enter the ~ (against sb),*** (fig) challenge (sb) or accept a challenge (from sb) to a contest. (喻)向人挑戰;接受挑戰。

lit /lɪt ; lɪt/ *pt, pp* of light⁴. ***lit up,*** (sl) drunk. (俚)喝醉。

lit·any /ˈlɪtənɪ ; ˈlɪtn̩ɪ/ *n* (*pl* -nies) form of prayer for use in church services, recited by a priest with responses from the congregation. 連禱;啓應式祈禱。**the L~,** that in the Book of Common Prayer of the Church of England. (英國國教公禱書中之)連禱文;啓應禱文。

lit·chi /ˈlaɪtʃiː ; ˈlitʃi/ = lychee.

liter /ˈliːtə(r) ; ˈlitɚ/ ⇨ litre.

lit·er·acy /ˈlɪtərəsɪ ; ˈlɪtərəsɪ/ *n* [U] ability to read and write. 會讀書和寫字。

lit·eral /ˈlɪtərəl ; ˈlɪtərəl/ *adj* **1** connected with, expressed in, letters of an alphabet: 與字母有關的;用字母表達的: *a ~ error,* a misprint. 字母上的錯誤(印刷錯誤)。**2** corresponding exactly to the original: 完全按照原文的: *a ~ transcript/copy of an old manuscript;* 一舊稿的精確的謄本; *a ~ translation.* 直譯。(Cf 參較 *free* translation.) **3** (contrasted with *figurative*) taking words in their usual and obvious sense, without allegory or metaphor: (與figurative相對)按照字義的;不是諷喻或比喻的: *I hear nothing in the ~ sense of the word,* (ie of the word 'hear') get no news by hearing people speak (though I may get news from letters, etc). 我並未'聽'到什麼(不過我也許自書信等中知道的)。**4** (of a person) prosaic; matter of fact; lacking in imagination: (指人)平凡的;求實際的;無想像力的: *He has a rather ~ mind.* 他的頭腦沒有什麼想像力。□ *n* ~ error; misprint. 字母上的錯誤;印刷錯誤。**~ly** /ˈlɪtərəlɪ ; ˈlɪtərəlɪ/ *adv* **1** word for word; strictly: 逐字地;嚴格地: *translate ~ly;* 直譯;逐字翻譯; *carry out orders too ~ly.* 過份嚴格執行命令。**2** (informal use, to intensify meaning) without exaggeration: (非正式用法,以加强含義)不誇張地;簡直: *The children were ~ly starving.* 孩子們簡直是在挨餓。

lit·er·ary /ˈlɪtərərɪ *US:* ˈlɪtərerɪ ; ˈlɪtəˌrerɪ/ *adj* of literature or authors: 文學的;作家的: *the ~ profession;* 著作業; *a ~ man,* either an author or a man interested in literature; 作家;文人;對文學有興趣的人; *~ style,* as used in literature contrasted with *colloquial,* etc. 文學體;文言(以別於白話等); **~ property,** the right of an author to fees, royalties, etc coming from his writings. (作者的)版權。

lit·er·ate /ˈlɪtərət ; ˈlɪtərɪt/ *adj* **1** able to read and write. 會讀書和寫字的。**2** cultured; well-read: 文雅的;博學的: *He's a remarkably ~ young man.* 他是個十分博學的青年。□ *n* ~ person. 會讀書和寫字的人。

lit·er·ati /ˌlɪtəˈrɑːtɪ ; ˌlɪtəˈretaɪ/ *n pl* the literary intelligentsia. 文學界;文人。

lit·era·ture /ˈlɪtrətʃə(r) *US:* -tʃʊər ; ˈlɪtərəˌtʃʊr/ *n* [U] **1** (the writing or the study of) books, etc valued as works of art (drama, fiction, essays, poetry, biography, contrasted with technical books and journalism). 文學;文學作品(之寫作或研究)。**2** (also with *indef art*) all the writings of a country (*French ~*) or a period (*18th century English ~*); books dealing with a special subject: (亦與不定冠詞連用)一國之文學(如法國文學);一時代之文學(如十八世紀英國文學); 關於某一專門科目的文獻: *travel ~;* 旅行文獻; *the ~ of poultry-farming.* 家禽飼養學的文獻。*There is now an extensive ~ dealing with the First World War.* 現在有大量關於第一次世界大戰的文獻。**3** printed material describing or advertising sth, eg pamphlets: 說明或廣告性質的印刷品(例如小冊子): *We shall be glad to send you some ~ about our refrigerators/package holidays.* 我們願意寄給你一些關於我們的冰箱(假日旅行)的說明。

lithe /laɪð ; laɪð/ *adj* (of a person, a body) bending, twisting or turning easily: (指人,身體)易彎曲的;柔軟的: *~ movements;* 柔軟的動作; *make one's muscles ~.* 使肌肉柔軟。

lith·ogra·phy /lɪˈθɒgrəfɪ ; lɪˈθɑgrəfɪ/ *n* [U] process of printing from parts of a flat stone or sheet of zinc or aluminium that are prepared to receive a greasy ink. 平版印刷術;石版印刷術;金屬板印刷術。**litho·graph** /ˈlɪθəgrɑːf *US:* -græf ; ˈlɪθəˌgræf/ *n* sth (esp a picture) printed by this process. 平版印刷物;(尤指)石版畫。□ *vt, vi* print by this process. 平版印刷;石版印刷。**litho·graphic** /ˌlɪθəˈgræfɪk ; ˌlɪθəˈgræfɪk/ *adj* of ~. 平版印刷術的;石版印刷術的。

liti·gant /ˈlɪtɪgənt ; ˈlɪtəgənt/ *n* person engaged in a lawsuit. 訴訟當事人。

liti·gate /ˈlɪtɪgeɪt ; ˈlɪtəˌget/ *vi, vt* **1** [VP2A] go to law; make a claim at a court of law. 訴訟;打官司。**2** [VP6A] contest (sth) at a court of law. 在法庭上爭論(某事物);訟爭。**liti·ga·tion** /ˌlɪtɪˈgeɪʃn ; ˌlɪtəˈgeʃən/ *n* [U] litigating; going to law. 訴訟;打官司;訟爭。**lit·igious** /lɪˈtɪdʒəs ; lɪˈtɪdʒɪəs/ *adj* **1** fond of going to law. 好訴訟的;愛打官司的。**2** that can be disputed at law. 可訴訟的。

lit·mus /ˈlɪtməs ; ˈlɪtməs/ *n* blue colouring-matter that is turned red by acid and can then be restored to blue by alkali. 石蕊(一種藍色素,遇酸變紅,再遇鹼恢復藍色)。**ˈ~-paper,** paper stained with ~ and used as a test for acids and alkalis. 石蕊試紙(試驗酸和鹼者)。

li·totes /ˈlaɪtəʊtiːz ; ˈlaɪtəˌtiz/ *n* understatement used ironically, esp using a negative to express the contrary, as 'I shan't be sorry when it's over' meaning 'I shall be very glad', or 'It was no easy matter' for 'It was very difficult'. 間接肯定法;意重語輕的反語法 (例如用 '此事結束後我不會難過' 代替 '我將很高興' 或 '此事不容易' 代替 '此事很困難')。

litre (US = **liter**) /ˈliːtə(r) ; ˈlitɚ/ *n* unit of capacity in the metric system. 1 ~ = about $1\frac{3}{4}$ pints. 升;公升(約合 $1\frac{3}{4}$ 品脫)。⇨ App 5. 參看附錄五。

lit·ter¹ /ˈlɪtə(r) ; ˈlɪtɚ/ *n* **1** (hist) couch or bed (often with a covering and curtains) in which a person may be carried about, eg on men's shoulders, and as used in ancient Rome. (史)轎;輿(如古羅馬所用者)。**2** sort of stretcher for carrying a sick or wounded person. 擔架;舁床。

lit·ter² /ˈlɪtə(r) ; ˈlɪtɚ/ *n* **1** [U] odds and ends, bits of paper, discarded wrappings, bottles, etc left lying about in a room or public place: (在室內或公共場所亂丟的)雜物;垃圾(如紙屑,不要的包裝紙,空瓶等): *Pick up your ~ after a picnic.* 野餐後將丟在地上的雜物收拾好。**ˈ~-bin/-basket** *n* bin, basket, into which to place ~. 垃圾箱;垃圾筒。**ˈ~-lout** *n* (colloq) person who leaves ~ about in public places. (俗)在公共場所亂丟雜物者。**2 a ~,** state of untidiness that results when things are left lying about instead of being put away: 雜亂;零亂: *Her room was in such a ~ that she was ashamed to* *ask me in.* 她的房間十分零亂，故而不好意思請我進去。 **3** [U] straw and dung of a farmyard; straw and similar material, eg dry bracken, used as bedding for animals or for protecting plants from frost. 農家院中的稻草和糞；廐肥；鋪給獸類睡眠或遮蓋植物以防霜的草薦。 **4** [C] all the newly born young ones of an animal: 一胎所生的小獸；一窩: *a ~ of puppies;* 一窩小狗； *ten little pigs at a ~.* 一窩十隻小豬。□ *vt, vi* **1** [VP6A, 15A, B, 14] ~ ***sth (up) with sth,*** make untidy with odds and ends; scatter ~(1): 使雜亂；使零亂；亂丟雜物: ~ *a desk with papers;* 將桌上零亂地堆滿了文件(或報紙)； ~ *up one's room.* 把房間弄得亂七八糟。 **2** [VP6A, 15B] ~ ***sth (down),*** supply (a horse, etc) with straw; make a bed for an animal: 給(馬等)以草薦；為獸作窩: ~ *down a horse/a stable.* 鋪草給馬(鋪草於馬廐)。 **3** [VP2A] (of animals, esp dogs and pigs) bring forth a ~ of young ones. (指動物，尤指狗和豬)產一窩小狗或小豬。

little /ˈlɪtl ; ˈlɪtl̩/ *adj* (In senses 1, 2 and 4 ~ has no real *comp* and *superl;* ~r and ~st are occasionally used but are better avoided; ⇨ less and least for senses 3 and 5.) (用於第 1, 2, 4 義，little 無眞正的比較級和最高級；littler 和 littlest 雖偶而可用，但最好避免用；第 3, 5 兩義請參看 less 和 least。) **1** small, or small in comparison: 小的: (as a distinctive epithet) (作區別性的形容詞) *the ~ finger/toe.* 小指(趾)。 **2** (often preceded by another *adj* with no connotation of smallness, to indicate affection, tenderness, regard, admiration, or the contrary, depending upon the preceding *adj*): (其前常與未有'小'之含義的形容詞連用，表示感情，親切，關心，羡慕或相反之義，視其前之形容詞而定): *Isn't he a ~ devil!* (indicating affectionate regard). 你看他是不是個小淘氣！(表示感情上的關切)。 *What a pretty ~ house!* 多麼漂亮的小房子啊！*That poor ~ girl!* (indicating sympathy). 那個可憐的小女孩！(表示同情)。 *What horrid ~ children!* 多麼討厭的小鬼！ *She's a nice ~ thing* (indicating tenderness or regard, but possibly patronage, or a feeling of superiority). 她是個可愛的小東西(含有親切或愛護之意，但亦可能表示屈尊或一種優越感)。*Such a dear ~ man* (suggesting benign patronage) *came round and fixed my central heating.* 這樣一個可愛的人(表示善意的屈尊)到這裏來裝修我的暖氣系統設備。*He's quite the ~ gentleman!* (suggesting patronage). 他可以說是個相當溫雅的人！(表示屈尊)。 ***the '~ people/folk,*** (esp in Ireland) fairies; elves. (尤用於愛爾蘭) 小仙；小神。 **3** short (in time, distance, stature): (指時間，距離，身材)短的；矮的: *Won't you stay a ~ time with me?* 你不願意陪我一會兒嗎？ *Come a ~ way with me.* 陪我走一小段路。 **4** young: 年輕的: *How are the ~ ones,* the children? 孩子們都好嗎？ *Here come the ~ Smiths,* the Smith children. 史密斯家的孩子們來了。 **5** not much: 很少的: *He gained ~ advantage from the scheme.* 他從這計畫中沒有獲得什麼利益。*I have very ~ time for reading.* 我很少有時間讀書。*He knows ~ Latin and less Greek.* 他對拉丁文懂得很少，對希臘文懂得更少。**6 a ~,** some but not much; a small quantity of: 少許的；少量的: *He knows a ~ French.* 他懂一點法文。 *A ~ care would have prevented the accident.* 稍微注意一點此一意外就不會發生了。*Will you have a ~ cake,* a piece or slice of cake? 你要吃一點糕嗎？(Cf 參較 *Will you have a cake,* one of tl ese cakes? 你要吃一塊糕嗎？) ***not a ~,*** (euphem) much: (委婉語)很多: *It has caused me not a ~ anxiety,* considerable anxiety. 此事曾使我相當焦慮。□ *adv* **1** not much; hardly at all; only slightly: 很少；幾乎一點也不；些微地: *He is ~ known.* 很少有人知道他。*She slept very ~ last night.* 她昨夜沒有睡什麼覺。*I see him very ~* (ie rarely) *nowadays.* 近來我很少看見他。*He left ~ more than an hour ago.* 他不過是一小時前離開的。*That is ~ short of* (= is almost) *madness!* 那幾近於瘋狂！ *He is ~ better than* (= is almost as bad as) *a thief.* 他和一個小偷沒有什麼差別。***a ~,*** (used *adverbially* meaning) (做副詞用，意為) rather; somewhat: 有幾分；稍微: *She seemed to be a ~ afraid.* 她好像有點害怕。 *This hat is a ~ too large for me.* 這帽子對我有點嫌大了。*He was not a ~ annoyed,* was considerably annoyed. 他相當苦惱。 **2** (with such *vv* as *know, think, imagine, guess, suspect, realize,* and always placed before the *v*) (用於 know, think, imagine, guess, suspect, realize 等動詞前) not at all: 毫不: *They ~ suspect/L~ do they suspect that their plot has been discovered.* 他們絲毫沒有想到他們的陰謀已被人發現了。*He ~ knows/L~ does he know that the police are about to arrest him.* 他一點也不知道警察就要逮捕他了。**~·ness** *n* [U] the quality of being ~. 小；少。□ *n* (⇨ less, least). **1** not much; only a small amount: 少許；少量: *You have done very ~ for us,* have not helped us much. 你沒有幫我們多少忙。*I see very ~ of him,* do not see him often or for long. 我很少看見他。*The ~ of his work that I have seen seems excellent.* 我所看到的他僅有的那一點工作似乎做得非常好。*I got ~ out of it,* not much advantage or profit. 我從這當中沒有得到什麼好處。*He did what ~ he could.* 他已盡到他僅有的一點力量了。*Every ~ helps.* 任何小東西都有用。~ ***by ~,*** gradually; by degrees. 逐漸；漸漸地。~ ***or nothing,*** hardly anything. 幾乎沒有東西。***in ~,*** on a small scale. 小規模的(地)。 **2 a ~,** a small quantity; something (*a ~* is positive; *~* is negative): 少許；一點(a little 是肯定的，little 含否定之義): *He knows a ~ of everything.* 他什麼都懂得一點。*A ~ makes some people laugh.* 只懂一點皮毛會招致某些人的譏笑。*Please give me a ~.* 請給我一點。***after/for a ~,*** after/for a short time or distance. 經過一段短時間或距離。

lit·toral /ˈlɪtərəl ; ˈlɪtərəl/ *n, adj* (part of a country which is) along the coast. 沿海岸的；沿海地區。

lit·urgy /ˈlɪtədʒɪ ; ˈlɪtɚdʒɪ/ *n* (*pl* -gies) [C, U] fixed form of public worship used in a church. 禮拜儀式。 **li·turgi·cal** /lɪˈtɜ:dʒɪkl ; lɪˈtɝdʒɪkl̩/ *adj*

liv·able, live·able /ˈlɪvəbl ; ˈlɪvəbl̩/ *adj* (of life) tolerable. (指生活)過得去的。 ~ ***(in),*** (of a house, room, climate, etc) fit to live in. (指房屋，房間，氣候等)適於居住的。 ~ ***(with),*** (of persons) easy to live with. (指人)易共同生活的；易處的。

live[1] /laɪv ; laɪv/ *adj* (rarely pred; ⇨ living and alive for pred uses). (罕作敍述用法；參看 living 和 alive 在述語中的用法)。 **1** having life: 有生命的；活的: ~ *fish;* 活魚； (joc) actual, not pretended: (諧)眞正的；不是假裝的: *There's a real ~ burglar under my bed!* 我床底下有一個眞正的竊賊！ **2** burning or glowing: 燃燒的；熾熱的: ~ *coals/embers;* 燃燒着的煤(餘燼)；unexploded: 未爆炸的: *a ~ shell/cartridge/bomb;* 未爆炸的砲彈(子彈，炸彈)；實彈；not used: 未用過的: *a ~ match;* 未用過的火柴；charged with electricity: 充電的: *a ~ rail,* carrying current for trains. 帶電的鐵軌。***a '~ wire,*** (fig) a lively energetic person. (喻) 精力充沛有生氣的人。 **3** (of sth broadcast) not recorded in advance (on tape or records): (指廣播內容)非預先錄音的；現場播出的: *It was a ~ broadcast, not a recording.* 那是現場廣播，不是錄音廣播。 **4 '~-birth** *n* (contrasted with *still-birth*) baby born alive: 生下後活着的嬰兒；活着生下來的嬰兒(與 still-birth 相對): *the ratio of ~-births to still-births.* 活產與死產之比率。 **5** full of energy, activity, interest, importance, etc: 充滿精力，活動力，興趣，重要性等的: *a ~ question/issue,* one in which there is great interest. 最為人關切的問題。□ *adv* (from 3 above): 現場播出地: *The concert will be broadcast ~.* 那音樂會將現場播出。

live[2] /lɪv ; lɪv/ *vi, vt* **1** [VP2A] have existence as a plant or animal; be alive (the more usu phrase: *He's still alive* is preferable to *He still ~s*). 生存；活着(be alive 較 live 常用，例如: He's still alive

較 He still lives 常用)。**2** [VP2A, B, C, 4A] continue to be alive; remain alive: 繼續活着;繼續生存: ~ *to be old/to a great age;* 活到老(高齡); ~ *to see all one's grandchildren married.* 活到看到自己的孫兒輩結婚。*She's very ill—the doctors don't think she will* ~. 她病得很重,醫生們認爲她不能活了。*Can he* ~ *through the night?* 他能活得過今夜嗎? ~ ***on,*** continue to ~: 繼續活着: *The old people died but the young people* ~*d on in the village.* 村子裡的老年人死了,但年輕人還繼續活着。 ~ ***through,*** experience and survive: 經歷…而未死: *He has* ~*d through two wars and three revolutions.* 他親歷兩次戰爭和三次革命。***You/We ~ and learn,*** phrase used when one hears sth new, esp sth surprising. 活到老學到老。~ ***and 'let ~,*** be tolerant; ignore the failings of others in order that one's failings may be ignored. 待人要容忍;待人寬容如待己。**3** [VP 3A] ~ ***by doing sth,*** earn one's livelihood by doing it. 以…爲生。~ ***by one's wits,*** get money by ingenious and irregular methods, not necessarily honest. 靠小聰明過日子(以機敏和不合常規的方法,但不一定是誠實的方法賺錢度日)。~ ***off the land,*** use its agricultural products for one's food needs. 以農產品爲食。~ ***on sth,*** have it as food or diet: 以…爲食: ~ *on fruit/a milk diet;* 以水果(規定的乳類飲食)爲食; depend upon for support, etc: 靠…過活: ~ *on one's salary/on £3000 a year/on one's wife's income.* 靠薪金(一年三千鎊,妻子的收入)過活。~ ***on one's name/reputation,*** keep one's position, continue to earn money, because one has been successful in the past. 靠好的名聲過活(由於過去有成就,故能繼續保持職位或賺錢度日)。 **4** [VP 2C, 3A] ~ ***(in/at),*** make one's home; reside: 居;住: ~ *in England;* 住在英國; ~ *at home;* 住在家裏; ~ *abroad;* 居於國外; ~ *in lodgings/an hotel.* 住在寄宿舍(旅館)。*Where do you* ~*?* 你住在那裏? ~ ***in/out,*** (esp of domestic servants, shop assistants, workers) lodge in/out of the building where one is employed. (尤指僕人,店員,工人)(不)住在主人家;(不)住在工作處。 ~ ***together,*** live in the same house, etc; (of two persons of opposite sex) live as if married: 住在一起;(指異性)同居: *I hear that Jane and Bill are living together.* 我聽說珍和比爾目前同居在一起。 **5** [VP6B, 2D] (with cognate object) spend, pass, experience: (與同源受詞連用)過;度過: ~ *a happy life/a virtuous life;* 過快樂的(有德性的)生活; ~ *a double life,* act two different parts in life. 過雙重生活。*He* ~*d the life of a Christian.* 他過着基督徒的生活。*He* ~*d and died a bachelor.* 他終生未娶。 **6** [VP 2C, D] conduct oneself; pass one's life in a specified way: 處身; 做人; 以某種方式生活: ~ *honestly/happily;* 誠實地(快樂地)生活; ~ *like a saint;* 像聖徒一般生活; ~ ***well,*** live a life satisfying all the appetites. 生活優裕。 ~ ***a lie,*** express a lie by one's manner of living. 過虛僞的生活。~ ***to oneself,*** in isolation, without trying to make friends. 過孤獨的生活。 **7** [VP15B] ~ ***sth down,*** live in such a way that (past guilt, scandal, foolishness, etc) is forgotten: 過新的生活以忘却(往日的罪惡,醜行,愚昧等): *He hopes to* ~ *down the scandal caused by the divorce proceedings.* 他希望藉新的生活忘却那因離婚而引起的醜聞。[VP2C] ~ ***up to sth,*** put (one's faith, principles, etc) into practice; reach the standard that may be expected: 實行(信仰,主義等);達到預期的標準: *It's difficult to* ~ *up to the principles of the Christian religion.* 實行基督教的教條是困難的。*He didn't* ~ *up to his reputation.* 他名不副實(徒有虛名)。 [VP3A] ~ ***with sth,*** accept and endure it: 接受並忍受某事物: *I don't like the noise of these jet aircraft, but I've learnt to* ~ *with it.* 我厭惡這些噴射機的噪音,但我已學會去忍受它了。 **8** [VP2A] (of things without life) remain in existence; survive: (指無生命的東西)繼續存在;仍在: *His memory will always* ~, *He will never be forgotten.* 他將永遠被人記得。*No ship could* ~ *in such a rough sea.* 任何船隻都不能在這洶湧的海上安然航行。 **9** [VP2A] enjoy life intensely: 享受人生: *'I want to* ~*', she said, 'I don't want to spend my days cooking and cleaning and looking after babies.'* '我要享受人生,'她說,'我不要把我的日子花費在燒飯,清洗和照顧孩子上。' ~ ***it up,*** live a life of hectic enjoyment. 享受人生。

live·li·hood /ˈlaɪvlɪhʊd ; ˈlaɪvlɪˌhʊd/ *n* means of living; way in which one earns money: 生計; 營生;謀生之道: *earn/gain one's* ~ *by teaching;* 靠教書爲生; *earn an honest* ~*;* 規規矩矩地謀生; *deprive a man of his* ~. 剝奪一人的生計。

live·long /ˈlɪvlɒŋ *US:* ˈlaɪvlɔːŋ ; ˈlɪvˌlɔŋ/ *adj* (only in) (僅用於) ***the ~ day/night,*** the whole length of the day/night (implying, according to context, weariness or delight). 整整的一天(夜)(含厭惡或喜悅之意,視上下文而定)。

live·ly /ˈlaɪvlɪ ; ˈlaɪvlɪ/ *adj* (-ier, -iest) **1** full of life and spirit; gay and cheerful: 有生氣的;活潑的;愉快的;快活的: *She's as* ~ *as a kitten.* 她快活得像隻小貓。*The patient seems a little livelier/a little more* ~ *this morning.* 那病人今晨似乎精神好些了。*He has a* ~ *imagination.* 他有活潑的想像力。*They had a* ~ *time,* exciting, perhaps with an element of danger. 他們有一段够刺激的(或許是驚險的)經歷。***look ~,*** move more quickly, show more energy. 較前活潑且精力充沛。***make things ~ for sb,*** make it exciting and perhaps dangerous for him. 使(某人)感到驚險刺激。 **2** (of colour) bright; gay. (指顏色)鮮明的;鮮豔的。 **3** (of non-living things) moving quickly or causing quick movement: (指無生命的東西)動作迅速的;引起迅速動作的: *a* ~ *ball;* 快速直球; *a* ~ *(cricket) pitch.* 迅速的(板球)一投。 **4** lifelike; realistic: 生動的;眞實的: *a* ~ *description of a football game;* 對一場足球比賽生動的描寫; *give sb a* ~ *idea of what happened.* 使某人對發生的事情有身歷其境的感覺。**live·li·ness** *n* [U] state of being ~. 有生氣;活潑;快活;鮮明;生動。

liven /ˈlaɪvn ; ˈlaɪvən/ *vt, vi* [VP15B, 2C] ~ ***up,*** make or become lively: 使有生氣;使活潑;活潑有力: *How can we* ~ *things up?* 我們怎樣能使事情有生氣呢? *The party is beginning to* ~ *up.* 這聚會現在開始活潑起來了。

liver[1] /ˈlɪvə(r) ; ˈlɪvɚ/ *n* **1** [C] large, reddish-brown organ in the body which secretes bile and purifies the blood. 肝臟。⇨ the illus at alimentary. 參看 alimentary 之挿圖。 **2** [U] animal's ~ as food. (動物的)肝(指做食物用者)。**~·ish** /-ɪʃ ; -ɪʃ/, **~y** *adjj* (colloq) suffering from ~ trouble; bilious. (俗)患肝病的;脾氣壞的。

liver[2] /ˈlɪvə(r) ; ˈlɪvɚ/ *n* person who lives in a specified way: 過某種生活者: *an evil/clean/loose* ~. 過着罪惡(淸白,放蕩)生活的人。

liver·wurst /ˈlɪvəwɜːst ; ˈlɪvɚˌwɝst/ *n* (US) sausage of chopped liver, popular in sandwiches. (美)肝製臘腸(常用於三明治)。

liv·ery /ˈlɪvərɪ ; ˈlɪvərɪ/ *n* (*pl* -ries) **1** special dress or uniform worn by men servants in a great household (esp of a king or noble) or by members of one of the city companies of London (trade or craft guilds). (帝王貴族等家庭僕從所穿的)僕從制服; (倫敦市某同業工會會員所穿的)會員制服。***in/out of ~,*** wearing/not wearing such dress or uniform. 穿(不穿)着制服。**'~ company,** one of the London trade guilds that has a distinctive uniform. (有特殊制服的)倫敦市同業工會之一。 **2** (fig, poet) dress; covering: (喻,詩) 衣服; 覆蓋物: *trees in the* ~ *of spring,* with new green leaves; 春季生出新葉的樹; *birds in their winter* ~. 長着冬季羽毛的鳥。 **3** **'~ (stable),** stable where horses are kept for their owners, fed and looked after for payment; stable from which horses may be hired. 馬房(付費後可寄馬和飼馬之處);租馬處。**liv·er·ied** /ˈlɪvərɪd ; ˈlɪvərɪd/ *adj* wearing ~(1). 穿特殊制

服的。**'~•man** /-mən ; -mən/ *n* (*pl* -men) **1** member of a ~ company. 倫敦市穿特殊制服的同業公會會員。 **2** keeper of, workers in, a ~ stable. 代人飼馬者;出租馬者。

lives /laɪvz ; laɪvz/ *pl* of life.

live•stock /'laɪvstɒk ; 'laɪv,stɑk/ *n* [U] (esp farm) animals kept for use or profit, eg cattle, sheep, pigs. 家畜(尤指農家者;例如牛,羊,豬等)。

livid /'lɪvɪd ; 'lɪvɪd/ *adj* of the colour of lead, blue-grey; (of a person or his looks) furiously angry: 鉛色的;藍灰色的;(指人或面容)狂怒的: *~ marks/bruises on the body;* 身上青灰色的斑記(瘀傷); *~ with cold/rage.* 凍(氣)得臉發青。**~•ly** *adv*

liv•ing¹ /'lɪvɪŋ ; 'lɪvɪŋ/ *adj* **1** alive, esp now existent: 活着的;(尤指)現存的: *~ languages.* 現行的語言。*No man ~* (= No man who is now alive) *could do better.* 當代的人沒有一個能做得比這更好的了。***within/in ~ memory,*** within the memory of people now alive. 在當今人的記憶中。 **2** (of a likeness) true to life: (指相似處或物)逼眞的;一模一樣的: *He's the ~ image of* (= is exactly like) *his father.* 他跟他父親長得一模一樣。 **3** strong; active; lively: 强烈的;活潑的;生動的: *a ~ hope/faith.* 强烈的希望(信心)。***the ~ theatre,*** the ordinary theatre (contrasted with the cinema, TV, etc). 舞臺劇(指一般的戲劇,以別於電影或電視劇等)。 □ *n* **the ~,** (with *pl v*) those now alive: (用複數動詞)現世的人: *He's still in the land of the ~.* 他尚活在人間。

liv•ing² /'lɪvɪŋ ; 'lɪvɪŋ/ *n* **1** means of keeping alive, of earning what is needed for life: 生存之道;生計: *earn/gain/get/make a ~ as a car salesman.* 做汽車推銷員以謀生。 **2** [U] manner of life: 生活方式: *good ~,* having good food, etc; 優裕的生活; *plain ~ and high thinking,* having plain, simple food and leading a philosophic life; 樸素的生活與崇高的思想(過簡樸曠達的生活); *the high cost/standard of ~ in the US;* 美國的生活費用(水準)很高; *the art of ~.* 生活的藝術。**,~ 'wage,** minimum wage for a worker and his family to live on. 使工人能夠維持一家人生活的工資。**'~-room** *n* room for general use during the day (often a general purpose room, used for meals, recreation, etc). 起居室;客廳。**'~-space** *n* area of land considered by a State as necessary for further expansion. 某一國家認爲未來擴展所必需的地區;生存空間。 **3** (Church of England) benefice. (英國教會)牧師的俸祿。

liz•ard /'lɪzəd ; 'lɪzərd/ *n* small, creeping, long-tailed, four-legged reptile. 蜥蜴;四脚蛇;石龍子。 ⇨ the illus at reptile. 參看 reptile 之插圖。

llama /'lɑːmə ; 'lɑmə/ *n* S American animal with a thick woolly coat, used as a beast of burden. 美洲駝;駱馬(南美洲產的一種毛厚的馱獸)。⇨ the illus at large. 參看 large 之插圖。

Lloyd's /lɔɪdz ; lɔɪdz/ *n* society of underwriters in London. 倫敦羅意德船舶協會。***A1 at ~,*** (dated sl) excellent. (過時俚語)第一流的;最好的。**~'s Register,** annual list of ships in various classes. 在羅意德協會每年登記的各種船舶名單。

lo /ləʊ ; lo/ *int* (old use) Look! See! (舊用法)看!瞧! ***Lo and behold!*** This will surprise you. 看啊!你瞧!

load¹ /ləʊd ; lod/ *n* [C] **1** that which is (to be) carried or supported, esp if heavy; (fig) weight of care, responsibility, etc: 負荷物;載荷物(尤指沉重者);(喻)負擔: *a heavy ~ on one's shoulders;* 肩上的重擔; *a 'coach-~ of passengers.* 一馬車乘客。***take a ~ off sb's mind,*** relieve him of anxiety, etc. 解除某人的憂慮等。 ***~s of,*** (colloq) a large amount of: (俗)大量的: *~s of friends/money/time.* 許多朋友(金錢,時間)。**'~-line** *n* = Plimsoll line. **2** amount which a cart, etc can take: 車等負載之量;裝載量: *a 'cart-~ of hay;* 一車乾草; *two 'lorry-~s of coal.* 兩卡車煤。 ⇨ also *payload* at pay¹. **3** amount of work that a dynamo, motor, engine, etc is required to do; amount of current supplied by a generating station or carried by an electric circuit. (發電機,發動機,引擎等之)載荷;(發電廠或電路的)負載;負荷。**'~-shedding** *n* cutting off the supply of current on certain lines when the demand for current is greater than the supply. (電源不勝負擔時)切斷某些電路的電源。

load² /ləʊd ; lod/ *vt, vi* **1** [VP6A, 14, 15A, B, 2A, C] ***~ sth into/on to sth/sb; ~ sth/sb (with sth); ~ sb/sth down (with sth),*** put a ~ in or on: 裝貨物於;裝載(貨物);使負擔: *~ sacks on to a cart/a donkey;* 裝貨於一車(驢); *~ a cart with coal;* 裝煤於車; *~ a lot of work on to one's staff;* 將許多工作交給下屬去做; *a poor old woman ~ed* (*down*) *with her shopping;* 揹着大包小包購物的可憐的老婦人; (fig) (喻) *~ a man with favours/honours;* 使一人備受恩寵(榮譽); *a heart ~ed with sorrow.* 滿懷悲傷的心。 ***~ (sth) up,*** fill with goods, materials, etc: 裝載貨物(於): *Have you finished ~ing up* (*the van*) *yet?* 你將貨物裝上(貨車)了嗎? **2** [VP6A, 2A] put a cartridge or shell into (a gun) or a length of film into (a camera): 裝彈於(槍砲);裝膠捲於(照相機): *Are you ~ed?* Is there a cartridge in your gun? 你的槍裏裝有子彈嗎? **3** [VP6A] weight with lead; add extra weight to: 塡鉛以加重;加重: *a ~ed cane/stick,* one having lead added to make the cane useful as a weapon; 鉛頭杖(用做武器); *~ed dice,* so weighted as to fall with a certain face, eg the six, uppermost. 塡有鉛的骰子(擲時某一面,例如六點,恆向上);假骰子。 ***~ the dice (against sb),*** (fig) do sth that gives one an unfair advantage (over him). (喻)使用欺詐手段(不利於某人)。 ***a ~ed question,*** one that is intended to trap a person into making an admission which may be harmful. 另有用意的問題(欲引誘某人作對其不利之承認的一個問題)。 **~ed** *adj* (sl) having much money. (俚)很有錢的。

load•star, load•stone ⇨ lode.

loaf¹ /ləʊf ; lof/ *n* (*pl* loaves /ləʊvz ; lovz/) **1** mass of bread cooked as a separate quantity: 一條麵包: *a two-pound ~.* 一條兩磅重的麵包。***Half a ~ is better than none/'no bread,*** It is better to take what one can get or is offered than to run the risk of having nothing. 半條麵包比沒有麵包强;聊勝於無。 **2** **'sugar-~** *n* [C] cone-shaped mass of sugar, as formerly made and sold. (昔時製來售賣的)圓椎形糖塊。**'~-sugar** *n* [U] sugar cut into small lumps. 小方塊糖。 **3** [C, U] (quantity of) food shaped and cooked: 一塊食物(之量): (*a*) *meat ~,* made of minced meat, eggs, etc. 剁碎之肉和蛋等製成的菜。 **4** (sl) ***use one's ~,*** think intelligently; reflect. (俚)動動腦筋;好好想一想。

loaf² /ləʊf ; lof/ *vi, vt* [VP2A, C, 15A, B] (colloq) waste time; spend time idly: (俗)浪費時間;虛擲光陰: *out-of-work men ~ing at street corners.* 在街道轉角處閒蕩的失業男子。*Don't ~ about while there's so much work to be done.* 當有這麼多工作要做時,不要閒着。*Don't ~ away your time.* 不要浪費你的時光。 □ *n* (*sing* only) ~ing. (僅用單數)虛擲光陰。 **~er** *n* person who ~s. 虛擲光陰者;游手好閒者。

loam /ləʊm ; lom/ *n* [U] rich soil with some sand or a little clay, and with much decayed vegetable matter in it. (含有少量沙或一點黏土及大量腐爛植物的)沃土;壤土。**~y** *adj* of or like ~: 上述沃土的;似上述沃土的: *~y land.* 沃地。

loan /ləʊn ; lon/ *n* **1** [C] sth lent, esp a sum of money: 借出物;(尤指)借款;貸款: *government ~s,* sum lent to the government; 公債; *domestic and foreign ~s.* 內債和外債。 **2** [U] lending or being lent. 借出。***have the ~ of sth; have sth on ~ (from sb),*** have it as a borrower: 借得某物: *May I have the ~ of your sewing-machine?* 我可以借用你的縫紉機嗎? *I have the book out on ~ from the library.* 我從圖書館裏借出那本書。**'~-collection** *n* number of pictures, etc lent by their owners for exhibition. 借自收藏家的展覽品。 **'~-office** *n* one for lending money to private borrowers. 代

款處。'～·**word** *n* word taken from another language. 外來語。□ *vt* [VP6A, 14] ～ ***sth (to sb)***, lend (which is the more usu word except in formal style). 借出;借(除正式文體外,lend 一字較常用)。

loath, loth /ləʊθ ; loθ/ *adj* (*pred* only) (僅作敍述用法) ～ ***to do sth***, unwilling. 不願意做某事。***nothing*** ～, quite willing. 十分樂意。

loathe /ləʊð ; loð/ *vt* [VP6A, C] **1** feel disgust for; dislike greatly: 厭惡; 嫌惡: *She was seasick, and ～d the smell of greasy food.* 她暈船,厭惡油膩食物的氣味。 **2** (colloq) dislike: (俗) 不喜歡: *He ～s travelling by air.* 他不喜歡坐飛機旅行。**loath·ing** *n* [U] disgust. 厭惡。**loath·ly**, (rare) (罕), **loath·some** /-səm ; -səm/ *adjj* disgusting; causing one to feel shocked: 可厭的; 令人震驚的: *a loathsome disease.* 討厭的疾病。

loaves /ləʊvz ; lovz/ *pl* of loaf[1].

lob /lɒb ; lɑb/ *vi, vt* (-bb-) [VP6A, 15A, 2C] strike or send (a ball) in a high arc (in tennis). (網球) 高擊(球)。□ *n* ball bowled underhand at cricket or hit high up into the air at tennis. (板球)下手球; (網球)高球。

lobby /'lɒbɪ ; 'lɑbɪ/ *n* (*pl* -bies) **1** porch, entrance-hall, anteroom, corridor: 門廊;入口的廳堂; 大廳; 通正室的接待室;走廊: *the ～ of a hotel／theatre.* 旅館(戲院)的休息室。 **2** (in the House of Commons, etc) large hall used for interviews between members and the public; group of people who try to influence members, eg of the House of Commons, the Senate in Washington, DC, to support or oppose proposed legislation. (下議院或參議院等中的) 民衆接待廳; 遊說議員的一群人。 **3 (di'vision)** ～, (House of Commons) one of two corridors to which members retire when a vote is taken in the House. (英國下議院分組表決時)議員前往投票的兩走廊之一。□ *vt, vi* [VP6A, 15A, 2A, C] (try to) influence the members of a law-making body; get (a bill) passed or rejected in this way: 遊說議員; 運動議員使(議案)通過或不通過: ～ *a bill through the Senate;* 運動議員使參議院通過一議案; *the National Union of Farmers ～ing in order to maintain subsidies／～ing for higher subsidies／～ing their MP's.* 爲維持補助金 (增加補助金) 而遊說議員的全國總農會。'～·**ist** /-ɪst ; -ɪst/ *n* person who lobbies. 遊說議員者;運動議員使議案通過或不通過者。

lobe /ləʊb ; lob/ *n* **1** lower rounded part of the external ear. 耳垂。⇨ the illus at ear. 參看 ear 之插圖。 **2** subdivision of the lungs or the brain. 肺葉;腦葉。⇨ the illus at respiratory. 參看 respiratory 之插圖。～**d** *adj* having ～s. 有耳垂的;有肺葉或腦葉的。

lob·ster /'lɒbstə(r) ; 'lɑbstɚ/ *n* **1** [C] shellfish with eight legs and two claws, bluish-black before and scarlet after being boiled. 龍蝦。⇨ the illus at crustacean. 參看 crustacean 之插圖。'～-**pot** *n* basket in which ～s are trapped. 捕捉龍蝦的籃或簍。 **2** [U] its flesh as food. 龍蝦肉(食用)。

lo·cal /'ləʊkl ; 'lokḷ/ *adj* **1** of, special to, a place or district: 地方的; 當地的; 本地的: *the ～ doctor*, living in the district; 當地的醫生; ～ *customs;* 地方風俗; *a column of ～ news;* 地方新聞欄; ～ *government.* 地方政府。～ **colour**, details of the scenes and period described in a story, added to make the story more real. 地方色彩(對地方背景和時代詳細的描述,以增加故事的眞實性)。～ **option／veto**, (in some countries) system by which people may decide, by voting, whether they do or do not want sth, eg the sale of alcoholic drink, in their district. (某些國家)地方人民的選擇 (否決) 權 (例如決定是否應販賣酒類)。～ **time**, time at any place in the world as calculated from the position of the sun: 地方時: *L～ time changes by one hour for every 15° longitude.* 經度每差十五度當地時間就差一小時。 **2** affecting a part, not the whole: 局部的: *a ～ pain／injury;* 局部疼痛(傷害); *a ～ anaesthetic.* 局部麻醉劑。□ *n* **1** (usu *pl*) inhabitant of a particular district. (通常用複數)當地人;本地人。 **2** item of ～ news in a newspaper. 地方新聞。 **3** (colloq) ～ public house: (俗) 當地酒店: *pop into the ～ for a pint.* 匆匆進入本地酒店去買一品脫酒。～**ly** /-kəlɪ ; -kəlɪ/ *adv*

lo·cale /ləʊ'kɑ:l *US:* -'kæl ; lo'kæl/ *n* [C] scene of an event; scene of a novel, etc. 事件的現場;小說等發生的地點。

lo·cal·ism /'ləʊkəlɪzəm ; 'lokḷ,ɪzəm/ *n* **1** [U] interest in a district, esp one's own; favouring of what is local; narrowness of ideas that may be the result of this. 對於地方(尤指自己的鄉土)的關心; 鄉土偏愛;(由鄉土偏愛產生的)思想的偏狹;地方主義。 **2** [C] local idiom, pronunciation, etc. 土話;方言;土音。

lo·cal·ity /ləʊ'kælətɪ ; lo'kælətɪ/ *n* (*pl* -ties) **1** [C] thing's position; place in which an event occurs; place, district, neighbourhood. 位置;發生地;所在地; 地方;地區。 **2** [U] faculty of remembering and recognizing places, features of the landscape, etc, esp as a help in finding one's way: 記憶地方的能力;辨認地方的能力: *She has a good sense of ～.* 她記憶地方的能力很强。

lo·cal·ize /'ləʊkəlaɪz ; 'lokḷ,aɪz/ *vt* [VP6A] **1** make local, not general; confine within a particular part or area: 使限於局部; 使限於一區域: *There is little hope of localizing the disease.* 沒有希望使疾病限於局部。 **2** invest with local characteristics. 使帶有地方色彩。**lo·cal·iz·ation** /,ləʊkəlaɪ'zeɪʃn *US:* -lɪ'z- ; ,lokḷə'zeʃən/ *n*

lo·cate /lə'keɪt *US:* 'ləʊkeɪt ; 'loket/ *vt* [VP6A, 15A] **1** discover, show, the locality of: 找出…的位置;指出…的位置: ～ *a town on a map.* 在地圖上找出一城市的位置。 **2** establish in a place: 在一地點設置: *a new school to be ～d in the suburbs.* 將設於郊區的一所新學校。*Where is the new factory to be ～d?* 新工廠將設於何處? **3 be ～d**, be situated. 位於。**lo·ca·tion** /ləʊ'keɪʃn ; lo'keʃən/ *n* **1** [U] locating or being ～d. 指出位置; 定位置。 **2** [C] position or place: 位置; 地方: *suitable locations for new factories.* 適於新建工廠的位置。 **3** place, not a film studio, where (part of) a cinema film is photographed. (電影之)外景拍攝地。***on location***, shooting film in this way. 拍外景。**4** (in S Africa) suburb where Africans are constrained to live. (南非)非洲土著被迫居住之城郊。

loch /lɒk ; lɑk/ *n* (Scot) (蘇) **1** long, narrow arm of the sea almost enclosed by land. 長窄的海灣。 **2** lake. 湖。

loci /'ləʊsaɪ ; 'losaɪ/ *pl* of locus.

lock[1] /lɒk ; lɑk/ *n* portion of hair that naturally hangs or clings together; (*pl*) hair of the head: 一綹頭髮;(複)頭髮: *my scanty ～s.* 我的稀少的頭髮。

lock[2] /lɒk ; lɑk/ *n* **1** appliance, mechanism, by which a door, gate, lid, etc may be fastened with a bolt that needs a key to work it. 鎖。***keep sth／put sth／be under ～ and key***, in sth fitted with a ～. 將某物鎖着(被鎖著)。'～·**smith** *n* maker and mender of ～s. 鎖匠。**2** mechanism by which a gun is fired. 槍機。～, ***stock and barrel***, the whole of the thing; completely. 全部;完全地。 **3** enclosed section of a canal or river at a point where the water level changes, for raising or lowering boats by the use of gates fitted with sluices. (運河或河流之)閘河。,～-'**gate**, gate on a lock. 閘門。'～-**keeper** *n* keeper of a canal or river ～, who opens and shuts the gates to allow boats to pass through. 水閘管理人。 **4** [U] condition of being fixed or jammed so that movement is impossible. 固定;塞緊。'～·**jaw** *n* [U] form of disease (tetanus) that causes the jaws to be firmly locked together. 牙關鎖閉症; 破傷風。'～·**nut** *n* extra nut screwed over another to prevent its turning. 鎖緊螺母(使另一螺母固定之螺母)。'～-**stitch** *n* sewing-machine stitch by which two

a canal lock

threads are firmly joined together. (縫紉機之)雙線連鎖縫法。⇨ also ***air*** ~ at air[1](7). **5** (motoring) extent of the turning arc of a steering wheel: (駕駛汽車)方向盤旋轉弧度: *full* ~, with the steering wheel turned (right or left) as far as it will go. (方向盤)可(左右)任意旋轉。

lock[3] /lɒk ; lɑk/ *vt, vi* **1** [VP6A, 15A, B] fasten a door, box, etc with a lock. 鎖(門,箱等)。~ ***the stable door after the horse has bolted/has been stolen,*** take precautions when it is too late. 亡羊補牢;賊去關門。~ ***sth away,*** put it away in a ~ed box, drawer, etc; (fig) keep securely: 將某物鎖藏起來;(喻)安全地保存: *have a secret safely ~ed (away) in one's breast.* 將一祕密隱藏在心底。~ ***sb in,*** put sb in a room of which the door is ~ed on the outside. 將某人鎖在房內。~ ***oneself in,*** ~ the door so that no one can enter from outside, or so that one cannot open it again. 將自己鎖在房內。~ ***sb out,*** keep him outside, prevent him from entering, by ~ing the gate or door(s) on the inside: 將某人鎖在房外: *If you don't get back before midnight, you'll be ~ed out.* 如果你在半夜以前還不回來,你將被鎖在房外。ˈ**~-out** *n* refusal of employers to allow workmen to enter their place of work until certain conditions are agreed to or demands given up. 閉廠;停業(雇主與工人間之條件未獲協議前抵制工人的行動)。⇨ strike[1]. ~ ***sth/sb up,*** **(a)** make safe by placing in sth that ~s: 鎖妥當;鎖好: *L~ up your jewellery before you go away.* 在你離開前把你的珠寶好好鎖藏起來。**(b)** shut up a house, etc by ~ing all the doors. 關鎖房門。**(c)** put (a person) in a ~ed room, a prison, a mental home, etc. 將(某人)鎖在房間、監獄、瘋人院等內。**(d)** invest (money) in such a way that it cannot easily or quickly be exchanged for cash: 使(資本)固定: *All his capital is ~ed up in land.* 他所有的資金都投資在土地上。ˈ**~-up** *n* place where prisoners may be kept temporarily; (colloq) any prison. 拘留所;(俗)監獄。▭ *adj* (attrib only) that can be ~ed: (僅作形容用法)可以鎖的: *a ~-up garage,* one, eg at a hotel, that can be ~ed. 可上鎖的汽車間(例如旅館中者)。**2** [VP2A] have a ~; become ~ed; be capable of being ~ed: 有鎖;鎖住;能被鎖上: *This trunk doesn't ~,* has no lock or has a lock that does not work. 這箱子沒有鎖(或有鎖而鎖不住)。*The door ~s easily.* 那門容易鎖。**3** [VP6A, 2A, C] (cause to) become fixed, unable to move: 使固定;固定: *His jaws were tightly ~ed.* 他的牙關緊閉。*He ~ed the wheels of the car to prevent its being stolen.* 他固定住汽車的輪胎以防被竊。*They were ~ed together in a fierce struggle.* 他們揪扭在一起猛烈地格鬪。*They were ~ed in each other's arms.* 他們緊緊擁抱着。*The parts ~ into each other,* interlock. 各部分互鎖着。**4** [VP2C] ~ ***on to,*** (of a missile, etc) find and automatically follow (a target) by radar. (指飛彈等)用雷達自動追踪(目標);鎖定(目標)。

locker /ˈlɒkə(r) ; ˈlɑkɚ/ *n* **1** small cupboard, esp one of a number used for keeping one's clothes, eg at a swimming-pool or golf-club. 有鎖的小橱櫃(尤指供儲放衣物用的許多小橱之一,例如游泳池或高爾夫球場附近者)。**2** box or compartment in a ship used for clothes, stores, ammunition, etc. 內務箱(船上儲放衣服,物品,軍火等的箱櫃或小艙)。***be in/go to Davy Jones's ~,*** be drowned at sea. 淹死在海中。

locket /ˈlɒkɪt ; ˈlɑkɪt/ *n* small (often gold or silver) case for a portrait, a lock of hair, etc, usu worn round the neck on a chain. (以項鍊懸於頸上的)小盒(裝畫像,或一綹頭髮等,常是金或銀質的)。

loco /ˈləʊkəʊ ; ˈloko/ *adj* (sl) mad. (俚)瘋的。

loco·motion /ˌləʊkəˈməʊʃn ; ˌlokəˈmoʃən/ *n* [U] moving, ability to move, from place to place. 運動;移動;運動力;移動力。**loco·mo·tive** /ˌləʊkəˈməʊtɪv ; ˌlokəˈmotɪv/ *adj* of, having, causing, ~. 移動的;有移動力的;引起運動的。▭ *n* self-propelled engine for use on railways: 火車機車;火車頭: *steam/Diesel/electric locomotives.* 蒸汽(柴油,電動)機車。

locum /ˈləʊkəm ; ˈlokəm/ (also ˌ~ ˈ**tenens** /ˈtiːnenz ; ˈtinɪnz/) *n* doctor or priest performing the duties of another who is away, eg on holiday. 臨時代理的醫師或牧師。

lo·cus /ˈləʊkəs ; ˈlokəs/ *n* (*pl* loci /ˈləʊsaɪ ; ˈlosaɪ/) exact place of sth. 所在地;場所。~ **classicus** /ˈklæsɪkəs ; ˈklæsɪkəs/, best known or most authoritative passage on a subject. 關於一問題最著名或最具權威的章節。

lo·cust /ˈləʊkəst ; ˈlokəst/ *n* **1** (kinds of) migratory African and Asian winged insect which flies in great swarms and destroys crops and vegetables. 蝗蟲。⇨ the illus at insect. 參看 insect 之挿圖。⇨ hopper[2](2). **2** ˈ**~(-tree),** (kind of) tree, esp *carob* and a N American tree, *false acacia.* 刺槐屬(尤指稻子豆及北美產刺槐)。

loc·ution /ləˈkjuːʃn ; loˈkjuʃən/ *n* [U] style of speech; way of using words; [C] phrase or idiom. 語風;語法;語句;慣用語。

lode /ləʊd ; lod/ *n* vein of metal ore. 礦脈。ˈ**~·star** *n* star by which a ship may be steered; the pole-star; (fig) guiding principle. 指示船航行方向之星;北極星;(喻)指導原則。ˈ**~·stone** *n* magnetized iron ore. 極磁鐵礦。

lodge[1] /lɒdʒ ; lɑdʒ/ *n* **1** small house, esp one at the entrance to the grounds of a large house, occupied by a gatekeeper, gardener or other employee of the estate. 小屋(尤指大宅第入口處守門人,園丁,或其他僕從所住者)。**2** country house used in the hunting or shooting season: 狩獵季節供人使用的房舍: *a* ˈ*hunting ~ in the Highlands;* 蘇格蘭高地供狩獵者用的房屋; (US) hut or cabin for temporary use: (美)暫時用的小屋: *a* ˈ*skiing ~.* 滑雪時用的小屋。**3** porter's room(s) in the chief gateway or entrance to a college, factory, block of flats, etc. 學院,工廠,公寓等的閽人室;門房。**4** (GB) residence of the head of a college. (英)大學院長之住宅。**5** (place of meeting for) members of a branch of a society such as the Freemasons. 會社(如共濟會) 支部的全體會員; 支部會員集會處。**6** beaver's lair. 海狸的巢穴。

lodge[2] /lɒdʒ ; lɑdʒ/ *vt, vi* **1** [VP6A, 15A] supply (sb) with a room or place to sleep in for a time; receive as a guest: 供以臨時住宿處;留宿: *The shipwrecked sailors were ~d in the school.* 那些遭船難的船員暫時住在學校裏。 **2** [VP3A] ~ ***at/with,*** live as a paying guest: 寄宿: *Where are you lodging now?* 你現在寄宿在何處? *I'm lodging at Mrs P's/with Mr and Mrs X.* 我現在寄宿在P太太(X夫婦)家。 **3** [VP3A] ~ ***in,*** enter and become fixed: 進入並固定: *The bullet ~d in his jaw.* 子彈射入他的顎。 **4** [VP6A, 15A] ~ ***(in),*** cause (sth) to enter and become fixed (*in*); put or place (in a particular place): 使進入並固定於(與 in 連用);置於(某一地方): ~ *a bullet in a man's brain.* 將一子彈射入某人的頭部。 **5** [VP6A, 15A] put (money, etc) for safety: 存放(金錢等): ~ *one's valuables in the bank while away from home on holiday.* 離家度假時將貴重物品存放在銀行裏。 **6** [VP6A, 14] ~ ***sth (with sb) (against sb),*** place (a statement, etc) with the proper authorities: 向當局提出(聲明等)(以控告某人): ~ *a complaint against one's neighbours with the authorities.* 向當局控訴鄰居。 **~r** *n* person paying for rooms, etc in sb's house: 房客;寄宿人: *The widow makes a living by taking in lodgers.* 那寡婦以收房客維持生活。

lodge·ment (also **lodg·ment**) /ˈlɒdʒmənt ; ˈlɑdʒmənt/ *n* **1** [U] act or process of lodging: 向當局提出: *the ~ of a complaint.* 控訴之提出。 ⇨ lodge[2] (6). **2** [C] sth that has accumulated or been deposited: 聚積物;沉澱物: *a ~ of dirt in a pipe.* 管內積存的髒物。 **3** [C] (mil) position gained in enemy territory: (軍)(在敵軍領土佔領的)立足點;據點: *gain a ~ on an enemy-held coast.* 在敵方海岸取得一據點。

lodg·ing /ˈlɒdʒɪŋ ; ˈlɑdʒɪŋ/ *n* (usu *pl*) room or rooms (not in a hotel) rented to live in: (通常用複數)出租的房間;寄宿舍: *It's cheaper to live in ~s than in a hotel.* 住寄宿舍比住旅館便宜。 *Where can we find ~s/a ~ for the night?* 我們今晚在那裏找一寄宿處? **ˈ~-house** *n* house in which ~s are let (usu by the week). 出租房間的公寓(通常按週出租);寄宿舍。

lo·ess /ˈləʊes; ˈlo·ɪs/ *n* [U] deposit of fine yellowish-grey soil, found esp in northern China, central USA and central Europe. (在中國北部,美國中部,以及歐洲中部一帶所見到的)黃土。

loft[1] /lɒft *US:* lɔːft ; lɔft/ *n* **1** room, place, used for storing things, in the highest part of a house, under the roof; space under the roof of a stable or barn, where hay or straw is stored. (屋頂下存放東西的)閣樓;頂樓;(貯放乾草的)廐樓。 **2** gallery in a church or hall: 教堂或廳堂的廊臺; 樓廂: *the ˈorgan-~.* 教堂內的風琴臺。

loft[2] /lɒft *US:* lɔːft ; lɔft/ *vt* [VP6A] (golf, cricket) hit (a ball) high: (高爾夫,板球)擊(球)高飛: ~ *a ball over the fielders' heads.* 將球擊出自外場員頭上飛過。

lofty /ˈlɒftɪ *US:* ˈlɔːftɪ ; ˈlɔftɪ/ *adj* (-ier, -iest) **1** (not used of persons) of great height: (不用以指人)極高的: *a ~ tower/mountain.* 高塔(山)。 **2** (of thoughts, aims, feelings, etc) distinguished; noble: (指思想,目的,情感等)高超的;高尚的: ~ *sentiments;* 高尚的情操; *a ~ style.* 高超的風格。 **3** haughty; proud; consciously superior: 高傲的;驕傲的;傲慢的: *a ~ appearance;* 高傲的樣子; *in a ~ manner.* 態度傲慢地。 **loft·ily** /-ɪlɪ ; -ɪlɪ/ *adv* **lofti·ness** *n*

log[1] /lɒg *US:* lɔːg ; lɔg/ *n* [C] rough length of tree-trunk that has fallen or been cut down; short piece of this for a fire: (未經刨削的)幹材;圓材;圓木;圓形短木柴: *a raft of logs,* floating down a river. (順流漂下之)圓木排。 ***like a log,*** unconscious; immovable. 無知覺的;不能動的。***sleep like a log,*** sleep soundly and with little or no movement. 酣睡; 熟睡得像塊木頭。 **ˌlog-ˈcabin** *n* cabin with walls and roof made of logs, not boards. 木屋(牆和屋頂均用圓木構成,而不用木板者)。 **ˈlog-jam** *n* mass of floating logs tightly mixed together; (US) deadlock. 河流中圓木阻塞;(美)僵局;停滯狀態。**ˈlog-rolling** *n* practice of giving support to others in return for support from them, eg by author-reviewers who praise each other's books. 互相標榜(例如作者兼書評家間的互捧)。**log·ging** *n* work of cutting down forest trees for timber: 伐木工作;伐木業: *a logging camp.* 伐木營。

log[2] /lɒg *US:* lɔːg ; lɔg/ *n* **1** device attached to a knotted line, trailed from a ship, to measure its speed through the water: (船隻的)測程儀: *sail by the log,* calculate a ship's position by means of information gained from the log. 用測程儀測量船的位置。 **2** (also 亦作 **ˈlog-book**) book with a permanent daily record or events during a ship's voyage (esp the weather, ship's position, speed, and distance as recorded by the log); (by extension) any record of performance, eg of a car or aircraft. 航海日誌;(引伸用法)任何進度記錄(例如汽車或飛機行駛里程,保養等記錄)。 **3** (colloq) registration book (of a motor-vehicle). (俗)汽車主登記表册。 □ *vt* (-gg-) [VP6A] enter (facts) in the log-book of a ship or aircraft. 記載(事實)於航海日誌或飛行日誌。

log[3] /lɒg *US:* lɔːg ; lɔg/ (colloq abbr for) logarithm. (俗)對數 (爲 logarithm 之略)。

lo·gan·berry /ˈləʊgənberɪ ; ˈlogənˌberɪ/ *n* (*pl* -ries) large dark-red berry from a plant that is a cross between a blackberry and a raspberry. 洛干楊莓;大楊莓(係黑莓與蘼莓子的交配種)。

log·ar·ithm /ˈlɒgərɪðəm *US:* ˈlɔːg- ; ˈlɔgəˌrɪðəm/ *n* (arith) one of a series of numbers set out in tables which make it possible to work out problems in multiplication and division by adding and subtracting. (算術)對數。

log·ger·heads /ˈlɒgəhedz ; ˈlɔgɚˌhɛdz/ *n* (only in) (僅用於) ***at ~ (with),*** disagreeing or disputing: (與…)不和;相爭: *He's constantly at ~ with his wife.* 他經常與妻子不和。

log·gia /ˈlɒdʒɪə ; ˈlɑdʒɪə/ *n* (I) open-sided gallery or arcade; part of a house with one side open to the garden. (義)涼廊;房屋敞向花園的部分。

logic /ˈlɒdʒɪk ; ˈlɑdʒɪk/ *n* [U] science, method, of reasoning; (person's) ability to argue and convince: 邏輯;論理學;理則學;(人之)辯論和說服的能力: *argue with learning and ~.* 有學問而且合邏輯地辯論。 **logi·cal** /-kl ; -kl/ *adj* in accordance with the rules of ~; able to reason correctly: 合邏輯的;條理分明的;能正確地推理的: *a ~al mind/argument/conclusion;* 有推理能力的頭腦(條理分明的辯論;合邏輯的結論); *~al behaviour.* 合理的行爲。 **logi·cally** /-klɪ; -klɪ/ *adv* **logi·cal·ity** /ˌlɒdʒɪˈkælətɪ ; ˌlɑdʒɪˈkælətɪ/ *n* [U] being ~al. 合乎邏輯;條理分明。 **lo·gician** /ləˈdʒɪʃn ; loˈdʒɪʃən/ *n* person skilled in ~. 邏輯學家;論理學家;理則學家。

lo·gis·tics /ləˈdʒɪstɪks ; loˈdʒɪstɪks/ *n* (with *sing v*) supply, distribution and replacement of materials and personnel, eg for the armed forces. (與單數動詞連用)後勤(學)。

loin /lɔɪn ; lɔɪn/ *n* **1** (*pl*) the lower part of the body on both sides of the spine between the ribs and the hip-bones. (複)腰;腰部。⇨ the illus at dog, domestic. 參看 dog, domestic 之挿圖。 ***gird (up) one's ~s,*** (biblical) prepare for a journey; make ready for action. (聖經)準備旅行;準備行動。 **ˈ~-cloth** *n* piece of cloth covering the middle of the body, folded between the legs, and fastened round the ~s. 纏腰布。 **2** joint of meat which includes the ~s: 腰肉: ~ *of mutton.* 羊腰肉。

loi·ter /ˈlɔɪtə(r) ; ˈlɔɪtɚ/ *vi, vt* [VP2A, C, 15B] go slowly and stop frequently on the way somewhere; stand about; pass (time) thus: 邊走邊停;閒蕩;徘徊;閒散以度過(時間): ~ *on one's way home;* 在回家路上邊走邊玩; ~ *the hours away;* 虛度時光; ~ *over a job.* 工作閒散。 **~er** *n* ~ing person. 閒

蕩者;閒散的人。

loll /lɒl ; lɑl/ *vi, vt* **1** [VP2A, C] ～ ***(about／around),*** rest, sit or stand (*about*) in a lazy way. 懶洋洋地躺臥,坐着或站着。 **2** [VP2C, 15B] ～ ***out,*** (of the tongue) (allow to) hang: (指舌)垂伸;任其垂伸: *The dog ～ed its tongue out.* 那狗垂伸着舌頭。*The dog's tongue was ～ing out.* 那狗的舌頭垂伸在外。

lol·li·pop /ˈlɒlɪpɒp ; ˈlɑlɪ͵pɑp/ *n* large sweet of boiled sugar on a stick, held in the hand and sucked. 棒棒糖。 **ˈ～ man／woman,** (colloq) one who carries a pole with a disc marked 'Stop! Children crossing', to conduct children across busy roads, eg outside a school. (俗)引導學童穿越鬧區馬路的男人或女人(手持一桿,桿頭有一圓盤狀板,上書「止步!孩子們在過馬路!」)。

lolly /ˈlɒlɪ ; ˈlɑlɪ/ *n* **1** (colloq) lollipop. (俗)棒棒糖。 **ice(d) ～,** quantity of frozen fruit juice on a stick. 冰棒。 **2** (sl) money, (esp money easily earned and lavishly spent). (俚)金錢(尤指容易賺得並揮霍掉者)。

lone /ləʊn ; lon/ *adj* (attrib only; ⇨ alone and lonely, which are more usu) solitary; without companions; unfrequented. (僅作形容用法; 參看 alone 和 lonely, 此二字較爲常用)孤單的;孤獨的;人跡罕至的。 ***play a ～ hand,*** (fig) do sth without the help or support of others, esp sth not very popular. (喻)獨力做某事(尤指不太普遍之事)。

lone·ly /ˈləʊnlɪ ; ˈlonlɪ/ *adj* (-ier, -iest) **1** without companions: 孤單的: *a ～ traveller.* 孤單的旅客。 **2** sad or melancholy because one lacks companions, sympathy, friendship: 孤寂的;寂寞的: *a ～-looking girl;* 樣子孤寂的女孩; *feel ～.* 感到寂寞。 **3** (of places) not often visited; far from inhabited places or towns: (指地點)人跡罕至的;偏僻的: *a ～ house;* 偏僻的房屋; *a ～ mountain village.* 荒涼的山村。 **lone·li·ness** *n* [U] state of being ～: 孤獨;孤寂;寂寞: *suffer from loneliness.* 備嘗孤寂之苦。

lone·some /ˈləʊnsəm ; ˈlonsəm/ *adj* **1** sad because alone: 寂寞的;孤寂的: *feel ～;* 感到寂寞; causing a feeling of loneliness: 令人感覺寂寞的: *a ～ journey.* 孤單的旅行。 **2** solitary, unfrequented: 偏僻的;人跡罕至的: *a ～ valley.* 人跡罕至的山谷。

long[1] /lɒŋ *US:* lɔːŋ ; lɔŋ/ *adj* (-nger /-ŋgə(r) ; -ŋgɚ/, -ngest /-ŋgɪst ; -ŋgɪst/) **1** of extent in space; measuring much from end to end: (指空間)長的: *How ～ is the River Nile?* 尼羅河有多長? *The new road is twenty miles ～.* 新路長達二十哩。*Your car is ～er than mine.* 你的汽車比我的長。 *What a lot of men have ～ hair nowadays!* 時下留長頭髮的男人眞多! *What a lot of ～-haired men we see today!* 今天我們看到留長頭髮的男人眞多啊! ***put on a ～ face,*** ⇨ face[1](3). **2** in phrases indicating (great) extent. 用於表示(廣大)範圍之片語中。***have a ～ arm,*** be able to make one's power felt far. 能使勢力遠伸。 ***the ～ arm of the law,*** its far-reaching power. 法律之遠及的力量。***make a ～ arm for sth,*** reach out for sth, eg at table. 伸手取物(例如用餐時)。 ***it's as broad as it's ～,*** ⇨ broad[1](9). **3** expressing duration or extent in time: (指時間)長的: *the ～ vacation,* the summer vacation of law courts and universities. 長的假期(如法院和大學的暑假)。*He was ill for a ～ time.* 他病了一段長時間。*How ～ are the holidays?* 假日有多久? *They're six weeks ～.* 有六週之久。 *He won't be ～ (in) making up his mind,* will soon do so. 他很快就會作決定。*Don't be too ～ about it,* Do it soon or quickly. 快點做。～ ***time no see!*** (colloq; as greeting) We haven't met for a long time. (俗;作爲寒暄語)好久不見了! **4** (of vowel sounds) usually taking more time to utter than others: (指母音)長音的: *'Sit' has a short vowel and 'seed' has a ～ vowel.* 'Sit' 有一短母音, 'seed' 有一長母音。 *The 'u' in 'rude' is ～.* 'rude' 中之 'u' 是長音。**5** (in phrases concerned with extent in time) (用於與期限有關的片語中) ～ **bond,** (fin) which mature in 20 years or more. (財政)長期債券(二十年以上到期者)。 ***take a ～ cool／hard look at sth,*** consider facts, problems shrewdly and at length. 明智細密地考慮事實或問題。***take the ～ view,*** consider events, factors, etc a ～ time ahead, rather than the present situation, etc. 眼光遠大。***in the ～ run,*** ⇨ run[1](7). ***in the ～ term,*** looking ahead for a ～ time. 長期。Hence, 由此產生, **͵～-ˈterm** *attrib adj* lasting for a ～ time: 長期的: *～-term agreements／contracts／investments.* 長期的協定(合約,投資)。**6** (compounds) (複合字) **ˈ～·boat** *n* sailing-ship's largest boat. 帆船所攜帶之最大的艇。 **ˈ～·bow** *n* bow drawn by hand, equal in length to the height of the archer, used with feathered arrows. 大弓;長弓(長度與射手身高相當,射出裝有羽毛的箭)。 ⇨ crossbow. ***draw the ～bow,*** tell exaggerated or invented stories. 說大話;吹牛。 **͵～-ˈdistance** *attrib adj* covering a ～ distance: 長距離的;長途的: *～-distance runners* (in sport); (運動)長途賽跑者; *a ～-distance telephone call;* 一次長途電話; *a ～-distance lorry driver.* 跑長途的卡車司機。～ ***drink*** *n* large quantity, eg of beer, served in a tall glass (contrasted with a *short drink,* eg neat whisky). 大量飲酒(例如用高杯飲啤酒; 以別於 short drink, 例如純威士忌)。 ***a ～ dozen,*** thirteen. 十三個。 **ˈ～·hand** *n* [U] ordinary handwriting (contrasted with *shorthand and typing*). 普通寫法(與shorthand 和 typing 相對)。 **͵～-ˈhaired** *adj* **(a)** ⇨ 1 above. 參看上列第1義。 **(b)** intellectual; artistic; unconventional. 有智力的;志趣高尙的;不守舊的。 ***a ～ haul,*** ⇨ haul. **͵～-ˈheaded** *adj* shrewd; having foresight. 精明的;有頭腦的;有先見的。 **the ˈ～ jump,** (athletic contest) measured along the ground for distance. (運動比賽)跳遠。⇨ *high jump* at high[1](12). ～ **measure,** ⇨ App 5. 參看附錄五。 ～ **metre** *n* [U] stanza of four eight-syllable lines. 長律(每節四行,每行有八音節的詩律)。 ～ **odds** *n pl* (in betting) very uneven, eg 50 to 1. (打賭)懸殊(例如 50 比 1)。 **͵～-play(ing) ˈdisc／ˈrecord** *n* (abbr 略作 **LP**) playing (at slow speed) for a ～er time than earlier kinds. 長時間唱片(以慢速放出)。 **ˈ～-range** *attrib adj* of ～ periods of time or ～ distances: 長期的;久遠的;長距離的;遠程的: *a ～-range weather forecast,* eg for one month ahead; 長期氣象預報(例如一月前所作); *～-range planning,* for a ～ time ahead, eg ten years; 遠程計畫(例如十年計畫); *～-range missiles.* 長程飛彈。 **ˈ～·shore·man** *n* man who works on shore (on wharves, in dockyards) loading and unloading ships. 碼頭上裝卸船貨的工人。 **a ～ shot,** ⇨ shot[1](2). **͵～-ˈsighted** *adj* able to see things a great distance away; (fig) prudent; having foresight. 能遠視的;(喻)審愼的;有遠見的。 **a ～ suit,** ⇨ suit[1](5). **ˈ～ stop** *n* [U] (cricket) player who fields straight behind the wicket-keeper. (板球)站在三柱門守門員正後方的外場員。 ⇨ the illus at cricket. 參看 cricket 之挿圖。 **ˈ～-time** *attrib adj* that has lasted for a long time: 長時間的: *a ～-time acquaintance.* 長時期的結識。～ **ton** *n* 2240 lb. 長噸(2240磅)。 **ˈ～ wave** *n* [U] (radio telegraphy) one having a wave-length of 1000 metres or over. (無線電)長波(波長在一千公尺以上者)。 **͵～-ˈwinded** *adj* tedious and diffuse in speaking or writing: (喻)冗長而令人生厭的: *a ～-winded and boring lecturer.* 冗長而令人生厭的演說者。Hence, 由此產生, **͵～-ˈwindedness.**

long[2] /lɒŋ *US:* lɔːŋ ; lɔŋ/ *n* **1** [U] ～ time or interval: 長期間: *I shall see you before ～.* 我不久就可以見到你了。*The work won't take ～.* 這工作不會花太長的時間。*Shall you be away for ～?* 你將離開很久嗎? ***at (the) ～est,*** to give the most distant date, etc: 最久;最長;最多: *I can wait only three days at ～est,* not after the third day from now. 我最多祇能等三天。 ***the ～ and the short of it,*** all that need be said; the general effect or result. 要言之;總之。 **2** [C] ～ syllable, esp in Latin verse:

長音節(尤指拉丁詩中者): *four ~s and six shorts.* 四個長音節和六個短音節。

long³ /lɒŋ *US:* lɔːŋ ; lɔŋ/ *adv* (-er /-ŋgə(r) ; -ŋgɚ/, -est /-ŋgɪst ; -ŋgɪst/) **1** ***(for) ~,*** for a long time: 長期地;長久地: *Stay (for) as ~ as you like.* 你願意停留多久皆可。*I've ~ wanted to meet her.* 我很久以來就想見她。***as/so ~ as,*** on condition that, provided that: 只要;如果: *You may borrow the book so ~ as you don't lend it to anyone else.* 只要你不把它借給別人,你可以借這本書。**2** (in numerous compounds): (用於許多複合字中): **ˌ~-drawn-ˈout** *adj* extended; unduly prolonged: 延長的;過分延長的: *a ~-drawn-out visit from my mother-in-law.* 我岳母的過長的訪期。**ˌ~-ˈlived** *adj* having a long life; living for a long time: 長壽的;長命的;長存的: *a ~-lived family.* 歷史悠久的家族。**ˌ~ ˈstanding** *adj* that has lasted for a long time: 存在已久的: *a ~-standing invitation to visit the Browns.* 爲時甚久的邀請去拜訪布朗一家人。**ˌ~-ˈsuffering** *adj* patient and uncomplaining in spite of trouble, provocation, etc: 能忍受的;長期受苦的: *his ~-suffering wife.* 他那位能吃苦的妻子。**3** at a long time (from a point of time): (自時間的某一點起)在長時間: *~ ago/before/after/since.* 很久以前(遠在…之前;遠在…之後;很久以來)。*That happened ~ ago.* 那事發生在很久以前。**4** (with *nn* indicating duration) throughout the specified time: (與表示持續時期的名詞連用)經過該段時間: *all day ~,* throughout the whole day; 整天; *all my life ~.* 我畢生;我一輩子。**5** ***no/any/much ~er,*** after a certain point of time: 在某一時刻以後: *I can't wait any/much ~er.* 我不能再等了(等太久)。*He's no ~er living here.* 他已不住在此處。

long⁴ /lɒŋ *US:* lɔːŋ ; lɔŋ/ *vi* [VP3A, 4C] ***~ for sth/for sb to do sth,*** desire earnestly; wish for very much: 渴望;渴慕: *She ~ed for him to say something.* 她渴望他說幾句話。*I'm ~ing to see you.* 我渴望着見你。*The children are ~ing for the holidays.* 孩子們渴望着假日。**~·ing** *n* [C, U] (an) earnest desire: 渴望;熱望: *a ~ing for home.* 思家。□ *adj* having or showing an earnest desire: 渴望的;表示渴望的: *a ~ing look;* 渴望的樣子;*with ~ing eyes.* 以渴望的眼神。**~·ing·ly** *adv*

lon·gev·ity /lɒnˈdʒevətɪ ; lɑnˈdʒɛvətɪ/ *n* [U] long life. 長壽;長命。

longi·tude /ˈlɒndʒɪtjuːd *US:* -tuːd ; ˈlɑndʒəˌtjud/ *n* distance east or west (measured in degrees) from a meridian, esp that of Greenwich, in London. 經度。⇨ the illus at projection. 參看 projection 之挿圖。**longi·tudi·nal** /ˌlɒndʒɪˈtjuːdɪnl *US:* -ˈtuːdnl ; ˌlɑndʒəˈtjudn̩l/ *adj* **1** of ~. 經度的。**2** of or in length. 長度的。**3** running lengthwise: 縱的: *longitudinal stripes,* eg in a flag. 縱條紋(例如旗幟上者)。

long·ways /ˈlɒŋweɪz *US:* ˈlɔːŋ- ; ˈlɔŋˌwez/, **long·wise** /ˈlɒŋwaɪz *US:* ˈlɔːŋ- ; ˈlɔŋˌwaɪz/ *adv* = lengthways.

loo /luː ; lu/ *n* (GB colloq) water-closet. (英俗)厠所。

loo·fah, loofa /ˈluːfə ; ˈlufə/ *n* [C] dried pod of a plant (kind of gourd or pumpkin) used as a sponge. 絲瓜絡。

look¹ /lʊk ; lʊk/ *vi, vt* (*pt, pp* ~ed) (For uses with *adverbial particles* and *preps* ⇨ 7 below.) (與副詞接語和介詞連用的用法,參看下列第7義。) **1** [VP2A, C, 3A, 4A] ***~ (at),*** use one's sight; turn the eyes in some direction; try to see: 看;視;望: *~ (up) at the ceiling;* (向上)看天花板; *~ (down) at the floor.* (向下)看地板。*We ~ed but saw nothing.* 我們看了,但沒有看見什麼。*I happened to be ~ing another way,* in a different direction. 我碰巧朝另一方向看。*L~ to see whether the road's clear before you cross.* 穿越以前看看路上是否安全。***to ~ at him/it, etc,*** judging by the outward appearance: 由外貌判斷: *To ~ at her you'd never guess that she was a university teacher.* 由外貌判斷你絕對想不到她是位大學敎師。***L~ before you leap,*** (prov) Avoid acting hastily, without considering the possible consequences. (諺)愼思而後行。**ˈ~·ing-glass** *n* mirror made of glass. 鏡子。**2** [VP2D, 4D] seem to be; have the appearance of being: 看來像是;現出某種樣子: *~ sad/ill/tired.* 面現愁容(病容,倦容)。*The town always ~s deserted on Sunday mornings.* 在星期日的早晨這座城市總顯得冷清清的樣子。*It ~s very suspicious to me,* I suspect that it is not strictly honest, straightforward, etc. 我覺得此事有點蹊蹺。*The girl ~ed puzzled.* 那女孩顯得很困惑。***(not) ~ oneself,*** (not) have one's normal appearance: 看起來跟平常一樣(不一樣): *You're not ~ing yourself today,* You're ~ing ill, worried, etc. 你看來有點異樣(像是病了,擔憂等)。*He's beginning to ~ himself again,* ~ well again, eg after an illness. 他開始復元了(例如病後)。***~ one's age,*** have an appearance that conforms to one's age: 看起來與年齡相符: *She ~s her age,* seems as old as she in fact is. 她看起來和她的年齡相符。*You don't ~ your age,* look younger than you are. 你看起來比你的實際年齡年輕。***~ one's best,*** appear to the greatest advantage: 最能顯現優點: *She ~s her best in jeans.* 她穿着牛仔褲最漂亮。***~ black (at),*** ~ angrily (at). 面帶怒色;怒目而視。***~ blue,*** appear sad or discontented. 面現憂傷或不滿之色。***~ good,*** **(a)** seem attractive, enticing, etc. 看來可愛,動人。**(b)** seem to be making satisfactory progress, doing well, etc: 似乎有令人滿意的進步;似乎做得不錯: *The horse I put my money on ~ed good until the last hundred metres.* 我賭的那匹馬在最後的一百公尺以前表現得不錯。Hence, 由此產生, **ˌgood-ˈ~ing** *adj* of fine appearance. 動人的;可愛的;好看的。***~ small,*** ~ mean or insignificant: 顯得卑鄙或不重要: *We made him ~ small,* exposed him as being insignificant. 我們使他顯得不重要了。***L~ alive!*** Get busy! Make haste! 趕快!快些! ***L~ here!*** often used to call attention to sth; or demand attention. 看這裏!(常用以引人注意或要人注意)。***L~ sharp!*** Hurry up! 趕快! ***~ well,*** **(a)** (of persons) be healthy in appearance. (指人)看來健康。**(b)** (of things) be attractive, pleasing, satisfactory: (指物)美觀;悅目;令人滿意: *Does this hat ~ well on me?* 我戴上這頂帽子好看嗎? **(c)** (of a person wearing sth) ~ attractive: (指穿着某衣物的人)看來動人;顯得漂亮: *He ~s well in naval uniform.* 他穿着海軍制服很漂亮。**3** [VP2C] ***~ like/as if,*** seem (to be): 似乎是;看來像是: *It ~s like salt and it is salt.* 它看來像鹽,而事實上也是鹽。*It ~s like* (= threatens to) *rain.* 天像是要下雨的樣子。*It ~s like being* (= promises to be) *a fine day.* 看來會是一個好天。*This ~s to me like a way in.* 在我看來這像是進去的路。*She ~s as if she were about to faint.* 她看來像是要暈倒的樣子。*You ~ as if you slept badly.* 你看來像是睡眠不足。*It doesn't ~ to me as if we shall get there in time.* 我看我們不能及時到達了。**4** [VP8] pay attention; learn by seeing: 注意;由觀看而知曉: *L~ where you're going!* 當心走路! *L~ who's here!* 看誰在這裏! *L~ (and see) whether the postman has been yet.* 去看看郵差來過沒有。**5** (= ~ at) ***~ sb/sth in the eye(s)/face,*** confront calmly and bravely: 鎮定勇敢地面對: *~ death/one's enemy in the face.* 鎮定勇敢地面對死亡(敵人)。**6** [VP6A] express by one's appearance: 露出…之表情;用臉色表示: *~ one's thanks/consent.* 露出感激(同意)的表情。**7** [VP2C, 3A, 15B] (uses with *adverbial particles* and *preps*): (與副詞接語和介詞連用的用法):

look about (for sth), be on the watch, in search of; examine one's surroundings, the state of affairs, etc: 警戒;看望;尋找;審視環境;查看情況: *Are you still ~ing about for a job?* 你仍在找工作嗎? ***~ about one,*** examine one's surroundings; give oneself time to make plans: 審視環境;找時間安排: *We hardly had time to ~ about us before we*

had to continue our journey. 我們幾乎沒有時間安排一下便不得不繼續旅行了。
look after sb/sth, (a) take care of; watch over; attend to: 照顧;照看;照料: *Who will ~ after the children while their mother is in hospital?* 在他們的母親住院期間,誰照顧這些孩子? *He needs a wife to ~ after him.* 他需要一個妻子照顧他。*He's well able to ~ after himself/to ~ after his own interests.* 他很會照顧自己(顧到自己的利益)。(b) follow with the eyes: 目送: *They ~ed after the train as it left the station.* 他們目送火車離站。
look at sth, (special uses) (特殊用法) **(a) not ~ at sth,** (usu with *will, would*) not consider: (通常與 will 或 would 連用)不考慮: *They wouldn't ~ at my proposal.* 他們不考慮我的建議。(b) examine: 檢查: *We must ~ at the question from all sides.* 我們必須從各方面檢討此問題。*Will you please ~ at the battery of my car?* 請你檢查一下我車上的電瓶好嗎? *Doctor, will you ~ at my ankle?* 醫師,請你檢查一下我的脚脖子好嗎? (c) in polite requests: 用於請求: *Will you please ~ at* (ie read) *this letter?* 請你讀一讀這封信好嗎? **good/bad, etc to ~ at,** of good, etc appearance: 外表美觀(不美觀等): *The hotel is not much to ~ at,* does not appear to be good from the outside. 這旅館的外表不太美觀。
look away (from sth), turn the eyes away. (自…)轉移目光。
look back (on/to sth), (fig) turn one's thoughts to sth in the past. (喻)追思;回顧。**never ~ back,** make uninterrupted progress. 不斷進步。
look down on sb/sth, despise; consider oneself superior to; show false contempt for: 輕視;瞧不起;蔑視: *When she married the boss, she ~ed down on the office girls she had worked with.* 她嫁給老板後,便瞧不起曾同她在一起辦公的女職員了。**~ down one's nose at sb/sth,** (colloq) regard with displeasure or contempt. (俗)對某人不悅或輕視。
look for sb/sth, (a) search for; try to find: 尋找;尋求: *Are you still ~ing for a job?* 你仍在找工作嗎? *That foolish fellow is ~ing for trouble,* is behaving in a way that will get him into trouble. 那個愚蠢的傢伙在自找麻煩。(b) expect: 期望: *It's too soon yet to ~ for results.* 現在便期望有結果爲時尚早。
look forward to sth, anticipate (usu with pleasure): 盼望;期待(通常以愉快的心情): *We're ~ing forward to seeing you again.* 我們盼望再見到你。
look in (on sb), make a short (usu casual) visit; pay a call: 便道過訪;拜訪: *Why don't you ~ in (on me) next time you're in town?* 你下次進城來請順便看看我好嗎? *The doctor will ~ in again this evening.* 醫生今晚將再來。**give sb/get a '~-in,** (colloq, sport, etc) chance (of winning, etc): (俗,運動等)給予某人(獲得)(得勝等的)機會: *You won't get a ~-in with such strong competition.* 在這種激烈的競爭下你沒有機會獲勝。
look into sth, (a) investigate; examine: 調查;檢查: *~ into a question.* 調查一問題。(b) dip into (a book, etc). 瀏覽(書等)。(c) ~ at the inside of, the depths of: 注視…的內部或深處: *He ~ed into the box/the mirror/her eyes.* 他注視箱底(鏡子,她的眼睛)。
look on, be a spectator; watch: 旁觀;觀望: *Why don't you play football instead of just ~ing on?* 你爲什麼不參加踢足球而祇是旁觀? Hence, 由此產生, **,~er-'on** *n* person who ~s on. 旁觀者。**~ on/upon sb/sth as,** regard as: 視作: *Do you ~ on him as an authority on the subject?* 你認爲他是這問題的權威嗎? **~ on/upon sb/sth with,** regard in the way specified: 以特殊方式看某人: *He seems to ~ on me with distrust.* 他似乎不信任我。**~ on to,** (of a place, room, etc) overlook, give a view of: (指地點,房間等)面對;瀕臨: *My bedroom ~s on to the garden.* 我的臥室面對着花園。
look out (of sth) (at sth): *He stood at the window and ~ed out (at the view).* 他站在窗前向外望(觀看景色)。*They were ~ing out of the window.* 他們正向窗外看。**~ out on (to)/over,** supply an outlook or view over: 供以瞭望的景色: *Our hotel room here ~s out on the sea front.* 我們的旅館房間面對海濱。**~ out (for sb/sth),** be prepared (for), be on the watch (for): 準備;警戒;當心;守候: *L~ out!* Be on the watch, be careful! 當心!小心! *Will you go to the station and ~ out for Mr Hill?* 請你到車站去等候希爾先生好嗎? Hence, 由此產生, **'~-out** *n* **(a) keep a good ~-out (for); be on the ~-out (for),** be watchful (for). 注意守望;嚴密注意。(b) [C] place from which to watch; person who has the duty of watching: 守望處;守望者: (attrib) (形容用法) *a ~-out post;* 監視哨所; *send ~-outs in advance.* 預先派出監視哨。(c) (*sing* only) prospect; what seems likely to come or happen: (僅用單數)遠景;前途: *It seems a bad ~-out for their children.* 他們的孩子們的前途似乎不佳。*That's your own ~-out,* sth you yourself must be responsible for. 那是你自己應負責任的事。**~ sth out (for sb),** select by making an inspection: 檢查以選出;挑選: *~ out some books for a friend in hospital.* 爲一住院友人挑選幾本書。
look over sth, inspect; examine: 檢閱;檢查: *We must ~ over the house before we decide to rent it.* 在決定租這房子前我們必須先看一下。**~ sth over,** inspect one by one or part by part: 逐一檢查;逐步檢閱: *Here's the correspondence; I've ~ed it over.* 這就是那封信,我已經檢查過。Hence, 由此產生, **'~-over** *n*: *give something a ~-over,* examine it. 檢查某物。
look round, (a) (fig) examine possibilities before deciding sth: (喻)事前仔細考慮: *Don't make a hurried decision; ~ round well first.* 不要急作決定,先好好考慮一下。(b) turn the head (to see): 轉首(欲看): *When I ~ed round for her, she was leaving the hall.* 當我轉過頭去看她時,她正離開大廳。**~ round (sth),** go sight-seeing, etc: 觀光;遊覽: *Have we time to ~ round (the town) before lunch?* 我們在中飯前有時間(在城裏)遊覽一下嗎?
look through sth, revise (a lesson, etc); study; examine: 仔細研讀(功課等);溫習;檢查: *L~ through your notes before the examination.* 考試前溫習你的筆記。*I must ~ through these bills and check them before I pay them.* 我必須在付款前審查和核對一下這些帳單。**~ sth through,** inspect carefully or successively: 仔細檢查;逐項審查: *He ~ed the proposals through before approving them.* 他在核准前仔細審查那些提議。
look to sth, be careful of or about: 注意: *The country must ~ to its defences.* 國家必須注意其防務。*L~ to your manners, my boy,* Don't be so rude. 注意你的態度,孩子。*L~ to it* (= Take care) *that this does not happen again.* 注意不要使此事再發生。**~ to sb for sth/to do sth,** rely on: 依賴: *They all ~ to you for help.* 他們全仰賴你的幫助。*They're ~ing to you for a solo/to sing to them.* 他們期待着你的獨唱(唱給他們聽)。**~ to/towards,** face: 面對: *a house ~ing towards the river/to the south.* 面臨河的(朝南的)一所房屋。
look up, (a) raise the eyes: 仰視: *Don't ~ up.* 不要向上看。(b) improve in price or prosperity: 漲價;繁榮: *Business is/Oil shares are ~ing up.* 商業(石油股票)呈現起色。**~ sth up,** search for (a word in a dictionary, facts in a reference book, etc): 查(字典中的字,參考書中的事實等): *Please ~ up a fast train to Leeds,* in a railway guide. 請查一下去里兹的快車(查一下火車時刻表)。**~ sb up,** pay a call on; visit: 拜訪;探訪: *Do ~ me up next time you're in London.* 你下次到倫敦時,務必請來訪我。**~ up to sb (as...),** respect: 尊敬: *They all ~ up to him as their leader.* 他們都尊他爲他們的領袖。**~ sb up and down,** examine him carefully or contemptuously. 上下打量某人;輕蔑地打量某人。

look² /lʊk; lʊk/ *n* [C] **1** act of looking: 看;望;視:

Let me have a ～at your new car. 讓我看一看你的新車。**2** facial expression; appearance: 表情；神色；外表；外觀：*A ～ of pleasure came to her face.* 她臉上顯出愉快的表情。*There were angry ～s from the neighbours.* 鄰人們有惱怒之色。*The town has a European ～.* 這城市的外貌有歐洲的風格。***give sth／get a new ～,*** a new and more up-to-date appearance: 給予(獲得)新面貌：*The High Street has been given a new ～.* 高街的外貌一新。**3** (*pl*) person's appearance: (複)容貌：*She's beginning to lose her ～s,* her beauty. 她的容顏漸老。**～er** *n*: *a ˌgood-ˈ～er,* a good-looking person. 美貌之人。

loom¹ /lu:m；lum/ *n* machine for weaving cloth. 織布機。

a hand loom

loom² /lu:m；lum/ *vi* [VP2C, D] ***loom (large),*** appear indistinctly and in a threatening way; (fig) appear great and fill the mind: 隱約地或威脅性地出現；(喻)龐然逼壓心頭：*The dark outline of another ship ～ed (up) through the fog.* 另一隻船的黑影在霧中隱現。*The threat of the H-bomb ～ed large in their minds.* 他們心中深受氫彈的威脅。

loon¹ /lu:n；lun/ *n* large diving-bird that lives on fish and has a loud, wild cry. 阿比(一種大潛水鳥，以魚爲食，鳴聲響亮)。

loon² /lu:n；lun/ *n* (Scot and archaic) foolish, idle, good-for-nothing person.(蘇，古)愚蠢、懶惰、無用的人。

loony /ˈlu:nɪ；ˈlunɪ/ *n, adj* (sl) lunatic. (俚)瘋子；狂人；瘋狂的。ˈ**～·bin** /-bɪn；-bɪn/ *n* (sl) mental home. (俚)瘋人院。

loop /lu:p；lup/ *n* **1** (shape produced by a) curve crossing itself as in the letters *l* and *h* in ordinary handwriting). 本身形成環的曲線；紐形弧；環形花樣(如手寫體中寫 l 和 h 所形成者)。**2** part of a length of string, wire, ribbon, etc in such a shape, eg as a knot or fastening; curved piece of metal as a handle; (colloq) ～-shaped intra-uterine contraceptive device. (繩，金屬線，絲帶等繞成的)環或圈(例如做結或繫物者)；金屬環柄；(俗)樂普(一種置於子宮內之避孕環)。**3** (also 亦作 ˈ**～-line**) railway or telegraph line that separates from the main line, runs in a curve, and then rejoins the main line farther on. 鐵軌或電報線之環狀側線；迴車道；迴線。**4** circuit in which an aviator, motor-cyclist, etc is for a time travelling in a ～ or in ～s: 飛機之翻圈飛行；觔斗；環飛；汽車等之環狀行駛：*The airman looped the ～ five times,* flew the shape of a ～ five times. 那飛行員做了五次觔斗飛行。□ *vt, vi* **1** [VP6A, 15B] form or bend into a ～ or ～s; supply with a ～ or ～s: 使成環或圈；形成環；圍以環或圈：*～ the curtains up／back;* 捲起窗簾；*～ things together.* 用環將物繫在一起。**2** [VP6A, 2A] perform a ～(4); make a ～ or ～s. 作環狀飛行或駕駛；觔斗飛行；環飛。

loop·hole /ˈlu:phəʊl；ˈlupˌhol/ *n* **1** narrow vertical opening in a wall for shooting or looking through, or to admit light and air (as in old forts, stockades, etc). (牆上供射擊，瞭望或通光通風用的)槍眼；窄窗；窗孔(如古堡壘，柵欄等中者)。**2** (fig) way of escape from control, esp one provided by careless and inexact wording of a rule: (喻)(因措詞欠妥而造成的法規上的)漏洞：*find a ～ in the law.* 找出法律上的漏洞。

loopy /ˈlu:pɪ；ˈlupɪ/ *adj* (sl) crazy. (俚)瘋狂的。

loose¹ /lu:s；lus/ *adj* (-r, -st) **1** free; not held, tied up, fastened, packed, or contained in sth: 無約束的；鬆開的；未受束縛的：*Many Englishmen carry their small change* (ie coins) *～ in their trouser pocket, not in a purse.* 許多英國人將零錢散置在褲子口袋內，而不放在錢袋內。*That dog is too dangerous to be left ～.* 那狗太危險，不可放開。***break／get ～,*** escape confinement: 自拘禁中逃出：*One of the tigers in the zoo has broken／got ～,* has escaped from its cage. 動物園中有一隻虎自籠中逃出來了。***let sth ～,*** allow it to be free from control: 任其自由；放任：*He let ～ his indignation,* did not control it. 他發洩他的憤慨。ˈ**～ box,** separate compartment in a stable or railway van, in which a horse can move about freely. (馬厩或運貨火車中之)馬匹自由活動間。ˌ**～-ˈleaf** *attrib adj* (of a notebook) with leaves that may be detached separately and replaced. (指筆記本)活頁的。**2** not close-fitting; not tight or tense: 不緊的；寬鬆的：*a ～ collar;* 寬鬆的衣領；*～-fitting clothes.* 寬大的衣服。**3** moving more freely than is right or usual: 不牢的；鬆弛的：*a ～ tooth;* 鬆動的牙齒；*～ bowels,* with a tendency to diarrhoea; 瀉肚；*a ～ thread;* 鬆弛的線；*a ～ window,* one that shakes or rattles in the wind. 不牢固的窗子。***come ～,*** (of a fastening, etc) come unfastened or insecure. (指縛繫物等)解開；變鬆。***have a ˈscrew ～,*** (colloq) be unsound in one's mind. (俗)心智不健全。***have a ～ tongue,*** be in the habit of talking too freely. 愛多嘴的；喜歡饒舌的。***ride with a ～ rein,*** **(a)** allow the horse freedom. 放鬆繮繩。**(b)** (fig) manage a person indulgently. (喻)放任；縱容。***work ～,*** (of a bolt, etc) become insecure, no longer tight. (指螺釘等)鬆弛。**4** not firmly or properly tied: 未繫牢的：*a ～ knot;* 未繫牢的結；*a ～ end of rope,* one that is not fastened. 繩子未繫牢的一端。***at a ～ end,*** (fig of a person) having nothing to do. (喻，指人)無事做的。**5** (of talk, behaviour, etc) not sufficiently controlled: (指言行等)不嚴謹的；放蕩的：*～ conduct;* 放蕩的行爲；*lead a ～ life;* 過放蕩的生活；*a ～* (= immoral) *woman.* 放蕩的女子。***(be) on the ～,*** (colloq) free from the restraints of morality or discipline; dissipated. (俗)放蕩；耽於遊樂。***play fast and ～ (with sb),*** behave dishonestly or in a deceitful manner. 欺騙；欺詐。**6** not strict; inexact; indefinite; (of translations) not close to the original: 不嚴格的；不精確的；不確定的；(指翻譯)不忠於原著的：*～ thinking;* 不嚴密的思想；*a ～ thinker;* 思想不嚴密的人；*a ～* (= badly constructed) *argument.* 不嚴密的論據。**7** not compact; not closely packed: 鬆散的；未包裝緊的：*～ soil;* 鬆土；*cloth with a ～ weave.* 織得鬆的布。**8** (of the human body) not closely knit: (指人體)不結實的：*a ～ frame;* 不結實的體格；*～ limbs,* rather awkward, ungainly in appearance; 笨拙難看的四肢；(of bodily actions) careless, bungling or inaccurate: (指身體動作)隨便的；笨拙的；不準確的：*～ bowling and fielding* (in cricket). (板球戲中)不準確的擲出與還擲。**～·ly** *adv* in a ～ manner: 鬆開地；寬鬆地；鬆弛地；不精確地；不嚴格地；放蕩地：*words ～ly employed,* ⇨ 6 above; 用得不精確的字(參看上列第6義)；*rules ～ly enforced.* 未嚴格執行的法規。

loose² /lu:s；lus/ *vt* [VP6A] make free or loose: 使無約束；使鬆弛：*Wine ～d his tongue,* made him talk freely (*loosen* is more usu). 酒使他多話 (loosen 較常用)。

loosen /ˈlu:sn；ˈlusn̩/ *vt, vi* [VP6A, 2A, 15B] ***～ (up),*** make or become loose or looser: 使鬆；放鬆；變鬆；鬆弛：*L～ the screw.* 把螺絲釘放鬆。*The screw has ～ed.* 螺絲釘鬆了。*This medicine may ～ your cough,* help to get up the phlegm. 此藥可減輕你的咳嗽(助你消痰)。*I must take some exercise and ~ up my muscles.* 我必須做點運動以放鬆我的肌肉。

loot /luːt; lut/ *n* [U] goods (esp private property) taken away unlawfully and by force, eg by thieves, or by soldiers in time of war. (盜賊的)贓物;(戰時士兵之)掠奪物;戰利品。□ *vt, vi* [VP6A, 2A] carry off ~ from: 搶劫;刼掠: *The brutal soldiers ~ed and massacred for three weeks.* 那些殘忍的士兵刼掠屠殺了三個星期。**~er** *n*

lop¹ /lɒp; lɑp/ *vt* (-pp-) [VP6A, 15B] ***lop (away/off)***, cut off, separate branches, etc from a tree. 砍去(樹枝等);砍掉。

lop² /lɒp; lɑp/ *vi* (-pp-) hang down loosely; (chiefly in compounds): 鬆弛地垂下;(主要用於複合字中): **ˈlop-ears** *n pl* drooping ears. 下垂的耳朵。**ˈlop-eared** *adj* having lop-ears: 耳朵下垂的: *a lop-eared rabbit.* 一隻垂着耳朵的兎子。**ˌlop-ˈsided** *adj* with one side lower than the other. 一邊低於另一邊的;一邊高一邊低的。

lope /ləʊp; lop/ *vi* [VP2A, C] move along with long, easy steps or strides (as a hare does). 大步慢跑;緩馳(如野兎所做者)。□ *n* step or stride of this kind: 大步慢跑;緩馳: *The deer went off at an easy ~.* 那鹿輕鬆地緩馳而去。

lo·qua·cious /ləˈkweɪʃəs; loˈkweʃəs/ *adj* talkative; fond of talking. 多嘴的;饒舌的。**~·ly** *adv* **~·ness, lo·quac·ity** /ləˈkwæsətɪ; loˈkwæsətɪ/ *nn* [U] being ~. 多嘴;饒舌;刺刺不休。

lo·quat /ˈləʊkwɒt; ˈlokwɑt/ *n* [C] (tree, common in China and Japan, with a) yellow or yellowish-red fruit that grows in clusters and has a sharp taste. 枇杷(樹)。⇨ the illus at fruit. 參看fruit之挿圖。

lor /lɔː(r); lɔr/ *int* (vulg substitute for) Lord! (= God). (鄙)主啊!天啊!

lord /lɔːd; lɔrd/ *n* **1** supreme male ruler: 最高統治者;君主: *our sovereign ~ the King.* 我們的君主。**2 the L~**, God; Christ. 上帝;基督。***L~! L~ God! Good L~! L~ knows! L~ bless us/me!*** exclamations of surprise, etc. 天啊!噯呀!哎喲! **Our L~,** Christ. 耶穌基督。**the ˈL~'s Day,** Sunday. 主日;星期日。**the ˌL~'s ˈPrayer,** that given by Jesus to his followers. 主禱文。**the ˌL~'s ˈSupper,** the taking of bread and wine to commemorate the last meal taken by Jesus Christ with his twelve disciples before his death. 聖餐(吃麵包和酒以紀念耶穌及其十二門徒共進最後晚餐之儀式)。**3** peer; nobleman: 貴族: *live/treat sb like a ~,* sumptuously. 過奢華的生活(把某人視做王公一般接待)。***as drunk as a ~,*** excessively drunk. 酩酊大醉。**the House of L~s,** (in GB) the upper division of Parliament, consisting of *the ~s spiritual* (the Archbishops and Bishops) and *the ~s temporal* (hereditary and life peers). (英國之)上議院(議員中包括主教和貴族)。**4** (in feudal times) superior. (封建時代之)領主。**the ~ of the manor,** man from whom vassals held land and to whom they owed service. 領主。**5** (joc, also 謔,亦作 *~ and master*) husband; great leader of industry: 丈夫;夫君;工業界領袖;實業巨子: *the ˈcotton ~s.* 棉業界領袖。(cf 參較 *ˈbeer barons*); *the ~s of creation,* mankind (contrasted with the animals). 人類(以別於動物)。**6** person in a position of authority: 權要: *the L~s of the Admiralty/Treasury,* the chief members of these Boards; (英)海軍部(財政部)的要員; *the First L~ of the Admiralty,* the president of this Board. 海軍部長。**7** first word in many official titles: 用作許多官銜的第一字: *the L~ Mayor of London;* 倫敦市長; *the L~ Chamberlain,* etc. 宮務大臣等。**8** title prefixed to names of peers and barons: 對貴族或男爵的尊稱;勛爵: *L~ Derby.* 德貝勛爵。Cf 參較 *the Earl of Derby.* 德貝伯爵。**9 *My ~,*** respectful formula for addressing certain noblemen and judges and bishops. 閣下(對某些貴族,法官及主教的尊稱)。□ *vt* (chiefly in) (主用於) ***~ it over sb,*** rule over like a ~: 作威作福;盛氣凌人;專橫霸道: *'I will not be ~ed over', she said to her husband.* '我不願受人主宰',她向她丈夫說。**~·less** *adj* without a ~. 無貴族的;無君王的;無主的。

lord·ly /ˈlɔːdlɪ; ˈlɔrdlɪ/ *adj* (-ier, -iest) **1** haughty; insolent. 傲慢的;無禮的。**2** like, suitable for, a lord; magnificent. 似貴族的;適於貴族的;堂皇的。**lord·li·ness** *n*

lord·ship /ˈlɔːdʃɪp; ˈlɔrdʃɪp/ *n* **1** [U] **~ over,** rule, authority. 統治;權威。**2** [C] ***His/Your L~,*** used when speaking of/to a lord. 閣下(對貴族的尊稱)。

lore /lɔː(r); lor/ *n* [U] learning or knowledge, esp handed down from past times, or possessed by a class of people: 學問或知識(尤指自過去傳下,或某一階級或民族所有者): *ˈIrish ~;* 愛爾蘭人的學問; *ˈgypsy ~;* 吉普賽人的學問; or of a special subject: 特殊科目的知識: *ˈfairy ~/ˈbird ~/ˈfolk ~.* 神話(飛禽學;民俗學)。

lor·gnette /lɔːˈnjet; lɔrnˈjɛt/ *n* pair of eye-glasses held to the eyes on a long handle. 長柄眼鏡。

lorn /lɔːn; lɔrn/ *adj* (poet or hum) forlorn; desolate: (詩或諧)孤單的;孤寂的: *a lone, ~ widow.* 寂寞孤單的寡婦。

lorry /ˈlɒrɪ *US:* ˈlɔːrɪ; ˈlɔrɪ/ *n* (*pl* -ries) (US 美 = *truck*) long, low, open motor-vehicle, for carrying goods by road. 載貨卡車。

lose /luːz; luz/ *vt, vi* (*pt, pp* lost /lɒst *US:* lɔːst; lɔst/) **1** [VP6A] no longer have; have taken away from one by accident, carelessness, misfortune, death, etc: 失去;損失;喪失: *~ one's money;* 損失金錢; *~ a leg,* eg in a road accident; 失去一腿(例如在車禍中); *~ a lot of money at the races* (by betting); 賭賽馬輸了很多錢; *~ one's balance,* fall over. 跌倒。*He lost two sons in the war,* They were killed. 他有兩個兒子在戰爭中陣亡。*She lost her husband,* He is dead. 她的丈夫已去世。*He has lost his job,* has been dismissed. 他失業了。*You're losing your hair,* getting bald. 你的頭髮漸漸脫落了。*She has lost her good looks,* is no longer good-looking. 她已失去她的美貌。*It was so cold that we lost the use of our hands,* could not use them. 天太冷,我們的手都凍僵了。*He's losing patience,* is becoming impatient. 他失去耐心了。***~ one's cool,*** (colloq) lose one's composure; be no longer calm or composed. (俗)失去鎭定;心情慌亂。***~ ground,*** ⇨ ground¹(2). ***~ one's head,*** ⇨ head¹(19). ***~ heart,*** ⇨ heart(2). ***~ one's heart to sb,*** ⇨ heart(2). ***~ interest (in sb/sth),*** cease to be interested in, attracted by. (對某人或某物)失去興趣;不再引起興趣。***~ one's reason/senses,*** become insane or wildly excited. 失去理性;發狂。***~ one's temper,*** become angry. 發怒。***~ A to B,*** have A taken away by B: A被B取而代之: *The little grocery shop is losing all its customers to the new supermarket.* 那個小雜貨店的顧客都跑到新開的超級市場去了。***~ touch (with),*** ⇨ touch¹(6). **2** (passive) be lost, disappear; die; be dead: (被動語態)失踪;死;死去: *The ship and all its crew were lost.* 該船及其所有船員皆失踪了。*Is letter-writing a lost art,* Has the art of writing (social) letters died, eg because of the use of the telephone? 通信術已被淘汰了嗎(例如由於電話之採用)? ***be lost to sth,*** be no longer affected by, be insensible to, eg all sense of shame, decency, honour, duty. 不爲(羞恥,體面,榮譽心,責任感等)所動;對…無感覺。***be lost in sth,*** be deeply occupied or filled with, eg thought, wonder, admiration. 沉入(思想,驚異,羡慕等)中。**3** [VP6A] (contrasted with *find, recover*) be unable to find: (與find, recover相對)遺失;失落;找不到: *I've lost the keys of my car.* 我的汽車鑰匙丢了。*The books seem to be lost/to have been lost.* 那些書好像不見了。*She lost her husband in the crowd.* 她和她丈夫在

人群中走散了。~ ***one's place,*** (in a book, etc) be unable to find the page, paragraph, etc where one stopped reading. (讀書等)忘記上次讀到的地方。~ ***oneself/one's way,*** get lost, be unable to find the right way, road, etc; not know where one is: 迷路: *The children lost their way in the forest.* 孩子們在森林中迷了路。*We lost our way in the dark.* 我們在黑暗中迷了路。*I hope the children haven't got lost/lost themselves.* 我希望孩子們沒有迷路。~ ***sight of sth,*** **(a)** overlook; fail to take account of: 忽視;忽略: *We mustn't ~ sight of the fact that....* 我們切不可忽視…之事實。**(b)** no longer be able to see: 看不見: *The early navigators disliked losing sight of land.* 早期的航海探險者嫌惡望不見陸地。*We lost sight of him in the crowd.* 我們在人群裏看不見他了。~ ***the thread of sth,*** eg an argument, ⇨ thread. 失去(例如議論的)條理。~ ***one's tongue,*** ⇨ tongue. ~ ***track of sth,*** ⇨ track. **4** [VP6A] (contrasted with *catch*) be too late for; fail to hear, see, etc: (與 catch 相對)未能趕上;未能聽到,看見等: ~ (more usu 較常用 *miss*) *one's train/the bus;* 未趕上火車(公共汽車); ~ *the post,* get to the post office, etc too late for the collection; 未趕上郵局收信的時間; ~ (= not hear) *the end of a sentence.* 沒聽見一句的末尾。*What he said was lost in the applause that greeted him.* 他的話被對他的喝采聲淹沒了。**5** [VP12C] cause (sb) the loss of: 使(某人)損失: *Such insolence will ~ you your situation.* 如此無禮的態度將會使你失去你的職位。*This remark lost him our sympathy.* 此話使我們對他失去了同情心。**6** [VP6A, 2A] fail to win, be defeated: 未能獲勝;輸;失敗: ~ *a game/a match/a battle/a war/a lawsuit/a prize;* 比賽輸了(賽輸;戰敗;敗訴;未能獲獎);~ *a motion,* fail to carry it in a debate. (辯論中)未能使一項動議獲得支持。***a lost cause,*** one that has already been defeated or is sure to be defeated. 已失敗或注定失敗的主義,運動等。***(play) a losing game,*** one in which defeat is likely or certain. (參加)多半或必定會輸的比賽。~ ***out (to),*** (colloq) be overcome and replaced (by): (俗)被取而代之: *Has the cinema lost out to TV?* 電影已被電視取代嗎? **7** [VP6A, 15A, 3A] ~ ***by/in/on sth,*** be or become worse: 受虧損;蒙損害: *You will ~ nothing by waiting,* will not suffer any loss. 等待不會使你吃虧。*Will the publisher ~ by it,* be worse off because of publishing the book? 出版商會爲(出版)這本書受損失嗎? *How much did he ~ on the transaction?* 該項交易使他受到多少虧損? *The story does not ~ in the telling,* is not made less interesting, is perhaps exaggerated. 這故事講起來照樣有趣(或許有些誇張)。**8** [VP2A, B] (of a watch or clock) go too slowly; fail to keep correct time because of this: (指鐘錶)走得太慢;因慢而不準確: *Does your watch gain or ~?* 你的錶快了還是慢了? *My watch ~s two minutes a day.* 我的錶一天慢兩分鐘。**9** [VP6A] spend time, opportunity, efforts to no purpose; waste: 浪費(時間,機會,努力): *There's not a moment to ~.* 沒有時間可浪費了。*I shall ~ no time in doing it,* shall do it at once. 我將卽刻做此事。***be lost upon sb,*** fail to influence or attract the attention of: 未能影響或引起注意: *My hints were not lost upon him,* They were noted. 我的暗示受到了他的注意。**10** ~ ***oneself in sth,*** (reflex) become engrossed in it: (反身)專心於某事;埋頭於某事: *She lost herself in a book,* became so deeply interested in it that she was unaware of other things. 她在埋頭讀一本書。~**r** *n* person who ~s or is defeated: 輸者;失敗者: *He's a good/bad ~r,* is cheerful/discontented when he ~s. 他是個輸得起(不起)的人。

loss /lɒs *US:* lɔːs ; lɔs/ *n* **1** [U] act or fact or process of losing: 損失;喪失;遺失: ~ *of blood;* 失血; ~ *of prestige.* 喪失聲望。*L~ of health is more serious than ~ of money.* 健康的喪失較金錢的損失尤爲嚴重。*The ~ of his heavyweight title doesn't seem to worry him.* 重量級拳王頭銜的喪失似乎並不使他煩惱。*The ~ of so many ships worried the Admiral.* 這麼多艦隻的損失使艦隊司令憂愁。**2** [U] (and with *indef art*) failure to keep, maintain or use: (與不定冠詞連用)未能保住;未保持;未能利用: *a heavy ~;* 嚴重損失; ~ *of opportunities;* 機會的失去; *without (any) ~ of time.* 未浪費時間。*There was a temporary ~ of power.* 暫時失去勢力。**3** [U] failure to win or obtain: 輸;未獲得: *the ~ of a contract.* 未獲承包。**4** [C] that which is lost: 損失物;喪失物;損耗: *sell sth at a ~;* 虧本賣出某物; *suffer heavy ~es in war,* men killed, wounded, captured; ships and aircraft lost. 戰爭中遭受重大損失(卽士兵傷亡或被俘,戰艦和飛機被毀)。⇨ gain[1], profit[1](2). ***a total ~,*** sth from which nothing can be saved: 完全損失: *The ship was wrecked and became a total ~.* 那條船失事,全部損失了。ˌ~-ˈ**leader** *n* (comm) article, etc sold at a ~ in order to attract customers to buy other goods. (商)爲招徠顧客虧本賣出的貨物。**5** (*sing* only) disadvantage or deprivation: (僅用單數)不利;剝奪: *Such a man is no great ~,* We need not regret losing his services. 損失這樣一個人並不遺憾。***be a dead ~,*** (colloq, of a person) be quite worthless: (俗,指人)毫無用處: *We'd better fire Smith—He's a dead ~.* 我們最好辭退史密斯——他毫無用處。**6** ***(be) at a ~ for sth/to do sth,*** be perplexed, uncertain: 困惑;不知所措: *He was at a ~ for words/to know what to say,* did not know how to express himself. 他不知道說些什麼好。

lost /lɒst *US:* lɔːst ; lɔst/ *pt, pp* of lose.

lot[1] /lɒt ; lɑt/ *n* (colloq) (俗) **1** ***the lot; the whole lot; all the lot,*** the whole number or quantity: 全體;全部;總量: *That's the lot,* That's all or everything. 全部都在此。*Take the (whole) lot.* 統統拿去。*Go away, the whole lot of you/all the lot of you,* (emphat for) 'all of you', 'every one of you'. 你們全都走開(較 'all of you', 及 'every one of you' 語氣猶重)。*She wants a new car, a fridge, and a colour TV—the lot!* 她要一部新汽車,一個冰箱,和一部彩色電視機——全套! **2** ***a lot (of); lots (and lots) (of),*** a great amount or number (of): 很多;許多: *What a lot of time you take to dress!* 你穿衣服費的時間眞多! *She spends a lot of money on clothes.* 她花很多錢添置衣服。*There were such a lot of people in the shops!* 商店裏的人眞多! *I want lots.* 我要很多。*I saw quite a lot of her* (= saw her often) *when I was in London last month.* 我上月在倫敦時常常看到她。*We don't see a lot of her nowadays.* 我們現今很少看到她。**3** (used *adverbially*) very much: (用作副詞)很多: *He's feeling a lot better today.* 他今天身體好多了。*A lot ˈyou care!* (ironic) You don't care at all! (反語)你才不關心哩! Cf 參較 *a good deal, a little.*

lot[2] /lɒt ; lɑt/ *n* [U] **1** (one of a set of objects used in) the making of a selection or decision by methods depending upon chance: 抽籤法;拈鬮法;籤;鬮: *divide property by lot.* 用抽籤法分財產。***draw/cast lots,*** eg by taking pieces of paper marked in some way from a box: 抽籤;拈鬮: *They drew lots as to who should begin.* 他們抽籤以決定由誰開始。**2** ***the lot,*** decision or choice resulting from this: 中籤;抽中: *The lot came to/fell upon me.* 我抽中了。**3** person's fortune or destiny: 命運;運氣: *His lot has been a hard one.* 他的命苦。*Such good fortune falls to the lot of few men.* 這種好運氣很少有人獲得。*It has fallen to my lot to oppose the President in the election.* 命中注定要我在選舉中對抗總統。***cast/throw in one's lot with sb,*** decide to share the fortunes of. 與某人禍福相共。**4** item, or number of items, (to be) sold at an auction sale: (拍賣品之)項目;組: *Lot 46, six chairs.* 第四十六項,椅子六把。**5** collection of objects of the same kind: 一批(同樣的東

西): *We have received a new lot of hats from the manufacturers.* 我們從製造商那裏收到了一批新帽子。**6** ***a bad lot,*** (colloq) a bad person. (俗)壞人；惡人。 **7** (cinema) studio and surrounding land. (電影)攝影場。 **8** plot of land: 一塊地；一塊地皮: (esp US) (尤美) *a 'parking lot,* for cars; 一塊停車場地；*a vacant lot,* a building site. 一塊空地皮。

loth /ləʊθ ; loθ/ *adj* ⇨ loath.

lo·tion /'ləʊʃn ; 'loʃən/ *n* [C, U] (kind of) medicinal liquid for use on the skin: (一種)洗劑: *a bottle of cleansing ~ for the face;* 一瓶洗面劑; *soothing ~s for insect bites.* 蟲咬鎮痛洗劑。

lot·tery /'lɒtərɪ ; 'lɑtərɪ/ *n* (*pl* -ries) [C] **1** arrangement to give prizes to holders of numbered tickets previously bought by them and drawn by lot: 發行獎券或彩票的辦法: (attrib) (形容用法) *'~ tickets.* 獎券；彩票。 **2** (fig) sth considered to be as uncertain as the winning of prizes in a ~: (喩)不定之事(如獎券之中獎): *Is marriage a ~?* 婚姻是可遇而不可求的嗎?

lot·to /'lɒtəʊ ; 'lɑto/ *n* [U] game of chance; bingo. 一種賭博性遊戲；賓果遊戲。

lo·tus /'ləʊtəs ; 'lotəs/ *n* (*pl* -es /-sɪz ; -sɪz/) (not often used in the *pl; '~ blooms* is preferred) (不常用複數形，複數多由 lotus blooms 表示) **1** (kinds of) water-lily, esp Egyptian and Asiatic kinds. 蓮；荷(尤指埃及和亞洲所產者)。⇨ the illus at flower. 參看 flower 之挿圖。 **2** (in old Gk legends) plant represented as bringing about a distaste for an active life. (古希臘傳說)忘憂樹(據傳可使人厭惡積極進取的生活)。**'~-eater** *n* person who gives himself up to indolent enjoyment. 貪圖安逸的人。

loud /laʊd ; laʊd/ *adj* (-er, -est) **1** not quiet or soft; easily heard: 高聲的；喧噪的；響亮的: *~ voices/cries/laughs.* 宏亮的嗓子(大聲的喊聲；哄然的笑聲)。*The bomb exploded with a ~ noise.* 那炸彈一聲巨響爆炸了。**,~-'hailer** *n* electronic device that enables a voice to be magnified and so be audible at a great distance: 强力揚聲器: *The naval officer called to the trawler by ~-hailer across the water.* 那海軍軍官以强力揚聲器向海面上的拖網漁船呼喊。**,~-'speaker** *n* (often shortened to 常略作 *speaker*) part of a radio receiving apparatus that converts electric impulses into audible sounds. 擴音器；揚聲器。 **2** (of a person's behaviour; of colours) of the kind that forces itself on the attention. (指人的行爲；指顏色)引人注目的；刺眼的。□ *adv* (after *talk, speak, laugh* etc) in a ~ manner: (用於 talk, speak, laugh 等動詞後)高聲地；大聲地；喧噪地: *Don't talk so ~.* 不要如此高聲談話。*They laughed ~ and long.* 他們大聲地笑了好一陣子。*Speak ~er!* 講大聲點！*Who laughed ~est?* 誰笑的聲音最大? **~·ly** *adv* in a ~ manner: 高聲地；喧噪地；刺目地: *Someone knocked ~ly at the door.* 有人大聲敲門。*What a ~ly dressed girl!* 這女孩穿的衣服多麼刺眼啊！**~·ness** *n*

lough /lɒk ; lɑx/ *n* (in Ireland) lake; arm of the sea. (愛爾蘭)湖；海灣。

lounge /laʊndʒ ; laʊndʒ/ *vi* [VP2A, C] sit, stand about (leaning against sth) in a lazy way: 懶洋洋地坐着或站着(倚靠某物): *idlers lounging at street corners;* 在街道轉彎處閒散的遊民; *lounging over a café table.* 懶洋洋地倚靠着咖啡館的桌子。**~r** *n* person who ~s. 懶洋洋地坐着或站着的人。□ *n* **1** act of lounging: 懶洋洋地坐着或站着: *have a ~.* 懶坐一會兒。 **2** comfortable sitting-room, esp in a club or hotel. 休息處；休息室(尤指俱樂部或旅館中者)。**'~-lizard** *n* (dated sl) professional dance-partner for women at dances in hotel ~s. (過時俚語)旅館休息室中陪婦女跳舞的職業舞伴。 **3** **'~-bar** *n* smartest bar in a public house. 酒館中最好的吧枱。**'~-chair** *n* comfortable easy-chair. 安樂椅；躺椅。**'~-suit** *n* man's ordinary suit of jacket, (waistcoat), and trousers. 男子平常穿的一套衣服(包括上衣，背心和褲子)。

lour, lower /'laʊə(r) ; laʊr/ *vi* [VP2A, 3A] **~ at/on/upon,** frown; look sullen or threatening; (of the sky, clouds) look dark, as if threatening a storm. 皺眉頭；作怒相；(指天氣，雲)變陰暗(好像預示暴風雨)。**~·ing·ly** *adv*

louse /laʊs ; laʊs/ *n* (*pl* lice /laɪs ; laɪs/) **1** small insect living on the bodies of animals and human beings under dirty conditions; similar insect living on plants. 蝨；(植物上的)寄生蟲。 **2** (sl) contemptible person: (俚)可鄙之人: *He's an absolute ~.* 他是個極爲可鄙的人。

lousy /'laʊzɪ ; 'laʊzɪ/ *adj* (-ier, -iest) infested with lice; (colloq) bad: 多蝨的；(俗)壞的: *a ~ dinner;* 很壞的一餐; (sl) well provided (*with*): (俚)有很多的(與 with 連用): *He's ~ with money.* 他有很多錢。

lout /laʊt ; laʊt/ *n* clumsy, ill-mannered person. 粗鄙的人。**'litter-~,** ⇨ litter²(1). **'~·ish** /-ɪʃ ; -ɪʃ/ *adj* of or like a ~: 粗鄙之人的；似粗鄙之人的: *~ish behaviour.* 粗鄙的行爲。

louvre (also **lou·ver**) /'lu:və(r) ; 'luvə/ *n* arrangement of fixed or moveable slats (in a door or window) for ventilation (like the slats in a Venetian blind). (通風用)門上百葉板窗；百葉板窗。**lou·vered** *adj* having ~s: 有百葉板窗的: *a ~ed door.* 有百葉板窗的門。

lov·able /'lʌvəbl ; 'lʌvəbl/ *adj* deserving or inspiring love; worthy of love: 可愛的；惹人愛的；值得愛的: *a ~ child;* 可愛的孩子; *a child's ~ ways.* 孩子可愛的地方。

love¹ /lʌv ; lʌv/ *n* **1** [U] warm, kind feeling; fondness; affectionate and tender devotion: 熱愛；喜愛；摯愛；鍾愛: *a mother's ~ for her children;* 母愛; *a ~ of learning/adventure;* 愛好學問(冒險); *~ of (one's) country,* patriotism; 愛國心; *show ~ towards one's neighbours.* 愛隣居。***give/send sb one's ~,*** give or send an affectionate greeting. 向某人致意。***play for ~,*** for the pleasure of the game, not for stakes. 爲娛樂(非爲賭錢)而玩。***not to be had for ~ or money,*** impossible to get by any means. 任何方法都得不到的。***There's ,no '~ lost between them,*** They dislike each other. 他們互相嫌惡。***a labour of ~,*** **(a)** sth that one enjoys doing for its own sake. 嗜愛的工作。 **(b)** one does for the ~ of sb. 爲他人所做的事。***for the ~ of,*** (in appeals, etc) for the sake of; in the name of: (用於懇求等)爲…的緣故；爲了: *Put that gun down, for the ~ of God!* 請看在上帝的面上放下那枝槍吧！**'~-feast** *n* meal taken by early Christians in token of brotherly ~; religious service imitating this. 愛席(早期基督教徒間表示兄弟愛的聚餐；教會倣此舉行之聚餐)。 **2** [U] warm, kind feeling between two persons; sexual passion or desire; this as a literary subject: 愛情；戀愛；性愛；肉慾；(文學上的)愛情主題: *a '~-story;* 愛情故事; *marry for ~, not for money.* 爲愛情而結婚，非爲金錢。***be in ~ (with sb),*** have ~ and desire (for): (與某人)戀愛；愛上(某人): *Hero and Leander were in ~. Leander was in ~ with Hero.* 希羅和麗安黛在戀愛。麗安黛愛上了希羅。***fall in ~ (with sb),*** come to feel ~ (for); begin to be in ~ (with). (與某人)戀愛；愛上(某人)。***make ~ (to sb),*** show that one is in ~ with sb; do the things that lovers do, eg kiss, caress, have sexual intercourse: (向某人)示愛；調情(例如接吻，撫愛，性交)；做愛: *Jane thinks it's more fun to make ~ than to make the beds.* 珍認爲做愛比鋪床有趣。*Make ~, not war!* 相愛，不要相戰！Hence, 由此產生，**'~-making** *n* **'~-affair** *n* instance of being in ~, often with a physical relationship: 戀愛；韻事: *a girl who had numerous ~-affairs before her marriage.* 婚前曾經多次戀愛的女子。**'~·bird** *n* small brightly coloured parrot said to pine away when it loses its mate; (*pl*) lovers very much in ~. 情鳥(顏色鮮明的小鸚鵡，據說喪偶後會憔悴)；(複)恩愛的情侶。**'~-child** *n* child of unmarried parents. 私生子。**'~-knot** *n* bow of ribbon, tied in a special way, formerly given or worn as a pledge of ~. 相思結;同心結(一種絲帶結,昔時贈送或佩帶表示愛的誓約)。 '~-**letter** *n* letter between persons in ~ and concerned with their ~. 情書。 '~•**lorn** /-lɔ:n; -,lɔrn/ *adj* unhappy because one's ~ is not returned; pining with ~. 失戀的;害相思病的。 '~-**match** *n* marriage made for love's sake, not an arranged marriage. 戀愛結婚(純爲愛情而結婚)。 '~-**philtre/-potion** *nn* magic drink supposed to make the person who drinks it fall in ~ with the person from whom it is received. 春藥;媚藥。 '~-**seat** *n* S-shaped bench with two seats facing in opposite directions. 情人座(一種兩人可面對相坐的 S 形座椅)。 '~•**sick** *adj* languishing because of ~. 害相思病的。 '~-**song** *n* song about or expressing ~. 情歌;戀歌。 '~-**story** *n* novel or story of which the main theme is ~. 愛情小說;戀愛故事。 '~-**token** *n* sth given as a symbol of ~. 象徵愛情的贈品。 **3** form of address between lovers, husband and wife, or to a child: 親愛的(愛人和夫妻間,或對孩子的稱呼): *Come here, my ~*. 過來,親愛的。 **4** (colloq) delightful or lovable person or thing: (俗)令人愉快或可愛的人或物: *Isn't she a little ~?* 她不是嬌小可愛嗎? *What a ~ of a cottage!* 多麼可愛的村舍啊! **5** person who is a sweetheart: 愛人: *She was an old ~ of mine years ago* (*flame* is more usu). 她是我多年前的舊情人 (flame 較常用)。 **6** personification of ~, ie a Cupid. 愛的化身;愛神。 **7** [U] (in games) no score, nothing, nil: (比賽)零分: *~ all*, no score for either side; 零比零; '*~ game*, one in which the loser did not score. 輸方無分的一局比賽。~•**less** *adj* unloving; unloved; without ~: 無愛情的: *a ~less marriage*. 無愛情的婚姻。

love² /lʌv; lʌv/ *vt* **1** [VP6A] have strong affection or deep tender feelings for: 愛;深愛;熱愛: *~ one's parents/one's country/one's husband*. 愛父母(國家,丈夫)。 **2** [VP6A] worship: 敬拜: *~ God*. 敬拜神(上帝)。 **3** [VP6A] have kind feelings towards: 以仁愛對待: *The Bible tells us to ~ all men*. 聖經告訴我們要愛所有的人。 **4** [VP6A, D, 7A, 17] (colloq) be very fond of; like; find pleasure in: (俗)喜好;喜歡: *~ comfort/mountain-climbing*. 喜好舒適(爬山)。 *She ~s to have/~s having a lot of dogs and young men round her*. 她喜歡有許多狗和青年男子在她周圍。 *'Will you come with me?'—'I should ~ to.'* '你跟我一起來好嗎?'—'我樂意奉陪。' *I'd ~ you to come with me*. 我喜歡你跟我一起來。

love•ly /'lʌvlɪ; 'lʌvlɪ/ *adj* **1** beautiful; attractive; pleasant: 美麗的;動人的;可愛的: *a ~ view*; 可愛的景色; *a ~ woman*; 美麗的女人; *~ hair/weather*. 美麗的頭髮(好天氣)。 **2** (colloq) enjoyable; amusing: (俗)令人愉快的;有趣的: *We had a ~ holiday*. 我們這個假日過得很快樂。 *What a ~ joke!* 這個笑話多麼有趣! *It's ~ and warm here*, ~ because warm. 這兒的天氣溫暖宜人。 **love•li•ness** *n*

lover /'lʌvə(r); 'lʌvɚ/ *n* **1** person who is fond of or devoted to (sth): 喜愛或專心於某一事物的人;愛好者: *a ~ of music/horses/good wine*. 音樂(馬匹,好酒)的愛好者。 **2** person in love with another; regular sexual partner. 愛人;情人;經常發生性關係之伴侶。 '~•**like** *adj* in the manner of a ~. 像愛人的。

lov•ing /'lʌvɪŋ; 'lʌvɪŋ/ *adj* feeling or showing love: 愛的;鍾情的;表示愛意的;親愛的: *a ~ friend*. 親愛的朋友。'~-**cup** *n* large wine-cup passed round from person to person so that everyone may drink from it. 愛杯(供多人輪流飲酒的大杯)。 ,~-'**kindness** *n* [U] tender consideration; mercy and kindness coming from love. 慈愛;出於愛心的憐憫與仁慈。 ~•**ly** *adv* in a ~ way: 親愛地: *Yours ~ly*, formula at the end of a letter, eg from a child to its parents. 你的親愛的(信末結語,如子女寫給父母親者)。

low¹ /ləʊ; lo/ *adj* (-er, -est) **1** not high; not extending far upwards: 低的;矮的: *a low wall/ceiling/shelf*; 矮的牆(天花板,架子); *a low range of hills*; 一列矮山; *low-rise housing*, of houses not many storeys high. 低層(層數不多)房屋。 *The moon was low in the sky*. 月亮低掛在天空。 *The glass is low*, The mercury in the barometer is low. 氣壓計所顯示的度數很低。 *He has a low brow*, short distance between the hair and the eyebrows. 他的前額很低。 *She was wearing a dress low in the neck/a 'low-necked dress*, one leaving the neck and (part of) the shoulders and breasts visible. 她穿着一件低領的衣服(開領很低,露出一部分肩膀和胸部者)。 **,low-re'lief**, ⇨ bas-relief. **2** below the usual or normal level or intensity: 低於通常或正常高度或强度的: *low-lying land*; 低地; *low pressure*, eg of the atmosphere, of gas or water from the mains; 低壓(例如氣壓,瓦斯或水壓); *a low-density housing estate*, with comparatively few houses to the acre. 低密度的宅地(房屋較少)。 *The rivers were low during the dry summer*. 乾旱的夏日裏河水低淺。 **low gear**, ⇨ gear(1). **low tide/water**, time when the tide is out and far from the shore or river bank. 低潮;低水位。 **,low-'water mark**, lowest points reached at low tide. 低潮點;低潮線;低水位線。 **be in low water**, (fig) short of money. (喻)缺少金錢。 **3** (of sounds) not loud; not high in pitch: (指聲音)不大的;不高的;不尖的;低的: *speak in a low voice*; 低聲說話; *the low notes of a cello*. 大提琴的低調。 *A tenor cannot get so low as a baritone*. 男高音不能唱得像男中音那樣低。 **,low-'keyed**, (fig) restrained in style or quality. (喻)在式樣或性質方面抑制的;不張揚的。 **,low-'pitched**, (music) low in pitch. (音樂)低調的。 **4** of or in inferior rank or social class: 身份或地位卑下的: *all classes of people, high and low*; 所有上下各階層的人們; *men of low birth*; 出身微賤的人; *have a low station in life*. 身份卑賤。 **be brought low**, be humbled. 被貶抑;被屈辱;敗落。 **5** commonplace; coarse; vulgar; little civilized: 平凡的;粗俗的;鄙陋的;鄙野的: *low manners*; 粗鄙的態度; *low company*; 下層社會的朋友; *low life*, of persons who are vulgar, coarse, etc; 下層生活; *low tastes*; 低級趣味; *low cunning*, cunning typical of sb who is mean or morally degraded. 卑鄙的狡詐。 *I never fell as low as that*, never let my standard of behaviour fall so low. 我的行爲從未那樣惡劣。 **6** feeble; lacking in strength of body or mind: 虛弱的;無力的;沒精神的: *in a low state of health*; 健康情形不佳; *feel low/in low spirits*, unhappy, depressed. 不高興(無精打采)。Hence, 由此產生, **,low-'spirited** *adj* **7** of small amount as measured by a scale or by degrees: 小量的;低度的: *a low temperature*; 低的溫度; *a low pulse*; 慢的脈搏; *low prices/wages/rates of pay*. 低的價格(工資,薪給)。 **low latitudes**, near the equator. 低緯度;靠近赤道地區。 ***have a low opinion of sb/sth***, think very little of him, his work, etc. 對某人(某事)評價很低。 ***at lowest***, at the least possible figure, quantity, etc. 至少。 **8** (of a supply of anything) (指供應物品) ***be/run low***, be/become nearly exhausted: 幾乎耗盡或用光的: *Our stock of coal is running low*. 我們的煤炭快燒完了。 *Food supplies were running low in the besieged town*. 這個被包圍的城鎮裏的糧食供應將盡。 **9** (of the position of the tongue when speaking) not raised: (指說話時舌頭位置)不抬高的;舌位低下的: *a low vowel*, one, eg the vowel /ɑ:/, made with the tongue low in the mouth. 低母音(例如壓低舌部所發出的母音/ɑ:/)。 **10** not highly developed: 低度發展的;低等的: *low forms of life*. 低等生物。 **11** **Low Church**, party in the Church of England giving a low place to the authority of bishops and priests, ecclesiastical organization, ritual, etc. (contrasted with *High Church*). 低派教會(英國國教中的一派,對主教和牧師的權威,教會組織,儀式等

不予重視;與 High Church 相對)。Hence, 由此產生, **Low Churchman,** supporter of this. 擁護低派教會者;低派教會之份子。 **12** (phrases) (片語) ***bring/lay sb/sth low,*** make low in health, wealth, position, etc; defeat; humble. 使健康情形,財富或地位等低落;挫敗;貶抑。 ***lie low,*** (fig) keep quiet or hidden; say nothing and wait: (喻)隱匿;靜待: *The escaped prisoners had to lie low for months.* 那些逃犯必須隱匿幾個月。 **13** (compounds) (複合字) **ˌlow-ˈborn** *adj* of humble birth. 出身低微的。 **ˌlow-ˈbred** *adj* having vulgar manners. 教養不良的;行爲粗野的。 **ˈlow·brow** *n, adj* (person) showing little interest in or taste for intellectual things, esp art, music, literature (contrasted with *highbrow*). 對文事(尤指藝術,音樂,文學)缺少興趣或修養的(人);知識程度低的(與 highbrow 相對)。 **lower case,** (in printing) small letters, not capitals. (印刷)小楷字母;小寫字體。 **Lower Chamber/House,** lower branch of a legislative assembly, eg the House of Commons in GB, the House of Representatives in US. 下議院(如英國之下議院,美國之衆議院)。 **low comedian,** person who acts in **low comedy,** kind of drama bordering on farce, with laughable situations, comic dialogue, etc. 滑稽劇演員;丑角 (low comedy 滑稽戲劇—由許多笑料,滑稽對話等構成,近乎鬧劇的一種喜劇)。 **the lower deck,** (in the Navy) the ratings; those who are not officers. (海軍中)全體士兵。 **ˈlow-down** *adj* (colloq) caddish; dishonourable: (俗)卑鄙的;下賤的;不光榮的: *~-down behaviour/tricks.* 卑鄙的行爲(詭計)。 ***give sb/get the low-down (on sth/sb),*** (colloq) give/get the true facts, inside information which is not generally known. (俗)給予某人(獲得)實情或內幕消息。 **ˈlow·lander** /-ləndə(r); -ləndɚ/ *n* person who lives in lowlands, esp (**L~**) one who lives in the Scottish Lowlands. 低地居民;(大寫時尤指)蘇格蘭低地居民。 **ˈlow·lands** /-ləndz; -ləndz/ *n pl* low level country: 低地: *the lowlands of Scotland.* 蘇格蘭的低地。 **Low Latin,** late, popular Latin (contrasted with classical Latin). 近代之通俗拉丁文(以別於古典拉丁文)。 **Low Mass,** (formerly) celebration of the Eucharist without a choir. (昔時)沒有唱詩班的彌撒;小彌撒。 **Low Sunday, Low Week,** coming after Easter Day and Easter Week. 復活節後的星期日,復活節後的下一週。 **ˈlow·ermost** *adj* lowest. 最低的。 **low·ness** *n*

low² /ləʊ; lo/ *adv* (-er, -est) in or to a low position; in a low manner: 在低下之位置;向低下之位置;低;卑下地: *aim/shoot low;* 向低處瞄準(射擊); *bow low to the Queen;* 向女王深深一鞠躬; *buy low* (= at low prices) *and sell high;* 低價買進高價賣出;賤買貴賣; *play low,* (in gambling) for small sums; 賭小錢; *speak low.* 低聲說話。

low³ /ləʊ; lo/ *n* sth low; low level or figure: 低的東西;低的水準或小的數目: *Several industrial shares reached new lows yesterday,* Their prices went down to a new low price (on the stock market). 昨天有一些工業股票落到新的低價。

low⁴ /ləʊ; lo/ *n* sound made by cattle. 牛叫聲;牛鳴。 □ *vi* (of cattle) make this characteristic sound. (指牛)鳴。

lower¹ /ˈləʊə(r); ˈloɚ/ *vt, vi* **1** [VP6A] let or bring down; cause to be down: 降低;降下;使跌落: *~ the sails/a flag.* 將帆(旗)降下。 ***~ away,*** (naut) lower a boat, sail, etc. (航海)放下小船,降下船帆等。 **2** [VP6A, 15A, 2A] make or become less high: 降低;減低;跌落: *~ the rent of a house.* 減低房租。 *The stocks ~ed in value.* 股票跌價。 *He ~ed his voice to a whisper.* 他把聲音降到耳語那麼低。 *We can't ~ the ceiling.* 我們不能降低天花板。 **3** [VP15A] ***~ oneself,*** degrade, disgrace: 降低品格;汚辱: *He would never ~ himself by taking bribes.* 他絕不會降低自己的品格去接受賄賂。 **4** [VP6A] weaken: 使弱;削弱;削減: *Poor diet ~s resistance to illness.* 營養太差的飲食會削弱對於疾病的抵抗力。

lower² /ˈlaʊə(r); ˈlaʊɚ/ *vi* = lour.

low·ly /ˈləʊlɪ; ˈlolɪ/ *adj* (-ier, -iest) humble; simple; modest. 謙卑的;卑微的;謙遜的。 **low·li·ness** *n*

loyal /ˈlɔɪəl; ˈlɔɪəl/ *adj* true and faithful (*to*): 忠誠的;(對…)忠貞的(與 to 連用): *~ subjects of the Queen;* 女王的忠誠臣民; *~ supporters;* 忠實的擁護者; *~ to one's country.* 忠於國家。 **ˈ~·ist** /-ɪst; -ɪst/ *n* person who is ~ to his ruler and government, esp one who supports the head of an established government during a revolt: 忠於政府的人;(尤指)暴亂時擁護政府元首者: (attrib) (形容用法) *the ~ist army/troops.* 忠於政府的軍隊。 **~·ly** /ˈlɔɪəlɪ; ˈlɔɪəlɪ/ *adv* **~·ty** *n* (*pl* -ties) **1** [U] being ~; ~ conduct. 忠誠;忠誠的行爲。 **2** (*pl*) kinds of ~ attachment: (複)忠義: *tribal loyalties.* 對種族或部落的效忠。

loz·enge /ˈlɒzɪndʒ; ˈlɑzɪndʒ/ *n* **1** four-sided, diamond-shaped figure. 菱形;菱形物。 **2** small tablet of flavoured sugar, esp one containing medicine: 小糖塊;(尤指)帶糖味的小藥片: *cough ~s.* 咳嗽藥片。

L-plate /ˈel pleɪt; ˈɛl plet/ *n* plate with a large capital L, fixed to a motor-vehicle being driven by a learner who has not passed his driving test. 學習駕駛牌(上書一大寫 L,固定於行駛中的車上,表示駕駛人在學習階段,尙未通過考試)。

LSD /ˌel es ˈdiː; ˌɛl ɛs ˈdi/ *n* [U] odourless, colourless and tasteless semi-synthetic substance causing hallucinations (often referred to as 'acid'). 迷幻藥。 ⇨ App 2. 參看附錄二。

£ s d /ˌel es ˈdiː; ˌɛl ɛs ˈdi/ *n* [U] term used, before British currency was decimalized, for pounds, shillings and pence; (colloq) money: 鎊,先令和辨士;(俗)金錢: *I'm short of £sd just now.* 我現在缺錢。 ⇨ App 5. 參看附錄五。

lub·ber /ˈlʌbə(r); ˈlʌbɚ/ *n* big, clumsy, stupid fellow. 大而蠢笨的人;笨漢。 ⇨ *land-~* at land¹(6). **~·ly** *adj*

lu·bri·cate /ˈluːbrɪkeɪt; ˈlubrɪˌket/ *vt* [VP6A] put oil or grease into (machine parts) to make (them) work easily; (fig) do sth that makes action, etc easier. 給(機件)加潤滑油使(它們)轉動順暢;使滑潤;加潤滑油;(喻)做出某事以使行動等順利進展。 **lu·bri·cant** /ˈluːbrɪkənt; ˈlubrɪkənt/ *n* [U, C] substance that ~s. 潤滑劑。 **lu·bri·ca·tion** /ˌluːbrɪˈkeɪʃn; ˌlubrɪˈkeʃən/ *n* [U, C] (instance of) lubricating or being ~d. 潤滑。

lu·cent /ˈluːsnt; ˈlusn̩t/ *adj* (liter) shining; translucent. (文)明亮的;半透明的。

lu·cerne /luːˈsɜːn; luˈsɝn/ *n* [U] (GB) clover-like plant used for feeding animals. (英)紫花苜蓿(供動物食用)。(US 美 = *alfalfa*).

lu·cid /ˈluːsɪd; ˈlusɪd/ *adj* **1** clear; easy to understand: 清楚的;容易了解的;明白的: *a ~ explanation;* 明白的解釋; *a ~ literary style;* 明暢的文體; *a ~ mind.* 清晰的頭腦。 **2** mentally sound: 神志清明的: *~ intervals,* periods of sanity between periods of insanity. 精神病患者之神志清明的時期。 **3** (poet) bright, clear, transparent. (詩)明亮的;清澈的;透明的。 **~·ly** *adv* **~·ity** /luːˈsɪdətɪ; luˈsɪdətɪ/ *n* [U] quality of being ~. 明白;清澄;透明;神志清明。

Luci·fer /ˈluːsɪfə(r); ˈlusəfɚ/ *n* **1** Satan, the chief rebel angel: 撒旦;魔鬼: *as proud as ~.* 極其傲慢。 **2** (the planet Venus as) the morning star. 金星;曉星;啓明星。

luck /lʌk; lʌk/ *n* [U] chance; fortune (good or bad); sth that is considered to come by chance: 機運;(好或壞的)運氣;不期而遇的事物: *have good/bad ~ in one's affairs;* 事情順利(不順利); *have hard ~,* be unfortunate. 遭遇不幸。 *As ~ would have it,...* Fortunately,... (or Unfortunately,... according to context). 幸運的是…;不幸的是…(視上下文而定)。 *It was hard ~ on you that...,* used to show sympathy. 你遭遇…眞是不幸(用以表示同情)。 *He tried his ~ at the gaming tables,* gambled, hoping for success. 他在賭枱上碰運氣。 *What rotten ~! Bad*

~! (used to show sympathy). 運氣眞不好！(用以表示同情)。*Good ~!* (used to encourage, express hopes of good fortune, etc). 祝你好運！(用以鼓勵,表示盼望有好運等)。*Just my ~!* I am unlucky, as usual. 我總是這樣倒霉！*My ~'s in / out,* I am / am not fortunate. 我是幸運(不幸)的。*I never have any ~.* 我從來沒有走過好運。*I had the ~* (= was fortunate enough) *to find him at home.* 我幸而在他家裏找到他。***be down on one's ~,*** (colloq) be unfortunate; suffer misfortune. (俗)運氣不好;倒霉。***be in / out of ~,*** have / not have good fortune. 運氣好(不好)。***for ~,*** to bring good fortune: 爲了討吉利;求福: *keep sth for ~.* 爲了討吉利而保有某種東西。***worse ~,*** (used parenthetically) more's the pity; unfortunately. (作挿語用)更不幸地;不幸地。**~·less** *adj* unfortunate; turning out badly: 運氣不佳的;不幸的;結果不好的: *a ~less day / attempt.* 倒霉的日子(未成功的嘗試)。

lucky /ˈlʌkɪ ; ˈlʌkɪ/ *adj* (-ier, -iest) having, bringing, resulting from, good luck: 有好運的;帶來好運的;由好運所造成的;幸運的: *a ~ escape / guess / man.* 僥倖的逃脫(僥倖的猜中;幸運的人)。*It's my ~ day,* one on which I am having good fortune. 今天我很走運。*You are ~ to be alive after being in that accident.* 你眞幸運,經過那場災禍而能生還。ˌ**~ ˈdip** *n* tub, etc containing articles of various values for which a person may dip in (taking the chance of getting sth of value) for a payment: 摸彩袋;幸運袋(袋中裝有價值不等之物,付錢卽可摸取): *L~ dip, 10p.* 摸彩,十辨士。**luck·ily** /ˈlʌkɪlɪ ; ˈlʌkɪlɪ/ *adv* in a ~ manner; fortunately: 幸運地;僥倖地;幸虧: *Luckily for me the train was late, so I just caught it.* 幸而火車誤點了,所以我剛好搭上。

lu·cra·tive /ˈluːkrətɪv ; ˈlukrətɪv/ *adj* profitable; bringing in money. 可獲利的;賺錢的。

lucre /ˈluːkə(r) ; ˈlukɚ/ *n* [U] (in a bad sense) profit or money-making (as a motive for action): (壞的意思)利益或賺錢 (作爲行爲的一種動機): *a man who would do anything for ~.* 爲了賺錢什麼都幹的人。

Lud·dite /ˈlʌdaɪt ; ˈlʌdaɪt/ *n* member of bands of workers who, in England, 1811-16, destroyed new machinery which, they thought, would cause unemployment. 1811-16 年間英國摧毀新機器的工人組織之一員(彼等認爲機器將導致失業)。

lu·di·crous /ˈluːdɪkrəs ; ˈludɪkrəs/ *adj* ridiculous; causing laughter. 荒謬的;可笑的。**~·ly** *adv*

ludo /ˈluːdəʊ ; ˈludo/ *n* [U] simple game played by moving counters on a special board after throwing dice. 一種骰子遊戲。

luff /lʌf ; lʌf/ *vt, vi* (naut) bring the head of a ship in a direction nearer to that of the wind; turn (the helm) so that this happens. (航海)轉船首順風行駛;爲達到此一目的而轉(舵)。

lug[1] /lʌg ; lʌg/ *vt* (-gg-) [VP6A, 15A, B] pull or drag roughly and with much effort: 用力拉或拖: *lugging two heavy suitcases up the stairs;* 拖着兩隻重衣箱上樓; *lug a handcart along.* 拉着一輛手車。□ *n* hard or rough pull. 用力拉;强拖。

lug[2] /lʌg ; lʌg/ *n* projecting part (of a metal casting) by which it is kept securely in place. (金屬鑄品的)突出部分(爲便於穩固放置之用);耳。

luge /luːʒ ; luʒ/ *n* (F) short toboggan for one person, as used in Switzerland. (法)一人乘的短雪橇(如用於瑞士者)。

lug·gage /ˈlʌgɪdʒ ; ˈlʌgɪdʒ/ *n* [U] bags, trunks, etc and their contents taken on a journey: 行李: *six pieces of ~;* 六件行李; *get one's ~ through the Customs.* (US 美 = *baggage.*) 使行李通過海關查驗。ˈ**~-carrier** *n* metal frame, eg one fixed behind the saddle of a bicycle, for ~. 行囊架(例如自行車後面放東西的架子)。ˈ**~-rack** *n* rack (above the seats) in a railway carriage, coach, etc, or on the roof of a motor-car, for ~. (火車等內座位上頭或汽車頂上的)行囊架。ˈ**~-van** *n* van for ~ on a railway train. (火車的)行李車。

lug·ger /ˈlʌgə(r) ; ˈlʌgɚ/ *n* small ship with one or more four-cornered sails set fore and aft. 四角縱帆帆船(有一個或多個四角帆的小船)。

lug·sail /ˈlʌgseɪl ; ˈlʌgˌsel/ *n* (naut) four-cornered sail. (航海)四角帆;斜桁用縱帆。

lu·gu·bri·ous /ləˈguːbrɪəs ; luˈgjubrɪəs/ *adj* (formal) dismal; mournful. (正式用語) 陰鬱的;悲哀的;陰沉的。**~·ly** *adv* **~·ness** *n*

luke·warm /ˌluːkˈwɔːm ; ˈlukˈwɔrm/ *adj* **1** (of liquids, etc) neither very warm nor cold. (指液體等)微溫的;不很熱也不冷的。**2** (fig) not eager either in supporting or opposing: (喩) 擁護或反對都不熱心的: *give only ~ support to a cause;* 對某一運動僅予以淡漠的支持; *~ friendship.* 淡薄的友誼。**~·ly** *adv* **~·ness** *n*

lull /lʌl ; lʌl/ *vt, vi* [VP6A, 15A, 2A] make or become quiet or less active: 使安靜或緩和;停息;平息;緩和: *~ a baby to sleep,* eg by rocking it and singing to it; 哄嬰孩入睡(如藉輕搖或唱催眠歌); *~ a person's fears / suspicions.* 消除一個人的恐懼(猜疑)。*The wind / sea was ~ed.* 風(海)已平息。*The wind ~ed.* 風已停息。□ *n* [C] interval of quiet; period of lessened activity, etc: 間歇;稍息;稍止: *a ~ in the storm / in the conversation.* 暴風雨的間歇(談話的中斷)。

lull·aby /ˈlʌləbaɪ ; ˈlʌləˌbaɪ/ *n* (*pl* -bies) song for lulling a baby to sleep; gentle, soft sound, eg made by wind in trees or by the running water of a brook. 催眠曲;搖籃曲;輕柔的聲音(如林間輕風或溪澗流水的聲音)。

lum·bago /lʌmˈbeɪgəʊ ; lʌmˈbego/ *n* [U] muscular pain in the lumbar regions. 腰肌痛;腰痛;腰風濕病。

lum·bar /ˈlʌmbə(r) ; ˈlʌmbɚ/ *adj* of the loins: 腰部的: *the ~ regions,* the lower part of the back. 腰背部位。

lum·ber[1] /ˈlʌmbə(r) ; ˈlʌmbɚ/ *n* [U] **1** roughly prepared wood; wood that has been sawn into planks, boards, etc. 木材;木料;木條;木板。ˈ**~·man** /-mən ; -mən/, ˈ**~·jack** *nn* man who fells trees; man who saws or transports ~. 伐木工人;鋸木材或運木材的人。ˈ**~-mill** *n* saw-mill. 鋸木廠。ˈ**~-yard** *n* place where ~ is stored. 木材堆置場。**2** (chiefly GB) useless or unwanted articles stored away or taking up space (eg old furniture, pictures). (主英) 無用的雜物 (例如舊傢具,圖畫等)。ˈ**~·room** *n* one in which ~ is stored. 破舊東西的儲存室。□ *vt* [VP6A, 14, 15A, B] ***~ sth (up) (with),*** (often in passive) fill with ~; fill space inconveniently; encumber: (常用被動語態)堆滿無用之物;零亂堆積;阻碍: *a room ~ed up with useless articles;* 堆滿無用物品的房間; (fig) (喩) *a mind that is ~ed (up) with useless bits of information.* 充滿無用資料的頭腦。

lum·ber[2] /ˈlʌmbə(r) ; ˈlʌmbɚ/ *vi* [VP2C] move in a heavy, clumsy, noisy way: 沉重,笨拙,而隆隆地行進: *The heavy army tanks ~ed along / by / past.* 重型戰車隆隆駛過。*What a big ~ing cart!* 一輛多麼大而笨重的載貨馬車！

lu·min·ary /ˈluːmɪnərɪ *US:* -nerɪ ; ˈluməˌnɛrɪ/ *n* (*pl* -ries) **1** star; the sun or moon; any light-giving body in the sky. 星;太陽;月亮;天上任何的發光體。**2** (fig) person who, because of his learning, is like a shining light; great moral or intellectual leader. (喩)領導人物;先知先覺者;學識卓越的人;道德或知識上偉大的領袖;泰斗。

lu·mi·nous /ˈluːmɪnəs ; ˈlumənəs/ *adj* **1** giving out light; bright: 發光的;明亮的: *~ paint,* as used on road signs, clocks and watches, visible in the dark. 發光塗料(如用於道路標誌,鐘錶上,暗中可見者)。**2** (fig) clear; easily understood: (喩)清楚的;容易了解的: *a ~ speaker / explanation.* 明晰的演說者(明白的解釋)。**lu·min·os·ity** /ˌluːmɪˈnɒsətɪ ; ˌluməˈnɑsətɪ/ *n* [U] quality of being ~. 發光;明亮;光輝;清晰;明白。

lummy, lumme /ˈlʌmɪ ; ˈlʌmɪ/ *int* (dated GB sl)

indicating surprise. (過時英俚)表示驚奇的感嘆詞。

lump[1] /lʌmp ; lʌmp/ *n* [C] **1** hard or compact mass, usu without a regular shape: 堆;塊;團(通常沒有一定形狀): *a ~ of clay;* 一塊泥土; *break a piece of coal into small ~s;* 把一塊煤打成一些小塊; *a ~ of sugar;* 一塊糖; ˈ*~ sugar,* sugar cut into cubes. 塊糖;方糖。***in the ~,*** added together; taken as a whole. 總計;全部;總括。***~ sum,*** one payment for a number of separate sums that are owed. 一次總付之款;總數。 **2** swelling or bump; bruise: 腫;隆起;傷痕: *He has a bad ~ on the forehead.* 他的額頭傷腫得很厲害。***have a ~ in one's/the throat,*** a feeling of pressure (as caused by strong emotion). 喉嚨哽住(如因情緒激動所致)。 **3** (colloq) heavy, dull person: (俗)笨拙遲鈍的人: *Get out of my way, you big fat ~ of a man!* 滾開,你這大笨豬! □ *vt, vi* **1** [VP6A, 15B] ~ ***(together),*** put together in one ~; include (a number of things) under one heading: 堆成一堆;合在一起;概括: *The boys agreed to ~ the expenses of their camping holiday.* 孩子們同意把露營費用合在一起而不分彼此。*Can we ~ all these items together under the heading 'incidental expenses'?* 我們能不能把所有這些項目歸納在'臨時費'項下? **2** [VP2A] form into ~s: 結塊: *This oatmeal ~s if you don't stir it well.* 假若你不好好攪動,這麥片粥會結塊。**~·ish** /-ɪʃ ; -ɪʃ/ *adj* (of a person) thickset; clumsy; stupid. (指人)矮胖的;笨拙的;愚蠢的。 **~y** *adj* (-ier, -iest) full of, covered with ~s: 多塊狀物的;覆有塊狀物的: *a ~y sauce;* 成團的醬; (of the surface of water) cut up by wind into small waves; choppy. (指水面)波浪起伏的。

lump[2] /lʌmp ; lʌmp/ *vt* (only in) (僅用於) ***~ it,*** (colloq) endure, put up with, sth unpleasant or unwanted: (俗)忍受(不愉快或不需要之事物): *If you don't like it you can ~ it.* 即使你不喜歡它,你也得忍受它。*Well, you'll just have to ~ it!* 哼,你就得忍受它!

lu·nacy /ˈluːnəsɪ ; ˈlunəsɪ/ *n* (*pl* -cies) **1** [U] madness; state of being a lunatic; mad or foolish behaviour: 瘋狂;精神錯亂;瘋狂或愚蠢的行為: *It's sheer ~.* 這完全是愚蠢的行為。**2** (*pl*) mad or very foolish acts. (複)瘋狂或愚蠢的行動。

lu·nar /ˈluːnə(r) ; ˈlunɚ/ *adj* of the moon: 月亮的: *a ~ month,* average time between successive new moons, about 29½ days; 恆星月;朔望月(約為二十九天半);陰曆一個月; *a ~ module,* detachable section of a spacecraft that orbits the moon and may descend to its surface; 登陸月球之小艇; *a ~ orbit* (by a spacecraft); (太空船)繞行月球之軌道; *a ~ year,* period of 12 ~ months. 陰曆一年。

lu·na·tic /ˈluːnətɪk ; ˈlunəˌtɪk/ *n* **1** mad person; mental patient (the preferred term). 瘋子;精神病人(mental patient 較好)。ˈ**~ asylum,** hospital (*mental home* and *mental hospital* are the names in present-day use) for the care and treatment of ~s. 瘋人院;精神病院(現今多用 mental home 和 mental hospital)。**2** (attrib) mad; extremely foolish: (形容用法)瘋狂的;極愚笨的: *a ~ proposal.* 極愚蠢的建議。ˌ**~ ˈfringe,** minority group with extreme views, or engaged in eccentric activities, eg in politics or literature. 極端份子(例如在政治或文學方面持極端意見或從事怪異活動之少數份子)。

lunch /lʌntʃ ; lʌntʃ/ *n* meal taken in the middle of the day: 午餐;中飯: *They were at ~ when I called.* 我去看他們的時候他們正在吃中飯。□ *vi, vt* eat ~; provide ~ for: 吃中飯;供給…午餐: *He ~ed me well at the Savoy.* 他在薩伏伊飯店招待我吃豐盛的午餐。**~eon** /ˈlʌntʃən ; ˈlʌntʃən/ *n* (formal word for) ~. (正式用語)午餐;午宴。

lung /lʌŋ ; lʌŋ/ *n* **1** either of the two breathing organs in the chest of man and other animals: 肺;肺臟: *the ˈ~ passages/tissues;* 肺臟通道(組織); *~ cancer.* 肺癌。*That opera singer has good ~s,* produces a great volume of sound. 那個歌劇演唱者聲音宏亮。⇨ the illus at respiratory. 參看 respiratory 之插圖。ˈ**~-power** *n* [U] power of voice. 發聲力;肺活量。 **2** (fig) open space in or close to a large city. (喻)大城市內或附近的空曠地方。

lunge /lʌndʒ ; lʌndʒ/ *n* sudden forward movement, eg with a sword, or forward movement of the body (eg when aiming a blow). (身體的)前衝;(以劍等的)衝刺;戳;擊。□ *vi* [VP2A, C] make a ~: 衝刺;前衝;戳;擊: *He ~d at his opponent/~d out suddenly.* 他突然向他的對手衝去(突然刺出)。

lu·pin (US = **lu·pine**) /ˈluːpɪn ; ˈlupɪn/ *n* garden or fodder plant with tall spikes of flowers of various colours. 羽扇豆。

lurch[1] /lɜːtʃ ; lɝtʃ/ *n* (only in) (僅用於) ***leave sb in the ~,*** leave him when he is in difficulties and needing help. 在某人危難時離棄不顧。

lurch[2] /lɜːtʃ ; lɝtʃ/ *n* sudden change of weight to one side; sudden roll or pitch: 突然傾斜;傾側: *The ship gave a ~ to starboard.* 船突然向右側傾斜。□ *vi* [VP2C] move along with a ~ or ~es: 蹣跚而行;東倒西歪地前進: *The drunken man ~ed across the street.* 那個醉漢蹣跚地穿過街道。

lurcher /ˈlɜːtʃə(r) ; ˈlɝtʃɚ/ *n* dog, a cross between a sheepdog and a greyhound, used for retrieving game (esp by poachers). 一種獵狗(牧羊犬和靈猩交配而生的雜種狗,用以尋回獵物,尤指盜獵之人所用者)。

lure /lʊə(r) ; lʊr/ *n* [C] bunch of brightly coloured feathers used to attract and recall a trained hawk; bait or decoy to attract wild animals; (fig) sth that attracts or invites; the attraction or interest that sth has: 用以喚回獵鷹的一束彩色羽毛;引誘野獸的餌; (喻)誘惑物;某事物所具有的吸引力或趣味: *the ~ of the sea;* 大海的誘惑; *the ~s used by a pretty woman to attract men.* 一個漂亮的女人用以吸引男人的魅力。□ *vt* [VP6A, 15B] attract, tempt: 吸引;誘惑: *~ sb away from his duty;* 引誘人離開職守; *be ~d on to destruction.* 被誘惑而走向毀滅。

lu·rid /ˈlʊərɪd ; ˈlʊrɪd/ *adj* **1** highly coloured, esp suggesting flame and smoke: 火紅的;紫紅的: *a ~ sky/sunset;* 火紅的天空(落霞); *~ thunderclouds.* 紫紅的雷雲。 **2** (fig) sensational; violent and shocking: (喻)聳人聽聞的;暴烈而驚人的: *~ details of a railway accident;* 火車失事的驚人詳情; *a ~ tale.* 可怖的故事。**~·ly** *adv* **~·ness** *n*

lurk /lɜːk ; lɝk/ *vi* [VP2C] be, keep, out of view, lying in wait or ready to attack: 潛伏;埋伏(等待或伺機出擊): *a suspicious-looking man ~ing in the shadows.* 一個形跡可疑的人潛伏在暗處。*Some suspicion still ~ed in his mind.* 他的心中仍然潛藏着懷疑。ˈ**~·ing-place** *n* hiding-place. 隱匿處;潛伏地點。

luscious /ˈlʌʃəs ; ˈlʌʃəs/ *adj* **1** rich and sweet in taste and smell, attractive: 味道與氣味甜美的;動人的: *~ peaches/lips.* 甜美的桃子(動人的嘴唇)。 **2** (of art, music, writing) very rich in ornament; suggesting sensual delights. (指藝術,音樂,寫作)鋪張華麗的;引起快感的。**~·ly** *adv* **~·ness** *n*

lush /lʌʃ ; lʌʃ/ *adj* (esp of grass and vegetation) growing luxuriantly: (尤指草木)茂盛的: *~ meadows;* 青草繁茂的草原; *a ~ growth of vegetation after the rains;* 雨後植物的茂盛生長; (fig) luxuriously comfortable. (喻)豪華舒適的。□ *n* (US sl) drunkard. (美俚)醉漢;酒鬼。

lust /lʌst ; lʌst/ *n* [U] violent desire to possess sth, esp strong sexual desire (*for*); passionate enjoyment (*of*): 慾望(尤指强烈的性慾);色慾;貪慾: *filled with ~;* 充滿慾望; [C] instance of this: 此種慾望的實例: *a ~ for power/gold;* 對權力(金錢)的慾望; *the ~s of the flesh.* 肉體的慾望。□ *vi* [VP3A] ***~ after/for,*** have ~ for: 貪求;渴望: *~ for/after gold;* 貪財; (biblical) (聖經) *~ after a woman,* have strong sexual desire. 貪戀女色。**~·ful** /-fl ; -fəl/ *adj* full of ~. 多貪慾的;好色的。 **~·fully** /-fəlɪ ; -fəlɪ/ *adv*

lustre (US = **lus·ter**) /ˈlʌstə(r) ; ˈlʌstɚ/ *n* **1** [U] quality of being bright, esp of a smooth or polished surface; sheen; soft reflected light: 光澤;光輝;光彩: *the ~ of pearls.* 珍珠的光澤。 **2** [U] (fig) glory; distinction: (喩)光榮;出色;卓越: *add ~ to one's name;* 使其聲名增輝; *deeds that shed ~ on an honoured family,* make its reputation more distinguished. 使光榮的家聲更爲顯耀的功業。 **3** (glass pendant of a) chandelier. 枝形吊燈;枝形吊燈之玻璃垂飾。 **lus·trous** /ˈlʌstrəs ; ˈlʌstrəs/ *adj* having ~: 有光澤的;光輝的: *lustrous pearls;* 光亮的珍珠; *her lustrous eyes.* 她明亮的眼睛。

lusty /ˈlʌstɪ ; ˈlʌstɪ/ *adj* healthy and strong; vigorous: 健壯的;精力充沛的;有力的: *a ~ girl from the country;* 鄉下來的一個健壯的女孩; *~ cheers.* 高聲的歡呼。 **lust·ily** /-ɪlɪ ; -əlɪ/ *adv*: *work/fight/shout lustily.* 起勁地工作(打鬪,叫喊)。

lute /luːt ; lut/ *n* stringed musical instrument (14th to 17th cc) associated with poets and poetry. 魯特琴(十四至十七世紀的一種絃樂器);琵琶。 **lu·tan·ist** /ˈluːtənɪst ; ˈlutn̩ɪst/ *n* player of the ~. 魯特琴彈奏者。

Lu·theran /ˈluːθərən ; ˈluθərən/ *adj, n* (follower) of Martin Luther; (member) of the Protestant Church named after Luther. 馬丁路德的(信徒);(起源於德國的一派基督教,以馬丁路德爲名)路德會的(教友);信義會的(教友)。

luxe /lʌks ; lʊks/ = de luxe.

lux·ur·iant /lʌgˈʒʊərɪənt ; lʌgˈʒʊrɪənt/ *adj* **1** strong in growth; abundant: 繁茂的;豐富的: *the ~ vegetation of the tropics;* 熱帶繁盛的草木; (fig) (喩) *a ~ imagination.* 豐富的想像力。 **2** (of liter and artistic style) richly ornamented; very elaborate. (指文體及藝術品之風格)華麗的;絢爛的。**~·ly** *adv* **lux·ur·iance** /-əns ; -əns/ *n* [U] ~ growth. 茂盛;豐富。

lux·ur·iate /lʌgˈʒʊərɪeɪt ; lʌgˈʒʊrɪˌet/ *vi* [VP3A] ~ *in,* take great delight in: 耽溺;盡情享受: *~ in the warm spring sunshine.* 盡情享受春天溫暖的陽光。

lux·ur·ious /lʌgˈʒʊərɪəs ; lʌgˈʒʊrɪəs/ *adj* **1** supplied with luxuries; very comfortable: 供有奢侈享受的;豪華的;非常舒服的: *live in ~ surroundings;* 生活在奢侈的環境中; *a ~ hotel.* 豪華的旅館。 **2** choice and costly: 精美昂貴的: *~ food.* 精美昂貴的食物。 **3** fond of luxuries; self-indulgent: 愛好奢侈的;放縱的: *~ habits.* 奢侈的習慣。**~·ly** *adv*

lux·ury /ˈlʌkʃərɪ ; ˈlʌkʃərɪ/ *n* (*pl* -ries) **1** [U] state of life in which, to an excessive degree, one has and uses things that please the senses (good food and drink, clothes, comfort, beautiful surroundings): 奢侈;豪華;奢華: *live in ~;* 過奢侈的生活; *a life of ~.* 奢侈的生活。 **2** (attrib use) enabling people to live this kind of life: (形容用法)豪華的: *a ~ hotel/ocean liner* (perhaps suggesting ostentation rather than real comfort, etc. ⇨ luxurious). 豪華旅社(海輪)(此處可能表示裝飾華美而非實際舒適等)。 **3** [C] sth not essential but which gives enjoyment and pleasure, esp sth expensive, out of season, etc: 奢侈品: *His salary is low and he gets few luxuries.* 他的薪水微薄,所以很少買奢侈品。

lycée /ˈliːseɪ *US:* liːˈseɪ ; ˌliˈse/ *n* state secondary school in France. 法國公立中等學校。

ly·ceum /laɪˈsiːəm ; laɪˈsiəm/ *n* (US) lecture hall; (building of an) association for organizing lectures, concerts, etc. (美)演講廳;舉行學術演講或音樂會等之社團;此種社團之建築物;學園;文苑。

ly·chee (also **li·chee, li·tchee, li·tchi**) /ˈlaɪtʃiː ; ˈlitʃi/ *n* fruit-tree, originally from China, widely grown in Bengal; its fruit consisting of a thin brown shell containing a white pulp round a single seed. 荔枝;荔枝樹。⇨ the illus at fruit. 參看 fruit 之插圖。

lych·gate *n* = lichgate.

lye /laɪ ; laɪ/ *n* alkali obtained by passing water through wood ashes, used in washing; any alkaline solution or detergent. 從木灰中濾出的鹼水(供洗滌用);灰汁;任何鹼水或清潔劑。

ly·ing /ˈlaɪɪŋ ; ˈlaɪɪŋ/ *pres p* of lie¹, lie².

lymph /lɪmf ; lɪmf/ *n* [U] colourless fluid in animal matter, like blood but without colouring matter. 淋巴;淋巴液。 **lym·phatic** /lɪmˈfætɪk ; lɪmˈfætɪk/ *adj* **1** of or carrying ~: 淋巴的;輸送淋巴的: *the ~atic vessels,* carrying ~ from the tissues with any waste matter. 淋巴管。 **2** (of persons) sluggish; slow in thought and action. (指人)遲鈍的;思想和行動緩慢的。

lynch /lɪntʃ ; lɪntʃ/ *vt* [VP6A] put to death (usu by hanging) without a lawful trial (sb believed to be guilty of crime). 不經合法審判而將(被認爲有罪之人)處死(通常用絞刑);施私刑。 □ *n* ˈ~ **law,** procedure of persons who executed a (supposed) criminal in this way. 私刑。

lynch·pin /ˈlɪntʃpɪn ; ˈlɪntʃpɪn/ = linchpin.

lynx /lɪŋks ; lɪŋks/ *n* short-tailed wild animal of the cat family, noted for its keen sight. 林狓;大山貓(一種短尾的貓科野獸,視力銳利)。⇨ the illus at cat. 參看 cat 之插圖。Hence, 由此產生, ˌ~-ˈ**eyed** *adj* keen-sighted. 眼光銳利的。

lyre /ˈlaɪə(r) ; laɪr/ *n* kind of harp with strings fixed in a U-shaped frame, used by the ancient Greeks. (古希臘人的)一種七弦琴;抱琴。 ˈ**~-bird** *n* Australian bird, the male having a long tail, shaped like a ~ when spread out. 澳洲產的琴鳥(雄者生有長尾,開展時狀似七弦琴)。

lyric /ˈlɪrɪk ; ˈlɪrɪk/ *adj* **1** of, composed for, singing. 吟唱的;供吟唱的。 **2** of poetry expressing direct personal feeling. 抒情詩的。 □ *n* [C] ~ poem; (*pl*) verses of a song, eg in a musical play. 抒情詩;(複)抒情的韻文(例如音樂劇中者)。

lyri·cal /ˈlɪrɪkl ; ˈlɪrɪkḷ/ *adj* **1** = lyric. **2** full of emotion; enthusiastic: 充滿感情的;熱情的: *She became/waxed quite ~ over the new dresses she had brought back from Paris.* 她從巴黎帶回來的新衣使她顯得興高采烈。 **~ly** /-klɪ ; -klɪ/ *adv*

ly·sol /ˈlaɪsɒl *US:* -sɔːl ; ˈlaɪsɑl/ *n* [U] (P) dark oily, liquid used as an antiseptic and disinfectant. (商標)來沙爾(防腐及消毒用的一種黑色油質藥水)。

Mm

M, m /em ; ɛm/ (*pl* M's, m's /emz ; ɛmz/) the 13th letter of the English alphabet; symbol for the Roman numeral 1000. 英文字母的第十三個字母;羅馬數字的 1000。⇨ App 4. 參看附錄四。

ma /mɑː ; mɑ/ *n* (colloq, abbr of) mamma. (俗)爲 mamma 之略。

ma'am /mæm ; mæm/ *n* madam, used in addressing a Queen. 對女王或皇后之尊稱。

mac /mæk ; mæk/ *n* (GB colloq, abbr of) mackintosh. (英俗)爲 mackintosh 之略。

ma·cabre /məˈkɑːbrə ; məˈkɑbrə/ *adj* gruesome; suggesting death. 可怕的;可怖的;表示死亡的。 **danse** /dɑːns ; dɑ̃s/ ~ *n* (F) dance of death. (法)死之舞;骷髏舞。

ma·cadam /məˈkædəm ; məˈkædəm/ *n* [U] ~ **road,** road with a surface of several layers of crushed rock or stone, each rolled hard before the next is put down. 碎石路(由幾層碎石壓成的道路)。**~·ize** /-aɪz ; -aɪz/ *vt* make or cover with such layers: 鋪以碎石;用碎石鋪成: *~ized roads.* 鋪碎石的道路。⇨ tarmac.

maca·roni /ˌmækəˈrəʊnɪ ; ˌmækəˈronɪ/ *n* [U] flour

paste made in the form of long tubes (often chopped into short pieces), prepared for eating by being boiled. 通心粉;通心麵。

ma·ca·roon /ˌmækəˈruːn ; ˌmækəˈrun/ *n* [C] small, hard, flat, sweet cake or biscuit made of sugar, white of egg, and crushed almonds or coconut. 蛋白杏仁餅或椰子餅(由糖、蛋白和杏仁或椰子粉製成的一種小甜餅或餅乾)。

ma·caw /məˈkɔː ; məˈkɔ/ *n* large, long-tailed parrot of tropical America. 鸚鵡(熱帶美洲產的一種長尾大鸚鵡);金剛鸚鵡。

mace¹ /meɪs ; mes/ *n* **1** large, heavy club, usu with a metal head covered with spikes, used as a weapon in the Middle Ages. 中古時代用作武器的一種釘頭鎚;鎚矛。 **2** ceremonial rod or staff (often very much ornamented) carried or placed before an official, eg a Mayor. 權杖(通常裝飾得很精美,持於或置於官員,如市長之前)。 **ˈ~-bearer** *n* person who carries an official ~. 持權杖的人。

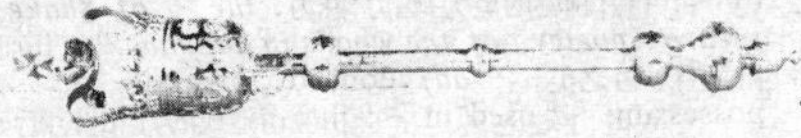

a ceremonial mace

mace² /meɪs ; mes/ *n* [U] dried outer covering of nutmegs, used as spice. 作香料用的乾荳蔻皮;荳蔻香料。

mac·er·ate /ˈmæsəreɪt ; ˈmæsəˌret/ *vt, vi* [VP6A, 2A] make or become soft by soaking in water or caustic potash. (在水或苛性鉀中)浸軟。

Mach /mɑːk ; mɑk/ *n* **ˈ~ number,** ratio of the air speed of an aircraft to the speed of sound: 馬赫值(飛行速度與音速之比例值): ~ *two,* twice the speed of sound. 二倍於音速。

ma·chete /məˈtʃetɪ *US:* -ˈʃetɪ ; mɑˈtʃete/ *n* cutlass (2); broad, heavy knife used in Latin America and the W Indies as a cutting tool and weapon. 種植可可及乾椰子者所用的大刀; 拉丁美洲和西印度群島人當作工具和武器的大刀。

mach·ia·vel·lian /ˌmækɪəˈvelɪən ; ˌmækɪəˈvɛlɪən/ *adj* showing or having no scruples in gaining what is wanted; of or like the ideas set out by Machiavelli, Italian statesman, who advocated putting expediency above political morality and the use of deceit in statecraft. 無所顧忌以求取得所想得到之物的;運用權術的;義大利政治家馬基維利所主張之權術觀念的;爲政治目的而不擇手段的。

machi·na·tion /ˌmækɪˈneɪʃn ; ˌmækəˈneʃən/ *n* [C, U] (esp evil) plot/plotting; scheme/scheming. 詭計或陰謀;圖謀不軌;設陰謀。

ma·chine /məˈʃiːn ; məˈʃin/ *n* [C] **1** appliance or mechanical device with parts working together to apply power, often steam or electric power (*a ˈprinting-~*), but also human power (*a ˈsewing-~*). 機器;機械(通常由蒸汽或電力推動,如印刷機等,亦有由人力推動者,如縫紉機等)。*We live in the ~ age,* the age in which ~s more and more replace hand labour. 我們生活於機器的時代(在這時代裏,機器越來越代替了人力)。 **ˈ~-gun** *n* gun that fires continuously while the trigger is pressed. 機關槍;機槍。 **ˌ~-ˈmade** *adj* made by ~ (contrasted with *handmade*). 機器製的(與hand-made相對)。 **ˈ~ tool,** tool, mechanically operated, for cutting or shaping materials. 機械用具;工作母機。 **2** persons organized to control a group: 操縱集團的核心組織: (US) (美) *the Democratic ~.* 民主黨核心人物。 □ *vt* [VP6A] operate on, make (sth) with, a ~ (esp of sewing and printing). 用機器製造(尤指用縫紉機和印刷機)。 **ma·chin·ist** /məˈʃiːnɪst ; məˈʃinɪst/ *n* one who makes, repairs or controls ~ tools; one who works a ~, esp a sewing-~. 製造機器的人;修理機器的人; 管理機器的人; 機械師; 機械工人; 操作機器的人(尤指使用縫紉機者)。

ma·chin·ery /məˈʃiːnərɪ ; məˈʃinərɪ/ *n* [U] **1** moving parts of a machine; machines collectively: 機器的轉動的部分;機械;機器(集合稱): *How much new ~ has been installed?* 安裝了多少新機器? (Cf 參較 *How many new machines have been installed?* 安裝了多少部新機器?) **2** methods, organization (eg of government). 方法;組織;機構(例如政府的)。

ma·chismo /məˈtʃɪzməʊ ; mɑˈtʃizmo/ *n* [U] exaggerated male pride; man's need to prove his virility. 誇張的男子氣概;證明男子氣概的需要。

mack·erel /ˈmækrəl ; ˈmækərəl/ *n* (*pl* unchanged) striped seafish used as food. (複數不變)鯖魚(亦稱青花魚)。 ~ **sky** *n* sky with bars of cloud like the stripes on a ~'s back. 鯖天(雲層似鯖魚鱗之天空)。

mack·in·tosh /ˈmækɪntɒʃ ; ˈmækɪnˌtɑʃ/ *n* (GB) rainproof coat made of cloth treated with rubber. (英)雨衣(橡皮布製成的)。

mac·ro·biotic /ˌmækrəʊbaɪˈɒtɪk ; ˌmækrobaɪˈɑtɪk/ *adj* prolonging life. 延長壽命的。 ~ **food,** containing pure vegetable substances grown and prepared without chemical assistance. 延長壽命的食物(生長與調製過程均不藉化學助力的純淨蔬菜)。

mac·ro·cosm /ˈmækrəʊkɒzəm ; ˈmækrəˌkɑzəm/ *n* the universe; any great whole. 宇宙;任何大而完整的實體。 ⇨ microcosm.

mad /mæd ; mæd/ *adj* (-dder, -ddest) **1** having, resulting from, a diseased mind; mentally ill. 瘋狂的;由於瘋狂的;精神錯亂的。 ***drive/send sb mad,*** cause him to be mad. 逼人發狂。 ***as mad as a March hare/as a hatter,*** very mad. 非常瘋狂。 **ˈmad·house** *n* (colloq) mental hospital. (俗)瘋人院。 **ˈmad·man** /-mən ; -ˌmæn/, **ˈmad·woman** *nn* person who is mad. 瘋人;瘋子;狂人。 **2** (colloq) much excited; filled with enthusiasm: (俗)非常激動的;充滿熱情的: *mad about pop music;* 對流行歌曲著迷; (esp US) angry: (尤用於美國)憤怒的: *mad about/at missing the train;* 未趕上火車氣得要命; wild: 激動的;狂亂的: *mad with pain.* 痛得發狂。*The dog was mad for water,* behaving wildly because it needed water; 這狗渴得要命; foolish: 愚蠢的: *What a mad thing to do!* 多麼愚蠢的一件事! ***be/go mad,*** be/become wildly excited, angry, upset, etc. 極爲激動、憤怒、不安等。 ***like mad,*** (colloq) with great energy; much: (俗)拚命地;猛烈地: *work/run/smoke like mad.* 拚命工作(奔跑,吸煙)。 **ˈmad-cap** /-kæp ; -ˌkæp/ *n* person acting recklessly or on impulse. 行動鹵莽的人; 做事衝動的人。 **3** (of a dog, etc) rabid. (指狗等)患狂犬病的;瘋的。 **mad·ly** *adv* in a mad manner; (colloq) extremely: 瘋狂地;(俗)極其: *madly excited/jealous.* 極其激動(嫉妒)。 **mad·ness** *n* [U] the state of being mad; mad behaviour: 瘋狂; 瘋狂的行爲: *It would be madness to try to climb the mountain in such a snowstorm.* 想在這樣大的暴風雪中去爬山簡直是瘋狂。 **mad·den** /ˈmædn ; ˈmædn̩/ *vt* [VP6A] make mad; irritate; annoy: 使瘋狂;激怒;使苦惱: *maddening delays.* 令人生氣的延誤。

madam /ˈmædəm ; ˈmædəm/ *n* **1** respectful form of address to a woman (whether married or unmarried): 夫人;女士(對婦女的尊稱): *Can I help you, ~?* (eg asked by a shop assistant); 我能爲妳效勞嗎,夫人? (例如店員所問); used in letters, as *Sir* is used to a man: 用於信件中,如對男人稱 Sir 一樣: *Dear M~.* 夫人(女士)臺鑒。 **2** (colloq) woman or girl who likes to order people about: (俗)喜歡指使他人的婦女: *She's a bit of a ~.* 她有點兒喜歡指使別人。*Isn't she a little ~!* 她不是個很喜歡指使旁人的女孩嗎! **3** (colloq) woman who manages a brothel. (俗)妓院女老板;鴇母。

Mad·ame /məˈdɑːm *US:* məˈdæm ; ˈmædəm/ *n* (abbr 略作 **Mme**) (*pl* Mesdames /meɪˈdɑːm ; meˈdɑm/) French title before the name of a married woman; also used before names of married women who are not British or American. 夫人(法國對已婚婦女之尊稱,置於姓名之前;亦用於非英美已婚婦女之姓名前)。

mad·der /ˈmædə(r) ; ˈmædɚ/ *n* [U] (red dye obtained from the root of a) herbaceous climbing

M

plant with yellowish flowers. 茜草(開黃花的一種草本攀緣植物)；茜草根製成的紅色染料。

made /meɪd ; med/ *pt, pp* of make¹.

Ma·deira /məˈdɪərə ; məˈdɪrə/ *n* white dessert wine from ~ (an island in the Atlantic Ocean). (大西洋 Madeira 島出產的)一種白葡萄酒。**ˈ~ cake** *n* kind of sponge-cake. 一種鬆軟蛋糕。

Mad·emoi·selle /ˌmædmwəˈzel ; ˌmædəməˈzɛl/ *n* (abbr 略作 **Mlle**) (*pl* Mesdemoiselles /ˌmeɪdmwəˈzel ; ˌmedəməˈzɛl/) French title used before the name of a young girl or an unmarried woman. 小姐(用於未婚女子姓名前之法語稱呼)。

Ma·donna /məˈdɒnə ; məˈdɑnə/ *n* **the ~,** (picture or statue of) Mary, Mother of Jesus Christ. 聖母(耶穌基督的母親)馬利亞(的畫像或影像)。**ˈ~ lily,** kind of pure white lily (as often shown in pictures of the ~). 白百合花(純白色,如常見於聖母像中者)。

mad·ri·gal /ˈmædrɪgl ; ˈmædrɪgl/ *n* part-song for several voices without instrumental accompaniment. 牧歌(一種無伴奏的多聲部歌謠)。

mael·strom /ˈmeɪlstrəm ; ˈmelstrəm/ *n* great whirlpool; (fig) violent or destructive force; whirl of events: 大漩渦;(喻)暴烈的或破壞性的力量;大動亂: *the ~ of war.* 戰爭的動亂。

mae·nad /ˈmiːnæd ; ˈminæd/ *n* priestess of Bacchus, the Greek god of wine; frenzied woman. 希臘酒神巴克斯的女祭司;狂亂的女人。

maes·tro /ˈmaɪstrəʊ ; ˈmaɪstro/ *n* (*pl* ~s or maestri /ˈmaɪstrɪ ; ˈmaɪstrɪ/) (I) eminent musical composer, teacher, or conductor. (義)著名的作曲家、音樂教師或指揮家;大師。

maf·fick /ˈmæfɪk ; ˈmæfɪk/ *vi* go in for wild public merry-making and rejoicing (eg in war, when there is news of a victory). 狂歡慶祝(如戰時獲悉勝利的消息時)。

Ma·fia /ˈmæfɪə *US:* ˈmɑːf- ; ˈmɑfiə/ *n* **the ~,** secret organization in Sicily, opposed to legal authority and engaged in crime; similar organization on the mainland of Italy and in US. 黑手黨(西西里島人的祕密組織,反對合法的當局,並從事犯罪行爲);義大利本土及美國類似的祕密組織。

mag /mæg ; mæg/ *n* (colloq abbr of) magazine(3): (俗)爲 magazine 之略: *the colour mags.* 彩色雜誌。

maga·zine /ˌmægəˈziːn *US:* ˈmægəziːn ; ˌmægəˈzin/ *n* **1** store for arms, ammunition, explosives, etc. 武器、彈藥、炸藥等的倉庫;軍火庫。 **2** chamber for holding cartridges to be fed into the breech of a rifle or gun; place for rolls or cartridges of film in a camera. (槍的)子彈鋏;彈倉;(照相機內的)軟片盒。⇨ the illus at rifle. 參看 rifle 之插圖。 **3** paper-covered (usu weekly or monthly, and illustrated) periodical, with stories, articles, etc by various writers. 雜誌(通常爲週刊或月刊,有插圖)。

ma·genta /məˈdʒentə ; məˈdʒɛntə/ *adj, n* bright crimson (substance used as a dye). 洋紅色(的);洋紅色染料。

mag·got /ˈmægət ; ˈmægət/ *n* larva or grub, esp of a kind of fly (the bluebottle) that lays its eggs in meat, and of the cheese-fly. 蛆;蠅的幼蟲。***have a ˈ~ in one's head,*** have a strange whim or fancy. 想入非非。**~y** *adj* having ~s: 有蛆的: *~y cheese.* 生蛆的乾酪。

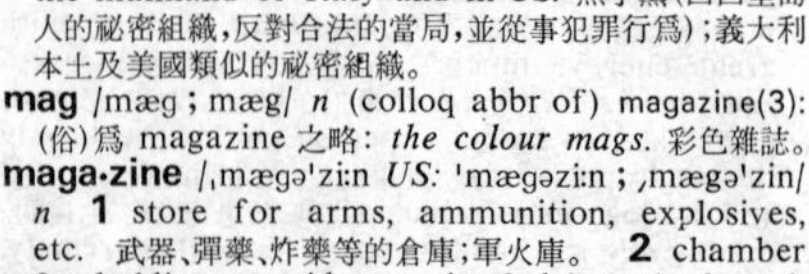

a maggot

Magi /ˈmeɪdʒaɪ ; ˈmedʒaɪ/ *n pl* **the M~,** the three wise men from the East who brought offerings to the infant Jesus. 由東方來朝見初生的耶穌的三個賢人(俗稱三博士)。⇨ Matt 2: 1. 參看新約聖經馬太福音第2章第1節。

magic /ˈmædʒɪk ; ˈmædʒɪk/ *n* [U] **1** art of controlling events by the pretended use of supernatural forces; witchcraft; primitive superstitious practices based on a belief in supernatural agencies. 魔法;巫術;基於相信超自然的力量之原始迷信行爲。***like ~; as if by ~,*** in a mysterious manner. 像藉魔法般地;不可思議地。**black/white ~,** ~ done with/without the help of devils. 藉(不藉)助於惡魔的巫術。 **2** art of obtaining mysterious results by tricks: 魔術;戲法: *The conjurer used ~ to produce a rabbit from his hat.* 魔術家用戲法從帽子裏變出一隻兔子。 **3** the identification of a symbol with the thing it stands for, as when the wearing of a lion's skin is thought to give the wearer a lion's courage. 將一標誌與其所代表的事物視爲同一(例如穿獅皮被認爲使穿者有獅子的勇氣)。 **4** (fig) mysterious charm; quality produced as if by ~: (喻)神祕的魔力;媚力;魅力: *the ~ of Shakespeare's poetry/of the woods in autumn.* 莎士比亞詩章(秋林)之美。□ *adj* done by, or as if by, ~; possessing ~; used in ~: 由魔術造成的;似出於魔術的;有魔力的;用於魔術的: *~ arts/words;* 魔術的技藝(魔術用語;具有魔力的言語); *a ~ touch.* 魔術的手法。**~ eye,** (colloq) name used for various electronic devices which control or indicate sth, eg the automatic opening and closing of doors, exact tuning of a radio set. (俗)魔眼;電眼(各種用以控制或指示之電子儀器,例如用於自動門之開關,收音機之精確調整者)。**~ lantern,** apparatus (now a toy) for throwing a magnified image of a picture, etc from a glass slide on to a white screen (*projector* is the name of the modern apparatus). 幻燈(現已用做玩具,現代幻燈稱爲 projector)。⇨ the illus at lantern. 參看 lantern 之插圖。**~ square,** large square divided into smaller squares, each with a number, so that the sum of each row, vertical, horizontal or diagonal is always the same 魔術方格(將一大方格分成若干小方格,每格上面均有數字,每行、每列或對角線上各數之和均相等)。**magi·cal** /-kl ; -kl/ *adj* of or like ~; (colloq) charming: 魔術的;似魔術的;不可思議的;(俗)迷人的: *a ~al stage set.* 迷人的舞臺佈景。 **magi·cally** /-klɪ ; -klɪ/ *adv* **ma·gician** /məˈdʒɪʃn ; məˈdʒɪʃən/ *n* person skilled in ~(2); wizard. 精於變戲法的人;魔術家;術士。

magis·terial /ˌmædʒɪˈstɪərɪəl ; ˌmædʒɪsˈtɪrɪəl/ *adj* of, conducted by, a magistrate; having or showing authority: 地方法官的;由地方法官辦的;有權威的;威風的: *~ rank;* 官吏的身份; *a ~ manner/opinion.* 威嚴的態度(權威的意見)。**~ly** /-ɪəlɪ ; -ɪəlɪ/ *adv*

magis·trate /ˈmædʒɪstreɪt ; ˈmædʒɪsˌtret/ *n* civil officer acting as a judge in the lowest courts; Justice of the Peace. 在地方法庭當法官的文官;地方官吏;地方法官;治安推事。**magis·tracy** /ˈmædʒɪstrəsɪ ; ˈmædʒɪstrəsɪ/ *n* (*pl* -cies) position of a ~. 地方法官或官吏的職位。**the magis·tracy,** ~s collectively. 地方法官或官吏的總稱。

mag·nani·mous /mægˈnænɪməs ; mægˈnænəməs/ *adj* having, showing, generosity. 寬宏大量的;慷慨的。**~·ly** *adv* **mag·na·nim·ity** /ˌmægnəˈnɪmətɪ ; ˌmægnəˈnɪmətɪ/ *n* [U] being ~; [C] (*pl* -ties) ~ act, etc. 寬宏大量;雅量;寬宏大量的行爲。

mag·nate /ˈmægneɪt ; ˈmægnet/ *n* wealthy leading man of business or industry; person who has power through wealth or position: 工商界大亨;工商界巨頭;因財富或地位而有權力的人物: *territorial ~s,* influential landowners. 大地主。

mag·nesia /mægˈniːʃə ; mægˈniʃə/ *n* [U] white, tasteless powder (carbonate of magnesium, **MgO**) used medicinally and in industry. 苦土;鎂氧(醫藥和工業用的一種無味的白色粉狀碳酸鎂,分子式爲 MgO)。

mag·nesium /mægˈniːzɪəm ; mægˈniʃɪəm/ *n* [U] silver-white metal (symbol **Mg**) used in the manufacture of aluminium and other alloys, fireworks and flash photography: 鎂(銀白色金屬元素,符號爲 Mg,用於製造鋁,其他合金及煙火,亦用於鎂光燈攝影): ~ *light*, bright light obtained by burning ~ wire. 鎂光(燃燒鎂線而發的亮光)。

mag·net /ˈmægnɪt ; ˈmægnɪt/ *n* [C] **1** piece of iron, often a horseshoe shape, able to attract iron, either natural (as in lodestone) or by means of an electric current. 磁鐵;磁石。 **2** (fig) person or thing that attracts. (喻)有吸引力的人或物。 **~·ic** /mægˈnetɪk ; mægˈnɛtɪk/ *adj* **1** having the properties of a ~; able to attract, etc: 有磁性的;能吸引的: *~ic field*, area in all parts of which a ~ic force may be detected; 磁場; *a ~ic mine*, submarine mine that is detonated when a large mass of iron (eg a ship) approaches it; 磁性水雷; *a ~ic needle*, one that points north and south; (指向南北的)磁針;指南針; *the ~ic north*, the point indicated by such a needle; 磁針所指之北;磁北; *a ~ic smile/personality*, attracting the attention of people. 吸引人的微笑(性格)。 **~ic tape**, kind of tape coated with iron oxide used for recording sound and vision. (錄音及錄影用)磁帶;錄音帶;錄影帶。 **2** of magnetism. 磁力學的;磁的。 **mag·neti·cally** /-klɪ ; -klɪ/ *adv*

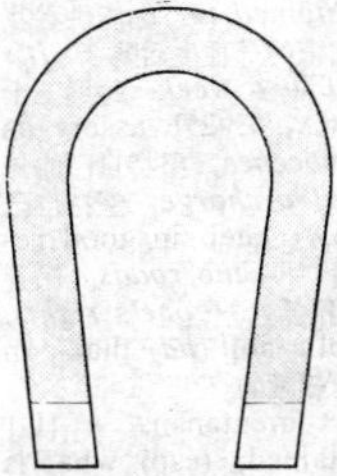

a magnet

a magnifying glass

mag·net·ism /ˈmægnɪtɪzəm ; ˈmægnəˌtɪzəm/ *n* [U] (the science of) magnetic phenomena and properties; (fig) personal charm and attraction. 磁的現象和性質;磁力現象;磁性;磁力學;磁學;(喻)人的魅力和吸引力。

mag·net·ize /ˈmægnɪtaɪz ; ˈmægnəˌtaɪz/ *vt* [VP6A] give magnetic properties to; (fig) attract as a magnet does, eg by personal charm, moral or intellectual power. 使生磁性;使有磁力;磁化;(喻)吸引(例如以外表魅力、品行或智慧力量等)。

mag·neto /mægˈniːtəʊ ; mægˈnito/ *n* (*pl* -tos /-təʊz ; -toz/) electric apparatus for producing sparks in the ignition system of an internal combustion engine. (內燃機內用以發生火花的)小型磁石發電機;久磁電機。

Mag·nifi·cat /mægˈnɪfɪkæt ; mægˈnɪfɪˌkæt/ *n* song of the Virgin Mary in Luke 1: 46—55. 馬利亞的讚美詩(指新約聖經路加福音第1章46到55節中,聖母馬利亞對上主的歌讚)。

mag·nifi·cent /mægˈnɪfɪsnt ; mægˈnɪfəsn̩t/ *adj* splendid; remarkable; important-looking: 壯麗的;不凡的;堂皇的;莊嚴的;看起來很了不起的: *a ~ house*; 華麗的房子; *his ~ generosity*. 他的了不起的寬宏大量。 **~·ly** *adv* **mag·nifi·cence** /-sns ; -sn̩s/ *n* [U].

mag·nify /ˈmægnɪfaɪ ; ˈmægnəˌfaɪ/ *vt* (*pt, pp* -fied) [VP6A] **1** make (sth) appear larger (as with a lens or microscope): 放大;擴大: *a ˈ~ing glass*, lens for this purpose. 放大鏡。 **2** exaggerate: 誇大: *~ dangers*. 誇大危險。 **3** extol; give praise to (God): 誇獎;讚美(上帝): *~ the Lord*. 讚美上帝。 **mag·ni·fier** /-faɪə(r) ; -ˌfaɪə/ *n* instrument, etc, that magnifies. 放大器;放大鏡。 **mag·ni·fi·ca·tion** /ˌmægnɪfɪˈkeɪʃn ; ˌmægnəfəˈkeʃən/ *n* (esp) power of ~ing, eg of a lens, a pair of binoculars. 放大;(尤指)放大率;倍率(如透鏡、雙眼望遠鏡等者)。

mag·nil·oquent /mægˈnɪləkwənt ; mægˈnɪləkwənt/ *adj* (of words, speech) pompous; (of a person) using pompous or high-sounding words. (指文字、言詞)誇大的;(指人)使用誇大的言詞的。**~·ly** *adv* **mag·nil·oquence** /-əns ; -əns/ *n*

mag·ni·tude /ˈmægnɪtjuːd *US:* -tuːd ; ˈmægnəˌtjud/ *n* [U] size; (degree of) importance; comparative brightness of stars. 大小;積;量;重要(的程度);星的光度。

mag·no·lia /mægˈnəʊlɪə ; mægˈnolɪə/ *n* tree with large, sweet-smelling wax-like flowers. 木蘭;木蓮。

mag·num /ˈmægnəm ; ˈmægnəm/ *n* (bottle containing) two quarts (of wine or spirit). 兩夸爾(酒或酒精);裝兩夸爾之瓶。

mag·pie /ˈmægpaɪ ; ˈmægˌpaɪ/ *n* noisy black-and-white bird which is attracted by, and often takes away, small, bright objects; (fig) person who chatters very much; (fig) petty thief. 鵲;(喻)多話的人;(喻)小偷。

Mag·yar /ˈmægjɑː(r) ; ˈmægjɑr/ *n, adj* (member, language) of the largest group of people in Hungary. 馬扎兒人(匈牙利的主要民族);馬扎兒語;馬扎兒人的。

Ma·ha·ra·ja(h) /ˌmɑːhəˈrɑːdʒə ; ˌmɑhəˈrɑdʒə/ *n* title of a prince in India, esp a sovereign ruler of one of the indigenous states. 印度某些君主的稱呼;大君。**Ma·ha·ra·nee** /ˌmɑːhəˈrɑːniː ; ˌmɑhəˈrɑni/ *n* wife of a ~; queen or princess with a position like that of a ~. 大君的妻子;女大君。

Ma·hatma /məˈhætmə ; məˈhætmə/ *n* (in India, etc) (title given to) one of a class of persons revered as having great high-mindedness and love of humanity. (印度等地)哲人;偉人;聖賢;聖雄(對某些智慧超群、愛心廣被之人的尊稱)。

mah·jong /ˌmɑːˈdʒɒŋ ; mɑˈdʒɔŋ/ *n* Chinese game for four persons played with 136 (or 144) pieces or tiles of wood, bone or ivory. 麻將(四個人玩的一種中國牌戲,共有136或144塊木、骨或象牙製的牌)。

ma·hog·any /məˈhɒgənɪ ; məˈhɑgənɪ/ *n* (tropical tree with) dark-brown wood much used for furniture. (做傢具用的)桃花心木;紅木;紅木樹(一種熱帶樹)。

maid /meɪd ; med/ *n* **1** (liter) girl. (文)少女。 **2** (old use) young, unmarried woman. (舊用法)年輕未婚女子。**old ~**, elderly woman who is considered unlikely to marry. 年老未婚女人;老處女。 **ˌ~ of ˈhonour**, **(a)** unmarried woman attending a queen or princess. 侍候皇后或公主的未婚女子;宮女。 **(b)** principal bridesmaid. 主要女儐相。 **3** (usu modern sense) woman servant: (通常爲現代含義)女佣人;女僕: *It's the ~'s day off;* 女佣人今天休假; (in compounds): (用於複合字): *ˈ~servant*, 女僕, *ˈhouse~*, 女管家;女佣人, *ˈnurse~*. 保姆。

maiden /ˈmeɪdn ; ˈmedn̩/ *n* (liter) girl; young unmarried woman. (文)少女;年輕未婚女子;處女。□ *adj* (attrib only) (僅作形容用法) **1** of a girl or woman. 少女的;女子的。 **ˈ~ name**, family name before marriage. 婚前姓氏。 **2** first or earliest: 首次的;初次的: *a ship's ~ voyage*. 船的處女航。**~ speech**, first speech in Parliament of a new member. (新議員在國會中發表的)首次演說。 **3 ~ (over)**, (cricket) one in which no runs are scored. (板球)未得分的投球。 **4** (of a woman) unmarried: (指女子)未婚的: *my ~ aunt*. 我未婚的姑姑(阿姨)。 **5** (compounds) (複合字) **ˈ~·hair** *n* (kinds of) fern with fine stalks and delicate fronds. 過壇龍;孔雀草(數種生細莖嫩葉的羊齒植物名)。 **ˈ~·head** /-hed ; -ˌhɛd/ *n* [U] the hymen; virginity. 處女膜;童貞。 **ˈ~·hood** /-hʊd ; -ˌhʊd/ *n* state of being a ~, period when one is a ~. 處女身分;少女時代。**ˈ~·like, ~·ly** *adjj* gentle; modest; of or like a ~. 文雅的;溫順的;少女的;像少女的。

mail¹ /meɪl ; mel/ *n* [U] body armour of metal rings or plates: 鎧甲: *a coat of ~;* 鎧甲; *ˈchain-~*. 鎖子甲。 **~ed** *adj* only in 僅用於 ***the ~ed fist***, (threat of) armed force. 武力(的威嚇)。

M

mail² /meɪl ; mel/ *n* **1** [U] government system of collecting, carrying and delivering letters and parcels: 郵政: *send a letter by air~;* 寄一封航空信; *the* '*~-coach,* (formerly) horse-drawn stage-coach for carrying ~. (昔時)郵件馬車;郵車。'**~-bag** *n* stout bag in which ~ is carried. 郵袋。'**~-boat** *n* one that transports ~. 郵件船。'**~-box** *n* (US) letter-box. (美)郵筒;信箱。'**~-man** /-mæn ; -ˌmæn/ *n* (*pl* -men) (US) postman. (美)郵差。ˌ~ '**order** *n* order for goods to be delivered by post; 郵購訂貨單;郵購; *a ~-order business,* one in which the buying and selling of goods is conducted by correspondence; 郵購業務; 函購商業; *a ~-order catalogue,* one with a price-list of goods. 郵購貨物價目單。'**~-train** *n* train that carries ~. 郵件火車。 **2** [C, U] letters, parcels, etc, sent or delivered by post; the letters, etc, sent, collected or delivered at one time: 信件;郵件;郵寄的包裹;某一時間內所投寄、收取或送遞的郵件: *Is there any ~ this morning?* 今早有郵件嗎? *I had a lot of ~ last week.* 上星期我收到好多信。*My secretary usually opens the ~.* 我的祕書通常爲我開啓信件。*The ship sank and the ~s were lost.* 船沉沒,郵件全遺失了。 □ *vt* [VP6A] (chiefly US; in GB *post* is more usu) send by ~. (主美,英國多用 post)郵寄。'**~ing-card,** (US) postcard. (美)明信片。'**~ing-list** *n* list of names of persons to whom sth, eg announcements of new books from a publisher, is regularly sent: 收郵件人的名單;郵寄名單(例如出版商經常將新書廣告寄給的某些人): *Please add my name to your ~ing-list.* 請將本人姓名列入貴處之郵寄名單內。

maim /meɪm ; mem/ *vt* [VP6A] wound or injure so that some part of the body is useless: 使殘廢;使受重傷: *He was seriously ~ed in the war.* 他在戰爭中重傷成殘。

main¹ /meɪn ; men/ *adj* (attrib only; no comp or superl) (僅作形容用法;無比較級或最高級) **1** chief; most important: 主要的; 最重要的: *the ~ thing to remember;* 所要記的主要東西; *the ~ street of a town;* 市內的主要街道; *the ~ line of a railway;* 鐵道的幹線; *the ~ point of my argument;* 我的議論的要點; *the ~ current/stream of traffic;* 交通的主線; *the ~ course of a meal.* 一餐的主菜。'**have an eye to the ~ chance,** ➪ chance¹(3). **2** exerted to the full. 盡全力的。**do sth by ~ force,** using one's strength to the utmost. 盡最大力量做某事。 **3** (compounds) (複合字) '**~ deck** *n* upper deck. 上層甲板;主甲板。'**~-land** /-lænd ; -ˌlænd/ *n* country, continent or land mass, without its islands. 大陸。'**~-mast** *n* principal mast of a sailing-ship. 帆船的主桅。'**~-spring** *n* **(a)** principal spring of a clock or watch. 鐘錶的主發條。**(b)** (fig) driving force or motive. (喻)推動的力量或動機。'**~-stay** /-steɪ ; -ˌste/ *n* rope from the top of the ~mast to the bottom of the foremast; (fig) chief support. 從主桅頂至前桅底的支索; 大桅支索; (喻)主要的支持。'**~-stream** *n* **1** dominant trend, tendency, etc: (潮流、傾向等之)主流: *the ~stream of political thought.* 政治思想的主流。 **2** style of jazz between traditional and modern. 傳統與現代爵士樂間之爵士樂。 **~-ly** *adv* chiefly; for the most part: 主要地; 大部分: *The people in the streets were ~ly tourists.* 街上的人大部分是遊客。*You are ~ly to blame.* 你應負大部分責任(應該受責備的是你)。

M

main² /meɪn ; men/ *n* **1** [C] (often 常作 **the ~s**) principal pipe bringing water or gas, principal wire transmitting electric current, from the source of supply into a building (contrasted with pipes from a cistern inside the building, etc); principal sewer to which pipes from a building are connected: (自來水、煤氣、電流、下水道等的)總管; 總線; 幹管; 幹線(以別於建築物內的支線): *My new house is not yet connected to the ~s.* 我的新房子(的水電)還沒有接上幹線。*We take our electric current from the ~s.* 我們從總電線接上電流。'**~s set,** radio set to be connected to the ~s for current, not a battery set. 用總線電流的收音機(不用電池的)。 **2 in the ~,** for the most part; on the whole. 大體上; 從全體看來; 就一般而論。 **3 with might and ~,** ➪ might². **4** (poet) sea, esp a wide expanse of sea. (詩)海; (尤指) 大海; 滄海。 **5 the Spanish M~,** that part of the NE coast of S America and the adjoining part of the Caribbean Sea, visited by the early Spanish navigators. 拉丁美洲大陸(指早年西班牙航海者所到達的南美洲東北海岸以及鄰近的加勒比海部分海面)。

main·tain /meɪnˈteɪn ; menˈten/ *vt* **1** [VP6A] keep up; retain; continue: 保持;維持;繼續: *~ friendly relations (with...);* (與…)保持友好關係; *~ prices,* keep them steady; 保持物價的平穩; *~ law and order,* 維持治安; *~ a speed of 60 miles an hour.* 保持一小時六十哩的速度。*The improvement in his health is being ~ed.* 他的健康仍然繼續在進步中。**~ an open mind on sth,** be ready to listen to and consider the views of others on a subject. 願意聽取他人對某事的意見。 **2** [VP6A] support: 供給;贍養: *~ a son at the university;* 供給一個兒子讀大學; *neglect to ~ one's family.* 忽略贍養家屬。*Can you ~ my daughter* (ie if you marry her) *in the style she has been accustomed to?* 你能供養我的女兒(如果你娶了她)過她所習慣的那種生活嗎? *It's difficult to ~ a family on £30 a week.* 每週三十鎊難以贍養一個家庭。 **3** [VP6A, 9, 25] assert as true: 堅持;主張: *~ one's innocence;* 堅持自己的無辜; *~ that one is innocent of a charge.* 堅持自己對某項罪名是無辜的。 **4** [VP6A] keep in good repair or working order: 保養: *~ the roads.* 保養道路。 **5** [VP6A] defend: 維護: *~ one's rights.* 維護自己的權利。 **~·able** /-əbl ; -əbl̩/ *adj* that can be ~ed. 可維持的;可支持的;可維護的。

main·ten·ance /ˈmeɪntənəns ; ˈmentənəns/ *n* [U] maintaining or being maintained; (esp) what is needed to support life. 維持或被維持;保養;(尤指)維持生活所需的東西;生活費用; 贍養費。 '**~ order** *n* (legal) order made by a court of law obliging sb to support sb, eg a husband to support his wife from whom he is separated. (法律)贍養令;扶養令(由法庭頒發的命令,判定某人須贍養某人,如夫婦分居時,丈夫應負擔妻子生活費用)。'**~ men/gang** *n* workmen who maintain roads and other public services. 道路或其他公共設施之修護工人; 修護大隊。ˌ**retail** ˌ**price** '**~,** practice of maintaining fixed retail prices. 保持固定零售價格;維持不二價。➪ *cut prices* at cut¹(9).

mai·son·nette /ˌmeɪzəˈnet ; ˌmezəˈnɛt/ *n* flat¹ on two floors¹(2). (二層樓)公寓。

maize /meɪz ; mez/ *n* [U] (also called 亦稱 *Indian corn*) sort of grain plant. 玉蜀黍;玉米。➪ the illus at cereal. 參看 cereal 之挿圖。

ma·jes·tic /məˈdʒestɪk ; məˈdʒɛstɪk/ *adj* having, showing, majesty. 有威嚴的;莊嚴的;高貴的;宏大的。 **ma·jes·ti·cally** /-klɪ ; -klɪ/ *adv*

maj·esty /ˈmædʒəstɪ ; ˈmædʒəstɪ/ *n* (*pl* -ties) **1** [U] kingly or queenly appearance, conduct, speech, causing respect; stateliness; royal power. 君王或皇后之令人敬仰的威儀、擧止、言詞;莊嚴;威嚴;王權。 **2** ***His/Her/Your M~; Their/Your Majesties,*** form used when speaking of or to a sovereign ruler or rulers. 陛下(對君王的稱呼)。

ma·jol·ica /məˈdʒɒlɪkə ; məˈdʒɑlɪkə/ *n* [U] (kinds of) Italian ornamented pottery; modern imitations of these, with white or coloured glazes. (數種)義大利的花飾陶器; 此類陶器的現代仿製品(塗有白色或彩色的釉)。

ma·jor¹ /ˈmeɪdʒə(r) ; ˈmedʒɚ/ *adj* **1** (contrasted with *minor*) greater or more important: (與minor相對)較大的;較重要的;主要的: *~ roads;* 要道; *the ~ portion;* 較大的部分; *a ~ operation,* (surgery) one that may be dangerous to the person's life. (外科)大手術。 **~ premise** *n* ➪ premise. **~ scale**

n (music) scale having two full tones between the key note and the third note. (音樂)大音階;長音階。~ **suit** *n* (cards, bridge) either spades or hearts. (紙牌、橋牌)大牌(黑桃或紅心)。 **2** (placed after a name) elder or first of two persons of the same name, eg in a school: (置於姓名後)同姓名的二人中較長的(例如在同一學校內): *Smith ~.* 較長的史密斯。 ⇨ minor, senior. □ *vi* [VP3A] **~ *in sth,*** specialize in (a certain subject) at college or university: 主修;專研(大學裏某一科目): *Christina ~ed in two subjects at Keele University.* 克里斯蒂納在基爾大學主修兩門科目。 *Brian ~ed in economics.* 布萊恩主修經濟學。□ *n* subject ~ed in. 主修學科。

ma·jor² /ˈmeɪdʒə(r) ; ˈmedʒɚ/ *n* army officer between a captain and a colonel. 陸軍少校。 **ˌ~-ˈgen·eral** *n* army officer next above a brigadier and under a lieutenant-general. 陸軍少將。

ma·jor-domo /ˌmeɪdʒə ˈdəʊməʊ ; ˈmedʒɚˈdomo/ *n* (*pl* ~s /-məʊz ; -moz/) head steward in a great household, esp of a prince in Italy or Spain in former times. (尤指昔時義大利或西班牙王公家中的)總管家。

ma·jor·ity /məˈdʒɒrətɪ *US:* -ˈdʒɔːr- ; məˈdʒɔrətɪ/ *n* (*pl* -ties) **1** (with *sing* or *pl v*) ***a/the ~ (of),*** the greater number or part (*of*): (動詞可用單數或複數)多數;大半: *The ~ of people seem to prefer watching games to playing games.* 大部分的人似乎都喜歡看比賽,而不喜歡參加比賽。 *The ~ were/was in favour of the proposal.* 多數人贊成這個建議。 **2** [C] number by which votes for one side exceed those for the other side: (投票時)超過對方的票數: *He was elected by a large ~/by a ~ of 3749.* 他以大多數票(超過對方3,749票)當選。*The Government's ~ was a small one.* 政府的多數票多得有限。 ***be in the/a ~,*** have the ~. 擁有多數;佔多數。 ***a ~ verdict,*** verdict of the ~ (of a jury, etc). (陪審團等的)多數判決。 **3** ***one's ~,*** **(a)** legal age of reaching manhood or womanhood: 達到成年的法定年齡: *He will reach his ~ next month.* 下個月他將達到法定年齡。 **(b)** army rank of major: 少校的階級: *obtain one's ~.* 獲授少校階級。

make¹ /meɪk ; mek/ *vt, vi* (*pt, pp* made /meɪd ; med/) (For uses with *nn,* ⇨ 25, 26 below; for uses with *adjj,* ⇨ 27 below; for uses with *adverbial particles* and *preps,* ⇨ 30 below.) (與名詞連用,參看下列25, 26義;與形容詞連用,參看27義;與副詞接語及介詞連用,參看30義。) **1** [VP6A, 14, 12B, 13B] ***~ sth from/(out) of sth; ~ sth into sth,*** construct or produce by combining parts or putting materials together; form or shape from material; bring into existence (esp by effort): 建造;製造;產生(尤指費力而做成): *~ bricks;* 造磚; *~ bread;* 製麵包; *~ a coat;* 做一件外衣; ~ (= manufacture) *paper.* 造紙。*She made* (= prepared) *coffee for all of us.* 她爲我們大家煮咖啡。*I made myself a cup of tea.* 我爲自己泡一杯茶。*Cloth is made of cotton, wool, silk and other materials.* 布是棉、毛、絲和其他原料製成的。 *Wine is made from grapes.* 葡萄酒是葡萄釀成的。 *We ~ bottles (out) of glass.* 我們用玻璃製造瓶子。 *Glass is made into bottles.* 玻璃可以製成瓶子。 *God made man.* 上帝創造了人。 ***show sb/let sb see what one is made of,*** show sb one's qualities, powers, abilities, etc. 讓人知道自己的品格、力量、能力等。 ***be as clever etc as they ~'em,*** be very clever etc. 非常精明等。⇨ come(10). **2** [VP6A] cause to appear by breaking, tearing, removing material: 藉打破、撕破、移去而形成: *~ a hole in the ground/a gap in a hedge.* 在地上挖一個洞(在樹籬上弄一缺口)。 ***~ a hole/dent in one's savings/reserves/finances etc,*** reduce them by a considerable amount. 用去大筆儲蓄(準備金,資金等)。 **3** [VP6A, 16A] enact; establish: 制定;規定: *The regulations were made to protect children.* 這些規則係爲保護兒童而制定的。*Who made this ridiculous rule?* 這個荒謬的規則是誰定的? **4** [VP6A] draft; draw up: 草擬;起草: *Father is making a fresh will.* 父親正重新立遺囑。*A treaty has been made with our former enemies.* 與我們過去的敵人間的一項條約業經擬定。*I'll get my solicitor to ~ a deed of transfer.* 我要找我的律師擬一讓渡書。 **5** [VP6A] eat, have (a meal): 吃;進(餐): *We made a good breakfast before leaving.* 我們在離開前吃了一頓豐富的早餐。*He made a hasty lunch.* 他匆匆吃了午飯。 **6** [VP6A, 13B] cause to be: 引起: *Why ~ a disturbance at this time of night?* 値此深夜爲何如此騷擾? *I don't want to ~ any trouble for you.* 我不想爲你惹麻煩。 **7** [VP16A] (passive only) be meant or intended: (僅作被動語態)預定;指定: *John and Mary seem to have been made for each other,* eg because they get on so well together. 約翰和瑪莉似乎是天生的一對。*In England we think bacon and eggs were made to be eaten together.* 在英國我們認爲醃肉和鷄蛋是配在一起食用的。 **8** [VP22, 24A] cause to be or become: 使;使成爲: *The news made her happy.* 這消息使她高興。*He made his meaning clear.* 他把他的意思說得很明白。*He made clear his objections/made it clear that he objected to the proposal.* 他明白表示他的異議(反對此項提議)。*His actions made him universally respected.* 他的行爲使他到處受尊敬。*He soon made himself understood.* 他立刻把他的意思說明白。 *Can you easily ~ yourself understood in English?* 你能用英語輕易地表明你的意思嗎? *The full story was never made known/public.* 全部情節從未公開過。*He couldn't ~ himself/his voice heard above the noise of the traffic.* 在交通的喧囂中他無法使他的聲音讓別人聽到。~ ***oneself useful*** (*about the house etc*), do sth to help: 做有用的事: *Don't stand about doing nothing—~ yourself useful!* 不要閑站在這裏——做點有用的事! ***~ it worth sb's while (to do sth),*** pay or reward him: 使某人值得(做某事);酬謝某人: *If you'll help me with this job, I'll ~ it worth your while.* 如果你願意幫我做這件工作,我會酬謝你。 ***~ sth good,*** ⇨ good¹(20). **9** [VP6A] earn; win; gain; acquire: 賺;贏;得;獲: *~ £5000 a year;* 一年賺五千鎊; *~ a profit/loss of £100.* 獲利(損失)一百鎊。 *He first made his name/reputation as a junior Minister.* 他以次長之職嶄露頭角。 *He made a name/reputation for himself at the Bar,* ie as a barrister. 做爲律師他贏得了好名譽。 *He soon made a fortune on the Stock Exchange.* 他不久便買賣股票發了財。 ***~ a pile/packet,*** (colloq) acquire a great deal of money. (俗)賺許多錢;發財。 ***~ one's living (as/at/by/from),*** have as one's work or livelihood: 謀生;(以做…)爲生: *He ~s his living by giving piano lessons.* 他以教授鋼琴爲生。 *Can you ~ a living from freelance journalism?* 你能靠在報上自由寫稿爲生嗎? *Does he ~ a living at it?* 他以此爲生嗎? **10** [VP2A, 6A] (various uses in card games, eg bridge) (在橋牌等紙牌戲中的各種用法) **(a)** win (a trick); play to advantage: 贏(一磴牌);打出能贏的(一張牌): *He made his Queen of Hearts.* 他打出紅心女王。 **(b)** (of a card) win a trick: (指紙牌)贏一磴: *Your ace and king won't make until you've drawn trumps.* 非等到你把王牌吊光,你的么點和老K贏不到牌。 **(c)** win (what one has set out to win): 贏得(所叫的分數或磴數);做成: *Little slam bid and made.* 叫小滿貫而做成了。 **(d)** shuffle, mix (the cards): 洗(牌): *Will you ~ the pack?* 請你洗牌好嗎? *My turn to ~.* 輪到我洗牌(該我洗牌)了。 **11** [VP6A] score (at cricket): (板球戲中)得分: *~ a century in a test match.* 在決賽中得一百分。*50 runs were made in the first hour.* 第一小時得五十分。 **12** [VP2A] (of the tide) begin to flow or ebb: (指潮)開始漲或退: *The tide is making fast.* 潮水正在很快地漲。*The ebb was now making,* The ebb tide was flowing. 正在退潮。 **13** ***~ or break/mar,*** either be successful or be ruined. 不是成功就

是失敗;孤注一擲。***a made man,*** one whose success has been assured: 確定會成功的人: *Get the Minister's help and you'll be a made man.* 去找部長幫忙,你一定會成功。 **14** [VP18B] compel; force; persuade; cause (sb) to do sth; cause (sth) to happen: 迫;强使;說服;使(某人)做某事;使(某事)發生: *They made me repeat/I was made to repeat the story.* 他們要我重述那個故事。*Can you ~ this old engine start?* 你能發動這個舊引擎嗎? *The children never behave well and no one ever tries to ~ them* (= ~ them behave well). 那些小孩子從不守規矩,也從沒有人要他們守規矩。*What ~s the grass grow?* 什麼東西使得青草生長? *I can't ~ anyone hear,* eg by ringing the doorbell, knocking, calling. 我沒法子使任何人聽得見(如按門鈴、敲門、叫喊)。*His jokes made us all laugh.* 他的笑話使我們都笑起來。***ˌ~ one's ˈblood boil; ~ one's ˈhackles rise,*** anger one. 使人大怒。***ˌ~ one's ˈhair stand on end,*** shock or frighten one: 使人毛髮竦然: *His ghost stories made our hair stand on end.* 他的鬼故事令我們毛髮竦然。***~ (sth) do; ~ do with sth,*** manage with it although it may not be really adequate or satisfactory: 用某種東西勉强應付;將就著用;湊合著用: *You'll have to ~ do with cold meat for dinner.* 晚餐你祇好將就一下吃冷肉了。*There's not much of it but I'll try to ~ (it) do.* 東西不多,但我會將就著用。***~ do and mend,*** manage without buying new articles, eg clothing, bed linen, household articles, esp by repairing and remaking old ones. (如衣服、床單、傢具等)修補好湊合使用。***~ sth go round,*** make it last or be enough: 使某物能維持或足够分配: *I don't know how she ~s the money go round.* 我不知道她如何能靠這筆錢維持。***~ believe (that.../to be...),*** pretend: 假裝;假扮: *Let's ~ believe that we're Red Indians.* 我們來假扮紅番。*The children made believe that they were/made believe to be shipwrecked on a desert island.* 孩子們假裝他們在荒島上遭遇船難。Hence, 由此產生, **ˈ~-believe** *n* [U] pretending; [C] pretence. 假裝;托辭;口實。 **15** [VP22, 18B, 23] represent as; cause to appear as; allege (to be, to do): 表現;使顯現爲;主張;斷定: *Olivier, in the film, ~s Hamlet a figure of tragic indecision.* 在該影片中,奧立佛把哈姆雷特演成了優柔寡斷的悲劇人物。 *Most of the old Chronicles ~ the king die in 1026,* give 1026 as the date of his death. 古史多半認爲那個國王死於1026年。*In the play the author ~s the villain commit suicide,* describe him as doing this. 在這部戲裏,作者讓歹徒自殺了。*You've made my nose too big,* eg in a drawing or painting. 你把我的鼻子畫得太大了。 **16** [VP6A, 25] estimate or reckon (to be); put (a total, etc) at: 估計;推斷;算定: *What time do you ~ it?* 你認爲現在幾點鐘了? *What do you ~ the time?* 你認爲現在幾點鐘? *How large do you ~ the audience?* 你估計觀衆(聽衆)有多少? *I ~ the total (to be) about £50.* 我算總數約爲五十鎊。*I ~ the distance about 70 miles.* 我估計那段距離大約有七十哩。 **17** [VP6A] come to, equal; add up to; constitute; amount to (in significance): 總計;合計;等於;構成: *Twenty shillings used to ~ one pound.* 二十先令在過去等於一鎊。*Twelve inches ~ one foot.* 十二吋等於一呎。*5 and 7 is 12, and 3 is 15, and 4 more ~s 19.* 五加七等於十二,再加三等於十五,再加四等於十九。*How many members ~ a quorum?* 多少人才構成法定人數? *His adventures ~ excellent reading.* 他的冒險故事是非常好的讀物。*The play ~s an excellent evening's entertainment.* 那劇是一極好的晚間娛樂。***~ (good/not much) sense,*** seem to have (plenty of/little) sense: 有意義(很有意義;沒有什麼意義): *His arguments have never made much sense.* 他的論據從來沒有什麼意義。***One swallow doesn't ~ a summer,*** ⇨ swallow[1]. **18** [VP6A] be (in a series); count as: 爲…之一份子;算爲: *This ~s the fifth time you've failed this examination.* 這次是你第五度參加這項考試失敗。*Will you ~ a fourth at bridge?* 我們打橋牌還缺一個人,你要不要參加?(你要不要做第四個打牌的人?) **19** [VP6A, 23] turn into; turn out to be; prove to be: 變爲;結果爲;證明爲: *If you train hard, you will ~ a good footballer.* 假若你加緊鍛鍊,你會成爲一個好的足球員。*He will ~ an excellent husband.* 他會成爲一個非常好的丈夫。*She will ~ him a good wife,* will be one. 她將成爲他的好妻子。*This length of cloth will ~ me a suit,* can be made up into one. 這塊布料够我做一套衣服。 **20** [VP6A] (colloq uses) travel over (a distance); reach, maintain (a speed); be in time to catch or reach; (US) gain the rank or place of: (俗語用法)旅行(某一路程);達到或維持(某一速度);趕上(火車等);到達(某地);(美)獲…之階級或地位: *We've made 80 miles since noon.* 從中午以來我們趕了八十哩的路。*We've made good time,* travelled the distance in good time, ie fast. 我們這一段路走得够快了。*The ship was making only nine knots.* 這艘船僅以每小時九浬的速度航行。*The disabled cruiser was only just able to ~ (= reach) port.* 那艘損壞的巡洋艦只能够到達港口。*The train leaves at 7.13; can we ~ it,* reach the station in time? 火車在七點十三分開,我們能趕得上嗎? *He's tired out already—he'll never ~ the summit.* 他已經疲倦了,他絕到不了山頂。*His new novel has made the best-seller list,* has sold enough copies to be on this list. 他的新小說被列爲暢銷書之一。*He'll never ~ (= win a place on) the team.* 他永遠沒有加入那個隊的機會。*Jones made (= reached the rank of) sergeant in six months.* 瓊斯經六個月後當了士官。 **21** [VP23] elect; appoint; nominate; raise to the dignity of: 選舉;被任命;派定;獲高位顯爵: *~ sb King/an earl/a peer.* 擁某人爲王(封某人爲伯爵;封某人爲貴族)。*Newton was made President of the Royal Society.* 牛頓被選爲皇家學會會長。*He was made General Manager by the directors.* 他被董事們推選爲總經理。*We ~ you our spokesman.* 我們指定你做我們的發言人。*He made her his wife,* married her. 他娶她爲妻。 **22** [VP12A, 13A] offer, propose, hold out (to sb): 提供;提出;出價: *M~ me an offer,* suggest a price! 請開價! *We made them two or three attractive proposals.* 我們向他們提供兩三個動人的建議。 *The Chairman of British Rail has made a new offer to the men,* eg of a rise in wages during a strike. 英國鐵路局主席向工人提出新的建議(例如在罷工時提出增加工資)。*I made him a bid for the antique table.* 我向他出價購買那張古老的桌子。 *I made her a present of the vase.* 我給她一個花瓶作禮物。 **23** ***~ sth of sb/sth; ~ sth/sb sth,*** cause sb/sth to be or become sth: 使某人(某物)成爲: *His parents want to ~ a doctor of him,* want him to be educated for the medical profession. 他的父母要他將來做醫生。*We must ~ an example of him,* eg by punishing him as a warning to others. 我們必須懲罰他以儆他人。 *Don't ~ a habit of it/Don't ~ it a habit,* Don't let it become a habit. 不要使它成爲習慣。*Don't ~ a hash/mess/muddle of it,* Don't do the job badly. 不要把事情弄糟了。*He has made a business of politics,* has made politics his chief concern. 他已經把政治作爲他的事業。 *Don't ~ an ass/fool of yourself,* behave foolishly. 不要像驢子那樣笨(不要做傻瓜)。 *Don't ~ a practice of cheating at exams.* 不要養成考試作弊的習慣。*Don't ~ cheating a practice.* 不要養成欺騙的習慣。 ⇨ *n* entries esp in 25 and 26 below for other examples of this pattern. 參看下列第25和26義中其他使用此一句型的例句。 **24** [VP2C] behave as if about to do sth: 做出…的舉動;好像要: *He made as if to strike me.* 他做出要打我的樣子。*He made to reply (= seemed to be about to do so) and then became silent.* 他好像要回答,然後又停住了。 **25** [VP6A, 14] (used with many *nn* where ~ + *n* have the same meaning as a *v* related in form to the *n*). (與許多名詞連用,其意義和該名詞的相關動詞的含義相同)。***~ allowance(s) (for),*** ⇨ allowance(3). ~

(an) application (to sb) (for sth), apply (to sb) (for sth). (向某人)申請。～ ***arrangements for,*** arrange for. 安排。 ～ ***a decision,*** decide. 決定。～ ***a guess (at),*** guess (at). 推測。～ ***an impression (on),*** impress. 予以印象。 ～ ***a request (to sb) (for sth),*** request (sth) (from sb). (向某人)要求。～ ***a success of sth,*** succeed with it/in doing it. 把…做得很成功。(For other phrases of this kind, ⇨ the *n* entries.) (其他此類片語參看各片語的名詞。) **26** [VP6A, 14] (used with a large number of *nn* in special senses; cf do²(2) for *nn* used with *do;* the examples below are a selection only; ⇨ the *n* entries): (與許多名詞連用形成特殊含義的片語；參較 do² 第 2 義中與 do 連用之名詞；以下各例僅爲選出的一部分；參看各片語中的名詞)： ～ *much* ado *(about);* 大忙一陣；費盡力氣； ～ advances *(to);* (向…)表示友好；(向…)獻慇懃； ～ amends *(to sb/for sth);* (爲某事)賠償(某人)； ～ *an* appointment; 約會； ～ *an* attempt; 嘗試；試圖； ～ *the* bed(s); 鋪牀； ～ *a* bee-line *(for);* 取捷徑前往；迅速前往； ～ *the* best *of;* 盡量利用； ～ *a* bid *(for);* 企圖獲得； ～ *no* bones *about;* 毫不猶豫； ～ *a* break *for it;* 逃脫；逃跑； ～ *a clean* breast *of;* 坦白供認； ～ capital *(out) of sth;* 利用； ～ *a* change; 改變； ～ *one's* day; 使某人非常快樂地過一天； ～ *a* deal *(with sb);* (與某人)做買賣；(與某人)妥協； ～ demands *(of/on);* 要求； ～ *some/little* difference; 甚爲重要(不大重要)； ～ *an* effort; 努力；盡力； ～ *an* excuse; 找藉口； ～ eyes *at;* 對…眉目傳情； ～ *a* face/faces *(at);* (向…)扮鬼臉； ～ fun *of;* 嘲弄；取笑； ～ *a* fuss *(of);* 小題大作；大驚小怪； ～ game *of;* 嘲弄；取笑； ～ *a* gesture; 作手勢；表示； ～ *a* go *of sth;* 使某事成功； ～ hay *of;* 使混亂； ～ head *or tail of;* 明白；了解； ～ *a* hit *(with);* 給予…良好印象； ～ inroads *into;* 侵犯；襲擊； ～ *a good/poor* job *of;* 把(某事)做好(弄糟)； ～ *a* man *of;* 使有男子氣；使成男子漢； ～ *one's* mark; 成名； ～ mincemeat *of;* 徹底擊敗(某人)；完全駁倒(某論點)； ～ mischief; 搬弄是非； ～ *a* mockery *of;* 嘲弄；愚弄； ～ money; 賺錢； ～ *the* most *of;* 充分利用； ～ *a mountain out of a* mole-hill; 小題大做； ～ much *of;* 瞭解；重視；誇張； ～ *a* name *for oneself;* 成名； ～ *a* night *of it;* 痛痛快快地玩一個晚上； ～ nonsense *of;* 破壞；使無效； ～ *a* pass *at;* 向…獻慇懃； ～ *one's* peace *(with);* (與…)和解； ～ *a* point *(of);* 堅持；決心； ～ room *(for);* 騰出空間； ～ *a* secret *of;* 隱瞞； ～ shift *with;* 盡量設法； ～ *a* song *and dance about;* 大驚小怪；小題大做； ～ war *(on);* (向…)開戰； ～ water; 小便；(指船)漏水； ～ *one's* way *in the world;* 有成就；發跡； ～ *heavy* weather *of;* 發現某事頗爲棘手； ～ *the* worst *of.* 對…做最壞的打算。 **27** [VP2D] (used with *adjj* in special senses; ⇨ the *adj* entries): (與形容詞連用的特殊用法；參看各片語中之形容詞)： ～ *so* bold *(as to);* 不揣冒昧； ～ certain *(of/that);* 弄清楚；弄確實； ～ *sth* fast; 繫牢； ～ free *with;* 隨意使用；擅用； ～ *sth* good; 補償；賠償；實現；證實；修復； ～ light *of;* 輕視； ～ merry; 作樂；行樂； ～ sure. 確信；查明。 **28** [VP2C, 3A] (of arguments, evidence, etc) point; tend: (指辯論、證據等)指向；趨於： *All the evidence ～s (points* is more usu) *in the same direction.* 所有的證據都指向同一方向 (point 一字較常用)。～ ***against,*** (rare) be contrary, unfavourable, prejudicial or harmful to: (罕)與…相反；不利於；有害於；有損於： *These dissipations ～ against your chance of success.* 這些不正當的消遣有損你成功的機會。 **29** (compounds) (複合字) **'～-believe** *n* ⇨ 14 above. 參看上列第 14 義。 **'～-shift** *n* sth used for a time until sth better is obtainable: 暫時的代用品： *use an empty crate as a ～shift for a table/as a ～shift table.* 用一個空箱子做桌子的代用品(代替桌子)。**'～-up** *n* (⇨ ～ *up* in 30 below) (參看下列第 30 義之 ～ up) **(a)** arrangement of type, etc on a printed page. (印刷品之字圖等的)編排；版面。**(b)** character, temperament: 性格；氣質： *people of that ～-up.* 那種性格的人。**(c)** [C, U] cosmetics, etc as used by actors; result of using these: 化粧品(如演員所用者)；使用化粧品的效果： *What a clever ～-up!* 多妙的化裝！ **(d)** [U] cosmetics as used on the face: 面部用的化粧品： *use too much ～-up/the wrong kind of ～-up.* 使用太多(不當的)化粧品。**'～-weight** *n* small quantity added to get the weight required; (fig) sth or sb of small value that fills a gap, supplies a deficiency. 補足重量的小量東西；(喻)塡補欠缺的不重要的人或物。 **30** [VP2C, 14, 15B, 3A] (uses with *adverbial particles* and *preps*): (與副詞接語及介詞連用的用法)：

make after sb, (formal) pursue; chase: (正式用語)追求；追趕： *She made after him like a mad woman.* 她像個瘋女人似地追趕他。

make at sb, move aggressively towards: 襲擊；攻擊： *The angry woman made at me with her umbrella.* 那個憤怒的女人用雨傘襲擊我。⇨ *come at* at come(16).

make away with oneself, commit suicide: 自殺： *Why did he ～ away with himself?* 他爲什麼自殺？ ***～ away with sth,*** destroy or steal it. 摧毀；竊取。

make for sb/sth, **(a)** move in the direction of; head for: 向某方向移動；走向： *The frigate made for the open sea.* 那艘巡防艦開向大海。 *It's late; we'd better turn and ～ for home.* 時間晚了，我們最好轉向回家。**(b)** charge at, rush towards: 攻擊；襲擊；衝向： *The bull made for me and I had to run.* 那隻公牛向我衝來，我不得不逃避。 *When the interval came everyone made for the bar,* ie to buy drinks. 休息時間一到，每個人都跑向酒吧。 **(c)** contribute to, tend towards: 有助於；傾向於： *Does early rising ～ for good health?* 早起對健康有益嗎？ *The improved lid of this jar ～s for easier opening.* 這個改良過的廣口瓶蓋子易於開啓。

make sth/sb into sth, change or convert to: 使變爲；轉變爲： *The huts can be made into temporary houses.* 這些簡陋的小屋可改裝爲臨時住宅。 *He wasn't always a bully—you made him into one.* 他並不老是個恃強凌弱的人，是你使他變成那樣的。

make sth of sb/sth, understand, interpret: 了解；解釋： *What do you ～ of it all?* 你對這一切作何解釋？ *What are we to ～ of his behaviour?* 我們怎麼解釋他的行爲？ *I can ～ nothing of all this scribble.* 這些潦草的筆跡我一點也看不懂。

make off, hurry away (esp in order to escape): 匆匆離開(尤指逃走)： *The get-away car made off at top speed.* 那輛逃走的汽車傾全速駛去。 ***～ off with sth,*** steal and hurry away: 捲逃： *The cashier made off with the firm's money.* 那個出納帶著公司裏的款逃走了。

make sth out, **(a)** write out; complete or fill in: 寫出；開出；塡寫： *～ out a cheque for £10;* 開出一張十英鎊的支票； *～ out a list for the grocer;* 把要向雜貨商購買的東西列成一張單子； *～ out a document in duplicate.* 將一文件寫成一式兩份。**(b)** manage to see, read (usu implying difficulty): 看出來；讀出來；認出來(通常含示經過困難)： *We made out a figure in the darkness.* 我們在黑暗裏看出一個人影。 *The outline of the house could just be made out.* 那屋子的輪廓勉强可以看出。 ***～ out that.../～ sb out to be,*** claim; assert; maintain: 聲稱；斷言；認定： *He made out that he had been badly treated.* 他聲稱他曾經受到虐待。 *He ～s himself out to be cleverer than he really is.* 他認爲他比實際上更聰明。 *He's not such a good lawyer as some people ～ out,* ie ～ him out to be. 他不是像某些人所說的那樣好的律師。 ***～ sb out,*** understand sb's nature: 了解某人的性情： *What a queer fellow he is! I can't ～ him out at all.* 他是多麼奇怪的一個人！我完全不能了解他。 ***～ it out; ～ (it) out if/whether,*** understand: 了解： *I can't ～ out what he wants.* 我不了解他要什麼。 *I couldn't ～ it out—did they want our help or not?* 我不了解——他們到底需不需要我們幫忙？ *How do you/does he, etc ～ that out?* How do you/does he reach that conclusion, support that contention? 你(他等)怎麼會得到那個結論(支持那個論

點)? ~ ***out (with sb),*** progress, get on: 進展: *How are things making out?* 一切事情進展如何? *How are you making out with Lucy?* How's your friendship progressing? 你和露西的友誼進展如何? ~ ***out a case for/against/that...,*** argue for/against: 爲贊成(反對)而爭論: *He has made out a strong case for prison reform.* 他爲監獄改革而力爭。*A case could be made out that Smith should be released/for Smith's release.* 我們主張史密斯應被釋放。

make sth/sb over, **(a)** change, transform, convert: 改變;變更;轉變: *The basement has been made over into a workshop.* 那地下室已改作工場。*You can't ~ over a personality in one day.* 一個人的個性非一日所能改變。**(b)** transfer the possession or ownership of: 轉讓所有權;移轉: *He has made over the whole of his property to the National Trust.* 他把全部財產交託給國立信託局。*How much did he ~ over?* 他轉讓多少?

make sth up, **(a)** complete: 完成;補足: *We still need £5 to ~ up the sum we asked for.* 我們還需要五英鎊,以補足我們所要求的數目。*They need ten more men to ~ up their full complement.* 他們尚需十個人員以補足。**(b)** supply; ~ good: 補充;彌補: *Our losses have to be made up with more loans.* 我們的損失必須靠更多的貸款來補充。**(c)** invent; compose (esp to deceive): 捏造;編造(尤指用於欺騙): *The whole story is made up.* 整個故事是虛構的。*It's all a made-up story.* 這完全是捏造的故事。*Stop making things up!* 不要再編造了! **(d)** arrange type, illustrations, etc in columns or pages for printing: 將鉛字、插圖等排成欄或頁;排版;整版: *Who is in charge of making up/the ~-up of the financial pages?* 誰負責排財務版? **(e)** form; compose; constitute: 合成;組成;組織: *Are all animal bodies made up of cells?* 所有動物的身體都是細胞組成的嗎? *What are the qualities that ~ up Hamlet's character?* 哈姆雷特的性格是由那些特質構成的? *I object to the way the committee is made up/to the ~-up of the committee.* 我反對這委員會的組織方式。**(f)** prepare, eg medicine, a prescription, tonic, by mixing ingredients: 配藥: *Ask the chemist to ~ this up for you.* 請藥商爲你配這服藥。**(g)** put together; shape: 整理;收拾: *~ up a bundle of old clothes for the church bazaar.* 整理出一包舊衣供教會義賣。*The grocer was making up the butter into packages of half a kilo.* 雜貨店老闆正在把奶油分成半公斤盒裝。*Have you made up Mrs Smith's order yet,* ie collected the items, articles, etc she ordered? 你把史密斯太太要的貨收拾好了沒有? **(h)** ~ (material, cloth, etc) into a garment: 把(布料等)縫製成衣服;裁製: *Customer's own materials made up.* 顧客自備材料,本店代爲縫製衣服。*Can you ~ up this suit length for me?* 你能用這塊料子爲我做成一套衣服嗎? *This material will ~ up into two dresses.* 這塊料子可裁製兩件衣服。**(i)** add fuel to, eg a fire in a fireplace or stove: 加燃料於(火或爐): *The fire needs making up,* needs to have more coal put on it. 這火需要添煤。*If the stove isn't made up, it will go out.* 如果爐子不加燃料,火會熄滅。**(j)** prepare (a bed) not at present in use (as for a new hospital patient); prepare (a new makeshift bed, eg on the floor): 準備(床鋪)以備用(例如爲醫院新病人);準備(臨時床鋪,如在地板上): *You can't go into the ward yet; your bed's still to be made up.* 你現在還不能進入病房,你的床鋪尚未備妥。*They made up a bed on the sofa for the unexpected visitor.* 他們爲那個不速之客在沙發上鋪個床鋪。~ ***sb/oneself up,*** prepare (an actor/oneself) for the stage by applying grease-paint, hair, etc to his/one's face or body; apply cosmetics to the face: 使某演員(自己)裝扮好準備登臺;化裝;打扮: *It takes him more than an hour to ~ up/do his ~-up for the part of Othello.* 他花費一個多小時化裝爲奧賽羅。*Isn't she badly made up!* 她化粧得多難看! Hence, 由此產生, **'~-up** *n* ~ ***up one's/sb's mind,*** come/cause sb to come to a decision: 下決心;決定;使某人下決心: *I've made up my mind.* 我已決定了。*My mind's made up.* 我的心意已定。*He needs someone to ~ up his mind for him.* 他需要別人替他作決定。~ ***up for sth,*** compensate for; outweigh: 補償;彌補;勝過: *Hard work can often ~ up for a lack of intelligence.* 勤能補拙。*Do you think her beauty could ~ up for her stupidity?* 你認爲她的美麗能彌補她的愚蠢嗎? ~ ***up for lost time,*** hurry, work hard, etc after losing time, starting late, etc. 加緊努力補回失去或落後的時間。~ ***up to sb for sth,*** atone; redress; ~ amends for: 爲某事而補償某人: *How can we ~ it up to them for what they have suffered?* 我們如何能補償他們所遭受的損害? ~ ***up to sb,*** ~ oneself pleasant to sb, to win favours: 向某人獻殷勤;向某人獻媚邀寵: *He's always making up to influential people.* 他經常向有勢力的人獻媚邀寵。*He doesn't welcome being made up to.* 他不喜歡別人向他獻殷勤。~ ***it up to sb,*** compensate sb for sth missed or suffered, or for money etc spent: 補償某人: *Thanks for buying my ticket—I'll ~ it up to you later,* by refunding you. 謝謝你爲我買票——我稍後會還你錢的。~ ***it up (with sb),*** end a quarrel, dispute or misunderstanding: (與某人)和解;和好: *They quarrel every morning and ~ it up every evening.* 他們每天早上吵架,晚上和好。*Why don't you ~ it up with her?* 你爲什麼不跟她和解?

make² /meɪk ; mek/ *n* [C, U] **1** way a thing is made; method or style of manufacture: 製造的方法;樣式: *cars of all ~s;* 各種廠牌的車; *an overcoat of first-class ~.* 第一流貨色的外套。*Is this your own ~,* made by you? 這是你自己做的嗎? ***on the ~,*** (sl) concerned with making a profit, gaining sth. (俚)急求得利;急求獲得某種東西。**2** (electr) completion of an electric circuit. (電)電路接通。

maker /ˈmeɪkə(r) ; ˈmekɚ/ *n* **1** ***the/our M~,*** the Creator; God. 創造者;造物主;上帝;神。**2** (esp in compounds) person or thing that makes: (尤用於複合字中)製造者;能製造的機器或工具: *'dress~.* 女裁縫。

mak·ing /ˈmeɪkɪŋ ; ˈmekɪŋ/ *n* **1** ***be the ~ of,*** cause the well-being of; cause to develop well: 爲…之成功(發展)的因素: *The two years he served in the Army were the ~ of him,* made him develop well (physically, etc according to context). 兩年軍中服役使他身心發展良好(體格或心智發展,視上下文而定)。**2** ***have the ~s of,*** have the necessary qualities for becoming: 有成爲… 所需的性質: *He has in him the ~s of a great man.* 他有成爲偉大人物的特質。

ma·lacca /məˈlækə ; məˈlækə/ *n* **ˌ~ 'cane,** cane walking-stick. 麻六甲手杖。

mala·chite /ˈmæləkaɪt ; ˈmæləˌkaɪt/ *n* [U] green mineral, a kind of stone used for ornaments, decoration, etc. 孔雀石(一種綠色礦物,用作首飾、裝飾等)。

mal·adjusted /ˌmæləˈdʒʌstɪd ; ˌmæləˈdʒʌstɪd/ *adj* badly adjusted; (esp of a person) unable to adapt himself properly to his environment, eg social or occupational. 不適應的;適應情形不良好的;(尤指人)不能適應(社會或職業)環境的。**mal·adjust·ment** *n* [U] condition of being ~. 不適應;適應不良;失調。

mal·adroit /ˈmælədrɔɪt ; ˌmæləˈdrɔɪt/ *adj* not adroit; clumsy; tactless. 不熟練的;笨拙的;無機智的。**~·ly** *adv* **~·ness** *n*

mal·ady /ˈmælədɪ ; ˈmælədɪ/ *n* (*pl* -dies) [C] disease; illness: 疾病: *a social ~;* 社會的病態(弊端); *spiritual maladies.* 道德敗壞;敗德。

mal·aise /mæˈleɪz ; mæˈlez/ *n* [U, C] feeling of bodily discomfort, but without clear signs of a particular illness: 身體不舒服;小病;微恙: (fig) (喻) *years of ~ in industrial relations.* 數年來勞資關係上的不愉快。

mala·prop·ism /ˈmæləprɒpɪzəm ; ˈmæləprɑpˌɪzəm/ *n* [C] misuse of a word, esp in mistake for one that resembles it, causing amusement, eg *'Come girls, this gentleman will exhort* (for *escort*) *us!'* 文字的錯用；誤用文字（尤指因相似而造成可笑的錯誤，例如將 escort 誤作 exhort）。

mal·apro·pos /ˌmælˌæprəˈpəʊ ; ˌmælæprəˈpo/ *adj, adv* inappropriate(ly); inopportune(ly). 不適當的（地）；不合時宜的（地）；不適合的（地）。

ma·laria /məˈleərɪə ; məˈlɛrɪə/ *n* [U] kinds of fever conveyed by mosquitoes, which introduce the germs into the blood. 瘧疾。**ma·lar·ial** /-ɪəl ; -ɪəl/ *adj* of ~; having ~: 瘧疾的；患瘧疾的: *a ~l patient;* 瘧疾病人; *a ~l district.* 瘧疾地區（瘧疾傳染病流行地區）。

Ma·lay /məˈleɪ ; məˈle/ *adj, n* (language, member) of the people living in the ~ peninsula and adjacent areas. 馬來人的；馬來的；馬來語；馬來人。

mal·con·tent /ˈmælkəntent ; ˈmælkənˌtɛnt/ *adj, n* [C] (person who is) discontented and inclined to rebel. 不滿的；反叛的；不滿者；意圖反叛者。

male /meɪl ; mel/ *adj* **1** of the sex that does not give birth to offspring; of or for this sex: 男性的；公的；雄的: *a ˌ~ voice ˈchoir,* of men and/or boys. 男聲唱詩班。**2** (of parts of tools, etc) designed for insertion into a bore or socket, the corresponding female part: （指工具的零件等）陽的: *a ~ screw.* 陽螺釘。□ *n* ~ person, animal, etc. 男人；公的動物；雄性動物等。

mal·edic·tion /ˌmælɪˈdɪkʃn ; ˌmæləˈdɪkʃən/ *n* [C] curse; prayer to God that sb or sth may be destroyed, hurt, etc. 詛咒。

mal·efac·tor /ˈmælɪfæktə(r) ; ˈmæləˌfæktɚ/ *n* wrongdoer; criminal. 作惡者；罪犯。

ma·lefi·cent /məˈlefɪsnt ; məˈlɛfəsn̩t/ *adj* hurtful (*to*). （對…）有害的；惡行的（與 to 連用）。

ma·levo·lent /məˈlevəlnt ; məˈlɛvələnt/ *adj* wishing to do evil or cause harm to others; spiteful (*to/towards*). 惡意的；惡毒的；（對…）懷恨的（與 to 或 towards 連用）。**~·ly** *adv* **ma·levo·lence** /-əns ; -əns/ *n* [U] ill will. 惡意；敵意；怨恨。

mal·feas·ance /ˌmælˈfiːzns ; ˌmælˈfizn̩s/ *n* [U] (legal) wrongdoing; [C] illegal act, esp an instance of official misconduct. （法律）惡事；惡行；（尤指公務員之）不法行爲；瀆職。

mal·for·ma·tion /ˌmælfɔːˈmeɪʃn ; ˌmælfɔrˈmeʃən/ *n* [U] state of being badly formed or shaped; [C] badly formed part: 畸形；不正常的部份: *a ~ of the spine.* 脊椎骨的畸形。**mal·formed** /ˌmælˈfɔːmd ; mælˈfɔrmd/ *adj* badly formed or shaped. 畸形的。

mal·func·tion /ˌmælˈfʌŋkʃn ; mælˈfʌŋkʃən/ *vi* [VP2A] fail to function in a normal or satisfactory manner. 發生故障；未起作用。□ *n* [U, C] failure of this sort. 發生故障。

mal·ice /ˈmælɪs ; ˈmælɪs/ *n* [U] ~ ***(towards),*** active ill will; desire to harm others: 敵意；惡意；怨恨: *bear sb no ~;* 不怨恨某人; *with ~ towards none.* 不對任何人懷惡意。***(with) ~ aforethought,*** (legal) (with) conscious intention to cause harm, do wrong. （法律）蓄意。**ma·licious** /məˈlɪʃəs ; məˈlɪʃəs/ *adj* feeling, showing, caused by, ~: 懷惡意的；出於惡意的；存心不良的: *malicious gossip.* 惡意的閒話。**ma·licious·ly** *adv*

ma·lign /məˈlaɪn ; məˈlaɪn/ *adj* (of things) injurious: （指事物）有害的: *exercise a ~ influence.* 運用不良的影響。□ *vt* [VP6A] speak ill of (sb); tell lies about: 誹謗（某人）；中傷；誣衊: *~ an innocent person.* 詆毀一個無辜的人。

ma·lig·nant /məˈlɪgnənt ; məˈlɪgnənt/ *adj* **1** (of persons, their actions) filled with, showing, a desire to hurt (~ is stronger in meaning than *malicious* and *malevolent*): （指人、其行爲）惡毒的；惡意的（malignant 的含義較 malicious 及 malevolent 强）: *~ fairies;* 惡毒的妖怪; *~ glances.* 兇惡的眼光。**2** (of diseases) harmful to life; violent: （指疾病）致命的；惡性的: *~ cancer.* 惡性的癌。**~·ly** *adv* **ma·lig·nancy** /-nənsɪ ; -nənsɪ/ *n* [U] the state of being ~. 惡毒；惡性；惡念。

ma·lig·nity /məˈlɪgnətɪ ; məˈlɪgnətɪ/ *n* (*pl* -ties) **1** [U] deep-rooted ill will; [C] instance of this; act, remark, etc, caused by such ill will. 極深的惡意；惡意的言行；憎恨。**2** (of diseases) malignant character. （指疾病）惡性。

ma·lin·ger /məˈlɪŋgə(r) ; məˈlɪŋgɚ/ *vi* [VP2A] pretend to be ill, protract an illness, in order to escape duty or work. 裝病以逃避責任；詐病。**~er** *n* person who ~s. 裝病以逃避責任的人；詐病者。

mal·lard /ˈmælɑːd *US:* ˈmælərd ; ˈmælɚd/ *n* kind of wild duck. 一種野鴨；鳧。

mal·leable /ˈmælɪəbl ; ˈmælɪəbl̩/ *adj* **1** (of metals) that can be hammered or pressed into new shapes. （指金屬）可鍛的；可壓製的；可鎚薄的；有展性的。**2** (fig, eg of a person's character) easily trained or adapted. （喻，如指人的性格）易訓練的；易適應的。**mal·lea·bil·ity** /ˌmælɪəˈbɪlətɪ ; ˌmælɪəˈbɪlətɪ/ *n*

mal·let /ˈmælɪt ; ˈmælɪt/ *n* **1** hammer with a wooden head, eg for striking the handle of a chisel. 木槌（如用於敲擊鑿子把柄者）。⇨ the illus at tool. 參看 tool 之插圖。**2** long-handled wooden-headed hammer for striking a croquet or polo ball. 球棍（玩槌球或馬球時用的）。

mal·low /ˈmæləʊ ; ˈmælo/ *n* wild plant with hairy stems and leaves and pink, mauve or white flowers; garden varieties of this. 錦葵；錦葵屬植物。

malm·sey /ˈmɑːmzɪ ; ˈmɑmzɪ/ *n* [U] a sweet wine from Greece, Spain, etc. （希臘、西班牙等國出產的）一種甜葡萄酒。

mal·nu·tri·tion /ˌmælnjuːˈtrɪʃn *US:* -nuː- ; ˌmælnjuˈtrɪʃən/ *n* [U] condition caused by not getting enough food or (enough of) the right kind(s) of food. 營養不良。

mal·odor·ous /ˌmælˈəʊdərəs ; mælˈodərəs/ *adj* (formal) ill-smelling. （正式用語）惡臭的。

mal·prac·tice /ˌmælˈpræktɪs ; mælˈpræktɪs/ *n* (legal) [U] wrongdoing; neglect of duty; [C] instance of this, eg the dishonest use of a position of trust for personal gain. （法律）不法行爲；怠忽職守；利用職位營私舞弊；瀆職。

malt /mɔːlt ; mɔlt/ *n* [U] grain (usu barley) allowed to germinate, used for brewing or distilling: 麥芽: (attrib) （形容用法） *~ liquors,* eg beer, stout. 麥芽酒（如啤酒、黑啤酒）。□ *vt, vi* **1** [VP6A] make (grain) into ~; [VP2A] (of grain) come to the condition of ~. 使（麥）發芽；（指麥）發芽。**2** [VP6A] prepare with ~: 以麥芽調製: *~ed milk.* 麥芽乳。

Mal·tese /mɔːlˈtiːz ; mɔlˈtiz/ *adj, n* (*pl* unchanged) (language, native) of Malta: （複數不變）馬爾他島的；馬爾他語；馬爾他人: ~ **cross,** ⇨ the illus at cross. 馬耳他式十字架（參看 cross 之插圖）。

Mal·thu·sian /mælˈθjuːzɪən *US:* -ˈθuːʒn ; mælˈθjuzɪən/ *adj, n* (supporter) of the principles of T R Malthus, who declared that the growth of the world's population would, unless checked, lead to a world shortage of food. 馬爾薩斯人口論的；擁護馬爾薩斯人口論者（馬爾薩斯宣稱，世界人口之增加如不加以節制，將導致糧食不足）。

mal·treat /ˌmælˈtriːt ; mælˈtrit/ *vt* [VP6A] treat roughly or cruelly. 惡待；虐待。**~·ment** *n* [U] ~ing or being ~ed. 虐待；被虐待。

malt·ster /ˈmɔːltstə(r) ; ˈmɔltˌstɚ/ *n* person who makes malt. 製麥芽者。

mal·ver·sa·tion /ˌmælvəˈseɪʃn ; ˌmælvɚˈseʃən/ *n* [U] (formal) corrupt administration (*of* public money, etc). （正式用語）（公款等的）濫用；貪汚；盜用（與 of 連用）。

mamba /ˈmæmbə ; ˈmɑmbə/ *n* black or green poisonous African snake. 非洲黑色或綠色毒蛇。⇨ the illus at snake. 參看 snake 之插圖。

mam(m)a /məˈmɑː *US:* ˈmɑːmə ; ˈmɑmə/ *n* familiar word for *mother.* 媽媽。

mam·mal /ˈmæml ; ˈmæml̩/ *n* any of the class of animals which feed their young with milk from the breast. 哺乳類動物。⇨ the illus at ape, cat, domestic, large, small. 參看 ape, cat, domestic, large, small 之插圖。

mam·mon /ˈmæmən ; ˈmæmən/ *n* [U] wealth (regarded as an evil influence). 財富(被視爲有壞影響)。**M～**, the god of greed: 貪慾之神;財神: *worshippers of M～*. 拜金主義者。

mam·moth /ˈmæməθ ; ˈmæməθ/ *n* large hairy kind of elephant now extinct; (attrib) immense: 猛獁(已絕種的古代有毛的大象);(形容用法)巨大的: *～ business enterprises*. 龐大的企業。

a mammoth

mammy /ˈmæmɪ ; ˈmæmɪ/ *n* (*pl* -mies) **1** (child's word for) mother. (小兒語) 媽咪。 **2** (US) (old use, now derog) ⚠ negro nursemaid for white children. (美) (舊用法,現爲貶抑語) (諱)照顧白人小孩的黑人褓姆。

man¹ /mæn ; mæn/ *n* (*pl* men /men ; mɛn/) **1** adult male human being. 男人;男子。 ***one's man of business***, one's agent or solicitor. 某人的經紀人或律師。 ***a man of letters***, a writer and scholar. 作家;文學家;文人。 ***a man about town***, one who spends much time in society, in clubs, at parties, theatres, etc. 到處遊樂的人;交際場中的人物。 ***a man of the world***, one with wide experience of business and society. 飽經世故的人;熟悉世情的人。 ***man and boy***, from boyhood onwards: 從小: *He has worked for the firm, man and boy, for thirty years.* 他從小就在這家公司工作,已有三十年之久。 **2** human being; person: 人(包含男女在內): *All men must die.* 所有人都會死亡。 *Growing old is something a man has to accept.* 變老是人必須接受的事實。 ***be one's own man***, be free to act or do as one pleases; be in full possession of one's own senses. 獨立自主;隨心所欲;神智健全。 ***every man for himself (and devil take the hindmost)***, all must see to their own safety. 爭先恐後。 ***the man in the street***, person looked upon as representing the interests and opinions of ordinary people. 普通人;一般人;世人。 ***to a man; to the last man***, all without exception: 毫無例外;全部: *They answered 'Yes' to a man.* 他們全體答'是'。 *They were killed to the last man.* 他們全被殺死,一個也不留。 **3** (*sing* only, no *article*) the human race; all mankind: (僅用單數,不加冠詞)人類;全人類: *Man is mortal.* 人都是會死的。 **4** husband (usu in *man and wife*). 丈夫(通常用於 man and wife 片語中)。 **5** male person under the authority of another; manservant or valet: (男性的)下屬;僕人;佣人: *masters and men*, employers and workers; 主人和僕人;雇主和雇員; *officers and men*, eg in the army. 官長和士兵。 **6** piece used in such games as chess. (西洋棋)一顆棋子。 **7** male person having the good qualities associated with men: 男子漢;大丈夫: *Be a man! Play the man!* Be brave! 做個大丈夫!要有男子氣概! *He's only half a man*, is lacking in spirit, strength, courage. 他沒有男子氣概(他缺少精神、力量、勇氣)。 *How can we make a man of him?* 我們怎樣使他成爲男子漢? **8** (as a vocative, to call attention; used in a lively or impatient way): (作爲促使注意的呼喊語;用於興奮或不耐煩的情況下): *Hurry up, man!* 趕快,趕快! *Nonsense, man!* 胡說八道! **9** (with *possessive adjj*) the person required: (與所有格形容詞連用)所需要的人: *If you want to sell your car, I'm your man*, I'll make an offer. 假如你要賣你的車子,我就是要買的人。 *If you want a good music teacher, here's your man*, here's someone suitable. 如果你需要一位良好的音樂教師,這就是你所需要的人。 **10** (as second element in compounds): (用於複合字中接他字之後): ˈ*clergyman*; ˈ*postman*; ˈ*fisherman*, etc. 教士;郵差;漁夫(等)。⇨ App 3. 參看附錄三。 **11** (compounds) (複合字) ˌ**man-at-ˈarms** *n* soldier, esp (in the Middle Ages) a mounted soldier with heavy armour and weapons. 士兵(尤指中古時代的重騎兵)。 ˈ**man-eater** *n* cannibal; man-eating tiger or shark. 吃人的野蠻人;吃人的老虎或鯊魚。 ˈ**man·handle** *vt* move by physical strength; handle roughly: 由人力操作;粗野地對付: *The drunken man was manhandled by the police.* 醉漢被警察以强硬手段制服了。 ˈ**man·hole** *n* opening (usu with a lid) through which a man may enter (an underground sewer, boiler, tank, etc) for inspection purposes. 出入口;人孔(通常有孔蓋,供工人進入檢查或修理用,如下水道、鍋爐、槽櫃等所設置者)。 ˈ**man-hour** *n* work done by one man in one hour. 工作時(一個人一小時的工作量)。 ˌ**man-of-ˈwar** *n* (old use) armed ship belonging to a country's navy. (舊用法)軍艦;戰鬥艦。 ˈ**man·power** *n* number of men available for military service, industrial needs, etc: 人力(可供軍事、工業等使用的人數): *a shortage of manpower in the coal-mines.* 煤礦坑裏缺少人力(人工)。 ˈ**man·servant** *n* male servant. 男僕;男佣人。 ˈ**man-sized** *adj* of a size or type right for a man; large-scale: 大小適合男人的;大的;大規模的: *a man-sized beefsteak.* 大塊牛排。 ˈ**man·slaughter** *n* [U] act of killing a human being unlawfully but not wilfully. 殺人;誤殺(非法但非故意的殺人);過失殺人。 ˈ**man·trap** *n* trap for catching trespassers, poachers, etc. 捕人的陷阱(用以捕捉侵入私宅,偷獵等之人者)。

man² /mæn ; mæn/ *vt* (-nn-) [VP6A] supply with person(s) for service or defence: 供以人員(用於工作或防衞): *man a fort/a ship*; 部署一個堡壘(給一艘船配置船員); *man a telephone switchboard.* 爲一電話總機配備人員。

man·acle /ˈmænəkl ; ˈmænəkl̩/ *n* (usu *pl*) fetter or chain for the hands or feet. (通常用複數)手銬;足鐐。□ *vt* [VP6A] fetter with ～s; (fig) restrain. 上手銬;加足鐐;(喻)束縛;妨碍。

man·age /ˈmænɪdʒ ; ˈmænɪdʒ/ *vt, vi* **1** [VP6A] control: 控制;駕馭;處理;管理: *～ a horse*; 駕馭一匹馬; *～ a sailing-boat*, handle the sails, etc, properly; 駕駛一艘帆船; *～ a business/household*; 開店(管理家務); *～ a naughty child/one's wife*; 駕馭頑童(妻子); *the managing director*, who controls the business operations of a company. 常務董事。 *Mrs Hill is a very managing woman*, one who likes to ～ or control other people. 希爾太太是個喜歡管別人的女人。 **2** [VP2A, C, 4A, 3A] ～ ***(to do sth)***; ～ ***(with/without sth/sb)***, succeed; contrive: 完成;設法辦到: *I shan't be able to ～ without help.* 沒有人協助我將不能辦到。 *If I can't borrow the money I shall have to ～ without.* 我若是借不到那筆錢,那就只好撐下去了。 *We can't ～ with these poor tools.* 我們無法用這些壞工具做工。 *In spite of these insults, she ～d to keep her temper.* 她雖然受盡侮辱,還是盡量克制自己的怒氣。 **3** [VP6A] (colloq, with *can, could, be able to*) make use of; eat: (俗,與 can, could, be able to 連用)使用;吃: *Can you ～ another slice of cake?* 你能不能再吃一塊蛋糕? ～-

M

able /-əbl ; -əbl̩/ *adj* that can be ~d; easily controlled. 能處理的;容易管理的。~**·abil·ity** /ˌmænɪdʒəˈbɪlətɪ ; ˌmænɪdʒəˈbɪlətɪ/ *n*

man·age·ment /ˈmænɪdʒmənt ; ˈmænɪdʒmənt/ *n* **1** [U] managing or being managed: 管理;處理;經營;支配: *The failure was caused by bad* ~. 這個失敗是因管理不善造成的。*The business is under new* ~. 這個商務現在用新的方式經營。 **2** [U] skilful treatment; delicate contrivance (and perhaps trickery): 手段;周密的策畫(或欺詐): *It needed a good deal of ~ to persuade them to give me the job.* 要用很多手段才能說服他們給我那個差事。 **3** [C, U] (with *sing* or *pl v*) all those concerned in managing an industry, enterprise, etc: (接單數或複數動詞)經理人員;(工業、企業等的)管理人員;主管階層;資方: *joint consultation between workers and* ~. 勞資聯席會議。*What this department store needs is a stronger* ~. 這家百貨公司所需要的是一個較健全的經理部。

man·ager /ˈmænɪdʒə(r) ; ˈmænɪdʒɚ/ *n* **1** person who controls a business, a hotel, etc. 經理。 **2** (usu with an *adj*) one who conducts business, manages household affairs, etc, in a certain way: (通常與形容詞連用)管理業務者;管理家務者: *My wife is an excellent* ~. 我內人是一個非常好的管家。~**·ess** /ˌmænɪdʒəˈres ; ˈmænɪdʒərɪs/ *n* woman ~(1). 女經理。

mana·gerial /ˌmænɪˈdʒɪərɪəl ; ˌmænəˈdʒɪrɪəl/ *adj* of managers: 經理的: *the '~ class,* people such as managers, directors, etc. 經理階級。

mana·tee /ˌmænəˈtiː ; ˌmænəˈti/ *n* large sea mammal with flippers and a broad, flat tail; sea-cow. 一種巨大的海洋哺乳動物;海牛。⇨ dugong.

man·da·rin /ˈmændərɪn ; ˈmændərɪn/ *n* **1** (old use) name for high Chinese government official. (舊用法)滿清高級官吏。 **2** standard spoken Chinese language. 中國國語。 **3** ~ **duck,** small Chinese duck with brightly coloured feathers. 鴛鴦。 **4** ~ **orange,** tangerine. 橘。 **5** person whose behaviour and language seems deliberately remote and difficult: 行爲和語言似乎故作隱祕艱澀的人: (attrib) (形容用法) *the ~ prose of some civil servants.* 某些文官之隱祕艱澀的文章。

man·date /ˈmændeɪt ; ˈmændet/ *n* [C] **1** order from a superior; command given with authority. 命令;訓令。 **2** (hist) authority to administer a territory authorized by the League of Nations after the First World War. (史)(第一次世界大戰後國聯所授予的)託管權。 **3** authority given to representatives by voters, members of a trade union, etc: 選舉人、工會會員等對代表的授權;代表所獲之權限: *the ~ given to us by the electors.* 選舉人授與我們的權限。□ *vt* [VP6A] put (a territory) under a ~(2): 將(某地)委託統治;託管: *the ~d territories.* 託管地。**man·da·tory** /ˈmændətrɪ *US:* -tɔːrɪ ; ˈmændəˌtorɪ/ *adj* of, conveying, a command; compulsory, obligatory: 命令的;含有命令的;委託的;强制性的;義務性的: *the mandatory power.* 受委託統治的國家;託管國。▭ *n* (also 亦作 **-tary** /-tərɪ *US:* -terɪ ; -ˌtɛrɪ/) person or state to whom a ~ has been given. 受託者;受委託統治的國家。

man·dible /ˈmændɪbl ; ˈmændəbl̩/ *n* **1** jaw, esp the lower jaw in mammals and fishes. 顎(尤指哺乳動物和魚的下顎)。 **2** either part of a bird's beak. 鳥嘴的上部或下部。 **3** (in insects) either half of the upper pair of jaws, used for biting and seizing. (昆蟲之)上顎之任一半;大顎(用於咬攫)。

man·do·lin /ˈmændəlɪn ; ˈmændl̩ˌɪn/ *n* musical instrument with 6 or 8 metal strings stretched in pairs on a rounded body. 曼陀林(一種六弦或八弦的樂器,每二弦爲一組,張緊於圓形共鳴箱上)。

man·drag·ora /mænˈdrægərə ; mænˈdrægərə/ *n* [U] poisonous plant used in medical preparations (as an emetic and for causing sleep). 曼陀羅華(可煉製催吐劑及催眠劑的有毒植物)。

man·drake /ˈmændreɪk ; ˈmændrɪk/ *n*=mandragora.

man·drill /ˈmændrɪl ; ˈmændrɪl/ *n* large baboon of West Africa. 山魈(一種大狒狒,產於西非)。

mane /meɪn ; men/ *n* [C] long hair on the neck of a horse, lion, etc; (colloq or hum) thick hair on a man's head. (馬、獅子等動物頸上的)鬃;(俗或諧)濃密的頭髮。⇨ the illus at cat, domestic. 參看 cat, domestic 之插圖。

manes /ˈmɑːneɪz ; ˈmeniz/ *n pl* (Lat) (among the ancient Romans) spirits of the dead, esp of ancestors worshipped as guardian influences. (拉)(古羅馬人所信的)陰魂;(尤指被崇奉爲守護神的)祖先的靈魂。

ma·neu·ver /məˈnuːvə(r) ; məˈnuvɚ/ *n, v* (US spelling of) manoeuvre. 爲 manoeuvre 之美國拼法。

man·ful /ˈmænfl ; ˈmænfəl/ *adj* brave; resolute; determined. 勇敢的;果斷的;堅決的。~**ly** /-fəlɪ; -fəlɪ/ *adv*

man·ga·nese /ˈmæŋgəniːz ; ˈmæŋgəˌnis/ *n* [U] hard, brittle, light-grey metal (symbol **Mn**) used in making steel, glass, etc. 錳(用以製鋼、玻璃等的一種堅硬易碎的淡灰色金屬,符號爲 Mn)。

mange /meɪndʒ ; mendʒ/ *n* [U] contagious skin disease, esp of dogs and cats. (狗貓所患的)皮膚病;畜疥。**mangy** /ˈmeɪndʒɪ ; ˈmendʒɪ/ *adj* **1** suffering from ~: 生瘡疥的: *a mangy dog.* 生疥的狗;癩狗。 **2** squalid; neglected. 汚穢的;被丢棄的。**mang·ily** /ˈmeɪndʒɪlɪ ; ˈmendʒəlɪ/ *adv*

man·gel-wur·zel /ˈmæŋgl wɜːzl ; ˈmæŋgl̩ˈwɝzl̩/ *n* [C] large round root, a kind of beet, used as cattle food. 飼料蒸菜(一種飼牛用的甜菜)。

manger /ˈmeɪndʒə(r) ; ˈmendʒɚ/ *n* long open box or trough for horses or cattle to feed from. 飼牛馬用的槽。***dog in the ~,*** ⇨ dog[1](2).

mangle[1] /ˈmæŋgl ; ˈmæŋgl̩/ *n* [C] machine with rollers for pressing out water from and for smoothing clothes, etc, that have been washed. (洗衣用的)軋乾機;輾壓機。□ *vt* [VP6A] put (clothes, etc) through a ~. 將(衣服等)用此種機器軋乾或軋平。

mangle[2] /ˈmæŋgl ; ˈmæŋgl̩/ *vt* [VP6A] **1** cut up, tear, damage, badly: 切碎;撕裂;毀壞: *He was knocked down by a lorry and badly ~d.* 他被一輛卡車撞倒而皮開肉綻。 **2** (fig) spoil by making bad mistakes: (喻)(因重大錯誤而)損壞;毀壞: *~ a piece of music.* 損害了一首樂曲。

mango /ˈmæŋgəʊ ; ˈmæŋgo/ *n* (*pl* ~es or ~s /-gəʊz ; -goz/) (tropical tree bearing) pear-shaped fruit with yellow flesh: 芒果;芒果樹: *~ chutney,* kind made with (green) unripe ~es. 芒果醬(用未成熟的芒果製成)。⇨ the illus at fruit. 參看 fruit 之插圖。

man·go·steen /ˈmæŋgəˌstiːn ; ˈmæŋgəˌstin/ *n* (E Indian tree bearing) fruit with thick red rind and white juicy pulp. (東印度群島之)山竹果樹;山竹果。

man·grove /ˈmæŋgrəʊv ; ˈmæŋgrov/ *n* [C] tropical tree growing in swamps and sending down new roots from its branches. 紅樹(一種熱帶樹,生於沼澤地,自枝上向下生長樹根)。

mangy /ˈmeɪndʒɪ ; ˈmendʒɪ/ ⇨ mange.

man·handle ⇨ man[1](11).

man·hat·tan /mænˈhætn ; mænˈhætn̩/ *n* (US) cocktail of whisky and vermouth. (美)曼哈坦鷄尾酒(由威士忌與苦艾酒合成)。

man·hood /ˈmænhʊd ; ˈmænhʊd/ *n* [U] **1** the state of being a man: (男子之)成年;成人: *reach ~;* 到達成年; *~ suffrage,* giving the vote to male citizens. 男性公民選舉權。 **2** manly qualities; courage; sexual virility. 男人氣質;勇氣;剛毅;男子氣概。 **3** all the men (collectively, *of* a country): 男人的總稱(指一國之男子,與 of 連用): *the ~ of Scotland.* 蘇格蘭男兒。

mania /ˈmeɪnɪə ; ˈmenɪə/ *n* **1** [U] violent madness. 癲狂;瘋狂;躁狂。 **2** [C] ~ ***(for),*** extreme enthusiasm (*for* sth): 熱中;狂熱: *a ~ for collecting china ornaments.* 收藏瓷器飾物癖。**maniac** /ˈmeɪnɪæk ; ˈmenɪˌæk/ *n* raving madman; (fig) extreme enthusiast. 叫囂的瘋子;(喻)極端狂熱者。**ma·niacal** /məˈnaɪəkl ; məˈnaɪəkl̩/ *adj* violently mad; (fig)

M

extremely enthusiastic. 瘋狂的;(喻)極端狂熱的。**ma·niacally** /mə'naɪəklɪ ; mə'naɪəklɪ/ *adv*

manic-depressive /ˌmænɪk dɪ'presɪv ; 'mænɪkdɪ'prɛsɪv/ *adj, n* (person) suffering from alternating periods of happy excitement and melancholic depression. 癲狂與抑鬱交替發作的(患者);躁鬱性精神病患者。

mani·cure /'mænɪkjʊə(r) ; 'mænɪˌkjʊr/ *n* [U] care of the hands and finger-nails: 修指甲: *have a course in ~;* 學修指甲; [C] treatment of this kind: 修指甲: *She has a ~ once a week.* 她每星期修指甲一次。□ *vt* [VP6A] give ~ treatment to; cut, clean and polish the finger-nails. 為…修指甲;修剪、洗淨及塗染(指甲)。**'mani·cur·ist** /-ɪst ; -ɪst/ *n* person who practises ~ as an occupation. 以修指甲為業的人。

mani·fest¹ /'mænɪfest ; 'mænəˌfɛst/ *n* list of a ship's cargo; list of passengers in an aircraft; list of trucks of a goods train. (船的)載貨單;(飛機的)旅客名單;(運貨火車的)無篷貨車清單。

mani·fest² /'mænɪfest ; 'mænəˌfɛst/ *adj* clear and obvious: 明白的;明顯的: *a ~ truth;* 明顯的眞理; *sth that should be ~ to all of you.* 你們全體應該明白的事情。□ *vt* [VP6A] **1** show clearly: 明白顯示;清楚表示: *~ the truth of a statement.* 明白顯示一項陳述的眞實性。**2** give signs of: 顯露(…的徵象): *She doesn't ~ much desire to marry him.* 她沒有顯露很想嫁給他的樣子。**3** (reflex) come to light; appear: (反身)顯明;顯現: *No disease ~ed itself during the long voyage.* 在這長久的航行中沒有發生任何疾病。*Has the ghost ~ed itself recently?* 最近那個鬼魂出現過了嗎? **mani·fes·ta·tion** /ˌmænɪfe'steɪʃn ; ˌmænəfɛs'teʃən/ *n* [U] ~ing; making clear; [C] act or utterance that ~s. 顯示;表明;明白表示的言行;發表。**~·ly** *adv* clearly; obviously. 明白地;顯然地。

mani·festo /ˌmænɪ'festəʊ ; ˌmænə'fɛsto/ *n* (*pl* ~s or ~es /-təʊz ; -toz/) public declaration of principles, policy, purposes, etc by a ruler, political party, etc or of the character, qualifications of a person or group. 宣言;聲明;布告。

mani·fold /'mænɪfəʊld ; 'mænəˌfold/ *adj* having or providing for many (uses, forms, parts etc); many and various. 有多種用途的;有多種形式的;多樣的;多方面的。□ *vt* [VP6A] (now usu *duplicate*) make a number of copies of (a letter, etc) on a machine. (現在通常用 duplicate) 用機器複印(信件等)。□ *n* pipe or chamber with several openings, for connections, eg for leading gases into or out of cylinders. 歧管;多支管(如用於使氣體通入或流出汽缸者)。

mani·kin /'mænɪkɪn ; 'mænəkɪn/ *n* **1** small, undersized man; dwarf. 矮人;侏儒。**2** anatomical model of the human body; figure of the human body used by artists, eg for drapery, clothes. 人體解剖模型;藝術家用的人體模型;模特兒(例如用於穿戴織物、衣服者)。

Ma·nilla (US also **Ma·nila**) /mə'nɪlə ; mə'nɪlə/ *n* **1 ~ (hemp),** plant fibre used for making ropes, mats, etc. 呂宋麻。**2 m~ paper,** strong, brown wrapping paper made from ~ hemp. 呂宋紙(呂宋麻製成的强靱的棕色包裝紙)。**m~ envelopes,** strong variety. 呂宋紙袋。**3** cheroot made in ~, the capital of the Philippine Islands. 呂宋煙(菲律賓首都馬尼拉製造的雪茄)。

M

ma·nipu·late /mə'nɪpjʊleɪt ; mə'nɪpjəˌlet/ *vt* [VP6A] **1** operate, handle, with skill: 熟練地使用;操縱: *~ the gears and levers of a machine.* 操縱機件。**2** manage or control (sb or sth) skilfully or craftily, esp by using one's influence or unfair methods: 操縱;控制;利用(尤指使用影響力或不公平手段者): *A clever politician knows how to ~ his supporters / ~ public opinion.* 一個聰明的政治家知道如何利用他的擁護者(輿論)。**ma·nipu·la·tion** /məˌnɪpjʊ'leɪʃn ; məˌnɪpjʊ'leʃən/ *n* [U] manipulating or being ~d; [C] instance of this: 操作;操縱;被操縱: *make a lot of money by clever manipulation of the Stock Market.* 由於巧妙的操縱股票市場而賺大錢。

man·kind *n* [U] **1** /ˌmæn'kaɪnd ; mæn'kaɪnd/ the human species. 人類。**2** /'mænkaɪnd ; 'mænˌkaɪnd/ the male sex (contrasted with *'womankind*). 男性(與 womankind 相對)。

man·like /'mænlaɪk ; 'mænˌlaɪk/ *adj* having the qualities (good or bad) of a man. 有男人(好或壞)氣質的;像男人的。

man·ly /'mænlɪ ; 'mænlɪ/ *adj* (-ier, -iest) having the good qualities expected of a man; (of a woman) having a man's qualities; (of things, qualities, etc) right for a man. 有男子氣概的;(指女人)有男人氣質的;男性化的;(指物品、性質等)適合於男人的。**man·li·ness** *n*

manna /'mænə ; 'mænə/ *n* [U] (in the Bible) food provided by God for the Israelites during their forty years in the desert (⇨ Exod 16); (fig) sth unexpectedly supplied or that gives spiritual refreshment. 嗎哪(聖經中以色列人在曠野四十年中所獲得的神賜食物;參看舊約出埃及記第十六章);(喻)不期而獲的東西;精神食糧。

man·ne·quin /'mænɪkɪn ; 'mænəkɪn/ *n* **1** woman employed to display new clothes for sale by wearing them (*model* is the usual word today). 時裝模特兒(現在通常多用 model)。**2** life-size dummy of a human body, used by tailors and in shops and shop-windows for the display of clothes. (裁縫、商店及櫥窗中用以展示衣服的)人體模型。

man·ner /'mænə(r) ; 'mænə/ *n* [C] **1** way in which a thing is done or happens: 方式;方法: *Do it in this ~.* 以這種方式來做。***(as) to the ~ born,*** as if knowing how to deal with a situation, practice, custom, etc from birth; naturally fitted for a position, duty, etc. 好像生來就知道如何應付某種情況、習俗等;天生適合於某種職位的。**2** (*sing* only) person's way of behaving towards others: (僅用單數)態度: *He has an awkward ~.* 他的舉止笨拙。*I don't like his ~.* 我不喜歡他的態度。**3** (*pl*) habits and customs; social behaviour: (複)習慣;風俗;社交行為;禮貌: *good / bad ~s;* 有(沒)禮貌; *He has no ~s at all,* is very badly behaved. 他毫無禮貌。*It is bad ~s to stare at people.* 瞪着眼睛看人是不禮貌的。*Aren't you forgetting your ~s, Mary?* (eg to a child who forgets to say 'Thank you' for a present). 瑪莉,你是不是忘記了禮貌?(例如小孩收了禮物忘記說'謝謝'時,問她這句話)。***comedy of ~s,*** play which is a satire on the customs of (a certain section of) society. 諷刺(某階層)社會風俗的喜劇。**4** style in literature or art: (文學或藝術的)風格;文體;作風: *a painting in the ~ of Raphael.* 一幅模仿拉斐爾作風的畫。**5** kind, sort: 種類: *What ~ of man is he?* 他是哪種人? ***all ~ of,*** every kind of. 各種的。***in a ~,*** in a certain degree; to a certain extent. 有幾分;有點兒;在某種意義上。***in a ~ of speaking,*** as one might say (used to weaken or qualify what one says). 可以說;可謂。***by 'no ~ of means,*** in no circumstances. 絕不;任何情況之下均不。**~ed** *adj* **1** (in compounds) (用於複合字中) ***ˌill- / ˌwell- / ˌrough-'~ed,*** having bad / good / rough ~s(3). 無禮貌的(有禮貌的;粗魯的)。**2** showing mannerisms. 表現出特殊習慣或奇癖的。

man·ner·ism /'mænərɪzəm ; 'mænəˌrɪzəm/ *n* [C] peculiarity of behaviour, speech, etc, esp one that is habitual; excessive use of a distinctive manner in art or literature. (行為、言語等的)特殊習慣;奇癖;(文學或藝術的)過份强調獨特風格。

man·ner·ly /'mænəlɪ ; 'mænəlɪ/ *adj* having good manners; polite. 有禮貌的;謙恭的;客氣的。

man·nish /'mænɪʃ ; 'mænɪʃ/ *adj* **1** (of a woman) like a man. (指女人)像男人的;巾幗鬚眉的。**2** more suitable for a man than for a woman: 較適合男人的(較不適合女人的): *a ~ style of dress;* 男式的

服裝；characteristic of a man. 男人特質的。

ma·noeuvre (US = **ma·neu·ver**) /mə'nu:və(r)；mə'nuvɚ/ *n* **1** planned movement (of armed forces); (*pl*) series of such movements, eg as training exercises: (軍隊的)調遣；機動(性)；(複)演習: *army／fleet ~s;* 陸軍(艦隊)演習； *troops on ~s.* 調動(或演習)中的部隊。 **2** movement or plan, made to deceive, or to escape from sb, or to win or do sth: 用於欺騙、逃避或取勝等的行動或計畫；策略；巧計: *the despicable ~s of some politicians.* 政客的卑鄙策略。□ *vi, vt* [VP2A, C, 6A, 15A] (cause to) perform ~s: 調遣；演習；計誘；策畫: *The fleet is manoeuvring off the east coast.* 艦隊正在東海岸外演習。*Can we ~ the enemy out of their strong position?* 我們能不能用計誘騙敵軍離開他們堅固的陣地？ *She ~d her car into a difficult parking space.* 她設法把車子開進了一個不方便停車的地方。 *Can you ~ me into a good job,* use your influence, etc in order to get a good job for me? 你能不能想辦法給我找個好差事？ *The yachts were manoeuvring for position,* moving about to get advantageous positions (in a race). 那些小艇正在移動以取得有利位置。 **ma·noeuvr·able** (US = **ma·neu·ver·able**) /-vrəbl；-vrəbḷ/ *adj* that can be ~d. 能調遣的；能演習的；可運用的；可操縱的。 **ma·noeuvr·abil·ity** (US = **-neu·ver-**) /mə͵nu:vrə'bɪlətɪ；mə͵nuvərə'bɪlətɪ/ *n* **~r** (US = **ma·neu·verer**) *n*

manor /'mænə(r)；'mænɚ/ *n* (in England) (在英國) **1** unit of land under the feudal system, part of which was used directly by the lord of the ~ (⇨ lord(4)) and the rest occupied and farmed by tenants who paid rent in crops and service. 封建制度下貴族的領地；采地；采邑(此種土地部分爲貴族自用，其餘租給佃農耕種)。 **2** (modern use) area of land with a principal residence (called 稱作 the **'~-house**). (現代用法)大宅邸的莊園。 **ma·nor·ial** /mə'nɔ:rɪəl；mə'norɪəl/ *adj* of a ~. 領地的；采邑的；領主田地的；莊園的。

man·sard /'mænsɑ:d；'mænsɑrd/ *n* **~ (roof),** roof with a double slope, the lower being steeper than the upper. 複折屋頂(下部分坡度比上部分陡)。

manse /mæns；mæns/ *n* church minister's house, esp in Scotland. 牧師住宅(尤指在蘇格蘭者)。

man·sion /'mænʃn；'mænʃən/ *n* **1** large and stately house. 大厦；巨宅；官邸。 **the 'M~ House,** the official residence of the Lord Mayor of London. 倫敦市長官邸。 **2** (*pl*, in proper names) block of flats: (複，用於專有名詞中)公寓大厦: *Victoria M~s.* 維多利亞公寓。

man·tel /'mæntl；'mæntl/ *n* structure of wood, marble, etc above and around a fireplace; (in modern houses, usu **'~piece**) shelf projecting from the wall above a fireplace. 壁爐上部及兩側的木石等構造；(現代房屋裏，通常稱 mantelpiece) 壁爐臺(壁爐上突出的架子)；壁爐前飾。

man·tilla /mæn'tɪlə；mæn'tɪlə/ *n* large veil or scarf worn by Spanish women to cover the hair and shoulders. (西班牙婦女披蓋頭髮和肩膀的) 披肩；頭紗；頭巾。

man·tis /'mæntɪs；'mæntɪs/ *n* **(praying) ~,** (kinds of) long-legged insect. 螳螂。⇨ the illus at insect. 參看 insect 之插圖。

mantle[1] /'mæntl；'mæntl/ *n* **1** loose, sleeveless cloak; (fig) covering: 無袖外套；斗篷；(喻)覆蓋物: *hills with a ~ of snow.* 覆着一層雪的山。 **2** lace-like cover fixed round the flame of a gas lamp and becoming incandescent, to provide bright light. (裝於煤氣燈火焰四周使燈光明亮的)白熱紗罩；燃罩。

mantle[2] /'mæntl；'mæntl/ *vt, vi* **1** [VP6A] cover in, or as in, a mantle: 覆蓋；套；罩；包: *an 'ivy-~d wall.* 爬滿常春藤的牆。 **2** [VP6A, 2C] (old use, or liter) (of blood) flow into the blood-vessels of; (of the face) flush: (舊用法或文學用語) (指血液)流入…之血管；(指臉)漲紅；發紅: *Blushes／Blood ~d (over) her cheeks.* 她的兩頰緋紅。 *Her face ~d with blushes.* 她滿臉羞紅。(fig) (喻) *Dawn ~d in the sky.* 朝輝抹紅了天際。

man·ual /'mænjʊəl；'mænjʊəl/ *adj* of, done with, the hands: 手的；手製的: *~ labour;* 手工；體力勞動； *~ training,* eg in schools, training in carpentry, metal work; 手工藝訓練(例如在學校內學習木工、金工等)； *~ exercises,* eg drill in handling a rifle. 操槍教練。□ *n* **1** handbook or textbook: 手册；教科書: *a shorthand ~.* 速記手册。 **2** keyboard of an organ, played with the hands. (風琴之)手鍵盤。 **~ly** /-jʊəlɪ；-jʊəlɪ/ *adv*

manu·fac·ture /͵mænjʊ'fæktʃə(r)；͵mænjə'fæktʃɚ/ *vt* [VP6A] **1** make, produce (goods, etc) on a large scale by machinery: 製造；以機器大量生產(貨物等)： *~ shoes／cement;* 製造鞋子(水泥)； *manufacturing industries;* 製造工業； *~d goods* (contrasted with raw materials, hand-made goods, etc). 機器製造物品；製造品(以別於原料、手工製品等)。 **2** invent (a story, an excuse, etc). 揑造(故事、託辭等)。□ *n* **1** [U] the making or production of goods and materials: 製造；生產: *firms engaged in the ~ of plastics;* 從事製造塑膠的公司； *goods of foreign ~.* 外國產品。 **2** (*pl*) ~d goods and articles. (複)機器製造物品；製造品；產品。 **manu·fac·turer** *n* person, firm, etc that ~s things. 製造者；製造商；製造廠；生產者。

manu·mit /͵mænjʊ'mɪt；͵mænjə'mɪt/ *vt* (-tt-) (in former times) set (a slave) free. (昔時)釋放(奴隸)。 **manu·mission** /͵mænjʊ'mɪʃn；͵mænjə'mɪʃən/ *n*

ma·nure /mə'njʊə(r)；mə'njʊr/ *n* [U] animal waste, eg from stables and cow barns, or other material, natural or artificial, spread over or mixed with the soil to make it fertile. 肥料(獸類糞便，或其他天然的及人造的物質，施於土壤上或混合於土壤中以使之肥沃)。⇨ *fertilizer,* the usu word for chemical or artificial manure, at fertilize. (fertilizer 通常指化學或人造肥料)。□ *vt* [VP6A] put ~ in or on (land／soil). 施肥於(土地、土壤)。

manu·script /'mænjʊskrɪpt；'mænjə͵skrɪpt/ *n* (shortened to 簡寫爲 **MS,** *pl* 複數簡寫爲 **MSS**) book, etc as first written out or typed: 手稿；原稿；草稿: *send a ~ to the printers.* 將一份原稿送往印刷商。 ***in ~,*** not yet printed: 尚未付印的: *poems still in ~.* 尚未付印的詩稿。

Manx /mæŋks；mæŋks/ *adj* of the Isle of Man. 曼島的。 **'~ cat,** tailless kind of cat. 曼島貓(一種無尾的貓)。□ *n* ~ language. 曼島語。

many /'menɪ；'mɛnɪ/ *adj, n* (contrasted with *few;* 與 few 相對；⇨ more, most) **1** (used with *pl nn;* 與複數名詞連用；⇨ much; in purely affirm sentences it is often preferable to use 在純粹的肯定句中，最好用 *a large number (of), numerous,* or (colloq) (俗) *a lot (of), lots (of), plenty (of)*): 許多(的): *Were there ~ people at the meeting?* 有很多人到會嗎？ *I have some, but not ~.* 我有一些，但是不很多。 *M~ people think so.* 很多人這麼想。 *M~ of them were broken.* 其中許多是破的。 *M~ of us left early.* 我們有很多人早離開了。 *How ~ do you want?* 你要多少？ *How ~ of them were absent?* 他們當中有多少人缺席呀？ *You gave me two too ~.* 你多給了我兩個。 *Do you need so ~?* 你需要這麼多嗎？ *He made ten spelling mistakes in as ~ lines,* ie in ten lines. 他在十行裏拼錯了十個字。 *I have six here and as ~ again* (ie six more) *at home.* 我這裏有六個，在家裏還有六個。 ***a great／good ~,*** a large number (of): 很多(的)： *I have a good ~ things to do today.* 我今天有很多事情要做。 ***one too ~,*** one more than the correct or needed number: 比正確的或所需要的多了一個；不需要的；多餘的: *I wish Jane would go away; she's one too ~ here,* We don't want her company. 我希望珍走開，她在這兒礙手礙脚。 *He's had one too ~ again,* is slightly drunk. 他又多喝了一點酒(有點醉了)。 ***be one too ~ for,*** be more than a match[2](2) for; get the better of; outwit: 優於；勝過: *He was one too ~ for you that*

M

time. 那次他勝過了你。**the ~,** the masses; the large number of ordinary people: 多數人;群衆: *Is it right that the ~ should starve while the few have plenty?* 多數人挨餓而少數人富足是應該的嗎? **2 ~ a,** (used with a *sing n;* rather liter, usu replaced by ~ and the *pl n* in ordinary style): (與單數名詞連用;比較有文學意味,在一般文體中通常由many 與多數名詞所取代): *M~ a man*(= M~ men) *would welcome the opportunity.* 許多人會很高興有這個機會。*I've been here ~ a time.* 我來過這兒好多次了。**~'s the sth/sb that/who...,** it/he has often... 此事曾時常…(他曾時常…)。**~'s the time (that) sth/sb...,** it/he often... 此事(他)時常…。**,~-'sided** *adj* having ~ sides; (fig) having ~ aspects, capabilities, etc: 多邊的;(喻)多方面的;多才多藝的: *a ~-sided problem.* 一個多方面的問題(牽扯很多的問題)。

Maori /'maʊrɪ; 'maʊrɪ/ *n* member, language, of the aboriginal race of New Zealand. 紐西蘭土人;毛利人;毛利語。

map /mæp; mæp/ *n* representation on paper, etc of the earth's surface or a part of it, showing countries, oceans, rivers, mountains, etc; representation of the sky showing positions of the stars, etc. 地圖;天體圖。⇨ the illus at projection. 參看 projection 之插圖。⇨ chart, plan. **on the map,** (fig) important, to be reckoned with. (喻)重要的;不可小看的。**off the map,** (colloq, of a place) inaccessible; (fig) unimportant. (俗,指地點)不能到達的;(喻)不重要的。**'map-reader** *n* (with an *adj*) person able to get information from maps: (與一形容詞連用)能利用地圖的人: *He's a good/poor map-reader.* 他是個會(不會)使用地圖的人。□ *vt* (-pp-) [VP6A] make a map of; show on a map; 繪製…的地圖;以地圖表示; [VP15B] **map out,** plan, arrange: 計畫;設計: *map out one's time.* 支配時間(計畫時間的利用)。

maple /'meɪpl; 'mepḷ/ *n* **1** [C] (sorts of) tree of the northern hemisphere, grown for timber and ornament. 楓樹;槭樹。⇨ the illus at tree. 參看 tree 之插圖。**~sugar/syrup** *n* sugar/syrup obtained from the sap of one kind of ~. 楓糖(楓蜜)。**'~-leaf** *n* emblem of Canada. 楓葉(加拿大的象徵)。**2** [U] wood of this tree. 楓木。

ma·quis /'mæki: *US:* 'mɑki:; ,mɑ'ki/ *n* **the ~,** the secret army of French patriots during World War II, fighting in France against the Germans. 第二次世界大戰中法國境內抗德游擊隊。

mar /mɑ:(r); mɑr/ *vt* (-rr-) [VP6A] injure; spoil; damage: 損傷;毀損;毀壞: *Nothing marred the happiness of our outing.* 沒有任何事物損害我們遠足的快樂。**make or mar,** make a great success of or ruin completely. 使大爲成功或徹底失敗。

mara·bou /'mærəbu:; 'mærə,bu/ *n* large W African stork; tuft of its soft feathers as trimming, eg for a hat. 產於西非的大鸛;(做帽子等裝飾用的)鸛毛。

mar·as·chino /,mærə'ski:nəʊ; ,mærə'skino/ *n* (*pl* ~s /-nəʊz; -noz/) sweet liqueur made from a small black kind of cherry. 黑櫻桃酒。

mara·thon /'mærəθən *US:* -θɒn; 'mærə,θɑn/ *n* **the M~,** long-distance race on foot (about 26 miles (or 41.8 kilometres) at modern sports meetings); (fig) test of endurance. 馬拉松賽跑(現代比賽全長約26哩或41.8公里);(喻)持久力的比賽;耐力的考驗。

ma·raud /mə'rɔ:d; mə'rɔd/ *vi* [VP2A] go about in search of plunder or prey: 到處搶劫;劫奪;劫掠: *The Roman Empire was attacked by ~ing Goths and Huns.* 羅馬帝國遭受到處搶劫的哥德人和匈奴人所攻擊。**~er** *n* person or animal that ~s. 劫掠的人或動物。

marble /'mɑ:bl; 'mɑrbl/ *n* **1** [U] (sorts of) hard limestone used, when cut and polished, for building and sculpture: 大理石: (attrib) (形容用法) *a ~ statue/tomb.* 大理石雕像(墓)。**2** (*pl*) works of art in ~; collection of ~ sculptures. (複)大理石藝術品;一批大理石雕刻品。**3** small ball of glass, clay or stone used in games played by children. (小孩玩的)玻璃彈子;泥彈子;石彈子;彈珠。**~s,** game played with these balls: 彈珠戲: *Let's have a game of ~s.* 我們來打彈珠。**4** (attrib) like ~: (形容用法)像大理石的: *a ~ brow,* smooth and white; 光滑而潔白的前額; *a ~ breast,* hard and unsympathizing personality. 冷酷無情的個性。**~d** /'mɑ:bld; 'mɑrbḷd/ *adj* stained or printed so as to look like variegated ~: (染印成)大理石花紋的: *a book with ~d edges.* 邊緣有大理石花紋的書。

March /mɑ:tʃ; mɑrtʃ/ *n* the third month of the year: 三月: *M~ hare,* ⇨ hare.

march¹ /mɑ:tʃ; mɑrtʃ/ *vi, vt* **1** [VP2A, B, C] walk as soldiers do, with regular and measured steps: 前進;齊步前進: *They have ~ed thirty miles today.* 他們今天已經行走了三十哩。*They ~ed into the town.* 他們進入那個城鎮了。*Quick ~!* (military command to begin ~ing). 快步走!(軍隊口令)。*The troops ~ed by/past/in/out/off/away.* 軍隊走過(走過,走進,出發,離開,開走)。*He ~ed impatiently up and down the station platform.* 他在月臺上不耐煩地踱來踱去。**'~ing orders,** orders for troops to leave for manoeuvres, for war, etc; (fig) dismissal. 出發令;開拔令;行軍命令;(喻)免職令;解雇通知。**2** [VP15A, B] cause to ~: 使前進: *They ~ed the prisoner away.* 他們把犯人押走。*He was ~ed off to prison.* 他被押去監獄。

march² /mɑ:tʃ; mɑrtʃ/ *n* **1** [U] act of marching (by soldiers, etc). (軍隊)進軍;前進。**on the ~,** marching. 在行進中;進軍中。**a line of ~,** a route followed by troops when ~ing: 行軍路線: *Scouts were sent out to discover the enemy's line of ~.* 斥候被派出去探查敵人行軍路線。**2** [C] instance of marching; distance travelled: 進軍或前進之實例;行程: *a ~ of ten miles.* 十哩的行程。**a ~ past,** ie of troops past a saluting point at a review. 分列式。**a forced ~,** one made more quickly than usual, or for a greater distance, in an emergency. 强行軍;兼程行軍。**steal a '~ on sb,** win a position of advantage by doing sth earlier than expected by him. 搶先某人;早某人一步。**3 the ~ of,** progress; onward movement: 進步;進展: *the ~ of events/time.* 事件的發展(時間的過去)。**4** [C] piece of music for marching to: 進行曲: *military ~es;* 軍隊進行曲; *a dead ~,* one in slow time for a funeral. 送葬曲;哀樂。**~er** *n*

march³ /mɑ:tʃ; mɑrtʃ/ *n* (usu *pl*) (hist) frontier areas (esp between England and Scotland or Wales), esp land that is in dispute: (通常用複數)(史)邊界;邊境(尤指英格蘭與蘇格蘭或威爾斯之間接壤的地帶);關糾紛的邊界: *riding round the ~es.* 在英格蘭與蘇格蘭的邊界駛車(騎馬)。□ *vi* [VP3A] **~ upon/with,** (archaic) (of countries, estates, etc) border upon; have a common frontier with: (古)(指國家、產業等)接鄰;毗連: *Our territory ~es with theirs.* 我們的土地和他們的毗鄰。

mar·chion·ess /,mɑ:ʃə'nes; 'mɑrʃənɪs/ *n* wife or widow of a marquis; woman who holds in her own right a position equal to that of a marquis. 侯爵夫人;侯爵未亡人;女侯爵。

Mardi Gras /,mɑ:dɪ 'grɑ:; 'mɑrdɪ'grɑ/ *n* (F) Shrove Tuesday; last day of carnival before Lent, celebrated in some places with parades and merry-making. (法)懺悔星期二;四旬齋前的狂歡節最後一日(某些地方以遊行和狂歡慶祝之)。

mare /'meə(r); mɛr/ *n* female horse or donkey. 母馬;母驢。**a '~'s nest,** a hoax; a discovery that turns out to be false or worthless. 戲弄人的事;假的或無價值的發現;一場空歡喜。

mar·gar·ine /,mɑ:dʒə'ri:n *US:* 'mɑ:rdʒərɪn; 'mɑrdʒə,rin/ *n* [U] food substance, used like butter, made from animal or vegetable fats. 人造奶油(以動物或植物脂肪製成的代用品)。

marge /mɑ:dʒ; mɑrdʒ/ *n* (colloq abbr for) margarine. (俗)爲 margarine 之略。

mar·gin /ˈmɑːdʒɪn ; ˈmɑrdʒɪn/ *n* [C] **1** blank space round the printed or written matter on a page: 空白邊;印刷品或書寫品每頁的空白邊緣: *wide/narrow ~s;* 寬(窄)邊; *notes written in the ~.* 寫在空白處的註解;眉批。 **2** edge or border: 邊;緣: *sit on the ~ of a lake/swimming pool;* 坐在湖邊(游泳池邊); *road ~s.* 路邊。 **3** amount (of time, money, etc) above what is estimated as necessary. (錢､時間等超出估計所需要之)餘裕;餘地。 **4** condition near the limit or borderline, below or beyond which sth is impossible: 邊際;極限: *a safety ~.* 安全限度。 *He escaped defeat by a narrow ~.* 他差一點兒失敗了。 **5** (comm) difference between cost price and selling price: (商)成本與售價的差額;盈餘;毛利: *an increase of a penny a gallon in the dealer's ~ on the price of petrol.* 在汽油的價格上商人的利潤每加侖增加一辨士。 **~al** /-nl ; -nl/ *adj* **1** of or in a ~(1): 頁邊的;空白處的: *~al notes.* 頁邊的註解。 **2** of a ~(4): 邊際的: *The differences between the employers and the workers are ~al.* 雇主與工人間的不同有限。 **~al land,** land which is not fertile enough for profitable farming except when prices of farm products are high. 邊際土地(不够肥沃，耕種無利可獲，非至農產價格高漲時不加利用)。 **~al seat/constituency,** one where the MP has been elected by a small majority. 邊際席位(選區)(超過對方票數很少而當選國會議員的席位或選區)。 **~·ally** /-nəlɪ ; -nḷɪ/ *adv*

Mar·grave /ˈmɑːgreɪv ; ˈmɑrgrev/ *n* hereditary title of certain princes in the Holy Roman Empire. (神聖羅馬帝國之)侯爵。

mar·guer·ite /ˌmɑːgəˈriːt ; ˌmɑrgəˈrit/ *n* kinds of daisy, esp the ox-eye daisy with white petals round a yellow centre. 延命菊;雛菊(尤指牛眼菊)。

mari·gold /ˈmærɪgəʊld ; ˈmærəˌgold/ *n* (kinds of) plant with orange or yellow flowers. 金盞草。

mari·juana, mari·huana /ˌmærɪˈwɑːnə ; ˌmærəˈwɑnə/ *n* (also called 亦稱作 *hashish, cannabis, pot*) dried leaves and flowers of Indian hemp, (esp) smoked in cigarettes (called *reefers or joints*) to induce euphoria. 印度大麻;乾的大麻葉和花(尤指混於煙葉當麻醉劑吸用者);大麻煙。

mar·imba /məˈrɪmbə ; məˈrɪmbə/ *n* musical instrument similar to the xylophone. 馬林巴(一種類似木琴的樂器)。

ma·rina /məˈriːnə ; məˈrinə/ *n* harbour designed for pleasure boats (small yachts, cabin cruisers, etc) often with hotels, etc. 遊艇停泊港(常有旅社等場所)。

mari·nade /ˌmærɪˈneɪd ; ˌmærəˈned/ *n* [U] pickle of wine, vinegar and spice; fish or meat pickled in this. (一種包含酒､醋､香料等的)醃泡汁;滷汁;泡在此種滷汁中的魚或肉。□ *vt* (also 亦作 **mari·nate** /ˈmærɪneɪt ; ˈmærəˌnet/) steep, make tender, in ~. (用此種醃汁)浸;使嫩。

mar·ine /məˈriːn ; məˈrin/ *adj* **1** of, by, found in, produced by, the sea: 海的;近海的;海中的;海產的: *~ products;* 海產; *a ˈ~ painter,* artist who paints seascapes. 海景畫家。 **2** of ships, sea-trade, the navy, etc: 船隻的;海運的;海軍的: *~ insurance,* of ships and cargo; 海上(運)保險; *~ stores,* materials and supplies for ships. 船用物品。 **ˈ~ corps,** body of soldiers serving on warships and trained for amphibious warfare. 海軍陸戰隊。□ *n* **1** ˌ**merchant/**ˌ**mercantile** ˈ~, all the merchant ships of a country. 一個國家的商船的總稱。 **2** [C] soldier of a ~ corps serving on a warship. 海軍陸戰隊軍官或士兵。 **the M~s,** country's general body of such soldiers. 一國之海軍陸戰隊。 ***Tell that to the ~s,*** (used to express disbelief in an impossible story). 誰會相信！沒有這回事！(表示不相信一件不可能的事)。

mari·ner /ˈmærɪnə(r) ; ˈmærənə/ *n* sailor, esp one who assists in navigating a ship: 水手;海員: *a ~'s compass.* 航海羅盤。 **master ~,** captain of a merchant ship. 商船船長。

mari·on·ette /ˌmærɪəˈnet ; ˌmærɪəˈnɛt/ *n* jointed doll or puppet moved by strings on a small stage. (用線牽動在小舞臺演出的)木偶;傀儡。 ⇨ the illus at puppet. 參看 puppet 之插圖。

mari·tal /ˈmærɪtl ; ˈmærətl/ *adj* of a husband; of marriage: 丈夫的;婚姻的: *~ obligations,* eg providing for one's wife. 丈夫的責任(如供養妻子)。

mari·time /ˈmærɪtaɪm ; ˈmærəˌtaɪm/ *adj* **1** connected with the sea or navigation: 海上的;航海的;海事的: *~ law;* 海事法; *the great ~ powers.* 海權强國。 **2** situated or found near the sea: 近海的;靠海的: *the ~ provinces of the USSR.* 蘇俄的沿海省份。

mar·joram /ˈmɑːdʒərəm ; ˈmɑrdʒərəm/ *n* [U] sweet-smelling herb used as seasoning in cooking and in medicine. 茉沃刺那(佐料及製藥用的唇形科薄荷植物)。

mark¹ /mɑːk ; mɑrk/ *n* **1** line, scratch, cut, stain, etc that spoils the appearance of sth: 痕跡;斑點;污點: *Who made these dirty ~s on my new book?* 誰在我的新書上弄了這些污跡？ **2** noticeable spot on the body by which a person or animal may be recognized: (人或動物身上可供識別用的)記號;標識;特徵: *a horse with a white ~ on its head;* 頭上有個白點的馬; *a ˈbirth~.* 胎記;生來就有的特徵。 **3** visible trace; sign or indication (of a quality, etc): 形跡;(性質等的)標誌;標示: *~s of suffering/old age.* 痛苦(年老)的標誌。 *Please accept this gift as a ~ of my esteem.* 請接受我這個表示敬意的禮物。 **4** figure, design, line, etc, made as a sign or indication: 符號;標誌: *ˌpunctuˈation ~s;* 標點符號; *ˈprice-~s,* on goods; 價目標籤; *ˈtrade ~s.* 商標。 **5** numerical or alphabetical symbol, eg β+, to indicate an award in an examination, or for conduct. 分數;評定考試成績或操行的符號(例如 β+)。 ***give sb/get/gain a good/bad, etc ~ (for sth):*** (爲某事)給某人(獲得)良好(不好)的成績: *get 72 ~s out of 100 for geography/full ~s for science.* 地理科考了72分(自然科學得了滿分)。 *He got the best ~s of his year.* 他是同年級中成績最好的。 **6** target; sth aimed at. 目標;目的物。 ***be/fall wide of the ~,*** be inaccurate, imprecise: 不準確;不正確: *Your guess/calculation is wide of the ~.* 你的猜測(計算)不對。 ***hit/miss the ~,*** (fig) succeed/fail in an attempt. (喩)嘗試成功(失敗)。 ***an easy ~,*** (colloq) person who is easily cheated, persuaded or ridiculed. (俗)易受騙，被說服或受嘲弄的人。 ***beside the ~,*** irrelevant. 不中肯;不切題。 **7** [U] distinction; fame: 顯赫;卓越;名譽: ***make one's ~,*** become distinguished. 成名。 **8 the ~, (a)** standard. 標準。 ***be up to/below the ~,*** equal to/below the required standard. 達到(低於)標準。 **(b)** what is normal. 常態。 ***not be/feel (quite) up to the ~,*** not in one's usual health. 健康情形欠佳。 **9** cross made on a document by an illiterate person: (文盲畫在文件上當作簽名的)十字畫押: *make one's ~.* 畫十字押。 *John Doe, his ~,* cross made by John Doe instead of a signature. 某甲，他的十字畫押。 **10** (athletics) line indicating the starting-point of a race: (體育)起點;起跑線: *On your ~s, get set, go!* (words used by the starter). 各就各位，預備，跑！ **11** (with numbers) model or type: (與數字連用)型;式: *Meteor M~ 3,* eg of an aircraft. 流星三型(如飛機的型式)。

mark² /mɑːk ; mɑrk/ *vt, vi* **1** [VP6A, 15A, B] ***~ sth on/with sth; ~ sth down/up,*** put or leave a ~ on sth by writing, stamping, etc: 加記號;加符號;作標誌;加標籤;標價格: *~ one's name on one's clothes/~ one's clothes with one's name.* 把名字寫在衣服上(把衣服寫上自己的名字)。 *All our stock has been ~ed down for the sales,* reduced in prices. 我們所有的存貨都減價廉售。 *The new tax made it necessary to ~ up all the goods in the shop,* put higher price ~s on them. 新稅迫使商店所有的貨物漲價。 Hence, 由此產生, **ˈ~-up** *n* amount by which a price is ~ed up: 價格增漲額: *a 10% ~-up.* 加價百分之十。'~·ing-ink *n* indelible ink for ~ing linen, etc. 不褪色墨水(在布等上標寫用的)。 **2** (passive) have natural ~s or visible signs: (用於被動語態)有天然的痕跡或可見的跡象: *A zebra is ~ed with stripes.* 斑馬身上有條紋。*His face is ~ed with smallpox,* has the scars of smallpox. 他的臉有天花疤痕(有麻子)。*Her face is ~ed with grief.* 她面露戚容。 **3** [VP6A] give ~s(5) to: 批分數;評成績: *~ examination papers;* 評閱考卷;評考試成績; *have twenty essays to ~/to be ~ed.* 有二十份論文要評分數。 **4** [VP22] indicate sth by putting a ~, eg a tick or a cross, on or against: 作記號以表示(例如以'√'或'+'等記號): *~ sth wrong;* 記下某事有問題; *~ a pupil absent.* 記下一學生缺席。 **5** [VP6A, 8, 10, 2A] pay attention (to): 注意: *M~ carefully how it is done/how to do it/how he does it.* 注意這是怎麼做的(怎麼做,他怎麼做)。***(You) m~ my words,*** Note what I say (and you will find, later, that I am right). 留心聽我所說的話(你以後會發現我是對的)。**a ~ed man,** one whose conduct is watched with suspicion or enmity. 嫌疑份子。 **6** [VP6A] be a distinguishing feature of: 爲…的特徵: *What are the qualities that ~ a great leader?* 偉大領袖的特質是甚麼? **7** [VP6A] signal; denote: 表示;指示: *His death ~ed the end of an era.* 他的逝世表示一個時代的結束。*There will be ceremonies to ~ the tenth anniversary of the Queen's accession.* 將有典禮以慶祝女王就位十週年。 **8** ***~ time,*** stamp the feet as when marching but without moving forward; (fig) wait until further progress becomes possible. 原地踏步;(喻)俟機;遷延。 **9** [VP 15B] (uses with *adverbial particles*) (與副詞接語連用) ***~ sth off,*** put ~s on (to show boundary lines, measurements, etc). 加標誌於某物(以示界線,測量等);以界線隔開。***~ sth out,*** put lines on sth to indicate limits, etc: 畫線表示界限: *~ out a tennis-court.* 用線畫出一個網球場。***~ sb out for sth,*** decide in advance that sb will receive sth: 事先決定(某人將接受某物): *~ sb out for promotion.* 內定某人升遷。*Peter was ~ed out for a special management course.* 彼得被選定接受一特別管理課程。 **~ed** /mɑ:kt ; mɑrkt/ *adj* clear; readily seen: 明顯的;顯著的: *a ~ed difference/improvement;* 顯著的不同(改良); *a man of ~ed ability.* 才能顯著的人。 **~·ed·ly** /'mɑ:kɪdlɪ ; 'mɑrkɪdlɪ/ *adv* in a ~ed manner. 顯著地;明顯地。**~·ing** *n* (esp) pattern of different colours of feathers, skin, etc. (尤指羽毛,皮膚等的)斑點;條紋;花紋。

mark[3] /mɑ:k ; mɑrk/ *n* unit of German currency. 馬克(德國錢幣單位)。

marker /'mɑ:kə(r) ; 'mɑrkɚ/ *n* **1** person or tool that marks, esp a person who marks the score at games, eg billiards. 作記號的人或器具;(尤指)(撞球等競賽中之)記分員;記分器。 **2** sth that marks or indicates, eg a flag or post on a playing field, a post showing distances. 作爲標誌之物(例如操場上的旗幟或標桿,表示距離的里程碑)。

mar·ket[1] /'mɑ:kɪt ; 'mɑrkɪt/ *n* **1** [C] public place (an open space or a building) where people meet to buy and sell goods; time during which such a meeting takes place: 市場;市集;市日: *She went to (the) ~ to buy food for the family.* 她去市場給家人購買食物。*There are numerous small ~s in the town.* 鎮裏有許多小市場。*The next ~ is on the 15th.* 下一次市日是在十五日。***bring one's eggs/hogs to a bad ~/to the wrong ~,*** fail in one's plans, fail because one goes to the wrong people for help. 計畫失敗;找錯了求援對象而失敗;失策;失算。***go to ~,*** go there for the purpose of shopping. 去市場購物。***go to a bad/good ~,*** be (un)successful. 失敗(成功)。'**~-day** *n* fixed day on which a ~ is held. 定期的交易日;市日。ˌ**~-'garden** *n* one where vegetables are grown for ~s. 種植蔬菜出售的菜園。Hence, 由此產生, ˌ**~-'gardening** *n* [U] the practice of doing this. 種植蔬菜出售的行業。'**~-place/-square** *n* square or open place in a town where a ~ is held. 市場(指空敞的地點);市集;商業集中地。'**~ hall,** (usu large) roofed area for a ~. 市場(指建築物)。'**~-town** *n* one where a ~ (esp one for cattle and sheep) is held. 市集(尤指有牛羊買賣的市鎮)。 **2** trade in a class of goods: 買賣某種貨物的行業: *the 'corn ~;* 穀物業(市場); *the 'coffee ~;* 咖啡業(市場); state of trade as shown by prices: 市況;行情;市價: *a dull/lively ~.* 蕭條的(繁榮的)市況。*The ~ rose/fell/was steady,* Prices rose/fell/did not change much. 行情上漲(下跌,平穩)。**~ price,** price for which sth, eg commodities/securities, is sold in the open ~. 市價;出售價格。'**down-/'up-~** *adjj* (trade use) low/high class. (貿易用語)低(高)級的。 **3** demand: 需求: *There's no/not much/only a poor ~ for these goods.* 這些貨品沒有銷路(銷路不好,銷路很差)。 **4** the ~, buying and selling. 買賣;交易。***be on/come on (to) the ~,*** be offered for sale: 出售: *This house will probably come on the market next month.* 這幢屋子可能下個月要出售。***be in the ~ for sth,*** be ready to buy or (fig) consider sth. 準備買某物;(喻)準備考慮某事。***play the ~,*** speculate (by buying and selling shares, commodities, etc). (買賣股票,商品等)投機。***put sth on the ~,*** offer it for sale. 出售某物。ˌ**~ re'search,** study of the reasons why people buy, or do not buy, certain goods, how sales are affected by advertising, etc. 市場調查(研究顧客購買或不願購買某些貨品的原因,以及廣告的效果等)。 **5** [C] area, country, in which goods may be sold. 推銷地區;市場: *We must find new ~s for our products.* 我們必須爲我們的產品找新的市場(推銷地區)。*Which countries are Brazil's best ~s for coffee?* 那些國家是巴西咖啡的最佳市場? ˌ**Common 'M~,** ⇨ common[1](1).

mar·ket[2] /'mɑ:kɪt ; 'mɑrkɪt/ *vi, vt* **1** [VP2A] buy or sell in a ~: (在市場)買;賣: *go ~ing.* 去市場買或賣東西。 **2** [VP6A] take or send to ~; prepare for (a/the) ~ and offer for sale. 帶或送貨到市場出售;銷售。**~·able** /-əbl ; -əbl/ *adj* that can be sold; fit to be sold: 可賣的;適合在市場出售的: *~able products.* 能銷的產品。**~·ing** *n* theory and practice of (large-scale) selling. (大規模)推銷原理和實務。

marks·man /'mɑ:ksmən ; 'mɑrksmən/ *n* (*pl* -men /-mən ; -mən/) person skilled in aiming at a mark, esp with a rifle. 善射手;名射手;(尤指)神槍手。**~ship** /-ʃɪp ; -ˌʃɪp/ *n* skill in shooting. 射擊術。

marl /mɑ:l ; mɑrl/ *n* [U] soil consisting of clay and carbonate of lime, used as a fertilizer. 泥灰(用作肥料)。

mar·line·spike /'mɑ:lɪnspaɪk ; 'mɑrlɪnˌspaɪk/ *n* pointed iron tool used for separating the strands of a rope which is to be spliced. 解索針;穿索鑽。

mar·ma·lade /'mɑ:məleɪd ; 'mɑrmḷˌed/ *n* [U] (bitter) jam made from citrus fruit (usu oranges). (苦味的)柑桔醬。

mar·mor·eal /mɑ:'mɔ:rɪəl ; mɑr'morɪəl/ *adj* (poet) white, cold or polished, like marble. (詩)像大理石般潔白,涼爽或光滑的。

mar·mo·set /'mɑ:məzet ; 'mɑrməˌzɛt/ *n* small, tropical American monkey with soft, thick hair and a bushy tail. 絹猴(中南美所產的一種小猴)。⇨ the illus at ape 參看 ape 之插圖。

mar·mot /'mɑ:mət ; 'mɑrmət/ *n* small animal of the squirrel family. 土撥鼠。

ma·ro·cain /'mærəkeɪn ; 'mærəken/ *n* [U] thin, fine dress material of silk or wool. 絲或毛的衣料;一種縐綢。

ma·roon[1] /mə'ru:n ; mə'run/ *adj, n* brownish-red (colour). 栗色;褐紅色;栗色的;褐紅色的。

ma·roon[2] /mə'ru:n ; mə'run/ *n* rocket, esp the kind used as a warning signal. 煙火(尤指示警用者)。

ma·roon[3] /mə'ru:n ; mə'run/ *vt* [VP6A] put (sb) on a desert island, uninhabited coast, etc, and

M

abandon him there. 放逐(某人)於荒島,無人煙的海邊等;棄(某人)於荒島。

marque /mɑːk ; mark/ *n* ˌ***letters of*** ˈ**~**, authority formerly given to private persons to fit out an armed ship and use it to attack, capture, and plunder. 捕拿特許狀(昔時頒給私人的特許,准其裝備武裝船隻並用以攻擊,緝捕和刼掠)。

mar·quee /mɑːˈkiː ; marˈki/ *n* large tent (as used for flower shows, garden parties, or for a circus). 大帳幕;大帳篷(如花展,園遊會,馬戲場所用者)。

mar·quetry /ˈmɑːkɪtrɪ ; ˈmarkətrɪ/ *n* [U] inlaid work (wood, ivory, etc) used for decorating furniture. (裝飾傢具的木或象牙等)鑲嵌細工。

mar·quis, mar·quess /ˈmɑːkwɪs ; ˈmarkwɪs/ *n* (GB) nobleman next in rank above an earl and below a duke; (in other countries) nobleman next in rank above a count. 侯爵(在英國高於 earl 而低於 duke; 在其他國家高於count)。⇨ marchioness.

mar·riage /ˈmærɪdʒ ; ˈmærɪdʒ/ *n* **1** [C, U] (instance of a) legal union of a man and woman as husband and wife; state of being married: 結婚;婚姻: *A ~ has been arranged between... and....* 某人與某人已準備結婚。*She has had an offer of ~.* 有人向她求婚。***give sb*** (esp one's daughter) ***in ~ (to sb)***, offer her as a wife. 把某人(尤指自己的女兒)嫁出去。***take sb in ~***, take as husband or wife. 嫁給某人; 娶某人爲妻。ˈ**~ certificate/licence/settlement**, ⇨ these words. 參看各該字。ˈ**~ lines**, (colloq) ~ certificate. (俗)結婚證書。**2** (usu 通常用 *wedding*) ceremony of being married: 結婚儀式;婚禮: *Was it a civil or a church ~?* 是普通婚禮還是在教堂行婚禮? ⇨ civil(1). **~·able** /-əbl ; -əbl̩/ *adj* (of a young person) old enough, fit for, ~: (指年輕人)已屆適婚年齡的;適合結婚的: *a girl of ~able age.* 到達適婚年齡的女子。**~·abil·ity** /ˌmærɪdʒəˈbɪlətɪ ; ˌmærɪdʒəˈbɪlətɪ/ *n*

mar·ried /ˈmærɪd ; ˈmærɪd/ *adj* united in marriage; of marriage: 結婚的;已婚的;婚姻的: *~ couples;* 夫婦; *~ life.* 婚姻生活。

mar·row /ˈmærəʊ ; ˈmæro/ *n* **1** [U] soft, fatty substance that fills the hollow parts of bones. 髓;骨髓。***chilled to the ~***, cold through and through. 寒冷徹骨。ˈ**~·bone** *n* bone containing edible ~. 髓骨(含有可吃的骨髓)。**2** [U] (fig) essence; essential part: (喻)精華;重要的部分: *the pith and ~ of his statement.* 他的聲明的要點。**3** [C] **(vegetable) ~**, vegetable of the gourd family (US 美=squash, like a large fat cucumber); [U] this as food, eg stuffed with minced meat: 葫蘆科蔬菜(似大黃瓜); (食用之) 葫蘆 (如填以碎肉者): *stuffed ~ for lunch.* 以葫蘆盅做午餐。⇨ the illus at vegetable. 參看 vegetable 之插圖。

marry /ˈmærɪ ; ˈmærɪ/ *vt, vi* (*pt, pp* -ried) **1** [VP6A, 2A, D, 4A] take as a husband or wife; have a husband or wife: 結婚;娶;嫁: *John is going to ~ Jane.* 約翰將要和珍結婚。*Tom and Alice are going to get married.* 湯姆和愛麗絲將要結婚。*Mary married young.* 瑪莉早婚。*Harry didn't ~ until he was over fifty.* 哈利過了五十歲才結婚。*She married again six months after the death of her first husband.* 她在前夫死後六個月又結婚了。*She married to get away from her tyrannical mother.* 她爲了脫離她那暴虐的母親而結婚。**2** [VP6A] (of a priest, a civil official) join as husband or wife: (指牧師,官員)主持…的婚禮;使結爲夫婦: *Which priest is going to ~ them?* 那一位牧師將要主持他們的婚禮? **3** [VP6A, 15B] **~ *(off)***, give in marriage: 嫁(女): *He married both his daughters to rich directors.* 他把兩個女兒都嫁給富有的董事。*She has married off all her daughters*, has found husbands for them. 她把她所有的女兒都嫁出去了。**4** [VP6A] obtain by ~ing: 由結婚而獲得: *~ money/wealth.* 由結婚而得到金錢(財富)。

Mars /mɑːz ; marz/ *n* **1** (Roman myth) the god of war. (羅馬神話)戰神。**2** (astron) planet fourth in order from the sun. (天文)火星。⇨ the illus at planet. 參看 planet 之插圖。

Mar·sala /mɑːˈsɑːlə ; marˈsala/ *n* [U] sweet white wine originally exported from Marsala, Sicily. 馬沙拉白葡萄酒(產於西西里島上馬沙拉地方)。

Mar·seil·laise /ˌmɑːsəˈleɪz ; ˌmarsl̩ˈez/ *n* French national anthem. 馬賽進行曲(法國國歌)。

marsh /mɑːʃ ; marʃ/ *n* [C, U] (area of) low-lying, wet land: 沼澤(地帶);濕地: *miles and miles of ~;* 濕地連連(表示面積甚大的沼澤地帶); *the Romney ~es.* 隆尼沼澤地區。ˈ**~ gas**, fire-damp; methane. 沼氣;甲烷。ˌ**~-ˈmallow** *n* **(a)** shrubby herb that grows near salt ~es. 藥蜀葵。**(b)** soft, spongy sweetmeat. 一種軟鬆糖果。**~y** *adj* (-ier, -iest) of or like a ~. 沼澤的;像沼澤的;多沼澤的。

mar·shal[1] /ˈmɑːʃl ; ˈmarʃəl/ *n* **1** Officer of highest rank: 最高級軍官;元帥: ˌ*Field-ˈM~*, (in the Army); 陸軍元帥; ˌ*Air-ˈM~*, (in the Air Force). 空軍中將。**2** official responsible for important public events or ceremonies, eg one who accompanies a High Court judge; an officer of the royal household. 司儀;司禮官;典禮官。**3** (US) official with the functions of a sheriff; head of a fire or police department. (美)地方法律執行官;消防隊長;警長。

mar·shal[2] /ˈmɑːʃl ; ˈmarʃəl/ *vt* (-ll-, US -l-) [VP6A, 15A, B] **1** arrange in proper order: 整理;序列: *~ facts/military forces.* 整理事實(軍隊)。ˈ**marshalling-yard** *n* railway yard in which goods trains, etc are assembled. (貨運火車)調車場。**2** guide or lead (sb) with ceremony: 按禮儀引導(某人): *~ persons into the presence of the Queen.* 引導人們覲見女王。

mar·su·pial /mɑːˈsuːpɪəl ; marˈsupɪəl/ *adj, n* (animal) of the class of mammals the females of which have a pouch in which to carry their young, which are born before developing completely, eg kangaroos. 有袋動物的;有袋動物(如袋鼠等)。

mart /mɑːt ; mart/ *n* **1** (liter) market-place; centre of commerce. (文)市場;商業中心。**2** auction room. 拍賣室。

mar·ten /ˈmɑːtɪn ; ˈmartɪn/ *n* [C] small animal of the weasel family; [U] its fur. 貂;貂皮。

mar·tial /ˈmɑːʃl ; ˈmarʃəl/ *adj* **1** of, associated with, war: 戰爭的;軍事的: *~ music;* 軍樂; *~ bearing.* 軍儀。ˌ**~ ˈlaw**, military government, by which ordinary law is suspended, eg during a rebellion: 戒嚴令: *declare ~ law;* 宣佈戒嚴令; *be under ~ law.* 在戒嚴期中;在戒嚴地區內。**2** brave; fond of fighting: 勇敢的;好戰的: *show a ~ spirit*, show eagerness for war. 表現尚武精神。**~ly** /-ʃəlɪ ; -ʃəlɪ/ *adv*

Mar·tian /ˈmɑːʃn ; ˈmarʃɪən/ *n, adj* (hypothetical inhabitant) of the planet Mars. 火星的;(假想的)火星人。

mar·tin /ˈmɑːtɪn *US:* -tn ; ˈmartɪn/ *n* **(ˈhouse-) ~**, bird of the swallow family that builds a mud nest on walls, etc. (築泥巢於牆壁等上的)一種燕子。

mar·ti·net /ˌmɑːtɪˈnet *US:* -tnˈet ; ˌmartn̩ˈɛt/ *n* person who requires and enforces strict discipline. 厲行嚴格紀律的人。

mar·tini /mɑːˈtiːnɪ ; marˈtinɪ/ *n* cocktail made of gin and dry vermouth. 馬丁尼酒(以杜松子酒和苦艾酒混合成的一種雞尾酒)。

mar·tyr /ˈmɑːtə(r) ; ˈmartɚ/ *n* person who is put to death or caused to suffer greatly for his religious beliefs or for the sake of a great cause or principle: 烈士;殉道者: *the early Christian ~s in Rome.* 在羅馬的早期基督教殉道者。*He died a ~ in the cause of science*, lost his life through his efforts to help forward the cause of science. 他爲科學而犧牲。***make a ~ of oneself***, sacrifice one's own wishes or advantage (or pretend to do so) in order to get credit or reputation. 犧牲(或假裝犧牲)自己的願望或利益以博得信用聲譽。***be a ~ to sth***, suffer greatly from: 遭受…的極大痛苦: *He's a ~ to rheumatism.* 他爲風濕症所苦。□ *vt* [VP

6A] put to death, cause to suffer, as a ~. (因其堅守所信而)殺害;使受苦。 '~·dom /-dəm ; -dəm/ *n* ~'s suffering or death: 殉道;犧牲;成仁;受難;受苦: *His wife's never-ending complaints made his life one long ~dom.* 他妻子無盡期的抱怨使他受罪一輩子。

mar·vel /'mɑːvl ; 'mɑrvḷ/ *n* [C] **1** wonderful thing; sth causing great surprise, pleased astonishment: 奇妙的事物;令人驚奇或驚喜的事物: *the ~s of modern science.* 近代科學的奇蹟。*It's a ~ to me that he escaped unhurt.* 他能安然無恙地逃脫,在我看來是件奇事。*The doctor's pills worked ~s,* had wonderful results. 那醫生的藥丸有神奇的效果。 **2** *~ of sth,* wonderful example: 奇異的例子;不凡的例子: *She's a ~ of patience.* 她的耐心是罕見的。*Your room is a ~ of neatness and order.* 你的房間是出奇的整潔。 □ *vi* (-ll-, US -l-) **1** [VP3A] *~ at sth,* be greatly surprised at: (對…)大爲驚訝;驚歎;驚異: *~ at sb's boldness.* 對某人的勇敢感到驚異。 **2** [VP3B] *~ that / why, etc,* wonder: 驚奇;驚異;詫異: *I ~ that she should agree to marry that man / ~ why she should want to marry him.* 我覺得奇怪她會同意嫁給那個人(爲什麼她要嫁給他)。 **~·lous,** (US = **~·ous**) /'mɑːvələs ; 'mɑrvḷəs/ *adj* astonishing; wonderful. 驚奇的;神妙的;不可思議的。 **~·lous·ly** (US = **~-ous·ly**) *adv*

Marx·ist /'mɑːksɪst ; 'mɑrksɪst/ *n* follower of Karl Marx, German economist and socialist: 馬克斯主義者: (attrib) (形容用法) *~ criticism;* 馬克斯主義的批評; *a ~ party.* 一個信奉馬克斯主義的政黨。 **Marx·ism** /'mɑːksɪzəm ; 'mɑrksɪzṃ/ *n* (esp) political and economic theory that class struggle has been the major force behind historical change, that the dominant class has exploited the other classes and that capitalism will inevitably be superseded by socialism and a classless society. 馬克斯主義(尤指其政治和經濟學說,認爲階級鬪爭是歷史演變的主力,當權階級曾自私地利用其他階級,資本主義將不可避免地被社會主義和一無階級社會所代替)。

mar·zi·pan /'mɑːzɪpæn ; 'mɑrzɪˌpæn/ *n* [U] thick paste of ground almonds, sugar, etc, made up into small cakes; [C] small cake made of this mixture. 杏仁粉和糖等所調成用以製小餅的濃醬;小杏仁餅。

mas·cara /mæ'skɑːrə *US:* -'skærə ; mæs'kærə/ *n* [U] cosmetic preparation for darkening the eyelashes. 染睫毛油;睫毛膏。

mas·cot /'mæskət ; 'mæskət/ *n* person, animal or object considered likely to bring good fortune. 吉祥的人,動物或東西(被認爲會帶來好運者)。

mas·cu·line /'mæskjʊlɪn ; 'mæskjəlɪn/ *adj* **1** of, like, the male sex: 男性的;像男性的: *a ~ style;* 男人的式樣; *a ~ woman.* 男性化的女人。 **2** of male gender: (文法)陽性的: *'He' and 'him' are ~ pronouns.* He 和 him 都是陽性代名詞。 **mas·cu·lin·ity** /ˌmæskjʊ'lɪnətɪ ; ˌmæskjə'lɪnətɪ/ *n* quality of being ~. 男性;陽性。 ⇨ feminine

ma·ser /'meɪzə(r) ; 'mezɚ/ *n* device for producing or amplifying microwaves. 微波器;微波放大器。

mash /mæʃ ; mæʃ/ *n* [U] **1** grain, bran, etc cooked in water for poultry, cattle or pigs. 由穀物、麥麩等煮成的家禽、牛或豬的飼料。 **2** [U, C] any substance softened and crushed, eg boiled potatoes beaten and crushed: 任何餬狀物(如搗爛的熟馬鈴薯): *a plate of sausage and ~.* 一盤香腸和馬鈴薯泥。 **3** mixture of malt and hot water used in brewing. 麥芽漿(釀啤酒用的熱水泡的麥芽)。 □ *vt* [VP6A] beat or crush into a ~: 搗碎成餬狀: *~ed turnips.* 搗爛的蘿蔔。 **~er** *n* cooking utensil for ~ing, eg potatoes. 搗碎機(如搗馬鈴薯器);搗碎器。

mask[1] /mɑːsk *US:* mæsk ; mæsk/ *n* **1** covering for the face, or part of it, eg a piece of silk or velvet for hiding the face; replica of the face carved in wood, ivory, etc; disguise. 面罩;面具;(以木頭、象牙等雕刻成的)面像摹製品;假面具;僞裝。 ***do sth under a / the ~ of friendship,*** while pretending to be a friend. 藉友誼之名(裝做朋友)做某事。 ***throw off one's ~,*** (fig) show one's true character and intentions. (喻)揭掉假面具;現出本來的面目。 **2 ('gas)·~,** breathing apparatus, in some cases for the whole of the head, worn as a protection against poisonous gas, smoke, etc, eg in coalmines, or by a fireman in a burning building. 防毒(火)面具(一種用以防止吸入毒氣、煙等的呼吸器具,有時遮住整個面部,如煤礦坑內工人,或救火員進入火場所用者)。 **3** pad of sterile gauze worn over the mouth and nose by eg doctors and nurses, eg for a surgical operation. (醫生或護士手術時所戴的紗布)口罩。 **4** replica of the face worn by an actor or actress. (演員所戴的)假面具。 **5** likeness of a face made by taking a mould in wax, etc. (用蠟等)模製的面像。 **'death ~,** one made by taking a mould of the face of a dead person. 照死人的臉面模製的面像。 **6** face or head of a fox. 狐狸的面或頭。

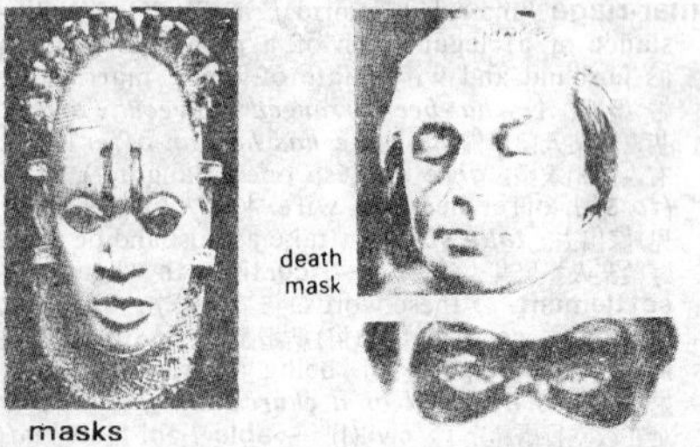

masks

mask[2] /mɑːsk *US:* mæsk ; mæsk/ *vt* [VP6A] **1** cover (the face) with a mask: 戴假面具;戴面罩: *a ~ed woman,* one wearing a mask; 戴著面罩的女人; *a ~ed ball,* one at which masks are worn. 化裝舞會。 **2** conceal: 隱蔽;遮掩: *~ one's enmity under an appearance of friendliness;* 把敵意隱藏在友善的外表之下; *~ed guns,* hidden from the enemy. 隱蔽的大砲。

maso·chism /'mæsəkɪzəm ; 'mæzəˌkɪzəm/ *n* [U] getting satisfaction (esp sexual pleasure) from pain or humiliation. 受虐狂(在痛苦或侮辱中獲得滿足或性快感);(尤指)受虐淫。 ⇨ sadism. **maso·chist** /-kɪst ; -kɪst/ *n* **maso·chis·tic** /ˌmæsə'kɪstɪk ; ˌmæzə'kɪstɪk/ *adj*

ma·son /'meɪsn ; 'mesṇ/ *n.* **1** stone-cutter; worker who builds or works with stone. 石匠;磚石匠;泥瓦匠。 **2** freemason. 互助會會員。 **~ic** /mə'sɒnɪk ; mə'sɑnɪk/ *adj* of freemasons. 互助會的;互助會會員的。 **~ry** /'meɪsnrɪ ; 'mesṇrɪ/ *n* **1** stonework; that part of a building made of stone and mortar. 石造物;石工;建築的石造部分。 **2** freemasonry. 互助會之制度。

Mason-Dixon line /ˌmeɪsn 'dɪksn laɪn ; 'mesṇ 'dɪksṇ laɪn/ *n* (US hist) boundary between Pennsylvania and Maryland, dividing the free and the slave States before the Civil War. (美史)南北分界線(美國內戰前在賓夕法尼亞州與馬里蘭州間之界線,將蓄奴與非蓄奴之各州分開)。

masque /mɑːsk *US:* mæsk ; mæsk/ *n* drama in verse, often with music, dancing, fine costumes and pageantry, esp as given in castles and great mansions in England during the 16th and 17th cc. 假面劇(一種詩劇,常伴以音樂、舞蹈、美觀劇裝及壯麗行列,尤指十六、十七世紀在英國城堡及巨宅中演出者)。

mas·quer·ade /ˌmɑːskə'reɪd *US:* ˌmæsk- ; ˌmæskə'red/ *n* **1** ball at which masks and other disguises are worn. 假面具舞會;化裝舞會。 **2** (fig) false show or pretence. (喻)假裝;僞裝。 □ *vi* [VP2A, C] *~ (as),* appear, be, in disguise: 假裝;喬裝;僞裝: *a prince who ~d as a peasant.* 一個喬裝爲農夫的王子。

mass /mæs ; mæs/ *n* **1** [C] *~ (of),* lump, quantity of matter, without regular shape; large number, quantity or heap: 塊;堆;大量;大堆: *~es of dark* *clouds in the sky.* 天上一朵朵的烏雲。*The azaleas made a ~ of colour in the garden.* 杜鵑花給花園裏添上一大片色彩。*A ~ of snow and rock broke away and started an avalanche.* 一大堆雪和岩石裂開了就開始雪崩。*The poor fellow was a ~ of bruises,* (colloq) was covered with bruises. (俗)那個可憐的人遍體鱗傷。**2 the ~es,** the proletariat; (manual) workers. 勞動階級;工人;群衆。***in the ~,*** in the main; as a whole: 大體而論;整體上: *The nation in the ~ was not interested in politics.* 這個國家的人民大體說來對政治不感興趣。~ **meeting,** large meeting, esp of people wishing, or requested, to express their views (protesting against sth, urging that sth be done, etc). 群衆大會(尤指發表意見以爲請願等的集會)。~ **com,munications;** ~ **media,** means (esp newspapers, radio, TV) of imparting information to, influencing the ideas of, enormous numbers of people. 大衆傳播工具(尤指報紙,無線電,電視等用以向大衆傳達消息或影響大衆意見者)。~ **observation,** study of the social customs of ordinary people. 對群衆的社會風俗的研究。~ **production,** manufacture of large numbers of identical articles by standardized processes. 大量生產(以標準化方法製造大量同樣的產品)。Hence, 由此產生, **~-produce** *vt* **3** [U] (science) quantity of material in a body measured by its resistance to change of motion. (科學)物體的質量。⇨ size¹(1). □ *vt, vi* [VP6A, 2A] form or collect into a ~: 集合;集結: *~ed bands,* number of bands(5) playing together. 混合大樂隊(集合在一起演奏的數個樂隊)。*Troops are ~ing/are being ~ed on the frontier.* 軍隊正在邊境集結。*The clouds are ~ing.* 雲朵密布。**~y** *adj* solid; massive. 結實的;巨大的。

Mass /mæs; mæs/ *n* [C, U] celebration (esp RC church) of the Eucharist: 彌撒(尤指天主教的領聖餐): *high/solemn ~,* with eg incense, music and considerable ceremony; 大彌撒(有燒香,奏樂,而儀式繁多者); *go to ~;* 去望彌撒; *hear ~.* 聽彌撒。*M~es were said for peace in the world.* 爲世界和平作彌撒。

mass·acre /ˈmæsəkə(r); ˈmæsəkɚ/ *n* [C] cruel killing of large numbers of (esp defenceless) people (occasionally used of animals). 大屠殺(尤指屠殺無防衛的人群,有時亦指獸類)。□ *vt* [VP6A] make a ~ of. 大屠殺。

mass·age /ˈmæsɑːʒ *US:* məˈsɑːʒ; məˈsɑʒ/ *n* [C, U] (instance of) pressing and rubbing the body, usu with the hands, esp the muscles and joints, in order to lessen pain, stiffness, etc. 按摩;揉捏(按摩身體上肌肉與關節以減少痛苦、僵硬等)。□ *vt* [VP6A] apply ~ to. 按摩;揉捏。**mass·eur** /mæˈsɜː(r); mæˈsɝ/, **mass·euse** /mæˈsɜːz; mæˈsɜz/ *nn* man, woman, who practises ~. 男按摩師;女按摩師。⇨ *physiotherapist* at physiotherapy.

massif /mæˈsiːf; ˈmæsɪf/ *n* compact group of mountain heights. 山嶽;山群。

mass·ive /ˈmæsɪv; ˈmæsɪv/ *adj* **1** large, heavy and solid: 大而重的;大塊的;巨大的: *a ~ monument.* 一個巨大的紀念碑。**2** (of the features) heavy-looking: (指容貌)粗大的: *a ~ forehead.* 寬大的前額。**3** (fig) substantial; impressive. (喻)結實的;予人深刻印象的。**~·ly** *adv* **~·ness** *n*

mast¹ /mɑːst *US:* mæst; mæst/ *n* **1** upright support (of wood or metal) for a ship's sails. (木製或金屬製的)船桅;檣。⇨ the illus at barque, ship. 參看 barque, ship 之插圖。***sail before the ~,*** work as an ordinary seaman (with a berth in the forepart of the ship). 做普通海員(鋪位在船之前部者)。**'~-head** *n* highest part of a ~, used as a look-out post. 桅頂(供瞭望用)。**2** tall pole (for a flag). (掛旗用的)長杆。**3** tall steel structure for aerials of a radio or television transmitter; (also 亦作 *'mooring-~*) tall tower to which an airship may be moored. 無線電或電視發射機的天線塔;飛艇繫留塔。

mast² /mɑːst *US:* mæst; mæst/ *n* [U] fruit of beech, oak and other forest trees (as food for pigs). 山毛櫸,橡樹等的果實(作豬的飼料)。

mas·ter¹ /ˈmɑːstə(r) *US:* ˈmæs-; ˈmæstɚ/ *n* **1** man who has others working for him or under him: 主人;雇主: *~ and man,* employer and workman (or manservant); 雇主與雇工; 主人與僕人; (attrib) skilled workman or one in business on his own account: (形容用法)熟練技工;能手;獨立經營者: *a ~ carpenter/builder, etc.* 木工能手(獨立經營的建築師或營造商等)。***be one's own ~,*** be free and independent. 獨立自主。**2** male head of a household: 家裏的男主人: *the ~ of the house.* 家長。***be ~ in one's own house,*** manage one's affairs without interference from others. 處理自己的事務不受他人干涉。**3** captain of a merchant ship: 商船的船長: *a ~ mariner;* 船長; *obtain a ~'s certificate,* one that gives the holder the right to be a ship's captain. 取得船長證書。**4** male owner of a dog, horse, etc. 狗,馬等的男主人。**5** male teacher: 男教師: *the ,matheˈmatics ~;* 數學教師; *'school~;* 教師;校長; *'house~,* ⇨ house¹(7); male teacher of subjects taught outside school: 擔任校外所授科目的男教師;教練: *a 'dancing/'fencing/'riding-~.* 舞蹈教師 (擊劍教練; 騎術教練)。**6 ~ of,** person who has control or who has (sth) at his disposal: 能控制或掌握某事物的人;能自由運用某事物的人;精通某事物的人: *He is ~ of the situation,* has it under control. 他能控制這個情況。*If only I could be ~ of this subject,* come to know it thoroughly. 我多麼希望能精通這個科目。*He has made himself ~ of the language,* has learnt it well, so that he can use it freely. 他已經精通這種語言。*You cannot be the ~ of your fate,* cannot decide your own destiny. 你不能決定你自己的命運。*He is ~ of a large fortune,* can use it as he wishes. 他能隨意處理一大筆財產。**7 the M~,** Jesus Christ. 主;耶穌基督。**,M~ of 'Arts/'Science, etc,** holder of the second university degree. 文學(理學等)碩士。⇨ bachelor. **8** (with a boy's name) young Mr: (與男孩的姓名連用)小主人;少爺: *M~ Charles Smith,* sometimes used when speaking of or to a boy up to about the age of 14. 查理史密斯少爺(有時用以對十四歲左右的男孩的尊稱)。**9** title of the heads of certain colleges: 某些學院的院長: *the M~ of Balliol,* Oxford. 牛津大學巴利奧學院院長。**10** great artists, esp **old ~s,** the great painters of the 13th to 17th cc; painting by one of these artists. 名家;大師(尤用於 old masters 中,指十三至十七世紀間的大畫家);大畫家之作品。**11** (attrib) commanding; superior: (形容用法) 主要的; 熟練的;高超的: *the work of a ~ hand,* a superior and skilful artist, etc. 能手的作品;名家的作品。*His ~ passion* (= The passion that dominates his thoughts, etc) *is motor-racing.* 他最大的愛好是賽車。**'~·mind** *n* person with superior brains (esp one who plans work to be carried out by others). 英才;老手;主腦(尤指計畫工作由別人執行的人物)。Hence, 由此產生, **'~-mind** *vt* plan, direct, a scheme: 策畫: *The whole affair was ~-minded by the publicity department.* 整個事情是由宣傳部門策畫的。**12** as title of various officials. 某些官員的頭銜。**M~ of the Horse,** official in the royal household. 御馬長官。**M~ of foxhounds,** man who controls them. 管獵狐狗的官員。**M~ of Ceremonies,** (abbr 略作 **MC**) person who superintends the forms to be observed on various social occasions, eg a public banquet. 司禮官;司儀。**13** (compounds) (複合字) **,~-at-'arms** *n* police officer in the Navy and in passenger ships of the merchant service. (海軍或商船上的)警衛長。**'~-key** *n* one that will open many different locks, each also opened by a separate key. 萬能鑰匙(可以開很多不同鎖的鑰匙)。**~·less** *adj* having no ~. 無主人的。**'~·piece** *n* sth made or done with very great skill. 傑作;名著。**'~·stroke** *n* surpassingly skilful act or piece (of policy, etc). (政策等)絕妙的行動;絕招。⇨ (for senses 1-5) mistress.

mas·ter² /ˈmɑːstə(r) *US:* ˈmæs- ; ˈmæstə/ *vt* [VP 6A] become the ~ of; overcome: 成爲…之主人;精通;征服;控制: *~ one's temper/feelings;* 控制脾氣(感情); *~ a foreign language/the saxophone.* 精通一種外國語(擅於吹奏薩克管)。

mas·ter·ful /ˈmɑːstəfl *US:* ˈmæs- ; ˈmæstəfəl/ *adj* fond of controlling others; dominating: 愛控制別人的;專橫的: *speak in a ~ manner.* 以專橫的態度說話。**~ly** /-fəlɪ ; -fəlɪ/ *adv*

mas·ter·ly /ˈmɑːstəlɪ *US:* ˈmæs- ; ˈmæstəlɪ/ *adj* worthy of a great master; very skilful: 巧妙的;精巧的: *with a few ~ strokes of the brush.* 用巧妙的幾筆。

mas·ter·ship /ˈmɑːstəʃɪp *US:* ˈmæs- ; ˈmæstəʃɪp/ *n* **1** [U] dominion; control. 主權;控制。 **2** [C] office, duties, of a (esp school-) master: 教師(尤指校長)的職位,職務: *He was offered an assistant-~* (now usu 現在通常作 *teaching post*) *in Bolton.* 他被邀請擔任波爾頓學校的助教。

mas·tery /ˈmɑːstərɪ *US:* ˈmæs- ; ˈmæstərɪ/ *n* [U] **1** *~ (of),* complete control or knowledge: 控制;熟練;精通: *his ~ of the violin;* 他拉小提琴的熟練; *get ~ of a wild horse.* 馴服一匹野馬。 **2** *~ (over),* supremacy: 控制權;優勢: *Which side will get the ~?* 那一邊將要取得控制權?

mas·ti·cate /ˈmæstɪkeɪt ; ˈmæstəˌket/ *vt* [VP6A] chew; soften, grind up (food) with the teeth. 咀嚼;咬碎(食物)。 **mas·ti·ca·tion** /ˌmæstɪˈkeɪʃn ; ˌmæstəˈkeʃən/ *n*

mas·tiff /ˈmæstɪf ; ˈmæstɪf/ *n* large, strong dog with drooping ears, much used as a watchdog. 獒(一種大猛犬,兩耳下垂,多作看守用)。

mas·to·don /ˈmæstədɒn ; ˈmæstəˌdɑn/ *n* large extinct elephant-like animal. 乳齒象(已絕種的古代似象的巨獸)。

mas·toid /ˈmæstɔɪd ; ˈmæstɔɪd/ *n* bone at the back of the ear. (耳後的)乳突。 **~·itis** /ˌmæstɔɪˈdaɪtɪs ; ˌmæstɔɪdˈaɪtɪs/ *n* inflammation of the ~. 乳突炎。

mas·tur·bate /ˈmæstəbeɪt ; ˈmæstəˌbet/ *vi, vt* [VP 2A, 6A] procure or provide sexual excitement by manual or other stimulation of the genital organs. 手淫。 **mas·tur·ba·tion** /ˌmæstəˈbeɪʃn ; ˌmæstəˈbeʃən/ *n*

mat¹ /mæt ; mæt/ *n* **1** piece of material (woven or plaited, of straw, rope, rushes, rags, fibre, etc) used for a floor covering, for sleeping on, or (a ˈ*doormat*) for wiping dirty shoes on. 蓆;墊(草、繩、燈心草、碎布、纖維等製成的織物,用以鋪地板、睡覺或作擦鞋墊 doormat 用)。 **2** small piece of material placed under vases, ornaments, etc, or (a ˈ*table-mat* of cork, asbestos, etc) under hot dishes on a table (to prevent injury to a varnished surface, etc). (用以墊瓶子,裝飾品,熱盤子等的)小墊。 **3** anything thickly tangled or twisted together: 纏結之物;一叢;一簇;一團: *a mat of weeds;* 一叢野草; *comb the mats out of a dog's thick hair.* 梳理一隻狗身上纏結的厚毛。□ *vt, vi* (-tt-) [VP6A] cover or supply with mats; [VP6A, 15A, 2A, C] (cause to) be or become tangled or knotted: 鋪蓆子;墊墊子;(使)纏結: *matted hair.* 亂蓬蓬的頭髮。

mat², matt (US also **matte**) /mæt ; mæt/ *adj* (of surfaces, eg paper) dull; not shiny or glossy: (指紙等之表面)不光滑的;粗糙的: *paint that dries with a ~ finish.* 乾後表面粗糙的漆。⇨ gloss¹(1).

M

mata·dor /ˈmætədɔː(r) ; ˈmætəˌdɔr/ *n* man whose task is to kill the bull in the sport of bull-fighting. 鬪牛士。

match¹ /mætʃ ; mætʃ/ *n* short piece of wood, pasteboard, wax taper, etc, with a head made of material that bursts into flame when rubbed on a rough or specially prepared surface (the second kind being called ˈ*safety ~es*): 火柴(有的火柴在粗糙表面摩擦卽生火,有的須在特製的表面摩擦始能生火,後者稱爲'安全火柴'): *strike a ~;* 劃火柴;擦火柴; *a box of ~es.* 一盒火柴。 **ˈ~·box** *n* box for holding ~es. 火柴盒。 **ˈ~·wood** *n* **(a)** wood suitable for making ~es. 適於製造火柴棒的木材。 **(b)** splinters or fragments of wood: 碎木;細木片: *smashed to ~wood,* completely broken up. 完全破碎;粉碎。

match² /mætʃ ; mætʃ/ *n* **1** contest; game: 比賽;競賽: *a ˈfootball/ˈwrestling ~;* 足球(角力)比賽; *a ˈboxing ~ of twenty rounds.* 二十回合的拳擊比賽。 **ˌ~-ˈpoint,** final point needed to win a ~, eg tennis. 最後決勝負的一分(如網球賽中)。 **2** person able to meet another as his equal in strength, skill, etc: 對手;敵手;在體力、技巧等方面相等的人: *find/meet one's ~.* 遇到對手。 *He is up against more than his ~,* has met sb who is his superior (in skill, etc). 他遇到比他高明的對手。 *You are no ~ for him,* are not strong, clever, etc enough to compete with him. 你不是他的對手(你敵不過他)。 **3** marriage: 婚姻;匹配: *They decided to make a ~ of it,* (of two persons) They decided to marry. 他倆決定結婚。 **ˈ~·maker** *n* (esp) person who is fond of arranging ~es(3) for others. 媒人;喜歡做媒的人。 **4** person considered from the point of view of marriage: 婚姻之對象;配偶: *He's a good ~,* is considered satisfactory or desirable as a possible husband. 他是個好配偶。 **5** person or thing exactly like, or corresponding to, or combining well with, another: 彼此完全相像的人或物;相配的人或物: *colours/materials that are a good ~.* 很相配的顏色(材料)。 **~·less** *adj* unequalled. 無比的;無雙的;無敵的。

match³ /mætʃ ; mætʃ/ *vt, vi* **1** [VP14] *~ sth/sb against/with,* put in competition: 使相競爭;使比賽: *I'm ready to ~ my strength with/against yours.* 我準備跟你比力氣。 **2** [VP6A] be equal to; be, obtain, a match(2) for: 和…匹敵;是…的對手;爲…找到對手: *a well-~ed pair,* eg boxers about equal in skill. 旗鼓相當的一對;勢均力敵的一對(例如拳擊手)。 *No one can ~ him in archery.* 在箭術方面沒有人能够和他相比。 *Can you ~ that story,* tell one that is equally good, amusing, etc? 你能講一個同樣精采的故事嗎? **3** [VP6A, 2A] be equal to or corresponding (with) (in quality, colour, design, etc): (在品質,顏色,設計等方面)(與…)相等;相當;相配: *The carpets should ~ the curtains.* 地毯該和窗簾相配。 *The curtains and carpets should ~.* 窗簾和地毯應該相配。 *She was wearing a brown dress with hat and gloves to ~.* 她穿着一件棕色的衣服,並有帽子和手套相配。⇨ clash(4). **4** [VP6A, 12B, 13B] find a material, etc that ~es(3) with (another): 找到和(另一件)相配的布料等: *Can you ~ (me) this silk?* 你能替我找到和這塊綢子相配的布料嗎?

match·et /ˈmætʃɪt ; ˈmætʃɪt/ *n* = machete.

match·lock /ˈmætʃlɒk ; ˈmætʃˌlɑk/ *n* old-fashioned style of musket. 舊式毛瑟槍;火繩槍。

mate¹ /meɪt ; met/ *n* **1** (colloq) friend; companion; fellow-worker (often as a form of address): (俗)朋友;伙伴;同事(常作稱呼用): *Where are you going, ~?* 老兄,你去哪兒? ⇨ *class-~* at class, *play~* at play¹(1). **2** ship's officer (not an engineer) below the rank of captain: 副船長;大副;副手(低於船長,但非輪機師): *the chief ~,* below the captain; 大副; *the first/second/third ~.* 大(二,三)副。 **3** helper: 助手: (in titles) (用於稱謂) *the cook's/gunner's/surgeon's ~;* 厨子的(砲手的,外科醫生的)助手; *a plumber's ~.* 鉛管工人的助手。 **4** one of a pair of birds or animals: 鳥獸之偶: *the lioness and her ~.* 母獅與其配偶。 **5** (colloq) partner in marriage, ie husband or wife: (俗)配偶(夫或妻): *She has been a faithful ~ to him.* 她一直都是他的忠實配偶。

mate² /meɪt ; met/ *vt, vi* [VP6A, 14, 2A, 3A] *~ (with),* (of birds or animals) (cause to) unite for the purpose of having sexual intercourse, producing young: (指鳥獸)使交配;交配: *the ˈmating* *season*, spring, when birds make their nests. 交配季節。*The zoo's camels have not ~d this year.* 動物園裏的駱駝今年還沒有交配。

mate[3] /meɪt ; met/ *n, v* (in chess) (下棋) =checkmate.

maté /ˈmɑːteɪ ; ˈmɑte/ *n* (tea made from) dried leaves of a S American evergreen holly shrub. 南美馬黛茶樹;馬黛茶。

ma·terial[1] /məˈtɪərɪəl ; məˈtɪrɪəl/ *adj* **1** (contrasted with *mental* and *spiritual*) made of, connected with, matter or substance: (與 mental 及 spiritual 相對)物質的;由物質構成的: *the ~ world;* 物質世界; *a ˈ~ noun,* naming a material, eg stone, wood, wool. 物質名詞(例如石頭,木材,毛織品)。**2** of the body; of physical needs: 身體的;肉體所需的: *~ needs,* eg food and warmth; 身體的需要(如食物與溫暖); *~ comforts and pleasures;* 使肉體得到安適與快樂的事物; *a ~ point of view,* worldly, considering only the things of the senses. (僅僅考慮感官之事物的)物慾的觀點。**3** (legal) important; essential: (法律)重要的;重大的: *~ evidence/testimony.* 重要的證據(證言)。*The judge warned the witness not to hold back ~ facts,* facts that might influence a decision. 法官警告證人不得隱瞞重要的事實。*Is this point ~ to your argument?* 這一點對你的議論很重要嗎? **~ly** /-ɪəlɪ ; -ɪəlɪ/ *adv* in a ~(3) manner; essentially. 重要地;重大地。

ma·terial[2] /məˈtɪərɪəl ; məˈtɪrɪəl/ *n* **1** [C, U] that of which sth is or can be made or with which sth is done: 材料;原料: *raw ~s,* not yet used in manufacture; 原料; *ˈdress ~s,* cloth; 衣料; fabrics from which dresses may be made: 織物;布料: *too much ~ for one overcoat;* 做一件大衣又太多的料子; *not enough ~ for two overcoats.* 做兩件大衣又不够的料子。**ˈwriting ~s,** pen, ink, paper, etc. 文具。**2** [U] (fig) facts, happenings, elements: (喻)事實;事件;要素;資料: *~ for a newspaper article;* 一篇報紙上的文章所需要的資料; *the ~ from which history is made.* 史料。

ma·teri·al·ism /məˈtɪərɪəlɪzəm ; məˈtɪrɪəlˌɪzəm/ *n* [U] **1** theory, belief, that only material things exist. 唯物主義;唯物論。**2** tendency to value, valuation of, material things (wealth, bodily comforts, etc) too much and spiritual, artistic and intellectual things too little. 物質主義;實利主義(過於重視物質方面的事物,如財富,肉體享受等,而輕視精神,藝術與智力方面的事物之傾向)。**ma·teri·al·ist** /-ɪst ; -ɪst/ *n* believer in ~; person who ignores religion, painting, music, etc. 唯物論(主義)者;物質主義者;實利主義者。**ma·teri·al·is·tic** /məˌtɪərɪəˈlɪstɪk ; məˌtɪrɪəlˈɪstɪk/ *adj* of ~ or materialists. 唯物(論)的;唯物主義者的。**ma·teri·al·is·ti·cally** /-klɪ ; -klɪ/ *adv*

ma·teri·al·ize /məˈtɪərɪəlaɪz ; məˈtɪrɪəlˌaɪz/ *vt, vi* [VP6A, 2A] (cause to) take material form; (cause to) become fact: (使)具體化;(使)實現: *Our plans did not ~,* came to nothing, were not carried out. 我們的計畫沒有實現。**ma·teri·al·iz·ation** /məˌtɪərɪəlaɪˈzeɪʃn *US:* -lɪˈz- ; məˌtɪrɪəlɪˈzeʃən/ *n*

ma·ternal /məˈtɜːnl ; məˈtɝnl̩/ *adj* of or like a mother: 母親的;似母親的: *~ care/instincts;* 母愛(母性); *my ~ grandfather/aunt, etc,* on my mother's side of the family. 我的外祖父(姨母等)。**~·ly** /-nəlɪ ; -nl̩ɪ/ *adv*

ma·tern·ity /məˈtɜːnətɪ ; məˈtɝnətɪ/ *n* [U] being a mother: 母性;母道: (attrib) (形容用法) *ˈ~ ward/hospital,* for women who are about to become mothers. 產科病房(醫院)。

matey /ˈmeɪtɪ ; ˈmetɪ/ *adj* **~ (with),** (colloq) sociable, familiar, friendly. (俗)友善的;親切的。

mathe·mat·ics /ˌmæθəˈmætɪks ; ˌmæθəˈmætɪks/ *n* (with *sing* or *pl v*) science of size and numbers (of which arithmetic, algebra, trigonometry and geometry are branches): (用單數或複數動詞)數學(包括算術,代數,三角與幾何等部門): *His ~ are weak.* 他的數學不好。*M~ is his weak subject.* 數學是他比較差的科目。**math·emat·ical** /ˌmæθəˈmætɪkl ; ˌmæθəˈmætɪkl̩/ *adj* of ~. 數學的。**math·emat·ically** /-klɪ ; -klɪ/ *adv* **math·ema·tician** /ˌmæθəməˈtɪʃn ; ˌmæθəməˈtɪʃən/ *n* expert in ~. 數學家。

maths (US = **math**) /mæθs *US:* mæθ ; mæθ/ *n* (colloq abbr of) mathematics. (俗)爲 mathematics 之略。

mati·née /ˈmætɪneɪ *US:* ˌmætnˈeɪ ; ˌmætn̩ˈe/ *n* [C] afternoon performance at a cinema or theatre: 電影院或戲院裏的下午演出;日戲: *ˈ~ idol,* much admired actor. 甚受愛慕的男明星。

mat·ins /ˈmætɪnz *US:* -tnz ; ˈmætɪnz/ *n pl* service of Morning Prayer in the Church of England; prayers recited at daybreak in the RC Church. 英國國教的晨禱;天主教的黎明禱告。

ma·tri·arch /ˈmeɪtrɪɑːk ; ˈmetrɪˌɑrk/ *n* woman head of a family or tribe. 女家長;女族長。**ma·tri·archy** /-ɑːkɪ ; -ɑrkɪ/ *n* social organization in which mothers are the heads of families. 母權制;母系制(以母親爲家長或族長的社會組織)。**ma·tri·ar·chal** /ˌmeɪtrɪˈɑːkl ; ˌmetrɪˈɑrkl̩/ *adj*

ma·tric /məˈtrɪk ; məˈtrɪk/ *n* (colloq abbr of) matriculation. (俗)爲 matriculation 之略。

ma·trices /ˈmeɪtrɪsiːz ; ˈmetrɪˌsiz/ *pl* of matrix.

mat·ri·cide /ˈmætrɪsaɪd ; ˈmætrəˌsaɪd/ *n* [U] killing of one's own mother; [C] instance of this; [C] person guilty of this. 弒母;弒母者。

ma·tricu·late /məˈtrɪkjʊleɪt ; məˈtrɪkjəˌlet/ *vt, vi* **1** [VP6A, 2A] (allow to) enter a university as a student, usu after passing an examination; admit, be admitted, as a member of a university. (准許)進入大學(通常指考試及格之後);註册入大學。**2** [VP 2A, C] (formerly) pass the final school examination. (昔時)通過期終考試。**ma·tricu·la·tion** /məˌtrɪkjʊˈleɪʃn ; məˌtrɪkjəˈleʃən/ *n* **1** [U] matriculating or being ~d; [C] instance of this. 准許進入大學;被准許進入大學;註册入學。**2** [U] (formerly) final school examination. (昔時)期終考試;大考。

mat·ri·mony /ˈmætrɪmənɪ *US:* -məʊnɪ ; ˈmætrəˌmonɪ/ *n* [U] state of being married: 婚姻;婚姻生活: *unite persons in holy ~.* 使人結成神聖的婚姻。**mat·ri·mo·nial** /ˌmætrɪˈməʊnɪəl ; ˌmætrəˈmonɪəl/ *adj* of ~: 婚姻的: *solicitors who help people who have matrimonial troubles,* eg persons wanting divorce. 幫助人們解決婚姻糾紛的律師。

ma·trix /ˈmeɪtrɪks ; ˈmetrɪks/ *n* (*pl* matrices /ˈmeɪtrɪsiːz ; ˈmetrɪˌsiz/, or ~es) **1** mould into which hot metal, or other material in a soft or liquid condition, is poured to be shaped, eg in the printing trade, or for making gramophone records. 鑄模;模型(例如印刷業所用的字模,紙型;製造唱片的原模)。**2** substance in which a mineral, etc is found embedded in the ground. 礦脈;母岩。**3** place where sth begins or develops. 創始地;發祥地。

ma·tron /ˈmeɪtrən ; ˈmetrən/ *n* **1** woman housekeeper in a school or other institution. (學校或其他機構的)女舍監;女總管。**2** woman who manages the domestic affairs and nursing staff of a hospital. 護士長。**3** married woman or widow (often used with a suggestion of dignity and social position): 已婚婦女;寡婦(常用以表示尊嚴及社會地位): (dressmaking) (女裝裁製) *styles suitable for ~s,* for middle-aged women. 適合中年婦女的式樣。**~·ly** *adj* of, like, suitable for, ~s: 女總管(等)的;似女總管(等)的;適合女總管(等)或已婚婦女的: *~ly duties;* 女總管(等)的責任; *a ~ly* (ie dignified) *manner.* 莊嚴的儀態。

matt /mæt ; mæt/ *adj* = mat[2].

mat·ted /ˈmætɪd ; ˈmætɪd/ *adj* ⇨ mat[1] *v.*

mat·ter[1] /ˈmætə(r) ; ˈmætɚ/ *n* **1** [U] substance(s) of which a physical thing is made (contrasted with mind, spirit, etc): 物質(與心,精神等相對): *organic/inorganic ~.* 有機(無機)物。**2** material for thought or expression; substance of a book, speech, etc contrasted with the form or style: 思想或表達的題材;書籍、演說等的內容(以別於形式或文

體): *The ~ in your essay is good but the style is deplorable.* 你文章的內容很好,但是體裁太糟糕了。 **3** [U] sth printed or written. 印刷或書寫之物。**'reading ~,** books, periodicals, etc. 讀物(書籍,刋物等)。**'postal ~,** everything sent by post. 郵件。**'printed ~,** (used on sth sent by post, to show that it goes out at a rate cheaper than for ordinary letters, etc). 印刷品(用於郵寄物品上,表示其郵資低於一般函件)。 **4** [C] sth to which attention is given; piece of business; affair: 事務;事情;問題: *'money ~s.* 金錢方面的事情。 *This is a ~ I know little about.* 這件事我不大知道。*There are several ~s to be dealt with at the committee meeting.* 有幾件事要在委員會的會議中討論。***a ~ of course,*** sth to be expected in the natural course of events. 理所當然的事。Hence, 由此產生, **ˌ~-of-'course** *adj* to be expected. 理所當然的;意料中的。***a ~ of opinion,*** sth about which opinions may differ. 觀點問題;看法不同的問題。***as a ~ of fact,*** in reality; although you may not know it or may be surprised. 事實上;實際上;其實。 Hence, 由此產生, **ˌ~-of-'fact** *adj* (of a person, his manner) unimaginative; ordinary; keeping to the facts. (指人,其態度)缺少想像力的;實際的;平凡的;拘泥事實的。***for 'that ~; for the ~ of that,*** so far as that is concerned. 就那件事而論;關於那件事。***in the ~ of,*** as regards, in what concerns: 至於;關於: *He is strict in the ~ of discipline.* 在紀律方面他是嚴格的。***a 'hanging ~,*** a crime for which the penalty may be death by hanging. 可處絞刑的罪。***no 'laughing ~,*** sth serious, sth not to be joked about. 正經的事;重要的事;不是開玩笑的事情。 **5** [U] importance. 重要;要緊。***(make/be) no ~,*** (be) of no importance: 無關緊要;不重要: *If you can't do it, no ~.* 你如果不能做,沒有關係。*It's no ~/it makes no ~ whether you arrive early or late.* 不論你早到或晚到都無關緊要。***no ~ who/what/where, etc,*** whoever (it is), whatever (happens, etc): 不論誰(什麼,在那裡等): *Don't trust him, no ~ what* (= whatever) *he says.* 不管他說什麼,你都不要信任他。*Don't believe the rumour, no ~ who* (= whoever) *repeats it/no ~ how often you hear it.* 不論是誰說的(不論你聽到多少次),都不要相信這謠言。 **6** ***be the ~ (with),*** be wrong (with): 有了毛病;發生困難: *What's the ~ with it?* (colloq) Surely this is all right, isn't it? (俗)這有什麼差錯嗎?(意謂:這不會有什麼差錯的,是不是?) *Is there anything the ~ with him,* Is he ill, in trouble, etc (according to context)? 他有什麼困難嗎?(是否生病,或遭遇困難等,視上下文而定)。 **7** ***a ~ of,*** approximately; only: 大約;僅有: *a ~ of 20 weeks/10 miles/£50;* 大約二十個星期(十哩,五十鎊); *within a ~ of hours.* 大約數小時內。

mat·ter² /ˈmætə(r); ˈmætɚ/ *vi* [VP2A, C] (chiefly in interr, neg and conditional sentences) be of importance: (主要用於疑問句,否定句和條件句中)關係重要;要緊: *What does it ~?* 有什麼關係? *It doesn't ~ much, does it?* 沒什麼大關係,是不是? *It hardly ~s at all.* 沒什麼要緊。*It doesn't ~ to me what you do or where you go.* 你做什麼或去什麼地方,對我都無關緊要。

mat·ting /ˈmætɪŋ; ˈmætɪŋ/ *n* [U] rough woven material used for floor covering and for packing goods: (用以覆蓋地板和包裝貨物的)粗糙織物;草蓆;蓆: *coconut-~.* 棕蓆。

mat·tins /ˈmætɪnz *US:* -tnz; ˈmætɪnz/ *n pl*=matins.

mat·tock /ˈmætək; ˈmætək/ *n* heavy tool with a long handle and an iron head, one end of which is pointed and the other blunt, used for breaking up hard ground, etc. 鶴嘴鋤;十字鎬。⇨ the illus at tool. 參看 tool 之插圖。

mat·tress /ˈmætrɪs; ˈmætrɪs/ *n* [C] long, thick, flat, oblong pad of wool, hair, feathers, foam rubber, etc on which to sleep. 床墊。**spring ~,** one with coiled wires fitted inside a padded cover of canvas or other frame of strong material. 彈簧床墊。

matu·rate /ˈmætjʊreɪt; ˈmætʃʊˌret/ *vi* [VP2A] become mature. 成熟。**matu·ra·tion** /ˌmætjʊˈreɪʃn; ˌmætʃʊˈreʃən/ *n* [U] process of becoming mature. 成熟的過程。

ma·ture /məˈtjʊə(r) *US:* -ˈtʊər; məˈtjʊr/ *vt, vi* [VP6A, 2A] **1** come or bring to full development or to a state ready for use: 成熟;使成熟: *His character ~d during these years.* 在這些年月裡他的性格發展成熟了。*These years ~d his character.* 這幾年使他的性格成熟了。*This wine has not ~d properly.* 這酒還沒有醸熟。 **2** (of bills) become due. (指票據)到期。□ *adj* **1** fully grown or developed; ripe with fully developed powers: 完全長成的;成熟的;具有充份發展之能力的: *persons of ~ years.* 成年人。 **2** careful; perfected: 愼重的;完善的;周密的: *after ~ deliberation;* 經過愼重考慮之後; *~ plans,* based on ~ deliberation. 周密的計畫。 **3** (comm, of bills) due for payment. (商,指票據)到期的。 **~·ly** *adv* **ma·tur·ity** /məˈtjʊərətɪ *US:* -ˈtʊə-; məˈtjʊrətɪ/ *n* [U] the state of being ~. 成熟;完成;到期。

ma·tuti·nal /məˈtjuːtɪnl *US:* -ˈtuːtnl; məˈtjutɪnl/ *adj* (formal) of, occurring in, the morning. (正式用語)早晨的;發生在早晨的。

maud·lin /ˈmɔːdlɪn; ˈmɔdlɪn/ *adj* sentimental or self-pitying in a silly or tearful way: 易傷感的;愛哭的: *The drunken man began to get ~.* 那個喝醉的人開始傷感落淚。

maul /mɔːl; mɔl/ *vt* [VP6A, 15B] hurt or injure by rough or brutal handling: 傷害;虐待;毆打: *~ed by a tiger.* 爲虎所傷。*Stop ~ing the cat.* 不要再虐待那隻貓了。*His latest novel has been ~ed by the critics,* They have written extremely adverse reviews. 他最近的一部小說被批評家挑剔得體無完膚。*Stop ~ing me about!* 不要再虐待我!

maul·stick /ˈmɔːlstɪk; ˈmɔlˌstɪk/ *n* light stick held by a painter's (left) hand as a support to the (right) hand that holds the brush. (畫家持於左手中以支持右手的)小杖;支手杖。

maun·der /ˈmɔːndə(r); ˈmɔndɚ/ *vi* [VP2A, C] talk in a rambling way; move or act in a listless way. 嘮嘮叨叨地講話;胡言亂語;沒精打采地行走或行動。

Maundy Thurs·day /ˌmɔːndɪ ˈθɜːzdɪ; ˈmɔndɪˈθɝzdɪ/ *n* Thursday before Easter, commemorating the Last Supper. 復活節前的星期四(紀念耶穌最後的晚餐)。⇨ lord(2); John 13: 14. 參看 lord 第 2 義及約翰福音第 13 章第 14 節。

mau·so·leum /ˌmɔːsəˈliːəm; ˌmɔsəˈliəm/ *n* magnificent and monumental tomb. 壯麗之墓;陵。

mauve /məʊv; mov/ *adj, n* bright but delicate pale purple. 淡紫色的;淡紫色。

mav·er·ick /ˈmævərɪk; ˈmævərɪk/ *n* (US) (美) **1** unbranded calf. 未打烙印的小牛。 **2** unorthodox person; person who dissents from the ideas, etc of an organized group: 意見等與衆不同者;持異議者;特立獨行者;自行其是者: *~ politicians.* 自行其是的政客。

ma·vis /ˈmeɪvɪs; ˈmevɪs/ *n* (poet) song-thrush. (詩)善鳴的畫眉鳥。

maw /mɔː; mɔ/ *n* animal's stomach or throat; (fig) devouring or destructive agency ready to swallow or engulf sth. 動物的胃或咽喉;(喻)隨時欲吞噬或毀滅他物之物。

mawk·ish /ˈmɔːkɪʃ; ˈmɔkɪʃ/ *adj* foolishly sentimental. 太容易傷感的;傷感到令人厭惡的。 **~·ly** *adv* **~·ness** *n*

maxi- /ˈmæksɪ; ˈmæksɪ/ *pref* of a large or long size, length, etc. (表示尺寸,長度等)大或長的。⇨ mini-.

maxim /ˈmæksɪm; ˈmæksɪm/ *n* widely accepted rule of conduct or general truth briefly expressed, eg *'Waste not, want not'.* 箴言;格言(如'不浪費,不窮困')。

maxi·mize /ˈmæksɪmaɪz; ˈmæksəˌmaɪz/ *vt* [VP6A] increase to a maximum: 使達最高限度;增至最大限度: *~ educational opportunities.* 盡量增加受教育機會。

maxi·mi·za·tion /ˌmæksɪmaɪˈzeɪʃn *US:* -mɪˈz- ; ˌmæksəmɪˈzeʃən/ *n*

maxi·mum /ˈmæksɪməm ; ˈmæksəməm/ *n, adj* (*pl* ~s or -ma /-mə ; -mə/) (opposite of *minimum*) (of) greatest possible or recorded degree, quantity, etc: 最大量(的);最高點(的);極點(的);極大(的)(為 minimum 之相反字): *the ~ temperature recorded in London;* 倫敦的最高溫度; *a ~ and minimum thermometer*, made so as to register ~ and minimum temperatures; 可指示最高溫與最低溫的溫度計; *obtain 81 marks out of a ~ of 100.* 得到最高分一百分當中的八十一分。*The ~ load for this lorry is one ton.* 這輛卡車最大載重量是一噸。

may /meɪ ; me/ *anom fin* (*pt* might /maɪt ; maɪt/) (*neg* may not, shortened to mayn't /ˈmeɪənt ; ment/ and might not shortened to mightn't /ˈmaɪtnt ; ˈmaɪtn̩t/) [VP5] **1** (used to indicate possibility or probability; as *might* is used to indicate a future condition, the perfect infinitive *might have* is used for past time): (用以表示'可能', '或許'; might 用來表示未來情況, might have + p.p. 用來表示過去): *That may or may not be true.* 那可能是眞的, 也可能不是眞的。*He may have* (= Perhaps he has) *missed his train.* 他或許沒趕上那班火車。*This medicine may/might cure your cough.* 這種藥可能治好你的咳嗽。*This might have cured your cough,* if you had taken it. 這藥可能已經治好了你的咳嗽(假如你以前吃過這種藥的話)。*You may walk* (= It is possible to walk) *for miles and miles among the hills without meeting anyone.* 你可能在山區走了許多哩路而遇不到任何人。**2** (used to indicate permission or request for permission; *might* suggests greater hesitation or diffidence. ⇨ can²(3)): (用以表示許可或請求許可; might 含有比較遲疑或缺乏自信之意): *May I come in?* 我可以進來嗎？*Might I make a suggestion?* 我可以提出一個建議嗎？*Well, if I may say so,....* 嗯, 假如我可以這麼說的話,…。*You may come if you wish.* 你要來就來好了。**3** (used to indicate uncertainty, and asking for information, or expressing wonder): (用以表示不確定, 詢問或表露驚愕): *Well, who may you be?* 啊,你會是誰呢？*How old may/might she be?* 她的年齡會有多大呢？**4** (used with *well* to suggest 'There is good reason'): (與 well 連用表示'有良好的理由'): *You may well say so.* 你很有理由這麼說。*Well may/might you be surprised!* 當然你會感到驚訝！*We may as well stay where we are,* It seems reasonable to do so. 我們留在現在的地方倒也不錯。*You might just as well go as not,* There is just as much to be said in favour of going as there is against. 你去也好,不去也好。⇨ well²(4). **5** (used to express wishes and hopes): (用以表示願望和希望): *May you both be happy!* 祝你們兩位幸福！*Long may she live to enjoy her good fortune!* 願她長壽以享幸福！**6** (used to express requests): (用以表示請求): *You might do me a favour,* Please do sth for me. 請你幫我一點忙。*I think you might at least offer to help.* 我想你至少總該表示要幫幫忙。**7** (in clauses) (used to express purpose, and after *wish, fear, be afraid,* etc): (在子句內)(用以表示目的,並用於 wish, fear, be afraid 等之後): *He died so that others might live.* 他死了,為了使旁人可以活下去。*I'll write to him today so that he may know when to expect us.* 我今天要寫信給他,好讓他知道我們什麼時候會去。*I'm afraid the news may be true.* 我恐怕這個消息可能是眞的。

May /meɪ ; me/ *n* **1** the fifth month of the year. 五月。**ˈMay Day,** 1st of May, celebrated as a spring festival and also as a day for socialist and labour demonstrations. 五朔節(五月一日,西洋的春節);勞動節(五月一日)。**ˈMay Queen,** girl crowned with flowers on May Day. 五朔節花后(五朔節以花冠加冕為后之少女)。**ˈmay-beetle, ˈmay-bug** *nn* cockchafer. 金龜子。**ˈmay·fly** *n* short-lived insect that appears in May. 蜉蝣(出現於五月)。**ˈmay·pole** *n* flower-decorated pole danced round on May Day. 五月柱(用花卉裝飾的柱子,於五朔節日供男女圍繞着跳舞者)。**2 m~,** hawthorn (blossom). 山楂花。

may·be /ˈmeɪbiː ; ˈmebɪ/ *adv* perhaps; possibly. 也許;可能。***as soon as maybe,*** as soon as possible. 儘可能地快。

may·day /ˈmeɪdeɪ ; ˈmeˌde/ *n* (radio telephony) (from French *m'aider,* help me) international signal (used by aircraft and ships) of distress: (無線電話)(飛機或船隻所發的)國際無線電求救呼號(由法文 m'aider '幫助我' 而來): *a ~ call from an airliner.* 一架客機發出的求救呼號。

May·fair /ˈmeɪfeə(r) ; ˈmeˌfɛr/ *n* fashionable district in the West End of London. 倫敦西區上流社會住宅區。

may·hem /ˈmeɪhem ; ˈmehɛm/ *n* **1** (old use, and US) crime of maiming. (舊用法,美國)傷人肢體罪。**2** state of violent disorder; havoc: 大混亂;大災害: *cause/create ~.* 造成大災害。

may·on·naise /ˌmeɪəˈneɪz *US:* ˈmeɪəneɪz ; ˌmeəˈnez/ *n* [U] thick dressing of eggs, cream, oil, vinegar, etc used on cold foods, esp salads; dish of food with this dressing: 蛋黃醬(一種調味醬,用蛋、奶油、植物油、醋等製成,用於調製涼菜,尤其是生菜);美乃滋;用此種醬汁調味的食物: *salmon ~.* 蛋黃醬鮭魚。

mayor /meə(r) *US:* ˈmeɪər ; ˈmeɚ/ *n* head of a municipal corporation of a city or borough. 市長。**~·ess** /meəˈres *US:* ˈmeɪərəs ; ˈmeərɪs/ *n* wife or female relative of a ~, helping in social duties; woman holding the office of ~. 市長夫人;(幫助市長做社交活動的)市長的女性親戚;女市長。**~·alty** /ˈmeərəltɪ *US:* ˈmeɪər- ; ˈmeərəltɪ/ *n* ~'s (period of) office. 市長之職位;市長之任期。

maze /meɪz ; mez/ *n* **1** network of lines, paths, etc; labyrinth: 錯綜複雜的曲徑;迷宮: *a ~ of narrow alleys.* 錯綜複雜的窄巷。**2** state of confusion or bewilderment (when faced by a confused mass of facts, etc). (面臨雜亂事物時所感到的)迷惘;困惑。***be in a ~,*** be puzzled, bewildered. 迷惘;困惑;不知所措。**mazed** *adj* bewildered. 迷惘的;困惑的。

ma·zurka /məˈzɜːkə ; məˈzɝkə/ *n* (piece of music for a) lively Polish dance for four or eight couples. 馬厝卡舞(一種輕快活潑的波蘭舞,供四對或八對男女共舞);馬厝卡舞曲。

Mc·Carthy·ism /məˈkɑːθɪɪzəm ; məˈkɑrθɪɪzm̩/ *n* (US, 1950's; after J R McCarthy, US politician) political policy of accusing persons of disloyalty (esp by saying they were pro-Communist); unscrupulous methods of investigation used for this purpose; witchhunt. 麥加錫主義(美國政治家麥加錫於1950年代主張的政策,即檢舉不忠於美國政府者,尤其是親共者);不正當的檢舉調查手段;(對不忠實者)檢舉並迫害。

me /miː ; mi/ *pron* object form for the pronoun *I*: 我(代名詞 I 的受格): *He saw me.* 他看見我。*Give me one.* 給我一個。*It's me* (now usu for 'It is I'). 是我(現在通常用以代替 'It is I')。

mead¹ /miːd ; mid/ *n* [U] alcoholic drink made from fermented honey and water. 蜂蜜酒。

mead² /miːd ; mid/ *n* [C] (poet) meadow. (詩)草地。

meadow /ˈmedəʊ ; ˈmɛdo/ *n* [C, U] (area, field, of) grassland, esp kept for hay. 草地(尤指生長畜類食用草秣者);牧場。

meagre (US = **mea·ger**) /ˈmiːgə(r) ; ˈmigɚ/ *adj* **1** thin; lacking in flesh: 瘦的;皮包骨的: *a ~ face.* 清瘦的臉。**2** insufficient; poor; scanty: 不足的;貧乏的;量少的: *a ~ meal;* 一頓簡單或不豐盛的飯食; *~ fare;* 簡陋的伙食; *a ~ attendance at the council meeting.* 議會會議席上出席人數甚少。**~·ly** *adv* **~·ness** *n*

meal¹ /miːl ; mil/ *n* [C] **1** occasion of eating: 餐;飯食: *three ~s a day;* 一日三餐; *breakfast, the first ~ of the day.* 早餐,一天的第一頓飯。**ˈ~·time** *n* usual time for taking a ~. (平常的)吃飯時間。

2 food that is eaten: 一餐所吃的食物: *have a good* ~. 吃豐富的一餐;飽餐一頓。

meal[2] /miːl ; mil/ *n* [U] grain coarsely ground: 粗略碾碎的穀物;(未經細磨的)粗粉: *'oat~;* 麥片; *'corn* ~, (US) ~ of maize or other grain. (美)玉蜀黍(或其他穀類之)粉。Cf 參較 *flour* for grain finely ground. flour 係碾細的穀粉。

mealie /'miːlɪ ; 'milɪ/ *n* (S Africa) (*pl*) maize; [C] an ear of maize. (南非洲)(複)玉蜀黍;玉米。

mealy /'miːlɪ ; 'milɪ/ *adj* (-ier, -iest) of, like, containing, covered with, meal; (of potatoes when boiled) dry and powdery. 粗粉的;粗粉狀的;含粗粉的;撒有粗粉的;(指煮過後的馬鈴薯)乾而易變成粉狀的。**'~-bug** *n* insect that infests vines, etc. 水臘蟲(葡萄樹等的害蟲)。**,~-'mouthed** *adj* too squeamish in the choice of words; tending to avoid plain speaking. 講話時選辭用字過於審愼的;不坦率的;油嘴滑舌的。

mean[1] /miːn ; min/ *adj* (-er, -est) **1** poor in appearance; shabby-looking: 粗陋的;破爛不堪的: *a ~ house in a ~ street.* 鄙陋街道上的鄙陋房屋。**2** (of behaviour) unworthy; discreditable: (指行爲)卑鄙的;丟臉的;不名譽的: *That was a ~ trick!* 那是一個卑鄙的詭計! *It was ~ of you to eat all the peaches!* 你把桃子全吃光了,眞不害羞! *He took a ~ advantage of me.* 他用卑鄙的手段欺騙了我。*What a ~ revenge!* 多麼卑鄙的報復! **3** (of persons, their character, etc) having or showing a fondness for ~ behaviour: (指人,人格等)卑賤的;卑鄙的: *a ~ rascal.* 卑鄙的流氓。*Don't be so ~ to your little brother,* Don't tease him, treat him unkindly, etc. 不要那樣惡待你的小弟弟(指揶揄他,或苛待他等)。*He's a ~-minded sort of fellow.* 他是一種心地卑下的人。**4** of low rank or humble birth: 地位卑下的;出身微賤的。**5** (of the understanding, the natural powers) inferior; poor: (指理解力,秉賦)低劣的;不如人的: *This should be clear even to the ~est intelligence.* 即使智力最低的人對此亦應瞭如指掌。*He is no ~ scholar,* is a good one. 他是個優秀的學者。**6** lacking in generosity; selfish: 吝嗇的;自私的: *Her husband is rather ~ over money matters.* 她的丈夫對錢財相當吝嗇。**7** (colloq) secretly ashamed: (俗)暗自慚愧的;不好意思的: *feel rather ~ for not helping more.* 因未多幫忙而感到很不好意思。**8** (US) nasty; vicious: (美)刻毒的;邪惡的: *He's a really ~ fellow—he likes to see people suffer.* 他眞是個邪惡的人──他喜歡看別人受苦。**~·ly** *adv* **~·ness** *n* **~ie, ~y** /'miːnɪ ; 'minɪ/ *nn* (colloq) ~-minded person: (俗)心地卑鄙的人;吝嗇或自私的人;吝嗇鬼: *What a ~ie you are!* 你眞是個吝嗇鬼! ⇨ 6 above. 參看上列第6義。

mean[2] /miːn ; min/ *adj* occupying the middle position between two extremes; average: (居於二極端之)中間的;平均的;中庸的: *the ~ annual temperature in Malta.* 馬爾他島的每年平均溫度。**Greenwich M~ Time,** ⇨ Greenwich. **~ price,** (fin, Stock Exchange) the average between the Stock jobber's buying and selling price; the market price of an investment. (財務,證券交易)股票經紀人買進賣出的平均價格;投資的市價。

mean[3] /miːn ; min/ *n* **1** [C] condition, quality, course of action, etc that is halfway between two extremes. 中間;居中;中庸。***the happy/golden ~,*** a moderate course of action. 中庸之道;折衷辦法。**2** (maths) term between the first and the last of a series; an average amount or value: (數學)比例中項;平均數;平均值: *In 1:3::3:9, the ~ is 3.* 在 1:3::3:9 中,比例中項是 3。*The ~ of 3, 5 and 7 is 5* (because 3 + 5 + 7 = 15 and 15 ÷ 3 = 5). 3, 5 和 7 的平均數是 5。

mean[4] /miːn ; min/ *vt* (*pt, pp* meant /ment ; mɛnt/) **1** [VP6A] (of words, sentences, etc) signify; import: (指字、句等)表示…的意思;含…之意: *A dictionary tries to tell you what words ~.* 字典告訴你語詞的含意。*The Latin word 'amo' ~s 'I love'.* 拉丁字 'amo' 的意思是 '我愛'。**2** [VP6A, C, 9] be a sign of; be likely to result in; entail: 爲…的徵兆;意謂;可能造成;使成爲必要: *This new frontier incident probably ~s war/that there will be war.* 這個新的邊境事件可能導致戰爭。*These new orders for our manufactures will ~ working overtime.* 這些訂購我們產品的新訂單意謂着要加班。**3** [VP6A, 9, 14, 16B, 17] **~ *(by),*** have as a purpose; contemplate; intend; refer to: 圖謀;計畫;意欲;企圖;意指: *What do you ~ by saying that?* What have you in mind? (or if the context allows) How dare you say that? 你那樣說是什麼意思?(你怎敢講那些話?視上下文而定)。*I wasn't serious—I ~t it/It was ~t as a joke.* 我不是認眞的──我是開玩笑的。*Do you ~* (= refer to) *Miss Elsie Smith or Miss Dora Smith?* 你是指艾爾絲·史密斯小姐還是指杜拉·史密斯小姐? *I didn't ~ you to read the letter.* 我並沒有打算要你讀那封信。*Is this figure ~t to be a 1 or a 7?* 這個數字是 1 還是 7? *I'm sorry if I hurt your feelings—I didn't ~ to.* 假如我傷了你的感情,眞對不起──我並不是故意的。*I ~ there to be/that there should be no argument about this,* won't allow any argument. 我的意思是不許對此事有任何爭論。*Is this valuable painting ~t for me,* Is the owner thinking of giving it to me? 這幅名貴的畫是要送給我的嗎? **~ *business,*** (colloq) be in earnest, ready to act (not merely talk). (俗)認眞要辦(非僅空談)。**~ *mischief,*** have in mind sth evil or injurious. 心存惡意;意欲傷害;存心搗亂。**4** [VP7A, 12A, 13A, 14, 17] **~ *(for),*** intend; be determined; destine: 意欲;決定;預定: *He ~s to succeed.* 他意欲獲致成功。*He ~s his son to succeed.* 他要他的兒子成功。*He ~s you no harm,* does not intend to hurt you. 他無意傷害你。*He ~s no harm to anyone.* 他無意傷害任何人。*I ~t this for my son,* intended to give it to him. 我打算把這個給我的兒子。*He seems obviously ~t for the army/~t to be a soldier,* is the sort of man destined for the army. 他似乎生來就適於做軍人。**5** [VP14] **~ *sth to sb,*** be of importance or value to: 對某人重要;對某人有價值: *Your friendship ~s a great deal to me,* I value it highly. 你的友誼對我極爲珍貴。*£20 ~s a lot to her,* is quite a large sum in her view. 二十英鎊對她是個大數目。*I can't tell you what Mary has ~t to me,* what a difference she has made in my life. 我沒法告訴你瑪莉對我的影響是多麼大。*The high cost of living ~s nothing to some people,* They do not worry about it (eg because they are very rich). 對某些人來說,高昂的生活費用算不得什麼。**6 ~ *well,*** have good intentions (though perhaps not the will or capacity to carry them out): 懷有善意(雖然不見得有意或有能力實踐): *Of course he ~s well.* 當然他是好意。**~ *well by sb,*** have kindly intentions towards sb: 對某人懷有善意: *We all know that he ~s well by you.* 我們都知道他對你是好意。**~·ing** *n* [C, U] what is ~t or intended: 意義;含意;企圖: *a word with many distinct ~ings;* 一個有許多不同意義的字; *a passage without much ~ing.* 一段沒有多大意義的文字。*He looked at me with ~ing.* 他意味深長地看着我。*What's the ~ing of this?* (asked, for example, by sb who thinks he has been badly treated, etc). 這是什麼意思?(例如某人認爲受不平待遇等而發問)。▭ *adj* full of ~ing: 有意義的;意味深長的: ***a ~ing look;*** 意味深長的表情; ***well-~ing,*** having good intentions. 善意的。**~·ing·ful** /-fl ; -fl/ *adj* significant; full of ~ing. 富有意義的;意味深長的。**~·ing·fully** /-fəlɪ ; -flɪ/ *adv* **~·ing·less** *adj* without ~ing or motive. 無意義的;無目的的。**~·ing·ly** *adv* with ~ing. 有意義地;意味深長地;故意地。

me·ander /mɪ'ændə(r) ; mɪ'ændɚ/ *vi* [VP2A, C] wander here and there; (fig) speak in an aimless way; (of a stream) follow a winding course, flowing slowly and gently. 漫遊;(喻)漫談;閒聊;(指河川)緩緩蜿蜒而流。**~·ings** /mɪ'ændrɪŋz ; mɪ'ændrɪŋz/ *n pl* winding path, course, etc. 曲折的路。

~·ing·ly /mɪˈændrɪŋlɪ ; mɪˈændrɪŋlɪ/ *adv*

means¹ /miːnz ; minz/ *n pl* (often treated as a *sing*, as in examples) method, process, by which a result may be obtained: (常作單數用,如例句中) 方法;手段: *a ~ to an end*, a way of achieving sth. 達到目的的手段。*There is/are no ~ of learning what is happening.* 我們無法知道現在有什麼事情發生。*Every ~ has/All possible ~ have been tried.* 每種(所有可能的)方法都嘗試過了。*Does the end always justify the ~*, If the aim or purpose is good, may any methods, even if bad, be employed? 目的正當就可以不擇手段嗎？ ***by ~ of***, through; with the help of: 藉;用: *Thoughts are expressed by ~ of words.* 思想藉文字表達出來。***by ˈall ~***, certainly. 當然;必定。***by ˈno ~***, not at all: 決不;一點也不: *These goods are by no ~ satisfactory.* 這些貨品一點也不令人滿意。***by ˈno manner of ~***, in no way. 決不;任何情況之下均不。***by some ~ or other***, somehow or other; if not in one way, then in another. 用某種方法;總有辦法。***by fair ~ or foul***, by any methods, just or unjust. 用任何方法;不擇手段。***ways and ~***, methods, esp of providing money by taxation for government needs. 方法;辦法;(尤指)政府稅收途徑。

means² /miːnz ; minz/ *n pl* money; wealth; resources: 金錢;財富;財源: *a man of ~*, a rich man; 富有的人; *a man of your ~*, with the money, etc you have at your disposal; 有你這樣財力的人; *have private ~*, an income from property, investments, etc (not earned as salary, etc). 有來自財產、投資等方面之收入。***live beyond/within one's ~***, spend more/less than one's income. 不能量入爲出(能量入爲出)。**ˈ~ test** *n* inquiry into the ~ of sb seeking help from the State or local authorities (eg if unemployed or too old to work). 個人經濟狀況調查 (如因失業或年老不能工作而向政府申請補助時而作者)。

meant /ment ; mɛnt/ *pt, pp* of mean⁴.

mean·time /ˈmiːntaɪm ; ˈmin,taɪm/ *adv, n* ***(in the) ~***, meanwhile. 其時;當其時。

mean·while /ˈmiːnwaɪl *US:* -hwaɪl ; ˈmin,hwaɪl/ *adv* in or during the time between. 其時;此際。

measles /ˈmiːzlz ; ˈmizlz/ *n* (with *sing v*) [U] infectious disease, marked by fever and small red spots that cover the whole body. (用單數動詞) 痲疹。

measly /ˈmiːzlɪ ; ˈmizlɪ/ *adj* (colloq) of little value; of poor quality; of small size or amount: (俗) 無價值的;劣質的;微小的;少量的: *What a ~ birthday present!* 一件多麼沒有價值的生日禮物！ *What a ~ helping of ice-cream!* 多麼少的一份冰淇淋！

measure¹ /ˈmeʒə(r) ; ˈmɛʒɚ/ *n* **1** [U] size, quantity, degree, weight, etc as found by a standard or unit. (由一個標準或單位所測定的)大小;數量;度量;重量。***give full/short ~***, give the full/less than the full amount. 給予足(不足)量。***made to ~***, (of clothes) specially made for sb after taking ~ments. (指衣服)量尺寸後做的;定做的。***get/take the ~ of sb***, (fig) form an estimate of his character, abilities, etc. (喻)估量某人的品格,能力等。 **2** [C] unit, standard or system used in stating size, quantity, or degree: 度量的單位,標準或制度: *liquid/dry ~*. 液(乾)量。*An inch is a ~ of length.* 吋是長度的單位。*Twenty ~s of wheat means twenty bushels.* 二十單位的小麥卽指二十蒲式耳。⇨ App 5. 參看附錄五。 **3** [C] sth with which to test size, quantity, etc: (用以測量大小,數量等的)量度器: *a pint ~*. 品脫量器。*A yardstick is a ~; so is a foot-rule.* 碼尺是量長短的器具,一呎長的直尺也是。*A chain's weakest link is the ~ of its strength.* 鏈條之强度以最弱之環爲準。*Words cannot always give the ~ of one's feelings*, cannot show the depth or strength of one's feelings. 言辭不一定總能表示出感情的程度 (卽不能表示出感情的深度或强度)。**ˈtape-~**, ⇨ tape. **ˌgreatest ˌcommon ˈ~**, (abbr 略作 GCM) largest number that will divide each of several given numbers exactly. 最大公約數。 **4** extent. 程度;範圍;限度。***beyond ~***, very great(ly): 逾限的;過度的;極其;非常: *Her joy was beyond ~.* 她高興逾常;她非常高興。***in ˈsome/ˈany ~***, to some/any extent or degree. 達某種(任何)範圍或程度;有幾分;稍許。***in great/large ~***, to a large extent: 很;大半;大部分: *Their success was in some ~/in great ~ the result of thorough preparation.* 他們的成功有幾分(大部分)是周密準備的結果。***set ~s to***, limit: 限制;約束: *set ~s to one's ambitions.* 約束某人的野心。 **5** [C] (proposed) law. 議案;法規。 **6** [C] proceeding; step: 處置辦法;步驟;措施: *What ~* (= plan) *do you propose?* 你建議用什麼辦法？ *They took strong ~s* (= acted vigorously) *against dangerous drivers.* 他們對危害公衆的駕駛採取强硬的措施。 **7** [U] verse-rhythm; metre; time of a piece of music; [C] (archaic) dance. 詩的韻律;音樂的拍子;(古)舞蹈。***tread a ~ (with sb)***, dance (with him). (與某人)跳舞。

measure² /ˈmeʒə(r) ; ˈmɛʒɚ/ *vt, vi* **1** [VP6A, 2A] find the size, extent, volume, degree, etc of (sth or sb): 量;度量;測量(某物或某人的大小,範圍,容量,程度等): *~ a piece of ground/the strength of an electric current/the speed of a car;* 測量一塊土地(一電流的强度,一輛汽車的速度); *tested for speed over a ~d mile.* 在整整一英里的路程上試驗過速度的。*The tailor ~d me for a suit.* 裁縫給我量尺寸做衣服。*Can you ~ accurately?* 你能準確地量嗎？ **2** [VP2B] be (a certain length, etc): 爲(某長度等);有…長(寬、高等): *This room ~s 10 metres across.* 這個房間有10公尺寬。 **3** [VP6A, 15A, B] ***~ out/off***, give a ~d quantity of: 配出…的一定之量: *~ out a dose of medicine;* 配出一服藥; mark out: 劃出;量好: *~ off 2 metres of cloth.* 量好(剪下)兩公尺布。 **4** ***~ one's length***, fall flat on the ground. 仆倒在地上。***~ swords against/with sb***, (fig) try out one's strength against him. (喻)與某人較量力氣;與人一較長短。***~ one's strength (with sb)***, try or test it. (與某人)比賽力氣。**meas·ured** *adj* **1** (of language) considered and weighed: (指言辭)愼重的;仔細考慮過的: *~d words.* 愼重考慮過的話語。 **2** in slow and regular rhythm: 緩慢而有韻律的: *with a ~d tread.* 步伐整齊。 **measur·able** /ˈmeʒərəbl ; ˈmɛʒrəbl̩/ *adj* that can be ~d: 可測量的;可衡量的: *We came within measurable distance of* (close to) *success.* 我們接近成功了。**measur·ably** /-əblɪ ; -əblɪ/ *adv* **~·less** *adj* immeasurable; limitless. 不可測量的;無限度的。**~·ment** *n* **1** [U] measuring: 測量;衡量: *the metric system of ~ment.* 十進法度量衡制;公制。**2** (*pl*) figures about length, breadth, depth, etc: (複)長度;寬度;深度;大小: *the ~ments of a room.* 房間的大小(長寬高)。

meat /miːt ; mit/ *n* **1** [U] flesh of animals used as food, excluding fish and birds: 食用的獸肉(不包括魚類,鳥類之肉): *~-eating animals;* 肉食動物; *cold ~*, meat that has been cooked and has then become cold; 凉了的熟肉;冷肉; *chilled/frozen ~*, meat chilled/frozen in order to keep it in good condition; 冷凍的肉; *fresh ~*, from a recently killed animal. 鮮肉。**ˈ~·ball** *n* small ball of minced meat or sausage-meat. 肉丸。**ˈ~-safe** *n* cupboard for storing ~, usu with sides of wire gauze. 貯肉的橱櫃(通常裝有鐵紗)。**~ pie** *n* ~ cooked with a covering of pastry. 肉煎餅;餡餅。**a ~ tea,** high tea with some kind of ~ dish included. 有肉類點心的下午茶。⇨ high¹(12). **2** (fig) important or substantial part of sth: (喻)重要部分;重要內容;實質: *There's not much ~ in this argument.* 這篇摘要沒有什麼內容。 **3** (old use) food in general: (舊用法)食物的總稱: *~ and drink.* 飲食。***One man's ~ is another man's poison,*** (prov) What one person likes is not necessarily liked by anyone else. (諺)甲所喜者未必爲乙所喜;利於甲者未必利於乙。**~·less** *adj* without ~: 沒有肉的: *~less days during the war.* 戰時無肉可吃的日子。**~y** *adj* (-ier,

-iest) (fig) full of substance; substantial. (喻)內容豐富的。

Mec·ca /ˈmekə; ˈmɛkə/ *n* **1** city in Saudi Arabia, birthplace of Muhammad and the spiritual centre of Islam. 麥加(沙烏地阿拉伯之一城,爲穆罕默德的誕生地及回教的精神中心)。 **2** goal of one's ambitions; place one is anxious to visit: 希望的目標;渴望前往的地方: *Stratford-on-Avon, the ~ of tourists in Britain.* 亞芬河畔的斯特拉福──英國的觀光勝地。

mech·anic /mɪˈkænɪk; məˈkænɪk/ *n* skilled workman, esp one who repairs or adjusts machinery and tools: 技工;(尤指)修理或調整機器的工人;機械工人: *a ˈmotor-~.* 汽車修理工人。

mech·an·ical /mɪˈkænɪkl; məˈkænɪkl̩/ *adj* **1** of, connected with, produced by, machines: 機械的;與機械有關的;由機械製成的: *~ power/transport/engineering.* 機械動力(汽車運輸,機械工程)。 **2** (of persons, their actions) like machines; automatic; as if done without thought: (指人,其動作)似機械的;呆板的;無意識的: *~ movements.* 機械般的行動。 **~ly** /-klɪ; -klɪ/ *adv* in a ~ way: 機械地;呆板地;無意識地: *~ly operated.* 用機械操作的。 ⇨ *manually* at manual.

mech·an·ics /mɪˈkænɪks; məˈkænɪks/ *n* **1** (usu with *sing v*) science of motion and force; science of machinery: (通常用單數動詞)力學;機械學: *M~ is taught by Mr MacHine.* 力學由麥克翰先生執教。 **2** (with *pl v*) (method of) construction: (用複數動詞)結構;構成法;技巧: *the ~ of play-writing.* 戲劇寫作方法。

mech·an·ism /ˈmekənɪzəm; ˈmɛkə,nɪzəm/ *n* [C] **1** working parts of a machine collectively; structure or arrangement of parts that work together as the parts of a machine do: 一部機器之各種機件之總稱;如機械般之結構或裝置;機構: *the ~ of the body;* 身體結構; *the ~ of government.* 政府之機構。 **2** way in which sth works or is constructed. (某物之)機械作用;結構方式。

mech·an·is·tic /ˌmekəˈnɪstɪk; ,mɛkəˈnɪstɪk/ *adj* **the ~ theory,** the theory that all changes in the universe and all living creatures are caused by physical and chemical forces only. 機械論(認爲宇宙和生物中所有的變化皆由物理和化學力量所造成)。

mech·an·ize /ˈmekənaɪz; ˈmɛkə,naɪz/ *vt* [VP6A] use machines in or for; give a mechanical character to: 在…中使用機械;爲…而使用機械;使機械化: *~d forces,* eg in the army, using motor transport instead of horses or mules. 機械化部隊(例如陸軍中運用汽車運輸,而不用馬騾等馱獸)。 **mech·an·iz·ation** /ˌmekənaɪˈzeɪʃn *US:* -nɪˈz-; ,mɛkənəˈzeʃən/ *n*

medal /ˈmedl; ˈmɛdl̩/ *n* flat piece of metal, usu shaped like a coin, with words and a design stamped on it, given as an award for bravery, to commemorate sth, or for distinction in scholarship. (金屬製,通常爲錢幣狀的)獎章;勳章;紀念章。 **~·list** (US 美 = **~·ist**) /ˈmedəlɪst; ˈmɛdl̩ɪst/ *n* person who has been awarded a ~, eg for distinction in literature, sport. 得過獎章的人;獎章持有人(例如因文學或運動方面的成就而得獎)。

me·dal·lion /mɪˈdælɪən; məˈdæljən/ *n* large medal; large, flat circular ornamental design, eg on a carpet or on a lace curtain. 大獎章;大而扁平的圓形裝飾圖案(如在地毯上或紗簾上者)。

meddle /ˈmedl; ˈmɛdl̩/ *vi* [VP2A, 3A] **~ (in sth),** busy oneself in sth without being asked to do so: 管閒事;干預: *Don't ~ in my affairs.* 不要干預我的事。 *Don't ~ in politics.* 不要干預政治。 **~ (with sth),** interfere: 妨碍;干擾;玩弄;亂弄: *Who's been meddling with my papers?* 誰動了我的文件? *You're always meddling.* 你老是多事。 **meddler** *n* person who ~s. 干預者;愛管閒事者。 **ˈ~·some** /-səm; -səm/ *adj* fond of, in the habit of, meddling. 愛管閒事的;好干預的。

me·dia /ˈmiːdɪə; ˈmidɪə/ *n* **the ~,** (usu with *sing v*) mass communications, eg television, radio, the press. (通常用單數動詞)大衆傳播工具(如電視,無線電,報紙)。 ⇨ mass(2), medium.

medi·aeval /ˌmedɪˈiːvl *US:* ˌmiːd-; ,midɪˈivl̩/ = medieval.

me·dial /ˈmiːdɪəl; ˈmidɪəl/ *adj* **1** situated in the middle. 中間的;中央的;居中的。 **2** of average size. 中等的;一般的;普通的。 **~ly** /-ɪəlɪ; -ɪəlɪ/ *adv*

me·dian /ˈmiːdɪən; ˈmidɪən/ *adj* situated in, passing through, the middle. 在中間的;通過中間的。 □ *n* ~ point, line, part, etc. 中點;中線;中部;中數。

me·di·ate /ˈmiːdɪeɪt; ˈmidɪ,et/ *vi, vt* **1** [VP2A, 3A] **~ (between),** act as go-between or peacemaker: 居中調停;斡旋: *~ between two warring countries/between employers and their workers.* 斡旋於兩交戰國之間(資方與勞方之間)。 **2** [VP6A] bring about by doing this: 居間促成: *~ a settlement/a peace.* 居間促成和解(和平)。 **me·di·ation** /ˌmiːdɪˈeɪʃn; ,midɪˈeʃən/ *n* [U] mediating: 調停;調解;斡旋: *All offers of mediation by a third party were rejected.* 第三方面所提有關調處之建議均遭拒絕。 **me·di·ator** /-tə(r); -tɚ/ *n* one who ~s. 調停者;斡旋者。

medic /ˈmedɪk; ˈmɛdɪk/ *n* (colloq abbr for) medical student. (俗)爲 medical student 之略。

medi·cal /ˈmedɪkl; ˈmɛdɪkl̩/ *adj* **1** of the art of medicine (the treatment of disease): 醫學的;醫術的;醫療的: *a ˈ~ examination,* to ascertain one's state of health; 體格檢查; *a ~ practitioner,* a qualified doctor; 合格醫生; *a ˈ~ school;* 醫學校; *ˈ~ students/knowledge;* 醫科學生(醫學知識); *~ jurisprudence,* legal knowledge required by a doctor. 法醫學。 **2** of the art of medicine (contrasted with *surgery*): 內科的: *~, not surgical, treatment.* 內科而非外科的治療。 *The hospital has a ~ ward and a surgical ward.* 這家醫院有一個內科病房和一個外科病房。 □ *n* **1** (colloq) ~ student. (俗)醫科學生。 **2** ~ examination. 體格檢查。 **~ly** /-klɪ; -klɪ/ *adv*

medic·ament /mɪˈdɪkəmənt; məˈdɪkəmənt/ *n* substance used in medical treatment, internally or externally. (內服或外用的)藥;藥劑。 ⇨ medicine(2).

Medi·care /ˈmedɪkeə(r); ˈmɛdɪ,kɛr/ *n* [U] (US) government programme providing medical care (esp for old persons.) (美)(政府辦的)醫療保險制度(尤指爲老年人所辦者)。

medi·cate /ˈmedɪkeɪt; ˈmɛdɪ,ket/ *vt* [VP6A] treat medically; permeate with a medicinal substance: 以藥物治療;以藥物處理;加以藥;摻以藥: *~d soap/gauze.* 藥皂(藥用紗布)。 **medi·ca·tion** /ˌmedɪˈkeɪʃn; ,mɛdɪˈkeʃən/ *n* [U] process of medicating: 藥物治療;藥物處理;摻入藥品: *mass medication,* eg, the addition of fluorine to public water supplies; the supply of vitamin tablets through the social services; 大衆藥物供應(例如加氟於自來水,經社會服務團體供應維他命丸等); [C] medicine. 藥品;藥。

med·ici·nal /mɪˈdɪsnəl; məˈdɪsn̩l/ *adj* having healing or curative properties: 有藥性的;醫藥的;治療的: *~ preparations for both internal and external use.* 供內服和外用的藥劑。

medi·cine /ˈmedsn *US:* ˈmedɪsn; ˈmɛdəsn/ *n* **1** [U] the art and science of the prevention and cure of disease: 醫學;醫術;內科學: *study ~ and surgery;* 研究內科與外科; *a ˌDoctor of ˈM~.* 醫學博士。 **2** [C, U] (kind of) substance, esp one taken through the mouth, used in ~: 藥;藥劑;(尤指)內服藥: *He's always taking ~s.* 他時常吃藥。 *He takes too much ~.* 他吃藥吃得太多。 *This is a good (kind of) ~ for a cough.* 這是(一種)治咳良藥。 (Note: 注意: for remedies not taken through the mouth, 非口服藥, ⇨ *injection* at inject, lotion, *medicinal preparation* at medicinal, ointment.) **ˈ~-ball** *n* large, heavy ball thrown and caught for physical exercise. (供運動用內有塡塞物之)實心皮球。 **ˈ~-chest** *n* chest with a selection of useful medicinal preparations. 藥箱;藥櫃。 **3** (fig) deserved punishment. (喻)應受的懲罰。 ***take one's ~,*** (fig) submit to what is unwelcome and unpleasant. (喻)忍受不喜歡或不愉快的事。**get some/a little of one's own ~,** be given the kind of unwelcome treatment that one has given to others. 自食其果。**4** [U] (among primitive peoples) spell; charm; fetish; magic. (原始民族所崇信的)符咒;咒文;物神(風,石等);巫術。'**~-man** /-mæn ; -mæn/ *n* (*pl* -men) witch-doctor. 巫醫。

med·ico /'medɪkəʊ ; 'mɛdɪ,ko/ *n* (*pl* ~s /-kəʊz ; -koz/) (colloq, hum) doctor or medical student. (俗,諧)醫生;醫科學生。

medi·eval (also **medi·aeval**) /,medɪ'i:vl *US:* ,mi:d- ; ,midɪ'ivl̩/ *adj* of the Middle Ages (about AD 1100–1500). 中古的;中世紀的(約在公元1100年至1500年之間)。

me·di·ocre /,mi:dɪ'əʊkə(r) ; 'midɪ,okə/ *adj* not very good; neither very good nor very bad; second-rate. 平庸的;普通的;第二流的;中等的。**me·di·oc·rity** /,mi:dɪ'ɒkrətɪ ; ,midɪ'ɑkrətɪ/ *n* (*pl* -ties) [U] quality of being ~; [C] person who is ~ (in qualities, abilities, etc): 平庸;普通;中等;平庸的人: *a Government of mediocrities.* 庸才政府。

medi·tate /'medɪteɪt ; 'mɛdə,tet/ *vt, vi* **1** [VP6A] think about; consider: 想;考慮: *~ revenge/mischief.* 圖謀報復(打算胡鬧)。 **2** [VP2A, 3A] ~ ***(up/upon),*** give oneself up to serious (esp religious) thought: (尤指在宗教上)沉思;冥想: *He sat there meditating upon his misfortunes.* 他坐在那兒沉思他的不幸遭遇。

medi·ta·tion /,medɪ'teɪʃn ; ,mɛdə'teʃən/ *n* **1** [U] meditating: 沉思;冥想;考慮: *deep in ~.* 陷於沉思之中。 **2** [C] instance of this: 沉思等的實例;深思探討某問題之演說或文章;沉思錄: *a ~ on the causes of aggression in man.* 一篇探討人類侵略的原因的文章。 **medi·tat·ive** /'medɪtətɪv *US:* -teɪt- ; 'mɛdə,tetɪv/ *adj* of ~; fond of ~. 沉思的;默想的;愛沉思的。 **medi·tat·ive·ly** *adv*

Medi·ter·ra·nean /,medɪtə'reɪnɪən ; ,mɛdətə'renɪən/ *adj* of, characteristic of, the M~ Sea or the countries, etc bordering this sea: 地中海的;地中海沿岸諸國的;地中海(地區)特有的: *~ climate.* 地中海的氣候。

me·dium /'mi:dɪəm ; 'midɪəm/ *n* (*pl* ~s or media /'mi:dɪə ; 'midɪə/) **1** that by which sth is expressed: 媒介;方法;手段: *Commercial television is a ~ for advertising.* 商業電視是一種廣告媒介。 *Vacant positions can be made known through the ~ of the press,* by putting announcements in newspapers. 職位空缺可藉報紙公諸大衆(即在報端刋登廣告)。*Oil paints and water colours are ~s for the creation of works of art.* 油畫顏料和水彩顏料是藝術創作的媒介。 ⇨ also mass(2). **2** middle quality or degree. 中庸;適度。**the happy ~,** avoidance of extremes, eg by being neither very lax nor very severe in maintaining discipline. 中庸之道(如維持紀律時不寬也不嚴)。 **3** (*pl* often 複數常作 media) substance, surroundings, in which sth exists or through which sth moves: 藉以生存之物或環境;媒介物;傳導體;介質: *Air is the ~ of sound.* 空氣是傳聲的媒介物。 **4** person who acts as a go-between, esp in spiritualism; person who claims to be able to receive messages from the spirits of the dead. 中間人;(尤指)關亡人;通靈之人。 □ *adj* coming halfway between; not extreme: 中庸的;中等的;普通的: *a man of ~ height;* 中等身材的人; *a ~-sized firm;* 中型規模的公司; *~ bonds,* maturing in a period between 15 and 20 years; 十五至二十年到期的債券; *the ~ income group,* those who have incomes between high and low. 中等收入的人們。 '**~ wave,** (radio telegraphy) one having a length of from 100 to 1000 metres. (無線電報)中波(波長爲100至1000公尺)。

med·lar /'medlə(r) ; 'mɛdlə/ *n* (tree with) fruit like a small brown apple, eaten when it begins to decay. 山楂;山楂樹。

med·ley /'medlɪ ; 'mɛdlɪ/ *n* (*pl* ~s) [C] mixture of things or persons of different sorts: 混合;混合物;雜處的人群: *the ~ of races in Hawaii.* 夏威夷各種族的大雜燴。

meed /mi:d ; mid/ *n* (poet) deserved portion (*of* praise, etc). (詩)(讚美等的)應得之份(與 of 連用)。

meek /mi:k ; mik/ *adj* (-er, -est) mild and patient; unprotesting (the contrary of *self-assertive*): 溫順的;謙和的(與 self-assertive 相反): *She's as ~ as a lamb.* 她像小羊一般的溫順。 **~·ly** *adv* **~·ness** *n*

meer·schaum /'mɪəʃəm ; 'mɪrʃəm/ *n* [U] white clay-like substance; [C] tobacco pipe with a bowl made of this. 海泡石;海泡石所製的煙斗。

meet[1] /mi:t ; mit/ *vt, vi* (*pt, pp,* met /met ; mɛt/) **1** [VP6A, 2A, C] come face to face with (sb or sth coming from the opposite or a different direction); come together from different points or directions: 遇見;碰見;相逢: *~ sb in the street.* 在街上遇見某人。 *We met (each other) quite by chance.* 我們的相遇十分偶然。 *Goodbye till we ~ again.* 珍重再見(道別時的用語)。 *The two trains ~* (= pass each other) *at Crewe.* 那二輛火車在克魯地方相遇(卽在該地錯車)。 *We write regularly but seldom ~,* see each other. 我們經常通信但却很少見面。*Can you ~* (= face) *misfortune with a smile?* 你能面對不幸的遭遇而一笑置之嗎? *The Debating Society ~s every Friday at 8 pm.* 辯論會每星期五下午八時開會。 **~ with, (a)** experience: 遭遇;受到: *~ with misfortune/an accident/great kindness.* 遭遇不幸(遇到意外;受到優遇)。**(b)** come upon by chance: 偶遇;碰到: *~ with obstacles;* 碰到阻礙; *~ with an old friend at a dinner party.* 在一個宴會上偶然遇到一位老友。**(c)** (US) have a meeting with. (美)和…會面。 **2** [VP6A, 2A] make the acquaintance of; be introduced to: 結識;被介紹: *I know Mrs Hill by sight, but have never met her/we've never met.* 我跟希爾夫人只是面熟,但並不認識她(從來沒人給我們介紹過)。(As a form of introduction) (作爲一種介紹用語) *M~ my wife.* 這是內子。*Pleased to ~ you.* 高興見到您;久仰久仰。 **3** [VP6A] go to a place and await the arrival of: 迎接: *Will you ~ me at the station?* 你要到車站接我嗎? *I'll ~ your train.* 我要到火車站接你。*The hotel bus ~s all the trains.* 旅館的汽車在火車站迎接各班車的旅客。 **4** [VP6A] satisfy (a demand, etc): 應付;滿足(要求等): *~ sb's wishes,* do what he wants. 滿足某人的願望。 *Can you ~ their objections/criticisms,* answer them in a satisfactory way? 你能圓滿答覆他們的抗議(批評)嗎? **~ *the case,*** be adequate, satisfactory: 適當;令人滿意: *I'm afraid your proposal hardly ~s the case.* 我恐怕你的提議不大合適。 **~ *sb halfway,*** (fig) compromise; give way to some extent in order to satisfy him. (喻)與人妥協;遷就某人。**~ *all expenses/bills, etc,*** pay them. 付全部費用(帳單等)。 **5** [VP6A, 2A] come into contact; touch: 接觸: *Their hands met.* 他們的手相觸。*His hand met hers.* 他的手碰到她的手。*My waistcoat won't ~,* is too small to be buttoned. 我的背心太小了,扣不上。 ***make (both) ends ~,*** make one's income and one's expenditure equal. 使收支相抵;量入爲出。 **6 ~ *the eye/ear,*** be visible/audible. 看得見(聽得到)。 ***There is more to/in sth/sb than ~s the eye,*** it/he has qualities, characteristics, etc that are not immediately seen. (喻)某事物(某人)的特性、特質等不是一眼看得出的。**~ *sb's eye,*** look in his eyes: 與某人目光相接: *She was afraid to ~ my eye.* 她怕與我目光相接。

meet[2] /mi:t ; mit/ *n* **1** (GB) gathering of riders and hounds at a fixed place (for foxhunting). (英) 出發獵狐前騎馬的獵者與獵犬的集合。 **2** (US) coming together of a number of people for a purpose: (美)集會;會: *an ath'letic ~;* 運動會; *a 'track/'swimming ~* (*meeting* is the usu word in GB). 田徑(游泳)比賽(英國通常用 meeting)。

meet[3] /mi:t ; mit/ *adj* (archaic) right; suitable; proper. (古)對的;適合的;適當的。

meet·ing /'mi:tɪŋ ; 'mitɪŋ/ *n* **1** coming together of a number of persons at a certain time and place, esp for discussion: 集會;(尤指)會議: *political ~s.* 政治集會;政治會議。*Mr Smith will now address the ~.* 史密斯先生現在要對大會演講。'**~-house** *n* building for ~s, esp those held by Quakers. 聚會所(尤指教友派的聚會所)。'**~-place** *n* place fixed for a ~. 集會地點;集合場所。**2** any coming together: 聚會;會晤: *a 'race-~;* 賽馬會; *a 'sports-~.* 運動會。*The ~ between the two families was a joyful one.* 這兩家人的聚會頗爲愉快。*She is shy at a first ~,* when she meets sb for the first time. 她與人初次見面時很害羞。

mega·cycle /ˈmegəsaɪkl ; ˈmɛgəˌsaɪkl/ *n* [C] one million cycles (of changes of radio current). (無線電頻率的)百萬周;兆周。

mega·death /ˈmegədeθ ; ˈmɛgəˌdɛθ/ *n* death of one million people (in nuclear war). 一百萬人之死亡(如核子戰中)。

mega·lith /ˈmegəlɪθ ; ˈmɛgəˌlɪθ/ *n* large stone, esp one used as a monument. 巨石;大石頭(尤指作紀念碑用者)。**mega·lithic** /ˌmegəˈlɪθɪk ; ˌmɛgəˈlɪθɪk/ *adj* made of ~s; marked by the use of ~s (esp in very early times). 巨石建造的;有使用巨石之特徵的(尤指遠古時代)。

megaliths

mega·lo·ma·nia /ˌmegələˈmeɪnɪə ; ˌmɛgələˈmenɪə/ *n* [U] form of madness in which a person has exaggerated ideas of his importance, power, wealth, etc: 自大狂;妄自尊大狂: *The dictator was obviously suffering from ~.* 那個獨裁者顯然有自大狂。**mega·lo·ma·niac** /-nɪæk ; -nɪˌæk/ *n* person suffering from ~. 有自大狂的人。

mega·phone /ˈmegəfəun ; ˈmɛgəˌfon/ *n* [C] horn for speaking through, carrying the voice to a distance. 擴音喇叭;傳聲筒。

mega·ton /ˈmegətʌn ; ˈmɛgəˌtʌn/ *n* explosive force equal to one million tons of T N T. 百萬噸級(相當於一百萬噸黃色炸藥之爆炸威力)。

me·grim /ˈmiːgrɪm ; ˈmigrɪm/ *n* (archaic) (古) **1** migraine. 偏頭痛。**2** (*pl*) low spirits. (複)沮喪;憂鬱。

mei·osis /maɪˈəusɪs ; maɪˈosɪs/ *n* = litotes.

mel·an·cholic /ˌmeləŋˈkɒlɪk ; ˌmɛlənˈkɑlɪk/ *adj* melancholy; with a tendency to melancholy. 憂鬱的;容易憂鬱的。

mel·an·choly /ˈmeləŋkɒlɪ ; ˈmɛlənˌkɑlɪ/ *n* [U] sadness; low spirits. 悲哀;憂鬱。□ *adj* sad; low-spirited; causing sadness or low spirits: 悲哀的;憂鬱的;引起悲哀或憂鬱的: *~ news;* 令人憂傷的消息; *a ~ occasion,* eg a funeral. 令人悲傷的場合(如葬禮)。**mel·an·cholia** /ˌmeləŋˈkəulɪə ; ˌmɛlənˈkolɪə/ *n* [U] mental illness marked by ~. 憂鬱症。

mé·lange /ˈmeɪlɑːnʒ *US:* meɪˈlɑːnʒ ; meˈlɑ̃ʒ/ *n* (F) mixture; medley. (法)混雜;混合物。

mê·lée /ˈmeleɪ *US:* meɪˈleɪ ; meˈle/ *n* (F) confused struggle; confused crowd of people. (法)混戰;亂鬪;混亂的羣衆。

meli·or·ate /ˈmiːlɪəreɪt ; ˈmiljəˌret/ *vt, vi* [VP6A, 2A] make or become better; improve. 改善;改良;變爲良好。**meli·or·ation** /ˌmiːlɪəˈreɪʃn ; ˌmiljəˈreʃən/ *n* process of improving. 改善;改良。**meli·or·ism** /ˈmiːlɪərɪzəm ; ˈmiljərɪzm̩/ *n* belief that mankind tends to ~, and that conscious human effort may further this tendency. 世界改善論(相信人類會改善,人類自覺的努力會加强此一趨勢)。

mel·lif·lu·ous /meˈlɪfluəs ; məˈlɪfluəs/ *adj* (of a person's voice or words, of music, etc) sweet-sounding; smooth-flowing. (指人的聲音,言語,音樂等)甜美的;流暢的。

mel·low /ˈmeləu ; ˈmɛlo/ *adj* (-er, -est) **1** soft and sweet in taste; soft, pure and rich in colour or sound: 軟而甜的;香醇的;(顏色)柔和的;(聲音)圓潤的: *a ~ wine;* 醇酒; *the ~ colours of the roofs in Dubrovnik.* 杜布洛尼港屋頂柔和的色彩。**2** made wise and sympathetic by age or experience: (因年齡或經驗而)成熟的;老練的: *~ judgement.* 成熟的判斷。**3** (colloq) genial; slightly intoxicated. (俗)高興的;和善的;微醉的。□ *vt, vi* [VP6A, 2A] make or become ~. (使)變香醇;(使)變柔美;(使)變成熟。**~·ly** *adv* **~·ness** *n*

mel·odic /mɪˈlɒdɪk ; məˈlɑdɪk/ *adj* of melody; melodious. 旋律的;音調悠揚的;音調美妙的。

mel·odi·ous /mɪˈləudɪəs ; məˈlodɪəs/ *adj* of, producing, melody; sweet-sounding: 旋律的;產生旋律的;聲調優美的;悅耳的: *the ~ notes of a thrush.* 畫眉鳥的美妙歌聲。**~·ly** *adv* **~·ness** *n*

melo·drama /ˈmelədrɑːmə ; ˈmɛləˌdrɑmə/ *n* **1** [C] exciting and emotional (often sensational, exaggerated) drama, usu with a happy ending; event or series of events, piece of behaviour or writing, which suggests a stage ~. 一種通俗鬧劇(刺激觀衆情感,常爲感人、誇大的,且通常以歡樂爲結局的戲劇);有此種戲劇性的事件、行爲或文章。**2** [U] language, behaviour, suggestive of plays of this kind. 具有通俗鬧劇性質的言語或行爲。**melo·dram·atic** /ˌmelədrəˈmætɪk ; ˌmɛlədrəˈmætɪk/ *adj* of, like, suitable for, ~. 通俗鬧劇的;通俗鬧劇般的;適於通俗鬧劇的。**melo·dram·ati·cally** /-klɪ ; -klɪ/ *adv*

mel·ody /ˈmelədɪ ; ˈmɛlədɪ/ *n* (*pl* -dies) **1** [U] sweet music; tunefulness; arrangement of notes in a musically expressive succession. 美妙的音樂;和諧的音調;音律。**2** [C] musical arrangement of words; song or tune: 歌曲;曲調: *old Irish melodies.* 古老的愛爾蘭歌曲。**3** [C] principal part or thread in harmonized music: 主調;旋律: *The ~ is next taken up by the flutes.* 這主調接着由橫笛合奏。

melon /ˈmelən ; ˈmɛlən/ *n* (kinds of) large, juicy round fruit growing on a plant that trails along the ground: (各種的)瓜: *a slice of ~.* 一片瓜。⇨ the illus at fruit. 參看 fruit 之插圖。

melt /melt ; mɛlt/ *vt, vi* (*pt, pp* ~ed; *pp* as *adj* (*of metal*) 過去分詞用作形容詞而指金屬時作 molten /ˈməultən ; ˈmoltn̩/) **1** [VP6A, 15B, 2A, C] (cause to) become liquid through heating: (使)融化;(使)熔化: *The ice will ~ when the sun shines on it.* 當太陽照到冰的時候,冰就融化。*The hot sun soon ~ed the ice.* 炎熱的太陽很快地把冰融化了。*It is easy to ~ butter.* 融化奶油很容易。**~ away,** become less, disappear, by ~ing: 融掉;融化而消失: *The snow soon ~ed away when the sun came out.* 太陽出來後不久,雪就融化掉了。*Her money seemed to ~ away in Paris.* 在巴黎,她的錢好像一會兒就花掉了。*The crowd quickly ~ed away* (= dispersed) *when the storm broke.* 暴風雨來襲,人羣很快地四散了。**~ sth down,** ~ (a metal article) in order to use the metal as raw material. 熔毀某物;熔化(金屬器,以作鑄造之材料)。**2** [VP2A, C] (of soft food) dissolve, be softened, easily: (指軟的食物)易於溶解或軟化: *This cake/pear ~s in the mouth.* 這蛋糕(梨)到嘴裡就軟化了。**3** [VP2A, 6A] (of a solid in a liquid) dissolve: (指液體中的固體)(使)溶解;溶於: *Sugar ~s in tea/Hot tea ~s sugar.* 糖溶於茶(熱茶使糖溶化)。**4** [VP6A, 2C] (of a person, heart, feelings) soften, be softened: (指人、人心、感情)(使)軟化;(使)感動: *Her heart ~ed with pity.* 她的心因憐憫而軟化。*Pity ~ed her heart.* 憐憫軟化了她的心。*She ~ed into tears.* 她感動得哭起來了。**5** [VP2C] fade; go (slowly) away: 褪色;逐漸消失;變淡: *One colour ~ed into another,* eg in the sky at sunset. 一種顏色漸漸變成另一種顏色(如在日落時之天空景色)。**~·ing** *adj* (fig) tender; sentimental: (喩)柔情的;感傷的: *in a ~ing voice/mood.* 以感傷的聲音(情緒)。'**~ing-point** *n* temperature at which a solid ~s. (固體的)熔點。*Lead has a lower ~ing-point than iron.* 鉛的熔點比鐵低。**'~ing-pot** *n* **(a)** pot in which metals, etc, are ~ed. 熔爐。***go into the ~ing-pot,*** (fig) undergo a radical change. (喻)徹底改變。**(b)** place, country, eg US, where immigrants from many different countries are assimilated. 各不同種族之移民受同化的地方或國家(如美國);大熔爐。

mem·ber /'membə(r) ; 'mɛmbɚ/ *n* **1** person belonging to a group, society, etc: (團體、學會等的)一份子;會員;成員: *a ~ of a club.* 俱樂部會員。*Every ~ of her family came to her wedding.* 她家裏的每一個人都來參加她的婚禮。**,M~ of 'Parliament,** (abbr 略作 **MP**) elected representative in the House of Commons. (下議院的)國會議員。**2** part of a human or animal body: 人或動物身體的某一部分;器官: *The tongue is sometimes called 'the unruly ~.'* 舌頭有時候被稱爲'難以控制的器官'。**~-ship** /-ʃɪp ; -,ʃɪp/ *n* **1** [U] the state of being a ~ (of a society, etc). (社團等的)會員的身份、資格。**2** (no *pl*) number of ~s: (無複數形式)會員的人數: *The society has a large ~ship/a ~ship of 80.* 該學會會員甚多(有八十個會員)。

mem·brane /'membreɪn ; 'mɛmbren/ *n* [C] soft, thin, pliable skin-like covering or lining, or connecting part, in an animal or vegetable body; [U] tissue of which such coverings, etc, are made. (動植物的)膜;薄膜;形成此等薄膜的組織。**mem·bra·nous** /'membrənəs ; 'mɛmbrənəs/ *adj* of or like ~. 膜的;膜狀的。

mem·ento /mɪ'mentəʊ ; mɪ'mɛnto/ *n* (*pl* ~s, ~es /-təʊz ; -toz/) sth that serves to remind one of a person or event. 紀念品;令人回憶起(某人或某事件)的東西。

memo /'meməʊ ; 'mɛmo/ *n* (*pl* ~s /-məʊz ; -moz/) short for memorandum. 爲 memorandum 之略。

mem·oir /'memwɑ:(r) ; 'mɛmwɑr/ *n* **1** record of events, esp by someone with first-hand knowledge. 傳記(尤指有第一手資料之人所寫者)。**2** (*pl*) person's written account of his own life or experiences: (複)自傳;回憶錄: *the flood of war ~s by generals and politicians.* 將軍和政治家們所寫的多如潮湧的戰爭回憶錄。

mem·or·able /'memərəbl ; 'mɛmərəbḷ/ *adj* deserving to be remembered. 值得紀念的。**mem·or·ably** /-əblɪ ; -əblɪ/ *adv*

mem·or·an·dum /,memə'rændəm ; ,mɛmə'rændəm/ *n* (*pl* -da /-də ; -də/ or ~s) (abbr 略作 memo) **1** note or record for future use: 備忘錄: *make a ~ of sth.* 記錄某事(以免遺忘)。**2** informal business communication, usu without a personal signature, on paper headed *M~* (or *Memo*). 非正式的商業文件;便條(通常私人不加簽名,紙上端並印有 Memorandum 或 Memo 字樣)。**3** (legal) record of an agreement that has been reached but not yet formally drawn up and signed. (法律)已經商妥但尚未正式起草簽署之協議的報告書;覺書;備忘錄。

mem·or·ial /mɪ'mɔ:rɪəl ; mə'morɪəl/ *n* **1** sth made or done to remind people of an event, person, etc: 紀念物;紀念品;紀念館;紀念碑;紀念儀式: *a ~ to the dead;* 對死者的紀念儀式; *a 'war ~,* a monument with the names of men killed in wars. 陣亡將士紀念碑。**2** (attrib use) serving to keep in mind: (形容用法)紀念性的: *a ~ tablet,* eg in the wall of a church, in memory of someone; 紀念牌匾(如在教堂牆上,用以紀念某人者); *a ~ service.* 追悼會;追思禮拜。**'M~ Day,** (US) day set aside by law for honouring the memory of members of the armed forces killed in war (30 May in most States). (美)陣亡將士紀念日(在大多數州爲五月三十日)。**3** (usu *pl*) historical records or chronicles. (通常用複數)歷史記錄;編年史。**4** (more usu 較常用 *petition*) written statement of facts, views, etc sent to authorities making a request or protest. 請願書;陳情書;抗議書。**~·ize** /-aɪz ; -,aɪz/ *vt* [VP6A] **1** (more usu 較常用 *petition*) present a ~(4) to. 向…上陳情書;向…呈遞請願書。**2** commemorate (which is the more usu word). 紀念(commemorate 爲較常用字)。

mem·or·ize /'meməraɪz ; 'mɛmə,raɪz/ *vt* [VP6A] learn by heart; commit to memory. 熟記;記住。

mem·ory /'memərɪ ; 'mɛmərɪ/ *n* (*pl* -ries) **1** [U] power of keeping facts in the conscious mind and of being able to call them back at will; preservation of past experience for future use. 記憶力;記憶。***commit sth to ~,*** learn it by heart. 記住某事物;熟記某事物。***speak from ~,*** ie without referring to notes, etc. 憑記憶講述。***to the best of my ~,*** as far as I can remember. 就我記憶所及;憑我所記得的。***in ~ of sb; to the ~ of sb,*** serving to recall sb, to keep him fresh in peoples' minds. 以紀念某人;爲了紀念某人。**2** [C] this power in an individual (also used, by extension, of the unit of a computer which stores data for future use): 個人的記憶力;記性;(亦可引申用以指電腦的)儲存器: *Some people have better memories than others.* 有些人的記憶力比別人好。*He has a bad ~ for dates.* 他對日期的記憶力很差。**3** [U] period over which the ~ can go back: 記憶的期限: *beyond/within the ~ of men.* 在人類有史以前(以來)。***within living ~,*** within the years that people now alive can remember. 在活着的人們所能記憶的年月裡。**4** [C] sth that is remembered; sth from the past stored in the ~: 記住的事情;留在記憶之中的往事: *memories of childhood.* 童年的回憶。**5** [U] reputation after death (esp of saints, great rulers): 死後的名望(尤指聖人、君王者): *the late king/pope, of blessed ~.* 先王(故教宗)(對已故國王、教宗的敬稱)。

mem·sa·hib /'memsɑ:b ; 'mɛm,sɑ·ɪb/ *n* (In India) (form of address to a) European woman. (在印度)歐洲婦女;太太(印度人對歐洲婦女之稱呼)。

men /men ; mɛn/ *n pl* of man¹.

men·ace /'menəs ; 'mɛnɪs/ *n* [C, U] danger; threat: 危險;威脅: *a ~ to world peace;* 對世界和平的威脅; *in a speech filled with ~.* 在一次滿口恫嚇的演說中。*That woman is a ~,* is a nuisance, is troublesome! 那女人眞討人厭(眞難纏)! □ *vt* [VP6A] threaten: 威脅;恐嚇: *countries ~d by/with war.* 受到戰爭威脅的國家。**men·ac·ing·ly** *adv* in a threatening manner. 威嚇地;脅迫地。

mé·nage /meɪ'nɑ:ʒ ; me'nɑʒ/ *n* (F) household. (法)家庭管理;家政;家務;家庭。

men·ag·erie /mɪ'nædʒərɪ ; mə'nædʒərɪ/ *n* collection of wild animals in captivity, esp for a travelling circus. 樊籠等之中的野獸;(尤指)馬戲團在各地表演時囚於籠中之獸羣;動物展覽。

mend /mend ; mɛnd/ *vt, vi* **1** [VP6A] remake, repair, set right (sth broken, worn out, or torn); restore to good condition or working order: 修補;修理: *~ shoes/a broken window.* 修補鞋子(破窗戶)。**2** [VP6A, 2A] (= *amend*) free from faults or errors: 修正;改良;改善: *That won't ~* (= improve) *matters.* 那無濟於事。***it's never too late to ~,*** (prov) reform one's way of living. (諺)改過不嫌遲;改過永遠不會太晚。**~ *one's ways,*** ⇨ way(10). **3** [VP2A] regain health; heal: 恢復健康;痊愈: *The patient is ~ing nicely.* 這病人康復得很快。**4** [VP6A] increase: 增加: *~ one's pace,* quicken it; walk faster; 加快脚步; *~ the fire,* (regional use) put more coal on it. (地方性用語)在火裡加煤炭;加添燃料。□ *n* damage or torn part, that has been ~ed: 補釘;修補處: *The ~s were almost invisible.* 修補的地方幾乎看不出來。***on the ~,*** improving in health or condition. 康復中;改進中。**~er** *n* (chiefly in compounds) one who ~s: (主用於複合字)修補者;修理者: *'road-~er.* 修路工人。**'~·ing** *n* (esp) work of ~ing (clothes, etc): 修補;(尤指衣服等的)補綴: *a basketful of ~ing,* of clothes, etc, to be ~ed; 一籃待補的衣物; *invisible ~ing,*

⇨ invisible. 織補。

men·da·cious /menˈdeɪʃəs ; mɛnˈdeʃəs/ *adj* (formal) false; untruthful: (正式用語)假的; 虛僞的: ~ *newspaper reports.* 不實的新聞報導。~·**ly** *adv* **men·dac·ity** /menˈdæsətɪ ; mɛnˈdæsətɪ/ *n* (formal) [U] untruthfulness; [C] (*pl* -ties) untrue statement. (正式用語)虛假;虛假之言語;謊言。

Men·delian /menˈdiːlɪən ; mɛnˈdilɪən/ *adj* of the theory of genetics of Mendel, the Czechoslovakian biologist. (捷克斯拉夫生物學家)孟德爾之遺傳學說的。

men·di·cant /ˈmendɪkənt ; ˈmɛndɪkənt/ *n, adj* (person) getting a living by asking for alms, or as a beggar: 靠救濟品過活的(人);行乞的(人): ~ *friars.* 托鉢僧(到處化緣的和尚)。

men·folk /ˈmenfəʊk ; ˈmɛnˌfok/ *n pl* (colloq) men, esp the men of a family: (俗)男人們(尤指一家之中的男人們): *The ~ have all gone out fishing.* 男人們都出去釣魚了。

me·nial /ˈmiːnɪəl ; ˈminɪəl/ *adj* suitable for, to be done by, a household servant: 適合於傭人的;由傭人做的: *such ~ tasks as washing pots and pans.* 洗鍋洗盆這類傭人所做的工作。□ *n* (usu derog) servant. (通常含貶抑意味)奴僕;賤僕。~**ly** /-ɪəlɪ ; -ɪəlɪ/ *adv*

men·in·gi·tis /ˌmenɪnˈdʒaɪtɪs ; ˌmɛnɪnˈdʒaɪtɪs/ *n* [U] (serious illness caused by) inflammation of any or all of the membranes enclosing the brain and spinal cord. 腦膜炎;腦膜炎症。

meno·pause /ˈmenəpɔːz ; ˈmɛnəˌpɔz/ *n* final cessation of the menses at the age of about 50 (colloq called *'change of life'*). 斷經;停經;斷經期;經絕期(俗稱'更年期',婦女之月經停閉約在五十歲左右)。

men·ses /ˈmensiːz ; ˈmɛnsiz/ *n pl* monthly bleeding from the uterus. 月經。

men·stru·ate /ˈmenstrʊeɪt ; ˈmɛnstrʊˌet/ *vi* [VP2A] discharge the menses. 月經來潮;行經。**men·stru·ation** /ˌmenstrʊˈeɪʃn ; ˌmɛnstrʊˈeʃən/ *n* [U] this process. 月經;行經。**men·strual** /ˈmenstrʊəl ; ˈmɛnstrʊəl/ *adj* of the menses or menstruation. 月經的。

men·sur·ation /ˌmensjʊˈreɪʃn ; ˌmɛnʃəˈreʃən/ *n* process of, mathematical rules for, finding length, area and volume. (長度、面積、體積之)測量;測量法;測量術。**men·sur·able** /ˈmensjʊrəbl ; ˈmɛnʃʊrəbl̩/ *adj* (rare) measurable. (罕)可測量的;可量度的。

men·tal /ˈmentl ; ˈmɛntl̩/ *adj* of or in the mind. 心智的;心理的;智力的;心中的。ˈ~ **age,** person's ~ level measured in terms of the average age of children having the same ~ standard. 心理年齡;心齡。ˌ~ **aˈrithmetic,** done in the mind without using written figures or a mechanical device. 心算。ˌ~ **deˈficiency,** subnormal development of intellectual powers, preventing a person from learning normally, looking after himself, etc. 心智缺陷(智力欠正常的發育,使患者不能正常學習、照料自己等)。ˈ~ **home/hospital,** one for ~ patients. 精神病院。ˌ~ ˈ**illness,** illness of the mind. 精神病。ˈ~ **patient,** person suffering an illness of the mind. 精神病人。ˌ~ **reserˈvation,** one concerning a statement, oath, etc present in the mind but not spoken in words. 心意保留(作一項陳述、誓言等時出現在心中但沒有說出的心意)。~**ly** /ˈmentəlɪ ; ˈmɛntl̩ɪ/ *adv*: *~ly deficient/defective,* suffering from ~ illness; unable to profit from the ordinary kind of school education; 患精神病的;智力不足的;心理有缺陷的; *~ly deranged,* (colloq 俗 = mad). 精神錯亂的;瘋的。

men·tal·ity /menˈtælətɪ ; mɛnˈtælətɪ/ *n* **1** [U] general intellectual character; degree of intellectual power: 心智;智力: *persons of average ~.* 智力普通的人。**2** [C] (*pl* -ties) characteristic attitude of mind: 心理狀態: *a war ~.* 戰爭心理。

men·thol /ˈmenθɒl ; ˈmɛnθol/ *n* [U] solid white substance obtained from oil of peppermint, used, eg by being rubbed on the skin, to relieve neuralgia, etc and as a flavouring, eg in ~ cigarettes. 薄荷腦(從薄荷油提煉出的一種白色固體,用於塗擦皮膚以減輕神經痛等,及用作香料,如薄荷香煙中所用者)。**men·tho·lated** /ˈmenθəleɪtɪd ; ˈmɛnθəˌletɪd/ *adj* containing ~. 含有薄荷腦的。

men·tion /ˈmenʃn ; ˈmɛnʃən/ *vt* [VP6A, C, 9, 13A] speak or write sth about; say the name of; refer to: 說到;寫到;提及: *He ~ed to me that he had seen you.* 他向我提到曾經見過你。*I shall ~ it to him.* 我將向他提到這件事。*Did I hear my name ~ed,* Was somebody talking about me? 是不是有人提到我的名字;是不是有人在談論我? ***not to ~; without ~ing,*** phrases used either to excuse ~ of sth unimportant or to emphasize sth important: 不用說;更不必說;遑論: *We're too busy to take a long holiday this year, not to ~ the fact that we can't afford it.* 我們今年太忙不能去度一個長的假期,更不必說我們出不起這筆錢。***Don't ~ it,*** phrase used to indicate that thanks, an apology, etc are unnecessary. 不必客氣;那裡那裡(對感謝及道歉的答語)。□ *n* **1** [U] ~ing or naming: 提到: *He made no ~ of your request.* 他沒有提到你的請求。**2** [C] brief notice or reference: 簡要的告示或提述: *Did the concert get a ~ in the paper?* 報上報導這次音樂會沒有? **-men·tioned** *adj* (with an *adv* prefixed): (字前附以副詞): *aˌbove-/beˌlow-ˈmentioned,* referred to above/below. 上述的(下述的)。

men·tor /ˈmentɔː(r) ; ˈmɛntɚ/ *n* wise and trusted adviser and helper (of an inexperienced person). (無經驗之人的)聰明可信賴的顧問;輔導者。

menu /ˈmenjuː ; ˈmɛnju/ *n* list of courses at a meal or of dishes available at a restaurant. 菜單。

Mephi·stoph·elian /ˌmefɪstəˈfiːlɪən ; ˌmɛfɪstəˈfilɪən/ *adj* of or like Mephistopheles /ˌmefɪˈstɒfəliːz ; ˌmɛfəˈstɑfəˌliz/ (the devil in a German legend); fiendish. (德國傳奇中之惡魔)麥斐斯托斐利的;像麥斐斯托斐利的;魔鬼的。

mer·can·tile /ˈmɜːkəntaɪl ; ˈmɝkəntɪl/ *adj* of trade, commerce and merchants. 貿易的;商業的;商人的。~ **marine,** country's merchant ships and seamen. 一國商船及海員的總稱。

Mer·cator's pro·jec·tion /məˌkeɪtəz prəˈdʒekʃn ; mɝˌketɚz prəˈdʒɛkʃən/ *n* method of making maps of the world in which meridians and parallels of latitude cross at right angles (so that areas far from the equator are exaggerated in size). 麥開托投影法(一種繪製世界地圖的方法,經緯線成直角相交,使遠離赤道的地區被放大)。⇨ the illus at projection. 參看 projection 之插圖。

mer·cen·ary /ˈmɜːsɪnərɪ *US:* -nerɪ ; ˈmɝsn̩ˌɛrɪ/ *adj* working only for money or other reward; inspired by love of money: 僅爲工錢或其他報酬而工作的;愛財所致的;圖利的: ~ *politicians;* 以金錢爲目的之政客; *act from ~ motives.* 所作所爲出自圖利的動機。□ *n* (*pl* -ries) soldier hired for pay to serve in a foreign army. 傭兵(爲金錢而受雇於外國軍隊中的士兵)。

mer·cer /ˈmɜːsə(r) ; ˈmɝsɚ/ *n* (GB) dealer in woven materials, esp silk and other textiles. (英)布商;(尤指)經銷綢緞及其他織物之商人。

mer·cer·ize /ˈmɜːsəraɪz ; ˈmɝsəˌraɪz/ *vt* [VP6A] treat (cotton threads) so that they are better able to take dyes and become glossy like silk: 處理(棉紗)使易於染色且具有絲綢光澤: *~d cotton.* 絲光棉布;府綢。

mer·chan·dise /ˈmɜːtʃəndaɪz ; ˈmɝtʃənˌdaɪz/ *n* [U] goods bought and sold; trade goods. 商品;貨品。

mer·chant /ˈmɜːtʃənt ; ˈmɝtʃənt/ *n* **1** (usu wholesale) trader, esp one doing business with foreign countries. (通常指批發)商人; (尤指)國際貿易商。**2** (chiefly attrib) of commercial shipping: (主作形容用法)海運商品的: (attrib) (形容用法) ~ *ships.* 商船。**the ~ navy/service/marine,** the ~ ships and seamen of a country collectively. 一國商船及船員的總稱。~ **seaman,** sailor in a ~ ship. 商船船員。

3 (as the second half of a compound *n*) person trading inside a country in the goods indicated: (用於複合字中接另一名詞後)經售某種貨品的商人: *a 'coal-~/'wine-~.* 煤炭商(酒商)。 **4** (GB sl) person who is very fond of (sth) or addicted to (sth): (英俚)狂熱於從事(某事物)的人;耽於(某事物)的人: *a 'speed ~,* person who likes to drive at high speeds. 好開快車的人。 **~·man** /-mən ; -mən/ *n* (*pl* -men) ~ ship. 商船。

mer·ci·ful /'mɜːsɪfl ; 'mɝsɪfəl/ *adj* ~ **(to)**, having, showing, feeling mercy (to). (對…)仁慈的;慈悲的。 **~·ly** /-fəlɪ ; -fəlɪ/ *adv*

mer·ci·less /'mɜːsɪlɪs ; 'mɝsɪlɪs/ *adj* ~ **(to)**, showing no mercy (to). (對…)無慈悲心的;無憐憫心的。 **~·ly** *adv*

mer·cur·ial /mɜː'kjʊərɪəl ; mɝ'kjurɪəl/ *adj* **1** of, like, caused by, containing, mercury: 水銀的;似水銀的;由水銀造成的;含水銀的: *~ ointment;* 含汞藥膏; *~ poisoning.* 水銀中毒。 **2** (fig) lively; quick-witted. (喻)活潑的; 機智的。 **3** (of persons) changeable; inconstant. (指人)多變的;三心二意的。

mer·cury /'mɜːkjʊrɪ ; 'mɝkjərɪ/ *n* [U] (also called 亦稱作 *quicksilver*) heavy, silver-coloured metal (symbol **Hg**) usu liquid, as in thermometers and barometers. 水銀;汞(銀色重金屬,化學符號 Hg, 通常爲液態,如溫度表及氣壓計中所用者)。

Mer·cury /'mɜːkjʊrɪ ; 'mɝkjərɪ/ *n* (Roman myth) messenger of the gods; (astron) planet nearest the sun. (羅神)莫丘利(衆神的使者);(天文)水星(最接近太陽)。 ⇨ the illus at planet. 參看 planet 之插圖。

mercy /'mɜːsɪ ; 'mɝsɪ/ *n* (*pl* -cies) **1** [U] (capacity for) holding oneself back from punishing, or from causing suffering to, sb whom one has the right or power to punish: 仁慈;憐憫;寬恕;慈悲心: *They showed little ~ to their enemies.* 他們對仇敵毫無憐憫之意。 *We were given no ~.* 我們沒有得到寬恕。 *He threw himself on my ~,* begged me to have ~ on him, not to punish him, etc. 他求我寬恕他。 *The jury brought in a verdict of guilty, with a recommendation to ~,* asking that the punishment should not be too severe. 陪審團宣判被告有罪附帶建議從輕量刑。 ***at the ~ of,*** in the power of; without defence against: 任由…擺佈;在…的掌握中;無法防禦…: *The ship was at the ~ of the waves,* was out of control, likely to be wrekced, etc. 船在浪濤中隨波漂流。 ***be left to the tender ~/mercies of,*** be exposed to the probably unkind, rough or cruel treatment of. 任憑…宰割。 **2** [C] piece of good fortune; sth to be thankful for; relief: 幸運;應感謝的事物;恩惠;減輕或解除痛苦之事物: *That's a ~!* 那眞幸運! *We must be thankful for small mercies.* 我們對小惠也應感激。 *His death was a ~,* eg of sb with a painful and incurable illness. 他的死亡是一種解脫(例如對一患痛苦而不治之症者)。 **'~ killing** *n* (colloq for) euthanasia. 無痛苦致死術;安死術(使患痛苦不治之症者無痛苦死亡;爲 euthanasia 之俗語)。 **3** *M~! M~ on us!* exclamations of surprise or (often pretended) terror. (表示驚愕或故作驚恐時的感嘆詞句)啊呀!我的天哪!

mere[1] /mɪə(r) ; mɪr/ *adj* not more than: 僅僅;祇不過: *She's a ~ child.* 她祇不過是個小孩而已。 *It's a ~/the ~st trifle,* nothing at all important, nothing of any value, etc. 那祇不過是件小事。 *M~ words* (= Words without acts) *won't help.* 光說(不做)無濟於事。 **~·ly** *adv* only; simply: 僅僅;祇;不過: *I ~ly asked his name.* 我祇問了問他的名字。 *I said it ~ly as a joke.* 我祇不過把它當做笑話說說而已。

mere[2] /mɪə(r) ; mɪr/ *n* pond; small lake. 池塘;小湖。

mer·etri·cious /ˌmerɪ'trɪʃəs ; ˌmɛrə'trɪʃəs/ *adj* attractive on the surface but of little value: 外表華麗而實際並無價值的;虛有其表的: *~ jewellery;* 僅供虛飾的珠寶; *a ~ style,* superficially attractive. 浮華不實的文體。 **~·ly** *adv* **~·ness** *n*

merge /mɜːdʒ ; mɝdʒ/ *vt, vi* **1** [VP2A, 3A, 6A, 14] ~ ***(in/into/with),*** (comm) (of business companies) (cause to) become one: (商)(指兩個或數個公司)(使)合併: *We are merging with the company that supplies components for our cars.* 我們卽將併入那家供應我們汽車配件的公司。 *The small banks ~d/were ~d into one large organization.* 這幾家小銀行合併成一個大機構。 **2** [VP3A] ~ ***into,*** fade or change gradually into: 逐漸消失而變成…;逐漸融入: *Twilight ~d into darkness.* 落日餘輝逐漸地融入了黑暗之中。 *His fear gradually ~d into curiosity to know what was happening.* 他的恐懼逐漸消失而變成欲知何事發生的好奇心。 **merger** /'mɜːdʒə(r) ; 'mɝdʒɚ/ *n* [U] merging; [C] instance of this; combining of estates, business companies, etc. 吞併;(產業、公司等的)合併;聯合組織。

mer·id·ian /mə'rɪdɪən ; mə'rɪdɪən/ *n* **1** (either half of a) circle round the globe, passing through a given place and the north and south poles: 子午線;子午圈;經線: *the ~ of Greenwich,* longitude 0°. 格林尼治子午線(地圖上的零度經線,卽經度起算處)。 **2** highest point reached by the sun or other star as viewed from a point on the earth's surface; 12 noon. 從地面觀測太陽或其他星球所到達的最高點;中天;中午十二時正;正午。 **3** (fig) period of greatest splendour, success, power, etc. (喻)(聲望、成就、權力等的)鼎盛時期;頂點。 **4** (attrib) of a ~: (形容用法)子午線(圈)的;正午的: *~ line/altitude;* 子午線(中天高度); (fig) (喻) *in his ~ splendour.* 在他最輝煌的時期。

mer·idi·onal /mə'rɪdɪənl ; mə'rɪdɪənl̩/ *adj* of the south; of the south of Europe, esp the south of France. 南方的;南歐的;(尤指)法國南部的。

me·ringue /mə'ræŋ ; mə'ræŋ/ *n* [U, C] whites of egg and sugar baked and used as a covering over pies, tarts, etc; small cake made of this mixture. (將蛋白與糖摻混而烘成、用以包覆果餡餅等之)餅皮;(用蛋白與糖混合做成的)蛋白甜餅。

mer·ino /mə'riːnəʊ ; mə'rino/ *n* (*pl* ~s /-nəʊz ; -noz/) **1** (also 亦作 **'~-sheep**) breed of sheep with long, fine wool. 麥利諾羊(一種毛細長的綿羊)。 **2** [U] yarn or cloth from this wool; soft wool and cotton material. 此種羊毛所製成的毛線或呢絨;柔軟的棉毛料子。

merit /'merɪt ; 'mɛrɪt/ *n* **1** [U] quality or fact of deserving well; worth; excellence: 功勞;勛績;價值;優點: *There isn't much ~ in giving away things you don't value or want.* 把你看不上或者不需要的東西給人,算不了什麼功德。 *Do men of ~ always win recognition?* 有功勞的人總會受到褒獎嗎? *She was awarded a certificate of ~ for her piano playing.* 她得到一張鋼琴演奏優異獎狀。 **2** [C] quality, fact, action, etc, that deserves reward: 應受獎賞的特質、事實、行動等: *We must decide the case on its ~s,* according to the rights and wrongs of the case, without being influenced by personal feelings. 我們必須按照事情的是非曲直來決定這個案件。 ***make a ~ of sth,*** represent it as deserving reward or praise: 誇稱某事值得獎賞或讚美;誇稱某事是件大功: *Don't make a ~ of being punctual—it's only what we expect of you.* 不要認爲你準時就有什麼了不起——那只是我們預期你應該做到的。 □ *vt* [VP6A] deserve; be worthy of: 應受;值得: *~ reward/punishment.* 該受獎賞(懲罰)。

meri·toc·racy /ˌmerɪ'tɒkrəsɪ ; ˌmɛrɪ'tɑkrəsɪ/ *n* (*pl* -cies) (system of government or control by) persons of high practical or intellectual ability. 具高度實幹能力或智力的人們; 才智卓越的人們; 能人治理;賢能政治(由才智卓越的人們執政的政治制度)。

meri·tori·ous /ˌmerɪ'tɔːrɪəs ; ˌmɛrə'torɪəs/ *adj* praiseworthy; deserving reward: 應受稱讚的;配受獎賞的;有功勞的;有勛績的: *a prize for ~ conduct.* 優良行爲或勛績之獎賞。 **~·ly** *adv*

mer·maid /'mɜːmeɪd ; 'mɝˌmed/ *n* (in children's stories, etc) woman with a fish's tail in place of legs. (童話等中之)美人魚(人身魚尾之女人)。**mer·man** /ˈmɜːmən ; ˈmɝ,mæn/ *n* (*pl* -men) male ～. 雄人魚(雄性之人魚)。

merry /ˈmerɪ ; ˈmɛrɪ/ *adj* (-ier, -iest) **1** happy; cheerful; bright and gay: 高興的;愉快的;歡樂的: *a ～ laugh;* 愉快的笑;*wish sb a ～ Christmas.* 祝某人聖誕快樂。***make ～,*** be gay and cheerful; laugh, talk, sing and feast. 作樂;行樂;宴樂。**ˈ～-maker** *n* person who does this. 作樂者;行樂者。**ˈ～-making** *n* [U] doing this. 作樂;行樂;歡樂。**ˈ～-go-round** *n* revolving machine with horses, cars, etc on which children ride at fun fairs, etc. 旋轉木馬(娛樂場所內供兒童乘坐的旋轉機械裝置，上有木馬，小車等)。 **2** (old use) pleasant: (舊用法)令人愉快的;令人快樂的;可愛的;美妙的: *the ～ month of May;* 可愛的五月;美好的五月; *M～ England.* 可愛的英格蘭;美麗英島。**mer·rily** /ˈmerəlɪ ; ˈmɛrɪlɪ/ *adv* **mer·ri·ment** /ˈmerɪmənt ; ˈmɛrɪmənt/ *n* [U].

mé·sal·liance /ˌmeɪˈzælɪɑːns ; meˈzælɪəns/ *n* marriage with a person of lower social position. 與社會地位較自己爲低的人所締結的婚姻;屈就的婚姻。

mes·cal /ˈmeskl ; mɛsˈkæl/ *n* **1** globe-shaped cactus of Mexico. 墨西哥仙人掌(呈球形)。 **2** Mexican liquor distilled from the juices of the agave plant. 墨西哥林酒(一種墨西哥烈酒，由蒸餾龍舌蘭液汁而製成)。**mes·ca·line** /ˈmeskəlɪn ; ˈmɛskəlɪn/ *n* [U] hallucinatory drug extracted from the ～ cactus. 麥司卡林(從墨西哥仙人掌汁中提煉出的一種迷幻藥)。

Mes·dames /meɪˈdɑːm ; meˈdɑm/ *n pl* of madame.

Mes·demoi·selles /ˌmeɪdmwəˈzel ; ˌmedmwəˈzɛl/ *pl* of mademoiselle.

me·seems /mɪˈsiːmz ; miˈsimz/ *vi* (old use) it seems to me. (舊用法)據我看來;我以爲。

mesh /meʃ ; mɛʃ/ *n* **1** one of the spaces in a net or wire screen: 網眼;篩孔: *a net with half-inch ～es;* 有半英寸網孔的網; spaces in other material. 其他材料上的空格。 **2** (*pl*) network: (複)網狀組織;網狀物: *the ～es of a spider's web;* 蜘蛛網的網狀組織; (fig) (喩) *entangled in the ～es of political intrigue.* 捲入政治陰謀。 **3** (mechanics) (機械) ***in ～,*** (of the geared teeth of wheels) engaged, interlocked. (指齒輪的齒)相嚙合。⇨ also synchromesh. □ *vt, vi* **1** [VP6A] catch (eg fish) in a net. 用網捕捉(魚等)。 **2** [VP2A, 3A] ～ ***(with),*** (of toothed wheels) interlock; be engaged (with others); (fig) harmonize: (指齒輪)(與其他齒輪)相嚙合;(喩)調和;和諧: *Our ways of looking at these problems don't ～.* 我們對這些問題的看法並不協調一致。

mes·mer·ism /ˈmezmərɪzəm ; ˈmɛsmə,rɪzəm/ *n* [U] (older name for) hypnotism. 催眠;催眠術(hypnotism 的較古名稱)。**mes·meric** /mezˈmerɪk ; mɛsˈmɛrɪk/ *adj* hypnotic. 催眠的。 **mes·mer·ist** /-ɪst ; -ɪst/ *n* hypnotist. 催眠者。**mes·mer·ize** /-aɪz ; -aɪz/ *vt* [VP6A] hypnotize. 施催眠術於(某人)。

me·son /ˈmiːsən ; ˈmisən/ *n* (phys) type of subatomic particle with a mass between that of an electron and a proton. (物理)介子。

mess¹ /mes ; mɛs/ *n* (with *indef art*, but rarely *pl*) state of confusion, dirt or disorder: (可與不定冠詞連用，但罕用複數)混亂;汚穢;雜亂: *The workmen cleaned up the ～ before they left.* 工人在離開之前把骯髒東西清理乾淨了。*Who's going to clear up the ～ made by the cat?* 誰去把貓弄亂的東西整理一下? *You've made a ～ of the job,* have done it very badly. 你已經把這事弄糟了。*He has got into another ～,* is in trouble again. 他又遇到麻煩了。*A nice ～ you've made of it,* You've spoilt it! 你把它弄得好糟糕! *I've never seen so much ～ and disorder!* 我從來沒有見過這麼亂七八糟的樣子! □ *vt, vi* **1** [VP6A, 15B] ～ ***sth (up),*** make a ～ of; put into disorder or confusion: 弄髒;弄亂;弄糟(某事物): *The late arrival of the train ～ed up all our plans.* 火車誤點把我們的計畫全弄糟了。Hence, 由此產生, **ˈ～-up** *n* (colloq) disorder or confusion: (俗)紊亂;混亂: *There's been a bit of a ～-up* (= a misunderstanding, a failure to do what was needed) *about booking seats for that concert.* 音樂會預定座位(卽預售門票)的情形有點兒紊亂。 **2** [VP2C, 15B] ～ ***(sth／sb) about,*** **(a)** do things with no very definite plan; behave foolishly. 瞎忙;亂做。**(b)** make a ～ or muddle (of sth); treat (sb) roughly or inconsiderately: 弄亂(某物); 粗魯地對待(某人): *Stop ～ing me about!* 別再對我粗魯! **～y** *adj* (-ier, -iest) dirty; in a state of disorder: 骯髒的;雜亂的;混亂的: *a ～y job,* eg one that makes the hands and clothes dirty. 骯髒的工作(如會把手和衣服弄髒的工作)。

mess² /mes ; mɛs/ *n* [C] company of persons taking meals together (esp in the Armed Forces); these meals; the room, etc in which the meals are eaten. 共餐者;伙食團(尤指軍中者);伙食;(供伙食團用之)膳廳: **ˈ～-jacket** *n* (uniform) jacket worn at ～. 軍官開飯時所穿的一種短上衣;用膳禮服或制服。**ˈ～-mate** *n* member of the same ～ (esp a ship's ～ in the Navy). 在同一伙食團用飯的人(尤指在海軍軍艦上者)。□ *vi* ～ ***with sb;*** ～ ***together,*** eat meals. 與某人共餐;會餐。*The five young men ～ together.* 那五個青年在一起吃飯。**ˈ～·ing allowance** *n* money allowed (in the Armed Forces) for cost of meals in a ～. (軍中)伙食津貼。

mess·age /ˈmesɪdʒ ; ˈmɛsɪdʒ/ *n* **1** piece of news, or a request, sent to sb: 消息;訊息: *Radio ～s told us that the ship was sinking.* 無線電訊告訴我們那艘船在下沉中。*Will you take this ～ to my brother?* 請把這消息帶給我哥哥(弟弟)好嗎? *Got the ～?* (sl) Have you understood? (俚)(你)懂了嗎? **2** social, moral or religious teaching: 教訓;寓意;宗教訓示: *the ～ of Muhammad to his age.* 穆罕默德對他那個時代的啓示。

mess·en·ger /ˈmesɪndʒə(r) ; ˈmɛsn̩dʒɚ/ *n* person carrying a message. 報信者;信差。

Mess·iah /mɪˈsaɪə ; məˈsaɪə/ *n* person expected by the Jews to come and set them free; Jesus Christ considered as this. 彌賽亞(猶太人所期待的救主);救世主;耶穌基督。

Mess·ieurs /meɪˈsjɜː(r) ; ˈmɛsɚz/ *n pl* of monsieur.

Messrs /ˈmesəz ; ˈmɛsɚz/ *n* (abbr of *Messieurs*) used as the *pl* of *Mr* before a list of men's names: (爲Messieurs 之略) Mr 的複數(用於一列男子姓名之前): ～ *Smith, Brown and Robinson;* 史密斯,布朗及魯賓遜諸先生;and before names of business firms: 亦可用於公司行號之前:～ *T Brown & Co.* 布朗公司。

mes·suage /ˈmeswɪdʒ;ˈmɛswɪdʒ/ *n* (legal) dwelling-house with the outbuildings and land that go with it. (法律)包括附屬建築與基地在內之住宅。

met /met ; mɛt/ *pt, pp* of meet.

Met /met ; mɛt/ *adj* (abbr of) Meteorological: 爲 Meteorological 之略: *get the latest ～ report,* issued by the ˈ*Met Office* on the weather. 獲得(氣象局發佈的)最新氣象報告。

me·tab·olism /mɪˈtæbəlɪzəm ; məˈtæbl̩ɪzəm/ *n* [U] process by which food is built up into living matter or by which living matter is broken down into simple substances. 新陳代謝。 **meta·bolic** /ˌmetəˈbɒlɪk ; ˌmɛtəˈbɑlɪk/ *adj* of ～. 新陳代謝的。

meta·car·pal /ˌmetəˈkɑːpl ; ˌmɛtəˈkɑrpl̩/ *adj, n* (anat) (of a) bone in the hand. (解剖)掌骨(的)。⇨ the illus at skeleton. 參看 skeleton 之插圖。

metal /ˈmetl ; ˈmɛtl̩/ *n* **1** [C] any of a class of mineral substances such as tin, iron, gold and copper: (某一種)金屬(如錫、鐵、金及銅等): *a worker in ～s.* 金屬工人;五金工人。**ˈ～-work** *n* artistic work in ～. 金屬工藝;五金工藝。 **ˈ～-worker** *n* one who shapes objects in ～. 金屬工人;金屬匠。 **2** [U] one of these (as a material *n*): 金屬(作物質名詞用): *Is it made of wood or ～?* 它是木頭還是金屬做成的? **3** [U] **(ˈroad-)～,** (GB) broken stone used for making roads or the beds of railways. (英)鋪馬路或鐵路路基所用的碎石。 **4** (*pl*) railway-lines: (複)火車軌道: *The train left/jumped the ~s.* 火車離(脫)軌。□ *vt* (-ll-; US -l-) [VP6A] make or repair a road with ~(3): 用碎石鋪或修補道路: *~led roads;* 用碎石修補過的道路; *a ~led road surface.* 用碎石修補的路面。

me·tal·lic /mɪˈtælɪk ; məˈtælɪk/ *adj* of or like metal: 金屬的; 似金屬的: *a ~ currency,* ie with metal coins; 硬幣;金屬錢幣; *~ compounds;* 金屬化合物; *~ sounds,* eg as made by brass objects struck together. 金屬聲音(例如銅器互擊的聲音)。

me·tal·lurgy /mɪˈtælədʒɪ *US:* ˈmetəlɜːrdʒɪ ; ˈmɛtl̩ˌɝdʒɪ/ *n* [U] science and technology of metals, eg of separating metal from ore, purifying it, and of working in metal. 冶金術;冶金學。**me·tal·lur·gist** /-dʒɪst ; -dʒɪst/ *n* expert in ~. 冶金家。**me·tal·lur·gi·cal** /ˌmetəˈlɜːdʒɪkl ; ˌmɛtl̩ˈɝdʒɪkl/ *adj* of ~. 冶金的;冶金學的。

meta·mor·phose /ˌmetəˈmɔːfəuz ; ˌmɛtəˈmɔrfoz/ *vt, vi* [VP6A, 14, 3A] ~ ***(sb/sth) (into),*** change in form, change the nature of (as by sorcery): 使…變形;使…變質: *Circe ~d the companions of Odysseus into swine.* 塞西把奧德賽的幾個同伴都變成了豬。

meta·mor·pho·sis /ˌmetəˈmɔːfəsɪs ; ˌmɛtəˈmɔrfəsɪs/ *n* (*pl* -oses /-əsiːz ; -əˌsiz/) change of form or character, eg by natural growth or development: 變形;變態;變質(如因自然成長或發展者): *the ~ in the life of an insect,* from the egg, etc; 昆蟲的蛻變; *social ~.* 社會變化。

meta·phor /ˈmetəfə(r);ˈmɛtəfɚ/ *n* [C, U] (example of) the use of words to indicate sth different from the literal meaning, as in 'I'll make him *eat* his words' or 'He has a heart *of stone*'. 隱喻(之例);暗喻(之例)(用言詞表示與其字面意義不同之某事物,例如 I'll make him eat his words 中的 eat, 或 He has a heart of stone 中的 of stone)。Cf 參較 *simile*: 明喻: 'a heart *like stone*'. **~i·cal** /ˌmetəˈfɒrɪkl *US:* -ˈfɔːr- ; ˌmɛtəˈfɔrɪkl/ *adj* of or like a ~; containing or using ~s. 隱喻的;似隱喻的;含有隱喻的;用隱喻的。**~i·cally** /-klɪ ; -klɪ/ *adv*

meta·phys·ics /ˌmetəˈfɪzɪks ; ˌmɛtəˈfɪzɪks/ *n* (with *sing v*) (用單數動詞) **1** branch of philosophy dealing with the nature of existence, truth and knowledge: 形而上學;玄學: *M~ deals with abstractions.* 玄學討論抽象的概念。*Do we need a new ~?* 我們需要一個新的玄學嗎? (Note: on the analogy of French and German, *metaphysic* is sometimes used, meaning 'system of ~'). (註:依法語及德語類推,此字有時寫作 metaphysic, 意指'玄學體系')。**2** (pop use) speculative philosophy; abstract talk. (通俗用法)思辨哲學;空泛的理論;空話。**meta·phys·ical** /ˌmetəˈfɪzɪkl ; ˌmɛtəˈfɪzɪkl/ *adj* of ~; based on abstract reasoning. 玄學的;形而上學的;根據抽象推理的。

meta·tar·sal /ˌmetəˈtɑːsl ; ˌmɛtəˈtɑrsl/ *adj, n* (anat) (of a) bone in the foot. (解剖)蹠骨(的)。⇨ the illus at skeleton. 參看 skeleton 之挿圖。

mete /miːt ; mit/ *vt* [VP15B] ~ ***out,*** portion or measure: 分配;衡量: *~ out rewards/punishments.* 給予報酬(處之以刑)。*Justice was ~d out to them.* 他們受到公平的賞罰。

me·teor /ˈmiːtɪə(r) ; ˈmitɪɚ/ *n* [C] small particle of matter that enters the earth's atmosphere from outer space and becomes bright (as a '*shooting star*' or '*falling star*') in the night sky as it is burnt up. 流星;隕星。

me·teoric /ˌmiːtɪˈɒrɪk *US:* -ˈɔːr- ; ˌmitɪˈɔrɪk/ *adj* **1** of the atmosphere or of atmospheric conditions; of meteors. 大氣的;大氣狀況的;流(隕)星的。**2** (fig) brilliant but brief: (喻)光輝但短暫的: *a ~ career.* 曇花一現的事業。

me·teor·ite /ˈmiːtɪəraɪt ; ˈmitɪərˌaɪt/ *n* [C] fallen meteor; fragment of rock or metal that has reached the earth's surface from outer space. 隕石。

me·teor·ol·ogy /ˌmiːtɪəˈrɒlədʒɪ ; ˌmitɪəˈrɑlədʒɪ/ *n* [U] science of the weather; study of the earth's atmosphere and its changes. 氣象學。**me·teor·ol·ogist** /ˌmiːtɪəˈrɒlədʒɪst ; ˌmitɪəˈrɑlədʒɪst/ *n* expert in ~. 氣象學家。**me·teoro·logi·cal** /ˌmiːtɪərəˈlɒdʒɪkl *US:* ˌmiːtɪɔːr- ; ˌmitɪərəˈlɑdʒɪkl/ *adj* of ~: 氣象(學)的: *weather forecasts from the Central Meteorological Office.* 中央氣象局的天氣預報。

me·ter[1] /ˈmiːtə(r) ; ˈmitɚ/ *n* [C] apparatus which measures, esp one that records the amount of whatever passes through it, or the distance travelled, fare payable, etc: 計量器;儀表(尤指記錄所通過之物的數量,行走之路程或應付之車費等者): *an ˌelecˈtricity-~;* 電表; *a ˈgas-~;* 煤氣表; *a ˈwater-~;* (自來水)水表; *an exˈposure-~,* for measuring the time needed for exposure of photographic film, etc; (照相用)曝光表; *a ˈparking-~,* one that measures the time during which a car is (for a fee) parked in a public place; 停車計時表(設置於公共場所用以計量停車時間,以收取停車費); *fares mounting up on the ~,* eg of a taxi-cab. (如計程車之)表上累積之費用。

an electricity meter

a metronome

me·ter[2] /ˈmiːtə(r) ; ˈmitɚ/ *n* (US) = metre.

meth·ane /ˈmiːθeɪn ; ˈmɛθen/ *n* [U] odourless, colourless inflammable gas **(CH_4)** that occurs in coalmines (as fire damp, causing explosions) and (as natural gas, marsh gas) on marshy areas. 甲烷;沼氣(煤礦中及沼澤地區之一種無臭、無色、可燃之氣體,化學符號爲 CH_4)。

me·thinks /mɪˈθɪŋks ; mɪˈθɪŋks/ *vi* (*pt* methought /mɪˈθɔːt ; mɪˈθɔt/) (old use) it seems to me. (舊用法)據我看來;我以爲。

method /ˈmeθəd ; ˈmɛθəd/ *n* **1** [U] system(3), orderliness: 規律;秩序: *He's a man of ~.* 他是個有條理的人。***There's ~ in his madness,*** His behaviour, etc is not so unreasonable as it seems. 他表面雖瘋狂,實有理性。 **2** [C] way of doing sth: 方法;辦法: *modern ~s of teaching arithmetic;* 現代教算術的方法; *~s of payment,* eg cash, cheques, monthly instalments. 付款辦法(如現金、支票、按月分期付款等)。 **~i·cal** /mɪˈθɒdɪkl ; məˈθɑdɪkl/ *adj* **1** done, carried out, with order or ~: 按次序做成的; 有條理的: *~ical work.* 井然有序的工作;按部就班所完成的工作。 **2** doing things with ~; having orderly habits: 做事有條理或有次序的;慣於有規律的: *a ~ical worker.* 有條不紊的工人。 **~i·cally** /-klɪ ; -klɪ/ *adv* **~·ol·ogy** /ˌmeθəˈdɒlədʒɪ ; ˌmɛθədˈɑlədʒɪ/ *n* [U] science or study of ~; [C] set of ~s used in working at sth. 方法學;研究法;一套方法。

Meth·od·ism /ˈmeθədɪzəm ; ˈmɛθədˌɪzəm/ *n* teaching, organization and manner of worship in the Christian denomination deriving from John Wesley. 衞理公會;美以美會(約翰衞理所創的一種基督教教派);衞理公會的教義、組織及禮拜方式。 **Meth·od·ist** /-ɪst ; -ɪst/ *n, adj* (member) of this denomination. 衞理公會的;衞理公會教友(信徒)。⇨ Wesleyan.

me·thought /mɪˈθɔːt ; mɪˈθɔt/ *pt* of methinks.

meths /meθs ; mɛθs/ *n pl* (colloq abbr for) methylated spirits. (俗)爲 methylated spirits 之略。

Me·thuse·lah /mɪˈθjuːzələ ; məˈθjuzlə/ *n* (in the Bible) man stated to have lived 969 years; (hence) man who lives to a great age. 瑪土撒拉(聖經中所述壽高969歲的老人);(由此產生)長壽的人;人瑞。⇨ Gen 5: 27. 參看舊約聖經創世記 5 章 27 節。

methyl /ˈmeθɪl ; ˈmɛθəl/ *n* ~ **alcohol**, kind of alcohol (also called 亦稱作 *wood spirit*) present in many organic compounds. 甲醇。ˈ**~·ated** /-eɪtɪd ; -etɪd/ *adj* **~ated spirit(s)**, [U] form of alcohol (made unfit for drinking) used for lighting and heating. 含甲醇酒精(不適於飲用,僅用作燃料)。

me·ticu·lous /mɪˈtɪkjʊləs ; məˈtɪkjələs/ *adj* ~ *(in)*, giving, showing, great attention to detail; careful and exact. 極注意細節的;仔細的;精確的。**~·ly** *adv*

mé·tier /ˈmetɪeɪ ; meˈtje/ *n* one's trade, profession or line of business. 職業;專業;行業。

metre[1] (US = **me·ter**) /ˈmiːtə(r) ; ˈmitɚ/ *n* unit of length in the metric system. 公尺;米。⇨ App 5. 參看附錄五。

metre[2] (US = **me·ter**) /ˈmiːtə(r) ; ˈmitɚ/ *n* [U] verse rhythm; [C] particular form of this; fixed arrangement of accented and unaccented syllables. (詩的)韻律;某種的韻律形式;步格(重音節與非重音節之一定的排列方式)。

met·ric /ˈmetrɪk ; ˈmɛtrɪk/ *adj* of the metre[1]: 公尺的;米制的: **the ˈ~ system**, the decimal measuring system based on the metre as the unit of length, the kilogram as the unit of mass and the litre as the unit of capacity. 十進制;公制(十進法的度量衡制,以公尺爲長度單位、公斤爲重量單位、公升爲容量單位)。~ **ton**, 1000 kilograms. 公噸(等於 1000 公斤)。**met·ri·cize** /ˈmetrɪsaɪz ; ˈmɛtrɪˌsaɪz/ *vt* convert to the ~ system. 將…改爲十進制;使變爲公制。

metri·cal /ˈmetrɪkl ; ˈmɛtrɪkḷ/ *adj* **1** of, composed in, metre[2] (contrasted with ordinary prose): 韻律的;有韻律的;詩體的(與'普通散文'相對): *a ~ translation of the Iliad.* 伊里亞特的詩體譯本。 **2** connected with measurement: 測量的: ~ *geometry.* 測量幾何。**~ly** /-klɪ ; -klɪ/ *adv*

metri·ca·tion /ˌmetrɪˈkeɪʃn ; ˌmɛtrɪˈkeʃən/ *n* conversion to the metric system. 十進化;公制化。

Metro /ˈmetrəʊ ; ˈmɛtro/ *n* **(the)** ~, the underground railway system in Paris. 巴黎的地下鐵道系統。Cf 參較 in London, 倫敦的 *Underground* or *tube.*

met·ro·nome /ˈmetrənəʊm ; ˈmɛtrəˌnom/ *n* (music) graduated inverted pendulum for sounding an adjustable number of beats per minute. (音樂)節拍器;節奏器(有刻度的倒置的擺桿,擺動而響出每分鐘的節拍數,節拍數可調整)。⇨ the illus at meter. 參看 meter 之插圖。

me·trop·olis /məˈtrɒpəlɪs ; məˈtrɑpḷɪs/ *n* (*pl* ~es) chief city of a country; capital; 大城市;大都會;首府;(in GB) (在英國) *the* ~, London. 倫敦。

metro·poli·tan /ˌmetrəˈpɒlɪtən ; ˌmɛtrəˈpɑlətn̩/ *adj* **1** of or in a capital city: 大城市的;大都會(中)的;首府的: *the ~ police* 首都警察。 **2** of an ecclesiastical province. 大主教教區的。~ **bishop**, one (usu an archbishop) having authority over the bishops in his province. 總主教(在其教區中有權管轄各主教者,通常爲大主教)。 **3 M~ France**, France itself as distinct from its dependencies overseas. 法國本土(別於其海外屬地)。□ *n* **1** person who lives in a metropolis. 大都市之居民。 **2 M~**, ~ bishop. 總主教;大主教。

mettle /ˈmetl ; ˈmɛtḷ/ *n* [U] quality, eg in persons, horses, of endurance and courage: (人、馬等之)忍耐力;勇氣: *a man of ~;* 有勇氣的人; *a horse that is full of ~;* 精力充沛的馬; *try sb's ~,* test his quality. 考驗某人的耐力或勇氣。***be on one's ~; put sb on his ~***, rouse oneself/him to do one's/his best, put oneself/him in a position that tests one's/his ~. (使某人)奮發起來;(使某人)鼓起勇氣。ˈ**~·some** /-səm ; -səm/ *adj* high-spirited. 有精神的;勇敢的。

mew /mjuː ; mju/ *n* (also 亦作 *miaow*) sound made by a cat or a seabird. 貓或海鳥叫的聲音;咪咪;喵喵。□ *vi* [VP2A] make this sound: 發此種的聲音;咪咪叫;喵喵地叫: *We heard the mewing of a cat.* 我們聽到貓在咪咪叫。

mews /mjuːz ; mjuz/ *n* (with *sing v*) (old use) square or street of stables behind a residential street; (modern use) such stables rebuilt for use as garages or converted into flats, etc: (用單數動詞)(舊用法)住宅街後面的一圈或一排馬廐;(現代用法)由此類馬廐改建而成之車房、公寓等: *living in a Chelsea ~.* 住在契爾西由馬廐改建而成的公寓裏。

mezza·nine /ˈmezəniːn ; ˈmɛzəˌnin/ *n, adj* (floor) between ground floor and first floor, often in the form of a balcony. 中樓(介於一樓與二樓之間,通常爲陽臺形式);中樓的。

mezzo /ˈmetsəʊ ; ˈmɛtso/ *adv* (musical direction) moderately; half: (樂譜說明)適中;半: ~ *forte,* moderately loud. 中强。**~-so·prano** /ˌmetsəʊsəˈprɑːnəʊ US: -ˈpræn- ; ˈmɛtsosəˈpræno/ *n* (person with, part for a) voice between soprano and contralto. 次高音;女中音;唱次高音或女中音的人;次高音部;女中音部。

mezzo·tint /ˈmetsəʊtɪnt ; ˈmɛtsəˌtɪnt/ *n* [C, U] (print produced by a) method of printing from a metal plate which has a rough surface of small dots scraped and polished to produce areas of light and shade. 金屬板印刷術;金屬板所印成之印刷品。

mi, me /miː ; mi/ *n* third note in the musical octave. 全音階的第三音。

mi·aou, mi·aow /miːˈaʊ ; mɪˈaʊ/ *n, vi* = mew.

mi·asma /mɪˈæzmə ; maɪˈæzmə/ *n* unhealthy mist rising from the ground; (fig) unhealthy environment or influence. 瘴氣(一種有害於健康的霧氣);(喻)不健康的環境或影響。

mica /ˈmaɪkə ; ˈmaɪkə/ *n* [U] transparent mineral substance easily divided into thin layers, used as an electrical insulator, etc. 雲母(一種易分爲薄片的透明礦物,用作電器的絕緣體等)。

mice /maɪs ; maɪs/ *n pl* of mouse.

Michael·mas /ˈmɪklməs ; ˈmɪklməs/ *n* 29 Sept, the feast of St Michael. 米迦勒節(九月廿九日,天使長米迦勒之節日)。ˌ~ ˈ**daisy**, perennial aster flowering in autumn, with blue, white, pink or purple flowers. 紫菀(多年生的園藝植物,秋季開藍、白、粉紅或紫色的花)。

mickey /ˈmɪkɪ ; ˈmɪkɪ/ *n* ***take the ~ (out of sb)***, (sl) hold (him) up to ridicule; mock or tease (him). (俚)使某人顯得可笑;嘲弄某人;揶揄某人。

mickle /ˈmɪkl ; ˈmɪkḷ/ (also 亦作 **muckle** /ˈmʌkl ; ˈmʌkḷ/) *n* (Scot) large amount: (蘇)大量: *Many a little makes a ~.* 積少成多;聚沙成塔。

microbe /ˈmaɪkrəʊb ; ˈmaɪkrob/ *n* tiny living creature that can be seen only with the help of a microscope, esp kinds of bacteria causing diseases and fermentation. 微生物;細菌;酵母菌。

micro·bi·ol·ogy /ˌmaɪkrəʊbaɪˈɒlədʒɪ ; ˌmaɪkrobaɪˈɑlədʒɪ/ *n* [U] study of micro-organisms. 微生物學。

micro-chip /ˈmaɪkrəʊtʃɪp ; ˈmaɪkrotʃɪp/ *n* chip used in an integrated circuit. 微積體電路。⇨ integrate(1).

micro·cosm /ˈmaɪkrəʊkɒzəm ; ˈmaɪkrəˌkɑzəm/ *n* [C] sth, (esp man, by the ancient philosophers) considered as representing (on a small scale) mankind or the universe; miniature representation (*of* a system, etc). (被古哲學家認作)代表人類或宇宙之縮影的某事物(尤指人);小天地;(制度,系統等之)縮圖(與 of 連用)。⇨ macrocosm.

micro·dot /ˈmaɪkrəʊdɒt ; ˈmaɪkrodɑt/ *n* photograph reduced to the size of a dot. 微粒照片(縮小至微粒大小的相片)。

micro-elec·tron·ics /ˌmaɪkrəʊɪˌlekˈtrɒnɪks ; ˌmaɪkroɪˌlɛkˈtrɑnɪks/ *n* (with *sing v*) design, construction and use of devices with extremely small (usu solid state) components. (用單數動詞)微電子學。

micro·fiche /ˈmaɪkrəʊfiːʃ ; ˈmaɪkrofiʃ/ *n* [C, U] sheet of microfilm. 一張縮影膠片。

micro·film /ˈmaɪkrəʊfɪlm ; ˈmaɪkrəˌfɪlm/ *n* [C, U] (roll, section, of) photographic film for small-scale reproduction of documentary material, etc. 縮影膠片(用於縮小攝製文件、書籍等);一捲或一段縮影膠片。□ *vt* [VP6A] photograph in this way: 縮小攝製;將…攝成縮影膠片: *~ old historical records/bank accounts.* 將舊日歷史紀錄(銀行帳目)攝製成縮影膠片。

mi·crom·eter /maɪˈkrɒmɪtə(r) ; maɪˈkrɑmətɚ/ *n* device for measuring very small objects. 測微器(測量極小物體的儀器);測微表;測微計。

mi·cron /ˈmaɪkrɒn ; ˈmaɪkrɑn/ *n* unit of length (symbol *μ*) equal to one millionth of a metre. 微米(長度單位,符號 *μ*,等於百萬分之一公尺)。

micro-or·gan·ism /ˌmaɪkrəʊˈɔːgənɪzəm ; ˌmaɪkro-ˈɔrgənˌɪzəm/ *n* organism so small as to be visible only under a microscope. (僅在顯微鏡下才看得見的)微生物。

micro·phone /ˈmaɪkrəfəʊn ; ˈmaɪkrəˌfon/ *n* instrument for changing sound waves into electrical current, as in telephones, radio, etc. 擴音器;麥克風(將音波化作電波之器具,如電話、無線電等所裝置者)。

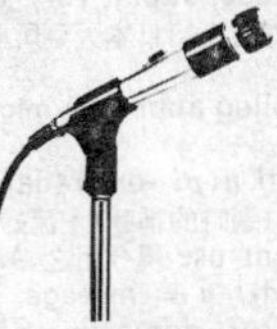

a microphone

a microscope

micro-pro·ces·sor /ˌmaɪkrəʊˈprəʊsesə(r) ; ˌmaɪ-kroˈprɑsɛsɚ/ *n* (comp) type of integrated circuit used in a computer. (電腦)(電子計算機中之)微處理機。⇨ integrate(1).

micro·scope /ˈmaɪkrəskəʊp ; ˈmaɪkrəˌskop/ *n* instrument with lenses for making very small near objects appear larger: 顯微鏡: *examine sth under the ~.* 在顯微鏡下檢查某物。**micro·scopic** /ˌmaɪ-krəˈskɒpɪk ; ˌmaɪkrəˈskɑpɪk/, **micro·scopi·cal** /-kl ; -kl̩/ *adjj* of the ~; too small to be visible except under a ~. 顯微鏡的;用顯微鏡方能看見的;極微小的。**micro·scopi·cally** /-klɪ ; -klɪ/ *adv*

micro·wave /ˈmaɪkrəʊweɪv ; ˈmaɪkrəˌwev/ *n* very short wave (as used in radio and radar). 微波(如無線電與雷達所用者)。

mid[1] /mɪd ; mɪd/ *adj* **1** in the middle of: 在…中間的: *from mid June to mid August;* 從六月中旬到八月中旬; *in mid winter;* 在仲冬時節; *a collision in mid Channel/in mid air.* 在英倫海峽中部(在半空中)相撞。 **2** (in compounds used attrib): (在作形容用法的複合字中): *a midwinter day;* 仲冬的一日; *mid-morning coffee.* (上午十時左右的)午前咖啡。**the ˌMidˈwest,** (also known as 亦通稱爲 **the ˌMiddle ˈWest**) that part of the US which is the Mississippi basin as far south as Kansas, Missouri and the Ohio River. (美國之)中西部(指包括密西西比河流域南至坎薩斯州、密蘇里州及俄亥俄河之地區)。 **3** (cricket) (板球) **ˌmid-ˈoff, ˌmid-ˈon,** fielder near the bowler on the off, on, side. 在投手左側右側的外場員。⇨ the illus at cricket. 參看 cricket 之插圖。 **mid·most** /ˈmɪdməʊst ; ˈmɪdˌmost/ *adj, adv* (*superl* of mid) (that is) in the very middle. (mid 的最高級)正中的(地);正中央的(地)。

mid[2] /mɪd ; mɪd/ *prep* (poet) amid; among. (詩)在…中。

mid·day /ˌmɪdˈdeɪ ; ˈmɪdˌde/ *n* noon: 中午: (attrib) (形容用法) *the ~ meal,* ie lunch. 午餐。

mid·den /ˈmɪdn ; ˈmɪdn̩/ *n* heap of dung or rubbish. 糞堆;垃圾堆。

middle /ˈmɪdl ; ˈmɪdl̩/ *n* **1 the ~,** point, position or part, which is at an equal distance from two or more points, etc or between beginning and end: 中間;中央;中部: *the ~ of a room;* 房間的中央; *in the ~ of the century;* 在這世紀的中葉; *in the very ~ of the night;* 就在午夜的時候; *standing in the ~ of the street;* 站在街的中央; *a pain in the ~ of the back.* 在後背當中部分的疼痛。*They were in the ~ of dinner* (= were having dinner) *when I called.* 我去拜訪他們的時候,他們正在吃飯。*I was in the ~ of reading* (= was busy reading) *when she telephoned.* 她打電話來的時候,我正在讀書。**ˌ~-of-the-ˈroad,** (attrib) (of policies, etc) avoiding extremes. (形容用法)(指政策等)中間路線的;不走極端的。 **2** (colloq) waist: (俗)腰部: *seize sb round the ~;* 攔腰抱住某人; *ˊfifty inches round the ~.* 腰圍五十吋。 **3** (attrib use) in the ~: (形容用法)在中間的: *the ~ house in the row.* 居於這一排當中的房子。**ˌ~ ˈage,** the period of life between youth and old age. 中年。Hence, 由此產生, **ˌ~-ˈaged** /-ˈeɪdʒd ; -ˈedʒd/ *adj* of ~ age: 中年的: *a ~-aged woman.* 中年婦人。 **ˌ~-age(d) ˈspread,** (colloq) corpulence that tends to come with ~ age. (俗)中年發胖。**the ˌM~ ˈAges,** the period (in European history) from about AD 1100 to 1500. (歐洲史上之)中世紀(約自公元 1100 年至 1500 年之期間)。**ˌ~ ˈclass,** class of society between the lower and upper classes (eg shopkeepers, business men, professional workers). 中產階級(例如店主、商人、專業人員等)。Hence, 由此產生, **ˌ~-ˈclass** *adj* of this class: 中產階級的;中層社會的: *a ~-class residential area.* 中層社會住宅區。***(take/follow) a ~ course,*** a compromise between two extreme courses (of action). (採)中間路線;(取)中庸之道。**the ˌ~ ˈdistance,** that part of a landscape, scene, painting, etc between the foreground and the background. 中距離;中景(風景、場面、繪畫等中介於前景與背景間之部份)。**the ˌ~ ˈear,** hollow space of the central part of the ear, in front of the ear-drum. 中耳。⇨ the illus at ear. 參看 ear 之挿圖。**the ˌM~ ˈEast,** ⇨ East. **ˌ~ ˈfinger,** the second. 中指。**the ˌM~ ˈKingdom,** (an old name for) China. 中國(China的舊稱)。**ˈ~·man** /-mæn ; -mæn/ *n* (*pl* -men) any trader through whose hands goods pass between the producer and the consumer. 中間人(貨品經其手由生產者傳至消費者手中的生意人);經紀人。**ˌ~ ˈname,** second of two given names, eg *Bernard* in *George Bernard Shaw.* 教名或所取名字中之第二個名字(如 George Bernard Shaw 中的 Bernard)。**ˈ~ school,** (in some countries) type of school between elementary school and high school. (某些國家的)初中。**the ˌ~ ˈwatch,** (on ships) between midnight and 4am. (船上)夜半値班;夜半更(自午夜至上午四時)。 **ˈ~·weight,** (esp) boxer weighing between 147 and 160 lb or (66·6 to 72·5 kg). 中量級;(尤指)中量級拳擊手(體重在 147 至 160 磅之間,或 66·6 至 72·5 公斤之間)。**the ˌM~ ˈWest,** ⇨ *Midwest* at mid[1](2).

mid·dling /ˈmɪdlɪŋ ; ˈmɪdlɪŋ/ *adj* of middle or medium size, quality, grade, etc: (大小、品質、等級等)中等的;普通的: *a town of ~ size.* 中型市鎮。*He says he's feeling only ~* (often 常作 ***fair to ~***), (colloq) in fairly good but not very good health. (俗) 他說他的健康還過得去(但並不是頂好)。□ *adv* (colloq) moderately: (俗)中等地;略爲;頗爲: *~ tall.* 頗高的。□ *n* (*usu pl*) goods of second or inferior quality, esp coarse-ground wheat flour mixed with bran. (通常用複數)二等貨;次等貨;(尤指)混有麥麩的粗麵粉。

middy /ˈmɪdɪ ; ˈmɪdɪ/ *n* (*pl* -dies) (colloq abbr of) midshipman. (俗)爲 midshipman 之略。**ˈ~ blouse,** loose blouse like that worn by naval seamen. 水兵式的寬外衣。

midge /mɪdʒ ; mɪdʒ/ *n* small winged insect like a gnat. 蚊蚋之類的小昆蟲;搖蚊。

midget /ˈmɪdʒɪt ; ˈmɪdʒɪt/ *n* extremely small person, eg one exhibited as a curiosity at a circus; (attrib) very small: 侏儒;矮人(例如馬戲班展出者); (形容用法)極小的: *a ~ submarine.* 極小型潛艇。

midi·nette /ˌmɪdɪˈnet ; ˌmɪdɪˈnɛt/ *n* Parisian shop-assistant, esp a milliner's assistant. 巴黎店員(尤指女帽店的店員)。

mid·land /ˈmɪdlənd ; ˈmɪdlənd/ *n* (often attrib) middle part of a country. (常作形容用法)一國的中部。**the M~s,** the ~ counties of England. 英格蘭中部諸郡。

mid·night /ˈmɪdnaɪt ; ˈmɪd,naɪt/ *n* **1** 12 o'clock at night: 午夜;子夜;夜半: *at/before/after ~.* 在午夜(在午夜前,在午夜後)。 **2** (attrib) during the middle of the night; at ~: (形容用法)在午夜的;在夜半的: *the ~ hours.* 午夜時分;午夜的那幾小時。***burn the ~ oil,*** sit up and work late at night. 工作到深夜;焚膏繼晷;開夜車。***the ~ sun,*** the sun as seen at ~ in summer within the Arctic or Antarctic Circle. (北極圈及南極圈內夏季所見到的)午夜太陽。

mid·riff /ˈmɪdrɪf ; ˈmɪdrɪf/ *n* **1** (anat) diaphragm. (解剖)横隔膜。**2** abdomen, belly: 腹部;肚子: (boxing) (拳擊) *a blow on the ~.* 對腹部的一擊。

mid·ship·man /ˈmɪdʃɪpmən ; ˈmɪd,ʃɪpmən/ *n* (*pl* -men) non-commissioned officer ranking below a sublieutenant in the Royal Navy; student training to be commissioned as an officer in the US Navy. 英國皇家海軍中階級低於尉官的非委任軍官;(美)海軍學校見習生。

mid·ships /ˈmɪdʃɪps ; ˈmɪd,ʃɪps/ *adv* = amidships.

midst /mɪdst ; mɪdst/ *n* (liter or archaic) middle part: (文或古)中部;中央;中間: *in/into/from/out of the ~ (of);* 在(到,從,從)(…的)中間; ***in our/your/their ~,*** among, with us etc. 在我們(你們,他們)中間。□ *prep* (liter or archaic) in the middle of; amidst. (文或古)在…中間;在…之間。

mid·stream /,mɪdˈstriːm ; ,mɪdˈstrim/ *n* [U] the part of a stream, river, etc away from both its banks. 中流。***in ~,*** in the middle of the action, event, etc. 在進行中。

mid·sum·mer /,mɪdˈsʌmə(r) ; ˈmɪdˈsʌmɚ/ *n* [U] period about 21 June. 仲夏(六月廿一日左右之期間)。**,M~ ˈday,** 24 June. 仲夏結帳日(六月廿四日)。**,~-ˈmadness,** the height of madness. 極度瘋狂。

mid·way /,mɪdˈweɪ ; ˈmɪdˈwe/ *adj, adv* **~ (between),** situated in the middle; halfway. 位於中間的(地);在中途的(地)。

mid·wife /ˈmɪdwaɪf ; ˈmɪd,waɪf/ *n* (*pl* midwives /-waɪvz ; -,waɪvz/) woman trained to help women in childbirth. 助產士;接生婆。**mid·wifery** /ˈmɪdwɪfrɪ ; ˈmɪd,waɪfərɪ/ *n* [U] profession and work of a ~; obstetrics: 助產士之職;助產學;產科學: *take a course in ~ry.* 選助產學課程。

mien /miːn ; min/ *n* (liter) person's appearance or bearing (as showing a mood, etc): (文)儀表;態度;風采;樣子;神態: *with a sorrowful ~;* 帶着憂傷的神色; *of pleasing ~;* 有惹人喜歡的儀表的; *the severity of his ~.* 他嚴肅的態度。

might¹ /maɪt ; maɪt/ *pt* of may.

might² /maɪt ; maɪt/ *n* [U] great power; strength: 强權;權力;力氣: *work with all one's ~;* 盡全力工作; *'M~ is right,' he said,* ie Having power to enforce one's will gives one the right to do so. 他說:'强權卽公理。' ***with ~ and main,*** using all one's physical force. 傾全力;竭盡體力。

mighty /ˈmaɪtɪ ; ˈmaɪtɪ/ *adj* (-ier, -iest) **1** (liter, biblical) powerful: (文,聖經)强而有力的;强大的: *a ~ nation.* 强大的國家。 **2** great; massive: 偉大的;巨大的: *the ~ ocean.* 浩大的海洋。***high and ~,*** very proud. 非常驕傲的。□ *adv* (colloq) very: (俗)很;非常: *think oneself ~ clever.* 認爲自己很聰明。**ˈmight·ily** /-ɪlɪ ; -ɪlɪ/ *adv* greatly; (dated colloq) extremely: 非常地;(過時俗語)極其;極端地: *mightily indignant.* 極爲氣憤的。

mignon·ette /,mɪnjəˈnet ; ,mɪnjənˈɛt/ *n* [U] garden plant with small, sweet-smelling, greenish-white flowers. 木犀草(園藝植物,開綠白色的芳香小花)。

mi·graine /ˈmiːgreɪn ; ˈmaɪgren/ *n* severe, frequently recurring, headache (usu on one side only of the head or face), often accompanied by nausea. 偏頭痛。

mi·grant /ˈmaɪgrənt ; ˈmaɪgrənt/ *n* one who migrates, esp a bird: 移居者;(尤指)候鳥: *Swallows are ~s.* 燕子是候鳥。**~ labour,** that available in a country from (short-term) immigrants. (短期)移民之勞工。

mi·grate /maɪˈgreɪt *US:* ˈmaɪgreɪt ; ˈmaɪgret/ *vi* [VP2A, 3A] **~ (from/to),** **1** move from one place to another (to live there). 遷移;遷居;移往。**2** (of birds and fishes) come and go with the season; travel regularly from one region to another. (指鳥,魚)隨季節之轉換而移棲;定期移棲。**mi·gra·tion** /maɪˈgreɪʃn ; maɪˈgreʃən/ *n* [U] migrating; [C] instance of this; [C] number of persons, animals, etc migrating together. 遷移;移動;移民;移棲;成群移棲的人或動物。**mi·gra·tory** /ˈmaɪgrətrɪ *US:* -tɔːrɪ ; ˈmaɪgrə,torɪ/ *adj* having the habit of migrating: 有遷移習慣的; 流動的; 漂泊的: *migratory birds.* 候鳥。

mi·kado /mɪˈkɑːdəʊ ; məˈkɑdo/ *n* (name formerly used outside, but not inside, Japan for) Emperor of Japan. 日本天皇(原爲外國人給日本天皇所取的名稱,日本人不用這名詞)。

mike /maɪk ; maɪk/ *n* (colloq abbr for) microphone. (俗)爲 microphone 之略。

mi·lady /mɪˈleɪdɪ ; mɪˈledɪ/ *n* (*pl* -dies) (dated form of address to a) lady. (過時的稱呼)上流婦女;貴婦;女士;夫人。Cf 參較 current use 現今用之 *My Lady.*

mi·lage /ˈmaɪlɪdʒ ; ˈmaɪlɪdʒ/ *n* = mileage.

milch /mɪltʃ ; mɪltʃ/ *adj* (of domestic mammals) kept for, giving, milk: (指家畜)爲取乳而飼養的;產乳的: *ˈ~ cows.* 乳牛。

mild /maɪld ; maɪld/ *adj* (-er, -est) **1** soft; gentle; not severe: 溫和的; 溫柔的; 和善的; 不嚴厲的: *~ weather;* 溫和的天氣; *~ punishments;* 輕微的懲罰; *a ~ answer.* 溫和的回答。*I'm the ~est man alive,* No one is gentler, etc than I am. 我是世上最和善的人。 **2** (of food, drink, tobacco) not sharp or strong in taste or flavour: (指食物、酒類、菸草)味道或氣味不濃的;不强烈的;淡的;順口的: *~ cheese;* 清淡的乳酪; *a ~ cigar;* 淡而順口的雪茄; *~ (ale) and bitter,* ~ and bitter beer mixed. 淡色啤酒與苦味啤酒混合起來的啤酒。***draw it ~,*** ⇨ draw²(4). **3** **~ steel,** tough and malleable, with a low percentage of carbon. 軟鋼(堅韌可鍛,含碳之百分比低)。**~·ly** *adv* in a ~ manner. 溫和地。***to put it ~ly,*** to say the least of it, to speak without exaggeration. 穩妥地說;委婉地說。**~·ness** *n*

mil·dew /ˈmɪldjuː *US:* -duː ; ˈmɪl,dju/ *n* [U] (usu destructive) growth of tiny fungi forming on plants, leather, food, etc in warm and damp conditions: (通常指破壞性的)霉;黴: *roses ruined by ~.* 給黴菌弄死了的玫瑰。□ *vt, vi* [VP6A, 2A] affect, become affected, with ~. 使發霉;發霉。

mile /maɪl ; maɪl/ *n* measure of distance, 1760 yards: 英里;哩(合 1760 碼): *For ~s and ~s there's nothing but desert.* 一連許多哩,除了沙漠以外,什麽也沒有。*It's a 30 ~/a 30 ~s' journey.* 那是一個長達三十哩的行程。*He ran the ~ in 4 minutes/a 4-minute ~.* 他四分鐘跑完了一哩。*She's feeling ~s better today,* (colloq) very much better. (俗)她今天覺得好得多了。*There's no one within ~s of him as a tennis player,* no one who can rival him. 沒有人網球打得比他好。⇨ nautical; ⇨ App 5. 參看附錄五。**~·om·eter** /maɪˈlɒmɪtə(r) ; maɪˈlɑmɪtɚ/ *n* device (in a motor-vehicle) recording the number of ~s travelled. (汽車等的)哩程表。**ˈ~·stone** *n* **(a)** stone set up at the side of a road showing distances. (立於路邊示明路程的)哩程碑。**(b)** (fig) (important) stage or event in history or in human life. (喻)歷史上或人生的(重要)階段或事件。

mile·age /ˈmaɪlɪdʒ ; ˈmaɪlɪdʒ/ *n* **1** distance travelled, measured in miles: 哩數;哩程: *a used car with a small ~,* one that has not run many miles. 還沒有跑多少哩的舊汽車。 **2** allowance for travelling expenses at so much a mile. 按哩計算的旅費津貼。

miler /ˈmaɪlə(r); ˈmaɪlɚ/ *n* (colloq) runner specializing in one mile races: (俗)專長於一哩賽跑的人(或馬): *He's our best* ~. 他是我們之中最擅長一哩賽跑的人。

mi·lieu /ˈmiːljɜː *US:* ˌmiːˈljɜː *the* ɜː *having no* r *quality* 此 ɜː 無 r 音; miˈljɸ/ *n* environment; social surroundings. 環境;社會環境。

mili·tant /ˈmɪlɪtənt; ˈmɪlətənt/ *adj* ready for fighting; actively engaged in or supporting the use of force or strong pressure: 好戰的;積極從事使用武力的;支持武力之使用的;尚武的: ~ *students/workers.* 好戰的學生(工人)。□ *n* ~ person, eg in trade unionism, politics. 好戰者;好戰份子(如在工會主義,政治等方面者)。**ˈmili·tancy** /-ənsɪ; -ənsɪ/ *n*

mili·tar·ism /ˈmɪlɪtərɪzəm; ˈmɪlətəˌrɪzəm/ *n* [U] belief in, reliance upon, military strength and virtues. 軍國主義; 黷武主義; 尚武精神。**mili·tar·ist** /ˈmɪlɪtərɪst; ˈmɪlətərɪst/ *n* supporter of, believer in ~. 軍國主義者;黷武主義者。**mili·tar·istic** /ˌmɪlɪtəˈrɪstɪk; ˌmɪlətəˈrɪstɪk/ *adj*

mili·tary /ˈmɪlɪtrɪ *US:* -terɪ; ˈmɪləˌterɪ/ *adj* of or for soldiers, an army; of or for all the armed forces: 軍人的;軍用的;陸軍的;軍事的;軍隊的: *in* ~ *uniform;* 穿軍服的; ~ *government;* 軍政府; *called up for* ~ *service,* eg to train or serve as a soldier. 被徵召受軍訓或服兵役。□ *n* [U] (with *sing* or *pl v*) (與單數或複數動詞連用) **the** ~, the soldiers; the army; the armed forces: 軍人;陸軍;軍隊;軍方: *The* ~ *were called in to deal with the rioting.* 軍隊被調來應付暴亂。

mili·tate /ˈmɪlɪteɪt; ˈmɪləˌtet/ *vi* [VP3A] ~ ***against,*** (of evidence, facts) have force, operate: (指證據,事實)對…發生影響;起作用;妨礙: *Several factors combined to* ~ *against the success of our plan.* 若干因素合在一起妨礙了我們計畫的成功。

mil·itia /mɪˈlɪʃə; məˈlɪʃə/ *n* (usu 通常用 **the** ~) force of civilians trained as soldiers but not part of the regular army. 國民自衛隊;民團。**~·man** /-mən; -mən/ *n* (*pl* -men) member of the ~. 國民自衛隊隊員;民兵。

milk¹ /mɪlk; mɪlk/ *n* [U] **1** white liquid produced by female mammals as food for their young, esp that of cows, drunk by human beings and made into butter and cheese: 乳;奶;(尤指)牛奶: ~ *fresh from the cow;* 剛從母牛擠出來的鮮奶; *tinned* ~; 罐頭牛奶; ~ *puddings,* eg rice, sago or tapioca baked with ~ in a dish. 牛奶布丁(由牛奶與米,西米或參茨澱粉烤製而成)。***the*** ~ ***of human kindness,*** the kindness that should be natural to human beings. 人類本性中的仁慈;天生的惻隱之心。***It's no use crying over spilt*** ~, over a loss or error for which there is no remedy. 為傾瀉的牛奶而痛哭是無用的;覆水難收,悔亦無益。~ ***and water,*** (fig) feeble discourse or sentiment. (喻)無味的言談;脆弱的情感。**2** (compounds) (複合字) **ˈ~-bar** *n* bar for the sale of drinks made from ~, ice-cream and other light refreshments. 牛奶吧臺(售賣牛奶、冰淇淋及其他點心的櫃臺);奶類飲食供應處。**ˈ~-churn** *n* large vessel fitted with a lid for carrying ~. 有蓋的大牛奶罐(此義不用於美國)。**ˈ~ loaf,** sweet-tasting white bread. 甜味的白麵包。**ˈ~·maid** *n* woman who milks cows and works in a dairy. 擠牛奶的女工。**ˈ~·man** /-mən; -mən/ *n* (*pl* -men) man who sells ~; man who goes from house to house delivering ~. 賣牛奶的人;(挨戶)送牛奶的人。**ˈ~-powder** *n* ~ dehydrated by evaporation. 奶粉。**ˈ~ round** *n* ~man's route from house to house, street to street. (從一條街到另一條街挨戶的)送牛奶路線。**ˈ~-shake** *n* beverage of ~ with ice-cream mixed into it and beaten up. 牛奶加冰淇淋攪打而成的飲料;泡沫奶。**ˈ~·sop** /-sɒp; -ˌsɑp/ *n* man or youth who is lacking in spirit, who is too soft and gentle. 懦弱的人或青年;懦夫;柔弱的人;沒骨氣的人。**ˈ~-tooth** *n* (*pl* -teeth) one of the first (temporary) teeth in young mammals. 乳齒。**ˌ~-ˈwhite** *adj* as white as ~. 乳白色的。**3** ~-like juice of some plants and trees, eg the juice inside a coconut. 乳狀樹液或果汁(如椰子所含之液汁)。**ˈ~·weed** *n* name used for several kinds of wild plant with a juice like ~. 乳草(有乳狀液之若干野生植物)。**4** ~-like preparation made from herbs, drugs, etc: (由草,藥等製成之)乳狀藥品;乳劑: ~ *of magnesia.* 乳劑氧化鎂。

milk² /mɪlk; mɪlk/ *vt, vi* **1** [VP6A] draw milk from a cow/ewe/goat, or juice from a plant, or venom from a snake; extract money, information, etc (by guile or dishonesty) from a person or institution. 擠(牛、綿羊、山羊)之奶;擠(植物)之乳液;擠(毒蛇)之毒液;(以詐術或不正當的手段)自(某人或某機構)榨取金錢,情報等;勒索。**2** [VP2A] yield milk: 產奶: *The cows are* ~*ing well.* 這些牛產奶很多。**ˈ~ing-machine** *n* apparatus for ~ing cows mechanically. 擠奶器。

milky /ˈmɪlkɪ; ˈmɪlkɪ/ *adj* (-ier, -iest) of or like milk; mixed with milk; (of a liquid) cloudy, not clear. 牛乳的;乳狀的;攙奶的;(指液體)混濁的;不清的。**the ˌM~ ˈWay,** the broad luminous band of stars encircling the sky; the Galaxy (as seen from earth). 銀河;天河。

mill¹ /mɪl; mɪl/ *n* **1** (building (ˈ*flour*-~) with) machinery or apparatus for grinding grain into flour (old style, ˈ*water*~, ˈ*wind*~). 磨粉機(舊式有: watermill 水力磨粉機, windmill 風力磨粉機);磨粉廠(亦稱 flour-mill);磨坊。***put sb/go through the*** ~, (cause to) undergo hard training or experience. 經歷(使某人經歷)磨鍊;(使)從痛苦經歷中學習。***run-of-the-~,*** ⇨ run¹(10). **ˈ~-dam** *n* dam built across a stream to make water available for a ~. 磨坊水壩(攔溪流所建使磨坊有水可用的水壩)。**ˈ~-pond** *n* water retained by a ~-dam, to flow to the ~: 磨坊貯水池(由磨坊水壩所攔貯的水而流入磨坊者): *like a* ~*-pond,* (of the sea) very calm. (指海洋)像磨坊貯水池那樣平靜;非常平靜。**ˈ~-race** *n* current of water that turns a ˈ~-wheel. 旋轉磨坊水車的水流。**ˈ~·stone** *n* one of a pair of circular stones between which grain is ground. 磨;石磨;磨石;兩片圓形石磨中之一片。***a*** ~***stone round one's neck,*** (fig) heavy burden: (喻)沉重的負擔;重擔: *That mortgage has been like a* ~*stone round my neck.* 那份抵押契據一直像塊磨石般壓在我的頸項上。***be between the upper and nether*** (= lower) ~***-stone,*** be subject to irresistible pressure. 被夾在上下兩片磨石之間(即受到無法抗拒的重壓)。**ˈ~-wheel** *n* wheel (esp a water-wheel) that supplies power to drive a ~. (推動磨粉機的)車輪;(尤指)水車車輪。**ˈ~-wright** *n* man who builds and repairs water~s and wind~s. 修建水力風力磨粉機的人。**2** building, factory, workshop, for industry: 工廠;工場: *a* ˈ*cotton-*/ˈ*paper-*/ˈ*silk-*/ˈ*steel-*~. 紗(紙,絲,鋼鐵)廠。**ˈ~-hand** *n* factory worker. 工廠工人。**ˈ~-girl** *n* girl who works in a ~, esp a cotton-~. 工廠女工;(尤指)紗廠女工。**3** small machine for grinding: 小型研磨機: *a* ˈ*coffee-*~; 咖啡研磨機; *a* ˈ*pepper-*~. 胡椒研磨機。

mill² /mɪl; mɪl/ *vt, vi* **1** [VP6A] put through a machine for grinding; produce by doing this: 碾碎;磨細;碾磨成: ~ *grain;* 碾磨穀粒; ~ *flour;* 磨製麵粉; ~ *ore,* crush it; 碾碎礦石; ~ *steel,* make it into bars. 碾壓鋼鐵而成鋼條。**2** [VP6A] produce regular markings on the edge of (a coin): 在(硬幣)上軋花邊: *silver coins with a* ~*ed edge.* 軋有花邊的銀幣。**3** [VP2C] ~ ***about/around,*** (of cattle, crowds of people) move in a confused way; move in a mass. (指牛群,人群)亂動;騷動;成群兜圈子。

mill·board /ˈmɪlbɔːd; ˈmɪlˌbord/ *n* [U] stout pasteboard used in binding books. (裝訂書籍用的)硬紙板。

mil·len·nium /mɪˈlenɪəm; məˈlɛnɪəm/ *n* (*pl* -nia /-nɪə; -nɪə/, ~s) **1** period of 1000 years. 一千年。**2** (fig) future time of great happiness and prosperity for everyone. (喻)未來的太平盛世。 **mil·len·arian** /ˌmɪlɪˈneərɪən ; ˌmɪləˈnɛrɪən/ *n* person who believes that the ~(2) will come. 相信太平盛世將會來臨的人。

mil·le·pede /ˈmɪlɪpiːd ; ˈmɪləˌpid/ *n* small worm-like creature with very many legs, usu in double pairs at each segment. 馬陸(一種多節足的蟲)。⇨ the illus at insect. 參看 insect 之插圖。

mil·ler /ˈmɪlə(r) ; ˈmɪlɚ/ *n* owner or tenant of a mill, esp the old-fashioned flour-mill worked by wind or water. 磨坊主人或租用人；磨粉廠廠主(尤指使用舊式風車或水車研磨麵粉者)。

mil·let /ˈmɪlɪt ; ˈmɪlɪt/ *n* [U] cereal plant growing 3 to 4 feet high and producing a large crop of small seeds; the seeds (as food). 粟；黍；小米。

milli- /ˈmɪlɪ ; ˈmɪlɪ/ *pref* (in the metric system) one-thousandth part of: (米突制)千分之一；毫: ˈ~-*gram;* 千分之一公分；毫克；公絲； ˈ~*metre.* 千分之一公尺；毫米；公厘。⇨ App 5. 參看附錄五。

mil·liard /ˈmɪlɪɑːd ; ˈmɪljɚd/ *n* (GB) thousand millions (1 000 000 000) (US 美 = *billion*). (英)十萬萬；十億。⇨ App 4. 參看附錄四。

mil·li·bar /ˈmɪlɪbɑː(r) ; ˈmɪlɪˌbɑr/ *n* unit of atmospheric pressure. 毫巴(大氣壓力的單位)。

mil·liner /ˈmɪlɪnə(r) ; ˈmɪlənɚ/ *n* person who makes and sells women's hats, and sells lace, trimmings, etc for hats. 女帽(及其飾物)商。 **~y** /-nərɪ *US:* -nerɪ ; -ˌnɛrɪ/ *n* [U] (the business of making and selling) women's hats, with lace, ribbons, etc. 女帽(及其飾物)類；女帽(及其飾物)業。

mil·lion /ˈmɪlɪən ; ˈmɪljən/ *n, adj* one thousand thousand (1 000 000). (Note: the *pl* is rarely used after a number): 一百萬(注意:在數字之後罕用其複數形): *~s of pounds;* 好幾百萬鎊； *six ~ people.* 六百萬人。 ***make a ~,*** make a ~ pounds/dollars, etc. 賺一百萬(鎊、元等)。 **~·aire** /ˌmɪlɪəˈneə(r) ; ˌmɪljənˈɛr/ *n* person who has a ~ dollars, pounds, etc; extremely rich man. 百萬富翁；大財主；大富豪。 ˈ**~·fold** *adv* a ~ times. 百萬倍地。 **mil·lionth** /-lɪənθ ; -ljənθ/ *n, adj* ⇨ App 4. 參看附錄四。

mil·li·pede /ˈmɪlɪpiːd ; ˈmɪləˌpid/ = millepede.

mil·ometer /maɪˈlɒmɪtə(r) ; maɪˈlɑmɪtɚ/ *n* = *mileometer.* ⇨ mile.

mi·lord /mɪˈlɔːd ; mɪˈlɔrd/ *n* (F word formerly used for) English lord; wealthy Englishman. (昔時法語用以稱呼)英國士紳；富有的英國人。

milt /mɪlt ; mɪlt/ *n* [U] (soft) roe of male fish; fish sperm. 雄魚之精液；魚精。

mime /maɪm ; maɪm/ *n* [U] (in the theatre, etc) use of only facial expressions and gestures to tell a story; [C] such a performance; actor in such drama. (在戲劇等中)只用面部表情及手勢的講述故事；此種戲劇的演出；滑稽啞劇演員。 □ *vi, vt* **1** [VP2A] act in a ~. 演滑稽模倣動作劇；演滑稽啞劇。 **2** [VP6A] express by ~. 以滑稽模倣動作劇表現。

mimeo·graph /ˈmɪmɪəgrɑːf *US:* -græf ; ˈmɪmɪəˌgræf/ *n* apparatus for making copies of written or typed material from a stencil. (蠟紙)油印機。□ *vt* [VP6A] make (copies) with a ~. 用油印機油印。

mi·metic /mɪˈmetɪk ; mɪˈmɛtɪk/ *adj* of, given to, imitation or mimicry. 模倣的；好模擬的。

mimic /ˈmɪmɪk ; ˈmɪmɪk/ *attrib adj* imitated or pretended: 模倣的；假裝的: ~ *warfare,* as in peace-time manoeuvres; 模擬戰；軍事演習； ~ *colouring,* eg of animals, birds and insects that have the colours of their natural surroundings. (動物,鳥類及昆蟲的)保護色。 □ *n* person who is clever at imitating others, esp in order to make fun of their habits, appearance, etc. 善於模倣的人(尤指爲取笑他人之習慣、外貌等而模倣者)。 □ *vt* (*pt, pp* ~ked) [VP6A] **1** ridicule by imitating: 以模倣而取笑；戲擬: *He was ~king his uncle's voice and gestures very cleverly.* 他把他叔父的聲音和姿態模仿得惟妙惟肖。 **2** (of things) resemble closely: (指物品)與…極相似: *wood painted to ~ marble.* 漆成酷似大理石的木料。 **~ry** *n* [U] ~king: 模倣；戲擬: *protective ~ry,* the resemblance of birds, animals and insects to their natural surroundings, giving some protection from enemies. 保護性的模擬；擬態；擬色(動物、鳥類、昆蟲模擬自然環境的形態或顏色,可幫助防止外敵之傷害)。

mim·osa /mɪˈməʊzə *US:* -ˈməʊsə ; mɪˈmosə/ *n* [U, C] shrub with clusters of small, ball-shaped, sweet-smelling yellow flowers. 含羞草。

min·aret /ˌmɪnəˈret ; ˌmɪnəˈrɛt/ *n* tall, slender spire, connected with a mosque, from the balconies of which people are called to prayer by a muezzin (or, often today, by loudspeaker). 回教寺院的尖塔(上有陽臺,供報時人站立呼喊回教徒作祈禱,現今則多在陽臺上裝置擴音器)。⇨ the illus at mosque. 參看 mosque 之插圖。

mina·tory /ˈmɪnətərɪ *US:* -tɔːrɪ ; ˈmɪnəˌtorɪ/ *adj* threatening. 恐嚇性的。

mince /mɪns ; mɪns/ *vt, vi* **1** [VP6A] cut or chop (meat, etc) into small pieces (with a knife, or a machine with revolving blades, called a ˈ*mincing machine* or *mincer*). 將(肉等)切碎；剁碎(用刀切或用機器絞碎,此種機器稱爲 mincing machine 或 mincer)。 ***not to ˈ~ matters/~ one's words,*** to speak plainly or bluntly in condemnation of sth or sb; not take pains to keep within the bounds of politeness. 直言不諱；率直地說。 **2** [VP6A] say (words) with an affectation of delicacy; [VP2A] put on fine airs when speaking or walking, trying to appear delicate or refined. 故作文雅地說(話)；言行矯飾；裝腔作勢。 □ *n* minced meat. 絞碎的肉；肉末。 ˈ**~·meat** *n* [U] mixture of currants, raisins, sugar, candied peel, apples, suet, etc for a ~-pie. 百果餡(由葡萄乾、糖、蜜餞菓皮、蘋果、板油等混合而成)。 ***make ~meat of,*** (colloq) defeat a person/an argument, etc. (俗)徹底擊敗(某人,一論據等)。 ˌ**~-ˈpie** *n* small round pie containing ~meat. 百果餡餅。 **mincer** *n* device for mincing food. 剁碎食物的機器；絞肉機。 ˈ**minc·ing** *adj*: *take mincing steps;* 裝模作樣地走； *an affected, mincing young girl,* 一個矯揉造作裝腔作勢的女孩,⇨ 2 above. 參看上列第 2 義。 ˈ**minc·ing·ly** *adv*

mind[1] /maɪnd ; maɪnd/ *n* **1** [U] memory; remembrance. 記憶；回憶。 ***bear/keep sth in ~,*** remember sth. 記住某事物。 ***bring/call sth to ~,*** recall it to the memory. 回憶某事。 ***go/pass from/out of one's ~,*** be forgotten. 被忘記；被遺忘。 ***put sb in ~ of sth,*** remind sb of, cause sb to think of sth. 提醒某人某事；使某人想起某事物。 ***Out of sight, out of ~,*** (prov) What is not seen is soon forgotten. (諺)離久情疏；看不見的人或東西很快地就會被遺忘。 **2** [U] (but with *indef art* or *pl* in some phrases, as shown below) what a person thinks or feels; way of thinking; conscious thoughts; feeling, wishing; opinion; intention; purpose: (但在某些片語中與不定冠詞連用,或用複數形,如下所列)一個人所思想或感覺者；思想；精神；想法；心意；意欲；感想；願望；意見；意向；目的: *Nothing was further from his ~,* his intentions. 那根本不是他的本意。 ***absence of ~,*** failure to think of what one is doing. 心不在焉。 ⇨ *absent-minded* at absent[1]. ***presence of ~,*** ability to act or decide quickly when this is needed. 當需要時能迅速採取行動或作決定的能力；應變才能；急智；鎮定。 ***be out of one's ~/not in one's right ~,*** mad. 發狂的；精神錯亂的。 ***be of one ~ (about sth),*** be in agreement; have the same opinion. (關於某事)意見一致；意見相同。 ***be of the same ~,*** **(a)** (of a number of persons) be in agreement. (指許多人)意見一致。 **(b)** (of one person) be unchanged in an opinion, decision, etc: (指一個人)不改變意見、決定等: *Is he still of the same ~?* 他仍然不改變初衷嗎？ ***be in two ~s about sth,*** feel doubtful, hesitate, about sth. 對某事感到懷疑；疑慮；猶豫不決；三心兩意。 ***bend one's ~,*** influence the ~ so that it is permanently affected (by beliefs, etc). (指信仰等)左右某人的思想使其永遠受影響。Hence, 由此產生, '~-**bending** *adj* ***blow one's ~,*** (colloq) (of drugs, extraordinary or sensational sights, sounds, etc) cause mental excitement, state of ecstasy, etc. (俗)(指藥物,非凡或感人的景象、聲音等)令人激動、狂喜、陶醉等;使人興奮。Hence, 由此產生, '~-**blowing** *adj* '~-**boggling** *adj* alarming; extraordinary. 可驚的;非常的。***change one's ~,*** change one's purpose or intention. 改變主意。***give one's ~ to sth,*** direct one's attention to sth. 注意某事物。***give sb a piece of one's ~,*** ⇨ piece¹(2). ***have a good ~ to do sth,*** be strongly disposed to do sth. 極有意做某事。***have half a ~ to do sth,*** be rather inclined to do sth. 有點想要做某事。***have sth on one's ~,*** be troubled about sth which, one feels, one ought to deal with. (某事該處理而未處理時)爲某事耿耿於懷;爲某事操心;爲某事焦慮。***keep one's ~ on sth,*** continue to pay attention to, not be diverted from: 繼續注意某事而不分心;專心於某事;留意着某件事: *Keep your ~ on what you're doing.* 注意你正在做的事情(勿分心)。***know one's own ~,*** know what one wants, have no doubts: 深知自己的需要: *He never knows his own ~,* often doubts, hesitates, about what to do. 他從不知道自己需要的是什麼(對要做什麼常遲疑不決)。***make up one's ~,*** **(a)** come to a decision: 決定;決心: *I've made up my ~ to be a doctor.* 我已決心當醫生。*Have you made up your ~ about what you'll do?* 你要做什麼,決定了沒有? **(b)** reconcile oneself to sth that cannot be changed, etc: 安於無法變更等的事情: *We're no longer a first-class power; we must make up our ~s to that.* 我們不再是第一等的强國;我們必須接受那事實。***read sb's ~,*** know what he is thinking. 知道某人在想什麼。Hence, 由此產生, '~ **reading,** guessing; knowing by intuition what sb is thinking. 猜測;測心術(憑直覺知道某人在想什麼)。Hence, 由此產生, '~-**reader** *n* ***set one's ~ on sth,*** want very much; be determined to have: 極想要某物;決心要有或要做某事物: *We've set our ~s on a holiday in France.* 我們已決定在法國度假一天。***speak one's ~,*** say plainly what one thinks. 坦率說出心中的話。***take one's/sb's ~ off sth,*** turn one's/sb's attention away from sth; distract from. 轉移自己(某人)的注意力;使自己(某人)分心。***in the ~'s eye,*** in imagination; in memory. 在想像中;在記憶中。***to 'my ~,*** according to my way of thinking: 照我的想法;依我之見: *To my ~, this is just a nonsense.* 依我看來,這簡直是胡鬧。 **3** [C, U] (person with) mental ability; intellect: 心智;智力;有才智的人: *He has a very good ~.* 他極有才智。*He has one of the great ~s of the age.* 他是當代最有頭腦的人物之一。*No two ~s think alike.* 沒有兩個人的想法是完全相同的。

mind² /maɪnd; maɪnd/ *vt, vi* **1** [VP6A, 9] take care of; attend to: 留心;注意: *Who is ~ing the baby?* 誰在照顧那嬰孩? *When Mr Green was called to the phone, his wife had to ~ the shop,* to attend to the shop. 當格林先生去聽電話時,其妻必須照顧店鋪。*M~ the step,* Watch out for it. 小心那臺階。*M~ your head,* (as a warning to stoop, eg at a low doorway). 注意不要碰到頭(走過矮門等時提醒屈身的警告)。*M~ the dog,* Beware of it. 注意那條狗。*M~ that you don't forget.* 注意不要忘記。***~ out (for sth),*** be careful (of it): 當心;小心;關注: *M~ out!* (as a warning). 當心!(作爲警告)。*Could you ~ out, please—I want to pass.* 請留神——我要過去。*When you go into the garden, remember to ~ out for the new seedlings.* 你走進花園時要當心那些幼苗。***~ one's P's and Q's,*** be careful and polite about what one says or does. 注意言行。***ˌM~ your ˌown 'business,*** Do not interfere in the affairs of others. 注意你自己的事;少管閒事。***~ 'you*** or ***~,*** used as an *int* meaning 'Please note': 注意;請注意(用做驚嘆語): *I have no objection, ~ (you) but I think it unwise.* 請注意,我並不反對,不過我認爲那樣做並不聰明。 **2** [VP6A, C, 2A, 19C] (usu in interr, neg and conditional sentences, and in affirm sentences that answer a question) be troubled by; feel objection to: (通常用於疑問句、否定句和條件句中,以及答覆詢問的肯定句中)介意;反對: *He doesn't ~ the cold weather at all.* 他對寒冷的天氣一點也不在乎。*Do you ~ if I smoke?* 我抽煙你介意嗎? *Do you ~ my smoking?* 你介意我抽煙嗎? *Would you ~ opening the window,* Will you please do this? 請你打開窗子好不好? *Would you ~ my opening the window,* Would you object if I did this? 我打開窗子你反對嗎? *'Do you ~ my leaving this payment until next year?'* — *'Yes, I do ~',* I object to that. '這筆帳我留到明年再付,你反對嗎?'—'當然反對。' *I shouldn't ~ a glass of iced beer,* I should like one. 來一杯冰啤酒也好(卽我想要一杯冰啤酒)。***Never ~,*** **(a)** It doesn't matter. 沒關係。 **(b)** Don't worry about it. 不必擔心。 **~er** *n* person whose duty it is to attend to sth: 看守人;守護人;照料者: (in compounds) (用於複合字中) *ma'chine-~er;* 守護機器的人; *'baby-~er.* 照看嬰兒的人。

minded /'maɪndɪd; 'maɪndɪd/ *adj* **1** (*pred* only) (僅作敍述用法) ***~ to do sth,*** disposed or inclined: 傾向於做某事;有意做某事: *He could do it if he were so ~.* 假如他想做,他就能做。*If she were ~ to help,....* 如果她有意幫忙,…。 **2** having the kind of mind indicated (by an *adj* or *adv* prefixed): (字前附以形容詞或副詞)有…頭腦的;有…心意的: *a 'strong-~ man;* 意志堅强的人; *'high-~ leaders;* 品格高尙的領袖們; *'evil-~ opponents;* 存心不良的對手; *com'mercially-~ men.* 有商業頭腦的人。 **3** conscious of the value or importance of (what is indicated by a *n* prefixed): (字前附以名詞)認識…的價值或重要性的: *He has become very 'food-~ since his holiday in France,* has become a gourmet. 自從他到法國度假以後,他就變得非常考究飲食了。

mind·ful /'maɪndfl; 'maɪndfəl/ *adj* ***~ of,*** giving thought and attention to: 留意;注意: *~ of one's duties/the nation's welfare.* 留意職責(國家的福祉)。 **~ly** /-fəlɪ; -fəlɪ/ *adv* **~·ness** *n*

mind·less /'maɪndlɪs; 'maɪndlɪs/ *adj* **1** ***~ of,*** paying no attention to; forgetful of: 不注意;忘却: *~ of danger.* 不注意危險;忘却危險。 **2** quite lacking in or not requiring intelligence: 智慧很差的;愚蠢的;不需要智慧的: *~ drudgery;* 不必花腦筋的討厭的苦工; *~ layabouts.* 愚蠢的遊蕩者。 **~·ly** *adv* **~·ness** *n*

mine¹ /maɪn; maɪn/ *poss pron* of or belonging to me: 我的: *Is this book yours or ~?* 這本書是你的還是我的? *He's an old 'friend of ~,* one of my old friends. 他是我的老友(之一)。 □ *poss adj* (in poet and biblical style only, before a vowel sound or *h*; sometimes placed after the *n*) my: (僅用於詩與聖經文體中,置於母音或 h 音之前;有時置於名詞之後)我的(= my): *~ eyes;* 我的眼睛; *~ heart;* 我的心; *O mistress ~;* 哦,我的(女)情人; *~ enemy.* 我的敵人。

mine² /maɪn; maɪn/ *n* **1** excavation with shafts, galleries, etc made in the earth from which coal, mineral ores, etc, are extracted. ⇨ quarry for stone or slate: 礦坑;坑道;礦: *'coal~;* 煤礦; *'gold~;* 金礦; (fig) rich or abundant source: (喻)豐富的資源: *A good encyclopedia/My grandmother is a ~ of information.* 一部好的百科全書(我的祖母)是知識的寶庫。 **2** (tunnel for) charge of high explosive (as used to destroy enemy fortifications); charge of high explosive buried and exploded, eg electrically, from a distance or laid on or just below the ground, exploded by contact with a vehicle, or a time fuse, etc: 地雷坑;地雷;觸發地雷;遙控地雷: *The lorry was destroyed by a buried ~.* 卡車被一枚埋在地下的地雷炸毀。 **3** (in war at sea) charge of high explosives in a metal case, placed in the sea, exploded on contact, or electrically, or magnetically. (海戰中的)水雷。 **4** '~-**detector** *n* electromagnetic device for finding ~s(2, 3). 測雷器(探測地雷及水雷的電磁裝置);地雷測探器。 '~-**disposal** *n* the making of ~s harmless (by defusing them, etc): 地雷處理(如拆除信管等使地雷不能爆炸): *~-disposal squads.* 地雷處理隊;拆雷小組。 '~-**field** *n* **(a)** area of land or sea where ~s(2, 3) have been laid. 雷區(設有地雷之地面區域);水雷區(佈有水雷之水域)。 **(b)** area of land where there are many ~s(1). 礦區。 '~-**layer** *n* ship or aircraft used for laying ~s at sea. 佈雷艇;佈雷飛機。 Hence, 由此產生, '~-**laying**, 佈雷, as in 如用於 *~-laying vessel.* 佈雷艇。 '~-**sweeper** *n* naval vessel (usu a trawler) employed for clearing the sea of ~s. 掃雷艇(通常爲拖撈船)。 Hence, 由此產生, '~-**sweeping** *n*

mine³ /maɪn ; maɪn/ *vt, vi* **1** [VP6A, 2A, 3A] ~ ***(for)***, dig (for coal, ores, etc) from the ground; obtain (coal, etc) from mines: 採掘(煤、礦砂等);開礦;採礦: ~ *(for) coal/gold;* 採煤(金); ~ *the earth for coal.* 挖地取煤。 *Gold is ~d from deep under ground.* 金(礦)自地下深處採掘出來。 **2** [VP 6A] (= *undermine*) make tunnels (in the earth) under: 在…下掘地道;挖坑: ~ *the enemy's trenches/forts.* 挖掘地道直通敵軍戰壕(堡壘)之下。 **3** [VP6A] lay mines (2, 3) in; destroy by means of these: 埋地雷於;佈水雷於;以地雷(水雷)炸毀: ~ *the entrance to a harbour.* 在進港處佈置水雷。 *The cruiser was ~d, and sank in five minutes.* 巡洋艦觸雷,五分鐘內即沉沒。 **4** [VP6A] (fig) weaken; undermine (which is the more usu word). (喻)使變弱;暗地破壞 (undermine 爲較常用字)。

miner /ˈmaɪnə(r) ; ˈmaɪnɚ/ *n* **1** man who works in a mine underground: 礦工: *'coal~s.* 煤礦工人。 **2** soldier trained to dig tunnels and lay mines under enemy trenches, etc. 地雷工兵;坑道工兵。

min·eral /ˈmɪnərəl ; ˈmɪnərəl/ *n* [C] natural substance (not vegetable or animal) got from the earth by mining, esp one that has a constant chemical composition: 礦物: *Coal and iron ore are ~s.* 煤與鐵礦是礦物。 □ *adj* of the class of ~s; containing, mixed with, ~s: 礦物的;含礦物的;混有礦物質的: ~ *ores.* 礦砂。 **the ~ kingdom**, natural substances of inorganic matter. 礦物界。 ⇨ animal and vegetable. '~ **oil**, any oil of ~ origin. 礦油(源於礦物的油類)。 '~ **pitch**, asphalt. 地瀝青;柏油。 '~ **water**, **(a)** water that naturally contains a ~ substance, esp one said to have medicinal value. 礦泉水(天然含有礦物質的水,尤指有醫藥價值者)。 **(b)** (GB) non-alcoholic drink (usu bottled, often flavoured) containing soda-water. (英)含蘇打水的非酒精性飲料(通常爲瓶裝,且常加有香料);碳酸水。 '~ **wool**, inorganic fibrous material (used for insulating, etc). 礦綿(無機物纖維質,用於絕緣等)。

min·er·al·ogy /ˌmɪnəˈrælədʒɪ ; ˌmɪnɚˈælədʒɪ/ *n* [U] the study and science of minerals. 礦物學。 **min·er·al·ogist** /ˌmɪnəˈrælədʒɪst ; ˌmɪnɚˈælədʒɪst/ *n* student of ~. 研究礦物學的人;礦物學家。

min·estrone /ˌmɪnɪˈstrəʊnɪ ; ˌmɪnəˈstronɪ/ *n* [U] (I) rich soup (of Italian origin) of mixed vegetables, vermicelli and meat broth. (義)(源於義大利的)含蔬菜,細麵條及肉之濃湯。

mingle /ˈmɪŋgl ; ˈmɪŋgl̩/ *vt, vi* [VP6A, 14, 2A, C] ~ ***(with)***, mix: 混合: *truth ~d with falsehood;* 混合著虛假的事實; ~ *with* (= go about among) *the crowds;* 混在人群中; *two rivers that join and ~ their waters.* 滙而爲一的兩條河。

mingy /ˈmɪndʒɪ ; ˈmɪŋdʒɪ/ *adj* (-ier, -iest) (GB colloq) mean, ungenerous, stingy: (英俗)小氣的;不慷慨的;吝嗇的: *a ~ fellow.* 吝嗇的傢伙;小氣鬼。

mini- /ˈmɪnɪ ; ˈmɪnɪ/ *pref* of small size, length, etc. ⇨ maxi-: 迷你(表示小、短等之義): *'~bus;* 迷你公車; *'~cab;* 迷你計程車; *'~skirt;* 迷你裙; *'~tour.* 短程旅行。

minia·ture /ˈmɪnɪtʃə(r) *US:* -tʃʊər ; ˈmɪnɪtʃɚ/ *n* **1** [C] very small painting of a person, esp one on ivory or vellum; [U] this branch of painting. 小型畫像(尤指刻於象牙或畫於犢皮紙上者);小型畫像繪畫術。 *in ~*, on a small scale. 小型的;縮小的。 **2** [C] small-scale copy or model of any object. 縮圖;縮影;縮小之模型。 **3** (attrib) on a small scale: (形容用法)小型的;縮小的: *a ~ railway;* (玩具用)小鐵道; *a ~ camera*, one for 35 mm or sub-standard size of film. 小型照相機(使用 35 公厘或小於標準規格之底片者)。 **minia·tur·ist** /ˈmɪnɪtʃərɪst ; ˈmɪnɪtʃərɪst/ *n* painter of ~s. 小型畫像畫家。

minim /ˈmɪnɪm ; ˈmɪnɪm/ *n* (music) note half the value of a semibreve. (音樂)二分音符;半音符。 ⇨ the illus at notation. 參看 notation 之插圖。

mini·mal /ˈmɪnɪml ; ˈmɪnɪml̩/ *adj* smallest in amount or degree: 最小量的;最低程度的;最小限度的: *On these cliffs vegetation is ~.* 在這些峭壁上極少植物生長着。

mini·mize /ˈmɪnɪmaɪz ; ˈmɪnəˌmaɪz/ *vt* [VP6A] reduce to, estimate at, the smallest possible amount or degree: 將…減至最小量或最低程度;將…作最低估計: ~ *an accident*, try to reduce its importance, say that it is not serious. 低估意外事件的嚴重性。

mini·mum /ˈmɪnɪməm ; ˈmɪnəməm/ *n, adj* (*pl* -ma /-mə ; -mə/, ~s) (opposite of *maximum*) (of) least possible or recorded amount, degree, etc: (爲 maximum 之相反字)最小量(的);最低額(的);最低程度(的): *reduce sth to a ~;* 將某物減至最少; *the ~ temperature;* 最低溫度; *a maximum and ~ thermometer;* 可記錄最高溫及最低溫之溫度計; *a ~ wage*, lowest wage that regulations allow to be paid. (規定的)最低工資。

min·ing /ˈmaɪnɪŋ ; ˈmaɪnɪŋ/ *n* the process of getting minerals, etc from mines: 採礦: *a '~ engineer;* 採礦工程師; *the '~ industry;* 採礦工業;礦業; *open-cast ~*, getting coal, etc that is near the surface, using mechanical shovels, etc. 露天採礦(法)。

min·ion /ˈmɪnɪən ; ˈmɪnjən/ *n* (derog) servant who, in order to win favour, obeys a master slavishly. (貶)寵信之僕人;唯命是從的奴僕。 ***the ~s of the law***, police, jailers. 警察;獄卒。

min·is·ter¹ /ˈmɪnɪstə(r) ; ˈmɪnɪstɚ/ *n* **1** person at the head of a Department of State (and often a member of the Cabinet): 部長(通常爲內閣閣員): *the M~ of Employment and Productivity;* 勞工生產部部長; *the Prime M~.* 首相。 **2** person representing his Government in a foreign country but of lower rank than an ambassador. 公使。 **3** Christian priest or clergyman, esp one in the Presbyterian and Nonconformist Churches. 基督教之牧師(尤指長老教會與獨立教會的牧師)。 Cf 參較 *priest* for the RC Church, and *vicar, rector, curate* for the Church of England. 天主教用 priest, 英國國教用 vicar, rector, curate。

min·is·ter² /ˈmɪnɪstə(r) ; ˈmɪnɪstɚ/ *vi* [VP3A] ~ ***to***, give help or service: 幫助;服侍: ~ *to the wants of a sick man;* 服侍病人;隨時照應病人之急需; *~ing to her husband's needs*, satisfying them. 滿足她丈夫的需要。

min·is·ter·ial /ˌmɪnɪˈstɪərɪəl ; ˌmɪnəsˈtɪrɪəl/ *adj* **1** of a Minister of State, his position, duties, etc: 部長的;部長之地位、職責等的: ~ *functions/duties.* 部長的權責(職務)。 **2** of or for a ministry(1) (or Cabinet): 部會的;內閣的: *the ~ benches.* (英國下議院中)執政黨閣員所坐的席次。 **~ly** /-ɪəlɪ ; -ɪəlɪ/ *adv*

min·is·trant /ˈmɪnɪstrənt ; ˈmɪnɪstrənt/ *attrib adj* (formal) administering. (正式用語)服侍的;給予濟助的。 □ *n* attendant; supporter or helper. 服侍者;濟助者。

min·is·tra·tion /ˌmɪnɪˈstreɪʃn ; ˌmɪnəˈstreʃən/ *n* [U] ministering or serving, eg in performing a religious service; [C] act of this kind: 幫助;服侍;行宗教儀式: *Thanks to the ~s* (= nursing, services) *of my devoted wife, I was restored to health.* 多虧愛妻的服侍,我終於恢復了健康。

min·is·try /ˈmɪnɪstrɪ ; ˈmɪnɪstrɪ/ *n* (*pl* -ries) **1** Department of State under a Minister: 部: *the 'Air*

M~; 空軍部; *the* ˌ*M~ of* ˈ*Finance.* 財政部。 **2 the ~,** the ministers of religion as a body: 全體牧師: *He was intended for the ~,* destined to be a minister, eg by his parents. 他注定(他的父母有意讓他)以後做牧師。 ***enter the ~,*** become a minister of religion. 做牧師。 **3** [C] office, duties, term of service, of a minister of religion. 牧師的職位、職責和任期。

mini·ver /ˈmɪnɪvə(r); ˈmɪnəvɚ/ *n* [U] ermine fur (as for the ceremonial robes of peers). 白貂皮(如用以製大典時貴族所穿的長袍)。

mink /mɪŋk; mɪŋk/ *n* [C, U] (valuable brown fur skin of a) small stoat-like animal: 貂; (褐色而貴重的) 貂皮: (attrib) (形容用法) *a ~ coat.* 貂皮大衣。

min·now /ˈmɪnəʊ; ˈmɪno/ *n* (sorts of) very small freshwater fish. 鰷魚。

mi·nor /ˈmaɪnə(r); ˈmaɪnɚ/ *adj* **1** smaller, less important: 較小的; 次要的: *~ repairs/alteration;* 小修理(修改); *a broken leg and ~ injuries.* 一條腿斷了,還有一些輕傷。 **2** comparatively unimportant: 比較不重要的: *the ~ planets,* the asteroids; 小行星; *~ poets;* 不太重要的詩人; *play only a ~ part in the play;* 僅擔任劇中的次要角色; (cards) (牌戲) *a ~ suit,* ie diamonds or clubs. 一副低花牌(指方塊或梅花)。 **3** (in schools) second or younger of two boys (esp in the same school) with the same surname: (學校中用語,尤指同學校中之)兩同姓男生中的老二或年齡較小的: *Smith ~.* (兩個史密斯中的)小史密斯。 **4** (music) (音樂) *a ~ third,* an interval of three semi-tones; 小三度(卽含三個半音的音程); *a ~ key,* in which the scale has a ~ third. 小調(卽有小三度之音階)。 ***in a ~ key,*** (fig) in a melancholy or depressed mood. (喩)帶有一種憂鬱或頹喪的心情。 ⇨ major. □ *n* (legal) person not yet legally of age. (法律)未成年者。

mi·nor·ity /maɪˈnɒrətɪ *US:* -ˈnɔːr-; məˈnɔrətɪ/ *n* (*pl* -ties) **1** [U] (legal) the state of being under age (in GB under 18). (法律)未成年(在英國指未滿十八歲)。 **2** [C] the smaller number or part, esp of a total of votes; small racial, religious, etc group in a community, nation, etc. 少數(尤指投票總數中的少數票); (在一社會、國家等中之)少數民族、少數宗教等。 ***be in a/the ~,*** be in the smaller of two groups: 屬於(兩個團體中之)較小團體; 是少數派: *We're in the ~,* More people are against us than with us. 我們是少數派(贊成我們的居少數)。 *I'm in a ~ of one,* have had support from no one. 贊成我的祇有我自己一票(沒有人支持我)。 **ˈ~ government,** one which has a ~ of the total number of seats in a legislative assembly. 少數黨政府(佔國會席次較少之黨所組成的政府)。 **ˈ~ programme,** (TV, radio) one viewed or listened to by a comparatively small proportion of the total viewers or listeners. (電視、無線電)收視(聽)率低的節目。 **ˈ~ report,** one made (after an official inquiry or investigation) by the ~, giving views, etc, different from those of the majority. (在一次正式調查後)由少數人提出的報告(與多數人所持之意見相異)。

Mino·taur /ˈmaɪnətɔː(r); ˈmɪnəˌtɔr/ *n* **the ~,** (Gk myth) monster, half man and half bull, fed with human flesh, kept in the labyrinth in Crete. (希神)牛頭人身怪物(食人肉,養於克里特的迷宮中)。

min·ster /ˈmɪnstə(r); ˈmɪnstɚ/ *n* large or important church, esp one that once belonged to a monastery: 大禮拜堂(尤指曾經一度屬於修道院者): *York ~.* 約克大教堂。

min·strel /ˈmɪnstrəl; ˈmɪnstrəl/ *n* **1** (in the Middle Ages) travelling composer, player and singer of songs and ballads. (中世紀時周遊四方並製作、演奏及演唱歌謠的)吟遊詩人。 **2** one of a company of public entertainers. 技藝團團員。 **~sy** /ˈmɪnstrəlsɪ; ˈmɪnstrəlsɪ/ *n* [U] the art, songs, etc of ~s(1). 吟遊詩人的技藝、歌謠等。

mint¹ /mɪnt; mɪnt/ *n* [U] (sorts of) plant whose leaves are used for flavouring (eg in drinks and in chewing-gum) and in making a sauce: 薄荷: *~ sauce,* chopped-up ~ leaves, in vinegar and sugar, as eaten with lamb. 薄荷醬(搗爛的薄荷葉,調以醋和糖,與羊肉同食)。

mint² /mɪnt; mɪnt/ *n* **1** place where coins are made, usu under State authority: 造幣廠: *coins fresh from the ~.* 剛出廠的硬幣。 **2** ***make/earn a ~ (of money),*** (colloq) a large amount. (俗)賺大錢。 **3** (attrib, of medals, stamps, prints, books, etc) unused. (形容用法,指獎章、郵票、印刷品、書籍等)未用過的。 ***in ~ condition,*** as if new; unsoiled; perfect. 嶄新的; 無汚損的; 完美的。 □ *vt* [VP6A] **1** make (coin) by stamping metal: 鑄造(錢幣): *~ coins of 50p.* 鑄造五十辨士的硬幣。 **2** (fig) invent a word, phrase, etc. (喩)創造(字、片語等)。

min·uet /ˌmɪnjʊˈet; ˌmɪnjʊˈɛt/ *n* [C] (piece of music for a) slow, graceful dance for groups of two couples (dating from the middle of the 17th c). 自十七世紀中葉流傳下來的一種緩慢而幽雅的雙人團體舞; 小步舞; 小步舞曲。

minus /ˈmaɪnəs; ˈmaɪnəs/ *adj* **1 the ˈ~ sign,** the sign —. 減號; 負號(—)。 ⇨ plus. **2** ⇨ positive. negative: 負的: *a ~ quantity,* a quantity less than zero (eg $-2x^2$). 負數(小於零的數,如 $-2x^2$)。□ *prep* less; with the deduction of: 減: *7 ~ 3 is 4;* 七減三等於四; (colloq) without: (俗)缺少; 無: *He came back from the war ~ a leg.* 他作戰回來,少了一條腿。□ *n* ~ sign or quantity. 減號; 負號; 負數。

min·us·cule /ˈmɪnəskjuːl; mɪˈnʌskjul/ *adj* tiny; very small. 微小的; 很小的。

min·ute¹ /ˈmɪnɪt; ˈmɪnɪt/ *n* **1** the sixtieth part of one hour: 分(一小時的六十分之一): *seven ~s to six;* 五點五十三分(差七分六點); *arrive ten ~s early.* 早十分鐘到達。 ⇨ App 4. 參看附錄四。 **ˈ~-gun** *n* one fired at intervals of a ~, eg at a grand funeral. 分砲(每隔一分鐘放一次砲,如在一隆重葬禮中施放者)。 **ˈ~-hand** *n* hand indicating the ~s on a watch or clock. (鐘錶上的)分針。 **ˈ~-man** /-mən; -ˌmæn/ *n* (*pl* -men) (US hist) militiaman ready to fight at a minute's notice. (美史)接獲命令立卽應召的民兵。 ***in a ~,*** soon: 立刻: *I'll come downstairs in a ~.* 我馬上下樓。 ***to the ~,*** exactly: 一分不差; 準確地: *The train arrived at 5 o'clock to the ~.* 那班列車在五點整到站。 ***the ~ (that),*** as soon as: 一…就: *I'll give him your message the ~ (that) he arrives.* 等他一到,我就把你的信給他。 ***up to the ~,*** most recent or fashionable. 最近的; 最新的; 時新的。 **ˌup-to-the-ˈ~** *attrib adj* most recent or fashionable: 最新的; 時髦的: *up-to-the-~ information/hairstyles.* 最新消息(時髦的髮式)。 **2** the sixtieth part of a degree (in an angle): (角度上)一度的六十分之一; 分: *37°30′,* 37 degrees 30 ~s. 37度30分。 **3** [C] official record giving authority, advice or making comments: 正式記錄; 備忘錄: *make a ~ of sth.* 記錄某事。 **4** (*pl*) summary, records, of what is said and decided at a meeting, esp of a society or committee: (複)會議記錄(尤指社團或委員會的會議記錄): *read and confirm the ~s of the last meeting.* 宣讀並追認上次會議記錄。 **ˈ~-book** *n* book in which ~s are written. 會議記錄簿。 □ *vt* [VP6A] record (sth) in the

a centaur

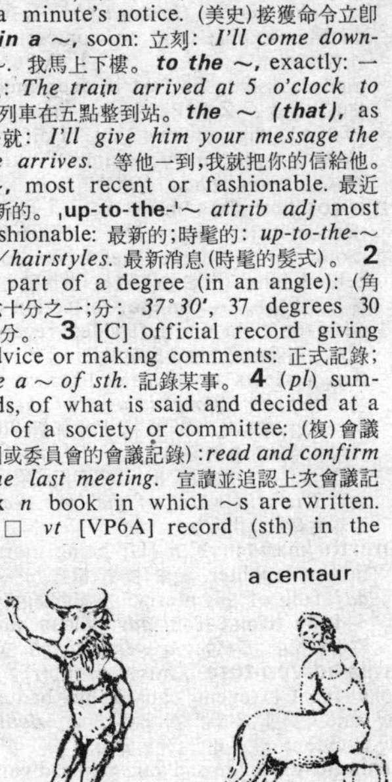

the Minotaur

~s(4); make a record of sth in a memorandum. 將(某事)列入會議記錄;將(某事)製成備忘錄。

mi·nute² /maɪˈnjuːt *US:* -ˈnuːt ; məˈnjut/ *adj* **1** very small: 極小的: *~ particles of gold dust.* 金粉的細小微粒。 **2** giving small details; careful and exact: 詳細的;仔細而準確的: *a ~ description;* 細膩的描寫; *the ~st details.* 最精確的細節。 **~·ly** *adv* **~·ness** *n*

mi·nu·tiae /maɪˈnjuːʃiː *US:* mɪˈnuːʃiː ; mɪˈnjuʃɪˌi/ *n pl* precise or trivial details. 細節;瑣事。

minx /mɪŋks ; mɪŋks/ *n* sly, impudent girl. 頑皮而冒失的女孩。

mir·acle /ˈmɪrəkl ; ˈmɪrəkl/ *n* **1** act or event (sth good or welcome) which does not follow the known laws of nature; remarkable and surprising event: 奇蹟(屬於好的一方面);特出而令人驚奇的事: *work/accomplish ~s.* 產生(造成)奇蹟。 *Her life was saved by a ~.* 她的命是奇蹟救活的。 *The doctors said that her recovery was a ~.* 醫師們說她的康復是件令人驚奇的事。 **ˈ~ play,** dramatic representation (in the Middle Ages) based on the life of Jesus or the Christian saints. 奇蹟劇;神蹟劇(中世紀的戲劇,根據耶穌或聖徒的生平事蹟而編寫)。 **2** **~ of,** remarkable example or specimen: (…的)特出事例: *It's a ~ of ingenuity.* 這是匠心獨運的驚人例子。 **mir·acu·lous** /mɪˈrækjʊləs ; məˈrækjələs/ *adj* like a ~; contrary to the laws of nature; surprising. 似奇蹟的;違反自然律的;不可思議的;令人驚奇的。 **mir·acu·lous·ly** *adv*

mi·rage /ˈmɪrɑːʒ *US:* mɪˈrɑːʒ ; məˈrɑʒ/ *n* [C] **1** effect, produced by hot air conditions, causing an optical illusion, esp the illusive appearance of a sheet of water eg in the desert. 海市蜃樓(因熱的大氣變化而造成的視覺上的幻景,尤指沙漠中所出現的水景幻象);蜃景。 **2** (fig) any illusion or hope that cannot be realized. (喻)(任何不能實現的)幻想;妄想。

mire /ˈmaɪə(r) ; maɪr/ *n* [U] swampy ground; soft, deep mud. 沼地;泥濘;泥坑。 ***be in the ~,*** (fig) be in difficulties. (喻)處於困境中;陷入困難之中。 ***drag sb/sb's name through the ~,*** bring disgrace on him, expose him to contempt. 使某人(某人之姓名)蒙受羞辱。 □ *vt, vi* **1** [VP6A] cover with mud; cause to be fast in deep mud. 使濺滿污泥;使陷入泥坑。 **2** [VP2A] sink in mud. 陷入泥中。 **3** [VP6A] (fig) involve (sb) in difficulties. (喻)使(某人)陷入困境。 **miry** /ˈmaɪərɪ ; ˈmaɪrɪ/ *adj* muddy: 泥濘的: *miry roads.* 泥濘的道路。

mir·ror /ˈmɪrə(r) ; ˈmɪrɚ/ *n* **1** polished surface that reflects images: 鏡子: *a ˈdriving ~, ~* in a motor-car to enable the driver to see what is behind him. (汽車之)反光鏡(供駕駛者觀看車後有無車輛行人之鏡)。 **ˌ~ ˈimage,** reflection or copy of sth with the right and left sides reversed. 鏡像(與某物左右兩邊相反之映像或摹製品);反像。 **2** (fig) sth that reflects or gives a likeness: (喻)反映眞象之物: *Pepys's 'Diary' is a ~ of the times he lived in.* 英國作家柏比斯的'日記'是他那個時代的一面鏡子(卽反映該時代社會情況的著作)。 □ *vt* [VP6A] (lit or fig) reflect as in a ~: (字面或喻)(像鏡子一樣)反映: *The still water of the lake ~ed the hillside.* 平靜的湖水映出山坡。

mirth /mɜːθ ; mɝθ/ *n* [U] being merry, happy and bright; laughter. 歡樂;快樂;歡笑。 **~·ful** /-fl ; -fəl/ *adj* full of ~; merry. 充滿歡樂的;快樂的;歡笑的。 **~·fully** /-fəlɪ ; -fəlɪ/ *adv* **~·less** *adj* without ~: 沒有歡樂的;憂愁的: *a ~less laugh.* 苦笑。

mis·ad·ven·ture /ˌmɪsədˈventʃə(r) ; ˌmɪsədˈvɛntʃɚ/ *n* [C, U] (event caused by) bad luck; misfortune. 惡運;不幸;不幸事件;災禍。 ***death by ~,*** by accident. 意外死亡;死於非命。

mis·ad·vise /ˌmɪsədˈvaɪz ; ˌmɪsədˈvaɪz/ *vt* [VP6A] (usu passive) advise wrongly. (通常用被動語態)謬誤地勸告。

mis·al·liance /ˌmɪsəˈlaɪəns ; ˌmɪsəˈlaɪəns/ *n* unsuitable alliance, esp marriage; mésalliance. 不適宜的結合(尤指結婚);不相匹配的婚姻。

mis·an·thrope /ˈmɪsnθrəʊp ; ˈmɪsənˌθrop/ *n* person who hates mankind; person who avoids society. 厭恨人類的人;厭世者。 **mis·an·thropic** /ˌmɪsnˈθrɒpɪk ; ˌmɪsənˈθrɑpɪk/ *adj* hating or distrusting mankind or human society. 厭恨人類的;厭世的。 **mis·an·thropy** /mɪsˈænθrəpɪ ; mɪsˈænθrəpɪ/ *n* [U] hatred of mankind. 厭恨人類;厭世。

mis·apply /ˌmɪsəˈplaɪ ; ˌmɪsəˈplaɪ/ *vt* (*pt, pp* -lied) [VP6A] apply wrongly; use for a wrong purpose, eg public funds. 誤用;濫用(如公款)。 **mis·ap·pli·ca·tion** /ˌmɪsæplɪˈkeɪʃn ; ˌmɪsæpləˈkeʃən/ *n* wrong or unjust use (*of*). 誤用;濫用(與 of 連用)。

mis·ap·pre·hend /ˌmɪsæprɪˈhend ; ˌmɪsæprɪˈhɛnd/ *vt* [VP6A] misunderstand. 誤解。 **mis·ap·pre·hen·sion** /ˌmɪsæprɪˈhenʃn ; ˌmɪsæprɪˈhɛnʃən/ *n* ***do sth/be under a misapprehension,*** do sth because of/have a failure to understand correctly. 出於誤解而做某事(誤解)。

mis·ap·pro·pri·ate /ˌmɪsəˈprəʊprɪeɪt ; ˌmɪsəˈproprɪˌet/ *vt* [VP6A] take and use wrongly; apply (sb else's money) to a wrong (esp one's own) use: 誤用; 濫用; 盜用(別人之錢,尤指盜爲己用): *The treasurer ~d the society's funds.* 這會計曾盜用該會的公款。 **mis·ap·pro·pri·ation** /ˌmɪsəˌprəʊprɪˈeɪʃn ; ˌmɪsəˌproprɪˈeʃən/ *n*: *misappropriation of public funds.* 盜用公款。

mis·be·got·ten /ˌmɪsbɪˈgɒtn ; ˌmɪsbɪˈgɑtn̩/ *adj* illegitimate; bastard; (colloq, as a term of scorn): 非婚生的; 私生的(俗,作爲罵人的用語): *Who's the author of these ~* (= ill-advised, worthless) *plans?* 誰定的這些莫名其妙(愚蠢無用)的計畫?

mis·be·have /ˌmɪsbɪˈheɪv ; ˌmɪsbɪˈhev/ *vt, vi* [VP6B, 2A] behave (oneself) improperly. 行爲不端;做不正當的事。 **mis·be·hav·iour** (US = **-ior**) /ˌmɪsbɪˈheɪvɪə(r) ; ˌmɪsbɪˈhevjɚ/ *n*

mis·cal·cu·late /ˌmɪsˈkælkjʊleɪt ; mɪsˈkælkjəˌlet/ *vt, vi* calculate (amounts, etc) wrongly. 誤算(數額等); 計算錯誤。 **mis·cal·cu·la·tion** /ˌmɪskælkjʊˈleɪʃn ; ˌmɪskælkjəˈleʃən/ *n*

mis·call /ˌmɪsˈkɔːl ; mɪsˈkɔl/ *vt* call by a wrong name: 誤稱;誤呼;叫錯: *King Robert, ~ed 'the Just'.* 被誤稱爲'公正者'的羅勃特王。

mis·car·riage /ˌmɪsˈkærɪdʒ ; mɪsˈkærɪdʒ/ *n* **1** [U] **~ of justice,** failure of a court to administer justice properly; mistake in judgement or in punishment; [C] instance of this. 誤審;誤判;誤罰;審判不公;誤審的案件;審判或量刑不公的案件。 **2** [U] failure to deliver to, or arrive at, the destination: 誤送;未能送達: *~ of goods;* 貨物誤送; [C] instance of this. 誤送的事例。 **3** [U] premature expulsion of a foetus from the womb; [C] instance of this: 流產;小產: *have a ~.* 流產;小產。

mis·carry /ˌmɪsˈkærɪ ; mɪsˈkærɪ/ *vi* (*pt, pp* -ried) [VP2A] **1** (of plans, etc) fail; have a result different from what was hoped for. (指計畫等)失敗;不順利;未達預期效果。 **2** (of letters, etc) fail to reach the right destination. (指書信等)誤投;未送達目的地。 **3** (of a woman) have a miscarriage(3). (指婦人)流產;小產。

mis·cast /ˌmɪsˈkɑːst *US:* -ˈkæst ; mɪsˈkæst/ *vt* (*pt, pp* miscast) [VP6A] (usu passive) (通常用被動語態)。 **1** (of an actor) be cast for a role for which he is unfitted: (指演員)被派扮演不適合的角色: *She was badly ~ as Juliet.* 她被派扮演朱麗葉,這角色對她非常不合適。 ⇨ cast¹(6). **2** (of a play) have the parts badly allocated to the actors and actresses. (指戲劇)角色被不當地分派給男女演員;亂派角色。

mis·cegen·ation /ˌmɪsɪdʒɪˈneɪʃn ; ˌmɪsɪdʒəˈneʃən/ *n* [U] mixture of races, the production of offspring by the sexual union of two people of different races. 人種混雜;異族通婚。

mis·cel·lan·eous /ˌmɪsəˈleɪnɪəs ; ˌmɪsl̩ˈenɪəs/ *adj* of mixed sorts; having various qualities and characteristics: 各式各樣的; 有不同性質與特徵的; 多方面的:

a ~ collection of goods; 一批雜貨; *Milton's ~ prose works.* 米爾頓的各種散文作品。 **mis·cel·lany** /mɪˈselənɪ *US:* ˈmɪsəleɪnɪ ; ˈmɪsḷˌenɪ/ *n* (*pl* -nies) collection, eg of writings on various subjects by various authors. 雜集(例如不同作者所寫不同題目的文集)。 **mis·cel·lanea** /ˌmɪsəˈleɪnɪə ; ˌmɪsəˈlenɪə/ *n pl* literary miscellany. (文學的)雜集;雜錄。

mis·chance /ˌmɪsˈtʃɑːns *US:* -ˈtʃæns ; mɪsˈtʃæns/ *n* [C, U] (piece of) bad luck: 不幸;壞運;不幸事件;災禍: *by ~;* 由於不幸;不幸地; *through a ~.* 因一不幸事件。

mis·chief /ˈmɪstʃɪf ; ˈmɪstʃɪf/ *n* **1** [U] injury or damage done by a person or other agent, esp on purpose: 傷害;損害(尤指故意造成者): *a storm that did much ~ to shipping.* 損害航運甚鉅的一次暴風雨。 ***do sb a ~,*** hurt him. 傷害某人。 **2** [U] moral harm or injury: 道德上的損害;精神上的傷害: *Such wild speeches may work great ~,* eg may rouse evil passions. 這種狂野的言論可能嚴重地危害人心。 ***make ~ (between...),*** cause discord or ill feeling. (在…之間)搬弄是非。Hence, 由此產生, **ˈ~-maker, ˈ~-making.** **3** [U] foolish or thoughtless behaviour likely to cause trouble; not very serious wrongdoing: 胡鬧;惡作劇: *Boys are fond of ~,* of playing tricks, etc. 男孩子們喜歡惡作劇。 *Tell the children to keep out of ~.* 告訴那些小孩不要胡鬧。 *He's up to ~ again,* planning some piece of ~. 他又在打算胡鬧了。 *She's always getting into ~.* 她老愛胡鬧。 **4** light-hearted, innocent desire to tease: 調皮;淘氣;嬉戲: *Her eyes were full of ~.* 她的兩眼充滿了調皮搗蛋的神情。 **5** [C] person who is fond of ~(3, 4): 好嬉戲的人;調皮搗蛋者: *Those boys are regular ~s.* 那幾個男孩子經常愛嬉鬧。 *Where have you hidden my book, you little ~?* 你這個小淘氣,把我的書藏到哪兒去了?

mis·chiev·ous /ˈmɪstʃɪvəs ; ˈmɪstʃɪvəs/ *adj* **1** causing mischief(2); harmful: 爲害的; 有害的: *a ~ letter/rumour.* 害人的信(謠言)。 **2** filled with, fond of, engaged in, mischief(3, 4); showing a spirit of mischief(3, 4): 胡鬧的; 惡作劇的;淘氣的;頑皮的;愛搗亂的: *~ looks/tricks;* 調皮的樣子(惡作劇的花樣); *as ~ as a monkey.* 像猴子一樣的頑皮。 **~·ly** *adv* **~·ness** *n*

mis·con·ceive /ˌmɪskənˈsiːv ; ˌmɪskənˈsiv/ *vt, vi* **1** [VP6A] understand wrongly. 誤解。 **2** [VP3A] ~ ***of,*** have a wrong conception of: 對…有錯誤觀念: *~ of one's duty.* 誤解個人的職責。 **mis·con·cep·tion** /ˌmɪskənˈsepʃn ; ˌmɪskənˈsɛpʃən/ *n* [U] misconceiving; [C] instance of this. 誤解;錯誤的觀念。

mis·con·duct /ˌmɪsˈkɒndʌkt ; mɪsˈkɑndʌkt/ *n* [U] **1** improper behaviour. 不規矩的行爲。 **2** bad management. 不當的處理;不善的管理。 □ *vt* /ˌmɪskənˈdʌkt ; ˌmɪskənˈdʌkt/ **1** [VP6B, 14] ~ ***oneself (with sb),*** behave badly. 行爲不規矩。 **2** [VP6A] manage badly: 處理不當;管理不善: *~ one's business affairs.* 對於個人的商務處置不當。

mis·con·struc·tion /ˌmɪskənˈstrʌkʃn ; ˌmɪskənˈstrʌkʃən/ *n* [U] false or inaccurate interpretation or understanding; [C] instance of this: 曲解;誤解: *Your words were open to ~.* 你的話容易被誤解。

mis·con·strue /ˌmɪskənˈstruː ; ˌmɪskənˈstru/ *vt* [VP6A] get a wrong idea of (sb's words, acts, etc): 誤解;誤會(某人的言語、行動等): *You have ~d my words.* 你誤會了我的話。

mis·count /ˌmɪsˈkaʊnt ; mɪsˈkaunt/ *vt, vi* [VP6A, 2A] count wrongly. 誤算;數錯。 □ *n* [C] wrong count, esp of votes at an election. 錯誤的計算(尤指選票的誤計)。

mis·cre·ant /ˈmɪskrɪənt ; ˈmɪskrɪənt/ *n* (dated) scoundrel; villain. (過時用語)無賴;惡徒。

mis·date /ˌmɪsˈdeɪt ; mɪsˈdet/ *vt* [VP6A] give a wrong date to an event, etc; put a wrong date on a letter, cheque, etc. 誤記(事件等)的日期;在(書信、支票等)之上塡錯日期。

mis·deal /ˌmɪsˈdiːl ; mɪsˈdil/ *vt, vi* (*pt, pp* -dealt /-ˈdelt ; -ˈdɛlt/) [VP6A, 2A] deal (playing-cards) wrongly. 發錯(紙牌)。 □ *n* error in dealing cards: 發牌錯誤: *I've got 14 cards; it's a ~.* 我有了十四張牌;這是發牌的錯誤。

mis·deed /ˌmɪsˈdiːd ; mɪsˈdid/ *n* wicked act; crime: 惡行;罪行: *be punished for one's ~s.* 因惡行而受罰。

mis·de·mean·our (US = **-meanor**) /ˌmɪsdɪˈmiːnə(r) ; ˌmɪsdɪˈminɚ/ *n* (legal) offence less serious than a felony. (法律)較輕的犯法行爲;輕罪;小罪。

mis·di·rect /ˌmɪsdɪˈrekt ; ˌmɪsdəˈrɛkt/ *vt* [VP6A] direct wrongly: 錯誤指示;寫錯地址;錯用: *~ a letter,* by failing to put the full or correct address on it; 寫錯一信的投遞地址; *~ one's energies or abilities,* eg by using them for a bad purpose; 錯用精力或能力(如用於爲非作歹); *~ a jury,* (of a judge in a law court) give the jury wrong information on a point of law. (指推事)在法律問題上對陪審團做錯誤的指示。 **mis·di·rec·tion** /ˌmɪsdɪˈrekʃn ; ˌmɪsdəˈrɛkʃən/ *n*

mis·doing /ˌmɪsˈduːɪŋ ; mɪsˈduɪŋ/ *n* (usu *pl*) misdeed. (通常用複數)惡行;罪行。

mise en scène /ˌmiːz ɒn ˈseɪn ; ˌmizɑ̃ˈsɛn/ *n* scenery and properties of an acted play; (fig) general surroundings of an event. 舞臺的佈景與道具;(喻)事件周遭之一般情況。

miser /ˈmaɪzə(r) ; ˈmaɪzɚ/ *n* person who loves wealth for its own sake and spends as little as possible. 守財奴;吝嗇的人。 **~·ly** *adj* like a ~; stingy. 似守財奴的;吝嗇的;小氣的。 **~·li·ness** *n*

mis·er·able /ˈmɪzrəbl ; ˈmɪzərəbḷ/ *adj* **1** wretched; very unhappy: 可憐的; 不幸的; 悲慘的; 愁苦的: *~ from cold and hunger;* 因飢寒而痛苦的; *the ~ lives of the refugees in Europe after the war.* 戰後歐洲難民的悲慘生活。 *He makes her life ~.* 他使她的生活苦不堪言。 **2** causing wretchedness and unhappiness: 造成不幸與痛苦的: *~ weather;* 惱人的天氣; *~ slums.* 令人難過的貧民區。 **3** poor in quality: 簡陋的;粗劣的: *What a ~ meal!* 多麼粗劣的一頓飯! *What a ~ pension after fifty years' hard work!* 五十年的辛苦工作祇拿到這麼可憐的一筆養老金! **mis·er·ably** /-əblɪ ; -əblɪ/ *adv*: *die miserably;* 悲慘地死去; *be miserably poor;* 窮得煞是可憐; *miserably underpaid.* 待遇奇低。

mis·ery /ˈmɪzərɪ ; ˈmɪzərɪ/ *n* (*pl* -ries) **1** [U] state of being miserable; great suffering (of mind or body): 悲慘;不幸;(心靈或身體上的)痛苦: *be in a ~/suffer ~ from the toothache;* 受牙痛之苦; *living in ~ and want,* in wretched conditions and poverty. 生活在貧窮困苦之中。 ***put the animal out of its ~,*** end its sufferings by killing it. 解除動物的痛苦(殺死它以結束其痛苦)。 **2** (*pl*) painful happenings; great misfortunes: (複)痛苦的事;大不幸: *the miseries of mankind.* 人類的大不幸。 **3** (colloq) person who is always miserable and complaining: (俗)總是不高興而抱怨的人: *I've had enough of your complaints, you little ~!* 我已經聽够了你的抱怨,你這個小嘮叨鬼!

mis·fire /ˌmɪsˈfaɪə(r) ; mɪsˈfaɪr/ *vi* [VP2A] (of a gun) fail to go off; (of a motor-engine) fail to ignite in a cylinder; (colloq of a joke, etc) fall flat; fail to have the intended result. (指槍砲)不發火;打不出;(指發動機)不着火;發不動;(俗,指笑話等)完全失敗;達不到目的。 □ *n* such a failure. 不發火;不能發動;未達到目的。

mis·fit /ˈmɪsfɪt ; ˈmɪsˌfɪt/ *n* article of clothing which does not fit well the person it is meant for; (fig) person not well suited to his position or his associates. 不合身的衣服;(喻)不甚稱職的人;不甚適合其地位的人;與夥伴合不來的人。

mis·for·tune /ˌmɪsˈfɔːtʃuːn ; mɪsˈfɔrtʃən/ *n* **1** [U] bad luck: 不幸: *suffer ~;* 遭受不幸; *companions in ~.* 患難中的友伴;患難之交。 **2** [C] instance of bad luck; unfortunate accident or happening: 災禍;不幸事故: *He bore his ~s bravely.* 他勇敢地忍受他所遭遇的災難。

mis·give /ˌmɪsˈgɪv ; mɪsˈgɪv/ *vt* (*pt* misgave /-ˈgeɪv; -ˈgev/, *pp* misgiven /-ˈgɪvn ; -ˈgɪvən/) (used impersonally; old use) cause to feel doubt, fear or anxiety: (無人稱用法;舊用法)使感到懷疑、恐懼或焦慮: *My mind/heart ~s me,* I am filled with suspicion or foreboding, I feel doubtful, troubled. 我感到疑慮不安。**mis·giv·ing** /ˌmɪsˈgɪvɪŋ ; mɪsˈgɪvɪŋ/ *n* [C, U] (feeling of) doubt, suspicion, distrust, etc: 懷疑;疑惑;擔憂: *a heart/mind full of misgiving(s).* 心中充滿疑慮;心中大感不安。

mis·gov·ern /ˌmɪsˈgʌvn ; mɪsˈgʌvən/ *vt* [VP6A] govern (the State, etc) badly. 治理(國家等)不當。**~·ment** *n* [U].

mis·guide /ˌmɪsˈgaɪd ; mɪsˈgaɪd/ *vt* [VP6A, 14] give wrong or misleading information or directions to: 給予錯誤的消息或指導;使誤入歧途: *We had been ~d into thinking that....* 我們受到錯誤的指導,認爲…。**mis·guided** *adj* foolish and wrong (because of bad or wrong guidance or influence): 愚昧而錯誤的 (因受不良或錯誤引導所致); 誤入歧途的: *~d conduct/zeal;* 愚昧的行爲 (錯用的熱心); *~d boys.* 被導入歧途的男孩們。

mis·handle /ˌmɪsˈhændl ; mɪsˈhændḷ/ *vt* deal with roughly, rudely or inefficiently. 粗暴地對待;虐待;瞎弄;處理不當。

mis·hap /ˈmɪshæp ; ˈmɪsˌhæp/ *n* [C] unlucky accident: 不幸的意外事故: *meet with a slight ~;* 遭遇到一件小意外事件; *arrive home after many ~s;* 歷經許多事故方才到家; [U] bad luck; accident: 不幸;意外: *arrive without ~.* 平安抵達。

mish·mash /ˈmɪʃmæʃ ; ˈmɪʃˌmæʃ/ *n* [U] confused mixture; hotchpotch. 雜亂的一堆;混雜。

mis·in·form /ˌmɪsɪnˈfɔːm ; ˌmɪsɪnˈfɔrm/ *vt* [VP6A] give wrong information to; mislead: 供給…錯誤消息;誤傳;誤引: *You've been ~ed.* 你所得到的消息不確。

mis·in·ter·pret /ˌmɪsɪnˈtɜːprɪt ; ˌmɪsɪnˈtɝprɪt/ *vt* [VP6A] give a wrong interpretation to; make a wrong inference from: 誤解;誤以爲;誤譯: *He ~ed her silence as giving consent.* 他把她的沉默誤認爲同意。

mis·judge /ˌmɪsˈdʒʌdʒ ; mɪsˈdʒʌdʒ/ *vt, vi* [VP6A, 2A] judge or estimate wrongly; form a wrong opinion of: (把…)判斷錯誤;(把…)估計錯誤;(將…)論斷錯誤: *You have ~d my motives.* 你把我的動機判斷錯了。*He ~d the distance and fell into the stream.* 他把距離估計錯誤,結果跌進小河裏去了。

mis·lay /ˌmɪsˈleɪ ; mɪsˈle/ *vt* (*pt, pp* mislaid /-ˈleɪd ; -ˈled/) [VP6A] put (sth) by an oversight where it cannot easily be found: 由於疏忽而把(某物)放在不容易找到的地方;誤置: *I've mislaid my passport.* 我忘了把護照放到哪裏去了。

mis·lead /ˌmɪsˈliːd ; mɪsˈlid/ *vt* (*pt, pp* misled /-ˈled ; -ˈlɛd/) [VP6A] lead wrongly; cause to be or do wrong; give a wrong idea to: 錯誤引領;使入歧途;使…有錯誤的想法;哄騙: *be misled by a guide,* during a journey; 被嚮導領錯了路; *misled by bad companions,* led into evil ways. 被不良夥伴領入歧途。*You misled me as to your intentions.* 你使我對於你的意向有錯誤的想法。*This information is rather ~ing,* gives a wrong impression. 這個消息容易引起誤解。

mis·man·age /ˌmɪsˈmænɪdʒ ; mɪsˈmænɪdʒ/ *vt* [VP6A] manage badly or wrongly. 管理不善;處理錯誤。**~·ment** *n*

mis·name /ˌmɪsˈneɪm ; mɪsˈnem/ *vt* [VP6A] (usu passive) call by a wrong or improper name. (通常用被動語態)誤稱;稱呼不當;取名不妥。

mis·nomer /ˌmɪsˈnəʊmə(r) ; mɪsˈnomɚ/ *n* [C] wrong use of a name or word: 錯用名稱;用字錯誤: *It's a ~ to call this place a first-class hotel.* 把這地方叫做第一流旅館是不當的。

mis·ogyn·ist /mɪˈsɒdʒɪnɪst ; mɪˈsɑdʒənɪst/ *n* hater of women. 憎恨女人的人。

mis·place /ˌmɪsˈpleɪs ; mɪsˈples/ *vt* [VP6A] **1** put in a wrong place. 錯放;誤置。**2** (usu passive) give love, affection wrongly or unwisely: (通常用被動語態)錯誤或愚昧地付出(愛情、情感): *~d confidence,* given to sb who does not deserve it or who misuses it. 錯誤付予的信任(卽對方不值得信任或胡亂利用此既得之信任)。

mis·print /ˌmɪsˈprɪnt ; mɪsˈprɪnt/ *vt* [VP6A] make an error in printing, eg *errors and omissions expected* for *errors and omissions excepted.* 誤印;印刷錯誤(如 errors and omissions excepted 誤印爲 errors and omissions expected)。□ *n* /ˈmɪsprɪnt ; mɪsˈprɪnt/ such an error. 誤印;排印上的錯誤。

mis·pro·nounce /ˌmɪsprəˈnaʊns ; ˌmɪsprəˈnaʊns/ *vt* [VP6A] pronounce wrongly. 發音錯誤;念錯。**mis·pro·nun·ci·ation** /ˌmɪsprəˌnʌnsɪˈeɪʃn ; ˌmɪsprəˌnʌnsɪˈeʃən/ *n*

mis·quote /ˌmɪsˈkwəʊt ; mɪsˈkwot/ *vt* [VP6A] quote wrongly. 引述錯誤。**mis·quo·ta·tion** /ˌmɪskwəʊˈteɪʃn ; ˌmɪskwoˈteʃən/ *n* [C, U].

mis·read /ˌmɪsˈriːd ; mɪsˈrid/ *vt* (*pt, pp* misread /-ˈred ; -ˈrɛd/) [VP6A] read or interpret wrongly: 錯讀;誤讀;將…解釋錯誤: *~ one's instructions.* 誤解訓令。

mis·rep·re·sent /ˌmɪsˌreprɪˈzent ; ˌmɪsrɛprɪˈzɛnt/ *vt* represent wrongly; give a false account of: 不正確地表達、解釋、描述; 不實地報導、敍述: *be grossly ~ed by the press.* 被報紙作粗鄙不實的報導。**mis·rep·re·sen·ta·tion** /ˌmɪsˌreprɪzenˈteɪʃn ; ˌmɪsrɛprɪzɛnˈteʃən/ *n* [C, U].

mis·rule /ˌmɪsˈruːl ; mɪsˈrul/ *n* [U] bad government; lawlessness; confusion. 苛政;暴政;無法無天;混亂;紊亂。

miss[1] /mɪs ; mɪs/ *n* [C] failure to hit, catch, reach, etc: 未打中;未捉到;沒達到;錯過;避過;省略: *ten hits and one ~.* 十次打中,一次未中。*That was a lucky ~,* a fortunate escape. 得免於難,眞是僥倖。***give sth a ~,*** (colloq) omit it, leave it alone: (俗)省略掉某物;不管它: *I'll give the fish course a ~.* 我不吃那道魚了。***A ~ is as good as a mile,*** (prov) A narrow escape is the same in effect as an escape by a wide margin. (諺)大錯小錯終歸是錯;死裡逃生與輕易逃脫結果相同。

miss[2] /mɪs ; mɪs/ *n* **1 M~,** title prefixed to the (first name +) surname of an unmarried woman: 小姐(對未婚女子之稱呼,加於姓或姓名前): *M~ (Gloria) Kelly.* (葛蘿麗亞)凱莉小姐。**M~ Jamaica,** eg as the title of a beauty queen. 牙買加小姐(選美會上優勝者的頭銜)。**2** (small *m,* usu playful or perhaps derog) young girl, schoolgirl: (小寫,通常含戲弄或輕蔑之意)少女;小妞;小女生: *She's a saucy ~.* 她是個孟浪的小妞。**3** (as a vocative, eg by schoolchildren to a woman teacher, also to shopkeepers, etc): (用作呼喚語,例如學童對女老師或商店女老闆等之稱呼): *Good morning, ~!* 小姐!您早哇! *Two cups of coffee, ~.* (來)兩杯咖啡,小姐(或老闆娘)。**4** (trade use, *pl*) young girls: (商業用語,複數)少女們: *shoes, coats, etc for Junior M~es,* (today, often replaced by *teenagers*). 供少女穿的鞋子、上衣等(此片語中之 Junior Misses 現常以 teenagers 一字代之)。

miss[3] /mɪs ; mɪs/ *vt, vi* (*pt, pp* missed) **1** [VP6A, B, C, 2A] fail to hit, hold, catch, reach, see, etc what it is desired to hit, hold, etc: 未打中;未抓住;未捉到;未達到;未看見;未趕上;錯過;避過: *fire at a tiger and ~ (it);* 開槍打虎但沒有打中(牠); *~ one's aim;* 沒達到目的; *~ the target.* 沒打中目標。*He ~ed his footing,* slipped, eg while climbing on rocks. 他失足滑了一下(如在攀登山石時)。*He ~ed the 9.30 train* (= was too late for it, did not catch it), *and therefore ~ed* (ie luckily escaped) *the accident.* 他沒趕上九時三十分的那班火車,也正因此而逃過那次車禍。*The house is at the next corner; you can't ~ it,* you'll certainly see it. 那房子就在下一個拐彎的地方,你不會看不見的。*He ~ed* (= failed to see) *the point of my joke.* 他沒聽懂我的笑話。*I ~ed* (= did not hear) *the first part of the speech.* 我沒聽到演說的第一部份。*We only just ~ed*

(= escaped) *having a nasty accident.* 我們僥倖逃過了一場大難。 *We ~ed seeing* (= didn't see, failed to see) *that film when it was at the local cinema.* 那影片在本地電影院上映時我們沒去看。 **2** [VP6A] realize, learn, feel regret at, the absence of: 發現遺失;得悉失掉;惋惜;懷念: *When did you ~ your purse,* realize that you no longer had it? 你什麼時候發現你的錢包不見了? *He's so rich that he wouldn't ~ £100.* 他非常有錢,不會因失掉一百鎊而覺得可惜。 *She'd ~ her husband if he died.* 假如她丈夫死了她會懷念他的。 *Old Smith won't be ~ed,* Nobody will feel regret at his absence, death, retirement, etc. 老史密斯要是不在了(死亡或者退休等),沒有人會感到遺憾。 **3** [VP2C] *~ out (on sth),* (colloq) lose an opportunity to benefit from sth, enjoy oneself: (俗)失去(自某事物)獲益的機會;失去享樂的機會: *If I don't go to the party, I shall feel that I'm ~ing out.* 如果我不去參加那舞會,我將會感到失去享樂的良機。 *I ~ed out on his offer of a free holiday in Spain.* 他讓我免費去西班牙度一天假,我却坐失良機。 [VP15B] *~ sth out,* omit; fail to put in or say: 省掉;遺漏;漏述: *The printers have ~ed out a word/line.* 印刷工人遺漏了一個字(一行)。 *I shall ~ out the sweet course,* ie at a meal, not take it. 我要省掉那道甜食(卽不吃它)。 *When we sing this song, ~ out the second and fourth verses,* don't sing them. 當我們唱這首歌的時候,大家省去第二節和第四節(卽不唱這兩節)。 **~·ing** *adj* not to be found; not in the place where it ought to be: 找不到的;失去的;失踪的: *a book with two pages ~ing;* 掉了兩頁的一本書; *the dead, wounded and ~ing,* ie soldiers in war; 傷亡與失踪的官兵; *~ing persons,* persons who cannot be traced. 行踪不明的人。 ***the ~ing link,*** ⇨ link¹(3).

mis·sal /ˈmɪsl ; ˈmɪsl/ *n* book containing the order of service for Mass in the RC Church; book of prayers and devotions. 天主教的彌撒書;祈禱書。

mis·shapen /ˌmɪsˈʃeɪpən ; mɪsˈʃepən/ *adj* (esp of the body or a limb) deformed; badly shaped. (尤指身體或四肢之一)殘廢的;畸形的。

mis·sile /ˈmɪsaɪl *US:* ˈmɪsl ; ˈmɪsḷ/ *n* object or weapon that is thrown (eg a stone), shot (eg an arrow) or projected (eg a rocket): 投出的東西或武器(如擲出的石頭、射出的箭矢或發射的火箭); 射體; 飛彈: (attrib) (形容用法) *~ sites/bases,* for ballistic ~s, etc. 飛彈發射場(基地)。 **guided ~,** eg from ground to air, for destroying aircraft, guided by electronic devices. 導向飛彈(如發自地面摧毀空中飛機之地對空電導飛彈)。 **inter-continental ballistic ~,** (abbr 略作 **ICBM**), long-range rocket with a warhead. 洲際彈道飛彈。

mission /ˈmɪʃn ; ˈmɪʃən/ *n* **1** (the sending out of a) number of persons entrusted with special work, usu abroad: (負有特殊任務通常派往國外的)代表團;工作團;使節團;此等團體之派遣: *a trade ~ to S America;* 派往南美的商務團(貿易考察團); *go/come/send sb on a ~ of inquiry;* 去(來,派遣某人去)擔任調查工作; *complete one's ~ successfully.* 成功地完成任務;達成任務。 **2** (the sending out of) religious teachers (*~aries*) to convert people by preaching, teaching, etc: 佈道團;佈道團之派遣: *Foreign M~s;* 國外佈道團; *Home M~s,* ie to preach to people in the home country, esp those not usu interested in religion. 國內佈道團。 **3** place where the work of a ~(2) is carried on; building(s), organization, etc needed for such work; settlement where charitable or medical work is carried on, esp among poor people. 傳道地區;傳道機構;傳道會;佈道所;慈善救濟機構;救濟所。 **4** ***~ in life,*** that work which a person feels called upon to do: 天職: *She feels her ~ in life is to reform juvenile delinquents.* 她覺得她的天職是改造少年罪犯。 **5** (esp US) special task, assigned to an individual or a unit of the armed forces: (尤美)(指派給某人或部隊單位的)特殊任務;作戰任務: *The group has flown twenty ~s.* 該小組已完成了二十次的特殊飛行任務。

mission·ary /ˈmɪʃənrɪ *US:* -nerɪ ; ˈmɪʃənˌɛrɪ/ *n* (*pl* -ries) person sent to preach his religion, esp among people who are ignorant of it; (attrib) of missions(2) or missionaries: 傳教士;(形容用法)傳道(團)的;傳教士的: *a ~ meeting,* at which a ~ talks about his work or one held to raise funds; 佈道會(會中由傳教士佈道或募集基金); *a ~ box,* in which money is collected for charitable missions. 慈善奉獻箱。

mis·sis /ˈmɪsɪz ; ˈmɪsɪz/ *n* ⇨ missus.

mis·sive /ˈmɪsɪv ; ˈmɪsɪv/ *n* (used hum for) (esp a long, serious-looking) letter. (詼諧的用法)書信(尤指長篇正式者);公文;公函。

mis·spell /ˌmɪsˈspel ; mɪsˈspɛl/ *vt* (*pt, pp* misspelled or misspelt /-ˈspelt ; -ˈspɛlt/) [VP6A] spell wrongly. 誤拼;拼錯。 **~·ing** *n*

mis·spend /ˌmɪsˈspend ; mɪsˈspɛnd/ *vt* (*pt, pp* misspent /-ˈspent ; -ˈspɛnt/) [VP6A] spend or use wrongly or foolishly (esp *pp*): 誤用;浪費;虛度(尤常用過去分詞形式): *a misspent youth,* (used of one who spends or has spent his early years only in foolish pleasures). 一位虛度光陰的靑年。

mis·state /ˌmɪsˈsteɪt ; mɪsˈstet/ *vt* [VP6A] state wrongly: 誤述;虛言;僞述: *He was careful not to ~ his case.* 他很小心,免得把他的事實講錯。 **~ment** *n*

mis·sus, mis·sis /ˈmɪsɪz ; ˈmɪsəz/ *n* (colloq or sl) (used with *the, my, his, your*) wife: (俗或俚)(與 the, my, his, your 連用)妻子: *How's the ~?* 尊夫人好嗎? *My ~ won't like that.* 內人不會喜歡那個。

missy /ˈmɪsɪ ; ˈmɪsɪ/ *n* (*pl* -sies) (colloq, familiar) young girl; miss: (俗,親暱語)小姑娘;小姐: *Well, ~, what do you want?* 喂,小姑娘,你要什麼?

mist /mɪst ; mɪst/ *n* **1** [C, U] (occasion when there is, an area with) water vapour in the air, at or near the earth's surface, less thick than fog and not so light as haze: 霧;靄(在地面上或近地面之霧,密度低於 fog 而高於 haze; 氣象學上名詞 fog =霧, mist =靄, haze =霾,但一般通稱爲霧);有霧之時;有霧地區: *Hills hidden/shrouded in ~;* 隱在霧中(爲霧所籠罩)的小山; (fig) (喩) *lost in the ~s of time;* 消失於時間的薄霧之中(時間久了,漸被遺忘); such vapour condensed on a surface, eg glass, clouding its appearance. 凝結於物體(如玻璃)表面上的水蒸氣;迷濛。 **2** [C] filmy appearance before the eyes (caused by tears, etc); (fig) sth that darkens the mind, makes understanding difficult, etc: (因流淚等而在眼前形成的)矇矓不清;(喩)蒙蔽心思之事物;使了解(力)困難之事物: *see things through a ~.* 模模糊糊地看事物。 □ *vi, vt* [VP2C, 6A] *~ (over),* cover, be covered, with ~: 籠罩以霧;被霧所籠罩;模糊不清: *The scene ~ed over.* 景色被霧籠罩着。 *The mirror ~ed over.* 那鏡子模糊不清。 *Her eyes (were) ~ed with tears.* 她的眼睛給眼淚迷濛了。 **~y** *adj* (-ier, -iest) **1** with ~: 有霧的;霧的: *a ~y evening;* 有霧的晚上; *~y weather;* 有霧的天氣; *a ~y view.* 霧景。 **2** not clear: 矇矓不清的;模糊的: *have only a ~y idea.* 只有一個模糊的觀念。 **~·ily** /-ɪlɪ ; -əlɪ/ *adv* **~i·ness** *n*

mis·take¹ /mɪˈsteɪk ; məˈstek/ *n* [C] wrong opinion, idea or act: (意見、想法或行爲上的)錯誤: *spelling ~s.* 拼字錯誤。 *We all make ~s occasionally.* 我們偶爾都會犯錯。 *There's some ~!* 有點兒錯! *There must be some ~!* 一定有些什麼錯了! ***by ~,*** as the result of carelessness, forgetfulness, etc; in error: 由疏忽、健忘等所致;由於錯誤;錯: *I took your umbrella by ~.* 我錯拿了你的雨傘。 ***and no ~,*** (colloq) without any doubt: (俗)毫無疑問;的確: *It's hot today and no ~!* 今天的確很熱!

mis·take² /mɪˈsteɪk ; məˈstek/ *vt, vi* (*pt* mistook /mɪˈstʊk ; mɪsˈtʊk/, *pp* mistaken /mɪˈsteɪkn ; məˈstekən/) **1** [VP6A, 10] be wrong, have a wrong idea, about: 弄錯;誤解: *~ sb's meaning.* 誤解某人的意思。 *We've ~n the house,* come to the wrong house. 我們走錯了房子。***There's no mistaking,*** no possibility of being wrong about: 不會弄錯的: *There's no mistaking what ought to be done.* 應該做什麼，是不會弄錯的。 **2** [VP14] ~ ***sb/sth for,*** wrongly suppose that sb or sth is (sb or sth else): 誤認某人或某物爲;錯把…當做: *Don Quixote mistook the windmills for giants.* 唐吉訶德錯把風車當巨人。*She is often ~n for her twin sister.* 她常常被誤認爲她的孿生姊姊(妹妹)。 **3** (older uses) (較舊用法) *If I ~ not,* unless I am wrong. 假如我沒錯的話;除非我錯了。*You ~, my dear,* you're wrong. 親愛的,你錯了。**mis·taken** (*pp* as 過去分詞用作) *adj* **1** in error; wrong in opinion: 錯誤的;見解上錯誤的: *a case of ~n identity;* 認錯人的事件;*~n ideas.* 錯誤的觀念。***be ~n (about sth),*** be in error: (對某事)持錯誤的見解;(把某事)弄錯: *If I'm not ~n, there's the man we met on the train.* 如果我沒弄錯，那個人就是我們在火車上碰到的。*You're ~n.* 你錯了。**2** ill-judged: 判斷錯誤的;不合時宜的: *~n kindness/zeal.* 用錯地方的慈愛(熱心)。**mis·tak·en·ly** *adv*

mis·ter /ˈmɪstə(r) ; ˈmɪstɚ/ *n* **1** (always written 總是寫成 **Mr**) title prefixed to a man's (first name +) surname when he has no other title: *Mr (Henry) Green,* or to his office: *Mr Secretary.* 先生(冠於沒有特殊銜稱的男人姓名或姓之前的稱呼，如 Mr (Henry) Green(亨利)格林先生,或冠於職務之前,如Mr Secretary 秘書先生)。⇨ Mrs; Ms. **2** (used without a person's name; sl, or used by children): (不附帶姓名的稱呼;俚,或孩童所用的稱呼)先生: *Listen to me, ~.* 聽我說,先生。*Please, ~, can I have my ball back?* 先生,請把我的球(扔)還給我好嗎?

mis·time /ˌmɪsˈtaɪm ; mɪsˈtaɪm/ *vt* (used esp in the *pp*) say or do sth out of season, at an unsuitable time: (尤用過去分詞)說不合時宜的話;做不合時宜的事: *a ~d* (= inopportune) *intervention.* 不合時宜的介入。

mistle·toe /ˈmɪsltəʊ ; ˈmɪsl̩,to/ *n* [U] parasitic evergreen plant (growing on fruit and other trees) with small white sticky berries (used in making bird-lime and as a Christmas decoration). 槲寄生(一種寄生於果樹等上的常青植物，其白色小漿果具粘性，用以製粘鳥膠,樹或枝則用作聖誕節之裝飾)。

mis·took /mɪˈstʊk ; mɪsˈtʊk/ *pt* of mistake.

mis·tral /ˈmɪstrəl ; ˈmɪstrəl/ *n* cold, dry wind blowing from the north through the Rhone valley in France. 吹過法國境內隆河流域的寒冷而乾燥的北風。

mis·trans·late /ˌmɪstrænzˈleɪt ; ˌmɪstrænsˈlet/ *vt* [VP6A] translate wrongly. 誤譯。**mis·trans·la·tion** /-ˈleɪʃn ; -ˈleʃən/ *n* [C, U].

mis·tress /ˈmɪstrɪs ; ˈmɪstrɪs/ *n* **1** woman at the head of a household or family; woman in authority who gives orders to servants: 主婦;女主人: *Servants willingly obey a kind ~.* 傭人願意聽從和善的女主人。*Is your ~ at home?* 你家太太在家嗎? **2** woman school teacher: 女教師: *the ˈFrench mistress,* teacher of French (but not necessarily a Frenchwoman); 女法文教師(但不一定是法國婦女); *the ˈgames ~,* in charge of games (hockey, etc). 女體育教員(負責曲棍球等者)。 **3** woman with a good knowledge or control of sth: 精通某事的婦女;能控制某情況的婦女: *a ~ of needlework.* 精於女紅的婦女。*She is ~ of the situation.* 她能控制這局面。*Venice used to be called the ~ of the Adriatic.* 威尼斯以前號稱亞得里亞海的門戶。 **4** (in stories, plays, etc dealing with periods before the 18th c, and still in Scotland by some people) title equivalent to the modern *Mrs* or *Miss.* (用於敍述十八世紀以前各代之故事、戲劇等,且仍爲蘇格蘭某些人民所沿用) 相當於現代所習用之'夫人' (Mrs) 或'小姐' (Miss) 的稱呼。 **5** (poet) woman loved and courted by a man: (詩)女愛人;女情人: *'O ~ mine!'* '哦,我的情人!' **6** woman having regular sexual intercourse with one man to whom she is not married. 情婦。Cf 參較 *paramour* (liter) (文學用語) and *concubine* (dated) (過時用語). ⇨ master.

mis·trial /ˌmɪsˈtraɪəl ; mɪsˈtraɪəl/ *n* (legal) trial which is made invalid because of some error in the proceedings. (法律)誤審(因程序錯誤而宣告無效的審判);無效審判。

mis·trust /ˌmɪsˈtrʌst ; mɪsˈtrʌst/ *vt* [VP6A] feel no confidence in: 不信任;不相信;懷疑: ~ *one's own powers.* 不相信自己的智能。□ *n* [U] (also with *indef art*) (亦與不定冠詞連用) ***(a) ~ (of),*** want of confidence or trust (in): 不信任;疑惑;懷疑: *She had a strong ~ of anything new and strange.* 她對任何新奇的事物都非常不信任。**~·ful** /-fl ; -fl/ *adj* suspicious (*of*). 疑惑的;疑心的(與 of 連用)。**~·fully** /-fəlɪ ; -fəlɪ/ *adv*

misty /ˈmɪstɪ ; ˈmɪstɪ/ ⇨ mist.

mis·un·der·stand /ˌmɪsˌʌndəˈstænd ; ˌmɪsʌndɚˈstænd/ *vt* (*pt, pp* -stood /-ˈstʊd ; -ˈstʊd/) [VP6A] take a wrong meaning from (instructions, messages, etc); form a wrong opinion of (sb or sth): 誤會;誤解: *His intentions were misunderstood.* 他的意向被誤解了。*She had always felt misunderstood.* 她先前總以爲被人誤解了。**~·ing** *n* [C, U] failure to understand rightly, esp when this has led or may lead to ill feelings: 誤會;誤解: *~ings between nations that may lead to war;* 可能導致戰爭的國際間的誤會; *clear up a ~ing.* 澄清誤會。

mis·use /ˌmɪsˈjuːz ; mɪsˈjuz/ *vt* [VP6A] use wrongly; use for a wrong purpose; treat badly. 誤用;錯用;濫用;虐待。□ *n* /ˌmɪsˈjuːs ; mɪsˈjus/ [U] using wrongly; [C] instance of this: 誤用;錯用;濫用;誤用之實例: *the ~ of power.* 濫用權力。

mite[1] /maɪt ; maɪt/ *n* **1** very small or modest contribution or offering: 極少的捐助或貢獻: *offer a ~ of comfort;* 給予一點安慰; *give one's ~ to a good cause.* 對善舉聊盡棉薄。 **2** tiny object, esp a small child (usu as an object of sympathy): 小東西(尤指小孩,通常爲可寄予同情之對象): *Poor little ~!* 可憐的小孩兒! *What a ~ of a child!* 一個多麼小的孩子!

mite[2] /maɪt ; maɪt/ *n* [C] small parasitic arachnid that may be found in food, eg *ˈcheese ~s,* and may carry disease. (發現於食物等中,可傳佈疾病之)節肢小寄生蟲(如 cheese mites 乳酪中之蛆)。

mi·ter /ˈmaɪtə(r) ; ˈmaɪtɚ/ *n* (US) = mitre.

miti·gate /ˈmɪtɪgeɪt ; ˈmɪtə,get/ *vt* [VP6A] make less severe, violent or painful. 使緩和;使減輕;使鎮靜。***mitigating circumstances,*** those that may make a mistake, crime, etc seem less serious. 似乎可減輕錯誤、犯罪等之嚴重性的情況; 有緩和作用的情勢。**miti·ga·tion** /ˌmɪtɪˈgeɪʃn ; ˌmɪtəˈgeʃən/ *n* [U].

mitre (US = **mi·ter**) /ˈmaɪtə(r) ; ˈmaɪtɚ/ *n* **1** tall head-dress worn by bishops at some ceremonies. 主教冠(主教在某些儀式進行時所戴者)。⇨ the illus at vestment. 參看 vestment 之插圖。 **2** **ˈ~(-joint),** joint whose line of junction bisects the angle between the two bevelled surfaces it joins. 斜榫; 斜接。

mitt /mɪt ; mɪt/ *n* **1** mitten. (拇指分開其他四指連在一起的)手套。 **2** baseball glove; (colloq) boxing-glove. 棒球手套;(俗)拳擊手套。 **3** (sl) hand; fist. (俚)手;拳。

mit·ten /ˈmɪtn ; ˈmɪtn̩/ *n* **1** kind of glove covering four fingers together and the thumb separately. (拇指分開，其他四指連在一起的)手套。 **2** covering for the back and palm of the hand only, leaving the thumb and fingers bare. 露指手套(僅套住掌心與手背)。

mix[1] /mɪks ; mɪks/ *vt, vi* **1** [VP6A, 12B, 13B, 14, 2A, C] (of different substances, people, etc) put, bring or come together so that the substances, etc are no longer distinct; make or prepare (sth) by doing this: (指不同物質、人等)混合;混在一起;藉混合以做成或調製成(某物): *mix flour and water.* 把麵粉和水混合在一起。*The doctor mixed me a bottle of medicine/mixed a bottle of medicine for me.* 醫生爲我配了一瓶藥。*We can sometimes mix* *business with pleasure.* 我們有時候能把工作和享樂合在一起。 *She was mixing* (= preparing) *a salad.* 她正在調拌沙拉(涼菜)。*Oil and water don't mix.* 油和水不相混合。*You can't mix oil with water.* 你不能使油與水相混合。*Many races are mixed in Hawaii.* 在夏威夷，許多人種混合在一起。 **2** [VP2A, 3A] ***mix (with),*** (of persons) come or be together in society: (指人)交往;相處: *He doesn't mix well,* doesn't get on well with people, esp people of different social classes or different interests. 他不善與人相處(尤指不善與社會階級不同或興趣不同的人相處)。 **3** [VP15B] ***ˌmix sth/sb up (with sth/sb),*** mix thoroughly (with); confuse in the mind (with); be unable to distinguish (from): 完全混合;使弄不清楚;不能分辨: *Mix up the salt with the pepper.* 把鹽和胡椒粉調合在一起。*Now you've mixed me up completely!* completely confused me! 你可把我完全弄糊塗了! *You're always mixing me up with my twin brother.* 你老是分辨不出我和我的孿生哥哥(弟弟)。 ***be/get mixed up in/with sth,*** be involved in/with: 參與: *Don't get mixed up in politics/mixed up with those politicians,* keep clear of them. 不要參與政治活動(不要和那些政客混雜在一起)。*I don't want to be mixed up in the affair,* I don't want to be connected with it in any way. 我不願被牽涉到那件事中。 **'mix-up** *n* confused state: 混亂;混雜: *What a mix-up!* 情形多混亂! *There's been a bit of a mix-up about who should be invited to the party,* some confusion and mistakes.應該請誰參加宴會已經有點兒弄不清楚了。 **'mixed-up** *adj* mentally confused; maladjusted: 糊塗的;不適應的: *He feels very mixed-up about life,* cannot see clearly what principles, etc to adopt. 他對人生感到很迷惘。*I'm sorry for these mixed-up kids,* children who are confused by social problems. 我爲這些無法適應社會的孩子們感到惋惜。

mix² /mɪks ; mɪks/ *n* (chiefly in trade and comm) ingredients, mixed or to be mixed, for a purpose, eg for plaster, mortar, concrete or kinds of food: (主用於貿易與商業)(爲了調製灰泥、混凝土或某些食品等而混好或待混的)混合成份: *an ice-'cream mix;* 冰淇淋粉; *a 'cake mix,* of flour, egg-powder, sugar, etc to be used in making cakes. 糕餅混合料(麵粉、蛋粉、糖等)。

mixed /mɪkst ; mɪkst/ *adj* of different sorts: 混合的;雜樣的: *~ biscuits/pickles;* 什錦餅乾(泡菜); *a ~ school,* for boys and girls; 男女兼收的學校; *a ~ company,* including people of different classes, tastes, etc. 一羣形形色色的人。 ***have ~ feelings (about sth),*** feel eg both sorrow and pleasure (about it). 對某事具混雜的感情(如亦悲亦喜);百感交集。 **ˌ~ 'blessing,** sth that has both advantages and disadvantages. 有利亦有弊之事。 **ˌ~ 'doubles,** (tennis, etc) with two players, one man and one woman, on each side. (網球等)男女混合雙打。 **ˌ~ 'farming,** eg dairy farming and cereals. 混合農作(例如兼營牛奶製品與穀物)。 **ˌ~ 'grill,** eg liver, kidney and bacon. 什錦烤肉 (例如由肝、腰子、醃肉等混雜而成)。 **ˌ~ 'marriage,** one between persons of different races or religions. 雜婚;異族通婚;不同宗教的通婚。 **ˌ~ 'metaphor,** two or more metaphors used inconsistently together, producing a ludicrous effect, eg 'The scourge of tyranny had burnt his fingers'. 混合隱喩(二個或更多的隱喩矛盾地用在一起，以收可笑之效,例如「暴虐的鞭笞已燒傷了他的手指」)。

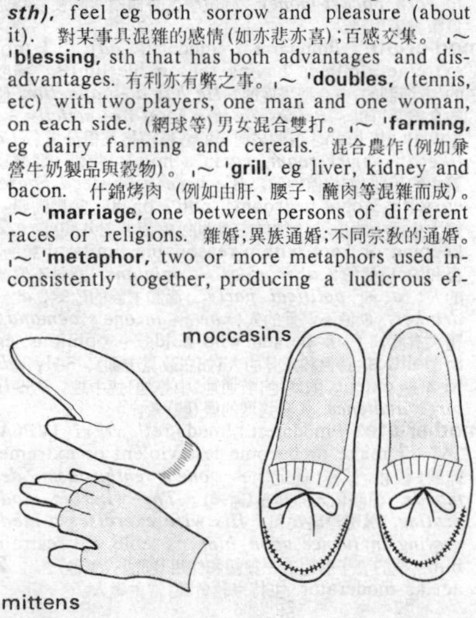

mixer /'mɪksə(r) ; 'mɪksɚ/ *n* **1** person or thing that mixes: 使混合的人或物;混合者;混合機;拌合機;攪拌器: *a ce'ment ~;* 水泥(混凝土)攪拌機; *an electric 'food-~;* 電動食物攪拌機; (TV, films) person or thing that combines shots on to one length of film or video-tape. (電視、電影)(電影膠片或電視錄影帶的)剪接者;剪接器。 **2** ***be a good ~,*** (colloq) one who is at ease with others on social occasions. (俗)是個善於交際的人(在社交場合上易於與人相處)。 ⇨ mix¹(2).

mix·ture /'mɪkstʃə(r) ; 'mɪkstʃɚ/ *n* **1** [U] mixing or being mixed. 混合;被混合。 **2** [C] sth made by mixing: 混合物: *a 'smoking ~,* made by blending different kinds of tobacco; 混合煙草; *a 'cough ~, ~* of several medicines. 咳嗽混合藥(藥水)。*Air is a ~, not a compound, of gases.* 空氣是氣體的混合物(而非化合物)。 ***the ~ as before,*** (colloq) the same procedure, treatment, etc as in the past. (俗)(手續、療法等)與以前一樣;照老辦法。

miz·zen, mizen /'mɪzn ; 'mɪzn̩/ *n* **1** **'~(-mast),** mast nearest the stern on a ship with three masts. 第三桅(三桅船上最靠近船尾的桅);後桅。 **2** **'~(-sail),** lowest square sail set on this mast. 後帆(第三桅上最低的方形帆);最後縱帆。 ⇨ the illus at barque. 參看 barque 之插圖。

mizzle /'mɪzl ; 'mɪzl̩/ *vi* (dial or colloq) [VP2A] rain in fine drops; drizzle. (方或俗)下毛毛雨;下細雨。

mne·monic /nɪ'mɒnɪk ; ni'mɑnɪk/ *adj* of, designed to help, the memory: 記憶的;幫助記憶的: *~ verses,* eg for remembering irregular declensions or conjugations. 幫助記憶的歌訣(如幫助記憶不規則名詞及形容詞等之語尾變化或動詞變化)。 **mne·mon·ics** *n pl* (with *sing v*) art of, system for, improving the memory. (與單數動詞連用)增進記憶的方法;記憶術。

mo /məʊ ; mo/ *n* (sl abbr of) moment: (俚) moment 之略: *half a mo.* 一會兒。

moan /məʊn ; mon/ *n* [C] low sound of pain or regret, or one suggesting suffering: 呻吟聲;嗚咽聲: *the ~s of the wounded;* 受傷者的呻吟; *the ~ of the wind on a winter evening.* 冬夜寒風的呼嘯聲。□ *vi, vt* [VP2A, C, 15B] utter ~s; say with ~s: 呻吟;悲嘆: *~ (out) a plea for help.* 哀哀求助。*What's she ~ing* (= complaining) *about now?* 她在抱怨些什麼?

moat /məʊt ; mot/ *n* deep, wide ditch filled with water, round a castle, etc as a defence. (防禦城堡等之)壕溝。⇨ the illus at drawbridge. 參看 drawbridge 之插圖。 **~ed** *adj* having a ~: 有壕溝的;囿有壕溝的: *a ~ed manor house.* 囿有壕溝的領主邸宅。

mob /mɒb ; mɑb/ *n* [C] **1** disorderly crowd, rabble, esp one that has gathered for mischief or attack: 無秩序之民衆;烏合之衆;(尤指)暴民;滋事的群衆: (attrib) (形容用法) *mob law, mob rule,* imposed or enforced by a mob. 暴民的法律;私刑。 **2** **the mob,** the masses: 民衆: *mob oratory,* the kind of speech-making that appeals to the emotions of the masses, not to the intellect. 煽動群衆的演講。 **3** gang of criminals. 犯罪集團;匪幫。 □ *vt* (-bb-) [VP6A] (of people) crowd round in great numbers, either to attack or to admire: (指民衆)包圍(爲攻擊或讚賞): *The pickpocket was mobbed by angry women.* 扒手被憤怒的婦女們包圍着。*The pop singer was mobbed by teenagers.* 那個流行歌曲歌手被少年男女包圍了。 **mob·ster** /'mɒbstə(r) ; 'mɑbstɚ/ *n* member of a gang or mob of rowdy persons. 暴徒或流氓集團的一份子。

mob·cap /'mɒbkæp ; 'mɑbˌkæp/ *n* (18th c) woman's indoor head-dress covering the whole of the hair. (十八世紀)室內用頭巾式女帽。

mo·bile /'məʊbaɪl *US:* -bl ; 'mobl̩/ *adj* **1** moving, able to be moved, easily and quickly from place to place: 易動的;可迅速移動的: ~ *troops/artillery*. 機動部隊(機動砲兵)。 **2** easily and often changing: 易變的;常變的: ~ *features*, quickly showing changes of thought and emotion. 迅速顯露思想與感情之轉變的面容。 □ *n* ornamental structure with parts that move in currents of air. 某些部份迎風轉動的裝飾性結構。 **mo·bil·ity** /məʊˈbɪlətɪ; moˈbɪlətɪ/ *n* [U] being ~. 可動性;流動性;移動性;易變性。

mo·bi·lize /ˈməʊbɪlaɪz; ˈmobl̩,aɪz/ *vt, vi* [VP6A, 2A] collect together for service or use, esp in war. 動員(尤指戰時人力物力等動員)。 **mo·bi·liz·ation** /ˌməʊbɪlaɪˈzeɪʃn *US:* -lɪˈz-; ˌmobl̩əˈzeʃən/ *n* mobilizing or being ~d: 動員: (attrib) (形容用法) *mobilization orders*. 動員令。

mob·ster /ˈmɒbstə(r); ˈmabstə/ *n* ⇨ mob.

moc·ca·sin /ˈmɒkəsɪn; ˈmakəsn̩/ *n* [U] soft leather made from deerskin; (*pl*) shoes made from this, as worn by N American Indians, or in similar style. 鹿皮製的軟革; (複) (北美印第安人等所穿的) 鹿皮鞋。⇨ the illus at mitten. 參看 mitten 之插圖。

mo·cha /ˈmɒkə *US:* ˈməʊkə; ˈmokə/ *n* [U] fine quality of coffee, originally shipped from the Arabian port of M~. 摩卡咖啡(一種精良咖啡,原係自阿拉伯摩卡港輸出者)。

mock /mɒk; mak/ *vt, vi* **1** [VP6A, 3A] ~ ***sb;*** ~ ***at sb,*** make fun of; ridicule (esp by copying in a funny or contemptuous way): 愚弄;嘲弄(尤指以可笑或侮慢的方式模倣): *The naughty boys ~ed the blind man.* 那些頑皮的男孩子愚弄那個盲人。*They ~ed at my fears.* 他們嘲弄我的恐懼。 **ˈ~·ing bird** *n* American bird of the thrush family that mimics the notes of other birds. 反舌鳥(美洲的一種畫眉鳥,善於模倣其他鳥類的聲調)。 **2** [VP6A] defy contemptuously: 使挫折;使徒勞無功: *The heavy steel doors ~ed the attempts of the thieves to open the safe.* 厚重的鐵門使盜賊開啓保險箱的企圖無法得逞。 **ˈ~-up** *n* **(a)** full-scale model, eg of an aircraft, made of wood, showing the appearance of a proposed machine (or any part of it). 實體模型(與實物同大小,如木製之飛機模型等)。 **(b)** lay-out of sth to be printed. 待印之某物的圖樣。□ *attrib adj* not real or genuine: 假的;模擬的: *a ~ battle;* 假想戰; *~-turtle soup*, made to imitate turtle soup; 充鼈湯(卽小牛頭湯); *ˌ~-ˈmodesty*, pretence of being modest; 假謙遜; *ˌ~-heˈroic*, making fun of heroic style in literature. 戲擬英雄詩體的;模倣英雄詩的。□ *n* (archaic) derision. (古)嘲笑。 ***make a ~ of,*** ridicule. 譏笑;嘲弄。 **~er** *n* person who ~s. 嘲弄者;作嘲弄性的模倣者。 **~·ing·ly** *adv*

mock·ery /ˈmɒkərɪ; ˈmakərɪ/ *n* (*pl* -ries) **1** [U] mocking; ridicule: 嘲弄;譏笑: *hold a person up to ~*. 嘲弄某人。 **2** [C] sb or sth that is mocked; occasion when sb or sth is mocked. 被嘲弄之人或事物;笑柄;受嘲弄的場合。 **3** [C] bad or contemptible example (of sth): (某事的)惡例;可蔑視之例: *His trial was a ~ of justice.* 他所受的審判是蔑視正義的惡例(他受到不公正的審判)。 *He received only the ~ of a trial.* 他只是受到一場不公正的審判。

mod /mɒd; mad/ *adj* (sl) up-to-date and smart (esp in dress). (俚)最新式的;時髦的(尤指服裝)。□ *n* **Mod,** (1960's in GB) young person wearing smart clothes and riding on motor-scooters: (1960 年代用於英國)馬德(指騎速克達機車,穿時髦服裝的青年): *Mods and Rockers*, ⇨ rock². 馬德與洛克。

mo·dal /ˈməʊdl; ˈmodl̩/ *adj* relating to mode or manner (contrasted with substance); (gram) relating to the mood of a verb: 形式上的;方式上的(與實質相對);(文法)動詞語氣的: ~ *auxiliaries*, eg *can, may*. 語氣助動詞(如 can, may 等是)。 **mo·dal·ity** /məʊˈdælətɪ; moˈdælətɪ/ *n* **1** [U] being ~. 形式。 **2** [C] way in which sth is done. 作法;方式。

mode /məʊd; mod/ *n* [C] **1** way in which sth is done; way of speaking or behaving: (做事、說話或行爲的)方式;方法: *a ~ of life/dressing the hair;* 一種生活方式 (一種髮型的梳理); fashion or style: 樣式;型;式: *the latest ~s* (of clothes). (服裝的)最新款式。 **2** (music) one of the two chief scale systems in modern music: (音樂)調式: *the major and the minor ~s.* 大調式及小調式。

model¹ /ˈmɒdl; ˈmadl̩/ *n* [C] **1** small-scale reproduction or representation of sth; design to be copied: 模型;模樣: ~ *of an ocean liner;* 一艘海輪的模型; *a clay or wax ~ for a statue,* to be copied in stone or metal; 塑像的泥質或蠟質模型(供製作石像或金屬像時模倣用); (attrib) (形容用法) ~ *aircraft/trains.* 模型飛機(火車)。 **2** person or thing to be copied: 供模倣的人或物;典範;模範: *He's a ~ of industry.* 他是勤勞的典範。 *Make yours on the ~ of your brother's.* 以你哥哥所做的爲模範。 **3** (colloq) person or thing exactly like another: (俗)極相似的人或物: *She's the ~/a perfect ~ of her mother.* 她(完全)像她的母親。 **4** person who poses for sculptors, painters or photographers. 模特兒(供雕塑家、畫家或攝影家用者)。 **5** person employed to wear clothes, hats, etc so that prospective buyers may see them; mannequin. 時裝模特兒(穿着衣帽等以示顧客);木頭或蠟製的時裝模特兒。 **6** article of clothing, hat, etc shown publicly by ~s(5). 模特兒表演時所穿着的衣帽等;模特兒身上所展示的服飾: *the latest Paris ~s,* clothes, etc from the Paris dressmakers. 最新巴黎時裝。 **7** design or structure of which many copies or reproductions are (to be) made: 產品的型式: *the latest ~s of Ford cars;* 最新型的福特汽車; *a ˈsports ~,* a car designed for fast driving. 跑車型汽車。 **8** (attrib) perfect; deserving to be imitated: (形容用法)完善的;值得做效的;典型的: ~ *behaviour;* 模範行爲; *a ~ wife.* 模範妻子。

model² /ˈmɒdl; ˈmadl̩/ *vt, vi* (-ll-, US -l-) **1** [VP6A, 14, 15A] ~ ***(in),*** shape (in some soft substance): (用某些軟物質)製作…的模型;塑造: ~ *sb's head in clay;* 用黏土製作某人頭部的塑像; (fig): (喻): *delicately ~led features.* 清秀的面貌。 **2** [VP2A, 6A] practise as a model(4, 5): 做模特兒: *She earns a living by ~ling clothes/hats.* 她做時裝模特兒以謀生(她的職業是時裝模特兒)。 **3** [VP14] ~ ***oneself on/upon sb,*** make from a model; take as a copy or example: 模倣;倣效;倣製: ~ *oneself on one's father.* 以父親爲模範而倣效之。 **~(l)er** *n* person who practises ~ling. 製作模型的人。 **~(l)ing** *n* [U] art of making ~s(1); way in which this is done; working as a ~(5): 模型製作術;製作模型的方法;當時裝模特兒: *She did some ~ling as a student to earn pocket-money.* 她做學生時偶爾當時裝模特兒以賺點零用錢。

mod·er·ate¹ /ˈmɒdərət; ˈmadərɪt/ *adj* **1** not extreme; limited; having reasonable limits: 適度的;有節制的;有合理限度的: *He has a ~ appetite.* 他的食慾還可以。 *Prices in this hotel are strictly ~,* not at all high. 這個旅館裏的各種價格都很公道。 *I'd like a ~-price room,* eg in a hotel. 我要一間價錢適中的房間(如旅館中的)。*We need a ~-sized house,* eg with 3 or 4 bedrooms, not 7 or 8. 我們需要一幢大小適中的房子(例如有三四間臥室而非七八間)。 **2** keeping or kept within reasonable limits: 中庸的;溫和的;穩健的: *a man of ~ opinions;* 意見不偏激的人; *a ~ political party;* 溫和主義的政黨; *a ~ drinker;* 飲酒不過量的人; *be ~ in one's demands.* 需求有度。 □ *n* person who holds ~ opinions, eg in politics. 持溫和意見的人(如在政見方面)。 **~·ly** *adv* to a ~ extent: 適度地;普通地;中等地;適中地: *a ~ly large audience.* 人數適度的觀(聽)衆。

mod·er·ate² /ˈmɒdəreɪt; ˈmadə,ret/ *vt, vi* [VP6A, 2A] **1** make or become less violent or extreme: 節制;緩和;減輕;穩定: ~ *one's enthusiasm/demands.* 節制個人的熱心(需求)。 *The wind is moderating.* 風勢漸趨緩和。 *His wife exercises a moderating influence upon him,* is able to restrain him. 他的妻子對他有一種緩和作用(卽能約束他)。 **2** act as moderator. 主持宗教會議;當主考人。

mod·er·ation /ˌmɒdəˈreɪʃn ; ˌmɑdəˈreʃən/ *n* **1** [U] quality of being moderate; freedom from excess: 適度;溫和;中庸: *My doctor has advised ~ in eating and drinking.* 我的醫師勸告我節制飲食。**in ~,** in a moderate manner or degree: 適度地: *Alcoholic drinks are not harmful taken in ~.* 適度飲酒不會有害。 **2** (*pl*) (shortened to 略作 **Mods**) first public examination for a degree in classical studies at Oxford. (複)牛津大學之古典文學研究之學位的初試。

mod·er·ator /ˈmɒdəreɪtə(r) ; ˈmɑdəˌretɚ/ *n* **1** Presbyterian minister presiding over a church court. 基督教長老會宗教會議的議長。 **2** presiding examiner at some university examinations. (某些大學之考試的)主考人。 **3** material in which neutrons are slowed down in an atomic pile. 減速劑;緩和劑(原子堆中使中子減速的物質)。

mod·ern /ˈmɒdn ; ˈmɑdɚn/ *adj* **1** of the present or recent times: 現代的;近代的: *~ history,* eg of Europe, from 1475 onwards; 近代史(如歐洲近代史,自1475年迄今); *~ languages,* those now spoken and written; 現代語言(現今所說所寫的各種語文); *M~ English,* from the 15th c onwards; 近代英語(十五世紀以後的英語); *~ inventions and discoveries.* 現代的發明與發現。ˌ**secondary ˈ~ school,** (GB; 1950's and 1960's) type of non-academic, semi-technical, secondary school. (英; 1950年代及1960年代)半工業技術中等學校。⇨ secondary. **2** new and up-to-date: 新近的;時髦的: *~ methods and ideas;* 新的方法與觀念; *a house with all ~ conveniences.* 有全部新式設備的房子。□ *n* person living in ~ times. 現代人。

mod·ern·ism /ˈmɒdənɪzəm ; ˈmɑdɚnˌɪzəm/ *n* [U] modern views or methods; (theology) subordination of tradition to modern thought. 現代的觀點或方法;現代思潮;(神學)現代主義。**mod·ern·ist** /-ɪst ; -ɪst/ *n* believer in, supporter of, ~. 現代主義者;擁護現代思潮者。**mod·ern·is·tic** /ˌmɒdəˈnɪstɪk ; ˌmɑdɚˈnɪstɪk/ *adj* of ~. 現代的;現代主義的。

mo·dern·ity /məˈdɜːnətɪ ; mɑˈdɝnətɪ/ *n* [U] being modern. 現代;現代性;現代作風。

mod·ern·ize /ˈmɒdənaɪz ; ˈmɑdɚnˌaɪz/ *vt* [VP6A] make suitable for present-day needs; bring up to date: 使適合現代需要;使現代化: *Ought we to ~ our spelling?* 我們應該把我們的拼字法現代化嗎? **mod·ern·iz·ation** /ˌmɒdənaɪˈzeɪʃn *US:* -nɪˈz- ; ˌmɑdɚnəˈzeʃən/ *n* [U].

mod·est /ˈmɒdɪst ; ˈmɑdɪst/ *adj* **1** having, showing, a not too high opinion of one's merits, abilities, etc. 謙遜的;客氣的;謙虛的: *be ~ about one's achievements;* 不誇耀一己之成就; *a ~ hero.* 一位謙遜的英雄。 **2** moderate; not large in size or amount: 適度的;適中的;質樸的: *He lives in a ~ little house,* not showy or splendid. 他住在一幢普通的小房子。*My demands are quite ~.* 我的要求不多。 *He is ~ in his requirements.* 他不過份要求。 **3** taking, showing, care not to do or say anything impure or improper: 謹慎的;莊重的;有禮貌的: *~ in speech, dress and behaviour.* 在言語、服裝、行爲方面謹慎。**~·ly** *adv* **mod·esty** /ˈmɒdɪstɪ ; ˈmɑdəstɪ/ *n* [U] state of being ~ (all senses): 謙遜;適度;謹慎;質樸;有禮貌;客氣: *Her ~y prevented her from making her feelings known to him.* 她的謹愼使她不敢向他表露感情。 ***in all ~y,*** without the least intention of boasting, etc. 一點也沒有自誇等的意思。

modi·cum /ˈmɒdɪkəm ; ˈmɑdɪkəm/ *n* (*sing* only) small or moderate amount: (僅用單數)小量;適量: *achieve success with a ~ of effort;* 稍微努力就獲得成功; *a simple meal with a ~ of wine.* 備有少量葡萄酒的一頓簡單餐食。

mod·ify /ˈmɒdɪfaɪ ; ˈmɑdəˌfaɪ/ *vt* (*pt, pp* -fied) [VP6A] **1** make changes in; make different: 修改;變更: *The industrial revolution modified the whole structure of English society.* 工業革命改變了整個英國社會的結構。 **2** make less severe, violent, etc: 減輕;緩和: *You'd better ~ your tone,* eg be less rude. 你最好說話文雅一點。*He won't ~ his demands,* reduce them. 他不減少他的要求。 **3** (gram) qualify the sense of (a word): (文法)修飾;限制(字)義: *Adjectives ~ nouns.* 形容詞修飾名詞。**modi·fier** /-faɪə(r) ; -ˌfaɪɚ/ *n* (gram) word that modifies, eg an *adj* or *adv.* (文法)修飾語(如形容詞或副詞)。 **modi·fi·ca·tion** /ˌmɒdɪfɪˈkeɪʃn ; ˌmɑdəfəˈkeʃən/ *n* [U] ~ing or being modified; [C] instance of this; change or alteration. 修改;修飾;減輕;緩和;變更;變化。

mod·ish /ˈməʊdɪʃ ; ˈmodɪʃ/ *adj* fashionable. 流行的;時髦的。**~·ly** *adv*

mo·diste /məʊˈdiːst ; moˈdist/ *n* (formal) milliner; dress-maker. (正式用語)女帽製造者;女衣縫製者。

modu·late /ˈmɒdjʊleɪt *US:* -dʒʊ- ; ˈmɑdʒəˌlet/ *vt, vi* **1** [VP6A] regulate; adjust; adapt; (music) make a change in the key of. 調節;調整;使適應;(音樂)改變…的調子;使變音;使變調。 **2** [VP2C] *~ from/to,* change from one key to another. 從一調變成另一調;變調;轉調。 **3** [VP6A] (radio) vary the frequency, amplitude or phase of a wave. (無線電)改變聲波的頻率、振幅或相位;調制;調變。⇨ modulation.

modu·la·tion /ˌmɒdjʊˈleɪʃn *US:* -dʒʊˈl- ; ˌmɑdʒəˈleʃən/ *n* **1** [U] process of modulating; state of being modulated; [C] change resulting from this; [U] (music) changing of key; [C] particular change of key. 調節;調整;因調節而產生的變化;(音樂)變調;轉調。 **2** (radio) variation in the amplitude, frequency or phase of a wave so that it is suitable for radio, eg of the human voice to a wave for radio or the telephone. (無線電)調制;調變(聲波之振幅、頻率或相位的改變使適合於無線電,例如人的聲音改變成無線電或電話的電波)。

mod·ule /ˈmɒdjuːl *US:* -dʒuːl ; ˈmɑdʒul/ *n* [C] **1** standard or unit of measurement as used in building. (建築方面所用的)標準尺寸;基本單位;模數。 **2** standard uniform component used in the structure of a building or in sectional furniture; unit of electronic components as used in the assembly of a computer: (建築物之構造或組合傢具中之)組件;(電子計算機等之)模組;單體: *a ˈmemory ~,* unit of components in a mechanical system. (機械系統中的)記憶單體。 **3** independent and self-contained unit of a spacecraft. 艙(太空船中具有一切必需配備的獨立單位)。**comˈmand ~,** for the astronaut in command. 指揮艙(供負責指揮太空探險之太空人乘坐者)。**ˈlunar ~,** to be separated for a moon landing. 登月小艇。**modu·lar** /ˈmɒdjʊlə(r) *US:* -dʒʊ- ; ˈmɑdʒʊlɚ/ *adj* based on a ~ or unit: 以組件爲基本的;以模組或單體爲基本的: *modular design/construction,* based on a ~ which is repeated throughout the design. 單體設計(構造物)(整個圖樣或構造物中以一單體之一再重覆而成)。

modus op·er·andi /ˌməʊdəs ˌɒpəˈrændiː ; ˈmodəsˌɑpəˈrændaɪ/ *n* (Lat) method of dealing with a piece of work; method of being operated. (拉)做法;方法;慣技。

modus vi·vendi /ˌməʊdəs vɪˈvendiː ; ˈmodəsvɪˈvendaɪ/ *n* (Lat) way of living; (way of getting a) temporary agreement (while awaiting the final settlement of a dispute, etc). (拉)生活方式;(在等待爭執等之最後解決時的)暫時協議;獲得暫時協議之途徑。

mo·gul /ˈməʊgl ; ˈmogʌl/ *n* (colloq) very rich or important person: (俗)非常富有或重要的人;鉅子;大亨: *Hollywood ~s.* 好萊塢大亨。

mo·hair /ˈməʊheə(r) ; ˈmoˌhɛr/ *n* [U] (thread, cloth, made from the) fine, silky hair of the Angora goat. 安哥拉山羊羊毛(質細而有光澤);此種羊毛所織成的毛線或毛料;馬海。

Mo·ham·medan /məˈhæmɪdən ; moˈhæmədən/ *n* ⇨ Muhammad.

moi·ety /ˈmɔɪətɪ ; ˈmɔɪətɪ/ *n* (*pl* -ties) (esp in legal sense) one of two parts into which sth is divided. (尤用於法律意義)一半;二分之一。

moil /mɔɪl ; mɔɪl/ *vi* (only in) (僅用於) ***toil and ~***, work hard. 辛勤工作。
moist /mɔɪst ; mɔɪst/ *adj* (esp of surfaces) slightly wet: (尤指表面)潮濕的;潤濕的: *eyes ~ with tears;* 爲淚水所潤濕的眼睛; *a ~ wind from the sea.* 海上吹來的一陣濕風。**~en** /ˈmɔɪsn ; ˈmɔɪsn̩/ *vt, vi* [VP6A, 2A] make or become ~: 使潤濕;變濕: *~en the lips,* eg by licking them; 舐濕嘴唇; *~en a sponge.* 把海綿沾濕。**~·ure** /ˈmɔɪstʃə(r) ; ˈmɔɪstʃɚ/ *n* [U] condensed vapour on a surface; liquid in the form of vapour. 潮濕;濕氣;水氣。
moke /məʊk ; mok/ *n* (GB sl) donkey. (英俚)驢。
mo·lar /ˈməʊlə(r) ; ˈmolɚ/ *n, adj* (one) of the teeth used for grinding food. 臼齒;臼齒的。⇨ the illus at mouth. 參看 mouth 之插圖。
mo·las·ses /məˈlæsɪz ; məˈlæsɪz/ *n* [U] thick dark syrup drained from raw sugar during the refining process. 糖蜜;糖漿。
mold, molder, mold·ing, moldy, ⇨ mould, etc.
mole[1] /məʊl ; mol/ *n* permanent, small, dark spot on the human skin. 痣;黑痣。
mole[2] /məʊl ; mol/ *n* small, dark-grey, fur-covered animal with tiny eyes, living in tunnels (or burrows) which it makes in the ground. 鼹鼠。⇨ the illus at small. 參看 small 之插圖。***blind as a ~***, having bad eye-sight. 視力很差的。**ˈ~-skin** *n* fur of a ~, used for making garments and hats. 鼹鼠皮(製衣帽等用)。**ˈ~-hill** *n* pile of earth thrown up by a ~ while burrowing. 鼹鼠丘(鼹鼠掘地洞時所堆積的泥土堆)。***make a mountain out of a ~-hill***, make a trivial matter seem important. 小題大做。
mole[3] /məʊl ; mol/ *n* stone wall built in the sea as a breakwater or causeway. 防波堤;堤道。⇨ the illus at breakwater. 參看 breakwater 之插圖。
mol·ecule /ˈmɒlɪkjuːl ; ˈmɑləˌkjul/ *n* smallest unit (one or more atoms) into which a substance can be divided without a change in its chemical nature. 分子(物質不改變其化學性質的最小單位,含一個或數個原子)。**mol·ecu·lar** /məˈlekjʊlə(r) ; məˈlɛkjəlɚ/ *adj* of or related to ~s: 分子的;與分子有關的: *molecular structure.* 分子結構。
mo·lest /məˈlest ; məˈlɛst/ *vt* [VP6A] trouble or annoy intentionally. 故意干擾;妨害;作弄;騷擾。**mol·es·ta·tion** /ˌməʊləˈsteɪʃn ; ˌmoləsˈteʃən/ *n* [U].
moll /mɒl ; mɑl/ *n* (sl) woman companion of a gangster, vagrant, etc; prostitute. (俚)匪徒、流氓等的情婦;妓女。
mol·lify /ˈmɒlɪfaɪ ; ˈmɑləˌfaɪ/ *vt* (*pt, pp* -fied) [VP6A] make (a person, his feelings) calmer or quieter: 使(人、其情緒)平靜;安慰;撫慰;緩和: *~ing remarks;* 安慰的話語; *~ sb's anger.* 緩和某人的憤怒。**mol·li·fi·ca·tion** /ˌmɒlɪfɪˈkeɪʃn ; ˌmɑləfəˈkeʃən/ *n* [U].
mol·lusc (US also **mol·lusk**) /ˈmɒləsk ; ˈmɑləsk/ *n* one of a class of animals with soft bodies (and often hard shells), eg oysters, mussels, cuttlefish, snails, slugs. 軟體動物(常有硬殼,如牡蠣、貽貝、烏賊、蝸牛、蛞蝓)。
molly·coddle /ˈmɒlɪkɒdl ; ˈmɑlɪˌkɑdl/ *n* person who takes too much care of his health, who pampers himself and likes others to pamper him. 過份當心自己健康的人;縱容自己並喜歡被別人縱容的人。□ *vt* [VP6A] (often reflex) pamper (sb, oneself). (常用反身式)溺愛;縱容(某人、自己)。
Mo·loch /ˈməʊlɒk ; ˈmolɑk/ *n* (in the Bible) god to whom children were sacrificed; (fig) dreadful thing, eg war, that requires great sacrifice of human life. (聖經中)摩洛(須以孩子爲祭品的神);(喻)需要犧牲人命的恐怖事物(如戰爭)。
molt /məʊlt ; molt/ ⇨ moult.
mol·ten /ˈməʊltən ; ˈmoltn̩/ *pp* of melt. **1** (of metals) in a melted (and therefore very hot) state: (指金屬)熔化的: *~ steel.* 鋼水。**2** made of metal that has been melted and cast: 由熔化金屬鑄造成的: *a ~ image,* eg of a god. 金屬鑄像(如神像)。
molto /ˈmɒltəʊ *US:* ˈməʊltəʊ ; ˈmolto/ *adv* (musical direction) very: (樂譜說明)很;甚;頗;極: *~ espressivo,* with much expression. 富於表情的;頗有表情似的。
mo·lyb·denum /məˈlɪbdənəm ; məˈlɪbdənəm/ *n* [U] silvery-white brittle metallic element (symbol **Mo**) used in alloys for making high-speed tools. 鉬(一種銀白色性脆的金屬元素,化學符號 Mo, 其合金用以製高速工具)。
mo·ment /ˈməʊmənt ; ˈmomənt/ *n* **1** [C] point or very brief period of time: 瞬間;片刻: *It was all over in a few ~s.* 沒多久就結束了。*Please wait a ~.* 請稍等。*Just a ~, please.* 請等一會兒。*He'll be here* (*at*) *any ~*, very soon now. 他立刻就要到了。*It was done in a ~.* 一會兒它便完成了。*He arrived at the last ~*, almost too late. 他在最後一刻才到達。*Study your notes at odd ~s*, whenever you have a few minutes to spare. 抽空研讀你的筆記。*I have just this ~/only this ~ heard the news,* heard it only a ~ ago. 我剛剛才聽到這消息。***Not for a ~***, never: 從來沒有: *'Have you ever thought of making your own dresses?'—'Not for a ~!'* '你曾否想到自己縫製衣服?'—'從來沒有!' ***man of the ~***, man who is important just now. 時下重要的人物。**2** ***the ~***, (used as a *conj*) as soon as; at the time when: (作連接詞用)一…就…;一當;就在那時: *I started the ~ your letter arrived.* 我一收到你的信就動身了。*The ~ I saw you I knew you were angry with me.* 我一看到你,就知道你在生我的氣。**3** [U] ***of (great, small, little, no, etc) ~***, of (great, small, etc) importance: (非常、沒什麼、不等)重要的: *an affair of great ~;* 非常重要的事情; *a matter of ~;* 重大的事; *men of ~.* 要人。

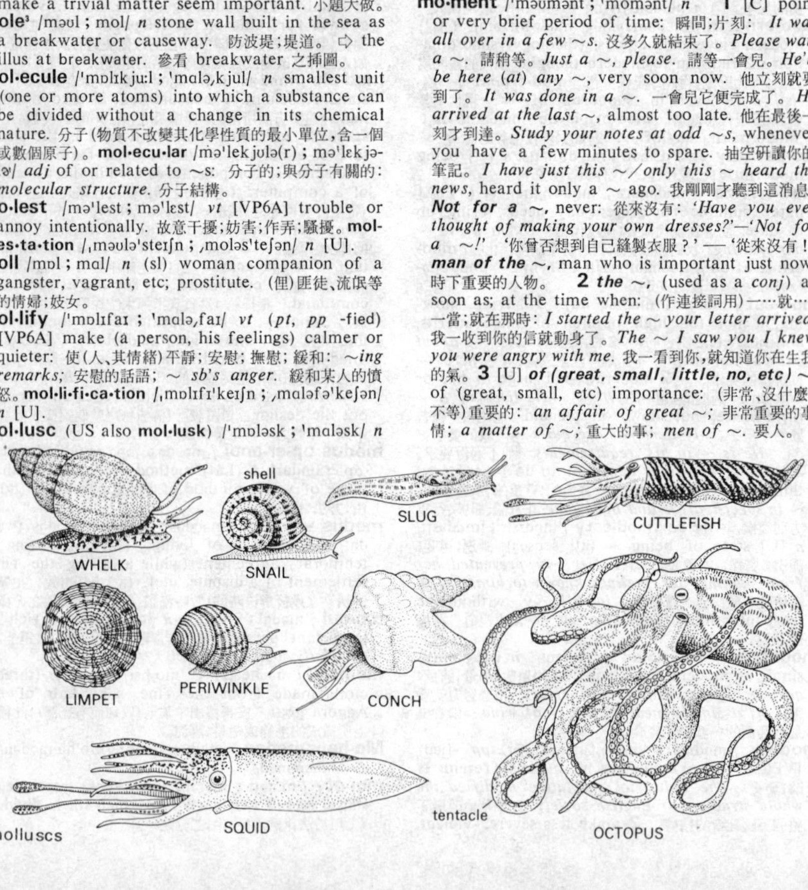

molluscs

mo·men·tary /ˈməʊməntrɪ *US:* -terɪ ; ˈmomənˌterɪ/ *adj* **1** lasting for, done in, a moment. 短暫的；瞬息間的；刹那的。 **2** at every moment: 隨時的: *with a learner at the wheel, and in ~ expectation of an accident.* 由一個初學的人駕駛，並且隨時都在準備着車禍的發生。 **mo·men·tar·ily** /ˈməʊməntrəlɪ *US:* ˌməʊmənˈterəlɪ ; ˈmomənˌterəlɪ/ *adv*

mo·men·tous /məˈmentəs ; moˈmɛntəs/ *adj* important; serious. 重要的；嚴重的。**~·ly** *adv* **~·ness** *n*

mo·men·tum /məˈmentəm ; moˈmɛntəm/ *n* [U] **1** (science) quantity of motion of a moving body (the product of its mass and velocity): (科學)動量(即物體之質量及速度的乘積): *Do falling objects gain ~?* 下落物體的動量是否增加？ **2** (fig, of events) impetus gained by movement: (喻，指事件)因動作而得到的衝力；動向；衝向: *lose／gain ~.* 失去(獲得)推動力；鬆弛(擴展)。

mon·arch /ˈmɒnək ; ˈmanɚk/ *n* supreme ruler (a king, queen, emperor or empress). 君主(國王、女王、皇帝或女皇)。 **mon·ar·chic** /məˈnɑːkɪk ; məˈnarkɪk/ *adj* of a ~ or a ~y. 君主的；帝王的；王朝的；君主制度的；君主政體的。⇨ absolute(2). **mon·ar·chism** /-kɪzəm ; -ˌkɪzəm/ *n* [U] system of government by a single ruler or ~. 君主制度。 **mon·ar·chist** /-ɪst ; -ɪst/ *n* supporter of ~ism. 擁護君主制度者。 **mon·archy** /ˈmɒnəkɪ ; ˈmanɚkɪ/ *n* [U] government by a ~; [C] (*pl* -chies) state ruled by a ~. 君主政體；君主國。⇨ limit².

mon·as·tery /ˈmɒnəstrɪ *US:* -sterɪ ; ˈmanəsˌterɪ/ *n* (*pl* -ries) place where monks live as a community under religious vows. 修道院。

mon·as·tic /məˈnæstɪk ; məˈnæstɪk/ *adj* of monks or monasteries: 修道士的；僧侶的；修道院的: *~ vows,* ie of poverty, chastity, and obedience; 修道誓願(即貧苦、貞潔與服從)； *~ architecture,* of the kind used for monasteries, abbeys, etc. 寺院式建築。 **mon·as·ti·cism** /məˈnæstɪsɪzəm ; məˈnæstəˌsɪzəm/ *n* [U] system of living as practised by monks in monasteries. 修道制度；修道生活。

mon·aural /ˌmɒnˈɔːrəl ; manˈɔrəl/ *adj* for one ear; (with trade abbr *mono*; of sound-reproducing equipment and recordings) not stereophonic. 爲一邊耳朶的；(商用略作 mono; 指放音設備及錄音)非立體音響的。

Mon·day /ˈmʌndɪ ; ˈmʌndɪ/ *n* second day of the week. 星期一。

mon·et·ary /ˈmʌnɪtrɪ *US:* -terɪ ; ˈmʌnəˌterɪ/ *adj* of money or a currency: 錢的；貨幣的: *a ~ policy,* of control over money; 貨幣政策； *~ reform,* eg to create a decimal coinage. 幣制改革。 *The ~ unit of the US is the dollar.* 美國的貨幣單位是'元'。 **mon·et·ar·ism** /-tərɪzəm ; -təˌrɪzəm/ *n* [U] policy of control over money as the chief method of managing a country's economy. 貨幣主義(以控制貨幣作爲管理國家經濟之主要方法的政策)。 **mon·et·ar·ist** /-tərɪst ; -tərɪst/ *n* person favouring monetarism. 貨幣主義者。

mon·et·ize /ˈmʌnətaɪz ; ˈmʌnəˌtaɪz/ *vt* [VP6A] **1** put (coins, notes) into circulation as money. 使(硬幣、鈔票)爲貨幣；定爲貨幣；發行貨幣。 **2** give (a currency) a fixed value 給予(貨幣)固定價值。

money /ˈmʌnɪ ; ˈmʌnɪ/ *n* **1** [U] coins stamped from metal (gold, copper, alloys), printed notes, given and accepted when buying and selling, etc: 錢；貨幣: *I keep my ~ in the bank.* 我把我的錢存在銀行。 *I could hear ~ jingling in his pocket.* 我聽見他口袋裏的錢玎璫地響。 ***be ˈcoining／ˈminting ~,*** be getting rich quickly. 迅速致富；暴富。 ***be in the ~,*** (sl) be rich. (俚)富有；有錢。 ***get one's ˈ~'s worth,*** get full value for ~ spent. 花錢得到應得的價值；撈回本兒。 ***make ~,*** earn it. 賺錢。 ***marry ~,*** marry a rich person. 娶(嫁)富有的人。 ***(pay) ~ down,*** (pay) in cash (contrasted with *credit*). 付現金(與 credit 相對)。 ***put ~ into sth,*** invest ~ in an enterprise, etc. 投資於某一企業等。 **ˌ~ of acˈcount,** ⇨ account¹(2). **ready ~,** cash (contrasted with *credit*, etc). 現款；現錢(與 credit 等相對)。 **2** (compounds) (複合字) **ˈ~-box** *n* closed box into which coins are dropped through a slit, used for savings or for collecting contributions (to charities, etc). 錢箱(儲蓄或收集捐款用)；撲滿。 **ˈ~-changer** *n* one whose business is to exchange ~ of one country for that of another country. 以兌換各國貨幣爲業的人；兌換業者。 **ˈ~-grubber** *n* person whose chief or only interest in life is making ~. 守財奴；唯利是圖的人。 **ˈ~-lender** *n* one whose business is to lend ~ at interest. 放債的人。 **the ˈ~-market** *n* the body of bankers, financiers, etc whose operations decide the rates of interest on borrowed capital. 金融市場。 **ˈ~ order** *n* order¹(7) bought from a post office for ~ to be paid by another post office to a named person. (郵政)滙票。 **ˈ~-spinner** *n* (colloq) book, play, etc that makes a lot of ~. (俗)賺大錢的書、戲劇等。 **3** (*pl*, moneys or monies /ˈmʌnɪz ; ˈmʌnɪz/) (legal or archaic) sums of ~: (法律或古)金額: *~s paid in／out;* 收進(付出)的錢數； *sundry ~s owing to the estate.* 來自財產的各項收益。 **~ed** /ˈmʌnɪd ; ˈmʌnɪd/ *adj* having (much) ~: 有錢的；富有的； *a ~ed man;* 富人； *the ~ed classes;* 有錢階級； *the ~ed interest,* the owners of capital. 金融業者；資本家；金融界。 **~·less** *adj* having no ~. 沒錢的。

mon·ger /ˈmʌŋgə(r) ; ˈmʌŋgɚ/ *n* (chiefly in compounds) trader, dealer: (主要用於複合字中)商人；販子: *ˈiron~;* 五金商； *ˈfish~;* 魚販； *ˈscandal-~.* 專事毀謗的人。

mon·gol·ism /ˈmɒŋgəlɪzəm ; ˈmaŋgəˌlɪzəm/ *n* [U] congenital condition in which a child is born with mental deficiency and a flattened broad skull and slanting eyes. 蒙古種型；蒙古人樣白癡(先天性之智力不足，頭顱平而寬，斜眼)。 **mon·gol** /ˈmɒŋgl ; ˈmaŋgəl/ *n, attrib adj* (person) suffering from ~: 患蒙古人樣白癡的；蒙古人樣白癡患者: *a mongol baby.* 患蒙古人樣白癡的嬰兒。

mon·goose /ˈmɒŋguːs ; ˈmaŋgus/ *n* (*pl* ~s /-sɪz ; -sɪz/) small Indian animal clever at destroying venomous snakes. 獴；貓鼬(善於捕殺毒蛇之小動物，產於印度)。⇨ the illus at small. 參看 small 之插圖。

mon·grel /ˈmʌŋgrəl ; ˈmʌŋgrəl/ *n* **1** dog of mixed breed. 雜種狗。 **2** any plant or animal of mixed origin. 雜種的動物或植物。□ *attrib adj* of mixed breed or origin. 雜種的；混種的。

mon·ies /ˈmʌnɪz ; ˈmʌnɪz/ *n pl* ⇨ money(3).

moni·tor /ˈmɒnɪtə(r) ; ˈmanətɚ/ *n* **1** pupil given authority over his fellows. 級長；班長。 **2** person employed to listen to and report on foreign broadcasts. 受雇監聽外國廣播的人員。 **3** apparatus for testing transmissions by radio or TV, for detecting radio-activity, for tracing the flight of missiles, etc. 稽查器；監測器；無線電或電視傳播偵測器；放射性偵察器；火箭追蹤器。 **ˈ~ (screen),** television screen used in a studio to check or select transmissions. 電視臺播送室中用以檢查或選擇播送的電視螢光幕。□ *vt, vi* act as ~(2). 監聽(外國廣播)。

monk /mʌŋk ; mʌŋk/ *n* member of a community of men living together under religious vows in a monastery. 僧侶；修道士。 **ˈ~·ish** /-ɪʃ ; -ɪʃ/ *adj* of or like ~s. (像)僧侶的；(像)修道士的。

mon·key /ˈmʌŋkɪ ; ˈmʌŋkɪ/ *n* (*pl* ~s) **1** member of the group of animals most closely resembling man. 猴；猿。⇨ the illus at ape. 參看 ape 之插圖。 ***be／get up to ˈ~ business／tricks,*** to mischief. 胡鬧；惡作劇；頑皮。 ***have a ˈ~ on one's back,*** (sl) (俚) **(a)** be a drug addict; 染上毒癮； **(b)** bear a grudge. 懷恨。 ***get one's ~ up,*** (sl) become angry. (俚)生氣；發怒。 ***put sb's ~ up,*** (sl) make him angry. (俚)使某人生氣。 **ˈ~-jacket** *n* short, close-fitting jacket as worn by some sailors. (某些水手等所穿的)緊身短上衣。 **ˈ~-nut** *n* groundnut. 落花生。 **ˈ~-puzzle** *n* Chilean pine-tree.

智利松。'~-**wrench** *n* wrench (spanner) with a jaw that can be adjusted to various lengths. 活動扳鉗;活口鉗。⇨ the illus at tool. 參看 tool 之插圖。**2** (playfully) person, esp a child, who is mischievous. (戲語)頑皮的人(尤指小孩)。 **3** (sl) £500 or $500. (俚)五百鎊;五百(美)元。□ *vi* [VP2C] ~ *about*, fool about. 胡鬧。

mono, mono- ⇨ monaural and App 3. 參看 monaural 及附錄三。

mono·chrome /'mɒnəkrəʊm ; 'mɑnə,krom/ *n* painting in (different tints of) one colour. 單色畫。□ *adj* having one colour. 單色的。

mon·ocle /'mɒnəkl ; 'mɑnəkl/ *n* eyeglass for one eye only, kept in position by the muscles round the eye. 單眼鏡。

mon·og·amy /mə'nɒgəmɪ ; mə'nɑgəmɪ/ *n* [U] practice of being married to only one person at a time. 一夫一妻制。 ⇨ polygamy. **mon·og·amist** /-ɪst ; -ɪst/ *n* person who practises ~. 實行一夫一妻制者。**mon·og·amous** /mə'nɒgəməs ; mə'nɑgəməs/ *adj* having only one wife or husband at a time. 一夫一妻(制)的。

mono·gram /'mɒnəgræm ; 'mɑnə,græm/ *n* two or more letters (esp a person's initials) combined in one design (used on handkerchiefs, notepaper, etc). 字母組合圖案(以二個或更多字母,尤其是姓名的起首字母,編成的圖案,用於手帕、私人信紙等上)。

a monogram

a monolith

mono·graph /'mɒnəgrɑːf *US:* -græf ; 'mɑnə,græf/ *n* detailed learned account, esp a published report on one particular subject. 專論;專文;專題研究報告。

mono·lin·gual /,mɒnə'lɪŋgwəl ; ,mɑnə'lɪŋgwəl/ *adj* using only one language: 只用一種語言的: *The OALDCE is a ~ dictionary.* 牛津高級當代英語字典是部只用一種語言的字典。

mono·lith /'mɒnəlɪθ ; 'mɑnḷ,ɪθ/ *n* single upright block of stone (as a pillar or monument). 獨石;獨立柱或碑。~**ic** /,mɒnə'lɪθɪk ; ,mɑnḷ'ɪθɪk/ *adj* of or like a ~. 獨石的;似獨石的。

mono·logue /'mɒnəlɒg *US:* -lɔːg ; 'mɑnḷ,ɔg/ *n* scene in a play, etc in which only one person speaks; dramatic composition for a single performer; soliloquy. 戲劇等中的獨白場景;獨演劇本;獨脚戲;自言自語;獨白。

mono·mania /,mɒnəʊ'meɪnɪə ; ,mɑnə'menɪə/ *n* [U] state of mind, sometimes amounting to madness, caused by the attention being occupied exclusively by one idea or subject; [C] instance of this. 偏執狂;對一事的狂熱;單狂;偏癖;其實例。⇨ paranoia. **mono·maniac** /,mɒnəʊ'meɪnɪæk ; ,mɑnə'menɪ,æk/ *n* sufferer from ~. 患偏執狂的人;有偏癖的人。

mono·plane /'mɒnəpleɪn ; 'mɑnə,plen/ *n* aircraft with one wing on each side of the fuselage. 單翼飛機。⇨ biplane.

mon·op·ol·ize /mə'nɒpəlaɪz ; mə'nɑpḷ,aɪz/ *vt* [VP 6A] get or keep a monopoly of; control the whole of, so that others cannot share: 專利;壟斷;獨佔: *Don't let me ~ the conversation.* 不要光讓我一個人講話。 **mon·op·ol·iz·ation** /mə,nɒpəlaɪ'zeɪʃn *US:* -lɪ'z- ; mə,nɑpḷə'zeʃən/ *n*

mon·op·oly /mə'nɒpəlɪ ; mə'nɑplɪ/ *n* (*pl* -lies) [C] **1** (possession of the) sole right to supply; the supply or service thus controlled. 專利權;專利權之佔有;專賣;獨佔事業。 **2** complete possession of trade, talk, etc: 商業、談話等的獨佔;壟斷: *In many countries tobacco is a government ~.* 在許多國家中,煙草是政府的專賣事業。 **3** anything over which one person or group has control and which is not or cannot be shared by others. 專利品;專賣品。 **mon·op·ol·ist** /-lɪst ; -lɪst/ *n* person who has a ~. 專利者;專賣者。 **mon·op·ol·is·tic** /mə,nɒpə'lɪstɪk ; mə,nɑpə'lɪstɪk/ *adj*

mono·rail /'mɒnəʊreɪl ; 'mɑnə,rel/ *n* single rail serving as a track for vehicles; railway system for vehicles using such a rail, or for vehicles suspended from one. (供車輛行駛的)單軌;單軌鐵道;單軌索道(供吊車行駛者)。

mono·syl·lable /'mɒnəsɪləbl ; 'mɑnə,sɪləbl/ *n* word of one syllable. 單音節的字。**mono·syl·labic** /,mɒnəsɪ'læbɪk ; ,mɑnəsɪ'læbɪk/ *adj* having only one syllable; made up of words of one syllable: 單音節的;由單音節的字組成的: *monosyllabic answers*, eg 'Yes' or 'No'. 單音字的回答(如答 Yes 或 No)。

mono·theism /'mɒnəʊθiːɪzəm ; 'mɑnəθi,ɪzəm/ *n* doctrine that there is only one God (contrasted with *polytheism*). 一神論;一神教(與 polytheism 相對)。 **mono·theist** /'mɒnəʊθiːɪst ; 'mɑnəθiɪst/ *n* believer in ~. 信一神教(論)者。**mono·the·istic** /,mɒnəʊθiː'ɪstɪk ; ,mɑnəθi'ɪstɪk/ *adj*

mono·tone /'mɒnətəʊn ; 'mɑnə,ton/ *n* (keeping a) level tone in talking or singing; utterance without change of pitch: 單調;音調無變化;平音: *speak in a ~.* 語調無變化地說話。

mon·ot·onous /mə'nɒtənəs ; mə'nɑtṇəs/ *adj* (uninteresting because) unchanging, without variety: 單調的;千篇一律的;單調乏味的: *a ~ voice*, one with little change of pitch; 單調的聲音; *~ work.* 單調乏味的工作。 **~·ly** *adv* **mon·ot·ony** /mə'nɒtənɪ ; mə'nɑtṇɪ/ *n* [U] the state of being monotonous; wearisome absence of variety. 單調;千篇一律。

mono·type /'mɒnətaɪp ; 'mɑnə,taɪp/ *n* (P) composing machine that casts, sets and assembles type letter by letter. (商標)單式自動鑄排機;自動鑄字機。

mon·ox·ide /mɒ'nɒksaɪd ; mɑn'ɑksaɪd/ *n* [C, U] oxide containing one oxygen atom in the molecule: 一氧化物: *carbon ~*, **(CO)**. 一氧化碳。

Mon·roe /mən'rəʊ ; mən'ro/ *n* ~ **doctrine**, (based on statements by James Monroe, US president (1817–1825) in 1823) US policy of opposing any interference by European powers in N and S America. 門羅主義(基於美國總統(1817—1825)詹姆士•門羅 1823 年所發表的言論,反對歐洲强國對南北美洲事務作任何干涉)。

Mon·sieur /mə'sjɜː(r) ; mə'sjɝ/ *n* (abbr 略作 **M**) (*pl* Messieurs /meɪ'sjɜː(r) ; 'mɛsɚz/) French title before the name of a man; Mr, sir, gentleman: (法)先生(冠於男子姓名前): *M~ Hercule Poirot;* 鄂居勒・布瓦后先生; *yes, ~.* 是的,先生。

Mon·si·gnor /mɒn'siːnjə(r) ; mɑn'sinjɚ/ *n* (title of honour given to) certain priests in the RC Church. 閣下(對某些天主教教士的尊稱)。

mon·soon /mɒn'suːn ; mɑn'sun/ *n* seasonal wind blowing in the Indian Ocean from SW from April to October (*wet ~*) and from NE during the other months (*dry ~*); the rainy season that comes with the wet ~. 季風(印度洋上四月至十月期間吹自西南的'濕季風',在其他月份中吹自東北的'乾季風');濕季風所帶來的雨季。

mon·ster /'mɒnstə(r) ; 'mɑnstɚ/ *n* **1** abnormally misshapen animal or plant; person or thing of extraordinary size, shape or qualities; (in stories) imaginary creature (eg half animal, half bird): 畸形的動物或植物;大小、形狀或癖性奇特的人或物;(故事中的)怪物;巨獸;怪獸(如半獸半鳥之怪物): *Mermaids, griffins and dragons are ~s.* 雌人魚、鷹頭獅身怪獸和龍都是怪物。 *A five-legged dog is a ~.* 五條腿的狗是一隻怪獸。 **2** person who is remarkable for some bad or evil quality: 惡人;殘忍的人: *a ~ of cruelty / ingratitude;* 極殘酷的人(忘恩負義的惡徒); *the Commissioners of Inland Revenue, those ~s* *of greed.* 國內稅務官,那些貪婪的惡吏。 **3** (attrib) huge: (形容用法)巨大的: *a ~ ship.* 大船。

mon·strance /ˈmɒnstrəns ; ˈmɑnstrəns/ *n* (in RC Church) vessel in which the Host is exposed for veneration. (天主教)聖餅匣。

mon·strous /ˈmɒnstrəs ; ˈmɑnstrəs/ *adj* **1** of or like a monster; of great size. (似)畸形之動物或植物的; (像)怪物的; 巨大的。 **2** atrocious; causing horror and disgust: 兇暴的;恐怖的;令人厭惡的: *~ crimes.* 恐怖的罪行。 **3** (colloq) quite absurd; incredible; scandalous: (俗) 荒誕的;難以置信的;可恥的: *It's perfectly ~ that men should be paid more than women for the same job.* 做相同的工作,而男人所得報酬比女人多,這簡直是荒誕透頂。 **~·ly** *adv*

mon·stros·ity /mɒnˈstrɒsətɪ ; mɑnˈstrɑsətɪ/ *n* (*pl* -ties) [U] state of being ~; [C] monster; hideous object, building, etc. 畸形;怪異;怪獸;怪物;令人恐怖的東西、建築物等。

mon·tage /ˈmɒntɑːʒ *US:* mɒnˈtɑːʒ ; mɑnˈtɑʒ/ *n* (F) [U] selection, cutting and arrangement of photographic film, etc to make a consecutive whole; process of using many pictures, designs, etc sometimes superimposed, to make a composite picture. (法)蒙太奇(把已經拍好的許多鏡頭等加以選擇、剪接及編排成連貫的影片);鏡頭剪輯;集錦剪輯(用許多圖片、圖案等,有時予以重叠,以拼湊成一幅集錦圖片的過程)。

month /mʌnθ ; mʌnθ/ *n* **calendar ~,** any of the twelve parts into which the year is divided; period of time from a day in one ~ to the corresponding day in the next ~ (eg 2 Jan to 2 Feb). 曆月;月;一個月的時間(如自一月二日至二月二日)。**lunar ~,** period in which the moon makes a complete revolution round the earth; period of 28 days: 太陰月(月球繞地球一週的期間);二十八天的期間: *a baby of three ~s/a three-~-old baby.* 三個月大的嬰孩。*In which ~ were you born?* 你是幾月生的? *I shall be back this day ~,* four weeks from today. 我將在下個月的今天回來。***a ~ of Sundays,*** a very long time: 很長的一段時間: *Never in a ~ of Sundays!* 決不!永不! **~·ly** *adj, adv* done, happening, published, etc, once a ~; valid for one ~: 每月一次的(地);每月出版一次的(地);有效一個月的(地): *a ~ly season ticket,* eg for railway travel. 月票(如乘火車用的)。 □ *n* **1** periodical issued once a ~. 月刊雜誌。 **2** (*pl* -lies) (colloq, dated use) occurrence of menstruation. (俗,過時用語)月經。

monu·ment /ˈmɒnjʊmənt ; ˈmɑnjəmənt/ *n* **1** building, column, statue, etc serving to keep alive the memory of a person or event: 紀念館;紀念碑;紀念像;紀念物: *a ~ to soldiers killed in the war.* 陣亡將士紀念碑。 **the M~,** the column in London that commemorates the Great Fire of London in 1666. 倫敦(1666年)大火紀念塔。 **2 Ancient M~s,** objects, of special historic interest, such as prehistoric fortifications and remains, old buildings and bridges (often preserved by official bodies). 古跡;名勝(例如史前的防禦工事和遺跡,古老的建築物和橋樑等,通常由政府機構保管之)。 **3** piece of scholarship or research that deserves to be remembered; work of literature or science of lasting value: 值得紀念的學術或研究成就; 有永久價值的文學作品或科學研究成果: *a ~ of learning.* 學術上的不朽成就。

monu·men·tal /ˌmɒnjʊˈmentl ; ˌmɑnjəˈmɛntl/ *adj* **1** of, serving for, a monument: 紀念物的;做爲紀念的: *a ~ inscription;* 碑銘; *~ masons,* eg making tombstones. 碑匠。 **2** (of books, studies, etc) of lasting value: (指著作、研究等)不朽的: *a ~ production,* eg *the Oxford English Dictionary.* 不朽的作品(如牛津英文字典)。 **3** (of qualities, buildings, tasks) very great: (指性質、建築物、工作)巨大的: *~ ignorance.* 極度的愚蠢。

moo /muː ; mu/ *n* sound made by a cow. 牛鳴聲。 □ *vi* (*pt* mooed) make the sound moo. 作牛鳴聲。 **ˈmoo-cow** *n* (child's word for) cow. (兒語)牛。

mooch /muːtʃ ; mutʃ/ *vi* [VP2C] **~ *about,*** (colloq) loiter about: (俗)徘徊;閒蕩: *out-of-work men ~ing about (the streets)* (在街上)閒蕩的失業男人。

mood[1] /muːd ; mud/ *n* [C] state of mind or spirits: 心境;情緒: *in a merry ~;* 心情快樂; *in the ~ for work,* inclined to work; 想工作; *not in the ~ for serious music.* 不想聽嚴肅的音樂。 *He's a man of ~s,* his ~s change often. 他是喜怒無常的人。 **~y** *adj* (-ier, -iest) **1** having ~s that often change. 心情變化不定的。 **2** gloomy; bad-tempered. 憂鬱的;易怒的。 **~·ily** /-ɪlɪ ; əlɪ/ *adv* **ˈ~i·ness** *n*

mood[2] /muːd ; mud/ *n* (gram) one of the groups of forms that a verb may take to show whether things are regarded as certain, possible, doubtful, etc: (文法)語氣(表示事物之確實性、可能性或可疑性等的動詞形式之一): *the indicative/imperative/subjunctive ~.* 直述(祈使,假設)語氣。

moon[1] /muːn ; mun/ *n* **1 the ~,** the body which moves round the earth once in a month and shines at night by light reflected from the sun: (指繞地球運行,並在夜間藉反射太陽的光而發亮的天體)月球: *Men have explored the surface of the ~.* 人類已經勘測了月球的表面。 *The ~ shone brightly.* 月光皎潔。***a + adj + ~,*** this body regarded as an object distinct from that visible in other times: (指某一時期出現而與其他時間所見有別的)月亮; 月: *a new/half/full ~.* 新月(半月;滿月)。⇨ new; ⇨ the illus at phase. 參看 phase 之插圖。***a/no ~,*** the ~ visible/invisible: 有(沒有)月亮: *There was no ~,* It was a night with no ~ visible in the sky. 那晚沒有月亮。 *Is there a ~ tonight?* 今晚有月亮嗎? ***cry for the ~,*** yearn for sth impossible. 渴望不可能的事物。 ***promise sb the ~,*** make extravagant promises. 許下過份的諾言。 **2** (compounds) (複合字) **ˈ~·beam** *n* ray of ~light. 一道月光。**ˈ~ buggy/rover** *n* vehicle for travelling on the ~. 月球車(行駛於月球上的一種單座車)。 **ˈ~·flower** *n* ox-eye daisy. 牛眼菊。 **ˈ~·light** *n* light of the ~; 月光; (often attrib) (常作形容用法) *go swimming in the ~light/by ~light;* 月光下去游泳; *a ~light night.* 月夜。**ˈ~·lit** *adj* lit by the ~: 被月光照亮的: *a ~lit scene/landscape.* 月夜的景色(風景)。 **ˈ~·shine** *n* **(a)** light of the ~. 月光。**(b)** foolish or idle talk, ideas, etc. 愚昧的言談;空談;妄想。**(c)** (US) whisky or other spirits illicitly distilled or smuggled. (美)私酒(私釀或走私的)。**ˈ~·stone** *n* semi-precious felspar. 月長石;月石。 **ˈ~·struck** *adj* wild and wandering in the mind (supposedly as the result of the ~'s influence). 發狂的(被認爲是受月光的影響)。 **3** [C] satellite of other planets: (除地球外其他行星的)衛星: *How many ~s has the planet Jupiter?* 木星有幾個衛星? **4** [C] (poet) month. (詩)一個月的時間。***once in a blue ~,*** (colloq) rarely or never. (俗)罕有;永無。 **~·less** *adj* without a visible ~: 沒有月亮的: *a dark, ~less night.* 無月光的黑夜。

moon[2] /muːn ; mun/ *vi, vt* **1** [VP2C] **~ *about/around,*** move or look listlessly. 閒蕩;茫然注視。 **2** [VP15B] **~ *away,*** pass (time) listlessly or aimlessly: 閒度(時光): *~ away the summer holidays.* 無所事事度過暑假。**~y** *adj* (-ier, -iest) given to ~ing away the time. 迷迷糊糊地過日子的。

moor[1] /mʊə(r) ; mʊr/ *n* [C, U] (area of) open, uncultivated land, esp if covered with heather (and often, in GB, used for preserving game, esp grouse). 荒野;曠野(尤指長有石南屬植物者,在英國常被保留作松鷄類獵物之繁殖地區);松鷄類獵物保留區。 **ˈ~·fowl, ˈ~·game** *nn* (*pl* unchanged) red grouse. (複數不變)紅松鷄。**ˈ~·cock** *n* male of this. 公紅松鷄。**ˈ~·hen** *n* **(a)** female of this. 母紅松鷄。**(b)** water-hen. 鷭;水鷄。⇨ the illus at water. 參看 water 之插圖。 **ˈ~·land** /-lənd ; -ˌlænd/ *n* land consisting of open ~ and covered with heather. (長有石南的)荒地。

moor[2] /mʊə(r) ; mʊr/ *vt* [VP6A, 15A] make (a boat, ship, etc) secure (to land or buoys) by means of cables, etc. 使(船)碇泊。'~·ing-mast *n* one for ~ing airships. 飛艇繫留塔。~·ings /'mʊərɪŋz ; 'mʊrɪŋz/ *n pl* **1** cables, anchors and chains, etc, by which a ship or boat is ~ed. 繫船的纜、錨、鏈等;繫船具;繫留錨;碇泊錨。 **2** place where a ship is ~ed. 繫船處;停船處。

Moor /mʊə(r) ; mʊr/ *n* member of the Muslim peoples of mixed Arab and Berber blood who now live in NW Africa; one of the Muslim Arabs who invaded Spain in the 8th c: 摩爾人(現居於非洲西北部之回教民族，具有阿拉伯人與柏柏人之血統;八世紀入侵西班牙之阿拉伯回教徒): *the conquest of Spain by the ~s.* 摩爾人之征服西班牙。

Moor·ish /'mʊərɪʃ ; 'mʊrɪʃ/ *adj* of the Moors and their culture: 摩爾人的;摩爾文化的: *~ palaces in Granada.* 在格拉那達的摩爾式宮殿。

moose /mu:s ; mus/ *n* (*pl* ~ or ~s /-sɪz ; -sɪz/) large sort of deer with coarse fleece and thick antlers, found in the forests of N America, and (where it is called an *elk*) in northern Europe and Asia. 麋(長有粗毛及厚角的一種大鹿,產於北美洲森林地帶,北歐及北亞,在北歐及北亞被稱爲 elk)。

moot /mu:t ; mut/ *adj* (only in) (僅用於) ***a ~ point/question,*** one about which there is uncertainty. 未決之點(問題)。□ *vt* [VP6A] raise or bring forward for discussion: 提出討論: *This question has been ~ed again.* 這問題已再度提出討論。

mop[1] /mɒp ; mɑp/ *n* **1** bundle of coarse strings, cloth, etc fastened to a long handle for cleaning floors, etc; similar material on a short handle for cleaning dishes, etc. (擦地板等用的)拖把;洗碗刷。 **2** mass of thick, untidy hair. 亂蓬蓬的頭髮。□ *vt* (-pp-) **1** [VP6A] clean with a mop: 用拖把洗擦: *mop the floor.* (用拖把)拖地板;擦地板。 **2** [VP6A, 15B] ~ ***(up),*** wipe (away) with, or as with, a mop: (用拖把等)擦;揩: *mop one's brow,* wipe away sweat, eg with a handkerchief; (如用手帕)擦額上的汗; *mop up a mess.* 擦掉一堆髒東西。***mop up,*** (colloq uses) finish off, make an end of: (俗)結束;做完: *mop up arrears of work;* 把耽誤的工作做完; *mopping-up operations* (in a military campaign, getting rid of defeated remnants of enemy troops). 掃蕩戰。***mop the floor with sb,*** defeat him completely, eg in a debate. 徹底擊敗某人(如在辯論中)。

mop[2] /mɒp ; mɑp/ *vi* (-pp-) (archaic or liter; only in) (古或文;僅用於) ***mop and mow,*** make grimaces. 扮鬼臉。

mope /məʊp ; mop/ *vi* [VP2A, C] pity oneself, give oneself up to sadness or low spirits: 鬱鬱不樂: *~ (about) in the house all day.* 整天在屋裏鬱鬱不樂。□ *n* **the ~s,** low spirits: 抑鬱;沮喪: *suffer from the ~s;* 抑鬱不樂; *have a fit of the ~s.* 突然沮喪起來。

mo·ped /'məʊped ; 'mopɛd/ *n* (GB) motor-cycle with pedals and a petrol engine of low power. (英)(裝有小型引擎的)機器脚踏車。

mo·quette /mə'ket *US:* məʊ- ; mə'kɛt/ *n* [U] synthetic fabric used for carpets and soft furnishings. 毛氈(地毯及柔軟傢具等用之一種合成纖維織物)。

mo·raine /mɒ'reɪn *US:* mɔ:- ; mo'ren/ *n* heap or mass of earth, gravel, rock, etc carried down and deposited by a glacier. 冰堆石;冰磧(由冰河夾帶並堆積的泥土沙石)。 ⇨ the illus at mountain. 參看 mountain 之插圖。

moral[1] /'mɒrəl *US:* 'mɔ:rəl ; 'mɔrəl/ *adj* **1** concerning principles of right and wrong: 有關是非之原則的;道德的: *~ standards;* 道德標準; *a ~ question;* 道德問題; *the ~ sense,* the power of distinguishing right and wrong; 是非感(分辨是非的能力); *~ law;* 道德律; *~ rights/obligations,* based on ~ law; (基於道德律的)道德上的權利(義務); *~ philosophy,* ethics, the study of right and wrong in human behaviour. 倫理學;道德哲學。 **2** good and virtuous: 品行端正的: *live a ~ life;* 過規矩的生活; *a ~ man.* 品行端正的人。 **3** able to understand the difference between right and wrong: 能明辨是非的: *At what age do we become ~ beings?* 我們要到什麼年齡才能辨別是非？ **4** teaching or illustrating good behaviour: 教導良好品德的;道德教育的;有寓意的: *a ~ book/story/talk.* 有寓意的書籍(故事,言談)。 **5** (contrasted with *physical* or *practical*) connected with the sense of what is right and just: (與 physical 或 practical 相對)精神上的;道義上的: *a ~ victory,* outcome of a struggle in which the weaker side is comforted because it has established the righteousness of its cause. 精神勝利。***a ~ certainty,*** sth so probable that there is little room for doubt. 確實可靠的事;非常可能的事。***~ courage/cowarpice,*** strength/lack of strength to face contempt or ridicule rather than do wrong. (缺少)寧受輕蔑或嘲笑而不肯做壞事的勇氣;道德上的勇氣(怯弱)。***give sb ~ support,*** help by saying that he has justice and right on his side. 給某人道義上(或精神上)的支持(如申言正義是在他這一邊)。~**ly** /-rəlɪ ; -rəlɪ/ *adv* in a ~ manner: 道德上: *M~ly he is all that she desired.* 就道德而言,她對他十分滿意。

moral[2] /'mɒrəl *US:* 'mɔ:rəl ; 'mɔrəl/ *n* **1** that which a story, event or experience teaches: 教訓;寓意: *And the ~ of this story is that a young girl should not speak to strange men.* 這個故事的教訓是年輕的女子不應和陌生男人談話。*You may draw your own ~ from this.* 你可以從這個找出對你自己的教訓。 **2** (*pl*) moral habits; standards of behaviour; principles of right and wrong: (複)品行;風化;行爲的標準;是非的原則;道德;倫理: *a man without ~s;* 沒有道德的人;不講是非的人; *a man of loose ~s;* 品行不佳的人; *improve the ~s of a country.* 改良一國的風氣。

mo·rale /mə'rɑ:l *US:* -'ræl ; mə'ræl/ *n* [U] state of discipline and spirit (in a person, an army, a nation, etc); temper, state of mind, as expressed in action: (個人、軍隊、國家等之)士氣;風氣;(表現於行爲的)性情;心境: *The army recovered its ~ and fighting power.* 這軍隊恢復了士氣與戰鬥力。*The failing ~ of the enemy* (= Their loss of confidence in themselves) *helped to shorten the war.* 敵軍士氣的衰落使戰爭縮短。

mor·al·ist /'mɒrəlɪst *US:* 'mɔ:r- ; 'mɔrəlɪst/ *n* person who points out morals(1); person who practises or teaches morality. 訓誨師;道德家;德育家。

mor·al·is·tic /ˌmɒrə'lɪstɪk *US:* ˌmɔ:r- ; ˌmɔrə'lɪstɪk/ *adj* concerned with morals(2). 注重道德的;說教的。

mor·al·ity /mə'rælətɪ ; mɔ'rælətɪ/ *n* (*pl* -ties) **1** [U] (standards, principles, of) good behaviour: 美德;道德;道義;倫理: *Have standards of political ~ improved in recent years?* 近年來政治道德標準改進了嗎？ *Is commercial ~ high in your country?* 貴國商業道德高不高？ **2** [C] particular system of morals: 某一倫理體系或道德律: *Muslim ~.* 回教的道德律。 **3** [C] '~ ***(play),*** form of drama, popular in the 16th c, teaching good behaviour, the chief characters being personifications of virtues and vices. 道德劇;寓意劇(流行於十六世紀,劇中主角爲善與惡之化身,主旨在於勸善規過)。

mor·al·ize /'mɒrəlaɪz *US:* 'mɔ:r- ; 'mɔrəlˌaɪz/ *vt, vi* **1** [VP2A, 3A] ~ ***(about/on/upon),*** deal with moral questions; talk or write on questions of duty, right and wrong, etc: 討論道德問題;作有關職責、是非等問題之談話或寫作;說教: *~ upon the failings of the young generation.* 討論年輕一代品行缺點的問題。*Oh, do stop moralizing! None of your moralizing!* Stop preaching at me! 哦！不要說教啦！ **2** [VP6A] give a moral interpretation of. 以道德意義解釋。

mo·rass /mə'ræs ; mo'ræs/ *n* [C] stretch of low, soft, wet land; marsh; (fig) entanglement. 低而柔軟的溼地;沼澤;(喻)困境。

mora·torium /ˌmɒrə'tɔ:rɪəm *US:* ˌmɔ:r- ; ˌmɔrə-

ˈtorɪəm/ *n* (*pl* ~s or -ria /-rɪə ; -rɪə/) [C] legal authorization to delay payment of debts; agreed deferment or delay. 延期償債(令);(經同意的)延期;延緩。

mor·bid /ˈmɔːbɪd ; ˈmɔrbɪd/ *adj* **1** diseased: 疾病的: *a ~ growth*, eg a cancer or tumour; 病態的生長(如癌或瘤); *~ anatomy*, the study of diseased organs in the body. 病理解剖學。 **2** (of sb's mind or ideas) unhealthy: (指人的心思或觀念)不健全的;病態的: *a ~ imagination*, one that dwells on horrible or nasty things. 病態的想像(只想到恐怖或卑鄙的事物)。 **~·ly** *adv* **~·ity** /mɔːˈbɪdətɪ ; mɔrˈbɪdətɪ/, **~·ness** *nn* state of being ~. 病態;不健康的狀況。

mor·dant /ˈmɔːdnt ; ˈmɔrdn̩t/ *adj* biting; sarcastic: 尖酸的;諷刺的: *~ criticism;* 尖刻的批評; *a ~ wit.* 一個機智而又尖刻的人。

more /mɔː(r) ; mor/ (contrasted with *less* and *fewer;* 與 less 及 fewer 相對;⇨ many, most¹, much¹) *adj* (independent comp) greater in number, quantity, quality, degree, size, etc; additional: (獨立比較級)數目更多的;更多量的;更佳的;程度更高的;更大的;附加的: *We need ~ men/help, etc.* 我們需要更多的人(幫助等)。 *Instead of fewer helpers, we want ~.* 我們需要更多的助手,而不是更少的助手。 *Have you any ~ paper?* 你還有紙嗎? *Would you like some/a little ~ soup/a little ~ of this soup?* 你要不要再喝一點湯? □ *n* a greater amount, number, etc; an additional amount: 更大的量、數等;額外數量: *What ~ do you want?* 你還要什麼? *There are still a few ~.* 還有一些。*There is hardly any ~.* 差不多没有了。 *That is ~ than enough.* 那是太多了。 *May I have one ~?* 我可以再要一個嗎? *I should like as many ~*, the same number again. 我願意照同樣的數目再要一些。 *I hope to see ~ of you,* to see you ~ often. 我希望以後時常和你見面。 □ *adv* **1** (forming the comparative degree of most *adjj* and *advv* of more than two syllables and of some of two syllables, esp if stressed on the first): (構成含有三個或三個以上音節的大多數形容詞及副詞的比較級;某些兩音節的字,尤指重音在前者,亦可用more): *~ beautiful/useful/interesting/serious* (*than...*); (比…)更美麗(更有用,更有趣,更嚴重); *~ easily/quietly/foolishly* (*than...*). (比…)更容易地(更安靜地,更愚昧地)。***and what is ~***, ~ important, serious, etc (according to context). 更重要者;更嚴重者;再者;更有甚者(視上下文而定)。 **2** to a greater extent; in a greater degree: 更多地;更大地: *You need to sleep ~*, ie ~ than you sleep now. 你需要更多的睡眠。 *You must attend to your work ~.* 你必須更專心於你的工作。 *He was ~ frightened than hurt.* 他沒有受什麼傷,倒是受驚不小。 *He likes summer ~ than autumn.* 他喜歡夏天甚於秋天。 **3** again: 再: *Once ~, please.* 請再來一次。*I shall not go there any ~*, ever again. 我再也不去那兒了。*We saw him no ~*, did not see him again. 我們再也沒看到他了。 **4** *~ and ~*, by ~ stages, degrees, etc: 越來越…: *The story gets ~ and ~ exciting.* 故事越來越動人。*Life is becoming ~ and ~ expensive.* 生活費用越來越昂貴。 ***~ or less***, about: 大約;多少有點兒: *It's an hour's journey, ~ or less.* 大約一小時的路程。 **5** (with a *n*, equivalent to an *adj*): (與名詞連用,相當於形容詞): *(The) ~ fool you to believe him,* You are, if you believe him, foolish in a higher degree. 假如你相信他,你就蠢不可言了。*It had ~ the characteristic* (= was ~ characteristic) *of a foolish dream than of a nightmare.* 說它是夢魘還不如說它是個荒謬的夢。*(The) ~'s the pity*, It is, to that extent, a greater pity. 那就更可惜了。⇨ also the (*adv*). ***no ~***, neither: 亦不;都不: *A: 'I can't understand this at all.' B: 'No ~ can I.'* 甲說:'我根本不懂這個。'乙說:'我也不懂。' ***no ~... than:*** 和…一樣不…;和…都不: *He's no ~ able to read Chinese than I am,* He is as unable to do so as I am. 他和我都看不懂中文。

mo·rello /məˈreləʊ ; məˈrɛlo/ *n* (*pl* ~s /-ləʊz ; -loz/) ~ **(cherry)**, bitter kind of cherry (used for jam). 黑櫻桃(味苦,作果醬用)。

more·over /mɔːˈrəʊvə(r) ; morˈovɚ/ *adv* further; besides; in addition (to this). 再者;此外;而且。

mores /ˈmɔːreɪz ; ˈmoriz/ *n pl* (formal) customs, usages, conventions, regarded as essential to a social group. (正式用語)某一社會團體的傳統習俗。

Mo·resque /mɔːˈresk ; məˈrɛsk/ *adj* (of style, design, decoration, architecture) Moorish. (指型式、設計、裝飾、建築)摩爾式的。

mor·ga·natic /ˌmɔːgəˈnætɪk ; ˌmɔrgəˈnætɪk/ *adj* ~ **marriage**, one between a man of high rank (eg a prince) and a woman of lower rank, who remains in her lower social station, the children having no claim to succeed to the property, titles, etc, of their father. 貴賤婚姻(貴族,如王子,和身份較低的女子的婚姻,女方保留原有較低身份,子女不得繼承父親財產、頭銜等)。

morgue /mɔːg ; mɔrg/ *n* **1** building in which bodies of persons found dead are kept until they are identified and claimed by members of their families. (待家人認領屍體的)陳屍所。⇨ mortuary. **2** file (in the office of a newspaper or magazine) with obituary notices of famous people still living (ready for use when they die). (報館或雜誌社資料室中的尚活着的)名人檔案(收集其生平簡傳,準備其死亡時登載訃聞之用)。

mori·bund /ˈmɒrɪbʌnd *US:* ˈmɔːr- ; ˈmɔrəˌbʌnd/ *adj* at the point of death; about to come to an end: 將死的;將要消滅的: *~ civilizations.* 即將消滅的文明。

Mor·mon /ˈmɔːmən ; ˈmɔrmən/ *n, adj* (member) of a religious organization founded in the US in 1830, officially called 'The Church of Jesus Christ of Latter-day Saints'. 摩門教派的;摩門教徒(摩門教是基督教的一個宗派,1830年創於美國,正式名稱爲'末世聖徒基督教會')。**~·ism** /-ɪzəm ; -ˌɪzəm/ *n*

morn /mɔːn ; mɔrn/ *n* (poet) morning. (詩)早晨。

morn·ing /ˈmɔːnɪŋ ; ˈmɔrnɪŋ/ *n* **1** [C, U] early part of the day between dawn and noon (or, more generally, before the midday meal): 早晨;上午: *in/during the ~;* 在早晨;在上午; *this ~;* 今早;今天上午; *yesterday/tomorrow ~;* 昨天(明天)早上; *every ~;* 每天上午; *on Sunday/Monday, etc ~;* 星期日(星期一等)上午; *the ~ of May the 1st;* 五月一日上午; *one ~ last week;* 上星期某一天上午; *one summer ~;* 一個夏天的早晨; *a few ~s ago;* 幾天前上午; *several ~s lately.* 最近幾個上午。*When he awoke it was ~.* 當他醒來時,已經是早晨了。 **2** (attrib) (形容用法): *a ~ walk;* 早晨的散步; *an early ~ swim.* 清晨的游泳。ˈ**~ coat**, long black coat with the front cut away. 常禮服上衣。ˈ**~ dress**, ~ coat with striped trousers. 常禮服(包含常禮服上衣及條紋褲)。ˌ**M~ ˈPrayer**, service used in the Church of England at ~ service. (英國國教會的)晨禱。**the ~ star**, Venus, or other bright star seen about dawn. 金星;晨星;曉星。**the ~ watch**, (at sea) period of duty, 4 a m to 8 a m. (航海)早班(上午4時至8時)。ˌ**~-ˈglory** *n* climbing plant of the convolvulus family, with flowers that fade by midday. 牽牛花。ˈ**~-room** *n* sitting-room for the ~. 上午用的起居間。ˈ**~ sickness** *n* (feeling of) nausea early in the morning, during the first few months of pregnancy. 孕婦晨吐;孕婦惡心(婦女懷孕最初幾個月期中早晨時的作嘔感覺)。

mo·rocco /məˈrɒkəʊ ; məˈrɑko/ *n* [U] soft leather made from goatskins. (山羊皮製成的)鞣皮;摩洛哥皮。

mo·ron /ˈmɔːrɒn ; ˈmorɑn/ *n* feeble-minded person (with a mental level not so low as imbeciles or idiots); (colloq) stupid person. 輕度低能者(智能程度高於 imbeciles 或 idiots 者);(俗)笨人;傻瓜。**~ic** /məˈrɒnɪk ; moˈrɑnɪk/ *adj*

mo·rose /məˈrəʊs ; moˈros/ *adj* sullen; ill-tempered; unsocial. 抑鬱的;壞脾氣的;不與人來往的;孤僻的。**~·ly** *adv* **~·ness** *n*

mor·pheme /ˈmɔːfiːm ; ˈmɔrfim/ *n* (ling) smallest

meaningful part into which a word can be divided: (語言)詞位(一個字可分割成的最小意義單位): *'Run-s' contains two ～s and 'un-like-ly' contains three.* runs 一字含兩個詞位(卽 run 和 s),unlikely 一字含三個詞位(卽 un, like 及 ly)。

Mor·pheus /ˈmɔːfɪəs ; ˈmɔrfɪəs/ *n* (Gk myth) god of dreams and sleep. (希神)睡夢之神。

mor·phia /ˈmɔːfɪə ; ˈmɔrfɪə/, **mor·phine** /ˈmɔːfiːn ; ˈmɔrfin/ *nn* [U] drug, usu in the form of a white powder, made from opium and used for relieving pain. 嗎啡(由鴉片製成的一種止痛劑,通常爲白色粉狀)。

mor·phol·ogy /mɔːˈfɒlədʒɪ ; mɔrˈfɑlədʒɪ/ *n* [U] **1** (biol) branch of biology dealing with the form and structure of animals and plants. (生物)生物形態學。 **2** (ling) study of the morphemes of a language and of how they are combined to make words. (語言)有關一語言的詞位及其組字的研究;字形學;語形學。⇨ syntax.

mor·ris dance /ˈmɒrɪs dɑːns *US:* ˈmɔːrɪs dæns ; ˈmɔrɪs dæns/ *n* old English folk-dance for men. 英國古時一種(男人)舞蹈。

mor·row /ˈmɒrəʊ *US:* ˈmɔːr- ; ˈmɔro/ *n* **1** (liter) the next day after the present or after any given day: (文)翌日;次日: *What had the ～ in store for them?* 他們後來的遭遇如何? **2** (archaic) morning: (古)早晨: *Good ～!* 早安!

Morse /mɔːs ; mɔrs/ *n* ˈ**～ (code)**, system of dots and dashes or short and long sounds or flashes of light, representing letters of the alphabet and numbers, to be signalled by lamp, radio, etc: 摩爾斯電碼(用點和線或長短的聲音、閃光代表字母及數字,可由燈光、無線電等發送): *a message in ～;* 用摩爾斯電碼傳達的消息; *the ～ alphabet.* 摩爾斯電碼。

mor·sel /ˈmɔːsl ; ˈmɔrsl/ *n* [C] tiny piece (esp of food); mouthful: 小塊;一小片(尤指食物);一口: *I haven't had a ～ of food since I left the house.* 我從家裏出來到現在還沒有吃過一點點東西。 *What a dainty／choice ～!* 多精美的一點食物!

mor·tal /ˈmɔːtl ; ˈmɔrtl/ *adj* **1** (contrasted with *immortal*) which must die; which cannot live for ever: (與 immortal 相對)必死的;不能永存的: *Man is ～,* All men must die. 人人必有一死;人是會死的。 *Here lie the ～ remains of...,* (eg on a tombstone) Here is buried what now remains of the body of.... …葬於此處(刻於墓碑等上的詞句)。 **2** causing death: 致命的: *a ～ wound.* 致命傷。 *His injuries proved ～.* 他的傷成了致命傷。 **～ sins,** causing spiritual death. 大罪;(宗教)使靈魂死亡的罪。 **3** lasting until death: 持續到死的: *～ hatred.* 終身的憎恨。 **～ combat,** only ended by the death of one of the fighters. 殊死戰;拚命的爭鬥;不死不休的戰鬥。 **～ enemies,** whose enmity will not end until death. 死敵;不共戴天的仇敵。 **4** accompanying death: 垂死的;臨終的: *in ～ agony.* 臨死的痛苦。 **5** (colloq) extreme; very great or long: (俗)極端的;極大的;極長的: *in ～ fear;* 極大的恐懼; *in a ～ hurry.* 非常匆促。 □ *n* human being. 人。**～ly** /-təlɪ ; -tlɪ/ *adv* **1** so as to cause death: 致命地: *～ly wounded.* 受了致命傷。 **2** deeply, seriously: 深重地;嚴重地: *～ly offended.* 極爲震怒。

mor·tal·ity /mɔːˈtælətɪ ; mɔrˈtælətɪ/ *n* [U] **1** state of being mortal. 必死的狀態;不可免的死亡。 **2** number of deaths caused by sth (eg a disaster or disease): 死亡數目(如災害或疾病所造成的): *an epidemic with a heavy ～,* a large number of deaths. 造成大量死亡的流行性傳染病。 **3** death-rate: 死亡率: ˈ**～ tables,** (insurance) tables showing how long people at various ages may expect to live. (保險)死亡率表。

mor·tar¹ /ˈmɔːtə(r) ; ˈmɔrtə/ *n* [U] mixture of lime, sand and water used to hold bricks, stones, etc together in building. (建築時用以黏接磚、石等的)砂漿;灰泥。ˈ**～-board** *n* **(a)** small, flat board with a short handle on the underside, used for holding a supply of ～ (while laying bricks, etc). 灰泥板;鏝板(砌磚時盛灰泥用的底面有短把手的小平板)。 **(b)** square cap worn as part of their academic costume by members of a college, etc. (大學生等所戴的)方頂禮帽;學位帽。 □ *vt* [VP6A] join (bricks, etc) with ～. 用灰泥黏接(磚等)。

mor·tar² /ˈmɔːtə(r) ; ˈmɔrtə/ *n* **1** bowl of hard material in which substances are crushed with a pestle. 臼;研鉢。⇨ the illus at pestle. 參看 pestle 之揷圖。 **2** (mil) cannon for firing shells at high angles. (軍)迫擊砲;臼砲。

mort·gage /ˈmɔːgɪdʒ ; ˈmɔrgɪdʒ/ *vt* [VP6A, 14] **～ *(to) (for),*** give sb a claim on (property) as a security for payment of a debt or loan: 抵押: *～ a house (to sb for £20 000);* 將一幢房子抵押(給某人,借款二萬鎊); *land that may be ～d.* 可以抵押的土地。 □ *n* act of mortgaging; agreement about this: 抵押;抵押單據(契約): *raise a ～ (on one's house) from a bank.* (把房子)抵押給銀行。 *I can buy the house only if a ～ for £20000 is obtainable.* 只要能抵押借到二萬鎊,我就能買這幢房子。 *We must pay off the ～ this year.* 我們今年必須還清抵押借款。***be ～d up to the hilt,*** have the maximum ～ possible (on property). (財產)抵押到可能的最高額。 **mort·gagee** /ˌmɔːgɪˈdʒiː ; ˌmɔrgɪˈdʒi/ *n* person to whom property is ～d. 承受抵押者;貸款人。 **mort·gagor** /ˌmɔːgɪˈdʒɔː(r) *US:* ˈmɔːrgɪdʒər ; ˈmɔrgɪdʒə/ *n* person who gives a ～ on his property. 抵押人;借款人。

mor·tice /ˈmɔːtɪs ; ˈmɔrtɪs/ *n* ⇨ mortise.

mor·ti·cian /mɔːˈtɪʃn ; mɔrˈtɪʃən/ *n* (US) funeral director; undertaker. (美)殯儀業者。

mor·tify /ˈmɔːtɪfaɪ ; ˈmɔrtəˌfaɪ/ *vt, vi* (*pt, pp* -fied) **1** [VP6A] cause (sb) to be ashamed, humiliated, or hurt in his feelings: 使(某人)蒙羞、受屈辱或感情受傷害: *mortified by sb's rudeness;* 被某人的粗暴所羞辱; *feel mortified at one's failure to pass an examination;* 因考試不及格而感到羞恥; *a ～ing defeat.* 屈辱的失敗。 **2** [VP6A] ***～ the flesh,*** discipline bodily passions, overcome bodily desires. 抑制肉體的情慾;克制肉體的慾望。 **3** [VP2A] (of flesh, eg round a wound) decay, be affected with gangrene. (指肌肉,如傷口周圍者)潰爛;生壞疽。 **mor·ti·fi·ca·tion** /ˌmɔːtɪfɪˈkeɪʃn ; ˌmɔrtəfəˈkeʃən/ *n* [U] ～ing or being mortified (all senses). 羞辱;屈辱;制慾;壞疽。

mor·tise, mor·tice /ˈmɔːtɪs ; ˈmɔrtɪs/ *n* hole (usu rectangular) cut in a piece of wood, etc to receive the end of another piece (the *tenon*). (通常爲長方形的)枘穴;榫眼。ˈ**～ lock,** secure lock which is fitted inside the woodwork (of a door, etc), not screwed on to the surface. (不在木器如門等表面上螺絲,而在其內部的)榫眼接合。 □ *vt* [VP15A, B] join or fasten in this way: 以枘穴接牢;上榫: *～ two beams together;* 把兩根梁用榫接在一起; *～ one beam to／into another.* 把一根梁接榫到另一根梁。

mor·tu·ary /ˈmɔːtʃərɪ *US:* -tʃʊerɪ ; ˈmɔrtʃʊˌɛrɪ/ *n* (*pl* -ries) room or building (eg part of a hospital) to which dead bodies are taken to be kept until burial; (attrib) of death or burial: 停屍處;太平間;(形容用法)死的;埋葬的: *～ rites.* 葬儀;葬禮。

mo·saic /məʊˈzeɪɪk ; moˈze·ɪk/ *n, adj* (form or work of art) in which designs, pictures, etc are made by fitting together differently coloured bits of stone, etc: 鑲嵌細工;鑲嵌的藝術品;鑲嵌細工的: *a design in ～;* 鑲嵌細工的圖案; *a ～ pavement／ceiling.* 嵌花的地面(天花板)。

Mo·saic /məʊˈzeɪɪk ; moˈze·ɪk/ *adj* of Moses. 摩西(舊約聖經中的先知)的。**(the) ～ law,** the first five books of the Old Testament. 摩西的律法(卽舊約聖經的前五卷)。

mo·selle /məʊˈzel ; moˈzɛl/ *n* dry, white wine from the valley of the River M～ (in W Germany). 莫塞爾酒(產於西德莫塞爾河流域的無甜味白葡萄酒)。

mosey /ˈməʊzɪ ; ˈmozɪ/ *vi* [VP2A, C] **～ *(along),*** (sl) amble aimlessly. (俚)漫步;徘徊。

Mos·lem /ˈmɒzləm ; ˈmɑzləm/ *n, adj* = Muslim.

mosque /mɒsk ; mɑsk/ *n* building in which Muslims worship Allah. 回教的寺院;清眞寺。

a mosque

mos·quito /məˈskiːtəʊ ; məˈskito/ *n* (*pl* ~es /-təʊz ; -toz/) small, flying, blood-sucking insect, esp the sort that spreads malaria. 蚊;(尤指)瘧蚊。⇨ the illus at insect. 參看 insect 之挿圖。**ˈ~-net** *n* net, hung over a bed, through which ~es cannot fly. 蚊帳。**ˈ~-craft** *n* (collective *pl*) small, armed ships with high speed and able to manoeuvre easily. (集合複數)迅速敏捷的小艦艇;蚊式艇。

moss /mɒs *US:* mɔːs ; mɔs/ *n* [U] sorts of small green or yellow plant growing in thick masses on wet surfaces: 苔;蘚: *~-covered rocks/roofs/tree-trunks.* 生滿了青苔的岩石(屋頂,樹幹)。***A rolling stone gathers no ~,*** (prov) A person who too frequently changes his occupation or who never settles in one place will not succeed in life. (諺)滾石不生苔,轉業不聚財(喻人若不能專心一事,時常改動,則難望有成)。**ˈ~-grown** *adj* covered with growing ~. 生苔的。**~y** *adj* (-ier, -iest) covered with ~; like ~: 生苔的;似苔的: *~y green.* 苔綠色。

most¹ /məʊst ; most/ (contrasted with *least* and *fewest;* 與 least 和 fewest 相對; ⇨ many, more, much¹) *adj, n* **1** (independent superl) (the) greatest in number, quantity, degree, etc: (獨立最高級)最多數的;最大量的;最高程度的: *Which is ~, 3, 13 or 30?* 那一個數目最大,3, 13, 還是 30? *Which of you has made (the) ~ mistakes?* 你們當中那一個犯錯誤最多? *Those who have (the) ~ money are not always (the) happiest.* 最有錢的人不一定是最快樂的。*Do the ~ you can.* 盡你所能去做。***at (the) ~; at the very ~,*** not more than: 至多: *I can pay only £10 at the ~.* 我最多只能付十英鎊。*There were only 30 people at the meeting at the very ~,* There were 30 or fewer. 最多只有三十個人參加那會議。***make the ~ of,*** use to the best advantage: 充分利用;善爲利用: *We have only a few hours so we must make the ~ of our time.* 我們只有幾小時,所以我們必須善爲利用我們的時間。*She's not really beautiful, but she makes the ~ of her looks.* 她並不十分漂亮,却很會打扮。***for the ˈ~ part,*** usually; on the whole: 通常地;大體說來: *Japanese TV sets are, for the ~ part, of excellent quality.* 大體說來,日本的電視機品質優良。**2** (not preceded by *def art* in this sense) the majority of; the greater part of: (用作此義時不加定冠詞)大多數;大部份: *M~ people fear pain.* 大多數人都怕痛。*He was ill ~ of the summer.* 那年夏天他大部份時間都在病中。□ *suff* (with *preps* or *adjj* of position): (與表示位置的介詞或形容詞連用): *top~,* highest; 最高的; *in(ner)~,* furthest in. 最內的。

most² /məʊst ; most/ *adv* **1** (forming the superlative degree of nearly all *adjj* and *advv* of more than one syllable): (與絕大部分兩音節或多音節的形容詞和副詞連用,形成最高級)最: *the ~ beautiful/interesting/useful, etc;* 最美麗的(最有趣的;最有用的等); *~ carefully/accurately, etc.* 最小心地(最準確地等)。**2** (modifying *vv*, but not to be placed between a *v* and its object): (修飾動詞,但不放在動詞和它的受詞之間): *What is troubling you ~?* 什麼事情最使你煩惱? *What ~ pleased me/What pleased me ~ was that....* 最令我高興的是…。**3** (intensive, modifying an *adj*; may be preceded by *indef art*) very; exceedingly: (用於加强語氣;修飾形容詞;前面可加不定冠詞): *This is a ~ useful book.* 這是一本極其有用的書。*He was ~ polite to me.* 他對我非常有禮貌。*Your news is ~ interesting.* 你的消息非常有趣。**4** (modifying an *adv*) quite: (修飾副詞)完全地;十分: *I shall ~ certainly go.* 我一定去。**5** (dial and US colloq) almost: (方,美俗)幾乎: *M~ everybody has gone home.* 幾乎所有的人都回家去了。**~·ly** *adv* chiefly; almost all; generally: 主要地;幾乎全部;大概: *The medicine was ~ly sugar and water.* 那種藥主要成份是糖和水。*The village is ~ly of mud houses.* 這個村莊裏的房子幾乎全是泥土造的。*We are ~ly out on Sundays,* are not at home on ~ Sundays. 星期天我們通常都不在家。

mote /məʊt ; mot/ *n* particle (of dust, etc): (灰塵等的)微粒: *~s dancing in a sunbeam.* 在陽光中飛揚的塵埃。***the ~ in sb's eye,*** the fault that he has committed (trifling if compared to one's own fault). 某人眼中的灰塵(意謂看見別人的小錯而忽視自己的大錯)。⇨ Matt 7: 3. 參看新約聖經馬太福音7章3節。

mo·tel /məʊˈtel ; moˈtɛl/ *n* motorists' hotel (with rooms or cabins, a parking area, service station, etc). 汽車旅館(供駕車旅客住宿,備有停車場、汽車修護站等)。

moth /mɒθ *US:* mɔːθ ; mɔθ/ *n* sorts of winged insect flying chiefly at night, attracted by lights. 蠹;蛾。⇨ the illus at insect. 參看 insect 之挿圖。**ˈ~-ball** *n* small ball (of camphor, etc) intended to discourage clothes-~s. 防蠹丸(樟腦等製成的)。⇨ *naphthalene* at naphtha. ***in ~-balls,*** (fig) in storage: (喻)貯存中: *After ten years in ~-balls the ships were sent to be broken up.* 經過十年的封存後,那些船隻被送去拆卸。**ˈclothes-~** *n* kind which breeds in cloth, fur, etc, its grub feeding on the cloth and making holes. 蠹魚(蛀衣服的蠹蟲)。**ˈ~-eaten** *adj* eaten or destroyed by clothes-~s; (fig) antiquated; out-of-date. 蠹魚蛀過的;(喻)古舊的;過時的。**ˈ~-proof** *adj* (of fabrics) treated chemically against damage by clothes-~s. (指織物)防蛀的。□ *vt* make ~-proof: 使有防蛀功能: *~-proof carpets.* 把地毯加以防蛀處理。

mother /ˈmʌðə(r) ; ˈmʌðɚ/ *n* **1** female parent; woman who has adopted a child; woman (often 常作 *ˈhousemother*) who is in charge of children in a boarding-school or home¹(2). 母親;養母;(寄宿學校或孤兒院中照管孩子們的)保姆。**2** quality or condition that gives rise to sth: 根本;起源: *Misgovernment is often the ~ of revolt.* 治理不善常常是叛亂的根源。***Necessity is the ~ of invention,*** (prov). (諺)需要爲發明之母。**3** head of a female religious community. 婦女宗教團體的首長。**M~ Superior,** head of a convent. 女修道院院長。**4** (various uses) (各種不同用法) **the ˈ~ country, (a)** one's native land. 祖國。**(b)** a country in relation to colonies, etc. (殖民地等的)母國。**~-in-law** /ˈmʌðər ɪn lɔː ; ˈmʌðərɪnˌlɔ/ *n* (*pl* ~s-in-law) ~ of one's wife or one's husband. 岳母;婆婆。**ˌ~-of-ˈpearl** *n* [U] hard, smooth, shiny, rainbow-coloured material that forms the lining of some shells, esp the pearl-oyster, used for making buttons, ornaments, etc. (貝殼,尤指珍珠貝的)珠母層;眞珠母(貝殼裏層堅硬光滑而發亮的彩色物質,可用於製造鈕扣、裝飾品等)。**~ ship** *n* one from which other ships (eg submarines) get supplies. 母艦(其他艦艇,如潛艇等,獲取補給的艦隻)。**~ tongue** *n* one's native language. 本國語言;家鄉話。**~ wit** *n* common sense; the intelligence with which one is born. 常識;天賦。**ˈ~·hood** /-hʊd ; -ˌhʊd/ *n* [U] state of being a ～. 母性；母權；母親的地位。**～·less** *adj* having no ～. 無母親的。**'～-like** *adj* in the manner of a ～. 似母親的。**～·ly** *adj* having, showing, the tender, kind qualities of a ～. 母親的；母性的；母愛的；慈愛的。**～·li·ness** *n* □ *vt* [VP6A] take care of (as a ～ does); protect or adopt (a child) as one's own. 對…盡母職；保護或收養(小孩)視同己子。

mo·tif /məʊ'ti:f ; mo'tif/ *n* [C] theme in music for treatment and development, often one which recurs; main feature in a work of art. (音樂或藝術品的)主題；主旨。

mo·tion /'məʊʃn ; 'moʃən/ *n* **1** [U] (manner of) moving: 運動；移動；動作；動態: *If a thing is in ～, it is not at rest.* 如果一個物體在運動中，它就不在靜止中。***put／set sth in ～,*** cause it to start moving or working. 使某物開始轉動或工作。～ **picture** *n* cinema film. 電影。Cf 參較 (colloq) (俗) *moving pictures; the movies.* **2** [C] gesture; particular movement; way of moving the hand, body, etc: 姿態；特別的動作；(手、身體等的)擺動方式: *If you watch my ～s carefully you will see how the trick is performed.* 假如你仔細看我的動作，你就會明白這個戲法是怎麼變的。*All her ～s were graceful.* 她的一舉一動都很優雅。***go through the ～s,*** (colloq) do sth (that one is expected or required to do) in a perfunctory or insincere manner. (俗)敷衍塞責。**3** [C] proposal to be discussed and voted on at a meeting: 提議；動議: *On the ～ of Mr X the committee agreed to....* 由於 X 先生的提議，委員會同意…。*The ～ was adopted／carried／rejected, etc by a majority of six.* 該項提議以六票的多數票被採納(通過，否決)。**4** [C] = movement(6). □ *vt, vi* **1** [VP17, 15A, B] direct (sb) by a motion or gesture: 以動作或手勢示意: ～ *sb in／away／to a seat.* 以手勢示意某人進來(離開，就坐)。*He ～ed me to enter.* 他示意叫我進去。**2** [VP3A] ***～ to sb (to do sth),*** indicate by a gesture: 打手勢表示；向某人打手勢(請他作某事): *He ～ed to me to come nearer.* 他打手勢叫我再走近一些。**～·less** *adj* not moving; still. 不動的；靜止的。

mo·ti·vate /'məʊtɪveɪt ; 'motə,vet/ *vt* [VP6A] be the motive of; give a motive or incentive to; act as an incentive. 為…的動機；引起動機；給予刺激；激發；促使。**mo·tiv·ation** /ˌməʊtɪ'veɪʃn ; ˌmotə'veʃən/ *n*

mo·tive /'məʊtɪv ; 'motɪv/ *adj* (attrib only) causing motion: (僅作形容用法) 發動的；起動的: ～ *power／force,* eg steam, electricity. 動力(如蒸汽，電)。□ *n* [C] **1** that which causes sb to act: 動機: *actuated by low and selfish ～s;* 出於卑下而自私的動機；*do sth from ～s of kindness.* 由於仁慈的動機而作某事。*Hatred was his ～ for attacking me.* 憎恨是他攻擊我的動機。**2** = motif. **～·less** *adj* without a ～. 無動機的；無主旨的；無目的的。

mot·ley /'mɒtlɪ ; 'mɑtlɪ/ *adj* **1** of various colours: 不同顏色的；雜色的: *a ～ coat,* eg that worn by a jester or fool in olden times. 雜色花衣(如古時弄臣或小丑所穿者)。**2** of varied character or various sorts: 不同性質的；不同種類的；混雜的: *a ～ crowd,* eg people of many different occupations, social classes, etc. 混雜的人群(如由許多不同職業、社會階級等的人們所形成的群衆)。□ *n* jester's dress. 弄臣的花衣；小丑的花衣。***wear the ～,*** play the part of a fool or jester. 扮演丑角。

mo·tor /'məʊtə(r) ; 'motə/ *n* **1** device which imparts or utilizes power (esp electric power) to produce motion, but not used of a steam engine: 發動機(尤指以電力發動者，但不用以指蒸汽引擎)；馬達: *fans driven by electric ～s.* 由電動機轉動的電扇。**2** (attrib, and in compounds) having, driven by, an internal combustion engine, a diesel engine, etc which generates mechanical power: (形容用法及用於複合字中)由產生機械動力之內燃機、柴油機等所推動的: *～-vehicles;* 機動車輛；摩托車輛；*a '～-boat／-coach／-scooter, etc.* 汽艇(公共汽車，速可達機車等)。**ˌ～-as'sisted** *adj* (eg of a pedal bicycle) having an engine to help propulsion. (如指脚踏車)有發動機輔助推進的。**'～·cade** *n* (US) procession of ～ vehicles. (美)機動車輛行列；(汽)車隊。**'～-car** (also **car**) *n* closed road vehicle on four wheels with a ～ engine, with seats usu both front and back, for 2—6 people. 汽車。**'～-cycle** (colloq 俗稱 **'～-bike**) *n* open road vehicle on two wheels with a ～ engine, with one seat for the driver, and usu with space for a passenger behind the driver.

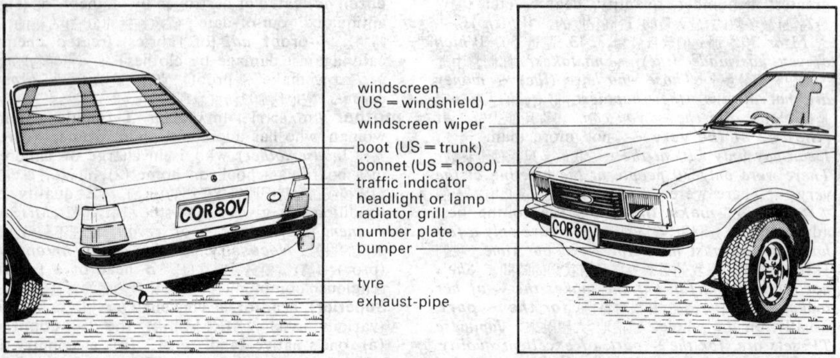

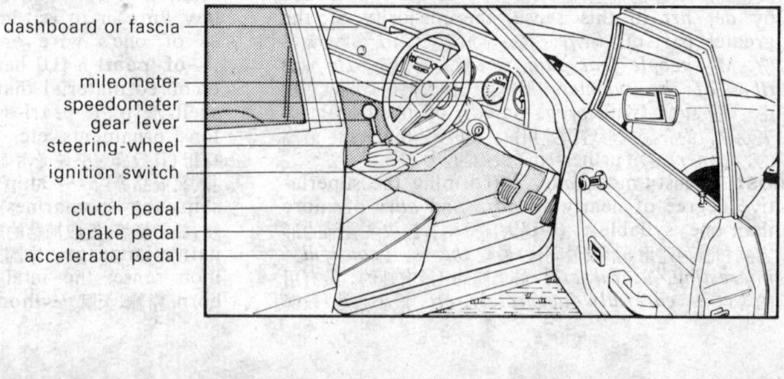

the motor-car

機車;摩托車。⇨ pillion. '~•man /-mæn ; -mən/ n (pl -men) driver of an electric vehicle. 電車或電動火車司機。'~•way n road designed and built especially for continuously moving fast traffic, with dual carriageways and going over or under other roads. 高速公路(供高速車輛行駛的雙線車道,高架於其他道路之上或穿過其他道路之下)。 **3** = ~-car (car is more usu) (car 較常用): *the '~ trade;* 汽車業; *the 'M~ Show.* 汽車展覽。 **4** muscle able to produce movement of a part of the body: 運動肌: ~ **nerve,** nerve that excites movements of a muscle or muscles. 運動神經。□ *vi* [VP2A, C] travel by ~-car: 乘汽車旅行: *~ from London to Brighton.* 乘汽車從倫敦去布來頓。 **~•ist** /-ɪst ; -ɪst/ *n* person who drives (and usu owns) a ~-car. 駕駛汽車(通常指自己的汽車)者;乘汽車旅行者。 **'~•ize** /-aɪz ; -ˌaɪz/ *vt* [VP6A] equip (troops, etc) with ~ transport. 摩托化;以汽車裝備(軍隊等)。

mottle /'mɒtl ; 'mɑtl/ *vt* [VP6A] (usu in *pp*) mark with spots or areas of different colours without a regular pattern: (通常用過去分詞)使成雜色;弄成斑駁: *the ~d skin of a snake;* 花斑紋的蛇皮; *linoleum with a ~d finish.* 有花斑紋的油地氈。

motto /'mɒtəʊ ; 'mɑto/ *n* (*pl* ~es or ~s /-təʊz ; -toz/) **1** short sentence or phrase used as a guide or rule of behaviour (eg *'Every man for himself', 'Always merry and bright'*). 箴言;座右銘(如'人人爲己各盡所能','永保喜樂')。 **2** short sentence or phrase written or inscribed on an object (eg a coat of arms) expressing a suitable sentiment; quotation prefixed to a book or chapter. (書於或刻於紋章等物品上以表示一適當之感懷的)銘辭;一本書或書中某章前面的引用句。

mou•jik /'muːʒɪk ; 'muʒɪk/ *n* (esp before the Revolution of 1917) Russian peasant. (尤指 1917 年革命前的)俄國農夫。

mould[1] (US = **mold**) /məʊld ; mold/ *n* [C] container, hollow form, into which molten metal or a soft substance is poured to cool into a desired shape; the shape or form given by this container; jelly, pudding, etc made in such a container. 鑄模;模子;由模子壓成的形狀;由模子製成的果凍、布丁等。 ***be cast in one/the same/a different, etc ~,*** (fig) have the same, different, etc (eg heroic, stubborn, rugged) character. (喩)由同一(相同、不同等)模子鑄出來的;具有一樣(相同、不同等)的性質(如英雄氣概,頑固,粗魯)。□ *vt* [VP6A, 14] ~ ***sth (in/from/out of sth),*** make sth in, or as in, a ~, from some material: 造型;(用…)鑄造;塑造: *~ a head out of/in clay;* 用黏土塑造一個頭; (fig) guide or control the growth of; influence: (喩)指導或控制…的生長;影響: *~ a person's character.* 塑造一個人的性格。

mould[2] (US = **mold**) /məʊld ; mold/ *n* woolly or furry growth of fungi appearing upon moist surfaces, eg leather, cheese or on objects left in a moist, warm atmosphere. 黴;霉。⇨ *iron~* at iron[1](3). □ *vi* [VP2A] (US) become covered with ~: (美)發黴;發霉: *Cheese ~s in warm, wet weather.* 乾酪在暖和潮溼的天氣裏會發黴。 **~y** *adj* (-ier, -iest) **1** covered with ~: 發黴的: *~y bread.* 發黴的麵包。 **2** stale; smelling of ~. 不新鮮的;發黴味的。 **3** (fig) out-of-date; old-fashioned; (sl, of a person) mean and obstructive; worthless. (喩)過時的;舊式的;(俚,指人)卑賤而礙事的;無用的。

mould[3] (US = **mold**) /məʊld ; mold/ *n* [U] soft, fine loose earth, esp from decayed vegetable matter, 鬆軟的泥土;沃土(尤指由腐敗的植物所變成者), eg 例如 *'leaf ~,* from decayed leaves fallen from trees. 腐葉土(由落葉腐敗而成的沃土)。

moulder (US = **molder**) /'məʊldə(r) ; 'moldə/ *vi* [VP2A, C] crumble to dust by natural decay: 由於自然腐爛而崩碎;腐朽: *the ~ing ruins of an old castle.* 古堡的腐朽遺跡。

mould•ing (US = **mold-**) /'məʊldɪŋ ; 'moldɪŋ/ *n* **1** [U] act of moulding or shaping; way in which sth is shaped. 鑄造;塑造;造型;鑄造或塑造方式。 **2** line of ornamental plaster, carved woodwork, etc round a wall or window, or in the cornices of a building, or on a pillar. 線脚(建築物之牆或窗戶四週,或檐板上,或柱上的裝飾性之灰泥線或木工嵌線)。⇨ the illus at column. 參看 column 之揷圖。

moult (US = **molt**) /məʊlt ; molt/ *vt, vi* [VP6A, 2A] (of birds) lose (feathers) before a new growth; (more rarely, of dogs and cats) lose hair. (指鳥)脫換(羽毛);(此義較少用,指狗貓)脫毛。□ *n* process or time of ~ing. 脫毛;換羽;脫毛(換羽)期。

mound /maʊnd ; maʊnd/ *n* [C] mass of piled up earth; small hill: 土墩;土堆;小山: *a 'burial-~,* of earth over a grave; 墓塚; *~s built for defensive purposes in olden times.* 古代爲防禦目的而建的掩體。

mount[1] /maʊnt ; maʊnt/ *n* (liter except in proper names) mountain, hill: (文,或用於專有名詞中)山;丘;峯: *Christ's sermon on the ~;* 基督的山上寶訓; (shortened to *Mt* before proper names): (用於專有名詞前簡寫爲 Mt): *Mt Etna.* 埃特納山。

mount[2] /maʊnt ; maʊnt/ *vt, vi* **1** [VP6A, 2A] go up (a hill, a ladder, etc); get on to (a horse, etc); supply (sb) with a horse; put (sb) on a horse: 爬上;走上;登上(山,梯等);騎上(馬等);供給(某人)馬匹;使(某人)騎上馬: *He ~ed (his horse) and rode away.* 他騎上馬走了。 *The ~ed police were called out to control the crowds.* 騎警隊(騎馬的警察)被召來控制那些群衆。 ~ ***the throne,*** become king, etc. 登極(成爲國王等)。 **2** [VP2A, C] ~ ***(up),*** become greater in amount: 增加;上升: *Our living expenses are ~ing up.* 我們的生活費用日漸增高。 *Bills soon ~ up at hotels.* 旅館裏帳單很快地增加。 **3** (of blood) rise into the cheeks: (指血液)上升到面頰: *A blush ~ed to* (= spread over) *the child's face.* 小孩的臉紅了。 **4** [VP6A] put and fix in position: 裝置: ~ *a gun,* on a gun-carriage; 裝置一門砲(於砲架上); ~ *pictures,* fix them with backings, margins, etc; 裱裝圖畫; ~ *jewels in gold;* 把珠寶鑲在金(製品)上; ~ *specimens,* eg on a slide for a microscope; 固定標本(於顯微鏡的承物玻璃片上等); ~ *insects,* eg for display or preservation in a museum. 把昆蟲作成標本。 **5** (mil uses): (軍語): ~ *an offensive/attack,* take the offensive, attack. 發動攻擊;攻擊。~ ***guard (at/over),*** act as a guard or sentinel: 站崗;守衞: *The Household Troops ~ guard at Buckingham Palace.* 近衞騎兵隊守衞白金漢宮。 **6** [VP6A] put (a play) on the stage: 上演(劇本): *The play was well ~ed,* was provided with good scenery, costumes, etc. 那齣戲配有很好的佈景,服裝等。 **7** (esp of large animals, eg a stallion) get up on (a female animal) in order to copulate. (尤指大的動物,如長成的牡馬)騎在(雌性動物身上)交配。□ *n* [C] that on which a person or thing is or may be ~ed (eg a card for a drawing or photograph, a glass slide for specimens, a horse for riding on, a gun-carriage, the ornamental metal part in which a jewel is fixed). 承載物(如畫或相片的襯紙板,承載標本的玻璃片,乘用的馬,砲架,鑲珠寶的金屬托等)。

moun•tain /'maʊntɪn *US:* -ntn ; 'maʊntn̩/ *n* **1** mass of very high land going up to a peak: 山;高山: *Everest is the highest ~ in the world.* 埃佛勒斯峯是世界上最高的山。 ~ **ash,** the rowan tree, with scarlet berries. 山梨;花楸樹。 ~ **chain,** series of ~s. 山脈。 ~ **dew,** (colloq) Scotch whisky. (俗)蘇格蘭威士忌酒。 ~ **range,** series of ~s more or less in a line. (約成直線延伸的)山脈。 **'~ sickness,** illness caused by rarefied air on high ~s. 高山病(因空氣稀薄所致)。 **2** (fig uses) sth immense: (比喩用法)巨大之物: *a ~ of debts/difficulties.* 債臺高築(困難重重)。 *The waves were ~ high,* very high. 波浪像山那麼高。 **~•eer** /ˌmaʊntɪ'nɪə(r) *US:* -ntn'ɪər ; ˌmaʊntn̩'ɪr/ *n* person who lives among ~s or is skilled at climbing ~s; 山地居民;善於爬

mountain features

山者; hence, 由此產生, **~·eer·ing** *n* [U] climbing ~s (as a sport). 登山(一種運動)。 **~·ous** /ˈmaʊntɪnəs *US:* -ntənəs ; ˈmaʊntn̩əs/ *adj* having ~s: 有山的;多山的: *~ous country;* 多山的地區; huge: 巨大的: *~ous waves.* 巨浪。

moun·te·bank /ˈmaʊntɪbæŋk ; ˈmaʊntəˌbæŋk/ *n* sb who tries to cheat people by clever talk. 巧言惑衆之人。

Mountie /ˈmaʊntɪ ; ˈmaʊntɪ/ *n* (colloq) member of the Royal Canadian Mounted Police. (俗) 加拿大的騎警。

mourn /mɔːn ; morn/ *vi, vt* [VP3A, 6A] ~ ***(for/over),*** feel or show sorrow or regret (for/over); grieve (for/over): 悲悼;哀悼;悲歎: *~ for a dead child;* 悲悼一個死去的小孩; *~ over the child's death;* 悲悼小孩的死亡; *~ the loss of one's mother.* 哀悼母親的逝世。 **~er** *n* person who ~s, esp one who attends a funeral as a relative or friend of the dead person. 哀悼者;送喪者。 **~·ful** /-fl ; -fəl/ *adj* sad; sorrowful. 悲哀的;悽慘的。 **~·fully** /-fəlɪ ; -fəlɪ/ *adv*

mourn·ing /ˈmɔːnɪŋ ; ˈmornɪŋ/ *n* [U] **1** grief. 悲哀;悲傷。 **2** ***go into/be in ~,*** (start to) wear black clothes as a sign of grief. 著喪服;戴孝。 **ˈ~-band** *n* band of black crepe worn round the sleeve. 喪章。 **ˈ~-ring** *n* (formerly) worn as a memorial of a dead person. (昔時)紀念死者的戒指。

mouse /maʊs ; maʊs/ *n* (*pl* mice /maɪs ; maɪs/) sorts of small rodent (*ˈhouse ~, ˈfield-~, ˈharvest-~*); (fig) shy, timid person. 鼠(家鼠,田鼠,巢鼠);(喻)羞怯或膽小的人。 **ˈ~-trap** *n* trap for catching mice: 捕鼠器: *~-trap cheese,* (hum) unpalatable kind of cheese. (諧)味道不佳的乾酪。□ *vi* [VP2A] (of cats) hunt for, catch, mice: (指貓)捕鼠: *Our cat ~s well.* 我們的貓很會捕鼠。 **mouser** /ˈmaʊzə(r); ˈmaʊzɚ/ *n* cat who does this. 會捕鼠之貓。 **mousy** /ˈmaʊsɪ ; ˈmaʊsɪ/ *adj* (-ier, -iest) (esp of hair) dull brown; (of a person) timid, shy. (尤指毛髮)暗褐色的;(指人)膽小的;羞怯的。

mousse /muːs ; mus/ *n* [C, U] (dish of) meat, fish, flavoured cream, etc beaten and served cold: (一盤)肉、魚、乳脂等攪勻後冷凍之食品; 奶油凍: *chocolate ~.* 巧克力奶油凍。

mous·tache (US = **mus·tache**) /məˈstɑːʃ *US:* ˈmʌstæʃ ; ˈmʌstæʃ/ *n* [C] hair allowed to grow on the upper lip. 髭(長在嘴唇上面的鬍子)。

mouth¹ /maʊθ ; maʊθ/ *n* (*pl* ~s /maʊðz ; maʊðz/) **1** opening through which animals take in food; space behind this containing the teeth, tongue, etc. 嘴;口。 ⇨ the illus here. 參看本條之插圖。 ***by word of ~,*** (of news, etc) orally (not in writing, etc). (指新聞等)口頭的(非書寫等的)。 ***down in the ~,*** sad, dejected. 悲哀的;沮喪的。 ***out of the ~s of babes and sucklings,*** (prov) innocent young people may speak wisely. (諺)黃口孺子也能說出至理名言。 ***laugh on the wrong side of one's ~,*** lament, be disappointed. 悲傷;失望。 ***look a gift-horse in the ~,*** accept sth ungratefully esp by examining it critically for faults. 接受禮物而不表感謝(尤指檢查禮物挑剔缺點)。 ***put words into sb's ~,*** **(a)** tell him what to say. 告訴某人說什麼。 **(b)** suggest or claim that he has said something. 暗示或聲稱某人曾說過什麼。 ***take the words out of sb's ~,*** say what he was about to say; anticipate his words. 說某人將要說的話;搶先說某人要說的話。 **~·ful** /-fʊl ; -ˌfʊl/ *n* as much as can be put into the ~ comfortably at one time: 一口的量: *swallow sth at a ~ful;* 一口吞下某物; *have only a ~ful of food.* 只有一口的食物。 **ˈ~-organ** *n* small musical wind-instrument with metal reeds, played by passing it along the lips and blowing; harmonica. 口琴。 **ˈ~-piece** *n* **(a)** that part of a tobacco pipe, a musical instrument, etc placed at or between the lips. (煙斗的)煙嘴;(樂器的)吹口;接口(管)。 **(b)** person, newspaper, etc, that expresses the opinions of others: 代言人;機關報;發言人: *Which newspaper is the ~piece of the Socialists?* 哪一家報紙是社會黨的機關報? **ˈ~-watering** *adj* ⇨ water²(3). **2** opening or outlet (of a bag, bottle, tunnel, cave, river, etc). (袋、瓶、隧道、洞穴、河流等的)口;開口處。

mouth² /maʊð ; maʊð/ *vt, vi* [VP6A, 2A] **1** speak with movement of the jaw but no sound. 以嘴唇的動作但不出聲地說出。 **2** utter pompously: 誇大地說話: *An actor who ~s his words is a poor actor.* 裝腔作勢背誦臺詞的演員是不好的演員。 **3** take (food) into the ~; touch with the ~. 把(食物)放進口中;用口接觸。

mov·able /ˈmuːvəbl ; ˈmuvəbl/ *adj* **1** that can be moved; (of property) that can be taken from place to place (eg furniture, contrasted with land and buildings, called *real* property or estate). 可移動的;(指財產)可搬動的(如傢具等,與土地、房屋等不動產相對);動產的。 ⇨ portable. **2** varying in date: 日期變動的: *Christmas is fixed but Easter* *is a ~ feast.* 聖誕節是固定的，而復活節是每年變動日期的節日。□ *n* (*pl*) personal property; articles that can be removed from the house (contrasted with *fixtures*). (複) 動產；可搬動的傢具 (與 fixtures 相對)。

move[1] /muːv ; muv/ *n* [C] **1** change of place or position, esp of a piece in chess or other games played on boards; player's turn to do this: 移動位置；(西洋棋或其他盤上遊戲之) 一步；(下棋等) 輪到走：*Do you know all the ~s in chess?* 你知道西洋棋的所有走法嗎？*Whose ~ is it?* 該誰走(棋)啦？ **2** sth (to be) done to achieve a purpose: (爲達到目的所採取的) 行動；步驟：*a ~ towards settling the strike.* 解決罷工的一個行動。*What's our next ~?* 我們的下一個步驟是什麼？ **3** ***on the ~,*** moving about: 在移動中：*Our planes reported that large enemy forces were on the ~.* 我們的飛機報告說大批敵軍在移動中。***make a ~,*** **(a)** ~ to a different place: 遷移：*Shall we make a ~ now?* 我們現在要不要遷移？ **(b)** begin to act: 開始行動：*Unless we make a ~ soon, we shall be in a hopelessly weak position.* 除非我們趕快開始行動，否則我們將處於劣勢。***get a ~ on,*** (sl) hurry up. (俚) 趕快。

move[2] /muːv ; muv/ *vt, vi* **1** [VP6A, 15A, B, 2A, C] (cause to) change position; put, cause to be, in a different place or attitude; (cause to) be in motion: (使) 改變位置；移動；搬動；開動：*M~ your chair nearer to the fire.* 把你的椅子挪近火爐一點。*It was calm and not a leaf ~d.* 平靜得連一片葉子也沒有動。*It's your turn to ~,* (in chess, etc) to ~ a piece from one square to another. (下棋等) 該你走了；輪到你走(棋)了。***~ heaven and earth,*** do one's utmost, use every possible means (*to do* sth). 盡最大力量；千方百計 (與不定詞連用)。 **2** [VP6A, 2C] ***~ (house),*** take one's furniture, etc to another house, flat, etc: 搬家；遷居：*We're moving (house) next week.* 我們下星期搬家。***~ in,*** take possession of a new dwelling-place. 搬進；遷入新居。***~ out,*** give up a dwelling-place: 搬出；遷出：*We ~d out on Monday and the new tenants ~d in on Tuesday.* 我們星期一遷出，新房客星期二就搬進來。 **3** [VP2C, 15B] ***~ on,*** ~ to another place or position (eg when ordered to do so by a policeman). 朝前走；走開 (如警察命令行人、車輛等移動)。***~ sb on,*** cause him to ~ by giving him the order 'M~ on, please'. 命令某人朝前走或走開。***~ along/down/up,*** ~ farther in the direction indicated so as to make space for others: 往前移動 (往下移動；往上移動；以讓出空間給別人)：*'M~ along, please', said the bus conductor.* 公共汽車收票員說，'請往前走'。 **4** [VP6A, 15A] arouse, work on, the feelings of; affect with pity, etc: 激動；煽動；感動：*be ~d with pity/compassion;* 爲憐憫之情所動；*be ~d to tears.* 感動得流淚。*We were all ~d by her entreaties.* 我們都被她的懇求所感動。*The story of their sufferings ~d us deeply.* 他們苦難的經歷深深地感動了我們。*It was a moving sight.* 那是個感人的情景。 **5** [VP17] cause (to do sth): 使做某事：*Nothing I said ~d him to offer his help.* 我說什麼都不能使他提供協助。*The spirit ~d him to get up and address the meeting,* He felt a desire to do this. 他覺得自己有一種願望，想要站起來對參加這個會的人們說話。*Who was the moving spirit in the enterprise,* Who started it and was most active? 誰是這個企業的主腦？ **6** [VP6A, 9] put forward for discussion and decision (at a meeting): (開會時) 提議：*Mr Chairman, I ~ that the money be used for library books.* 主席，我提議把那筆錢用來增購圖書館的藏書。⇨ motion(3). **7** [VP3A] ***~ for,*** make formal application for: 正式要求；請求：*The noble Lord ~d for papers,* ie in a debate in the House of Lords. (英) 這位上議院議員正式要求查看一些文件。 **8** [VP2A, C] make progress; go forward: 進步；前進：*Time ~s on.* 時光流逝。*The work ~s slowly.* 工作進展緩慢。*Things are not moving as rapidly as we had hoped.* 事情進行沒有像我們希望的那麼快。 **9** [VP2A, C] take action: 採取行動：*Nobody seems willing to ~ in the matter.* 似乎沒有人願意對這件事採取行動。 **10** [VP2C] live one's life; pass one's time: 生活；度日子：*They ~ in the highest society.* 他們和上流社會人士交往。 **11** [VP6A, 2A] cause (the bowels) to act, to empty; (of the bowels) be emptied. 使(腸)通便；(指腸)通便。

move·ment /ˈmuːvmənt ; ˈmuvmənt/ *n* **1** [U] moving or being moved; activity (contrasted with quiet and rest): 移動；運動；活動 (與安靜及靜止相對)：*He lay there without ~.* 他一動也不動地躺在那裏。*The novel/play lacks ~,* ie there is not enough action in it. 那部小說(戲)情節呆滯。 **2** [C] act of changing position, esp a military evolution: 移動 (尤指軍事調動)：*By a series of rapid ~s the general placed his forces in an advantageous position.* 經一連串的迅速調動，將軍把他的軍隊置於有利的地位。 **3** [C] moving part of a machine or mechanism or a particular group of such parts: 機器、機械裝置等的運轉部分：*the ~ of a clock or a watch.* 鐘或錶的運轉部分。 **4** [C] united actions and efforts of a group of people for a special purpose: (一群人爲某種目的而聯合起來的) 運動：*the ~ to abolish slavery.* 廢除奴役的運動。**the ˈLabour M~,** organized(2) (manual) workers. 勞工運動；勞工工會。 **5** [C] (music) principal division of a musical work with a distinctive structure of its own: (音樂) 樂章：*the final ~ of the Ninth Symphony.* 第九交響曲的最後樂章。 **6** [C] emptying of the bowels. 通便。 **7** [U] activity (in a stock market, etc) for some commodity: (股票市場等的) 交易活動；變動：*not much ~ in oil shares.* 油類股票沒有什麼波動。

mover /ˈmuːvə(r) ; ˈmuvə/ *n* (esp) person who moves(6) a proposal. (尤指) 提議人。***the prime ~,***

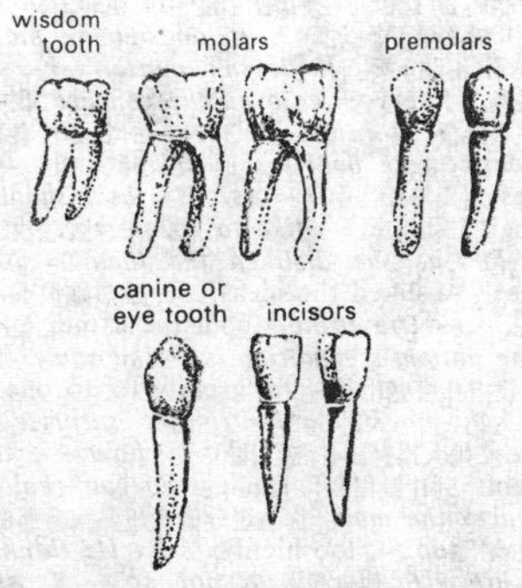

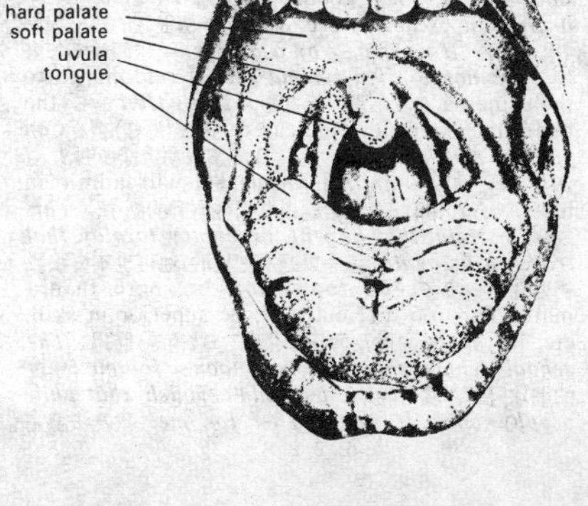

the mouth

the person chiefly responsible for starting sth. 主要負責創辦某事物的發起人;創辦人。

movie /ˈmuːvɪ; ˈmuvɪ/ *n* (colloq) (俗) **1** motion picture. 電影。 **2 the ~s,** the cinema; the cinema industry: 電影院;電影;電影業: *How often do you go to the ~s?* 你多久看一次電影?

mow[1] /məʊ; mo/ *vt, vi* (*pt* mowed, *pp* mown /məʊn; mon/ or mowed) **1** [VP6A, 2A] cut (grass, etc) with a scythe or a machine: 用鐮刀或刈草機割(草等): *mow the lawn;* 修剪草地; *new-mown hay;* 新割下的乾草; *mow a field.* 割除田裏的草。 **2** [VP15B] **mow down,** cut down like grass; destroy as if by sweeping movements: (像刈草一樣)刈除;掃除: *Our men were mown down by the enemy's machine-gun fire.* 我們的士兵被敵人的機槍掃射倒地。 **mower** /ˈməʊə(r); ˈmoɚ/ *n* person or machine that mows: 割草人;刈草機: *a ˈlawn-mower.* 刈草機。

mow[2] /məʊ; maʊ/ *n* [C] heap of hay, straw, etc; place in a barn where hay, etc is stored. 草堆;禾堆;(穀倉之)禾草堆積處。

mow[3] /maʊ; maʊ/ *vi* **mop and mow,** ⇨ mop[2].

Mr /ˈmɪstə(r); ˈmɪstɚ/ title prefixed to the (first name and the) surname of a man: 先生(冠於男子之姓或姓名前的稱呼): *Mr (John) Brown.* (約翰•)布朗先生。

Mrs /ˈmɪsɪz; ˈmɪsɪz/ title prefixed to the (first name and the) surname of a married woman: 夫人; 太太(冠於已婚婦女之姓或姓名前之稱呼): *Mrs (Jane) Brown;* (珍•)布朗太太; (formal): (正式用語): *Mrs John Brown.* 約翰•布朗太太。

Ms /mɪz; mɪz/ title prefixed to the (first name and the) surname of a woman, whether married or unmarried: 女士(冠於已婚或未婚女子之姓或姓名前之稱呼): *Ms (Mary) Green.* (瑪莉•)格林女士。

much[1] /mʌtʃ; mʌtʃ/ (more, most. ⇨ little) *adj, n* (~ is used with *sing nn,* uncountable. Cf *many,* used with *pl nn.* In purely affirm sentences it is often preferable to use *plenty (of), a lot (of), a large quantity (of), a good/great deal (of). M~* is often used in affirm sentences when it is (a part of) the subject, and when used with *how, too, so,* or *as*): (much 與單數不可數名詞連用。參較 many, 與複數名詞連用。純粹肯定句中最好用 plenty (of), a lot (of), a large quantity (of), a good (great) deal (of)。much 作主詞(或其一部份)或與 how, too, so, as 等連用時,常用於肯定句): *There isn't ~ food in the house.* 家裏食物不多了。 *He never eats ~ breakfast.* 他早餐從來吃得不多。 *Did you have ~ difficulty in finding the house?* 你找那房子很困難嗎? *M~ of what you say is true.* 你所說的大部份是眞實的。 *We have ~ to be thankful for.* 我們有很多應該感謝的。 *You have given me too ~.* 你已經給我太多了。 **come to ~,** ⇨ come(3). **how ~,** **(a)** what quantity: 多少: *How ~ flour* (= What weight) *do you want?* 你要多少麵粉? **(b)** what price: 什麼價格: *How ~ a kilo is that beef?* 那牛肉一公斤多少錢? **be up to ~,** be worth ~: 很有價值: *I don't think his work is up to ~,* ie it is not good. 我不以爲他的作品很有價值。 **not ~ of a,** not a good: 不算好的: *He's not ~ of a linguist/scholar, etc.* 他不是一個很好的語言學家(學者等)。 *It wasn't ~ of a dinner.* 這頓飯並不怎麼好。 *I'm not ~ of a cinema-goer,* I seldom go to the cinema. 我不常去看電影。 **this/that ~,** the quantity, extent, etc indicated: 這樣(那樣)多: *Can you let me have this ~?* 你能讓我拿這樣多嗎? *I will say this ~ in his favour...,* I will admit in his favour that.... 我要說這些對他有利的話…。 *This ~ is certain, that he will never try to play that trick on us again.* 這一點是有把握的,他再也不會跟我們要那個把戲了。 **be too ~ for,** be more than a match for, too difficult for; be superior in skill, etc, to: 非…能力所及;對…太難了;(技術等)勝過: *The school tennis champion was too ~ for me.* 學校的網球冠軍非我所能敵。 *I couldn't finish that philosophy book, it was too ~ for me.* 我無法讀完那本關於哲學的書,那本書對我是太難了。 **make ~ of,** **(a)** understand: 瞭解;明白: *I didn't make ~ of that lecture.* 我不瞭解那篇演講。 **(b)** attach importance to; exaggerate: 重視;誇張: *We mustn't make too ~ of this incident.* 我們不必太重視這個事件。 *He makes (too) ~ of his connections with rich people.* 他(過份)誇張他與有錢人的關係。 **think ~ of,** have a good opinion of: 認爲佳: *I don't think ~ of my English teacher.* 我覺得我的英文老師不怎麼高明。 **as ~ (as),** the same (as): 與…相同;與…同樣: *Give me as ~ again,* the same quantity again. 再給我同樣的份量。 *I thought as ~,* That is what I thought. 我也這樣想。 *You have always helped me and I will always do as ~ for you,* will always help you. 你總是幫助我,我將要同樣地幫助你。 *It is as ~ your responsibility as mine,* You and I are equally responsible. 你和我對這件事都要負責。 *It was as ~ as he could do to* (= He could do no more than) *pay his way.* 他只能做到不負債的地步。 *That is as ~ as to say* (= is the same thing as saying) *that I am a liar.* 那無異是說我是個說謊的人。 **(with) not/without so ~ as,** not even: 甚至不: *He left without so ~ as saying 'Thank you'.* 他走了,甚至連'謝謝'都沒說。 *He rushed past me with not so ~ as a 'By your leave',* without any apology. 他從我身邊衝過去,連一聲'借過'也沒說。 *He hadn't so ~ as his fare home.* 他甚至連回家的車費都沒有。 ⇨ also *so ~ (many), not so ~ as, so ~ so that, so ~ for,* under so[1](6).

much[2] /mʌtʃ; mʌtʃ/ *adv* **1** (modifying comparatives and superlatives, preceding the *def art*): (修飾比較級與最高級,置於定冠詞之前): *He is ~ better today.* 他今天好得多了。 *You must work ~ harder.* 你必須更加努力。 *This is ~* (= by far) *the best.* 這是最好的了。 *He's not ~ the worse for his fall into the canal.* 他並沒有因爲跌到運河裏而受到什麼損傷。 **~ more/less,** (used to indicate that what has been stated about sth applies with greater force to the following statement): (用以表示前句含義加强後句含義)更加;更沒有;遑論;何況: *It is difficult to understand his books, ~ more his lectures.* 他的書難懂,而他的演講更難懂。 *I didn't even speak to him, ~ less discuss your problems with him.* 我甚至沒有跟他說話,當然更沒有與他討論你的問題。 **2** (modifying passive *participles* and *pred adjj* such as *afraid.* Cf *very,* used to modify passive and *present participles* which are true *adjj* as *very frightened*): (修飾被動的分詞及afraid等敍述形容詞。參較 very, 用於修飾成爲眞正形容詞的被動與現在分詞,如 very frightened): *I am very ~ afraid that...;* 我非常害怕…; *I shall be ~ surprised if he succeeds.* 假如他成功的話,我將極爲驚奇。 *I hope you will not be ~ inconvenienced.* 我希望你將不會太不方便。 **3** (When *much* modifies a *v* phrase, it may occur within the *v* phrase or in end position, but may not occur between this *v* phrase and its object): (當 much 修飾一動詞片語時,其位置可在動詞片語之中或在句末,但不可置於動詞片語與其受詞之間): *It doesn't ~ matter.* 不大要緊;不關重要。 *It doesn't matter very ~.* 沒什麼大要緊。 *I very ~ enjoyed the concert.* 我非常喜歡那個音樂會。 *I enjoyed it very ~.* 我非常喜歡它。 *He doesn't like beef ~.* 他不頂喜歡牛肉。 **4** (in phrases) (用於片語中) **~ as:** *M~ as I should* (= Although I should ~) *like to go,...;* 雖然我很想去,…; *M~ as she disliked the idea* (= Although she ~ disliked the idea),.... 雖然她很不喜歡那種意見,…。 **~ the same,** about the same: 差不多一樣: *The patient's condition is ~ the same.* 那病人的情況沒有什麼變化。 **~ to,** greatly to; to one's great...: 大爲;對…大爲: *M~ to her surprise/regret, etc.* 她大爲驚訝(深感遺憾)…。 **how ~,** to what extent: 到什麼程度: *How ~ do you really want to marry the man?* 你有幾分眞意想要嫁給那個人? ⇨ much[1]. **too ~,** too highly: 太高: *He thinks too ~ of himself.* 他自視過高。 **not so ~ X as**

Y, Y rather than X: 與其說X，不如說 Y: *Oceans don't so ~ divide the world as unite it,* They serve to unite countries rather than to divide them. 與其說海洋分隔了世界，不如說海洋聯結了世界。 **~ness** *n* (only in the colloq phrase) (僅用於口語片語中) ***~ of a ~ness,*** ~ the same; almost alike. 差不多相同；幾乎同様。

mu·ci·lage /ˈmju:sɪlɪdʒ; ˈmjuslɪdʒ/ *n* [U] kinds of vegetable glue (obtained from plants, seaweed, etc), used as an adhesive. 植物質膠水；黏液(從植物、海草等提取者)。

muck /mʌk; mʌk/ *n* [U] **1** dung; farmyard manure (the droppings of animals). 糞；糞肥。**ˈ~-heap** *n* heap of farmyard ~. (農家園院中的)糞肥堆。**ˈ~-raker** *n* (usu fig) person who is always looking for scandal, corruption, etc. (通常爲喻)經常探聽醜聞、貪汚等的人。Hence, 由此產生，**ˈ~-raking** *n* **2** dirt; filth; (colloq) anything disgusting or dirty. 髒物；汚物；(俗)任何令人討厭或不潔的東西。 ***make a ~ of sth,*** (colloq) make a mess of it; make it dirty; spoil it. (俗)把某事弄得一團糟；弄亂；弄髒；弄壞某事物。□ *vt, vi* **1** [VP6A, 15B] ***~ sth (up),*** (colloq) make a mess of it; spoil it. (俗)弄髒某事物；弄壞；弄糟。 **2** [VP2C] ***~ about,*** (GB sl) do useless or unnecessary things; go about, spend time, aimlessly: (英俚)作無用或無必要之事；混日子；虛擲光陰: *'What's he up to?'—'Oh, just ~ing about.'* '他在幹什麼？'—'哦，不過混日子而已。' **3** [VP2C, 15B] ***~ out,*** clean out (stables, etc) by removing dung: 掃除糞便以清理(馬廐等): *She ~s out (the stables) every morning.* 她每天早晨清掃(馬廐)。**~y** *adj* (-ier, -iest) dirty. 髒的。

muckle /ˈmʌkl; ˈmʌkḷ/ *n* ⇨ mickle.

mu·cous /ˈmju:kəs; ˈmjukəs/ *adj* of, like, covered with, mucus. 黏液的；似黏液的；佈滿黏液的。 ***the ~ membrane,*** the moist skin that lines the nose, mouth and food canal. 黏膜。

mu·cus /ˈmju:kəs; ˈmjukəs/ *n* [U] sticky, slimy substance produced by the mucous membrane; similar slimy substance: (由黏膜分泌的)黏液；類似黏液的物質: *Snails and slugs leave a trail of mucus.* 蝸牛和蛞蝓行進時會留下一道黏液。

mud /mʌd; mʌd/ *n* [U] soft, wet earth: 軟濕的泥土: *Rain turns dust into mud.* 雨將塵土弄成軟泥。 ***throw/fling/sling mud at sb,*** speak evil of him, try to damage his reputation. 說某人壞話；企圖破壞某人名譽。Hence, 由此產生，**ˈmud-slinger** *n.* ***sb's name is mud,*** he is in disgrace. 某人聲名狼藉。**ˈmud-bath** *n* bath in mud of mineral springs (eg for treating rheumatism). 泥浴(在含有礦泉的泥中沐浴，如作爲治風濕病的一種醫療法)。**ˈmud flat** *n* muddy land covered by the sea at high tide and not covered at low tide. 泥灘(高潮時爲海水所浸，低潮時不爲海水所浸的軟泥地)。**ˈmud·guard** *n* curved cover over a wheel (of a bicycle, etc). (脚踏車等的彎形)擋泥蓋；擋泥板。⇨ the illus at bicycle. 參看 bicycle 之插圖。□ *vt* (-dd-) [VP6A] cover with mud: 覆以泥: *You've mudded the carpet.* 你把地毯弄得都是泥巴了。**muddy** *adj* (-ier, -iest) **1** full of, covered with, mud: 多泥的；覆着泥巴的: *muddy roads/shoes.* 泥濘的路(沾滿泥巴的鞋)。 **2** mud-coloured; like mud because thick: 泥色的；(因其濃稠)似泥的: *a muddy stream;* 混濁的溪流； *a muddy skin;* 泥土色的皮膚； *muddy coffee;* 泥色的咖啡； *muddy* (fig, = confused) *ideas.* (喻)混亂的意念。□ *vt* (*pt, pp* -died) [VP6A] make muddy. 使多泥；使覆着軟泥。

muddle /ˈmʌdl; ˈmʌdḷ/ *vt, vi* **1** [VP6A, 15B] ***~ (up),*** bring into a state of confusion and disorder; make a mess of: 使混亂；弄成一團糟: *You've ~d the scheme completely.* 你已經把這個計畫完全弄糟了。*A glass of whisky soon ~s him.* 一杯威士忌很快就會把他醉得迷迷糊糊。*Don't ~* (= mix) *things up (together).* 不要把東西弄亂(在一起)。 ***~ sth/sb up with sth/sb,*** (colloq) be unable to distinguish sth/sb from sth/sb else. (俗)不能分辨某兩物(人)；把兩物(人)弄混。 **2** [VP2C] ***~ along/on,*** get on in a foolish or helpless way, with no clear purpose or plan: 漫無目的而糊裡糊塗地混: *He's still muddling on/along.* 他仍然是糊裡糊塗地混日子。 ***~ through,*** reach the end of an undertaking in spite of inefficiency, obstacles of one's own making, etc. 混過去。□ *n* (usu 通常作 **a ~**) ~d state; confusion of ideas: 混亂；意念的紊亂: *Everything was in a ~ and I couldn't find what I wanted.* 每一件東西都是亂糟糟的，我找不到我所要的東西。*You have made a ~ of it,* mismanaged it, bungled it. 你已經把它弄糟了。**ˈ~-headed** *adj* confused in mind; stupid. 頭腦不清楚的；愚笨的。

muesli /ˈmju:zlɪ; ˈmjuzlɪ/ *n* [U] breakfast food of a mixture of uncooked cereal, nuts, dried fruit, etc. 一種由未經烹煮的穀類，堅果，乾果等混合製成的早餐食品。

mu·ez·zin /mu:ˈezɪn *US*: mju:-; mjuˈɛzɪn/ *n* man who proclaims the hours of prayers from the minaret of a mosque. (在回教寺院的尖塔上)呼報祈禱時刻的人。

muff[1] /mʌf; mʌf/ *n* covering, usu a cylindrical padded bag of fur, open at both ends, used to keep the hands warm; similar covering for the foot. (通常爲圓筒形、皮製、兩端開口的)暖手袋；皮手筒；(類似皮手筒的)暖足套。

muff[2] /mʌf; mʌf/ *n* person who is awkward or clumsy, esp in games (eg by failing to catch the ball at cricket). 笨拙的人(尤指遊戲時笨手笨脚的人，如板球戲中接球失誤者)。□ *vt* [VP6A] bungle; fail to catch; miss: 笨拙地作；接不住；漏接: *~ a ball;* 漏接一球； *~ an easy catch.* 沒接住一個容易接的球。

muf·fin /ˈmʌfɪn; ˈmʌfɪn/ *n* small, light, flat, round cake, usu eaten hot with butter. 小鬆餅(通常加奶油趁熱吃)。

muffle /ˈmʌfl; ˈmʌfḷ/ *vt* **1** [VP6A, 15B] ***~ (up),*** wrap or cover for warmth or protection: 包；覆；圍裹: *~ oneself up well;* 把自己圍裹妥當； *~ one's throat,* eg by putting a scarf round it; 把頸部圍起來(如用圍巾)； *~d up in a heavy overcoat.* 圍裹在厚重的大衣裏。 **2** [VP6A] make the sound of sth (eg a bell or a drum) dull by wrapping it up in cloth, etc: 將某物(如鐘或鼓)包住使之聲音低沉；使發悶音；使消音: *~ the oars of a boat,* to deaden the sound of their touching the water; 把船的槳包紮起來(使划船時能消音)； *~d voices,* eg from persons whose mouths are covered. 悶住的聲音(如蒙住口之人所發出者)。

muf·fler /ˈmʌflə(r); ˈmʌflɚ/ *n* **1** cloth, scarf, worn round the neck for warmth. 圍巾；領巾。 **2** (US) silencer. (美)消音器；滅音器。

mufti /ˈmʌftɪ; ˈmʌftɪ/ *n* (usu 通常用於 *in ~*) plain, ordinary clothes worn by someone (eg an official, an army officer) who has the right to wear uniform. 便衣；便裝(指有權穿制服之官員、軍官等所穿的普通服裝)。

mug[1] /mʌg; mʌg/ *n* **1** (usu straight-sided) drinking vessel of china or metal with a handle, for use without a saucer; its contents: (通常周邊垂直，不用杯托之)有把手的瓷杯或金屬杯；(該杯的)一杯容量: *a ˈbeer-mug;* 啤酒杯； *a mug of milk.* 一大杯牛奶。 **2** (sl) face; mouth. (俚)臉；嘴。

mug[2] /mʌg; mʌg/ *n* (sl) simpleton; easily deceived person. (俚)愚人；容易受騙的人。 ***a ˈmug's game,*** sth unlikely to bring profit or reward. 不大可能獲利或得到報酬的事物。

mug[3] /mʌg; mʌg/ *vt* (-gg-) [VP15B] ***mug sth up,*** (colloq) (try to) become quite familiar with sth on which one is to be tested. (俗)(試圖)把要測驗的事物讀得很熟；勤習；苦讀。

mug[4] /mʌg; mʌg/ *vt* (-gg-) [VP6A] (colloq) attack (sb) violently and rob (eg in a dark street, a lift, an empty corridor, etc). (俗)(如在黑暗的街道上，電梯中，空無人在的通道中)猛烈襲擊並搶刼(某人)。

mug·ger *n* **mug·ging** *n* [U, C].

mug·gins /ˈmʌgɪnz ; ˈmʌgɪnz/ *n* (colloq) fool. (俗)愚人;傻瓜;笨蛋。

muggy /ˈmʌgɪ ; ˈmʌgi/ *adj* (-ier, -iest) (of the weather, a day, etc) damp and warm; close and sticky: (指天氣、某天等)濕而熱的;悶人的;悶熱的: *~ days during the rainy season.* 雨季裏的悶熱日子。**muggi·ness** *n*

mug·wump /ˈmʌgwʌmp; ˈmʌg,wʌmp/ *n* (US) conceited person; person who has a high opinion of his own importance. (美)自負的人;自以爲了不起的人。

Mu·ham·mad /məˈhæmɪd ; muˈhæməd/ *n* Prophet and Founder of Islam. 穆罕默德 (回教的先知及創始者)。**~an** /-ən ; -ən/ *n, adj* Muslim. 回教的;回教徒。**Mu·ham·ma·dan·ism** /məˈhæmɪdənɪzəm ; muˈhæmədən,ɪzəm/ *n* Islam (the preferred name). 回教;伊斯蘭教 (Islam 爲較爲人所喜用之名稱)。

mu·latto /mjuːˈlætəʊ *US:* məˈl- ; məˈlæto/ *n* (*pl* ~s, ~es /-təʊz ; -toz/) person who has one parent of black race and one of white race. (白人與黑人所生的)黑白混血兒。

mul·berry /ˈmʌlbrɪ *US:* ˈmʌlberɪ ; ˈmʌl,bɛrɪ/ *n* (*pl* -ries) [C] tree with broad, dark-green leaves on which silkworms feed; its fruit (dark purple or white). 桑樹;桑葚(桑樹所結之深紫色或白色的果實)。

mulch /mʌltʃ ; mʌltʃ/ *n* [C] protective covering of peat, spread over the roots of trees and bushes, to retain moisture, smother weeds, etc. 護根(鋪於樹木根部上之泥煤，有保持潮濕及遏制雜草生長等功用)。□ *vt* cover (ground) with a ~. 在(地面)上覆以護根。

mulct /mʌlkt ; mʌlkt/ *vt* [VP12C, 14] **~ (in/of)**, (rare) punish by means of a fine; take (sth) away from: (罕)處以罰金;自…奪取(某物): *~ a man £5;* 罰某人五鎊; *~ a man in £5;* 罰某人五鎊; *be ~ed of one's money.* 某人的錢被搶去。

mule[1] /mjuːl ; mjul/ *n* **1** animal that is the offspring of an ass and a mare. 騾。***as obstinate/stubborn as a ~***, very obstinate/stubborn. 像騾子一樣的固執(頑固);非常固執(頑固)。**2** (colloq) stubborn person. (俗)頑固的人。**3** kind of spinning-machine. 走錠精紡機。**mu·le·teer** /,mjuːləˈtɪə(r) ; ,mjuləˈtɪr/ *n* ~-driver. 馭騾者。**mul·ish** /-ɪʃ ; -ɪʃ/ *adj* stubborn; obstinate. 頑固的;執拗的。**mu·lish·ly** *adv* **mu·lish·ness** *n*

mule[2] /mjuːl ; mjul/ *n* heelless slipper. 無後側鞋幫的便鞋。

mull[1] /mʌl ; mʌl/ *vt* [VP6A] make (wine, beer) into a hot drink with sugar, spices, etc: 加糖、香料等溫熱(葡萄酒,啤酒): *~ed claret.* 加糖、香料等溫熱的紅葡萄酒。

mull[2] /mʌl; mʌl/ *n* (Scot) (in place-names) promontory: (蘇) (與地名連用)海角;岬: *the M~ of Kintyre.* 琴泰岬。

mull[3] /mʌl ; mʌl/ *vt* [VP15B] ***~ sth over; ~ over sth,*** ponder over it. 思索;沉思(某事)。

mul·lah /ˈmʌlə ; ˈmʌlə/ *n* Muslim learned in theology and sacred law. 回教的神學家。

mul·lein /ˈmʌlɪn ; ˈmʌlɪn/ *n* kinds of plant with leaves covered with grey hairs, and small yellow flowers. 毛蕊花。

mul·let /ˈmʌlɪt ; ˈmʌlɪt/ *n* kinds of seafish used as food, esp *red ~* and *grey ~*. 刀魚 (數種食用之海魚,尤指緋鯢鰹與鯔)。

mul·li·ga·tawny /,mʌlɪgəˈtɔːnɪ ; ,mʌlɪgəˈtɔnɪ/ *n* **~ (soup)**, thick, highly seasoned soup with curry powder in it, often with boiled rice added. 咖哩濃湯(常加有米飯);咖哩燴飯。

mul·lion /ˈmʌlɪən ; ˈmʌljən/ *n* vertical stone division between parts of a window. (某些窗之)石質中框;直欞。⇨ the illus at window. 參看 window 之挿圖。**~ed** /ˈmʌlɪənd ; ˈmʌljənd/ *adj* having ~s. 有石質中框的;有直欞的。

multi- /ˈmʌltɪ ; ˈmʌltɪ/ *pref* having many of (eg *~-coloured*, of many colours; *a ,~-,millioˈnaire*, person having 2 or more millions of money); 多(如 multi-coloured 多色的; a multi-millionaire, 數百萬富翁); *a ,~-,stage ˈrocket,* with parts that ignite (and then fall away) in stages; 多節火箭; *a ,~-,racial ˈcountry,* with many races of people. 多種族的國家。

mul·ti·far·ious /,mʌltɪˈfeərɪəs ; ,mʌltəˈfɛrɪəs/ *adj* many and various: 各種各樣的;五花八門的: *his ~ duties;* 他的各種各樣的職責; having great variety. 多樣性的。**~·ly** *adv*

mul·ti·form /ˈmʌltɪfɔːm ; ˈmʌltə,fɔrm/ *adj* having many forms or shapes. 各式各樣的;形式繁多的。

mul·ti·lat·eral /,mʌltɪˈlætərəl ; ,mʌltɪˈlætərəl/ *adj* involving two or more participants: 多邊的; 多方面的: *~ disarmament,* after agreement between two or more countries; 多邊裁軍; *~ trade,* carried on between many or all countries without the need for pairs of countries to balance payment between themselves. 多邊貿易;多國貿易。

mul·tiple /ˈmʌltɪpl ; ˈmʌltəpḷ/ *adj* having many parts or elements: 複合的;多樣的;多數的: *a man of ~ interests;* 有多方面興趣的人; *a ~ shop/store,* one with many branches, cf *chain store,* the more usu term; 聯號商店(參較比較常用的 chain store); *a ~-unit train,* made up of several coaches (eg Diesel coaches) each of which can run independently. 聯列火車或電車(例如每節可單獨行駛之柴油列車)。□ *n* quantity which contains another quantity a number of times without remainder: 倍數: *28 is a ~ of 7.* 28 是 7 的倍數。*30 is a common ~ of 2, 3, 5, 6, 10 and 15.* 30 是 2, 3, 5, 6, 10 和 15的公倍數。**least/lowest common ~**, (abbr 略作 **LCM**) least quantity that contains two or more given quantities exactly: 最小公倍數: *12 is the LCM of 3 and 4.* 12 是 3 和 4 的最小公倍數。⇨ factor(1).

mul·ti·plex /ˈmʌltɪpleks ; ˈmʌltə,plɛks/ *adj* having many parts or forms; of many elements. 有很多部份的;多種形式的;多種成分的。

mul·ti·pli·ca·tion /,mʌltɪplɪˈkeɪʃn ; ,mʌltəpləˈkeʃən/ *n* **1** [U] multiplying or being multiplied: 增多;倍加;乘;被乘;乘法;繁殖: *The symbol × stands for ~.* 符號 × 代表乘法。ˈ**~ table**, list of numbers, usu 1 to 12, showing the results of multiplying by the same number successively. 乘法表;乘數表。**2** [C] instance of this: 相乘之實例;乘算: *3 × 11 is an easy ~.* 3×11 是一個容易的乘算。

mul·ti·plic·ity /,mʌltɪˈplɪsətɪ ; ,mʌltəˈplɪsətɪ/ *n* [U] being great in number: 多;多樣;繁多: *the ~ of small city states into which ancient Greece was divided;* 古希臘分割成的許多小城邦; *a ~ of duties.* 繁多的職責。

mul·ti·ply /ˈmʌltɪplaɪ ; ˈmʌltə,plaɪ/ *vt, vi* (*pt, pp* -lied) **1** [VP14] ***~ sth by sth,*** add (a given quantity or number) a given number of times: 乘: *~ 3 by 5,* to make 15. 用 5 來乘 3 (得 15)。*6 multiplied by 5 is 30,* 6 × 5 = 30. 6乘以5等於 30。**2** [VP6A] produce a large number of; make greater in number: 提出大量的…;增多;增加: *~ instances,* produce a larger number of examples. 舉出更多的例證。**3** [VP2A] increase in number by procreation: 繁殖:*Rabbits ~ rapidly.* 兎子繁殖甚快。

mul·ti·tude /ˈmʌltɪtjuːd *US:* -tuːd ; ˈmʌltə,tjud/ *n* **1** [C] great number (esp of people gathered together). 多數;大批(尤指集結的人群)。**2 the ~,** the common people; the masses: 群衆;大衆: *demagogues who appeal to the ~.* 煽動群衆的政客。**3** [U] greatness of number: 大量: *like the stars in ~.* 像繁星(那麼多)。**multi·tud·in·ous** /,mʌltɪˈtjuːdɪnəs *US:* -ˈtuːdənəs ; ,mʌltəˈtjudṇəs/ *adj* very numerous; great in number. 非常多的;衆多的;大量的。

mul·tum in parvo /,mʊltəm ɪn ˈpɑːvəʊ ; ˈmʌltəm ɪn ˈpɑrvo/ *n* (Lat) much in a small space. (拉)形體小而內容多。

mum[1] /mʌm ; mʌm/ *int, n* Silence! 安靜! ***Mum's***

the word! Say nothing about this. 別說出去！□ *adj* ***keep mum,*** silent. 保持安靜。

mum[2] /mʌm ; mʌm/ *n* (colloq) mother. (俗)媽；母親。

mumble /ˈmʌmbl ; ˈmʌmbl/ *vt, vi* [VP6A, 2A, C] **1** say sth, speak one's words, indistinctly: 喃喃而言；言語不清；咕噥: *The old man was mumbling away to himself.* 那個老人不停地喃喃自語。*Don't ~ your words.* 別喃喃而言。 **2** bite or chew as with toothless gums. 如無齒般地咀嚼；癟着嘴咀嚼。

mumbo-jumbo /ˌmʌmbəʊ ˈdʒʌmbəʊ ; ˈmʌmbo-ˈdʒʌmbo/ *n* meaningless or obscure ritual; gibberish. 無意義或曖昧難解的宗教儀式；無意義的聲音。

mum·mer /ˈmʌmə(r) ; ˈmʌmɚ/ *n* actor in an old form of drama without words. 啞劇演員。**~y** *n* (*pl* -ries) **1** [C] performance by ~s; dumb show. 啞劇演員的表演；啞劇。 **2** [U] foolish or unnecessary ceremonial (esp religious); [C] instance of this. 愚昧或無必要的儀式(尤指宗教的)。

mum·mify /ˈmʌmɪfaɪ ; ˈmʌmɪˌfaɪ/ *vt* (*pt, pp* -fied) [VP6A] preserve (a corpse) by embalming; shrivel. 用香料防腐法保存(屍體)；使皺縮。**mum·mi·fi·ca·tion** /ˌmʌmɪfɪˈkeɪʃn ; ˌmʌmɪfəˈkeʃən/ *n*

mummy[1] /ˈmʌmɪ ; ˈmʌmɪ/ *n* (*pl* -mies) body of a human being or animal embalmed for burial; dried-up body preserved from decay (as in early Egypt). 爲埋葬而塗有香料以防腐的人或獸的屍體；(經過防腐處理的)乾屍(如古埃及所爲者)；木乃伊。

a mummy in a sarcophagus

mummy[2] /ˈmʌmɪ ; ˈmʌmɪ/ *n* (*pl* -mies) (chiefly child's word for) mother. (主要爲小兒語)媽咪；媽媽。

mumps /mʌmps ; mʌmps/ *n* (with *sing v*) contagious disease with painful swellings in the neck. (用單數動詞)耳下腺炎；腮腺炎。

munch /mʌntʃ ; mʌntʃ/ *vt, vi* [VP6A, 2A, C] chew with much movement of the jaw: 用力咀嚼；大聲咀嚼: *~ing away at a hard apple;* 用力咬嚼一個硬蘋果; *cattle ~ing their fodder.* 正在大聲咀嚼草料的牛群。

mun·dane /mʌnˈdeɪn ; ˈmʌnden/ *adj* **1** worldly (contrasted with *spiritual* or *heavenly*): 世俗的；塵世的(與 spiritual 或 heavenly 相對): *When a man is near death he loses interest in ~ affairs.* 人快要死的時候，對世事都失去興趣。 **2** dull, ordinary: 平凡的: *~ occupations/speeches.* 平凡的職業(演說)。**~·ly** *adv*

mu·nici·pal /mjuːˈnɪsɪpl ; mjuˈnɪsəpḷ/ *adj* of a town or city having self-government: 市的；市政的；自治城市的: *~ buildings,* eg the town hall, public library; 市屬建築物(如市政廳，公共圖書館)；*~ undertakings,* eg the supply of water, tram and bus services; 市營事業(如自來水之供應，公共電車及公共汽車之營運)；*the ~ debt.* 市債。 **~ly** /-pəlɪ ; -pḷɪ/ *adv* **~·ity** /mjuːˌnɪsɪˈpælətɪ ; ˌmjunɪsəˈpælətɪ/ *n* (*pl* -ties) town, city, district, with local self-government; governing body of such a town, etc. 自治市；自治區；市政府。

mu·nifi·cent /mjuːˈnɪfɪsnt ; mjuˈnɪfəsṇt/ *adj* (formal) extremely generous; (of sth given) large in amount or splendid in quality. (正式用語)非常慷慨的；寬厚的；(指給與之物)大量的；精美的。**~·ly** *adv* **mu·nifi·cence** /-sns ; -sṇs/ *n* [U] great generosity. 慷慨；大度；寬厚；寬大。

mu·ni·ments /ˈmjuːnɪmənts ; ˈmjunəmənts/ *n* (legal) documents kept as evidence of rights or privileges. (法律)契據；證書。

mu·ni·tion /mjuːˈnɪʃn ; mjuˈnɪʃən/ *n* (*pl* except when attrib) military supplies, esp guns, shells, bombs, etc: (用複數，但作形容用法時用單數)軍火；軍需品(尤指槍砲、砲彈、炸彈等): *The war was lost because of a shortage of ~s/a ~ shortage.* 戰事因爲缺乏軍火而失敗。□ *vt* [VP6A] provide with ~s: 供以軍火: *~ a fort.* 以軍火供應一個堡壘。

mural /ˈmjʊərəl ; ˈmjʊrəl/ *adj* of, like, on, a wall: 牆壁的；似壁的；在壁上的: *a ~ painting.* 一幅壁畫。□ *n* [C] wall-painting; fresco. 壁畫。

mur·der /ˈmɜːdə(r) ; ˈmɝdɚ/ *n* **1** [U] unlawful killing of a human being on purpose; [C] instance of this: 謀殺；謀殺案: *commit ~;* 犯殺人罪; *be declared guilty of ~;* 被宣判犯殺人罪; *six ~s in one week.* 一星期內有六起殺人案。 ***cry blue ~,*** (colloq) shout loudly and in alarm. (俗)大聲而驚慌地喊叫。***ˌM~ will ˈout,*** (prov) cannot be hidden. (諺)謀殺案終必敗露；紙包不住火。⇨ homicide, manslaughter, regicide, etc. **2** [U] unjustifiable sacrifice of life (eg in war): (戰時等之)無端殺害；濫殺無辜；屠殺: *Nothing could justify the bombing of the town; it was sheer ~.* 實在沒有理由轟炸這個城市；這簡直是屠殺。□ *vt* [VP6A] **1** kill (a human being) unlawfully and on purpose. 謀殺。 **2** spoil by lack of skill or knowledge: (因缺乏技術或知識而)糟塌: *~ a piece of music,* play it very badly. 把一支曲子演奏得糟透了。*Do you ever ~ the English language?* 你有沒有胡亂使用英語？ **~er** *n* person guilty of ~. 謀殺犯；兇手。 **~·ess** /-ɪs ; -ɪs/ *n* woman ~er. 女謀殺犯；女兇手。 **~·ous** /ˈmɜːdərəs ; ˈmɝdərəs/ *adj* planning, suggesting, designed for, ~: 計畫、暗示或設計來殺人的；謀殺的；要人命的；兇殘的: *a ~ous-looking villain;* 一臉兇殺相的惡棍; *a ~ous burst of fire from the enemy's guns.* 敵人槍砲冒出的兇惡火焰。 **~·ous·ly** *adv*

murk /mɜːk ; mɝk/ *n* [U] darkness; gloom. 黑暗；陰暗。**~y** *adj* (-ier, -iest) dark; gloomy: 暗的；陰暗的: *a ~y night;* 黑夜; (of darkness) thick. (指黑暗)深的；濃的。**~·ily** /-ɪlɪ ; -əlɪ/ *adv*

mur·mur /ˈmɜːmə(r) ; ˈmɝmɚ/ *n* **1** low, continuous, indistinct sound, rising and falling very little in pitch: 低沉連續而極少高低變化的模糊聲: *the ~ of bees in the garden;* 花園中蜜蜂的嗡嗡聲; *the ~ of a distant brook/of distant traffic.* 遠方溪流的潺潺聲(遠處車輛的隆隆聲)。 **2** softly spoken word(s): 低語；輕語: *a ~ of conversation from the next room.* 隔壁房間裏傳來的輕微的談話聲。 **3** subdued expression of feeling: 表示感情的細語；怨言: *a ~ of delight.* 表示愉快的細語。*They paid the higher taxes without a ~,* ie without complaining. 他們毫無怨言地付了更高的稅。□ *vi, vt* **1** [VP2A, C] make a ~(1): 發低沉連續的模糊聲: *a ~ing brook.* 潺潺的小溪。 **2** [VP2A, C, 3A] ~ ***(at/against),*** complain in a ~(3): (對…)低聲抱怨: *~ at injustice;* 抱怨不公平; *~ against new taxes.* 抱怨新的稅捐。 **3** [VP6A] utter in a low voice: 低聲說: *~ a prayer.* 低聲作禱告。

murphy /ˈmɜːfɪ ; ˈmɝfɪ/ *n* (*pl* -phies) (sl) potato. (俚)馬鈴薯。

mur·rain /ˈmʌrɪn ; ˈmʌrɪn/ *n* **1** [U] infectious disease of cattle. 牛瘟；牛疫。 **2** (old use): (舊用法): *A ~ on you!* A plague on you! Curse you! 該死的！天咒你！

mus·ca·tel /ˌmʌskəˈtel ; ˌmʌskəˈtɛl/ *n* [U] rich, sweet wine made from musk-flavoured kinds of grape. 麝香葡萄酒。

muscle /ˈmʌsl ; ˈmʌsl/ *n* [C, U] (band or bundle of) elastic substance in an animal body that can be tightened or loosened to produce movement: (一束)肌肉: *When you walk you exercise your leg ~s.* 你走路時就會使你腿上的肌肉得到運動。 *Physical exercises develop ~.* 運動鍛鍊肌肉。 *Don't move a ~,* stay perfectly still. 不要動。 **ˈ~-man** /-mæn ; -ˌmæn/ *n* (*pl* -men) man of great muscular development. 肌肉發達的人；力氣大的人。 **ˈ~-bound** *adj* having stiff ~s as the result of over-training or excessive exercise. (因過度運動而)肌肉僵硬的。□ *vi* [VP2C] ~ '*in (on sth)*, (colloq) use force to get a share (of sth considered advantageous). (俗)强取;奪取;用强制手段取得(一份利益)。

Mus·covy /ˈmʌskəvɪ ; ˈmʌskəvɪ/ *n* (old name for) Russia. (舊名稱)俄羅斯。**Mus·co·vite** /ˈmʌskəvaɪt ; ˈmʌskəˌvaɪt/ *n, adj* (citizen) of Moscow. 莫斯科人;莫斯科的。

mus·cu·lar /ˈmʌskjʊlə(r) ; ˈmʌskjələ/ *adj* **1** of the muscles: 肌肉的: ~ *tissue / rheumatism.* 肌肉組織(肌肉風濕病)。 **2** having strong muscles. 肌肉發達的。

muse[1] /mju:z ; mjuz/ *n* **1 the M~s,** (Gk myth) the nine goddesses, daughters of Zeus, who protected and encouraged poetry, music, dancing, history and other branches of art and learning. (希神)繆司女神(宙斯的九個女兒,爲保護並鼓勵詩歌、音樂、舞蹈、歷史和其他藝術與學術的女神);文藝女神。 **2 (the) M~,** poet's genius; spirit that inspires a poet. 詩才;詩人的靈感;詩興。

muse[2] /mju:z ; mjuz/ *vi* [VP2A, 3A] ~ *(over / on / upon)*, think deeply or dreamily, ignoring what is happening around one: 沉思;冥想: *musing over memories of the past.* 緬懷往事。**mus·ing·ly** *adv*

mu·seum /mju:ˈzɪəm ; mjuˈziəm/ *n* building in which objects illustrating art, history, science, etc are displayed. 博物館。*a* '~ *piece*, fine specimen suitable for a ~; (fig) sth or sb antiquated. 適合陳列於博物館中的精緻標本;(喻)過時的人或物;舊思想的人。

mush /mʌʃ ; mʌʃ/ *n* [U] soft, thick mixture or mass; (US) boiled corn meal. 軟而濃的混合物或塊物;(美)玉蜀黍粥。**~y** *adj* like ~; (colloq) weakly sentimental. 像濃粥的;糊狀的;(俗)多愁善感的。

mush·room /ˈmʌʃrʊm *US:* -ru:m ; ˈmʌʃrum/ *n* [C] fast-growing fungus of which some kinds can be eaten: 蕈;菌;蘑菇: (attrib) (形容用法) *the* ~ (= rapid) *growth of London suburbs.* 倫敦郊區的迅速發展。*The* ~ *cloud* (because of its ~ shape) *of a nuclear explosion.* 核爆所生的蕈狀雲。⇨ the illus at fungus. 參看 fungus 之插圖。□ *vi* **1** *go ~ing,* go out into the fields to gather ~s. 採蘑菇去。 **2** [VP2C] spread or grow rapidly: 迅速發展或生長: *English language schools are ~ing in Bournemouth.* 英語學校像雨後春筍般紛紛在波芳斯市設立。

mu·sic /ˈmju:zɪk ; ˈmjuzɪk/ *n* [U] art of making pleasing combinations of sounds in rhythm, harmony and counterpoint; the sounds and composition so made; written or printed signs representing these sounds: 作曲法;音樂;樂曲;樂譜: (attrib) (形容用法) *a* ~ *lesson / teacher.* 音樂課(老師)。 *face the ~,* face one's critics; face difficulties boldly. 面對批評者;勇敢地面對困難。*set / put sth to ~,* provide words, eg of a poem, with ~. 將…配上音樂。'**~-box** *n* (US) musical-box, ⇨ musical. (美)音樂匣。 '**~-hall** *n* (GB) hall or theatre used for variety entertainment (eg songs, acrobatic performances, juggling). (英)雜耍戲院;歌廳。⇨ *concert-hall* at concert[1](1). '**~-stand** *n* light (usu folding) framework for holding sheets of printed music. 樂譜架。'**~-stool** *n* seat without a back (usu adjustable in height) used when playing a piano. 琴櫈(彈奏鋼琴時用的無靠背櫈子,通常可調節高低)。⇨ the illus at brass, keyboard, notation, percussion, string. 參看 brass, keyboard, notation, percussion, string 之插圖。

mu·si·cal /ˈmju:zɪkl ; ˈmjuzɪkl/ *adj* of, fond of, skilled in, music: 音樂的;愛好音樂的;精於音樂的: ~ *instruments,* eg the violin, piano, harp; 樂器(如小提琴,鋼琴,豎琴); *She's not at all* ~, does not enjoy or understand music. 她不喜歡音樂;她不懂音樂。'**~-box** *n* box with a mechanical device that produces a tune when the box is opened. 音樂匣(盒內有機械裝置,匣蓋開啓時卽鳴奏簡單音樂)。 ˌ~ '**chairs,** game in which players go round a row of chairs one fewer than the number of players. Each time the music stops, the players sit down and the one left without a chair is eliminated. 佔椅子遊戲(參加遊戲者繞着一排椅子而走,椅子數比遊戲人數少一。每一次音樂停止時,參加者佔一椅子坐下,佔不到椅子的人被淘汰)。ˌ~ '**comedy,** a light, amusing play with songs and dancing. 喜歌劇;歌舞劇。□ *n* [C] **1** musical comedy. 喜歌劇;歌舞劇。**2** cinema film in which songs have an essential part. 音樂片(以音樂爲主的電影片)。**~ly** /-klɪ ; -kl̩ɪ/ *adv*

mu·si·cian /mju:ˈzɪʃn ; mjuˈzɪʃən/ *n* person skilled in music; composer of music. 精於音樂的人;樂師;音樂家;作曲家。**~·ship** *n* [U] art and skill in (performing) music. 音樂家的技巧。

musk /mʌsk ; mʌsk/ *n* [U] **1** strong-smelling substance produced in glands by male deer, used in the manufacture of perfumes. 麝香(雄鹿腺體所分泌的物質,具强烈香味,用以製香水)。'**~-deer** *n* small hornless deer of central Asia. 麝;麝香鹿(產於中亞的一種體小的無角鹿)。'**~-rat** (or 或作 *musquash*) *n* large rat-like water animal of N America, valuable for its fur. 麝香鼠(北美產的一種似鼠的大水生動物,其毛皮甚爲珍貴)。 **2** kinds of plant with musky smell. 麝香植物。'**~ melon** *n* sweet juicy kind of melon. 一種香瓜;甜瓜;金瓜。'**~-rose** *n* rambling rose with large, sweet-smelling flowers. 麝香玫瑰。**~y** *adj* (-ier, -iest) having the smell of ~. 有麝香味的。

mus·ket /ˈmʌskɪt ; ˈmʌskɪt/ *n* firearm used by foot-soldiers (16th to 19th cc) now replaced by the rifle. (十六世紀至十九世紀步兵所用的)舊式步槍;滑膛槍(今已爲來復槍所取代)。**~·eer** /ˌmʌskɪˈtɪə(r) ; ˌmʌskəˈtɪr/ *n* foot-soldier armed with a ~. 裝備滑膛槍的步兵。**~ry** /ˈmʌskɪtrɪ ; ˈmʌskɪtrɪ/ *n* [U] **1** (science of, instruction in) shooting with rifles. 步槍射擊(術);步槍射擊教練。**2** (old use) troops armed wtih ~s. (舊用法)裝備滑膛槍的軍隊。

Mus·lim /ˈmʊzlɪm *US:* ˈmʌzləm ; ˈmʌzləm/ *n* one who professes Islam; follower of Muhammad; (attrib) of ~s and Islam: 回教徒;(形容用法)回教徒的: ~ *historians / holidays.* 回教歷史家(回教節日)。

mus·lin /ˈmʌzlɪn ; ˈmʌzlɪn/ *n* [U] thin, fine, cotton cloth, used for dresses, curtains, etc. (做衣服、窗帷等用的)細薄棉布。

mus·quash /ˈmʌskwɒʃ ; ˈmʌskwɑʃ/ *n* (fur of the) musk-rat. 麝香鼠;麝香鼠皮。⇨ musk (1).

muss /mʌs ; mʌs/ *n* (US) [U] disorder; [C] muddle. (美)混亂;雜亂。□ *vt* [VP6A, 15B] ~ *(up)*, put into disorder: 使混亂: *Don't ~ up my hair!* 別弄亂我的頭髮!

mus·sel /ˈmʌsl ; ˈmʌsl̩/ *n* (sorts of) mollusc with a black shell in two parts. 貽貝;淡菜。⇨ the illus at bivalve. 參看 bivalve 之插圖。

must[1] /mʌst ; mʌst/ *n* [U] grape-juice before fermentation has changed it into wine. 發酵前的葡萄汁。

must[2] /*usual form:* məst ; məst; *strong form:* mʌst; mʌst/ *aux v, anom fin* (No infinitive, no participles, no inflected forms; ~ *not* may be contracted to ~n't /ˈmʌsnt ; ˈmʌsn̩t/.) (無不定詞,無分詞,亦無字形變化; must not 可縮寫爲 mustn't。) [VP5] **1** (expressing an immediate or future obligation or necessity; ~ *not* expresses a prohibition. Cf the use of *may* to express permission and of *need not* to express non-obligation. Cf the use of *had to* for a past obligation and *shall / will have to* for a future obligation): (表示立卽的或將來的義務或必需;must not 表示禁止。參較 may 表示許可,與 need not 表示無義務的用法。參較 had to 爲過去義務,與 shall 或 will have to 爲將來義務的用法): *You ~ do as you're told.* 你必須照着吩咐去做。*Soldiers ~ obey orders.* 軍人必須服從命令。*Cars ~ not be parked in front of the entrance.* 車輛不可停在入口處。*You ~n't do that.* 你不可以做那件事。*We ~n't be late, ~ we?* 我們不可以遲到,是嗎? *A: 'M~ you go so soon?' B: 'Yes, I*

~.' (or) *'No, I needn't.'* 甲:'你必須這麼早去嗎?' 乙:'是的,我必須這麼早去。' (或) '不,我不需要這麼早去。' **2** (= *had to*, used to indicate what was necessary or obligatory at a time in the past): (用以表示過去的必要或義務): *She said she ~ have a new hat for Easter.* 她說復活節時她必須要有一頂新帽子。*As he had broken it, he agreed that he ~ buy a new one.* 由於他把它弄破了,他答應要買一個新的。*On the other side of the wood was a field that he ~ cross.* 森林的另一邊有一片他必須穿過的田野。**3** (with less emphasis on necessity; stressing what is desirable or advisable): (不太强調必要;着重想做或該做之事)應該:*We ~ see what can be done.* 我們應該看看能做些什麼。*I ~ ask you not to do that again.* 我應該勸你不要再做那種事情。 **4** (expressing certainty): (表示確定)一定: *Don't bet on horse-races, you ~ lose* (= will certainly lose) *in the long run.* 不要賭賽馬,你終久必輸。 **5** (expressing strong probability): (表示極大的可能性)必定;必然: *You ~ be hungry after your long walk.* 你走了遠路後必定會餓。*This ~ be* (= very probably is) *the book you want.* 這一本一定是你要的書。*You ~ have known* (= Surely you knew) *what she wanted.* 你當時一定知道她要什麼。 *You ~ be joking!* You can't be serious! 你一定是在開玩笑罷! **6** (indicating the occurrence of sth unwelcome, sth contrary to what was wanted): (表示發生不受歡迎或不需要之事): *He ~ come and worry her with questions, just when she was busy cooking the dinner!* 正當她在忙着做飯的時候,偏巧他來了,問一些問題麻煩她! □ *n* (colloq) sth that ~ be done, seen, heard, etc: (俗)必須做、看、聽等的事: *Green's new novel is a ~ for all lovers of crime fiction.* 格林新出版的小說是愛好罪犯小說者所必須看的一本書。

mus·tache /ˈmʌstæʃ ; ˈmʌstæʃ/ *n* (US) = moustache.

mus·tachio /məˈstɑːʃɪəʊ *US:* -ˈstæʃ- ; məˈstɑʃo/ *n* (*pl* ~s /-ɪəʊz ; -oz/) a large (usu long-haired) moustache. 大片的(通常很長的)髭。

mus·tang /ˈmʌstæŋ ; ˈmʌstæŋ/ *n* small wild or half-wild horse of the American plains. 產於美國平原的小野馬或半野馬。

mus·tard /ˈmʌstəd ; ˈmʌstɚd/ *n* [U] **1** plant with yellow flowers and seeds (black or white) in long, slender pods. 芥。 **2** fine, yellow powder made from the seeds of this plant; this powder made into hot-tasting sauce. 芥末;芥粉;芥子醬。ˈ~ **gas** *n* kind of liquid poison with vapour that burns the skin (used in World War I). 芥子氣(第一次世界大戰中用的一種糜爛皮膚的毒氣)。ˈ~ **plaster** *n* poultice made with ~. 芥末硬膏。***as keen as ~,*** very keen. 很起勁;很感興趣。 ***grain of ˈ~ seed,*** sth very small capable of developing into sth very large. 一粒芥菜種(喻可以長得很大的小東西)。⇨ Matt 13: 31. 參看聖經馬太福音 13 章 31 節。

mus·ter /ˈmʌstə(r) ; ˈmʌstɚ/ *n* assembly or gathering of persons, esp for review or inspection. 人員的集合;集中(尤指爲檢閱或檢查而召集者)。 ***pass ˈ~,*** be considered satisfactory; be good enough for the purpose or occasion. 被認爲滿意;合格。□ *vt, vi* [VP6A, 15B, 2A] ~ ***(up),*** call, collect or gather together: 召集;集合;集中: *Go and ~ all the men you can find.* 去把能找到的人都集合起來。*They ~ed (up) all their courage.* 他們鼓起所有的勇氣。

musty /ˈmʌstɪ ; ˈmʌstɪ/ *adj* (-ier, -iest) **1** stale; smelling or tasting mouldy: 有霉味的;發霉的: ~ *books;* 發霉的書; *a ~ room.* 有霉味的房間。 **2** (fig) stale; out-of-date: (喻)陳舊的;過時的: *a professor with ~ ideas.* 觀念陳舊的教授。 **musti·ness** /ˈmʌstɪnɪs ; ˈmʌstɪnɪs/ *n*

mu·table /ˈmjuːtəbl ; ˈmjutəbl̩/ *adj* liable to change; likely to change. 可變的;易變的;不定的。 **mu·ta·bil·ity** /ˌmjuːtəˈbɪlətɪ ; ˌmjutəˈbɪlətɪ/ *n* [U].

mu·ta·tion /mjuːˈteɪʃn ; mjuˈteʃən/ *n* [U] change; alteration; [C] instance of this: 變化;更換;轉變: *Are ~s in plants caused by cosmic rays?* 植物的變種是宇宙射線所造成的嗎?

mu·ta·tis mu·tan·dis /muːˌtɑːtɪs muːˈtændɪs ; mjuˈtetɪs mjuˈtændɪs/ *adv* (Lat) with necessary alterations or changes (when comparing cases). (拉)(就實際情形)已作必要改變或修正。

mute /mjuːt ; mjut/ *adj* **1** silent; making no sound: 沉默的;無聲的: *staring at me in ~ amazement.* 目瞪口呆地凝視着我。 **2** (of a person) dumb; unable to speak. (指人)啞吧的;不能說話的。 **3** (of a letter in a word) not sounded: (指字中的字母) 不讀音的;不發音的: *The 'b' in 'dumb' is ~.* 'dumb' 字中的 'b' 是不讀音的。□ *n* **1** dumb person. 啞子;啞吧。 **2** piece of bone or metal used to soften the sounds produced from a stringed instrument; pad placed in the mouth of a wind instrument for the same purpose. 弱音器 (置於樂器上使聲音變柔和的裝置,在弦樂器上者爲骨片或金屬小片;在管樂器上者爲管口的塞頭)。□ *vt* [VP6A] deaden or muffle the sound of (esp a musical instrument). 減弱或減低(尤指樂器)的聲音。~**·ly** *adv*

mu·ti·late /ˈmjuːtɪleɪt ; ˈmjutl̩ˌet/ *vt* [VP6A] damage by breaking, tearing or cutting off a necessary part; destroy the use of (a limb, etc). 使殘缺不全;使殘廢;殘害;毀壞;切斷(手足等)。**mu·ti·la·tion** /ˌmjuːtɪˈleɪʃn ; ˌmjutl̩ˈeʃən/ *n* [U] mutilating or being ~d; [C] injury or loss caused by this. 毀傷;殘害;由此種殘害所造成的損傷或損失。

mu·ti·nous /ˈmjuːtɪnəs ; ˈmjutn̩əs/ *adj* guilty of mutiny; rebellious: 反叛的;叛變的;反抗的: ~ *sailors;* 叛變的水手; ~ *behaviour.* 背叛的行爲。

mu·tiny /ˈmjuːtɪnɪ ; ˈmjutn̩ɪ/ *n* (*pl* -nies) [U] (esp of soldiers and sailors) open rebellion against lawful authority; [C] instance of this. (尤指軍人和水手)譁變;抗命;叛變;兵變。□ *vi* [VP2A, 3A] ~ ***(against),*** be guilty of ~; revolt. 叛變;反抗。**mu·tin·eer** /ˌmjuːtɪˈnɪə(r) ; ˌmjutn̩ˈɪr/ *n* person guilty of ~. 反叛者;叛兵;反抗者。

mutt /mʌt ; mʌt/ *n* (sl) (俚) **1** ignorant blunderer: 笨蛋: *You silly big ~!* 你這大笨蛋! **2** mongrel dog. 雜種狗。

mut·ter /ˈmʌtə(r) ; ˈmʌtɚ/ *vt, vi* [VP6A, 14, 2A, C] speak, say (sth), in a low voice not meant to be heard; grumble in an indistinct voice: 輕聲低語;喃喃而語;咕噥地抱怨: *He was ~ing away to himself.* 他不停地喃喃自語。 *Are you ~ing threats at me?* 你是在咕噥咕噥地對我說威脅話嗎? *We heard thunder ~ing in the distance.* 我們聽到遠處隆隆的雷聲。□ *n* ~ed utterance or sound. 喃喃低語;呢喃低語聲。~**er** *n* person who ~s. 喃喃低語者。

mut·ton /ˈmʌtn ; ˈmʌtn̩/ *n* [U] flesh of fully grown sheep: 羊肉: *a leg/shoulder of ~;* 羊腿(羊的肩膀肉); *roast ~;* 烤羊肉; *a ~ chop,* piece of ~ rib. 羊排(帶肋骨的一片羊肉)。 ***as dead as ~,*** quite dead. 死翹翹了。~ ***dressed as lamb,*** used of an elderly person dressed in a style suitable for a young person. (指作年輕人打扮的老年人)老來俏。ˈ~**-head** *n* (colloq) dull, stupid person. (俗)愚人;笨人。

mu·tual /ˈmjuːtʃʊəl ; ˈmjutʃʊəl/ *adj* **1** (of love, friendship, respect, etc) shared; exchanged equally; (of feelings, opinions, etc) held in common with others: (指愛情、友誼、尊敬等)共有的;相互的;(指感情、意見等)與旁人共同持有的: ~ *suspicion/affection.* 互相猜疑(互愛)。 **2** each to the other(s): 彼此的;相互的: ~ *enemies/well-wishers;* 互相敵對的人(互相祝福者); ~ *aid.* 互助。~ **funds,** (US) (美) = unit trusts. **a** ˌ~ **inˈsurance company,** one in which some or all of the profits are divided among the policy-holders. 互助保險公司 (部份或全部的營利由投保人分享的保險公司)。 **3** common to two or more persons: 爲兩人或更多人所共有的; 共同的: *our ~ friend Smith,* ie Smith, a friend of both of us. 我們共同的朋友史密斯。~**ly** /-ʊəlɪ ; -ʊəlɪ/ *adv*

muzzle /ˈmʌzl ; ˈmʌzl̩/ *n* **1** nose and mouth of an animal (eg dog or fox); guard of straps or wires placed over this part of an animal's head to prevent it biting, etc. (狗或狐等的) 鼻和嘴；動物的口套；口絡。⇨ the illus at dog. 參看 dog 之揷圖。**2** ⇨ the illus at cannon. 參看 cannon 之揷圖。open end or mouth of a fire-arm: 槍口；砲口：*a ~-loading gun.* 前膛裝塡的槍或砲。**'~-velocity,** speed of a projectile as it leaves the ~. (彈丸離開槍砲口時的) 初速；槍(砲)口速度。⇨ breech. □ *vt* [VP 6A] put a ~ on (a dog, etc); (fig) prevent (a person, society, newspaper, etc) from expressing opinions freely. 戴口絡於(狗等)的口部；(喻)禁止(人、會社、報紙等)自由發表意見。

muzzy /ˈmʌzɪ ; ˈmʌzɪ/ *adj* (-ier, -iest) **1** confused in mind; spiritless; stupid from drinking. 迷糊的；沒精神的；醉得發呆的。**2** blurred. 弄污的；模糊不清的。

my /maɪ ; maɪ/ *poss adj* **1** belonging to me: 我的：*Where's my hat?* 我的帽子在哪裏？ *This car is my own.* 這部汽車是我自己的。**2** as a part of a form of address: 作爲稱呼的一部份：*Yes, my dear.* 是的，我親愛的。*My dear fellow!* 我親愛的夥伴！ **3** in exclamations: 用於驚歎語中：*My goodness!* 天呀！ *Oh, my!* 啊呀！

my·col·ogy /maɪˈkɒlədʒɪ ; maɪˈkɑlədʒɪ/ *n* [U] science or study of fungi. 眞菌學；黴菌學。

my·el·itis /ˌmaɪəˈlaɪtɪs ; ˌmaɪəˈlaɪtɪs/ *n* (path) inflammation of the spinal cord. (病理)脊髓炎。

my·na(h) /ˈmaɪnə ; ˈmaɪnə/ *n* **'~ (bird),** (kinds of) starling of SE Asia, known for their ability to mimic human speech. (產於東南亞之能模倣人語的)燕八哥。⇨ the illus at rare. 參看 rare 之揷圖。

my·opia /maɪˈəʊpɪə ; maɪˈopɪə/ *n* [U] short-sightedness. 近視。**my·opic** /maɪˈɒpɪk ; maɪˈɑpɪk/ *adj* short-sighted. 近視的。

myr·iad /ˈmɪrɪəd ; ˈmɪrɪəd/ *n* [C] ~ ***(of),*** very great number. 極大數量。

myr·mi·don /ˈmɜːmɪdən *US:* -dɒn ; ˈmɝməˌdɑn/ *n* (contemptuous or humorous term for a) person who carries out any kind of order without questions: (輕蔑或詼諧用語)毫不遲疑奉行任何命令的人：*~s of the law,* eg bailiffs. 法律執行官；警察。

myrrh /mɜː(r) ; mɝ/ *n* [U] sweet-smelling, bitter-tasting kind of gum or resin obtained from shrubs, used for making incense and perfumes. 沒藥(一種有香氣、帶苦味的樹脂，用以製造香料)。

myrtle /ˈmɜːtl ; ˈmɝtl̩/ *n* (kinds of) evergreen shrub with shiny leaves and sweet-smelling white flowers. 桃金孃(數種常綠灌木，葉發亮，開有香味的白花)。

my·self /maɪˈself ; maɪˈsɛlf/ *pron* (reflex and emphat): (反身及强勢語)我自己：*I hurt ~.* 我傷了自己。*I can do it (all) by ~,* ie without help. 我能獨自做。*I tired ~ out.* 我疲倦極了。*I ~ said so.* 我親口這麼說的。*I said so ~.* 我親口這麼說的。*I'm not ~ today,* am not feeling so well as I usually do. 我今天有點不舒服(或失常)。

mys·teri·ous /mɪˈstɪərɪəs ; mɪsˈtɪrɪəs/ *adj* full of, suggesting, covered in, mystery: 神秘的；難解的；隱秘的：*a ~ crime;* 神秘的罪行；*a ~-looking parcel.* 一個樣子很神秘的包裹。**~·ly** *adv*

mys·tery /ˈmɪstərɪ ; ˈmɪstərɪ/ *n* (*pl* -ries) **1** [C] sth of which the cause or origin is hidden or impossible to understand: 神秘的事物；不可思議的事物；難解的事物：*The murder remained an unsolved ~.* 那件謀殺案仍然是個解不開的謎。**2** [U] condition of being secret or obscure: 秘密；神秘：*The origin of this tribe is lost in ~,* It has been impossible to learn anything about it. 這個種族的來源是個難解的謎。**3** (*pl*) secret religious rites and ceremonies (of ancient Greeks, Romans, etc). (複)(古希臘、羅馬等的)秘密的宗教儀式。**4** [C] **'~ (play),** medieval drama based on episodes in the life of Jesus. 神蹟劇(以耶穌一生事蹟爲本的中古戲劇)。

mys·tic /ˈmɪstɪk ; ˈmɪstɪk/ *adj* of hidden meaning or spiritual power; causing feelings of awe and wonder: 神秘的；不可思議的；令人敬畏而驚奇的：*~ rites and ceremonies;* 神秘的儀式；*~ teachings.* 神秘的教義。□ *n* person who seeks union with God and, through that, realization of truth beyond men's understanding. 尋求接近上帝藉以了解人類所不能明白的眞理的人；神秘主義者。**mys·ti·cal** /ˈmɪstɪkl ; ˈmɪstəkl̩/ *adj* = mystic.

mys·ti·cism /ˈmɪstɪsɪzəm ; ˈmɪstəˌsɪzəm/ *n* [U] beliefs, experiences, of a mystic; teaching and belief that knowledge of God and of real truth may be obtained through meditation or spiritual insight, independently of the mind and the senses. 神秘主義；相信不用思考力與感官而藉默想與心靈內省可以認識上帝與眞理的學說。

mys·tify /ˈmɪstɪfaɪ ; ˈmɪstəˌfaɪ/ *vt* (*pt, pp* -fied) [VP6A] puzzle; bewilder. 使迷惑；使困惑。**mys·ti·fi·ca·tion** /ˌmɪstɪfɪˈkeɪʃn ; ˌmɪstəfəˈkeʃən/ *n* [U] ~ing or being mystified; [C] sth that mystifies. 迷惑；困惑；令人迷惑的事物。

mys·tique /mɪˈstiːk ; mɪsˈtik/ *n* **1** esoteric character of a person, institution, etc caused by mystical devotion and veneration: (由於不可思議的熱愛與崇拜所造成的個人、團體等的)神秘性：*the ~ of the monarchy in Great Britain.* 英國君主政治的奧秘。**2** incommunicable quality; skill known only to a few practitioners. 不可言傳的性質；奧妙；秘訣。

myth /mɪθ ; mɪθ/ *n* **1** [C] story, handed down from olden times, esp concepts or beliefs about the early history of a race, explanations of natural events, such as the seasons: 神話(由古相傳的故事，尤指有關一民族早期歷史的觀念或信仰、自然現象如季節等的解釋)：*ancient Greek ~s.* 古希臘的神話。**2** [U] such stories collectively: 神話(集合用法)：*famous in ~ and legend.* 在神話與傳奇中有名的。**3** [C] person, thing, etc, that is imaginary, fictitious, or invented: 想像、虛構或創造的人或事物：*That rich uncle of whom he boasts is only a ~.* 他所誇耀的那位闊叔叔不過是個虛構的人物。**~·ical** /ˈmɪθɪkl ; ˈmɪθɪkl̩/ *adj* **1** of ~; existing only in ~: 神話的；僅存在於神話中的：*~ical heroes;* 神話中的英雄；*~ical literature.* 神話文學。**2** imaginary; fictitious: 想像的；虛構的：*~ical wealth.* 想像中的財富。

myth·ol·ogy /mɪˈθɒlədʒɪ ; mɪˈθɑlədʒɪ/ *n* (*pl* -gies) **1** [U] study or science of myths. 神話學。**2** [U] myths collectively: 神話(集合用法)：*Greek ~;* 希臘神話；[C] body or collection of myths: 神話集：*the mythologies of primitive races.* 原始民族的神話集。**myth·ol·ogist** /mɪˈθɒlədʒɪst ; mɪˈθɑlədʒɪst/ *n* student of ~. 研究神話者；神話學家。**mytho·logi·cal** /ˌmɪθəˈlɒdʒɪkl ; ˌmɪθəˈlɑdʒɪkl̩/ *adj* of ~ or myths; unreal. 神話學的；神話的；非眞實的；假的。

myxo·ma·to·sis /ˌmɪksəməˈtəʊsɪs ; ˌmɪksəməˈtosɪs/ *n* [U] infectious fatal disease of rabbits. 兎瘟；兎疫。

Nn

N, n /en ; ɛn/ (*pl* N's, n's /enz ; ɛnz/) the 14th letter of the English alphabet. 英文字母的第十四個字母。

nab /næb ; næb/ *vt* (-bb-) (colloq) catch in wrong-doing; seize: (俗)逮捕；捉：*The thief was nabbed by the police.* 小偷被警察逮住了。

na·bob /ˈneɪbɒb ; ˈnebɑb/ *n* (18th c use) wealthy, luxury-loving person. (十八世紀用語)富有而喜愛奢華的人。

na·celle /næˈsel ; nəˈsɛl/ *n* outer casing for an engine of an aircraft or airship. (飛機的)發動機短

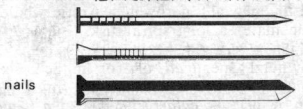

艙；(飛艇的)吊艙。⇨ the illus at air. 參看 air 之挿圖。

nacre /ˈneɪkə(r) ; ˈnekɚ/ *n* [U] mother-of-pearl. 珠母層；眞珠母。⇨ mother(4).

na·dir /ˈneɪdɪə(r) ; ˈnedɚ/ *n* point of the heavens directly beneath an observer; (fig) lowest, weakest, point: 天底；(喩)最低點；最弱點: *at the ~ of one's hopes.* 希望極爲渺茫。⇨ zenith.

nag[1] /næg ; næg/ *n* (colloq) (usu old) horse. (俗)(通常指老的)馬；駑馬。

nag[2] /næg ; næg/ *vt, vi* (-gg-) [VP6A, 2A, C, 3A] ***nag (at) (sb),*** find fault with continuously; worry or annoy by scolding: 不斷地挑剔(某人)；以責罵來惱人: *She nagged (at) him all day long.* 她整天嘮嘮叨叨地責罵他。**nag·ger** *n*

naiad /ˈnaɪæd ; ˈneæd/ *n* (*pl* ~s, ~es /-diːz ; -ˌdiz/) (Gk myth) water-nymph. (希神)水神。

nail /neɪl ; nel/ *n* **1** layer of hard substance over the outer tip of a finger (**ˈfinger-~**) or toe (**ˈtoe-~**). 指甲 (finger-nail 手指甲, toe-nail 脚趾甲)。⇨ the illus at arm, leg. 參看 arm, leg 之挿圖。***fight tooth and ~,*** with all one's strength, making every possible effort to win. 盡全力攻擊以求勝。**ˈ~·brush** *n* for cleaning the ~s. 指甲刷。⇨ the illus at brush. 參看 brush 之挿圖。**ˈ~-file,** small, flat file for shaping the ~s. 指甲銼。**ˈ~-scissors** *n* for trimming the ~s. 指甲剪刀。**ˈ~-varnish/-polish** *n* for giving a shiny tint to the ~s. 指甲油。 **2** piece of metal, pointed at one end and with a head at the other, (to be) hammered into articles to hold them together, or into a wall, etc to hang sth on. 釘；鐵釘；鋼釘。***drive a ~ into sb's coffin,*** ⇨ coffin. ***as hard as ~s,*** (of a person) (指人) **(a)** in first-rate physical condition. 身體極爲健壯的；最佳健康狀況中的。 **(b)** pitiless; unsympathetic. 無情的；無同情心的；冷酷的。***hit the ~ on the head,*** pick out the real point at issue; give the true explanation. 一針見血；說中；解釋正確；中肯。***right as ~s,*** quite right. 完全對的。***(right) on the ~,*** at once. 立即；立刻。□ *vt* [VP15A, B] **1** make fast with a ~ or ~s: 用釘釘牢: *~ a lid on a box.* 把箱蓋釘牢。*~ **sb down (to sth),*** make him say clearly what he intends to do (about sth). 使某人明白說出他打算做的事；使某人負責。*~ **sth down,*** make (eg a carpet, a cover) secure by using nails. 用釘子釘牢(如地毯、遮蓋物等)。*~ **sth up,*** make (a door, window, etc) secure with ~s. 用釘子釘住或釘牢(門、窗等)。*~ **one's colours to the mast,*** ⇨ colour[1](8). *~ **a lie (to the counter),*** prove that a statement is false. 證實某些話是假的；拆穿謊言。 **2** hold fast, keep fixed (a person, sb's attention, etc): 使固定；使不動；捉牢；吸引(人、某人的注意力等): *He ~ed me in the corridor.* 他在走廊纏住我(不讓我走開)。

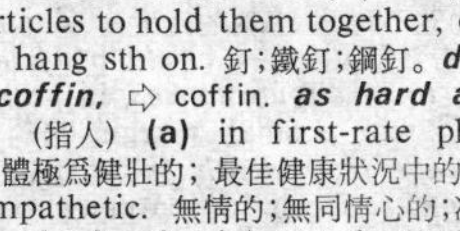

nails

nain·sook /ˈneɪnsʊk ; ˈnensʊk/ *n* [U] fine cotton cloth. 細棉布。

naira /ˈnaɪrə ; ˈnaɪrə/ *n* [C] unit of Nigerian currency, = 100 kobos. 奈拉(奈及利亞貨幣單位，合 100 科博)。

naïve, naive /naɪˈiːv ; nɑˈiv/ *adj* natural and innocent in speech and behaviour (eg because young or inexperienced); amusingly simple: 言行自然而天眞的(如因年輕或無經驗所致)；質樸的: *~ remarks/tourists.* 天眞的話(觀光客)。**~·ly** *adv* **~té** /-teɪ ; -te/, **~ty** /-tɪ ; -tɪ/ *n* [U] artlessness; being ~; [C] ~ remark, etc. 天眞；質樸；天眞的話等。

naked /ˈneɪkɪd ; ˈnekɪd/ *adj* **1** without clothes on: 裸體的: *as ~ as the day he was born.* 像他初生時那樣赤裸裸的。 **2** without the usual covering: 沒有通常的遮蓋物的: *a ~ sword,* without its sheath; 無鞘之劍; *fight with ~ fists,* without boxing-gloves; 不帶拳擊手套的打鬪; *~ trees,* without leaves; 光禿禿(無葉)的樹; *a ~ light,* not protected from the wind by glass, without a lampshade. 沒有燈罩的燈。***see sth with the ~ eye,*** without using a microscope, telescope or other aid to seeing. 用肉眼看某物(不用顯微鏡、望遠鏡或任何其他助視器)。***the ~ truth,*** not disguised, softened, ornamented. 原原本本的事實；赤裸裸的事實。**~·ly** *adv* **~·ness** *n*

namby-pamby /ˌnæmbɪ ˈpæmbɪ ; ˈnæmbɪˈpæmbɪ/ *adj* (of persons, talk) foolishly sentimental. (指人、言談)感傷得可笑的。□ *n* person of this sort. 感傷得可笑之人。

name[1] /neɪm ; nem/ *n* **1** word(s) by which a person, animal, place, thing, etc is known and spoken to or of: 名字；名稱: *A person of the ~ of Smith* (= Someone who is called Smith) *wants to see you.* 有個名叫史密斯的人要見你。*He writes under the ~ of Nimrod,* uses Nimrod instead of his real name. 他用尼蒙洛這個名字發表著作。*I know the man by ~,* only by hearsay, not by personal acquaintance. 我只知道這個人的名字。*The teacher knows all the pupils in his class by ~,* knows them individually. 該教師知道他班上全部學生的名字。***in the ~ of,*** **(a)** with the authority of: 憑…的權威: *Stop! in the Queen's ~.* 停住！憑女王的名義(命令你)。*In the ~ of the law....* 憑法律…。**(b)** in the cause of (used when making an appeal): 爲…的緣故(在提出一項懇求時使用): *In the ~ of common sense, what are you doing?* 你究竟在幹什麼？***call sb ~s,*** call him insulting ~s (eg liar, coward). 辱罵某人(爲說謊者、懦夫等)。***enter/put down one's ~ for,*** (a school, college, etc), apply for entry (at a future date). 申請 (於將來某一日期) 入(學校、大學等)。***not have a penny to one's ~,*** be without money. 沒有錢；一文不名。***lend one's ~ to,*** (an enterprise, etc), allow it to be quoted in support or in favour of (the enterprise, etc). 讓自己的名字被列爲(一項事業等) 的贊助人。***take sb's ~ in vain,*** use a ~ (esp God's) disrespectfully. 濫用某人的名字(尤指上帝之名)。**ˈ~-day** *n* feast day of the Saint whose ~ one was given at christening. 命名日(本人敎名所紀念的聖徒的節日)。**ˈ~-dropping** *n* the practice of casually mentioning the ~s of important people to impress. 隨便地提起重要人物的名字給人印象以提高身份。Hence, 由此產生, **ˈ~-drop** *vi* [VP2A] talk in this way. 隨便提起要人名字以提高身份。**ˈ~-part** *n* title-role of a play: 戲名角色: *Who will play the ~-part in 'Hamlet'?* 誰將飾演'哈姆雷特'中的哈姆雷特？**ˈ~·plate** *n* plaque (on the door of a building, room, etc) with the ~ of the occupant. 名牌(掛於建築物、房間等門上的金屬板，上有使用人的姓名)。**ˈ~·sake** *n* person or thing with the same ~ as another. 同名的人或物。**2** (*sing* only) reputation; fame. (僅用單數)名譽；聲譽。***make/win a ~ for oneself,*** become well-known. 使自己成名；爲自己贏得名聲。*The firm has a ~ for good workmanship.* 這家公司以手藝精良著稱。 **3** famous person: 著名的人物: *the great ~s of history.* 歷史上的偉人。

name[2] /neɪm ; nem/ *vt* **1** [VP6A, 14, 23] *~ **(after/** (US) **for),*** give a ~ to: 命名: *They ~d the child John.* 他們給小孩取名爲約翰。*The child was ~d after its father,* given its father's first ~. 這個小孩以他父親的名字爲名字。*Tasmania was ~d after its discoverer, A J Tasman.* 塔斯曼尼亞是以它的發現者塔斯曼爲名。 **2** [VP6A] say the ~(s) of: 說出…的名字: *Can you ~ all the plants and trees in this garden?* 你能說出這花園裏所有花草樹木的名稱嗎？ **3** make an offer of (price, etc): 提出(價格等): *N~ your price,* Say what price you want. 開出你的價格。 **4** state (what is desired, etc): 說出；指定；訂定 (所欲求者等): *Please ~ the day,* say on what date you will be willing to (eg marry). 請指定日期。 **5** [VP6A, 14] *~ **(for),*** nominate for, appoint to, a position: 提名;任命: *Mr X has been ~d for the directorship.* 某先生已經被提名擔任董事職務。

name·less /ˈneɪmlɪs ; ˈnemləs/ *adj* **1** not having a name; having an unknown name: 無名的;不知名的: *a ~ grave;* 沒有名字的墓; *a well-known person who shall be ~,* whose name I shall not mention. 姑隱其名的某一名人。 **2** too bad to be named: 太惡劣而不宜說明的: *~ vices.* 不堪說明的惡行。 **3** difficult or impossible to name or describe: 難以名狀的;無法描述的: *a ~ longing/horror.* 一種無可名狀的渴望(恐懼)。

name·ly /ˈneɪmlɪ ; ˈnemlɪ/ *adv* that is to say: 即;就是: *Only one boy was absent, ~ Harry.* 只有一個男孩缺席,就是哈利。

nan·keen /nænˈkiːn ; nænˈkin/ *n* [U] kind of cotton cloth, originally made of naturally yellow cotton. 南京棉布;原色棉布。

nanny /ˈnænɪ ; ˈnænɪ/ *n* (*pl* -nies) = nurse¹(1).

nanny-goat /ˈnænɪ gəʊt ; ˈnænɪˌgot/ *n* female goat. 母山羊;牝山羊。⇨ billy-goat.

nap¹ /næp ; næp/ *n* [C] short sleep (esp during the day, not necessarily in bed): 小睡;打盹(尤指在白天,不一定要躺在床上): *have/take a nap after lunch on a hot day.* 熱天午飯後小睡片刻。□ *vi* (-pp-) (rare, except in) (罕,除非用於) ***catch sb napping,*** find him asleep; catch him unawares (in error, etc). 看到某人在打盹;乘某人不備而抓到他的過錯等。

nap² /næp ; næp/ *n* [U] surface of cloth, felt, etc, made of soft, short hairs or fibres, smoothed and brushed up. (絨布、呢等上面的一層)細毛。

nap³ /næp ; næp/ *n* (GB) name of a card-game. (英)一種紙牌戲。

na·palm /ˈneɪpɑːm ; ˈneˌpɑm/ *n* [U] jellied petroleum used in making fire-bombs. 膠化汽油;納磅油(用以製造燒夷彈)。

nape /neɪp ; nep/ *n* back (of the neck). 頸背。⇨ the illus at head. 參看 head 之插圖。

na·pery /ˈneɪpərɪ ; ˈnepərɪ/ *n* [U] (old use) household linen, esp table linen (tablecloths and napkins). (舊用法)布巾;(尤指)桌布;餐巾。

naph·tha /ˈnæfθə ; ˈnæpθə/ *n* [U] kinds of inflammable oil obtained from coaltar and petroleum. 石油精; 石腦油 (從煤焦油和石油中提煉出來的可燃油)。 **~·lene** /-liːn ; -ˌlin/ *n* [U] strong-smelling substance made from coaltar and petroleum, used in the manufacture of dyes and (in the form of white 'moth balls') to put among clothes. 萘;臭樟腦;辟瘟腦;駢苯(從煤焦油和石油中提煉出來一種氣味濃烈的物質,用以製造染料及防蛀丸等)。

nap·kin /ˈnæpkɪn ; ˈnæpkɪn/ *n* [C] **1** (**ˈtable**) **~,** piece of cloth used at meals for protecting clothing, for wiping the lips, etc. 餐巾。**ˈ~-ring** *n* ring to hold and distinguish a person's ~. 套餐巾的小環。⇨ serviette. **2** (US 美 = *diaper*) (*nappy* is more usu) towel folded round a baby's bottom and between its legs, to absorb excreta. 嬰孩的尿布 (nappy 較常用)。

Na·po·leonic /nəˌpəʊlɪˈɒnɪk ; nəˌpolɪˈɑnɪk/ *adj* of or like Napoleon Bonaparte, ruler of France. (法國統治者)拿破崙一世的;似拿破崙一世的。

nappy /ˈnæpɪ ; ˈnæpɪ/ *n* (*pl* -pies) (GB colloq) (英俗) = napkin(2).

nar·ciss·ism /ˈnɑːsɪsɪzəm ; nɑrˈsɪsˌɪzəm/ *n* [U] (psych) obsessive and exclusive interest in one's own self. (心理)自體觀窺慾;自戀;自愛慾。

nar·cissus /nɑːˈsɪsəs ; nɑrˈsɪsəs/ *n* (*pl* ~es /-səsɪz ; -səsɪz/ or -cissi /-sɪsaɪ ; -sɪˌsaɪ/) sorts of bulb plant (daffodil, jonquil, etc), esp the kind having heavily scented white or yellow flowers in the spring. 水仙花。

nar·cotic /nɑːˈkɒtɪk ; nɑrˈkɑtɪk/ *n, adj* (kinds of drug) producing sleep, often blunting the senses and, in large doses, producing complete insensibility: 痲醉劑;痲醉的;催眠的: *Opium is a ~ drug.* 鴉片是一種痲醉藥。*The use of ~s by teenagers is a problem in many countries;* 青少年服痲醉藥在許多國家中是一個問題; (person) addicted to ~s. 耽於服用痲醉藥的(人);癮君子。

nark¹ /nɑːk ; nɑrk/ *n* (GB sl) police decoy or spy. (英俚)協助警察誘捕人犯的人;線民。

nark² /nɑːk ; nɑrk/ *vt* (GB sl) annoy: (英俚)煩擾;使苦惱: *feel ~ed at unjust criticism.* 對不公正的批評感到苦惱。

nar·rate /nəˈreɪt ; næˈret/ *vt* [VP6A] tell (a story); give an account of: 講(故事);敍述: *~ one's adventures.* 敍述奇遇。**nar·rator** /-tə(r) ; -tɚ/ *n* person who ~s. 講述者;敍述者。 **nar·ra·tion** /nəˈreɪʃn ; næˈreʃən/ *n* [U] telling of a story, etc; [C] story; account of events. 講述;故事;敍述。

nar·ra·tive /ˈnærətɪv ; ˈnærətɪv/ *n* **1** [C] story or tale; orderly account of events; [U] (composition that consists of) story-telling. 故事;敍述;講述;敍事體。 **2** (attrib) in the form of, concerned with, story-telling: (形容用法)敍述的;敍事體的: *~ literature,* stories and novels; 敍事文學(故事及小說); *~ poems;* 敍事詩; *a writer of great ~ power,* able to describe events well. 富有敍述能力的作家。

nar·row /ˈnærəʊ ; ˈnæro/ *adj* (-er, -est) (opposite of *wide*) (爲 wide 之相反字) **1** measuring little across in comparison with length: 窄的: *a ~ bridge.* 窄橋。*The road was too ~ for cars to pass.* 這條路太窄了,車輛過不去。*A ~-gauge railway is one with rails less than 4 ft 8 in apart.* 窄軌鐵路是軌寬不到四呎八吋的鐵路。 **2** small, limited: 狹小的;有限制的: *a ~ circle of friends;* 交遊狹小; *living in ~ circumstances,* in poverty. 生活於貧窮中。 **3** with a small margin: 所餘不多的;勉强的: *a ~ escape from death.* 勉强逃過死亡;九死一生。***a ~ squeak,*** (colloq) sth barely avoided or escaped from. (俗)倖免於難。*elected by a ~ majority,* eg when voting is 67 to 64. 以差距甚小之多數當選(如以 67 票對 64 票當選)。 **4** strict; exact: 嚴格的;精確的: *a ~ search.* 嚴密的搜查。*What does the word mean in the ~est sense?* 就最精確含義來說,這個字是什麼意思? **5** limited in outlook; having little sympathy for the ideas, etc, of others. 褊狹的;度量小的。**ˌ~-ˈminded** /ˈmaɪndɪd ; ˈmaɪndɪd/ *adj* not easily seeing or sympathizing with the ideas of others. 胸襟褊狹的;度量小的。 **ˌ~-ˈminded·ly** *adv* **ˌ~-ˈminded·ness** *n* □ *vt, vi* [VP6A, 2A] (cause to) become ~. 使窄小;變窄。□ *n* (usu *pl*) ~ strait or channel between two larger bodies of water; ~ place in a river or pass. (通常用複數)海峽;江峽;狹路。**~·ly** *adv* **1** only just; with little to spare: 僅僅;勉强地: *He ~ly escaped drowning.* 他差一點兒淹死。 **2** closely; carefully: 嚴密地;仔細地: *Watch that fellow ~ly.* 注意看着那傢伙。**~·ness** *n*

nar·whal /ˈnɑːwəl ; ˈnɑrhwəl/ *n* Arctic whale with (in the male) a long spiral tusk. 一角魚;角鯨(一種產於北極的鯨魚,雄者有一螺旋形的長牙)。

na·sal /ˈneɪzl ; ˈnezl̩/ *adj* of, for, in the nose: 鼻的;爲鼻子的; 在鼻中的: *~ sounds,* eg /m, n, ŋ/; 鼻音(如 /m, n, ŋ/); *~ catarrh;* 鼻黏膜炎; *a ~ douche.* 鼻孔灌洗;鼻孔灌洗器。□ *n* [C] nasal sound. 鼻音。 **~·ize** /ˈneɪzəlaɪz ; ˈnezl̩ˌaɪz/ *vt* [VP6A] make (a sound) with the air stream, or part of it, passing through the nose. 使鼻音化。

nascent /ˈnæsnt ; ˈnæsn̩t/ *adj* (formal) coming into existence; beginning to exist. (正式用語)初生的;初期的。

nas·tur·tium /nəˈstɜːʃəm *US:* næ- ; næˈstɝʃəm/ *n* [C] garden plant with red, orange or yellow flowers, round-shaped leaves, and seeds that may be pickled and eaten. 蔊菜;金蓮花。

nasty /ˈnɑːstɪ *US:* ˈnæ- ; ˈnæstɪ/ *adj* (-ier, -iest) **1** dirty; disgusting; unpleasant: 髒的;令人厭惡的;令人不快的: *medicine with a ~ smell and a nastier taste.* 既難聞而且更難吃的藥。 **2** morally dirty and unpleasant: 在道德上令人不快的; 淫猥的; 卑鄙的: *a* *man with a ~ mind;* 心思卑鄙的人；*~ stories.* 下流的故事。 **3** showing ill will and spite: 表示惡意的；壞心眼的：*a ~ temper.* 壞脾氣。 **4** dangerous; threatening: 危險的；帶有威脅意味的；威脅人的：*There was a ~ sea when we got out of the harbour.* 我們離港後，海上風浪險惡。*There was a ~ look in his eye.* 他的眼中露出威脅的眼光。 **5** causing difficulty or danger; awkward: 引起困難或危險的；難應付的：*That's a ~ corner for a car that's travelling fast.* 那是個開快車不容易通過的街角。 **nas·tily** /-ɪlɪ ; -əlɪ/ *adv* **nas·ti·ness** *n*

na·tal /ˈneɪtl ; ˈnetl̩/ *adj* of, from, one's birth. 誕生的；初生的；生來的。

na·tion /ˈneɪʃn ; ˈneʃən/ *n* [C] large community of people associated with a particular territory usu speaking a single language and usu having a political character or political aspirations: 國家；民族：*the ~s of Western Europe;* 西歐諸國；*the United N~s Organization,* UNO. 聯合國組織。⇨state¹(2). ˌ**~·ˈwide** *adj, adv* throughout a ~; concerning, expressed by, all citizens. 遍及全國(的)；有關全國公民的；由全國人民所表示的；全國性的。

na·tion·al /ˈnæʃnəl ; ˈnæʃənl̩/ *adj* of a/the nation; common to a/the whole nation; characteristic of a/the nation: 國家的；國有的；全國普遍的；國民的；民族的；某國家或民族特有的：*a ~ theatre,* one supported by the State; 國立劇院；國家劇院；*~ opposition to a government policy,* expressed by all citizens. 全國人民對政府某項政策的普遍反對。ˌ**~ ˈanthem,** song or hymn of a nation (eg 'God Save the Queen' in GB). 國歌(如英國國歌'天佑吾王')。**the ˌN~ ˈDebt,** total money owed by the State to those who have lent it money. 國債；公債。ˌ**~ ˈmonument,** structure, landmark, site of historic interest (often one maintained by the government). 國家古跡（通常由政府所維護）。ˌ**~ ˈpark,** area of land declared to be public property, for the use and enjoyment of the people. 國家公園。ˌ**~ ˈservice,** period of compulsory service in the armed forces. 國民兵役。ˌ**N~ ˈTrust,** (in GB) society founded in 1895 to preserve places of natural beauty or historic interest for the nation. (英)國家信託社(創立於1895年，替國家保護天然風景區或歷史古蹟)。**the ˌGrand ˈN~,** the chief steeplechase in GB, run in March. (每年三月舉行的)英國大賽馬。□ *n* citizen of a particular nation: (某一國之)公民；國民：*One of a consul's duties is to help his own ~s,* his fellow countrymen. 領事職責之一是協助他自己的同胞。**~ly** /ˈnæʃnəlɪ ; ˈnæʃənl̩ɪ/ *adv*

na·tion·al·ism /ˈnæʃnəlɪzəm ; ˈnæʃənl̩ˌɪzəm/ *n* [U] **1** strong devotion to one's own nation; patriotic feelings, efforts, principles. 愛國心；國家主義；民族主義。 **2** movement for political/economic, etc independence (in a country controlled by another). 政治(經濟等)獨立運動(指受他國管制的國家內的)。

na·tion·al·ist /ˈnæʃnəlɪst ; ˈnæʃənl̩ɪst/ *n* supporter of nationalism(2): 政治獨立運動的擁護者：*Scottish ~s,* those who want Scotland to have more self-government. 蘇格蘭自治論者。□ *adj* (also 亦作 **~ic** /ˌnæʃnəˈlɪstɪk ; ˌnæʃənl̩ˈɪstɪk/) favouring, supporting, nationalism: 國家主義的；民族主義的；政治獨立運動的；擁護國家主義的：*~ movements in Zimbabwe.* 辛巴威的民族獨立運動。

na·tion·al·ity /ˌnæʃəˈnælətɪ ; ˌnæʃənˈælətɪ/ *n* (*pl* -ties) [C, U] being a member of a nation: 國籍：*What is your ~?* 你是哪一國的人？ *There were men of all nationalities in Geneva.* 在日內瓦有各種國籍的人。

na·tion·al·ize /ˈnæʃnəlaɪz ; ˈnæʃənl̩ˌaɪz/ *vt* [VP6A] **1** transfer from private to State ownership: 使歸為國有；國有化：*~ the railways/the coal-mines/the steel industry.* 使鐵路(煤礦，鋼鐵工業)歸為國有。 **2** make (a person) a national: 使(某人)歸化為一國的國民；使歸化：*~d Poles and Greeks in the US.* 已歸化為美國人的波蘭人與希臘人。 **3** make into a nation: 使成為國家：*The Poles were ~d after the war of 1914–18,* They became an independent nation. 在1914至1918年戰爭後，波蘭獲得獨立。**na·tion·ali·zation** /ˌnæʃnəlaɪˈzeɪʃn *US:* -lɪˈz ; ˌnæʃənl̩ɪˈzeʃən/ *n* nationalizing or being ~d: 收歸國有；國有化；歸化：*the nationalization of the railways.* 鐵路國有化。

na·tive /ˈneɪtɪv ; ˈnetɪv/ *n* **1** person born in a place, country, etc and associated with it by birth: (生於該地且與該地有淵源的)某地人；某國人：*a ~ of London/Wales/India/Kenya.* 倫敦(威爾斯，印度，肯亞)人。 **2** such a person as distinguished from immigrants, residents, visitors, tourists, etc from other countries, usu when the race to which he belongs is different in culture: (別於從外國來的移民、居民、遊客、觀光客等的)當地人；土人(通常指文化迥異者)：*the first meetings between Captain Cook and the ~s* (= the aboriginal inhabitants) *of Australia.* 科克船長與澳洲土著最初幾次的會面。 **3** animal or plant natural to and having its origin in a certain area: 原產於某地域的動物或植物；土生的動(植)物：*The kangaroo is a ~ of Australia.* 袋鼠是澳洲的土產動物。 **4** (GB) oyster reared wholly or partly in British waters, esp in artificial beds: (英)全部或部份養殖於英國水域的蠔（尤指生長於人工養殖場者）：*Whitstable ~s.* 威玆特布土產的蠔。□ *adj* **1** associated with the place and circumstances of one's birth: 出生地的；與出生地有關聯的：*your ~ land/place.* 你的祖國(故鄉)。 **2** of ~s (2 above): 當地的；土著的：*~ customs.* 土著的風俗。 **3** (of qualities) belonging to a person by nature, not acquired through training, by education, etc: (指性質)本性的；天賦的；天然的：*~ ability/charm.* 天賦才能(魅力)。 **4** *~* **to,** (of plants, animals, etc) having their origin in: (指動植物等)原屬於…的；源於…的；土產的；原產於：*plants ~ to America,* eg tobacco, potatoes. 原產於美洲的植物(如煙草、馬鈴薯)。*One of the animals ~ to India is the tiger.* 老虎是印度土產動物之一。 **5** (of metals) found in a pure state, uncombined with other substances: (指金屬)天然純淨的：*~ gold.* 原金。

na·tiv·ity /nəˈtɪvətɪ ; neˈtɪvətɪ/ *n* (*pl* -ties) birth, esp (**the N~**) of Jesus Christ; picture of the N~ of Christ. 誕生；(尤指)耶穌基督的誕生；基督誕生圖。**a ˈN~ Play,** one about the N~. 基督誕生劇。

nat·ter /ˈnætə(r) ; ˈnætɚ/ *vi* [VP2A, C] (GB colloq) chatter, grumble (esp to oneself): (英俗)(尤指對自己)喋喋不休；發怨言；抱怨：*What's she ~ing (on) about now?* 她在抱怨什麼？

natty /ˈnætɪ ; ˈnætɪ/ *adj* (-ier, -iest) (colloq) (俗) **1** neat; smart and tidy: 整潔的；漂亮乾淨的：*new and ~ uniforms for bus conductresses.* 給公車女售票員穿的整潔的新制服。 **2** quick and skilful. 敏捷而靈巧的。**nat·tily** /-ɪlɪ ; -əlɪ/ *adv*

natu·ral /ˈnætʃrəl ; ˈnætʃərəl/ *adj* **1** of, concerned with, produced, by nature: 自然的；有關自然的；天然產生的：*animals living in their ~ state,* wild, not domesticated; 生活於自然環境中的動物；*a country's ~ resources,* its minerals, forests, etc; 一國之天然資源；*land in its ~ state,* not used for industry, farming, etc. 未用於工業或未加耕種的土地。ˌ**~ ˈforces/pheˈnomena,** the forces of nature, such as storms, thunder and lightning. 自然力量(現象)(如暴風雨、雷電等)。ˌ**~ ˈgas,** gas occurring with petroleum deposits, eg North Sea gas. 天然氣(蘊藏於石油層中，如北海天然氣)。ˌ**~ ˈhistory,** botany and zoology; (formerly) scientific study of all nature. 動植物學；(昔時)博物學(研究自然界萬物的科學)。ˌ**~ ˈlaw,** rules for behaviour considered as innate and universal. 自然法則；被認為是天生且普遍化的行為準則；天理。ˌ**~ phiˈlosophy,** (name formerly used for) the science of physics, or physics and dynamics. (舊名稱)物理學；物理學與力學。ˌ**~ reˈligion,** religion and ethics based on reason (contrasted

N

with religion from divine revelation). 自然宗教(基於理性的宗教及倫理，與出自神啓的宗教相對)。ˌ~ seˈlection, evolutionary theory that animals and plants survive or become extinct in accordance with their ability to adapt themselves to their environment. 天擇；自然淘汰(動植物的生存或絕種係視其對環境的適應力而定的進化論)。**2** of, in agreement with, the nature(4) of a living thing: 本性的；天性的：~ *gifts／abilities.* 天賦。**3** (of persons) possessing qualities by nature(4); born with qualities or powers: (指人)天生賦有某些性質的；生而具有某些性質或能力的：*He's a ~ orator,* makes speeches easily. 他是天生的演說家。*She's a ~ linguist,* learns languages easily. 她是個天生的語言學家(善於學習語言)。*It comes ~ to her.* 那事對於她不學自會。⇨ come(10). **4** ordinary; normal; to be expected: 普通的；正常的；預期的：*die a ~ death,* not as the result of an accident, violence, etc. 自然死亡(並非意外或橫死)；壽終正寢。*It is ~ for a bird to fly.* 鳥會飛是自然的。*He was sentenced to prison for the term of his ~ life,* ie until he died. 他被處無期徒刑(終身監禁)。**5** simple; not cultivated or self-conscious: 自然的；不造作的：~ *behaviour;* 自然的行爲(非故意的)；*speak in a ~ voice,* not affected. 用自然(不造作)的聲調說話。*It was a ~ piece of acting,* with no exaggeration. 那是自然的演出(毫無誇張的)。**6** (music) neither sharp nor flat: (音樂)本位音的；自然的：*B ~* (cf 參較 *B sharp, B flat*). 本位 B 調。⇨ the illus at notation. 參看 notation 之插圖。**7** (of a son or daughter) illegitimate: (指子女)不合法的；私生的。□ *n* **1** (music) ~ note; musical note that is not a sharp or a flat; the sign (♮) placed before a note (in printed music) to make it a ~. (音樂)本位音；本位音符；鍵盤上之白鍵；(樂譜上之)本位記號(♮)。**2** person born without ordinary intelligence; person feeble-minded from birth. 低能之人；白癡。**3** (colloq) (俗) ***a ~ for sth,*** person naturally fitted or qualified: 天生適合(作某事)的人：*He's a ~ for the job／the part.* 他是天生適合做那件工作(擔任那個職位)的人。

natu·ral·ism /ˈnætʃrəlɪzəm；ˈnætʃərəlˌɪzəm/ *n* [U] **1** adherence to nature in literature and art; drawing and painting things in a way true to nature. (文學及藝術的)自然主義；寫實主義；寫實。**2** (phil) system of thought which rejects the supernatural and divine revelation and holds that natural causes and laws explain all phenomena. (哲學)自然主義(反對超自然及神啓，主張天然因素現象及法則解釋一切現象)。

natu·ral·ist /ˈnætʃrəlɪst；ˈnætʃərəlɪst/ *n* person who makes a special study of animals or plants. 博物學者；研究動(植)物的人。

natu·ral·is·tic /ˌnætʃrəˈlɪstɪk；ˌnætʃərəlˈɪstɪk/ *adj* of naturalism: 自然主義的；寫實派的：*a ~ painter.* 寫實派畫家。⇨ abstract¹(1), cubism, surrealism.

natu·ral·ize /ˈnætʃrəlaɪz；ˈnætʃərəlˌaɪz/ *vt, vi* **1** [VP6A] give (sb from another country) rights of citizenship: 予(外國人)公民權；使歸化；使入籍：*She was ~d in Japan,* was made a Japanese subject. 她歸化爲日本人。**2** [VP6A] take (a word) from one language into another: 將(某一語言中之字或詞)採用於另一種語言：*English sporting terms have been ~d in many languages.* 英語的運動名詞已經被許多語言所採用。**3** [VP6A] introduce and acclimatize (an animal or plant) into another country. 移殖(動物)；移植(植物)。**4** [VP6A] plant (bulbs, etc) in woodland areas so that the flowers appear to be growing wild or naturally. 把(鱗莖等)種植於森林地區使其花卉自然生長。**5** [VP2A] become ~d. 歸化。**natu·ral·iz·ation** /ˌnætʃrəlaɪˈzeɪʃn *US:* -lɪˈz-；ˌnætʃrəlɪˈzeʃən/ *n* [U] naturalizing or being ~d: 歸化；入籍；移殖；移植：*Naturalization papers,* the documents that prove that a person has been admitted to citizenship of another country. 歸化證書(證明一個人已取得他國公民權之文件)。

nat·urally /ˈnætʃrəlɪ；ˈnætʃərəlɪ/ *adv* **1** by nature(4): 天性地；天生地：*She's ~ musical.* 她天性喜愛音樂。**2** of course; as might be expected: 當然；必然地：*'Did you answer her letter?'—'N~!'* '你回了她的信嗎？'—'當然囉！' **3** without artificial help, special cultivation, etc: 無人工幫助或特別培植等地；天然地：*Her hair curls ~.* 她的頭髮自然捲曲。*Plants grow ~ in such a good climate.* 在這麼好的氣候裡，植物能自然生長。**4** without artifice: 不用手段地；自然地：*She speaks and behaves ~.* 她的言談和舉止都很自然。

na·ture /ˈneɪtʃə(r)；ˈnetʃɚ/ *n* **1** [U] the whole universe and every created thing: 自然；自然界；宇宙萬物：*Is ~ at its best in spring?* 自然界在春天最美好嗎？ˈ~ **study,** the study of animals, plants, insects, etc. 動植物、昆虫等的研究；自然研究。ˈ~ **worship,** the worship of trees, oceans, the winds, etc. 自然崇拜(對樹、海洋、風等之自然崇拜)。**2** [U] force(s) controlling the phenomena of the physical world: 自然力；控制物質世界現象的力量：*Man is engaged in a constant struggle with ~.* 人類不斷地與大自然競爭。*Miracles are contrary to ~.* 奇蹟是與自然力相反的。ˈ~ **cure,** form of therapy relying upon natural remedies (sunlight, diet, exercise). 自然療法(靠天然治療物如日光、食物、運動的一種療法)。***pay the debt of ~; pay one's debt to ~,*** die. 死亡。***in the course of ~,*** according to the ordinary course of things. 根據事物的常理。**3** [U] simple life without civilization; outdoor, animal-like existence: 自然的生活；無文明的簡單生活；戶外的似獸類的生活：*Some 18th-century writers were in favour of a return to ~,* to the simple and primitive life that people were thought to have led before mankind became civilized. 有些十八世紀作家贊成回返自然的生活(文明前的原始生活)。***be in a state of ~,*** be completely naked (as in a nudist camp). 全裸著(如天體營中者)。**4** [C, U] qualities and characteristics, physical, mental and spiritual, which belong to a person or thing: 本性；天性；性質：*It is the ~ of a dog to bark.* 吠是狗的天性。*Cats and dogs have quite different ~s.* 貓和狗有相當不同的天性。*That man is proud by ~.* 那個人天生驕傲。*Chemists study the ~ of gases.* 化學家研究氣體的性質。ˌ**human** ˈ~, the qualities possessed by man (in contrast with animals). 人性(與獸性相對)。**good ~,** unselfishness; willingness and readiness to help; kind-heartedness. 善良的本性(無私、樂於助人、仁慈等)。Hence, 由此產生，ˌ**good-**／ˌ**ill-**ˈ**~ed,** having a good／ill ~. 本性善良(邪惡)的。**5** qualities of non-material things (eg art, knowledge, language). 不具體之物(例如藝術、知識、語言)的性質。**6** sort; kind: 種類：*Things of this ~ do not interest me.* 這類事物不會使我感興趣。*His request was in the ~ of a command,* could not be ignored. 他的要求就是一種命令。

na·tur·ism /ˈneɪtʃərɪzəm；ˈnetʃərɪzəm/ *n* nudism. 裸體主義。**na·tur·ist** /-ɪst；-ɪst/ *n* nudist. 裸體主義者。

naught /nɔːt；nɔt/ *n* = nought(1).

naughty /ˈnɔːtɪ；ˈnɔtɪ/ *adj* (-ier, -iest) **1** (of children, their behaviour, etc) bad; wrong; disobedient; causing trouble: (指兒童、其行爲等)壞的；錯的；不聽從的；惹麻煩的；頑皮的；淘氣的：*a ~ child.* 頑皮的小孩。*It was ~ of you to pull the cat's tail.* 你拉貓的尾巴太頑皮了。**2** taking pleasure in shocking, intended to shock, people: 以令人震驚或反感爲樂的；企圖令人震驚或反感的；猥褻的：*a ~ novel(ist);* 猥褻的小說(小說家)；~ *stories.* 猥褻的故事。**naught·ily** /-ɪlɪ；-əlɪ/ *adv* **naughti·ness** *n*

nausea /ˈnɔːsɪə *US:* ˈnɔːz-；ˈnɔʒə/ *n* [U] feeling of sickness (eg as caused by bad food) or disgust; seasickness: 作嘔；惡心；暈船：*overcome by ~ after eating octopus;* 吃了章魚後感到惡心；*filled with ~ at the sight of cruelty to animals.* 看到虐待動物心中充滿厭惡。**naus·eate** /ˈnɔːsɪeɪt *US:* ˈnɔːz-；ˈnɔʒɪ-

ˌet/ *vt* [VP6A] cause ~: 使作嘔;使惡心: *nauseating food;* 令人作嘔的食物; *a nauseating sight.* 令人惡心的情景。 **naus·eous** /ˈnɔːsɪəs *US:* ˈnɔːʃəs ; ˈnɔʒəs/ *adj* disgusting; causing ~. 令人厭惡的;令人作嘔的。

nautch /nɔːtʃ ; nɔtʃ/ *n* performance by a professional dancing-girl (**ˈ~-girl**) in India, etc. (印度等之)職業舞女的表演;印度舞。

nauti·cal /ˈnɔːtɪkl ; ˈnɔtɪkḷ/ *adj* of ships, sailors or navigation: 船舶的;船員的;航海的: *~ terms,* used by sailors; 海員用語;航海用語; *a ~ almanac.* with information about the sun, moon, tides, etc; 航海曆書(上載日、月、潮水等資料); *a ~ mile,* 1／60 of a degree, 6080 ft (= 1852 metres). 一海里;一浬(爲一緯度的六十分之一,計 6080 呎或 1852 公尺)。

nauti·lus /ˈnɔːtɪləs *US:* ˈnɔːtələs ; ˈnɔtḷəs/ *n* (*pl* ~es /-ləsɪz ; -ḷəsɪz/) small sea animal of which the female has a very thin shell. 鸚鵡螺(小海生動物,雌者殼極薄)。

na·val /ˈneɪvl ; ˈnevḷ/ *adj* of a navy; of warships: 海軍的;軍艦的: *~ officers／battles.* 海軍軍官(海戰)。

nave /neɪv ; nev/ *n* central part of a church where the people sit. 教堂的正廳(會衆所坐的部份)。 ⇨ the illus at church. 參看 church 之插圖。

na·vel /ˈneɪvl ; ˈnevḷ/ *n* small depression in the middle of the surface of the belly (left by the severance of the umbilical cord). 肚臍。 ⇨ the illus at trunk. 參看 trunk 之插圖。 ~ **orange,** large orange with a ~-like formation in the top. 臍柑(頂端形狀像肚臍)。

navi·gable /ˈnævɪgəbl ; ˈnævəgəbḷ/ *adj* **1** (of rivers, seas, etc) that can be navigated; suitable for ships: (指江河、海洋等) 可航行的; 適於行船的: *The Rhine is ~ from Strasbourg to the sea.* 萊茵河從斯特拉斯堡到海這一段可以通航。 **2** (of ships, etc) that can be steered and sailed: (指船等)可駕駛的;可航行的: *not in a ~ condition.* 不能航行。 **navi·ga·bil·ity** /ˌnævɪgəˈbɪlətɪ ; ˌnævəgəˈbɪlətɪ/ *n*

navi·gate /ˈnævɪgeɪt ; ˈnævəˌget/ *vt, vi* [VP6A, 2A] **1** plot the course, find the position, etc of a ship or aircraft, etc, using maps and instruments. 利用地圖及儀器測定(船隻或飛機等)的航道、航綫及位置等;測航。 **2** steer (a ship); pilot (an aircraft); (fig) direct: 駕駛(船隻、飛機);(喩)指導;使通過: *~ a Bill through the House of Commons.* 使一個法案在下議院通過。 **3** sail over (a sea); sail up or down (a river). 航行於(海)上;沿(河)向上游或下游航行。 **navi·gator** /-tə(r) ; -tə/ *n* **1** person who ~s(1). 測航者。 **2** sailor with skill and experience who has taken part in many voyages; (esp) early explorer: 精於航海術且富有航海經驗的海員;航海者;(尤指)早期的探險者: *the 16th c Spanish and Portuguese navigators.* 十六世紀的西班牙與葡萄牙航海家。

navi·ga·tion /ˌnævɪˈgeɪʃn ; ˌnævəˈgeʃən/ *n* [U] **1** the act of navigating. 航行;航海;航空。 **2** the art or science of navigating. 航行學;航海術;航空術。 **3** the making of voyages on water or of journeys through the air: 水路航行;空中航行: *inland ~,* by river and canal. 內河航行。 *There has been an increase in ~ through the Panama Canal,* more ships use it. 通過巴拿馬運河的船隻一直在增加中。

navvy /ˈnævɪ ; ˈnævɪ/ *n* (*pl* -vies) (GB) unskilled workman. (英)無技術的工人;粗工;小工。

navy /ˈneɪvɪ ; ˈnevɪ/ *n* (*pl* -vies) **1** (**a／the**) ~, (with *sing* or *pl v*) that part of a country's military forces that is organized for fighting at sea: (與單數或複數動詞連用)海軍: *join the ~;* 參加海軍; *an officer／sailor in the Royal N~.* 皇家海軍之軍官(水兵)。 ˌ~ ˈ**blue,** dark blue as used for naval uniforms. (海軍制服用的)深藍色。 **2** a country's warships collectively: (集合用法)海軍(指一國之艦艇): *a small ~.* 艦艇爲數甚少之海軍。

nay /neɪ ; ne/ *adv* (old use) no; (rhet) not only that, but also: (舊用法)不;否;(修辭)不僅如此,而且: *I suspect, nay, I am certain, that he is wrong.* 我不僅猜想而且確信他錯了。

Nazi /ˈnɑːtsɪ ; ˈnɑtsɪ/ *n, adj* (member) of the German National Socialist Party founded by Hitler. 納粹黨(希特勒所創的德國國家社會黨)的;納粹黨員。 **Nazism** /ˈnɑːtsɪzəm ; ˈnɑtsˌɪzəm/ *n* the ideology of the ~s. 納粹黨的思想方式;納粹主義。

Ne·an·der·thal /niːˈændətɑːl ; nɪˈændəˌtɑl/ *adj* ~ **man,** extinct type of man of the stone age. 尼安得塔爾人(已絕種的石器時代原始人)。

neap /niːp ; nip/ *n* ˈ~(**-tide**), tide when high water is at its lowest level of the year. 一年中的最低潮;小潮。 ⇨ *spring tide* at spring[1] (3).

Nea·poli·tan /nɪəˈpɒlɪtən ; ˌniəˈpɑlətṇ/ *n, adj* **1** (inhabitant) of Naples. 拿坡里的; 拿坡里人。 **2** (small *n*) with many flavours and colours: (小寫) 多種味道及顏色的: *~ ice-cream.* 三色冰淇淋。

near[1] /nɪə(r) ; nɪr/ *adj* (-er, -est) **1** not far from; close in space or time: 不遠的;(空間或時間上) 接近的: *The post office is quite ~.* 郵局距離這兒很近。 *Christmas is ~.* 聖誕節快到了。 *Come ~er.* 再走近些。 *Can you tell me the ~est* (= shortest) *way to the station?* 你能告訴我去車站最近的路嗎? *She was ~ to tears,* was almost crying. 她幾乎哭了。 ***the ~ distance,*** that part of a scene between the foreground and the background. 近景。 ***a ~ miss,*** eg of a bomb or shell, not a direct hit, but close enough to the target to cause damage. (指炸彈或砲彈等)近似命中 (雖非直接命中,但極接近目標而造成毀壞)。 ***a ~ thing,*** a narrow escape. 勉强的逃脫;九死一生。 ˌ~-ˈ**sighted** *adj* short-sighted; seeing well only when sth, eg a book, is held close to the eyes. 近視的。 **2** close in relation or affection: 近親的;親密的;親近的: *a ~ relation,* eg a mother, a son or daughter; 近親(例如母親、子或女); *friends who are ~ and dear to us.* 我們極親近的朋友。 **3** (contrasted with *off*) (of parts of animals and vehicles, or of horses in a team, when on a road, etc) the left side: (與 off 相對) (指行走在路上等的動物及車輛或一組馬匹)左邊的: *the ~ foreleg;* 左前腿; *the ~ front wheel of a car.* 汽車的左前輪。 ˈ**~·side** *n* side ~est the kerb: 最靠近人行道的一邊;(最)左邊: *the ~side lane of traffic.* 最左邊的車道。 **4** niggardly (contrasted with *generous*): 慳吝的(與 generous 相對): *He's very ~ with his money.* 他對金錢很吝嗇。 □ *vt, vi* [VP6A, 2A] come or draw ~ (to); approach: 走近;靠近;行近: *The ship was ~ing land.* 那隻船正在攏岸。 *He's ~ing his end,* is dying. 他快要死了。 *The road is ~ing completion.* 那條路快完成了。 **~·ness** *n*

near[2] /nɪə(r) ; nɪr/ *adv* not far; to or at a short distance in space or time: 不遠;(空間或時間上) 至近距離;在近距離: *We searched far and ~* (= everywhere) *for the missing child.* 我們到處尋找那失蹤的孩子。 ***as ~ as,*** nearly: 接近地: *As ~ as I can guess* (= My ~est or best guess is that) *there were forty people present.* 就我所能猜測,有四十個人出席。 *He was as ~ as could be to* (= only just escaped, narrowly escaped) *being knocked down by the bus.* 他差點被公共汽車撞倒。 ***as ~*** (= nearly) ***as makes no difference,*** with no difference worth considering: 接近到幾乎沒什麼兩樣: *They're the same height, or as ~ as makes no difference.* 他們身高相同,或是說接近到幾無兩樣。 ***~ at hand,*** **(a)** within easy reach: 在近旁: *Always have your reference books ~ at hand.* 要經常把參考書擺在手邊。 **(b)** not far distant in the future: 在不久的將來: *The examinations are ~ at hand.* 考試快到了。 ***~ on／upon,*** not far in time from; almost: 將近;幾近: *It was near upon midnight.* 將近午夜。 ***nowhere／***(colloq) (俗) ***not ~,*** far from: 離…很遠: *The concert hall was nowhere ~ full.* 那音樂廳離滿座還差得遠。 *She's nowhere ~ as old as her husband.* 她遠不如她丈夫那麼老(比她丈夫小得多)。 ***~ by,*** not far off. 不遠;在附近。Hence, 由此產生, ˈ**~·by** *adj*

near[3] /nɪə(r) ; nɪr/ *prep* (equivalent to *near*[1] with *to*) close to (in space, time, relationship, etc): (等於 near¹ 與 to 連用之用法) (空間、時間、關係等) 接近;靠近: *Come and sit ~ me.* 來靠近我坐。*It's convenient living so ~ the station.* 住在離車站這麼近實在很方便。

near·ly /ˈnɪəlɪ ; ˈnɪrlɪ/ *adv* **1** almost: 幾乎;將近: *It's ~ one o'clock/~ time to start.* 將近一點鐘了 (差不多是開始的時刻)。*I'm ~ ready.* 我差不多準備好了。⇨ hardly, scarcely. **2** closely: 密切地;親近地: *We're ~ related,* are near relations. 我們是近親。**3** ***not ~,*** far from: 相差甚遠: *I have £20, but that isn't ~ enough for my journey, I shall need much more.* 我有二十鎊,但是遠不够我旅行用,我還需要更多(錢)。

neat /niːt ; nit/ *adj* (-er, -est except 5 below 下列第 5 義除外) **1** (liking to have everything) tidy; in good order with nothing out of place; done carefully: (喜愛) 整潔的;整齊的;小心做成的;精巧的: *~ work;* 精巧的製作品; *a ~ worker;* 靈巧的工人;乾淨的工人; *a ~ desk;* 整齊的書桌; *~ writing.* 工整的筆跡。**2** simple and pleasant; in good taste: 簡潔的;雅致的: *a ~ dress.* 雅致的衣服。**3** pleasing in shape and appearance: 形態優雅的;勻稱的: *a ~ figure.* 優雅的身材。**4** cleverly said or done: 巧妙的: *a ~ answer/conjuring trick.* 巧妙的回答(魔術)。**5** (of wines and spirits) unmixed with water; undiluted: (指酒類) 沒攙水的;純的: *drink one's whisky ~.* 喝純威士忌。**~·ly** *adv* **~·ness** *n*

'neath /niːθ ; niθ/ *prep* (poet) beneath. (詩) 在…下面。

neb·ula /ˈnebjʊlə ; ˈnɛbjələ/ *n* (*pl* ~e /-liː ; -ˌli/ or ~s) [C] cluster of very distant stars, diffuse mass of gas, seen in the night sky as an indistinct patch of light. 星雲 (夜晚天空所見之片狀光霧,係由極遙遠之恆星群及散佈之氣團所形成)。**nebu·lar** /-lə(r) ; -lɚ/ *adj* of ~s. 星雲的。

nebu·lous /ˈnebjʊləs ; ˈnɛbjələs/ *adj* cloud-like; hazy; indistinct; vague. 似雲的;雲霧狀的;模糊不清的;含糊的。

necess·ar·ily /ˌnesəˈserəlɪ ; ˈnɛsəˌsɛrəlɪ/ *adv* as a necessary result; inevitably: 必要地;必然地;必定地: *Big men are not ~ strong men.* 大塊頭的人不一定就是强壯的人。

necess·ary /ˈnesəsərɪ *US:* -serɪ ; ˈnɛsəˌsɛrɪ/ *adj* which has to be done; which must be; which cannot be done without or escaped from: 必須做的;必要的;必然的;必需的;必定的;難以逃避的: *Sleep is ~ to health.* 睡眠對健康是必要的。*Is war a ~ evil in this world?* 戰爭是世上難以避免的災禍嗎? *Is it ~ for you to be/Is it ~ that you should be so economical?* 你非要如此節省不可嗎? □ *n* [C] (usu *pl*) things ~ (for living). (通常用複數) (生活) 必需品。

ne·cessi·tate /nɪˈsesɪteɪt ; nəˈsɛsəˌtet/ *vt* [VP6A, C] make necessary: 使成爲必要: *Your proposal ~s borrowing money.* 你的提議使借款成爲必要。*The increase in population ~s a greater food supply.* 人口的增加需要更多的食物供應。

ne·cessi·tous /nɪˈsesɪtəs ; nəˈsɛsətəs/ *adj* (formal) poor; needy: (正式用語) 窮的;貧困的: *in ~ circumstances,* in poverty. 處於貧困之境。

ne·cess·ity /nɪˈsesətɪ ; nəˈsɛsətɪ/ *n* (*pl* -ties) **1** [U] urgent need; circumstances that compel sb to do sth; natural laws that direct human life and action: 急需;迫使某人作某事的情況;支配人類生活與行動的自然律;必需;必要: *He was driven by ~ to steal food for his starving children.* 他迫不得已爲他飢餓的兒女偷竊食物。*The doctor asked us not to call him during the night except in case of ~,* eg unless the patient's condition changed very much for the worse. 醫生吩咐我們除非必要不要在夜裡叫他。***be under the ~ of. . . ,*** be compelled by. . . . 不得已而…。***bow to ~,*** do what one is compelled to do. 做不得已的事。***make a virtue of ~,*** accept credit without protest; claim credit for doing sth that one cannot help doing. 認可而不加抗議;把不得不做的事當做應當做的事。***of ~,*** as a matter of ~. 必然;必定;不得已。**2** [C] sth that is necessary: 必需品: *The necessities of life,* food, clothing and shelter. 生活必需品(食物、衣服及住所)。**3** [C] sth of which the absence or non-occurrence cannot be imagined: 必然的事;絕不可無的事物: *Is it a logical ~ that the cost of living will go up if wages go up?* Can the one be considered possible without the other? 假如工資增加,生活費用也要增加,這是不是邏輯上必然的結果?

neck /nek ; nɛk/ *n* **1** part of the body that connects the head and the shoulders: 頸;脖子: *wrap a scarf round one's ~.* 在頸上圍一條圍巾。⇨ the illus at head. 參看 head 之插圖。***break one's ~,*** work extremely hard to achieve sth. 拚命地幹以完成某事。⇨ breakneck. ***breathe down sb's ~,*** (colloq) be close behind, almost touching, eg in a race; be watching closely. (俗) 緊跟在某人後頭(至幾乎能觸及的程度,如在賽跑中);緊迫地盯住某人。***get it in the ~,*** (sl) suffer a severe or a fatal blow; have a painful experience. (俚)遭受嚴重的或致命的打擊;有痛苦的經驗。***have the ~*** (more usu 較常用 *nerve*) ***to do sth,*** (sl) be impudent, cheeky enough to do it. (俚)厚著臉皮做某事。***save one's ~,*** escape hanging; (fig) escape the results of being foolish, etc. 免受絞刑;(喻)免於遭受由愚昧等所造成的結果。***stick one's '~ out,*** (sl) do or say sth that may bring severe criticism, or result in a painful experience. (俚) 做出(說出)會使自己受到嚴厲批評或遭受痛苦的事(話);自找麻煩。***win/lose by a ~,*** (horse-racing) by the length of a horse's ~; (fig) by a narrow margin. (賽馬)以一頸之差獲勝(失敗);(喻)險勝(小敗)。***~ and crop,*** headlong; altogether; bag and baggage: 匆促地;全部地;完全;帶着全部東西: *throw him out ~ and crop.* 要他帶著全部東西滾蛋。***~ and ~,*** (of horse-racing, and fig) side by side, with no advantage over the other in a race or struggle. (指賽馬,亦作比喻用法) 並駕齊驅;不分上下。***~ or nothing,*** taking desperate risks; venturing everything. 冒一切危險;拚命。**2** flesh of an animal's ~ as used for food, esp *~ of mutton.* 作食物用的動物的頸肉;(尤指)羊頸肉。**3** sth like a ~ in shape or position: 形狀或部位像頸之物;頸狀物;頸部: *the ~ of a bottle;* 瓶頸; *a narrow ~ of land,* eg an isthmus. 狹窄的地帶(如地峽)。**4** (compounds) (複合字) **'~·band** *n* part of a shirt, etc that goes round the ~. (襯衣等的) 領圈(裝領的部分)。**'~·cloth** *n* cravat. 舊式領帶。**~·er·chief** /ˈnekətʃɪf ; ˈnɛkɚtʃɪf/ *n* (old use) cloth or scarf worn round the ~. (舊用法) 圍巾;領巾。**'~·lace** /-lɪs ; -lɪs/ *n* string of beads, pearls, etc worn round the ~ as an ornament. 項鍊。**'~·let** /-lɪt ; -lɪt/ *n* ornament (eg of beads) for the ~. 頸飾;項珠;小項鍊。**'~·line** *n* (of fashions for women's clothes) line of a garment at or near the ~: (指女裝的款式) 領口;開領: *This year the ~line is up and the hemline is down.* 今年流行的女裝款式領口高下襬低。**'~·tie** *n* (now usu 今通常稱 *tie*) band of material worn round the ~ and knotted in front. 領帶。**'~·wear** /-weə(r) ; -ˌwɛr/ *n* [U] (term used by shopkeepers for) collars and ties. (商人所用的名詞) 領子和領帶。□ *vi* (sl) (of couples) exchange kisses, caresses and hugs: (俚) (指一對男女) 互相親吻、撫愛、擁抱: *sitting on park benches petting and ~ing in the dark.* 坐在公園長櫈上在黑暗中互相親吻、撫愛、擁抱。

nec·ro·mancy /ˈnekrəmænsɪ ; ˈnɛkrəˌmænsɪ/ *n* [U] art or practice of communicating by magic with the dead in order to learn about the future. 施魔法問未來於亡魂的法術;巫術;關亡術。**nec·ro·man·cer** /-sə(r) ; -sɚ/ *n* person who practises ~. 問未來於亡魂的法師;巫師;行關亡術者。

ne·crop·olis /nɪˈkrɒpəlɪs ; nɛˈkrɑpəlɪs/ *n* (*pl* ~es /-lɪsɪz ; -lɪsɪz/) cemetery, esp a large one in an ancient town. 墓地；公墓；(尤指)(古城市中的)大墓地。

nec·tar /ˈnektə(r); ˈnɛktə/ *n* [U] **1** (in old Gk stories) the drink of the gods. (古希臘傳說)神的飲料；瓊漿玉液。⇨ ambrosia. **2** sweet liquid in flowers, collected by bees; any delicious drink. 花蜜；任何美味的飲料。

nec·tar·ine /ˈnektərɪn; ˈnɛktəˌrin/ *n* kind of peach with thin, smooth skin and firm flesh. 油桃(桃的一種，皮薄而光滑，果肉堅實)。

née /neɪ; ne/ *adj* (F) born (put after the name of a married woman and before her father's family name): (法)本姓；娘家姓…的(用於已婚婦女姓氏之後，娘家姓氏之前，表示其娘家的姓氏): *Mrs J Smith, née Brown.* 娘家姓布朗的史密斯夫人。

need¹ /ni:d; nid/ *anom fin* (no *inf*, no participles, *3rd p sing* present tense is *need*, not *needs*; used in *interr* and *neg* followed by *inf* without *to*; need not contracted to needn't /ˈni:dnt; ˈnidn̩t/) (無不定詞，無分詞，第三人稱單數現在式是 need 而非 needs；用於疑問句及否定句中後接沒有 to 的不定詞；need not 縮寫爲 needn't) [VP5] **1** be obliged; be necessary: 必要；必須：*N~ you go yet? No, I ~n't. Yes, I must.* 你一定要去嗎？不，我不必去。是的，我必須去。*You ~n't go yet, ~ you?* 你不一定要去，是嗎？ *I ~ hardly tell you* (= You must already know or guess) *that....* 不用我說你也知道…。 **2** (followed by a *perfect infinitive*, ~ indicates that although sth may have occurred or been done in the past, it was or may have been unnecessary): (後接完成式不定詞，表示雖然某事可能在過去曾經發生或已做了，但此事並不需要)：*N~ it have happened?* 難道當時沒法避免嗎？ *We ~n't have hurried,* We hurried but now we see that this was unnecessary. 我們當時實在不必那麼匆忙。Cf 參較 *We didn't ~ to hurry,* We didn't hurry because it was unnecessary. 我們當時無須匆忙(我們當時並沒匆忙)。⇨ need³(2). **~·ful** /-fl; -fəl/ *adj* ~ed; necessary: 需要的；必須的：*do what is ~ful.* 做所必須做的事。***do the ~ful,*** (colloq) provide the money, perform the action, that is required. (俗)供所需的錢；採取必要的行動。**~·fully** /-fəlɪ; -fəlɪ/ *adv* **~·less** *adj* not ~ed; unnecessary: 不需要的；不必要的：*~less work/trouble.* 不必要的工作(麻煩)。*N~less to say, he kept his promise.* 不用說，他信守了他的諾言。**~·less·ly** *adv*

need² /ni:d; nid/ *n* **1** [U] ***~ (for),*** circumstances in which sth is lacking, or necessary, or requiring some course of action: 困乏之境；缺乏；需要；必須：*There's no ~ (for you) to start yet.* (你)現在還不必動身。*There's no/not much ~ for anxiety.* 不必(太)焦慮。*There's a great ~ for a book on this subject.* 非常需要有一本關於這題目的書。***if ~ be,*** if necessary. 如果需要的話。**2** (used in *pl*) requirement; sth felt to be necessary: (用複數)要求；需要之物：*He earns enough to satisfy his ~s,* ie to buy food, clothing, etc. 他賺得的錢足够滿足他的需要。*My ~s are few.* 我的需求很少。*£10 will meet my immediate ~s.* 十鎊足以應付我目前的需要。**3** [U] poverty; misfortune; adversity: 貧窮；不幸；逆境：*He helped me in my hour of ~.* 他在我困難的時候幫助過我。***A friend in ~ is a friend indeed,*** (prov) A friend who helps when one is in trouble is a real friend. (諺)患難之交才是眞正的朋友。**~y** *adj* (-ier, -iest) very poor; lacking the necessities of life: 非常貧窮的；缺乏生活必需品的：*a ~y family;* 貧窮家庭；*help the poor and ~y.* 幫助貧窮的人。

need³ /ni:d; nid/ *vt* **1** [VP6A, E] want; require: 需要；要：*The garden ~s rain.* 花園需要雨水。*Does he ~ any help?* 他需要幫助嗎？ *It only ~s good will from both sides.* 它只要雙方的善意。*This chapter ~s rewriting/~s to be rewritten.* 這一章需要重寫。**2** [VP7A] be under a necessity or obligation: 必要；必須：*He didn't ~ to be reminded about it.* 不必向他提醒那事情。*Does he ~ to know?* 他一定要知道嗎？ *It ~s to be done carefully.* 此事必須仔細地做。*He ~s to be kept informed about developments.* 他必須隨時獲知有關發展的情形。 **3** [VP6A] deserve; ought to have: 值得；該有：*What he ~s is a good whipping!* 應該狠狠地給他一頓鞭打！

needle /ˈni:dl; ˈnidl̩/ *n* **1** small, thin piece of polished steel, pointed at one end and with a small hole at the other end for thread, used in sewing and darning. 針；縫衣針。***look for a ~ in a haystack,*** (prov) engage in a hopeless search. (諺)從事無希望的搜索；海底撈針。***as sharp as a ~,*** quick-witted; observant. 非常機警；非常敏銳。**ˈ~-woman** *n* (*pl* -women) woman who sews. 善縫紉的婦女；善女紅的婦女。**ˈ~·craft, ˈ~·work** *nn* [U] sewing; embroidery. 縫紉；刺繡；女紅。**ˌpins and ˈ~s,** ⇨pin¹(1). **2** long, thin piece of polished wood, bone or metal (without an eye), with a pointed end (for knitting) or a hook (for crocheting). (木質、骨質或金屬的無針孔的)編織針；鉤針(一端有鉤，鉤織用)。 **3** thin steel pointer in a compass, showing the magnetic north; similar pointer in a telegraphic instrument. 磁針；指南針；電報機上之針。 **4** sth like a ~(1) in shape, appearance or use (eg the thin, pointed leaves of pine-trees; a sharp, pointed peak or rocky summit; the sharp, hollow end of a syringe used for giving injections). 針狀物(如松樹之針狀葉、尖峯、注射針)。⇨ the illus at tree; syringe. 參看 tree, syringe 之挿圖。 **5** stylus used in recording and playing gramophone records. (唱機用的)唱針。Cf 參較 *sapphire and diamond styluses.* **6 the ~,** (sl) nervous excitement: (俚)激動；興奮：*give sb the ~*, provoke or excite him; 激怒或刺激某人；*get the ~*, be provoked. 被激怒。**7** obelisk: 方尖石碑；方尖塔；方尖柱碑：*Cleopatra's ~*, in London. (倫敦的)克利奧佩特拉尖塔。□ *vt* **1** [VP6A, 15A] sew, pierce, operate on, with a ~; thread (one's way) between or through things. 用針縫、刺穿或施手術；穿過。 **2** (colloq) goad, provoke (sb, esp by making cruel comments, etc). (俗)刺激或激怒(某人，尤指以殘酷的批評等)。

needs /ni:dz; nidz/ *adv* (now used only with *must*) of necessity. (現在只與 must 連用)必要地；一定；務必。***N~ must when the devil drives,*** (prov) Circumstances may compel us to act in a certain way. (諺)情勢所迫，只好如此。(When the *adv* follows *must*, as in 'He must ~', the sense is usu sarcastic, as here): (當此副詞用於 must 之後時，例如 'He must needs'，通常含有諷刺之意，如下例)：*He must ~ go away just when I want his help,* He foolishly or stupidly insisted on going away.... 我正需要他協助的時候，他偏要走開(他愚昧地堅持要走開)。

ne'er /neə(r); nɛr/ *adv* (poet) never. (詩)永不；決不；從未。**~-do-well** /ˈneə du: wel; ˈnɛrduˌwɛl/ *n* useless or good-for-nothing person. 無用之人。

nef·arious /nɪˈfeərɪəs; nɪˈfɛrɪəs/ *adj* (formal) wicked; unlawful. (正式用語)邪惡的；不法的。**~·ly** *adv* **~·ness** *n*

ne·gate /nɪˈgeɪt; ˈniget/ *vt* [VP6A] (formal) deny; nullify. (正式用語)否定；使無效。

ne·ga·tion /nɪˈgeɪʃn; nɪˈgeʃən/ *n* [U] **1** (opp of *affirmation*) (爲 affirmation 之相反字) act of denying: 否定；否認：*Shaking the head is a sign of ~.* 搖頭是否認的表示。 **2** absence of any positive or real quality or meaning: 實質或眞義的不存在；虛無：*The life of an evil man is a moral ~.* 惡人的生命毫無道德價值。

nega·tive /ˈnegətɪv; ˈnɛgətɪv/ *adj* **1** (opp of *affirmative*) (爲 affirmative 之相反字) (of words and answers) indicating *no* or *not*: (指字句及回答)否定的(含'不'之義)：*give sb a ~ answer.* 給某人一個否定的答覆。 **2** (opp of *positive*) (爲 positive 之相反字) expressing the absence of any positive character; that stops, hinders or makes powerless: 消極的；反對的：*~ criticism,* that does not help by building up, making suggestions; 消極的批評；*~ praise*, not finding fault; 消極的稱讚(即不找錯)；*~ virtue*, doing nothing wrong, but doing nothing good or right, either. 消極的美德(不做好事，也不做壞事)。 **3** (maths) of a number or quantity that has to be subtracted (數學)負的(eg 如 $-x^2y$). **4** of that kind of electricity produced by rubbing wax, vulcanite, etc; of or from the cathode: (電)負的；陰的；陰性的: *the ~ plate in a battery*, from which electrons will flow to the positive plate. 電池中的陰(極)板。 **the ~ pole**, (made of zinc) in a cell. 電池內的陰極(鋅製成)。 **5** (photo) having lights and shades reversed. (攝影)明暗相反的；底片的。□ *n* [C] **1** word or statement that denies: 否定字；否定句；否定；否認: *'No', 'not' and 'neither' are ~s.* no, not 及 neither 都是否定詞。*The answer is in the ~,* is 'No'. 答覆是否定的。 **2** (maths) a minus quantity (數學)負數；負值 (eg 如 $-5x$). **3** (photo) developed plate or film on which lights and shades are reversed. (攝影)底片。□ *vt* [VP6A] **1** prove (a theory, etc) to be untrue: 否定(理論等)的眞實性；推翻；駁斥: *Experiments ~d his theory.* 實驗否定了他的理論。 **2** reject; refuse to accept; neutralize (an effect). 拒絕；否決；抵銷。 **~·ly** *adv*

the negative of the photograph at *ski*

ne·glect /nɪ'glekt ; nɪ'glɛkt/ *vt* **1** [VP6A] pay no attention to; give no or not enough care to: 疏忽；忽略: *~ one's studies／children／health.* 疏忽學業(子女，健康)。 **2** [VP7A, 6C] omit or fail (*to do* sth); leave undone (what one ought to do): 遺漏(與不定詞連用)；漏做；忘記做(該做的事): *He ~ed to write and say 'Thank you'.* 他忘了寫信道謝。*Don't ~ writing to your mother.* 不要忘了寫信給你母親。□ *n* [U] ~ing or being ~ed: 疏忽；忽略；遺漏: *He lost his job because of ~ of duty.* 他因爲疏忽職責而失去工作。*The garden was in a state of ~.* 那花園疏於整理。 **~·ful** /-fl ; -fəl/ *adj* in the habit of ~ing things: 疏忽的；忽視的；不留心的: *boys who are ~ful of their appearance.* 不注意自己儀表的男孩們。 **~·fully** /-fəlɪ ; -fəlɪ/ *adv* **~·ful·ness** *n*: *He has a tendency to ~fulness.* 他有疏忽的傾向。

nég·ligé, neg·li·gee /'neglɪʒeɪ *US*: ˌneglɪ'ʒeɪ ; ˏnɛglɪ'ʒe/ *n* [C, U] (condition of being in a) loose, free style of informal dress. 寬鬆的便服；穿着寬鬆便服的狀態。

neg·li·gence /'neglɪdʒəns ; 'nɛglədʒəns/ *n* [U] **1** carelessness; failure to take proper care or precautions: 不留心；疏忽；不注意；粗心大意: *The accident was due to ~.* 這次意外是由於疏忽。 **2** neglected condition or appearance: 隨便；不注意儀表: *~ of dress.* 衣着隨便；衣冠不整。

neg·li·gent /'neglɪdʒənt ; 'nɛglədʒənt/ *adj* taking too little care, guilty of neglect: 不注意的；疏忽的；隨便的: *He was ~ in* (= in respect of) *his work.* 他不注意工作。*He was ~ of his duties.* 他疏忽職責。 **~·ly** *adv*

neg·li·gible /'neglɪdʒəbl ; 'nɛglədʒəbl̩/ *adj* that need not be considered; of little or no importance or size: 不需要加以考慮的；不重要的；很小的: *a ~ quantity.* 小量；小數目。

ne·go·ti·able /nɪ'gəʊʃɪəbl ; nɪ'goʃɪəbl/ *adj* **1** that can be negotiated(2): 可商議的；可談判處理的: *Is the dispute ~?* 那爭執可由談判加以解決嗎？ **2** that can be changed into cash, or passed from person to person instead of cash: 可兌換現金的；可轉讓的；可流通的: *~ securities／instruments,* eg cheques, promissory notes. 可轉讓的證券或票據。 **3** (of roads, rivers, etc) that can be passed over or along. (指道路、河流等)可通行的。

ne·go·ti·ate /nɪ'gəʊʃɪeɪt ; nɪ'goʃɪˏet/ *vi, vt* **1** [VP2A, 3A] *~ (with sb),* discuss, confer, in order to come to an agreement: (與某人)商議；談判；磋商: *We've decided to ~ with the employers about our wage claims.* 我們已經決定和雇主談判關於我們的工資要求。 **2** [VP6A, 14] *~ sth (with sb),* arrange by discussion: (與某人)藉商議處理某事；商訂: *~ a sale／a loan／a treaty／peace.* 商訂售賣(貸款，條約，和約)。 **3** [VP6A] get or give money for (cheques, bonds, etc). 買賣；讓渡(支票、債券等)。 **4** [VP6A] get past or over: 通過；越過: *This is a difficult corner for a large car to ~.* 這個拐角大的汽車很難通過。*My horse ~d* (ie jumped over) *the fence very well.* 我的馬輕易地跳過了柵欄。 **ne·go·ti·ator** /-tə(r) ; -tɚ/ *n* one who ~s. 談判者；商議者。

ne·go·ti·ation /nɪˌgəʊʃɪ'eɪʃn ; nɪˏgoʃɪ'eʃən/ *n* [C, U] negotiating: 商議；談判；讓與；流通: *enter into／open／start／carry on／resume ~s with sb;* 與某人着手(展開，開始，進行，恢復)談判; *be in ~ with sb.* 與某人商議。*The price is a matter of ~.* 價格是可商議的事。

Ne·gress /'ni:gres ; 'nigrɪs/ *n* Negro woman or girl. 女黑人；黑妞。

Ne·gro /'ni:grəʊ ; 'nigro/ *n* (*pl* ~es /-rəʊz ; -roz/) member (or, outside Africa, descendant) of one of the black-skinned African peoples south of the Sahara. 黑人(非洲撒哈拉沙漠以南的黑種人，或在非洲以外此種人的後代)。

Ne·groid /'ni:grɔɪd ; 'nigrɔɪd/ *adj* of or akin to Negroes or the Negro race. 黑人的；黑種人的；類似黑種人的。□ *n* person of the ~ race. 黑種人；黑人。

ne·gus /'ni:gəs ; 'nigəs/ *n* hot, sweetened wine, lemon juice, nutmeg and water. 尼加斯酒(甜酒、檸檬汁、荳蔻末及水混合成的一種熱酒)。

Ne·gus /'ni:gəs ; 'nigəs/ *n* (title of the) ruler of Ethiopia. 衣索比亞王(的稱號)。

neigh /neɪ ; ne/ *vi, n* (make the) cry of a horse. (作)馬叫；馬嘶。

neigh·bour (US = **-bor**) /'neɪbə(r) ; 'nebɚ/ *n* person living in a house, street, etc near another; person, thing or country that is near(est) another: 隣人；隣居；隣近的人或物；隣國: *We're nextdoor ~s,* Our houses are side by side. 我們是隔壁隣居。*We were ~s at dinner,* We sat together at table. 我們在用餐時坐在一起。*When the big tree fell, it brought down two of its smaller ~s,* two smaller trees near it. 當那棵大樹倒下來的時候，它把附近的兩棵小樹也壓倒了。*Britain's nearest ~ is France.* 英國最近的隣國是法國。□ *vt, vi* [VP6A, 3A] *~ (on／upon),* (chiefly in the form *~ing*) be near to: (主要用於現在分詞形式)隣接；相隣: *~ing countries;* 隣國; *in the ~ing village.* 在隣近的村莊裡。 **'~·hood** /-hʊd ; -ˏhʊd/ *n* **1** (people living in a) district; area near the place, etc referred to: 地區；某一地區的人們；隣近地區；附近地方: *There's some beautiful scenery in our ~hood.* 在我們附近地方有一些美麗的景色。*He was liked by the whole ~hood.* 他爲隣近的人們所喜愛。*He wants to live in the ~hood of London.* 他要住在倫敦附近。 **2** condition of being near: 隣近；大約: *The ~hood of this noisy airport is a serious disadvantage.* 和這嘈鬧的飛機場隣近是一個嚴重的缺點。*He lost a sum in the ~hood of £500.* 他丟了大約五百鎊的錢。 **~·ly** *adj* kind; friendly. 親切的；友善的。 **~·li·ness** *n* [U] friendly feeling, help, that is expected from ~s. (隣人間應有的)友善；和睦；睦隣。

nei·ther /'naɪðə(r) *US*: 'ni:ð- ; 'niðɚ/ *adj, pron* (used with a *sing n* or *pron*; 與單數名詞或代名詞連用; cf 參較 *either*) not one nor the other (of two): (兩

者)都不: *N~ statement is true.* 兩種說法都不是眞的。*N~ (one) is satisfactory.* 兩個都不令人滿意。*I like ~ of them.* 他們兩個我都不喜歡。*I can agree in ~ case.* 兩種情形我都不能同意。*In ~ case can I agree.* 兩種情形我都不能同意。□ *adv, conj* **1** ~... **nor...,** not... and not...: 既不…也不…: *He ~ knows nor cares what happened.* 他既不知道也不在乎發生了什麼。*It's ~ pleasant to eat nor good for you.* 它既不好吃也對你沒有好處。*N~ you nor I could do it.* 你和我都不能做這件事。*The cat has not been fed; ~ has the dog* 貓還沒餵;狗也沒餵(or)(或) *N~ the cat nor the dog has been fed.* 貓和狗都還沒餵。**2** (after a negative *if*-clause, etc) (用於否定的 if 子句等之後) and not: 亦不;也不: *If you don't go, ~ shall I.* 假如你不去,我也不去。*As he won't help you, ~ will I.* 既然他不會幫助你,我也不會幫助你。*I haven't been to the Exhibition; ~ do I* (= and I do not) *intend to go.* 我還沒去看展覽會;我也不想去。*A: 'I don't like it'—B: 'N~ do I'* 甲:'我不喜歡它'——乙:'我也不喜歡' Cf 參較 *Nor do I. No more do I.*

Nelly /ˈnelɪ ; ˈnɛlɪ/ *n* (only in) (僅用於) ***not on your ~,*** (GB sl) certainly not! (英俚)決不!

nem con /ˌnem ˈkɒn ; ˌnɛm ˈkɑn/ *adv* (abbr Lat) unanimously; without any objection being raised: (略,拉)全體一致地;無異議地: *The resolution was carried ~.* 決議案無異議通過。

nem·esis /ˈneməsɪs ; ˈnɛməsɪs/ *n* (*pl* -eses /-əsiːz ; -əˌsiz/) (formal) (正式用語) **1** deserved fate; just punishment for wrong-doing. 報應;公正的懲罰。**2 N~,** goddess of vengeance. 復仇女神。

neo- /ˈniːəʊ ; ˌnio/ *pref* new; modern. 新的;新近的;現代的。⇨ App 3. 參看附錄三。

neo-col·onial·ism /ˌniːəʊ kəˈləʊnɪəlɪzəm ; ˌniokəˈlonɪəˌlɪzəm/ *n* control by powerful countries of former colonies, or less developed countries by economic pressure. 新殖民主義(强國對以前的殖民地或尙未完全開發的國家施以經濟壓力的控制)。

neo·lithic /ˌniːəˈlɪθɪk ; ˌnioˈlɪθɪk/ *adj* of the new or later stone age: 新石器時代的: *~ man.* 新石器時代的人。

neol·ogism /niːˈɒlədʒɪzəm ; niˈɑləˌdʒɪzəm/ *n* [U] coining or using of new words; [C] newly coined word. 新字的創造或使用;新創的字。

neon /ˈniːɒn ; ˈniɑn/ *n* [U] colourless gas forming a very small proportion of the earth's atmosphere. 氖(一種無色氣體元素,在地球的大氣中所佔比例極小)。**~ light** *n* coloured light produced when an electric current passes through this gas in a low-pressure bulb or tube. 霓虹光;霓虹燈。**~ sign** *n* advertisement, etc in which ~ light is used. 霓虹燈廣告。

neo·phyte /ˈniːəfaɪt ; ˈnioˌfaɪt/ *n* person who has newly been converted to some belief or religion. 剛改奉某種信仰的人;新近才改信某一宗教的人;新信徒;新入教者。

neo·plasm /ˈniːəʊplæzəm ; ˈnioˌplæzəm/ *n* (path) tumor. (病理)贅瘤;贅疣;贅生物。

nephew /ˈnevjuː *US:* ˈnefjuː ; ˈnɛfju/ *n* son of one's brother or sister. 姪兒;外甥。

neph·ri·tis /nɪˈfraɪtɪs ; nɪˈfraɪtɪs/ *n* [U] inflammation of the kidneys. 腎臟炎。

ne plus ultra /ˌniːˌplʌsˈʌltrə ; ˈniplʌsˈʌltrə/ *n* (Lat) farthest point attained or attainable; highest point, culmination (*of*). (拉)(已達到或可達到的)最遠點;最高點;至高;至上(與 of 連用)。

nep·ot·ism /ˈnepətɪzəm ; ˈnɛpəˌtɪzəm/ *n* [U] the giving of special favour (esp employment) by a person in high position to his relatives. 袒護親戚;重用親人;族閥主義。

Nep·tune /ˈneptjuːn *US:* -tuːn ; ˈnɛptʃun/ *n* **1** (Roman god of) the sea. (羅馬神話中之)海神;海洋。**2** one of the farthest planets of the solar system. 海王星。⇨ the illus at planet. 參看 planet 之插圖。

ne·reid /ˈnɪərɪɪd ; ˈnɪrɪɪd/ *n* (Gk myth) sea-nymph. (希神)海的女神。

nerve /nɜːv ; nɝv/ *n* **1** [C] fibre or bundle of fibres carrying feelings and impulses between the brain and all parts of the body. 神經。**ˈ~-cell** *n* cell that conducts impulses. 神經細胞。**ˈ~-centre** *n* group of closely connected ~-cells; (fig) centre of control. 神經中樞;(喻)控制中心。**2** (*pl*) condition of being easily excited, worried, irritated: (複)神經過敏;神經緊張: *He is suffering from ~s,* quickly and easily becomes excited, frightened, etc. 他患神經過敏的病。*That man doesn't know what ~s are,* is never worried, upset, etc by events. 那個人不知神經緊張爲何物(即從不爲某些事情而憂慮、不安等)。*He has ~s of iron,* is never upset, etc. 他從不緊張。***get on one's ~s,*** worry or annoy: 使某人心煩;打擾某人;使煩惱: *That noise gets on my ~s.* 那聲音吵得我心煩。**war of ~s,** campaign in which an attempt is made to weaken an opponent by destroying his morale. 神經戰;心理戰(破壞對方士氣以減弱其實力的活動)。**ˈ~-racking** *adj* inflicting strain on the ~s. 傷腦筋的;令人緊張的。**3** [U] quality of being bold, self-reliant, etc: 膽量;勇氣;自信心: *A test pilot needs plenty of ~.* 飛機的試飛員需要大量勇氣。*What a ~!* What cheek! 多無恥啊!臉皮眞厚! ***have the ~ to do sth,*** **(a)** have the necessary courage, self-reliance: 有足够的勇氣(自信心)去做某事: *have the ~ to drive a racing car.* 有勇氣駕駛競賽用的汽車。**(b)** (colloq) be impudent enough: (俗)厚顏;魯莽: *He had the ~ to suggest that I was cheating.* 他竟敢說我在欺騙。***have a ~,*** (colloq) be self-assured or audacious: (俗)自信;大膽: *He's got a ~, going to work dressed like that!* 他眞大膽,竟敢穿着那樣的衣服去工作! ***lose/regain one's ~,*** lose/recover one's courage and self-assurance. 失去(恢復)勇氣及自信。**4** [C] (old use) sinew, tendon. (舊用法)腱;筋。***strain every ~ to do sth,*** make great efforts. 盡全力做某事。**5** (bot) rib, esp mid-rib, of a leaf. (植物)葉脈;(尤指)葉的中脈。□ *vt* [VP6A, 14, 16A] ***~ oneself for sth/to do sth,*** summon up one's strength (physical or moral): 喚起(肉體或精神的)力量去做某事;鼓起勇氣: *~ oneself for a task;* 鼓起勇氣去做某件工作; *~ oneself ready to face troubles.* 鼓起勇氣準備面對困難。**~·less** *adj* (from ~(4)) lacking in vigour or spirit; without energy: (由上列第4義而來)沒精神的;沒勁兒的;沒氣力的: *The knife fell from his ~less hand.* 那把刀從他那沒氣力的手中掉了下來。**~·less·ly** *adv*

nerv·ous /ˈnɜːvəs ; ˈnɝvəs/ *adj* **1** of the nerves(1): 神經的: *the ~ system of the human body.* 人體的神經系統。**a ˌ~ ˈbreakdown,** neurasthenia. 神經衰弱症。**2** tense; excited: 神經緊張的;神經過敏的: *Are you ~ in the dark?* 你在暗處會神經緊張嗎? *What's she so ~ about?* 她爲着什麼而神經緊張? **3** having strong sinews; vigorous: 剛健的;有力的: *full of ~ energy;* 精力充沛; *a ~ style of writing.* 有力的文體。**~·ly** *adv* **~·ness** *n*

nervy /ˈnɜːvɪ ; ˈnɝvɪ/ *adj* **1** (GB colloq) suffering from nervous strain. (英俗)神經緊張的。**2** (sl) impudent. (俚)厚臉皮的;魯莽的。

nes·cience /ˈnesɪəns ; ˈnɛʃɪəns/ *n* [U] (formal) absence of knowledge. (正式用語)無知。**nes·cient** /-ənt ; -ənt/ *adj* without knowledge. 無知的。

ness /nes ; nɛs/ *n* (usu in place names) promontory; headland. (通常用於地名)海角;岬;岬角。

nest /nest ; nɛst/ *n* **1** place made or chosen by a bird for its eggs. 鳥巢;鳥窠。⇨ the illus at prey. 參看 prey 之插圖。***feather one's ~,*** ⇨ feather²(1). ***foul one's own ~,*** abuse(2) one's own family, home, etc. 罵自己的家庭等;家醜外揚。**ˈ~-egg** *n* (fig) sum of money saved for future use. (喻)爲將來之用而儲蓄的錢。**2** place in which certain living things have and keep their young: 某些生物育幼之處: *a ˈwasps' ~;* 黃蜂窩; *a ˈturtle's ~.* 海龜窠。**3** comfortable place: 舒適之處: *make oneself a ~*

of cushions. 用墊子給自己做個舒適的地方。 **4** number of like things (esp boxes, tables) fitting one inside another. 一套相似物(一個比一個小,可以重疊在一起,尤指箱、桌等)。 **5** (fig) shelter; hiding-place; secluded retreat: (喩)庇護所;隱蔽所;隱退處: *a ~ of crime/vice/pirates;* 罪惡的淵藪(罪惡的隱蔽所;海盜窠); *machine-gun ~s,* where they are hidden from direct view. 機槍巢(機槍在該處被隱蔽起來,不能直接看見)。 □ *vi* [VP2A, C] **1** make and use a ~: 做窠;築巢: *The swallows are ~ing in the woodshed.* 燕子正在柴房裡做巢。 **2** *go ~ing,* search for the ~s of wild birds and take the eggs. 找鳥巢(尋找野鳥的巢並取其蛋)。

nestle /ˈnesl ; ˈnɛsl/ *vt, vi* **1** [VP2C] ~ ***(down),*** settle comfortably and warmly: 舒適而溫暖地安頓下來: ~ *down among the cushions;* 舒適地坐在墊子堆裡; ~ *down in bed.* 舒適地躺臥在床上。 **2** [VP 2C] ~ ***up (against/to),*** press oneself lovingly to: 偎依;挨靠: *The child was nestling closely up to her mother.* 小孩緊緊地偎依著她的母親。 **3** [VP 15A] cradle: 抱;懷抱: *She ~d the baby in her arms.* 她把嬰兒抱在懷裡。

nest·ling /ˈnestlɪŋ ; ˈnɛstlɪŋ/ *n* [C] bird too young to leave the nest. 雛鳥。

Nes·tor /ˈnestɔ(r) ; ˈnɛstɚ/ *n* wise, old counsellor (the name of one of the Greeks in Homer's *Iliad*). 賢明的長者;聰明的老年忠告者(荷馬史詩"伊里亞德"中一希臘人的名字)。

net¹ /net ; nɛt/ *n* [U] **1** open-work material of knotted string, hair, wire, etc; [C] such material made up for a special purpose: (繩、毛髮、鐵絲等編成的)網;(爲某一特殊目的用的)網織品: *a mosˈquito-net,* for use over a bed; 蚊帳; *ˈfishing-nets;* 魚網; *ˈtennis nets,* ⇨ the illus at tennis; 網球網(參看 tennis 之插圖); *ˈhair-nets* (used by women to keep the hair in place). (女人用以保護頭髮不亂的)髮網。 **2** (fig) moral or mental snare. (喩)(精神或心理上的)羅網;陷穽;圈套。 **3** **ˈnet·ball** *n* girls' game in which a ball has to be thrown so that it falls through a net fastened to a ring on the top of a post. 落網球戲(一種女子球戲,繫網於柱頂的網圈上,投球進網始能得分)。 **the nets,** (cricket) wickets set up inside a net for practice: (板球)(練習用之)張網的三柱門: *have an hour at the nets.* 在張了網的三柱門前練習一小時。 **ˈnet·work** *n* **(a)** complex system of lines that cross: 網狀組織;網形系統: *a network of railways/canals.* 鐵路網(運河網)。 **(b)** connected system: 連接的系統: *An intelligence/spy network.* 情報(間諜)網;情報(間諜)系統。 *A world communications network,* eg for radio and TV, using satellites. 世界通訊系統(例如利用人造衛星的無線電及電視通訊網)。 □ *vt* (-tt-) [VP6A] **1** catch (fish, animals, etc) with or in a net. 用網捕(魚、獸等)。 **2** cover (eg fruit trees) with a net or nets: 用網覆蓋(果樹等): *net strawberries/currant bushes,* against birds. 用網覆蓋草莓(紅醋栗樹)(防鳥啄食)。 **3** put nets in place in: 佈網於: *net a river.* 佈網於河。

net², nett /net ; nɛt/ *adj* remaining when nothing more is to be taken away: 淨的;純淨的: *net price,* off which discount is not to be allowed; (不能再打折扣的)實價; *net profit,* when working expenses have been deducted; 淨利;純利; *net weight,* of the contents only, excluding the weight of packing, the container, etc. (包裝重量除外的)實重;淨重。 □ *vt* (-tt-) [VP6A] gain as a net profit: 淨得;淨賺: *He netted £5 from the deal.* 該筆買賣他淨賺五鎊。

nether /ˈneðə(r) ; ˈnɛðɚ/ *adj* **1** (archaic) lower: (古)下面的;較下的: *the ~ regions/world,* the world of the dead; hell. 冥府;陰間;地獄。 **2** (joking style) (戲謔語) ~ *garments,* trousers. 褲子。 **~·most** /-məʊst ; -ˌmost/ *adj*

Neth·er·lander /ˈneðəlændə(r) ; ˈnɛðɚˌlændɚ/ *n* native of the Netherlands (Holland). 荷蘭人。 ⇨ App 6. 參看附錄六。

nett ⇨ net².

net·ting /ˈnetɪŋ ; ˈnɛtɪŋ/ *n* [U] **1** making or using nets. 製網;用網。 **2** netted string, thread or wire: 網狀編織物;(由繩、金屬線等織成的)網: *five yards of wire ~;* 五碼金屬網; *windows screened with ~.* 裝有紗窗或鐵網的窗戶。

nettle /ˈnetl ; ˈnɛtl/ *n* [C] common wild plant which has on its leaves hairs that sting and redden the skin when touched. 蕁麻。 **ˈ~·rash** *n* eruption on the skin with red patches like those caused by ~s. 蕁麻疹;風疹塊。 □ *vt* [VP6A] sting (oneself) with ~s; (fig) make rather angry; annoy: 用蕁麻刺(自己);(喩)激怒;使煩惱: *She looked ~d by my remarks.* 她看來被我的話語激怒了。

net·work ⇨ net¹.

neu·ral /ˈnjʊərəl *US:* ˈnʊərəl ; ˈnjʊrəl/ *adj* of the nerves. 神經的。

neu·ral·gia /njʊəˈrældʒə *US:* nʊ- ; njʊˈrældʒə/ *n* [U] sharp, jumping pain in the nerves, esp of the face and head. 神經痛(尤指面部及頭部的)。 **neu·ral·gic** /njʊəˈrældʒɪk ; njʊˈrældʒɪk/ *adj* of ~. 神經痛的。

neur·as·thenia /ˌnjʊərəsˈθiːnɪə *US:* ˌnʊr- ; ˌnjʊrəsˈθinɪə/ *n* [U] exhausted condition of the nervous system; low state of health, general weakness, accompanying this condition. 神經衰弱;(此症所帶來的)身體虛弱。 **neur·as·thenic** /-ˈθenɪk ; -ˈθɛnɪk/ *adj* suffering from, related to, ~. (患)神經衰弱的。 □ *n* person suffering from ~. 患神經衰弱的人。

neur·itis /njʊəˈraɪtɪs *US:* nʊ- ; njʊˈraɪtɪs/ *n* [U] inflammation of a nerve or nerves. 神經炎。

neur·ol·ogy /njʊəˈrɒlədʒɪ *US:* nʊ- ; njʊˈrɑlədʒɪ/ *n* [U] branch of medical science that is concerned with nerves. 神經學(醫學中有關神經的一門)。 **neur·ol·ogist** /njʊəˈrɒlədʒɪst *US:* nʊ- ; njʊˈrɑlədʒɪst/ *n* expert in ~. 神經學家。

neur·osis /njʊəˈrəʊsɪs *US:* nʊ- ; njʊˈrosɪs/ *n* (*pl* -oses /-əʊsiːz ; -osiz/) functional derangement caused by disorder of the nervous system or by something in the subconscious mind. 神經官能病;精神神經病。 **neur·otic** /njʊəˈrɒtɪk *US:* nʊ- ; njʊˈrɑtɪk/ *adj* (of a person) suffering from a ~; of abnormal sensitivity; obsessed. (指人)患神經官能病的;患精神神經病的;神經過敏的;有强迫觀念的。 □ *n* neurotic person. 患神經官能病者;患精神神經病者。

neu·ter /ˈnjuːtə(r) *US:* ˈnuː- ; ˈnjutɚ/ *adj* **1** (gram; of gender) neither feminine nor masculine. (文法;指性)中性的;無性的。 **2** (of plants) without male or female parts. (指植物)無雌雄之別的;無性的。 **3** (of insects, eg worker ants) sexually undeveloped; sterile. (指昆蟲,如工蟻)性器官發育不完全的;不能生育的。 □ *n* **1** ~ noun or gender. 中性名詞;中性。 **2** sexually undeveloped insect; castrated animal: 性器官發育不完全的昆蟲;經閹割的動物: *My cat is an enormous ginger ~.* 我的貓是一隻閹割過的薑黃色的大貓。 □ *vt* castrate: 閹割: *a ~ed tomcat.* 經閹割過的雄貓。

neu·tral /ˈnjuːtrəl *US:* ˈnuː- ; ˈnjutrəl/ *adj* **1** helping neither side in a war or quarrel: (他國戰爭或他人爭吵時)中立的;不協助任何一方的: ~ *nations;* 中立國; *be/remain ~.* 守(保持)中立。 **2** of a country that remains ~ in war: 中立國的: ~ *territory/ships.* 中立國的地區(船隻)。 **3** having no definite characteristics; not clearly one (colour, etc) or another: 無確定性質的;不屬於某一顏色的;中色的: ~ *tints.* 不明顯的顏色(如淺灰色等)。 **4** (chem) neither acid nor alkaline. (化學)非酸非鹼的;中性的。 **5** (of gear mechanism) of the position in which no power is transmitted: (指齒輪機械)空檔的;不傳動的: *leave a car in ~ gear.* 讓車子放空檔。 □ *n* ~ person, country, etc; ~ position of gears: 中立的人;中立國;(齒輪的)空檔位置: *slip the gears into ~.* 把齒輪推到空檔。 **~·ity** /njuːˈtrælətɪ *US:* nuː- ; njuˈtrælətɪ/ *n* [U] state of being ~, esp in war: 中性;(尤指戰爭中的)中立: *armed ~ity,* readiness to fight if attacked, but remaining ~ unless or until this happens. 武裝中立(保持中立,但如遭攻擊隨時可以應戰)。 **~·ize** /-aɪz; -ˌaɪz/ *vt* [VP6A] **1** make ~; declare by agreement that (a place) shall be treated as ~ in war; exempt or exclude from hostilities. 使中立;經協議宣告(某地)爲中立;免除或排除敵對行爲。 **2** take away the effect or special quality of, by means of sth with an opposite effect or quality: 使無效;中和: *~ize a poison.* 中和一種毒物。**~·iz·ation** /ˌnjuːtrəlaɪˈzeɪʃn *US:* -lɪˈz-; ˌnjutrələˈzeʃən/ *n*

neu·tron /ˈnjuːtrɒn *US:* ˈnuː-; ˈnjutrɑn/ *n* particle carrying no electric charge, of about the same mass as a proton, and forming part of the nucleus of an atom. 中子(構成原子核的一部份,質量約與質子相同,但不帶電荷)。

never /ˈnevə(r); ˈnɛvɚ/ *adv* **1** at no time; on no occasion: 從未;未曾: *She ~ goes to the cinema.* 她從來不去看電影。*He has ~ been abroad.* 他從未出過國。*They say that he ~ told a lie.* 據說他從來沒有撒過謊。*I'm tired of listening to your ~-ending complaints.* 我聽膩了你那永遠沒完的抱怨。(Front position for emphasis): (never 放在句首表示强調語氣): *N~ in all my life have I heard such nonsense!* 我這輩子從沒聽過這種廢話! (modifying *again* and *before*): (修飾 again 與 before): *I shall ~ again stay at that hotel.* 我絶對不再住那家旅館。*Such a display has ~ before been seen/has ~ been seen before.* 這一種展覽以前從未見過。 **2** (used as an emphatic substitute for *not*): (用作 not 的强調代用字): *That will ~ do,* won't do at all. 那絕對不行。*I ~ slept a wink all night.* 我整夜沒合過眼(一會兒也沒睡)。*He ~ so much as smiled,* didn't smile even once. 他甚至連笑也不笑。 **3** (phrases) (片語) ***Well, I ˈ~ (did)!*** expressing surprise. 我從來不曾聽見或看見過此類事(表示驚訝)!哇,眞沒想到! ***N~ mind!*** Don't worry! Don't trouble about it. 不要緊!不必介意!沒關係! ***the ˌN~ ˈN~ Land,*** imaginary land. 想像中的地方。 ***on the ˌ~-ˈ~,*** (sl) on the hire-purchase system: (俚) 以分期付款方式(購買某物): *buy sth on the ~-~.* 分期付款購買某物。 **~·more** /ˌnevəˈmɔː(r); ˌnɛvɚˈmor/ *adv* ~ again. 永不再;決不再。

never·the·less /ˌnevəðəˈles; ˌnɛvɚðəˈlɛs/ *adv, conj* however; in spite of that; still: 然而;雖然如此;依然: *There was no news; ~, she went on hoping.* 沒有消息;然而她繼續存着希望。

new /njuː *US:* nuː; nju/ *adj* (-er, -est) **1** not existing before; seen, heard of, introduced, for the first time; of recent origin, growth, manufacture, etc: 從未有過的;初見到的;初聽到的;新產的;新的: *a new school/idea/film/novel/invention;* 新學校(觀念,影片,小說,發明); *new potatoes,* lifted from the soil early in the season; 早收的馬鈴薯; *new clothes/furniture;* 新衣服(傢具); *new* (= freshly baked) *bread;* 剛出爐的麵包; *the newest* (= latest) *fashions;* 最新的款式; *new members of Parliament,* elected to Parliament for the first time. 初次當選的國會議員。 **new look,** ⇨ look²(2). **the New Testament,** (abbr 略作 NT) the second part of the Bible. (聖經中的)新約。 **2** already in existence, but only now seen, discovered, etc: 已經存在但現在才被看到、發現等的; 初見的; 新發現的: *learn new words in a foreign language;* 學外國語的生字; *discover a new star.* 發現一顆新星。 **the New World,** N and S America. 新大陸;新世界(指北美洲與南美洲)。 **3** ***new to,*** unfamiliar with; not yet accustomed to: 對…不熟悉;尙未習慣於…: *I am new to this town.* 我不熟悉此城。*They are still new to the work/trade.* 他們對這個工作(行業)還沒習慣。 ***new from,*** freshly or recently arrived from: 剛自…來到: *an office boy new from school;* 一個剛出校門的辦公室工友; *a person new from the provinces.* 剛自外地來的人。 **4** (with *def art*) later, modern, having a different character. (與定冠詞連用) 新近的;現代的;與衆不同的。 ***the new poor/rich,*** those people recently made poor/rich by social changes, etc. 新形成的窮人(富人)。 ***the new woman,*** (as used in the first half of the 20th c) woman having or claiming independence, social freedom, etc. 新女性(二十世紀前半期的名詞,指已具有或主張獨立、社交自由等的婦女)。 ***a new deal,*** ⇨ deal⁴(1). **5** beginning again. 再開始的。 ***lead a new life,*** give up old habits, etc. (摒棄舊習慣等)過新生活。 ***a/the new moon,*** seen as a thin crescent. 新月。 ***wish sb a Happy New Year,*** ie on **New Year's Day,** 1 Jan, or on **New Year's Eve,** 31 Dec. (在一月一日元旦,或十二月卅一日除夕)祝某人新年快樂。 □ *adv* (preceding, joined or hyphened to, the word it qualifies) recently: (置於所修飾的字之前,與該字連合,或接以'連字號')新近地: *a newborn baby;* 新生嬰孩; *new-laid eggs;* 剛下的蛋; *new-fallen snow;* 新降的雪; *new-made graves.* 新建的墳墓。 **ˈnew-comer** *n* person who has recently arrived in a place. 新來者。 **ˌnew-ˈfangled** /-ˈfæŋgld; -ˈfæŋgḷd/ *adj* newly come into use or fashion (and, for this reason, disliked by some): 剛被採用的; 新流行的(因此有些人不喜歡的): *new-fangled ideas about education.* 有關教育的新奇見解。 **new·ly** *adv* **1** recently: 新近地: *a newly married couple;* 新婚夫婦; *her newly awakened curiosity.* 她的新近激起的好奇心。 **ˈnewly-wed** *n* newly married person. 新婚的人。 **2** in a new, different way: 以一種新方式: *newly arranged furniture.* 以新方式排列的傢具。 **new·ness** *n*

newel /ˈnjuːəl *US:* ˈnuːəl; ˈnjuəl/ *n* centre pillar of a winding stair; post supporting a hand-rail at the top, bottom or turn of a staircase. (旋梯的)中柱;(樓梯頂部、底部或轉彎處的)欄杆柱。

new-fangled /ˌnjuː ˈfæŋgld *US:* ˌnuː; ˌnjuˈfæŋgḷd/ *adj* ⇨ new.

New·found·land /ˈnjuːfəndlənd *US:* ˈnuː-; ˈnjufəndlənd/ *n* large breed of spaniel, originally from ~, a large island in Canada, noted for its intelligence and swimming powers. 紐芬蘭狗(原產於加拿大之大島紐芬蘭,體大,性機敏,善泳)。

New·mar·ket /ˈnjuːmɑːkɪt *US:* ˈnuː-; ˈnjuˌmɑrkɪt/ *n* English town noted for horse-races; kind of card-game. 紐馬克(英國一城鎮,以賽馬聞名);一種紙牌戲。

news /njuːz *US:* nuːz; njuz/ *n sing* [U] new or fresh information; report(s) of what has most recently happened: 新聞;消息;新聞報導: *What's the latest ~?* 有什麼最新的消息? (TV and radio): (電視及無線電): *Here is the ~.* 現在報告新聞。*Here are the ~ headlines.* 現在報告新聞標題。*Here is a ~ summary/a summary of the ~.* 現在報告新聞提要。*Here are some interesting items/pieces/bits of ~.* 現在報告幾件有趣的新聞。*That's no ~ to me,* I already know that. 我早就知道啦(對我不是新聞)。*Sandra is in the ~,* is being written about in the papers. 桑德拉現在是新聞人物(報紙正登載她的消息)。*The ~ that the enemy were near alarmed the citizens.* 敵軍迫近的消息使市民驚慌。*Have you any ~ of* (= concerning) *where your brother is staying?* 你有沒有你哥哥(弟弟)現在何處的消息? ***ˌNo ~ is ˈgood ~,*** (prov) If there were bad ~ we should hear it. (諺)沒有消息就是好消息(如果有壞消息我們就會聽到了)。 **ˈ~ agency** *n* agency that collects ~ and sells it to the press. 通訊社(收集並賣新聞給報紙的機構)。 **ˈ~·agent** *n* shopkeeper who sells ~papers, periodicals, etc. 賣報紙雜誌等的店商。 **ˈ~·boy** *n* boy who sells ~papers in the streets. (沿街的)賣報童;報童。 **ˈ~·cast** *n* broadcast of ~. 新聞廣播。 **ˈ~·caster** *n* person who does this. 新聞廣播員。 **ˈ~ cinema/theatre,** cinema showing ~reels, cartoons, and other short films. 放映新聞片,卡通片及其他短片之電影院。 **ˈ~·dealer,** (US) (美) = ~agent. **ˈ~·letter** *n* letter or circular sent out to members of a society, etc.

N

(對一會社之會員等發行的)通訊;簡訊。 **'~·monger** *n* person who gossips. 喜歡說閒話的人;饒舌的人。 **'~·paper** /'nju:speɪpə(r) *US:* 'nu:z- ; 'njuz,pepə/ *n* printed publication, usu issued every day, with ~, advertisements, etc. 報紙;新聞紙。 **'~·paper-man** /-mæn ; -,mæn/ *n* (*pl* -men) journalist. 新聞工作者;新聞記者。 **'~·print** *n* [U] paper for printing ~-papers on. 白報紙。 **'~·reel** *n* cinema film of recent events. 新聞影片。 **'~·room** *n* room (in a library, etc) where ~papers and other periodicals may be read. (圖書館等中之)閱報室(閱讀報紙、雜誌等的房間)。 **'~·sheet** *n* simple form of ~paper. 單頁報紙;單張報紙。 **'~·stand** *n* stall for the sale of ~papers, etc. 報攤;雜誌攤;書報攤。 **'~·vendor** *n* seller of ~papers. 賣報者。 **'~·worthy** *adj* sufficiently interesting for reporting, eg in a newspaper. 有趣而值得在報紙上發表的;值得報導的;有報導價值的。 **~·less** *adj* without ~. 沒有消息的;無新聞的。 **~y** *adj* (colloq) full of ~ or gossip: (俗)多新聞的;饒舌的: *a ~y letter.* 滿紙新聞的信。

newt /nju:t *US:* nu:t ; njut/ *n* (kinds of) small lizard-like animal which spends most of its time in the water. 水蜥;蠑螈。⇨ the illus at amphibian. 參看 amphibian 之挿圖。

New·to·nian /nju:'təunɪən *US:* nu:- ; nju'tonɪən/ *adj* related to Sir Isaac Newton, and his theories, esp his law of gravity. 牛頓的;牛頓學說的;(尤指)牛頓萬有引力律的。□ *n* follower of Newton and his system. 牛頓及其學說的信徒。

next /nekst ; nɛkst/ *adj, n* **1** ~ ***(to sth/sb),*** coming immediately after, in order or space: 僅次的;其次的;下次;下一個;與…隣接的: *What's the ~ thing to do?* 其次要做的是什麼? *Take the ~ turning to the right.* 前面向右轉彎。 *Miss Green was the ~ (person) to arrive.* 下一個來到的(人)是格林小姐。 *Come and sit down ~ to me.* 來坐在我旁邊。 *Which is the town ~ to London in size?* 大小僅次於倫敦的是哪一個城? ***the ~ best (thing),*** that which is chosen or accepted if the first choice fails: 第二好的;次好的事物: *There are no tickets left for the Circus: the ~ best thing is the Zoo.* 看馬戲的票沒有了,次好的去處是動物園。 ***~ to nothing,*** scarcely anything; almost nothing: 幾乎沒有: *No wonder she's ill! She eats ~ to nothing.* 怪不得她病了!她幾乎什麼都沒吃。 ***~ door,*** in the ~ house: 隣家;隔壁: *He lives ~ door (to me).* 他住在(我的)隔壁。 *The people ~ door are very noisy.* 隔壁的人很吵鬧。 *We are ~-door neighbours.* 我們是隔壁隣居。 ***~ door to,*** (fig) almost; not far from: (喻)幾乎;近乎;差不多: *Such ideas are ~ door to madness.* 這種主意近乎瘋狂。 ***next of kin,*** ⇨ kin. **2** (of time; *def art* needed if the reference is to a time that is future in relation to a time already mentioned): (指時間;假如所指的時間是在已提到的時間的未來,則須加定冠詞): *I shall go there ~ Friday/week/year.* 下星期五(下星期,明年)我要到那裡去。 *We shall be in France by this time ~ week.* 下星期這個時候我們將在法國了。 *He will spend the first week of his holiday in France and the ~ (week) in Italy.* 他將要在法國度他的假期的第一週,而在義大利度第二週。 *We arrived in Turin on a Monday; the ~ day we left for Rome.* 我們星期一抵達了杜林;次日我們去羅馬。 *That summer was very wet; the ~ summer was even wetter.* 那年夏天雨很多;次年夏天雨更多。 *Is he coming this weekend* (ie the coming weekend) *or ~ weekend* (ie the following weekend)? 他是本週末要來還是下週末要來?□ *adv* **1** after this/that; then: 在這(那)以後;然後: *What are you going to do ~?* 你接著要做什麼? *When I ~ saw her she was dressed in green.* 我再度看到她時,她穿着綠色衣服。 ***come ~,*** follow: 隨着;跟着: *What comes ~,* what's the ~ thing (to do, etc). 接下去(要做的等)是什麼? **2** used to express surprise or wonder: 用於表示驚訝: *What will he be saying ~?* 他下一步又要說什麼呢? *A new motor-car! What ~?* 一輛新車!還要什麼(含諷刺意味)? □ *prep* (archaic) (古) = next to.

nexus /'neksəs ; 'nɛksəs/ *n* (*pl* ~es /-səsɪz ; -səsɪz/) connection; bond; connected series. 關係;連結;連繫;連結的系列。

nib /nɪb ; nɪb/ *n* split pen-point (to be) inserted in a pen-holder. 鋼筆尖。

nibble /'nɪbl ; 'nɪbl/ *vt, vi* [VP6A, 2A, 3A] ~ ***(at),*** **1** take tiny bites: 細咬;輕咬: *fish nibbling (at) the bait.* 輕咬魚餌的魚。 **2** (fig) show some inclination to accept (an offer), agree to (a suggestion, etc), but without being definite. (喻)表示有意(但未確定地)接受(提議),贊同(建議等)。□ *n* [C] act of nibbling: 輕咬;細咬: *I felt a ~ at the bait.* 我覺得有魚輕輕地咬了一下魚餌。

nice /naɪs ; naɪs/ *adj* (-r, -st) **1** (contrary to *nasty*) pleasant; agreeable; kind; friendly; fine: (與 nasty 相反)令人愉快的;宜人的;良好的;友善的;優美的: *a ~ day;* 好天氣;美好的一天; *~ weather;* 好天氣; *a ~ little girl;* 可愛的小女孩; *~ to the taste/the feel, etc;* 味道佳美(摸起來覺得柔細等)的; *medicine that is not ~ to take.* 不好吃的藥。 ***~ and + adj,*** ~ because...: 因爲…而宜人: *~ and warm by the fire;* 在火邊溫暖而舒適; *~ and cool in the woods.* 在森林裡很涼快。 **2** needing care and exactness; sensitive; subtle: 需要愼重和精確的;精微的;敏感的;狡黠的: *a ~ point of law,* one that may be difficult to decide; 法律上難以決定之處; *~ (= delicate) shades of meaning.* 意義的微妙區別。 **3** (ironic) difficult; bad: (反語)困難的;壞的: *You've got us into a ~ mess.* 你使我們陷入困境了。 **4** hard to please; having or showing delicate tastes: 難以取悅的;難侍候的;講究的: *too ~ in one's dress.* 衣着過份講究。 **5** punctilious; scrupulous: 謹愼的;多顧慮的: *He's not so ~ in his business methods.* 他的經營方法不太愼重。 **~·ly** *adv* **1** in a ~ manner. 美好地;宜人地;精細地;講究地;謹愼地。 **2** (colloq) very well; all right: (俗)很好;相宜: *That will suit me ~ly.* 那會剛好適合我。 *The patient is doing ~ly,* is making good progress. 那個病人好得很快。 **~·ness** *n*

nicety /'naɪsətɪ ; 'naɪsətɪ/ *n* (*pl* -ties) **1** [U] accuracy; exactness: 準確;精確: *~ of judgement;* 判斷的準確; *a point of great ~,* one needing most careful and exact consideration. 需要仔細考慮之處。 **2** [C] delicate distinction: 細微的區別: *the niceties of criticism.* 批評的細微之處。 ***to a ~,*** exactly right: 正確地;恰好地: *He judged the distance to a ~.* 他判斷那段距離甚爲精確。

niche /nɪtʃ ; nɪtʃ/ *n* [C] **1** (usu shallow) recess (often with a shelf) in a wall, eg for a statue or ornament. (通常爲淺的)壁龕(常有框架,用以放置塑像或裝飾品等)。 ***have a ~ in the temple of fame,*** have achievements that will not be forgotten. 流芳百世。 **2** (fig) suitable or fitting position: (喻)適當的位置;恰當的場所: *He found the right ~ for himself,* a place where he could do what he wanted to do, comfortably and happily. 他找到了適當的職位。

nick[1] /nɪk ; nɪk/ *n* **1** small V-shaped cut (made in sth), eg as a record. V形的小刻痕(例如作記錄者)。 **2** ***in the ~ of time,*** only just in time; at the critical or opportune time. 剛來得及;在恰好的時候;正當危急之際。 **3** ***in the ~,*** (sl) in prison. (俚)在監獄中;在監禁中。□ *vt* make a ~ in: 刻痕於: *~ one's chin,* while shaving; (刮鬍子時)在下巴處留下一道割痕; cut a notch in. 刻V形缺口於。

nick[2] /nɪk ; nɪk/ *n* (sl) (only in) (俚)(僅用於) ***in good/poor ~,*** in good/poor health or condition: 健康情形良好(不好);情況良好(不好): *feeling in very good ~.* 感覺健康情形非常良好。 *The house is in pretty poor ~.* 那幢房子的情況糟透了。

Nick /nɪk ; nɪk/ *n* short for *Nicholas.* 爲 Nicholas 的簡寫。 **Old N~,** the devil. 魔鬼。

nickel /'nɪkl ; 'nɪkl/ *n* **1** [U] hard, silver-white metal (symbol **Ni**) used in the form of ~-plating and in alloys (ˌ~-ˈ*steel*, ˌ~-ˈ*silver*). 鎳(一種銀白色的堅硬金屬，用於鍍鎳及鎳鋼、鎳銀等合金中)。 **2** US coin, value 5 cents. 美國的鎳幣(值五分錢)。□ *vt* (-ll-, US = -l-) coat with ~. 鍍鎳於。

nick·nack /ˈnɪknæk ; ˈnɪkˌnæk/ *n* = knick-knack.

nick·name /ˈnɪkneɪm ; ˈnɪkˌnem/ *n* name given in addition to or altered from or used instead of the real name (eg *Fatty* for a fat person; *Shorty* humorously for a very tall person). 綽號；渾名(例如叫胖的人'胖子'; 對非常高的人詼諧地稱爲'矮子')。□ *vt* [VP6A, 23] give a ~ to: 加綽號於；給…起綽號: *They ~d him Hurry.* 他們給他起個綽號'慌張'。

nic·otine /ˈnɪkətiːn ; ˈnɪkəˌtin/ *n* [U] poisonous, oily substance in tobacco-leaves: 尼古丁(菸葉中所含的有毒的油質成分): *~-stained fingers;* 被尼古丁薰黃的手指; *cigarettes with a low ~ content.* 含尼古丁成分低的香煙。

niece /niːs ; nis/ *n* daughter of one's brother(-in-law) or sister(-in-law). 姪女；甥女。

niff /nɪf ; nɪf/ *n* (GB sl, dial) (unpleasant) smell. (英俚，方)臭味。**~y** *adj* (sl) having a bad smell. (俚)有臭味的。

nifty /ˈnɪftɪ ; ˈnɪftɪ/ *adj* (sl) (俚) **1** smart; stylish. 漂亮的；時髦的。 **2** having an unpleasant smell. 有臭味的。 **3** quick, efficient: 迅速敏捷的: *Look ~!* 趕快！ (more usu 較常用 *Look nippy!*)

nig·gard /ˈnɪgəd ; ˈnɪgɚd/ *n* mean, stingy person. 小氣鬼；吝嗇鬼。**~·ly** *adj* giving, given, unwillingly, in small amounts; miserly: 吝嗇的；小氣的: *~ly contributions.* 小氣的捐助。**~·li·ness** *n*

nig·ger /ˈnɪgə(r) ; ˈnɪgɚ/ *n* ⚠ (impolite and offensive word for) Negro. (諱)黑鬼(指黑人，爲不禮貌及侮蔑用語)。

niggle /ˈnɪgl ; ˈnɪgḷ/ *vi* give too much time or attention to unimportant details; complain about trivial matters. 過份爲小事費時或操心；爲瑣事發牢騷。**nig·gling** *adj* trifling; lacking in boldness of effect. 瑣碎的；無關重要的；微小的；不顯目的。

nigh /naɪ ; naɪ/ *adv, prep* (-er, -est) (archaic and poet) near (to). (古及詩)近；靠近。

night /naɪt ; naɪt/ *n* [C, U] **1** dark hours between sunset and sunrise or twilight and dawn: 夜: *in/during the ~;* 在夜裡; *on Sunday ~;* 在星期日夜裡; *on the ~ of Friday, the 13th of June;* 在六月十三日星期五晚上; *a late-~ show at the cinema,* one given much later than the usual shows. 夜晚最後一場電影。*He stayed three ~s with us,* slept at our house three ~s. 他在我們家裡住了三夜。*Can you stay over ~,* spend the ~ with us? 你能在我們家裡過夜嗎？*What a dirty ~ it has been,* how stormy, rainy, etc the ~ has been! 這一夜風雨好大！ ***~ after ~,*** for many ~s in succession. 一夜又一夜；連着幾夜。***all ~ (long),*** throughout the whole ~. 整夜裡；徹夜；終夜。***~ and day,*** continuously: 日以繼夜；不斷地: *travel ~ and day for a week.* 晝夜不停地旅行一星期。***at ~,*** when ~ comes; during the ~: 夜裡: *6 o'clock at ~,* 6pm. 下午六時。***by ~,*** during the ~: 夜裡；夜間: *travel by ~.* 夜間旅行。***get/have/take a ~ off,*** a ~ free from work usually done at ~. 一夜不做(通常在夜間做的)工作；一夜不當班。***have a good/bad ~,*** sleep well/badly. (夜裡)睡得好(不好)。***have a ~ out,*** spend an evening and ~ in pleasure, eg by having dinner out, followed by a visit to the cinema. 在外頭玩一個晚上(如在外面吃飯，接着去看電影等)。***make a ~ of it,*** spend all ~ in pleasure-making, esp at a party. 痛痛快快地玩一個晚上。***turn ~ into day,*** do at ~ what is usu done during the day. 以夜作晝(把通常在日間做的工作放在晚上做)；日夜顛倒。***work ~s,*** work on ~ shift: 上夜班: *My husband's working ~s this week.* 我丈夫這星期當夜班。⇨ shift¹(2). **2** (compounds) (複合字) **ˈ~-bell** *n* bell (eg on the street door, at a doctor's house) to be used at ~. (醫師住宅等大門上所裝的)夜間門鈴。**ˈ~-bird** *n* **(a)** bird (eg an owl) which is active at ~. 夜鳥(夜間活動的鳥，如貓頭鷹)。 **(b)** person (usu disreputable) who goes about at ~. 夜遊人(通常指品行不良之人)。**ˈ~·cap** *n* **(a)** cap (formerly) worn in bed. (昔時睡覺戴的)睡帽。 **(b)** (usu alcoholic) drink taken before going to bed. 睡前的飲料(通常指酒類)；睡前酒。 **ˈ~-club** *n* club open until the early hours of the morning to members for dancing, supper, entertainment, etc. 夜總會。**ˈ~·dress** *n* long, loose garment worn by a woman or child in bed. (婦女和小孩的)睡袍；睡衣。**ˈ~·fall** *n* [U] the coming of ~; evening. 日暮；傍晚；黃昏。**ˈ~·gown** *n* = ~dress. **~ie, ~y** *n* (colloq) (俗) = ~dress. **ˈ~·jar** *n* ~-flying bird that resembles a swift. 歐夜鷹。**ˈ~ life,** entertainment, eg cabaret, ~clubs, available in a town late at ~. 夜生活(城市中深夜裡的娛樂，如餐飲場所的歌舞表演、夜總會等)。**ˈ~-light** *n* light (eg a short, thick candle, or a small electric bulb) kept burning in a bedroom at ~ (esp for a small child or an invalid). 通夜不熄的燈；通宵燈(如粗短的蠟燭或小電燈，尤指爲小孩或病者而點者)。**ˈ~-line** *n* line left in a river, lake, etc with baited hooks, to catch fish by ~. 夜釣繩(夜間放在水中以釣魚，繩端裝有上了餌的鈎)。**ˈ~-long** *adj* lasting the whole ~. 通宵的；徹夜的。**ˈ~·mare** /-meə(r) ; -ˌmɛr/ *n* [C] **(a)** terrible, frightening dream. 夢魘；惡夢。**(b)** haunting fear; sth dreaded; (memory of a) horrible experience: 縈繞於心的恐懼；可怕的事物；可怕經驗(的記憶): *Travelling on those bad mountain roads was a ~mare.* 在那些崎嶇山路上旅行是可怕的事。**ˈ~-porter** *n* hotel porter on duty during the ~. 旅館夜間當班的門房。**ˈ~ safe** *n* facility or opening like a letter-box in a wall of a bank, so that valuables, money, etc may be deposited after banking hours. 夜間保險箱(裝置於銀行牆上像信箱的開口，供客戶於銀行下班後存放珍貴物品、金錢等)。**ˈ~ school** *n* one that gives lessons to persons who are unable to attend classes during the day. 夜校。**ˈ~·shade** *n* [U] name of various wild plants with poisonous berries. 龍葵(結有毒漿果的數種野生植物)。 **ˈ~ shift,** ⇨ shift¹(2). **ˈ~·shirt** *n* boy's or man's long shirt for sleeping in. 男睡衣。**ˈ~-soil** *n* contents of earth-closets and cess-pools, removed during the ~. 糞坑和糞池中的糞便(通常在夜間運走)。**ˈ~ stop** *n,* **ˈ~-stop** *n* break in a journey for a night. 夜間停留過夜。**ˈ~-time** *n* time of darkness: 夜間: *in the ~-time,* by ~. 在夜間；夜裡。**ˌ~-ˈwatch** *n* (person or group of persons keeping) watch by ~. 守夜；守夜者。***in the ~-watches,*** during the wakeful, restless, or anxious periods of ~. 在夜裡睡不着，不安或焦急的那幾段時間中。**ˌ~-ˈwatchman** /-mən ; -mən/ *n* (*pl* -men) man employed to keep watch (eg in a factory) at ~. (工廠等所雇用的)守夜者。**ˈ~·work** *n* work that is done, or must be done, by ~. 夜間工作；夜工。**~·ly** *adj, adv* (taking place, happening, existing) in the ~ or every ~: 在夜裡；夜間發生、存在等的；每夜(的): *~ly performances;* 夜間演出；每晚演出; *a film show twice ~ly;* 每晚放映兩次的電影; *do something ~ly.* 每天晚上都要做點事。

night·in·gale /ˈnaɪtɪŋgeɪl *US:* -tng- ; ˈnaɪtṇˌgel/ *n* small, reddish-brown migratory bird that sings sweetly by night as well as by day. 夜鶯。⇨ the illus at bird. 參看 bird 之插圖。

ni·hil·ism /ˈnaɪɪlɪzəm ; ˈnaɪəlˌɪzəm/ *n* [U] total rejection of current political institutions and religious and moral beliefs. 無政府主義；虛無主義。**ni·hil·ist** /-ɪst ; -ɪst/ *n* believer in ~. 無政府主義者；虛無主義者。 **ni·hil·is·tic** /ˌnaɪɪˈlɪstɪk ; ˌnaɪəˈlɪstɪk/ *adj* relating to ~. 無政府主義的；虛無主義的。

nil /nɪl ; nɪl/ *n* nothing: 無；零: *The result of the game was three nil/three goals to nil,* ie 3–0. 比賽結果是三比零。

Ni·lotic /naɪˈlɒtɪk ; naɪˈlɑtɪk/ *adj* of the Nile, the Nile region, or its inhabitants. 尼羅河的；尼羅河流

域的;尼羅河流域之居民的。

nimble /ˈnɪmbl ; ˈnɪmbḷ/ *adj* **1** quick-moving: 敏捷的;迅速的: *as ~ as a goat.* 像山羊一樣敏捷。**2** (of the mind) sharp; quick to understand. (指頭腦)敏銳的;聰明的。**nim·bly** /ˈnɪmblɪ ; ˈnɪmblɪ/ *adv* **~·ness** *n*

nim·bus /ˈnɪmbəs ; ˈnɪmbəs/ *n* (*pl* ~es /-bəsɪz ; -bəsɪz/, -bi /-baɪ ; -baɪ/) **1** bright disc round or over the head of a saint (in a painting, etc). (在畫等之中,聖者頭部四周或上面的)光環;光輪;光雲。⇨ halo. **2** rain-cloud. 雨雲。

nim·iny-pim·iny /ˌnɪmɪnɪ ˈpɪmɪnɪ; ˈnɪmənɪˈpɪmənɪ/ *adj* affected; mincing; prim. 做作的;矯飾的;拘泥形式的。

Nim·rod /ˈnɪmrɒd ; ˈnɪmrɑd/ *n* great hunter. 大獵人寧錄。⇨ Gen 10: 8, 9. 參看創世記 10 章 8 節和 9 節。

nin·com·poop /ˈnɪŋkəmpuːp ; ˈnɪnkəmˌpup/ *n* foolish, weak-minded person. 愚人;傻子。

nine /naɪn ; naɪn/ *n, adj* the number 9, ⇨ App 4. 九;九個;九個的(參看附錄四)。***a ~ days' wonder,*** sth that attracts attention for a few days and is then forgotten. 一時引人注意不久卽被遺忘的事物。***dressed up to the ~s,*** (colloq) dressed very elaborately or extravagantly. (俗)穿着非常考究或奢侈。***~ times out of ten,*** very often. 十有八九。**nine·pence** /ˈnaɪnpəns *US:* -npens ; ˈnaɪnpəns/ *n* 九辨士。**nine·penny** /ˈnaɪnpənɪ *US:* -npenɪ ; ˈnaɪnˌpɛnɪ/ *adj* 九辨士的。**~·teen** /ˌnaɪnˈtiːn ; naɪnˈtin/ *n, adj* the number 19. 十九;十九的。***(talk) ~teen to the dozen,*** (talk) continually. 不停地(說話);喋喋不休。**~·teenth** /ˌnaɪnˈtiːnθ ; naɪnˈtinθ/ *n, adj* the next after the 18th, one of 19 equal parts. 第十九(的);十九分之一。**~·ti·eth** /ˈnaɪntɪəθ ; ˈnaɪntɪɪθ/ *n, adj* the next after the 89th; one of 90 equal parts. 第九十(的);九十分之一。**~ty** /ˈnaɪntɪ ; ˈnaɪntɪ/ *n, adj* the number 90. 九十(的)。***~ty-~ times out of a hundred,*** almost always. 一百次中有九十九次;幾乎總是如此。**the ~ties,** 90-99. 90至99之數。**ˈ~·fold** /-fəʊld ; -ˌfold/ *adj, adv* ~ times as many or much. 九重的(地);九倍的(地)。**ninth** /naɪnθ ; naɪnθ/ *n, adj* the next after the 8th; one of 9 equal parts. 第九(的);九分之一。**ninth·ly** *adv*

nine·pins /ˈnaɪnpɪnz ; ˈnaɪnˌpɪnz/ *n pl* (with *sing v*) (與單數動詞連用) **1** game in which a ball is rolled along the floor at nine bottle-shaped pieces of wood. 九柱戲(沿地面滾球撞擊九根瓶狀木柱的一種遊戲)。⇨ tenpins. **2** (*sing*) one of these pieces. (單)(九柱戲中的一根)瓶狀木柱;柱。***go down like a ninepin,*** fall heavily. 重重跌倒(像九柱戲中的木柱般跌倒)。

ninny /ˈnɪnɪ ; ˈnɪnɪ/ *n* (*pl* -nies) fool; simpleton. 愚人;傻子。

Niobe /ˈnaɪəbɪ ; ˈnaɪəbɪ/ *n* (Gk myth) woman who was changed into a stone fountain while weeping for her children who had been killed; woman who weeps and cannot be comforted. (希神)尼奧比(當哀哭其子女被殺時,被化爲石泉之女人);哀泣而無法安慰的婦女。

nip /nɪp ; nɪp/ *vt, vi* (-pp-) **1** [VP6A, 15A, B] pinch; press hard (eg between finger and thumb, or with the claws, as a crab does, or with the teeth, as a dog or horse might do): 捏;箝;掐;夾(例如人用大姆指與食指,蟹等用螯,狗馬等用牙): *A crab nipped my toe while I was swimming.* 當我游泳的時候,一隻螃蟹箝住了我的脚指頭。*He nipped his finger in the door,* ie between the door and the door-post. 他的手指給門縫夾了。*The gardener was nipping off* (= pinching out) *the side shoots from his chrysanthemums;* 園丁正在把菊花的邊芽掐掉; (sewing) alter the size slightly: (縫級)略爲修改: *The dress fits me now that I've nipped in the sides a little,* reduced the width by altering the seams. 這件衣服兩邊略爲修改後很合我的身。**2** [VP 6A, 15A] (of frost, wind, etc) stop the growth of; damage. (指霜、風等)傷害;摧殘。***nip sth in the bud,*** stop its development. 在萌芽時摘取;阻止某事物的發展;防患於未然。**3** [VP2A] perform the action of biting or pinching. 咬;夾;捏。**4** (colloq) [VP2C] hurry: (俗)趕快;急忙: *nip along.* 急忙前進。*He nipped in* (= got in quickly) *just in front of me.* 他就在我前面挿進來。*I'll nip on ahead and open the door.* 我要趕到前面去打開那個門。□ *n* [C] **1** sharp pinch or bite: 捏;箝;夾;咬: *a cold nip in the air,* a feeling of frost. 空氣裡刺骨的寒冷。**2** small drink (esp of spirits): 少量(尤指烈酒): *a nip of brandy.* 少量的白蘭地。**ˈnip·ping** *adj* (of the air or wind) sharp; biting cold. (指空氣或風)凜冽的;刺骨的;嚴寒的。⇨ nippy(1).

nip·per /ˈnɪpə(r) ; ˈnɪpɚ/ *n* **1** (*pl;* colloq) pincers, forceps or other tool for gripping. (複;俗)鑷子;鉗子;拔鉗;任何夾東西的工具。**2** crustacean's claw. 甲殼類動物的螯。**3** (GB colloq) small child. (英俗)小孩。

nipple /ˈnɪpl ; ˈnɪpḷ/ *n* **1** part of the breast through which a baby gets its mother's milk; similar small projection on the breast of a human male. (人類的)乳頭;奶頭。Cf 參較 *teat* for other mammals. 其他哺乳動物的奶頭用 teat。**2** (more usu 較常用 *teat*) rubber mouth-piece of a baby's feeding bottle. (奶瓶上的)橡皮奶頭。**3** sth shaped like a ~: 似奶頭之物: *ˈgreasing ~s,* through which grease is injected. 加脂乳頭(滑脂經由其灌入)。

Nip·pon·ese /ˌnɪpəˈniːz ; ˌnɪpənˈiz/ *adj* of Nippon /ˈnɪpɒn ; ˈnɪpɑn/ (= Japan). 日本的。

nippy /ˈnɪpɪ ; ˈnɪpɪ/ *adj* (-ier, -iest) (colloq) (俗) **1** (GB) biting cold. (英)刺骨的;嚴寒的。**2** nimble. 敏捷的;迅速的。***look ~,*** be quick. 趕快。

nir·vana /nɪəˈvɑːnə ; nɜˈvænə/ *n* (in Buddhism) state in which individuality becomes extinct by being absorbed into the supreme spirit. (佛教的)涅槃(個體藉融入最高之精神體而寂滅之境界)。

nisi /ˈnaɪsaɪ ; ˈnaɪsaɪ/ *conj* (Lat, legal) unless. (拉,法律)除非。**decree ~,** decree (of divorce, etc) valid unless cause is shown for rescinding it before the time when it is made absolute. 在指定時日以前不提出反對理由卽行生效的(離婚等的)判決。

Nis·sen hut /ˈnɪsn hʌt ; ˈnɪsṇ hʌt/ *n* prefabricated semicircular hut of sheets of corrugated iron, erected over a concrete floor. 尼森式小屋(建於混凝土地面上,用波狀鐵皮預造的半圓形小屋)。

nit[1] /nɪt ; nɪt/ *n* egg of a louse or other parasitic insect. 虱或其他寄生蟲的卵。

nit[2] /nɪt ; nɪt/ *n* = nitwit.

ni·ter /ˈnaɪtə(r) ; ˈnaɪtɚ/ ⇨ nitre.

ni·trate /ˈnaɪtreɪt ; ˈnaɪtret/ *n* salt formed by the chemical reaction of nitric acid with an alkali, esp *potassium* ~ and *sodium* ~, used as fertilizers. 硝酸鹽(尤指作肥料用的硝酸鉀與硝酸鈉)。(Used in *pl* for 'kinds of ~'). (複數指各類的硝酸鹽)。

nitre (US = **niter**) /ˈnaɪtə(r) ; ˈnaɪtɚ/ *n* [U] potassium or sodium nitrate (also called 亦稱作 *salt-petre*). 硝酸鉀(卽硝石);硝酸鈉。

ni·tric /ˈnaɪtrɪk ; ˈnaɪtrɪk/ *adj* of, containing, nitrogen. 氮的;含氮的。**ˌ~ ˈacid, (HNO_3),** clear colourless, powerful acid that eats into and destroys most substances. 硝酸(無色強酸,能侵蝕大多數物質,分子式爲 HNO_3)。

ni·tro-chalk /ˌnaɪtrəʊˈtʃɔːk ; ˌnaɪtroˈtʃɔk/ *n* [U] fertilizer used in spring to encourage growth of grass. 白堊硝(春季裡用以加速青草生長的肥料)。

ni·tro·gen /ˈnaɪtrədʒən ; ˈnaɪtrədʒən/ *n* [U] gas (symbol **N**) without colour, taste or smell, forming about four-fifths of the atmosphere. 氮(化學符號 N,無色、無味、無臭的氣體,大約佔空氣的五分之四)。

ni·tro·glycer·ine, -glycerin /ˌnaɪtrəʊˈglɪsəriːn *US:* -rɪn ; ˌnaɪtrəˈglɪsrɪn/ *n* [U] powerful explosive made by adding glycerine to a mixture of nitric and sulphuric acids. 硝化甘油;炸藥油;硝化甘油炸藥。

ni·trous /ˈnaɪtrəs ; ˈnaɪtrəs/ *adj* of, like, nitre. 硝石的;似硝石的。**~ oxide,** gas **(N_2O)** (also called *laughing-gas*) sometimes used by dental surgeons to make a person unconscious while having a tooth or teeth pulled out. 氧化亞氮 (亦稱笑氣，分子式爲N_2O，牙醫拔牙時作麻醉劑用)。

nitty-gritty /ˌnɪtɪ ˈgrɪtɪ ; ˌnɪtɪˈgrɪtɪ/ *n* [U] **the ~,** (colloq) the basic fact(s) of a matter. (俗)事情的基本事實。

nit·wit /ˈnɪtwɪt ; ˈnɪtˌwɪt/ *n* (colloq) person with very little intelligence. (俗)笨人。Hence, 由此產生, **~·ted** /ˌnɪtˈwɪtɪd ; ˌnɪtˈwɪtɪd/ *adj* unintelligent. 愚昧的。

nix /nɪks ; nɪks/ *n* (sl) nothing. (俚)無物。

no /nəʊ ; no/ *adj* **1** not one; not any: 無;沒有: *She had no friends.* 她沒有朋友。*The poor boy had no money.* 那可憐的男孩沒有錢。*No words can describe the scene.* 那景色非筆墨所能形容。*There was no end to our troubles,* They were endless. 我們的麻煩是沒完的。***no end of,*** (colloq) a large number or quantity of; very great: (俗)多的;大量的;極大的: *He spends no end of money on clothes.* 他花大量的錢在衣着上。*We had no end of a good time,* a very enjoyable time. 我們玩得極爲愉快。(Note that *no* precedes numerals and *other*): (注意 no 放在數字與 other 之前): *No one man could have done it,* No man could have done it by himself. 沒有一個人能單獨完成那件事。*No two men think alike.* 沒有兩個人想法是一樣的。*No other man could do the work.* 沒有別的人能做那個工作。 **2** (implying the opposite of the following word): (表示隨在後面那個字的相反的意思): *He's no friend of mine.* 他不是我的朋友。*The task is no easy one.* 那工作是不容易的。*This nightclub is no place for a young and innocent girl.* 這家夜總會不是年輕純潔的女孩應該去的地方。*Matilda is no beauty,* is not at all beautiful. 麥狄達一點也不漂亮。 **3** (in the pattern: 用於下列句型: *there + be + no + gerund*): *There's no saying* (= It is impossible to say) *what he'll be doing next.* 他接下去將要做什麼,很難斷言。*There's no denying* (= We cannot deny) *that....* 無可否認的…。 **4** (in elliptical constructions): (用於省略結構): *No smoking* (= Smoking is not allowed). 禁止吸煙。*No surrender!* 絕不投降! *It's raining hard and no mistake,* and there can be no doubt about it. 現在正下着大雨,這是千眞萬確的。 **5** (phrases) (片語) ***It's no go,*** (colloq) can't be done, won't succeed. (俗)行不通;不行;不成。***be no good/use,*** useless: 無用;沒有用: *It's no good crying over spilt milk.* 牛奶灑了,哭也無益。⇨ milk¹(1). ***be no wonder (that),*** not surprising (that). 怪不得(…);(…)是不足爲奇的。 ***by 'no means,*** ⇨ means¹. ***in 'no time,*** very soon, very quickly. 立刻。**ˌno-ˈball,** unlawfully delivered ball in cricket. 玩板球時所投的不合規則的球。**ˌno-ˈgo area,** (colloq) (usu urban) area barricaded to prevent the police or security force from entering. (俗) (通常指都市的) 設有障礙物的地區 (阻止警察或保安部隊進入者)。 **ˈno-man's-land,** (in war) ground between the fronts of two opposing armies. (戰爭時兩軍陣前之)無人地帶。**ˈno one, ˈno-one,** *pron* = nobody. □ *adv* **1** (used with comparatives): (與比較級形容詞或副詞連用): *We went no farther than* (= only as far as) *the bridge.* 我們只走到橋邊。*I hope you're feeling no worse this morning.* 我希望你今早不會覺得更不舒服。*I have no more money.* 我沒有更多的錢了。 **2** (phrases) (片語) ***no more...than,*** ⇨ more(5). ***no such,*** ⇨ such. **3** ***whether or no,*** = whether or not: *Whether or no you like it, you've got to do it.* 不論你是否喜歡它,你都得去做。□ *particle* **1** (opposite of 'Yes'): (Yes之相反字): *Is it Monday today?—No, it isn't.* 今天是星期一嗎?—不,今天不是星期一。*Isn't it Monday today?—No, it isn't.* 今天不是星期一嗎?—不,今天不是星期一。*Aren't you busy?—No, I'm not.* 你不忙嗎?—不,我不忙。 **2** (used with *not* or *nor* to emphasize a negative): (與 not 或 nor 連用以加强否定語氣): *One man couldn't lift it; no, nor half a dozen.* 這玩意兒一個人舉不起來;就是六個人也不行。□ *n* [C] refusal; denial: 拒絕;否認: *The noes* /nəʊz ; noz/ *have it,* Those voting 'no' are in the majority. 反對的佔多數。

Noah's ark /ˌnəʊəz ˈɑːk ; ˌnoəzˈɑrk/ *n* model of the ark in which Noah and his family were saved from the Flood, with small animal and human figures. 挪亞方舟(挪亞及其家人從大洪水中逃生所乘方舟的模型,上有小動物及人物的形像)。⇨ Gen, chap 5-9. 參看舊約聖經創世記第5至9章。

nob¹ /nɒb ; nɑb/ *n* (sl) head. (俚)頭。

nob² /nɒb ; nɑb/ *n* (sl) member of the upper classes; person of high rank. (俚)上流社會的人物;地位高的人。

nobble /ˈnɒbl ; ˈnɑbl̩/ *vt* (GB sl) (英俚) [VP6A] **1** tamper with (a race-horse) to lessen its chance of winning. 暗害(賽跑的馬)以減少其獲勝機會。 **2** (colloq) get the attention of (in order to gain an advantage, etc); get sth dishonestly or by devious means. 引起…的注意(以期獲得好處等);詐取;騙取;以不正當手段取得某物。

Nobel Prize /nəʊˌbel ˈpraɪz ; ˈnoˌbɛl ˈpraɪz/ *n* any of the prizes awarded each year by the Nobel Foundation for outstanding achievements in literature, science and the promotion of world peace (after A B Nobel, Swedish inventor of dynamite who established the awards). 諾貝爾獎(每年由諾貝爾基金會頒獎給在文學、科學及促進世界和平方面有卓越成就者;該獎係由瑞典炸藥發明家 A B Nobel 所設立)。

no·bil·ity /nəʊˈbɪlətɪ ; noˈbɪlətɪ/ *n* [U] **1** quality of being noble; noble character, mind, birth, rank. 高尚;高貴;高尚的性格、思想、出身、地位。 **2** (usu with *def art*) the nobles as a class: (通常與定冠詞連用) 貴族: *a member of the ~;* 貴族階級的人; *marry into the ~.* 嫁給貴族。

noble /ˈnəʊbl ; ˈnobl/ *adj* **1** having, showing, high character and qualities: 高尚的;崇高的;偉大的: *a ~ leader;* 偉大的領袖; *~ sentiments;* 高尚的情操; *a ~ mind.* 高尚的思想。 Hence, 由此產生, **ˌ~-ˈminded** /ˈmaɪndɪd ; ˈmaɪndɪd/ *adj* **ˌ~-ˈminded·ness** *n* **2** of high rank, title or birth: 貴族的;高貴的: *a man of ~ rank/birth.* 身份(出身)高貴的人。 **3** splendid; that excites admiration: 卓越的;輝煌的: *a building planned on a ~ scale;* 設計宏偉的建築物; *a ~ horse;* 一匹駿馬; *~ metals,* eg gold, silver, platinum, that do not easily tarnish in air or water. 貴金屬(例如在空氣或水中不易失去光澤的金、銀、鉑)。□ *n* person of ~ birth. 出身高貴的人;貴族。 **ˈ~·man** /-mən ; -mən/ *n* (*pl* -men) (GB) peer; person of parallel rank in other countries. (英)貴族; 在其他國家內相當於英國貴族身份的人。 **nobly** /ˈnəʊblɪ ; ˈnoblɪ/ *adv* in a ~ manner; splendidly. 高尚地;高貴地;華貴地。

no·blesse /nəʊˈbles ; noˈblɛs/ *n* (F) class of nobles. (法)貴族階級。 **ˌ~ oˈblige** /əˈbliːʒ ; oˈbliʒ/ (prov) privilege entails responsibility. (諺)位高任重。

no·body /ˈnəʊbədɪ ; ˈnoˌbadɪ/ *pron* (*pl* -dies) **1** not anybody; no person: 沒有人;無人: *We saw ~ we knew.* 我們沒有看到我們認識的人。*He said he would marry me or ~.* 他說他要娶我否則就不結婚。*N~ could find their luggage* (colloq for *his or her luggage*). 沒有人能找到自己的行李(本句的 their 爲口語用法,代替 his 或 her)。*N~ else* (= No other person) *offered to help.* 沒有其它的人願意協助。 **2** (used in the *sing* with the *indef art,* and in the *pl*) unimportant or unimpressive person: (單數與不定冠詞連用,且可用複數)不重要的人;小人物: *Don't marry a ~ like James.* 不要嫁給像詹姆士那樣庸碌的人。

noc·tam·bu·list /nɒkˈtæmbjʊlɪst ; nɑkˈtæmbjəlɪst/ *n* sleepwalker. 夢遊者。

noc·tur·nal /nɒkˈtɜːnl ; nɑkˈtɝnəl/ *adj* of or in the night; done, active, or happening, in the night: 夜的;在夜間的;在夜間做的; 在夜間活動的; 發生於夜裡的: *a man of ~ habits;* 有夜生活習慣的人; *~ birds,* eg owls. 夜鳥(如貓頭鷹)。

N

noc·turne /ˈnɒktɜːn ; ˈnɑktɝn/ *n* [C] **1** painting of a scene at night. (畫的)夜景。 **2** soft, dreamy piece of music. 夜曲;夢幻曲。

nod /nɒd ; nɑd/ *vi, vt* (-dd-) **1** [VP2A, 3A, 4A] ***nod (to/at),*** bow the head slightly and quickly as a sign of agreement or as a familiar greeting: 點頭(表示同意或招呼): *He nodded to me as he passed.* 他走過的時候向我點頭打招呼。 *He nodded to show that he understood.* 他點頭表示他明白了。 ***have a nodding acquaintance with,*** ⇨ acquaintance. **2** [VP2A, 2C] ***nod (off),*** let the head fall forward when sleepy or falling asleep; make a mistake as if asleep or half asleep: 垂着頭打瞌睡;打盹;(在類似打瞌睡的狀態下)犯錯: *She sat nodding by the fire.* 她坐在火爐邊打盹。*She often nods off* (=falls asleep) *during the afternoon.* 她下午常常打瞌睡。 *The teacher caught one of her pupils nodding,* falling asleep, or so sleepy as to make mistakes. 那老師發現她的一個學生在打瞌睡(或因昏昏欲睡而犯錯)。 ***Homer sometimes nods,*** (prov) Even the greatest may make a small mistake. (諺)荷馬有時也打瞌睡;最偉大的人也可能犯小錯誤;智者千慮,必有一失。 **3** [VP2C, 6A, 12A, 13A] indicate by nodding: 以點頭表示: *He nodded approval/in approval/approvingly.* 他點頭表示贊成。*He nodded me a welcome/nodded a welcome to Mary.* 他對我點頭表示歡迎(向瑪莉點頭歡迎)。 □ *n* **1** nodding of the head: 點頭: *He gave me a nod as he passed.* 他走過時對我點頭。 **2** ***the Land of Nod,*** sleep. 睡鄉。 **3** ***on the ~,*** (US sl) on credit. (美俚)憑信用(賒購)。

noddle /ˈnɒdl ; ˈnɑdl̩/ *n* (colloq) head. (俗)頭。

node /nəʊd ; nod/ *n* [C] **1** (bot) point on the stem of a plant where a leaf or bud grows out. (植物)莖節(長葉或發苞的部位)。 **2** (phys) point or line of rest in a vibrating body. (物理)波節(不受振動之點或線)。 **3** (fig) point at which the parts of sth begin or meet. (喻)起點;交點。

nod·ule /ˈnɒdjuːl *US:* ˈnɒdʒuːl ; ˈnɑdʒul/ *n* small rounded lump; small knob or swelling. 小圓塊;小結節;小瘤。 **nod·u·lar** /-lə(r) ; -lɚ/, **nod·u·lat·ed** /-leɪtɪd ; -letɪd/ *adjj* having ~s. 有小圓塊的;有結節的;有瘤塊的。

Noel /nəʊˈel ; noˈɛl/ *n* Christmas. 聖誕節。

nog·gin /ˈnɒgɪn ; ˈnɑgɪn/ *n* small measure, usu $\frac{1}{4}$ pint, of liquor; (sl) head. 酒類的小量名 (通常爲 $\frac{1}{4}$ 品脫);(俚)頭。

no·how /ˈnəʊhaʊ ; ˈnoˌhaʊ/ *adv* (colloq) in no way; not at all. (俗)決不;毫不。

noise /nɔɪz ; nɔɪz/ *n* [C, U] loud and unpleasant sound, esp when confused and undesired: 聲音;噪音;喧聲;鬧聲: *the ~ of jet aircraft;* 噴射機的噪音; *Don't make so much ~/such a loud ~!* 不要那麼吵鬧! *What's that ~?* 那是什麼聲音? *What are those strange ~s?* 那些奇怪的聲音是什麼聲音? ***make a ~ (about sth),*** talk or complain in order to get attention. (爲某事而)高聲談論或抱怨(以引起別人的注意)。 ***make a ˈ~ in the world,*** become famous, be much talked about. 成名;成爲人們談論的對象。 **a ˈbig ~,** (sl) important person. (俚)要人。 □ *vt* ***~ sth abroad,*** make public: 宣揚;哄傳;謠傳: *It was ~d abroad that he had been arrested.* 盛傳他已經被逮捕了。 **~·less** *adj* making little or no ~: 無聲的;靜的: *with ~less footsteps.* 以無聲的腳步。 **~·less·ly** *adv* **~·less·ness** *n*

noi·some /ˈnɔɪsəm ; ˈnɔɪsəm/ *adj* offensive; (esp, of smell) disgusting. 令人不快的; (尤指氣味)令人討厭的;難聞的。

noisy /ˈnɔɪzɪ ; ˈnɔɪzɪ/ *adj* (-ier, -iest) **1** making, accompanied by, much noise: 吵鬧的;發吵聲的: *~ children;* 吵鬧的小孩; *~ games.* 喧鬧的遊戲。 **2** full of noise: 喧嘩的;嘈雜的: *a ~ classroom.* 喧嚣的教室。 **nois·ily** /-ɪlɪ ; -ɪlɪ/ *adv* **noisi·ness** *n*

no·mad /ˈnəʊmæd ; ˈnomæd/ *n* member of a tribe that wanders from place to place, with no fixed home. 遊牧部落的人; 流浪者。 **~ic** /nəʊˈmædɪk ; noˈmædɪk/ *adj* of ~s: 遊牧部落的: *a ~ic society.* 遊牧部落的社會。

nom de plume /ˌnɒm də ˈpluːm ; ˈnɑmdəˌplum/ *n* (*pl* noms /nɒm ; nɑm/ de plume) (F) pen-name. (法)筆名。

no·men·cla·ture /nəˈmenklətʃə(r) *US:* ˈnəʊmənkleɪtʃər ; ˈnomənˌkletʃɚ/ *n* [C] (formal) system of naming: (正式用語)命名法;專門名辭;術語: *botanical ~;* 植物的命名法; *the ~ of chemistry.* 化學的專門名辭。

nom·inal /ˈnɒmɪnl ; ˈnɑmənl̩/ *adj* **1** existing, etc, in name or word only, not in fact: 名義上的;有名無實的: *the ~ ruler of the country;* 名義上的國家統治者; *the ~ value of the shares.* 股份的面值(股票的票面價值,並非市場價值)。 **2** of little importance or value: 不重要或無價值的: *a ~ sum;* 極小的數目; *a ~ rent,* one very much below the actual value of the property. 名義租金(極少的象徵性租金)。 **3** (gram) of a noun or nouns. (文法)名詞的。 **4** of, bearing, a name: 名字的;帶有名字的;記名的: *a ~ roll.* 名簿。**~ly** /-nəlɪ ; -nl̩ɪ/ *adv*

nomi·nate /ˈnɒmɪneɪt ; ˈnɑməˌnet/ *vt* [VP6A, 14, 23] **1** ~ ***sb (for),*** put forward for election to a position: 提名某人(爲…候選人): *~ a man for the Presidency;* 提名一個人競選總統; *~ Mr X for Mayor.* 提名X先生爲市長候選人。 **2** ~ ***sb (to),*** appoint to office: 任命某人(做…);指定;指派: *a committee of five ~d members and eight elected members.* 由五個指派的委員和八個選出的委員組成的委員會。 **nomi·nee** /ˌnɒmɪˈniː ; ˌnɑməˈni/ *n* person who is ~d for an office or appointment. 被提名的候選人;被任命者。

nomi·na·tion /ˌnɒmɪˈneɪʃn ; ˌnɑməˈneʃən/ *n* **1** [U] nominating; [C] instance of this: 提名;任命: *How many ~s have there been* (= How many persons have been nominated) *so far?* 到現在有多少人被提名? **2** [U] right of nominating sb for an office or position. 提名權;任命權。

nomi·na·tive /ˈnɒmɪnətɪv ; ˈnɑmənətɪv/ *adj, n* (of the) form of a word (eg the pronoun *we*) when it is the grammatical subject: 主格; 主格的 (例如 we): *the ~ case.* 主格。 ⇨ case¹(3).

nomi·nee /ˌnɒmɪˈniː ; ˌnɑməˈni/ *n* ⇨ nominate.

non- /ˌnɒn ; nɑn/ *pref* who or which is not, does not, etc: 不;非;無:

ˌnon-agˈgression *n* not attacking; not starting hostilities: 不侵略;不攻擊;不挑釁: *a ˌnon-agˈgression pact.* 不侵略協定。

ˌnon-aˈlignment *n* principle or practice of not joining either of the great power blocs. 不結盟(不與世界上大集團任何一方結盟的原則或做法)。

ˌnon-ˈcombatant *n* person (esp in the armed forces, eg a surgeon or chaplain) who does not take part in the fighting. 非戰鬥人員(尤指軍中的醫官或牧師等不參與戰鬥的人員)。

ˌnon-comˈmissioned *adj* (esp of army officers such as sergeants and corporals) not holding commissions(4). 無委任狀的; 非受任命的(尤指軍中士官)。

ˌnon-comˈmittal *adj* not committing oneself to a definite course or to either side (in a dispute, etc): (在爭論等中) 不表示確定意見或立場的;不明確的: *give a non-committal answer.* 給一個不明確的回答。

ˌnon-comˈpliance *n* refusal to comply (with an order, etc). 不順從(命令等)。

ˌnon-conˈductor *n* substance that does not conduct heat or electric current. 非導體(不傳熱或電的物質)。

ˌnon·conˈformist *n* **1** person who does not conform to society's standards. 不遵奉社會標準者。 **2** (in England) member of a sect that has separated from the Church of England. (在英國)與英國國教分離的教派的教友。

ˌnon-conˈformity *n* **1** failure to conform. 不遵從;不適合;不一致。 **2** (beliefs and practices of) nonconformists as a body. 非國教教徒(之信仰與慣例)。

ˌ**non-con'tentious** *adj* not likely to cause contention. 不會引起爭論的。
ˌ**non-e'vent** *n* (colloq) planned event which turns out to be unworthy of what it was expected or hoped to be. (俗) 經計畫但結果却不如當時所預料那樣有價值的事件。
ˌ**non-'fiction** *n* [U] prose books other than writings (eg novels, stories, plays) which deal with fictitious events and persons. 非小說性的散文文學(不像小說、故事、戲劇中之事件與人物均係虛構者)。
ˌ**non-'flammable** *adj* (in official use, contrary to *inflammable*) having no tendency to burst into flames. (正式用字,與 inflammable 相對)不燃燒的。
ˌ**non-ˌinter'ference, ˌnon-ˌinter'vention** *nn* principle or practice, esp in international affairs, of keeping out of other people's disputes. 不干預;不干涉(尤指在國際事務中避免捲入他國爭執之原則或做法)。
ˌ**non-'moral** *adj* that cannot be considered or judged as either moral or immoral. 非道德的(既非有道德的,亦非不道德的);與道德無關的。
ˌ**non-ob'servance** *n* failure to observe (a rule, etc). 不遵從;違反(規則等)。
ˌ**non-'payment** *n* failure or neglect to pay (a debt, etc). 不支付;未償付(債務等)。
ˌ**non-'resident** *adj* who does not reside in: 非住在(某地)的: *a non-resident priest*, not living where he performs his duties. 不住在其執行職務地區的牧師。▭ *n* person not staying at a hotel, etc: 非住宿於旅館等中的人: *Meals served to non-residents.* 餐食供應非住宿本旅館之客人。
ˌ**non-'skid** *adj* (of tyres) designed to prevent or reduce the risk of skidding. (指輪胎) 防滑的; 不打滑的。
ˌ**non-'smoker** *n* person who does not smoke tobacco; place, eg a train compartment, where smoking is forbidden. 不抽煙的人; 禁煙的場所(例如火車的隔間)。
ˌ**non-'starter** *n* horse which, although entered for a race, does not run; (fig) person who has no chance of success in sth he undertakes to do. 雖參加但未出賽的馬;(喻)雖從事某工作但無成功機會的人。
ˌ**non-'stick** *adj* (eg of a pan) made so that food, etc will not stick to its surface. (指鍋等)不黏食物的。
ˌ**non-'stop** *adj, adv* without a stop: 中途不停的: *a non-stop train from London to Brighton;* 從倫敦到布來頓的直達火車; *fly non-stop from New York to Paris.* 從紐約直飛巴黎。
ˌ**non-'U** *adj* ⇨ App 2. 參看附錄二。
ˌ**non-'union** *adj* not belonging to a trade union; not observing trade union rules: 沒參加工會的;不遵守工會規章的: *non-union labour.* 沒參加工會的工人。
ˌ**non-'violence** *n* policy of rejecting violent means (but using peaceful protest, etc) to gain a political or social objective. 反暴力(政策) (不以暴力手段,而以和平方式的抗議等,以達到政治或社會的目的)。

non·age /'nəunɪdʒ ; 'nɑnɪdʒ/ *n* [U] = minority(1); immaturity. 未成年;未成熟。

nona·gen·arian /ˌnɒnədʒɪ'neərɪən ; ˌnɑnədʒə'nɛrɪən/ *n, adj* (person who is) between 89 and 100 years old. 九十到九十九歲的(人)。

nonce /nɒns ; nɑns/ *n* (old use, or liter; only in) (舊用法,或文;僅用於) ***for the ~,*** for the present time only. 暫時;目前。'**~-word** *n* word coined for one occasion. 臨時語(爲某一場合而臨時創造的詞語)。

non·cha·lant /'nɒnʃələnt ; 'nɑnʃələnt/ *adj* not having, not showing, interest or enthusiasm; deliberately casual. 不感興趣的;冷漠的;不熱心的;故意漠不關心的。**~·ly** *adv* **non·cha·lance** /-ləns ; -ləns/ *n* [U].

non com·pos men·tis /ˌnɒn ˌkɒmpəs 'mentɪs ; 'nɑnˌkɑmpəs'mɛntɪs/ (Lat) (legal) not legally responsible because not of sound mind; (colloq) confused in one's mind. (拉) (法律) 因精神不正常而不負法律上責任的;心神喪失的;(俗)心亂如麻的。

non·de·script /'nɒndɪskrɪpt ; 'nɑndɪˌskrɪpt/ *n, adj* (person or thing) not easily classed, not having a definite character; uninteresting. 不易分類的;沒有特徵的;難以區別的; 難以形容的人或物; 難以區別的人或物;無趣味的。

none /nʌn ; nʌn/ *pron* **1** not any, not one: 毫無;一個也沒有: *I wanted some string but there was ~ in the house.* 我需要一些繩子,但家裡一根也沒有。*N~ of this money is mine.* 這筆錢沒有一點是我的。*'Is there any coal left?' 'No, ~ at all.'* '還有煤炭嗎?' '沒有,一點兒也沒有。' *There are faults from which ~ of us* (= not one of us, or not any of us) *is/are free.* 有一些錯誤我們任何人均不能避免。*N~ of them has/have come back yet.* 他們之中還沒有一個人回來。*He is aware, ~ better than he* (ie no one is better aware than he), *that....* 沒有一個人比他更知道…。***~ the less,*** nevertheless. 然而;雖然如此;依然。***~ but,*** only: 僅;只: *They chose none but the best.* 他們只挑最好的。***~ other than***: 就是: *The new arrival was ~ other than the President* (emph for *the President himself*). 剛到達的就是總統本人(爲 the President himself 的强調說法)。**2** (in constructions equal to an imperative): (用在相當於祈使句的結構中): *N~ of that!* Stop that! 不要那樣! *N~ of your impudence!* Don't be impudent! 不得無禮!別那麼不要臉! **3** (separated from its *n*, in liter or rhet style): (在文學或修辭體裁中,與所代表的名詞分開使用): *They looked down on the plain, but village there was ~.* 他們往下看那原野,但是那兒一個村莊也沒有。*Sounds there were ~* (= There were no sounds) *except the murmur of the bees.* 除了蜜蜂的嗡嗡聲以外,沒有別的聲音。▭ *adv* by no means; in no degree; not at all: 絕不;決不;毫不: *I hope you're ~ the worse for that fall from your horse.* 你從馬上跌下來,我希望你沒有受傷。*I'm afraid I'm ~ the wiser for your explanation.* 我恐怕聽了你的解釋我還是不明白。*The salary they pay me is ~ too high.* 他們付給我的薪水一點也不高。***There are ˌ~ so ˌdeaf as those who will not 'hear,*** (prov) who refuse to hear. (諺)最聾的莫過於那些不願意聽話的人。

non·en·tity /nɒ'nentətɪ ; nɑn'ɛntətɪ/ *n* (*pl* -ties) [C] **1** unimportant person. 不重要的人。**2** thing that does not really exist or that exists only in the imagination. 並不眞正存在之事物;想像中的事物。

none·such, non·such /'nʌnsʌtʃ ; 'nʌnˌsʌtʃ/ *n* person or thing without equal; paragon. 無雙之人或物;絕品;模範。

non·pareil /ˌnɒn pə'reɪl *US:* -'rel ; ˌnɑnpə'rɛl/ *adj, n* (formal) unique or unrivalled (person or thing). (正式用語)獨特的;無匹的;獨特的人或物。

non·plus /nɒn'plʌs ; nɑn'plʌs/ *vt* (-ss-, US -s-) [VP6A] (usu passive) surprise or puzzle (sb) so much that he does not know what to do or say: (通常用被動語態)使(某人) 驚訝或困窘而不知所措; 使狼狽: *I was completely ~sed when she said 'No' to my proposal of marriage.* 她拒絕我的求婚時,我感到十分狼狽。

non·sense /'nɒnsns *US:* -sens ; 'nɑnsɛns/ *n* (usu 通常作[U]) meaningless words; foolish talk, ideas, behaviour: 無意義的話;廢話;愚昧的思想;愚蠢的行爲: *You're talking ~!* 你在胡說八道! *I want no more of your ~.* 我不許你再胡鬧。*What (a) ~!* 簡直是一派胡言! **non·sen·si·cal** /nɒn'sensɪkl ; nɑn'sɛnsɪkḷ/ *adj* not making sense: 無意義的: *nonsensical remarks.* 無意義的言詞。

non sequi·tur /ˌnɒn'sekwɪtə(r) ; nɑn'sɛkwɪtɚ/ *n* (Lat) (logic) conclusion which does not follow from the premises; illogical step. (拉) (邏輯)非由前提推演出的結論;與前提不符的結論;不合邏輯的步驟。

non·such ⇨ nonesuch.

noodle¹ /'nu:dl ; 'nudḷ/ *n* fool. 笨人。

noodle² /'nu:dl ; 'nudḷ/ *n* (usu *pl*) type of paste of flour and water or flour and eggs prepared in long, narrow strips and used in soups, with a sauce, etc. (通常用複數) 麵條。

nook /nʊk ; nʊk/ *n* out-of-the-way place; inside

corner: 偏僻之處；角落；內隅: *search every ~ and cranny*, everywhere. 搜查每個角落和裂隙（搜遍每一個地方）。

noon /nu:n ; nun/ *n* midday; 12 o'clock in the middle of the day: 中午；正午: *at ~;* 在中午; *the ~ gun.* 午砲。**'~·day** /-deɪ ; -ˌde/, **'~·tide** /-taɪd ; -ˌtaɪd/ *nn* = ~.

no-one, no one /ˈnəʊ wʌn ; ˈnoˌwʌn/ *pron* = nobody(1).

noose /nu:s ; nus/ *n* ⇨ the illus at knot. 參看 knot 之插圖。loop of rope (with a running knot) that becomes tighter when the rope is pulled: 索套；活結；活圈: *the hangman's ~.* 絞刑吏的索套。***put one's head in the ~,*** (fig) allow oneself to be caught. (喻)自投羅網。□ *vt* catch with a ~; make a ~ on a cord, rope, etc. 用索套捕捉；在索、繩等上結成活套。

nope /nəʊp ; nop/ *int* (sl) No! (俚)不！沒！

nor /nɔ:(r) ; nɔr/ *conj* **1** (after *neither* or *not*) and not: (用在 neither 或 not 之後)也不: *I have neither time nor money for skiing.* 我既沒有時間也沒有錢去滑雪。*Not a flower nor even a blade of grass will grow in this desert.* 沒有一朵花甚至也沒有一片草將會生長在這沙漠裡。**2** and... not: 而…也不: *He can't do it; nor can I, nor can you, nor can anybody.* 他不能做；我也不能，你也不能，任何人都不能。*Nor was this all,* And this was not all. 這也不是全部；不僅此也。*Nor will I* (=And I will not) *deny that....* 我也不否認…。

nor'- /ˌnɔ:(r) ; nɔr/ *pref* ⇨ north.

Nor·dic /ˈnɔ:dɪk ; ˈnɔrdɪk/ *n, adj* (member) of the European type marked by tall stature, blond hair, and blue eyes, esp in Scandinavia. 北歐人（身材高大、金髮藍眼的種族，尤指居住於斯堪的納維亞半島的人）；北歐人的。

Nor·folk /ˈnɔ:fək ; ˈnɔrfək/ *n* English county. 諾福克（英國的郡名）。~ **jacket,** man's loose-fitting jacket with a waistband. 諾福克夾克（寬鬆有腰帶的男上衣）。

norm /nɔ:m ; nɔrm/ *n* **1** standard; pattern; type (as representative of a group when judging other examples). 標準；典型；模範（當評判某類中之其他例子時所用的代表）。**2** (in some industries, etc) amount of work required or expected in a working day: (在某些工業等中)每一工作日所要求或預期的工作量: *set the workers a ~;* 給工人定個標準工作量; *fulfil one's ~.* 達到一個人的標準工作量。

nor·mal /ˈnɔ:ml ; ˈnɔrml/ *adj* in agreement with what is representative, usual, or regular: 正常的；常態的；平常的；正規的: *the ~ temperature of the human body.* 人體的正常溫度。**'~ school,** (in some countries, not in GB) one for the training of teachers (usu in elementary grades). (在若干國家，但不在英國) 師範學校（通常指培育小學師資者）。□ *n* [U] usual state, level, standard, etc: 通常情況；常態；通常的標準: *above/below ~.* 高於（低於）常態。**~ly** /ˈnɔ:məlɪ ; ˈnɔrml̩ɪ/ *adv* **~·ity** /nɔ:ˈmæləti ; nɔrˈmæləti/, **~cy** /ˈnɔ:mlsɪ ; ˈnɔrml̩sɪ/ *nn* [U] the state of being ~. 正常；常態；標準。**~·ize** /ˈnɔ:məlaɪz ; ˈnɔrml̩ˌaɪz/ *vt* make ~. 使正常；正常化。**~·iz·ation** /ˌnɔ:məlaɪˈzeɪʃn *US:* -lɪˈz- ; ˌnɔrml̩əˈzeʃən/ *n*

Nor·man /ˈnɔ:mən ; ˈnɔrmən/ *n* inhabitant or native of Normandy; descendant of the mixed Scandinavian and Frankish race established there in the 9th c. 法國諾曼第人；第九世紀以來住在諾曼第的斯堪的納維亞和法蘭克混血種族的後代。□ *adj* of the ~s, esp those who conquered England in the 11th c: 諾曼第人的；（尤指）第十一世紀征服英格蘭之諾曼第人的: *the ~ Conquest;* 諾曼第人的征服（英國）; *~ architecture.* 諾曼第式建築。

nor·ma·tive /ˈnɔ:mətɪv ; ˈnɔrmətɪv/ *adj* setting a standard: 定標準的: *a ~, prescriptive grammar of the English language.* 英語之標準、合乎慣例的文法；標準英語慣用法文法。

Norse /nɔ:s ; nɔrs/ *n* the Norwegian language. 挪威語。□ *adj* of Norway. 挪威的。

north /nɔ:θ ; nɔrθ/ *n* **1** one of the four cardinal points of the compass, lying to the left of a person facing the sunrise; part of any country lying farther in this direction than other parts: 北；北方；北部: *the ~ of England;* 英格蘭北部; *cold winds from the ~.* 寒冷的北風。⇨ the illus at compass. 參看 compass 之插圖。**2** (attrib) situated in, living in, pertaining to, coming from, the ~: (形容用法) 位於北部的；居於北方的；屬於北方的；來自北方的: *the N~ Star,* the pole-star; 北極星; *the ~ pole;* 北極; *a ~ wind;* 北風; *a ~ light,* from the ~, as usu desired by artists in studios; 從北面來的光線（畫家在畫室中所希望的光線來源方向）。*the 'N~ Country,* ~ part of England; 英格蘭的北部; *a ˌN~ 'countryman* /-mən ; -mən/, a native of the ~ of England. 英格蘭北部的人。□ *adv* to or towards the ~: 在北方；向北方: *sailing ~.* 向北航行。**ˌ~-'east, ˌ~-'west** (abbr 略作 NE, NW) *nn, adjj, advv* (sometimes, esp naut, 有時作，尤指航海用語，**nor'-east** /ˌnɔ:rˈi:st ; nɔrˈist/, **nor'-west** /ˌnɔ: ˈwest ; nɔrˈwɛst/) (regions) midway between ~ and east, ~ and west. 東北（地區）；西北（地區）；東北的；西北的；在東北；向東北；在西北；向西北。**the ˌN~-west 'Passage,** the sea route from the Atlantic to the Pacific along the ~ coast of Canada and Alaska. 西北航路（自大西洋至太平洋沿加拿大及阿拉斯加北方海岸之海洋航線）。**ˌ~-~·'east, ˌ~-~·'west** (abbr 略作 NNE, NNW) *nn, adjj, advv* (sometimes, esp naut, 有時作，尤指航海用語，**nor'-nor'-east** /ˌnɔ: nɔ:r ˈi:st ; ˌnɔr nɔr ˈist/, **nor'-nor'-west** /ˌnɔ: nɔ: ˈwest ; ˌnɔr nɔr ˈwɛst/) (regions) midway between ~ and ~east, ~west. 北北東（地區）；北北西（地區）；北北東的；北北西的；在北北東；向北北東；在北北西；向北北西。**ˌ~·'easter** *n* strong wind, storm, or gale, from the ~east. 強烈的東北風；東北風暴。**ˌ~·'easter·ly** *adj* (of wind) blowing from the ~east; (of direction) towards the ~ east. （指風）吹自東北的；（指方向）向東北的。**ˌ~·'wester** *n* strong wind from the ~west. 強烈的西北風。**ˌ~·'wester·ly** *adj* (of wind) from the ~west; (of direction) towards the ~west. （指風）吹自西北的；（指方向）向西北的。**ˌ~-'eastern** /-ˈi:stən ; -ˈistən/ *adj* of, from, situated in, the ~east. 東北的；來自東北的；在東北的。**ˌ~-'western** /-ˈwestən ; -ˈwɛstən/ *adj* of, from, situated in the ~west. 西北的；來自西北的；在西北的。**'N~·man** /-mən ; -mən/ *n* (*pl* -men) (hist) Viking; native of Scandinavia. (史)古代北歐人；八至十世紀北歐之海盜；斯堪的納維亞人。**~·wards** /ˈnɔ:θwədz ; ˈnɔrθwədz/ *adv* towards the ~. 向北方。

north·er·ly /ˈnɔ:ðəlɪ ; ˈnɔrðəlɪ/ *adj, adv* (of winds) from the north; towards the north; in or to the north. （指風）來自北方；向北方；在北方；往北方。

north·ern /ˈnɔ:ðən ; ˈnɔrðən/ *adj* in or of the north: 在北方的；北方的: *the ~ hemisphere.* 北半球。**the ~ lights,** streamers and bands of light appearing in the ~ sky; the aurora borealis. 北極光；北光。**~er** /ˈnɔ:ðənə(r) ; ˈnɔrðənə/ *n* person born in or living in the ~ regions of a country. 北方人（出生或居於一國家之北部地區的人）。**'~·most** /-məʊst ; -ˌmost/ *adj* lying farthest north. 最北的；極北的。

Nor·we·gian /nɔ:ˈwi:dʒən ; nɔrˈwidʒən/ *n, adj* (native, language) of Norway. 挪威人；挪威語；挪威的。

nose[1] /nəʊz ; noz/ *n* **1** part of the face above the mouth, through which breath passes, and serving as the organ of smell: 鼻: *hit a man on the ~* (note *def art*). 打一個人的鼻子（注意用定冠詞）。⇨ the illus at head. 參看 head 之插圖。***bite/snap sb's ~*** (*head* is more usu) ***off,*** answer him sharply and angrily. 氣勢洶洶地回答(head 較常用)。***count/tell ~s,*** (*heads* is more usu) (heads 較常用) count the number of persons (esp supporters, when voting to decide sth). 數人數；計算人數（尤指投票決定某事時，計算支持的人數）。***cut off one's ~ to spite one's face,*** damage one's own interests in an attempt at revenge on sb. 因企圖報復而危害了自己。 ***follow one's ~,*** go straight forward; be guided by instinct. 向前直走;由本能引導;憑本能行動。 ***keep a person's ~ to the grindstone,*** make him work hard without rest. 使人勞動不息。 ***lead sb by the ~,*** ⇨ lead³(2). ***look down one's ~ at sb,*** treat haughtily. 傲慢地對待某人。 ***pay through the ~,*** pay an excessive price. 付出太多的代價。 ***poke/stick one's ~ into*** (sb else's business), intrude; ask questions without being asked to do so. 干預(他人的事);問長問短。 ***put sb's ~ out of joint,*** ⇨ joint²(2). ***turn one's ˈ~ up at,*** show disdain for. 瞧不起;鄙視。 ***as plain as the ~ on one's face,*** obvious; easily seen. 淸楚明白的;顯而易見的。 ***(right) under one's very ~,*** **(a)** directly in front of one. 就在某人的面前。 **(b)** in one's presence, and regardless of one's disapproval. 當著某人的面前,而不顧其反對。 **2** sense of smell: 嗅覺: *a dog with a good ~;* 嗅覺靈敏的狗; (fig) (喩) *a reporter with a ~ for news/scandal/a story.* 善於採探新聞(醜聞,故事)的記者。 **3** sth like a ~ in shape or position, eg the open end of a pipe, bellows or retort; the most forward part of the fuselage of an aircraft. 形狀或位置似鼻子的東西;鼻形物(例如管的開口處、風箱口、蒸餾器的管口);機身的最前端;機首。 **4** (compounds) (複合字) **ˈ~-bag** *n* bag for food (oats, etc) fastened on a horse's head. 掛在馬首的糧秣袋。 **ˈ~·bleed** *n* bleeding from the ~. 流鼻血;鼻出血。 **ˈ~·cone** *n* most forward section of a rocket or guided missile, usu separable. (火箭或飛彈最前部的)鼻錐體(通常可分離)。⇨ the illus at capsule. 參看 capsule 之插圖。 **ˈ~·dive** *n* sharp vertical descent made by an aircraft. 飛機的俯衝。 ▭ *vi* (of an aircraft) come down steeply with the ~ pointing to earth. (指飛機)俯衝。 **ˈ~-flute** *n* musical instrument blown with the ~, as used in some Asian countries. 鼻笛(用鼻子吹的笛子,爲亞洲某些國家用的樂器)。 **ˈ~·gay** *n* bunch of cut (esp sweet-scented) flowers. 花束(尤指有香味的花)。 **ˈ~·ring** *n* ring fixed in the ~ of a bull, etc, for leading it. 牛的鼻環(供人牽引者)。 **ˈ~·wheel,** the front landing-wheel under the fuselage of an aircraft. 鼻輪(飛機機首下的着陸前輪)。 **-nosed** *suff* (in compounds) having the kind of ~ indicated: (用於複合字中)有某種鼻子的: *red-~d;* 紅鼻子的; *long-~d.* 長鼻子的。

nose² /nəʊz ; noz/ *vt, vi* **1** [VP15A] go forward carefully, push (one's way): 小心地向前推進;謹愼地前進;挺進: *The ship ~d its way slowly through the ice.* 那艘船緩慢地破冰前進。 **2** [VP15B] ***~ sth out,*** discover by smelling: 嗅出;嗅到: *The dog ~d out a rat.* 那隻狗嗅到一隻老鼠的氣味。 *That man will ~ out a scandal anywhere.* 那個人在任何地方都會探聽出醜聞。 **3** [VP2C, 3A] ***~ about (for sth),*** smell for; (fig) pry or search for. 嗅;聞; (喩)探聽;搜查;偵查。 ***~ into sth,*** pry into: 探聽;打聽: *a man who is always nosing into other people's affairs.* 常常打聽别人事情的人。

nosey, nosy /ˈnəʊzɪ ; ˈnozɪ/ *adj* (-ier, -iest), *n* (sl) inquisitive (person). (俚)好打聽别人事情的(人);好管閒事的(人)。 **ˈ~ parker** *n* (colloq) inquisitive person. (俗)好打聽别人事情的人;好管閒事者。

nosh /nɒʃ ; nɑʃ/ *n* [U] (GB sl) food. (英俚)食物。 **ˈ~-up** *n* a good meal. 豐盛的一餐。 □ *vi* (colloq) eat. (俗)吃。

nos·tal·gia /nɒˈstældʒə ; nɑˈstældʒɪə/ *n* [U] homesickness; wistful longing for sth one has known in the past. 思鄉病;鄉愁;留戀過去;懷舊。 **nos·tal·gic** /nɒˈstældʒɪk ; nɑˈstældʒɪk/ *adj* of, feeling or causing, ~. 思鄉病的;懷舊的;感到或引起鄉愁的。 **nos·tal·gi·cally** /-klɪ ; -klɪ/ *adv*

nos·tril /ˈnɒstrəl ; ˈnɑstrəl/ *n* either of the two external openings into the nose. 鼻孔。⇨ the illus at head. 參看 head 之插圖。

nos·trum /ˈnɒstrəm ; ˈnɑstrəm/ *n* [C] (usu contemptuous) medicine, etc, prepared by the person who recommends it; quack remedy; scheme for political or social reform (called a ~ by its opponents). (通常爲輕蔑語)密醫的藥;江湖郎中的藥;騙人的療法;政治或社會改革的方案(被反對者稱之爲騙人的方案)。

not /nɒt ; nɑt/ *adv* **1** (used to make negative one of the 24 *anom fin vv* listed in the Introduction under 'Anomalous Verbs': *is not; must not; could not;* often contracted to -n't /-nt ; -n̩t/; *hasn't* /ˈhæznt ; ˈhæzn̩t/, *needn't* /ˈniːdnt ; ˈnidn̩t/.) (用於使本字典序言中所列之 24 個變則定動詞成爲否定:如 is not; must not; could not; 常縮寫爲 -n't: 如 hasn't, needn't。) **2** (used with non-finite *vv*): (與非限定動詞連用): *He warned me not to be late.* 他警告我不要遲到。 *You were wrong in not making a protest.* 你錯在沒有提出抗議。 **3** (used after certain *vv*, esp *think, suppose, believe, expect, fear, fancy, trust, hope, seem, appear, be afraid,* as equivalent to a *that*-clause): (用於某些動詞之後,尤指 think, suppose, believe, expect, fear, fancy, trust, hope, seem, appear 和 be afraid 之後,相當於一個由 that 所引導的子句): *'Can you come next week?'—'I'm afraid not.'* I'm afraid that I cannot come. '你下星期能來嗎?'—'我恐怕不能。' *'Will it rain this afternoon?'—'I hope not.'* '今天下午會下雨嗎?'—'我希望不會。' **4** (used elliptically, in phrases.) (省略地用於片語中) ***as likely as not,*** probably: 可能;也許;說不定: *He'll be at home now, as likely as not.* 說不定他現在在家。 ***as soon as not,*** ⇨ soon(5). ***not at all,*** /ˌnɒt əˈtɔːl ; ˌnɑt əˈtɔl/ used as a polite response to thanks, enquiries after sb's health, etc: 别客氣;沒關係;不要緊;沒什麼(回答感謝、問安等客氣話): *'Thank you very much.'—'Not at all',* No need to mention it. '非常謝謝你。'—'别客氣。' *'Are you tired?'—'Not at all',* Not in the least. '你累了嗎?'—'沒什麼。' ***ˈnot that,*** it is not suggested that: 並非意指: *If he ever said so—not that I ever heard him say so—he told a lie.* 假如他是那麼說—並不是指我聽到他那麼說—他就是撒謊。 ***ˈnot but what,*** nevertheless; although: 雖然…但是;雖然: *I can't do it; not but what a younger man might be able to do it.* 我不能做;但是一個比較年輕的人也許能做。 **5** (in understatements): (用於謹愼的陳述): *not a few,* many; 不少;許多; *not seldom,* often; 常常; *not without reason,* with good reason; 不無理由;有充分理由; *not half,* (sl) exceedingly; (俚)非常地; *in the not-so-distant* (=recent) *past.* 不久以前。 **6** (used to indicate the absence, opposite, or negative of sth): (用以指不在,相反或否定): *not here;* 不在這裡; *not anything;* 什麼也沒有; *not clean/hot/good;* 不淸潔(熱,好); *not he/John/my son.* 不是他(約翰,我的兒子)。

nota bene /ˌnəʊtə ˈbeneɪ ; ˈnotəˈbinɪ/ *v imper* (Lat) (拉) (abbr 略作 **NB, nb** /ˌen ˈbiː ; ˌɛn ˈbi/) observe carefully. 注意。

no·table /ˈnəʊtəbl ; ˈnotəbl̩/ *adj* deserving to be noticed; remarkable: 値得注意的;顯著的;著名的: *~ events/speakers/artists.* 著名的事件(演說家,藝術家)。 □ *n* eminent person. 名人。 **no·tably** /ˈnəʊtəblɪ ; ˈnotəblɪ/ *adv* **nota·bil·ity** /ˌnəʊtəˈbɪlətɪ ; ˌnotəˈbɪlətɪ/ *n* (*pl* -ties) **1** [U] the condition of being ~. 顯著;著名。 **2** [C] ~ person. 名人。

no·tary /ˈnəʊtərɪ ; ˈnotərɪ/ *n* (*pl* -ries) (often 常作 **ˌ~ ˈpublic**) official with authority to perform certain kinds of legal transactions, esp to record that he has witnessed the signing of legal documents. (法律上的)公證人。

no·ta·tion /nəʊˈteɪʃn ; noˈteʃən/ *n* **1** [C] system of signs or symbols representing numbers, amounts, musical notes, etc. (代表數字、數量等的)一套符號;(音樂之)樂譜,記譜法。 **2** [U] representing of numbers, etc by such signs or symbols. (以此等符號)表記;記號法;符號法;記法;符記。

notch /nɒtʃ ; nɑtʃ/ *n* V-shaped cut (*in* or *on* sth);

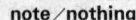

musical notation

(US) narrow pass through mountains; defile². (在某物上的) V 形切痕(與 in 或 on 連用,後接某物); (美) 山間小徑; 隘路。 □ *vt* **1** [VP6A] make or cut a ~ or ~es in or on, eg a stick, as a way of keeping count. 刻 V 形凹痕於(例如刻在棒上作爲記數用)。 **2** [VP15B] ~ ***up,*** (colloq) achieve; score: (俗) 完成; 得分: *~ up a new record.* 締造新記錄。

note¹ /nəʊt ; not/ *n* **1** short record (of facts, etc) made to help the memory: 筆記; 摘記: *He spoke for an hour without a ~/without ~s.* 他不用草稿演講了一小時。 **'~·book** *n* book in which to write ~s. 筆記簿。 **2** short letter: 短信; 短簡: *a ~ of thanks;* 謝函; *an exchange of ~s between two governments.* 兩國政府間的函件往返。 **'~·paper** *n* [U] paper for (esp private) correspondence. 信紙(尤指私人的)。 **3** short comment on or explanation of a word or passage in a book, etc: 評註; 註釋: *a new edition of 'Hamlet', with copious ~s.* 有詳細註解的'哈姆雷特'新版本。 ⇨ *footnote* at foot¹ (8). **4** observation (not necessarily written): 觀察所得; 評論(不一定是書面的): *He was comparing ~s with a friend,* exchanging views, comparing experiences, etc. 他和一個朋友交換意見。 **5** (US 美 = *bill*) piece of paper money; bank~: 紙幣; 鈔票: *a £5 ~.* 一張五鎊的紙幣。 **'~·case** *n* wallet. 皮夾。 **6** single sound of a certain pitch and duration: 單音; 鳴聲; 音調; 調: *the blackbird's merry ~;* 山鳥的輕快鳴聲; sign used to represent such a sound in manuscript or printed music ⇨ the illus at notation; any one of the keys of a piano, organ, etc. (樂譜上的) 音符(參看 notation 之挿圖); (鋼琴, 風琴等的) 鍵。 ***sound a ~ of warning (against sth),*** warn against sth. (就某事物) 提出警告。 ***strike the right ~,*** (fig) speak in such a way that one wins the approval or sympathy of one's listeners. (喻) 說話使聽的人贊同或同情; 說話適當; 說話得體。 ***strike/sound a false ~,*** (fig) do or say sth that causes one to lose sympathy or approval. (喻) 說某些話或做某件事而致失去他人的同情或贊許; 做錯事; 說錯話。 **7** quality (esp of voice) indicating the nature of sth (usu *sing* with the *indef art*): 聲調; 語氣; 特徵(通常爲單數, 與不定冠詞連用): *There was a ~ of self-satisfaction in his speech.* 在他的話語中有一種自滿的語氣。 **8** [U] distinction; importance: 著名; 重要: *a singer of ~.* 著名的歌唱家。 **9** [U] notice; attention: 注意: *worthy of ~.* 值得注意的。 *Take ~ of what he says,* pay attention to it. 注意他所說的。

note² /nəʊt ; not/ *vt* **1** [VP6A, 8, 9, 10] notice; pay attention to: 注意; 留心: *Please ~ my words.* 請注意我的話。 *N~ how to do it/how I did it.* 注意看怎麼做(我是怎麼做的)。 *She ~d that his hands were dirty.* 她注意到他的手是髒的。 **2** [VP6A, 15B] ~ ***sth (down),*** make a ~ of; write down in order to remember: 記下(某事); 記錄: *The policeman ~d down every word I said.* 警察記下我所說的每一句話。 **noted** *adj* celebrated (*for, as*): 著名的(與 for, as 連用): *a town ~d for its pottery/~d as a health resort.* 以出產陶器聞名(以療養地著名)的城鎮。 **'~·worthy** *adj* deserving to be ~d; remarkable. 値得注意的; 顯著的。

noth·ing /ˈnʌθɪŋ ; ˈnʌθɪŋ/ *n* **1** (with *adj, inf,* etc, following) not anything: (後接形容詞、不定詞等) 沒什麼; 沒什麼東西; 無物: *There's ~ interesting in the newspaper.* 報紙上沒有什麼有趣的新聞。 *He's had ~ to eat yet.* 他還沒有東西吃。 *N~ (that) I could say had any influence on her.* 我所能說的任何話都不會對她發生任何影響(說什麼也沒用)。 *N~ ever pleases her.* 沒有任何東西能取悅她。 *He's five foot ~,* exactly five foot tall. 他整整五英尺高。 *There's little or ~ wrong with him,* very little wrong. 他沒有什麼不正常。 *There's ~ like leather* (= ~ is so good as leather) *for shoes.* 做鞋用皮革再好沒有了。 **2** (phrases) (片語) ***be ~ to,*** **(a)** be a matter of indifference to: 對…無關重要: *She's ~ to him,* He is indifferent to, uninterested in, her. 她在他心目中算不了什麼。 **(b)** be as ~ if compared: 假如比較起來等於沒有: *My losses are ~ to yours.* 我的損失和你的比起來算不了什麼。 ***come to ~,*** fail; be without result. 失敗; 無結果。 ***go for ~,*** be without reward, result, value: 沒有報酬; 沒有結果; 沒有價值: *Six months' hard work all gone for ~.* 六個月的辛勞工作毫無結果。 ***have ~ to do with,*** **(a)** avoid; have no dealings with: 避免; 不與…來往: *I advise you to have ~ to do with that man.* 我勸你不要跟那個人來往。 **(b)** not to be the business or concern of: 與…無關: *This has ~ to do with you.* 這跟你沒有關係。 ***make ~ of,*** be unable to understand. 不能了解。 ***mean ~ to,*** **(a)** have no meaning for: 對…沒有意義: *These technical words mean ~ to me.* 這些專門術語對我毫無意義。 **(b)** be sth or sb that sb has no concern or interest in: 不爲…所關心或感興趣: *He used to like Jane but she means ~ to him now.* 他以前喜歡過珍, 但現在對她不感興趣了。 ***to say ~ of,*** not to mention: 更不用說; 更不待言: *He had his wife and seven children with him in the car, to say ~ of* (= as well as) *two dogs, a cat and a parrot.* 他的車裡載着他的太太和七個孩子, 更不用說二隻狗、一隻貓和一隻鸚鵡了。 ***think ~ of,*** consider as ordinary, usual or unremarkable: 認爲平常; 認爲…算不了什麼: *He thinks ~ of a twenty-mile walk/of asking me to lend him £20.* 他認爲走二十哩(向我借二十鎊)不算一回事。 ***think ~ 'of it,*** friendly reply to sb who offers thanks, an apology, etc: 這算不了什麼(對致謝、道歉等的友善的回答): *'You didn't mind my using your typewriter?'*—

'*Of course not! Think ~ of it!*' '你沒介意我用了你的打字機嗎?'—'當然沒有！這算得了什麼!' **for ~,** **(a)** free; without payment. 免費;不要錢的。**(b)** without a reward or result; to no purpose: 沒有酬勞;無結果;無收獲: *It was not for ~ that he spent three years studying the subject.* 他花了三年時間研究這題目並非毫無收獲。**next to ~,** ⇨ next. **~ but,** merely: 僅僅;祇不過;只: *N~ but doubts can prevent you from succeeding;* '僅僅是疑慮就會阻礙你成功; only: 只有: *N~ but a miracle can save him.* 只有奇蹟能挽救他。**There's ~ 'for it but to...,** The only thing we can do is to.... 我們唯一能做的是…。**N~ doing!** (colloq) expression used to indicate refusal of a request, etc. (俗)(用於表示拒絕請求等)不行！□ *adv* not at all; in no way: 毫不;決不: *The house is ~ near as large as I expected.* 那幢房屋遠不如我預期的那麼大。*His new book is ~ like as good as his earlier books.* 他的新作遠不如他以前的作品那麼好。**~·ness** *n* [U] being ~; the state of non-existence: 空;無;不存在: *pass into ~ness.* 化爲烏有;消滅。

no·tice /ˈnəʊtɪs ; ˈnotɪs/ *n* **1** [C] (written or printed) news of sth about to happen or sth that has happened: (手寫的或印刷的)佈告; 公告; 告示; 消息: *put up a ~;* 張貼佈告; *~s of births, deaths and marriages in the newspapers.* 報紙上出生、死亡和結婚的啓事。**'~-board** *n* one provided for ~s to be affixed to. 佈告板。**2** [U] warning (of what will happen): 警告;通知: *give a member of staff a month's ~,* tell him that he must leave one's employment at the end of one month; 通知一職員一個月後解雇; (of a tenant) (指租戶) *receive two months' ~ to quit,* to vacate a house, etc; 收到兩個月後遷離的通知; (of an employee) (指受雇者) *give one's employer ~ that one intends to leave;* 告知雇主打算辭職; *leave without ~,* without giving any warning. 沒有預先通知就離去。**(do sth) at short ~,** with little warning, little time for preparation, etc. (沒有警告、沒作準備等)突然(做某事)。**3** [U] attention. 注意。**be beneath one's ~,** be sth one should ignore: 不爲某人所理會;不足取;不值一顧: *Their insults should be beneath your ~.* 你不要理會他們的侮慢。**bring sth to sb's ~,** call sb's attention to sth. 使某人注意某事物。**come to sb's ~,** have one's attention called to sth: 受到某人的注意: *It has come to my ~ that...,* I have learnt that.... 我已經注意到…。**sit up and take ~,** (of sb who is ill, etc) show signs of recovery from illness. (指病者等)顯示康復的跡象; 病況轉佳。**make sb sit up and take ~,** make sb keenly aware of events: 使某人提高警覺; 使某人特別留神: *This new process should make our competitors sit up and take ~.* 這種新方法必使我們的競爭者提高警覺。**take no ~ (of sth),** pay no attention to sth: 不注意(某事物);不理: *Take no ~ of what they're saying about you.* 別理會他們對你的微詞。**4** [C] short review of a new book, play, etc in a periodical. (雜誌上關於新的書籍、戲劇等的)短評;評介。□ *vt, vi* **1** [VP6A, 8, 9, 10, 18A, 19A, 2A] take ~ (of); observe: 注意(到);看到: *I didn't ~ you.* 我沒注意到你。*I ~d that he left early.* 我注意到他提早離開了。*I wasn't noticing.* 我那時候沒有注意。*Did you ~ him pause?* 你有沒有注意到他停頓? *Did you ~ his hand shaking?* 你有沒有注意到他的手發抖? *He was too proud to ~ me.* 他太傲慢了,連理都不理我。**2** [VP6A] say or write sth about (a book, play, etc). 評介(書, 戲劇等)。**~·able** /-əbl ; -əbl̩/ *adj* easily seen or ~d. 易見的;顯明的;顯著的。**~·ably** /-əblɪ ; -əblɪ/ *adv*

no·ti·fi·able /ˈnəʊtɪfaɪəbl ; ˈnotəˌfaɪəbl̩/ *adj* that must be notified (esp of certain diseases that must be notified to public health authorities). 應通知的;應報告的(尤指必須通知衞生當局的某些疾病)。

no·tify /ˈnəʊtɪfaɪ ; ˈnotəˌfaɪ/ *vt* (*pt, pp* -fied) [VP 6A, 14, 11] **~ sb of sth; ~ sth to sb,** give notice of; report: 通知;報告: *~ the police of a loss;* 向警察局報告損失情形; *~ a loss to the police;* 向警察局報告損失情形; *~ a birth;* 公告出生; *~ the authorities that....* 報告當局…。**no·ti·fi·ca·tion** /ˌnəʊtɪfɪˈkeɪʃn ; ˌnotəfəˈkeʃən/ *n* [U] ~ing; [C] instance of this (eg to the authorities, of births, deaths, cases of infectious disease). 通知;報告(如向當局報告出生、死亡、傳染病例等)。

no·tion /ˈnəʊʃn ; ˈnoʃən/ *n* [C] **1** idea; opinion: 觀念;意見: *I have no ~ of what he means.* 我不明白他的意思。*Your head is full of silly ~s.* 你滿腦子都是蠢想法。*He has a ~ that I'm cheating him.* 他認爲我在欺騙他。**2** (*pl*) (US) small miscellaneous goods. (複)(美)小雜物。⇨ novelty(3). **~al** /-ʃənl ; -ʃənl̩/ *adj* **1** (of knowledge, etc) speculative; not based on experiment or demonstration. (指知識等)思辨的; 理論的; 不是根據實驗或證明的。**2** nominal; token. 名義上的;象徵的。

no·tori·ous /nəʊˈtɔːrɪəs ; noˈtorɪəs/ *adj* widely known (esp for sth bad): (尤指因壞事)著名的;聲名狼藉的: *a ~ criminal;* 聲名狼藉的罪犯; *~ for his goings-on;* 以他的行爲不檢而著名; *~ as a rake.* 以浪子的身份聞名。**~·ly** *adv* **no·tor·iety** /ˌnəʊtəˈraɪətɪ ; ˌnotəˈraɪətɪ/ *n* [U] state of being ~. 狼藉的聲名; 惡名;著名。

not·with·stand·ing /ˌnɒtwɪθˈstændɪŋ ; ˌnɑtwɪθˈstændɪŋ/ *prep* in spite of. 雖然;儘管。□ *adv* nevertheless; all the same. 雖然;仍然。□ *conj* although. 雖然。

nou·gat /ˈnuːgɑː *US:* ˈnuːgət ; ˈnugət/ *n* sort of hard sweet made of sugar, nuts, etc. 一種用糖、核果等製成的堅硬甜點;杏仁糖。

nought /nɔːt ; nɔt/ *n* **1** nothing. 無。**bring sb/sth to ~,** ruin; baffle. 毀滅某人(某物);難倒。**come to ~,** be ruined; fail. 毀了;失敗。**set sb/sth at ~,** disregard; defy; despise. 不顧;不服從;蔑視。**2** the figure 0; zero: 零: *point ~ one,* ie ·01. 點零一(卽·01)。**~s and crosses,** game played by writing ~s (zero signs) and crosses on lines of vertical and horizontal squares. 在直線和橫線構成的方格上面畫○和×的遊戲。

noun /naʊn ; naʊn/ *n* (gram) word (not a *pron*) which can function as the subject or object of a *v*, or the object of a *prep;* word which is marked *n* in this dictionary. (文法)名詞。

nour·ish /ˈnʌrɪʃ ; ˈnɜɪʃ/ *vt* [VP6A] **1** keep (sb) alive and well with food; make well and strong; improve (land) with manure, etc: 滋養;使健壯;用肥料等改良(土地): *~ing food;* 滋養的食物; *~ the soil.* 給土地施肥。**2** have or encourage (feelings): 懷有或抱有(情緒): *~ feelings of hatred;* 懷恨; *~ hope in one's heart.* 心中抱着希望。**~·ment** *n* [U] food. 食物;營養品。

nous /naʊs ; nus/ *n* [U] (Gk) (希) **1** (phil) intellect; (divine) reason. (哲)智力;(神的)理性。**2** (GB colloq) common sense; gumption. (英俗)常識。

nou·veau riche /ˌnuːvəʊ ˈriːʃ ; nuvoˈriʃ/ *n* (usu in *pl* nouveaux riches, pronunciation unchanged) (通常用複數形,發音不變) (F) person who has recently become rich, esp one who is ostentatious. (法)暴發戶。

nova /ˈnəʊvə ; ˈnovə/ *n* (*pl* ~s, -vae /-viː ; -vi/) (astron) star that suddenly increases its brilliance for a period. (天文)新星(在一段時間中突然增强其光度的星)。

novel[1] /ˈnɒvl ; ˈnɑvl̩/ *adj* strange; of a kind not previously known: 奇異的;新奇的: *~ ideas.* 新奇的想法。

novel[2] /ˈnɒvl ; ˈnɑvl̩/ *n* story in prose, long enough to fill one or more volumes, about either imaginary or historical people: 小說: *the ~s of Dickens.* 狄更斯的小說。**,~'ette** /-ˈet ; -ˈɛt/ *n* short ~. 中篇小說。**'~·ist** /-ɪst ; -ɪst/ *n* writer of ~s. 小說家。

nov·elty /ˈnɒvltɪ ; ˈnɑvl̩tɪ/ *n* (*pl* -ties) **1** [U] newness; strangeness; quality of being novel: 新鮮;奇

異;新奇: *The ~ of his surroundings soon wore off*, He become accustomed to them. 他對於環境的新奇不久就覺得平淡了。 **2** [C] previously unknown thing, idea, etc; sth strange or unfamiliar. 新奇的事物、觀念等;奇異或不熟悉的事物。 **3** (*pl*) miscellaneous manufactured goods of low cost, eg toys, small ornaments. (複)各種廉價製品(如玩具、小裝飾品等)。

No·vem·ber /nəʊˈvembə(r) ; noˈvɛmbɚ/ *n* the eleventh month of the year, with thirty days. 十一月。

nov·ice /ˈnɒvɪs ; ˈnɑvɪs/ *n* person who is still learning and who is without experience, esp a person who is to become a monk or a nun. 生手;初學者;(尤指) 見習修士或修女。 **no·vi·ci·ate, no·vi·ti·ate** /nəˈvɪʃɪət ; noˈvɪʃɪɪt/ *nn* period or state of being a ~. 初學;做見習修士或修女;見習期。

now /naʊ ; naʊ/ *adv* **1** at the present time; in the present circumstances: 現在;目前: *Where are you now living/living now?* 你現在住在什麼地方? *Now is the best time to visit Devon.* 現在是遊覽得文最好的時候。 *I cannot now* (ie in the circumstances, after what has happened, etc) *ever believe you again.* 我現在不能再相信你了。 **2** (used after a *prep*): (用於介詞之後): *He will be in London by now.* 他這時將到達倫敦。 *Up to/till/until now we have been lucky.* 直到如今我們一直是幸運的。 *From now onwards I shall be stricter.* 從今以後我將要更嚴格。 **3** (phrases) (片語) ***(every) now and then/again,*** occasionally; from time to time: 有時候;偶而: *We go to the opera now and then.* 我們有時候去看歌劇。 ***now... now/then...,*** at one time..., at another time...: 時而…時而…: *What mixed weather, now fine, now/then showery!* 多難捉摸的天氣,時而晴朗,時而陣雨! **4** at once; immediately: 立刻;馬上: *Do it now.* 馬上做。 *Now or never!* 機會難再! ***just now,*** ⇨ just²(6). **5** (used without reference to time, to indicate the mood of the speaker, to explain, warn, comfort, etc): (與時間無關,係用以表示說話者的語氣,或解釋、警告、安慰等): *Now what happened was this* (explanatory). 所發生的事情就是這樣(解釋性的)。 *Now stop quarrelling and listen to me* (entreaty or reproof). 別吵鬧,聽我說(請求或斥責)。 *No ˈnonsense, now* (warning). (警告)別胡扯啦。 ***now, ˈnow; ˈnow then,*** (used at the beginning of a sentence, often as a protest or warning, or simply to call attention): (用於句首,常作抗議或警告,或僅僅引人注意): *Now then, what's troubling you?* 喂,你有什麼苦惱呀? □ *conj* as a consequence of the fact (that): 既然: *Now (that) you mention it, I do remember.* 你這樣一說,我想起來了。 *Now (that) you're grown up, you must stop this childish behaviour.* 你既然長大了,就必須停止這種幼稚的行爲。

now·adays /ˈnaʊədeɪz ; ˈnaʊə,dez/ *adv* at the present time (and often used in contrasts between present day manners, customs, etc, and those of past times): 時下;現今(常用於現今與舊時之禮俗、習慣等的對比中): *N~ children prefer TV to reading.* 現今兒童喜歡看電視而不喜歡讀書。

no·where /ˈnəʊweə(r) *US:* -hweər ; ˈno,hwɛr/ *adv* not anywhere: 無處: *The boy was ~ to be found.* 到處都找不到那個男孩。 *Such methods will get you ~,* will not produce results. 這些方法將不會產生結果。 *£50 is ~ near enough,* not nearly enough. 五十鎊根本就不够。 ***come (in)/be ~,*** fail to win or get a place (in a competition). (比賽時)輸了;沒得到名次。

no·wise /ˈnəʊwaɪz ; ˈno,waɪz/ *adv* (old use) not at all; in no way. (舊用法)決不;毫不。

noxious /ˈnɒkʃəs ; ˈnɑkʃəs/ *adj* harmful: 有害的;有毒的: *~ gases.* 有毒的氣體。 **~·ly** *adv* **~·ness** *n*

nozzle /ˈnɒzl ; ˈnɑzl̩/ *n* metal end of a hose or bellows, through which a stream of liquid or air is directed. 管嘴(水管的金屬管口);噴嘴(風箱的金屬噴氣口)。⇨ the illus at hosepipe. 參看 hosepipe 之插圖。

nuance /ˈnjuːɑːns *US:* ˈnuː- ; njuˈɑns/ *n* [C] delicate difference in, or shade of, meaning, opinion, colour, etc. 意義、意見、顏色等的細微差異。

nub /nʌb ; nʌb/ *n* **1** small lump or knob (eg of coal). (煤等的)小塊。 **2** (colloq, fig) gist or point (of a story, affair). (俗,喻)(故事、事情的)要旨;要點。

nu·bile /ˈnjuːbaɪl *US:* ˈnuːbl ; ˈnjubl̩/ *adj* (of girls) marriageable; old enough to marry. (指女子)及笄的;到出嫁年齡的。

nu·clear /ˈnjuːklɪə(r) *US:* ˈnuː ; ˈnjuklɪɚ/ *adj* of a nucleus, esp of a heavy atom, with release of energy: 核心的;(尤指)原子核的;核子的: *~ energy,* obtained by ~ fission; 核能(由核子分裂而得); *a ~ power station;* 核能發電廠; *~-powered submarines;* 核子動力潛艇; *~ bombs/missiles;* 核子炸彈(飛彈); *~ disarmament,* the renunciation of ~ weapons. 放棄核子武器的協議。

nu·cleic /njuːˈkleɪɪk *US:* nuː- ; njuˈkliɪk/ *adj* **~ acid,** one of two complex compounds occurring in all living cells. 核酸。

nu·cleus /ˈnjuːklɪəs *US:* ˈnuː- ; ˈnjuklɪəs/ *n* (*pl* nuclei /-klɪaɪ ; -klɪ,aɪ/) central part, round which other parts are grouped or round which other things collect; (esp) central part of an atom, consisting of protons and neutrons. 中心;核心;(尤指)原子核;核子(包括質子和中子)。

nude /njuːd *US:* nuːd ; njud/ *adj* naked. 裸體的。□ *n* [C] ~ human figure (esp in art). 裸體人像(尤指藝術的)。 ***in the ~,*** unclothed: 未穿衣的;裸露的: *pose in the ~ for an artist.* 裸體擺成姿勢供畫家作畫。 **nu·dist** /-ɪst ; -ɪst/ *n* person who believes that exposure of the naked body to sun and air is good for the health. 裸體主義者(認爲曝露裸體於陽光及空氣中對健康有益)。 **ˈnudist camp/colony,** place where nudists practise their beliefs. 天體營(裸體主義者實行其信條的場所)。 **nu·dism** /-ɪzəm ; -ɪzəm/ *n* the practice of going ~. 裸體主義。 **nu·dity** /ˈnjuːdətɪ *US:* ˈnuː- ; ˈnjudətɪ/ *n* nakedness. 裸體;裸露。

nudge /nʌdʒ ; nʌdʒ/ *vt* [VP6A] touch or push slightly with the elbow in order to draw sb's attention privately. 以肘輕碰或輕推,暗中促人注意。□ *n* push given in this way. 此種輕碰或輕推。

nu·ga·tory /ˈnjuːgətərɪ *US:* ˈnuːgətɔːrɪ ; ˈnjugə,torɪ/ *adj* (formal) trifling; worthless; not valid. (正式用語)微小的;無價值的;無效的。

nug·get /ˈnʌgɪt ; ˈnʌgɪt/ *n* lump of metal, esp gold, as found in the earth. 礦塊(尤指天然金塊);塊金。

nui·sance /ˈnjuːsns *US:* ˈnuː- ; ˈnjusn̩s/ *n* [C] thing, person, act, etc that causes trouble or offence: 討厭的事物、人、行爲等: *The mosquitoes are a ~.* 蚊子是討厭的東西。 *What a ~ that child is!* 那個小孩多討厭!

null /nʌl ; nʌl/ *adj* of no effect or force. 無效的;無力量的。 ***~ and void,*** (legal) without legal effect; invalid. (法律)法律上無效的;無效的。 **nul·lify** /ˈnʌlɪfaɪ ; ˈnʌlə,faɪ/ *vt* (*pt, pp* -fied) [VP6A] make ~ and void. 使無效。 **nul·li·fi·ca·tion** /,nʌlɪfɪˈkeɪʃn ; ,nʌləfəˈkeʃən/ *n* [U] making ~. 使無效。 **nul·lity** /ˈnʌlətɪ ; ˈnʌlətɪ/ *n* being ~; invalidity: 無效;無力: *nullity of marriage;* 婚姻無效; *a ˈnullity suit,* one that asks for ~ity of marriage. 請求宣判婚姻無效的訴訟。

numb /nʌm ; nʌm/ *adj* without ability to feel or move: 失去感覺的;麻木的: *fingers ~ with cold.* 凍僵了的手指。□ *vt* [VP6A] make ~; deaden: 使麻木;使失去感覺: *~ed with grief.* 因悲傷而變得麻木的。 **~·ly** *adv* **~·ness** *n*

num·ber /ˈnʌmbə(r) ; ˈnʌmbɚ/ *n* **1** *3, 13, 33 and 103 are ~s.* 3, 13, 33 和 103 都是數字。⇨ App 4. 參看附錄四。 **2** quantity or amount: 數量;總數: *a large ~ of people.* 很多人。 *N~s of people* (= Very many people) *came from all parts of the country to see the exhibition.* 許許多多人從國內各地來參觀這個展覽。 *The ~ of books missing from the library is large.* 圖書館遺失的書籍數量很大。 *A*

～ *of books* (= Some books) *are missing from the library*. 圖書館裡有一些書不見了。 ***His／Your, etc ～ is up,*** (colloq) He is／You are, etc ruined, going to die, to pay a penalty, etc. (俗)他(你等)完了(要死了，要受罰了等)。 ***in ～:*** 總共: *They were fifteen in ～,* There were fifteen of them. 他們總共是十五個。 ***to the ～ of,*** mounting to. 達到…數目；總數爲。 ***without ～,*** too many to be counted. 無數的；太多而數不清的。 ***times without ～,*** very often; so often that counting is impossible. 常常；經常；無數次地。 **'～-plate** *n* plate showing the licence number of motor vehicles, the ～ of a house, etc. (汽車等的)牌照；門牌；標示數字編號的牌子。 ⇨ the illus at motor. 參看 motor 之插圖。 **3** (attrib use before a definite ～(1), usu shortened to **No**, *pl* **Nos**): (置於數字之前，作形容用法，表示號數，通常縮寫爲 No, 複數作Nos): *Room No 145*, eg in a hotel; 145 號房間(如旅館中的)；*living at No 4*, house number four. 住在四號房屋。 **No 10 (Downing Street),** official residence of the British Prime Minister. (唐寧街)十號(英國首相官邸)。 ***look after／take care of ～ one,*** (colloq) look after oneself and one's own interests. (俗)照顧自己和自己的利益。 **4** one issue of a periodical, esp for one day, week, etc: 期刊的一期: *the current ～ of 'Punch';* 最近一期的 Punch 雜誌; *back ～s* (=earlier issues) *of 'Nature'*. 舊的 Nature 雜誌。 ***a back ～,*** (fig) out of date or old-fashioned. (喻)落伍者；過時者。 **5** part of an opera indicated by a ～; dance, song, etc for the stage. (以號數代表的)歌劇的一段；舞臺演出的舞蹈、歌曲等的一個節目。 **6** (gram) variations in the forms of *nn, vv,* etc according to whether only one or more than one is to be indicated: (文法)數(依據所指者僅是一個或爲多個而決定的名詞、動詞等形式的變化): *Man／men, does／do and I／we illustrate grammatical ～ in English.* Man 和 men, does 和 do, I 和 we 都是說明英文文法上數的變化。 **7** (*pl*) numerical superiority: (複)數量上的優勢: *The enemy won by ～s／by force of ～s.* 敵人以人多獲勝。 **8** (*pl*) arithmetic: (複)算術: *He's not good at ～s.* 他不擅長算術。 □ *vt, vi* **1** [VP6A, 14] give a ～ to: 編號: *Let's ～ them from 1 to 10.* 給他們從一到十編號。 **2** amount to; add up to: 計有；總共: *We ～ed 20 in all.* 我們共計二十個人。 **3** [VP14] ***～ sb／sth among,*** include; place: 包括(某人或某事物於其中)；置…於…中；計入；算爲: ～ *sb among one's friends.* 把某人算爲一個朋友。 **4** (passive) be restricted in ～: (被動語態) 在數目方面受到限制: *His days are ～ed,* He has not long to live. 他活不久了。 **5** [VP2C] ***～ off,*** (mil) call out one's ～ in a rank of soldiers: (軍)報數: *The company ～ed off from the right.* 該連士兵從右開始報數。

nu·mer·able /ˈnjuːmərəbl *US:* ˈnuː- ; ˈnjumərəbl/ *adj* that can be numbered or counted. 可數的；可計算的。

nu·meral /ˈnjuːmərəl *US:* ˈnuː ; ˈnjumrəl/ *n, adj* (word, figure or sign) standing for a number; of number. 代表數目的(字、數字或符號)；數字的。 **Arabic ～s,** 1, 2, 3, etc. 阿拉伯數字 (1, 2, 3 等)。 **Roman ～s,** I, II, III, etc. 羅馬數字 (I, II, III 等)。 ⇨ App 4. 參看附錄四。

nu·mer·ate /ˈnjuːmərət *US:* ˈnuː- ; ˈnjumərɪt/ *adj* (of a person) having a good basic competence in mathematics and science. (指人)對數學及科學具有良好之基本能力的。 ⇨ literate. **nu·mer·acy** /ˈnjuːmərəsɪ *US:* ˈnuː- ; ˈnjumərəsɪ/ *n*

nu·mer·ation /ˌnjuːməˈreɪʃn *US:* ˌnuː- ; ˌnjuməˈreʃən/ *n* method or process of numbering or calculating; expression in words of numbers written in figures. 計算(法)；命數(法)；讀數法。

nu·mer·ator /ˈnjuːməreɪtə(r) *US:* ˈnuː- ; ˈnjuməˌretɚ/ *n* number above the line in a vulgar fraction, eg 3 in $\frac{3}{4}$. 分數中的分子(如 $\frac{3}{4}$ 中的3)。 ⇨ denominator.

nu·meri·cal /njuːˈmerɪkl *US:* nuː- ; njuˈmɛrɪkḷ/ *adj* of, in, denoting, numbers: 數字的；數字上的；表示數量的: ～ *symbols.* 數字符號。 **～ly** /-klɪ ; -klɪ/ *adv*: *The enemy were ～ly superior.* 敵方在數量上佔優勢。

nu·mer·ous /ˈnjuːmərəs *US:* ˈnuː- ; ˈnjumrəs/ *adj* great in number; very many: 極多的；甚多的: *her ～ friends.* 她的許多朋友。

nu·min·ous /ˈnjuːmɪnəs *US:* ˈnuː- ; ˈnjumɪnəs/ *adj* awe-inspiring; divine. 令人敬畏的；神聖的。

nu·mis·mat·ics /ˌnjuːmɪzˈmætɪks *US:* ˌnuː- ; ˌnjumɪzˈmætɪks/ *n* (with *sing v*) the study of coins, coinage and medals. (用單數動詞)對錢幣、鑄幣及獎章之研究；錢幣學。 **nu·mis·ma·tist** /njuːˈmɪzmətɪst *US:* nuː- ; njuˈmɪzmətɪst/ *n* expert in ～; collector of coins and medals. 錢幣學家；錢幣及獎章收藏家。

num·skull /ˈnʌmskʌl ; ˈnʌmˌskʌl/ *n* stupid person. 笨人。

nun /nʌn ; nʌn/ *n* woman who, after taking religious vows, lives, with other women, in a convent, a life in the service of God. 修女；尼姑。 **nun·nery** /ˈnʌnərɪ ; ˈnʌnərɪ/ *n* (*pl* -ries) house of nuns; convent. 女修道院；尼姑庵。 ⇨ monk, monastery.

nun·cio /ˈnʌnsɪəʊ ; ˈnʌnʃɪˌo/ *n* (*pl* ～s) ambassador or representative of the Pope in a foreign country. 羅馬教宗的(駐外)使節。

nup·tial /ˈnʌpʃl ; ˈnʌpʃəl/ *adj* of marriage or weddings: 婚姻的；婚禮的: ～ *happiness;* 婚姻的快樂; *the ～ day.* 結婚之日。 **nup·tials** *n pl* wedding. 結婚；婚禮。

nurse[1] /nɜːs ; nɝs/ *n* **1** **('～-)maid,** woman or girl employed to look after babies and small children. 保姆；照顧小孩的女用人。 ⇨ nanny. **2** **('wet-)～,** woman employed to suckle another's infant. 奶媽。 **3** [U] nursing or being nursed: 看護；受照顧: *put a child to ～.* 把小孩交保姆看護。 **4** person, usu trained, who cares for people who are ill or injured: 護士: *hospital ～s;* 醫院護士; *Red Cross ～s;* 紅十字會護士; *male ～s,* eg in a mental home for men. 男護士(如精神病院中看護男病人者)。 **5** country, college, institution, etc which protects or encourages a certain quality: 保護或鼓勵某一特質的國家、大學、機構等；保護者；贊助者: *Iceland, the ～ of liberty.* 冰島，自由的保護者。

nurse[2] /nɜːs ; nɝs/ *vt* [VP6A] **1** take charge of and look after (persons who are ill, injured, etc) (but not used as in the sense of nurse[1](1)): 看護；護理(病人、傷患等) (不用以指做保姆照顧小孩): (gerund) (動名詞) *the nursing profession;* 護理的職業; *take up nursing as a career.* 以護理爲職業。 *Careful nursing will be needed.* 需要細心的看護。 **'nursing-home** *n* building, usu privately owned and smaller than a hospital, where persons who are ill may be cared for, operated on, etc. 療養院(通常爲私立且比醫院小，病人在院中可獲得照料、接受手術等)。 **2** feed (a baby) at the breast; suckle. 哺乳；給 (嬰孩) 餵奶。 **3** hold (a baby, a child, a pet dog) on the knees; clasp caressingly. 抱(嬰孩，小孩，愛犬)在膝上；擁抱。 **4** give special care to: 特別照料；養育；保護: ～ *young plants.* 培養幼苗。 ⇨ nursery(2); ～ ***a constituency,*** keep in touch with the voters (to obtain or retain their support). 維護選舉區(與選民保持接觸，以獲得或保有他們的支持)。 ～ ***a cold,*** stay at home, keep warm, in order to cure it. 待在家裡保持溫暖以使傷風痊癒。 **5** have in the mind, think about a great deal: 蓄；懷: ～ *feelings of revenge.* 蓄意復仇。

nurse·ling, nurs·ling /ˈnɜːslɪŋ ; ˈnɝslɪŋ/ *n* infant, esp in relation to its nurse. 嬰孩(尤指由保姆或奶媽撫養者)。

nurs·ery /ˈnɜːsərɪ ; ˈnɝsrɪ/ *n* (*pl* -ries) **1** room for the special use of small children. 幼兒室。 **'day ～,** building where mothers who go out to work may leave babies and young children. (日間)托兒所。 **'～ rhymes,** poems or songs (usu traditional) for young children. 兒歌；童謠。 **'～ school,** for children of 2 to 5; pre-primary school. 托兒所(收納二至五歲的小孩); 幼稚園。 ~ **slope,** (skiing) slope suitable for learners. (滑雪)適合初學者的坡地。 **2** place where young plants and trees are raised (for transplanting later, and usu for sale). 植物育苗場;苗圃;苗床。 **'~·man** /-mən ; -mən/ *n* (*pl* -men) man who works in a ~(2). 苗圃主人;苗圃工人。

nur·ture /ˈnɜːtʃə(r) ; ˈnɝtʃɚ/ *n* [U] (formal) care, training; education (of children). (正式用語)(兒童的)養育;教養;訓練;教育。□ *vt* bring up; give ~ to: 養育;教養: *a delicately ~d girl.* 一個經悉心教養的女孩。

nut /nʌt ; nʌt/ *n* **1** fruit consisting of a hard shell enclosing a kernel that can be eaten. 堅果(有硬殼,內含可吃的果肉)。 ***a hard nut to crack,*** a problem difficult to solve. 不易解決的難題。 **'nut-brown** *adj* (eg of ale) coloured like ripe hazelnuts. (指啤酒等)栗色的。 **ˌnut-'butter** *n* butter substitute made from nuts (eg *peanut butter*). 堅果奶油(奶油的代用品,如花生醬)。 **'nut-crackers** *n pl* device for cracking nuts open. 堅果鉗; 胡桃鉗。 **'nut·shell** *n* hard outside covering of a nut. 堅果殼。 ***(put sth) in a nutshell,*** (fig) in the fewest possible words. (喻)用最少的幾句話(說明某事物)。 **2** small piece of metal with a threaded hole for screwing on to a bolt. 螺母;螺帽。 ⇨ the illus at bolt. 參看 bolt 之插圖。 **3** (sl) head (of a human being). (俚)(人的)頭。 ***off one's nut,*** (sl) insane. (俚)瘋狂的。 **'nut house** *n* (sl) mental hospital. (俚)精神病院;瘋人院。 **4** (*pl*) small lumps of coal. (複)小煤塊。□ *vi* ***go nutting,*** look for, gather nuts (eg hazel-nuts in the woods and hedges). 採集堅果(例如在樹林或樹籬中採集榛果)。

nut·meg /ˈnʌtmeg ; ˈnʌtmɛg/ *n* **1** [C] hard, small, round; sweet-smelling seed of an E Indian evergreen. 荳蔻;肉荳蔻。 **2** [U] this seed grated to powder, used as a flavouring. 荳蔻末(用作香料)。

nu·tria /ˈnjuːtrɪə *US:* ˈnuː- ; ˈnjutrɪə/ *n* skin or fur of the small S American rodent called coypu. (南美產的)河鼠毛皮。

nu·tri·ent /ˈnjuːtrɪənt *US:* ˈnuː- ; ˈnjutrɪənt/ *adj* (formal) serving as or providing nourishment. (正式用語)營養的;滋養的。

nu·tri·ment /ˈnjuːtrɪmənt *US:* ˈnuː- ; ˈnjutrəmənt/ *n* (formal) nourishing food. (正式用語)營養品;營養的食物。

nu·tri·tion /njuːˈtrɪʃn *US:* nuː- ; njuˈtrɪʃən/ *n* (formal) [U] the process of supplying and receiving nourishment; the science of food values: (正式用語)營養(作用);營養學: *the care and ~ of children.* 兒童的照顧與營養。

nu·tri·tious /njuːˈtrɪʃəs *US:* nuː- ; njuˈtrɪʃəs/ *adj* (formal) nourishing; having high value as food. (正式用語)營養的;多滋養的。

nu·tri·tive /ˈnjuːtrɪtɪv *US:* ˈnuː- ; ˈnjutrɪtɪv/ *adj* (formal) serving as food; of nutrition. (正式用語)用作食物的;營養的。

nuts /nʌts ; nʌts/ *adj* (sl) crazy; insane. (俚)瘋狂的;發瘋的。 ***be ~ about/over sb/sth,*** be in love with, infatuated with. 迷戀某人(熱愛某事物)。

nutty /ˈnʌtɪ ; ˈnʌtɪ/ *adj* (-ier, -iest) **1** tasting like nuts. 有堅果味的。 **2** (sl) mad; crazy. (俚)瘋的;狂的。 **3** containing, made up of, nuts(4): 含小塊煤的;小塊煤構成的: *~ slack coal.* 小塊的鬆煤。

nuzzle /ˈnʌzl ; ˈnʌzḷ/ *vt, vi* **1** [VP6A] press the nose against: 以鼻推壓: *The horse ~d my shoulder.* 那匹馬用鼻子摩我的肩膀。 **2** [VP2C] ***~ up (against/to),*** rub or push with the nose: 用鼻子摩擦或推壓: *The horse ~d up against my shoulder.* 那匹馬用鼻子摩我的肩膀。

ny·lon /ˈnaɪlɒn ; ˈnaɪlɑn/ *n* **1** [U] synthetic fibre used for hosiery, rope, brushes, etc: 尼龍(一種合成纖維,用以製衣襪、繩索、刷等): *~ stockings/blouses, etc.* 尼龍襪子(短衫等)。 **2** (*pl*) ~ stockings. (複)尼龍長襪。

nymph /nɪmf ; nɪmf/ *n* **1** (in old Gk and Roman stories) one of the lesser goddesses, living in rivers, trees, hills, etc; (liter) beautiful young woman. (希臘與羅馬神話)居住河上、林中、山上等的仙女;(文)美麗的少女。 **2** pupa; chrysalis. 蛹。

nym·phet /nɪmˈfet ; nɪmˈfɛt/ *n* (colloq) young girl looked upon as sexually desirable. (俗)性感的少女。

nym·pho /ˈnɪmfəʊ ; ˈnɪmfo/ *n* (*pl* ~s /-fəʊz ; -foz/) (colloq abbr of) nymphomaniac. (俗) nymphomaniac 之略。

nym·pho·mania /ˌnɪmfəˈmeɪnɪə ; ˌnɪmfəˈmenɪə/ *n* [U] abnormal sexual desire in women. 女子淫狂;女花癡。 **nym·pho·maniac** /-ˈmeɪnɪæk ; -ˈmenɪæk/ *n, adj* (woman) suffering from ~. 女子淫狂者;花癡女;女子淫狂的。

Oo

O, o /əʊ ; o/ (*pl* O's, o's /əʊz ; oz/) the 15th letter of the English alphabet; O-shaped sign or mark; (in quoting telephone numbers) 6033, 'six O double three'. 英文字母的第十五個字母;O 形的符號或標記;(報電話號碼)零 (6033 讀作 six O double three)。 ⇨ App 4. 參看附錄四。

O, oh /əʊ ; o/ *int* cry of surprise, fear, pain, sudden pleasure, etc. 啊;呀(表示驚訝、恐懼、痛苦、突然的高興等的感歎詞)。

o' /ə ; ə/ (abbr of) *of,* as in *o'clock, man-o'-war.* of 的略寫(如 o'clock, man-o'-war 中之 o')。

oaf /əʊf ; of/ *n* (*pl* ~s or, rarely 罕作 oaves /əʊvz ; ovz/) awkward lout. 笨拙的粗人;蠢漢。 **'oaf·ish** /-ɪʃ ; -ɪʃ/ *adj* roughly behaved; loutish. 行爲粗野的;粗鄙的。

oak /əʊk ; ok/ *n* [C] sorts of large tree with tough, hard wood, common in many parts of the world, ⇨ the illus at tree; [U] the wood of this tree: 橡樹(參看 tree 之插圖);橡木: *a forest of oak(s)/oak-trees;* 橡林; *an oak door;* 橡木門; *oak panels.* 橡木鑲板。 **'oak-apple** *n* growth on an oak leaf or stem caused by an insect. 長於橡樹葉或莖上的蟲癭;伍倍子;沒食子。 **the Oaks,** name of a classic horse-race, run at Epsom, near London. 在倫敦附近艾普孫舉行的著名的賽馬會。 **oaken** /ˈəʊkən ; ˈokən/ *adj* made of oak. 橡木做的。

oa·kum /ˈəʊkəm ; ˈokəm/ *n* [U] loose fibre or threads obtained by picking old ropes, used for filling up spaces between the boards of a ship. (從舊索中解得的)麻絮;麻絲(用於填塞船縫)。

oar /ɔː(r) ; or/ *n* pole with a flat blade, pulled by hand against a pin, rowlock or other support on the side of a boat, in order to propel the boat through the water. 槳;櫓。 ⇨ the illus at eight, row. 參看 eight, row 之插圖。 ***pull a good oar,*** be a good oarsman. 是一個好槳手。 ***put/shove one's oar in,*** (colloq) interfere. (俗)干涉;干預。 ***rest on one's oars,*** stop working for a time. 停工休息一會兒。 **oars·man** /ˈɔːzmən ; ˈorzmən/ *n* (*pl* -men), **'oars·woman** *n* (*pl* -women) rower. 男划手;女划手。Hence, 由此產生, **'oars·man·ship** *n*

oasis /əʊˈeɪsɪs ; oˈesɪs/ *n* (*pl oases* /-siːz ; -siz/) fertile place, with water and trees, in a desert; (fig) experience, place, etc which is pleasant in the midst of what is dull, unpleasant, etc. 沙漠中的綠洲;(喻)在枯燥、不愉快等情況中的愉快經驗、宜人的地方等。

oast /əʊst ; ost/ *n* kiln for drying hops. 烘蛇麻子的

爐。'~·**house** *n* building containing an ~. 蛇麻子烘乾所。

oat /əut ; ot/ *n* (usu *pl*) (通常用複數) **1** (grain from a) hardy cereal plant grown in cool climates as food (*oats* for horses, *oatmeal* for human beings). 燕麥 (燕麥供馬食用，麥片 oatmeal 供人食用)。⇨ the illus at cereal. 參看 cereal 之插圖。***feel one's oats,*** (colloq) feel gay, lively, ready for activity, active. (俗)覺得愉快而精力充沛；輕鬆活躍。***sow one's wild oats,*** lead a life of pleasure and gaiety while young before settling down seriously. 年輕時縱情玩樂。'**oat·cake** *n* (esp in Scot and N England) thin, unleavened cake made of oatmeal. (尤指在蘇格蘭及英格蘭北部)燕麥餅；麥片餅。'**oat·meal** *n* meal made from oats, used in porridge and oatcakes. 麥片；燕麥片(用於煮麥片粥及製麥片餅)。**2** (*pl* with *sing v*) oatmeal porridge: (複數，與單數動詞連用)麥片粥；燕麥粥：*Is Scotch ~s on the breakfast menu?* 早餐菜單上有蘇格蘭燕麥粥嗎？

oath /əuθ ; oθ/ *n* (*pl* ~s /əuðz ; oðz/) **1** solemn undertaking with God's help to do sth; solemn declaration that sth is true. 誓約；誓。***be on/under ~,*** (legal) having sworn to tell the truth: (法律)已宣誓說實話；宣誓不作僞證：*The judge reminded the witness that he was still under ~.* 那法官提醒證人他已宣誓不作僞證 (其誓言仍然有效)。***put sb under ~,*** (legal) require sb to swear an ~. (法律)使某人宣誓(或立誓)。***swear/take an ~,*** promise solemnly to give (one's loyalty, allegiance, etc). 發誓；宣誓；立誓(忠誠，效忠等)。***on one's ~,*** (non-legal) used to emphasize that one is telling the truth: (非法律用語) ··· 發誓 (用以强調所說的話絕對眞實)：*I didn't say anything to him about you, on my ~.* 我發誓，我沒有對他說任何關於你的事。**2** wrongful use of God's name or of sacred words to express strong feeling; swear-word; piece of profanity. 表示强烈情緒的咒語；詛咒；褻瀆的言語。

ob·bli·gato /ˌɒblɪ'gɑːtəu ; ˌɑblɪ'gato/ *n* (*pl* ~s /-təuz ; -toz/), *adj* (music) (音樂) **1** (to be) performed without any omissions (opp to *ad libitum*). 全部演奏的(爲 ad libitum 之相反字)。**2** (accompanying part) forming an integral part of a composition. 必須的或不可缺少的(伴奏)。

ob·du·rate /'ɒbdjuərət *US:* -dər- ; 'ɑbdjərɪt/ *adj* (formal) stubborn; impenitent. (正式用語)執拗的；頑固的；不悔悟的。~·**ly** *adv* **ob·du·racy** /'ɒbdjuərəsɪ *US:* -dər- ; 'ɑbdjərəsɪ/ *n* [U].

obedi·ent /ə'biːdɪənt ; ə'bidɪənt/ *adj* doing, willing to do, what one is told to do: 服從的；遵從的；聽話的：*~ children.* 聽話的孩子們。***your ~ servant,*** formula used at the end of letters of an official or public nature. 正式或公開的書信中所用結尾套語；頓首；敬啓。~·**ly** *adv* **obedi·ence** /-əns ; -əns/ *n* [U] being ~: 服從；遵從；聽話：*Soldiers act in obedience to the orders of their superior officers.* 軍人服從上級軍官的命令而行動。

obeis·ance /əu'beɪsns ; o'besn̩s/ *n* [C] (formal) deep bow (of respect or homage): (正式用語)(表示尊敬或臣服的)深深的鞠躬：*do/pay ~ to a ruler,* show respectful homage or submission. 向統治者表示臣服。

ob·elisk /'ɒbəlɪsk ; 'ɑbl̩ˌɪsk/ *n* tall, pointed, tapering, four-sided stone pillar, set up as a monument or landmark. 方尖形的石碑(作紀念碑或路標用)；方尖塔；方尖柱碑。

obese /əu'biːs ; o'bis/ *adj* (of persons) very fat. (指人)非常肥胖的。**obes·ity** /əu'biːsətɪ ; o'bisətɪ/ *n* [U] being ~. 肥胖。

obey /ə'beɪ ; ə'be/ *vt, vi* [VP6A, 2A] do what one is told to do; carry out (a command): 服從；執行(命令)：*~ an officer;* 服從官長；*~ orders.* 服從命令。

ob·fus·cate /'ɒbfəskeɪt ; ɑb'fʌsket/ *vt* [VP6A] (formal) darken or obscure (the mind); bewilder. (正式用語)使(心靈)迷惑；使困惑。

obi /'əubɪ ; 'obɪ/ *n* (*pl* obis) (Japanese) broad sash (often ornamental) fastened round the waist so that there is a large bow. (日)(圍紮和服，常作裝飾用的)寬腰帶。

obiter dic·tum /ˌɒbɪtə 'dɪktəm ; 'ɑbɪtɚ'dɪktəm/ *n* (*pl* dicta) /'dɪktə ; dɪktə/) (Lat) incidental remark or statement. (拉)附帶的陳述；附言。

obitu·ary /ə'bɪtʃuərɪ *US:* -tʃuerɪ ; ə'bɪtʃuˌɛrɪ/ *n* (*pl* -ries) printed notice of sb's death, often with a short account of his life; 訃聞(常附有死者的傳略)；(attrib) (形容用法) *~ notices,* eg in a newspaper. 訃聞(如報紙上所刊載者)。

ob·ject¹ /'ɒbdʒɪkt ; 'ɑbdʒɪkt/ *n* **1** sth that can be seen or touched; material thing: 看得見或摸得到的東西；物體；物品：*Tell me the names of the ~s in this room.* 告訴我這屋裡各件東西的名稱。'~ **lesson,** **(a)** one (to be) taught or learnt from an example, or from specimens, etc placed before or shown to the learner. 實物教學。**(b)** practical illustration of some principle, often given or used as a warning. 用作警戒的某種行爲準則的實例；殷鑑。'~ **glass/lens** *n* = objective *n*(2). **2** person or thing to which action or feeling or thought is directed; thing aimed at; end; purpose: 對象；目的物；目標；目的：*an ~ of pity/admiration,* sb or sth pitied/admired; 憐憫(欽佩)的對象；*with no ~ in life;* 沒有生活的目標；*work with the ~ of earning fame;* 爲了要想成名而工作；*fail/succeed in one's ~.* 未達到(達到)目的。***no ~,*** no hindrance; not important: 無障礙；不重要：***money/time/distance, etc no ~,*** (in advertisements, eg for jobs) the person answering may make his own terms about money, time, etc. 待遇(時間，距離遠近等)不計 (如報紙徵聘人員的廣告中，可由應徵者開列自己所要求的待遇、時間等)。**3** person or thing of strange appearance, esp if ridiculous, pitiful or contemptible: 樣子怪異的人或物 (尤指可笑、可憐或可鄙者)：*What an ~ you look in that old hat!* 你戴著那頂舊帽子顯得多麼滑稽啊！**4** (gram) *n* or *n* equivalent (eg a clause) towards which the action of the *v* is directed, or to which a preposition indicates some relation, as in (direct object) 'He took *the money*' or 'He took *what he wanted*' or (indirect ~) 'I gave *him* the money' or (prepositional ~) 'I gave the money to *the treasurer*'. (文法) 受詞 (由名詞或名詞相等詞，如名詞子句，所構成，作爲動詞之動作或介詞表示某種關係的對象，如 He took the money 中的 money 或 He took what he wanted 中的 what he wanted 均爲直接受詞，I gave him the money 中的 him 爲間接受詞，I gave the money to the treasurer 中的 the treasurer 爲介詞受詞)。

ob·ject² /əb'dʒekt ; əb'dʒɛkt/ *vi, vt* **1** [VP2A, 3A] ~ ***(to),*** say that one is not in favour of sth; be opposed (to); make a protest against: 不贊成；反對：*I ~ to all this noise/to being treated like a child.* 我反對所有這種鬧聲 (被當做小孩看待)。*He stood up and ~ed in strong language.* 他站起來以强硬的言詞抗議。**2** [VP9] ~ ***(against sb) that,*** give as a reason against: 提出…作爲反對 (某人)的理由：*I ~ (against him) that he is too young for the position.* 我反對(他)的理由是他太年輕不適合那個職位。**ob·jec·tor** /-tə(r) ; -tɚ/ *n* person who ~s. 反對者；抗議者。**conscientious ~or,** ⇨ conscientious.

ob·jec·tion /əb'dʒekʃn ; əb'dʒɛkʃən/ *n* **1** [C, U] statement or feeling of dislike, disapproval or opposition: 厭惡；不贊成；反對：*He has a strong ~ to getting up early.* 他强烈地反對早起。*O~s to the plan will be listened to sympathetically.* 對本計畫的異議將予以考慮。***take ~ to,*** object to. 反對。**2** [C] that which is objected to; drawback; defect. 被反對的事物；缺點；缺陷。~·**able** /-əbl ; -əbl/ *adj* likely to be objected to; unpleasant: 可能會引起反對的；令人不愉快的：*an ~able smell;* 難聞的味道；*~able remarks.* 可能會引起反對的言詞。~·**ably** /-əblɪ ; -əblɪ/ *adv*

ob·jec·tive /əb'dʒektɪv ; əb'dʒɛktɪv/ *adj* **1** (in

O

philosophy) having existence outside the mind; real. (哲學) 客觀的；眞實的。 ⇨ subjective. **2** (of persons, writings, pictures) uninfluenced by thought or feeling; dealing with outward things, actual facts, etc uninfluenced by personal feelings or opinions. (指人，著作，圖畫) 客觀的；實體的；不受個人的感情或意見所影響的。 **3** (gram) of the object(4): (文法)受詞的: *the ~ case*, in Latin and other inflected languages. (拉丁文及其他有字形變化的文字中)受格。□ *n* **1** object aimed at; purpose; (esp mil) point to which armed forces are moving to capture it: 目標；目的；(尤指軍語)攻擊目標: *All our ~s were won.* 我們所有的目的都達到了。 **2** lens of a microscope or telescope closest to the object being looked at. (顯微鏡或望遠鏡中最接近目的物的)物鏡；接物鏡。 **~·ly** *adv* in an ~(2) manner. 客觀地。 **ob·jec·tiv·ity** /ˌɒbdʒekˈtɪvətɪ ; ˌɑbdʒɛkˈtɪvətɪ/ *n* state of being ~; impartial judgement; ability to free oneself from personal prejudice. 客觀；公平的判斷；大公無私；無偏見。

ob·jur·gate /ˈɒbdʒəgeɪt ; ˈɑbdʒɚˌget/ *vt* [VP6A] (liter) scold; rebuke. (文) 罵；叱責。 **ob·jur·ga·tion** /ˌɒbdʒəˈgeɪʃn ; ˌɑbdʒɚˈgeʃən/ *n* [C, U] scolding; rebuke. 罵；叱責。

ob·late /ˈɒbleɪt ; ˈɑblet/ *adj* (geom) flattened at the poles: (幾何) 兩極扁平的；扁圓的: *The earth is an ~ sphere.* 地球是一扁圓球體。

ob·la·tion /əˈbleɪʃn ; ɑbˈleʃən/ *n* [C] offering made to God or a god. 祭物；獻神物；牲禮。

ob·li·gate /ˈɒblɪgeɪt ; ˈɑbləˌget/ *vt* [VP17] **~ *sb to do sth,*** (formal) bind (a person, esp legally) (usu passive): (正式用語) (通常用被動語態) 强制 (某人，尤指依法) 作某事: *He felt ~d to help.* 他覺得有責任去幫助。

ob·li·ga·tion /ˌɒblɪˈgeɪʃn ; ˌɑbləˈgeʃən/ *n* [C] promise, duty or condition that indicates what action ought to be taken (eg the power of the law, duty, a sense of what is right): 義務；職責；責任: *the ~s of good citizenship/of conscience;* 好公民的義務 (良心上的責任)； *fulfil/repay an ~*, eg by returning hospitality that one has received. 履行義務 (報恩)。 ***be/place sb under an ~,*** be/make sb indebted to another. 受人恩惠；負有義務 (對某人施恩惠；使某人負有義務)。

ob·li·ga·tory /əˈblɪgətrɪ *US:* -tɔːrɪ ; əˈblɪgəˌtorɪ/ *adj* that is required by law, rule or custom: (法律，規則或習俗上) 要求的；必須的；必須做的: *Is attendance at school ~ or optional in that country?* 在那個國家裡，上學是强制的還是隨意的？ *It is ~ on café owners to take precautions against fire.* 餐館老闆必須作防火的措施。

ob·lige /əˈblaɪdʒ ; əˈblaɪdʒ/ *vt* **1** [VP17] **~ *sb to do sth,*** require, bind (sb) by a promise, oath, etc: 要求 (某人作某事)；以諾言、誓約等束縛 (某人): *The law ~s parents to send their children to school.* 法律要求父母送子女入學。 **2** [VP17] (esp in passive) ***be ~d to do sth,*** compel: (尤用於被動語態) 强迫: *They were ~d to sell their house in order to pay their debts.* 他們被迫出賣他們的房子來還債。 ⇨ have³(1). **3** [VP6A, 14] do sth for sb as a favour or in answer to a request: 施惠；答應要求而作: *Please ~ me by closing the door.* 請替我關上那個門。 *Can you ~ me with...,* lend or give me...? 能借我 (或給我)…嗎？ *I'm much ~d to you,* I'm grateful for what you've done. 我非常感激你。 **oblig·ing** *adj* willing to help: 願意協助的: *obliging neighbours.* 熱心助人的鄰居。 **oblig·ing·ly** *adv*

ob·lique /əˈbliːk ; əˈblik/ *adj* **1** sloping; slanting: 歪的；斜的: *an ~ angle,* any angle that is not a right angle (ie not 90°). 斜角 (非九十度的角，包括銳角和鈍角)。 **2** indirect: 間接的: *an ~ reference to sth.* 間接提及某事物。 **~·ly** *adv* **ob·li·quity** /əˈblɪkwətɪ ; əˈblɪkwətɪ/ *n* (*pl* -ties) **1** [U] state of being ~. 歪；斜。 **2** [C, U] (instance of) moral perversity. 邪惡 (的實例)；不正的行爲。

ob·lit·er·ate /əˈblɪtəreɪt ; əˈblɪtəˌret/ *vt* [VP6A] rub or blot out; remove all signs of; destroy. 擦掉；塗掉；除去；毀滅。 **ob·lit·er·ation** /əˌblɪtəˈreɪʃn ; əˌblɪtəˈreʃən/ *n* [U].

ob·liv·ion /əˈblɪvɪən ; əˈblɪvɪən/ *n* [U] state of forgetting or being quite forgotten: 遺忘或完全被遺忘的狀態；湮沒: *sink/fall into ~;* 湮沒無聞; (colloq) unconsciousness. (俗) 失去知覺。

ob·livi·ous /əˈblɪvɪəs ; əˈblɪvɪəs/ *adj* **~ *of,*** unaware, having no memory: 不注意的；忘記的: *~ of one's surroundings/of what was taking place.* 忘了周圍的一切 (沒注意到所發生的事)。

ob·long /ˈɒblɒŋ *US:* -lɔːŋ ; ˈɑblɔŋ/ *n, adj* (figure) having four straight sides and angles at 90°, longer than it is wide. 長方形；長方形的。

ob·loquy /ˈɒbləkwɪ ; ˈɑbləkwɪ/ *n* [U] public shame or reproach; abuse; discredit. 公開的辱罵；咒罵；汚辱；不名譽。

ob·nox·ious /əbˈnɒkʃəs ; əbˈnɑkʃəs/ *adj* nasty; very disagreeable (*to*). 可憎的；非常討厭的 (與 to 連用)。 **~·ly** *adv* **~·ness** *n*

oboe /ˈəʊbəʊ ; ˈobo/ *n* woodwind instrument of treble pitch with a double-reed mouthpiece. 雙簧管；奧博管 (一種高音的木管樂器)。 ⇨ the illus at brass. 參看 brass 之挿圖。 **obo·ist** /-ɪst ; -ɪst/ *n* player of the ~. 吹奏雙簧管的人。

ob·scene /əbˈsiːn ; əbˈsin/ *adj* (of words, thoughts, books, pictures, etc) morally disgusting; offensive; likely to corrupt and deprave (esp by regarding or describing sex indecently). (指文字、思想、書籍、圖畫等) 猥褻的；(尤指由於對於性活動的看法或描寫不正當而) 淫穢的。 **~·ly** *adv* **ob·scen·ity** /əbˈsenətɪ ; əbˈsɛnətɪ/ *n* (*pl* -ties) [U] being ~; ~ language, etc; [C] instance of this. 猥褻；淫穢；猥褻或淫穢的話；猥褻或淫穢的實例 (行爲)。

ob·scure /əbˈskjʊə(r) ; əbˈskjʊr/ *adj* **1** dark; hidden; not clearly seen or understood: 暗的；隱藏的；不清楚的；含糊難解的: *an ~ view/corner.* 朦朧的景色 (昏暗的角落)。 *Is the meaning still ~ to you?* 那意義對你還是含糊難懂嗎？ **2** not well known: 不著名的: *an ~ village/poet.* 無名的村莊 (詩人)。 □ *vt* [VP6A] make ~: 使暗；使不明顯: *The moon was ~d by clouds.* 月亮被雲遮暗了。 *Mist ~d the view.* 霧使景色迷濛不清。 **~·ly** *adv* **ob·scur·ity** /əbˈskjʊərətɪ ; əbˈskjʊrətɪ/ *n* (*pl* -ties) **1** [U] state of being ~: 含糊；朦朧；默默無聞；不顯揚: *content to live in obscurity.* 安於默默無聞的生活。 **2** [C] sth that is ~ or indistinct: 晦澀或不明之事物: *a philosophical essay full of obscurities.* 一篇充滿晦澀文字的有關哲學的文章。 **ob·scur·ant·ism** /ˌɒbskjʊˈræntɪzəm ; əbˈskjʊrəntˌɪzəm/ *n* [U] **1** opposition to enlightenment. 反啓蒙主義。 **2** deliberate vagueness. 故意含混不明。 **ob·scur·ant·ist** /-ɪst ; -ɪst/ *n* person who practises obscurantism. 反啓蒙主義者。

ob·sequies /ˈɒbsɪkwɪz ; ˈɑbsɪkwɪz/ *n pl* funeral ceremonies. 葬禮。

ob·sequi·ous /əbˈsiːkwɪəs ; əbˈsikwɪəs/ *adj* **~ *(to/towards),*** too eager to obey or serve; showing excessive respect (esp from hope of reward or advantage): 逢迎的；卑躬的 (尤指希望藉以得到報酬或好處者): *~ to the Manager.* 對經理卑躬屈節。 **~·ly** *adv* **~·ness** *n*

ob·serv·able /əbˈzɜːvəbl ; əbˈzɝvəbḷ/ *adj* that can be seen or noticed; deserving to be observed. 看得見的；值得注意的。 **ob·serv·ably** /-əblɪ ; -əblɪ/ *adv*

ob·serv·ance /əbˈzɜːvəns ; əbˈzɝvəns/ *n* **1** [U] the keeping or observing(2) of a law, custom, festival, etc: (法律、習俗、節日等的) 遵守；奉行: *the ˌLord's ˌDay Obˈservance Society,* ie for seeing that proper respect is paid to Sunday; 守主日會; *the ~ of the Queen's birthday.* 女王誕辰之慶祝。 **2** [C] act performed as part of a ceremony, or as a sign of respect or worship. 慶典儀節；宗教儀式；表示尊敬之禮節。

ob·serv·ant /əbˈzɜːvənt ; əbˈzɝvənt/ *adj* **1** quick at noticing things: 善於觀察的; 注意的; 機警的: *an ~ boy.* 機警的男孩。 **2** careful to observe(2) laws, customs, etc: 小心遵奉 (法律、習俗等)的: *~ of the rules.* 遵守規則。 **~·ly** *adv*

ob·ser·va·tion /ˌɒbzəˈveɪʃn ; ˌɑbzəˈveʃən/ *n* **1** [U] observing or being observed: 觀察; 注意: *~ of natural phenomena;* 自然現象的觀察; *escape ~.* 不爲人所注意; 沒有被察覺。 ***be/come under ~,*** be observed. 被觀察中; 被看到。 ***keep sb under ~,*** watch him carefully (eg a suspected criminal by the police; a hospital patient by the medical staff). 注意觀察某人 (如警察對可疑的罪犯; 醫護人員對醫院中的病人)。 **ˈ~ car,** (in a railway train) one with wide windows through which to watch the scenery, etc. (火車之) 瞭望車 (有寬濶的窗戶以供觀賞風景等者)。 **ˈ~ post,** (mil) post as near to the enemy's lines as possible, from which reports of the enemy's movements may be obtained. (軍) 觀測所; 監視哨; 瞭望哨。 **2** [U] power of taking notice: 觀察力: *a man of little ~.* 觀察力極差的人。 **3** [U] (usu *pl*) collected and recorded information: (通常用複數) 經收集並作記錄的資料; 觀測報告: *Has he published his ~s on bird life in the Antarctic yet?* 他已經把觀察南極鳥類生活的報告出版了嗎? **4** ***take an ~,*** take the altitude of the sun or other heavenly body in order to find the latitude and longitude of one's position. 測天 (測量太陽或其他天體的高度, 藉以測定本身所處位置的經緯度)。

ob·serv·atory /əbˈzɜːvətrɪ *US:* -tɔːrɪ ; əbˈzɝvəˌtorɪ/ *n* (*pl* -ries) building from which natural phenomena (eg the sun and the stars, volcanic activity, marine life) may be observed. 天文臺; 氣象臺; 瞭望臺。

an astronomical observatory

ob·serve /əbˈzɜːv ; əbˈzɝv/ *vt, vi* **1** [VP6A, 8, 9, 10, 25, 2A, and 18A, 19A, in passive 用被動語態] see and notice; watch carefully: 看; 觀察: *~ the behaviour of birds.* 觀察鳥類的行爲。 *The accused man was ~d to enter the bank/trying to force the lock of the door.* 被告被看到進入銀行 (企圖撬開門鎖)。 *I have never ~d him do otherwise.* 我從來沒有看到他別的做法。 *He ~d that it had turned cloudy.* 他發覺天已經轉陰。 *He ~s keenly but says little.* 他觀察敏銳但很少說話。 **2** [VP6A] pay attention to (rules, etc); celebrate (festivals, birthdays, anniversaries, etc): 遵守 (規則等); 慶祝 (節日, 生日, 週年等); 守; 過: *Do they ~ Christmas Day in that country?* 那個國家的人過聖誕節嗎? **3** [VP6A, 9] say by way of comment: 評論; 評述; 說: *He ~d that we should probably have rain.* 他說也許會下雨。 **~r** *n* **1** one who ~s(1): 觀察者: *an ~r of nature.* 自然界的觀察者。 **2** one who observes(2): 遵行者; 奉行者: *an ~r of the Sabbath.* 守安息日的人。 **3** person who attends a conference, etc to listen but who does not otherwise take part. 會議等的觀察員 (出席會議等, 但僅旁聽而不參加)。 **ob·serv·ing** *adj* quick to notice. 善於觀察的; 注意的。 **ob·serv·ing·ly** *adv*

ob·sess /əbˈses ; əbˈsɛs/ *vt* [VP6A] (usu passive, ***~ed by/with***) (of a fear, a fixed or false idea) occupy the mind of; continually distress: (通常用被動語態) (指恐懼, 固執的或錯誤的觀念) 佔據心思; 不斷地困擾: *~ed by/with fear of unemployment.* 被失業的恐懼所困擾。 **~·ion** /əbˈseʃn ; əbˈsɛʃən/ *n* **1** [U] state of being ~ed. 被困擾; 纏繞。 **2** [C] ***~ion (about/with sth/sb),*** sth that ~es; fixed idea that occupies one's mind. 縈繞於心的事物; 成見; 頑念。 **~·ive** /əbˈsesɪv ; əbˈsɛsɪv/ *adj* of or like an obsession. 縈繞的; 似縈繞於心之事物的。

ob·sid·ian /əbˈsɪdɪən ; əbˈsɪdɪən/ *n* dark volcanic rock like the glass of which some bottles are made. 黑曜岩。

ob·sol·escent /ˌɒbsəˈlesnt ; ˌɑbsəˈlɛsn̩t/ *adj* becoming out of date; passing out of use. 過時的; 已廢的。 **ob·sol·escence** /-ˈlesns ; -ˈlɛsn̩s/ *n* [U] being ~. 過時; 作廢。

ob·sol·ete /ˈɒbsəliːt ; ˈɑbsəˌlit/ *adj* no longer used; out of date. 作廢的; 過時的。

ob·stacle /ˈɒbstəkl ; ˈɑbstəkl̩/ *n* sth in the way that stops progress or makes it difficult: 障礙; 妨害物: *~s to world peace.* 世界和平的障礙。 **ˈ~ race,** one in which ~s, natural or artificial, eg ditches, hedges, have to be crossed. 障礙賽跑。

ob·stet·ric /əbˈstetrɪk ; əbˈstɛtrɪk/ (also 亦作 **ob·stet·ri·cal** /-kl ; -kl̩/) *adj* of obstetrics: 產科的: *the ~ ward* (in a hospital). (醫院中之) 產科病房。 **ob·stet·rics** *n pl* (with *sing v*) branch of medicine and surgery connected with childbirth, its antecedents and sequels. (與單數動詞連用) 產科醫學; 接生術。 **ob·ste·trician** /ˌɒbstɪˈtrɪʃn ; ˌɑbstɛˈtrɪʃən/ *n* expert in obstetrics. 產科醫生。

ob·sti·nate /ˈɒbstɪnət ; ˈɑbstənɪt/ *adj* **1** not easily giving way to argument or persuasion: 頑固的; 不易說服的; 倔强的: *an ~ character/streak.* 頑固的性格 (倔强的性情)。 **2** not easily overcome: 不易屈服的; 難克服的: *~ resistance;* 頑强的抵抗; *an ~ disease.* 難治的病。 **~·ly** *adv* **ob·sti·nacy** /-nəsɪ ; -nəsɪ/ *n* [U] being ~; stubbornness. 頑固; 倔强; 固執。

ob·strep·er·ous /əbˈstrepərəs ; əbˈstrɛpərəs/ *adj* unruly; noisily resisting control: 難駕馭的; 吵鬧不服管束的; 暴躁的: *~ behaviour/children.* 難駕馭的行爲 (吵鬧不服管束的孩子們)。 **~·ly** *adv* **~·ness** *n*

ob·struct /əbˈstrʌkt ; əbˈstrʌkt/ *vt* [VP6A] **1** be, get, put, sth in the way of; block up (a road, passage, etc): 阻隔; 阻塞; 遮斷 (道路、通道等): *The mountain roads were ~ed by falls of rock.* 山路被落下的石頭所阻塞。 *Trees ~ed the view.* 樹木遮蔽了視野。 **2** make (the development, etc of sth) difficult: 使 (事物發展等) 困難; 妨礙: *~ the progress of a Bill through the House of Commons.* 阻礙一個法案在下議院中的審議。

ob·struc·tion /əbˈstrʌkʃn ; əbˈstrʌkʃən/ *n* **1** [U] obstructing or being obstructed: 阻礙; 障礙; 封鎖: *The Opposition adopted a policy of ~.* 反對黨採取一種阻礙政策。 **2** sth that obstructs: 阻礙物; 障礙物: *~s on the road,* eg trees blown down in a gale. 路上的障礙物 (如被强風吹倒的樹)。 **~·ism** /-ɪzəm ; -ˌɪzəm/ *n* systematic ~ of plans, legislation, etc. (對計畫、立法等之) 有系統的阻礙。 **~·ist** /-ɪst ; -ɪst/ *n*

ob·struc·tive /əbˈstrʌktɪv ; əbˈstrʌktɪv/ *adj* causing, likely or intended to cause, obstruction: 阻礙的; 妨害的: *a policy ~ to our plans.* 妨害我們計畫的政策。 **~·ly** *adv*

ob·tain /əbˈteɪn ; əbˈten/ *vt, vi* **1** [VP6A] get; secure for oneself; buy; have lent or granted to oneself: 取得; 獲得; 買到; 借到: *~ what one wants.* 獲得所要的東西。 *Where can I ~ the book?* 在什麼地方我可以買到這本書? **2** [VP2A] (of rules, customs) be established or in use: (指規則, 習俗) 制定; 通行; 流行: *The custom still ~s in districts.* 這種風俗在某些地區仍然流行。 **~·able** /-əbl ; -əbl̩/ *adj* that can be ~ed. 可獲得的; 能取得的。

ob·trude /əbˈtruːd ; əbˈtrud/ *vt, vi* [VP14, 2A] ***~ (upon),*** push (oneself, one's opinions, etc) for-

O

ward, esp when unwanted. 强入;闖入;强使(某人)接受(自己,自己的意見等)。**ob·trus·ive** /əbˈtruːsɪv; əbˈtrusɪv/ *adj* inclined to ~. 强入的;强人接受己見的;闖入的。**ob·trus·ive·ly** *adv*

ob·tuse /əbˈtjuːs *US:* -ˈtuːs; əbˈtus/ *adj* **1** blunt. 鈍的。 **2** (of an angle) between 90° and 180°. (指角度)在90度與180度之間的;鈍角的。 ⇨ the illus at angle. 參看 angle 之插圖。 **3** slow in understanding; stupid. 遲鈍的;愚笨的。 **~·ly** *adv* **~·ness** *n*

ob·verse /ˈɒbvɜːs; ˈabvɝs/ *n* side of a coin or medal having on it the head or principal design, ⇨ reverse; face of anything intended to be presented; counterpart: (錢幣、獎章等的)正面;表面;(事實等的)對應部份: (attrib) (形容用法) *the ~ side.* 正面。

ob·vi·ate /ˈɒbvɪeɪt; ˈabvɪˌet/ *vt* [VP6A] get rid of; clear away; anticipate: 排除;消除;預防: *~ dangers/difficulties.* 預防危險(排除困難)。

ob·vi·ous /ˈɒbvɪəs; ˈabvɪəs/ *adj* easily seen or understood; clear; plain. 顯而易見的;清楚的;明白的。 **~·ly** *adv* **~·ness** *n*

oca·rina /ˌɒkəˈriːnə; ˌakəˈrinə/ *n* small, egg-shaped musical wind-instrument (with holes for the finger-tips) made of porcelain, plastic or metal. 洋壎(一種陶器、塑膠或金屬的卵形吹奏樂器)。

oc·ca·sion /əˈkeɪʒn; əˈkeʒən/ *n* **1** [C] time at which a particular event takes place; right time (*for* sth): (發生特殊事情的)時機;機會(與 for 連用,後接某事物): *on this/that ~...;* 在這個(那個)時機…;*on the present/last ~...;* 在這次(上次)…; *on one ~,* once; 曾經;有一次; *on rare ~s.* 很少;不常。 *I have met Mr White on several ~s.* 我曾經見過懷特先生幾次。 *This is not an ~* (= a suitable time) *for laughter.* 這不是歡笑的時候。 *He has had few ~s to speak French.* 他很少有機會說法語。 ***on ~,*** now and then; whenever the need arises. 不時地;必要時。 ***rise to the ~,*** show that one is equal to what needs to be done. 顯出有應付特殊事故的能力。 ***take this/that ~ to say sth,*** avail oneself of the opportunity. 利用這(那)機會說某事。 **2** [U] reason; cause; need: 理由;原因;需要: *I've had no ~ to visit him recently.* 我最近沒有必要去看他。 *You have no ~ to be angry.* 你沒有生氣的理由。 **3** [C] immediate, subsidiary or incidental cause of sth: 某事的近因,附帶原因或偶因: *The real causes of the strike are not clear, but the ~ was the dismissal of two workmen.* 罷工的眞正原因並不清楚,但近因是由於兩個工人的被開除。 □ *vt* [VP6A, 12A, 13A] be the cause of: 引起;惹起: *The boy's behaviour ~ed his parents much anxiety.* 那孩子的行爲使他父母大爲着急。

oc·ca·sional /əˈkeɪʒənl; əˈkeʒənḷ/ *adj* **1** happening, coming, seen, etc from time to time, but not regularly: 偶爾的;偶然的: *He pays me ~ visits.* 他偶爾來看我。 *There will be ~ showers during the day.* 今天將會有陣雨。 ***the ~ + n,*** = an ~ + *n: He pays me the ~ visit,* an ~ visit. 他偶爾來看我。 **2** used or meant for a special event, time, purpose, etc: 應時的;應景的: *~ verses,* eg written to celebrate an anniversary. 應景詩(如慶祝週年紀念者)。 **~·ly** /-nəlɪ; -nḷɪ/ *adv* now and then; at times: 偶爾地;間或: *He visits me ~ly.* 他偶爾來看我。

Oc·ci·dent /ˈɒksɪdənt; ˈaksədənt/ *n* **the ~,** (liter) the countries of the West, ie Europe and America, contrasted with *the Orient.* (文)西方(包括歐洲與美洲,與東方 the Orient 相對)。 **Oc·ci·den·tal** /ˌɒksɪˈdentl; ˌaksəˈdɛntḷ/ *n, adj* (native) of the ~ or a country in the ~. 西方的;西方國家的;西方人。

oc·cult /ɒˈkʌlt *US:* əˈkʌlt; əˈkʌlt/ *adj* **1** hidden; secret; only for those with special knowledge. 隱密的; 秘密的; 神秘的; 玄奧的。 **2** supernatural, magical: 超自然的;秘術的: *~ sciences,* eg astrology. 秘術(例如占星術)。 **the ~,** that which is ~. 神秘的事物;奥秘。

oc·cu·pant /ˈɒkjʊpənt; ˈakjəpənt/ *n* person who occupies a house, room or position; person in actual possession of land, etc. (房屋、地位等的)佔據者; 居住者;佔有者;(土地等的)實際擁有者。 **oc·cu·pancy** /-pənsɪ; -pənsɪ/ *n* act, fact, period of occupying a house, land, etc by being in possession. (房屋、土地等的)據有;居住;佔有;佔有期間;居住期間。

oc·cu·pa·tion /ˌɒkjʊˈpeɪʃn; ˌakjəˈpeʃən/ *n* **1** [U] act of occupying(1); taking and holding possession of: 佔有;據有;佔領;居住;擁有: *the ~ of a house by a family;* 某屋爲一個家庭所居住; *an army of ~,* one that occupies conquered territory until peace is made. 佔領軍。 **2** [U] period during which land, a building, etc is occupied. (土地、建築物等的)佔有期;居住期。 **3** [C] business, trade, etc; that which occupies one's time, either permanently or as a hobby, etc: 事業;職業;行業;工作(永久的或作爲嗜好而佔據某人之時間的): *useful ~s for long winter evenings.* 消磨漫長冬夜的有用的工作。 **~al** /-ʃənl; -ʃənḷ/ *adj* arising from, connected with, a person's ~. 職業的;因職業而有的;與職業有關的。 **ˌ~al ˈhazards,** risks that arise from a person's ~ (eg explosions in coalmines). 職業上的危險(如煤礦坑中的爆炸)。 **ˌ~al ˈtherapy,** treatment of illness, etc by activity in creative or productive employment. 職業療法(由從事創造性或生產性的工作來治療疾病等)。

oc·cu·pier /ˈɒkjʊpaɪə(r); ˈakjəˌpaɪɚ/ *n* occupant; person in (esp temporary or subordinate) possession of land or a building (contrasted with the owner or tenant). 土地或建築物的佔據者(尤指暫時的佔有者;與地主、房東、佃戶或租戶相對)。

oc·cupy /ˈɒkjʊpaɪ; ˈakjəˌpaɪ/ *vt* (*pt, pp* -pied) [VP6A] **1** live in, be in possession of (a house, farm, etc). 居住; 擁有(房屋、田園等)。 **2** take and keep possession of (towns, countries, etc, in war): 佔領(城鎮、國家等): *~ the enemy's capital.* 佔領敵人的首都。 **3** take up, fill (space, time, attention, the mind): 佔;塡滿;盤據(空間、時間、注意力、心思): *The dinner and speeches occupied three hours.* 餐宴和演講佔了三小時。 *Many anxieties ~ my mind.* 許多憂慮盤據我的心頭。 *He is occupied in translating/occupied with a translation of a French novel.* 他正忙於翻譯一本法文小說。 **4** hold, fill: 佔;充任: *My sister occupies an important position in the Department of the Environment.* 我姊姊在環境處充任要職。

oc·cur /əˈkɜː(r); əˈkɝ/ *vi* (-rr-) **1** [VP2A] take place; happen: 發生: *Don't let this ~ again.* 不要讓這件事再發生。 *When did the accident ~?* 那意外事故是什麼時候發生的? **2** [VP3A] *~* ***to,*** come into (sb's mind): 想起;想到: *An idea has ~red to me.* 我想到了一個主意。 *Did it ever ~ to you that...,* Did you ever have the idea that...? 你有沒有想到…? **3** [VP2C] exist; be found: 存在;被發現: *Misprints ~ on every page.* 每一頁都有印刷的錯誤。

oc·cur·rence /əˈkʌrəns; əˈkɝəns/ *n* **1** [C] happening; event: 發生;事件: *an everyday ~;* 每日發生的事件; *an unfortunate ~.* 不幸的事件。 **2** [U] fact or process of occurring: 發生的事實或過程: *of frequent/rare ~,* happening frequently/rarely. 經常(極少)發生的。

ocean /ˈəʊʃn; ˈoʃən/ *n* **1** the great body of water that surrounds the land masses of the earth: 海洋;大海: *an ~ voyage.* 海洋航行。 *~-going ships,* (contrasted with *coastal* ships). 遠洋船隻(與近海船隻相對)。 **2** one of the main divisions of this: 世界上的大洋之一: *the Atlantic/Pacific/Indian O~.* 大西洋(太平洋;印度洋)。 **the ~ lanes,** the routes regularly used by ships. 海洋航線;遠洋航線。 **3** (colloq) great number or quantity: (俗)極多的數目或數量;大量: *~s of time/money.* 極多的時間(金錢)。 **~ic** /ˌəʊʃɪˈænɪk; ˌoʃɪˈænɪk/ *adj* of, like, living in, the ~. 海洋的;似海洋的;生活於海洋中的。

ochre (US also **ocher**) /ˈəʊkə(r); ˈokɚ/ *n* [U] sorts of earth used for making pigments varying from light yellow to brown; pale yellowish-brown colour. 赭石;赭土石(用以製作自淡黃色至棕褐色之顏料);淡黃褐色;赭石色。

o'clock /ə'klɒk ; ə'klak/ *particle* (= of the clock) used in asking and telling the time (to specify an hour): 點鐘: *He left at five ~/between five and six ~.* 他於五點鐘離開(五點鐘與六點鐘之間離開)。 ⇨ App 4. 參看附錄四。

oc·ta·gon /'ɒktəgən *US:* -gɒn ; 'aktə,gan/ *n* plane figure with eight sides and angles. 八邊形;八角形。 **oc·tag·onal** /ɒk'tægənl ; ak'tægənḷ/ *adj* eight-sided. 八邊的。

oc·tane /'ɒkteɪn ; 'akten/ *n* paraffin hydro-carbon: 辛烷: *high ~,* (of fuels used in internal-combustion engines) having good anti-knock properties; (指內燃機用的燃料)高辛烷的;具有良好抗爆性的; *'~ rating,* measure of these properties, esp of petrol. 辛烷等級(尤指汽油之抗爆性能數)。 ⇨ knock²(3).

oc·tave /'ɒktɪv ; 'aktev/ *n* **1** (music) the note that is six whole tones above or below a given note; the interval of five whole tones and two semitones (*do, re, mi, fa, so, la, ti, do*); note and its ~ sounded together. (音樂)第八音;第八音程;八度音程;八度和音。 ⇨ scale²(7). **2** (poetry) first eight lines of a sonnet; stanza of eight lines. (詩)商籟詩(十四行詩)的起首八行;八行的詩節。

oc·tavo /ɒk'teɪvəʊ ; ak'tevo/ *n* (abbr 略作 **8vo**, or **oct**; *pl* ~s /-vəʊz ; -voz/) (size of a) book or page produced by folding sheets of paper three times or into eight leaves. 八開本的書;八開的紙;八開;八開大小。

oc·tet, oc·tette /ɒk'tet ; ak'tɛt/ *n* **1** (piece of music for) eight singers or players. 八重唱(曲);八重奏(曲)。 **2** = octave(2).

Oc·to·ber /ɒk'təʊbə(r) ; ak'tobɚ/ *n* the tenth month of the year, with 31 days. 十月。

oc·to·gen·arian /,ɒktədʒɪ'neərɪən ; ,aktədʒə'nɛrɪən/ *n, adj* (person) of an age from 80 to 89. 八十多歲的(人)。

oc·to·pus /'ɒktəpəs ; 'aktəpəs/ *n* (*pl* ~es /-pəsɪz ; -pəsɪz/) sea animal with a soft body and eight arms (*tentacles*) provided with suckers. 章魚。 ⇨ the illus at mollusc. 參看 mollusc 之插圖。

oc·troi /'ɒktrwɑː *US:* ɒk'trwɑː ; 'aktrɔɪ/ *n* [C] duty levied (in some European countries) on goods brought into a town; place where, officials by whom, the levy is collected. (某些歐洲國家之)貨物入市稅;入市稅徵收處;入市稅徵收員。

ocu·lar /'ɒkjʊlə(r) ; 'akjələ/ *adj* of, for, by, the eyes; of seeing: 眼睛的; 適於眼睛的; 用眼睛的; 視覺的: *~ proof/demonstration.* 顯而易見的證據。

ocu·list /'ɒkjʊlɪst ; 'akjəlɪst/ *n* specialist in diseases of the eye. 眼科醫生。

oda·lisque /'əʊdəlɪsk ; 'odḷ,ɪsk/ *n* Eastern female slave or concubine, eg in a seraglio in olden times. 東方的女奴或婢妾(例如古代土耳其皇宮中的奴婢)。

odd /ɒd ; ad/ *adj* **1** (of numbers) not even; not exactly divisible by two: (指數字)奇數的;不能用二除盡的: *1, 3, 5 and 7 are odd numbers.* 1, 3, 5 和 7 都是奇數。 **2** of one of a pair when the other is missing: 一雙中的單個的: *an odd shoe/boot/glove.* 單隻鞋子(靴子,手套)。 **3** of one or more of a set or series when not with the rest: 一套中的單個的: *two odd volumes of an encyclopaedia;* 一部百科全書中的兩本; *an odd player,* (in a game) an extra player above the number actually needed. (比賽中之)額外選手。 ***odd man out,*** **(a)** person or thing left when the others have been arranged in pairs. 無配對的人或物(其他的全已成双配對而剩下的一個); 落單的人或物。 **(b)** (colloq) person who stands aloof from, or cannot fit himself into, the society, community, etc, of which he is a member. (俗)社會團體中不能與他人相處的人; 獨來獨往的人。 **4** with a little extra: 零頭的;少量剩餘的: *five 'hundred odd,* a number greater than 500; 五百多; *'thirty-odd years,* between 30 and 40; 三十幾歲; *twelve'-'pounds odd,* £12 and some pence extra. 十二鎊多。 **5** not regular, habitual, or fixed; occasional: 非經常的;非固定的;臨時的: *make a living by doing odd jobs;* 靠做零工生活; *weed the garden at odd times/moments,* at various and irregular times. 在空閒的時候除去花園裡的雜草。 ***the odd + n,*** = an odd + *n*: *The landscape was bare except for the odd cactus.* 那片地上除了零星的仙人掌外什麼也沒有。 **6** (-er, -est) strange; peculiar: 奇怪的;古怪的: *He's an odd/odd-looking old man.* 他是一個古怪(樣子古怪)的老人。 *How odd!* 好奇怪! **odd·ly** *adv* in an odd manner: 成奇數;單個地;零星地;非經常地;奇怪地: *oddly enough,* strange to say. 說來奇怪。

odd·ity /'ɒdɪtɪ ; 'adətɪ/ *n* (*pl* -ties) **1** [U] quality of being odd(6); strangeness: 奇怪;古怪;怪異: *~ of behaviour/dress.* 行爲(服裝)的怪異。 **2** [C] queer act, thing or person: 怪異的行爲;怪事;怪物;怪人: *He's something of an ~,* is unusual in some ways. 他在某些方面異於常人。

odd·ment /'ɒdmənt ; 'admənt/ *n* [C] **1** remnant; sth left over; odd piece: 殘餘之物;零頭;零碎: *The chair was sold as an ~ at the end of the auction.* 拍賣結束時那把椅子單獨賣掉了。 **2** (*pl*) odd pieces. (複)零零碎碎的東西;零星雜物。 ⇨ *odds and ends* at odds(5).

odds /ɒdz ; adz/ *n pl* **1** the chances in favour of or against sth happening: 可能的機會;成敗的可能性: *The ~ are against us,* We are unlikely to succeed. 我們成功的機會甚小。 *The ~ are in your favour,* You are likely to succeed. 你們有成功的可能。 *The ~ are that...,* It is probable that...; 可能是…。 *They were fighting against heavy ~.* 他們和優勢的敵人作戰。 ***It makes no ~,*** makes no difference, will not influence the outcome. 沒有關係; 沒有差別。 ***What's the ~?*** (colloq) What does it matter? (俗)有什麼要緊? ***give/receive ~,*** give/receive an equalizing allowance (eg a number of strokes in golf, when a player is known to be stronger or weaker than another). 比賽時讓與(接受)有利條件(例如高爾夫球比賽中的讓桿)。 **2** things that are not even; inequalities: 不平均之事物;不平等: *make ~ even.* 使不平均之事物平均;使不均衡之事物均衡。 **3** (betting) difference in amount between the money staked on a chance and the money that will be paid if the chance is successful: (打賭)賭注與付款的差額: *~ of ten to one.* 十賭一(輸時付十,贏時只得一,即輸贏爲十與一之比)。 **fixed ~,** (eg football pools) with a promise to pay agreed odds, eg 100—1, regardless of the number of punters, gamblers. (足球賽之賭注等)固定比數(不管下注者的人數,以允諾的比數付款,如輸百贏一)。 **lay ~ of,** offer ~ of: 提出…的差額比數: *I'll lay ~ of three to one that....* 我將以三比一(輸三贏一)打賭…。 **long ~,** eg 20 to 1. 長差比數(例如二十比一)。 **short ~,** eg 3 to 1. 短差比數(例如三比一)。 **,~-'on,** better than even (chance). 有一半以上的(成功機會);有一半以上的勝算。 **4** ***be at ~ (with sb) (over/on sth),*** be quarrelling or disagreeing. (爲某事)(與某人)爭吵;爭論。 **5** ***~ and ends,*** small articles, bits, and pieces, of various sorts and usu of small value. 零星雜物;零碎雜物。

ode /əʊd ; od/ *n* poem, usu in irregular metre and expressing noble feelings, often in celebration of some special event. 頌;歌(通常爲不規則韻律和表達高尚情感的詩,常常爲慶祝某一特殊事情而寫的)。

odi·ous /'əʊdɪəs ; 'odɪəs/ *adj* hateful; repulsive. 可恨的;討厭的。 **~·ly** *adv*

odium /'əʊdɪəm ; 'odɪəm/ *n* [U] general or widespread hatred; strong feeling against sth: 普遍的憎恨;討厭: *behaviour that exposed him to ~.* 使他被人憎恨的行爲。

odor·ifer·ous /,əʊdə'rɪfərəs ; ,odə'rɪfərəs/ *adj* (formal) fragrant. (正式用語)香的。

odor·ous /'əʊdərəs ; 'odərəs/ *adj* (chiefly poet) fragrant. (主要用於詩歌)香的。

odour (US = **odor**) /ˈəʊdə(r) ; ˈodɚ/ *n* **1** [C] smell (pleasant or unpleasant). (香或臭的)氣味。 **2** [U] reputation; approval; favour. 名譽;稱讚;好感。 ***be in good／bad ～ (with sb),*** enjoy／not enjoy his favour or approval. (在某人心目中)有良好(不良)的聲譽。～**·less** *adj*·

od·ys·sey /ˈɒdɪsɪ ; ˈɑdəsɪ/ *n* long, adventurous journey or series of adventures (from the voyage of Odysseus /əˈdɪsɪəs ; oˈdɪsɪəs/ after the siege of Troy, in Homer's epic). 長久的冒險旅行;一連串的冒險(源出荷馬史詩奧德修斯圍攻特洛伊後的航海歷程)。

oecu·meni·cal /ˌi:kju:ˈmenɪkl ; ˌɛkjʊˈmɛnɪkl̩/ *adj* = ecumenical.

Oedipus complex /ˈi:dɪpəs kɒmpleks *US:* ˈed- ; ˈɛdəpəs ˈkɑmplɛks/ *n* (psych) sexual love of an infant for the parent of the opposite sex, with jealousy of the other parent. (心理)戀母情結(兒子對母親的性愛及對父親的嫉妒); 戀父情結(女兒對父親的性愛及對母親的嫉妒)。

o'er /ɔ:(r) ; or/ *adv, prep* (poet) (詩) = over.

oesoph·agus /i:ˈsɒfəgəs ; iˈsɑfəgəs/ *n* = esophagus.

of /*usual form:* əv ; əv; *strong form:* ɒv ; ɑv/ *prep* **1** (indicating separation in space or time): (表示空間與時間的距離): *five miles south of Leeds;* 里玆以南五哩; *within a hundred yards of the station;* 距車站一百碼以內; *within a year of his death;* 他死後一年內; (US) (美) *five minutes／a quarter of* (= before) *two* (GB 英 = 'five minutes／a quarter *to* two'). 差五分(一刻鐘)兩點。 **2** (indicating origin, authorship): (表示來源,作者): *a man of humble origin;* 出身低微的人; *of royal descent;* 皇家後裔的; *the works of Shakespeare;* 莎士比亞的著作; *the Iliad of Homer.* 荷馬的伊里亞特。 **3** (indicating cause): (表示原因): *die of grief／hunger, etc;* 悲傷(飢餓等)而死; *do sth of necessity／of one's own choice／of one's own accord;* 做必要的(自己選擇的,出於本意的)事; *sick／proud／ashamed／afraid／glad／tired, etc of sth or sb;* 對某事物或某人感到厭惡(驕傲,羞恥,害怕,高興,厭倦等); *taste／smell, etc of sth;* 某物的味道(氣味等); *because of;* 因爲;由於; *for fear of.* 因爲怕…。 *The explosion couldn't have happened of itself,* ie without an external cause. 那爆炸不會無緣無故發生的。 **4** (indicating relief, deprivation, riddance): (表示解除、剝奪、免除): *cure sb of a disease／a bad habit, etc;* 治癒某人的病(矯正某人的壞習慣等); *rid a warehouse of rats;* 清除倉庫裡的老鼠; *be／get rid of sth or sb;* 擺脫某事物(或某人); *rob sb of his money;* 搶某人的錢; *relieve sb of anxiety;* 解除某人的憂慮; *clear oneself of an accusation;* 證明自己無罪; *destitute of sense;* 無感覺的; *trees bare of leaves;* 沒有葉子的樹; *free of customs duty;* 免關稅的; *independent of help;* 不依賴幫助的; *short of money.* 缺錢的。 **5** (indicating material or substance): (表示材料或質料): *a table of wood;* 木桌; *a house of stone;* 石屋; *a dress of silk;* 綢衣; *made of steel and concrete;* 鋼筋混凝土造成的; *built of brick.* 磚造的。 **6** (forming *adj* phrases; descriptive genitive): (構成形容詞片語;描述的所有格): *goods of our own manufacture;* 我們自己製造的貨物; *tomatoes of my own growing,* that I have grown myself; 我自己種的番茄; *a girl of ten years,* a girl ten years old, a ten-year-old girl; 十歲的女孩子; *a man of foreign appearance;* 外國人模樣的男人; *a man of genius;* 有天才的人; *a man of ability,* an able man; 能幹的人; *a woman of no importance,* an unimportant woman; 不重要的女人; *the vice of drunkenness,* the vice that is drunkenness; 酗酒之害; *a coat of many colours,* a many-coloured coat; 一件彩色的上衣; *the city of Dublin;* 都柏林市; *the Isle of Wight.* 威特島。 **7** (in the pattern 'noun¹ *of* noun²' = noun² that is noun¹): (在 'noun¹ of noun²' 的句型中,表示 noun² 具有 noun¹ 的屬性): *They live in a palace of a house,* a house that is a palace, a palatial house. 他們住在一棟宮殿似的房子裡。 *He has the devil of a temper,* a devilish temper. 他的脾氣非常壞。 *Where's that fool of an assistant,* that foolish assistant? 那個笨助手在哪裡? *What a mountain of a wave,* a mountainous wave! 山一般高的浪濤! *She's a fine figure of a woman,* a woman with a fine figure. 她是個身裁很美的女人。 *Where's your rascal of a husband,* your rascally husband? 你的流氓丈夫在哪兒? **8** (objective genitive): (受格的所有格): *a maker of pots,* a man who makes pots; 製鍋者; *the love of study;* 愛好研究; *the writing of a letter;* 信件的寫作; *loss of power／appetite;* 權力(胃口)的失去; *great eaters of fish,* people who eat much fish; 愛吃魚的人; *the fear of God,* ie felt by men towards God. 人對上帝的敬畏。 **9** (subjective genitive): (主格的所有格): *the love of God,* God's love for mankind, 上帝對世人的愛, (⇨ 8 above, 參看上列第8義 *the fear of God*); *the love of a mother,* a mother's love, the love that a mother has for her children. 母愛。 Cf 參較 *his love of* (ie for) *his mother.* 他對母親的愛。 **10** (indicating connection, reference or relation): (表示連接、關連或關係): *the cause of the accident;* 意外事件的原因; *the result of the debate;* 辯論的結果; *a topic of conversation;* 話題; *the first day of June;* 六月的第一天;六月一日; *the manners of the present day;* 時下的習俗; *those of the middle classes;* 那些中產階級的人; *the master of the house;* 一家之主; *the wall of the garden,* the garden wall; 花園的圍牆; *the leg of the table,* the table leg; 桌子的腿; *the opposite of what I intended;* 和我所計畫的相反; *Doctor of Medicine;* 醫學博士; *Master of Arts;* 文學碩士; *think well of sb;* 重視某人;對某人印象甚好; *admitting／allowing of no doubt;* 不容懷疑; *accused／suspected／convicted of a crime;* 被控有(涉嫌,被判有)某一罪狀; *speaking／talking／dreaming of sth;* 說(談,夢)到某事物; *sure／certain／confident／fond／guilty／innocent, etc of sth;* 確信有把握得到(確定,深信,喜歡,觸犯,沒有犯)某事物; *hard of hearing,* deaf; 重聽; *blind of* (= in respect of) *one eye;* 瞎了一隻眼睛; *at thirty years of age.* 三十歲。 *What of* (= about) *the risk?* 有什麼危險? *Well, what of it?* 嗯,這有什麼關係? **11** (indicating partition, inclusion, measure): (表示區分、包含、分量): **(a)** *a sheet of paper;* 一張紙; *a roll of cloth;* 一匹布; *a pint of milk;* 一品脫牛奶; *a ton of coal;* 一噸煤; *3 acres of land;* 三英畝的土地; *2 yards of cloth;* 二碼布; *some of that cake;* 那個蛋糕的一部份; *one／a few／all of us;* 我們當中的一個(我們當中的幾個;我們全體); *a lot／a great deal／not much of this stuff;* 這種材料很多(甚多,不多); *no more of that.* 那個沒有了;不要再來那個了。 *The car won't hold the six of us.* 這輛車載不了我們六個人。 **(b)** (after superlatives): (在最高級的形容詞後面): *He is the most dangerous of enemies.* 他是仇敵中最兇惡的。 *You have had the best of teachers,* the best of those teachers who were available. 你有了最好的教師。 **(c)** (= out of): *It surprises me that you, of all men, should be so foolish.* 在所有的人之間,偏偏你那麼笨,眞令我驚奇。 *On this day of all days.* 就在這一天。 **(d)** (intensive): (加强語氣): *the song of songs;* 歌中之歌; *the Holy of Holies,* best deserving the name. 至聖所。 **12** (in the pattern *n + of + possessive*) (在 n + of + possessive 的句型中): **(a)** from among the number of: 其中的一部份;出自…之中: *a friend of mine;* 我朋友中的一個;我的一個朋友; *no business of yours;* 沒你的事兒; *reading a volume of Ruskin's,* a book, one of a number of which Ruskin was the author; 讀一本羅斯金的著作; *a painting of the king's,* one of a number belonging to, or painted by, the king. 國王所有的圖畫中的一幅。 Cf 參較 *a portrait of the king,* a painting to show the king's appearance. 國王的肖像。 **(b)** (used when the *n* is modified by a demonstrative or other word that cannot be combined with a possessive): (用於當名詞被指示詞或其他不能與所有格連用的字所修飾時): *that long nose of his;* 他那個長鼻子; *this essay of Green's;* 格林這篇短論; *that foolish young wife of yours;* 你那位年輕無知的太太; *that queer-looking hat of hers.* 她那頂怪模樣的帽子。 **13** (in the pattern *adj* + *of* + *n*／*pron*): (用於 adj + of + n／pron 之句型中): *How kind of you to help!* 非常謝謝你的幫助! *It was good of your brother to come.* 謝謝令兄(令弟)的光臨。 **14** (indicating time): (表示時間): *in days of old／of yore,* in the past; 以前的日子; *of late,* recently; 近來; *of late years,* during recent years. 最近幾年。 *What do you do of a Sunday,* on Sundays? 你星期天都做什麼? *He sometimes comes in of an evening,* in the evenings. 他有時候晚上來。 **15** by: 等於 by 的含義: *beloved of all.* 被大家所愛。

off¹ /ɒf *US:* ɔːf ; ɔf/ *adj* **1** (contrasted with *near*) (of horses, vehicles) on the right-hand side: (與 near 相對) (指馬、車)右邊的: *the off front wheel;* 右前輪; *the off hind leg of a horse;* 馬的右後腿; *the off horse* (of a pair). (一對中的)右邊的馬。 **2** (remotely) possible or likely. (極少)可能的;不大可能的。 ***on the off chance,*** ⇨ chance¹(2). **3** inactive; dull: 不活動的;沉悶的;清淡的;蕭條的: *the 'off season,* ⇨ season.

off² /ɒf *US:* ɔːf ; ɔf/ *adverbial particle* (For special uses with *off* as an *adverbial particle* such as *go off: turn sth off* ⇨ the *v* entries.) (off 作副詞接語的特殊用法如 go off, turn sth off, 參看 go, turn 等動詞。) **1** (indicating distance in space or time) departure, removal, separation at or to a distance; away: (表示空間或時間的距離)離去;移去;除去;離開;在遠處;至遠處: *The town is five miles off.* 那個城在五哩外。 *We're still some way off,* from our destination. 我們距離目的地還有一些路。 *The holidays are not far off.* 假期不遠了。 *Why don't you have that long beard off,* cut off, shaved off? 你爲什麼不把那麼長的鬍子剃掉(或剪短)? *He's off to London.* 他到倫敦去了。 *It's time I was off／I must be off now,* I must leave now. 是我該走的時候了(我得走啦)。 *We're off／Off we go!* We've started／We're starting! 我們走啦(我們要走啦)! *They're off!* (in racing) The race has started! (賽跑)比賽已經開始了! 他們已經起跑了! *Off with him!* Take him away! 把他趕走! *Off with his head!* Cut his head off! 砍掉他的頭! **2** (contrasted with *on*) indicating the ending of sth arranged, planned, etc: (與 on 相對)表示經安排、計畫等之事的結束: *Their engagement* (ie to marry) *is off／broken off,* ended. 他們的婚約取消了。 *The miners' strike is off,* will not now take place. 礦工罷工已經取消了。 **3** (contrasted with *on*) disconnected; no longer available: (與 on 相對)中斷的;沒有了: *The water／gas／electricity is off.* 自來水(煤氣,電)沒有了;自來水(煤氣,電)停了。 *Are the brakes off?* 煞車鬆開了嗎? *The central heating is off.* 中央暖氣系統停了。 *That dish is off,* (in a restaurant) no more of that dish is available (even though it is on the menu). (餐館中)那一樣菜沒有了(雖然菜單上列有)。 **4** indicating absence or freedom from work or duty: 表示缺席、不在、不工作或責任的免除: *I think I'll take the afternoon off,* not do my usual work, etc. 我想我下午要休假。 *The manager gave the staff a day off,* a day's holiday. 經理放全體職員一天假。 *You mustn't take time off* (= stay away from work) *just because you want to see a football match.* 你不可以只是爲了想看一場足球賽而休假。 **5** (of food) no longer fresh: (指食物)不新鮮: *This fish has gone slightly off,* is beginning to smell or taste rather bad. 這魚有點不新鮮了。 **6** (in a theatre) behind or at the side(s) of the stage: (戲院中)在舞台後方或兩旁: *Noises off,* eg as a stage direction in a printed play. 舞台外發出聲音(如劇本中的舞台說明)。 **7** (phrases) (片語) ***off of,*** (US) (美) = off (*prep*). ***on and off; off and on,*** from time to time; now and again; irregularly: 不時; 斷斷續續地; 間歇地; 不規則地: *It rained on and off all day.* 整天斷斷續續地下着雨。 ***badly／comfortably／well off,*** ⇨ these adverbs. 參看各副詞。 ***better／worse off,*** ⇨ better²(1), worse *adv*(1). ***right／straight off,*** at once; immediately. 立刻;立即。

off³ /ɒf *US:* ɔːf ; ɔf/ *prep* **1** not on; down from; away from: 不在…上; 從…下來; 離開: *fall off a ladder／a tree／a horse.* 從梯子(樹,馬)上跌下來。 *The rain ran off the roof.* 雨水從屋頂流下來。 *The ball rolled off the table.* 球從桌上滾下來。 *Keep off the grass.* 勿踐踏草地。 *Cut another slice off the loaf.* 再切一片麵包。 *Can you take something off* (ie reduce) *the price?* 你能減點價錢嗎? **2** (of a road or street) extending or branching from: (指路或街道)自…延伸或分叉: *a narrow lane off the main road;* 大路邊的一條小巷; *a street off the Strand,* branching from the street called the Strand. 自斯特蘭街分叉出的一條街。 **3** at some distance from: 離…一些距離: *a house off the main road;* 離大路不遠處的一幢房子; a short distance seaward of: 離…不遠的海上: *an island off the Cornish coast;* 康瓦耳海岸外的一個島; *a ship anchored off the harbour entrance.* 下碇在港口外的一艘船。 *The battle was fought off Cape Trafalger.* 海戰在特拉法加角附近海面上進行。 **4** (colloq) feeling averse to; not taking or indulging in: (俗)對…感覺討厭;嫌惡;不吃;不飲;不抽;不耽溺於: *I'm off my food,* have little or no appetite, don't enjoy it. 我沒有食慾(胃口不好)。 *She's off smoking／drugs,* does not smoke／take drugs any more. 她不再抽煙(不再服麻醉藥)。

off⁴ /ɒf *US:* ɔːf ; ɔf/ *pref* (used in numerous compounds) (用於許多複合字中) ⇨ the entries below. 參看下列各條。

of·fal /ˈɒfl *US:* ˈɔːfl ; ˈɔfl̩/ *n* [U] those parts, eg heart, head, kidneys, which are considered less valuable than the flesh when an animal is cut up for food. 動物屠宰後被認爲食用價值較少的部份(如心、頭、腰子);腸肚雜碎。

off-beat /ˌɒf ˈbiːt *US:* ˌɔːf ; ˈɔfˌbit/ *adj* (colloq) unusual; unconventional: (俗)不平常的;非傳統的: *an ~ TV comedy.* 新奇的電視喜劇。

off-day /ˈɒf deɪ *US:* ˈɔːf ; ˈɔf de/ *n* (colloq) day when one is unlucky, when one does things badly, clumsily, etc: (俗)倒楣的日子(運氣不佳的一天,笨手笨脚什麼事都做不好等): *I'm afraid this is one of my ~s.* 我恐怕這又是我倒楣的一天。

of·fence (US = **of·fense**) /əˈfens ; əˈfɛns/ *n* **1** [C] ***an ~ against,*** crime, sin, breaking of a rule: 過錯;罪;犯法;罪過: *an ~ against the law／against good manners;* 違犯法律(沒有規矩); *be charged with a serious ~.* 被控告犯嚴重的罪。 **2** [U] the hurting of sb's feelings; condition of being hurt in one's feelings. 傷人感情;觸怒;不悅。 ***give／cause ~ (to sb);*** 觸怒(某人); ***take ~ (at sth):*** (因某事物而)發怒: *He is quick to take ~,* is easily offended. 他很容易生氣。 ***No ~!*** (phrase used to say) I did not intend to hurt your feelings. 我無意傷你感情! **3** [U] attack: 攻擊: *weapons of ~.* 攻擊性的武器。 *They say that the most effective defence is ~.* 據說最有效的防禦就是攻擊。 **4** [C] that which annoys the senses or makes sb angry: 令人討厭或生氣的事物: *That cesspool is an ~ to the neighbourhood.* 那個污水坑是令附近隣居氣惱的東西。 **~·less** *adj* without ~; not giving ~. 無罪的;無咎的;不攻擊的;不觸怒的。

of·fend /əˈfend ; əˈfɛnd/ *vi, vt* **1** [VP3A] ***~ against,*** do wrong; commit an offence: 犯法;犯罪;違犯: *~ against good manners／the law／traditions, etc.* 違犯禮貌(法律,傳統等)。 **2** [VP6A] hurt the feelings of; give offence to: 傷…的感情;觸怒: *I'm sorry if I've ~ed you.* 假如我冒犯了你,我很抱歉。

He was ~ed at/by my remarks. 他被我的話觸怒了。*She was ~ed by/with her husband.* 她被她丈夫觸怒了(她生她丈夫的氣)。 **3** [VP6A] displease; annoy: 使不愉快;煩擾: *sounds that ~ the ear;* 刺耳的聲音; *ugly buildings that ~ the eye.* 難看的醜陋建築物。**~er** *n* person who ~s, esp by breaking a law: 冒犯者;(尤指)犯罪者;犯人: *first ~ers,* found guilty for the first time and not usu treated severely; 初犯; *an old ~er,* one who has often been found guilty. 累犯;慣犯。

of·fense /əˈfens ; əˈfɛns/ ⇨ offence.

of·fen·sive /əˈfensɪv ; əˈfɛnsɪv/ *adj* **1** causing offence to the mind or senses; disagreeable: 令人不快的;討厭的: *fish with an ~ smell;* 有難聞氣味的魚; *~ language.* 無禮的言語。 **2** used for, connected with, attack: 攻擊(性)的: *~ weapons/wars.* 攻擊性的武器(攻擊戰)。 ⇨ defensive. □ *n* attack; an attitude of attack. 攻擊;攻勢。 ***go into/take the ~,*** go into attack. 進攻;採取攻勢。 **a peace ~,** (modern jargon) sustained effort the declared aim of which is to lessen the risk of war. (現代術語)和平攻勢。**~·ly** *adv* **~·ness** *n*

of·fer /ˈɒfə(r) *US:* ˈɔːf- ; ˈɔfɚ/ *vt, vi* **1** [VP6A, 7A, 12A, 13A, 14] ***~ sth to sb; ~ sb sth; ~ sth for sth,*** hold out, put forward, to be accepted or refused; say what one is willing to pay, give or exchange: 提供;提出;出價: *They ~ed a reward for the return of the jewels that had been lost.* 他們懸賞尋找失去的珠寶。*I have been ~ed a job in Japan.* 有人提供我一個在日本的工作機會。*He ~ed to help me.* 他表示要幫助我。*He ~ed me his help.* 他給我幫助。*We ~ed him the house for £20000/~ed him £20000 for the house.* 我們索(出)價二萬英鎊賣給(買)他那幢房子。***~ battle,*** give the enemy an opportunity of fighting. 給敵人一個戰鬥的機會;挑戰。***~ one's hand,*** hold it out (to shake hands). 伸出手來(準備握手)。***~ one's hand (in marriage),*** make a proposal of marriage to a woman. 向女人求婚。 **2** [VP6A, 12A, 13A, 15B] ***~ sth (up) (to God),*** present (to God): (向上帝)奉獻: *~ prayers to God;* 向上帝祈禱; *~ up a sacrifice.* 奉獻犧牲;獻祭。 **3** [VP6A, 7A, 14] ***~ (to),*** attempt; give signs of: 企圖;表示: *~ no resistance to the enemy.* 表示不抵抗敵人。 **4** [VP2A] occur; arise: 發生;出現: *Take the first opportunity that ~s,* that there is. 抓住第一個出現的機會。 ***as occasion ~s,*** when there is an opportunity. 有機會時;機會來到時。□ *n* [C] statement ~ing to do sth or give sth; that which is ~ed: 提供;提議;提出之物;提供的機會;出價: *an ~ of help;* 援助的提議; *your kind ~ to help;* 你的援助的好意; *an ~ of marriage,* a proposal. 求婚。*I've had an ~ of £20 000 for the house.* 有人已經出價二萬英鎊要買我那幢房子。*Make me an ~.* 給我出個價。 ***be open to an ~,*** be willing to consider a price to be named by a buyer. 願意考慮買主的出價。***(goods) on ~,*** for sale at a certain price. 出售的(貨品)。 **~·ing** /ˈɒfərɪŋ *US:* ˈɔːf- ; ˈɔfərɪŋ/ *n* **1** [U] act of ~ing: 提供;奉獻: *the ~ing of bribes.* 提出賄賂;行賄。 **2** [C] sth ~ed or presented: 提供之物: *a ˈpeace ~ing,* sth ~ed in the hope of restoring friendship after a quarrel, etc. 謝罪之禮 (爭吵等之後爲求恢復友誼而奉送之禮物)。

of·fer·tory /ˈɒfətrɪ *US:* -tɔːrɪ ; ˈɔfɚˌtorɪ/ *n* (*pl* -ries) [C] gifts collected in church during, or at the end of, a service. (教堂做禮拜時所收的)奉獻金。

off-hand /ˌɒf ˈhænd *US:* ˌɔːf ; ˈɔfˈhænd/ *adj* **1** without previous thought or preparation; extempore: 事先未加思索或未作準備的;臨時的;即席的: *~ remarks.* 隨口說出的話。 **2** (of behaviour, etc) casual; curt: (指行爲等) 隨便的;唐突的: *in an ~ way.* 隨便地;唐突地。□ *adv* without previous thought: 事先未加思索地;隨便地: *I can't say ~.* 我不能隨便說。**ˌoff-ˈhanded(ly)** *adj, adv* = ~.

of·fice /ˈɒfɪs *US:* ˈɔːf- ; ˈɔfɪs/ *n* [C] **1** (often *pl*) room(s) used as a place of business: (常用複數)辦公處;辦公室;事務所;營業所: *a lawyer's ~;* 律師事務所; *working in an ~,* in business, eg as a clerk or typist; 做辦公室的工作 (如當辦事員或打字員); *our London ~,* our branch in London; 我們的倫敦分公司(辦事處或分行); (US) surgery. (美)(醫師或牙醫的)診所。**ˈbooking ~,** ⇨ book²(2). **ˈbox-~,** ⇨ box¹(2). **ˈ~-block,** (usu large) building containing ~s (often of more than one company or firm). 辦公大樓(通常爲高樓大廈,內有許多辦公室,常爲數家公司者)。**ˈ~-boy** *n* boy employed to do less important duties in an ~. (辦公室的)工友。 **2** (buildings of a) government department, including the staff, their work and duties: 政府機關、部、局、處等;其建築物: *the ˈForeign O~.* 外交部。 **3** the work which it is sb's duty to do, esp in a public position of trust and authority: 職位;職務;公職: *enter upon/leave/accept/resign ~,* esp of positions in the government service. 擔任(離開,接受,辭去)公職。*Which party will be in ~ after the next general election?* 哪一黨會在下次大選後執政? *The Liberals have been out of ~ for a long time now.* 自由黨已經很久沒有執政了。**ˈ~-bearer** *n* person who holds an ~. 公務員;官吏。 **4** duty: 職責;任務: *the ~ of host/chairman.* 主人(主席)的職責。 **5** (*pl*) attentions, services, help: (複)慇懃;服務;幫助: *through the good ~s* (= kind help) *of a friend;* 藉着一個朋友好意的協助; *perform the last ~s for...,* conduct the burial service of.... 爲…舉行葬禮。**Divine O~,** certain forms of worship in the Roman Catholic and Episcopal Churches. (天主教和聖公會的)禮拜儀式。

of·fi·cer /ˈɒfɪsə(r) *US:* ˈɔːf- ; ˈɔfəsɚ/ *n* **1** person appointed to command others in the armed forces, in merchant ships, aircraft, the police force, etc usu wearing special uniform with indications of rank: 軍官;高級船員;高級航空人員;警官: *commissioned and non-commissioned ~s;* 軍官與士官; *~s and crew.* 高級船員與水手。 **2** person with a position of authority or trust, engaged in active duties, eg in the government: 官員;官吏;公務員: *executive/clerical ~s,* in the civil service; 行政官員(文書官); *a customs ~;* 海關人員; *~s of state,* ministers in the government; 部長; *the ~s of the Debating Society,* ie the President, Secretary, Treasurer; 辯論會職員(卽主席、秘書、財務); *the Medical O~ of Health;* 衞生官員; *ˈWelfare O~s.* 福利官員。 **3** form of address to a policeman. 警官(對警察的稱呼)。

of·fi·cial /əˈfɪʃl ; əˈfɪʃəl/ *adj* **1** of a position of trust or authority; said, done, etc with authority: 公務的;憑職權所說、所做等的;職權上的;官方的;正式的: *~ responsibilities/records;* 公務(正式記錄); *in his ~ uniform;* 穿着他的制服; *~ statements.* 正式聲明。*The news is not ~.* 這消息不是正式的。 **2** characteristic of, suitable for, persons holding office: 官式的;官僚的: *written in ~ style.* 用官式體裁寫成的。□ *n* person holding public office (eg in national or local government): 公務員;官員: *government ~s.* 政府官員。**~ly** /-ʃəlɪ ; -ʃəlɪ/ *adv* in an ~ manner; with ~ authority. 正式地;官方地;憑職權地。 **~·dom** /-dəm ; -dəm/ *n* ~s collectively; the ways of doing business of (government) ~s. (集合稱) 官員; 官場; 官僚作風。 **~ese** /əˌfɪʃəˈliːz ; əˌfɪʃəˈliz/ *n* [U] language characteristic of the writing of some government ~s (considered to be too formal or obscure). (一般認爲太正式或含糊難解的)公文術語;公文用語。⇨ *journalese* at journal.

of·fici·ate /əˈfɪʃɪeɪt ; əˈfɪʃɪˌet/ *vi* [VP2A, C, 3A] ***~ (as) (at),*** perform the duties of an office or position: 執行職務: *~ as chairman;* 擔任主席; *~ as host at a dinner party;* 作宴會的主人; *~ at a marriage ceremony,* (of a priest) perform the ceremony. (指神父)主持結婚儀式。

of·fi·cious /əˈfɪʃəs ; əˈfɪʃəs/ *adj* too eager or ready to help, offer advice, use authority. 過份慇懃的;好管閒事的;好用權威的。~**·ly** *adv* ~**·ness** *n*

off·ing /ˈɒfɪŋ US: ˈɔːf- ; ˈɔfɪŋ/ *n* part of the sea distant from the point of observation but visible: 視界範圍內的遠處海面: *a ship in the ~;* 在看得見的遠處海面上的一艘船; (fig) (喻) *a quarrel in the ~,* one that appears likely to break out. 即將發生的爭吵。

off·ish /ˈɒfɪʃ US: ˈɔːf- ; ˈɔfɪʃ/ *adj* (colloq) inclined to aloofness; distant in manner. (俗)疏遠的;冷淡的。⇨ *stand-offish* at stand²(10).

off-li·cence /ˈɒf laɪsns US: ˈɔːf ; ˈɔfˌlaɪsns/ *n* licence to sell beer and other alcoholic drinks for consumption off the premises; shop, part of a public house, where such drinks may be bought and taken away. (英) 賣酒執照(所賣之酒應攜出店外喝);賣酒店(爲酒館中的一部份,所賣之酒可攜帶出外)。

off-peak /ˈɒf piːk US: ˈɔːf ; ˈɔfˈpik/ *attrib adj* ⇨ peak¹(4).

off-print /ˈɒf prɪnt US: ˈɔːf ; ˈɔfˌprɪnt/ *n* [C] separate printed copy of an article in part of a larger publication. 出版物中單篇印刷的文章;抽印本;選刊。

off-put·ting /ˌɒf ˈpʊtɪŋ US: ˌɔːf ; ˈɔfˌpʊtɪŋ/ *adj* (colloq) disconcerting. (俗)令人不安的;使人慌亂的。⇨ *put off* at put¹(11).

off-scour·ings /ˈɒf skaʊərɪŋz US: ˈɔːf ; ˈɔfˌskaʊrɪŋz/ *n pl* (usu fig) refuse; dregs. (通常爲喻)垃圾;渣滓。

off·set /ˈɒfset US: ˈɔːf- ; ɔfˈsɛt/ *vt* (-tt-) [VP 6A, 14] balance, compensate for: 抵銷;彌補: *He has to ~ his small salary by living economically.* 他薪水微薄,不得不節儉度日。□ *n* **1** ~ **(process),** method of printing in which the ink is transferred from a plate to a rubber surface and then on to paper. 橡皮版印刷術;透印版印刷術。**2** = offshoot.

off·shoot /ˈɒfʃuːt US: ˈɔːf- ; ˈɔfˌʃut/ *n* [C] stem or branch growing from a main stem (lit or fig): (樹木的)旁枝;分枝(字面或喻): *an ~ of a plant/a mountain range/a family.* 植物的分枝(山脈的支脈;家族的旁系)。

off-shore /ˌɒf ˈʃɔː(r) US: ˌɔːf ; ˈɔfˈʃor/ *adj* **1** in a direction away from the shore or land: 自海岸的;從陸上的: *~ breezes.* 吹向海洋的微風。**2** at a short way out to sea: 在近海處的: *~ islands/fisheries.* 近海島嶼(漁場)。**3** ~ **purchases,** (US) goods purchased by the US for countries in receipt of economic or military aid, but which do not come from the US directly, eg aluminium shipped from Canada to Europe. (美)國外採購(美國向國外購買以援助他國的經援或軍援物資,例如向加拿大購買鋁運往歐洲國家)。

off·side /ɒfˈsaɪd US: ɔːf ; ˈɔfˈsaɪd/ *attrib adj, adv* (football, hockey) (of a player) in a position on the field in relation to the ball which is debarred by the rules: (足球、曲棍球)(指球員)越位(的): *~ play;* 越位踢球; *the ~ rule.* 越位的規則。

off·spring /ˈɒfsprɪŋ US: ˈɔːf- ; ˈɔfˌsprɪŋ/ *n* (*pl* unchanged) child; children; young of animals: (複數不變)子孫;後代;後裔;(動物的)幼仔: *He is the ~ of a scientific genius and a ballet dancer.* 他是一位天才科學家和一位巴蕾舞蹈家的後代。*Their ~ are all slightly mad.* 他們的子孫都有一點瘋狂。

off-street /ˈɒf striːt US: ˈɔːf ; ˈɔfˈstrit/ *attrib adj* not on the main streets: 不在大街上的: *~ parking,* of motor vehicles; 不在大街上停車; *~ (un)loading,* eg of lorries at the rear entrances of buildings. 不在大街上裝貨(卸貨)(例如載貨卡車在建築物後門的裝貨或卸貨)。

off-white /ˌɒf ˈwaɪt US: ˌɔːf ˈhwaɪt ; ˈɔfˈhwaɪt/ *adj* not pure white, but with a pale greyish or yellowish tinge. 灰白色的;米色的。

oft /ɒft US: ɔːft ; ɔft/ *adv* (in poetry) often: (詩)時常: *an oft-told tale;* 常講的故事; *many a time and oft,* very often. 常常。**ˈoft-times** *adv* (archaic) often. (古)時常。

of·ten /ˈɒfn US: ˈɔːfn ; ˈɔfən/ *adv of frequency* (usu occupying mid-position (ie with the *v*); may occupy front-position or end-position for emphasis (esp when modified by *very* or *quite*), or for contrast; comp and sup either *~er, ~est,* or *more ~, most ~.*) (通常置於句子中間,即與動詞連用;亦可置於句首或句末,作加强語氣用,尤其被 very 或 quite 所修飾時,或作對比用;比較級或最高級可寫爲 ~er, ~est 或 more ~, most ~。) **1** many times; in a large proportion of the instances: 時常;常常: *We ~ go there.* 我們常常去那兒。*We have ~ been there.* 我們時常去那兒。*We've been there quite ~.* 我們經常到那兒去。*It very ~ rains here in April.* 這兒四月間經常下雨。**2** (in phrases) (在片語中) ***how ~:*** 多少時候一次;多久一次: *How ~ do the buses run?* 公車多久有一班? ***as ~ as,*** each time that: 每一次: *As ~ as I tried to ring him the line was engaged.* 每次我想打電話給他,總是有人在講話。***as ~ as not; more ~ than not,*** very frequently: 常常;極常;屢屢: *During foggy weather the trains are late more ~ than not.* 有霧的時候火車常常誤點。***every so ~,*** from time to time. 時時。***once too ~,*** once more than is wise, safe, etc: 又一次;再一次;次數太多(即超過明智、安全等的限度,而發生問題): *He exceeded the speed limit once too ~ and was fined £50.* 他又一次超速,被罰了五十英鎊。

ogle /ˈəʊgl ; ˈogl̩/ *vi, vt* [VP3A, 6A] ~ ***(at),*** look at (suggesting lust or longing): 色迷迷地看;向…送秋波;向…拋媚眼: *ogling all the pretty girls.* 色迷迷地看著所有漂亮的女郎。

ogre /ˈəʊgə(r) ; ˈogɚ/ *n* [C] (in fables) cruel man-eating giant. (寓言中)殘忍的吃人巨妖。**ogress** /ˈəʊgres ; ˈogrɛs/ *n* female ~. 女的吃人巨妖。**ˈ~·ish** /-ɪʃ ; -ɪʃ/ *adj* like an ~. 似吃人巨妖的;兇暴的;可怕的。

oh /əʊ ; o/ *int* exclamation of surprise, fear, etc. 啊;噢;呀(表示驚訝、恐懼等的驚歎詞)。

ohm /əʊm ; om/ *n* [C] unit of electrical resistance (symbol Ω). 歐姆(電阻的單位,符號Ω)。

oho /əʊˈhəʊ ; oˈho/ *int* exclamation of surprise or triumph. 表示驚奇或得意的感歎詞。

oil /ɔɪl ; ɔɪl/ *n* [C, U] **1** (sorts of) (usu easily burning) liquid which does not mix with water, obtained from animals (eg *whale-oil*), plants (*coconut oil, ˌolive-ˈoil, oil of peppermint, essential oils*), or found in rock underground (*mineral oil, petroleum*): (各種)油類;油(通常爲易燃的液體,不與水混合,取自動物者,如鯨油 whale-oil, 取自植物者,如椰子油 coconut oil, 橄欖油 olive-oil, 薄荷油 oil of peppermint, 揮發油 essential oils, 或自地下岩層中所採得者,如礦物油 mineral oil, 石油 petroleum): *cod-liver oil;* 魚肝油; *salad oil;* 沙拉油; *hair oil.* 髮油。**2** (phrases) (片語) ***burn the midnight oil,*** sit up late at night to study, etc. 讀書等直到深夜;開夜車。***paint in oils,*** paint with oil-colours (⇨ below). 用油畫顏料畫(參看下列之 oil-colours)。***pour oil on the flame(s),*** make anger more intense, make a quarrel more bitter, etc. 火上加油;煽動。***pour oil on troubled waters,*** act or speak in such a way as to end quarrelling, bitterness, etc. 調解爭端;勸人息怒。***smell of the midnight oil,*** bear marks of study (as if done late at night by the light of an oil-lamp). 有用功的痕跡(似乎曾在油燈旁熬夜用功)。***strike oil,*** find petroleum in the ground by sinking a shaft, etc; (fig) become very prosperous or successful. 掘得石油;(喻)發大財;極爲成功。**3** (compounds) (複合字) **ˈoil-bearing** *adj* (eg rock strata) containing mineral oil. (例如岩層)含(礦)油的。**ˈoil-burner** *n* engine, ship, heater, etc that uses oil as fuel. 以油爲燃料的發動機、船隻、生熱器等。**ˈoil-cake** *n* [U] cattle food made from seeds after the oil has been pressed out. 油渣餅;油粕(植物種子經榨油後製成的家畜飼料)。**ˈoil-can** *n* can with a long nozzle, used for oiling machinery. 加油壺;

加油器。 **'oil·cloth** *n* [U] cotton material waterproofed and used as a covering for shelves, etc. (防水的)油布。 **'oil-colours, oils** *n pl* paints made by mixing colouring matter in oil. 油畫顏料。 **'oil-field** *n* area where petroleum is found. 油田(發現有石油的地區)。 **'oil-fired** *adj* (eg of a furnace) burning oil as fuel: (指火爐等)以油爲燃料的; 燒油的: *oil-fired central heating.* 燒油的中央暖氣系統。 **'oil-painting** *n* [U] art of painting in oil-colours; [C] picture painted in oil-colours. 油畫術; 油畫。 **'oil-palm** *n* tropical palm tree yielding oil. 油棕櫚(產油的熱帶棕櫚樹)。 **'oil-paper** *n* paper made transparent and waterproof by being treated with oil. (用油處理透明而防水的)油紙。 **'oil-rig** *n* structure and machinery for drilling (eg in the sea-bed) for oil. 鑽油機械裝置(如用於海底者)。 ⇨ derrick (2). **'oil-silk** *n* silk cloth treated with oil to make it air-tight and water-tight, used for making raincoats, etc. 油質綢(上油的綢布，不透氣不漏水，用以製雨衣等)。 **'oil-skin** *n* [C, U] (coat etc, made of) cloth treated with oil to make it waterproof; (*pl*) suit of clothes made of this material, as worn by sailors, etc. 油衣; 防水布; (複)(水手等所穿的)一套油布衣; 防水衣。 **'oil-slick,** ⇨ slick. **'oil-tanker** *n* ship, large vehicle, for carrying oil (esp petroleum). 油輪; 運油車。 **'oil-well** *n* well from which petroleum is obtained. 油井。 □ *vt* [VP6A] put oil on or into (eg to make a machine run smoothly): 加油於; 上油在; 塗油於: *oil a lock / bicycle;* 給鎖(自行車)上油; *oil the wheels / works,* (fig) make things go smoothly by being tactful; (喻)用圓滑手段使事情順利進展; *oil* (more usu 較常用 *grease*) *sb's palm,* give him a bribe. 賄賂某人。 **oiled** *adj* (usu 通常作 *well-oiled*) (sl) rather drunk. (俚)相當醉的。

an oil-tanker

oiler /'ɔɪlə(r) ; 'ɔɪlə/ *n* **1** ship built for carrying oil; oil-tanker. 油輪; 運油車。 **2** oil-can for oiling machinery. 加油壺; 加油器。 **3** person who oils machinery, eg in the engine-room of a ship. 爲機器加潤滑油的人(例如船上輪機室中的油工)。

oily /'ɔɪlɪ ; 'ɔɪlɪ/ *adj* (-ier, -iest) **1** of or like oil: 油的; 似油的: *an ~ liquid.* 油質液體。 **2** covered or soaked with oil: 塗有油的; 浸過油的: *~ fingers.* 沾着油的手指。 **3** (of speech or manner) too smooth; fawning; trying by fawning to win favour. (指言語或態度)太圓滑的; 奉承的; 拍馬屁討好的; 油腔滑調的。 **'oili·ness** *n* also ⇨ oleaginous.

oint·ment /'ɔɪntmənt ; 'ɔɪntmənt/ *n* [C, U] (sorts of) medicinal paste made from oil or fat and used on the skin (to heal injuries or roughness, or as a cosmetic). (各種)藥膏; 油膏。

okapi /əʊ'kɑːpɪ ; o'kɑpɪ/ *n* rare forest ruminant animal of Central Africa. 奧卡皮(產於非洲中部的一種罕見森林反芻動物)。

okay /ˌəʊ'keɪ ; 'o'ke/ (abbr 略作 **OK**) *adj, adv* (colloq) all right; correct; approved. (俗)好; 對的; 行。 □ *vt* [VP6A] agree to; approve of. 同意; 贊成; 贊同。 □ *n* agreement; sanction: 同意; 許可: *Have they given you their OK?* 他們同意你了嗎?

okra /'əʊkrə ; 'okrə/ *n* (tropical and semi-tropical plant with) edible green seed pods used as a vegetable. 秋葵(熱帶及亞熱帶植物); 秋葵莢(呈綠色，作蔬菜食用)。

old /əʊld ; old/ *adj* (-er, -est) ⇨ also elder¹, eldest. **1** (with a period of time, and with *how*) of age: (與一段時間，或與 how 連用)年歲的: *He's forty years old.* 他四十歲。 *At fifteen years old he left home to become a sailor.* 他十五歲時離家去當水手。 *How old are you?* 你幾歲了? *He is old enough to know better.* 他已經大了，應該更懂事些。 *Ought a seven-year-old child to be able to read?* 七歲的小孩應該會讀書嗎? **2** (contrasted with *young*) having lived a long time; no longer young or middle-aged: (與 young 相對)老的; 年老的; 年長的: *Old people cannot be so active as young people.* 老年人不能像年輕人那麼活躍。 *He's far too old for a young girl like you to marry.* 他太老了，像你這樣年輕的女孩子不適於嫁給他。 *What will he do when he grows / is / gets old?* 當他老的時候，他要做什麼? **the old,** old people. 老人們。 **young and old,** everyone. 每個人; 無論老少。 **old age,** the latter part of life. 晚年; 老年。 **old age pension,** (abbr 略作 **OAP**), (or 或作 *retirement pension*) pension paid by the State to old persons. (國家發給老年人的)養老金。 Hence, 由此產生, **old age pensioner** *n* (or 或作 *senior citizen*). 領養老金者; 領退休金者。 **the old man,** (colloq) (俗) **(a)** one's husband or father. 老頭(指丈夫或父親)。 **(b)** (among sailors) the captain of a ship. (水手間用語)船長。 **the old woman,** (colloq) one's wife. (俗)老婆(指妻子)。 **ˌold-'womanish** *adj* fussy and timid. 大驚小怪而膽怯的。 **an old maid,** ⇨ maid. **ˌold-'maidish** *adj* precise, tidy, fidgety. 嚴謹、整潔、煩躁的。 **3** (contrasted with *new, modern, up-to-date*) belonging to past times; having been in existence or use for a long time: (與 new, modern, up-to-date 相對)古老的; 舊的; 用久的: *old customs / families / civilizations;* 古老的習俗(家庭，文明); *old houses / clothes.* 舊房子(衣服)。 ***one of the 'old school,*** conservative; old-fashioned. 保守的(人等); 舊派的; 守舊的; 老式的。 **the Old World,** Europe, Asia and Africa. 舊世界(指歐、亞、非三洲)。 **ˌold-'fashioned** *adj* **(a)** out of date: 舊式的; 老式的: *old-fashioned styles / clothes.* 老式的樣子(衣服)。 **(b)** keeping to old ways, ideas, customs, etc: 守舊的: *an old-fashioned aunt;* 守舊的姑媽; *an old-fashioned child,* one who behaves like a much older person. 老成的孩子。 **(c)** (of glances) reproving: (指目光)譴責的: *She gave him an old-fashioned look.* 她瞪他一眼。 □ *n* (US) kind of cocktail made with whiskey. (美)用威士忌調成的鷄尾酒。 **old fogey** *n* ⇨ fogey. **old hat,** (colloq) out of date. (俗)舊式的; 老式的; 過時的。 **'old-time** *adj* belonging to, typical of, past times: 古時的; 往昔的: *old-time dances.* 古時的舞蹈。 **'old-world** *adj* belonging to, typical of, past times; not modern: 古時的; 老式的; 古色古香的: *an old-world cottage / garden.* 老式的小屋(花園)。 **4** long known or familiar: 熟悉的; 親密的: *an old friend of mine,* one who has been a friend for a long time (but not necessarily old in years). 我的一個老朋友。 **Old Glory,** used by Americans of the flag of the US. 美國國旗(美國人用語)。 **5** former; previous (but not necessarily old in years). 從前的; 早先的; 以前的(不一定是古老的)。 **'old boy / girl,** former member of the school in question. 校友; 畢業生。 **the 'old country,** one's mother country (used esp when one has left it to settle elsewhere). 祖國(尤爲定居於國外者之用語)。 **the / one's old school,** the school one attended as a boy / girl. 幼年時代所上的學校; 母校。 **the / one's old school tie, (a)** tie worn by former pupils. 昔時小學生所結的領帶。 **(b)** feeling of solidarity, wish to give mutual help, among former pupils of the same school or similar types of school. (同一小學或同類小學)校友間之團結互助感。 **6** having much experience or practice: 老經驗的; 老練的: *a man who is old in diplomacy.* 富有外交經驗的人; 外交界元老。 **the old guard,** long-standing faithful supporters. 長期的忠實擁護者。 **old offender,** person who has often been convicted of crime. 累犯; 慣犯。 **an old hand (at sth),**

person with long experience. (做某事的)老手;熟手。 **old-'timer** *n* person who has for many years lived in a place, been associated with (a club, occupation, etc). 久居一地、久爲會員或久任一職的人;老資格的人;老前輩。 ***come the old soldier (over sb),*** (colloq) claim, because of long experience, to have superior knowledge or ability. (俗)因有長久經驗而(向某人)聲稱具有較高的學識或能力;(對某人)擺老資格。 **7** (colloq) used in addressing persons, and with names (and nicknames) giving intimacy, or in joking style: (俗)用於稱呼而與姓名(或綽號)連用,表示親切或戲謔: *'Good old John!'* '老約翰!' *'Listen, old man.'* '老兄,請聽。' *'Hullo, old thing!'* '喂,老兄!' ***the 'old one; the old gentleman; old Harry/Nick/Scratch,*** the devil. 惡魔;老魔頭。 **8** (sl) used as an intensive: (俚)用於加重語氣: *We're having a high old time,* a very good time. 我們過得非常愉快。 *Any old thing* (= Anything whatever) *will do.* 什麼東西都行。 □ *n* the past: 往昔;昔時;古時: *in days of old;* 在往昔的日子裡; *the men of old.* 昔時的人。 **old·ish** /-ɪʃ; -ɪʃ/ *adj* rather old. 稍老的;稍舊的。

olden /'əʊldən; 'oldn̩/ *adj* (archaic, liter) of a former age: (古,文)往昔的;古老的: *in ~ times/days.* 往昔(昔日)。

old·ster /'əʊldstə(r); 'oldstɚ/ *n* (colloq) (opposite to *youngster*) old person: (俗)老人 (爲 youngster 之相反字): *Some of us ~s have more energy than the youngsters.* 咱們有些老人比年輕小伙子更有精力。

ole·agi·nous /ˌəʊlɪ'ædʒɪnəs; ˌolɪ'ædʒənəs/ *adj* having properties of oil; producing oil; fatty; greasy. 油質的;產油的;多脂肪的;油膩的。

ole·an·der /ˌəʊlɪ'ændə(r); ˌolɪ'ændɚ/ *n* [C] evergreen shrub with tough leaves and red, pink or white flowers growing in clusters. 夾竹桃。

ol·fac·tory /ɒl'fæktərɪ; ɑl'fæktərɪ/ *adj* concerned with smelling: 嗅覺的: *the ~ nerves.* 嗅覺神經。

oli·garchy /'ɒlɪgɑːkɪ; 'ɑlɪˌgɑrkɪ/ *n* (*pl* -chies) [C, U] (country with) government by a small group of all-powerful persons; such a group. 寡頭政治;行寡頭政治的國家;寡頭政治的執政團。 **oli·garch** /'ɒlɪgɑːk; 'ɑlɪˌgɑrk/ *n* member of an ~. 寡頭政治的執政者。

ol·ive /'ɒlɪv; 'ɑlɪv/ *n* **1** ⇨ the illus at tree. 參看 tree 之插圖。 **'~(-tree),** (evergreen tree common in S Europe bearing a) small oval fruit with a hard stone-like seed and a bitter taste, yellowish-green when unripe and bluish-black when ripe; used for pickling, to be eaten as a relish, and for oil, **(ˌ~-'oil),** which is used for cooking, dressing salads, etc. 橄欖樹(盛產於南歐);橄欖(呈橢圓形,果核堅如石,味苦,未成熟時爲黃綠色,成熟時呈藍黑色;用之醃泡以製成美味食品,所製成之橄欖油 olive-oil 用於烹調、調生菜等)。 **2** leaf, branch or wreath of ~ as an emblem of peace. 作爲和平象徵的橄欖葉、橄欖枝或橄欖枝葉圈。 ***ˌhold out the '~-branch,*** show that one is ready to discuss peace-making. 表示願意講和。 □ *adj* the colour of the unripe fruit, yellowish-green or yellowish-brown. 橄欖色的;黃綠色的;黃褐色的。

Olym·piad /ə'lɪmpɪæd; o'lɪmpɪˌæd/ *n* period of four years between celebrations of the Olympic Games. 兩次奧林匹克運動會之間的四年期間。

Olym·pian /ə'lɪmpɪən; o'lɪmpɪən/ *adj* (of manners, etc) magnificent; god-like: (指儀態等)高貴的;莊嚴的;似神的: *~ calm.* 莊嚴的靜肅。 □ *n* one of the greater gods of ancient Greece; person with god-like qualities. 奧林巴斯神(古希臘重要神祇之一);有神性的人。

Olym·pic /ə'lɪmpɪk; o'lɪmpɪk/ *adj* **the ~ Games,** **(a)** the contests held at Olympia in Greece in ancient times. 古時在希臘奧林比亞舉行的競賽會。 **(b)** the international athletic competitions held in modern times every four years in a different country. (近代每四年在不同國家舉行的)世界運動會。

om·buds·man /'ɒmbʊdzmæn; 'ɑmbədzmən/ *n* **the O~,** (in GB officially called 在英國正式名稱爲 *Parliamentary Commissioner*) experienced person having authority to inquire into and pronounce upon grievances of citizens against public authorities. 國會民間冤情調查委員(經驗豐富、有權調查並斷定人民對政府行政當局的訴願者)。

omega /'əʊmɪgə *US:* əʊ'megə; o'mɛgə/ *n* the last letter (Ω) of the Greek alphabet, ⇨ App 4; final development. 希臘字母中最末一個字母(Ω)(參看附錄四);終局;結局。 ***Alpha and O~,*** the beginning and the end. 始與終;首尾;始末。

om·elette, om·elet /'ɒmlɪt; 'ɑmlɪt/ *n* [C] eggs beaten together and fried, often flavoured with cheese or containing herbs, etc or (*sweet ~*) jam, sugar. 煎蛋捲(常常以乳酪作調味,或以香草等作餡;甜煎蛋捲 sweet omelet 則以果醬、糖等作餡)。

omen /'əʊmen; 'omɪn/ *n* [C, U] (thing, happening, regarded as a) sign of sth good or warning of evil fortune: 徵兆;預兆;視爲預兆之事物: *an ~ of success;* 成功的預兆; *an event of good/bad ~.* 一件被視爲好(壞)徵兆的事。 □ *vt* [VP6A] be an ~ of. 爲…的徵兆;顯出…的預兆。

om·in·ous /'ɒmɪnəs; 'ɑmənəs/ *adj* of bad omen; threatening: 惡兆的;不祥的: *an ~ silence;* 一陣不祥的靜寂; *~ of disaster.* 預示災禍的。 **~·ly** *adv*

omission /ə'mɪʃn; o'mɪʃən/ *n* **1** [U] act of omitting, leaving out or undone: 省略;刪除;遺漏: *sins of ~,* leaving undone those things that ought to be done. 該做的事而未做之過失;疏忽罪。 **2** [C] sth that is omitted. 省略之事物;刪除之事物;遺漏之事物。

omit /ə'mɪt; o'mɪt/ *vt* (-tt-) **1** [VP7A, 6C] ***~ to do/doing sth,*** fail: 疏忽;怠忽: *~ to do/~ doing a piece of work.* 忘記做一件事(漏做一件事)。 **2** [VP6A] fail to include; leave out: 遺漏;省略: *This chapter may be ~ted.* 這一章可以省掉。

om·ni·bus /'ɒmnɪbəs; 'ɑmnəˌbʌs/ *n* (*pl* ~es /-bəsɪz; -bəsɪz/) **1** (former name for a) bus; (in names): (以前的名稱)公共汽車(用於名稱中): *The ˌMidland 'O~ Co.* 中部公共汽車公司。 **2** (attrib) for, including, many purposes: (形容用法)爲着許多目的的;包含多項目標的: *an ~ volume,* a large book in which a number of books, eg by the same author, are reprinted. 彙編;選集。

om·nip·otence /ɒm'nɪpətəns; ɑm'nɪpətəns/ *n* [U] infinite power: 全能: *the ~ of God.* 上帝的全能。 **om·nip·otent** /-ənt; -ənt/ *adj* having infinite power: 全能的: *the O~,* God. 全能者(上帝)。

om·niscience /ɒm'nɪsɪəns; ɑm'nɪʃəns/ *n* [U] (formal) infinite knowledge. (正式用語)全知;無所不知。 **om·niscient** /-sɪənt; -ʃənt/ *adj* having infinite knowledge. 全知的;無所不知的。

om·niv·or·ous /ɒm'nɪvərəs; ɑm'nɪvərəs/ *adj* (formal) eating all kinds of food; (fig) reading all kinds of books, etc: (正式用語)什麼都吃的;雜食的;(喻)無所不讀的: *an ~ reader.* 無所不讀的讀者。

on¹ /ɒn; ɑn/ *adverbial particle* (For special uses with *on* as an *adverbial particle* such as *go on, go on sth,* ⇨ the *v* entries.) (on 作副詞接語用之特殊用法,如 go on, go on something 等,參看各動詞。) **1** (expressing the idea of progress, advance, continued activity; ⇨ *v* entries for special uses): (表示進展、向前、繼續活動的觀念;特殊用法參看各動詞): *Come on!* 來呀! *They hurried on.* 他們匆匆前進。 *I will follow on,* come after you. 我會跟上來的。 *He's getting on in years,* growing old. 他漸漸老了。 *The war still went on,* did not end. 戰爭仍在進行中。 *How can you work on* (= continue working) *so long without a rest?* 你怎麼能不休息而繼續工作那麼久? *On with the show!* Let the show begin! Let the show continue! 開始表演!繼續表演! ***and 'so on,*** and other things of the same kind; et cetera. 等等。 ***later on,*** at, during, a later time. 後來;過些時。 ***on and on,*** without stopping: 不停地: *We walked on and on.* 我們不停地行走。 **2** (corresponding in meaning to on²(1)): (相當於 on² 第1義): *On* *with your coat,* Put it on. 穿上你的外衣。*Your hat is not on straight.* 你的帽子沒有戴正。*He had nothing on,* was naked. 他什麼也沒穿。*Has he got his spectacles on?* Is he wearing them? 他戴眼鏡了嗎？ **on to, onto** *prep* to a position on: 達於…上;向而及於: *She fainted and fell on to the floor.* 她暈倒在地板上。*The actor stepped onto the stage.* 那演員走上舞台。*We ran out of the sea and on to the beach.* 我們跑出海水,跑上海灘。 **3** (contrasted with off²(3)) (與 off² 第 3 義相對) **(a)** in action; in use; functioning; flowing, running, etc: 行動中;使用中;操作中;流動中: *The lights were all full on,* giving their maximum light. 燈光全亮着。*Someone has left the bathroom tap on,* running. 有人沒關掉洗澡間的水龍頭。 *I can smell gas—is one of the taps on,* is gas escaping from one of them? 我聞到煤氣味 —— 是不是有一個煤氣栓開着？ *Be sure the handbrake is on before you leave the car.* 你離開車子以前,務必要拉手煞車。*The performance is on,* has begun. 表演已經開始了。*The strike of postal workers is still on,* has not ended yet. 郵政工作者的罷工仍在進行中。**(b)** available or procurable when or if needed: 需要時可獲得的;可得到的: *Is the water on yet?* Is a supply available from the mains? 水管接通了嗎？ **4** (combined with *be* and *have* in various meanings): (與 be 和 have 連用,表各種含義): *What's on?* What's the programme? What's happening? 有什麼節目？發生了什麼事？ *What's on* (= What films are being shown) *at the local cinema this week?* 這個星期本地電影院上演什麼片子？ *There's nothing on tomorrow, is there,* eg no meeting I ought to attend, no engagement I ought to carry out? 明天沒事兒,是嗎？ *Have you anything on this evening,* any engagements, plans, etc? 你今晚有事兒嗎？ ***be 'on about sth,*** (colloq) talk or grumble about it: (俗)談論;抱怨: *What's he on about now?* 他現在談些什麼？ ***be 'on at sb,*** (colloq) nag or pester him (*about* or *to do* sth). (俗)嘮叨地責罵或糾纏(與 about 或不定詞連用)。 ***be 'on to sb/sth,*** **(a)** be in contact with: 與…連絡: *I've been on to the President, and he told me that....* 我曾與總統連絡,他告訴我說…。**(b)** be aware of the plans, actions, importance etc of; be in pursuit of: 知曉…的計畫,行動,重要性等;追蹤: *be on to a conspiracy/scandal/murderer.* 得悉一陰謀(得悉一醜行;追蹤一兇手)。 ***be ,on to a good 'thing,*** be lucky or successful. 幸運;成功。 **5** towards: 向着;朝向: *a ship broadside on to the dock gates,* with its side facing towards the gates; 舷側朝向船塢閘門的一條船; *end on,* ie with the end forward. 末端向前。

on² /ɒn; ɑn/ *prep* **1** supported by; fastened or attached to; covering or forming part of (a surface); lying against; in contact with: 支承在…上;繫於;附於;蓋在(表面);構成(表面)一部份;靠在;與…接觸;在…上面: *a carpet on the floor;* 鋪在地板上的地毯; *the jug on the table;* 桌上的水罐; *pictures on the wall;* 掛在牆上的圖畫; *the words (written) on the blackboard;* (寫)在黑板上的字; *flies on the ceiling;* 天花板上的蒼蠅; *a blister on the sole of my foot;* 我脚掌上的一個水泡; *put a roof on the shed;* 給棚子蓋一個頂; *sit on the grass;* 坐在草地上; *floating on the water;* 漂在水上; *write on paper;* 寫在紙上; *hang sth on a peg/a nail;* 掛某物於釘子上; *stick a stamp on the envelope;* 貼一張郵票於信封上; *live on the Continent,* 住在歐洲大陸上, Cf 參較 live *in* Europe; 住在歐洲; *have a hat on one's head/a ring on one's finger;* 頭上戴着一頂帽子 (手指上戴着一個戒指); *carry a coat on/over one's arm;* 手臂上掛着一件外衣; *be/go on board a ship;* 在船上(上船); *have lunch on the train;* 在火車上吃午餐; *continued on page five,* 下接第五頁, Cf 參較 *in* a book, magazine, etc. *Have you a match/any money on you,* ie in your pockets, etc? 你(口袋裡等)帶了火柴(錢)沒？ **2** (indicating time) (指時間) **(a)** *on Sunday(s);* 在星期日; *on the 1st of May;* 在五月一日; *on the evening of May the first,* 在五月一日晚上, Cf 參較 *in* the evening; *on New Year's Day/Eve;* 在元旦(除夕); *on a sunny day in July,* ⇨ one¹(4); 在七月裡一個晴朗的日子; *on that day;* 在那一天; *on this occasion.* 在這一次。**(b)** at the time of: 在…之時: *on the death of his parents,* when they died; 在他父母親逝世的時候; *on my arrival home;* 在我到家的時候;當我抵家時; *payable on demand;* 來取即付的;見票即付的;(指票據)即期的; *on (my) asking for information.* 在(我)詢問消息時。**(c)** *on time, on the minute,* ie punctually. 準時。 **3** about; concerning: 關於;論及: *speak/lecture/write on international affairs;* 演說(演講,撰寫)國際形勢; *a lecture on Shakespeare;* 關於莎士比亞的演講; *be keen/bent/determined/set on sth/on doing sth.* 渴望(一心;決心;決定)要某物(作某事)。 **4** (indicating membership): (表示爲…之一份子): *He is on the committee/the jury/the staff.* 他是委員會 (陪審團,幕僚) 中之一員。*He's on 'The Daily Telegraph',* is a member of the staff of this newspaper. 他在 '每日電訊報' 工作。 **5** (indicating direction) towards: (指方向)向: *marching on the enemy's capital;* 向敵人首都進軍; *turn one's back on sb;* 不理睬某人; *smile/frown on sb;* 向某人微笑(皺眉頭); *draw a knife on sb,* ie to attack him; 拔刀攻擊某人; *a ship drifting on(to) the rocks;* 漂向礁石的船; *hit sb on the head,* (note: not *his* head); 擊打某人的頭(注意:此語中不可用 his head); *give sb a box/blow on the ear.* 打某人一個耳光。 **6** (expressing the basis, ground or reason for sth): (表示某事物的根據或理由): *on this/that/no account;* 爲了這個緣故(爲了那個緣故;無緣無故); *a story based on fact;* 根據事實寫成的故事; *have sth on good authority;* 從可靠方面獲悉某事; *act on your lawyer's advice;* 依照你的律師的意見行事; *arrested on a charge of theft;* 被控偷竊而逮捕的; *retire on a pension;* 領取養老金而退休; *on penalty of death;* 以死刑作爲懲罰; *on an average;* 平均算來; *swear sth on the Bible;* 手按聖經發誓; *be on one's oath/one's honour.* 發誓(以人格保證)。 **7** (indicating a charge or imposition): (指費用或徵稅): *put a tax on tobacco;* 徵煙草稅; *charge interest on money;* 索取利息; *place a strain on the economy.* 加重經濟負擔。 **8** (indicating proximity) close to; against: (表示接近)接近;靠近: *Henley-on-Thames;* 泰晤士河邊的恆利城; *a town on the coast;* 海邊的一個城市; *a house on the main road;* 大路邊的一幢房子; *a village on the frontier;* 在邊境的一個村莊; *on both sides of the river;* 在河的兩岸; *on my right/left;* 在我右(左)邊; *just on* (= almost) *2 o'clock;* 差不多兩點鐘; *just on a year ago;* 差不多一年前; *just on £10.* 差不多十英鎊。 **9** (followed by a *n,* or *adj*) (indicating an activity, action, manner, state): (後接名詞或形容詞,表示活動、行動、態度、情況): *on business,* engaged in business; 因商務;因公;有事; *on holiday;* 度假; *on tour,* touring; 在旅行; *go on an errand;* 辦差事;跑腿; *on the way;* 在途中; *on the sly,* in a sly manner; 秘密地;暗暗地; *buy sth on the cheap,* (colloq) at a low price; (俗)廉價買進某物; *on his best behaviour,* behaving very well; 表現他最好的行爲;行爲檢點; *be on the look-out for sb,* watching for him; 注意某人; *on fire,* burning; 着火;失火; *on sale;* 出售; *on loan.* 出借。 **10** added to: 加添: *suffer disaster on disaster/insult on insult.* 遭受一次又一次的災禍(一次又一次的侮辱)。

once /wʌns; wʌns/ *adv* **1** (usu end position) for one time, on one occasion, only: (通常置於句末)一次: *I have been there ~.* 我到過那兒一次。*This clock needs winding ~ a week.* 這個時鐘一星期只需要上一次發條。*He goes to see his parents in Wales ~ (in) every six months.* 他每六個月去威爾斯看他父母一次。*We go to the cinema ~ a week/a fortnight,* every week/every two weeks.

我們每星期(每兩星期)去看一次電影。~ **more,** again; another time. 再一次;再來一次。~ **or twice;** ~ **and again;** ~ **in a while,** now and again; occasionally; a few times. 一兩次;一再;有時;偶爾。**(for) this** ~**; (just) for** ~**,** on this one occasion only, as an exception. 只此一次(下不爲例)。~ **(and) for all,** ⇨ all[5](5). ~ **in a blue moon,** ⇨ blue[1]. **2** (often mid position) at some indefinite time in the past; formerly: (常置於句子中間)曾經;從前;昔時: *He* ~ *lived in Persia.* 他從前住在波斯。*This novel was* ~ *very popular but nobody reads it today.* 這本小說曾經一度很受人歡迎,但是現在沒有人讀它了。ˌ~ **upon a ˈtime,** (in story-telling style): (講故事用語): *O*~ *upon a time there was a giant with two heads.* 從前有個兩頭巨人。**3** (in negative, conditional or indefinite clauses) ever; at all; even for one time: (用於否定子句、條件子句或不定子句中)曾;全然;一旦: *He didn't* ~ *offer/He never* ~ *offered to help.* 他從沒有提供過幫助。*O*~ (= If you ~, As soon as) *you understand this rule, you will have no further difficulty.* 你一旦瞭解這個規則,就不會再有困難。 **4** **at** ~**, (a)** without delay; immediately: 立刻;馬上: *I'm leaving for Rome at* ~. 我馬上就去羅馬。*Come here at* ~! 立刻到這兒來!**(b)** at the same time: 同時: *Don't all speak at* ~! 不要全體同時說!*I can't do two things at* ~. 我不能同時做兩件事。*The book is at* ~ *interesting and instructive.* 這本書既有趣又有益。**all at** ~**,** suddenly: 突然: *All at* ~ *I saw a rabbit dart across the road.* 突然間我看到一隻兔子急速越過道路。**get/give sb/sth the** ~**-over,** (colloq) get/give sb/sth a rapid inspection or examination. (俗)被迅速檢查一遍;將某人(某物)迅速檢查一遍。

on·com·ing /ˈɒnkʌmɪŋ; ˈɑnˌkʌmɪŋ/ *adj* advancing; approaching: 即將來臨的;接近的: *the* ~ *shift,* the shift (of workers) coming on duty (in a factory); (工廠中的)下一班(工人); ~ *traffic.* 迎面而來的行人車輛。□ *n* approach: 來臨: *the* ~ *of winter.* 冬天的來臨。

one[1] /wʌn; wʌn/ *numeral adj, pron* **1** the number 1, ⇨ App 4. 一;一個(參看附錄四)。**(a)** as in the series: 如用於一系列數目中: *one pen, two pencils and three books;* 一枝鋼筆,兩枝鉛筆,三本書; as in: 如用於下列場合: *one from twenty leaves nineteen;* 二十減一剩下十九; *one is enough;* 一個够了; *one o'clock;* 一點鐘; as in: 如用於下列場合: ˌ*twenty-ˈone,* ˌ*thirty-ˈone,* etc. 二十一、三十一等。**(b)** as in: 如用於下列場合: *one hundred, one thousand, one million;* 一百,一千,一百萬; *one half, one third,* etc. 一半,三分之一等。(Except in formal, precise or legal style, *a year and a half* or *eighteen months* is preferred to *one and a half years; a million and a half* to *one and a half millions; a pound of tea* to *one pound of tea.*) (除非用於正式的、精確的或法律的文體, a year and a half 或 eighteen months 較 one and a half years 爲佳; a million and a half 較 one and a half millions 爲佳; a pound of tea 較 one pound of tea 爲佳。) **(c)** as in: 如用於下列場合: *one pound ten,* one pound and ten pence. 一鎊十辨士。 **2** (as a *n,* with *pl* ones) the symbol or figure 1: (作爲名詞,複數用 ones) 表示'一'的符號或數字: *a row of ones,* ie 1 1 1 1. 一排的'一' (卽 1 1 1 1)。 **3** as in: 如用於下列場合: *Book One, Chapter One,* the first book, the first chapter. 第一册,第一章。 **4** as in: 如用於下列場合: *one day/morning/afternoon/evening/night,* 有一天(早上,下午,晚上,夜晚), (similar in function to the *indef art,* but with the difference that the *prep 'on'* is used before the *indef art.* 此種用法其功用與不定冠詞相似,所不同者,不定冠詞前應加介詞 on。⇨ on[2](2a). Cf 參較 *one summer evening* and *on a summer evening; one morning in June* and *on a June morning*). **5** (*One* is used to indicate a contrast (expressed or implied) with *the other,* or *another,* or *other(s)*): (one 用以表示與 the other, 或 another, 或 other(s) 的對比(表明的或暗示的)): *The two girls are so much alike that it is difficult for strangers to tell (the) one from the other.* 這兩個女孩是如此相像,以致陌生人難以辨別她們。*He did not know which to admire more, the one's courage or the other's determination.* 他不知道比較欽佩何者,那個人的勇氣呢,還是另一個人的決心。*Well, that's one way of doing it, but there are other and better ways.* 不錯,那是做這件事的一種方法,但是還有其他更好的方法。*I, for one, don't like the idea,* suggesting 'and there may also be others who do not like it'. 拿我來說,我就不喜歡這個主意(暗示可能還有其他的人不喜歡它)。**for ˈone thing,** for one reason (out of several or many): 擧個理由;一則: *I can't help you. For one thing, I've no money.* 我不能幫你的忙,理由之一是我沒有錢。 **6** (always stressed; used for emphasis): (總是重讀;用以加强語氣): *There's only ˈone way to do it.* 做這事只有一個方法。*That's the ˈone thing needed.* 那是唯一需要的東西。*No ˈone of you could lift it,* ie two or more of you would be needed. 你們當中沒有人能單獨把它擧起來(卽需要兩個或更多的人才能擧起)。*They went forward as one man,* ie all together, in a body. 他們一同前進。 **7** (before a family name, with or without a title; ⇨ a[2](9)) (用在姓氏之前,可以和或不和稱呼連用; 參看 a[2] 第9義) a certain: 某一: *I heard the news from one (Mr) Smith,* (dated formal) from a certain person named Smith. (過時正式用語)我從一位史密斯(先生)那兒聽到這消息。(Note that if *one* is replaced by the *indef art* a title must be used: 注意:假如以不定冠詞代替 one, 則必須用稱呼: *A Mr Smith has called to see you* 有位史密斯先生來過,他要見你). **8** (as *adj*) the same: (作形容詞用)同樣的: *They all went off in one direction.* 他們都往同一方向去了。**be at ˈone (with sb),** be in agreement: 意見一致; 同意: *I'm at one with you on this subject/We are at one on this subject,* Our opinions are the same. 關於這問題,我和你的意見是一致的(我們對這問題的意見是一致的)。**It's all one (to sb),** It's all the same, it makes no difference: (對某人)都是一樣,沒有什麼不同: *It's all one to me whether you go or don't go.* 你去不去,對我都是一樣。**one and the same,** (emph for) the same: 一樣的 (the same 的强調用法): *One and the same idea occurred to each of them.* 他們每一個人都想起同樣的念頭。**become one; be made one,** be united; be married. 團結一致; 結合; 結婚。 **9** (phrases) (片語) **one and all,** everyone. 每一個人。**(all) in one,** combined: 合在一起: *He is President, Chairman and Secretary in one.* 他一身兼董事長、主席和秘書三職。**one or two,** a few: 一兩個;一些: *I shall be away only one or two days.* 我只要離開這兒一兩天。**by ones and twos,** one or two at a time: 一次一兩個;三三兩兩: *People began to leave the meeting by ones and twos.* 人們開始三三兩兩地離開會場。**be one ˈup (on sb),** have an advantage over him, be one step ahead of him. (比某人)佔優勢;(比某人)領先一步。Hence, 由此產生, **ˌone-ˈup·man·ship** /-mənʃɪp; -mənˌʃɪp/ *n* technique of being one up. 佔優勢或領先的技巧。**ˌnumber ˈone,** (colloq) oneself; one's own interests: (俗)自己;自己的利益: *He's always thinking of 'number one',* of himself, his own welfare. 他總是想到自己(自己的利益)。**10** (with an *of* -adjunct) a single person or thing of the sort indicated or supplied (with *some, any, several,* etc for the *pl;* ⇨ a[2](3) and one[2](1)): (與 of 片語連用)表示同類中的一人或物(與 some, any, several 等連用表示多數): *One of my friends* (*pl* 複 *some* of my friends) *arrived late.* 我的朋友中有一個遲到了。*If one of them* (*pl* 複 *any* of them) *should need help....* 假如他們當中有一個需要幫助的話…。*I borrowed one of your books* (= a book of yours; *pl* 複 *some* of your books) *last week.* 上個星期我借了你的一本書。(Note the use of *his, her, herself* and *himself* in these

O

examples): (注意下面這些例句中的 his, her, herself, 及 himself 的用法): *One of the boys/girls lost his/her shoe.* 男(女)孩子中有一個丟了一隻鞋。 *One of the girls/boys has hurt herself/himself.* 女(男)孩子中有一個弄傷了自己。 **11** (compounds) (複合字) **ˌone-ˈarmed** *adj* having only one arm. 只有一隻手臂的;獨臂的。 **ˌone-armed ˈbandit** *n* (colloq) coin-operated gambling machine (also called 亦稱 a *fruit-machine*). (俗)吃角子老虎(一種投硬幣操作的賭博機器)。 **ˌone-ˈeyed** *adj* having only one eye. 只有一隻眼睛的;獨眼的。 **ˌone-ˈhorse** *adj* **(a)** drawn or worked by a single horse. 由一匹馬拖拉或工作的;單馬的。 **(b)** (fig, sl) poorly equipped: (喻,俚)簡陋的: *a one-horse town,* a small provincial town with few attractions, etc. 一個簡陋的小鎮。 **ˌone-iˈdea'd** *adj* possessed by a single idea. 只有一種思想的;心目中只有一個觀念的;思想狹隘的。 **ˌone-ˈsided** *adj* having one side only; occurring on one side only; partial; unfair; prejudiced: 只有一邊的;單方面的;偏袒的;不公平的;偏見的: *a one-sided argument;* 片面的議論; *a one-sided account of a quarrel.* 對於一場紛爭的片面之詞。 **ˈone-time** *adj* former: 從前的;昔時的: *a one-time politician.* 一位昔時的從政者。 **ˌone-track ˈmind** *n* one dominated by one interest, subject, etc. 偏狹的思想。 **ˌone-way ˈstreet** *n* street in which traffic may proceed in one direction only. 單行道。

one² /wʌn ; wʌn/ *indef pron* (used in place of a preceding or following *n* standing for a member of a class) (用以代替前述或後述名詞,代表同類中的一個) **1** (with an *of*-adjunct, indicating inclusion; equivalent to *among;* ⇨ a²(3); no corresponding *pl* word): (與 of 片語連用,表示包括在內之意;此處 of 相當於 among; 此種用法無相當的複數字): *Mr Smith is not one of* (= not numbered or included among) *my customers.* 史密斯先生並不是我的顧客之一。 Cf for *pl*: 參較複數用法: *Mr Green and Mr Smith are not customers of mine.* 格林先生和史密斯先生都不是我的顧客。 *This problem is one of great difficulty* (*pl*: *These problems are of great difficulty*). 這個問題是一個大難題(複:這些問題是大難題)。 *We have always treated her as one* (= as a member) *of the family* (*pl*: *We have always treated them as members of the family*). 我們總是把她當作家中一份子來看待(複: 我們總是把他們當作家裡人看待)。 *One of my friends was ill* (*pl*: *Some of my friends were ill*). 我的一個朋友病了(複:我有幾個朋友病了)。 ⇨ one¹(10). **2** (Cf *one* and *it*. *One* replaces a *n* modified by the *indef art* or a *pl n* modified by *some* or *any*. *It* replaces a *n* made definite in some way, eg a *n* modified by *the, this, that*): (參較 one 與 it。one 代替由不定冠詞所修飾的名詞或由 some 或 any 所修飾的複數名詞; it 代替經以某種方式所確定的名詞,例如由 the, this, that 所修飾的名詞): *I haven't a pen. Can you lend me one?* 我沒有鋼筆。你能借我一枝嗎? *I haven't any stamps. Will you please give me one?* 我沒有郵票。請給我一張好嗎? Cf 參較 *I'd like to look at that atlas. May I borrow it?* 我想看那本地圖集。我可以借它嗎? *Where's the railway timetable? Have you seen it?* 火車時間表在哪兒?你有沒有看到它? **3** (the *pron* 'one', *pl* 'ones', is used, in colloq style, equivalent to *that, those*): (代名詞 one, 複數爲 ones, 用於口語文體中相當於 that 與 those): *I drew my chair nearer to the one* (= to that) *on which Mary was sitting.* 我把我的椅子拉到靠近瑪莉坐的椅子旁邊。 *It's in that drawer—the one* (= that) *with the key in the lock.* 它是在那個抽屜裡——有鑰匙插在鎖孔的那一個。 *The students who do best in examinations are not always the ones* (= those) *with the best brains.* 考試考得最好的學生不一定都是聰明的學生。 **4** (when the *pron 'one'* is used after the *def art,* or after an *adj* (or a *n* used as an *adj*), it may be called a 'prop-word'. As an *adj* cannot stand alone for one or more members of a class, *one* is used to support or 'prop up' the *adj,* as in): (當代名詞 one 用於定冠詞之後,或形容詞(或當作形容詞的名詞) 之後,它可以稱爲'墊字'。由於形容詞不能單獨代表某一類中的一個或數個, one 就被用來支助或'支墊'那個形容詞,如下列所用者): *a better one;* 更好的一個; *that one;* 那個; *my old ones.* 我的幾個舊的。 *Your plan is a good one on paper.* 你的計畫在理論上是個好計畫。 *There's a right answer and a wrong one.* 有一個對的答案和一個錯的答案。 *Yours may be the right answer and mine the wrong one.* 你的答案可能是對的,而我的可能是錯的。 *The chance was too good a one to let pass.* 這是一個不能放過的好機會。 *He keeps his postage-stamps—he has some very rare ones—in a fire-proof safe.* 他把他的郵票——他有一些珍貴的郵票——放在防火的保險箱裡。 **5** (The 'prop-word' *one* is not used, except in colloquial style, after a possessive (eg *your, Mary's*) unless there is also an *adj.* It is not used after *own*): (除用於口語中外,'墊字' one 不可用於所有格如 your, Mary's 之後,除非還有一個形容詞。one 不可用於 own 之後): *This is my hat and that is my brother's.* 這頂帽子是我的,那頂是我哥哥(弟弟)的。Not: 不可寫作: *my brother's one. Tom's exercise book is neater than John's.* 湯姆的練習簿比約翰的整潔。Not: 不可寫作: *John's one. Do you rent the house or is it your own?* 那幢房子是你租的還是你自己的? Not: 不可寫作: *your own one.* (With an *adj*): (與形容詞連用): *My cheap camera seems to be just as good as John's expensive one.* 我這架便宜的照相機似乎跟約翰那架名貴的同樣好。 *Your old suit looks as smart as your brother's new one.* 你這套舊衣服看起來跟你哥哥(弟弟)那套新衣服同樣漂亮。 **6** (In formal or written style it is preferable to avoid the use of the 'prop-word' *one,* esp when there are two *adjj* indicating a contrast. The *n* is placed after only one of the *adjj*): (在正式或寫作文體中,最好避免使用'墊字' one, 尤其當兩個形容詞表示相對的意義時。僅在其一個形容詞之後放置名詞卽可): *If we compare British with American universities* (better than: 不宜寫爲: *If we compare British universities with American ones*).... 假如我們把英國和美國的大學作一比較…。 Cf 參較 *Don't praise the younger child in the presence of the elder.* 不要在大的孩子面前稱讚小的孩子。 *I put my right arm through Mary's left.* 我把我的右手臂穿過瑪莉的左臂彎。 *At home Hanako prefers Japanese to European-style clothes.* 花子在家裡比較喜歡穿日本式衣服,不大喜歡穿西式衣服。 *What the teacher said seemed to go in at one ear and out at the other.* 老師所說的話好像由一邊耳朵進去,再從另一邊耳朵出來。 **7** (*One* is used after *this* and *that,* but is better avoided, in formal or written style, after *these* and *those*): (one 可用於 this 和 that 之後,但是在正式或寫作文體中最好避免用於 these 和 those 之後): *Will you have this* (*one*) *or that* (*one*)*?* 你要這(一)個或是那(一)個? *Will you have these or those?* 你要這些或是那些? (With an *adj, 'one'* is necessary): (與形容詞連用時,需要 one): *Will you have this green one/these green ones or that blue one/those blue ones?* 你要這個(這些)綠色的還是那個(那些)藍色的? **8** (The 'prop-word' *one* is used with *which,* esp to distinguish *sing* from *pl*): ('墊字' one 可與which 連用,尤用於分別單數與複數): *Here are some books on European history. Which one(s) do you want?* 這兒有一些關於歐洲歷史的書。你要哪一本(哪幾本)?

one³ /wʌn ; wʌn/ *pers pron* **1** (used, always with a qualifying word or phrase, for a particular person or creature): (總是與修飾字或片語連用,以指某種人或生物): *the ˈHoly One,* God; 上帝; *the ˈEvil One,* Satan, the Devil; 撒旦;魔鬼; *the absent one,* eg the absent member of the family; 缺席者; *the little ones,* the children; 小孩子們; *a nest with five young ones,* young birds; 一個有五隻小鳥的巢; *my sweet one,* as a term of endearment. 我親愛的人兒。 **2** (used, in liter style, with a following *adj*, phrase or clause): (在文學體裁中,與隨後的形容詞、片語或子句連用): *He lay there like one dead*, as if he were dead. 他像死人一樣躺在那兒。*He worked like one possessed*, like a man possessed by a spirit. 他着了魔一般地工作。*He was one* (= the sort of person) *who never troubled about his personal comfort.* 他是一個從來不爲自己舒適而操心的人。*He's not one to be* (= not a man who is) *easily frightened.* 他不是一個輕易被嚇倒的人。 **3** ***one another***, (used like *each other*, to indicate mutual action or relation; may be the object of a *v* or a *prep*; possessive form is *one another's*; both words usu unstressed): 彼此;互相(用法類似 each other, 表示彼此的行爲或關係; 可作動詞或介詞的受詞; 所有格作 one another's; 兩字通常都不重讀): *They don't like one another.* 他們彼此不喜歡。*They have quarrelled and no longer speak to one another.* 他們吵過架而彼此不再講話。 *They were fighting with cudgels, trying to break one another's heads.* 他們用棍子打架,都想打破對方的頭。

one[4] /wʌn; wʌn/ *impers pron* (standing for any person, including the speaker or writer. 代表任何人,包括說者或寫者在內。Cf 參較 French *on*, German *man.* 法文的 on, 德文的 man。Possessive: 所有格爲: *one's*, reflexive: 反身代名詞爲:*oneself.* ⇨ one[1](10)): *One cannot always find time for reading.* 人不一定能常常有時間閱讀。*If one wants a thing done well, one had best do it oneself.* 一個人如果要事情做得好,最好自己去做。*One doesn't like to have one's word doubted.* 人不喜歡自己的話被別人懷疑。(In colloq style it is more usual to employ 在口語中通常多用 *you, we, people*) Cf 參較 *We live and learn.* (我們)活到老學到老。*You never can tell.* 很難說。*What's a chap/a fellow to do in such a situation?* 一個人在這種情況下應該怎麼辦? (In American usage, *one* may be followed by *he, him, his, himself* instead of by *one, one's, oneself*): (美國用法, one 之後可以使用 he, him, his, himself 代替 one, one's, oneself): *One does not like to have his word doubted.* 誰也不願讓自己的話受到懷疑。

on·er·ous /ˈɒnərəs; ˈɑnərəs/ *adj* needing effort; burdensome (*to*): 苛煩的;繁重的: *~ duties.* 繁重的職務。**~·ly** *adv*

one·self /wʌnˈself; wʌnˈsɛlf/ *reflex, emphat pron* one's own self: 自己; 自身: *wash/dress oneself.* 洗澡(穿衣服)。 *One should not live for oneself alone.* 人不應該專爲自己而活。

on-go·ing /ˈɒn gəʊɪŋ; ˈɑnˌgoɪŋ/ *adj* ⇨ *go on* at go[1](29).

onion /ˈʌnɪən; ˈʌnjən/ *n* [C] **1** vegetable plant with a round bulb of many concentric coats, a strong smell and flavour, used in cooking and pickled: 洋葱; *spring-~s;* 春季洋葱; *Spanish ~s;* 西班牙洋葱; [U] this plant as food: (作爲食物的)洋葱: *too much ~ in the salad;* 生菜裡洋葱太多; *the ~-domed churches of Austria*, having ~-shaped domes. 奧地利的洋葱形屋頂的教堂。⇨ the illus at vegetable. 參看 vegetable 之挿圖。***know one's ~s***, (sl) be clever (because experienced). (俚)(因經驗豐富而)聰明;精明練達。 **2** (sl) head. (俚)頭。***off his ~***, (sl) mentally unbalanced. (俚)精神錯亂;神智失常。

on·looker /ˈɒnlʊkə(r); ˈɑnˌlʊkɚ/ *n* person who looks on at sth happening. 旁觀者。***The ~ sees most of the game***, (prov) The spectator is in a better position to judge than those who are taking part. (諺)旁觀者淸。

only[1] /ˈəʊnlɪ; ˈonlɪ/ *adj* **1** (with a *sing n*) that is the one specimen of its class; single: (與單數名詞連用)獨一的;唯一的: *Smith was the ~ person able to do it.* 史密斯是唯一能做那事的人。*Harry is an ~ child*, has no brothers or sisters. 哈利是個獨子。*Her ~ answer was a shrug.* 她唯一的回答是聳一下肩膀。 **2** (with a *pl n*) that are all the specimens or examples: (與複數名詞連用) 僅有的: *We were the ~ people there.* 只有我們在那裡。 **3** best; most or best worth consideration: 最佳的;最值得考慮的: *He's the ~ man for the position.* 他是這個職位的最佳人選。*She says holidays in Ireland are the ~ thing these days.* 她說在愛爾蘭度假是目前最稱心的事。

only[2] /ˈəʊnlɪ; ˈonlɪ/ *adv* solely; and no one, nothing, more. 單獨地;僅僅;只。 **1** (modifying a single word, and placed, in written or formal style, close to the word it modifies; in speech the stress-pattern may indicate this, so that *only* may have various positions): (修飾一個字,在書寫或正式文體中,only 與其所修飾的字緊隣;在說話中,重音型式可表明其所修飾的字,故 only 可置於不同的位置): *I ˌ~ saw ˈMary*, I saw Mary and no one else (= written style, *I saw ~ Mary*). 我只看到瑪利一個人(only 與 Mary 重讀,表示除了瑪利外我沒看到別人;如爲書寫文體,應作 I saw only Mary)。Cf 參較 *I ˌ~ ˈsaw Mary*, I saw her but didn't speak to her. 我僅僅是看到瑪利而已(only 與 saw 重讀,表示我只是看到她而沒有跟她講過話)。*O~ the teachers are allowed to use this room.* 只有教員可以使用這房間。*O~ five men were seriously hurt in the accident.* 那次意外事件中只有五個人重傷。*We've ~ half an hour to wait now.* 現在我們只要等半個小時。*Ladies ~*, eg on a compartment in a railway carriage. 僅限婦女(例如指火車車廂中之一隔間)。*We can ~ guess* (= We cannot be certain about) *what happened.* 我們祇能猜測發生了什麼事。 **2** ***~ too***, (with an *adj* or *pp*) very: (與形容詞或過去分詞連用)極: *I shall be ~ too pleased to get home.* 我回到家裡將非常高興。*The news was ~ too true*, was really true, and not, as might be hoped or expected, untrue. 這消息是極眞實的。***if ~***, expressing a wish or assumption. 但願。⇨ if(8).

only[3] /ˈəʊnlɪ; ˈonlɪ/ *conj* but then; it must, however, be added that: 但是;不過;可是: *The book is likely to be useful, ~ it's rather expensive.* 這本書可能很有用,只是相當貴。 *He's always ready to promise help, ~ he never keeps his promises.* 他總是輕易允諾協助,但是他從來不守諾言。***~ that***, with the exception that; were it not that: 若不是;若非: *He would probably do well in the examination, ~ that he gets rather nervous.* 若不是他有點緊張,他可能考得很好。

ono·mato·poeia /ˌɒnəˌmætəˈpɪə; ˌɑnəˌmætəˈpiə/ *n* [U] formation of words in imitation of the sounds associated with the thing concerned (as *cuckoo* for the bird that utters this cry). 擬聲造字法(如 cuckoo 一字卽由模擬布穀鳥的鳴聲而造成的)。

on·rush /ˈɒnrʌʃ; ˈɑnˌrʌʃ/ *n* strong, onward rush or flow. 猛衝;急流。

on·set /ˈɒnset; ˈɑnˌsɛt/ *n* attack; vigorous start: 進攻;有力的開始: *at the first ~;* 在最初著手時; *the ~ of a disease.* 疾病的起始;起病。

on·shore /ˈɒnʃɔː(r); ˈɑnˌʃor/ *adj, adv* toward the shore. 向岸的(地)。

on·slaught /ˈɒnslɔːt; ˈɑnˌslɔt/ *n* [C] furious attack (*on*). 猛攻;突擊(與 on 連用)。

onto /*before consonants:* ˈɒntə; ˈɑntə; *before vowels or finally:* ˈɒntuː; ˈɑntu/ *prep* ⇨ on[1](2).

on·tol·ogy /ɒnˈtɒlədʒɪ; ɑnˈtɑlədʒɪ/ *n* [U] department of metaphysics concerned with the nature of existence; [C] specific theory of this. 實體論;本體論。

onus /ˈəʊnəs; ˈonəs/ *n* ***the ~***, responsibility for, burden of, doing sth: 責任;負擔: *The ~ of proof rests with you*, It is for you to supply proof. 提出證據的責任在你。

on·ward /ˈɒnwəd; ˈɑnwɚd/ *adj* forward: 前進的;向前的: *an ~ march/movement.* 前進(向前移動)。 □ *adv* (also 亦作 **~s**) towards the front; forward: 向前;前進地: *move ~(s).* 向前移動。

onyx /ˈɒnɪks; ˈɑnɪks/ *n* [U] (sorts of) quartz in layers of different colours, used for ornaments, etc. (各種)截子瑪瑙(作裝飾品等用)。

oodles /ˈuːdlz ; ˈudl̩z/ *n pl* (sl) ~ ***of***, great amounts or sums: (俚)大量;多量: ~ *of money.* 大量金錢。

oomph /ʊmf ; ʊmf/ *n* (sl) energy; sex appeal. (俚)精力;性感。

O

ooze /uːz ; uz/ *n* [U] soft liquid mud, esp on a river-bed, the bottom of a pond, lake, etc. 泥漿; (尤指河床、湖底等的)淤泥;軟泥。□ *vi, vt* **1** [VP2C] (of moisture, thick liquids) pass slowly through small openings: (指水份、濃液)慢慢地滲流: *Blood was still oozing from the wound.* 血仍然從傷口徐徐滲出。(fig) (喻) *Their courage was oozing away.* 他們的勇氣慢慢地消失。 **2** [VP6A] pass out; emit: 流出;滲出: *He was oozing sweat.* 他在流汗。**oozy** *adj* of or like ~; slimy. 軟泥的;泥漿的;像軟泥的;像黏泥的。

opac·ity /əʊˈpæsətɪ ; oˈpæsətɪ/ *n* [U] (quality of) being opaque. 不透明(性);晦暗;愚鈍。

opal /ˈəʊpl ; ˈopl̩/ *n* semi-precious stone in which changes of colour are seen, often used as a gem. 蛋白石;貓眼石。**opal·escent** /ˌəʊpəˈlesnt ; ˌopl̩ˈɛsn̩t/ *adj* like an ~. 像蛋白石的;發乳白光的。

opaque /əʊˈpeɪk ; oˈpek/ *adj* not allowing light to pass through; that cannot be seen through; dull. 不透光的;不透明的;晦暗的;愚鈍的。**~·ly** *adv* **~·ness** *n*

op art /ˈɒp ɑːt ; ˈap ɑrt/ *n* form of modern abstract art using geometrical patterns which produce optical illusions. 歐普藝術(一種現代抽象藝術,利用幾何圖案使人產生視覺上的錯覺)。

open¹ /ˈəʊpən ; ˈopən/ *adj* **1** not closed; allowing (things, persons) to go in, out, through: 開着的;開放的;開的: *sleep with ~ windows;* 開着窗戶睡覺; *leave the door ~.* 讓門開着。ˌ**~-ˈeyed** *adj* with ~ eyes; watchful; surprised. 睜着眼睛的;留心的;驚訝的。ˌ**~-ˈmouthed** /-ˈmaʊðd ; -ˈmaʊðd/ *adj* **(a)** showing greed (for food, etc). 貪吃的;貪婪的。**(b)** showing great surprise or stupidity. 驚訝的;發呆的。**~ vowel,** one made with the roof of the mouth and the tongue fairly wide apart, eg /ɑː, ɒ ; ɑr, ɑ/. 開母音(如 /ɑː, ɒ ; ɑr, ɑ/)。ˈ**~-work** *n* [U] pattern (in metal, lace, etc) with spaces: (金屬、花邊等)網狀細工;透孔鏤刻: *~-work lace;* 透孔花邊; *~-work stockings.* 網狀長襪。 **2** not enclosed, fenced in, barred or blocked: 開闊的;空曠的: *the ~ country,* land affording wide views, without forests, etc. 空曠之地;曠野。**the ~ sea,** not a bay or harbour, not closed in by land. 大海;公海。**an ~ river,** not barred by ice, mudbanks, etc. 暢通的河流。**~ water,** navigable, free from ice. (沒有冰的)可航行的水域。**an ~ prison,** one with fewer restrictions than usual, esp one where prisoners with good records come and go freely to work outside. 開放式監獄(比一般監獄較少禁制,尤指紀錄良好之囚犯可自由出外工作者)。 **3** not covered in or over: 無遮蓋的;敞開的: *an ~ boat,* one without a deck; 無甲板的敞船; *an ~ car,* with no roof, or a roof that is folded back; 無篷或未張篷的汽車; *an ~ drain／sewer,* in the form of a ditch, not in pipes under the ground; 明溝; *an ~ sandwich,* single slice of bread with meat, etc on top; 單片三明治(只用一片麵包,上有肉等); *in the ˌ~ ˈair,* out of doors. 在戶外;在野外。ˈ**~-air** *attrib adj* taking place out of doors; fond of life in the ~ air: 戶外的;喜歡野外生活的: *an ˌ~-air ˈtheatre.* 露天戲院。 **4** spread out; unfolded: 開放的;開啓的;張開的: *The flowers were all ~.* 那些花都開了。*The book lay ~ on the table.* 那本書攤開着擺在桌子上。*His mind was／His thoughts were an ~ book,* It was easy to read his thoughts. 他的思想像一本攤開的書(易於被人瞭解)。***with ~ hands,*** generously. 慷慨地。Hence, 由此產生, ˌ**~-ˈhanded** *adj* generous; giving freely. 慷慨的;好施捨的。ˌ**~-ˈhearted** *adj* sincere; frank. 誠摯的;坦白的。 ***with ~ arms,*** with affection or enthusiasm. 熱誠地。**~ order,** (of troops), with wider space than usual between ranks. (指軍隊的)散開隊形(列與列間之距離較平常爲大)。**5** public; free to all; not limited to any special persons, but for anyone to enter: 公開的;公共的;不限制任何人的: *an ~ competition／championship／scholarship;* 公開競爭(公開競爭的錦標; 公開競爭的獎學金); *tried in ~ court,* of a law case, the public being freely admitted to hear the trial. 在法庭公開審判的。*The position is still ~,* No one has yet been chosen to fill it. 這個職位仍然虛懸着。**the ~ door,** policy of free trade or freedom from tariffs; admission of foreign traders. 門戶開放(自由貿易或免除關稅的政策)。**~ shop,** workshop, factory, etc where members and non-members of trade unions work on equal terms. 開放工廠(工會會員及非工會會員以平等之條件雇用者)。⇨ *closed shop* at close⁴(2). ***keep ~ house,*** offer hospitality to all comers. 歡迎所有來客。**6** not settled or decided: 未解決的;未決定的: *leave a matter ~.* 留下一件事沒解決。ˌ**~-ˈended** *adj* (of a discussion, a subject for debate, etc) having a variety of possible solutions; on which no decision or agreement is reached, expected or required. (指討論、辯論之主題等)無固定答案的;具多種不同之解決辦法的;達不到、不期望有或不必有決定或一致意見的; 可廣泛解釋的。**an ~ question,** with no decision, answer. 未解決的問題。**an ~ verdict,** jury's verdict of the fact and cause of a death, but not saying whether it is natural, accidental, suicide or murder. 存疑裁決(陪審團對死亡案件的判決,但未說明是自然死亡、意外死亡、自殺抑或謀殺)。***have／keep an ~ mind (on sth),*** be ready to consider sth further, to listen to new evidence, agreements, etc. (對某事)準備再加思考,聽取新的證據、協議等;虛心研討(某事)。Hence, 由此產生, ˌ**~-ˈminded** *adj* unprejudiced. 無偏見的;虛心的。 **7** ready for business or for the admission of the public: 開放營業的;開着可以進去的;開放的: *Are the shops ~ yet?* 商店開始營業了嗎? *Doors ~ at 7.00pm,* eg of a theatre. 下午七點鐘開門或開始營業(如指戲院)。 **8** known to all; not secret or disguised; frank: 公開的;無秘密的;坦白的: *an ~ quarrel／scandal;* 公開的爭吵(醜聞); *an ~ character／countenance.* 坦率的性格(面容)。*Let me be quite ~ (= frank) with you.* 讓我坦白對你說。**an ~ letter,** one that is addressed to an individual or group but sent to and published in a periodical, usu in protest against sth. 公開信(寫給某人或某一團體,送往期刊公開登載的信,通常爲對某事提出抗議者)。**9** unprotected; unguarded; vulnerable. 不設防的;未加防護的;易受攻擊的。***be／lay oneself ~ to sth,*** behave so that one is vulnerable to sth: 易受(使自己易受)某事物的傷害或攻擊: *Don't lay yourself ~ to ridicule／attack.* 不要使自己易招致嘲笑(攻擊)。**10** not settled, finished or closed: 未解決的;未完成的;未結束的: *keep one's account ~ at a bank;* 在銀行裡開着一個戶頭; *be ~ to an offer,* willing to consider one. 願意考慮某一提議。 **11** (phrases) (片語) ˈ**~-cast** *adj* surface: 表面的: *~-cast coal;* 地面煤炭;表層煤炭; *~-cast mining,* from strata near the earth's surface (contrasted with production from deep mines). 露天採礦(法);表層採礦(法)(從靠近地面之礦層採礦,與深坑採礦相對)。**an ~ cheque,** one that is not crossed and which may be cashed at the bank on which it is drawn. 普通支票(向銀行提示即可兌現的支票,非劃線支票)。 **the ˈ~ season,** (fishing and shooting) when there are no restrictions. (漁獵)開放季節。⇨ close¹(11). **an ~ secret,** sth supposed to be a secret but in fact known to all people. 公開的秘密(被認爲是一秘密,事實上是大家全都知道的事)。**the O~ University,** (GB) university (founded in 1971) whose students live at home and get tuition by correspondence, textbooks and special radio and TV programmes. (英)空中大學(創辦於 1971 年,學生在家裡藉函授、教科書和特殊無線電廣播及電視節目而上課)。**~ weather, an ~ winter,** free from severe frost and snow, so that it is possible to get about. 和暖的天氣,和暖的多天。□ *n* **the ~,** the ~ air. 戶外;野外。⇨ 3 above. 參看上列第3義。***come (out) into the ~,*** (fig) come into public view; make one's ideas, plans, etc, known. (喻)成爲公開;現身;把意見、計畫等公開。**~·ly** *adv* without secrecy; frankly; publicly: 公然地;坦白地;公開地: *speak ~ly;* 公開說; *go ~ly into a place,* eg where one might be expected to go secretly. 公開地進入某一場所(例如該場所可能被認爲宜秘密進入者)。**~·ness** *n* [U].

open² /ˈəupən ; ˈopən/ *vt, vi* **1** [VP6A, 14, 16A, 12C] make open or cause to be open; unfasten: 開;打開;開啓: *~ a box.* 打開盒子。*He ~ed the door for me to come in/to let me in.* 他開門讓我進去。*O~ the window a fraction/crack/bit, please.* 請將窗子打開一點點。**~ *one's eyes,*** express surprise. 睜大眼睛(表示驚訝)。**~ *(sb's) eyes to sth,*** cause him to realize sth, eg how he has been deceived. 使(某人)明白或醒悟某事。 **2** [VP6A, 15A, B] cut or make an opening in or a passage through: 開口;打通;開通: *~ a mine/a well;* 開礦(鑿井); *~ a new road through a forest;* 開一條新路穿過森林。*O~ up!* command to ~ a door, etc. 開門!打開! **~ *sth up,*** make ~; make accessible; make possible the development of: 打開某物;打通;開展: *~ up a wound/a mine/undeveloped land/a new territory to trade.* 打開傷口(開礦;開發未墾土地;開拓新的貿易地區)。 **3** [VP6A, 15A, B] spread out; unfold: 展開;解開;張開: *~ one's hand/a book/a newspaper/a parcel;* 張開手(翻開書;打開報紙;解開包裹); *~ out a folding map.* 展開一幅摺叠的地圖。**~ *one's mind/heart to sb,*** make known one's ideas/feelings. 對某人吐露心意(眞情)。 **4** [VP6A] start: 開始: *~ an account,* eg at a bank, shop; (在銀行、店鋪等)開個戶頭; *~ a debate/a public meeting.* 開始辯論(會議)。**~ *the bidding,*** make the first bid (at an auction, at bridge). (在拍賣場)作第一次叫價;開價;(在橋牌戲中)作第一次叫牌;開叫。**~ *fire (at/on),*** start shooting. (向…)開火。 **5** [VP6A] declare, indicate, that business, etc may now start: 開業;開張: *~ a shop;* 開一家店鋪; *~ Parliament.* 主持國會開幕。 **6** [VP2A, C] become open; be ~ed; allow of being ~ed: 開着;被開啓;展開: *The flowers are ~ing.* 花正開着。*This shop does not ~ on Sundays.* 這家店鋪星期天不開門(營業)。*The door ~ed and a man came in.* 門開了,一個人走進來。*Does this door ~ inwards or outwards?* 這個門朝裡還是朝外開?*The two rooms ~ into one another,* have a door between them. 這兩個房間有門相通。*This door ~s on to the garden.* 這個門通向花園。 **7** [VP3A] **~ *with,*** start: 開始: *The story ~s with a murder.* 這故事以一個謀殺案件開始。 **8** [VP2A, C] **~ *(out),*** become visible: 展示;顯現: *The view ~ed (out) before our eyes.* 景色顯現在我們眼前。**~er** *n* person or thing that ~s: 開啓的人或工具: (chiefly in compounds) (主要用於複合字中) *ˈpew-~er;* 教堂中引人入座者; *ˈtin-~er;* 開罐器; *ˈbottle-~er.* 開瓶蓋工具;開瓶器。**ˈeye-opener,** ⇨ eye¹(3).

open·ing /ˈəupənɪŋ ; ˈopənɪŋ/ *n* **1** open space; way in or out: 口;穴;孔;洞;通路: *an ~ in a hedge.* 籬笆上的一個洞口。 **2** beginning: 開始;開端: *the ~ of a book/speech.* 書(演講)的開端。**the ~ night,** eg on which a new play/film is performed/shown for the first time, and to which dramatic critics are invited. (戲劇或電影的)上演第一夜;首映夜。**~ time,** eg at which public houses open and begin to serve drinks. 開放時間;開始營業時間。 **3** process of becoming open: 張開;開的過程: *watch the ~ of a flower.* 看一朵花開。 **4** position (in a business firm) which is open or vacant; opportunity: (公司行號中職位的)空缺;機會: *an ~ in an advertising agency.* 廣告代理處的空缺。□ *adj* first: 第一次的;開頭的: *his ~ remarks.* 他的開場白。

op·era /ˈɒprə ; ˈɑpərə/ *n* **1** [C] dramatic composition with music, in which the words are sung. 歌劇。**comic ~,** humorous, with spoken dialogue and a happy ending. 喜歌劇(有對白及喜劇結尾者)。**grand ~,** serious, with no spoken dialogue. 大歌劇;莊歌劇(無對白者)。**light ~,** not serious. 輕歌劇。⇨ cantata, oratorio. **2** [U] dramatic works of this kind as entertainment: 歌劇作品;歌劇: *fond of ~;* 喜歡歌劇; *the ~ season.* 歌劇季節。**ˈ~-cloak** *n* lady's cloak for wearing with evening dress. 配合晚禮服穿的女披風。**ˈ~-glasses** *n pl* small binoculars for use in a theatre. 看戲用的小型雙眼望遠鏡。**ˈ~-hat** *n* man's tall, black silk hat, made so that it folds flat. 可摺扁的男用高頂絲質黑禮帽。**ˈ~-house** *n* theatre for performances of ~s. 歌劇院。**op·er·atic** /ˌɒpəˈrætɪk ; ˌɑpəˈrætɪk/ *adj* of or for an ~: 歌劇的: *~tic music/singers.* 歌劇音樂(演唱者)。

op·er·ate /ˈɒpəreɪt ; ˈɑpəˌret/ *vt, vi* **1** [VP6A, 2A, C, 4A] (cause to) work, be in action, have an effect; manage: (使)運轉;操作;起作用;管理;經營: *~ a machine;* 操縱一部機器; *machinery that ~s night and day.* 日夜運轉的機器。*The company ~s three factories and a coal-mine.* 那家公司經營三個工廠和一個煤礦。*The lift was not operating properly.* 那電梯操縱不靈。*The lift is ~d by electricity.* 那升降機(電梯)是用電操作的。*This new law ~s* (= produces an effect) *to our advantage.* 這條新法律對我們有利。*Several causes ~d to bring about the war.* 若干原因引起這次戰爭。 **2** [VP2A, 3A] **~ *(on sb) (for sth),*** perform a surgical operation: 動手術;開刀: *The doctors decided to ~ at once.* 醫師們決定立刻動手術。**ˈoperating-table/-theatre** *n* for use in surgical operations. 手術檯(室)。 **3** [VP2A, C] (of an army) carry out various movements: (指軍隊)作軍事行動: *operating on a large scale.* 作大規模軍事行動。 **4** [VP2A, C] (of a stockbroker) buy and sell, esp in order to influence prices. (指股票經紀人)買賣以左右股票價格;做價;操縱市場。**op·er·able** /ˈɒpərəbl ; ˈɑpərəbl̩/ *adj* that can be treated by means of a surgical operation. 可動手術的。

op·er·ation /ˌɒpəˈreɪʃn ; ˌɑpəˈreʃən/ *n* **1** [U] working; way in which sth works. 運轉;操作;作用;運行法。***be in/bring sth into/come into ~,*** be/cause to be/become effective: 生效中(使生效;生效): *When does the plan come into ~?* 該計畫何時開始生效?*Is this rule in ~ yet?* 這條規則開始生效了嗎? **2** [C] piece of work; sth (to be) done: 工作;(待)完成的事: *begin ~s;* 開始工作; *the ~s of nature,* changes brought about by natural forces. 自然力量的作用;大自然之變化。 **3** (usu *pl;* 通常用複數; colloq abbr 俗語略作 **ops**) movements of troops, ships, aircraft, etc in warfare or during manoeuvres. (作戰或演習中的)軍事行動;作戰行動。**ˈ~s room,** from which ~s are controlled; (*sing*) in code names for military campaigns (*O~ Overlord*) and, by extension, for planned campaigns in industry, commerce, etc: 作戰指揮室;(單)用於代號表示戰役或演習名稱(如 Operation Overlord);(工商界等的)有計畫行動: *building/banking ~s;* 有計畫的建屋(存款)行動; *~s research,* to promote greater efficiency in industry. (提高工業效率的)營運研究;作業研究。 **4** [C] ***an ~ (on sb) (for sth),*** act performed by a surgeon on any part of the body, esp by cutting to take away or deal with a diseased part: 手術: *an ~ for appendicitis.* 闌尾手術;割除闌尾。 **5** (maths) addition, subtraction, multiplication, division, etc. (數學)加、減、乘、除等;運算。**~al** /-ʃənl ; -ʃənl̩/ *adj* **1** of, for, used in, ~s. 操作的;管理的;工作的;軍事行動的;手術的;適於操作(等)的;用於操作(等)的。**~al costs/expenditure,** needed for operating (machines, aircraft, etc). 營運成本(費用)。**~al research,** into the best ways of using, improving, etc new weapons, machinery, etc. (新武器、機器等的)更新研

究;營運研究。 2 ready for use: 卽可使用的: *When will the newly designed airliner be ~al?* 新設計的客機何時啓用?

op·er·at·ive /ˈɒpərətɪv *US:* -reɪt- ; ˈɑpəˌretɪv/ *adj* **1** operating; having an effect: 操作的;運轉的;有效的: *This law became ~ on 1 May.* 這條法律五月一日生效。 **2 ~ words,** those having legal effect in a deed, etc; (loosely) most significant words. 在契約等中有法律效力的文字;(泛指)最重要的文字。 **3** of surgical operations: 外科手術的: *~ treatment.* 手術治療。□ *n* worker; mechanic: 工人;機械人員;技工: *cotton ~s.* 棉花工人。

O

op·er·ator /ˈɒpəreɪtə(r) ; ˈɑpəˌretɚ/ *n* **1** person who operates or works sth: 操作者;工作者: *telephone / telegraphy ~s;* 電話接線生(無線電報報務員); *private ~s in civil aviation,* privately owned companies (contrasted with state-owned corporations). 民營航空公司(與國營航空公司相對)。 **2** (sl) confident, efficient man (in business, love affairs, etc): (俚)(在事業、愛情等方面)自信而又能幹的人;精明的人: *He's a smooth / slick ~.* 他是個精明圓滑的傢伙。

op·er·etta /ˌɒpəˈretə ; ˌɑpəˈrɛtə/ *n* one-act, or short, light musical comedy. (獨幕或短而輕鬆的)小歌劇;輕歌劇。

oph·thal·mia /ɒfˈθælmɪə ; ɑfˈθælmɪə/ *n* [U] inflammation of the eye. 眼炎。 **oph·thal·mic** /-mɪk ; -mɪk/ *adj* of the eyes; afflicted with ~. 眼睛的; 眼炎的。 **oph·thal·mo·scope** /ɒfˈθælməskəʊp ; ɑfˈθælməˌskop/ *n* instrument with a mirror (having a hole in the centre) through which the eye may be examined. 檢眼鏡。

opi·ate /ˈəʊpɪət ; ˈopɪˌet/ *n* [C] drug containing opium, used to relieve pain or to help sb to sleep. 鴉片劑(用以止痛或安眠)。

opine /əˈpaɪn ; oˈpaɪn/ *vt* [VP9] **~ *that,*** (formal) have or express the opinion. (正式用語)認爲;以爲。

opin·ion /əˈpɪnɪən ; əˈpɪnjən/ *n* **1** [C] belief or judgement not founded on complete knowledge: 意見;看法;主張: *political ~s.* 政見。 *What's your ~* (= view) *of the new President?* 你對新總統的看法如何? *Those are my ~s about the affair.* 那些就是我對這事的意見。 ***in my, your, etc ~; in the ~ of sb,*** it is my, your, etc view that...: 我的(你的等)意見是…;我(你等)認爲…: *In my ~ / In the ~ of most people, the scheme is unsound.* 我認爲(大部份的人認爲)這個計畫不完善。 ***act up to one's ~s,*** act according to them. 照自己的主張行事。 ***be of the ~ that...,*** feel, believe, that.... 覺得…;相信…;認爲…。 ***have a good / bad / high / low ~ of sb / sth,*** think well / badly, etc of. 對某人(某事物)的評價很好(壞、高、低)。 **2** [U] views, beliefs, of a group: 團體的意見;團體的看法;群衆的見解: *O~ is shifting in favour of stiffer penalties for armed robbery.* 群衆的意見趨向於贊成對武裝搶刼處以較嚴厲的刑罰。 **public ~,** what the majority of people think: 大衆意見;輿論: *Public ~ is against the proposed change.* 輿論反對擬議中的更動。 **ˈ~ poll,** ⇨ poll¹(2). **3** [C] professional estimate or advice: 專業性的鑑定或意見: *get a lawyer's ~ on the question.* 聽取律師關於這問題的意見。 *You had better have another ~ before you let that man take out all your teeth.* 在讓那個人拔掉你全部牙齒之前,你最好先聽取其他的意見。 **~·ated** /-eɪtɪd ; -etɪd/, **~·at·ive** /-ətɪv *US:* -eɪtɪv ; -etɪv/ *adjj* obstinate in one's ~s; dogmatic. 固執己見的;武斷的。

opium /ˈəʊpɪəm ; ˈopɪəm/ *n* [U] substance prepared from poppy seeds, used to relieve pain, cause sleep, and as a narcotic drug. 鴉片。 **ˈ~-den** *n* place where ~ smokers can obtain and use this drug. 鴉片煙館。

opos·sum /əˈpɒsəm ; əˈpɑsəm/ (also 亦作 **possum** /ˈpɒsəm ; ˈpɑsəm/) *n* kinds of small American animal that lives in trees. 鼴;負鼠。

op·po·nent /əˈpəʊnənt ; əˈponənt/ *n* person against whom one fights, struggles, plays games, or argues. 對手;敵手;反對者。

op·por·tune /ˈɒpətjuːn *US:* -tuːn ; ˌɑpɚˈtjun/ *adj* **1** (of time) suitable, favourable; good for a purpose: (指時間)合適的;恰好的: *arrive at a most ~ moment.* 在最適當的時刻到達。 **2** (of an action or event) done, coming, at a favourable time: (指行動或事件)適時的;及時的: *an ~ remark / speech.* 合時宜的話(演說)。 **~·ly** *adv*

op·por·tun·ism /ˌɒpəˈtjuːnɪzəm *US:* -ˈtuːn- ; ˌɑpɚˈtjunɪzəm/ *n* [U] being guided by what seems possible, or by circumstances, in determining policy; preferring what can be done to what should be done. 機會主義;投機。 **op·por·tun·ist** /-ɪst ; -ɪst/ *n* person who acts on this principle; person who is more anxious to gain an advantage for himself than to consider whether he is trying to get it fairly. 機會主義者;唯利是圖的投機者。

op·por·tun·ity /ˌɒpəˈtjuːnətɪ *US:* -ˈtuːn- ; ˌɑpɚˈtjunətɪ/ *n* (*pl* -ties) [C, U] **~ *(for sth / of doing sth / to do sth),*** favourable time or chance: 機會;時機: *to make / find / get an ~;* 製造(尋找,獲得)機會; *have few opportunities of meeting interesting people;* 遇見有趣的人的機會並不多; *have no / little / not much ~ for hearing good music.* 沒有(很少,沒有多少)機會聽到好的音樂。 *I had no ~ to discuss the matter with her.* 我沒有機會和她討論那件事。 *The ~ came early one morning.* 有一天清早機會來了。

op·pose /əˈpəʊz ; əˈpoz/ *vt* **1** [VP6A] set oneself, fight, against (sb or sth): 反對;反抗(某人或某事物): *~ the Government;* 反對政府; *~ a scheme.* 反對某一計畫。 *I am very much ~d to your going abroad,* I am against the plan. 我非常反對你出國。 **2** [VP14] **~ *(against / to),*** put forward as a contrast or opposite; set up against: 使對立;使相對;使對照;以…對抗: *~ your will against mine / your views to mine;* 把你的意向與我的意向(你的觀點與我的觀點)對照一下; *~ a vigorous resistance to the enemy.* 猛烈抵抗敵人。 ***as ~d to,*** in contrast with. 與…對照;與…成對比。

op·po·site /ˈɒpəzɪt ; ˈɑpəzɪt/ *adj* **1 ~ *(to),*** facing; front to front or back to back (with): 朝向…的; (與…)面對面的; (與…)背對背的; 對立的; 相對的: *the house ~ (to) mine;* 與我的房子相對的那幢房子; *on the ~ side of the road.* 在路的對面。 **2** entirely different; contrary: 完全不同的;相反的: *in the ~ direction.* 朝相反的方向。 **3** similarly placed elsewhere. 對當的。 **one's ~ number,** person occupying the same or a similar position in another group, etc: 與其地位相等或相當的人: *The British Foreign Minister is in Washington discussing problems with his ~ number.* 英國外相正在華盛頓與其身份相等的人(美國國務卿)討論問題。□ *n* word or thing that is ~: 相反字;相對的事物: *Black and white are ~s.* 黑與白相反。 *I thought quite the ~.* 我想的剛好相反。

op·po·si·tion /ˌɒpəˈzɪʃn ; ˌɑpəˈzɪʃən/ *n* **1** [U] the state of being opposite or opposed: 反對;敵對;相反;相對: *The Socialist Party was in ~,* formed the O~. 社會黨是國會中的反對黨。 ⇨ 2 below. 參看下列第2義。 ***be in ~ to,*** opposing: 反對;與…相反: *We found ourselves in ~ to our friends on this question.* 我們發現我們對於這個問題和我們的朋友意見(立場)相反。 **2** (*sing*) MP's of the political party or parties opposing the Government: (單)國會中的反對黨(與執政黨敵對的政黨): *Her Majesty's O~;* 女王(英國政府,即執政黨)的反對黨; *the leader of the O~;* 反對黨的領袖; *the O~ benches.* (國會中的)反對黨席。 *We need a stronger O~.* 我們需要一個更強大的反對黨。 **3** [U] resistance: 抵抗: *Our forces met with strong ~ all along the front.* 我軍在前線遭遇到全面的強烈抵抗。

op·press /əˈpres ; əˈprɛs/ *vt* [VP6A] **1** rule unjustly or cruelly; keep down by unjust or cruel government. 壓迫;壓制。 **2** (fig) weigh heavily on; cause to feel troubled, uncomfortable: (喻)重壓;使煩惱;使難受: *~ed with anxiety/with a foreboding of misfortune;* 因焦慮(因不幸的預感)而煩惱; *feel ~ed with the heat.* 悶熱難耐。**~or** /-sə(r) ; -sɚ/ *n* person who ~es; cruel or unjust ruler. 壓迫者;暴君。**op·pression** /ə'preʃn ; ə'prɛʃən/ *n* **1** [U] the condition of being ~ed: 壓抑;鬱悶: *a feeling of ~ion.* 鬱悶之感。**2** [U] ~ing or being ~ed: 壓迫;被壓迫: *victims of ~ion;* 受壓迫的苦難者; [C] instance of this; cruel or unjust act. 壓迫或被壓迫的實例;暴虐或不公平的行爲。**op·press·ive** /ə'presɪv ; ə'prɛsɪv/ *adj* **1** unjust: 不公平的;暴虐的;壓迫的: *~ive laws/rules.* 不公平的法律(規則)。**2** hard to endure; over-powering: 難以忍受的;壓制的: *~ive weather/heat/taxes.* 難以忍受的天氣(悶熱,苛稅)。**op·press·ive·ly** *adv*

op·pro·bri·ous /ə'prəubrɪəs ; ə'probrɪəs/ *adj* (formal) (of words, etc) showing scorn or reproach; abusive. (正式用語)(指文字等)辱罵的;侮辱的。**~·ly** *adv* **op·pro·brium** /-brɪəm ; -brɪəm/ *n* (formal) [U] scorn; disgrace; public shame. (正式用語)輕蔑;耻辱;不名譽。

op·pugn /ə'pju:n ; ə'pjun/ *vt* [VP6A] (formal) call in question; be contrary to. (正式用語)反對;反駁;質問。

opt /ɒpt ; ɑpt/ *vi* **1** [VP3A] ***opt for sth,*** choose; decide on: 選擇;挑選: *Fewer students are opting for science courses nowadays.* 時下很少學生選擇科學課程。 **2** ***opt out of,*** choose to take no part in: 決定不參加;決定退出: *young people who have opted out of society,* chosen not to be conventional members of society. 決定退出現社會的年輕人(不爲社會的傳統份子)。

op·tat·ive /'ɒptətɪv ; 'ɑptətɪv/ *adj, n* (of) verbal form expressing desire: 表願望的;祈願的;祈願式: *~ mood,* eg in Greek, but not in English. 祈願語氣(如希臘文中者,但英文中無此名稱)。

op·tic /'ɒptɪk ; 'ɑptɪk/ *adj* of the eye or the sense of sight: 眼睛的;視覺的: *the ~ nerve,* from the eye to the brain. 視覺神經。⇨ the illus at eye. 參看 eye 之插圖。**~s** *n* (with *sing v*) science of light and the laws of light. (與單數動詞連用)光學。

op·tical /'ɒptɪkl ; 'ɑptɪkl/ *adj* **1** of the sense of sight. 視覺的。**an ~ illusion,** sth by which the eye is deceived: 光幻視;視錯覺;錯視: *A mirage is an ~ illusion.* 海市蜃樓是一種視錯覺。 **2** for looking through; to help eyesight: 用以使人看得清楚的;幫助視力的: *~ instruments,* eg microscopes, telescopes; 幫助視力的工具;光學儀器(如顯微鏡、望遠鏡); *~ glass,* the kind used for ~ instruments. (用於光學儀器的)光學玻璃。**~·ly** /-klɪ ; -klɪ/ *adv*

op·ti·cian /ɒp'tɪʃn ; ɑp'tɪʃən/ *n* person who makes or supplies optical instruments, esp lenses and spectacles. 光學儀器(尤指透鏡及眼鏡)製造者或售賣者;光學儀器商。

op·ti·mism /'ɒptɪmɪzəm ; 'ɑptə,mɪzəm/ *n* [U] (opp of *pessimism*) belief that in the end good will triumph over evil; tendency to look upon the bright side of things; confidence in success. (爲 pessimism 之相反字)樂觀;樂天;樂觀主義;對成功的信心。**op·ti·mist** /-mɪst ; -mɪst/ *n* person who is always hopeful and looks upon the bright side of things, who believes that all things happen for the best. 樂觀的人;樂觀主義者。**op·ti·mis·tic** /,ɒptɪ'mɪstɪk ; ,ɑptə'mɪstɪk/ *adj* expecting the best; confident: 樂觀的;有信心的: *an optimistic view of events.* 對事情樂觀的看法。**op·ti·mis·ti·cally** /-klɪ ; -klɪ/ *adv*

op·ti·mum /'ɒptɪməm ; 'ɑptəməm/ *n* (attrib) best or most favourable: (形容用法)最佳的;最適宜的;最有利的: *the ~ temperature for the growth of plants.* 對植物生長的最佳溫度。

op·tion /'ɒpʃn ; 'ɑpʃən/ *n* **1** [U] right or power of choosing. 選擇權;選擇力。***have no/little, etc ~,*** have no/little, etc choice: 無選擇餘地;不能作選擇: *I haven't much ~ in the matter,* cannot choose. 對這件事我不能選擇。*I had no ~,* was forced to act as I did. 我沒有選擇的餘地。*He was given six months' imprisonment without the ~ of a fine.* 他被判監禁六個月而不得易以罰金。**local ~,** right of people (in some towns, districts) to decide, by voting, whether or not to have or allow sth, eg the sale of alcoholic liquor. 地方居民選擇權(例如由投票決定是否可賣酒等)。 **2** [C] thing that is or may be chosen: 選擇之事物;可選擇之事物: *None of the ~s is satisfactory.* 所選之物無一令人滿意。***leave one's ~s open,*** not commit oneself. 不作選擇;不作承諾。 **3** [C] (comm) right to buy or sell sth at a certain price within a certain period of time: (商)(在某一期間內可以某種價格)買賣某物的權利: *have an ~ on a piece of land.* 對某塊土地有買賣權。**'~al** /-ʃənl ; -ʃənḷ/ *adj* which may be chosen or not as one wishes; not compulsory: 可選擇的;非强制的;隨意的: *~al subjects at school.* 學校的選修課。**~·ally** /'ɒpʃənəlɪ ; 'ɑpʃənḷɪ/ *adv*

opu·lence /'ɒpjʊləns ; 'ɑpjələns/ *n* [U] (formal) wealth; abundance. (正式用語)富裕;豐富。**opu·lent** /-ənt ; -ənt/ *adj* rich; wealthy; luxuriant: 富足的;富有的;華麗的;繁茂的: *~ vegetation.* 茂盛的草木。**opu·lent·ly** *adv*

opus /'əupəs ; 'opəs/ *n* (*pl* opera /'ɒpərə ; 'ɑpərə/, rarely used) separate musical composition (abbr 略作 **op**, used in citing a composition by number, as *Beethoven, Op 112*). (複數作 opera, 罕用)樂曲;作品(用以表示作品編號,如 Beethoven, Op 112)。**,magnum '~,** great artistic undertaking, completed or in course of being completed. 鉅著;傑作。

or /ɔ:(r) ; ɔr/ *conj* **1** (introducing an alternative): (引出另一個代替的事物,表示兩者居其一) 或;抑: *Is it green or blue?* 它是綠的還是藍的? *Are you coming or not?* 你來還是不來? ***either... or,*** ⇨ either. ***whether... or:*** 是…還是…;不論…或…: *I don't care whether he stays or goes.* 我不在乎他留下來還是離去。***or else,*** otherwise: 否則: *Hurry up or else you'll be late.* 趕快,否則你就會遲了。*Pay up, or else!* (as a threat). 將款付清,否則的話!(作爲一種威脅)。 **2** (introducing all but the first of a series of alternatives): (引出除首項事物外之一系列的代替者,表示其中任何一個): *I'd like it to be black, (or) white or grey.* 我希望它是黑的,(或者)白的或者灰的。 **3** (introducing a word that explains, or means the same as, another): (表示一個字可解釋另一字的含義或與該字同義)換言之卽;也就是: *an English pound, or one hundred pence;* 一個英鎊,也就是一百個辨士; *a dugout, or a canoe made by hollowing out a tree trunk;* 獨木舟,也就是挖空樹幹造成的小舟; *geology, or the science of the earth's crust.* 地質學,換句話說就是研究地殼的科學。 **4** ***or so,*** (often equivalent to *about*) suggesting vagueness or uncertainty about quantity: (常等於 about; 表示數量不確定)大約: *There were twenty or so.* 有二十個左右。***or somebody/something/somewhere; somebody/something/somewhere or other,*** (colloq) (expressing uncertainty about who/what/where): (俗)(表示不能確定是誰,是何事物或是何地方)某人;某事物;某地: *I put it in the cupboard or somewhere,* ie somewhere, perhaps in the cupboard. 我大概是把它放在櫥櫃裏或是其他什麼地方了。*'Who told you?'—'Oh, somebody or other, I've forgotten who.'* '誰告訴你的?'—'噢,有個人告訴我的,我忘記是誰了。'

or·acle /'ɒrəkl *US:* 'ɔ:r- ; 'ɔrəkḷ/ *n* **1** (in ancient Greece) (answer given at) place where questions about the future were asked of the gods; priest(ess) giving the answers: (古希臘)神諭;祈求神諭的廟;傳神諭的祭司(女祭司): *consult the ~.* 詢求神諭。 **2** person considered able to give reliable guidance. 被認爲能給予可靠指導的人。**oracu·lar** /ə'rækjʊlə(r) ;

ɔ'rækjələ/ *adj* of or like an ~; with a hidden meaning: 神諭的;像神諭的;有隱意的: *oracular utterances.* 玄奧難解的話。

oral /'ɔːrəl ; 'orəl/ *adj* **1** using the spoken, not the written, word: 口說的;口頭的: *an ~ examination.* 口試。 **2** (anat) of, by, for, the mouth: (解剖)口的;用口的;適於口的: *~ contraceptives,* ⇨ pill(2). 口服避孕藥。□ *n* (colloq) ~ examination. (俗)口試。**~ly** /'ɔːrəlɪ ; 'orəlɪ/ *adv* by spoken words; by the mouth: 口頭上;用口: *not to be taken ~ly,* (eg of medical preparations) not to be swallowed; for external use only. (如指藥劑)不可口服;外用的;外敷的。

or·ange /'ɒrɪndʒ *US:* 'ɔːr- ; 'ɔrɪndʒ/ *n, adj* [C] ⇨ the illus at fruit. 參看 fruit 之插圖。(evergreen tree with a) round, thick-skinned juicy fruit, green and usu changing to a colour between yellow and red; [U] (of the) usu colour of this fully-ripened fruit. 柑(樹);橙(樹);橘(樹);橙黃色(的)。**~·ade** /ˌɒrɪndʒ'eɪd *US:* ˌɔːr- ; ˌɔrɪndʒ'ed/ *n* [U] drink made of ~ juice. 柑汁飲料;橘子水。

Or·ange·man /'ɒrɪndʒmæn *US:* 'ɔːr- ; 'ɔrɪndʒmən/ *n* (*pl* -men) member of a Protestant political society in Ulster, Northern Ireland. 奧蘭治黨員(北愛爾蘭阿爾斯特省擁護新教之政治社團中之一員)。

orang-outang /ɔːˌræŋ uː'tæŋ *US:* əˌræŋ ə'tæŋ ; o'ræŋʊˌtæŋ/ (also **-utan, -outan** /-'tæn ; -ˌtæn/) *n* large, long-armed ape of Borneo and Sumatra. (產於婆羅洲和蘇門答臘的)長臂巨猿;猩猩。⇨ the illus at ape. 參看 ape 之插圖。

orate /ɔː'reɪt ; 'oret/ *vi* [VP2A] speak publicly. 演說;演講。

ora·tion /ɔː'reɪʃn ; o'reʃən/ *n* [C] formal speech made on a public occasion: 正式演講;演說: *a funeral ~.* 弔辭。

ora·tor /'ɒrətə(r) *US:* 'ɔːr- ; 'ɔrətə/ *n* person who makes speeches (esp a good speaker). 演說者;(尤指出色的)演說家。**~·i·cal** /ˌɒrə'tɒrɪkl *US:* ˌɔːrə'tɔːr-; ˌɔrə'tɔrɪkl/ *adj* of speech-making and ~s: 演說的;演說家的: *~ical phrases/gestures;* 演說家的辭令(演說的手勢); *an ~ical contest.* 演講比賽。

ora·torio /ˌɒrə'tɔːrɪəʊ *US:* ˌɔːr- ; ˌɔrə'torɪo/ *n* (*pl* ~s) [C] musical composition for solo voices, chorus and orchestra, usu with a religious subject: 聖樂;神劇(包括獨唱、合唱及管弦樂,通常以宗教爲主題): *the ~s of Handel;* 韓德爾的聖樂; [U] musical compositions of this kind collectively: 聖樂的總稱: *Do you like ~?* 你喜歡聖樂嗎? ⇨ cantata, opera.

ora·tory¹ /'ɒrətrɪ *US:* 'ɔːrətɔːrɪ ; 'ɔrəˌtorɪ/ *n* (*pl* -ries) [C] small chapel for private worship or prayer. 小禮拜堂;祈禱室。

ora·tory² /'ɒrətrɪ *US:* 'ɔːrətɔːrɪ ; 'ɔrəˌtorɪ/ *n* [U] (art of) making speeches; rhetoric. 演說(術);修辭。

orb /ɔːb ; ɔrb/ *n* globe, esp the sun, moon or one of the planets; jewelled globe with a cross on top, part of a sovereign's regalia. 球體;(尤指)星球(太陽、月亮或行星);王權寶球(鑲珠寶的球,球頂有十字架,爲王權標誌之一)。⇨ the illus at regalia. 參看 regalia 之插圖。

or·bit /'ɔːbɪt ; 'ɔrbɪt/ *n* path followed by a heavenly body, eg a planet, the moon, or a man-made object, eg a spacecraft, round another body: (一天體,如行星、月球或太空船等人造飛行物,繞行另一天體的)軌道: *the earth's ~ round the sun.* 地球繞行太陽的軌道。*How many satellites have been put in ~ round the earth?* 有多少個人造衛星已被射入環繞地球的軌道? □ *vt, vi* [VP6A, 2A, C] put into, (cause to) move in, ~ (round): 使進入軌道;(使)循軌道運行: *When was the first man-made satellite ~ed?* 第一顆人造衛星是何時射入軌道的? *How many spacecraft have orbited the moon?* 有多少艘太空船在繞月球軌道運行? **~al** /'ɔːbɪtl ; 'ɔrbɪtl/ *adj* of an ~: 行星(衛星)軌道的: *a spacecraft's ~al distance from the earth.* 太空船軌道與地球的距離。**~ velocity,** minimal velocity needed to place sth in ~. 軌道速度(使某物進入軌道所需的最低速度)。

or·chard /'ɔːtʃəd ; 'ɔrtʃəd/ *n* [C] piece of ground (usu enclosed) with fruit-trees: 果園(通常指圍起來的): *apple-~s.* 蘋果園。

or·ches·tra /'ɔːkɪstrə ; 'ɔrkɪstrə/ *n* **1** group of persons playing musical instruments together: 管絃樂隊;管絃樂團: *a dance/string/symphony ~.* 舞蹈樂隊(絃樂隊;交響樂團)。⇨ *brass band* at brass(3). **2 ~ (pit),** place in a theatre for an ~. (劇院中的)樂隊席。**~ stalls,** front seats on the floor of a theatre. 劇院正廳的前座。**3** semicircular space in front of the stage of a theatre in ancient Greece, where the chorus sang and danced. 合唱舞蹈席(古希臘劇場中舞臺前的半圓場地,爲合唱隊歌唱舞蹈之處)。**or·ches·tral** /ɔː'kestrəl ; ɔr'kɛstrəl/ *adj* of, for, by, an ~: 管絃樂隊的;適於管絃樂隊的;管絃樂隊所演奏的: *orchestral instruments/performances.* 管絃樂隊所用的樂器(管絃樂演奏)。

or·ches·trate /'ɔːkɪstreɪt ; 'ɔrkɪsˌtret/ *vt* [VP6A] compose, arrange, score, for orchestral performances. 把…作成管絃樂;把…編成管絃樂;把…譜入管絃樂。**or·ches·tra·tion** /ˌɔːkɪ'streɪʃn ; ˌɔrkɪs'treʃən/ *n*

or·chid /'ɔːkɪd ; 'ɔrkɪd/ (also **or·chis** /'ɔːkɪs ; 'ɔrkɪs/) *n* [C] sorts of plant of which the English wild kinds (usu *orchis*) have tuberous roots, and the tropical kinds (usu *orchid*) have flowers of brilliant colours and fantastic shapes. 蘭花(英國野生蘭通常稱爲 orchis,有塊狀根;熱帶蘭通常稱爲 orchid,開艷麗奇狀的花)。⇨ the illus at flower. 參看 flower 之插圖。

or·dain /ɔː'deɪn ; ɔr'den/ *vt* **1** [VP6A, 23] make (sb) a priest or minister: 立(某人)爲神父或牧師: *He was ~ed priest.* 他被立爲神父。**2** [VP9] **~ that,** (of God, law, authority) decide; give orders (that); destine: (指上帝、法律、當局)決定;命令;注定: *God has ~ed that all men shall die.* 上帝注定所有的人終必死亡。

or·deal /ɔː'diːl ; ɔr'dil/ *n* severe test of character or endurance: 對於品格或耐力的嚴酷考驗: *pass through terrible ~s.* 經歷可怕的考驗。

or·der¹ /'ɔːdə(r) ; 'ɔrdə/ *n* **1** [U] way in which things are placed in relation to one another: 次序;順序: *names in alphabetical ~;* 照字母順序排列的名字; *in chronological ~,* ie according to dates. 按年代順序。**in ~ of,** arranged according to: 照…排列: *in ~ of size/merit/importance, etc.* 依大小(功績,重要性等)次序排列。**2** [U] condition in which everything is carefully arranged; working condition. 有規律的狀況;工作狀況。***(not) in ~,*** (not) as it should be: 處於(不)正常狀況中;情況良好(不良): *Is your passport in ~,* Has it all the necessary entries to satisfy the authorities? 你的護照辦好了嗎? *He put/left his affairs/accounts/papers in ~ before he left the country.* 他出國前把他的事務(帳目,文件)都整理好了。*Get your ideas into some kind of ~ before beginning to write.* 在動筆之前先把你的概念作一整理。***in good ~,*** without any confusion: 整齊;不亂;井然有序;情況良好: *The troops retired in good ~,* Their retreat was orderly, disciplined. 軍隊秩序井然地撤退。***in good/bad/running/working ~,*** (esp of machines) working well/badly/smoothly, etc: (尤指機器)運轉良好(不佳,正常): *The engine has been tuned and is now in perfect running ~.* 發動機已經調整過,現在運轉十分良好。***out of ~,*** (of a machine, a bodily organ) not functioning properly: (指機器、身體器官)壞了;有毛病;不能適當地起效用: *The lift/phone is out of ~.* 電梯(電話)壞了。*My stomach is out of ~.* 我的胃有點毛病。**3** [U] (condition brought about by) good and firm government, obedience to law, rules, authority: 秩序;良好與穩固的管理;對法律、規則、權威的遵守: *The army restored law and ~.* 軍隊使法律與秩序恢復。*It is the business of the police to keep ~.* 維持秩序(治安)是警察的事。*Some teachers find it difficult to* *keep ~ in their classes／to keep their classes in ~.* 有些教師發現很難維持教室秩序。⇨ disorder. **4** [U] rules usual at a public meeting; rules accepted, eg in Parliament, committee meetings, by members and enforced by a president, chairman, or other officer. 會議規則;(國會,委員會會議等所遵守的)議事規則;會議程序;會場秩序。***call (sb) to ~,*** (of the Speaker in the House of Commons, the chairman of a meeting, etc) request (a member, etc) to obey the rules, the usual procedures. (指英國下議院議長、會議主席等)請(某人)遵守會場秩序。***be in ~ to do sth,*** be according to the rules, etc: 依照規定等做某事: *Is it in ~ to interrupt?* 打岔(插嘴)合規矩嗎？ ***on a point of ~,*** on a point (= question) of procedure. 在程序問題上。***O~! O~!*** (used to call attention to a departure from the usual rules of debates or procedures). 守秩序！守秩序！ ***~ of the day,*** programme of business to be discussed. 當日議程。**'~-paper** *n* written or printed ~ of the day. 當日議程表。**standing ~s,** ⇨ standing *adj*(1). **5** [C] command given with authority: 命令: *Soldiers must obey ~s.* 軍人必須服從命令。*He gave ~s for the work to be started／that the work should be started at once.* 他下令立刻開始工作。***be under ~s (to do sth),*** have received ~s: 奉命(做某事): *He is under ~s to leave for Finland next week.* 他奉命下星期前往芬蘭。***by ~ of,*** according to directions given by proper authority of: 奉…之命: *by ~ of the Governor.* 奉省(州)長之命。***under the ~s of,*** commanded by. 受…指揮。***under starters' ~s,*** ⇨ start². **6** [C] request to supply goods; the goods (to be) supplied: 定購;定單;定貨;(待)交付之貨: *an ~ for two tons of coal;* 二噸煤的定單; *give a tradesman an ~ for goods;* 向商人定購貨物; *fill an ~,* supply the goods asked for. 交付定貨。*The butcher has called for ~s,* to ask what is wanted. 肉商來問需要什麼肉。***on ~,*** requested but not yet supplied. 定購中。***made to ~,*** made according to the customer's special requirements or instructions. 定做的。⇨ *ready-made* at ready. **a large／tall ~,** (colloq) sth difficult to do or supply. (俗)難做的事;難供應之物。**'~-book** *n* one in which a tradesman, commercial traveller, manufacturer, etc writes down ~s for goods: 定貨簿: *The company has full ~-books,* orders for large quantities of goods. 該公司有多本滿滿的定貨簿(有大量的定貨)。**'~-form** *n* printed form with blank spaces to be filled in by the customer. 定貨單。 **7** [C] written direction to a bank (**'banker's ~**) or post office (**'postal ~**) to pay money, or giving authority to do sth: (銀行或郵局之)滙票;授權憑證: *an ~ on O'Reilly's Bank;* 歐來利銀行滙票; *a postal ~ for £9;* 九鎊的郵政滙票; *an ~ to view,* eg from an estate-agent to inspect a house that is for sale. 察看許可書 (例如房地產經紀人所開讓人察看出售房屋者)。 **8** [U] purpose, intention. 目的;意向。***in ~ to do sth,*** with the purpose of doing sth, with a view to doing sth: 欲作某事; 爲了做某事: *in ~ (for you) to see clearly.* 爲着(使你)看得清楚。 ***in ~ that,*** with the intention that; so that: 爲了;以便: *in ~ that he may／might／shall／should arrive in time.* 以便他能及時到達。 **9** [C] group of people belonging to or appointed to a special class (as an honour or reward): 屬於或被列入某一特殊等級(作爲一種榮譽或報酬)的一批人: *the O~ of Merit／of Knights／of the Bath／of the Golden Kite, etc;* 獲得殊功勳位(爵士勳位，巴斯勳位，金鳶勳位等)的一批人; badge, sign, etc worn by members of such an ~:(有此類勳位者所佩帶的)勳章;勳位標誌: *wearing all his ~s and decorations.* 佩帶着他所有的勳章和獎章。 **10** (*pl*) authority given by a bishop to perform church duties. (複)主敎所授予以便履行敎會職責的權力;牧師職。***be in／take (holy) ~s,*** be／become a priest. 擔任牧師(受聖職;就任牧師職)。 **11** [C] class of persons on whom holy ~s have been conferred: 聖職人員階級: *the O~ of Deacons／Priests／Bishops.* 執事(牧師,主敎)階級。 **12** [C] group of persons living under religious rules: 敎團;修道會: *the monastic ~s;* 修士會; *the ~ of Dominicans.* 聖多明尼克敎會。 **13** [C] method of treating architectural forms, esp of columns (pillars) and capitals, esp the classical ~s (*Doric, Ionic, Corinthian*). (尤指柱子與柱冠的)建築形式;柱範;柱式(尤指古典柱式) (Doric order, 希臘 Doris 地方流行的一種最古樸的柱式; Ionic order, 希臘 Ionia 地方流行的一種雕刻較精的柱式; Corinthian order, 希臘 Corinth 地方流行雕刻最華麗的柱式)。⇨ the illus at column. 參看 column 之插圖。 **14** (biol) [C] highest division under *class* in the grouping of animals, plants, etc: (生物)目(生物分類中僅次於 '綱' 的分類): *The rose and the bean families belong to the same ~.* 薔薇科與豆科屬於同一個目。 **15** [C] kind; sort: 種;類: *intellectual ability of a high ~.* 高等的智能。 **16** [U] arrangement of military forces: 軍隊的排列;隊形;序列: *advance in review ~,* on parade; (閱兵中)以分列式行進; *advance in extended ~,* in battle. (戰鬥中) 以疏開隊形前進。***advance in open／close ~,*** with wide／with only slight spaces between the men, etc. 以散開(密集)隊形前進。

or·der² /'ɔ:də(r) ; 'ɔrdɚ/ *vt* **1** [VP6A, 9, 12B, 13B, 15A, B, 17] give an order (5, 6, 7) *to* (sb) or *for* sth: (對某人或爲某事)命令;指令;定購;滙寄;授權: *The doctor ~ed me to (stay in) bed.* 醫生吩咐我臥床休息。*The disobedient boy was ~ed out of the room.* 那個不聽話的男孩被趕出房間。*The chairman ~ed silence.* 主席命令保持肅靜。*The regiment was ~ed to the front.* 該團奉令開赴前線。*The judge ~ed that the prisoner should be remanded.* 法官諭令被告還押。*The doctor has ~ed me absolute quiet.* 醫生囑我要絕對安靜。*She ~ed herself two dozen oysters and a pint of stout.* 她自己點了兩打牡蠣和一品脫黑啤酒。*I've ~ed lunch for 1.30.* 我已經下令一點三十分開午飯。*The regiment was ~ed up (to the front).* 該團奉令出發(開赴前線)。***~ sb about,*** keep on giving orders to him. 不斷驅使某人。 **2** [VP6A, 15A] arrange; direct: 安排;指導;管理: *~ one's life according to strict rules.* 依嚴格的規律安排自己的生活。 **~·ing** *n* (from 2 above) (出自上列第 2 義) arrangement. 安排;佈置。

or·der·ly /'ɔ:dəlɪ ; 'ɔrdɚlɪ/ *adj* **1** well arranged; in good order; tidy: 有秩序的;有順序的;整齊的: *an ~ room／desk;* 整齊的房間(書桌); methodically inclined: 有條理的: *a man with an ~ mind.* 思想有條不紊的人。 **2** well behaved; obedient to discipline: 守秩序的;守規律的: *an ~ crowd.* 守秩序的群衆。 **3** (army use, attrib only) concerned with carrying out orders: (軍隊用語,僅作形容用法)執行命令的: *the ~ officer,* the officer on duty for the day; 值日官;值勤官; *the '~ room,* room in barracks where the clerical work is done. (營房內之)辦公室;文書室。 □ *n* (*pl* -lies) (army) officer's messenger. (軍語)傳令兵。 **medical ~,** attendant in a military hospital. 醫務兵。 **or·der·li·ness** *n*

or·di·nal /'ɔ:dɪnl *US:* -dənl ; 'ɔrdn̩əl/ *n, adj* [C] (number) showing order or position in a series. 序數;順序的;依次的。~ **numbers,** eg *first, second, third.* 序數(例如第一,第二,第三)。⇨ cardinal; App 4. 參看 cardinal 及附錄四。

or·di·nance /'ɔ:dɪnəns ; 'ɔrdn̩əns/ *n* [C] order, rule, statute, made by authority or decree: 法令;條例: *the ~s of the City Council.* 市議會頒佈的法令。

or·di·nand /ˌɔ:dɪ'nænd *US:* 'ɔ:rdənænd ; 'ɔrdənænd/ *n* candidate for ordination. 聖職候選人。

or·di·nary /'ɔ:dɪnrɪ *US:* 'ɔ:rdənerɪ ; 'ɔrdn̩ɛrɪ/ *adj* normal; usual; average: 正常的;通常的;普通的: *an ~ day's work;* 日常的工作; *in ~ dress.* 穿着平常的衣服。***in an ~ way,*** if the circumstances were ~ or usual. 若按常情;就通常情形。***in the ~ way,*** in the usual or customary way. 通常地;通例地;慣常地;一般。***in ~***, by permanent appointment, not temporary or extraordinary: 常任的; 非臨時的: *physician in ~ to Her Majesty.* 女王的常任醫師;御醫。***out of the ~***, unusual. 不平常的。~ **seaman**, (abbr 略作 **OS**) one who has not yet received the rank of *able seaman* (abbr 略作 *A B*). 二等水兵(一等水兵爲 able seaman)。**or·di·nar·ily** /ˈɔːdɪnərəlɪ *US:* ˌɔːdnˈerəlɪ; ˌɔrdnˈɛrəlɪ/ *adv* in an ~ way: 通常地;正常地;一般: *behave quite ordinarily.* 行爲十分平常。

or·di·na·tion /ˌɔːdɪˈneɪʃn *US:* -dnˈeɪʃn; ˌɔrdnˈeʃən/ *n* [U] ceremony of ordaining (a priest or minister); [C] instance of this. 任命(神父或牧師)的儀式;聖職的任命。

ord·nance /ˈɔːdnəns; ˈɔrdnəns/ *n* [U] artillery; munitions. 砲;軍火。**Royal Army ˈO~ Corps**, (US 美 = **O~ Corps**), that which is responsible for military supplies. 皇家陸軍兵工署(部隊)。**the O~ Survey**, (the preparation of) accurate and detailed maps of GB. 精確詳細的英國地圖;此種地圖之測繪。

or·dure /ˈɔːdjʊə(r) *US:* -dʒər; ˈɔrdʒɚ/ *n* [U] excrement; dung; filth. 排泄物;糞;汚物。

ore /ɔː(r); or/ *n* [C, U] (kinds of) rock, earth, mineral, etc from which metal can be mined or extracted: 礦石;礦沙;礦塊: *iron ore;* 鐵礦; *a district rich in ores.* 礦產豐富的地區。

or·gan /ˈɔːgən; ˈɔrgən/ *n* **1** any part of an animal body or plant serving an essential purpose: (動植物的)器官: *the ~s of speech*, the tongue, teeth, lips, etc; 語言器官(如舌、牙、唇等);發音器官; *the ˈnasal ~*, the nose; 鼻器官; *the reproductive ~s.* 生殖器官。⇨ the illus at alimentary, ear, eye, respire, reproduce. 參看 alimentary, ear, eye, respire, reproduce 等字之插圖。**2** means of getting work done; organization: 工作機關;組織: *Parliament is the chief ~ of government.* 國會是政府的主要機關。**3** means for making known what people think: 傳播工具;報紙: *~s of public opinion*, newspapers, radios, TV, etc. 輿論的喉舌(報紙,無線電廣播,電視等)。**4** musical instrument from which sounds are produced by air forced through pipes, played by keys pressed with the fingers and pedals pressed with the feet (in US also called 美亦稱 a **ˈpipe-~**). 風琴。⇨ the illus at church. 參看 church 之插圖。**ˈreed/Aˈmerican ~**, harmonium (with reeds instead of pipes). 簧風琴(以簧代管的風琴)。**ˈ~-blower** *n* person who works the bellows of an ~. 操作風琴風箱的人。**ˈ~-grinder** *n* person who plays a barrel-~. 操作筒風琴的人。⇨ barrel. **ˈ~-loft** *n* gallery (in some churches, etc) where the ~ is placed. (某些教堂等中的)風琴臺。**ˈ~·ist** /-ɪst; -ɪst/ *n* person who plays an ~(4). 風琴演奏家。

or·gan·die (US also **-dy**) /ɔːˈgændɪ; ˈɔrgəndɪ/ *n* [U] kind of fine translucent muslin. 蟬翼紗(一種透明的細棉布)。

or·ganic /ɔːˈgænɪk; ɔrˈgænɪk/ *adj* **1** of an organ or organs of the body: 器官的: *~ diseases*, affecting the structure of these organs, not only their functions. 器官性病;機質性病。**2** (opp *inorganic*) having bodily organs: (爲 inorganic 之相反字)有機(體)的: *~ life.* 有機的生物。~ **chemistry**, dealing with carbon compounds. 有機化學。**3** made of related parts; arranged as a system: 有組織的;有系統的: *an ~* (ie organized) *whole;* 有組織的整體; *an ~* (ie structural) *part.* 一個組成部份。**or·gani·cally** /-klɪ; -kl̩ɪ/ *adv.*

or·gan·ism /ˈɔːgənɪzəm; ˈɔrgənˌɪzəm/ *n* [C] living being with parts which work together; individual animal or plant; any system with parts dependent upon each other: 生物;個別的動物或植物;有機體;組織: *the social ~.* 社會;社會組織。

or·gan·iz·ation /ˌɔːgənaɪˈzeɪʃn *US:* -nɪˈz-; ˌɔrgənəˈzeʃən/ *n* **1** [U] act of organizing; condition of being organized: 組織的行動; 被組織的狀況; 組織: *He is engaged in the ~ of a new club.* 他正忙着組織一個新俱樂部。*An army without ~ would be useless.* 無組織的軍隊是沒用的。**2** [C] organized body of persons; organized system: 機構;組織;有組織的系統: *The human body has a very complex ~.* 人體有很複雜的組織。

or·gan·ize /ˈɔːgənaɪz; ˈɔrgənˌaɪz/ *vt, vi* [VP6A, 2A] **1** put into working order; arrange in a system; make preparations for: 組合;組織;籌畫;籌辦;創辦: *~ an army/a government/a political party/an expedition to the South Pole/one's work/oneself.* 編組軍隊(組織政府;組織政黨;組織南極探險隊;籌畫工作;使自己心裡有準備)。**2** (of workers, etc) form into, join, a trade union. (指工人等)組成工會;參加工會。**or·gan·ized** *adj* **1** ordered; orderly. 有組織的;有秩序的。**2** furnished with organs; made into a living organism: 有器官的;作成生物的: *highly ~d forms of life.* 器官發達的生物。**3** (of workers) in a trade union. (指工人)加入工會的。**or·gan·izer** *n* person who ~s things. 組織者;創辦者。

or·gasm /ˈɔːgæzəm; ˈɔrgæzəm/ *n* [C] violent (esp erotic) excitement; the climax of sexual excitement. 激烈的(尤指性的)興奮;性慾高潮;性慾亢進。

or·gi·as·tic /ˌɔːdʒɪˈæstɪk; ˌɔrdʒɪˈæstɪk/ *adj* of the nature of an orgy; frenzied. 狂歡的;狂亂的。

orgy /ˈɔːdʒɪ; ˈɔrdʒɪ/ *n* [C] (*pl* orgies) **1** occasion of wild merry-making; (*pl*) drunken or licentious revels. 狂歡;(複)醉酒或淫佚的宴樂;喝花酒。**2** (colloq) excessive amount: (俗)過量;過多: *an ~ of parties/concerts/spending.* 過多的聚會(音樂會,花費)。

oriel /ˈɔːrɪəl; ˈorɪəl/ *n* **1** part of a room projecting from an upper storey and supported from the ground or on corbels and having a window in it. 樓房懸凸壁外而帶窗的部份。**2** ˈ~ **(window)**, window of an ~. 凸窗;突窗。⇨ the illus at window. 參看 window 之插圖。

orient[1] /ˈɔːrɪənt; ˈorɪˌɛnt/ *n* **the O~**, (liter) the countries of the East, ie Asia, contrasted with *the Occident.* (文)東方諸國(卽亞洲,與 the Occident 相對)。□ *adj* (poet) Eastern; (of the sun) rising: (詩)東方的;(指太陽)上昇的: *the ~ sun.* 上昇的太陽;朝陽。

orient[2] /ˈɔːrɪənt; ˈorɪˌɛnt/ *vt* = orientate.

orien·tal /ˌɔːrɪˈentl; ˌorɪˈɛntl/ *adj* of the Orient: 東方(諸國)的: *~ civilization/art/rugs.* 東方文明(藝術,地毯)。□ *n* **O~**, inhabitant of the Orient, esp China and Japan. 東方人(尤指中國人與日本人)。**~·ist** /-ɪst; -ɪst/ *n* person who studies the languages, arts, etc of ~ countries. 研究東方語言、藝術等的人。

orien·tate /ˈɔːrɪənteɪt; ˈorɪɛnˌtet/ *vt* [VP6A] **1** place (a building, etc) so as to face east; build (a church) with the chancel end due east. 使(建築物等)朝向東方;建築(教堂)使其聖壇在東端。**2** place or exactly determine the position of (sth) with regard to the points of the compass; (fig) bring into clearly understood relations: 照指南針安置或決定(某物)之位置;(喻)使認清情勢: *~ oneself*, make oneself familiar with a situation, determine how one stands in relation to one's surroundings, etc. 認識環境,確定立場(使自己認識環境,決定自己在所處環境中的立場,並使自己能够適應)。**orien·ta·tion** /ˌɔːrɪenˈteɪʃn; ˌorɪɛnˈteʃən/ *n* [U] orientating or being ~d. 朝向東方;使在東端;定方向;定方位;朝向;認識環境。

ori·fice /ˈɒrɪfɪs *US:* ˈɔːr-; ˈɔrəfɪs/ *n* outer opening; mouth (of a cave, etc). 外孔;(洞穴等的)口;洞口。

ori·gin /ˈɒrɪdʒɪn *US:* ˈɔːrədʒɪn; ˈɔrədʒɪn/ *n* [C, U] starting-point: 起源;開端: *the ~ of a quarrel;* 爭吵的起因; *the ~(s) of civilization;* 文明的起源; *a man of humble ~*, parentage; 出身寒微的人; *words of Latin ~.* 字源出自拉丁文的字。

orig·inal /əˈrɪdʒənl; əˈrɪdʒənl̩/ *adj* **1** first or earliest: 原先的;最早的;最初的: *the ~ inhabitants of the country.* 這個國家最早的居民。*The ~ plan was better than the plan we followed.* 原先的計畫優於我

們所實行的計畫。 ~ **sin**, ⇨ sin. **2** newly formed or created; not copied or imitated: 新創的;創舉的;非抄襲的;非模仿的: ~ *ideas;* 創見; *an ~ design.* 別出心裁的設計。 **3** able to produce new ideas, etc; inventive: 能產生新見解的; 有創見的: *an ~ thinker/writer;* 富創見的思想家(作家); *an ~ mind.* 獨具卓見的人。□ *n* **1** [C] that from which sth is copied: 原作品;原物: *This is a copy; the ~ is in the Prado in Madrid.* 這是仿造品,原作是在馬德里的國家美術館。 **2 the ~,** language in which sth was first composed: 原文: *read Homer in the ~,* in ancient Greek; 讀原文(即古希臘文)的荷馬作品; *study Don Quixote in the ~,* in Spanish. 研讀原文(即西班牙文)的唐吉訶德。 **3** [C] person with an original(3) mind. 有創見的人。 **~ly** /-nəlɪ; -nl̩ɪ/ *adv* **1** in an ~ manner: 新穎地;獨特地;別出心裁地: *speak/think/write ~ly.* 別出心裁地說話(思想,寫作)。 **2** from or in the beginning: 原先;起始: *The school was ~ly quite small.* 這個學校原先是相當小的。 **~·ity** /əˌrɪdʒəˈnælətɪ; əˌrɪdʒəˈnælətɪ/ *n* [U] state or quality of being ~(2): 創新; 創造性; 創造力;獨特: *work that lacks ~ity,* is copied or imitated. 缺少創造性的作品(抄襲或模仿的作品)。

orig·inate /əˈrɪdʒɪneɪt; əˈrɪdʒəˌnet/ *vi, vt* **1** [VP2C, 3A] *~ from/in sth; ~ from/with sb,* have as a cause or beginning: 發源;發起;發生: *The quarrel ~d in rivalry between two tribes.* 爭論是由兩個部落之間的競爭而起的。 *With whom did the scheme ~?* 這計畫是誰發起的? **2** [VP6A] be the author or creator of: 創作;發明: *~ a new style of dancing.* 創造一種新的舞步。 **orig·in·ator** /-tə(r); -tɚ/ *n*

ori·ole /ˈɔːrɪəʊl; ˈorɪˌol/ *n* **(golden) ~,** kinds of bird with black and yellow feathers. 金鶯。

ori·son /ˈɒrɪzn *US:* ˈɔːr-; ˈɔrɪzn̩/ *n* [C] (archaic) prayer. (古)祈禱。

or·lop /ˈɔːlɒp; ˈɔrlɑp/ *n* **'~ (deck),** lowest deck of a ship with three or more decks. (具有三層或更多層甲板之船的)最下層甲板。

or·molu /ˈɔːməluː; ˈɔrməˌlu/ *n* [U, C] (article made of, or decorated with) gilded bronze or a gold-coloured alloy of copper, zinc and tin: 金色黃銅(鍍金的黃銅或金色的銅、鋅、錫合金);金色黃銅製品;用金色黃銅裝飾的物品: *an ~ clock.* 金色黃銅時鐘。

or·na·ment /ˈɔːnəmənt; ˈɔrnəmənt/ *n* **1** [U] adorning or being adorned; that which is added for decoration: 裝飾;裝飾物: *add sth by way of ~;* 加添某物作爲裝飾; *an altar rich in ~.* 裝飾華麗的祭壇。 **2** [C] sth designed or used to add beauty to sth else: 裝飾品: *a shelf crowded with ~s,* eg small vases, statuettes, pieces of china. 擺滿裝飾品的架子。 **3** [C] person, act, quality, etc that adds beauty, charm, etc: 添加光彩的人;增添優美或韻味的動作、品質等: *He is an ~ to his profession.* 他是一個爲他職業增光的人。□ *vt* /ˈɔːnəment; ˈɔrnəˌmɛnt/ [VP6A, 14] be an ~ to; make beautiful: 裝飾;修飾: *~ a dress with lace.* 用花邊裝飾衣服。 **or·na·men·tal** /ˌɔːnəˈmentl; ˌɔrnəˈmɛntl̩/ *adj* of or for ~. 裝飾的;爲着裝飾的。 **or·na·men·ta·tion** /ˌɔːnəmenˈteɪʃn; ˌɔrnəmɛnˈteʃən/ *n* [U] ~ing or being ~ed; that which ~s: 裝飾;被裝飾;裝飾物: *a church with no ~ation.* 沒有裝飾的教堂。

or·nate /ɔːˈneɪt; ɔrˈnet/ *adj* richly ornamented; (of liter style) full of flowery language; not simple in style or vocabulary. 裝飾華麗的;(指文學體裁)詞藻華美的;文詞繁複的。 **~·ly** *adv* **~·ness** *n*

or·nery /ˈɔːnərɪ; ˈɔrnərɪ/ *adj* (US colloq) ill-tempered; perverse and stubborn. (美俗)壞脾氣的;倔强頑固的。

or·ni·thol·ogy /ˌɔːnɪˈθɒlədʒɪ; ˌɔrnəˈθɑlədʒɪ/ *n* [U] scientific study of birds. 鳥類學。 **or·ni·thol·ogist** /-dʒɪst; -dʒɪst/ *n* expert in ~. 鳥類學家。 **or·ni·tho·logi·cal** /ˌɔːnɪθəˈlɒdʒɪkl; ˌɔrnɪθəˈlɑdʒɪkl/ *adj*

oro·tund /ˈɔːrəʊtʌnd; ˈɔrəˌtʌnd/ *adj* (formal) (正式用語) **1** imposing; dignified. 宏壯的;莊嚴的。 **2** pompous; pretentious. 誇大的;矯飾的。

or·phan /ˈɔːfn; ˈɔrfən/ *n* person (esp a child) who has lost one or both of its parents by death: 父親、母親或雙親死亡的人;(尤指)孤兒: (attrib) (形容用法) *an ~ child.* 孤兒。□ *vt* [VP6A] cause to be an ~: 使成爲孤兒: *~ed by war.* 因戰爭而成爲孤兒的。 **~·age** /-ɪdʒ; -ɪdʒ/ *n* home for ~s. 孤兒院。

or·ris·root /ˈɒrɪsruːt *US:* ˈɔːr-; ˈɔrɪsˌrut/ *n* fragrant root of some kinds of iris, used in perfumes and cosmetics. 鳶尾根(某些鳶尾屬植物之藍紫色香根,用以製香水及化粧品)。

or·tho·dox /ˈɔːθədɒks; ˈɔrθəˌdɑks/ *adj* (having opinions, beliefs, etc which are) generally accepted or approved: 持有正統或純正之見解、信仰等的;正統的;純正的;公認的;傳統的: *an ~ member of the Church;* 正統教會的教友; *~ beliefs;* 正統的信仰; *~ behaviour.* (公認的)正當的行爲。 ⇨ heterodox. **the O~ Church,** the Eastern Church, recognizing the Patriarch of Constantinople (= *Istanbul*) as chief bishop; the communion of the autonomous churches of the Soviet Union, Romania, Greece, etc. 東正教;希臘正教。 **~y** /ˈɔːθədɒksɪ; ˈɔrθəˌdɑksɪ/ *n* (*pl* ~ies) [U] being ~; [C] ~ belief, character, practice. 正統;純正; 正教; 傳統的說法;正統的信仰、性格、常規。

or·thogra·phy /ɔːˈθɒgrəfɪ; ɔrˈθɑgrəfɪ/ *n* [U] (system of) spelling; correct or conventional spelling. 拼字(法); 正確的拼字; 傳統的拼字。 **or·tho·graphic** /ˌɔːθəˈgræfɪk; ˌɔrθəˈgræfɪk/ *adj*

or·tho·paedic (also **-pedic**) /ˌɔːθəˈpiːdɪk; ˌɔrθəˈpidɪk/ *adj* of the curing of deformities and diseases of bones: 矯形(畸形及骨病之治療)的: *~ surgery.* 矯形外科;整形外科。 **or·tho·paed·ics** (also 亦作 **-ped·ics**) *n* (with *sing v*) branch of surgery dealing with bone deformities and diseases. (用單數動詞)矯形學。

or·to·lan /ˈɔːtələn; ˈɔrtələn/ *n* small wild bird valued as a table delicacy. 蒿雀(可作美味食品)。

oryx /ˈɒrɪks *US:* ˈɔːr-; ˈɔrɪks/ *n* African antelope with long, straight or arching horns. 非洲大羚羊(角長而直或彎成拱形)。

Os·car /ˈɒskə(r); ˈɔskɚ/ *n* the annual US award for what is judged to be a great achievement in cinema: 奧斯卡金像獎(美國每年一度頒給電影藝術之偉大成就獎): *be nominated for/win an ~.* 被提名競選(獲得)奧斯卡金像獎。

os·cil·late /ˈɒsɪleɪt; ˈɑslˌet/ *vi, vt* **1** [VP2A] swing backwards and forwards as the pendulum of a clock does; (fig) waver or change between extremes of opinion, etc. 來回擺動;(喻)意見等游移不定;躊躇。 **2** [VP6A] cause to swing to and fro. 使來回擺動;使動搖。 **3** (electr, of current) undergo high frequency alternations; (of radio receivers) radiate electromagnetic waves; experience interference (in reception) from this. (電學,指電流)振盪;(指無線電接收器)發射電磁波;(接收時由於電磁波而)受干擾;發雜音。 **oscillating current,** current whose direction is periodically reversed. 振盪電流。 **os·ci·la·tion** /ˌɒsɪˈleɪʃn; ˌɑslˈeʃən/ *n* oscillating or being ~d; [C] one swing of a pendulum or other object or of an electric charge. 來回擺動; 振盪; (鐘擺等的) 一次擺動。 **os·cil·lator** /-tə(r); -tɚ/ *n* (esp) device for producing electric oscillations (eg for wireless telegraphy). (尤指)使電振盪的工具;發振器;振盪器(如無線電報等中所用者)。

os·cillo·graph /əˈsɪləgrɑːf *US:* -græf; əˈsɪləˌgræf/ *n* (electr) instrument for recording oscillations. (電)示波記錄器(記錄振盪的儀器)。

os·cillo·scope /əˈsɪləskəʊp; əˈsɪləˌskop/ *n* (electr) instrument which shows on the screen of a cathode ray tube (like a TV screen) variations of current as a wavy line. (電)示波器(在陰極射線管屏幕上,如電視之螢光幕,顯出波動曲線以表示電流變動之儀器)。

osier /ˈəʊzɪə(r) *US:* ˈəʊʒə(r); ˈoʒɚ/ *n* [C] kind of willow-tree, the twigs of which are used in basket-work. 一種柳樹(其枝用於編結筐籃)。

os·prey /ˈɒsprɪ; ˈɑsprɪ/ *n* (*pl* ~s) large kind of

hawk that preys on fish. 鶚(一種食魚的大鷹)。

osseous /ˈɒsɪəs ; ˈɑsɪəs/ *adj* consisting of bone; having a bony skeleton. 含骨的;有骨骼的。

oss·ify /ˈɒsɪfaɪ ; ˈɑsəˌfaɪ/ *vt, vi* (*pt, pp* -fied) [VP6A, 2A] (formal) make or become hard like bone; change into bone; (fig) make or become rigid, unprogressive, unable to change. (正式用語)(使)硬化如骨;(使)骨化;成爲骨;(喻)(使)僵化或不進展;(使)不改變。**ossi·fi·ca·tion** /ˌɒsɪfɪˈkeɪʃn ; ˌɑsəfəˈkeʃən/ *n* [U] ~ing or being ossified; that part of a structure that is ossified. 骨化;硬化;硬化部份。

os·ten·sible /ɒˈstensəbl ; ɑsˈtɛnsəbl̩/ *adj* (of reasons, etc) put forward in an attempt to hide the real reason; apparent. (指理由等)假裝的;表面的。**os·ten·sibly** /-əblɪ ; -əblɪ/ *adv*

os·ten·ta·tion /ˌɒstenˈteɪʃn ; ˌɑstənˈteʃən/ *n* [U] display (of wealth, learning, skill, etc) to obtain admiration or envy: (財富、學識、技術等的)誇耀;虛飾;賣弄: *the ~ of the newly rich.* 暴發戶的誇耀。

os·ten·ta·tious /ˌɒstenˈteɪʃəs ; ˌɑstənˈteʃəs/ *adj* fond of, showing, ostentation: 好誇耀的;招搖的;炫耀的;賣弄的: *~ jewellery;* 外觀華麗的珠寶; *in an ~ manner.* 以誇張的態度。**~·ly** *adv*

os·te·opathy /ˌɒstɪˈɒpəθɪ ; ˌɑstɪˈɑpəθɪ/ *n* [U] treatment of certain diseases by manipulation of the bones and muscles. 骨療法(以按摩骨骼與肌肉以治療某些疾病的方法);按骨術;療骨術。**os·teo·path** /ˈɒstɪəpæθ ; ˈɑstɪəˌpæθ/ *n* person who practises ~. 按骨術士;施行骨療者。

os·tler /ˈɒslə(r) ; ˈɑslɚ/ *n* (old use) stableman (man who looks after horses) at an inn. (舊用法)小旅店中的馬夫。

os·tra·cize /ˈɒstrəsaɪz ; ˈɑstrəˌsaɪz/ *vt* [VP6A] **1** shut out from society; refuse to meet, talk to, etc: 放逐;排斥;擯棄: *People who hold very unorthodox opinions are sometimes ~d.* 持非正統意見的人有時會遭受排斥。 **2** (in ancient Greece) banish by popular vote for ten or five years. (在古希臘)由公民投票放逐十年或五年;流放。**os·tra·cism** /-sɪzəm ; -ˌsɪzəm/ *n* [U] ostracizing or being ~d. 放逐;排斥;擯棄。

os·trich /ˈɒstrɪtʃ ; ˈɔstrɪtʃ/ *n* fast-running bird, the largest in existence, unable to fly, bred for its valuable tail feathers: 鴕鳥: *have the digestion of an ~*, be able to digest almost anything. 有鴕鳥那樣的消化力(幾乎能消化任何東西)。 ⇨ the illus at rare. 參看 rare 之插圖。

other /ˈʌðə(r) ; ˈʌðɚ/ *adj, pron* (person or thing) not already named or implied. 其他的(人或物);另外的(人或物);其餘的(人或物);別的(人或物)。 **1 the ~,** (*sing*) the second of two: (單)(指兩者中之第二個)另一(個): *The twins are so much alike that people find it difficult to tell (the) one from the ~.* 那一對孿生子那麼地相像,使人們難以分辨彼此。*One of them is mine; the ~ is my sister's.* 兩個之中一個是我的,另一個是我姐姐(妹妹)的。*The post office is on the ~ side of the street.* 郵局在街的另一邊。*Where are the ~ boys?* 其他的男孩子在哪兒? ***on the ˈ~ hand,*** used (sometimes, but not always, after *on the one hand*) to introduce sth in contrast to an earlier statement, etc: (有時用在 on the one hand 之後,但並非總是如此)另一方面: *It's cheap, but on the ~ hand the quality is poor.* 它是便宜的,但在另一方面,質料很差。 **2 the ~s,** (*pl*) when the reference is to two or more: (複)其他的(指兩個或更多的人、物等);其餘的(人、物): *Six of them are mine; the ~s are John's.* 其中六個是我的,其餘是約翰的。 *Where are the ~s?* 其他的人在哪兒? **3** (with the *indef art,* written and printed as one word, **an~** /əˈnʌðə(r) ; əˈnʌðɚ/) an additional (one); a different one. (與不定冠詞連用,寫成或印成一個字,即 another) 再一;又一(個);另一個。 ⇨ another. *Will you have an~ cup of tea?* 你再來一杯茶好嗎? *I won't say an~ word about it.* 我不願再談這件事。*I don't like this one; can you show me an~?* 我不喜歡這一個;你能給我看另外一個嗎? (The *pl* of *an~* is *some/any ~s* or *some/any more*): (another 的複數是 some/any others 或 some/any more): *I don't like these. Have you any ~s/any more?* 我不喜歡這些。你還有沒有其他的呢? *Please let me see some ~s/some more.* 請另外拿一些給我看。 **4** (when one member of a group is compared with any ~ member of the group, *other* is usu used): (當一群中某一份子與該群中其他份子比較時,通常用 other): *Green is far better as a bowler than any ~ member of the team.* 身爲板球投手,格林比隊裡其他隊員强得多。 **5** (phrases) (片語) ***each ~,*** ⇨ each(4). ***every ~,*** **(a)** all the ~s: 所有其他的: *John is stupid; every ~ boy in the class knows the answer.* 約翰很笨;班上所有其他的男孩都知道這答案。 **(b)** alternate: 間隔的;交替的: *Write only on every ~ line.* 務必隔行書寫。 ***one an~,*** ⇨ one[3](3). ***one after the ~; one after an~,*** in succession, not together. 一個接一個地;相繼地。 ***... or ~,*** used to suggest absence of certainty or precision: 用以表示不肯定或不精確之意: *I shall be coming again some day or ~*, one of these days. 我大約過幾天還會再來。 *I'll get there somehow or ~*, by one means if not by an~. 我無論如何會到那兒。*Someone or ~* (= Some unknown person) *has left the gate open.* 有人沒關上門。 ***~ things being equal,*** if conditions are/were the same or alike except for the point in question: 如果其他情形都一樣: *O~ things being equal, Alice would marry Jim, not Tom, but Jim is poor and Tom is rich.* 如果其他情形都一樣,愛麗絲會嫁給吉姆,不會嫁給湯姆,可是吉姆貧窮而湯姆富有。 ***the ~ day,*** a few days ago. 幾天前。 **6** different: 不同的: *I do not wish her ~ than she is.* 我不希望她改變現狀。*The question must be decided by quite ~ considerations.* 這個問題必須根據完全不同的因素來決定。 **~·worldly** /ˌʌðəˈwɜːldlɪ ; ˈʌðɚˈwɝldlɪ/ *adj* concerned with, thinking of, another world, of sth mystic rather than with this world. 來世的;凝想來世的;超脫世俗的。 □ *adv* (= *otherwise*) in a different way: 用別的方法;不那樣: *I could not do it ~ than hurriedly.* 我只好匆匆忙忙地做那件事。

other·wise /ˈʌðəwaɪz ; ˈʌðɚˌwaɪz/ *adv* **1** in another or different way: 用其他的方法;不同地;不那樣: *You evidently think ~.* 你顯然有不同的想法。*He should have been working but he was ~ engaged,* but he was doing sth different. 他應該已經在工作,但是他却在忙別的事。 **2** in other or different respects; in different conditions: 在其他方面;在不同方面;在不同的情況之下: *The rent is high, but ~ the house is satisfactory.* 租金昂貴,但在其他方面這屋子還令人滿意。□ *conj* if not; or else: 否則;不然: *Do what you've been told; ~ you will be punished.* 照所吩咐的做,否則你將受罰。

oti·ose /ˈəʊʃɪəʊs ; ˈoʃɪˌos/ *adj* (formal) serving no practical purpose; not required; functionless. (正式用語)沒用處的;不需要的;無效的。

ot·ter /ˈɒtə(r) ; ˈɑtɚ/ *n* [C] fur-covered, fish-eating aquatic animal with four webbed feet and a flat tail; [U] its fur. (水)獺;獺皮。 ⇨ the illus at small. 參看 small 之插圖。

ot·to·man /ˈɒtəmən ; ˈɑtəmən/ *n* long cushioned seat without back or arms, often used as a box, eg for storing bedding. 無椅背和扶手而有軟墊的長椅(常用做放置寢具等的箱子)。

ou·bli·ette /ˌuːblɪˈet ; ˌublɪˈɛt/ *n* secret dungeon (underground prison) with an entrance only by a trapdoor in the roof. (只有頂上有孔出入的)地下密牢。

ouch /aʊtʃ ; aʊtʃ/ *int* used to express sudden pain. 哎唷(表示突然疼痛)!

ought /ɔːt ; ɔt/ *anom fin* [VP7B] **~ to,** (defective; no infinitive, no particles, no inflected forms; *ought not* is contracted to oughtn't /ˈɔːtnt ; ˈɔtn̩t/; for past time, *ought* is used with a perfect infinitive; in reported speech, the perfect infinitive is not always necessary; *ought to* = *should* as found at shall (3,8,9)). (變化不完全的動詞;無不定詞,無分詞,無字形變化; ought not 縮寫爲 oughtn't; 表示過去時, ought 與完成式的不定詞連用;在間接引語時,完成式的不定詞並不一定需要; ought to = should, 參看 shall 第3, 8, 9義)。 **1** (indicating duty or obligation): (表示責任或義務): *You ~ to start at once.* 你應該立刻開始。*Such things ~ not to be allowed, ~ they?* 這類事不應該准許,是嗎? *'O~ I to go?' —'Yes, I think you ~ (to).'* '我應該去嗎?'—'是的,我認爲你應該去。' *You ~ to have done that earlier.* 你早就應該做那事了。*I told him (that) he ~ to do it,* ie now, or in future. 我對他說他應該去做。*I told him (that) he ~ to have done it,* ie in the past. 我對他說他早就應該去做了。 **2** (indicating what is advisable, desirable or right): (表示適當、合意或應該): *There ~ to be more buses during the rush hours.* 在上下班交通擁擠的時刻,公共汽車應增加班次。*You ~ (ie I advise you) to see that new film at the Odeon.* 你應該去看在奧登電影院上映的那部新影片。*Coffee ~ to be drunk while it is hot.* 咖啡應該趁熱喝。*Your brother ~ to have been a doctor,* He would probably have been a good doctor. 你的哥哥(弟弟)過去應該學醫才對。 **3** (indicating probability): (表示可能性): *If he started at nine, he ~ to be here now.* 假如他在九點出發的話,現在大概到達這兒了。*That ~ to be enough fish for three people, I think.* 我想大概有够三個人吃的魚。*Harry ~ to win the race.* 哈利可能會在這場競賽中獲勝。

ouija /ˈwiːdʒə ; ˈwidʒə/ *n* **ˈ~(-board)**, board lettered with the alphabet, and with other signs, used in seances to obtain messages said to come from the spirits of the dead. 靈應盤 (寫有字母及其他符號的板,降神會時用作傳達所謂來自亡魂的訊息)。

ounce /aʊns ; aʊns/ *n* (abbr 略作 **oz**) unit of weight, one sixteenth of a pound avoirdupois or one twelfth of a pound troy. 盎斯;英兩;唡(常衡爲 1/16 磅,金衡爲1/12磅)。⇨ App 5. 參看附錄五。

our /ɑː(r), ˈaʊə(r) ; aʊr/ *adj* of or belonging to us, that we are concerned with, etc: 我們的;屬於我們的: *We have done our share.* 我們已經做完我們那一份。**Our Father,** God. 天父(上帝)。**Our Lady,** the Virgin Mary. 聖母馬利亞。**Our Lord,** Jesus Christ. 我們的主(耶穌基督)。

ours /ɑːz, ˈaʊəz ; aʊrz/ *pron, pred adj* (the one or ones) belonging to us: 我們的(東西);屬於我們的(東西): *This house is ~.* 這幢房子是我們的。*Don't stay at their house; stay at ~.* 不要住在他們家;住在我們家。*O~ is larger than theirs.* 我們的比他們的大。*Let me show you some of ~.* 我給你看一些我們的。*This dog of ~ never wins any prizes.* 我們的這隻狗從沒有得到任何獎。*The land became ~ by purchase.* 那塊地經購買而成爲我們的。

our·selves /ɑːˈselvz, aʊə'- ; aʊrˈsɛlvz/ *pron* **1** (reflex): (反身)我們自己: *It's no use worrying ~ about that.* 我們爲那件事著急是沒用的。*We shall give ~ the pleasure of visiting you soon.* 我們不久將很高興去拜訪你。 **2** (emphat): (強勢語): *We ~ have often made that mistake/We've often made that mistake ~.* 我們自己常常犯那個錯誤。*We'd better go and see the house (for) ~,* not be content to rely upon what others say. 我們最好親自去看一看那幢房子(不要聽信別人所說的就認爲滿意)。***(all) by ~,*** **(a)** without help. 無他人幫助的。**(b)** alone, without company: 單獨的;無他人在一起的: *Come in; we're all by ~,* there are no visitors, etc. 進來,我們沒有外人。

oust /aʊst ; aʊst/ *vt* [VP6A, 14] ***~ sb (from),*** drive or push (sb) out (from his employment, position, etc): 驅逐(某人);趕走(某人): *~ a rival from office.* 罷黜敵對者。

out /aʊt ; aʊt/ *adv part* (For special uses in combination with *vv*, ⇨ the *v* entries. Specimens only are given here.) (與動詞連用的特殊用法,參看各動詞。此處僅提供一些範例。) **1** away from, not in or at, a place, the usual or normal condition, etc: 離去;在外;出外: *go out;* 出外; *run out;* 跑出; *walk out;* 走出; *take sb out;* 帶某人出去; *find one's way out;* 想出辦法來; *lock sb out;* 把某人鎖在外面; *throw sth out.* 把某物丟出。*Out you go!* Go out! 滾出去! *Out with it!* Bring it out! Say it! 把它拿走!坦白說出!從實招來! **2** (with *be*, various meanings): (與 be 連用,表不同的含義): *Mrs White is out,* not at home. 懷特太太不在家。*The manager is out,* not in the office. 經理出去了。*The dockers are out again,* on strike. 碼頭工人又罷工了。*The book I wanted was out,* ie had been borrowed; was not in the library. 我要的那一本書已被借走了。*The tide is out,* low. 潮退了。*The ship was four days out from Lisbon,* had sailed from Lisbon four days earlier. 那艘船已離開里斯本四天了。*The Socialist party was out,* out of office; not in power. 社會黨下臺了。*Short skirts are out,* not fashionable. 短裙過時了。***be out and about,*** (of a person who has been in bed through illness or injury) able to get up, go outdoors, etc. (指因病或受傷臥床的人)能起床走動。 **3** (in various phrases to indicate absence from home): (在不同的片語中表示不在家): *We don't go out much.* 我們不常外出。*Let's have an evening out,* eg at a cinema or discotheque, or having dinner at a restaurant, etc. 我們出去玩一個晚上吧(如看電影,去狄斯可舞廳跳舞或吃館子等)。 **4** (with *advv* and *adv* phrases, to emphasize the idea of distance): (與副詞及副詞片語連用,強調距離觀念): *He lives out in the country.* 他住在很遠的鄉下。*My brother is out in Australia.* 我的哥哥(弟弟)遠在澳洲。*He lived out East for many years.* 他遠在東方住過許多年。*The fishing boats are all out at sea.* 所有漁船都出海了。*What are you doing out there?* 你在那裏做什麼? **5** (indicating liberation from confinement or restraint; into the open; exposed; discovered): (表示脫離限制或約束;公開;暴露;被發現): *The secret is out,* discovered, known. 秘密洩露了。*The apple blossom is out,* open. 蘋果花開了。*The sun is out,* not hidden by cloud. 太陽出來了。*His new book is out,* published. 他的新書出版了。*There's a warrant out* (ie issued) *against him.* 逮捕他的拘票已經發出。*Out with it!* Tell the news! Explain it! etc, according to context. 說出來呀!講講看!從實招來!(此等含義視上下文而定)。*It's the best game out,* the best ever invented. 這是最妙的策略。 **6** (indicating exhaustion, extinction): (表示耗盡,消滅): *The fire/gas/candle, etc is out,* not burning. 火(煤氣,蠟燭等)熄滅了。*The fire has burnt out.* 火已經燒完了。*The lease/copyright is out,* has reached the end of its term. 租約(著作權)到期了。*The warships steamed towards the enemy with all lights out.* 軍艦熄滅全部燈火向敵方駛去。*Put that cigarette out!* 把香煙熄掉! *The wind blew the candles out.* 風把蠟燭吹滅了。*The candle blew out.* 蠟燭吹滅了。 **7** (to or at an end; completely) (used with many *vv*, as): (結束;完全地)(與許多動詞連用,如): *hear sb out;* 聽完某人的話; *work out a problem;* 解決一個難題; *supplies running out;* 供應品快完了; *fight it out,* settle the dispute by fighting. 決鬥以解決爭端。*I'm tired out.* 我精疲力竭了。*He'll be here before the week is out.* 本星期內他會來這兒。*Let her have her sleep out,* have all the sleep she needs. 讓她睡個够。***cry one's 'eyes out,*** continue crying until this brings relief. 痛哭。***have it out with sb,*** ⇨ have[4](9). ***out and out,*** thorough(ly); surpassing(ly): 完全的(地);徹底的(地);超越的(地): *He's a crook out and out/an out-and-out crook.* 他是個十足的惡棍。***out and away,*** by far: 遠;甚: *I was out and away the handsomest man in the room.* 我是房間裏最漂亮的男人。 **8** (indicating error): (表示錯誤): *I'm out in my calculations/reckoning.* 我的計算錯誤。*We're ten pounds out in our accounts.* 我們把帳算錯了十鎊。*You're not far out,* not much in error; almost right. 你幾乎沒什麼錯誤。*Your guess was a long way out*, badly in error. 你的猜測差太遠了。*You've put me out*, distracted me, upset the thread of my ideas, etc. 你分散了我的注意力。*My watch is five minutes out* (more usu five minutes *slow* or *fast*). 我的錶差了五分鐘(較常用 slow 或 fast 代替 out, 表示慢或快五分鐘)。 **9** (indicating clearness or loudness): (表示清楚或響亮): *call／cry／shout out;* 大聲叫(嚷,喊); *say sth out loud*, in a loud voice; 大聲地把某事說出來; *speak out*, clearly, or without hesitation; 明白地說; 直截了當地說出; *bring out* (= make clearer) *the meaning of a paragraph by paraphrasing it;* 用意譯把一段的意思寫出來; *tell sb sth straight out／right out*, without keeping anything back, without ambiguity. 明白而徹底地將某事告訴某人。 **10** (in phrases) (用於片語中) ***be out for,*** be engaged in seeking, interested in obtaining: 企求;想獲得: *I'm not out for compliments.* 我並不想得到稱讚。*He's out for your blood*, anxious to attack you. 他要打你。***out to***+*inf*, trying or hoping to: 企圖;希望: *I'm not out* (= It is not my aim) *to reform the world.* 我並不企圖改革世界。*The firm is out to capture the Canadian market.* 該公司有意獲得加拿大市場。 ***all out,*** exerting the maximum power or effort: 全力地: *His new car does 80 miles an hour when it's going all out.* 他的新車全速行駛時每小時跑八十哩。*What is needed is an all-out effort.* 所需要的是全力以赴。 **11** (cricket) (of a batsman) no longer batting; having been bowled, caught, etc: (板球) (指擊球員) 出局;退場: *The captain was out for three.* 隊長出局三次。 *Kent all out, 137*, innings ended for 137 runs. 肯特隊賽畢,獲得137分。 **12** ***out of,*** *prep* (contrasted with *in* and *into*. ⇨ the *n* and *v* entries for special uses, eg *out of date* at date[1](3), *out of the way* at way(2).) (與 in 及 into 相對。 特殊用法參看連用的名詞及動詞各條,例如 date[1] 第3義之 out of date, way 第2義之 out of the way。) **(a)** (of place): (指地點): *Fish cannot live out of water.* 魚離水便不能活。*Mr Green is out of town this week.* 格林先生這星期不在城裡。*This plant is not found out of* (= is found only in) *a small area in Central Asia.* 這種植物只在亞洲中部一小片地區才有。**(b)** (of movement): (指動作): *He walked out of the shop.* 他從店鋪裡走出來。 *He jumped out of bed.* 他從床上跳下來。*We pulled the cart out of the ditch.* 我們把車子拖出壕溝。**(c)** (indicating motive or cause): (表示動機或原因): *It was done out of mischief／spite.* 這是由於惡作劇(惡意)所造成的。 *They helped us out of pity／kindness.* 他們基於同情(仁慈)而幫助我們。*She asked only out of curiosity.* 她只是出於好奇而探問。**(d)** from among: 從…中: *Choose one out of these ten.* 從這十個當中挑選一個。 *It happens in nine cases out of ten.* 十次有九次如此。 *This is only one instance out of several.* 這不過是若干例子中的一個。 **(e)** by the use of; from: 利用;從: *The hut was made out of old planks.* 這小屋是用舊木板造的。*She made a hat out of bits of old material.* 她用零星舊布料做了一頂帽子。*Can good ever come out of evil?* 惡能生善嗎? **(f)** without: 無;不;沒有: *out of breath*, breathless; 喘不過氣來; *out of work*, unemployed; 失業; *out of patience;* 不耐煩; (*born*) *out of wedlock*, of unmarried parents. 非婚生的; 私生的;庶出的。*We're out of tea／petrol*, We have no tea／petrol left. 我們沒有茶葉(汽油)了。 *This book is out of stock*, There are no copies left in the shop. 這本書賣完了(沒有存貨了)。**(g)** (indicating condition): (表示情況): *out of fashion;* 不流行; *out of control;* 失去控制; *out of order;* 壞了;發生故障; 出毛病;弄亂; *out of danger.* 脫離危險。⇨ the *n* entries. 參看各片語中的名詞。**(h)** (indicating origin or source): (表示起源或來源): *a scene out of a play;* 戲裡的一場(景); *drink out of a cup／a bottle;* 從一隻杯(瓶)裡喝; *copy sth out of a book;* 從一本書裡抄錄某些東西; *steps cut out of the solid rock;* 由堅固岩石鑿成的梯級; *paid for out of the housekeeping money;* 由家用款項開支的; *a dog and a cat eating out of the same dish.* 一隻狗和一隻貓用同一個盤子吃東西。**(i)** (indicating result): (表示結果): *talk sb out of doing sth*, talk to him with the result that he does not do it; 勸某人不做某事; *reason sb out of his fears;* 說服某人使他不再恐懼; *cheat sb out of his money;* 騙走某人的錢; (colloq) (俗) *be done* (= cheated) *out of sth;* 被騙去某物; *frighten sb out of his wits.* 嚇得某人不知所措。 **(j)** at a certain distance from: 距;離: *The ship sank ten miles out of Singapore.* 該船在距新加坡十哩處沉沒了。***out of it,*** **(a)** not invited to be a member of a party, etc; sad for this reason: 未被邀請;因未被邀請而難過: *She felt out of it as she watched the others set off on the picnic.* 當她看着別人出發去野餐時, 因爲自己未被邀請而感到難過。**(b)** not concerned with, not involved in, sth: 與某事物無關;不牽連在內: *It's a dishonest scheme and I'm glad to be out of it.* 那是個陰謀,我很高興自己與它無關。 **13** (used as *n*) (用作名詞) ***the ins and (the) outs,*** **(a)** those in office and those out of office; the Government and the Opposition. 執政黨與在野黨;政府與反對黨。 **(b)** the details (of procedure, etc). (程序等的)細節。 □ *vt* (sl or colloq) eject by force. (俚或俗)驅逐;趕走。

out·back /ˈaʊtbæk ; ˈaʊtbæk/ *adj, n* (eg in Australia) (of) the more remote and sparsely populated areas. (澳洲等地)偏僻而人口稀少的地區(的);內陸(的);內地(的)。

out·bal·ance /aʊtˈbæləns ; aʊtˈbæləns/ *vt* [VP6A] weigh down; outweigh. 重過; 重量上勝過; 比…來得重要。

out·bid /aʊtˈbɪd ; aʊtˈbɪd/ *vt* (-dd-) (*pt, pp* -bid) [VP6A] go beyond in bidding ; bid higher than (another person) at an auction, etc. 出價或叫牌超過;(拍賣等中)出價高於(他人)。

out·board /ˈaʊtbɔːd ; ˈaʊtˌbord/ *attrib adj* placed on or near the outside of a ship or boat. 在船外的;舷外的。 ~ **motor** *n* detachable engine that is mounted at the stern, outside the boat. 裝於船尾外的馬達。

out·bound /ˈaʊtbaʊnd ; ˈaʊtˈbaʊnd/ *adj* (of a ship) outward bound; going away from a home port. (指船)往外地的;離開船籍港的。

out·brave /aʊtˈbreɪv ; aʊtˈbrev/ *vt* [VP6A] defy: 奮勇抵抗;以勇氣勝過: ~ *the storm.* 勇敢地抵抗暴風雨。

out·break /ˈaʊtbreɪk ; ˈaʊtˌbrek/ *n* [C] breaking out: 爆發;發生: *an ~ of anger／fever／hostilities.* 發怒(發燒;開戰)。

out·build·ing /ˈaʊtbɪldɪŋ ; ˈaʊtˌbɪldɪŋ/ *n* building, eg a shed or stable, separate from the main building: (與正屋分開的)附屬建築物(如棚或畜舍);庫房: *a ten-roomed farmhouse, with useful ~s.* 一幢十間房的農舍,附有若干有用的庫房。

out·burst /ˈaʊtbɜːst ; ˈaʊtˌbɝst/ *n* [C] bursting out (of steam, energy, laughter, anger, etc). (蒸氣、能量、笑聲、怒氣等的)爆發;突發。

out·cast /ˈaʊtkɑːst *US:* -kæst ; ˈaʊtˌkæst/ *n, adj* (person or animal) driven out from home or society ; homeless and friendless. 被逐出家庭或社會的(人或動物);流浪者;無家可歸且無親友的;被遺棄的。

out·caste /ˈaʊtkɑːst *US:* -kæst ; ˈaʊtˌkæst/ *n, adj* (eg in India) (person) having lost, or been expelled from, or not belonging to, a caste. (在印度等地)失去階級的(人);被驅出階級的(人);無階級的(人)。

out·class /aʊtˈklɑːs *US:* -ˈklæs ; aʊtˈklæs/ *vt* [VP6A] be much better than; surpass: 遠勝過;遠超過: *He was ~ed from the start of the race*, His competitors were much better. 比賽一開始他就落後許多。

out·come /ˈaʊtkʌm ; ˈaʊtˌkʌm/ *n* [C] effect or result of an event, or of circumstances. 結果;成果;結局。

out·crop /ˈaʊtkrɒp；ˈaʊtˌkrɑp/ *n* [C] that part of a layer or vein (of rock, etc) which can be seen above the surface of the ground. (岩石等)露出地面的部份；露出地面的地層或礦層；露頭。

out·cry /ˈaʊtkraɪ；ˈaʊtˌkraɪ/ *n* (*pl* -cries) **1** [C] loud shout or scream (of fear, alarm, etc). (恐懼、警告等的)大聲喊叫；尖叫。 **2** [C, U] public protest (*against* sth). 公開反對(與 against 連用，後接某事物)。

out·dated /aʊtˈdeɪtɪd；aʊtˈdetɪd/ *adj* made out of date (by the passing of time). 過時的；不流行的。

out·dis·tance /aʊtˈdɪstəns；aʊtˈdɪstəns/ *vt* [VP6A] travel faster than, and leave behind: 在行進上快過；超過；把…拋在後頭: *Tom ~d all his competitors in the mile race.* 湯姆在一哩賽跑中勝過所有競爭者。

out·do /aʊtˈduː；aʊtˈdu/ *vt* (*3rd person sing pres t* -does /-ˈdʌz；-ˈdʌz/, *pt* -did /-ˈdɪd；-ˈdɪd/, *pp* -done /-ˈdʌn；-ˈdʌn/) [VP6A] do more or better than: 勝過；優於: *Not to be outdone* (ie not wanting to let someone do better than he himself had done), *he tried again.* 爲了不讓別人勝過自己，他再試一次。

out·door /ˈaʊtdɔː(r)；ˈaʊtˌdor/ *attrib adj* done, existing, used, outside a house or building: 戶外的；在戶外的；用於戶外的: *leading an ~ life*, eg of a person fond of open-air activities and sport; 過着戶外的生活(如指某人喜歡戶外活動和運動)； *~ dress／clothes*, worn outside the house; 戶外服裝(衣服)； *~ sports* (*cf* 參較 *indoor games*) 戶外運動。

out·doors /ˌaʊtˈdɔːz；ˈaʊtˈdorz/ *adv* in the open air; outside: 在戶外；戶外: *It's cold ~.* 屋外寒冷。 *In hot countries it's possible to sleep ~.* 在炎熱的國家裡可以睡在屋外。 *Farm workers spend most of their time ~.* 農場工人大部份時間在戶外。

outer /ˈaʊtə(r)；ˈaʊtə/ *adj* of or for the outside, ⇨ inner; farther from the middle or inside: 外的；外面的；外部的；外邊的: *~ garments.* 外衣。⇨ underwear; *the ~ suburbs;* 郊外； *journeys to ~ space,* eg to the planet Mars; 太空旅行(例如前往火星)； *the ~ man,* his personal appearance, dress, etc. 人的外表；外貌。 **ˈ~·most** /-məʊst；-most/ *adj* farthest from the inside or centre. 最外的；離內面或中心最遠的。

out·face /ˌaʊtˈfeɪs；aʊtˈfes/ *vt* [VP6A] face boldly; stare at (sb) until he turns his eyes away; cause (sb) to be embarrassed. 大膽地面對；逼視(某人)直至其眼睛轉開；使(某人)侷促不安。

out·fall /ˈaʊtfɔːl；ˈaʊtˌfɔl/ *n* place where water falls or flows out (of a lake, river, etc); outlet; river mouth. (湖泊，河流等的)出口；排洩口；河口。

out·field /ˈaʊtfiːld；ˈaʊtˈfild/ *n* (usu 通常作 **the ~**) (cricket and baseball) part of the field farthest from the batsmen; the fielders there. (板球及棒球)外場；外野；外場員；外野手。**~er** *n*

out·fight /ˌaʊtˈfaɪt；aʊtˈfaɪt/ *vt* (*pt, pp* -fought /-ˈfɔːt；-ˈfɔt/) [VP6A] fight better than: 戰勝；打敗: *The champion outfought his opponent.* 那位衞冕者打敗了他的對手。

out·fit /ˈaʊtfɪt；ˈaʊtˌfɪt/ *n* [C] all the clothing or articles needed for a purpose: (爲某一目的所需要的)服裝；裝備；用具: *a camping ~*, tent, etc; 露營裝備； *a boy's ~ for school;* 男孩上學的用具； *a carpenter's ~*, his tools, etc. 木匠的工具。□ *vt* (-tt-) fit out (chiefly in the *pp* 主要用過去分詞形式 ~ted). 裝備。**~ter** *n* shopkeeper selling clothes. 售賣服裝的商人。

out·flank /ˌaʊtˈflæŋk；aʊtˈflæŋk/ *vt* [VP6A] go or pass round the flank of (the enemy): 包圍(敵人)的側翼；包抄: *an ~ing movement.* 包圍側翼的調動。

out·flow /ˈaʊtfləʊ；ˈaʊtˌflo/ *n* [C] flowing out: 流出；外流: *an ~ of water／bad language;* 水的流出(滔滔不絕的粗話)； *the ~ of gold bullion.* 金塊外流。

out·fox /ˌaʊtˈfɒks；aʊtˈfɑks/ *vt* [VP6A] get the better of by being cunning. 以計勝過。

out·go /ˈaʊtgəʊ；ˈaʊtˌgo/ *n* (*pl* ~es /-gəʊz；-goz/) (opp of *income*) that which goes out or is paid out; expenditure. (爲 income 之相反字)消耗；支出；付出；開支。

out·go·ing /ˈaʊtgəʊɪŋ；ˈaʊtˌgoɪŋ/ *adj* (attrib only) going out; leaving: (僅作形容用法)外出的；離開的: *the ~ tenant*, the one who is giving up the house, etc; 即將遷出的房客； *an ~ ship／tide.* 離港出航的船(退落的潮水)。 **out·go·ings** *n pl* expenditure; outlay. 支出；開支。

out·grow /ˌaʊtˈgrəʊ；aʊtˈgro/ *vt* (*pt* -grew /-ˈgruː；-ˈgru/, *pp* -grown /-ˈgrəʊn；-ˈgron/) [VP6A] grow too large or too tall for, eg one's clothes; grow faster or taller than, eg one's brother; leave behind, as one grows older (bad habits, childish interests, opinions, etc): 長得太大或太高而不適於(原有的衣服等)；長得比(本人的哥哥等)更快或更高；因長大而放棄(壞習慣，兒時的興趣，幼稚的意見等)： *~ one's strength,* grow too quickly (during childhood), so that the health suffers. 個子長得太快而體力趕不上。

out·growth /ˈaʊtgrəʊθ；ˈaʊtˌgroθ/ *n* [C] **1** natural development or product. 自然的發展；自然的產物。 **2** that which grows out of sth; offshoot: 生出之物；枝條；分枝: *an ~ on a tree.* 樹的分枝。

out-herod /ˌaʊtˈherəd；aʊtˈhɛrəd/ *vt* [VP6A] *~ **Herod,*** be more cruel, violent, etc than King Herod (ruler of Palestine when Jesus was born). 比希律王更暴虐(希律是耶穌誕生時巴勒斯坦的統治者)。

out·house /ˈaʊthaʊs；ˈaʊtˌhaʊs/ *n* (*pl* -houses /-haʊzɪz；-ˌhaʊzɪz/) small building adjoining the main building (eg a shed, barn, or stable); (US) outdoor lavatory. 附屬的建築物(如棚，倉，畜舍)；庫房；(美)戶外厠所。

out·ing /ˈaʊtɪŋ；ˈaʊtɪŋ/ *n* [C] holiday away from home; pleasure trip: 出外度假；遠足；旅行: *go for an ~;* 去遠足； *an ~ to the seaside.* 到海濱小遊。

out·land·ish /aʊtˈlændɪʃ；aʊtˈlændɪʃ/ *adj* looking or sounding odd, strange or foreign: 看起來或聽起來怪異的；古怪的；異國風格的: *~ dress／behaviour／ideas.* 奇裝異服(怪異的行爲；怪主意)。 **~·ly** *adv* **~·ness** *n*

out·last /ˌaʊtˈlɑːst *US:* -ˈlæst；aʊtˈlæst/ *vt* [VP6A] last or live longer than. 比…耐久；比…活得長。

out·law /ˈaʊtlɔː；ˈaʊtˌlɔ/ *n* (hist) person punished by being placed outside the protection of the law; criminal. (史)被剝奪法律保障的人；罪犯；亡命之徒。□ *vt* [VP6A] make (sb) an ~; drive out from society. 使(某人)失去法律保障；將(某人)逐出社會。**~·ry** /ˈaʊtlɔːrɪ；ˈaʊtˌlɔrɪ/ *n* [U] being an ~; being ~ed. 逐出法外；被放逐；法律保障的喪失。

out·lay /ˈaʊtleɪ；ˈaʊtˌle/ *n* [U] *~ **(on),*** spending; laying out money; [C] sum of money that is spent: 開支；花費；費用；花費數目: *a large ~ on／for scientific research.* 科學研究的大量費用。

out·let /ˈaʊtlet；ˈaʊtˌlɛt/ *n ~ **(for),*** **1** way out for water, steam, etc: (水流、蒸氣等的)出口；出路: *an ~ for water;* 出水口； *the ~ of a lake.* 湖泊的出水口。 **2** (fig) means of or occasion for releasing (one's feelings, energies, etc): (喻)發洩(情感，精力等)的方法或機會: *Children need an ~ for their energies.* 孩子們需要發洩精力的機會。

out·line /ˈaʊtlaɪn；ˈaʊtˌlaɪn/ *n* [C] **1** line(s) showing shape or boundary: 外形；輪廓: *an ~ map of Great Britain;* 大不列顛的略圖； *draw sth in ~.* 畫某物的輪廓。 **2** statement of the chief facts, points, etc: 要點；大綱；綱要: *an ~ for an essay／a lecture;* 一篇短論(演講)的要點； *An O~ of European History,* title of a book with a summary of the chief events, etc. 歐洲史大綱。□ *vt* [VP6A] draw in ~; give an ~ of: 畫…的輪廓；敍述…的要點: *~ Napoleon's Russian campaign.* 概述拿破崙的征俄戰役。

out·live /ˌaʊtˈlɪv；aʊtˈlɪv/ *vt* [VP6A] **1** live longer than: 活得比…長久: *~ one's wife.* 比妻子活得久。 **2** live until sth is forgotten: 活到某事物被遺忘；活久而忘了: *~ a disgrace.* 時久而淡忘了恥辱。

out·look /ˈaʊtlʊk；ˈaʊtˌlʊk/ *n* **1** view on which one looks out: (所眺望之)景色；光景: *a pleasant ~*

over the valley; 山谷的宜人景色; *an ~ on to roofs and chimneys.* 看得見屋頂和烟囪的景色。 **2** what seems likely to happen: 展望;前途;遠景: *a bright ~ for trade;* 商業的光明遠景; (weather forecast): (氣象預報): *further ~, dry and sunny.* 未來天氣展望,乾燥而晴朗。 **3** person's way of looking at sth: 對事物的看法: *a man with a narrow ~ on life.* 人生觀狹窄的人。

out·lying /ˈaʊtlaɪɪŋ; ˈaʊtˌlaɪɪŋ/ *adj* far from the centre: 邊遠的;遠離中心的: *~ villages, with poor communications.* 交通不便的邊遠村莊。

out·man·oeuvre (US = **-ma·neu·ver**) /ˌaʊtməˈnuːvə(r); ˌaʊtməˈnuvɚ/ *vt* [VP6A] overcome, get the better of, by being superior in manoeuvring. 以戰略取勝;以謀略取勝。

out·march /ˌaʊtˈmɑːtʃ; aʊtˈmɑrtʃ/ *vt* [VP6A] surpass by marching faster or longer. 以行進較快或較久而超過;趕過。

out·match /ˌaʊtˈmætʃ; aʊtˈmætʃ/ *vt* [VP6A] be more than a match for; excel: 勝過;超過;優於: *be ~ed in skill and endurance.* 技術與耐力不如人。

out·moded /ˌaʊtˈməʊdɪd; aʊtˈmodɪd/ *adj* out of fashion. 過時的;不流行的。

out·most /ˈaʊtməʊst; ˈaʊtˌmost/ *adj* = outermost.

out·num·ber /ˌaʊtˈnʌmbə(r); aʊtˈnʌmbɚ/ *vt* [VP 6A] be greater in number than. 數量上勝過;比…多。

out-of-date /ˈaʊt əv deɪt; ˈaʊtəvˈdet/ *adj* not modern; not fashionable: 過時的: *~ styles/methods/slang.* 過時的式樣(方法,俚語)。

out-of-door /ˌaʊt əv ˈdɔː(r); ˈaʊtəvˈdor/ *attrib adj* = outdoor.

out-of-doors /ˌaʊt əv ˈdɔːz; ˈaʊtəvˈdorz/ *adv* = outdoors.

out-of-the-way /ˌaʊt əv ðə ˈweɪ; ˈaʊtəvðəˈwe/ *adj* **1** remote; secluded: 荒僻的;對外隔絕的;人跡罕至的: *an ~ cottage.* 一個偏遠的村舍。 **2** not commonly known: 不尋常的; 非一般人所知的: *~ items of knowledge.* 一些不尋常的知識。

out·patient /ˈaʊtpeɪʃnt; ˈaʊtˌpeʃənt/ *n* person visiting a hospital for treatment but not staying there. 不住院的病人;門診病人。

out·play /ˌaʊtˈpleɪ; aʊtˈple/ *vt* [VP6A] play better than: (在比賽等中)打敗;勝過: *The English team was ~ed by the Brazilians.* 英國隊被巴西隊打敗。

out·point /ˌaʊtˈpɔɪnt; aʊtˈpɔɪnt/ *vt* [VP6A] (in boxing, etc) score more points than; defeat on points: (拳擊等)得分多於;以積分勝過;以點數勝過: *The British champion was ~ed by the Mexican.* 英國衛冕者以點數輸給了墨西哥對手。

out·port /ˈaʊtpɔːt; ˈaʊtˌport/ *n* port or harbour away from a central custom-house or centre of trade. (離開主要海關或貿易中心的)外港。

out·post /ˈaʊtpəʊst; ˈaʊtˌpost/ *n* **1** (soldiers in an) observation post at a distance from the main body of troops. 前哨;哨兵。 **2** any distant settlement: 遙遠的殖民地;邊遠地區: *an ~ of the Roman Empire.* 羅馬帝國的邊遠地區。

out·pour·ing /ˈaʊtpɔːrɪŋ; ˈaʊtˌporɪŋ/ *n* [C] pouring out; (usu *pl*) expression of feeling: 傾倒;流出;(通常用複數)感情流露: *~s of the heart.* 傾訴衷曲。

out·put /ˈaʊtpʊt; ˈaʊtˌpʊt/ *n* (*sing* only) (僅用單數) **1** quantity of goods, etc, produced: 生產量: *the ~ of a gold mine/a factory;* 金礦(工廠)的產量; *the literary ~ of the year,* the books, etc published. 本年的出版物數量。 **2** power, energy, etc produced; information produced from a computer. 輸出的動力、功能等; 輸出物; (電子計算機資料的)輸出; 輸出資料。 ⇨ input.

out·rage /ˈaʊtreɪdʒ; ˈaʊtˌredʒ/ *n* [U, C] **1** (act of) extreme violence or cruelty: 極度暴烈或殘忍; 殘暴;暴行: *never safe from ~;* 永不能免受迫害; *~s committed by a drunken mob.* 一群酒鬼犯的暴行。 *Would the use of H-bombs be an ~ against humanity?* 使用氫彈是違背人道的暴行嗎? **2** act that shocks public opinion. 使輿論震驚的行爲。□ *vt* [VP6A] treat violently; be guilty of an ~ upon; violate: 虐待;侵害;觸犯;違犯: *~ public opinion;* 違反民意; *~ one's sense of justice.* 違反某人的正義感。

out·rage·ous /aʊtˈreɪdʒəs; aʊtˈredʒəs/ *adj* shocking; very cruel, shameless, immoral: 駭人的;暴虐的;無恥的;不道德的: *~ behaviour;* 暴行; *an ~ price/remark.* 駭人的價格(談話)。 **~·ly** *adv*

out·range /ˌaʊtˈreɪndʒ; aʊtˈrendʒ/ *vt* [VP6A] have a greater range than: 射程超過: *Our guns were ~d by those of the enemy's cruisers.* 我們大砲的射程不如敵人巡洋艦的砲。

out·rank /ˌaʊtˈræŋk; aʊtˈræŋk/ *vt* [VP6A] rank higher than. 階級高於;地位高於。

outré /ˈuːtreɪ *US:* uːˈtreɪ; uˈtre/ *adj* outside the bounds of what is conventionally correct; contrary to what is decorous: 超出常軌的;越禮的;過分的: *~ behaviour.* 超出常軌的行爲。

out·ride /ˌaʊtˈraɪd; aʊtˈraɪd/ *vt* (*pt* -rode /-ˈrəʊd; -ˈrod/, *pp* -ridden /-ˈrɪdn; -ˈrɪdn̩/) [VP6A] ride better or faster than: 騎得比…好或快: *~ one's pursuers.* 騎得比追趕者快。

out·rider /ˈaʊtraɪdə(r); ˈaʊtˌraɪdɚ/ *n* person on horseback, a motor-cycle, etc, accompanying a vehicle, as an attendant or guard. (隨護車輛的)騎馬的侍從;駕機車的警衛。

out·rig·ger /ˈaʊtrɪgə(r); ˈaʊtˌrɪgɚ/ *n* (boating) beam, spar or structure projecting from or over the side of a boat for various purposes (eg for the rowlock in a racing shell, or to give stability to a canoe or yacht). (駕舟)舷外木(鐵)桿(裝在舷外的梁架,帆桅或其他裝置,例如賽船上的槳架或獨木舟、遊艇的穩定裝置);叉架。 **out·rigged** /ˈaʊtrɪgd; ˈaʊtˌrɪgd/ *adj* (of a boat) having an ~ or ~s. (指船)有舷外裝置的;有叉架的。

out·right /ˈaʊtraɪt; ˈaʊtˌraɪt/ *adj* **1** thorough; positive: 完全的;確實的;斷然的: *an ~ denial;* 斷然否認;明白的拒絕; *~ wickedness;* 十足的邪惡; *an ~ manner,* ie thoroughly frank. 徹底坦白的態度。 **2** clear; unmistakable: 明白的;顯然的;無疑的: *On the voting for secretary, Smith was the ~ winner.* 關於投票選幹事,史密斯是無疑的當選者。 □ *adv* **1** openly, with nothing held back: 公然地;率直地: *tell a man ~ what one thinks of his behaviour.* 坦白告訴某人自己對他的行爲的看法。 **2** completely; at one time: 完全地;一次;立即: *buy a house ~,* ie not by instalments; 一次付款買下房屋; *be killed ~ by a blow.* 當場一擊致命。

out·rival /ˌaʊtˈraɪvl; aʊtˈraɪvl̩/ *vt* (-ll-, US also -l-) [VP6A] be or do better than (sb) as a rival. 競爭中勝過(某人)。

out·run /ˌaʊtˈrʌn; aʊtˈrʌn/ *vt* (*pl* -ran /-ˈræn; -ˈræn/, *pp* -run; -nn-) [VP6A] run faster or better than; go beyond: 跑得比…快;跑得比…好;超過: *His ambition outran his ability,* He was ambitious to do more than he was able to do. 他的野心超過了他的才能(他眼高手低)。

out·sail /aʊtˈseɪl; aʊtˈsel/ *vt* [VP6A] sail faster than. 航行得比…快。

out·set /ˈaʊtset; ˈaʊtˌsɛt/ *n* start. 開始。 ***at/from the ~,*** at/from the beginning: 在(從)開始時: *at the ~ of his career.* 在他事業的初期。

out·shine /ˌaʊtˈʃaɪn; aʊtˈʃaɪn/ *vt* (*pt, pp* -shone /-ˈʃɒn; -ˈʃon/) [VP6A] shine more brightly than. 照得比…更亮。

out·side /ˌaʊtˈsaɪd; ˈaʊtˈsaɪd/ *n* (contrasted with *inside*) (與 inside 相對) **1** the outer side or surface; the outer part(s): 外面;外部: *The ~ of the house needs painting.* 房子外部需要油漆。 *Don't judge a thing from the ~,* from the external appearance. 不可憑外表判斷事物。 **2** ***at the (very) ~,*** at the most; at the highest reckoning: 至多;充其量: *There were only fifty people there at the ~,* certainly not more than fifty. 那兒最多不過五十個人。 *He earns £10000 a year at the ~.* 他一年至多賺一萬鎊。□ /ˈaʊtsaɪd; ˈaʊtˈsaɪd/ *adj* (or attrib use of *n*) (或名詞作形容詞用) **1** of or on, nearer, the ~: 外面的;在外面的;外頭的;外部的: ~ *repairs*, ie to the ~ of a building; (建築物的)外部修理; ~ *measurements*, eg of a box; (盒子等的)外部尺寸; *an* ~ *broadcast*, from a place ~ the studios. 室外廣播(非在播音室中所作者)。 **2** greatest possible or probable: 可能性最大的;最可能的: *an* ~ *estimate／price*. 最高的估計(價格)。 **3** not connected with or included in a group, organization, etc: 局外的;外界的: *We shall need* ~ *help* (= extra workers) *for this job*. 我們這項工作需要外界的協助。 *She doesn't like meeting the* ~ *world*, people not belonging to the close circle of her family and friends. 她不喜歡與外人結識。□ *adv* on or to the ~: 在外面;在外頭;在外部: *The house is painted green* ~. 那幢房子外面漆成綠色。*The car is waiting* ~. 車子在外面等着。□ *prep* **1** at or on the outer side of: 在…的外面;在…的外邊: ~ *the house*; 在屋子外面; *a ship moored* ~ *the harbour*. 一艘停泊在港外的船。 **2** beyond the limits of: 超出…的範圍: *We cannot go* ~ *the evidence*. 我們不得超出證據的範圍。*He has no occupation* ~ *his office work*. 除了上班以外,他沒有別的工作。

out·sider /ˌaʊtˈsaɪdə(r) ; ˌaʊtˈsaɪdɚ/ *n* **1** person who is not, or who is not considered to be, a member of a group, society, etc; (colloq) ill-mannered person not socially acceptable. 非會員;局外人;(俗)社交上不受歡迎的粗俗人。 **2** (racing) horse that is thought to have little chance of winning a race. (賽馬)獲勝機會甚微的馬;冷門馬。

out·size /ˈaʊtsaɪz ; ˈaʊtˌsaɪz/ *adj* (esp of articles of clothing, etc) larger than the usual size. (尤指衣服等)大於通常尺碼的;特大的。

out·skirts /ˈaʊtskɜːts ; ˈaʊtˌskɝts/ *n pl* borders or outlying parts (esp of a town): 邊界;(尤指)市郊: *on the* ~ *of Lille*. 在里耳的郊區。

out·smart /ˌaʊtˈsmɑːt ; aʊtˈsmɑrt/ *vt* [VP6A] (colloq) be smarter (= cleverer, more cunning) than. (俗)比…更聰明;以機智勝過。

out·span /ˌaʊtˈspæn ; aʊtˈspæn/ *vi, vt* (-nn-) [VP 6A, 2A] (S Africa) unyoke; unharness. (南非)解除牛軛;卸下馬具。

out·spoken /ˌaʊtˈspəʊkən ; ˈaʊtˈspokən/ *adj* saying freely what one thinks; frank: 直言的;坦白的: ~ *comments*; 坦率的批評; *be* ~ *in one's remarks*. 說話直率。~**·ly** *adv* ~**·ness** *n*

out·spread /ˌaʊtˈspred ; aʊtˈsprɛd/ *adj* spread or stretched out: 張開的;伸開的: *with* ˌ~ ˈ*arms*; 伸開雙臂地; *with arms* ~. 兩臂伸開着。

out·stand·ing /ˌaʊtˈstændɪŋ ; ˈaʊtˈstændɪŋ/ *adj* **1** in a position to be easily noticed; attracting notice: 傑出的;顯著的;引人注意的: *the* ~ *features of the landscape*; 風景特別引人注意之處; *an* ~ *landmark*. 顯著的陸標。*The girl who won the scholarship was quite* ~. 那個獲得獎學金的女孩是相當傑出的。 **2** (of problem, work, payments, etc) still to be attended to: (指問題,工作,債務等)尚未解決的: ~ *debts／liabilities*; 未償的債務; *a good deal of work still* ~. 尚待完成的一大堆工作。 **3** /ˈaʊtstændɪŋ ; ˈaʊtˈstændɪŋ/ sticking out: 突出的;伸出的: *a boy with big*, ~ *ears*. 兩耳大而突出的男孩。~**·ly** *adv* to a high degree: 高度地: ~*ly intelligent*. 非常聰明。

out·station /ˈaʊtsteɪʃn ; ˈaʊtˌsteʃən/ *n* remote station(2). 遠方的駐所;遠方支部。

out·stay /ˌaʊtˈsteɪ ; aʊtˈste/ *vt* [VP6A] stay longer than: 居留比…長久;停留較…長久: ~ *the other guests*. 停留的時間比其他客人長久。~ ***one's welcome***, stay too long, until one is no longer a welcome guest. 停留太久而致令主人生厭。

out·stretched /ˌaʊtˈstretʃt;aʊtˈstrɛtʃt/ *adj* stretched or spread out: 伸開的;展開的: *with* ~ *arms*; 伸開雙臂地; *lie* ~ *on the grass*. 手脚伸開地躺臥草地上。

out·strip /ˌaʊtˈstrɪp ; aʊtˈstrɪp/ *vt* (-pp-) [VP6A] do better than; pass (sb) in a race, etc: 做得比…好;(在賽跑等中)超過(某人): *The hare was* ~*ped by the tortoise*. 兎子被烏龜超過了。

out·vie /ˌaʊtˈvaɪ ; aʊtˈvaɪ/ *vt* [VP6A] do better than in competition. (在競賽中)勝過;擊敗。

out·vote /ˌaʊtˈvəʊt ; aʊtˈvot/ *vt* [VP6A] win, obtain, more votes than. 比…得更多選票;得票超過。

out·ward /ˈaʊtwəd ; ˈaʊtwɚd/ *adj* **1** of or on the outside: 外面的;在外面的: *the* ~ *appearance of things*; 東西的外表; *the* ~ *man* (contrasted with the spiritual nature, the soul). 人的軀殼;肉體(與精神,靈魂相對)。 **2** going out: 出去的;外出的: *during the* ~ *voyage*. 在出航期間。□ *adv* (also 亦作 **out·wards** /-wədz ; -wɚdz/) towards the outside; away from home or the centre: 向外;在外: *The two ends must be bent* ~*s*. 兩端必須向外彎。*The ship is* ~ *bound*, sailing away from its home port. 這艘船是開往外埠的。~**·ly** *adv* on the surface; apparently: 表面上;外表上: *Though badly frightened she appeared* ~*ly calm*. 雖然大受驚嚇,她外表上還是顯得很鎮靜。

out·wear /ˌaʊtˈweə(r) ; aʊtˈwɛr/ *vt* (*pt* -wore /-ˈwɔː(r) ; -ˈwor/ *pp* -worn /-ˈwɔːn ; -ˈworn/) [VP 6A] **1** last longer than: 比…耐穿;比…經久: *Well-made leather shoes will* ~ *two pairs of these cheap rubber shoes*. 做得好的皮鞋比兩雙這種便宜的膠鞋還耐穿。 **2** wear out; use up; exhaust (esp in the *pp* when attrib): 穿破;用壞;用完;使無力或疲憊(過去分詞作形容用法時,尤作此解): *outworn quotations*, used so often that they no longer strike the listener or reader; 陳舊的引語; *outworn* (= out-of-date) *practices in industry*. 工業界落伍的慣例。

out·weigh /ˌaʊtˈweɪ ; aʊtˈwe/ *vt* [VP6A] be greater in weight, value or importance than: 比…更重;比…更有價值;比…更重要;重量、價值或重要性超過…: *Do the disadvantages* ~ *the advantages?* 弊多於利嗎?

out·wit /ˌaʊtˈwɪt ; aʊtˈwɪt/ *vt* (-tt-) [VP6A] get the better of by being cleverer or more cunning than: 以機智勝過;以狡計擊敗: *The thief* ~*ted the police and got away with his loot*. 小偷以狡計騙過警察帶著贓物逃跑了。

out·wore /ˌaʊtˈwɔː(r) ; aʊtˈwor/, **out·worn** /ˌaʊtˈwɔːn ; aʊtˈworn/ ⇨ outwear.

out·work /ˈaʊtwɜːk ; ˈaʊtˌwɝk/ *n* part of a military defence system away from the centre: 軍事的外圍防禦工事;外堡;外壘: *the* ~*s of a castle*. 城堡的外壘。

ouzel /ˈuːzl ; ˈuzḷ/ *n* kinds of small bird of the thrush family. 黑鶇。

ouzo /ˈuːzəʊ ; ˈuzo/ *n* [U] aniseed-flavoured Greek liqueur, drunk with water. 茴香烈酒(產於希臘,與水攙飲)。

ova /ˈəʊvə ; ˈovə/ *n pl* of ovum.

oval /ˈəʊvl ; ˈovḷ/ *n, adj* (plane figure or outline that is) egg-shaped; shaped like an ellipse. 卵形的;橢圓的;橢圓形。

ovary /ˈəʊvərɪ ; ˈovərɪ/ *n* (*pl* -ries) either of the two reproductive organs in which ova are produced in female animals; seed-vessel in a plant. (雌性動物的)卵巢;(植物的)子房。 ⇨ ovum. ⇨ the illus at flower, reproduce. 參看 flower, reproduce 之插圖。

ova·tion /əʊˈveɪʃn ; oˈveʃən/ *n* [C] enthusiastic expression of welcome or approval: 熱烈歡迎;大喝采: *The leader was given a standing* ~, The audience stood to clap, etc. 那樂隊指揮受到聽衆的起立歡呼。

oven /ˈʌvn ; ˈʌvən/ *n* **1** enclosed box-like space which is heated for cooking food: 烤爐;烤箱: *Bread is baked in an* ~. 麵包是在烤爐裡烘成的。 **2** small furnace or kiln used in chemistry, etc. (化學等方面所用的)小烘爐;小窰。ˈ~**·ware** /-weə(r) ; -ˌwɛr/ *n* heat-proof dishes for use in an ~: (經得起在烤箱中烘烤的)耐熱盤碗。~*ware pottery*. 耐熱陶器。

over¹ /ˈəʊvə(r) ; ˈovɚ/ *adv* (⇨ the *v* entries for special combinations, eg *give over*. Specimens only are given here.) (與動詞連用的特殊用法，例如 give over, 參看各動詞條。本條中僅提供若干例句。) **1** (indicating movement from an upright position, from one side to the other side, or so that a different side is seen, etc): (表示從直立位置倒下，從一邊到另一邊，或使不同之一邊被看見等的動作)： *He fell ~ on the ice.* 他跌倒在冰上。*Don't knock that vase ~.* 不要把那隻花瓶碰倒。*A slight push would send it ~.* 輕輕一推會把它弄倒。*He gave me a push and ~ I went,* I fell. 他推我一下，我就跌倒了。*Turn the patient ~ on his face and rub his back.* 把病人翻過去俯臥，按摩他的背部。*Turn ~ the page.* 把這一頁翻過去。 *It rolled ~ and ~,* made a series of revolutions. 它一再滾動。*He turned ~ in bed.* 他在床上翻身。 **2** (indicating motion upwards and outwards): (表示向上及向外的動作)： *The milk boiled ~.* 牛奶沸溢出來了。 *He was boiling ~ with rage.* 他正在發怒。 **3** from beginning to end; through: 自始至終；遍及： *I'll look the papers ~,* look or read through them. 我要把這些文件全部看過。*You should think it ~,* consider the matter carefully. 你應該把它仔細考慮一下。 **4** (indicating repetition) again: (表示重複)再： *Count them ~,* a second time. 再把它們數一數。 ***(all) ~ again,*** a second time (from the beginning): 再一次： *He did the work so badly that I had to do it all ~ again myself.* 他把那項工作做得那麼糟我自己還得再做一次。***~ and ~ again,*** repeatedly; many times: 一再地；許多次： *I've warned you ~ and ~ again not to do that.* 我一再警告你不要做那件事。 **5** across (a street, an open space, a distance, etc): 越過(街道，空地，一段距離等)： *Take these letters ~ to the post office.* 把這些信送到郵局去。*Let me row you ~ to the other side of the lake.* 讓我把你划到湖的那一邊去。*Ask him ~,* Ask him to come here／to pay a visit. 請他到這裡來。*He's ~ in／has gone ~ to France.* 他到法國去了。*Come ~ and see me some time,* Come to visit me some time. 那一天請過來看我。*Some wild geese have just flown ~.* 有幾隻雁剛剛飛過。***~ against,*** (lit or fig) (字面或喻) **(a)** opposite to. 與…相對；在…對面。**(b)** in contrast with. 與…相比。 **6** remaining; not used after part has been taken or used: 剩餘；餘下： *Seven into thirty goes four times and two ~.* 三十除以七得四餘二。 *If there's any meat (left) ~, give it to the dog.* 如果有肉剩下的話，把它餵狗。*I've paid all my debts and have £15 ~.* 我把欠債都還清了還剩下十五鎊。 **7** in addition; in excess; more: 加之；超過；更多： *children of fourteen and ~;* 十四歲以上的孩子們；*10 metres and a bit ~.* 十公尺多一點。 **8** ended; finished; done with: 結束；完畢；完成： *The meeting will be ~ before we arrive if we don't hurry.* 假如我們不趕快的話，不等我們到達，就已經散會了。*The storm is ~.* 風暴已經過去了。*His sufferings will soon be ~.* 他的痛苦不久就要過去了。*It's all ~ with him,* He's ruined, sure to die soon, etc, according to context. 他一切都完了(垮了，卽將死亡等，其意義視上下文而定)。 **9** more than is right, usual, wise, etc: 太過；過份： *~ anxious;* 太焦急的；過於憂慮的； *~ polite.* 太多禮的；過份客氣的。*If she grieves ~ much, she may fall ill.* 假如她過度悲傷，她可能會生病。 *He's not ~ strong,* not so strong as is desirable. 他並不太强壯。*He hasn't done it ~ well,* He has done it rather badly. 他做得不大好。 ⇨ over- below. 參看下列之 over-。 **10** (indicating transference or change from one person, party, etc to another): (表示移轉或更換)： *He has gone ~ to the enemy,* joined them. 他已經投向敵人。*He made his business ~ to his son,* made his son the owner. 他把事業移轉給他的兒子。*Hand that weapon ~ to me.* 把那武器交給我。 *Over (to you)!* (in radio telegraphy, etc) It is now your turn to speak. (無線電報等用語)請回話！ **11** on the whole surface; in all parts: 遍佈；到處： *He was aching all ~.* 他全身都痛。*This pianist is famous all the world ~.* 這位鋼琴家聞名全世界。*Your clothes are all ~ dust／are dusty all ~.* 你的衣服到處都是灰塵。*Paint the old name ~,* cover it with paint. 把舊名字全部用油漆塗蓋起來。*That's Smith all ~,* It's characteristic of him, what he might be expected to do. 史密斯就是這麼一個人。

over² /ˈəʊvə(r) ; ˈovɚ/ *prep* **1** resting on the surface of and covering, partly or completely (not, in this sense, replaceable by *above*): 在…上面(部份或全部蓋着)(用作此義時，不能以 above 代替)： *He spread his handkerchief ~ his face to keep the flies off.* 他把手帕蓋在臉上阻擋蒼蠅。*Spread a cloth ~ the table.* 鋪一塊布在桌上。*Tie a piece of paper firmly ~ the top of the jar.* 在瓶口緊緊地紮上一張紙。*I knocked the man's hat ~ his eyes,* so that he couldn't see. 我把那人的帽子碰到他臉上，遮住了他的眼睛。 **2** at or to a level higher than, but not touching (in this sense often replaceable by *above*): 在…之上(但未接觸)(用作此義，常可被 above 代替)： *Attendants held a large umbrella ~／above the chief's head.* 隨從們把一支大傘撐在首領的頭頂上。*The sky is ~／above our heads.* 天在我們的頭頂上。*These telegraph wires ~ the streets are ugly.* 街道上空這些電報線很難看。*The balcony juts out ~ the street.* 陽臺向大街伸展出去。*There was a lamp ~ the table.* 桌子上方有一盞燈。 **3** (indicating superiority in rank, authority, etc): (表示階級高，權力大等)： *He reigns ~ a great empire.* 他統治一個大帝國。*He has jurisdiction ~ three provinces.* 他管轄三個省。*These people need a firm ruler ~ them.* 這些人民需要一個堅定的統治者管理他們。*He has no command ~ himself／~ his passions.* 他控制不了自己(自己的情感)。 *Mr White is ~ me in the office.* 懷特先生的職位比我高。 **4** in or across every part of: 在…的各部份；遍及…的各部份： *Snow is falling ~ the north of England.* 英格蘭北部到處都在下雪。*He is famous all ~ the world.* 他聞名全世界。 ⇨ over¹(11). *He has travelled all ~ Europe.* 他已經遊遍歐洲。 **5** from one side to the other of; to or at the other side of: 從一邊到…的另一邊；到或在…的另一邊： *He escaped ~ the frontier.* 他逃過邊界了。*She spoke to me ~ her shoulder.* 她轉過頭對我說話。*Look ~ the hedge.* 看圍籬的那一邊。*We heard voices from ~ the fence.* 我們聽到從籬笆那一邊傳來的聲音。*Who lives in that house ~ the way,* on the opposite side of the road or street? 誰住在路對面的那一幢屋子裡？ **6** (of time): (指時間)： *Can you stay ~ Sunday,* until Monday? 你能够停留在這裡過了星期日再走嗎？ **7** so as to be ~ and on the other side of: 越過；過到…的另一邊： *climb ~ a wall;* 爬過一道牆； *jump ~ a brook.* 跳過一條小溪。 **8** (opp of *under*) more than: (爲 under 之相反字)超過： *He spoke for ~ an hour.* 他說了一個多鐘頭。*He stayed in London (for) ~ a month.* 他在倫敦停留一個多月。*She is ~ 40 inches round the waist.* 她的腰圍四十幾吋。*The river is ~ fifty miles long.* 這條河長五十多哩。*He's ~ fifty.* 他五十多歲了。***~ and above,*** besides; in addition to: 除…之外： *The waiters get good tips ~ and above their wages.* 侍者們除了工資外，還有可觀的小費。 **9** in connection with; while engaged in; concerning: 與…有關；從事…之際；關於： *He went to sleep ~ his work,* while doing it. 他在工作時睡着了。*How long will he be ~ it?* How long will it take him to do it, get there, etc? 他要多久才會做完(到達等)？ *We had a pleasant chat ~ a cup of tea,* while drinking tea. 我們一邊喝茶，一邊愉快地聊天。*We all laughed ~ the affair.* 我們都爲那件事情而發笑。

over³ /ˈəʊvə(r) ; ˈovɚ/ *n* (cricket) number of balls bowled in succession by each bowler in turn. (板球)每個投手一次連續所投出的球數。

over- /ˌəʊvə(r) ; ˌovɚ/ *pref* too (much): 太(多)： *ˌ~-poˈlite;* 太多禮的；太拘禮的； *ˌ~-ˈtired;* 太疲倦的； *ˌ~-ˈheated.* 加熱過度的；過度激昂的。 (Note: compounds not entered below have the same stress pattern as the examples below.) (注意:未列在下面的複合字,其重音型式一如以下各例。) The meanings of the *adjj* below may be obtained by putting *too* in place of *over*. 下列形容詞的含義可以 too 代替 over 來表示,即'太過…'之意。

ˌ~-aˈbundant	**ˌ~-exˈcited**
ˌ~-ˈactive	**ˌ~-faˈmiliar**
ˌ~-amˈbitious	**ˌ~-ˈfond**
ˌ~-ˈanxious	**ˌ~-ˈfull**
ˌ~-ˈbold	**ˌ~-ˈgenerous**
ˌ~-ˈbusy	**ˌ~-ˈgreedy**
ˌ~-ˈcareful	**ˌ~-ˈhasty**
ˌ~-ˈcautious	**ˌ~-ˈjealous**
ˌ~-ˈconfident	**ˌ~-ˈmodest**
ˌ~-ˈcredulous	**ˌ~-ˈnervous**
ˌ~-ˈcritical	**ˌ~-ˈproud**
ˌ~-ˈcurious	**ˌ~-ˈripe**
ˌ~-ˈdelicate	**ˌ~-ˈsensitive**
ˌ~-ˈeager	**ˌ~-ˈserious**
ˌ~-eˈmotional	**ˌ~-susˈpicious**
ˌ~-enˌthusiˈastic	**ˌ~-ˈzealous**

The meanings of the *nn* below may be obtained by putting *too much* in place of *over*. 下列名詞的含義可以 too much 代替 over 來表示,即'太多…'之意。

ˌ~-aˈbundance	**ˌ~-inˈdulgence**
ˌ~-anˈxiety	**ˌ~-ˈpayment**
ˌ~-ˈconfidence	**ˌ~-ˌpopuˈlation**
ˌ~-creˈdulity	**ˌ~-proˈduction**
ˌ~-exˈertion	**ˌ~-ˈstrain**
ˌ~-exˈposure	**ˌ~-ˈtolerance**

The meaning of the *vv* below may be obtained by putting *too much* after the *v* in place of *over*. 下列動詞的含義可以 too much 接該動詞之後代替 over 來表示,即'…得太過'或'…得太多'之意。

ˌ~-ˈburden	**ˌ~-ˈheat**
ˌ~-ˈcook	**ˌ~-inˈdulge**
ˌ~-ˈeat	**ˌ~-ˈpraise**
ˌ~-ˈemphasize	**ˌ~-proˈduce**
ˌ~-ˈestimate	**ˌ~-ˈsimplify**
ˌ~-exˈert	**ˌ~-ˈstrain**
ˌ~-exˈpose	**ˌ~-ˈvalue**

over·act /ˌəuvərˈækt ; ˈovəˈækt/ *vi, vt* [VP2A, 6A] act²(4) in an exaggerated way: 演得過火;演得太誇張: *~ing (in) his part.* 把他的角色演得太誇張。

over·all¹ /ˌəuvərˈɔ:l ; ˈovəˌɔl/ *adj* including everything; containing all: 包含一切的;全部的: *the ~ measurements of a room;* 一個房間的全部面積; *coal burnt at an ~ efficiency of only 18 per cent.* 只用百分之十八的全效能燃燒的煤。

over·all² /ˈəuvərɔ:l ; ˈovəˌɔl/ *n* **1** (GB) loose-fitting garment that covers other garments (eg as worn by small children during play). (英)罩衫;罩衣(如小孩遊戲時所穿者)。 **2** (*pl*) loose-fitting trousers, with the front extended above the waist, with shoulder straps, and made of heavy, strong material, worn over other clothes to protect them from dirt, etc. (複)工作褲;工裝褲。

over·arch /ˌəuvərˈɑ:tʃ ; ˌovəˈartʃ/ *vt, vi* [VP6A, 2A] form an arch (over): (在…上面)形成拱形: *Trees ~ed the road.* 樹木在道路上方形成拱形。

over·arm /ˈəuvərɑ:m ; ˈovəˌarm/ *adj, adv* (sport, eg cricket) with the arm swung over the shoulder: (運動,如板球)舉臂過肩的(地): *bowling ~;* 舉臂過肩地投球; *an ~ bowler.* 舉臂過肩的投手。

over·awe /ˌəuvərˈɔ: ; ˌovəˈɔ/ *vt* [VP6A] awe completely; awe through great respect, etc: 使畏縮;使敬畏;威壓;威嚇: *~ sb into submission.* 使某人敬畏而屈服。

over·bal·ance /ˌəuvəˈbæləns ; ˌovəˈbæləns/ *vt, vi* **1** [VP6A, 2A] (cause to) lose balance; fall over: (使)失去平衡;跌倒: *He ~d and fell into the water.* 他失去平衡跌入水中。 *Don't ~ the canoe.* 不要使獨木舟失去平衡。 **2** [VP6A] outweigh: 重過;價值超過;超過: *The gains ~ the losses.* 利潤多於虧損。

over·bear /ˌəuvəˈbeə(r) ; ˌovəˈbɛr/ *vt* (*pt* -bore /-ˈbɔ:(r) ; -ˈbor/, *pp* -borne /-ˈbɔ:n ; -ˈborn/) [VP6A] overcome (by forcible arguments, strong force, or authority): (以有力的論據,强力,權威)壓服;克服;鎮懾: *My objections were overborne in the argument.* 我的異議都在辯論中被壓服。 **~·ing** *adj* masterful; forcing others to one's will: 專橫的;强人聽從的;壓倒的: *an ~ing manner.* 盛氣凌人的態度。 **~·ing·ly** *adv*

over·bid /ˌəuvəˈbɪd ; ˌovəˈbɪd/ *vt, vi* (*pt, pp* -bid; -dd-) **1** [VP6A] (at an auction) bid higher than (another person). (拍賣時)出價高過(他人)。 **2** [VP6A, 2A] bid more than the value of (sth offered for sale). 出價高過(待售之物)的價值;出價過高。 **3** [VP6A, 2A] (bridge) make a higher bid than (one's partner) or than one's hand is worth. (橋牌戲)叫牌高過(伙伴的叫牌,或自己手上的牌力);叫牌過高。 □ *n* /ˈəuvəbɪd ; ˈovəˌbɪd/ act of ~ding. 出價過高;叫牌過高。

over·blown /ˌəuvəˈbləun ; ˌovəˈblon/ *adj* (of flowers) too fully open; past their best. (指花)開得過盛的;盛開期已過的。

over·board /ˈəuvəbɔ:d ; ˈovəˌbord/ *adv* over the side of a ship or boat into the water: 越過船邊落入水中: *fall/jump ~;* 從船上跌(跳)入水中; *throw sb ~,* (fig) get rid of him, stop supporting him, etc. (喻)擺脫某人;停止支持某人;拋棄某人。

over·bore /ˌəuvəˈbɔ:(r) ; ˌovəˈbor/, **over·borne** /ˌəuvəˈbɔ:n ; ˌovəˈborn/ ⇨ overbear.

over·bur·den /ˌəuvəˈbɜ:dn ; ˈovəˌbɝdn̩/ *n* surface soil, etc which must be moved away to get at coal, etc underneath. 地層表土(採礦時必須挖去的地表土石層)。□ *vt* [VP6A] burden too heavily: 使負擔過重;使裝載太多: *~ed with grief.* 悲傷過度。

over·call /ˌəuvəˈkɔ:l ; ˈovəˈkɔl/ *vt, vi* = overbid(3).

over·capi·tal·ize /ˌəuvəˈkæpɪtəlaɪz ; ˈovəˈkæpətl̩ˌaɪz/ *vt* fix or estimate the capital of (a company) too high. 將(某一公司)的資本定得或估計過高。 **over·capi·tal·iz·ation** /ˌəuvəˌkæpɪtəlaɪˈzeɪʃn *US:* -lɪˈz- ; ˈovəˌkæpətl̩ɪˈzeʃən/ *n*

over·cast /ˌəuvəˈkɑ:st *US:* -ˈkæst ; ˈovəˌkæst/ *adj* (of the sky) darkened (as) by clouds; (fig) gloomy; sad. (指天空)因多雲而陰暗的;多雲的;陰沉的;(喻)憂鬱的;悲哀的。□ *n* (*sing* only) cloud-covered sky: (僅作單數)多雲的天;密雲: *Breaks in the ~ will give sunny periods.* 密雲,偶爾出現陽光;陰偶晴。

over·charge /ˌəuvəˈtʃɑ:dʒ ; ˈovəˈtʃardʒ/ *vt, vi* **1** [VP6A, 2A] charge (sb) too high a price: (向某人)索價太高: *We were ~d for the eggs.* 我們的雞蛋買貴了。 *That grocer never ~s.* 那個雜貨商從來不亂索價。 **2** [VP6A] fill or load too heavily: 使裝塡過多;使裝載過多;使超載: *~ a gun;* 使槍砲彈藥裝塡過多; *~ an electric circuit.* 使電路荷電太多。□ *n* /ˈəuvətʃɑ:dʒ ; ˈovəˌtʃardʒ/ [C] charge that is too high or great, eg of electric current, explosive or for a purchase. 荷電太多;超載;索價太高;炸藥裝塡過多。

over·cloud /ˌəuvəˈklaud ; ˌovəˈklaud/ *vt, vi* [VP6A, 2A] cover, become covered, with clouds or shadows; (fig) make or become gloomy. 以或被雲掩蔽;以或被陰影遮住;(使)變陰暗;(喻)使憂鬱;變爲憂鬱。

over·coat /ˈəuvəkəut ; ˈovəˌkot/ *n* long coat worn out of doors over ordinary clothes in cold weather. 大衣。

over·come /ˌəuvəˈkʌm ; ˌovəˈkʌm/ *vt* (*pt* -came /-ˈkeɪm ; -ˈkem/, *pp* -come) [VP6A] **1** get the better of; be too strong for: 勝過;壓倒;克服: *~ the enemy;* 擊敗敵人; *~ a bad habit;* 克服一種惡習; *~ temptation.* 克制誘惑。 **2** make weak: 使弱;使無能力: *be ~ by fatigue/emotion/liquor/fumes.* 筋疲力竭(不勝感觸;酒醉;被煙薰倒)。

over·crop /ˌəuvəˈkrɒp ; ˌovəˈkrap/ *vt* (-pp-) [VP6A] take too many crops from (land) (so that it loses fertility). 把(農地)使用過度;耕種過多以致使(地)變貧瘠。

over·crowd /ˌəuvəˈkraud ; ˌovəˈkraud/ *vt* [VP6A]

crowd too much: 使過度擁擠：~*ed buses／trains;* 擁擠不堪的公共汽車(火車)；*the ~ing of large cities.* 大城市的擁擠。

over·do /ˌəuvəˈduː ; ˈovɚˈdu/ *vt* (*pt* -did /-ˈdɪd ; -ˈdɪd/, *pp* -done /-ˈdʌn ; -ˈdʌn/) [VP6A] **1** do too much; exaggerate; overact: 做太多或過份;過份誇張;演得過火：*The comic scenes in the play were overdone.* 這戲的滑稽場面太誇張了。*He overdid his part in the play.* 在那齣戲裡他把他的角色演得太過火了。*~ it,* **(a)** work, etc too hard: 太用功;努力過度：*You should work hard, but don't ~ it and make yourself ill.* 你應該努力工作,但不可過度把自己累病了。**(b)** exaggerate; go too far in order to achieve one's object: 誇張;過火：*He showed sympathy for us, but didn't he rather ~ it?* 他對我們表同情,但是否稍嫌過火？ **2** cook too much: 煮過度;燒太久：*overdone beef.* 煮太久的牛肉。

over·dose /ˈəuvədəus ; ˈovɚˌdos/ *n* too great an amount (of a drug) taken at one time: (指藥物)過度劑量;過量：*take an ~;* 服藥過量；*die of an ~ of morphine.* 死於服用過量嗎啡。□ /ˌəuvəˈdəus ; ˈovɚˈdos/ *vt* [VP6A, 14] *~ sb (with sth),* give him an ~ (of sth). 使服用過量(某物)。

over·draft /ˈəuvədrɑːft *US:* -dræft ; ˈovɚˌdræft/ *n* amount of money by which a bank account is overdrawn. 超支銀行存款的金額;透支。

over·draw /ˌəuvəˈdrɔː ; ˈovɚˈdrɔ/ *vt, vi* (*pt* -drew /-ˈdruː ; -ˈdru/, *pp* -drawn /-ˈdrɔːn ; -ˈdrɔn/) [VP6A, 2A] **1** draw a cheque for a sum in excess of (one's credit balance in a bank): 開支票超過(在銀行之存款額);透支;超支：*an ~n account.* 透支了的帳戶。 **2** exaggerate: 誇張：*The characters in this novel are rather ~n,* are not true to life. 這部小說中的人物有點誇張(不够逼眞)。

over·dress /ˌəuvəˈdres ; ˈovɚˈdrɛs/ *vt, vi* [VP6A, 2A] dress (oneself, etc) too richly or more showily than is suitable for the occasion. 打扮(自己等)太考究;過度裝飾(不適於某場合)。

over·drive /ˈəuvədraɪv ; ˈovɚˌdraɪv/ *n* mechanism fitted into the normal gear-box of a motor vehicle to reduce the power output while maintaining the driving speed. 加速傳動裝置(加裝於汽車齒輪箱中的裝置,用以減低動力輸出量而又能維持行車速度)。

over·due /ˌəuvəˈdjuː *US:* -ˈduː ; ˈovɚˈdju/ *adj* beyond the time fixed (for arrival, payment, etc): 過時(到達,付款等)的;遲到的;過期的：*The train is ~,* is late. 火車誤點了。*These bills are all ~,* ought to have been paid before now. 這些帳單過期了還沒付。*The baby is two weeks ~,* still not born two weeks after the expected date of birth. 那胎兒已超過預產期兩個星期了。

over·flow /ˌəuvəˈfləu ; ˌovɚˈflo/ *vt, vi* (*pt, pp* ~ed) **1** [VP6A, 2A] flow over; flow over the edges or limits; flood; spread beyond the ordinary or usual area: 淹沒;氾濫;溢出;漫出：*The river ~ed its banks.* 河水淹沒兩岸。*The lake is ~ing.* 湖水正在氾濫。*The crowds were so big that they ~ed the barriers.* 人太多了,以致擠出柵欄。 **2** [VP3A] *~ with,* be more than filled: 充溢;洋溢：*a heart ~ing with gratitude;* 充滿着感激的心；*a friend ~ing with kindness.* 洋溢着慈愛的朋友。□ *n* /ˈəuvəfləu ; ˈovɚˌflo/ [C] flowing over of liquid; flood; that which flows over or is too much for the space, area, etc available: 溢流;氾濫;洪水;無法容納而溢出或過多之物：*new suburbs for the ~ of population;* 爲着人口過剩而闢的新郊區；*an ~ meeting,* one held for those unable to find room in the hall, etc where the principal meeting is held. 增設之會場(因主要會場人滿而加設者)。

over·grown /ˌəuvəˈgrəun ; ˈovɚˈgron/ *adj* **1** having grown too fast: 長得太快的：*an ~ boy.* 長得太快的男孩。 **2** covered with sth that has grown over: 覆着蔓生之物的;長滿的：*a garden ~ with weeds;* 長滿野草的花園；*walls ~ with ivy.* 爬滿着常春藤的牆。

over·growth /ˈəuvəgrəuθ ; ˈovɚˌgroθ/ *n* **1** [U, C] that which has grown over: 蔓生或滋蔓之物：*an ~ of weeds.* 蔓生的野草。 **2** [U] growth that is too fast or excessive: 生長過速;生長過度；*weakness due to ~.* 由於生長過速所致的虛弱。

over·hand /ˈəuvəhænd ; ˈovɚˈhænd/ *adj* (cricket, etc) overarm; (in swimming) with the hand and arm raised out of the water: (板球等)擧臂過肩的;(游泳)手和胳臂伸出水面的;兩手交拍水面的：*the ~ stroke.* 兩手交拍水面的泳法。

over·hang /ˌəuvəˈhæŋ ; ˌovɚˈhæŋ/ *vt, vi* (*pt, pp* -hung /-ˈhʌŋ ; -ˈhʌŋ/) [VP6A, 2A] **1** hang over; be over; project over, like a shelf: 懸於…之上;懸垂;伸出;突出於…之上：*The cliffs ~ the stream.* 那些峭壁懸在溪流之上。*The ledge ~s several feet.* 這個突出部份伸出好幾呎。 **2** threaten; be likely to come: 威脅;逼近;可能來到：*~ing dangers.* 逼近的危險。□ *n* /ˈəuvəhæŋ ; ˈovɚˌhæŋ/ part that ~s: 突出部份;懸垂部份：*the ~ of a roof／cliff.* 屋頂(峭壁)的懸垂部份。

over·haul /ˌəuvəˈhɔːl ; ˌovɚˈhɔl/ *vt* [VP6A] **1** examine thoroughly in order to learn about the condition of: 細密檢查;徹底檢查以期了解…之狀況;檢修：*have the engine of a car ~ed;* 將汽車引擎徹底檢修；(colloq) (俗) *go to one's doctor to be ~ed,* physically examined. 到醫生那裏去徹底檢查身體。 **2** overtake; catch up with: 追上;趕上：*The fast cruiser soon ~ed the old cargo boat.* 那艘快速的巡洋艦不久就趕上了那老舊的貨輪。□ *n* /ˈəuvəhɔːl ; ˈovɚˌhɔl/ [C] examination for the purpose of repairing, cleaning, etc. (爲修理、清潔等而作的)徹底檢查;檢修。

over·head /ˌəuvəˈhed ; ˈovɚˈhɛd/ *adv* above one's head; in the sky: 在頭頂上;在上空：*the people in the room ~;* 在頭頂上那個房間裡的人；*the stars ~.* 天上的星星。□ *adj* /ˈəuvəhed ; ˈovɚˌhɛd/ **1** raised above the ground: 離地面的;懸空的;高架的：*~ wires／cables;* 飛線;架空線(纜)；*an ~ railway,* built at a level higher than that of the streets. 高架鐵道。 **2** (business): (貿)：*~ expenses／charges* (or, *n pl,* 或作複數名詞 ~s), those expenses, etc needed for carrying on a business, eg rent, advertising, salaries, light, heating, not manufacturing costs. 經常費;營業費用(維持商業所需要的費用,如租金、廣告、薪水、照明、暖氣等,非指製造成本)。

over·hear /ˌəuvəˈhɪə(r) ; ˌovɚˈhɪr/ *vt* (*pt, pp* -heard /-ˈhɜːd ; -ˈhɝd/) [VP6A, 18A, 19A] hear without the knowledge of the speaker(s); hear what one is not intended to hear; hear by chance. 偷聽;無意中聽到;偶然聽到。

over·joyed /ˌəuvəˈdʒɔɪd ; ˈovɚˈdʒɔɪd/ *adj* greatly delighted (*at* one's success, etc). 大爲高興的;極開心的(與 at 連用,後接成功等)。

over·kill /ˈəuvəkɪl ; ˈovɚˌkɪl/ *n* capacity exceeding what is needed to destroy. 超過所需的殺傷威力。

over·land *adj* /ˈəuvəlænd ; ˈovɚˌlænd/, *adv* /ˌəuvəˈlænd ; ˈovɚˌlænd/ across the land (contrasted with the sea): 經過陸地的;陸上的;經陸路(與海路相對)：*the ~ route used by Marco Polo;* 馬哥孛羅所走的陸上路線；*travel ~.* 作陸上旅行。

over·lap /ˌəuvəˈlæp ; ˌovɚˈlæp/ *vt, vi* (-pp-) [VP 6A, 2A] **1** partly cover by extending beyond one edge: 部份重疊：*tiles that ~ one another;* 彼此部份重疊的瓦片；*~ping shingles;* 部份重疊的屋頂板；*~ping boards.* 部份重疊的牆板;魚鱗板。 **2** (fig) partly coincide; involve duplication: (喻)部份相同;重複：*His duties／authority and mine ~.* 他的職責(權力)和我的有一部份相同。*His visit and mine ~ped.* 他的訪問和我的正好在同一時間。 □ *n* /ˈəuvəlæp ; ˈovɚˌlæp/ [C] ~ping part; [U] fact or process of ~ping. 重疊或重複的部份;重疊;重複。

over·lay /ˌəuvəˈleɪ ; ˌovɚˈle/ *vt* (*pt, pp* -laid /-ˈleɪd ; -ˈled/) put a coating over the surface of: 覆蓋;包;鍍：*wood overlaid with gold.* 包一層金的木料。□ *n* /ˈəuvəleɪ ; ˈovɚˌle/ thing laid over sth. 覆蓋之物。

over·leaf /ˌəuvəˈliːf ; ˈovɚˈlif/ *adv* on the other side of the leaf (of a book, etc). 在(書等的)某面

的背面;在反面。

over·leap /ˌəʊvəˈliːp; ˌovɚˈlip/ *vt* (*pt, pp* ~ed or -leapt /-ˈlept; -ˈlɛpt/) [VP6A] leap over; (fig) go too far, attempt too much: 跳過;(喻)做得過份;企圖太多: *Ambition often ~s itself.* 野心太大常招致失敗。

over·load /ˌəʊvəˈləʊd; ˌovɚˈlod/ *vt* [VP6A] put too great a load on; (electr) put too great a charge into. 使過量載重;使超載;(電)使超量負載;使過量負荷。

over·look /ˌəʊvəˈlʊk; ˌovɚˈlʊk/ *vt* [VP6A] **1** have a view of from above: 俯視;俯瞰: *From my study window I ~ the bay and the headlands.* 從我書房的窗口,我可以俯瞰海灣和海岬。 *Our garden is ~ed from the neighbours' windows,* They can look down on to our garden from their windows. 從鄰居的窗口可以看到我們的花園。 **2** fail to see or notice; pay no attention to: 忽視;忽略;沒注意到: *~ a printer's error.* 看漏了一個印刷錯誤。 *His services have been ~ed by his employers,* They have not properly rewarded him. 他的服務一直未得到他雇主的重視(即未獲得適當的報酬)。 **3** pass over without punishing: 寬恕: *~ a fault.* 寬恕一個過失。 **4** superintend; supervise. 監督;指導。

over·lord /ˈəʊvəlɔːd; ˈovɚˌlɔrd/ *n* (in feudal times) nobleman in relation to his vassals; superior from whom men held land and to whom they owed service. (在封建時代)大封主;大地主。

over·ly /ˈəʊvəlɪ; ˈovɚlɪ/ *adv* to an excessive degree: 過度地;極度: *~ cautious.* 極度小心。 Cf 參較 *over-cautious.*

over·man·tel /ˈəʊvəmæntl; ˈovɚˌmæntl̩/ *n* structure (wood or stone, carved or decorated) over a mantlepiece. 壁爐上的飾架(木質或石質,刻有花紋或加有其他裝飾)。

over·mas·ter /ˌəʊvəˈmɑːstə(r) *US:* -mæs-; ˌovɚˈmæstɚ/ *vt* [VP6A] overcome, overpower: 勝過;壓服: *an ~ing passion,* a passion so strong that it is difficult to subdue it. 一種難以壓制的强烈情感。

over·much /ˌəʊvəˈmʌtʃ; ˈovɚˈmʌtʃ/ *adj, adv* too great(ly): 太多: *give children ~ homework;* 給兒童太多的作業; *an author who has been praised ~.* 受到過份讚揚的作者。

over·night /ˌəʊvəˈnaɪt; ˈovɚˈnaɪt/ *adv* **1** on the night before: 在前一夜: *get everything ready for the journey ~;* 在旅行的前一夜把一切都準備好; *make preparations ~.* 前一夜做準備。 **2** for, during, the night: 一夜(間): *stay ~ at a friend's house,* sleep there for the night. 在朋友家裡過夜。 *The situation changed ~.* 一夜之間情況改變了。 □ /ˈəʊvənaɪt; ˈovɚˈnaɪt/ *adj* during or for the night: 晚上的;夜裡的: *an ~ journey;* 夜間旅行; *an ~ stop at Rome.* 在羅馬停留過夜。

over·pass /ˈəʊvəpɑːs *US:* -pæs; ˈovɚˌpæs/ *n* bridge or road that carries a road over a highway or motorway. (架設於公路或快車道之上的)天橋;陸橋;高架道路。 ⇨ flyover, underpass.

over·pay /ˌəʊvəˈpeɪ; ˈovɚˈpe/ *vt* (*pt, pp* -paid /-ˈpeɪd; -ˈped/) [VP6A, 14] pay too much or too highly: 多付;給付過高: *Has Jack been overpaid for his work?* 傑克的工作報酬是否過高?

over·play /ˌəʊvəˈpleɪ; ˌovɚˈple/ *vt* ~ **one's hand,** (gambling, cards) take risks that are not justified (by overestimating one's own strength). (賭博,牌戲)(由於高估自己手中的牌力而)冒不應當冒的險。

over·plus /ˈəʊvəplʌs; ˈovɚˌplʌs/ *n* [C] amount which is surplus or in excess. 剩餘數量;超出的數量。

over·power /ˌəʊvəˈpaʊə(r); ˌovɚˈpaʊɚ/ *vt* [VP6A] overcome; be too strong for; defeat by greater strength or numbers: 克服;壓服;以力量或數目勝過: *The criminals were easily ~ed by the police.* 那些犯人輕易地被警察鎮壓住。 *He was ~ed by the heat.* 他受不住熱。 **~·ing** *adj* too strong; very powerful: 太强的;强烈的;難抗拒的: *an ~ing stink;* 强烈的惡臭; *~ing grief.* 難以抑制的悲傷。

over·print /ˌəʊvəˈprɪnt; ˌovɚˈprɪnt/ *vt* [VP6A] print additional matter on (an already printed surface, eg of postage stamps). 在(印刷品,如郵票)上加印;覆印。 □ *n* /ˈəʊvəprɪnt; ˈovɚˌprɪnt/ thing ~ed. 加印之物;覆印之物。

over·rate /ˌəʊvəˈreɪt; ˈovɚˈret/ *vt* [VP6A] put too high a value on: 高估;估計…過高: *~ sb's abilities;* 高估某人的能力; *an ~d book.* 一本評價太高的書。

over·reach /ˌəʊvəˈriːtʃ; ˌovɚˈritʃ/ *vt* [VP6A] **1** get the better of (by trickery). (以詭計)勝過。 **2** *~ oneself,* fail in one's object, damage one's own interests, by being too ambitious. 因野心太大而失敗;因操之過急而蒙受損失。

over·ride /ˌəʊvəˈraɪd; ˌovɚˈraɪd/ *vt* (*pt* -rode /-ˈrəʊd; -ˈrod/, *pp* -ridden /-ˈrɪdn; -ˈrɪdn̩/) [VP6A] prevail over (sb's opinions, decisions, wishes, claims, etc): 不顧;藐視;不理(某人的意見,決定,願望,要求等): *They overrode my wishes,* set them aside without consideration. 他們不顧我的願望。

over·rule /ˌəʊvəˈruːl; ˌovɚˈrul/ *vt* [VP6A] decide against (esp by using one's higher authority): 反對;拒絕;(尤指利用較高職權)否決;駁回: *~ a claim or objection.* 不准某項要求或異議。 *The judge ~d the previous decision.* 法官宣佈撤銷原判。 *We were ~d by the majority.* 我們被多數所否決。

over·run /ˌəʊvəˈrʌn; ˌovɚˈrʌn/ *vt* (*pt* -ran /-ˈræn; -ˈræn/, *pp* -run) [VP6A] **1** spread over and occupy or injure: 蔓延;佔領;侵害: *a country ~ by enemy troops;* 被敵軍佔據的國家; *warehouses ~ with rats;* 老鼠猖獗的貨棧; *a garden ~ with weeds.* 雜草蔓生的花園。 **2** go beyond (a limit): 超過;超出(某一範圍): *speakers who ~ the time allowed them.* 講話超過規定時間的演講者。 *The broadcast overran the allotted time.* 廣播超過了排定的時間。

over·sea(s) /ˌəʊvəˈsiː(z); ˈovɚˈsi(z)/ *adj* (at, to, from, for, places) across the sea: (在,到,來自,爲)海外的: *~(s) trade;* 海外貿易; *an ~(s) broadcast programme.* 國外廣播節目。 □ *adv: go/live ~(s),* across the sea; abroad. 到海外去(住在國外)。

over·see /ˌəʊvəˈsiː; ˌovɚˈsi/ *vt* (*pt* -saw /-ˈsɔː; -ˈsɔ/, *pp* -seen /-ˈsiːn; ˈsin/) [VP6A] look after, control (work, workmen). 監察;監督(工作,工人)。 **over·seer** /ˈəʊvəsɪə(r); ˈovɚˌsiɚ/ *n* foreman; person whose duty it is to take charge of work and see that it is properly done. 工頭;監工(管理工作並負責該工作妥善完成的人)。

over·sexed /ˌəʊvəˈsekst; ˌovɚˈsɛkst/ *adj* having sexual desire in excess of what is normal; obsessed by sex. 性慾過强的;好色的;淫蕩的。

over·shadow /ˌəʊvəˈʃædəʊ; ˌovɚˈʃædo/ *vt* [VP6A] throw a shade over; (fig) render less conspicuous; cause to seem less important. 遮蔽;使蒙上陰影;(喻)使不顯著;使顯得較不重要。

over·shoe /ˈəʊvəʃuː; ˈovɚˌʃu/ *n* [C] rubber shoe worn over an ordinary one for protection against wet and mud. 套鞋(套在普通鞋上的橡皮鞋,以防雨水及泥土)。 ⇨ galoshes.

over·shoot /ˌəʊvəˈʃuːt; ˌovɚˈʃut/ *vt* (*pt, pp* -shot /-ˈʃɒt; -ˈʃɑt/) [VP6A] shoot over or beyond (a mark); (lit, fig) go too far: 射擊高過或超過(標的);(字面,喻)超過;把…做得過份: *The aircraft overshot the runway.* 那架飛機降落時超出了跑道(進場過高)。

over·shot /ˌəʊvəˈʃɒt; ˌovɚˈʃɑt/ *adj* ~ **wheel,** water wheel driven by the pressure of water falling on to it from above. 上射式水車(水由上沖下而推動者)。

over·side /ˈəʊvəsaɪd; ˈovɚˌsaɪd/ *adv* over the side (of a ship, etc): 越過(船隻等之)邊緣地;從船邊: *discharge cargo ~,* eg into lighters, not on to the quay. 從船邊卸貨(如卸貨於駁船而非卸於碼頭上)。

over·sight /ˈəʊvəsaɪt; ˈovɚˌsaɪt/ *n* **1** [U] failure to notice sth; [C] instance of this: 失察;疏忽: *Through an unfortunate ~ your letter was left unanswered.* 由於令人遺憾的疏忽,沒有給你回信。 **2** [U] watchful care: 小心照顧: *under the ~ of a nurse.* 在護士小心照顧之下。

over·sim·plify /ˌəʊvəˈsɪmplɪfaɪ; ˌovɚˈsɪmpləˌfaɪ/ *vt, vi* [VP6A, 2A] state (problem, fact, etc) too imply for the truth to be fully told. 過於簡單地陳述(問題、事實等)。 **over·sim·pli·fi·cation** /ˌəʊvəˌsɪmplɪfɪˈkeɪʃn ; ˌovɚˌsɪmpləfəˈkeʃən/ *n* [U, C] (instance of) oversimplifying. 過於簡單的陳述。

over·skirt /ˈəʊvəskɜːt ; ˈovɚˌskɝt/ *n* one worn over a skirt. (穿在裙子外面的)外裙;上裙。

over·sleep /ˌəʊvəˈsliːp ; ˈovɚˈslip/ *vi* (*pt, pp* -slept /-ˈslept ; -ˈslɛpt/) [VP2A] sleep too long; continue sleeping after the proper time for waking: 睡得太久;睡過該醒的時刻;睡過頭: *He overslept and was late for work.* 他睡過了頭而上班遲到了。

over·spill /ˈəʊvəspɪl ; ˈovɚˌspɪl/ *n* sth that spreads into surrounding areas; (esp) excess population: 遍佈於周圍地區之物;溢出物;(尤指) 過剩的人口: *build new towns for London's* ~. 爲倫敦過剩的人口設置新市鎮。

over·state /ˌəʊvəˈsteɪt ; ˈovɚˈstet/ *vt* [VP6A] express or state too strongly; state more than is true about: 誇大敍述;言過其實: *Don't* ~ *your case.* 不要誇張你的實情。 ~**·ment** /ˈəʊvəsteɪtmənt ; ˈovɚˈstetmənt/ *n* [U] exaggeration; [C] exaggerated statement. 誇張;誇張的敍述。

over·stay /ˌəʊvəˈsteɪ ; ˈovɚˈste/ *vt* [VP6A] stay too long. 停留太久而超過…之期限。 ~ ***one's welcome,*** stay until one is no longer a welcome guest. 停留過久而令人生厭。

over·step /ˌəʊvəˈstep ; ˌovɚˈstɛp/ *vt* (-pp-) [VP6A] go beyond: 踰越;越過: ~ *one's authority.* 越權。

over·stock /ˌəʊvəˈstɒk ; ˌovɚˈstɑk/ *vt* [VP6A] supply with too large a stock: 供以過多的存貨;供給過多;使過剩: ~ *a farm with cattle,* with more cattle than there is food or space for. 供給某一農場過多的牛。

over·strung /ˌəʊvəˈstrʌŋ ; ˈovɚˈstrʌŋ/ *adj* **1** (of a person, his nerves) intensely strained; easily excited; too sensitive. (指人,人的神經)過度緊張的;容易激動的;過敏的。 **2** (of a piano) with strings crossing obliquely to save space. (指鋼琴)爲節省空間把琴絃斜向交叉裝置的。

over·stuffed /ˌəʊvəˈstʌft ; ˈovɚˈstʌft/ *adj* (of seats, etc) made soft and comfortable by very thick padding. (指座位等)因用厚墊而柔軟舒適的。

over·sub·scribed /ˌəʊvəsəbˈskraɪbd ; ˈovɚsəbˈskraɪbd/ *adj* (fin) (of an issue of shares, etc) with applications in excess of what is offered. (財政) (指股份等之發行)認購逾額的;求過於供的。

overt /ˈəʊvɜːt *US:* əʊˈvɜːrt ; oˈvɝt/ *adj* done or shown openly, publicly: 公然的;公開的: ~ *hostility.* 公然的敵意。 ~**·ly** *adv* ⇨ covert.

over·take /ˌəʊvəˈteɪk ; ˌovɚˈtek/ *vt* (*pt* -took /-ˈtʊk ; -ˈtʊk/, *pp* -taken /-ˈteɪkən ; -ˈtekən/) [VP6A] **1** come or catch up with; outstrip: 趕上;追上;超過: ~ *other cars on the road;* 追過路上的其他車輛; ~ *arrears of work.* 趕補躭擱的工作。 **2** (of storms, troubles, etc) come upon (sb) suddenly, by surprise: (指暴風雨,麻煩等)突然降臨 (某人);意外地臨到(某人): *be* ~*n by/with fear/surprise/events;* 突然感到恐懼(突然感到驚愕,突然節外生枝); *be* ~*n by a storm.* 突然受到暴風雨的襲擊。

over·tax /ˌəʊvəˈtæks ; ˈovɚˈtæks/ *vt* [VP6A] tax too heavily; put too heavy a burden or strain on: 課稅過重;加過重負擔於: ~ *one's strength/sb's patience.* 過於用力(使某人失去耐心)。

over·throw /ˌəʊvəˈθrəʊ ; ˌovɚˈθro/ *vt* (*pt* -threw /-ˈθruː ; -ˈθru/, *pp* -thrown /-ˈθrəʊn ; -ˈθron/) [VP6A] defeat; put an end to; cause to fall or fail: 擊敗;使毁滅;傾覆;推翻;打倒: ~ *the government.* 推翻政府。 □ *n* /ˈəʊvəθrəʊ ; ˈovɚˌθro/ ruin; defeat; fall. 毁滅;擊敗;打倒;推翻;傾覆。

over·time /ˈəʊvətaɪm ; ˈovɚˌtaɪm/ *n* [U], *adv* (time spent at work) after the usual hours: 超出的時間;額外的時間;加班的時間;超出時間地: *working* ~; 加班工作; *be paid extra for* ~; 因加班而得到額外給付; *be on* ~, ie working ~; 在加班工作中; ~ *pay.* 加班費。

over·tone /ˈəʊvətəʊn ; ˈovɚˌton/ *n* (music) higher note more faintly heard than the main note produced from a string, pipe, etc; (often *pl*) (fig) implication. (音樂)泛音(高於而較弱於主音的音); (常用複數) (喻)含意;暗示。

over·top /ˌəʊvəˈtɒp ; ˌovɚˈtɑp/ *vt* (-pp-) [VP6A] be higher than; rise above: 高於;高過;高於…之上: ~*ped by the new skyscraper.* 在新建的摩天樓之下。

over·trump /ˌəʊvəˈtrʌmp ; ˌovɚˈtrʌmp/ *vt* [VP6A] (whist, bridge) play a higher trump than. (惠斯特牌戲,橋牌戲)以更大的王牌取勝。

over·ture /ˈəʊvətjʊə(r) ; ˈovɚtʃɚ/ *n* **1** (often *pl*) approach made (*to* sb) with the aim of starting discussions: (常用複數)提議;建議 (與 to 連用,後接某人): *peace* ~*s;* 和平建議; *make* ~*s to sb.* 向某人提議。 **2** musical composition played as an introduction to an opera, or as a separate item at a concert. (音樂的)序樂;序曲。

over·turn /ˌəʊvəˈtɜːn ; ˌovɚˈtɝn/ *vt, vi* [VP6A, 2A] (cause to) turn over; upset: 使傾覆;顛覆;翻倒;推翻: *He* ~*ed the boat.* 他弄翻了那隻船。*The boat* ~*ed.* 船翻了。

over·ween·ing /ˌəʊvəˈwiːnɪŋ ; ˈovɚˈwinɪŋ/ *adj* having, marked by, excessive self-confidence or conceit: 過份自信的;自負的;傲慢的: ~ *ambition/vanity.* 自負的雄心(虛榮心)。

over·weight /ˈəʊvəweɪt ; ˈovɚˌwet/ *n* excess of weight above what is usual or legal: 過重;超重: *Shopkeepers rarely give* ~. 店家很少給超過應得的重量。□ *adj* /ˌəʊvəˈweɪt ; ˈovɚˈwet/ exceeding the weight allowed or normal: 過重的;超重的: *an* ~ *bag.* 過重的袋子。*If your luggage is* ~ *you'll have to pay extra.* 假如你的行李過重,你得付額外的運費。*Your suitcase is five kilograms* ~. 你的小提箱超重五公斤。⇨ underweight. ~**ed** /ˌəʊvəˈweɪtɪd ; ˈovɚˈwetɪd/ *part adj* carrying too much weight: 超載的;載重過多的: ~*ed with packages.* 包裹裝載過多的。

over·whelm /ˌəʊvəˈwelm *US:* -ˈhwelm ; ˌovɚˈhwɛlm/ *vt* [VP6A] weigh down; submerge, cover completely by flowing over or pouring down on; crush; destroy; cause to feel confused or embarrassed: 壓倒;浸沒;淹沒;使粉碎;擊潰;使不安;使困窘: *be* ~*ed by the enemy/by superior forces;* 被敵軍(被優勢兵力)所擊潰; *an* ~*ing victory;* 勢如破竹的勝利;壓倒性的勝利; ~*ing sorrow;* 極度的悲哀; *be* ~*ed by a flood;* 被洪水淹沒; *be* ~*ed with grief/gratitude.* 不勝悲哀(感激)。

over·work /ˌəʊvəˈwɜːk ; ˈovɚˈwɝk/ *vt, vi* [VP6A, 2A] (cause to) work too hard or too long: (使)工作過勞或太久;過度工作: ~ *oneself;* 操勞過度; ~ *a horse.* 使馬工作過度。*It's foolish to* ~. 工作過度是愚蠢的。□ *n* /ˈəʊvəwɜːk ; ˈovɚˈwɝk/ [U] working too much or too long: 過多或過久的工作;過度工作;過勞: *ill through* ~. 因過勞而生病。

over·wrought /ˌəʊvəˈrɔːt ; ˈovɚˈrɔt/ *adj* tired out by too much work or excitement; in a state of nervous excitement. 過勞的;過份緊張而疲倦的;神經緊張的。

ovi·duct /ˈəʊvɪdʌkt ; ˈovɪˌdʌkt/ *n* (also called 亦稱作 *Fallopian tube*) either of two tubes through which ova pass from the ovary to the uterus. 輸卵管。⇨ the illus at reproduce. 參看 reproduce 之插圖。

ovip·ar·ous /əʊˈvɪpərəs ; oˈvɪpərəs/ *adj* producing young from eggs which hatch outside the body. 卵生的。

ovoid /ˈəʊvɔɪd ; ˈovɔɪd/ *adj, n* egg-shaped (object). 卵形的;卵形物。

ovum /ˈəʊvəm ; ˈovəm/ *n* (*pl* ova /ˈəʊvə ; ˈovə/) female germ or sex cell in animals, capable of developing into a new individual when fertilized by male sperm. 卵;卵子;卵細胞。

owe /əʊ ; o/ *vt, vi* **1** [VP6A, 12A, 13A, 2A, 3A] ***owe sb sth; owe sth to sb; owe for sth,*** be in debt to (sb) (for sth): 欠;負(某人)債: *He owes* *his father £50.* 他欠他父親五十鎊。*He owes £50 to his father.* 他欠他父親五十鎊。*I have paid all that was owing.* 我已經把所有的欠債還清。*He still owes for the goods he had last month.* 他仍然欠上個月買東西的帳。 **2** [VP12A, 13A] be under an obligation to, feel the necessity of gratitude to: 受到…的恩惠;感激: *I owe a great deal to my parents and teachers.* 我深受父母及師長之恩。*I owe it to you that I am still alive.* 我感激你的救命之恩。 **3** [VP12A, 13A] be bound to give as a duty: 按責任或義務須給;應盡;負有: *owe reverence and obedience to the Pope.* 應該尊敬並服從教宗。 **4** [VP14] ***owe sth to sth,*** be indebted to as the source of: 應該把…歸功於: *He owes his success to good luck more than to ability.* 他的成功多半靠幸運,較少靠能力。*To whom do we owe the discovery of penicillin?* 盤尼西林的發現該歸功於誰?

ow·ing /ˈəʊɪŋ ; ˈo·ɪŋ/ *adj* still to be paid: 未付的;欠着的: *large sums still ~.* 尚未償付的大批款項。 ~ ***to*** *prep* because of; on account of: 因爲;由於: *O~ to the rain the match was cancelled.* 因爲下雨,比賽取消了。

owl /aʊl ; aʊl/ *n* night-flying bird that lives on small birds and animals, eg mice. 貓頭鷹;梟。 ⇨ the illus at prey. 參看 prey 之插圖。**ow·let** /ˈaʊlɪt ; ˈaʊlɪt/ *n* young owl. 小貓頭鷹。**owl·ish** /ˈaʊlɪʃ ; ˈaʊlɪʃ/ *adj* of or like an owl; looking, or trying to look, solemn and wise. 貓頭鷹的;似貓頭鷹的;顯得嚴肅而聰明的;裝着嚴肅而聰明的。**owl·ish·ly** *adv*

own¹ /əʊn ; on/ *adj, pron* **1** (used with possessives, either attributively or predicatively, to give emphasis to the idea of personal possession, to the peculiar or individual character of sth): (與所有格連用,可作形容用法或敍述用法,强調個人所有或某事物的特性)自己的: *I saw it with my own eyes.* 我親眼看到它。*It was her own idea.* 那是她自己的意思。*This is my own house/This house is my own,* belongs to me, is not rented. 這是我自己的房子(這房子是我自己的)。*This fruit has a flavour all its own,* is not to be compared to the flavour of any other fruit. 這種水果有它特有的味道。*May I have it for my very own,* Are you willing to let me be the sole owner, so that I need not share it? 我可以把它據爲己有嗎? *My time is my own,* I can spend it as I wish. 我的時間是我自己的(我可以自由支配)。*For reasons of his own* (= For particular reasons, reasons perhaps only known to him), *he refused to join the club.* 爲了個人的理由,他拒絕參加那俱樂部。***(be) (all) on one's own,*** **(a)** alone: 單獨;獨自: *I'm all on my own today.* 今天就只有我一個人。*She lives on her own,* alone, not with family or friends. 她獨自一個人住(沒和家人或朋友同住)。**(b)** independently of an employer; without supervision: 獨立地;不受雇於人地;不受監督地: *He's (working) on his own.* 他現在獨立工作。*He can be left to work on his own.* 可以讓他獨自工作。**(c)** outstanding; excellent: 傑出的;極佳的: *For craftsmanship, Smith is on his own,* has no equal. 論到手藝,史密斯是傑出無匹的。***own brother/sister,*** with both parents the same, not a half-brother/sister. 親兄弟(姐妹);胞兄弟(姐妹)。***be one's own man/master,*** be independent; be self-employed. 獨立自主;自己做老板。***come into one's own,*** receive what rightly belongs to one, the credit, fame, etc that one deserves: 得到自己應得之物;獲得應得的信譽等: *Along unpaved and rutted tracks, this sturdy car really comes into its own,* shows what it is capable of. 在這些未經鋪設而且轍跡很深的路上,這部結實的車眞正表現了它獨到的性能。***get one's 'own back,*** have one's revenge. 報仇。***hold one's 'own (against sb/sth),*** **(a)** maintain one's position against attack; not be defeated. (對某人或某事物)固守立場;不爲所敗。**(b)** not lose strength: 支撐;硬挺: *The patient is holding her own.* 這個女病人還在支撐着。 **2** (used to indicate the idea of personal activity; done or produced by and for oneself): (用以表示個人的行動;自己做的;爲自己而做的): *She makes all her own clothes.* 她所有的衣服都是自己縫製的。*I can cook my own meals.* 我能够自己煮飯。*It's unwise to try to be your own lawyer.* 你想當你自己的律師是不智的。

own² /əʊn ; on/ *vt, vi* **1** [VP6A] possess; have as property: 據有;擁有: *This house is mine; I own it.* 這屋子是我的;我擁有它。*Who owns this land,* To whom does it belong? 這塊地爲誰所有? **2** [VP6A, 9, 2C, 3A, 25] ~ ***(to),*** agree; confess; recognize: 同意;坦承;承認: *own that a claim is justified;* 同意某一要求是正當的; *own to having told a lie;* 承認曾撒一次謊; *own one's faults;* 坦承錯誤; *own oneself (to be) defeated;* 承認失敗; *own the force of an argument.* 承認一項論據令人折服。*The man refused to own the child,* would not admit that he was its father. 那個人拒絕承認自己是那小孩的父親。*I must own myself no* (= confess that I am not a) *supporter of reform.* 我必須坦白承認我不是擁護改革者。***own up (to sth),*** confess fully and frankly. 完完全全地坦白供認。

owner /ˈəʊnə(r) ; ˈonɚ/ *n* person who owns sth: 所有者;擁有人: *Who's the ~ of this house?* 誰是這房子的房主? ˌ**~-'driven** *adj* (of a vehicle) driven regularly by the ~. (指車輛)車主經常駕駛的。ˌ**~-'driver** *n* motorist who drives a car which he owns. 開自己車子的駕駛人。**~·less** *adj* without an ~; not known to belong to anyone: 無主的;不知屬於誰的: *~less dogs.* 無主的狗。ˌ**~-'occupied** *adj* (of a house, etc) lived in by the ~ (not rented to sb else). (指房子等)主人自己住的; 自用的。ˌ**~-'occupier** *n* one who owns the house he lives in. 住自己房子的居住人。**'~·ship** /-ʃɪp ; -ˌʃɪp/ *n* state of being an ~; right of possessing: 物主身分;主權;所有權: *land of uncertain ~ship.* 所有權不詳的土地。

ox /ɒks ; ɑks/ *n* (*pl* oxen /ˈɒksn ; ˈɑksn̩/) **1** general name for domestic cattle. 牛(家畜的牛的通稱)。⇨ bull¹(1), bullock, cow¹. ⇨ the illus at domestic. 參看 domestic 之插圖。 **2** (esp) fully grown castrated bullock, used as a draught animal. (尤指作駄獸用而去勢的)大公牛。**'ox-eye** *n* name (often used *attrib*) of several kinds of plants (daisies, wild chrysanthemums, etc). (常作形容用法)牛眼菊。ˌ**ox-'eyed** *adj* with large, round eyes like those of an ox. 長着像牛眼一般大而圓的眼睛的。**'ox-tail** *n* tail of ox, much used for soup, etc. 牛尾(常用以作羹湯等)。

Ox·bridge /ˈɒksbrɪdʒ ; ˈɑksˌbrɪdʒ/ *n* (invented name for) Oxford and/or Cambridge (contrasted with *Redbrick,* ⇨ red(3)). (創造的名詞)牛橋(指"牛津"及(或)"劍橋")(與 Redbrick 相對)。

Ox·ford /ˈɒksfəd ; ˈɑksfɚd/ *n* (university city in England). 牛津 (英格蘭的一個大學城)。 ~ **bags,** trousers with very wide legs. 牛津袋褲(褲腿特別寬大的褲子)。~ **blue,** dark, purplish blue. 略帶紫色的深藍色。 **the ~ Movement,** religious movement (19th c) advocating the revival of Catholicism within the Anglican Church. 牛津運動(十九世紀的宗教運動,主張在英國國教內恢復天主教教義與儀式)。~ **shoes,** low shoes lacing over the instep. 牛津鞋(在鞋面繫帶的淺口低跟鞋)。

ox·ide /ˈɒksaɪd ; ˈɑksaɪd/ *n* [C, U] compound of oxygen: 氧化物: *iron ~;* 氧化鐵; *~ of tin.* 氧化錫。**oxi·dize** /ˈɒksɪdaɪz ; ˈɑksəˌdaɪz/ *vt, vi* [VP6A, 2A] (cause to) combine with oxygen; make or become rusty. (使)氧化;(使)生銹。**oxi·diz·ation** /ˌɒksɪdaɪˈzeɪʃn *US:* -dɪˈz- ; ˌɑksədɪˈzeʃən/ *n*

Ox·on·ian /ɒkˈsəʊnɪən ; ɑksˈonɪən/ *n, adj* (member) of the University of Oxford. 牛津大學的(學生或教師)。

oxy·acety·lene /ˌɒksɪəˈsetəli:n ; ˌɑksɪəˈsɛtl̩ˌin/ *adj, n* (of a) mixture of oxygen and acetylene: 氧乙炔(的): *~ torch/blowpipe,* tool burning ~; 氧炔焰噴燈(氧炔吹管); *~ welding,* by means of a

oxyacetylene welding

hot flame of ~. 汽焊；氧乙炔焊接。

oxy·gen /ˈɒksɪdʒən ; ˈɑksədʒən/ *n* [U] chemical element (symbol **O**), gas without colour, taste, or smell, present in the air and necessary to the existence of all forms of life. 氧；氧氣（符號爲 O）。 **ˈ~ mask,** mask placed over the nose and mouth to supply ~, eg in an aircraft at a great altitude. 氧氣面具（戴於口鼻上以供給氧氣，高空飛行等人員用之）。 **ˈ~ tent,** small tent or canopy placed over the head and shoulders of a patient who needs an extra supply of ~. 氧氣帳（罩於需要加量氧氣之病人身上的小帳幕）。 **ˈ~·ate** /-eɪt ; -ˌet/, **ˈ~·ize** /-aɪz ; -ˌaɪz/ *vt* supply, treat, or mix, with ~. 給…氧；用氧處理；使與氧混合。

oyez /əʊˈjez ; ˈojɛz/ (also **oyes** /əʊˈjes ; ˈojɛs/) *int* cry meaning 'Listen', repeated three times by (hist) a town-crier, or (in a law court) by an usher to demand silence and attention. '聽'；'靜聽'；'肅靜'（昔時由街頭公告員或在法庭上由法警呼喊三次，促人安靜並注意）。

oy·ster /ˈɔɪstə(r) ; ˈɔɪstə/ *n* kinds of shellfish much used as food, usu eaten uncooked. 蠔；牡蠣。⇨ the illus at bivalve. 參看 bivalve 之插圖。 **ˈ~-bar** *n* counter (in a restaurant, etc) where ~s are served. （菜館等內的）供應蠔肉的櫃檯。 **ˈ~-bed, ˈ~-bank** *nn* part of the seabottom where ~s breed or are bred. 養蠔場。 **ˈ~-catcher** *n* wading seabird. 蠣鷸。

ozone /ˈəʊzəʊn ; ˈozon/ *n* [U] form of oxygen with a sharp and refreshing smell; (fig) exhilarating influence; (colloq) pure refreshing air as at the seaside. 臭氧；（喻）使人高興的力量；（俗）（海邊等的）新鮮空氣。

Pp

P, p /piː ; pi/ (*pl* **P's, p's** /piːz ; piz/) the 16th letter of the English alphabet. 英文字母的第十六個字母。 ***mind one's p's and q's,*** be careful not to offend against propriety. 謹慎行事；留心言行。

pa /pɑː ; pɑ/ *n* (colloq) short for *papa.* （俗）爲 papa 之略。

pabu·lum /ˈpæbjʊləm ; ˈpæbjələm/ *n* [U] food (usu fig): 食物（通常作喻）: *mental ~,* food for thought. 精神食糧。

pace /peɪs ; pes/ *n* [C] **1** (distance covered by the foot in a) single step in walking or running. （走或跑的）一步；一步的距離。 **2** rate of walking or running, or (fig) progress. 走或跑的速度；（喻）進步的速度。 ***go at a good ~,*** go fast. 快速地行走。 ***go the ~,*** **(a)** go at great speed. 飛快地行進。 **(b)** (fig) spend money freely (esp on pleasure or in dissipated ways). （喻）隨便花錢（尤指花在享樂或放蕩方面）。 ***keep ~ (with sb／sth),*** (lit or fig) go forward at the same rate: （字面或喻）同速前進；（與某人）並駕齊驅: *He finds it hard to keep ~ with all the developments in nuclear physics.* 他發現要趕上核子物理學上所有的發展很難。 ***set the ~ (for sb),*** set a speed for sb. 定速度（讓某人隨從）。 **ˈ~-maker** *n* **(a)** (also 亦作 **ˈ~-setter**) rider, runner, etc who sets the ~ for another in a race. 競賽時爲別人定步調的人；帶步人。 **(b)** electronic device (with radioactive core) to correct weak or irregular heart beats. 電子心臟定調器（用以糾正微弱或不規則之心跳）。 **3** (esp of horses) way of walking, running, etc. （尤指馬的）步態；步法。 ***put a person through his ~s,*** test his abilities, etc. 試驗某人之本領等。 □ *vi, vt* **1** [VP2A, C] walk with slow or regular steps: 緩慢而行；以規律的步伐行走；踱: *~ up and down;* 來回走動；(of a horse) amble; go at an easy, unhurried ~. （指馬）溜蹄；緩馳。 **2** [VP6A] move across in this way: 以緩慢或規律的步伐走過: *~ a room;* 在房間裡踱來踱去; *pacing the station platform.* 在火車站月臺上踱着。 **3** [VP15B] ***~ sth off／out,*** measure it by taking ~s: 以走步測量: *~ off a distance of 30 metres;* 用走步測出三十公尺的距離; *~ out a room.* 用走步測一房間之大小。 **4** [VP6A] set the ~ for (a rider or runner in a race). 爲（騎士或賽跑者）定步調；定步速。

pachy·derm /ˈpækɪdɜːm ; ˈpækəˌdɝm/ *n* (kinds of) thick-skinned, four-footed animal, eg an elephant. 厚皮四足動物（如象）；厚皮類。

pa·ci·fic /pəˈsɪfɪk ; pəˈsɪfɪk/ *adj* peaceful; making or loving peace. 和平的；和解的；愛好和平的。 **pa·ci·fi·cally** /-klɪ ; -klɪ/ *adv*

paci·fi·ca·tion /ˌpæsɪfɪˈkeɪʃn ; ˌpæsəfəˈkeʃən/ *n* [U] making or becoming peaceful; bringing about a state of peace. 媾和；和平；平定。

paci·fism /ˈpæsɪfɪzəm ; ˈpæsəˌfɪzəm/ *n* [U] principle that war should and could be abolished. 和平主義；綏靖主義；反戰主義。 **paci·fist** /-ɪst ; -ɪst/ *n* believer in ~. 和平主義者；反戰論者。

pac·ify /ˈpæsɪfaɪ ; ˈpæsəˌfaɪ/ *vt* (*pt, pp* -fied) [VP6A] calm and quieten; end violence in. 使平靜；撫慰；平定；綏靖。

pack¹ /pæk ; pæk/ *n* **1** bundle of things tied or wrapped up together for carrying; (US) packet: 捆；包裹；（美）小包: *a ~ of cigarettes.* 一包香煙。 **ˈ~-horse, ˈ~-animal** *nn* one used for carrying ~s. 馱馬；馱獸。 **ˈ~-saddle** *n* one with straps for supporting ~s. 馱鞍。 **ˈ~-thread** *n* [U] strong thread for sewing or tying up ~s or canvas bags. 包裹繩；包裝線；包紮繩。 **2** number of dogs kept for hunting (*a ~ of hounds*) or of wild animals that go about together: （獵狗或野獸）一羣 (a ~ of hounds 一羣獵犬): *Wolves hunt in ~s.* 狼成羣獵食。 **3** (usu contemptuous) number of things or persons: （通常爲輕蔑用語）（人或事物的）羣；集團；套；幫: *a ~ of thieves／liars／lies.* 一羣賊（一羣騙子；一套謊言）。 **4** complete set (usu 52) of playing-cards. 一副紙牌（通常爲 52 張）。 **5** (Rugby football) a side's forwards. （橄欖球）（一隊之）全體前衛。 **6** **ˈ~-ice** *n* [U] mass of large pieces of floating ice in the sea. 海上大堆浮冰。 **7** quantity of fish, meat, fruit, etc packed in a season: 一季中裝成罐頭的魚、肉、水果等的數量: *this year's ~ of salmon.* 今年鮭魚的裝罐量。⇨ pack²(5).

pack² /pæk ; pæk/ *vt, vi* **1** [VP6A, 14, 15A, B, 2A, C] ***~ (up) (in／into),*** put (things) into a box, bundle, bag, etc; fill (a bag, box, etc) with things; get ready for a journey by doing this: 包紮；捆紮；包裝（東西）；裝（袋、盒等）；整理行裝: *~ clothes into a trunk;* 把衣服裝進衣箱內; *~ a trunk with clothes.* 把衣服裝進衣箱內。 *Have you ~ed (up) your things?* 你把行李收拾好了沒有？ *You must begin ~ing at once.* 你必須立刻動手整理行裝。 *These books ~ easily,* It is easy to ~ them. 這些書很容易包裝。 *Her husband takes a ~ed lunch* (eg sandwiches, etc ~ed into a box or other container) *to work every day.* 她的丈夫每天帶裝盒的午餐（如裝在盒子或其他容器中的三明治等）去工作。 ***~ one's bags,*** (lit or fig) prepare to leave. （字面或喻）準備離開。 ***~ it***

in, (sl) give up doing sth; end it. (俚)放棄做某事;結束某事。 ~ ***up,*** (colloq) put one's tools, etc away; stop working: (俗)收拾工具;停止工作;收工: *It's time to ~ up.* 是收工的時候了。*One of the aircraft's engines ~ed up,* (sl) failed. (俚)飛機的一個引擎壞了。 **2** [VP14, 3A] ~ ***into,*** crush or crowd together (into a place or period of time): 塞進;擠進(某一地方或某一段時間): *~ing people into an already overcrowded bus;* 使人們擠進已經太擁擠的公共汽車; *crowds ~ing into the cinemas on a wet day.* 在雨天擠進電影院的大羣人。*She managed to ~ a lot of sightseeing into the short time she had in London.* 她在倫敦逗留的短短時間中,緊湊地安排了一連串的觀光活動。 **3** [VP6A, 15A] put soft material into or round (sth) to keep it safe, or to prevent loss or leakage: (用柔軟材料)填塞;包墊(以保護物品,或防止損失或破漏): *glass ~ed in straw;* 包紮於稻草中的玻璃器皿; *~ a leaking joint.* 填塞漏裂的接頭。 **4** ~ ***sb off; send sb ~ing,*** send him away quickly and unceremoniously (because he is troublesome, etc): 急忙而唐突地打發某人離去;辭退某人: *I wish you'd ~ yourself off,* go away. 我眞希望你快點離開這兒。 **5** [VP6A] prepare and put (meat, fruit, etc) in tins for preservation. 把(肉類、水果等)裝罐;製成罐頭。⇨ pack[1](7). **6** [VP6A] choose (the members of a committee, etc) so that their decisions are likely to be in one's favour. 挑選(委員會的委員等)以使他們的決定對自己有利;籠絡;糾集。~**er** *n* person or machine that ~s; (esp, usu *pl*) person who ~s meat, fruit, etc for market. 包裝者;包裝機;(尤指,通常用複數)罐頭食品工人。

pack·age /ˈpækɪdʒ; ˈpækɪdʒ/ *n* [C] parcel of things, packed together; (fig, colloq) detailed plan. 捆;束;包;包裹;(喻,俗)詳細的計畫。~ **deal/offer** *n* (colloq) number of proposals for discussion or acceptance. (俗)整批交易(指必須同時討論或接受之若干提議)。ˈ~ **tour,** (colloq) holiday tour with many details arranged in advance by travel agents and sold at a fixed price. (俗)一切由旅行社代辦且費用固定的假日旅遊。□ *vt* place in a ~; make a ~ of. 包裝;打包;捆紮。

packet /ˈpækɪt; ˈpækɪt/ *n* **1** small parcel or bundle: 小包;小捆: *a ~ of letters;* 一捆信件; *a postal ~;* 郵政包裹; *a ~ of 20 cigarettes.* 二十支裝的一包香煙。 **2** ˈ~**(-boat),** mailboat. 郵船。 **3** (sl) considerable sum of money: (俚)大筆款項: *make/cost a ~.* 賺(花)大錢。 **4** (army sl) trouble of some sort: (軍俚)麻煩;不幸的事;困難: *catch/stop/get a ~,* (esp) be severely wounded. 惹上麻煩;(尤指)受了重傷。

pack·ing /ˈpækɪŋ; ˈpækɪŋ/ *n* [U] process of packing (goods); materials used in packing(3), eg for closing a leaking joint. 包裝(貨物的過程);填塞;填塞或包紮的材料(如填塞裂漏之接頭用者)。ˈ~**-case** *n* one of rough boards in which goods are packed for shipment. 裝運貨物的粗木箱。ˈ~**-needle** *n* large needle used for sewing up canvas packages, etc. 縫包裝袋的粗針。

pact /pækt; pækt/ *n* compact; agreement: 協定;公約: *the P~ of Locarno;* 羅加諾協定; *a new Peace P~.* 新的和平公約。

pad[1] /pæd; pæd/ *n* **1** mass of, container filled with, soft material, used to prevent damage, give comfort or improve the shape of sth. (用以防止損壞,增加舒適或改進物品形狀的)墊塞物;墊子。 **2** guard for the leg or other parts of the body (in cricket and other games). (打板球或做其他運動時)保護腿部或身體其他部份的墊子;護脛;護胸;護膝(等)。 ⇨ the illus at cricket. 參看 cricket 之插圖。 **3** number of sheets of writing-paper fastened together along one edge. 拍紙簿。 **4** (also 亦作 ˈ**ink-pad**) absorbent material (usu in an oblong box) used for inking rubber stamps. 橡皮圖章用的印色(通常裝於長方形的盒子中);印色盒;打印臺。 **5** soft, fleshy underpart of the foot (of a dog, fox, etc). (狗、狐等的)肉趾;爪褥(足底的軟肉部份)。 **6** (usu 通常作 ˈ**launching-pad**) platform from which missiles are launched into outer space. 飛彈(火箭)發射臺。⇨ the illus at rocket. 參看 rocket 之插圖。 **7** (sl) bed; room to sleep in; apartment. (俚)床;臥室;房間。□ *vt* (-dd-) **1** [VP6A] put pads(1) in or on (to prevent injury, to give comfort, or to fill out hollow spaces, etc): 加墊子於;塞填料於(以防受傷、增加舒適或填補低淺部份等): *a jacket with padded shoulders;* 有墊肩的上裝; *a padded cell,* one with padded walls (in a mental hospital). (精神病院裡的)牆壁裝有護墊的小房間。 **2** [VP6A, 15B] ***pad sth out,*** make (a sentence, essay, book, etc) longer by using unnecessary material: (以不必要的材料)拉長(句子、文章、書等);添湊;過事鋪陳: *an essay padded out with numerous quotations.* 用許多引語添湊起來的短論。 **pad·ding** /ˈpædɪŋ; ˈpædɪŋ/ *n* [U] material used for making pads(1) or for padding(*v*, 2). 填塞的材料;添湊語;補白。

pad[2] /pæd; pæd/ *vi, vt* (-dd-) [VP2A, C] travel on foot: 步行;走路: *padding along;* 向前走去; [VP6A] tramp (the roads) on foot: 走(路): *He lost all his money and had to pad it home.* 他的錢都丟了,不得不步行回家。

paddle[1] /ˈpædl; ˈpædl/ *n* **1** short oar with a broad blade at one or (*double ~*) at both ends, used (without a rowlock) to propel a canoe through the water. (一端或兩端有寬濶槳葉而不用槳架的)短槳。⇨ the illus at canoe. 參看 canoe 之插圖。 **2** (in rowing) act or period of propelling a boat with light, easy strokes. (划船時的)划槳;盪槳。 **3** ˈ~**-box** *n* wooden covering for the upper part of a ~-wheel. 明輪轂(明輪上部的木蓋)。 ˈ~**-steamer** *n* steam vessel propelled by ~-wheels. 明輪船(用明輪推進的船)。ˈ~**-wheel** *n* one of a pair of wheels, each with boards round the circumference which press backwards against the water and propel a ~-steamer. (裝有翼板用以擊水推進輪船的)明輪;蹼輪。 **4** ~-shaped instrument (eg one used for beating, stirring or mixing things). 槳形工具(如用於擊打、攪拌或混合物品者);槳形板。□ *vt, vi* [VP6A, 2A] send (a canoe) through the water by using a ~ or ~s; row with light, easy strokes. 以槳划動(小船);盪槳。~ ***one's own canoe,*** (colloq) depend on oneself alone. (俗)靠自己;自立;自力更生。

paddle[2] /ˈpædl; ˈpædl/ *vi* [VP2A] walk with bare feet in shallow water (as children do at the seaside): 涉水;玩水: *a ˈpaddling pool,* shallow pool (eg in a public park) where children ~. 淺水池(如公園內供兒童玩水的小池子)。□ *n* act or period of paddling. 涉水;玩水。

pad·dock /ˈpædək; ˈpædək/ *n* **1** small grass field, esp one used for exercising horses. 小牧場(尤指用來溜馬的草地)。 **2** (at a race-course) enclosed area of grassland where horses are assembled and paraded before a race. (賽馬場中)比賽前供馬匹聚集及受檢閱的圍場。

paddy[1] /ˈpædɪ; ˈpædɪ/ *n* [U] rice that is still growing; rice in the husk. (生長中的)稻;(未碾磨的)榖。ˈ~**-field** *n* rice-field. 稻田。

paddy[2] /ˈpædɪ; ˈpædɪ/ *n* (*pl* -dies) (colloq) rage; fit of bad temper: (俗)憤怒;發脾氣: *She's in one of her paddies,* one of the fits of bad temper to which she is subject. 她在發脾氣。

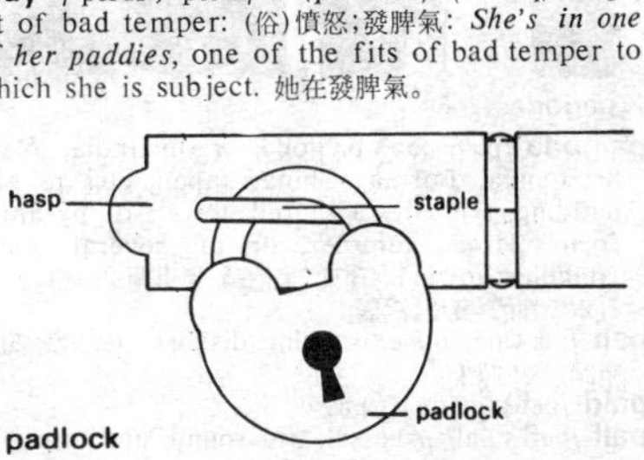

a padlock

Paddy /ˈpædɪ; ˈpædɪ/ *n* (nickname for an) Irishman. 愛爾蘭人(綽號)。 **ˈ~-wagon,** (US sl) police van for taking persons suspected of crime into custody. (美俚)逮捕嫌犯用的警車。

pad·lock /ˈpædlɒk; ˈpæd,lɑk/ *n* lock of the kind shown here. 掛鎖;釦鎖。 □ *vt* [VP6A] fasten with a ~: 鎖以掛鎖: *The gate was ~ed.* 那門有掛鎖鎖着。

padre /ˈpɑːdreɪ; ˈpɑdrɪ/ *n* (army and navy colloq) chaplain; (GB colloq) priest; parson. (陸海軍俗語)隨軍牧師;(英俗)傳教士;牧師。

paean, (US) **pean** /ˈpiːən; ˈpiən/ *n* song of thanksgiving, praise or triumph. 感恩歌;讚美歌;凱歌。

paed·er·asty /ˈpedəræstɪ; ˈpɛdə,ræstɪ/ *n* = pederasty.

paedi·at·rics /ˌpiːdɪˈætrɪks; ,pidɪˈætrɪks/ *n* = pediatrics.

pae·ony /ˈpiːənɪ; ˈpiənɪ/ *n* = peony.

pa·gan /ˈpeɪɡən; ˈpeɡən/ *n, adj* (person who is) not a believer in any of the chief religions of the world. 不是世界上任一主要宗教之教徒的;異教徒的;異教徒: **~·ism** /-ɪzəm; ,ɪzəm/ *n* [U] beliefs, practices, of ~s. 異教徒的信仰與習俗。

page[1] /peɪdʒ; pedʒ/ *n* one side of a leaf of paper in a book, periodical, etc; entire leaf of a book, etc: (書籍、期刊等的)一面; 頁; (書等的)一張(兩頁): *Several ~s have been torn out.* 好幾頁被撕掉了。□ *vt* number the ~s of. 標明…的頁數。

page[2] /peɪdʒ; pedʒ/ *n* **1** (also 亦作 **ˈ~ boy**) boy servant, usu in uniform, in a hotel, club, etc. 僮僕(指旅館、俱樂部等內通常穿制服的男侍)。 **2** (in the Middle Ages) boy in training for knighthood and living in a knight's household. (中古)住在騎士家中的學習騎士。□ *vt* [VP6A] call by name, by means of, or as if by means of (eg over a loudspeaker), a page(1). (派僮僕或以擴音器等)在公共場所呼喊(某人)名字以尋找。

pag·eant /ˈpædʒənt; ˈpædʒənt/ *n* **1** public entertainment, usu outdoors, in which historical events are acted in the costume of the period. 歷史事蹟之表演(通常在戶外舉行,着古裝演出)。 **2** public celebration, esp one in which there is a procession of persons in fine costumes (eg a coronation). 慶典(尤指含有盛裝行列者,如加冕典禮)。 **~ry** /ˈpædʒəntrɪ; ˈpædʒəntrɪ/ *n* [U] rich and splendid display. 華麗的展示;盛觀。

pagi·na·tion /ˌpædʒɪˈneɪʃn; ,pædʒəˈneʃən/ *n* [U] (figures used for the) numbering of the pages of a book. 標記頁數(的數字)。

pagodas

pa·goda /pəˈɡəʊdə; pəˈɡodə/ *n* (in India, Nepal, Sri Lanka, Burma, China, Japan, etc) religious building, typically a sacred tower of pyramidal form (Hindu temple), or of several storeys (Buddhist tower). (印度、尼泊爾、斯里蘭卡、緬甸、中國、日本等地的)寶塔;浮屠。

pah /pɑː; pɑ/ *int* expressing disgust. (表示憎惡的感嘆詞)呸!哼!

paid /peɪd; ped/ ⇨ pay[2].

pail /peɪl; pel/ *n* vessel, usu round and open, of metal or wood, for carrying liquid: 桶;鐵桶;木桶: *a ~ of milk.* 一桶牛奶。 **ˈ~·ful** /-fʊl; -,fʊl/ *n* as much as a ~ holds. 一桶之量。

pail·lasse, pal·li·asse /ˈpælɪæs *US:* ˌpælɪˈæs; ,pælɪˈæs/ *nn* mattress filled with straw. 草褥;草薦。

pain /peɪn; pen/ *n* **1** [U] suffering of mind or body: (心或身的)痛苦;痛;疼: *be in (great) ~;* (深爲)痛苦; *cry with ~;* 痛得大叫; *feel some/no/not much/a great deal of ~.* 覺得有點痛(不痛,不頂痛,非常痛)。 **ˈ~-killer** *n* medicine for lessening ~. 止痛藥。 **2** [C] particular or localized kind of bodily suffering: 身體某部份的痛: *a ~ in the knee;* 膝蓋痛; *~s in the back;* 背痛; *stomach ~s.* 胃痛。 ***a ~ in the neck,*** (sl) irritating person. (俚)令人感到不舒服的人;討厭的傢伙。 **3** [U, C] (old use) punishment; penalty: (舊用法)罰;刑罰: (legal phrases) (法律用語): *~s and penalties.* 刑罰。 ***on/under ~ of death,*** at the risk of being sentenced to death. 冒着被處死刑的危險。□ *vt* [VP6A] cause ~ to: 使痛苦: *Doesn't your laziness ~ your parents?* 你的懶惰不會使你父母親難過嗎? *My foot is still ~ing me.* 我的脚還在痛。 **~ed** *adj* distressed: 痛苦的;難過的: *She looked ~ed when I refused to help.* 當我拒絕幫助她時,她顯得很痛苦。 *She had a ~ed look.* 她的表情悲痛。 **ˈ~·ful** /-fl; -fəl/ *adj* causing ~: 痛的;使痛苦的;會痛的: *This duty is ~ful to me.* 這責任使我很痛苦。 **ˈ~·fully** /-fəlɪ; -fəlɪ/ *adv* **~·less** *adj* without ~; causing no ~: 無痛的;不會痛的: *~less extractions,* (of teeth). 無痛的拔牙。 **~·less·ly** *adv*

pains /peɪnz; penz/ *n pl* trouble; effort: 勞苦;辛勞;煩勞: *work hard and get very little for all one's ~.* 辛勤工作而所得極微。 ***be at ~ to do sth,*** make a great effort, work hard, to do it. 努力做某事;費盡心機做某事。 ***spare no ~,*** do everything possible. 不辭辛勞。 ***take (great) ~ (over sth/to do sth),*** take great trouble: 煞費苦心(做某事);(爲某事)費盡心機: *take great ~ to please one's lover.* 煞費苦心使愛人高興; 費盡心機取悅愛人。 **ˈ~·taking** *adj* careful; industrious. 小心的;辛勤的。

paint /peɪnt; pent/ *n* **1** [U] solid colouring matter (to be) mixed with oil or other liquid and used to give colour to a surface: 油漆;塗料: *give the doors two coats of ~.* 把門塗上兩層油漆。 **2** [U] material used to colour the face. 香粉;胭脂。 **3** (*pl*) collection of tubes or cakes of colouring materials. (複)(管裝或塊狀的一組)顏料。 **ˈ~-box** *n* box with such a collection. (裝有一組顏料的)顏料盒。 **ˈ~-brush** *n* brush for applying ~. 畫筆;油漆刷。 ⇨ the illus at palette. 參看 palette 之插圖。 □ *vt, vi* **1** [VP6A, 22] coat with paint: 油漆;漆: *~ a door;* 漆一扇門; *~ the gate green.* 把大門油漆成綠色。 ***~ the town red,*** (colloq) go out and have a lively, exciting time esp when celebrating sth. (俗)逛遊尋歡作樂(尤指當慶賀某事時)。 **2** [VP6A, 15A, B, 2A, C] make a picture (of) with paint: (用顏料)畫;繪畫: *~ flowers/a landscape;* 畫花卉(風景); *~ in oils/in water-colours.* 畫油畫(水彩畫)。 ***~ sth in,*** add to a picture: 畫某物於圖中: *~ in the foreground.* 畫出前景。 ***~ sth out,*** cover up or hide by using paint. 用顏料或油漆塗去。 **3** [VP 6A, 22] (fig) describe vividly in words. (喻)逼眞地描述;生動地描寫。 ***not so black as one is ~ed,*** not so bad as one is represented to be. 並不像所形容的那樣壞。

painter[1] /ˈpeɪntə(r); ˈpentɚ/ *n* **1** person who paints pictures; artist. 畫圖者;畫家。 **2** workman who paints woodwork, walls, buildings, ships, etc. 油漆工人;油漆匠。

painter[2] /ˈpeɪntə(r); ˈpentɚ/ *n* rope fastened to the bow of a boat by which it may be tied to a ship, pier, etc. 艇頭索;繫索(連於小艇首部的纜索,用以連繫他船、碼頭等)。 ⇨ the illus at sail. 參看 sail 之插圖。 ***cut the ~,*** **(a)** set (a boat, etc) adrift. 使(船等)漂流。 **(b)** (fig), effect a separation; become independent. (喻)和…脫離關係;獨立。

paint·ing /ˈpeɪntɪŋ ; ˈpentɪŋ/ *n* **1** [U] using paint; occupation of a painter. 油漆;繪畫;油漆業;繪畫業。 **2** [C] painted picture. 圖畫;油畫。

pair /peə(r) ; pɛr/ *n* **1** two things of the same kind (to be) used together: 一雙;一對: *a ~ of shoes／gloves;* 一雙鞋(手套); *two ~s of socks.* 兩雙短襪。 **2** single article with two parts always joined: 由兩部份合在一起的單件物品: *a ~ of trousers／tights／scissors／tongs.* 一條褲子(一件緊身衣;一把剪刀;一把鉗子)。 **3** two persons closely associated, eg an engaged or married couple: 兩個關係密切的人(如已訂婚的男女或夫妻): *the happy ~,* eg two newly married persons. 快樂的一對(如新婚夫婦)。 ***in ~s,*** in twos. 成雙的;成對的。 **4** two animals of opposite sex; two horses harnessed together. 雌雄一對的動物;套在同一馬具上的兩匹馬。 **5** (in Parliament) two persons of opposite political parties who absent themselves from a division(6) by mutual agreement; one member willing to do this: (國會中)分屬兩敵對政黨而約好對某項表決放棄投票權的兩個議員;約好願意放棄投票權的一方: *The member for Lewisham couldn't find a ~.* 路易薩姆的議員找不到對方也願意放棄投票的人。□ *vt, vi* [VP 6A, 15B, 2A, C] form a ~ or ~s; join in ~s; (of animals) mate. (使)成對;配合;(指動物)交配。 **~ *off,*** put in ~s; go off in ~s; (in Parliament) make a ~(5). 配成對;成雙;(國會中)敵對雙方同意放棄投票。

pais·ley /ˈpeɪzlɪ ; ˈpezlɪ/ *n* (soft wool fabric with) curved patterns in bright colours: 帕斯力圖案(色彩鮮明的弧曲圖案);帕斯力毛料(上有此種圖案的柔軟毛織品): *a ~ shawl.* 帕斯力披肩。

pa·ja·mas /pəˈdʒɑːməz ; pəˈdʒæməz/ *n pl* ⇨ pyjamas.

pal /pæl ; pæl/ *n* (colloq) comrade; friend. (俗)同志;朋友。□ *vi* (-ll-) ***pal up (with sb),*** become friendly. (與某人)要好起來;(與某人)結交。 **pally** /ˈpælɪ ; ˈpælɪ/ *adj* (colloq) friendly. (俗)親密的;友好的。

pal·ace /ˈpælɪs ; ˈpælɪs/ *n* **1** official residence of a sovereign, archbishop or bishop; any large and splendid house; large, splendid building for entertainment. 皇宮;宮殿;(大主教或主教的)官邸;豪華大厦;豪華的娛樂大厦。 **2 the ~,** influential persons at the ~ of a sovereign ruler. 宮廷權貴。 **~ revolution,** overthrow of sb in a position of great power, eg a President, by high-ranking colleagues or close subordinates. 宮廷革命(攬大權者,如總統,被其高級同僚或親信屬僚所推翻的革命)。

pala·din /ˈpælədɪn ; ˈpælədɪn/ *n* any of the twelve Peers of the court of Emperor Charlemagne; knight errant; notable champion. 查理曼大帝的十二武士之一;遊俠;著名的鬥士。

palaeo- /ˌpælɪəʊ- *US:* ˌpeɪlɪəʊ- ; ˈpelɪo-/ *pref* (in compounds, etc) (用在複合字等中) = paleo-.

palan·quin, palan·keen /ˌpælənˈkiːn ; ˌpælənˈkin/ *nn* covered litter for one person, carried on poles by two or more men, as formerly used in India and other Eastern countries. (印度及其他東方國家昔時所用的由二人或更多人抬的)單座轎子。

pal·at·able /ˈpælətəbl ; ˈpælətəbl̩/ *adj* agreeable to the taste or (fig) to the mind. 可口的;美味的;(喻)怡人的。

pala·tal /ˈpælətl ; ˈpælətl̩/ *n, adj* (sound) made by placing the tongue against or near (usu the hard) palate (eg /j, ʒ, ʃ, dʒ/); of the palate. 舌頭接觸口蓋所發的(音);顎音(如 /j, ʒ, ʃ, dʒ/ 等音);上顎的。

pal·ate /ˈpælət ; ˈpælɪt/ *n* **1** roof of the mouth: 上顎;口蓋: *the hard／soft ~,* its front／back part. 硬(軟)顎。 ˌ**cleft** ˈ**~,** ⇨ cleave¹(3). ⇨ the illus at mouth. 參看 mouth 之插圖。 **2** sense of taste: 味覺: *have a good ~ for fine wines.* 精於品評上等酒類。

pa·la·tial /pəˈleɪʃl ; pəˈleʃəl/ *adj* of or like a palace; magnificent: 宮殿的;像宮殿的;堂皇的;莊嚴的: *a ~ residence.* 富麗堂皇的居所。

pa·lat·in·ate /pəˈlætɪnət *US:* -tənət ; pəˈlætn̩ˌet/ *n* territory ruled over by an earl or count having some royal privileges. 有王權伯爵的領地。

pal·aver /pəˈlɑːvə(r) *US:* -ˈlæv- ; pəˈlævɚ/ *n* [C] (hist) talk or conference, esp one between traders or explorers and the people of the country; [U] idle talk; [U, C] (colloq) bother. (史)商談;交涉;談判(尤指外來商旅與當地人之間所作者);閒談;(俗)麻煩。□ *vi* [VP2A] talk idly for a long time. 長時間閒談;閒聊。

pale¹ /peɪl ; pel/ *adj* (-r, -st) **1** (of a person's face) having little colour; bloodless: (指臉色)蒼白的;沒有血色的: *He turned ~ at the news.* 他聽到那消息面容失色。 *You're looking ~ today.* 你今天臉色蒼白。 ˈ**~-face** *n* name said to have been used by N American Indians for a European white person. 白臉人(據說北美印第安人從前用此名稱指歐洲的白種人)。 **2** (of colours) not bright; faintly coloured: (指顏色)暗淡的;淺淡的: *~ blue.* 淡藍色。□ *vi* [VP2A, C] grow ~; lose colour. 變淡;變暗淡;失色。**~ *before／by the side of,*** (fig) be far outdone by; appear weak when seen with. (喻)遠遜於;(與…在一起)相形見絀;黯然失色。 **~·ly** /ˈpeɪllɪ ; ˈpellɪ/ *adv* **~·ness** *n*

pale² /peɪl ; pel/ *n* pointed piece of wood used for fences; stake. 圍籬用的尖木條;樁。 ⇨ paling.

pale³ /peɪl ; pel/ *n* (hist) area around Dublin (in Ireland) controlled by the English. (史)愛爾蘭都柏林周圍的英屬地域。 Now, only in: 今僅用於: ***beyond／outside the ~,*** socially unacceptable or unreasonable: 社交上不爲人所接受的或不當的: *His remarks put him quite outside the ~.* 他所說的話使他被遠拒於社交圈子外。

paleo·lithic (also **palaeo-**) /ˌpælɪəʊˈlɪθɪk *US:* ˌpeɪl- ; ˌpelɪəˈlɪθɪk/ *adj* of the period marked by the use of primitive stone implements. 舊石器時代的。

pale·on·tol·ogy (also **palae-**) /ˌpælɪɒnˈtɒlədʒɪ *US:* ˌpeɪl- ; ˌpelɪɑnˈtɑlədʒɪ/ *n* [U] study of fossils as a guide to the history of life on earth. 古生物學;化石學。 **pale·on·tol·ogist** (also **palae-**) /-ədʒɪst ; -ədʒɪst/ *n*

pal·ette /ˈpælɪt ; ˈpælɪt/ *n* board (with a hole for the thumb) on which an artist mixes his colours. (畫家用的)調色板。 ˈ**~-knife** *n* thin steel blade with a handle, used (by artists) for mixing (and sometimes spreading) oil colours, (by potters) for moulding clay, and in cookery. (畫油畫用的)調色刀;(陶工用的)塑陶土刀;(烹飪用的)烹飪刀。

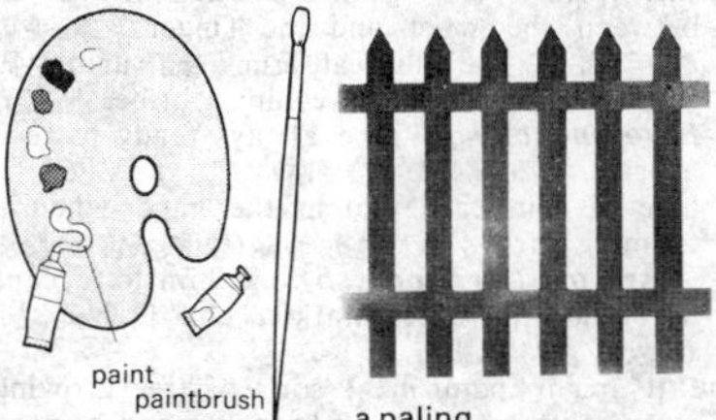

a palette　　a paling

pal·frey /ˈpɔːlfrɪ ; ˈpɔlfrɪ/ *n* (*pl* -freys) (old use, and in poetry) saddle-horse for riding, esp one for a woman. (舊用語及詩中用語)供乘騎的馬(尤指供婦女乘用者)。

pal·imp·sest /ˈpælɪmpsest ; ˈpælɪmpˌsɛst/ *n* [C] piece of parchment or other writing material from which the original writing has been erased to make room for new writing, esp as a source for lost works of the remote past. 刮去舊字以供書寫新字的羊皮紙或其他書寫材料(尤指作爲古代佚失作品之來源者)。

pal·in·drome /ˈpælɪndrəʊm ; ˈpælɪnˌdrom/ *n* word, verse, etc that reads the same backwards as forwards, eg *madam.* 迴文(正讀反讀都一樣的字、詩句等,如 madam)。

pal·ing /ˈpeɪlɪŋ ; ˈpelɪŋ/ *n* fence made of pales[2]. 用樁圍成的柵;木柵;圍籬。

pali·sade /ˌpælɪˈseɪd ; ˌpæləˈsed/ *n* **1** fence of strong, pointed wooden stakes (eg as used to defend a building in former times). 木柵(用堅固的尖木樁圍成,如昔時用於防衛建築物者)。 **2** (*pl*) (US) line of high, steep cliffs (esp along a river). (複)(美)一列高聳的峭壁(尤指沿河者)。 □ *vt* [VP6A] enclose or fortify with a ~(1). 用柵圍繞;用柵防衛。

pal·ish /ˈpeɪlɪʃ ; ˈpelɪʃ/ *adj* somewhat pale. 略帶蒼白的。

pall[1] /pɔːl ; pɔl/ *n* **1** heavy cloth spread over a coffin. 柩衣。 **ˈ~-bearer** *n* person who helps to carry, or who walks alongside, a coffin at a funeral. (出殯時)扶棺者;護柩者。 **2** (fig) any dark, heavy covering: (喻)任何深色而厚重的覆蓋物: *a ~ of smoke.* 一片濃煙。

pall[2] /pɔːl ; pɔl/ *vi* [VP2A, 3A] ~ ***(on/upon),*** become distasteful or boring because done, used, etc for too long a time: (久而)乏味;令人生厭;掃興: *pleasures that ~ after a time;* 久而令人生厭的娛樂; *a long lecture that ~ed upon most of the listeners.* 令大多數聽衆生厭的長篇講演。

pal·let /ˈpælɪt ; ˈpælɪt/ *n* **1** straw-filled mattress for sleeping on. 稻草牀墊;草薦。 **2** large tray or platform for moving loads (by means of slings, etc), eg from a lorry into a train or on to a ship, and so save handling of separate items. (利用吊索等從貨車上運貨至火車或船上的)輸送臺。

pal·li·asse /ˈpælɪæs *US:* ˌpælɪˈæs ; ˌpælɪˈæs/ *n* = paillasse.

pal·li·ate /ˈpælɪeɪt ; ˈpælɪˌet/ *vt* [VP6A] (formal) lessen the severity of (pain, disease); excuse the seriousness of (a crime, etc). (正式用語)減輕;緩和(痛、病);掩飾(罪等)。 **pal·li·ation** /ˌpælɪˈeɪʃn ; ˌpælɪˈeʃən/ *n* [U] the act of palliating; the state of being ~d; [C] that which ~s; excuse. 減輕;緩和;掩飾;使減輕或緩和之物;辯解;掩飾之詞;託辭;藉口。 **pal·li·ative** /ˈpælɪətɪv ; ˈpælɪˌetɪv/ *n, adj* (sth) serving to ~. 減輕的;緩和的;掩飾的;用以減輕、緩和或掩飾之物。

pal·lid /ˈpælɪd ; ˈpælɪd/ *adj* pale; ill-looking. 蒼白的;有病容的。 **~·ly** *adv* **~·ness** *n*

pal·lor /ˈpælə(r) ; ˈpælɚ/ *n* [U] paleness, esp of the face. 蒼白;(尤指)臉色蒼白。

pally ⇨ pal.

palm[1] /pɑːm ; pɑm/ *n* inner surface of the hand between the wrist and the fingers. 掌;手掌;掌心;手心。 ⇨ the illus at arm. 參看 arm 之插圖。 ***grease/oil sb's ~,*** give him a bribe. 賄賂某人。 ***have an itching ~,*** be always ready to receive a bribe. 貪賄;隨時準備接受賄賂。 □ *vt* [VP6A, 15B] hide (a coin, card, etc) in the hand when performing a trick. (表演魔術時)藏(硬幣、紙牌等)於掌中。 ***~ sth off (on/upon sb),*** get him to accept it by fraud, misrepresentation, etc. 以欺騙的方式使(某人)接受某物;騙賣。

palm[2] /pɑːm ; pɑm/ *n* **1** sorts of tree growing in warm climates, with no branches and a mass of large wide leaves at the top: 棕櫚: *the ˈdate-~;* 棗椰樹; *the ˈcoconut ~.* 椰子樹。 **ˈ~-oil** *n* [U] oil obtained from the nuts of a W African ~. 棕櫚油。 **ˈ~ wine** *n* [U] W African alcoholic drink, the sap of ~ trees. 棕櫚酒(非洲西部由棕櫚樹液製成的一種酒)。 **ˌP~-ˈSunday,** the Sunday before Easter. 棕櫚主日(復活節前的禮拜天)。 **2** leaf of a ~ as a symbol of victory. (象徵勝利的)棕櫚葉。 ***bear/carry off the ~,*** be victorious. 得勝。 ***yield the ~ (to sb),*** admit defeat (by sb). 承認(被某人)打敗;(向某人)認輸。 **~y** *adj* (-ier, -iest) flourishing; prosperous: 繁盛的;興盛的: *in my ~y days.* 在我的全盛時代。 **~er** *n* (formerly) pilgrim returning from the Holy Land with a ~-leaf. (昔時)帶着棕櫚葉自聖地歸來的朝聖者。

pal·metto /pælˈmetəʊ ; pælˈmɛto/ *n* (*pl* ~s or ~es /-təʊz ; -toz/) kinds of small palm with fan-shaped leaves, common in the West Indies and the S E coast of the US. (產於西印度群島及美國東南沿海一帶,有扇形葉的)小棕櫚。

palm·ist /ˈpɑːmɪst ; ˈpɑmɪst/ *n* person who claims to tell a person's future by examining the lines on his palm. 手相家。 **palm·is·try** /ˈpɑːmɪstrɪ ; ˈpɑmɪstrɪ/ *n* art of doing this. 手相術。

pal·pable /ˈpælpəbl ; ˈpælpəbḷ/ *adj* that can be felt or touched; clear to the mind: 可觸知的;摸得出的;明顯的;明白的: *a ~ error.* 一個明顯的錯誤。 **pal·pably** /-əblɪ ; -əblɪ/ *adv*

pal·pi·tate /ˈpælpɪteɪt ; ˈpælpəˌtet/ *vi* [VP2A, C] (of the heart) beat rapidly and irregularly; (of a person, his body) tremble (with terror, etc). (指心臟)急速而不規則地跳動;悸動;(指人、人體)(因恐懼等)發抖。 **pal·pi·ta·tion** /ˌpælpɪˈteɪʃn ; ˌpælpəˈteʃən/ *n* palpitating of the heart (from disease, great efforts, etc). (由於疾病,用力等所致的)心臟急跳;心悸;悸動;忐忑。

palsy /ˈpɔːlzɪ ; ˈpɔlzɪ/ *n* [U] paralysis: 痲痺;癱瘓;中風: *suffering from cerebral ~.* 患大腦性癱瘓。 ⇨ spastic. □ *vt* paralyse. 使痲痺;使癱瘓。

pal·ter /ˈpɔːltə(r) ; ˈpɔltɚ/ *vi* [VP3A] ~ ***with,*** be insincere when dealing with; trifle with: 不誠懇地對待或處理;敷衍;馬馬虎虎應付: *Don't ~ with the question,* Do treat it seriously. 不要馬馬虎虎處理這個問題。

pal·try /ˈpɔːltrɪ ; ˈpɔltrɪ/ *adj* (-ier, -iest) worthless; of no importance; contemptible. 無價值的;不重要的;微不足道的;可鄙的。

pam·pas /ˈpæmpəs *US:* -əz ; ˈpæmpəz/ *n pl* extensive, flat, grassy, treeless plains of S America. 南美的大草原。 ⇨ prairie, savanna, steppe, veld. **ˈ~-grass** *n* [U] tall grass with sharp-edged blades and a silvery plume-like flower. 一種桿莖高大,葉片銳利,生銀色羽狀花的草;銀葦。

pam·per /ˈpæmpə(r) ; ˈpæmpɚ/ *vt* [VP6A] indulge too much; be unduly kind to: 縱容;嬌養: *a ~ed poodle.* 一隻嬌生慣養的獅子狗。 *She sometimes ~s herself and has a day in bed.* 她有時縱容自己,一整天躺在床上。

pamph·let /ˈpæmflɪt ; ˈpæmflɪt/ *n* [C] small paper-covered book, esp on a question of current interest. 小册子(尤指有關於時事問題者)。 **~·eer** /ˌpæmfləˈtɪə(r) ; ˌpæmflɪˈtɪr/ *n* writer of ~s. 小册子作者。

pan[1] /pæn ; pæn/ *n* **1** flat dish, usu shallow and without a cover, used for cooking and other domestic purposes. (烹飪及其他家事用途的)無蓋淺鍋;平底鍋;盤子;盆子。 **ˈpan·cake** *n* **(a)** batter cooked on both sides until brown and (usu) eaten hot. 薄煎餅。 **ˈPancake Day,** = Shrove Tuesday. **(b)** **pancake landing,** emergency landing in which the aircraft drops flat to the ground. 平墜着陸(飛機平落地面之緊急降落)。 **(c)** cosmetic face-powder pressed into a flat cake, used without a foundation cream. (化粧用的)粉餅。 **2** receptacle with various uses: (各種用途的)容器: *the pan* (= bowl)

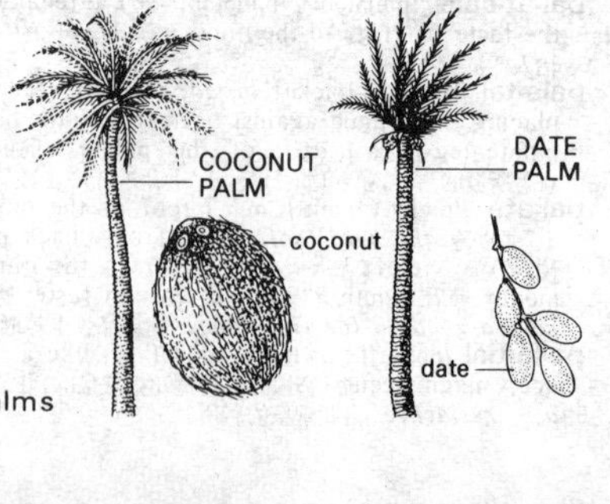

palms

of a lavatory; (盥洗室中的)洗臉盆。*a* ˈ*bedpan,* ⇨ bed¹(6). **3** (natural or artificial) depression in the ground: (地面上天然或人工的)窪穴;坑: *a* ˈ*salt-pan,* where salt water is evaporated. 晒鹽池。 **4** ˈ**brain-pan,** upper part of the skull, enclosing the brain. 頭蓋。 **5** either of the dishes on a pair of scales. (天平的)秤盤。⇨ the illus at balance. 參看 balance 之挿圖。 **6** open dish for washing gravel, etc to separate gold ore or other metals. 汰鉢;淘金盤(用以將金或其他金屬與砂石分開)。 **7** (in flintlock guns) cavity in the lock that holds the gunpowder. (舊式燧發槍中的)火藥池。***a flash in the pan,*** ⇨ flash¹(1). **8** [U] (ˈ**hard-)pan,** hard subsoil. 硬的底土;磐;硬磐。 **9** (sl) face. (俚)臉;面。□ *vt, vi* (-nn-) **1** [VP15B, 3A, 2C] ***pan sth off/out,*** wash (gold-bearing gravel, etc) in a pan. 用淘金盤淘洗(金砂等)。***pan for,*** wash gravel, etc for eg gold. 淘洗金砂等以取(金)。 ~ ***out,*** **(a)** yield gold. 產金。**(b)** (fig) succeed; turn out: (喻)成功;結果: *How did things pan out?* 事情的結果如何? *The scheme panned out well.* 那計畫結果甚佳。 **2** [VP6A] (colloq) criticize harshly. (俗)嚴厲批評;苛評。

pan² /pæn; pæn/ *vi, vt* (cinema and TV) turn a camera right or left to follow a moving object or get a panoramic effect. (電影及電視)左右轉動攝影機使鏡頭能對着移動的目的物或收到攝取全景的效果;轉動(鏡頭)。⇨ zoom(2).

pan- *pref* ⇨ App 3. 參看附錄三。

pana·cea /ˌpænəˈsɪə; ˌpænəˈsiə/ *n* remedy for all troubles, diseases, etc. 解決一切弊病的方法;萬靈藥。

pa·nache /pæˈnæʃ *US:* pə-; pəˈnæʃ/ *n* [U] confident and flamboyant manner: 自信,浮華的態度;誇耀: *There was an air of ~ about everything he did.* 他做每一件事都帶着浮誇的態度。

pa·nama /ˈpænəmɑː; ˈpænəˌmɑ/ *n* ~ **(hat),** hat made from fine pliant straw-like material from the leaves of a plant of S and Central America. 巴拿馬草帽。

pana·tella /ˌpænəˈtelə; ˌpænəˈtɛlə/ *n* [C] long slender cigar. 細長的雪茄煙。

pan·chro·matic /ˌpænkrəˈmætɪk; ˌpænkroˈmætɪk/ *adj* (photo) equally sensitive to all colours: (攝影)對所有顏色都同樣感應的;全色的;泛色的: *~ film.* 全色軟片。

pan·creas /ˈpæŋkrɪəs; ˈpænkrɪəs/ *n* [C] gland near the stomach, discharging a juice which helps digestion. 胰;胰腺。⇨ the illus at alimentary. 參看 alimentary 之挿圖。**pan·cre·atic** /ˌpæŋkrɪˈætɪk; ˌpænkrɪˈætɪk/ *adj* of the ~. 胰(腺)的。

panda /ˈpændə; ˈpændə/ *n* bear-like mammal of Tibet, with black legs and a black and white body. 猫熊(產於西藏,似熊,脚黑色,身體爲黑白色)。ˈ**P~ car** *n* (GB) police patrol car. (英)警察巡邏車。ˈ**P~ crossing** *n* (GB) road crossing controlled by flashing lights, operated by pedestrians who press a button on a post. (英)(由行人按鈕控制紅綠燈的)行人穿越道。

pan·demic /pænˈdemɪk; pænˈdɛmɪk/ *n, adj* (disease) prevalent over the whole of a country or continent. 流行全國或全洲的(疾病);流行性的;大流行病。

pan·de·mo·nium /ˌpændɪˈməʊnɪəm; ˌpændɪˈmonɪəm/ *n* [C, U] (scene of) wild and noisy disorder. 大混亂;嘈雜;騷動(的場面)。

pan·der /ˈpændə(r); ˈpændɚ/ *vi* [VP3A] ~ ***to,*** **1** give help or encouragement (to sb, to his base passions and desires): 幫助;鼓勵;煽動(與 to 連用,後接某人或卑鄙的情慾): *newspapers that ~ to the public interest in crime;* 煽動讀者對犯罪感興趣的報紙。*~ to low tastes.* 迎合低級趣味。 **2** act as a go-between (eg to sb's sexual desires). 作淫媒;拉皮條。⇨ procure(3), the more usu word now. (今較常用 procure)。□ *n* person who ~s(2). 淫媒;拉皮條者。

pane /peɪn; pen/ *n* single sheet of glass in (a division of) a window. 窗上的單塊玻璃;窗玻璃片。⇨ the illus at window. 參看 window 之挿圖。

pan·egyric /ˌpænɪˈdʒɪrɪk; ˌpænəˈdʒɪrɪk/ *n* [C] speech, piece of writing, praising a person or event. 頌詞;頌文;褒詞。

panel /ˈpænl; ˈpænḷ/ *n* **1** separate part of the surface of a door, wall, ceiling, etc usu raised above or sunk below the surrounding area. 門、牆、天花板等的鑲板;嵌板;方格(通常高出或低於其周圍部份)。 **2** piece of material of a different kind or colour inserted in a dress. 衣服上所縫綴的不同質料或顏色的布塊;飾塊。 **3** board or other surface for controls and instruments: 裝控制開關及儀器的板或面;儀錶板: ˈ*instrument ~,* of an aircraft or motor-vehicle; (飛機或汽車的)儀錶板; *conˈtrol ~,* on a radio or TV set. (收音機或電視機上的)控制板。 **4** list of names, eg of men who may be summoned to serve on a jury. 名單(例如陪審員名單)。 **5** group of speakers, esp one chosen to speak, answer questions, take part in a game, before an audience, eg of listeners to a broadcast: (廣播等中的)座談小組;答問小組;遊戲小組: (attrib) (形容用法) *a* ˈ*~ discussion/game.* 小組討論(小組遊戲)。□ *vt* (-ll-, US -l-) furnish or decorate with ~s(1, 2): 鑲板於;以方格裝飾;飾以嵌板;縫飾塊於: *a ~led room/wall/wainscot.* 嵌板房間(格子牆;方格壁板)。**~·ling** *n* [U] series of ~s on a wall, etc. 牆壁等的鑲板。

pang /pæŋ; pæŋ/ *n* sharp, sudden feeling of pain, remorse, etc. 突然的劇痛、懊悔等;悲痛。

panga /ˈpæŋgə; ˈpɑŋgə/ *n* large chopping knife used by African workers. (非洲工人用的)大斧頭;大砍刀。

pan·handle /ˈpænhændl; ˈpænˌhændḷ/ *n* (US) narrow strip of land projecting from a larger area. (美)鍋柄地帶(突出於一塊大地域的狹長地帶)。□ *vi* (US colloq) beg, esp on the streets. (美俗)行乞;(尤指)在街上行乞。

panic /ˈpænɪk; ˈpænɪk/ *n* [C, U] **1** unreasoning, uncontrolled, quickly spreading fear: 驚慌;恐慌: *There is always danger of (a) ~ when a cinema catches fire.* 電影院着火時總是有引起驚慌的危險。ˈ**~-stricken** *adj* terrified; overcome by ~: 爲驚慌所襲的;極度受驚的;驚慌失措的: *The crowd was ~-stricken,* filled with ~. 羣衆極爲驚慌。 **2** (attrib) unreasoning: (形容用法)沒理由的: *~ fear.* 沒理由的恐懼。□ *vi* (-ck-) be affected with ~: 受驚;驚慌: *Don't ~! There's no danger!* 不要驚慌!沒有危險! **pan·icky** /ˈpænɪkɪ; ˈpænɪkɪ/ *adj* (colloq) easily affected by ~; in a state of ~. (俗)容易受驚的;驚慌的。

pan·jan·drum /pænˈdʒændrəm; pænˈdʒændrəm/ *n* name applied jokingly to an exalted personage or to a pompous official. 大老爺(戲謔地加諸大人物或自大的官員的稱謂)。

pan·nier /ˈpænɪə(r); ˈpænjɚ/ *n* one of a pair of baskets placed across the back of a horse or donkey; one of a pair of bags on either side of the back of a (motor-)cycle. (掛在馱馬或馱驢兩

cycle panniers

donkey panniers

側的)馱籃;(掛在脚踏車或機車後座兩旁的)裝物袋。

pan·ni·kin /ˈpænɪkɪn ; ˈpænəkɪn/ *n* (GB) small metal cup; its contents. (英)小金屬杯;一小杯之量。

pan·oply /ˈpænəplɪ ; ˈpænəplɪ/ *n* (*pl* -plies) complete suit of armour; (fig) splendid array. 全副甲胄;(喩)華麗的衣服。Hence, 由此產生, **pan·oplied** /ˈpænəplɪd ; ˈpænəplɪd/ *adj* provided with a ~. 披甲胄的;全身披甲的;盛裝的。

pan·op·tic /pænˈɒptɪk ; pæˈnɑptɪk/ *adj* giving a complete view, eg by diagram, illustration, of sth. (以圖解、插圖等)表示某物全貌的。

pan·or·ama /ˌpænəˈrɑːmə *US:* -ˈræmə ; ˌpænəˈræmə/ *n* wide, uninterrupted view; constantly changing scene: 全景;全圖;活動畫景;連續轉換之景: *the ~ of London life.* 倫敦生活的形形色色。**pan·or·amic** /ˌpænəˈræmɪk ; ˌpænəˈræmɪk/ *adj*

pan-pipes /ˈpæn paɪps ; ˈpænˌpaɪps/ *n pl* musical instrument made of a series of reeds or pipes, played by blowing across the open ends. 排簫;潘神簫(蘆桿製的樂器)。

pansy /ˈpænzɪ ; ˈpænzɪ/ *n* (*pl* -sies) **1** flowering herbaceous plant. 三色紫羅蘭。 **2** ⚠ (derog, offensive term for) effeminate man; homosexual. (諱)(貶抑及侮蔑語)女性化的男子;同性戀的男人。

pant /pænt ; pænt/ *vi, vt* **1** [VP2A, C] take short, quick breaths; gasp: 喘氣;喘息: *The dog ~ed along behind its master's horse.* 那隻狗喘着氣跟在主人的馬後。 **2** [VP6A, 15B] say while ~ing: 喘着氣說: *He ~ed out his message.* 他氣喘吁吁地說出他的口信。 **3** [VP3A] ~ ***for,*** (old use) have a strong wish for. (舊用法)切望;渴望。□ *n* short, quick breath; gasp. 喘氣;喘息。**~·ing·ly** *adv*

pan·ta·loon /ˌpæntəˈluːn ; ˌpæntl̩ˈun/ *n* **1** (in pantomime) foolish character upon whom the clown plays tricks. (啞劇中)爲丑角取笑對象的愚蠢角色。 **2** (*pl*) (now hum, or US) = pants. (複)(諧,美)褲子。

pan·tech·ni·con /pænˈteknɪkən ; pænˈtɛknɪˌkɑn/ *n* (GB) large van for removing furniture. (英)傢具搬運車。

pan·the·ism /ˈpænθɪɪzəm ; ˈpænθiˌɪzəm/ *n* [U] belief that God is in everything and that everything is God; belief in and worship of all gods. 宇宙卽神論;汎神論;多神崇拜。**pan·the·ist** /-ɪst ; -ɪst/ *n* believer in ~. 宇宙卽神論者;汎神論者;多神崇拜者。**pan·the·is·tic** /ˌpænθɪˈɪstɪk ; ˌpænθiˈɪstɪk/ *adj* of ~. 宇宙卽神論的;汎神論的;崇拜多神的。

pan·theon /ˈpænθɪən *US:* -θɪɒn ; ˈpænθɪən/ *n* temple dedicated to all the gods: 萬神殿;萬神廟: *the P~ in Rome;* 羅馬萬神殿; all the gods of a nation collectively: 一國的衆神: *the (ancient) Egyptian ~;* (古代)埃及的衆神; building in which the illustrious dead are buried or have memorials. 偉人祠;先賢祠(內有名人墳墓或紀念碑的建築物)。

pan·ther /ˈpænθə(r) ; ˈpænθɚ/ *n* black leopard; (US) puma. 黑豹;(美)山豹。⇨ the illus at cat. 參看 cat 之插圖。

pan·ties /ˈpæntɪz ; ˈpæntɪz/ *n pl* **1** short trousers worn by children. 兒童所穿的短褲。 **2** (woman's or girl's) close-fitting short drawers. (婦人或少女的)內褲。

pan·tile /ˈpæntaɪl ; ˈpænˌtaɪl/ *n* curved roof tile: 波形瓦: (attrib) (形容用法) *a ~ roof.* 波形瓦屋頂。

panto /ˈpæntəʊ ; ˈpænto/ *n* (colloq abbr of) pantomime. (俗)爲 pantomime 之略。

pan·to·graph /ˈpæntəgrɑːf *US:* -græf ; ˈpæntəˌgræf/ *n* **1** device for copying a plan, etc on a different scale. 比例尺;放大尺;伸縮繪圖器;縮放繪圖器。 **2** device for carrying electric current to a vehicle from overhead wires. (電車頂之)電桿架。

pan·to·mime /ˈpæntəmaɪm ; ˈpæntəˌmaɪm/ *n* **1** [C, U] (example of a) kind of English drama based on a fairy tale or traditional story, with music, dancing and clowning. 取材於童話或傳說,有音樂、舞蹈及滑稽表演的一種英國戲劇;啞劇。 **2** [C] acting without words. 表意動作;手勢。

pan·try /ˈpæntrɪ ; ˈpæntrɪ/ *n* (*pl* -tries) **1** room (in a large house, hotel, ship, etc) in which silver, glass, table-linen, etc are kept. (大房子、旅館、船等的)餐具室。ˈ**~·man** /-mən ; -mən/ *n* (*pl* -men) butler or his assistant. 飯廳管理員;飯廳管理員的助手。 **2** larder; room (in a house) in which food is kept. 食品室;備餐室。

pants /pænts ; pænts/ *n pl* (GB) underpants; (US) trousers. (英)內褲;(美)褲子。***bore/scare/talk, etc the ˈ~ off one,*** bore, etc one extremely. 極端令人厭煩(極爲使人驚嚇;談話使人極爲厭煩等)。***catch sb with his ˈ~ down,*** find him in an unprepared state. 出其不意;乘其不備。

panty-hose /ˈpæntɪ həʊz ; ˈpæntɪ hoz/ *n* = tights.

pan·zer /ˈpæntsə(r) ; ˈpænzɚ/ *attrib adj* (G) armoured: (德)裝甲的;配有裝甲車輛及武器的: *ˈ~ divisions/troops.* 裝甲師(裝甲部隊)。

pap /pæp ; pæp/ *n* [U] soft or semi-liquid food for very young children or invalids; (fig) easy, trivial reading matter. (嬰兒或病人食用的)柔軟或半流質食物;(喩)淺易娛樂性讀物。

papa /pəˈpɑː *US:* ˈpɑːpə ; ˈpɑpə/ *n* (child's word for) father. (兒語)父親;爸爸。

pa·pacy /ˈpeɪpəsɪ ; ˈpepəsɪ/ *n* (*pl* -cies) position of, authority of, the Pope; system of government by Popes. 羅馬教宗的職位或權柄;教宗治理的制度;教宗政治。**pa·pal** /ˈpeɪpl ; ˈpepl̩/ *adj* of the Pope or the ~. 羅馬教宗的;羅馬教宗之職位、權柄或制度的。

pa·paw, paw·paw /pəˈpɔː *US:* ˈpɔːpɔː ; ˈpɔpɔ/ *n* **1** tropical tree with a straight trunk like that of a palm; its large edible fruit with yellow pulp inside. 木瓜樹;木瓜。⇨ the illus at fruit. 參看 fruit 之插圖。 **2** small N American evergreen tree with small fleshy edible fruit (also called 亦稱作 *custard apple*). 蕃荔枝;釋迦果。

pa·paya /pəˈpaɪə ; pəˈpaɪə/ *n* = papaw.

pa·per /ˈpeɪpə(r) ; ˈpepɚ/ *n* **1** [U] substance manufactured from wood fibre, rags, etc in the form of sheets, used for writing, printing, drawing, wrapping, packing, etc: 紙: *a sheet of ~;* 一張紙; *a ~ bag.* 一個紙袋。***(be/look) good on ~,*** (be/look) good when judged from written or printed evidence, eg plans, proposals, diplomas, testimonials: 照書面的情形看來很好(如計畫,提議,文憑,證明書): *a good scheme on ~* (but not yet tested). 好的書面計畫(但尚未經過考驗)。*This applicant looks good on ~,* has good ~ qualifications. 照書面資料看來,這個申請人的資歷很不錯。***put pen to ~,*** (dated for) begin to write, eg a letter. (過時用語)開始寫(信等)。ˈ**~·backed** *adj* (of books) bound in paper covers. (指書)以紙作封面的;平裝的。Hence, 由此產生, ˈ**~·back** *n* such a book and such a form: 平裝書;平裝: *Has the book appeared in ~back?* 此書的平裝本出來了嗎? ˈ**~-chase** *n* ⇨ *hare and hounds,* at hare. ˈ**~-clip** *n* = clip¹(1). ˈ**~-hanger** *n* man whose trade is to paste ~ on the walls of rooms. 貼壁紙的工人。ˈ**~-knife** *n* one for cutting open the leaves of books, opening envelopes, etc. (用於割開書頁,信封等的)裁紙刀;拆信刀。ˈ**~-mill** *n* one where ~ is made. 造紙廠。ˌ~ ˈ**tiger** *n* person, group of persons, etc which seems to be, but is not, powerful. 外强中乾的人;紙老虎。ˈ**~-weight** *n* weight placed on loose ~s to prevent them from being blown away. 紙壓;書鎭。ˈ**~-work** *n* [U] written work (in an office, etc, eg filling in forms, correspondence, contrasted with practical affairs, dealing with people): 文書業務;文書工作: *He's good at ~-work.* 他擅長文書工作。 **2** [C] newspaper: 報紙: *today's ~s;* 今天的報紙; *the evening ~.* 晚報。 **3** [U] ~ **(money),** banknotes, etc used as currency. 鈔票;紙幣。 **4** (*pl*) documents showing who sb is, what authority he has, etc: (複)身分證明文件;證件: *send in one's ~s,* (mil) resign. (軍)辭職;提出辭呈。 **5** [C] set of printed examination questions on a given subject: 試卷;

試題：*The biology ~ was difficult.* 生物學試題很難。**6** [C] essay, esp one to be read to a learned society: 論文(尤指在學會宣讀者)：*a ~ on currency reform.* 一篇關於通貨改革的論文。□ *vt* [VP6A, 15B] paste ~ on (walls, etc): 貼紙於(牆上等)：*~ the dining-room;* 用紙裱糊餐廳；cover with ~. 用紙覆蓋；用紙包。***~ over the cracks,*** (fig) cover up, conceal, faults, etc. (喻)隱瞞、掩飾過錯等。***~ the house,*** (fig) issue free tickets for a theatre, etc (to give the impression of success). (喻)戲院等發行招待券(以顯示其成功)。

pa·pier-mâché /ˌpæpɪeɪ ˈmæʃeɪ *US:* ˌpeɪpər məˈʃeɪ; ˈpepəˈməˈʃe/ *n* [U] paper pulped and used as a plastic material for making trays, boxes, etc. 混凝紙(用於製造盤、盒等的可塑紙料)。

pa·pist /ˈpeɪpɪst; ˈpepɪst/ *n, adj* (unfriendly word, as used by some Protestants) (member) of the Roman Catholic Church. (某些基督教徒等所用的不友善用語)天主教的；天主教徒。

pa·poose /pəˈpuːs *US:* pæˈpuːs; pæˈpus/ *n* (word used by Indians of N America for a) baby; framed bag (like a rucksack) for carrying a young baby on sb's back. (北美印地安人用語)嬰孩；(背嬰兒用的)背囊。

pap·rika /ˈpæprɪkə *US:* pəˈpriːkə; pæˈprikə/ *n* [U] sweet red pepper used in cooking. (烹調用的)辣椒。⇨ the illus at vegetable. 參看 vegetable 之插圖。

pa·py·rus /pəˈpaɪərəs; pəˈpaɪrəs/ *n* **1** [U] (kind of paper made in ancient Egypt from) tall water plant or reed. 紙草；(古埃及用紙草製成的)紙草紙。**2** [C] (*pl* papyri /pəˈpaɪəraɪ; pəˈpaɪraɪ/) manuscript written on this paper. 寫在此種紙上的文稿。

par¹ /pɑː(r); pɑr/ *n* [U] **1** average or normal amount, degree, value, etc. 平均數量；正常數量；一般程度；常態。***above／below／at par,*** (of shares, bonds, etc), above／below／at the original price or face value. (指股票、證券等)高於(低於，照)原價或票面價值。***on a par (with),*** equal (to). 等於。***up to par,*** (colloq) as good／well as usual. (俗)達正常標準。**par of exchange,** normal rate of exchange between two currencies, eg the £ and the US $. 滙兌平價(如英鎊和美元之滙率)。**par value,** nominal or face value of a share. 面值；股票的面值。**2** (golf) number of strokes considered necessary for a good player to complete a hole or course. (高爾夫球)(一洞或一場球的)標準桿數。

par² /pɑː(r); pɑr/ ⇨ parr.

par·able /ˈpærəbl; ˈpærəbl/ *n* simple story designed to teach a moral lesson: 寓言；比喻：*speak in ~s.* 以比喻來說。*Jesus taught in ~s.* 耶穌以比喻講道。**para·boli·cal** /ˌpærəˈbɒlɪkl; ˌpærəˈbɑlɪkl/ *adj* of, expressed in, ~s. 寓言的；以比喻說明的。

par·ab·ola /pəˈræbələ; pəˈræbələ/ *n* plane curve formed by cutting a cone on a plane parallel to its side, so that the two arms get farther away from one another. 抛物線。**para·bolic** /ˌpærəˈbɒlɪk; ˌpærəˈbɑlɪk/ *adj* of, like, a ~. 抛物線的；似抛物線的。

para·chute /ˈpærəʃuːt; ˈpærəˌʃut/ *n* apparatus used for a jump from an aircraft or for dropping supplies, etc: 降落傘：(attrib) (形容用法) *'~ troops／flares／mines.* 傘兵部隊(附傘照明彈；傘投水雷)。□ *vt, vi* [VP2A, C, 6A, 15A, B] drop, descend, from an aircraft by means of a ~: (用降落傘)空降；空投：*men ~d behind the enemy lines.* 空降敵後的部隊。**para·chut·ist** /-ɪst; -ɪst/ *n* person who jumps with a ~. 跳傘人；傘兵。

par·ade /pəˈreɪd; pəˈred/ *vt, vi* **1** [VP6A, 2A] (of troops) (cause to) gather together for drilling, inspection, etc; march in procession. (指部隊)(爲訓練、檢閱等而)集結；列隊行進；(指人群)遊行。**2** [VP 6A] make a display of; try to attract attention to: 誇示；炫耀：*~ one's abilities.* 炫耀個人的能力。□ *n* **1** [U] parading of troops: 閱兵；(軍隊的)分列式；遊行：*be on ~;* 在遊行；[C] instance of this. 閱兵或遊行之實例。**2** [C] **'~-ground,** area of ground on which ~s are held. 閱兵場；遊行地區。**3** [C] display or exhibition. 陳列；展覽。***make a ~ of one's virtues,*** try to impress people by showing them. 誇示個人的優點。**4** public promenade; wide, often ornamented pathway, esp on a sea-front. 公共散步場所；(尤指海邊之)寬濶且常有裝飾物的人行道。

para·digm /ˈpærədaɪm; ˈpærəˌdɪm/ *n* example or pattern, esp of the declension of a noun, the conjugation of a verb, etc. (名詞、動詞等的)變化例；變化表。

para·dise /ˈpærədaɪs; ˈpærəˌdaɪs/ *n* **1** the Garden of Eden, home of Adam and Eve. 伊甸園；(亞當和夏娃之)樂園。ˌ**bird of '~,** bird (of New Guinea) with beautiful feathers. (新幾內亞產的)極樂鳥；風鳥。**2** heaven. 天堂；天國。**3** [C] any place of perfect happiness; [U] condition of perfect happiness. 樂土；極樂的地方；極樂；至福。**a fool's ~,** ⇨ fool¹(1). **para·dis·iac** /ˌpærəˈdɪzɪæk; ˌpærəˈdɪsɪˌæk/, **para·disia·cal** /ˌpærədɪˈzaɪəkl; ˌpærədɪˈsaɪəkl/ *adj* of or like ~: (似)樂園的；天堂的；極樂的：*Adam and Eve in their paradisiac state,* in their pristine innocence. 樂園中天眞無邪的亞當和夏娃。

para·dox /ˈpærədɒks; ˈpærəˌdɑks/ *n* [C] statement that seems to say sth opposite to common sense or the truth, but which may contain a truth (eg 'More haste, less speed'). 似非而是的雋語(如'欲速則不達')；反論。**~i·cal** /ˌpærəˈdɒksɪkl; ˌpærəˈdɑksɪkl/ *adj* **~i·cally** /-klɪ; -klɪ/ *adv*

par·af·fin /ˈpærəfɪn; ˈpærəfɪn/ *n* [U] **1 '~ (oil),** (GB) oil obtained from petroleum, coal, etc used as a fuel (in lamps, heating and cooking-stoves). (英)(從石油、煤等提煉出來的)煤油；石蠟油(用作油燈、暖爐及炊爐的燃料)。(US 美 = *kerosene*). **2 ~ (wax),** wax-like substance used for making candles. (製造蠟燭用的)石蠟。**3 (ˌliquid) '~,** odourless, tasteless form of ~ used as a laxative. (無臭無味，作通便劑用的)液狀石蠟。

para·gon /ˈpærəgən *US:* -gɒn; ˈpærəˌgɑn/ *n* model of excellence; apparently perfect person or thing: 模範；完美的人或物：*I make no claim to be a ~ of virtue.* 我並不認爲自己是個美德的典範。

para·graph /ˈpærəgrɑːf *US:* -græf; ˈpærəˌgræf/ *n* [C] **1** division (usu a group of several sentences dealing with one main idea) of a piece of writing, started on a new line (and usu indented); the mark (¶) used to show where a new ~ is to begin, and as a mark of reference. 段；節(文章的段，通常包含若干句子表達某一要旨，每段新起一行且通常縮進若干字母)；表示新段落或參考某一附註之符號(¶)。**2** small item of news in a newspaper. (報紙上新聞的)小節。□ *vt* divide into ~s. 將…分段。

para·keet /ˈpærəkiːt; ˈpærəˌkit/ *n* small, long-tailed parrot of various kinds. 長尾小鸚鵡。⇨ the illus at rare. 參看 rare 之插圖。

par·al·lel /ˈpærəlel; ˈpærəˌlɛl/ *adj* (of lines) continuing at the same distance from one another; (of one line) having this relation (*to* or *with* another): (指線條)彼此間保持等距離的；平行的；(指一線)與他線相平行的(後接 to 或 with)：*a road running ~ to／with the railway;* 與鐵路平行的一條路；*in a ~ direction (with...).* 朝着(與…)平行的方向。ˌ**~ 'bars,** pair of ~ bars on posts for gymnastic exercises. (運動用的)雙槓。□ *n* **1 ~ of latitude,** line on a map ~ to, and passing through all places the same distance north or south of, the equator. 緯線；緯圈。⇨ the illus at projection. 參看 projection 之插圖。***in ~,*** (of the components of an electrical circuit) with the supply of current taken to each component independently, not in series. (指電路結構)並聯的。⇨ series. **2** [U, C] person, event, etc precisely similar: 極相似的人或物：*a brilliant career without (a) ~ in modern times.* 近世無匹的輝煌事蹟。**3** comparison: 比較；對比：

draw a ~ between.... 在…之間作一比較。□ *vt* (-l- or (GB) -ll-) [VP6A] **1** quote, produce or mention sth ~ or comparable. 比較。 **2** be ~ to: 與…相似;與…平行: *His experiences ~ mine in many instances.* 他的經歷在許多方面與我的相似。*The street ~s the railway.* 這條街與鐵路平行。 **~·ism** /-ɪzəm ; -ˌɪzəm/ *n* (lit or fig) being ~. (字面或喻)平行;相似;相同;類似。 **~o·gram** /ˌpærəˈleləgræm ; ˌpærəˈlɛləˌgræm/ *n* four-sided plane figure whose opposite sides are ~. 平行四邊形。 ⇨ the illus at quadrilateral. 參看 quadrilateral 之插圖。

par·al·ysis /pəˈrælәsɪs ; pəˈræləsɪs/ *n* [U] loss of feeling or power to move in any or every part of the body; (fig) state of utter powerlessness. 麻痺;癱瘓;(喻)毫無力量;無能力。 **para·lyt·ic** /ˌpærəˈlɪtɪk ; ˌpærəˈlɪtɪk/ *n, adj* **1** (person) suffering from ~: 麻痺的;癱瘓的;麻痺患者: *a paralytic stroke;* 中風; (fig) helpless: (喻)無助的;無用的;無能爲力的: *paralytic laughter.* 不能自已的笑聲。 **2** (person who is) very drunk. 酩酊大醉;酩酊大醉之人。 **para·lyse,** (US = **-lyze**) /ˈpærəlaɪz ; ˈpærəˌlaɪz/ *vt* [VP6A] **1** affect with ~. 使麻痺;使癱瘓。 **2** make helpless: 使無助;使無能爲力: *paralysed with fear.* 嚇得癱軟。

par·ameter /pəˈræmɪtə(r) ; pəˈræmətɚ/ *n* characteristic or determining feature. 特色;特點。

para·mili·tary /ˌpærəˈmɪlɪtrɪ *US:* -terɪ ; ˌpærəˈmɪlɪˌtɛrɪ/ *adj* having a status or function ancillary or similar to that of regular military forces: 有輔助正規軍之地位或功能的;準軍事性的: *~ organizations.* 準軍事性的組織。

para·mount /ˈpærəmaʊnt ; ˈpærəˌmaʊnt/ *adj* (formal) supreme, superior in power: (正式用語)最高的;至上的: *~ chiefs;* 最高首領; pre-eminent: 超越其他的;卓越的: *of ~ importance;* 最重要的; superior. 優於;勝過。 **~cy** /-tsɪ ; -tsɪ/ *n*

para·mour /ˈpærəmʊə(r) ; ˈpærəˌmʊr/ *n* (archaic) illicit partner of a married man or woman. (古)情夫;情婦。

para·noia /ˌpærəˈnɔɪə ; ˌpærəˈnɔɪə/ *n* [U] mental disorder (usu incurable), marked by fixed delusions, eg of persecution or grandeur. 妄想狂(一種精神病,通常無法醫治)。 **para·noiac** /ˌpærəˈnɔɪæk ; ˌpærəˈnɔɪæk/, **para·noid** /ˈpærənɔɪd ; ˈpærəˌnɔɪd/ *nn, adjj* (person) suffering from ~. 妄想狂患者;患妄想狂的。

para·pet /ˈpærəpɪt ; ˈpærəpɪt/ *n* **1** (usu low) protective wall at the edge of a flat roof, side of a bridge, etc. (平屋頂之邊緣、橋之側旁等處之)扶牆;欄杆;矮垣。 **2** defensive bank of earth, stone, etc along the front edge of a trench (in war). (戰壕的)前牆;護牆;胸牆。

para·pher·nalia /ˌpærəfəˈneɪlɪə ; ˌpærəfəˈnelɪə/ *n* [U] numerous small possessions, tools, instruments, etc esp concerning sb's hobby or technical work. 個人財物;工具;行頭(尤指與某人之嗜好或技術性工作有關者)。

para·phrase /ˈpærəfreɪz ; ˈpærəˌfrez/ *vt* [VP6A], *n* (give a) restatement of the meaning of (a piece of writing) in other words. 釋義;意譯;解述(一作品)之意義。

para·ple·gia /ˌpærəˈpli:dʒə ; ˌpærəˈplidʒɪə/ *n* [U] (path) paralysis of the lower part of the body, including both legs, caused by injury to the spinal cord. (病理)下身癱瘓;截癱(因脊髓受傷所致)。 **para·plegic** /ˌpærəˈpli:dʒɪk ; ˌpærəˈplɛdʒɪk/ *n, adj* (person) suffering from ~. 下身癱瘓患者;下身癱瘓的。

para·site /ˈpærəsaɪt ; ˈpærəˌsaɪt/ *n* **1** animal (eg *louse, hookworm*) or plant (eg *mistletoe*) living on or in another and getting its food from it. 寄生動物;寄生蟲;寄生植物。 **2** person supported by another and giving him nothing in return. 靠他人爲生的人;食客。 **para·sitic** /ˌpærəˈsɪtɪk ; ˌpærəˈsɪtɪk/, **para·siti·cal** /ˌpærəˈsɪtɪkl ; ˌpærəˈsɪtɪkḷ/ *adjj* caused by, living as, a ~. 寄生物引起的;寄生的;靠他人爲生的。

para·sol /ˈpærəsɒl *US:* -sɔ:l ; ˈpærəˌsɔl/ *n* umbrella used to give shade from the sun. 陽傘。

para·troops /ˈpærətru:ps ; ˈpærəˌtrups/ *n pl* troops trained for being dropped by parachute. 傘兵部隊。 **para·trooper** /ˈpærətru:pə(r) ; ˈpærəˌtrupɚ/ *n* one of these. 傘兵。

para·typhoid /ˌpærəˈtaɪfɔɪd ; ˌpærəˈtaɪfɔɪd/ *n* [U] kind of fever in some ways like typhoid but milder and caused by a different bacterium. 副傷寒。

par·boil /ˈpɑ:bɔɪl ; ˈpɑrˌbɔɪl/ *vt* [VP6A] boil (food) until partially cooked; (fig) make uncomfortably hot. 將(食物)煮到半熟;(喻)使過熱;使熱得難受。

par·cel /ˈpɑ:sl ; ˈpɑrsḷ/ *n* [C] **1** thing or things wrapped and tied up for carrying, sending by post, etc: 包裹;小包;郵包: *She left the shop with an armful of ~s.* 她抱著一抱小包離開店鋪。 **ˈ~ post** *n* [U] system, method, etc of carrying ~s by post. 包裹郵遞(之系統、方法等);包裹郵務部;包裹郵件。 **2** ***part and ~ of,*** an essential part of. …的主要部分。 ***a ~ of land,*** an area of land (esp part of an estate). 一塊地(尤指產業之一部分)。□ *vt* (-ll-, US also -l-) [VP6A, 15B] **~ *out,*** divide into portions. 分爲數份;分配。 **~ *up,*** make (books, etc) into a ~. 將(書等)捆成包裹;打包。

parch /pɑ:tʃ ; pɑrtʃ/ *vt* [VP6A] **1** (of heat, the sun, etc) make hot and dry: (指熱、陽光等)使焦乾: *the ~ed deserts of N Africa.* 北非的乾燥沙漠。 **2** dry or roast by heating: 烤乾;烘乾: *~ed peas.* 乾炒豌豆。

parch·ment /ˈpɑ:tʃmənt ; ˈpɑrtʃmənt/ *n* **1** [C, U] (manuscript on) writing material prepared from the skin of a sheep or goat. 羊皮紙;寫在羊皮紙上的文件或手稿。 **2** [U] kind of paper resembling ~. 類似羊皮紙的紙。

par·don /ˈpɑ:dn ; ˈpɑrdṇ/ *n* **1** [U] forgiveness: 寬恕;赦免: *ask for ~;* 懇求寬恕; [C] instance of this. 寬恕或赦免的實例。 **2** [U] indulgence; forbearance. 原諒;寬容。 ***beg sb's ~,*** excuse oneself, eg for disagreeing with what sb says, or apologize, eg for not hearing or understanding what sb says: 請原諒,不敢苟同; 對不起請再說一遍: *I beg your ~!* 對不起請再說一遍! ⇨ excuse²(3); sorry(2). **3** (archaic) indulgence(4). (古)赦罪;免罪符。□ *vt* [VP6A, 12B, 13B] ***~ sb for sth; ~ sb sth,*** forgive; excuse; overlook: 饒恕;寬恕;原諒: *~ sb for doing wrong;* 寬恕某人犯了過錯; *~ sb an offence.* 原諒某人的罪過。*P~ me for / P~ my contradicting you.* 原諒我反駁你。 **~·able** /ˈpɑ:dnəbl ; ˈpɑrdṇəbḷ/ *adj* that can be ~ed. 可寬恕的;可原諒的。 **~·ably** /-əblɪ ; -əblɪ/ *adv* (formal) in a way that can be ~ed: (正式用語)可原諒地;難怪地: *She was ~ably proud of her wonderful cooking.* 她的烹調非常高明,難怪她會那麼驕傲。 **~er** *n* (in the Middle Ages) person who had been licensed to sell papal indulgences(4). (中古時代)獲准售賣天主教免罪符的人。

pare /peə(r) ; pɛr/ *vt* [VP6A, 15B] cut away the outer part, edge or skin of: 剝;削;切去…的外部、外邊或外皮: *~ one's (finger-)nails;* 剪指甲; *~ the claws of an animal;* 切掉獸爪; ~ (= peel) *an apple;* 削蘋果皮; (fig) (喻) *~ down* (= reduce) *one's expenses.* 削減開支。 **par·ings** /ˈpeərɪŋz ; ˈpɛrɪŋz/ *n pl* that which is ~d off: 削去之物;剝去之物;切去之物: *ˈnail-parings.* 剪下的指甲。

par·egoric /ˌpærəˈgɒrɪk *US:* -ˈgɔ:r- ; ˌpærəˈgɔrɪk/ *n* [U] soothing medicine containing opium and flavoured with aniseed. (含有鴉片而帶茴香味的)鎮痛劑;緩和劑。

par·ent /ˈpeərənt ; ˈpɛrənt/ *n* father or mother; ancestor: 父;母;祖先: *the ~ birds;* 親鳥; *the ~ plant.* 母樹。 *May I introduce you to my ~s?* ie to my father and mother. 我把你介紹給我的父母好嗎? **~ company,** (comm) one that controls another, eg by owning more than half its shares or because of the composition of its Board of Directors. (商)母公司(因擁有較多股份或因董事會的結構而控制另一公司者)。 ˈ~·age /-ɪdʒ ; -ɪdʒ/ *n* [U] fatherhood or motherhood; origin; birth: 父親的身分;母親的身分;根本;出身: *of unknown ~age,* having unknown ~s. 身世不明的。 **~al** /pəˈrentl ; pəˈrɛntl̩/ *adj* of ~(s): 父的;母的: *~al anxieties;* 父母的憂慮; *children who lack ~al care.* 缺乏父母照顧的孩子們。 **~·ally** /-təlɪ ; -tl̩ɪ/ *adv*

par·enth·esis /pəˈrenθəsɪs ; pəˈrɛnθəsɪs/ *n* (*pl* -eses /-əsi:z ; -əˌsiz/) sentence within another sentence, marked off by commas, dashes or brackets; (*sing* or *pl*) round brackets () for this. 挿句(用逗點、破折號或括弧加以分開);(用單數或複數)圓括弧。⇨ bracket². ⇨ App 9. 參看附錄九。 *in ~,* between parentheses; (fig) taking (sth) separately. 括在括弧裡;(喩)附帶。 **par·en·thetic** /ˌpærənˈθetɪk ; ˌpærənˈθɛtɪk/, **par·en·theti·cal** /-ɪkl ; -ɪkl/ *adjj* of, relating to, used as, a ~. 挿句的;括弧的;作爲挿句的。 **par·en·theti·cally** /-klɪ ; -klɪ/ *adv*

par ex·cel·lence /ˌpɑ:r ˈeksəlɑ:ns *US:* ˌeksəˈlɑ:ns ; pɑrˈɛksəˌlɑns/ *adv* (F) by virtue of special excellence; in the highest degree. (法)出類拔萃地;卓越地。

pa·riah /pəˈraɪə ; pəˈraɪə/ *n* (India) person of low caste or of no caste; (fig) social outcast. (印度)最下級或無階級的人;(喩)流浪者;無賴漢。 ˈ**~-dog** *n* (India) ownerless dog of mixed breed. (印度)無主的雜種狗。

pari-mu·tuel /ˌpærɪ ˈmju:tjʊel *US:* ˈmju:tʃʊəl ; ˈpærɪˈmjutʃʊəl/ *n* (F) form of betting (on races) in which the winners divide the stakes of the losers, less a percentage for management expenses. (法)賽馬賭博的一種分彩法(獲勝者除去付出百分之一的手續費外將所有輸者的賭注平分)。

pari passu /ˌpærɪ ˈpæsu: ; ˌpærɪˈpæsju/ *adv* (Lat) simultaneously and equally; at an equal rate of progress. (拉)同時而同等地;同一步調地;並行地。

par·ish /ˈpærɪʃ ; ˈpærɪʃ/ *n* (GB) division of a county with its own church and priest: (英)教區(郡以下的區分,有屬於本區的教堂和牧師): *the ~ church;* 教區禮拜堂; *the ~ council.* 教區會議。 **~ clerk,** official with various duties connected with the ~ church. 教區執事。 ˌ**~-ˈpump,** (used attrib) of local interest only: (作形容用法)區域性的;地區性的: *~-pump affairs/politics.* 地區性的事務(政治)。 **~ register,** book with records of christenings, marriages and burials. 教區記事錄(記錄本區居民之洗禮、命名以及婚喪等事)。 **civil ~,** division of a county for local government. 郡以下的地方行政區。 **~ioner** /pəˈrɪʃənə(r) ; pəˈrɪʃənɚ/ *n* inhabitant of a ~. 一教區內的居民。

Pa·ris·ian /pəˈrɪzɪən *US:* -ɪʒn ; pəˈrɪʒən/ *n, adj* (native, inhabitant) of Paris. 巴黎人;巴黎居民;巴黎的。

par·ity /ˈpærətɪ ; ˈpærətɪ/ *n* [U] equality; being equal; being at par: 同等; 相等; 平等: *Should teachers in secondary schools and teachers in primary schools receive ~ of pay?* 中學教師和小學教師應否接受同等的薪水? *The two currencies have now reached ~,* are at par. 這兩種貨幣現在已達到同等價值。 ˌ**~ of exˈchange,** rates of currency exchange officially determined by Governments. (政府所訂定之)匯率。

park¹ /pɑ:k ; pɑrk/ *n* **1** public garden or public recreation ground in a town. 公園。 ˈ**ball ~,** (US) playing-field. (美)球場;運動場;兒童遊戲場。 **2** area of grassland (usu with trees) round a large country house or mansion. 庭園;邸園(鄉村巨宅或大廈周圍之草地,通常有樹木)。 **3** ˈ**car-~,** place where motor-vehicles may be left for a time. 停車場。 **4** ˌ**national** ˈ**~,** area of natural beauty, eg mountains, forests, lakes, set apart by the State for public enjoyment, and where industrial and urban development is forbidden or limited. 國家公園;國立公園。 **5** place used by the military for artillery, stores, etc. 軍隊的槍砲、軍需品等的放置場。

park² /pɑ:k ; pɑrk/ *vt, vi* **1** [VP6A, 2A] put (a motor-vehicle) for a time, unattended: 停(車等)於;停車: *Where can we ~ (the car)?* 我們可以在那裡停車? **2** [VP6A, 15A] (colloq) put (sth or sb) somewhere: (俗)將(某人或某物)放置在某處: *Where can I ~ my luggage?* 我可以在那裡放行李? *P~ yourself in that chair while I make you a cup of tea.* 請在那張椅子上坐,我去給你泡茶。

parka /ˈpɑ:kə ; ˈpɑrkə/ *n* (US) waterproof jacket with a hood attached (as worn for skiing, mountain-climbing, etc). (美)帶兜帽的防水短外套(如滑雪,爬山等所穿着者)。(GB 英 = *anorak*).

parking /ˈpɑ:kɪŋ ; ˈpɑrkɪŋ/ *n* [U] (area for the) ~ of motor-vehicles: 停車;停車區;停車處: *No ~ between 9am and 6pm.* 上午九時至下午六時不准停車。 ˈ**~ lot,** (US) area for the ~ of motor-vehicles. (美)停車場。 ˈ**~ meter,** coin-operated meter beside which a car may be parked in a public place, eg a street. 停車計時器。 ˈ**~ orbit,** temporary orbit for a spacecraft. (太空船的)駐留軌道。

Parkinson's /ˈpɑ:kɪnsnz ; ˈpɑrkɪnsənz/ *adj* ˈ**~ disease,** (path) chronic progressive disease of old people, with muscular tremors, muscular rigidity and general weakness. (病理)巴金生氏病;震顫麻痺(老年人因肌肉僵硬或身體衰弱而引起的慢性震顫症)。 ˈ**~ law,** (hum) suggestion that work will always last as long as the time available for it. (諧)巴金生氏定律(只要時間許可,工作總會拖到最後)。

parky /ˈpɑ:kɪ ; ˈpɑrkɪ/ *adj* (sl) (of the air, weather) chilly. (俚)(指空氣、天氣)寒冷的。

par·lance /ˈpɑ:ləns ; ˈpɑrləns/ *n* use or choice of words; way of speaking: 用語;說法: *common/legal ~.* 一般說法(法律用語)。

par·ley /ˈpɑ:lɪ ; ˈpɑrlɪ/ *n* (*pl* -leys) [C] conference, esp between leaders of two opposed forces. 會談;談判(尤指敵對兩軍領袖所作者)。 □ *vi* [VP2A, 3A] *~ (with sb),* discuss terms, hold a conference. (與某人)談判;討論。

par·lia·ment /ˈpɑ:ləmənt ; ˈpɑrləmənt/ *n* (in countries with representative government) supreme law-making council or assembly, esp of GB, formed of the House of Commons and the House of Lords: (在代議政體的國家內)國會;議會(尤指英國由上議院及下議院所構成者): *enter P~;* 成爲國會議員; *ˌMembers of ˈP~;* 國會議員; *summon/adjourn P~;* 召開國會(宣佈國會休會); *P~ sits/rises;* 國會開會(休會); *open P~,* (of the Sovereign) declare it open with traditional ceremonial. (指君王)宣佈議會開會。 **par·lia·men·tarian** /ˌpɑ:ləmənˈteərɪən ; ˌpɑrləmɛnˈtɛrɪən/ *n* person skilled in the rules and procedures of ~, who is a good debater, etc. 精於議會法規與程序的人;議會中的雄辯家。 **par·lia·men·tary** /ˌpɑ:ləˈmentrɪ ; ˌpɑrləˈmɛntərɪ/ *adj* of ~: 議會的;國會的: *~ary debates;* 議會辯論; *~ary language,* polite, civil language, as required in ~ary debates. (如議會辯論時所用的)愼重有禮的言語。

par·lour (US = -lor) /ˈpɑ:lə(r) ; ˈpɑrlɚ/ *n* **1** ordinary sitting-room for the family in a private house (now more usu called sitting-room or living-room). 起居室 (現多稱作 sitting-room 或 living-room). ˈ**~ games,** games played in the home (competitions, guessing, etc). 室內遊戲或比賽(如競爭、猜測等)。 **2** official room for the reception of visitors: 會客室;接待室: *the Mayor's ~,* in a town hall, etc. 市長的會客室。 **3** (esp US) room for customers and clients: (尤美)接待顧客的房間: *a ˈbeauty ~;* 美容院; *a ˈhairdresser's ~.* 女子美髮店。 ˈ**~-car** *n* (US) luxurious railway coach with individual reserved seats. (美)豪華的鐵路客車。

par·lous /ˈpɑ:ləs ; ˈpɑrləs/ *adj* (formal) perilous. (正式用語)危險的。

Par·me·san /ˈpɑ:mɪzæn ; ˌpɑrməˈzæn/ *n* kind of cheese made at Parma and elsewhere in N Italy. (義大利北部巴馬等地所製的)巴馬乾酪。

par·ochial /pəˈrəʊkɪəl ; pəˈrokɪəl/ *adj* of a parish;

P

(fig) limited, narrow: 教區的;(喻)有限的;狹小的: *a ~ outlook / mind / point of view.* 狹隘的見地(思想,觀點)。**~ly** /-kɪəlɪ ; -kɪəlɪ/ *adv* **~·ism** /-ɪzəm ; -ˌɪzəm/ *n*

par·ody /ˈpærədɪ ; ˈpærədɪ/ *n* (*pl* -dies) **1** [C, U] (piece of) writing intended to amuse by imitating the style of writing used by sb else. (模仿他人文體所作的)遊戲詩文;諷刺詩文。 **2** [C] weak imitation. 拙劣的仿造物。□ *vt* [VP6A] make a ~ of: 藉模仿…而作遊戲詩文;歪改;拙劣地模仿: *~ an author / a poem.* 模仿某作家而作成一篇遊戲文字;歪改某一首詩。 **par·odist** /-ɪst ; -ɪst/ *n* person who writes parodies. 藉模仿而作遊戲詩文的人。

P

pa·role /pəˈrəul ; pəˈrol/ *n* [U] prisoner's solemn promise, on being given certain privileges, that he will not try to escape. 囚犯為獲得某些特許而作的不企圖逃脫的誓言。**on ~,** liberated after making such a promise. 發誓後而假釋的。**break one's ~,** (try to) escape while on ~. 違誓;發誓而假釋後(企圖)逃脫。□ *vt* [VP6A] set (a prisoner) free on ~. 使(囚犯)宣誓後假釋。

paro·quet /ˈpærəkiːt ; ˈpærəˌkɛt/ *n* = parakeet.

par·ox·ysm /ˈpærəksɪzəm ; ˈpærəksˌɪzəm/ *n* [C] sudden attack or outburst (of pain, anger, laughter, etc). (痛苦、憤怒、笑等之)突然發作。

par·quet /ˈpɑːkeɪ *US:* pɑːrˈkeɪ ; pɑrˈke/ *n* flooring of wooden blocks fitted together to make a pattern. 木塊拼花地板;嵌木地板。

parr, par /pɑː(r) ; pɑr/ *n* young salmon. 幼鮭。

par·ri·cide /ˈpærɪsaɪd ; ˈpærəˌsaɪd/ *n* [C, U] (person guilty of the) murder of one's father or near relation. 弒父;弒親;弒君;弒親者;弒君者。

par·rot /ˈpærət ; ˈpærət/ *n* **1** sorts of bird with a hooked bill and (usu) brightly coloured feathers, some kinds of which can be trained to imitate human speech. 鸚鵡。⇨ the illus at rare. 參看 rare 之插圖。**ˈ~ fever,** = psittacosis. **2** person who repeats, often without understanding, what others say. 重覆他人之言而常不解其義的人。

parry /ˈpærɪ ; ˈpærɪ/ *vt* (*pt, pp* -ried) [VP6A] turn aside (a blow); (fig) evade (a question). 擋開或閃避(打擊);(喻)避開(問題)。□ *n* [C] act of ~ing, esp in fencing and boxing. 擋開;閃避(尤指擊劍與拳擊時的動作)。

parse /pɑːz *US:* pɑːrs ; pɑrs/ *vt* [VP6A] describe (a word) grammatically; point out how the words of a sentence are related. 將(某字)作文法上的分析;指出句中各字的關係。

Par·see /pɑːˈsiː ; pɑrˈsi/ *n* member of a religious group in India, the members being descended from Persians who settled in India in the 8th c. (印度的)祆教徒(為第八世紀定居印度的波斯人的後裔)。

par·si·mony /ˈpɑːsɪmənɪ *US:* -məunɪ ; ˈpɑrsəˌmonɪ/ *n* [U] (formal) (usu as a bad quality) excessive carefulness in using money or (fig) immaterial things. (正式用語) 吝嗇; 小氣; 過份節省; (喻) 過於節約非物質之物。 **par·si·moni·ous** /ˌpɑːsɪˈməunɪəs ; ˌpɑrsəˈmonɪəs/ *adj* too economical; miserly. 太節省的;吝嗇的;小氣的。

pars·ley /ˈpɑːslɪ ; ˈpɑrslɪ/ *n* [U] garden plant with crinkled green leaves, used in seasoning and sauces and for garnishing food. 芫荽菜;香菜。

pars·nip /ˈpɑːsnɪp ; ˈpɑrsnəp/ *n* [C] long, white or pale-yellow root, cooked as a vegetable. (可煮食的)防風草根。

par·son /ˈpɑːsn ; ˈpɑrsn̩/ *n* parish priest; (colloq) any clergyman. 教區長;(俗)牧師。**~'s nose,** (colloq) rump of a cooked fowl. (俗)烹調過的禽類的尾部;雞鴨等的屁股。**ˈ~·age** /-ɪdʒ ; -ɪdʒ/ *n* ~'s house. 教區長住宅。

part¹ /pɑːt ; pɑrt/ *n* [C] **1** (often *sing* without *indef art*) some but not all of a thing or a number of things; something less than the whole: (常為單數,不用不定冠詞)部分: *We spent (a) ~ of our holiday in France / in a ~ of the country we had never visited before.* 我們假期的一部分是在法國(以前沒去過的地方)度過。*P~s of the book are interesting.* 這本書有些部分很有趣。*The greater ~ of what you heard is only rumour.* 你所聽到的大部分不過是謠言而已。**for the ˈmost ~,** in most cases; mostly. 一般地;大抵;大半。**in ~,** in some degree. 一部分;有幾分。**ˌ~-ˈowner** *n* person who owns sth in common with others. (財物之)共有人。**ˌ~-ˈtime** *adj, adv* for only a ~ of the working day or week: 部分時間的(地);一天或一週中工作一部分時間的(地);兼任的(地): *be employed ~-time;* 受雇從事部分時間的工作; *~-time teaching,* eg two days a week. 部分時間的教學;兼任教學(如每週兩天)。Hence, 由此產生, **ˌpart-ˈtimer** *n.* 部分時間工作者;兼任者;兼差者。 **2** (*pl*) region; district: (複)地區;區域: *in these / those ~s.* 在這些(那些)地區。 **3** any one of a number of equal divisions: 若干等分之一;…分之一: *A minute is the sixtieth ~ of an hour.* 一分鐘是一小時的六十分之一。**4** person's share in some activity; his duty or responsibility; what an actor in a play, film, etc says and does: (某人在某一活動中所擔任的)職務;職責;本分;(戲劇、電影等中之)角色,臺詞及動作: *a man with a ~ in a play / in a conference.* 劇中扮演一個角色的人(參加某一會議的人)。*He spoke / acted his ~ very well.* 他的臺詞唸得(他的戲演得)很好。*Do the actors all know their ~s?* 演員們都熟悉他們的臺詞及動作嗎? *I had only a small ~ in these events.* 在這些事件中我只盡了一小部分力量。**play a (big, small, etc) ~ (in sth),** be concerned in sth, make a contribution: 與(某事)有(極大或一點)關係; 對(某事)有(極大或一點)貢獻: *He had an important ~ to play in ensuring the success of the scheme.* 為確保該計畫的成功他作過重大貢獻。**take ~ (in),** have a share (in); help: 參加;協助: *Are you going to take ~ in the discussion,* Do you intend to speak? 你要參加討論嗎? **5** side in a dispute, transaction, agreement, mutual arrangement, etc. (辯論、交易、合約、雙方協議等之)一方。**take sb's ~; take the ~ of sb,** support sb: 支持某人;袒護某人: *He always takes his brother's ~.* 他總是袒護他哥哥(弟弟)。**for ˈmy ~,** as far as I am concerned: 就我而論: *For my ~ I am quite happy about the division of the money.* 就我來說,我對於那筆錢的分配感到相當滿意。**on ˈmy / ˈhis / ˈyour, etc ~; on the ~ of (Mr A, etc),** proceeding from, done by, me / him / you / Mr A, etc: 在我(他、你等)來說;在(A先生等)來說;在我(他、你等)的方面;在(A先生等)的方面: *There was no objection on his ~ / on the ~ of the owner of the land,* He did not object. 在他(地主)來說,不表示反對。*The agreement has been kept on my ~ but not on his.* 我遵守了協議,而他却沒有。 **6** ***take sth in good ~,*** not be offended at it. 樂意接受某事物。**7** division of a book; each issue of a work published in instalments: (書的)部;篇;卷;(連續出版物的)期: *a new encyclopaedia to be issued in monthly ~s.* 將按月分期出版的一套新百科全書。 **8** essential piece or section of sth. 重要部分。 **(spare) ~,** extra piece, etc to be used when needed, when sth breaks or wears: (機器的)備份零件;備用器材: *When can I get a ~ for my pump?* 我何時才能獲得我的唧筒的零件? **9** (music) each of the melodies that make up a harmony; the melody for a particular voice or instrument: (音樂)樂曲的一部分;適於某一人聲演唱或某一樂器演奏的部分;聲部: *orchestra ~s;* 管弦樂部分; *sing in three ~s.* 三部合唱。**ˈ~-singing, ˈ~-song** *n* singing, song, with three or more voice ~s. (三部或三部以上的) 無伴奏合唱; 合唱曲。 **10** (gram) **ˌ~ of ˈspeech,** one of the classes of words, eg noun, verb, adjective. (文法)詞類(如名詞、動詞、形容詞)。 **11** ***a man / woman of (many) ~s,*** of (many) abilities; talented. 有(極有)才幹的男人(女人)。□ *adv* (usu ~...~...) in some degree: 部分地;一部分: *made ~ of iron and ~ of wood.* 部分用鐵部分用木材造成的。**~·ly** *adv* in some degree.

部分地；有幾分。

part² /pɑːt ; pɑrt/ *vt, vi* **1** [VP6A, 2A, D] (cause to) separate or divide: (使)分離；分開: *The policemen ~ed the crowd.* 警察排開群衆。*We tried to ~ the two fighters.* 我們試圖把兩個打架的人拉開。*Let us ~ friends,* leave each other with no feeling of enmity. 讓我們和和氣氣地分手。*The crowd ~ed and let us through.* 人羣分開來讓我們通過。**~ *company (with sb),*** **(a)** end a relationship. (與…)斷絕關係。**(b)** leave; separate from. 各自東西；各奔前程。**(c)** disagree: 意見不合: *On that question I am afraid I must ~ company with you.* 關於那個問題，我恐怕要和你分道揚鑣了。 **2** [VP3A] **~ *with,*** give up, give away: 放棄；捨棄: *He hates to ~ with his money,* doesn't like to spend it or give it away. 他極不喜歡花錢。 **3** [VP6A] **~ *one's hair,*** make a dividing line by combing the hair in opposite ways. 分頭髮(把頭髮梳向兩邊)。**~·ing** *n* **1** [C] line where the hair is combed in opposite ways. 頭髮的分梳線。**2** [C, U] departure; leave-taking: 離開；分別: (attrib) (形容用法) *his ~ing injunctions,* those given on taking leave. 他的臨別訓諭。***at the ~ing of the ways,*** at the point where the road divides or forks; (fig) when one has to choose between courses of action. 在路的分歧處；在十字路口；(喻)到了必須抉擇的時候。 **~·ing shot** = *Parthian shot,* ⇨ Parthian.

par·take /pɑːˈteɪk ; pɚˈtek/ *vi* (*pt* -took /-ˈtʊk ; -ˈtʊk/, *pp* -taken /-ˈteɪkən ; -ˈtekən/) [VP3A] **~ *of sth,*** (dated formal) (過時的正式用語) **1** take a share in: 分享；分擔；參與: *They partook of our triumph.* 他們分享我們的勝利。*They were partaking of our simple meal.* 他們跟我們一起吃便飯。 **2** have some of (the nature or characteristics of): 帶有幾分(…的性質或特性): *His manner ~s of insolence.* 他的態度帶有幾分侮慢。

par·terre /pɑːˈteə(r) ; pɑrˈtɛr/ *n* **1** (in a garden) level space with lawns and flower-beds. (庭園之)花壇。 **2** (in a theatre) part of the auditorium behind the orchestra. (戲院之)樓下正廳。

par·theno·gen·esis /ˌpɑːθɪnəʊˈdʒenəsɪs ; ˌpɑrθənoˈdʒɛnəsɪs/ *n* [U] reproduction of offspring without fertilization by sexual union. 孤雌生殖；單性生殖。

Par·thian /ˈpɑːθɪən ; ˈpɑrθɪən/ *adj* of Parthia, ancient country of N E Iran conquered by the Persians in AD 226. 安息(伊朗東北一古國)的。 **~ *shot/shaft,*** (fig) sth said or done as a final reply, argument, etc at the moment of parting. (喻)臨去時所說的話或所做的事；回馬槍；回馬箭。

par·tial /ˈpɑːʃl ; ˈpɑrʃəl/ *adj* **1** forming only a part; not complete: 部分的；不完全的: *a ~ success;* 部分的成功; *a ~ eclipse of the sun.* 日偏蝕。 **2 ~ *(towards),*** showing too much favour to one person or side: 偏心的；偏袒的: *examiners who are ~ towards pretty women students.* 偏袒漂亮女生的主考人員。 **3 ~ *to,*** having a liking for: 對…偏愛的: *~ to French cuisine.* 偏愛法國烹調。**~ly** /ˈpɑːʃəlɪ ; ˈpɑrʃəlɪ/ *adv* **1** partly; not completely. 部分地；不完全地。 **2** in a ~(2) manner. 偏袒地。**~·ity** /ˌpɑːʃɪˈælətɪ ; pɑrˈʃælətɪ/ *n* **1** [U] being ~(2) in treatment of people, etc; bias; favouritism. 偏袒；偏心；偏見；徇私。 **2 *~ity for,*** [C] fondness: 喜愛: *a ~ity for moonlight walks.* 喜歡在月光下散步。

par·tici·pate /pɑːˈtɪsɪpeɪt ; pɚˈtɪsəˌpet/ *vi* [VP2A, 3A] **~ *(in),*** have a share, take part (in): 分享；參與: *~ in sb's suffering/in a plot.* 分擔某人的痛苦(參與某一圖謀)。 **par·tici·pant** /pɑːˈtɪsɪpənt ; pɚˈtɪsəpənt/ *n* person who ~s (*in* sth). 分享者；參與者(與 in 連用後接某事物)。**par·tici·pa·tion** /pɑːˌtɪsɪˈpeɪʃn ; pɑrˌtɪsəˈpeʃən/ *n* [U] act of participating. 分享；參與。

par·ti·ciple /ˈpɑːtɪsɪpl ; ˈpɑrtəsəpl̩/ *n* (gram) verbal *adj* qualifying *nn* but retaining some properties of a *v*: (文法)分詞(動詞變成的形容詞，可修飾名詞，但尚保有動詞的某些特性): *'Hurrying'* and *'hurried'* *are the present and past ~s of 'hurry'.* hurrying 和 hurried 是 hurry 的現在分詞和過去分詞。**par·ti·cip·ial** /ˌpɑːtɪˈsɪpɪəl ; ˌpɑrtəˈsɪpɪəl/ *adj* of a ~: 分詞的: *a participial adjective,* eg 'loving' in 'a loving mother'. 分詞形容詞(如 a loving mother 中的 loving)。

par·ticle /ˈpɑːtɪkl ; ˈpɑrtɪkl̩/ *n* **1** very small bit: 極小之物；粒子；微粒；質點: *~s of dust;* 塵埃; smallest possible quantity: 極小量: *She hasn't a ~ of sense.* 她一點兒腦筋也沒有。**elementary ~,** (phys) one of the constituents of an atom, not yet known to be composed of simpler ~s, eg an electron. (物)元質點。 **2** (gram) minor part of speech, eg an article (*a, an, the*), a preposition or adverb (*up, in, out*), a conjunction (*or*), an affix (*un-, in-, -ness, -ly*). (文法)質詞(如冠詞 a, an, the; 介詞或副詞 up, in, out; 連接詞 or; 字首或字尾 un-, in-, -ness, -ly)。

parti-col·oured, (US = **-col·ored**) /ˈpɑːtɪ kʌləd ; ˈpɑrtɪˌkʌlɚd/ *adj* differently coloured in different parts. 雜色的；斑駁的。

par·ticu·lar /pəˈtɪkjʊlə(r) ; pɚˈtɪkjəlɚ/ *adj* **1** relating to one as distinct from others: 單獨的；特殊的: *in this ~ case.* 在這種特殊情況(事件)中。 **2** special; worth notice; outstanding: 特別的；值得注意的；突出的: *for no ~ reason.* 沒有特別理由。*He took ~ trouble to get it right.* 他特別費力把它弄好。***in ~,*** especially: 特別地；尤其: *I remember one of them in ~.* 我特別記得其中一個。 **3** very exact; scrupulous: 極精確的；嚴謹的: *a full and ~ account of what we saw.* 關於我們所見情形完整而精確的記述。 **4 ~ *(about/over),*** hard to satisfy; fastidious: 難以滿足的；挑剔的；吹毛求疵的: *She's ~ about what she wears.* 她對於穿着很講究。*He's too ~ over what he will eat and drink.* 他對於吃喝太講究了。□ *n* detail. 細節；瑣碎；細項。***go into ~s,*** give details. 詳細列出。**~·ly** *adv* in a ~ manner: 特別地；顯著地: *His good humour was ~ly noticeable.* 他的好脾氣是顯而易見的。*I ~ly mentioned that point.* 我特地提到那一點。**~·ity** /pəˌtɪkjʊˈlærətɪ ; pɚˌtɪkjəˈlærətɪ/ *n* [U] exactness; attention to detail. 精確；考究；詳細；特質。**~·ize** /-aɪz ; -ˌaɪz/ *vt, vi* [VP6A, 2A] name specially or one by one. 逐一列舉；特別提出。

part·ing /ˈpɑːtɪŋ ; ˈpɑrtɪŋ/ ⇨ part².

par·ti·san /ˌpɑːtɪˈzæn *US:* ˈpɑːrtɪzn ; ˈpɑrtəzn̩/ *n* **1** person devoted to a party, group or cause. 同黨人；幫夥；黨羽。 **2** (esp) member of an armed resistance movement in a country occupied by enemy forces: (尤指)淪陷區的抗敵分子；游擊隊員: *~ troops.* 游擊隊。□ *adj* uncritically devoted to a cause: 效忠的；獻身的；盲目推崇的: *His loyalties are too ~.* 他的忠心太盲目。**'~·ship** /-ʃɪp ; -ˌʃɪp/ *n*

par·ti·tion /pɑːˈtɪʃn ; pɑrˈtɪʃən/ *n* **1** [U] division into parts: 分割；畫分；分配；瓜分: *the ~ of India in 1947.* 1947年印度的分割。 **2** [C] that which divides, esp a thin wall between rooms, etc. 分隔物；隔牆。**3** [C] part formed by dividing; section. 分割的部分；區分。□ *vt* [VP6A, 15B] **~ *(sth off),*** divide into sections, etc; separate by means of a ~(2). 分割；瓜分；區分；隔開。

par·ti·tive /ˈpɑːtɪtɪv ; ˈpɑrtətɪv/ *n, adj* (word) denoting part of a collective whole: 表示部分的詞；表示部分的: *'Some' and 'any' are ~s.* some 和 any 都是表示部分的詞。

part·ner /ˈpɑːtnə(r) ; ˈpɑrtnɚ/ *n* **1** person who takes part with another or others in some activity, esp one of the owners of a business: 夥伴；合作者；(尤指經商之)合夥人: *~s in crime;* 共犯; *profits shared equally among all the ~s;* 合夥人平均分享的利潤; *active ~,* one taking part in the affairs of the business. 參與業務的合夥人。**sleeping ~,** ⇨ sleep²(2). **2** one of two persons dancing together, playing tennis, cards, etc together; husband or wife. 舞伴；(打網球、玩紙牌等的)同邊者；搭檔；夫或妻。□ *vt* [VP6A, 15A] be a ~ to; bring (people) together as ~s. 做…的夥伴;使(人們)成爲夥伴。 '~**·ship** /-ʃɪp; -ʃɪp/ *n* [U] state of being a ~; [C] joint business: 合夥;合股;合股經營的生意: *enter into ~ship* (*with* sb); 與(某人)合夥; *be in ~ship*. 入夥;合夥。

par·took /pɑ:'tʊk; pɑr'tʊk/ ⇨ partake.

par·tridge /'pɑ:trɪdʒ; 'pɑrtrɪdʒ/ *n* [C] sorts of bird of the same family as the pheasant; [U] its flesh as food. 雉;鷓鴣;松雞;雉肉。⇨ the illus at fowl. 參看 fowl 之挿圖。

par·tur·ition /ˌpɑ:tjʊ'rɪʃn *US:* -tʃʊ-; ˌpɑrtʃʊ'rɪʃən/ *n* [U] childbirth. 分娩。

P

party /'pɑ:tɪ; 'pɑrtɪ/ *n* (*pl* -ties) **1** [C] group of persons united in policy and opinion, in support of a cause, esp in politics: 團體;黨派;政黨: *the Conservative, Liberal and Socialist parties.* 保守黨、自由黨和社會黨。 **2** [U] (esp attrib use) government based on political parties: (尤作形容用法) 政黨政治: *the '~ system;* 政黨制度; *~ politics,* politics of and within a ~, eg manoeuvres designed to win influence or power; 政黨策略(如意在爭取影響力或權力的策略); *Should a politician put public interest before ~ interest?* 政治家應該把公共利益放在政黨利益之前嗎? ***follow the ~ line;*** **~ line,** ⇨ line¹(11). **~ machine,** ⇨ machine(2). **ˌ~-'spirit,** enthusiasm for, devotion to, a (political) ~. 黨性(對政黨的熱心)。 Hence, 由此產生, **ˌ~-'spirited** *adj* 熱衷(政)黨的;黨性强的。 **3** one of the persons or sides in a legal agreement or dispute. (契約或爭論的)一方;當事人。**ˌ~-'wall,** one that divides two properties and is the joint responsibility of the owners of these properties. 共有隔牆;界牆。 **4** group of persons travelling or working together, or on duty together: 同行的一羣人;共同工作的人;一同值班的人: *a 'firing-~,* of soldiers, at a military funeral or execution. (軍事葬禮之)鳴槍班;(執行死刑之)行刑班。 **5** gathering of persons, by invitation, for pleasure: 集會;聚會: *a 'dinner/'birthday ~;* 宴會;慶生會; *give a ~,* arrange one and be the host(ess); 舉辦集會;請客; (attrib) (形容用法) *a ~ dress.* 宴會服裝。***lack the ~ spirit,*** be without enthusiasm for a ~. 對宴會不熱心;對宴會不起勁。***make up a ~,*** join together to form a ~. 聚會;參加聚會。 **6** person taking part in and approving of or being aware of what is going on: 參與人;贊同人;關係人: *a ~ to a conspiracy;* 參與陰謀的人; *an innocent ~.* 無辜的關係人。 **7** (hum) person: (諧)人: *Who's the old ~ in blue,* the old person dressed in blue? 穿藍衣服的那個老頭兒是誰? **8** **'~-coloured,** = parti-coloured.

par·venu /'pɑ:vənju: *US:* -nu:; 'pɑrvəˌnju/ *n* person who has suddenly reached higher economic or social status from a lower status. 暴發戶;崛起者。

pas·chal /'pæskl; 'pæskl/ *adj* **1** of the Jewish Passover. (猶太人之)踰越節的。**2** of Easter. 復活節的。

pasha /'pɑ:ʃə *US:* 'pæʃə; 'pæʃə/ *n* (hist) title of honour placed after the name of a Turkish officer of high rank or the governor of a province. (史)帕夏(從前土耳其高級官員或省長的頭銜或尊稱,通常置於人名之後)。

pass¹ /pɑ:s *US:* pæs; pæs/ *n* **1** success in an examination, esp (in university degree examinations) success in satisfying the examiners but without distinction or honours¹(7): 考試及格;考試通過(尤指大學學位考試達到及格標準,但並無特別優異的成績): *get a ~;* 及格; *a '~ degree.* 達到及格標準的學位。 **2** ***come to/reach a pretty/sad/strange, etc ~,*** reach such a state or condition. 遭遇困難;陷入困境。 **3** ***bring to ~,*** accomplish, carry out. 完成;實行。***come to ~,*** happen: 發生: *How exactly did that come to ~?* 那事到底是怎麼發生的? **4** (paper, ticket, etc giving) permission or authority to travel, enter a building, occupy a seat in a cinema, etc: 通行或出入許可;通行證;入場券: *a free ~,* ticket giving free travel on the railways, etc. (如火車之)免費乘車證;免票證。 *All ~es to be shown at the barrier,* eg in a station. 所有通行證都要在(車站等的)柵口出示。*No admittance without a ~.* 沒有通行證不准進入。⇨ ~-book below. 參看下列之 pass-book。 **5** act of kicking, throwing, or hitting the ball from one player to another player (of the same team): 傳球(給本隊的隊員): *a clever ~ to the forward.* 給前鋒的一個妙傳。 **6** movement of the hand over or in front of sth (as in conjuring or juggling, or in mesmerism). 手在某種東西上面或前面的動作(如玩魔術、變戲法或行催眠術時手的動作)。 **7** forward movement, blow (in fencing, etc). (擊劍等之)刺;戳。***make a ~ at sb,*** (sl) make (possibly unwelcome) amorous advances. (俚)向(某人)做出非禮的舉動。 **8** narrow way over or through mountains; such a way viewed as the entrance to a country. 山間隘路;狹路;進入一個國家的通路。⇨ the illus at mountain. 參看 mountain 之挿圖。***hold the ~,*** (fig) defend a cause. (喻)捍衛某一目標(主義或運動)。 ***sell the ~,*** (fig) betray a cause; yield up a position. (喻)背叛某一目標(主義或運動);放棄立場。 **9** (card games) act of passing. (紙牌戲)放棄出牌或叫牌。⇨ pass²(15). **10** (compounds) (複合字) **'~·book** *n* **(a)** book supplied by a bank to a customer with records of his account. 銀行存摺。**(b)** (S Africa) booklet, document, allowing a black African person to be in a certain area. (南非)(准許非洲黑人在某地居留的)小册子,證明文件。 **'~·key** *n* private key to a gate, etc; key which opens a number of locks; master key. 大門鑰匙;(能開啓若干鎖的)總鑰匙;萬能鑰匙。 **'~·word** *n* secret word or phrase which enables a person to be recognized as a friend by sentries: (哨兵等藉以辨別敵友的)口令;密語: *give/demand the ~word.* 答(問)口令。

pass² /pɑ:s *US:* pæs; pæs/ *vi, vt* (*pp* ~ed, or, as *adj* past /pɑ:st *US:* pæst; pæst/) (For special uses with *advv* and *preps,* ⇨ 19 below.) (與副詞及介詞連用的特殊用法參看下列第19義。) **1** [VP2A, C] move towards and beyond, proceed (*along, through, down, etc*): 前進;通過;穿過(與 along, through, down 等連用): *~ through a village.* 經過一個村莊。*Please let me ~.* 請讓我過去。*The road was too narrow for cars to ~.* 這條路太窄,車子過不去。*The two ships ~ed each other during the night.* 那兩艘船在夜間錯過了。*I glanced at her and ~ed on.* 我看了她一眼,繼續往前走。*He ~ed in front of/behind me.* 他從我前面(後面)經過。*They ~ed by,* went past. 他們走過去了。Hence, 由此產生, **ˌ~er-'by** *n* (*pl* passers-by) person who ~es sb or sth: 過路人;偶然經過的人: *The purse was picked up by a ~er-by.* 錢包被路人撿到了。 **2** [VP6A] leave (a person, place, object, etc) on one side or behind as one goes forward: 經過: *Turn right after ~ing the Post Office.* 經過郵局後向右轉。*I ~ed Miss Green in the street.* 我在街上遇見格林小姐。 **3** [VP6A] go through, across, over or between: 通過: *The ship ~ed the channel.* 船駛過海峽。*No complaints ~ed her lips.* 她毫無怨言。 **4** [VP2A] (of time) go by; be spent: (指時間)過去;消逝: *Six months ~ed and still we had no news of them.* 六個月過去了,而我們還沒有他們的消息。*The time ~ed pleasantly.* 很愉快地度過了那一段時間。 **5** [VP6A] spend (time): 消磨(時間): *How shall we ~ the evening?* 我們如何消磨今晚的時間? *What can we do to ~ the time?* 我們能做什麼來消磨時間? **6** [VP3A] **~ *(from...) (to/into...),*** change from one state of things to another; change into another state of things: 改變事物的狀況;變成另一種狀況: *Water ~es from a liquid to a solid state when it freezes.* 水凍結時由液體變成固體。 *When water boils it ~es into steam.* 水煮沸時變爲蒸氣。 **7** [VP6A, 15B, 12A, 13A] give by handing: 傳遞: *Please ~ (me) the butter.* 請把奶油遞過來(給我)。*The letter was ~ed on/round to all the members of the family.* 那封信

給全家人傳閱。*The note was ~ed round the table.* 那字條由桌子周圍的人傳閱。 **8** [VP6A] utter: 說出: *~ a remark,* say sth. 說一些話。 *~* ***the time of day with sb,*** engage them in light conversation. 跟某人寒暄或打招呼。 **9** [VP6A, 2A, C] (cause to) circulate: (使)流通;傳布: *He was imprisoned for ~ing forged banknotes.* 他因使用僞鈔而被監禁。*He ~es under the name of Mr Green,* is known and accepted as Mr Green. 他用格林先生這個名字。 **10** [VP6A, 2A] examine and accept; be examined and accepted: 審查通過;考試及格: *Parliament ~ed the Bill.* 國會通過那個法案。*The Bill ~ed and became law.* 那個法案已經通過成爲法律。 *The examiners ~ed most of the candidates.* 主考人讓大部分參加考試的人及格。*The candidates ~ed (the examination).* 參加考試的人都及格了。*Will the play ~ the censor?* 那個劇本會通過檢查嗎? *We have to ~ the Customs before we leave.* 我們在離開以前,得先通過海關檢查。 **11** [VP2A, C] take place; be said or done (between persons): 發生;(在人們之間)說出或做出: *Did you see/hear what was ~ing?* 你有沒有看見(聽到)所發生的事情? *Tell me everything that ~ed between you.* 把你們之間的一切情形告訴我。 **12** [VP6A] be beyond the range of: 超過;超出…之範圍: *a story that ~es belief.* 無法令人相信的故事。*It ~es my comprehension.* 那是我所不能了解的。 **13** [VP14] *~* ***sth on sth/sb,*** give (an opinion, judgement, sentence on sth or sb): (對某事物或某人)表示(意見);作(判斷);處(刑): *~ sentence on an accused man.* 將被告判刑。*I can't ~ an opinion on your work without seeing it.* 我沒有看到你的作品,不能發表意見。 **14** [VP2A] be accepted without rebuke or blame; go unnoticed or unreproved: 不受非難而被接受;被寬大的放過;不被注意或不被譴責: *His rude remarks ~ed without comment.* 他那些粗魯的話沒有受到批評。*I don't like it, but I'll let it ~,* will not make objections, etc. 我不喜歡它,但我並不會表示反對。*Such conduct may ~ in certain circles but cannot be tolerated here.* 這種行爲在某些圈子裡也許沒有問題,在此地却不允許。 ~ **muster,** ⇨ muster. **15** [VP2A] (card games) let one's turn go by without playing a card or making a bid. (紙牌戲)放棄出牌或叫牌。 **16** [VP15A] move; cause to go: 使移動;使進行: *He ~ed his hand across his forehead/his fingers through his hair.* 他用手撫摸額頭(用手指梳理頭髮)。*I ~ed a rope round the barrel.* 我把一根繩子繞在桶上。*Will you please ~ your eye (= glance) over this note.* 這張條子請你過目一下。 ~ ***water,*** (euphem) urinate. (委婉語)小便。 **17** (in football, hockey, etc) kick, hand or hit (the ball) to a player of one's own side. (足球、曲棍球等)傳(球)給本隊的球員。 **18** [VP 6A, 15A] cause (troops) to go by: 使(部隊)走過: *~ troops in review.* 檢閱時使部隊成分列式走過。 **19** [VP2C, 15B] (special uses with *adverbial particles* and *preps*): (與副詞接語及介詞連用的特殊用法):

pass away, (euphem) die: (委婉語)逝世;去世;過世: *He ~ed away peacefully.* 他安詳地逝世了。

pass sb/sth by, pay no attention to; disregard: 不注意;忽視: *I can't ~ the matter by without a protest.* 我不能忽視此事而不提出抗議。

pass for sb/sth, be accepted as: 被認爲;被當做: *In this small village, he ~ed for a learned man.* 在這個小村子裡,他被視爲學識豐富的人。*Do I speak French well enough to ~ for a Frenchman?* 我的法文能說得好到讓人把我當成法國人嗎?

pass in; pass into sth, gain admission (to): 獲准入學;獲准進入: *He ~ed into the Military College with no difficulty.* 他毫無困難地獲准就讀軍事學院。

pass off, **(a)** (of events) take place, be carried through: (指事件)發生;進行: *The meeting of the strikers ~ed off quietly.* 罷工者的會議進行得很平靜。**(b)** (of pain, a crisis) end: (指痛苦、危機)結束: *Has your toothache ~ed off yet?* 你的牙疼好了沒有? ~ ***sth off,*** turn attention from: 不注意;把注意力從…移到他處: *~ off an awkward situation.* 不去注意一個尷尬的處境。~ ***sth/sb off as sth/sb,*** represent falsely to be: 把某事物或某人假裝爲;冒充: *He tried to ~ himself off as a qualified doctor.* 他試圖冒充合格醫生。

pass on, (euphem) die: (委婉語)逝世;去世: *I'm grieved to learn that your dear mother has ~ed on.* 聽說令堂去世我非常難過。~ ***sth on,*** hand or give it (to sb else, to others). 將(某物)交給(別人)。

pass out, (colloq) faint; lose consciousness. (俗)昏厥;失去知覺。~ ***out (of sth),*** leave college, etc having ~ed one's examinations. 畢業;通過考試。Hence, 由此產生, **ˌ~ing-ˈout (ceremony/parade),** esp for cadets who have completed their training. 畢業(典禮,遊行)(尤指爲已完成訓練的軍校學生所舉行者)。

pass sb over, overlook; fail to notice: 忽視;不注意: *They ~ed me over* (eg failed to promote me) *in favour of young Hill.* 他們忽視我(例如未提升我),而看重年輕的希爾。

pass through sth, experience it. 經歷;體驗。

pass sth up, (colloq) neglect it; not take advantage of it: (俗)忽略;放過(某事物): *~ up an opportunity.* 放過一次機會。

pass·able /ˈpɑːsəbl *US:* ˈpæs- ; ˈpæsəbl̩/ *adj* **1** (of roads, etc) that can be passed over or crossed: (指道路等)可通過的: *Are the Alpine roads ~ yet?* 阿爾卑斯山上的路暢通了嗎? **2** that can be accepted as fairly good but not excellent: 還好的;尚可的;過得去的: *a ~ knowledge of German.* 粗通德文。 **pass·ably** /-əblɪ ; -əblɪ/ *adv*

pass·age /ˈpæsɪdʒ ; ˈpæsɪdʒ/ *n* **1** [U] passing; act of going past, through or across; right to go through: 通過;經過;穿過;通過權: *the ~ of time.* 時光的流逝。**bird of ~, (a)** migratory bird. 候鳥。**(b)** person who passes through a place without staying there long. 到處漂泊的人。 **2** [C] voyage; journey from point to point by sea or air: 航行;(從一地到他地之間乘船或乘飛機的)旅行: *book one's ~ to New York.* 定去紐約的船(飛機)票。***work one's ~,*** ⇨ work²(4). **3** [C] way through: 通路: *force a ~ through a crowd.* 在人群中擠出一條通路。 **4** [C] **ˈ~·(way),** corridor in a house. (屋內之)通道;走廊。 **5** [C] short extract from a speech or piece of writing, quoted or considered separately. (演講詞或文章的)一段;一節。 **6** passing of a Bill so that it becomes law. 法案的通過。 **7** (*pl*) what passes between two persons in conversation: (複)(兩個人談話中)彼此所說的話: *have angry ~s with an opponent during a debate.* 在辯論過程中與對方惡言相向。 **8** **ˌ~ of ˈarms,** (lit, fig) combat; dispute. (字面,喻)交戰;爭論。

pass·book *n* ⇨ pass¹(10).

passé /ˈpæseɪ *US:* pæˈseɪ ; pæˈse/ *adj* (fem 陰性作 **passée**) (F) past his/her/its best; no longer current; out of date. (法)已過盛年的;過時的。

pas·sen·ger /ˈpæsɪndʒə(r) ; ˈpæsn̩dʒɚ/ *n* **1** person being conveyed by bus, taxi, tram, train, ship, aircraft, etc. (公共汽車、計程車、電車、火車、船、飛機等的)乘客。 **2** (colloq) member of a team, crew, etc who does no effective work. (俗)(一隊、一組等單位中)工作表現不佳的人;無能的選手。

passe·par·tout /ˌpæspɑːˈtuː ; ˌpæsparˈtu/ *n* **1** master-key. 萬能鑰匙。 **2** kind of adhesive tape used eg as a mounting for a picture, etc (to form a frame). (鑲照片等用的)膠(紙)帶。

passer-by /ˌpɑːsəˈbaɪ *US:* ˈpæsər ; ˈpæsɚˈbaɪ/ ⇨ pass²(1).

pas·sim /ˈpæsɪm ; ˈpæsɪm/ *adv* (Lat) (of allusions, phrases, etc to be found in a book or author) frequently; in every part: (拉)(指出現在某書或某作者的作品中的引述或詞句等)時常;到處: *This occurs in Milton ~.* 這個在米爾頓的作品中到處可見。

pas·sing /ˈpɑːsɪŋ *US:* ˈpæs- ; ˈpæsɪŋ/ *adj* going by; not lasting: 經過的;目前的;短暫的: *the ~ years.* 目

前的幾年。□ *adv* (old use) very: (舊用法)極其;很: ~ *rich.* 極其富有。□ *n* [U] the act of going by: 逝去;過去: *the ~ of the old year,* ie on New Year's Eve. 舊年的逝去(卽在除夕)。

passion /ˈpæʃn ; ˈpæʃən/ *n* **1** [U, C] strong feeling or enthusiasm, esp of love, hate or anger: 熱情;激情;强烈的感情(尤指愛、恨或怒): *be filled with ~* (ie love) *for sb;* 充滿對某人的愛; *choking with ~,* ie anger or hate. 因生氣或憤恨而說不出話來。*P~s were running high,* People were filled with strong feeling. 群情激昂。 **2 a ~,** outburst of strong feeling: 强烈感情的突發: *fly into a ~,* become very angry; 勃然大怒; *be in a ~.* 在生氣;發怒。 **3 the P~,** the suffering and death of Jesus. 耶穌的受難。**ˌP~ ˈSunday,** the fifth Sunday in Lent. 受難主日(封齋期中的第五個星期日,亦卽復活節前第二個星期日)。**ˈP~ Week,** the week between P~ Sunday and Palm Sunday. 受難週(復活節前第二週)。**ˈP~ play,** drama dealing with the P~. 受難劇(描寫耶穌受難的戲劇)。 **ˈ~-flower** *n* kinds of (usu climbing) plants with flowers that are thought to resemble the crown of thorns placed on the head of Jesus. 西番蓮(此花被認爲與耶穌受難時所戴的荆棘冠冕相似)。**ˈ~ fruit,** edible fruit of the ~-flower. 西番蓮果實(可食用)。**~·less** *adj*

passion·ate /ˈpæʃənət ; ˈpæʃənɪt/ *adj* easily moved by passion; filled with, showing, passion: 易動情的;熱情的;多情的: *a ~ nature;* 熱情的天性; *~ language.* 熱情的言語。**~·ly** *adv* in a ~ manner: 熱情地;深情地: *She is ~ly fond of tennis.* 她熱愛網球。

pass·ive /ˈpæsɪv ; ˈpæsɪv/ *adj* **1** acted upon but not acting; not offering active resistance: 被動的;消極的: *~ obedience.* 消極的服從。*In spite of my efforts the boy remained ~,* showed no signs of interest, activity, etc. 儘管我費了很多力,那男孩還是不起勁。**ˌ~ reˈsistance,** resistance that takes the form of not obeying orders, the law, etc but without active measures of opposition. 消極抵抗。**ˌ~ reˈsister,** persons who practise this. 消極抵抗者。 **2 the ~ (voice),** (gram) the form in italic type in the sentence 'The letter *was written* yesterday,' ie the verb phrase containing *be + pp.* (文法)被動語態(如 The letter was written yesterday 一句中的 was written 就是被動語態,亦卽 be + 過去分詞)。⇨ active. □ *n* ~ voice. 被動語態。**~·ly** *adv* **~·ness, pass·iv·ity** /pæˈsɪvətɪ ; pæˈsɪvətɪ/ *nn* [U] the state or quality of being ~. 被動;被動性;消極;不抵抗。

pass·key ⇨ pass¹(10).

Pass·over /ˈpɑːsəʊvə(r) *US:* ˈpæs- ; ˈpæsˌovə/ *n* Jewish religious festival commemorating the liberation of the Jews from slavery in Egypt. ⇨ Exod 12. 踰越節(猶太人的宗教節日,紀念其祖先在埃及爲奴被釋放;參看舊約聖經出埃及記第12章)。

pass·port /ˈpɑːspɔːt *US:* ˈpæs- ; ˈpæsˌport/ *n* government document to be carried by a traveller abroad, giving personal particulars; (fig) sth that enables one to win or obtain sth: 護照(往外國旅行者所持的政府證明文件,載明持用人的個人資料); (喻)使人獲得某物之物;達到某一目的之手段: *Is flattery a ~ to success?* 阿諛是成功的手段嗎?

pass·word ⇨ pass¹(10).

past¹ /pɑːst *US:* pæst ; pæst/ *adj* (Cf 參較 *passed,* *pp* of pass²) of the time before the present; gone by in time: 過去的;已過的: *for the ~ few days/weeks, etc;* 過去的幾天(幾週等); *during the ~ week;* 在過去的一週裡; *in times ~;* 在過去;好久以前; *for a long time ~;* 在過去的一段長時間中; *~ generations;* 過去的幾代; *the ~ tense;* (動詞的)過去式; *a ~ participle,* eg passed, taken, gone. 過去分詞(如 passed, taken, gone)。**~ master,** one who has a thorough mastery (*of* or *in* a subject, *at* doing sth). 能手;老手;專家(與 of 或 in 連用,後接專長的項目,與 at 連用,後接動名詞)。□ *n* **1 the ~,** ~ time: 往時;昔時;過去: *We cannot change the ~.* 我們不能改變過去。 *Memories of the ~ filled her mind.* 她的腦海裡充滿了過去的回憶。 **2** person's ~ life or experiences, esp when these are not reputable: 過去的生活或經驗(尤指不名譽者): *We know nothing of his ~.* 我們不知道他過去的生活情形。*She's a woman with a ~.* 她過去是個生活放蕩的女人。

past² /pɑːst *US:* pæst ; pæst/ *prep* **1** beyond in time; after: 在時間上超過;在…之後: *half ~ two;* 兩點半; *ten (minutes) ~ six;* 六點十分; *buses every twenty minutes ~ the hour,* ie at 1.20, 2.20, 3.20, etc; 公共汽車每小時過廿分開一班(卽一點二十分、兩點二十分、三點二十分等各一班); *stay out until ~ 11 o'clock;* 留在外面到十一點過後(才回來); *an old man ~ seventy;* 七十多歲的老人; *a woman ~ middle age.* 過了中年的婦人。 **2** beyond in space; up to and farther than: 在空間上超過;經過;經由: *He walked ~ the house.* 他走過那房子。*He hurried ~ me without stopping to speak.* 他匆忙地從我身旁走過,沒有停下來說話。*The driver took the bus ~ the traffic signal.* 司機開着公車通過交通號誌。 **3** beyond the limits, power or range of: 超過…之限制、權力或範圍: *The old man is ~ work,* too old, weak, etc to work. 這老人再也不能工作了。*She's ~ child-bearing,* too old to bear a child. 她不能再生育了。*The pain was almost ~ bearing,* too severe to be endured. 這種痛苦實在叫人受不了。*He's ~ praying for,* There's no hope of cure, improvement, etc. 他已經沒救了。*She's ~ caring what happens,* has reached the stage of complete indifference, is quite resigned to ill fortune, etc. 她對一切都不在乎了。***be/get ~ it,*** (colloq) be no longer able to do the things one could formerly do: (俗)再也不能做過去所能做的事了: *My gardener is over seventy-five and I'm afraid he's getting ~ it.* 我的園丁已超過七十五歲,恐怕已力不從心了。***wouldn't put sth ˈ~ sb,*** consider him capable of doing sth disreputable, unusual, etc: 認爲某人會做出不名譽或不尋常等的事來: *You may say that he is honest but I wouldn't put it ~ him to run off with the money.* 你可以說他很誠實,但我認爲他會携款潛逃。□ *adv* (in the sense of 2 above): (照上列第2義): *walk/march/go/run/hurry ~.* 走過(齊步走過;經過;跑過;匆匆走過)。

pasta /ˈpæstə *US:* ˈpɑːstə ; ˈpɑstə/ *n* [U] (I) (dish of food prepared from a dough of) flour, eggs and water mixed and dried, eg macaroni, spaghetti, ravioli. (義)麵食(如通心麵、細麵條、餛飩等)。

paste /peɪst ; pest/ *n* [U] **1** soft mixture of flour, fat, etc for making pastry. (做點心用的)麵團;麵糊。 **2** preparation of food-stuffs, cut up and pounded to a soft, moist mass: (食物搗爛的)糊;醬: *ˈanchovy ~;* 鯷魚醬; *ˈfish-~.* 魚糊。**3** mixture of flour and water used for sticking things together, esp paper on walls and boards: 漿糊: *a bottle of ~.* 一瓶漿糊。**ˈ~·board** *n* [U] stiff board-like material made by pasting sheets of paper together; cardboard. 硬紙板;紙板。 **4** substance (a glass-like material) used in making artificial diamonds, etc. 製造假鑽石等的原料(一種似玻璃的物質)。□ *vt* **1** [VP6A, 15A, B] stick with ~(3). (用漿糊)黏貼。**~ *sth down,*** fasten down with ~. 黏貼某物。**~ *sth up,*** **(a)** fasten with ~ to a surface: 把某物黏貼在平面上;把某物貼起來: *~ up a notice.* 張貼告示。**(b)** seal or cover using ~: 用漿糊封閉或遮蓋: *~ up cracks with paper.* 用紙貼補裂縫。**(c)** fasten sheets or strips of paper on larger sheets, eg to design pages for a magazine, book, etc. 把小紙條貼在較大張的紙上(如設計雜誌、書籍等的版頁)。Hence, 由此產生, **ˈ~-up** *n.* **2** [VP6A] (colloq) thrash; beat. (俗)鞭笞;打。Hence, 由此產生, **pasting** *n* (colloq) severe beating: (俗)痛打;毒打: *Get/Give sb a pasting.* 把某人痛打一頓。

pas·tel /ˈpæstl *US:* pæˈstel ; pæsˈtɛl/ *n* **1** (picture drawn with) coloured chalk made into crayons. 彩色粉筆;蠟筆;彩色粉筆畫;蠟筆畫。 **2** (attrib) (形容用法) *~ shades,* soft, light, delicate shades of colour. 輕淡柔和的色彩。

pas·tern /ˈpæstən ; ˈpæstɚn/ *n* part of a horse's foot between the fetlock and the hoof. (馬足部的)骹。⇨ the illus at domestic. 參看 domestic 之插圖。

pas·teur·ize /ˈpɑːstʃəraɪz ; ˈpæstə͵raɪz/ *vt* [VP6A] rid (milk, etc) of disease-producing bacteria by using the heating method of Louis Pasteur. 以巴斯德法除去(牛奶等的)病菌。**pas·teur·iz·ation** /ˌpɑːstʃəraɪˈzeɪʃn *US:* -rɪˈz- ; ͵pæstərəˈzeʃən/ *n*

pas·tiche /pæˈstiːʃ ; pæsˈtiʃ/ *n* [C] literary or other work of art composed in the style of another author, etc; musical composition made up from various sources. (文學或藝術的)模仿作品;(音樂的)混成曲。

pas·tille /ˈpæstɪl *US:* pæˈstiːl ; pæsˈtil/ *n* [C] small flavoured tablet to be sucked, eg one containing medicine for the throat. (含治喉疾藥物等的)錠劑;喉片。

pas·time /ˈpɑːstaɪm *US:* ˈpæs- ; ˈpæs͵taɪm/ *n* [C] anything done to pass time pleasantly; game: 消遣;娛樂;遊戲: *Photography is her favourite ~.* 攝影是她最喜歡的消遣。

pas·tor /ˈpɑːstə(r) *US:* ˈpæs- ; ˈpæstɚ/ *n* minister(3), esp of a nonconformist church. 牧師(尤指非英國國教的牧師)。

pas·toral /ˈpɑːstərəl *US:* ˈpæs- ; ˈpæstərəl/ *adj* **1** of shepherds and country life: 牧人及田園生活的: *~ poetry.* 田園詩。**2** of a pastor; (esp) of a bishop: 牧師的;(尤指)主教的: *a ~ letter,* one to the members of a bishop's diocese; 主教給教區教友的書信; *~ staff,* bishop's emblem, like a shepherd's crook, carried by or before bishops ceremonially. 主教的權杖(牧杖)。**3** of (duties towards) a priest's or a minister's flock: 傳教士或牧師之教徒的;牧師對教徒之職責的: *~ care/responsibilities.* 牧師對教徒的照顧(責任)。□ *n* ~ poem, play, letter, etc. 田園詩;牧歌;田園劇;主教給教區教友的書信(等)。

pas·tor·ate /ˈpɑːstərət *US:* ˈpæs- ; ˈpæstərɪt/ *n* **1** office of a pastor; time during which he holds it. 牧師職務;牧師任期。**2** body of pastors. 牧師團。

pas·try /ˈpeɪstrɪ ; ˈpestrɪ/ *n* (*pl* -ries) **1** [U] paste of flour, fat, etc baked in an oven; pie-crust. 用麵粉和油脂等做成的麵團所烤成的點心; 餡餅皮。**2** [C] article of food made wholly or partly of this, eg a pie or tart; [U] such articles collectively: 全部或部分此種原料製成的食物(如餡餅或果糕); 此種食物之總稱;麵製糕餅: *eat less ~.* 少吃糕餅。**ˈ~-cook** *n* person who makes ~, esp for public sale. 糕餅點心製造人(尤指製造以供出售者)。

pas·ture /ˈpɑːstʃə(r) *US:* ˈpæs-;ˈpæstʃɚ/ *n* [U] grassland for cattle; grass on such land, ⇨ meadow; [C] piece of land of this kind. 牧地;草原;草地;牧草;牧場。□ *vt, vi* **1** [VP6A] (of persons) put (cattle, sheep, etc) to graze: (指人)放牧;牧(牛、羊等): *~ one's sheep on the village common;* 在村莊的公地上放羊; (of cattle, etc) eat down grassland. (指牛等)在牧場上吃草。**2** [VP2A] graze. 吃草。**pas·tur·age** /-ɪdʒ ; -ɪdʒ/ *n* [U] (right to graze cattle on) ~ land. 牧場;牧草;放牧權。

pasty¹ /ˈpeɪstɪ ; ˈpestɪ/ *adj* (-ier, -iest) like paste (1): 如麵團的: *a ~ complexion,* white and unhealthy. 蒼白的臉色。

pasty² /ˈpæstɪ ; ˈpæstɪ/ *n* (*pl* -ties) pie of meat, jam, etc enclosed in paste and baked without a dish: 肉餡餅;餡餅: *a Cornish ~.* 康瓦爾餡餅。

pat¹ /pæt ; pæt/ *adv* at the right moment; at once and without hesitation: 適時地;立刻而不猶豫地: *The answer came pat.* 那個回答適時答出(來得正好)。*He had his excuse pat.* 他正好有個藉口。***stand pat,*** stick to one's decision; refuse to change. 堅持自己的決定;拒絕改變。

pat² /pæt ; pæt/ *vt, vi* (-tt-) **1** [VP6A, 15A] tap gently with the open hand or with sth flat: (用掌或扁平物)輕拍: *pat a dog;* 輕拍一隻狗; *pat a ball,* so that it bounces up and down. 拍球(使其上下跳動)。***pat sb/oneself on the back,*** (fig) express approval, congratulate, etc. (喻)表示贊成、恭賀等。**2** [VP2A] carry out the action of patting. 拍;輕拍。□ *n* [C] **1** tap with the open hand, eg as a caress or to show sympathy. 輕拍(如作爲愛撫動作或表示同情)。**2** small mass of sth, esp butter, formed by patting. 一小團東西(尤指拍成的奶油)。**3** light sound made by striking sth with a flat object. 輕拍聲。

patch¹ /pætʃ ; pætʃ/ *n* **1** small piece of material put on over a hole or a damaged or worn place: 補釘;補片: *a coat with ~es on the elbows;* 肘部有補釘的上衣; *a ~ on the inner tube of a tyre.* 車內胎的一塊補片。**ˌ~-ˈpocket** *n* one made by sewing a piece of cloth on to the outside of a garment. 縫在衣服外面的口袋。**2** piece of plaster put over a cut or wound. 貼傷口的膏藥(膠帶)。**3** pad worn to protect an injured eye. 保護受傷眼睛的眼罩。**4** small, irregular, differently coloured part of a surface: 表面上顏色不同的小斑塊: *a dog with a white ~ on its neck.* 一隻頸上有一塊白斑的狗。**5** small area (of ground, esp for garden vegetables): 小塊土地(尤指作菜園用的): *the ˈcabbage ~;* 捲心菜菜圃; small area of anything: 任何小片的東西: *~es of fog;* 幾片濃霧; *small ~es of blue in a cloudy sky.* 雲天中的幾片小小的藍天。**6** ***not a ~ on,*** not nearly so good as. 遠不如;比…差得遠。**7** ***go through/hit/strike a bad ~,*** be in/reach a period of bad luck, difficulty, unhappiness. 遭遇不幸、困難或不愉快;倒楣。**ˈ~·work** *n* [U] **1** piece of material made up of bits of cloth of various sizes, shapes and colours: 各形各色小布片縫綴而成的料子;補綴品: (attrib) (形容用法) *a ~work quilt.* 補綴布面的棉被。**2** (fig) piece of work made up of odds and ends. (喻)拼湊之物;雜湊之物。

patch² /pætʃ ; pætʃ/ *vt* [VP6A] **1** put a patch on; (of material) serve as a patch for. 補綴;縫補;(指布料等)作爲…的補片。**2** [VP15B] ~ ***up,*** repair; make roughly ready for use: 修理;草率做成: *an old, ~ed-up motor-cycle;* 一輛修好的舊機器脚踏車; (fig) (喻) *~ up a quarrel,* settle it for a time. 暫時止息口角。**~y** *adj* (-ier, -iest) made up of ~es; not regular or uniform; of uneven quality: 補綴的;不規律的;不畫一的;質地不均的: *~y work/knowledge.* 零星的工作(零碎的知識)。*The fog was ~y.* 霧散落各處。**~·ily** /-ɪlɪ ; -əlɪ/ *adv* **~i·ness** *n*

patch·ouli /ˈpætʃulɪ ; ˈpætʃulɪ/ *n* [U] (perfume derived from an) Asiatic plant. 亞洲產的一種薄荷;薄荷香水。

pate /peɪt ; pet/ *n* (colloq) head: (俗)頭: *a bald ~.* 禿頭。

pâté /ˈpæteɪ *US:* pɑːˈteɪ ; pɑˈte/ *n* **1** pie; patty. 餡餅;小麵餅。**2** paste. 製餡餅的麵團。**~ de foie gras** /ˌ- də fwɑː ˈgrɑː ; ˈ-də͵fwɑˈgrɑ/, (F) (patty of) goose-liver paste. (法)製鵝肝餅的麵團;鵝肝餅。

pa·tella /pəˈtelə ; pəˈtɛlə/ *n* (anat) kneecap. (解剖)膝蓋骨。

pat·ent¹ /ˈpeɪtnt *US:* ˈpætnt ; ˈpetnt/ *adj* **1** evident, easily seen: 顯著的;明顯的: *It was ~ to everyone that he disliked the idea.* 每個人都看得出來他不喜歡這個主意。**2** **ˌletters ˈ~** /ˈpætnt ; ˈpætnt/, government authority to manufacture sth invented and protect it from imitation. 專利權狀;專利證。**3** protected by letters ~: 有專利的;受專利權保護的: *~ medicines,* made by one firm or person only. 專利藥品。**4** **~ leather,** leather with a hard, smooth, shiny surface. 漆皮(通常爲黑色)。**~·ly** *adv* clearly; obviously. 清晰地;顯然地。

pat·ent² /ˈpeɪtnt *US:* ˈpætnt ; ˈpetnt/ *n* [C] **1** (privilege granted by) letters patent: 專利證;專利權: *take out a ~ to protect a new invention.* 取得專利權以保護一項新發明。**P~** (usu 通常讀 /ˈpætnt ; ˈpætnt/) **Office,** government department which issues ~s. 專利局(政府中主管頒發專利權狀,註册商標

等事務的機構)。 **2** that which is protected by letters ~; invention or process. 受到專利證保護之物;發明物或方法。□ *vt* [VP6A] obtain a ~ for (an invention or process). 取得(發明物或方法)之專利權。 **~ee** /ˌpeɪtnˈtiː *US:* ˌpætn- ; ˌpætn̩ˈti/ *n* person to whom a ~ is issued. 獲有專利權者。

pater·fa·mil·ias /ˌpeɪtəfəˈmɪlɪæs *US:* ˌpæt- ; ˈpetɚfəˈmɪlɪˌæs/ *n* (hum) father or head of a family. (諧)父親或家長。

pa·ter·nal /pəˈtɜːnl ; pəˈtɝnl̩/ *adj* **1** of or like a father: 父親的;似父親的: ~ *care.* 父親的照顧。 **2** related through the father: 父系的: *my ~ grandfather.* 我的祖父。 **~ly** /-nəlɪ ; -nl̩ɪ/ *adv* **~·ism** /-ɪzəm ; -ˌɪzəm/ *n* [U] (practice of) governing or controlling people in a ~ way (providing for their needs but giving them no responsibility). 仁慈的專制政治; 家長政治 (供給人民所需而不賦予任何義務)。

pa·ter·nity /pəˈtɜːnətɪ ; pəˈtɝnətɪ/ *n* [U] fatherhood; being a father; origin on the father's side: 父性;父道;父職;父系: *of unknown ~.* 生父不明。

pater·nos·ter /ˌpætəˈnɒstə(r) ; ˈpetɚˈnɑstɚ/ *n* (Lat 拉 for 意爲 'Our Father') **1** (recital of) the Lord's Prayer. 主禱文(的誦讀)。 **2** bend in a rosary at which the Lord's Prayer is repeated. 念珠串上主禱文重覆之處。 **3** lift(2) with a series of doorless cars(3) moving on a continuous belt so that passengers can step on or off at each floor. 連鎖式電梯(有一串無門的梯箱,由一條轉動的鏈帶牽動,使乘客在每樓上下)。

path /pɑːθ *US:* pæθ ; pæθ/ *n* (*pl* ~s /pɑːðz *US:* pæðz ; pæðz/) **1** **ˈ~·(way), (ˈfoot)·~,** way, track made (across fields, through woods, etc) by or for people walking: 小路;小徑(田野、林中等由行人踩成者): *Keep to the ~ or you may lose your way.* 沿着這條小路走,否則你可能會迷路。 **ˈ~-finder** *n* explorer; sb sent on ahead to find a route, etc; pioneer. 探路者;探險者;開拓者;先驅。 **2** track specially made for foot or cycle racing (usu 通常作 *cinder track*). (競走或脚踏車比賽的)跑道。 **3** line along which sth or sb moves: 軌道;路線: *the moon's ~ round the earth;* 月亮繞行地球的軌道; *the ˈflight ~ of a spacecraft;* 太空船飛行的軌道; *the ~ of a tornado.* 颶風經過的路線。 **~less** *adj* having no ~s: 無路的: *~less jungles.* 無路可走的叢林。

pa·thetic /pəˈθetɪk ; pəˈθɛtɪk/ *adj* **1** able to be considered sad, pitiful, or (colloq) contemptible: 悲哀的;可憐的;(俗)可鄙的: *a ~ sight;* 悲慘的景象; *~ ignorance.* 可憐的無知。 **2 the ~ fallacy,** the error of imaginatively endowing inanimate objects with life, human feelings, etc. 感情的謬誤;在想像中把生命、感情等賦予無生命的東西。 **pa·theti·cally** /-klɪ ; -klɪ/ *adv*

pa·thol·ogy /pəˈθɒlədʒɪ ; pæˈθɑlədʒɪ/ *n* [U] science of diseases. 病理學。 **path·ol·ogist** /pəˈθɒlədʒɪst ; pæˈθɑlədʒɪst/ *n* student of, expert in, ~. 研究病理學者;病理學家。 **path·o·logi·cal** /ˌpæθəˈlɒdʒɪkl ; ˌpæθəˈlɑdʒɪkl̩/ *adj* of ~; of the nature of disease. 病理學的; 與疾病有關的; 由疾病引起的。 **path·o·logi·cally** /-klɪ ; -klɪ/ *adv*

pa·thos /ˈpeɪθɒs ; ˈpeθɑs/ *n* [U] quality in speech, writing, etc which arouses a feeling of pity, sympathy or tenderness. (演講、文章等)哀婉動人的性質。

pa·tience /ˈpeɪʃns ; ˈpeʃəns/ *n* [U] **1** (power of) enduring trouble, suffering, inconvenience, without complaining; ability to wait for results, to deal with problems calmly and without haste: 容忍;忍耐;耐心;耐性;忍耐力: *I haven't the ~ to hear your complaints again.* 我沒有耐心再聽你的抱怨。 *She has no ~ with people who are always grumbling,* cannot endure them. 她不能容忍那些常常發牢騷的人。 ***be out of ~ (with),*** be unable to endure further. 對…忍無可忍。 **the ~ of Job,** very great ~: 極度的忍耐: *His behaviour would try* (= test) *the ~ of Job.* 他的行爲考驗最有耐性的人(意即:連最有耐性的人也無法忍受)。 **2** (GB) kind of card game, usu for one player (US 美=*solitaire*). (英)一種一個人玩的紙牌遊戲。

pa·tient[1] /ˈpeɪʃnt ; ˈpeʃənt/ *adj* ~ ***(with sb),*** having or showing patience (with him): 有耐性的;忍耐的;容忍的: *be ~ with a tired child.* 對疲倦的小孩要有耐性。 ***be ~ of sth,*** (archaic) (古) **(a)** be able to endure it ~ly. 能忍受。 **(b)** admit(5). 容許有。 **~·ly** *adv*: *wait/sit/listen ~ly.* 耐心地等(坐,聽)。

pa·tient[2] /ˈpeɪʃnt ; ˈpeʃənt/ *n* [C] person who has received, is receiving, or is on a doctor's list for, medical treatment: 病人: *The Smiths are ~s of Dr Quack.* 庫瓦克醫生替史密斯全家人看病。 **~·ly** *adv*

pat·ina /ˈpætɪnə ; ˈpætɪnə/ *n* (usu) green, glossy surface formed on old bronze or copper; glossiness of old woodwork, etc. 古銅上所生的(通常爲)綠色光滑的表面;銅綠;古老木器等的光澤;古色。

patio /ˈpætɪəʊ ; ˈpɑtɪˌo/ *n* (*pl* ~s /-əʊz ; -oz/) **1** courtyard, open to the sky, within the walls of a Spanish or Spanish American house. (西班牙或使用西班牙語之美洲各國的)屋內庭院;天井。 **2** (modern use) paved area near a house, used for recreation. (現代用法)房屋附近用磚石等鋪平的遊樂場地。

pa·tis·serie /pəˈtiːsərɪ ; pəˈtisərɪ/ *n* (F) shop, bakery, specializing in (French) pastry and cakes. (法)(專門製售法國點心的)麵包店。

pat·ois /ˈpætwɑː ; ˈpætwɑ/ *n* dialect of the common people of a district, differing from the standard language of the country. 方言;土話。

pa·trial /ˈpeɪtrɪəl ; ˈpetrɪəl/ *n* person who has qualifications which give him the right to be considered legally a British citizen. 有英國公民資格的人。

patri·arch /ˈpeɪtrɪɑːk *US:* ˈpæt- ; ˈpetrɪˌɑrk/ *n* **1** venerable old man. 年高德劭的人。 **2** male head of a family or tribe. (男性)家長;族長。 **3** bishop among the early Christians; (in the RC Church) high-ranking bishop; (in Eastern Churches) bishop of highest honour: 早期基督教徒中的監督;(羅馬天主教的)高級主教;(東正教的)大主教: *the P~ of Antioch/Jerusalem.* 安提阿(耶路撒冷)的大主教。 **~al** /ˌpeɪtrɪˈɑːkl *US:* ˌpæt- ; ˌpetrɪˈɑrkl̩/ *adj* of or like a ~. (似)家長的;(似)族長的;(似)監督的;(似)大主教的。 **ˈ~·ate** /-eɪt ; -ɪt/ *n* position, see², residence, of a Church ~. 主教的職位、轄區、住所。

pa·tri·cian /pəˈtrɪʃn ; pəˈtrɪʃən/ *n, adj* (person) of noble birth (esp in ancient Rome); aristocrat(ic). 出身高貴的;(尤指古羅馬時)出身高貴的人;貴族;貴族的。

pat·ri·cide /ˈpætrɪsaɪd ; ˈpætrɪˌsaɪd/ *n* [U] killing of one's own father; [C] instance of this; [C] person guilty of this. 弒父;此種行爲之實例;弒父者。

pat·ri·mony /ˈpætrɪmənɪ *US:* -məʊnɪ ; ˈpætrəˌmonɪ/ *n* (*pl* -nies) [C] property inherited from one's father or ancestors; endowment. 世襲的財產;祖傳的產業;捐贈的財產。 **pat·ri·mo·nial** /ˌpætrɪˈməʊnɪəl ; ˌpætrəˈmonɪəl/ *adj* of a ~. 世襲財產的;祖傳產業的;捐贈財產的。

pa·triot /ˈpætrɪət *US:* ˈpeɪt- ; ˈpetrɪət/ *n* person who strongly supports his country. 愛國者。 **ˈ~·ism** /-ɪzəm ; -ˌɪzəm/ *n* [U] the feelings and qualities of a ~. 愛國心;愛國精神。 **~ic** /ˌpætrɪˈɒtɪk *US:* ˌpeɪt- ; ˌpetrɪˈɑtɪk/ *adj* having, showing, the qualities of a ~. 愛國的;有愛國心的。 **~i·cally** /-klɪ ; -klɪ/ *adv*

pa·trol /pəˈtrəʊl ; pəˈtrol/ *vt, vi* (-ll-) [VP6A, 2A] go round (a camp, town, the streets, roads, etc) to see that all is well, to look out (for wrong-doers, persons in need of help, the enemy, etc). 巡邏;巡查。□ *n* **1** [U] the act of ~ling: 巡邏;巡查: *soldiers on ~;* 在巡邏中的士兵; *maintain a constant sea and air ~,* eg looking for submarines during a war; 維持不斷的海空巡邏(如在戰時搜索潛水艇); (attrib) (形容用法) *a police ˈ~ car,* eg on a motorway. 警察巡邏車(如在公路上者)。 **2** [C] person(s), ship(s) or aircraft on ~ duties: 巡邏者;巡邏員;巡邏船;巡邏機: *We were helped by an AA* (= Automobile Association) *~(man),* scout. 我們

受到汽車協會巡邏員的協助。 **3** (US) (美) **'~ wagon** *n* one used by the police for conveying prisoners or persons who have been arrested. (運送犯人用的)警車;囚車。**'~·man** /-mən ; -mən/ *n* (*pl* -men) (esp) policeman who ~s an area. (尤指)巡警。

pa·tron /'peɪtrən ; 'petrən/ *n* **1** person who gives encouragement, moral or financial support, to a person, cause, the arts, etc: (對某人,某種目標,藝術等之)贊助人;資助人:*Modern artists have difficulty in finding wealthy ~s.* 現代藝術家們難以找到富有的贊助人。**,~ 'saint,** saint regarded as the special protector (*of* a church, town, travellers, etc). (教堂、城鎮、旅行者等的)守護神。 **2** regular customer at a shop. 主顧。**'~·ess** /-ɪs ; -ɪs/ *n* woman ~. 女贊助人;女主顧。

pa·tron·age /'pætrənɪdʒ *US:* 'peɪt- ; 'petrənɪdʒ/ *n* [C] **1** support, encouragement, given by a patron: 支持;贊助;資助: *with/under the ~ of the Duke of X.* 在某公爵的贊助之下。 **2** right of appointing sb to a benefice or office, to grant privileges, etc: 任命聖職之權;委派職務之權;給予權力之權: *He's an influential man, with a great deal of ~ in his hands.* 他是個有影響力的人,握有任免大權。 **3** customer's support (to a shopkeeper, etc): (顧客的)惠顧: *take away one's ~ because of poor service.* 因服務欠佳,不再惠顧。 **4** patronizing manner. 施恩的態度。⇨ patronize(2).

pa·tron·ize /'pætrənaɪz *US:* 'peɪt- ; 'petrən,aɪz/ *vt* [VP6A] **1** act as patron towards: 光顧;惠顧;照顧;贊助: *~ a young musician/a dressmaker.* 贊助一個年輕的音樂家(光顧一個裁縫師)。**2** treat (sb whom one is helping, talking to, etc) as if he were an inferior person; be condescending towards. 以恩賜的態度對待(所贊助的人或談話的對象); 對…表現屈尊的樣子。**pat·ron·iz·ing** *adj* **pat·ron·iz·ing·ly** *adv*

pat·ro·nymic /,pætrə'nɪmɪk ; ,pætrə'nɪmɪk/ *n, adj* (name) derived from that of a father or ancestor, eg *Robertson; MacNeil; O'Neil.* 取自父親或祖上名字的; 取自父親或祖上名字的姓 (如: Robertson 意即 son of Robert; MacNeil 意即 son of Neil; O'Neil 意即 son of Neil)。

pat·ten /'pætn ; 'pætn̩/ *n* clog, wooden shoe, mounted on a metal framework to keep the wearer's foot above the mud. (防泥用的)木套鞋。

pat·ter¹ /'pætə(r) ; 'pætɚ/ *n* [U] **1** kind of talk used by a particular class of people: 行話;切口;暗語: *thieves' ~;* 小偷們的暗語; *the ~ of an auctioneer.* 拍賣人的行話。**2** rapid talk of a conjuror or comedian; rapid speech introduced into a song (*a '~ song*). 魔術家或喜劇演員的喋喋快語;歌(快調滑稽歌)中的快調插詞。□ *vt, vi* [VP6A] recite, say, repeat (prayers, etc) very quickly or in a mechanical way; [VP2A] talk fast or glibly. 喋喋背誦;喋喋地說;喋喋地重複(祈禱等);快速或敏捷地講。

pat·ter² /'pætə(r) ; 'pætɚ/ *n* [U] sound of quick, light taps or footsteps: 急速的輕拍聲;輕快的脚步聲: *the ~ of rain on a roof;* 雨打屋頂的滴答聲; *the ~ of footsteps.* 脚步的啪噠啪噠聲。□ *vi* [VP2A, C] make this sound: 發出急速輕拍聲;滴答地響;啪噠地響: *rain ~ing on the window-panes.* 雨點啪噠地打在玻璃窗上。

pat·tern /'pætn ; 'pætɚn/ *n* [C] **1** excellent example; sb or sth serving as a model: 模範;典型;作爲典範的某人或某事物: *She's a ~ of all the virtues.* 她是一切美德的典範。(attrib) (形容用法) *He has a ~* (*model* is the usu word) *wife.* 他有個模範的妻子(本義通常用 model)。 **2** sth serving as a model, esp shape of a garment, cut out in paper, used as a guide in dressmaking, etc; model from which sth is to be cast and from which a mould is made (in a foundry, etc): (做衣服等用的)紙樣;式樣;(鑄造工廠等用的)模子;模型: *'~-maker;* 製模工人; *'~-shop,* in a foundry. (鑄造工廠中的)製模房。 **3** sample, esp a small piece of cloth: 樣品;(尤指)布樣: *a bunch of ~s from the tailor.* 裁縫給的一束布樣。 **4** ornamental design, eg on a carpet, on wallpaper, curtain material: (地毯、壁紙、窗簾布等的)圖案;花樣;式樣: *a ~ of roses;* 玫瑰的圖案; *geometrical ~s.* 幾何圖案。 **5** way in which sth happens, develops, is arranged, etc: 方式: *new ~s of family life,* eg when married women, instead of keeping house, go out to work and add to the family income. 家庭生活的新方式(例如已婚婦女不做家事而外出工作,以增加家庭收入)。 □ *vt* **1** [VP14] **~ *sth/oneself upon/after sth/sb,*** model: 仿造;模仿: *a dress ~ed upon a Paris model.* 仿照巴黎式樣的衣服。 *He ~s himself upon his father.* 他仿傚他的父親。 **2** decorate with a ~. 以圖案裝飾;加花樣。

patty /'pætɪ ; 'pætɪ/ *n* (*pl* -ties) little pie or pasty: 小餡餅;小麵餅: *oyster patties.* 牡蠣餅。**'~-pan** *n* pan for baking a ~ in. 餡餅鍋。

pau·city /'pɔːsətɪ ; 'pɔsətɪ/ *n* [U] (formal) smallness of number or quantity. (正式用語)少數;少量。

Paul /pɔːl ; pɔl/ *n* ***rob Peter to pay ~,*** ⇨ Peter. **~ Pry,** an inquisitive person. 愛管閒事的人。

paunch /pɔːntʃ ; pɔntʃ/ *n* belly, esp if fat: 腹(尤指肥大的肚子): *a ~ like that of Falstaff.* 像孚斯塔夫那樣的大肚子。 *He was getting quite a ~,* getting wide round the waist. 他的腰圍越來越粗了。**~y** *adj* having a large ~. 肚子大的;大腹便便的。**~i·ness** *n*

pau·per /'pɔːpə(r) ; 'pɔpɚ/ *n* person with no means of livelihood, esp one who is supported by charity. 窮人;貧民(尤指靠施捨度日者)。 **'~·ism** /-ɪzəm ; -,ɪzəm/ *n* [U] state of being a ~; existence of ~s: 貧窮;窮困: *abolish ~ism.* 消除貧窮。 **'~·ize** /-aɪz ; -,aɪz/ *vt* [VP6A] bring to the state of being a ~. 使貧窮;使成爲窮人。**~·iz·ation** /,pɔːpəraɪ'zeɪʃn *US:* -rɪ'z- ; ,pɔpərə'zeʃən/ *n*

pause /pɔːz ; pɔz/ *n* **1** short interval or stop (while doing or saying sth): 中止;暫停: *during a ~ in the conversation;* 在會談中停頓的時候; *a ~ to take breath.* 停下來喘口氣。 ***give ~ to,*** cause (a person) to hesitate, to stop and think. 使(人)躊躇。 **2** (music) sign (𝄐 or 𝄑) over or under a note or rest to show that it is to be prolonged. (音樂) 延長記號(𝄐或𝄑,置於音符或休止符上或下,以示該符號應予延長)。□ *vi* [VP2A, 4A] make a ~: 暫停;中止: *~ to look round.* 停下來看看四周。

pave /peɪv ; pev/ *vt* [VP6A] put flat stones, bricks, etc on (a path, etc): 鋪石板、磚等於(道路等): *a path ~d with brick;* 鋪磚的小路; (fig) (喻) *a career ~d with* (= full of) *good intentions.* 充滿善意的生涯。 ***~ the way for,*** make conditions easy or ready for. 爲…作準備; 使…容易進行; 爲…鋪路。 **'paving-stone** *n* slab of stone for paving. 鋪路用的石板。

pave·ment /'peɪvmənt ; 'pevmənt/ *n* **1** (GB) paved way at the side of a street for people on foot (US 美=*sidewalk*). (英) (街邊的)人行道。**'~ artist,** one who draws pictures on a ~ with coloured chalks (to get money from passers-by). 馬路畫家(用彩色粉筆在人行道上畫圖向行人討錢者)。 **2** (US) hard surface for streets, roads, etc. (美) (街道,道路等的)硬路面。 **crazy ~,** ⇨ crazy(4).

pa·vil·ion /pə'vɪlɪən ; pə'vɪljən/ *n* **1** building on a sports ground for the use of players, spectators, etc. 運動場上供運動員、觀衆等使用的建築物。**2** ornamental building for concerts, dancing, etc. 供音樂會、舞蹈等使用的裝飾華美的建築物。 **3** large tent, eg as used for a flower exhibition. 大帳篷(如供花展使用者)。

paw /pɔː ; pɔ/ *n* animal's foot that has claws or nails (contrasted with *hoof*): (動物有爪的)脚掌;脚爪(異於 hoof): *a dog's paw,* ⇨ the illus at dog; 狗掌;狗爪(參看 dog 之插圖); (colloq, hum) hand. (俗,諧)手。□ *vt* [VP6A, 15B] **1** (of animals) feel or scratch with the paw(s); (of a horse) strike (the ground) with a hoof. (指動物)以掌摸或抓;(指馬)以蹄扒(地)。 **2** (of persons) touch with the hands, awkwardly, rudely or with improper familiarity. (指人)用手粗笨地摸;毛手毛脚地摸。

pawky /ˈpɔːkɪ ; ˈpɔkɪ/ *adj* (Scot) sly; arch: (蘇)狡猾的;頑皮的: ~ *humour.* 俏皮的幽默。 **pawk·ily** /ˈpɔːkɪlɪ ; ˈpɔkɪlɪ/ *adv*

pawl /pɔːl ; pɔl/ *n* **1** lever with a catch for the teeth of a ratchet wheel or rod, to prevent slipping or movement in the opposite direction. (防止棘齒輪逆轉的)撐手;倒齒;爪。 **2** short bar used to prevent a capstan or windlass from recoiling. (防止絞盤退轉的)掣轉桿。

P

pawn¹ /pɔːn ; pɔn/ *n* least valuable piece in the game of chess; person made use of by others for their own advantage. 兵;卒(西洋棋中最不重要的棋子);被別人利用的人。⇨ the illus at chess. 參看 chess 之插圖。

pawn² /pɔːn ; pɔn/ *vt* [VP6A] **1** deposit (clothing, jewellery, etc) as a pledge for money borrowed: 典當;質押(衣物、珠寶等): *The medical student ~ed his microscope to pay his rent.* 那個醫學院學生典當他的顯微鏡付房租。 **2** (fig) pledge: (喻)以…爲保證: ~ *one's life/honour.* 以生命(榮譽)擔保。 □ *n* [U] ***in*** ~, in a state of being ~ed: 當掉;押掉: *My watch is in* ~. 我的錶當掉了。 **ˈ~·broker** *n* person licensed to lend money at interest on the security of goods left with him. 開當鋪者;當鋪老闆。 **ˈ~·shop** *n* ~broker's place of business. 當鋪。 **ˈ~-ticket** *n* ~broker's receipt for goods pledged with him. 當票;質押單據。

paw·paw /pəˈpɔː *US:* ˈpɔːpɔː ; ˈpɔpɔ/ *n* = papaw.

pax /pæks ; pæks/ *n* (in church) kiss or sign of peace. (教會)表示和平之吻或聖號。 **Pax Romana** /ˌpæks rəʊˈmɑːnə ; ˈpæks roˈmenə/, peace enforced on states in the ancient Roman Empire. 羅馬帝國統治下的和平。

pay¹ /peɪ ; pe/ *n* [U] money paid for regular work or services, esp in the armed forces (*Pay* is used instead of *wages* and *salary* in the Navy, Army and Air Force): 工資;薪餉(在海、陸、空軍中用 pay 而不用 wages 與 salary): *draw one's pay;* 領薪餉; *get an increase in pay.* 獲得加薪。 ***in the pay of,*** employed by (often with a suggestion of dishonour, eg *in the pay of the enemy*). 受雇於(常指不名譽者,如被敵方收買)。 **ˈpay-claim** *n* = *wage-claim,* ⇨ wage. **ˈpay-day** *n* **(a)** day on which wages, salaries, etc are (to be) paid. 發薪日。 **(b)** day (on the Stock Exchange) on which transfer of stock has to be paid for. (證券市場的)交割日。 **ˈpay-dirt** [U] (US) earth in which there is ore of a grade high enough to make mining profitable. (美)(含量具有開採價值的)礦土;礦砂。 **ˈpay·load** *n* **(a)** that part of the load (of a ship, aircraft, etc) for which payment is received, eg passengers and cargo, but not fuel. (船、飛機等)收費的載重;酬載(如旅客與貨物,但使用的燃料不計在內)。 **(b)** bomb in a missile. 飛彈所載之炸彈。 **(c)** crew and instruments of a spacecraft. 太空船中的人員和儀器。 **ˈpay·master** *n* official responsible for paying troops, workers, etc. (負責發放薪餉的)軍需官;出納員;發款員。 **ˌpay·master ˈgeneral,** officer at the head of a department of the Treasury. (英國財政部的)會計長。 **ˈpay-off** *n* (colloq) (time of) full and final settlement of accounts or of final retribution or revenge. (俗)總結算(的時刻);報復(的時刻);報應(的時刻)。 **ˈpay-packet** *n* envelope or packet containing pay. 薪水袋。 **ˈpay-phone/-station** *nn* (US) coinoperated telephone call-box. (美)(投硬幣的)公共電話(亭)。 **ˈpay-roll/-sheet** *nn* **(a)** list of persons to be paid and the amounts due to each. 薪餉表;工資單(載明每人應得的薪額)。 **(b)** total amount of wages, salaries, etc to be paid to them. 所有員工薪給的總數。 **ˈpay-slip** *n* slip of paper included in a pay-packet, showing how pay has been calculated, deductions for tax, etc. (放在薪水袋內註明薪資核算方法、扣稅額等的)薪資核算單。

pay² /peɪ ; pe/ *vt, vi* (*pt, pp* paid /peɪd ; ped/) (For special uses with *adverbial particles* and *preps,* ⇨ 6 below.) (與副詞接語及介詞連用的特殊用法,參看下列第6義。) **1** [VP6A, 12A, 13A, 14, 3A] ***pay sb; pay for sth; pay sb for sth; pay sb sth; pay sth (to sb) (for sth),*** give (sb) money for goods, services, etc: 付給;付款;付還;償付(某人): *You must pay me what you owe.* 你必須把你所欠我的付給我。 *You must pay for what you eat and drink.* 你必須付你吃喝的費用。 *Have you paid the milkman this month?* 你這個月付款給賣牛奶的人了嗎? *I paid you the money last week.* 我上星期把錢還(付)給你了。 *He paid £600 to a dealer for that car.* 他花了六百鎊向汽車商人買了那輛車子。 *I pay £5 a week for guitar lessons.* 我每週爲吉他課付五鎊學費。 **2** [VP2A, 14, 12A, 13A] give (sb) reward or recompense: 給(某人)報酬;報償;補償: *He says that sheep farming doesn't pay,* that it isn't profitable. 他說養羊不賺錢。 *He has been amply paid for his trouble.* 他的辛勞已經獲得很豐富的報酬。 *They say it pays to advertise.* 他們說登廣告很有用。 **3** [VP6A] settle (debts, etc): 償還;付清(債務等): *Have you paid all your debts yet?* 你償還你全部的債了嗎? *He has paid his bills/dues/subscriptions/taxes.* 他已付清帳單(應付之款,訂閱費,稅金)。 ***put ˈpaid to sth,*** (colloq) settle it; end it so that it gives no more trouble. (俗)解決某事物;結束某事物以免再有麻煩。 **4** [VP6A, 12A, 13A] ~ ***(to),*** give, eg attention, respect, etc to: 給予;付出(如注意力、敬意等): *Please pay more attention to your work.* 請更加注意你的工作。 *He has called to pay* (= offer) *his respects.* 他曾經前來拜訪致敬。 *He seldom pays his wife any compliments,* seldom compliments her. 他很少稱讚他的太太。 *I look forward to paying you a visit* (= visiting you) *next week.* 我期待着下星期去拜訪你。 **5** (phrases) (片語) ***pay one's way,*** not get into debt. 不負債。 ***pay through the nose,*** ⇨ nose¹(1). **ˌpay-as-you-ˈearn,** (abbr 略作 **PAYE**), method of collecting income tax (in GB) by requiring employers to deduct it from earnings. 預扣所得稅(英國的一種徵收所得稅的方法,要求雇主在發薪時就扣繳所得稅)。 **pay·able** /ˈpeɪəbl ; ˈpeəbl̩/ *adj* which must or may be paid. 應付的;可付的。 **payee** /peɪˈiː ; peˈi/ *n* person to whom sth is (to be) paid. 受付人;受款人。 **payer** *n* person who pays or who is to pay. 付款人;付給者。 **6** [VP15B, 3A, 2C] (special uses with *adverbial particles* and *preps*): (與副詞接語及介詞連用的特殊用法):

pay sth back, return (money, etc) that has been borrowed. 歸還;償還。 ***pay sb back/out (for sth),*** punish him; have one's revenge: 懲罰某人;向某人報復: *I've paid him out for the trick he played on me.* 我已經報復他對我的愚弄。

pay for, **(a)** ⇨ 1 above. 參看上列第1義。 **(b)** suffer pain or punishment for: 爲…受痛苦或懲罰: *He'll have to pay for this foolish behaviour.* 他將爲這種愚蠢行爲而得到報應。

pay sth in; pay sth into sth, deposit (money) with a bank, to one's own or another's account: 將錢存入(自己或他人的)銀行帳戶: *Please pay this sum into my/my wife's account.* 請把這筆錢存入我的(我太太的)帳戶。

pay sb off, **(a)** pay sb his wages and discharge him. 給薪解僱;遣散。 **(b)** pay in full and be free from obligation: 全部還清: *pay off one's creditors;* 把所有債權人的債都還清; *pay off the crew of a ship.* 發清全船船員的薪水。 ⇨ *pay-off* at pay¹.

pay sth out, **(a)** give money, eg in settlement of expenses: 付錢(如付清費用): *When you move into a new house you really have to start paying out (money).* 當你遷入新居,你就得開始付錢了。 **(b)** (naut) allow (rope) to run out freely through the hands; slacken (rope) so that it runs freely. (航海)放鬆(繩子)使其順手滑出。

pay up, pay in full what is owing: 付清;繳清: *If you don't pay up, I'll take you to court.* 如果你不

還清欠款,我就到法院告你。

pay·ment /ˈpeɪmənt; ˈpemənt/ *n* **1** [U] paying or being paid: 支付;繳納;報酬: *demand prompt ~;* 要求即時付款; *a cheque in ~ for services rendered.* 償付所作服務的支票。 **2** [C] sum of money (to be) paid: 付出的款額;(應)支付的款額: *£50 cash down and ten monthly ~s of £5.* (交貨時)先付五十鎊現款,然後分十個月攤付,每月五鎊。 **3** [C, U] (fig) reward; punishment. (喻)報償;懲罰。

pay·nim /ˈpeɪnɪm; ˈpenɪm/ *n* (archaic) pagan; heathen; (esp during the Crusades to the Holy Land) Saracen. (古) 異教徒;不信基督教者;(尤指十字軍東征時的)回教徒。

pea /piː; pi/ *n* [C] plant with seeds in pods, used for food. 豌豆。⇨ the illus at vegetable. 參看 vegetable 之插圖。 ***as like as two peas (in a pod),*** exactly alike. 完全相似;一模一樣。 **ˈpea-chick, ˈpea-fowl, ˈpea-hen** *nn* ⇨ peacock. **ˈpea-flour** *n* [U] meal made from dried peas. 豌豆粉。 **ˈpea-green** *adj, n* bright light-green colour of young peas. 青豆色(的);淺綠色(的)。 **ˈpea-shooter** *n* (toy) tube from which dried peas are shot by blowing through the tube. (玩具)豆子槍(由管中吹出乾豌豆的一種玩具)。 **ˌpea-ˈsoup** *n* thick soup made from dried peas. 豌豆湯。 **ˌpea-ˈsouper** *n* (colloq) thick yellow fog. (俗)黃色濃霧。

peace /piːs; pis/ *n* [U] (not used in *pl*, but see examples for use of *indef art*) (不用作複數,但與不定冠詞連用者見以下例句) **1** state of freedom from war: 和平: *be at ~ with neighbouring countries.* 與鄰國和平相處。*After a brief ~* (= a brief period of ~) *war broke out again.* 經過短暫的和平,戰爭又爆發了。***make ~ (with),*** bring about ~ (with). (跟…)講和;(與…)重新和好。 **2** (often 常作 **P~**) treaty of ~: 和約: *P~/A P~ was signed between the two countries.* 兩國簽訂了和約。 **3** freedom from civil disorder. (社會的)安定;安寧;治安。 ***break the ~,*** cause civil disorder, rioting, etc. 破壞治安;妨害安寧。 ***keep the ~,*** obey the laws and refrain from disorder and strife. 維持治安;遵守法紀。 **breach of the ~,** a disturbance or riot. 妨害治安;騷亂;暴動。 **the King's/Queen's ~,** the general ~ of the country, as secured by law. (某王國的)社會安寧;治安。 **Justice of the P~,** (abbr 略作 **JP**) a magistrate. 保安官;地方執法官。 **4** rest; quiet; calm: 安穩;安靜;寧靜: *the ~ of the countryside;* 鄉間的寧靜; *~ of mind.* 心境的安寧。***at ~ (with),*** in a state of friendship or harmony: (與…)保持友好、和諧;平靜: *He's never at ~ with himself,* is always restless. 他老是坐立不安。 ***in ~,*** peacefully: 平安地;和平地: *live in ~ with one's neighbours.* 與鄰居和睦相處。***hold one's ~,*** keep silence; stop talking or arguing. 保持緘默;停止說話或爭論。 ***make one's ~ (with sb),*** settle a quarrel. (與某人)和解。 **ˈ~·maker** *n* person who restores friendly relations. 調停人;和事佬。 **ˈ~-offering** *n* sth offered to show that one is willing to make ~. 表示願意和解而獻出的東西。

peace·able /ˈpiːsəbl; ˈpisəbl/ *adj* not quarrelsome; free from fighting or uproar. 溫和的;和平的;平靜的。 **peace·ably** /-əblɪ; -əblɪ/ *adv*

peace·ful /ˈpiːsfl; ˈpisfəl/ *adj* **1** loving peace: 愛好和平的: *~ nations.* 愛好和平的國家。 **2** calm; quiet: 安詳的;寧靜的;和平的: *a ~ evening;* 寧靜的夜晚; *a ~ death.* 安詳的死亡。 **~ly** /-fəlɪ; -fəlɪ/ *adv* **~·ness** *n*

peach[1] /piːtʃ; pitʃ/ *n* **1** (tree with) juicy, round fruit with delicate yellowish-red skin and a rough stone-like seed; yellowish-red. 桃;桃樹;桃色。⇨ the illus at fruit. 參看 fruit 之插圖。 **2** (sl) person or thing greatly admired. (俚)極受愛慕的人或物。

peach[2] /piːtʃ; pitʃ/ *vi, vt* [VP2A, 3A, 6A] ~ ***(against/on/upon) (sb),*** (sl) inform (against); betray. (俚)告密;告發;出賣。

pea·cock /ˈpiːkɒk; ˈpiˌkɑk/ *n* large male bird noted for its fine tail feathers. 雄孔雀。⇨ the illus at rare. 參看 rare 之插圖。 **ˌ~-ˈblue** *adj, n* bright blue (colour). 孔雀藍(的);鮮藍色(的)。 **ˈpea-chick** *n* young pea-fowl. 小孔雀。 **ˈpea-fowl** *n* ~ or pea-hen. 孔雀。 **ˈpea-hen** *n* female of the ~. 雌孔雀。

pea-jacket /ˈpiː dʒækɪt; ˈpiˌdʒækɪt/ *n* short double-breasted overcoat of thick woollen cloth, as worn by sailors. 粗呢短外衣(如水手所穿着者)。

peak[1] /piːk; pik/ *n* **1** pointed top, esp of a mountain; point, eg of a beard. 尖頂;(尤指)山峯;(鬍鬚等的)尖端。⇨ the illus at mountain. 參看 mountain 之插圖。 **ˈP~ District,** area in Derbyshire, England having many ~s. (英國德貝郡的)山巒地區。 **2** pointed front part of a cap; projecting brim (to shade the eyes). 帽舌;帽簷。 **3** narrow part of a ship's hold at the bow (*ˈfore~*) or stern (*ˈafter~*). 船首艙(forepeak);船尾艙(afterpeak)。 **4** highest point in a record of figures that fluctuate: (升降不定之數字紀錄的)最高點: *~ hours of traffic,* times when the traffic is heaviest; 交通最頻繁的尖峯時刻; *industry's ~ hours,* when consumption of electric current, etc is highest; 工業用電等最多的尖峯時刻; *off-~ periods,* when traffic, consumption of current, etc is light; 非尖峯時刻(指交通量較小、用電量較小等的時間); *off-~ flights to Rome,* during the less busy times, eg during hours of darkness. 飛往羅馬的不擁擠班次(如夜間班次)。 **peaked** *adj* having a ~: 有尖頂的;有帽簷的: *~ed cap/roof.* 有簷的帽子(尖的屋頂)。

peak[2] /piːk; pik/ *vi* [VP2A] **1** reach the highest point, value, etc: 達於頂點: *Property prices have ~ed.* 房地產價格已達最高點。 **2** *~* ***and pine,*** waste away. 消瘦;憔悴。 **peaked** *pp* sharp-featured; thin, pale and weak-looking. 消瘦的;憔悴的。 **peaky** *adj* = peaked.

peal /piːl; pil/ *n* [C] **1** loud ringing of a bell or of a set of bells with different notes; changes rung upon a set of bells; set of bells tuned to each other. 響亮的鐘聲;一組鐘的變奏法;彼此諧音的一組鐘。 **2** loud echoing noise: 宏亮的回響聲;隆隆聲: *a ~ of thunder;* 雷聲隆隆; *~s of laughter.* 一陣大笑聲;哄堂大笑。 □ *vi, vt* **1** [VP2A, C] sound forth in a ~; ring out loudly. 隆隆地響;大聲鳴響。 **2** [VP6A] cause to ring or sound loudly. 使大聲鳴響。

pean /ˈpiːən; ˈpiən/ (US) (美) = **paean.**

pea·nut /ˈpiːnʌt; ˈpiˌnʌt/ *n* groundnut. 花生;落花生;花生米。 **ˌ~ ˈbutter,** paste of roasted ground ~s. 花生醬。 **ˌ~ ˈoil,** oil pressed from ~s, used in cooking, etc. 花生油。 **~s,** (sl, derog) small amount of money. (俚,貶)少數的錢;很少的錢。

pear /peə(r); pɛr/ *n* [C] (tree with) sweet, juicy fruit, usu tapering towards the stalk. 梨;梨樹。⇨ the illus at fruit. 參看 fruit 之插圖。

pearl /pɜːl; pɝl/ *n* **1** silvery-white or bluish-white spherical formation found inside the shells of some oysters, valued as a gem: 珍珠;蚌珠: *a necklace of ~s;* 珍珠項鍊; *a ~ necklace.* 珍珠項鍊。 **ˈ~-diver** *n* one who dives for ~-oysters. 潛水採珍珠貝的人。 **ˈ~-fishery** *n* place where ~-oysters are fished up. 珍珠貝採集場;養珠場。 **ˈ~-oyster** *n* kind in which ~s are found. 珍珠貝。 **2** = mother-of-~: 貝殼之珠母層: *~ buttons.* 貝殼鈕扣。⇨ mother. **3** small round fragment of various substances. 小圓形物。 **ˌ~-ˈbarley/-ˈsago** *nn* barley/sago rubbed into small ~-like grains. 珍珠麥(西米);被揉搓得像珠粒的大麥(西米)。 **4** sth that looks like a ~, eg a dew-drop; sb or sth very precious: 像珍珠之物(如露珠);極重要之人;極珍貴之物: *She's a ~ among women.* 她是婦女中的傑出者。 ***cast ~s before swine,*** (prov) offer sth valuable or beautiful to those who cannot appreciate it. (諺)把珍美之物獻給不能賞識者;對牛彈琴。 □ *vi* fish for ~s: 採珠: *go ~ing.* 去採珠。 **~y** *adj* of, like, ornamented with, ~s. 珠的;似珠的;以珍珠裝飾的。 **P~y**

King/Queen, costermonger wearing pearlies. 穿著飾有貝殼鈕扣衣服的小販。 **~·ies** *n pl* (the now festive) dress of some London costermongers, ornamented with many mother-of-~ buttons. (目前節日時) 倫敦某些小販所穿的衣服 (上面飾有許多貝殼鈕扣)。

pear·main /ˈpeəmeɪn ; ˈpɛrmen/ *n* variety of apple. 一種蘋果。

peas·ant /ˈpeznt ; ˈpɛznt/ *n* (not GB or US) countryman working on the land, either for wages or on a very small farm which he either rents or owns: (不用於英國或美國) 小農；佃農；農夫: (attrib) (形容用法) ~ *labour,* ⇨ for GB, *smallholder,* at small and, for US, *sharecropper* at share¹(1). 農工。 **~ry** /ˈpezntrɪ ; ˈpɛzntrɪ/ *n* the ~s of a country; ~s as a class. 一國的農民；農民階級。

pease /piːz ; piz/ *n* **~-pudding** *n* pudding of boiled peas. 豌豆布丁。

peat /piːt ; pit/ *n* [U] plant material partly decomposed by the action of water, found in bogs, used in horticulture, and as a fuel: 泥炭(用於園藝，並用作燃料): *a bag/bale of ~;* 一袋(包)泥炭; *a* ˈ*~-bog,* a marshy place where ~ is found; 泥炭田; *a ~ fire,* one on which cut pieces of ~ are burnt as fuel. 泥炭火。 **~y** *adj* of, like, smelling of, ~. 泥炭的；似泥炭的；有泥炭味的。

pebble /ˈpebl ; ˈpɛbl/ *n* small stone made smooth and round by the action of water, eg in a stream or on the seashore. (河裡或海邊的) 小圓石；卵石。 **peb·bly** /ˈpeblɪ ; ˈpɛblɪ/ *adj* covered with ~s: 覆有小圓石的: *a pebbly beach.* 遍布小圓石的海灘。

pe·can /pɪˈkæn *US:* pɪˈkɑːn ; pɪˈkɑn/ *n* [C] (nut of a) kind of hickory tree growing in the Mississippi region of the USA. (產於美國密西西比河流域的) 山核桃；山核桃樹。

pec·cable /ˈpekəbl ; ˈpɛkəbl/ *adj* (formal) liable to sin. (正式用語) 易犯罪的。

pec·ca·dillo /ˌpekəˈdɪləʊ ; ˌpɛkəˈdɪlo/ *n* (*pl* ~es or ~s /-ləʊz ; -loz/) small weakness in a person's character; small sin or fault. 性格上的小缺點；小過失。

pec·cary /ˈpekərɪ ; ˈpɛkərɪ/ *n* (*pl* -ries) kind of wild pig found in America. 美洲的一種野豬。

peck¹ /pek ; pɛk/ *n* measure of capacity for dry goods (= 2 gallons or approx 9 litres): 配克(乾貨容量單位，等於兩加侖或者約九公升): *a ~ of beans;* 一配克的豆; (fig) a lot: (喻) 許多: *a ~ of troubles.* 許多麻煩。 ⇨ App 5. 參看附錄五。

peck² /pek ; pɛk/ *vi, vt* **1** [VP2A, C, 3A, 6A] ~ *(at),* (try to) strike with the beak: 以喙啄: *hens ~ing at the corn;* 啄食穀粒的母雞; *cocks ~ing (at) the hens;* 啄母雞的公雞; (colloq) (俗) *~ at one's food,* (of a person) eat only small bits of food; eat without appetite. (指人) 只吃少量食物；吃東西沒有胃口。 ˈ**~·ing order,** order (within a flock of poultry) in which each bird submits to ~ing and domination by stronger birds and itself ~s and dominates weaker birds; any similar arrangement in a group of human beings: (一羣家禽中，强者啄欺弱者的) 强弱順序; (一羣人中) 强弱的順序: *Poor Tom! He's at the bottom of the ~ing order,* is dominated by all the members of his group. 可憐的湯姆！他是他們那羣人中最受氣的一個。 **2** [VP6A] get or make by striking with the beak: 啄食；啄到；啄成: *~ corn.* 啄食穀粒。 *The hens ~ed a hole in the sack.* 母雞在袋上啄了一個洞。 **3** (colloq) kiss hurriedly from habit or a sense of duty rather than from affection. (俗) 匆忙而敷衍地吻。 □ *n* **1** stroke with the beak; mark made by this. 啄擊；啄痕。 **2** (colloq) hurried, unemotional kiss. (俗) 匆忙而敷衍的吻。 **~er** *n* (GB sl) human nose; (fig) courage; spirits. (英俚) (人的) 鼻子; (喻) 勇氣；精神。 ˌ*keep your* ˈ*~er up,* stay cheerful; don't let your spirits droop. 保持愉快；打起精神來。 ˈ**~·ish** /-ɪʃ ; -ɪʃ/ *adj* (colloq) hungry. (俗) 飢餓的。

pec·tin /ˈpektɪn ; ˈpɛktɪn/ *n* [U] (chem) compound similar to sugar, formed in fruits by ripening process and by heating, eg when fruit is made into jam. (化學) 果膠(水果由成熟過程或加熱製醬等時所產生的一種似糖的黏膠質)。 **pec·tic** /ˈpektɪk ; ˈpɛktɪk/ *adj* of ~; producing ~: 果膠的；產生果膠的: *pectic acid.* 果膠酸。

pec·toral /ˈpektərəl ; ˈpɛktərəl/ *adj* **1** of, for, the chest or breast: 胸的；爲着胸部的: *a ~ muscle/fin.* 胸肌(胸鰭)。 **2** worn on the chest or breast: 佩於胸前的: *a ~ cross,* as worn by a bishop. 佩於胸前的十字架(如主教所佩者)。

pecu·late /ˈpekjʊleɪt ; ˈpɛkjəˌlet/ *vi, vt* embezzle. 侵吞；盜用；挪用(公款)。 **pecu·la·tion** /ˌpekjʊˈleɪʃn ; ˌpɛkjəˈleʃən/ *n* [U] peculating; [C] instance of this. 侵吞；盜用；挪用(公款)。

pe·cu·liar /pɪˈkjuːlɪə(r) ; pɪˈkjuljɚ/ *adj* **1** ~ *(to),* belonging exclusively; used, adopted, practised, only by: 特有的；獨特的；僅由…使用、採納、實行的: *customs ~ to these tribes;* 這些部落所特有的習俗; *a style ~ to the 18th century.* 十八世紀特有的風格。 **2** strange; unusual; odd. 奇怪的；罕有的；奇異的。 **3** particular; special: 特殊的；特別的: *a matter of ~ interest.* 特別有趣的事。 **~·ly** *adv* in a ~ manner: 獨特地；特別地；奇異地: *~ly annoying,* more than usually annoying. 特別惱人的。 **~·ity** /pɪˌkjuːlɪˈærətɪ ; pɪˌkjulɪˈærətɪ/ *n* (*pl* -ties) **1** [U] the quality of being ~. 獨特性；特質；特色。 **2** [C] sth distinctive or characteristic. 獨特之處；特徵；特點。 **3** [C] sth odd or strange: 奇異之事物；怪癖: *~ities of speech/dress/behaviour.* 言語(服裝，行爲)的怪異。

pe·cuni·ary /pɪˈkjuːnɪərɪ *US:* -ɪerɪ ; pɪˈkjunɪˌɛrɪ/ *adj* (formal) of money: (正式用語) 錢的: *~ aid;* 金錢援助; *work without ~ reward.* 沒有金錢報酬的工作。

peda·gogue (US also **-gog**) /ˈpedəgɒg ; ˈpɛdəˌgɑg/ *n* (formal) schoolmaster; (colloq) pedantic teacher. (正式用語) 教師; (俗) 賣弄學問的教師。 **peda·gogy** /ˈpedəgɒdʒɪ ; ˈpɛdəˌgodʒɪ/ *n* [U] science of teaching. 教學法。 **peda·gog·ic** /ˌpedəˈgɒdʒɪk ; ˌpɛdəˈgɑdʒɪk/, **peda·gogi·cal** /-ɪkl ; -ɪkl/ *adjj* of pedagogy. 教學法的。

pedal¹ /ˈpedl ; ˈpɛdl/ *n* lever (eg on a bicycle, sewing-machine, organ or piano) worked by the foot or feet: (如脚踏車、縫級機、風琴或鋼琴的) 踏板: (attrib) (形容用法) *~ cyclist;* 騎脚踏車者; *~ boat,* propelled by ~s. 用脚踩動的船。 ⇨ the illus at bicycle, church, key. 參看 bicycle, church, key 之插圖。 □ *vi, vt* (-ll-, US also -l-) [VP2A, C, 6A] use a ~ or ~s (for playing an organ, riding a bicycle, etc); move or work by the use of a ~ or ~s: 踩踏板；踩踏板轉動或操作(如彈風琴、騎脚踏車等): *The boy ~led away on his tricycle.* 那男孩踩着他的三輪脚踏車走了。

pedal² /ˈpedl ; ˈpɛdl/ *adj* (zool) of the foot or feet. (動物) 脚的。

ped·ant /ˈpednt ; ˈpɛdnt/ *n* person who lays too much stress on book-learning, technical knowledge, rules and adherence to rules. 太過强調書本學問、專門知識、規則等的人；拘泥於規則的人；迂腐的人；書獃子；學究。 **~ry** /ˈpedntrɪ ; ˈpɛdntrɪ/ *n* [U] tiresome and unnecessary display of learning; too much insistence upon formal rules; [C] instance of this. 賣弄學問；過於拘泥形式上的規則。 **pe·dan·tic** /pɪˈdæntɪk ; pɪˈdæntɪk/ *adj* of or like a ~. 學究的；迂腐的。 **pe·dan·ti·cally** /-klɪ ; -klɪ/ *adv*

peddle /ˈpedl ; ˈpɛdl/ *vi, vt* **1** [VP2A] be a pedlar; go from house to house trying to sell small articles. 做小販；沿街叫賣；挨家兜售。 **2** [VP6A] deal out in small quantities: 零售；散播: *She loves to ~ gossip round the village.* 她喜歡在村裡到處說閒話。 **ped·dler** *n* = pedlar. **ped·dling** *adj* petty; trivial: 細小的；瑣碎的: *peddling details.* 瑣碎的細節。

ped·er·asty /ˈpedəræstɪ ; ˈpɛdəˌræstɪ/ *n* [U] amorous or sexual relations between a man and a boy. 雞姦；男色(指男人與男童之間的色情或性關係)。 **ped·er·ast** *n* man who practices ~. 雞姦者；男色者。

ped·estal /ˈpedɪstl ; ˈpɛdɪstl/ *n* base of a column; base for a statue or other work of art; each of the two supports of a knee-hole writing-desk. 柱基;(塑像或藝術品的)墊座;(基座式書桌的)基座。Hence, 由此產生，ˈ~ *desk.* 基座式書桌。***knock sb off his ~,*** show that he is no longer highly regarded. 不再推崇某人;不再看重某人。***set sb on a ~,*** make him an object of high regard. 把某人當做偶像崇拜;把某人理想化。

pe·des·trian /pɪˈdestrɪən ; pəˈdɛstrɪən/ *n* person walking in a street, etc: 行人;走路的人: *~s killed in traffic accidents.* 車禍中死亡的行人。**~ crossing,** street crossing specially marked, where ~s have priority over traffic. 行人穿越道。**~ precinct,** ⇨ precinct. □ *adj* **1** connected with walking. 步行的。 **2** (of writing, a person's way of making speeches, etc) prosaic; dull; uninspired. (指文章、演說的方式等)平淡的;單調的;沉悶的。

pedi·at·rics /ˌpiːdɪˈætrɪks ; ˌpidɪˈætrɪks/ *n* (with *sing v*) branch of medicine concerned with children and their illnesses. (用單數動詞)小兒科;兒科學。**pedia·tric·ian** /ˌpiːdɪəˈtrɪʃn ; ˌpidɪəˈtrɪʃən/ *n* physician who specializes in ~. 小兒科醫師。

pedi·cab /ˈpedɪkæb ; ˈpɛdɪˌkæb/ *n* (in some Asian countries) tricycle with one seat for the man in charge and a seat behind for two passengers, used as a form of public transport. (在某些亞洲國家內用的)三輪車;三輪人力車。

pedi·cure /ˈpedɪkjʊə(r) ; ˈpɛdɪˌkjur/ *n* treatment of the feet, esp toe-nails, corns, bunions, etc. 修脚指甲;脚上雞眼、蹈囊炎腫等的治療;脚病的治療。

pedi·gree /ˈpedɪgriː ; ˈpɛdəˌgri/ *n* **1** [C] line of ancestors: 家系;家譜: *proud of their long ~s;* 爲他們長遠的家系而驕傲; [U] ancestry, esp ancient descent. 世系;門第;出身。 **2** (attrib) having a line of descent that has been recorded: (形容用法)有血統紀錄的: *~ cattle;* 純種牛; *a ~ poodle.* 有血統書的貴賓狗。

pedi·ment /ˈpedɪmənt ; ˈpɛdəmənt/ *n* (in Gk architecture) triangular part over the front of a building; similar part over the portico of a building in other styles of architecture. (希臘建築)正面上方的三角牆;門廊上方的三角頂。⇨ the illus at column. 參看 column 之挿圖。

ped·lar, ped·dler /ˈpedlə(r) ; ˈpɛdlɚ/ *n* person who travels about selling small articles. 小販。

ped·ometer /pɪˈdɒmɪtə(r) ; pɪˈdɑmətɚ/ *n* device which measures the number of steps taken by a walker, and the approximate distance he walks. (步行者計步數及距離的)計步表;步程計;萬步表。

pee /piː ; pi/ *vi* [VP2A] (colloq) urinate: (俗)解小便: *Do you want to pee?* 你要解小便嗎? □ *n* [U] urine: 尿: *a puddle of pee;* 一灘尿; [C] act of urinating: 解小便: *I must go for/must have a pee.* 我必須去小便。

peek /piːk ; pik/ *vi* **~ at,** peep at. 窺視;偷看。□ *n* quick look: 一瞥;匆忙看過: *have a quick ~ over the fence.* 匆匆地看了籬牆那邊一眼。

peek-a-boo /ˌpiːk ə ˈbuː ; ˈpikəˌbu/ *n* game for amusing a small child, in which one covers and then uncovers the face, repeatedly, saying '~!' as one does this. 躲躲猫(面孔一隱一現以逗小孩之遊戲)。

peel /piːl ; pil/ *vt, vi* **~ *(off),*** **1** [VP6A, 15B] take the skin off (fruit, etc): 剝;削(水果等的)皮: *~ a banana;* 剝一根香蕉的皮; *~ potatoes.* 削馬鈴薯的皮。 **2** [VP2A, C] come off in strips or flakes: 剝落;脫皮: *These potatoes ~ easily,* the skin comes off them easily. 這些馬鈴薯容易脫皮。*The wall-paper is ~ing off.* 壁紙開始脫落了。*After a day in the hot sun my skin began to ~/my face ~ed.* 曬了一天炎熱的太陽後,我的皮膚開始脫皮了(我的臉脫皮了)。*The bark of plane-trees ~s off regularly.* 法國梧桐的樹皮會定時脫落。*It was so hot that we all ~ed off* (= undressed) *and jumped into the lake.* 天氣太熱，我們全都脫光了衣服跳入湖中。 □ *n* [U] skin of fruit, some vegetables, young shoots, etc. (水果、蔬菜、嫩枝等的)皮。⇨ the illus at fruit. 參看 fruit 之挿圖。**candied ~,** ⇨ candy. 蜜餞果皮。**~er** *n* (in compounds) device used for ~ing, eg potatoes. (用於複合字中)(用來削馬鈴薯皮等的)刨刀;水果刀。 **~·ings** *n pl* parts ~ed off (esp of potatoes). 削下的皮(尤指馬鈴薯皮)。

peep¹ /piːp ; pip/ *n* **1** short, quick look, often one taken secretly or inquisitively; incomplete view: 偷看;瞥見;窺視;不完全的景象;隱約看見: *have a ~ at sb through the window.* 從窗口偷看某人。**ˈ~-hole** *n* small opening in a wall, partition, etc through which one can have a ~. 窺孔。 **ˈ~-show** *n* exhibition of small pictures to be seen through a magnifying lens in a small opening. 西洋鏡(從裝有放大鏡的小孔看箱中的小圖片)。 **2** the first light (of day): (一天的)破曉: *~ of day,* dawn. 黎明。□ *vi* [VP2A, C] **1 ~ *(at),*** take a ~ (at); look slyly or cautiously: 窺視;偷看: *~ through a key-hole at sth;* 從鑰匙孔偷看某事物; *neighbours ~ing at us from behind curtains.* 隣人從窗簾後偷看我們。**ˌ~ing ˈTom,** name used of a prurient person who spies on people who think they are alone; voyeur. 愛偷看別人的好色男子;窺淫狂者。 **2** come slowly or partly into view: 微現;慢慢露出: *The moon ~ed out from behind the clouds.* 月亮從雲後慢慢露出。**~er** *n* **1** person who ~s. 窺視者;偷看者。**2** (sl) eye. (俚)眼睛。

peep² /piːp ; pip/ *n* [C] weak, shrill sound made by mice, young birds, etc. (鼠、小鳥等的)吱吱聲;啾啾聲。□ *vi* make this sound. 吱吱地叫;啾啾地叫。

pee·pul, pi·pal /ˈpiːpəl ; ˈpipəl/ *n* large Indian fig-tree. (印度產的)菩提樹。

peer¹ /pɪə(r) ; pɪr/ *n* **1** equal in rank, merit or quality: 同輩;同等之人;同儕;匹敵: *It will not be very easy to find his ~.* 不太容易找到與他匹敵的人。 **2** (in GB) member of one of the degrees of nobility, eg duke, marquis, earl, viscount, baron. (英)貴族;公侯伯子男(爵)中之任一個。**~ of the realm,** person with the right to sit in the House of Lords. 可成爲上議院議員的貴族。**ˈlife ~,** one elected to the House of Lords for life only (contrasted with a **heˈreditary ~**). 終身職上議院議員(此等被選爲上議院議員者只能任職一生,而不能傳後; 與 hereditary peer '世襲上議院議員' 相對)。**~·ess** /ˈpɪəres ; ˈpɪrɪs/ *n* woman ~; wife of a ~(2). 女貴族;女上議院議員;貴族夫人;上議院議員夫人。 **~·less** *adj* without a ~(1); without equal. 無匹敵的;無雙的。

peer² /pɪə(r) ; pɪr/ *vi* [VP2A, 3A] **~ *(at/into),*** look closely, as if unable to see well: 凝視;盯着看;瞇着眼看: *~ into dark corners;* 凝視黑暗的角落; *~ing at her over his spectacles.* 從他的眼鏡上方盯着她。

peer·age /ˈpɪərɪdʒ ; ˈpɪrɪdʒ/ *n* **1** the whole body of peers; rank of peer(2). 全體貴族;貴族爵位;上議院議員的地位、身分。***raise sb to the ~,*** elect sb to the ~. 封一個人爲貴族。 **2** book containing a list of peers(2) with their ancestry. 貴族名鑑(記載所有貴族及其世系)。

peeve /piːv ; piv/ *vt* (colloq) vex; annoy. (俗)使氣惱;使惱怒。**~d** *adj* (colloq) annoyed. (俗)氣惱的;惱怒的。

pee·vish /ˈpiːvɪʃ ; ˈpivɪʃ/ *adj* irritable. 易怒的;脾氣乖張的。**~·ly** *adv* **~·ness** *n*

pee·wit /ˈpiːwɪt ; ˈpiwɪt/ = pewit.

peg¹ /peg ; pɛg/ *n* **1** wooden or metal pin or bolt, usu pointed at one end, used to fasten parts of woodwork together. (木或金屬的)栓;釘。***a square peg in a round hole,*** a person unsuited to the position he fills. 不稱職的人。 **2** pin driven into the ground to hold a rope (*a ˈtent-peg*), or fastened to a wall or door (*ˈhat and ˈcoat pegs*), or to mark a position or boundary. 繫帳篷的樁;掛衣帽的釘;定位置或界限的樁。***(buy sth) off the peg,*** (colloq) (buy clothes) ready-made (as if off a peg in a shop). (俗)(買)現成的(衣服),(好像從店裡的衣服釘上取下來的一樣)。 **3** **ˈclothes-peg,**

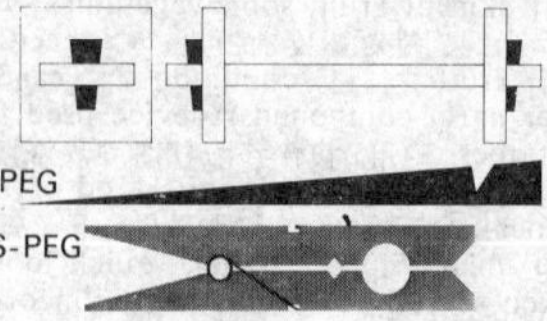

device for holding laundered clothes in place on a line. 曬衣服的夾子。 **4** (fig) theme, pretext or excuse: (喻)主題; 遁詞; 藉口: *a peg on which to hang a speech.* 演說的主題。 **5** wooden screw for tightening or loosening the string of a violin, etc. (提琴等用於調整弦線鬆緊的)軫; 木栓。 ⇨ the illus at string. 參看 string 之插圖。 ***ˌtake sb ˈdown a peg (or two),*** humble him. 抑某人的傲氣; 挫某人的銳氣; 煞某人的威風。 **6** piece of wood for stopping the vent of a cask, etc. (塞桶孔等的)木塞。 **7** (colloq) wooden leg. (俗)木腿; 義腿。

peg² /peg ; pɛg/ *vt, vi* (-gg-) **1** [VP6A, 15B] ***peg sth (down),*** fasten with pegs: 以栓、釘、樁等釘牢或繫緊: *peg a tent down.* 把帳篷用木樁繫牢在地上。 ***peg sb down,*** (fig) make him keep to a certain line of action, restrict him to the rules, etc. (喻)約束某人; 管住某人。 **2** [VP15B] ***peg sth out,*** mark by means of pegs fixed in the ground; show (a score, esp at cribbage) by means of pegs. 以木樁釘在地上標出; 以木樁畫分; (尤指一種紙牌戲中)以木釘在有孔的木板上記(分)。 ***level pegging,*** (often fig) making progress at the same rate. (常作比喻用法)以相同比率進展; 以同樣速度進步。 **3** [VP6A, 15B] (comm) keep (prices, etc) steady by buying and selling (stocks) freely at fixed prices; keep (wages) steady: (商)以固定價格隨時買賣股票以穩定(價格等); 使(工資)穩定: *wage-pegging efforts that failed.* 業已失敗的穩定工資的努力。 **4** [VP2C] ***peg away at,*** keep on working at. 繼續做。 ***peg out,*** (colloq) die. (俗)死亡。

pei·gnoir /ˈpeɪnwɑ:(r) ; penˈwɑr/ *n* woman's loose dressing gown. 婦女梳妝時所著的寬袍; 女用浴袍; 女用寬大便服。

pe·jor·at·ive /pɪˈdʒɒrətɪv *US:* -ˈdʒɔ:r- ; ˈpidʒəˌretɪv/ *adj* depreciatory; disparaging; deteriorating in use or meaning. 輕視的; 蔑視的; (意義或用法)有貶抑意味的。 **~·ly** *adv*

peke /pi:k ; pik/ *n* short for *pekinese (dog).* 哈巴狗(簡稱)。

pe·kin·ese /ˌpi:kɪˈni:z ; ˌpikɪnˈiz/ *n* small Chinese dog with long, silky hair. 哈巴狗。 ⇨ the illus at dog. 參看 dog 之插圖。

pe·koe /ˈpi:kəʊ ; ˈpiko/ *n* [U] high grade of black tea. 白毫(一種上等紅茶)。

pelf /pelf ; pɛlf/ *n* [U] (usu contemptuous use) money. (通常爲輕蔑用語)錢。

peli·can /ˈpelɪkən ; ˈpɛlɪkən/ *n* large water-bird with a large bill under which hangs a pouch for storing food. 塘鵝; 鵜鶘。 ⇨ the illus at water. 參看 water 之插圖。

pe·lisse /peˈli:s ; pəˈlis/ *n* mantle. 無袖外套; 斗篷。

pel·let /ˈpelɪt ; ˈpɛlɪt/ *n* **1** small ball of sth soft, eg wet paper, bread, made, for example, by rolling between the fingers. (用手指將濕的紙或麵包等撚成的)小團; 小球; 小丸。 **2** slug of small shot, eg as used from an air-gun. 小彈丸(如氣槍所用者)。 **3** pill. 藥丸。

pell-mell /ˌpelˈmel ; ˈpɛlˈmɛl/ *adv* in a hurrying, disorderly manner. 匆忙雜亂地; 混亂地; 亂七八糟地。

pel·lu·cid /peˈlu:sɪd ; pəˈlusɪd/ *adj* (lit, fig) very clear. (字面, 喻)清澈的; 清晰的。 **~·ly** *adv*

pel·met /ˈpelmɪt ; ˈpɛlmɪt/ *n* strip (of wood, cloth, etc) above a window or door to conceal a curtain rod. (窗簾或門簾上方用以遮蔽簾子拉桿的)狹長木框、短帷幔等。

pe·lota /pəˈləʊtə ; pəˈlotə/ *n* [U] ball game popular in Spain, Latin America and the Phillippines, the players using a long basket strapped to the wrist to hit the ball against a wall. 回力球(西班牙、拉丁美洲和菲律賓風行之一種球戲)。

pelt¹ /pelt ; pɛlt/ *n* animal's skin with the fur or hair on it. 帶毛的獸皮; 毛皮。

pelt² /pelt ; pɛlt/ *vt, vi* **1** [VP6A, 14] ***~ sth (at sb); ~ sb (with sth),*** attack by throwing things at: 投擲; 投擊: *~ sb with stones/snowballs/mud.* 以石頭(雪球, 泥巴)擲向某人。 **2** [VP2C] (of rain, etc) beat down; fall heavily: (指雨等)急降; 下得很大: *It was ~ing with rain.* 大雨傾盆而降。 *The rain was ~ing down.* 大雨傾盆。 *The hail was ~ing against the roof.* 冰雹猛打着屋頂。 □ *n* ~ing. 投擲; 投擊; 急降。 ***at full ~,*** (running) as fast as possible. (跑步)儘速地; 儘快地。

pel·vis /ˈpelvɪs ; ˈpɛlvɪs/ *n* (*pl* ~es or pelves /ˈpelvi:z ; ˈpɛlviz/) (anat) bony frame within the hip-bones and the lower part of the backbone, holding the kidneys, rectum, bladder, etc. (解剖)(人體的)骨盤; 骨盆。 ⇨ the illus at skeleton. 參看 skeleton 之插圖。 **pel·vic** /ˈpelvɪk ; ˈpɛlvɪk/ *adj* of the ~. 骨盤的; 骨盆的。

pem·mi·can /ˈpemɪkən ; ˈpɛmɪkən/ *n* [U] dried lean meat beaten and mixed into cakes (as by N American Indians). 乾肉餅(如北美洲印地安人所製者)。

pen¹ /pen ; pɛn/ *n* **1** (formerly) quill-feather, pointed and split at the end, for writing with ink; (mod use) instrument with a pointed piece of split metal (*ˈpen-nib*) fixed into a holder (*ˈpen-holder*) of wood or other material; ballpoint-pen; fountain-pen, ⇨ *ball(point)-pen* at ball¹(1) and *fountain-pen* at fountain. (昔時之)鵝毛筆(用翎羽削尖剪裂爲筆, 蘸墨水書寫); (現在之)蘸水筆(用金屬筆尖 'pen-nib, 固定於木製或其他材料製成之筆管 'pen-holder 而成); 原子筆; 鋼筆。 **2** (style of) writing: 寫作; 文體: *make a living with one's pen.* 靠寫作爲生。 **3** **ˌpen-and-ˈink,** (attrib) drawn with these: (形容用法)用鋼筆墨水畫出的: *a pen-and-ink sketch.* 鋼筆畫素描。 **ˈpen-friend** *n* person (eg in another country) with whom one has a friendship through exchanges of letters. 筆友。 **ˈpen·knife** *n* small folding knife, usu carried in the pocket. (可以摺起來放在口袋裡攜帶的)小刀; 削鉛筆刀。 **pen·man·ship** /ˈpenmənʃɪp ; ˈpɛnmənˌʃɪp/ *n* [U] art or style of handwriting. 書法; 筆跡。 **ˈpen-name** *n* name used by a writer instead of his real name. 筆名。 **ˈpen-pusher** *n* (derog) clerk. (貶)書記; 抄寫員。 □ *vt* (-nn-) write (a letter, etc). 寫(信等)。

pen² /pen ; pɛn/ *n* **1** small enclosure for cattle, sheep, poultry, etc or other purposes. (牛、羊、家禽等的)圈; 圍欄; 檻。 **2** **(ˈplay)-pen,** portable enclosure for a very small child to play in safety. (供幼兒遊玩於其中的)安全圍欄。 **3** bomb-proof shelter for submarines. (供潛水艇停泊的)防彈掩體(如修理潛水艇之船塢, 上有厚混凝土頂蓋者)。 □ *vt* (-nn-) [VP15A, B] ***pen up/in,*** shut up in, or as in, a pen. 關入欄中; 把…關起來。

penal /ˈpi:nl ; ˈpinḷ/ *adj* connected with punishment: 刑罰的; 刑事的: *~ laws;* 刑法; *a ~ offence,* one for which there is legal punishment. 刑事罪。 **ˌ~ ˈservitude,** imprisonment with hard labour. 勞役監禁。 **ˈ~ settlement/colony,** one used as a place of punishment. 監禁地; 充軍地。 **~ly** /ˈpi:nəlɪ ; ˈpinḷɪ/ *adv*

pe·nal·ize /ˈpi:nəlaɪz ; ˈpinḷˌaɪz/ *vt* **1** [VP6A] make (sth) penal; declare to be punishable by law. 規定(某事物)應罰; 宣告有罪應罰。 **2** [VP6A, 14] ***~ sb (for sth),*** place at a disadvantage; give a penalty(2) to (a player, competitor, etc). 使不利; 處罰(運動員、比賽者等)。 **pe·nal·iz·ation** /ˌpi:nəlaɪˈzeɪʃn *US:* -lɪˈz- ; ˌpinḷɪˈzeʃən/ *n*

pen·alty /ˈpenltɪ ; ˈpɛnḷtɪ/ *n* (*pl* -ties) **1** [U] punishment for wrongdoing, for failure to obey rules or keep an agreement; [C] what is imposed (imprisonment, payment of a fine, etc) as punishment; (fig) suffering which a wrongdoer brings upon himself or others: 懲罰;刑罰;處罰(如服刑、罰款等);(喻)報應: *Spitting forbidden*: ~ *£5*. 禁止吐痰:違者罰款五鎊。*The* ~ (eg in a business agreement) *for non-performance of contract is heavy*. 不履行契約的罰款很重。'~ **clause**, (comm) clause in a contract requiring payment for breaking it. (商)合約中違約罰款之條款; 罰款規定。 ***on/under ~ of (death, etc)***, with (death, etc) as the ~: 違者處(死刑等): *forbidden under* ~ *of death*. 違者處以死刑的;以死刑嚴禁的。 **2** (in sport, competitions, etc) disadvantage to which a player or team must submit for breaking a rule: (運動、競賽等)犯規的處罰: *The referee awarded a* ~. 裁判員判罰球。'~ **area**, (football) part of the ground in front of the goal where a breach of the rules by defenders gives the opposing team the right to a free kick (*a* '~ *kick*) at the goal. (足球)罰球區(如守方球員在此區內犯規,則應由對方罰十二碼球 a penalty kick)。 **3** handicap imposed upon a player or team for winning a previous contest. (對上次比賽中獲勝者或獲勝隊給予的)困難;障礙。

pen·ance /ˈpenəns ; ˈpɛnəns/ *n* [U] **1** punishment which one imposes upon oneself to show repentance, eg upon the advice of a priest. (表示懺悔的)自我懲罰;(贖罪的)苦行。***do ~ (for sth)***, perform an act of ~ (for sth). (爲…)苦行贖罪。 **2** (RC Church) name for the sacrament that includes contrition, confession and penance. (天主教)告解。

pence /pens ; pɛns/ *n* ⇨ penny.

pen·chant /ˈpɑːnʃɑːn *US:* ˈpentʃənt ; ˈpɛntʃənt/ *n* (F) ***a ~ (for)***, taste, liking, inclination: (法)喜愛;愛好;傾向: *have a* ~ *for marshmallows*. 喜愛藥蜀葵根製成的甜食。

pen·cil /ˈpensl ; ˈpɛnsl̩/ *n* instrument for drawing or writing with, esp of graphite or coloured chalk enclosed in wood or fixed in a metal holder; stick of cosmetic material: 鉛筆;彩色畫筆;眉筆: *an* ˈ*eyebrow* ~. 一枝眉筆。□ *vt* (-ll-, US also -l-) [VP6A] write, draw, mark, with a ~: 用鉛筆畫、寫、作記號: ~*led eyebrows*. 畫過的眉毛。

pen·dant /ˈpendənt ; ˈpɛndənt/ *n* **1** ornament which hangs down, esp one attached to a necklet, bracelet, etc; lustre attached to a chandelier, etc. (項鍊、手鐲、枝形吊燈架等的)墜子;垂環;垂飾。**2** (naut) (航海) = pennant.

pen·dent /ˈpendənt ; ˈpɛndənt/ *adj* (formal) (正式用語) **1** hanging; overhanging: 下垂的;懸掛的;吊着的: ~ *rocks*. 懸岩。 **2** = pending.

pend·ing /ˈpendɪŋ ; ˈpɛndɪŋ/ *adj* waiting to be decided or settled: 待決的; 未決的: *The lawsuit was then* ~. 那件訴訟那時尚未解決。□ *prep* **1** during: 當…的時候;在…期間: ~ *these discussions*. 在討論期間。 **2** until: 直到…;在…之前: ~ *his decision*. 在他決定之前。

pen·du·lous /ˈpendjʊləs *US:* -dʒʊləs ; ˈpɛndʒələs/ *adj* (formal) hanging down loosely so as to swing freely: (正式用語)下垂的;懸垂而搖擺不定的: *the* ~ *nests of the weaver-birds*. 鸞鳥的垂巢。

pen·du·lum /ˈpendjʊləm *US:* -dʒʊləm ; ˈpɛndʒələm/ *n* weighted rod hung from a fixed point so that it swings freely, esp one to regulate the movement of a clock. 擺;擺錘;(尤指)鐘擺。 ***the swing of the ~***, (fig) the movement of public opinion from one extreme to the other. (喻)輿論之自一個極端轉變到另一個極端。

pen·etrable /ˈpenɪtrəbl ; ˈpɛnətrəbl̩/ *adj* (formal) that can be penetrated. (正式用語)能穿入的;能滲透的;能透過的。 **pen·etra·bil·ity** /ˌpenɪtrəˈbɪlətɪ ; ˌpɛnətrəˈbɪlətɪ/ *n*

pen·etrate /ˈpenɪtreɪt ; ˈpɛnəˌtret/ *vt, vi* **1** [VP6A, 3A] ***~ (into/to/through)***, make a way into, etc; (fig) see into, etc: 進入; 貫穿; (喻)看穿;透視: *The cat's sharp claws ~d my skin*. 貓的尖爪刺入我的皮膚。*The mist ~d (into) the room*. 霧滲入房間。*He ~d their thoughts*. 他看穿了他們的心思。*Our eyes could not ~ the darkness*. 我們的眼睛在黑暗裡看不見。*We soon ~d his disguise*, saw through it, knew who he really was. 我們很快地看穿了他的僞裝。 **2** ***be ~d with***, be filled with: 充滿: *be ~d with a desire for mystical experiences*. 充滿了要獲得神秘經驗的欲望。 **pen·etrat·ing** *adj* **1** (of a person, his mind) able to see and understand quickly and deeply. (指人、其思想)聰慧的;有眼光的;敏銳的。 **2** (voices, cries, etc) piercing; loud and clear. (指聲音、喊叫等)尖銳的;響亮的。 **pen·etrat·ing·ly** *adv*

pen·etra·tion /ˌpenɪˈtreɪʃn ; ˌpɛnəˈtreʃən/ *n* [U] **1** penetrating: 穿入;浸入;滲透;貫穿: *peaceful* ~, acquiring influence, control, etc without the use of force, eg by trade, supplying a country with capital. 和平的滲透。 **2** mental quickness; ability to grasp ideas. (心智的)敏銳;洞察力。

pen·etra·tive /ˈpenɪtrətɪv *US:* -treɪtɪv ; ˈpɛnəˌtretɪv/ *adj* able to penetrate; intelligent. 能穿入的;能滲透的;能貫穿的;敏銳的;有眼光的;聰慧的。

pen-friend /ˈpen frend ; ˈpɛnˌfrɛnd/ ⇨ pen[1](3).

pen·guin /ˈpeŋgwɪn ; ˈpɛŋgwɪn/ *n* seabird of the Antarctic with wings used for swimming. 企鵝(南極產海鳥,有用於游泳之翼)。⇨ the illus at water. 參看 water 之插圖。

peni·cil·lin /ˌpenɪˈsɪlɪn ; ˌpɛnɪˈsɪlɪn/ *n* [U] antibiotic drug that, by changing the chemical environment of germs, prevents them from surviving or multiplying. 盤尼西林;青黴素(一種抗生素)。

pen·in·sula /pəˈnɪnsjʊlə *US:* -nsələ ; pəˈnɪnsələ/ *n* area of land, eg Italy, almost surrounded by sea and projecting far into the sea. 半島。**pen·in·su·lar** /-lə(r) ; -lɚ/ *adj* of or like a ~. 半島的;似半島的;半島形的。

pe·nis /ˈpiːnɪs ; ˈpinɪs/ *n* organ of urination and copulation of a male animal. (雄性動物的)生殖器;陰莖。

peni·tence /ˈpenɪtəns ; ˈpɛnətəns/ *n* [U] ***~ (for)***, sorrow and regret (for wrongdoing, sin). 懺悔;悔罪;後悔(所犯之錯、所犯之罪)。

peni·tent /ˈpenɪtənt ; ˈpɛnətənt/ *adj* feeling regret; showing regret or remorse. 懺悔的;悔罪的;後悔的。 **~·ly** *adv*

peni·ten·tial /ˌpenɪˈtenʃl ; ˌpɛnəˈtɛnʃəl/ *adj* of penitence or penance. 悔悟的;後悔的;贖罪苦行的。**~·ly** /-ʃəlɪ ; -ʃəlɪ/ *adv*

peni·ten·tiary /ˌpenɪˈtenʃərɪ ; ˌpɛnəˈtɛnʃərɪ/ *n* (*pl* -ries) (US) prison for persons guilty of serious crimes, esp one in which reform of the prisoners is the main aim. (美)監獄(尤指以感化犯人爲主要目的者);感化院。□ *adj* of reformatory treatment. 感化的。

pen-name /ˈpen neɪm ; ˈpɛnˌnem/ ⇨ pen[1](3).

pen·nant /ˈpenənt ; ˈpɛnənt/ *n* flag (usu long and narrow) used on a ship for signalling, identification, etc. (船上用的)信號旗;小旗(通常爲狹長者)。⇨ the illus at barque. 參看 barque 之插圖。

pen·ni·less /ˈpenɪlɪs ; ˈpɛnlɪs/ *adj* without any money: 一文不名的;分文沒有的;貧窮的: *I'm ~ until pay-day*. 在發薪日以前我分文沒有。

pen·non /ˈpenən ; ˈpɛnən/ *n* **1** long, narrow (usu triangular) flag, as used by a knight on his lance, by soldiers in lancer regiments, and on ships, eg in signalling. (騎士矛上的)小三角旗;(槍騎兵團士兵所用的)小三角旗; (船上用的)小旗(如發信號所用者)。 **2** (US) flag of this shape as a school banner, with the school's name or initials on it. (美)長三角形校旗。

penn'orth /ˈpenəθ ; ˈpɛnɚθ/ *n* = *pennyworth*; ⇨ penny(5).

penny /ˈpenɪ ; ˈpɛnɪ/ *n* (*pl* pence /pens ; pɛns/ when combined with numbers, as in ˈ*sixpence*, 'tenpence, ˌeighteen'pence; pl pennies /'penɪz; 'pɛnɪz/ when used of individual coins: 與數目字連用時,複數爲 pence, 如 sixpence 六辨士, tenpence 十辨士, eighteenpence 十八辨士; 指硬幣的個數時,複數爲 pennies: *Please give me ten pennies for this tenpence piece.* 請把這個十辨士的銅幣換成十個辨士。) ⇨ App 5. 參看附錄五。 **1** (until 1971) British bronze coin (abbr 略作 **d**) worth one twelfth of a shilling. (到1971年爲止)辨士(價值十二分之一先令的英國銅幣)。 **2** (since decimal coinage was introduced, 1971) British bronze coin (abbr 略作 **p**) worth one hundredth of a pound: (1971年採用十進位幣制之後)(新)辨士(價值百分之一英鎊): *These cigarettes are 70 pence a packet.* 這些香煙賣七十辨士一包。 **3** (US colloq) cent. (美俗)一分(等於 cent)。 **4** (phrases, all pre-1971 in origin) (片語用法,全部沿用 1971 年以前用法) ***(cost) a pretty ~,*** a large sum of money. (值)很多錢。 ***in for a ~, in for a pound,*** sth that one has begun must be finished, whatever the cost may be. 一不做,二不休;一旦開始,無論如何必須完成。 ***~ wise and pound foolish,*** careful in small matters and wasteful in large matters. 小處節省,大處浪費;小處聰明,大處糊塗;明於小事而昧於大事。 ***turn an honest ~,*** earn a little money honestly. 正正當當地賺一點錢。 **5** (compounds) (複合字) ˌ~ **'dreadful,** (colloq) cheap, sensational, popular novel, etc. (俗)聳人聽聞而且很流行的廉價小說等。 '~ **pincher,** (colloq) miser. (俗)守財奴;吝嗇鬼。'~ **pinching** *adj* mean; miserly. 吝嗇的。 '**~·weight** *n* 24 grains, one-twentieth of an ounce Troy. (英國金衡制)英錢(二十四喱或二十分之一兩重)。 ⇨ App 5. 參看附錄五。 ˌ~ **'whistle,** simple, cheap musical pipe. 一種簡單、便宜的小笛。'**~·worth** (also 亦作 **penn'orth** /'penəθ; 'pɛnɚθ/) *n* as much as can be bought for a ~. 一辨士之值;值一辨士之物。 ***a good／bad ~worth,*** a good／bad bargain. 合算(不合算)的交易。 **6** (from the use of pennies in coin-operated machines, locks on doors, etc). (下列用法源出於投辨士開轉的機器、門鎖等)。 ***spend a ~,*** (colloq) urinate. (俗)小便。 ***The ~ dropped,*** The desired result was achieved, the meaning of a remark, etc was understood. 目的已達到;話已聽明白。

pe·nol·ogy /piː'nɒlədʒɪ; pi'nɑlədʒɪ/ *n* [U] study of the problems of legal punishment and prison management. 刑罰學;監獄管理學。

pen·sion¹ /'penʃn; 'pɛnʃən/ *n* [C] regular payment made by the State to sb old (*Re'tirement P~,* or *old-'age ~*), disabled (eg *'war ~*) or widowed, or by a former employer to an employee after long service. (國家定期付給老年人的) 養老金 (亦作 Retirement Pension 或 old-age pension); (國家定期付給殘廢者或寡婦的)撫卹金(如 war pension);(原雇主給予長久服務後之人員的)退休金;年金。 ***draw a／one's ~,*** receive it on one occasion or regularly. 領退休金。 ***on (a) ~,*** receiving a ~: 領退休金;領養老金: *be／go／retire on (a) ~.* 領養老金退休。 □ *vt* [VP15B] ***~ sb off,*** grant or pay a ~ to; dismiss or allow to retire with a ~. 發給(某人)養老金、退休金、撫卹金; 發給(某人)養老金而令其退休。 **~·able** /-əbl; -əbl̩/ *adj* (of services, posts, age, work, etc) entitling one to a ~. (指服務、職位、年齡、工作等)有資格領退休金的。 **~er** *n* person who is receiving a ~. 領養老金者;領撫卹金者;領退休金者。

pen·sion² /'pɒnsɪɒn; 'pɑnsɪˌɑn/ *n* (in Europe, but not GB) boarding-house at which fixed rates are charged (by the week or month). (在歐洲但英國除外,按週或按月付固定之食宿費的) 公寓; 供膳的宿舍。 ***en ~*** /ɒn 'pɒnsɪɒn; ɑn'pɑnsɪˌɑn/, as a boarder. 在公寓寄宿。

pen·sive /'pensɪv; 'pɛnsɪv/ *adj* deep in thought; seriously thoughtful: 沈思的;愁眉苦臉的: *a ~ look;* 沈思狀; *look ~.* 顯得愁眉苦臉。 **~·ly** *adv* **~·ness** *n*

pen·stock /'penstɒk; 'pɛnˌstɑk/ *n* flood-gate; sluice. 洪水閘門;水門。

pen·ta·gon /'pentəgən *US:* -gɒn; 'pɛntəˌgɑn/ *n* plane figure with five sides and five angles. 五角形;五邊形。 **the P~,** building in Arlington, Virginia, headquarters of the US Armed Forces. 五角大厦(美國國防部辦公處,位於維吉尼亞州的阿靈頓郡)。 **pen·tag·onal** /pen'tægənl; pɛn'tægənl̩/ *adj*

pen·tam·eter /pen'tæmɪtə(r); pɛn'tæmətɚ/ *n* (in English verse) line of five iambic feet. (英詩中之)五音步詩行(爲抑揚格)。

Pen·ta·teuch /'pentətjuːk; 'pɛntəˌtjuk/ *n* **the ~,** the first five books of the Bible. 聖經的首五卷;摩西五經。

pen·tath·lon /pen'tæθlən; pɛn'tæθlən/ *n* (modern Olympic Games) contest in which each competitor takes part in five events (running, horse-back riding, swimming, fencing and shooting with a pistol). (現代奧林匹克運動會中)五項運動(賽跑、騎馬、游泳、擊劍和手槍射擊)。

Pente·cost /'pentɪkɒst *US:* -kɔːst; 'pɛntɪˌkɔst/ *n* [U] **1** Jewish harvest festival, fifty days after the Passover. (猶太人的) 五旬節 (踰越節後五十天)。 **2** (esp US) Whit Sunday, the seventh Sunday after Easter. (尤美) 聖靈降臨節 (復活節後第七個星期日)。 **~al** /ˌpentɪ'kɒstl *US:* -'kɔːstl; ˌpɛntɪ'kɔstl/ *adj*

pent·house /'penthaʊs; 'pɛntˌhaʊs/ *n* **1** sloping roof supported against a wall, esp one for a shelter or shed. 庇檐;披屋(靠牆的斜屋頂,尤指用於避雨處或棚舍者)。 **2** apartment built on the roof of a tall building. (建於大厦屋頂的)樓頂房屋。

pent-up /ˌpent 'ʌp; 'pɛnt'ʌp/ *adj* repressed: 被幽禁的;被抑制的: *~ feelings／fury.* 被抑制的情緒(憤怒)。

pen·ul·ti·mate /pen'ʌltɪmət; pɪ'nʌltəmɪt/ *n, adj* (word, syllable, event, etc which is) the one before the last one. (指字、音節、事件等)倒數第二個(的)。

pen·um·bra /pɪ'nʌmbrə; pɪ'nʌmbrə/ *n* partly shaded region around the shadow of an opaque body (esp round the total shadow of the moon or earth in eclipse). 黑影周圍的半陰影 (尤指日月蝕周圍的半陰影)。

pen·uri·ous /pɪ'njʊərɪəs *US:* -'nʊr-; pə'nʊrɪəs/ *adj* (formal) poor; grudging; stingy: (正式用語) 貧窮的;缺乏的;吝嗇的: *a man who is ~ in his habits.* 吝嗇成性的人。 **~·ly** *adv* **~·ness** *n* **pen·ury** /'penjʊərɪ; 'pɛnjərɪ/ *n* [U] (formal) poverty: (正式用語)貧窮: *living in penury;* 過着貧窮的生活; *reduced to penury.* 陷於貧困。

peon /'piːən; 'piən/ *n* **1** (in Latin America) unskilled farm worker, esp one who is not wholly free. (拉丁美洲的)不熟練的農場工人(尤指不太自由者); 被迫以勞役償債的工人。 **2** (in India and Pakistan) office messenger; orderly. (印度及巴基斯坦的) (機關的)信差;傳令兵。 '**~·age** /-ɪdʒ; -ɪdʒ/ *n* [U] system of employing ~s(1); (legal) use of indebtedness to compel sb to work. 勞役償債制度; (法律)勞役償債。

peony /'piːənɪ; 'piənɪ/ *n* (*pl* -nies) [C] garden plant with large round pink, red or white flowers. 牡丹;芍藥。

people /'piːpl; 'pipl̩/ *n* [U] (collective, with *pl v.* Note that for one human being, it is preferable to use *man, woman, boy, girl* and not *person,* which, although useful in definitions, may be derogatory or formal). (集合名詞,與複數動詞連用。注意: 當指一個人的時候,最好用 man, woman, boy, girl, 而不用 person; person 雖可用於定義中,但可能是貶抑或正式的用法)。 **1** persons in general: 人;一般的人: *streets crowded with ~.* 擠滿人的街道。 *Some ~ are very inquisitive.* 有些人很愛管閒事。 **2** those persons belonging to a place, or forming a social class: 某地區的人;某階層的人: *The ~ in the village like the new doctor.* 村裡的人喜歡那位新來的醫生。 *Some ~ spend a lot of money on clothes.* 有些人花很多錢在衣着上。 **3** all the persons forming a State: 全國的人;民衆;人民: *government of the ~, by the ~, for the ~.* 民有、民治、民享的政府。 **4** those persons who are not nobles, not high in rank, position, etc. 平民；黎民；庶民。 **5** (colloq) one's near relations: (俗)家人；親屬: *You must come home with me and meet my ~, darling.* 親愛的，你一定要跟我一起回家會見我的家人。 **6** [C] (not collective) race, tribe, nation: (非集合用法) 種族；民族: *the ~s of Asia;* 亞洲各民族; *a brave and intelligent ~.* 勇敢而有智慧的民族。□ *vt* [VP6A] fill with ~; put ~ in: 供以人民；使人民居於: *a thickly ~d district.* 人口稠密的地區。

pep /pep ; pɛp/ *n* [U] (sl) vigour; spirit. (俚)精力；精神。 **ˈpep pill,** one that stimulates the nervous system (usu one containing amphetamine). 興奮藥丸；提神藥丸(通常含有刺激中樞神經的安非他命)。 **ˈpep talk,** one intended to fill the listener(s) with spirit and energy. 鼓勵的話；精神訓話。□ *vt* (-pp-) [VP15B] ***pep up,*** give energy to; liven up. 激勵；鼓舞；使有活力。

pep·per /ˈpepə(r) ; ˈpɛpɚ/ *n* **1** [U] hot-tasting powder made from the dried berries of certain plants, used to season food. 胡椒粉。 **ˌ~-and-ˈsalt** *n* (colour of) cloth of dark and light wools woven together, with small dark and light dots. (雜有深色和淺色細點的)椒鹽色；椒鹽色的毛料。 **ˈ~·corn** *n* the dried, black berry of the plant; (fig) this as a nominal rent. 乾胡椒子；(喻)空有其名的象徵性租金。 **ˈ~-mill** *n* container in which ~corns are ground to powder and sprinkled on food. 碾胡椒子的小罐。 **ˈ~·mint** *n* **(a)** [U] kind of mint grown for its essential oil, used in medicine and confectionery. (一種製藥與作糖果香料用的)薄荷。 **(b)** [C] sweet of boiled sugar flavoured with ~mint. 薄荷糖。 **ˈ~-pot** *n* small container with a perforated top from which ~ is sprinkled on food. 胡椒盒；胡椒罐；胡椒瓶。 **2** (garden plant with a) red or green seed pod (eg capsicum) which is used as a vegetable: 辣椒；生辣椒之植物: *stuffed ~s.* 內有填塞物的辣椒。□ *vt* [VP6A] **1** put ~ on (food). 灑胡椒粉於(食物)上。 **2** pelt (sb) (with stones, shot, questions, etc). (以石頭)投擲(某人)；(以子彈)射擊(某人)；(以問題) 質問 (某人)。 **~y** *adj* tasting of ~; (fig) hot-tempered: 胡椒味的；(喻)暴躁的；易怒的；性子急的: *a ~y old colonel.* 暴躁的老上校。

pep·sin /ˈpepsɪn ; ˈpɛpsɪn/ *n* [U] liquid (an enzyme) produced in the stomach for helping to digest food. 胃液素；胃蛋白酶。 **pep·tic** /ˈpeptɪk ; ˈpɛptɪk/ *adj* digestive; of digestion or the digestive system: 消化的；消化系統的: *a peptic ulcer.* 胃潰瘍；消化性潰瘍。

per /pɜː(r) ; pɝ; *weak form* pə(r) ; pɚ/ *prep* **1** (when comparing two amounts; when quoting a *rate*¹(1)) for each: (比較兩種數量或引述一種比率時) 每一；每: *per annum* /ˈænəm ; ˈænəm/, for each year; 每年; *per diem* /ˈdiːem ; ˈdiəm/, for each day; 每天; *per pound;* 每磅; *15 rounds of ammunition per man;* 每人十五發子彈; *interest at 6 per cent,* (6%); 百分之六的利息; *30 miles per gallon,* (abbr 略作 **m p g**). 每加侖(油)跑三十英里。⇨ to¹(12). **2** by means of: 由；經；靠: *per post/rail.* 由郵寄(鐵路)。 ***as per,*** (colloq) following: (俗)按照；根據: *as per instructions.* 按照指示。 ***as per usual,*** (colloq) as usual. (俗)照常。

per·ad·ven·ture /ˌpɜːrədˈventʃə(r) ; ˌpɝədˈvɛntʃɚ/ *adv* (archaic) (古) **1** perhaps. 也許。 **2** (after *if* and *lest*) by chance: (用在 if 及 lest 之後) 偶爾；萬一: *If ~ you fail.* 萬一你失敗了。

per·am·bu·late /pəˈræmbjʊleɪt ; pɚˈæmbjəˌlet/ *vi, vt* [VP6A, 2A] (liter) walk through or over; walk up and down. (文)巡行；巡迴；漫步；徘徊。 **per·am·bu·la·tion** /pəˌræmbjʊˈleɪʃn ; pɚˌæmbjəˈleʃən/ *n*

per·am·bu·la·tor /pəˈræmbjʊleɪtə(r) ; pɚˈæmbjəˌletɚ/ *n* (common colloq abbr 俗語用法常略作 **pram** /præm ; præm/) four-wheeled carriage, pushed by hand, for a baby; baby-carriage (the usu word in US). 四輪嬰兒車；嬰兒車(美國通常用 baby-carriage)。

per·ceive /pəˈsiːv ; pɚˈsiv/ *vt* [VP6A, 8, 9, 10, 18A, 19A, 25] (formal) become aware of, esp through the eyes or the mind: (正式用語)感覺；察覺；看出: *On entering his house, we at once ~d him to be/~d that he was a man of taste.* 我們一進他的房子，立刻感覺到他是個高雅的人。 **per·ceiv·able** /-əbl ; -əbl̩/ *adj*

per·cen·tage /pəˈsentɪdʒ ; pɚˈsɛntɪdʒ/ *n* **1** rate or number per cent (= for each hundred). 百分比；百分率。 **2** proportion: 部份；比率: *What ~ of his income is paid in income tax?* 他所繳的所得稅佔他的收入的百分之幾？

per·cep·tible /pəˈseptəbl ; pɚˈsɛptəbl̩/ *adj* (formal) that can be perceived. (正式用語)能感覺到的；看得出的；可察覺的；顯而易見的。 **per·cep·tibly** /-əblɪ ; -əblɪ/ *adv* **per·cep·ti·bil·ity** /pəˌseptəˈbɪlətɪ ; pɚˌsɛptəˈbɪlətɪ/ *n*

per·cep·tion /pəˈsepʃn ; pɚˈsɛpʃən/ *n* [U] (formal) process by which we become aware of changes (through the senses of sight, hearing, etc); act or power of perceiving. (正式用語)感覺；知覺；了解；領悟力；理解力。

per·cep·tive /pəˈseptɪv ; pɚˈsɛptɪv/ *adj* (formal) having, connected with, perception; able to perceive; discerning. (正式用語)有知覺的；與感覺有關的；有理解力的；有悟性的。 **~·ly** *adv*

perch¹ /pɜːtʃ ; pɝtʃ/ *n* (*pl* unchanged) kinds of freshwater fish with spiny fins, used as food. (複數不變)鱸魚。

perch² /pɜːtʃ ; pɝtʃ/ *n* **1** bird's resting-place, eg a branch; bar or rod provided, eg in a bird-cage, a hen-roost, for this purpose. 鳥的棲息之所(如樹枝)；(鳥籠或雞籠中的)棲木。 **2** (colloq) high position occupied by a person; elevated and secure position: (俗)某人所居的高位；高而安全的地位: *come off your ~,* (colloq) stop being so superior (in manner, etc); (俗) 別趾高氣揚; *knock sb off his ~,* stop sb being too confident and superior. 打敗某人；挫某人銳氣。 **3** (also 亦作 *pole, rod*) measure of length, esp for land, $5\frac{1}{2}$ yds; 桿(長度單位，尤用於丈量土地，等於 $5\frac{1}{2}$ 碼); *square ~,* $30\frac{1}{4}$ sq yds. 平方桿(等於 $30\frac{1}{4}$ 平方碼)。⇨ App 5. 參看附錄五。□ *vi, vt* **1** [VP2C] alight: 棲息；棲止；停歇: *The birds ~ed upon the television aerial.* 鳥棲在電視天線上。 **2** [VP2C] (of a person) take up a position (usu on sth high): (指人) 就位(於高處): *~ed on stools at the bar.* 坐在酒吧間裡的欖子上。 **3** (chiefly in *pp*) (of buildings) be situated (on sth high): (主要用過去分詞) (指建築物) 位於 (高處): *a castle ~ed on a rock.* 位於岩上的堡壘。

per·chance /pəˈtʃɑːns *US:* -ˈtʃæns ; pɚˈtʃæns/ *adv* (archaic) by chance; possibly. (古)偶然；可能地。

per·cipi·ent /pəˈsɪpɪənt ; pɚˈsɪpɪənt/ *adj* (formal) perceiving (quickly and keenly). (正式用語)知覺的；感覺的；感覺敏銳的。

per·co·late /ˈpɜːkəleɪt ; ˈpɝkəˌlet/ *vi, vt* [VP6A, 2A, 3A] ~ ***(through),*** (of liquid) (cause to) pass slowly; filter: (指液體)(使)滲透過；濾；濾過: *Water ~s through sand.* 水由沙中濾過；水滲入沙中。 *I make coffee by percolating boiling water through ground coffee.* 我藉滾水濾過磨碎的咖啡來煮咖啡。 *I'll ~ some coffee.* 我將用過濾法煮一點咖啡。 **per·co·lator** /-tə(r) ; -tɚ/ *n* (esp) kind of coffee pot in which boiling water ~s through coffee (in a container near the top). (尤指)(滾水過濾咖啡的)煮咖啡壺。

per·cussion /pəˈkʌʃn ; pɚˈkʌʃən/ *n* the striking together of two (usu hard) objects; sound or shock produced by this. 撞擊；碰撞；震動；撞擊聲。 **the ˈ~ (section),** musical instruments played by ~, eg drums, cymbals. 打擊樂器(例如鼓、銅鈸)。 **ˈ~ cap,** ⇨ cap *n* (4). **~·ist** /-ɪst ; -ɪst/ *n* player of ~ instruments. 打擊樂器演奏者。

per·di·tion /pəˈdɪʃn ; pɚˈdɪʃən/ *n* [U] (formal)

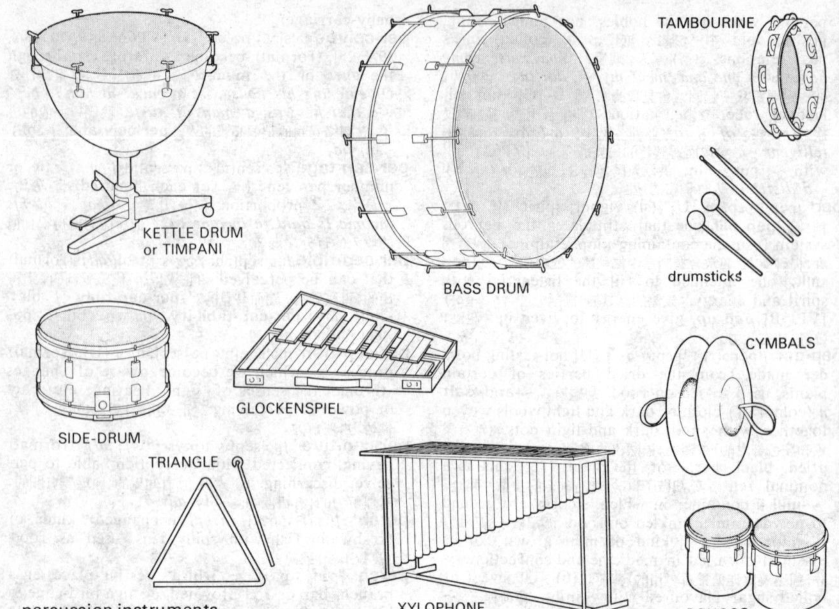

percussion instruments

complete ruin; everlasting damnation. (正式用語) 全毀;永死;萬刼不復。

per·egri·na·tion /ˌperɪgrɪˈneɪʃn ; ˌpɛrəgrɪˈneʃən/ *n* [U] (formal) travelling; [C] journey. (正式用語) 旅行;旅程。

per·emp·tory /pəˈremptərɪ *US:* ˈperəmptɔːrɪ ; pəˈrɛmptərɪ/ *adj* (formal) (of commands) not to be disobeyed or questioned; (of a person, his manner) (too) commanding; insisting upon obedience. (正式用語) (指命令) 不許違反的; 不容疑問的; (指人、態度) 威風凜凜的; 專橫的。 ～ **writ,** (legal) one that compels a defendant to appear in court. (法律) 强制令狀 (强迫被告出庭之傳票)。 **per·emp·torily** /-trəlɪ *US:* -tɔːrəlɪ ; -tərəlɪ/ *adv*

per·en·nial /pəˈrenɪəl ; pəˈrɛnɪəl/ *adj* **1** continuing throughout the whole year. 終年的; 一年到頭的; 四季不斷的。 **2** lasting for a very long time. 長久的;持久的。 **3** (of plants) living for more than two years. (指植物) 多年生的 (超過兩年的)。 □ *n* ～ plant: 多年生植物: *hardy*(1) *～s.* 耐寒的多年生植物。 *～***ly** /-nɪəlɪ ; -nɪəlɪ/ *adv*

per·fect¹ /ˈpɜːfɪkt ; ˈpɝfɪkt/ *adj* **1** complete with everything needed. 完全的; 完備的。 **2** without fault; excellent: 完美的; 無瑕的; 極佳的: *a ～ performance of a play.* 一個劇的完美的演出。 **3** exact; accurate: 正確的;準確的: *a ～ circle.* 一個正圓。 **4** having reached the highest point in training, skill, etc: 技術精湛的;熟練的: *～ in the performance of one's duties.* 克盡自己的責任。 **5** ～ **tenses,** those composed of *have* + *pp,* eg 'He *has/had/will have written* the letter' (present, past, future ～). 完成式 (由 have + pp 形成的時態, 如 'He *has/had/will have written* the letter' 中的斜體字就是現在、過去、未來三種完成式)。 **6** (attrib only) complete; utter; unqualified: (僅作形容用法) 完全的;全然的;絕對的: *a ～ stranger/fool;* 完全陌生的人 (十足的笨蛋); *～ nonsense.* 完全胡說八道;一派胡言。 *～***ly** *adv* **1** quite; quite well; completely: 十分地;美好地;完全地: *～ly happy/satisfied.* 十分快樂 (滿意)。 **2** in a ～ way: 完美地;極佳地: *Your trousers fit ～ly.* 你的褲子極爲合身。

per·fect² /pəˈfekt ; pəˈfɛkt/ *vt* [VP6A] make ～: 使完美;使完善;改善: *She's ～ing her Arabic before taking up her job in Cairo.* 她去開羅任職前,一直在增進她的阿拉伯文。 *～***·ible** /-əbl ; -əbl̩/ *adj* that can be ～ed. 可使之完美的;可臻完善的;可改善的。 *～***·i·bil·ity** /pəˌfektəˈbɪlətɪ ; pəˌfɛktəˈbɪlətɪ/ *n*

per·fec·tion /pəˈfekʃn ; pəˈfɛkʃən/ *n* [U] **1** perfecting or being perfected: 完成: *busy with the ～ of detail.* 忙於細節的完成。 **2** perfect quality or example: 完善之性質或典型: *It was the very ～ of beauty.* 它是美的極致。 **3** best possible state; highest point attainable: 完美;十全十美: *bring something to ～.* 使某事物達到十全十美。 **4** (with *pl*) accomplishment(3). (用複數) 成就;才藝;優點。 *～***·ist** /-ɪst ; -ɪst/ *n* **1** person who believes that moral ～ may be attained, that it is possible to live without sinning. 至善論者 (認爲道德上的十全十美可以達到,無過錯的生活乃屬可能)。 **2** (colloq) person who is satisfied with nothing less than what he thinks to be perfect. (俗) 凡事求其完美的人。

per·fer·vid /pɜːˈfɜːvɪd ; pɝˈfɝvɪd/ *adj* (formal) extremely zealous or eager. (正式用語) 非常熱心的; 熱烈的。

per·fidi·ous /pəˈfɪdɪəs ; pəˈfɪdɪəs/ *adj* (formal) treacherous; faithless (*to*). (正式用語) 不義的; (對…) 不忠心的 (與 to 連用)。 *～***·ly** *adv* *～***·ness** *n*

per·fidy /ˈpɜːfɪdɪ ; ˈpɝfədɪ/ *n* [U] (*pl* -dies) (formal) treachery; breaking of faith; [C] instance of this. (正式用語) 不義;不忠;背信;不義、不忠、背信之實例。

per·for·ate /ˈpɜːfəreɪt ; ˈpɝfəˌret/ *vt* [VP6A] make a hole or holes in; make rows of tiny holes (in paper) so that part may be torn off easily: 打洞於;穿孔於; (在紙上) 打孔狀接縫: *a ～d sheet of postage stamps;* 一大張有齒孔的郵票 (指許多張郵票連在一起); *a ～ed ulcer.* 穿孔性潰瘍。 **per·for·ation** /ˌpɜːfəˈreɪʃn ; ˌpɝfəˈreʃən/ *n* **1** [U] perforating or being ～d. 打洞;穿孔;貫穿。 **2** [C] series of small holes made in paper, etc eg as between postage stamps. 孔狀接縫 (如郵票與郵票之間的齒孔)。

per·force /pəˈfɔːs ; pəˈfors/ *adv* of necessity. 必要

地；必需地；不得已地。

per·form /pəˈfɔːm ; pɚˈfɔrm/ *vt, vi* **1** [VP6A] do (a piece of work, sth one is ordered to do, sth one has promised to do): 執行；履行： *~ a task.* 做工作。 **2** [VP6A, 2A] act (a play); play (music); sing, do tricks, etc before an audience: 演出（戲劇）；演奏（音樂）；唱；表演（戲法等）： *~ 'Hamlet';* 演出'哈姆雷特'； *~ skilfully on the flute.* 熟練地吹奏橫笛。 *The seals ~ed well at the circus.* 海豹在馬戲團裡表演精彩。 *Do you enjoy seeing ~ing animals?* 你喜歡看動物表演嗎？ **~er** *n* one who ~s, esp at a concert or other entertainment. 執行者；履行者；（尤指）演奏者；表演者。

per·form·ance /pəˈfɔːməns ; pɚˈfɔrməns/ *n* **1** [U] performing: 執行；履行： *faithful in the ~ of his duties.* 忠於他的職守。 **2** [C] notable action; achievement: 成績；表現；成就： *His innings of 150 was a fine ~.* 他打一場板球得 150 分是很好的成績。 *Are you satisfied with the ~ of your new car?* 你對你的新車的性能滿意嗎？ **3** [C] performing of a play at the theatre; public exhibition; concert: 戲劇的演出；展覽；音樂演奏會： *two ~s a day;* 一天演兩場； *tickets for the afternoon ~.* 下午表演的入場券。 *What a ~!* (derog) What shocking behaviour! （貶）多麼驚人的行爲！

per·fume /ˈpɜːfjuːm ; ˈpɝfjum/ *n* [C, U] (kinds of prepared liquid with) sweet smell, esp from an essence of flowers. 香味；香水。 □ *vt* /pəˈfjuːm ; pɚˈfjum/ [VP6A] give a ~ to; put ~ on. 使有香味；加香味於；洒香水於。 **~r** *n* person who makes and sells ~s. 香水製造商；香料商。

per·func·tory /pəˈfʌŋktərɪ ; pɚˈfʌŋktərɪ/ *adj* **1** done as a duty or routine but without care or interest: 敷衍的；塞責的；馬虎的： *a ~ inspection.* 馬虎的視察。 **2** (of persons) doing things in this way. （指人）做事敷衍塞責的。 **per·func·torily** /-trəlɪ *US:* -tɔːrəlɪ ; -tərəlɪ/ *adv*

per·gola /ˈpɜːgələ ; ˈpɝgələ/ *n* structure of posts (forming an arbour, or over a garden path) for climbing plants. （構成涼亭，或架於花園通道上的）蔓籐花棚；籐架。

per·haps /pəˈhæps ; pɚˈhæps/ *adv* possibly; maybe. 也許；可能。

peri /ˈpɪərɪ ; ˈpɪrɪ/ *n* (in Persian myth) beautiful girl or woman; fairy; elf. （波斯神話中的）美女；小仙子；精靈。

peri·gee /ˈperɪdʒiː ; ˈpɛrəˌdʒi/ *n* point in an orbit of a planet or spacecraft at which it is closest to the earth. 近地點（行星或太空船的軌道上最接近地球之點）。

peri·helion /ˌperɪˈhiːlɪən ; ˌpɛrɪˈhilɪən/ *n* point in a planet's orbit at which it is nearest to the sun. 近日點（行星軌道上最接近太陽之點）。

peril /ˈperəl ; ˈpɛrəl/ *n* **1** [U] serious danger: 危險： *in ~ of one's life;* 冒着生命的危險； *do sth at one's ~,* at one's own risk. 冒險做某事。 **2** [C] sth that causes danger: 危險的事物： *the ~s of the ocean,* storm, shipwreck, etc. 海洋上的危險（如暴風雨，海難等）。 □ *vt* (-ll-, US also -l-) (liter, poet) (= *imperil,* which is more usu) put or bring into danger. （文學，詩）（等於 imperil，但 imperil 較爲常用）置於險境。 **~·ous** /ˈperələs ; ˈpɛrələs/ *adj* dangerous; full of risk. 危險的；多險的。 **~·ous·ly** *adv*

per·imeter /pəˈrɪmɪtə(r) ; pəˈrɪmətɚ/ *n* [C] (length of the) outer boundary of a closed figure, a military position, an airfield, etc. （封閉圖形、陣地、機場等的）周圍；周界；周邊；外緣；周圍之長度；周長。

period /ˈpɪərɪəd ; ˈpɪrɪəd/ *n* [C] **1** length or portion of time marked off by events that recur, eg hours, days, months and years, fixed by events in nature: 一段時間（如時、日、月、年等）；周期： *20 teaching ~s a week;* 一星期授課二十節； *a lesson ~ of 45 minutes.* 四十五分鐘的一節課。 **2** portion of time in the life of a person, a nation, a stage of civilization, etc; division of geological time: 時代；時期；（地質）紀： *the ~ of the French Revolution.* 法國大革命時期。 *The actors will wear costumes of the ~/~ costumes,* ie of the time when the events of the play took place. 演員們將穿着劇中時代的服裝。 *The house is 18th century and has ~ furniture,* ie of the same century. 那屋子是十八世紀的，而且也有那時代的家具。 **3** full pause at the end of a sentence; full stop (.) marking this in writing and print: 一句話結束時的完全停頓；句點(.)（一個句子結束時的標點）： *put a ~ to sth,* bring it to an end. 結束某事物。 ⇨ App 9. 參看附錄九。 **4** (gram) complete sentence or statement, usu complex; (*pl*) rhetorical or flowery language. （文法）完全句（通常爲複句）；（複）矯飾或華美的言詞。 **5** time during which a disease runs its course; stage in the course of a disease: （疾病的）期；時期；（疾病進行的）階段： *the ~ of incubation,* the time during which it is latent. 潛伏期。 **6** (astron) time taken to complete one revolution. （天文）週期；運轉一周的時間。 **7** occurrence of menstruation. 月經期。

peri·odic /ˌpɪərɪˈɒdɪk ; ˌpɪrɪˈɑdɪk/ *adj* occurring or appearing at regular intervals: 定期的；週期的： *~ attacks of malaria;* 瘧疾的週期性發作； *the ~ revolution of a heavenly body.* 星球的週期性運轉。 **ˌ~ ˈtable,** (chem) tabular arrangement of the elements according to their atomic weights and common properties. （化學）週期表。 **peri·od·ical** /-kl ; -kḷ/ *adj* = ~. □ *n* magazine or other publication which appears at regular intervals, eg monthly, quarterly. 期刊（定期如每月或每季出版的雜誌或其他刊物）。 **peri·od·ically** /-klɪ ; -klɪ/ *adv*

peri·pa·tetic /ˌperɪpəˈtetɪk ; ˌpɛrəpəˈtɛtɪk/ *adj* going about from place to place; wandering: 走來走去的；徘徊的；漫遊的；巡遊的： *the ~ religious teachers of India.* 印度的遊方宗教教師。

pe·riph·ery /pəˈrɪfərɪ ; pəˈrɪfərɪ/ *n* (*pl* -ries) external boundary or surface. 外圍；表面。 **pe·riph·eral** /-ərəl ; -ərəl/ *adj* of, on, forming, a ~. 外圍的；表面的；在外圍上的；形成外圍的。

pe·riph·ra·sis /pəˈrɪfrəsɪs ; pəˈrɪfrəsɪs/ *n* (*pl* -ases /-əsiːz ; -əˌsiz/) roundabout way of speaking; circumlocution; (gram) using an auxiliary word in place of an inflected form, eg *'It does work'* for *'It works', 'the word of God'* for *'God's word'.* 紆迴的說法；繞圈子的陳述；（文法）紆說法（用助動詞代替字尾的變化，如用 'It does work' 代替 'It works', 'the word of God' 代替 'God's word'）。 **peri·phras·tic** /ˌperɪˈfræstɪk ; ˌpɛrəˈfræstɪk/ *adj* of ~. 紆迴的；轉彎抹角的；用紆說法表示的。

peri·scope /ˈperɪskəʊp ; ˈpɛrəˌskop/ *n* instrument with mirrors and lenses arranged to reflect a view down a tube, etc so that the viewer may get a view as from a level above that of his eyes; used in submarines, trenches, etc. （潛水艇、戰壕等中所用的）潛望鏡。

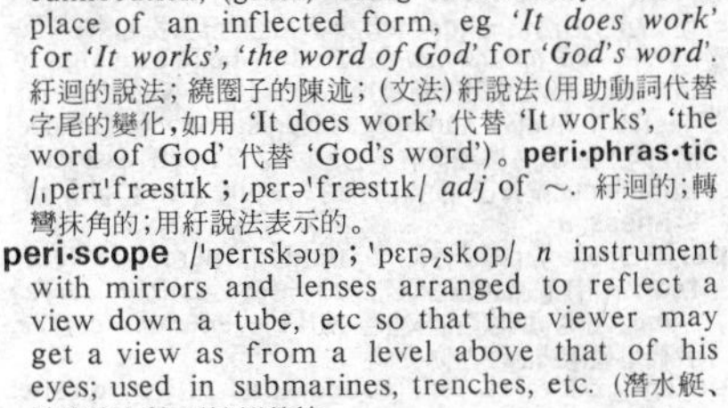

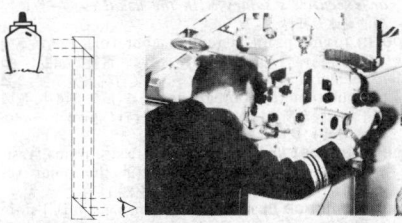

a submarine periscope

per·ish /ˈperɪʃ ; ˈpɛrɪʃ/ *vi, vt* **1** [VP2A, C] (liter or journalism) be destroyed, come to an end, die: （文或新聞學）毀滅；死亡： *Hundreds of people ~ed in the earthquake.* 數以百計的人死於那次地震。 *I shall do it or ~ in the attempt.* 我要拼死一試。 ***P~ the thought!*** May even the thought die!

死了這條心吧！千萬不要存這種念頭！ **2** [VP6A] (of cold or exposure; usu passive) reduce to distress or inefficiency: (指寒冷或暴露;通常用被動語態)使陷於痛苦或無能: *We were ~ed with cold/hunger.* 我們凍(餓)得要死。 **3** [VP6A, 2A] (cause to) lose natural qualities; decay: (使)失去本質; (使)損壞: *The rubber belt on this machine has ~ed,* has lost its elasticity. 這機器上的橡皮帶已失去彈性。*Oil on your car tyres will ~ them.* 在你車胎上的油將會使車胎損壞。 **~·able** /-əbl ; -əbḷ/ *adj* (esp of food) quickly or easily going bad. (尤指食物)易壞的。**~·ables** *n pl* (esp) goods that go bad if delayed in transit, eg fish, fresh fruit. (尤指)易壞的物品(如魚、新鮮水果)。**~er** *n* (sl) person who is unpleasant and disliked; naughty child. (俚)討厭鬼;頑皮的孩子。

peri·style /ˈperɪstaɪl ; ˈpɛrə,staɪl/ *n* (archit) row of columns surrounding a temple, court, etc; space so surrounded. (建築)(寺廟、宮殿等的)周圍列柱;列柱廊;列柱中庭。

per·ito·ni·tis /ˌperɪtəˈnaɪtɪs ; ˌpɛrətəˈnaɪtɪs/ *n* [U] inflammation of the membrane lining the walls of the abdomen. 腹膜炎。

peri·wig /ˈperɪwɪg ; ˈpɛrə,wɪg/ *n* = wig.

peri·winkle[1] /ˈperɪwɪŋkl ; ˈpɛrə,wɪŋkḷ/ *n* creeping, evergreen plant with light-blue flowers. 長春花(一種開淡藍色花的常綠蔓生植物)。

peri·winkle[2] /ˈperɪwɪŋkl ; ˈpɛrə,wɪŋkḷ/ *n* [C] edible sea snail with a spiral shell. 玉黍螺(一種可食海螺)。⇨ the illus at mollusc. 參看 mollusc 之插圖。

per·jure /ˈpɜːdʒə(r) ; ˈpɝdʒɚ/ *vt* [VP6A] (reflex) *~ oneself,* knowingly make a false statement after taking an oath to tell the truth. (反身)作僞證。**~r** /ˈpɜːdʒərə(r) ; ˈpɝdʒərɚ/ *n* person who has ~d himself. 作僞證者。**per·jury** /ˈpɜːdʒərɪ ; ˈpɝdʒərɪ/ *n* [U] act of perjuring oneself; [C] (*pl* -ries) wilful false statement. 作僞證;僞證罪;僞證。

perk[1] /pɜːk ; pɝk/ *vi, vt* **1** [VP2C] *~ up,* (of a person) become lively and active (after depression, illness, etc). (指人)(在愁苦、疾病等之後)活潑起來;振作起來。 **2** [VP15B] *~ sb/sth up,* smarten; raise (head); make (sb) lively: 打扮起來; 擧(首); 使(某人)活潑: *~ oneself up.* 把自己打扮起來。*The horse ~ed up its head,* lifted its head as a sign of interest. 那匹馬興緻勃勃地昂起頭來。**~y** *adj* (-ier, -iest) **1** lively; showing interest or confidence. 活潑生動的; 有興趣或有信心的。 **2** self-assertive; impudent. 堅持己見的;鹵莽的。**~·ily** /-ɪlɪ ; -əlɪ/ *adv* **~i·ness** *n*

perk[2] /pɜːk ; pɝk/ *vi, vt* (colloq) percolate (coffee): (俗)過濾(咖啡); (指咖啡)滲濾: *Is the coffee ~ing yet?* 咖啡還在滲濾嗎？*We ~ed some coffee.* 我們用過濾法煮了些咖啡。

perk[3] /pɜːk ; pɝk/ *n* (colloq; usu *pl*) perquisite: (俗;通常用複數)額外津貼; 小帳; 獎金; 賞錢; 額外利益: *an executive's salary with the usual ~s.* 一位總經理的薪水及津貼。

perm /pɜːm ; pɝm/ *n* (colloq abbr for) (俗,爲下列各詞的略稱) **1** permanent wave: 電燙的頭髮: *go to the hairdresser's for a ~.* 到美容院去燙頭髮。 **2** permutation (in football pools). (足球賽賭注)選擇若干足球隊名所做成之任一組合。 □ *vt* give a ~ to. 電燙(頭髮);選擇並組合(足球隊名)。

per·ma·frost /ˈpɜːməfrɒst *US:* -frɔːst ; ˈpɝmə,frɔst/ *n* permanently frozen subsoil (in the polar regions). (在南、北極地區的)永久凍土;永凍層。

per·ma·nence /ˈpɜːmənəns ; ˈpɝmənəns/ *n* [U] state of being permanent. 永久; 恒久。 **per·ma·nency** /-nənsɪ ; -nənsɪ/ *n* (*pl* -cies) **1** [U] =permanence. **2** permanent thing, person or position: 永久性的事物、人或職位: *Is your new job a permanency or merely temporary?* 你的新工作是永久性的,還是暫時性的？

per·ma·nent /ˈpɜːmənənt ; ˈpɝmənənt/ *adj* not expected to change; going on for a long time; intended to last: 長久的; 永久的; 恒久的: *my ~ address;* 我的永久地址; *a ~ position in the Civil Service.* 一個永久性的文官職位。⇨ temporary. **~ wave,** style of hairdressing in which artificial waves or curls are put in the hair so that they last several months. 電燙頭髮。**~·ly** *adv*

per·manga·nate /pəˈmæŋgəneɪt ; pɝˈmæŋgə,net/ *n* **~ of potash, potassium ~,** (**$KMnO_4$**) dark-purple crystalline salt which is used, dissolved in water, as an antiseptic and disinfectant. 高錳酸鉀(深紫色結晶鹽,溶於水中可用作防腐劑及消毒劑)。

per·meate /ˈpɜːmɪeɪt ; ˈpɝmɪ,et/ *vt, vi* [VP6A, 3A] *~ (through/among),* pass, flow or spread into every part of: 瀰漫;散佈;普及;滲透: *water permeating (through) the soil;* 水滲透到泥土裡面; *new ideas that have ~d (through/among) the people.* 已普及民間的新觀念。 *The smell of cooking ~d (through) the flat.* 烹飪的氣味瀰漫整層公寓。 **per·meation** /ˌpɜːmɪˈeɪʃn ; ˌpɝmɪˈeʃən/ *n* [U] permeating or being ~d. 瀰漫;普及;散佈;滲透。**per·meable** /ˈpɜːmɪəbl ; ˈpɝmɪəbḷ/ *adj* that can be ~d by fluids; porous. 可滲透的;可透過的。**per·mea·bil·ity** /ˌpɜːmɪəˈbɪlətɪ ; ˌpɝmɪəˈbɪlətɪ/ *n*

per·mis·sible /pəˈmɪsəbl ; pɚˈmɪsəbḷ/ *adj* that may be permitted. 可允許的。**per·mis·sibly** /-əblɪ ; -əblɪ/ *adv*

per·mission /pəˈmɪʃn ; pɚˈmɪʃən/ *n* [U] act of allowing or permitting; consent: 許可;准許;允許;同意: *with your ~,* if you will allow me; 如果你許可的話; *give sb ~ to do sth.* 允許某人做某事。*You have my ~ to leave.* 我准許你離開;你可以走了。*By whose ~ did you enter this building?* 是誰准許你進入這建築物的？

per·miss·ive /pəˈmɪsɪv ; pɚˈmɪsɪv/ *adj* giving permission: 許可的;准許的;允許的: *~ legislation,* that gives powers to do sth but does not order that it shall be done. 伸縮性立法(賦予權力可做某事但非必須完成該事)。 **the ~ society,** (in GB, 1967 onwards) term used for social changes, including greater sexual freedom, homosexual law reform, abolition of censorship in the theatre, frank discussion of hitherto taboo subjects, etc. 寬容的社會(指英國自 1967 年以後社會的變遷,包括更多的性自由,改革同性戀法律, 廢止對影劇院的檢查, 自由談論避諱的事等)。**~·ness** *n*

per·mit /pəˈmɪt ; pɚˈmɪt/ *vt, vi* (-tt-) **1** [VP6A, C, 17, 19C] allow: 允許;許可: *weather ~ting.* 如果天氣好的話;要是天氣許可的話。*Smoking not ~ted in this cinema.* 本電影院禁止吸煙。*Circumstances do not ~ me to help you/do not ~ my helping you.* 情況不許可我幫助你。 **2** [VP3A] *~ of,* (formal) admit of: (正式用語)容許: *The situation does not ~ of any delay,* There must be no delay. 這種情況不容許有任何躭擱。 □ *n* /ˈpɜːmɪt ; ˈpɝmɪt/ [C] written authority to go somewhere, do sth, etc: 通行證;許可證: *You won't get into the atomic research station without a ~.* 你一定要有通行證才能進入原子研究站。

per·mu·ta·tion /ˌpɜːmjuːˈteɪʃn ; ˌpɝmjəˈteʃən/ *n* (maths) [U] change in the order of a set of things arranged in a group; [C] any one such arrangement: (數學)排列; 置換; 排列成之任一組: *The ~s of x, y and z are xyz, xzy, yxz, yzx, zxy, zyx.* x, y 和 z 的排列是 xyz, xzy, yxz, yzx, zxy, zyx。

per·mute /pəˈmjuːt ; pɚˈmjut/ *vt* [VP6A] change the order of. 改變…的序列;排列。

per·ni·cious /pəˈnɪʃəs ; pɚˈnɪʃəs/ *adj ~ (to),* harmful, injurious: (對…)有害的;傷害性的: *~ habits;* 有害的習慣; *~ to the welfare of society;* 對社會福利有害的; *~ anaemia,* a severe kind, often fatal. 惡性貧血。**~·ly** *adv* **~·ness** *n*

per·nick·ety /pəˈnɪkətɪ ; pɚˈnɪkɪtɪ/ *adj* (colloq) fussy; worrying about trifles. (俗)好挑剔的;過於顧慮瑣事的;吹毛求疵的。

per·or·ation /ˌperəˈreɪʃn ; ˌpɛroˈreʃən/ *n* (formal)

last part of a speech; summing up. (正式用語) (演說的) 結尾; 總結; 結論。

per·ox·ide /pəˈrɒksaɪd; pəˈrɑksaɪd/ *n* (hydrogen ~; ~ of hydrogen (H_2O_2)) colourless liquid used as an antiseptic and to bleach hair. 過氧化氫(H_2O_2, 無色液體,用作防腐劑及漂染頭髮)。**~ blonde,** person with hair bleached with ~. 頭髮染爲金黃色的人。

per·pen·dicu·lar /ˌpɜːpənˈdɪkjʊlə(r); ˌpɝpənˈdɪkjələ/ *adj* **1** ~ *(to),* at an angle of 90° (to another line or surface). (與另一線或面)成直角的; 正交的。**2** upright; crossing the horizontal at an angle of 90°; (archit; **P~**) of the style of English Gothic architecture of the 14th and 15th cc, marked by vertical lines in the tracery of its windows. 垂直的; 與水平線成直角的; (建築) 垂直式的 (指十四、十五世紀英國哥德式建築, 其特徵爲窗上用垂直線飾花圖案)。□ *n* [C] ~ line; [U] ~ position: 垂直線; 垂直位置: *The wall is a little out of the ~.* 這牆有點傾斜。**~·ly** *adv*

per·pe·trate /ˈpɜːpɪtreɪt; ˈpɝpəˌtret/ *vt* [VP6A] commit (a crime, an error); be guilty of (sth wrong or sth considered outrageous): 犯 (罪、錯誤); 做 (錯事、殘暴或不道德之事): *~ a crime/a blunder/a frightful pun.* 犯罪(犯錯; 亂講惡劣的雙關語)。**per·pe·tra·tor** /-tə(r); -tɚ/ *n* **per·pe·tra·tion** /ˌpɜːpɪˈtreɪʃn; ˌpɝpəˈtreʃən/ *n*

per·pet·ual /pəˈpetʃʊəl; pɚˈpɛtʃʊəl/ *adj* **1** never-ending; going on for a long time or without stopping. 永久的; 持久的。**ˌ~ ˈmotion,** the motion of a machine, if such could be invented, which would go on for ever without an external source of energy. 永久運動(一種假想的機械運動, 雖無持續的能源亦能永遠運轉)。**2** continual; often repeated: 不斷的; 一再重覆的: *She's tired of their ~ chatter.* 她對他們沒完沒了的閒談感到厭倦。**~ly** /-tʃʊəlɪ; -tʃʊəlɪ/ *adv*

per·petu·ate /pəˈpetʃʊeɪt; pɚˈpɛtʃʊˌet/ *vt* [VP6A] preserve from being forgotten or from going out of use: 使永存; 使不被遺忘; 使不朽: *~ the memory of a great statesman by erecting a statue of him.* 藉建造一座塑像來紀念一位偉大的政治家。**per·petu·ation** /pəˌpetʃʊˈeɪʃn; pɚˌpɛtʃʊˈeʃən/ *n*

per·petu·ity /ˌpɜːpɪˈtjuːətɪ *US:* -ˈtuː-; ˌpɝpəˈtjuətɪ/ *n* (*pl* -ties) **1** [U] state of being perpetual. 永恆; 永存; 不朽。*in ~,* for ever. 永遠。**2** [C] (legal) perpetual annuity or possession. (法律) 終身年金; 永久產業。

per·plex /pəˈpleks; pɚˈplɛks/ *vt* [VP6A, 14] ~ *(with),* **1** puzzle; bewilder: 使困惑; 使迷惑: *~ sb with questions.* 以問題使某人困惑。**2** make more complex or intricate: 使更複雜: *Don't ~ the issue.* 不要把這問題弄得更複雜。**~ed** *adj* puzzled; complicated. 困惑的; 複雜的。**~·ed·ly** /-ɪdlɪ; -ɪdlɪ/ *adv* **~·ity** /-ətɪ; -ətɪ/ *n* (*pl* -ties) **1** [U] ~ed condition; mental difficulty caused by doubt: 困惑: *He looked at us in ~ity.* 他困惑地看着我們。**2** [C] perplexing thing; cause of bewilderment. 令人困惑的事物; 迷惑的原因。

per·qui·site /ˈpɜːkwɪzɪt; ˈpɝkwəzɪt/ *n* [C] profit, allowance, etc given or looked upon as one's right, in addition to regular wages or salary: (正式薪資以外的) 津貼; 賞錢; 小帳; 獎金; 額外收入; 額外利益: *The salesman's ~s include the use of his firm's car out of business hours.* 這推銷員的額外津貼包括在下班後使用公司的車子。*Politics in Britain used to be the ~ of the great landowners.* 在英國, 參政曾經是大地主的一項額外利益。⇨ perk³.

perry /ˈperɪ; ˈpɛrɪ/ *n* [U] drink made from the fermented juice of pears. 梨酒。⇨ cider.

per se /ˌpɜːˈseɪ; ˈpɝˈsi/ *adv* (Lat) (of sth) considered alone. (拉) (指事物) 本身; 本質上。

per·se·cute /ˈpɜːsɪkjuːt; ˈpɝsɪˌkjut/ *vt* **1** [VP6A] punish, treat cruelly, esp because of religious beliefs. (尤指因宗教信仰不同而) 迫害; 懲罰。**2** allow no peace to; worry: 煩擾; 困擾: *~ a man with questions.* 以問題困擾一個人。**per·se·cu·tor** /-tə(r); -tɚ/ *n* **per·se·cu·tion** /ˌpɜːsɪˈkjuːʃn; ˌpɝsɪˈkjuʃən/ *n* **1** [U] persecuting or being ~d: 迫害; 煩擾: *suffer persecution for one's religious beliefs.* 爲了宗教信仰而遭受迫害。**2** [C] instance of this (in history, etc): (歷史等中的) 迫害事件: *the numerous persecutions of the Jews.* 對猶太人的許多迫害。

per·se·vere /ˌpɜːsɪˈvɪə(r); ˌpɝsəˈvɪr/ *vi* [VP2A, 3A] ~ *(at/in/with),* keep on steadily, continue (esp sth difficult or tiring): 堅忍; 堅持; 固守 (尤指困難或令人厭倦的事): *~ in one's studies.* 孜孜不倦地研讀。**per·se·ver·ing** *adj* **per·se·ver·ing·ly** *adv* **per·se·ver·ance** /-rəns; -rəns/ *n* [U] constant effort to achieve sth; steadfastness. 毅力; 堅忍; 不屈不撓。

Per·sian /ˈpɜːʃn *US:* ˈpɜːrʒn; ˈpɝʒən/ *n, adj* (inhabitant) of Persia (now Iran); language of the people of Persia (now Iran): 波斯的; 波斯人; 波斯語 (波斯即現在的伊朗): *~ carpets;* 波斯地毯; *~ cats,* with long, silky hair. 波斯貓。

per·si·flage /ˈpɜːsɪflɑːʒ; ˈpɝsɪˌflɑʒ/ *n* [U] banter; light, good-humoured teasing. 嘲弄; 戲謔; 挖苦。

per·sim·mon /pəˈsɪmən; pɚˈsɪmən/ *n* (tree bearing) soft yellow fruit which becomes sweet when completely ripe, esp when softened by frost. 柿子; 柿子樹。

per·sist /pəˈsɪst; pɚˈzɪst/ *vi* **1** [VP3A] ~ *in sth/in doing sth,* refuse, in spite of argument, opposition, failure, etc to make any change in (what one is doing, one's beliefs, etc): 堅持; 固執 (所爲、所信等): *She ~s in wearing that old-fashioned hat.* 她堅持要戴那頂舊式的帽子。*~ with,* continue to work hard at. 繼續努力。**2** [VP2A] continue to exist: 持續; 存留: *The fog is likely to ~ in most areas.* 可能大部分地區還有霧。**~·ence** /-əns; -əns/ *n* [U] ~-ing or being ~ent: 堅持; 固執; 持續; 存留: *The ~ence of a high temperature in the patient puzzled the doctor.* 這病人一直發燒使醫生困惑。**~·ent** /-ənt; -ənt/ *adj* ~ing; continuing; occurring again and again: 堅持的; 固執的; 持續的; 一再發生的: *~ent attacks of malaria.* 瘧疾的持續發作。**~·ent·ly** *adv*

per·son /ˈpɜːsn; ˈpɝsn̩/ *n* **1** man, woman (which are the preferred words; *people* is preferred to ~s for the *pl;* ~ is often derog except when official or impersonal): 人 (指一個人時, man 或 woman 比 person 更常用; 指許多人時 people 比 persons 更常用; 除了用於公務或非特指某一個人以外, person 常有輕蔑之意): *Who is this ~?* 這傢伙是誰? *There's a young ~ to see you.* 有個年輕人來看你。*Any ~* (= Anyone) *leaving litter in the park will be prosecuted.* 任何人在公園裡丟垃圾將被告發。*in the ~ of,* in the man/woman who is: 在…人那裡; 在…人身上: *She found a good friend in the ~ of her landlady,* Her landlady became her good friend. 她的女房東變成了她的好朋友。**ˌ~-to-ˈ~ call,** (of a telephone call) made (via the operator) to a particular ~ and charged for only from the time that ~ answers the phone. 叫人電話(自接話人答話時開始計算費用者)。**2** living body of a human being: 人身: *Offences against the ~* (eg assaults, bodily attacks) *are punished severely.* 對人身的攻擊處罰很重。*in ~,* physically present: 親身; 親自: *I shall be present at the meeting in ~,* I shall be there myself (instead of sending sb to represent me). 我將親自出席那個會議。*Will you apply for the position by letter or in ~?* 你要親自去申請那個工作, 還是寫信去申請? **3** (gram) each of three classes of personal pronouns: (文法) 人稱; 身: *the first ~* (I, we), *the second ~* (you) *and the third ~* (he, she, it, they). 第一人稱 (I, we), 第二人稱 (you), 和第三人稱 (he, she, it, they)。

per·sona /pɜːˈsəʊnə; pɚˈsonə/ *n* (psych) role that a person assumes to show his conscious intentions to himself and others. (心理) (一個人爲了對自己及他人表示自己的意向而扮演的) 人物角色。**ˌ~ ˈgrata** /ˈgrɑːtə; ˈgretə/, (Lat) person who is acceptable, esp a diplomat who is acceptable to a foreign government. (拉)受歡迎的人;被接受的人(尤指被外國政府所接受的外交官)。ˌ~ ˌ**non 'grata** /ˌnɒn-'grɑːtə ; ˏnɑn'gretə/, one who is not acceptable in this way. 不受歡迎的人;不被接受的人(外交官)。

per·son·able /'pɜːsənəbl ; 'pɝsn̩əbl/ *adj* handsome; pleasing in manner. 英俊的;美貌的;風度好的。

per·son·age /'pɜːsənɪdʒ ; 'pɝsn̩ɪdʒ/ *n* (important) person; person of distinction. (要)人;名士;顯要。

per·sonal /'pɜːsnl ; 'pɝsn̩l/ *adj* **1** private; individual; of a particular person: 私人的;個人的;某一個人的: *my ~ affairs/needs/opinions;* 我個人的事(需要,意見); *your ~ rights.* 你個人的權利(你的人權)。*I have something ~ to discuss with you,* either my own or your intimate affairs. 我有點私事和你商量(有關我個人的事或與你切身的事)。'~ **column,** (in a newspaper, etc) column in which private messages or advertisements appear. (報紙等的)人事廣告欄。 **2** done or made by a person himself: 本人所做的;親身的: *a ~ interview.* 親自晤談。*The Prime Minister made a ~ appearance at the meeting,* appeared himself, instead of sending one of his colleagues. 首相親自參加會議。 **3** done or made for a particular person: 爲了某人的;爲某人所做的: *provide a ~ service for sb;* 爲某人提供服務; *give sb one's ~ attention.* 予某人以關注。*He did me a ~ favour,* one directed to me and by him. 他親自幫了我一個忙。ˌ~ **as'sistant** (abbr 略作 **PA**), one who helps an official, etc in an office, government department, etc usu doing more than a secretary, eg by making travel arrangements, interviewing people. 私人助理(在辦公室,政府機關等中協助官員等之人,其職務通常超過一般秘書,如安排旅行、接見訪客等)。 **4** of the body: 人身的;身體的: *P~ cleanliness is important to health as well as to appearance.* 個人清潔對健康及儀表同樣重要。 **5** of the nature of a human being: 人性的: *Do you believe in a ~ God?* 你相信有人性的神嗎? **6** of or about a person in a critical or hostile way: 涉及私人的; 攻擊個人的: *I object to such highly ~ remarks.* 我反對這種純粹是攻擊個人的批評。*Let's not be too ~.* 我們別過於涉及私人。 **7** ˌ~ **'property/e'state,** (legal) temporal or movable property, not land. (法律)動產。 ⇨ *real estate* at real¹(2). **8** ˌ~ **'pronoun,** pronoun for the three persons(3): 人稱代名詞: *I, we; you; he, she, it; they.* 我、我們;你(你們);他、她、它;他們。 □ *n* [C] short newspaper item about a particular person. 有關個人的短聞。 **~ly** /-ənəlɪ ; -ənlɪ/ *adv* **1** in one's own person, not through an agent: 本人;親自: *He conducted me ~ly through the mansion.* 他親自帶我到大厦各處參觀。*She likes ~ly conducted tours,* holiday tours with a courier or guide who accompanies those making the tour. 她喜歡有人嚮導的旅行。 **2** speaking for oneself; for one's own part: 就自己而言;爲自己地: *P~ly I see no objection to your joining us.* 就我個人而言,我不反對你加入我們。

per·son·al·ity /ˌpɜːsə'nælətɪ ; ˏpɝsn̩'ælətɪ/ *n* (*pl* -ties) **1** [U] state of being a person; existence as an individual: 人格;個人的存在: *respect the ~ of a child.* 尊重兒童的人格。 **2** [C, U] qualities that make up a person's character: 個性: *a man with little ~;* 沒有什麼個性的人; *a woman with a strong ~.* 個性强的女人。*They both have striking personalities.* 他們兩人都有突出的個性。**3** [C] (mod use) person, esp one who is well known in certain circles (though perhaps quite unknown in other circles): (現代用法)人物; (某些圈子中的)名人: *personalities of the stage and screen;* 影劇界名人; *a TV ~,* sb known to television viewers. 電視明星。'~ **cult,** practice of giving fervent admiration, devotion, etc to a ~, esp a political leader. 人物崇拜(尤指對政治領袖的崇拜)。 **4** (*pl*) impolite remarks about sb's looks, habits, etc: (複)對某人的容貌、習慣等的不客氣批評;對某人的攻擊: *indulge in personalities,* utter such remarks. 任意誹謗他人。

per·son·al·ize /'pɜːsənəlaɪz ; 'pɝsn̩l͵aɪz/ *vt* [VP6A] have (sth) printed with one's address (*~d stationery*) or given a monogram (with one's initials) (*~d shirts, handkerchiefs*). 印個人地址於(信紙等上);印個人姓名的第一個字母於(襯衫、手帕等上)。

per·son·alty /'pɜːsənltɪ ; 'pɝsn̩l̩tɪ/ *n* [U] (legal) personal estate. (法律)動產。

per·son·ate /'pɜːsəneɪt ; 'pɝsn̩͵et/ *vt* [VP6A] **1** play the part of (a character in a drama). 扮演;飾演(戲中某一角色)。 **2** = impersonate (the more usu word). (impersonate 較爲常用)。 **per·son·ation** /ˌpɜːsə'neɪʃn ; ˏpɝsn̩'eʃən/ *n*

per·son·ify /pə'sɒnɪfaɪ ; pɚ'sɑnə͵faɪ/ *vt* (*pt, pp* -fied) [VP6A] **1** regard or represent (sth) as a person: 擬(某物)爲人;視(某物)爲人: *~ the sun and moon,* by using 'he' and 'she'. 把太陽和月亮看作人(以'他'和'她'稱呼之)。 **2** be an example of (a quality): 爲(某性質)的實例;爲…的化身: *That man personifies avarice/is avarice personified.* 那個人是貪婪的化身。**per·soni·fi·ca·tion** /pəˌsɒnɪfɪ'keɪʃn ; pɚ͵sɑnəfə'keʃən/ *n* **1** [U] ~ing or being personified; [C] instance of this. 擬人;人格化。 **2** *the ~ of,* a striking example of a quality of: 典型;化身;活例: *He's the personification of selfishness.* 他是自私的化身。

per·son·nel /ˌpɜːsə'nel ; ˏpɝsn̩'ɛl/ *n* (with *sing* or *pl v*) staff; persons employed in any work, esp public undertakings and the armed forces: (與單數或複數動詞連用)職員;人員(尤指公職和軍職人員): *There were five airline ~ on the plane that crashed.* 失事的飛機上有五位工作人員。'~ **officer/manager,** one employed to deal with relationships between individual employees, their problems, grievances, etc. 人事官(人事主任)。

per·spec·tive /pə'spektɪv ; pɚ'spɛktɪv/ *n* **1** [U] the art of drawing solid objects on a flat surface so as to give the right impression of their relative height, width, depth, distance, etc; [C] drawing so made. 透視法;透視繪圖法;透視圖。*in/out of ~,* drawn/not drawn according to the rules of ~. 按照(未按照)透視法畫的。 **2** [U] apparent relation between different aspects of a problem. (問題之不同方面的) 明顯關係。*in the/its right/wrong ~,* in the right/wrong relationship; with/without exaggeration or neglect of any aspects: 正確地(不正確地): *You must get the story in (its right) ~.* 你必須正確地了解這故事。*He sees things in their right ~.* 他正確地察覺事物;他對事物有正確的觀點。 **3** [C] (lit, fig) view; prospect: (字面,喻)景色;遠景;看法;前途: *a distorted ~ of the nation's history.* 對這國家歷史的歪曲看法。

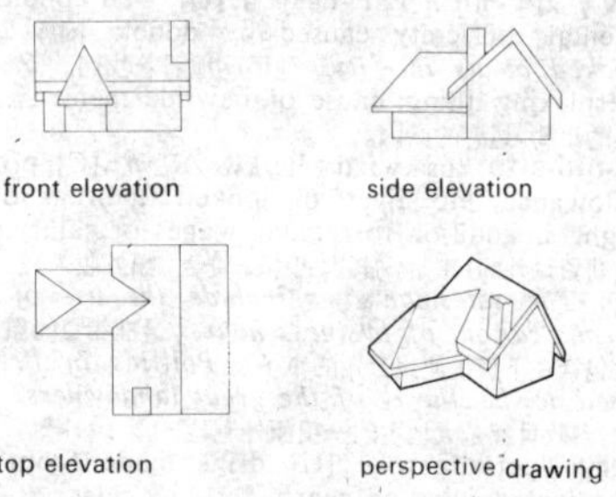

per·spex /'pɜːspeks ; 'pɝ͵spɛks/ *n* [U] (P) tough plastic material that will not splinter, used as a substitute for glass (eg in the windscreens of cars). (商標)不碎透明塑膠(如汽車的擋風屏)。

per·spi·ca·cious /ˌpɜːspɪ'keɪʃəs ; ˏpɝspɪ'keʃəs/ *adj* (formal) quick to judge and understand. (正式用語)敏於判斷與了解的;敏銳的;聰明的。**per·spi·cac·ity**

/ˌpɜ:spɪˈkæsətɪ ; ˌpɜspɪˈkæsətɪ/ *n* [U].

per·spicu·ous /pəˈspɪkjʊəs ; pəˈspɪkjʊəs/ *adj* (formal) expressed clearly; expressing things clearly. (正式用語)意思明白的;說明清楚的; 明晰的。**~·ly** *adv* **~·ness** *n* **per·spi·cu·ity** /ˌpɜ:spɪˈkju:ətɪ ; ˌpɜspɪˈkjuətɪ/ *n*

per·spire /pəˈspaɪə(r) ; pəˈspaɪr/ *vi* [VP2A] sweat. 出汗; 流汗。**per·spir·ation** /ˌpɜ:spəˈreɪʃn ; ˌpɜspəˈreʃən/ *n* [U] sweat; sweating. 汗;流汗。

per·suade /pəˈsweɪd ; pəˈswed/ *vt* **1** [VP11, 14] *~ sb that...; ~ sb of sth,* convince (sb): 使(某人)相信: *How can I ~ you of my sincerity/that I am sincere?* 我如何能够使你相信我的誠意 (我是誠意的)? **2** [VP17] cause (sb) by reasoning (to do sth): 說服;勸說: *We ~d him/He was ~d to try again.* 我們勸他 (他被勸說)再度嘗試。 **3** [VP14] ***~ sb into/out of (doing) sth,*** cause sb to do/stop doing sth: 勸某人做(不做)某事: *Can you ~ her out of her foolish plans?* 你能勸她放棄那些愚蠢的計畫嗎? *Who ~d you into writing that letter?* 誰勸你寫那封信? **per·suad·able** /-əbl ; -əbl/ *adj*

per·sua·sion /pəˈsweɪʒn ; pəˈsweʒən/ *n* **1** [U] persuading or being persuaded; power of persuading. 說服;勸說;被說服;說服力。**2** [U] conviction; belief (the usu word): 確信;信念 (belief 為常用字): *It is my ~ that....* 我相信…;我認為…。 **3** [C] group or set holding a particular belief: 持某信仰的宗派: *men of various (religious) ~s.* 持各種不同(宗教)信仰的人們。

per·sua·sive /pəˈsweɪsɪv ; pəˈswesɪv/ *adj* able to persuade; convincing: 有說服力的; 能勸說的; 令人信服的: *She has a ~ manner.* 她有令人信服的態度。**~·ly** *adv* **~·ness** *n*

pert /pɜ:t ; pɜt/ *adj* **1** saucy; not showing proper respect: 魯莽的;無禮的: *a ~ child/answer.* 無禮的小孩(回答)。 **2** (US) lively; sprightly. (美)活潑的;輕快的。**~·ly** *adv* **~·ness** *n*

per·tain /pəˈteɪn ; pəˈten/ *vi* [VP3A] ***~ to,*** (formal) belong as a part or accessory; have reference; be appropriate: (正式用語)屬於;關於;適合於: *the enthusiasm ~ing to youth;* 屬於年輕人的熱情; *the mansion and the lands ~ing to it.* 大廈及所附屬的土地。

per·ti·na·cious /ˌpɜ:tɪˈneɪʃəs *US:* -tnˈeɪʃəs ; ˌpɜtn̩ˈeʃəs/ *adj* (formal) not easily giving up (what has been started); determined. (正式用語) 頑固的; 執拗的; 固執的; 堅決的。 **~·ly** *adv* **per·ti·nac·ity** /ˌpɜ:tɪˈnæsətɪ *US:* -tnˈæ- ; ˌpɜtn̩ˈæsətɪ/ *n* [U].

per·ti·nent /ˈpɜ:tɪnənt *US:* -tənənt ; ˈpɜtn̩ənt/ *adj* ***~ (to),*** (formal) referring directly; relevant: (正式用語)有關的;中肯的: *remarks not ~ to the subject under discussion;* 與討論中的題目無關的談話; *a ~ reply.* 恰當的回答。**~·ly** *adv* **per·ti·nence** /-əns ; -əns/ *n* [U].

per·turb /pəˈtɜ:b ; pəˈtɜb/ *vt* [VP6A] (formal) trouble; make anxious: (正式用語) 煩擾; 使焦急: *~ing rumours;* 令人不安的謠言; *a man who is never ~ed.* 從來不煩惱的人。**per·tur·ba·tion** /ˌpɜ:təˈbeɪʃn ; ˌpɜtəˈbeʃən/ *n* [U] ~ing or being ~ed. 擾亂;不安;焦慮;煩惱。

pe·ruke /pəˈru:k ; pəˈruk/ *n* long wig. 長假髮。

pe·ruse /pəˈru:z ; pəˈruz/ *vt* [VP6A] (formal) read carefully. (正式用語)細讀。**pe·rusal** /pəˈru:zl ; pəˈruzl̩/ *n* [C, U] act of reading carefully. 細讀。

Peru·vian /pəˈru:vɪən ; pəˈruvɪən/ *adj* of Peru: 秘魯的: *~ bark,* of the cinchona tree, the source of quinine. 金雞納皮(為製奎寧的原料)。□ *n* native of Peru. 秘魯人。

per·vade /pəˈveɪd ; pəˈved/ *vt* [VP6A] spread through every part of: 蔓延;遍及;瀰漫;滲透;充滿: *The subversive ideas that ~ all these periodicals may do great harm.* 遍佈所有這些雜誌中的顛覆思想可能造成很大的危害。**per·va·sion** /pəˈveɪʒn ; pəˈveʒən/ *n* [U] pervading or being ~d. 蔓延;遍佈;瀰漫;滲透。

per·va·sive /pəˈveɪsɪv ; pəˈvesɪv/ *adj* tending to pervade: 蔓延的;遍佈的;瀰漫的;滲透的: *~ influences.* 普遍性的影響;深入各處的影響。**~·ly** *adv* **~·ness** *n*

per·verse /pəˈvɜ:s ; pəˈvɜs/ *adj* **1** (of persons) wilfully continuing in wrongdoing; wilfully choosing a wrong course. (指人)剛愎的;故意作惡的;怙惡不悛的;邪惡的。 **2** (of circumstances) contrary (to one's wishes). (指環境) 與意願相違的。 **3** (of behaviour) contrary to reason. (指行為) 背理的;荒謬的。**~·ly** *adv* **~·ness** *n*

per·ver·sion /pəˈvɜ:ʃn *US:* -ʒn ; pəˈvɜʒən/ *n* **1** [U] perverting or being perverted. 誤用;濫用;墮落。 **2** [C] turning from right to wrong; change to sth abnormal, unnatural, etc: 歪曲;曲解;倒錯;顛倒; 反常: *a ~ of justice;* 歪曲正義; *a ~ of the appetite,* eg a desire to eat grass, as Nebuchadnezzar had; 食慾反常(如古代巴比倫國王尼布加尼撒之吃草慾); *sexual ~s.* 性慾倒錯;性變態。

per·ver·sity /pəˈvɜ:sətɪ ; pəˈvɜsətɪ/ *n* (*pl* -ties) [U] being perverse; [C] perverse act. 剛愎;怙惡不悛;邪惡;背理;荒謬;反常的行為。

per·vert /pəˈvɜ:t ; pəˈvɜt/ *vt* [VP6A] **1** turn (sth) to a wrong use. 誤用;濫用(某事物)。 **2** cause (a person, his mind) to turn away from right behaviour, beliefs, etc: 使(人、心智)墮落; 誘(人)入邪道: *~ (the mind of) a child.* 使小孩(的心智)走上邪道。*Did Socrates really ~ the youth of Athens?* 蘇格拉底真的使雅典的青年誤入歧途嗎? *Do pornographic books ~ those who read them?* 色情書籍會使讀者墮落嗎? □ *n* /ˈpɜ:vɜ:t ; ˈpɜvɜt/ ~ed person; person whose behaviour deviates from what is normal, eg in sexual practices. 墮落的人;入邪道的人;行為反常的人;乖癖者;性慾倒錯者;性變態者。

pe·seta /pəˈseɪtə ; pəˈsetə/ *n* (*pl* ~s) unit of currency in Spain. 西班牙的貨幣單位。

pesky /ˈpeskɪ ; ˈpɛskɪ/ *adj* (colloq) troublesome; annoying. (俗)麻煩的;惱人的。

peso /ˈpeɪsəʊ ; ˈpeso/ *n* (*pl* ~s) unit of currency in many Latin American countries and the Philippines. 比索(拉丁美洲許多國家及菲律賓的貨幣單位)。

pes·sary /ˈpesərɪ ; ˈpɛsərɪ/ *n* (*pl* -ries) (med) any of various devices placed and left in the vagina to support the uterus or prevent conception. (醫)子宮壓定器;子宮托;子宮套;通經器。

pes·si·mism /ˈpesɪmɪzəm ; ˈpɛsəˌmɪzəm/ *n* [U] (opp of *optimism*) tendency to believe that the worst thing is most likely to happen, that everything is essentially evil. (為 optimism 之相反字)悲觀;悲觀主義。**pes·si·mist** /-ɪst ; -ɪst/ *n* person subject to ~. 悲觀者。**pes·si·mis·tic** /ˌpesɪˈmɪstɪk ; ˌpɛsəˈmɪstɪk/ *adj* **pes·si·mis·ti·cally** /-klɪ ; -klɪ/ *adv*

pest /pest ; pɛst/ *n* troublesome or destructive thing, animal, etc; (colloq) person who is a nuisance: 令人討厭或有害之物、動物等;(俗)惹人討厭的人;討厭鬼: *garden ~s,* eg insects, mice, snails; 園中害物(如昆蟲、老鼠、蝸牛); *'~ control,* the use of various methods to get rid of ~s. 害物控制。**pes·ti·cide** /ˈpestɪsaɪd ; ˈpɛstɪˌsaɪd/ *n* substance used to destroy ~s, esp insects. 除蟲藥;殺蟲劑;滅鼠藥。

pes·ter /ˈpestə(r) ; ˈpɛstə/ *vt* [VP6A, 17, 14] ***~ sb (with sth/for sth/to do sth),*** annoy; trouble: 使困惱;使苦惱;煩擾: *be ~ed with flies/with requests for help;* 為蒼蠅(為求助)所擾; *~ sb for money;* 纏著某人要錢; *~ sb to help.* 麻煩某人去幫助。

pes·tif·er·ous /peˈstɪfərəs ; pɛsˈtɪfərəs/ *adj* causing disease; morally dangerous. 引起疾病的;邪惡的;傷風敗俗的。

pes·ti·lence /ˈpestɪləns ; ˈpɛstl̩əns/ *n* [C, U] (any kind of) fatal epidemic disease, esp bubonic plague. (任何一種) 瘟疫; 惡疫 (尤指腺鼠疫)。**pes·ti·lent** /-ənt ; -ənt/, **pes·ti·len·tial** /ˌpestɪˈlenʃl ; ˌpɛstl̩ˈɛnʃəl/ *adjj* **1** like a ~; carrying infection. 似瘟疫的;似惡疫的;傳染的。 **2** (colloq) extremely annoying or objectionable: (俗)極其惱人的;極討厭的;最可惡的: *These pestilential flies/children give* *me no peace.* 這些可惡的蒼蠅(小孩子)使我不得安寧。

pestle /ˈpesl; ˈpɛsḷ/ *n* stick with a thick end used in a mortar for pounding or crushing things. (搗研用的)杵。□ *vt* crush in (or as in) a mortar. (在臼等中)以杵搗;研碎。

pet[1] /pet; pɛt/ *n* **1** (often attrib) animal, etc kept as a companion, treated with care and affection, eg a cat or a dog: (常作形容用法)寵愛的動物;愛物;寵物(如貓或狗): *a ˈpet shop,* one where pets, eg dogs, canaries, tortoises are sold. 寵物店(如出售狗、金絲雀、烏龜等者)。 **2** person treated as a favourite: 受寵愛的人: *Mary is the teacher's pet.* 瑪莉是受老師寵愛的學生。 **3** sb specially loved or lovable: 特別受愛護的人;可愛的人: *make a pet of a child.* 寵愛小孩。 *She's a perfect pet,* (colloq) has very winning ways, is very lovable. (俗)她是最可愛的人兒。 **pet aversion,** sth or sb most disliked: 最令人厭惡的物或人: *Cowboy films are her pet aversion.* 她最討厭看西部牛仔片。 **ˈpet name,** name other than the real name, used affectionately. 愛稱;暱稱。□ *vt* (-tt-) fondle; treat with affection; kiss and caress: 撫弄;愛撫;親吻: *silly women petting their poodles.* 愛撫着捲毛狗的愚蠢婦人。

pet[2] /pet; pɛt/ *n* fit of ill temper, esp about sth trifling: 發怒;發脾氣(尤指爲着小事生氣): *in one of her pets.* 在她某次發脾氣時。

petal /ˈpetl; ˈpɛtḷ/ *n* one of the leaf-like divisions of a flower: 花瓣: *ˈrose ~s.* 玫瑰花瓣。⇨ the illus at flower. 參看 flower 之插圖。**pet·alled** (US **pet·aled**) /ˈpetld; ˈpɛtḷd/ *adj* having ~s. 有花瓣的。

pe·tard /peˈtɑːd; pɪˈtɑrd/ *n* kind of bomb used in former times to break down doors, gates, walls, etc. (昔時用以爆破城門、圍牆等的)炸藥筒。***hoist with one's own ~,*** (prov) caught or injured by what one intended as a snare for others. (諺)作法自斃;害人反害己。

peter /ˈpiːtə(r); ˈpitɚ/ *vi* [VP2C] **~ *out,*** (of supplies, etc) come gradually to an end. (指供應品等)漸漸耗盡;漸漸消失。

Peter /ˈpiːtə(r); ˈpitɚ/ *n* ***rob ˌ~ to pay ˈPaul,*** take from one to give to another. 取諸甲償諸乙;借債還債;剜肉補瘡。**ˌblue ˈpeter,** blue flag with a white square, flown by a ship before leaving port. 開船旗(船離港時所懸的藍底白方格旗)。

pe·tit bour·geois /ˌpetɪ ˈbʊəʒwɑː; ˌpɛtɪˈbʊrʒwɑ/ *n* (F) member of the lower middle class: (法)小資產階級;中下層階級一份子: (attrib) (形容用法) *~ habits/opinions.* 小資產階級的習慣(思想)。⇨ *middle class* at middle(3); ⇨ bourgeois.

pe·tite /pəˈtiːt; pəˈtit/ *adj* (of a person) small, slender, neat and dainty. (指人)嬌小玲瓏的。

pe·ti·tion /pɪˈtɪʃn; pəˈtɪʃən/ *n* [C] **1** prayer; earnest request; appeal (esp a written document signed by a large number of people). 祈禱;懇求;請願;(尤指多人簽名的)請願書;陳情書。 **2** formal application made to a court of law. (向法庭呈出的)訴狀。□ *vt, vi* **1** [VP6A, 17, 11, 14] **~ *sb (for sth/to do sth/that...),*** make a ~ to, eg the authorities: 向(當局等)請求: *~ Parliament to redress grievances.* 向國會請求解除疾苦。 **2** [VP3A] **~ *for,*** ask earnestly or humbly: 祈求;懇求;請求: *~ for a retrial.* 請求再審。 **~er** *n* one who ~s, esp the plaintiff in a divorce suit. 請求人;請願人;原告(尤指離婚訴訟的原告)。

pet·rel /ˈpetrəl; ˈpɛtrəl/ *n* long-winged black and white seabird. 海燕。⇨ the illus at water. 參看 water 之插圖。 **stormy ~,** (fig) person whose coming causes (eg social or industrial) unrest. (喻)一來就造成(社會或工業等)不安的人。

pet·rify /ˈpetrɪfaɪ; ˈpɛtrəˌfaɪ/ *vt, vi* (*pt, pp* -fied) [VP6A, 2A] (cause to) change into stone; (fig) take away power to think, feel, act, etc (through terror, surprise, etc): (使)變爲石頭;(使)石化;(喻)使無思考、感覺、行動等能力;使發呆(因恐懼、驚嚇等之故): *petrified with terror.* 被嚇呆了。 **pet·ri·fac·tion** /ˌpetrɪˈfækʃn; ˌpɛtrəˈfækʃən/ *n* ~ing or being petrified; petrified substance. 石化;嚇呆;化石。

petro- /ˌpetrəʊ-; ˈpɛtrə-/ *pref* of rocks or of petroleum. 表示'岩石'或'石油'。**~-chemical** *n* chemical substance derived from petroleum or natural gas. 石油化學產品。

pet·rol /ˈpetrəl; ˈpɛtrəl/ *n* [U] refined petroleum used as a fuel in internal combustion engines (US 美 = *gasoline*): 汽油: *fill up with ~;* 灌滿汽油; *stop at the next ˈ~ station;* 停在下一個加油站; *the ˈ~ tank.* (汽)油箱。

pe·tro·leum /pɪˈtrəʊlɪəm; pəˈtrolɪəm/ *n* [U] mineral oil (vegetable in origin, from forests in prehistoric times) found underground and obtained from wells; used in various forms (petrol, paraffin, etc) for lighting, heating and driving machines. 石油。**ˌ~ ˈjelly** *n* [U] semi-solid substance obtained from ~, used as a lubricant and in ointments. 礦脂;凡士林。

pe·trol·ogy /pɪˈtrɒlədʒɪ; piˈtrɑlədʒɪ/ *n* [U] the study of rocks. 岩石學。

pet·ti·coat /ˈpetɪkəʊt; ˈpɛtɪˌkot/ *n* woman's underskirt. (婦女的)襯裙。

pet·ti·fog·ging /ˈpetɪfɒgɪŋ; ˈpɛtɪˌfɑgɪŋ/ *adj* (of a person) worrying about small and unimportant details; (of a method) unnecessarily concerned with small matters. (指人)爲不重要小節而煩惱的;(指方法)小題大作的;不必要地注意小事的。

pet·tish /ˈpetɪʃ; ˈpɛtɪʃ/ *adj* **1** (of a person) having short and often repeated fits of ill temper, like a spoiled child. (指人)易怒的;使性子的;愛鬧脾氣的。 **2** (of a remark, act) said or done in a fit of ill temper. (指言語、行爲)發怒時說出的;發脾氣時做的。 **~·ly** *adv* **~·ness** *n*

petty /ˈpetɪ; ˈpɛtɪ/ *adj* (-ier, -iest) **1** small; unimportant: 小的;不重要的: *~ troubles/details;* 小毛病(瑣碎細節); *~ regulations enforced by officials.* 小公務員執行的瑣細的法規。 **2** on a small scale: 小規模的;小型的: *~ farmers/shopkeepers.* 小農(小店主)。 **3** having or showing a narrow mind; mean: 小器的;卑鄙的: *~ spite.* 卑鄙的惡意。 **4** **~ cash,** (business) money for or from small payments. (商)小額收支的現金;零用現金。**~ larceny,** theft of articles of little value. 輕竊盜罪。**~ officer,** highest rank of non-commissioned officer in the navy. 海軍上士。 **pet·tily** /ˈpetɪlɪ; ˈpɛtɪlɪ/ *adv* **pet·ti·ness** *n*

petu·lant /ˈpetjʊlənt *US:* -tʃʊ-; ˈpɛtʃələnt/ *adj* unreasonably impatient or irritable. 性急的;暴躁的。 **~·ly** *adv* **petu·lance** /-əns; -əns/ *n* [U].

pe·tu·nia /pɪˈtjuːnɪə *US:* -ˈtuː-; pəˈtunjə/ *n* [C] garden plant with funnel-shaped flowers of various colours. 撞羽朝顏屬;毽子花(一種園藝植物,開各色漏斗狀花)。

pew /pjuː; pju/ *n* bench with a back, usu fixed to the floor, in a church: (教堂裡)有靠背的長椅: *empty pews at morning service;* 早晨禮拜時空的長椅; (colloq) seat: (俗)座位: *Take a pew!* 請坐! ⇨ the illus at church. 參看 church 之插圖。**ˈpew-opener** *n* person who conducted persons to their seats when, in former times, family pews were enclosed and had doors. (從前教堂裡的)領座人(當時教堂裡的家族席位是隔開的,並且有門扉)。

pe·wit, pee·wit /ˈpiːwɪt; ˈpiwɪt/ *n* lapwing; kind of mountain plover, named after its cry. 田鳧;京燕(一種山鷸,英文名字得自其鳴聲)。

pew·ter /ˈpjuːtə(r); ˈpjutɚ/ *n* [U] grey alloy of lead and tin; kitchen vessels made of this: 白鑞(鉛與錫的合金);白鑞所製成的容器: *a good collection of ~;* 可觀的白鑞器皿收藏; (attrib) (形容用法) *~ mugs/dishes.* 白鑞製成的杯(盤子)。

pe·yote /peɪˈəʊtɪ; peˈotɪ/ *n* Mexican cactus from which is derived a drug (*mescaline*) which causes hallucinations. 一種墨西哥產仙人掌(此種仙人掌所製

成之毒瞼能使人產生幻覺)。

pfen·nig /ˈfenɪg; ˈfɛnɪg/ *n* German copper coin, one hundredth of a mark. 德國銅幣(值百分之一馬克)。

phae·ton /ˈfeɪtn *US:* ˈfeɪətən ; ˈfeətn̩/ *n* (hist) light, four-wheeled open carriage, usu drawn by a pair of horses. (史) 輕快四輪敞篷馬車 (通常由兩匹馬拉之)。

phago·cyte /ˈfægəsaɪt ; ˈfægəˌsaɪt/ *n* sort of leucocyte (blood cell) capable of guarding the system against infection by absorbing microbes. 吞噬細胞 (藉吞噬微生物而能保護身體以抵抗疾病的一種白血球)。

phal·anx /ˈfælæŋks ; ˈfelæŋks/ *n* (*pl* ~es or phalanges /fəˈlændʒiːz ; fəˈlændʒiz/) **1** (in ancient Greece) body of soldiers in close formation for fighting. (古希臘) 排成作戰密集隊形的軍隊;方陣。**2** number of persons banded together for a common purpose. 爲共同目標而結合的一羣人。**3** (anat) bone in a finger or toe. (解剖) 指骨;趾骨。⇨ the illus at skeleton. 參看 skeleton 之插圖。

phal·lus /ˈfæləs ; ˈfæləs/ *n* image of the erect penis, as a symbol of generative power. 陰莖像(作爲生殖力的象徵)。**phal·lic** /ˈfælɪk ; ˈfælɪk/ *adj* of a ~: 陰莖像的: *phallic symbols/emblems.* 陰莖象徵。

phan·tasm /ˈfæntæzəm ; ˈfæntæzəm/ *n* phantom. 幻影;幻像;幽靈;空想。**phan·tas·mal** /fænˈtæzməl ; fænˈtæzməl/ *adj* of or like a ~. 幻影的;似幻影的;幻覺的;幽靈的;非眞實的。**phan·tas·ma·goria** /ˌfæntæzməˈgɒrɪə *US:* -ˈgɔːrɪə ; ˌfæntæzməˈgorɪə/ *n* changing group of images, real or imagined figures, etc eg as seen in a dream. 變幻不定的成羣影像;變幻不定的許多眞實的或幻想的人物(如夢中所見者)。

phan·tasy /ˈfæntəsɪ ; ˈfæntəsɪ/ *n* = fantasy.

phan·tom /ˈfæntəm ; ˈfæntəm/ *n* [C] ghost; sth without reality, as seen in a dream or vision: 幽靈;幻像;幻影;夢幻: (attrib) (形容用法) ~ *ships.* 鬼船。

Phar·aoh /ˈfeərəʊ ; ˈfɛro/ *n* title of the kings of ancient Egypt. 法老(古埃及國王的稱謂)。

Phari·see /ˈfærɪsiː ; ˈfærəˌsi/ *n* member of an ancient Jewish sect known for strict obedience to written laws and for pretensions to sanctity; (small **p**) hypocritical and self-righteous person. 法利賽人(古猶太人中的一派,以嚴格遵守成文法律及自命聖潔見稱); (小寫 p) 自以爲正直的僞善者。**phari·saic** /ˌfærɪˈseɪɪk ; ˌfærəˈse·ɪk/, **phari·sai·cal** /-kl ; -kl̩/ *adjj* of or like a ~ or the ~s. (似)法利賽人的;自以爲正直的;僞善的。

phar·ma·ceuti·cal /ˌfɑːməˈsjuːtɪkl *US:* -ˈsuː- ; ˌfɑrməˈsjutɪkl̩/ *adj* of, engaged in, pharmacy; of medicinal drugs: 製藥的;配藥的;藥物的;醫藥的: *the ~ industry.* 製藥業;製藥工業。

phar·ma·cist /ˈfɑːməsɪst ; ˈfɑrməsɪst/ *n* person professionally qualified to prepare medicines. 藥劑師。⇨ chemist, druggist.

phar·ma·col·ogy /ˌfɑːməˈkɒlədʒɪ ; ˌfɑrməˈkɑlədʒɪ/ *n* [U] science of pharmacy. 藥物學;藥理學。**pharma·col·ogist** /-ədʒɪst ; -ədʒɪst/ *n* expert in, student of, ~. 藥物學家;研習藥物學的人。

phar·ma·co·poeia /ˌfɑːməkəˈpiːə ; ˌfɑrməkəˈpiə/ *n* (officially published) book with list of medicinal preparations and directions for their use. (官方出版的) 藥典;藥方書。

phar·macy /ˈfɑːməsɪ ; ˈfɑrməsɪ/ *n* (*pl* -cies) **1** [U] preparation and dispensing of medicines and drugs. 製藥;配藥。**2** [C] dispensary; (part of a) shop where medical goods are sold. (US 美 = *drugstore*). 藥房;藥店。

pharos /ˈfeərɒs ; ˈferɑs/ *n* lighthouse; beacon for sailors. 燈塔;航線標燈。

phar·ynx /ˈfærɪŋks ; ˈfærɪŋks/ *n* cavity (with the muscles, etc that enclose it) at the back of the mouth, where the passages to the nose, mouth and larynx begin. 咽。⇨ the illus at head. 參看 head 之插圖。**phar·yn·gi·tis** /ˌfærɪnˈdʒaɪtɪs ; ˌfærɪnˈdʒaɪtɪs/ *n* [U] inflammation of the mucous membrane of the ~. 咽炎。

phase /feɪz ; fez/ *n* [C] **1** stage of development: 階段;時期;局面: *a ~ of history;* 歷史的一個階段; *the critical ~ of an illness;* 疾病的危險期; *enter upon a new ~ of one's career;* 開始自己事業的新局面; stage in a cycle. 相;周相。***in/out of ~,*** having/not having the same ~ at the same time; in/out of harmony. 同(異)相;和(不和)諧。**2** (of the moon) amount of bright surface visible from the earth (new moon, full moon, etc). (指月亮)位相;盈虧(新月、滿月等)。□ *vt* [VP6A, 15B] plan, carry out, by ~s: 分期計畫;按階段執行: *a ~d withdrawal,* one made by stages. 分期撤出。***~ in,*** introduce, one stage at a time. 逐步採用;逐步實施。***~ out,*** withdraw, one stage at a time. 逐步結束;逐步撤出。

crescent half moon gibbous full moon

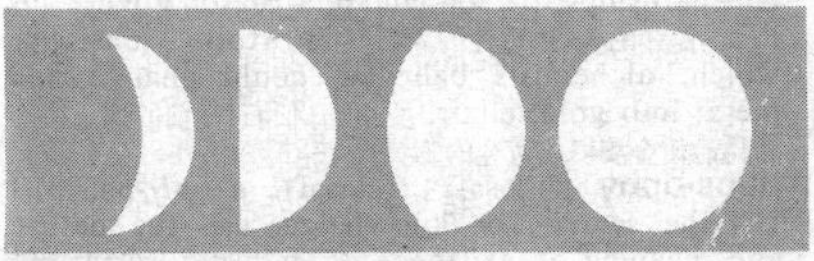

the phases of the moon

pheas·ant /ˈfeznt ; ˈfɛznt̩/ *n* [C] long-tailed game bird; [U] its flesh as food. 雉;雉肉。⇨ the illus at fowl. 參看 fowl 之插圖。

pheno·bar·bi·tone /ˌfiːnəʊˈbɑːbɪtəʊn ; ˌfinoˈbɑrbɪˌton/ *n* [U] drug used to calm the nerves and induce sleep. 苯基巴比特魯(一種鎮靜劑及安眠藥)。

phe·nol /ˈfiːnɒl ; ˈfinɔl/ *n* [U] (comm, science) carbolic acid (as used in disinfectants). (商,科學) 石碳酸;酚(用作消毒劑)。

phe·nom·enal /fɪˈnɒmɪnl ; fəˈnɑmənl/ *adj* **1** perceptible to the senses. 感覺得到的。**2** concerned with phenomena. 關於現象的。**3** prodigious; extraordinary. 奇異的;非常的。**~ly** /-nəlɪ ; -nl̩ɪ/ *adv*

phe·nom·enon /fɪˈnɒmɪnən *US:* -nɒn ; fəˈnɑməˌnɑn/ *n* (*pl* -ena /-ɪnə ; -ənə/) **1** thing that appears to or is perceived by the senses: 現象: *the phenomena of nature.* 自然的現象。**2** remarkable or unusual person, thing, happening, etc. 非凡的或特殊的人、物、事件等。

phew /fjuː ; fju *or a less precise puffing noise* 或是一種不太清楚的吹氣聲/ *int* natural cry indicating astonishment, impatience, discomfort, disgust, etc according to context. 呸!啐!(表示驚訝、不耐煩、不舒服、憎厭等的感嘆聲,其意義視上下文而定)。

phial /ˈfaɪəl ; ˈfaɪəl/ *n* small bottle, esp one for liquid medicine; vial. 小瓶;(尤指)小藥水瓶。

phil·an·der /fɪˈlændə(r) ; fəˈlændɚ/ *vi* [VP2A] be in the habit of making love without serious intentions; flirt. 用情不專;調情。**~er** *n* person who does this. 用情不專者;調情者。

phil·an·thropy /fɪˈlænθrəpɪ ; fəˈlænθrəpɪ/ *n* [U] love of mankind; practical sympathy and benevolence. 博愛;慈善;同情;仁慈。**phil·an·thro·pist** /-ɪst ; -ɪst/ *n* person who helps others, esp those who are poor or in trouble. 博愛者;慈善家。**phil·an·thropic** /ˌfɪlənˈθrɒpɪk ; ˌfɪlənˈθrɑpɪk/ *adj* of ~; benevolent; kind and helpful: 博愛的;慈善的;助人的: *philanthropic institutions,* eg for blind people or orphans. (爲盲人或孤兒等所設的) 慈善機構。**phil·an·thropi·cally** /-klɪ ; -klɪ/ *adv*

phil·at·ely /fɪˈlætəlɪ ; fəˈlætl̩ɪ/ *n* postage-stamp collecting. 集郵。**phil·at·el·ist** /-ɪst ; -ɪst/ *n* person who collects postage-stamps; person with expert knowledge of them. 集郵者;集郵專家。

phil·hel·lene /fɪlˈhiːliːn ; fɪlˈhɛlin/ *n, adj* (person) friendly to the Greeks. 對希臘人友善的;希臘之友。**phil·hel·lenic** /ˌfɪlheˈliːnɪk *US:* -ˈlenɪk ; ˌfɪlhɛˈlɛnɪk/ *adj*

Phi·lis·tine /ˈfɪlɪstaɪn *US:* -stiːn ; fəˈlɪstɪn/ *n* **1**

(Biblical) one of the warlike people in Palestine who were the enemies of the Israelites. (聖經)非利士人(古以色列人的仇敵，居於巴勒斯坦，好戰)。**2** (mod use; small **p**) uncultured person; person whose interests are material and commonplace: (現代用法，小寫 p)沒教養的人；庸俗的人：(attrib) (形容用法) ～ *neighbours.* 缺乏教養的鄰居。

phil·ol·ogy /fɪˈlɒlədʒɪ ; fɪˈlɑlədʒɪ/ *n* [U] study of the development of language, or of particular languages. 語文學；(舊用法)語言學。⇨ linguistics. **phil·ol·ogist** /fɪˈlɒlədʒɪst ; fɪˈlɑlədʒɪst/ *n* student of, expert in, ～. 語文學家；研究語文學的人。**philo·logi·cal** /ˌfɪləˈlɒdʒɪkl ; ˌfɪləˈlɑdʒɪkl̩/ *adj* of ～. 語文學的。

phil·os·opher /fɪˈlɒsəfə(r) ; fəˈlɑsəfɚ/ *n* **1** person studying or teaching philosophy, or having a system of philosophy. 哲學家；研究或教授哲學的人。**2** person whose mind is untroubled by passions and hardships; person who lets reason govern his life. 豁達的人；重理性的人。**～'s stone,** substance which, alchemists believed, could change any metal into gold; elixir. 點金石；仙石(從前的煉金術士認爲能使金屬變成黃金的物質)。

phil·os·ophy /fɪˈlɒsəfɪ ; fəˈlɑsəfɪ/ *n* (*pl* -phies) **1** [U] the search for knowledge, esp the nature and meaning of existence. 哲學；學問的研究(尤指對存在之性質及意義所作之探討)。**moral ～,** the study of the principles underlying the actions and behaviour of men; ethics. 倫理學。**natural ～,** (old use) physics. (舊用法)物理學。**2** [C] system of thought resulting from such a search for knowledge: (由此研究所得之)思想體系；原理；原則；人生觀：*conflicting philosophies;* 互相矛盾的思想體系；*a man without a* ～, with no views upon the problems of life. 沒有人生觀的人。**3** [U] calm, quiet attitude towards life, even in the face of unhappiness, danger, difficulty, etc. 達觀；冷靜；沉着。**philo·sophi·cal** /ˌfɪləˈsɒfɪkl ; ˌfɪləˈsɑfɪkl̩/ *adj* **1** of, devoted to, guided by, ～. 哲學的；專心於哲學的；以哲理爲準則的。**2** resigned; of or like a philosopher(2). 忍從的；逆來順受的；豁達的。**philo·sophi·cally** /-klɪ ; -klɪ/ *adv* **phil·os·ophize** /fɪˈlɒsəfaɪz ; fəˈlɑsəˌfaɪz/ *vi* [VP2A] think or argue like a philosopher; discuss, speculate about, a theory in ～. 像哲學家那樣思考或辯論；討論哲理；默想哲理。

philtre (US = **phil·ter**) /ˈfɪltə(r) ; ˈfɪltɚ/ *n* [C] love-potion. 春藥；媚藥。

phleb·itis /flɪˈbaɪtɪs ; flɪˈbaɪtɪs/ *n* inflammation of a vein. 靜脈炎。

phlegm /flem ; flɛm/ *n* [U] **1** thick, semi-fluid substance forming abnormally in the respiratory passages, and brought up by coughing. 痰。**2** quality of being slow to act, or to feel and show emotion or interest. 遲鈍；冷漠；冷靜。**phleg·matic** /flegˈmætɪk ; flɛgˈmætɪk/ *adj* having the quality of ～(2): 遲鈍的；冷漠的；冷靜的：*Not all English people are ～atic.* 並非所有英國人都是冷漠的。**phleg·mat·i·cally** /-klɪ ; -klɪ/ *adv*

phlox /flɒks ; flɑks/ *n* [U] kinds of garden plant with clusters of flowers in various colours. 草夾竹桃。

pho·bia /ˈfəʊbɪə ; ˈfobɪə/ *n* morbid or pathological fear and dislike; aversion. (病態的)恐懼；憎惡；恐怖症。

phoe·nix /ˈfiːnɪks ; ˈfinɪks/ *n* mythical bird which, after living hundreds of years in the Arabian desert, burnt itself on a funeral pile and rose from the ashes young again, to live for another cycle. 長生鳥(神話中的鳥，在阿拉伯沙漠活了數百年後，自焚於火葬柴堆，復自灰中新生，再開始另一循環)。

phone[1] /fəʊn ; fon/ *n, vt, vi* (colloq abbr for) telephone. (俗)爲 telephone 之略。**ˈ～·booth** *n* telephone kiosk; call-box. 電話亭；公共電話間。**ˈ～·call** *n* telephone call. 打電話。**ˈ～-in** *n* radio/television programme in which listeners/viewers participate by telephone. 由聽(觀)衆藉電話參與的廣播(電視)節目。

phone[2] /fəʊn ; fon/ *n* (ling) single speech-sound (vowel or consonant). (語言)單音(母音或子音)。

pho·neme /ˈfəʊniːm ; ˈfonim/ *n* [C] (ling) unit of the system of sounds of a language. (語言)音位；音素(某一語言的語音系統中的一個單元)：*English has 24 consonant ～s.* 英語中有二十四個子音音素。**pho·nemic** /fəˈniːmɪk ; foˈnimɪk/ *adj* (of transcriptions) providing one symbol for each ～ of the language transcribed (as with the pronunciations in this dictionary). (指標音)音位的(只用一個符號表示一個音素的，如本字典所用的音標)。**pho·nem·ics** *n* (with *sing v*) study and description of the phonemic systems of languages. (用單數動詞)音位學；音素學。

pho·netic /fəˈnetɪk ; foˈnɛtɪk/ *adj* (ling) (語言) **1** concerned with the sounds of human speech. 語音的；語音學的。**2** (of transcriptions) providing not only a symbol for each phoneme of the language transcribed but with additional symbols for differences between variations of the same phoneme in different situations. (指音標)表實際語音的(不僅以一個符號表示一個音素，而且用附加符號表示此音素在不同情況下之不同發音的)。**3** (of a language) having a system of spelling that approximates closely to the sounds represented by the letters used: (指語言)拼字與發音相似的：*Spanish spelling is ～.* 西班牙文的拼字與發音相似。**pho·net·ics** *n* (with *sing v*) study and science of speech sounds, their production, and the signs used to represent them. (用單數動詞) 語音學。**pho·neti·cally** /-klɪ ; -klɪ/ *adv* **pho·neti·cian** /ˌfəʊnɪˈtɪʃn ; ˌfonəˈtɪʃən/ *n* expert in ～s. 語音學家。

pho·ney, phony /ˈfəʊnɪ ; ˈfonɪ/ *adj* (colloq) sham; unreal; not genuine. (俗)假的；假冒的；不眞實的。□ *n* ～ person: 虛假的人；冒充的人；騙子：*He's a complete ～.* 他是個十足的騙子。

pho·nic /ˈfɒnɪk ; ˈfɑnɪk/ *adj* of sound; of vocal sounds. 聲音的；語音的。**～s** *n* (with *sing v*) the use of elementary phonetics in the teaching of reading. (用單數動詞)看字讀音法(一種教初學者按照字母及音節的基本語音讀出單字的方法)。

pho·no·graph /ˈfəʊnəgrɑːf *US:* -græf ; ˈfonəˌgræf/ *n* (US) record player. (美)唱機；留聲機。

pho·nol·ogy /fəˈnɒlədʒɪ ; foˈnɑlədʒɪ/ *n* [U] (ling) scientific study of the organization of speech sounds (including phonemes), esp in particular languages. (語言) 音韻學 (對某些語言的語音結構之研究)。**pho·no·logi·cal** /ˌfəʊnəˈlɒdʒɪkl ; ˌfonəˈlɑdʒɪkl̩/ *adj*

phooey /ˈfuːɪ ; ˈfuɪ/ *int* exclamation of contempt, disbelief or disappointment. 呸！啐！(表示輕視、不信或失望的感嘆字)。

phos·gene /ˈfɒzdʒiːn ; ˈfɑsdʒin/ *n* [U] colourless gas (**$COCl_2$**), used as a poison gas and in industry. 氯化碳醯；二氯化碳；氯代氯化甲醯；光氣(一種毒氣)。

phos·phate /ˈfɒsfeɪt ; ˈfɑsfet/ *n* any salt of phosphoric acid, esp one of the numerous artificial fertilizers containing or composed of various salts of this kind, used widely in agriculture. 磷酸鹽；(尤指)含有磷酸鹽的肥料；磷肥。

phos·pho·res·cence /ˌfɒsfəˈresns ; ˌfɑsfəˈrɛsn̩s/ *n* [U] the giving out of light without burning, or by gentle burning without heat that can be felt. 發燐光；燐光性；燐光；燐火；鬼火。**phos·pho·res·cent** /-snt ; -sn̩t/ *adj* giving out light without burning. 發燐光的；燐光性的。

phos·phorus /ˈfɒsfərəs ; ˈfɑsfərəs/ *n* [U] yellowish, nonmetallic, poisonous wax-like element (symbol **P**) which catches fire easily and gives out a faint light in the dark; red, non-poisonous form used in the manufacture of safety matches. 燐；黃燐；赤燐。**phos·phoric** /fɒsˈfɒrɪk *US:* -ˈfɔːr- ; fɑsˈfɔrɪk/, **phos·phor·ous** /ˈfɒsfərəs ; ˈfɑsfərəs/ *adjj* relating to or containing ～. 燐的；含燐的。

photo /ˈfəʊtəʊ ; ˈfoto/ *n* (*pl* ～s /-təʊz ; -toz/) (colloq abbr for) photograph. (俗)爲 photograph 之略。

photo- /ˈfəʊtəʊ; ˈfoto/ *pref* of light or of photography. 表示 '光' 或 '攝影'。 **ˈ~·copy** *vt, n* [VP6A] (make a) copy of (a document, etc) by a photographic method. (用照相法)影印(文件等); 影印本。Hence, 由此產生, **ˈ~·copier** *n* (用照相法之)影印機;複印機。 **ˌ~·eˈlectric** *adj*: 光電的: *~electric cell*, cell or device which emits an electric current when light falls on it, used for many purposes, eg to measure light for photography, to cause a door to open when someone approaches it, to count objects passing before it. 光電管;光電儀(遇到光線卽產生電流的裝置,用途甚廣,如照相時測光,使門在有人接近時自動開啓,計算通過其前面的物體等)。 **ˌ~ ˈfinish** *n* (horse-racing) finish so close that only a photograph of the horses as they pass the winning-post can decide the winner. (賽馬)攝影終局(指比賽的馬匹到達終點時,先後非常接近,唯有從馬匹跑過終點標桿時所攝的照片,才能判斷獲勝者)。 **ˌ~-ˈgenic** /-ˈdʒenɪk; -ˈdʒɛnɪk/ *adj* suitable for being photographed; photographing well or effectively. 適於拍照的; 可照得好的; 上像的。 **ˌ~-ˈsensitize** *vt* make (sth) sensitive to light. 使(某物)感光靈敏。

photo·graph /ˈfəʊtəgrɑːf *US:* -græf; ˈfotəˌgræf/ *n* [C] picture recorded by means of the chemical action of light on a specially prepared glass plate or film in a camera, transferred to specially prepared paper. 照片;相片。□ *vt, vi* **1** [VP6A] take a ~ of. 拍…的照片;攝影。 **2** *~ well/badly*, come out well/badly when ~ed. 上(不上)像;照相照得好(不好)。 **photo·grapher** /fəˈtɒgrəfə(r); fəˈtɑgrəfɚ/ *n* person who takes ~s: 攝影者: *amateur and professional ~ers*. 業餘的和職業的攝影者。Cf 參較 *camera man*, for cinema and TV. 電影及電視的攝影師。 **photo·gra·phy** /fəˈtɒgrəfɪ; fəˈtɑgrəfɪ/ *n* [U] art or process of taking ~s. 攝影術;攝影。 **photo·graphic** /ˌfəʊtəˈgræfɪk; ˌfotəˈgræfɪk/ *adj* of, related to, used in, taking ~s: 攝影的;攝影用的;與攝影有關的: *photographic apparatus/goods/periodicals, etc.* 攝影的器械(器材,雜誌等)。 **photo·graphi·cally** /-klɪ; -kḷɪ/ *adv*

photo·gra·vure /ˌfəʊtəgrəˈvjʊə(r); ˌfotəgrəˈvjʊr/ *n* [U] process of producing a picture on a metal plate from a photographic negative so that the plate can be used in printing; [C] picture printed from such a plate. 照相製版法;照相版印成的圖畫。

photo·li·tho·gra·phy /ˌfəʊtəʊlɪˈθɒgrəfɪ; ˌfotəlɪˈθɑgrəfɪ/ *n* [U] process of reproducing on plates (stone or zinc) by means of photography. 照相石(鋅)版術;影印石(鋅)版術。

photo·meter /fəʊˈtɒmɪtə(r); foˈtɑmətɚ/ *n* device for measuring the intensity of light. 測光表;曝光表。

photon /ˈfəʊtɒn; ˈfotɑn/ *n* (phys) unit of quantity of energy in light. (物理)光量子;光子。

photo·stat /ˈfəʊtəstæt; ˈfotəˌstæt/ *vt, n* (P) (商標) = photocopy.

photo·syn·thesis /ˌfəʊtəʊˈsɪnθəsɪs; ˌfotəˈsɪnθəsɪs/ *n* [U] process by which the energy of sunlight is used by a green plant to keep it growing. 光合作用。

phrase /freɪz; frez/ *n* [C] **1** group of words (often without a finite *v*) forming part of a sentence, eg *in the garden, in order to*. 片語(常無限定動詞,構成句的一部分,如 in the garden, in order to)。 **ˈ~-book** *n* one containing and explaining (or giving equivalents of in another language) ~s of a language: 片語集(收集片語並加以解釋,或與其他語言中的片語對照): *an English-Polish ~-book*. 英波片語集。 **2** striking, clever way of saying sth. (簡明的)警句。 **3** (music) short, independent passage forming part of a longer passage. (音樂)樂句;分句。□ *vt* [VP6A] express in words: 用話表示;措詞: *a neatly ~d compliment*. 措辭簡潔的讚語。 **phrasal** /ˈfreɪzl; ˈfrezḷ/ *adj* in the form of a ~: 片語的;片語形式的: *phrasal verbs*, eg *go in for, fall over, blow up*. 片語形式的動詞(如 go in for, fall over, blow up)。 **phras·eol·ogy** /ˌfreɪzɪˈɒlədʒɪ; ˌfrezɪˈɑlədʒɪ/ *n* [U] choice of words; wording. 措辭;用字;用語。

phren·etic /frəˈnetɪk; frɪˈnɛtɪk/ *adj* = frenetic.

phren·ol·ogy /frəˈnɒlədʒɪ; frɛˈnɑlədʒɪ/ *n* [U] the judging of a person's character, capabilities, etc from an examination of the shape of his skull. 顱相學(由顱骨的形狀判斷一個人的性格,能力等)。 **phren·ol·ogist** /-ɪst; -ɪst/ *n* person who practises ~. 顱相學家。

phthi·sis /ˈθaɪsɪs; ˈθaɪsɪs/ *n* [C] tuberculosis of the lungs. 肺癆;肺結核。

phut /fʌt; fʌt/ *adv* **go ~**, (lit or fig) (colloq) collapse; break down: (字面或喻)(俗)崩潰;破裂;壞掉: *My record player has/holiday plans have gone ~*. 我的唱機壞了(度假計畫泡湯了)。

phylum /ˈfaɪləm; ˈfaɪləm/ *n* (biol) highest division in the animal kingdom. (生物)門(爲動物之最高分類)。

physic /ˈfɪzɪk; ˈfɪzɪk/ *n* **1** (archaic) medicine. (古)藥。 **2** (*pl*) (複) = physics.

physi·cal /ˈfɪzɪkl; ˈfɪzɪkḷ/ *adj* **1** of material (contrasted with moral and spiritual) things: 物質的(與道德的及精神的相對): *the ~ world/universe;* 外界;物質世界; *~force*. 物質的力量。 **2** of the body; bodily: 身體的;肉體的: *~ exercise*, eg walking, playing football; 運動(如散步、踢足球); *~ education*. 體育。 **3** of the laws of nature: 自然律的: *It's a ~ impossibility to be in two places at once.* 同時在兩地是自然律上不可能的事。 **4** of the natural features of the world: 地球之自然特徵的: *~ geography*, of the earth's structure. 地文學;自然地理。 **~ly** /-klɪ; -kḷɪ/ *adv*

phys·ician /fɪˈzɪʃn; fəˈzɪʃən/ *n* person qualified to practise both medicine and surgery. 醫生。

physi·cist /ˈfɪzɪsɪst; ˈfɪzəsɪst/ *n* expert in, student of, physics. 物理學家;研究物理學之人。

phys·ics /ˈfɪzɪks; ˈfɪzɪks/ *n* (with *sing v*) group of sciences dealing with matter and energy (eg heat, light, sound), but usu excluding chemistry and biology: (用單數動詞) 物理學: *P~ is taught by Professor Molecule*. 物理學是茅立逑爾教授教的。

physi·og·nomy /ˌfɪzɪˈɒnəmɪ *US:* -ˈɒgnəʊmɪ; ˌfɪzɪˈɑgnəmɪ/ *n* (*pl* -mies) [C, U] (art of judging character from the features of) the face; general features of a country. 相面術;相貌;臉;國家的地勢。

physi·ol·ogy /ˌfɪzɪˈɒlədʒɪ; fɪzɪˈɑlədʒɪ/ *n* [U] science of the normal functions of living things, esp animals. 生理學; (尤指)動物生理學。 **physi·ol·ogist** /-ɪst; -ɪst/ *n* expert in, student of, ~. 生理學家;研究生理學的人。 **physio·logi·cal** /ˌfɪzɪəˈlɒdʒɪkl; ˌfɪzɪəˈlɑdʒɪkḷ/ *adj*

physio·ther·apy /ˌfɪzɪəʊˈθerəpɪ; ˌfɪzɪoˈθɛrəpɪ/ *n* [U] treatment of disease by means of exercise, massage, the use of light, heat, electricity and other natural forces. 物理治療法(藉運動、按摩或使用光、熱、電及其他自然力量治療疾病之法)。 **physio·thera·pist** *n* person trained to give such treatment. 物理治療師;物理治療家。

phy·sique /fɪˈziːk; fɪˈzik/ *n* [U, C] structure and development of the body: 體格;身體的構造與發育: *a man of strong ~*. 體格强壯的人。

pi /paɪ; paɪ/ *n* the Greek letter p (π), esp (maths) as a symbol of the ratio of the circumference of a circle to its diameter (ie 3·14159). 希臘字母 p (π); (尤指)(數學)圓周率(爲圓周與直徑之比,其值爲 3·14159)的符號。⇨ App 4. 參看附錄四。

pi·ano¹ /ˈpjɑːnəʊ; pɪˈɑno/ *adv, adj* (music) soft(ly). (音樂)弱;輕;柔和;溫和。 **pia·nis·simo** /pjæˈnɪsɪməʊ; ˌpiəˈnɪsəˌmo/ *adv, adj* very soft(ly). 最輕;最弱。

pi·ano² /pɪˈænəʊ; pɪˈæno/ *n* (*pl* ~s /-nəʊz; -noz/) musical instrument in which stretched metal strings are struck by hammers operated by keys. 鋼琴。⇨ the illus at keyboard. 參看 keyboard 之插圖。 **cottage ~**, small upright ~. 豎式小鋼琴。 **grand ~**, ~ with horizontal strings. 大鋼琴(卽平

台鋼琴)。**upright** ~, one with vertical strings. 豎式鋼琴。**pia·nist** /ˈpɪənɪst ; pɪˈænɪst/ *n* person who plays the ~. 鋼琴彈奏者;鋼琴家。**piano·forte** /pɪˌænəʊˈfɔːtɪ *US:* pɪˈænəfɔːrt ; pɪˈænəˌfort/ *n* (full name, now formal, for) ~. 鋼琴(鋼琴的全名,現在爲鋼琴的正式名稱)。**pia·nola** /pɪəˈnəʊlə ; ˌpiəˈnolə/ *n* (P) ~ operated mechanically. (商標)一種附有自奏機的鋼琴;自動鋼琴。

pi·astre (US = **pi·as·ter**) /pɪˈæstə(r) ; pɪˈæstə/ *n* unit of currency in some countries in the Middle East. 中東某些國家的貨幣單位。

pi·azza /pɪˈætsə ; pɪˈæzə/ *n* **1** public square or market-place, esp in an Italian town. (尤指義大利城市內的)公共廣場;市場。**2** (US) veranda. (美)走廊。

pi·broch /ˈpiːbrɒk ; ˈpibrɑk/ *n* piece of martial music for the bagpipes. 風笛變奏曲。

pica /ˈpaɪkə ; ˈpaɪkə/ *n* printer's unit for the size of type¹(3). 派卡(印刷商計算活字大小的單位,等於 12 point);十二磅因大的活字。

pica·dor /ˈpɪkədɔː(r) ; ˈpɪkəˌdɔr/ *n* man (mounted on a horse) who uses a lance to incite and weaken bulls in the sport of bull-fighting. (以矛刺牛使之激怒及衰弱的)騎馬的鬪牛士。

pic·ar·esque /ˌpɪkəˈresk ; ˌpɪkəˈrɛsk/ *adj* (of a style of fiction) dealing with the adventures of rogues and vagabonds. (指小說文體)以惡徒及流浪者之冒險事蹟爲題材的。

pic·ca·lilli /ˌpɪkəˈlɪlɪ ; ˌpɪkəˈlɪlɪ/ *n* [U] kind of hot-tasting pickle made of chopped vegetables, spices in mustard, vinegar, etc. 辛辣的泡菜(以切碎的蔬菜、香料、芥末、醋等製成)。

pic·ca·ninny /ˌpɪkəˈnɪnɪ *US:* ˈpɪkənɪnɪ ; ˈpɪkəˌnɪnɪ/ *n* (*pl* -nies) (old use) small child, esp a Negro baby. (舊用法)小孩;(尤指)黑人小孩。

pic·colo /ˈpɪkələʊ ; ˈpɪkəˌlo/ *n* (*pl* ~s /-ləʊz ; -loz/) small flute producing notes an octave higher than those of the ordinary flute. 短笛(其音度較長笛高出一倍)。⇨ the illus at brass. 參看 brass 之挿圖。

pick¹ /pɪk ; pɪk/ *n* picking; selection. 挑選;選擇。***the ~ of***, the best (part) of a collection of things or people. 最優部份;最優秀的份子。

pick² /pɪk ; pɪk/ *n* **1** **'~(-axe)**, heavy tool with an iron head having two pointed ends, used for breaking up hard surfaces. 鎬;尖鋤;鶴嘴鋤。⇨ the illus at tool. 參看 tool 之挿圖。**2** small, sharp-pointed instrument: 尖銳的小工具: *an 'ice-~;* 冰鑿子; *a 'tooth~.* 牙籤。

pick³ /pɪk ; pɪk/ *vt, vi* (For special uses with *adverbial particles* and *preps*, ⇨ 7 below.) (與副詞接語及介詞連用的特殊用法參看下列第 7 義。) **1** [VP6A] take up, remove, pull away, with the fingers: (以手指)採;摘;取去: ~ *flowers,* gather flowers; 摘花;採花; ~ *fruit,* take fruit from the bush or tree; 摘水果; ~ *a thread from one's coat;* 從外套上拔下一根線; ~ *one's nose,* remove bits of dried mucus from the nostrils. 挖鼻孔。~ ***sb's brains,*** get ideas and information from sb. 剽竊某人的思想。~ ***sb's pocket,*** steal sth from it. 竊取某人口袋內的東西;扒某人的口袋。Hence, 由此產生, **'~·pocket** *n* person who ~s pockets. 扒手。~ ***and steal,*** pilfer. 扒竊。**2** [VP6A] tear or separate; use a pointed instrument to clean, etc: 撕;扯;剔;挖: ~ *rags,* tear them to small pieces; 撕破布; ~ *one's teeth,* get bits of food from the spaces between them, etc by using a pointed stick of wood (*a 'toothpick*); (以牙籤 toothpick)剔牙; ~ *a lock,* use a pointed tool, a piece of wire, etc to unlock it without a key; 撬開鎖; ~ *a bone,* get all the meat from it. 啃骨頭(啃食骨頭上的肉)。***have a 'bone to ~ with sb,*** ⇨ bone(1). **3** [VP6A] choose; select: 挑選;選擇: ~ *only the best;* 只挑最好的; ~ *one's words,* choose those words that express one's meaning best, that will not cause offence, etc (according to context); 愼選最適當的字眼;注意措詞; ~ *one's way along a muddy road;* 在泥濘的路上選擇可走的路; ~ *sides,* choose players for the two teams in a game (of football, cricket, etc) or competition; (足球、板球等比賽或競賽時)挑選兩隊選手; ~ *the winning horse/~ the winner,* make a successful guess at the winner (before the race). (賽馬之前)挑中獲勝的馬(獲勝者)。~ ***a quarrel with sb,*** bring about a quarrel intentionally. 向某人挑釁;故意和某人爭吵。**4** [VP6A] make by ~ing: 剔成;挖成;鑿成: ~ *holes in sth.* 在某物上鑿洞。~ ***holes in an argument,*** (fig) find its weak points. (喻)在辯論中找漏洞。**5** [VP6A] (of birds) take up (grain, etc) in the bill; peck; (of persons) eat (food, etc) in small amounts; (指鳥) 啄食(穀物等);(指人)一點一點地吃(食物等)。[VP3A] ~ ***at,*** eat without interest or appetite: 不感興趣或沒食慾地吃: *She only ~ed at her food.* 她只吃了一點點食物。**6** (US) pluck (the strings of): (美)彈奏;撥奏(琴絃): ~ *a banjo/the strings of a banjo.* 彈奏五絃琴。**7** [VP3A, 15B] (special uses with *adverbial particles* and *preps*): (與副詞接語及介詞連用的特殊用法):

pick at sb, (colloq) nag at; find fault with: (俗)挑剔;找毛病: *Why are you always ~ing at the poor child?* 你爲什麼總是找那個可憐的小孩的毛病?

pick sth off, take or pluck off. 摘去。~ ***sb off,*** shoot him with deliberate aim: 瞄準射死某人: *A sniper behind the bushes ~ed off three of our men.* 藏在樹叢後面的一個狙擊手射死了我方三個人。

pick on sb, single out, esp for sth unpleasant: 挑選某人(尤指挑選去做不愉快的事): *Why should you ~ on me to do the chores?* 你爲什麼要挑我去做那些雜務?

pick sb/sth out, **(a)** choose. 選擇;選拔。**(b)** distinguish from surrounding persons, objects, etc: 分辨出: ~ *out one's friends in a crowd.* 在人羣中辨出自己的朋友。~ ***sth out,*** **(a)** make out, see, (the meaning of a passage, etc) by careful study. 了解;領會(一段文字的含義等)。**(b)** play (a tune) by ear on a piano, etc. 憑聽過後的記憶而彈奏(曲子)。**(c)** relieve (one colour, the ground colour) with touches of a different colour: 襯托;使(一種顏色、底色)明顯: *green panels ~ed out with brown.* 以褐色襯托的綠鑲板。

pick sth over, examine and make a selection from: 檢查並從中挑選: ~ *over a basket of strawberries,* eg to throw out any that are bad. 揀選一籃草莓(把壞的挑掉)。

pick sth up, **(a)** break up (ground) with a pick-axe. 用尖鋤掘(地)。**(b)** take hold of and lift: 拾起;撿起: ~ *up one's hat/parcels, etc.* 拾起帽子(包裹等)。**(c)** gain; acquire: 得到;獲得: ~ *up a foreign language,* learn it without taking lessons or studying; 自然學得一種外文; ~ *up a livelihood by selling things from door to door;* 靠挨家售賣東西謀生; ~ *up bits of information;* 得到一些消息;獲得點滴的資料; ~ *up a bargain at an auction sale.* 在拍賣時買到便宜貨。*The locomotive ~s up current from a third rail.* 火車機車從第三軌獲得電力。**(d)** succeed in seeing or hearing (by means of apparatus): (藉着儀器)看到;聽到;偵得: *enemy planes ~ed up by our searchlights/radar installations, etc.* 被我們的探照燈照到(雷達測得等)的敵機。**(e)** recover; regain: 恢復;重獲: *You'll soon ~ up health when you get to the seaside.* 你到了海濱,就會很快地恢復健康。~ ***sb up,*** **(a)** make the acquaintance of casually: 偶然結識: *a girl he ~ed up on the street.* 他在街上邂逅的女孩子。**(b)** take (persons) along with one: 搭載(人);帶(人)走: *He stopped the car to ~ up a young girl who was hitch-hiking across Europe.* 他停下車來搭載一個乘便車旅行歐洲的年輕女郎。*The escaped prisoner was ~ed up* (= seen and arrested) *by the police at Hull.* 逃犯在赫爾被警察逮到了。~ ***oneself up,*** raise (oneself) after a fall: 跌倒後自己站起來: *She slipped and fell, but quickly ~ed herself up.* 她滑了一跤,但是很快地站

了起來。~ ***up (health),*** recover health; improve: 恢復健康;健康進步: *He's beginning to ~ up now.* 他現在已開始康復了。~ ***up speed,*** gain speed. 加速。~ ***up with sb,*** make acquaintance with: 結識;與…交朋友: *Where did you ~ up with that queer fellow?* 你在什麼地方結識那個怪傢伙的?'**~-up** *n* (*pl* ~-ups) **(a)** that part of a record-player that holds the stylus. 唱頭(電唱機之裝置唱針的部分)。**(b)** small general-purpose van or truck, open and with low sides, (eg as used by builders, farmers, etc, for carrying merchandise). 小型輕便汽車(如建築商、農夫等用於載貨的車子)。**(c)** (sl) person whose acquaintance is made casually. (俚)偶然認識的人。**(d)** acceleration: 加速: *an engine/car with a good ~-up.* 加速效能良好的引擎(車子)。**~-me-up** /ˈpɪk mɪ ʌp; ˈpɪkmɪʌp/ *n* sth, eg a drink, that gives new strength and cheerfulness. 增加精力或使人愉快之物(如飲料);提神酒。

picka·back /ˈpɪkəbæk; ˈpɪkəˌbæk/ *adv* (eg of the way a child is carried) on the shoulders or back like a bundle. 在肩上;在背上(如背小孩的方式)。

picker /ˈpɪkə(r); ˈpɪkɚ/ *n* person or thing that picks (chiefly in compounds): 採摘者;撿拾器(主要用於複合字中): *'hop-~s;* 蛇麻子採集人(機); *'rag-~s.* 拾荒者;撿破爛的人。

pick·erel /ˈpɪkərəl; ˈpɪkərəl/ *n* (*pl* unchanged) young pike. (複數不變)小梭魚。

picket /ˈpɪkɪt; ˈpɪkɪt/ *n* **1** pointed stake, etc set upright in the ground (as part of a fence, or to tether a horse to). (籬笆間或繫馬用的)尖樁。**2** small group of men on police duty, or sent out to watch the enemy. 排哨;哨兵。**3** worker, or group of workers, stationed at the gates of a factory, dock-yard, etc during a strike, to try to persuade others not to go to work: 罷工時守在工廠等門口勸阻他人上班的工人;罷工糾察員: *a '~ line,* line of ~s, eg outside a factory. 罷工時在工廠外面等勸阻他人上班的一排工人;一排罷工糾察員。**flying ~,** ~ formed of workers who do not work at the place where the ~ is stationed. 由他處工人組成的罷工糾察員。□ *vt, vi* [VP6A, 2A] **1** put ~s(1) round; tether (a horse) to a ~(1). 圍以尖樁;繫(馬)於尖樁。**2** place ~s(2) in or round; station (men) as ~s. 配置哨兵於;放哨;派(人)爲哨兵。**3** place ~s(3) at: 配置罷工糾察員於: *~ a factory;* 在一家工廠配置罷工糾察員; act as a ~(3). 擔任罷工糾察員。

pick·ing /ˈpɪkɪŋ; ˈpɪkɪŋ/ *n* **1** [U] act of picking. 採摘;竊取;選擇;鑿掘。~ ***and stealing,*** stealing cheap things. 扒竊(廉價物品);偷竊。**2** (*pl*) things left over from which profits may be made; these profits; profits made from stealing cheap things. (複)尙可獲得利益的剩餘物;從剩餘物所獲得之利益;由扒竊廉價物所得的利益。

pickle /ˈpɪkl; ˈpɪkl̩/ *n* **1** [U] salt water, vinegar, etc for keeping meat, vegetables, etc, in good condition. (醃肉、泡菜等的)醃汁;泡菜水。***have a rod in ~ for sb,*** ⇨ rod. **2** (usu *pl*) vegetables kept in ~: (通常用複數)泡菜: *onion ~s.* 泡洋葱。**3** ***in a sad/sorry/nice ~,*** in a sad, etc plight. 處於困難的境地;處境困難。□ *vt* [VP6A] **1** preserve in ~: 醃;泡: *~d onions/walnuts.* 醃泡的洋葱(胡桃)。**2** **~d** *pp* (sl) drunk. (俚)醉的。

pic·nic /ˈpɪknɪk; ˈpɪknɪk/ *n* **1** pleasure trip on which food is carried to be eaten outdoors: 野餐: *have/go for a ~;* 舉行(去)野餐; (attrib) (形容用法) *a '~ hamper,* one for holding food, dishes, etc. 野餐用的籃子。**2** (colloq) sth easy and enjoyable: (俗)輕鬆而愉快的事物: *It's no ~,* is not an easy job. 那不是容易的工作。□ *vi* (-ck-) take part in a ~: 參加野餐;去野餐: *~ in the woods.* 在森林中野餐。**pic·nicker** *n* person who ~s. 野餐者。

pic·ric /ˈpɪkrɪk; ˈpɪkrɪk/ *adj* **~ acid,** acid used in dyeing, explosives and antiseptics. 苦味酸(用於染物、製造炸藥、防腐等)。

pic·tor·ial /pɪkˈtɔːrɪəl; pɪkˈtorɪəl/ *adj* of, having, represented in, pictures: 圖畫的;有圖的;以圖畫表示的: *a ~ record of the wedding.* 婚禮的圖片紀錄。□ *n* periodical in which pictures are the main feature. 畫刊;畫報;圖畫雜誌。

pic·ture /ˈpɪktʃə(r); ˈpɪktʃɚ/ *n* **1** painting, drawing, sketch, of sth, esp as a work of art. 畫;圖畫(尤指藝術作品)。'**~-book** *n* book consisting mainly of ~s, esp one for children. 圖畫書(尤指供兒童閱讀者)。'**~-card** *n* (in playing cards) court-card; one with a king, queen or knave on it. (紙牌中)花牌(上面有 king, gueen 或knave 之牌)。'**~-gallery** *n* room or building in which ~s are exhibited. 圖畫陳列室;畫廊。'**~ hat,** woman's hat with a very wide brim. (女人戴的)寬邊帽。**2** beautiful scene, object, person, etc. 美麗的景色、物品、人等。**3** type or embodiment. 典型;化身。***be the ~ of health,*** appear to have it in a high degree. 健康良好。**4** (fig) account or description that enables sb to see in his mind an event, etc. (喻)(使人明白某事件等的)陳述;描寫。***be/put sb in the ~,*** be/cause sb to be well informed, aware of all the facts of a situation. (使某人)了解實情。**5** film (to be) shown in a cinema. 影片;電影。**the ~s,** the cinema: 電影: *We don't often go to the ~s.* 我們不常去看電影。**6** what is seen on a television screen: 電視畫面: *a set free from ~ distortion.* 畫面不會失眞的電視機。□ *vt* **1** [VP6A] make a ~ of; paint. 繪;畫。**2** [VP14] ***~ sth to oneself,*** imagine: 想像: *He ~d to himself what it might be like to live in Java.* 他想像生活在爪哇的情況。

pic·tur·esque /ˌpɪktʃəˈresk; ˌpɪktʃəˈrɛsk/ *adj* **1** having the quality of being like, or of being fit to be, the subject of a painting: 如畫的;可入畫的: *a ~ village.* 風景如畫的村莊。**2** quaint; vivid; graphic: 有趣的;逼眞的;生動的: *~ language.* 生動的語言。**3** (of a person, his character) striking; original. (指人、性格)引人注意的;獨特的。**~·ly** *adv* **~·ness** *n*

piddle /ˈpɪdl; ˈpɪdl̩/ *vi, n* (colloq) (pass) urine. (俗)(解)小便。

pid·dling /ˈpɪdlɪŋ; ˈpɪdlɪŋ/ *adj* trifling; insignificant: 微小的;不重要的: *~ jobs.* 小差事;瑣碎的工作。

pidgin /ˈpɪdʒɪn; ˈpɪdʒɪn/ *n* **1** any of several languages resulting from contact between European traders and local peoples, eg in West Africa and the Far East, containing elements of the local language(s) and English, French or Dutch, still used for internal communication. 洋涇濱語;不純正的英、法或荷蘭語(原爲西非及遠東地區的人與歐洲商人交談時用的不純正英語、法語或荷蘭語,現仍用於其國內)。**2** **'one's ~,** (colloq) one's job or concern: (俗)自己的事;與自己有關的事: *Don't ask me; that's 'your ~.* 別問我,那是你的事。

pie /paɪ; paɪ/ *n* [C, U] meat or fruit covered with pastry and baked in a deep dish: 以肉或水果爲餡的烤餅;餡餅: *fruit pies;* 水果餡餅; *a meat pie;* 肉餡餅; *eat too much pie.* 吃太多餡餅。⇨ flan, tart². ***have a finger in the/every pie,*** be concerned in the/every matter (esp in an officious way). 干預某事;參與某事;管閒事。***as easy as pie,*** (sl) very easy. (俚)極容易。***pie in the sky,*** happiness in Heaven; unrealistic hopes. 天堂之樂;不切合實際的希望;空頭支票。'**pie-crust** *n* [U] baked paste of a pie. 餡餅皮。

pie·bald /ˈpaɪbɔːld; ˈpaɪˌbɔld/ *adj* (of a horse) having white and dark patches of irregular shape. (指馬)黑白斑駁的。

piece¹ /piːs; pis/ *n* **1** part or bit of a solid substance (complete in itself, but broken, separated or made from a larger portion): 塊;片;段;斷片;部分: *a ~ of paper/wood/glass/chalk.* 一張紙(一塊木頭;一片玻璃;一枝粉筆)。*Will you have another ~ (= slice) of cake?* 你要不要再吃一塊蛋糕? *This*

~ *of string is too short.* 這根繩子太短。***(be) in ~s,*** broken; dismantled: 破碎了;拆散了: *The vase is in ~s.* 這花瓶破了。***break (sth) to ~s,*** be in ~s as the result of an accident: 打破;打碎: *The teapot fell and was broken to ~s.* 茶壺掉在地上打碎了。***come/take (sth) to ~s,*** divide (sth) into the parts which make it up: 拆開;分散: *Does this machine come/take to ~s?* 這部機器能拆開嗎? ***go (all) to ~s,*** (colloq) (of a person) break up physically, mentally or morally. (俗)(指人的身體、精神或道德)崩潰。***a ~ of cake,*** (sl) sth very easy. (俚)容易的事。***~ by ~,*** one at a time. 一塊一塊地;一片一片地。***of a ~ (with sth),*** (fig) of the same character (as); consistent (with); in keeping (with). (喻)(與…)同性質的;(與…)一致的。**2** separate instance or example: 個別的事例: *a ~ of news/luck/advice/information, etc;* 一條新聞(一件幸事;一項忠告;一項消息等); single article: 一件東西: *a ~ of furniture.* 一件家具。***give sb a ~ of one's mind,*** tell him candidly what one thinks of him. 坦白告訴某人對他的看法。***say one's ~,*** say what one has to say, sth one has learnt to say, eg a poem to be recited. 說出自己準備說的話(如誦讀一首詩)。**3** standard length or quantity in which goods are prepared for distribution: (指物品長度或數量標準的)件;個;份;塊: *a ~ of wall-paper* (usu 12 yds); 一張壁紙(通常爲十二碼); *a ~ of cloth;* 一塊布; *sold only by the ~.* 只論個或件賣的。'**~-goods** *n pl* textile fabrics (esp cotton and silk) made in standard lengths. (標準長度的)布匹(尤指棉和絲的布匹)。**4** single composition (in art, music, etc): (藝術品、音樂等的)幅;篇;首: *a fine ~ of work/music/poetry;* 一件完美的作品(一支優美的音樂;一首好詩); *a dramatic ~.* 一部劇本。**5** single thing out of a set: (一套中的)件;個: *a dinner service of 50 ~s;* 一套五十件的餐具; one of the wooden, metal, etc objects moved on a board in such games as chess. (棋類等的)棋子。**6** coin: 硬幣: *a ten-pence ~;* 十辨士的硬幣; *a five cent ~;* 五分的硬幣; *a ~ of eight,* an old Spanish silver coin. 西班牙昔時的一種銀幣(等於 8 reals)。**7** gun: 槍砲: *a fixed-~,* field-gun; 野戰砲; *a 'fowling-~,* for shooting game. 鳥槍。**8** (fixed or agreed) amount of work (to be) done: (工作的)件: *pay a workman by the ~,* according to the work produced (not by the time taken). 按件計酬。Hence, 由此產生, '**~-work** *n* ⇨ *time-work* at time¹(13). **9** (in compounds) (用於複合字中) **(a)** (player of a) musical instrument: 樂器(的演奏者): *a six-~ jazz group.* 六人組成的爵士樂隊。**(b)** item in collection: 一套: *a 25-piece dinner service,* ⇨ service(7).

piece² /piːs ; pis/ *vt* [VP6A, 15A, B] ***~ (together),*** put (parts, etc) together; make by joining or adding (pieces) together: 湊合;湊成: *~ together odds and ends of cloth;* 把零碎的布拼湊在一起; *~ a quilt,* make one by putting ~s together; 拼湊布頭而縫成一牀棉被; *~ one thing to another.* 把一件東西拼合到另一件東西上。***~ sth out,*** make (a story, theory, etc) complete by connecting the parts. 藉串連各部分而完成(故事、理論等)。

piece·meal /'piːsmiːl ; 'pis,mil/ *adv* piece by piece; a part at a time: 一件一件地;零碎地: *work done ~.* 零碎做成的工作。□ *adj* coming, done, etc piece by piece. 一件一件的;零碎的。

pied /paɪd ; paɪd/ *adj* of mixed colours, of black and white, eg of birds. (指鳥等)雜色的;黑白的。

pied-à-terre /,pjeɪd ɑː 'teə(r) ; ,pjeda'tɛr/ *n* (F) extra room(s) or house which one keeps for use when needed: (法)備用的房屋;臨時休息處: *He lives in the country, and has a ~ in London.* 他住在鄉間,而在倫敦有個臨時的住所。

pier /pɪə(r) ; pɪr/ *n* **1** structure of wood, iron, etc built out into the sea as a landing-stage; similar structure for walking on for pleasure (often with a pavilion, restaurant, etc). 碼頭(供旅客、貨物上下或供人散步遊樂用,常附有帳篷、餐館等)。**2** pillar supporting a span of a bridge, etc. 橋墩;橋臺。**3** wall between windows or other openings. 窗間壁;戶間壁。'**~-glass** *n* large, long mirror in which one can see the whole of oneself. 可照全身的長鏡;穿衣鏡。

a pier

pierce /pɪəs ; pɪrs/ *vt, vi* **1** [VP6A] (of sharp-pointed instruments) go into or through; make (a hole) by doing this: (指尖銳工具)戳入;刺穿;穿(洞);穿(孔): *The arrow ~d his shoulder.* 箭刺入他的肩膀。*She had her ears ~d in order to be able to wear earrings.* 她爲了能戴耳環而把耳朵穿孔。**2** [VP 6A] (fig, of cold, pain, sounds, etc) force a way into or through; affect deeply: (喻,指寒冷、痛苦、聲音等)刺入;穿透;響徹;深深感動: *Her shrieks ~d the air.* 她的尖叫聲響徹長空。*A ray of light ~d the darkness.* 一道光線穿透黑暗。**3** [VP2C] penetrate (*through, into,* etc): 進入;穿入;突破(與 through, into 等連用): *Our forces ~d through the enemy's lines.* 我軍突破了敵人的防線。**~·ing** *adj* (esp of cold, voices) sharp; penetrating: (尤指寒冷、聲音)刺骨的;尖銳的: *a piercing wind.* 刺骨的風。**~·ing·ly** *adv: a piercingly cold wind.* 刺骨的寒風。

pier·rot /'pɪərəʊ ; ,piə'ro/ *n* **1** character in French pantomime. (法國啞劇中的)丑角。**2** member of a group of entertainers (esp at seaside resorts), dressed in loose white clothes and with a whitened face. 穿寬鬆白衣面塗白色的表演者(尤指在海濱遊樂場所獻藝者)。

pietà /,piːeɪ'tɑː ; pje'tɑ/ *n* (I) painting or sculpture of the Virgin Mary holding the dead body of Jesus in her lap. (義)聖母馬利亞抱耶穌屍體於膝上的畫像或雕像。

piety /'paɪətɪ ; 'paɪətɪ/ *n* **1** [U] devotion to God and good works; being pious. 虔敬;虔誠。**filial ~,** correct behaviour towards a parent. 孝道;孝順。**2** [C] (*pl* -ties) act, etc that shows ~. 虔敬的行爲;孝行。

piffle /'pɪfl ; 'pɪfḷ/ *n* [U] (colloq) nonsense. (俗)廢話;無聊的話;胡說八道。□ *vi* talk ~. 胡說;胡扯。**pif·fling** /'pɪflɪŋ ; 'pɪflɪŋ/ *adj* trivial; worthless. 瑣屑的;無價值的;無聊的。

pig /pɪg ; pɪg/ *n* **1** [C] domestic and wild animal, ⇨ the illus at domestic; 猪(參看 domestic 之插圖); ⇨ boar, hog, sow¹, swine; [U] its flesh (esp *roast pig*) as meat. 猪肉(尤指烤猪肉)。⇨ bacon, ham, pork. ***bring one's pigs to the wrong market,*** fail in an undertaking (to sell sth). 賣東西吃虧。***buy a pig in a poke,*** buy sth without seeing it or knowing its value, which turns out to be worth less than one paid for it. 亂買;瞎買。***pigs might fly,*** (expressing disbelief) wonders might happen. (表示不相信)奇蹟很少發生;不可能的。'**pig·boat** *n* (US sl) submarine. (美俚)潛水艇。,**pig-'headed** *adj* stubborn. 頑固的;倔强的。,**pig-'headedly** *adv* ,**pig-'headedness** *n* '**pig·skin** *n* [U] (leather made of a) pig's skin; (sl) saddle. 猪皮;猪革;(俚)馬鞍。'**pig-sticking** *n* [U] the sport of hunting wild boars with spears. 用矛獵野猪。'**pig·sty** /-staɪ ; -staɪ/ *n* **(a)** small building for pigs. 小猪舍;猪欄;猪圈。**(b)** dirty hovel. 骯髒的住處。'**pig-tail** *n* plait of hair hanging down over the back of the neck and shoulders. 髮辮;辮子。**'pig·wash, 'pig·swill** *nn* [U] waste food (from a brewery or kitchen) given to pigs as food. (給豬吃的)殘食;泔脚;豬食。**2** (colloq) dirty, greedy or ill-mannered person. (俗)骯髒的人;貪婪的人;粗野的人。***make a 'pig of oneself,*** eat or drink to excess. 過分地吃喝。**3 'pig-iron** *n* [U] oblong mass of iron extracted from ore and shaped in a mould. 生鐵塊。□ *vi* (-gg-) ***pig it; pig together,*** live or herd together in dirty conditions. 住在骯髒的環境裡;羣居於骯髒的地方。**'piggish** /-ɪʃ ; -ɪʃ/ *adj* like a pig; dirty, greedy. 像豬的;髒的;貪婪的。**pig·gish·ly** *adv* **pig·gish·ness** *n* **piggery** /'pɪgərɪ ; 'pɪgərɪ/ *n* (*pl* -ries) pig-breeding establishment; pig-farm. 養豬的地方;養豬場。**piggy** /'pɪgɪ ; 'pɪgɪ/ *n* little pig. 小豬。□ *adj* (colloq) greedy. (俗)貪婪的。**'piggy·back,** (US) (美) = pickaback. **'piggy bank** *n* model (of a pig) with a slot for coins, used by a child for saving coin money. (小孩儲蓄錢用的)撲滿。

pigeon /'pɪdʒɪn ; 'pɪdʒən/ *n* **1** bird, wild or tame, of the dove family: 鴿子: *'carrier-~, 'homing-~,* kind trained to carry messages or bred for sport. 傳信鴿。⇨ the illus at bird. 參看 bird 之插圖。**'~-breasted** *adj* (of a person) having a bulging, convex chest. (指人)有鴿胸的;有雞胸的。**'~-toed** *adj* (of a person) having the toes turned inwards. (指人)脚趾向內彎的;足內翻的。**'~·hole** *n* one of a set of small open boxes for keeping papers in. 文件架的格架。□ *vt* put (papers, etc) in a ~hole and ignore or forget them; postpone consideration of: 將(文件)放在架中並置之不理;擱置: *The scheme was ~holed.* 那計畫被擱置了。**2 clay ~,** disc thrown up into the air as a mark for shooting. 飛靶(抛到空中作射擊目標的泥餅)。**3** simpleton; easily deceived person. 愚人;容易受騙的人。**4 ('stool-) ~,** ⇨ stool. **5 'one's ~,** = *one's pidgin,* ⇨ pidgin(2).

pig-iron /'pɪg aɪən ; 'pɪgaɪən/ *n* ⇨ pig(3).

pig·let /'pɪglɪt ; 'pɪglɪt/ *n* young pig. 小豬。

pig·ment /'pɪgmənt ; 'pɪgmənt/ *n* **1** [U] colouring matter for making dyes, paint, etc; [C] particular substance used for this. (用於製造染料、油漆等用的)顏料。**2** [U] the natural colouring matter in the skin, hair, etc of living beings. (生物之皮、毛髮等的)色素。**pig·men·ta·tion** /ˌpɪgmen'teɪʃn ; ˌpɪgmən'teʃən/ *n* colouring of tissues by ~. 染色;着色;色素形成。

pigmy /'pɪgmɪ ; 'pɪgmɪ/ *n* = pygmy.

pike[1] /paɪk ; paɪk/ *n* long wooden shaft with a spearhead, formerly used by soldiers fighting on foot. 矛;槍(昔時步兵用的武器)。**'~·staff** *n* wooden shaft of a ~. 矛桿;矛柄。***as plain as a ~staff,*** quite plain; easy to see or understand. 非常明顯的;顯而易見的。

pike[2] /paɪk ; paɪk/ *n* (*pl* unchanged) large, fierce, freshwater fish. (複數不變)梭子魚(一種兇猛的大淡水魚)。

pike[3] /paɪk ; paɪk/ *n* **1** turnpike road. 收費的公路。**2** toll-bar; toll. 收通行費的關卡;通行費。

pike[4] /paɪk ; paɪk/ *n* (dialect, N of England) peaked top of a hill: (方,英國北部)山峯;尖峯: *Langdale P~.* 蘭德爾峯。

pi·laf(f) /pɪ'læf *US:* -'lɑːf ; pə'lɑf/ = pilau.

pi·las·ter /pɪ'læstə(r) ; pə'læstɚ/ *n* rectangular column, esp an ornamental one that projects from a wall into which it is set. 長方柱;(尤指一半嵌在牆裡的)壁柱;半柱。

pi·lau /pɪ'laʊ ; pɪ'laʊ/ (also **pi·laf(f)** /pɪ'læf *US:* -'lɑːf ; pə'lɑf/) *n* [U] oriental dish of steamed rice with meat, etc. 肉飯。

pil·chard /'pɪltʃəd ; 'pɪltʃɚd/ *n* small sea-fish resembling the herring. 類似鯡魚的一種小海魚。

pile[1] /paɪl ; paɪl/ *n* [C] heavy beam of timber, steel, concrete, etc driven into the ground, esp under water, as a foundation for a building, a support for a bridge, etc. (作屋基、橋基等的)木樁、鐵樁、水泥樁等。**'~-driver** *n* machine for driving ~s into the ground. 打樁機。**'~-dwelling** *n* (also called 亦稱作 *lake-dwelling*) house resting on ~s, esp at the side of a lake. 建於樁上的房屋(尤指建於湖濱者)。□ *vt* [VP6A] supply with ~s. 供以樁;打樁於。

pile[2] /paɪl ; paɪl/ *n* **1** number of things lying one upon another: 堆;排;疊: *a ~ of books.* 一堆書。**2 funeral ~,** heap of wood, etc on which a corpse is burnt. 火葬的柴堆。**3** (colloq) large amount of money. (俗)大量的錢。***make a/one's ~,*** earn a lot of money. 發財;賺大錢。**4** large high building or group of buildings. 高大的建築物;一堆建築物。**5** dry battery for producing electric current. 一種乾電池;電堆。**atomic ~,** apparatus for the controlled release of atomic energy; nuclear reactor. 核子反應器;原子爐。

pile[3] /paɪl ; paɪl/ *vt, vi* **1** [VP6A, 15A, B] make into a ~; put on or in a ~: 堆起;堆疊: *~ logs;* 堆木頭; *~ up dishes on a table;* 將盤子堆在桌上; *~ a table with dishes;* 將盤子堆在桌子上; *~ more coal on (the fire).* 添煤於(火爐)…。***~ arms,*** place (usu four) rifles together with butts on the ground and muzzles touching. 架槍(通常爲四枝步槍,槍托觸地,槍口靠在一起)。***~ it on,*** (colloq) exaggerate. (俗)誇張。***~ on the agony,*** (colloq) make a description of a painful event more agonizing than is necessary. (俗)把一件慘事描寫得格外悲慘。**2** [VP2C] ***~ up,*** **(a)** accumulate: 累積: *My work keeps piling up,* There is more and more work for me to do. 我的工作愈積愈多。**(b)** (of a number of vehicles) crash into each other, forming a ~. (指若干車輛)碰撞在一起。Hence, 由此產生, **'~-up** *n*: *another bad ~-up on the motorway during thick fog.* 濃霧中高速公路上又發生了一件嚴重的連環車禍。**3 *~ into/out of sth,*** enter/leave in a disorderly way: 蜂湧而入(出): *They all ~d into/out of the car/cinema.* 他們一窩蜂地湧進(出)汽車(電影院)。

pile[4] /paɪl ; paɪl/ *n* [U] soft, thick, hair-like surface of velvet, some carpets, etc. (天鵝絨,某些地毯等的)絨面;軟絨。

piles /paɪlz ; paɪlz/ *n* [U] hemorrhoids. 痔瘡。

pil·fer /'pɪlfə(r) ; 'pɪlfɚ/ *vt, vi* [VP6A, 2A] steal, esp in small quantities: (尤指小量地)偷竊: *~ed during transit by rail.* 在火車輸送時被竊。**~er** *n* **~·age** /-ɪdʒ ; -ɪdʒ/ *n* [U] act of ~ing; loss by ~ing. 偷竊;失竊。

pil·grim /'pɪlgrɪm ; 'pɪlgrɪm/ *n* person who travels to a sacred place as an act of religious devotion: 往聖地朝拜者;朝山進香者: *~s to Mecca;* 去麥加聖地朝拜者; *the Canterbury ~s,* in England, during the Middle Ages. (英國中古時)往坎特布里的朝聖者。**the P~ Fathers,** English Puritans who went to America in 1620 and founded the colony of Plymouth, Massachusetts. 1620年往美洲建立普里茅斯殖民地的英國清教徒。**~·age** /-ɪdʒ ; -ɪdʒ/ *n* journey of a ~: 朝聖者的旅程: *go on a ~age to Benares.* 往貝那拉斯朝聖。

pill /pɪl ; pɪl/ *n* **1** small ball or tablet of medicine for swallowing whole. 藥丸。***a bitter ~ (to swallow),*** ⇨ bitter. ***sugar/sweeten the ~,*** make sth disagreeable seem less so. 使令人不愉快之事物較易爲人接受。**'~·box** *n* **(a)** small cylindrical box for holding ~s. 裝藥丸的小圓筒。**(b)** (army use) small (often partly underground) concrete fort. (陸軍用語)槍堡(常爲部分建於地下者);掩體。**2 the ~,** oral contraceptive. 口服避孕藥。***be/go on the ~,*** be taking/start to take such ~s regularly. 按時服用(開始服用)避孕藥丸。

pil·lage /'pɪlɪdʒ ; 'pɪlɪdʒ/ *n, vt* plunder, esp in war. 掠奪;(尤指在戰爭中)搶刼。**pil·lager** /-ɪdʒə(r) ; -ɪdʒɚ/ *n* one who ~s. 掠奪者;搶刼者。

pil·lar /'pɪlə(r) ; 'pɪlɚ/ *n* **1** upright column, of

stone, wood, metal, etc as a support or ornament. 柱子(作支持或裝飾用的石柱、木柱、金屬柱等)。 ⇨ the illus at church, column. 參看 church, column 之插圖。 ***from ~ to post,*** (fig) from one resource to another, to and fro. (喻)從一個地方到另一個地方;走投無路。 **2** (fig) ***~ of,*** strong and important supporter: (喻)堅强而重要的支持者;支柱;棟樑: *a ~ of the establishment.* 這組織的一位强力支持者。 **3** **'~-box** *n* cylindrical container (in GB, scarlet) about 5 feet high, standing in a public place, in which letters are posted. 郵筒(英,深紅色)。 **4** sth in the shape of a ~, eg a column of fire, smoke, cloud or, in a coalmine, of coal left to support the roof. 柱形物(如火柱、煙柱、雲柱或煤礦中留着支持礦頂的煤柱)。

pil·lion /ˈpɪlɪən ; ˈpɪljən/ *n* seat for a second rider behind the rider of a horse; saddle for a passenger behind the driver of a motor-bike: 馬鞍後附加的座位;機器脚踏車的後座: *riding ~;* 騎在後座; *the ~ passenger.* 後座的乘客。

pil·lory /ˈpɪlərɪ ; ˈpɪlərɪ/ *n* (*pl* -ries) wooden framework in which the head and hands of wrongdoers were, in olden times, secured whilst they were ridiculed. 枷(古代的刑具,係木材製成,可將犯人的頭手夾在其中)。

pil·low /ˈpɪləʊ ; ˈpɪlo/ *n* soft cushion for the head, esp when lying in bed. 枕頭。**'~-case / -slip** *n* washable cover for a ~. 枕套。**'~-fight** *n* child's game of fighting with ~s. 枕頭戰(兒童互擲枕頭的遊戲)。 □ *vt* [VP6A] rest, support, on or as on a ~; serve as a ~ for. 擱在枕頭上;枕於;作爲…的枕頭。

pi·lot /ˈpaɪlət ; ˈpaɪlət/ *n* **1** person trained and licensed to take ships into or out of a harbour, along a river, through a canal, etc. 領港員;領航員。 ***drop the ~,*** (fig) dismiss a trusted adviser. (喻)開革可靠的顧問;不聽忠告。 **2** person trained to operate the controls of an aircraft. 飛機駕駛員。 **P~ Officer,** lowest commissioned rank in the Royal Air Force, below that of Flying Officer. 英國皇家空軍少尉。 **3** (attrib) experimental; used to test how sth on a larger scale will work, how it may be improved, etc: (形容用法)實驗的;以小規模作試驗的: *a '~ census / survey / scheme;* 實驗性的人口調查(測量,計畫); *a '~ plant,* for a manufacturing process; 小規模實驗的工廠; *a '~ tunnel.* 試驗性的隧道。 **4** (compounds) (複合字) **'~-boat** *n* one which takes ~s to ships. 領港船;運送領航員到船上的小船。 **'~-cloth** *n* [U] blue woollen cloth used for overcoats, etc. (製大衣等的)藍色呢絨。**'~-engine** *n* railway engine that goes in advance (eg to check for safety). (鐵道上作安全檢查等而先行的)清路機車;前導機車。**'~-fish** *n* small fish which often swims in company with larger fish, eg sharks, or sometimes ships. (常伴隨鯊魚或船隻等游動的)鰤類海魚。 **'~-light / -burner** *n* small flame in a gas cooker or lamp, kept burning continuously, which lights large burners, etc when the gas is turned on. (煤氣爐或燈中之)點火苗(爲着準備點燃大的燈頭而不停地燃着的小火種)。 □ *vt* [VP6A, 15A] act as a ~ to: 領航;駕駛: *~ ships through the Panama Canal.* 引領船隻通過巴拿馬運河。

pi·mento /pɪˈmentəʊ ; pɪˈmɛnto/ *n* (*pl* ~s /-təʊz ; -toz/) **1** [U] dried aromatic berries of a West Indian tree, also called *Jamaica pepper* and *allspice.* 產於西印度羣島的一種胡椒(亦稱 Jamaica pepper 與 all-spice);牙買加胡椒;甘椒。 **2** [C] tree that produces the berries. 牙買加胡椒樹;甘椒樹。

pimp /pɪmp ; pɪmp/ *n* pander(2). 淫媒;拉皮條者;妓院老闆。□ *vi* [VP2A, 3A] ***~ (for sb),*** act as a ~. 作淫媒;拉皮條。

pim·per·nel /ˈpɪmpənel ; ˈpɪmpəˌnɛl/ *n* small annual plant growing wild in wheatfields and on waste land, with scarlet, blue or white flowers. 紫蘩蔞。

pimple /ˈpɪmpl ; ˈpɪmpl̩/ *n* small, hard, inflamed spot on the skin. 丘疹;粉刺;面皰。 **pim·pled** *adj* having ~s. 有丘疹的;長粉刺的;長面皰的。 **pim·ply** /ˈpɪmplɪ ; ˈpɪmplɪ/ *adj* (-ier, -iest) having ~s: 有丘疹的;長粉刺的: *a pimply boy / face.* 長丘疹的男孩(臉)。

pin¹ /pɪn ; pɪn/ *n* **1** short, thin piece of stiff wire with a sharp point and a round head, used for fastening together parts of a dress, papers, etc. 大頭針。 ***don't care a pin,*** don't care at all. 一點也不在乎。 ***neat as a new pin,*** very neat. 非常整潔。 ***pins and needles,*** tingling sensation in a part of the body caused by blood flowing again after its circulation has been checked for a time. (身體某部血液受阻一段時間後,再行流動時所感到的)發痲;刺痲。 **2** similar piece of wire with an ornamental head for special purposes: 飾針;別針: *a 'tie-pin;* 領帶別針; *a 'hat-pin.* 帽子飾針。 **'safety-pin,** pin bent with a guard at one end to protect and hold fast the point at the other end. 安全別針。 ⇨ the illus at safety. 參看 safety 之插圖。 **3** peg of wood or metal for various purposes. (木製的或金屬的)栓;釘;針。⇨ *drawing-pin* at drawing, *hairpin* at hair(2), ninepins, *rolling-pin* at roll²(10); peg round which a string of a musical instrument is fastened. (樂器上繫絃的)木栓。 **'pin-ball** *n* game played with a small ball which has to be electrically struck against one of several upright knobs, and guided into one of several numbered holes on a sloping board. 彈球戲(斜板上置若干標有數字的洞,電動彈球進洞時需觸及釘於板上的釘頭)。**'pin-table** *n* table used in pin-ball. 彈球臺。 **4** (*pl*) (sl) legs: (複)(俚)腿: *He's quick on his ~s.* 他走(跑)得快。 **5** (compounds) (複合字) **'pin-cushion** *n* pad into which (a dressmaker's) pins are stuck. (裁縫揷針用的)針墊。**'pin·head** *n* (colloq) very stupid person. (俗)非常愚蠢之人;傻瓜。 **'pin-money** *n* [U] money allowance to, or money earned by, a woman for dress, small personal necessities, etc. (給婦女的)零用錢;(婦女的)私房錢。 **'pin-point** *n* sth very small; (attrib, of targets) requiring accurate and precise bombing or shelling. 極小之物;(形容用法,指目標)需要精確轟擊的。 □ *vt* find, hit, such a target with the required accuracy: 精確地找到(目標);精確地轟擊(目標): *Our planes pin-pointed the target.* 我們的飛機精確地炸中目標。 **'pin-prick** *n* (fig) small act, remark, etc causing annoyance. (喻)令人氣惱的小動作、話語等。**'pin-stripe** *adj* (of dress material) with many very narrow stripes. (指衣料)帶有許多細窄條紋的。

pin² /pɪn ; pɪn/ *vt* (-nn-) [VP15A, B] **1** fasten (things *together, up, to* sth, etc) with a pin or pins: (用針)別住;釘住(東西,後接 together, up, to 等): *pin papers together;* 將文件用針別起來; *pin up a notice,* eg with drawing-pins on a notice-board. 釘上一張告示(如用圖釘釘在佈告板上)。 ***pin sth on sb,*** make him appear responsible; place the blame for sth on sb. 讓某人對某事負責;將責任推到某人身上。 ***pin one's hopes on sb,*** have strong hope that he will help; rely on him unquestioningly. 將希望寄託在某人身上;毫不懷疑地依賴某人。 **'pin-up** *n* picture of a favourite or much admired person, pinned up on a wall: 釘在牆上的最令人喜歡或十分令人愛慕的人物的照片: (attrib) (形容用法) *a 'pin-up girl.* 其照片常被人釘在牆上的漂亮女孩子。 **2** make unable to move: 阻止;扣牢;止住: *He was pinned under the wreckage / the wrecked car.* 他被壓在殘骸(破車子)底下。*He pinned his assailant against the wall,* held him there and prevented him from moving. 他把攻擊他的人按在牆上。 *The troops were pinned down by accurate fire,* were unable to advance or withdraw. 部隊被準確的炮火所困(無法前進或後退)。 ***pin sb down,*** (fig) get him to commit himself, to state his intentions, etc: (喻)使某人履行其義務(說明其意圖等): *He's a difficult man to pin down.* 他是個不易就範的人。***pin sb down to sth,*** get him to agree to keep, eg a promise, an agreement. 使某人信守諾言(遵守合約)。

pina·fore /ˈpɪnəfɔ:(r); ˈpɪnə,for/ *n* loose article of clothing worn over a dress to keep it clean. 圍裙;圍兜;涎布。

pince-nez /ˈpæns neɪ; ˈpæns,ne/ *n* pair of spectacles with a spring to clip the nose (instead of a frame that fits round the ears). 夾鼻眼鏡(不用鉤住耳朵者)。

pin·cers /ˈpɪnsəz; ˈpɪnsɚz/ *n pl* **(pair of) ~. 1** instrument for gripping things, pulling nails out of wood, etc. 鉗子;手鉗。⇨ the illus at tool. 參看 tool 之插圖。ˈ**pincer movement,** (mil) attack by two converging forces. (軍)鉗形攻勢。**2** pincer-shaped claws of certain shellfish. (蟹、蝦等的)螯。⇨ the illus at crustacean. 參看 crustacean 之插圖。

pinch /pɪntʃ; pɪntʃ/ *vt, vi* **1** [VP6A, 15A, B] take in a tight grip between the thumb and finger; have in a tight grip between two hard things which are pressed together: 捏;掐;夾;擠: *He ~ed the boy's cheek.* 他掐那男孩的面頰。*He ~ed the top of the plants off/~ed out the side shoots.* 他把植物的頂端掐掉(把旁邊的新芽摘掉)。*I ~ed my finger in the doorway.* 我在門口夾到了手指頭。**2** [VP 6A, 2A] be too tight; hurt by being too tight: 緊壓;擠痛: *These shoes ~ (me).* 這雙鞋子會夾腳。***(see, etc) where the shoe ~es,*** (fig) where the difficulty or hardship lies. (喩)(找出)困難所在。**3** (in passive) suffer; feel the effects of: (用於被動語態)遭受;嚐到: *be ~ed with cold/poverty.* 遭受寒冷(貧窮)之苦。***be ~ed for money,*** be short of money. 缺少錢;經濟拮据。**4** [VP6A] (colloq) steal; take without permission: (俗)偷;竊;未經許可而取用: *Who's ~ed my dictionary?* 誰拿了我的字典? **5** [VP2A] be niggardly; be very mean; live sparingly or economically: 小氣;吝嗇;節省: *parents who have to ~ and scrape in order to save money for a child's clothes.* 必須格外節儉以便爲孩子買衣服的父母。**6** (sl) (of the police) take into custody; arrest: (俚)(指警察)逮捕;捉住: *You'll be ~ed if you're not careful.* 你如果不小心,將會被逮捕。□ *n* **1** act of ~ing; painful squeeze: 捏;擠;夾: *He gave her a spiteful ~.* 他狠狠地擰她一下。**2** (fig) stress: (喩)重壓;壓迫: *feel the ~ of poverty.* 感到貧窮的痛苦。**3** amount which can be taken up with the thumb and finger: 一撮或一捻之量: *a ~ of salt/snuff.* 一撮鹽(鼻煙)。***take sth with a ~ of salt,*** ⇨ salt. **4** ***at a ~; if it comes to the ~,*** if there is need and if there is no other way: 必要時: *We can get six people round the table at a ~.* 必要時我們可以使六個人坐在一桌。

pinch·beck /ˈpɪntʃbek; ˈpɪntʃbɛk/ *n* alloy of copper and zinc, simulating gold, used in cheap jewellery, etc. 用於廉價珠寶等的合金;金色銅。□ *adj* sham. 假的。

pine¹ /paɪn; paɪn/ *n* [C] kinds of evergreen tree with needle-shaped leaves (ˈ**~-needles**) and cones (ˈ**~-cones**); [U] the wood of this tree. 松樹;松木。⇨ the illus at tree. 參看 tree 之插圖。

pine² /paɪn; paɪn/ *vi* **1** [VP2A, C] waste away through sorrow or illness: 消瘦;憔悴: *pining from hunger.* 餓瘦了。**2** [VP3A, 4C] ***~ for sth; ~ to do sth,*** have a strong desire: 渴望;渴慕: *exiles pining for home/to return home.* 渴望回家的流亡者。

pin·eal /ˈpaɪnɪəl; ˈpɪnɪəl/ *adj* shaped like a pine-cone: 松果形的: *~ gland,* gland in the brain. 松果腺。

pine·apple /ˈpaɪnæpl; ˈpaɪn,æpl/ *n* [C] (tropical plant with) sweet, juicy fruit; [U] this as food: 鳳梨樹;鳳梨(亦名波羅): *~ juice;* 鳳梨汁; *tinned ~.* 罐頭鳳梨。⇨ the illus at fruit. 參看 fruit 之插圖。

ping /pɪŋ; pɪŋ/ *n* short, sharp, ringing sound as of elastic being stretched and released or a rifle bullet in the air or striking a hard substance. 砰(短促尖銳的響聲,如槍彈在空中的響聲,或擊中硬物的響聲)。□ *vi* make this sound. 發出砰聲。

ping·pong /ˈpɪŋpɒŋ; ˈpɪŋ,pɑŋ/ *n* (colloq) table tennis. (俗)乒乓球;桌球。

pin·ion¹ /ˈpɪnɪən; ˈpɪnjən/ *n* **1** bird's wing, esp the outer joint; flight-feather of a bird. 鳥翼(尤指末端的一段);翮。**2** (poet) wing: (詩)翼;翅: *an eagle's ~s.* 鷹的翅膀。□ *vt* [VP6A] **1** cut off a ~ of (a wing or bird) to hamper flight. 剪掉(翼)之尖端或(鳥)之羽翼使不能飛。**2** [VP15A, B] ***~ (to/together),*** bind the arms of (a person); bind (sb's arms); bind (sb) fast (to sth). 綁住(一人)的手臂;綁住(某人的手臂);將(某人)綁在(某物)上。

pin·ion² /ˈpɪnɪən; ˈpɪnjən/ *n* small cogwheel with teeth fitting into those of a larger cogwheel. (接合大齒輪的)小齒輪;齰輪;副齒輪。⇨ the illus at gear. 參看 gear 之插圖。

pink¹ /pɪŋk; pɪŋk/ *n* **1** [U] pale red colour of various kinds (*rose ~, salmon ~*). 淡紅色;粉紅色(玫瑰紅、橙紅)。**~ gin,** portion of gin with angostura. 苦味杜松子酒。**2** [C] garden plant with sweet-smelling white, ~, crimson or variegated flowers. 石竹;石竹花。**3** ***in the ~ (of health),*** (colloq) very well. (俗)(健康)良好;甚佳。□ *adj* **1** of pale red colour. 淡紅的;粉紅的。**2** (colloq) inclined to be left wing in politics. (俗)(政治上)左傾的。⇨ red. **~·ish** /-ɪʃ; -ɪʃ/ *adj* rather ~. 略帶淡紅色的。

pink² /pɪŋk; pɪŋk/ *vt* **1** [VP6A] pierce with a sword. 以劍刺。**2** [VP6A, 15B] ***~ (out),*** decorate (leather, cloth) with small holes, etc. 以小孔等裝飾(皮革、布)。ˈ**~·ing scissors/shears** *n pl* sewing scissors with serrated edges, used to prevent edges of cloth from fraying. 有鋸齒形刃的剪刀(用以剪布邊以防其脫散)。

pink³ /pɪŋk; pɪŋk/ *vi* (of an internal combustion engine) make high-pitched explosive sounds; knock(3). (指內燃機)發響爆聲;發格達格達的響聲。

pin·nace /ˈpɪnɪs; ˈpɪnɪs/ *n* big ship's small motor-boat. 附屬於大船的小汽艇。

pin·nacle /ˈpɪnəkl; ˈpɪnəkl̩/ *n* **1** tall, pointed ornament built on to a roof or buttress. (屋頂上的)尖頂;尖塔。⇨ the illus at church. 參看 church 之插圖。**2** high, slender mountain peak. 尖峯;高峯。**3** (fig) highest point: (喩)最高點;頂點: *at the ~ of his fame.* 在他聲望最高的時候。□ *vt* set (as) on a ~; supply with ~s. 置於尖頂上;築尖頂於;建尖塔於。

pin·nate /ˈpɪneɪt; ˈpɪnet/ *adj* (bot) (of a leaf) formed of small leaves on opposite sides of a stem. (植物)(指葉)由葉柄兩旁對稱的小葉構成的;羽狀的。

pinny /ˈpɪnɪ; ˈpɪnɪ/ *n* (*pl* -nies) (child's name for a) pinafore. (兒語)圍兜;涎布。

pint /paɪnt; paɪnt/ *n* unit of measure for liquids and certain dry goods, one-eighth of a gallon or about ·57 of a litre: 品脫(容量單位,等於八分之一加侖或約 0·57 公升): *a ~ of milk/beer/lentils.* 一品脫的牛奶(啤酒,扁豆)。⇨ App 5. 參看附錄五。

pion·eer /,paɪəˈnɪə(r); ,paɪəˈnɪr/ *n* **1** person who goes into a new or undeveloped country to settle or work there; first student of a new branch of study, etc; explorer. 拓荒者;開闢者;(新學科等的)先驅;探險者。**2** (mil) one of an advance party of soldiers (eg clearing or making roads). (軍)先遣兵;工兵(擔任清除道路障礙或開通道路等任務)。□ *vi, vt* [VP2A] act as a ~; [VP6A] open up (a way, etc); show (new methods, etc) to others. 作先驅;作拓荒者;開闢(道路等);提倡(新法等)。

pious /ˈpaɪəs; ˈpaɪəs/ *adj* **1** having, showing, deep devotion to religion. 虔誠的;虔敬的。**2** (old use) dutiful to parents. (舊用法)孝順的。**~·ly** *adv*

pip¹ /pɪp; pɪp/ *n* seed, esp of a lemon, orange, apple or pear. 種子(尤指檸檬、柑、蘋果或梨的種子)。⇨ the illus at fruit. 參看 fruit 之插圖。

pip² /pɪp; pɪp/ *n* **the pip,** disease of poultry; (sl) fit of depression or irritation. 家禽的舌病;(俚)沮喪;厭煩。***have/get/give sb the pip:*** 感到(使某人感到)厭煩: *That man gives me the pip.* 那人使我感

到厭煩。

pip³ /pɪp ; pɪp/ *n* note of a time-signal on the telephone or radio: (電話或收音機的)報時響聲: *The last of the six pips gives the time to the second.* 六個響聲的最後一響表示準確的時刻。

pip⁴ /pɪp ; pɪp/ *n* **1** each spot on playing-cards, dice and dominoes. (紙牌、骰子、骨牌上的)點。 **2** (GB colloq) star (1 to 3 according to rank) on an army officer's shoulder-strap. (英俗)陸軍軍官肩章上的星(一至三顆,視階級而定)。

pip⁵ /pɪp ; pɪp/ *vt* (-pp-) [VP6A] (GB colloq) hit with a gunshot. (英俗)以子彈射擊。***pipped at the post,*** defeated at the last moment. 於最後時刻被擊敗;功敗垂成。

pi·pal /ˈpiːpəl ; ˈpipəl/ ⇨ peepul.

pipe¹ /paɪp ; paɪp/ *n* **1** tube through which liquids or gases can flow: (供液體或氣體流動的)管: *ˈwater-~s;* 水管; *ˈgas-~s;* 煤氣管; *ˈdrain~s.* 排水管。 **ˈ~-line** *n* line of connected ~s, often underground, for conveying eg petroleum to distant places. (通常埋設於地下用以輸送石油等的)管道;管線。 ***in the ~line,*** (of any kind of goods or proposals) on the way; about to be delivered in a schedule, list, etc to receive attention. (指任何貨物或提議)運輸中;遞送中;即將遞送。 **2** musical wind-instrument (a single tube with holes stopped by the fingers); each of the tubes from which sound is produced in an organ; (*pl*) bag~s. 管樂器(如笛、簫等);(風琴中的)音管;(複)風笛。 **3** (sound of the) whistle used by a boatswain. (水手長用的)笛子;(水手長的)笛聲。 **4** song or note of a bird. (鳥的)鳴聲。 **5** tubular organ in the body: (身體內的)管狀器官: *ˈwind~.* 氣管。 **6 (toˈbacco) ~,** tube with a bowl, used for smoking tobacco; quantity of tobacco held in the bowl: 煙斗;一煙斗的煙絲: *smoke a ~.* 抽煙斗。 *Give me a ~ of tobacco, please.* 請給我一煙斗的煙絲。 ***Put ˈthat in your ~ and smoke it,*** (colloq) That is sth for you to reflect upon and accept if you can. (俗)你好好考慮一下吧。 **ˈ~·clay** *n* [U] fine, white clay formerly used for making tobacco ~s, and (by soldiers) for whitening leather belts and other pieces of equipment. 煙斗泥;管土(昔時用以製煙斗及士兵用來擦皮帶等裝備的上等白黏土)。 **ˈ~·dream** *n* plan, idea, etc that is fantastic and impracticable. 狂想;幻想;不切實際的計畫、觀念等。 **ˈ~-rack** *n* rack for tobacco ~s. 煙斗架。 **7** cask for wine (equal to about 105 gallons). 大酒桶(約裝 105 加侖)。 **ˈ~·ful** /-fʊl ; -ˌfʊl/ *n* as much as a ~(6) holds. 一煙斗的量。

pipe² /paɪp ; paɪp/ *vi, vt* **1** [VP6A, 15A] convey (water, etc) through pipes: 以管輸送(水等): *~ water into a house.* 以管輸送水到屋裡。 **2** [VP6A, 2A] play (a tune) on a pipe; whistle; utter or sing in a thin, treble voice. 以管樂器吹奏(曲調);吹哨子;(以尖細的聲音)說或唱。 [VP2C] ***~ up,*** (colloq) begin to play, sing or speak. (俗)開始吹奏;開始唱;開始說。 *~* ***down*** (colloq) be quiet; be less noisy or cocksure. (俗)安靜下來;壓低過高的聲音;不再過於自信。 **3** [VP15A] (naut) summon (sailors) by blowing a boatswain's pipe: (航海)吹水手長的笛子召集(水手): *~ all hands on deck;* 吹笛子召集所有的水手到甲板上; lead or welcome (sb) by the sound of a boatswain's pipe: 以水手長的笛聲引領或歡迎(某人): *~ the captain on board.* 以笛聲歡迎船長登船。 **4** [VP6A] trim (a dress), ornament (a cake, etc) with piping. 以管狀窄條裝飾(衣服);以糖線裝飾(蛋糕等)。⇨ piping(2).

piper /ˈpaɪpə(r) ; ˈpaɪpɚ/ *n* one who plays on a pipe, esp a player of the bagpipes. 吹管樂器者;(尤指)吹風笛者。 ***pay the ~ (and call the tune),*** bear the cost of an undertaking (and have control of what is done). 負擔費用(而取得控制權)。

pip·ette /pɪˈpet ; pɪˈpɛt/ *n* slender tube for transferring small quantities of liquid, esp in chemistry. 吸量管(用以輸送小量液體的細管,尤指作化學實驗時所用者);球管;移液管。

pip·ing /ˈpaɪpɪŋ ; ˈpaɪpɪŋ/ *n* [U] **1** length of pipes(1), esp for water and drains: 管道;管系(尤指水管和排水管);某管系的總長: *ten feet of lead ~.* 十呎長的鉛管。 **2** narrow cord-like material used to ornament the edges of some garments; cord-like lines of icing-sugar used to decorate cakes, etc. (裝飾衣服邊的)管狀窄條;(裝飾糕餅等的)糖線。 **3** action of playing on a pipe; sound produced from a pipe. 吹笛;笛聲。 □ *adj* like the sound from a pipe(2): 似笛聲的;尖聲的: *a ~ voice.* 尖叫聲。 ***the ~ time(s) of peace,*** time(s) when there is peaceful music instead of martial music. 承平的時代。 □ *adv ~* ***hot,*** (of liquids, food) hissing or steaming hot. (指液體、食物)滾燙的。

pip·pin /ˈpɪpɪn ; ˈpɪpɪn/ *n* kinds of apple. 數種蘋果的統稱。

pip·squeak /ˈpɪpskwiːk ; ˈpɪpskwik/ *n* (sl) insignificant or contemptible person or thing. (俚)不重要的人或物;可輕視的人或物。

pi·quant /ˈpiːkənt ; ˈpikənt/ *adj* pleasantly sharp to the taste: 辛辣而開胃的: *a ~ sauce;* 辣醬; (fig) pleasantly exciting to the mind: (喻)刺激的;令人興奮的: *a ~ bit of gossip.* 有趣的閒話。 **~·ly** *adv* **pi·quancy** /-ənsɪ ; -ənsɪ/ *n* the quality of being ~. 辛辣;刺激;興奮。

pique /piːk ; pik/ *vt* [VP6A] **1** hurt the pride or self-respect of. 傷害…的自尊心;激怒;使生氣。 **2** stir (the curiosity); stir the curiosity of (sb). 激起(好奇心);激起(某人的)好奇心。 **3** *~* ***oneself on sth,*** pride oneself on; feel proud about: 以…自豪;對…感到自傲: *He ~d himself on being punctual.* 他以能準時自傲。 □ *n* [U, C] pride; feeling one has when one's curiosity is unsatisfied; resentment: 驕傲;(好奇心未能滿足時的)不高興;憤慨: *go away in a fit of ~;* 不高興地走開; *take a ~ against sb.* 生某人的氣。

pi·quet /pɪˈket ; pɪˈkɛt/ *n* card game for two players with a pack of 32 cards. 兩人玩的一種紙牌戲(用 32 張紙牌)。

pi·ranha /pɪˈrɑːnjə ; pɪˈrɑnjə/ *n* (kinds of) tropical American freshwater fish, noted for attacking and eating live animals. 產於南美洲的一種淡水魚,會攻擊並吞食活的動物。

pi·rate /ˈpaɪərət ; ˈpaɪrət/ *n* **1** sea-robber; sea-robber's ship. 海盜;海盜船。 **2** person who infringes another's copyright, who broadcasts without a licence, usurps trading rights, etc. (不顧著作權的)盜印者;無照設立廣播電台者;侵犯專利權者。 □ *vt* [VP6A] use, reproduce (a book, a recording, another's work, etc) without authority and for one's own profit. 盜印(書籍);盜製(唱片、錄音帶等)。 **pi·rati·cal** /ˌpaɪəˈrætɪkl ; paɪˈrætɪkl/ *adj* of, in the manner of, a ~. 海盜的;海盜作風的;盜印的;盜製的。 **pi·rati·cally** /-klɪ ; -klɪ/ *adv* **pi·racy** /ˈpaɪərəsɪ ; ˈpaɪrəsɪ/ *n* (*pl* -cies) [U] robbery by ~s; pirating of books, etc; [C] instance of either of these. 海上搶劫;盜印書籍;盜製唱片、錄音帶等。

pir·ou·ette /ˌpɪrʊˈet ; ˌpɪrʊˈɛt/ *n* [C] ballet-dancer's rapid turn on the ball of the foot or on the point of the toe. (芭蕾舞蹈者的)單足旋轉;趾尖旋轉。 □ *vi* dance a ~ or ~s. (跳芭蕾舞時)用單足旋轉;用趾尖旋轉。

pis al·ler /ˌpiːz ˈæleɪ *US:* ˌpiːz æˈleɪ ; ˌpizaˈle/ *n* (F) the last resort; course of action taken because there seems to be nothing better. (法)最後的手段。

pis·ca·tor·ial /ˌpɪskəˈtɔːrɪəl ; ˌpɪskəˈtorɪəl/ *adj* of fishing; addicted to fishing. 捕魚的;嗜好釣魚的。

Pis·ces /ˈpaɪsiːz ; ˈpɪsiz/ *n* twelfth sign of the zodiac (also called 亦稱作 *the fish*). (十二宮中的)雙魚宮。⇨ the illus at zodiac. 參看 zodiac 之插圖。

piss /pɪs ; pɪs/ *vt, vi* ⚠ (not in polite use) pass urine; discharge (blood) with urine; wet with urine. (諱)(不雅的用法)小便;排尿帶血;尿濕: ***P~ off!*** (vulg) Go away! (鄙)走開!滾蛋! **~ed** *adj* (vulg) very drunk. (鄙)大醉的。**~ed off,** (vulg) annoyed. (鄙)厭煩的。□ *n* urine. 尿。

pis·ta·chio /pɪˈstɑːtʃɪəʊ *US:* -tæʃɪəʊ ; pɪsˈtɑʃɪ,o/ *n* (*pl* ~s /-tʃɪəʊz ; -ʃɪoz/) (tree yielding) nut with a green edible kernel; colour of this kernel. 阿月渾子樹;阿月渾子(其綠色果仁可吃);其果仁的綠色。

pis·til /ˈpɪstl ; ˈpɪstl̩/ *n* seed-producing part of a flower. 雌蕊。⇨ the illus at flower. 參看 flower 之挿圖。

pis·tol /ˈpɪstl ; ˈpɪstl̩/ *n* [C] small firearm held and fired in one hand. 手槍。***hold a ~ to sb's head,*** try, by using threats, to make him do what one wants. 以恐嚇方式使某人從命。

pis·ton /ˈpɪstən ; ˈpɪstn/ *n* round plate or short cylinder of wood or metal, fitting closely inside another cylinder or tube in which it moves up and down or backwards and forwards, used in engines, pumps, etc to impart or receive motion by means of a rod, called a ˈ*~-rod.* (引擎、抽水機等中的)活塞(藉活塞桿 piston-rod, 以傳遞或承受運動)。⇨ the illus at motor. 參看 motor 之挿圖。**ˈ~ engined,** (of aircraft) having engines with ~s (contrasted with jet engines). (指飛機)裝活塞引擎的(與噴射引擎相對)。**ˈ~ ring** *n* split metal ring used in a ~ to make a gastight joint. 活塞脹圈;活塞環。

pit¹ /pɪt ; pɪt/ *n* **1** hole in the earth, usu with steep sides, esp one from which material is dug out (*a ˈchalk-pit; a ˈclay-pit; a ˈcoal-pit*) or for industrial purposes (*a ˈsaw-pit*). 坑(尤指挖掘後所留的坑，如 chalk-pit 白堊坑，clay-pit 黏土坑，coal-pit 煤坑;或爲着工業目的所掘成的坑,如 saw-pit 鋸木坑)。**ˈpit·head** *n* entrance of a coalmine: 煤礦坑入口: *pithead baths.* 在煤礦坑口的浴室。**ˈpit·man** /-mən ; -mən/ *n* (*pl* -men) collier; worker in a coal-pit. 礦工;煤礦工。**ˈpit pony** *n* pony kept underground in coalmines. 煤礦坑裡運輸用的小馬。**ˈpit-prop** *n* prop used to support the roof of a gallery in a mine pit. 用以支持坑道頂部的支柱。**ˈpit·saw** *n* saw used in a saw-pit. 鋸木坑內用的鋸。⇨ saw². **2** covered hole as a trap for wild animals, etc. (捕獸等的)陷阱。**ˈpit·fall** *n* covered pit as a trap for animals; (more usu, fig) unsuspected snare or danger. 陷坑;(更常作比喻用)誘惑物;圈套;暗伏的危險。**3** hollow in an animal or plant body. 動物或植物體的凹陷處。***the pit of the stomach,*** the depression in the belly between the ribs. 心窩。⇨ also *armpit* at arm¹(1). **4** scar left on the body after smallpox. 生天花後的疤痕;痲子。 **5** (GB, not US) seats on the ground floor of a theatre behind the stalls; people occupying these seats. (英,不用於美國)(戲院中之)正廳後座;正廳後座的觀衆。 **6** (US) part of the floor of an exchange used for a special commodity: (美)交易所供特定貨品交易的地方: *the ˈwheat-pit.* 小麥交易處。 **7 the pit,** (rhet, biblical) hell. (修辭,聖經用語)地獄。 **8** hole in the floor (of a garage, workshop) from which the underside of a motor-vehicle can be examined and repaired; place (at a race-course) at which racing cars stop for fuel, new tyres, etc, during a race. (修車場內)檢修汽車底部的地上凹坑;(賽車場內)比賽中供汽車加油或換車胎等的地方。 **9** = cockpit. □ *vt* **1** [VP6A] mark with pits(4) or with hollows in the ground: 使有痘痕;使有痲子;使有凹陷: *a face pitted with smallpox;* 痲臉; *the surface of the moon, pitted with craters.* 佈滿岩坑的月球表面。**2** [VP14] ~ ***against,*** cause to struggle against: 使與…相鬪: *pit one's wits against the Income Tax Office.* 以智力對抗所得稅務局。

pit² /pɪt ; pɪt/ *n* (US) hard, stone-like seed (of such fruits as cherries, plums, peaches, dates). (美)(櫻桃、李、桃、棗等水果的)核。□ *vt* (-tt-) (US) remove pits from. (美)除去…之核。

pit-a-pat /ˌpɪt ə ˈpæt ; ˈpɪtə,pæt/ *adv* with quick beating, with the sound of light, quick taps or steps: 畢畢卜卜地;有輕快之拍擊或步伐聲地: *Her heart／feet went ~.* 她的心卜卜地跳(她的脚噼啪噼啪地走)。

pitch¹ /pɪtʃ ; pɪtʃ/ *n* **1** place where sb (esp a street trader) usu does business, where a street entertainer usu performs. (街上零售商的)售貨攤;(街上賣藝人的)路邊表演場。***queer sb's ~,*** upset his plans; thwart him. 破壞某人的計畫;阻撓某人。 **2** (cricket) part of the ground between the wickets; manner in which the ball is delivered in bowling; (baseball) manner or act of pitching the ball; (football) ground, field (the usual words) on which the game is played. (板球)柱與柱間的場地;投球式;(棒球)投球式;投球;(足球)足球場 (ground, field 較常用)。 **3** act of pitching or throwing anything; distance to which sth is thrown. 投擲;所投的距離。 **4** (music and speech) degree of highness or lowness; quality of sound. (音樂與說話)音高;音質。 **5** degree: 程度: *at the lowest ~ of his (ill) fortune.* 在他最不幸的時候。*Excitement rose to fever ~.* 興奮達到極點。 **6** amount of slope (esp of a roof). 斜度(尤指屋頂的斜度)。 **7** (of a ship) process of pitching(5). (指船)上下顛簸。

pitch² /pɪtʃ ; pɪtʃ/ *n* [U] black substance made from coal-tar, turpentine or petroleum, sticky and semi-liquid when hot, hard when cold, used to fill cracks or spaces, eg between planks forming a floor or ship's deck, make roofs waterproof, etc. 瀝青(由煤焦油或松節油提煉的黑黏物,遇熱成黏性半液體,遇冷變硬,用以塡塞板面等之間的裂縫或使屋頂防水等)。***as black／dark as ~,*** completely black／dark. 漆黑的;極暗的。**ˌ~-ˈblack／-ˈdark** *adjj* completely black／dark. 漆黑的;極暗的。**ˈ~-blende** *n* [U] black, shining mineral ore (oxide of uranium) yielding radium. 瀝青鈾礦。**ˈ~ pine** *n* specially resinous kinds of pine-tree or its wood. 脂松;脂松木。

pitch³ /pɪtʃ ; pɪtʃ/ *vt, vi* **1** [VP6A] set up, erect (a tent, camp); [VP2A] set up one's tent or camp. 搭架(帳幕);紮(營);搭帳篷;紮營。 **2** [VP6A, 15A, B] throw (a ball, etc); throw (sb or sth *out, aside,* etc), esp with impatience or energetic dislike: 投;擲(球等);抛;丢棄(某人或某物,後接 out, aside 等): *Let's ~ the drunkard out.* 我們來把那個醉鬼攆出去。*The men were ~ing hay,* lifting it, eg into a wagon, with forks. 那些人正在用叉擲乾草(於車裡)。**ˈ~·fork** *n* long-handled fork with sharp prongs for lifting hay, etc. (叉乾草等用的)長柄叉。□ *vt* lift or move with a fork; (fig) thrust (a person) forcibly (*into* a position, etc). 以叉叉起;以叉叉去;(喻)强挿(某人)(於某一位置等,與 into 連用)。 **3** [VP15A] (music) set in a certain pitch(4) or key: (音樂)定爲某調: *~ a tune too high／in a lower key.* 把一歌曲的調子定得太高(較低)。*This song is ~ed too low for me.* 這支歌的調子對我是太低了。 **4** [VP2C, 15A, B] (cause to) fall heavily forwards or outwards: (使)向前傾跌;(使)向外摔: *He ~ed on his head.* 他頭朝地跌倒了。*The carriage overturned and the passengers were ~ed out.* 車子翻了,乘客都被摔出來。 **5** [VP2A, C] (of a ship) move up and down as the bows rise and fall. (指船)上下顛簸。⇨ roll²(6). **6** ~ ***in,*** set to work with energy. 開始努力工作。~ ***into,*** **(a)** attack violently: 猛烈攻擊: *They ~ed into him.* 他們猛烈攻擊他。**(b)** get busy with: 着手;忙於做某事: *We ~ed into the work.* 我們開始忙於那件工作。*The hungry boy ~ed into the meatpie,* began to eat it. 那個飢餓的男孩開始大吃肉餡餅。~ ***upon,*** select by chance; light or pick upon: 偶然選中;偶然發現: *~ upon the most suitable man for the job.* 碰巧選到最適當的人做那工作。**7 *~ed battle,*** one that is fought with troops arranged in prepared positions, not a casual encounter. 陣地戰(並非偶然的遭遇戰)。 **8** [VP15B, 22] (cricket) cause (the ball) to strike the ground near or around the wicket: (板球)使(球)碰到三柱門附近的地面: *~ the ball short;* 擊短球; *~ the ball* *up a bit;* 球投得高一點; (baseball) throw (the ball) to the batter. (棒球)將(球)投向打擊手。~ ***wickets,*** (cricket) fix the stumps in the ground with the bails in place. (板球)固定三柱門於地上。**9** (sl) tell (a yarn, a story). (俚)講(故事)。**10** **ˌ~-and-ˈtoss** *n* game of skill and chance in which coins are ~ed at a mark. 一種向標的擲錢的遊戲。

pitcher[1] /ˈpɪtʃə(r);ˈpɪtʃɚ/ *n* large (usu earthenware) vessel with a handle and lip for holding liquids; large jug. 大水罐(通常爲陶製品,有柄和嘴);大壺;盂。

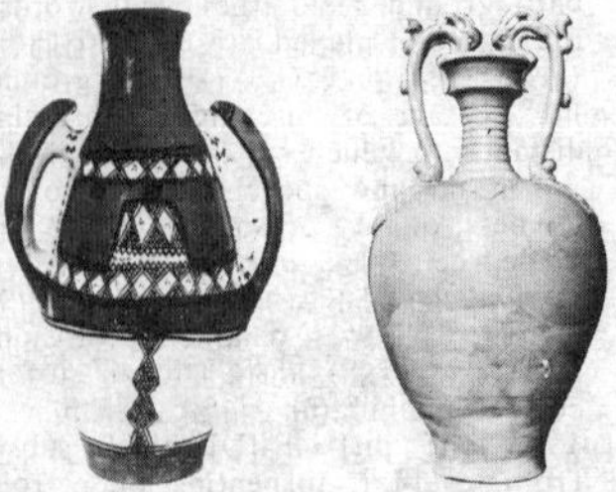

pitchers

pitcher[2] /ˈpɪtʃə(r) ; ˈpɪtʃɚ/ *n* (baseball) player who throws the ball. (棒球)投手。⇨ the illus at baseball. 參看 baseball 之挿圖。

pit·eous /ˈpɪtɪəs ; ˈpɪtɪəs/ *adj* arousing pity. 令人同情的;可憐的。**~·ly** *adv*

pit·fall /ˈpɪtfɔːl ; ˈpɪtˌfɔl/ ⇨ pit[1](2).

pith /pɪθ ; pɪθ/ *n* [U] **1** soft substance that fills the stems of some plants (eg reeds); similar substance lining the rind of oranges, etc. (某些植物莖中的)木髓;(柑橘等果皮內)類似木髓的柔軟組織。**ˈ~ hat／helmet,** light sun hat made of dried ~. 木髓製的輕便遮陽帽。**2** (fig) essential part: (喻)重要部分: *the ~ of his argument／speech, etc.* 他的辯論(演講等)的重點。**3** vigour; force. 精力;力量。**~y** *adj* (-ier, -iest) **1** of, like, full of, ~. 木髓的;似木髓的;多木髓的。**2** forcible; full of meaning: 有力的;簡潔的: *~y sayings.* 簡潔的諺語。**~·ily** /-ɪlɪ ; -ɪlɪ/ *adv*

piti·able /ˈpɪtɪəbl ; ˈpɪtɪəbḷ/ *adj* exciting pity; deserving only contempt: 令人憐憫的;可憐的;可憐又可鄙的: *a ~ attempt.* 可憐又可鄙的企圖。**piti·ably** /-əblɪ ; -əblɪ/ *adv*

piti·ful /ˈpɪtɪfl ; ˈpɪtɪfəl/ *adj* **1** feeling pity; compassionate. 同情的;慈悲的。**2** causing pity: 令人同情的;可憐的: *a ~ sight.* 可憐的景象。**3** arousing contempt. 可鄙的。**~ly** /-fəlɪ ; -flɪ/ *adv*

piti·less /ˈpɪtɪlɪs ; ˈpɪtɪlɪs/ *adj* showing no pity. 無憐憫心的;無情的。**~·ly** *adv*

pi·ton /ˈpiːtɒn ; ˈpitɑn/ *n* metal spike driven into rock, with a hole for rope, used as a hold in mountain climbing. (一頭有孔可穿繩,尖端可釘入岩石,爬山時用以抓握之)長釘;岩釘。

pit·tance /ˈpɪtns ; ˈpɪtṇs/ *n* low, insufficient payment or allowance (for work, etc): 微薄的薪資或津貼: *work all day for a mere ~.* 爲着一點薄酬而整天工作。

pitter-patter /ˈpɪtə pætə(r) ; ˈpɪtɚˌpætɚ/ *n* patter: 啪嗒聲(輕拍聲、脚步聲等): *the ~ of rain on the roof.* 雨落在屋頂上的啪嗒聲。

pi·tu·itary /pɪˈtjuːɪtərɪ *US:* -ˈtuːəterɪ ; pɪˈtjuəˌtɛrɪ/ *adj* **ˈ~ gland,** small ductless gland at the base of the brain, secreting hormones that influence growth, etc. 腦垂體;腦下腺。□ *n* ~ gland. 腦垂體;腦下腺。

pity /ˈpɪtɪ ; ˈpɪtɪ/ *n* (*pl* -ties) **1** [U] feeling of sorrow for the troubles, sufferings, etc of another person: 同情;憐憫: *be filled with／feel ~ for sb.* 同情某人。***have／take ~ on sb,*** help sb in trouble, etc. 因同情而幫助某人。***for ~'s sake,*** (used as a form of entreaty): 發發慈悲(作懇求的用語): *For ~'s sake try to stop this persecution.* 發發慈悲停止這種迫害吧。***out of ~,*** because of a feeling of ~: 出於同情;因爲覺得可憐: *give a beggar a few coins out of ~.* 出於同情而給乞丐幾個硬幣。**2** (with *indef art,* but not in *pl* except as below) (event which gives) cause for regret or sorrow: (與不定冠詞連用,但除了下面例句的用法外不用複數)令人遺憾的事;可悲的事: *What a ~* (= How unfortunate) *(that) you can't come with us!* 你不能跟我們一起去,眞可惜! *It's a ~ (that) he can't swim.* 眞遺憾,他不會游泳。*The ~ is that...,* The thing to be regretted is that.... 遺憾的是…;可惜…。*It's a thousand pities that...,* is most unfortunate that.... 最不幸的是…。□ *vt* (*pt, pp* -tied) [VP6A] feel genuine ~ for; feel contemptuous ~ for: 同情;憐憫;對…覺得可憐又可鄙: *He is much to be pitied.* 他很可憐;他值得同情。*I ~ you if you think that you deserve to be helped.* 如果你以爲你配接受幫助,我會覺得你可憐。**~·ing** *adv* expressing ~. 表示同情的。**~·ing·ly** *adv*

pivot /ˈpɪvət ; ˈpɪvət/ *n* **1** central pin or point on which sth turns, ⇨ the illus at balance; (fig) sth on which an argument or discussion depends. 軸;樞軸;支點(參看 balance 之挿圖);(喻)辯論或討論的要點;中心點。**2** (mil) man or unit on whom a body of troops turns or wheels when changing front or direction. (軍)基準兵;標兵;標軸單位。□ *vt, vi* **1** [VP3A] ~ ***on,*** turn as on a ~. (以某事物爲軸心而)旋轉;以…爲轉移;由…而定。**2** [VP6A] place on a ~; supply with a ~. 放在軸上;裝置樞軸。**~al** /-tl ; -tḷ/ *adj* of, forming, a ~; (fig) of great importance because other things depend upon it. 軸的;作爲旋軸的;(喻)(因被其他事物所依靠而)非常重要的;關鍵性的。

pixi·lated /ˈpɪksɪleɪtɪd ; ˈpɪksəˌletɪd/ *adj* (dial) slightly crazy. (方)有點瘋狂的;瘋瘋癲癲的。

pixy, pixie /ˈpɪksɪ ; ˈpɪksɪ/ *n* (*pl* -xies) small elf or fairy. 小精靈;小仙子。

pizza /ˈpiːtsə ; ˈpitsə/ *n* (I) dish of food made by baking a layer of dough covered with a mixture of tomatoes, cheese, etc. (義)(上面覆有番茄醬及乳酪等的)煎餅。

piz·zi·cato /ˌpɪtsɪˈkɑːtəʊ ; ˌpɪtsɪˈkɑto/ *adj, adv* (I) (music) (played) by plucking the strings (of a violin, etc) instead of using the bow. (義)(音樂)用指彈撥(提琴等)的(地);撥奏的(地)。

plac·ard /ˈplækɑːd ; ˈplækɑrd/ *n* written or printed announcement (to be) publicly displayed; poster. 公告;佈告;招貼;海報。□ *vt* [VP6A] put ~s on (walls, etc); make known by means of ~s. 貼公告於(牆上等);(以佈告)宣佈;(以招貼)公告。

pla·cate /pləˈkeɪt *US:* ˈpleɪkeɪt ; ˈpleket/ *vt* [VP6A] soothe; pacify. 安慰;撫慰。

place[1] /pleɪs ; ples/ *n* **1** particular part of space occupied by sb or sth: 地方;所在地: *I can't be in two ~s at once.* 我不能同時在兩個地方。**2** city, town, village, etc: 城市;鎮;村: *visit ~s and see things,* travel as a tourist. 到各地旅行觀光。***ˈgo ~s,*** (colloq) have increasing success. (俗)成功;勝利;表演精彩。**ˈ~-name** *n* name of a city, town, village, hill, lake, etc: 地名(城鎮、村莊、山、湖等之名稱): *an expert on the origin of ~-names.* 詳識地名起源之專家。**3** building or area of land used for some particular purpose that is specified: (用作某種特殊目的的)建築物;場所: *a ~ of worship,* a church, etc; 禮拜的場所(如教堂等); *~s of amusement,* theatres, discotheques, cinemas, etc; 娛樂場所; *a ˈmarket-~;* 市場; *a ~ of business.* 營業處。**4** particular ~ on a surface: 表面上的某部分: *a sore ~ on my neck.* 我脖子上痛的地方。**5** passage, part, in a book, etc: 書籍等中的段落或部分: *I've lost my ~,* can't find the ~ where I stopped reading. 我找不到原來讀的地方了。*Use a book-mark to keep your ~ instead of turning down the corner of the page.* 用一個書籤指明你所讀到的地方,而不要把書頁摺角。**6** rank or station (in society, etc): 地位;

(社會上的)階級: *keep/know one's ~.* 保持(了解)自己的身分或地位。 **7** (in a race) position among those competitors who are winners: (競賽時)獲勝者的名次: *Whose horse got the first ~?* 誰的馬獲得第一名? *I shall back* (= bet some money on) *the favourite for a ~,* ie to be one of the first three past the winning-post. 我要賭那匹最有希望獲得前三名的馬。Hence, 由此產生, **'~-bet** *n* **8** (maths) position of a figure in a series as indicating its value in decimal or other notation: (數)位: *calculated to five ~s of decimals/to five decimal ~s,* eg 6·57132. 計算到小數點後五位(如6·57132)。**9** single step or stage in an argument, etc. (議論等的)步驟; 層次。***in the first/second, etc ~,*** firstly/secondly, etc. 第一(第二等)點; 首先(其次等)。**10** proper or natural position: 適當的位置; 天然的位置: *A tidy person likes to have a ~ for everything and everything in its ~.* 一個整潔的人喜歡每一樣東西都有其位置,而每一樣東西都在其應在的位置。*Please take your ~s,* eg ready for a dance. 請就位(如準備跳舞)。*Go back to your ~,* eg your seat. 回到你的位子去。*There's always a ~ for you around our table,* You will always be a welcome guest. 我們的餐桌總是有你的位子(隨時歡迎你來)。***in ~,*** **(a)** in the right or proper ~: 在對的位置; 在適當的位置: *I like to have everything in ~.* 我喜歡一切都在其適當的位置。**(b)** (fig) suitable; appropriate: (喻)適合的; 適當的: *The proposal is not quite in ~.* 那提議並不十分適當。***out of ~,*** **(a)** not in the right or proper ~. 不在應在的位置; 不在適當的位置。**(b)** (fig) unsuitable; inappropriate: (喻)不適合的; 不適當的: *Your remarks were rather out of ~.* 你的話有點不恰當。***in ~ of,*** instead of. 代替。***give ~,*** yield. 屈服; 讓步。***give ~ to,*** be succeeded by. 讓位於。***make ~ for,*** **(a)** make room (which is the more usu word) for. 騰出空位給…(room 較常用)。**(b)** yield precedence to. 讓…在先。**(c)** be superseded by. 被…所取代。***put sb in his (proper) ~; put oneself in sb's/sb else's ~,*** ⇨ put¹(2). ***take the ~ of,*** be substituted for: 代替; 取代: *Who will take the ~ of Mr X/take Mr X's ~?* 誰將要代替某先生? *Plastics have taken the ~ of many materials.* 塑膠已經取代了許多材料。***take ~,*** happen: 發生; 舉行: *The wedding/party/celebration took place yesterday.* 婚禮(宴會,慶祝會)在昨日舉行。***pride of ~,*** position of superiority. 高位; 尊位。**11** office, employment, esp a government appointment; duties of an office-holder: 職位(尤指公職); 職責: *It's your ~ to see that the junior members of the staff do not arrive late.* 你的職責是使下級職員不遲到。*He will get a ~ in the Oxford boat,* will be chosen to be a member of the crew. 他將被選爲牛津校船上的一名划手。**'~·man, '~-seekers,** man looking for favoured positions, eg in government. 鑽營職位的人(尤指官吏)。**12** estate; house; home: 地產; 房屋; 住所: *He has a nice little ~ in the country.* 他在鄉間有所漂亮的小房屋。*Come round to my ~ one evening.* 隨便那天晚上請到舍下來。**13** (in proper names) alternative name for *Street, Square,* etc in a town: (與專有名詞連用)城市之 Street, Square 等的代稱: *St James's P~.* 聖詹姆斯街。**14** **'~-kick** *n* (Rugby football) kick made when the ball is previously placed for that purpose on the ground. (橄欖球)定位踢(由另外球員預先將球置於地上然後踢出)。

place² /pleɪs; ples/ *vt* [VP6A, 15A, B] **1** put (sth) in a certain place; arrange (things) in their proper places: 放(某物)於某一位置; 放置; 安排(各物)於適當的位置; 安置: *P~ them in the right order.* 把它們按順序放好。 **2** appoint (sb) to a post; put in office or authority: 任命(某人); 給予職務或職權: *He was ~d in command of the Second Army.* 他被任命指揮第二軍團。 **3** put, invest (money): 存(款); 投(資): *~ £500 in Saving Bonds;* 買了五百鎊的儲蓄公債; *~ £100 to sb's credit in the bank.* 將一百鎊存入某人在銀行的戶頭。 **4** put (an order for goods, etc) with a business firm: 發出(訂單): *~ an order for books with Blackwell's.* 向布萊克威爾公司訂購書籍。**5** dispose of (goods) to a customer: 售出(貨物): *How can we ~ all this surplus stock?* 我們怎樣才能夠賣出全部剩餘存貨? **6** have, fix, repose: 寄託; 信賴: *~ confidence in a leader.* 信賴一個領袖。**7** recognize or estimate (sb) by connecting him with past experience; fully identify: 認出或估計(某人); 完全認定: *I know that man's face, but I can't ~ him.* 我認得那人的面孔,但我認不出來他是誰。*He's a difficult man to ~.* 難以判斷他是何許人物。**8** (racing) state the position of runners (in a race), contestants (in an athletic contest). (賽跑等)定出(選手的)名次。***be ~d,*** be among the first three: 列入前三名: *The Duke's horse wasn't ~d.* 公爵的馬沒進入前三名。

pla·cebo /plə'siːbəʊ; plə'sibo/ *n* (*pl* ~s) sth not containing medicine given to soothe, not to cure, a patient. 安慰劑(安慰病患用之非藥劑性物品); 寬心丸。

pla·centa /plə'sentə; plə'sɛntə/ *n* (zool) organ lining the womb during pregnancy, by which the foetus is nourished. It is expelled with the foetus and the umbilical cord following birth. (動物)胎盤; 胎衣。⇨ the illus at reproduce. 參看 reproduce 之挿圖。

pla·cid /'plæsɪd; 'plæsɪd/ *adj* calm; untroubled; (of a person) not easily irritated. 安靜的; 平靜的; (指人)溫和的; 沉着的。**~·ly** *adv* **~·ity** /plə'sɪdətɪ; plə'sɪdətɪ/ *n* [U].

placket /'plækɪt; 'plækɪt/ *n* opening in a woman's skirt to make it easier to put on and take off; pocket inside this. 女裙的開口; 此種開口內的口袋。

plage /plɑːʒ; plɑʒ/ *n* (F) sea beach (esp at a fashionable seaside resort). (法)海灘(尤指在時髦人物常去的海濱遊樂地)。

pla·giar·ize /'pleɪdʒəraɪz; 'pledʒɪəˌraɪz/ *vt, vi* [VP 2A, 6A] take and use (sb else's ideas, words, etc) as one's own. 抄襲(他人的思想、文字等); 剽竊。**pla·giar·ism** /-ɪzəm; -ɪzəm/ *n* [U] plagiarizing; [C] instance of this. 抄襲; 剽竊。**pla·giar·ist** /-ɪst; -ɪst/ *n* person who ~s. 抄襲者; 剽竊者。

plague /pleɪg; pleg/ *n* **1 the ~,** = *bubonic plague,* ⇨ bubonic. **'~-spot** *n* **(a)** spot on the skin characteristic of ~. 疫斑。**(b)** district infected with ~. 瘟疫區。**(c)** centre, source or symptom of moral evil. 罪惡的中心、根源或徵兆。 **2** cause of trouble, annoyance or disaster: 麻煩、困擾或災禍的原因; 禍患: *a ~ of locusts/flies.* 蝗蟲(蒼蠅)的災禍。*What a ~ that boy is!* What a nuisance he is! 那小孩多麼討厭! □ *vt* [VP6A, 14] ***~ (with),*** annoy (esp with repeated requests or questions). 煩擾(尤指以一再請求或詢問來困擾)。**plaguy** /'pleɪgɪ; 'plegɪ/ *adj* (colloq) annoying. (俗)煩擾的; 麻煩的。**pla·guily** /-ɪlɪ; -əlɪ/ *adv* annoyingly; provokingly. 煩擾地; 惱人地。

plaice /pleɪs; ples/ *n* (*pl* unchanged) edible flat-fish. (複數不變)鰈(一種可食的比目魚)。⇨ the illus at fish. 參看 fish 之挿圖。

plaid /plæd; plæd/ *n* **1** [C] long piece of woollen cloth worn over the shoulders by Scottish Highlanders. (蘇格蘭高地人所披的)肩巾。 **2** [U] cloth, usu with a chequered or tartan pattern, used for this article of dress. (用作肩巾的)方格呢; 格子花呢。

plain¹ /pleɪn; plen/ *adj* (-er, -est) **1** easy to see, hear or understand: 明白的; 清楚的; 易了解的: *~ English;* 簡明英語; *in ~ speech;* 以明白的言詞; *~ language,* (of telegrams, etc) not in code. (指電報等)明碼。*The meaning is quite ~.* 這意義十分清楚。**ˌ~ 'sailing,** (fig) course of action that is simple and free from difficulties: (喻)一帆風順: *After we engaged a guide, everything was ~ sailing.* 我們僱到一個嚮導之後,一切都順利了。**2** simple; ordinary; without luxury or ornament: 簡單的; 平凡的; 樸素的: *a ~ blue dress,* of blue material without a design on it, or without trimmings, etc; 一件純藍的女裝; *in ~ clothes*, (esp of policemen) in ordinary clothes, not in uniform; (尤指警察)穿便服的; *~ food/cooking;* 簡單的食物(烹飪); *a ~ cook*, one who can prepare ~ meals. 能烹調簡單餐食的廚子。 **3** (of persons, their thoughts, actions, etc) straightforward; frank: (指人、思想、行爲等) 直截了當的; 坦白的: *in ~ words*, frankly; 坦白地; *~ dealing*, honesty, sincerity. 誠實;眞摯。 ***to be '~ with you,*** to speak openly. 坦白對你說。 **ˌ~-ˈspoken** *adj* frank in speech. 說話坦白的;直言的。 **4** (of a person's appearance) not pretty or handsome. (指人的容貌) 不漂亮的; 不美的。 **5 '~-song/-chant** *n* music for a number of voices in unison, used in the Anglican and Roman Catholic Church services. (英國國教及天主教禮拜式中所唱的)齊唱的歌曲;素歌。□ *adv* clearly: 清楚地;明白地: *learn to speak ~;* 學習說清楚; entirely: 完全地: *You are ~ wrong.* 你完全錯了。**~·ly** *adv* clearly: 清楚地: *The rock stuck out ~ly;* 那岩石清楚地突了出來; obviously: 顯然地: *You are ~ly wrong.* 你顯然錯了。**~·ness** *n*

plain² /pleɪn ; plen/ *n* area of level country: 平原; 平地: *the wide ~s of Canada.* 加拿大的廣大平原。 **'~s·man** /-zmən ; -zmən/ *n* (*pl* -men) inhabitant of a ~. 平原居民。

plain³ /pleɪn ; plen/ *n* simple stitch in knitting. (編織時的)正編;上針。⇨ purl¹. □ *vt, vi* knit this stitch. 正編;用上針織。

plaint /pleɪnt ; plent/ *n* **1** (legal) charge; accusation. (法律)告訴;控訴。 **2** (poet) complaint; lamentation. (詩)訴怨;悲嘆。

plain·tiff /ˈpleɪntɪf ; ˈplentɪf/ *n* person who brings an action at law. 原告。⇨ defendant.

plain·tive /ˈpleɪntɪv ; ˈplentɪv/ *adj* sounding sad; sorrowful. 哀傷的;悲哀的。**~·ly** *adv* **~·ness** *n*

plait /plæt ; plet/ *vt* [VP6A] weave or twist (three or more lengths of hair, straw, etc) under and over one another into one rope-like length. 編(頭髮)成辮;編(草)爲繩。□ *n* sth made by ~ing: 編成物;髮辮;辮子;緶: *wearing her hair in a ~.* 將她的頭髮編成一條辮子。

plan /plæn ; plæn/ *n* **1** outline drawing (of or for a building) showing the relative size, positions, etc of the parts, esp as if seen from above: (建築物的)設計圖;圖面; 平面圖: *~s for a new school.* 一所新學校的平面圖。⇨ elevation(5); ⇨ the illus at perspective. 參看 perspective 之插圖。 **2** diagram (of the parts of a machine). (機器各部的)圖解;說明圖。 **3** diagram showing how a garden, park, town or other area of land has been, or is to be, laid out. (花園、公園、城鎮或其他地區的)詳圖;計畫圖。 Cf *map* for a large area of land. (參較 map 表示大地區的地圖)。 **4** arrangement for doing or using sth, considered in advance: 計畫;策略;方案: *make ~s for the holidays;* 作度假的計畫; *a ~ to encourage saving;* 鼓勵儲蓄的方案; *a five-year ~*, eg for a country's economic and industrial development. 五年計畫(例如爲國家的經濟和工業發展而擬訂者)。 ***(go) according to ~,*** (happen) as planned. 照計畫進行。□ *vt* (-nn-) **1** [VP6A] make a ~ of or for: 設計;作…的計畫;繪…的設計圖: *~ a house/garden.* 設計一座房子(花園)。 **2** [VP7A] **~ *to do sth,*** make ~s: 計畫(做某事): *We're ~ning to visit Europe this summer.* 我們正計畫今年夏天去歐洲旅行。 **3** [VP6A, 15B] ***~ (out),*** consider and arrange in advance: 策畫;籌畫: *~ (out) a military campaign.* 策畫一個戰役。**a ~ned economy,** economic system ~ned by government authorities. 計畫經濟。⇨ town(2). **~·ner** *n* one who makes ~s. 設計者;策畫者。**~·less** *adj* without a ~. 沒有計畫的。

plan·chette /plɑːnˈʃet *US:* plænˈʃet ; plænˈʃɛt/ *n* small board supported by two castors, with a vertical pencil said to trace marks on paper at spiritualistic seances without conscious direction by hand. 扶乩寫字板;乩板。

plane¹ /pleɪn ; plen/ *n* **'~(-tree),** one of several kinds of tree with spreading branches, broad leaves and thin bark, which comes off in flakes. 篠懸木;法國梧桐。

plane² /pleɪn ; plen/ *n* tool for trimming the surface of wood by taking shavings from it. 鉋刀;鉋子。⇨ the illus at tool. 參看 tool 之插圖。□ *vt, vi* [VP2A, 15B, 2D, 22] use a ~; make smooth with a ~: 用鉋子;用鉋鉋平: *~ sth smooth.* 將某物鉋平滑。 ***~ away/down,*** remove irregularities with a ~. 鉋去不平之處。

plane³ /pleɪn ; plen/ *n* **1** flat or level surface; surface such that the straight line joining any points on it is touching it at all points; imaginary surface of this kind; 平面;幾何平面;想像中的絕對平面; (attrib) (形容用法) **ˌ~ geˈometry,** geometry of figures on a ~. 平面幾何學。**ˌ~ ˈsailing,** the art of determining a ship's position on the theory that the ship is moving on a ~. 平面航行術(依據船隻在一平面上航行之理論以決定一船的位置)。⇨ *plain sailing* at plain¹(1). **2** main supporting surface of an aeroplane. 機翼。 **3** (fig) level or stage (*of* development, etc): (喻)(發展等的)水準; 階段: *on the same ~ as a savage;* 跟野蠻人同樣階段; *on a higher social ~.* 在更高的社會水準。□ *vi* ***~ (down),*** (of aeroplanes) travel, glide. (指飛機)航行;下滑。

plane⁴ /pleɪn ; plen/ *n* (colloq abbr for) aeroplane. (俗)爲 aeroplane 之略。

planet /ˈplænɪt ; ˈplænɪt/ *n* one of the heavenly bodies (eg *Mars, Venus*) which moves round a star such as the sun and is illuminated by it. 行星(如火星、金星)。 **plan·et·ary** /ˈplænɪtrɪ *US:* -terɪ ; ˈplænəˌtɛrɪ/ *adj* relating to, moving like, a ~. 行星的; 有關行星的; 運行像行星的。 **plan·et·ar·ium** /ˌplænɪˈteərɪəm ; ˌplænəˈtɛrɪəm/ *n* (building with a) device for representing the movements of the stars and ~s by projecting spots of light on the inner surface of a large dome that represents the sky. 行星運行儀;太陽系儀(將光點投射於代表天空的大圓頂內面以表示星球運行的儀器);裝有此種儀器的建築物;假天;天文館。

plan·gent /ˈplændʒənt ; ˈplændʒənt/ *adj* (formal) (of sounds) resounding; vibrating. (正式用語)(指聲音)回響的;震顫的。

plank /plæŋk ; plæŋk/ *n* **1** long, flat piece of timber, 2 to 6 inches thick, 9 or more inches wide; board. 厚木板(厚二吋到六吋,寬九吋以上);板。**'~-bed** *n* one of boards, without mattresses. 木板床。 ***walk the ~,*** ⇨ walk²(4). **2** basic principle in a political platform. 政綱的準則;政綱的基本條款。□ *vt* **1** [VP6A] furnish with ~s; cover (a floor, etc) with ~s. 供以厚板;以厚板鋪(地面等)。 **2** [VP15B] **~ *sth down,*** (colloq) put down (esp money); pay at once. (俗)放下(尤指錢);立刻付款。 **~·ing** *n* [U] ~s put down to form a floor. (用以鋪地板之)板材;鋪板。

plank·ton /ˈplæŋktən ; ˈplæŋktən/ *n* [U] the (chiefly microscopic) forms of organic life that drift in or float on the water of the oceans, lakes, rivers, etc. 浮游生物(主要爲微生物)。

plant¹ /plɑːnt *US:* plænt ; plænt/ *n* **1** living organism which is not an animal, esp the kind smaller than trees and shrubs: 植物;(尤指小於喬木及灌木的)花草;苗木: *garden ~s;* 庭園中的花木;園藝植物; *a tobacco ~.* 一株菸草。**'~-louse** *n* kinds of insect pest that attack ~s, esp aphis. 危害植物的昆蟲;(尤指)蚜蟲。 **2** [U] apparatus, fixtures, machinery, etc used in an industrial or manufacturing process: 用於工業生產中之儀器、設備、機器等: *We get our tractors and bulldozers from a ~-hire firm.* 我們向一家機器出租公司租用牽引機和推土機。*The farm has its own lighting ~*, eg a generator for producing electric current. 這農場有自己的發電設備。 **3** [U] (US) factory; buildings and equip-

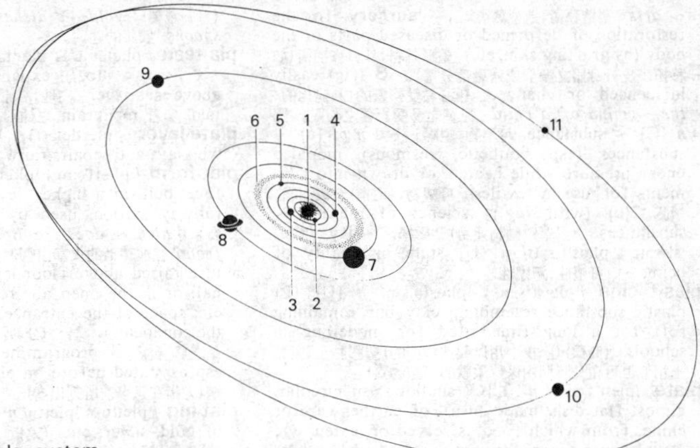

the planets of our solar system

ment of an institution. (美)工廠;一個機構的建築物與設備。 **4** (sl) planned swindle; hoax; person who joins a gang of criminals to get evidence against them. (俚)騙局; 欺詐; 參加犯罪集團以套取可資控告之證據的人。

plant² /plɑːnt *US:* plænt ; plænt/ *vt* [VP6A, 15A, B] **1** put ~s, bushes, trees, etc in (a garden, etc): 栽植花木、灌木、喬木等於(庭園等)中: *~ a garden with rose-bushes;* 在花園裡栽植玫瑰花; *set up a monument and ~ it round with trees/~ trees round it.* 設立紀念碑並在其四週栽種樹木。 **2** put (plants, trees, etc) in the ground to grow; (fig) cause (an idea) to take root in sb's mind: 種植(花木、樹等); (喻)灌輸(觀念)於某人心中: *~ (out) strawberry runners/pansies.* 種植草莓的藤蔓(三色紫羅蘭)。 ⇨ sow². **3** place firmly in position; take up a position or attitude: 安置;處於某一位置;採取某一姿勢: *He ~ed his feet firmly on the ground.* 他把腳穩踏在地上。*He ~ed himself in front of the fire.* 他站在爐火的前面。 *He ~ed his feet wide apart.* 他兩脚跨得很開地站著。 **4** establish, found (a community, colony, etc); settle (a person) in a place as a colonist, etc. 建立;設立(社區、殖民地等);使(某人)爲殖民等; 安置(某人)。 **5** deliver (a blow, etc) with deliberate aim: 打出(一擊等);瞄擊: *~ a blow on sb's ear.* 打某人的耳光。 **6** (sl) hide (esp in order to deceive sb, to cause an innocent person to seem guilty, etc): (俚)隱藏(尤指爲了欺騙某人、使無辜者蒙受不白之寃等);栽(贓): *~ stolen goods on sb.* 栽某人的贓。~**er** *n* **1** person who grows crops on a plantation: 種植者;栽培者: *'tea/'rubber-~ers.* 種茶(橡膠)者。**2** machine for ~ing. 種植機;播種機。

plan·tain¹ /ˈplæntɪn ; ˈplæntɪn/ *n* tree-like tropical plant bearing fruit similar to that of the banana-palm; its fruit. (熱帶產的)大蕉; 大蕉之果實。 ⇨ the illus at vegetable. 參看 vegetable 之挿圖。

plan·tain² /ˈplæntɪn ; ˈplæntɪn/ *n* common wild plant with broad leaves and seeds much used for cage-birds. 車前草。

plan·ta·tion /plænˈteɪʃn ; plænˈteʃən/ *n* **1** area of land planted with trees: 造林地; 森林: *~s of fir and pine.* 樅樹及松樹的森林。 **2** large estate on which tea, cotton, sugar, tobacco or other commercial crop is cultivated: 大農場;大種植園: *'~ songs,* songs sung by Negroes who formerly worked as slaves on cotton ~s in N America. 昔時北美洲棉花農場上黑奴所唱的歌。

plaque /plɑːk *US:* plæk ; plæk/ *n* flat metal or porcelain plate fixed on a wall as an ornament or memorial. 裝在牆上作裝飾或紀念用的薄金屬板或瓷片;飾板。

plash /plæʃ ; plæʃ/ *n* (*sing* only) light splashing sound: (僅用單數)輕輕的拍水聲: *the ~ of oars in water.* 槳拍在水上的激濺聲。 □ *vt, vi* [VP6A, 2A] strike the surface of (water) gently; splash. 輕拍(水)面;激濺。

plasm /ˈplæzəm ; ˈplæzəm/ *n* [U] genetic material of a cell. (細胞的)原漿;原生質;胞漿。

plasma /ˈplæzmə ; ˈplæzmə/ *n* **(ˈblood) ~,** [U] clear, yellowish fluid in which the blood-cells are carried. 血漿。

plas·ter /ˈplɑːstə(r) *US:* ˈplæs- ; ˈplæstɚ/ *n* **1** [U] soft mixture of lime, sand, water, etc used for coating walls and ceilings. 灰泥(用於塗牆及天花板)。 **ˌ~ of ˈParis** *n* [U] white paste made from gypsum, that becomes very hard when dry, used for making moulds, etc. 燒石膏;熟石膏。 **ˈ~ cast** *n* **(a)** mould made with gauze and ~ of Paris to hold a broken or dislocated bone in place. (用於固定折骨或脫臼之骨的)石膏繃帶; 石膏夾。 **(b)** mould (eg for a small statue) made of ~ of Paris. 石膏模型(如製小雕像者)。 **ˈ~·board** *n* [U] board made of gypsum and thick paper or cardboard, used for inside walls and ceilings instead of plastering. 石膏厚紙板(用作內牆及天花板而無需塗灰泥)。 **2** [C] piece of fabric spread with a medicinal substance, for application to part of the body, to relieve pain, cover a wound, etc. 膏藥。 **3** **(ˈsticking-)~,** [U, C] material treated with some substance so that it will stick to the skin, used for covering a cut, blister, burn, for holding a bandage in position, etc. 橡皮膏;絆創膏(用於包覆輕傷、固定繃帶等)。 □ *vt* [VP6A, 14] **1** cover (a wall, etc) with ~(1); put a ~(2) on (the body). 塗灰泥於(牆等); 敷膏藥於(身體)。 **2** *~ sth with sth; ~ sth on sth,* cover thickly: 厚厚地塗蓋: *hair ~ed with oil;* 油塗得很厚的頭髮; *an old suitcase ~ed with hotel labels.* 貼滿了旅館標籤的一隻舊手提箱。~**ed** *adj* (colloq) drunk. (俗)醉的。~**er** *n* workman who ~s walls and ceilings. 塗灰泥於牆壁及天花板的工人;泥水匠。

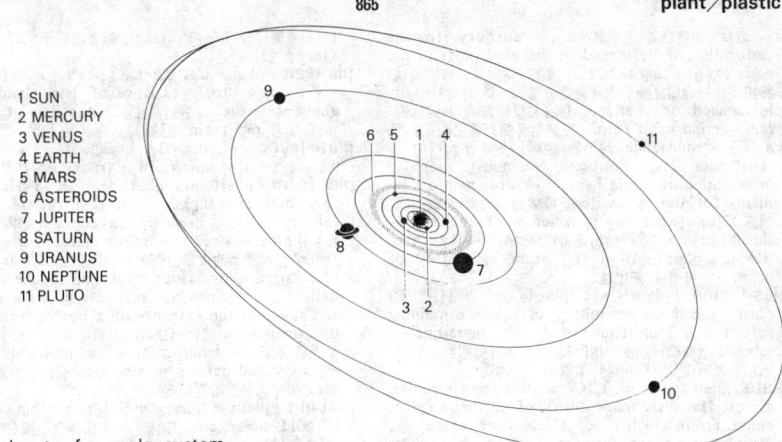

plas·tic /ˈplæstɪk ; ˈplæstɪk/ *adj* **1** (of materials) easily shaped or moulded: (指物質)易做成各種形態的;易塑的: *Clay is a ~ substance;* 黏土是易塑的物質; (of goods) made of such materials, esp synthetic resinous substances: (指貨物)由易塑物質做成的;(尤指)合成樹脂做成的;塑膠做成的: *~ raincoats/flowers/cups/spoons.* 塑膠雨衣(花,杯,匙)。**ˌ~ exˈplosive,** kind that is easily moulded around the object it is to destroy. 可塑炸藥。**ˌ~ˈbomb,** one made of such explosive. 可塑炸藥製成的炸彈; 塑膠炸彈。 **2** of the art of modelling: 塑造術的: *the*

~ *arts.* 塑造藝術;造型藝術。ˌ~ ˈ**surgery,** for the restoration of deformed or diseased parts of the body (by grafting skin, etc). 整形外科;外科修補術(如移植表皮於身體之畸形或病患部分等)。 **3** (fig) easily influenced or changed: (喻)易受影響的;易變化的: *the ~ mind of a child.* 兒童之易受影響之心靈。□ *n* [C] ~ substance. 可塑物;塑膠。**~s** *n pl* **(a)** ~ substances (esp synthetic, resinous) moulded under pressure while heated, or drawn into filaments for use in textiles. 可塑物;(尤指)合成樹脂;塑膠。**(b)** (with *sing v*) science of making ~ substances. (與單數動詞連用)塑膠學。**~·ity** /plæˈstɪsətɪ ; plæsˈtɪsətɪ/ *n* [U] state or quality of being ~. 可塑性;適應性。

plas·ti·cine /ˈplæstɪsiːn ; ˈplæstəˌsin/ *n* [U] (P) plastic substance resembling clay but remaining soft for a long time, used for modelling in schools. (商標)(學校中用以製造模型的)塑膠黏土(與黏土相似但可在長時期內保持柔軟的可塑物質)。

plate[1] /pleɪt ; plet/ *n* **1** [C] shallow, usu circular, almost flat dish, made (usu) of earthenware or china, from which food is served or eaten: 盤; 碟: *a dinner/soup/dessert ~;* 餐(湯,水果或甜點)盤; contents of this: 盤或碟所盛之物: *a ~ of beef and vegetables.* 一盤牛肉和青菜。***hand/give sb sth on a ~,*** (colloq) give, allow sb to have, sth without his having to make any effort. (俗)使某人輕易得到某物;給某人送上門去。***on one's ~,*** to occupy one's time: 佔據時間: *He has enough/a lot/too much on his ~.* 他的時間排了够多(很多,太多)的活動或工作。ˈ**~-rack** *n* rack in which ~s are kept or placed to drain after being washed. 餐具架(放置盤碟或盤碟洗過後晾乾用的架子)。 **2** [C] similar vessel or dish (usu of metal) used for collection of money in churches: (教會中的)奉獻盤(通常爲金屬製): *put only a dime in the ~.* 只放一角錢在奉獻盤上。 **3** [U] (collective) gold or silver articles, eg spoons, dishes, bowls, for use at meals: (集合用法)金質或銀質的餐具(如匙、碟、碗): *a fine piece of ~,* one of these articles. 一件精緻的金質或銀質餐具。⇨ plate[2](2). ˈ**~-powder** *n* [U] powder for cleaning and polishing ~. 擦亮金屬餐具之粉;擦銀粉。 **4** [C] flat, thin sheet of metal, glass, etc eg steel ~s for building ships: 金屬、玻璃等薄片(如用以造船的薄鋼板): *ˈboiler ~s.* 鍋爐鋼板。ˌ**~-ˈglass** *n* [U] thick and very clear glass in sheets for windows, mirrors, doors, etc. 平板玻璃(透明的厚玻璃板,用以做窗玻璃、鏡子、門等)。 **5** [U, C] sheet of glass coated with sensitive film for photography: (照相用的玻璃質)感光板; 底片: *ˈwhole-~,* 全張感光板, *ˈhalf-~,* 對開感光板, *ˈquarter-~,* the usual sizes. 四開感光板(通常用的尺碼)。 **6** [C] oblong piece of metal (usu brass) with a person's name, etc on it, fixed to the door or gate (as used by doctors, solicitors and other professional persons). 名牌;招牌(長方形的金屬板,通常爲銅製,上有姓名,懸於門旁,醫生、律師等專業人員多用之)。 **7** sheet of metal, plastic, rubber, etc from which the pages of a book are printed; book illustration (usu photographic) printed separately from the text. (印書之)金屬、塑膠或橡皮板;書中插圖(與書之本文分開印刷,通常爲照相者)。 **8** ˈ**dental ~,** (also called 亦稱作 a *denture*) thin piece of plastic material, moulded to the shape of the gums, with artificial teeth attached to it. 假牙床。 **9** [C] silver or gold cup as a prize for a horse-race; the race. (作爲賽馬獎品之)金盃;銀盃;(以金盃或銀盃作獎品之)賽馬。 **10** (in baseball) (also 亦作 **home ~**) home base of the batting side. (棒球)本壘。ˈ**~·ful** /-fʊl ; -ˌfʊl/ *n* amount that a ~ holds. 一盤或一碟之量。

plate[2] /pleɪt ; plet/ *vt* [VP6A, 14] ~ ***(with),*** **1** cover (esp a ship) with metal plates(4). 以薄金屬板覆蓋;(尤指)以薄鋼板包被(船)。 **2** cover (another metal) with gold, silver or tin: 以金、銀、銅或錫鍍(另一金屬): *gold-~d dishes;* 鍍金的碟子; *silver-~d spoons.* 鍍銀的匙。

pla·teau /ˈplætəʊ *US:* plæˈtəʊ ; plæˈto/ *n* (*pl* ~s or ~x /-təʊz ; -ˈtoz/) expanse of level land high above sea-level. 高地;高原。⇨ the illus at mountain. 參看 mountain 之插圖。

plate·layer /ˈpleɪtleɪə(r) ; ˈpletˌleɚ/ *n* workman who lays and repairs railway tracks. (鐵路之)路工。

plat·form /ˈplætfɔːm ; ˈplætˌfɔrm/ *n* **1** flat surface built at a higher level than the track in a railway station, used by travellers: (火車站之)月台: *Which ~ does the Bournemouth train leave from?* 往波茅斯的火車由哪個月台開出? **2** flat structure raised above floor-level for speakers in a hall or in the open air, teachers in a classroom, etc; space at the entrance of a bus or tram (for the conductor). 講台;(公共汽車或電車入口處剪票員所站之)平台。 **3** programme of a political party, esp as stated before an election. (政黨之)政綱;黨綱(尤指在選舉前所列出者)。

plat·ing /ˈpleɪtɪŋ ; ˈpletɪŋ/ *n* [U] (esp) thin coating of gold, silver, etc. (尤指)一層極薄之金屬(如金、銀等)鍍層;鍍金;鍍銀。⇨ plate[2](2).

plati·num /ˈplætɪnəm ; ˈplætn̩əm/ *n* [U] grey untarnishable metal (symbol **Pt**) used for jewellery and alloyed with other metals for use in industry. 鉑;白金(符號爲 Pt)。ˌ**~ ˈblonde,** (colloq) woman with silvery-white hair (but not used of a hair that has turned white with age). (俗)銀白色頭髮的女人(非指因年老而頭髮變白者)。

plati·tude /ˈplætɪtjuːd *US:* -tuːd ; ˈplætəˌtjud/ *n* **1** [C] statement that is obviously true, esp one often heard before, but uttered as if it were new. 平凡陳腐的話;陳腔濫調。**2** [U] quality of being commonplace. 平凡; 陳腐。 **plati·tudi·nous** /ˌplætɪˈtjuːdɪnəs *US:* -ˈtuːdənəs ; ˌplætəˈtjudn̩əs/ *adj* commonplace: 平凡的; 陳腐的: *platitudinous remarks.* 平凡的話。

Pla·tonic /pləˈtɒnɪk ; pleˈtɑnɪk/ *adj* of Plato or his teachings: 柏拉圖的;柏拉圖哲學的: *~ love/friendship,* between two people without a desire for physical love. 柏拉圖式的愛情(友誼)(卽兩人之間不摻雜色情或肉慾成分的愛情或友誼);精神戀愛;純潔友誼。

pla·toon /pləˈtuːn ; plæˈtun/ *n* body of soldiers, subdivision of a company, acting as a unit and commanded by a lieutenant. 排(軍隊中連以下的單位)。

plat·ter /ˈplætə(r) ; ˈplætɚ/ *n* **1** (US) large, shallow dish for serving food, esp meat and fish. (美)(盛食物,特別是盛肉及魚的)大淺盤。 **2** (archaic in GB) flat dish, often of wood. (古英)扁平之盤碟(常爲木製)。

platy·pus /ˈplætɪpəs ; ˈplætəpəs/ *n* (*pl* ~es /-pəsɪz ; -pəsɪz/) **(ˌduck·billed)** ˈ**~,** (also called 亦稱作 *duckbill*) small Australian animal which suckles its young but lays eggs (called *duckbill* because it has a bill like that of a duck). 鴨嘴獸(產於澳洲的小獸,哺乳但卵生,因其嘴似鴨,故名)。⇨ the illus at small. 參看 small 之插圖。

plau·dit /ˈplɔːdɪt ; ˈplɔdɪt/ *n* (usu *pl*) cry, clapping or other sign of approval: (通常用複數)喝采;鼓掌;稱讚: *gratified at the ~s of the audience.* 因觀衆之喝采而感到高興。

plaus·ible /ˈplɔːzəbl ; ˈplɔzəbl̩/ *adj* **1** seeming to be right or reasonable: 似眞實的;似合理的: *a ~ excuse/explanation.* 似乎合理的藉口(解釋)。 **2** (of persons) clever at producing convincing arguments, etc: (指人)能言善辯的;嘴巧的;花言巧語的: *a ~ rogue.* 花言巧語的歹徒。**plaus·ibly** /-əblɪ ; -əblɪ/ *adv* **plausi·bil·ity** /ˌplɔːzəˈbɪlətɪ ; ˌplɔzəˈbɪlətɪ/ *n* [U] state of being ~; [C] (*pl* -ties) ~ excuse, argument, etc. 似眞;似合理;似合理的藉口、議論等。

play[1] /pleɪ ; ple/ *n* **1** [U] (what is done for) amusement; recreation: 遊玩; 遊戲; 娛樂: *The children are at ~,* engaged in playing. 孩子們在遊戲。*What*

I said was only in ~, not intended to be taken seriously. 我所說的話不過是開玩笑而已。 ***a ~ on words,*** a pun. 雙關語;俏皮話。 **ˈchild's-~** *n* [U] sth simple and easy. 簡易之事。 **ˈ~-box** *n* box to hold toys. 玩具箱;玩具盒。 **ˈ~·boy** *n* rich young man chiefly interested in enjoying himself. 花花公子;主要興趣在享樂的年輕人。 **ˈ~·fellow/mate** *nn* companion in ~. 玩伴。 **ˈ~·ground** *n* piece of ground used for ~, eg one at a school or in a public park (cf 參較 *playing-field* below). (學校或公園內之)運動場。 **ˈ~-group** *n* = ~-school. **ˈ~-pen** *n* portable enclosure in which a baby or small child may be left to ~. (可將小孩放在裡面玩的)輕便圍欄。 **ˈ~·room** *n* one in a house for children to ~ in. (兒童的)遊戲室;娛樂間。 **ˈ~-school** *n* group of young children who play together regularly under supervision. 幼稚園;托兒所。 **ˈ~-suit** *n* loose garment(s) to be worn (eg on a beach) by a child while playing. (幼兒在海濱等地遊戲時所穿着之)運動裝;運動衫。 **ˈ~·thing** *n* toy; (fig) sb treated as a mere toy. 玩具;(喻)被玩弄取樂的人;玩物。 **ˈ~·time** *n* period for ~. 遊戲時間;休閒時間。 **2** [U] the playing of a game; manner of playing: 競賽;運動;遊戲或競賽的方式: *There was a lot of rough ~ in the football match yesterday.* 昨天的足球比賽很粗野。 *That was expert ~/an expert bit of ~!* 那場競賽漂亮極了! ***in/out of ~,*** (of the ball in football, cricket, etc) in/not in a position where the rules of the game allow it to be played. (指足球、板球等比賽中的球)位(未位)於比賽規則允許之處;(不是)死球。 **fair ~,** (fig) justice, equal conditions and treatment for all: (喻)公正;公平;平等對待;公平處置: *I will see fair ~,* I will ensure that both sides are treated justly. 我將公平處理之。 **foul ~,** ~ contrary to the rules; (fig) treachery; violence: 犯規;(喻)奸詐;暴力: *Do the police suspect foul ~?* 警方懷疑其中有奸詐嗎? **3** [U] turn or move in a game (eg chess): (下棋等之)輪到;移動;走棋: *It's your ~,* You are to make the next move. 該你(走)了。 **4** [U] gaming; gambling: 賭;賭博: *lose £50 in one evening's ~;* 一晚上賭博輸掉五十鎊; *high ~,* ie for high stakes. 輸贏很大的賭博。 **5** [C] drama for the stage: 劇本;戲劇: *the ~s of Shakespeare.* 莎士比亞的劇本。 *Let's go to a ~* (= theatre) *this evening.* 我們今晚去看戲吧。 ***as good as a ~,*** amusing, interesting. 很好玩的;有趣的。 **ˈ~-acting** [U] *n* performance of ~s; (fig) pretence. 戲劇的演出;表演;(喻)假裝;矯飾。 **ˈ~-actor** *n* (old use) actor. (舊用法)演員;伶人。 **ˈ~-bill** *n* bill announcing the performance of a ~. 戲單;戲碼。 **ˈ~·goer** /-gəʊə(r); -ˌgoɚ/ *n* person who often goes to the theatre. 常去看戲的人。 **ˈ~·house** *n* theatre. 戲院。 **ˈ~·wright** *n* dramatist. 劇作家。 **6** [U] light, quick, fitful movement: 輕快而斷續的動作: *the ~ of sunlight upon water.* 陽光在水面上的閃爍。 **7** [U] (space for) free and easy movement; scope for activity: 自由活動;自由活動的空間;活動的範圍: *allow full ~ to one's curiosity;* 讓好奇心自由發展; *give free ~ to one's fancy/emotions;* 縱情想像(任感情氾濫); *a knot with too much ~,* one that is not tight enough. 不够緊的結。 *Give the rope more ~,* keep it less taut. 把繩子放鬆一些。 **8** [U] activity; operation: 活動;運轉;作用: *the ~ of forces.* 力的作用。 ***be in full ~,*** be fully operating or active. 在全力運轉(活動)中。 ***bring sth into ~,*** make use of it; bring it into action. 利用某物;使某物發生作用。 ***come into ~,*** begin to operate or be active. 開始活動。

play² /pleɪ; ple/ *vt, vi* (*pt, pp* ~ed /pleɪd; pled/) (For special uses with *adverbial particles* and *preps,* ⇨ 15 below.) (與副詞接語及介詞連用的特殊用法,參看下列第 15 義。) **1** [VP2A, B, C] (contrasted with *work*) have fun; do things to pass the time pleasantly, as children do: (與 work 相對)玩耍;遊樂: *The children are ~ing in the park.* 孩子們正在公園裡玩耍。 *Let's go out and ~.* 我們出去玩吧。 ***~ with,*** amuse oneself with: 以…自娛: *~ with the kitten.* 以逗小猫自娛。 **2** [VP3A, 6A] ***~ (at doing sth),*** pretend, for fun, to be sth or do sth: 假裝;假扮: *Let's ~ (at being) pirates.* 我們來假扮海盜吧。 *The children were ~ing at keeping shop.* 孩子們在假裝開店鋪。 **3** [VP6A, 14, 12C] ***~ a joke/prank/trick (on sb),*** trick him. 開玩笑;戲謔某人。 **4** [VP6A, 14, 2A, C, 3A] (be able to) take part in a game, eg of cricket, football, golf, cards: 參加(板球、足球、高爾夫球、紙牌等)遊戲;打(球);玩(遊戲): *Do you ~ cricket?* 你打板球嗎? *He ~s (football) for Stoke/England.* 他參加斯都克市隊(英國隊)(踢足球)。 *On Saturday France ~s (Rugby) against Wales/~s Wales at Rugby.* 星期六法國隊和威爾斯隊比賽橄欖球。 *They were ~ing bridge.* 他們在玩橋牌。 *Will you ~ me at chess/~ chess with me?* 你願意和我下棋嗎? *He went on ~ing* (= gambling) *until he had lost everything.* 他繼續賭博直到輸得精光。 **5** [VP2C, 3A, 6A] ***~ (as/at),*** fill a particular position in a team: 在隊中擔任某一職務: *I've never ~ed (as/at) centre-forward before.* 我從來沒有擔任過中鋒。 *Who's ~ing in goal/as goalkeeper?* 誰做守門員? [VP6A, 15A, 16B] ***~ sb (as/at),*** include in a team: 起用某人參加比賽;使包括在某隊中: *I think we should ~ Smith in the next match.* 我認爲我們應該在下一場比賽中起用史密斯。 *Who shall we ~ as goalkeeper?* 我們將派誰擔任守門員? **6** [VP15A, B] (cricket, football, etc) strike (the ball) in a specified manner: (板球、足球等)以某種方式打或踢(球): *~ the ball to mid-on;* 把球打至投手右側外場員的附近; *~ (the ball) on to one's own wicket* (and so put oneself out). 將(球)打到自己的三柱門(而使自已出局)。 *In soccer only the goalkeeper may ~ the ball with his hands.* 踢足球時,只有守門員可以用手拿球。 ***~ ball (with),*** (fig, colloq) be ready to act in partnership; co-operate: (喻,俗)(和…)合夥;合作: *The French President refused to ~ ball,* eg to co-operate with the leader of another country. 法國總統拒絕合作。 [VP2C] (cricket, of the ground) be in good, poor, etc condition for ~ing: (板球)(指球場)適合(不適合)打球: *The pitch is ~ing well/badly.* 柱間的場地適合(不適合)打球。 **7** [VP6A] move (a piece) in chess: 移動;走(棋子): *~ a pawn;* 移動小卒; take (a playing-card) from one's hand (in whist, bridge, etc) and lay it down face upwards when one's turn comes: (在惠斯特、橋牌等中)出(牌): *~ one's ace of hearts/a trump.* 出紅心么點牌(一張王牌)。 ***~ one's cards well/badly,*** (fig) make good/bad use of opportunities. (喻)善(不善)於利用機會。 **8** ***~ fair,*** fairly; in accordance with the rules. 公平地玩;規規矩矩地玩。 ***~ hard,*** (of a player) ~ vigorously. (指球員、比賽者)賣力地比賽(打球等)。 ***~ the ball, not the man,*** kick the ball, not one's opponent. 踢球而非踢人(對手)。 ***~ the game,*** observe the rules of the game; (fig) be fair and honest; observe the code of honour. 遵守運動規則;(喻)公正誠實;遵守社交禮法。 **9** [VP6A, 2A, 12B, 13B] perform on (a musical instrument), perform (music); cause (music) to be heard (by operating a record-player or taperecorder): 演奏(樂器);彈;拉;吹;演奏(樂曲);(用唱機或錄音機)放出: *~ the piano/flute/violin, etc;* 彈鋼琴(吹笛子;拉小提琴等); *~ a Beethoven sonata.* 演奏貝多芬的奏鳴曲。 *Won't you please ~ me some Chopin/~ some Chopin for me?* 請你爲我演奏一些蕭邦的作品好嗎? *He was ~ing an old tune on his guitar.* 他在用吉他彈奏一首老曲子。 *We ~ed a lot of reggae at our party.* 我們在宴會中放了很多西印度羣島的流行音樂。 *P~ me Pat Simon's latest disc.* 給我放些派特•賽門最近灌製的唱片。 [VP15B] ***~ sth back,*** reproduce (music, speech, etc) from a tape or disc after it has been recorded: 播放(錄下的音樂、演講等): *The discussion was recorded on tape and then ~ed back.* 討論的內容被

錄音,然後再播放出來。Hence, 由此產生, **ˈ~-back** *n* **(a)** the device on a tape-recorder which ~s back recorded material. (錄音機上的)放音裝置。**(b)** occasion when this is done. 放音。 ***~ second fiddle (to sb),*** ⇨ fiddle. ***~ sth by ear/at sight,*** ⇨ ear¹(2), *at/on sight* at sight¹(2). ***~ it cool,*** ⇨ cool¹(5). **10** [VP6A, 2A] perform (a drama on the stage); act (a part in a drama); (of a drama) be performed: 演(戲);扮演(角色);(指戲劇)上演: *~ 'Twelfth Night';* 演出'第十二夜'; *~ Shylock;* 扮演 '威尼斯商人' 中的夏洛克; *the National Theatre, where 'Hamlet' is now ~ing,* = being ~ed. 正在上演'哈姆雷特'的國家戲院。 ***~ the fool,*** act foolishly. 行爲愚蠢;幹傻事。 ***~ the man,*** act like a man; be manly. 行爲像男人;有男子氣概。 ***~ a (big/small, etc) part (in sth),*** ⇨ part¹(4). **11** [VP2A, C, 15A] move about in a light or capricious manner; direct (light) (*on, over, along,* etc sth): 輕快或不定地活動;投射(光線)(到某物上): *sunlight ~ing on the water.* 在水面閃爍的陽光。*They ~ed coloured lights over the dance floor.* 他們把彩色燈光投射到舞池上。*A smile ~ed on her lips.* 她的唇上露出一絲微笑。*His fancy ~ed round the idea of entering a monastery.* 他一心想着進修道院。*They ~ed searchlights on the clouds/along the road.* 他們用探照燈照射雲(沿路照射)。 **12** [VP2A, 6A, 15A] operate continuously; discharge in a steady stream: 繼續或持續地操作;規律地放出;發射: *The fountains in the park ~ on Sundays.* 公園裡的噴泉星期天才噴水。*The firemen ~ed their hoses on the burning building.* 消防隊員用水管向着火的建築物噴水。 **13** [VP14, 3A] ***~ (sth) on/upon sth,*** fire: 射擊;開火: *We ~ed our guns on the enemy's lines.* 我們對着敵人的陣線射擊。*Their guns ~ed on the fort.* 他們的砲朝着城堡發射。 **14** ***~ a fish,*** (when angling with a rod and line) allow a fish to exhaust itself by pulling against the line. 讓魚拉動釣線以致疲乏。 **15** [VP2C, 3A, 15B] (special uses with *adverbial particles* and *preps*): (與副詞接語及介詞連用的特殊用法):

play at sth, **(a)** ⇨ 2, 5 above. 參看上列第 2, 5 義。**(b)** engage in sth in a trivial or half-hearted way, or merely for pleasure: 不經心地做某事;純粹爲了好玩而做某事: *Go for him properly—you're only ~ing at boxing!* 好好地和他打——你簡直是在玩弄拳擊!

play sth back, ⇨ 9 above. 參看上列第 9 義。

play down to sb, deliberately talk to or behave towards sb so that he does not feel inferior, in order to win support or favour. (爲了免得對方覺得自卑,或是爲了贏得支持或好感而) 和善地與某人講話;和善地對待某人。 ***~ sth down,*** deliberately minimize its importance. 故意減低某事物的重要性。

play sb in; play sb into a place, ~ music while he is entering (the place). 在某人進入(某地)時奏樂;奏樂歡迎某人。

play into sb's hands/the hands of sb, act so as to give him an advantage or benefit: 爲某人謀方便;有利於某人: *My opponent ~ed into my hands.* 我的對手做出了有利於我的行動。

play one person off against another, oppose him against another, esp for one's own advantage; stimulate rivalry between them. 挑撥離間;使雙方鬧翻以坐收漁利。 ***~ (sth) off,*** ~ again (eg a football match that was drawn): (足球等比賽結束雙方積分相等時)延長比賽;加賽: *~ off a draw/tie.* 打成平手後延長比賽以決勝負。*Leeds and Liverpool ~ off (their tie) tomorrow.* 里玆隊和利物浦隊明天將加賽一場以決勝負。 Hence, 由此產生, **ˈ~-off** *n* such a match. 延長比賽;加賽。

play on/upon sth, try to rouse or make use of (sb's feelings, incredulity, etc): 激起或利用(某人的感情、不信任等): *He tried to ~ on her sympathies.* 他想利用她的同情心。 ***~ on/upon words,*** make puns. 說雙關語;說俏皮話。

play sth out, ~ it to the end (usu fig): 結束(通常作比喻用法): *The long struggle between the strikers and their employers is not yet ~ed out.* 罷工者和雇主間的長期鬥爭尚未結束。 ***be ~ed out,*** be exhausted of energy or usefulness; be out of date: 衰竭;無用;過時: *His horse was ~ed out when the day's hunting was over.* 打了一天獵之後,他的馬筋疲力竭了。*Is that theory ~ed out,* no longer worth considering? 那種理論已落伍了嗎?

play up, **(a)** (esp in the imper) (sport) ~ vigorously, energetically. (尤用於祈使句中)(運動)使勁參加比賽;加油。**(b)** (colloq) behave mischievously: (俗)行爲頑皮;惡作劇: *Don't let the children ~ up.* 別讓孩子們淘氣。 ***~ sth up,*** give excessive importance to: 特別重視;過度重視: *Don't let him ~ up his illness,* eg by making it an excuse for doing nothing. 別讓他過於重視他的病(如以病爲藉口而無所事事)。 ***~ (sb) up,*** (colloq) give trouble (to): (俗)給某人麻煩;使人困擾: *This sciatica has been ~ing me up again.* 我這坐骨神經痛又使我煩惱了。 ***~ up to sb,*** **(a)** act in a drama so as to support another actor. 擔任另一演員的配角。 **(b)** (colloq) flatter (to win favour for oneself): (俗)諂媚;拍馬屁: *He always ~s up to his political bosses.* 他老是拍他政界上司的馬屁。

play with sb, **(a)** ⇨ 1 and 4 above. 參看上列第 1 義及第 4 義。**(b)** trifle with; consider lightly: 輕視;忽畧;玩弄: *It's wrong for a man to ~ with a woman's affections.* 男子玩弄女子的情感是不對的。*He's ~ing with the idea of emigrating to Canada.* 他目前不太重視移民到加拿大的想法。

player /ˈpleɪə(r); ˈpleɚ/ *n* **1** one who plays a game. 遊戲者;運動者。**2** actor. 演員;伶人。**3** person who plays a musical instrument; mechanical device for producing musical sounds: 演奏樂器者;產生樂聲之機器: *a ˈrecord-~.* 電唱機。 **ˈ~-piano** *n* piano fitted with a mechanism which enables the piano to be played automatically. 自奏鋼琴;自動鋼琴。

play·ful /ˈpleɪfl; ˈplefəl/ *adj* full of fun; in a mood for play; not serious: 十分有趣的;愛遊戲的;嬉戲的;頑皮的: *as ~ as a kitten;* 像小猫一樣頑皮; *a ~ manner.* 嬉戲的態度。**~ly** /-fəlɪ; -flɪ/ *adv* **~·ness** *n*

play·ing /ˈpleɪɪŋ; ˈpleɪŋ/ *n* **ˈ~-card,** ⇨ card¹(3). **ˈ~-field** *n* field for such games as football and cricket; field for children's games. (足球、板球遊戲等的)球場;操場;兒童遊戲場。

play·let /ˈpleɪlɪt; ˈplelɪt/ *n* short dramatic piece. 短劇。

plaza /ˈplɑːzə *US:* ˈplæzə; ˈplæzə/ *n* market-place; open square (esp in a Spanish town). 市場;(尤指西班牙城市的)廣場。

plea /pliː; pli/ *n* [C] **1** (legal) statement made by or for a person charged in a law court. (法律)(法庭中被告之)答辯;抗辯;辯護。 **2** request: 懇求;請求: *~s for mercy.* 懇求慈悲。 **3** reason or excuse offered for wrongdoing or failure to do sth, etc: (爲做錯事或未做某事等所做的)辯解;藉口: *on the ~ of ill health.* 以健康不佳爲藉口。

pleach /pliːtʃ; plitʃ/ *vt* [VP6A] interlace: 交錯;編結: *~ed hedges,* made by intertwining growing branches. 交錯的樹籬。

plead /pliːd; plid/ *vt, vi* (*pt, pp* ~ed, or, US pled, /pled; plɛd/) **1** [VP3A] (legal) ***~ for/against sb,*** address a court of law as an advocate on behalf of either the plaintiff or the defendant. (法律)爲某人辯護(反駁某人);抗辯;答辯。 ***~ guilty/not guilty,*** admit/deny that one is guilty: 承(否)認有罪;服(不服)罪: *'How do you ~?'—'Not guilty, my Lord.'* '你服罪嗎?'—'不服罪,法官。' **2** [VP6A] (legal) (of a lawyer) present the case of (to a court of law); put forward as a plea: (法律)(指律師)(向法庭)提出抗辯;辯護: *You should get a lawyer to ~ your case.* 你該請一位律師爲你的案子辯護。*Her counsel ~ed insanity,* declared that his client was insane, and therefore not legally responsible for her actions. 她的律師辯護說她的精神不健全(故對她的

行爲不負法律責任)。 **3** [VP3A] ~ ***(with sb) (for sth/to do sth),*** ask earnestly: 懇求;祈求: ~ *(with sb) for mercy.* (向某人)祈求寬恕。*He ~ed with his son to be less trouble to his mother.* 他求他的兒子少給他母親添麻煩。 **4** [VP6A] offer as an explanation or excuse: 以…爲口實;以…爲託詞: *The thief ~ed poverty.* 那賊以貧窮爲託詞。 *She ~ed ignorance of the law.* 她以不諳法律爲藉口。 **5** [VP6A] argue in favour of; advance reasons for (a cause, etc): 主張;爲…辯護;提出(運動等)的理由: ~ *the cause of the political prisoners.* 爲政治囚犯辯護。 **~·ings** *n pl* (legal) formal (usu written) statements, replies to accusations, etc, made by the parties in a legal action. (法律)(原告的)訴狀;(被告的)答辯狀。 **~·ing·ly** *adv*

pleas·ance /ˈplezns ; ˈplɛzn̩s/ *n* [C] (archaic) pleasure; pleasure-ground. (古)遊樂;遊樂園。

pleas·ant /ˈpleznt ; ˈplɛzn̩t/ *adj* giving pleasure; agreeable; friendly: 可喜的;愉快的; 適意的; 友愛的: *a ~ afternoon/taste/wine/surprise/companion;* 愉快的下午(合意的味道; 美味的葡萄酒; 驚喜; 友愛的伴侶); *make oneself ~ to visitors;* 親切週到地待客; ~ *to the taste.* 好吃;可口。**~·ly** *adv* **~·ness** *n* [U].

pleas·ant·ry /ˈplezntrɪ ; ˈplɛzn̩trɪ/ *n* (*pl* -ries) **1** [U] being jocular; humour. 詼諧; 幽默。 **2** [C] humorous or joking remark: 詼諧的笑話; 幽默話: *The girls smiled dutifully at the headmistress's pleasantries.* 女生們對於女校長所說的笑話發出應付的微笑。

please /pliːz ; pliz/ *vi, vt* **1** (imper) (abbr of *if you ~*) (used as a polite form of request): (祈使用法) (if you ~ 之略) (用作請求的客套話): *Come in, ~.* 請進來。*P~ come in.* 請進來。*Two coffees, ~.* 請來兩杯咖啡。*P~ don't do that.* 請別做那件事。 **2** [VP6A] give satisfaction to; be agreeable to: 使滿足;取悅;合…之意: *That will ~ you.* 那將會合你的意。 *It's difficult to ~ everybody.* 很難使每人滿意。*Are you ~d with your new clothes?* 你對你的新衣服滿意嗎? *We're very ~d to see you here.* 我們很高興在這裡見到你。*I shall be ~d to come.* 我將樂意來。 **ˌP~ yourˈself,** Do as you like. 隨你的意思;隨便你。 **3** [VP2A] think fit; choose: 認爲合適;選擇: *I shall do as I ~.* 我將隨我的意思去做。*Take as many as you ~.* 你要取多少就取多少。*You may do as you ~.* 你可以照你的意思做。 **4** ***if you ~,*** (used with the ironical implication that nothing could be more reasonable): (用作反語)眞是怪事;竟然: *'And now, if you ~, I'm to get nothing for all my work!'* '眞是怪事,我做了這麼多工作,却將一無所獲!' ~ ***God,*** if it be pleasing to God: 如果上帝願意;如果幸運: *War may be abolished one day, ~ God.* 如果幸運,戰爭將有一天會被廢止。 **~d** *adj* glad; feeling or showing satisfaction: 欣喜的; 愉快的;感到或表示滿足的: *He looked ~d with himself.* 他看起來對自己感到滿足(怡然自得)。*I'm very (much) ~d with what he has done.* 我對他所做的事感到高興。 **pleas·ing** *adj* affording pleasure (*to*); agreeable. 令人喜愛的(與 to 連用); 合意的。 **pleas·ing·ly** *adv*

pleas·ure /ˈpleʒə(r) ; ˈplɛʒɚ/ *n* **1** [U] feeling of being happy or satisfied: 快樂;享樂;愉快;滿足: *It gave me much ~ to hear of your success.* 聽到你成功我很快樂。*Is this a ~-seeking age?* 這是尋歡作樂的時代嗎? *Has he gone abroad for ~ or on business?* 他出國是爲遊樂,還是爲業務? *May we have the ~ of your company for lunch?* 請和我們共進午餐好嗎? *'Will you join us?'—'Thank you, with ~.'* '你願和我們一起嗎?'—'謝謝,非常願意。' *His life is given to ~,* to sensuous enjoyments. 他躭於逸樂。 ***take (no/great, etc) ~ in sth,*** experience (no, etc) enjoyment: 對…感到樂趣 (對…不感樂趣;對…感到極大樂趣等): *Some boys take great ~ in teasing their little sisters.* 有些男孩很喜歡逗弄他們的小妹妹。 **ˈ~-boat/-craft** *n* one used for ~ only. 遊艇(專供遊樂用的飛機)。 **ˈ~-ground** *n* amusement park; recreation ground. 遊樂場;娛樂場。 **2** [U] will; desire: 意志;願望: *We await your ~.* 我們聽候你的意思。 *We needn't consult his ~.* 我們不必跟他商量。*You may go or stay at your ~,* as you wish. 去留悉聽尊便。 **3** [C] thing that gives happiness: 使人愉快的事物;樂趣: *the ~s of friendship.* 友誼的樂趣。 **pleas·ur·able** /ˈpleʒərəbl ; ˈplɛʒrəbl̩/ *adj* giving ~. 悅人的;愉快的。**pleas·ur·ably** /-əblɪ ; -əblɪ/ *adv*

pleat /pliːt ; plit/ *n* fold made by doubling cloth on itself. (衣服上的)褶。□ *vt* [VP6A] make ~s in: 打褶於: *a ~ed skirt.* 褶裙。

pleb /pleb ; plɛb/ *n* (colloq abbr for) plebeian. (俗)爲 plebeian 之略。

pleb·eian /plɪˈbiːən ; plɪˈbiən/ *n, adj* (person who is) of the lower social classes (originally in ancient Rome); coarse; ignoble. (源自古羅馬)下層社會的(人);平民(的);粗俗的;鄙賤的。

plebi·scite /ˈplebɪsɪt *US:* -saɪt ; ˈplɛbəˌsaɪt/ *n* [C] (decision made upon a political question by) the votes of all qualified citizens. 公民投票;公民投票對政治問題所作的決定。

plec·trum /ˈplektrəm ; ˈplɛktrəm/ *n* small piece of metal, bone or ivory attached to the finger for plucking the strings of some stringed instruments, eg the mandolin, guitar. (戴於手指以撥動曼陀林、吉他等絃樂器之絃的)撥子;琴撥。

pled /pled ; plɛd/ ⇨ plead.

pledge /pledʒ ; plɛdʒ/ *n* **1** [C] sth left with sb to be kept by him until the giver has done sth which he is under an obligation to do; article left with a pawnbroker. 抵押品;典當品。 **2** [U] state of being left with sb on these conditions: 抵押;典當: *goods lying in ~;* 作抵押的貨物; *put/hold sth in ~;* 以(收下)某物作抵押; *take sth out of ~.* 贖出某物。 **3** [C] sth given as a sign of love, approval, etc: (表示愛、讚許等的)信物;保證物: *a ~ of friendship;* 表示友誼的信物; (fig) (喩) *the ~ of their youthful love,* their child. 他們年輕時愛情的信物(卽他們的孩子)。 **4** [U] agreement; promise: 信約;誓約;承諾: *under ~ of secrecy.* 在誓守秘密之下。 ***take/sign the ~,*** (esp) make a written promise to abstain from alcoholic drink. (尤指)作書面保證戒酒;立誓戒酒。□ *vt* [VP6A] **1** give as security; put in pawn. 以…作擔保;抵押;典當。 **2** give; engage; make an undertaking (to do sth): 提出;誓言;保證: *be ~d to secrecy;* 誓守秘密; ~ *one's word/honour.* 保證;發誓。 **3** drink the health of: 舉杯祝…健康: ~ *the bride and bridegroom.* 舉杯祝新娘和新郎健康。

ple·nary /ˈpliːnərɪ ; ˈplinərɪ/ *adj* **1** (of powers, authority) unlimited; absolute. (指權力、權威) 無限制的;絕對的。 **2** (of meetings) attended by all who have a right to attend: (指會議) 全體出席的: *a ~ session.* 一項全體出席的會議。**plen·ar·ily** /ˈpliːnərəlɪ ; ˈplinərəlɪ/ *adv*

pleni·po·ten·tiary /ˌplenɪpəˈtenʃərɪ ; ˌplɛnəpəˈtɛnʃərɪ/ *n* (*pl* -ries), *adj* (person, eg a representative, an ambassador) having full power to act, make decisions, etc (on behalf of his government, etc). (代表其政府等之) 全權代表(大使等);有全權的。

pleni·tude /ˈplenɪtjuːd *US:* -tuːd ; ˈplɛnəˌtjud/ *n* (*sing* only) (formal) fullness; abundance: (僅用單數) (正式用語) 充足; 豐饒: *in the ~ of his powers.* 在他權力的最高峯。

plen·teous /ˈplentɪəs ; ˈplɛntɪəs/ *adj* (chiefly poet) plentiful. (主要用於詩中)充足的;豐富的。 **~·ly** *adv*

plen·ti·ful /ˈplentɪfl ; ˈplɛntɪfəl/ *adj* in large quantities or numbers; abundant. 大量的;豐富的。 **~·ly** /-fəlɪ ; -fl̩ɪ/ *adv*

plenty /ˈplentɪ ; ˈplɛntɪ/ *n* [U] ***~ (of),*** as much as or more than is needed or desired; a large number or quantity: 富足;充裕;大量: *There are ~ of eggs in the house.* 家裡有很多蛋。 *There's ~*

more (*of it*). (這東西) 尚有許多。*We must get to the station in ~ of time.* 我們必須及早動身以便從容抵達車站。*Six will be ~*, as many as I need. 六個足够了。*I've had ~, thank you.* 我已經够了，謝謝你。**in ~**, in a large quantity: 大量的；許多：*There was food and drink in ~.* 有許多食物和飲料。□ *adv* (colloq) quite: (俗) 十分；充分地：*It's ~ big enough.* 它實在够大了。

pleo·nasm /ˈplɪənæzəm ; ˈpliəˌnæzəm/ *n* [C, U] (instance of the) use of more words than are needed to express the meaning, eg 'each of the *two* twins'; 'divide sth into *four* quarters'. 冗言或贅言之使用；冗言或贅言使用之實例；冗言；贅言 (如 twins 之前加 two, quarters 之前加 four)。

pleth·ora /ˈpleθərə ; ˈplɛθərə/ *n* (formal) (正式用語) **1** glut; (over-)abundance. 過量供應；過剩；充斥。**2** (med) unhealthy condition of the body marked by an excess of red corpuscles in the blood. (醫) 多血症；紅血球過多症。

pleur·isy /ˈplʊərəsɪ ; ˈplʊrəsɪ/ *n* [U] serious illness with inflammation of the delicate membrane of the thorax and the lungs, marked by pain in the chest or sides. (醫) 肋膜炎；胸膜炎。

plexus /ˈpleksəs ; ˈplɛksəs/ *n* (*pl* ~es /-səsɪz ; -səsɪz/ or ~) (anat) network of fibres or vessels in the body: (解剖) (纖維或血管之) 叢：*the solar ~*, in the abdomen. 腹腔叢；太陽神經叢。

pli·able /ˈplaɪəbl ; ˈplaɪəbl/ *adj* easily bent, shaped or twisted; (of the mind) easily influenced; open to suggestions. 易曲折的；柔順的；(指思想) 易受影響的；能接受意見的。**pli·abil·ity** /ˌplaɪəˈbɪlətɪ ; ˌplaɪəˈbɪlətɪ/ *n* [U].

pli·ant /ˈplaɪənt ; ˈplaɪənt/ *adj* = pliable. **~·ly** *adv* **pli·ancy** /ˈplaɪənsɪ ; ˈplaɪənsɪ/ *n*

pli·ers /ˈplaɪəz ; ˈplaɪəz/ *n pl* **(pair of) ~**, kind of pincers with long, flat jaws, used for holding, bending, twisting or cutting wire, etc. (鉗鋼絲等的) 鉗子；老虎鉗。⇨ the illus at tool. 參看 tool 之插圖。

plight¹ /plaɪt ; plaɪt/ *n* serious and difficult condition: 嚴重和困難的情況；困境；苦境：*His affairs were in a terrible ~.* 他的事情陷入嚴重的情況。*What a ~ to be in!* 處境多壞啊！

plight² /plaɪt ; plaɪt/ *vt* [VP6A] (archaic) (古) **1** pledge, promise: 保證；誓約：*one's ~ed word.* 某人的誓言。**2** *~ one's troth; ~ oneself*, engage oneself to be married. 訂婚。

Plim·soll /ˈplɪmsəl ; ˈplɪmsl/ *n* **'~ line/mark**, line on the hull of a ship to mark how far it may legally go down in the water when loaded. (船身上的) 法定載貨吃水線；普紹索標；裝載水線標。

plim·solls /ˈplɪmsəlz ; ˈplɪmslz/ *n pl* rubber-soled canvas shoes (US 美 = *sneakers*). (輕便的) 橡皮底帆布鞋。

plinth /plɪnθ ; plɪnθ/ *n* square base or block on which a column or statue stands. (柱或雕像的) 基脚；基礎；基座。⇨ the illus at column. 參看 column 之插圖。

plod /plɒd ; plɑd/ *vi, vt* (-dd-) [VP2C] continue walking, working, etc slowly and wearily but without resting: 緩慢、疲倦但不休息地繼續步行，工作等；孜孜從事：*~ on one's way;* 緩慢而不停地行走；*~ away at a dull task.* 孜孜不息地做着沉悶的工作。**~·der** *n* person who ~s; slow but earnest person. 緩慢而不休息的步行者、工作者；動作緩慢而有熱忱者；孜孜從事者。**~·ding** *adj* **~·ding·ly** *adv*

plonk¹ /plɒŋk ; plɑŋk/ *n* sound of sth dropping (esp into liquid). 墜落聲；(尤指某物落入水中的) 撲通聲。□ *adv* with a ~. 撲通一聲。□ *vt* **~ (down)**, drop sth with a ~ing sound: 撲通一聲墜落；發出落水聲：*~ the fish down on the table.* 啪達一聲把魚丟在桌子上。

plonk² /plɒŋk ; plɑŋk/ *n* [U] (sl) cheap wine. (俚) 便宜的酒。

plop /plɒp ; plɑp/ *n* [C] sound (as) of a small smooth object dropping into water without a splash. (光滑的小物件落入水中而未濺潑的) 落水聲；撲通聲。□ *adv* with a ~. 撲通一聲地。□ *vi* (-pp-) make a ~; fall with a ~. 發出落水聲；撲通地墜落。

plo·sive /ˈpləʊsɪv ; ˈplosɪv/ *n, adj* (phon) (consonant sound) with a complete closing of the air passage followed by an audible release of the air compressed behind the closure, eg /t/ and /p/ in *top*. (語音) 爆裂的；爆裂音 (使氣流全部閉塞然後再清晰可聞地吐氣所發的子音，如 top 中的 /t/ 及 /p/)。

plot¹ /plɒt ; plɑt/ *n* piece of ground (usu small): (通常指小的) 一塊地：*a building ~;* 建地；*a ~ of vegetables.* 一塊做菜園用的地。□ *vt* (-tt-) **1** [VP6A] make a plan, map or diagram of; mark (the position of sth) on a diagram by connecting points on a graph: 製…之圖、地圖或圖解；在圖解上標明 (某物之位置)：*~ a temperature curve;* 繪製溫度曲線；*~ aircraft movements by radar.* 藉雷達標示飛機的動向。**2** [VP6A, 15B] *~ (out)*, divide into ~s. 分成小塊地。

plot² /plɒt ; plɑt/ *n* [C] **1** secret plan (good or bad); conspiracy: 密謀 (好的或壞的)；陰謀：*a ~ to overthrow the government.* 推翻政府的陰謀。**2** plan or outline (of the events of a story, esp of a novel or drama). (尤指小說或戲劇之故事的) 情節；結構。□ *vt, vi* (-tt-) [VP2A, 3A, 4A, 6A, 8, 10] make secret plans; form, take part in, a ~: 密謀；計畫；參與陰謀：*~ with sb against the government.* 與某人密謀反對政府。**~·ter** *n* person who ~s; conspirator. 密謀者；陰謀者。

plough (US = **plow**) /plaʊ ; plaʊ/ *n* **1** implement for cutting furrows in soil and turning it up, drawn by animals or (more usually) a tractor. 犂 (由獸力或曳引機拖動)。***put one's hand to the ~***, (fig) undertake a task. (喻) 着手工作。**'~·boy** *n* boy who leads the horses that pull a ~. 牽引犂田之馬的孩子；耕童。**'~·man** /-mən ; -mən/ *n* (*pl* -men) man who guides a ~. 以犂耕田者；農夫。**'~·share** *n* broad blade of a ~. 犂鏵。**2** kinds of implement resembling a ~. 犂形器具。**'snow-~** *n* one for clearing away snow from roads and railways. 除雪機；排除道路上及鐵道上積雪的器具。**3** [U] ploughed land: 耕地；耕過的地：*100 acres of ~.* 一百畝耕地。**4 the P~**, (astron) the group of stars called *Charles's Wain, the Big Dipper* or *the Great Bear.* (天文) 北斗七星 (又稱爲 Charles's Wain, the Big Dipper 或 the Great Bear)。□ *vt, vi* **1** [VP6A, 15B] *~ (back)*, break up (land) with a ~: 犂 (地)；耕 (田)：*~ a field;* 耕田；(fig) (喻) *~ back the profits of a business,* reinvest them. 以利潤作爲資本投資；再投資。***~ a lonely furrow***, (fig) work without help or support. (喻) 孤獨無援地工作。***~ the sand***, (fig) do useless work. (喻) 做無用之事；徒勞無功。**2** [VP3A] ***~ through***, force a way through; advance laboriously: 費力穿過；艱苦前進：*a ship ~ing through the heavy waves;* 冒著大浪前進的一條船；*~ (one's way) through the mud;* 在泥濘中費力前行；*~ through a dull textbook.* 很費力地閱讀一本枯燥的教科書。**3** [VP6A] (sl) reject (a candidate) in an examination: (俚) 在考試中淘汰 (應試者)；當掉 (應試者)：*The examiners ~ed half the candidates.* 主考人員刷掉

a plough

了一半的應試者。

plover /ˈplʌvə(r) ; ˈplʌvɚ/ *n* sorts of long-legged, short-tailed land bird that frequents marshy ground near the sea, esp (in England) the golden ~, the green ~, and the lapwing or peewit. 千鳥；鴴；雎鳩(長足短尾之陸上禽類，常見於靠近海洋的沼澤地帶，在英格蘭尤指黃鴴、綠鴴及田鳧)。

plow /plaʊ ; plaʊ/ (US) = plough.

ploy /plɔɪ ; plɔɪ/ *n* [C] manoeuvre; sth said or done, eg in a game, to win an advantage over one's opponent. 策略；手法(例如在比賽時爲了戰勝對方而採取者)。

pluck /plʌk ; plʌk/ *vt, vi* **1** [VP6A] pull the feathers off (a hen, goose, etc): 拔去(雞、鵝等)的毛: *Has this goose been ~ed?* 這隻鵝的毛拔過了嗎？ **2** [VP6A] pick (flowers, fruit, etc). 摘(花、果等)。[VP15B] ~ ***sth out/up,*** pull (weeds, etc, up or out). 拔(野草等)。 **3** [VP3A] ~ ***at,*** snatch at; take hold of and pull: 拉；拽；抓住: *The child was ~ing at its mother's skirt.* 那孩子抓住母親的裙子。 **4** ~ ***up courage,*** summon one's courage; overcome one's fears. 鼓起勇氣；克服恐懼。 **5** [VP6A] (sl) swindle (esp a young or inexperienced person, eg in gambling). (俚) 詐欺 (尤指年輕或無經驗之人，如在賭博中)。 □ *n* **1** [U] courage; spirit. 勇氣；精神。 **2** [U] that which is ~ed out, esp the heart, liver and lungs of an animal that has been killed. 被摘除或拔除之物；(尤指從被殺死之動物所取出之)心、肝和肺；內臟。 **3** [C] short, sharp pull. 短急的拉；拽。 **~y** *adj* (-ier, -iest) brave; having ~(1). 勇敢的；有膽量的。 **~·ily** /-ɪlɪ ; -əlɪ/ *adv*

plug /plʌg ; plʌg/ *n* **1** piece of wood, metal, rubber etc used to stop up a hole (eg in a barrel, wash-basin, bath, cistern, etc) (US 美 = *stopper*). (用於塞大桶，臉盆，浴盆等之洞的)栓；塞子。 **ˈ~-hole,** hole for a ~ (US 美 = *drain*). 排水洞。 **2** device for making a connection with a supply of electric current: 電插頭: *a three-/two-pin ~;* 三(二)脚的電插頭; *put the ~ in the socket/outlet.* 把插頭插在插座內。 ⇨ also *sparking-~* at spark¹. **3** cake of pressed or twisted tobacco; piece of this cut off for chewing. 煙餅；板煙；口嚼煙(切開之煙餅供咀嚼者)。 **4** (sl) piece of favourable publicity (eg in a radio or TV programme) for commercial product. (俚)(廣播或電視的)一則商業廣告。⇨ 5 below. 參看下列第5義。 □ *vt, vi* (-gg-) **1** [VP6A, 15B] ~ ***(up),*** stop or fill (up) with a ~: 以塞子塞住: *~ a leak.* 塞住漏洞。 **2** [VP2C] (colloq) (俗) ~ ***away at,*** work hard at. 孜孜從事。 **3** [VP2C, 15B] ~ ***(sth) in,*** make a connection with a ~(2): 插上(某物)的插頭通電: *~ in the TV set.* 插上電視機的插頭。 **4** [VP6A] (US, sl) hit; shoot. (美，俚)打；射擊。 **5** [VP6A] (sl) cause (sth) to be widely known by giving repeated publicity: (俚)藉反覆宣傳使(某事物)爲大衆所知；大事宣傳: *~ a new song,* eg on radio or TV. 宣傳一首新歌(如藉無線電廣播或電視反覆播放)。

plum /plʌm ; plʌm/ *n* **1** (tree having) soft round, smooth-skinned fruit with a stone-like seed. 梅子(樹)；李子(樹)。 ⇨ the illus at fruit. 參看 fruit 之挿圖。 **2** ˌ~ ˈ**cake,** kind containing dried raisins, currants, etc. 葡萄乾糕餅。ˌ~ ˈ**duff,** boiled pudding containing dried raisins, currants, etc. 葡萄乾布丁。ˌ~-ˈ**pudding,** rich boiled pudding containing dried fruits and spices, part of traditional Christmas food. 乾果布丁(相沿爲聖誕節食品之一部分)。 **3** (colloq) sth considered good and desirable, esp a well-paid position. (俗)被認爲理想之事物(尤指待遇好的職務)；肥缺；好差事。

plum·age /ˈpluːmɪdʒ ; ˈplumɪdʒ/ *n* [U] bird's feathers: 鳥羽；羽毛: *tropical birds in their brightly coloured ~.* 羽毛鮮艷的熱帶鳥。

plumb /plʌm ; plʌm/ *n* ball or piece of lead tied to the end of a cord or rope **(a ˈ~-line)** for finding the depth of water or testing whether a wall is vertical. 垂球；鉛垂；測垂(固定於鉛垂線 ˈplumb-line 之一端，以測定水深或牆是否垂直的鉛球或鉛塊)。 ***out of ~,*** not vertical. 不垂直的。 □ *adv* **1** exactly. 正確地；精確地。 **2** (US, colloq) quite: (美，俗)非常；全然: *~ crazy.* 非常瘋狂。 □ *vt* [VP6A] (fig) get to the root of: (喻)追根究底；查明: *~ the depths of a mystery.* 查明某項神秘事物的底細。

plum·bago¹ /plʌmˈbeɪgəʊ ; plʌmˈbego/ *n* [U] black substance, graphite, used for pencils, etc and mixed with clay for making crucibles. 黑鉛；石墨(用於製鉛筆等，與黏土混合可製坩堝)。

plum·bago² /plʌmˈbeɪgəʊ ; plʌmˈbego/ *n* (*pl* ~s /-gəʊz ; -goz/) blue-flowered plant. 磯松屬植物(一種琉璃茉莉，開藍花)。

plumber /ˈplʌmə(r) ; ˈplʌmɚ/ *n* workman who fits and repairs water-pipes, water-tanks, cisterns, etc in a building. 裝修水管的工人；鉛管工人。

plumb·ing /ˈplʌmɪŋ ; ˈplʌmɪŋ/ *n* [U] **1** the work of a plumber. 鉛管工；裝修水管業。 **2** the water-pipes, water-tanks, cisterns, etc in a building: (建築物之)水管裝置(水管、水槽等): *The ~ is out of order.* 水管裝置出了毛病。

plume /pluːm ; plum/ *n* feather, esp a large one used as a decoration; ornament of feathers; sth suggesting a feather by its shape: 羽毛(尤指作裝飾用的大羽毛)；羽毛飾；羽毛狀的東西: *a ~ of smoke/steam.* 一縷煙(水氣)。 ⇨ the illus at rare. 參看 rare 之挿圖。 ***borrowed ~s,*** (fig) finery displayed as one's own but borrowed from someone. (喻)穿着借來的華美衣服而誇爲己有。 □ *vt* [VP6A] (of a bird) smooth (its feathers); preen (itself, its wings). (指鳥)整刷(其羽毛)；以喙整理(自己，其翅膀)。 ~ ***oneself (on sth),*** (fig) congratulate oneself. (喻)(爲某事)自慶；自鳴得意。

plum·met /ˈplʌmɪt ; ˈplʌmɪt/ *n* (weight attached to a) plumb-line; weight attached to a fishing-line to keep the float upright. 鉛垂線；鉛錘；釣絲上的墜子(能使浮子垂直)。 □ *vi* (-tt-) [VP2A] fall, plunge, steeply: 垂直落下；筆直下墜: *Share prices have ~ted.* 股票價格直線下跌。

plummy /ˈplʌmɪ ; ˈplʌmɪ/ *adj* (-ier, -iest) (colloq) good; desirable: (俗)好的；理想的: *~ jobs;* 理想的工作; affected, snobbish: 矯揉做作的；勢利的: *a ~ voice.* 矯揉做作的聲音。

plump¹ /plʌmp ; plʌmp/ *adj* (esp of an animal, a person, parts of the body) rounded; fat in a pleasant-looking way: (尤指動物、人、身體之各部分)圓胖的；豐滿的: *a baby with ~ cheeks.* 面龐肥肥胖胖的嬰兒。 □ *vt, vi* [VP6A, 2A, 15B, 2C] ~ ***(out/up),*** make or become rounded: 使圓胖；使膨脹；變圓胖；變膨脹: *His cheeks are beginning to ~ up/out.* 他的面頰胖起來了。 *She ~ed up the pillows.* 她把枕頭塡得鼓鼓的。

plump² /plʌmp ; plʌmp/ *vi, vt* **1** [VP2C, 15B] ~ ***(sb/oneself/sth) down,*** (cause to) fall or drop, suddenly and heavily: (使)突然而沈重地落下: *~ (oneself) down in a chair;* 猛一下坐在椅子上; *~ down a heavy bag.* 撲通一聲把一隻沈重的袋子放下。 **2** [VP3A] ~ ***for,*** vote for, choose, with confidence: 充滿信心地支持或選擇；極力支持；衷心擁護: *~ for the Liberal candidate.* 極力支持自由黨候選人。 □ *n* abrupt, heavy fall. 突然而沈重的落下。 □ *adv* **1** suddenly, abruptly: 突然地；驀地: *fall ~ into the hole.* 突然落入洞中。 **2** bluntly: 率直地: *I told him ~ that....* 我率直地告訴他…。 □ *adj* unqualified; direct: 絕對的；直接的: *give sb a ~ 'No' for an answer.* 直截了當地以'不'回答某人。

plun·der /ˈplʌndə(r) ; ˈplʌndɚ/ *vt, vi* [VP6A, 14, 2A] ~ ***(of),*** rob (people), esp during war or civil disorder; take goods from (places) by force: (尤指在作戰或內亂時)搶刧(人)；搶奪(某地)的東西: *~ a palace of its treasures;* 刧掠宮廷的財寶; *~ the citizens of a conquered town.* 搶刧淪陷市鎮的市民。 □ *n* [U] ~ing; goods taken: 搶刧；搶奪；搶奪物；戰利品: *live by ~;* 以搶刧爲生; *wagon-loads of ~.*

一車車的掠奪物。~**er** *n*

plunge /plʌndʒ; plʌndʒ/ *vt, vi* **1** [VP6A, 14, 2A, C] ~ ***(into),*** put (sth), or go suddenly and with force, into: 投入(某物);使陷入;突入: ~ *one's hand into cold water/a hole;* 將手伸入冷水(洞)中; ~ *a country into war;* 使一國陷入戰爭; ~ *a room into darkness,* eg by cutting off the current; 使一房間陷入黑暗中(如切斷電源); ~ *into a swimming-pool;* 跳入游泳池; ~ *into an argument;* 突然開始爭論; *be ~d into grief.* 陷入悲哀的境地。**2** [VP2A, C] (of a horse) move forward and downward quickly; (of a ship) thrust its bows into the water; (sl) gamble deeply; run into debt. (指馬)顛躍;(指船)顛簸;(俚)狂賭;負債。□ *n* act of plunging (eg from a diving-board into water); violent thrust or other movement. 投入;陷入;跳入(如從跳臺跳水);突進。***take the ~,*** (fig) take a critical step; do sth decisive. (喻)採取重大步驟,做決定性的事。**plunger** *n* (esp) part of a mechanism that moves with a plunging motion, eg the piston of a pump; suction device for clearing a blocked pipe. (尤指機器之)活柱頂塞(如唧筒的活塞);柱塞。

plunk /plʌŋk; plʌŋk/ = plonk¹.

plu·per·fect /ˌpluːˈpɜːfɪkt ; ˌpluˈpɝfɪkt/ *n, adj* (gram) (tense) expressing action completed before some past time stated or implied (and in English conveyed by *had* and a *pp,* as in 'As he *had* not *received* my letter, he did not come'). (文法)過去完成的;過去完成式(在英語中以 had 及過去分詞表示之,如 As he had not received my letter, he did not come 中的 had received)。

plu·ral /ˈplʊərəl ; ˈplʊrəl/ *n, adj* (form of word) used with reference to more than one: 複數(式);複數的;多於一個的: 'The ~ of *child* is *children.*' 'child 的複數是 children。' ~ **society,** one with more than one race, eg Kenya, with Africans, Asians and Europeans. 複性社會(多數人種組成的社會,如肯亞有非洲人、亞洲人和歐洲人)。~ **voter,** person who has a vote in more than one constituency. 有權利在一個以上的選區投票的人;有複投票權者。

plu·ral·ism /ˈplʊərəlɪzəm ; ˈplʊrəlɪzm̩/ *n* [U] the quality of being plural; the holding of more than one office at one time. 複數性;多元性;兼職。**plu·ral·ist** /-ɪst ; -ɪst/ *n* supporter of ~. 贊成兼職者。

plu·ral·ity /plʊəˈrælətɪ ; plʊˈrælətɪ/ *n* (*pl* -ties) **1** [U] state of being plural; [C] large number; majority (*of* votes, etc). 複性;衆多的狀態;大量;多數;(選票等的)過半數(與 of 連用)。**2** [U] holding of more than one office at a time; [C] office held with another. 兼職;所兼之職位。

plus /plʌs ; plʌs/ *prep* with the addition of: 加;加上: *Two ~ five is seven,* 2 + 5 = 7. 二加五等於七。ˌ~-ˈ**fours** *n pl* wide, loose knickerbockers. 一種寬鬆的燈籠褲。□ *adj* positive: 正的: *a ~ quantity,* one greater than zero. 正數。⇨ minus. □ *n* the sign +; (colloq, fig) positive quality. 加號;正號(+);(俗,喻)利益;優點。

plush /plʌʃ ; plʌʃ/ *n* [U] kind of silk or cotton cloth with a soft nap. 一種有軟絨的棉布或綢布。□ *adj* (also ~**y** (-ier, -iest)) (sl) smart; sumptuous: (俚)漂亮的;華美的: *a ~(y) restaurant.* 豪華餐館。

Pluto /ˈpluːtəʊ ; ˈpluto/ *n* **1** (Roman myth) god of the underworld. (羅神)冥府之神;閻羅王。**2** (astron) planet farthest from the sun. (天文)冥王星。⇨ the illus at planet. 參看 planet 之插圖。

plu·toc·racy /pluːˈtɒkrəsɪ ; pluˈtɑkrəsɪ/ *n* (*pl* -cies) [C, U] (government by a) rich and powerful class. 富豪階級;財閥階級;富豪政治;財閥政治。**plu·to·crat** /ˈpluːtəkræt ; ˈplutəˌkræt/ *n* person who is powerful because of his wealth. 有錢有勢的人;富豪;財閥。**plu·to·cratic** /ˌpluːtəˈkrætɪk ; ˌplutəˈkrætɪk/ *adj* of ~ or a plutocrat. 富豪階級的;富豪政治的;富豪的。

plu·to·nium /pluːˈtəʊnɪəm ; pluˈtonɪəm/ *n* [U] (artificially produced) radioactive element (symbol Pu) derived from uranium, used in nuclear reactors and weapons. 鈽(以人工方法自鈾形成的放射性元素,符號 Pu, 用於核子反應器及核子武器中)。

ply¹ /plaɪ ; plaɪ/ *n* [C] **1** layer of wood or thickness of cloth: (木的)板層;(布的)厚度: *three-ply wood,* made by sticking together three layers with the grain of each at a right angle to that of the next. 三夾板。ˈ**ply·wood** *n* [U] board(s) made by gluing together thin layers of wood. 合板;夾板。**2** one strand in wool, rope, etc: (毛線、繩等的)綯;股;縷: *four-ply wool for knitting socks.* 織襪子的四股毛線。

ply² /plaɪ ; plaɪ/ *vt, vi* (*pt, pp* plied /plaɪd ; plaɪd/) **1** [VP6A] (formal) work with (an instrument): (正式用語)使用(器具): *ply one's needle,* work busily with it. 忙於針黹。**2** [VP2C] (of ships, buses, etc) go regularly to and fro: (指船、公共汽車等)定期往來;定時往來: *ships that ply between Glasgow and New York;* 在格拉斯哥與紐約之間定期往來的班船; *ferry-boats plying across the Channel.* 定時往來英吉利海峽的渡船。**3** ***ply a trade,*** work at it. 經營一商業;從事一行業。***ply sb with sth,*** keep him constantly supplied with (food and drink); attack him constantly with (questions, arguments, etc). 經常以(食物和飲料)供給某人;經常以(問題、議論等)攻擊某人。

pneu·matic /njuːˈmætɪk *US:* nuː- ; njuˈmætɪk/ *adj* worked or driven by compressed air: 由壓縮空氣操作或推動的: ~ *drills;* 氣鑽;風鑽; filled with compressed air: 充氣的;裝有壓縮空氣的: ~ *tyres.* 充氣的輪胎。**pneu·mati·cally** /-klɪ ; -klɪ/ *adv*

pneu·monia /njuːˈməʊnɪə *US:* nuː- ; njuˈmonjə/ *n* [U] serious illness with inflammation of one or both lungs. 肺炎。

poach¹ /pəʊtʃ ; potʃ/ *vt* [VP6A] cook (an egg) by cracking the shell and dropping the contents into boiling water; simmer (eg fish) in liquid (eg wine). 煮(荷包蛋);在液體(如酒)中燉(如魚)。

poach² /pəʊtʃ ; potʃ/ *vt, vi* [VP6A, 2A, 3A] ~ ***on/for,*** **1** (go on sb else's property and) take (hares, pheasants, salmon, etc) illegally: (侵入他人之土地)非法獵取或捕取(野兎、野雞、鮭等);盜獵;盜捕: ~ *hares;* 非法獵野兎; ~ *for salmon;* 盜捕鮭; *go out ~ing;* 出外偷獵; ~ *on a neighbour's land.* 侵入隣人的土地非法狩獵。**2** (fig) be active in some kind of work that properly belongs to another (or that he considers to be his preserve): (喻)在他人的領域內活動;侵害他人的領域: *Don't ~ on my preserves.* 不要侵入我的領域。~**er** *n*

pock /pɒk ; pɑk/ *n* spot on the skin caused by smallpox. 痘疱;痘痕;麻子。ˈ~-**marked,** with marks left after smallpox. 有痘痕的;麻臉的。~**ed** *adj* ***be ~ed with,*** have holes or depressions in: 有凹洞的: *The moon's surface is ~ed with small craters.* 月球的表面佈滿了隕石坑。

pocket /ˈpɒkɪt ; ˈpɑkɪt/ *n* **1** small bag sewn into and forming part of an article of clothing, for carrying things in: 口袋;衣袋: *trouser/waistcoat, etc ~.* 褲(背心等)口袋。***pick sb's ~,*** steal from sb's ~. 扒竊某人的口袋。***put one's pride in one's ~,*** do sth that would normally make one feel mortified. 忍辱。***put one's hand in one's ~,*** be ready to spend or give money. 願意花錢;願意出錢。ˈ~-**book** *n* **(a)** notebook. 小記事簿;袖珍記事册。**(b)** (US) leather case for paper money (GB 英 = *wallet*). (美)錢包;皮夾子。**(c)** (US) woman's purse or handbag. (美)(女人的)手提包;錢袋。ˌ~-ˈ**handkerchief** *n* one to be carried in the ~; (attrib) of small size: 手巾;手絹;(形容用法)小型的: *a ~-handkerchief rug.* 小塊地毯。ˈ~-**knife** *n* small knife with one or more folding blades. (可摺合的)小刀。ˈ~-**money** *n* [U] money for small needs, esp money given to children. 零用錢(尤指給與小孩者)。**2** money resources; money: 財源;錢: *He will suffer in his ~,* will lose financially. 他將在錢財方面有所損失。

in/out of ~, having gained/lost money as the result of doing sth: 因做某事而賺(虧)錢: *The deal left him hundreds of dollars out of ~.* 那筆生意使他虧了好幾百元。**out-of-~ expenses,** actual outlay incurred; what one has actually spent. 實際花費;現金支出。 **3** bag, hollow, cavity, eg a string pouch at the corner of a billiard or pool table; small cavity in the ground or in rock, containing gold or ore; partial vacuum in the atmosphere (*an 'air-~*) affecting the flight of an aircraft; cavity of air (*an 'air-~*) in a mine²(1), eg when a shaft is flooded; isolated area: 袋;洞(如撞球臺角的網袋);(地面或岩石中的)礦穴;礦脈瘤;空中陷阱;氣潭(大氣中部分眞空之現象,影響飛機飛行,亦稱作 'air-~);礦穴裡的氣坑(亦稱做 'air-~);孤立地區: *enemy ~s,* eg occupied by enemy forces; 孤立的敵人佔領區; *~s of resistance;* 孤軍抵抗地區; *~s of unemployment in the Midlands.* 英格蘭中部諸郡的失業地區。 **4** (attrib) of a size suitable for a ~: (形容用法)袖珍的;小型的: *a ~ guide/dictionary/edition;* 袖珍指南(字典,版本); *a ~-size camera.* 袖珍照相機。 **'~·ful** /-fʊl; -ˌfʊl/ *n* amount which a ~ holds. 一袋之量;滿袋。□ *vt* [VP6A] **1** put into one's ~: 放入袋中;納入袋中: *He ~ed the money.* 他把錢納入口袋。 **~ an insult,** endure it without protest. 忍受侮辱。 **~ one's pride,** suppress or hide one's feelings of mortification. 壓抑或掩飾自已的屈辱感覺。 **2** appropriate for oneself (usu but not necessarily dishonestly): 據爲已有;(通常指)侵吞;僭取: *He ~ed half the profits.* 他把一半的利潤據爲己有。*He was given £5 for expenses, but ~ed most of it.* 他得到五鎊的經費,但侵吞了大部分。 **3** send (a ball) into a ~ on a billiard or pool table. (撞球)把(球)打進網袋。

pod /pɒd; pɑd/ *n* [C] long seed-vessel of various plants, esp peas and beans. 莢;莢;(尤指)豆莢。⇨ the illus at vegetable. 參看 vegetable 之插圖。□ *vt, vi* (-dd-) **1** [VP6A] take (peas, etc) out of pods. 剝掉(豌豆等)之莢。 **2** [VP2A, C] **~ *(up)*,** form pods: 結莢;生莢: *The peas are podding (up) well.* 豌豆結莢良好。

podgy /ˈpɒdʒɪ; ˈpɑdʒɪ/ *adj* (-ier, -iest) (of a person) short and fat. (指人)矮胖的。

podi·atry /pəˈdaɪətrɪ; poˈdaɪətrɪ/ *n* [U] (US) (美) = chiropody.

po·dium /ˈpəʊdɪəm; ˈpodɪəm/ *n* platform, eg for the conductor of an orchestra, a lecturer, etc. 高臺;(樂隊的)指揮臺;講臺。

poem /ˈpəʊɪm; ˈpo·ɪm/ *n* [C] piece of creative writing in verse form, esp one expressing deep feeling or noble thought in beautiful language, composed with the desire to communicate an experience; piece of prose writing in elevated style: (一篇或一首)詩;韻文;風格高尚的散文: *a 'prose ~.* 散文詩。

po·esy /ˈpəʊɪzɪ; ˈpo·ɪsɪ/ *n* [U] (archaic) poetry. (古)詩。

poet /ˈpəʊɪt; ˈpo·ɪt/ *n* writer of poems. 詩人。ˌ~ **'laureate,** ⇨ laureate. **'poet·ess** /-es; -ɛs/ *n* woman ~. 女詩人。

po·etic /pəʊˈetɪk; poˈɛtɪk/ *adj* of poets and poetry: 詩人的;詩的;韻文的;詩意的: *in ~ form;* 以詩的形式; *~ genius.* 詩才。ˌ~ **'justice,** ideal justice, with proper distribution of rewards and punishments. 理想的因果報應;詩的正義。ˌ~ **'licence,** ⇨ licence. **po·eti·cal** /-kl; -kḷ/ *adj* = ~: *~al works of Keats,* his poetry. 濟慈的詩。**po·eti·cally** /-klɪ; -klɪ/ *adv*

po·etry /ˈpəʊɪtrɪ; ˈpo·ɪtrɪ/ *n* [U] **1** the art of a poet; poems. 作詩法;詩(總稱)。 **2** quality that produces feelings as produced by poems: 詩情;詩意;詩或似詩的性質: *the ~ of motion,* eg in ballet or some kinds of athletics. (如芭蕾舞或若干其他運動之)動作的韻律。

po·grom /ˈpɒgrəm *US:* pəˈgrɒm; ˈpogrəm/ *n* [C] organized persecution or killing and plunder (of a group or class of people). (對某一團體或階層之人的)有組織的屠殺或刦掠;集體迫害。

poign·ant /ˈpɔɪnjənt; ˈpɔɪnənt/ *adj* distressing to the feelings; deeply moving; keen: 痛切的;傷心的;深刻的: *~ sorrow/regret/memories.* 深切的悲哀(痛悔;傷心的回憶)。 **~·ly** *adv* **poign·ancy** /-ənsɪ; -ənsɪ/ *n* [U] state or quality of being ~. 痛切;傷心;深刻。

poin·set·tia /pɔɪnˈsetɪə; pɔɪnˈsɛtɪə/ *n* tropical plant with small, greenish-yellow flowers surrounded by large scarlet leaves. 猩猩木;聖誕紅(熱帶植物,生鮮紅的大葉,開綠黃色的小花)。

point¹ /pɔɪnt; pɔɪnt/ *n* **1** [C] sharp tip (of a pin, pencil, knife, etc). (針、鉛筆、刀等的)尖。 ***not to put too fine a ~ on it,*** to speak bluntly, to tell the plain truth. 坦白地說;老實說。 **2** [C] tapering end; tip: 尖端: *the ~ of the jaw,* eg as the place for a knockout in boxing; 顎端(拳賽中擊倒對方之處); headland or promontory; piece of land that stretches out into the sea, a lake, etc: 崎;岬;(伸入海、湖等之地角: *a ~ of land;* 陸地的地角; *Pagoda P~,* in Burma. 寶塔角(在緬甸)。 **3** dot made by or as with the ~ of a pen, etc: (用筆尖等畫的或類似的)點: *a decimal ~;* 小數點; *four ~ six (4.6);* 四點六; *a full ~,* a full stop, the sign. 句點。 **4** [C] real or imaginary mark of position, in space or time: (在空間或時間眞實的或想像的)點: *a ~ of departure.* 起點。 ***a/the ~ of no return,*** ⇨ return¹(1). **~ of view,** position from which sth is viewed; (fig) way of looking at a question. 觀察點;着眼點;(喻)觀點。 ⇨ angle¹(2) (US). ***at 'this ~,*** at this place or moment. 在此地;在此刻。 ***be at the ~ of death,*** be dying. 彌留時刻。 ***be on the ~ of doing sth,*** be about to do sth. 正要做某事。 ***if/when it comes to the ~,*** if/when the moment for action or decision comes: 如果(當)時機到來(時): *When it came to the ~, he refused to help.* 到了需要他幫忙的時候,他却拒絕幫忙。 **'~-duty** *n* [U] duty of a policeman stationed at a particular ~ to control traffic. (警察指揮交通的)值勤;站崗。 **'turning-~,** ⇨ turning. ˌ**~-to-'~ race,** race (by persons riding horses) across country, from one ~ to another (these being recognized by certain landmarks). (騎馬者所作之)越野賽馬(途中各點藉各種界標指明)。 **5** [U] (printing) unit of measurement for type: (印刷)磅因(計算活字大小的單位): *6-~ is small and 18-~ is large.* 六磅因的活字小而十八磅因的活字大。*Is this sentence printed in 8-~?* 這個句子是用八磅因的活字印的嗎? **6** [C] mark on a scale; unit of measuring; degree: 量器等上之刻度;點;度: *the 'boiling-~ of water;* 水的沸點; *the 'melting-~ of lead.* 鉛的鎔點。*The cost of living went up several ~s last month,* eg from 105 to 110, with 100 as a standard fixed earlier. 上個月的生活費用指數上升了好幾點(如以過去某時的生活費用爲標準,定爲100,而從105漲到110)。*Oil shares rose several ~s* (ie on the Stock Exchange) *yesterday.* 昨天石油股票漲了數點(卽證券交易)。 ***Possession is nine ~s*** (= nine-tenths) ***of the law,*** is strong evidence in favour of the person in possession of sth. 現實佔有之物主在法律上佔有九分道理(終必繼續佔用)。 **7** [C] unit of scoring in some games and sports, in measuring the quality, etc of exhibits in a show: (運動及比賽,評量展覽物之品質時的)分;點: *score twenty ~s.* 獲得二十分。 ***give sb ~s; give ~s to sb,*** be able to offer him advantages and still win: 讓(某人)分數而仍然獲勝: *He can give me ~s at golf,* give me odds; is a better player. 打高爾夫球他讓我分數仍然能贏(打得比我好)。 ***score a ~ (against/off/over sb),*** ⇨ score²(3). ***win/be beaten on ~s,*** (boxing) win/be beaten by the ~s awarded, there being no knockout. (拳賽)由積分獲勝(被擊敗)(並非由於擊倒)。 **8** [C] one of the thirty-two marks on the circumference of a compass; one of the divisions (11° 15′) between two such consecutive marks. 羅盤上

三十二個刻度之一；方位(相連二刻度間的區劃之一,等於 $11\frac{1}{4}$ 度)。⇨ the illus at compass. 參看 compass 之插圖。 **9** [C] chief idea of sth said, done or planned; single item, detail or particular: (所說、所做、所計畫之某事物的)要點；論點；主旨: *There are ~s on which we've agreed to differ.* 有幾個論點我們已經同意保持異議。*Let me explain the theory ~ by ~.* 讓我一點一點地說明這理論吧。*What was the first ~ in his argument?* 他所爭論的第一點是什麼？ ***carry/gain one's ~,*** persuade sb to agree to one's objective. 說服別人同意自己的目標；達到目的。 ***come to/get to/reach the ~,*** give the essential fact or part of what one is trying to say, ignoring what is irrelevant. 說明重點。***get/see/miss the ~ of sth,*** see/fail to see what sb is trying to make clear, etc: 明白(不明白)重點；抓得(不)到要點: *I don't quite get the ~.* 我抓不到要點。*She missed the ~ of the story/joke.* 她沒有聽懂故事或笑話的重點。***make one's ~,*** win acceptance for an argument, establish what one is proposing. 論點獲得認可；立論成立。***make a ~ of doing sth,*** regard or treat it as important or necessary. 認爲(做)某事是必要的；堅持(做)某事。***stretch a ~,*** go beyond what is normally allowable on a question of principle, etc: 通融；變通: *Can't you stretch a ~ in my favour?* 你不能爲我通融一下嗎？***take sb's ~,*** (during a discussion) understand, appreciate what sb is proposing, etc. (在討論中)明白或喜歡某人的建議。***(get/wander) away from/off the ~,*** (say sth) not relevant to what is being discussed. 離題。***a case in ~,*** one connected with the subject being discussed: 與討論有關的事例；適當的例子: *Let me give you a case in ~*, an example that illustrates my argument. 讓我給你一個適當的例子。 ***in ~ of fact,*** in reality; indeed. 事實上；實際上。***a ~ of honour/conscience,*** sth of great importance to one's honour/conscience. 關係榮譽(良心)之事。***on a ~ of order,*** ⇨ order[1](4). **10** [U] reason. 理由。***no/not much ~ in doing sth,*** no good reason, little reason, for doing it: 沒有做某事的理由: *There's very little ~ in protesting*, It won't help much. 抗議沒有什麼用處。 ***What's the ~?*** Why bother? (It's irrelevant, useless, etc). 有什麼關係？別管它！ **11** [C] marked quality; characteristic: 特徵；特點: *What are her best ~s as a secretary?* 作爲一個秘書,她的長處是什麼？ *He has many good ~s and few bad ~s.* 他有許多優點而很少缺點。*Singing is not my best ~*, I don't sing well. 唱歌非我所擅長。 **12** [C] (GB) socket or outlet for electric current. (英)電插座。 **13** (*pl*) tapering movable rails by which a train can move from one track to another. (複)(鐵路上之)轉轍器；路閘(一端尖細的活動軌道,火車可藉此換軌)。 **'~s·man** /-smən；-smən/ *n* (*pl* -men) worker in charge of ~s on a railway, to keep them in order, see that they are moved as needed, etc. (鐵路之)轉轍手；搬閘夫。 **14** [U] effectiveness; urgency: 有效；有力；鋒利: *His remarks lack ~.* 他的評語不够犀利。

point[2] /pɔɪnt；pɔɪnt/ *vt, vi* **1** [VP2A, 3A] ***~ (to),*** direct attention to; show the position or direction of; be a sign of: 指向；顯示…之位置或方向；表明；表示: *The needle of a compass ~s to the north.* 羅盤針指向北方。*He ~ed to the door.* 他指着門。*It's rude to ~.* 用手指人是不禮貌的。*Both the hour hand and the minute hand ~ed to twelve*, It was noon. 時針和分針都指着十二；是正午的時候。*All the evidence ~s to his guilt.* 一切證據均表明他有罪。 **2** [VP14] ***~ sth at/towards,*** aim or direct (at, towards): 瞄準；對着: *~ a gun at sb;* 以槍瞄準某人； *~ a telescope at the moon;* 以望遠鏡對着月亮； *~ing his forefinger at me reprovingly.* 他譴責地以食指指着我。 **3** [VP15B] ***~ sth out,*** show; call or direct attention to: 指出；使注意: *~ out a mistake;* 指出錯誤； *~ out to sb the stupidity of his behaviour.* 促使某人注意其愚行。*Can you ~ (me) out the man you suspect?* 你能把你懷疑的那個人指出來嗎？ *He ~ed out the finest pictures to me.* 他把最好的圖畫指給我看。*I must ~ out that delay is unwise.* 我必須指出,拖延是不智的。 **4** [VP6A] make a point on (eg a pencil); (fig) give force to (advice, a moral). 削尖(鉛筆)；(喻)增强(忠言,教訓)之力量；强調。 **5** [VP6A] fill in the joints of (brickwork, etc) with mortar or cement, using a trowel to smooth the material. 以灰泥或水泥塡塞(砌磚工程等)的接合處；用泥刀抹平。 **6** (of a dog) take up a position with the body steady and the head ~ing in the direction of game. (指犬)站住以頭指向獵物。 ⇨ pointer(3). **~ed** *adj* **1** (fig) directed clearly against a particular person or his behaviour: (喻)明指某人或其行爲的；直截了當的；率直的: *a ~ed reproof.* 率直的責備。*Jack was showing ~ed attentions to the glamorous film star.* 傑克特別對那位迷人的電影明星獻慇懃。 **2** (of wit) incisive. (指機智)銳敏的；犀利的。 **~·ed·ly** *adv*

point-blank /ˌpɔɪnt ˈblæŋk；ˈpɔɪntˈblæŋk/ *adj* **1** (of a shot) aimed, fired, at very close range: (指彈丸)極近距離瞄準、射出的；零距離的；零分畫的: *fired at ~ range.* 在最近距離內射擊的。 **2** (fig, of sth said) in a manner that leaves no room for doubt: (喻,指所說的話)無疑慮之餘地的；坦白的；率直的: *a ~ refusal.* 率直的拒絕。□ *adv* in a ~ manner: 近射地；坦白地；率直地: *fire ~ at sb;* 對着某人近射； *ask sb ~ whether he intends to help;* 率直地問某人是否有意幫助； *refuse ~ to help.* 坦白地拒絕幫助。

pointer /ˈpɔɪntə(r)；ˈpɔɪntɚ/ *n* **1** stick used to point to things on a map, etc. (指示地圖等的)指示棒；指示物；教鞭。 **2** indicator on a dial or balance. (標度盤或天平上的)指針。 **3** large, short-haired hunting dog trained to stand still with its nose pointing in the direction of game it scents. 一種短毛大獵犬(訓練後可站住以鼻指向所嗅出之獵物的方向)。

point·less /ˈpɔɪntlɪs；ˈpɔɪntlɪs/ *adj* **1** (fig) with little or no sense, aim or purpose: (喻)無意義的；無目標的；無方針的: *It seemed ~ to go on until they were certain of being on the right road.* 在他們確定未走錯路以前,繼續前進似乎漫無目標。 **2** without points scored: 未得分的: *a ~ draw.* 雙方均未得分之平手(卽零比零)。**~·ly** *adv*

poise /pɔɪz；pɔɪz/ *vt, vi* **1** [VP2C] be or keep balanced; (fig) be ready: 均衡；保持平衡；(喻)準備好: *~d in mid-air/on the brink/for action.* 在半空中保持平衡(在峭壁頂端的邊緣保持平衡；準備好行動)。 **2** [VP6A, 15A] balance; support in a particular place or manner: 使平衡；在某地方或以某姿式支持: *He ~d himself on his toes.* 他用脚尖站立使自己保持平衡。*Note the way he ~s his head.* 注意他使頭部保持平衡的方式。□ *n* **1** [U] balance, equilibrium; [C] way in which one carries oneself, holds one's head, etc. 平衡；均衡；(身體、頭部等的)姿態。 **2** [U] quiet self-confidence; self-possession. 泰然自若；鎭靜。

poi·son /ˈpɔɪzn；ˈpɔɪzn̩/ *n* [C, U] **1** substance causing death or harm if absorbed by a living thing (animal or plant): 毒藥；毒物(動植物吸收後可能致死或受害): *'rat-~;* 毒老鼠藥； *~ for killing weeds on gravel paths;* 除去碎石路上野草的藥物； *commit suicide by taking ~.* 服毒自殺。 **ˌ~-'gas** *n* deadly gas used in warfare. (戰時用的)毒氣。 **ˌ~-'ivy** *n* N American shrub or vine which causes painful spots if brought into contact with a person's skin. 野葛(一種北美灌木或攀爬植物,如與人的肌膚接觸,會造成使人覺得疼痛之斑點)。 **'~ pen,** person who writes anonymous letters full of malice, slander, etc. 寫匿名誹謗信者。 **ˌ~ 'pen letter,** letter of this kind. 匿名誹謗信。 **2** (fig) evil principle, teaching, etc considered harmful to society. (喻)敗壞社會之有害的主義、敎訓等。□ *vt* [VP6A] **1** give ~ to; put ~ on or in; kill with ~; infect: 使中毒；置毒於；毒殺；毒害；使感染: *~ a cat;* 將猫毒死； ~

the wells; 置毒物於井中; *a ~ed hand,* inflamed because of an infected cut, etc. (因切傷等感染病菌而)發炎的手。 **2** injure morally: (在道德上)敗壞; 沾汚: *~ a person's mind against sb;* 使對某人發生惡感; *an experience which ~ed his whole life,* which spoilt or ruined his life. 一種毀了他一生的經驗。**~er** *n* (esp) person who murders by means of ~. (尤指) 毒殺者; 放毒者。**~·ous** /ˈpɔɪzənəs ; ˈpɔɪznəs/ *adj* **1** acting as ~; causing death or injury if taken into the system: 有毒的; 進入身體組織內會造成死亡或傷害的: *~ous plants.* 有毒的植物。**2** morally injurious: 敗德的;在道德上有害的: *a ~ous play/novel/doctrine;* 敗德的戲劇(小說,教條); *a man with a ~ous tongue,* one who spreads evil reports, wicked scandal, etc. 口舌惡毒之人。**~·ously** *adv*

poke[1] /pəʊk ; pok/ *vt, vi* **1** [VP6A, 15A, B] push sharply, jab (with a stick, one's finger, etc): (以棍、手指等)撥;推: *~ a man in the ribs,* nudge him in a friendly way; 友善地輕觸一個人的肋骨(以促其注意); *~ the fire,* move the coals, to make the fire burn up. 撥火(撥動煤塊使火燃旺)。**2** [VP15A] put, move (sth) in a given direction, with a sharp push: 戳;刺(洞);穿;塞: *Don't ~ your umbrella through the bars of the lion's cage.* 別把傘伸進獅檻中去。*She ~d a toffee into my mouth.* 她把一塊太妃糖塞進我的口中。*Don't let your boy ~ his head out of the (train) window—it's dangerous!* 別讓你的孩子把頭伸出(火車)窗外—太危險了! **~ fun at sb,** ridicule him. 嘲弄某人。**~ one's nose into sth,** (colloq) interfere in (sb's business, affairs). (俗)干預(別人的事)。**3** [VP2C] **~ (about),** search, feel about: 到處撥動;尋求: *He was poking (about) at the rubbish.* 他撥動垃圾。*Who's that poking about in the attic?* 誰在小閣樓上翻動東西? **4** [VP 6A, 15A] make (a hole) by poking: 刺(洞);穿(洞): *~ a hole in a paper screen.* 在紙屏上戳一個洞。□ *n* act of poking; nudge: 撥;推;戳;刺: *give the fire a ~;* 撥一撥火; *give sb a ~ in the ribs.* 輕觸某人的肋骨(以促其注意)。

poke[2] /pəʊk ; pok/ *n* sack 袋;囊 (now dial, except in 現爲方言,祇用於) ***buy a pig in a ~,*** ⇨ pig.

poke-bonnet /ˌpəʊk ˈbɒnɪt ; ˌpokˈbɑnɪt/ *n* bonnet with a broad projecting brim. 有寬撑邊的女帽。

poker[1] /ˈpəʊkə(r) ; ˈpokɚ/ *n* strong metal rod or bar for stirring or breaking up the coal in the fire. 撥火鐵棒;火鉗;火鉤。

poker[2] /ˈpəʊkə(r) ; ˈpokɚ/ *n* [U] card game for two or more persons in which the players bet on the value of the cards they hold. 撲克牌(供二人或多人玩的一種紙牌遊戲)。**ˈ~-face** *n* (colloq) (person with a) face that betrays no emotion. (俗)無表情的面孔;面無表情的人。

poky /ˈpəʊkɪ ; ˈpokɪ/ *adj* (-ier, -iest) (of a place) small; limited in space: (指地方) 窄小的;有限的: *a ~ little room.* 窄小的房間。

po·lar /ˈpəʊlə(r) ; ˈpolɚ/ *adj* **1** of or near the North or South Pole: 北極的; 南極的; 近北極或南極的: *the ~ circles,* the Arctic and Antarctic Circles. 北極圈和南極圈。**ˈ~ bear,** the white kind living in the north ~ regions. 北極熊。⇨ the illus at bear. 參看 bear 之插圖。**2** directly opposite. 正相反的。**~·ity** /pəˈlærətɪ ; poˈlærətɪ/ *n* [U, C] state in which there are two opposite, conflicting or contrasting qualities, principles or tendencies. (性質,原則或傾向之)正相反。

po·lar·ize /ˈpəʊləraɪz ; ˈpoləˌraɪz/ *vt* [VP6A] cause to concentrate about two opposite, conflicting or contrasting positions. 賦與極性;使極化。**po·lar·iz·ation** /ˌpəʊləraɪˈzeɪʃn *US:* -rɪˈz- ; ˌpolərəˈzeʃən/ *n* act of polarizing; state of being ~d. 生極性;得極性;極化;成極作用。

po·lar·oid /ˈpəʊlərɔɪd ; ˈpoləˌrɔɪd/ *n* [U] (P) thin transparent film used in sun-glasses, car windows, etc to lessen sun glare: (商標) (太陽眼鏡、汽車窗子等的)偏光板;偏光片: *~ camera,* one able to produce positive prints within seconds after the picture has been taken. 拍立得(立即顯影)照相機。

pole[1] /pəʊl ; pol/ *n* **1 North/South P~,** either of the two ends of the earth's axis. 北極(南極)。**2 North/South Magnetic P~,** either of the two points near the North P~ or South P~ to which the compass needle points. 北磁極;南磁極(磁針所指接近南北極之點)。**3 North/South P~,** (astron) either of the two points in the celestial sphere about which the stars appear to turn. (天文)天球北極; 天球南極 (假想之地軸延伸線與天球所交之兩點,衆星似繞此兩極轉動)。**ˈ~-star** *n* the North Star or **Polaris** /pəʊˈlærɪs ; poˈlɛrɪs/, almost coinciding with the true north of the celestial sphere. 北極星(幾與天球之正北相合)。**4** either of the two ends of a magnet or the terminal points of an electric battery: 磁極;電極: *the negative/positive ~.* 陰(陽)極。**5** (fig) each of two opposite, conflicting or contrasting principles, etc. (喻)二相反原則等之一;二極端之一。***be ~s apart,*** be widely separated: 相距甚遠: *The employers and the trade union leaders are still ~s apart,* are far from reaching an agreement or compromise, eg about wages. 雇主們與工會領袖們的意見仍然相差太遠(如有關工資問題)。

pole[2] /pəʊl ; pol/ *n* **1** long, slender, rounded piece of wood or metal, esp as a support for a tent, telegraph wires, etc or for flying a flag. 細長的圓木棒或金屬棒(尤指用於支撐帳篷,電線等,或張懸旗幟者); 柱; 桿; 竿。***under bare ~s,*** (naut) with all sails furled. (航海)不張帆。***up the ~,*** (sl) **(a)** in a difficulty. (俚)在困難中。**(b)** slightly mad; eccentric. 微狂的; 古怪的。**ˈ~-jumping** *n* (athletic contest) jumping with the help of a long ~ held in the hands. 撐竿跳。**ˈ~-vault** *n* jump of this kind over a bar which can be raised or lowered. (越過可升降之橫竿的) 撐竿跳高。**2** measure of length (also called 亦稱作 *rod* or *perch*), 5½ yds or about 5 metres. 桿(長度單位名,合 5½ 碼或 5 公尺左右)。⇨ App 5. 參看附錄五。

Pole /pəʊl ; pol/ *n* native of Poland. 波蘭人。

pole-axe, pole-ax /ˈpəʊl æks ; ˈpolˌæks/ *n* **1** (hist) axe for use in war, with a long handle. (史)長柄戰斧;鉞。**2** butcher's implement for slaughtering cattle. (殺牲畜用的)屠斧。□ *vt* [VP6A] strike down with a ~; (fig) slaughter; destroy. 以斧砍倒;(喻)屠殺;摧毀。

pole·cat /ˈpəʊlkæt ; ˈpolˌkæt/ *n* small, dark-brown, fur-covered animal of the weasel family which gives off an unpleasant smell, native of Europe. 雞貂(一稱臭猫,覆有深褐色毛皮之鼬類小動物,發臭氣,原產於歐洲)。

pol·emic /pəˈlemɪk ; poˈlɛmɪk/ *n* [C] (formal) dispute; argument; (*pl*) art or practice of carrying on arguments. (正式用語)爭論;辯論;(複)辯論法。□ *adj* of ~s. 引起爭論的;好辯論的;辯論法的。**pol·emi·cally** /-klɪ ; -klɪ/ *adv*

po·lice /pəˈliːs ; pəˈlis/ *n* (collective *n*, always *sing* in form, used with *pl v*) **(the) ~,** men and women belonging to a department of government concerned with the keeping of public order: (集合用法,形式上永遠是單數,與複數動詞連用)警察當局;警察: *Several hundred ~ were on duty at the demonstration.* 在示威運動中有數百名警察值勤。*Extra ~ are needed here.* 這裡需要加派警察。*The ~ have not made any arrests.* 警方尚未逮捕人。**ˌ~ ˈconstable** *n* ~-officer of ordinary rank. 普通警員。**ˈ~ dog** *n* dog trained to track or attack suspected criminals. 警犬。**ˈ~ force** *n* body of ~-officers of a country, district or town. (一個國家、地區或城鎮所有的)警察;警力。**ˈ~·man** /-mən ; -mən/ *n* (*pl* -men) male member of the ~ force. 警員;警察。**ˈ~-office** *n* headquarters of the ~ in a city or town. (市,鎮)警察局。**ˈ~-officer** *n* ~man or ~woman.

警官;警察。'~ **state** *n* one controlled by political ~, usu a totalitarian state. 警察國家(通常爲極權國家)。'~-**station** *n* office of a local ~ force: (當地的)警察分局;派出所: *The drunken driver was taken to the ~-station.* 酒醉駕車者被帶進派出所。'~-**woman** *n* (*pl* -women) female member of the ~ force. 女警員。□ *vt* [VP6A] keep order in (a place) with ~ or as with ~; control: 以警察管治(一地方); 統治: *United Nations forces ~d the Gaza strip for a long period.* 聯合國軍隊在加薩走廊管轄過一段很長的時期。

pol·icy[1] /ˈpɒləsɪ; ˈpɑləsɪ/ *n* (*pl* -cies) **1** [U, C] plan of action, statement of aims and ideals, esp one made by a government, political party, business company, etc: (尤指政府、政黨、公司等的)方針;政策: *British foreign ~,* official relations between the British government and other governments. 英國的外交政策。*Is honesty the best ~?* 誠實爲最上策嗎? **2** [U] wise, sensible conduct; art of government. 明智的行爲;治術;權謀。

pol·icy[2] /ˈpɒləsɪ; ˈpɑləsɪ/ *n* written statement of the terms of a contract of insurance: 保險單: *a* ˈ*fire-insurance ~;* 火險保險單; *a* ˈ*~-holder.* 投保人;保險客戶。

po·lio /ˈpəʊlɪəʊ; ˈpolɪo/ *n* [U] (colloq abbr for) poliomyelitis: (俗)脊髓灰白質炎(爲 poliomyelitis 之略): ˈ*~ victims;* 小兒痲痺症患者; ˌ*anti-*ˈ*~ injections.* 預防小兒痲痺症的注射。

polio·my·eli·tis /ˌpəʊlɪəʊˌmaɪəˈlaɪtɪs; ˌpolɪoˌmaɪəˈlaɪtɪs/ *n* [U] infectious, virus-caused disease with inflammation of the grey matter of the spinal cord, often resulting in physical disablement; formerly called 'infantile paralysis'. 脊髓灰白質炎(由濾過毒引起的一種傳染病,常導致身體的殘廢); (昔時稱爲)小兒痲痺症。

polish /ˈpɒlɪʃ; ˈpɑlɪʃ/ *vt, vi* **1** [VP6A, 15B, 2A] ~ *(up),* make or become smooth and shiny by rubbing (with or without a chemical substance): 磨光;擦光;使光滑;變光滑: *~ furniture/shoes;* 擦光傢具(擦鞋); *~ sth up.* 將某物擦亮。*This wood won't ~.* 這種木材無法磨光。**2** [VP6A] (usu in *pp*) improve in behaviour, intellectual interests, etc; make refined or elegant: (通常用過去分詞)在行爲,雅趣各方面改進;使優雅;文飾: *a ~ed speech/performance.* 優雅的演說(演奏)。**3** [VP15B] ~ ***sth off,*** finish quickly: 很快結束: *~ off a large plateful of pie;* 很快吃完一大盤餡餅; *~ off arrears of correspondence.* 儘快趕完積欠的回信。□ *n* **1** [U, C] (shiny surface, etc obtained by) ~ing: 磨光;擦亮;光滑的表面等: *shoes/tables with a good ~.* 擦亮的鞋(桌)。**2** [U, C] substance used for ~ing: 擦亮劑;上光劑: ˈ*shoe/*ˈ*furniture/*ˈ*floor ~;* 鞋油(傢具擦光油;地板蠟); *a tin of metal ~.* 一罐金屬擦亮劑。**3** [U] (fig) refinement; elegance. (喻)優雅;精良。~**er** *n* workman skilled in ~ing wood or metal. 精於磨光木器或金屬器的工人;磨擦匠。

Pol·ish /ˈpəʊlɪʃ; ˈpolɪʃ/ *adj* of Poland or the Poles. 波蘭的;波蘭人的。□ *n* [U] language of the Poles. 波蘭語。

pol·it·buro /ˈpɒlɪtbjʊərəʊ; ˈpɑlɪtbjʊro/ *n* (*pl* ~s /-rəʊz; -roz/) chief executive committee of a political (esp the Communist) party. 政黨(尤指共黨)的執行委員會;政治局。

pol·ite /pəˈlaɪt; pəˈlaɪt/ *adj* **1** having, showing the possession of, good manners and consideration for other people: 有禮貌的;客氣的: *a ~ boy;* 有禮貌的男孩; *a ~ remark.* 客氣話。**2** refined: 文雅的;優雅的: *~ society;* 上流社會; *~ literature.* 純文學。~·**ly** *adv* ~·**ness** *n*

poli·tic /ˈpɒlətɪk; ˈpɑləˌtɪk/ *adj* **1** (of persons) acting or judging wisely; prudent. (指人)有智慮的;明達的;精明的。**2** (of actions) well judged; prudent: (指行爲)有策略的;得當的;審愼的: *follow a ~ course;* 採取審愼的方針; *make a ~ retreat.* 作策略上的退却。**3 the** ˌ**body** ˈ**~,** the state as an organized group of citizens. 國家;政治體。

pol·iti·cal /pəˈlɪtɪkl; pəˈlɪtɪkḷ/ *adj* **1** of the State of government; of public affairs in general: 政府的;政治的;行政的: *~ liberties;* 政治自由; *for ~ reasons.* 爲了政治上的理由。ˌ~ **a'sylum,** protection given by a State to sb who has left his own country for ~ reasons: 政治庇護: *a sailor who deserted his ship and asked for ~ asylum.* 一個棄船要求政治庇護的水手。ˌ~ **e'conomy,** study of the ~ problems of government. 政治經濟學。ˌ~ **ge'ography,** dealing with boundaries, communications, etc. 政治地理學。Cf 參較 *physical* and *economic* geography. 地文地理學及經濟地理學。ˌ~ **'prisoner,** one who is imprisoned because he opposes the (system of) government. 政治犯。**2** of politics: 政治學的;政治上的: *a ~ crisis.* 政治上的危機。~**ly** /-klɪ; -klɪ/ *adv*

poli·ti·cian /ˌpɒlɪˈtɪʃn; ˌpɑləˈtɪʃən/ *n* person taking part in politics or much interested in politics; (in a bad sense) person who follows politics as a career, regardless of principle: 從政者;熱心政治者; (壞的意義)政客: *party ~s.* 搞黨務的政客。*Is your leader a ~ or a statesman?* 你的首領是個政客還是位政治家?

pol·iti·cize /pəˈlɪtɪsaɪz; pəˈlɪtəˌsaɪz/ *vt, vi* [VP6A, 2A] become or cause to become politically conscious or organized. (使)具有政治意義;(使)政黨化。

poli·tick /ˈpɒlətɪk; ˈpɑləˌtɪk/ *vi* [VP2A] engage in politics. 從事政治活動。

poli·tics /ˈpɒlətɪks; ˈpɑləˌtɪks/ *n pl* (with *sing* or *pl v*) the science or art of government; political views, affairs, questions, etc: (用單數或複數動詞)政治學;政治;政治策略;政見;政務;政治問題等: *party ~;* 政黨政治; *local ~.* 地方行政。*What are your ~?* 你的政見是什麼? *'P~ is much more difficult than physics,' said Einstein.* 愛因斯坦說:'政治比物理難得多。'

pol·ity /ˈpɒlətɪ; ˈpɑlətɪ/ *n* (*pl* -ties) [U] form or process of government; [C] society as an organized State. 政府;國家;政體;行政;國體。

polka /ˈpɒlkə *US:* ˈpəʊlkə; ˈpolkə/ *n* [C] (piece of music, of E European origin, for a) lively kind of dance. 波爾卡舞(源自東歐的一種輕快舞蹈); 波爾卡舞曲。ˈ~ **dots,** regular pattern of large dots on cloth: (布料上的)圓點花樣: (attrib) (形容用法) *a ~-dot scarf.* 有圓點花樣的圍巾。

poll[1] /pəʊl; pol/ *n* **1** voting at an election; list of voters; counting of the votes; place where voting takes place: 選舉之投票;投票者之名册;投票之計算;投票處: *a light/heavy ~,* voting by a small/large proportion of the voters; 低(高)的投票率; *awaiting the result of the ~;* 等候開票的結果; *go to the ~s* (= ~ing-booths), vote; 到投票處去;前往投票; *exclude people from the ~;* 不許人們投票; *be successful at the ~;* 競選獲勝;當選; *head the ~,* have the largest number of votes; 得票最多; *declare the ~,* announce the result. 宣布選舉結果。**2** survey of public opinion by putting questions to a representative selection of persons: 民意調查: *a public opinion ~;* 民意調查或測驗; *the Gallup ~.* 蓋洛普民意測驗。⇨ *straw vote* at straw. **3** (old use) head: (舊用法)頭: (hum) (諧) *a grey ~,* a grey-haired person. 白髮人。ˈ~-**tax** *n* tax levied on every person in a community. 人頭稅。

poll[2] /pəʊl; pol/ *vt, vi* **1** [VP2A, C] vote at an election; [VP6A] receive (a certain number of) votes; take the votes of electors in (a constituency): (在選舉時)投票;獲得(某數之)選票;得到(一選區之)選舉人票: *Mr Hill ~ed over 3000 votes.* 希爾先生獲得三千多選票。*The constituency was ~ed thoroughly.* 這選區的選舉人票盡被得去。ˈ~·**ing-booth/-station** *nn* place where voters go to record votes. 投票處;投票所。ˈ~·**ing-day** *n* day appointed for a ~. 投票日。**2** [VP6A] cut off the top of (the horns of cattle): 切短(牛角): *~ed cattle;* 角被切短的牛; cut off the top of (a tree)

(= pollard). 剪去(樹)梢。

poll[3] /pɒl ; pal/ *n* (also 亦作 '~*parrot*) conventional name for a parrot. 鸚鵡的俗稱。

pol·lard /'pɒləd ; 'palɚd/ *vt* [VP6A] cut off the top of (a tree) so that a thick head of new branches grows out. 剪去(樹)梢;使成截頭樹。□ *n* ~ed tree. 截頭樹。

pol·len /'pɒlən ; 'palən/ *n* [U] fine powder (usu yellow) formed on flowers which fertilizes other flowers when carried to them by the wind, insects, etc. 花粉(通常爲黃色,結於花上,由風、昆蟲等帶至其他花上使之受精)。'~ **count**, figure of the ~ in the atmosphere in a given volume of air during 24 hours, from deposits on slides, as a guide to possible attacks of hay fever, etc. 花粉數量(在定量空氣中,二十四小時之內,可能引起花粉熱等症的花粉數量)。

pol·lin·ate /'pɒlɪneɪt ; 'palə,net/ *vt* [VP6A] make fertile with pollen. 授以花粉;使受精。**pol·li·na·tion** /,pɒlɪ'neɪʃn ; ,palə'neʃən/ *n* [U].

poll·ster /'pəʊlstə(r) ; 'polstɚ/ *n* (colloq) person who conducts public opinion polls. (俗) 民意測驗者;民意調查者。

pol·lute /pə'lu:t ; pə'lut/ *vt* [VP6A] make dirty; destroy the purity or sanctity of: 使髒;污染;褻瀆: *rivers ~d with filthy waste from factories;* 爲工廠污穢廢物所污染的河流; *~d water*, unfit to drink. 污水(不宜飲用)。**pol·lu·tant** /-ənt ; -ənt/ *n* anything that ~s, eg exhaust fumes from motor-vehicles. 污染物(如機動車輛排出之廢氣)。**pol·lu·tion** /pə'lu:ʃn ; pə'luʃən/ *n* [U] polluting or being ~d; that which ~s. 弄髒;褻瀆;污染;污穢物。

polo /'pəʊləʊ ; 'polo/ *n* [U] ball game played on horse-back with mallets. (用球棍在馬上玩的)馬球。'**water-~** *n* game played by swimmers with a large ball. 水球。'**~-neck**, *adj* = *turtle-neck(ed)*. ⇨ turtle[1].

pol·on·aise /,pɒlə'neɪz ; ,polə'nez/ *n* (piece of music for a) slow processional dance of Polish origin. 波羅奈斯舞(一種起源於波蘭的慢步舞);波羅奈斯舞曲。

po·lony /pə'ləʊnɪ ; pə'lonɪ/ *n* [U] sausage of partly cooked pork. (由半熟豬肉做成的)臘腸。

pol·ter·geist /'pɒltəgaɪst ; 'poltɚ,gaɪst/ *n* [C] (in folklore, etc) noisy, mischievous spirit(2). (民間傳說等中的)吵鬧頑皮的鬼。

pol·troon /pɒl'tru:n ; pal'trun/ *n* coward. 卑怯者;懦夫。**~·ery** /-ərɪ ; -ərɪ/ *n* cowardice. 卑怯;懦弱。

poly /'pɒlɪ ; 'palɪ/ *n* (colloq abbr for) polytechnic. (俗)爲 polytechnic 之略。

poly·an·dry /'pɒlɪændrɪ ; 'palɪ,ændrɪ/ *n* [U] custom of having more than one husband at the same time. 一妻多夫;一妻多夫制。**poly·an·drous** /,pɒlɪ'ændrəs ; ,palɪ'ændrəs/ *adj* **1** of, practising, ~. 一妻多夫的;實行一妻多夫制的。**2** (bot) (of plants) having numerous stamens. (植物)(指植物)多雄蕊的。

poly·an·thus /,pɒlɪ'ænθəs ; ,palɪ'ænθəs/ *n* (*pl* ~es /-θəsɪz ; -θəsɪz/ for individual plants) (複數指個別的植物) kinds of cultivated primrose with several flowers on one stalk. 數種在同一莖上開數朶花的栽培櫻草;黃花九輪草;夜香蘭。

poly·gamy /pə'lɪgəmɪ ; pə'lɪgəmɪ/ *n* [U] custom of having more than one wife at the same time. 一夫多妻;一夫多妻制。**poly·ga·mist** /-ɪst ; -ɪst/ *n* man who practises ~. 有多妻的人;實行一夫多妻制的人。**poly·ga·mous** /pə'lɪgəməs ; pə'lɪgəməs/ *adj* of, practising, ~. 一夫多妻的;實行一夫多妻制的。

poly·glot /'pɒlɪglɒt ; 'palɪ,glat/ *adj* knowing, using, written in, many languages. 通曉或使用多種語言的;用多種語言寫成的。□ *n* ~ person or book. 通曉多種語言的人;用多種語言寫成的書。

poly·gon /'pɒlɪgən *US:* -gɒn ; 'palɪ,gan/ *n* plane figure with many (usu five or more) straight sides. (有五邊或多於五邊的)平面多邊形;多角形。

poly·mor·phous /,pɒlɪ'mɔ:fəs ; ,palɪ'mɔrfəs/, (also 亦作 **poly·mor·phic** /-fɪk ; -fɪk/) *adj* having, passing through, many stages (of development, growth, etc). 多形的;多態的;複式的。

polyp /'pɒlɪp ; 'palɪp/ *n* (zool) very simple form of animal life found in water; polypus. (動物)水螅;(病)黏膜瘤;息肉。

poly·ph·ony /pə'lɪfənɪ ; pə'lɪfənɪ/ *n* [U] (music) counterpoint. (音樂)多音曲;複調音樂;對位法。**poly·phonic** /,pɒlɪ'fɒnɪk ; ,palɪ'fanɪk/ *adj* (music) contrapuntal. (音樂)複調的;對位法的。

poly·pus /'pɒlɪpəs ; 'paləpəs/ *n* (*pl* ~es /-pəsɪz ; -pəsɪz/, -pi /-paɪ ; -paɪ/) (path) kinds of tumour (eg in the nose) usu with many stems like tentacles, extending down into the tissue. (病)息肉;黏膜瘤(生於鼻子等中,通常有許多似觸鬚之莖,伸入組織內)。

poly·sty·rene /,pɒlɪ'staɪri:n ; ,palɪ'staɪrin/ *n* [U] type of light, firm plastic material (a good insulator), used esp for making boxes etc. 聚苯乙烯(一種又輕又硬的塑膠物質,也是一種良好的絕緣體,特別用於製造箱匣等)。

poly·syl·lable /'pɒlɪsɪləbl ; 'palə,sɪləbl/ *n* word of several (usu more than three) syllables. 多音節字(通常多於三個音節)。**poly·syl·labic** /,pɒlɪsɪ'læbɪk ; ,paləsɪ'læbɪk/ *adj* 多音節的。

poly·tech·nic /,pɒlɪ'teknɪk ; ,palə'tɛknɪk/ *n* (colloq abbr 俗略作 **poly** /'pɒlɪ ; 'palɪ/) institution for advanced full-time and part-time education, esp in scientific and technical subjects. 工藝學校。

poly·theism /'pɒlɪθi:ɪzəm ; 'paləθi,ɪzəm/ *n* [U] belief in, worship of, more than one god. 多神論;多神教;多神崇拜。**poly·theis·tic** /,pɒlɪθi:'ɪstɪk ; ,paləθi'ɪstɪk/ *adj* 多神論的;多神教的;信多神教的。

poly·thene /'pɒlɪθi:n ; 'paləθin/ *n* [U] plastic material widely used for waterproof packaging, insulation, etc. (普遍用於防水包裝,絕緣等的)塑膠。

pom /pɒm ; pam/ *n* (abbr) (略) = pommy.

po·made /pə'mɑ:d *US:* pəʊ'meɪd ; po'med/ *n* [U] perfumed ointment for use on the hair. (香的)髮油;髮臘。□ *vt* put ~ on. 塗髮油於…上。

pom·egran·ate /'pɒmɪgrænɪt ; 'pʌm,grænɪt/ *n* (tree with) thick-skinned round fruit which, when ripe, has a reddish centre full of seeds. 石榴;石榴樹。

pom·elo /'pɒmɪləʊ ; 'paməlo/ *n* (*pl* ~s /-ləʊz ; -loz/) kind of large grapefruit; shaddock. 柚子;朱欒。

pom·mel /'pɒml ; 'pʌml/ *n* **1** the rounded part of a saddle which sticks up at the front. 鞍頭,前鞍(鞍最前端向上突起之圓形部分)。⇨ the illus at harness. 參看 harness 之插圖。**2** rounded knob on the hilt of a sword. (劍柄之)圓頭;欛頭。□ /'pʌml ; 'pʌml/ *vt* (-ll-, US also -l-) = pummel.

pommy /'pɒmɪ ; 'pamɪ/ *n* (*pl* -mies) (sl) British immigrant in Australia or New Zealand; British person. (俚)(澳大利亞或紐西蘭之)英國移民;英國人。

pomp /pɒmp ; pamp/ *n* [U] splendid display, magnificence, esp at a public event: 壯觀;壯麗;盛況(尤指公開之盛大事件): *the ~ and ceremony of the State Opening of Parliament.* 國會正式揭幕的盛況。

pom·pon /'pɒmpɒn ; 'pampan/ *n* ornamental tuft or bunch of feathers, silk, ribbon, etc worn on a hat or dress or shoes; ball of wool worn on eg a soldier's cap. (帽、女裝或鞋上所綴之裝飾性)絨球;絲球;(軍帽的)毛球。

pom·pous /'pɒmpəs ; 'pampəs/ *adj* full of, showing, self-importance: 自大的;誇大的;虛誇的;華而不實的: *a ~ official;* 自大的官員; *~ language*, full of high-sounding words. 浮誇不實的言詞。**pom·pos·ity** /pɒm'pɒsətɪ ; pam'pasətɪ/ *n* [U] being ~; [C] (*pl* -ties) instance of this. 自大;誇大;虛誇;自大或誇大的實例。

ponce /pɒns ; pans/ *n* man who lives with a prostitute and lives on her earnings. 與妓女同居且靠其收入爲生的男子。

pon·cho /'pɒntʃəʊ ; 'pantʃo/ *n* (*pl* ~s /-tʃəʊz ; -tʃoz/) large piece of cloth with a slit in the middle for the head, worn as a cloak; similar garment in waterproof material used by hikers, cyclists, etc.一種斗篷(一塊長布,中間開縫以伸出頭部);(徒步,騎單車的人所穿之)斗篷式雨衣。

pond /pɒnd ; pand/ *n* small area of still water, esp one used or made as a drinking place for cattle. 池塘(尤指供家畜飲水者)。

pon·der /ˈpɒndə(r) ; ˈpandɚ/ *vt, vi* [VP6A, 2A, 8, 10, 3A] ~ ***(over)***, consider; think over: 考慮;沉思: *We ~ed many things.* 我們考慮了許多事情。*He ~ed over the incident.* 他沉思那事件。

pon·der·able /ˈpɒndərəbl ; ˈpandərəbl/ *adj* (phys) that can be weighed or measured. (物)可衡量的;能估計的。□ *n* (*pl*) events, conditions, etc that can be taken into account and estimated. (複)可予考慮及估計的事件,情況等。

pon·der·ous /ˈpɒndərəs ; ˈpandərəs/ *adj* **1** heavy; bulky; unwieldy: 沉重的;龐大的;笨重的: ~ *movements,* eg of a heavy man. 笨重的動作(如魯鈍的人所表現者)。**2** (of style) dull; laboured. (指文體)沉悶的;艱澀的。~**·ly** *adv*

pone /pəʊn ; pon/ *n* (also 亦作 **ˈcorn ~**) maize bread, esp as made by N American Indians. 玉米麵包(尤指北美印第安人做的)。

pon·gee /pɒnˈdʒiː ; panˈdʒi/ *n* [U] kind of soft silk cloth, usu unbleached so that it has the natural colour (brownish yellow). 繭綢;府綢(通常未漂白,故爲天然的淡褐黃色)。

pon·iard /ˈpɒnjəd ; ˈpanjɚd/ *n* (archaic or poet) dagger. (古或詩)匕首;短劍。

pon·tiff /ˈpɒntɪf ; ˈpantɪf/ *n* **1** the Pope. 教皇;教宗。**2** (old use) bishop; high priest; chief priest. (舊用法)主教;高僧;教長;大祭司。

pon·tifi·cal /pɒnˈtɪfɪkl ; panˈtɪfɪkl/ *adj* **1** of or relating to the Pope or a bishop. 教皇的;教宗的;有關教皇的;主教的。**2** authoritative (in a pompous way). 權威的;傲慢武斷的。□ *n* (*pl*) vestments and insignia used by bishops and cardinals at some church functions and ceremonies. (複)(主教及紅衣主教在教會的若干儀典中所用的)法衣及徽章。

pon·tifi·cate /pɒnˈtɪfɪkət ; panˈtɪfɪkɪt/ *n* office of a pontiff, esp of the Pope; period of this. 主教,高僧,大祭司,(尤指)教皇的職位;其任期。□ *vi* /-keɪt ; -ket/ [VP2A] assume airs of infallibility. 裝作絕無錯誤的樣子;武斷。

pon·toon[1] /pɒnˈtuːn ; panˈtun/ *n* flat-bottomed boat; one of a number of such boats, or a floating hollow metal structure, supporting a roadway over a river: 平底船;躉船;用以支撐橋路的平底船或金屬浮筒: *a ~ bridge.* 浮橋。⇨ the illus at bridge. 參看 bridge 之插圖。

pon·toon[2] /pɒnˈtuːn ; panˈtun/ *n* [U] kind of card game. 一種紙牌戲。

pony /ˈpəʊnɪ ; ˈponɪ/ *n* (*pl* -nies) **1** horse of small breed. 小馬;駒。**ˈ~-tail** *n* style of girls' hairdressing which became popular in the 1950's with long hair tied in a bunch at the back of the head. (女孩的髮型)馬尾(流行於 1950 年代)。**ˈ~-trekking** *n* [U] the making of a journey for pleasure by riding on ponies. (以玩樂爲目的的)騎小馬旅遊。**2** (GB sl) £25. (英俚)二十五鎊。**3** (US sl) (美俚) = crib²(2).

poodle /ˈpuːdl ; ˈpudl̩/ *n* kind of dog with thick curling hair, often clipped and shaved into fantastic patterns. 一種有鬈曲厚毛之獅子狗;貴賓狗(其厚毛常剪成各種花樣)。⇨ the illus at dog. 參看 dog 之插圖。

poof /puːf ; puf/ *n* = pouf(2).

pooh /puː ; pu/ *int* expressing impatience or contempt or disgust at a bad smell. 呸!啐!(表示不耐煩、輕蔑或厭惡臭味)。

pooh-pooh /ˌpuː ˈpuː ; ˈpuˈpu/ *vt* [VP6A] treat (an idea, etc) with contempt. 藐視(意見等)。

pool[1] /puːl ; pul/ *n* **1** small area of still water; esp one naturally formed: (尤指自然形成的)小池;水塘;水坑: *After the rainstorm there were ~s on the roads.* 驟雨後路上有水坑。**2** quantity of water or other liquid lying on a surface: 一灘水或其他液體: *The corpse was lying in a ~ of blood.* 屍體躺在血泊中。**3** (**ˈswimming-**)**~,** large paved hole filled with water to swim in. 游泳池。**4** part of a river where the water is quiet and deep. 河水靜止而且很深的地方;淵;潭。

pool[2] /puːl ; pul/ *n* **1** (gambling) total of money staked by a number of gamblers. (賭博)(參與賭博者所下的)全部賭金;總賭注。**the (ˈfootball) ~s,** organized gambling on the results of football matches: 以足球比賽之輸贏賭博: *hoping to win a fortune on the ~s.* 希望在足球比賽的賭博中贏一大筆錢。**2** arrangement by business firms to share business and divide profits, to avoid competition and agree on prices. 公司行號爲避免競爭而協議價格並共同經營且分享利潤的措施;聯營。**3** common fund, supply or service, provided by or shared among many: (由衆人出資或共有的)共同的基金,供應物或服務: *a ˈtyping ~,* arrangement by which many persons share the services of typists instead of each having the services of his or her own typist. 聯合打字服務(許多人共用打字員,而非各人有其打字員的措施)。**4** [U] (US) game for several players played on a billiard-table with six pockets (GB 英 = *snooker*): (美)撞球;彈子: *to shoot* (= play) *~.* 打撞球;打彈子。**ˈ~-room** *n* place, room, in which the game of ~ is played. 撞球場。□ *vt* [VP6A] share in common; put (money, resources, etc) together for the use of all who contribute: 共有;分享;集中(錢,資源等)共同使用;聯營: *They ~ed their savings and bought a used car.* 他們用他們的積蓄合資買了一部舊汽車。

poop /puːp ; pup/ *n* (raised deck at the) stern of a ship. 船尾;船尾高甲板;船尾樓。⇨ the illus at barque. 參看 barque 之插圖。

poor /pʊə(r) ; pʊr/ *adj* (-er, -est) **1** having little money; not having and not able to get the necessaries of life. 無錢的;貧窮的;衣食不足的。**the ~** *n pl* ~ people. 窮人。**ˈ~-box** *n* (formerly, in a church) box in which money may be placed to be given to the ~. (昔時教堂的)濟貧捐款箱;慈善箱。**ˈ~-house** *n* (formerly) building where ~ people were maintained at the public expense. (昔時)公立貧民院;救濟院。**ˈ~ law** *n* (formerly) group of laws relating to the relief and care of the ~ (now replaced by Social Security Services). 濟貧法(昔時英國之法律,現由社會救濟服務法取代之)。**ˈ~-rate** *n* (formerly) rate (= local tax) for the relief of the ~. (昔時)濟貧稅。**ˌ~ ˈwhite,** (in southern US and S Africa) one of a class of socially inferior white people. (美國南方及南非之)社會地位低的白人。**2** deserving or needing help or sympathy: 值得或需要幫助或同情的;可憐的: *The ~ little puppy had been abandoned.* 那可憐的小狗已被遺棄了。**3** (often hum or ironic) humble; of little value: (常爲諧或反語)不足道的;無價值的: *in my ~ opinion.* 鄙見以爲。**4** small in quantity: 少量的;稀少的: *a ~ supply of well-qualified science teachers;* 資格好的自然科學教師的缺乏; *a country ~ in minerals.* 缺乏礦產的國家。**5** low in quality: 質劣的;壞的: *~ soil;* 貧瘠的土地; *~ food;* 差的食物; *in ~ health.* 健康不佳。**ˌ~-ˈspirited** *adj* lacking in courage; timid. 無勇氣的;膽怯的。

poor·ly /ˈpʊəlɪ ; ˈpʊrlɪ/ *pred adj* (colloq) unwell: (俗)身體不適的;不舒服的: *He's rather ~ this morning.* 他今晨頗感不適。□ *adv* **1** in a poor manner; badly; with little success: 貧乏地;拙劣地;結果不佳地: *~ lighted streets;* 燈光不足的街道; *~ dressed.* 穿得不好的。**2 ~ off,** having very little money: 無錢的;貧困的: *She's been ~ off since her husband died.* 丈夫死後她一直是貧困的。

poor·ness /ˈpʊənɪs ; ˈpʊrnɪs/ *n* [U] lack of some desirable quality or element (note that *poverty* is usu for being poor(1)): 貧乏;不足;可憐;拙劣(注意:

poverty 通常是指無錢或貧窮): *the ~ of the soil.* 土壤的貧瘠。

pop¹ /pɒp; pɑp/ *n* **1** short, sharp, explosive sound: 短而尖銳的爆裂聲;砰的一聲: *the pop of a cork.* 瓶塞的砰然聲。 **2** [U] (sl) bottled drink with gas in it: (俚)加有氣體的瓶裝飲料;汽水;啤酒;香檳酒: *ginger pop,* ginger beer; 薑汁啤酒; *a bottle of pop.* 一瓶汽水。 **3** (sl) ***in pop,*** in pawn. (俚)被典當;在質押中。 □ *adv* with the sound of popping: 砰然;發爆裂聲地: *I heard it go pop.* 我聽到它砰然一響。*Pop went the cork!* 瓶塞砰地一聲跳出來了!

pop² /pɒp; pɑp/ *n* (US abbr for) poppa. (美)爲 poppa 之略。

pop³ /pɒp; pɑp/ *adj* (colloq abbr for) popular: (俗, popular 之略)通俗的;流行的;大衆的: *'pop music;* 流行音樂; 通俗音樂; 熱門音樂; *'pop singers;* 流行歌曲歌手; 熱門音樂歌手; 紅歌星; *'pop groups,* (singers and players) (esp) those whose records sell in large numbers and who are most popular on radio, TV and in discotheques. 熱門音樂團;流行歌曲合唱團。 **'pop art,** the depiction of scenes of everyday life, using comic strips, commercial technique, etc. 以漫畫或廣告技巧描繪現實生活的藝術;普普藝術。 **'pop concert,** of popular music. 大衆音樂會;流行音樂會;熱門音樂會。 **'pop festival,** large, usu outdoor, gathering of people to hear pop singers and musicians. (通常在室外舉行的)大衆音樂欣賞會;熱門音樂會。 □ *n* [U] (colloq) pop music, pop art, etc; [C] pop song: (俗)流行音樂;普普藝術等;流行歌曲: *top of the pops,* disc, etc which (calculated by sales) is most popular during a given period of time. (某一段時期內)最暢銷的唱片;冠軍歌曲;金唱片。

pop⁴ /pɒp; pɑp/ *vt, vi* (-pp-) **1** [VP6A, 15B, 2C] (cause to) make a sharp, quick sound (as when a cork comes out of a bottle): (使)發出短促的砰聲 (如軟木塞拔出瓶子時所發出者); 發爆裂聲: *Champagne corks were popping (away) on all sides.* 到處都是打開香檳酒塞子的砰砰聲。***pop the question,*** (sl) propose marriage. (俚)求婚。 **'pop-eyed** *adj* having bulging eyes or eyes very wide open (with surprise, etc). (因驚奇等)眼睛睜大的;突眼的。 **'pop-gun** *n* child's toy gun which fires a cork with a popping sound. 玩具氣槍。 **2** [VP15A, B, 2A, C] (uses with *adverbial particles* and *preps*) (與副詞接語及介詞連用) ***pop across to,*** ⇨ pop over below. 參看下列之 pop over。***pop in/out (of),*** (cause to) go or come in/out quickly (giving the idea of rapid or unexpected movement or activity: (使)突然地進出;突然地活動: *He popped his head in at the door.* 他突然將頭伸進門內。*Pop in and see me some time.* 找一個時候來看我。 *The neighbours' children are always popping in and out,* are very frequent visitors. 隣居的孩子們總是走進走出的(是走動很勤的常客)。 *His eyes almost popped out (of his head) in surprise.* 他因驚訝而睜大着眼睛(他的眼睛因驚訝而幾乎脫眶而出)。 ***pop sth into sth,*** quickly put it there: 將某物很快地放於某處: *She popped the gin bottle into the cupboard as the vicar entered the room.* 牧師進入房間時,她很快地把杜松子酒瓶放進櫥櫃。 ***pop off,* (a)** go away. 忽然離去。 **(b)** (sl) die: (俚)死掉: *I don't intend to pop off yet.* 我還不想死呢。 ***pop over/across to,*** make a quick, short visit to: 突然造訪;匆促前往: *She has just popped over/across to the grocer's.* 她剛剛匆促地往雜貨店去了。 **3** (sl) [VP2C] shoot: (俚)射殺;開槍: *They were popping away at the pigeons.* 他們用槍打鴿子。 **4** (sl) pawn: (俚)典當: *I'll pop my watch and take you to the cinema.* 我要把手錶當掉,請你看電影。 **5** (US) parch (maize) until it bursts open and puffs out. (美)爆玉米花。 **'pop·corn** *n* maize treated in this way. 玉米花。

Pope /pəʊp; pop/ *n* (often 常作 **the ~**) the Bishop of Rome as chief bishop of the Roman Catholic Church. (天主教的)教宗;教皇。 **pop·ery** /ˈpəʊpərɪ; ˈpopərɪ/ *n* [U] (in hostile use) Roman Catholicism; papal system. (含有敵意的用法)天主教之教義;教皇制度。 **pop·ish** /ˈpəʊpɪʃ; ˈpopɪʃ/ *adj* (in hostile use) of popery. (含有敵意的用法)天主教之教義或教皇制度的。 **pop·ish·ly** *adv*

pop·in·jay /ˈpɒpɪndʒeɪ; ˈpɑpɪnˌdʒe/ *n* conceited person, esp one who is vain about clothes. 自大者;(尤指)講究衣著者;紈袴子。

pop·lar /ˈpɒplə(r); ˈpɑplɚ/ *n* [C] tall, straight, fast-growing tree; [U] its wood. 白楊;白楊樹;白楊木。

pop·lin /ˈpɒplɪn; ˈpɑplɪn/ *n* [U] (formerly) cloth of silk and wool with a ribbed surface; (now, usu) kind of strong, shiny cotton cloth used for shirts, etc. (昔時之)毛葛(絲與羊毛合織的一種起稜的布料);(現在通常指)一種用於製襯衣等之堅實發光的棉布。

poppa /ˈpɒpə; ˈpɑpə/ *n* (US) = papa.

pop·pet /ˈpɒpɪt; ˈpɑpɪt/ *n* (GB) used as a term of endearment (usu to a child): (英)小乖乖;小寶貝(通常用做對小孩的暱稱): *Isn't she a ~?* 她不是一位可愛的人兒嗎? *And how's my little ~ this morning?* 我的小寶貝今天早上好嗎?

poppy /ˈpɒpɪ; ˈpɑpɪ/ *n* (*pl* -pies) sorts of plant, wild and cultivated, with large flowers, esp red, and a milky juice: 罌粟(野生或栽培的植物,開大花,尤多紅色,果含漿汁): *'opium ~,* kind from which opium is obtained. 產鴉片的罌粟。

poppy·cock /ˈpɒpɪkɒk; ˈpɑpɪˌkɑk/ *n* [U] (sl) nonsense. (俚)胡說;廢話。

popu·lace /ˈpɒpjʊləs; ˈpɑpjəlɪs/ *n* (formal) the common people; the general public; the masses. (正式用語)平民;大衆;民衆;老百姓。

popu·lar /ˈpɒpjʊlə(r); ˈpɑpjəlɚ/ *adj* **1** of or for the people: 人民的;民衆的;爲了人民的: *~ government,* by the elected majority of all those who have votes. 民治的政府。 **ˌ~ ˈfront,** (in politics) coalition of parties opposed to reaction and fascism. (政治) (反對保守派及法西斯主義的) 聯合陣線;民衆陣線。 **2** suited to the tastes, needs, educational level, etc of the general public: 適於大衆之愛好,需要,教育水準等的; 一般的; 通俗的: *~ science;* 大衆科學;通俗科學; *meals at ~ (= low) prices.* 廉價餐。 **3** liked and admired: 受愛慕的;被擁戴的;有名氣或人望的: *a ~ hero;* 一般民衆崇拜的英雄; *~ film stars;* 有名氣的影星; *a man who is ~ with his neighbours.* 一位受鄰居歡迎的人。 ⇨ pop³. **~·ly** *adv*

popu·lar·ity /ˌpɒpjʊˈlærətɪ; ˌpɑpjəˈlærətɪ/ *n* [U] quality of being popular(3): 受愛慕;被擁戴;聲望;普遍: *win ~;* 得人心;得名望; *the ~ of baseball in Japan.* 日本人對棒球的普遍愛好。

popu·lar·ize /ˈpɒpjʊləraɪz; ˈpɑpjələˌraɪz/ *vt* [VP 6A] make popular: 使普及;使通俗;使得人心: *~ a new method of teaching spelling.* 推廣一種教拼字的新方法。 **popu·lar·iz·ation** /ˌpɒpjʊləraɪˈzeɪʃn *US:* -rɪˈz; ˌpɑpjələrɪˈzeʃən/ *n*

popu·late /ˈpɒpjʊleɪt; ˈpɑpjəˌlet/ *vt* [VP6A] supply with people; inhabit; form the population of: 殖民於;居住於;構成…之人口: *thinly ~d;* 人口稀少; *the densely ~d parts of India.* 印度人口稠密的地方。

popu·la·tion /ˌpɒpjʊˈleɪʃn; ˌpɑpjəˈleʃən/ *n* (number of) people living in a place, country, etc or a special section of them: (地方,國家等之全部或一部分的)人口;人口數: *a fall/rise in ~;* 人口的減少(增加); *the ~ of London;* 倫敦的人口; *the working-class ~.* 工人階級的人口數。

popu·lism /ˈpɒpjʊlɪzəm; ˈpɑpjəlɪzm̩/ *n* [U] government or politics based on an appeal to popular sentiments or fears. 民粹主義。 **popu·list** /-ɪst; -ɪst/ *n* supporter or promoter of ~. 民粹黨黨員;擁護或提倡民粹主義者。

popu·lous /ˈpɒpjʊləs; ˈpɑpjələs/ *adj* thickly populated. 人口稠密的。

por·ce·lain /ˈpɔːsəlɪn; ˈporslɪn/ *n* [U] (articles, eg cups and plates, made of a) fine china with a coating of translucent material called *glaze.* 瓷

(其表面塗有透明的釉);瓷器(如杯盤)。

porch /pɔːtʃ; portʃ/ *n* **1** built-out roofed doorway or entrance to a building. 門廊。 **2** (US, also) veranda. (美國亦指)走廊。

por·cine /ˈpɔːsaɪn; ˈpɔrsaɪn/ *adj* of or like a pig. 猪的;似猪的。

por·cu·pine /ˈpɔːkjʊpaɪn; ˈpɔrkjəˌpaɪn/ *n* small rat-like animal covered with spines that the animal can stick out if attacked. 豪猪(又名箭猪,似鼠之小動物,體生硬刺毛,遇敵時可豎立以自衛)。

pore¹ /pɔː(r); por/ *n* tiny opening (esp in the skin of an animal body) through which fluids (eg sweat) may pass: 小孔;(尤指動物身體上的)毛孔: *He was sweating at every ~.* 他的每一個毛孔都在出汗。

pore² /pɔː(r); por/ *vi* [VP3A] **~ *over sth,*** study it with close attention: 仔細研讀某物;熟讀: *~ over a letter/book.* 仔細研讀一信(書)。

pork /pɔːk; pork/ *n* [U] flesh of a pig (usu fresh, not salted or cured) used as food: 猪肉(通常指未加鹽或燻醃的鮮肉): *a leg of ~;* 猪腿; *a ~ chop;* 猪排; *roast ~.* 烤猪肉。⇨ bacon, ham(1). **ˈ~-barrel** *n* (US, sl) money from State or Federal taxes, etc spent to confer local benefits for political reasons. (美俚)爲了政治因素由州或聯邦的賦稅等中撥出而花費於地方福利的經費;政治分肥。 **ˈ~-butcher** *n* one who kills pigs for sale as food, makes ~ sausages, ~ pies, etc. 屠戶;猪肉商。 **ˌ~ˈpie** *n* minced ~, highly seasoned, in a container of pie-crust. 猪肉餅。**~er** *n* pig raised for food, esp one fattened for killing. 猪;(尤指養肥後宰食之)肉猪。

porn /pɔːn; pɔrn/ *n* (colloq abbr of) pornography. (俗)爲 pornography 之略。**ˈ~ shop** *n* shop where pornographic books, etc are sold. 色情書報店。

por·nogra·phy /pɔːˈnɒgrəfɪ; pɔrˈnɑgrəfɪ/ *n* [U] treatment of obscene subjects, in writing, pictures, etc; such writings, etc. (寫作、圖畫等中之)淫穢題材的處理; 誨淫; 色情文學; 色情畫; 春畫; 春宮。 **por·nogra·pher** /pɔːˈnɒgrəfə(r); pɔrˈnɑgrəfɚ/ *n* person who makes or deals in ~. 撰寫色情文學者;製作色情書畫者;推銷色情書畫者。 **por·no·graphic** /ˌpɔːnəˈgræfɪk; ˌpɔrnəˈgræfɪk/ *adj*

po·rous /ˈpɔːrəs; ˈporəs/ *adj* **1** full of pores. 多孔的。 **2** allowing liquid to pass through: 能浸透的;可滲水的: *Sandy soil is ~.* 沙土會滲水。**~·ness, po·ros·ity** /pɔːˈrɒsətɪ; poˈrɑsətɪ/ *nn* quality or condition of being ~. 孔;多孔;多孔性;滲水性。

por·phyry /ˈpɔːfɪrɪ; ˈpɔrfərɪ/ *n* [U] hard, red kind of rock with red and white crystals bedded in it, polished and made into ornaments. 斑岩(有紅色和白色結晶嵌於其中的一種堅硬的紅岩石,磨光後可做成裝飾品);細紋硬石。

por·poise /ˈpɔːpəs; ˈpɔrpəs/ *n* sea animal rather like a dolphin or small whale. 海豚。⇨ the illus at sea. 參看 sea 之插圖。

por·ridge /ˈpɒrɪdʒ *US:* ˈpɔːr-; ˈpɔrɪdʒ/ *n* [U] soft food made by boiling a cereal, eg oatmeal, in water or milk: (用麥片等穀類加水或牛奶煮成的)粥; 麥片粥: *a bowl/plate of ~.* 一碗(盤)麥片粥。

por·rin·ger /ˈpɒrɪndʒə(r) *US:* ˈpɔːr-; ˈpɔrɪndʒɚ/ *n* small bowl with a handle (for a child) from which porridge, soup, etc is eaten. (小孩用的、有柄的)小湯碗;粥碗。

port¹ /pɔːt; port/ *n* **1** harbour: 港;港口: *a naval ~;* 軍港; *reach ~.* 靠港。 **2** town or city with a harbour, esp one where customs officers are stationed. 港市(尤指有海關官員駐征關稅者)。**free ~,** one open for the merchandise of all countries to load and unload in; one where there is exemption of duties for imports or exports. 自由港(各國商品皆可裝卸而無進出口稅之港口)。 **3** (fig) refuge. (喻)避難所;休息處。***any ~ in a storm,*** in time of difficulty help or safety may be sought anywhere. 危難時可尋求幫助或安全的任何處所。***~ after stormy seas,*** rest after struggles. 掙扎後的休息。

port² /pɔːt; port/ *n* (naut) opening in the side of a ship for entrance, or for loading and unloading cargo; ~hole(b). (航海)(船的)艙門;上下貨口;舷窗。**ˈ~·hole** *n* **(a)** opening in a ship's side for admission of light and air. 船側供採光通氣的窗孔。 **(b)** small glass window in the side of a ship or aircraft. 舷側或機側之小玻璃窗;舷窗。

port³ /pɔːt; port/ *n* left-hand side of a ship or aircraft as one faces forward: (船的)左舷;(飛機的)左側: *put the helm to ~;* 把舵朝向左舷(使船首向右轉); (attrib) (形容用法) *on the ~ bow/quarter.* 在左舷船首(船尾)。⇨ starboard; ⇨ the illus at ship. 參看 ship 之插圖。 □ *vt* [VP6A] turn (the ship's helm) to ~. 把(船舵)轉向左舷。

port⁴ /pɔːt; port/ *n* [U] strong, sweet, dark-red or white wine of Portugal. (葡萄牙產的)暗紅色或白色濃而甜的葡萄酒。

port⁵ /pɔːt; port/ *n* ***at the ~,*** (mil) position of a rifle on porting arms. (軍)作端槍的姿勢。 □ *vt* carry (a rifle or other weapon) diagonally across and close to the body ready for inspection by an officer: 握持(槍)使槍管斜交於身體,以備檢查; 端槍: *P~ arms!* command for this to be done. (軍隊口令)端槍!

port·able /ˈpɔːtəbl; ˈportəbl/ *adj* that can be carried about; not fixed: 可攜帶的;手提式的;能移動的: *~ radios/typewriters.* 手提收音機(打字機)。 **port·abil·ity** /ˌpɔːtəˈbɪlətɪ; ˌportəˈbɪlətɪ/ *n* [U] being ~: 可攜帶;能移動;輕便: *The portability of my tape-recorder is exaggerated.* 我這錄音機的輕便性是誇大其詞的。

port·age /ˈpɔːtɪdʒ; ˈportɪdʒ/ *n* [C, U] (cost of) carrying goods, esp when (eg in forest country in Canada) goods have to be carried overland between two rivers or parts of a river; place where this is done. 貨物搬運; 搬運費; (尤指) 兩河之間或一河的兩部分之間的陸上運送 (如在加拿大的林區); 兩水路之間的陸上運送地點。

por·tal /ˈpɔːtl; ˈportl̩/ *n* doorway, esp an imposing one of a large building. 入口; 大門; (尤指大建築物的)正門。

port·cul·lis /ˌpɔːtˈkʌlɪs; portˈkʌlɪs/ *n* (hist) iron grating that could be raised or lowered to protect the gateway of a castle. (史)(保護城堡入口之可升降的)鐵門;城堡吊門。⇨ the illus at drawbridge. 參看 drawbridge 之插圖。

porte-cochère /ˌpɔːt kəˈʃeə(r); ˌportkəˈʃɛr/ *n* (F) gateway at the entrance to a building to give shelter to persons entering or leaving cars, etc. (法)(建築物大門前供人進入或下車等之)有頂蓋的通道。

por·tend /pɔːˈtend; porˈtɛnd/ *vt* [VP6A] (formal) be a sign or warning of (a future event, etc): (正式用語)預示;爲(未來事件等)之徵兆: *This ~s war.* 這是戰爭的預兆。

por·tent /ˈpɔːtent; ˈportɛnt/ *n* thing, esp sth marvellous or mysterious, that portends sth; omen. (尤指奇特或神秘的) 預兆;徵兆。 **por·ten·tous** /pɔːˈtentəs; porˈtɛntəs/ **1** ominous; threatening. 預示的;不祥的。 **2** marvellous; extraordinary. 奇特的; 可驚的;非常的。**por·ten·tous·ly** *adv*

por·ter¹ /ˈpɔːtə(r); ˈportɚ/ *n* **1** person whose work is to carry luggage, etc at railway stations, airports, hotels, etc. (火車站、飛機場、旅館等處搬運行李之)脚夫。 **2** person carrying a load on his back or head (usu in country where there are no roads for motor-vehicles). (在無汽車道路地區以背或頭負物之)挑夫;馱夫。 **3** (US) attendant in a sleeping-car or parlour-car on a train. (美)(鐵路之臥車或特等客車上的)侍者;服務員。**ˈ~·age** /-ɪdʒ; -ɪdʒ/ *n* [U] (the charge for) carrying of luggage, etc by a ~. 搬運行李;行李搬運費。

por·ter² /ˈpɔːtə(r); ˈportɚ/ *n* doorkeeper (at a hotel, public building, etc) (US 美 = *doorman*):(旅館、公共建築等之)門房;守門者: *The hotel ~ will call a taxi for you.* 旅館的門房將爲你叫一部計程車。**~'s**

lodge, ⇨ lodge¹(3).

por·ter³ /ˈpɔːtə(r) ; ˈportɚ/ *n* [U] dark-brown bitter beer. 一種黑褐色的苦啤酒。

por·ter·house /ˈpɔːtəhaʊs ; ˈportɚˌhaʊs/ *n* ~ **(steak)**, choice cut of beefsteak. 上等牛排。

port·folio /pɔːtˈfəʊlɪəʊ ; portˈfolɪˌo/ *n* (*pl* ~s /lɪəʊz ; -lɪoz/) **1** flat case (usu leather) for keeping loose papers, documents, drawings, etc. 公事包(通常爲皮製)。 **2** position and duties of a minister of state: 大臣(部長)的職位和職責: *He resigned his* ~. 他辭去部長職務。*Mr X is minister without* ~, not in charge of any particular department. 某先生是不管部大臣(部長)。 **3** list of securities and investments (stocks, shares, etc) owned by an individual, a bank, etc. 有價證券類。

port·hole *n* ⇨ port².

port·ico /ˈpɔːtɪkəʊ ; ˈportɪˌko/ *n* (*pl* ~es or ~s /-kəʊz ; -koz/) roof supported by columns, esp at the entrance of a building. 柱廊;(尤指)有圓柱的門廊。

a portico

port·ière /ˌpɔːtɪˈeə(r) ; ˌportɪˈɛr/ *n* (F) heavy curtain hung over a door(way). (法)門帷;門簾。

por·tion /ˈpɔːʃn ; ˈporʃən/ *n* **1** part, esp a share, (to be) given when sth is distributed: 部份;(尤指某物被分配時之)一份: (of a railway ticket) *this* ~ *to be given up;* (指火車票)此聯須繳回; (of a railway train) *the through* ~ *for Liverpool*, the coaches for Liverpool (passengers in which will not need to change trains); (指火車)直達利物浦的一部份車廂; *a marriage* ~, dowry. 嫁資;妝奩。 **2** quantity of any kind of food served in a restaurant: (餐館食物的)一份: *a generous* ~ *of roast duck*. 一大份烤鴨。 **3** (*sing*) one's lot or fate: (單)命運: *Brief life is here our* ~. 短暫的人生是我們今世的命運。□ *vt* **1** [VP15B] ~ ***sth out (among/between)***, divide into ~s, share. 分配。 **2** [VP14] ~ ***sth to sb***, provide a ~ of (sth to sb). 把(某物)之一份給某人。

Port·land /ˈpɔːtlənd ; ˈportlənd/ *n* ~ **stone**, yellowish-white limestone (quarried near ~, Dorset), used for building. 一種微黃色石灰石(建築用,產於英國 Dorset 郡的 Portland);波特蘭石。~ **cement**, cement used for concrete that resembles ~ stone in colour. 波特蘭水泥(用此種水泥和成之混凝土,其顏色似波特蘭石)。

port·ly /ˈpɔːtlɪ ; ˈportlɪ/ *adj* (usu of elderly persons) stout; round and fat: (通常指長者) 壯碩的;肥胖的: *a* ~ *city councillor*. 一位肥胖的市議員。

port·man·teau /pɔːtˈmæntəʊ ; portˈmænto/ *n* (*pl* ~s or ~x /-təʊz ; -toz/) oblong, square-shouldered leather case for clothes, opening on a hinge into two equal parts. 一種裝衣服的皮箱(長方形,肩部平正,以鉸鏈連合,打開時成爲相同的兩部分)。 ~ **word**, one made by using two or more words and combining their meanings, eg *shamateur* (from *sham* and *amateur*). 用兩個以上的字並結合其意義所造成的字(如 shamateur, 係由 sham 及 amateur 所構成)。

por·trait /ˈpɔːtrɪt ; ˈportret/ *n* **1** painted picture, drawing, photograph, of a person or animal. 人或動物之畫像或照片;肖像;人像。 **2** vivid description in words. 生動之文字描寫。ˈ~·**ist** /-ɪst ; -ɪst/ *n* maker of ~s. 人像畫家;人像攝影師。 ˈ~·**ure** /-tʃə(r) *US:* -tʃʊə(r) ; -tʃɚ/ *n* [U] art of making ~s; ~. 人像或肖像畫法;人像攝影;人像;肖像;描寫。

por·tray /pɔːˈtreɪ ; porˈtre/ *vt* [VP6A] **1** make a picture of. 作…之畫像;描畫。 **2** describe vividly in words. (以文字生動地)描寫。 **3** act the part of (in a play). 扮演;飾演…之角色。 ~**al** /pɔːˈtreɪəl ; porˈtreəl/ *n* [U] ~ing; [C] description. 畫像;描畫;描寫。

pose /pəʊz ; poz/ *vt, vi* **1** [VP6A] put (sb) in a desired position before making a portrait, taking a photograph, etc: (在作畫、攝影等之前)使(某人)擺成所要求之姿勢: *The artist* ~*d his model carefully.* 那畫家仔細地把他的模特兒的姿勢擺好。*All the subjects are well* ~*d.* 所有的人都擺好了姿勢。 **2** [VP 2A, 3A] ~ ***(for)***, take up a position (for a portrait, etc): (爲畫像等)擺姿勢: *Are you willing to* ~ *for me?* 你願意擺個姿勢讓我爲你拍照(畫像)嗎? **3** [VP6A] put forward for discussion; create; give rise to: 提出討論;造成;引起: *The increase in student numbers* ~*s many problems for the universities.* 學生人數的增加給大學帶來許多問題。 **4** [VP 2C] ~ ***as***, set oneself up as, claim to be: 使自己成爲;以…身份出現;佯裝: ~ *as an expert on old coins.* 佯裝爲古錢幣專家。 **5** [VP2A] behave in an affected way, hoping to impress people: 態度做作(以使人印象深刻);矯揉造作: *She's always posing*, is never natural in her behaviour. 她總是矯揉造作。□ *n* **1** position taken up for a portrait, photograph, etc: (爲繪畫、照相等所做的)姿勢: *a striking and unusual* ~. 顯眼而不尋常的姿勢。 **2** attitude, unnatural way of behaving, intended to impress people; affectation: 姿態;不自然的態度;裝腔作勢(爲使人印象深刻所做者): *That rich man's socialism is a mere* ~. 那位富人標榜社會主義只是一種姿態。**poser** *n* awkward or difficult question. 難題。

po·seur /pəʊˈzɜː(r) ; poˈzɝ/ (fem) (陰) **po·seuse** /pəʊˈzɜːz ; poˈzɝz/ *n* person who poses(5); affected person. 態度做作的人;裝腔作勢的人。

posh /pɒʃ ; pɑʃ/ *adj* (colloq) smart; first-class: (俗)漂亮的;頭等的: *a* ~ *hotel;* 頭等旅館; ~ *clothes;* 華服; *her* ~ *friends.* 她的出衆的朋友。□ *vt* [VP15B] ~ ***up***, make ~: 打扮: *We must* ~ *ourselves up for the party.* 我們必須打扮得漂亮一點去參加宴會。

posit /ˈpɒzɪt ; ˈpɑzɪt/ *vt* [VP6A] postulate. 假設;假定。

po·si·tion /pəˈzɪʃn ; pəˈzɪʃən/ *n* **1** [C] place where sth or sb is or stands, esp in relation to others: 位置: *fix a ship's* ~, eg by observation of the sun or stars; (藉觀察太陽或星球)確定船隻的位置; *secure a* ~ *where one will get a good view of the procession;* 找一個能看清楚遊行的位置; *storm the enemy's* ~*s*, the places they occupy. 猛攻敵軍的陣地。***in/out of*** ~, in/not in the right place. 在(不在)適當位置。 **2** [U] state of being advantageously placed (in war or any kind of struggle): (在戰爭或任何鬪爭中之)有利之地位或陣勢: *They were manoeuvring for* ~. 他們在用策略以取得有利之陣勢。 **3** [C] way in which sb or sth is placed; attitude or posture: 某人或某物被安置的方式;姿勢: *sit/lie in a comfortable* ~. 舒適地坐(躺)着。 **4** [C] person's place or rank in relation to others, in employment, in society, etc: 階級;地位: *a pupil's* ~ *in class;* 一個學生在班上的名次; *a high/low* ~ *in society.* 高(低)的社會地位。 **5** [C] job; employment: 工作;職位: *apply for the* ~ *of assistant manager.* 申請副經理的職位。 **6** [C] condition; circumstance: 狀況;環境: *placed in an awkward* ~. 處於困窘之境地。*I regret I am not in a* ~ (= am unable) *to help you.* 我很抱歉無力幫助你。 **7** [C] attitude; opinion: 態度;見解;主張: *What's your* ~ *on this problem?* 你對這問題的意見如何? □ *vt* [VP 6A] place (sth or sb) in ~; determine the ~ of. 安置(某物或某人)在適當的位置;決定…之位置。

posi·tive /ˈpɒzətɪv ; ˈpɑzətɪv/ *adj* **1** definite; sure;

leaving no room for doubt: 確定的;確實的;無疑的: *give a man ~ orders／instructions;* 給某人明確的命令(指示); *~ knowledge.* 確定的知識。 **2** (of persons) quite certain, esp about opinions: (指人)極有把握的;確信的(尤指在見解上): *Are you ~ (that) it was after midnight?* 你能斷定是在午夜後(發生的)嗎？ *Can you be ~ about what you saw?* 你能確定你所見到的是眞的嗎？ **3** practical and constructive; that definitely helps: 實際而有建設性的;確有助益的: *a ~ suggestion;* 積極的建議; *~ help;* 實際的幫助; *~ criticism.* 建設性的批評。 **4** (colloq) downright; out and out: (俗)完全的;徹底的: *That man is a ~ fool／nuisance.* 那傢伙是一個徹頭徹尾的傻瓜(討厭鬼)。*It's a ~ crime to drink and drive.* 醉酒駕車絕對有罪。 **5** (maths) greater than zero: (數學)正的;正數的: *the ~ sign* (+). 正號。 **6** (of electricity) of the sort produced by rubbing glass with silk; of the sort caused by deficiency of electrons: (指電)陽;正: *a ~ charge.* 陽電荷;正電荷。~ **pole,** anode. 陽極。 **7** (photo) showing light and shadows as in nature, not reversed (as in a *negative*). (攝影)正片的。 **8** (gram, of *adjj* and *advv*) of the simple form, not the comparative or superlative. (文法,指形容詞及副詞)原級的(非比較級或最高級的)。□ *n* ~ degree, adjective, quantity, etc; photograph printed from a (negative) plate or film. 原級;原級形容詞;正量;正數;(照相之)正片。**~·ly** *adv* definitely; certainly. 確定地;斷然地;絕對地。**~·ness** *n* [U] confidence. 確實;確信。

posi·tiv·ism /ˈpɒzɪtɪvɪzəm ; ˈpɑzətɪvˌɪzəm/ *n* philosophical system of Auguste Comte, based on observable phenomena and positive facts rather than speculation. 實證哲學;實證論(爲法國哲學家孔德所倡,其體系基於可觀察之現象及實在之事實)。 **logical ~,** modern (20th c) development of this philosophy mainly concerned with linguistic analysis and verification of empirical statements by observation. 邏輯實證論;論理實證法。 **posi·tiv·ist** /-ɪst ; -ɪst/ *n*

posse /ˈpɒsɪ ; ˈpɑsɪ/ *n* (chiefly US) body of constables or other men having authority who can be summoned by a sheriff to help him in maintaining order, etc. (主美)保警隊;地方團隊(郡執行官可召集以維持治安等)。

pos·sess /pəˈzes ; pəˈzɛs/ *vt* [VP6A] **1** own, have: 有;具有: *~ nothing;* 一無所有;身無長物; *lose all that one ~es.* 失去一個人所擁有的全部財物。 **2** keep control over: 控制;抑制;克制: *~ one's soul in patience,* be patient. 竭力忍耐。⇨ *self-~ed* at self-. **3 ~ *oneself of,*** (old use) become the owner of. (舊用法)持有;爲…之主人。 ***be ~ed of,*** have: 有;握有;據有: *He is ~ed of great natural ability.* 他很有天才。 **4 *be ~ed,*** be mad, be controlled by an evil spirit: 瘋狂;着魔: *She is surely ~ed.* 她確是發瘋了。*He fought like one ~ed,* like a person having a devil inside him. 他像着了魔似地打鬪。 **5** occupy (the mind); dominate: 佔據(心);擺佈;支配: *What ~ed you to do that?* What influenced or dominated your mind and caused you to do that? 什麼使你做出那種事的？ *He is ~ed with the idea that someone is persecuting him.* 他心裡老想着有人要害他。 **~or** /-sə(r) ; -sɚ/ *n* owner; person who ~es sth. 持有者;所有人。

pos·session /pəˈzeʃn ; pəˈzɛʃən/ *n* **1** [U] possessing; ownership: 持有;具有;所有權: *come into ~ of a large estate;* 獲得一大筆地產; *get ~ of sth,* succeed in getting ~ of it. 拿到;占有;占領。 *The players fought for／won ~ of the ball.* 球員們爭奪(搶到)球。*Who is in ~ of the property?* 誰持有那財產？ *The information in my ~ is strictly confidential.* 我握有的情報是極度機密的。*You can't take ~ of the house* (= move into it) *until all the papers have been signed.* 在各項證件簽字以前,你不能住進那房屋。*Is the woman in full ~ of her senses?* Is she quite sane? 那女人神志健全嗎？ **2** [C] (often *pl*) sth possessed; property: (常用複數)所有物;財產: *lose all one's ~s;* 失去所有的財產; *a man of great ~s.* 富人。*Most of Britain's ~s overseas* (= her former colonies, etc) *are now independent countries.* 英國昔日的海外屬地如今大部分已成爲獨立的國家。

pos·sess·ive /pəˈzesɪv ; pəˈzɛsɪv/ *adj* **1** of possession or ownership: 所有的;所有權的: *He has a ~ manner,* seems to assert claims, eg to the attention of people. 他有一種想要慑服人的態度(如想引起旁人注意)。*She has a ~ nature,* is eager to acquire things or wants the whole of (someone's) love or attention. 她有一種愛佔有的天性。 **2** (gram) showing possession: (文法)表示所有的;所有格的: *the ~ case,* eg *Tom's, the boy's, the boys';* 所有格(如Tom's, the boy's, the boys'); *~ pronouns,* eg *yours, his.* 所有格代名詞(如 yours, his)。**~·ly** *adv*

pos·set /ˈpɒsɪt ; ˈpɑsɪt/ *n* drink of warm milk with ale or wine and spices in it, formerly much used as a remedy for colds. 牛奶酒(熱牛奶加淡啤酒或葡萄酒及香料而成之飲料,昔時多用以治療受寒)。

pos·si·bil·ity /ˌpɒsəˈbɪlətɪ ; ˌpɑsəˈbɪlətɪ/ *n* (*pl* -ties) **1** [U] state of being possible; (degree of) likelihood: 可能;可能性;可能的程度: *Is there any／much ~ of your getting to London this week?* 本週你(很)有可能到倫敦去嗎？ *I admit the ~ of your being right.* 我承認你可能是對的。*Help is still within the bounds of ~.* 援助的可能性仍然存在。 **2** [C] sth that is possible: 可能之事;可能發生之事物: *I see great possibilities in this scheme,* It can have great success in many ways. 我看這計畫很可能成功。*Don't neglect the ~ that his train has been delayed／the ~ of an accident.* 不要忽略他所搭的火車有誤點的可能(可能發生意外事故)。

poss·ible /ˈpɒsəbl ; ˈpɑsəbl/ *adj* **1** that can be done; that can exist or happen: 可能的;可能存在或發生的: *Come as quickly as ~.* 儘快來。*Frost is ~, though not probable, even at the end of May.* 卽使在五月底,下霜也是可能的,雖然可能性不大。 *Are you insured against all ~ risks?* 你投保了一切可能發生的危險嗎？ **2** that is reasonable or satisfactory: 合理的;令人滿意的: *a ~ answer to a problem,* one that may be accepted, though not, perhaps, the best. 對於一個問題較合理的解答。*He is the only ~ man for the position.* 他是該職位唯一合適的人選。□ *n* ~ person or thing: 可能的人或物: *A trial game was arranged between ~s and probables.* 預備隊員之間安排了一次預賽。**poss·ibly** /-əblɪ ; -əblɪ/ *adv* **1** in accordance with what is ~: 可能地: *I will come as soon as I possibly can.* 我儘可能早來。*Can you possibly lend me £5?* 你可能借我五鎊錢嗎？ **2** perhaps: 或者;或許;也許: *'Will they put your salary up?'—'Possibly.'* '他們會提高你的薪水嗎？'—'也許會。'

pos·sum /ˈpɒsəm ; ˈpɑsəm/ *n* (colloq abbr of) opossum. (俗)爲 opossum 之略。***play ~,*** pretend to be asleep, unaware, etc so as to deceive sb (from the ~'s habit of feigning death when attacked). 裝睡;裝病;裝迷糊(由鼴被襲擊時裝死之習慣而來)。

post[1] /pəust ; post/ *n* [C] **1** place where a soldier is on watch; place of duty: 哨所;崗位: *The sentries are all at their ~s.* 哨兵們都在崗位上。 **2** place occupied by soldiers, esp a frontier fort; the soldiers there. 軍隊駐紮地;營區;(尤指)邊疆堡壘;屯兵。⇨ outpost. **3** trading station, esp one in a country where law and order are not yet firmly established: (尤指法治尚未充分建立之國家的)貿易站: *trading ~s in northern Canada a hundred years ago.* 一百年前在加拿大北部的貿易站。 **4** position or appointment; job: 職位;工作: *get a better ~;* 得到一個更好的工作; *be given a ~ as general manager.* 獲得總經理之職。□ *vt* [VP6A, 15A] **1** put at a ~(1): 佈置於哨站: *~ sentries at the gates of the camp.* 在軍營的大門口佈置哨兵。 **2** send to a ~(1, 2, 4): 派往哨站或駐紮地;指派: *~ an officer* *to a unit.* 指派一軍官至某單位。*I hope to be ~ed to Damascus next year.* 我希望明年被派往大馬士革。

post² /pəʊst ; post/ *n* (mil) bugle-call sounded at sunset; (軍)日落時所吹之號音: (esp) (尤指) **the first/last ~,** (The last ~ is also sounded at military funerals). 就寢或熄燈預備號(熄燈號)(熄燈號在軍隊葬禮中亦吹之)。

post³ /pəʊst ; post/ *n* **1** (hist) one of a number of men placed with horses at intervals, the duty of each being to ride with letters, etc to the next stage; letter-carrier; mail-cart. (史)騎驛馬送信件等之人; 信差; 郵車。 ˌ~-ˈ**chaise** *n* (hist) travelling carriage hired from stage to stage or drawn by ~-horses hired from stage to stage. (史)驛車。 ˈ**~-horse** *n* (hist) horse kept at inns, etc for the use of men carrying letters, etc and for other travellers. (史)驛馬。 **2** (GB) transport and delivery of letters, etc; one collection of letters, etc; one delivery or distribution of letters, etc (US 美=*mail*): (英)郵政;郵務;一批郵件;一次投遞或分送的郵件: *miss/catch the ~,* be too late/in time for one of the regular clearances of letters. 未趕上(趕上)郵局收信的時間。*Has the ~ come yet?* Has there been a delivery of letters, etc? 郵件來過沒有? *I will send you the book by ~.* 我將把這本書郵寄給你。*Please reply by return of ~,* by the next ~ (from your town, etc to mine). 回信請交下一班郵遞。**the P~ (Office),** public corporation set up to perform these duties, responsible to the Ministry of ~s and Telecommunications. 郵政總局。 **3 the ~,** ~ box or ~ office: 郵筒;郵局: *take letters to the ~.* 去郵局寄信。**4** (compounds) (複合字) ˈ**~·bag** *n* = mailbag. ˈ**~·box,** box into which letters are dropped for collection. 郵筒;郵箱。 ˈ**~·card** *n* card, one side of which is usu a photograph or picture, used instead of a letter. 明信片。 ˈ**~·code,** (US 美 = *zipcode*) group of letters and numbers, eg W1X4AH, used to make the sorting and delivery of mail easier (by use of a computer). 郵遞區號(用字母和數字表示,如W1X 4AH, 藉電腦處理,以便於郵件之分類及遞送)。ˌ~-ˈ**free** *adj, adv* carried free of charge by ~, or with postage prepaid; (of a price) including the charge for postage. 免付郵費(的);郵資已預付(的);(指價格)郵費包括在內(的)。ˈ**~·man** /-mən ; -mən/ *n* (*pl* -men) man employed to deliver letters, etc (US 美 = *mailman*). 郵差;信差。ˈ**~·mark** *n* official mark stamped on letters, cancelling postage stamp(s) and giving the place, date, and time of collection. 郵戳。□ *vt* mark (an envelope, etc) with this. 以郵戳蓋於(信封等)。ˈ**~·master,** ˈ**~·mistress** *nn* official in charge of a ~ office. 郵政局長;女郵政局長。ˈ**~ office** *n* office, building, etc where ~al business is carried on, together with the business of telegraphs and telephones, payment of state pensions, etc. (包含電報、電話等業務的)郵局。 ˈ**~ office** (abbr 略作 **PO**) **box** *n* numbered box in a ~ office for ~ addressed to an individual or company. (在郵局內爲私人或公司所開的)郵政信箱。ˌ~-ˈ**paid** *adj, adv* with postage already paid. 郵資已付(的)。

post⁴ /pəʊst ; post/ *vt, vi* **1** [VP6A] put (letters, etc) into a postbox or take (them) to a post office to be forwarded (US 美 = *mail*). 郵寄(信件等);投寄。 **2** [VP3A] (hist) travel (*from/to*) by stages, using relays of horses. (史)騎驛馬旅行(與 to 或 from 連用)。⇨ post³(1). ˌ~-ˈ**haste** *adv* in great haste. 急速地;火速地。 **3** [VP6A, 15B] ~ ***(up),*** (book-keeping) write items in (a ledger); transfer (items) from a day-book to a ledger: (簿記)登錄於(分類帳);從日記簿過(帳)於分類帳: *~ (up) export sales;* 過外銷帳於分類帳; *~ up a ledger.* 記入分類帳。***keep sb ~ed,*** (fig) keep him supplied with news. (喻)不斷供給某人消息。

post⁵ /pəʊst ; post/ *n* upright piece of wood, metal, etc supporting or marking sth: (木、金屬等的)柱;支柱;標竿: *ˈgate~s;* 門柱; *the ˈstarting/ˈwinning-~,* marking the starting and finishing points in a race; (賽跑用之)起(終)點標; *ˈbed~s* (in the old-fashioned kind of bed which had curtains round it); (舊式床用以支撐帷幕之)床柱; *ˈlamp-~s,* poles in towns, etc with electric lamps for street-lighting. (市鎮等之)燈柱;電燈桿。□ *vt* [VP6A, 15A, B] **1** ~ ***(up),*** display publicly in a public place by means of a paper, placard, etc: (以報紙、招貼等在公共地方)公佈: *P~ no bills* (warning that notices, advertisements, etc, must not be pasted on the wall, etc). 禁止招貼(警告不得在牆壁等處張貼告示、廣告等)。*The announcement was ~ed up on the wall of the town hall.* 該通告公佈在市政廳的牆上。 **2** ~ ***(over),*** cover with bills, placards, etc: (以告示、招貼等)張貼於: *~ a wall (over) with placards.* 貼招貼紙於牆上。 **3** make known by means of a ~ed notice: 告示;揭示: *a ship ~ed as missing.* 公告失蹤的一隻船。

post- /pəʊst ; post/ *pref* after. 在後。⇨ App 3. 參看附錄三。

post·age /ˈpəʊstɪdʒ ; ˈpostɪdʒ/ *n* [U] payment for the carrying of letters, etc: 郵費;郵資: *What is the ~ for an air-letter?* 寄一封航空郵簡的郵費要多少? ˈ**~ stamp** *n* stamp (to be) stuck on letters, etc with a specified value, showing the amount of ~ paid. 郵票。

postal /ˈpəʊstl ; ˈpostl/ *adj* of the post³(2): 郵政的;郵局的: *ˈ~ rates;* 郵費; *ˈ~ workers;* 郵政人員; *a ~ vote,* sent by post to decide a ballot; 通訊選票;通訊選舉; *~ union,* agreement by governments of most countries for the regulation of international postal business. 萬國郵政協會。ˈ**~ order,** 郵政滙票。⇨ order¹(7).

post·date /ˌpəʊstˈdeɪt ; ˌpostˈdet/ *vt* [VP6A] **1** put (on a letter, cheque, etc) a date later than the date of writing. (在信件、支票等上)填遲日期;預填日期。 **2** give (to an event) a date later than its actual date. 把(一事件)的日期塡遲;寫遲日期。

poster /ˈpəʊstə(r) ; ˈpostɚ/ *n* **1** placard displayed in a public place (announcing or advertising sth); large printed picture. (張貼於公共場所的)海報;告示;廣告;印成的大照片。 **2 (ˈbill-)~,** person who posts bills or placards on walls, hoardings, etc. 張貼告示或廣告的人。

poste res·tante /ˌpəʊst ˈrestɑːnt *US:* reˈstænt ; ˌpostrɛsˈtɑnt/ *n* [U] (F) post office department to whose care letters may be addressed, to be kept until called for. (法)(郵局之)待領郵件部。

pos·terior /pɒˈstɪərɪə(r) ; pɑsˈtɪrɪɚ/ *adj* **1** ~ ***(to),*** later in time or order. (時間或順序上)在後的;較遲的;較晚的。⇨ prior¹. **2** placed behind. 位於後部的;後面的。□ *n* (hum) buttocks: (諧)屁股;臀部: *kick his ~.* 踢他的屁股。

pos·ter·ity /pɒˈsterətɪ ; pɑsˈtɛrətɪ/ *n* [U] **1** person's descendants (his children, their children, etc). (某人之)後裔;子孫。 **2** future generations: 後代;後世: *plant trees for the benefit of ~.* 爲謀後代之利益而種樹。

pos·tern /ˈpɒstən ; ˈpostɚn/ *n* side way or entrance; (esp, in former times) concealed entrance to a castle or fortress: 旁門;便門;後門;便道;邊道;(尤指昔時通往城堡的)暗道: (attrib) (形容用法) *~ door/gate.* 後門。

Post Exchange /ˌpəʊst ɪkˈstʃeɪndʒ ; ˌpostɪkˈstʃendʒ/ *n* (abbr 略作 **PX**) (US) store at a military base where personnel and their families may buy services and tax-free goods. (美)(在軍事基地所設立的免稅)福利社;販賣部。

post·gradu·ate /ˌpəʊstˈgrædʒʊət ; postˈgrædʒʊɪt/ *adj* (of studies, etc) done after taking a first academic degree. (指學科研究等)大學畢業後所做的;研究院的。□ *n* person engaged in ~ studies. (大學畢業後的)研究生。

post·hum·ous /ˈpɒstjʊməs ; ˈpɑstʃuməs/ *adj* **1** (of a child) born after the death of its father. (指小孩)父死後出生的;遺腹的。**2** coming or happening after death: 死後出現或發生的;身後的: *~ fame;* 死後的聲譽; *a ~ novel,* published after the author's death; 作者死後出版的小說; *the ~ award of a Victoria Cross.* 死後頒贈的維多利亞十字勳章。**~·ly** *adv*

pos·til·ion (also **pos·til·lion**) /pɒˈstɪlɪən ; poˈstɪljən/ *n* man riding on one of the two or more horses pulling a carriage or coach. 馬車騎手(騎在拉曳馬車之兩匹或多匹馬中的一馬上面者);騎在左馬上的御者。

post·mas·ter /ˈpəʊstmɑːstə(r) *US:* -mæs- ; ˈpost-ˌmæstɚ/ *n* **ˌP~ ˈGeneral,** the Minister at the head of a country's Post Office Department. 郵政總長。⇨ post[3](4).

post meri·diem /ˌpəʊst məˈrɪdɪəm ; ˈpostməˈrɪdɪ-ˌɛm/ *adv* (*abbr* 略作 **pm**) time between noon and midnight: 午後;下午: *7.30 pm.* 午後七時半。⇨ am at ante meridiem; ⇨ App 4(6). 參看附錄四之六。

post-mor·tem /ˌpəʊst ˈmɔːtəm ; ˌpostˈmɔrtəm/ *n, adj* **1** (medical examination) made after death: 死後所做的(醫學檢驗);驗屍: *A ~ showed that the man had been poisoned.* 驗屍顯示那人是被毒死的。**2** (colloq) review of an event, etc in the past. (俗)(對過去事件的)檢查;檢討。

post·pone /pəˈspəʊn ; postˈpon/ *vt* [VP6A, C] put off until another time: 展緩;延擱: *~ a meeting;* 展緩會期; *~ sending an answer to a request.* 延擱對一請求的答覆。**~·ment** *n* [U] postponing; [C] instance of this: 展緩;延擱: *after numerous ~-ments.* 在無數次的延擱之後。

post·pran·dial /ˌpəʊstˈprændɪəl ; postˈprændɪəl/ *adj* (usu hum) after dinner: (通常爲詼諧用法)飯後的;餐後的: *~ oratory.* 餐後演說。

post·script /ˈpəʊsskrɪpt ; ˈpostskrɪpt/ *n* **1** (abbr 略作 **PS**) sentence(s) added (*to* a letter) after the signature. (信件的)附筆;又及;再啓(與 to 連用,後接某信)。**2** additional or final information. 附加或最後的消息。

pos·tu·lant /ˈpɒstjʊlənt *US:* -tʃʊ- ; ˈpɑstʃələnt/ *n* candidate, esp for admission to a religious order. 志願人;候選人;(尤指)聖職志願人;牧師志願人。⇨ novice.

pos·tu·late /ˈpɒstjʊleɪt *US:* -tʃʊ- ; ˈpɑstʃəˌlet/ *vt* [VP6A] demand, put forward, take for granted, as a necessary fact, as a basis for reasoning. (認作必然的事實或推理的基礎而)要求;假設;假定;公設;以…爲前提。□ *n* sth ~d; sth that may be considered axiomatic: 要求事項;基本要求;假設;公設;公理: *the ~s of Euclidean geometry,* eg the possibility of drawing a straight line between any two points. 歐幾里德幾何學的假設(如任何二點之間可作一直線的可能性)。

pos·ture /ˈpɒstʃə(r) ; ˈpɑstʃɚ/ *n* **1** [C] attitude of, way of holding, the body: (身體的)姿勢;體態: *The artist asked his model to take a reclining ~.* 藝術家要求他的模特兒作斜躺的姿勢。*Good ~ helps you to keep well.* 好的姿勢幫助你保持健康。**2** [U] state or condition: 狀態;情況: *in the present ~ of public affairs.* 在目前的世事情況之下。**3** frame of mind; attitude: 心境;態度: *Will the Government alter its ~ over aid to the railways?* 政府會改變其對補助鐵路方面的態度嗎?. □ *vt, vi* **1** [VP6A] put or arrange in a ~: 令取某種姿勢: *~ a model.* 令模特兒擺某種姿勢。**2** [VP2A] adopt a vain, pretentious ~: 擺姿勢;裝模作樣: *The vain girl was posturing before a tall mirror.* 那個愛虛榮的女郎對着大鏡子擺姿勢。**pos·tur·ing** *n* [U, C] (from the *v*(2)): (由動詞第2義轉變而來): *All this posturing must stop!* 所有這些裝模作樣都必須停止!

posy /ˈpəʊzɪ ; ˈpozɪ/ *n* (*pl* -sies) small bunch of cut flowers. 小花束。

pot[1] /pɒt ; pɑt/ *n* **1** round vessel of earthenware, metal or glass, for holding liquids or solids, for cooking things in, etc; contents of such a vessel: 罐;壺;盆;瓶;鍋(作容器、烹調等用);一罐(鍋等)之物;一罐(鍋等)之量: *a ˈjam-pot;* 果醬罐; *eat a whole pot of jam;* 吃整罐的果醬; *a ˈteapot;* 茶壺; *a ˈcoffee-pot;* 咖啡壺; *a ˈflower-pot;* 花盆; *a ˈchamber-pot.* 便壺;夜壺。⇨ the *nn* forming the first element of such compounds. 參看構成上列複合字前一部分的名詞。**2** (phrases and provs) (片語與諺語) ***go to pot,*** (sl) be ruined or destroyed. (俚)毀滅;毀壞。***keep the ˈpot boiling,*** earn enough money to buy one's food, etc; keep sth, eg a children's game, going briskly. 餬口;謀生;使事情(如兒童遊戲)保持生氣勃勃。***take ˌpot ˈluck,*** whatever is available (without choice); whatever is being prepared for a meal: 有什麼吃什麼;吃便飯: *Come home with me and take pot luck.* 跟我回家吃便飯吧。***the ˌpot calling the ˌkettle ˈblack,*** the accuser having the same fault as the accused. 五十步笑百步;一丘之貉。**3** (colloq) large sum: (俗)大量: *make a pot/pots of money.* 賺大錢。**4** ***a big pot,*** (colloq) an important person. (俗)大人物。**5** (colloq) prize in an athletic contest, esp a silver cup: (俗)(運動會的)獎品;(尤指)銀杯: *all the pots he won when he was young.* 他年輕時所贏得的全部獎品。**6** (sl) marijuana. (俚)大麻煙。**7** (compounds) (複合字) **ˈpot-belly** *n* (person with a) large, prominent belly. 大腹;有大腹之人。**ˌpot-ˈbellied** *adj* (of a person) having a pot-belly; (of a stove) having a rounded container in which fuel, eg wood, burns. (指人)大腹的;(指爐灶)有燃燒燃料之圓肚的。**ˈpot-boiler** *n* book, picture, etc produced merely to bring in money. 僅爲賺錢而作的書、圖畫等。**ˈpot-bound** *adj* (of a plant) having roots that have filled its pot. (指植物)根生滿一花盆的。**ˈpot-boy, ˈpot-man** /-mən ; -mən/ (*pl* -men) *nn* (hist) one who helps in a public house by filling pots with beer, etc. (史)酒館侍役(幫助斟啤酒等)。**ˈpot hat** *n* (sl) bowler hat. (俚)高頂禮帽。**ˈpot-head** *n* (sl) habitual marijuana user. (俚)吸食大麻煙上癮者。**ˈpot-herb** *n* plant, etc whose leaves or stems, or whose roots or tubers, are used in cooking. 蔬菜類植物(其葉、莖或根、塊莖用於烹飪);調味用之植物。**ˈpot-hole** *n* **(a)** hole in a road made by rain and traffic. (道路因雨及行車所形成的)坑;穴。**(b)** deep cylindrical hole worn in rock (eg in limestone caves) by water. 地壺(石灰巖穴等內之岩石上爲水侵蝕成的圓筒狀深洞)。**ˈpot-holer** *n* person who explores pot-holes in caves. (在巖穴內)探勘地壺之人。**ˈpot-hook** *n* **(a)** hook, often S-shaped, which can be raised or lowered on a metal bar, for holding pots, etc over a fireplace. 鍋鉤;掛鉤(可上下挪動,用以懸掛火爐上之鍋、壺等)。**(b)** curved or wavy stroke made by children when learning to write their letters. (兒童學寫字母時所作之)彎形筆畫。**ˈpot-house** *n* (old use) low-class public house; ale-house: (舊用法)低級酒店;啤酒店: *pot-house manners,* vulgar manners. 粗鄙之舉止。**ˈpot-hunter** *n* **(a)** sportsman who shoots anything he comes across, thinking only of food for the pot or profit. (只想到獵取食物或牟利的)亂獵者。**(b)** person who takes part in contests merely for the sake of the prizes. 僅爲贏取獎品而參加競賽的人。⇨ 5 above. 參看上列第5義。**ˈpot roast** *n* beef, etc browned in a pot and cooked slowly with very little water. 燜燒牛肉等。**ˈpot-shot** *n* shot aimed at a bird or animal that is near, so that careful aim is not needed; random shot. (鳥獸距離甚近無需仔細瞄準的)近距離射擊;隨意射擊;亂射。**ˈpot-trained** *adj* (of a small child) trained to use a chamber-pot. (指小孩)會使用便壺便溺的。

pot[2] /pɒt ; pɑt/ *vt, vi* (-tt-) **1** [VP6A] put (meat, fish paste, etc) in a pot to preserve it: 裝(肉、魚醬等)於罐內以保存之: *potted shrimps/ham.* 罐裝小蝦(火腿)。**2** [VP6A, 15B] ***pot (up),*** plant in a flower-pot: 種在花盆內: *pot (up) chrysanthemum* *cuttings*. 把菊花的插枝種在花盆內。 **3** [VP6A] kill with a pot-shot: 近距離射殺: *pot a rabbit;* 近距離射殺一隻兔子; [VP3A] ***pot at,*** shoot at: 射擊;射殺: *~ at a hare.* 射野兔。 **4** (billiards) drive a ball into a pocket. (撞球)擊球入袋。 **5** (colloq) put (a baby) on a chamber-pot. (俗)置(嬰兒)於便壺上便溺。

pot·able /ˈpəutəbl ; ˈpɔtəbḷ/ *adj* fit to drink. 可以喝的。

pot·ash /ˈpɒtæʃ ; ˈpɑtˌæʃ/ *n* [U] common name for various potassium salts, used in the manufacture of fertilizers, soap, and various chemicals. 鉀鹼(數種鉀鹽之通用名稱,用以製造肥料、肥皂及各種化學品)。

po·tass·ium /pəˈtæsɪəm ; pəˈtæsɪəm/ *n* [U] soft, shining, white metallic element (symbol **K**), vital to all living matter, occurring in the form of mineral salts and in rocks. (化)鉀(柔軟而有光澤的白色金屬元素,爲一切生物所必需,存在於礦鹽及岩石中;符號爲K)。

po·ta·tion /pəuˈteɪʃn ; poˈteʃən/ *n* (liter) drink. (文)飲料。

po·tato /pəˈteɪtəu ; pəˈteto/ *n* (*pl* ~es /-təuz ; -toz/) plant with rounded tubers eaten as a vegetable; one of the tubers: 馬鈴薯(一種植物,其圓形塊莖可作蔬菜): *baked ~es;* 烤馬鈴薯; *mashed ~(es);* 馬鈴薯泥; *~ soup;* 馬鈴薯湯; (US) (美) *~ chips* (= GB 英 *crisps*). 炸馬鈴薯片。 ⇨ the illus at vegetable. 參看 vegetable 之挿圖。 **ˌsweet ˈ~,** tropical plant with long tuberous roots used for food. 紅薯;甘薯。 **ˈ~ beetle,** beetle that destroys the leaves of ~ plants. 薯蟲(傷害馬鈴薯葉的甲蟲)。

po·teen /pɒˈtiːn ; poˈtin/ *n* [U] Irish whisky from an illicit still. (愛爾蘭的)私造威士忌酒。

po·tent /ˈpəutnt ; ˈpotn̩t/ *adj* (not of persons or machines) powerful: (不指人或機器)有力的;有效的: *~ reasons/arguments/charms/drugs/remedies;* 有力的理由(有力的論據;有效的符咒;有效的藥物;有效的治療法); (of males) not sexually impotent. (指男人)有性交能力的。 **~·ly** *adv* **po·tency** /-nsɪ ; -nsɪ/ *n*

po·ten·tate /ˈpəutnteɪt ; ˈpotn̩ˌtet/ *n* powerful person; monarch; ruler. 有權威的人;君王;統治者。

po·ten·tial /pəˈtenʃl ; pəˈtɛnʃəl/ *adj* **1** that can or may come into existence or action: 可能的;潛在的: *~ wealth/resources;* 潛在的財富(資源); *~ energy* (waiting to be released); (物理)位能;勢能(待放出之能); *the ~ sales of a new book.* 一本新書的可能銷售量。 **2 ~ mood,** (gram) indicating possibility. (文法)可能語氣。 □ *n* **1** [C] that which is ~; possibility; [U] what sb or sth is capable of: 可能之事物; 可能; 可能性; 潛力; 潛勢; 潛能: *He hasn't realized his full ~ yet.* 他尙未完全發揮他的潛力。 **2** (gram) ~ mood. (文法)可能語氣。 **3** (electr) energy of an electric charge, expressed in volts: (電)電勢; 電位 (以電壓之實用單位伏特表示之): *a current of high ~.* 高壓電。 **~ly** /-ʃəlɪ ; -ʃəlɪ/ *adv a ~ly rich country,* eg one with rich but undeveloped natural resources. 具開發潛力的國家; 蘊藏豐富資源的國家。 **~·ity** /pəˌtenʃɪˈælətɪ ; pəˌtɛnʃɪˈælətɪ/ *n* (*pl* -ties) power or quality which is ~, and needs development; latent capacity: 可能性;潛能;潛力: *a situation/a country with great potentialities.* 大有發展的情況(潛力大的國家)。

pother /ˈpɒðə(r) ; ˈpɑðɚ/ *n* trouble; commotion. 騷動;喧擾。

po·tion /ˈpəuʃn ; ˈpoʃən/ *n* [C] dose of liquid medicine or poison, or of sth used in magic: (液體藥物或毒物的)一劑;一服;(魔術中所用之某物的)一份: *a ˈlove ~.* 可以引起愛情的魔藥;春藥;媚藥。

pot-pourri /ˌpəu ˈpuəriː *US:* pəˈriː ; pɑtˈpurɪ/ *n* **1** mixture of dried rose-petals and spices, kept in a jar for its perfume. 乾玫瑰花瓣及香料的混合物(置於瓶中以聞其香味)。 **2** musical or literary medley. (音樂之)雜曲;混成曲;(文學作品之)雜集。

pot·sherd /ˈpɒt-ʃɜːd ; ˈpɑtˌʃɝd/ *n* broken piece of pottery (esp in archaeology). (尤指考古學上的)陶器碎片。

pot·tage /ˈpɒtɪdʒ ; ˈpɑtɪdʒ/ *n* (old use) thick soup. (舊用法)濃湯。

potted /ˈpɒtɪd ; ˈpɑtɪd/ *adj* **1** ⇨ pot². **2** (of a book, etc) inadequately summarized: (指書等)摘要的;簡略的: *a ~ version of a classical novel.* 一本古典小說的簡易本。

pot·ter¹ /ˈpɒtə(r) ; ˈpɑtɚ/ (US = **put·ter** /ˈpʌtər ; ˈpʌtɚ/) *vi, vt* **1** [VP2A, C] work with little energy; move about from one little job to another: 懶散地工作;各處走動做些瑣碎事情: *~ing about in the garden.* 在花園各處做些瑣碎的工作。 **2** [VP15B] waste (time) in ~ing: 虛度(時間): *~ away a whole afternoon.* 浪費整個下午。 **~er** *n* person who ~s. 懶散的工作者;各處走動做些瑣屑工作者;虛擲光陰者。

pot·ter² /ˈpɒtə(r) ; ˈpɑtɚ/ *n* maker of pots. 製陶工人;陶工。 **~'s wheel,** horizontal revolving disc on which pots are shaped. (製陶器用之)橫式轉盤;拉坯輪車。 **pot·tery** *n* (*pl* -ries) [U] earthenware; pots; [C] ~'s workshop. 陶器; 瓦器; 陶器場。 **the Potteries,** district in Staffordshire, England where ~y is the chief industry. 帕特利斯(英國斯塔福郡之陶器出產地)。

a potter's wheel

potty¹ /ˈpɒtɪ ; ˈpɑtɪ/ *adj* (-ier, -iest) (GB dated colloq) (英國過時俗語) **1** petty; unimportant; insignificant: 細小的; 不重要的; 瑣碎的: *~ little details/jobs.* 瑣碎的細節(工作)。 **2 ~ *(about sb/sth),*** (of a person) foolish, crazy: (指人)胡塗的;瘋癲的;著迷的: *She's quite ~,* mad. 她瘋了。 *He's ~ about his new gramophone.* 他迷上了他新買的唱機。

potty² /ˈpɒtɪ ; ˈpɑtɪ/ *n* (*pl* -ties) child's chamber-pot. (小孩的)便壺。

pouch /pautʃ ; pautʃ/ *n* **1** small bag carried in the pocket (*a toˈbacco-~*) or fastened to the belt (a soldier's *ˌammuˈnition-~*). 小袋;小包 (或攜帶於口袋中,如煙草袋;或固定於束帶上,如兵士的彈藥包)。 **2** bag-like formation, eg that in which a female kangaroo carries her young. 袋狀物(如雌袋鼠裝幼仔的肚袋)。 ⇨ the illus at large. 參看 large 之挿圖。 **3** puffy area of skin, eg under the eyes of a sick or old person. 皮膚之腫脹處 (如病人或老人眼下之眼包)。 □ *vt* **1** [VP6A] put into a ~. 裝入袋中。 **2** [VP6A] make (part of a dress, etc) like a ~; [VP2A] hang like a ~. 把(衣服等之一部分)做成袋狀;似袋般懸掛;懸垂如袋。

pouf, pouffe /puːf ; puf/ *n* **1** large, thick cushion used as a seat. 大而厚的坐墊;蒲團。 **2** /pʊf ; puf/ ⚠ (derog sl) male homosexual. (諱)(貶抑俚語)男同性戀者。

poul·terer /ˈpəultərə(r) ; ˈpoltərɚ/ *n* (GB) dealer in poultry and game, eg hares. (英)家禽販;鷄販;獵物販(如賣野兎者)。

poul·tice /ˈpəultɪs ; ˈpoltɪs/ *n* [C] soft heated mass of eg linseed, mustard, spread on a cloth, and put on the skin to relieve pain, etc. 糊藥;膏藥(以亞麻子、芥子末等做成的軟糊而敷於布上者,加熱軟化後貼於皮膚以減痛等)。 □ *vt* [VP6A] put a ~ on. 敷糊藥於。

poul·try /ˈpəultrɪ ; ˈpoltrɪ/ *n* (collective *n*) (集合名詞) **1** (with *pl v*) large domestic fowl (eg hens, ducks, geese, turkeys) kept for eating or for egg-laying: (用複數動詞)(養來吃或下蛋之)家禽(如雞、鴨、鵝、火雞等): *The ~ are being fed.* 家禽正在吃飼

料。 **2** (with *sing v*) these considered as food: (用單數動詞)鷄肉;鴨肉;鵝肉;家禽肉: *P~ is expensive this Christmas.* 今年聖誕節的禽肉很貴。 ⇨ the illus at fowl. 參看 fowl 之挿圖。

pounce /paʊns ; paʊns/ *vi* [VP3A] ~ ***on/at,*** make a sudden attack or downward swoop on: 突襲;猛撲: *The hawk ~d on its prey.* 鷹向着牠的捕食對象猛撲。*The tiger ~d savagely on the goat.* 那虎兇暴地突襲那隻山羊。(fig) (喻) *He ~d at* (= seized) *the first opportunity to inform against his colleague.* 他抓住第一個機會去密告他的同事。□ *n* such an attack. 突襲;猛撲。

pound[1] /paʊnd ; paʊnd/ *n* (⇨ App 5) (參看附錄五) **1** unit of weight, 16 ounces avoirdupois, 12 ounces troy. 磅(重量單位,常衡時等於16盎斯,金衡時等於12盎斯)。 **2** ~ **(sterling),** British unit of money: 鎊(英國貨幣單位): *five ~s,* written £5; 五鎊(書作£5); *a five-~ note,* banknote for £5. 五鎊之紙幣。***penny wise, ~ foolish; in for a penny, in for a ~,*** ⇨ penny. **3** monetary unit of various other countries. 鎊(許多其他國家之幣制單位。)

pound[2] /paʊnd ; paʊnd/ *n* **1** enclosed area in a village where, in olden times, cattle that had strayed were kept until claimed by their owners. (昔時鄉村中)收留迷失牲畜以待失主認領的獸欄。 **2** (mod use) place where stray dogs and cats, and motor-vehicles left in unauthorized places, are kept until claimed. (現代用法)收留迷失之犬猫及隨意放置之摩托車以待認領的地方。

pound[3] /paʊnd ; paʊnd/ *vt, vi* [VP6A, 15A, 2C, 3A] ~ ***(away) (at/on),*** **1** strike heavily and repeatedly; thump: 連續重擊;重擊發聲;砰砰地打: *Our heavy guns ~ed (away at) the walls of the fort.* 我們的重砲轟擊堡壘的牆(對着堡壘的牆轟擊)。*Who is ~ing (on) the piano?* 誰在用力彈鋼琴? *Someone was ~ing at the door with a heavy stick.* 有人在用粗棍敲門。*I could hear feet ~ing on the stairs.* 我聽到樓梯上的沉重脚步聲。*She could feel her heart ~ing as she finished the 100 metres race.* 結束一百公尺的賽跑後,她感到心臟跳動得很厲害。 **2** crush to powder; break to pieces: 搗成粉;擊碎: *~ crystals in a mortar;* 搗碎研鉢中的結晶體; *a ship ~ing/being ~ed to pieces on the rocks.* 在岩石上撞碎的一隻船。 **3** ride, run, walk, heavily: 沉重地騎、跑、走: *He ~ed along the road.* 他沿着大路沉重地跑。

pound·age /ˈpaʊndɪdʒ ; ˈpaʊndɪdʒ/ *n* [U] commission or fee of so much (eg 5p) per pound sterling (£1) or payment of so much (eg 3 oz) per pound weight (1 lb). 按每鎊五辨士等所抽取的佣金或費用;按每磅三盎司等所付之價款。

pounder /ˈpaʊndə(r) ; ˈpaʊndɚ/ *n* (usu in compounds) sth weighing so many pounds: (通常用於複合字中)有…磅重之物: *a three-~,* eg a fish weighing 3 lb; 一件三磅重之物(如魚); gun that fires a shot of so many pounds: 發射…磅砲彈的砲: *an eighteen-~.* 發射十八磅砲彈的大砲。

pour /pɔː(r) ; por/ *vt, vi* **1** [VP6A, 12B, 13B, 15A, B, 14] cause (a liquid or a substance that flows like a liquid) to flow in a continuous stream: 使(液體或流動似液體之物)流動;灌;澆;注;倒: *P~ yourself another cup of tea.* 你再倒杯茶喝吧。*Please ~ a cup of tea for me, too.* 請你也為我倒一杯茶。*He ~ed the coffee out of the saucepan into the jug.* 他把咖啡從深平底鍋倒進壺中。(fig) (喻) *He ~ed out his tale of misfortunes.* 他傾訴自己的不幸遭遇。*The underground stations ~ thousands of workers into the streets between 8 and 9.30 each morning.* 每日早晨八時至九時半之間,成千成萬的工人從地下火車站出來到各街道去。~ ***cold water on sth,*** discourage (a person's plan, zeal or enthusiasm). 使沮喪;(對某人之計畫或熱心)澆冷水。~ ***oil on troubled waters,*** try to calm a disturbance or quarrel with soothing words. 調解爭端。 **2** [VP2C] flow in a continuous stream; come freely (*out/off, etc*): 流;瀉;湧入;湧出(與 out, off 等連用): *The sweat was ~ing off him.* 他汗流浹背。*Tourists ~ into London during the summer months.* 在夏季遊客湧入倫敦。*The crowds were ~ing out of the football ground.* 群衆正自足球場蜂湧而出。*Letters of complaint ~ed in.* 抱怨的信件源源而來。 **3** (of rain) come down heavily: (指雨)傾注: *The rain ~ed down.* 大雨傾盆而下。*It was a ~ing wet day.* 那是一個大雨天。***It never rains but it ~s,*** a saying used when (usu unwelcome) things come or events happen in quick succession. 事情(通常指不利的事)不發生則已,一發生就接二連三地來;禍不單行。

pout /paʊt ; paʊt/ *vt, vi* [VP6A, 2A] (as a sign of displeasure) push out (the lips). (作為不悅之表示)噘(嘴)。□ *n* such a pushing out of the lips. (不悅時的)噘嘴。**~·ing·ly** *adv* sulkily. 繃着臉地;不悅地。

pov·erty /ˈpɒvətɪ ; ˈpɑvɚtɪ/ *n* [U] state of being poor: 貧窮: *live in ~;* 過窮日子; *fall into ~;* 變窮; lack, inferiority: 缺乏;低劣: *an essay which shows ~ of ideas.* 缺乏思想的一篇文章。**ˈ~-stricken** *adj* affected by ~: 窮困的;貧窮的;為貧窮所苦惱的: *~-stricken homes.* 貧苦的家庭。

pow·der /ˈpaʊdə(r) ; ˈpaʊdɚ/ *n* **1** [C, U] (kind of) substance that has been crushed, rubbed or worn to dust; special kind of this, eg for use on the skin (*a tin of ˈtalcum-~*), or as a medicine (*take a ~ every morning*), for cleaning things (*ˈsoap-~, ˈbleaching-~*), or for cooking (*ˈbaking-~*). 粉;細粉;粉末;特別調製的粉末(如 a tin of talcum-~, 一罐搽皮膚用的爽身粉; take a ~ every morning, 每天早晨服用藥粉; soap-~, 肥皂粉; bleaching-~, 漂白粉; baking-~, 烹調用的酸粉)。**ˈ~-puff** *n* soft pad used for applying cosmetic ~ to the skin. 粉撲。**ˈ~-room** *n* ladies' room in an hotel, restaurant, cinema, etc with wash-basins and lavatories. (旅館、餐館、電影院等的)女用盥洗室;化粧室。 **2** = gunpowder, ⇨ gun. ***not worth ~ and shot,*** not worth fighting for. 不值得浪費彈藥(一戰)。**ˈ~-flask/-horn** *n* (hist) for carrying gun~. (史)火藥筒(角製火藥筒)。**ˈ~-magazine** *n* place where gun~ is stored. 火藥庫。□ *vt, vi* **1** [VP6A] put ~ on (the face, etc). 搽粉於(臉等)。 **2** [VP2A] use face-powder. 搽粉。**~ed** *adj* reduced to ~; dehydrated: 弄成粉的;脫水的: *~ed milk/eggs.* 奶(蛋)粉。**~y** *adj* of, like, covered with, ~: 粉的;粉狀的;敷粉的: *~y snow;* 粉狀的雪; *a ~y nose.* 敷着粉的鼻子。

power /ˈpaʊə(r) ; ˈpaʊɚ/ *n* **1** [U] (in living things, persons) ability to do or act: (生物或人之)做事或行動的能力: *It is not within/It is beyond/outside my ~ to help you,* I am unable, or am not in a position, to do so. 我沒有能力幫助你。*This animal, the chameleon, has the ~ of changing its colour.* 變色蜥蜴這種動物能變更自體的顏色。*I will do everything in my ~ to help.* 我願(就我的能力範圍內)儘量協助。 **2** (*pl*) faculty of the body or mind: (複)體力;智力;精力: *His ~s are failing,* He is becoming weak. 他的體力在衰退中。*You are taxing your ~s too much.* 你在耗費太多的精力。*He's a man of great intellectual ~s.* 他是一位大智者。 **3** [U] strength; force: 力;力氣: *the ~ of a blow.* 一擊之力。***More ~ to your elbow!*** (phrase used to encourage sb). 努力做! 祝你成功! (用以鼓勵人的片語)。 **4** [U] energy of force that can be used to do work: 動力;機力: *ˈwater ~;* 水力; *eˈlectric ~.* 電力。**ˈhorse~,** ⇨ horse. (attrib) (形容用法) *ˈ~-lathe/-loom/-mill,* operated by mechanical ~, not by hand labour. 動力車床(織布機,磨坊)。**ˈ~-boat,** one with an engine; motorboat (esp one used for racing; or towing water-skiers). 汽艇(尤指比賽或拖曳滑水者所用之汽艇)。**ˈ~-dive** *vt, n* (put an aircraft into a) steep dive with the engines working. (使飛機) 動力俯衝; 開油門俯衝。**ˈ~-house/-station,** building where electric ~ is generated for distribution. 發電所。**ˈ~-point,** socket on a wall, etc for a plug to connect an electric circuit. 電插座。 **5** [U] right; control; authority: 權;權力;勢力: *the ~ of the law;* 法律的力量; *the ~ of Congress;* 國會的權力; *have a person in one's ~,* be able to do what one wishes with him; 能左右一個人; *have ~ over sb;* 對某人有控制力; *Spain at the height of her ~;* 全盛時期的西班牙; *fall into sb's ~.* 落入某人的控制中。 ***in ~,*** (of a person or political party) in office. (指人或政黨) 當權; 秉政。 **~ politics,** diplomacy backed by force. 以武力爲後盾的外交;權力政治;强權政治。 **6** [C] right possessed by, or granted to, a person or group of persons: (個人或團體所獲有的) 權限;職權: *Are the ~s of the Prime Minister defined by law?* 首相的權限法律有明文規定嗎? *The President has exceeded his ~s,* has done more than he has authority to do. 總統已逾越他的職權。 **7** [C] person or organization having great authority or influence: 很有權力或影響力的人或組織;當權者: *Is the press a great ~ in your country?* Are the newspapers influential, etc? 貴國的報界有很大的影響力嗎? ***the ~s that be,*** (hum) those who are in authority. (諧)當局。 **8** [C] State having great authority and influence in international affairs. 强國。 **the Great P~s,** the largest and strongest States. 列强。 **9** [C] (maths) result obtained by multiplying a number or quantity by itself a certain number of times: (數學)乘方;乘冪;冪: *the second, third, fourth, etc ~ of x* (= x^2, x^3, x^4, *etc*); x的二次、三次、四次等冪; *the fourth ~ of 3* (= 3 × 3 × 3 × 3 = 81). 三的四次冪(=81)。 **10** [U] capacity to magnify: 放大力: *the ~ of a lens;* 透鏡的放大力; *a telescope of high ~.* 高倍望遠鏡。 **11** (colloq) large number or amount: (俗) 許多;大量: *This brandy is doing me a ~ of good!* 這種白蘭地酒對我助益甚大。 **12** [C] god, spirit, etc: 神;幽靈;鬼怪: *Preserve us from the ~s of darkness.* 保佑我們不受魔鬼的侵害。 **pow·ered** *adj* having, able to exert or produce, mechanical energy: 有動力的;能產生機械力的: *a new aircraft ~ed by Rolls Royce engines;* 一架以勞斯萊斯引擎爲動力的新飛機; *a high-~ed car;* 一部大馬力引擎的汽車; (fig) (喻) *a high-~ed salesman,* one with great ~s of persuasion. 很有說服力的推銷員。

power·ful /ˈpaʊəfl; ˈpaʊɚfəl/ *adj* having or producing great power: 有力的;强的: *a ~ blow/enemy;* 强有力的一擊(敵人); *a ~ remedy for constipation.* 便秘的特效藥。 **~ly** /-fəlɪ; -fəlɪ/ *adv*

power·less /ˈpaʊəlɪs; ˈpaʊɚlɪs/ *adj* without power; unable (*to do* sth): 無力的;無權的;不能(做某事)的(與不定詞連用): *render sb ~;* 使某人無能爲力; *be ~ to resist.* 無力抵抗。 **~·ly** *adv*

pow·wow /ˈpaʊwaʊ; ˈpaʊˌwaʊ/ *n* conference of N American Indians; (colloq) any other kind of conference. 北美印第安人的會議;(俗)任何集會。□ *vi* hold a conference (*about* sth). (爲某事)舉行會議(與 about 連用)。

pox /pɒks; pɑks/ *n* (colloq, usu 俗,通常作 **the ~**) syphilis: 梅毒: *catch/give sb the pox.* 染上梅毒(把梅毒傳染給某人)。

prac·ti·cable /ˈpræktɪkəbl; ˈpræktɪkəbl/ *adj* that can be done or used or put into practice: 可做的;可用的;可實行的: *methods that are not ~;* 不可實行的措施; *a mountain pass that is ~ only in summer.* 僅在夏季可通行的山路。 **prac·ti·cably** /-əblɪ; -əblɪ/ *adv* **prac·ti·ca·bil·ity** /ˌpræktɪkəˈbɪlətɪ; ˌpræktɪkəˈbɪlətɪ/ *n*

prac·ti·cal /ˈpræktɪkl; ˈpræktɪkḷ/ *adj* **1** concerned with practice (contrasted with *theoretical*): 實際的;實行上的(與 theoretical 相對): *overcome the ~ difficulties of a scheme;* 克服某計畫的實際困難; *a suggestion/proposal with little ~ value;* 甚少實際價值的建議; *a ~ joke,* ⇨ joke. **2** (of persons, their character, etc) clever at doing and making things; preferring activity and action to theorizing: (指人,其性格等)做事靈敏的;喜實際工作的;不好理論的: *a ~ young wife;* 做事靈敏的年輕妻子; *ideas that appeal to ~ minds.* 合乎實事求是者的主意(切合實際的想法)。 **3** useful; doing well what it is intended to do: 有用的;實用的: *Your invention is ingenious, but not very ~.* 你的發明物很精巧,但是不很實用。 **~ly** /-klɪ; -kḷɪ/ *adv* **1** in a ~ manner. 實際地;實用地。 **2** almost: 幾乎: *We've had ~ly no fine weather this month.* 這個月可以說沒有好天氣。 *He says he is ~ly ruined.* 他說他幾乎破產了。 **~·ity** /ˌpræktɪˈkælətɪ; ˌpræktɪˈkælətɪ/ *n* (*pl* -ties): *Let's get down to ~ities,* to considering ~ proposals. 我們來考慮實際的問題吧。

prac·tice /ˈpræktɪs; ˈpræktɪs/ *n* **1** [U] performance; the doing of sth (contrasted with *theory*): 實施;實行;應用(與 theory 相對): *put a plan into ~,* carry it out, do what has been planned. 實行某計畫。 *The idea would never work in ~,* may seem good theoretically, but would be useless if carried out. 那主意不能實現(理論上或許是好的)。 **2** [C] way of doing sth that is common or habitual; sth done regularly: 習慣; 常例: *the ~ of closing shops on Sundays;* 星期日休業的慣例; *Christian/Protestant/Catholic ~s,* ceremonies or observances; 基督教(新教,天主教)的教規或儀式; *an aperitif before dinner, as is my usual ~.* 飯前喝一杯酒,那是我的習慣。 ***make a ~ of (sth),*** do it habitually: 養成…之習慣;慣常做(某事): *boys who make a ~ of cheating at examinations.* 以考試作弊爲常事的男孩子們。 **3** [U] frequent or systematic repetition, repeated exercise, in doing sth (esp an art or craft): 經常或有系統的重複; 練習(尤指在藝術或手藝方面): *Piano-playing needs a lot of ~.* 彈鋼琴需要多練習。 *That is a stroke,* eg in golf, *that needs a lot of ~.* 那是需要經常練習的打法(如打高爾夫球)。 *It takes years of ~ to acquire the skill of an expert.* 要想獲得專家的技術,需要多年的練習。(attrib) (形容用法) *Let's have a ~ game.* 我們作一場練習賽吧。 ***in/out of ~,*** having/not having given enough time recently to ~: 近來勤(疏)於練習;練習充足(不足): *Please don't ask me to play the piano for you: I'm out of ~.* 請勿要我爲你彈鋼琴: 我近來疏於練習。 **4** [U] work of a doctor or lawyer: (醫生或律師之)業務: *retire from ~;* 從業務中退休; *no longer in ~;* 不再執業; [C] (collective) (number of) persons who regularly consult a doctor or lawyer: (集合用法)醫生或律師之經常主顧;此種主顧之數目: *a doctor with a large ~;* 求診者很多的一位醫生; *sell one's ~,* sell (to another doctor) the connection one has (of regular patients); 轉讓主顧(如把經常求醫的病人轉讓給另一醫生); *a doctor in general ~,* ⇨ *general practitioner* at practitioner. **5 sharp ~,** [U] not strictly honest or legal ways of doing business. 做生意不很規矩的方式。

prac·ti·cian /prækˈtɪʃn; prækˈtɪʃən/ *n* = practitioner.

prac·tise (US = **-tice**) /ˈpræktɪs; ˈpræktɪs/ *vt, vi* [VP6A, C, 2A, B] **1** do sth repeatedly or regularly in order to become skilful: 練習;實習: *~ the piano;* 練習彈鋼琴; *~ making a new vowel sound;* 練習一個新母音的發音; *~ (for) two hours every day.* 每日練習兩小時。 **2** make a habit of: 慣做;常爲;養成…的習慣: *~ early rising.* 養成早起的習慣。 ***~ what one preaches,*** make a habit of doing what one advises others to do. 教誨他人之事必先自己實踐;躬行己說。 **3** exercise or follow (a profession, etc): 操持(專業等): *~ medicine/the law,* work as a doctor/lawyer. 執業爲醫生(律師); 開業做醫生(律師)。 **4** [VP3A, 4A] ***~ on/upon; ~ to do sth,*** (old use) take advantage of (sb's credulity, etc); set oneself: (舊用法)利用(某人之輕信等);竭力想: *~ to deceive.* 竭力想行騙。**~d** (US = **-ticed**) *adj* skilled; having had much practice. 熟練的;練習充分的。

prac·ti·tioner /prækˈtɪʃənə(r); prækˈtɪʃənɚ/ *n* **1** one who practises a skill or art. 實習者;練習者;練習生。 **2** professional man, esp in medicine and the law. 從業者;(尤指)開業醫生;律師。 ˌ**general** ˈ~ (abbr 略作 **GP**), doctor who is qualified in both medicine and minor surgery (also called 亦稱作 *a family doctor*) who sees patients either in his surgery or in their homes. 全科醫生(在其診所或出診看病者)。

prae·sid·ium /prɪˈsɪdɪəm ; prɪˈsɪdɪəm/ *n* = presidium.

prae·tor (also **pre·tor**) /ˈpriːtə(r) ; ˈpritɚ/ *n* annually elected magistrate in ancient Rome. 古羅馬每年選出的執政官。 **prae·tor·ian** /prɪˈtɔːrɪən ; prɪˈtorɪən/ *adj* of, having the rank of, a ~; of the bodyguard of a Roman commander or Emperor. 古羅馬之執政官的;具有執政官之地位的;古羅馬統帥或皇帝之衞隊的。

prag·matic /prægˈmætɪk ; prægˈmætɪk/ *adj* concerned with practical results and values; treating things in a matter-of-fact or practical way. 關心實際之效果及價值的;實事求是的;實用主義的;重實效的。 **prag·mati·cally** /-klɪ ; -klɪ/ *adv*

prag·ma·tism /ˈprægmətɪzəm ; ˈprægməˌtɪzəm/ *n* [U] **1** (phil) belief or theory that the truth or value of a conception or assertion depends upon its practical bearing upon human interests. (哲)實用主義(認爲概念或主張之眞理或價值,係以其對人生利益之實效爲依歸)。 **2** dogmatism; officiousness; pedantry. 獨斷;好管閒事;裝腔作勢。 **prag·ma·tist** /-tɪst ; -tɪst/ *n* believer in ~(1). 實用主義者。

prairie /ˈpreərɪ ; ˈprɛrɪ/ *n* wide area of level land with grass but no trees, esp in N America. (尤指北美洲無樹木的)大草原。 ⇨ pampas, savanna, steppe, veld.

praise /preɪz ; prez/ *vt* [VP6A] **1** speak with approval of; say that one admires: 稱讚;讚美: *~ a man for his courage.* 讚美一個人的英勇。*Our guests ~d the meal as the best they had had for years.* 我們的客人稱讚說,這是他們多年來所吃過的最好的一頓飯。**2** give honour and glory to (God). 讚頌(神)。 □ *n* **1** [U] act of praising: 稱讚;讚美: *His heroism is worthy of great ~/is beyond* (= too great for) ~. 他的英勇值得大大讚揚(是讚不盡的)。*The leader spoke in ~ of the man who had given his life for the cause.* 領袖稱讚那位爲主義捐軀的人。 **2** (*pl*) (複) ***sing sb's/one's own ~s,*** ~ him/oneself enthusiastically. 熱烈頌揚某人(自己)。 **3** [U] worship; glory: 崇拜;榮耀: *P~ be to God.* 榮耀歸於上帝。*P~ be!* Thank goodness! 謝天謝地! ˈ**~worthy** /-wɜːðɪ ; -ˌwɝðɪ/ *adj* deserving ~. 值得稱讚的; 值得讚美的。 ˈ**~·worth·ily** /-ɪlɪ ; -əlɪ/ *adv* ˈ**~·worthi·ness** *n*

pram /præm ; præm/ *n* (GB) (short for, and the usu word for) perambulator. (英) perambulator 之常用略語。

prance /prɑːns *US:* præns ; præns/ *vi* [VP2A, C] ~ ***(about),*** **1** (of a horse) move forwards jerkily, by raising the forelegs and springing from the hind legs. (指馬)(前足離地而以後足向前)騰躍。 **2** (fig) move, carry oneself, in an arrogant manner; dance or jump happily and gaily. (喻)昂然而行;擧止驕傲;歡躍。□ *n* prancing movement. (馬的)騰躍;(喻)昂然而行;歡躍。

prank /præŋk ; præŋk/ *n* [C] playful or mischievous trick: 開玩笑;惡作劇: *play ~s on sb.* 戲弄某人。

prate /preɪt ; pret/ *vi* [VP2A, C] talk (foolishly); talk too much: 談;空談;瞎談;喋喋不休: *a silly young fellow prating about a subject of which he knows nothing.* 對自己一無所知的題目大談特談的一位愚昧的年輕人。

prattle /ˈprætl ; ˈprætl/ *vi* [VP2A, C] (of a child) talk in a simple, artless way; (of adults) talk in a childish, simple way; chatter. (指小孩)自然而天眞地談話; (指成人) 像小孩一般天眞地談話; 喋喋不休。 □ *n* [U] such talk. 自然而天眞的談話;孩子氣的話。 **prat·tler** /ˈprætlə(r) ; ˈprætlɚ/ *n* one who ~s. 談話天眞者;喋喋不休者。

prawn /prɔːn ; prɔn/ *n* [C] edible shellfish like a large shrimp: 大蝦;斑節蝦: *a dish of curried ~s.* 一盤咖哩大蝦。□ *vi* fish for ~s: 捕大蝦: *go ~ing.* 去捉大蝦。

pray /preɪ ; pre/ *vt, vi* **1** [VP2A, 3A] ~ ***(to God) (for sth),*** commune with God; offer thanks, make requests known: 祈禱;禱告;感恩;祈求: *~ to God for help.* 祈求神賜予援助。*They knelt down and ~ed.* 他們跪下祈禱。 *The farmers are ~ing for rain.* 農夫正在求雨。*He's past ~ing for,* There now seems to be little hope for his recovery, eg from illness, or from some fault, etc. 他已無藥可救了(爲他禱告是無用的,如已病入膏肓,或積重難返等)。 **2** [VP17, 14, 11] ~ ***sb for sth/to do sth,*** (liter, rhet) ask sb as a favour: (文,修辭)乞求;懇求(某人)幫忙做(某事): *I ~ you to think again.* 我求你再想一想。 *We ~ you for mercy/to show mercy.* 我們懇求你發慈悲。 *We ~ you that the prisoner may be set free.* 我們懇求你釋放犯人。 **3** (formal request equivalent to) please: (正式的請求,相當於 please)請: *P~ don't speak so loud.* 請勿大聲說話。

prayer /preə(r) ; prɛr/ *n* **1** [U] act of praying to God: 祈禱;禱告: *He knelt down in ~.* 他跪下禱告。 **2** [U] form of church worship: 敎堂之祈禱式: *Morning/Evening P~.* 早(晚)禱。 **3** [C] form of words used in praying: 祈禱文: *the Lord's P~.* 主禱文。 ⇨ lord; request or petition (spoken or unspoken) to God: 對上帝之懇求或祈禱(包括說出或未說出的): *say one's ~s;* 祈禱;禱告; *family ~s;* 家庭禱告; *a ~ for rain.* 求雨。 ˈ**~-book** *n* book containing ~s for use in church services, etc. 祈禱書。 **the** ˈ**P~ Book,** (also called 亦稱作 *Book of Common P~*) the one used in Church of England services. (英國國敎的)祈禱書。ˈ**~-meeting** *n* meeting at which those present offer up ~s to God in turn. 祈禱會(參加者輪流向神祈禱)。 ˈ**~-rug/-mat** *n* small rug used by Muslims to kneel on when they pray. 回敎徒跪下祈禱時所用的小塊氈子(墊子)。ˈ**~-wheel** *n* revolving cylinder inscribed with or containing ~s, used by the Buddhists of Tibet. (西藏喇嘛敎徒所用的)祈禱輪;地藏車。

pre- /priː ; pri/ *pref* before; beforehand: 在…之先;前;預先: *pre-war;* 戰前的; *a pre-amplifier;* 前置放大器; *pre-natal;* 出生前的;胎兒期的; *pre-arrange.* 預先安排。 ⇨ App 3. 參看附錄三。

preach /priːtʃ ; pritʃ/ *vt, vi* **1** [VP6A, 2A, B, C, 3A] ~ ***(to),*** deliver (a sermon); make known (a religious doctrine, etc); give a talk (esp in church) about religion or morals: 講(道);傳佈(敎旨等);(尤指在敎堂)佈道;傳敎: *~ the gospel;* 傳佈福音; *~ Buddhism;* 宣揚佛敎; *~ against covetousness;* 講道指摘貪婪; *~ for two hours.* 講道達二小時。 **2** [VP3A, 12A, 13A] ~ ***(to),*** give moral advice: 勸誡;說敎: *the headmaster ~ing to his pupils.* 對學童們諄諄勸誡的校長。 *Don't ~ me a sermon about being lazy now, please.* 請勿現在對我講有關懶惰的大道理。 **3** [VP6A] urge; recommend (as right or desirable): (認爲正當或有價值而)鼓吹;倡導: *The Dictator ~ed war as a means of making the country great.* 那位獨裁者鼓吹戰爭爲强國的一種手段。**~er** *n* one who ~es (esp sermons). 說敎者;鼓吹者;(尤指)傳敎者;講道者。ˈ**~·ify** /-ɪfaɪ ; -əˌfaɪ/ *vi* (*pt, pp* -fied) ~, esp(2); moralize in a tedious way. 講道;(尤指)勸誡;說敎;嘮叨地敎誨。

pre·amble /priːˈæmbl ; ˈpriæmbl/ *n* introduction or preliminary statement (esp to a formal document). 序言;(尤指法律文件的)序文。

pre·arrange /ˌpriːəˈreɪndʒ ; ˌpriəˈrendʒ/ *vt* arrange in advance. 事前安排。**~·ment** *n*

preb·end /ˈprebənd ; ˈprɛbənd/ *n* (eccles) part of the revenue of a church granted as a stipend to a priest. (敎會)敎會之收入中撥爲牧師或神父薪俸之部分。 **preb·en·dary** /ˈprebəndrɪ *US:* -derɪ ; ˈprɛbəndˌɛrɪ/ *n* (*pl* -ries) priest who receives a ~. 受俸牧師或神父。

pre·cari·ous /prɪˈkeərɪəs ; prɪˈkɛrɪəs/ *adj* (formal)

uncertain; unsafe; depending upon chance: (正式用語)不穩定的;不確定的;危險的;隨機會而定的: *make a ~ living as an author.* 當一名作家,維持着不穩定的生計。~**·ly** *adv*

pre·cast /ˌpriːˈkɑːst *US:* -ˈkæst ; prɪˈkæst/ *adj* (of concrete) cast into blocks ready for use in building. (指水泥)預凝成塊的;預鑄的。

pre·caution /prɪˈkɔːʃn ; prɪˈkɔʃən/ *n* [U] care taken in advance to avoid a risk; [C] instance of this: 預防;防備;預防或防備的實例: *take an umbrella as a ~;* 帶傘以爲防備; *take ~s against fire;* 採取防火的措施; *insure one's house as a measure of ~.* 給房屋保險作爲預防的措施。~**·ary** /ˌprɪˈkɔːʃənərɪ *US:* -nerɪ ; prɪˈkɔʃənˌɛrɪ/ *adj* for the sake of ~. 爲了預防的;防備的。

pre·cede /prɪˈsiːd ; prɪˈsid/ *vt, vi* [VP6A, 2A] come or go before (in time, place or order): (在時間,位置或順序上) 在前;居先;先於: *the calm that ~d the storm;* 暴風雨前的平靜; *the Mayor, ~d by the mace-bearer;* 市長,由持權杖者前導; *in the preceding paragraph/the paragraph that ~s.* 在前一段裡(在上一段裡)。**pre·ced·ing** *adj* existing or coming before. 在前的;在先的。

pre·ced·ence /ˈpresɪdəns ; prɪˈsidn̩s/ *n* [U] (right to a) priority, or to a senior place. 在前;居先;優越;優先權。***have/take ~ (over)***: 在…之上;優於: *questions which take ~ over all others,* which must be considered first. 必須在所有其他問題之先加以考慮的一些問題(必須優先考慮的問題)。

pre·ced·ent /ˈpresɪdənt ; ˈprɛsədənt/ *n* earlier happening, decision, etc taken as an example or rule for what comes later. 先例;前例。***set/create/establish a ~ (for sth)***: 開創(某事的)先例: *Is there a ~ for what you want me to do?* 你要我做的事有前例可援嗎? ~**ed** *adj* having, supported by, a ~. 有先例的;有前例可援的。

pre·cen·tor /prɪˈsentə(r) ; prɪˈsɛntɚ/ *n* (eccles) person in general control of the singing. (教會)領唱之人。

pre·cept /ˈpriːsept ; ˈprisɛpt/ *n* **1** [U] moral instruction: 道德上的箴言;告誡;教訓: *Example is better than ~.* 以身作則勝於口頭告誡(言教不如身教)。**2** [C] rule or guide, esp for behaviour. (尤指行爲的)規範;教訓;戒律;格言。

pre·cep·tor /prɪˈseptə(r) ; prɪˈsɛptɚ/ *n* (formal) teacher; instructor. (正式用語)教師;導師。

pre·cession /prɪˈseʃn ; priˈsɛʃən/ *n* ***~ of the equinoxes,*** change by which the equinoxes occur earlier in each successive year. 歲差(每年二分點提早發生之變化)。

pre·cinct /ˈpriːsɪŋkt ; ˈprisɪŋkt/ *n* [C] **1** space enclosed by outer walls or boundaries, esp of a cathedral or church: (尤指教堂的)界域;境域: *within the sacred ~s.* 在(教堂之)神聖的境域內。**2** (US) subdivision of a county or city or ward: (美)郡,市或區的次級區分;轄區: *an eˈlection ~;* 選舉區; *a poˈlice ~.* 警察的轄區。**3** (*pl*) neighbourhood or environs (of a town). (複)(城市的)附近;周圍;市郊。**4** boundary: 界限;範圍: *within the city ~s.* 在市區範圍內。**5** area of which the use is in some way restricted. 使用上受限制的地區。**pedestrian ~,** where vehicles are not allowed. 行人區;不准車輛行駛之地區。**ˈshopping ~,** for shops only. 商店區。

pre·ci·os·ity /ˌpreʃɪˈɒsətɪ ; ˌprɛʃɪˈɑsətɪ/ *n* [U] over-refinement; being precious(4); [C] (*pl* -ties) instance of this. (言語,手藝等之)過於講究;過於細心;過於細膩;矯揉造作。

precious /ˈpreʃəs ; ˈprɛʃəs/ *adj* **1** of great value and beauty: 貴重的;寶貴的: *the ~ metals,* gold, platinum; 貴金屬(金,鉑); *~ stones,* diamonds, rubies, etc. 寶石(鑽石,紅寶石等)。**2** highly valued; dear: 珍愛的;可愛的: *Her children are very ~ to her.* 她極疼愛她的孩子。**3** (colloq) (as in intensive) complete: (俗)(用於加强語氣)完全的;徹底的: *a ~ fool.* 大傻瓜。*It cost a ~ sight more than I could afford,* very much more. 它的價格遠超出我所能負擔的。**4** (of language, workmanship, etc) over-refined; affected. (指言語,手藝等)過於講究的;過於細心的;矯揉造作的。□ *adv* (colloq) very: (俗)很;甚: *I have ~ little* (= hardly any) *money left.* 我沒剩下什麼錢了。~**·ly** *adv* ~**·ness** *n*

preci·pice /ˈpresɪpɪs ; ˈprɛsəpɪs/ *n* vertical or very steep face of a rock, cliff or mountain. 懸崖;絕壁。

pre·cipi·tate /prɪˈsɪpɪteɪt ; prɪˈsɪpəˌtet/ *vt* [VP6A, 14] **1** throw or send (sb or sth) violently down from a height. (自高處)將(某人或某物)猛然摔下;猛投。***~ sb/sth into sth,*** thrust violently into (a condition): 使突然陷入某種狀態: *~ the country into war.* 使國家突然陷入戰爭。**2** cause (an event) to happen suddenly, quickly, or in haste: 使(事件)突然,迅速或急促地發生: *~ a crisis;* 突然引起危機; *events that ~d his ruin.* 使其突然破產的事件。**3** (chem) separate (solid matter) from a solution. (化學)使(固體)沉澱。**4** condense (vapour) into drops which fall as rain, dew, etc. 使(水氣)凝爲雨,露等。□ *n* that which is ~d as solid matter, rainfall, etc. 沉澱物;凝結物(如雨等)。□ *adj* /prɪˈsɪpɪtət ; prɪˈsɪpəˌtet/ violently hurried; hasty; (doing things, done) without enough thought. 急促的;匆忙的;鹵莽的;未多加考慮的。~**·ly** *adv*

pre·cipi·ta·tion /prɪˌsɪpɪˈteɪʃn ; prɪˌsɪpəˈteʃən/ *n* **1** (esp) fall of rain, sleet, snow or hail; amount of this: (尤指)雨,霙,雪或雹之下降;其降量;雨量: *the annual ~ in the Lake District;* 大湖區每年的雨量; *a heavy ~.* 一陣大雨。**2** [U] violent haste or being violently hurried: 急促;鹵莽: *act with ~,* without enough thought or consideration of the consequences. 鹵莽行事。**3** act of precipitating. 猛擲;猛投;加速;促進;沉澱;凝結。

pre·cipi·tous /prɪˈsɪpɪtəs ; prɪˈsɪpətəs/ *adj* (formal) like a precipice; very steep. (正式用語)似懸崖的;陡峭的;險峻的。~**·ly** *adv*

pré·cis /ˈpreɪsiː *US:* preɪˈsiː ; preˈsi/ *n* (*pl* unchanged in spelling, pronunciation /-iːz ; -iz/) restatement in shortened form of the chief ideas, points, etc of a speech or piece of writing. (複數的拼法不變,讀作 /ˈpreɪsiːz ; preˈsiz/) (演說或文章之)摘要;大綱;梗概。□ *vt* make a ~ of. 寫大綱;摘要。

pre·cise /prɪˈsaɪs ; prɪˈsaɪs/ *adj* **1** exact; correctly and clearly stated; free from error: 精確的;敍述正確的;明白的;無誤的: *~ measurements;* 精確的尺寸; *~ orders;* 嚴格的命令; *at the ~ moment when I lifted the receiver.* 正好在我拿起聽筒的時刻。**2** taking care to be exact, not to make errors: 小心謹愼的;注意不犯錯的: *a very ~ man;* 非常嚴謹的人; too careful, fussy, about details: 對細節過於小心或挑剔的;斤斤計較的: *prim and ~ in his manner.* 他在態度上拘泥而斤斤計較。~**·ly** *adv* **1** in a ~ manner; exactly: 精確地;明白地;謹慎地;無錯誤地;斤斤計較地: *state the facts ~ly;* 明白地敍述事實; *at 2 o'clock ~ly.* 恰好在兩點鐘。**2** (as a response, agreeing with sb) quite so. (用作同意某人之答語)對;正是如此;一點不錯。~**·ness** *n*

pre·ci·sion /prɪˈsɪʒn ; prɪˈsɪʒən/ *n* [U] accuracy; freedom from error: 精確(度);正確: (attrib) (形容用法) *~ instruments/tools,* those, used in technical work, that are very precise (for measuring, etc); 精密儀器(工具); *~ bombing.* 正確轟炸;精密轟炸。

pre·clude /prɪˈkluːd ; prɪˈklud/ *vt* [VP6A, C, 14] ***~ sb from doing sth,*** prevent; make impossible: 阻止某人做某事;使不可能: *~ all doubts/misunderstanding.* 排除所有疑慮(誤解)。**pre·clu·sion** /prɪˈkluːʒn ; prɪˈkluʒən/ *n*

pre·co·cious /prɪˈkəʊʃəs ; prɪˈkoʃəs/ *adj* **1** (of a person) having developed certain faculties earlier than is normal: (指人)早熟的: *a ~ child,* eg one who reads well at the age of three. 早熟的孩子(如三歲時即能閱讀書籍)。**2** (of actions, knowledge, etc) marked by such development. (指行爲,知識等)早熟的;像大人的;過早的。~**·ly** *adv* ~**·ness, pre·coc·ity**

/prɪˈkɒsətɪ ; prɪˈkɑsətɪ/ *nn* [U] being ~. 早熟。

pre·cog·ni·tion /ˌpriːkɒɡˈnɪʃn ; ˌprikɑɡˈnɪʃən/ *n* [U] knowledge of sth before it occurs. 預知;先知。

pre·con·ceive /ˌpriːkənˈsiːv ; ˌprikənˈsiv/ *vt* [VP6A] form (ideas, opinions) in advance (before getting knowledge or experience): 預想;(在未獲得對某事物之知識或經驗前)預先形成(概念，意見): *visit a foreign country with ~d ideas.* 懷着成見訪問外國。 **pre·con·cep·tion** /ˌpriːkənˈsepʃn ; ˌprikənˈsɛpʃən/ *n* [U, C] ~d idea. 預想;先入之見;成見。

pre·con·certed /ˌpriːkənˈsɜːtɪd ; ˌprikənˈsɝtɪd/ *adj* (formal) agreed in advance: (正式用語)事先同意的;預定的: *following ~ plans.* 依照預定的計畫。

pre·con·di·tion /ˌpriːkənˈdɪʃn ; ˌprikənˈdɪʃən/ *n* = prerequisite.

pre·cur·sor /ˌpriːˈkɜːsə(r) ; prɪˈkɝsɚ/ *n* [C] (formal) person or thing coming before, as a sign of what is to follow. (正式用語)先驅;先兆。 **pre·cur·sory** /-sərɪ ; -sərɪ/ *adj* preliminary; anticipating. 前驅的;先鋒的;預兆的;前兆的。

preda·tory /ˈpredətrɪ *US:* -tɔːrɪ ; ˈprɛdəˌtorɪ/ *adj* (formal) (正式用語) **1** (of people) plundering and robbing: (指人)搶刼的;掠奪的: *~ tribesmen/habits;* 以掠奪爲生的部族(掠奪的習慣); *~ incursions,* raids made for plunder. 掠奪性的侵襲。 **2** (of animals) preying upon others. (指動物)食肉的。 **pred·ator** /-tə(r) ; -tɚ/ *n* ~ animal. 食肉動物。

pre·de·cease /ˌpriːdɪˈsiːs ; ˌpridɪˈsis/ *vt* (legal) die before (another person). (法律)死於(某人)之先。

pre·de·cessor /ˈpriːdɪsesə(r) *US:* ˈpredɪ- ; ˌprɛdɪˈsɛsɚ/ *n* **1** former holder of any office or position: (某職位的)前任: *Mr Green's ~ in office.* 格林先生所任職位的前任。 **2** thing to which another has succeeded: 原有的事物: *Is the new proposal any better than its ~?* 新提議比原提議好嗎?

pre·des·ti·nate /ˌpriːˈdestɪneɪt ; prɪˈdɛstənɪt/ *adj* foreordained by God; fated. 神預先安排的;命中注定的。□ *vt* = predestine(1).

pre·des·ti·na·tion /ˌpriːdestɪˈneɪʃn ; prɪˌdɛstəˈneʃən/ *n* **1** theory or doctrine that God has decreed from eternity that part of mankind shall have eternal bliss and part eternal punishment. 命定論;宿命論(認爲神早已預定某部分人類將得永遠幸福,某部分人類將萬刼不復)。 **2** destiny; doctrine that God has decreed everything that comes to pass. 命運;一切事物均已由神定說。

pre·des·tine /ˌpriːˈdestɪn ; prɪˈdɛstɪn/ *vt* **1** [VP14, 17] (often passive) (常用被動語態) ~ **sb to sth/to do sth,** (of God, fate) decide, ordain, beforehand; cause (sb) to behave, etc in a certain way. (指神、命運)注定某人做某事;預定。 **2** [VP17] ~ **sb to do sth,** decide or make inevitable: 注定某人做某事: *Everything took place as if he was ~d to succeed.* 他一切順利,似乎注定該成功。 *These events were clearly ~d (to happen).* 這些事件顯然是注定(要發生)的。

pre·de·ter·mine /ˌpriːdɪˈtɜːmɪn ; ˌpridɪˈtɝmɪn/ *vt* (formal) (正式用語) **1** [VP6A] decide in advance: 預先決定: *The social class into which a child is born often seems to ~ his later career.* 嬰兒所出生的社會階層往往能決定他以後的事業。 **2** [VP17] ~ **sb to do sth,** persuade or impel sb in advance to do sth: 預先說服或驅使某人做某事: *Did an unhappy childhood ~ him to behave as he did?* 是否係不愉快的童年驅使他這麼做? **pre·de·ter·mi·na·tion** /ˌpriːdɪˌtɜːmɪˈneɪʃn ; ˌpridɪˌtɝməˈneʃən/ *n*

pre·dica·ment /prɪˈdɪkəmənt ; prɪˈdɪkəmənt/ *n* difficult or unpleasant situation from which escape seems difficult: 苦境; 困境; 窮境; 險境: *be in an awkward ~.* 處於困境中。

predi·cate[1] /ˈpredɪkət ; ˈprɛdɪkɪt/ *n* (gram) part of a statement which says sth about the subject, eg 'is short' in 'Life is short'. (文法)述語;述詞(如 'Life is short' 中之 'is short' 卽爲述詞)。

predi·cate[2] /ˈpredɪkeɪt ; ˈprɛdɪˌket/ *vt* (formal) (正式用語) **1** [VP6A, 17, 9] declare to be true or real: 宣稱…爲眞實;斷言: *~ of a motive that it is good;* 斷言某動機是好的; *~ a motive to be good.* 斷言某動機是好的。 **2** [VP6A] make necessary as a consequence: 使成爲必然的結果: *These policies were ~d by Britain's decision to join the Common Market.* 這些措施是英國決定加入共同市場的必然結果。

pre·di·cat·ive /prɪˈdɪkətɪv *US:* ˈpredɪkeɪtɪv ; ˈprɛdɪˌketɪv/ *adj* (gram, of an *adj* or *n*, opposed to *attrib*) forming part or the whole of the predicate. (文法,指形容詞或名詞,與 attributive 相反)敍述的;表述的。 ~ **adjective,** one used only in the predicate, eg *asleep, alive.* (僅用於述詞中的)敍述形容詞(如 asleep, alive)。

pre·dict /prɪˈdɪkt ; prɪˈdɪkt/ *vt* [VP6A, 9, 10] say, tell in advance: 預言;預測;預示: *~ a good harvest;* 預示豐收; *~ that there will be an earthquake.* 預測將有地震。 **pre·dic·tion** /prɪˈdɪkʃn ; prɪˈdɪkʃən/ *n* [U] ~ing; [C] sth ~ed; prophecy. 預言;預示;預言或預示將要發生之事物。 **~·able** /-əbl ; -əbl/ *adj* that can be ~ed. 可預言的; 可預測的; 可預示的。 **~or** /-tə(r) ; -tɚ/ *n* instrument or device that ~s, eg one used in war to determine when to open anti-aircraft fire. 測位器;位置預測器(如戰時用的高射瞄準器)。 **~a·bil·ity** /prɪˌdɪktəˈbɪlətɪ ; prɪˌdɪktəˈbɪlətɪ/ *n*

pre·di·gest /ˌpriːdaɪˈdʒest ; ˌpridəˈdʒɛst/ *vt* treat (food) so that it is easily digested: 處理(食物)以便容易消化: *~ed food for babies.* 經過處理而容易消化的嬰兒食物。

pre·di·lec·tion /ˌpriːdɪˈlekʃn *US:* ˌpredlˈek- ; ˌpridl̩ˈɛkʃən/ *n* [C] **a ~ for,** special liking, mental preference. 偏愛;偏好。

pre·dis·pose /ˌpriːdɪˈspəʊz ; ˌpridɪsˈpoz/ *vt* [VP14, 17] ~ **sb to sth/to do sth,** (formal) cause (sb) to be inclined or liable before the event: (正式用語) 使先傾向於; 使先偏向於; 使偏愛; 使易罹染: *His early training ~d him to a life of adventure/to travel widely.* 他早年所受的教養使他偏愛冒險生活(到處旅行)。 *I find myself ~d in his favour,* inclined to favour him. 我發現自己對他有所偏愛。

pre·dis·posi·tion /ˌpriːdɪspəˈzɪʃn ; ˌpridɪspəˈzɪʃən/ *n* [C] ~ **to sth/to do sth,** state of mind or body favourable to: (身心的)傾向;愛好;偏好;癖性;易…之體質: *a ~ to arthritis;* 易罹關節炎的體質; *a ~ to find fault.* 吹毛求疵的癖性。

pre·domi·nant /prɪˈdɒmɪnənt ; prɪˈdɑmənənt/ *adj* ~ **(over),** (formal) having more power or influence than others; prevailing, conspicuous: (正式用語)有勢力的;優勢的; 主要的;卓越的; 支配的;流行的;顯著的: *The ~ feature of his character was pride.* 他的性格的主要特色是驕傲。 **~·ly** *adv* in a ~ manner: 有較大之力量或影響地;主要地;卓越地;顯著地: *a ~ly brown-eyed race.* 棕色眼睛佔大多數的民族。 **pre·domi·nance** /-əns ; -əns/ *n* [U] superiority in strength, numbers, etc; state of being ~. (力量,數量等的)優越;卓越;支配;顯著。

pre·domi·nate /prɪˈdɒmɪneɪt ; prɪˈdɑməˌnet/ *vi* [VP2A, 3A] ~ **(over),** (formal) have or exert control (over); be superior in numbers, strength, influence, etc: (正式用語)統治; 支配; (在數量,力量,勢力等上)佔優勢: *a forest in which oak-trees ~.* 橡樹爲主的森林。

pre-emi·nent /ˌpriːˈemɪnənt ; prɪˈɛmənənt/ *adj* excelling others; best of all: 超羣的;最好的;優秀的;卓越的: *~ above all his rivals.* 超越他所有的敵手。 **~·ly** *adv* **pre-emi·nence** /-əns ; -əns/ *n* [U].

pre-empt /ˌpriːˈempt ; prɪˈɛmpt/ *vt* [VP6A] (formal) (正式用語) **1** obtain by pre-emption. 以優先購買權取得。 **2** (US) occupy (public land) so as to have the right of pre-emption. (美)佔用(公地)以取得優先購買權。 **pre-emp·tion** /ˌpriːˈempʃn ; prɪˈɛmpʃən/ *n* [U] (formal) purchase by one person, etc before others are offered the chance to buy; right to purchase in this way; the obtaining of sth in advance. (正式用語)先買(權);優先購買(權);搶

先取得。**pre·emp·tive** /-tɪv ; -tɪv/ *adj* relating to pre-emption: 先買(權)的；優先的： *a ~ bid,* (in bridge) one intended to be high enough to prevent further bidding; (橋牌)爲吃住對方儘量叫大牌； *a ~ 'air strike,* eg by bombing, against forces considered likely to attack. 先發制人之空襲(爲預防敵人攻擊而先向敵人實施的轟炸等)。

preen /priːn ; prin/ *vt* **1** [VP6A] (of a bird) smooth (itself, its feathers) with its beak. (指鳥)以喙整理(羽毛)。 **2** [VP6A, 14] (of a person) tidy (oneself). (指人)打扮(自己)。 *~ **oneself on,*** (fig) pride oneself (on); show self-satisfaction. (喻)以…自傲；顯出自滿。

pre-exist /ˌpriː ɪɡˈzɪst ; ˌpriɪɡˈzɪst/ *vi* [VP2A] exist beforehand; live a life before this life. 先存；先在；存在於前世。 **~·ence** /-əns ; -əns/ *n* life of the soul before entering its present body or this world. 前生；前世 (靈魂進入今生前的生命)。 **~·ent** /-ənt ; -ənt/ *adj* existing in a former life or previously. 在前世存在的；以前存在的。

pre·fab /ˈpriːfæb *US:* ˌpriːˈfæb ; ˌpriˈfæb/ *n* [C] (colloq abbr of) prefabricated house. (俗)活動房屋；預鑄房屋(爲 prefabricated house 之略)。

pre·fab·ri·cate /ˌpriːˈfæbrɪkeɪt ; priˈfæbrəˌket/ *vt* [VP6A] manufacture the parts, eg roofs, walls, fitments, of a building, a ship, etc before they are put together on the site, in the yards, etc: 預先建造(房屋，船等的)組成部分(如房頂，牆，鑲造部分)以便在基地，工場等處裝架： *~d houses;* 活動房屋；預鑄房屋； *a ~d school.* 活動校舍。 **pre·fab·ri·ca·tion** /ˌpriːfæbrɪˈkeɪʃn ; prɪˌfæbrɪˈkeʃən/ *n*

pref·ace /ˈprefɪs ; ˈprɛfɪs/ *n* [C] author's explanatory remarks at the beginning of a book; preliminary part of a speech: (書籍之)序言；序文；(演講之)開場白；開端： *write a ~ to a book.* 寫一本書的序言。 □ *vt* [VP14] *~ **sth with sth/by doing sth,*** provide with a ~; begin (a talk, etc) with a ~: 給…作序；以…作(講話等的)開端： *The chairman ~d his remarks with some sharp raps on the table.* 主席重重地敲了幾下桌子，然後開始講話。 **prefa·tory** /ˈprefətrɪ *US:* -tɔːrɪ ; ˈprɛfəˌtorɪ/ *adj* of or in the nature of a ~: 序言的；開端的；序言或開端性質的： *after a few prefatory remarks.* 在幾句開場白之後。

pre·fect /ˈpriːfekt ; ˈprifɛkt/ *n* **1** (in ancient Rome) title of various civil and military officers; governor. (古羅馬)某些文武官員的頭銜；行政長官；司令官。 **2** (in France, Japan) title of the chief administrative officer of a department; head of the Paris police. (法國及日本之)最高行政長官；首長；巴黎的警察局長。 **3** (in some English schools) one of a number of senior pupils given responsibility, eg for keeping order. (英國若干學校之)級長；領導生；(負責維持紀律等的)高年級生。

pre·fec·ture /ˈpriːfektjʊə(r) *US:* -tʃər ; ˈprifɛktʃə/ *n* **1** administrative area in some countries, eg France, Japan. (法，日等國之)省；郡；州(最大的地方行政區劃)。 ⇨ county (in GB). **2** (in France) place or office where a prefect(2) works; his official residence. (法國) 省長或巴黎警察局長之官署；其官邸。 **3** position of a prefect(1); period of office. (古羅馬)行政長官或司令官之職位；其任期。 **pre·fec·tural** /priːˈfektʃərəl; prɪˈfɛktʃərəl/ *adj* of a ~: 省(州)的；省長 (或巴黎警察局長) 之官署或官邸的；古羅馬地方行政長官之職位或任期的： *the prefectural offices.* 地方官署。

pre·fer /prɪˈfɜː(r) ; prɪˈfɝ/ *vt* (-rr-) **1** [VP6A, D, 7A, 9, 14, 17] *~ **(to),*** choose rather; like better: 較喜歡；寧願： *Which would you ~, tea or coffee?* 你比較喜歡喝茶，還是喝咖啡？ *I ~ walking to cycling.* 我喜愛步行勝過騎單車。 *He ~s to write his letters rather than dictate them.* 他喜歡自己寫信，不願口授自己的信。 *I should ~ to wait until evening.* 我願意等到天黑。 *I should ~ you not to go/that you did not go there alone.* 我倒希望你不要單獨前往。 **2** [VP6A, 14] *~ **a charge/charges (against sb),*** put forward, submit: 提出控告；告發(某人)： *~ a charge against a motorist,* ie accuse him of sth. 控告駕駛汽車者。 **3** [VP6A, 14] *~ **sb (to sth),*** appoint (sb) (to a higher position). 擢陞(某人)(至較高之職位)。 **~·able** /ˈprefrəbl ; ˈprɛfrəbl̩/ *adj* (not used with *more*) *~ **(to),*** superior; to be ~red. (不可與 more 連用)優越的；較好的；較合人意的。 **~·ably** /ˈprefrəblɪ ; ˈprɛfrəblɪ/ *adv*

pref·er·ence /ˈprefrəns ; ˈprɛfərəns/ *n* **1** [C, U] act of preferring: 較喜歡；寧願；喜愛： *have a ~ for French novels.* 喜讀法國小說。 *I should choose this in ~ to any other.* 我寧願選擇這個而不要其他的。 **2** [C] that which is preferred: 喜愛物；嗜好物： *What are your ~s?* 你喜愛些什麼？ **3** [U] the favouring of one person, country, etc more than another (in business relations, etc esp by admitting imports at a lower import duty); [C] instance of this: (在商務關係上給予某人，某國等的)優先權；優待；(尤指准許課以較低之進口稅的)特惠；優待或特惠的實例： *give sb ~ (over others).* 給某人(較他人)優待。 **4** **'P~ Stock,** stock on which dividend payments must be made before profits are distributed to holders of Ordinary Stock. 優先股(對股利之分配較普通股享有優先權)。

pref·er·en·tial /ˌprefəˈrenʃl ; ˌprɛfəˈrɛnʃəl/ *adj* of, giving, receiving preference; (eg of import duties, etc) favouring particular countries: 優先的；給予優先的；得到優先的；(指進口稅等之)特惠的： *get ~ treatment.* 享受優先的待遇。

pre·fer·ment /prɪˈfɜːmənt ; prɪˈfɝmənt/ *n* [U] act of preferring(3); promotion or advancement: 擢陞；晉級： *~ to a directorship.* 擢陞爲董事。

pre·fig·ure /ˌpriːˈfɪɡə(r) *US:* -ɡjər ; priˈfɪɡjə/ *vt* (formal) (正式用語) **1** [VP6A] represent beforehand; show (what is coming). 預表；預示。 **2** [VP 6A, 9, 10] imagine, picture to oneself, beforehand. 預想。

pre·fix /ˈpriːfɪks ; ˈpriˌfɪks/ *n* **1** (abbr *pref* in this dictionary) word or syllable, eg *pre-, co-,* placed in front of a word to add to or change its meaning. (本字典略爲 pref)字首(加於一字之前，以增加或改變其意義的字或音節，如 pre-, co-)。 ⇨ App 3. 參看附錄三。 **2** word used before a person's name, eg Mr, Dr. 人名前用的尊稱(如 Mr, Dr)。 □ *vt* /ˌpriːˈfɪks ; priˈfɪks/ [VP6A, 14] *~ **sth (to sth),*** add a ~ to or in front of; add at the beginning: 置字首或尊稱於…之前；加在前頭： *~ a new paragraph to Chapter Ten.* 在第十章的前頭新加一段。

preg·nant /ˈpregnənt ; ˈprɛgnənt/ *adj* **1** (of a woman or female animal) having in the uterus offspring in a stage of development before birth. (指女人或雌性動物) 懷孕的；有胎的。 **2** (of words, actions) significant; full of promise. (指文字，行動)重要的；富有意義的；可望成功的。 *~ **with,*** filled with: 充滿着： *words ~ with meaning;* 富有意義之言辭； certain or likely to have: 一定或可能會有的： *political events ~ with consequences.* 可能會產生重大後果的政治事件。 **preg·nancy** /-nənsɪ ; -nənsɪ/ *n* [U] the state of being ~; (fig) fullness; depth; significance; [C] instance of being ~: 懷孕；(喻)豐富；深刻；重大；富有意義；此等之實例： *She's had six pregnancies in six years.* 她在六年中懷孕六次。

pre·hen·sile /ˌpriːˈhensaɪl *US:* -sl ; prɪˈhɛnsl̩/ *adj* (of a foot or tail, eg a monkey's) able to seize and hold. (指猴等的足或尾)能握住的；適於捲纏的。

pre·his·toric /ˌpriːhɪˈstɒrɪk *US:* -tɔːrɪk ; ˌprɪɪsˈtɔrɪk/, **-tori·cal** /-kl ; kl̩/ *adjj* of the time before recorded history. 史前的。 **pre·his·tory** /ˌpriːˈhɪstrɪ ; priˈhɪstrɪ/ *n*

pre·judge /ˌpriːˈdʒʌdʒ ; priˈdʒʌdʒ/ *vt* [VP6A] make up one's mind about a person, cause, action, etc before hearing the evidence, making a proper inquiry, etc. 未經詳究而對(某人，主張，行動等)作判斷；未獲充分證據而作判斷；預斷。 **~·ment** *n*

preju·dice /ˈpredʒʊdɪs ; ˈprɛdʒədɪs/ *n* **1** [U] opinion, like or dislike, formed before one has adequate knowledge or experience; [C] instance of this: 偏見；成見；偏見或成見的實例: *have a ~ against/in favour of modern jazz;* 對現代爵士樂有偏見(偏愛)；*listen to new poems without ~;* 未存成見地聆聽新詩；*racial ~*, against members of other races. 種族偏見；種族歧視。**2** [U] (legal) injury that may or does arise from some action or judgement: (法律)傷害；損害；不利(由某種行爲或判斷所造成或可能造成者): *to the ~ of sb's rights*, with (possible) injury to them. 損及(或可能損及)某人的權利。***without ~ (to)***, without injury to any existing right or claim. (對任何現有的權益)無損害。□ *vt* [VP6A, 15A] ***~ sb (against/in favour of sb/sth)***, **1** cause sb to have a ~(1). 使某人(對某人或某物)有偏見(偏愛)。**2** injure or weaken (sb's interests, etc): 傷害；損害(某人之利益等): *He ~d his claim by asking too much.* 他因需索過度而影響到他所作的要求。**preju·di·cial** /ˌpredʒʊˈdɪʃl ; ˌprɛdʒəˈdɪʃəl/ *adj* ***~ (to)***, causing ~ or injury. 造成偏見或損害的。

prel·acy /ˈpreləsɪ ; ˈprɛləsɪ/ *n* (*pl* -cies) **1** office, rank, see, of a prelate. 主教或高級教士之職位，階級或教區。**2 the ~**, the whole body of prelates. 主教或高級教士團；主教或高級教士(集合用法)。

prel·ate /ˈprelət ; ˈprɛlɪt/ *n* bishop or other churchman of equal or higher rank. 主教；高級教士(與主教平行或高於主教)。

pre·lim /prɪˈlɪm ; prɪˈlɪm/ *n* (colloq abbr for preliminary) (俗，爲 preliminary 之略) **1** preliminary examination. 初試。**2** (*pl*) /ˈpriːlɪmz ; ˈprilɪmz/ pages (with title, contents, etc) preceding the actual text (in a book). (複)(書中)正文前的幾頁(包括書名、目錄等)。

pre·limi·nary /prɪˈlɪmɪnərɪ *US:* -nerɪ ; prɪˈlɪməˌnɛrɪ/ *adj* coming first and preparing for what follows: 初步的；開始的: *a ~ examination;* 初試；*after a few ~ remarks.* 在幾句開場白之後。□ *n* (*pl* -ries) (usu *pl*) ~ actions, measures, etc: (通常用複數)初步的行動，措施等: *the usual preliminaries to a Geneva conference*, eg the wrangling about procedures and agenda. 日內瓦會議之預備會(如對程序和議程的折衝)。

prel·ude /ˈpreljuːd ; ˈprɛljud/ *n* [C] ***~ to***, action, event, etc that serves as an introduction to (another); (music) introductory movement (to a fugue or as part of a suite). 先驅；前奏；序幕；(音樂)序曲；前奏曲。□ *vt* [VP6A] serve as, be, a ~ to. 作爲…之前奏，序幕，先驅。

pre·mari·tal /ˌpriːˈmærɪtl ; priˈmærətl/ *adj* before marriage. 婚前的。

pre·ma·ture /ˈpremətjʊə(r) *US:* ˌpriːməˈtʊər ; ˌpriməˈtjʊr/ *adj* done, happening, doing sth, before the right or usual time: 太早的；未成熟的: *~ decay of the teeth;* 牙齒之過早齲腐；*~ birth;* 早產；*a ~ baby*, one born at less than 38 weeks of pregnancy. 早產的嬰兒(懷孕不到 38 週而產下之嬰兒)。**~·ly** *adv*

pre·medi·tate /ˌpriːˈmedɪteɪt ; prɪˈmɛdəˌtet/ *vt* [VP 6A] consider, plan, (sth) in advance: 預謀；預先考慮或計畫(某事): *a ~d murder.* 預謀的兇殺。**pre·medi·ta·tion** /ˌpriːmedɪˈteɪʃn ; ˌprimɛdəˈteʃən/ *n* [U].

pre·mier /ˈpremɪə(r) *US:* ˈpriːm- ; ˈprimɪɚ/ *adj* first in position, importance, etc. 第一的；首要的。□ *n* prime minister; head of the government. 首相；內閣總理。**ˈ~·ship** /-ʃɪp ; -ˌʃɪp/ *n*

pre·mière /ˈpremɪeə(r) *US:* prɪˈmɪər ; prɪˈmɪr/ *n* first performance of a play or (*ˈfilm-~*) first public showing of a cinema film. (戲劇之)首次公演；(影片之)首次放映(亦作 film-première)。

prem·ise, prem·iss /ˈpremɪs ; ˈprɛmɪs/ *n* **1** statement on which reasoning is based. (爲推理之根據的)前提。**2** each of the two first parts of a syllogism: (三段論法的)前提: *the major ~*, eg 'Boys like fruit'; *the minor ~*, eg 'You are a boy'; the conclusion being 'Therefore you like fruit'. 大前提(如'男孩喜歡水果')；小前提(如'你是男孩')；結論是'所以你喜歡水果'。**3** (*pl*) house or building with its outbuildings, land, etc: (複)房屋連同附屬建築，土地等；房產: *business ~s*, the building(s), offices, etc where a business is carried on; 事務所；辦公室；*to be consumed on the ~s*, eg of alcoholic drinks in a public house or hotel which has no 'off-licence'. 限在店內喝完(如指某些酒店或旅館中出售的酒不得携出飲用)。**4** (*pl*) (legal) details of property, names of persons, etc in the first part of a legal agreement. (複)(法律)契約之緣起或要件(契約的開頭部分記述讓渡財產之詳情、當事人姓名等)。□ *vt* [VP6A, 9] ***~ (sth/that...)***, state by way of introduction. 提論；預述；立前提。

pre·mium /ˈpriːmɪəm ; ˈprimɪəm/ *n* (*pl* ~s) **1** amount or instalment paid for an insurance policy. 保險費(總額或分期攤付之額)。**2** reward; bonus: 報酬；獎金: *a ~ for good conduct.* 品行優良獎。**ˈP~ Bond**, (GB) government bond that offers the chance of prizes (in a draw) instead of the more usual interest¹(6). (英)以抽獎代替一般利息的公債。***put a ~ on sth***, make it advantageous for sb (to behave in a certain way, to do sth): 誘發；鼓勵(某種行爲，行動): *Does high taxation put a ~ on business dishonesty?* 重稅會誘使人做生意不規矩嗎？**3** addition to ordinary charges, wages, rent, etc; bonus: (一般費用，工資，租金等之外的)額外費用；賞金: *He had to pay the agent a ~ before he could rent the house*, an extra sum above the rent. 租用那幢房子以前，他得先付代理人一筆佣金。**4** fee (to be) paid by a pupil to a professional man, eg an accountant or architect, for instruction and training. (生徒付給會計師或建築師等專業人員的)學費；束脩。**5** (of stocks and shares) amount above par value: (指公債及股票)超過票面的價值；溢價: *The shares are selling at a ~.* 這些股票溢價出售。***at a ~***, (fig) highly valued or esteemed. (喻)非常寶貴的；甚受尊敬的。

pre·mon·ition /ˌpriːməˈnɪʃn ; ˌpriməˈnɪʃən/ *n* [C] feeling of uneasiness considered as a warning (of approaching danger, etc): (對於即將來到之危險等的)預感；前兆: *have a ~ of failure.* 有失敗之預感。**pre·moni·tory** /prɪˈmɒnɪtərɪ *US:* -tɔːrɪ ; prɪˈmɑnəˌtorɪ/ *adj*

pre·natal /ˌpriːˈneɪtl ; priˈnetl/ *adj* preceding birth. 出生前的；胎兒期的。

pren·tice /ˈprentɪs ; ˈprɛntɪs/ *n* (old use, short for *apprentice*) (舊用法，爲 apprentice 之略) ***try his ~ hand***, make an unskilled or novice's attempt. 初次嘗試。

pre·oc·cu·pa·tion /ˌpriːɒkjʊˈpeɪʃn ; priˌɑkjəˈpeʃən/ *n* [U] state of mind in which sth takes up all a person's thoughts; [C] the subject, etc that takes up all his thoughts: 全神貫注；出神；使人全神貫注的事物；急務: *His greatest ~ was how to find money for a holiday in Europe.* 他的首急之務是如何籌錢去歐洲度假。

pre·oc·cupy /priːˈɒkjʊpaɪ ; priˈɑkjəˌpaɪ/ *vt* (*pt, pp* -pied) [VP6A] take all the attention of (sb, his mind) so that attention is not given to other matters: 使全神貫注；盤據(心頭)；迷住: *preoccupied by family troubles;* 心神被家庭糾紛盤據着；*preoccupied with thoughts of the coming holidays.* 一心一意想着即將來臨之假期。

pre·or·dain /ˌpriːɔːˈdeɪn ; ˌpriɔrˈden/ *vt* [VP6A, 9] decree or determine in advance. 預先注定；預定。

prep /prep ; prɛp/ *n* (schoolboy slang for) (學童俚語) **1** preparation(3). 課外作業。**2** preparatory school. 預備學校；先修班。

pre-pack·aged /ˌpriːˈpækɪdʒd ; priˈpækɪdʒd/, **pre-packed** /ˌpriːˈpækt ; priˈpækt/ *adjj* (of products) wrapped, packed, before being supplied to shops, etc where they are to be sold. (指產品)(在送往商店等出售前)預先包裝好的。

prep·ara·tion /ˌprepəˈreɪʃn ; ˌprɛpəˈreʃən/ *n* **1** [U] preparing or being prepared: 準備；預備: *The meal* *is in* ~. 飯菜在預備中。*We're getting things together in ~ for the journey*. 我們在收拾東西準備旅行。*Don't try to do it without* ~. 沒準備就不要試着去做。**2** [C] (usu *pl*) things done to get ready for sth: (通常用複數)準備之事務: *~s for war;* 戰備; *make ~s for a voyage.* 做航海之準備。**3** [U] (colloq abbr *prep*) homework. (俗略作 prep)課外作業。**4** [C] kind of medicine, food, etc specially prepared: (特別調製的) 藥劑,食物等;配製品: *pharmaceutical ~s.* 藥劑。

pre·para·tory /prɪˈpærətrɪ *US:* -tɔːrɪ ; prɪˈpærəˌtorɪ/ *adj* introductory; needed for preparing: 初步的;預備的;準備上需要的: ~ *measures/training.* 初步的措施(訓練)。~ ***to,*** in readiness for; before. 作為…之準備;在…之先。ˈ~ **school,** (esp in England) private school where pupils are prepared for entry to a higher school (esp a public school); (US) (usu private) school where pupils are prepared for college. (英國之) 預備學校;預科(尤指使學生準備升入公立學校的私立學校); (美) 大學先修班(通常為私立)。

pre·pare /prɪˈpeə(r) ; prɪˈpɛr/ *vt, vi* **1** [VP6A, 7A, 14, 3A] ~ ***(for),*** get or make ready: 預備;準備: ~ *a meal/one's lessons/a sermon;* 預備飯(功課,講道); ~ *pupils for an examination,* coach them; 指導學生準備考試; ~ *for an attack,* get ready to repel an attack; 準備應付攻擊; ~ *to attack,* get ready to make an attack; 準備攻擊; *be ~d for anything to happen.* 準備好對付任何可能發生的事件。**2** ***be ~d to,*** be able and willing to: 有能力而且願意: *We are ~d to supply the goods you ask for.* 我們能夠而且願意供應你要的貨物。**~d·ness** /prɪˈpeərɪdnɪs ; prɪˈpɛrɪdnɪs/ *n* [U] being ~d: 預備;準備: *Everything was in a state of ~dness.* 一切都準備好了。

pre·pay /ˌpriːˈpeɪ ; priˈpe/ *vt* (*pt, pp* -paid /-ˈpeɪd ; -ˈped/) [VP6A] pay in advance: 預付;先付: *send a telegram with reply prepaid.* 發一電報並預付回電費用。

pre·pon·der·ant /prɪˈpɒndərənt ; prɪˈpɑndərənt/ *adj* (formal) greater in weight, number, strength, etc. (正式用語) (在重量,數量,力量等上)佔優勢的。**~·ly** *adv* **pre·pon·der·ance** /-əns ; -əns/ *n*

pre·pon·der·ate /prɪˈpɒndəreɪt ; prɪˈpɑndəˌret/ *vi* [VP2A, C] (formal) be greater in weight, number, strength, influence, etc: (正式用語) (在重量,數量,力量,影響等上)超過;勝過;壓倒: *reasons that ~ over other considerations.* 需要優先考慮的理由。

prep·osi·tion /ˌprepəˈzɪʃn ; ˌprɛpəˈzɪʃən/ *n* word or group of words (eg *in, from, to, out of, on behalf of*) often placed before a *n* or *pron* to indicate place, direction, source, method, etc. 介詞;前置詞(置於名詞或代名詞之前,以表示位置,方向,來源,方法等,如 in, from, to, out of, on behalf of)。**~al** /-ʃənl ; -ʃənl/ *adj* of, containing, a ~. 介詞的;含有介詞的。**~al phrase, (a)** phrase made up of a group of words used as a ~, (用作介詞之) 介詞片語, eg 如 *in front of, on top of.* **(b)** ~ + the *n* or *n phrase* following it, (用作形容詞或副詞之)介詞片語, eg 如 *in the night, on the beach.*

pre·pos·sess /ˌpriːpəˈzes ; ˌpripəˈzɛs/ *vt* [VP6A, 15A] (formal) give (a person) a feeling (about sth), usu favourable; fill (a person *with* or *by* an idea, a feeling): (正式用語)使有好感;使(某人)充滿(某種思想,感情): *I was ~ed by his appearance and manners,* They made a favourable impression upon me. 他的儀表與舉止給我留下了好印象。**~·ing** *adj* attractive; making a good impression: 吸引人的;給人良好印象的: *a girl of ~ing appearance.* 儀表動人的女郎。**pre·pos·session** /ˌpriːpəˈzeʃn ; ˌpripəˈzɛʃən/ *n* [C] favourable feeling experienced in advance. 預先懷有的好感;偏愛。

pre·pos·ter·ous /prɪˈpɒstərəs ; prɪˈpɑstərəs/ *adj* completely contrary to reason or sense; absurd. 完全與理性或常識相反的;荒謬的;反常的。**~·ly** *adv*

pre·puce /ˈpriːpjuːs ; ˈpripjus/ *n* (anat) foreskin. (解剖)包皮。

pre·re·cord /ˌpriːrɪˈkɔːd ; ˌprirɪˈkɔrd/ *vt* [VP6A] record, eg a radio or TV programme, in advance on tape or discs. 預先錄音或錄影(如廣播或電視節目)。

pre·requi·site /ˌpriːˈrekwɪzɪt ; priˈrɛkwəzɪt/ *n, adj* (thing) required as a condition for sth else: 首要的(事物);必備的(事物);先決條件: *Three passes at 'A' level are a ~ for university entrance/are ~ for university entrance.* 必須有三個科目達到 A 的標準才能進大學。

pre·roga·tive /prɪˈrɒgətɪv ; prɪˈrɑgətɪv/ *n* [C] special right(s) or privilege(s), esp of a ruler: 特權;(尤指)統治者的特權: *the ~ of pardon,* eg to pardon a condemned criminal. 赦免(罪犯)權。**the Royal P~,** (GB) the (theoretical) right of the sovereign to act independently of Parliament. (英)皇室的特權。

pre·sage /ˈpresɪdʒ ; ˈprɛsɪdʒ/ *n* [C] (formal) presentiment; sign looked upon as a warning. (正式用語)預知;預感;預示;預兆。□ *vt* /prɪˈseɪdʒ ; prɪˈsedʒ/ [VP6A] foretell; be a sign of: 預言;預示: *The clouds ~ a storm.* 密雲為暴風雨的先兆。

pres·by·ter /ˈprezbɪtə(r) ; ˈprɛzbɪtɚ/ *n* elder (person in authority) in some Protestant churches, esp the Presbyterian Church. (若干新教,尤指長老會中的)長老;教會監督人。

Pres·by·terian /ˌprezbɪˈtɪərɪən ; ˌprɛzbəˈtɪrɪən/ *adj* ~ **Church,** one governed by elders, all of equal rank (in England, since 1972, united with the Congregational Church to form the United Reformed Church) (⇨ episcopal, governed by bishops). 基督教長老會(由長老監督之,在英國自 1972 年起與公理會合併成聯合改革教會)(參看 episcopal, 由主教監理之英國國教)。□ *n* member of the ~ Church. 長老會教友。**~·ism** /-ɪzəm ; -ˌɪzəm/ *n* the ~ system of church government; the beliefs of ~s. 長老會制;長老會之教義。

pres·by·tery /ˈprezbɪtrɪ *US:* -terɪ ; ˈprɛzbəˌtɛrɪ/ *n* (*pl* -ries) [C] **1** (in a church) eastern part of the chancel beyond the choir; sanctuary. (教堂中之)祭司席;內殿。**2** (regional) administrative court of the Presbyterian Church. 長老會之 (地區性的) 教務評議會。**3** residence of a Roman Catholic parish priest. 天主教神父的居所。

pre·sci·ent /ˈpresɪənt ; ˈprɛʃɪənt/ *adj* (formal) knowing about, able to see into, the future. (正式用語)預知的;有先見的。**~·ly** *adv* **pre·sci·ence** /-əns ; -əns/ *n*

pre·scribe /prɪˈskraɪb ; prɪˈskraɪb/ *vt, vi* **1** [VP6A, 14] ~ ***sth (for sth),*** advise or order the use of: 勸告或吩咐使用;開(藥方): *~d textbooks,* books which pupils are required to use. 指定的教科書。*The doctor ~d a long rest.* 醫生吩咐作長期的休息。*What do you ~ for this illness?* 你對此病開什麼方子呢? **2** [VP6A, 8, 10, 21, 2A, 3A] say, with authority, what course of action is to be followed: 指示所應遵循的行動方針;指揮;規定: *penalties ~d by the law.* 法律規定的懲罰。*Complete the ~d form.* 填好規定的表格。

pre·script /ˈpriːskrɪpt ; ˈpriskrɪpt/ *n* ordinance; command. 規定;法律;命令。

pre·scrip·tion /prɪˈskrɪpʃn ; prɪˈskrɪpʃən/ *n* [U] act of prescribing; [C] that which is prescribed; (esp) doctor's written order or direction for the making up and use of a medicine; the medicine itself: 吩咐;指定;指示;規定;所規定之事物;(尤指)醫生開的處方;處方上的藥: ~ *charges,* (in GB) charges made under National Health Service requirements for ~s. 處方收費 (英國國民保健制度規定之處方統一收費標準)。

pre·scrip·tive /prɪˈskrɪptɪv ; prɪˈskrɪptɪv/ *adj* giving orders or directions; authorized; prescribed by custom: 規定的;指示的;慣例的: *a ~ grammar of the English language,* one telling the reader how he ought to use the language. 說明如何使用英語之文法書。⇨ descriptive.

pres·ence /ˈprezns ; ˈprɛzn̩s/ *n* [U] **1** being present in a place, etc: 出席;在場: *in the ~ of his friends,* with his friends there. 在他朋友的面前。*Your ~ is requested at the annual general meeting,* Please be there. 敬請光臨一年一度的大會。*He was calm in the ~ of danger.* 危險當前,他鎮定自若。**~ of mind,** ⇨ mind¹(2). **2** bearing; person's way of carrying himself: 儀容;態度: *a man of noble ~.* 儀態高貴的人。

pres·ent¹ /ˈpreznt ; ˈprɛzn̩t/ *adj* **1** being in the place in question: 出席的;在場的: *the Smiths, and other people ~* (= who were ~). 史密斯夫婦以及其他在場的人。*Were you ~ at the ceremony?* 你參加了典禮嗎? ***~ company excepted,*** (colloq) used to show that one's remarks do not apply to anyone who is ~. (俗)在場的人不算;在座的諸位除外。⇨ absent¹(1). **2** being discussed or dealt with; now being considered: 在討論或處理中的;正在考慮中的: *in the ~ case,* this case. 在這事件中;此際;當下。**3** existing now: 現在的;現存的: *the ~ government.* 現在的政府。 **4 ~ to,** felt, remembered by: 由…所感覺或記憶的: *~ to the mind/imagination.* 記憶猶新(呈現於想像中)。**5** (archaic) ready at hand: (古)在手邊的;應急的;隨時的: *'a very ~ help in trouble'.* '在患難中隨時的幫助'。□ *n* **1 the ~,** the ~ time, the time now passing: 現在;目前: *the past, the ~, and the future;* 過去,現在和未來; (gram) (文法) *the ~ tense.* 現在式。**at ~,** now: 現在: *We don't need any more at ~.* 我們現在不需要更多的了。**for the ~,** for the time being, as far as the ~ is concerned: 目前;暫且: *That will be enough for the ~.* 暫且够用。**2 by these ~s,** (legal) by this document. (法律)根據本文件。

pres·ent² /ˈpreznt ; ˈprɛzn̩t/ *n* gift: 禮物;贈品: *'birthday ~s;* 生日禮物; *I'm buying it for a ~* (= as a gift), *so please wrap it up nicely.* 我買這東西作禮物,請好好地包裝。***make sb a ~ of sth,*** give sb sth: 把某物贈送某人: *I'll make you a ~ of my old car.* 我將把我的舊車送給你。

pre·sent³ /prɪˈzent ; prɪˈzɛnt/ *vt* **1** [VP14, 15A] ***~ sth to sb; ~ sb with sth,*** give; offer; put forward; submit: 給;贈;交出;提出;呈遞: *~ the village with a bus-shelter/~ a bus-shelter to the village;* 贈送一座公共汽車候車亭給該村莊; *the clock that was ~ed to me when I retired;* 我退休時贈給我的鐘; *~ a petition to the Governor;* 向總督呈遞請願書; *~ a cheque at the bank,* ie for payment; 向銀行兌支票; *~ one's compliments/greetings, etc to sb,* (polite phrases). (客套語)恭維(問候)某人。**2** [VP6A, 14, 15A] ***~ sb to sb,*** introduce formally. 引見;介紹。 **3** [VP15A] (reflex) appear; attend: (反身式)出現;出席: *~ oneself at a friend's house;* 到朋友家中; *~ oneself for trial/for examination.* 出席受審(參加考試)。 **4** [VP6A] show; reveal: 呈現;顯示;顯出: *He ~ed a bold front to the world,* showed that he was facing his difficulties, etc bravely. 他勇敢地面對困難等。*This case ~s some interesting features.* 這事件顯出若干有趣的特色。*A good opportunity has ~ed itself for doing what you suggested.* 照你的建議去做的好機會已經到了。 **5** [VP6A] (of a theatrical manager or company) produce (a play); cause (an actor) to take part in a play: (指戲院經理或劇團)演出(戲劇);使(演員)參加演出: *The Mermaid Company will ~ 'Hamlet' next week/will ~ Tom Hill as Brutus in 'Julius Caesar'.* 美人魚劇團將於下週演出'哈姆雷特'(將由湯姆•希爾演出'朱利阿斯•凱撒'中的布魯塔斯)。**6** [VP14] ***~ sth at sb,*** aim (a weapon) at him; hold out (a weapon) in position for aiming at him: 以(武器)瞄準;舉槍瞄準: *The intruder ~ed a pistol at me.* 闖入者用手槍對準我。**7** [VP6A] hold (a rifle, etc) vertically in front of the body as a salute, etc. 舉(槍等)敬禮。***P~ arms!*** (the order to do this). (口令)舉槍敬禮! □ *n* position of a weapon in a salute: 敬禮時槍的位置: *at the ~,* with the weapon held in a perpendicular position. 槍直舉着。

pre·sent·able /prɪˈzentəbl ; prɪˈzɛntəbl̩/ *adj* fit to appear, be shown, in public: 適於公然出現或展示的: *Is this old suit still ~?* 這套舊衣服還穿得出去嗎? *Is the girl he wants to marry ~,* the sort of girl he can introduce to his friends and family? 他要娶的那個女孩能見得人嗎(卽教養,出身等良好嗎)? **pre·sent·ably** /-əblɪ ; -əblɪ/ *adv*

pres·en·ta·tion /ˌprezn̩ˈteɪʃn *US:* ˌpriːzen- ; ˌprɛzn̩ˈteʃən/ *n* [U] presenting or being presented; [C] sth presented: 贈送;提出;引見;介紹;出席;呈現;演出;被贈送、提出等之物: *the ~ of a new play;* 新劇的演出; *a ~ copy,* a book given as a present, esp by the author. (尤指作者送的)贈閱本。*The cheque is payable on ~,* ie at the bank. 此支票交銀行卽可兌現。

pre·sen·ti·ment /prɪˈzentɪmənt ; prɪˈzɛntəmənt/ *n* [C] (formal) vague feeling that sth (esp unpleasant or undesirable) is about to happen. (正式用語)預感(尤指感覺壞事卽將發生)。

pres·ent·ly /ˈprezntlɪ ; ˈprɛzn̩tlɪ/ *adv* **1** soon: 不久;卽刻: *I'll be with you ~.* 我不久就可陪你。 **2** (US) at the present time: (美)現在: *The Secretary of State is ~ in Africa.* 國務卿目前正在非洲。

pres·er·va·tion /ˌprezəˈveɪʃn ; ˌprɛzəˈveʃən/ *n* [U] **1** act of preserving: 保護;貯藏;維持;留存: *the ~ of food/one's health;* 食物的保存(健康的維護); *the ~ of peace;* 和平的維持; *the ~ of wild life.* 保護野生動物。 **2** condition of sth preserved: 某物被保存的狀況: *old paintings in an excellent state of ~.* 保存得很好的古畫。

pre·serv·ative /prɪˈzɜːvətɪv ; prɪˈzɝvətɪv/ *n, adj* (substance) used for preserving: 保護的;保存的;防腐的;保護物;防腐劑: *fresh cream free from ~s,* with no substances added to preserve the cream. 未加防腐劑的新鮮奶油。

pre·serve /prɪˈzɜːv ; prɪˈzɝv/ *vt* [VP6A, 14] ***~ (from),*** **1** keep safe from harm or danger: 保護;防護: *social activities preserving old people from the loneliness of old age.* 防止老年人寂寞的社交活動。*God ~ us all!* 上帝保佑我們全體! **2** keep from decay, risk of going bad, etc (by pickling, making into jam, etc): (藉醃漬,製成果醬等而)保藏;貯存: *~ fruit/eggs, etc.* 保藏水果(蛋等)(卽製成果醬,醃成鹹蛋等)。 **3** keep from loss; retain (qualities, etc): 使不損失;維持(品質等): *~ one's eyesight;* 保護視力; *a well-~d old man,* one who shows few signs of the usual weaknesses of old age. 保養得好的老人。 **4** care for and protect land, rivers, lakes, etc with the animals, birds and fish, esp to prevent these from being taken by poachers: 禁止漁獵並保護土地,河,湖等: *The fishing in this stream is strictly ~d.* 此河嚴禁捕魚。 **5** keep alive (sb's name or memory); keep extant: 使(某人的名字或名聲)流傳;使留存: *Few of his early poems are ~d.* 他早期的詩很少保存下來。□ *n* **1** (usu *pl*) jam. (通常用複數)果醬;蜜餞。 **2** woods, streams, etc where animals, birds and fish are ~d: 漁獵禁地: *a 'game ~.* 禁獵地。***poach on another's ~,*** (fig) take a share in activities, interests, etc looked upon as associated especially with sb else. (喩)侵害他人的活動,利益等的領域。 **pre·serv·able** /-əbl ; -əbl̩/ *adj* that can be ~d. 可保護的;可貯藏的;可維持的;可留存的。**~r** *n* person or thing that ~s. 保護之人或物;貯藏食品者;禁獵地管理者。

pre·side /prɪˈzaɪd ; prɪˈzaɪd/ *vi* [VP2A, C, 3A] **~ at,** be chairman: 作主席: *The Prime Minister ~s at meetings of the Cabinet.* 首相在內閣會議中當主席。**~ over,** be the head or director of: 主持;管理: *The city council is ~d over by the mayor.* 市政會議由市長主持。

presi·dency /ˈprezɪdənsɪ ; ˈprɛzədənsɪ/ *n* (*pl* -cies) **1 the ~,** the office of president. 總統,部會首長,

董事長,總經理,院長,校長,社長,主席,會長等的職位。 **2** term of office as a president: 上述各職位的任期: *during the ~ of Lincoln.* 在林肯當總統的期間。

presi·dent /'prezɪdənt ; 'prɛzədənt/ *n* **1** (elected) head of the government in the US and other modern republics. (美國及其他現代共和國民選的)總統。 **2** head of some government departments (*P~ of the Board of Trade*), of some business companies, colleges, societies, etc. 若干政府機關的首長(如商務部長);若干商行,大學,會社等的首長;董事長;總經理;校長;院長;社長;會長;主席。 **presi·den·tial** /ˌprezɪ'denʃl ; ˌprɛzə'dɛnʃəl/ *adj* of a ~ or his duties: 總統的;首長(等)的;其職務的: *the ~ial election;* 總統選舉; *the ~ial year,* (in US) the year of the ~ial elections. (美國的)總統選舉年;大選年。

pre·sid·ium /prɪ'sɪdɪəm ; prɪ'sɪdɪəm/ *n* executive committee of the administration, and of various organisations, in some socialist countries; group of presiding persons. (某些社會主義國家的政府及其各種組織的)常務委員會;主席團。

press[1] /pres ; prɛs/ *n* **1** act of pressing: 壓;按;擠;搾;緊握;擁抱: *a ~ of the hand;* 緊握手; *give sth a light ~.* 輕按某物。 **2** machine or apparatus for pressing: 壓搾機;壓力機;夾具;(網球拍等的)夾子: *a 'wine-~;* (搾汁做酒的)搾葡萄機; *a 'cider-~;* 蘋果汁搾取器; *keep one's (tennis) racket in a ~;* 把(網球)球拍放在球拍夾子中; *a hydraulic ~.* 水壓機。 **3** (usu 常作 **the ~**), printed periodicals; the newspapers generally; journalists: 定期刊物;雜誌;報紙(集合稱);新聞記者;新聞界: *The book was favourably noticed by the ~/had a good ~,* was favourably reviewed by the literary critics. 這書曾得報章雜誌的好評。*There was a ~ campaign against him,* He was attacked in the newspapers. 各報對他發動了一場攻擊。*The liberty/freedom of the ~* (= The right of newspapers to report events, express opinions, etc freely) *is a feature of democratic countries.* 出版自由是民主國家的特徵。 **'~-agent** *n* person employed by a theatre, actor, musician, etc to arrange for publicity in the newspapers. (戲院、演員,音樂家等雇來設計做報紙宣傳的) 宣傳員;公共關係人員。Hence, 由此產生, **'~-agency** *n* **'~-box** *n* place reserved for reporters at a football or cricket match, etc. (足球或板球比賽等的)新聞記者席。 **'~ conference** *n* one of newspaper reporters, convened by a minister, government official, etc who talks about policy, achievements, etc. 記者招待會。 **'~-cutting/-clipping** *nn* paragraph, article, etc cut out from a newspaper or other periodical. 從報紙雜誌剪下的資料;剪報。 **'~-gallery** *n* gallery reserved for reporters, esp in the House of Commons. (尤指英國下議院的)新聞記者席。 **'~-lord** *n* powerful newspaper proprietor. 報業鉅子。 **'~-photographer** *n* newspaper photographer. 攝影記者。 **4** business for printing (and sometimes publishing) books or periodicals: 印刷業;出版業;出版社: *Oxford University P~;* 牛津大學出版社;(also 亦作 **'printing-~**) machine for printing: 印刷機: *in the ~,* being printed; 印刷中; *send a manuscript to the ~,* send it to be printed; 把原稿付印; *go to ~,* start printing; 付印;開始印刷; *correct the ~,* correct errors in printing, be a proof-reader. 校對印刷稿。 **5** crowd: 羣衆;人叢: *lost in the ~;* 在人羣中走失; *fight one's way through the ~.* 拚命擠過人叢。 **6** pressure: 緊迫;壓力: *the ~ of modern life;* 現代生活的壓力; *because of the ~ of business.* 由於事忙 (事情之急待處理)。 **7** cupboard with shelves for clothes, books, etc usu in a recess in a wall. (放衣服、書籍等之)櫥(通常爲嵌入牆壁的凹處者)。 **'~-mark** *n* mark or number in a book showing its place in a library shelf. (書本上表示其在圖書館位置的)書架號碼。 **8 ~ of sail/canvas,** (naut) as much sail as the wind will allow. (航海)吃滿風的帆;滿帆。

press[2] /pres ; prɛs/ *vt, vi* **1** [VP6A, 15B] push steadily against: 壓;按;扣: *~ the trigger of a gun;* 扣槍的扳機; *~ (down) the accelerator pedal* (of a car); 踩(下)(汽車的)加速器踏板; *~ the button,* eg of an electric bell. 按鈕(如按電鈴)。 **'~-up** *n* (*pl* ~-ups) exercise in which one stretches out face down on the floor, the arms being straightened and bent by ~ing against the floor with the palms of one's hands to raise and lower one's body. 伏地挺身(運動)。 **'~-stud** ⇨ snap(5). **2** [VP6A, 15B, 22] use force or weight to get sth smooth or flat, to get sth into a smaller space, to get juice out of fruit, etc: 壓平;熨平;塞進較小的空間;壓緊;搾出果汁(等): *~ a suit/skirt, etc,* with an iron, to remove creases, etc; (用熨斗)燙平一套衣服(一條裙子等); *~ grapes,* when making wine; (製酒時)壓搾葡萄; *~ the juice out of an orange;* 擠出橘子汁; *~ed beef,* beef that has been boiled and pressed into shape for packing in tin boxes. (煮熟並壓成某形狀以便裝罐的)罐頭牛肉;牛肉乾。 **3** [VP6A, 15A, B] keep close to and attack; bear heavily on: 接近而攻擊;進逼: *~ the enemy hard,* attack with determination; 進逼敵人;果敢襲擊敵人; *~ (home) an attack,* carry it out with determination; 强襲;緊攻; *~ a point* (in an argument, debate) *-home,* (fig) obtain support, agreement, etc by a determined, articulate, speech; (喻)(在辯論中)因堅決清晰的言辭而獲得支持或贊成; *be hard ~ed,* be under determined attack. 被緊攻;被强襲。 **4 ~ for,** make repeated requests for; demand urgently: 反覆請求;緊急要求: *~ for an inquiry into a question.* 反覆要求調查某一問題。 **5 be ~ed for,** have barely enough of: 缺少;缺乏: *~ed for time/money/space.* 缺少足够的時間(金錢,空間)。 **6** [VP2C] push, crowd, with weight or force: 用力推;推進;擁擠: *crowds ~ing against the barriers/~ing round the royal visitors.* 向柵欄推擠(擁擠在王室賓客周圍)的羣衆。 **7** [VP3A, 4A, 14, 17] **~ (sb) for sth; ~ (sb) to do sth,** urge; insist on: 敦促;催促;力勸;堅持: *~ (sb) for an answer;* 敦促(某人)作答; *~ sb for a debt/to pay a debt.* 催促某人還債。*He did not need much ~ing.* 他並不需要多加催逼。*They are ~ing for a decision to be made.* 他們堅持要作一決定。 **~ sth on/upon sb,** insist that sb takes it: 堅持要某人接受某事物: *He ~ed the money on me,* insisted on my accepting it. 他堅持要我接受那筆錢。 *Don't ~ your opinions upon her,* Don't insist that she should accept them. 不要逼她接受你的意見。 **8** [VP2A] demand action or attention: 急迫;亟需行動或注意: *The matter is ~ing,* is urgent. 事情緊急。 **9 Time ~es,** There is no time to lose. 時間緊迫。 **10** [VP6A, 15A] squeeze (sb's hand, arm, etc) as a sign of affection or sympathy; draw (sb) to oneself in an embrace: 緊握(某人之手、臂等,表示關切或同情);擁抱: *He ~ed her to his side.* 他把她擁向身邊。 **11** [VP2C] **~ (down) on/upon sb,** weigh; oppress: 使負重擔;壓迫: *His responsibilities ~ heavily upon him.* 他的責任沉重地壓在他身上。 *The new taxes ~ed down heavily on the people.* 新稅使人民不勝負荷。 **12** [VP2C] **~ on/forward (with sth),** hurry, continue in a determined way: 加緊;決心要繼續: *~ on with one's work.* 加緊自己的工作。*It was getting dark, so the travellers ~ed forward.* 天快黑了,因此旅客們儘快趕路。 **~·ing** *n* one of many identical gramophone records made from the same matrix: 同一模型做出來的許多唱片之一;唱片: *make and sell 10 000 ~ings of a symphony.* 製造並銷售一萬張某交響樂的唱片。 ▭ *adj* **1** urgent; requiring immediate attention: 緊急的;急迫的;需要立卽處理的: *~ing business.* 急事。 **2** (of persons, their requests, etc) insistent: (指人、其要求等)堅持的;執拗的: *a ~ing invitation;* 懇切的邀請; *as you are so ~ing.* 你旣然這樣堅持。 **~·ing·ly** *adv*

press[3] /pres ; prɛs/ *vt* [VP15A] **1** (hist) force (a man) to serve in the navy or army. (史)强迫(人)

服兵役。**'~-gang** *n* (hist) body of men employed to ~ men. (史)兵士强募隊;(强拉他人服役之)拉伕隊。**2** take (sth) for public use; requisition. 徵用(某物);徵發。**~ *into service,*** make use of because of urgent need: 因急需而使用: *Even my thirty-year-old car was ~ed into service to take voters to the polling-station.* 甚至我那部卅年的老爺車也用來載送選民前往投票所。

press·ure /ˈpreʃə(r) ; ˈprɛʃɚ/ *n* [C, U] **1** pressing; (the amount of) force exerted continuously on or against sth by sth which touches it: 壓;壓力;施諸某物的壓力之量: *a ~ of 6 lb to the square inch;* 加於每平方吋上的六磅的壓力; *see that the tyre ~ is right;* 注意要使輪胎的壓力正常; *atmospheric ~/the ~ of the atmosphere,* the ~ of weight of air, as measured by a barometer. 大氣的壓力(如氣壓計所測量者)。**'blood-~** *n* tension of the blood-vessels. 血壓。**'~ cabin** *n* cabin (in an aircraft) that is pressurized. (飛機上的)壓力艙。**'~-cooker** *n* airtight container for cooking quickly with steam under ~. 快鍋;壓力鍋(利用蒸氣在其壓力下快速烹煮的緊密的容器)。**'~-gauge** *n* apparatus or device for measuring the ~ of a liquid or gas at a given point. (測量液體或氣體在某一點上壓力的)壓力計。**2** compelling force or influence: 强制力;影響力: *He pleaded ~ of work/family ~s and resigned his place on the committee.* 他以工作繁重(家庭負擔)爲由而辭掉在委員會的職位。***be/come under ~,*** feel/be caused to feel strongly compelled (to act): 受到壓力;在壓力之下: *He's under strong ~ to vote with the government on this issue.* 他受到强大的壓力而投票贊成政府的這項主張。*He always works best under ~,* when he has to. 他總是在迫不得已時工作成績才最好。***bring ~ to bear on sb (to do sth); put ~ on sb/put sb under ~ (to do sth),*** use force or influence on sb. 壓迫某人;對某人施壓力。**'~ group,** organized group, eg an association of manufacturers such as brewers, farmers, which tries to exert influence or lobby for the benefit of its members. 壓力集團(藉施壓力或遊說,以爲其會員謀取福利的集團,如造酒公會、農會)。**3** sth that oppresses or weighs down: 壓迫物;困苦;艱難;重荷: *the ~ of taxation;* 稅的重負; *under the ~ of poverty/necessity.* 在貧困(需要)的壓迫下。**4** ***(at) high ~,*** (with) great energy and speed: 拚命(地);很有衝勁(的): *work at high ~;* 拼命地工作; *a high-~ salesman.* 很有衝勁的推銷員。□ *vt* = pressurize.

press·ur·ize /ˈpreʃəraɪz ; ˈprɛʃəˌraɪz/ *vt* **1** [VP6A] apply pressure to. 加壓力於。**2** [VP6A, 14, 17] ~ ***sb (into doing sth/to do sth),*** use force (of persuasion, influence, etc) to make him do it: 迫使某人(做某事): *~ the President into resigning/to resign.* 迫使總統辭職。**3** (usu *pp*) (of an aircraft, a submarine, etc) construct so that the internal air pressure can be controlled and kept normal: (通常用過去分詞)使(飛機、潛艇等之內部)增壓: *a ~d cabin.* 增壓艙。

presti·digi·ta·tor /ˌprestɪˈdɪdʒɪteɪtə(r) ; ˌprɛstɪˈdɪdʒɪˌtetɚ/ *n* juggler; conjuror. 變戲法者;演幻術者。**pres·ti·digi·ta·tion** /ˌprestɪˌdɪdʒɪˈteɪʃn ; ˌprɛstɪˌdɪdʒɪˈteʃən/ *n*

pres·tige /preˈstiːʒ ; ˈprɛstɪdʒ/ *n* [U] **1** respect that results from the good reputation (of a person, nation, etc); power or influence coming from this: (指人、國家等的)聲望;威望;勢力;威力: *behaviour that would mean loss of ~.* 可能會降低聲望的行爲。**2** distinction, glamour, that comes from achievements, success, possessions, etc: (由於成就、成功、財富等而產生的)顯赫;魅力;烜赫: (attrib) (形容用法) *the ~ value of living in a fashionable district/of owning a Rolls-Royce.* 居住於高級住宅區(擁有勞斯萊斯汽車)之顯赫價值。**pres·tig·ious** /preˈstɪdʒəs ; prɛsˈtɪdʒɪəs/ *adj* bringing ~. 帶來聲望的;有聲望的。

pres·tis·simo /preˈstɪsɪməʊ ; prɛsˈtɪsəˌmo/ *adj, adv* (I; music) very quick(ly); as quickly as possible. (義;音樂)極快的(地);儘快地。

presto /ˈprestəʊ ; ˈprɛsto/ *adj, adv* (I; music) quick(ly). (義;音樂)急速的;急速地。***Hey ~!*** words used by a conjuror when performing a trick. 快,快!變!(變戲法時用語)。

pre·stressed /ˌpriːˈstrest ; priˈstrɛst/ *adj* (of concrete) strengthened by having stretched cables inserted. (指混凝土)預力的;藉嵌入拉緊的鋼筋以加强的。

pre·sum·able /prɪˈzjuːməbl *US:* -ˈzuː- ; prɪˈzjuməbl/ *adj* that may be presumed. 可假定的;可能的。**pre·sum·ably** /-əblɪ ; -əblɪ/ *adv*

pre·sume /prɪˈzjuːm *US:* -ˈzuːm ; prɪˈzjum/ *vt, vi* **1** [VP6A, 9, 25] take for granted; suppose (to be true): 以爲;認定;推測;假定(爲眞實): *In Britain an accused man is ~d (to be) innocent until he is proved guilty.* 在英國被告在未證實有罪以前,仍被認作是無辜的。*Let us ~ that....* 讓我們假定…。*Dr Livingstone, I ~.* 我想,你是李文斯頓博士。**2** [VP7A] venture; take the liberty: 敢於;擅敢;冒昧: *I won't ~ to disturb you.* 我不敢打擾你。*May I ~ to advise you?* 我可以向你進一言嗎?**3** [VP3A] ~ ***upon sth,*** (formal) make a wrong use of, take an unfair advantage of: (正式用語)錯用;不當地利用: *~ upon sb's good nature,* take advantage of it by asking for help, etc; 利用某人性情好(而要求幫助等); *~ upon a short acquaintance,* treat sb familiarly even though one has known him for only a short time. 憑着一面之交就和人親熱起來。**pre·sum·ing** *adj* having, showing, a tendency to ~, to take liberties. 冒昧的;不客氣的;僭越的。

pre·sump·tion /prɪˈzʌmpʃn ; prɪˈzʌmpʃən/ *n* **1** [C] sth presumed(1); sth which seems likely although there is no proof: 被認定之事物;雖無證明而似合理之事物;推測;假定;推定: *on the false ~ that the firm was bankrupt;* 基於該公司破產之謬誤的推測; *the ~ that he was drowned.* 他被淹死的假定。**2** [U] arrogance; behaviour that is too bold: 傲慢;僭越;過於大膽的行爲;冒昧: *If you will excuse my ~, I should like to contradict what you have just said.* 請恕我冒昧,我要反駁你剛才說的話。

pre·sump·tive /prɪˈzʌmptɪv ; prɪˈzʌmptɪv/ *adj* based on presumption(1): 基於推測的;假定的;推定的: *~ evidence;* 推定的證據; *the ~ heir/the heir ~,* person who is heir (to the throne, etc) until sb with a stronger claim is born. (王位等之)推定繼承人(在更具有繼承權的人誕生以前的繼承者)。**~·ly** *adv*

pre·sump·tu·ous /prɪˈzʌmptʃʊəs ; prɪˈzʌmptʃuəs/ *adj* (formal) (of behaviour, etc) too bold or self-confident. (正式用語)(指行爲等)膽大妄爲的;僭越的;自大的;專擅的。**~·ly** *adv*

pre·sup·pose /ˌpriːsəˈpəʊz ; ˌprisəˈpoz/ *vt* [VP6A, 9] **1** assume beforehand. 預想;預先假定;事先推測。**2** imply; require as a condition: 含示;以…爲先決條件: *Sound sleep ~s a mind at ease.* 心情舒暢才能酣睡。**pre·sup·po·si·tion** /ˌpriːsʌpəˈzɪʃn ; ˌprisʌpəˈzɪʃən/ *n* [C] sth ~d; [U] presupposing. 預想之事;預先假定之事;先決條件;預想;推測;含示。

pre·tence (US = **-tense**) /prɪˈtens ; prɪˈtɛns/ *n* **1** [U] pretending; make-believe: 虛假;僞裝;掩飾: *do sth under the ~ of friendship/religion/patriotism.* 以友誼(宗教,愛國)爲掩飾而做某事。*It's all ~.* 那全是虛假。**2** [C] pretext or excuse; false claim or reason: 藉口;託辭;口實;僞稱: *He calls for the night porter on the slightest ~.* 他有一點點藉口就把夜班侍者召來。*It is only a ~ of friendship.* 那不過是以友誼爲口實罷了。***false ~s,*** (legal) acts intended to deceive: (法律)詐欺: *obtain money by/on/under false ~s.* 藉詐欺搞錢。**3** [C] claim (to merit, etc); [U] ostentation: 自稱(有優點、功績等);誇耀;虛飾: *a man without ~.* 實事求是的人。

pre·tend /prɪˈtend ; prɪˈtɛnd/ *vt, vi* **1** [VP7A, 9] make oneself appear (to be sth, to be doing sth), either in play or to deceive others: 佯裝;僞

裝(為某身份,正做某事,或出於嬉戲,或欲欺騙他人): ~ *to be asleep;* 假裝睡着; *boys ~ing that they are pirates.* 佯裝海盜的男孩們。*Let's ~ we are cowboys.* 我們假裝牛仔吧。*They ~ed not to see us.* 他們佯裝沒看見我們。**2** [VP6A] say falsely that one has (as an excuse or reason, or to avoid danger, difficulty, etc): (作為藉口或理由,或想避免危險、困難等而)僞稱;佯稱有: ~ *sickness.* 佯稱有病。*He ~ed ignorance, hoping to avoid being fined for breaking the law.* 他僞稱不知情以避免違法罰鍰。**3** [VP3A] ~ ***to,*** put forward a claim to: 自稱;自認;覬覦;爭: *There are not many persons who ~ to an exact knowledge of the subject.* 自認對那題目有確切了解的人不多。*Surely he does not ~ to intelligence!* 當然他不會自以為聰明! *The young man ~ed to the throne,* claimed it (falsely). 那青年覬覦王位。**~·ed·ly** *adv* **~er** *n* person whose claim (to a throne, a title, etc) is disputed. 覬覦(王位、爵位、名份等)者;佯裝者;僞稱者。

pre·tense /prɪˈtens ; prɪˈtɛns/ ⇨ pretence.

pre·ten·sion /prɪˈtenʃn ; prɪˈtɛnʃən/ *n* **1** [C] (often *pl*) (statement of a) claim: (常用複數)要求;主張;權利: *He makes no ~s to expert knowledge of the subject.* 他未自詡對那問題具有專家的學識。*Has he any ~s to being considered a scholar?* 他有被認為是學者的資格嗎? *She has some social ~s,* claims some place in high society. 她自稱在上流社會頗有地位。**2** [U] being pretentious. 自負;驕傲。

pre·ten·tious /prɪˈtenʃəs ; prɪˈtɛnʃəs/ *adj* claiming (without justification) great merit or importance: (無正當理由)自命不凡的;自負的;驕傲的: *a ~ author/book/speech;* 自誇的作者(書,演說); *use ~ language.* 使用矯飾的言詞。**~·ly** *adv* **~·ness** *n*

pret·er·ite (also **-erit**) /ˈpretərɪt ; ˈprɛtərɪt/ *n, adj* ~ ***(tense),*** (gram) (tense) expressing a past action or state. (文法)過去的;過去式;過去時態。

pre·ter·natu·ral /ˌpriːtəˈnætʃrəl ; ˌpritəˈnætʃərəl/ *adj* out of the regular course of things; not normal or usual. 逸出事物之常軌的;異常的;奇特的;不可思議的。**~·ly** *adv*: *~ly solemn.* 異常肅穆的。

pre·text /ˈpriːtekst ; ˈpritɛkst/ *n* [C] false reason (*for* an action, etc): (行動等的)藉口;託辭: *On/Under the ~ of asking for my advice, he called and borrowed £10 from me.* 以向我討教為藉口,他來我處借去十鎊。*Can we find a ~ for refusal/refusing the invitation?* 我們能找到拒絕(不接受邀請)的託辭嗎?

pre·tor /ˈpriːtə(r) ; ˈpritə/ *n* ⇨ praetor.

pret·tify /ˈprɪtɪfaɪ ; ˈprɪtɪˌfaɪ/ *vt* (*pt, pp* -fied) [VP6A] make pretty, esp in an insipid way. 使美;美化;(尤指)平淡無奇地裝飾。

pretty /ˈprɪtɪ ; ˈprɪtɪ/ *adj* (-ier, -iest) **1** pleasing and attractive without being beautiful or magnificent: 悅人的;可愛的;漂亮的;精緻的(非華麗或堂皇的): *a ~ girl/garden/picture/piece of music.* 漂亮的女郎(漂亮的花園;美麗的圖畫;優美的樂曲)。ˈ**~-~** *adj* (colloq) superficially ~ or charming. (俗)裝飾過分的;打扮得俗氣的;矯揉造作的。**2** fine; good: 好的;優良的: *a ~ wit.* 一個有才氣的人。(ironic) (反語) *A ~ mess you've made of it!* 你把它弄得多糟啊! **3** (colloq) considerable in amount or extent. (俗)相當多的;相當大的。***a ~ penny,*** quite a lot: 很多錢;相當多的錢: *It will cost you a ~ penny.* 它會花費你不少錢。***come to/reach a ~ pass,*** reach a difficult position. 陷入困境。***a ˈ~ kettle of fish,*** ⇨ fish[1] (1). □ *adv* fairly, moderately: 相當地;頗: *The situation seems ~ hopeless.* 這情況似乎沒有多大希望了。*It's ~ cold outdoors today.* 今天戶外頗冷。~ ***much,*** very nearly: 幾乎;差不多: *The result of the ballot is ~ much what we expected.* 投票的結果和我們預料的差不多。~ ***nearly,*** almost: 幾乎;差不多: *The car is new, or ~ nearly so,* almost new. 這汽車是新的,或近乎新的。~ ***well,*** almost: 幾乎;差不多: *We've ~ well finished the work.* 我們已經差不多完成這工作。***sitting ~,*** (colloq) well off; favourably placed for future developments, etc. (俗)小康;所處地位有利於未來發展等。□ *n* (*pl* -ties) *my ~,* my ~ one (used of a child). 我的好孩子。**pret·tily** /ˈprɪtɪlɪ ; ˈprɪtɪlɪ/ *adv* in a ~ or charming way. 悅人地;可愛地。**pret·ti·ness** *n*

pret·zel /ˈpretsl ; ˈprɛtsl/ *n* (G) crisp, salt-flavoured biscuit, made in the shape of a knot or stick. (德)鬆脆的椒塩餅乾(做成紐結狀或棒狀)。

pre·vail /prɪˈveɪl;prɪˈvel/ *vi* **1** [VP2A, 3A] ~ ***(over/against),*** gain victory (over); fight successfully (against): 獲勝;戰勝: *Truth will ~.* 眞理將獲勝。*We ~ed over our enemies.* 我們勝過敵人。**2** [VP 2A] be widespread; be generally seen, done, etc: 盛行;流行: *the conditions now ~ing in Africa.* 非洲目前普遍的狀況。*The use of opium still ~s in the south.* 吸鴉片在南方仍甚盛行。**3** [VP3A] ~ ***on/upon sb to do sth,*** persuade: 勸導: *~ upon a friend to lend you £10.* 勸朋友借給你十鎊錢。**~·ing** *adj* most frequent or usual: 最常有的;最普通的;流行的: *the ~ing winds/fashions in dress.* 最常颳的風(流行的服式)。

preva·lent /ˈprevələnt ; ˈprɛvələnt/ *adj* (formal) common, seen or done everywhere (at the time in question): (正式用語)(在談論之時)普遍的;流行的: *the ~ fashions;* 流行的服裝式樣; *the ~ opinion on the proposed reforms.* 對於提議中的改革之一般意見。*Is malaria still ~ in that country?* 瘧疾在那個國家仍然流行嗎? **preva·lence** /-əns ; -əns/ *n* [U] being ~: 普遍;流行: *I'm shocked at the prevalence of bribery among these officials.* 這些官員普遍的受賄使我深感驚愕。

pre·vari·cate /prɪˈværɪkeɪt ; prɪˈværəˌket/ *vi* [VP 2A] (formal) make untrue or partly untrue statements; try to evade telling the (whole) truth. (正式用語)作不實或部分不實之言;支吾;搪塞。**pre·vari·ca·tion** /prɪˌværɪˈkeɪʃn ; ˌprɪværəˈkeʃən/ *n* [U] prevaricating; [C] instance of this. 支吾;搪塞;其實例。

pre·vent /prɪˈvent ; prɪˈvɛnt/ *vt* **1** [VP6A, 14, 19C] ~ ***sb (from doing sth);*** ~ ***sth (from happening),*** stop or hinder: 阻止;妨礙;預防: *~ a disease from spreading.* 防止一疾病蔓延。*Who can ~ us from getting married/~ our getting married now that you are of age?* 既然你已成年,誰能阻止我們結婚呢? *Your prompt action ~ed a serious accident.* 你即時的行動防止了一次嚴重的事故。**2** (old use) go before as a guide: (舊用法)前行而引導;帶領: *'P~ us, O Lord, in all our doings.'* '主啊,求您帶領我們的所做所為。' **~·able** /-əbl ; -əbl/ *adj* that can be ~ed. 可阻止的;能防止的。

pre·ven·ta·tive /prɪˈventətɪv ; prɪˈvɛntətɪv/ *adj, n* = preventive.

pre·ven·tion /prɪˈvenʃn ; prɪˈvɛnʃən/ *n* [U] act of preventing: 阻止;妨礙;預防: *the Society for the P~ of Cruelty to Animals.* 防止虐待動物協會。*P~ is better than cure.* 預防勝於治療。

pre·ven·tive /prɪˈventɪv ; prɪˈvɛntɪv/ *adj* serving or designed to prevent; precautionary. 阻止性的;預防的。~ **custody,** imprisonment of sb considered unlikely to be reformed, so that he may not commit further crimes. 防範性的監禁(施於被認為無法改過之罪犯,以防止其再犯罪)。~ **detention,** detention without trial because a person is thought likely to commit crime or (in some countries) oppose the government. 預防羈押;預防拘留(未經審判而拘留以防止其犯罪或(在某些國家)反抗政府)。~ **medicine,** research into means of warding off disease, illness, eg hygiene, working conditions. 預防醫學。□ *n* sth (eg medicine) to prevent or ward off sth. 預防物;預防劑;預防藥。

pre·view /ˈpriːvjuː ; ˈpriˌvju/ *n* [C] view of a film, play, etc before it is shown to the general public. (電影之)預映;試映;(戲劇等之)預演;試演。□ *vt* have/give a ~ of. 預映;預演。

pre·vi·ous /ˈpriːvɪəs ; ˈprivɪəs/ *adj* **1** coming earlier in time or order: (時間或順序上)在前的;早先的: *on a ~ occasion;* 在早先的一個場合; *~ convictions,* convictions for earlier offences, taken into account by a judge when passing sentence upon sb convicted of a further offence. 先前的判罪;前科(法官對某人再犯罪時作爲量刑的參考)。*I regret that a ~ engagement prevents me from accepting your kind invitation.* 我有約在先,故不能接受你好意的邀請,實在很遺憾。 **2** too hasty: 過急的;太快的: *Aren't you rather ~ in supposing that I will marry you?* 你以爲我會嫁給你,那不是言之過早嗎? **3** *~ **to,*** before. 在…以前。**~·ly** *adv*

pre·vi·sion /ˌpriːˈvɪʒn; prɪˈvɪʒən/ *n* [U] foresight; [C] instance of this: 預見;預知;其實例: *have a ~ of danger.* 預知危險。

prey /preɪ; pre/ *n* (*sing* only) animal, bird, etc hunted for food: (僅用單數)被捕食之動物(獸、禽等): *The eagle was devouring its ~.* 鷹在吞食捕獲物。***be/fall a ~ to,*** **(a)** be seized, caught by: 被…捕獲;被…捕食: *The zebra fell a ~ to the lion.* 那斑馬被獅子所捕食。 **(b)** be greatly troubled by: 深爲…所苦;深爲…所折磨: *be a ~ to anxiety and fears.* 深爲憂慮和恐懼所折磨。**ˌbeast/ˌbird of ˈ~,** one that kills and eats others, eg tigers, eagles. 食肉獸(鳥);猛獸(禽)(如虎、鷹)。 □ *vi* [VP3A] *~ **on/upon,*** **1** take, hunt, as ~(1): 捕食;攫食: *hawks ~ing on small birds.* 捕食小鳥的老鷹。 **2** steal from; plunder: 掠奪;劫掠: *Our coasts were ~ed upon by Viking pirates.* 我們的海岸曾被威金族的海盜劫掠。 **3** (of fears, etc) trouble greatly: (指恐懼等)使苦惱: *anxieties/losses that ~ upon my mind.* 使我心中苦惱的憂慮(損失)。

price /praɪs; praɪs/ *n* **1** [C] sum of money for which sth is (to be) sold or bought; that which must be done, given or experienced to obtain or keep sth: 價格;價錢;代價: *What ~ are you asking?* 你要價多少? *P~s are rising/falling/going up/going down.* 物價正上漲(下跌)。*I won't buy it at that ~.* 我不會以那價錢買它的。*He sold the house at a good ~.* 他以高價賣了那房子。*Loss of independence was a high ~ to pay for peace.* 喪失獨立來換取和平是一項重大的代價。***at a ~,*** at a fairly high price: 以高價: *There's fresh asparagus in the shops—at a ~!* 店裡有新鮮的蘆筍,價錢奇高! ***Every man has his ~,*** can be bribed. 人人都可能受到利誘。***put a ˈ~ on sb's head,*** offer a reward for his capture (dead or alive). 懸賞緝拿某人(無論死活)。**ˈasking ~,** (for a house, etc) price stated by the vendor: 開價;初價: *accept an offer of £200 below the asking ~.* 接受低於初價二百鎊的交易。**ˈ~-control** *n* control or fixing of ~s by authorities, manufacturers, etc. (由當局、廠商等所定的)物價管制;定價。Hence, 由此產生, **ˈ~-controlled** *adj.* 限價的。**ˈ~-list** *n* list of current ~s of goods for sale. 定價表;價目表。**ˈlist-~** *n* ~ recommended by the manufacturer, etc but not always compulsory. 廠商等提供之價格;報價;定價。 **2** [U] value; worth: 價值: *a pearl of great ~.* 極貴重的珍珠。***beyond/above/without ~,*** so valuable that buying is impossible. 非任何價錢所能購買的;無價的;極貴重的。**3** [C] (betting) odds. (賭博)賭注與贏款的差額。***What ~...?*** (sl) (俚) **(a)** What is the chance of...? …的勝算如何?…的機會如何? **(b)** (used to sneer at the failure of sth): (用以嘲笑某事物的失敗): *What ~ peace now?* 和平現在有什麼用? **ˈstarting ~,** odds offered by bookmakers as the race is about to start. 賽馬將開始時賭業者所開出的賠錢的比例。□ *vt* **1** [VP6A] fix, ask about, the ~ of sth; mark (goods) with a ~: 定…之價;問…之價;以價格標明(貨物): *All our goods are clearly ~d.* 我們所有的貨品都標明了價格。 **2** *~ **oneself/one's goods out of the market,*** (of manufacturers, producers) fix ~s so high that sales decline or stop. (指廠商、製造者)定價過高以致銷路減少或停頓。**~y** /ˈpraɪsɪ; ˈpraɪsɪ/ *adj* (sl) expensive. (俚)貴的;昂貴的。**~·less** *adj* **1** too valuable to be ~d: 無價的;極貴重的: *~less paintings.* 極貴重的畫。 **2** (sl) absurd: (俚)荒謬的: *a ~less old fellow;* 不像話的老傢伙; very amusing: 非常有趣的: *a ~less joke.* 極有趣的笑話。

prick¹ /prɪk; prɪk/ *n* **1** small mark or hole caused by the act of pricking: (穿刺之)小洞;刺痕: *~s made by a needle.* 以針穿刺的小孔。 **2** pain caused by pricking: 刺痛;扎痛: *I can still feel the ~.* 我仍能感到那刺痛。*He feels the ~ of conscience/remorse,* mental uneasiness. 他感到良心不安。**ˈpin-**

birds of prey

~, (fig) sth small that irritates. (喻)小刺激;小煩惱。 **3** (old use) goad for oxen. (舊用法)驅牛之刺棒。 ***kick against the ~s,*** (fig) hurt oneself by useless resistance. (喻) 作無謂之抵抗徒使自己受到損害;螳臂當車。 **4** ⚠ (vulg) penis; (vulg) term of abuse: (諱) (鄙)陽物;陰莖;辱罵人的話: *He's a stupid ~!* 他是個傻蛋!

prick² /prɪk ; prɪk/ *vt, vi* **1** [VP6A] make a hole or a mark in (sth) with a sharp point: 以尖物在(某物)上刺洞或作記號;穿;刺: *~ a toy balloon;* 在玩具氣球上刺洞; *~ a blister,* on the skin; 穿刺(皮膚上的)水泡; *~ holes in paper.* 在紙上穿洞。 **2** [VP 6A] hurt, cause pain to, with a sharp point or points: 以尖物刺傷;刺痛: *~ one's finger with/on a needle.* 用針刺傷手指。*The thorns on these roses ~ed my fingers.* 這些玫瑰上的刺刺痛了我的手指。(fig) (喻) *His conscience ~ed him.* 他的良心使他不安。 **3** [VP2A] feel sharp pain: 感到劇痛: *My fingers are ~ing.* 我的手指感到刺痛。 **4** [VP15B] ***~ sth out/off,*** put (seedlings) in the earth (in holes made with a pointed stick, etc): 移植(幼苗)(於以尖棒等所挖的地洞中): *~ out young cabbage plants.* 移植甘藍菜的幼苗。 **5** [VP15B] ***~ up one's ears,*** (esp of dogs, horses) raise the ears; (fig, of persons) pay sharp attention to sth being said. (尤指犬、馬)豎起耳朵;(喻,指人)豎耳靜聽。**~er** *n* person who, thing which, ~s; instrument for piercing holes, eg a bradawl. 刺者(人或物);刺洞之用具(如打眼鑽)。**~·ing** *n* act of ~ing; ~ing sensation. 刺;刺傷;刺痛。

prickle /ˈprɪkl ; ˈprɪkl̩/ *n* [C] (usu small) pointed growth on the stem, etc of a plant, or on the skin of some animals, eg hedgehogs; thorn. (植物之莖等上,或猬等動物之皮上的)尖刺;小刺;荊棘。□ *vt, vi* give or have a pricking sensation. 刺痛;感覺刺痛。**prick·ly** /ˈprɪklɪ ; ˈprɪklɪ/ *adj* **1** covered with ~s. 多刺的。 **prickly pear,** cactus covered with ~s and having pear-shaped fruit. 霸王樹 (一種多刺的仙人掌,結梨形之果實)。 **2** **prickly heat,** inflammation of the sweat glands, marked by a pricking sensation, common in the tropics during the hot-weather season. 痱子(汗腺之發炎,有刺痛感,常見於熱帶之炎熱季節)。 **3** (colloq) easily irritated or angered: (俗)易生氣的;易發脾氣的: *You're a bit prickly today.* 你今天很容易發脾氣。

pride /praɪd ; praɪd/ *n* **1** [U] feeling of satisfaction arising from what one has done, or from persons, things, etc one is concerned with: (因曾做某事,或因某些人、物等與自己有關而生的)得意之感;自豪: *look with ~ at one's garden.* 得意地看着自己的花園。***take (a) ~ in sb/sth; take no/little, etc ~ in sb/sth,*** have some/no/little, etc ~ about him/it: 對…感到(不感,很少感到)自豪: *take (a) great ~ in one's achievements/in the success of one's children.* 對自己的成就 (孩子的成功)感到自豪。***~ of place,*** a position of superiority. 高位;優越的位置。 **2** [U] (also 亦作 **proper ~**) self-respect; knowledge of one's worth and character: 自尊;自尊心: *He has no ~.* 他沒有自尊心。 *His ~ prevents him from doing anything dishonourable.* 他的自尊使他未做出任何不名譽的事。*Don't say anything that may wound his ~.* 不要說任何可能傷他自尊心的話。**false ~,** mistaken feeling of this kind; vanity. 妄自尊大;虛榮心。 **3** [U] object of ~(1): 引以自豪的對象: *a girl who is her mother's ~ and joy.* 一位使她的母親感到自豪與欣喜的女孩。 **4** [U] too high an opinion of oneself, one's position, possessions, etc; arrogance: 自大;傲慢;驕傲: *the sin of ~;* 傲慢罪(宗教或道德方面者); *be puffed up with ~.* 充滿傲氣。***P~ goes before a fall,*** (prov) ⇨ *go before* at go¹(29). (諺)驕者必敗。 **5** ***the ~ of,*** the prime, flower, of: 全盛;精華: *in the full ~ of youth.* 正值少壯時期。 **6** [C] group: 羣:(esp) (尤用於) *a ~ of lions/peacocks.* 一羣獅子(孔雀)。□ *vt* (reflex) ***~ oneself on/upon sth,*** take ~ in; be pleased and satisfied about: (反身式)以…自豪;自負;自傲;得意於: *He ~s himself upon his skill as a pianist.* 他對於自己的鋼琴技巧感到很得意。

prie-dieu /ˈpriː djɜː ; priˈdjø/ *n* small piece of furniture at which to kneel when praying to God. 禱告臺;禱告椅。

priest /priːst ; prist/ *n* **1** ordained minister of a Christian Church, esp one who is between a deacon and a bishop in the Anglican, Orthodox or Roman Catholic Church. 基督教的教士;牧師;神父;(尤指英國國教,東正教或天主教位於執事與主教之間的)僧侶。⇨ the illus at vestment. 參看 vestment 之挿圖。*Clergyman* is usu in the Anglican Church, except in official use, *minister* in the nonconformist Churches. 在英國國教中,除正式用法外,clergyman 是此義的通用字,不遵奉英國國教的基督新教中用 minister 一字。**ˈ~-ridden** *adj* ruled by, under the subjection of, ~s. 受教士支配的;僧侶統治的。 **2** (of non-Christian religions) person trained to perform special acts of religion, to serve the deity, give advice, etc. (指基督教以外之宗教)訓練來擔任宗教之特別活動、伺奉神等的祭司;術士;和尙。**~·ess** /ˈpriːstes ; ˈpristɪs/ *n* woman ~(2). 女祭司;女術士;尼姑。**ˈ~·craft** *n* [U] ambitious or worldly policy of ~s. 僧侶之謀略(謀求遂行野心或干預俗務者)。 **~-hood** /-hʊd ; -hʊd/ *n* the whole body of ~s of a Church: 教會之全體教士、牧師或僧侶: *the Irish ~-hood.* 愛爾蘭的教士們。**~·ly, ~·like** *adjj* of or for a ~; like a ~. 教士的;適於教士的;似教士的。

prig /prɪg ; prɪg/ *n* [C] smug, self-satisfied, self-righteous person. 自滿的人;沾沾自喜的人;自以爲正直的人。**~·gish** /-ɪʃ ; -ɪʃ/ *adj* behaving like, typical of, a ~; full of self-satisfaction. 一本正經的;沾沾自喜的。**~·gish·ly** *adv* **~·gish·ness** *n*

prim /prɪm ; prɪm/ *adj* (-mmer, -mmest) neat; formal: 整潔的;整齊的: *a ~ garden;* 整齊的花園; (of persons, their manner, speech, etc) disliking, showing a dislike of, anything rough, rude, improper: (指人、其儀態、言詞等)不喜歡或厭惡粗魯、無禮或不規矩之事物的;拘謹的;規矩的;正經的: *a very ~ and proper old gentleman.* 一位非常規矩有禮的老紳士。□ *vt* (-mm-) put (the face, lips) into a ~ expression. 使(面部、唇)作出正經的表情。**~·ly** *adv* **~·ness** *n*

prima /ˈpriːmə ; ˈprimə/ *adj* (I) first. (義)第一的;主要的。 **ˌ~ ˌballeˈrina** /ˌbæləˈriːnə ; ˌbæləˈrinə/, leading woman performer in ballet. 芭蕾舞之首席女演員。**ˌ~ ˈdonna** /ˈdɒnə ; ˈdɑnə/, leading woman singer in opera; (colloq) arrogant, temperamental person. 歌劇中的首席女歌手;首席女聲;(俗)傲慢和性情多變的人。

pri·macy /ˈpraɪməsɪ ; ˈpraɪməsɪ/ *n* (*pl* -cies) **1** pre-eminence. 首要;首位。 **2** position of an archbishop. 大主教之職位。

pri·mae·val /praɪˈmiːvl ; praɪˈmivl̩/ *adj* ⇨ primeval.

prima facie /ˌpraɪmə ˈfeɪʃiː ; ˈpraɪməˈfeʃɪˌi/ *adv, adj* (Lat) (based) on the first impression: (拉)乍看起來;據初次印象: *have ~ a good case.* 遇到初看起來似乎眞實的事件; (法律) 遇到乍看起來證據充分的案件。 **~ evidence,** (legal) sufficient to prove something (unless refuted). (法律)初步的證據。

pri·mal /ˈpraɪml ; ˈpraɪml̩/ *adj* (formal) primeval; chief; first in importance. (正式用語) 最初的;原始的;主要的;首要的。

pri·mary /ˈpraɪmərɪ *US:* -merɪ ; ˈpraɪˌmɛrɪ/ *adj* **1** leading in time, order or development: 在時間、次序或發展上領先的; 第一的; 基本的; 主要的: *of ~ (= chief) importance;* 首要的; *a ˈ~ school,* (GB) for junior pupils (5 to 11 years); 小學(英國,五歲至十一歲兒童就讀的學校); *~ rocks,* of the lowest series of strata; 原成岩(最下層的岩石);結晶岩; *the ~ meaning of a word,* the earliest and original meaning. 字的原始意義(本義)。 **2** ***~ colours,*** red, blue and yellow, from which all other colours can be obtained by mixing two or more. 原色(即

紅、藍、黃三色，由混合二種或二種以上之原色可得所有其他顏色)。□ *n* (*pl* -ries) (US) meeting of electors to name candidates for a coming election. (美) 提名候選人的預選會。 **pri·mar·ily** /ˈpraɪmərəlɪ *US:* praɪˈmerəlɪ ; ˈpraɪˌmɛrəlɪ/ *adv* in the first place; essentially. 首先;主要地;基本地。

pri·mate¹ /ˈpraɪmeɪt;ˈpraɪmɪt/ *n* archbishop. 大主教。

pri·mate² /ˈpraɪmeɪt ; ˈpraɪmɪt/ *n* one of the highest order of mammals (including men, apes, monkeys and lemurs). 靈長類動物(最高級之哺乳動物,包括人、猿、猴及狐猴)。

prime¹ /praɪm ; praɪm/ *adj* **1** chief; most important: 主要的;最重要的: *his ~ motive.* 他的主要動機。**P~ Minister,** chief minister of a Government. 首相;內閣總理。**2** excellent; first-rate: 最佳的;第一流的: *~ (cuts of) beef.* 上等牛肉(片)。 **3** fundamental; primary. 基本的;根本的。~ **cost,** cost of production not including overhead charges, margin for profit, etc. 主要成本(不包含間接費用、賺頭等的製造成本)。 ~ **meridian,** the zero meridian, that of Greenwich. 本初子午線。~ **mover,** primary source of motive power, eg wind, water; (fig) person who initiates a plan, action, etc. 主推動力;原動力(如風、水等);(喻)發起人;發動者。~ **number,** (maths) one which cannot be divided exactly except by itself and the number 1 (eg 7, 17, 41). (數學)質數;素數(除本身和1以外，不能被其他數目除盡的數，如 7, 17, 41 等)。

prime² /praɪm ; praɪm/ *n* [U] **1** state of highest perfection; the best part: 最完美的狀態;最佳部分: *in the ~ of youth;* 正值少壯時期; *in the ~ of life.* 在壯年。*When is a man in his ~?* 何時是一個人的盛年？*He is past his ~.* 他的盛年已過。**2** first or earliest part: 第一部分;最初部分: *the ~ of the year,* spring. 春季。 **3** church service at 6am or sunrise. (教堂在早晨六時或日出時舉行的)早課;晨禱。

prime³ /praɪm ; praɪm/ *vt* [VP6A] **1** get ready for use or action: 把…準備好以便使用或行動: *~ a gun,* (hist) put in gunpowder, etc; (史)裝火藥等於槍砲; *~ a pump,* wet it, pour in water, to get it started. 倒水於抽水機(使能發生吸力開始抽水)。~ ***the pump,*** (fig) put money into an inactive industry, etc or into the economy, to stimulate it to growth. (喻)將錢投入不景氣的工業等,或作經濟投資,以刺激其成長。 **2** supply with facts, etc: 供以事實等: *The witness had been ~d by a lawyer.* 這證人曾經受到律師的指點。*The Socialist candidate had been well ~d with facts by Party headquarters.* 社會黨的候選人已由該黨總部供給各種事實。**3** (colloq) fill (a person) with food or drink: (俗)以食物或飲料塞飽(某人): *well ~d with liquor.* 喝足了酒。 **4** cover (a surface) with the first coat of paint, oil, varnish, etc. 以頭道油漆等塗(表面)。

primer¹ /ˈpraɪmə(r) ; ˈprɪmɚ/ *n* first school textbook: 兒童的啓蒙讀物;初級讀本;入門書: *a Latin ~.* 拉丁文入門。

primer² /ˈpraɪmə(r) ; ˈpraɪmɚ/ *n* [C] **1** small quantity of explosive, contained in a cap or cylinder, for igniting the powder in a cartridge, bomb, etc. 底火;火帽;雷管;起爆劑(裝在帽形或棒形容器內的少量炸藥,用以引發彈藥筒、炸彈等)。⇨ the illus at cartridge. 參看 cartridge 之插圖。 **2** priming (of paint). (油漆的)底塗;底層漆。

pri·me·val (also **-mae·val**) /praɪˈmiːvl ; praɪˈmivl̩/ *adj* **1** of the earliest time in the world's history. 世界史之最初期的;太古的。 **2** very ancient: 古老的;原始的: *~ forests,* natural forests in which no trees have ever been felled. (從未加以砍伐的)原始森林;原生林。

prim·ing /ˈpraɪmɪŋ ; ˈpraɪmɪŋ/ *n* **1** gunpowder used to fire the charge of a gun, bomb, mine, etc. 點火藥;起爆劑。 **2** mixture used by painters for a first coat. 油漆底子;底漆。

primi·tive /ˈprɪmɪtɪv ; ˈprɪmətɪv/ *adj* **1** of the earliest times; of an early stage of social development: 上古的;原始的;社會發展之早期的: *~ man;* 原始人;初民; *~ culture.* 原始文化。 **2** simple; old-fashioned; having undergone little development: 簡單的;原始性的;不發達的: *~ weapons,* eg bows and arrows, spears. 原始性的武器(如弓、箭、矛)。□ *n* painter or sculptor of the period before the Renaissance; example of his work. 文藝復興以前之畫家或雕刻家;其作品。**~·ly** *adv* **~·ness** *n*

pri·mo·geni·ture /ˌpraɪməʊˈdʒenɪtʃə(r) *US:* -tʃʊər ; ˌpraɪməˈdʒɛnətʃɚ/ *n* fact of being the firstborn of the children of the same parents. 長子身份。**right of ~,** (legal) system by which all real estate passes on from a father to the eldest son. (法律)長子繼承權(所有不動產由父親傳給長子之制度)。

pri·mor·dial /praɪˈmɔːdɪəl ; praɪˈmɔrdɪəl/ *adj* in existence at or from the beginning; primeval. 原生的;原始的;最初的。

primp /prɪmp ; prɪmp/ *vt* = prink.

prim·rose /ˈprɪmrəʊz ; ˈprɪmˌroz/ *n* [C] common wild plant with pale yellow flowers; the flower; its colour. 櫻草(開淡黃色花);櫻草花;櫻草色;淡黃色。***the ~ way/path,*** (fig) the pursuit of reckless pleasure. (喻)追求使人墮落的享樂。

prim·ula /ˈprɪmjʊlə ; ˈprɪmjʊlə/ *n* kinds of perennial herbaceous plants with flowers of various colours and sizes (including the primrose and polyanthus). 櫻草屬 (多年生的草本植物,其花之顏色及大小各不相同,包括櫻草及黃花九輪草)。

pri·mus /ˈpraɪməs ; ˈpraɪməs/ *n* (*pl* ~es /-məsɪz ; -məsɪz/) (P) kind of cooking stove that burns vaporized oil. (商標)一種燃燒汽化油的爐子。

prince /prɪns ; prɪns/ *n* **1** ruler, esp of a small state. (尤指小國的)君主;諸侯。 **2** male member of a royal family, esp (in GB) a son or grandson of the Sovereign. 太子;王子(在英國尤指君主的兒子或孫子)。 **3 the ~ of darkness,** Satan. 撒旦;魔鬼。**the P~ of Peace,** Jesus. 和平之君(耶穌)。**P~ Consort,** husband of a reigning queen. 女王之夫。**~·dom** /-dəm ; -dəm/ *n* rank or dignity of, or area ruled by, a ~(1). 小國君主的地位,領地。**~·ly** *adj* (-ier, -iest) (worthy) of a ~; splendid; generous: 君主的;王侯的;與王侯相稱的;壯麗的;慷慨的: *a ~ly gift.* 豐厚的禮物。**prin·cess** /prɪnˈses ; ˈprɪnsɪs/ *n* wife of a ~; daughter or granddaughter of a sovereign. 王妃;公主。

prin·ci·pal /ˈprɪnsəpl;ˈprɪnsəpl̩/ *adj* highest in order of importance: 主要的;首要的;重要的: *the ~ rivers of Europe;* 歐洲的主要河流; *the ~ food of the people of Java.* 爪哇人的主食。 ~ **boy,** person (traditionally, in GB, an actress, not an actor) who takes the leading part in a pantomime. 啞劇裡的主角 (在英國，一向由女伶而非男伶擔任)。□ *n* **1** title of some heads of colleges and of some other organizations. (學校或機關之主管的稱謂)校長;首長。 **2** person for whom another acts as agent in business: (代理人所代表的)本人;委託人: *I must consult my ~.* 我必須跟我的委託人商量。 **3** main girder or rafter in a roof. (屋頂的)主樑;主椽。 **4** (fin) money lent, put into a business, etc on which interest is payable. (財政) (生息之) 本金;資本。 **5** (legal) person directly responsible for a crime (distinguished from an abetter or accessory). (法律)主犯(有別於教唆犯或從犯)。 **~ly** /-plɪ ; -pl̩ɪ/ *adv* for the most part; chiefly. 大抵;主要地。

prin·ci·pal·ity /ˌprɪnsɪˈpælətɪ ; ˌprɪnsəˈpælətɪ/ *n* (*pl* -ties) country ruled by a prince. 公國;侯國。**the P~,** Wales. 英國威爾斯之別名。

prin·ciple /ˈprɪnsəpl ; ˈprɪnsəpl̩/ *n* [C] **1** basic truth; general law of cause and effect: 原理;原則;一般因果律: *the (first) ~s of geometry/political economy/navigation.* 幾何學(政治經濟學,航海學)的(首要)原理。 **2** guiding rule for behaviour: 行爲的準則: *moral ~s;* 道義;道德規範;節操; *~s of conduct;* 行爲的準則; *live up to one's ~s;* 照自己的標準行事;言行一致; (collective *sing*) (集合單數) *a man of high*

~. 操守好的人。***in ~,*** (contrasted with *in detail*) in general. 大體上 (與 in detail 相對)。***on ~,*** from conviction, from a settled moral motive: 根據信念;由於一種固定的道德上的動機;根據原則: *He refused on ~ to understate his income for taxation purposes.* 他由於一種道德上的動機,拒絕爲了少納稅而少報收入。 **3** general law shown in the working of a machine, etc: 機器等的運轉原理: *These machines work on the same ~.* 這些機器按照相同的原理運轉。 **~d** *adj* (in compounds) following, having, the kind of ~(2) indicated: (用於複合字中)遵守行爲準則的;有節操的: *a most high-~d woman, unhappily married to a low-~d man.* 一位很有節操的女子,不幸與一位沒有節操的男人結婚。⇨ unprincipled.

prink /prɪŋk ; prɪŋk/ *vt* ~ ***oneself (up),*** make oneself look smart or spruce. 把自己打扮得漂亮。

print[1] /prɪnt ; prɪnt/ *n* **1** [U] mark(s), letters, etc in printed form: 印刷符號,字母等;印刷體;版: *clear ~;* 清晰的印刷; *in large/small ~.* 用大(小)鉛字;以大(小)字體印刷。***in ~,*** (of a book) printed and on sale. (指書)已出版;出售中;在銷行。***out of ~,*** (of a book) no more printed copies available from the publisher. (指書)絕版。***rush into ~,*** (of an author) hasten to publish sth he has written. (指作者)急於把作品付印。 **2** [C] (usu in compounds) mark left on a surface preserving the form left by the pressure of sth: (通常用於複合字中)印跡;痕跡: *'finger-~s;* 指紋;指印; *'foot-~s.* 足跡;足印。 **3** [U] printed cotton fabric: 印花棉布: (attrib) (形容用法) *a ~ dress.* 印花布的衣服。 **4** [C] picture, design, etc made by ~ing from a block, plate, etc: (由印模,感光版等) 印成的畫片,圖案等;版畫;印畫: *old Japanese ~s;* 古老的日本版畫; photograph ~ed from a negative. 印出之照片。**'blue·~,** ⇨ blue²(7). **'~-seller** *n* man who sells engravings, etchings, etc. 版畫售賣者。 **'~-shop** *n* shop of a ~-seller. 版畫店。 **5** [C] (now chiefly US) ~ed publication, esp a newspaper (現在主用於美)印刷物;出版物;(尤指)報紙。

print[2] /prɪnt ; prɪnt/ *vt, vi* **1** [VP6A] make marks on (paper), etc by pressing it with inked type, etc; make books/pictures, etc in this way; (of a publisher, an editor, an author) cause to be ~ed: 印符號於(紙等上);印刷(書,圖畫等);(指出版者,編輯,作者)出版;編印;刊行: *~ 6000 copies of a novel.* 印刷某小說六千册。*Do you intend to ~ your lectures/have your lectures ~ed?* 你有意把你的講稿印行嗎? (fig) (喻) *The incidents ~ed themselves on her memory.* 那些小事深深地印在她的記憶中。 **'~ed matter/papers,** (as on envelopes, wrappers, etc) circulars, prospectuses, etc to be charged for postage at a reduced rate. 印刷品(註於郵件上以獲得郵資之優待)。 **'~-out** *n* the ~ed output of a computer. (電子計算機之)輸出資料。 **2** [VP6A] shape (one's letters), write (words), in imitation of ~ed characters (instead of ordinary joined handwriting). 照印刷體寫(字母,字)。 **3** [VP 6A, 15B] ~ ***(off),*** make (a photograph) on paper, etc from a negative film or plate: 用底片印(相片)於紙上等: *How many copies shall I ~ (off) for you from this negative?* 你要我用這張底片洗出多少張相片? **4** [VP2A] (of a plate or film) produce a picture; be produced as the result of ~ing(3): (指感光板或底片)印相片;被印出來: *This film/plate/picture hasn't ~ed very well.* 這膠捲(感光板,照片)印出來不清楚。 **5** [VP6A] mark (a textile fabric) with a coloured design. 印彩色圖案於(織物)。 **~·able** /-əbl ; -əbḷ/ *adj* that can be ~ed, or ~ed from; fit to be ~ed. 可印刷的;可由其印出的;適於印行的。 **~er** *n* workman who ~s books, etc; owner of a ~ing business. 印刷工人;印刷業者。 **~·ing** *n* (in verbal senses): (按動詞各義): **'~ing-ink,** kind of ink used for ~ing books, etc. 印刷用油墨。 **'~ing-machine, '~ing-press** *nn* machine for ~ing books, etc. 印刷機。 **'~ing office** *n* place where ~ing is done. 印刷廠。

prior[1] /'praɪə(r) ; 'praɪɚ/ *adj* ~ ***(to),*** earlier in time, order or importance: 較早的;順序在先的;更重要的: *have a ~ claim to sth.* 對某事物有優先權。 **~ to,** *prep* (formal) before: (正式用語)在…之前: *~ to any discussion of this matter.* 在討論這事之前。*The house was sold ~ to auction,* before the day of the auction. 這房子在拍賣日之前業已售出。

prior[2] /'praɪə(r) ; 'praɪɚ/ *n* head of a religious order or house; (in an abbey) next below an abbot. 教派的首長;小修道院院長;(大修道院的)副院長;副主持。 **~ess** /'praɪərɪs ; 'praɪərɪs/ *n* woman ~. 小女修道院院長; 大女修道院副院長。 **~y** /'praɪərɪ ; 'praɪərɪ/ *n* religious house governed by a ~ or ~ess. 小修道院或女修道院。

pri·or·ity /praɪ'ɒrətɪ *US:* -'ɔːr- ; praɪ'ɔrətɪ/ *n* (*pl* -ties) **1** [U] ~ ***(over),*** being prior; right to have or do sth before others: 較早;順序在先;優先權: *I have ~ over you in my claim.* 我的請求比你優先。*The proceeds of the sale* (eg of the property of a bankrupt) *will be distributed according to ~.* 售賣所得 (如拍賣破產者之財產) 將按優先順序分配。 **2** [C] claim to consideration; high place among competing claims: 被考慮的權利;佔優先的位置;需要優先考慮的事物: *Road building is a first ~* (or, colloq, 俗, *a top ~*). 築路爲第一優先。*The Government gave ~ to housing after the War.* 政府在戰後優先考慮房屋問題。

prise /praɪz ; praɪz/ *vt* = prize³.

prism /'prɪzəm ; 'prɪzəm/ *n* **1** solid figure with similar, equal and parallel ends, and with sides which are parallelograms. 壔;稜柱(各對應邊平行,各面爲平行四邊形之立體圖形)。 **2** body of this form, usu triangular and made of glass, which breaks up white light into the colours of the rainbow. 稜柱體;(通常指)三稜鏡;稜鏡。

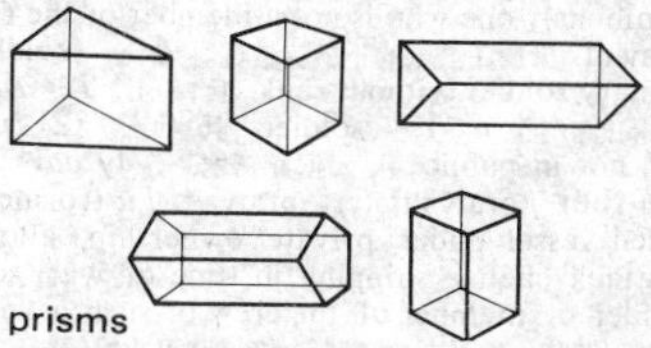

prisms

pris·matic /prɪz'mætɪk ; prɪz'mætɪk/ *adj* **1** like, having the shape of, a prism. 似稜柱或三稜鏡的;稜柱或三稜鏡形的。 **2** (of colours) brilliant and varied. (指顏色)光彩奪目的;五光十色的。

prison /'prɪzn ; 'prɪzṇ/ *n* [C] building in which wrongdoers are kept locked up; place where a person is shut up against his will; [U] confinement in such a building: 監獄;牢房;監禁;禁錮: *escape/be released from ~;* 逃出 (被放出) 監獄; *be in/go to/send sb to ~.* 坐牢(入獄;把某人關進監牢)。 **'~-breaking** *n* the illegal act of escaping from ~. 越獄。 **~er** *n* person kept in ~ for crime or until tried in a law court; person, animal or bird kept in confinement: 囚犯;犯人;刑事被告;被禁閉的人,動物或鳥: *a bird kept ~er in a cage.* 被關在籠中的鳥。 **ˌ~er of 'conscience,** political ~er, 政治(囚)犯, ⇨ political(1). **ˌ~er of 'war,** person captured in war and (usu) kept in a camp for the duration of the war. 戰俘;俘虜。

pris·tine /'prɪstiːn ; 'prɪstin/ *adj* (formal) primitive; of early times; unchanged by later developments; fresh as if new: (正式用語)原始的;初期的;未受後來發展之影響的;像新的一般鮮明的: *Who would want to get back to the ~ simplicity of Anglo-Saxon days?* 誰會想要回復盎格魯撒克遜時代原始的質樸呢?

prithee /'prɪðɪ ; 'prɪðɪ/ *int* (archaic) I pray thee; please: (古)請你;請: *P~, keep silent.* 請君保持安靜。*Tell me, ~,....* 請告訴我…。

priv·acy /ˈprɪvəsɪ *US:* ˈpraɪv- ; ˈpraɪvəsɪ/ *n* [U] **1** state of being away from others, alone and undisturbed: 隱退;靜居; 獨處而不受干擾: *the invasion of ~ by the press and TV.* 報紙和電視對靜居的侵擾。*I should hate to live in a household where ~ was impossible.* 我討厭住在沒法靜居的家中。*I don't want my ~ disturbed.* 我不願私生活受干擾。 **2** secrecy (opp to *publicity*): 祕密(與 publicity 相反): *They were married in strict ~.* 他們在極度祕密下結婚。

pri·vate /ˈpraɪvɪt ; ˈpraɪvɪt/ *adj* **1** (opp of *public*) of, for the use of, concerning, one person or group of persons, not people in general: (爲 public 之相反字)私人的;私用的;私有的: *a ~ letter,* about personal matters; 私人信件; *for ~ reasons,* not to be explained to everybody. 爲了私人的理由。ˌ**~ ˈenterprise,** the management of industry, etc by ~ individuals, companies, etc (contrasted with State ownership or control). 私人企業(與國營企業相對)。ˌ**~ ˈmeans,** income not earned as a salary, etc but coming from personal property, investments, etc. 私產所得(指來自個人之財產,投資等,而非來自薪金之收入)。ˌ**~ ˈschool,** one at which fees are paid (contrasted with a school financially supported by the State, etc). 私立學校(與公立學校相對)。 **2** secret; kept secret: 祕密的;保持祕密的: *a letter marked 'P~';* 標有'密'字的信件; *have ~ information about sth.* 得到有關某事的祕密消息。**~ parts,** external sex organs. 私處;陰部。 **3** having no official position; not holding any public office: 無官職的;平民的: *do sth in one's ~ capacity,* not as an official, etc; 以平民資格做某事; *his ~ life,* the life he leads away from business or public affairs. 他的私生活(與業務或公務無關者)。***retire into ~ life,*** retire after a public career. 退休(從公職退休)。**~ member** (of the House of Commons), one who is not a member of the Government. 未擔任公職的下議院議員。 **4 ~ (soldier),** ordinary soldier without rank: 兵;兵士: *P~ Dodd.* 兵士陶德。☐ *n* **1** ~ soldier. 兵;兵士。 **2** *in ~,* ~ly, not in public. 私下地;祕密地。**~·ly** *adv*

pri·va·teer /ˌpraɪvəˈtɪə(r) ; ˌpraɪvəˈtɪr/ *n* (formerly) armed vessel under private ownership, allowed to attack enemy shipping in time of war; commander or member of the crew of such a vessel. 私掠船(昔時一種私有的武裝船,在戰時可攻擊敵船);私掠船的指揮官或船員。

pri·va·tion /praɪˈveɪʃn ; praɪˈveʃən/ *n* **1** [U, C] lack of the necessaries of life; destitution: 生活必需品的缺乏;窮困: *fall ill through ~;* 因缺乏生活必需品而生病;貧病交加; *suffering many ~s.* 備嘗艱辛。 **2** [C] state of being deprived of sth (not necessarily sth essential): 被剝奪某物(不一定爲必需品);喪失;不便: *He found it a great ~ not being allowed to smoke in prison.* 他覺得在監獄中禁止吸煙是一件很大的不便。

privet /ˈprɪvɪt ; ˈprɪvɪt/ *n* [U] evergreen shrub, bearing small white flowers, much used for garden hedges: 水蠟樹;女貞(一種常綠灌木,開小白花,多用作園籬): *clipping the ~ hedges.* 修剪水蠟樹樹籬。

pri·vi·lege /ˈprɪvəlɪdʒ ; ˈprɪvl̩ɪdʒ/ *n* **1** [C] right or advantage available only to a person, class or rank, or the holder of a certain position, etc: (某人,某階級或地位,或擔任某職位者等的)特權; 特惠: *the ~s of birth,* eg that come because one is born into a wealthy family. 與生俱來的特權 (例如因爲生於富家)。 **2** [C] special favour or benefit: 特殊的榮幸,恩惠或利益: *grant sb the ~ of fishing in a privately owned trout stream.* 特許某人在私有的產鱒的河中捕魚。*It was a ~ to hear her sing.* 聽她唱歌是一樁很榮幸的事。 **3** [C, U] right to do or say things without risk of punishment, etc (as when Members of Parliament may say things in the House of Commons which might result in a libel case if said outside Parliament). 做或說某事而不致受罰的權利;特權(例如國會議員可在下議院內發表的某些言論,如在國會以外說出可能招致毀謗罪)。**~d** /ˈprɪvəlɪdʒd ; ˈprɪvl̩ɪdʒd/ *adj* having, granted, a ~ or ~s. 有特權的;獲得特殊利益的。**the ~d classes,** those who enjoy the advantages of the best education, of wealth, and secure social position. 特權階級。ˌ**under-ˈ~d,** suffering from poverty. 貧苦的。

privy /ˈprɪvɪ ; ˈprɪvɪ/ *adj* **1** (old use, except legal) secret; private. (除法律用語外爲舊用法) 祕密的;私有的。**~ *to,*** having secret knowledge of: 與聞…之機密: *charged with having been ~ to the plot against the prince.* 被控曾參與背叛王子的陰謀。 **2 the P~ Council,** committee of persons appointed by the Sovereign, advising on some State affairs, but membership now being chiefly a personal dignity. 英國樞密院(英國國君任命之組織,咨議國事,但樞密顧問之身份現在主要爲個人的一種尊榮而已)。**P~ Councillor/Counsellor,** member of the P~ Council. 樞密顧問官。**P~ Purse,** allowance of money from the public revenue for the Sovereign's private expenses. 國家歲收中撥爲君主私用的錢財。**P~ Seal,** State seal affixed to documents of minor importance. (英)御璽。☐ *n* (*pl* -vies) (old use) water-closet. (舊用法) 舊式厠所; 茅坑。**priv·ily** /-ɪlɪ ; -ɪlɪ/ *adv* privately; secretly. 私下地;祕密地。

prize¹ /praɪz ; praɪz/ *n* **1** sth (to be) awarded to one who succeeds in a competition, lottery, etc: 獎品;贈品;獎金: *be awarded a ~ for good conduct;* 因品行優良獲獎; *draw a ~-winning ticket in a lottery;* 抽到一張得獎的彩票;中獎; *carry off most of the ~s at the village flower show;* 奪得該村花展的大部分獎品; *win first ~ on the pools;* 贏得總賭注的頭獎; *consolation ~s,* given to console those who do not win the good ~s; 精神獎;安慰獎(用以安慰未獲大獎者); *~ cattle,* cattle that have been awarded ~s; 獲獎的牛; *a ~ scholarship,* one awarded as a ~. 成績優良獎學金。 **2** (fig) anything struggled for or worth struggling for: (喻)奮鬪爭取的東西;值得奮鬪爭取的東西: *the ~s of life.* 人生之目的。 **3** ˈ**~-fight** *n* boxing match for money.(以營利爲目的之)職業性拳賽。Hence, 由此產生, ˈ**~-fighter,** ˈ**~-fighting** *nn* ˈ**~-ring** *n* the enclosed area (now usu a square) in which boxing-matches are fought; the sport of ~-fighting. 職業性拳擊場(現在通常爲方形);職業性拳擊。 **4** ˈ**~·man** /-mən ; -mən/ *n* (*pl* -men) winner of a ~ (usu with the name of the ~ or scholarship prefixed). 得獎者;得獎學金者(通常其前冠以獎品或獎學金之名稱)。☐ *vt* value highly: 珍視;重視: *my most ~d possessions.* 我最珍視的財產。

prize² /praɪz ; praɪz/ *n* [C] sth, esp a ship or its cargo, captured at sea during a war. 戰時在海上捕獲之物 (尤指船或船貨); 海上戰利品。ˈ**~-money** *n* money realized by the sale of a ~ (and divided up among those who captured it). 捕獲賞金(出售海上捕獲物所得之錢,由捕獲者分享之)。

prize³ (also **prise**) /praɪz ; praɪz/ *vt* [VP15A, B] use force to get sth, eg a box, lid, *open/up/off.* 撬開;撐起(如箱,蓋) (與 open, up, off 連用)。

pro¹ /prəʊ ; pro/ *n* [C] (usu only in) (通常僅用於) ***the ~s and cons (of sth),*** the arguments for and against (sth). 贊成論與反對論; 正反雙方的理由。☐ *adv* ***pro and con,*** for and against: 贊成與反對: *argue pro and con.* 從正反兩方辯論。

pro² /prəʊ ; pro/ *n* (*pl* pros) (colloq) (short for) professional (player): (俗)爲 professional (player) 之略: *a golf pro.* 高爾夫球職業選手。

pro- /ˌprəʊ ; prə/ *pref* supporting; favouring: 支持的;贊成的;親善的: *pro-British;* 親英的; acting for: 代理的: *pro-consul;* 代理領事; 副領事; *pro-vice-chancellor.* 代理副校長。⇨ App 3. 參看附錄三。

prob·abil·ity /ˌprɒbəˈbɪlətɪ ; ˌprɑbəˈbɪlətɪ/ *n* (*pl* -ties) **1** [U] quality of being probable. 或然;大概。***in all ~,*** most probably. 大概;多半;十之八九。

2 [U] likelihood: 可能性: *There is no/little/not much ~ of his succeeding/that he will succeed.* 他不(很少,不大)可能會成功。 **3** [C] (most) probable event or outcome: (最)可能發生的事件或結果: *What are the probabilities?* 成算怎樣?

prob·able /'prɒbəbl ; 'prɑbəbl/ *adj* likely to happen or to prove true or correct: 可能發生或證實的;或然的;大概的: *the ~ result;* 可能的結果; *a ~ winner.* 有希望的得勝者。*Rain is possible but not ~ before evening.* 在傍晚前下雨是可能的,但是不一定會下。 *It seems ~ that....* 很可能是;恐怕要…。□ *n* person who will most likely be chosen, eg for a team, or do sth; ~ candidate, winner, etc. 最可能被選出(參加球隊)的人;有希望的候選人、得勝者等。**prob·ably** /-əblɪ ; -əblɪ/ *adv* most likely: 或許;大概: *Jim's late—he's probably stuck in a traffic jam.* 吉姆晚了—他大概被交通阻塞困住了。

pro·bate /'prəubeɪt ; 'probet/ *n* **1** [U] the official process of proving the validity of a will: 遺囑之認證: *take out ~ of a will;* 取得某遺囑的認證; *grant ~ of a will.* 通過某遺囑的認證。 **2** [C] copy of a will with a certificate that it is correct. 經認證的遺囑。□ *vt* (US) establish the validity of a will (GB 英 = *prove*). (美)認證遺囑的效力。

pro·ba·tion /prə'beɪʃn *US:* prəu- ; pro'beʃən/ *n* [U] **1** testing of a person's conduct, abilities, qualities, etc before he is finally accepted for a position, admitted into a society, etc: (在決定給予某人一職位,准許某人加入某會社等之前的)試驗;試用;見習: *two years on ~,* ie undergoing such testing; 試用兩年; *an officer on ~.* 見習官。 **2 the '~ system,** (legal) that by which (esp young) offenders are allowed to go unpunished for their first offence while they continue to live without further breaking of the law: (法律)緩刑;緩刑制: *three years' ~ under suspended sentence of one year's imprisonment.* 判刑一年,緩刑三年。**'~ officer,** one who watches over the behaviour of offenders who are on ~. 緩刑監視官(對緩刑期間犯人之行爲加以監視者)。**~·ary** /prə'beɪʃnrɪ *US:* prəu'beɪʃənerɪ ; pro'beʃən,ɛrɪ/ *adj* relating to ~. 試驗的;試用的;緩刑的。**~er** *n* **1** hospital nurse receiving training and still on ~(1). (醫院中的)見習護士。 **2** wrongdoer who has been released on ~(2). 緩刑期中的罪犯。

probe /prəub ; prob/ *n* **1** slender instrument with a blunt end, used by doctors for learning about the depth and direction of a wound, etc. 探針(一種鈍頭之細長工具,醫生用以探測傷處等之深度及方向者)。 **2** (journalism) investigation (*into* a scandal, etc). (新聞用語)刺探;偵察(醜聞等,與 into 連用)。□ *vt* [VP6A] **1** examine with a ~. 用探針檢查;探查。 **2** investigate or examine thoroughly (sb's thought, the causes of sth). 偵察;細察(某人的思想,某事的原由)。

prob·ity /'prəubətɪ ; 'probətɪ/ *n* [U] (formal) uprightness of character; integrity. (正式用語)性格之剛直;誠正。

prob·lem /'prɒbləm ; 'prɑbləm/ *n* [C] question to be solved or decided, esp sth difficult: 問題;難題: *mathematical ~s;* 數學問題; *the ~s of youth.* 青少年的問題。**'~ child,** one whose behaviour offers a difficult ~ to his parents, teachers, etc. 問題兒童。**~ picture,** one in which the artist's intention is obscure. (藝術家意向不明的)問題圖畫。 **~ play/novel,** one dealing with a social or moral ~. (處理社會或道德問題的)問題劇(小說)。 **~·atic** /,prɒblə'mætɪk ; ,prɑblə'mætɪk/ *adj* (esp of a result) doubtful; that cannot be seen or foretold. (尤指結果)有疑問的;不能看出或預知的。 **~·ati·cally** /-klɪ ; -klɪ/ *adv*

pro·bos·cis /prə'bɒsɪs ; pro'bɑsɪs/ (*pl* ~es /-sɪsi:z ; -sɪsɪz/) *n* **1** elephant's trunk. 象鼻。 **2** elongated part of the mouth of some insects. (若干昆蟲的)長嘴;吻部。

pro·cedure /prə'si:dʒə(r) ; prə'sidʒə/ *n* [C, U] (the regular) order of doing things, esp legal and political: 做事的(一般)手續;(尤指)訴訟程序;議事程序: *the usual ~ at committee meetings;* 委員會會議的一般程序; *stop arguing about (questions of) ~ and get down to business.* 停止爭辯程序(問題)而致力於議事。**pro·cedural** /prə'si:dʒərəl ; prə'sidʒərəl/ *adj* of ~. 手續的;訴訟程序的;議事程序的。

pro·ceed /prə'si:d ; prə'sid/ *vi* **1** [VP2A, 3A, 4C] ~ *to sth/to do sth,* go forward; go on: 前進;着手;繼續進行: *Let us ~ to business/to the next item on the agenda.* 我們着手工作吧(我們繼續進行議程上的下一個項目吧)。*He ~ed to inform me that....* 他開始告訴我…。*They ~ed* (more usu 較常用 *went*) *from London to Leeds.* 他們由倫敦前往里玆。 **~ with sth,** start or continue with it: 開始;繼續: *Please ~ with your explanation.* 請繼續解釋。 **2** [VP3A] **~ from sth,** come, arise from: 來到;發生: *famine, plague and other evils that ~ from war.* 因戰爭而引起的饑饉,瘟疫及其他弊害。**3** [VP3A] **~ against sb,** take legal action. 控訴;起訴。 **4** [VP3A] **~ to sth,** go on from a lower university degree: (在獲得較低的大學學位後)繼續攻讀: *~ to the degree of MA.* 攻讀文學碩士學位。

pro·ceed·ing /prə'si:dɪŋ ; prə'sidɪŋ/ *n* **1** [U] course of action; (way of) behaving: 動作之過程;進行;舉止;行徑: *What is our best way of ~?* 我們最好的進行方式是什麼? **2** [C] sth done; piece of conduct: 做過之事;行爲;行動;處置: *What he did was a rather high-handed ~.* 他的所做所爲是一種相當專橫的行爲。*The ~s at the meeting were rather disorderly.* 會議的進展頗爲紊亂。*There have been suspicious ~s in committee meetings.* 委員會會議中有可疑的處置。 **3** (*pl*) (複) ***take/start legal ~s (against sb),*** take legal action. (對某人)提起訴訟;控訴。 **4** (*pl*) records (of the activities of a society, etc); minutes: (複)(會社等活動的)記錄;議事錄: *the ~s of the Kent Archaeological Society.* 肯特考古學會的活動記錄。

pro·ceeds /'prəusi:dz ; 'prosidz/ *n pl* financial results, profits, of an undertaking: 所得;贏利;收入: *hold a bazaar and give the ~ to local charities.* 舉行義賣,所得捐給當地的慈善機構。

pro·cess[1] /'prəuses *US:* 'prɒses ; 'prɑsɛs/ *n* **1** [C] connected series of actions, changes, etc esp such as are involuntary or unconscious: 相互關聯的一系列的活動、變化等(尤指不隨意的或不自覺的);進行;經過;過程: *the ~es of digestion, reproduction and growth.* 消化,生殖及生長的過程。 **2** [C] series of operations deliberately undertaken: 一系列審慎採取的步驟;手續;程序: *Unloading the cargo was a slow ~.* 卸船貨的程序是緩慢的。 **3** [C] method, esp one used in manufacture or industry: (尤指用於生產或實業中的)方法;製法: *the 'Bessemer ~,* in steel manufacture. 英人 Henry Bessemer 的製鋼法。 **4** [U] forward movement; progress: 前進;進展: *The glasses were broken during the ~ of removal.* 在拆除的過程中眼鏡片破了。***in ~ of,*** during: 在…期間: *a building in ~ of construction;* 建造中的房屋; *in ~ of time,* as time goes on. 隨着時間的進展;逐漸地。 ***in ~,*** in course of being done. 進行中。 **5** [C] (legal) action at law; formal commencement of this; summons or writ ordering a person to appear in a law court. (法律)訴訟;正式提起訴訟;訴訟程序;傳票。**'~-server** *n* sheriff's officer who delivers writs. 送達傳票的司法人員。□ *vt* [VP6A] treat (material) in order to preserve it: 處理(原料)以保存之: *~ leather;* 鞣製皮革; put (esp food) through a special ~(3): 特別處理(尤指食物);加工: *~ed cheese;* 加工奶酪; (photo) (攝影) *~ film,* develop it, etc; 冲洗軟片; (computers) (電腦) *~ tape/information,* put it through the system in order to obtain the required information. 處理資料帶(資訊)。

pro·cess[2] /prə'ses ; pro'sɛs/ *vi* walk in or as if in procession. 列隊進行;如列隊之進行。

pro·ces·sion /prəˈseʃn ; prəˈsɛʃən/ *n* [C] number of persons, vehicles, etc moving forward and following each other in an orderly way: (人,車輛等的)進行行列;隊伍: *a ˈfuneral ~;* 送葬行列; [U] act of moving forward in this way: 列隊進行: *walking in ~ through the streets.* 排成隊伍走過街道。**~al** /-ʃənl ; -ʃənl/ *adj* of, for, used in, ~s: 行列的; 隊伍的; 適於行列或隊伍的; 用於行列或隊伍的: *a ~al chant,* sung by persons taking part in a religious ~. 行列聖歌(在宗教的遊行隊伍中由參加者唱之)。

pro·claim /prəˈkleɪm ; proˈklem/ *vt* [VP6A, 9, 23, 25] **1** make known publicly or officially: 宣告; 公佈;正式宣佈: ~ (= declare) *war/peace;* 宣戰(宣告和平); *~ a public holiday;* 宣佈節日;宣佈公定假日; *~ a republic;* 宣佈一共和國的成立; *~ a man (to be) a traitor/~ that he is a traitor.* 宣佈某人為叛徒。*He ~ed Anne his heir.* 他宣佈安為他的繼承人。**2** reveal, show: 顯示; 顯露: *His accent ~ed him a Scot/that he was a Scot.* 他的口音顯示他是蘇格蘭人。**proc·la·ma·tion** /ˌprɒkləˈmeɪʃn ; ˌprɑkləˈmeʃən/ *n* [U] act of ~ing: 宣告;公佈: *by public proclamation;* 公開宣告; [C] that which is ~ed: 宣言;布告;文告: *issue/make a proclamation.* 發表文告。

pro·cliv·ity /prəʊˈklɪvətɪ ; proˈklɪvətɪ/ *n* (*pl* -ties) [C] **~ *(to/towards sth/to do sth),*** (formal) tendency, inclination. (正式用語)傾向;癖性。

pro·con·sul /ˌprəʊˈkɒnsl ; proˈkɑnsl/ *n* (in ancient Rome) governor of a Roman province; (rhet, mod use) governor of a colony or dominion. (古羅馬之)地方總督; (修辭,現代用法) 殖民地或自治領的總督。**pro·con·su·lar** /ˌprəʊˈkɒnsjʊlə(r) *US:* -səl- ; proˈkɑnsḷɚ/ *adj* **pro·con·su·late** /-lət ; -lɪt/ *n* position of a ~; his term of office. 地方總督或殖民地總督的職位;其任期。

pro·cras·ti·nate /prəʊˈkræstɪneɪt ; proˈkræstəˌnet/ *vi* [VP2A] (formal) delay action; keep on putting off: (正式用語)耽擱;拖延;遲滯: *He ~d until it was too late.* 他拖延得太遲了。**pro·cras·ti·na·tion** /prəʊˌkræstɪˈneɪʃn ; proˌkræstəˈneʃən/ *n* [U]: ***Procrastination is the thief of time,*** (prov) procrastinating wastes time. (諺)拖延乃時間之賊。

pro·create /ˈprəʊkrɪeɪt ; ˈprokrɪˌet/ *vt* [VP6A] beget, generate (offspring). 生育;生殖;產(子)。**pro·cre·ation** /ˌprəʊkrɪˈeɪʃn ; ˌprokrɪˈeʃən/ *n*

proc·tor /ˈprɒktə(r) ; ˈprɑktɚ/ *n* **1** (at Oxford and Cambridge) university official with various duties, including the maintenance of discipline among students. (牛津及劍橋大學的)學監;訓導員(其職務包括維持學生的紀律)。**2 Queen's/King's P~,** official whose duty is to watch the parties in certain kinds of legal cases, eg divorce, and to intervene if there are irregularities, eg collusion or suppression of facts. 王室的訟監(在某些法律案件如離婚等中,監視訴訟當事人,不使有串騙或隱匿事實等情者)。

procu·ra·tor /ˈprɒkjʊreɪtə(r) ; ˈprɑkjəˌretɚ/ *n* **1** agent, esp one who has a power of attorney. 代理人;(尤指)訴訟代理人;代訴人。**2 ~ fiscal,** public prosecutor of a district in Scotland. 蘇格蘭的地方檢察官。

pro·cure /prəˈkjʊə(r) ; proˈkjʊr/ *vt* [VP6A, 12B, 13B] **1** obtain, esp with care or effort: 獲得;(尤指用心或費力)取得: *Can you ~ me some specimens?* 你可以為我取得一些標本嗎? *The book is out of print and difficult to ~.* 那書已絕版,難於獲得。**2** (old use) bring about; cause: (舊用法)促成;引致: *~ sb's death by poison.* 毒死某人。**3** obtain clients for a prostitute. 介紹娼妓;為…拉皮條。**pro·cur·able** /-əbl ; -əbḷ/ *adj* obtainable. 可獲得的。**~·ment** *n* procuring: 獲得; 得到: *the ~ment of military supplies.* 獲得軍用物資; 獲得補給。**~r** *n* (esp) pander. (尤指)淫媒;拉皮條者。**pro·cur·ess** /-rɪs ; -rɪs/ *n* woman ~r. 老鴇;鴇母。

prod /prɒd ; prɑd/ *vt, vi* (-dd-) [VP6A, 3A] **~ *(at),*** push or poke with sth pointed; (fig) urge (to action): 以尖物推或刺;(喻)促(採取行動);激起: *The cruel boys were ~ding (at) the bear through the bars of the cage.* 那些殘忍的孩子們隔着籠子的欄杆以尖物刺那隻熊。□ *n* poke or thrust: 刺;戳: *She gave the man a ~ with her umbrella.* 她用傘戳了那男人一下。

prodi·gal /ˈprɒdɪgl ; ˈprɑdɪgḷ/ *adj* **~ *(of),*** wasteful; spending or using too much: 浪費的; 揮霍的; 不吝惜的: *a ~ administration,* spending public funds too freely. 浪費(公帑)的政府。*Nature is ~ of her gifts.* 大自然不吝惜其恩賜。**the ~ son,** wasteful and improvident man (in one of the parables of Jesus) who repents of his actions. 浪子(見於耶穌的寓言之一)。⇨ Luke 15:11. 參看路加福音第 15 章第 11 節。□ *n* [C] person who is wasteful. 浪費之人;浪子。**~·ly** /-gəlɪ ; -glɪ/ *adv* in a ~ manner: 浪費地; 揮霍地; 不吝惜地: *a man who gives ~ly to charities.* 不吝捐贈慈善事業的人。**~·ity** /ˌprɒdɪˈgælətɪ ; ˌprɑdɪˈgælətɪ/ *n* [U] (in a good sense) being ~: (好的意思)不吝惜;慷慨: *the ~ity of the sea,* ie in supplying fish; 海洋的慷慨(卽大量供應魚產); (in a bad sense) extravagance; wasteful spending. (壞的意思)浪費;揮霍。

pro·di·gious /prəˈdɪdʒəs ; prəˈdɪdʒəs/ *adj* enormous; surprisingly great; wonderful: 巨大的; 大得驚人的; 奇異的: *a ~ sum of money.* 鉅款。**~·ly** *adv*

prod·igy /ˈprɒdɪdʒɪ ; ˈprɑdədʒɪ/ *n* (*pl* -gies) sth wonderful because it seems to be contrary to the laws of nature; person who has unusual or remarkable abilities or who is a remarkable example of sth: 似乎與自然律相抵觸的奇怪事物;了不起的事物; 不凡之人; 典型人物: *a ~ of learning;* 飽學之士; *prodigies of nature.* 大自然的瑰寶。**infant ~,** extremely talented child, eg one who plays the piano well at six. 神童(具有非常才智之兒童,如六歲卽善彈鋼琴)。

pro·duce /prəˈdjuːs *US:* -ˈduːs ; prəˈdjus/ *vt, vi* [VP6A, 2A] **1** put or bring forward to be looked at or examined: 提出;呈出: *~ proofs of a statement;* 提出說明的證據; *~ one's railway ticket when asked to do so.* 繳驗火車票。*The conjuror ~d a rabbit from his hat.* 魔術師從帽中取出一隻兔子。**2** manufacture; make; grow; create: 製造; 生產; 出產;生長;創造: *~ woollen goods;* 生產毛織品; *fields which ~ heavy crops.* 產量豐富的田地。*We must ~ more food for ourselves and import less.* 我們必須增產糧食減少進口。*This artist ~s very little.* 這位藝術家作品甚少。**3** give birth to; lay (eggs). 生;產(卵)。**4** cause; bring about: 引起;導致: *success ~d by hard work and enthusiasm;* 由努力工作及熱忱導致的成功; *a film that ~d a sensation.* 轟動一時的影片。**5** (maths) make (a line) longer (*to* a point). (數學)引長(線段至某點)。**6** bring before the public: 演出;出版: *~ a new play,* organize it and put it on the stage; 演出新戲; *a well-~d book,* one that is well printed, bound, etc. 印刷、裝訂等都很好的書。□ *n* /ˈprɒdjuːs *US:* -duːs ; ˈprɑdjus/ [U] that which is ~d, esp by farming: 生產品; 出產品; (尤指)農產品: *garden/farm/agricultural ~.* 農圃(農場,農業)的產品。

pro·ducer /prəˈdjuːsə(r) *US:* -ˈduː- ; prəˈdjusɚ/ *n* **1** person who produces goods (contrasted with the *consumer*). 生產者(與 consumer 相對)。**2** person responsible for presenting a play in the theatre or for the production of a film (apart from the directing of the actors); person in charge of a broadcast programme (radio or TV). (戲劇)演出人;(影片)製片人;(廣播或電視節目的)製作人。⇨ director. **3 ˈ~ gas,** gas obtained by passing air through red-hot carbon or air and steam through hot coal or coke. 發生爐煤氣(使空氣通過紅熱之碳,或使空氣與水氣通過熾熱之煤或焦炭所得者)。

prod·uct /ˈprɒdʌkt ; ˈprɑdəkt/ *n* [C] **1** sth produced (by nature or by man): (天然或人造的)產品;生產物: 'farm ~s; 農產品; the chief ~s of Scotland; 蘇格蘭的主要產物; the ~s of genius, eg great works of art. 天才的產品(如偉大的藝術作品)。**2** (maths) quantity obtained by multiplication; (chem) substance obtained by chemical reaction. (數學)積;乘積;(化學)生成物。

pro·duc·tion /prəˈdʌkʃn; prəˈdʌkʃən/ *n* **1** [U] process of producing: 製造;生產: *the ~ of crops/manufactured goods, etc.* 農作物(工業品等)的生產。**mass ~,** ⇨ mass. **2** [U] quantity produced: 產量: *increase ~ by using better methods and tools;* 利用更好的方法和工具增加生產; *a fall/increase in ~.* 產量的減少(增加)。**3** [C] thing produced: 製造品;生產品: *epic ~s at the cinema;* 以英雄事蹟爲題材的影片; *his early ~s as a writer,* his first novels, plays, etc. 他的早期作品(小說,戲劇等)。

pro·duc·tive /prəˈdʌktɪv; prəˈdʌktɪv/ *adj* **1** able to produce; fertile: 能生產的;肥沃的: *~ land.* 肥沃的土地。**2** *~ of,* tending to produce; resulting in: 有生產或導致…之傾向的;可能產生…的: *~ of happiness;* 可產生幸福的; *discussions that seem to be ~ only of quarrels.* 似乎只會導致口角的討論。**3** producing things of economic value: 生產有經濟價值之東西的: *~ labour.* 有生產價值的勞動。**~·ly** *adv*

pro·duc·tiv·ity /ˌprɒdʌkˈtɪvətɪ; ˌprodʌkˈtɪvətɪ/ *n* [U] being productive; power of being productive: 能生產;多產;生產力: *increase ~,* increase efficiency and the rate at which goods are produced; 增加生產力; *a ~ bonus for workers.* 工人的增產紅利。**'~ agreement,** (as part of a wage settlement) better pay and conditions for an increased output. 增產協議(生產增加時則提高工人的薪資或改善工作環境)。

pro·fane /prəˈfeɪn *US:* prəʊ-; prəˈfen/ *adj* **1** (contrasted with *sacred, holy*) worldly: 凡俗的;世俗的(與 sacred, holy 相對): *~ literature,* (opp *biblical*). 世俗文學(爲 biblical 之相反字)。**2** having or showing contempt for God and sacred things: 瀆神的;褻瀆的;不敬神的: *~ language/words/practices;* 褻瀆神的言語(話,習慣); *a ~ man.* 不敬神的人。□ *vt* [VP6A] treat (sacred or holy places, things) with contempt, without proper reverence: 褻瀆;玷污(聖地,聖物): *~ the name of God.* 褻瀆上帝之名。**~·ly** *adv* **~·ness** *n* **profa·na·tion** /ˌprɒfəˈneɪʃn; ˌprɑfəˈneʃən/ *n* [C, U] instance of profaning. 褻瀆神聖;褻瀆之事例。**pro·fan·ity** /prəˈfænətɪ *US:* prəʊ-; prəˈfænətɪ/ *n* (*pl* -ties) **1** [U] *~* conduct or speech; use of *~* language. 褻瀆的行爲或言語;褻瀆神聖;不敬語的使用。**2** (*pl*) *~* phrases, utterances: (複)褻瀆的詞句、話: *A string of profanities came from his lips.* 從他的口裡說出了一連串褻瀆的話。

pro·fess /prəˈfes; prəˈfɛs/ *vt, vi* **1** [VP6A] declare that one has (beliefs, likes, ignorance, interests, etc): 公開承認;公言;明言具有(信念,喜好,愚昧,興趣等): *He ~es a distaste for modern music.* 他聲言不喜歡現代音樂。*He ~ed a great interest in my welfare.* 他明白表示非常關心我的幸福。**2** [VP6A] affirm one's faith in, allegiance to, (a religion, Christ): 表白信仰(某宗教,基督): *~ Islam.* 表白信仰回教。**3** [VP6A] (formal) have as one's profession or business: (正式用語)以…爲業;執業: *~ law/medicine;* 做律師(醫生); teach as a professor: 教;教授: *~ history/modern languages.* 教授歷史(現代語)。**4** [VP6A, 7A, 9, 25] claim; represent oneself: 聲稱;自稱: *I don't ~ to be an expert on that subject.* 我不自認爲是那問題的專家。*He ~ed himself satisfied.* 他聲稱感到滿意。*She ~ed that she could do nothing unaided.* 她自稱無法獨力做任何事。**~ed** *adj* **1** self-acknowledged: 自認的;明言的: *a ~ed atheist.* 自認的無神論者。**2** falsely claiming to be: 詐稱的;自稱的: *a ~ed friend.* 表面上的朋友。**3** having taken religious vows: 已立誓修行的;已受戒的: *a ~ed nun.* 已受戒的女尼。**~·ed·ly** /-ɪdlɪ; -ɪdlɪ/ *adv* according to one's own claims or admissions: 根據其聲言或承認;公言地;表面上地;詐稱地: *He is ~edly a Communist.* 他自稱是共產黨徒。

pro·fes·sion /prəˈfeʃn; prəˈfɛʃən/ *n* [C] **1** occupation, esp one requiring advanced education and special training, eg the law, architecture, medicine, accountancy: 職業;(尤指需接受高深教育及特殊訓練的)專門職業(例如律師,建築師,醫師,會計師的職業): *He is a lawyer by ~.* 他的職業是律師。**2** *~ of,* statement or declaration of belief, feeling, etc: (信念,感情等的)表白;宣佈: *~s of faith/loyalty.* 信仰(忠誠)的表白。*She does not believe in his ~s of passionate love.* 她不相信他所表白的熱愛。**3** *the ~,* the body of persons engaged in a particular ~(1). 某專業的團體;同業。

pro·fes·sional /prəˈfeʃənl; prəˈfɛʃənl̩/ *adj* **1** of a profession(1): 專門職業的;職業上的: *~ skill;* 專門職業上的技術; *~ etiquette,* the special conventions, forms of politeness, etc associated with a certain profession; 某行業特有的禮儀;行規; *~ men,* eg doctors, lawyers. 從事專門職業的人(如醫生,律師)。**2** doing or practising sth as a full-time occupation or for payment or to make a living (opp of *amateur*): 職業性的;專業的(與 amateur 相對): *~ football;* 職業足球賽; *~ tennis-players;* 職業網球選手; *a ~ politician.* 以從政爲職業的人。□ *n* (contrasted with *amateur*) (與 amateur 相對) **1** (often abbr to 常略作 *pro* /prəʊ; pro/) person who teaches or engages in some kind of sport for money. 爲賺錢而從事某種運動的人;職業教練;職業選手。**2** person who does sth for payment that others do (without payment) for pleasure: 爲賺錢而從事某種遊藝的人;職業藝人: *~ musicians.* 職業樂師;職業樂手;職業音樂家。**turn ~,** become a ~. 成爲職業的(選手、演員等)。**~·ly** /-nəlɪ; -nl̩ɪ/ *adv* in a ~ manner or capacity. 專業地;在職業上。**~·ism** /-əlɪzəm; -əlɪzm̩/ *n* **1** mark or qualities of a profession(1). 某專門職業的標記或特性。**2** the practice of employing ~s to play games. 雇用職業選手參加比賽。

pro·fes·sor /prəˈfesə(r); prəˈfɛsɚ/ *n* **1** university teacher of the highest grade, holding a chair of some branch of learning; (in US, also) teacher or instructor. (大學)教授;(在美國,亦作)教師;講師。**2** title assumed by instructors of various subjects: 若干科目之教師的稱謂;專家;教授: *P~ Pate, the renowned phrenologist.* 培德教授,著名的顱相學家。**3** one who makes a public profession(2): 公開表白其信仰等之人: *a ~ of pacifism/Catholicism.* 信守和平主義(信奉天主教義)之人。**prof·es·sorial** /ˌprɒfɪˈsɔːrɪəl; ˌprofəˈsorɪəl/ *adj* relating to a ~: (大學)教授的;有關教授的: *his ~ial duties.* 他的教授職務。**~·ship** /-ʃɪp; -ʃɪp/ *n* ~'s post at a university: (大學的)教授職位: *be appointed to a ~ship.* 被聘爲大學教授。

prof·fer /ˈprɒfə(r); ˈprɑfɚ/ *vt* [VP6A, 7A] offer. 提供;提出。□ *n* offer. 提供;提出。

pro·fi·cient /prəˈfɪʃnt; prəˈfɪʃənt/ *adj* ~ *(in),* skilled; expert. 熟練的;精通的。**~·ly** *adv* **pro·fi·ciency** /-nsɪ; -nsɪ/ *n* ***proficiency (in),*** [U] being ~: 熟練;精通: *a certificate of proficiency in English.* 熟諳英語的證書。

pro·file /ˈprəʊfaɪl; ˈprofaɪl/ *n* **1** [U, C] side view, esp of the head: 側面;側面像: *a portrait drawn in ~.* 側面畫像。**2** edge or outline of sth seen against a background. (背景襯出之)輪廓;外形。**3** brief biography, as given in an article in a periodical or a broadcast talk. 對於人物之簡短的描述;人物素描(如雜誌或廣播中所作者)。□ *vt* draw, show, in ~: 作…之側面像;描繪…之輪廓: *a line of hills ~d against the night sky.* 以夜空爲背景的羣山的輪廓。

profit¹ /ˈprɒfɪt; ˈprɑfɪt/ *n* **1** [U] advantage or good obtained from sth: 利益;裨益: *gain ~ from one's studies;* 從讀書獲得益處; *study sth to one's ~.* 學習某事以獲益。**2** [C, U] money gained in business, etc: 利潤;贏利: *make a ~ of ten pence on* *every article sold;* 每賣一物獲利十辨士; *sell sth at a ~;* 賺錢賣出某物; *do sth for ~.* 爲贏利做某事。 ˌ**~ and ˈloss account,** (book-keeping) one that shows the trading ~ or loss for a definite period. (簿記)損益帳。 **ˈ~-margin** *n* difference between cost of purchase or production and selling price. 盈餘;成本與售價之差額。 **ˈ~-sharing** *n* [U] the sharing of ~s between employers and employees: (雇主與雇員間的) 分紅; 分紅制: *start a ~-sharing scheme.* 開始一項分紅制度。**~·less** *adj* **~·less·ly** *adv*

profit² /ˈprɒfɪt ; ˈprɑfɪt/ *vt, vi* **1** [VP3A] ~ ***from/by,*** (of persons) be benefited or helped: (指人) 獲益;獲利: *Have you ~ed by the experience?* 你是否曾自該經驗中獲益? *I have ~ed from your advice.* 我從你的勸告得到好處。 **2** [VP6A, 13A] (old use) (of things) be of advantage to: (舊用法) (指事物) 有利;對…有益: *What can it ~ him?* 此事對他有什麼利益呢? *It ~ed him nothing.* 此事對他毫無益處。

prof·it·able /ˈprɒfɪtəbl ; ˈprɑfɪtəbl/ *adj* bringing profit; beneficial: 賺錢的;獲利的;有益的: *~ investments;* 有利的投資; *a deal that was ~ to all of us.* 對大家有利的一樁買賣。**prof·it·ably** /-əblɪ ; -əblɪ/ *adv*

profi·teer /ˌprɒfɪˈtɪə(r) ; ˌprɑfəˈtɪr/ *vi* [VP2A] make large profits, esp by taking advantage of times of difficulty or scarcity, eg in war. 獲暴利;賺大錢(尤指利用困難或缺乏之時機,如在戰時)。□ *n* person who does this. 獲暴利者;投機商人。

prof·li·gate /ˈprɒflɪgət ; ˈprɑfləgɪt/ *adj* **1** (of a person, his behaviour) shamelessly immoral. (指人,其行爲)放蕩的;淫佚的。 **2** (of the spending of money) reckless; very extravagant: (指花錢) 恣意的;極其浪費的: *~ of one's inheritance.* 揮霍遺產。□ *n* ~(1) person. 放蕩的人;淫佚者。 **prof·li·gacy** /ˈprɒflɪgəsɪ ; ˈprɑfləgəsɪ/ *n* [U] being ~. 放蕩;淫佚;恣意浪費。

pro forma /ˌprəʊ ˈfɔːmə ; proˈfɔrmə/ *adj, adv* (Lat) as a formality only. (拉)僅爲形式之故;僅爲官樣文章。 **~ invoice,** one that notifies the value of goods dispatched but does not ask for payment. 估價單。

pro·found /prəˈfaʊnd ; prəˈfaund/ *adj* **1** deep: 深的;淵深的: *a ~ sleep/sigh/bow;* 熟睡(深長的嘆息; 深深的鞠躬); *take a ~ interest in sth;* 對某事物深感興趣; *listen with ~ interest.* 深感興趣地聆聽。 **2** needing, showing, having, great knowledge: 需要,顯示或具有淵博知識的;深奧的;博學的: *~ books/authors/thinkers;* 深奧的書(著作者,思想家); *a man of ~ learning.* 博學的人。 **3** needing much thought or study to understand: 需要多加思索或研究才能了解的;奧妙的: *~ mysteries.* 奧秘。 **~·ly** *adv* in a ~ manner: 深深地;深奧地;奧妙地: *~ly* (= deeply) *grateful/disturbing.* 深爲感激的(極爲擾人的)。 **pro·fun·dity** /prəˈfʌndətɪ ; prəˈfʌndətɪ/ *n* (*pl* -ties) [U] depth: 深;淵深: *the profundity of his knowledge;* 他的學問的淵深; [C] (chiefly in non-material senses) that which is deep or abstruse; (*pl*) depths of thought or meaning. (主要用作非物質的意思)有深度的東西;深奧之事物;(複)思想或意義的深奧。

pro·fuse /prəˈfjuːs ; prəˈfjus/ *adj* **1** very plentiful or abundant: 非常豐富的;大量的: *~ gratitude.* 千恩萬謝。 **2** ~ ***in,*** lavish or extravagant: 浪費的;奢侈的: *He was ~ in his apologies,* apologized almost to excess. 他一再道歉(幾達過份程度)。 **~·ly** *adv* **~·ness** *n* **pro·fu·sion** /prəˈfjuːʒn ; prəˈfjuʒən/ *n* [U] abundance; great supply: 豐富;大量: *roses growing in profusion;* 大量盛開的玫瑰; *make promises in profusion.* 作過多的允諾。

pro·geni·tor /prəʊˈdʒenɪtə(r) ; proˈdʒɛnətɚ/ *n* (formal) ancestor (of a person, animal or plant); (fig) political or intellectual predecessor. (正式用語)(人,動植物的)祖先;(喻)政治上或學術上的前輩。

progeny /ˈprɒdʒənɪ ; ˈprɑdʒənɪ/ *n* (formal) (collective *sing*) offspring; descendants, children. (正式用語)(集合單數)子孫;後裔;小孩。

prog·no·sis /prɒgˈnəʊsɪs ; prɑgˈnosɪs/ *n* (*pl* -noses /-nəʊsiːz ; -nosiz/) (med) forecast of the probable course of a disease or illness. (醫) 病狀之預斷; 預後。⇨ diagnosis.

prog·nos·tic /prɒgˈnɒstɪk ; prɑgˈnɑstɪk/ *adj* (formal) predictive (*of*). (正式用語)預兆的; 預後的;病狀預斷的(與 of 連用)。□ *n* pre-indication (*of*): 預示;預兆(與 of 連用): *a ~ of failure.* 失敗的預兆。

prog·nos·ti·cate /prɒgˈnɒstɪkeɪt ; prɑgˈnɑstɪˌket/ *vt* [VP6A, 9] (formal) foretell; predict: (正式用語)預言;預示;預測: *~ trouble.* 預示困難。 **prog·nos·ti·ca·tion** /prɒgˌnɒstɪˈkeɪʃn ; prɑgˌnɑstɪˈkeʃən/ *n* [U] prognosticating; [C] sth which ~s. 預言;預示;預測;前兆;徵候。

pro·gramme (also **-gram**) /ˈprəʊgræm ; ˈprogræm/ *n* **1** list of items, events, etc, eg for a concert, or to be broadcast for radio or TV, or for a sports meeting; list of names of actors in a play, singers in an opera, etc. 節目單(例如音樂會,廣播,電視或運動會中者);程序表;(戲劇或歌劇等中之)演員名單。 **ˈ~ music,** music designed, in sound, to suggest to the listener a known story, picture, etc. 效果音樂;背景音樂;標題音樂。 **ˈ~ note,** short account, in a ~, eg of a musical work, a performer, etc. (對樂曲,表演者等的)簡短介紹。 **2** plan of what is to be done: 工作計畫;預定表: *a political ~.* 政治綱領。 *What's the ~ for tomorrow?* What are we/you going to do? 明天要做什麼? **3** coded collection of information, data, etc fed into an electronic computer. (電腦)程式。□ *vt* [VP6A] make a ~ of or for; supply (a computer) with a ~; plan. 排…之節目單;擬…之計畫;以一批相關的資料供給(電腦)作爲計算資料;設計。 **~d course,** (education) one in which the material to be learnt is presented (in books or a machine) in small, carefully graded amounts. (教育) 編序課程。 **~d learning,** self-instruction using such courses. 編序教學;編序學習。 **pro·gram·mer** *n* person who prepares a computer ~. 電腦程式設計人;程式師。

prog·ress /ˈprəʊgres *US:* ˈprɒg- ; ˈprɑgrɛs/ *n* **1** [U] forward movement; advance; development: 進步;進展;改進;發展: *making fast ~;* 進步神速; *make ~ in one's studies;* 學業有進步; *~ in civilization.* 文明的進展。 *An inquiry is now in ~,* being made. 一項調查目前正在進行中。 *The patient is making good ~,* is improving. 這個病人的病情大有起色。 **2** [C] (old use) state journey: (舊用法) 王侯的視察; 巡行: *a royal ~ through Cornwall.* 國王巡行康瓦耳。□ *vi* /prəˈgres ; prəˈgrɛs/ [VP2A, C] make ~: 進步;進行: *The work is ~ing steadily.* 工作正在穩定地進行中。 *She is ~ing in her studies.* 她在學業上有進步。

pro·gression /prəˈgreʃn ; prəˈgrɛʃən/ *n* **1** [U] progress; moving forward: 進步;前進;行進: *modes of ~,* eg crawling, walking. 行進的方式(如爬、步行)。 **2** (maths) (數學) ⇨ arithmetic, geometry.

pro·gress·ive /prəˈgresɪv ; prəˈgrɛsɪv/ *adj* **1** making continuous forward movement. 前進的。 **the ~ tenses,** (gram) forms of the verb (using the ending *-ing*) that express action that continues over a period of time, as in 'I am/was/will be/have been writing.' (Also called 亦稱作 *continuous tenses.*) (文法)進行式 (be + -ing 之形式,表示動作持續一段時間,如 I am/was/will be/have been writing)。 **2** increasing by regular degrees or advancing in successive stages: 累進的;遞增的;循序漸進的: *~ education/schools;* 循序漸進的教育(學校); *~ taxation,* with an increase of the rate of tax as the incomes increase; 累進課稅; *~ cancer,* becoming steadily worse. 繼續惡化的癌;擴散性癌。 **3** undergoing improvement; getting better, eg in civilization; supporting or favouring progress: 改進的;上進的;進步的(如在文明方面);支持或贊成進步的: *a ~ policy;* 進步的政策; *a ~ political party.* 提倡改革的政黨。□ *n* person supporting a ~ policy. 支持進步政策者;進步論者。 **~·ly** *adv* **~·ness** *n*

pro·hibit /prəˈhɪbɪt *US:* prəʊ- ; proˈhɪbɪt/ *vt* [VP6A, 14] ~ ***sb (from doing sth),*** forbid (esp by rules or regulations); say that sth must not be done, that sb must not do sth: 禁止;阻止: *Smoking strictly ~ed.* 嚴禁吸煙。*Children are ~ed from buying cigarettes.* 禁止兒童購買香煙。

pro·hib·ition /ˌprəʊɪˈbɪʃn ; ˌproəˈbɪʃən/ *n* **1** [U] prohibiting; (esp) prohibiting by law the making or sale of alcoholic drinks (esp, US, the period 1920–33): 禁止;(尤指美國 1920–33 期間) 禁止造酒或賣酒: *the ~ law(s);* 禁酒法; *in favour of/opposed to ~.* 贊成(反對)禁酒。**2** [C] edict or order that forbids: 禁令;禁律: *a ~ against the sale of cigarettes to children.* 禁止售賣香煙給兒童之命令。**~·ist** /-ɪst ; -ɪst/ *n* person who favours the ~ of sth, esp the sale of alcoholic drink. 贊成禁止某物者;(尤指)贊成禁酒者。

pro·hibi·tive /prəˈhɪbətɪv *US:* prəʊ- ; proˈhɪbɪtɪv/ *adj* tending to, intended to, prevent the use or abuse or purchase of sth: 禁止的;意欲阻止使用,濫用或購買某物的: *a ~ tax;* 寓禁稅; *books published at ~ prices.* 以高至令人不敢問津的價格所發行的書。

pro·hibi·tory /prəˈhɪbɪtərɪ *US:* prəʊˈhɪbɪtɔːrɪ ; proˈhɪbəˌtorɪ/ *adj* designed to prohibit sth: 有禁止之意的;爲禁止某物而設計的: *~ laws.* 查禁的法令。

pro·ject[1] /ˈprɒdʒekt ; ˈprɑdʒɛkt/ *n* [C] (plan for a) scheme or undertaking: 設計;計畫;事業;企業: *a ~ to establish a new national park;* 建立一座新的國家公園的計畫; *form/carry out/fail in a ~.* 擬訂一計畫(執行一計畫;計畫失敗)。

pro·ject[2] /prəˈdʒekt ; prəˈdʒɛkt/ *vt, vi* **1** [VP6A] make plans for: 計畫;設計: *~ a new dam/waterworks.* 設計新水壩(自來水廠)。**2** [VP6A, 14] ~ ***sth (on (to) sth),*** cause a shadow, an outline, a picture from a film, slide, etc to fall on a surface, etc: 使(影子,輪廓,影片,幻燈片等之圖像)投落在表面等上;投射;放映; *~ a picture on a screen;* 將影片放映於銀幕上; *~ a beam of light on to sth.* 投射一道光線在某物上。**3** [VP14] ~ ***sth on to sb,*** attribute unconsciously (usu unpleasant feelings such as guilt, inferiority) to other people (often as a means of self-justification or self-defence): 歸咎;將某事歸罪某人;(心理)投射: *She always ~s her own neuroses on to her colleagues,* describes them as suffering from them. 她總是將自已的神經病投射到她的同事身上。**4** [VP6A] make known the characteristics of: 使…之特色爲人所知;表達…的特色: *Do the BBC External Services adequately ~ Great Britain,* give listeners right ideas about British life, etc? 英國廣播公司的海外廣播部能使聽衆對英國有正確認識嗎? **5** [VP6A, 15A] throw; hurl: 拋;投;射: *an apparatus to ~ missiles into space.* 發射飛彈進入太空的裝置。**6** [VP6A] represent (a solid thing) on a plane surface by drawing straight lines through every point of it from a centre; make (a map) in this way. 藉投影圖表示(某立體物);以投影法製作(地圖)。**7** [VP2A, C] stick out; stand out beyond the surface nearby: 突出;伸出附近之平面: *~ing eyebrows;* 突出的眉毛; *a balcony that ~s over the street.* 伸到街上的陽臺。

pro·jec·tile /prəˈdʒektaɪl *US:* -tl ; prəˈdʒɛktl/ *n* sth (to be) shot forward, esp from a gun; self-propelling missile, eg a rocket. 拋射物;投射物;(尤指)彈丸;火箭;飛彈。□ *adj* able to send sth, or be sent, forward through air, water, etc: 能(被)拋射通過空氣,水等的;拋射的;發射的: *a ~ missile/torpedo.* 發射飛彈(魚雷)。

pro·jec·tion /prəˈdʒekʃn ; prəˈdʒɛkʃən/ *n* [U] the act of projecting (all senses); [C] sth that projects or has been projected; prominence. 計畫;投射;投拋;投影;突出;投射作用;所計畫,投射,投拋,投影之物;突出部分。ˈ**~ room,** (in a cinema) room from which pictures are projected on to the screen. (電影院)放映室。⇨ Mercator's projection. **~·ist** /-ɪst ; -ɪst/ *n* (in a cinema) person who projects the pictures on to the screen. (電影院)放映電影者;放映技師。

pro·jec·tor /prəˈdʒektə(r) ; prəˈdʒɛktɚ/ *n* [C] apparatus for projecting pictures by rays of light on to a screen: 影像放映機: *a ˈcinema/ˈslide ~.* 電影(幻燈片)放映機。

pro·lapse /prəʊˈlæps ; prəˈlæps/ *vi* (med, eg of the bowel or uterus) slip forward or down out of place. (醫,如指腸或子宮)脫出;脫垂。□ *n* /ˈprəʊ-

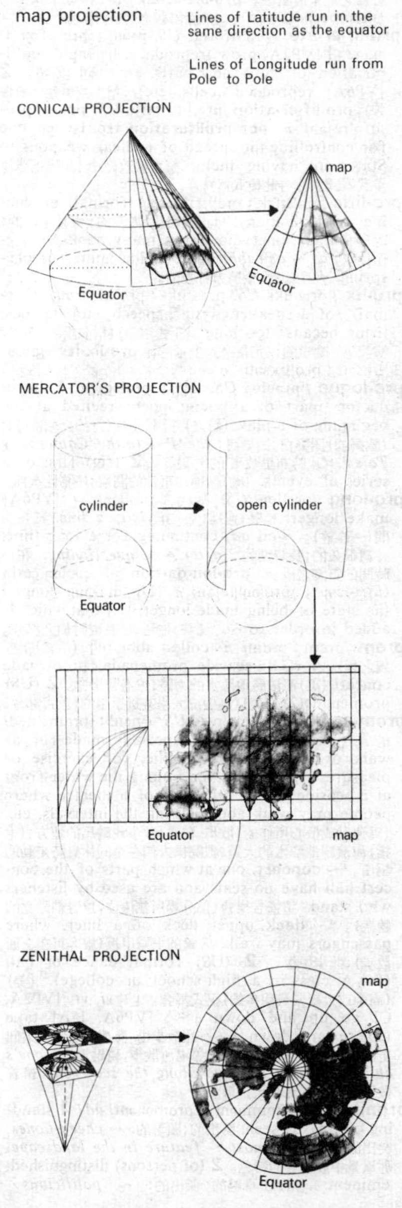

læps ; ˈprolæps/ such a movement. 脫出;脫垂。

prole /prəʊl ; prol/ *n* (colloq) member of the proletariat. (俗)無產階級者。

pro·let·ariat /ˌprəʊlɪˈteərɪət ; ˌproləˈtɛrɪət/ *n* **1** the whole body of wage-earners (esp manual workers) contrasted with the owners of industry (the bourgeoisie): 無產階級;勞動階級(尤指勞工,與'資產階級'相對): *the dictatorship of the ~,* as a Communist aim or ideal. 無產階級專政。 **2** (in ancient Rome) the lowest class of the community. (古羅馬)社會之最下層階級。 **pro·let·arian** /-ɪən ; -ɪən/ *n, adj* (member) of the ~. 無產階級者;無產階級的。

pro·lif·er·ate /prəˈlɪfəreɪt *US:* prəʊ- ; proˈlɪfəˌret/ *vi, vt* **1** [VP2A] grow, reproduce, by rapid multiplication of cells, new parts, etc. 增生;繁殖。 **2** [VP6A] reproduce (cells, etc). 增生或繁殖(細胞等)。**pro·lif·er·ation** /prəˌlɪfəˈreɪʃn *US:* prəʊ- ; proˌlɪfəˈreʃən/ *n.* **non-proliferation treaty,** eg one for controlling the spread of nuclear weapons to States not having them. 禁止擴散條約(如防止非核子武器國家擁有此種武器)。

pro·lific /prəˈlɪfɪk ; prəˈlɪfɪk/ *adj* (formal) producing much or many: (正式用語)多產的;大量生產的: *a ~ author,* one who writes many books, etc; 多產作家; *as ~ as rabbits,* producing numerous offspring. 多產如兎;生殖力特强的。

pro·lix /ˈprəʊlɪks *US:* prəʊˈlɪks ; proˈlɪks/ *adj* (formal) (of a speaker, writer, speech, etc) tedious; tiring because too long. (正式用語)(指演說者,作家,演說等)嚕囌的;冗長令人生厭的。 **pro·lix·ity** /prəʊˈlɪksətɪ ; proˈlɪksətɪ/ *n*

pro·logue /ˈprəʊlɒg *US:* -lɔːg ; ˈprolɔg/ *n* **1** introductory part of a poem; poem recited at the beginning of a play: (詩之)序詞;序詩(詩的介紹部分); (戲劇的)開場白;開場詩: *the 'P~' to the 'Canterbury Tales'.* '坎特布里故事'的'序詩'。 **2** (fig) first of a series of events. (喩)一連串事件的開端;序幕性事件。

pro·long /prəˈlɒŋ *US:* -ˈlɔːŋ ; prəˈlɔŋ/ *vt* [VP6A] make longer: 延長;拖延: *~ a visit/a line.* 延長訪問(一條線)。**~ed** *adj* continuing for a long time: 持續很久的;長時期的: *after ~ed questioning.* 在長時間的質詢之後。 **pro·lon·ga·tion** /ˌprəʊlɒŋˈgeɪʃn *US:* -lɔːŋ- ; ˌprolɔŋˈgeʃən/ *n* [U] making longer; the state of being made longer; [C] that which is added in order to ~. 延長;拖延;延長或附加之部分。

prom /prɒm ; prɑm/ *n* (colloq abbr of) (俗,以下各義之畧) **1** (GB) seaside promenade; promenade concert. (英)海濱勝地臨水的大路;逍遙音樂會。**2** (US) promenade(2). (美)(高中或大學某班學生的)正式舞會。

prom·en·ade /ˌprɒməˈnɑːd *US:* -ˈneɪd ; ˌprɑməˈned/ *n* **1** (place suitable for, specially made for, a) walk or ride taken in public, for exercise or pleasure, esp a broad road along the water-front at a seaside resort, or a part of a theatre where people may walk about during the intervals, etc. (爲運動或散心所作的)散步;騎馬;散步或騎馬的地方;(尤指)海濱勝地臨水的大道;戲院供人們在幕間休息時走動的場所。**ˈ~ concert,** one at which parts of the concert hall have no seats and are used by listeners who stand. 逍遙音樂會(部分場所無座位,以容納站立的聽衆)。**ˈ~ deck,** upper deck of a liner, where passengers may walk. 客輪的上層甲板(旅客可在上面散步);散步甲板。 **2** (US) formal dance or ball (for a class in a high-school or college). (美)(高中或大學某班學生的)正式舞會。□ *vi, vt* [VP2A, C] go up and down a ~; [VP6A, 15A] take (sb) up and down a ~: 在散步場、海濱大道等處來回走動;散步;帶着(某人)在此等場所散步,騎馬等。*~ one's children/one's husband along the sea-front.* 帶着孩子(丈夫)在海濱大道散步。

promi·nent /ˈprɒmɪnənt ; ˈprɑmənənt/ *adj* **1** standing out; easily seen: 突出的;顯著的: *~ cheek-bones;* 突出的顴骨; *the most ~ feature in the landscape.* 那風景中最顯著的特色。**2** (of persons) distinguished; eminent: (指人)卓越的;傑出的: *~ politicians/scientists.* 卓越的政治家(科學家)。 **3** important; conspicuous: 重要的;引人注目的: *occupy a ~ position;* 居高位;居要職; *play a ~ part in civic life.* 在市民生活中扮演重要的角色。**~·ly** *adv* **promi·nence** /-əns ; -əns/ *n* **1** [U] the state of being ~. 突出;顯著;卓越;重要。***bring sth/come into prominence,*** (cause to) become ~. (使某物)變得顯著,重要。 **2** [C] ~ part or place: 突出的部分或地方: *a ~ in the middle of a plain.* 平原中央突起的部分。

pro·mis·cu·ous /prəˈmɪskjʊəs ; prəˈmɪskjʊəs/ *adj* **1** confused and disorderly; unsorted: 雜亂的;混淆的;一團糟的: *in a ~ heap.* 成爲雜亂的一堆。 **2** indiscriminate; casual: 不加選擇的;隨便的: *~ friendships,* made without careful choice; 交友不加選擇; *~ sexual intercourse.* 亂交;雜交。**~·ly** *adv* **prom·is·cu·ity** /ˌprɒmɪˈskjuːətɪ ; ˌprɑmɪsˈkjuətɪ/ *n* (state of) being ~; confusion caused by being ~. 雜亂;不加選擇;雜交;混亂。

prom·ise¹ /ˈprɒmɪs ; ˈprɑmɪs/ *n* **1** [C] written or spoken undertaking to do, or not to do, sth: 諾言;約定: *~s of help;* 幫助的諾言; *make/give/keep/carry out/break a ~;* 許下(提出,信守,履行,違背)諾言; *under a ~ of secrecy.* 在保守秘密的承諾之下。 **2** [C] that which one undertakes to do: 約定或承諾要做的事: *I claim your ~,* require you to do what you said you would do. 我要求你履行諾言。 **3** [U] (sth that gives) hope of success or good results: (有成功或良好結果的)希望;有希望的事物: *boys who don't show much ~,* do not seem likely to succeed; 沒有多大前途的男孩們; *a writer of ~;* 有希望的作家; *the land of ~.* 想望之福地。

prom·ise² /ˈprɒmɪs ; ˈprɑmɪs/ *vt, vi* **1** [VP6A, 7A, 9, 11, 12A, 13A, 17] make a promise(1) to: 答應;允諾;約定: *They ~d an immediate reply.* 他們答應卽刻回覆。 *He ~d (me) to be here/that he would be here at 6 o'clock.* 他和我約好六點鐘到此。 *I ~d myself a quiet weekend.* 我決定要過一個平靜的週末。 *'Will you come?' — 'Yes, I ~.'* '你會來嗎?'—'是的,我會的。' **the P~d Land,** the land of promise: **(a)** the fertile country ~d to the Israelites by God; Canaan. 上帝答應給以色列人的肥沃土地;迦南。 **(b)** any state of future happiness. 未來的幸福境界。**2** [VP6A, 2A] give cause for expecting: 有…希望;預示: *The clouds ~ rain.* 陰雲預示有雨。 *It ~s to be warm this afternoon.* 今天下午可望轉暖。***~ well,*** show signs of success. 大有希望;顯示成功的跡象。**prom·is·ing** *adj* full of promise(3); seeming likely to succeed, have good results, etc. 有希望的;有前途的;大有可爲的。

prom·iss·ory /ˈprɒmɪsərɪ *US:* -sɔːrɪ ; ˈprɑməˌsorɪ/ *adj* conveying a promise. 約定的;應許的。**ˈ~ note,** signed promise to pay a stated sum of money to a specified person or to the bearer on a specified date or on demand. 期票;本票。

prom·on·tory /ˈprɒməntrɪ *US:* -tɔːrɪ ; ˈprɑmənˌtorɪ/ *n* [C] headland; high point of land standing out from the coastline. 岬;海角。

pro·mote /prəˈməʊt ; prəˈmot/ *vt* **1** [VP6A, 14] ~ ***(to),*** give (sb) a higher position or rank: 擢升: *He was ~d sergeant/to sergeant/to the rank of sergeant.* 他被升做士官。 **2** [VP6A] help to organize and start; help the progress of; help to found or organize: 協辦;籌設;提倡;促進;創設: *~ a new business company;* 籌設一家新的商行; *~ a bill in Parliament;* 促使議案在國會通過; *try to ~ good feelings (between...).* 設法促進(…彼此間的)好感。 **pro·mo·ter** *n* (esp) person who ~s new trading companies, professional sports, etc. (尤指)新公司的發起人;籌設者;職業性運動的倡導人;贊助人。

pro·mo·tion /prəˈməʊʃn ; prəˈmoʃən/ *n* **1** [U] promoting or being promoted: 擢升;晉級;協辦;籌設: *win/gain ~.* 獲得晉級。 *Ought ~ to go by seniority or by merit and abilities?* 擢升應以年資,還是以功績和能力爲準? **2** [C] instance of promoting or being promoted: 擢升、協辦等的實例: *He resigned* *from the firm because ~s were few and far between.* 他辭去那家公司的差事,因爲升遷少,而每升一級又要隔很長時間。 **3** encouragement by publicity, etc: 以廣告推銷;促銷: *the ~ of a new commercial product/a new book;* 一種新商品(一本新書)的推銷; *sales ~,* advertising, publicising one's products. 以廣告推銷;宣傳產品。

prompt[1] /prɒmpt; prɑmpt/ *adj* acting, done, sent, given, without delay: 迅速的;敏捷的;即時的: *a ~ reply;* 迅速的回答; *~ payment;* 即時付錢; *men who are ~ to volunteer;* 敏於自告奮勇的人; *at 6 pm ~* (= ~ly). 下午六時正。 **~·ly** *adv* **~·ness** *n*

prompt[2] /prɒmpt; prɑmpt/ *vt* **1** [VP6A, 17A] be the reason causing (sb to do sth): 促使(某人做某事);激勵;鼓勵;喚起;驅使: *He was ~ed by patriotism.* 他爲愛國心所激勵。 *What ~ed him to be so generous?* 什麼使得他如此大方呢? **2** [VP6A] follow the text of a play and, when an actor forgets his words, say quietly some of these to him. 提示臺詞給(演員);提詞。 □ *n* action of ~ing (an actor): 提詞: *wait for a ~.* 等候提詞。 **'~-box** *n* place where the ~er sits. 提詞者的座位。 **'~-copy** *n* text of a play, used by a ~er. 提詞者用的劇本。 **~er** *n* person who ~s actors. 提詞者。

promp·ti·tude /'prɒmptɪtju:d *US:* -tu:d; 'prɑmptə,tjud/ *n* [U] promptness; readiness to act. 迅速;敏捷;機敏行事。

prom·ul·gate /'prɒmlgeɪt; prə'mʌlget/ *vt* [VP6A] **1** make public, announce officially (a decree, a new law, etc). 宣佈;公佈;頒佈(命令,新法律等)。 **2** spread widely beliefs, knowledge, opinions, etc. 傳播;散播(信念,知識,意見等)。 **prom·ul·ga·tion** /,prɒml'geɪʃn; ,promʌl'geʃən/ *n* [U].

prone /prəun; pron/ *adj* **1** (stretched out, lying) face downwards; prostrate: 面向下的;俯伏的;俯臥的: *in a ~ position;* 成俯伏的姿勢;臥姿地; *fall ~.* 面朝下跌倒。 **2** **~ to,** liable, inclined: 易於…的;有…之傾向的: *~ to accidents/error/anger/idleness/superstition* (and other generally undesirable things). 容易發生意外事故(犯錯,發怒,偷懶,迷信以及其他令人不快的事物)的。 **'accident-~** *adj* often experiencing accidents: 時常發生意外事故的: *Some people seem to be accident-~.* 有些人似乎時常發生意外事故。 **~·ness** *n*

prong /prɒŋ *US:* prɔ:ŋ; prɔŋ/ *n* each one of the long, pointed parts of a fork. 叉(之一)股;叉尖;叉頭。 **~ed** *adj* (in compounds) having the kind or number of ~s indicated: (用於複合字中)有某種或某數量之叉股的: *a ,three-~ed 'fork;* 一把三股的叉子; *a ,three-~ed at'tack,* (mil) one made by three attacking forces. (軍)三路進攻。

pro·nomi·nal /prəu'nɒmɪnl; prə'nɑmənl/ *adj* of (the nature of) a pronoun. 代名詞的;有代名詞性質的。

pro·noun /'prəunaun; 'pronaun/ *n* word used in place of a *n* or *n phrase,* eg *he, it, hers, me, them.* 代名詞(如 he, it, hers, me, them)。

pro·nounce /prə'nauns; prə'nauns/ *vt, vi* **1** [VP6A, 9, 22, 25] declare, announce (esp formally, solemnly or officially): 宣稱;宣佈(尤指正式,嚴肅或官方地): *The doctors ~d him to be/~d that he was out of danger.* 醫生們宣稱他已脫離危險。 *Has judgement been ~d yet?* 判決已宣佈了嗎? **2** [VP9, 25] declare as one's opinion: 斷言;聲言: *The wine was tasted and ~d excellent.* 那葡萄酒已被嘗過並被認定爲好酒。 *He ~d himself in favour of the plan.* 他聲言贊成那計畫。 **3** [VP3A] **~ for/against sb,** (legal) pass judgement (in a law court). (法律)(在法院)判決有利(不利)某人。 **~ on/upon,** give one's opinion on, eg a proposal. 對(如某提議)表示意見。 **4** [VP6A, 2A] utter, make the sound of (a word, etc): 發出(字等的)聲音;發音: *He ~s badly.* 他發音不好。 *How do you ~ p-h-l-e-g-m?* 你怎樣讀 p-h-l-e-g-m 這字? *The 'b' in 'debt' is not ~d.* debt 中的 b 不發音。 **~·able** /-əbl; -əbl/ *adj* (of sounds, words) that can be ~d. (指聲音,字)可發音的。 **~d** *adj* definite; strongly marked: 確切的;明白表示的: *a man of ~d opinions.* 有堅定意見的人。 **~·ment** *n* [C] formal statement or declaration. 公告;文告;聲明。

pronto /'prɒntəu; 'prɑnto/ *adv* (sl) quickly; at once. (俚)很快地;立刻;馬上。

pro·nun·cia·mento /prə,nʌnsɪə'mentəu; prə,nʌnsɪə'mɛnto/ *n* (*pl* ~s /-təuz; -toz/) manifesto or proclamation. 宣言;檄文;佈告。

pro·nun·ci·ation /prə,nʌnsɪ'eɪʃn; prə,nʌnsɪ'eʃən/ *n* **1** [U] way in which a language is spoken: (一種語言的)發音;發音法: *lessons in ~;* 發音課程; *study the ~ of English.* 研究英語的發音法。 **2** [U] person's way of speaking a language, or words of a language: (一個人的)發音;發音方式: *His ~ is improving.* 他的發音在進步中。 **3** [C] way in which a word is pronounced: (一字的)讀法: *Which of these three ~s do you recommend?* 這三種讀法你認爲那一種好?

proof[1] /pru:f; pruf/ *n* **1** [U] evidence (in general), or [C] a particular piece of evidence, that is sufficient to show, or helps to show, that sth is a fact: (一般的)證據;證明文件;證言;物證: *We shall require ~(s) of that statement.* 我們將需要那項聲明之證據。 *Is there any ~ that the accused man was at the scene of the crime?* 有沒有證據證明被告在犯罪的現場? *They gave him a gold watch as (a) ~ of their regard.* 他們送他一個金錶,以表示敬意。 *Can you give ~ of your nationality/~ that you are British?* 你能證明你的國籍(你是英國人)嗎? **2** [U] demonstrating; testing of whether sth is true, a fact, etc: 證明;驗證: *Is life on the planet Mars capable of ~?* 火星上有生物存在的說法能驗證嗎? *He produced documents in ~ of his claim.* 他提出文件以證明他的所有權。 **3** [C] test, trial, examination: 考驗;試驗;測驗: *put sth to the ~,* test it. 試驗某事物。 *It has stood the ~,* has passed the test. 它已通過了試驗(經得起考驗)。 ***The ~ of the pudding is in the eating,*** (prov) The real test is practical, not theoretical. (諺)布丁之美味吃時方知;空言不如實驗。 **4** [C] trial copy of sth printed or engraved, for approval before other copies are printed: (印刷物的)校樣;校稿: *pass the ~s for press,* approve them, agree that printing may be begun. 看完校樣同意付印。 **'~-read** *vi, vt* [VP2A, 6A] read and correct ~s. 校對。 **'~-reader** *n* person employed to read and correct ~s. 校對員;改正校稿者。 **5** [U] standard of strength of distilled alcoholic liquors: (酒的)標準酒精度: *This rum is 30 per cent below ~.* 這蘭酒的酒精度低於標準百分之三十。 **~ spirit,** alcoholic mixture which is up to standard. 標準强度的酒;合度酒。

proof[2] /pru:f; pruf/ *adj* **~ *(against),*** giving safety or protection; able to resist or withstand: 防止的;耐…的;有耐力的;不能透入的;堅固的: *~ against bullets;* 防彈的; *'bullet-~;* 防彈的; *'water~;* 防水的; *'sound~;* 隔音的; *'splinter-~;* 防彈片的;防碎片的; *'shatter-~;* 防破碎的;不碎的; (fig) (喻) *~ against temptation.* 能抵抗誘惑的。 **'fool-~** *adj* incapable of failure; involving no risk. 永不會失敗的;安全無比的;萬無一失的。 □ *vt* [VP6A] make (sth) ~ (esp make a fabric water~). 使(某物)禁得住;(尤指)使(布)防水。

prop[1] /prɒp; prɑp/ *n* **1** support used to keep sth up: 支持物;支柱;撐材: *'pit-~s,* supporting the roof in a coalmine; 煤礦的坑道支柱; *a 'clothes-~,* holding up a line on which laundered clothes are drying. 晾衣繩支柱。 **2** person who supports sth or sb: 支持者;後援者;倚靠人: *He is the ~ of his parents in their old age.* 他是父母年老時的奉養者。 □ *vt* (-pp-) [VP6A, 15A, B, 22] **~ sth (up),** support; keep in position: 支持;維持;使…保持某一位置: *Use this box to ~ the door open.* 用這箱子撐門,使之開着。 *The nurse ~ped her patient (up) on* *the pillows.* 護士使病人倚靠在枕頭上。*I ~ped the ladder against the wall.* 我把梯子靠着牆放。(fig) (喩) *He can't always expect his colleagues to ~ him up.* 他不能老期望他的同事們支持他。

prop² /prɒp; prɑp/ *n* (colloq abbr of) propeller. (俗)爲 propeller 之略。⇨ turboprop.

prop³ /prɒp; prɑp/ *n* (colloq abbr of) (stage) property: (俗)爲 (stage) property 之略: *Who's in charge of the ~s?* 誰負責管理道具?⇨ property (5).

propa·ganda /ˌprɒpəˈgændə; ˌprɑpəˈgændə/ *n* [U] information; (derog) doctrines, opinions, official statements: 宣傳資料; (貶)宣傳(指教條,言論,官方聲明): *~ by government departments for public health, better driving, etc;* 政府機構爲公共衞生、駕駛安全等所作的宣傳; *political ~;* 政治宣傳; (attrib) (形容用法) *~ plays/films.* 宣傳劇(電影)。**the Congregation/College of the P~,** a committee of RC cardinals in charge of foreign missions. 天主教的傳道總會(負責海外傳教由紅衣主教組成的委員會)。**propa·gan·dist** /-dɪst; -dɪst/ *n* person who spreads ~. 宣傳者;宣傳家。**propa·gan·dize** /-daɪz; -daɪz/ *vi* spread ~. 宣傳;傳播;傳教。

propa·gate /ˈprɒpəgeɪt; ˈprɑpəˌget/ *vt, vi* (formal) (正式用語) **1** [VP6A] increase the number of (plants, animals, diseases) by natural process from the parent stock: 繁殖;增殖(植物,動物);使(疾病)蔓延: *~ plants by taking cuttings.* 藉插枝繁殖植物。*Trees ~ themselves by seeds.* 樹木藉種子繁殖。**2** [VP6A] spread more widely: 傳播: *~ news/knowledge.* 傳播消息(知識)。**3** [VP6A] transmit; extend the operation of: 傳導;傳送: *vibrations ~d through rock.* 由岩石傳導的震動。**4** [VP2A] (of animals and plants) reproduce; multiply. (指動植物)繁殖;增殖。**propa·ga·tor** /-tə(r); -tɚ/ *n* **propa·ga·tion** /ˌprɒpəˈgeɪʃn; ˌprɑpəˈgeʃən/ *n* [U] propagating: 繁殖;增殖;傳播;傳導: *the propagation of disease by insects/of plants by cuttings.* 由昆蟲傳播疾病(藉插枝繁殖植物)。

pro·pane /ˈprəʊpeɪn; ˈpropen/ *n* [U] colourless gas **(C_3H_8)** (in natural gas and petroleum) used as a fuel. 丙烷(取自天然煤氣和石油的無色氣體,用作燃料)。

pro·pel /prəˈpel; prəˈpɛl/ *vt* (-ll-) [VP6A, 15A] drive forward: 推進;推動: *mechanically ~led vehicles;* 機械力推進的車輛; *a boat ~led by oars;* 以槳操作的船; *a ~ling pencil,* with lead that is ~led forward as the outer case is turned. 自動鉛筆(轉動筆桿,鉛心卽向前推進)。**~·lant, ~·lent** /-ənt; -ənt/ *adj, n* ~ling (agent); explosive substance that ~s a bullet from a fire-arm; fuel that burns to ~ a rocket, etc. 推進的;推動的;推進者;推動物;發射彈丸的火藥;發射火箭的燃料。**~·ler** *n* two or more spiral blades, fixed to a revolving shaft, for driving a ship or aircraft. 推進器;螺旋槳。⇨ *air-screw* and the illus at air¹. 參看 air¹ 之 air-screw 及插圖。

pro·pen·sity /prəˈpensətɪ; prəˈpɛnsətɪ/ *n* [C] (*pl* -ties) *~ to/towards sth/to do sth/for doing sth,* natural tendency: 傾向;習性;嗜好: *a ~ to exaggerate;* 誇大的習性; *a ~ for getting into debt.* 好欠債的習性。

proper /ˈprɒpə(r); ˈprɑpɚ/ *adj* **1** right, correct, fitting, suitable: 正當的;正確的;適合的;適當的: *clothes ~ for such an occasion;* 適合此種場合的衣服; *not a ~ time for merrymaking.* 不是作樂的適當時候。*Are you doing it the ~ way?* 你是在用正確的方法做那事嗎? *Is this the ~ tool for the job?* 這是做那工作的適當工具嗎? *We must do the ~ thing by him,* treat him in the right way, be fair or loyal to him. 我們必須合理對待他(對他公平或忠實)。**2** in conformity with, paying regard to, the conventions of society; respectable: 遵守或注重社會習尚的;可敬的;高尙的: *~ behaviour.* 高尙的行爲。*He's not at all a ~ person for a young girl to know.* 他根本不是適於少女結識的男子。*That's not a ~ thing to do in the public park.* 那是不適於在公園中做的事。**3** *~ to,* (formal) belonging especially; relating distinctively: (正式用語)專屬的;獨特的;專述的;專爲…的: *the books ~ to this subject;* 專論本問題的書; *the psalms ~ to this Sunday.* 這個禮拜天專用的聖詩。**4** (placed after the *n*) strictly so called; genuine: (置於名詞之後)嚴格而言的;眞正的;本來的: *architecture ~,* excluding, for example, the question of water-supply, electric current, etc. 建築物的本身(例如不包括水電裝置等)。**5** (colloq) great; thorough: (俗)大的;徹底的: *We're in a ~ mess.* 我們眞是一團糟。*He gave the burglar a ~ hiding,* beat him thoroughly. 他痛毆那竊賊。**~ fraction,** (eg $\frac{1}{2}$, $\frac{3}{4}$) one in which the number above the line is smaller than that below the line. (數學)眞分數(如 $\frac{1}{2}$, $\frac{3}{4}$)。**~ noun/name,** (gram) name used for an individual person, town, etc eg *Mary, Prague.* (文法)專有名詞(如 Mary, Prague)。**~·ly** *adv* **1** in a ~ manner: 正當地;適合地;可敬地;專屬地;眞正地: *behave ~ly.* 行爲正當。*Do it ~ly or not at all.* 好好地做,否則就別做。*He is not ~ly* (= strictly) *speaking a chemist.* 嚴格地說,他不是一位化學家。**2** (colloq) thoroughly: (俗)徹底地: *The American boxer was ~ly beaten by the new world champion.* 那位美國拳擊手被本屆世界冠軍打得慘敗。

prop·erty /ˈprɒpətɪ; ˈprɑpɚtɪ/ *n* (*pl* -ties) **1** [U] (collectively) things owned; possessions: (集合用法)財產;資產;擁有之物: *Don't interfere with these tools—they're not your ~.* 不要亂弄這些工具——那不是你的東西。**man of ~,** wealthy man. 富人;財主。**common ~,** known to, possessed by, many people. 公物;人所共知之事。**personal ~,** movable belongings. 動產。**real ~,** land, buildings. 不動產。**2** [C] estate; area of land or land and buildings: 地產;房地產: *He has a small ~* (ie land and a house) *in Kent.* 他在肯特有一筆小小的房地產。**3** [U] ownership; the fact of owning or being owned: 所有權;所有: *There is no ~ in the seashore,* it cannot be privately owned. 海岸不能據爲私有。*P~ has its obligations,* eg if you own farmland, etc, you have the duty of keeping it free from weeds, etc. 有財產就有其義務(例如你擁有農田,就有不使之荒蕪的義務)。**4** [C] special quality that belongs to sth: 特性;屬性;性質: *the chemical properties of iron;* 鐵的化學性質; *herbs with healing properties.* 有治療性能的藥草。**5** (theatre) (abbr 略作 *prop*) article of dress or furniture or other thing (except scenery) used on the stage in the performance of a play. (戲劇)服裝或道具(佈景以外的一切舞臺用具)。**ˈ~-man/-master,** (also 亦作 *props-man/-master*), *n* man in charge of stage properties. (舞台的)道具、服裝等之管理人。**prop·er·tied** /ˈprɒpətɪd; ˈprɑpɚtɪd/ *adj* owning ~, esp land: 有財產的; (尤指)有地產的: *the propertied classes,* the landowners. 地主階級。

proph·ecy /ˈprɒfəsɪ; ˈprɑfəsɪ/ *n* (*pl* -cies) **1** [U] power of telling what will happen in the future: 預言能力: *have the gift of ~.* 有預言的天才。**2** [C] statement that tells what will happen: 預言: *His ~ was fulfilled.* 他的預言應驗了。

proph·esy /ˈprɒfɪsaɪ; ˈprɑfəˌsaɪ/ *vt, vi* (*pt, pp* -sied) **1** [VP6A, 9, 10] foretell; say (what will happen in the future): 預告;預言(未來將發生之事): *~ war/that war will break out.* 預言戰爭將爆發。**2** [VP2A, C] speak as a prophet: 預言;預告: *He prophesied of strange things to come.* 他預言有奇事要發生。*Does he ever ~ right?* 他的預言應驗嗎?

prophet /ˈprɒfɪt; ˈprɑfɪt/ *n* **1** person who teaches religion and claims that his teaching comes to him directly from God: 先知;代神發言者: *the ~ Isaiah;* 先知以賽亞; *Muhammad, the P~ of Islam.* 回教先知穆罕默德。**the P~s,** the prophetical books of the Old Testament. 舊約聖經中的預言書。**2** pioneer of a new theory, cause, etc; advocate: 新理論、主義等的鼓吹者;提倡者: *William Morris, one* *of the early ~s of socialism.* 威廉·毛禮斯，社會主義早期的鼓吹者之一。**3** person who tells, or claims to tell, what will happen in the future: 預言者: *I'm not a good weather-~.* 我不大會預測天氣。**~·ess** /-es ; -ɪs/ *n* woman ~. 女先知；女提倡者；女預言者。

pro·phetic /prəˈfetɪk ; prəˈfɛtɪk/ *adj* of a prophet or prophecy; containing a prophecy: 先知的；預言者的；預言的；預示的: *accomplishments which were ~ of her future greatness.* 預示她來日之偉大之成就。**pro·pheti·cal** /-kl ; -kḷ/ *adj* = ~. **pro·pheti·cally** /-klɪ ; -klɪ/ *adv*

pro·phy·lac·tic /ˌprɒfɪˈlæktɪk ; ˌprofəˈlæktɪk/ *n, adj* [C] (substance, treatment, action) serving or tending to protect from disease or misfortune. 預防疾病的；預防藥(劑)；預防處理；預防災禍之行動；預防法。**pro·phy·lax·is** /-ˈlæksɪs ; -ˈlæksɪs/ *n* [U] preventive treatment of disease. 疾病之預防處理；疾病之預防法。

pro·pin·quity /prəˈpɪŋkwətɪ ; proˈpɪnkwətɪ/ *n* [U] (formal) nearness (in time, place, relationship); similarity (of ideas). (正式用語)(時間，地點，關係上之)接近；(觀念之)相近；類似。

pro·pi·ti·ate /prəˈpɪʃɪeɪt ; prəˈpɪʃɪˌet/ *vt* [VP6A] (formal) do sth to take away the anger of: (正式用語)勸解；慰解: *offer a sacrifice to ~ the gods.* 供奉祭品以慰諸神。**pro·pi·ti·ation** /prəˌpɪʃɪˈeɪʃn ; prəˌpɪʃɪˈeʃən/ *n* [U] propitiating; atoning. 勸解；慰解；贖罪。**pro·pi·ti·atory** /prəˈpɪʃɪətrɪ *US:* -tɔːrɪ ; prəˈpɪʃɪəˌtorɪ/ *adj* serving to, intended to, ~: 勸解的；慰解的；意欲慰解等的: *With a propitiatory smile he offered her a large bunch of roses.* 他帶着歉然的微笑，送給她一大束玫瑰。

pro·pi·tious /prəˈpɪʃəs ; prəˈpɪʃəs/ *adj* ~ ***to sb／for sth,*** favourable; well-disposed: 順遂的；有利的；善意的；慈悲的: *~ omens;* 吉兆；*weather that was ~ for our enterprise.* 有利於我們事業的天氣。**~·ly** *adv*

pro·pon·ent /prəˈpəʊnənt ; prəˈponənt/ *n* person who proposes sth: 提議者；建議者: *a ~ of a theory／a course of action.* 一項理論(行動)之提出者。

pro·por·tion /prəˈpɔːʃn ; prəˈporʃən/ *n* **1** [U] relation of one thing to another in quantity, size, etc; relation of a part to the whole: (一物與他物在量、大小等方面的)比例；比率；部分與整體的關係: *The ~ of imports to exports* (= The excess of imports over exports) *is worrying the government.* 進出口的比率(入超)令政府擔憂。***in ~ to,*** relative to: 按着…的比例；與…成比例: *wide in ~ to the height;* 就其高度的比例而言是很寬的；*payment in ~ to work done, not in ~ to the time taken to do it.* 薪資與工作量成比例，並非與花費的時間成比例。***get sth／be out of (all／any) ~ (to),*** (make sth) bear no relation (to): (使)與…不相稱；(使)與…不成比例: *His earnings are out of all ~ to his skill and ability,* He earns much more than is right for his skill and ability. 他的收入和他的技術能力不相稱(收入多，本事小)。*When you're angry, you may get things out of ~,* have an exaggerated or distorted view of things. 你在氣憤時可能會歪曲事實。**2** (often *pl*) the correct relation of parts or of the sizes of the several parts: (常用複數)均衡；相稱: *a room of good ~s.* 各方面很相稱的房間。*The two windows are in admirable ~.* 兩扇窗子非常相稱。**3** (*pl*) size; measurements: (複)大小；面積；體積: *a ship of majestic ~s;* 一艘巨船；*build up an export trade of substantial ~s.* 建立相當規模的輸出貿易。**4** [C] part; share: 部份；份: *You have not done your ~ of the work.* 你沒做完你的那份工作。**5** (maths) equality of relationship between two sets of numbers; statement that two ratios are equal (eg 4 is to 8 as 6 is to 12. $\frac{5}{8}$ and $\frac{10}{16}$ are in ~). (數學)比例；二比相等之敍述(如4比8等於6比12，$\frac{5}{8}$ 和 $\frac{10}{16}$ 成比例)。□ *vt* [VP6A, 14] ~ ***(to),*** put into ~ or right relationship: 使均衡；使相稱；使成比例: *Do you ~ your expenditure to your income?* 你量入爲出嗎？*What a well-~ed room!* 多麼相稱調和的房間！**~·able** /-ʃənəbl ; -ʃənəbḷ/ *adj* = ~al.

pro·por·tional /prəˈpɔːʃənl ; prəˈporʃənḷ/ *adj* ~ ***(to),*** (formal) in proper proportion; corresponding in degree or amount: (正式用語)成適當比例的；相稱的: *payment ~ to the work done;* 和所做之工作相稱的薪資；*compensation ~ to his injuries.* 與他所受傷害相稱的賠償。ˌ~ ˌ**represenˈtation,** ⇨ *representation* at representˈ. **~ly** /-ənəlɪ ; -ənḷɪ/ *adv*

pro·por·tion·ate /prəˈpɔːʃənət ; prəˈporʃənɪt/ *adj* (formal) (正式用語) = proportional. **~·ly** *adv*

pro·po·sal /prəˈpəʊzl ; prəˈpozḷ/ *n* **1** [U] proposing. 提議；建議。**2** [C] sth proposed; plan or scheme: 所提議之事；計畫: *a ~ for peace;* 和平建議；*~s for increasing trade between two countries.* 促進兩國間貿易的計畫。**3** offer (esp of marriage): 求婚: *a girl who had five ~s in one week.* 一星期中受到五次求婚的女郎。

pro·pose /prəˈpəʊz ; prəˈpoz/ *vt, vi* **1** [VP6A, D, 7A, 9] offer or put forward for consideration, as a suggestion, plan or purpose: 提議；建議: *I ~ starting early／an early start／to start early／that we should start early.* 我建議(我們)早些動身。*We ~ leaving at noon.* 我們提議中午離開。*The motion was ~d by Mr X and seconded by Mr Y.* 那動議由X先生提出，Y先生附議。~ ***a toast／sb's health,*** ask persons to drink sb's health or happiness. 提議爲某人乾杯(以祝福某人健康或快樂)。**2** [VP6A, 2A] ~ ***(marriage) (to sb),*** offer marriage. (向某人)求婚。**3** [VP6A, 14] ~ ***sb (for sth),*** put forward (sb's name) for an office／for membership of a club, etc: 提出(某人之名)(充任某職或成爲俱樂部會員等)；推薦: *I ~ Mr Smith for chairman.* 我提名史密斯先生做主席。*Will you please ~ me for your club?* 請推薦我加入你們的俱樂部好嗎？**pro·poser** *n*

prop·osi·tion /ˌprɒpəˈzɪʃn ; ˌprɑpəˈzɪʃən/ *n* [C] **1** statement; assertion: 聲明；主張: *a ~ so clear that it needs no explanation.* 非常清楚而無需解釋的主張。**2** question or problem (with or without the answer or solution): (已有解答或尚無解答的)問題；(能解決或未能解決的)難題；命題；定理: *a ~ in Euclid.* 歐幾里得幾何學中的一項定理。*Tunnelling under the English Channel is a big ~.* 在英吉利海峽海底鑿隧道是一個大問題。**3** proposal; suggestion. 提議；建議。**4** (colloq) matter to be dealt with. (俗)要處理的事。***a tough ~,*** (colloq) sb or sth difficult to deal with. (俗)難對付的人或事物。□ *vt* [VP6A] (colloq) make a (esp illegal or immoral) ~(3) to: (俗)向…提議；(尤指)向…作不合法或不道德的要求: *She was ~ed by her boss.* 她的老闆向她作非分的要求。

pro·pound /prəˈpaʊnd ; prəˈpaund/ *vt* [VP6A] (formal) put forward or offer for consideration or solution: (正式用語)提出以供考慮或解決: *~ a theory／a riddle.* 提出一學理(謎語)。

pro·pri·etary /prəˈpraɪətrɪ *US:* -terɪ ; prəˈpraɪəˌtɛrɪ/ *adj* **1** (abbr (P) used in this dictionary) owned or controlled by sb; held as property: (本字典署爲P)獨佔的；專利的；所有的: *~ medicine,* patented; 專賣藥品；*~ rights;* 所有權；*a ~ name,* eg Kodak for cameras and films. 專利商標名(如柯達照相機及軟片)。**2** of or like a proprietor or owner: 所有人的: *He walked round his estate with ~ solicitude.* 他以業主關懷的心情在地產的四處走動。

pro·pri·etor /prəˈpraɪətə(r) ; prəˈpraɪətɚ/ *n* owner, esp of a hotel, store, land or patent: 業主；(尤指旅館，商店，土地或專利的)所有人: *the ~s of the hotel／this patent medicine.* 旅館的所有人(此種藥品的專利所有人)。**pro·pri·e·tress** /prəˈpraɪətrɪs ; prəˈpraɪətrɪs/ *n* woman ~. 女業主；女性所有人。

pro·pri·ety /prəˈpraɪətɪ ; prəˈpraɪətɪ/ *n* (*pl* -ties) (formal) (正式用語) **1** [U] state of being correct in behaviour and morals: 行爲和道德之正當；禮；禮貌: *a breach of ~;* 失禮；(*pl*) details of correct social behaviour: (複)禮節；禮儀；規矩: *observe the* *proprieties;* 遵守禮儀; *offend against the proprieties.* 違反禮節。 **2** [U] reasonableness; fitness: 合理;適當: *I question the ~ of granting such a request,* doubt whether it is right to do so. 我懷疑答應這項請求是否適當。

pro·pul·sion /prəˈpʌlʃn ; prəˈpʌlʃən/ *n* [U] propelling force. 推進力。 **jet ~,** by means of jet engines. 噴射引擎推進。 **pro·pul·sive** /prəˈpʌlsɪv ; prəˈpʌlsɪv/ *adj* propelling; serving to propel. 推進的;有推進功能的。

pro rata /ˌprəʊ ˈrɑːtə ; proˈretə/ *adv* (Lat) in proportion; according to the share, etc of each. (拉)成比例;按比例。

pro·rogue /prəʊˈrəʊg ; proˈrog/ *vt* [VP6A] bring (a session of Parliament) to an end without dissolving it (so that unfinished business may be taken up again in the next session). 使(國會會期)休會;閉會。 **pro·ro·ga·tion** /ˌprəʊrəˈgeɪʃn ; ˌprorəˈgeʃən/ *n*

pro·saic /prəˈzeɪɪk ; proˈzeɪk/ *adj* dull; uninteresting; commonplace: 無聊的;沒趣的;平凡的: *a lively woman with a ~ husband;* 一個嫁了平凡丈夫的活躍女人; *the ~ life of the ordinary housewife.* 一般家庭主婦的枯燥無味的生活。 **pro·sai·cally** /-klɪ ; -klɪ/ *adv*

pro·scenium /prəˈsiːnɪəm ; proˈsinɪəm/ *n* (in a theatre) that part of the stage between the curtain and the orchestra. (戲院中之)舞臺前部(指幕及樂隊之間的部分);前臺。 **~ arch,** arch above this space. 承幕的拱架。

pro·scribe /prəˈskraɪb *US:* prəʊ- ; proˈskraɪb/ *vt* [VP6A] **1** (old use) publicly put (a person) out of the protection of the law. (舊用法)公然摒棄(某人)於法律保護之外;褫奪(某人)人權。 **2** denounce (a person, practice, etc) as dangerous. 指摘(某人,慣例等)爲危險;排斥。 **pro·scrip·tion** /prəˈskrɪpʃn *US:* prəʊ- ; proˈskrɪpʃən/ *n* [U] proscribing or being ~d; [C] instance of this. 剝奪人權;排斥;此等之實例。

prose /prəʊz ; proz/ *n* [U] language not in verse form: 散文: (attrib) (形容用法) *the ~ writers of the 19th century.* 十九世紀的散文作家。 ⇨ poetry.

pros·ecute /ˈprɒsɪkjuːt ; ˈprɑsɪˌkjut/ *vt* **1** [VP6A] (formal) continue with: (正式用語)繼續從事;進行: *~ a war/one's studies/an inquiry.* 進行作戰(研究學問,查詢)。 **2** [VP6A, 14] **~ sb (for sth),** start legal proceedings against: 告發;檢舉;起訴: *~d for exceeding the speed limit.* 因行車超速而被檢舉。 *Trespassers will be ~d.* 閒人免進,違者法辦。 **pros·ecu·tor** /ˈprɒsɪkjuːtə(r) ; ˈprɑsɪˌkjutɚ/ *n* person who ~s(2). 檢舉人;告發人;起訴人。 **ˌPublic ˈProsecutor,** legal official who ~s criminal cases on behalf of the State or the public. 檢察官;檢控官。

pros·ecu·tion /ˌprɒsɪˈkjuːʃn ; ˌprɑsɪˈkjuʃən/ *n* **1** [U] act of prosecuting(1): 繼續從事;進行: *In the ~ of his duties he had to interview people of all classes.* 在執行職務時他必須接見各階層的人。 **2** [U] prosecuting or being prosecuted(2): 告發;檢舉;起訴;被告發(等): *make oneself liable to ~;* 使自己可能遭受檢舉; [C] instance of this: 告發或檢舉等的實例: *start a ~ against sb.* 檢舉某人。 **the Director of Public P~s,** Public Prosecutor. 檢察官。 ⇨ prosecute. **3** (collective) person who prosecutes(2), together with his advisers: (集合用法)原告;告發人及其律師: *the case for the ~.* 對原告有利的案子。 ⇨ defence(3).

pros·elyte /ˈprɒsəlaɪt ; ˈprɑsl̩ˌaɪt/ *n* person who has been converted from his religious, political or other opinions or beliefs to different ones. 改變宗教、政治或其他的信仰者;改宗者;改入他黨者。 **pros·elyt·ize** /ˈprɒsəlɪtaɪz ; ˈprɑsəlɪtˌaɪz/ *vt, vi* [VP6A, 2A] make, try to make, converts to a religion or cause; make a ~ of (sb). 使皈依另一宗教或主義;使(某人)改變宗教信仰或改入他黨。

pros·ody /ˈprɒsədɪ ; ˈprɑsədɪ/ *n* [U] science of verse rhythms or metres; (of a language) rhythm, pause, tempo, stress and pitch features. 詩體論;韻律學;作詩法;(語言的)抑揚頓挫等特性。

pros·pect¹ /ˈprɒspekt ; ˈprɑspɛkt/ *n* **1** [C] wide view over land or sea or (fig) before the mind, in the imagination. (陸或海之)景色;(喻)(心靈或想像中的)景象;概觀;縱覽。 **2** (*pl*) sth expected, hoped for, looked forward to: (複)期望,希望,盼望之事物: *The ~s for the wine harvest are poor this year.* 今年的葡萄收成不會好。 *The manager held out bright ~s to me if I would accept the position.* 如果我願意接受那個職位,經理答應給我光明的前途。 **3** [U] expectation; hope: 期望;希望: *I see no/little/not much ~ of his recovery.* 我看他沒有(甚少)痊癒的希望。 *Is there no ~ of your visiting us soon?* 你不可能馬上來看我們嗎? *He is out of work and has nothing in ~* (=no expectation of finding work) *at present.* 他已失業,現在也沒有找到工作的希望。 **4** [C] possible customer or client; sb from whom one hopes to gain something: 可能的主顧或委託人;可能使人獲得利益之人: *He's a good/bad ~.* 他可能是個好(壞)顧客。

pros·pect² /prəˈspekt *US:* ˈprɒspekt ; ˈprɑspɛkt/ *vi* [VP2A, 3A] **~ (for),** search (for): 尋找;探勘: *~ing for gold.* 探勘金礦。 **pros·pec·tor** /-tə(r) ; -tɚ/ *n* person who explores a region looking for gold or other valuable ores, etc. 探勘礦藏的人;探礦者。

pros·pec·tive /prəˈspektɪv ; prəˈspɛktɪv/ *adj* hoped for; looked forward to; which or who will or may be: 有望的;預期的;未來的: *~ advantages/wealth;* 預期的利益(財富); *a ~ buyer;* 可能的買主; *my ~ bride;* 我未來的新娘; *the ~ Labour candidate.* 未來的工黨候選人。

pro·spec·tus /prəˈspektəs ; prəˈspɛktəs/ *n* (*pl* ~es /-təsɪz ; -təsɪz/) printed account giving details of and advertising sth, eg a university, a new business enterprise, a book about to be published. (創辦大學,新企業等的)計畫書;發起書;募股書;(即將出版之書的)內容說明;大綱。

pros·per /ˈprɒspə(r) ; ˈprɑspɚ/ *vi, vt* **1** [VP2A] succeed; do well: 成功;興隆;昌盛: *The business ~ed.* 生意興隆。 *Is your son ~ing?* 你的兒子諸事順遂嗎? **2** [VP6A] (liter or rhet) (of God) cause to ~: (文或修辭)(指上帝)使成功;使昌隆: *May God ~ you!* 願上帝使你成功!

pros·per·ity /prɒˈsperətɪ ; prɑsˈpɛrətɪ/ *n* [U] state of being successful; good fortune: 成功;幸運;昌隆;繁榮: *a life of happiness and ~;* 幸福而成功的一生; *live in ~.* 過着富足的生活。 *The ~ of this industry depends upon a full order book.* 這種工業的繁榮要依靠大批的訂貨。

pros·per·ous /ˈprɒspərəs ; ˈprɑspərəs/ *adj* successful; flourishing: 成功的;繁榮的;昌隆的: *a ~ business;* 興隆的生意; *~ years.* 繁榮的年代。 **~·ly** *adv*

pros·tate /ˈprɒsteɪt ; ˈprɑstet/ *n* **~ (gland),** (anat) gland in male mammals at the neck of the bladder. (解剖)前列腺;攝護腺。

pros·ti·tute /ˈprɒstɪtjuːt *US:* -tuːt ; ˈprɑstəˌtjut/ *n* person who offers herself/himself for sexual intercourse for payment. 娼妓;妓女;男娼。 □ *vt* **1** [VP6A] (reflex) make a ~ of (oneself). (反身)使(自己)賣淫;賣身。 **2** [VP6A] put to wrong or unworthy uses: 濫用: *~ one's energies/abilities;* 濫用精力(才能); *~ one's honour,* lose it for money basely gained. 圖利而出賣名譽。 **pros·ti·tu·tion** /ˌprɒstɪˈtjuːʃn *US:* -ˈtuːʃn ; ˌprɑstəˈtjuʃən/ *n* [U] practice of prostituting oneself, one's talents, etc. 賣淫;操淫業;濫用才能。

pros·trate /ˈprɒstreɪt ; ˈprɑstret/ *adj* **1** lying stretched out on the ground, usu face downward, eg because exhausted, or to show submission, deep respect. 平臥的;俯臥的;臥倒的;臥拜的(如出於疲乏,或表示順從,深摯的敬意)。 **2** (fig) overcome (with grief, etc); conquered; overthrown. (喻)爲(悲傷等)征服的;降伏的;瓦解的;沮喪的。 □ *vt* /prɒˈstreɪt *US:* ˈprɒstreɪt ; ˈprɑstret/ **1** [VP6A] cause to be ~: 使臥;弄倒: *trees ~d by the gale.* 被疾風

吹倒的樹。**2** [VP6A] (reflex) make (oneself) ~: (反身)使(自己)平臥;俯伏: *The wretched slaves ~d themselves before their master.* 可憐的奴隸們拜倒在他們的主人面前。 **3** (usu passive) overcome; render helpless: (通常用被動語態)克服;使無能爲力: *Several of the competitors were ~d by the heat.* 數位競爭者熱得昏倒了。 *She is ~d with grief.* 她悲傷不已。 **pros·tra·tion** /prɒˈstreɪʃn ; prɑˈstreʃən/ n **1** [U] state of extreme physical weakness; complete exhaustion: 身體極度虛弱;筋疲力盡;虛脫;衰弱: *Two of the runners in the Marathon race collapsed and were carried off in a state of prostration.* 兩位馬拉松賽跑的選手倒下,並在虛脫的狀態中被抬走。 **2** [C] act of bowing or lying face downwards to show submission or humility. 拜倒;俯身致敬。

prosy /ˈprəʊzɪ ; ˈprozɪ/ *adj* (-ier, -iest) (of authors, speakers, books, speeches, style, etc) dull; tedious; unimaginative. (指作者,演說者,書,演說,文體等)單調的;乏味的;囉嗦的;缺乏想像的。 **pro·sily** /-əlɪ ; -əlɪ/ *adv* **prosi·ness** *n*

pro·tag·on·ist /prəˈtægənɪst ; proˈtægənɪst/ *n* (formal) chief person in a drama; (by extension) chief person in a story or factual event. (正式用語)戲劇中之主角;(廣義)故事或實事中的主角。

pro·tean /ˈprəʊtɪən ; ˈprotɪən/ *adj* versatile; easily and quickly changing (like Proteus /ˈprəʊtɪəs ; ˈprotjus/, the Greek sea-god who took various shapes). 變化自如的;易變的;多變的(似希臘神話中之海神 Proteus 能變多種形態的)。

pro·tect /prəˈtekt ; prəˈtɛkt/ *vt* [VP6A, 14] ~ ***sb/sth (from/against)*, 1** keep safe (from danger, enemies; against attack); guard: 防禦(危險,敵人,與 from 連用);襲擊,與 against 連用);保護;警戒: *well ~ed from the cold/against the weather.* 防護良好而不受凍(不被惡劣氣候侵襲)。 **2** guard (home industry) against competition by taxing imports. (以進口稅)保護(國內工業)。

pro·tec·tion /prəˈtekʃn ; prəˈtɛkʃən/ *n* [U] **1** protecting or being protected: 防禦;保護;警戒: *travel under the ~ of a number of soldiers.* 在一些兵士的保護下旅行。 *These tender plants need ~ against the weather.* 這些幼小的植物需要保護,以免受惡劣氣候的侵害。 **ˈ~ (money)**, money demanded by or paid to, gangsters for ~ against acts of violence, etc. (爲免受暴力侵害,付給歹徒或由其索取的)保護費。 **2** [U] system of protecting home industry against foreign competition. 保護國內工業之制度。 **3** [C] person or thing that protects: 保護者;保護物: *wearing a heavy overcoat as a ~ against the cold.* 穿著厚大衣禦寒。 **~·ism** /-ɪzəm ; -ɪzm̩/ *n* [U] system of giving ~(2) to home industry. 保護國內工業之制度;保護貿易主義。 **~·ist** /-ɪst ; -ɪst/ *n* supporter of, believer in, ~ism. 保護貿易主義者。

pro·tec·tive /prəˈtektɪv ; prəˈtɛktɪv/ *adj* **1** giving protection: 給予保護的;防護的: *a ~ covering;* 保護性的覆蓋物; *a ~ tariff,* ie on imported goods; (加於進口貨物之)保護關稅; *~ sheath,* ⇨ sheath. **ˌ~ ˈclothing**, clothes that safeguard the wearer against such risks as burns, contamination and radiation. 防護衣(能防止灼傷、污染、放射線等)。 **ˌ~ ˈcolouring**, ie of animals, birds, insects, causing them to be seen with difficulty in their natural surroundings, thus protecting them from their enemies. (獸,禽,昆蟲的)保護色(使其在所處的自然環境中難以辨認,俾防敵攻擊)。 **ˌ~ ˈfoods**, foods that safeguard health, eg kinds with a good supply of essential vitamins. 保健的食物(如含有充分主要維他命者)。 **2 ~ *(towards)*,** (of persons) with a wish to protect: (指人)有保護意願的: *A mother naturally feels ~ towards her children.* 一位做母親的自然會保護她的孩子。 **~·ly** *adv*

pro·tec·tor /prəˈtektə(r) ; prəˈtɛktə/ *n* **1** person who protects; sth made or designed to give protection. 保護者;防禦者;保護物;保護裝置。 **2** (GB hist) **the P~**, official title of Oliver and Richard Cromwell. (英史)護國公(英國共和政治時奧立佛・克倫威爾及其子理查・克倫威爾的稱號)。

pro·tec·tor·ate /prəˈtektərət ; prəˈtɛktərɪt/ *n* **1** country under the protection of another. 保護國(受他國保護的國家);保護領地。 **2 the P~**, period (1653–59) of rule of Oliver and Richard Cromwell. 攝政時期(奧立佛・克倫威爾和理查・克倫威爾攝政之時期,1653–59)。

pro·tégé (fem **-gée**) /ˈprɒtɪʒeɪ *US:* ˌprəʊtɪˈʒeɪ ; ˈprotəˌʒe/ *n* (F) person to whom another gives encouragement and help (usu over a long period). (法)被保護者;被提拔者(通常須經過一段長時期)。

pro·tein /ˈprəʊtiːn ; ˈprotin/ *n* [U, C] body-building substance essential to good health, in such foods as milk, eggs, meat. 蛋白質(促進身體發育之物質,爲健康所必需,見於牛奶、蛋類、肉類等食物中)。

pro tem·pore /ˌprəʊ ˈtempərɪ ; proˈtɛmpəˌri/ *adv* (Lat) (often shortened to 常略作 **pro tem**) for the time being; for the present only: (拉)暫時;目前: *I'm in charge of the office pro tem.* 我暫時任此職務。

pro·test[1] /ˈprəʊtest ; ˈprotɛst/ *n* **1** [C, U] (statement of) disapproval or objection: 抗議;反對: *make/lodge/enter a ~ (against sth).* (對某事)提出抗議。 *The Government's policy gave rise to vigorous ~s.* 政府的決策引起了强烈的反對。 *He paid the tax demand under ~,* unwillingly and after declaring that what he was doing was not right or just. 他抗議着,滿心不服地照稅額繳付了。 *He gave way without ~,* without making any objection. 他無異議地讓步。 **2** (attrib) expressing ~: (形容用法)表示抗議: *a ˈ~ movement;* 抗議運動; *a ˈ~ march,* eg by persons objecting to official policy. 抗議遊行(如反對官方決策之人所舉行者)。

pro·test[2] /prəˈtest ; prəˈtɛst/ *vt, vi* **1** [VP6A, 9] affirm strongly; assert against opposition: 堅決聲明;力言;矢言: *He ~ed that he had never been near the scene of the crime.* 他堅持說他從未在犯罪現場附近。 *He ~ed his innocence,* asserted his innocence by ~ing. 他力言無罪。 **2** [VP2A, 3A] ~ ***(against)*,** raise an objection, say sth (*against*): 抗議;反對: *I ~ against being called an old fool.* 我抗議被稱爲老傻瓜。 *The children ~ed loudly* (= cried out in disapproval) *when they were told to go to bed early.* 當孩子們被吩咐早睡覺的時候,他們大聲抗議。 **~er** *n* **~·ing·ly** *adv*

Prot·es·tant /ˈprɒtɪstənt ; ˈprɑtɪstənt/ *n, adj* (member) of any of the Christian bodies that separated from the Church of Rome at the time of the Reformation (16th c), or their later branches. 新教(十六世紀宗教改革時脫離天主教,或其後來另行分出教派)的;基督教的;新教徒;基督教徒。 **~·ism** /-ɪzəm ; -ˌɪzəm/ *n* [U] systems, beliefs, teaching, etc of the ~s; ~s as a body. 新教徒的制度,信仰,教義等;基督教(教會);新教。

prot·esta·tion /ˌprɒteˈsteɪʃn ; ˌprɑtəsˈteʃən/ *n* [C] (formal) solemn declaration: (正式用語)鄭重聲明;力言: *~s of innocence/friendship.* 鄭重聲明無罪(友好)。

pro·to·col /ˈprəʊtəkɒl *US:* -kɔːl ; ˈprotəˌkɑl/ *n* **1** [C] first or original draft of an agreement (esp between States), signed by those making it, in preparation for a treaty. (尤指國與國間的)條約草案;草約;議定書。 **2** [U] code of behaviour; etiquette as practised on diplomatic occasions: 禮規;外交禮儀: *Were the seating arrangements for the dinner party according to ~,* Were rules of precedence, etc properly observed? 餐會座位的安排合乎禮規嗎?

pro·ton /ˈprəʊtɒn ; ˈprotɑn/ *n* positively charged particle forming part of an atomic nucleus. 質子(構成原子之一部分而帶有陽電荷的單位)。 ⇨ electron.

pro·to·plasm /ˈprəʊtəplæzəm ; ˈprotəˌplæzəm/ *n* [C] colourless, jelly-like substance which is the material basis of life in animals and plants. 原

生質;原形質(無色之膠狀物,爲動植物生命之物質基礎)。

pro·to·type /ˈprəʊtətaɪp ; ˈprotəˌtaɪp/ *n* [C] first or original example, eg of an aircraft, from which others have been or will be copied or developed. 原型(其他同類物由此模倣或發展而來,例如飛機的原始樣式)。

pro·to·zoa /ˌprəʊtəˈzəʊə ; ˌprotəˈzoə/ *n pl* (division of the animal kingdom consisting of) animals of the simplest type formed of a single cell (and usu microscopic). 原生動物(由單細胞組成的最簡單之動物,通常爲微生物);原生動物門。

pro·tract /prəˈtrækt *US:* prəʊ- ; proˈtrækt/ *vt* [VP 6A] prolong; lengthen the time taken by: 延長;拖延時間: *a ~ed visit/argument.* 拖延的訪問(辯論)。**pro·trac·tion** /prəˈtrækʃn *US:* prəʊ- ; proˈtrækʃən/ *n* lengthening out. 延長;拖延;擴張。

pro·trac·tor /prəˈtræktə(r) *US:* prəʊ- ; proˈtræktɚ/ *n* instrument, usu in the form of a semicircle, and graduated (0° to 180°), for measuring and drawing angles. 量角器;分度規;分度器;半圓規。

pro·trude /prəˈtruːd *US:* prəʊ- ; proˈtrud/ *vi, vt* [VP2A, 6A] (cause to) stick out or project: (使)伸出;突出: *a shelf that ~s from a wall;* 自牆壁伸出的架子; *protruding eyes/teeth.* 凸眼(暴牙)。**pro·tru·sion** /prəˈtruːʒn *US:* prəʊ- ; proˈtruʒən/ *n* [U] protruding; [C] sth that ~s. 伸出;突出;伸出(突出)之物;隆起物。**pro·trus·ive** /prəˈtruːsɪv *US:* prəʊ- ; proˈtrusɪv/ *adj* protruding. 伸出的;突出的。

pro·tu·ber·ant /prəˈtjuːbərənt *US:* prəʊˈtuː- ; proˈtjubərənt/ *adj* (formal) curving or swelling outwards; bulging. (正式用語)突出的;隆起的。**pro·tu·ber·ance** /-əns ; -əns/ *n* [U] being ~; [C] sth that is ~; bulge or swelling. 突出;隆起;突出之物;隆起之物。

proud /praʊd ; praʊd/ *adj* (-er, -est) **1** (in a good sense) having or showing a proper pride or dignity: (好的意義)具有或顯出適度驕傲或尊嚴的;自重的;自尊的;感到光榮或得意的: *~ of their success/of being so successful;* 對於他們的成功(如此的成功)感到驕傲; *~ to belong/that they belonged to such a fine team.* 對隸屬(他們隸屬)這麼好的一個隊感到光榮。 **2** (in a bad sense) arrogant; having or showing too much pride: (壞的意義)傲慢的;過於驕傲的: *He was too ~ to join our party.* 他太驕傲,不屑參加我們的集會。 **3** arousing justifiable pride; of which one is or may be properly ~; splendid; imposing: 足以誇耀的;令人感到得意的;壯麗的;堂皇的: *soldiers in ~ array.* 排成壯麗陣式的兵士。*It was a ~ day for the country when its team won the championship.* 該國的球隊獲得冠軍的那一天,全國都感到光榮。*His rose garden was a ~ sight.* 他的玫瑰園壯觀極了。 **4** *~ flesh,* overgrown flesh round a healing wound. (傷口長好後所結的)贅肉;疤;浮肉。**5** (compounds) (複合字) **ˈhouse-~,** of one's house, of the care with which it is looked after, cleaned, etc. 誇耀自己的家的;以用心照顧或清理家爲榮的。**ˈpurse-~,** arrogant because of one's wealth. 以富驕人的。 **6** (*adv* use; colloq) ***do sb ~,*** honour greatly, entertain splendidly. (副詞用法;俗)十分禮遇(某人);厚待(某人);給面子。**~·ly** *adv* in a ~ manner; splendidly. 自重地;驕傲地;傲慢地;壯麗地;光榮地。

prove /pruːv ; pruv/ *vt, vi* (*pp* ~d, or, as 1 below, 第一義並作 ~n /ˈpruːvn ; ˈpruvən/) **1** [VP6A, 9, 14, 25] *~ (to),* supply proof of; show beyond doubt to be true: 證明;證實: *~ sb's guilt/that he is guilty.* 證明某人有罪。*His guilt was clearly ~d.* 他的罪明確地證實了。*I shall ~ to you that the witness is quite unreliable.* 我將向你證明,證人十分不可靠。*Can you ~ it to me?* 你能對我證實嗎? ***The exception ~s the rule,*** shows that the rule is valid in most cases. 例外證明了本規則的適用性。 ***not ~n,*** (in a criminal trial in Scotland) jury's decision that as the charge cannot be ~d, the accused may be released (although he may not be innocent). 證據不足(蘇格蘭的刑事審判中,陪審團對不能證明的指控所作的一種裁決,被告縱然有罪,亦可被開釋)。 **2** [VP6A] establish the genuineness of: 確定…之眞實性;查驗: *~ a will;* 查驗遺囑; test the quality or accuracy of: 考驗品質或正確性: *~ a man's worth.* 考驗一個人的價值。 **3** [VP4D, 25] ***~ (oneself) (to be),*** be seen or found in the end (to be): 終被發現(是);表現出: *The new typist ~d (to be) useless.* 那位新打字員終於被發現是不能幹的。 *He ~d (himself) to be a coward.* 他表現出是一個儒夫。*Our wood supply ~d (to be) insufficient.* 我們的木材供應顯得不够。**prov·able** /-əbl ; -əbl̩/ *adj* that can be ~d. 可證明的;可查驗的。

prov·enance /ˈprɒvənəns ; ˈprɑvənəns/ *n* [U] (place of) origin: 起源;出處: *antique furniture of doubtful ~,* eg that may not be genuinely antique. 出處不明的古董家具(如可能並非眞爲古代所製)。

prov·en·der /ˈprɒvɪndə(r) ; ˈprɑvəndɚ/ *n* [U] food, eg hay, oats, for horses and cattle; (colloq) food of any kind. 牛和馬的飼料;糧草;秣料;(俗)任何食物。

prov·erb /ˈprɒvɜːb ; ˈprɑvɝb/ *n* **1** popular short saying, with words of advice or warning, eg 'It takes two to make a quarrel'. 諺語;格言(如'一個巴掌拍不響')。 **2** **(the Book of) P~s,** one of the books of the Old Testament. (舊約的)箴言(書)。 **3** sb or sth so well known that he/it has become notorious: 惡名遠播的人或事;話柄;笑柄: *He is a ~ for meanness.* 他因卑鄙而惡名遠播。*His meanness is a ~.* 他的卑鄙盡人皆知。 **~·ial** /prəˈvɜːbɪəl ; prəˈvɝbɪəl/ *adj* **1** of or expressed in a ~: 諺語的;格言的;用諺語表達的: *~ sayings/wisdom.* 諺語(格言所表示的智慧)。 **2** widely known and talked about; admitted by everyone: 衆所周知的;大家公認的: *His stupidity is ~ial.* 他的愚蠢是衆所周知的。 **~i·ally** *adv*: *He is ~ially stupid.* 他是出名地愚蠢。

pro·vide /prəˈvaɪd ; prəˈvaɪd/ *vi, vt* **1** [VP3A] ***~ for sb/sth,*** make ready, do what is necessary, for: 準備;籌備;(爲…)做必須之事;扶養: *He has a large family to ~ for.* 他要養一大家子。*We must ~ for our visitors,* get in supplies of food, etc. 我們要準備好東西款待客人。*He died without providing for his widow,* leaving nothing for her to live on. 他死了,沒有爲他的寡妻留下任何東西維生。 ***~ against sth,*** take steps to guard against: 防備;預防: *Have you ~d against a coal shortage next winter?* 對於下一個冬季的煤荒你已有所防備嗎? **2** [VP6A, 14] ***~ sth (for sb); ~ sb with sth,*** give, supply (what is needed, esp what a person needs in order to live): 供給;供應;備辦(所需物,尤指生活必需品): *~ one's children with food and clothes;* 供應孩子們的衣食; *~ food and clothes for one's family.* 供應一家人的衣食。 **3** [VP9] stipulate: 約定;規定: *A clause in the agreement ~s that the tenant shall bear the cost of all repairs to the building.* 合約中有一條規定,房客將負擔修理房屋的一切費用。 **~r** *n* person who provides. 準備者;籌備者;供應者;備辦者。

pro·vided /prəˈvaɪdɪd ; prəˈvaɪdɪd/ *conj* ***~ (that),*** on condition (that). 假若;倘使。

provi·dence /ˈprɒvɪdəns ; ˈprɑvədəns/ *n* **1** [U] (old use) thrift; being provident or prudent (about future needs, etc). (舊用法)節約;愼重;深謀遠慮。 **2** **P~,** God; God's care for human beings and all he has created; (small *p*) particular instance of this care: 上帝;天佑; (小寫 p) 天佑的特殊實例: *the mysterious working of divine ~.* 上蒼保佑的神秘方式。*A special ~ preserved him from the tragic fate of his companions.* 上天的特別保佑使他未遭受到他的同伴所遇到的刼數。

provi·dent /ˈprɒvɪdənt ; ˈprɑvədənt/ *adj* (careful in) providing for future needs or events, esp in old age: (小心)爲未來的需要或事件而預做準備的;顧及未來的;(尤指)爲老年的需要而儲蓄的: *Our firm has a ~ fund for the staff.* 我們的公司設有員工福利基金。 **~·ly** *adv*

provi·den·tial /ˌprɒvɪˈdenʃl ; ˌprɑvəˈdɛnʃəl/ *adj* of, by, through, coming from, Providence(2): 神的;

由神做出的;藉神力做出的;由神而來的; 天佑的; 幸運的: *a ~ escape.* 一次幸運的逃脫。**~·ly** /-ʃəlɪ; -ʃlɪ/ *adv*

pro·vid·ing /prəˈvaɪdɪŋ; prəˈvaɪdɪŋ/ *conj* **~ (that),** =provided (that): *I will go ~ (that) my expenses are paid.* 要是我的費用有人代付我就去。

prov·ince /ˈprɒvɪns; ˈprɑvɪns/ *n* **1** large administrative division of a country. 省(一個國家的大行政區)。**2 the ~s,** all the country outside the capital: 地方(首都以外的全部地區): *people from the ~s visiting London.* 自全國各地到倫敦來遊玩的人。*The pop group is now touring the ~s.* 流行樂團正在各省旅行表演。 **3** district under an archbishop. 大主教轄區;總主教區。**4** area of learning or knowledge; department of activity: 學問中之部門;範圍;知識範疇: *That is outside my ~,* not sth with which I can or need deal. 那是我研究範圍以外的東西。*Doesn't your question fall outside the ~ of science?* 你的問題不是超出科學範圍了嗎?

prov·in·cial /prəˈvɪnʃl; prəˈvɪnʃəl/ *adj* **1** of a province(1): 省的: *~ taxes;* 省的稅收; *~ government.* 省政府。**2** of the provinces(2): 外省的;地方的: *~ roads.* 地方道路。 **3** narrow in outlook; having, typical of, the speech, manners, views, etc of a person living in the provinces (esp in former times when communications were poor): 見解偏狹的; 地方居民所特有的 (尤指以前交通不便時): *a ~ accent.* 地方口音。□ *n* person from the provinces; countrified person. 地方居民;鄉下佬。**~ly** /-ʃəlɪ; -ʃəlɪ/ *adv* **~·ism** /-ɪzəm; -ˌɪzəm/ *n* [C] example of ~ manners, speech, behaviour, etc; [U] attachment to one's province and its customs, etc rather than to one's country. 地方居民特有的態度、語言、行爲等之實例; 對於本鄉及其習俗的濃厚情感; 鄉土觀念。

pro·vi·sion /prəˈvɪʒn; prəˈvɪʒən/ *n* **1** [U] providing, preparation (esp for future needs): 準備;防備(尤指爲未來的需要者);供應: *the ~* (=supply) *of water and gas to domestic consumers;* 爲家庭用戶供應水和煤氣; *make ~ for one's old age,* eg by saving money; 爲老年預做準備(如儲蓄錢); *make ~ against sth,* guard against it. 防備某事。 **2** [C] amount (*of* sth) provided: 準備之量;供應品: *issue a ~ of meat to the troops.* 撥發肉類供應品給軍隊。 **3** (*pl*) food; food supplies: (複)食物;食物供應: *lay in a store of ~s;* 貯存大量的食物; (attrib, *sing*) (形容用法,單數) *a ~ merchant,* a grocer; 雜貨商; *a wholesale ~ business.* 食品批發店。 **4** [C] condition in a legal document, eg a clause in a will: (法律文件中之)規定;條款(如遺囑中之某一條): *if there is no ~ to the contrary.* 如無相反之條款。□ *vt* [VP6A] supply with ~s(3) and stores: 供以食物及必需品: *~ a ship for a voyage to the Antarctic.* 供應開往南極的船所需的食物及必需品。

pro·vi·sional /prəˈvɪʒənl; prəˈvɪʒənḷ/ *adj* of the present time only, and to be confirmed or changed or replaced later: 臨時的;暫時性的: *a ~ government/contract, etc.* 臨時政府(草約等)。**~ly** /-nəlɪ; -nlɪ/ *adv*

pro·viso /prəˈvaɪzəʊ; prəˈvaɪzo/ *n* (*pl* ~s, US also 美亦作 ~es /-zəʊz; -zoz/) (clause containing a) limitation, esp in a legal document: 附文;條件;但書;限制條款(尤指法律文件中者): *with the ~ that,* on condition that; 以…爲條件;但須…; *subject to this ~,* with this limitation. 附有此一條件。**pro·vi·sory** /prəˈvaɪzərɪ; prəˈvaɪzərɪ/ *adj* depending upon a ~. 有附文的;附有條件的。

Provo /ˈprəʊvəʊ; ˈprovo/ *n* (*pl* ~s /-əʊz; -oz/) (colloq) member of a group (*the Provisional IRA*) fighting for the political unification of Ireland. (俗)(爲爭取愛爾蘭統一之)愛爾蘭共和軍之一員。

pro·vo·ca·tion /ˌprɒvəˈkeɪʃn; ˌprɑvəˈkeʃən/ *n* **1** [U] provoking or being provoked: 激怒; 被激怒; 刺激; 被刺激: *wilful ~ of public disorder;* 故意激起公衆的騷動; *do sth under ~,* when provoked. 被激怒而做某事;在憤怒下做某事。*She flares up at/on the slightest ~,* Very little things make her anger break out. 一點點小事都會使她突然發怒。**2** [C] sth that provokes or annoys. 激怒之原因;令人發怒之事。

pro·voca·tive /prəˈvɒkətɪv; prəˈvɑkətɪv/ *adj* causing, likely to cause, anger, argument, interest, etc: 激怒的;引起議論,興趣等的;激起的;刺激的: *~ remarks;* 煽動性的言論;使人惱怒的談話; *a ~ dress.* 一件撩人的衣服。**~·ly** *adv*

pro·voke /prəˈvəʊk; prəˈvok/ *vt* **1** [VP6A] make angry; vex: 激怒;招惹: *He was ~d beyond endurance.* 他怒不可遏。*If you ~ the dog, it will attack you.* 如果你去招惹那隻狗,牠會咬你。 **2** [VP6A] cause; arouse: 致使;引起: *~ laughter/a smile/a riot.* 引起大笑(微笑,一場暴亂)。**3** [VP17, 14] **~ sb to do sth/into doing sth,** cause or compel them: 驅使;迫使(某人做某事): *His impudence ~d her into slapping his face.* 他的鹵莽迫使她打他耳光。*He was ~d to answer rudely.* 他受激而無禮地回答。**pro·vok·ing** *adj* annoying: 惱人的; 氣人的; 叫人煩惱的: *provoking of sb to be late.* 因爲某人晚到而氣惱。**pro·vok·ing·ly** *adv*

pro·vost /ˈprɒvəst *US:* ˈprəʊ-; ˈprɑvəst/ *n* **1** title of some heads of university colleges, etc. (大學中某些學院的)院長。**2** (in Scotland) head of a municipal corporation or burgh (= mayor). (蘇格蘭)市長。**3 ~ marshal** /prəˌvəʊ ˈmɑːʃl *US:* ˌprəʊvəʊ; ˈprovoˈmɑrʃəl/, head of the military police. 憲兵司令。

prow /praʊ; praʊ/ *n* pointed front of a ship or boat. 船首。⇨ the illus at barque. 參看 barque 之插圖。

prow·ess /ˈpraʊɪs; ˈpraʊɪs/ *n* [U] bravery; valour; unusual skill or ability. 勇敢;英勇;超凡的技術或能力。

prowl /praʊl; praʊl/ *vi, vt* **1** [VP2A, C] go about cautiously looking for a chance to get food (as wild animals do), or to steal, etc. 悄悄潛行以尋找食物(如野獸所做者),或偸竊等。**2** [VP6A] go about (the streets) in this way. 逡巡於(街上)。□ *n* **be on the ~, ~**ing. 在逡巡或徘徊中。**ˈ~ car,** (US) (美) ⇨ *squad car* at squad. **~er** *n* animal or person that ~s. 潛行者;徘徊者;逡巡者。

prox /prɒks; prɑks/ ⇨ proximo.

proxi·mate /ˈprɒksɪmət; ˈprɑksəmɪt/ *adj* (formal) nearest, before or after. (正式用語)最接近的;前後的。

prox·im·ity /prɒkˈsɪmətɪ; prɑkˈsɪmətɪ/ *n* [U] (formal) nearness: (正式用語) 接近: *in (close) ~ to,* (very) near to (which is usu preferable). 非常接近於(通常較常用 very near to)。**~ fuse,** one that explodes the shell to which it is fitted when near the target, eg an enemy aircraft. 近發引信(使砲彈在接近敵機等目標時爆炸者)。

prox·imo /ˈprɒksɪməʊ; ˈprɑksɪmo/ *adj* (abbr 略作 **prox**) (comm or official style, better avoided) of next month: (商業或公務上的文體,最好不用) 下月的;次月的: *on the 22nd prox.* 下月二十二日。

proxy /ˈprɒksɪ; ˈprɑksɪ/ *n* (*pl* -xies) [C] (document giving) [U] authority to represent or act for another (esp in voting at an election); [C] person given a ~: 代理權;代表權(尤指在選舉中代表他人投票); 委託書; 委託投票書; 代理人; 代表者: *vote by ~;* 由代理人投票; *make one's wife one's ~.* 以妻爲自己的代表。

prude /pruːd; prud/ *n* person of extreme or exaggerated propriety (often affected) in behaviour or speech. 極端或過份拘禮的人; 裝得規規矩矩的人。**pru·dery** /ˈpruːdərɪ; ˈprudərɪ/ *n* (*pl* -ries) [U] extreme propriety; [C] prudish act or remark. 過份的禮儀;極端拘謹;過份拘禮的行動或言詞。**prud·ish** /ˈpruːdɪʃ; ˈprudɪʃ/ *adj* of or like a ~; excessively modest; easily shocked. 過份拘禮者的;像過份拘禮者的;過於謙遜的;裝模作樣的;易於驚恐的。**pru·dish·ly** *adv*

pru·dent /ˈpruːdnt; ˈprudṇt/ *adj* careful; acting only after careful thought or planning: 審愼的;三思而後行的: *a ~ housekeeper.* 一位謹愼的女管家。**~·ly** *adv* **pru·dence** /-dns; -dṇs/ *n* [U] being

~; careful forethought. 審愼;事先仔細的考慮。

pru·den·tial /pruːˈdenʃl ; pruˈdɛnʃəl/ *adj* relating to, marked by, prudence. 審愼的;有智慮的。

prune¹ /pruːn ; prun/ *n* dried plum; (colloq) silly person. 乾梅子;梅乾;(俗)傻瓜。

prune² /pruːn ; prun/ *vt* [VP6A, 14, 15B] ~ ***sth from sth; ~ sth off sth; ~ sth away,*** cut away parts of (trees, bushes, etc) in order to control growth or shape; (fig) take out unnecessary parts from: 修剪(樹,灌木等);(喩)自…刪除不必要的部份: ~ *the rose-bushes;* 修剪玫瑰樹叢; ~ *away unwanted growth;* 剪掉不要的枝葉等; ~ *an essay of superfluous matter;* 刪去文章中多餘的部分; ~ *away unnecessary adjectives.* 刪去不必要的形容詞。 **prun·ing** *n* [U]: *The roses need pruning,* ought to be ~d. 這些玫瑰需要修剪了。 **ˈpruning-knife/-hook/-saw/-scissors/-shears,** kinds of tool used for pruning. 修剪用的刀(彎刀,鋸,剪,大剪)。 **pruners** *n pl* pruning-scissors. 修剪用的剪刀。

pru·ri·ent /ˈprʊərɪənt ; ˈprʊrɪənt/ *adj* having, showing, an excessive and unhealthy interest in matters of sex. 好色的;貪淫的;對淫穢之事特別感興趣的。 **~·ly** *adv* **pru·ri·ence** /-əns ; -əns/, **pru·ri·ency** /-ənsɪ ; -ənsɪ/ *nn* state of being ~. 淫亂;好色。

Prus·sian /ˈprʌʃn ; ˈprʌʃən/ *n, adj* (inhabitant, native) of Prussia. 普魯士居民;普魯士人;普魯士的。 ~ **blue,** deep blue colour. 深藍色;普魯士藍。

prus·sic /ˈprʌsɪk ; ˈprʌsɪk/ *adj* ˌ~ **ˈacid,** violent and deadly poison. 氫氰酸;普魯士酸(烈性毒物)。

pry¹ /praɪ ; praɪ/ *vi* (*pt, pp* pried /praɪd ; praɪd/) [VP2A, 3A] ***pry (into),*** inquire too curiously (into other people's affairs); 偵察;刺探;打聽(別人之事); [VP2C] ***pry about,*** look or peer (about) inquisitively. 到處窺探。 **pry·ing·ly** *adv*

pry² /praɪ ; praɪ/ *vt* [VP22, 15A, B] (= *prize³*) get (sth *open*) (eg with a lever); lift (sth *up*): (以槓桿等)撬開(與 open 連用);舉起(某物,與 up 連用): (fig) (喩) *pry a secret out of sb.* 探知某人之秘密。

psalm /sɑːm ; sɑm/ *n* sacred song or hymn, esp **(the P~s)** those in the Bible. 聖歌;聖詩;讚美詩;(尤指聖經之)詩篇(the Psalms)。 **~·ist** /-ɪst ; -ɪst/ *n* person who writes ~s, esp **the P~ist,** David, said to be the author of ~s in the Bible. 聖歌作者;(尤指)大衛王(據說爲聖經詩篇之作者)。 **~·ody** /ˈsɑːmədɪ ; ˈsɑmədɪ/ *n* (*pl* -dies) **1** [U] practice or art of singing ~s. 唱讚美詩;唱讚美詩之技巧。 **2** [C] arrangement of ~s for singing; book of ~s with their musical settings. (附樂譜之)讚美詩集。

psal·ter /ˈsɔːltə(r) ; ˈsɔltə/ *n* Book of Psalms; copy of the Psalms, esp one designed for use in public worship. (聖經之)詩篇;(尤指禮拜時所用之)詩篇集。

psal·tery /ˈsɔːltərɪ ; ˈsɔltrɪ/ *n* (*pl* -ries) musical instrument (ancient and medieval times) with strings over a sound-board, played by plucking the strings. 薩泰里琴(古代和中世紀的一種絃樂器)。

pse·phol·ogy /seˈfɒlədʒɪ *US:* siː- ; siˈfɑlədʒɪ/ *n* scientific study of election trends, eg by means of opinion polls. (利用民意測驗等研究選舉趨勢的)選舉學。 **pse·phol·ogist** /-ɪst ; -ɪst/ *n*

pseud /sjuːd *US:* suːd ; sud/ *n* (colloq) (俗) = pseudo(*n*).

pseudo /ˈsjuːdəʊ *US:* ˈsuː- ; ˈsjudo/ *adj* (colloq) sham; insincere: (俗)冒充的;騙人的;虛假的;僞善的: *I've always found him very* ~. 我一直覺得他很虛僞。□ *n* sham person. 虛僞之人。

pseudo- /ˌsjuːdəʊ *US:* ˌsuː- ; ˌsjudo/ *pref* false; spurious: 僞的;假的: ~*-scientific.* 假科學的。⇨ App 3. 參看附錄三。

pseu·do·nym /ˈsjuːdənɪm *US:* ˈsuː- ; ˈsjudn̩ˌɪm/ *n* name taken, esp by an author, instead of his real name. 假名;(尤指)筆名。 **pseud·ony·mous** /sjuːˈdɒnɪməs *US:* suː- ; sjuˈdɑnəməs/ *adj* writing, written, under an assumed name. 以筆名寫作的;用筆名的。

pshaw /pʃɔː ; ʃɔ *or similar 'burst' of noise* 或類似之'突發'聲/ *int* exclamation to indicate contempt or impatience. (表示不耐煩及輕蔑等之感嘆聲)呸!啐!

psit·ta·co·sis /ˌsɪtəˈkəʊsɪs ; ˌsɪtəˈkosɪs/ *n* [U] (also called 亦稱作 *'parrot fever'*) contagious virus disease (caught from parrots and related birds) producing fever and other complications (as in pneumonia). 鸚鵡熱;鸚鵡病。

psyche /ˈsaɪkɪ ; ˈsaɪkɪ/ *n* **1** human soul or spirit. 人之靈魂或精神。 **2** human mind; mentality. 人之心靈;心智。

psyche·delic /ˌsaɪkɪˈdelɪk ; ˌsaɪkɪˈdɛlɪk/ *adj* **1** (of drugs) hallucinatory: (指藥)使人產生幻覺的: *Mescalin and LSD are ~ drugs.* Mescalin 和 LSD 是迷幻藥。 **2** (of visual and sound effects) acting on the mind like ~ drugs: (指視覺和聲音效果)引起心神渙散的;引起幻覺的: ~ *music.* 迷魂音樂。

psy·chia·try /saɪˈkaɪətrɪ *US:* sɪ- ; saɪˈkaɪətrɪ/ *n* [U] the study and treatment of mental illness. 精神病學;精神病治療法。 **psy·chia·trist** /-ɪst ; -ɪst/ *n* expert in ~. 精神病專家;精神病醫師。 **psy·chi·atric** /ˌsaɪkɪˈætrɪk ; ˌsaɪkɪˈætrɪk/ *adj* of ~: 精神病學的;精神病治療的: *a psychiatric clinic.* 精神病醫療診所。

psy·chic¹ /ˈsaɪkɪk ; ˈsaɪkɪk/ *n* [C] person apparently, or claiming to be, responsive to occult powers; (popular term for a) medium(4). 通靈之人;巫師;(自稱能與鬼魂通訊息的)關亡人。

psy·chic² /ˈsaɪkɪk ; ˈsaɪkɪk/, **psy·chi·cal** /ˈsaɪkɪkl ; ˈsaɪkɪkl̩/ *adjj* **1** of the soul or mind. 靈魂的;心靈的。 **2** of phenomena and conditions which appear to be outside physical or natural laws: 超自然的;與通靈有關的: ~ *research,* the study and investigation of such phenomena, eg telepathy, second sight. 心靈研究(對心靈感應、千里眼等現象的研究)。

psy·cho-an·aly·sis /ˌsaɪkəʊ əˈnæləsɪs ; ˌsaɪkoəˈnæləsɪs/ *n* [U] **1** method of healing mental illnesses by tracing them, through interviews, to events in the patient's early life, and bringing those events to his consciousness. 精神分析(一種治療精神病的方法,藉談話以追溯患者早年生活中的事件,並使之重現在他的意識之中)。 **2** body of doctrine based on this method concerned with the investigation and treatment of emotional disturbances. 精神分析學。 **psy·cho-ana·lyst** /ˌsaɪkəʊ ˈænəlɪst ; ˌsaɪkoˈænl̩ɪst/ *n* person who practises ~. 從事精神分析的人;精神分析家。 **psy·cho-ana·lytic(al)** /ˌsaɪkəʊ ˌænəˈlɪtɪk(l) ; ˌsaɪkoˌænl̩ˈɪtɪk(l̩)/ *adj* relating to ~. 精神分析的;精神分析學的。 **psy·cho-ana·lyse** (US = **-lyze**) /ˌsaɪkəʊ ˈænəlaɪz ; ˌsaɪkoˈænl̩ˌaɪz/ *vt* treat (sb) by ~. 用精神分析法治療(某人)。

psy·chol·ogy /saɪˈkɒlədʒɪ ; saɪˈkɑlədʒɪ/ *n* [U] **1** science, study, of the mind and its processes: 心理學: *abnormal/animal/child/industrial* ~, branches of this science. 變態(動物,兒童,工業)心理學。 **2** [C] (colloq, unscientific use) mental nature, processes, etc of a person: (俗,但非科學的用法)心理(指一個人的心理狀態、過程等): *She understands her husband's ~ very well.* 她非常了解她丈夫的心理。 **psy·chol·ogist** /-ɪst ; ɪst/ *n* student of, expert in, ~. 研究心理學者;心理學家。 **psy·cho·logi·cal** /ˌsaɪkəˈlɒdʒɪkl ; ˌsaɪkəˈlɑdʒɪkl̩/ *adj* of ~; of the mind. 心理學的;心理的。 **the psychological moment,** the most appropriate time; the time when one is most likely to achieve the desired end. 最適當的時機;最能獲得所期望之目的的時刻。 **psy·chological warfare,** waged by trying to influence people's ideas and beliefs. 心理戰(用以影響人們的思想和信仰者)。 **psy·cho·logi·cally** /-klɪ ; -klɪ/ *adv*

psy·cho·path /ˈsaɪkəʊpæθ ; ˈsaɪkəˌpæθ/ *n* person suffering from severe emotional derangement, esp one who is aggressive and antisocial, with little or no moral sense. 精神變態者;精神病患者(尤指性好爭吵毆鬪、反社會、無道德感的人)。 **~ic** /ˌsaɪkəʊˈpæθɪk ; ˌsaɪkəˈpæθɪk/ *adj* of, suffering from, severe emotional or mental disorder. 精神變態的;患精神病的。

psy·cho·sis /saɪˈkəʊsɪs ; saɪˈkosɪs/ *n* (*pl* -choses

/-ˈkəʊsiːz ; -ˈkosiz/) severely abnormal or diseased mental state. 精神變態；精神病。

psy·cho·so·matic /ˌsaɪkəʊsəˈmætɪk ; ˌsaɪkosoˈmætɪk/ *adj* (of disease) caused by mental stress; (of medicine) concerned with such disease. (指疾病)由心理壓力引起的；(指醫學)研究由心理壓力引起之疾病的；心身性的。

psy·cho·therapy /ˌsaɪkəʊˈθerəpɪ ; ˌsaɪkoˈθɛrəpɪ/ *n* [U] treatment by psychological methods of mental, emotional and nervous disorders. 心理療法；精神療法。

ptar·mi·gan /ˈtɑːmɪgən ; ˈtɑrməgən/ *n* bird of the grouse family with black or grey feathers in summer and white in winter. 雷鳥(松鷄類禽鳥，夏季羽毛爲黑或灰色，冬季則爲白色)。

ptero·dac·tyl /ˌterəˈdæktɪl ; ˌtɛrəˈdæktɪl/ *n* extinct flying reptile. 翼手龍(一種已絕跡的會飛的爬蟲)。

pto·maine /ˈtəʊmeɪn ; ˈtomen/ *n* (sorts of) poison which is found in decaying food: 屍毒(腐敗食物上所產生的各種毒素)：*ill with ~ poisoning.* 因中屍毒而生病。

pub /pʌb ; pʌb/ *n* (abbr for) public house: 爲 public house 之略：*go round to the pub for a drink.* 到酒館去喝酒。**ˈpub-crawl,** ⇨ crawl *n*(1).

pu·berty /ˈpjuːbətɪ ; ˈpjubətɪ/ *n* [U] stage at which a person becomes physically able to become a parent; maturing of the sexual functions: 青春期；發情期；性官能的成熟：*reach the age of ~.* 已屆青春期。

pu·bic /ˈpjuːbɪk ; ˈpjubɪk/ *adj* of the lower part of the abdomen: 陰部的：*~ hair.* 陰毛。

pub·lic /ˈpʌblɪk ; ˈpʌblɪk/ *adj* (opp of *private*) of, for, connected with, owned by, done for or done by, known to, people in general: (爲 private 之相反字)公衆的；爲公衆的；與公衆有關的；由公衆所有的；爲公衆而做或由公衆所做的；爲公衆所知的：*a ~ library/park;* 公共圖書館(公園)；*a matter of ~ knowledge,* sth known to everyone; 人人皆知的事；*enter ~ life,* engage in the affairs or service of the people, eg in government; 從事公務；*~ elementary and secondary schools,* government-controlled schools providing free education. 公立小學和中學。**ˌ~-adˈdress system** *n* (abbr 略作 **PA system**) system of microphones and loud speakers for broadcasting in ~ areas. 擴音系統(包括麥克風和揚聲喇叭等)。**ˌ~ ˈbar,** ordinary bar in a ~ house or hotel. (酒館或旅館內的)賣酒櫃臺；普通酒吧。⇨ *saloon bar* at saloon. **ˌ~ ˌcorpoˈration,** (legal) corporation providing services for the public, eg in GB *the British Broadcasting Corporation, the BBC.* (法律)服務大衆的公司(如英國廣播公司 BBC)。**ˌ~ ˈenemy,** person thought to be a danger to the ~, to the whole community. 國民公敵。**ˌ~ ˈhouse** *n* (GB) (formal) (colloq abbr 俗略作 **pub** /pʌb ; pʌb/) house (not a club, hotel, etc) licensed to sell alcoholic drinks to be consumed on the premises but not offering accommodation. (英)(正式用語)酒館。**ˌ~ ˈnuisance,** (legal) illegal act harmful to people in general rather than to an individual; (colloq) sb who is a nuisance to a community. (法律)對公衆的妨害；公害；(俗)對公衆造成妨害之人。**ˌ~ oˈpinion poll,** ⇨ poll¹(2). **ˌ~ ˈownership,** ownership by the State, eg of the railways. 國有(如鐵路國有)。**ˌP~ ˈProsecutor,** ⇨ *prosecutor* at prosecute. **ˌ~ reˈlations** (abbr 略作 **PR**) *n pl* (esp) relations between a government department or authority, business organization, etc with the general ~, usu through the distribution of information. 公共關係(尤指政府各部門或當局，商業機構等透過消息發佈而與公衆建立的關係)。**ˌ~ reˈlations officer** (abbr 略作 **PRO**) person employed in ~ relations. 公共關係人員。**ˈ~ school, (a)** (GB) private school for older fee-paying pupils, usu a boarding school, supported partly by endowments and managed by a board of governors. (英國)私立學校；公學(爲年齡較大且繳付學費的學生設立，通常爲寄宿學校，部分經費來自基金，而由董事會管理之)。⇨ *preparatory school* (for younger pupils) at preparatory. **(b)** (US and Scot) school providing free education, supported by ~ funds. (美國及蘇格蘭)公立學校。**ˌ~ ˈspirit,** readiness to do things that are for the good of the community. 熱心公益；爲公衆服務的精神。Hence, 由此產生，**ˌ~-ˈspirited** *adj* **ˌ~ ˈtransport,** transport systems (road and rail) owned by ~ corporations, eg city and town authorities: 公共交通系統；公共交通設施(如公路、鐵路等)：*travel by ~ transport,* contrasted with privately owned systems, one's own car, etc. 搭乘公共交通工具旅行。**~ trustee,** ⇨ trustee. **ˌ~ uˈtilities,** organizations which supply services and commodities, eg water, gas, electricity, transport, communications, to the general ~. 公用事業(如水、煤氣、電、交通設施、電信等)。***go ~,*** (of a business organization) offer shares for purchase (on the Stock Exchange) by the ~: (指商業機構)公開發售股票；股票上市：*Rolls-Royce, after its bankruptcy in 1971, went ~ in 1972.* 勞斯萊斯在 1971 年破產之後，於 1972 年公開發售股票。□ *n* **1 the ~,** members of the community in general: 公衆；民衆：*the British ~.* 英國民衆；一般英國人。*The ~ are not admitted.* 一般民衆不得擅自進入。*The ~ is/are requested not to leave litter in the park.* 民衆請勿在公園中拋棄廢物。***in ~,*** openly, not in private. 公開地；公然地。**2** particular section of the community: 社會上的某一部分人：*the theatre-going ~,* those who attend theatres; 愛看戲的人；*the reading ~,* those who read books, etc; 讀者羣；*a book that will appeal to a large ~,* to many readers. 會吸引很多讀者的書。**~·ly** /-klɪ ; -klɪ/ *adv*

pub·li·can /ˈpʌblɪkən ; ˈpʌblɪkən/ *n* **1** (GB) keeper of a public house. (英)酒館老闆。**2** (in Roman times and in the New Testament) tax-gatherer. (在羅馬帝國時代和在新約聖經中指)收稅員；稅吏。

pub·li·ca·tion /ˌpʌblɪˈkeɪʃn ; ˌpʌblɪˈkeʃən/ *n* **1** [U] act of making known to the public, of publishing sth: 發佈；出版：*the ~ of a report;* 一篇報告的公佈；*date of ~.* 出版日期。**2** [C] sth published, eg a book or a periodical. 出版物(如書或期刊)。

pub·li·cist /ˈpʌblɪsɪst ; ˈpʌblɪsɪst/ *n* newspaper man who writes on current topics of public interest, eg a political journalist; person who publicizes. (報紙或通訊社等之)時事評論家；政論作家；宣揚者；宣傳者。

pub·lic·ity /pʌbˈlɪsətɪ ; pʌbˈlɪsətɪ/ *n* [U] **1** the state of being known to, seen by, everyone: 爲人人所知所見之情況；出風頭：*an actress who seeks/avoids ~;* 一位想出風頭(避免出風頭)的女伶；*heads of state who live their lives in the full blaze of ~.* 在衆目睽睽之下過生活的國家元首們。**2** (business of) providing information to win public interest: 廣告；宣傳；宣傳業務：*give a new book/play, etc wide ~;* 對新書(劇等)廣事宣傳；*conduct a ˈ~ campaign.* 從事一項宣傳運動。**ˈ~ agent,** person employed to keep the name of a person, eg an actor, or product constantly before the public. 宣傳員(其工作在於使某人，如某演員，或某產品的名字經常出現於大衆之前)。

pub·li·cize /ˈpʌblɪsaɪz ; ˈpʌblɪˌsaɪz/ *vt* [VP6A] give publicity to: bring to the attention of the public. 宣揚；引起大衆注意；宣傳。

pub·lish /ˈpʌblɪʃ ; ˈpʌblɪʃ/ *vt* [VP6A] **1** have (a book, periodical, etc) printed and announce that it is for sale. 出版(書、期刊等)。**2** make known to the public: 公佈；宣佈：*~ the news;* 發佈消息；*~ the banns of marriage,* announce formally in a church the names of persons shortly to be married. (在教堂中)公佈結婚預告。**~er** *n* person whose business is the ~ing of books. 出版商；出版者。

puce /pjuːs ; pjus/ *n* [U] purple-brown. 紫褐色。

puck¹ /pʌk ; pʌk/ *n* (in folklore) mischievous

sprite or goblin. (民間傳說中之)愛惡作劇的精靈或惡鬼。～·ish /-ɪʃ ; -ɪʃ/ *adj* mischievous: 惡作劇的: *a ～ish smile.* 淘氣的微笑。～·ish·ly *adv*

puck² /pʌk ; pʌk/ *n* hard rubber disc used instead of a ball in ice-hockey. (冰上曲棍球戲中用以代替球的)橡皮圓盤。⇨ the illus at hockey. 參看 hockey 之插圖。

pucker /ˈpʌkə(r) ; ˈpʌkɚ/ *vt, vi* [VP6A, 15B, 2A, C] ～ *(up),* draw or come together into small folds or wrinkles: 摺疊;皺起;縮攏: *～ up one's brows/ lips.* 皺起眉頭(雙唇)。*This coat ～s (up) at the shoulders.* 這件外衣的肩部皺了。□ *n* wrinkle. 皺紋。

pud /pʊd ; pʊd/ *n* [U] (sl) pudding. (俚)布丁。

pud·den /ˈpʊdn ; ˈpʊdn̩/ *n* (colloq) (only in) (俗)(僅用於) **ˈ～-head** *n* slow, stupid person. 笨人;愚鈍者。

pudding /ˈpʊdɪŋ ; ˈpʊdɪŋ/ *n* [C, U] **1** (dish of) food, usu a soft, sweet mixture, served as part of a meal, generally eaten after the meat course: 布丁(一種鬆軟的甜食,爲正餐之一部分,通常在主菜後食用): *milk ～s,* of some kind of grain, eg rice, cooked with milk and flavourings. 牛奶布丁(米等同牛奶和香料製成者)。**ˈ～-face,** large fat face. 大而胖的臉。**2** kind of sausage. 一種臘腸。**ˈblack ～,** intestine of pig stuffed with oatmeal, blood, etc. 黑臘腸(由燕麥片、血等塞入豬腸中製成)。**3** sth like a ～ in appearance. 外貌若布丁之物。**4** **ˈ～ stone,** rock composed of rounded pebbles in a kind of stone like concrete. 礫岩;布丁岩(由小卵石組成,形似混凝土)。

puddle /ˈpʌdl ; ˈpʌdl/ *n* **1** [C] small pool of water. 小水潭。**2** [U] wet clay and sand mixed to a paste, used as a watertight covering for embankments, etc. (濕黏土與沙混拌成泥漿,用以塗塞堤防等以免漏水的)窯泥;膠泥。□ *vt* **1** mix (wet clay and sand) into a thick paste. 混拌(濕黏土與沙)而成厚泥漿。**2** stir (molten iron) to produce wrought iron by expelling carbon. 攪動(熔鐵)以排除碳而煉出鍛鐵。**pud·dler** /ˈpʌdlə(r) ; ˈpʌdlɚ/ *n* worker who ～s clay, etc or molten iron. 混拌泥漿者;攪鍊熔鐵者。

pu·denda /pjuːˈdendə ; pjuˈdɛndə/ *n pl* (formal) external genital organs, esp of the female. (正式用語)陰部;(尤指)女陰。

pudgy /ˈpʌdʒɪ ; ˈpʌdʒɪ/ *adj* (-ier, -iest) short, thick and fat: 矮胖的;短而粗的: *～ fingers.* 短而粗的手指。

pueblo /ˈpwebləʊ ; ˈpwɛblo/ *n* (*pl* ～s /-ləʊz ; -loz/) communal village dwelling of adobe and stone, as built by American Indians in Mexico and the south-western US. (墨西哥和美國西南部之印第安人)用泥磚和石塊建的村落。

puer·ile /ˈpjʊəraɪl *US:* -rəl ; ˈpjuə,rɪl/ *adj* trivial; suitable only for a child: 瑣屑的;只適於小孩的;幼稚的: *ask ～ questions.* 問些幼稚的問題。**puer·il·ity** /ˌpjʊəˈrɪlətɪ ; ˌpjuəˈrɪlətɪ/ *n* [U] childishness; foolishness; [C] childish or foolish act, idea, utterance, etc. 幼稚;愚蠢;幼稚或愚蠢的言行思想等。

pu·er·peral /pjuːˈɜːpərəl ; pjuˈɝpərəl/ *adj* of, due to, childbirth: 分娩的;因分娩而起的: *～ fever.* 產褥熱。

puff¹ /pʌf ; pʌf/ *n* [C] **1** (sound of a) short, quick sending out of breath, air, etc; amount of steam, smoke, etc sent out at one time: (呼吸、空氣等)短而快的噴送;噴送聲;一次噴出之(蒸汽、煙等的)量: *～s from a steam-engine;* 蒸汽機噴出之氣; *have a ～ at a pipe.* 吸一口煙斗。**2** **(ˈpowder-)～,** piece or ball of soft material, for putting powder on the face. 粉撲。**3** round, soft mass of material used on an article of dress as an ornament: (衣服上用做裝飾的)圓而鬆的疊縐;褶襉: *～ sleeves,* swelling out like balloons. (寬鬆而鼓起的)燈籠袖。**4** **～ pastry,** light, flaky pastry. 多層酥餅;千層餅。**5** quantity of ～ pastry filled with jam, whipped cream, etc: (包有果醬、奶油等的)酥皮點心: *jam ～s.* 果醬酥皮點心。**6** review of a book, play, etc, praising it extravagantly. (對書、戲劇等之)過份誇獎的評論;吹噓。**7** **ˈ～-adder** *n* poisonous African viper which inflates the upper part of its body when excited. 鼓腹蝰(非洲產的一種毒蛇,受到刺激時身體上半部卽脹大)。**ˈ～-ball** *n* kind of fungus shaped like a ball which when ripe breaks open and sends out ～s of dust-like spores. 塵菌;馬勃菌(形如球,成熟時卽裂開,並噴散出塵土狀孢子)。**～y** *adj* (-ier, -iest) short of breath; easily made short of breath (by running, climbing, etc); swollen: 喘息的;易喘息的;膨脹的: *a red face, ～y under the eyes.* 一張紅紅的臉,眼睛下面腫脹的。**～i·ness** *n* [U] state of being ～y. 喘息;易喘息或膨脹的狀態。

puff² /pʌf ; pʌf/ *vi, vt* **1** [VP2A, C] move along with puffs (1); breathe quickly (as after running); (of smoke, steam, etc) come out in puffs: 噴送着氣(蒸汽、煙等)而行進;喘息(如跑後);(指煙、蒸汽等)陣陣噴出: *The old steam-engine ～ed out of the station.* 那輛舊的蒸汽機車噴着陣陣的煙駛出了車站。*He was ～ing hard when he jumped on to the bus.* 他跳上公共汽車時喘息不已。*He was ～ing (away) at his cigar.* 他一口一口地噴着雪茄煙。*Smoke ～ed up from the crater of the volcano.* 煙從火山口一陣陣地噴出。**2** [VP15A, B] send out in puffs: 陣陣噴出: *He ～ed smoke into my face.* 他向著我的臉噴煙。*He managed to ～ out a few words.* 他喘息着說出幾句話。*He was rather ～ed* (= out of breath) *after running to the bus stop.* 跑到公共汽車站後,他喘息不已。**～ed up,** filled with pride; conceited. 傲慢的;自負的。**3** [VP15B] ～ *sth out,* **(a)** blow out: 吹熄: *He ～ed out the candle.* 他吹熄蠟燭。**(b)** cause to swell with air: 使脹(使因有空氣而脹起): *He ～ed out his chest with pride.* 他傲氣十足地挺起胸膛。**4** [VP6A] praise (a book, etc) in an advertisement or review, esp in an exaggerated way. 在廣告或書評中(尤指過分)稱讚(某書等);吹捧。

puf·fin /ˈpʌfɪn ; ˈpʌfɪn/ *n* N Atlantic seabird with a large bill. 善知鳥;海鴨(產於北大西洋的一種大嘴海鳥)。⇨ the illus at water. 參看 water 之插圖。

pug /pʌg ; pʌg/ *n* (also亦作 **ˈpug-dog**) small breed of pug-nosed dog. 哈巴狗。**ˈpug-nose(d)** *adj, n* (with a) short, squat or snub nose. 獅子鼻(短、扁、微向上翻的鼻子);有獅子鼻的。

pu·gil·ist /ˈpjuːdʒɪlɪst ; ˈpjudʒəlɪst/ *n* (formal) boxer. (正式用語)拳擊家。**pu·gil·ism** /-ɪzəm ; -ɪzəm/ *n* [U] boxing. 拳擊。**pu·gil·is·tic** /ˌpjuːdʒɪˈlɪstɪk ; ˌpjudʒəˈlɪstɪk/ *adj* of ～s or pugilism. 拳擊家的;拳擊的。

pug·na·cious /pʌgˈneɪʃəs ; pʌgˈneʃəs/ *adj* (formal) fond of, in the habit of, fighting. (正式用語)好戰的;好鬪的。**～·ly** *adv* **pug·nac·ity** /pʌgˈnæsətɪ ; pʌgˈnæsətɪ/ *n* [U].

puis·sant /ˈpjuːɪsnt ; ˈpjuɪsn̩t/ *adj* (archaic) having great power or influence. (古)具有極大力量或影響的。**puis·sance** /-sns ; -sn̩s/ *n* [U] strength. 力量。

puke /pjuːk ; pjuk/ *vi, vt, n* [U] (sl) vomit. (俚)嘔吐。

pukka /ˈpʌkə ; ˈpʌkə/ *adj* (dated sl) genuine; authentic; superior. (過時俚語)眞正的;可靠的;優良的。

pul·chri·tude /ˈpʌlkrɪtjuːd *US:* -tuːd ; ˈpʌlkrɪ,tjud/ *n* [U] (formal) physical beauty. (正式用語)美麗;漂亮;外在美。**pul·chri·tudi·nous** /ˌpʌlkrɪˈtjuːdɪnəs *US:* -ˈtuːdənəs ; ˌpʌlkrɪˈtjudn̩əs/ *adj*

pule /pjuːl ; pjul/ *vi* [VP2A] (eg of a baby) cry feebly; whimper. (指嬰兒等)微弱地哭泣;低泣;嗚咽。

pull¹ /pʊl ; pʊl/ *n* **1** [C] act of pulling: 拖;拉;扯;曳;吸: *give a ～ at a rope;* 拉繩子; [C] act of deep drinking: 大口喝: *take a ～ at a bottle,* drink deeply from it. 從瓶中喝一大口。**2** [C, U] attraction: 吸引力: *the ～ of the life of a sailor/ singer/tramp.* 船員(歌星,流浪者)生活的吸引力。**3** [C] effort of moving: 費力;奮力: *a hard/long ～ up the hill.* 吃力的(漫長而費力的)爬山。**4** [C, U] (colloq) power to get help or attention through influence, eg with people in high positions: (俗)勢力;影響力: *He has a strong ～/a great deal of ～ with the Managing Director.* 他對總經理頗有影響力。**5** handle, etc which is to be pulled. 拉手;把手。**6** (printing) proof; single impression.

(印刷)校樣;校稿。

pull² /pʊl; pul/ *vt, vi* (For special uses with *adverbial particles* and *preps,* ⇨ 7 below.) (與副詞接語及介詞連用的特殊用法,參看下列第7義。) **1** [VP 6A, 15A, B, 22, 2A] (contrasted with *push*) use force upon (sth or sb) so as to draw towards or after one, or in the direction indicated: (與push 相對)拉;扯;拖: *The horse was ~ing a heavy cart.* 馬在拉重的車。*How many coaches can that locomotive ~?* 那個火車頭能拉多少節客車? *Would you rather push the barrow or ~ it?* 你願推還是願拉手推車? *The baby was ~ing its father's beard.* 那嬰兒在扯他父親的鬍子。*P~ your chair up to the table.* 把你的椅子拖近桌邊。*She ~ed her tights/gloves on/off.* 她把她的緊身衣(手套)穿(戴)上(脫下)。*He ~ed my ears/~ed me by the ears.* 他扯我的耳朵。*I'm going to the dentist to have a bad tooth ~ed out.* 我要到牙醫那裏拔掉一顆壞牙。*Stop ~ing, please!* 請別拉了! ***~ sth to pieces,*** use force to separate its parts or to break it up into parts; (fig) criticize severely by pointing out the weak points or faults: 用力將某物扯成碎片或拆散;(喩)指出缺點或錯誤而加以嚴厲地批評: *He ~ed my proposals/theory to pieces.* 他把我的建議(理論)批評得體無完膚。**2** [VP6A, 15A, B, 2A, C] move (a boat) by ~ing an oar or a pair of oars; (of a boat) be rowed (by): 划(船);(指船)被划動: *Now, all ~ together, please!* 現在請大家一起划! *The men/boat ~ed for the shore.* 那些人(該船)划向岸邊。***~ together,*** (fig) work together; co-operate. (喩)一起工作;合作。***~ one's weight,*** exert oneself so as to do a fair share of the work: 盡力做好自己的一份工作;盡自己的本分: *Either you ~ your weight or we replace you.* 你要是不盡力做好你的工作,我們便換人做你的事。**3** [VP3A] ***~ at/on sth,*** **(a)** give a tug: 拖曳: *~ at/on a rope.* 拖曳繩子。**(b)** draw or suck: 吸;吮: *~ing at his pipe,* drawing in breath and smoke through his (tobacco) pipe; 吸他的煙斗; *~ at a bottle,* have a drink from one. 從瓶中喝一口。⇨ pull¹(1). **4** ***~ a 'fast one,*** (colloq) deceive sb. (俗)欺騙某人;欺詐。***~ a muscle,*** strain it. 拉傷肌肉。***~ a proof,*** take an impression (from type); print a proof. 印刷校稿。For other uses with *nn,* ⇨ the *n* entries, eg 與名詞連用的其他用法參看各名詞,如 ***~ a face/faces; ~ sb's leg; ~ one's punches; ~ strings; ~ wires; ~ the 'wool over sb's eyes.*** **5** (in games, sport) (用於遊戲、運動) (golf) hit (the ball) wrongly to the left, Cf 參較 *slice*(4); (高爾夫球)擊(球)偏向左方; (cricket) strike (the ball) forward and to the left of the wicket, by striking across the ball's path; (板球)擊(球)向前至三柱門的左方; (horse-racing) ~ in the reins (of a horse) to prevent it from winning. (賽馬)(故意要輸而)勒住馬。**6** (sl) raid; rob: (俚)襲擊;搶劫: *~ a bank;* 搶劫銀行; steal: 偷竊: *~ a few thousand quid.* 偷竊幾千鎊。**7** [VP15B, 2C] (special uses with *adverbial particles* and *preps*): (與副詞接語和介詞連用的特殊用法):

pull sb/sth about, ~ in different directions; treat roughly. 拖着某人或某物到處跑;拖來拖去;虐待某人或某物。

pull sth apart, tear or ~ into its parts. 扯斷;拆開;撕開。

pull sth down, destroy or demolish, eg an old building. 摧毀;拆除(如舊的建築物)。***pull sb down,*** (of illness, etc) weaken; lower the spirits of: (指疾病等)使虛弱;使精神不振: *An attack of influenza soon ~s you down.* 害一次流行性感冒很快就使你虛弱下來。

pull in, **(a)** (of a train) enter a station: (指火車)進站: *The express from Rome ~ed in on time.* 從羅馬來的快車準時進站。**(b)** (of a motor-vehicle or boat) move in towards: (指車輛或船)移向;駛向: *The boat ~ed in to the bank/shore.* 該船向岸靠攏。*The lorry driver ~ed in to the side of the road.* 卡車司機把車子駛向路邊。Hence, 由此產生, **'~-in** *n* place at which to ~ in 可停車之處 (also ⇨ *~-up* below). (亦參看下列之 ~-up)。***~ sb in,*** **(a)** attract, draw: 吸引: *The new play at the National Theatre is ~ing in large audiences.* 在國家戲院上演的新劇吸引了大批觀衆。**(b)** (colloq, of the police) detain; arrest: (俗,指警察)拘留;逮捕: *He was ~ed in for questioning/loitering.* 他被逮捕審問(他因遊蕩而遭拘留)。***~ sth in,*** (colloq) earn: (俗)賺進: *How much money is he ~ing in, do you think?* 你認爲他賺進多少錢? ***~ oneself in,*** draw in the stomach muscles (so as to be upright, less flabby). 收縮腹肌(保持身體正直,減少腹肌鬆弛)。

pull sth off, **(a)** drive a motor-vehicle into a layby or hard shoulder. 將車開入大路旁的停車處。Hence, 由此產生, **'~-off** *n* (US) (美) = layby. **(b)** succeed in a plan, in winning sth: (某項計畫)獲得成功;得到某物: *~ off a good speculation;* 在一宗投機生意中大獲成功; *~ off some good wins at the races,* make successful bets. 在賽馬中贏了可觀的賭注。

pull out, **(a)** move or row out: 駛出;划出: *The boat ~ed out into midstream.* 該船划出而進入中流。*The driver of the car ~ed out from behind the lorry.* 該車的司機把車子開出行車的行列以便超越那輛卡車。**(b)** detach, eg from a periodical: 分開;分離(如從一期刊中):(attrib) (形容用法) *a '~-out supplement,* part of a magazine, etc which can be ~ed out and kept separately. (雜誌等之可取下單獨保存的)增刊。Hence, 由此產生, **'~-out** *n* ***~ out of sth,*** leave: 離開;離去;脫離: *The train ~ed out of Euston right on time.* 火車準時離開尤斯頓。*Sam ~ed out of the scheme at the last moment.* 山姆於最後一刻退出那計畫。***~ (sb) out (of sth),*** (cause to) leave a place or situation which is too difficult to manage: (使某人)脫離困境: *Troops are being ~ed out/are ~ing out of these troubled areas.* 軍隊被調離(正離開紛亂地區)。Hence, 由此產生, **'~-out** *n*: *The ~-out was planned to spread over a month.* 撤離的工作計畫在一個月的時間內進行。

pull (sth) over, (cause a vehicle, boat, etc to) move or steer to one side, eg to let another vehicle or boat pass: (將車、船等)開向一邊讓其他車、船超越: *P~ (your car) over and let me pass!* (將你的車子)開到一邊讓我超越!

pull (sb) round, (help to) recover from illness, weakness, a faint, etc: 康復;復元;協助某人使康復、清醒等: *You'll soon ~ round here in the country.* 住在這鄉間你不久即可康復。*Have this brandy; it will ~ you round.* 把這點白蘭地喝下;它會使你(從暈眩等中)復元。

pull through, **(a)** = *~ round.* **(b)** succeed in avoiding difficulties, dangers, etc; avoid failure. 在逃避困難、危險等方面成功;免於失敗。***~ sb through,*** **(a)** help to recover from illness, etc: 幫助(某人)恢復健康等: *The doctors ~ed me through.* 醫生們幫助我恢復了健康。**(b)** help to avoid failure, help to pass an examination, etc: 協助(某人)免於失敗;幫助(某人)通過考試等: *David's tutor did what he could to ~ him through.* 大衛的家庭教師盡力幫助他通過考試。**'~-through** *n* oily rag attached to a cord, ~ed through the barrel of a rifle, etc to clean it. 槍膛清掃布(結於繩上之油布,用以拉過槍筒而擦淨之)。

pull together, ⇨ 2 above. 參看上列第2義。***~ onself together,*** get control of oneself, of one's feelings, etc. 控制自己、自己的感情等。

pull (sth) up, bring or come to a stop: 使停止;停止: *The driver ~ed up when he came to the traffic lights.* 司機遇到交通燈時將車停下來。*He ~ed up his car at the entrance.* 他把他的汽車停在大門口。Hence, 由此產生, **'~-up** *n* place at which to ~ up: (路旁)飲食店等(可停車於附近者): *'Good ~-up for lorry-drivers',* eg as a sign outside a roadside café (also ⇨ *~-in* above). '貨車司機的理想飲

食處'(如路邊飲食店所掛的招牌)(亦參看上列之pull-in)。 **~ sb up,** check; reprimand: 阻止;申斥: *He was ~ed up by the chairman.* 他為主席所阻止。**~ up to / with sb / sth,** improve one's relative position (in a race, etc): 改善相對的地位(如在賽馬等中);追上: *The favourite soon ~ed up with the other horses.* 那匹有希望贏得競賽的馬不久追上了其他的馬。

pul·let /ˈpʊlɪt; ˈpʊlɪt/ *n* young hen, esp at the time she begins to lay eggs. 小母鷄(尤指開始生蛋者)。

pul·ley /ˈpʊlɪ; ˈpʊlɪ/ *n* (*pl* ~s) grooved wheel(s) for ropes or chains, used for lifting things. 滑輪;滑車。ˈ**~-block** *n* wooden block in which a ~ is fixed. 滑車組。

Pull·man /ˈpʊlmən; ˈpʊlmən/ *n* **1** (also 亦作 ˈ**~ car**) sleeping-car on a railway train. (火車上的)臥車。**2** especially comfortable railway carriage. (特別舒適的火車)客車。

pull·over /ˈpʊləʊvə(r); ˈpʊl,ovɚ/ *n* knitted outer garment, with or without sleeves, pulled on over the head. 套頭毛衣;套頭毛背心。⇨ jersey, jumper, sweater.

pul·lu·late /ˈpʌljʊleɪt; ˈpʌljə,let/ *vi* breed, multiply, rapidly; swarm. 繁殖;增殖;充滿;羣集。

pul·mon·ary /ˈpʌlmənərɪ *US:* -nerɪ; ˈpʌlmə,nɛrɪ/ *adj* of, in, connected with, the lungs: 肺的;肺部的;與肺有關的: *~ diseases;* 肺病; *the ~ arteries,* conveying blood to the lungs. 肺動脈。

pulp /pʌlp; pʌlp/ *n* **1** [U] soft, fleshy part of fruit: 果肉: *ˈapple ~.* 蘋果的果肉。**2** [U, C] soft mass of other material, esp of wood fibre as used for making paper: 柔軟的材料;(尤指用於造紙,由木材纖維製成的)木漿;紙漿。*reduce to (a) ~,* destroy the shape of by beating up and making soft. 打成稀爛如漿。**~ magazines / literature,** (term applied disparagingly to) cheap, popular periodicals, etc. (輕蔑語,指)廉價而流行的雜誌(作品)。□ *vt, vi* [VP6A, 2A] make into, become like, ~; remove ~ from: 製成漿;變成如漿之物;取出…之果肉或柔軟部分: *~ old books.* 把舊書做成造紙的紙漿。**~y** *adj* (-ier, -iest) like or consisting of ~. 像果肉或漿的;有果肉或漿的。

pul·pit /ˈpʊlpɪt; ˈpʊlpɪt/ *n* (usu small) raised and enclosed structure in a church, used by a clergyman, esp when preaching. 教堂中佈道的講壇(通常指小者)。**the ~,** the clergy. 教士職;聖職;教士(總稱)。⇨ the illus at church. 參看 church 之插圖。

pul·que /ˈpuːlkeɪ; ˈpʊlkɪ/ *n* [U] fermented milky drink made in Mexico from some kinds of agave. (墨西哥的)龍舌蘭酒。

pul·sar /ˈpʌlsɑː(r); ˈpʌlsar/ *n* star (in a galaxy) detected by pulsating radio signals only. 僅由脈動無線電信號所測出的銀河系星球;脈冲星。

pul·sate /pʌlˈseɪt *US:* ˈpʌlseɪt; ˈpʌlset/ *vt, vi* **1** [VP2A] beat or throb; expand and contract rhythmically; vibrate; quiver. 跳動;悸動;有節奏地擴張與收縮;震動;震顫;脈動。**2** [VP6A] cause to vibrate; agitate. 使震動;激動;使脈動。**pul·sa·tion** /pʌlˈseɪʃn; pʌlˈseʃən/ *n* **1** [C] single beat or throb; heartbeat. 一次跳動;悸動;心臟跳動。**2** [U] pulsating; throbbing. 震動;有韻律的悸跳;脈動。

pulse¹ /pʌls; pʌls/ *n* **1** the regular beat of the arteries, eg as felt at the wrist, as the blood is pumped through them by the heart: 脈搏: *The patient has a weak / strong / low / irregular ~.* 這位病人脈搏很弱(强,低,不規律)。**feel sb's ~,** feel the artery at the wrist and count the number of beats per minute. 診脈(按觸腕部動脈,並計算其每分鐘跳動次數)。**2** (fig) throb or thrill of life or emotion: (喻)生命或感情的激動: *an event that stirred my ~s,* roused my emotion, excited me. 一件使我感情激動的事件。□ *vi* [VP2C] beat; throb: 跳動;震動: *the life pulsing through a great city;* 大城市中緊張紛亂的生活; *news that sent the blood pulsing through his veins.* 使他的血液沸騰的消息。

pulse² /pʌls; pʌls/ *n* [U] (collective *sing,* sometimes with *pl v*) seeds growing in pods, eg peas, beans and lentils, used as food. (集合單數,有時用複數動詞)用作食物的豆;豆類(如豌豆、蠶豆、扁豆)。

pul·ver·ize /ˈpʌlvəraɪz; ˈpʌlvə,raɪz/ *vt, vi* **1** [VP6A] grind to powder; smash completely: 研磨成粉;澈底摧毁: (fig) (喻) *~ an opponent's arguments.* 澈底粉碎對方的論調。**2** [VP2A] become powder or dust. 變成粉狀或塵埃。

puma /ˈpjuːmə; ˈpjumə/ *n* large brown American animal of the cat family 美洲山豹;美洲獅 (also called 亦稱作 a *cougar* and *mountain lion*). ⇨ the illus at cat. 參看 cat 之插圖。

pum·ice /ˈpʌmɪs; ˈpʌmɪs/ *n* [U] ˈ**~(-stone),** light, porous stone (lava) used for cleaning and polishing. (輕而多孔的)浮石(可用以擦淨或磨光東西)。

pum·mel /ˈpʌml; ˈpʌml/ *vt* (-ll-, US also -l-) [VP 6A, 15B] beat repeatedly with the fists: 以拳連擊: *give sb a good ~ling.* 把某人好好揍一頓。

pump¹ /pʌmp; pʌmp/ *n* machine or device for forcing liquid, gas or air into, out of or through sth, eg water from a well, petrol from a storage tank, air into a tyre, oil through a pipe-line: 唧筒;抽水機;抽油機;打氣筒;幫浦: *a row of ˈpetrol ~s;* 一排汽油泵; *a ˈbicycle ~.* 脚踏車打氣筒。⇨ the illus at bicycle. 參看 bicycle 之插圖。⇨ also *parish-pump* at parish. ˈ**~-room** *n* (at a spa) room where medicinal water is dispensed. (有礦泉水之療養地的)藥用水調配室。□ *vt, vi* **1** [VP6A, 15A, B, 22] force, eg water, etc *out / up / into / through* sth, by using a ~: 以唧筒打(水等)(與 out, up, into, through 連用,後接某物): *~ water up / out;* 用唧筒把水抽上(出)來; *~ a well dry,* ~ until there is no water left in the well; 把井中的水抽乾; *~ air into a tyre;* 爲輪胎打氣; *~ up the tyres;* 把輪胎打足氣; (fig) (喻) *~ information out of sb;* (經盤問而)從某人口中獲得消息; *~ facts into the heads of dull pupils;* 把事實塞進笨學生的腦子裏; *a ˈ~ing station,* eg on a pipe-line carrying petroleum. (如輸油線上的)供油站;抽水站。**2** [VP2A, C] use a ~: 使用唧筒或打氣筒: *He was ~ing away.* 他正用唧筒抽水。

pump² /pʌmp; pʌmp/ *n* kind of light, soft shoe worn for sport, dancing, etc; (US) woman's low-heeled shoe without a fastening. 一種輕軟的運動或舞蹈等所穿的鞋;(美)無繫帶(扣)的低跟女鞋。

pum·per·nickel /ˈpʌmpənɪkl; ˈpʌmpɚ,nɪkl/ *n* [U] wholemeal rye bread. 裸麥粗麵包。

pump·kin /ˈpʌmpkɪn; ˈpʌmpkɪn/ *n* large, round orange-yellow fruit with many seeds in it, used as a vegetable and (US) as a filling for pies. 南瓜。

pun /pʌn; pʌn/ *n* [C] humorous use of different words which sound the same or of two meanings of the same word, 雙關諧語(卽用同音異義或一字二義之語以爲詼諧之用), eg 如 'A cannon-ball took off his *legs,* so he laid down his *arms.*' '一砲彈打斷他的腿,所以他放下他的武器。' □ *vi* (-nn-) [VP2A, 3A] **~ (on / upon),** make a pun or puns (on / upon a word). 用雙關諧語;將(某字)用作雙關諧語。

punch¹ /pʌntʃ; pʌntʃ/ *n* **1** tool or machine for cutting holes in leather, metal, paper, etc; tool for forcing nails beneath a surface, or bolts out of holes. 打洞器;鑽孔機;(壓或起)釘器。**2** tool for stamping designs on surfaces. 打印器。□ *vt* **1** [VP6A] make a hole (in sth) with a ~: 用打洞器打洞(於某物): *~ holes in a sheet of metal;* 在金屬板上鑽孔; *~ a train-ticket;* 軋洞於火車票上; *~ed cards,* as used in filing systems or computers; 打孔卡片(如用於檔案或電腦處理中者); *~d (paper) tape,* used by computer programmers. (電腦程式師所用的)打孔(紙)帶。**2** [VP15B] **~ sth in / out,** drive sth in or out with a ~. 以釘器打進或起出。

punch² /pʌntʃ; pʌntʃ/ *n* [U] drink made of wine or spirits mixed with hot water, sugar, lemons, spice, etc: 五味酒(用酒同熱水,糖,檸檬,香料等混合成的飲料);潘趣酒: *rum ~.* 蘭五味酒。ˈ**~-bowl** *n* bowl in which ~ is mixed. 五味酒鉢;潘趣酒鉢。

punch[3] /pʌntʃ ; pʌntʃ/ *vt* [VP6A, 15A] strike hard with the fist: 以拳重擊: ~ *a man on the chin.* 以拳重擊某人之下顎。*He has a face I'd like to ~.* 他有一張我很想飽以老拳的臉。□ *n* **1** [C] blow given with the fist: 用拳的一擊: *give sb a ~ on the nose;* 用拳擊某人的鼻子; *a boxer with a strong ~,* the ability to deliver strong ~es. 出拳很重的拳擊手。***pull one's ~es,*** attack less vigorously than one is able to. 沒有用盡力氣打;故意不用力打。**'~-ball, '~·ing-ball** *nn* inflated or stuffed ball hung up and ~ed with the fists for exercise. 拳球;梨形球(練習拳擊的吊球)。**,~-'drunk** *adj* (in boxing) dazed by ~es received in a fight; (fig) confused. (在拳擊中)因受拳擊而暈眩的; (喻)惶惑的。**'~ line** *n* climax of a story (where the point is made, where laughter comes). 故事的高潮;滑稽故事中使人發笑的地方;妙語。**'~-up** *n* (colloq) fight with the fists: (俗)用拳頭打鬪: *The quarrel ended in a ~-up.* 爭論釀成了拳鬪。**2** [U] (fig) energy: (喻)力量;精力;效果;魄力: *a speech with plenty of ~ in it.* 有力的演說。

Punch /pʌntʃ ; pʌntʃ/ *n* grotesque hump-backed figure in the traditional puppet-show called **P~ and Judy**. (傳統傀儡戲 Punch and Judy 中)滑稽的駝背木偶。***as pleased/proud as P~,*** greatly pleased/very proud. 非常快樂(驕傲)。

punc·tilio /pʌŋk'tɪlɪəʊ ; pʌŋk'tɪlɪ,o/ *n* (*pl* ~s /-lɪəʊz ; -lɪoz/) **1** [C] particular point of good conduct, ceremony, honour. (良好行爲、儀式、榮譽的)特殊細節。**2** [U, C] formality; (point of) etiquette (esp when it is not really important): 拘泥形式;禮儀(的細節);(尤指)無謂的禮儀(的細節): *stand upon ~s,* insist too much upon protocol(2). 過份拘泥於禮儀。

punc·tili·ous /pʌŋk'tɪlɪəs ; pʌŋk'tɪlɪəs/ *adj* (formal) very careful to carry out correctly details of conduct and ceremony; careful in performing duties. (正式用語)留心細節的;小心執行任務的: **~·ly** *adv* **~·ness** *n*

punc·tual /'pʌŋktʃʊəl ; 'pʌŋktʃʊəl/ *adj* neither early nor late; coming, doing sth, at the time fixed: 準時的;守時的: *be ~ for the appointment/in payment of one's rent.* 準時赴約(準時付租金)。**~ly** /-ʊəlɪ ; -ʊəlɪ/ *adv* in a ~ manner: 準時地;守時地: *The train arrived ~ly.* 火車準時到站。**~·ity** /,pʌŋktʃʊ'ælətɪ ; ,pʌŋktʃʊ'ælətɪ/ *n* [U] being ~. 準時;守時。

punc·tu·ate /'pʌŋktʃʊeɪt ; 'pʌŋktʃʊ,et/ *vt* **1** [VP6A] put full-stops, commas, etc, (eg. , ; : ? !) into a piece of writing. 加標點於。**2** [VP15A] interrupt from time to time: 不時打斷;不時介入: *a speech ~d with cheers;* 不時被歡呼聲打斷的演講; *~ one's remarks with thumps on the table.* 談話中不時以拳頭擊桌。**punc·tu·ation** /,pʌŋktʃʊ'eɪʃn ; ,pʌŋktʃʊ'eʃən/ *n* [U] punctuating; art or practice of punctuating. 標點;標點使用法。⇨ App 9. 參看附錄九。

punc·ture /'pʌŋktʃə(r) ; 'pʌŋktʃɚ/ *n* [C] small hole made by sth sharp, esp one made accidentally in a pneumatic tyre. 小洞;小孔(尤指充氣車胎偶然被刺穿者)。□ *vt, vi* **1** [VP6A] make a ~ in: 穿孔於;刺穿: ~ *an abscess/a motor-car tyre;* 刺破膿腫(汽車胎); (fig) deflate: (喻)減低;挫…之銳氣: *She likes to ~ her husband's ego,* lessen his self-conceit. 她喜歡煞她丈夫的威風。**2** [VP2A] experience a ~: 被刺孔: *Two of my tyres ~ed while I was on that stony road.* 我在那碎石路上開車時,有兩個輪胎被刺破了。

pun·dit /'pʌndɪt ; 'pʌndɪt/ *n* very learned Hindu; authority on a subject; (hum) learned teacher; pedant. 極有學問的印度人;某一學科之權威;(諧)有學問的教師;腐儒。

pun·gent /'pʌndʒənt ; 'pʌndʒənt/ *adj* (of smells, tastes; fig of remarks) sharp; biting; stinging: (指氣味,味道)刺鼻的;辛辣的;(喻,指批評)尖刻的: *a ~ sauce;* 辣醬油; ~ *remarks/satire/criticism.* 尖刻的評語(諷刺,批評)。**~·ly** *adv* **pun·gency** /-nsɪ ; -nsɪ/ *n* [U] ~ quality. 辛辣;尖刻。

Pu·nic /'pju:nɪk ; 'pjunɪk/ *adj* of ancient Carthage and its people. 古迦太基及其人民的。**the ~ Wars,** the wars between Rome and Carthage. 羅馬與迦太基間之戰爭。**~ faith,** treachery. 背信;背叛。

pun·ish /'pʌnɪʃ ; 'pʌnɪʃ/ *vt* [VP6A, 14] ~ ***sb (with/by sth) (for sth),*** **1** cause (sb) suffering or discomfort for wrongdoing; cause suffering or discomfort to sb (for wrongdoing): 處罰;懲罰: ~ *a man with/by a fine.* 處某人以罰金。*How would you ~ stealing/sb for stealing/sb who steals?* 你如何處罰偷竊(懲罰偷竊的人)? **2** treat roughly; knock about: 粗魯地對待;痛擊: *The champion ~ed his opponent severely,* (boxing) gave him severe blows. (拳擊)那位冠軍痛擊他的對手。*Chapman ~ed the bowling,* (cricket) scored freely (from poor or weak bowling). (板球)(因對方投球失誤)查普曼連連得分。**3** (colloq) eat, drink, use up, deal with, etc, much of: (俗)猛吃;猛喝;大量消耗: ~ *the cold beef/the cider cask.* 猛吃冷牛肉(猛喝蘋果酒)。**~·able** /-əbl ; -əbl/ *adj* that can be ~ed (by law). 能(由法律)懲罰的。**~·ment** *n* [U] ~ing or being ~ed: 處罰;被處罰: *escape without ~ment;* 免受懲罰; [C] penalty inflicted for wrongdoing: 因犯罪而受的懲罰: *make the ~ment fit the crime;* 使某種處罰適用於某種罪行;因罪量刑; *inflict severe ~ments on criminals.* 對罪犯施以嚴厲處罰。

pu·ni·tive /'pju:nɪtɪv ; 'pjunətɪv/ *adj* (intended for) punishing: (用以)處罰的;懲罰性的: *a ~ expedition,* a military expedition with the purpose of punishing rebels, etc. 懲罰叛逆者的征伐;討逆。

punk /pʌŋk ; pʌŋk/ *n* **1** [U] (US) partly decayed wood; rotten wood used as tinder. (美)半朽之木;(做引火物用的)朽木。**2** [U] (colloq) worthless stuff; rubbish: (俗)廢物;無意義的話: *He talked a lot of ~.* 他說了許多廢話。~ **rock** *n* [U] (late 1970's) loud, fast, violent style of rock[3] music. (1970年代末期之)一種喧囂激烈的搖滾樂。**3** [C] (sl) worthless person. (俚)無用的人;不中用的人。**4** [C] (late 1970's) fan[3] (of bizarre appearance) of ~ rock music. (1970年代末期)(外表古怪的)搖滾樂迷。

pun·kah /'pʌŋkə ; 'pʌŋkə/ *n* (India) large piece of cloth on a frame, kept moving by means of a cord and pulley, used to keep the air in movement (as an electric fan does). (印度)布風扇(係繫於架上的大塊布,由繩索及滑車使之擺動,以使空氣保持流通,如電扇所爲者)。

pun·net /'pʌnɪt ; 'pʌnɪt/ *n* small basket, made of very thin wood, plastic, etc esp as a measure for fruit: (用薄木片等所做之)小籃(尤指用以計量水果者): *strawberries, 20p a ~.* 草莓每籃二十辨士。

pun·ster /'pʌnstə(r) ; 'pʌnstɚ/ *n* person who has the habit of making puns. 好做雙關語者。

punt[1] /pʌnt ; pʌnt/ *n* flat-bottomed, shallow boat with square ends, moved by pushing the end of a long pole against the river-bed. 方頭平底淺船(以長篙撐之使前進)。□ *vt, vi* [VP6A, 2A] move (a ~) in this way; carry (sb or sth) in a ~; go in a ~. 以長篙撐之使(方頭平底淺船)前進;以此等船載運(人或物);乘此等船。**punter** *n*

punt[2] /pʌnt ; pʌnt/ *vt* [VP6A] kick (a football) after it has dropped from the hands and before it reaches the ground. 踢(從手中落下而未着地之足球)。□ *n* such a kick. 踢懸空球。

punt[3] /pʌnt ; pʌnt/ *vi* [VP2A] (in some card-games) lay a stake against the bank; bet on a horse, etc. (在某些牌戲中)對莊家下賭注;對一賽馬等下賭注。**~er** *n* person who ~s or bets. 下賭注的人。

puny /'pju:nɪ ; 'pjunɪ/ *adj* (-ier, -iest) small and weak: 小而弱的: *What a ~ little creature!* 一個多麼小而弱的人啊! *My ~ efforts are not worth much.* 我這小小的努力算不得甚麼。**pun·ily** /'pju:nɪlɪ ; 'pjunɪlɪ/ *adv*

pup /pʌp ; pʌp/ *n* **1** young dog; young of some other animals, eg the seal. 小狗;幼犬;其他動物(如

海豹)的幼子。***sell sb a pup,*** (colloq) swindle him, esp by selling him sth which, he is made to believe, may have greatly increased value in the future. (俗)欺騙某人;(尤指)賣給人某種使他相信價值將會大增的東西。 **2** conceited young man. 自負的年輕人。

pupa /ˈpjuːpə ; ˈpjupə/ *n* (*pl* ~s, or ~e /-piː ; -pi/) chrysalis. 蛹。⇨ the illus at butterfly. 參看 butterfly 之插圖。

pu·pil¹ /ˈpjuːpl ; ˈpjupḷ/ *n* young person who is learning in school or from a private teacher. 學生(中小學生)。

pu·pil² /ˈpjuːpl ; ˈpjupḷ/ *n* (anat) circular opening in the centre of the iris of the eye, regulating the passage of light. (解剖)瞳孔;瞳人。⇨ the illus at eye. 參看 eye 之插圖。

pup·pet /ˈpʌpɪt ; ˈpʌpɪt/ *n* **1** doll, small figure of an animal, etc with jointed limbs moved by wires or strings, used in plays or shows called '*~-plays / -shows;* marionette; ('*glove-~*) doll of which the body can be put on the hand like a glove, the arms and head being moved by the fingers of the operator. 木偶戲('~-plays 或 '~-shows) 中的木偶; 傀儡;以手牽動線而使做各種動作之木偶;牽動木偶;布袋戲中的木偶;指動木偶。 **2** person, group of persons, whose acts are completely controlled by another: 行動完全受他人控制之人或團體;傀儡: (attrib) (形容用法) *a ~ government / State.* 一個傀儡政府(國家)。

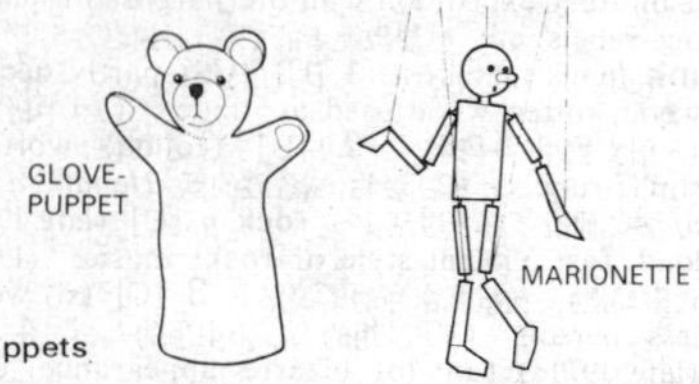

puppets

puppy /ˈpʌpɪ ; ˈpʌpɪ/ *n* (*pl* -pies) **1** young dog. 小狗;幼犬。 **'~ fat** *n* [U] the kind of fat that boys and girls sometimes have before adolescence. 男女孩子在青春期前所顯現的肥胖。 **'~ love** *n* [U] first love affair(s). 初戀。 **2** conceited young man. 自負的年輕人。

pur·blind /ˈpɜːblaɪnd ; ˈpɝˌblaɪnd/ *adj* partly or nearly blind; (fig) stupid. 半盲的;幾乎全瞎的;(喻)愚蠢的。

pur·chase¹ /ˈpɜːtʃəs ; ˈpɝtʃəs/ *n* **1** [U] buying: 購買: '*~-money,* price (to be) paid. 買價。 **'~ tax** *n* (US 美 = *sales tax*) tax on the retail price of goods, collected by the retailer and paid by him to the State (GB since 1973 replaced by value-added tax.) 購物稅; 貨物稅(由零售商在顧客購物時收繳政府)(英國自1973年起由增值稅 value-added tax 取代。) ⇨ value. **2** [C] sth bought: 購買之物: *He filled the car with his ~s.* 他把買的東西裝滿一車。 *I have some ~s to make.* 我要買些東西。 **3** (*sing* only) firm hold or grip (for pulling or raising sth, or to prevent sth from slipping): (僅用單數)緊握;緊抓(以便拉或舉某物,或防止其落下): *get a / any / some ~ on sth.* 緊抓住某物。 **4** [U] value or worth, esp as reckoned in annual yield or return: 價值(尤指以每年之收益爲準所計算者): *sold at thirty years' ~,* (of land, etc) sold for the equivalent of thirty years' rent. (指土地等)以相當於三十年租金的價格賣出。*His life is not worth a day's ~,* He is on the point of death. 他命在旦夕。

pur·chase² /ˈpɜːtʃəs ; ˈpɝtʃəs/ *vt* [VP6A] buy (which is much more usu): 購買(buy 更爲常用): *a dearly ~d victory,* eg a battle in which many lives are lost. 代價甚高(如在戰爭中傷亡慘重)的勝利。 **pur·chas·able** /-əbl ; -əbḷ/ *adj* that can be ~d. 可購買的。 **~r** *n* buyer. 購買者;買主。

pur·dah /ˈpɜːdə ; ˈpɝdə/ *n* [U] (esp in Muslim communities) curtain for, convention of, keeping women from the sight of strangers, esp men: (尤指回教社會中) 使婦女不被男人看見的簾或幃幔; 深閨的習俗: *live / be in ~.* 生活於深閨中。

pure /pjʊə(r) ; pjʊr/ *adj* (-r, -st except 5, 6 below) (下列第 5, 6 兩義無比較級和最高級) **1** unmixed with any other substance, etc: 未同其他物質等混合的;純淨的: *~ water / milk / gold;* 純水(牛奶,金); *~ air,* free from smoke, fumes, etc. 純淨的空氣。 **2** of unmixed race: 血統純的;未與他族混血的: *~ blood;* 純的血統; *a ~ Negro;* 純黑人; *a ~bred* (= *thoroughbred,* which is more usu) *Alsatian dog.* 純種的亞爾撒森狗(德國牧羊犬)(thoroughbred 較常用)。 **3** clean; without evil or sin: 純潔的;無惡或罪的: *~ in body and mind;* 身心純潔; *~ thoughts;* 純潔的思想; *the ~ in heart.* 心地純潔的人。 **4** (of sounds) clear and distinct: (指聲音)清亮的: *a ~ note.* 一個清亮的鳴聲。 **5** dealing with, studied for the sake of, theory only (not *applied*): 純理論的(非實用的): *~ mathematics / science.* 理論數學(純科學)。 **6** mere; nothing but: 純粹的;完全的: *~ mischief;* 純粹的惡作劇; *a ~ waste of time;* 純粹浪費時間; *spread unkind gossip out of ~ malice.* 純屬惡意地散佈刻薄的閒話。***sth ~ and simple,*** it alone: 完全的;純粹的;十足的: *laziness ~ and simple,* sheer laziness. 十足的懶惰。 **~·ly** *adv* (esp) entirely; completely; merely: (尤指)全然地;澈底地;僅僅地: *~ly by accident;* 完全出於偶然; *a ~ly formal request.* 一個非常正式的請求。 **~·ness** *n* = purity (which is more usu). (purity 較常用)。

pu·rée /ˈpjʊəreɪ *US:* pjʊəˈreɪ ; pjʊˈre/ *n* thick liquid made of vegetables, etc boiled to a pulp and pressed through a sieve; fruit similarly treated. (蔬菜等煮成漿狀並由篩壓榨出的)濃菜汁;濃果汁。

pur·ga·tion /pɜːˈgeɪʃn ; pɝˈgeʃən/ *n* [U] (formal) purging or purification. (正式用語)滌淨;洗淨。

pur·ga·tive /ˈpɜːgətɪv ; ˈpɝgətɪv/ *n, adj* (substance) having the power to purge or cleanse the bowels. 能洗滌或淨腸的(物質);瀉藥。

pur·ga·tory /ˈpɜːgətrɪ *US:* -tɔːrɪ ; ˈpɝgəˌtorɪ/ *n* (*pl* -ries) **1** (esp in RC doctrine) condition after death in which the soul is purified in preparation for heaven; place where souls are so purified. (尤指天主教教義中)死後靈魂需要受滌淨以備上天堂之情況;滌罪;滌罪所;煉獄。 **2** any place of temporary suffering or expiation. 暫時受苦或贖罪之所。 **pur·ga·torial** /ˌpɜːgəˈtɔːrɪəl ; ˌpɝgəˈtorɪəl/ *adj* of ~. 滌罪的;煉獄的。

purge /pɜːdʒ ; pɝdʒ/ *vt* [VP6A, 14, 15A, B] ***~ sb (of / from sth); ~ sth (away) (from sb),*** **1** make clean or free (of physical or moral impurity): 使淨或免於(身體或道德上的)不潔;清除;洗滌: *be ~d of / from sin;* 被滌除罪; *~ away one's sins.* 洗除罪惡。 **2** empty (the bowels) of waste matter by means of medicine. 以藥物洗淨(腸);瀉。 **3** clear (oneself, a person, of a charge, of suspicion); (legal) atone for (an offence, etc) by submission. 洗雪(自己或某人的罪名、嫌疑);(法律)藉認錯或接受刑罰而補償(一項犯罪等)。 ***~ one's contempt,*** (legal) do what is right after showing contempt of court. (法律)於蔑視法庭後表示認錯或接受改正。 **4** rid (a political party, etc) of members who are considered undesirable. 整肅;排除(政黨等中的)異己份子。□ *n* [C] **1** purging, clearing out or away: 整肅;清除: *the political ~s that followed the overthrow of the government.* 繼推翻政府後之政治上的整肅。 **2** medicine used for purging (2). 瀉藥。

pu·rify /ˈpjʊərɪfaɪ ; ˈpjʊrəˌfaɪ/ *vt* (*pt, pp* -fied) [VP 6A, 14] ***~ sth (of),*** make pure; cleanse: 使純淨;淨化: *an air-~ing plant* (eg for providing pure air in a factory). 淨化空氣的設備(如在工廠中用以使空氣清新者)。 **pu·ri·fi·ca·tion** /ˌpjʊərɪfɪˈkeɪʃn ; ˌpjʊrəfəˈkeʃən/ *n* [U] ~ing, eg as a religious ceremony. 洗淨;淨化;洗罪;齋戒。

pu·rist /ˈpjʊərɪst ; ˈpjʊrɪst/ *n* person who pays great attention to correct procedures (eg in the arts). (在藝術等方面)力求純正之人。

puri·tan /ˈpjʊərɪtən ; ˈpjʊrətn̩/ *n* **1 P~,** (16th and 17th cc, in England) member of a division of the Protestant Church which wanted simpler forms of church ceremony. (十六世紀和十七世紀在英國的)清教徒(爲基督新教之一派,主張較單純之宗教儀式)。 **2** person who is strict in morals and religion, who looks upon fun and pleasure as sinful, and who believes that all people should work hard always. 道德與宗教觀念嚴格者(視享樂爲罪惡,並主張人類應永遠辛苦工作)。 □ *adj* of or like a P~ or a ~. 清教徒的;似清教徒的;道德及宗教觀念嚴格(之人)的。 **~·ism** /-ɪzəm ; -ˌɪzəm/ *n* practices and beliefs of a P~ or a ~. 清教徒之習俗及教義;嚴格的道德及宗教觀念。 **puri·tani·cal** /ˌpjʊərɪˈtænɪkl ; ˌpjʊrəˈtænɪkl̩/ *adj* very strict and severe, like a ~. 在道德及宗教方面嚴格的;嚴謹的。 **puri·tani·cally** /-klɪ ; -klɪ/ *adv*

pu·rity /ˈpjʊərətɪ ; ˈpjʊrətɪ/ *n* [U] state or quality of being pure. 純淨;純正;純粹。

purl¹ /pɜːl ; pɝl/ *n* (knitting) inverted stitch, which produces a ribbed appearance (the opp of *plain*). (編織)反針法;倒織(可織出稜線形狀,爲plain之相反字)。 □ *vt, vi* invert (stitches); invert stitches of (sth being knitted). 反(針);倒織;以反針織(所織之物)。

purl² /pɜːl ; pɝl/ *vi* (poet) (of a small stream) flow with a murmuring sound. (詩)(指小溪)潺潺而流。□ *n* this sound. 潺潺流水聲。

pur·lieus /ˈpɜːljuːz ; ˈpɝluz/ *n pl* outskirts; outlying parts: 郊區;外緣部分: *the ~ of the camp.* 營地之外緣。

pur·loin /pɜːˈlɔɪn ; pɝˈlɔɪn/ *vt* [VP6A] (formal) steal. (正式用語)偷竊。

purple /ˈpɜːpl ; ˈpɝpl̩/ *n, adj* (colour) of red and blue mixed together: 紫色;紫色的: *a ~ sunset;* 紫色的落霞; *become ~ with rage.* 氣得臉色發紫。**the ~,** the ~ robes of a Roman emperor or a cardinal. 羅馬皇帝或羅馬天主教樞機主教所著之紫袍。***born in the ~,*** a member of a royal family. 生於王室。***raise sb to the ~,*** make him a cardinal. 升某人爲樞機主教。**ˌ~ ˈheart** *n* **(a)** (GB) heart-shaped tablet containing amphetamine, used as a stimulant. (英)一種心形的興奮劑藥片。**(b)** (US 美 **P~ Heart**) medal awarded to a soldier wounded in battle. 紫心章(頒給作戰負傷之軍人)。**pur·plish** /ˈpɜːpəlɪʃ ; ˈpɝplɪʃ/ *adj* somewhat ~. 略帶紫色的。

pur·port /ˈpɜːpət ; ˈpɝport/ *n* [U] (formal) general meaning or intention of sth said or written; likely explanation of a person's actions: (正式用語)主旨;意義;一個人的行動之可能解釋: *the ~ of what he said.* 他所說的話的含意。□ *vt* /pəˈpɔːt ; pəˈport/ **1** [VP6A, 9] seem to mean: 似乎意思是;意謂: *The statement ~s that....* 這一聲明主旨係謂…。 **2** [VP 7A] claim: 聲稱;聲言: *The book ~s to be an original work but is really a compilation.* 該書聲稱是本有獨創見解的著作,但實際上是一本編輯的書。

pur·pose /ˈpɜːpəs ; ˈpɝpəs/ *n* **1** [C] that which one means to do, get, be, etc; plan; design; intention: 目的;計畫;意圖;意向: *For what ~(s) do you want to go to Canada?* 你要去加拿大的目的何在？ *I wouldn't go to London for/with the mere ~ of buying a new tie.* 我不會只爲買一條新領帶而去倫敦。 *This van is used for various ~s.* 這貨車可用於不同的目的。*This is a novel with a ~,* one written eg to explain or defend a doctrine, not merely to amuse. 這是一本爲闡釋或辯護某種理論等而寫的小說(並非僅供消遣)。**ˌ~-ˈbuilt** *adj* made to serve a particular function. 爲了達成某種目的的;爲了某種特殊作用的。 **2** [U] determination; power of forming plans and keeping to them: 決心;形成與堅守計畫的力量: *weak of ~;* 沒有決心; *wanting in ~.* 缺乏果斷力。 **3** (phrases) (片語) ***on ~,*** by intention, not by chance: 故意地;不是偶然地: *You sometimes hurt yourself by accident but you don't hurt yourself on ~.* 你有時會偶然傷害自己,但你不會故意傷害自己。*He has left the book here on ~ for you to read.* 他有意把這本書留在這兒讓你讀。*He came here on ~ to borrow money from you.* 他特地來這裡向你借錢。*She sometimes does things on ~ just to annoy me.* 她有時故意做些事來使我生氣。***of set ~,*** deliberately; not accidentally. 有意地;蓄意地;非偶然地。***to the ~,*** useful for one's ~; relevant: 合乎目的的;中肯的;切題的: *The reply was so little to the ~ that it was not worth our consideration.* 這答覆一點也不中肯,所以不值得我們考慮。***to little/no/some ~,*** with little/no/some result or effect. 有很少(毫無,有一些)結果或效果。***serve/answer one's ~,*** be satisfactory; do what is required. 令人滿意;適合目的。□ *vt* [VP6A, D, 7, 9] (liter) have as one's ~: (文)意欲;意圖: *They ~ (making/to make) a further attempt.* 他們意圖做進一步的嘗試。**~·ful** /-fl ; -fʊl/ *adj* having a conscious ~; full of meaning. 蓄意的;有意義的。**~·fully** /-fəlɪ ; -fʊlɪ/ *adv* **~·less** *adj* lacking ~; having no object in view. 缺乏意義的;沒有目的的。**~·less·ly** *adv.* **~·ly** *adv* on ~; intentionally. 故意地;蓄意地。**pur·pos·ive** /ˈpɜːpəsɪv ; ˈpɝpəsɪv/ *adj* having, serving, done with, a ~: 有目的的;合於目的的;故意而爲的: *purposive movements;* 有目的的行動; (of a person, his conduct) having, showing, ~ and determination. (指人、其行爲)有決心的;表現決心的;果斷的。

purr /pɜː(r) ; pɝ/ *vi, vt* **1** [VP2A, C] (of a cat) make a low, continuous vibrating sound expressing pleasure; (of a car engine) make a vibrating sound; (fig, of a person) indicate contentment by using a pleasant tone: (指貓)發出低的連續顫動的嗚嗚聲(表示愉快);(指汽車引擎)發出震顫的聲音;(喻,指人)以愉快聲調表示滿意: *Mrs Black ~ed with delight on receiving the invitation to dine with the duchess.* 布拉克太太接到與公爵夫人共餐的約請時,發出愉快滿足的聲音。 **2** [VP6A] express (contentment, etc) thus: 以愉快聲調表示(滿足等): *She ~ed her approval of the suggestion.* 她很高興地表示贊同此一建議。□ *n* ~ing sound. 滿足而低沉的聲音。

purse /pɜːs ; pɝs/ *n* **1** small bag for money (originally closed by drawing strings together, now usu closed with a clasp): 小錢袋;小錢夾(原來多用拉索合起,現在通常用按鈕): *That big car is beyond my ~,* costs more than I can afford. 那輛大轎車非我財力所能買得起。**ˈ~-proud** *adj* ⇨ proud(5). ***hold the ˈ~-strings,*** have control of expenditure. 控制錢袋;控制開支。***tighten/loosen the ˈ~-strings,*** reduce/increase expenditure; be economical/generous. 緊縮(增加)開支;節省用錢(隨便花錢)。 **2** money; funds. 金錢;基金。**Privy P~,** ⇨ privy. **the public ~,** the national treasury. 國庫。 **3** sum of money collected or offered as a prize, gift, etc: 捐贈之款項(作爲獎金,賞金等): *make up a ~;* (爲慈善事業)募捐; *give/put up a ~,* eg for the winner of a boxing match. 捐贈獎金(如捐給拳擊比賽優勝者)。 **4** (US) handbag. (美)女用手提包。□ *vi, vt* [VP2A, C, 6A, 15B] ~ ***(up);*** ~ ***(up) the lips,*** draw the lips together in tiny folds or wrinkles. 皺起嘴唇;噘嘴。

purser /ˈpɜːsə(r) ; ˈpɝsɚ/ *n* officer responsible for a ship's accounts and stores, esp in a passenger liner. 船(尤指客輪)上的事務長。

pur·su·ance /pəˈsjuːəns *US:* -ˈsuː- ; pɚˈsuəns/ *n* ***in ~ of,*** (formal) in the carrying out of or the performance of (one's duties, a plan, etc). (正式用語)在實施或執行(一個人的職務、計畫等)時。**pur·su·ant** /-ənt ; -ənt/ *adj* ***pursuant to,*** (formal) in accordance with; in agreement with: (正式用語)依照;遵循: *pursuant to your instructions.* 依照閣下指示。

pur·sue /pəˈsjuː *US:* -ˈsuː ; pɚˈsu/ *vt* [VP6A] **1** go after in order to catch up with, capture or kill: 追趕;追逐;追捕;追殺: *pursuing a robber/a bear;* 追捕盜賊(熊); *make sure that you are not being ~d.* 弄清楚沒有人在追捕你。 **2** (fig) (of consequences, penalties, etc) persistently follow: (喻)(指後果、處罰等)永遠跟隨;一再伴隨: *His record as a criminal ~d him wherever he went.* 不論他到哪裏,他的犯罪記錄卽隨之而至。*He has been ~d by misfortune.* 不幸一直尾隨着他(他連遭不幸)。**3** go on with; work at: 繼續做;做: *~ one's studies after leaving school.* 離開學校後仍繼續研究。**4** have as an aim or purpose: 以…爲目的或目標;追求: *~ pleasure.* 追求享樂。**~r** *n* person who ~s (1). 追捕者。

pur·suit /pəˈsjuːt *US:* -ˈsuːt ; pɚˈsut/ *n* **1** [U] ***(in) ~ (of),*** act of pursuing: 追逐;追捕;追殺;追求: *a dog in ~ of rabbits;* 一隻追逐兎子的狗; *a fox with the hounds in hot ~;* 一隻被獵犬窮追的狐狸; *in his ~ of happiness;* 在他追求幸福方面; (attrib) (形容用法) *a ~ plane,* one that pursues and fights enemy planes. 驅逐機。**2** [C] sth at which one works or to which one gives one's time: 職業;工作;消遣: *engaged in scientific/literary ~s.* 從事科學(文學)的研究。

pursy[1] /ˈpɜːsɪ ; ˈpɝsɪ/ *adj* (old use) (of a person) fat and short-winded. (舊用法)(指人)肥胖而喘息的。

pursy[2] /ˈpɜːsɪ ; ˈpɝsɪ/ *adj* (old use) puckered: (舊用法)皺起的;有皺紋的: *~ eyes.* 皺起的眼睛。⇨ purse, *v.*

puru·lent /ˈpjʊərələnt ; ˈpjurələnt/ *adj* of, containing, discharging, pus. 膿的;含有膿的;流膿的。**puru·lence** /-əns ; -əns/ *n*

pur·vey /pəˈveɪ ; pɚˈve/ *vt, vi* **1** [VP6A, 14] ***~ (to),*** (formal) provide, supply (food, as a trader): (正式用語)(商人等)供給;供應(食物): *A butcher ~s meat to his customers.* 肉商供應顧客肉類。**2** [VP 3A] ***~ for,*** supply provisions for: 爲…供應食物等: *a firm that ~s for the Navy.* 一個負責供應海軍糧食的公司。**~or** /-ə(r) ; -ɚ/ *n* person whose business is to supply provisions on a large scale, eg for the Army or Navy, for large public dinners. 大量供應食糧者;承辦公衆伙食者。**~·ance** /-əns ; -əns/ *n*

pur·view /ˈpɜːvjuː ; ˈpɝvju/ *n* (formal) range of operation or activity; scope; extent: (正式用語)工作或活動的範圍;視界;區域: *These are questions that lie outside/that do not come within the ~ of our inquiry.* 這些問題是在我們的調查範圍之外的。

pus /pʌs ; pʌs/ *n* [U] thick yellowish-white liquid formed in and coming out from a poisoned place in the body: 膿(在身體受感染的部位形成後流出之黃白色濃液): *It is unwise to squeeze a boil to force the pus out.* 硬把瘡子的膿擠出是不智之舉。

push[1] /pʊʃ ; puʃ/ *n* **1** [C] act of pushing: 推;推動: *Give the door a hard ~.* 用力推那門。*He opened the gate with/at one ~.* 他一下子就把門推開了。**2** [C] vigorous effort: 奮力: *We must make a ~ to finish the job this week.* 我們必須奮力把這件事在本週內做完。*The enemy made a ~* (= an attack in force) *to capture the city.* 敵人對該城發動猛攻。**3** ***get the ~,*** (sl) be dismissed (from one's employment, etc). (俚)被解雇。***give sb the ~,*** (sl) dismiss him. (俚)解雇某人。**4** [U] determination to make one's way in life, to attract attention, etc: 努力上進,吸引注意等之決心;毅力: *He hasn't enough ~ to succeed as a salesman.* 他沒有做成功的推銷員所需要的毅力。**5** ***at a ~,*** if compelled by need or circumstances: 若爲需要或環境之所迫;不得已時: *We can sleep seven or eight people in the house at a ~.* 在不得已的時候,我們能讓七個或八個人住在此屋內。***if/when/until it comes to the ~,*** if/when/until one is compelled by need or circumstances, when an effort is needed: 假如(在,直到)爲需要或環境所迫而不能不奮力時;在(直到)情勢緊急之際: *He seemed a satisfactory man until it came to the ~; then he failed us.* 在陷入緊急情勢之前,他似乎一直是個令人滿意的人;到情勢緊急時,他却使我們甚爲失望。

push[2] /pʊʃ ; puʃ/ *vt, vi* (For special uses with *adverbial particles* and *preps,* ⇨ 9 below.) (與副詞接語及介系詞連用的特殊用法參看下列第9義。) **1** [VP 6A, 15A, B, 22, 2A, C] (contrasted with *pull*) use force on (sth/sb) to cause forward movement; exert pressure against: (與 pull 相對)推(某人或某物);推(某人或某物)使之移動;擠: *Please ~ the table nearer to the wall.* 請把這桌子推得靠牆一點。*If you'll ~ the car, I'll steer it.* 如果你來推車,我就來駕車。*You can pull a rope, but you can't ~ it!* 你可以拉繩子,但不能推繩子! *We had to ~ our way* (= go forward by ~ing) *through the crowd.* 我們必須從人羣中擠過去。*Stop ~ing at the back!* 别在後面推! *He ~ed the door open.* 他把門推開。*The football crowds ~ed past me.* 看足球的觀衆從我旁邊擠過去。**2** [VP6A] persuade others to recognize, eg claims, or buy, eg goods: 勸使他人承認(某要求等)或購買(商品等): *Unless you ~ your claims you'll get no satisfaction.* 如果你不努力爭取,你就得不到賠償。*You must ~ your wares if you want better sales.* 如果你想要銷路好,你必須强行推銷你的商品。*Haven't you a friend who can ~ you,* use his influence to help you? 你難道沒有一個能够提拔你的朋友嗎? ***~ oneself,*** show energy, etc to win recognition: 驅策自己;發憤: *You'll never get anywhere if you don't ~ yourself.* 你如果不策勵自己,將永遠沒有成就。⇨ also *~ oneself forward* in 9 below. 參看下列第9義之 ~ oneself forward。**3** [VP6A] sell (illicit drugs) by acting as a link between large suppliers and the drug addicts. (做中盤)販賣(毒品)。⇨ pusher below. 參看下列之 pusher。**4** [VP14] ***~ sb for sth,*** press sb hard (to get sth): 催迫某人(以獲得某物): *We're ~ing them for payment/an answer to our request.* 我們正催促他們付款(答覆我們的請求)。***be ~ed for sth,*** have difficulty in finding: 困於…;爲…所迫;短少: *I'm rather ~ed for money/time just now.* 我目前頗拮据(時間迫促)。**5** [VP14, 17] ***~ sb/oneself to sth/to do sth,*** drive or urge: 驅策某人(自己)做某事: *Tony had to ~ himself to go on doing such dull work.* 湯尼不得不驅策自己繼續做這種單調無趣的事。*She'll ~ him to the verge of suicide.* 她將會把他逼到自殺的地步。**6** [VP6A] press: 按: *~ a button,* eg to ring a bell; 按鈕(如按電鈴); *~-button warfare,* war in which missiles, eg with atomic warheads, are fired by pressing buttons. 按鈕戰爭(按鈕卽可發射帶原子彈頭等的飛彈之戰爭)。**7** ***be ~ing thirty/forty, etc,*** (colloq) be nearing the age indicated: (俗)接近三十歲(四十歲等)。*She wouldn't like you to think so, but she's ~ing thirty.* 她不願讓你知道,其實她已快三十歲了。**8** (compounds) (複合字) **ˈ~-bike** *n* one that is worked by pedalling (not a *moped* or *motor-bike*). 自行車(以脚踏動而非用發動機者)。**ˈ~-cart** *n* small cart ~ed by a man. 手推車。**ˈ~-chair** *n* carriage for a child, like a chair on wheels (used when a child is old enough to sit up). 嬰兒推車(在嬰兒會坐時使用)。**~er** *n* **1** (colloq) person who ~es himself/herself forward: (俗)進取的人;鑽營的人: *Isn't she a ~er!* (said of someone who takes every opportunity of gaining an advantage for herself). 她眞是個善於鑽營的人! **2** (sl) pedlar of illicit drugs. (俚)販毒者。⇨ 3 above. 參看上列第3義。**~·ful** /-fl ; -fʊl/, **~·ing** *adjj* having a tendency to ~ oneself: 有進取心的;愛出風頭的: *He's too ~ing with strangers,* tries too much to force himself upon their attention. 他太愛在陌生人面前出風頭。**9** [VP15A, B, 2C] (special uses with *adverbial particles* and *preps*): (與副詞接語及介詞連用的特殊用法):

push along, (colloq) leave sb/a place: (俗)離開某人(某地): *I'm afraid it's time I was ~ing along,* time for me to go. 恐怕是我該走的時候了。

push sb around, (colloq) bully him; order him about: (俗)威脅某人;驅使某人;擺佈某人: *I'm not going to be ~ed around by you or anybody!* 我將不受你或任何人擺佈!

push forward/on (to a place), go on resolutely with a journey, one's work, etc: 堅决地繼續旅

行、工作等: *It's getting dark; we must ~ on to our destination.* 天漸漸黑了，我們必須趕到目的地。 *We must ~ on with our work,* hurry and finish it. 我們必須趕快做完我們的工作。 **~ oneself forward,** ambitiously draw attention to oneself, eg at work, in society: 極力表現自己(如在工作上或社交上); 强出風頭: *He never ~es himself forward,* is modest, doesn't try to attract attention. 他從不强出風頭(他是一個謙遜的人)。

push off, (colloq) leave; go away: (俗)離去;走開: *Tell that rude fellow to ~ off!* 叫那個無禮的傢伙走開！ *It's time we ~ed off.* 是我們離去的時候了。 **~ (a boat, etc) off,** (of sb in a boat) ~ against the bank, etc, eg with an oar or pole, to get the boat moving in the current, etc. (指船中的人)以槳或篙頂岸等使(船)進入水流中等。

push (a boat, etc) out, = ~ off.

push sb/sth over, cause to fall; overturn: 推倒; 使傾覆: *Don't ~ me over!* 不要把我推倒。 *Several children were ~ed over in the stampede.* 有幾個小孩在驚慌逃奔中絆倒了。 **'~-over** *n* (sl) sth very easy to do; person who is easily overcome or controlled. (俚)容易做的事;易於征服或控制的人。

push sb through (sth), enable sb (esp sb needing help) to succeed in sth: 促使某人(尤指需要幫助者)成功: *~ a weak student through an exam.* 幫助一個成績差的學生通過考試。 **~ sth through,** bring sth to the final stage by special efforts: 努力完成某事: *~ legislation through,* get it passed. 使立法通過。 *We must ~ the matter through.* 我們必須把這件事辦妥。

push sth up, force, eg prices, to rise. 强使(物價等)上升。 **~ up the daisies,** (sl) be buried in a grave. (俚)被埋葬。

pu·sil·lani·mous /ˌpjuːsɪˈlænɪməs; ˌpjuslˈænəməs/ *adj* (formal) timid; easily frightened. (正式用語)膽怯的;易受驚的。 **pu·sil·la·nim·ity** /ˌpjuːsɪləˈnɪmətɪ; ˌpjusḷəˈnɪmətɪ/ *n* [U].

puss /pʊs; pus/ *n* **1** cat; word used to call a cat. 猫;用以喚猫的字。 **2** (colloq) girl: (俗)女孩: *She's a sly ~.* 她是個狡猾的女孩。 **~y** /ˈpʊsɪ; ˈpusɪ/ *n* (*pl* -sies) (also 亦作 **'~y-cat**) (child's word for a) cat. (小兒語)猫。 **'~y·foot** *vi* [VP2A, C] (colloq) move about in a quiet, stealthy way (as a cat does): (俗)輕輕地,偷偷地走(如猫所爲者): *Was that you ~y-footing about in the corridor last night?* 昨晚是你躡手躡脚地在走廊上走動嗎? (fig) act too cautiously or timidly. (喻)過於謹愼或膽小地行事。 **'~y willow** *n* tree with soft silky catkins. 一種生有絨球花的柳樹。

pus·tule /ˈpʌstjuːl *US:* -tʃuːl; ˈpʌstʃul/ *n* (med) pimple or blister, esp one filled with pus. (醫)膿疱。

put[1] /pʊt; put/ *vi, vt* (*pt, pp* put, *pres part* -tt-) (For special uses with *adverbial particles* and *preps,* ⇨ 11 below.) (與副詞接語及介詞連用的特殊用法,參看下列第11義。) **1** [VP6A, 15A] move (sth) so as to be in a certain place or position: 置放於某處;使處於某種位置: *He put the book on the table.* 他把書放在桌子上。 *He put his hands in(to) his pockets.* 他把手放在口袋中。 *He put the corpse down the well.* 他把屍體拋進井中。 *Did you put milk in my tea?* 你在我的茶中加了牛奶嗎? *It's time to put the baby to bed.* 是讓嬰兒睡覺的時候了。 *Will you please put* (= sew) *a patch on these trousers?* 請爲這條褲子補綴一塊布好嗎? *He put* (= fastened) *a new handle to the knife.* 他給刀子裝上新柄。 *He put* (= pushed) *a knife into me/between my ribs.* 他把刀刺進我的身體(刺進我的肋骨間)。 *I'll put a bullet through your head,* kill you. 我將以子彈射穿你的腦袋。 *They've put a satellite into orbit round Mars.* 他們已將一人造衞星射進圍繞火星的軌道。 *They've put men on the moon.* 他們已把人類送上月球。 *He put* (= pushed) *his fist through the window,* broke it by doing this. 他用拳頭擊破窗子。 *He put his pen through the word,* struck the word out. 他用鋼筆刪掉那個字。 **put pen to paper,** start writing. 開始寫。 **put one's foot in it,** ⇨ foot[1] (1). **2** [VP15A] cause (sb/oneself) to be in some relationship, eg as an employee, client, with sb. 使(某人,自己)與某人有某種關係(如成爲雇員,雇客等)。 **put oneself/sth in/into sb's hands,** let him deal with one's problems, etc: 把自己(某事)交給某人處理;託付: *I put myself entirely in your hands.* 我把自己完全託付給你。 *I shall put the matter into the hands of my solicitors.* 我將把此事交給幾位律師去處理。 **put sb in his (proper) place,** make him humble. 使某人謙卑。 **put oneself in sb's/sb 'else's position,** imagine oneself in his position: 設身處地;站在他人的立場設想: *How would you feel (about the matter)?—Just put yourself in my/her position!* 你(對這事)作何感想?——只要站在我(她)的立場設想就行了! **3** [VP14] make sb bear (the particular nervous or moral strain indicated). 使某人承受(精神或道德的壓力)。 **put the blame on sb,** blame him: 歸咎於某人: *Don't put all the blame on me.* 不要完全歸咎於我。 **put pressure on sb (to do sth),** strongly urge him: 對某人施壓力迫使: *They're putting great pressure on him* (= pressing him hard) *to resign.* 他們對他大施壓力迫他辭職。 **put (a) strain on sb/sth,** make him/it suffer from hard work or use: 使某人(某物)不勝負荷: *All this work is putting (a) great strain on him.* 所有這些工作使他不勝負荷。 **4** [VP15A] affect the progress of. 影響…的進展。 **put an end/a stop to sth,** end or abolish it.結束或廢除某事物。 **put an end to one's life,** commit suicide. 自殺。 **put the brake(s) on sth,** (fig, colloq) slow it down. (喻,俗)使緩慢。 **5** [VP15A] cause to pass into or suffer the emotional, physical etc state indicated by the phrase that follows. 使成爲…狀態;使遭受感情或身體上的某種情況。 **put oneself to death,** commit suicide. 自殺。 **put sb to death,** kill him. 殺死或處死某人。 **put sb at his ease,** cause him to feel relaxed, free from anxiety, etc. 使某人感到自在,不緊張;使放心。 **put sb to (great) expense,** cause him to spend (a lot). 使某人花(很多)錢。 **put sb to (great) inconvenience,** cause him (great) inconvenience. 使某人感到(極爲)不便。 **put sb to the indignity of doing sth,** cause him to do sth involving loss of dignity. 使某人忍辱做某事。 **put sb in mind of sb/sth,** recall or remind him of sb/sth. 使某人想起(某人或某事物)。 **put sb/sth out of his/its misery,** relieve him/it of anxiety, pain, etc; kill (eg an animal in pain). 解除某人(某動物)的焦慮、痛苦等;使解脫;殺死(痛苦的動物等)。 **put sb on (his) oath,** make sb swear on oath; bind him to tell the truth. 使某人立誓或說實話。 **put sb/sth to the test,** test him/it. 考驗某人(某事物)。 **put sb in the wrong,** cause him to appear to be wrong. 嫁禍於某人;歸咎於某人。 **6** [VP22] cause sb/sth to become (what is indicated by the *adj*): 使某人(某事物)成…樣子(根據下面所接形容詞所表示的狀態): *That picture on the wall is crooked—I must put it straight.* 牆上那幅畫掛歪了——我必須把它擺正。 **put sth right,** correct it: 糾正某事: *A short note put the matter right,* ended any misunderstanding. 一封短函把這件事解釋清楚了。 **put sb right/straight,** correct an error he has made; give him correct information: 改正某人的錯誤;告訴某人正確的消息: *We had taken a wrong turning, but a policeman put us right,* told us which way to go. 我們轉錯了彎,但一位警察指示了我們正確的方向。 **7** [VP15A] write; indicate; mark: 寫;指出;標明: *put a tick against a name/a price on an article/one's signature to a will.* 在名字旁邊勾一下(在一件物品上標明價碼;在遺囑上簽字)。 **8** [VP14] **put sth to sb; put it to sb (that),** submit; propound; express: 呈交;提出;表示: *put a proposal to the Board of Directors;* 向董事會提出一建議; *put a question to the vote/a resolution to the meeting.* 將問題付諸表決(將議案提交會議討論)。 *I put it to you that...,* invite you to agree with me that.... 我

請你同意…。*You have put the case very clearly.* 你已把這事情解釋得很清楚。*Put it* (= submit the matter) *to her so as not to offend her.* 把這事情交給她以免使她不快。*How can I put it*, express it? 我該怎樣說才好呢？*How would you put* (= express, translate) *this in Danish?* 這個意思在丹麥語裡怎麼說？*That can all be put in a few words.* 那件事可以用簡單幾句話說明白。*Please put all questions to the chairman.* 請向主席提出所有的問題。**put the question**, ⇨ question¹(2). **9** [VP14] **put a price/value/valuation on sth**, state or estimate the value: 估計某物的價錢(價值,評價): *The experts refused to put a price on the Rubens painting.* 專家們拒絕估計魯賓斯的畫的價錢。*What value do you put on her advice?* 你對她的建議做何評價？**put sth at (a figure)**, say that, eg sb's age, sth's value, weight, is: 估計作(後接數目字,如表示年齡,價值,重量): *I would put her age at about sixty.* 我猜測她的年齡大約是六十歲。*I put her fur coat at £200.* 我估計她的皮外衣值二百鎊。**10** [VP6A] throw with an upward and outward movement of the arm. 以胳臂向上並向前拋擲。**put the shot**, ⇨ shot¹(3). Hence, 由此產生, **'shot-put** *n* this as an event at an athletic meeting. 推鉛球(爲運動會的項目之一)。**11** [VP15B, 2C, 14] (special uses with *adverbial particles* and *preps*): (與副詞接語及介詞連用的特殊用法):

put (a ship) about, (cause to) change direction: (使)(船)改變方向: *The captain put the ship about.* 船長改變了船的航行方向。**put oneself about**, (chiefly Scots) trouble, distress, oneself: (主要用於蘇格蘭)使自己煩惱,痛苦: *He was very much put about by these false allegations.* 他甚爲這些僞辯所苦惱。**put sth about**, spread, eg rumours: 散佈(如謠言): *Don't believe all these stories that are being put about.* 不要相信所有這些謠傳。

put sth across (to sb), **(a)** communicate sth successfully: 使(某人)瞭解或接受某事物; 溝通: *a teacher who quickly puts his ideas across to his students.* 很快和學生溝通觀念的教師。**(b)** (colloq) make a success of: (俗)使獲得成功: *Put a business deal across* (more usu *through*). 使一樁交易成功(through 比 across 常用)。**put sth across sb**, (colloq) deceive; trick: (俗)欺騙;欺詐: *You can't put that across me*, make me believe or accept it. 你不能騙我接受(相信)那件事。

put sth aside, **(a)** lay down: 放下: *put aside one's book*; 把書放下; *put one's work aside.* 把工作擱下。**(b)** save: 儲蓄: *He has put aside a good sum of money.* 他已經儲蓄了很多錢。**(c)** disregard; ignore: 不顧;忽視: *Put aside for a moment the fact that the man has been in prison.* 暫時先別管那人曾坐牢的事。

put sth away, **(a)** put in the usual place of storage, eg a drawer, box: 將某物放置於慣常保存之處(如抽屜,盒子): *Put your books/toys away.* 把你的書(玩具)收好。**(b)** save: 儲存;儲蓄: *put money away for one's old age.* 爲老年而儲蓄。**(c)** (colloq) eat or drink (to excess): (俗)(過度地)吃或喝: *How can that boy put away so much pie and ice-cream?* 那個男孩如何能吃那麼多餡餅和冰淇淋呢？**(d)** give up; renounce: 放棄;棄絕: *He's had to put away all ideas of becoming a concert pianist.* 他只好放棄做鋼琴演奏家的一切念頭。**put sb away**, **(a)** (colloq) put into confinement, eg in a mental home: (俗)囚禁;監禁(如囚於精神病院): *He was acting so strangely that he had to be put away.* 他的行爲十分怪異,所以不得不被禁錮起來。**(b)** (colloq, of pets) put to death (because of age, illness): (俗,指寵愛的動物)(因年老或疾病而被)弄死: *The dog was so old and weak that it had to be put away.* 這隻狗既老且病,所以不得不把牠弄死。

put back, (naut) return: (航海)歸來: *The ship/We put back to harbour.* 該船(我們)回到港內。**put sth back**, **(a)** replace: 放回原處: *Put the reference books back on the shelf when you've finished with them.* 參考書看完後放回原來的書架。**(b)** move backwards: 向後移;撥回: *That clock is fast; I'd better put it back five minutes*, move the minute hand back. 那鐘太快了,我最好撥回五分鐘。**(c)** (fig) check the advance of, cause delay to: (喩)阻礙;阻止;使遲滯: *put back the efforts of the reformers.* 阻礙改革家們的努力。*The strike at the car factory put back production badly.* 汽車工廠的罷工大大妨礙了生產。

put sth by, save for future use: 爲將來而儲蓄: *Has she any money put by?* 她有沒有存錢？

put (sth) down, **(a)** land: (使)着陸: *He put down (his glider) in a field.* 他在原野中降落(他的滑翔機)。**(b)** set or place down: 放下: *Put down that gun!* 把槍放下！**(c)** press down: 按下;壓下;踩下: *When you get on the motorway, you can really put your foot down*, press the accelerator pedal down. 當你到了高速公路上時,就可眞正地踩下油門。**put one's foot down**, ⇨ foot¹(1). **(d)** place in storage: 儲藏: *put down eggs*, eg by packing in isinglass. 把蛋儲藏起來(如放於魚膠中)。*He has put down a good supply of port and claret.* 他已經儲藏了很多紫葡萄酒和紅葡萄酒。**(e)** suppress by force or authority: 鎮壓;平定;消除;撲滅: *put down a rebellion*; 敉平叛亂; *put down gambling and prostitution.* 消除賭博與娼妓。**(f)** write down; make a note of: 寫下;記下: *Here's my address—put it down before you forget it.* 這是我的地址──寫下來,免得忘了。**put sb down**, **(a)** allow to alight: 讓(某人)下車: *The bus stopped to put down passengers.* 公共汽車停下來讓乘客下車。**(b)** snub; reduce to silence: 輕待;奚落;制止;使沉默: *put down hecklers at a political meeting.* 制止政治會議上詰難的人。Hence, 由此產生, **'put-down** *n* snub. 輕待;奚落。**(c)** make humble: 使卑微; 貶抑;挫: (biblical) (聖經) *put down the mighty from their seats.* 降低强者的地位;使强者謙恭。**put sb down as**, consider that sb is: 認爲某人是: *They put me down as a fool.* 他們認爲我是個傻瓜。**put sb down for**, write his name on a list as willing to give, eg to a charity or other fund: 登記名字認捐: *You can put me down for £5*; 你可以寫上我認捐五鎊; put sb's name down as an applicant, participant, etc: 登記姓名(如成爲申請者、參與者等): *They put him down for Eton/the school football team.* 他們爲他登記進入伊頓公學(參加學校足球隊)。**put sth down to sth**, **(a)** charge to an account: 記在…帳上: *Put the shoes down to my account.* 把這雙鞋子記在我的帳上。*You can put the cost of the petrol down to business expenses.* 你可以把汽油的費用記在業務費用的帳下。**(b)** attribute to: 歸於;諉於: *The cholera outbreak was put down to bad drinking water.* 那次霍亂的發生歸因於不潔的飲水。*Can we put it down to his ignorance?* 我們能把此事歸因於他的無知嗎？

put sth forth, (formal) send out: (正式用語)發出;長出: *The trees are putting forth new leaves.* 這些樹正在長出新葉子。

put sth forward, **(a)** advance; put before people for consideration: 提出;建議: *put forward a new theory.* 提出一新理論。**(b)** move on: 撥快: *put forward the hands of a clock*, eg when it is stopped or slow. (如時鐘停或慢時)撥快鐘針。**put sb forward**, propose: 推薦: *put oneself/a friend forward as a candidate.* 推薦自己(一位朋友)爲候選人。

put in, exclaim (often as an interruption): 喊叫(通常用於打岔);插嘴: *'But what about us?' he put in.* '可是我們怎麼辦？'他喊道。**put in/into**, (naut) (of a boat, its crew) enter: (航海)(指船或水手)進入;駛進;入港: *The boat put in at Malta/put into Malta for repairs.* 該船駛到馬爾他修理。**put in for sth**, apply formally for: 正式申請: *put in for the position of manager.* 申請經理之職位。**put in for leave**, request permission to be absent from duty, work, etc. 請假。**put sth in**, **(a)** cause to be in: 使在內: *He put his head in at the window.* 他從窗口把頭伸進來。**(b)** submit; present formally: 提出;正式提呈: *put in a claim for damages;* 提出賠償損失之要求; *put in a document* (in a law case); (在法律案件中)提出證明文件; *put in a plea of not guilty.* 提出無罪之抗辯。**(c)** manage to strike or utter: 擊出或說出: *put in a blow／word.* 加以打擊(說出一句話)。***put sth in／into sth,*** devote; give: 獻身於;付出;花費: *put a lot of work into improving one's French.* 下很大的工夫進修法文。***put sb in for sth,*** recommend sb for promotion, an award, etc: 推薦某人晉升、得獎等: *The commanding officer is putting Sergeant Green in for the Victoria Cross.* 指揮官推薦格林士官得維多利亞十字勳章。***put in a good word for sb,*** say sth on his behalf, to help him. 爲某人說好話。**(d)** do, perform: 做;履行: *put in an hour's work before breakfast;* 早餐之前做一小時的工作。*put in an hour's piano practice.* 練習彈鋼琴一小時。**(e)** pass (time): 消磨;度過(時間): *There's still an hour to put in before the pubs open.* 酒館再過一小時才開門。***put sb in,*** **(a)** give duties to: 任命;使就任: *put in a caretaker／bailiff.* 任用一管理員(一監守官)。**(b)** elect to office: 選爲執事;選爲執政: *Which party will be put in at the next general election?* 下一次大選中那一黨會當選執政? ***put sb in mind of sb／sth,*** ⇨ 5 above. 參看上列第5義。⇨ the *n* entries for 參看下列各片語中之名詞 ***put in an appearance; put the boot in; put one's oar in; put a sock in it.***

put off, (of a boat or crew) leave: (指船或船員)離岸: *We put off from the pier.* 我們駛離碼頭。***put sth off,*** **(a)** postpone: 延期: *put off a meeting;* 把會議延期; *put off going to the dentist.* 延期去看牙醫。**(b)** (usu of nonmaterial things, *take off* being usual for clothes) get rid of: (通常指非物質的東西;脫衣服通常多用 take off)消除;袪除: *You must put off your doubts and fears.* 你必須袪除你的疑慮和恐懼。***put sb off,*** **(a)** put to a later date an arrangement, etc: 把約會等延後: *We shall have to put the Smiths off till next week.* 我們須把同史密斯夫婦之約會延到下星期。**(b)** make excuses and try to avoid, eg sth one has promised to do, a duty: 閃避;敷衍;推諉(已答應做的事,責任): *He tried to put me off with vague promises.* 他企圖以含混的允諾來敷衍我。*I won't be put off with such flimsy excuses,* won't accept them. 我不會被這些薄弱的藉口敷衍過去的。***put sb off (sth),*** hinder or distract him (from sth): 妨礙或勸阻: *put sb off his game,* eg distract him when he is about to strike the ball at golf. 妨礙一個人比賽(如在他將擊球時分散他的注意力)。*The mere smell of garlic put him off his supper,* caused him not to want supper. 他一聞到蒜味就對晚餐倒了胃口。***put sb off his stroke,*** distract him; cause him to pause. 使某人分心;使某人停止。

put sth on, **(a)** (contrasted with *take off*) clothe oneself with: (與 take off 相對)穿;戴: *put one's hat／shoes, etc on.* 戴上帽子(穿上鞋子等)。**(b)** assume; pretend to have: 假裝;僞稱有: *put on an air of innocence.* 裝出一派天眞純樸的樣子。*Her modesty is all put on,* she's only pretending to be modest, eg about her ability or skill. 她的謙遜只是裝出來的。**(c)** increase; add: 增加;添上: *put on more steam／pressure;* 添加更多蒸汽(壓力); *put on speed.* 增加速度。*He's putting on weight／flesh,* is getting heavier／fatter.他的體重在增加(他愈來愈胖)。*Marks and Sparks put on sixty runs,* (cricket) together added sixty to the score. (板球戲)馬克斯和史巴克斯合起來多得了60分。**(d)** add to: 增添;增加: *This policy will put pounds on the cost of living,* will make it much higher. 這項措施將使生活費用增高。**(e)** arrange for; make available: 安排;準備;使可利用: *put on extra trains during the rush hours;* 在乘客擁擠時加開火車; *put a play on,* arrange for it to be shown at a theatre. 安排一戲劇的演出。**(f)** advance: 撥快: *put the clock on one hour,* move the hands forward, eg for Summer Time. 把鐘撥快一小時(如夏令時間)。***put sb on,*** (colloq) deceive him: (俗)欺騙: *He's not really interested; he's putting you on.* 他不是眞有興趣;他只是在欺騙你。Hence, 由此產生, **ˈput-on** *n* deception: 欺騙: *What a put-on!* 好一個騙局! ***put it on,*** (colloq) (俗) **(a)** exaggerate a show of feeling; pretend to be more important, etc than is justified or warranted; talk or behave in a pretentious way. 誇張感情的表現;裝得過份重要;裝模作樣地講話或行動。**(b)** overcharge: 索價過高: *Some of the hotels put it on during the holiday season.* 在假日季節有些旅館提高收費。***put sb on (to bowl),*** (cricket) arrange for him to bowl at least one over. (板球戲)安排某人至少投球一次。***put money on sb／sth,*** stake (horse-racing, etc): 賭(賽馬等): *I've put a pound on the favourite.* 我在有獲勝希望的馬身上賭一鎊。

put out (from), (naut) (of a boat or crew) move out, leave, eg from harbour. (航海)(指船或船員)(從港口)駛出。***put sth out,*** **(a)** extinguish; cause to stop burning: 撲滅;熄滅;使停止燃燒: *put out the lights／the candle／the gas／the gas-fire.* 熄滅燈(燭,煤氣,煤氣暖爐)。*The fireman soon put the fire out.* 消防隊員不久卽撲滅那場火。**(b)** cause to be out of joint; dislocate: 使脫關節;使脫臼: *She fell off a horse and put her shoulder out.* 她從馬上跌下,肩膀脫臼了。**(c)** give (sth) to be done off the premises: 把(某事物)送到外面去做: *All repairs are done on the premises and not put out.* 全部修繕都在家裡進行,不送到外面去做。*We put out the washing,* send it to a laundry instead of having it done at home. 我們把要洗的衣服送到洗衣店去洗。**(d)** lend (money) at interest: 放利息;放帳: *He has £1 000 put out at 5 per cent.* 他以百分之五的利息放款一千鎊。**(e)** produce: 生產: *The firm puts out 1 000 bales of cotton sheeting every week.* 這家公司每週出產一千包棉質被單布。⇨ output. **(f)** issue; broadcast: 發佈;廣播: *The Health Department has put out a warning about dangerous drugs.* 衞生部就危險藥品發佈警告。***put one's ˈhand out,*** hold it out in welcome, for caning as a punishment, etc. 伸出手(以示歡迎,罰打手心等)。***put one's ˈtongue out,*** show it, eg for a doctor, or at sb, as a rude act. (向醫生,或不雅地向某人)伸出舌頭。***put sb out,*** **(a)** disconcert; cause to be confused or worried: 使困惑不安;使迷惑或憂煩: *The least thing puts him out,* he is easily upset. 一點兒小事就會使他不安。*She was very much put out by your rudeness.* 你的魯莽使她受窘。**(b)** inconvenience: 使感不便: *Would it put you out to lend me £5 until Friday?* 借給我五鎊,(下)星期五歸還,對你有什麼不方便嗎? *He was very much put out by the late arrival of his guests.* 他的客人們姍姍來遲使他大感不便。***put sb out (of),*** expel; drive out. 驅逐;趕出。

put over, (naut) (of a boat or crew) move over: (航海)(指船或船員)駛過: *put over to the other side of the harbour.* 駛向港的對面。***put sth over to sb,*** (colloq) = put sth across to sb.

put sth through, carry it out: 實行;完成: *put through a business deal.* 完成一樁交易。***put sb／sth through,*** connect (by telephone): 接通(電話): *Please put me／this call through to the Manager.* 請替我接經理。***put sb through sth,*** cause him to undergo, eg an ordeal, a test: 使受(考驗,試驗): *The police put him through a severe examination.* 警方對他嚴加詢問。*The trainees were put through an assault course.* 受訓人員接受突擊訓練課程。***put a person through his paces,*** ⇨ pace *n*(3). ***put sb ˈthrough it,*** (colloq) test or examine him thoroughly, eg by giving him a medical examination, or by inflicting suffering on him to get a confession. (俗)徹底地檢查或審訊某人。

put sth to sb, ⇨ 8 above. 參看上列第8義。***be hard ˈput to it to do sth,*** find difficulty in doing sth: 非常爲難;做某事有困難: *I'd be hard put to it to say exactly why I disliked him.* 我很難啓齒説明我到底爲什麼不喜歡他。*He was hard put to it to satisfy his creditors.* 他爲償清對債主之欠款感到爲難。***put sth together,*** construct (a whole) by combining parts: 結合各部分而構成(一整體);裝配: *It's easier to take a machine to pieces than to put it together again.* 拆卸一機器比重新裝配起來容易。*I must put my thoughts/ideas together before I go on the platform,* collect my ideas, etc before I give my address, speech, etc. 在踏上講臺講演之前,我必須把我的思緒整理一下。***put our/your/their 'heads together,*** consult one another. 彼此商量;共同商討。***put two and two together,*** ⇨ two. ***put up (at),*** obtain lodging and food: 獲得食宿: *put up (at an inn) for the night.* (在客棧)過夜。***put up (for sth),*** offer oneself for election: 競選: *Are you going to put up for Finchley again,* ie as a prospective member of Parliament? 你還要競選代表芬赤利市的國會議員嗎? ***put sth up,*** **(a)** raise; hold up: 舉起;抬起: *put up one's hands,* eg over one's head, as a sign that one is ready to surrender, or with fists clenched, ready to fight; 舉起手(如舉過頭以示投降,或握緊拳頭準備打架); *put up a flag/a sail.* 升旗(張帆)。***put one's 'hair up,*** (of long hair) wear it coiled on the head instead of letting it fall over the neck and shoulders. 把頭髮挽於頭上。**(b)** build, erect: 建立;豎立: *put up a shed/a tent.* 搭起一小棚(一帳篷)。**(c)** publish (banns); place so as to be seen: 公佈(結婚預告);公告: *put up a notice.* 公佈一通知。**(d)** raise, increase: 提高;增加: *put up the rent by 50p (a week).* 將房租(每週)提高五十辨士。**(e)** pack (in parcels, boxes, etc): 包裝(於小包,盒等): *herrings put up in barrels.* 裝於桶中的青魚。*The hotel will put us up some sandwiches,* prepare and pack some for us. 旅館將爲我們準備一些三明治並且包好。**(f)** offer, make: 給予;施以: *put up a stout resistance/a good fight.* 予以頑强之抵抗(挺身奮戰)。**(g)** supply (a sum of money for an undertaking): 提供(一筆錢做一事業): *I will supply the skill and knowledge if you will put up the £2 000 capital.* 如果你提供兩千鎊的資本,我願貢獻技術與知識。**(h)** (old use) sheathe (a sword). (舊用法)插(刀)入鞘。**(i)** cause (wild birds or animals) to leave shelter or cover: 使(野禽野獸)離巢穴: *put up a partridge.* 把一隻鷓鴣趕出巢。***put sb's back up,*** ⇨ back¹(1). ***put sth up for auction/sale,*** offer it to be auctioned/sold: 提出以供拍賣(出售): *Has the house been put up for auction?* 那房子是否要拍賣? ***a ˌput-up 'job,*** sth done in order to give a false impression, to swindle sb, etc. 意圖蒙混之事(爲了給人錯誤印象或欺騙他人而爲者)。***put sb up,*** provide lodging and food (for): 供以食宿(與 for 連用): *We can put you up for the weekend.* 周末我們能供你食宿。***put sb up (for sth),*** propose, nominate sb for a position: 推薦或提名某人就任某職務: *She was put up for the position of secretary,* eg of a society; 她被推薦擔任秘書職務; *put sb up for a club.* 推薦(提名)某人爲一俱樂部之會員。***put sb 'up to sth,*** suggest sth to sb, esp urge him to do sth mischievous or wrong: 向某人建議做某事(尤指促其做壞事或錯事);教唆: *Who put you up to all these tricks?* 誰教唆你做這些騙人的事? ***put 'up with sb/sth,*** endure without protest; bear patiently: 容忍;忍受: *There are many inconveniences that have to be put up with when you are camping.* 在你露營時,有很多不方便處必須忍受。

put² /pʌt ; pʌt/ *n, vi, vt* = putt.

pu·ta·tive /ˈpjuːtətɪv ; ˈpjutətɪv/ *adj* commonly reputed to be: 一般公認的;推定的: *his ~ father.* 他那位一般公認的父親。

pu·trefy /ˈpjuːtrɪfaɪ ; ˈpjutrəˌfaɪ/ *vt, vi* (*pt, pp* -fied) [VP6A, 2A] (cause to) become putrid. (使)腐敗。**pu·tre·fac·tion** /ˌpjuːtrɪˈfækʃn ; ˌpjutrəˈfækʃən/ *n* ~ing; sth which has putrefied. 腐敗;腐敗物。

pu·tres·cent /pjuːˈtresnt ; pjuˈtrɛsnt/ *adj* becoming putrid; in the process of rotting. 變爲腐敗的;正在腐敗的。**pu·tres·cence** /-sns ; -sns/ *n*

pu·trid /ˈpjuːtrɪd ; ˈpjutrɪd/ *adj* **1** having become rotten; decomposed and ill-smelling: 已變爲腐爛的;腐爛且有臭味的: *~ fish.* 腐爛的臭魚。**2** (sl) very distasteful or unpleasant: (俚)非常令人不快的: *~ weather.* 很壞的天氣。**~·ity** /pjuːˈtrɪdətɪ ; pjuˈtrɪdətɪ/ *n* [U] decomposed matter; ~ state. 腐爛物;腐爛。

putsch /pʊtʃ ; pʊtʃ/ *n* (G) revolutionary attempt; insurrection. (德)革命的企圖;起義;反叛。

putt /pʌt ; pʌt/ *vi, vt* [VP2A, 6A] strike (a golf-ball) gently with a club so that it rolls across the ground towards or into a hole: 以球棍小心輕擊(高爾夫球)使滾過場地滑向或滾進一洞: *spend an hour practising ~ing.* 花一小時練習輕擊高爾夫球。**ˈ~·ing-green** *n* smooth area of lawn around a hole. 高爾夫球穴周圍的草地;穴周之平坦的輕打區域。**ˈ~·ing-iron** *n* club for ~ing. 輕擊高爾夫球之球棍。□ *n* stroke as described above. 上述的一擊;輕擊。

put·tee /ˈpʌtɪ ; ˈpʌtɪ/ *n* long band of cloth wound round the leg from ankle to knee, for protection and support. 裹腿;綁腿。

put·ter /ˈpʌtə(r) ; ˈpʌtɚ/ *vt, vi* = potter.

putty /ˈpʌtɪ ; ˈpʌtɪ/ *n* [U] soft paste of white powder and oil used for fixing glass in window frames, etc. 白灰同油混合的柔軟糊狀物;油灰(用以黏玻璃於窗框等者)。□ *vt* [VP6A, 15B] fill or make fast with ~: 以油灰填塞或黏牢: *~ up a hole.* 以油灰補塞一個洞。

puzzle /ˈpʌzl ; ˈpʌzl̩/ *n* [C] **1** question or problem difficult to understand or answer. 難理解或回答之問題。**2** problem (eg *a ˈcrossword-~*) or toy (eg *a ˈjigsaw-~*) designed to test a person's knowledge, skill, patience or temper. 用以測驗人之知識,技術,耐心或脾氣而設計的問題(如縱橫字謎)或玩具(如拼圖板);謎。**3** (*sing* only) state of bewilderment or perplexity: (僅用單數)迷惑;困惑: *be in a ~ about sth.* 對某事物深感迷離不解。□ *vt, vi* **1** [VP6A] cause (sb) to be perplexed; make hard thought necessary to (sb): 使(某人)困惑;使苦思: *This letter ~s me.* 這封信使我困惑不解。*He was ~d what to do next/how to answer the letter.* 他不知道下一步怎麼辦(如何回這封信)。*He ~d his brains* (= thought hard) *to find the answer.* 他絞盡腦汁以尋求答案。**2** [VP3A] ***~ over sth,*** think deeply about it. 深思(某事)。**3** [VP15B] ***~ sth out,*** (try to) find the answer or solution by hard thought. 苦思而找出答案或解決某問題。**~·ment** *n* state of being ~d. 困惑;苦思。**puzz·ler** *n* puzzling question: 難解之問題: *ask sb a few ~rs.* 問某人一些難題。*That's a real ~r!* 那眞是個難題!

pygmy, pigmy /ˈpɪgmɪ ; ˈpɪgmɪ/ *n* (*pl* -mies) **1** P~, member of a dwarf people in Equatorial Africa. 赤道非洲之侏儒種族。**2** very small person; dwarf. 十分矮小的人;侏儒。**3** (attrib) very small. (形容用法)非常小的。

py·ja·mas (US = **pa·ja·mas**) /pəˈdʒɑːməz *US:* -ˈdʒæm- ; pəˈdʒæməz/ *n pl* **1** (also 亦作 **a pair of ~**) loose-fitting jacket and trousers for sleeping in (*sing* when attrib): 寬鬆之睡衣褲(作形容用法時用單數): *pyjama top/jacket/bottom/trousers.* 睡衣上身(上衣,下身,褲子)。**cat's ~** = *cat's whiskers,* ⇨ whisker(2). **2** loose trousers tied round the waist, worn by Muslims of both sexes in India and Pakistan. (印度與巴基斯坦回教徒穿的一種圍腰而繫的)寬鬆的褲子。

py·lon /ˈpaɪlən ; ˈpaɪlɑn/ *n* **1** tower (steel framework) for carrying overhead high-voltage electric cables. 架高壓電纜之鐵塔。**2** gateway to an ancient Egyptian temple; tall structure erected as a support, boundary or decoration. 古埃及廟宇的大門;作爲支柱,界線或裝飾用之高大建築。

py·or·rhoea (also **-rhea**) /ˌpaɪəˈrɪə ; paɪəˈriə/ *n*

pylons

[U] inflammation of the gums causing them to shrink, with loosening of the teeth. 齒槽膿溢；牙周病(牙齦發炎，能使牙齦萎縮，牙齒鬆動)。

pyra·mid /ˈpɪrəmɪd ; ˈpɪrəmɪd/ *n* structure with a triangular or square base and sloping sides meeting at a point, esp one of those built of stone in ancient Egypt; pile of objects in the shape of a ~. 角錐；錐體；(尤指古埃及之)金字塔；角錐形之一堆東西。⇨ the illus at Sphinx. 參看 Sphinx 之插圖。 **~ selling,** (comm) method of selling goods whereby distributors pay a premium for the right to sell a company's goods and then sell part of that right to other distributors. (商)分層銷售(銷售商品的方法，即由經銷商付權利金取得某商品之經銷權，再將部分經銷權轉賣給其他經銷商)。

pyre /ˈpaɪə(r) ; paɪr/ *n* large pile of wood for burning, esp a funeral pile for a corpse. 大堆供燃燒之木料；(尤指)火葬用之柴堆。

py·rites /ˌpaɪəˈraɪtiːz *US:* pɪˈr- ; pəˈraɪtiz/ *n* [U] **copper ~,** sulphide of copper and iron. 黃銅礦(銅與鐵之硫化物)。 **iron ~,** either of two sulphides of iron, gold in colour. 黃鐵礦(鐵之兩種硫化物之任一種，色金黃)。

pyro·tech·nics /ˌpaɪrəˈteknɪks ; ˌpaɪrəˈtɛknɪks/ *n pl* art of making or using fireworks; public display of fireworks; (fig, often ironic) brilliant display of oratory, wit, etc. 煙火製造術或使用法；放煙火；(喻，常作反語)辯才，機智等之炫耀。 **py·ro·tech·nic** *adj* of ~. 煙火製造術或使用法的；放煙火的；誇大炫耀的。

Pyr·rhic /ˈpɪrɪk ; ˈpɪrɪk/ *adj* **~ victory,** one gained at too great a cost. 付出過大代價而獲取之勝利。

py·thon /ˈpaɪθn ; ˈpaɪθɑn/ *n* large snake that kills its prey by twisting itself round it and crushing it. 一種大蟒(將身體盤繞捕獲物，將其絞死)。⇨ the illus at snake. 參看 snake 之插圖。

pyx /pɪks ; pɪks/ *n* (eccles) vessel in which consecrated bread used at Holy Communion is kept. (教會)聖體容器；聖餅盒。

Qq

Q, q /kjuː ; kju/ (*pl* Q's, q's /kjuːz ; kjuz/) the seventeenth letter of the English alphabet. 英文字母之第十七個字母。 ***mind one's p's and q's,*** ⇨ P,p. ***on the qt,*** ⇨ quiet(5).

qua /kweɪ ; kwe/ *conj* (Lat) as; in the character or capacity of. (拉)作爲；以…之身份或資格。

quack[1] /kwæk ; kwæk/ *vi, n* [VP2A] (make the) cry of a duck. (作出)鴨叫聲；(指鴨)呷呷地叫。 **ˈ~-~** *n* (child's name for a) duck. (兒語)鴨。

quack[2] /kwæk ; kwæk/ *n* person dishonestly claiming to have knowledge and skill (esp in medicine); (attrib) of, used by, sold by, such persons: 僞稱具有知識與技能的人；冒充內行的人；(尤指)庸醫；江湖郎中；(形容用法)冒充內行者的，所用的，所賣的；庸醫的：*a ~ doctor;* 庸醫；江湖郎中；*~ remedies.* 江湖郎中的藥物。 **ˈ~·ery** /-ərɪ ; -ərɪ/ *n* [U] methods, practices, etc of ~s; (*pl*) instances of the use of such methods, etc. 庸醫的醫術、治療等；(複)使用上述醫術等之實例。

quad /kwɒd ; kwɑd/ *n* (colloq abbr of) (俗，爲下列二字之略) **1** quadrangle. **2** quadruplet.

quad·rangle /ˈkwɒdræŋgl ; ˈkwɑdræŋgl/ *n* **1** plane figure with four sides, esp a square or a rectangle. 四邊形(尤指正方形或長方形)。 **2** (abbr 略作 *quad*) space in the form of a ~, wholly or nearly surrounded by buildings, esp in a college, eg at Oxford. 內圍；方庭(尤指牛津大學等之學院中者)。 Cf 參較 *court* at Cambridge. **quad·ran·gu·lar** /kwɒˈdræŋgjʊlə(r) ; kwɑdˈræŋgjʊlə/ *adj* in the form of a ~. 四邊形的。

quad·rant /ˈkwɒdrənt ; ˈkwɑdrənt/ *n* **1** fourth part of a circle or its circumference. 象限；圓或其圓周的四分之一。⇨ the illus at circle. 參看 circle 之插圖。 **2** graduated strip of metal, etc shaped like a quarter-circle, for use in measuring angles (of altitude) in astronomy and navigation. 象限儀；四分儀。

quad·ratic /kwɒˈdrætɪk ; kwɑdˈrætɪk/ *adj* (maths) **~ equation,** one in which the second and no higher power of an unknown quantity is used, eg $x^2 + 2x - 8 = 0$. (數學)二次方程式(如 $x^2 + 2x - 8 = 0$)。

quad·ri·lat·eral /ˌkwɒdrɪˈlætərəl ; ˌkwɑdrəˈlætərəl/ *adj, n* four-sided (plane figure). 四邊的；四邊形。

qua·drille /kwəˈdrɪl ; kwəˈdrɪl/ *n* [C] (music for an) old-fashioned square dance for four couples. 瓜德利爾舞(一種舊式的由四對組成之方塊舞)；其舞曲。

quad·ril·lion /kwɒˈdrɪlɪən ; kwɑdˈrɪljən/ *n* **1** (GB) fourth power of one million (1 followed by 24 ciphers). (英)一百萬之四次方；1後加24個零之數。 **2** (US) fifth power of one thousand (1 followed by 15 ciphers). (美)一千之五次方；1後加15個零之數。⇨ App 4. 參看附錄四。

quad·ro·phony /kwɒˈdrɒfənɪ ; kwɑˈdrɑfənɪ/ *n* [U] recording or reproduction of sound using four channels. 四聲道錄音或放音。 **quad·ro·phonic** /ˌkwɒdrəˈfɒnɪk ; ˌkwɑdrəˈfɑnɪk/ *adj*

quad·ru·ped /ˈkwɒdrʊped ; ˈkwɑdrəˌpɛd/ *n* four-footed animal. 四足獸。

quad·ru·ple /ˈkwɒdruːpl *US:* kwɒˈdruːpl; ˈkwɑdrʊpl/ *adj* **1** made up of four parts. 由四部分組成的。 **2** agreed to by four persons, parties, etc: 由四個人或四方面同意的：*a ~ alliance,* of four Powers. 四國聯盟。□ *n* number or amount four times as great as another: 四倍：*20 is the ~ of 5.* 20 爲 5 之 4 倍。□ *vt, vi* /kwɒˈdruːpl ; kwɑdˈrupl/ [VP6A,

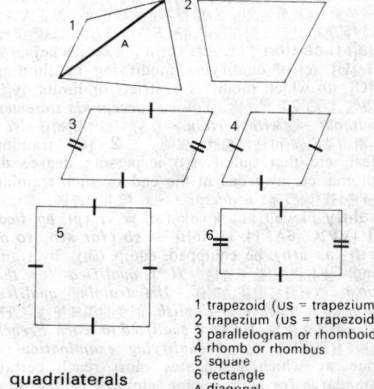

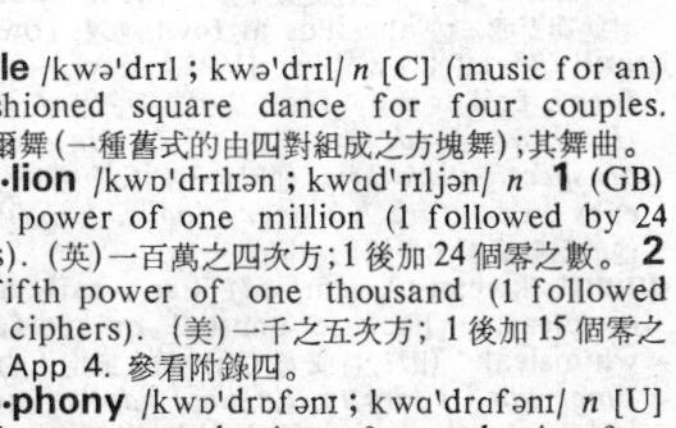

quadrilaterals

2A] multiply by 4: 以 4 乘之;四倍之: *He has ~d his income/His income has ~d in the last four years.* 他的收入在過去四年中增加了四倍。

quad·ru·plet /ˈkwɒdruːplət *US:* kwɒˈdruːp-; ˈkwɑdrʊˌplɪt/ *n* (common abbr 常略作 *quad*) one of four babies at a birth (usu *pl*: *one of the ~s* is commoner than *one ~*). 一胎四嬰中之一個 (通常用複數: one of the quadruplets 較 one quadruplet 常用)。

quad·ru·pli·cate /kwɒˈdruːplɪkət ; kwɑdˈruplɪkɪt/ *adj* four times repeated or copied. 重覆四次的; 抄寫四份的。□ *n* ***in ~,*** in four exactly similar examples or copies. 以四個同樣之例證;以四份同樣之文件;一式四份地。□ *vt* /kwɒˈdruːplɪkeɪt; kwɑdˈruplɪˌket/ [VP6A] make four specimens of. 四次重覆之;作成…之四個範例或四份文件;把…作成一式四份。

Q

quaff /kwɒf *US:* kwæf ; kwæf/ *vt, vi* [VP6A, 15B, 2A] (liter) drink deeply: (文)痛飲;暢飲: ~ *(off) a glass of wine.* 飲盡一杯酒。

quagga /ˈkwægə ; ˈkwægə/ *n* (now extinct) S African quadruped related to the ass and the zebra. 泥馬(南非產的一種四足獸,與驢及斑馬同屬,現已絕種)。

quag·mire /ˈkwægmaɪə(r) ; ˈkwægˌmaɪr/ *n* [C] area of soft, wet land; bog; marsh. 沼澤;沼地。

Quai d'Or·say /ˌkeɪ dɔːˈseɪ ; ˌkedɔrˈse/ *n* (F) (used for) French Foreign Office; French foreign policy. (法) (用以指)法國外交部;法國外交政策。

quail¹ /kweɪl ; kwel/ *n* small bird, similar to a partridge, valued as food: 鶉: (unchanged in the collective *pl*) (集合複數不變) *shoot ~ and duck.* 射鶉與野鴨。⇨ the illus at fowl. 參看 fowl 之挿圖。

quail² /kweɪl ; kwel/ *vi* [VP2A, 3A] ~ ***(at/before),*** feel or show fear: 感到或顯露恐懼;膽怯;畏縮: *His heart ~ed.* 他心裡感到恐懼。*He ~ed at the prospect before him.* 他對自己的前途感到惶恐。*His eyes ~ed before her angry looks.* 在她的怒容之前,他的眼睛裏顯出畏懼的神情。

quaint /kweɪnt ; kwent/ *adj* (-er, -est) attractive or pleasing because unusual or old-fashioned; whimsical: (因奇特或老式而) 誘人或悅人的;古怪的: *American visitors to England admire our ~ villages/ customs.* 來英國的美國遊客對於我們的古老鄉村(風俗)甚爲稱讚。**~·ly** *adv* **~·ness** *n*

quake /kweɪk ; kwek/ *vi* [VP2A, C] **1** (of the earth) shake: (指地)顫動;震動: *The ground ~d under his feet.* 地在他脚下震動。 **2** (of persons) tremble: (指人)戰慄;顫抖: *quaking with fear/cold.* 因恐懼(寒冷)而戰慄。□ *n* (colloq abbr for) earthquake. (俗)爲 earthquake 之略。

Quaker /ˈkweɪkə(r) ; ˈkwekɚ/ *n* member of the Society of Friends, a Christian group that holds informal meetings instead of formal church services and is opposed to violence or war under any circumstances. 教友派的信徒; 貴格會員(教友派,亦稱貴格會,爲基督教之一支,舉行非正式集會而不做正式教會禮拜儀式,此派反對在任何情形下使用暴力或訴諸戰爭)。

quali·fi·ca·tion /ˌkwɒlɪfɪˈkeɪʃn ; ˌkwɑləfəˈkeʃən/ *n* **1** [U] act of qualifying, modifying or limiting; [C] sth which modifies, restricts or limits: 修飾; 限制;修飾或限制之物: *You can accept his statement without ~/with certain ~s.* 你可以不附帶任何條件(附帶某些條件)地接受他的聲明。 **2** [C] training, test, etc that qualifies(1) a person; degree, diploma, etc awarded at the end of such training: 資格;條件;資歷: *a doctor's ~s.* 醫生的資格。

qual·ify /ˈkwɒlɪfaɪ ; ˈkwɑləˌfaɪ/ *vt, vi* (*pt, pp* -fied) **1** [VP2C, 6A, 14, 17, 16B] ~ ***sb (for sth/to do sth/as sth),*** be equipped, equip (sb) by training: 使有資格;給予資格: *He's qualified for this post.* 他有資格擔任這工作。*His training qualifies him as a teacher of English.* 他受的訓練使他有資格做一個英文教師。*He's not qualified to teach French.* 他沒有資格教法文。*A qualifying examination* (= one at which candidates must reach certain standards for a profession, etc) *will be held next week.* 一次甄審考試將於下星期舉行。 **2** [VP17, 4A, 3A] ~ ***sb to do sth,*** entitle: 使某人有資格做某事: *He's the manager's son but that does not ~ him to criticize my work.* 他是經理的兒子,但這並不足以使他有資格批評我的工作。~ ***for sth,*** be entitled to: 有…的資格: *Do you ~ for the vote/to vote?* 你有投票的資格嗎? **3** [VP6A] limit; make less inclusive, less general: 限制; 使包括較少; 使較不籠統: *The statement 'Boys are lazy' needs to be qualified,* eg by saying 'Some boys' or 'Many boys'. '男孩子懶惰' 這句話需要斟酌 (例如改說 '某些男孩' 或 '很多男孩')。 **4** [VP6A] (gram) limit the meaning of; name the qualities of: (文法)限制…之意義;指明…之性質;修飾;形容: *Adjectives ~ nouns.* 形容詞修飾名詞。 **5** [VP16B] ~ ***sb as,*** describe: 描寫; 將…描述爲: *~ a man as an ambitious self-seeker.* 把一個人描述成有野心的自私自利者。**quali·fied** *adj* **1** having the necessary qualifications: 具必需條件的;合格的: *a qualified doctor.* 一位合格的醫生。 **2** limited: 限制的: *give a scheme one's qualified approval.* 對一計畫給予有限度的贊同。 **quali·fier** /-faɪə(r) ; -ˌfaɪɚ/ *n* (gram) ~ing word, eg an adjective or adverb. (文法)修飾詞(如形容詞或副詞)。

quali·tat·ive /ˈkwɒlɪtətɪv *US:* -teɪt- ; ˈkwɑləˌtetɪv/ *adj* relating to quality: 與性質有關的;定性的: *~ analysis.* 定性分析。⇨ quantitative.

qual·ity /ˈkwɒlətɪ ; ˈkwɑlətɪ/ *n* (*pl* -ties) **1** [C, U] (degree, esp high degree, of) goodness or worth: 質;品質;(尤指)高級品質;優良品質: *goods of first-rate ~.* 第一等品質的貨物。*Poor ~ goods won't sell easily.* 品質差的貨物不易賣出。*We aim at ~ rather than quantity,* aim to produce superior goods, not large quantities. 我們的目標是重質不重量。*We manufacture goods of various qualities.* 我們製造各種不同品質的貨物。*He is a man with many good qualities.* 他是一位有很多優點的人。*Give us a taste of your ~,* show us what accomplishments you have. 讓我們瞧瞧你的才藝吧。 **2** [C] sth that is special in, or that distinguishes, a person or thing: 性質;特質: *One ~ of pine-wood is that it can be sawn easily.* 松木的一種特質是它容易被鋸開。*He has the ~ of inspiring confidence.* 他有激發別人對他信任的特質。 **3** [U] (archaic) high social position: (古)很高的社會地位: *a lady of ~.* 一位貴婦。

qualm /kwɑːm ; kwɑm/ *n* [C] **1** feeling of doubt (esp about whether one is doing or has done right); misgiving: 疑慮 (尤指對所做或已做的事是否正確所感覺者);疑惑;不安: *He felt no ~s about borrowing money from friends.* 他對於向朋友們借錢未感到絲毫不安。 **2** temporary feeling of sickness in the stomach: 胃中暫時之不適;噁心: *~s which spoilt his appetite during the first few days of the voyage.* 在航海的頭幾天使他沒有食慾的噁心。

quan·dary /ˈkwɒndərɪ ; ˈkwɑndrɪ/ *n* [C] (*pl* -ries) state of doubt or perplexity: 疑慮;困惑: *be in a ~ about what to do next.* 對下一步該怎麼辦感到困惑。

quango /ˈkwæŋgəʊ ; ˈkwæŋgo/ *n* *qu*asi-*a*utonomous *n*on-*g*overnmental *o*rganisation. 半自治的非政府組織(此字係由 *qu*asi-*a*utonomous *n*on-*g*overnmental *o*rganisation 一詞中每字起首字母組成)。

quan·tify /ˈkwɒntɪfaɪ ; ˈkwɑntəˌfaɪ/ *vt* [VP6A] express or measure the quantity of. 表示或測定…之量。

quan·ti·tat·ive /ˈkwɒntɪtətɪv *US:* -teɪt- ; ˈkwɑntəˌtetɪv/ *adj* relating to quantity: 與量有關的;定量的: *~ analysis.* 定量分析。⇨ qualitative.

quan·tity /ˈkwɒntətɪ ; ˈkwɑntətɪ/ *n* (*pl* -ties) **1** [U] the property of things which can be measured, eg size, weight, number: 物之能衡量之屬性(如大小、重量、數量);量: *I prefer quality to ~.* 我重質不重量。*Mathematics is the science of pure ~.* 數學是研究純量之科學。 **2** [C] amount, sum or number: 數量: *There's only a small ~* (ie not much or not many) *left.* 只剩下少量。*What ~ do you want?* 你要多少? **3** (often *pl*) large amount or number: (常用複數)大量: *We've had quantities of rain this summer.* 今年夏天雨下得很多。*He buys things in ~/in large quantities.* 他總是大宗採購東西。 **4 an unknown ~,** (maths) symbol (usu *x*) representing an unknown ~ in an equation; (fig) person or thing whose action, ability etc cannot be foreseen. (數學)在一個方程式中代表一未知數的符號(通常用 x 表示);未知數; (喩)其行動、能力等難以預測的人或事物。 **~ surveyor,** expert who estimates quantities of materials needed in building, their cost, etc. 建築積算師;建築估料師。 **bill of ~,** one prepared by a ~ surveyor. 建築工程清單。

quan·tum /ˈkwɒntəm ; ˈkwɑntəm/ *n* (*pl* quanta /-tə ; -tə/) amount required or desired. (所需或所欲之)量;額。ˈ**~ theory,** (phys) the hypothesis that in radiation the energy of electrons is discharged not continuously but in certain fixed amounts (or *quanta*). (物理)量子論(物理學上的一個假說,即在輻射中,電子的能量不是接續不斷而是以某固定之量 'quanta' 放出的)。

quar·an·tine /ˈkwɒrəntiːn *US:* ˈkwɔːr- ; ˈkwɔrən-ˌtin/ *n* [U] (med) (period of) separation from others until it is known that there is no danger of spreading disease: (醫) (防止疾病傳染所施行的)隔離;檢疫;檢疫期: *be in ~ for a week;* 隔離一週; *be out of ~;* 解除檢疫; (attrib) of the system of ~: (形容用法)隔離制度的: *the ~ regulations.* 隔離管制條例。*How long will my dog be kept in ~?* 我的狗要被隔離多久? □ *vt* [VP6A] put in ~: 使受隔離: *~d because of yellow fever.* 因黃熱病而被隔離。

quark /kwɑːk ; kwɑrk/ *n* (phys) kind of elementary particle. (物理)夸克(一種最基本的粒子)。

quar·rel /ˈkwɒrəl *US:* ˈkwɔːrəl ; ˈkwɔrəl/ *n* [C] **1** angry argument; violent disagreement: 口角;爭論: *have a ~ with sb about sth.* 爲某事同某人爭論。*They made up their ~,* ended it and became friendly. 他們於爭吵後言歸於好。*He's always fighting other people's ~s,* helping them, eg to get social justice. 他總是幫着別的人吵架(例如爲主持公道)。 **2** cause for being angry; reason for protest or complaint: 口角的原因;抗議或抱怨之理由: *I have no ~ with/against him.* 我沒有跟他爭吵的理由。 ***pick a ~ (with sb),*** find or invent some occasion or excuse for disagreement, etc. (向某人)尋釁。□ *vi* (-ll-, US also -l-) **1** [VP2A, C, 3A] ***~ (with sb) (about sth),*** have, take part in, a ~: 爭論;爭吵: *The thieves ~led with one another about how to divide the loot.* 盜賊們爲了如何分贓而彼此爭吵起來。 **2** [VP3A] ***~ with,*** disagree with; refuse to accept; complain about: 不同意;拒絕接受;抱怨: *It's not the fact of examinations I'm ~ling with; it's the way they're conducted.* 我並非對考試這件事本身有異議,而是不贊成考試的方式。ˈ**~·some** /-səm ; -səm/ *adj* quick-tempered; fond of ~s. 急躁的;愛爭吵的。

quarry[1] /ˈkwɒrɪ *US:* ˈkwɔːrɪ ; ˈkwɔrɪ/ *n* (*pl* -ries) (usu *sing*) animal, bird, etc which is hunted; anything eagerly pursued. (通常用單數) 被追獵的獸、禽鳥等;獵物;任何被熱烈追求之物。

quarry[2] /ˈkwɒrɪ *US:* ˈkwɔːrɪ ; ˈkwɔrɪ/ *n* [C] (*pl* -ries) place (not underground like a mine) where stone, slate, etc is obtained (for building, road-making, etc). 採石場(非如在地下之礦坑)。□ *vt, vi* **1** [VP6A, 15A, B] get from a ~: 從採石場開採: *~ limestones;* 開採石灰石; *~ (out) a block of marble;* 挖出一大塊大理石; (fig) search for (facts, etc) in old books, records, etc. (喩)在舊書、記錄等中探索(事實等)。 **2** [VP2A, C] engage in work of this kind: 從事尋找資料之工作: *~ in old manuscripts.* 在舊手稿中尋找資料。ˈ**~·man** /-mən ; -mən/ *n* (*pl* -men) man who works in a ~. 採石工人。

quart /kwɔːt ; kwɔrt/ *n* measure of capacity equal to two pints or about 1·14 litre. 夸(脫)(容量之單位,等於二品脫或約 1·14 公升)。⇨ App 5: 參看附錄五: *drink a ~ of beer.* 喝一夸脫的啤酒。***put a ~ into a pint pot,*** make the less contain the greater; attempt the impossible. 欲使較小者裝較大者;大脚穿小鞋;做不可能之事。

quar·ter /ˈkwɔːtə(r) ; ˈkwɔrtɚ/ *n* **1** fourth part (¼); one of four equal or corresponding parts: 四分之一;四等分或四相關部分之一: *a ~ of a mile;* 四分之一哩; *a mile and a ~;* 一又四分之一哩; *a ~ of an hour,* 15 minutes; 一刻鐘;十五分鐘; *an hour and a ~;* 一小時又十五分鐘; *the first ~ of this century,* ie 1901-25. 本世紀的前二十五年。*We've come a ~ of the distance now.* 我們現在已走了全程的四分之一。*Divide the apples into ~s.* 把這些蘋果分爲四分。 ***a bad ~ of an hour,*** a short but unpleasant experience (eg in a dentist's chair). 一段短暫而不愉快的經驗(如坐在牙醫的椅上)。 **2** point of time 15 minutes before or after any hour: (任何小時之前或後的)一刻鐘: *a ~ to* (US 美 = *of*) *two;* 差一刻兩點; *a ~ past six.* 六點一刻。*It isn't the ~ yet.* 還不到一刻鐘。*This clock strikes the hours, the half-hours, and the ~s.* 這時鐘每逢點鐘、半點鐘和一刻鐘均敲響。 **3** three months, esp as a period for which rent and other payments are made: 三個月;一季 (尤指房地租或其他款項償付之時期): *owe several ~s' rent;* 欠好幾季的房(地)租; *pay one's rent at the end of each ~.* 在每季之末付房(地)租。ˈ**~-day** *n* first day of a legal ~ of the year, on which rents and other three-monthly accounts are paid (in England, 25 Mar; 24 June; 29 Sept; 25 Dec). 四季結帳日(卽一年中各法定季的第一日,爲付房地租及其他按季付款之日,在英國爲三月廿五日;六月廿四日;九月廿九日;十二月廿五日)。 ˈ**~ sessions,** ⇨ *court of ~ sessions* at court[1](1). **4** (US) 25 cents; a ~ of a dollar. (美)兩角五分;四分之一元;兩角五分的硬幣。 **5** joint of meat including a leg: 包括一條腿在內的一大塊肉: *a ~ of beef;* 有條腿在內的一大塊牛肉; also used of the living animal (usu in compounds, as *ˈfore-~s; ˈhind-~s*). 也用以指活的動物(通常用於複合字中,如 fore-~s 前半身; hind-~s 後半身)。 **6** direction; district; source of supply, help, information, etc: 方向;區域;供應、援助、消息等之來源: *men running from all ~s/from every ~;* 從四面八方(從各方)跑來的人們; *travel in every ~ of the globe,* everywhere. 在世界各地旅行。*From what ~ does the wind blow?* 風從甚麼方向吹來? *As his father was penniless, he could expect no help from that ~.* 因爲他父親身無分文,他不能希望從他父親那裏得到援助。*The suggestion did not find favour in the highest ~s,* was not welcomed by those at the head of affairs. 這建議沒有得到最高階層的贊同。 **7** division of a town, esp one of a special class of people, etc: 一城市中的一區(尤指屬於某一特殊階層者): *the Chinese ~ of San Francisco;* 舊金山的華人區; *the manufacturing/residential ~.* 工廠(住宅)區。 **8** one-fourth of a lunar month; the moon's phase at the end of the first or third week: 陰曆一個月的四分之一;在第一或第三週末月亮之位相: *the moon at the first ~/in its last ~.* 上弦(下弦)月。⇨ the illus at phase. 參看 phase 之插圖。 **9** (*pl*) lodging; (mil) place where soldiers, etc are lodged or stationed: (複)住所;寓所;(軍)營房;軍營: *take up ~s, lodge;* 住宿; *return to ~s.* 回到住所。⇨ *headquarters* at head[1](20). **married ~s,** place where soldiers, etc lodge with their families. 軍眷區。 **single ~s,** place where unmarried soldiers, etc lodge. (未婚官兵住宿之)單身營房。 **10** ***at close ~s,*** (seen) from very near. 非常接近;從很近的地方(看的)。 **11** (*pl*) positions taken up by sailors on duty on a ship, esp for fighting: (複) (海員在船上於擔任職務時,尤指海軍在作戰時,所佔之)崗位: *Officers and men at once took up their ~s.* 官兵立卽各就其崗位。 **12** [U] ***ask for/give ~,*** mercy to an enemy; life granted to a defeated enemy who is willing to surrender: 請求(給予)饒恕;寬恕敵人;給自願投降之敵人活路: *No ~ was asked for and none given,* There were no prisoners. 無

人求饒，未予饒恕(未留俘虜)。 **13** (naut) rear part of a ship's side: (航海)船舷之後部；船尾: *on the port／starboard ~.* 在左(右)舷後部。 **'~-deck** *n* part of the upper deck between the stern and the aftermast of a warship, reserved for officers; officers of a warship or navy. 軍艦上船尾與後檣間的上甲板部分；後甲板(係供軍官所用者)；戰艦上或海軍之全體軍官。 ⇨ *lower deck* at low¹(13), forecastle. **14** (GB) fourth part of a hundredweight, 28 lb; (US) 25 lb; grain-measure of eight bushels. 夸特(英爲 28 磅；美爲 25 磅；穀量單位爲 8 蒲式耳)。 ⇨ App 5. 參看附錄五。 **15** one of the four parts of a shield used in armorial bearings. 紋章中所用的盾形的四分之一。 **16** (compounds) (複合字) **,~-'final** *n* (sport) one of four competitions or matches, the winners of which play in the semi-finals. (運動)預賽(四場比賽之一，獲勝者參加準決賽)。 **'~-light** *n* triangular section at the front or back window of a car, opened to admit air. (車輛的)邊窗。 **'~-master** *n* **(a)** (army) (abbr 略作 **QM**) officer in charge of the stores, etc of a battalion. (陸軍)經理官。 **(b)** (navy) petty officer in charge of steering the ship, signals, etc. (海軍) 航信士官。 **,~-master-'general** *n* (abbr 略作 **QMG**) staff officer in charge of supplies for a whole army. 經理署長；軍需監。 **'~-plate** *n* photographic plate $3\frac{1}{4}$ inches × $4\frac{1}{2}$ inches; photograph made from it. $3\frac{1}{4}$吋 × $4\frac{1}{2}$ 吋大的照相感光板；由此種感光板照的相片。 **'~-staff** *n* strong pole, 6 to 8 ft long, formerly used as a weapon and in a rough kind of fencing. 長六呎到八呎的堅實木棒 (以前用作一種武器，並用於一種粗野的擊劍術中)。 □ *vt* **1** [VP6A] divide into ~s: 分…爲四份；四分之: *~ an apple;* 把一蘋果分爲四份； (in former times) divide (a traitor's body) into ~s: (昔時)將(叛國賊之屍體)肢解: *condemned to be hanged, drawn* (= disembowelled) *and ~ed.* 被判決處以絞刑，取出腸子，並肢解之。 **2** [VP6A, 15A] find lodgings for (troops); place (troops) in lodgings: 爲(軍隊)找駐屯處；安置(軍隊)於駐紮地: *~ troops in the villages.* 安置軍隊駐屯於村中。 **~·ing** *n* method of arranging two or more coats of arms, to show alliances with or descent from various families; coat of arms resulting from this. 排列兩個或兩個以上之紋章以示與不同家族之聯姻或爲不同家族之後代的方法；由此種方法排列成之紋章。

quar·ter·ly /ˈkwɔːtəlɪ ; ˈkwɔrtɚlɪ/ *adj, adv* (happening) once in each three months: 每三個月(發生)一次的(地)；按季的(地): *~ payments／subscriptions;* 按季付款(訂閱費)； *to be paid ~.* 按季付款。□ *n* (*pl* -lies) periodical published ~. 季刊(每三個月出版一次的期刊)。

quar·tet /kwɔːˈtet ; kwɔrˈtɛt/ *n* (piece of music for) four players or singers: 四個演奏者或歌唱者組成之一組；四重奏；四重唱；四部合奏(唱)曲: *a string ~,* for (usu) two violins, viola and cello; 絃樂四重奏(通常爲二小提琴，一中音提琴和一大提琴): *a piano ~,* for piano and three stringed instruments. 鋼琴四重奏(由鋼琴和三件絃樂器合奏)。

quarto /ˈkwɔːtəʊ ; ˈkwɔrto/ *n* (*pl* ~s /-təʊz ; -toz/) (also written 亦書作 **4to**) size given by folding a sheet of paper twice (making four leaves or eight pages); book made of sheets so folded (usu about 9 by 12 in): 四開(將一張紙摺兩次，摺成四張八頁)；四開本的書(通常爲 9×12 吋): *the first ~ of 'Hamlet'.* 哈姆雷特的第一四開本。

quartz /kwɔːts ; kwɔrts/ *n* [U] sorts of hard mineral (esp crystallized silica), including agate and other semi-precious stones. 石英(尤指結晶之矽石，包括瑪瑙及其他次等寶石)。 *~* **clock,** one of very great accuracy, with ~ oscillators. (一種裝有石英晶體振盪器的非常準確的)石英鐘。

quasar /ˈkweɪzɑː(r) ; ˈkwezɑr/ *n* (astron) very distant source of radio or light waves. (天文)類星體(極遠的無線電波或光波來源)。

quash /kwɒʃ ; kwɑʃ/ *vt* [VP6A] put an end to, annul, reject as not valid (by legal procedure): 以法律程序)停止；廢止；宣告無效: *~ a verdict／decision.* 宣告一判決(決定)無效。

quasi- /ˈkweɪsaɪ ; ˈkwesaɪ/ *pref* (with a *n* or *adj*) to a certain extent; seeming(ly): (與名詞或形容詞連用)有相當程度；準；類似的: *a ~-official position.* 一個半官方的職位。 ⇨ App 3. 參看附錄三。

quas·sia /ˈkwɒʃə ; ˈkwɑʃɪə/ *n* [U] (bitter drug used medicinally and obtained from) wood or bark of a S American tree; the tree. 南美所產一種苦木科植物的木材與樹皮； 苦木； 從苦木中提煉出的一種苦味藥；苦木樹。

quat·er·cen·ten·ary /ˌkwɒtəsenˈtiːnərɪ *US:* -ˈsentənerɪ ; ˌkwɑtɚˈsɛntɪˌnɛrɪ/ *n* 400th anniversary: 四百周年紀念: *the ~ celebrations in 1964 of Shakespeare's birth.* 在1964年舉行的莎士比亞誕生四百周年紀念之慶祝活動。

quat·rain /ˈkwɒtreɪn ; ˈkwɑtren/ *n* verse of four lines, usu rhyming *a b a b.* 四行詩 (其韻脚通常是 a b a b)。

quat·tro·cento /ˌkwætrəʊˈtʃentəʊ ; ˌkwɑtroˈtʃɛnto/ *n* (I) the 15th century as a period of Italian art and literature. (義) (做爲義大利藝術與文學一個時代的)第十五世紀。

qua·ver /ˈkweɪvə(r) ; ˈkwevɚ/ *vt, vi* **1** [VP2A] (of the voice or a sound) shake; tremble: (指聲音)顫抖；震顫: *in a ~ing voice;* 以一種震顫的聲音； *in a voice that ~ed.* 以一種震顫的聲音。 **2** [VP6A, 15B] say or sing in a shaking voice: 以震顫的聲音說出或唱出: *She ~ed (out／forth) her little song.* 她以震顫的聲音唱出她的小調。□ *n* [C] **1** ~ing sound. 震顫的聲音。 **2** musical note with one-half the time value of a crotchet. 八分音符。 ⇨ the illus at notation. 參看 notation 之插圖。

quay /kiː ; ki/ *n* solid, stationary landing-place usu built of stone or iron, alongside which ships can be tied up for loading and unloading. 碼頭；横碼頭。

queasy /ˈkwiːzɪ ; ˈkwizɪ/ *adj* (-ier, -iest) **1** (of food) causing a feeling of sickness in the stomach. (指食物)令人作嘔的。 **2** (of the stomach) easily upset. (指胃)易嘔吐的。 **3** (of a person) easily made sick; feeling sick. (指人)容易不舒服的；感覺不舒服的。 **4** (fig, of a person or his conscience) over-scrupulous, tender or delicate. (喻，指人或其良心)過於小心的；善感的；敏感的。 **queas·ily** /-ɪlɪ ; -əlɪ/ *adv* **queasi·ness** *n*

queen /kwiːn ; kwin/ *n* **1** woman ruler in her own right: 女王: *the Q~ of England;* 英國女王； *Q~ Elizabeth II.* 女王伊利莎白二世。 **2** wife of a king: 皇后: *King George VI and Q~ Elizabeth.* 英王喬治六世與伊利莎白皇后。 **3** ~ **dowager,** widow of a king. 孀居之皇后；太后。 ~ **mother,** ~ dowager who is the mother of a reigning Sovereign. 皇太后；母后。 **4** woman regarded as first of a group: 一羣婦女中之第一名；美女；佳麗: *the ~ of the May;* 五月皇后； *'May Q~,* girl chosen as ~ in old-time May Day ceremonies; 五月皇后(舊時在 May Day 慶祝時節選出者)； town or place regarded as occupying a leading position: 居於首要地位的城市或地方；首邑: *Venice, the ~ of the Adriatic.* 威尼斯，亞得里亞海沿岸的首要都市。 **'beauty ~,** winner of a beauty contest. 選美皇后。 **5** ~ **ant／bee／wasp,** fertile, egg-producing ant etc. 蟻王(蜂王，黃蜂王)。 **6** (chess) most powerful piece for attack or defence, ⇨ the illus at chess; (棋)攻守最有力的棋子；后棋(參看 chess 之挿圖)； (cards) one with the picture of a ~: (紙牌)后牌: *the ~ of spades／hearts.* 黑桃(紅心)后牌。 **7** ⚠ (GB derog sl) effeminate male homosexual. (諱)(英俚，貶)女性化的男子同性戀者。□ *vt* ~ ***it (over sb),*** act like a ~; assume the leadership. 行動若一女王；擔起領導責任。 **~·ly** *adj* like a ~; fit for a ~; majestic; generous: 像女王的；適於女王的；威嚴的；慷慨的: *~ly robes;* 女王穿的袍； *her ~ly duties.* 她做女王的職責。

queer /kwɪə(r); kwɪr/ *adj* **1** strange; unusual: 奇怪的;不平常的: *a ~ way of talking.* 一種古怪的講話方式。 **2** causing doubt or suspicion: 引起疑慮或懷疑的: *a ~ character;* 一個可疑的人; *~ noises in the attic.* 頂樓中可疑的鬧聲。 **3** (colloq) unwell; faint: (俗)不適的;眩暈的: *feel very ~.* 感覺非常不適。 **4** ⚠ (derog sl) homosexual. (諱)(貶俚)同性戀的。 **5** ***in 'Q~ Street,*** (GB sl) in debt; in trouble. (英俚)負債;在困難中。□ *n* ⚠ (derog sl) homosexual. (諱)(貶俚)同性戀者。□ *vt* [VP6A] (sl) put out of order; cause to go wrong, (俚)破壞;使失敗, esp 尤用於 *~ sb's pitch,* ⇨ pitch¹(1). **~·ly** *adv* **~·ness** *n*

quell /kwel; kwɛl/ *vt* [VP6A] (poet and rhet) suppress, subdue (a rebellion, rebels, opposition). (詩,修辭)鎮壓;壓制(叛亂、叛徒、反對)。

quench /kwentʃ; kwɛntʃ/ *vt* [VP6A] **1** put out (flames, fire). 熄滅(焰、火)。 **2** satisfy (thirst). 解除(口渴)。 **3** put an end to (hope). 結束;滅絕(希望)。 **4** cool in water: 使在水中變冷;淬火;冷浸: *~ steel.* 淬鋼。 **~·less** *adj* (liter) that cannot be, or is never, ~ed: (文)無法或永不熄滅、解除、結束的: *a ~less flame.* 一個無法熄滅的火焰。

quern /kwɜːn; kwɝn/ *n* hand-mill for grinding corn; small hand-mill for pepper, etc. (磨穀粉之)手磨;(研胡椒等之)小型手磨。

queru·lous /ˈkwerʊləs; ˈkwɛrələs/ *adj* full of complaints; fretful: 多牢騷的;愛抱怨的;易怒的: *in a ~ tone.* 以抱怨的語調。 **~·ly** *adv* **~·ness** *n*

query /ˈkwɪərɪ; ˈkwɪrɪ/ *n* [C] (*pl* -ries) **1** question, esp one raising a doubt about the truth of sth: 疑問(尤指對某事物的眞實性發生懷疑者): *raise a ~.* 發問。 **2** the mark (?) put against sth, eg in the margin of a document, as a sign of doubt. (畫於某物旁邊表示懷疑之)問號(?)(例如畫於一文件的邊上者)。□ *vt* **1** [VP10] ***~ whether/if,*** inquire: 詢問: *I ~ whether his word can be relied on.* 我懷疑他的話是否可靠。 **2** [VP6A] express doubt about: 對…表示懷疑: *~ a person's instructions.* 懷疑一個人的指示。 **3** [VP6A] put the mark (?) against. 畫問號(?)於。

quest /kwest; kwɛst/ *n* [C] (rhet) search or pursuit: (修辭)尋求;追求: *the ~ for gold.* 尋找金子。 ***in ~ of,*** (old or liter use) seeking for, trying to find: (舊用法或文學用法)尋找; 設法找到: *He went off in ~ of food.* 他出去找食物。□ *vi* [VP3A] ***~ for,*** (esp of dogs) look for; (rhet) go about in ~ of: (尤指狗)尋找;(修辭)到處尋找: *~ing for further evidence.* 到處尋找更多的證據。

ques·tion¹ /ˈkwestʃən; ˈkwɛstʃən/ *n* **1** sentence which by word-order, use of interrogative words (*who, why,* etc) or intonation, requests information, an answer, etc: 疑問句;問題;詢問;質問: *ask a lot of ~s;* 詢問很多問題; *put a ~ to sb.* 向某人提出一疑問。 **'~-mark** *n* the mark (?). 問號(?)。⇨ App 9. 參看附錄九。 **'~-master** *n* (in panel games) chairman. (廣播或電視等中之)答問節目主持人。 **'~ time,** (in the House of Commons) period of time during which ministers answer ~s put to them by members. 質詢時間;質詢期(英國內閣閣員答覆下議院議員之質詢時間)。 **2** sth about which there is discussion; sth which needs to be decided; inquiry; problem; affair: 討論中之事物;需要決定之事物;查詢;問題;事件: *a difficult/vexed ~;* 一個困難的(爭論不休的)問題; *economic ~s.* 經濟問題。 *Success is only a ~ of time,* will certainly come sooner or later. 成功僅係時間問題(遲早會成功)。 *The ~ is...,* What we want to know, what we must decide, is.... 問題是…;我們要知道的是…;我們必須決定的是…。 *That's not the ~,* not the matter being discussed. 那不在討論範圍之內。 ***in ~,*** being talked about: 正被談論的: *Where's the man in ~?* 我們談論的那個人在哪裏? ***out of the ~,*** impossible; not to be discussed at all: 不可能;根本不必討論: *We can't go out in this weather; it's out of the ~.* 我們不能在這種天氣下出去,這事免談了。 ***be some/no, etc ~ of,*** some/no, etc discussion of: 對…有些(沒有等)討論: *There was no ~ of my being invited to become Chairman,* that was not discussed or proposed. 我被邀請擔任主席這件事並未被討論或提出。 ***beg the ~,*** ⇨ beg(2). ***come into ~,*** be discussed, become of practical importance: 被討論;變爲有實際重要性: *If sending me in a spacecraft to the moon ever comes into ~, I shall refuse without hesitation.* 如果提出以太空船送我到月球的話,我將毫不猶疑地拒絕。 **Q~!** (at a public meeting) used to warn a speaker that he is not keeping to the subject being discussed, or (less correctly) to express doubt about the truth of sth he has said. (在公共集會上用以警告發言者說話離題)不要扯到題外去!(較不精確用法;對發言者所說的話的眞實性表示疑問)有問題! ***put the ~,*** (at a meeting) ask those present to record their votes for or against the proposal. (在集會上)要求出席者投票決定;提付表決。 **3** [U] (the putting forward of) doubt, objection: 懷疑;反對;懷疑或反對之提出: *There is no ~ about/some ~ as to his honesty.* 他的誠實毫無(有些)問題。 *There is no ~ but that he will* (= He will undoubtedly) *succeed.* 他會成功是確然無疑的事。 ***beyond (all)/without ~,*** certain(ly); without doubt: 毫無疑問: *His integrity is beyond all ~.* 他的廉正是毋庸置疑的。 *Without ~, he's the best man for the job.* 毫無疑問的,他是做這工作的最佳人選。 ***call sth in ~,*** raise objections to, express doubt about, it: 對…提出反對,對…表示懷疑: *No one has ever called my honesty in ~.* 沒有人對我的誠實有所懷疑。 *His conduct was called in ~.* 他的行爲被人懷疑。

ques·tion² /ˈkwestʃən; ˈkwɛstʃən/ *vt* **1** [VP6A] ask a ~ or ~s of; examine: 詢問;審問: *a two-hour ~ing session.* 兩小時的審問庭期。 *He was ~ed by the police.* 他被警方審問。 *They ~ed the Conservative candidate on his views.* 他們詢問保守黨候選人的意見。 **2** [VP6A, 10] ***~ (whether/if),*** express or feel doubt about: 對…表示或感到懷疑: *~ sb's veracity;* 懷疑某人的誠實; *~ the value* (or *importance*) *of compulsory games at school.* 懷疑學校中强迫運動的價值(重要性)。 *I ~ whether his proposal will be approved.* 我懷疑他的提議是否會被批准。 **~·able** /-əbl; -əbl̩/ *adj* which may be ~ed(2): 可疑的;有問題的;引起爭論的: *a ~able assertion.* 一個頗有問題的主張。 **~·ably** /-əblɪ; -əblɪ/ *adv* **~er** *n* person who ~s(1). 詢問者;審問者。 **~·ing·ly** *adv* in a ~ing manner. 詢問地;表示疑問地。

ques·tion·naire /ˌkwestʃəˈneə(r); ˌkwɛstʃənˈɛr/ *n* list of (usu printed) questions to be answered by a group of people, esp to get facts or information, or for a survey. 調查表;問題單;問卷(由一些人來回答,以獲得資料或進行全面的調查)。

quet·zal /ˈkwetsl *US:* ketˈsæl; kɛtˈsɑl/ *n* beautiful bird of Central America; monetary unit of Guatemala. 中美產的一種美麗的鳥;瓜地馬拉的貨幣單位。

queue /kjuː; kju/ *n* **1** line of people waiting for their turn (eg to enter a cinema, get on a bus, buy sth): 一排等待(進入電影院、上公共汽車、購物等)的人;長龍: *form a ~;* 排長龍; *stand in a ~.* 排隊。 ***jump the ~,*** ⇨ jump²(6). **2** line of vehicles waiting to proceed: 等待前進的一列車輛: *a ~ of cars held up by the traffic lights.* 爲交通燈所攔住的一長列汽車。 **3** plait of hair hanging down over the back of the neck (eg part of a wig, as worn by men in Europe in former times). 辮子(如從前歐洲男人所戴假髮的一部分)。□ *vi* [VP2A, C, 3A] ***~ (up) (for sth),*** get into, be in, a ~: 排成長隊: *~ing for a bus;* 排長隊等公共汽車; *~ up to buy tickets for the film.* 排隊買電影票。

quibble /ˈkwɪbl; ˈkwɪbl/ *n* [C] evasion of the main point of an argument, attempt to escape giving an honest answer, by using a secondary or doubtful meaning of a word or phrase. 避開議論之重

點;避重就輕的回答;支吾;遁辭。□ *vi* ~ ***(over),*** use ~s; argue about small points or differences: 用遁辭;爭辯不重要之點或異見: ~ *over trivialities.* 爭辯瑣屑之事。**quib·bler** *n* **quib·bling** *adj*

quiche /kiːʃ ; kiʃ/ *n* open tart with savoury filling; flan. 一種餡餅。

quick /kwɪk ; kwɪk/ *adj* (-er, -est) **1** moving fast; able to move fast and do things in a short time; done in a short time: 快的;迅速的;動作敏捷的;在短時間內做的: *a ~ train／worker;* 行駛快速的火車(動作敏捷的工人); *walking at a ~ pace;* 快步行走; *have a ~ meal;* 吃一頓快餐; *find ~ ways of doing sth／getting somewhere.* 發現做某事(到某地)之捷徑。*Be ~ about it!* Hurry up! 趕快! *Try to be a little ~er.* 設法快一點兒。*She's as ~ as lightning.* 她迅如閃電。*The flashes of lightning came in ~ succession,* at very short intervals of time. 閃電頻頻接續而來。*We just have time for a ~ one,* (usu = a ~ (alcoholic) drink). 我們時間不多,只能快飲。***(in) ~ time,*** (at) the ordinary rate of marching for soldiers (about four miles an hour). (以)齊步(行軍的普通速度,約每小時四哩)。~ ***march*** *int* (command to) begin marching in ~ time. (口令)齊步走。 **ˈ~·step** *n* ballroom dance with both quick and slow steps. 社交舞中的活潑舞步。ˌ**~-ˈchange** *attrib adj* (of an actor, etc) ~ly changing his appearance, costume, etc to play another part: (指演員等)迅速換裝以演另一脚色的: *a ~-ˈchange artist.* 一個換裝迅速的藝人。**ˈ~-freeze** *vt* freeze (food) very ~ly so as to keep the natural flavours unchanged: 快速冷凍(食物)以保持其原有味道: *~-frozen foods.* 速凍的食物。 **2** lively; bright; active; prompt: 活潑的;伶俐的;機敏的;立即的: ~ *to understand;* 敏於領悟的; *a ~ ear for music;* 對音樂感受靈敏的耳朵; ~ *to make up one's mind／to seize an opportunity;* 敏於下決心(抓住機會); ~ *at figures;* 敏於計算數字; *a* ~ (= intelligent) *child;* 一個聰穎的小孩; *not very ~,* (colloq, of a child) rather dull or stupid; (俗,指兒童)相當遲鈍或笨的; *a ~ temper,* soon aroused. 性情急躁。ˌ**~-ˈeared／-ˈeyed／-ˈsighted／-ˈtempered／-ˌwitted** *adjj* having ~ ears／eyes／sight, etc. 聽覺靈敏的(眼力敏銳的;眼快的;性情急躁的;才思敏捷的)。**3** (old use) living. (舊用法)活的。***the ~ and the dead.*** 生者與死者。□ *n* [U] tender or sensitive flesh below the skin, esp the nails: 皮下(尤指指甲下)的細嫩或敏感的肉: *bite one's nails to the ~.* 咬指甲直咬到下面的肉。***cut／touch sb to the ~,*** hurt his feelings deeply. 深深傷害某人的感情。□ *adv* (-er, -est) **1** (common in colloq use for *quickly,* always placed after the *v*): (在口語中常用以代替 quickly, 總是放在動詞後面): *You're walking too ~ for me.* 你走得太快了,我追不上。*Can't you run ~er?* 你不能跑快一點兒嗎? *He wants to get rich ~.* 他想很快地發財。*I don't know any get-rich-~ methods.* 我不知道任何迅速致富的方法。**2** (in compounds, for ~*ly*): (在複合字中,代替 quickly): *a ~-firing gun.* 速射槍。**~·ly** *adv* in a ~ manner: 迅速地;快地: *You speak too ~ly.* 你說得太快。*He ~ly changed his clothes.* 他迅速地換衣服。**~·ness** *n*

quicken /ˈkwɪkən ; ˈkwɪkən/ *vt, vi* [VP6A, 2A] **1** make or become quick(er): 使(較)快;變為(較)快: *We ~ed our pace.* 我們加快腳步。*Our pace ~ed.* 我們的腳步加快了。 **2** make or become more lively, vigorous or active: 使或變為更活潑、有力或敏捷: *Good literature ~s the imagination.* 好的文學作品能激發想像力。*His pulse ~ed.* 他的脈搏加快。*The child ~ed in her womb,* She felt its movement for the first time. 她第一次感到胎兒在她的子宮中動。

quickie /ˈkwɪkɪ ; ˈkwɪkɪ/ *n* (colloq) sth made or done very quickly. (俗)倉促製成的物品。

quick·lime /ˈkwɪklaɪm ; ˈkwɪkˌlaɪm/ *n* unslaked lime. 生石灰。⇨ lime¹(1).

quick·sand /ˈkwɪksænd ; ˈkwɪkˌsænd/ *n* [C] (area of) loose, wet, deep sand which sucks down men, animals, vehicles, etc that try to cross it. 流沙(區)。

quick·set /ˈkwɪkset ; ˈkwɪkˌsɛt/ *adj* (of hedges) formed of living plants, esp hawthorn, set in the ground to grow. (指樹籬)插樹做成的; (尤指) 插山楂樹做成的。

quick·sil·ver /ˈkwɪksɪlvə(r) ; ˈkwɪkˌsɪlvɚ/ *n* [U] mercury. 水銀;汞。

quick·step /ˈkwɪkstep ; ˈkwɪkˌstɛp/ *n* ⇨ quick(1).

quid¹ /kwɪd ; kwɪd/ *n* lump of chewing tobacco. 含在口中咀嚼的煙草塊。

quid² /kwɪd ; kwɪd/ *n* (GB, sl; *pl* unchanged) pound: (英俚,複數不變)鎊: *earning fifty quid* (= £50) *a week.* 每週賺五十鎊。

quid pro quo /ˌkwɪd prəʊ ˈkwəʊ ; ˌkwɪdproˈkwo/ *n* (Lat) sth given or returned as the equivalent of sth else. (拉)補償物;交換物。

qui·esc·ent /kwaɪˈesnt ; kwaɪˈɛsnt/ *adj* at rest; motionless; passive. 安靜的;靜止的;不活動的。**~·ly** *adv* **qui·esc·ence** /-sns ; -sns/ *n*

quiet /ˈkwaɪət ; ˈkwaɪət/ *adj* (-er, -est) **1** with little or no movement or sound: 靜止的;寧靜的: *a ~ sea;* 一片平靜無浪的海; *a ~ evening;* 一個寧靜的傍晚; ~ *footsteps.* 輕輕的脚步。 **2** free from excitement, trouble, anxiety: 沒有激動、煩惱、憂慮的;心情寧靜的: *live a ~ life in the country;* 在鄉間過一種悠然自在的生活; *have a ~ mind;* 有寧靜心境; ~ *times.* 平靜的時代。**3** gentle; not rough (in disposition, etc): 溫柔的;嫻靜的: ~ *children;* 溫雅的孩子; *a ~ old lady.* 一位嫻靜的老婦。 **4** (of colours) not bright. (指顏色)樸素的。 **5** not open or revealed: 未予公開或洩露的;隱密的: *harbouring ~ resentment.* 暗含憤懣。***keep sth ~,*** keep it secret. 對某事保密。***on the ~,*** (or, sl, 或俚, ***on the qt*** /ˌkjuː ˈtiː ; ˌkjuˈti/), secretly: 秘密地;偷偷地: *have a drink on the ~;* 偷偷地喝杯酒; *tell sb sth on the ~,* in confidence. 秘密地將某事告訴某人。□ *n* [U] state of being ~ (all senses): 靜止、寧靜、嫻靜、樸素、隱密等的狀態: *in the ~ of the night;* 在夜闌人靜時; *have an hour's ~,* an hour free from activity, disturbance, etc; 享受一小時的清靜; *live in peace and ~;* 生活於和平寧靜中; *a period of ~ after an election,* free from all the activity, etc that usu accompanies an election. 選舉後一段平靜的日子。□ *vt, vi* (more usu 較常用 **~en** /ˈkwaɪətn ; ˈkwaɪətn/) [VP6A, 15B, 2C] make or become ~: 使或變為平靜: *~(en) a fretful child;* 讓一個急躁的孩子平靜下來; *~(en) sb's fears／suspicions.* 消除某人的恐懼(疑慮)。*The city ~ed／~ened down after the political disturbances.* 在政治騷亂後這個城市平靜下來。**~·ly** *adv* **~·ness** *n*

quiet·ism /ˈkwaɪɪtɪzəm ; ˈkwaɪətɪzm/ *n* [U] (as a form of religious mysticism) the abandoning of all desire, with a passive acceptance of whatever comes. 寂靜主義(棄絕一切慾望,消極接受發生的一切,為一種神秘的宗教運動)。**quiet·ist** /-ɪst ; -ɪst/ *n* person who follows this principle. 寂靜主義者。

quiet·ude /ˈkwaɪɪtjuːd *US:* -tuːd ; ˈkwaɪəˌtjud/ *n* (liter) stillness; tranquillity. (文)寂靜;平靜;寧靜。

qui·etus /kwaɪˈiːtəs ; kwaɪˈitəs/ *n* (formal) final settlement (eg of a debt); release from life; extinction: (正式用語) 解除; 清除(例如債務); 根絕生命; 滅絕;死: *give sb his ~,* put an end to his life. 結束某人的生命。

quiff /kwɪf ; kwɪf/ *n* lock of hair brushed up above the forehead. 梳在額上的鬈髮。

quill /kwɪl ; kwɪl/ *n* **1** **ˈ~(-feather),** large wing or tail feather; (hollow stem of) such a feather as formerly used for writing with: 翼或尾上的大羽毛、羽莖;翮;(昔時)此等羽莖做的筆: *a ~ pen.* 羽筆。 **2** long, sharp, stiff spine of a porcupine. 豪豬的長而尖硬的刺。

quilt /kwɪlt ; kwɪlt/ *n* thick bed-covering of two layers of cloth padded with soft material kept in place by crossed lines of stitches. 被;棉被。

duvet. □ *vt* make in the form of a ~, ie with soft material between layers of cloth: 製成被狀(卽在兩層布間加輕而軟的東西): *a ~ed dressing-gown.* 中間襯有輕軟之物的晨衣。

quin /kwɪn ; kwɪn/ *n* (colloq abbr of) quintuplet. (俗) 爲 quintuplet 之略。

quince /kwɪns ; kwɪns/ *n* (tree with) hard, acid, pear-shaped fruit, deep yellow when ripe, used in jams and jellies. 榲桲(爲一種硬、酸、梨形水果,成熟後爲深黃色,用於製果醬與凍子);榲桲樹。

quin·cen·ten·ary /ˌkwɪnsen'ti:nərɪ *US:* -'sentənerɪ ; kwɪn'sɛntɪˌnɛrɪ/ *adj, n* (of the) 500th anniversary. 五百周年紀念(的)。

quin·ine /kwɪ'ni:n *US:* 'kwaɪnaɪn ; 'kwaɪnaɪn/ *n* [U] bitter liquid made from the bark of a tree and used as a medicine for fevers and a flavouring in drinks. 奎寧;金雞納(從一種樹皮中提煉的苦味液體,用爲治療發燒的藥物及飲料中的調味物)。

Quin·qua·ges·ima /ˌkwɪŋkwə'dʒesɪmə ; ˌkwɪnkwə'dʒɛsəmə/ *n* the Sunday before Lent. 四旬齋前的星期日。

quinsy /'kwɪnzɪ ; 'kwɪnzɪ/ *n* [U] inflammation of the throat with discharge of pus from the tonsils. 扁桃腺發炎;(膿性)咽門炎。

quin·tal /'kwɪntl ; 'kwɪntl̩/ *n* unit of weight, 100 or 112 lb or 100 kilograms. 重量單位(100或112磅,或100公斤)。

quin·tes·sence /kwɪn'tesns ; kwɪn'tɛsn̩s/ *n* **1** perfect example: 最完美的榜樣: *the ~ of virtue／politeness.* 美德(禮貌)的最好榜樣。**2** essential part. 精華;本質。

quin·tet /kwɪn'tet ; kwɪn'tɛt/ *n* (piece of music for) group of five players or singers: 五位演奏者或歌唱者組成之一組;五重唱(曲);五重奏(曲): *piano ~,* string quartet and piano; 鋼琴五重奏(絃樂四重奏和鋼琴合奏); *string ~,* string quartet and an additional cello or viola; 絃樂五重奏(絃樂四重奏再加上一大提琴或中音提琴); *wind ~,* bassoon, clarinet, flute, horn and oboe. 管樂(巴頌管、豎笛、笛、喇叭和雙簧管)五重奏。

quin·tu·plet /'kwɪntjuːplet *US:* kwɪn'tu:plɪt ; 'kwɪntəplɪt/ *n* (common abbr 通常略作 *quin*) one of five children at a birth. (usu *pl: two of the ~s* is commoner than *two ~s*). 五胞胎中之一個(常用複數: two of the ~s 比 two ~s 常用)。

quip /kwɪp ; kwɪp/ *n* clever, witty or sarcastic remark or saying; quibble. 妙語;警語;諷刺語;雙關語;遁辭。□ *vi* (-pp-) make ~s. 譏諷;作妙語、警語、遁辭。

quire /'kwaɪə(r) ; kwaɪr/ *n* twenty-four sheets of writing-paper: 二十四張爲一帖的寫字紙: *buy／sell paper by the ~／in ~s.* 成帖(二十四張)買(賣)紙。

quirk /kwɜ:k ; kwɝk/ *n* habit or action peculiar to sb／sth; foible: 特有的習性或行爲;怪癖: *One of his ~s is sleeping with his socks on.* 他的怪癖之一是穿着襪子睡覺。

quis·ling /'kwɪzlɪŋ ; 'kwɪzlɪŋ/ *n* person who co-operates with the authorities of an enemy country who are occupying his country. (與佔領本國之敵人當局合作的)賣國賊;通敵者。

quit[1] /kwɪt ; kwɪt/ *pred adj* free, clear: 免除的;清除的: *We are well ~ of him,* fortunate to be rid of him. 我們幸而把他擺脫開了。

quit[2] /kwɪt ; kwɪt/ *vt, vi* (-tt-, US also -t-; *pt, pp* ~ted or ~) **1** [VP6A, 2A] go away from; leave: 離開;離去: *I ~ted him in disgust.* 我懷着嫌惡離開了他。*We've had notice to ~,* a warning that we must give up the house we rent. 我們已得到搬家的通知。*I've given my secretary notice to ~,* told her that she must leave my service. 我已通知我的秘書離職。 **2** [VP6A, D] stop: 停止: *~ work when the siren sounds;* 汽笛響時停止工作; *~ grumbling.* 停止抱怨。*Q~ that!* Stop doing that! 停止做那事! **3** (old use; reflex) acquit: (舊用法;反身式)行動;處己: *They ~ted themselves like heroes.* 他們的行爲像英雄。**~·ter** *n* (colloq) person who does not finish what he has started, esp sth undertaken as a duty. (俗)半途而廢之人;虎頭蛇尾之人;(尤指)放棄職責者。

quite /kwaɪt ; kwaɪt/ *adv* **1** completely; altogether: 完全地;澈底地: *He has ~ recovered from his illness.* 他已完全康復。*I ~ agree／understand.* 我十分同意(了解)。 *She was ~ alone.* 她非常孤獨。*See that your watch is ~* (= exactly) *right.* 務必要把你的錶對得非常準確。*That man is not ~ acceptable.* 那個人不大受歡迎。*It was ~* (= at least) *six weeks ago.* 至少是六週以前。*That's ~ another* (ie a completely different) *story.* 那完全是另外一回事。 *~ **the thing,*** (colloq) what is considered correct, fashionable, etc: (俗) 被認爲是正確、流行等的東西: *These Italian dress materials are ~ the thing this summer.* 這些義大利衣料今夏很流行。**2** to a certain extent; more or less; in some degree: 到某種範圍;或多或少;在某種程度內;相當地: (preceding articles and *adjj*) (放在冠詞和形容詞之前) *~ a good player.* 一個相當不錯的運動員。*It's ~ warm today.* 今天的天氣相當暖和。 *He was ~ polite, but he wasn't ready to help me.* 他相當客氣,但他並不願意幫助我。 *She ~ likes him, but not enough to marry him.* 她相當喜歡他,但還不到跟他結婚的程度。 **3** really; truly: 眞正地;眞實地: *They are both ~ young.* 他們倆都很年輕。*She's ~ a beauty.* 她眞是個美人。*I believe they're ~ happy together.* 我認爲他們在一起的確很幸福。 **4** (used to indicate agreement, understanding, polite acquiescence): (用以表示同意、了解、禮貌的默許): A: *'It's a difficult situation.'* B: *'Q~ (so)!'* 甲:'那是個很棘手的情勢。' 乙:'的確如此!' A: *'I'm so sorry; I'm afraid I've taken your seat.'* B: *'Oh, that's ~ all right.'* 甲:'眞抱歉,我恐怕坐在你的座位上了。' 乙:'哦,沒關係。'

quits /kwɪts ; kwɪts/ *pred adj* ***be ~ (with sb),*** be on even terms (by repaying a debt of money, punishment, etc): (由償付債務、給予處罰等而)與某人處於平等的關係;不分勝負;兩相抵消: *We're ~ now.* 我們現在兩不相欠(不分勝負)。 *I'll be ~ with him,* will have my revenge. 我要向他報復。 ***call it ~,*** agree that things are even, that a dispute or quarrel may cease. 同意不分勝負而使爭論或爭吵結束。***double or ~,*** ⇨ double[3] (1).

quit·tance /'kwɪtns ; 'kwɪtn̩s/ *n* (document giving) release from an obligation or debt. 免除義務或債務(之文件)。

quiver[1] /'kwɪvə(r) ; 'kwɪvɚ/ *n* archer's sheath for carrying arrows. 箭囊。

quiver[2] /'kwɪvə(r) ; 'kwɪvɚ/ *vt, vi* [VP6A, 2A] (cause to) tremble slightly or vibrate: (使)微震;震顫: *a ~ing leaf.* 一片顫動的葉子。*The moth ~ed its wings.* 蛾顫動其翼。□ *n* ~ing sound or movement. 震顫的聲音或動作。

qui vive /ˌki: 'vi:v ; ˌki 'viv/ *n* (only in) (僅用於) ***on the ~,*** on the alert; watchful. 警戒中;警覺的。

quix·otic /kwɪk'sɒtɪk ; kwɪk'sɑtɪk/ *adj* generous, unselfish, imaginative, in a way that disregards one's own welfare. (不顧自己利益地)慷慨,不自私或富於幻想的。**quix·oti·cally** /-klɪ ; -klɪ/ *adv*

quiz /kwɪz ; kwɪz/ *vt* (-zz-) [VP6A] **1** ask questions of, as a test of knowledge. (對知識等之)測驗;小考。 **2** (archaic) make fun of; tease; stare at. (古)戲弄;嘲弄;注視。□ *n* **1** general knowledge test; (broadcasting) game in which members of a panel undergo such a test. 一般知識測驗;小考;(廣播)猜謎或答問節目;益智節目。**'~-master,** = question-master. **2** (archaic) amused, supercilious look. (古)高興而又傲慢的樣子。

quiz·zi·cal /'kwɪzɪkl ; 'kwɪzɪkl̩/ *adj* questioning and teasing: 探詢的;嘲弄的;揶揄的: *a ~ smile.* 一個嘲弄的微笑。**~ly** /-klɪ ; -klɪ/ *adv*

quoin /kɔɪn ; kɔɪn/ *n* exterior angle in the brickwork or stonework of a building; cornerstone. (磚石等建築物之)突角;外角;角石;隅石。

quoit /kɔɪt *US:* kwɔɪt ; kwɔɪt/ *n* ring (of metal,

rubber, rope) to be thrown at a peg so as to encircle it; (*pl*) this game (as often played on the deck of a ship). (擲環套樁遊戲等中用之)鐵圈;橡皮圈;繩圈;(複)(在甲板等上玩的)擲環套樁遊戲;扔環遊戲;丟繩圈。

Quonset /ˈkwɒnsɪt ; ˈkwɑnsɪt/ *n* **ˈ~ (hut),** (US) (P) large prefabricated hut, usu of corrugated iron, semicircular at each end and with a rounded roof, similar to, but much larger than, a Nissen hut. (美)(商標)活動房屋(一種很大的簡單房屋，通常用波狀鐵皮做成，每端均呈半圓形，有一圓形屋頂，同 Nissen hut 形式相似，但大得多)。

quo·rum /ˈkwɔːrəm ; ˈkworəm/ *n* (*pl* ~s) number of persons who must, by the rules, be present at a meeting (of a committee, etc) before its proceedings can have authority: 法定人數: *have/form a ~.* 够(構成)法定人數。

quota /ˈkwəʊtə ; ˈkwotə/ *n* (*pl* ~s) limited share, amount or number, esp a quantity of goods allowed to be manufactured, sold, etc or number, eg of immigrants allowed to enter a country: 配額;限額(尤指貨物之製造，出售或移民入境之定額): *The village was unable to raise its ~ of men for the army.* 該村無法徵集到所分配的壯丁名額。*The ~ of immigrants for this year has already been filled.* 本年的移民額已滿。

quo·ta·tion /kwəʊˈteɪʃn ; kwoˈteʃən/ *n* **1** [U] quoting(1). 引述;引用。 **2** [C] sth quoted(1): 引用文;引用語: *~s from Shakespeare.* 引自莎士比亞的作品中的文句。**ˈ~ marks,** the marks " " or ' ' enclosing words quoted. 引號。⇨ App 9. 參看附錄九。 **3** [C] statement of the current price of an article, etc: 物品等的時價;行市;行情表: *the latest ~s from the Stock Exchange.* 來自證券交易所的最近的行情。 **4** [C] estimate of the cost of a piece of work: 報價單: *Can you give me a ~ for building a garage?* 你能不能給我一張建造一汽車間的報價單?

quote /kwəʊt ; kwot/ *vt* **1** [VP6A, 14] **~ *(from)*,** repeat, write (words used by another); repeat or write words (from a book, an author, etc): 引述(他人的話);引用(一書，作者等): *~ a verse from the Bible;* 引用聖經中的一節; *~ the Bible.* 引述聖經。*Is Shakespeare the author most frequently ~d from?* 莎士比亞是最常被引用的作家嗎? *He is ~d as having said that there will be an election this autumn.* 有人引述他的話說今秋將舉行選舉。 **2** [VP6A,13A] give (a reference, etc) to support a statement: 提供(引證等)以支持一陳述: *Can you ~ (me) a recent instance?* 你能舉出一個最近的例證嗎? **3** [VP6A] name, mention (a price): 提出(價格);報(價): *This is the best price I can ~ you.* 這是我能向你提出的最好的價錢了。*The shares are ~d on the Stock Exchange at 80p.* 證券交易所公佈的這些股票的價格是八十辨士。□ *n* (colloq) sth ~d, esp sth witty, unusual, etc; quotation (2, 3, 4). (俗)引述的話(尤指富有機智，不平常者);引用文;行情表;報價單。**quot·able** /-əbl ; -əbḷ/ *adj* that can be, or deserves to be, ~d. 能够或值得引用，引證，報價的。**quo·ta·bil·ity** /ˌkwəʊtəˈbɪlətɪ ; ˌkwotəˈbɪlɪtɪ/ *n* [U].

quoth /kwəʊθ ; kwoθ/ *vt* (1st and 3rd person *sing, pt* only) (archaic) said: (古)說(僅用於第一和第三人稱，單數，過去式): *~ I/he/she.* 我(他，她)說過。*Q~ the raven, 'Nevermore!'* 大烏鴉說，'永遠不再!'

quo·tid·ian /kwəʊˈtɪdɪən ; kwoˈtɪdɪən/ *adj* (of a fever) recurring every day. (指熱病)每日發作的。

quo·tient /ˈkwəʊʃnt ; ˈkwoʃənt/ *n* (maths) number obtained by dividing one number by another. (數學)商數;商。

Rr

R, r /ɑː(r) ; ɑr/ (*pl* R's, r's) the eighteenth letter of the English alphabet. 英文字母之第十八個字母。**the three R's,** reading, (w)riting and (a)rithmetic as the basis of an elementary education. 讀、寫、算(為初等教育之基礎)。

rabbi /ˈræbaɪ ; ˈræbaɪ/ *n* teacher of the Jewish law; (title of a) spiritual leader of a Jewish congregation. 猶太法學專家;猶太教教士(的頭銜);(猶太人的)先生;老師。**rab·bini·cal** /rəˈbɪnɪkl ; ræˈbɪnɪkḷ/ *adj* of ~s, their learning, writings, etc. 猶太法學專家的;猶太法學專家之學問、著作等的。

rab·bit /ˈræbɪt ; ˈræbɪt/ *n* **1** small burrowing animal of the hare family, brownish-grey in its natural state, black or white or bluish-grey in domestic varieties. 兔。⇨ the illus at small. 參看 small 之插圖。**ˈ~-hole/-burrow** *nn* hole in which wild ~s live. 野兔洞;野兔穴。**ˈ~-hutch** *n* wooden cage for domestic ~s. 兔籠;兔檻。**ˈ~-punch** *n* punch on the back of the neck. 打在頸背的一拳。**ˈ~-warren** *n* area of land full of ~-burrows; (fig) area of narrow, winding streets or rooms and passages. 野兔繁殖區;(喻)有很多狹窄彎曲街道之地區;有很多房間及走道之地區。**Welsh ~,** = rarebit. **2** (colloq) poor performer at any game, esp tennis. (俗)技術拙劣的運動員(尤指網球員)。□ *vi* (-tt-) hunt ~s: 獵兔: *go ~ting.* 去獵兔。

rabble /ˈræbl ; ˈræbḷ/ *n* **1** disorderly crowd; mob. 烏合之眾;暴民。**ˈ~-rousing** *adj* inciting, designed to rouse, the passions of the mob: 激發或煽動暴民之情緒的: *~-rousing speeches/speakers.* 煽動暴民之演說(演說者)。**2 the ~,** (contemptuous) the lower classes of the populace. (輕蔑語)下層階級之人民。

Rab·elais·ian /ˌræbəˈleɪzɪən *US:* -eɪʒn ; ˌræbḷˈezɪən/ *adj* of or like the writings, marked by coarse humour and satire, of Rabelais, French writer. 法國幽默諷刺作家拉伯雷及其作品的;拉伯雷式的;作品粗俗幽默而又諷刺的。

rabid /ˈræbɪd ; ˈræbɪd/ *adj* **1** affected with rabies; mad. 患恐水症的;患狂犬病的;瘋狂的。 **2** furious; fanatical; violent: 狂怒的;狂熱的;狂暴的: *~ hate;* 痛恨; *a ~ Socialist/Conservative,* one with extreme views, violently expressed. 一個思想偏激的社會(保守)主義者。

ra·bies /ˈreɪbiːz ; ˈrebiz/ *n* [U] infectious disease causing madness in wolves, dogs and other animals; hydrophobia. 恐水症;狂犬病。

rac·coon = racoon.

race¹ /reɪs ; res/ *n* [C] **1** contest or competition in speed, eg in running, swimming or to see who can finish a piece of work, or get to a certain place, first: 速度競賽;比賽;賽跑: *a ˈhorse-~;* 賽馬; *a ˈboat-~;* 賽舟; *a half-ˈmile ~;* 半英里賽跑; *run a ~ with sb;* 同某人賽跑; *a ~ for a train,* an effort to catch it. 趕火車。***a ~ against time,*** an effort to do sth before a certain time or possible event. 努力在某特定時間或可能事件前做某事;爭取時間。**ˈ~-card** *n* programme of a ~-meeting with a list of ~s and names of horses. (賽馬大會中的)賽馬節目單。**ˈ~-course** *n* ground where horse-~s are run. 賽馬場。**ˈ~-horse** *n* horse specially bred for running ~s. 供賽馬用的馬。**ˈ~-meeting** *n* occasion when a number of horse-~s are held on a certain ~-course on a certain day, or a number of successive days: 賽馬會: *the Epsom ~-meeting.* 在英國艾普孫每年一度的賽馬會。**the ~s,** ~-meeting. 賽馬大會。 **2** strong, fast current of water in the sea, a river, etc: (海，河等中的)急流: *a ˈmill-~,* the channel carrying water to the wheel of a water-mill. 引水到水力磨坊之水車的溝渠。 **3** (liter) course of the sun or moon, or (fig) of life: (文)太陽或月亮的運行；(喻)人生之路程：*His ~ is nearly run,* He is near the end of his life. 他的人生路程快走完了(他快走到生命盡頭了)。□ *vi, vt* **1** [VP2A, C, 3A, 4A] ~ ***(with/against sb),*** compete in speed, have a ~; move at full speed: 競賽速度；賽跑；比賽；全速行進：~ *along;* 快步前行；~ *over the course;* 在跑道中賽跑；*boys racing home from school;* 從學校跑回家的孩子們；~ *to see what is happening;* 跑着去看發生了甚麼事情；~ *against time;* 爭取時間；~ *with sb for a prize.* 爲一獎品同某人競賽。*I'll ~ you home,* (colloq) ~ against you to get home first. (俗)我要和你比賽誰先到家。**2** [VP2A, 6A] own or train horses for racing and take part in ~-meetings; cause (a horse) to compete in ~s: 擁有或訓練賽馬用之馬，並參加賽馬大會；以賽馬爲業；使(馬)參加競賽：*He ~s at all the big meetings.* 他參加所有大規模的賽馬會。*Are you going to ~ your horse at Newmarket next week?* 你要讓你的馬參加下週在紐馬克特的賽馬會嗎？**3** [VP6A, 15A] cause (sth or sb) to move at full speed: 使(某物或某人)全速行進：*He ~d me to the station in his car.* 他用他的車子全速把我送到車站。*The Government ~d the bill through the House,* pushed it through the House of Commons at great speed. 政府使該法案在下議院很快地通過。*Don't ~ your engine,* cause the engine to run very fast when it is not doing any work. 不要快速空轉引擎。[VP2A] *Don't let the engine ~.* 不要讓這引擎空轉太快。**racing** *n* [U] (esp) the hobby, sport or profession of running horses or motor-cars in races: (尤指)賽馬或賽車的嗜好，運動或職業：*a 'racing man;* 賽馬(車)迷；*keep a racing stable;* 有一羣比賽用的馬；*a 'racing car/yacht,* designed for racing. 競賽用的跑車(快艇)。**~r** *n* horse, boat, car, etc designed for racing. 比賽用之馬，舟，汽車等。

race² /reɪs ; res/ *n* **1** [C, U] any of several subdivisions of mankind sharing certain physical characteristics, esp colour of skin, colour and type of hair, shape of eyes and nose: 種族；人種：*the Caucasian/Mongolian/Negroid ~;* 高加索(蒙古，黑色)人種；*people of mixed ~;* 具有混血種的人們；*people of the same ~ but different culture.* 種族相同而文化不同的人們。**2** [C] (used loosely for) group of people having a common culture, history and/or language: (泛指)一羣有共同文化、歷史和(或)語言的人；民族：*the ˌAnglo-'Saxon ~;* 盎格魯·撒克遜人；*the 'German ~.* 日耳曼民族。**3** (attrib) of, between, ~s(1, 2): (形容用法)種族的；種族之間的：*Can ~ relations be improved by legislation?* 立法能改善種族關係嗎？**4** [U] ancestry; descent: 祖先；祖籍；世系：*a man of ancient and noble ~.* 一個古老貴族的後代。**5** [C] main division of any living creatures: 任何生物的種屬；族類：*the human ~,* mankind; 人類；*the 'feathered ~,* (joc) birds; (謔)鳥類；*the 'finny ~,* (joc) fish. (謔)魚類。

ra·ceme /ræ'siːm *US:* reɪ- ; re'sim/ *n* (botany) flower cluster with the separate flowers on short equal stalks springing from a main central stem, the lowest flowers opening first. (植物)串狀花；總狀花序。

racial /'reɪʃl ; 'reʃəl/ *adj* relating to race²(1, 2): 種族的；人種上的：~ *conflict/hatred/pride;* 種族的衝突(仇恨，自尊心)；~ *minorities;* 少數民族；少數種族；~ *discrimination.* 種族歧視。**~ly** /-ʃəlɪ ; -ʃəlɪ/ *adv* **~·ism** /-ʃəlɪzəm ; -ʃəlˌɪzəm/ *n* [U] tendency to ~ conflict; antagonism between different races; belief that one's own race is superior. 種族衝突；種族仇視；種族偏見；種族主義；種族優越感。**~·ist** /-ɪst ; -ɪst/ *n* person who stirs up ~ism. 煽動種族衝突者；種族主義者。

rac·ily, raci·ness ⇨ racy.

rac·ism /'reɪsɪzəm ; 'resɪzəm/ *n* racialism; belief that human abilities are determined by race. 種族主義；種族偏見；種族優越感。**rac·ist** /-ɪst ; -ɪst/ *n* racialist; believer in racialism or racism. 種族主義者；種族偏見者。

rack¹ /ræk ; ræk/ *n* **1** wooden or metal framework for holding food (esp hay) for animals (in a stable or in the fields). (在馬廐或田野中)盛動物飼料(尤指乾草)的木質或金屬架；裝草架。**2** framework with bars, pegs, etc for holding things, hanging things on, etc: 放置或掛東西用的架子：*a 'plate-~;* 盤碟架；*a 'hat-~;* 帽架；*a 'tool-~.* 工具架。**3** shelf over the seats of a railway-carriage, air-liner, bus, etc for light luggage: (火車，客機，公共汽車等座位上方放輕便行李之)行李架：*a 'luggage-~.* 行李架。**4** rod, bar or rail with teeth or cogs into which the teeth on a wheel (or pinion) fit (as used on special railways up a steep hillside). 齒條；齒軌(俾輪上或小齒輪上之齒嵌於其中，如爬陡山坡的特殊鐵軌上使用者)。⇨ the illus at gear. 參看 gear 之插圖。**'~-railway** *n* one with a third rail with cogs between the two rails on which the wheels of trains are supported. 齒軌鐵道(在承載火車輪的兩鐵軌間設有有齒的第三軌者)。

rack² /ræk ; ræk/ *n* (usu 通常作 **the ~**) instrument of torture consisting of a frame with rollers to which a person's wrists and ankles were tied so that his joints were stretched when the rollers were turned. 拷問臺(一種刑具，架上有滾輪，受刑者之腕與踝縛於滾輪上，輪轉動時，其關節卽被拉扯)。***on the ~,*** undergoing severe suffering (physical or mental). 受(身心的)極端痛苦。□ *vt* [VP6A, 15A] **1** torture by placing on the ~; (of a disease or of mental agony) inflict torture on: 置於拷問臺上折磨；(指疾病或精神痛苦)使痛苦：*~ed with pain;* 痛苦難忍；*a ~ing headache;* 劇烈的頭疼；*~ed with a bad cough;* 爲很厲害的咳嗽所苦；*~ed by remorse.* 悔恨交加。**2** ~ ***one's brains (for),*** make great mental efforts (for, in order to find, an answer, method, etc). (爲一答案，方法等)絞盡腦汁。**3** oppress (tenants) with excessive rent. 向(租戶)索取過高的租金。Hence, 由此產生，**'~-rent** *n* exorbitant rent. 過高的租金。

rack³ /ræk ; ræk/ *n* [U] (liter) drifting cloud. (文)流雲；飛雲；浮雲。

rack⁴ /ræk ; ræk/ *n* (only in) (僅用於) ***go to ~ and ruin,*** fall into a ruined state. 毀壞；朽壞；衰敗。

racket¹ /'rækɪt ; 'rækɪt/ *n* **1** (*sing* only, with *indef art* or [U]) uproar, loud noise: (僅用單數，與不定冠詞連用，或爲不可數名詞)喧囂；鬧聲：*What a ~!* 多麼大的吵鬧聲！*The drunken men in the street kicked up no end of a ~,* were very noisy and boisterous. 那些醉漢在街上大嚷大鬧。**2** [U] (time of) great social activity, hurry and bustle: 繁忙的社交活動；繁忙；繁忙的時間：*the ~ of a politician's life.* 從政者生活的繁忙。**3** [C] (colloq) dishonest way of getting money (by deceiving or threatening people, selling worthless goods, etc): (俗)詐騙；勒索：*be in on a ~,* have a share in it, be one of those who make money from it. 參與詐騙勒索。**4** [C] ordeal or trying experience. 嚴格的考驗；痛苦或難熬的經驗。***stand the ~,*** **(a)** come successfully through a test (of sth). 成功地通過(某事物的)考驗。**(b)** accept, be responsible for, the consequences (of sth); take the blame; pay the costs. 接受(某事的)後果；對(某事的)後果負責；承擔過錯；付帳。□ *vi* [VP2A, C] ~ ***(about),*** make a ~(1, 2). 喧鬧；過繁忙的社交生活：**~·eer** /ˌrækə'tɪə(r) ; ˌrækɪt'ɪr/ *n* person who is engaged in a ~(3). 詐騙者；勒索者。**~·eer·ing** *n* [U] the actions of ~eers. 詐騙、勒索的行爲。

racket², rac·quet /'rækɪt ; 'rækɪt/ *n* **1** light bat used for hitting the ball in tennis, badminton, etc. (網球，羽毛球等之)球拍。⇨ the illus at badminton, tennis. 參看 badminton, tennis 之插圖。**2** (*pl*) ball-game for two or four players in a court with four walls. (複)二或四人在四面有圍牆的球場玩的一種球戲。

rac·on·teur /ˌrækɒn'tɜː(r) ; ˌrækɑn'tɜ/ *n* person

R

who tells anecdotes or stories with skill and wit: 善於講逸事或故事的人: *a good* ～. 一個說故事的高手。
rac·oon, rac·coon /rə'ku:n *US:* ræ-；ræ'kun/ *n* small, flesh-eating animal of N America with a bushy, ringed tail; (US) its fur. 浣熊(北美產,食肉,有多毛而呈環狀花紋之尾巴)；(美)浣熊之毛皮。
rac·quet = racket².
racy /'reɪsɪ；'resɪ/ *adj* (-ier, -iest) **1** (of speech or writing) vivid; spirited; vigorous: (指言詞或寫作)生動的;活潑的;有力的: *a* ～ *style*. 一種爽朗活潑的風格。 **2** having strongly marked qualities: 有顯著特徵的;道地的: *a* ～ *flavour*. 道地的口味。 **～ *of the soil***, showing traces of origin; direct, lively and stimulating. 顯出原有之特徵的;活潑而富刺激的。 **rac·ily** /-ɪlɪ；-ɪlɪ/ *adv* **raci·ness** *n*
radar /'reɪdɑ:(r)；'redɑr/ *n* [U] (the use of) apparatus that indicates on a screen (by means of radio echoes) solid objects that come within its range, used (eg by pilots of ships, aircraft or spacecraft) in fog or darkness and which gives information about their position, movement, speed, etc: 雷達(一種無線電裝置,藉無線電回波而在一螢光幕上指示進入其探測範圍的物體;船,飛機或太空船之駕駛員在大霧或黑夜中使用,藉以測知方位,動向,速度等)；雷達之使用: *follow the flight of an aircraft by* ～; 藉雷達追踪一飛機之飛行; (attrib) (形容用法) *'～ installation;* 雷達裝置; *on the '～ screen*. 在雷達幕上。
radial /'reɪdɪəl；'redɪəl/ *adj* relating to a ray, rays or a radius; (of spokes in a bicycle wheel, ect) from a centre; arranged like rays or radii. 光線的; 半徑的;(指自行車輪子的輻條)輻射狀的; 像光線或半徑般排列的。□ *n* **～ (tyre)**, tyre designed (by having the material inside the tyre wrapped in a direction ～ to the hub of the wheel) to give more grip on road surfaces, esp when cornering or when roads are wet. 防滑輪胎; 加力輪胎。**～ly** /-ɪəlɪ；-ɪəlɪ/ *adv*
radi·ant /'reɪdɪənt；'redɪənt/ *adj* **1** sending out rays of light; shining: 光芒四射的;光輝燦爛的: *the* ～ *sun*. 光輝燦爛的太陽。**2** (of a person, his looks, eyes) bright; showing joy or love: (指人,其面容,眼睛)明亮的;流露喜悅或熱情的: *a* ～ *face;* 一張容光煥發的臉; *the* ～ *figures in the paintings of Renoir*. 雷諾瓦繪畫上喜氣洋洋的人物。 **3** (phys) transmitted by radiation: (物理)輻射的: ～ *heat／energy*. 輻射熱(能)。**～·ly** *adv* **radi·ance** /-əns；-əns/ *n* [U] ～ quality. 發光;閃爍;輻射。
radi·ate /'reɪdɪeɪt；'redɪ,et/ *vt, vi* **1** [VP6A] send out rays of (light or heat): 發射(光或熱): *a stove that* ～*s warmth;* 一個發射熱的火爐; (fig) spread abroad, send out: (喻)散發;發出: *a woman who* ～*s happiness;* 一個洋溢着快樂的婦人; *an orator who* ～*s enthusiasm for the cause he supports*. 一個對其所支持的主義散發出熱情的演說家。 **2** [VP 2A, 3A] ～ ***(from)***, come or go out in rays; show: 射出;表現: *heat that* ～*s from a stove／a fireplace;* 從火爐(壁爐)散發出來的熱; *the happiness that* ～*s from her eyes*. 從她眼睛裡流露出來的快樂。 **3** [VP2A, 3A] ～ ***(from)***, spread out like radii: 輻射;向各方伸展: *the avenues that* ～ *from the Arc de Triomphe in Paris*. 在巴黎以凱旋門爲中心向四方伸展的街道。
radi·ation /,reɪdɪ'eɪʃn；,redɪ'eʃən/ *n* **1** [U] radiating; the sending out of energy, heat, etc in rays. 發射; 放射; 能,熱等之輻射。 **'～ sickness**, illness caused by gamma rays or rays from radioactive dust (as from nuclear weapons). 輻射症(由加瑪射線或核子武器等之輻射塵所引起的病症)。 **2** [C] sth radiated: 放射出之物;輻射線;輻射能: ～*s emitted by an X-ray apparatus*. X光裝置所放射出來的輻射線。
radi·ator /'reɪdɪeɪtə(r)；'redɪ,etɚ/ *n* [C] **1** apparatus for radiating heat, esp heat from steam or hot water supplied through pipes or from electric current. 暖氣爐;放熱器。 **2** device for cooling the cylinders of the engine of a motor-vehicle: (汽車引擎的) 冷却器; 水箱: *This car has a fan-cooled* ～. 這部汽車有一個由風扇散熱的冷却器。⇨ the illus at motor. 參看 motor 之插圖。
rad·ical /'rædɪkl；'rædɪkl̩/ *adj* **1** of or from the root or base; fundamental: 根本的;基本的: ～ (= thorough and complete) *reforms;* 徹底而完全的改革; *make* ～ *changes in a scheme*. 對一個計畫做徹底的改變。 **2** (politics) favouring fundamental reforms; advanced in opinions and policies: (政治) 贊成根本改革的; 激進的; 意見和政策上急進的: *a member of the R～ Party*. 激進黨黨員。 **3** (maths) relating to the root of a number or quantity: (數學)根的: *the* ～ *sign* (√). 根號(√)。□ *n* **1** person with ～(2) opinions; member of the R～ Party. 激進份子;激進黨黨員。 **2** (maths) the ～ sign; a quantity expressed as the root of another. (數學)根號;根數;根。 **～ly** /-klɪ；-klɪ/ *adv* **～·ism** /-kəlɪzəm；-klɪzm̩/ *n* beliefs and policies of ～(2) people. 激進主義;激進政策。**～·ize** /-kəlaɪz；-kl̩,aɪz/ *vt* [VP6A] cause to become ～(2). 使激進。
rad·icle /'rædɪkl；'rædɪkl̩/ *n* embryo root (eg of a pea or bean). (豌豆或豆子的)幼根;胚根。
radii /'reɪdɪaɪ；'redɪ,aɪ/ ⇨ radius.
radio /'reɪdɪəʊ；'redɪ,o/ *n* (*pl* ～s /-dɪəʊz；-dɪ,oz/) **1** [U] (communication by) use of electromagnetic waves without a connecting wire: 無線電: *send a message by* ～. 以無線電傳遞消息。 **2** [U] broadcasting by this means: 無線電廣播: *hear something on the* ～; 在無線電廣播中聽到某消息; *talk over the* ～; 在無線電廣播中講話; (attrib) (形容用法) *the* ～ *programme*. 無線電廣播節目。 **3** [C] **'～(-set)**, apparatus, eg on ships, aircraft, for transmitting and receiving ～ messages or (as in the home) for receiving sound broadcast programmes: (船,飛機等的)無線電收發報機; (家庭等的)收音機: *a portable* ～; 手提式收音機; *the latest types of* ～*s／*～*-sets*. 最新型的收音機。 **4 '～ beacon**, station for transmitting signals to help aircraft pilots. 無線電導航信標(發信號以協助飛機駕駛員)。**'～ beam**, beam of ～ signals from a ～ beacon. 無線電領航信號。 **'～ frequency**, frequency between 10 kilocycles per second to 300 000 megacycles per second. 射(電)頻(率)(自每秒十仟週至每秒三十萬兆週)。**'～ link**, (sound broadcasting) programme in which speakers in widely separated towns are linked by the same programme. (廣播)相距甚遠城市中的不同演講者，在同一節目中以無線電聯繫起來的一種節目。
radio- /,reɪdɪəʊ；,redɪo/ *pref* of rays or radium. 光的;鐳的。 **,～·'ac·tive** *adj* (of such metals as radium and uranium) having atoms that break up and, in so doing, send out rays in the form of electrically charged particles capable of penetrating opaque bodies and of producing electrical effects: (指鐳和鈾等金屬)有放射性的;有輻射能的(此等金屬之原子具分裂性，在分裂時射出帶電微粒之射線,能穿透不透明體,並產生電效應): ～*active carbon;* 放射性碳;輻射碳; ～*active dust*, dust (eg as carried by winds) from explosions of nuclear bombs, etc; 放射塵(由核彈等爆炸所產生之塵，由風帶往他處); ～*active waste*, waste material from nuclear power stations, etc. (由核能發電廠等排出的)放射性廢料。Hence, 由此產生, **,～·ac'tiv·ity** *n* [U]. **'～·gram** *n* **1** (abbr of) ～-gramophone. 爲 ～-gramophone 之略。 **2** X-ray photograph. X光照片。 **,～-'gramophone** *n* combined ～ receiver and record-player. 收音電唱機。**'～·graph** *n* X-ray photograph. X光照片。 **,radi·'ogra·phy** /,reɪdɪ'ɒgrəfɪ；,redɪ'ɑgrəfɪ/ *n* [U] production of X-ray photographs. X光攝影。 **,radi·'ogra·pher** *n* person trained to take ～graphs. X光攝影師。**,～·'iso·tope** *n* ～active form of an element, used in medicine, industry, etc to study the path and speed of substances through bodies and objects. 放射同位素(一元素的放射性之形式,用於醫學,工業等方面，以研究物質穿過人體

及物體的途徑與速度)。ˌ~-lo'cation *n* radar. 無線電定位;雷達。ˌradi'ology /ˌreɪdɪ'ɒlədʒɪ; ˌredɪ'alədʒɪ/ *n* [U] scientific study of X-rays and other radiation (esp as used in medicine). 放射學;(尤指醫學中)放射線科。ˌradi'ologist *n* expert in ~logy. 放射線專家。ˌ~ 'telescope *n* apparatus that detects stars by means of ~ waves from outer space and tracks spacecraft. (藉太空無線電波偵察星球和追蹤太空船的)無線電望遠鏡。ˌ~-'therapy *n* treatment of disease by means of X-rays or other forms of radiation, eg of heat. X光治療法;放射療法。ˌ~-'therapist *n* expert in ~-therapy. 放射療法專家。

a radio telescope

rad·ish /'rædɪʃ; 'rædɪʃ/ *n* salad plant with a white or red edible root. (一種做生菜的)蘿蔔。

radium /'reɪdɪəm; 'redɪəm/ *n* [U] radioactive metallic element (symbol **Ra**) used in the treatment of some diseases, eg cancer. 鐳(放射性金屬元素,符號爲 Ra, 用以治療某些疾病,如癌)。

radius /'reɪdɪəs; 'redɪəs/ *n* (*pl* -dii /-dɪaɪ; -dɪˌaɪ/) **1** (length of a) straight line from the centre of a circle or sphere to any point on the circumference or surface. 半徑。⇨ the illus at circle. 參看 circle 之插圖。 **2** circular area measured by its ~: 以半徑度量之圓形面積: *The police searched all the fields and woods within a ~ of two miles.* 警方搜查半徑兩英里範圍內所有的田野和森林。**3** (anat) outer of the two bones in the forearm.(解剖)橈骨。⇨ the illus at skeleton. 參看 skeleton 之插圖。

raf·fia /'ræfɪə; 'ræfɪə/ *n* [U] fibre from the leaf-stalks of a kind of palm-tree, used for making baskets, hats, mats, etc. 拉菲亞纖維(由拉菲亞棕櫚樹之葉柄做成,用於製籃子、帽子、蓆子等)。

raff·ish /'ræfɪʃ; 'ræfɪʃ/ *adj* disreputable; dissipated: 聲名狼藉的;放蕩的: *a ~ young man;* 一個聲名狼藉的年輕人; *with a ~ air.* 具有一副放蕩的樣子。**~·ly** *adv*

raffle /'ræfl; 'ræfl/ *n* [C] sale of an article by a lottery, often for a charitable purpose: (常爲慈善目的之)抽籤售賣: *buy '~ tickets/tickets for a ~.* 購買抽籤售物的彩劵。□ *vt* [VP6A, 15B] **~ *sth* (*off*),** sell in a ~: 以抽籤法售賣: *~ (off) a motor-scooter.* 以抽籤法賣一部速克達機車。

raft /rɑːft *US:* ræft; ræft/ *n* **1** number of tree trunks fastened together to be floated down a river. (綁在一起俾順流漂下的)一排樹幹; 木排。 **2 ('life-)~,** flat, floating structure of rough timber, barrels, etc as a substitute for a boat or for the use of swimmers: (用原木、木桶等做成的)筏;救生筏: *The sailors got away from the wrecked ship on a ~.* 水手們乘救生筏離開失事的船。□ *vt, vi* **1** [VP6A, 15A, B] carry on a ~; cross (a stream) on a ~. 以筏運送;乘筏過(河)。 **2** [VP2C] go on a ~: 乘筏航行: *~ down the stream.* 乘筏順流而下。**~er, 'rafts·man** /-mən; -mən/ (*pl* -men) *nn* man who ~s timber. 運送木排者。

rafter /'rɑːftə(r) *US:* 'ræf-; 'ræftɚ/ *n* one of the sloping beams of the framework on which the tiles or slates of a roof are supported. 椽。**raft·ered** /'rɑːftəd *US:* ræf-; 'ræftɚd/ *adj* provided with ~s: 裝有椽的: *a ~ed roof,* (esp) one of which the ~s are visible from beneath, eg in a hall that has no ceiling. 椽架屋頂(尤指屋子沒有天花板,從內部可以望見椽木者)。

rag¹ /ræg; ræg/ *n* [C] **1** odd bit of cloth: 零頭布;碎布: *a rag to polish the car with.* 用來擦車的碎布。**2** piece of old and torn cloth; (*pl*) old and torn clothes: 破布;(複)破舊衣服: *dressed in rags;* 穿著破爛; *My coat was worn to rags.* 我的外套破爛不堪了。**the 'rag trade,** (sl) the business of making and selling clothes. (俚)製造及售賣成衣。**'glad rags,** ⇨ glad. **3** scrap; irregular piece. 碎屑;一點點;不規則的碎片。**'rag-bag** *n* **(a)** bag in which scraps of fabric are stored. 儲放碎布或破布的袋子。**(b)** motley collection; confused mass. 雜亂的一堆;雜湊。**(c)** (sl) untidily dressed person. (俚)衣着不整之人。 **4** (*pl*) old, waste pieces of cloth from which a good quality of paper (*'rag paper*) is made. (複)做紙漿用的舊布片(可製成上等紙,稱爲 rag paper)。 **5** (used contemptuously for a) newspaper: (含輕蔑意義)報紙: *Why do you read that worthless rag?* 你爲什麼看那種沒有價值的報紙?

rag² /ræg; ræg/ *vt* (-gg-) [VP6A] (colloq) tease; play practical jokes on; be noisy and boisterous. (俗)揶揄;戲弄;喧鬧。□ *n* (colloq) rough, noisy disturbance; carnival with side-shows, a procession of amusing floats¹(3), etc, eg as held by college students. (俗)粗魯而喧鬧的滋擾;(包括雜耍、花車遊行等的)狂歡會(例如大學生所舉行者)。**'rag-day,** day (usu annually) on which students hold a rag, and often collect money for charity. (通常一年一度的)學生狂歡會(通常爲了募集慈善基金)。

raga·muf·fin /'rægəmʌfɪn; 'rægəˌmʌfɪn/ *n* dirty, disreputable person, esp a small boy dressed in rags. 骯髒而名譽不佳的人;(尤指)衣著襤褸的小男孩。

rage /reɪdʒ; redʒ/ *n* **1** [C, U] (outburst of) furious anger; violence: 盛怒(之暴發);狂暴: *livid with ~;* 氣得臉色發青; *the ~ of the sea,* its violence during a storm. 怒海澎湃。***be in/fly into a ~,*** be, become, violently angry. 勃然大怒。**2** [C] ***~ (for),*** strong desire: (對某事物之)强烈慾望: *He has a ~ for collecting butterflies.* 他極好搜集蝴蝶。 **3 *be (all) the ~,*** (colloq) sth for which there is a widespread but temporary enthusiasm; sth very fashionable: (俗)風靡一時之物;極爲流行之物: *The new musical comedy at Drury Lane is all the ~.* 特魯利街戲院新推出的喜歌劇風靡一時。 *These white handbags from Italy are (all) the ~ this summer.* 這些由義大利進口的白色手提包今年夏季甚爲風行。□ *vi* [VP2A, C] be violently angry; (of storms, etc) be violent: 發怒;(指暴風雨等)狂暴: *He ~d and fumed against me for not letting him have his own way.* 他對我發怒因爲我沒有讓他自行其道。 *The storm ~d all day.* 暴風雨竟日肆虐不已。 *The wind ~d round the house.* 風在房屋四周狂吹。 *Flu ~d through the country.* 流行性感冒在全國各地猖獗。

rag·ged /'rægɪd; 'rægɪd/ *adj* **1** (with clothes) badly torn or in rags: 衣服破爛的;衣衫襤褸的: *a ~ coat;* 一件破外套; *a ~ old man.* 衣衫襤褸的老人。**2** having rough or irregular edges or outlines or surfaces: 邊緣、外形或表面不平滑或參差不齊的: *a dog with a ~ coat of hair;* 一身毛長短不齊的狗; *a sleeve with ~ edges/which is ~ at the cuff;* 袖口破爛不齊的袖子; *~ rocks;* 嶙峋之石; *~ clouds driven by the gale.* 被狂風吹飄的殘雲。 **3** (of work, etc) imperfect; lacking smoothness or uniformity: (指工作等)不完美的; 不流暢的;不一致的: *a ~ performance,* eg of a theatrical rôle, a piece of music. 雜亂的表演;不流暢的音樂演奏。**~·ly** *adv* **~·ness** *n*

rag·lan /'ræglən; 'ræglən/ *n* (usu attrib) sweater or coat without shoulder seams (so that the seams for the sleeves go up from the armpit to the neckline). (通常爲形容用法)一種無肩縫的毛線衫或大衣(兩袖連到頸部)。

ra·gout /'ræguː *US:* ræ'guː; ræ'gu/ *n* (dish of) meat and vegetable stew. (一道)菜燉肉。

R

rag·tag /ˈrægtæg ; ˈræg,tæg/ *n* ***(the)*** ***ˌ~ and ˈbobtail,*** the riff-raff; disreputable people. 流氓;賤民;聲名狼藉之輩。

rag·time /ˈrægtaɪm ; ˈræg,taɪm/ *n* [U] (1920's) popular music and dance of US Negro origin, the accent of the melody falling just before the regular beat of the accompaniment. 繁音拍子(起源於美國黑人的一種流行音樂和舞蹈,旋律中的重音落在伴奏的規則拍子前,流行於1920年代);一種早期的爵士樂。

rah /rɑː ; rɑ/ *int* hurrah (as used, in US) in cheers at a sports meeting, etc: (美)(運動會等中的)歡呼聲:*Rah, rah, rah!* 加油!加油!加油!

raid /reɪd ; red/ *n* **1** surprise attack made by troops, ship(s) or aircraft: (部隊,艦艇或飛機所作之)襲擊;突襲: *make a ~ upon the enemy's camp;* 突擊敵軍軍營; *killed in an ˈair-~* (attack by aircraft). 在空襲中喪生。 **2** sudden visit by police to make arrests: (警察的)突然搜查;搜捕: *a ~ on a gambling-den.* 警察搜查賭窟。 **3** sudden attack or inroad for the purpose of taking money: 搶劫;盜用: *a ~ on a bank by armed men;* 持械暴徒搶劫銀行; *a ~ on the bank's reserves,* when they are to be used by the directors for expansion, etc. 盜用銀行之儲備金(如董事們爲擴張業務等所爲者)。□ *vt, vi* [VP6A, 2A] make a ~ on or into; carry out a ~: 襲擊;侵入;搶劫: *Boys have been ~ing my orchard,* visiting it to steal fruit. 孩子們老跑到我的果園偸果子。**~er** *n* person, ship, aircraft, etc that makes a ~. 襲擊之人,艦艇,飛機等;侵入者。

R

rail¹ /reɪl ; rel/ *n* **1** horizontal or sloping bar or rod or continuous series of bars or rods, of wood or metal, as part of a fence, as a protection against contact or falling over: 橫檔;欄杆;圍欄: *wooden ~s round a field;* 圍着一塊地的木欄杆; *metal ~s round a monument;* 圍繞一紀念碑的鐵欄杆; *build a ~ fence.* 裝一圍欄。 *He was leaning on the ship's ~, looking over the water.* 他斜倚着船的欄杆眺望水面。 *One of the horses was forced to the ~s,* (in a horse-race) pressed so close to the ~s of the race-course that it was at a disadvantage. (賽馬中)一匹馬被擠近圍欄而無法快跑。 **2** similar bar or rod placed for things to hang on: 掛東西用的橫桿: *a ˈtowel-~,* eg at the side of a wash-basin. 掛毛巾的桿子。 **3** steel bar or continuous line of such bars, laid on the ground as one side of a track for trains or trams: 鐵軌: *send goods by ~,* by ~way; 由火車運貨; *a ~ strike,* of railway workers. 鐵路工人罷工。***off the ~s,*** (of a train) off the track; (fig) out of order, out of control; disorganized; (colloq) eccentric; neurotic; mad. (指火車)出軌;(喻)失靈的;失常的;失去控制的;雜亂無章的;(俗)怪誕的;神經過敏的;瘋狂的。 **ˈ~·road** *n* (US) (美) = ~way. □ *vt* (colloq) [VP15A, B] rush (sb or sth) unfairly (*to, into, through, etc*): (俗)使(某人或某事物)草草了事;使(議案等)草草通過(與 to, into, through 等連用): *~road a bill through Congress.* 使一議案在國會中草草通過。 **ˈ~·way** *n* **1** road or track laid with ~s on which trains run: 鐵路: *build a new ~way.* 修築一條新鐵路。 **2** system of such tracks, with the locomotives, cars, wagons, etc and the organization controlling the system: 鐵路界(包括鐵路,機車,車廂,貨車等,以及管理鐵路之機構): *work on the ~way.* 在鐵路局工作。 *The ~ways in many countries are owned by the State.* 在許多國家,鐵路爲國有。 **3** (attrib) (形容用法) *ˈ~way station/bridge/carriage/engineer/contractors/transport, etc.* 火車站(鐵路橋樑;火車車廂;鐵路工程師;鐵路承建者;鐵路運輸等)。 **ˈ~-car** *n* single coach or car, with its own motive power, used on a ~way. (由本身動力在鐵軌上行駛的)單節機動車。 **ˈ~·head** *n* farthest point reached by a ~way under construction. 修築中的鐵路的最遠點。□ *vt* [VP6A, 15B] ***~ off/in,*** put ~s(1) round; shut (in, off) separate, by means of ~s(1): 以欄杆圍起來;以欄杆隔開: *~ off a piece of ground;* 以欄杆圍起一塊地; *fields that are ~ed off from the road.* 以欄杆同道路隔離的田地。 **~·ing** *n* [C] (often *pl*) fence made with ~s, eg as a protection at the side of a series of steps. (常用複數)(樓梯等的)欄杆;扶手;圍欄。

rail² /reɪl ; rel/ *vi* [VP2A, 3A] ~ ***(at/against),*** (liter) find fault; utter reproaches: (文)挑剔;抱怨;責罵: *It's no use your ~ing at fate.* 你抱怨命運沒有用。 **~·ing** *n* [U] act of finding fault, complaining, protesting, etc; (*pl*) utterances of this kind.挑剔;抱怨;抗議(等);(複)挑剔,抱怨,抗議等之言辭。

rail·lery /ˈreɪlərɪ ; ˈrelərɪ/ *n* [U] (liter) good-humoured teasing; [C] (*pl* -ries) instance of this. (文)善意的嘲弄;此種嘲弄之實例。

rai·ment /ˈreɪmənt ; ˈremənt/ *n* [U] (liter) clothing. (文)衣服。

rain¹ /reɪn ; ren/ *n* **1** [U] condensed moisture of the atmosphere falling in separate drops; fall of such drops: 雨;下雨: *It looks like ~,* as if there will be a fall of ~. 好像要下雨的樣子。*Don't go out in the ~.* 不要冒着雨出去。*Come in out of the ~.* 快進來,不要在外面淋雨。*The farmers want ~.* 農民需要雨。***~ or shine,*** whether the weather is wet or sunny. 無論晴雨;晴雨無阻。 **~·bow** /ˈreɪnbəʊ ; ˈren,bo/ *n* arch containing the colours of the spectrum, formed in the sky opposite the sun when ~ is falling or when the sun shines on mist or spray. 虹。 **ˈ~·bow trout,** food fish with reddish bands and black spots. 虹鱒魚。 **ˈ~·coat** *n* light coat of waterproof or tightly-woven material. 雨衣。 **ˈ~-drop** *n* single drop of ~. 雨點。 **ˈ~·fall** *n* amount of ~ falling within a given area in a given time, (eg measured in cm of depth per annum). 雨量(指某一地區在某一期間內的降雨量言,例如以每年多少公分深量測之)。 **ˈ~ forest,** hot, wet forest in tropical areas, where ~fall is heavy and there is no dry season. (熱帶的)雨林。 **ˈ~-gauge** *n* instrument for measuring ~fall. 雨量器;雨量計。 **ˈ~·proof** *adj* able to keep ~ out. 防雨的。 **ˈ~·water** *n* water that has fallen as ~ and has been collected as ~ (contrasted with *well-water,* etc); soft water. 雨水(與 well-water 等相對);軟水。 **2** ***a*** + *adj* + **~,** fall or shower of ~: 落雨;陣雨: *There was a heavy ~ last night.* 昨晚下過一場大雨。 **the ~s,** the season in tropical countries when there is heavy and continuous ~. (熱帶地區之)雨季。 **3** (use 通常用 **a ~**) descent of sth that comes like ~: 如雨般之降落: *a ~ of arrows/bullets;* 箭(彈)如雨下; *a ~ of ashes,* eg from a volcano; (來自火山等之)陣陣落塵; (fig) (喻) *a ~ of congratulations.* 一連串的祝賀。

rain² /reɪn ; ren/ *vi, vt* **1** (impers): (無人稱): *It was ~ing, ~* was falling. 正在下雨。 *It has ~ed itself out,* has stopped ~ing. 雨停了。***~ cats and dogs,*** ~ very hard. 降傾盆大雨。***It never ~s but it pours,*** (prov) Things, usu unwelcome, do not come singly but in numbers, eg if one disaster happens, another will follow. (諺)雨不下則已,一下傾盆;災禍接踵而至;禍不單行。 **2** [VP2C] fall in a stream: 灑落: *Tears ~ed down her cheeks.* 她淚流滿面。 *Misfortunes have ~ed heavily upon the old man.* 那老人接連遭遇不幸。 **3** [VP14] ***~ sth on/upon,*** send or come down on: 使降下;落下: *He ~ed blows/Blows ~ed on the door.* 他(有人)連連敲門。 *The people ~ed gifts upon the heroes returning from the war.* 人們紛紛送禮物給那些戰罷歸來的英雄。

rainy /ˈreɪnɪ ; ˈrenɪ/ *adj* (-ier, -iest) having much rain: 多雨的: *~ weather;* 多雨的天氣; *a ~ day/climate;* 雨天(多雨的氣候); *the ˈ~ season.* 雨季。 ***save/provide/put away/keep sth for a ~ day,*** save (esp money) for a time when one may need it. 儲蓄以備未來之需;未雨綢繆。

raise /reɪz ; rez/ *vt* [VP6A, 15A, B] **1** lift up; move from a low(er) to a high(er) level; cause to rise: 舉起;升起: *~ a sunken ship to the surface of the* *sea;* 把一艘沉船吊到海面上來; ~ *one's hat to sb,* as a sign of respect; 向某人舉帽致敬; ~ *one's glass to one's lips;* 舉杯到唇邊; ~ *prices;* 抬高物價; ~(= build, erect) *a monument.* 建一紀念碑。~ ***one's glass to sb,*** drink his health. 向某人舉杯祝賀健康; 向某人敬酒。~ ***one's hand to sb,*** move as if to give him a blow. 向某人伸拳(好像要打他的樣子)。~ ***sb's hopes,*** make him more hopeful. 燃起某人的希望。~ ***a man to the peerage,*** make him a peer. 封某人爲貴族。~ ***the temperature,*** **(a)** make a place warmer. 使溫度升高。**(b)** (fig) increase tension, eg by losing one's temper. (喻)使氣氛緊張(如因發脾氣所致)。~ ***one's voice,*** speak more loudly or in a higher tone: 提高聲音;提高嗓子: *voices ~d in anger.* 咆哮的聲音。 **2** cause to be upright: 使直立;扶直: ~ *a man from his knees;* 扶起一跪着的人; ~ *the standard of revolt.* 揭竿而起。~ ***sb from the dead,*** restore him to life. 使某人復生。 **3** cause to rise or appear: 引起;掀起;惹起;使出現: ~ *a cloud of dust;* 揚起一片塵土; ~ *the spirits of the dead;* 使死者的靈魂出現; *shoes that ~ blisters on my feet;* 把我的脚磨起水泡的鞋; *a story that might ~ a blush on a young girl's cheeks;* 一個可能使少女聽了臉紅的故事; *a long, hot walk that ~d a good thirst,* caused the walker to be thirsty. 使人口渴的又長又熱的步行。~ ***a dust/commotion,*** (fig) cause a disturbance. (喻)惹起一場紛擾;引起騷動。~ ***a laugh,*** do sth to cause laughter. 惹起一陣大笑。 ~ ***Cain/hell/the devil/the roof,*** (sl) cause an uproar; start a big row or disturbance. (俚)興風作浪;惹起騷亂;鬧出問題。**4** bring up for discussion or attention: 提出(以便討論或引起注意): ~ *a new point/a question/a protest/an objection.* 提出一新論點(問題,抗議,異議)。**5** grow or produce (crops); breed (sheep, etc); rear, bring up (a family). 種植或出產(作物);飼養(羊等);養(家);撫育(子女)。**6** get or bring together; manage to get: 集結;召集;籌措: ~ *an army;* 召募一支軍隊; ~ *a loan;* 借款; ~ *money for a new undertaking;* 爲一新事業籌款; ~ *funds for a holiday,* eg by pawning one's jewels. 籌集度假費用(例如典當珠寶首飾等)。**7** ~ ***a siege/blockade,*** end it. 解除包圍(封鎖)。~ ***an embargo,*** remove it. 解除禁運。**8** ~ ***land,*** (naut) come in sight of land that appears to rise above the horizon: (航海)看見陸地: *The ship ~d land the next morning.* 翌晨該船卽見陸地。□ *n* (esp US, cf GB, *rise*) increase in salary, etc. (尤美,參較英國用法之 rise) 薪資等之提高;加薪。~**r** *n* (in compounds) one who, that which, ~s (in various senses): (用於複合字) 舉起者;扶直者;升起者;提出者;種植者;養育者;募集者;解除者: *'cattle-~rs;* 養牛業者; *'curtain-~r,* short introductory play; 開臺戲(正戲前之配戲); *'fire-~rs,* arsonists. 縱火者;放火者。

raisin /ˈreɪzn; ˈrezn̩/ *n* [C] dried sweet grape, as used in cakes, etc. 葡萄乾。

raison d'être /ˌreɪzɒn ˈdetrə; ˈrezɒnˈdɛt/ *n* (*sing only*) (F) reason for, purpose of, a thing's existence. (僅作單數)(法)存在之理由或目的。

raj /rɑːdʒ; rɑdʒ/ *n* sovereignty: 統治;主權: *the ending of the British raj in India.* 英國統治印度之結束。

ra·jah /ˈrɑːdʒə; ˈrɑdʒə/ *n* Indian prince; Malayan chief. 印度王公;馬來亞之酋長。

rake[1] /reɪk; rek/ *n* **1** long-handled tool with prongs used for drawing together straw, dead leaves, etc or for smoothing soil or gravel, ⇨ the illus at tool; similar kinds of tool on wheels, drawn by a horse or tractor. 耙子(參看 tool 之插圖);(由馬或牽引機拖拉的)耙機。**2** implement used by a croupier for drawing in money or chips at a gaming-table. 在賭桌上負責收取或償付賭注者用以耙取賭金或籌碼的小耙。□ *vt, vi* **1** [VP6A, 22] use a ~ (on); make smooth with a ~: 以耙子耙;以耙子耙平: ~ *garden paths;* 以耙子耙花園的小路; ~ *the soil smooth for a seedbed.* 耙平土壤設一苗圃。**2** [VP6A, 15A, B, 14] get (sth *together, up, out, etc*) with or as with a ~: 用耙子等耙(某物)(與 together, up, out 等連用): ~ *together dead leaves;* 把枯葉耙在一起; ~ *out a fire,* get the ashes or cinders out from the bottom of a grate, etc; 把灰或炭渣從爐底耙出; ~ *up hay;* 把乾草耙在一起; ~ *the dead leaves off the lawn.* 把枯葉從草地上耙除。~ ***sth in,*** (fig) earn, make, much money: (喻)賺大錢;發財: *The firm is very successful—they're raking it in/raking in the money.* 這公司非常成功——他們賺了很多錢。**'~-off** *n* (sl) (usu suggesting dishonesty) commission; share of profits: (俚)(通常暗示不正當之)佣金;回扣;贏利之一份: *If I put this bit of business in your way, I expect a ~-off.* 如果我把這筆生意交給你做,我希望能得到一些回扣。~ ***sth up,*** (esp) bring to people's knowledge (sth forgotten, esp sth which it is better not to recall to memory): (尤指)重新提起(某件被遺忘的事,尤指最好不要記起的事): ~ *up old quarrels/accusations/slanders/grievances.* 重新提起舊日的爭吵(控訴,誹謗,冤情)。 *Don't ~ up the past.* 不要把過去的事都翻出來。 **3** [VP6A, 15A, B, 2C, 3A] ~ ***(over/through) sth,*** search for facts, etc: 在…搜尋事實等: ~ *through old manuscripts for information;* 在舊原稿中搜求資料; ~ *one's memory;* 從記憶中搜覓; ~ *about among old documents.* 在舊文件中尋找。**4** [VP6A, 15A] fire with guns at, from end to end: 掃射;縱射: ~ *a ship;* 縱射一船; ~ *a trench with machine-gun fire.* 以機關槍向一戰壕掃射。

rake[2] /reɪk; rek/ *n* dissolute man. 浪子;放蕩的人。

rake[3] /reɪk; rek/ *vi, vt* [VP2A, 6A] (of a ship, or its bow or stern) project beyond the keel; (of the funnel, masts) (cause to) slope towards the stern; (of the stage of a theatre) slope down (towards the audience). (指船,船首或船尾)突出於龍骨之外;傾斜; (指煙囱,桅)(使)向船尾傾斜; (指劇院中之舞台)(向觀衆)傾斜。□ *n* degree of slope: 傾斜度: *the ~ of a ship's masts/of the stage of a theatre.* 船桅(戲院舞台)的傾斜度。

rak·ish[1] /ˈreɪkɪʃ; ˈrekɪʃ/ *adj* **1** of or like a rake[2]; dissolute: 浪子的;像浪子的;放蕩的;淫樂的: *a ~ appearance.* 放蕩的樣子。**2** jaunty: 自信和自滿的;揚揚得意的;俏皮的: *set one's hat at a ~ angle* (from *rake*[3]). 俏皮地歪戴帽子。~**·ly** *adv* in a ~ manner: 放蕩地;揚揚得意地;俏皮地: *with his hat tilted ~ly.* 俏皮地歪戴着他的帽子。~**·ness** *n*

rak·ish[2] /ˈreɪkɪʃ; ˈrekɪʃ/ *adj* (of a ship) looking smart and as if built for speed (and therefore, in olden times, suggesting that she might be a pirate ship). (指船)外形靈巧、速度似乎很快的(因此在昔時含示這船可能是海盜船)。

ral·len·tando /ˌrælənˈtændəʊ; ˌrælənˈtændo/ *adj, adv* (music) gradually slower. (音樂)逐漸緩慢(的)。 ⇨ accelerando.

rally[1] /ˈrælɪ; ˈrælɪ/ *vt, vi* (*pt, pp* -lied) [VP6A, 15A, 2A, C] **1** (cause to) come together, esp after defeat or confusion, or in the face of threats or danger, to make new efforts: (使)重新集結在一起做新的努力(尤指在失敗或混亂後或是面對威脅或危險時); 重整旗鼓: *The troops rallied round their leader.* 軍隊重新集結於他們的指揮官左右。*The leader rallied his men.* 指揮官重整其部屬。*My supporters are ~ing round me again.* 擁護我的人再度集合起來幫助我。 *They rallied to the support of the Prime Minister.* 他們協力支持首相。 **2** give new strength to; (cause to) recover health, strength, firmness: 給予新力量;(使)恢復健康,力量,決心: ~ *one's strength/spirits;* 恢復一個人的力量(快樂心境); ~ *from an illness.* 從疾病中復元。*The boy rallied his wits.* 這男孩恢復了理智。*The market rallied,* eg of the Stock Exchange, prices stopped dropping and became firm. (指股票市場等)價格止跌回穩。□ *n* (*pl* -lies) [C] **1** act or process of ~ing; coming together after being dispersed; recovery of strength; improvement during illness. 集結或重整的行動或

過程；被擊潰後之再集結；力量之恢復；疾病之復元。 **2** (tennis) exchange of several strokes before a point is scored. (網球得分前的)連續對打。 **3** gathering or assembly, esp to encourage fresh effort: 集會(尤指鼓舞新的努力者)：*a po'litical ~;* 政黨集會；*a 'peace ~,* one to urge the necessity of ending or avoiding war. 和平集會(爲力陳結束或避免戰爭之必要而舉行者)。 **4** competition of motor vehicles over public roads. 汽車競賽會；公路賽車。

rally² /'rælɪ ; 'rælɪ/ *vt* (*pt, pp* -lied) [VP6A] tease; chaff good-humouredly. 揶揄；善意地戲弄。

ram /ræm ; ræm/ *n* **1** uncastrated male sheep. (未去勢之)公羊；牡羊。 **2** one of various implements or devices for striking or pushing with great force, eg the falling weight of a pile-driving machine; form of water-pump in which a heavy fall of water is used to force a smaller quantity to a higher level. 各種撞擊工具或裝置之一(如打樁機的下落重槌)；水力泵；水力揚水機(抽水機的一種，利用水之大量下降而壓使較少量之水達於一較高平面上)。 **3** ⇨ *batteringram* at batter¹. **4** metal projection on a warship's bow for piercing the side of an enemy ship. (用以撞穿敵人艦舷的)艦首金屬撞角。□ *vt* (-mm-) **1** [VP6A, 15A, B] strike and push heavily: 力擊；夯擊；力衝，撞：*ram down the soil,* eg when building roads or embankments; (在築路建堤時)把土搗固；*ram piles into a river bed;* 把樁打入河床；*ram a charge home / into a gun;* 把火藥塡好(塡入一槍砲)；(colloq) (俗) *ram one's clothes into a suitcase.* 把衣服塞進衣箱中。 ***ram sth down sb's throat,*** (fig) say sth repeatedly so as to impress it upon sb, get him to learn it or recognize its truth. (喻)一再敍述某事以使某人獲得深刻印象，使之學會或認識其眞相；向某人灌輸某事。 **2** [VP 6A] (of a ship) strike with a ram(4): (指船)以撞角撞擊：*ram and sink a submarine.* 以撞角撞沉一潛水艇。 **3** **'ram-jet** *n* jet engine in which the air is rammed or forced through the engine and compressed by the speed of flight. 衝壓式噴射發動機(由飛行速度逼使空氣由發動機流過並產生壓縮之效果)。 **'ram-rod** *n* iron rod for ramming the charge into old (muzzle-loading) guns. 槍杵；搠杖；推彈桿(舊式槍砲裝火藥時用的鐵棒)。

Rama·dan /ˌræməˈdɑːn *US:* -ˈdæn ; ˏræməˈdɑn/ *n* ninth month of the Muslim year, when Muslims fast between sunrise and sunset. 拉馬丹月(回教曆的第九個月，這期間回教徒在日出之後到日落之前齋戒)；齋月。

ramble /'ræmbl ; 'ræmbl̩/ *vi* [VP2A, C] **1** walk for pleasure, with no special destination; (fig) wander in one's talk, not keeping to the subject. 漫步；漫遊；(喻)漫談。 **2** (of plants) grow with long shoots that trail or straggle. (指植物)蔓生。□ *n* rambling walk: 漫步：*go for a country ~.* 去鄉間漫遊。 **ram·bler** *n* person or thing that ~s: 漫步者；漫談者；蔓生植物：(attrib) (形容用法) *~r roses.* 攀緣薔薇。 **ram·bling** *adj* **1** (esp of buildings, streets, towns), extending in various directions irregularly, as if built without planning. (尤指建築物，街道，城市)排列凌亂無序的(向各方延伸，好像建築時一無計畫)。 **2** (of a speech, essay, etc) disconnected. (指演講詞，文章等)蕪雜散漫的。

ram·bunc·tious /ræmˈbʌŋkʃəs ; ræmˈbʌŋkʃəs/ *adj* boisterous. 狂暴的；猛烈的；(指人，其行爲)喧鬧的；粗野的。

ram·ify /'ræmɪfaɪ ; 'ræməˏfaɪ/ *vi, vt* (*pt, pp* -fied) [VP2A, 6A] form or produce branches; make or become a network: (使)形成枝節；(使)分出枝節；(使)組織或形成一網狀系統：*a ramified system.* 一種網狀系統。 **rami·fi·ca·tion** /ˌræmɪfɪˈkeɪʃn ; ˏræməfəˈkeʃən/ *n* [C] subdivision of sth complex or like a network: 分枝；分支；支脈；支流；支線；枝節；細節：*the widespread ramifications of trade / a plot / an argument.* 廣佈各處的商業分支機構(一計畫之細節，一論據之枝節)。

ram·jet ⇨ ram(3).

ramp¹ /ræmp ; ræmp/ *n* sloping way from one level to another, eg instead of, or in addition to, stairs or steps in a hospital, so that beds can be wheeled from one floor to another, or, at a kerb in a many-storeyed garage, so that cars can be driven up and down; change of level during road repairs. 坡道；斜坡；滑行道；匝道(從一水平面到另一水平面的斜路或坡道，如醫院中代替樓梯或除樓梯外另設的盤道，使病床能從建築物之一層推到另一層；或如立體停車場中所用者，汽車可以直接開上駛下；或如修路所設者)。

ramp² /ræmp ; ræmp/ *n* (GB, sl) dishonest attempt to obtain an exorbitant price; swindle. (英，俚)詐取過高的價錢；敲詐。

ramp³ /ræmp ; ræmp/ *vi* [VP2C] ~ ***about,*** (now usu joc) storm, rage or rush. (現通常爲謔)暴跳；狂怒；猛衝。

ram·page /ræmˈpeɪdʒ ; ræmˈpedʒ/ *vi* [VP2A] rush about in excitement or rage. 雀躍不已；暴跳如雷。□ *n* /'ræmpeɪdʒ ; 'ræmpedʒ/ ***be / go on the ~,*** be / go rampaging. 亂衝亂跑；暴怒。 **ram·pa·geous** /ræmˈpeɪdʒəs ; ræmˈpedʒəs/ *adj* excited and noisy. 興奮而喧鬧的。

ram·pant /'ræmpənt ; 'ræmpənt/ *adj* **1** (of plants, etc) rank; luxuriant: (指植物等) 蔓延的；繁茂的：*Rich soil makes some plants too ~,* causes them to spread too thickly, to have too much foliage, etc. 肥沃的土壤使某些植物過於繁茂。 **2** (of diseases, social evils, etc) unchecked; beyond control: (指疾病，社會弊端等) 不能制止的；猖獗的；不能控制的：*Cholera was ~ among them.* 他們之中很多人都得了霍亂。 **3** (of animals, esp of a lion in heraldry) on the hind legs. (指動物，尤指紋章上的獅子) 舉前肢以後腿站立的。 **~·ly** *adv*

ram·part /'ræmpɑːt ; 'ræmpɑrt/ *n* [C] **1** wide bank of earth, often with a wall, built to defend a fort or other defensive work. 壁壘 (保護堡壘或其他防禦物的厚土牆)。 **2** (fig) defence; protection. (喻)防禦；保護。

ram·rod /'ræmrɒd ; 'ræmˏrɑd/ ⇨ ram(3).

ram·shackle /'ræmʃækl ; 'ræmˏʃækl̩/ *adj* almost collapsing; nearly at breaking-point: 要倒塌的；近於崩潰的：*a ~ house;* 一座搖搖欲倒的房子；*a ~ old bus;* 一輛快報廢的公共汽車；*their ~ empire.* 他們那即將解體的帝國。

ran /ræn ; ræn/ *pt* of run².

ranch /rɑːntʃ *US:* ræn- ; ræntʃ/ *n* (US) large farm, esp one with extensive lands for cattle, but also for fruit, chickens, etc. (美)大農場；(尤指兼種果樹養鷄等的)大牧場。 **'~ house,** (US) rectangular bungalow type of house. (美)長方形的平房。 **'~ wagon,** (US) (美) = station-wagon. **~er** *n* person who owns, manages or works on, a ~. 大農(牧)場主人，管理人或工人。

ran·cid /'rænsɪd ; 'rænsɪd/ *adj* with the smell or taste of stale, decaying fat or butter; (of fat) having gone bad; ill smelling: 有腐臭脂肪或奶油的氣味或味道的；(指脂肪) 敗壞的；惡臭的：*This butter smells ~ / has gone ~.* 這奶油有臭味(已變臭)。

ran·cour (US = **-cor**) /'ræŋkə(r) ; 'ræŋkɚ/ *n* [U] deep and long-lasting feeling of bitterness; spitefulness: 怨恨；積怨；懷恨：*full of ~ (against sb).* (對某人) 懷恨在心。 **ran·cor·ous** /'ræŋkərəs ; 'ræŋkərəs/ *adj*

rand /rænd ; rænd/ *n* monetary unit of the Republic of S Africa, divided into 100 cents. 南非共和國的貨幣單位。

ran·dom /'rændəm ; 'rændəm/ *n* **1** ***at ~,*** without aim or purpose: 無目的或目標：*shooting / dropping bombs at ~;* 胡亂射擊(投彈)；*hit out at ~.* 隨便攻擊；無的放矢。 **2** (attrib) done, made, taken, at ~: (形容用法)隨便做的、造的、選取的：*~ remarks;* 隨便說的話；*a ~ sample / selection;* 隨意抽取的樣品(隨意選擇之物)；*~ sampling.* 隨意抽樣。

randy /'rændɪ ; 'rændɪ/ *adj* (-ier, -iest) **1** (Scot) boisterous; aggressively noisy. (蘇)吵鬧的；喧囂的。

2 full of sexual lust. 淫蕩的;好色的。

ranee, rani /ˈrɑːniː; ˈrɑnɪ/ *n* Hindu queen or princess; wife of a rajah. (印度之)女王;王妃;(王公之)妻室。

rang /ræŋ; ræŋ/ *pt* of ring².

range¹ /reɪndʒ; rendʒ/ *n* [C] **1** row, line or series of things: (指物)排;行;系列; *a magnificent ~ of mountains;* 巍巍壯麗的山脈; *a 'mountain-~;* 山脈; *a long ~ of cliffs.* 一長列絕壁。**2** area of ground with targets for shooting at: 靶場;射擊場: *a 'rifle-~;* 步槍靶場; area in which rockets and missiles are fired. (火箭及飛彈之)發射場。 **3** distance to which a gun will shoot or to which a shell, etc can be fired: 射程: *at a ~ of five miles;* 五哩的射程; *in/within/out of/beyond ~;* 在射程之內(外); distance between a gun, etc and the target: 槍砲等與靶間的距離: *fire at short/long ~.* 短(長)距離射擊。ˈ**~-finder** *n* **(a)** instrument for finding the distance of sth to be fired at. 測距器(用於測定被射擊目標之距離者)。**(b)** device fitted in some cameras for measuring distances. (攝影機中的)測距儀。**4** distance at which one can see or hear, or to which sound will carry. 視域;聽域;聲音可及的距離。 **5** extent; distance between limits: 範圍;幅度;差距: *the annual ~ of temperature,* eg from −10°C to 40°C; 每年之溫度差距(如從攝氏 −10° 到 40°); *a long-~ weather forecast,* for a long period; 長期天氣預告; *a narrow ~ of prices;* 價格差距很小; *cotton fabrics in a wide ~ of colours;* 顏色種類很多的棉織物; *the ~ of her voice,* ie between her top and bottom notes; 她的音域(她能唱出的最高音與最低音間之差距); (fig) (喩) *a subject that is outside my ~,* one that I have not studied; 在我研究範圍之外的題目; *a wide ~ of interests.* 廣泛的興趣。 **6** (US) area of grazing or hunting ground. (美)放牧場;狩獵場。 **7** area over which plants are found growing or in which animals are found living: 動植物生長之地區: *What is the ~ of the nightingale in this country?* 在這個國家甚麼地方有夜鶯? **8** cooking-stove, usu with ovens, a boiler, and a surface with openings or hotplates for pans, kettles, etc: 爐竈: *a kitchen ~.* 厨房中的爐竈。

range² /reɪndʒ; rendʒ/ *vt, vi* **1** [VP6A, 15A] place or arrange in a row or rows; put, take one's place, in a specified situation, order, class or group: 排列成行;安置或列身於某一特定的情況,次序,類或羣: *The general ~d his men along the river bank.* 將軍令其士兵沿河岸排隊。*They were ~d against us/among the rebels.* 他們站在反對我們的一邊(加入了叛徒之列)。*The spectators ~d themselves along the route of the procession.* 觀衆沿遊行行列的路線列隊佇立。**2** [VP2C, 3A, 6A] **~ (through/over),** go, move, wander: (在…)漫遊;(在…)徘徊: *animals ranging through the forests;* 在森林中漫遊的動物; *~ over the hills;* 在小山上漫遊; *~ the seas/hills, etc;* 漫遊於海洋(山丘等); (fig) (喩) *researches that ~d over a wide field;* 涉及範圍很廣的研究; *a speaker who ~d far and wide,* spoke on many topics; 一位講辭包羅萬象的演說者; *a wide-ranging discussion.* 廣泛的討論。 **3** [VP2C] extend, run in a line: 延伸;綿延: *a boundary that ~s north and south/from A to B.* 南北延展(從 A 延伸到 B)的界限。 **4** [VP2C] vary between limits: (在某一範圍內)變化;變動;造成差異: *prices ranging from £7 to £10/between £7 and £10.* 從七鎊到十鎊(在七鎊與十鎊間)的各種價格。 **5** (of guns, projectiles) carry: (指槍砲,彈丸)射程爲: *This gun ~s over six miles,* can fire to this distance. 這砲射程超過六哩。

ranger /ˈreɪndʒə(r); ˈrendʒɚ/ *n* **1** (US) forest guard. (美)森林看守人。 **2** (US) one of a body of mounted troops employed as police (eg in thinly populated areas). (美)(在人口稀少等地區擔任警察的)騎兵巡邏隊隊員;遊騎兵。**3** (US) commando. (美)突擊隊員。 **4** (GB) keeper of a royal park, who sees that the forest laws are observed. (英)(皇家公園的)守衛員(負責森林法之執行)。

rani /ˈrɑːniː; ˈrɑni/ ⇨ ranee.

rank¹ /ræŋk; ræŋk/ *n* **1** [C] line of persons or things: (指人或物)一列;一排;一行: *a 'cab-~.* 一長列出租汽車。*Take the taxi at the head of the ~,* the first one in the line. 乘坐排在前頭的那部計程車。 **2** number of soldiers placed side by side (on parade, usu in three lines, called the *front, centre* and the *rear ~s*). 士兵列成之橫排(閱兵時,通常爲三排,稱爲'前排'、'中排'及'後排')。 ***keep/break ~,*** remain/fail to remain in line. 保持隊形(出列;掉隊)。 **3 *the ~s; the ~ and file; other ~s,*** ordinary soldiers, ie privates, corporals, etc contrasted with officers. 士兵(與軍官相對)。 ***be reduced to the ~s,*** (of a non-commissioned officer, eg a sergeant) made an ordinary private soldier (as a punishment). (指士官)降級爲士兵(做爲一種處罰)。 ***rise from the ~s,*** (of an ordinary soldier) be given a commission as an officer. (指普通士兵)被任命爲軍官。 **4** [C, U] position in a scale; distinct grade in the armed forces; category or class: 等級;軍隊中的官階;種屬;階層: *promoted to the ~ of captain;* 擢升到上尉軍階; *above/below a major in ~;* 在階級上高於(低於)少校; *officers of high ~;* 高級軍官; *hold the ~ of colonel;* 保有上校軍階; *persons of high ~,* of high social position; 社會地位甚高的人; *people of all ~s and classes;* 各階層的人; *be in the ~s of the unemployed;* 屬於失業者羣; *a painter of the first ~;* 第一流的畫家; *a second-~* (more usu 較常用 *second-rate*) *dancer.* 第二流的舞蹈家。 ***pull ~ on sb,*** use one's superior position to gain an advantage over him. 利用職權壓制某人。□ *vt, vi* **1** [VP6A, 15A, 16B] put or arrange in a ~ or ~s; put in a class: 排列成行;列屬某類: *Where/How do you ~ Addison as an essayist?* 你把阿狄生列爲那一類的散文家? *Would you ~ him among the world's great statesmen?* 你會把他列爲世界上偉大政治家之一嗎? **2** [VP3A] have a place: 佔有一地位: *Does he ~ among/with the failures?* 他該算是一個失敗者嗎? *A major ~s above a captain.* 少校階級高於上尉。*Will my shares ~ for the next dividend?* 我的股份可以分到下次的股息嗎? **3 *~ing officer,*** (US) the officer of highest ~ present. (美)在場的最高級軍官。

rank² /ræŋk; ræŋk/ *adj* **1** (of plants, etc) growing too luxuriantly, with too much leaf: (指植物等)繁茂的;過於茂盛的: *~ grass;* 叢生的雜草; *roses that grow ~;* 過於茂盛的玫瑰; (of land) choked with weeds or likely to produce a lot of weeds: (指土地)長滿雜草的;可能生長很多雜草的: *~ soil;* 雜草叢生的土壤; *a field that is ~ with nettles and thistles.* 一塊長滿蕁蔴和薊的地。 **2** smelling or tasting bad; offensive: 氣味或味道不好的;令人不快的: *~ tobacco.* 氣味可厭的煙草。 **3** unmistakably bad; possessing a bad quality to an extreme degree: 顯然很壞的;壞到極點的: *a ~ traitor;* 罪大惡極的叛國者; *~ injustice.* 極端的不公正。*These fungi are ~ poison.* 這些菌類是最烈性的毒物。 **~·ly** *adv* **~·ness** *n*

ranker /ˈræŋkə(r); ˈræŋkɚ/ *n* commissioned officer who has risen from the ranks. 出身行伍的軍官。⇨ rank¹(3).

rankle /ˈræŋkl; ˈræŋkḷ/ *vi* [VP2A] continue to be a painful or bitter memory: 繼續成爲痛苦或傷心的回憶;使人痛心: *The insult ~d in his mind.* 那次侮辱使他痛心。

ran·sack /ˈrænsæk *US:* rænˈsæk; ˈrænsæk/ *vt* **1** [VP6A, 14, 16A] ***~ sth (for sth/to do sth),*** search (a place) thoroughly (for sth): 遍搜(某地)(找某物): *~ a drawer;* 搜抽屜; *~ a dictionary to find just the right word.* 遍查字典找尋合適的字。 **2** [VP6A, 14] ***~ sth (of sth),*** rob; plunder: 搶劫;掠奪: *The house had been ~ed of all that was worth anything.* 屋裏一切有點兒價值的東西都被搶去了。

ran·som /ˈrænsəm; ˈrænsəm/ *n* [U] freeing of a

R

captive on payment; [C] sum of money, etc, paid for this. 付贖金贖救;贖金。***hold a man to*** ~, keep him as a captive and ask for ~. 擄人待贖;綁票。***worth a king's*** ~, worth a very large sum of money. 值一筆鉅額的金錢。□ *vt* [VP6A] obtain the freedom of (sb), set (sb) free, in exchange for ~: 贖回;贖出(某人);取贖金而釋放(某人): ~ *a kidnapped diplomat.* 贖回遭綁架的外交官。

rant /rænt ; rænt/ *vi, vt* [VP2A, 6A] use extravagant, boasting language; say or recite (sth) noisily and theatrically: 用狂言壯語;喧囂而誇大地說出或背誦(某事物): *an actor who ~s his part.* 一個過份誇張其脚色的演員。□ *n* piece of ~ing talk. 狂言;壯語。**~er** *n* person who ~s. 說狂言壯語者;說話過份誇張者。

rap[1] /ræp ; ræp/ *n* [C] **1** (sound of a) light, quick blow: 輕敲(聲);急拍(聲): *I heard a rap on the door.* 我聽見敲門聲。***give sb a rap on/over the knuckles,*** reprove him. 譴責某人。**2** (colloq) blame; consequences. (俗)責備;後果。***take the rap (for sth),*** be reproved or reprimanded (esp when innocent). (因某事而)受責備;(尤指)背黑鍋。**3** (US sl) conversation; discussion. (美俚)談話;討論。□ *vt, vi* (-pp-) [VP6A, 15B, 2A, C] **1** give a rap to; make the sound of a rap: 輕敲;做出輕敲聲: *rap (on) the table;* 敲桌子; *rap (at) the door.* 敲門。**2** ***rap sth out,*** **(a)** say sth suddenly or sharply: 突然或厲聲說出某事: *rap out an oath.* 厲聲發誓。**(b)** (of spirits at a seance) express by means of raps: (指降神會上的靈魂)以輕敲表達: *rap out a message.* 以輕敲表達鬼魂之意。**3** (US sl) talk; discuss. (美俚)談話;討論。

rap[2] /ræp ; ræp/ *n* ***not care/give a rap,*** not care at all. 全然不介意。

ra·pa·cious /rəˈpeɪʃəs ; rəˈpeʃəs/ *adj* (formal) greedy (esp for money). (正式用語)貪婪的(尤指貪錢)。**~·ly** *adv* **ra·pac·ity** /rəˈpæsətɪ ; rəˈpæsətɪ/ *n* [U] greed; avarice. 貪婪;貪心。

rape[1] /reɪp ; rep/ *n* [U] plant grown as food for sheep and pigs; plant grown for the oil obtained from its seeds. 蕓薹;油菜(作爲羊與猪之飼料,或從其種子榨油)。

rape[2] /reɪp ; rep/ *vt* [VP6A] **1** seize and carry off by force. 强奪;搶劫。**2** commit the crime of forcing sexual intercourse on (a woman or girl). 强姦(婦女)。□ *n* act of raping. 强奪;搶劫;强姦。**rap·ist** /ˈreɪpɪst ; ˈrepɪst/ *n*

rapid /ˈræpɪd ; ˈræpɪd/ *adj* **1** quick; moving, occurring with great speed: 迅速的;敏捷的;快速的: *a ~ decline in sales;* 銷售量急遽下降; *a ~ pulse/river/worker;* 跳動很快的脈搏(水流湍急的河;敏捷的工人); (of action) done quickly: (指動作)很快完成的: *~-fire questions,* in ~ succession. 連珠砲似的問題。**2** (of a slope) steep; descending steeply. (指斜坡)急陡的;陡峭下斜的。□ *n* (usu *pl*) part of a river where a steep slope causes the water to flow fast. (通常用複數)急灘;湍流。**~·ly** *adv* **rap·id·ity** /rəˈpɪdətɪ ; rəˈpɪdətɪ/ *n* [U].

rapier /ˈreɪpɪə(r) ; ˈrepɪɚ/ *n* light sword used for thrusting in duels and the sport of fencing. 在決鬥中或劍術中所用的一種輕劍。**ˈ~-thrust,** (fig) a delicate or witty retort. (喻)靈敏或機智的反駁。

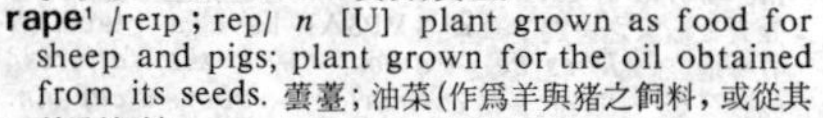

a rapier

rap·ine /ˈræpaɪn *US:* ˈræpɪn ; ˈræpɪn/ *n* (liter or rhet) [U] plundering. (文或修辭)搶劫;强奪。

rap·port /ræˈpɔː(r) *US:* -ˈpɔːrt ; ræˈport/ *n* [U, C] sympathetic relationship. 密切,融洽,和諧的關係。***be in ~ (with),*** (or, as in French, 法文作 ***en*** /ɑːn- ; ɑn-/ ~), in close relationship or sympathy (with). (與…)關係密切或融洽。

rap·proche·ment /ræˈprɒʃmɒŋ *US:* ˌræprəʊʃˈmɒŋ ; raprɔ̃ʃˈmɑ̃/ *n* [C] coming together again (of persons, parties, States) in friendly relations; renewal of friendship. (人,黨派,國家)重建友誼關係;重歸舊好;恢復友誼;復交。

rap·scal·lion /ræpˈskælɪən ; ræpˈskæljən/ *n* (old use) rascal; rogue. (舊用法)流氓;惡徒。

rapt /ræpt ; ræpt/ *adj* so deep in thought, so carried away by feelings, that one is unaware of other things; enraptured: 全神貫注的;心移神馳的;着迷的;狂喜的: *listening to the orchestra with ~ attention;* 聚精會神地聽管絃樂隊演奏; *~ in contemplation of the scenery;* 出神地欣賞風景; *~ in a book.* 潛心於一書。

rap·ture /ˈræptʃə(r) ; ˈræptʃɚ/ *n* **1** [U] state of being rapt; ecstatic delight: 精神貫注;着迷;狂喜: *gazing with ~ at the face of the girl he loved.* 癡癡地望着他喜愛的那個女孩的臉。**2** (*pl*) (複) ***be in/go into/be sent into ~s (over/about),*** be/become extremely happy, full of joy and enthusiasm: 極度喜愛;狂喜;充滿喜悅與熱忱: *She went into ~s over the dresses they showed her.* 她對他們給她看的衣服喜愛若狂。**rap·tur·ous** /ˈræptʃərəs ; ˈræptʃərəs/ *adj* inspiring or expressing ~. 引起或表示狂喜的。**rap·tur·ous·ly** *adv*

rare[1] /reə(r) ; rɛr/ *adj* (-r, -st) **1** unusual; uncommon; not often happening, seen, etc: 罕有的;稀罕的;不常發生或看見的: *a ~ occurrence;* 罕有的事件; *a ~ book,* one of which few copies are obtainable. 善本書;珍本書。*It is very ~ for her to arrive late.* 她是很難得遲到的。**2** (dated colloq) unusually good: (過時俗語)非常好的: *We had a ~ time/~ fun.* 我們玩得非常開心。**3** (of a substance, esp the atmosphere) thin; not dense: (指物質,尤指大氣)稀薄的;不密的: *the ~ air of the mountains in the Himalayas.* 喜馬拉雅山上稀薄的空氣。**~·ly** *adv* **1** seldom: 罕有地;不常地: *I ~ly eat in restaurants.* 我很少在飯館吃飯。*He visits us only ~ly nowadays.* 如今他很少來看望我們。**2** excellently. 極;非常地。**~·ness** *n*

rare[2] /reə(r) ; rɛr/ *adj* (of meat) underdone; cooked so that the redness and juices are retained: (指肉)未煮熟的;半熟的: ~ *steak.* 煎成半生的牛排。

rare·bit /ˈreəbɪt ; ˈrɛrˌbɪt/ *n* [C] **Welsh ~** (also, colloq, 俗亦作 *rabbit*), melted or toasted cheese on toasted bread. 塗於烤過的麵包上的溶化的或烘烤過的乳酪。

rarefy /ˈreərɪfaɪ ; ˈrɛrəˌfaɪ/ *vt, vi* (*pt, pp* -fied) [VP6A, 2A] make or become less dense; purify: 使或變爲稀薄;使純淨;使純: *the rarefied air of the mountain tops;* 山頂上變稀薄的空氣; refine; make subtle: 淨化;精煉: *rarefied ideas/theories.* 千錘百鍊的思想(理論)。**rare·fac·tion** /ˌreərɪˈfækʃn ; ˌrɛrəˈfækʃən/ *n* [U] ~ing. 使或變爲稀薄;使純淨;精煉。

rar·ing /ˈreərɪŋ ; ˈrɛrɪŋ/ *adj* (colloq) full of eagerness: (俗)興致勃勃的;十分渴望的: *They're ~ to go.* 他們亟欲前往。

rar·ity /ˈreərətɪ ; ˈrɛrətɪ/ *n* (*pl* -ties) **1** [U] rareness. 罕有;稀薄。**2** [C] sth rare, uncommon or unusual; sth valued because rare: 罕見之物;珍貴之物: *Rain is a ~ in Upper Egypt.* 在上埃及雨是罕見的。

ras·cal /ˈrɑːskl *US:* ˈræskl ; ˈræskl/ *n* **1** dishonest person. 不忠實的人;流氓。**2** (playfully) mischievous person (esp a child), fond of playing tricks. 好惡作劇的人;喜歡開玩笑的人;(尤指)小淘氣。**~ly** /-kəlɪ ; -klɪ/ *adj* of or like a ~; mean; dishonest: 流氓的;像流氓的;卑鄙的;欺詐的: *a ~ly trick.* 一個卑鄙的騙局。

rase /reɪz ; rez/ *vt* ⇨ raze.

rash[1] /ræʃ ; ræʃ/ *n* (breaking out of, patch of) tiny red spots on the skin: 疹子;發疹;一片紅疹: *a ˈheat-~;* 熱疹; *ˈnettle-~;* 蕁麻疹; (fig) (喻) *a ~ of new red brick bungalows on a country road.* 鄉間大道旁一片新的紅磚平房。*If a ~ appears, the child may have (the) measles.* 如果有一片紅疹出現,這孩子可能是出痲疹。

rash[2] /ræʃ ; ræʃ/ *adj* too hasty; overbold; done,

rare or exotic birds

doing things, without enough thought of the consequences: 太匆忙的；太鹵莽的；輕率而未想及後果的：*a ~ act/statement;* 一個輕率的行動(聲明)；*a ~ young man.* 一個鹵莽的年輕人。**~·ly** *adv* **~·ness** *n*

rasher /ˈræʃə(r) ; ˈræʃə/ *n* slice of bacon or ham (to be) fried:(煎的或待煎的)鹹肉片；火腿片：*eat three ~s and two fried eggs for breakfast.* 早餐吃三片鹹肉和兩個煎蛋。

rasp /rɑːsp *US:* ræsp ; ræsp/ *n* [C] metal tool like a coarse file with a surface or surfaces having sharp points, used for scraping; rough, grating sound produced by this tool. 粗銼刀；銼磨的粗厲刺耳聲。□ *vt, vi* **1** [VP6A, 15A, B, 22] *~ sth (away/off),* scrape with a ~; scrape. 以粗銼刀銼；銼掉。**2** [VP6A] (fig) grate upon, have an irritating effect upon: (喻)激怒；刺激：*~ sb's feelings/nerves.* 刺激某人的感情(神經)。**3** [VP15B] *~ out,* utter in a way that grates or sounds like the noise of a ~: 以使人不快或刺耳的聲音說出：*~ out orders/insults.* 厲聲發出命令(侮辱的話)。**4** [VP2A, C] make a harsh, grating sound: 發出粗厲刺耳之聲：*a learner ~ing (away) on his violin;* 在提琴上拉出刺耳之音的初學者；*a ~ing voice.* 粗厲刺耳的聲音。**~·ing·ly** *adv*

rasp·berry /ˈrɑːzbrɪ *US:* ˈræzberɪ ; ˈræzˌbɛrɪ/ *n* (*pl* -ries) **1** bush with small, sweet, yellow or red berries, wild or cultivated: 覆盆子植物；蕉莓(野生或栽種灌木，其漿果小而甜，呈黃或紅色)：(attrib) (形容用法) *~ jam/canes;* 蕉莓果醬(覆盆子的枝)；one of these berries. 覆盆子之果實；蕉莓。**2** (sl) contemptuous noise made with the tongue and lips, or a gesture indicating dislike, derision or disapproval: (俚)(表示憎惡、嘲弄或不贊成的)咂舌聲或姿態：*give/blow sb a ~;* 咂舌嘲弄某人；*get a ~.* 受人咂舌嘲弄。

rat /ræt ; ræt/ *n* **1** animal like, but larger than, a mouse; person who deserts a cause that he thinks is about to fail (from the belief that rats desert a ship that will sink or be wrecked). 鼠(較 mouse 大者)；見風轉舵的人；變節者(出自鼠會捨棄將沉沒或遇難的船之說法)。⇨ the illus at small. 參看 small 之插圖。***smell a rat,*** suspect that sth wrong is being done. 懷疑其中有詭詐。***(look) like a drowned rat,*** wet and miserable; soaked to the skin. (顯得)濕而可憐的；全身濕透的。**the ˈrat race,** ceaseless and undignified competition for success in one's career, social status, etc as among office workers, etc. 激烈競爭。**2** (fig) cowardly traitor; strike-breaker. (喻)懦弱的叛逆者；破壞罷工者。**Rats!** (dated sl, as an exclamation) Nonsense! (過時俚語，作驚嘆詞用)胡說！□ *vi* (-tt-) **1** [VP2A] hunt rats: 捕鼠：*go ratting.* 去捕鼠。**2** [VP2A, 3A] *~ (on sb),* break a promise, withdraw from an undertaking. 背叛(某人)(如不履行諾言或退出一事業)。 **rat·ter** *n* man, dog or cat that catches rats: 捕鼠之人、狗或猫：*Are terriers good ratters?* 㹴是善捕鼠的狗嗎？ **rat·ty** *adj* (-ier, -iest) (colloq) irritable; snappish. (俗)易怒的；暴躁的。

rat·able, rate·able /ˈreɪtəbl ; ˈretəbḷ/ *adj* liable to payment of municipal rates: 應徵地方稅的：*~ property;* 應徵地方稅的財產；*the ~ value of a house,* its value as assessed for the levying of rates. 一棟房屋之課稅現值。**rat·abil·ity, rate·abil·ity** /ˌreɪtəˈbɪlətɪ ; ˌretəˈbɪlətɪ/ *n* [U].

rat·an /ræˈtæn ; ræˈtæn/ ⇨ rattan.

rat-a-tat-tat /ˌræt ə ˌtæt ˈtæt ; ˌrætəˌtætˈtæt/ ⇨ rat-tat.

ratch /rætʃ ; rætʃ/ *n* = ratchet.

ratch·et /ˈrætʃɪt ; ˈrætʃɪt/ *n* toothed wheel provided with a catch (*pawl*) that prevents the wheel from slipping back and allows it to move in only one direction. 棘輪；棘輪機(一種有齒之輪，裝有一掣子，用以防止輪子滑回，而只許向一個方向移動)。

rate¹ /reɪt ; ret/ *n* **1** [C] standard of reckoning, obtained by bringing two numbers or amounts into relationship: 比率；率：*walk at the ~ of 3 miles an hour;* 以每小時三哩的速度走路；*a train* *travelling at a/the ~ of 50 miles an hour;* 以時速五十哩行駛的火車; *an aircraft with a good ~ of climb;* 一種爬升率甚高的飛機; *at a great/fearful, etc ~,* at great speed; 以高速度; *buy things at the ~ of 55p a hundred.* 以每一百個五十五辨士的價格買東西。*What is the airmail letter ~ to Peru?* 寄航空信件到祕魯的郵資是多少? ⇨ per; to¹(12). **'birth/'marriage/'death, etc ~,** the number of births, etc in relationship to a period of time and a number of people: 出生(結婚, 死亡等)率: *a death-~ of 2.3 per 1000 (per year).* (每年)千分之 2.3 的死亡率。 **~ of exchange,** relationship between two currencies (eg US dollars and F francs). 兩種貨幣間的兌換率。 **the 'discount ~, the 'bank ~,** the officially announced percentage at which a country's central bank is prepared to discount Bills. 貼現率(銀行準備對期票貼現的官方公布之百分率)。 **2** (phrases) (片語) ***at 'this/'that ~,*** if this/that is true, if we may assume that this/that is the case; if this/that state of affairs continues. 如果此(彼)種情形是眞實的話; 如果我們可以假定情形如此(彼); 如此(彼)種情形繼續下去。 ***at 'any ~,*** in any case; whatever happens. 在任何情形下; 無論如何。 **3 (the) ~s,** (GB) tax on property (land and buildings), paid to local authorities for local purposes: (英)地方徵收之財產(土地與建築物)稅: *an extra penny on the ~s for the public library,* ie a charge of one penny on each pound of the assessment. 爲興建公立圖書館而在財產稅每鎊中附徵的一辨士。 **~s and taxes,** payments to local authorities and taxes levied by the national government. 地方稅與中央稅。 **'~-payer** *n* person liable to have ~s exacted from him. (地方稅之)納稅人。⇨ also *water-~* at water¹(7). **4** (with ordinal numbers) class or grade: (與序數連用)等級: *first ~,* excellent; 第一等; 最好的; *second ~,* fairly good; 第二等; 尙好; *third ~,* (rather) poor; 第三等; (頗)差; (attrib, with a hyphen) (形容用法, 加連字符號) *a first-~ teacher.* 第一流的教師。Hence, 由此產生, *ˌfirst-'rater, ˌsecond-'rater, etc.* 一流, 二流等的人或物。

rate² /reɪt; ret/ *vt, vi* **1** [VP6A, 14, 15A, 16B] ~ ***(at),*** judge or estimate the value or qualities of: 估價; 評價; 評估: *What do you ~ his fortune at?* 你估計他的財產有多少? *He was a man whom all his friends ~d as kind and hospitable.* 所有他的朋友都認爲他是一個仁慈而好客的人。 *Do you ~* (= consider) *Mr X among your friends?* 你認爲X先生是你的朋友嗎? **2** [VP6A, 14] ~ ***sth (at),*** (GB) value (property) for the purpose of assessing rates(3) on: (英)評估(財產之)課稅現值: *My property was ~d at £100 per annum.* 我的財產估計每年應繳稅一百鎊。 *Should private houses be more heavily ~d than factories?* 私人房產應該比工廠課更重的稅嗎? **3** [VP16B] ~ ***sb as,*** (naut) place in a certain class: (航海)定出等級: *He was ~d as a midshipman.* 他被定爲海軍學校見習生的等級。 **4** [VP2D, C] (colloq) be ~ed: (俗)被定出等級: *He ~s high/as a midshipman.* 他的等級很高(被定爲海軍學校見習生)。

rate·able /'reɪtəbl; 'retəbl̩/ *adj* ⇨ ratable.

rather /'rɑːðə(r) *US:* 'ræ-; 'ræðɚ/ *adv* **1** more willingly; by preference or choice (usu 通常作 ***would/had ~... than;*** also with inversion 也可顚倒作: ***~ than...would***): 更爲情願地; 寧願: *I would ~ you came tomorrow than today.* 我寧願你明天來, 不要今天來。 *She would ~ have the small one than the large one.* 她寧願要小的一個而不要大的。 *Wouldn't you ~ be liked than feared?* 你不是寧願受人愛戴, 不願讓人懼怕嗎? *He resigned ~ than take part in such a dishonest transaction.* 他寧願辭職也不願參與這種欺詐的交易。 *A: 'Will you join us in a game of cards?'—B: 'Thank you, but I'd ~ not.'* 甲:'你願參加我們的牌戲嗎?'—乙:'謝謝, 我不想參加。' **2** more truly, accurately or precisely: 更眞實, 正確或精密地: *He arrived very late last night or ~ in the early hours this morning.* 他昨晚深夜到達, 或更精確地說, 在今天凌晨到達。 **3** (to be distinguished from *fairly²*; note that *fairly* is not used with comparatives, *too, nn,* and *vv*) (應與 fairly² 區分; 注意: fairly² 不與比較級, too, 名詞和動詞連用) in a certain degree or measure; more (so) than not; somewhat; 相當地; 多多少少; 有一點; **(a)** (with *adjj,* preceding or following the *indef art,* following the *def art*): (與形容詞連用; 放在不定冠詞之前或後, 放在定冠詞之後): *a ~ surprising result/~ a surprising result;* 一個相當驚人的結果; *the ~ tall boy in the corner.* 在牆角那個相當高的男孩子。 **(b)** (with comparatives): (與比較級的形容詞或副詞連用): *My brother is ~ better today.* 我哥哥(弟弟)今天好得多了。 *This hat is ~ more expensive than that.* 這頂帽子比那一頂貴得多。 **(c)** (with *too*): (與 too 連用): *This book is ~ too difficult for the juniors and ~ too easy for the seniors.* 這本書對低年級學生太難, 對高年級學生又太容易。 **(d)** (with *nn*): (與名詞連用): *It's ~ a pity, ~* regrettable. 令人相當惋惜。 *She's ~ a dear, ~* lovable. 她是個相當可愛的人。 *£100 is ~ a lot to pay for a dress, isn't it?* 一百鎊買一件女裝太貴了點, 不是嗎? **(e)** (with *vv* and *pp*): (與動詞及過去分詞連用): *I ~ think you may be mistaken.* 我倒認爲你可能錯了。 *The rain ~ spoiled our holiday.* 我們的假日適逢下雨, 頗爲掃興。 *We were all ~ exhausted when we got to the top of the mountain.* 我們到達山頂時, 都相當疲倦了。 **(f)** (with *advv*): (與副詞連用): *You've done ~ well/~ better than I had expected.* 你做得很好(比我預期的要好得多)。 **4** (colloq; GB /ˌrɑː'ðɜː(r); 'rɑðɚ/) (in answers) most certainly. (俗)(用於回答中)確實如此; 當然; 一定。

rat·ify /'rætɪfaɪ; 'rætəˌfaɪ/ *vt* (*pt, pp* -fied) [VP6A] confirm (an agreement) by signature or other formality. 批准。 **rati·fi·ca·tion** /ˌrætɪfɪ'keɪʃn; ˌrætəfə'keʃən/ *n* ~ing or being ratified. 批准; 被批准。

rat·ing /'reɪtɪŋ; 'retɪŋ/ *n* **1** [C] act of valuing property for the purpose of assessing rates, ⇨ rate²(2); amount or sum fixed as the municipal rate. 評估財產之課稅現值; 地方稅額。 **2** [C] class, classification, eg of yachts by tonnage, motor-cars by engine capacity or horse-power; popularity of radio or TV programmes as estimated by asking a selected group. 等級; 類別; 分類(例如遊艇按噸數分類, 汽車按馬力分類); (根據抽樣調查所得廣播或電視節目的)收視(聽)率。 **3** (navy) person's position or class as recorded in the ship's books; noncommissioned sailor: (海軍) 艦艇記錄上所記載的職別或等級; 兵類: *officers and ~s.* 海軍官兵。

ra·tio /'reɪʃɪəʊ; 'reʃo/ *n* (*pl* ~s /-ʃɪəʊz; -ʃoz/) [C] relation between two amounts determined by the number of times one contains the other: 比; 比率: *The ~s of 1 to 5 and 20 to 100 are the same.* 1 與 5 和 20 與 100 的比率是相同的。

rati·oc·in·ation /ˌrætɪˌɒsɪ'neɪʃn *US:* ˌræʃɪ-; ˌræʃɪˌɑsn̩'eʃən/ *n* [U] the process of methodical reasoning, esp by the use of syllogisms. 推論(尤指使用三段論法者)。

ration /'ræʃn; 'ræʃən/ *n* fixed quantity, esp of food, allowed to one person; (*pl*) fixed allowance served out to, eg members of the armed forces: 定量(尤指配給個人之食物的定額); (複)口糧; 配給(如配給三軍人員者): *go and draw ~s.* 去領取配給。 **'~ card/book,** one that entitles the holder to ~s, eg for a civilian when there is a food shortage during or immediately after a war. 配給卡(簿)。 ***be on short ~s,*** be allowed or able to have less than the usual quantity of food. 糧食配給不足; 糧食缺乏。□ *vt* **1** [VP6A] limit (sb) to a fixed ~. 定量配給(某人)。 **2** [VP6A, 15B] ~ ***(out),*** limit (food, water, etc): 限制使用(食物、水等): *We'll have to ~ the water.* 我們將限制用水。 *He ~ed out* (= distributed ~s of) *the bread.* 他分發麵包。

ra·tional /ˈræʃnəl ; ˈræʃənl/ *adj* **1** of reason or reasoning. 理性的;推理的。 **2** able to reason; having the faculty of reasoning. 能推理的;有推理能力的。 **3** sensible; that can be tested by reasoning: 明達的;合理的: ~ *conduct/explanations.* 合理的行爲(解釋)。 **~ly** /-ʃnəlɪ ; -ʃənlɪ/ *adv* **~·ity** /ˌræʃəˈnælətɪ ; ˌræʃəˈnælətɪ/ *n* quality of being ~; reasonableness. 理性;明達;推理能力。

ration·ale /ˌræʃəˈnɑːl ; ˌræʃəˈnæl/ *n* fundamental reason, logical basis (of sth). (某事物的)基本理由;理論基礎。

ration·al·ism /ˈræʃnəlɪzəm ; ˈræʃənlˌɪzəm/ *n* [U] the practice of treating reason as the ultimate authority in religion as in other subjects of study. 理性主義;唯理主義。**ration·al·ist** /-ɪst ; -ɪst/ *n* person who accepts reason as the ultimate authority in religion, ethics, etc. 理性主義者;唯理論者。 **ration·al·is·tic** /ˌræʃnəˈlɪstɪk ; ˌræʃənlˈɪstɪk/ *adj* of ~ or rationalists. 理性主義的;理性主義者的。

ration·al·ize /ˈræʃnəlaɪz ; ˈræʃənlˌaɪz/ *vt* **1** [VP6A] bring into conformity with reason; (attempt to) treat or explain in a rational manner: 使合理;(試圖)以合理態度處理或解釋: ~ *one's fears/behaviour.* 合理解釋自己的恐懼(行爲)。 **2** [VP6A] reorganize (an industry, etc) so as to lessen or get rid of waste (in time, labour, materials, etc). 改組(工業等)以減少或消除(時間、人工、材料等之)浪費。 **ration·al·iz·ation** /ˌræʃnəlaɪˈzeɪʃn *US:* -lɪˈz- ; ˌræʃənəlɪˈzeʃən/ *n*

rat·lin, rat·line /ˈrætlɪn ; ˈrætlɪn/ *n* (usu *pl*) small rope fixed across the shrouds of a ship (like a rung on a ladder) used as a step by a sailor climbing up or down. (通常用複數)索梯(船上橫着固定在護桅索上的細繩,類似梯階,供船員爬上爬下之用)。

rat·tan, ratan /ræˈtæn ; ræˈtæn/ *n* **1** [C] (East Indian palm-tree with a) cane-like stem. 省籐(東印度所產之棕櫚樹);籐。 **2** [C] walking-stick or cane made from a ~ stem. 籐杖。 **3** [U] ~ stems (collectively), as used for building, basketwork, furniture, etc: (集合用法)(用於建築、籃狀編製品、傢具等之)籐條: *a chair with a ~ seat.* 一把有籐座的椅子。

rat-tat /ræ ˈtæt ; ˌræˈtæt/ (also 亦作 **rat-a-tat-tat** /ˌræt ə ˌtæt ˈtæt ; ˌrætəˌtætˈtæt/) *n* sound of rapping or knocking, esp on a door. 砰砰敲擊聲;(尤指)敲門聲。

rattle /ˈrætl ; ˈrætl/ *vt, vi* **1** [VP6A, 15A, 2A, C] (cause to) make short, sharp sounds quickly, one after the other: (使)急速、連續地發出短促尖銳的聲音;發嘎嘎聲: *The wind ~d the windows.* 風吹得窗子嘎嘎作響。 *The windows were rattling in the wind.* 窗子在風中嘎嘎作響。 *The hailstones ~d on the tin roof.* 冰雹砰砰地落在洋鐵皮屋頂上。 *The old bus ~d along over the stony road.* 那輛老爺公共汽車在石子路上嘎嘎地往前行駛。 **2** [VP2C, 15B] ~ ***away;*** ~ ***sth off,*** talk, say or repeat (sth) quickly and in a thoughtless or lively way: 疾速而不加思索地談,說或重述(某事物);喋喋而言: *The boy ~d off the poem he had learnt.* 那男孩將他學到的那首詩背得滾瓜爛熟。 *The children ~d away merrily.* 這些孩子愉快地喋喋不休地說話。 □ *n* **1** [U] rattling sound: 嘎嘎聲;喋喋聲: *the ~ of bottles from a milkman's van;* 送牛奶者的貨車裏發出的奶瓶碰擊聲; *the ~ of hail on the window-panes.* 冰雹打在玻璃窗上的砰砰聲。 **2** [C] baby's toy for producing a rattling sound; similar device whirled (eg by spectators at a football match) to make a noisy clatter. 撥浪鼓(能發出嘎嘎聲的玩具);發出嘎嘎聲的手搖物(如足球觀衆所持者)。 **3** [U] lively flow of talk; chatter. 喋喋不休的談話;饒舌。 **4** [C] series of horny rings in a ~snake's tail. (響尾蛇尾部的)一列響環。 **ˈ~·snake** *n* poisonous American snake that makes a rattling noise with its tail. 響尾蛇(美洲產的一種毒蛇,其尾常發出聲響)。 ⇨ the illus at snake. 參看 snake 之插圖。 **5 (ˈdeath-)~,** rattling sound sometimes produced in the throat immediately before death. 死前喉間有時發出的咯咯聲。 **6 ˈ~-brain, ˈ~-pate** *nn* person with an empty head; silly chatterer. 沒有思想的蠢人;愚蠢而又嘮叨的人。 Hence, 由此產生, **ˈ~-brained, ˈ~-pated** *adjj* **rat·tler** /ˈrætlə(r) ; ˈrætlɚ/ *n* person or thing that ~s, esp a ~snake. 發出嘎嘎、喋喋等聲的人或物;(尤指)響尾蛇。 **rat·tling** /ˈrætlɪŋ ; ˈrætlɪŋ/ *adj* (sl) quick(-moving); first-rate; excellent: (俚)(行動)很快的;第一流的;卓越的: *travelling at a rattling rate;* 以極快速度旅行; *a rattling breeze;* 颯颯之微風; *have a rattling* (= enjoyable) *time.* 度過一段非常愉快的時光。 ▭ *adv* (sl) very: (俚)非常: *a rattling good speech.* 一篇極好的演說。

ratty /ˈrætɪ ; ˈrætɪ/ *adj* ⇨ rat.

rau·cous /ˈrɔːkəs ; ˈrɔkəs/ *adj* (of sounds) harsh; rough; hoarse: (指聲音)粗厲的;沙啞的: *the ~ cries of the crows;* 烏鴉的粗啞的叫聲; *a ~ voice;* 沙啞的聲音; ~ *laughter.* 沙啞的笑聲。 **~·ly** *adv*

rav·age /ˈrævɪdʒ ; ˈrævɪdʒ/ *vt* [VP6A] **1** destroy; damage badly: 毀壞;嚴重的損壞: *forests ~d by fire;* 被大火損毀的森林; *a face ~d by disease,* eg covered with marks after smallpox. 爲病所毀的面容(如患天花後留有麻子)。 **2** (of armies, etc) rob, plunder, with violence: (指軍隊等)搶刼;掠奪: *They had ~d the countryside.* 他們已把鄉間洗刼一空。 □ *n* **1** [U] destruction; devastation. 破壞;蹂躪。 **2** (*pl*) (複) **~s of,** destructive effects: 破壞的結果: *the ~s of time,* eg on a woman's looks; 時間的摧殘(如在婦女之容貌上所造成者); *the ~s of torrential rains.* 暴雨造成的災情。

rave /reɪv ; rev/ *vi, vt* **1** [VP2A, C, 3A] ~ ***(at/against/about sth),*** talk wildly, violently, angrily: 狂野地、粗暴地、憤怒地講;發狂言或譫語: *The patient* (eg someone with a high fever) *began to ~.* 病人(如發高燒者)開始胡言亂語。 *When he was accused of stealing he ~d wildly against me.* 當他被控犯偷竊罪時,他氣呼呼地把我臭罵一頓。 **2** [VP3A] ~ ***about sb/sth,*** talk or act with (often) excessive enthusiasm: 過分熱心地說或做: *She ~d about the food she had had in France.* 她過分誇張地談她在法國吃過的食物。 **3** [VP15B] ~ ***it up,*** (sl) take part in a very noisy, enjoyable party. (俚)參加一熱鬧愉快的聚會。Hence, 由此產生, **ˈ~-up** *n* lively party. 熱鬧的聚會。 □ *n* **1** (colloq, often attrib) enthusiastic praise: (俗,常作形容用法)熱烈的誇獎;大捧特捧: *a ~ review,* eg of a book. (對一本書等之)大捧特捧的評論。 **2** (sl) wild, exciting party, dance, outing, etc. (俚)狂熱的宴會、舞會、遠足等。 **3** (sl) great enthusiasm: (俚)極端的熱心: *be in a ~ about sb.* 對某人極端的熱心。 **raver** *n* (colloq) sb who ~s(3). (俗)過分熱心地說或做的人。**rav·ing** *adj* talking wildly: 發狂言譫語的: *a raving lunatic.* 一個說狂話的瘋子。▭ *adv* to the point of talking wildly: 近乎放肆地狂言: *You're raving mad!* 你簡直在說瘋話! **rav·ings** *n pl* foolish or wild talk: 愚蠢或狂野的談話: *the ravings of a madman.* 狂人的囈語。

ravel /ˈrævl ; ˈrævl/ *vt, vi* (-ll-, US also -l-) **1** [VP2A, C] (of knitted or woven things) separate into threads; become untwisted; fray: (指編織物)綻線;綻裂;散開;磨散: *Bind the edge of the rug so that it won't ~.* 把地毯邊鑲好以免它綻線。 **2** [VP6A] cause (threads, hair, etc) to be twisted together, knotted, etc; (fig) make confused. 使(線,髮等)糾結一起;(喻)使混亂。 **3** [VP6A, 15B] ~ ***(out),*** disentangle: 解開;清理: ~ (*out*) *a rope's end.* 解開繩之一端。 ⇨ unravel.

raven /ˈreɪvn ; ˈrevən/ *n* **1** large, black bird like a crow, popularly regarded as a bird of ill omen. 渡鳥(一種大烏鴉,一般視爲不吉之鳥)。 **2** (attrib) glossy, shining black: (形容用法)烏溜溜的: ~ *locks,* black hair. 烏溜溜的頭髮。

rav·en·ing /ˈrævənɪŋ ; ˈrævənɪŋ/ *adj* fierce; savage; crazy for food: 兇猛的;野蠻的;貪吃的: *a ~ wolf.* 一隻兇猛的餓狼。

R

rav·en·ous /ˈrævənəs ; ˈrævənəs/ *adj* **1** very hungry. 很餓的。 **2** greedy: 貪婪的: *a ~ appetite;* 貪婪的食慾; *~ hunger;* 極度飢餓; *~ for power.* 貪圖權力。 **~·ly** *adv* hungrily; greedily: 飢餓地;貪婪地: *eat ~ly.* 貪婪地吃。

ra·vine /rəˈviːn ; rəˈvin/ *n* deep, narrow valley. 深而狹的谷;峽谷。

ravi·oli /ˌrævɪˈəʊlɪ ; ˌrævɪˈolɪ/ *n* (I) dish of small cases of pasta containing chopped meat, etc usu served with a sauce. (義)一種類似餃子的點心。

rav·ish /ˈrævɪʃ ; ˈrævɪʃ/ *vt* [VP6A] **1** fill with delight; enchant: 使狂喜;使陶醉: *a ~ing view;* 醉人的景色; *~ed by the view;* 爲美景所陶醉; *~ed with her beauty.* 爲她的美所傾倒。 **~·ing·ly** *adv* **~·ment** *n* ~ing or being ~ed. 狂喜;陶醉。 **2** (archaic or poet) seize and carry off: (古或詩)攫奪;掠刼: *~ed from the world by death.* 被死亡刼去; 死。 **3** (archaic) rape (a woman or girl). (古)强姦(婦女)。

raw /rɔː ; rɔ/ *adj* **1** uncooked: 未煮過的: *raw meat;* 生肉; *eat oysters raw.* 吃生蠔。 **2** in the natural state, not manufactured or prepared for use: 天然狀態的;未經製造或加工的: *raw hides,* not yet tanned; 生牛皮(未硝的); *raw sugar,* not yet refined; 粗糖(未精煉過的); *the raw materials of industry,* eg coal, ores; 工業用的原料(如煤,原礦); *raw spirit,* undiluted alcohol. 未稀釋之酒精。 ***in the raw,*** unrefined; in the natural state; (fig) naked. 純眞的; 天然的;(喻)裸體的。 **ˈraw·hide** *adj* made of untanned hide: 生牛皮做的: *rawhide boots.* 生牛皮做的皮靴。 **3** (of persons) untrained; unskilled; inexperienced: (指人)未受訓練的;不熟練的;無經驗的: *raw recruits,* for the army, etc. 新兵。 **4** (of the weather) damp and cold: (指天氣)潮濕而冷的: *a raw February morning;* 一個陰冷的二月的早晨; *raw winds.* 陰寒的風。 **5** (of wounds) unhealed; bloody; (of a place on the flesh) with the skin rubbed off; sore and painful. (指傷)未癒的;流血的;(指肉上一處)擦掉皮的;疼痛的。 **ˌraw-ˈboned** *adj* having little flesh on the bones: 骨瘦如柴的: *a raw-boned horse.* 一匹瘦馬。 **6** artistically crude: 技藝上不成熟的: *His literary style is still rather raw.* 他的文學風格還相當不成熟。 **7** (colloq) harsh; unjust; (俗)嚴苛的;不公的; (esp) (尤用於) ***a raw deal,*** harsh or cruel treatment. 嚴苛或殘酷的對待。 □ *n* raw place on the skin, esp on a horse's skin. 皮膚(尤指馬的皮膚)上的擦傷之處。 ***touch sb on the raw,*** (fig) wound a person's feelings, wound him on the question, topic, etc on which he is most sensitive. (喻)傷害到某人的感情;觸及某人的痛處。

ray[1] /reɪ ; re/ *n* [C] **1** line, beam, of radiant light, heat, energy: (輻射的光、熱、能的)線;射線: *the rays of the sun;* 太陽的光線; *ˈX-rays; X* 射線; *ˈheat-rays;* 熱射線; (fig) (喻) *a ray of hope.* 一線希望。 **2** any one of a number of lines coming out from a centre. 從一中心射出之許多線中之一。□ *vi, vt* send out or come out in rays. 呈線狀射出。

ray[2] /reɪ ; re/ *n* kinds of large sea-fish with a broad, flat body, eg *skate.* 魟魚;鰩魚(數種大海魚,身體寬而扁,如耙魟等)。

rayon /ˈreɪɒn ; ˈreɑn/ *n* [U] silk-like material made from cellulose: 嫘縈;人造絲: (attrib) (形容用法) *~ shirts.* 人造絲做的襯衫。

raze, rase /reɪz ; rez/ *vt* [VP6A] destroy (towns, buildings) completely, esp by making them level with the ground: 徹底破壞(城市、建築物);(尤指)夷爲平地: *a city ~d by an earthquake.* 一個被地震摧毀的城市。

razor /ˈreɪzə(r) ; ˈrezɚ/ *n* instrument with a sharp blade or cutters (some electrically driven) used for shaving hair from the skin. (電動)刮鬍刀;剃刀。 **ˈsafety ~** *n* kind in which a thin blade is fitted between metal guards. 安全剃刀。 **ˈ~-back** *n* kind of whale. 剃刀鯨。 **ˈ~-backed** *adj* having a thin, sharp back: 有尖突脊背的: *a ~-backed pig.* 一隻脊背尖突的瘦豬。 **ˈ~-blade** *n* disposable blade for a safety ~. 刮鬍刀片。 **ˌ~-ˈedge** *n* sharp line of division; critical situation. 明顯的分界線;危險的情勢;危機。 □ *vt* (rare, except in *pp*): (罕,僅用過去分詞): *a well-~ed chin,* well shaved. 剃得很光的下巴。

razors

razzle /ˈræzl ; ˈræzl̩/ *n* (also 亦作 **ˌ~-ˈdazzle**) ***be/go on the ~,*** (sl) be/go on a spree. (俚)狂飲。 ⇨ spree.

re[1] /riː ; ri/ *prep* (in legal style) in the matter of; concerning. (法律用語)關於。

re[2] /reɪ ; re/ *n* second note in the musical octave. 八度音程中之第二音。

re- /riː- ; rɪ-/ *pref* **1** again: 再;重: *reappear, refloat, replay.* 再出現; 再浮起; 重賽。 **2** in a different way: 以不同之方式: *rearrange.* 重新安排。⇨ App 3. 參看附錄三。

reach /riːtʃ ; ritʃ/ *vt, vi* **1** [VP2C, 3C, 15B] *~ (out) (for),* stretch out: 伸出: *He ~ed out his hand for the knife, but it was too far away.* 他伸出手取那刀子,但太遠了,搆不著。 *He ~ed (out) for the dictionary.* 他伸出手拿字典。 **2** [VP6A, 15B, 12B, 13B] stretch out the hand for and take (sth); get and give (sth) to: 伸手取(某物);把(某物)遞給: *Can you ~ that book for your brother?* 你能把那本書遞給你哥哥(弟弟)嗎? *Please ~ me that book.* 請把那本書遞給我。 *He ~ed down the atlas from the top shelf.* 他從書架的頂層取下地圖集來。 **3** [VP6A] (lit or fig) get to, go as far as: (字面或喻)抵達;到: *~ London;* 抵達倫敦; *~ the end of the chapter.* 看到這章的末尾。 *Can you ~ the branch with those red apples?* 你能搆到那根結有紅蘋果的枝子嗎? *Not a sound ~ed our ears.* 我們沒有聽到任何聲音。 **4** [VP2C] extend; go; pass: 延伸;通到;傳達: *My land ~es as far as the river.* 我的地一直延伸到河邊。 *The speaker's voice did not ~ to the back of the hall.* 講演者的聲音不能傳到大廳的後邊。 *I haven't been able to reach Kate for days,* ie get into contact with her, eg by telephone. 我已好些天沒有聯絡到凱蒂了(如以電話聯絡)。 ***as far as the eye can ~,*** to the horizon. 就目力之所及;遠及地平線;極目。 **5** **ˈ~-me-downs** *n pl* (sl) second-hand clothes. (俚)估衣。□ *n* **1** (*sing* only) act of ~ing or stretching out (a hand, etc): (僅用單數) (手等之)伸出;延伸: *get sth by a long ~.* 把手伸長取某物。 **2** [U] extent to which a hand, etc can be ~ed out, a movement carried out or one's mental powers extended or used: (手、活動、心力等所及的)範圍: *This boxer has a long ~.* 這位拳擊手的手搆得很遠。 ***within/out of/beyond ~:*** *I like to have my reference books within my ~/within easy ~,* so near that I can get them quickly and easily. 我喜歡把參考書放在我伸手可取的範圍內 (順手可取的地方)。 *Put that bottle of weed-killer out of the children's ~/out of ~ of the children.* 把那瓶除草藥放在孩子們拿不到的地方。 *The hotel is within easy ~ of the beach.* 這家旅館距離海濱很近。 *The village is within ~ of London.* 該村莊就在倫敦附近。 *He was beyond ~ of human aid,* No one could do anything to help him. 任何人都幫不上他的忙。 **3** [C] continuous extent, esp of a river or canal, that can be seen between two bends or locks. 連續不斷的地區;(尤指河或運河的兩彎間可見的)河段。⇨ lock[2](3): *one of the most beautiful ~es of the Thames.* 泰晤士河最美麗的河段之一。

re·act /rɪˈækt ; rɪˈækt/ *vi* **1** [VP2A, 3A] ~ ***on/upon,*** have an effect (on the person or thing acting): 對(行動中的人或進行中的事)有影響: *Applause ~s upon a speaker,* eg has the effect of giving him confidence. 鼓掌對一個演說者有影響(例如給他信心)。 **2** [VP3A] ~ ***to,*** respond; behave differently, be changed, as the result of being acted upon: 反應;因受影響而改變行動: *An orator ~s to applause.* 一個演說家對於鼓掌有反應。 *Do children ~ to kind treatment by becoming more self-confident?* 對孩子們和善是否會使他們更有自信? **3** [VP3A] ~ ***against,*** respond to sth with a feeling: 反抗;反對: *Will the people one day ~ against the political system that oppresses them?* 人們有一天會反抗壓迫他們的政治制度嗎? **4** [VP3A] ~ ***on,*** (chem) (of one substance applied to another) have an effect: (化學) (指加於他種物質之某種物質) (對…)起反應: *How do acids ~ on metals?* 酸對金屬會引起怎樣的化學反應?

re·ac·tion /rɪˈækʃn ; rɪˈækʃən/ *n* [C, U] **1** action or state resulting from, in response to, sth, esp a return to an earlier condition after a period of the opposite condition: 反應;反動;反作用: *action and ~.* 作用與反作用。 *After these days of excitement there was a ~,* eg a period when life seemed dull. 經過這些天的興奮之後又有一段沉悶生活。 *Higher wages affect costs of production and then comes the ~ of costs on prices.* 較高的工資會影響生產成本,而生產成本又會影響售價。 **2** retrograde tendency, esp in politics; opposition to progress: 倒退之傾向(尤指政治方面);反動;反進步: *The forces of ~ made reform difficult.* 反動力量使改革困難。 **3** responsive feeling: 反應: *What was his ~ to your proposal?* 他對你的建議有何反應? **4** (science) action set up by one substance in another; change within the nucleus of an atom. (科學)化學反應;核子反應。 **~·ary** /rɪˈækʃənrɪ *US:* -ənerɪ ; rɪˈækʃənˌɛrɪ/ *n* (*pl* -ries), *adj* (person) opposing progress or reform. 反對進步或改革的(人);反動的(人)。

re·ac·tor /rɪˈæktə(r) ; rɪˈæktɚ/ *n* **nuclear ~,** apparatus for the controlled production of nuclear energy; atomic pile. 核子反應器(一種控制核能生產的裝置);原子爐。

read /riːd ; rid/ *vt, vi* (*pt, pp* read /red ; rɛd/) **1** [VP6A, 2A] (used in the simple tenses or with *can/be able*) look at and (be able to) understand (sth written or printed): (用作簡單時態或與can, be able 連用時)讀;看懂: *Can you ~ Chinese characters/French/a musical score?* 你能看懂中文字(法文,樂譜)嗎? *A motorist must be able to ~ traffic signs.* 駕車者必須能看懂交通標誌。 *Can the child ~ the time/the clock yet?* 這孩子會看時間(鐘)嗎? *I can't ~ your shorthand notes.* 我看不懂你的速記符號。 *The boy can neither ~ nor write.* 這男孩既不會讀也不會寫。 **2** [VP6A, 12A, 13A, 15B, 2A, C] (simple or continuous tenses) reproduce mentally or vocally the words of (an author, book, etc): (用於簡單式或進行式)閱讀;默讀;朗誦: *R~ the letter aloud, please.* 請大聲唸這封信。 *She was ~ing the letter silently/to herself* 她正在默讀那封信。 *She was ~ing a story to the children.* 她正在唸一篇故事給孩子們聽。 *I haven't enough time to ~/for ~ing.* 我沒有足够的時間閱讀。 *He ~ the letter through six times.* 他把那封信從頭到尾看了六次。 *Please ~ me the letter.* 請把那封信唸給我聽。 *She ~ out the letter to all of us.* 她向我們大家朗誦那封信。 *The old man ~ me a lesson/~ me a severe lecture,* reproved me. 那老人教訓了我一番。 *The play was ~* (ie each actor ~ his part aloud) *before the cast went on the stage.* 劇本在上演之前先(由演員)誦讀臺詞。 **3** [VP6A, 15A, B] study (a subject, esp at a university): 研究;攻讀(一學科,尤指大學中者): *He's ~ing physics/~ing for a degree in physics/~ing for a physics degree at Cambridge.* 他在劍橋大學攻讀物理(攻讀物理學位)。 *He's ~ing for the Bar,* studying law in order to become a barrister. 他在攻讀法律準備當律師。 *You had better ~ the subject up,* make a special study of it. 你最好對這科目作深入的研究。 **4** [VP6A] interpret mentally; learn the significance of: 解釋;解答;領會…的意義: *~ a riddle/dream;* 解謎(詳夢); *~ sb's thoughts.* 了解某人之思想。 *The gipsy offered to ~ my hand/palm,* tell me about myself and the future by examining the lines on the palm of my hand. 那個吉卜賽人要爲我看手相。 **5** [VP2C] give a certain impression; seem (good, etc) when ~: 給予某種印象;讀起來似乎(不錯等): *The play ~s better than it acts,* is better for ~ing than for performance on the stage. 這個劇本讀起來要比上演好得多。 **6** [VP16B] assume, find implications in (what is read, etc): 假定或找出(所讀之物等中)的含意: *Silence mustn't always be ~ as consent,* We must not always assume that a person means 'Yes' when no answer is given to a request, etc. 沉默不能永遠被假定爲同意。 ~ ***into,*** add more than is justified: 加上某種含意;自以爲有某種含意: *You have ~ into her letter more sympathy than she probably feels.* 你自以爲她信中的同情比她可能感覺到的要多。 ~ ***between the lines,*** look for or discover meanings that are not actually expressed. 找出字裏行間的言外之意。 **7** [VP2B] (of instruments) indicate: (指儀器)指示: *What does the thermometer ~?* 溫度計指多少度? **8** [VP15A] bring into a specified state by ~ing: 由閱讀而進入某種狀態: *She ~ herself to sleep.* 她看書看得睡着了。 **9** (*pp* with an *adv*) having knowledge gained from books, etc: (過去分詞與副詞連用)有從書中得來的知識的;有書本知識的: *a well-~ man;* 學問淵博的人; *deeply ~ in the classics.* 精通古典文學。 □ *n* period of time given to ~ing: 專注閱讀的一段時間: *have a good ~ in the train;* 在火車上好好看一會兒書; *have a quiet ~.* 靜靜地看一會兒書。 **~·able** /ˈriːdəbl ; ˈridəbl̩/ *adj* **1** that is easy or pleasant to ~. 易讀的;讀來令人愉快的。 **2** that can be ~. 能够被讀的;可讀的;清楚的。 ⇨ legible, the more usu word. (legible 較常用)。 **~·abil·ity** /ˌriːdəˈbɪlətɪ ; ˌridəˈbɪlətɪ/ *n*

re·ad·dress /ˌriː əˈdres ; ˈriəˈdrɛs/ *vt* [VP6A] change the address on (a letter, etc). 更改(信等)上的地址。

reader /ˈriːdə(r) ; ˈridɚ/ *n* **1** person who reads, esp one who spends much time in reading; (*publisher's ~*) person employed to read MSS offered for publication and say whether they are good, etc; printer's proof-corrector; (*lay ~*) person appointed to read aloud parts of a service in church. 讀者(尤指花很多時間於閱讀者);(出版者雇用的)審閱原稿的人; 校對員; (在教堂儀式中被指定)朗誦經文者。 **2** (GB) university teacher of a rank immediately below a professor: (英) 階級低於教授的大學教師;講師: *R~ in English Literature.* 英國文學講師。 **3** textbook for reading in class; book with selections for reading by students of a language: 教科書; (學習語言者的) 讀本: *a Latin R~.* 拉丁文讀本。 **4** person who can interpret what is hidden or obscure, 釋疑者;解答者;闡明者, esp 尤指 *a 'mind-/'thought-~.* 測心術者;讀心術者。 **'~·ship** /-ʃɪp ; -ʃɪp/ *n* **1** position of a ~(2). 大學講師之職位。 **2** (of a periodical) number of persons who read it (which may be larger than its circulation). (指期刊)讀者羣(讀者人數可能大於發行數量)。

read·ily, readi·ness ⇨ ready.

read·ing /ˈriːdɪŋ ; ˈridɪŋ/ *n* **1** [U] act of one who reads. 閱讀或朗誦的動作。 **'~ desk,** lectern. (教堂中的)讀經檯。 **'~-glasses** *n* glasses for ~ (contrasted with glasses for long-distance use). 讀書時戴用之眼鏡 (與看遠距離所用者相對)。 **'~-lamp** *n* shaded table-lamp used to read by. (閱讀用的)有罩檯燈。 **'~-room** *n* room (eg in a club or public library) set apart for ~. 閱覽室。 **2** [U] know-

R

ledge, esp of books: 知識(尤指書本知識): *a man of wide ~.* 學識淵博的人。 **3** [C] way in which sth is interpreted or understood: 某事物被解釋或理解之方式: *my solicitor's ~ of this clause in the agreement,* what he says it means. 我的律師對該契約中這一條文之解釋。 **4** [C] figure of measurement, etc as shown on a dial, scale, etc: 讀數(刻度盤,尺等上所指出的度數): *The ~s on my thermometer last month were well above the average.* 上月我的溫度計所指示出的度數遠超過平均溫度。 **5** [C] variant reading of a text that occurs in copying or printing from time to time: 出現於不同抄本或版本行文略有出入的同一篇文字: *The ~ of the First Folio is the true one.* 第一對摺本的文字是眞正的原文。 **6** [C] entertainment in which sth is read to an audience; passage so read: (向聽衆朗誦某種讀物的)朗誦會;朗誦的章節: *R~s from Dickens.* 狄更斯作品朗誦會;狄更斯朗誦選。 **'play-~,** recital of the text of a play by a group. 劇本誦讀。 **7** [C] (in Parliament) one of the three stages through which a Bill must pass before it is ready for royal assent. (在議會中)一法案三讀過程中之任何一次。

R

re·ad·just /ˌriːəˈdʒʌst ; ˌriəˈdʒʌst/ *vt, vi* [VP6A, 3A, 15A] ~ ***(oneself) (to),*** adjust again: 再整理;再調整;重新適應: *It's sometimes difficult to ~ (oneself) to life in Britain after working abroad.* 在國外工作過之後,有時很難再適應英國的生活方式。**~·ment** *n* ~ing or being ~ed; [C] instance of this. 再整理;再調整;重新適應;被再整理或再調整;再整理、再調整、重新適應之實例。

ready /ˈredɪ ; ˈrɛdɪ/ *adj* (-ier, -iest) **1** (*pred* only) (僅作敍述用法) ~ ***(for sth/to do sth),*** in the condition needed for use; in the condition for doing sth; willing: 在準備使用之狀態的; 在準備做某事之狀態的;自願(做某事)的; 準備妥當的; 準備就緒的: *~ for work;* 爲工作準備就緒; 準備好了,可以工作了; *get ~ for a journey;* 準備旅行; *be ~ to start.* 準備出發。 *He's always ~ to help his friends.* 他總是樂意幫助朋友。***make ~,*** prepare. 預備;準備。**2** quick; prompt: 迅速的;立卽的: *Don't be so ~ to find fault.* 不要動不動就吹毛求疵。*He always has a ~ answer.* 他永遠有現成的答案。*You are too ~ with excuses.* 你總是有藉口。*He has a ~ wit.* 他有機智。 **3** within reach; easily procured: 在可及之範圍內的;易於取得的: *keep a revolver ~,* near at hand. 把一手槍放於身邊。**~ money,** money in the form of coins or notes, which can be used for payment at the time when goods are bought (contrasted with *credit*). 現款; 現錢 (與 credit 相對)。 **~ reckoner,** book of answers to various common calculations needed in business, etc. 計算便覽;算術表。 **4** (*adv* use, with *pp*) prepared beforehand: (作副詞用,與過去分詞連用)事先準備好的: *buy food ~ cooked.* 買做好的食品。**ˌ~-ˈmade** *adj* **(a)** ~ to wear or use: 現成的;做好的: *~-made clothes,* made in standard sizes, not to measurements of customers. 成衣(按標準尺碼做成者)。 **(b)** (fig) not original; of standard pattern, etc: (喩)非獨創的;陳腐的;老套的: *come to a subject with ~-made ideas.* 以陳腐的想法來處理一件事。□ *n* (only in) (僅用於) ***at the ~,*** (of a rifle) in the position for aiming and firing. (指步槍)準備射擊;瞄準。 **read·ily** /-ɪlɪ ; -ɪlɪ/ *adv* **1** without showing hesitation or unwillingness. 毫不遲疑地;欣然。 **2** without difficulty. 容易地;無困難地。 **readi·ness** /ˈredɪnɪs ; ˈrɛdɪnɪs/ *n* [U] **1** ***in readiness (for),*** in a ready or prepared state: 準備好的狀態: *have everything in readiness for an early start.* 爲及早出發而把一切準備好。 **2** willingness: 情願: *a surprising readiness to accept the proposal.* 出奇爽快地接受該項提議。 **3** promptness; quickness: 敏捷;迅速: *readiness of wit.* 機智;機敏。

re·af·firm /ˌriːəˈfɜːm ; ˌriəˈfɝm/ *vt* [VP6A, 9] affirm again; repeat an affirmation: 重申;再肯定;再斷定;再證實: *~ one's loyalty.* 重申個人的忠誠。

re·af·for·est /ˌriːəˈfɒrɪst *US:* -ˈfɔːr- ; ˌriəˈfɔrəst/, (US = **re·for·est** /ˌriːˈfɒrɪst *US:* -ˈfɔːr- ; riˈfɔrɪst/) *vt* replant (an area of land) with forest trees. 再植樹;再造林。 **re·af·for·est·ation** /ˌriːəˌfɒrɪˈsteɪʃn *US:* -ˌfɔːr- ; ˌriəfɔrəsˈteʃən/, (US = **re·for·est·ation** /ˌriːˌfɒr- *US:* -ˌfɔːr- ; ˌrifɔrɪsˈteʃən/) *n*

re·agent /riːˈeɪdʒənt ; riˈedʒənt/ *n* [C] (chem) substance used to detect the presence of another by reaction; reactive substance or force. (化學)試劑;試藥;反應物;反應劑;反應力。

real[1] /rɪəl ; ˈriəl/ *adj* **1** existing in fact; not imagined or supposed; not made up or artificial: 事實上存在的;非想像或假設的;非虛構的;眞實的: *Is this ~ gold or pinchbeck?* 這是眞金還是合金(金色銅)? *Is this ~ silk or rayon?* 這是眞絲還是人造絲? *Was it a ~ man you saw or a ghost?* 你看見的是眞的人還是鬼魂? *The doctors could not effect a ~* (= genuine, complete) *cure.* 這些醫生都不能予以根治。 *Things that happen in ~ life are sometimes stranger than things that occur in fiction.* 發生於現實生活中的事有時比小說中虛構的事還要離奇。 *Who is the ~ manager of the firm?* 誰是這家商號眞正的經理? *Tell me the ~* (= true) *reason.* 把眞正理由告訴我。 **~ ale,** (GB 1970s) ale that is made, stored and served in traditional, careful ways. 眞正淡色啤酒(英國 1970 年代,以傳統而又細心的方式釀製、儲存及飲用之淡色啤酒)。 **2 '~ estate,** (legal) immovable property consisting of land, any natural resources, and buildings (contrasted with *personal estate*). (法律)房地產; 不動產 (與 personal estate 相對)。 **3** (US colloq as *adv*) really, very: (美俗,作副詞用)眞正地;非常地: *We had a ~ good time.* 我們玩得非常盡興。*I'm ~ sorry.* 我的確很抱歉。**~ly** /ˈrɪəlɪ ; ˈriəlɪ/ *adv* **1** in fact; without doubt; truly: 事實上;無疑地;眞正地: *What do you ~ly think about it?* 你對那件事到底做何想法? *It was ~ly not my fault.* 那的確不是我的錯。 *I'm ~ly sorry.* 我確實很抱歉。 **2** (as an expression of interest, surprise, mild protest, doubt, etc according to context): (用以表示興趣、驚訝、溫和的抗議、懷疑等,其意義依上下文而定): *'We're going to Mexico next month.'—'Oh, ~ly!'* (or) *'Not ~ly?'* '我們下個月要去墨西哥。'—'啊!眞的呀!'(或'不是眞的吧?') *You ~ly shouldn't say that about her!* 你眞不該說她那種話!

real[2] /reɪˈɑːl ; ˈriəl/ *n* [C] silver coin and unit of currency formerly used in Spanish-speaking countries. 昔時西班牙語國家所使用之銀幣和貨幣單位。

real·ism /ˈrɪəlɪzəm ; ˈriəlˌɪzəm/ *n* [U] **1** (in art and literature) showing of real life, facts, etc in a true way, omitting nothing that is ugly or painful, and idealizing nothing. (藝術與文學) 寫實主義(以忠實的方式表現眞實生活、事實等,不略去醜惡或痛苦的事,亦不理想化任何事)。 **2** behaviour based on the facing of facts and disregard of sentiment and convention. 就事論事或面對事實的態度。 **3** (phil) theory that matter has real existence apart from our mental perception of it. (哲學)實在論;唯實論(認爲物質眞正存在,不受我們對它認知的影響)。⇨ idealism. **real·ist** /-ɪst ; -ɪst/ *n* person who believes in ~ in art, philosophy, social problems, etc; person who believes himself to be without illusions. 寫實主義者;實在論者;腳踏實地的人。**real·is·tic** /ˌrɪəˈlɪstɪk ; ˌriəˈlɪstɪk/ *adj* **1** marked by, relating to, ~ in philosophy or art. 實在論的;寫實主義的。 **2** practical; not moved by sentiment: 實際的;現實的;不爲感情所動的: *realistic politics.* 現實的政治。 **real·is·ti·cally** /-klɪ ; -klɪ/ *adv*

re·al·ity /rɪˈælətɪ ; rɪˈælətɪ/ *n* (*pl* -ties) **1** [U] the quality of being real; real existence; that which underlies appearance: 眞實;實存;現實;眞相: *belief in the ~ of miracles;* 相信奇蹟之眞實性; *the search after God and ~.* 追求上帝與眞實。***bring sb back to ~,*** get him to stop dreaming, being sentimental, etc. 使某人面對現實。***in ~,*** really, in actual fact. 實際上;事實上。 **2** [C] sth real; sth actually seen or experienced: 眞實之物;眞正被看到或經驗過

的事或物：*the grim realities of war,* contrasted with romantic ideas, etc. 戰爭的冷酷事實(與戰爭的幻想相對)。 **3** [U] realism(1). 寫實主義。

real·ize /ˈrɪəlaɪz ; ˈriəˌlaɪz/ *vt* **1** [VP6A, 9, 10] be fully conscious of; understand: 完全認知；了解：*Does he ～ his error yet／～ that you must have help?* 他知道他的錯(你需要幫忙)嗎？ **2** [VP6A] convert (a hope, plan, etc) into a fact: 使(希望、計畫等)實現：*～ one's hopes／ambitions.* 實現一個人的希望(野心)。 **3** [VP6A] exchange (property, business shares, etc) for money: 變賣(財產、股票等)：*Can these shares／bonds, etc, be ～d at short notice?* 這些股票(債券等)能隨時變賣成現款嗎？ **4** [VP6A, 14] **～ *(on),*** (of property, etc) obtain as a price for or as a porfit: (指財產等)做爲代價或收益而獲得；賣得(若干錢)：*The furniture ～d a high price at the sale.* 在拍賣時傢具賣到很高的價錢。*How much did you ～ on the paintings you sent to the sale?* 你送去賣的畫賣了多少錢？ **real·iz·able** /-əbl ; -əbl/ *adj* that can be ～d. 可認知的；可實現的；可實行的；可變賣的。 **real·iz·ation** /ˌrɪəlaɪˈzeɪʃn *US:* -lɪˈz- ; ˌrɪələˈzeʃən/ *n* [U] realizing (of a plan, one's ambitions or hopes); act of exchanging property for money. (計畫，野心或希望的)實現；變賣。

realm /relm ; rɛlm/ *n* **1** (poet, rhet or legal use) kingdom: (詩，修辭，法律用語)王國：*the defence of the R～;* 保衛國家；*a Peer of the R～.* 國家的貴族。 **2** region (fig): (喻)區域；領域：*the ～ of the imagination;* 想像的領域；*in the ～s of fancy.* 在幻想的領域中。

Re·al·tor/ ˈrɪəltə(r) ; ˈrɪəltɚ/ *n* (US) person engaged in real estate business who is a member of the National Association of Real Estate Boards and subscribes to its standards of ethical conduct (GB 英 = *estate agent*). (美)房地產經紀人(全國房地產委員會之會員)。

re·alty /ˈrɪəltɪ ; ˈriəltɪ/ *n* (*pl* -ties) (legal) real estate. (法律)房地產；不動產。

ream /ri:m ; rim/ *n* measure for paper, 480 (or US 500) sheets or 20 quires; (colloq, *pl*) great quantity (of writing): 令(量紙的單位，480張(美500張)或20帖)；(俗，複)大量(的寫作)：*She has written ～s of verse.* 她寫了無數的詩。

re·ani·mate /ri:ˈænɪmeɪt ; riˈænəˌmet/ *vt* [VP6A] fill with new strength, courage or energy. 使充滿新力量、勇氣或活力。

reap /ri:p ; rip/ *vt, vi* [VP6A, 2A] cut (grain, etc), gather in a crop of grain from (a field, etc): 收割；收穫：*～ a field of barley;* 收割田中大麥；*～ the corn;* 收割穀物；(fig) (喻) *～ the reward of virtue;* 得到美德的報酬；*～ where one has not sown,* profit from work done by others. 不勞而獲。***(sow the wind and) ～ the whirlwind,*** (prov) suffer for one's foolish conduct. (諺)因做出愚蠢行爲而自食其惡果。 **ˈ～·ing-hook** *n* sickle. 鐮刀。 **～·er** *n* **1** person who ～s. 收割者。 **2** ～ing-machine for cutting grain (and in some cases binding it into sheaves). 收割機。

re·appear /ˌri:əˈpɪə(r) ; ˌriəˈpɪr/ *vi* [VP2A] appear again (esp after disappearing). 再出現(尤指消失後再出現)。 **～·ance** /-rəns ; -rəns/ *n*

re·apprais·al /ˌri:əˈpreɪzl ; ˌrɪəˈprezḷ/ *n* new examination and judgement: 再評價；再鑑定；再研判：*a ～ of our relations with China.* 我們同中國的關係的再研判。

rear¹ /rɪə(r) ; rɪr/ *n* **1** back part: 後部；背面：*The kitchen is in the ～ of the house.* 廚房在房子的後部。*The garage is at the ～ of* (US 美 *in the ～ of*) *the house.* 車房在房子的後邊。 **2** (attrib) in or at the ～: (形容用法)在後部的：*the ～ wheels／lamps,* of a car, etc; (汽車等的)後輪(尾燈)；*leave the bus by the ～ entrance;* 從後門下公共汽車；*a ～-view mirror,* driving mirror (in a motor-vehicle) for seeing out of the back window. (汽車之)後視鏡。 **3** last part of any army, fleet, etc: (軍隊，艦隊等的)後陣；後尾：*attack the enemy in the ～.* 從背後攻擊敵人。***bring up the ～,*** come／be last. 殿後。 **4** ˌ**～-ˈadmiral** /ˌrɪər ˈædmərəl ; ˌrɪrˈædmərəl/ *n* naval officer below a vice-admiral. 海軍少將。 **ˈ～·guard** *n* body of soldiers given the duty of guarding the ～ of an army. 後衛。***a ～guard action,*** fight between an army in retreat and the enemy. 後衛戰鬪。 **～·most** /ˈrɪəməʊst ; ˈrɪrˌmost/ *adj* farthest back. 最後面的。 **～·ward** /ˈrɪəwəd ; ˈrɪrwɚd/ *n*: *to ～ward of,* some distance behind; 遙遙在後的；*in the ～ward,* at the back. 在後面。 **～·wards** /ˈrɪəwədz ; ˈrɪrwɚdz/ *adv* towards the ～. 向後面地。

rear² /rɪə(r) ; rɪr/ *vt, vi* **1** [VP6A] cause or help to grow; bring up: 使或助之生長；養育；飼養：*～ poultry／cattle;* 飼養家禽(家畜)；*～ a family* (US usu 美通常作 *raise a family*). 養育子女。 **2** [VP2A, C] (esp of a horse) rise on the hind legs. (尤指馬)後腿站立。 **3** [VP6A, 15B] raise; lift up: 抬起；擧起：*The snake ～ed its head.* 蛇擧起了頭。*The horse ～ed itself up.* 馬用後腿直立。 **4** [VP6A] set up: 建立；豎立：*～ a monument.* 建一紀念碑。

re·arm /ˌri:ˈɑ:m ; riˈɑrm/ *vt, vi* [VP6A, 2A] supply (an army, etc) with weapons again, or with weapons of new types, etc. 再武裝；重整軍備；重新裝備；配以新式武器。 **re·arma·ment** /ri:ˈɑ:məmənt ; riˈɑrməmənt/ *n*

rea·son¹ /ˈri:zn ; ˈrizṇ/ *n* **1** [C, U] (fact put forward or serving as) cause of or justification for sth: 理由；原因；緣故：*There is ～ to believe that he is dishonest.* 有理由相信他不誠實。*Is there any ～ why you should not help?* 你有甚麼理由不幫忙？ *He complains with ～* (= rightly) *that he has been punished unfairly.* 他抱怨所受處罰不公平是有理由的。*Give me your ～s for doing it.* 告訴我你做那件事的理由。*My ～ is that the cost will be too high.* 我的理由是費用太高。*The ～ why he's late is that／because there was a breakdown on the railway.* 他遲到的原因是鐵路出了毛病。***by ～ of,*** because of: 因爲；由於：*He was excused by ～ of his age.* 他因爲年齡的關係而被原諒。 **2** [U] power of the mind to understand, form opinions, etc: 理解；理智；理性：*Only man has ～.* 只有人類有理性。***lose one's ～,*** go mad: 發瘋：*The poor old fellow has lost his ～.* 那個可憐的老人瘋了。 **3** [U] what is right or practicable; common sense; sensible conduct: 正確或可行之事；道理；常識；明智的行爲：*He's not amenable to ～.* 他不講理。***bring sb to ～,*** persuade him to give up foolish activities, useless resistance, etc. 說服某人放棄愚蠢的活動，無用的抵抗等；使遵從道理。***do anything in／within ～,*** anything sensible or reasonable: 做任何合理明智的事：*I'm willing to do anything in ～.* 我願做任何合理的事。***listen to／hear ～,*** allow oneself to be persuaded; pay attention to common-sense, advice, etc. 聽從道理。***lose all ～,*** become irrational, illogical. 失去理智的；不合常理的。***without rhyme or ～,*** ⇨ rhyme(1). ***It stands to ～ (that...),*** is obvious to sensible people (that...); most people will agree (that...). 明眼人一望而知；大多數人會同意…；合於道理；按照常情。 **～·less** *adj* lacking ～. 缺乏理性的；沒有理智的；不合道理的。

rea·son² /ˈri:zn ; ˈrizṇ/ *vi, vt* **1** [VP2A] make use of one's reason(2); exercise the power of thought: 推理；思考：*Man's ability to ～ makes him different from the animals.* 人的思考能力使人異於禽獸。 **2** [VP3A] ***～ with sb,*** argue in order to convince him: (爲說服某人而)與某人辯論：*She ～ed with me for an hour about the folly of my plans.* 她同我爭辯了一小時，想使我明白我的計畫多荒唐。 **3** [VP9] ***～ that...,*** say by way of argument: 爭辯著說：*He ～ed that if we started at dawn, we could arrive before noon.* 他爭辯著說如果我們黎明卽出發，中午之前就能抵達。 **4** [VP6A] express logically or in the form of an argument: 合邏輯地或以議論形式表達：

a well-~ed statement/manifesto. 一個非常合邏輯的陳述(宣言)。 **~ *sth out,*** find an answer by considering successive arguments, etc: 推論出某事物的答案: *~ out the answer to a question.* 推論出某問題的答案。 **5** [VP14] **~ *sb into/out of sth,*** persuade by argument to do/not to do sth: 說服某人做(不做)某事: *~ a person out of his fears,* show him that his fears are groundless; 說服某人使祛除其恐懼; *~ sb out of a false belief;* 說服某人放棄一錯誤信仰; *~ sb into a sensible course of action.* 說服某人採取合理的行動。 **~·ing** *n* [U] process of reaching conclusions by using one's reason: 推理的過程: *He surpasses most of us in power of ~ing,* is better at drawing conclusions from facts, etc. 他的推理能力超過我們大多數人。 *There's no ~ing with that woman,* She won't listen to reason. 那個女人不可理喻。

rea·son·able /ˈriːznəbl ; ˈriznəbḷ/ *adj* **1** having ordinary common sense; able to reason; acting, done, in accordance with reason; willing to listen to reason: 有普通常識的; 能推理的; 行爲或做事合乎道理的;服理的;講理的: *You're not very ~ if you expect a child to understand sarcasm.* 你如果希望一個小孩子能懂得諷刺,那就太不明理了。 *Is the accused guilty beyond ~ doubt?* 被告是毫無疑問地有罪嗎? **2** moderate; neither more nor less than seems right or acceptable: 適度的;不多不少的;公道的: *a ~ price/offer.* 公道的價格(出價)。 **3** fair; just; not absurd: 公平的;正當的;不荒謬的: *a ~ excuse;* 一個合理的藉口; *be ~ in one's demands.* 要求合理。 **~·ness** *n* **rea·son·ably** /-əblɪ ; -əblɪ/ *adv*

R

re·as·sure /ˌriːəˈʃʊə(r) ; ˌriəˈʃʊr/ *vt* [VP6A] remove the fears or doubts of: 祛除對…之恐懼或疑慮;使安心: *She felt ~d after the police had told her that her children were safe.* 警察告訴她她的孩子們很安全後,她就安心了。 **re·as·sur·ance** /-rəns ; -rəns/ *n* [U, C]. **re·as·sur·ing** *adj* comforting: 安慰的; 令人安心的: *a reassuring glance/word/pat.* 令人安心的一瞥(話,輕拍)。 **re·as·sur·ing·ly** *adv*

re·bar·ba·tive /rɪˈbɑːbətɪv ; rɪˈbɑrbətɪv/ *adj* (formal) stern; repellent. (正式用語)嚴厲的;討人厭的。

re·bate /ˈriːbeɪt ; ˈribet/ *n* [C] sum of money by which a debt, tax, etc may be reduced; discount: 債務、租稅等可獲減免的款額; 寬減額; 折扣; 折讓; 議減: *There is a ~ of £1.50 if the account is settled before 31 Dec.* 如果帳目在十二月三十一日前結清,可減收一鎊半。

rebel[1] /ˈrebl ; ˈrɛbḷ/ *n* **1** person who takes up arms against, or refuses allegiance to, the established government; person who resists authority or control: 武裝反抗或不服從政府的叛徒; 抗拒權威或控制的人: *a ~ in the home,* eg a child who resists the authority of its parents. 家庭的叛徒(如不服從父母權威的孩子)。 **2** (attrib) relating to ~s; of the nature of a rebellion: (形容用法)叛徒的;反叛的: *the ~ forces.* 叛軍。

re·bel[2] /rɪˈbel ; rɪˈbɛl/ *vi* (-ll-) [VP2A, 3A] **~ *(against),*** **1** take up arms to fight (against the government). 武裝反抗(政府);造反;反叛。 **2** show resistance; protest strongly: 抵抗;强烈抗議: *The prisoners ~led against having no physical exercise.* 囚犯們抗議沒有運動的機會。 *Such treatment would make anyone ~.* 這樣的對待會使任何人起而反抗。

re·bel·lion /rɪˈbelɪən ; rɪˈbɛljən/ *n* [U] **~ *(against),*** rebelling, esp against a government: 反叛 (尤指反叛政府): *rise in ~;* 舉起反叛;揭竿而起; [C] instance of this: 反叛之實例;叛亂: *five ~s in two years;* 兩年之內五次叛亂; *a ~ against the dictator.* 對獨裁者的反叛。

re·bel·li·ous /rɪˈbelɪəs ; rɪˈbɛljəs/ *adj* **1** acting like a rebel; taking part in a rebellion: 反叛的;參與反叛的: *~ subjects;* 反叛的臣民; *~ behaviour.* 反叛行爲。 **2** not easily controlled: 不易控制的: *a child with a ~ temper.* 一個脾氣倔强的孩子。 **~·ly** *adv* **~·ness** *n*

re·bind /ˌriːˈbaɪnd ; riˈbaɪnd/ *vt* (*pt, pp* -bound /-ˈbaʊnd ; -ˈbaʊnd/) [VP6A] put a new binding on (a book, etc). 重新裝訂(書等)。

re·birth /ˌriːˈbɜːθ ; riˈbɝθ/ *n* **1** spiritual change, eg by conversion or enlightenment, causing a person to lead a new kind of life. (由信仰之改變或啓蒙等而使人過一種新生活的) 精神改變; 新生; 再生。 **2** revival: 復生;復興: *the ~ of learning.* 文藝復興。

re·born /ˌriːˈbɔːn ; riˈbɔrn/ *adj* (fig) born again, ie spiritually. (喻)再生的;新生的。

re·bound /rɪˈbaʊnd ; rɪˈbaʊnd/ *vi* [VP2A, 3A] **1 ~ *(from),*** spring or bounce back after hitting sth: 躍回;彈回: *The ball ~ed from the wall into the lily pond.* 球從牆上彈回掉到蓮花池中。 **2 ~ *on/upon,*** (fig) come back upon the agent; happen as the consequence of one's own action: (喻)自食其果;報應: *The evil you do may ~ upon yourselves.* 你們所做的惡可能回報到你們自己的身上;你們會自食惡果。 **3** *pt, pp* of rebind. □ *n* /ˈriːbaʊnd ; ˈriˌbaʊnd/ ***on the ~,*** **(a)** while bouncing back: 彈回時: *hit a ball on the ~.* 擊彈回之球。 **(b)** (fig) while still reacting to depression or disappointment: (喻)沮喪或失望之餘: *She quarrelled with Paul and then married Peter on the ~.* 她和保羅爭吵之後憤而嫁給彼得。

re·buff /rɪˈbʌf ; rɪˈbʌf/ *n* [C] ***meet with/suffer a ~ (from sb),*** unkind or contemptuous refusal of, or show of indifference to (an offer of or request for help, friendship, etc); snub. (對提供或要求援助、友誼等表示的)嚴峻或輕蔑的拒絕; 輕待; 冷落。 □ *vt* [VP6A] give a ~ to. 嚴拒。

re·build /ˌriːˈbɪld ; riˈbɪld/ *vt* (*pt, pp* -built /-ˈbɪlt ; -ˈbɪlt/) [VP6A] build or put together again: 再建; 重新裝組: *a rebuilt typewriter.* 一架重裝的打字機。

re·buke /rɪˈbjuːk ; rɪˈbjuk/ *vt* [VP6A, 14] **~ *sb (for sth),*** reprove, speak severely to (officially or otherwise): 指責;非難: *~ a subordinate for being impudent.* 指責一屬下的鹵莽。□ *n* [C] reproof: 指責;非難: *administer ~s to sb.* 予某人以指責(責難某人)。 **re·buk·ing·ly** *adv*

re·bus /ˈriːbəs ; ˈribəs/ *n* puzzle in which a word or phrase has to be guessed from pictures or diagrams that suggest the syllables that make it. 畫謎;字謎。

re·but /rɪˈbʌt ; rɪˈbʌt/ *vt* (-tt-) [VP6A] prove (a charge, piece of evidence, etc) to be false; refute. 證明(控訴、證據等)爲僞;反駁。 **~·tal** /-tl ; -təl/ *n* act of ~ting; evidence that ~s a charge, etc. 反駁;反證。

re·cal·ci·trant /rɪˈkælsɪtrənt ; rɪˈkælsɪtrənt/ *adj* disobedient; resisting authority or discipline. 不服從的;反抗權威或紀律的。 **re·cal·ci·trance** /-əns ; -əns/, **re·cal·ci·trancy** /-ənsɪ ; -ənsɪ/ *nn* [U] being ~. 不服從;反抗。

re·call /rɪˈkɔːl ; rɪˈkɔl/ *vt* **1** [VP6A, 14] **~ *sb (from/to),*** summon back: 召回: *~ an ambassador (from his post/to his own country).* (從其駐在地)召回一大使(返國)。 **2** [VP6A, C, 8, 9, 10, 19C] bring back to the mind; recollect: 記起; 憶起: *I don't ~ his name/face/meeting him/where I met him.* 我不記得他的名字(他的臉,見過他,在甚麼地方見過他)。 *Can you ~ your schooldays?* 你能憶起學生時代的情形嗎? **3** [VP6A] take back; revoke (an order, a decision). 撤銷;取消(訂單、決定)。□ *n* **1** summons to return; (esp) summons to an ambassador to return to his own country: 召回;喚回;(尤指)召回大使: *letters of ~.* 召回大使之函件;解任狀。 **2** [U] ability to remember: 回憶;回想: *a man gifted with instant ~.* 一個天生有敏捷記憶力的人。 **3** [U] possibility of recalling. 召回,記起或撤銷之可能性。 ***beyond/past ~,*** that cannot be brought back or revoked. 不能召回的; 記不起的; 不能撤銷的。 **4** [C] signal, eg a bugle call, to troops, etc to return: 軍隊等的召回訊號;收操(工)號: *sound the ~.* 吹收操(工)號。

re·cant /rɪˈkænt; rɪˈkænt/ *vt, vi* [VP6A, 2A] give up (an opinion, a belief); take back (a statement) as being false: 放棄(意見,信仰);(因其不實而)撤銷(一聲明): *The torturers could not make the man ~*, give up his beliefs, eg religious or political. 施酷刑者不能使那個人放棄其(宗教或政治)信仰。**re·can·ta·tion** /ˌriːkænˈteɪʃn; ˌrikænˈteʃən/ *n* [U] ~ing; [C] instance of this; statement disavowing former beliefs. 放棄信仰或意見;撤銷聲明;放棄或撤銷之實例;放棄原信仰的聲明。

re·cap¹ /ˈriːkæp; ˈrikæp/ *vt, vi, n* (colloq abbr of) recapitulate, recapitulation. (俗)爲 recapitulate, recapitulation 之略。

re·cap² /ˌriːˈkæp; riˈkæp/ *vt* (-pp-) (US) retread (a tyre). (美)翻新(輪胎)。

re·cap·itu·late /ˌriːkəˈpɪtʃʊleɪt; ˌrikəˈpɪtʃəˌlet/ *vt, vi* [VP6A, 2A] repeat, go through again, the chief points of (sth that has been said, discussed, argued about, etc). 對(已說過,討論過,辯論過的東西等)做一扼要說明或重述;摘要重述。**re·cap·itu·la·tion** /ˌriːkəˌpɪtʃʊˈleɪʃn; ˌrikəˌpɪtʃəˈleʃən/ *n* [U] recapitulating; [C] instance of this. 扼要說明;重述要點。

re·cap·ture /ˌriːˈkæptʃə(r); riˈkæptʃɚ/ *vt* [VP6A] **1** capture again. 再捕獲。 **2** recall: 回憶: *try to ~ the past.* 試着回憶過去。

re·cast /ˌriːˈkɑːst *US:* -ˈkæst; riˈkæst/ *vt* [VP6A] **1** cast or fashion anew: 重鑄;再鑄: *~ a gun/a bell;* 重新鑄造一砲(一鐘); *~* (= rewrite) *a sentence/paragraph/chapter.* 重寫一個句子(一段,一章)。 **2** change the cast of a play, ie find different actors or give actors different parts. 改變一齣戲的演員陣容(卽找不同的演員或給演員不同的脚色)。

recce /ˈrekɪ; ˈrɛki/ *n* (mil; colloq abbr of) reconnaissance. (軍;俗)爲 reconnaissance 之略。

re·cede /rɪˈsiːd; rɪˈsid/ *vi* [VP2A, 3A] *~ (from),* **1** (appear to) go back from the observer or from an earlier position: (顯得)後退: *As the tide ~d we were able to explore the rocky pools on the beach.* 潮退的時候,我們得以探察海灘上的石水潭。*As our ship sailed out to sea the coast slowly ~d.* 我們的船駛向大海時,海岸離我們越來越遠。 **2** slope away from the front or from the observer: 向後傾斜: *a receding chin/forehead.* 向後傾斜的下顎(額頭)。

re·ceipt /rɪˈsiːt; rɪˈsit/ *n* **1** [U] receiving or being received: 收到;被收到: *on ~ of the news.* 當收到消息時。*I am in ~ of your letter of the 3rd,* (pompous for) I have received.... 我已收到你三日寫的信(是 I have received... 的浮誇說法)。 **2** (*pl*) money received (in a business, etc, contrasted with *expenditure*). (複)收到之款;進款;收入(與 expenditure 相對)。 **3** [C] written statement that sth (money or goods) has been received: 收據;收條: *get a ~ for money spent;* 收到一張開支收據; *sign a ~;* 在收據上簽名; *a ˈ~ book,* one with forms and counterfoils for writing out ~s. 收據簿。□ *vt* [VP6A] write out and sign or stamp a ~(3): 寫並簽署或蓋章於一收據;立收據: *~ a hotel bill,* put 'Paid' or 'Received with thanks' on it. 在旅館帳單上簽字或蓋章表示該款業已付淸。

re·ceiv·able /rɪˈsiːvəbl; rɪˈsivəbḷ/ *adj* **1** that can be received; fit to be received. 可接收的;適於接收的。 **2** (comm; of bills, accounts, etc) on which money is to be received. (商;指票據,帳款等)待收款的;應收的。***bills ~,*** contrasted with *bills payable.* 應收票據(與 bills payable 相對)。

re·ceive /rɪˈsiːv; rɪˈsiv/ *vt, vi* [VP6A, 2A] **1** accept, take, get (sth offered, sent, etc): 接受;接收;領取: *When did you ~ the letter/news/telegram, etc?* 你何時接到那封信(消息,電報等)? *He ~d a good education.* 他受過良好教育。*We ~d nothing but insults.* 我們甚麼也沒有得到,只受到侮辱。*You will ~ a warm welcome when you come to England.* 你到英國時會受到熱烈歡迎。*He was caught receiving* (ie taking possession of stolen property) *soon after his release from prison.* 他被釋出獄不久卽因收受贓物而被捕。**reˈceiving-set** *n* radio receiver. 接收機。 **2** allow to enter; (formally) see, welcome or entertain (friends, guests, etc): 准予進入;(正式地)接待;招待;款待(朋友、客人等): *The hotel is now open to ~ guests.* 該旅館現在已開業招待客人。*He was ~d into the Church,* admitted as a member. 他被准許入教。*Lady Snooks ~s on Monday afternoons,* is at home to her friends and acquaintances then. 斯努克斯夫人每星期一下午在家見客。**~d** *adj* widely accepted as correct: 被認爲正確而普遍接受的;公認爲正確的: *the ~d version/text/view/opinion/pronunciation.* 公認爲正確之譯本(正文,看法,意見,讀音)。

re·ceiver /rɪˈsiːvə(r); rɪˈsivɚ/ *n* **1** person who receives, esp who knowingly receives stolen goods. 接受者;(尤指)收贓者。 **2 (Official) R~,** official appointed to take charge of the property and affairs of a bankrupt, or to administer property in dispute. 破產管理官(被指派負責管理破產財務或有爭議之財產者)。 **3** part of an apparatus for receiving sth, eg that part of a telephone that is held to the ear; apparatus for receiving broadcast signals: 一裝置中能接收某種東西的部分;接收器(如電話之聽筒);收音機: *a ˈradio-~.* 無線電接收機。**~·ship** /-ʃɪp; -ˌʃɪp/ *n* office of a ~(2); his period of office. 破產管理官之職務或任期。

re·cent /ˈriːsnt; ˈrisṇt/ *adj* (having existed, been made, happened) not long before; begun not long ago: 不久前(才存在,才做成,才發生)的;不久前開始的;最近的: *~ news;* 最近的消息; *a ~ event;* 不久前發生的事件; *within ~ memory.* 在最近的記憶之中。*Ours is a ~ acquaintance,* We have been acquainted for only a short time. 我們是最近才認識的。**~·ly** *adv* lately; not long ago: 最近地;不久之前地: *until quite ~ly.* 直到最近。

re·cep·tacle /rɪˈseptəkl; rɪˈsɛptəkḷ/ *n* container or holder in which things may be put away or out of sight. 容器。

re·cep·tion /rɪˈsepʃn; rɪˈsɛpʃən/ *n* **1** [U] receiving or being received: 接待;被接待: *prepare rooms for the ~ of guests;* 準備房間以接待嘉賓; *ˈ~ area/camp/centre,* one where persons, eg evacuees, refugees, are received and accommodated; (撤退者,難民等的)接待區(營,中心); *a ˈ~ committee.* 接待委員會。*The house has two ~ rooms* (rooms for the ~ of guests, but this usu means living-rooms), *a kitchen, and three bedrooms.* 這座房子有兩間接待室(通常等於起居室),一間廚房,三間臥房。**ˈ~-desk,** (in a hotel) counter where guests are received, where they ask for rooms, etc. (旅館中的)接待處(卽接待客人,客人詢問房間等事務的櫃檯)。**ˈ~ clerk,** (US) person at a ~-desk, who attends to inquiries from guests. (美)在接待處負責答覆客人詢問的接待人員。 **2** [C] formal party or welcome: 正式招待會或歡迎會: *Mrs X holds a ~ every Monday.* 某太太每星期一都接見賓客(或舉行一個招待會)。*There was a ~ after the wedding ceremony.* 結婚典禮之後有宴會。 **3** [C] welcome or greeting of a specified kind; demonstration of feeling toward sb or sth: 某種的歡迎或招呼;對某人或某事物表示的感情: *The new book had a favourable ~,* was welcomed by the critics, the public, etc. 這本新書頗受歡迎。*The President was given an enthusiastic ~.* 總統受到熱烈的接待。 **4** [U] receiving of radio, etc signals; degree of efficiency of this: (無線電等信號的)接收;接收力: *Is radio ~ good in your district?* 在你們那一區收音機聽得清楚嗎? *R~ of TV programmes is unsatisfactory here.* 這裡電視節目的接收情形不佳。**~·ist** /-ɪst; -ɪst/ *n* person employed in a hotel, or by a hair-dresser, dentist or other professional person, to receive clients. 接待員;招待員(旅館,美容師,牙醫或其他專業人員雇用以招待客人者)。

re·cep·tive /rɪˈseptɪv; rɪˈsɛptɪv/ *adj* quick or ready

to receive suggestions, new ideas, etc: 敏於接受建議,新思想等的: *a ~ mind;* 易於接受新思想的頭腦; *~ to new ideas.* 易於接受新的觀念。**~·ly** *adv* **re·cep·tiv·ity** /ˌriːsepˈtɪvətɪ ; rɪˌsɛpˈtɪvətɪ/ *n*

re·cess /rɪˈses *US:* ˈriːses ; rɪˈsɛs/ *n* **1** (US 美 = *vacation*) period of time when work or business is stopped, eg when Parliament, the law courts, are not in session. 暫歇時期;休業期;休會期(例如議會之休會期,法院之休庭期)。**2** part of a room where the wall is set back from the main part; alcove or niche: 室內牆壁之凹處;凹室;壁龕: *a ~ with a writing-desk and a chair in it.* 一個置有一書桌和一椅的凹室。**3** secret place; place difficult of access: 隱密地方;難進入的地方: *the dark ~es of a cave;* 洞穴中隱密的暗處; *a mountain ~;* 山之深處;山隈; (fig) (喻) *in the innermost ~es of the heart/mind.* 心之最深處。□ *vt* [VP6A] **1** place in a ~; set back: 置於凹室或壁龕內;置於隱密處;做成凹處: *~ a wall/a ~ed wall.* 在牆上做一壁龕(有壁龕的牆)。**2** provide with ~es. 供以隱密處。

re·ces·sion /rɪˈseʃn ; rɪˈsɛʃən/ *n* **1** [U] withdrawal; act of receding. 撤回;退回;退後。**2** [C] slackening of business and industrial activity: 工商業之衰退;不景氣: *The ~ caused a lot of unemployment.* 不景氣造成了大量的失業。

R

re·ces·sional /rɪˈseʃənl ; rɪˈsɛʃənəl/ *n* **~ (hymn),** hymn sung while the clergy and choir withdraw after a church service. (禮拜儀式完畢後在牧師和唱詩班退出時唱的)退場讚美詩。□ *adj* **1** of a recession: 撤回的;退出的: *ˈ~ music.* (禮拜儀式結束時所奏之)退場樂。**2** relating to a Parliamentary recess. 議會休會期的。

re·ces·sive /rɪˈsesɪv ; rɪˈsɛsɪv/ *adj* **1** having a tendency to recede or go back. 退後的;倒退的;有倒退之傾向的。**2** (biol) exhibiting weak characteristics (the stronger ones are called *dominant*) which are passed on by means of genes to later generations, eg blue eyes and blond hair. (生物)隱性的;潛性的。

ré·chauffé /reɪˈʃəʊfeɪ *US:* ˌreɪʃəʊˈfeɪ ; ˌreˌʃoˈfe/ *n* dish of food warmed up again; rehash. 再煮熱的(剩)菜;改成新形式的舊材料。

re·cher·ché /rəˈʃeəʃeɪ ; rəˈʃɛrʃe/ *adj* devised or selected with (too much) care; too studied or far-fetched. 精心設計的;精選的;用心推敲的;過於造作牽强的;不自然的。

re·cidi·vist /rɪˈsɪdɪvɪst ; rɪˈsɪdəvɪst/ *n* person who habitually relapses into crime; one who apparently cannot be cured of criminal tendencies; persistent offender. 常犯罪的人;無法改正犯罪傾向的人;累犯。**re·cidi·vism** /-ɪzəm ; -ɪzəm/ *n*

recipe /ˈresəpɪ ; ˈrɛsəpɪ/ *n* [C] *~ (for),* direction for preparing (a cake, a dish of food, a medical remedy) or for getting (any result): 烹飪法;食譜;處方;祕訣: *a ~ for a fruit cake.* 水果餅製法。*Have you a ~ for happiness?* 對於幸福快樂你有甚麼祕訣嗎?

re·cipi·ent /rɪˈsɪpɪənt ; rɪˈsɪpɪənt/ *n* person who receives sth. 接受者。

re·cip·ro·cal /rɪˈsɪprəkl ; rɪˈsɪprəkḷ/ *adj* **1** given and received in return; mutual: 互惠的;交互的;相互的: *~ affection/help.* 相互的喜愛(幫助)。**2** corresponding, but the other way round: 相對的;彼此相反的: *a ~ mistake,* eg I thought he was a waiter and he thought I was a guest, but I was a waiter and he was a guest. 彼此相反的錯誤(例如我以爲他是侍者,他想我是客人,但事實上我是侍者而他是客人)。**3** (gram) **~ pronouns,** those expressing mutual action or relation, eg *each other, one another.* (文法)相互代名詞(表示相互行動或關係者,例如 each other, one another)。**~·ly** /-klɪ ; -kḷɪ/ *adv*

re·cip·ro·cate /rɪˈsɪprəkeɪt ; rɪˈsɪprəˌket/ *vt, vi* [VP 6A, 2A] **1** give in return; give and receive, each to and from each: 回報;報答;交換;互惠: *I ~ your good wishes.* 我也同樣祝福您。*He ~d by wishing her a pleasant journey.* 他祝福她旅途愉快,以爲回報。**2** (of parts of a machine) (cause to) move backwards and forwards in a straight line (eg the piston of an engine): (指機件)(使)沿直線來回移動(如引擎的活塞): *a reciprocating engine/saw.* 往復式引擎(鋸子)。⇨ rotatory. **re·cip·ro·ca·tion** /rɪˌsɪprəˈkeɪʃn ; rɪˌsɪprəˈkeʃən/ *n* [U].

reci·proc·ity /ˌresɪˈprɒsətɪ ; ˌrɛsəˈprɑsətɪ/ *n* [U] principle or practice of give and take, of making mutual concessions; the granting of privileges in return for similar privileges: 予與取,相互讓步之原則或實施;互惠: *~ in trade (between two countries).* (兩國間之)貿易互惠。

re·cital /rɪˈsaɪtl ; rɪˈsaɪtḷ/ *n* [C] **1** detailed account of a number of connected events, etc: (一連串相關連事件的)詳述: *We were bored by the long ~ of his adventures.* 我們對他的冒險經歷的長篇敍述感到厭煩了。**2** performance of music by a soloist or small group, or of the works of one composer: 音樂演奏會;獨奏會;獨唱會;個人作品發表會: *a piˈano ~;* 鋼琴獨奏會; *a ~ of songs.* 歌曲演唱會。

reci·ta·tion /ˌresɪˈteɪʃn ; ˌrɛsəˈteʃən/ *n* **1** [U] the act of reciting(2): 列舉;詳述: *the ~ of his grievances.* 詳述其苦難。**2** [U] public delivery of passages of prose or poetry learnt by heart; [C] instance of this: 背誦;當衆吟誦;背誦之實例: *a ˈDickens ~,* of dramatic extracts from the novels. 狄更斯小說中若干精采段落的朗誦。**3** [C] piece of poetry or prose (to be) learnt by heart and recited. 背誦(用)的詩文。**4** (US) [U] repetition of a prepared lesson by a pupil to his teacher; [C] instance of this. (美)學生向老師背書;其實例。

reci·ta·tive /ˌresɪtəˈtiːv ; ˌrɛsətəˈtiv/ *n* **1** [U] style of music between singing and talking, many words being spoken or sung on the same note, used for the narrative and dialogue parts of some operas. 朗誦調;宣敘調(介於唱與說話之間的一種音樂體裁,許多字句以同樣調子說或唱,用於某些歌劇中之敘述或對白部分)。**2** [C] passage (in an opera or oratorio) (to be) rendered thus. (歌劇或神劇中的)宣敘部。

re·cite /rɪˈsaɪt ; rɪˈsaɪt/ *vt, vi* [VP6A, 15A, 2A] **1** say (esp poems) aloud from memory: 背誦;吟誦;(尤指)吟詩: *The mayor ~d to the Queen a long and tedious speech of welcome.* 市長向女王背了一篇又長又臭的歡迎詞。**2** give a list of, tell one by one (names, facts, etc): 列舉一連串(名字、事實等);詳述: *~ one's grievances;* 詳述一個人的苦難; *~ the names of all the capital cities of Europe.* 列舉歐洲各國首都的名字。

reck·less /ˈreklɪs ; ˈrɛklɪs/ *adj* **~ (of),** rash; not thinking of the consequences: 鹵莽的;不考慮後果的: *a ~ spender;* 亂花錢者; *~ of danger/the consequences;* 不管危險(後果); *fined £10 for ~ (= dangerous) driving.* 因鹵莽駕駛而被罰款十鎊。**~·ly** *adv* **~·ness** *n*

reckon /ˈrekən ; ˈrɛkən/ *vt, vi* **1** [VP6A, 15B, 2A] calculate; find out (the quantity, number, cost, etc) by working with numbers: 計算;算出(量,數,成本等): *~ the cost of a holiday.* 計算假期費用。*Hire charges are ~ed from the date of delivery.* 租金是從交貨日開始計算的。*The child can't ~ yet.* 這孩子還不會計算。**~ sth in,** include, take into account, when ~ing: 把…計算在內: *Did you ~ in the cost of a taxi across London?* 你把穿過倫敦的出租汽車車資計算在內了嗎? **~ sth up,** find the total of: 總計;結算: *~ up the bill.* 把帳單上各項目加起來。**2 ~ with sb, (a)** deal with; settle accounts with: 處理;清算: *When the fighting is over, we'll ~ with the enemy's sympathizers.* 戰爭結束之後,我們就要處理通敵的人。**(b)** take into account; consider: 斟酌;考慮: *He is certainly a man to be ~ed with,* a man who cannot be ignored, who may be a serious competitor, opponent, etc (according to context). 他確實是個不可忽視的人物(是個有力的競爭者、對手等,意義視上下文而定)。**~ without sb,** not take into account; not consider. 未將某人算在內;未在考慮之中。 **3** ~ ***on/upon sb/sth,*** depend on, base one's hopes on: 依賴;寄望於: *I ~ on your help.* 我寄望於你的幫助。 *The proprietors of the Casino ~ on human foolishness and greed,* can depend, for making profit, on the foolishness and greed of those who gamble. 賭場老闆全靠人類的愚蠢和貪婪(而獲利)。*He's the sort of man you can ~ on in a crisis.* 他是那種在危急時你能信賴的人。 **4** [VP9, 16B, 25, 7A] ~ ***sb/sth as/to be;*** ~ ***that...,*** be of the opinion, suppose; consider: 以爲;認定;認爲: *One-quarter of the country is ~ed as unproductive.* 該國四分之一的土地被認爲是不能生產的。 *She was ~ed (to be) the prettiest girl in the village.* 她被認爲是那村子裡最漂亮的女孩。*Do you still ~ him among/as one of your friends?* 你還認爲他是你的朋友嗎? *I ~ he is rather too old to marry again.* 我認爲他年齡太大,不適於再婚。 **5** [VP 9, 7A] estimate; calculate: 估計: *I ~ to arrive in Delhi at noon.* 我估計正午抵達德里。 **6** [VP9] (US colloq) assume: (美俗)假定;以爲: *I ~ we'll go next week.* 我以爲我們下星期會去。 **~er** /ˈrekənə(r); ˈrɛkənɚ/ *n* person or thing that counts. 計算者;計算表。 **ready ~er,** ⇨ ready. **~·ing** /ˈrekənɪŋ; ˈrɛkənɪŋ/ *n* (esp) (尤指) **1** [C] (totalled) account of items to be paid for, eg at a hotel or restaurant: (結算)總帳(旅社或飯店等的費用): *pay the ~ing.* 付帳。 *There'll be a heavy ~ing to pay if he continues this wild life,* He will have to suffer for it. 如果他仍繼續過這種荒唐的生活,他就得付出一大筆帳(就要自食惡果)。 ***day of ~ing,*** time when sth must be atoned for. 報應來到的日子;清算日。 **2** [U] calculation, eg of a ship's position by observation of the sun, stars, etc. (由觀測太陽、星辰等而對船的位置所做的)推算。 ***dead ~ing,*** method of calculating the position of a ship or aircraft from a known earlier position, and later course and distance, when observations of the sun, etc are impossible. 推算航行法(在不可能觀測太陽或星辰時,僅憑船隻或飛機早先的位置以及後來的航向和距離所做的推算)。 ***out in one's ~ing,*** mistaken in one's calculations. 計算不確;估計錯誤。

re·claim /rɪˈkleɪm; rɪˈklem/ *vt* [VP6A] **1** bring back (waste land, etc) to a useful condition, a state of cultivation, etc. 開拓(荒地等使之成爲有用、可耕植之狀態);墾殖。 **2** reform (a person): 改正;矯正(人): *~ a man from error/vice;* 糾正某人之錯誤(邪惡); *a ~ed drunkard.* 一個改邪歸正的酒鬼。 **3** demand that sth be given back. 要求歸還。 **rec·la·ma·tion** /ˌrekləˈmeɪʃn; ˌrɛkləˈmeʃən/ *n* [U].

re·cline /rɪˈklaɪn; rɪˈklaɪn/ *vi, vt* [VP2A, C, 15A] place oneself, be, in a position of rest; put (one's arms, etc) in a resting position; lie back or down: 處於休息位置;置(臂等)於休息位置;躺臥;斜倚: *~ on a couch;* 斜臥榻上; *~ one's arms on the table;* 把胳臂靠在桌上; *a reclining chair,* one with a back that tilts. 躺椅;臥椅。

re·cluse /rɪˈkluːs; ˈrɛklus/ *n* person who lives alone and avoids other people: 遁世者;隱士: *live the life of a ~,* live like a hermit, avoiding meeting people. 過隱居的生活。

rec·og·ni·tion /ˌrekəgˈnɪʃn; ˌrɛkəgˈnɪʃən/ *n* [U] recognizing or being recognized: 認出;被認出;承認;被承認;認識;識別: *~ signals;* 識別信號; *aircraft ~.* 飛行識別。 *He was given a cheque for £25 in ~ of his services.* 他得到一張二十五鎊的支票作爲對他服務的報酬。 *R~ of the new State is unlikely,* It is unlikely that diplomatic relations will be established with it. 那個新國家不大可能獲得承認。 ***alter/change beyond/out of (all) ~,*** change so much that ~ is impossible: 改變得使人認不出: *The town has changed out of all ~ since I was there ten years ago.* 自從十年前我離開之後,這城鎮變得認不得了。

re·cog·ni·zance /rɪˈkɒgnɪzns; rɪˈkɑgnɪzəns/ *n* [C] (legal) (法律) **1** bond by which a person is bound to appear before a court of law at a certain time, or to observe certain conditions, and to forfeit a certain sum if he fails to do so. 保證書;具結。 ***enter into ~s,*** sign such a bond. 具結。 **2** sum of money (to be) paid as surety for observing such a bond. (交付法院的)保證金;抵押金;保釋金。

rec·og·nize /ˈrekəgnaɪz; ˈrɛkəgˌnaɪz/ *vt* **1** [VP6A, 16A] know, (be able to) identify again (sb or sth) that one has seen, heard, etc before: 認識;認出;(能)認明(某人或某物)係曾見過、聽到過等: *~ a tune/an old acquaintance.* 認出一聽過的歌曲(舊相識)。 **2** [VP6A] be willing to accept (sb or sth) as what he or it claims to be or has been in the past: 承認;認可: *refuse to ~ a new government/~ sb as lawful heir.* 拒絕承認一新政府(某人爲合法繼承人)。 **3** [VP6A, 9] be prepared to admit; be aware: 自認;知道: *He ~d that he was not qualified for the post/~d his lack of qualifications.* 他承認他沒有資格擔任那職位(承認缺乏資格)。 **4** [VP 6A, 9, 25] acknowledge: 公認;賞識: *Everyone ~d him to be the greatest living authority on ancient Roman coins.* 大家公認他是當今古羅馬錢幣的最傑出的行家。 *His services to the State were ~d,* eg he was made a knight. 他對國家的貢獻獲得賞識(如被封爲爵士)。 **rec·og·niz·able** /ˈrekəgnaɪzəbl; ˈrɛkəgˌnaɪzəbḷ/ *adj* that can be ~d. 可認出的;可辨認的;可承認的。 **rec·og·niz·ably** /-əblɪ; -əblɪ/ *adv*

re·coil /rɪˈkɔɪl; rɪˈkɔɪl/ *vi* **1** [VP2A, 3A] ~ ***(from),*** draw or jump back; shrink: 撤回;跳回;退縮: *~ from doing sth* (in fear, horror, disgust, etc). (因憂慮,恐懼,厭惡等)做某事畏縮不前。 **2** [VP2A] (of a gun) kick back (when fired). (指槍砲)(射擊時)彈回;反衝;後坐。 **3** [VP3A] ~ ***on/upon,*** (fig) rebound; react: (喻)報應;反應: *His meanness ~ed upon his own head.* 他的卑鄙回報到他自己頭上。*Revenge may ~ upon the person who takes it.* 報復者常身受其報。 □ *n* act of ~ing. 退縮;彈回;報應;反應。

rec·ol·lect /ˌrekəˈlekt; ˌrɛkəˈlɛkt/ *vt, vi* [VP6A, C, 8, 10, 9, 2A] call back to the mind; succeed in remembering: 記起;憶起;記得: *~ childhood days;* 記起童年時代的日子; *~ meeting the King;* 記起會見國王的事; *~ how to do sth/how sth was done.* 記得如何做某事(某事是如何做的)。 *As far as I ~,....* 就我所能記憶,…。

rec·ol·lec·tion /ˌrekəˈlekʃn; ˌrɛkəˈlɛkʃən/ *n* **1** [U] act or power of recollecting: 回憶;記憶力: *scenes which arise in quiet ~ of the past;* 在對往事靜靜回憶中出現的情景; *to the best of my ~,* so far as I can recollect; if I remember correctly. 就我所能記憶;如我記得不錯。 **2** [U] time over which the memory goes back: 記憶所及的時間: *Such a problem has never arisen within my ~.* 這樣的一個問題從來不曾在我記憶中出現過。 **3** [C] sth recollected; that which is remembered: 回憶的事物;記起的事物: *The old letters brought many ~s to my mind.* 這些舊信使我想起許多往事。

rec·om·mend /ˌrekəˈmend; ˌrɛkəˈmɛnd/ *vt* **1** [VP 6A, 14, 12A, 13A, 16A] ~ ***sth (to sb) (for sth);*** ~ ***sb sth;*** ~ ***sb (for sth/as sth),*** speak favourably of; say that one thinks sth is good (for a purpose) or that sb is fitted (for a post, etc as...): 推薦;介紹: *I can ~ this soap.* 我可以推薦這種肥皂。*He has been ~ed for first class honours.* 他被推薦爲優等。*What would you ~ for getting ink stains from my blouse?* 你看用甚麼可以洗掉我上衣上的墨水污痕呢? *Can you ~ me a good novel?* 你能介紹一本好的小說給我嗎? *Can you ~ Miss Hill as a good typist?* 你能推薦希爾小姐說她是個好打字員嗎? **2** [VP17, 6C, 9] suggest as wise or suitable; advise: 建議;勸告: *I have been ~ed to try these pills for sea-sickness.* 有人建議我試服這些藥丸來治暈船。 *I ~ you not to/that you do not disobey your officers.* 我勸你不要反抗你的長官。 *Do you ~ raising the school-leaving age?* 你建議提高離校年齡嗎? **3** [VP6A, 14] ~ ***sb (to sb),*** (of a quality, etc) cause to be or appear pleasing, satisfactory; make acceptable: (指某種性質,特質等)使之或使看來可愛、令人滿意;使受歡迎: *Behaviour of that sort will not ~ you.* 那樣的行爲不會使別人對你有好感。**4** [VP 14] **~ sb to sb,** commend (the more usu word): 託付;交付 (commend 較常用): *~ oneself/one's soul to God;* 把自己(自己的靈魂)交給上帝; *~ a child to sb's care.* 把一個孩子託付某人看顧。**rec·om·men·da·tion** /ˌrekəmenˈdeɪʃn ; ˌrɛkəmɛnˈdeʃən/ *n* **1** [U] ~ing: 推薦;介紹;建議;勸告;託付: *speak in ~ation of sb or sth;* 推薦某人或某物; *buy sth on the ~ation of a friend,* because he has ~ed it. 由一位朋友的推薦而買某物。**2** [C] statement that ~s sb or sth: 推薦書;介紹信: *My bank manager has sent me a list of ~ations,* eg names of stocks which he ~s me to buy. 我的銀行經理給了我一張推薦單子(例如他建議我買的股票名稱)。*The jury brought in a verdict of guilty, with a ~ation to mercy.* 陪審團宣判被告有罪,附帶建議從輕量刑。**3** [C] sth which causes a person to be well thought of: 使人受到重視的性質;可取之處: *Is a sweet disposition a ~ation in a wife?* 溫和的性情是作妻子的可取之處嗎?

rec·om·pense /ˈrekəmpens ; ˈrɛkəmˌpɛns/ *vt* [VP 6A, 14] **~ sb (for sth),** reward or punish; make payment to: 賞或罰;報償: *~ sb for his trouble;* 酬答某人之煩勞; *~ good with evil;* 以怨報德; *~ sb for a loss.* 賠償某人的損失。□ *n* [C, U] reward; payment; satisfaction given for injury: 報償;報償金;賠償: *receive a ~ for one's services;* 接受酬勞; *work hard without ~;* 沒有報酬地努力工作; *in ~ for your help.* 爲報償你的幫助。

rec·on·cile /ˈrekənsaɪl ; ˈrɛkənˌsaɪl/ *vt* **1** [VP6A, 14] **~ sb (with sb),** cause (persons) to become friends after they have quarrelled: 使(人)在爭吵後再和好;使和解;使復交: *We became ~d.* 我們已言歸於好。*He refused to become ~d with his brother.* 他拒絕同他的兄弟和解。**2** [VP6A] settle, arrange (a quarrel, difference of opinion, etc). 調解;調停(口角,歧見等)。**3** [VP6A, 14] **~ sth (with sth),** bring into harmony with; cause to agree with: 使和諧;使一致: *How can this decision be ~d with justice?* 這個決定如何才能符合公道呢? *I can't ~ what you say with the facts of the case.* 我看不出你所說的與該案件諸事實相符合。**4** [VP14] **~ oneself to sth; be ~d to sth,** overcome one's objections to; resign oneself to: 安於;順從(於);聽從(於): *You must ~ yourself to a life of hardship and poverty.* 你必須安於艱苦貧窮的生活。**rec·on·cil·able** /-əbl ; -əbḷ/ *adj* **rec·on·cili·ation** /ˌrekənˌsɪlɪˈeɪʃn ; ˌrɛkənˌsɪlɪˈeʃən/ *n* [U] reconciling or being ~d; [C] instance of this: 和解;復交;調停;調解;和諧;一致;順從;聽從: *bring about a reconciliation between friends who have quarrelled.* 使爭吵的朋友重修舊好。

rec·on·dite /ˈrekəndaɪt ; ˈrɛkənˌdaɪt/ *adj* **1** (of subjects of knowledge) out of the way; little known; abstruse: (指知識的學科)深奧的;鮮爲人知的: *~ studies.* 深奧的學問。**2** (of an author) having ~ knowledge. (指作家)有深奧學問的。

re·con·di·tion /ˌriːkənˈdɪʃn ; ˌrikənˈdɪʃən/ *vt* [VP 6A] put into good condition again: 使恢復良好狀態;修復: *a car with a ~ed engine.* 一輛整修過引擎的汽車。

re·con·nais·sance /rɪˈkɒnɪsns ; rɪˈkɑnəsəns/ *n* **1** [U] act of reconnoitring: 偵察;搜索: *~ in force,* made with sufficient troops to resist any enemy forces that may be encountered. 威力偵察;威力搜索。**2** [C] instance of reconnoitring; survey, made by troops or a group of scouting vessels or aircraft, of an enemy's position or whereabouts; (fig) survey of any kind of work before it is started: 偵察或搜索的實例;由部隊或偵察艦或偵察機對敵人位置所做的觀測; (喩)任何一件工作開始前所做之通盤考慮或考查;勘查: *make a ~ of the work to be done.* 在工作開始前做一番考查。

re·con·noitre (US = **-ter**) /ˌrekəˈnɔɪtə(r) ; ˌrikəˈnɔɪtɚ/ *vt, vi* [VP6A, 2A] go to or near (a place or area occupied by enemy forces) to learn about their position, strength, etc: 進至或接近(敵人佔據之地方或地區)以探究其陣地、兵力等;偵察;搜索: *~ the ground.* 偵察地形。

re·con·struct /ˌriːkənˈstrʌkt ; ˌrikənˈstrʌkt/ *vt* [VP 6A] **1** construct again. 重建;再建。**2** build up a complete structure or description of (sth of which one has only a few parts or only partial evidence): 將(只有幾部分或部分證據的事物)組成完整的結構或敍述;重整: *~ a ruined abbey.* 重建一被毀之寺院。*The detective tried to ~ the crime,* picture to himself how it had been committed. 那偵探試圖根據該案之已知事實,設想出完整的犯罪經過。**re·con·struc·tion** /ˌriːkənˈstrʌkʃn ; ˌrikənˈstrʌkʃən/ *n*

rec·ord[1] /ˈrekɔːd *US:* ˈrekərd ; ˈrɛkɚd/ *n* **1** [C] written account of facts, events, etc: 記錄: *a ~ of school attendances/of road accidents;* 學生出席(車禍)記錄; *the* (ˌ*Public*) ˈ*R~ Office,* one in London where public documents with accounts of events, official acts, etc written down at the time they occur, are stored. (公共)檔案局(在倫敦,該局保存事件或官方行動等發生時所記錄之文件)。**2** [U] state of being ~ed or preserved in writing, esp as authentic evidence of sth: 記載;存證: *a matter of ~,* sth that is established as fact by being ~ed. 有記錄可查的事件。**be/go/put sb on ~:** 有記錄;列入記錄;將…列入記錄: *It is on ~ that the summer was the wettest for 50 years.* 根據記錄今(該)夏是五十年來雨量最多的季節。*I don't want to go on ~/don't want you to put me on ~ as saying that I think the Prime Minister a fool.* 我不願你把我所說'我認爲首相是傻瓜'之事列入記錄。**off the ~,** (colloq) not for publication or for recording: (俗)不公開的;不發表的;不記載的;非正式的: *What the President said at his press conference was off the ~,* not to be repeated by the newspaper men there, and not to be used in their reports or articles. 總統在記者招待會上所說的話是不准報紙引述或刋登的。**3** [C] facts known about the past of sb or sth: 有關某人或某事物的過去的已知事實;履歷;個案記錄: *He has an honourable ~ of service/a good ~.* 他有光榮的服務記錄(良好的記錄)。*Your ~ is in your favour,* What we know about your past is favourable to you. 你的履歷對你有利。*That airline has a bad ~,* eg has had many accidents to its aircraft. 那家航空公司記錄不佳(如曾有多次飛機失事)。**4** [C] sth that provides evidence or information: 供給證據或資料的東西: *Our museums are full of ~s of past history.* 我們的博物館有很多過去歷史的資料。*R~s of ancient civilizations are still being excavated.* 古代文明的遺跡仍在不斷出土。**5** [C] disc on which sound has been registered; what is ~ed on such a disc: 唱片: ˈ*gramophone ~s.* 留聲唱片。⇨ recording. ˈ**~-player** *n* instrument for reproducing sound from discs (often one connected to an external loud-speaker). (電)唱機。**6** [C] limit, score, point, attainment, mark, etc (high or low), not reached before; (esp in sport) the best yet done: 以前從未達到的(高或低)限制、得分、點、成就、分數等;(尤指運動方面)最高記錄: *Which country holds the ~ for the marathon?* 哪一個國家保持馬拉松賽跑的最快記錄? *Two ~s fell during the sports meeting at Oslo last week.* 上星期在奧斯陸舉行的運動會上有兩項記錄被打破了。(attrib) (形容用法) *Hill made a ~ score in the match against Kent,* (cricket) scored a total that was a ~. 在對抗肯特的板球比賽中希爾得到刷新記錄的得分。*There was a ~ rice crop in Thailand that year.* 那一年泰國的稻穀收成創下了最高記錄。**break/beat the ~,** do better than has been done before. 打破記錄。Hence, 由此產生, ˈ**~-breaking** *adj*

re·cord[2] /rɪˈkɔːd ; rɪˈkɔrd/ *vt* [VP6A] **1** set down in writing for reference; preserve for use, by writing or in other ways, eg on a disc, magnetic tape, video-tape, film, etc: 寫下以作參考；記錄；(以書寫或其他方式,如圖片、磁帶、錄影帶、影片等)記錄: *This volume ~s the history of the regiment.* 這部書記錄了該團的歷史。*The programme was ~ed.* 該節目被錄下來了。Cf 參較 *a 'live' broadcast.* 實況廣播。*The tape-recorder has ~ed his voice and the camera has ~ed his features.* 錄音機錄下了他的聲音,攝影機留下了他的面貌。**~ing angel,** angel who, it is said, ~s men's good and bad actions. 傳說中負責記錄人之善惡的天使。**2** (of an instrument) mark or indicate on a scale: (指儀器)標明或指示刻度: *The thermometer ~ed 40°C.* 寒暑表上指明是攝氏 40°。

re·corder /rɪˈkɔːdə(r) ; rɪˈkɔrdɚ/ *n* **1** (GB) judge with a certain criminal and civil jurisdiction. (英)民刑推事。**2** apparatus that records. 記錄器。**ˈtape-~,** one that records sound on magnetic tape. 錄音機。**ˈvideo tape-~,** one that records vision and sound on magnetic tape. 錄影機。**3** wooden musical instrument with finger holes, played by blowing it at one end. 直笛(一種木管樂器)。⇨ the illus at brass. 參看 brass 之插圖。

re·cord·ing /rɪˈkɔːdɪŋ ; rɪˈkɔrdɪŋ/ *n* (esp in sound or TV broadcasting, and for record-players, etc) programme, piece of music, etc registered on a disc, magnetic tape, film, etc for reproduction: 錄製(尤指廣播、電視、錄音等)節目: *It wasn't a 'live' performance but a B B C ~.* 那不是現場播出而是英國國家廣播公司的錄音節目。*I have a good ~ of this opera on three discs.* 我有這齣歌劇的三張錄製得很好的唱片。⇨ the illus at tape. 參看 tape 之插圖。

re·count /rɪˈkaʊnt ; rɪˈkaʊnt/ *vt* [VP6A] give an account of; tell: 敍述;講述: *He ~ed to them the story of his adventures in Mexico.* 他向他們講述他在墨西哥的冒險經過。

re-count /ˌriː ˈkaʊnt ; ˌriˈkaʊnt/ *vt* [VP6A] count again: 再算;重計: *~ the votes.* 重計票數。□ *n* /ˈriː kaʊnt ; ˈriˌkaʊnt/ another count: 重新計算;第二次計算: *One of the candidates demanded a ~.* 候選人中有一位要求重計票數。

re·coup /rɪˈkuːp ; rɪˈkup/ *vt* [VP6A, 14] ~ ***(for),*** compensate (sb, oneself, *for* a loss, etc); make up for: 賠償;補償(某人、自己之損失等): *~ one's losses;* 補償個人的損失; *~ oneself for one's losses.* 補償個人之損失。

re·course /rɪˈkɔːs ; rɪˈkors/ *n* [U] **1** ***have ~ to,*** turn to for help; seek help from: 求助於;求援於: *I don't advise you to have ~ to the money-lenders.* 我勸你不要求援於放利者。**2** sth turned to for help: 求助之事物: *Your only ~ is legal action against them.* 你只有借助法律行動對付他們。

re·cover /rɪˈkʌvə(r) ; rɪˈkʌvɚ/ *vt, vi* **1** [VP6A] get back (sth lost, etc); get back the use of: 尋回;取回(遺失之物等);恢復: *~ what was lost;* 尋回失去的東西; *~ consciousness* (after fainting); (昏倒後)恢復知覺; *~ one's sight/hearing.* 恢復視力(聽力)。*I am ~ing my strength,* getting well (after an illness). 我(病後)正在復元。*We soon ~ed lost time.* 我們很快就彌補了浪費的時間。*They have ~ed their losses.* 他們已經補償了他們的損失。**2** [VP2A, 3A] ~ ***(from),*** become well; get back to a former position of prosperity, state of health, mental condition, etc: 病後復元;恢復以前的繁榮、健康、心理狀況等: *He is slowly ~ing from his illness.* 他正慢慢從病中復元。*I doubt whether he will ~.* 我不知道他是否會康復。*I haven't yet ~ed from my astonishment.* 我還驚魂未定。*Has the country ~ed from the effects of the war yet?* 那個國家已從戰爭的影響中恢復過來了嗎？ **3** [VP6A] regain control of oneself; become calm or normal: 重新控制自己;變得平靜或正常;恢復正常: *He almost fell, but quickly ~ed (himself).* 他幾乎跌倒,但很快又站穩了。*He ~ed his balance/composure.* 他恢復了平衡(平靜)。**~·able** /-əbl ; -əbl/ *adj* that can be ~ed(1): 能尋回的;能取回的;能恢復的: *Is the deposit I've paid ~able?* 我所付的定金能取回嗎？ **re·cov·ery** *n* [U] ~ing or being ~ed: 尋回;被尋回;恢復;復元;痊癒: *make a quick ~y,* get well again quickly or quickly regain one's position after losing for a time in a game, athletic match, etc; 很快康復;很快趕上(比賽中失去的分數等); *~y from influenza;* 患流行性感冒後復元; *the ~y of a lost article,* getting it back again. 尋回失掉的物件。

re-cover /ˌriː ˈkʌvə(r) ; ˌriˈkʌvɚ/ *vt* [VP6A] supply with a new cover: 裝以新的蓋或封面: *This cushion/quilt needs to be ~ed.* 這個墊子需要換套子(這床棉被需要換被面)。

rec·re·ant /ˈrekrɪənt ; ˈrɛkrɪənt/ *adj, n* (liter) cowardly, unfaithful or traitorous (person): (文)懦弱的;不忠的;叛逆的;懦弱者;叛徒: *a ~ lover.* 一個不忠的愛人。

rec·re·ation /ˌrekrɪˈeɪʃn ; ˌrɛkrɪˈeʃən/ *n* [C, U] (form of) play or amusement; refreshment of body and mind; sth that pleasantly occupies one's time after work is done: (一種)遊戲或娛樂;身心的休閑;工作之餘的消遣活動: *walk and climb mountains for ~.* 爲消遣而走路和爬山。*Is gardening a ~ or a form of hard work?* 園藝是一種休閑活動呢,還是一種勞苦的工作？ *Flirting is an innocent ~, perhaps.* 調情取樂或許可說是一種無害的娛樂。**ˈ~ ground,** land, eg in a public park, set aside for games, etc. 供遊戲活動的場地;遊樂場。**~al** /-ʃənl ; -ʃənl/ *adj* of ~: 遊戲或娛樂的;休閑的;消遣的: *provide more ~al facilities,* eg sports grounds, swimming pools. 提供更多消遣活動的設備(如運動場,游泳池)。

re·crimi·na·tion /rɪˌkrɪmɪˈneɪʃn ; rɪˌkrɪməˈneʃən/ *n* [C, U] accusation made in return for one already made; countercharge: 反控訴;反訴;反責: *indulge in ~(s).* 互相責備對方;反訴罪狀。**re·crimi·nate** /rɪˈkrɪmɪneɪt ; rɪˈkrɪməˌnet/ *vi* [VP2A, 3A] ~ ***(against sb),*** accuse (sb) in return. 反控訴;反責(某人)。**re·crimi·na·tory** /rɪˈkrɪmɪnətrɪ *US:* -tɔːrɪ; rɪˈkrɪmənəˌtorɪ/ *adj* of ~. 反控訴的;反責的。

re·cru·des·ence /ˌriːkruːˈdesns ; ˌrikruˈdɛsn̩s/ *n* (of disease, violence, etc) new outburst; breaking out again: (指疾病,暴行等)新發作;再發作: *a ~ of civil disorder;* 內亂的再爆發; *the ~ of influenza.* 流行性感冒的再發生。

re·cruit /rɪˈkruːt ; rɪˈkrut/ *n* new member of a society, group, etc, esp a soldier in the early days of his training: (會社,團體等中之)新份子;新會員;新黨員;(尤指)新兵: *gain a few ~s to one's party,* eg in politics; 吸收幾個新黨員(如在政治方面); *~s being drilled on the parade ground.* 正在校閱場操練的新兵。□ *vt, vi* **1** [VP6A] get ~s for; enlist (persons) as ~s (for the army, a cause, etc): 爲…吸收新份子; (爲軍隊、某一目標) 徵募(人員)做新份子;徵募新兵: *a ˈ~ing officer;* 徵募新兵之軍官; *~ a new political party from the middle classes.* 從中層階級中爲新的政黨吸收新份子。*Were men for the Navy ~ed from men on merchant ships?* 海軍的人員是從商船的人員中徵募的嗎？ **2** [VP6A] get a sufficient quantity or store of; bring back to what is usual or normal: 獲得…的足量;補充;使恢復平常的或正常的狀態: *~ supplies;* 補充供應品; *~ one's health/strength.* 恢復健康(體力)。**~·ment** *n*

rec·tal /ˈrektəl ; ˈrɛktl̩/ *adj* of the rectum. 直腸的。

rec·tangle /ˈrektæŋgl ; ˈrɛktæŋgl̩/ *n* [C] plane four-sided figure with four right angles, esp one with adjacent sides unequal. 方形;(尤指)長方形;矩形。⇨ the illus at quadrilateral. 參看 quadrilateral 之插圖。**rec·tangu·lar** /rekˈtæŋgjʊlə(r) ; rɛkˈtæŋgjəlɚ/ *adj* in the shape of a ~. 長方形的。

rec·tify /ˈrektɪfaɪ ; ˈrɛktəˌfaɪ/ *vt* (*pt, pp* -fied) [VP6A] **1** put right; take out mistakes from: 改正;矯正: *~ abuses;* 改正惡習弊端; *mistakes that cannot be rectified.* 無法改正的錯誤。**2** purify or refine by repeated distillation or other process: 以連續蒸餾或其他過程淨化或精煉;精餾: *rectified spirits.* 精餾酒精。**rec·ti·fier** *n* person or thing that rectifies;

(electr) device which converts alternating current to direct current. 改正者;矯正器;精餾器;(電)整流器。 **rec·tifi·ca·tion** /ˌrektɪfɪˈkeɪʃn ; ˌrɛktəfəˈkeʃən/ *n* [U] ~ing or being rectified: 改正;被改正;精餾;被精餾: *the rectification of errors/alcohol;* 錯誤之改正(酒精之精餾); [C] instance of this; sth that has been rectified. 改正或精餾之實例;被改正或精餾過之物。

rec·ti·lin·ear /ˌrektɪˈlɪnɪə(r) ; ˌrɛktəˈlɪnɪɚ/ *adj* in or forming a straight line; bounded by, characterized by, straight lines. 直線的;形成直線的;由直線圍起的;有直線特徵的。

rec·ti·tude /ˈrektɪtjuːd *US:* -tuːd ; ˈrɛktəˌtjud/ *n* [U] honesty; upright or straightforward behaviour. 忠實;正直或坦率的行爲。

recto /ˈrektəʊ ; ˈrɛkto/ *n* (*pl* ~s /-təʊz ; -toz/) any right-hand page of a book. 書的右頁。⇨ verso.

rec·tor /ˈrektə(r) ; ˈrɛktɚ/ *n* **1** (C of E) clergyman in charge of a parish, the tithes of which were not withdrawn (eg to a college), at or after the time when the English Church separated from the Church of Rome. (英國教會)仍保留什一稅的教區之教區長。⇨ vicar. **2** head of certain universities, colleges, schools or religious institutions. 某些大學、學院、學校、宗教機構之首長; 校長; 院長。 **~y** /ˈrektərɪ ; ˈrɛktərɪ/ *n* (*pl* -ries) ~'s residence. 教區長、某些學校校長等之住宅。

rec·tum /ˈrektəm ; ˈrɛktəm/ *n* lower and final part of the large intestine. 直腸。⇨ the illus at alimentary. 參看 alimentary 之插圖。

re·cum·bent /rɪˈkʌmbənt ; rɪˈkʌmbənt/ *adj* (esp of a person) lying down: (尤指人)臥倒的; 躺臥的: *a ~ figure on a tomb,* statue or carving in a ~ position. 墳墓上的一個橫臥影像。

re·cu·per·ate /rɪˈkuːpəreɪt ; rɪˈkjupəˌret/ *vt, vi* [VP 6A, 2A] make or become strong again after illness, exhaustion or loss: (使)於病後或疲倦後恢復體力;休養;彌補損失: *~ one's health;* 恢復健康; *go to the seaside to ~.* 到海濱去休養。 **re·cu·per·ation** /rɪˌkuːpəˈreɪʃn ; rɪˌkjupəˈreʃən/ *n* recuperating. 復元;休養;恢復。 **re·cu·per·at·ive** /rɪˈkuːpərətɪv ; rɪˈkjupəˌretɪv/ *adj* helping, relating to, recuperation. 有助於或關於休養、恢復的。

re·cur /rɪˈkɜː(r) ; rɪˈkɝ/ *vi* (-rr-) **1** [VP2A] come, happen, again; be repeated: 再來; 再發生; 重複: *a problem which ~s periodically;* 一個定期發生的問題; *~ring decimals,* figures in decimal fractions that ~ in the same order, as 3·999... (written 3·9̇), 4·014014...(written 4·0̇14̇)。循環小數,如 3·999··· (寫作 3·9̇), 4·014014... (寫作 4·0̇14̇). **2** [VP3A] ~ *to,* go back (to sth) in words or thought: 在談話或思想中重回(到某事物): *~ring to what you said yesterday;* 回到你昨天所說的話題上; *if I may ~ to your idea.* 如果我可以再談談你的意見。 **3** [VP3A] ~ *to,* (of ideas, events etc) come back: (指思想,事件等)重現: *My first meeting with her often ~s to my memory.* 我同她首次會面的情景時常重現在我的記憶中。 **re·cur·rence** /rɪˈkʌrəns ; rɪˈkɝəns/ *n* [C, U] ~ring; repetition: 再發生;再回到;重現;重覆: *Let there be no ~rence of this error.* 不要再有這種錯誤發生。 *The frequent ~rence of these headaches made her life miserable.* 頭痛經常復發使她生活十分痛苦。 **re·cur·rent** /-ənt ; -ənt/ *adj* (of events, fevers etc) ~ring frequently or regularly: (指事件,發燒等)經常發生的;週期性發生的: *allow £35 a month for ~rent expenses,* eg rent, lighting and heating. 每月留三十五鎊作爲經常的費用(如房租,照明,暖氣)。

re·curve /ˌriːˈkɜːv ; rɪˈkɝv/ *vt, vi* curve or bend backwards or downwards. (使)向後或向下彎曲;折回。

recu·sant /ˈrekjʊznt ; ˈrɛkjuznt/ *n, adj* (person) refusing to submit to authority or to comply with regulations, esp (hist) a Roman Catholic who refused to attend Church of England services. 拒絕向權威屈服或遵從規則的(人);(尤指,史)拒絕參與英國國教禮拜式的天主教徒。 **recu·sancy** /-znsɪ ; -znsɪ/ *n* [U].

re·cycle /ˌriːˈsaɪkl ; rɪˈsaɪkl/ *vt* [VP6A] treat (substances already used for industry, etc) so that further use is possible: 處理(廢物)使成爲有用之物: *~ old newspapers,* by de-inking and pulping them. 以除墨和化成紙漿等方式處理舊報紙。

red /red ; rɛd/ *adj* (-der, -dest) **1** of the colour of fresh blood, rubies, human lips, the tongue, maple leaves in autumn, post-office pillar boxes in GB; of shades varying from crimson to bright brown (as of iron rust): 紅色的(如鮮血,紅寶石,唇,舌,秋日楓葉,英國郵筒等之顏色);從深紅到鮮褐(如鐵銹色)間之不同色調的: *red with anger/embarrassment,* flushed in the face; 氣(窘)得滿臉通紅; *with red hands,* with hands stained with blood; 雙手染有血跡; *with red eyes,* eyes red with weeping. 哭得眼睛發紅。 **ˌ~ ˈcarpet,** one laid out for the reception of an important visitor. (接待貴賓所鋪設的)紅地毯。 ***paint the town red,*** go on a spree and indulge in noisy, rough behaviour. 狂歡作樂。 ***see red,*** lose control of oneself through anger, or indignation. 怒不可遏。 **2** Russian; Soviet; Communist: 俄國的;蘇維埃的; 共黨的: *The Red Army.* 紅軍。 **3** (various uses in compounds, etc): (在複合字等中的各種用法): **ˈred·breast** *n* (also 亦作 *robin redbreast*) bird called the robin. 知更鳥;紅襟鳥。 **ˈRed·brick** *adj* (GB) name applied to the English universities founded near the end of the 19th c (contrasted chiefly with Oxford and Cambridge—known as *Oxbridge*). (英)(十九世紀末設立之)大學(主要以別於牛津和劍橋——合稱'牛橋')。 **ˈred·cap** *n* (GB) member of the military police; (US) railroad porter. (英)憲兵; (美)(火車站的)脚夫。 **ˈred·coat** *n* (old name for) British soldier. (舊名稱)英國兵。 **ˌRed ˈCrescent** *n* (emblem of an) organization in Muslim countries corresponding to the Red Cross. 紅新月會(回教國家相當於紅十字會的組織);其標記。 **ˌRed ˈCross** *n* (emblem of the) international organization concerned with the relief of suffering caused by natural disasters, etc and for helping the sick and wounded and those taken prisoner in war. 紅十字會;紅十字會的標記(紅十字會係一國際組織,辦理因天災等造成的災民救濟工作,以及協助戰爭中之傷患及戰俘)。 **ˌred ˈdeer** *n* kind of deer native to the forests of Europe and Asia. (歐洲和亞洲森林中產的)赤鹿。 **ˌred ˈensign** (or colloq, **ˌred ˈduster**) *n* red flag with the Union Jack in one corner, used by British merchant ships. (英國商船上懸掛的在一角有英國國旗之)紅旗。 **ˌred ˈflag** *n* **(a)** flag used as a symbol of danger (eg on railways, by workers on the roads). (鐵路上、道路工人等所用的) 作爲危險信號的紅旗。 **(b)** symbol of revolution. (作爲革命象徵的)紅旗。 **(c) the ˌRed ˈFlag,** revolutionary socialist song. 革命之歌;紅旗歌(社會主義者等唱之)。 ***(catch sb) ˌred-ˈhanded*** *adj* in the act of committing a crime. 趁其犯罪時(逮捕某人);當場(逮捕某人)。 **ˌred ˈhat** *n* cardinal's hat. 樞機主教之帽子。 **ˈred·head** *n* person having red hair. 有紅髮的人。 **ˌred ˈherring** *n* **(a)** smoke-cured herring. 燻青魚。 **(b)** (fig) irrelevant matter introduced to distract attention from the subject being discussed. (喻)用以分散對本題之注意力的不相干的東西。 ***neither fish, flesh, nor good red herring,*** of a doubtful or ambiguous nature, which cannot be defined. 性質可疑或不明的東西;非驢非馬。 ***draw a red herring across the trail,*** introduce irrelevant matter to distract attention from the subject being discussed. 提出不相干的問題去分散對本題的注意力。 **ˌred-ˈhot** *adj* (of a metal) heated until it is red; (fig) highly excited, furious: (指金屬)熾熱的;(喻)極端興奮的;猛烈的: *red-hot enthusiasm.* 非常的熱心。 **ˌRed ˈIndian** *n* (old use, now impolite) American Indian. (舊用法,現爲不禮貌用語)美洲印第安人。 **ˌred ˈlead** *n* [U] pigment made from red oxide of lead. 鉛丹(一種顏料)。 **ˌred-ˈletter day,** important or memorable day. 重要或值得紀念的日

子。ˌ**red 'light** *n* **(a)** danger signal on railways, etc; 'stop' signal on roads. 鐵路等上的危險信號;道路上'停'的標誌。***see the red light,*** realize the nearness of danger or disaster. 看到了紅燈(知道危險或災難之將臨)。 **(b)** ***red-light district,*** part of a town where there are brothels. (城市中之)紅燈區;風化區。ˌ**red 'meat** *n* [U] beef and mutton (contrasted with *white* meat, ie veal, pork, poultry). 牛羊肉(與 white meat, 卽小牛肉,豬肉,家禽肉相對)。ˌ**red 'pepper** *n* red fruit of the capsicum plant. 紅辣椒。ˌ**red 'rag** *n* ***like a red rag to a bull,*** sth that excites a person's anger or passion. (如刺激公牛發怒之紅布) 能激起憤怒或强烈感情之事物。**'red·skin** *n* (old use, now impolite) American Indian. (舊用法,現爲不禮貌用語)美洲印第安人。**the ˌRed 'Star,** symbol of the USSR and other Communist States. 紅星(蘇俄和其他共產國家的標誌)。ˌ**red 'tape** *n* [U] (fig) excessive use of formalities in public business; too much attention to rules and regulations: (喩)繁文縟節;官樣文章;官僚習氣: *red tape in government offices.* 政府機關中的官僚習氣。**'red·wing** *n* name used of kinds of thrush and other birds with red wing-feathers. 畫眉鳥;紅翼鶇。**'red·wood** *n* name used of kinds of tree with reddish wood, esp an evergreen Californian tree, some of which are of great height. 紅杉 (各種有紅色木質之樹,尤指美國加州產的一種常青樹,有些紅杉長得極高)。□ *n* **1** [C, U] (shade of) red colour: (深淺程度不同的)紅色: *too much red in the painting;* 這畫中用的紅色太多; *the reds and browns of the woods in autumn,* the red and brown shades of the leaves. 秋林中各種紅色和褐色樹葉。**2** red clothes: 紅衣服: *dressed in red.* 穿紅衣。**3** (colloq) person favouring or supporting Communism or the Soviet system. (俗)贊成或支持共產主義或蘇維埃制度的人;赤色份子。**4 the red,** debit side of business accounts. 赤字;虧空。***be in/get into the red,*** have/get liabilities that exceed assets. 負債。***be/get out of the red,*** reach the position when one is no longer in the red. 不再虧空。⇨ black *n* (5).

re·dact /rɪ'dækt ; rɪ'dækt/ *vt* [VP6A] (formal) edit. (正式用語)編輯。**re·dac·tion** /rɪ'dækʃn ; rɪ'dækʃən/ *n* [U, C].

red·den /'redn ; 'rɛdn̩/ *vt, vi* [VP6A, 2A] make or become red; blush. 使紅;變紅;臉色變紅;赧顏。

red·dish /'redɪʃ ; 'rɛdɪʃ/ *adj* rather red. 微紅的;略帶紅色的。

re·deem /rɪ'di:m ; rɪ'dim/ *vt* [VP6A, 14] ~ ***(from),*** **1** get (sth) back by payment or by doing sth: 贖回;挽回: ~ *a pawned watch/a mortgage;* 贖回一典當的錶(抵押品); ~ *one's honour.* 挽回一個人的名譽。**2** perform (a promise or obligation). 踐約;實踐(義務)。**3** set free by payment; rescue: 贖救;拯救: ~ *a slave/prisoner;* 贖出一奴隸(囚犯); (by Jesus) make free from sin. (由耶穌)贖罪。**4** compensate; make amends for: 賠償;補救: *his ~ing feature,* the feature or quality that balances his faults, etc. 能彌補他的缺點等的特質。*The acting barely ~s the play,* The play is poor and the acting not very good. 該劇的演出未能補救劇本的缺點(劇本差勁,演得也不好)。**~·able** /-əbl ; -əbl̩/ *adj* that can be ~ed. 可贖回的;可實踐的;可拯救的;可補償的。**(the) Re·dee·mer** *n* Jesus Christ. 救世主(耶穌基督)。

re·demp·tion /rɪ'dempʃn ; rɪ'dɛmpʃən/ *n* [U] redeeming or being redeemed: 贖回;被贖回;實踐;被實踐;補償;被補償: *the ~ of a promise;* 諾言的實踐; deliverance or rescue (esp from evil ways): 救出;贖救 (尤指從罪惡中救出): *past/beyond ~,* too bad to be redeemed. 無可救藥。

re·demp·tive /rɪ'demptɪv ; rɪ'dɛmptɪv/ *adj* serving to redeem; relating to redemption. 適合於或關於贖回等的;挽回的;實踐的;拯救的;補償的。

re·de·ploy /ˌri:dɪ'plɔɪ ; ˌridɪ'plɔɪ/ *vt* [VP6A] (of troops, workers in industry, etc) withdraw and rearrange so as to use more efficiently. (指軍隊,產業工人等)重新部署;轉用;調動。**~·ment** *n* [U, C] ~ing: *the ~ment of labour.* 勞工的調配。

re·dif·fu·sion /ˌri:dɪ'fju:ʒn ; ˌridɪ'fjuʒən/ *n* [U] system of using broadcast programmes (sound and television) in public places (eg cinemas). 在公共場所(如電影院)播放(廣播電台及電視)廣播節目之系統。

re·do /ˌri:'du: ; ri'du/ *vt* (*pt* -did /-'dɪd ; -'dɪd/, *pp* -done /-'dʌn ; -'dʌn/) [VP6A] do again: 再做: *We must have the walls redone,* repapered, recoloured, etc according to context. 我們必須把這些牆再整理一番(例如重新糊紙、改換顏色等,其意義視上下文而定)。

redo·lent /'redələnt ; 'rɛdl̩ənt/ *adj* ~ ***of,*** (formal) having a strong smell, esp one that is reminiscent of sth: (正式用語)有濃烈氣味的;(尤指)具有使想起某種東西之强烈氣味的: *bed sheets ~ of lavender;* 有薰衣草芳香氣味的床單; (fig) (喩) *a town ~ of age and romance.* 使人想起古代和傳奇的一個城市。**redo·lence** /-əns ; -əns/ *n*

re·double /rɪ'dʌbl ; ri'dʌbl̩/ *vt, vi* [VP6A, 2A] **1** make or become greater or stronger: 使或變得更大或更强;增添: *They ~d their efforts.* 他們加倍努力。*Her zeal ~d.* 她的熱心倍增。**2** (bridge) double again a bid already doubled by an opponent. (橋牌)再賭倍(把已由對方賭倍的叫牌再予賭倍)。⇨ double[4](6).

re·doubt /rɪ'daʊt ; rɪ'daʊt/ *n* [C] strong point in a system of fortifications: 稜堡;角面堡;安全退避處;防守據點: *attack and capture a ~.* 攻擊並佔領一防守重鎭。

re·doubt·able /rɪ'daʊtəbl ; rɪ'daʊtəbl̩/ *adj* (liter) to be feared; formidable: (文)可怕的;令人畏懼的: *those ~ ladies, the suffragettes.* 那些頑强的女士們,指二十世紀初葉鼓吹英國婦女有參政權的婦女。

re·dound /rɪ'daʊnd ; rɪ'daʊnd/ *vi* [VP3A] ~ ***to,*** (formal) contribute greatly in the end; promote: (正式用語)有助於;促進: *Your success will ~ to the fame of the college.* 你的成功將提高該大學的聲譽。*It ~s to your honour.* 這事提高你的榮譽。

re·dress /rɪ'dres ; rɪ'drɛs/ *vt* [VP6A] **1** set (a wrong) right again; make up for, do sth that compensates for (a wrong): 改正;修正;矯正;補償: *You should confess and ~ your errors.* 你應該懺悔並改正你的錯誤。**2** ~ ***the balance,*** make things equal again. 使再平衡。□ *n* [U] act of ~ing or correcting (abuses, etc); sth that ~es: 改正或矯正(惡習等);有改正或補償等作用的事物;賠償: *seek ~;* 求賠償;革除惡習; *go to a lawyer to get legal ~.* 找律師以期獲得合法賠償。

re·duce /rɪ'dju:s *US:* -'du:s ; rɪ'djus/ *vt, vi* [VP6A, 14] ~ ***(to),*** **1** make less; make smaller in size, number, degree, price, etc: 使較少;使(體積)變小;減少(數目);降低(程度);減低(價格)等: ~ *speed/pressure/costs;* 減低速度(壓力,成本); ~ *one's expenses;* 減縮開支; ~ *one's weight by ten pounds/from X pounds to Y pounds.* 減輕體重十磅(自 X 磅減爲 Y 磅)。*He is ~d almost to a skeleton,* has become very thin. 他瘦得幾乎變成了一個骨頭架子。[VP2A, B] (colloq): (俗): *She has been reducing for the last few weeks,* has been dieting (or trying other methods) in order to ~ her weight. 最近幾個星期她一直在節食(或以其他方法)減輕體重。**2** bring or get to a certain condition, way of living, etc: 促成或達到某種情況、生活方式等: ~ *a class of noisy children to order;* 使一班吵鬧的孩子恢復秩序; ~ *sb to silence,* cause him to stop talking; 使某人不再講話; ~ *sth to order;* 使某事物有規律; ~ *the rebels to submission;* 使叛徒屈服; ~ *a sergeant to the ranks.* 將一士官貶爲士兵。*They were ~d to begging or starving,* They became so poor that they had either to beg or go hungry. 他們窮得不行乞便挨餓。*They are living in ~d circumstances,* in (comparative) poverty. 他們過着(相當)貧困的生活。**3** change (to another form): 改變(成另一形式,與 to 連用): ~ *an equation/argument/state-*

ment to its simplest form; 把一方程式(論據,陳述)化成最簡單形式; ~ *water by electrolysis,* separate it into oxygen and hydrogen; 以電解法分解水(卽分解爲氧與氫); ~ (*sth*) *to an absurdity,* make, eg a scheme or argument, appear absurd by removing whatever hides its real nature; (揭露其眞實性質)使(某一計畫或論據等)顯得荒謬可笑; ~ *wood logs to pulp.* 把木材化成紙漿。**re·duc·ible** /-əbl; -əbḷ/ *adj* that can be ~d. 能減低或變小的;能變形的;能化簡的;能分解的。

reductio ad absurdum /rɪˌdʌktɪəʊ ˌæd əbˈsɜ:dəm; rɪˈdʌkʃɪoˌædæbˈsɝdəm/ (Lat) the disproof of a proposition by showing that its conclusion can only be absurd. (拉丁)歸謬法;反證論法(指出某一命題結論之荒謬,以證明該命題爲誤之方法)。

re·duc·tion /rɪˈdʌkʃn; rɪˈdʌkʃən/ *n* **1** [U] reducing or being reduced; [C] instance of this: 減少;減低;使變形;被減少;被減低;變形: *a ~ in/of numbers;* 數目方面的減少; *great ~s in prices; price ~s.* 大減價。 **2** [C] copy, on a smaller scale, of a picture, map, etc. (圖畫,地圖等之)縮版;縮圖。

re·dun·dant /rɪˈdʌndənt; rɪˈdʌndənt/ *adj* superfluous; not needed: 過多的;多餘的;不需要的: *a paragraph without a ~ word;* 沒有一個廢字的一段文章; ~ *labour,* unneeded or surplus workers. 過剩的勞工。*With the decreasing demand for coal many thousands of miners may become ~.* 由於煤的需要量減少,成千上萬的礦工可能成爲過剩的勞工。**re·dun·dance** /-əns; -əns/, **re·dun·dancy** /-ənsɪ; -ənsɪ/ *nn* [U] being ~: 過多;過剩: *redundancy among clerks caused by the increasing use of computers;* 因電子計算機的使用日漸增加而造成職員的過剩。[C] (*pl* -cies) instance of this: 過多或過剩之實例: *more redundancies in the docks.* 船塢中有過多的船。**reˈdundancy pay,** money paid by an employer to a ~ worker, the sum depending upon age and length of service. 遣散費。

re·dupli·cate /rɪˈdju:plɪkeɪt *US:* -ˈdu:-; rɪˈdjupləˌket/ *vt* [VP6A] double; repeat. 加倍;重複。**re·dupli·ca·tion** /rɪˌdju:plɪˈkeɪʃn *US:* -ˌdu:-; rɪˌdjupləˈkeʃən/ *n*

re-echo /ri: ˈekəʊ; riˈɛko/ *vi* [VP2A] echo again and again. 回響;再發回聲。□ *n* (*pl* ~es /-əʊz; -oz/) echo of an echo. 回聲之回響;再回聲。

reed /ri:d; rid/ *n* [C] **1** (tall, firm stem or stalk of) kinds of coarse, firm-stemmed, jointed grasses growing in or near water; [U] (collective) mass of such grasses growing together; (*pl*) dried stalks used for thatching. 蘆葦(桿);(集合用法)蘆葦叢;(複)乾蘆桿(用於蓋屋頂)。 ***a broken ~,*** (fig) an unreliable person or thing. (喻)不可靠的人或物。 **2** (in some wind-instruments, eg the oboe, bassoon, clarinet and in some organ-pipes) strip of metal, etc that vibrates to produce sound. (某些管樂器,如雙簧管,低音管,豎笛,某些風琴管中之)顫動以發出聲音的部分;簧。**the ~s,** ~ instruments of this sort. 簧樂器。 **~y** *adj* **1** abounding in ~s(1). 多蘆葦的。 **2** (of sounds, voices) shrill; piping. (指聲音)細而尖的;尖銳的。

reef¹ /ri:f; rif/ *n* that part of a sail which can be rolled up or folded so as to reduce its area: 縮折帆葉(帆的能捲起或摺起以減少面積的部分): *take in a ~,* shorten sail; (fig) go forward more cautiously. 捲疊一部分帆;(喻)加倍小心前進。**ˈ~-knot** *n* ordinary double knot (US = *square knot*). 平結;方結;拱結。⇨ the illus at knot. 參看 knot 之插圖。□ *vt* [VP6A] reduce the area of (a sail) by rolling up or folding a part. 縮(帆)(由捲起或摺疊而減少帆的面積)。

reef² /ri:f; rif/ *n* ridge of rock, shingle etc just below or above the surface of the sea: 礁;暗礁: *wrecked on a coral ~.* 撞及珊瑚礁而破船的。⇨ the illus at atoll. 參看 atoll 之插圖。

reefer /ˈri:fə(r); ˈrifɚ/ *n* **1** close-fitting double-breasted jacket of thick cloth, as worn by sailors. 一種緊身、雙排扣的粗布外衣(如海員等所穿者)。 **2** (sl) kind of cigarette containing marijuana. (俚)含有印度大麻的香煙。

reek /ri:k; rik/ *n* [U] **1** strong, bad smell: 濃烈的臭味: *the ~ of stale tobacco smoke.* 發霉煙草的臭煙味。 **2** (liter and Scot use) thick smoke or vapour: (文學及蘇格蘭用語)濃煙或蒸汽: *the ~ of a peat fire.* 泥炭火的濃煙。□ *vi* **1** [VP3A] **~ of,** smell unpleasantly of: 有臭味: *He ~s of whisky/garlic.* 他有威士忌(大蒜)的臭味。*The room ~ed of stale cigar smoke.* 這房裏瀰漫着發霉雪茄的臭煙味。 **2 ~ with,** be covered (with sweat, blood, etc); show signs or traces of: 爲(汗、血等)浸染;有…跡象: *a horse ~ing with sweat;* 一匹混身汗水的馬; *a murderer whose hands still ~ed with blood.* 手上仍然血跡斑斑的一個殺人犯。

reel¹ /ri:l; ril/ *n* **1** cylinder, roller or similar device on which cotton, thread, wire, photographic film, magnetic tape, hose (for water, etc), a fishing line, is wound. 線軸;捲筒;捲軸;捲盤。***(straight) off the ~,*** (colloq) without a hitch or pause, in rapid succession. (俗)迅速不停地。 **2** (cinema) length of positive film rolled on one ~: (電影)(影片的)一捲;一本: *a six-~ film,* a complete film on six ~s. 一部有六大本的電影片。⇨ spool. □ *vt* [VP6A, 15A, B] roll or wind (thread, a fishing line, etc) on to, or with the help of, a ~; wind (thread, etc) *off*: 捲或纏(線,釣線等)於軸上;藉軸而捲或纏;抽出(線等,與 off 連用): *~ in the line;* 捲線; *~ up a fish;* 收釣線拉魚; *~ the silk thread off cocoons.* 從繭中抽出絲。**~ sth off,** tell, say or repeat sth without pause or apparent effort: 滔滔不絕地說出或背出: *~ off the verses of a long poem;* 滔滔不絕地背出一首長詩的各節; *~ off a list of names.* 連續地講出一串人名。

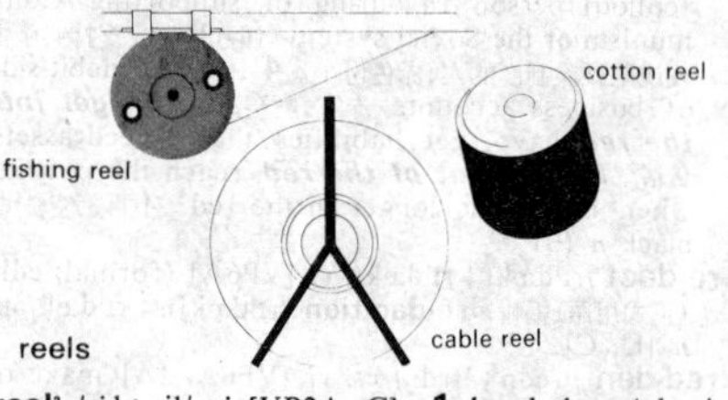

reels

reel² /ri:l; ril/ *vi* [VP2A, C] **1** be shaken (physically or mentally) by a blow, a shock, rough treatment, etc: (身體或心理方面)因打擊或驚訝或粗魯對待等而震顫: *His mind ~ed when he heard the news.* 他聽到那消息時,內心感到一陣震顫。 **2** walk or stand unsteadily, moving from side to side; sway: 不穩地走或站;來回地搖擺;搖晃: *He ~ed like a drunken man.* 他搖搖晃晃,像個醉漢。*He went ~ing down the road.* 他搖搖擺擺地沿大路走去。 **3** seem to sway; appear to move or shake: 似乎搖晃;看來搖動或震顫: *The street ~ed before his eyes.* 街道似乎在他眼前搖動起來。

reel³ /ri:l; ril/ *n* [C] (music for a) lively Scottish dance, usu for two couples. 利爾舞(一種輕快的蘇格蘭舞,通常由兩對共舞);利爾舞曲。

re-en·try /ˌri: ˈentrɪ; riˈɛntrɪ/ *n* (*pl* -ries) act of re-entering; return of a spacecraft into the earth's atmosphere. 再進入;再登記;(太空船)重回大氣層。

reeve /ri:v; riv/ *n* **1** (hist) chief magistrate of a town or district. (史)市邑長官;地方官。 **2** (Canada) president of a village or town council. (加拿大)(鄉鎭議會之)議長。

re·face /ˌri:ˈfeɪs; riˈfes/ *vt* put a new surface on. 重裝新面;重修表面。

re·fec·tion /rɪˈfekʃn; rɪˈfɛkʃən/ *n* [U] refreshment in the form of food and drink; [C] light meal. 茶點;點心;便餐;小吃。

re·fec·tory /rɪˈfektərɪ; rɪˈfɛktərɪ/ *n* (*pl* -ries) dining-hall (in a monastery, convent or college). (修道院,尼庵或大學中的)餐廳。

re·fer /rɪˈfɜː(r); rɪˈfɝ/ *vt, vi* (-rr-) **1** [VP14, 15B] *~ sb/sth (back) (to sb/sth),* send, take, hand over (*to, back to*) to be dealt with, decided, etc: 送交;呈交;提交(某人或某機構)處理或決定: *The dispute was ~red to the United Nations.* 該項爭執已提交聯合國處理。*I was ~red to the Manager/to the Inquiry Office.* 我被吩咐去向經理(問訊處)接洽。*The question was ~red back,* was deferred. 該問題被擱置。 **2** [VP3A] *~ to,* (of a speaker, what is said, etc) speak of, allude to; apply to: (指講話者,所談及之事等)談及;提及;應用於: *When I said that some people are stupid I wasn't ~ring to you.* 當我說某些人很愚蠢的時候,我並不是指你。*Don't ~ to this matter again, please.* 請不要再提這件事了。*What I have to say ~s to all of you.* 我要說的這一切和你們大家有關。*Does that remark ~ to me?* 那批評的話是指我說的嗎? **3** [VP3A] *~ to,* turn to, go to, for information, etc: 參考;諮詢: *The speaker often ~red to his notes.* 那位講演者一再參考他的大綱。**ref·er·able** /rɪˈfɜːrəbl; ˈrɛfrəbḷ/ *adj* that can be ~red. 可歸因於…的。

ref·eree /ˌrefəˈriː; ˌrɛfəˈri/ *n* **1** person to whom disputes, eg in industry, between workers and employers, are referred for decision. 糾紛的仲裁者;調停者(如調停勞資雙方間的糾紛者)。 **2** (in football, boxing, etc) person who controls matches, judges points in dispute, etc. (足球、拳擊等的)裁判員。⇨ umpire. □ *vt, vi* [VP6A, 2A] act as ~: 裁判: *~ a football match.* 爲足球比賽做裁判。

ref·er·ence /ˈrefrəns; ˈrɛfrəns/ *n* **1** [C, U] (instance of) referring: 送交;交付;談到;提及;參考;諮詢;提及等之實例: *You should make ~ to a dictionary.* 你應該參考字典。*The book is full of ~s to places that I know well.* 這本書裏提到很多我所熟知的地方。ˈ**~ book, book of ~,** one that is not read through but consulted for information, eg a dictionary or encyclopaedia. 參考書(例如字典或百科全書)。ˈ**~ library,** one containing ~ books, to be consulted there but not to be taken away. 參考書閱覽室(室內藏書可供參閱,但不得外借)。 ***terms of ~,*** (of a commission, etc) scope or range given to an authority: (指委員會等)委託的範圍;授權的範圍: *Is this question outside our terms of ~,* one that we are not required to investigate? 這個問題不在我們調查的範圍內嗎? **2** [C] (person willing to make a) statement about a person's character or abilities: (有關一個人的品格或能力的)證明書;介紹書;(願提供證明書的)證明人;介紹人: *excellent ~s from former employers.* 以前的雇主們給的很好的證明書。*The shop will open a credit account for you if you supply a banker's ~,* a note from your bank stating that your financial position is sound. 如果你能提出銀行給你的證明書,這家商店就會爲你開一個信用帳戶。 **3** [C] note, direction, etc telling where certain information may be found: 附註;旁註;參照註: *He dislikes history books that are crowded with ~s to other books.* 他不喜歡有很多參考其他書籍的附註的歷史書。ˈ**~ marks,** marks, eg *, †, ‡, §, used to refer the reader to the place, eg a footnote, where information may be found. 參照符號(用以指示讀者參看資料來源的符號)。 ˌ**cross-ˈreference,** ⇨ cross-~. **4** [U] ***in/with ~ to,*** concerning; about. 關於;有關。 ***without ~ to,*** irrespective of; having no connection with. 不顧;無關。 **ref·er·en·tial** /ˌrefəˈrenʃl; ˌrɛfəˈrɛnʃəl/ *adj* having ~ to. 參考的;參看的;諮詢的;有關的。

ref·er·en·dum /ˌrefəˈrendəm; ˌrɛfəˈrɛndəm/ *n* (*pl* ~s; -da /-də; -də/) [C] the referring of a political question to a direct vote of the electorate. 複決權;複決投票;公民投票。

re·fill /ˌriːˈfɪl; riˈfɪl/ *vt* fill again. 再充滿;再注滿。□ *n* /ˈriːfɪl; ˈriˌfɪl/ that which is used to ~; a container: 用以再注滿之物;新補充物;容器: *two ~s for a ball-point pen.* 原子筆的兩支替換筆心。

re·fine /rɪˈfaɪn; rɪˈfaɪn/ *vt, vi* **1** [VP6A, 2A] free from other substances; make or become pure: 淨化;使純淨;變純淨;精煉: *~ sugar/oil/ores.* 精煉糖(石油,礦石)。 **2** [VP6A] cause to become more cultured, polished in manners; get rid of what is coarse or vulgar: 使文雅高尚;袪除粗俗的行爲,言語等: *~ a language;* 使一語言純淨高雅; *~d language/manners/speech/taste.* 高雅的言語(態度,言談,趣味)。 **3** *~ upon,* improve by giving great attention to details: 由特別注意細節而改良;精益求精: *~ upon one's methods.* 改良個人的方法。

re·fine·ment /rɪˈfaɪnmənt; rɪˈfaɪnmənt/ *n* **1** [U] refining or being refined. 精煉;改良;被精煉;被改良。 **2** [U] purity of feeling, taste, language, etc; delicacy of manners: (感情,趣味,語言等的)純潔;高尚;(態度的)嫻雅: *a lady of ~;* 一位嫻雅的女士; *lack of ~,* ie vulgarity; 缺乏教養; *aim at acquiring ~.* 以達到高尚嫻雅爲目的。 **3** [C] ingenious or remarkable example of such purity of tastes, etc; delicate or clever development of sth: (趣味等)純潔高尚之巧妙的或顯著的例子;某事物之細緻的或巧妙的發展: *~s of meaning/cruelty;* 意義的精微巧妙處(殘酷虐待的妙法); *all the ~s of the age.* 這個時代所有高尚的事物。

re·finer /rɪˈfaɪnə(r); rɪˈfaɪnɚ/ *n* **1** person whose business is to refine sth: 精煉者;精製者: *sugar ~s.* 精煉糖者。 **2** machine for refining metals, sugar, etc. (金屬,糖等之)精煉機。**~y** /-nərɪ; -nərɪ/ *n* place, building, etc where sth is refined: 精煉場;精煉廠;精製廠: *a ˈsugar ~y;* 煉糖廠; *an ˈoil ~y.* 煉油廠。

re·fit /ˌriːˈfɪt; riˈfɪt/ *vt, vi* (-tt-) [VP6A] make (a ship, etc) ready for use again by renewing or repairing parts; [VP2A] (of a ship) be made fit for further voyages: 重新裝配或修理(船等);改裝;整修;(指船)被修理或裝配: *The ship put into Cardiff to ~.* 該船駛入加地夫修理。□ *n* /ˈriːfɪt; riˈfɪt/ refitting. 再裝配;修理。

re·flate /ˌriːˈfleɪt; rɪˈflet/ *vt* [VP6A] restore to a previous economic or currency state: 使(通貨)再膨脹;使(經濟或貨幣)恢復原先狀態: *plans to ~ the economy.* 計畫恢復經濟。

re·fla·tion /riːˈfleɪʃn; rɪˈfleʃən/ *n* [U] inflation of currency after a deflation, to restore the system to its previous condition. 通貨再膨脹(使通貨恢復原先狀態)。

re·flect /rɪˈflekt; rɪˈflɛkt/ *vt, vi* **1** [VP6A] (of a surface) throw back (light, heat, sound); (of a mirror) send back an image of: (指表面)反射(光,熱,聲);(指鏡)反映…之像: *The sunlight was ~ed from the water.* 日光由水面反射出來。*Look at the trees ~ed in the lake.* 看湖中倒映的樹影。*The moon shines with ~ed light.* 月以反射之光照耀。*The sight of my face ~ed in the mirror never pleases me.* 我永遠不喜歡看自己在鏡中反映出的臉孔。ˈ**~ing telescope,** one in which the image is ~ed in a mirror and magnified. 反射望遠鏡。 **2** [VP6A] express; show the nature of: 表達;表現…之性質: *Her sad looks ~ed the thoughts passing through her mind.* 她憂戚的面容反映出她內心的思想。*Does the literature of a nation ~ its politics?* 一個國家的文學反映出它的政治嗎? **3** [VP14] *~ sth on/upon sb,* (of actions, results) bring (credit or discredit upon): (指行動,結果)帶給(榮譽或玷辱): *The results ~ the greatest credit upon all concerned.* 這些成績帶給所有有關人員最大的榮譽。*Such behaviour can only ~ discredit upon you.* 這樣的行爲只能給你帶來恥辱。 **4** [VP3A] *~ on/upon,* bring discredit upon; hurt the good reputation of: 不信任;玷辱名譽: *I do not wish to ~ upon your sincerity,* suggest that you are not sincere. 我不希望懷疑你的誠意。*Your rude behaviour ~s only upon yourself,* You are the only person whose reputation is hurt by it. 你的粗魯行爲只會損及你自己的名譽。 **5** [VP2A, 3A, 9, 8, 10] *~ (on/upon),* consider; think on: 考慮;思考: *I must ~ upon what answer to give/how to answer that* *question.* 我必須思考一下如何答覆(如何答覆那個問題)。*He ~ed how difficult it would be to escape.* 他在想逃走會有多麼困難。

re·flec·tion (GB also **re·flexion**) /rɪˈflekʃn; rɪˈflɛkʃən/ *n* **1** [U] reflecting or being reflected: 反射;被反射;反映: *the ~ of heat.* 熱之反射。 **2** [C] sth reflected, esp an image reflected in a mirror or in still water: 被反射或反映之物;(尤指)鏡中或靜水中之映像: *see one's ~ in a mirror;* 看自己在鏡中的映像; *the ~ of trees in (the water of) a lake.* 湖(水)中樹的倒影。 **3** [U] thought; (re)consideration: 思想;沉思;(再)考慮: *lost in ~;* 陷於沉思中; *do sth without sufficient ~.* 未經過深思熟慮卽做某事。***on*** ~, after reconsidering the matter. 經再三考慮。 **4** [C] expression of a thought in speech or writing; idea arising in the mind: (在言談或寫作中的)思想之表達; 心中產生的意念: *~s on the pleasures of being idle.* 對閑散生活之樂趣的看法。 **5** [C] expression of blame: 非難;責備: *I intended no ~ on your character,* did not want to suggest that you are blameworthy. 我無意對你的品格有何責難。*How dare you cast ~s on my motives?* 你怎敢責難我的動機? **6** [C] sth that brings discredit: 帶來恥辱之事物: *This is a ~ upon your honour.* 這對你的名譽是一種損害。

re·flec·tive /rɪˈflektɪv; rɪˈflɛktɪv/ *adj* thoughtful; in the habit of reflection(3). 沉思的;時常思考的。 **~·ly** *adv*

re·flec·tor /rɪˈflektə(r); rɪˈflɛktɚ/ *n* sth that reflects heat, light or sound, esp a piece of glass or metal for reflecting light, etc in a required direction. 反射熱、光、聲的東西(尤指向一指定方向反射光等之玻璃或金屬面);反射器;反射鏡;反射體。ˈ**~ studs,** (GB) studs inserted in a road surface to help drivers by reflecting light from headlamps (= colloq 俗 *cat's eyes*). (英)反光釘(鋪於路面,藉反射車輛前燈之燈光以幫助駕駛人員)。⇨ the illus at bicycle. 參看 bicycle 之插圖。

re·flex /ˈriːfleks; ˈriflɛks/ *adj* **1** ˈ**~ action,** action that is independent of the will, being an involuntary response to a stimulation of the nerves, eg shivering, sneezing. 反射動作(不受意志力所控制,係對神經感受刺激的自動反應,如發抖,打噴嚏等)。**2** ˈ**~ camera,** hand camera in which, by means of a mirror, the reflected image of the object or scene to be photographed can be seen and focused up to the moment of exposure. 反射式照相機(一種手提照相機,藉一鏡之助,待拍攝之景物的反射映像可在曝光前被看見並集中在焦點上)。□ *n* ~ action. 反射動作;反射。

re·flexion /rɪˈflekʃn; rɪˈflɛkʃən/ *n* = reflection.

re·flex·ive /rɪˈfleksɪv; rɪˈflɛksɪv/ *n, adj* (word or form) showing that the agent's action is upon himself. 反身的(字或形式)。 ~ **verb,** eg He *cut* himself. 反身動詞(如 He cut himself 中的 cut)。~ **pronoun,** eg *myself, themselves.* 反身代名詞(如 myself, themselves)。

re·float /ˌriːˈfləʊt; riˈflot/ *vt, vi* [VP6A, 2A] cause (sth) to float again after it has gone aground, been sunk, etc; float again. 使(某物)在擱淺或沉沒後再浮起;再浮起。

re·flux /ˌriːˈflʌks; ˈrɪˌflʌks/ *n* flowing back; ebb: 回流;倒流;退潮: *flux and ~.* 潮之漲落;事之榮枯。

re·for·est /ˌriːˈfɒrɪst *US:* -ˈfɔːr-; riˈfɔrɪst/ *vt* ⇨ reafforest. **re·for·es·ta·tion** /ˌriːˌfɒrɪˈsteɪʃn *US:* -ˌfɔːr-; ˌrifɔrɪsˈteʃən/ *n*

re·form /rɪˈfɔːm; rɪˈfɔrm/ *vt, vi* [VP6A, 2A] make or become better by removing or putting right what is bad or wrong: 改革;改進;改造;改善: *~ a sinner/one's character/the world;* 改造一罪人(一個人的品格,世界); *~ oneself;* 改過自新; *a ~ed man,* one who has given up his bad ways and is now living a good life. 一個改過自新的人。□ *n* **1** [U] ~ing; removal of vices, imperfections, etc: 改革; 改造; 改進; 改善; 革除惡習,缺點等: *agitate for social or political ~;* 鼓吹社會或政治的革新; *the Reˈform Bill ˈof 1832,* (GB) that which extended the franchise and improved parliamentary representation. 1832年英國的改革法案(擴大投票權及改革議會代表方式的法案)。 **2** [C] instance of ~; change made in order to remove imperfections: 改革之實例;爲革除缺點所作的改變: *a ~ in teaching methods.* 教學法之改進。 **~er** *n* person actively engaged in advocating or carrying out ~s. 從事改革運動者;改革家。

re-form /ˌriːˈfɔːm; ˌriˈfɔrm/ *vt, vi* form again; (of soldiers) get into ranks, etc again. 再形成;(指士兵)重編隊。 **re-for·ma·tion** /ˌriː fɔːˈmeɪʃn; ˌrifɔrˈmeʃən/ *n*

ref·or·ma·tion /ˌrefəˈmeɪʃn; ˌrɛfɚˈmeʃən/ *n* **1** [U] reforming or being reformed; [C] radical change for the better in social, political or religious affairs. 改革; 被改革; (社會、政治或宗教事務上的)革新。 **2 the R~,** the 16th-century movement for reform of the Roman Catholic Church, resulting in the establishment of the Reformed or Protestant Churches. 宗教改革(十六世紀改革羅馬天主教會的運動,結果產生了新教)。

re·forma·tory /rɪˈfɔːmətrɪ *US:* -tɔːrɪ; rɪˈfɔrməˌtorɪ/ *adj* tending or intending to produce reform. 趨於或意欲改革的;改善的;改進的。□ *n* (*pl* -ties) (formerly) school or institution for reforming young offenders against the law by means of special training, mental, moral and physical (usu, in GB, called 在英國通常稱爲 an *approved school* or *community house*). (昔時)少年感化院。

re·fract /rɪˈfrækt; rɪˈfrækt/ *vt* [VP6A] cause (a ray of light) to bend aside where it enters, eg water, glass, obliquely: 使(光線)在斜進(水,玻璃等)的地方屈折;使折射: *Light is ~ed when it passes through a prism.* 光經過稜鏡便折射了。**re·frac·tion** /rɪˈfrækʃn; rɪˈfrækʃən/ *n* ~ing or being ~ed. 折射;被折射。

re·frac·tory /rɪˈfræktərɪ; rɪˈfræktərɪ/ *adj* **1** resisting control, discipline, etc; wilful: 難控制的; 難馴御的;任性的;剛愎的: *as ~ as a mule;* 倔强得像匹騾子; (of diseases) not yielding to treatment. (指疾病)難醫治的。 **2** (of substances, esp metals) hard to melt, fuse or work. (指物質,尤指金屬)難熔的;不易處理的。

re·frain[1] /rɪˈfreɪn; rɪˈfren/ *n* [C] lines of a song which are repeated, esp at the end of each verse: (歌曲的)重疊句(尤指每節收尾的疊句);副歌: *Will you all join in singing the ~, please?* 請大家一齊來唱副歌好嗎?

re·frain[2] /rɪˈfreɪn; rɪˈfren/ *vi* [VP2A, 3A] ~ ***(from),*** hold oneself back: 抑制;克制: *Please ~ from spitting in public places.* 請勿在公共場所吐痰。*Let's hope they will ~ from hostile action.* 希望他們不採取敵對行動。

re·fresh /rɪˈfreʃ; rɪˈfrɛʃ/ *vt* [VP6A] **1** give new strength to; make fresh: 給予新力量;使精神爽快: *~ oneself with a cup of tea/a warm bath.* 喝杯茶(洗個熱水澡)提神。 **2** ~ ***one's memory,*** call things back to the memory by referring to notes, etc. 喚起記憶。 **3** take sth to eat or drink: 吃東西;喝飲料: *They stopped at a pub to ~ themselves.* 他們在酒館停下來,喝幾杯酒。*They felt much ~ed.* 他們覺得喝够(吃飽)了。**~·ing** *adj* **1** strengthening; giving rest and relief: 給人力量的;使人恢復體力的;使人精神爽快的: *a ~ing breeze/sleep.* 使人心曠神怡的微風(使人恢復體力的睡眠)。 **2** welcome and interesting because rare or unexpected: (因稀罕或出乎意料而)令人欣喜的;新奇的: *~ing innocence,* eg of children to older, sophisticated persons. 令人喜愛的天眞。**~·ing·ly** *adv*

re·fresher /rɪˈfreʃə(r); rɪˈfrɛʃɚ/ *n* **1** (legal) extra fee paid to counsel[1](3) while a case is proceeding in the law courts. (法律)(訴訟進行中)律師之額外訟費。**2** (colloq) drink. (俗)飲料。**3** (attrib) (形容

用法) '~ **course,** course providing instructions, eg to teachers already in service, on modern methods, newer professional techniques, etc. 進修課程(如對在職教師提供有關現代方法,較新的專門技術等的課程)。

re·fresh·ment /rɪ'freʃmənt ; rɪ'frɛʃmənt/ *n* **1** [U] refreshing or being refreshed: 精神爽快;心曠神怡: *feel ~ of mind and body.* 身心均感爽快。 **2** [U] (often *pl*) that which refreshes, esp food and drink: (常用複數)提神的東西(尤指食物和飲料): *order some light ~(s),* snacks; 叫一些點心; '~ *room,* one where one can buy food and drink, eg at a railway station. (火車站等處的)飲食店;餐室。*R~s were provided during the interval.* 在休息時間有點心供應。

re·frig·er·ate /rɪ'frɪdʒəreɪt ; rɪ'frɪdʒə,ret/ *vt* [VP6A] make cool or cold; keep (food) in good condition by making and keeping it cold. 使涼或冷;冷藏(食物)。**re·frig·er·ant** /-ənt ; -ənt/ *n, adj* (substance) serving to ~, eg liquid carbon dioxide. 冷凍的;清涼劑;冷却劑;冰凍劑。**re·frig·er·ation** /rɪ,frɪdʒə'reɪʃn ; rɪ,frɪdʒə'reʃən/ *n* (esp) the cooling or freezing of food in order to preserve it: (尤指)食物之冷藏: *the refrigeration industry.* 冷藏工業。**re·frig·er·ator** /rɪ'frɪdʒəreɪtə(r) ; rɪ'frɪdʒə,retɚ/ *n* [C] (colloq abbr 俗語略作 *fridge*) cabinet or room in which food is kept cold. (電)冰箱;冷凍庫。

reft /reft ; rɛft/ *pp* = bereft.

re·fuel /,riː'fjuːəl ; ri'fjuəl/ *vt, vi* (-ll-; US also -l-) [VP6A, 2A] supply with, take on, a fresh quantity of fuel: 供以或取得新燃料;加添燃料: *The plane came down to ~.* 飛機降落加油。

ref·uge /'refjuːdʒ ; 'rɛfjudʒ/ *n* [C, U] (place giving) shelter or protection from trouble, danger, pursuit, etc: 庇護; 避難; 避難所: *seek ~ from the floods;* 躲避洪水; *take ~ in the cellar;* 在地下室避難; (fig) (喻) *take ~ in silence,* eg to avoid answering impertinent questions. 以沉默來逃避(回答無禮或不相干的問題等)。*Books are a ~ of the lonely.* 書籍乃孤獨者的慰藉物。

refu·gee /,refjʊ'dʒiː *US:* 'refjʊdʒiː ; ,rɛfjʊ'dʒi/ *n* person who has been forced to flee from danger, eg from floods, war, political persecution: 避難者;難民: (attrib) (形容用法) *,refu'gee camps.* 難民營。

re·ful·gent /rɪ'fʌldʒənt ; rɪ'fʌldʒənt/ *adj* (formal) shining; brilliant. (正式用語)光亮的;燦麗的。**re·ful·gence** /-əns ; -əns/ *n* [U].

re·fund /rɪ'fʌnd ; rɪ'fʌnd/ *vt* [VP6A] pay back (money to sb): 退還(錢給某人): *~ the cost of postage.* 退還郵費。□ *n* /'riːfʌnd ; 'ri,fʌnd/ [C, U] repayment: 退還;退款: *obtain a ~ of a deposit.* 得到保證金之退款。

re·fur·bish /,riː'fɜːbɪʃ ; ri'fɝbɪʃ/ *vt* [VP6A] make clean or bright again; make (as if) like new. 弄新;刷新;革新;翻修;使清潔。

re·fusal /rɪ'fjuːzl ; rɪ'fjuzḷ/ *n* **1** [U] act of refusing; [C] instance of this: 拒絕;不願;固辭;推却: *the ~ of an invitation;* 對邀請的謝絕; *his ~ to do what I asked.* 他之拒絕做我所請求之事。**2** **(the)** ~, right of deciding whether to accept or refuse sth before it is offered to others: 優先決定權;取捨權;先買權: *If you ever decide to sell your car, please give me (the) first ~.* 如果你決定把汽車賣掉,請給我優先購買權。

ref·use[1] /'refjuːs ; 'rɛfjus/ *n* [U] waste or worthless material: 棄物;垃圾;廢物: *a '~ dump,* eg place where town ~ (collected from houses, etc) is dumped. 垃圾場;垃圾堆。'~-**collector** *n* dustman. 清除垃圾工人。

re·fuse[2] /rɪ'fjuːz ; rɪ'fjuz/ *vt, vi* [VP6A, 7A, 12C, 2A] say 'no' to (a request or offer); show unwillingness to accept (sth offered), to do (sth that one is asked to do): 拒絕(一項請求或提供);不願接受(所提供之某物)或做(被請求之事);固辭;推却: *~ a gift;* 拒受禮物; *~ one's consent;* 不同意;不承認; *~ to help.* 不願幫助。*They ~d me permission.* 他們拒絕答應我的要求。*I was ~d admittance.* 我未獲准進入。

re·fute /rɪ'fjuːt ; rɪ'fjut/ *vt* [VP6A] prove (statements, opinions, etc) to be wrong or mistaken; prove (sb) wrong in his opinions: 證明(陳述、意見等)爲誤;證明(某人)看法不對;駁斥;駁倒;反駁: *~ an argument/an opponent.* 駁斥一論據(對手)。**re·fut·able** /-əbl ; -əbl/ *adj* that can be ~d. 可駁斥的;可辯駁的。**refu·ta·tion** /,refjuː'teɪʃn ; ,rɛfjʊ'teʃən/ *n* [U] refuting; [C] counter-argument. 駁斥;駁倒;反駁。

re·gain /rɪ'geɪn ; rɪ'gen/ *vt* [VP6A] **1** get possession of again: 恢復;復得: *~ consciousness;* 恢復知覺;蘇醒; *~ one's freedom.* 重獲自由。 **2** get back to (a place or position): 重回;復至(某地方或位置): *~ one's footing,* recover one's balance after slipping or falling. (滑跤或跌倒後)恢復身體的平衡;重站起來。

re·gal /'riːgl ; 'rigḷ/ *adj* of, for, fit for, by, a monarch; royal: 君王的;適於君王的;由於君王的;王室的: *~ dignity/splendour/power.* 帝王的莊嚴(豪華,權力)。**~ly** /-gəlɪ ; -gḷɪ/ *adv*

re·gale /rɪ'geɪl ; rɪ'gel/ *vt* [VP6A, 14] **~ *oneself/sb (with/on sth),*** give pleasure or delight to: 使喜悅;歡娛;款待: *~ oneself with a cigar;* 享用雪茄; *regaling themselves and their friends on caviar and champagne.* 以魚子醬及香檳酒供他們自己及朋友們享用。

re·galia /rɪ'geɪlɪə ; rɪ'gelɪə/ *n pl* [C] (often with a *sing v*) (常用單數動詞) **1** emblems (crown, orb, sceptre, etc) of royalty, as used at coronations. 王權的標識(王冠、寶球、王杖等,如用於加冕禮中)。 **2** emblems or decorations of an order(9), eg of the Freemasons. 任何團體(如共濟會)之標識或徽章。

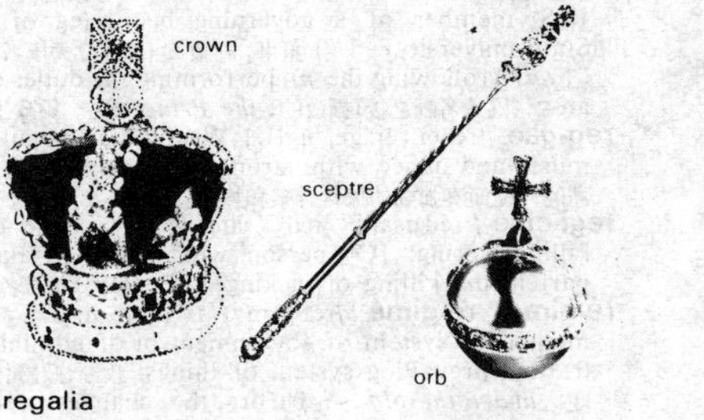

regalia

re·gard[1] /rɪ'gɑːd ; rɪ'gɑrd/ *n* **1** (liter or old use) long, steady or significant look. (文或舊用法)注視;凝視。 **2** [U] point attended to; relation. 注意之點;關係。***in 'this ~,*** in respect of (= regarding) this point. 在這一點上; 關於此事。***in/with ~ to,*** with respect to; concerning. 關於。 **3** [U] attention; concern; consideration: 注意;關心;顧慮: *You'll get into trouble if you continue to behave without ~ to decency.* 如果你繼續不顧禮法行事,你會招來麻煩的。*He has very little ~ for the feelings of others.* 他不大顧慮別人的感情。*More ~ must be paid to safety on the roads.* 應多注意道路安全。 **4** [U] esteem; consideration; respect: 敬重; 敬意; 尊敬: *hold sb in high/low ~;* 極爲(不大)尊敬某人; *have a high/low ~ for sb's judgement.* 非常(不大)尊重某人的判斷。 **5** (*pl*) kindly thoughts and wishes: (複)問候;致意: (at the end of a letter) (用於信尾) *with kind ~s, yours sincerely,....* 謹致問候之意,…敬啓。*Please give my kind ~s to your brother.* 請代我問候令兄(令弟)。**~·ful** /-fl ; -fəl/ *adj* ***~ful (of),*** full of ~(3): 注意的;關心的: *Be more ~ful of your own interests.* 祈多注意你自己的利益。**~·less** *adj* ***~less of,*** paying no attention to: 不顧;不注意: *~less of the consequences;* 不顧後果; *~less of expense.* 不顧慮費用。

re·gard[2] /rɪ'gɑːd ; rɪ'gɑrd/ *vt* **1** [VP6A] (liter or old use) look closely at. (文或舊用法)注視;凝視。**2** [VP16B] **~ *sb/sth as,*** consider: 視爲;認作: *~ sb as a hero;* 認爲某人是英雄; *~ sth as a crime.*

把某事認作一種罪行。*He's ~ed as the best dentist in town.* 他被認爲是城內最好的牙醫師。 **3** [VP6A, 14] ~ ***(with),*** look upon mentally: 在心理上以…看待;對待: *I ~ his behaviour with suspicion/horror.* 我對他的行爲感到懷疑(恐懼)。*How is he ~ed locally?* 當地的人對他看法如何? *He is ~ed with disfavour/unfavourably.* 他不受喜愛。 **4** [VP6A] pay attention to (chiefly neg and interr): 注意;尊敬(主要用於否定句及疑問句中): *He seldom ~s my advice.* 他不大尊重我的忠言。*Why do you so seldom ~ my wishes?* 你爲何老是不尊重我的願望呢? **as ~s, ~ing** *prep* with reference to; concerning. 關於;有關。

re·gatta /rɪ'gætə ; rɪ'gætə/ *n* meeting for boat races (rowing boats or yachts). 賽船會;賽艇會。

re·gency /'ri:dʒənsɪ ; 'ridʒənsɪ/ *n* (*pl* -cies) the office of a regent; regent's period of office. 攝政職位;攝政期間。**the R~,** (in GB) the period 1810-20. (英國之)攝政時期(自1810年至1820年)。

re·gen·er·ate /rɪ'dʒenəreɪt ; rɪ'dʒɛnə,ret/ *vt, vi* [VP 6A, 2A] **1** reform spiritually; raise morally. 在精神上改造;在道德上提高;改過自新。 **2** give new strength or life to; restore lost qualities to. 賦與新力量或生命;恢復…所喪失的性質。 **3** grow again. 重生;再生。□ *adj* /rɪ'dʒenərət ; rɪ'dʒɛnərɪt/ spiritually reborn: 精神重生的;更生的;革新的: *a ~ society.* 革新的社會。**re·gen·er·ation** /rɪ,dʒenə'reɪʃn ; rɪ,dʒɛnə'reʃən/ *n* [U] being ~d. 精神重生;更生;再生;更新;革新。

re·gent /'ri:dʒənt ; 'ridʒənt/ *n* **1** person appointed to perform the duties of a ruler who is too young, old, ill, etc or who is absent. 攝政者。 **2** (US) member of a governing board (eg of a State university). (美)董事;評議員(如州立大學者)。□ *adj* (following the *n*) performing the duties of a ~: (置於名詞之後)攝政的: *the Prince R~.* 攝政王。

reg·gae /'regeɪ ; 'rɛge/ *n* [U] West Indian popular music and dance with strong rhythms. 西印度群島的一種節奏强勁的流行音樂和舞蹈。

regi·cide /'redʒɪsaɪd ; 'rɛdʒə,saɪd/ *n* [U] crime of killing a king; [C] person who kills, or takes part in the killing of, a king. 弑君;(參與)弑君者。

ré·gime, re·gime /reɪ'ʒi:m ; rɪ'ʒim/ *n* [C] **1** method or system of government or of administration; prevailing system of things: 政制;政體;制度: *under the old ~,* before the changes were made, etc (according to context). 在舊的制度下(依據上下文而決定其意義)。 **2** = regimen.

regi·men /'redʒɪmən ; 'rɛdʒə,mɛn/ *n* [C] set of rules for diet, exercise, etc for promoting one's health and physical well-being. 養生之道;攝生法。

regi·ment /'redʒɪmənt ; 'rɛdʒəmənt/ *n* [C] (cavalry and artillery) unit divided into squadrons or batteries and commanded by a colonel; (GB infantry) organization usu based on a city or county, with special traditions and dress, represented in the field by battalions: (騎兵和砲兵)團;(英國步兵)通常根據城市或郡所構成的軍事組織,以營爲單位,各有其獨特的傳統和服裝: *the 1st battalion of the Manchester R~.* 曼徹斯特步兵團的第一營。~ ***of,*** large number: 多數;大羣: *whole ~s of starlings.* 一羣羣的歐椋鳥。□ *vt* [VP6A] organize; discipline: 組織;控制: *~ the workers of a country.* 組織一國的工人。**reg·i·men·ta·tion** /,redʒɪmen'teɪʃn ; ,rɛdʒəmɛn'teʃən/ *n* [U] subjection to control; strict political discipline (as in a police state). 統制;(如警察國家中的)嚴格管制。

regi·men·tal /,redʒɪ'mentl ; ,rɛdʒə'mɛntl/ *adj* of a regiment: 團的: *the ~ tie,* in the colours of the regiment. 團服之領帶。□ *n* (*pl*) dress worn by the men of a regiment; military uniform: (複)團服;軍服: *in full ~s,* in full dress. 著全副戎裝。

Re·gina /rɪ'dʒaɪnə ; rɪ'dʒaɪnə/ *n* (abbr 略作 **R**) reigning queen: 女王: (used in signatures to proclamations) (用於宣言或布告之簽字中) *Elizabeth ~;* 伊利莎白女王; (legal) (used in titles of lawsuits): (法律)(用於訟案的名稱中): *~ v Hay,* the Crown against Hay. 女王對黑伊的訟案。⇨ Rex.

re·gion /'ri:dʒən ; 'ridʒən/ *n* [C] area or division with or without definite boundaries or characteristics: 地方;區域;地區: *the Arctic ~s;* 北極地區; *the forest ~;* 林區; *the lower ~s,* hell; 地獄; *the ~ of metaphysics;* 玄學的領域; *the abdominal ~.* 腹部。**~al** /-nl ; -nl/ *adj* of a ~: 地方的;區域的;地區的: *the ~al wines of France;* 法國各地區產的不同種類的葡萄酒; *a ~al geography.* 區域地理。**~·ally** /-nəlɪ ; -nlɪ/ *adv*

reg·is·ter[1] /'redʒɪstə(r) ; 'rɛdʒɪstɚ/ *n* [C] **1** (book containing a) record or list: 記錄;名單;登記簿;名簿: *a parish ~,* one with records of baptisms, marriages and funerals; 教區記事簿(包括受洗,結婚及喪葬記錄); *Lloyd's ~,* of shipping; 羅意德船舶協會出版的年鑑; *the R~ of voters, the Parliamentary R~,* of persons qualified to vote at elections. 選擧人名簿;大選名簿。 **2** range of the human voice or of a musical instrument; part of this range: (人聲或樂器的)音域;音域的一部分: *the upper/middle ~;* 上(中)聲域; *the lower ~ of the clarinet.* 豎笛的下音域。 **3** mechanical device for indicating and recording speed, force, numbers, etc. (表示速度、力量、數目等的)記錄器。**'cash ~,** as used for recording cash payments in shops, etc. (商店等中所用的)現金出納機。⇨ the illus at cash. 參看 cash 之插圖。 **4** adjustable metal plate or grating for widening or narrowing the size of an opening and so regulating the passage of air, etc through it: 調節氣流等的金屬片或格柵裝置: *a hot-air ~,* one controlling the flow of hot air, eg in a building heated from a basement furnace. 調節暖氣的裝置。**5** = registry. **6** (linguistics) vocabulary, grammar, etc used by speakers in particular circumstances or contexts, eg legal, commercial. (語言學)(說話者在法律、商業等特別的情況或上下文中所用之)語法與字彙。

reg·is·ter[2] /'redʒɪstə(r) ; 'rɛdʒɪstɚ/ *vt, vi* [VP2A, 3A, 6A, 14] ~ ***(sth/oneself) (with sth/sb) (for sth),*** **1** make a written and formal record of, in a list: 記錄;登記;註册: *~ one's car/the birth of a child/a new trade-mark;* 登記汽車(小孩的出生,新的商標); *a State R~ed Nurse,* one who is officially ~ed. 已向政府登記的護士;正式護士。*I am a foreigner here; must I ~ (myself) with the police?* 我在此地是外國人;我必須向警方登記嗎?*Where can I ~ for the Arabic course?* 我選阿拉伯文一科到那裡註册? **2** put or get (sb's name, one's own name) on a register. 登記(姓名)。**3** (of instruments) indicate; record: (指儀器)指示;記出: *The thermometer ~ed only two degrees above freezing-point.* 寒暑表顯示僅高於冰點兩度。 **4** (of sb's face) show (emotion, etc): (指人的面孔)顯出;表示(某種情緒等): *Her face ~ed surprise.* 她的臉上現出驚訝之色。 **5** send (a letter or parcel) by special post, paying an extra charge which ensures compensation if it is lost: 以掛號寄送(信或包裹): *It's wise to ~ letters containing banknotes.* 用掛號信郵寄附有鈔票的信是明智的。

reg·is·trar /,redʒɪ'strɑ:(r) ; 'rɛdʒɪ,strɑr/ *n* person whose duty is to keep records or registers, eg for a town council or a university. 記錄員;登記員;主管註册者(如市鎮議會的記錄官或大學的註册主任)。

reg·is·tra·tion /,redʒɪ'streɪʃn ; ,rɛdʒɪ'streʃən/ *n* **1** [U] registering; recording: 登記;掛號;註册: *~ of letters/luggage;* 信件(行李)之掛號; *~ of students for an examination/an academic course;* 學生之報名考試(選課登記); *the '~ number* (eg of a car). (汽車等之)登記號碼。 **2** [C] entry; record of facts. 登記之項目;事實之記錄。

reg·is·try /'redʒɪstrɪ ; 'rɛdʒɪstrɪ/ *n* (*pl* -tries) **1** (sometimes 有時作 *register*) place where registers are kept: 登記處;註册處: *a ship's port of ~;* 某船

之船籍港; *married at a* '~ *office*, before a registrar (without a religious ceremony). 在婚姻註册處結婚(不舉行宗教儀式)。 **2** [U] = registration.

reg·nant /'regnənt ; 'rɛgnənt/ *adj* reigning: 統治的: *Queen* ~, one who is ruling in her own right and not as a consort. 執政女王;當朝女王。

re·gress /rɪ'gres ; rɪ'grɛs/ *vi* [VP2A] return to an earlier or more primitive form or state. 退步;退化;退回;倒退;復歸;回歸。**re·gression** /rɪ'greʃn ; rɪ'grɛʃən/ *n* ~ing. 退步;退化;退回;倒退;復歸;回歸。**re·gressive** *adj* tending to ~. 回歸的;逆行的;退化的;退步的。

re·gret[1] /rɪ'gret ; rɪ'grɛt/ *n* **1** [U] feeling of sadness at the loss of sth, or of annoyance or disappointment because sth has or has not been done: 悲悼;惋惜;懊悔;抱憾;抱歉: *express* ~ *at not being able to help;* 爲幫不上忙而表示抱歉; *hear with* ~ *that a friend is ill.* 遺憾地聽到一位朋友生病了。 *Much to my* ~ *I am unable to accept your kind invitation.* 我不能接受你盛意的邀請,深感抱歉。**2** (*pl*) (in polite expressions of refusal, etc): (複)(用作禮貌的謝絕語等): *Please accept my* ~*s at having to refuse.* 不能奉約,謹致歉意。 *He refused with many* ~*s/with much* ~. 他非常客氣地拒絕了。 *I have no* ~*s*, do not feel sorry (about what I did, etc). 我不感到遺憾;我毫不後悔。 **~·ful** /-fl ; -fl/ *adj* sad; sorry. 哀惜的;遺憾的;抱歉的。**~·fully** /-fəlɪ ; -flɪ/ *adv* sadly; with ~. 哀惜地;遺憾地;抱歉地。

re·gret[2] /rɪ'gret ; rɪ'grɛt/ *vt* (-tt-) [VP6A, D, 7A, 9] **1** be sorry for the loss of; wish to have again: 以喪失…爲憾;悲悼;惋惜: ~ *lost opportunities.* 惋惜失去的機會。 *He died* ~*ted by all.* 他死了,大家深感痛惜。 **2** feel sorry for; be sorry (*to say, etc; that...*): 爲…感到遺憾;懊悔;抱憾;抱歉(後接 to say 等,或 that…): *I* ~ *being unable to help/*~ *that I cannot help.* 我幫不上忙甚爲抱歉。 *I* ~ *to say that....* 我很抱歉…。 *It is to be* ~*ted that...*, is a pity that.... 眞可惜…;…爲一憾事。 *I* ~ *my child's ignorance.* 我爲孩子的無知感到遺憾。 **~·table** /-əbl ; -əbl/ *adj* to be ~ted: 令人遺憾的;可惜的;可悲的;不幸的: ~*table failures.* 不幸的失敗。**~·tably** /-əblɪ ; -əblɪ/ *adv*: *a* ~*tably small attendance.* 出席者少得可憐。

re·group /ˌri:'gru:p ; ri'grup/ *vt, vi* [VP6A, 2A] form again into groups; form into new groups. 重行編制;重新編組;整編;重新組合。

regu·lar /'regjʊlə(r) ; 'rɛgjələ/ *adj* **1** evenly arranged; symmetrical; systematic: 整齊的;端正的;對稱的;有系統的: ~ *teeth;* 整齊的牙齒; ~ *features*, eg of the face; 端正的面貌; *a* ~ *figure;* 勻稱的身材; *a* ~ *nomenclature.* 有系統的命名法。**2** coming, happening, done, again and again at even intervals: 習慣性的;有規律的;不變的;經常的;定期的: *a man with* ~ *habits*, doing the same things at the same times every day; 生活習慣有規律的人; *keep* ~ *hours*, eg leaving and returning home, getting up and going to bed, at the same times every day; 按時作息;過規律生活; ~ *breathing;* 均勻的呼吸; *have a* ~ *pulse;* 脈搏跳動正常; *walking up and down with* ~ *steps.* 以規律的步子走來走去。 *He has no* ~ *work*, no continuous occupation.他沒有固定的工作。**3** properly qualified; recognized; trained; full-time or professional: 合格的;認可的;有訓練的;專任的;職業性的: ~ *soldiers*, not volunteers or militia; 常備兵;正規兵; *the* ~ *army*, made up of ~ soldiers. 常備軍;正規軍。**4** conforming to a standard of etiquette; in agreement with what is considered correct procedure or behaviour: 合於禮儀標準的;合於正確之手續或行爲的: *I doubt whether your procedure would be considered* ~ *by the authorities.* 我懷疑當局是否會認爲你的手續合乎規定。**5** (gram, of *vv, nn*, etc) having normal inflections: (文法,指動詞、名詞等)變化有規則的: *The verb 'go' is not* ~. 動詞 go 的變化不規則。 **6** (eccles) bound by, living under, religious rule (opp of *secular*): (教會)受教規約束的;按教規生活的;屬於教團的(爲 secular 之相反字): *the* ~ *clergy*, eg monks but not parish priests. 屬於教團的僧侶(但並非教區教士)。 **7** (colloq) thorough; complete: (俗)徹底的;完全的: *He's a* ~ *hero/rascal.* 他是十足的英雄(流氓)。 **8** ordinary; normal: 普通的;一般的: *Do you want king size cigarettes or* ~ *size?* 你要長枝的還是一般長短的香煙? **9** (colloq) likeable; good: (俗)可愛的;好的: *He's a* ~ *guy.* 他是個好人。□ *n* **1** soldier of the ~ army. 常備兵;正規兵。 **2** (colloq) ~ customer or client, eg at a hairdresser's or a pub. (俗)常客;老主顧(如美容院或酒館中者)。 **~·ly** *adv* in a ~ manner; at ~ intervals or times: 整齊地;端正地;有規律地;經常地;定期地: *a garden* ~*ly laid out;* 設計得很整齊的花園; *as* ~*ly as clockwork.* (像鐘錶裝置一般)非常規律地。**~·ity** /ˌregjʊ'lærətɪ ; ˌrɛgjə'lærətɪ/ *n* [U] state of being ~: 整齊;端正;規律;經常;定期: *win a prize for* ~*ity of attendance.* 因全勤而獲獎。

regu·lar·ize /'regjʊləraɪz ; 'rɛgjələˌraɪz/ *vt* [VP6A] make lawful or correct: 使合法化;調整;整理;使有組織;使有秩序: ~ *the proceedings.* 調整程序。**regu·lar·iz·ation** /ˌregjʊləraɪ'zeɪʃn *US:* -rɪ'z- ; ˌrɛgjələrɪ'zeʃən/ *n*

regu·late /'regjʊleɪt ; 'rɛgjəˌlet/ *vt* [VP6A] **1** control systematically; cause to obey a rule or standard: 有系統地管理;節制;使遵守規則或合標準: ~ *one's conduct/expenditure;* 節制行爲(花費); ~ *the traffic.* 管理交通。 *Accidents happen even in the best* ~*d families.* 卽使在管理最好的家庭也會發生事故。 **2** adjust (an apparatus, mechanism) to get the desired result: 調節;校準(儀器,機械): ~ *a clock;* 對鐘; ~ *the speed of a machine.* 調節機器的速度。**regu·la·tor** /-tə(r) ; -tə/ *n* person or thing that ~s, eg a device that ~s a mechanical movement, esp in a clock. 調整之人或物;調節器;(尤指校準鐘錶的)整時器。

regu·la·tion /ˌregjʊ'leɪʃn ; ˌrɛgjə'leʃən/ *n* **1** [U] regulating or being regulated: 管理;節制;調節;校準: *the* ~ *of affairs/of a clock.* 事務的管理(鐘的校準)。 **2** [C] rule; order; authoritative direction: 規則;規定;法令;命令: '*safety* ~*s*, eg in factories; (工廠等中之)安全條例; '*traffic* ~*s*, made by the police for drivers of vehicles; 交通規則; *contrary to* ~*s;* 違反規定; *Queen's/King's* ~*s*, those governing the conduct of the armed forces. (英國女王或國王頒佈之)三軍行爲條例。 **3** (attrib) as required by rules; correct:(形容用法)規定的;正規的: ~ *dress/uniform;* 正式的衣服(制服); *application forms of the* ~ *size.* 合於規定大小的申請表格。

re·gur·gi·tate /ri:'gɜ:dʒɪteɪt ; ri'gɝdʒəˌtet/ *vi, vt* [VP2A, 6A] (of liquid, etc) gush back; bring (swallowed food) up again to the mouth. (指液體等)湧回;流回;把(吃下的食物)吐出;反胃。

re·ha·bili·tate /ˌri:ə'bɪlɪteɪt ; ˌriə'bɪləˌtet/ *vt* [VP 6A] **1** restore (eg old buildings) to a good condition. 恢復;修復(舊房屋等)。 **2** restore (sb) to former rank, position or reputation: 恢復(某人)原有的地位,職位或名譽: *He has been* ~*d in public esteem.* 公衆已恢復了對他的敬重。**3** bring back (sb who is physically disabled or delinquent) to a normal life by special treatment. 藉特殊的方法使(身體有缺陷或犯過的人)恢復正常生活。 **re·ha·bili·ta·tion** /ˌri:əˌbɪlɪ'teɪʃn ; ˌriəˌbɪlə'teʃən/ *n* rehabilitating: 恢復;修復;恢復原有地位,正常生活等: *a rehabilitation centre*, place where persons are ~d(3). 傷殘重建中心。

re·hash /ˌri:'hæʃ ; ri'hæʃ/ *vt* take (eg old literary material) and use again in a new form: 以新的形式改寫(舊文稿等);改作;重講: ~ *last term's lectures for the coming term.* 改編上學期的講稿在下學期使用。□ *n* /'ri:hæʃ ; 'riˌhæʃ/ [C] ~ed material. 改編過的教材;改寫品。

re·hear /ˌri:'hɪə(r) ; ri'hɪr/ *vt* [VP6A] hear, consider, again (a case, plea etc in a law court). 再審;覆審。**re·hear·ing** *n* instance of this. 再審之事例。

re·hearse /rɪˈhɜːs ; rɪˈhɝs/ *vt, vi* [VP6A, 2A] **1** practise (a play, music, programme, etc) for public performance: 演習;預演;排演;演練(戲,樂曲,節目等): *~ the parts in a play;* 排演一齣戲的各角色; *~ an opera.* 排演一歌劇。**2** say over again; give an account of: 複述;詳述: *~ the events of the day;* 詳述當日的諸事件; *~ one's grievances.* 反覆述說苦況。**re·hearsal** /-sl ; -sl̩/ *n* **1** [U] rehearsing: 演習;排演;複述;詳述: *put a play into rehearsal.* 排演一部戲。**2** [C] trial performance of a play or other entertainment: 排演;預演;試演: *a ˈdress rehearsal,* one in which the actors wear the costumes and use the props as for public performances. (演員穿著演出時之服裝的)彩排。

re·house /ˌriːˈhaʊz ; riˈhaʊz/ *vt* [VP6A] provide with a new house (esp in place of one officially condemned): 供以新房屋 (尤指代替被官方認爲不適於居住者): *The people in these slums will have to be ~d.* 在這些貧民窟裏居住的人們勢須供以新房屋。

Reich /raɪk ; raɪk/ *n* the German Commonwealth as a whole. 德國;(德意志)帝國。**the First R~,** the Holy Roman Empire, 9th c to 1806. 第一帝國(九世紀至 1806 年之神聖羅馬帝國)。 **the Second R~,** 1871–1918. 第二帝國(1871 年至 1918 年之德意志帝國)。 **the Third R~,** the Nazi regime, 1933–45. 第三帝國(1933 年至 1945 年之納粹德國)。

reign /reɪn ; ren/ *n* [C] (period of) sovereignty, rule; dominance: 主權;統治;統治時代;朝代;王朝: *during five successive ~s;* 在接連五個朝代的期間; *in the ~ of King Alfred;* 在阿佛列王統治時期; *the ~ of law/reason;* 法治(以理性治理); *the R~ of Terror,* (in France, 1793–94, during the Revolution). 恐怖時代(指法國大革命時期 1793 年至 1794 年的一段時間)。 □ *vi* [VP2A, 3A] ***~ (over).*** **1** hold office as a monarch: 爲王;爲君;當朝;統治: *The king ~ed but he did not rule or govern.* 那國王當朝,但並不治理國事。*He ~ed over the country for ten years.* 他統治該國有十年之久。**2** be influential; prevail: 有勢力;佔優勢;盛行: *the ~ing beauty,* woman acknowledged to be most beautiful for the time in question. 當時的第一美人;絕代佳人。*Silence ~ed everywhere.* 到處寂靜無聲。

re·im·burse /ˌriːɪmˈbɜːs ; ˌriɪmˈbɝs/ *vt* [VP6A, 12A, 13A, 14] ***~ sth (to sb); ~ sb (for) sth,*** pay back (sb who has spent money, the money spent): 償還;補償(花錢之人,所花之錢): *We must ~ him the costs of the journey.* 我們必須把旅費償還給他。*You will be ~d (for) your expenses.* 你的花費將得到償還。 **~·ment** *n* [C, U] repayment (of expenses). (費用的)償還;補償。

rein /reɪn ; ren/ *n* (often *pl* in the same sense as the *sing*) long, narrow strap fastened to the bit of a bridle for controlling a horse. (常用複數,與單數同義)韁繩。 ⇨ the illus at harness. 參看 harness 之插圖。***assume/drop the ~s of government,*** enter upon/give up office. 掌握(放棄)政權。***draw ~,*** (lit and fig) pull up; go slower. (字面及喻)勒韁;緩行。***give free ~/the ~s to sb/sth,*** (lit and fig) allow freedom to: (字面及喻)放鬆韁繩;給予自由;放任: *give a horse the ~s;* 讓馬自由奔馳; *give the ~(s) to one's imagination,* allow it great freedom. 任想像馳騁奔放。***hold/take the ~s,*** (lit and fig) have/take control: (字面及喻)握着韁繩;統馭;支配;控制;執掌: *hold the ~s of government.* 執掌政權。***keep a tight ~ on sb/sth,*** (lit and fig) be firm with; allow little freedom to. (字面及喻)勒緊韁繩;嚴格要求;抑制(某人或某事物)。 □ *vt* [VP6A, 15B] control with, or as with, ~s: 駕馭;控制: *~ in a horse,* restrain it; check it; 勒住馬;控制馬; *~ up/back a horse,* pull it up or back with the ~s. 勒馬躍起(後退)。

re·in·car·nate /ˌriːɪnˈkɑːneɪt ; ˌriɪnˈkarnet/ *vt* give a new body to (a soul). 賦予(靈魂)新肉體;使再生。 □ *adj* /ˌriːɪnˈkɑːneɪt ; ˌriɪnˈkarnet/ born again in a new body. 賦予新肉體而再生的。**re·in·car·na·tion** /ˌriːɪnkɑːˈneɪʃn ; ˌriɪnkarˈneʃən/ *n* [U] religious doctrine that the soul enters, after death, into another (human or animal) body; [C] instance of this; new body inhabited by the soul. 人死後靈魂投入另一(人或動物)軀體的宗教學說;再生說;轉世說;再生的實例;靈魂附着的新軀體;化身。

rein·deer /ˈreɪndɪə(r) ; ˈrenˌdɪr/ *n* (*pl* unchanged) kind of large deer with branched antlers, used in Lapland for transport and kept in herds for its milk, flesh and hide. (複數不變)馴鹿。 ⇨ the illus at large. 參看 large 之插圖。

re·in·force /ˌriːɪnˈfɔːs ; ˌriɪnˈfors/ *vt* [VP6A] make stronger by adding or supplying more men or material; increase the size, thickness, of sth so that it supports more weight, etc: 增援;加强;增加…之大小,厚度等: *~ an army/a fleet;* 增援一支軍隊(艦隊); *~ a garment,* by adding an extra thickness of cloth in places; 加厚一件衣服; *~ a bridge.* 加强一座橋。**~d concrete,** concrete strengthened with steel bars or metal netting embedded in it. 鋼筋混凝土。 **~·ment** *n* [U] reinforcing or being ~d; (esp *pl*) that which ~s; (esp) men, ships, etc sent to ~. 增援;加强;(尤用複數)增援或加强之物;(尤指)援兵,援艦等。

re·in·state /ˌriːɪnˈsteɪt ; ˌriɪnˈstet/ *vt* [VP6A, 14] ***~ sb (in),*** replace (sb) (in a former position or condition): 使(某人)恢復(原位或原狀): *~ sb in his former office.* 使某人復職。 **~·ment** *n*

re·in·sure /ˌriːɪnˈʃʊə(r) ; ˌriɪnˈʃʊr/ *vt* [VP6A] insure again (esp of an underwriter who relieves himself of some or all of a risk by taking out an insurance with another underwriter or insurance company). 再保險;(尤指某保險商爲了減輕部分或全部風險而與另一保險商或保險公司共同承保的)轉保險。**re·in·sur·ance** /-rəns ; -rəns/ *n*

re·is·sue /ˌriːˈɪʃuː ; riˈɪʃʊ/ *vt* [VP6A] issue again after temporary discontinuance: 再發行: *~ stamps/books.* 再發行郵票(書)。 □ *n* sth ~d, esp a reprint of a book with a change of format or price. 再發行之物;(尤指形式或價格改變的) 再版圖書。Cf 參較 *new edition,* in which changes are made in the text. 修訂版。

re·iter·ate /riːˈɪtəreɪt ; riˈɪtəˌret/ *vt* [VP6A] say or do again several times: 反覆地說或做: *~ a command.* 重申一項命令。**re·iter·ation** /riːˌɪtəˈreɪʃn ; riˌɪtəˈreʃən/ *n* [U] act of reiterating; [C] instance of this; repetition. 反覆的說或做;反覆的話或動作;重複。

re·ject¹ /ˈriːdʒekt ; ˈridʒɛkt/ *n* sth ~ed: 被棄之物: *export ~s,* articles made for export but ~ed because of a flaw or imperfection. 因有瑕疵而被打回的輸出品。

re·ject² /rɪˈdʒekt ; rɪˈdʒɛkt/ *vt* [VP6A] **1** put aside, throw away, as not good enough to be kept: 拋棄;丟棄: *~ fruit that is over-ripe.* 拋棄過熟的水果。**2** refuse to accept: 拒絕;不接受: *~ an offer of help;* 拒絕別人提供的幫助; *~ a heart transplant,* (of the body) fail to adapt to the new heart; (指身體)排斥新移植的心臟; *a ~ed suitor.* 未被接受的求婚者。*The army doctors ~ed him,* would not accept him as medically fit. 軍醫們未接受他(認爲他身體不合格)。**re·jec·tion** /rɪˈdʒekʃn ; rɪˈdʒɛkʃən/ *n* [U] ~ing or being ~ed; [C] instance of this; sth ~ed: 拋棄;被棄;拒絕;被拒;拋棄或拒絕的實例;被拋棄或拒絕之物: *ˈ~ion slip,* printed or written note from an editor or publisher ~ing an offered article, novel etc. 退稿附條(由編輯或出版人所發之印刷或書寫的說明)。

re·jig /ˌriːˈdʒɪɡ ; ˌriˈdʒɪɡ/ *vt* (-gg-) [VP6A] supply (a factory, etc) with new mechanical equipment. 以新的機械設備供應(工廠等)。

re·joice /rɪˈdʒɔɪs ; rɪˈdʒɔɪs/ *vt, vi* **1** [VP6A] make glad; cause to be happy: 使喜;使樂: *The boy's success ~d his mother's heart.* 這男孩的成功使他母親衷心歡喜。**2** [VP2A, C, 3A, B, 4C] ***~ (at/over),*** feel great joy; show signs of great happiness: 欣喜;高興;快樂: *~ over a victory;* 爲勝利而欣喜; *~ at* *sb's success.* 爲某人的成功而高興。*I ~ to hear that you are well again/~ that you have recovered so quickly.* 聽到你已痊癒(你已很快復元)我很高興。*He ~s in the name of Bloggs,* humorous for 'His name is Bloggs'. (詼諧語)他名叫 Bloggs。Note: in colloq style 'be glad' and 'be pleased' are commoner than 'rejoice'. 注意:在口語中, be glad 及 be pleased 比 rejoice 更爲通用。**re·joic·ing** *n* [U] happiness; joy; (*pl*) celebrations; merry-making. 快樂;欣喜;高興;(複)慶祝;歡宴。

re·join[1] /rɪˈdʒɔɪn ; rɪˈdʒɔɪn/ *vt, vi* [VP6A, 2A] answer; reply; (legal) answer a charge or plea. 回答;應答;(法律)答辯。**~·der** /-də(r) ; -dɚ/ *n* [C] what is said in reply; retort. 答語;回答;還口;反駁。

re·join[2] /ˌriːˈdʒɔɪn ; ˌriˈdʒɔɪn/ *vt* [VP6A] join the company of again: 重返;再加入: *~ one's regiment/ship.* 重新回到團裏(船上)。

re-join /ˌriːˈdʒɔɪn ; ˌriˈdʒɔɪn/ *vt* [VP6A] join (together) again. 再接;再接合。

re·ju·ven·ate /riːˈdʒuːvəneɪt ; rɪˈdʒuvəˌnet/ *vt, vi* [VP6A, 2A] make or become young or vigorous again in nature or appearance. (使)變得年輕;(使)恢復活力。**re·ju·ven·ation** /rɪˌdʒuːvəˈneɪʃn ; rɪˌdʒuvəˈneʃən/ *n*

re·kindle /ˌriːˈkɪndl ; riˈkɪndl̩/ *vt, vi* [VP6A, 2A] kindle again: 再燃;再點火: *~ a fire.* 再把火點起來。*Our hopes ~d.* 我們的希望之火又燃起來了。

re·laid /ˌriːˈleɪd ; riˈled/ *pt, pp* of relay².

re·lapse /rɪˈlæps ; rɪˈlæps/ *vi* [VP2A, 3A] **~ *(into),*** fall back again (into bad ways, error, illness, silence etc): 故態復萌;重犯(壞習慣、錯誤);(疾病)復發;恢復(沉靜等): *He ~d into smoking twenty cigarettes a day.* 他又每天吸二十支香煙了。□ *n* [C] falling back, esp after recovering from illness: 故態復萌;重犯;(尤指疾病之)復發: *The patient has had a ~.* 病人舊疾復發。

re·late /rɪˈleɪt ; rɪˈlet/ *vt, vi* **1** [VP6A, 14] **~ *(to),*** (formal) tell (a story, etc to sb); give an account of (facts, adventures etc): (正式用語)(對某人)講(故事等);敍述(事實、奇遇等): *He ~d to his wife some amusing stories about his employer.* 他對太太述說有關他僱主的一些趣事。*Strange to ~, I once met Christopher in Katmandu.* 說來奇怪,有一次我在加德滿都碰見克利斯多夫。 **2** [VP14] **~ *to/with,*** connect in thought or meaning: 在思想或意義上使有關聯: *It is difficult to ~ these results with/to any known cause.* 這些結果很難與任何已知的原因相關聯。 **3** [VP3A] **~ *to,*** have reference (to): 與…有關係: *She is a girl who notices nothing except what ~s to herself.* 她是一個只注意與她有關的事的女孩。 **4 *be ~d (to),*** be connected by family (to): (與…)有親戚關係: *I am not ~d to him in any way.* 我和他無任何親戚關係。*He and I are not ~d.* 他和我無親戚關係。*She says she is ~d to the royal family.* 她說她與王室有親戚關係。

re·la·tion /rɪˈleɪʃn ; rɪˈleʃən/ *n* **1** [U] the act of relating(1), narrating or telling: 講;說;敍述: *the ~ of his adventures;* 敍述他的奇遇; [C] that which is narrated; tale or narrative. 所述說之事物;故事。 **2** [U] (= ~ship) connection; what there is between one thing, person, idea, etc and another or others: 關聯;(物、人、意念等與他者的)關係: *the ~ between mother and child/between weather and the crops.* 母親與子女(天氣與作物)間的關係。*The effort and expense needed for this project bore no ~/were out of all ~ to the results,* were not proportional to the results. 此計畫所需付出的努力和費用,與其成果(完全)不稱(卽花費過多)。***in/with ~ to,*** as regards; concerning. 關於;有關。 **3** (usu *pl*) dealings; affairs; what one person, group, country etc, has to do with another: (通常用複數)交往;事務;(人、團體、國家等與他者的)關係;利害關係;外交關係: *have business ~s with a firm in Stockholm;* 與斯德哥爾摩的一家商號有生意上的來往; *the friendly ~s between my country and yours;* 貴我兩國間的友好關係; *diplomatic ~s.* 外交關係。*I have broken off all ~s with that fellow,* I have nothing to do with him now. 我已和那傢伙斷絕一切關係。 **ˌpublic reˈlations officer,** ⇨ public, *adj.* **4** [U] kinship (now usu *~ship*); [C] kinsman or kinswoman; relative(2): 親戚關係(現在通常用 ~ship); 男女親戚;親屬: *He's a near ~ of mine.* 他是我的一位近親。*She's a ~ by marriage.* 她是一位姻親。 **~·ship** /-ʃɪp ; -ˌʃɪp/ *n* **1** ~(2): 關係: *He admitted his affair with Susan could never develop into a lasting ~ship.* 他承認他和蘇珊的愛情絕不會發展成持久的關係。 **2** [U] (=~(4)) condition of belonging to the same family; being connected by birth or marriage. 屬於同一家族之關係;血親或姻親關係。 **3** [C] instance of being related; particular connection or ~ (*between/to/with*). 有關係之實例;某種關係(與 between, to, with 連用)。

rela·tive /ˈrelətɪv ; ˈrɛlətɪv/ *adj* **1** comparative: 比較的;相對的: *the ~ advantages of two methods/of gas and electricity for heating.* 二種方法(煤氣取暖及電氣取暖)相對的優點。*They are living in ~ comfort,* ie compared with other people or with themselves at an earlier time. 他們現在生活得比較舒服。 **2 ~ *to,*** referring to; having a connection with: 關於…的;與…有關的: *the facts ~ to this problem;* 與此問題有關的事實; *the papers ~ to the case.* 關於此案件的文件。 **3** (gram) (文法) **~ adverb** (eg *where* in 'the place where the accident occurred'). 關係副詞(例如 the place where the accident occurred 中的 where)。**~ clause,** one joined by a ~ *pron* or *adv* to the antecedent of the ~ word. 關係子句 (藉關係代名詞或副詞與其先行詞相連接的子句)。 **~ pronoun** (eg *whom* in 'the man whom we saw'). 關係代名詞(例如 the man whom we saw 中的 whom)。□ *n* [C] **1** ~ word, esp a ~ pronoun. 關係詞;(尤指)關係代名詞。 **2** person to whom one is related (eg an uncle or aunt, a cousin, a nephew or niece). 親戚;親屬(如叔、嬸、表親、姪子、姪女等)。 **~·ly** *adv* comparatively; in proportion to: 比較地;成比例地;(與…)相對而言: *In spite of her dull husband she is ~ly happy.* 儘管她的丈夫遲鈍,她還算快樂。*The matter is unimportant, ~ly speaking,* if we think of this matter in proportion to other matters. 比較地說,此事不重要。

rela·tiv·ity /ˌreləˈtɪvətɪ ; ˌrɛləˈtɪvətɪ/ *n* [U] (esp) Einstein's theory of the universe, based on the principle that measures of motion, space and time are relative. (尤指)相對論(愛因斯坦對宇宙的理論,係以'運動、時、空之度量乃相對的'原理爲基礎)。

re·lax /rɪˈlæks ; rɪˈlæks/ *vt, vi* **1** [VP6A] cause or allow to become less tight, stiff, strict or rigid: 使鬆弛;放鬆;鬆解: *~ one's grip/hold on sth;* 放鬆對某物的執握; *~ the muscles;* 鬆弛肌肉; *~ discipline;* 鬆解紀律; *a ~ed throat,* a form of sore throat; 一種咽喉炎; *a ~ing climate,* (opp of *bracing*) one that causes an inclination to feel sluggish, lacking in energy. (爲 bracing 之相反字)使人懶洋洋的氣候。 **2** [VP2A, C] become less tense, rigid, energetic, strict: 鬆弛;放鬆;鬆解: *His severity ~ed.* 他的嚴肅緩和了。*His face ~ed in a smile.* 他的表情在一笑中變輕鬆了。*Let's stop working and ~ for an hour.* 我們停工休息一小時吧。*He's feeling ~ed now,* free from nervous anxiety, disturbing tensions, etc. 他現在覺得輕鬆多了。**~·ation** /ˌriːlækˈseɪʃn ; ˌrilæksˈeʃən/ *n* **1** [U] ~ing or being ~ed: 鬆弛;放鬆: *~ation of the muscles.* 肌肉的放鬆。 **2** [U] recreation; [C] sth done for recreation: 消遣;娛樂: *Fishing and mountain-climbing are his favourite ~ations.* 垂釣和爬山是他最喜愛的消遣。

re·lay[1] /ˈriːleɪ ; ˈrile/ *n* [C] **1** supply of fresh horses to take the place of tired horses; gang or group of men, supply of material, similarly used: 替換倦馬的一批新馬;人員、物資等之類似的補充;替班;接力: *working in/by ~s.* 輪班工作。 **ˈ~ race** *n* one between teams, each member of the team running, swimming, etc one section of the total distance. (賽跑、游泳等的)接力賽。 **2** (telegraphy, broadcasting) device which receives messages, radio programmes, etc and transmits them with greater strength, thus increasing the distance over which they are carried. (電報、無線電廣播)替續器；中繼器。 **'~ station,** place from which radio programmes are broadcast after being received from another station. 轉播站；中繼站。 **3** (short for) ~ race; ~ed broadcast programme. (簡稱)接力賽；轉播的無線電廣播節目。 □ *vt* /rɪ'leɪ; rɪ'le/ (*pt, pp* ~ed) send out (a broadcast programme received from another station). 轉播(自另一臺收到的廣播節目)。

re·lay² /ˌriː'leɪ; ˌri'le/ *vt* (*pt, pp* -laid /-'leɪd; -'led/) lay (a cable, carpet, etc) again. 重新放置；再鋪設(電纜、地毯等)。

re·lease /rɪ'liːs; rɪ'lis/ *vt* [VP6A, 14] ~ ***(from),*** **1** allow to go; set free; unfasten: 放行；釋放；免除；解開；解放： ~ *one's hold of sth;* 鬆開對某物之執握； ~ *a man from prison / from a promise;* 釋放某人出獄(不要求某人履行諾言)； ~ *a bomb* (*from an aircraft*), allow it to fall; (自飛機)投炸彈； ~ *a monk from his vows;* 准許一僧侶還俗； ~ *sb from his suffering;* 解除某人的痛苦； ~ *the handbrake* (*of a car*). 放開(汽車的)手煞車。 **2** allow (news) to be known or published; allow (a film) to be exhibited or (goods) to be placed on sale: 發佈(新聞)；發行(影片)；發售(貨物)： *recently ~d films / discs.* 最近推出之影片(唱片)。 **3** (legal) give up or surrender (a right, debt, property) to another. (法律)放棄；讓與(權利、債務、財產)。 □ *n* **1** [U] releasing or being ~d; [C] instance of this: 放行；釋放；免除；發佈；發行；放棄；讓與；其實例： *obtain* (*a*) *~ from an obligation;* 獲准免除某義務； *an order for sb's ~ from prison;* 釋放某人出獄的命令； *the ~ of a film for public exhibition;* 一影片之發行； *a 'press ~,* ie to the newspapers; 發佈新聞(給各報紙)； *a feeling of ~,* ie of freedom; 解脫的感覺； *the newest ~s,* eg films / discs; 最新的發行物(如影片、唱片)； *on general ~,* (of cinema films) available for seeing at the usual network of local cinemas. (指影片)普遍發行的。 **2** [C] handle, lever, catch, etc that ~s part of a machine: (鬆開某機件的)把手、槓桿、掣子等；鬆放柄；放鬆桿；釋放器： *the 'carriage ~* (on a typewriter); (打字機的)機頭平行放鬆鈕； (attrib) (形容用法) *'~ gear;* 釋放裝置； *the '~ button / knob.* 釋放按鈕(轉螺)。

rel·egate /'relɪgeɪt; 'rɛləˌget/ *vt* [VP14] ~ ***sth / sb to sth,*** **1** delegate². 委託；付託；移送。 **2** dismiss to a lower position or condition: 貶謫；貶黜；使歸屬於較低的地位或狀況： *He ~d his wife to the position of a mere housekeeper.* 他把太太貶低到管家者的地位。 (League football) (足球聯賽) *Will our team be ~d to the second division?* 我們的球隊會落入第二組嗎？ **rel·ega·tion** /ˌrelɪ'geɪʃn; ˌrɛlə'geʃən/ *n* [U].

re·lent /rɪ'lent; rɪ'lɛnt/ *vi* [VP2A] become less severe; give up unkind or cruel intentions: 變溫和；變寬厚；動憐憫： *At last their mother ~ed and allowed the children to stay up and watch TV.* 最後母親發了慈悲，准許孩子們不睡覺看電視節目。 **~·less** *adj* without pity: 無慈悲的；不憐憫的： *~less persecution.* 殘忍的迫害。 **~·less·ly** *adv*

rel·evant /'reləvənt; 'rɛləvənt/ *adj* ~ ***(to),*** (closely) connected with what is happening, being discussed, done, etc: (與…)有關的；切題的；中肯的： *have all the ~ documents ready;* 把所有有關的文件準備妥當； *supply the facts ~ to the case.* 提供與該案件相關的事實。 **~·ly** *adv* **rel·evance** /-əns; -əns/, **rel·evancy** /-ənsɪ; -ənsɪ/ *nn*

re·liable /rɪ'laɪəbl; rɪ'laɪəbḷ/ *adj* that may be relied or depended upon: 可靠的；可信賴的： ~ *tools / assistants / information / witnesses.* 可靠的工具(助手，消息，證人)。 **re·li·ably** /-əblɪ; -əblɪ/ *adv* **re·lia·bil·ity** /rɪˌlaɪə'bɪlətɪ; rɪˌlaɪə'bɪlətɪ/ *n* [U] state or quality of being ~. 可靠；可信賴。

re·li·ance /rɪ'laɪəns; rɪ'laɪəns/ *n* **1** [U] ~ ***on / upon,*** trust; confidence: 信任；信賴；信心： *Do you place much ~ on your doctor?* 你很信任你的醫生嗎？ *There is little ~ to be placed on his promises.* 他的諾言不甚可靠。 **2** person or thing depended upon. 所信賴的人或物。 **re·li·ant** /-ənt; -ənt/ *adj* having ~; trusting. 有信心的；信任的。

relic /'relɪk; 'rɛlɪk/ *n* [C] **1** part of the body, dress, etc of a saint or sth that belonged to him or was connected with him, kept after his death, as an object of reverence, and in some cases said to have miraculous powers. 聖者的部分遺骸、衣物等(在其死後保存以作爲崇敬的東西，據說在某些情形中具有神奇的力量)；聖物。 **2** sth that has survived from the past and that serves to keep memories alive: 紀念物；遺物： *a ~ of early civilization,* eg a stone implement; 早期文明的遺物(如石器等)； *~s of superstition.* 迷信的遺俗。 **3** (*pl*) person's dead body or bones; what has survived destruction or decay. (複)遺骸；遺跡；廢墟。

re·lict /'relɪkt; 'rɛlɪkt/ *n* (legal) widow: (法律)寡婦： *Alice, ~ of Arthur Williams.* 愛麗絲，亞瑟·威廉茲的未亡人。

re·lief¹ /rɪ'liːf; rɪ'lif/ *n* [U] (used with the *indef art* as in examples, but not normally in the *pl*) (如例句所示與不定冠詞連用，惟一般都不用複數) **1** lessening or ending or removal of pain, distress, anxiety, etc: (痛苦、困苦、憂慮等的)減輕；解除： *The doctor's treatment gave / brought some / not much ~.* 醫生的治療使(稍使，未能使)病情減輕。 *A doctor's task is to work for the ~ of suffering.* 醫生的工作是解除病痛。 *She heaved a sigh of ~ when she was told that the child's life was not in danger.* 當她聽到孩子無生命危險時，才鬆了一口氣。 *To my great ~ the difficulties were all overcome.* 使我大爲欣慰，困難全都克服了。 *It was a great ~ to find the children safe.* 發現孩子們平安無事，覺得很放心。 **2** that which brings ~(1); help given to those in need; food, clothes, money, etc for persons in trouble: 減輕或解除痛苦之事物；給予貧者或需要者的幫助；救濟物(食品、衣服、金錢等)： *send ~ to people made homeless by floods;* 送救濟品給那些因水災而變爲無家可歸的人們； *provide ~ for refugees;* 賑濟難民； *a '~ fund;* 救濟基金；賑款； *a '~ road,* alternative road for one that has heavy traffic. 爲減輕原來道路之擁擠交通而設的另一道路；間道。 **3** sth that makes a change from monotony or that relaxes tension: (冲淡單調或鬆弛緊張的)調劑： *We crossed wide stretches of moorland without ~,* with no change of scenery. 我們走過一大片景色單調的荒野。 *Shakespeare introduced comic scenes into his tragedies by way of ~.* 莎士比亞把喜劇的情節穿插於悲劇中，使觀衆的心情放鬆。 **4** ~ ***(of),*** reinforcement of a beseiged town; raising (of a siege): (圍城的)救援；解圍： *The general hastened to the ~ of the fortress.* 將軍火速前往救援該堡壘。 **5** (replacing of a person, persons, on duty by a) person or persons appointed to go on duty: 換班；接替；換班者；接替者： *on duty from 8am to 8pm with only two hours' ~;* 從上午八時到晚上八時值班，中間只有兩小時的替換； *happy to know that the ~ is on the way;* 聽到接替者要來了很高興； (attrib) (形容用法) *a '~ driver.* 輪替的駕駛員。

re·lief² /rɪ'liːf; rɪ'lif/ *n* ⇨ bas-~. **1** [U] method of carving or moulding in which a design stands out from a flat surface: 凸雕法；浮彫： *a profile of Julius Caesar in ~;* 凱撒之側面浮彫； *in high / low ~,* with the background cut out to a deep / shallow degree. 高(薄)浮彫的。 **2** [C] design or carving made in this way. 浮彫品。 **3** [U] (in drawing, etc) appearance of being done in ~ by the use of shading, colour, etc. (繪畫等)用明暗法、色彩等使人或物凸現。 **'~ map,** one showing hills, valleys, etc by shading or other means, not only by contour lines. (除了用等高線，並用明暗度或其他方法顯示丘陵、盆地等的)地形圖；立體地圖。 **4** [U] (lit and fig) vividness; distinctness of outline.(字面及喻)生動;輪廓顯著。***be/stand out in ~ against,*** be in contrast to: 與…成爲强烈的對照: *The hills stood out in sharp ~ against the morning sky.* 在晨空的映襯之下,羣山的輪廓極爲明顯。*His behaviour stood out in strong ~ against his declared principles.* 他的行爲與他所標榜的原則成了强烈的對照。

re·lieve /rɪˈliːv ; rɪˈliv/ *vt* [VP6A] **1** give or bring relief¹ to; lessen or remove (pain or distress): 給予救濟;援助;減輕或解除(痛苦或困難): *We were ~d to hear that you had arrived safely.* 聽到你已安全到達,我們安心了。*The fund is for relieving distress among the flood victims.* 這基金是用於賑濟水災災民的。~ ***one's feelings,*** provide an outlet for them (eg by shedding tears, or by using strong language, behaving violently). 發洩感情;洩憤(如藉流淚、破口大罵、行爲粗暴等)。~ ***oneself,*** empty the bladder or bowels. 大便;小便。⇨ relief¹(3). **2** take one's turn on duty: 換班;接替: ~ *the guard/the watch/a sentry.* 接替守衛(看守者,哨兵)。*You will be ~d at noon.* 中午會有人來換你的班。⇨ relief¹(5). **3** ~ ***sb of sth,*** **(a)** take it from him: 從某人手中接取某物: *Let me ~ you of your suitcase,* carry it for you (which is more usu). 讓我替你拿手提箱。**(b)** (joc) steal from: (諧) 偷;自…竊去: *The thief ~d him of his watch.* 那賊偷去他的手錶。**(c)** dismiss from: 開除;解除: *He was ~d of his post.* 他被解除職務。**4** bring into relief²; make (sth) stand out more clearly (*against* a dark background, etc). 使凸起;使(某物)更清晰地顯出(藉黑暗的背景襯托等,與 against 連用)。

re·lig·ion /rɪˈlɪdʒən ; rɪˈlɪdʒən/ *n* **1** [U] belief in the existence of a supernatural ruling power, the creator and controller of the universe, who has given to man a spiritual nature which continues to exist after the death of the body. 宗教信仰。**2** [C] one of the various systems of faith and worship based on such belief: 宗教: *the great ~s of the world,* eg Christianity, Islam, Buddhism. 世界之大宗教(如基督教、回教、佛教)。**3** [U] life as lived under the rules of a monastic order: 修道生活: *Her name in ~ is Sister Mary,* This is her name as a nun. 她的道名是瑪莉修女。**4** matter of conscience; sth that one considers oneself bound to do: 良心所安之事;自認須做之事: *She makes a ~ of keeping her house clean and tidy.* 她認爲保持房子整潔是她分內的事。

re·lig·ious /rɪˈlɪdʒəs ; rɪˈlɪdʒəs/ *adj* **1** of religion. 宗教的;宗教信仰的。**2** (of a person) devout; God-fearing. (指人)虔誠的;敬畏神的。**3** of a monastic order: 教團的;修道的: *a ~ house,* a monastery or convent. 修道院;僧院。**4** scrupulous; conscientious: 謹愼的;憑良心的: *do one's work with ~ care/exactitude.* 嚴謹地做事。□ *n* **a** ~, person bound by monastic vows; monk or nun; 僧侶;尼姑;修士;修女;(*pl,* unchanged in form) (複數,字形不變) *the/some/several ~,* persons bound by monastic vows. 全體(若干,幾位)僧尼。**~·ly** *adv*

re·line /ˌriːˈlaɪn ; riˈlaɪn/ *vt* put a new lining in, eg a garment. 加新襯裏於(衣服上等)。

re·lin·quish /rɪˈlɪŋkwɪʃ ; rɪˈlɪŋkwɪʃ/ *vt* **1** [VP6A] give up: 放棄: ~ *a hope/a habit/a belief.* 放棄希望(習慣,信仰)。~ ***one's hold of/over sb/sth,*** give up control. 放手不管(某人,某事物)。**2** [VP14] ~ ***sth (to sb),*** surrender: 將某事物讓與(某人): ~ *one's rights/shares to a partner.* 把權利(股份)讓給合夥人。

reli·quary /ˈrelɪkwərɪ *US:* -kwerɪ ; ˈrɛləˌkwɛrɪ/ *n* (*pl* -ries) box, casket, or other receptacle for a relic or relics. 聖骨箱(匣、盒);聖物箱(匣、盒);遺物箱(匣、盒)。

rel·ish /ˈrelɪʃ ; ˈrɛlɪʃ/ *n* **1** [C, U] (sth used to give, or which has, a) special flavour or attractive quality: 特別風味;美味;吸引力;調味品;作料;引起興趣之事物: *Hunger is the best ~ for food.* 肚子餓的時候什麼都好吃。*Some pastimes lose their ~ when one grows old.* 一個人年紀大了,對某些娛樂就會不感興趣。**2** [U] liking (*for*); zest: 喜好(與 for 連用);熱心;興趣: *I have no further ~ for active pursuits now that I am 90.* 我已經九十歲了,對於積極的工作或活動沒有多大興趣了。□ *vt* [VP6A, D] enjoy; get pleasure out of: 享受;愛好;喜好: *I would ~ a lobster and a bottle of wine.* 我願享受一隻龍蝦和一瓶酒。*She won't ~ having to get up before dawn to catch that train.* 在黎明前須起床趕那班火車,她不會喜歡的。

re·live /ˌriːˈlɪv ; riˈlɪv/ *vt* live through, undergo, again: 再經驗;再體驗: *That was an experience I should not like to ~.* 那種經驗我不願再領略了。

re·lo·cate /ˌriːləʊˈkeɪt *US:* ˌriːˈləʊkeɪt ; riˈloket/ *vt, vi* establish, become established, in a new place or area. 設置於新的地方;建造於新的地方;遷建;遷徙。**re·lo·ca·tion** /ˌriːləʊˈkeɪʃn ; ˌriloˈkeʃən/ *n* [U] putting in, moving to, a new place or area: 放置於新地方;遷徙於新地方: *the relocation of industry;* 工業區之遷徙; *the relocation of population;* 人口之遷移; compulsory evacuation of persons from military areas during a war, with resettlement in a new area. 戰時之强迫人們撤離軍事地區(另定居於新地方)。

re·luc·tant /rɪˈlʌktənt ; rɪˈlʌktənt/ *adj* ~ ***(to do sth),*** (slow to act because) unwilling or disinclined; offering resistance: 不願(做某事)的;因不願而遲緩的;勉强的;頑抗的;難駕馭的: ~ *helpers;* 不情願的幫助者; *a ~ recruit into the army.* 勉强入伍的新兵。*He seemed ~ to help us.* 他似乎不願幫助我們。**~·ly** *adv* **re·luc·tance** /-əns ; -əns/ *n* [U].

rely /rɪˈlaɪ ; rɪˈlaɪ/ *vi* (*pt, pp* -lied) [VP3A] ~ ***on/upon,*** depend upon with confidence, look to for help: 信賴;依賴: *He can always be relied upon for help.* 他的幫助是永遠可依賴的。*You may ~ upon my early arrival.* 你放心好了,我會早到的。*You may ~ upon it that he will be early.* 你放心好了,他一定會早到的。

re·main /rɪˈmeɪn ; rɪˈmen/ *vi* **1** [VP2A] be still present after a part has gone or has been taken away: 剩下;遺留: *After the fire, very little ~ed of my house.* 火燒後,寒舍所剩無幾。*If you take 3 from 8, 5 ~s.* 八減三剩五。*Much ~s to be settled.* 待解決的事尙多。**2** [VP2A, B, C, 4A] continue in some place or condition; continue to be: 停留;保持;依然;繼續存在: *How many weeks shall you ~* (=stay) *here?* 你將在此地停留幾個星期?*Let things ~ as they are.* 一切聽其自然吧。*He ~ed silent.* 他仍然緘默。*I shall ~* (*stay* is more usu) *to see the end of the game.* 我將留下來看比賽的結果(stay 較常用)。*Man ~ed a hunter for thousands of years,* ie before beginning to cultivate crops, etc. 人類的狩獵時期有數千年之久。

re·main·der /rɪˈmeɪndə(r) ; rɪˈmendɚ/ *n* that which remains; persons or things that are left over: 剩餘物;剩下的人或物: *Twenty people came in and the ~* (= the rest, the others) *stayed outside.* 二十個人進來,其餘的留在外面。

re·mains /rɪˈmeɪnz ; rɪˈmenz/ *n pl* **1** what is left: 所剩下或遺留者: *the ~ of a meal;* 殘羹剩飯; *the ~* (= ruins) *of an old abbey/of ancient Rome.* 古寺院(古羅馬)之遺跡。**2** dead body; corpse: 屍體;遺骸: *His mortal ~ are buried in the churchyard.* 他的屍體埋葬於教堂的墓地。

re·make /ˌriːˈmeɪk ; riˈmek/ *vt* (*pt, pp* -made /-ˈmeɪd ; -ˈmed/) make again. 再做;重做;改做;再製;重造。□ *n* /ˈriːmeɪk ; ˈriˌmek/ sth made again: 重做之物;再製品: *a ~ of a film.* 影片的再攝製。

re·mand /rɪˈmɑːnd *US:* -ˈmænd ; rɪˈmænd/ *vt* [VP 6A] send (an accused person) back (from a court of law) into custody so that more evidence may be obtained: 還押(將被告自法庭送回監禁以待更多證據): *~ed for a week.* 在押一星期。□ *n* [U] ~ing or being ~ed: 在押;還押: *detention on ~.* 在押;還押。ˈ~ ***centre/home,*** institution to which law-breaking children and adolescents are sent while inquiries are being made, or until the courts have decided their future treatment. 青少年拘留所(在進行調查中,或法院判決前,犯法之兒童或青少年被送往拘留的機構)。

re·mark /rɪˈmɑːk; rɪˈmɑrk/ *vt, vi* **1** [VP6A, 9] say (*that*): 談起; 述及 (後接名詞子句): *He ~ed that he would be absent the next day.* 他談到他次日不克出席。*'I thought it was curious,' he ~ed.* '我認爲那是稀奇的,' 他說。 **2** [VP3A] ~ ***on/upon,*** say sth by way of comment. 談論;評論: *It would be rude to ~ upon her appearance.* 談論她的容貌是不禮貌的。 **3** [VP6A, 9, 10] (formal, old use) notice; see: (正式用語,舊用法)注意;留意;看: *Did you ~ the similarity between them?* 你注意到他們之間的相似之處嗎? □ *n* **1** [C] comment; sth said: 評論;談話: *pass rude ~s about sb;* 用粗魯的話批評某人; *make a few ~s,* give a short talk. 說幾句話;作短評。 **2** [U] notice; looking at: 注意;留意;看: *There was nothing worthy of ~ at the Flower Show.* 花展中沒有值得一看的東西。**~·able** /-əbl; -əbl̩/ *adj* out of the ordinary; deserving or attracting attention: 不平常的;值得注意的: *a ~able event;* 不平常的事件; *a boy who is ~able for his stupidity.* 笨得驚人的男孩。**~·ably** /-əblɪ; -əblɪ/ *adv*

re·marry /ˌriːˈmærɪ; riˈmærɪ/ *vt, vi* (*pt, pp* -ried) marry again. 再婚;再與…結婚。**re·mar·riage** /ˌriːˈmærɪdʒ; riˈmærɪdʒ/ *n*

rem·edy /ˈremədɪ; ˈrɛmədɪ/ *n* [C, U] (*pl* -dies) ~ ***(for),*** cure (for a disease, evil, etc); method of, sth used for, putting right sth that is wrong: (疾病之)治療;(壞事等之)矯正;補救;治療法;矯正法;藥物;補救物: *a good ~ for colds.* 治傷風的良藥。*The ~ seems to be worse than the disease.* 服用這種藥物無異於飲酖止渴。 *Your only ~* (= way to get redress) *is to go to law.* 你唯一的補救辦法是訴諸法律。*The evil is past/beyond ~,* cannot be cured. 這弊害無藥可救。□ *vt* [VP6A] put right; provide a ~ for (evils, defects): 治療;矯正(壞事、缺點): *Your faults of pronunciation can be remedied.* 你的發音毛病是可以矯正的。 **re·medial** /rɪˈmiːdɪəl; rɪˈmidɪəl/ *adj* providing, or intended to provide, a ~: 治療的;矯正的;用於治療或矯正的: *remedial measures;* 補救辦法; *remedial education/classes,* eg for children suffering disadvantages. 矯治教育(班)。 **re·medi·able** /rɪˈmiːdɪəbl; rɪˈmidɪəbl̩/ *adj* that can be remedied. 可治療或矯正的;可補救的。

re·mem·ber /rɪˈmembə(r); rɪˈmɛmbɚ/ *vt, vi* **1** [VP 6A, C, 7A, 8, 9, 10, 14, 16B, 19C] have or keep in the memory; call back to mind the memory of: 記得;憶及: *I can't ~ his name.* 我記不起他的名字。*I ~ed* (= did not forget) *to post your letters.* 我(那時)未忘記要爲你寄信。*I ~ posting your letters* (= have the memory of that act in my mind). 我記得爲你寄過信。 *I ~ having heard you speak on that subject.* 我記得曾聽你談論那題目。 *Do you ~ where you put the key?* 你記得把鑰匙放在何處嗎? *I ~ her* (= picture her in my mind) *as a slim young girl.* 我想起她那時還是個纖弱的小女孩。*Please don't ~ this unfortunate affair against me,* don't bear it in mind and, for that reason, be unfriendly to me. 請不要把這不幸的事記在心裡怨恨我。 *'Have you ever met my brother?'—'Not that I ~.'* I don't ~ having met him. '你見過我哥哥(弟弟)嗎?'—'我不記得曾見過他。' **2** [VP6A] make a present to: 贈與: *Please ~ the waiter,* don't forget to tip him. 別忘了賞侍者小費。*I hope you'll ~ me in your will,* leave me sth. 我希望你在遺囑中對我有所遺贈。 **3** [VP14] ~ ***sb to sb,*** convey greetings: 問候;致意: *Please ~ me to your brother.* 請代向令兄(弟)問候。

re·mem·brance /rɪˈmembrəns; rɪˈmɛmbrəns/ *n* **1** [U] remembering or being remembered; memory: 回想;記憶;記憶力: *to the best of my ~;* 就我記憶所及; *have no ~ of sth;* 不記得某事物; *a service in ~ of those killed in the war.* 紀念陣亡者的儀式。**R~ Day/Sunday,** (GB) Nov 11th, or the nearest Sunday, on which those killed in the two World Wars are commemorated. (英)陣亡將士紀念日(紀念在兩次世界大戰中的死難者,在十一月十一日或最近該日的星期天)。 **2** [C] sth given or kept in memory of sb or sth: 紀念物: *He sent us a small ~ of his visit.* 他送給我們一個他造訪的小紀念物。 **3** (*pl*) regards; greetings (⇨ regard¹(5)): (複)問候;致意: *Give my kind ~s to your parents.* 請爲我向令尊令堂致意。

re·mili·tar·ize /ˌriːˈmɪlɪtəraɪz; riˈmɪlətəˌraɪz/ *vt* [VP6A] provide, occupy, again with armed forces and military equipment. 使重整軍備;使重新武裝。 **re·mili·tar·iz·ation** /ˌriːˌmɪlɪtəraɪˈzeɪʃn *US:* -rɪˈz-; ˌrimɪlətərɪˈzeʃən/ *n*

re·mind /rɪˈmaɪnd; rɪˈmaɪnd/ *vt* [VP6A, 11, 14, 17, 20, 21] ~ ***sb (to do sth/that...);*** ~ ***sb of sth/sb,*** cause (sb) to remember (to do sth, etc); cause (sb) to think (of sth): 提醒(某人)(做某事等,與不定詞或名詞子句連用);使(某人)想起(某事物或某人,與 of 連用): *Please ~ me to answer that letter.* 請提醒我回覆那封信。*Travellers are ~ed that inoculation against yellow fever is advisable.* 旅客們被提醒,注射黃熱病預防針是明智的。*He ~s me of his brother.* 他使我想起他哥哥(弟弟)。*This ~s me of what we did together during our holidays.* 這使我想起我們在假日一同做的事。*That ~s me,...,* What you have just said ~s me..., I've just remembered..., etc. 這使我想起…。 **~er** *n* sth (eg a letter) that helps sb to remember sth: 使人記起某事之事物(例如信函): *He hasn't paid me that money yet—I must send him a ~er,* ie a letter to ~ him about it. 他還未付我那筆錢——我必須寫一封信提醒他。

remi·nisce /ˌremɪˈnɪs; ˌrɛməˈnɪs/ *vi* [VP2A, 3A] ~ ***(about),*** think or talk about past events and experiences. 回憶;話舊;緬懷往事。

remi·nis·cence /ˌremɪˈnɪsns; ˌrɛməˈnɪsn̩s/ *n* ~ ***(of),*** **1** [U] reminiscing; recalling of past experiences. 回憶;話舊;懷舊。 **2** (*pl*) remembered experiences; narrative, spoken or written, of what sb remembers: (複)所追懷的經驗;舊事;回憶錄;經驗談: *~s of my days in the Navy.* 我在海軍那一段日子的回憶。**3** sth that is suggestive (*of* sth else): 令人聯想(其他事物)的東西(與 of 連用): *There is a ~ of his father in the way he walks.* 他走路的樣子使人聯想到他的父親。

remi·nis·cent /ˌremɪˈnɪsnt; ˌrɛməˈnɪsn̩t/ *adj* ~ ***(of),*** **1** reminding one of; suggestive of: 使人想起的;暗示的: *Your face is ~ of your mother's.* 你的面孔使人想起你母親的面孔。 **2** recalling past experiences: 回憶的;懷舊的: *become ~.* 開始懷舊。**~·ly** *adv*

re·miss /rɪˈmɪs; rɪˈmɪs/ *adj* ~ ***in,*** careless of duty: 疏忽職守的: *You have been ~ in your duties.* 你已疏忽職守。~ ***of,*** negligent, lax: 鬆懈的;怠慢的;隨便的: *That was very ~ of you.* 你對那件事太疏忽了。 **~·ness** *n* [U].

re·mission /rɪˈmɪʃn; rɪˈmɪʃən/ *n* **1** [U] pardon or forgiveness (of sins, by God). (上帝對罪過的)赦免;寬恕。**2** [U] freeing (from debt, punishment, etc): (債務、處分等之)免除;放棄: *~ of a claim;* 對一項要求權利之放棄; [C] instance of this: 免除或放棄之實例: ~ (from a prison sentence) *for good conduct;* 因行爲良好而減免徒刑; *No ~s of examination fees are allowed.* 檢查費不減免。 **3** [U] lessening or weakening (of pain, efforts, etc): (痛苦、努力等之)緩和;減輕: *~ of a fever.* 熱度之減退。

re·mit /rɪˈmɪt; rɪˈmɪt/ *vt, vi* (-tt-) **1** [VP6A] (of God) forgive (sins). (指上帝)赦(罪)。 **2** [VP6A] excuse (sb) payment (of a debt, a punishment): 免除(某人之債);赦免(某人之刑罰): *The taxes have been ~ted.* 稅已免除了。*Your fees cannot be ~ted.* 你的費用不能豁免。**3** [VP12A, 13A, 2C] send (money, etc) by post: 滙(錢等): *When can you ~ me the money?* 你何時能滙錢給我? *Kindly ~ by cheque,* send a cheque for the sum owing. 祈惠寄支票付款。**4** [VP6A] make or become less: 緩和;減輕: ~ *one's efforts.* 鬆懈努力。**5** [VP14] ~ ***sth to sb,*** take or send (a question to be decided) (to some authority):將(待決之問題)送呈(有關當局): *The matter has been ~ted to a higher tribunal.* 那事件已送呈上一級法院裁決。**~·tance** /-ns.; -ṇs/ *n* [U] the ~ting, of money; [C] sum of money sent. 滙款;所滙款額。

re·mit·tent /rɪˈmɪtnt ; rɪˈmɪtṇt/ *adj* (esp of a fever) that abates in severity at intervals. (尤指熱病)忽輕忽重的;間歇性的。

rem·nant /ˈremnənt ; ˈrɛmnənt/ *n* [C] **1** small part that remains: 剩下之小部分;殘餘;剩餘: *~s of a banquet;* 筵席之剩菜; *~s of former glory.* 往昔光榮之遺跡。**2** (esp) length of cloth offered at a reduced price after the greater part has been sold: (尤指減價出售的)零頭布: *a ~ sale.* 零頭布的減價出售。

re·mon·strance /rɪˈmɒnstrəns ; rɪˈmɑnstrəns/ *n* [U] remonstrating (*with*); [C] protest (*against*). 抗辯;規諫(與 with 連用);抗議(與 against 連用)。

re·mon·strate /ˈremənstreɪt ; rɪˈmɑnstret/ *vi* [VP 2A, 3A] ~ ***with sb (about sth/that...),*** make a protest; argue in protest: 抗議;抗辯;規諫: *~ with sb about his foolish behaviour;* 就其愚行規諫某人; *~ against cruelty to children.* 抗議對孩子的虐待。

re·morse /rɪˈmɔːs ; rɪˈmɔrs/ *n* [U] **1** ~ ***(for),*** deep, bitter regret for wrongdoing: 懊悔;悔恨: *feel/be filled with ~ for one's failure to help sb;* 因未能幫助某人而感到懊悔; *in a fit of ~.* 在一陣懊悔中。**2** compunction: 良心的不安: *without ~,* merciless(ly). 無情的(地)。**~·ful** /-fl ; -fəl/ *adj* feeling ~. 懊悔的;良心不安的。**~·fully** /-fəlɪ ; -fəlɪ/ *adv* **~·less** *adj* without ~. 不知懊悔的。**~·less·ly** *adv*

re·mote /rɪˈməʊt ; rɪˈmot/ *adj* (-r, -st) ~ ***(from),*** **1** far away in space or time: (在空間或時間上)遙遠的: *in the ~st parts of Asia;* 在亞洲的遙遠的地方; *live in a house ~ from any town or village;* 居住於遠離任何城鎮或村莊的房子; *in the ~ past/future.* 在遙遠的過去(未來)。**~ control,** control of apparatus, eg in an aircraft, a rocket, from a distance by means of radio signals. 遙控(如在遠處用無線電波對飛機、火箭之控制)。**2** widely separated (in feeling, interests, etc *from*): (在感情、興趣等方面)距離很大的;關係甚遠的(與 from 連用): *Some of your statements are rather ~ from the subject we are discussing.* 你有一些話與我們所談論的問題關係不甚密切。**3** distant in manner; aloof. 疏遠的;冷淡的。**4** (esp in the superl) slight: (尤用於最高級)些微的;輕的: *a ~ possibility;* 極小的可能性; *have not the ~st idea of what sth means.* 一點不知道某事物的含義。**~·ly** *adv* in a ~ manner: 遙遠地;關係甚遠地: *Gillian and I are ~ly related.* 吉蓮和我是遠親。**~·ness** *n*

re·mount¹ /ˌriːˈmaʊnt ; riˈmaʊnt/ *vt, vi* [VP6A, 2A] get on (a horse, bicycle, etc) again; go up (a ladder, hill, etc) again. 再上(馬、單車等);再爬(梯、山等)。

re·mount² /ˌriːˈmaʊnt ; riˈmaʊnt/ *vt* [VP6A] **1** supply (a man, a regiment) with a fresh horse or horses. 以新馬供給(某人、某團)。**2** put (a photograph, etc) on a new mount. 放(照片等)於新襯紙上;重新安裝。□ *n* /ˈriːmaʊnt ; ˈriˌmaʊnt/ fresh horse; supply of fresh horses. 新馬;新補充之馬。

re·move¹ /rɪˈmuːv ; rɪˈmuv/ *vt, vi* **1** [VP6A, 14] ~ ***(from),*** take off or away from the place occupied; take to another place: 自原來位置拿開;取去;移動: *~ one's hat/coat;* 脫帽(上衣); *~ one's hand from sb's shoulder;* 把放在某人肩上的手移開; *~ the cloth from the table;* 把桌上的桌布拿掉; *~ a boy from school,* eg because of ill health. 使一男孩休學(如因健康不佳)。**2** [VP6A, 14] ~ ***(from),*** get rid of: 除去;排除: *~ doubts/fears.* 消除疑慮(恐懼)。*What do you advise for removing grease/ink stains, etc from clothes?* 你有什麼好辦法除去衣服上的油漬(墨水漬等)? **3** [VP6A, 14] ~ ***(from),*** dismiss: 免職;開除: *~ a man from office;* 免除一人之職務; *~ a Civil Servant.* 將一公務員革職。**4** [VP2A, C] go to live in another place (move is more usu): 移居(move 比 remove 常用): *We're removing into the country next week/removing from London to the country.* 我們將於下週遷到鄉下(從倫敦遷到鄉下)。**5** **~d from,** distant or remote from: 遠離的;關係甚遠的: *a dialect equally ~d from French and Spanish;* 與法語和西班牙語關係同樣疏遠的一種方言; *an explanation far ~d from the truth.* 與事實相距甚遠的一種解釋。**6** **~d,** (of cousins) different by a generation: (指堂、表親)相隔一代的: *first cousin once ~d,* first cousin's child. 堂姪;表姪。**re·mov·able** /-əbl ; -əbḷ/ *adj* that can be ~d (esp of a magistrate or other official who can be ~d from office at any time). 可移動的;可除去的;(尤指官員)可撤任的;可免職的。**~r** *n* **1** (esp) person who follows the business of moving furniture when people ~(4). (尤指)搬場業者;搬運傢具者。**2** (in compounds) sth that ~s(2): (用於複合字中)用以除去或排除之物: *superfluous hair ~r.* 除去多餘毛髮的藥劑。**re·moval** /-vl ; -vḷ/ *n* [U] act of removing: 移動;除去;搬家;免職: *the removal of furniture;* 傢具之搬運; (attrib) (形容用法) *a reˈmoval van* (for furniture); 搬運車; *the removal of dissatisfaction;* 不滿情緒之排除; [C] instance of removal. 移動、除去、移居、搬家、免職等之實例。

re·move² /rɪˈmuːv ; rɪˈmuv/ *n* stage or degree: 階段;程度: *only a few ~s from....* 與…僅差少許。

re·mun·er·ate /rɪˈmjuːnəreɪt ; rɪˈmjunəˌret/ *vt* [VP 6A, 14] ~ ***sb (for sth),*** pay (sb) (for work or services); reward. (因工作或服務而)酬勞(某人);報酬。**re·mun·er·ation** /rɪˌmjuːnəˈreɪʃn ; rɪˌmjunəˈreʃən/ *n* [U] payment; reward. 酬勞;報酬。**re·mun·er·ative** /rɪˈmjuːnərətɪv *US:* -nəreɪtɪv ; rɪˈmjunəˌretɪv/ *adj* profitable. 有酬勞的;有利益的。

re·nais·sance /rɪˈneɪsns *US:* ˈrenəsɑːns ; rɪˈnesṇs/ *n* **1** **the R~,** (period of) revival of literature, painting, etc in Europe in the 14th, 15th and 16th cc, based on ancient Greek learning: (歐洲十四,十五及十六世紀之)文藝復興;文藝復興時期: (attrib) (形容用法) *~ art.* 文藝復興時期的藝術。**2** [C] any similar revival. 任何類似的復興;再生。

re·nal /ˈriːnl ; ˈrinḷ/ *adj* (anat) of or in the (region of the) kidneys: (解剖)腎臟的;腎臟中的;腎部的: *~ artery.* 腎動脈。

re·name /ˌriːˈneɪm ; riˈnem/ *vt* [VP6A] give a new name to; name again. 予以新名;再命名。

re·nas·cence /rɪˈnæsns; rɪˈnæsṇs/ *n*=renaissance(2). **re·nas·cent** /-snt ; -sṇt/ *adj* springing up anew; reviving; being reborn. 再生的;復活的;重生的。

rend /rend ; rɛnd/ *vt* (*pt, pp* rent /rent ; rɛnt/) [VP 6A, 14, 15A] (liter) (文) **1** pull or divide forcibly; penetrate: 用力拉或分開;分裂;刺破: *a country rent (in two) by civil war.* 因內戰分裂(爲二)的國家。*Loud cries rent the air.* 吼聲震雲霄。**2** tear or pull (*off, away*) violently: 扯裂;强使分離(與 off, away 連用)。*Children were rent from their mothers' arms by the brutal soldiers.* 兇暴的兵士强使孩子離開母親的懷抱。

ren·der /ˈrendə(r) ; ˈrɛndɚ/ *vt* **1** [VP6A, 14, 12A, 13A, 15A, B] ~ ***sth (to sb),*** give in return or exchange, or as sth due: 報答;回報;歸還;給予: *~ thanks to God;* 答謝上帝; *~ good for evil;* 以德報怨; *~ help to those in need;* 予貧困者以幫助; *~ a service to sb/~ sb a service;* 爲某人服務(幫某人忙); *~ up* (= surrender) *a fort to the enemy;* 把堡壘放棄給敵人; *a reward for services ~ed.* 酬謝服務的獎金。**2** [VP6A] present; offer; send in (an account for payment): 呈遞;提供;開出(帳單催促付款): *an account ~ed,* previously presented but not yet paid. 已開來而尚未付款的帳單;交驗帳;付款催單。*You will have to ~ an account of your expenditure.* 你的開支必須報帳。**~ *an account of oneself/one's behaviour,*** explain, justify oneself/

it. 爲自己(自己的行爲)辯護;說明理由。 **3** [VP22] cause to be (in some condition): 使成;致使(處於某狀況): *~ed helpless by an accident.* 因意外而束手無策。 **4** [VP6A, 14] give a performance of (eg a drama, a character in a drama); express in another language: 演出(戲劇,劇中之角色等);扮演;演奏;翻譯: *The piano solo was well ~ed.* 那支鋼琴獨奏曲彈得很好。*'Othello' was ~ed rather poorly.* '奧賽羅'一劇演出頗差。*There are many English idioms that cannot be ~ed into other languages.* 有許多英文慣用語無法翻譯成其他文字。 **5** [VP6A, 15B] ~ ***sth (down),*** melt and make clear: 煎熬(脂肪): *~ down fat/lard.* 熬脂肪(豬油)。 **6** [VP6A] cover (stone, brick) with the first layer of plaster. 塗第一層灰泥於(石,磚)。 **~·ing** /ˈrendərɪŋ ; ˈrɛndərɪŋ/ *n* **1** [C] way of performing, playing, translating, sth, ⇨ ~(4): 演出,演奏,翻譯之方式: *a ~ing of the Bible.* 聖經的翻譯。 **2** [U] first layer of plaster, ⇨ ~(6). 第一層灰泥。

ren·dez·vous /ˈrɒndɪvuː; ˈrɑndəˌvu/ *n* (*pl* ~ /-z ; -z/) [C] **1** (place decided upon for a) meeting at a time agreed upon. 約會;集會;約會地點;集會地點;會合點。 **2** place where people often meet: 人們常聚會之處: *This café is a ~ for writers and artists.* 這家咖啡館是作家和藝術家們經常聚會的地方。 □ *vi* [VP2A, C] meet at a ~: 約見;聚會;在約好的地方相見: *~ in a café/beside a lake.* 經約好在一咖啡館(湖濱)相見。

ren·di·tion /renˈdɪʃn ; rɛnˈdɪʃən/ *n* [C] interpretation or rendering (*of* a song, etc). (歌曲等的) 解釋;演唱;演奏;演出;翻譯(與 of 連用)。

ren·egade /ˈrenɪgeɪd ; ˈrɛnɪˌged/ *n* [C] person who changes his religious beliefs; person who deserts his political party; traitor: 背教者;叛黨者;叛徒: (attrib) (形容用法) *a ~ priest.* 一位背教的傳教士。 □ *vi* turn ~. 成爲背教者,叛黨者或叛徒。

re·nege, re·negue /rɪˈniːg ; rɪˈnig/ *vi* **1** (in card games) revoke(2). (紙牌戲)手中有可跟之牌而違例不跟。 **2** [VP3A] ~ ***on,*** fail to keep (one's word). 違背(諾言);背信。

re·new /rɪˈnjuː *US:* -ˈnuː ; rɪˈnju/ *vt* [VP6A] **1** make (as good as) new; put new life and vigour into; restore to the original condition: 使新;更新;注入新生命和精力;使恢復: *~ one's youth;* 恢復青春; *with ~ed enthusiasm.* 以重新燃起的熱情。 **2** get, make, say or give, again: 再得;再做;再說;再給;重新開始: *~ a lease/contract;* 續訂租約(契約); *~ one's subscription to a periodical;* 續訂一期刊; *~ an attack;* 再行攻擊; *~ one's complaints.* 再提告訴;再度抱怨。 **3** replace (with the same sort of thing, etc): 換新;補充: *We must ~ our supplies of coal.* 我們必須補充煤的儲藏量。*Snakes cast off and ~ their skins.* 蛇蛻皮復長新皮。 **~·able** /-əbl ; -əbl/ *adj* that can be ~ed. 可更新的;可重新開始的;可換新的。 **~al** /-ˈnjuːəl *US:* -ˈnuːəl ; -ˈnuəl/ *n* [U] ~ing or being ~ed: 更新;重新開始;換新: *delighted at the ~al of negotiations;* 對恢復談判感到高興; *urban ~al,* eg slum clearance for the provision of better housing; 都市更新;都市改建; [C] sth ~ed. 更新,重新開始,換新等之事物。

ren·net /ˈrenɪt ; ˈrɛnɪt/ *n* [U] preparation used in curdling milk for making cheese, etc. 凝乳素(用於製乾酪等用)。

re·nounce /rɪˈnaʊns ; rɪˈnaʊns/ *vt* [VP6A] **1** declare formally that one will no longer have anything to do with, that one no longer recognizes (sb or sth having a claim to one's care, affection, etc): 正式宣稱(與某人或某事物)斷絕關係;棄絕: *~ one's faith/religion;* 棄絕信仰(宗教); *~ the world,* give up meeting people socially, begin to lead the life of a hermit, etc. 脫離社會;遁世。 **2** consent formally to give up (a claim, right, possession): 正式同意放棄(要求,權利,財產): *~ one's claim to the throne/a peerage.* 放棄王位的繼承權(貴族的地位)。 **3** disown; refuse to recognize: 否認;拒絕承認: *He ~d his sons because they were criminals.* 他拒絕承認他們是他的兒子,因爲他們是罪犯。

reno·vate /ˈrenəveɪt ; ˈrɛnəˌvet/ *vt* [VP6A] restore, eg old buildings, oil paintings, to good or strong condition. 修理;恢復(舊房屋,油畫)至良好狀況。 **reno·va·tor** /-tə(r) ; -tɚ/ *n* person who ~s. 修理者;使舊房屋,油畫等恢復至良好狀況者。 **reno·va·tion** /ˌrenəˈveɪʃn ; ˌrɛnəˈveʃən/ *n* [U] renovating; [C] instance of this: 修理;恢復;修理或恢復之實例: *costly renovations of old college buildings at Oxford.* 花費很大的牛津大學舊校舍修復工程。

re·nown /rɪˈnaʊn ; rɪˈnaʊn/ *n* [U] fame: 名望;聲譽: *win ~;* 獲得聲譽; *a man of high ~.* 極有名望的人。 **~ed** *adj* famous; celebrated: 有名的;著名的: *~ed as a portrait painter;* 是個著名的人像畫家; *~ed for his skill.* 以其技巧著名的。

rent¹ /rent ; rɛnt/ *n* [C, U] regular payment for the use of land, a building, a room or rooms, machinery, etc; sum of money paid in this way: (土地,建築物,房舍,機器等之)定期的租費; 租金總額: *owe three weeks' ~ for one's house;* 欠三星期的房租; *live in a house free of ~,* without paying ~; 居住不收租金的房屋; *pay a heavy/high ~ for farming land;* 繳付農地之昂貴租金; *collect the ~s.* 收租。 **ˈ~-collector** *n* person who goes from house to house to collect ~s for the owner(s). (爲房地主挨戶)收租者。 **ˌ~-ˈfree** *adj, adv*: *a ~-free house,* for which no ~ is charged to the tenant; 不收租金的房子; *occupy a house ~-free.* 居住不收租金的房屋。 **ˌ~-ˈrebate** *n* rebate, based on earnings and the amount of ~ payable, given by a local government authority on ~ paid, esp by council tenants. 租金寬減額;房租之寬減。 **ˈ~-roll** *n* **(a)** register of a person's land and buildings with the ~s due from them. 租摺;房地租帳。 **(b)** total income from ~s. 房地租總收入。 □ *vt, vi* **1** [VP6A, 14] ~ ***(from/to),*** occupy or use (land, buildings, etc) for ~; allow (land, buildings, etc) to be used or occupied in return for ~: 租用;出租(土地,建築物等): *We don't own our house, we ~ it from Mr Gay.* 我們住的房子不是自己的,是向蓋伊先生租的。 *Mr Hill ~s this land to us at £50 a year.* 希爾先生把這塊地租給我們,每年五十鎊。 **2** [VP2A, C] be ~ed: 出租: *The building ~s at £150 a year.* 這建築物每年以一百五十鎊出租。 **~·able** *adj* that may be ~ed; able to yield a ~. 可租的;可收租金的。 **~al** /ˈrentl ; ˈrɛntl/ *n* [C] amount of ~ paid or received; income from ~s. 租金額;租金收入。

rent² /rent ; rɛnt/ *n* [C] **1** torn place in cloth, etc; split: (布等之)破裂處;裂縫: *~ in his shirt.* 他襯衫上的裂縫。 **2** (fig) division or split (in a political party, etc). (喻)(政黨等的)分裂;分歧。

rent³ /rent ; rɛnt/ *pt, pp* of rend.

rent·ier /ˈrɒntɪeɪ ; ˈrɑntje/ *n* person whose income comes from investments and/or rents from property. 靠投資收入和(或)房地產租金度日者。

re·nunci·ation /rɪˌnʌnsɪˈeɪʃn ; rɪˌnʌnsɪˈeʃən/ *n* [U] renouncing, self-denial. 棄絕;放棄;否認;自制;克己。

re·open /riːˈəʊpən ; riˈopən/ *vt, vi* [VP6A, 2A] open again after closing or being closed: 重開;再開始: *~ a shop;* 重新開一商店; *~ a discussion.* 再予討論。 *School ~s on Monday.* 星期一恢復上課。

re·or·gan·ize /riːˈɔːgənaɪz ; riˈɔrgəˌnaɪz/ *vt, vi* organize again or in a new way. 重新組織;改組;整頓。

re·orien·tate /riːˈɔːrɪənteɪt ; riˈɔrɪɛnˌtet/ (also 亦作 **re·orient** /riːˈɔːrɪənt ; riˈɔrɪˌɛnt/) *vt, vi* orient(ate) again or anew. 再使朝向東方;再使在東端;再定方向;再定方位。

rep¹, **repp** /rep ; rɛp/, **reps** /reps ; rɛps/ *n* [U] textile fabric used in upholstery. (室內裝飾品用的)一種織物。

rep² /rep ; rɛp/ *n* (colloq abbr of) representative (*n*(2)) of a commercial firm; commercial traveller. (俗)公司代表(爲 representative of a commercial firm 之略);旅行推銷員。

rep[3] /rep ; rɛp/ *n* (colloq abbr of) repertory company or theatre: (俗)時常換演員或戲目的劇團或戲院(爲 repertory company 或 theatre 之略): *act in rep.* 在時常換演員或戲目的劇團或戲院演戲。

re·pair[1] /rɪˈpeə(r) ; rɪˈpɛr/ *vt* [VP6A] **1** restore (sth worn or damaged) to good condition: 修補; 修理(破舊或損壞之物): *~ the roads/a puncture/a watch/a shirt.* 修路(補洞;修錶;補襯衣)。**2** put right again: 補救; 糾正: *~ an error.* 糾正一錯誤。□ *n* **1** [U] ~ing or being ~ed: 修理;補救: *road under ~.* 在修補中的道路。**2** (*pl*) work or process of ~ing: (複)修理、補救等的工作或過程: *The shop will be closed during ~s.* 整修期間該店將暫停營業。*The ~s needed before we can occupy the house will be considerable.* 那幢房子在我們搬進之前需要大事整修一番。**3** [U] relative condition for using or being used: 使用中的相對狀況: *The machine is in a bad state of ~/in good ~.* 這機器情況不佳(情況良好)。**~·able** /-əbl ; -əbḷ/ *adj* that can be ~ed. 可修理的;可修補的;可補救的。**~er** *n* one who ~s things: 修補者: *boot and shoe ~ers.* 修鞋匠。

re·pair[2] /rɪˈpeə(r) ; rɪˈpɛr/ *vi* [VP3A] *~ to*, (formal) go to (esp go frequently, go in large numbers to): (正式用語)(尤指)常去;衆多人去: *~ to the seaside resorts for the summer.* 大夥去海濱勝地避暑。

rep·ar·able /ˈrepərəbl ; ˈrɛpərəbḷ/ *adj* (of a loss, etc) that can be made good. (指損失等)能補救的;可補償的。

rep·ar·ation /ˌrepəˈreɪʃn ; ˌrɛpəˈreʃən/ *n* [U] act of compensating for loss or damage; (*pl*) compensation for war damages, demanded from a defeated enemy. 補償;(複)戰敗者之賠償;賠款。

rep·ar·tee /ˌrepɑːˈtiː ; ˌrɛpɚˈti/ *n* [C] witty, clever retort; [U] the making of such retorts: 巧妙的應答或反駁;作巧妙的應答或反駁: *He's good at ~.* 他善作巧妙的應答。

re·past /rɪˈpɑːst *US:* -ˈpæst ; rɪˈpæst/ *n* (formal) meal: (正式用語)餐;食事: *The guests partook of a luxurious ~ in the banqueting hall.* 賓客們在大餐廳參加一次盛宴。

re·pat·ri·ate /riːˈpætrɪeɪt *US:* -ˈpeɪt- ; riˈpetrɪˌet/ *vt* [VP6A] send or bring (sb) back to his own country: 遣返;遣送(某人)回國: *~ refugees after a war.* 戰後遣送難民回國。□ *n* ~d person. 被遣返者。 **re·pat·ri·ation** /ˌriːpætrɪˈeɪʃn *US:* -ˌpeɪt- ; ˌripetrɪˈeʃən/ *n*

re·pay /rɪˈpeɪ ; rɪˈpe/ *vt, vi* (*pt, pp* -paid /-ˈpeɪd ; -ˈped/) **1** [VP6A] pay back (money): 付還(錢): *If you'll lend me 75p, I'll ~ you next week.* 你若借我七十五辨士,我下星期就還你。**2** [VP6A, 14] *~ sth; ~ sb (for sth)*, give in return: 報答; 回報: *~ sb's kindness;* 報答某人的恩惠; *~ sb for his kindness.* 報答某人的恩惠。*I have been repaid (for the help I gave) only with ingratitude.* (對於我給予的幫助)我祇得到不義的報答。**3** [VP2A] give equal favour (or justice) in return: 報應;報復: *God will ~*, eg will punish injustice. 上天會給予報應的。**~·able** /-əbl ; -əbḷ/ *adj* that can or must be repaid. 可付還或回報的;必須付還或回報的。**~·ment** *n* [U] ~ing; [C] instance of this: 付還;回報: *bonds due for ~ment.* 到期該償還的債券。

re·peal /rɪˈpiːl ; rɪˈpil/ *vt* [VP6A] revoke, annul (a law, etc). 撤銷;廢止(法令等)。□ *n* ~ing. 撤銷;廢止。

re·peat /rɪˈpiːt ; rɪˈpit/ *vt, vi* **1** [VP6A, 9] say or do again: 重說;重做;重複: *~ a word/a mistake.* 重複一字(錯誤)。*I ~ that I cannot undertake the task.* 我再說一遍,我不能擔任這工作。*Don't ~ yourself,* say or do the same thing more than once (usu without being aware of doing so). 不要重複(勿說或做同樣的事)。*Does history ~ itself,* Do similar events or situations recur? 歷史會重演嗎? **ˈ~ing rifle,** ⇨ repeater below. 參看下列之 repeater。**2** [VP6A] say (what sb else has said or what one learnt by heart): 轉述; 複誦; 背誦: *You must not ~ what I've told you; it's very confidential.* 你切不可轉述我告訴你的事,那是很機密的。*His language won't bear ~ing,* eg contained too many curses, swear words, etc. 他的話不堪重述(例如含有太多的咒語,粗話等)。**3** [VP2A] (of food) continue to be tasted after being eaten: (指食物)吃後仍留有味道: *Do you find that onions ~?* 你發現吃過洋葱後口裡仍留有味道嗎? **4** [VP2A] (of numbers, eg decimals) recur: (指數字,如小數)循環: *The last two figures ~.* 最後二位數字循環。**5** [VP6A] (comm) supply a further consignment of: (商)再供應(託售之物): *We regret that we cannot ~ this article.* 抱歉我們無法再供應此物。□ *n* **1** [C] ~ing (eg of an item in a programme) of a performance: 動作或行爲的重複; (節目等的) 重複表演: (attrib) (形容用法) *a ~ performance;* 重複的表演; *a ~ order,* (comm) an order for a further consignment of goods similar to an earlier one. (商)再供給同樣貨品的訂單。*There will be a ~* (= another broadcast) *of this talk on Friday.* 星期五將重播此次的談話。**2** (music) mark indicating a passage intended to be repeated. (音樂) 反覆記號。**~·ed** *part adj: ~ed questioning/banging.* 再三詢問(猛擊)。**~·ed·ly** *adv* again and again. 反覆地;再三地。**~er** *n* revolver or rifle which can be fired a number of times without being reloaded (now usu a *(semi-)automatic* or *self-loading rifle*). 轉輪手槍; 連發步槍(現在通常爲(半)自動或自動裝彈步槍)。

re·pel /rɪˈpel ; rɪˈpɛl/ *vt* (-ll-) [VP6A] **1** drive back or away; refuse to accept: 逐退;驅開;拒絕: *~ the enemy/temptation;* 擊退敵人(拒絕誘惑); *~ a young man's advances,* discourage him. 拒絕一位年輕人的友誼或求愛。**2** cause a feeling of dislike in: 使厭惡;使不愉快: *His long, rough beard ~led her.* 他的長而粗的鬍子使她厭惡。 **~·lent** /-ənt ; -ənt/ *adj* tending to ~; unattractive; uninviting: 逐退的;驅開的;討人嫌的;討厭的: *~lent work/food.* 討厭的工作(食物)。*His manner is rather ~lent.* 他的態度頗令人厭惡。▭ *n* [U] sth that ~s, esp a preparation that ~s insects: 令人厭惡之物;(尤指)驅蟲劑: *Smear some of this mosquito ~lent on your legs.* 搽一些驅蚊劑在你的腿上。

re·pent /rɪˈpent ; rɪˈpɛnt/ *vi, vt* [VP2A, 3A, 6A, D] *~ (of)*, think with regret or sorrow of; be full of regret (about); wish one had not done (sth): 悔悟;懊悔;痛悔;後悔曾做(某事): *He ~ed of what he had done.* 他懊悔他的所作所爲。*Don't you ~ (of) having wasted your money so foolishly?* 你不後悔如此糊塗亂花錢嗎? *He has bitterly ~ed his folly.* 他痛悔他的愚行。*Have you nothing to ~ of?* 你沒有可懊悔的事嗎? **~·ance** /-əns ; -əns/ *n* [U] regret for wrongdoing: 悔悟;懊悔;痛悔;後悔: *show ~ance (for sth).* (對某事)表示悔悟。**~·ant** /-ənt ; -ənt/ *adj* feeling or showing ~ance: 悔悟的;懊悔的: *a ~ant sinner;* 悔悟的罪人; *~ant of his folly;* 懊悔其愚行; *the righteous and the ~ant.* 正直者與悔悟者。**~·ant·ly** *adv*

re·per·cussion /ˌriːpəˈkʌʃn ; ˌrɪpɚˈkʌʃən/ *n* **1** [U] springing back; driving or throwing back; [C] sth thrown or driven back; echoing sound: 彈回; 逐回;擊退;反響;反射;逐回或擊退之物;回聲: *the ~ of the waves from the rocks.* 從岩石上擊回的逆浪。**2** [C] (usu *pl*) far-reaching and indirect effect (of an event, etc): (通常用複數,指事件等之)久遠而間接的影響;反應: *The assassination of the President was followed by ~s throughout the whole country.* 總統被暗殺之後,全國均有反應。

rep·er·toire /ˈrepətwɑː(r) ; ˈrɛpɚˌtwɑr/ *n* [C] all the plays, songs, pieces, etc which a company, actor, musician, etc, is prepared to perform, etc: (劇團,演員,音樂家等所預備表演的)全部戲,歌,節目等;戲目;曲目: *She has a large ~ of songs.* 她能演唱很多歌。

rep·er·tory /ˈrepətrɪ *US:* -tɔːrɪ ; ˈrɛpɚˌtorɪ/ *n* (*pl* -ries) [C] **1** = repertoire. **ˈ~ company/theatre,**

(common abbr 常略作 *rep*) one in which the actors/plays are changed regularly (instead of having long runs as in most London theatres). 時常換演員或戲目的劇團 (戲院) (非如倫敦的大多數戲院作長期連續的演出)。 **2** store or collection, esp of facts, information, etc: (尤指事實,知識等之) 蒐集; 貯積: *My father is a ~ of useful information.* 家父是實用知識的寶庫。

rep·eti·tion /ˌrepɪˈtɪʃn ; ˌrɛpɪˈtɪʃən/ *n* **1** [U] repeating or being repeated; [C] instance of this: 重說; 重做; 重複; 複誦; 背誦; 循環: *after numerous ~s.* 在無數次的重複後。 **2** [C] further recurrence: 復現; 再發生: *Let there be no ~ of this,* Don't do it again. 不要再做這種事。 **3** [C] piece (of poetry, etc) set to be learnt by heart and repeated. 背誦文(詩等)。 **rep·eti·tious** /ˌrepɪˈtɪʃəs ; ˌrɛpɪˈtɪʃəs/, **re·peti·tive** /rɪˈpetətɪv ; rɪˈpɛtɪtɪv/ *adjj* characterized by ~: 重複的; 反覆的: *the repetitive work of a factory's production line.* 工廠生產線之反覆性的工作。

re·pine /rɪˈpaɪn ; rɪˈpaɪn/ *vi* [VP2A, 3A] ~ ***(at),*** (formal) be discontented with: (正式用語) (對…) 不滿: *~ at misfortune.* 怨懟不幸的遭遇。 ~ ***against,*** fret against: 抱怨: *~ against Providence.* 怨天。

re·place /rɪˈpleɪs ; rɪˈples/ *vt* **1** [VP6A, 15A] put back in its place: 放回; 置於原處: *~ a dictionary on the shelf;* 把字典放回架上; *~ the receiver,* ie after telephoning. (打電話後) 置聽筒於原處。 **2** [VP 6A] take the place of: 代替; 取代: *Have buses ~d trams in your town?* 在你居住的城市裡, 公共汽車已取代電車了嗎? *Can anything ~ a mother's love and care?* 有什麼東西能取代母親的愛和關懷嗎? **3** [VP14] ~ ***sb/sth by/with,*** supply as a substitute for: 以…代替: *~ coal by/with oil.* 以油替換煤。 **~·able** /-əbl ; -əbl̩/ *adj* that can be ~d. 可放回原處的; 可替換的。 **~·ment** *n* [U] replacing or being ~d: 放回; 代替; 替換: *the ~ment of worn-out parts;* 磨損零件的替換; [C] sb or sth that ~s: 替換之人或物: *get a ~ment* (ie sb to do one's work) *while one is away on holiday.* 外出度假時找一位代理工作的人。

re·play /ˌriːˈpleɪ ; riˈple/ *vt* [VP6A] play (eg a football match that was drawn) again. 重賽(如賽成平手的足球賽); 再播放。 □ *n* /ˈriːpleɪ ; ˈriˌple/ [C] ~ed match; ~ing of a record, etc. 重賽; (唱片等的) 重放。

re·plen·ish /rɪˈplenɪʃ ; rɪˈplɛnɪʃ/ *vt* [VP6A, 14] ~ ***(with),*** fill up (sth) again; get a new supply of or for: 再裝滿; 補充: *I must ~ my wardrobe.* 我必須添置衣服。 **~·ment** *n*

re·plete /rɪˈpliːt ; rɪˈplit/ *adj* ~ ***(with),*** (formal) filled with; holding as much as possible: (正式用語) 裝滿的; 充盈的; 飽足的: *~ with food;* 吃得飽飽的; *feeling ~;* 覺得飽; *a home ~ with every modern convenience.* 有各種現代設備的家庭。 **re·ple·tion** /rɪˈpliːʃn ; rɪˈpliʃən/ *n* [U] (formal) state of being ~: (正式用語) 裝滿; 充盈; 飽足: *Is it wrong to eat to repletion?* 吃得過飽是不是不好?

rep·lica /ˈreplɪkə ; ˈrɛplɪkə/ *n* [C] exact copy (esp one made by an artist of one of his own pictures): 複製品; 摹寫品 (尤指藝術家對自己作品的複製): *make a ~ of a painting.* 照一幅畫臨摹一次。

re·ply /rɪˈplaɪ ; rɪˈplaɪ/ *vi, vt* (*pt, pp* -plied) [VP2A, 3A, B, 9] ~ ***(to),*** give as an answer to, in words or action: (以話語或行動) 回答; 答覆: *He failed to ~ (to my question).* 他無法回答(我的問題)。 *'Certainly not,' he replied.* '當然不會啦,'他回答。 *He replied that I could please myself.* 他回答說我可以隨我自己的意思。 *The enemy replied to our fire,* fired in return. 敵人向我們還擊。 *David Jones rose to ~ for* (= speak on behalf of) *the guests.* 大衛·瓊斯站起來代表來賓致答辭。 □ *n* act of ~ing; what is replied: 回答; 答覆: *He made no ~.* 他沒有回答。 *What did he say in ~?* 他如何答覆? ˌ**~-ˈpaid,** (of a telegram, letter, etc) with the cost of the ~ prepaid by the sender. (指電報等) 回電費用 (回郵等) 已付。

re·point /riːˈpɔɪnt ; riˈpɔɪnt/ *vt* [VP6A] point (brickwork, etc) again. 將(建築物的砌磚部分等之)接縫處再度用水泥或灰泥填塞起來。 ⇨ point²(5).

re·port¹ /rɪˈpɔːt ; rɪˈport/ *n* **1** [C] account of, statement about, sth heard, seen, done, etc: (對所聞,所見,所做等的) 報導; 報告; 記事: *~s on the state of the roads,* eg from an automobile association; 關於路況的報告; *the annual ~ of a business company;* 一商號的年度報告; *the chairman's ~,* ⇨ *chairman* at chair; ˈ*law ~s,* ie of trials, etc, in the law courts; 判決錄 (報導法庭審理案件的情形等); *a school ~,* eg by teachers about a pupil, with his examination marks, etc; 學生成績報告單; *newspaper ~s.* 新聞報導。 **2** [U] common talk; rumour; [C] piece of gossip: 傳聞; 謠言; 閒話: *R~ has it that...,* People are saying that.... 據說…。 *We have only ~(s)* (ie no reliable news) *to go on.* 我們只有一些傳聞可資依據。 *Don't listen to idle ~s.* 勿聽信閒話。 **3** [U] (formal) repute; way a person or thing is spoken about: (正式用語) 名譽; 名聲: *of good/evil ~.* 名譽好(壞)的。 **4** [C] sound of an explosion: 爆炸聲: *the ~ of a gun.* 槍砲聲。 *It went off with a loud ~.* 它砰然一聲爆炸了。

re·port² /rɪˈpɔːt ; rɪˈport/ *vt, vi* **1** [VP6A, D, 9, 25, 3A, 15B] give an account of (sth seen, heard, done, etc); give as news: 報導; 報告 (所見,所聞,所做等的事物); 當作新聞敘述: *The discovery of a new planet has been ~ed.* 據報導已發現一顆新行星。 *It is ~ed that another earth satellite has been put into orbit.* 據報導另一地球衛星已被射入軌道。 *They ~ed the enemy to be ten miles away.* 他們說敵人在十哩外。 *He ~ed having seen the escaped convict.* 他稱述曾看見那個逃犯。 ~ **on sth,** give news about or comment on it: 報導某事; 評論某事: *Jim's been sent to Hong Kong to ~ on the situation there.* 吉姆已被派往香港報導該地之情形。 ~ **sth out,** (US) return it with comment: (美) 送回並附審查意見: *The committee ~ed the proposal out in record time.* 委員會以無比的快速送回該提案並附加審查意見。 ~ ***progress,*** state what has been done so far. 報告經過或進展情形。 **~·ed·ly** *adv* according to report(s). 據報導; 據說。 **2** [VP6A, 2A] take down (eg in shorthand) the words of speeches, etc for newspapers, etc: 為報館等記錄 (如用速記) 演說詞等: *~ a speech/a Parliamentary debate;* 寫新聞稿報導演說 (國會辯論); *~ for 'The Times',* be a correspondent on its staff. 擔任'泰晤士報'的記者。 **~ed speech,** = indirect speech. ⇨ indirect. **3** [VP3A, 14, 15A] ~ ***(oneself) (to sb/sth) (for sth),*** go (somewhere), and announce that one has come, that one is ready for work, duty, etc: (向某處) 報到; 到差; 復命: *~ for duty at the office;* 到辦公室報到; *~ to the Manager.* 向經理復命。 *The officer was told to ~ (himself) to headquarters.* 那軍官奉命前往司令部報到。 **4** [VP6A, 14] ~ ***sb/sth (to sb) (for sth),*** make a complaint against sb (to authorities): (向當局) 告發; 檢舉: *~ an official for insolence.* 告發一官員無禮。 *I shall have to ~ your unpunctuality to the Manager.* 我勢將向經理舉發你不守時。 **~·age** /ˌrepɔːˈtɑːʒ ; rɪˈportɪdʒ/ *n* [U] (typical style of) ~ing events for newspapers. 新聞報導; 新聞報導式的文體。 **~·er** *n* person who ~s for a newspaper, for radio or TV. 記者; 通訊員。

re·pose¹ /rɪˈpəʊz ; rɪˈpoz/ *vt* [VP14] ~ ***sth in sth/sb,*** (formal) place (trust, confidence, etc) in: (正式用語) 把 (信用,信心等) 寄託於: *Don't ~ too much confidence in that man/his honesty/his promises, etc.* 不要對那人 (他的誠實,他的諾言等) 過於相信。

re·pose² /rɪˈpəʊz ; rɪˈpoz/ *vt, vi* (formal) (正式用語) **1** [VP6A, 15A, 2A, C] rest; give rest or support to: 休息; 使休息或依靠: *a girl reposing in a hammock;* 在吊床上休息的女郎; *~ one's head on a cushion;* 將頭靠在墊子上; *~ onself.* 休息; 歇息。 *Below this stone ~ the mortal remains of....* 在此石塊下長眠的是…的遺骸。 **2** [VP3A] ~ ***on,*** be based or supported on. 依靠。□ *n* [U] (formal) (正式用語) **1** rest; sleep: 休息;睡眠: *earn a night's ~;* 獲得一夜的睡眠; *disturb sb's ~.* 打擾某人的安眠。*Her face is beautiful in ~.* 她的面貌在睡眠中很美。 **2** peaceful, restful or quiet behaviour or appearance: 安靜的行爲或外表: *His attitude lacked ~*, ease of manner. 他的態度不安詳。**~·ful** /-fl; -fḷ/ *adj* calm; quiet. 安靜的;沉靜的。

re·posi·tory /rɪˈpɒzɪtrɪ *US:* -tɔːrɪ; rɪˈpɑzəˌtorɪ/ *n* [C] (*pl* -ries) place where things are or may be stored: 貯藏物品的地方;倉庫;棧房: *The drawers in my desk are repositories for all sorts of useless papers.* 我書桌的抽屜是各種無用之文件的貯存處。*My grandfather is a ~ of interesting facts.* 我的祖父有滿腹的有趣的事實。

re·pot /ˌriːˈpɒt; riˈpɑt/ *vt* transfer (a plant) from one pot to another (usu larger) pot. 將(植物)自一盆移植到另一(較大的)盆。

rep·re·hend /ˌreprɪˈhend; ˌrɛprɪˈhɛnd/ *vt* [VP6A] rebuke, reprove: 責難;譴責: *~ sb's conduct.* 指責某人的行爲。**rep·re·hen·sible** /ˌreprɪˈhensəbl; ˌrɛprɪˈhɛnsəbḷ/ *adj* deserving to be ~ed. 應受責難的;該當譴責的。

rep·re·sent¹ /ˌreprɪˈzent; ˌrɛprɪˈzɛnt/ *vt* **1** [VP6A] be, give, make, a picture, sign, symbol or example of: 表示;表現;象徵: *Phonetic symbols ~ sounds.* 音標表示聲音。*This painting ~s a hunting scene.* 這是一幅出獵圖。*The new ambassador ~s the best traditions of his country.* 這位新大使表現了其國家最好的傳統。 **2** [VP16A, 25, 9] declare to be; describe (*as*); allege (that...): 聲稱;宣稱(與as連用): *He ~ed himself as an expert.* 他聲言自己是一位專家。*I am not what you have ~ed me to be.* 我並不是像你所說的那種人。 **3** [VP6A, 9, 14] *~ sth (to sb),* explain; make clear: 說明;使明白: *Let me try to ~ my ideas to you in another way/in different terms.* 讓我試用另外一種方式(不同的說法)向你說明我的想法。 **4** [VP6A, 14, 9] *~ sth (to sb),* convey; express: 傳達;表達: *They ~ed their grievances to the Governor.* 他們向總督陳情。*I will ~ to him the risks he is running.* 我將向他說明他所冒的危險。*He ~ed to the magistrates that the offender was only a child.* 他向地方法官說明犯罪者僅是個小孩子。 **5** [VP6A] act or speak for; be MP for; be agent for: 代表;爲…國會議員;代理: *members* (ie MP's) *~ing Welsh constituencies.* 代表威爾斯各選區的國會議員們。*Many countries were ~ed by their ambassadors at the Independence Day celebrations.* 慶祝美國獨立紀念日時,許多國家都派其大使代表參加。*Our firm is ~ed in India and Pakistan by Mr Hall.* 本商號在印度和巴基斯坦的代表是賀爾先生。 **6** [VP6A] act (a play, etc); play the part of, on the stage. 演出(戲等);扮演…角色。**~·ation** /ˌreprɪzenˈteɪʃn; ˌrɛprɪzɛnˈteʃən/ *n* **1** [U] ~ing or being ~ed; [C] that which is ~ed: 表示;象徵;聲言;陳述;說明;代表;演出;扮演;所表示、聲言、說明、代表、扮演等之事物: *no taxation without ~ation,* ie citizens should not be taxed without being ~ed (in Parliament, etc); 議會中無代表者不應納稅; *an unusual ~ation of 'Hamlet'.* 一次不同凡響的'哈姆雷特'的演出。 **proportional ~ation,** an electoral system designed so that minority parties, etc are ~ed (in a legislative assembly) in proportion to their strength. 比例代表制(少數黨按其實力之大小推選代表的一種選舉制度)。 **2** [C] (esp) polite protest or remonstrance: (尤指)有禮貌的抗議;陳情: *make ~ations to the Inspector of Taxes about an excessive assessment.* 就過高估稅向稅務稽查官陳情。

re·pre·sent² /ˌriːprɪˈzent; ˌriprɪˈzɛnt/ *vt* submit again: 再送;再提出: *Your cheque has been returned; please ~ it when you have funds in your account.* 你的支票被退回了,請在你的帳戶內有存款時再開一張。

rep·re·sen·ta·tive /ˌreprɪˈzentətɪv; ˌrɛprɪˈzɛntətɪv/ *adj* **1** *~ (of),* serving to portray or show; serving as an example of a class or group; containing examples of a number of classes or groups: 表明的;象徵的;代表的: *manuscripts ~ of monastic life;* 說明寺院生活的文稿; *a ~ collection of domestic utensils of the Middle Ages.* 所收藏的一批具有代表性的中世紀家庭用具。 **2** consisting of elected deputies; based on representation by such elected deputies: 由選出之代表組成的;代議制的: *~ government/institutions.* 代議政府(制度)。□ *n* [C] *~ (of),* **1** example; typical specimen (of a group or class). 例子;(一羣或一類的)典型。 **2** person elected or appointed to represent or act for others: 代表: *send a ~ to a conference;* 派代表參加會議; *sole ~s of the XYZ Petrol Company in Cardiff;* XYZ 石油公司派駐加地夫的總代理; *~s of the press,* newspaper reporters; 新聞記者; *our ~* (= MP) *in the House of Commons.* 我們在下議院的代表(國會議員)。 **the House of R~s,** the lower house of the US Congress or of a state legislature. (美)(國會之)衆議院;(州議會之)下院。

re·press /rɪˈpres; rɪˈprɛs/ *vt* [VP6A] keep or put down or under; prevent from finding an outlet: 鎮壓;抑制;阻止: *~ a revolt;* 鎮壓暴動; *~ sedition;* 消弭叛變; *~ a sneeze;* 抑止噴嚏; *~an impulse;* 抑制衝動; *~ed emotions.* 壓抑的情緒。**~ed** *adj* suffering from repression(b). 受壓制的;被抑制的。**re·pres·sion** /rɪˈpreʃn; rɪˈprɛʃən/ *n* **1** [U] ~ing or being ~ed. 鎮壓;抑制。 **2** [U] (psych) forcing into the unconscious of impulses and desires, esp those in conflict with accepted standards of conduct, often resulting in abnormal behaviour; [C] impulse or instinct ~ed in this way. (心理)壓抑(把本能的衝動和欲望,尤其是與一般公認的行爲標準相衝突者,壓抑於非意識中,往往因而導致行爲異常);被壓抑的行爲或本能。**re·pres·sive** /rɪˈpresɪv; rɪˈprɛsɪv/ *adj* serving or tending to ~: 鎮壓的;抑制的;壓抑的: *~ive legislation.* 鎮壓性的立法。*The ~ive measures taken by the police were condemned in Parliament.* 警方所採取的鎮壓措施在國會中受到抨擊。

re·prieve /rɪˈpriːv; rɪˈpriv/ *vt* [VP6A] postpone or delay punishment (esp the execution of sb condemned to death); (fig) give relief for a short time (from danger, trouble, etc). 暫緩處決(被判死刑的人);(喻)暫時減輕(危險,困難等)。□ *n* [C] (order giving authority for) postponement or remission of punishment (esp by death); (fig) delay or respite: 暫緩處決;暫緩處決的命令;(喻)暫緩;暫止: *grant (sb) a ~.* 准許(某人)暫緩受處決。

re·pri·mand /ˈreprɪmɑːnd *US:* -mænd; ˈrɛprəˌmænd/ *vt* [VP6A] rebuke (sb) severely and officially (for a fault, etc). 申斥;懲戒(某人)。□ *n* [C] official rebuke. (當局的)申斥;懲戒。

re·print /ˌriːˈprɪnt; riˈprɪnt/ *vt* [VP6A] print again; print a new impression of: 重印;再版: *The book is ~ing,* being ~ed. 該書在重印中。□ *n* /ˈriːprɪnt; ˈriˌprɪnt/ [C] new impression of sth printed (usu without alterations). 再版;再版本(通常未加修訂)。⇨ edition.

re·prisal /rɪˈpraɪzl; rɪˈpraɪzḷ/ *n* **1** [U] paying back injury with injury: 以牙還牙;報復: *do sth by way of ~.* 出於報復而做某事。 **2** (*pl*) acts of retaliation, esp of one country on another during a war. (複)報復行爲(尤指在戰時一國對他國所做者)。

re·proach /rɪˈprəʊtʃ; rɪˈprotʃ/ *vt* [VP6A, 14] *~ sb (for/with sth),* find fault with (sb, usu with a feeling of sorrow, or suggesting the need for sorrow): 責備(某人,通常帶着難過的心情,或含示需要感到難過): *~ sb with extravagance/for being late.* 責備某人浪費(遲到)。*We have nothing to ~ ourselves with,* have done nothing we need regret. 我們沒有值得自責的事。□ *n* **1** [U] ~ing: 責備: *a term/look of ~.* 責備的話(眼光)。 **2** [C] instance of ~ing; word, phrase, etc that ~es: 責備之實例;責備的字、詞句等: *She heaped ~es upon her sister.*

她狠狠地責備她的妹妹。 **3** [U] state of disgrace or discredit: 恥辱;不名譽: *bring ~ upon oneself.* 自取其辱。***above／beyond ~,*** perfect; blameless. 無可訾議的;無瑕疵的。 **4** [C] ~ ***(to),*** sth that brings disgrace or discredit (to): 帶來不名譽的事物: *slums that are a ~ to the city council.* 給市議會帶來不名譽的貧民窟。 **~·ful** /-fl ; -fl/ *adj* full of ~; expressing ~: 責備的;表示譴責的: *a ~ful look.* 責備的眼光。 **~·fully** /-fəlɪ ; -fəlɪ/ *adv*

rep·ro·bate /ˈreprəbeɪt ; ˈrɛprəˌbet/ *vt* [VP6A] express or feel strong disapproval of. 非難;責備;拒絕;反對。 □ *n* depraved person; person with no respect for moral behaviour. 墮落的人;惡棍;無賴。 **rep·ro·ba·tion** /ˌreprəˈbeɪʃn ; ˌrɛprəˈbeʃən/ *n* [U].

re·pro·duce /ˌri:prəˈdju:s *US:* -ˈdu:s ; ˌriprəˈdjus/ *vt, vi* **1** [VP6A] cause to be seen, heard, etc again: 使再被見到,聽到等;使重現;播放;放映;複製: *~ music from magnetic tape.* 播放錄音帶上的音樂。 *This record／record-player ~s every sound perfectly.* 這唱片(電唱機)完美地放出聲音。 *The artist has ~d your features very well in this portrait.* 這藝術家在此畫像中把你的容貌表現得維妙維肖。 **2** [VP6A, 2A] bring forth as offspring; bring about a natural increase: 生殖;繁殖: *~ one's kind;* 繁殖;生殖; *plants that ~ by spores,* eg ferns. 由芽胞繁殖的植物(如羊齒植物)。 **3** [VP6A] grow anew (a part that is lost, etc): 再生(已損失的部分等): *Can lizards ~ their tails?* 蜥蜴的尾巴斷了以後能再生嗎? *Human beings cannot ~ lost limbs.* 人類的肢體斷掉以後不能再生。 **~r** *n* one who, that which, ~s. 複製者;複製器;有再生能力的動物。 **re·pro·duc·ible** /-əbl ; -əbl/ *adj* that can be ~d. 可複製的;可再生的;可重現的。 **re·pro·duc·tion** /ˌri:prəˈdʌkʃn ; ˌriprəˈdʌkʃən/ *n* [U] process of reproducing; [C] sth ~d; copy of sth, esp a work of art. 複製;再生;重現;生殖;複製或再生之物;(尤指藝術作品的)複製品。 **re·pro·duc·tive** /ˌri:prəˈdʌktɪv ; ˌriprəˈdʌktɪv/ *adj* reproducing; for, relating to, reproduction: 複製的;再生的;生殖的;適於,有關複製或再生的: *reproductive organs.* 生殖器官。

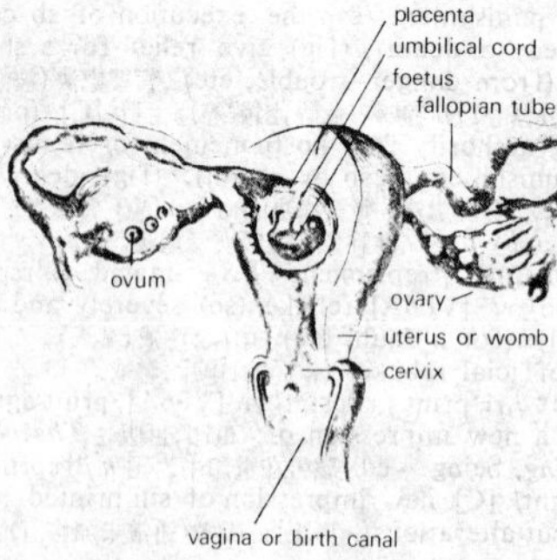

the female reproductive organs in early pregnancy

re·proof[1] /rɪˈpru:f ; rɪˈpruf/ *n* **1** [U] blame; finding fault: 譴責;非難: *a glance of ~;* 譴責的一瞥; *conduct deserving of ~.* 該受責備的行爲。 **2** [C] expression of blame or disapproval: 譴責之詞: *administer sharp ~s.* 作嚴厲的譴責。

re·proof[2] /ˌri:ˈpru:f ; ˌriˈpruf/ *vt* [VP6A] make (a coat, etc) waterproof again. 使(外衣等)再能防水。

re·prove /rɪˈpru:v ; rɪˈpruv/ *vt* [VP6A, 14] ***~ sb (for sth),*** find fault with; say sharp words to: 非難;責罵;譴責: *The priest ~d the people for not attending church services.* 牧師責備那些人不上教堂做禮拜。 **re·prov·ing·ly** *adv*

rep·tile /ˈreptaɪl *US:* -tl ; ˈrɛptl/ *n* cold-blooded egg-laying animal that creeps or crawls, eg *a lizard, tortoise, crocodile, snake.* (冷血的卵生)爬行動物;爬蟲(如蜥蜴,龜,鱷魚,蛇)。 ⇨ the illus here and at snake. 參看 snake 之插圖。 **rep·til·ian** /repˈtɪlɪən ; rɛpˈtɪlɪən/ *adj* of, or like a ~. 爬蟲類的;似爬蟲類的。

re·pub·lic /rɪˈpʌblɪk ; rɪˈpʌblɪk/ *n* **1** (country with a) system of government in which the elected representatives of the people are supreme, with an elected head (the President), as eg in the US, France, India. 共和國;共和政體。 (in France) (法國) **the First R~,** 1789–1804; 第一共和, 1789–1804; **the Second R~,** 1848–1852; 第二共和, 1848–1852; **the Third R~,** 1871–1940; 第三共和, 1871–1940; **the Fourth R~,** 1947–1958; 第四共和, 1947–1958; **the Fifth R~,** from 1958. 第五共和, 1958–。 **2** any society in which the members have equal rights and privileges: (組成分子享有平等權利的)任何社團: *the ~ of letters,* literary men as a class. 文學界;文壇。

re·pub·li·can /rɪˈpʌblɪkən ; rɪˈpʌblɪkən/ *adj* of, relating to, supporting the principles of, a republic. 共和國的;共和政體的;有關共和的;贊成共和的。 □ *n* **1** person who favours ~ government. 擁護共和政體者。 **2 R~,** member of one of the two main political parties in the US (the other is *Democrat*). (美國兩大政黨中之)共和黨員(另一爲'民主黨員')。 **~·ism** /-ɪzəm ; -ˌɪzəm/ *n* [U] (adherence to) ~ principles. 共和主義;對共和主義的擁護。

re·pudi·ate /rɪˈpju:dɪeɪt ; rɪˈpjudɪˌet/ *vt* [VP6A] **1** disown; say that one will have nothing more to do with: 不承認與…有關; 與…斷絕關係: *~ an old friend／a wicked son.* 棄絕一位老友(一個敗家子)。 **2** refuse to accept or acknowledge: 拒絕接受或承認;否認: *~ the authorship of an article,* declare that one did not write it. 否認爲某篇文章的作者。 **3** refuse to pay (an obligation or debt). 拒償(債務)。 **re·pudi·ation** /rɪˌpju:dɪˈeɪʃn ; rɪˌpjudɪˈeʃən/ *n*

re·pug·nant /rɪˈpʌgnənt ; rɪˈpʌgnənt/ *adj* ~ ***(to),*** distasteful; causing a feeling of dislike or opposition: 討厭的;令人不悅或起反感的: *I find his views／proposals ~.* 我發覺他的觀點(提議)令人起反感。 *All food was ~ to me during my illness.* 生病時所有的食物都使我感到厭惡。 **re·pug·nance** /-nəns ; -nəns/ *n* [U] ~ ***(to),*** strong dislike or distaste: 嫌棄;討厭: *a great repugnance to accept charity;* 對接受濟助的厭惡; *the repugnance she has to writing letters.* 她對寫信的厭惡。

re·pulse /rɪˈpʌls ; rɪˈpʌls/ *vt* [VP6A] **1** repel; drive back (the enemy); resist (an attack) successfully. 驅逐; 逐退(敵人); 擊退(攻擊)。 **2** (not replaceable by *repel*) refuse to accept (sb's help, friendly offers, etc); discourage (a person) by unfriendly treatment. (不可用 repel 代替)拒絕接受(某人的幫助,友好的建議等);排斥(某人)。 □ *n* repulsing or being ~d. 擊退;被擊退;拒絕;排斥。 **re·pul·sion** /rɪˈpʌlʃn ; rɪˈpʌlʃən/ *n* [U] **1** feeling of dislike or distaste: 厭惡;嫌忌: *feel repulsion for sb.* 厭惡某人。 **2** (phys) (opp of *attraction*) tendency of bodies to repel each other. (物理)推斥;斥力(爲 attraction 之相反字)。

re·pul·sive /rɪˈpʌlsɪv ; rɪˈpʌlsɪv/ *adj* **1** causing a feeling of disgust: 令人厭惡的; 討厭的: *a ~ sight;* 使人厭惡的景象; *a ~-looking beggar.* 樣子令人討厭的乞丐。 **2** (phys) repelling; exercising repulsion(2): (物理)拒斥的;推斥的: *~ forces.* 斥力;推力。 **~·ly** *adv* in a ~ manner: 討厭地;拒斥地: *~ly ugly.* 醜惡得令人厭惡。

repu·table /ˈrepjʊtəbl ; ˈrɛpjətəbl/ *adj* respected; of good repute: 受尊敬的;名譽好的: *~ occupations;* 高尚的職業; *a ~ wine merchant.* 名譽好的酒商。 **repu·tably** /-əblɪ ; -əblɪ/ *adv*

repu·ta·tion /ˌrepjʊˈteɪʃn ; ˌrɛpjəˈteʃən/ *n* [U, C] the general opinion about the character, qualities, etc of sb or sth: 名聲;名譽: *a man of high ~;* 名譽很好的人; *have a good ~ as a doctor;* 是個很有名望的醫生; *have a ~ for courage;* 以勇敢著稱; *make a ~ for oneself;* 爲自己博得名聲; *have the ~ of*

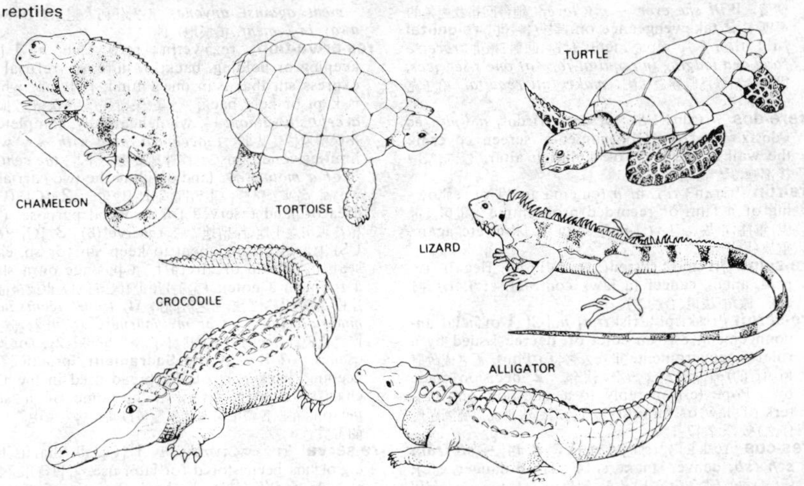

being a miser. 有守財奴之稱。 ***live up to one's ~,*** live in the way that people expect (because of one's ~). 行爲與聲譽相符;不負衆望。

re·pute /rɪ'pju:t ; rɪ'pjut/ *vt* [VP25] (usu *passive*) (通常用被動語態) ***be ~d as/to be,*** be generally considered or reported (to be), be thought of as: 被認爲;被當作: *He is ~ed (to be) very wealthy.* 他被認爲很富有。 *He is ~d (as/to be) the best surgeon in Paris.* 一般認爲他是巴黎最好的外科醫生。 *He is well/ill/highly ~d,* thought or spoken of. 他的名譽好(不好,很好)。 **~d** *attrib adj* generally considered to be (but with some element of doubt): 一般認爲的;號稱的(帶有若干懷疑的成分): *the ~d father of the child;* 據說是那孩子的父親的人; *his ~d learning.* 他那被公認的學問。 **re·put·ed·ly** *adv* □ *n* [U] **1** reputation (good or bad): (好的或壞的)名聲;名譽: *know a man by ~;* 由某人的名聲而知其人; *be held in high ~;* 享有好名聲; *be in bad ~ with sb.* 對某人喪失信譽。 **2** good reputation: 美名;聲望: *wines of ~;* 名酒; *a doctor of ~.* 名醫。

re·quest /rɪ'kwest ; rɪ'kwɛst/ *n* **1** [U] asking or being asked: 請求;被求: *We came at your ~/at the ~ of Mr X.* 我們應你(X 先生)的請求而來。 *Buses stop here by ~,* if signalled to do so. 有人招呼,公共汽車才在這裡停車。 *This is a ~ stop.* 這是個招呼站。 *Catalogues of our books will be sent on ~.* 我們的書目函索卽寄。 **2** [C] expression of desire for sth: 請求;請求書: *repeated ~s for help;* 一再請求幫助; *make a ~ for quiet;* 請求安靜; *your ~ that I should lecture on Pakistan.* 你要我以巴基斯坦爲題作演講的要求。 **3** [C] thing asked for: 所請求之事物: *You shall have your ~.* 你就會得到你所要的東西。 *All my ~s were granted.* 我所請求之事全被允准了。 **4** [U] state of being in demand, sought after. 需要。 ***in ~,*** often asked for. 有必要;受歡迎。 □ *vt* [VP6A, 9, 17] ***~ sth (from/of sb); ~ sb to do sth,*** make a ~: (向某人)請求某事物;請求(某人做某事): *Visitors are ~ed not to touch the exhibits,* as a notice in a museum, etc. 來賓請勿動展覽品(如博物館等中之告示)。 *All I ~ of you is that you should be early.* 我對你的唯一請求是要你早點到。 *I ~ed him to use/~ed that he (should) use his influence on my behalf.* 我請求他爲我施用他的影響力。

requiem /'rekwɪəm ; 'rikwɪəm/ *n* [C] (musical setting for a) special mass for the repose of the soul of a dead person. (爲死者擧行的)追思彌撒;安靈彌撒;安魂曲;鎭魂曲;奠祭曲。

re·quire /rɪ'kwaɪə(r) ; rɪ'kwaɪr/ *vt* **1** [VP6A, D, 9] need; depend on for success, fulfilment, etc: 需要;依靠…而成功,完成等: *We ~ extra help.* 我們需要額外的幫助。 *Does this machine ~ much attention?* 這機器需要經常照料嗎? *The situation there ~s that I should be present.* 那邊的情況需要我到場。 **2** [VP6A, 9, 14, 17] ***~ sth (of sb); ~ sb to do sth; ~ that...,*** (often passive) (formal) order; demand; insist upon as a right or by authority: (常用被動語態)(正式用語)命令;要求;(作爲權利或依據權利而)堅持: *Students are ~d to take three papers in English literature.* 按規定所有學生都要答三份英國文學的試卷。 *What do you ~ of me?* 你對我有何要求? *It is ~d that you arrive at 8 am.* 你必須上午八時到達。 *I have done all that is ~d by law.* 我已照法律所規定的一切做了。 *These books are ~d reading,* must be read, eg for an examination. 這些書是指定的讀物。 **~·ment** *n* sth ~d or needed: 要求或需要之物;需求;必要條件;規定: *fulfil the ~ments of the law;* 履行法律之規定; *meet sb's ~ments,* do what he wants done. 滿足某人的要求。

requi·site /'rekwɪzɪt ; 'rɛkwəzɪt/ *n, adj* ***~ (for),*** (thing) needed or required by circumstances or for success: 必需品;需要物;需要的;必要的: *We supply every ~ for travel/all travelling ~s.* 我們供應一切旅行用的必需品。 *They lack the ~ capital for expanding their business.* 他們缺乏擴大營業的必要資金。

requi·si·tion /ˌrekwɪ'zɪʃn ; ˌrɛkwə'zɪʃən/ *n* [U] act of requiring or demanding; [C] formal and usu written demand (*for* sth or *that* sth should be done): 需要;要求;徵用;(通常指書面的)正式要求或請求;申請或徵用文書(與 for 或名詞子句連用): *a ~ for supplies,* eg by army authorities during a war; 徵發補給的文書; *make a ~ on the citizens for stores.* 向民衆徵用軍需品。 *The hotel bus was in constant ~ (= was needed all the time) for bringing visitors from, and taking them back to, the railway station.* 旅館的公用汽車經常應需要往返火車站接運旅客。 □ *vt* [VP6A, 14] ***~ (for),*** make a ~ for: 要求;徵用;徵發: *~ food for the troops;* 徵發供應部隊的食物; *~ sb's services;* 徵調某人服務; *~ a town for supplies/lodgings,* eg during a war. 向一城市徵用補給品(住處)(例如在戰時)。

re·quite /rɪ'kwaɪt ; rɪ'kwaɪt/ *vt* [VP6A, 14] ***~ sth/sb (with sth),*** (formal) (正式用語) **1** repay; give in return: 付還;回報;酬謝: *~ kindness with ingratitude;* 以怨報德; *~ an obligation.* 報恩;還人

情債。*Will she ever ~ my love?* 她會回報我對她的愛嗎？ **2** take vengeance on. 報復；報仇。**re·qui·tal** /-tl ; -tl/ *n* [U] repayment: 付還；回報；報仇：*receive food and lodging in requital for/of one's services;* 得到食宿以爲服務之報酬；*make full requital.* 給予充分的酬答。

rere·dos /ˈrɪədɒs *US:* ˈrerədɒs ; ˈrɪrdɑs/ *n* (*pl* ~es /-dɒsɪz ; -dɑsɪz/) [C] ornamental screen covering the wall at the back of a church altar. (教堂祭壇後部遮覆牆壁的)裝飾屏風。

re·run /ˈriːrʌn ; riˈrʌn/ *n* (cinema and TV) reshowing of a film or recorded programme. (電影及電視)重播；重放。□ *vt* (-nn-) show a film, etc again. 重放(影片等)。

re·scind /rɪˈsɪnd ; rɪˈsɪnd/ *vt* [VP6A] (legal) repeal, annul, cancel (a law, contract, etc). (法律)廢止；撤銷(法規、合約等)。

re·script /ˈriːskrɪpt ; ˈriskrɪpt/ *n* [C] **1** official announcement, esp an edict or decree issued by a ruler or government. 正式公告；(尤指由統治者或政府所頒行的)佈告；敕令；政令；法令。 **2** decision made by a Pope (esp in reply to a question on matters of law or morality). (教宗對法律或道德問題所作之)敕答；咨覆書。

res·cue /ˈreskjuː ; ˈrɛskju/ *vt* [VP6A, 14] **~ *sb from sth/sb,*** deliver, make safe (from danger, etc); set free: (從危險等中)救出；解救；使免於：*~ a child from drowning;* 救出一小孩免於溺斃；*~ a man from captivity;* 營救一人免於被俘；*~ a drunkard,* persuade him to give up drinking; 勸服一醉漢不再酗酒；*~ sb's name from oblivion,* prevent his name from being quite forgotten. 使某人的名聲不致湮沒。□ *n* [U] rescuing or being ~d. 救出；解救。***come/go to the ~/to sb's ~,*** help him; [C] instance of this: 援救(救助某人)；救出或解救的實例：*three ~s from drowning in one afternoon.* 在一個下午三人獲救而免於溺斃。**res·cuer** *n*

re·search /rɪˈsɜːtʃ *US:* ˈriːsɜːtʃ ; ˈrisɝtʃ/ *n* [U, C] (not usu with *many* or numerals) investigation undertaken in order to discover new facts, get additional information, etc: (通常不與 many 或數字連用)研究；調查；探索：*be engaged in ~;* 從事研究；*busy with ~ work;* 忙於研究工作；*carry out (a) ~/~es into the causes of cancer.* 作癌症之起因的研究工作。*His ~es have been successful.* 他的研究工作很成功。*R~ students usually supplement their income by teaching.* 研究生通常以兼課來貼補收入。*R~ workers are examining the problem.* 研究人員在審查該問題。□ *vi* [VP2A, 3A] ***~ (into),*** make ~es (into a problem, etc). 從事(對某問題等的)研究。**~er** *n*

re·seat /ˌriːˈsiːt ; riˈsit/ *vt* [VP6A] **1** supply with a new seat: 供以新座位或座部：*~ an old pair of trousers/a cane chair.* 換舊褲(籐椅)的座部。 **2** sit on a seat again: 再就座：*She stood up and then ~ed herself more comfortably.* 她站起來，然後又更舒服地坐下去。

re·sem·blance /rɪˈzembləns ; rɪˈzɛmbləns/ *n* **1** [U] likeness; similarity: 相似；類似：*There's very little ~ between them.* 他們之間的相似處很少。 **2** [C] point or degree of likeness or similarity: 相似之點或程度：*The boys show great ~s—are they twins?* 這兩個男孩有許多相像之處——他們是雙胞胎嗎？

re·semble /rɪˈzembl ; rɪˈzɛmbl/ *vt* [VP6B] be like; be similar to: 相似；類似：*She ~s her mother.* 她像她母親。*They ~ each other in shape but not in colour.* 它們的形狀相似，但顏色不同。

re·sent /rɪˈzent ; rɪˈzɛnt/ *vt* [VP6A, C, 19C] feel bitter, indignant or angry at: 對…感覺不愉快；憤恨；怨恨：*~ criticism.* 怨恨批評。*Does he ~ my being here?* 我在此地他感覺不愉快嗎？ **~·ful** /-fl ; -fl/ *adj* feeling or showing ~ment; inclined to ~. 憤恨的；怨恨的；易起怨恨的。**~·fully** /-fəlɪ ; -fəlɪ/ *adv* **~·ment** *n* [U] feeling that one has when insulted, ignored, injured, etc: 憤恨；怨恨：*bear/feel no ~ment against anyone;* 不對任何人抱怨恨；*walk away in ~ment.* 憤恨地走開。

res·er·va·tion /ˌrezəˈveɪʃn ; ˌrɛzɚˈveʃən/ *n* **1** [U] keeping or holding back; failure or refusal to express sth that is in one's mind; [C] that which is kept or held back: 隱藏；保留；隱藏或保留之事物：*accept sth without ~,* wholeheartedly, completely; 不保留地接受某事物；*accept a plan with ~s,* with limiting conditions; 有條件地接受一計畫；*the central ~ of a motorway,* land dividing the two carriageways. 高速公路雙向車道間的分隔地帶。 **2** [C] (US) area of land reserved for a special purpose. (美)留待專用之土地；保留地。⇨ reserve¹(5). **3** [C] (esp US) travel arrangement to keep sth for sb, eg a seat in a train or aircraft, a passage on a ship, a room in a hotel: (尤美)預定；保留(如火車或班機之座位、輪船之艙位、旅館之房間)：*My travel agents have made all the ~s for my journey.* 我的旅行經紀人已爲我把行程中的一切安排好了。⇨ book²(2), for GB usages. **4 R~ of the Sacrament,** practice of keeping back part of the bread used in the Eucharist for later use, eg at the home of a sick person. 在聖餐禮中保留部分麵包以備在病人家中等食用的習慣。

re·serve¹ /rɪˈzɜːv ; rɪˈzɝv/ *n* **1** [C] sth that is being or has been stored for later use: 貯以待用之物：*a ~ of food;* 存糧；*the bank's ~s,* ie of money; 銀行的儲備金；*the company's ~s,* its undivided profits; 商行之公積金(未分派之利潤)；*the 'gold ~,* ie to cover the issue of notes; (銀行發行鈔票之)黃金準備；(attrib) (形容用法) *a '~ fund;* 準備金；預備金；*his ~ strength.* 他所儲存的氣力。 **2** (mil) military forces kept back for use when needed. (軍)預備隊；後備軍。 **3 the R~,** forces outside the regular Navy, Army and Air Force, liable to be called out if needed. (正規之海陸空軍以外的)後備海軍、陸軍及空軍；預備役。 **4** [U] ***in ~,*** kept back unused, but available if needed: 儲藏；保留：*have/hold a little money in ~.* 儲存一些錢。 **5** [C] place or area reserved for some special use or purpose: 留待專用的地方或區域：*a 'game ~,* eg in Africa, for the preservation of wild animals; 獵物保留地；禁獵區(如非洲之野生動物保護區)；*a 'forest ~.* 森林保留地；保留林。 **6** [C, U] (instance of) limitation or restriction; condition that limits or restricts: 限制；節制；限制或節制的實例、狀況：*We accept your statement without ~,* believe it completely. 我們完全相信你的陳述。*He has put a ~ price on his house,* has fixed a price less than which will not be accepted. 他已替他的房子定下最低售價。*He has placed a ~ on the painting,* ie a ~ price. 他已定下那張畫的最低售價。 **7** [U] self-control in speech and behaviour; keeping silent or saying little; not showing one's feelings: 言行之自制；緘默；含蓄；冷淡：*~ of manner;* 態度之冷淡；*break through sb's ~,* get him to talk and be sociable. 打破某人之緘默(使之說話而隨和)。**re·serv·ist** /rɪˈzɜːvɪst ; rɪˈzɝvɪst/ *n* soldier or sailor belonging to the Army or Navy R~. (後備陸海軍之)後備兵；預備人員。⇨ 3 above. 參看上列第 3 義。

re·serve² /rɪˈzɜːv ; rɪˈzɝv/ *vt* [VP6A, 14] **1** store, keep back, for a later occasion: 貯備；保留；延遲：*R~ your strength for the climb.* 留點力氣爬山吧。*The judge ~d his judgement,* deferred announcing it until a future time. 法官延期宣判。 **2** keep for the special use of, or for a special purpose: 留作專用：*The first three rows of the hall are ~d for special guests.* 大廳的前三排留給特別來賓。 **3** secure possession of, or the right to use, eg by advance payment: 預定(例如以先付錢之方式)：*~ rooms at a hotel.* 預定旅館的房間。***All seats ~d,*** ie the seats (in a theatre, concert hall, etc) can be obtained only by booking them in advance. 所有座位必須預定。***All rights ~d,*** (legal) secured or kept (for the owners of property, etc). (法律)

擁有全部權利;保障所有權。 **4** set apart, destine: 撥出;留給;注定: *A great future is ~d for you.* 光明的前程正等待着你。~**d** *adj* (of a person, his character) slow to reveal feelings or opinions; uncommunicative: (指人、其性格)有所保留的;含蓄的;緘默的: *He is too ~d to be popular.* 他太沈默寡言,不會受人歡迎。~**d·ly** /rɪˈzɜːvɪdlɪ; rɪˈzɝvɪdlɪ/ *adv*

res·er·voir /ˈrezəvwɑː(r); ˈrɛzɚˌvwɔr/ *n* [C] **1** place (often an artificial lake) where water is stored, eg for supplying a town; anything for holding a liquid: 貯水池;水庫(常爲人工的,如用於供應一城市);任何貯存液體的東西: *the ~ of a fountain-pen/an oil lamp.* 鋼筆的蓄水管(油燈的盛油壺)。 **2** (fig) supply (of facts, knowledge, etc). (喻)(事實、知識等的)貯積。

re·set /ˌriːˈset; riˈsɛt/ *vt* (*pt, pp* reset; -tt-) [VP6A] **1** sharpen again: 再磨快: *~ a saw.* 再把鋸子磨快。 **2** place in position again: 重新放置;重嵌: *~ a diamond in a ring,* 重鑲鑽石於戒指中; *~ a broken bone.* 重接斷骨。 **3** (printing) set the type again. (印刷)重新排版;重排。⇨ set²(9).

re·settle /ˌriːˈsetl; riˈsɛtl̩/ *vt, vi* [VP6A, 2A] (esp of refugees) (help to) settle again in a new country: (尤指難民)(幫助)在新國家再定居下來: *~ war refugees in Canada.* 將戰時的難民安頓在加拿大。~**·ment** *n*

re·shuffle /ˌriːˈʃʌfl; riˈʃʌfl/ *vt* [VP6A] shuffle again: 重新洗(牌);轉變;改組: *~ the cards.* 重洗紙牌。□ *n* shuffling again: 重新洗牌;轉變;改組: *a Cabinet ~,* a redistribution of Cabinet posts among the same persons. 內閣改組。

re·side /rɪˈzaɪd; rɪˈzaɪd/ *vi* **1** [VP2C, 3A] *~ (in/at),* live (the more usu word), have one's home: 住;居留 (live 較常用): *~ abroad;* 居於國外; *~ at 10 Railway Terrace.* 住在鐵路街10號。 **2** [VP3A] *~ in,* (of power, rights, etc) be the property of, be present in: (指權力、權利等)爲…所有;存在於: *The supreme authority ~s in the President.* 最高權力掌握於總統手中。

resi·dence /ˈrezɪdəns; ˈrɛzədəns/ *n* **1** [U] residing: 住;居留: *take up one's ~ in a new house,* go and live in it. 遷入新居。 ***in ~,* (a)** (of an official, etc) living in the house officially provided for him. (指官員等)住公家宿舍的;駐於任所的。 **(b)** (of students, etc) residing in a college, etc: (指大學等的學生)住校的: *The students are not yet in ~.* 學生尚未住校。 **2** place where one resides; house (esp a large or dignified one): 住處;住宅(尤指大的或堂皇的): (as used by house-agents) (房屋經紀人用語) *town and country ~s;* 城市及鄉村住宅; *this desirable family ~ for sale.* 吉屋出售。

resi·dency /ˈrezɪdənsɪ; ˈrɛzədənsɪ/ *n* [C] (*pl* -cies) official residence of a Resident(2). 駐紮官的官邸。

resi·dent /ˈrezɪdənt; ˈrɛzədənt/ *adj* residing: 居住的;居留的: *the ~ population of the town* (contrasted with visitors, tourists, etc); 該城的居民人口(與 visitor, tourist 等相對); *a ~ tutor,* one who lives in the household as a member of the family; 住家家庭教師; *a ~ physician,* one who lives in the hospital, etc where he works. 住院醫師。□ *n* **1** person who resides in a place (contrasted with a visitor). 居民(與 visitor 相對)。 **2 R~,** official sent to another country to act as adviser to the administration, etc. (派駐外國充當行政顧問之)駐紮官。

resi·den·tial /ˌrezɪˈdenʃl; ˌrɛzəˈdɛnʃəl/ *adj* **1** of residence: 居住的;居留的: *the ~ qualifications for voters,* ie requiring that they should reside in the constituency. 選民之居住資格(卽選民必須居住於該選區之規定)。 **2** of, with, private houses: 住宅的;私宅的;有住宅的: *a ~ suburb;* 有住宅的郊區; *~ parts of the town* (contrasted with business or industrial parts). 該城之住宅區(與商業區或工業區相對)。

re·sid·ual /rɪˈzɪdjʊəl *US:* -dʒʊ-; rɪˈzɪdʒʊəl/ *adj* remaining; of, forming, a residue. 剩餘的;殘餘的;構成剩餘物的。

re·sidu·ary /rɪˈzɪdjʊərɪ *US:* -dʒʊerɪ; rɪˈzɪdʒʊˌɛrɪ/ *adj* of a residue; (legal) relating to the residue of an estate: 剩餘的;殘餘的;(法律)剩餘財產的;餘產的: *the ~ legatee,* the person to whom the residue of an estate is left. 餘產受贈者;剩餘遺產繼承人。

resi·due /ˈrezɪdjuː *US:* -duː; ˈrɛzəˌdju/ *n* [C] that which remains after a part is taken or used; (legal) that part of an estate which is left after all particular bequests, debts, etc have been settled. 剩餘物;殘餘;(法律)剩餘財產;餘產。

re·sign /rɪˈzaɪn; rɪˈzaɪn/ *vt, vi* **1** [VP6A, 2A, 3A] ***~ (from),*** give up (a post, claim, etc): 辭(職);放棄(要求等): *~ one's job;* 辭去工作; *~ one's position as secretary of the club;* 辭去俱樂部秘書之職位; *~ from the Cabinet.* 辭去閣員之職。*The Minister of Education has ~ed.* 教育部長已辭職。 **2** [VP14] ***~ sb/oneself to sb/sth,*** hand over: 委託;交給: *I ~ my children to your care/myself to your guidance.* 我把我的孩子委託你照顧(我聽從你的指導)。 **3** [VP14] ***~ oneself to sth/be ~ed to sth,*** be ready to accept or endure uncomplainingly: 聽任;順從: *be ~ed to one's fate.* 聽天由命。*We must ~ ourselves to leaving the country.* 我們只好離開國家了。~**ed** *adj* having or showing patient acceptance of sth: 聽任的;順從的: *with a ~ed look.* 帶着順從的臉色。 ~**·ed·ly** /-ɪdlɪ; -ɪdlɪ/ *adv* in a ~ed manner. 聽任地;順從地。

res·ig·na·tion /ˌrezɪɡˈneɪʃn; ˌrɛzɪɡˈneʃən/ *n* **1** [U] resigning(1); [C] instance of this; letter (to one's employers, superior, etc) stating this: 辭職;放棄;辭職或放棄的實例;(給雇主、上級等的)辭呈: *offer/send in/hand in one's ~.* 提出(遞)辭呈。 **2** [U] state of being resigned to conditions, etc; uncomplaining acceptance or endurance: 聽任;順從: *accept failure with ~.* 順從地接受失敗。

re·sil·ience /rɪˈzɪlɪəns; rɪˈzɪlɪəns/, **re·sil·iency** /-nsɪ; -nsɪ/ *nn* [U] quality or property of quickly recovering the original shape or condition after being pulled, pressed, crushed, etc: 彈性(能);彈力;回彈;回能: *the ~ of rubber;* 橡皮的彈性; (fig) power of recuperating quickly; buoyancy: (喻)迅速恢復的力量;復元力;愉快: *the ~ of the human body.* 人體的復元力。**re·sil·ient** /-nt; -nt/ *adj* having or showing ~; (of persons) buoyant in disposition. 有或顯出彈性的;(指人)性情開朗的。

resin /ˈrezɪn *US:* ˈrezn; ˈrɛzn̩/ *n* [C, U] sticky substance that flows out from most plants when cut or injured, esp from fir and pine trees, hardening in air, used in making varnish, lacquer, etc; kind of similar substance (plastics) made chemically, widely used in industry. 樹脂(尤指樅脂與松香);合成樹脂;塑膠。⇨ rosin. ~**·ated** /ˈrezɪneɪtɪd *US:* -zən-; ˈrɛzn̩ˌetɪd/ *adj* flavoured, permeated, with ~. 加樹脂香料的;摻入樹脂的。~**·ous** /ˈrezɪnəs *US:* ˈrezənəs; ˈrɛzn̩əs/ *adj* of or like ~. 樹脂的;似樹脂的。

re·sist /rɪˈzɪst; rɪˈzɪst/ *vt, vi* [VP6A, C, 2A] **1** oppose; use force against in order to prevent the advance of: 抵抗;對抗;用武力阻止…之前進: *~ the enemy/an attack/authority/the police.* 抵抗敵人(攻擊,權勢,警察)。*He could ~ no longer.* 他再也無法抗拒了。 **2** be undamaged or unaffected by: 未受…之損害或影響;耐得住: *a kind of glass dish that ~s heat,* that does not break or crack in a hot oven. 一種耐熱的玻璃盤。 **3** try not to yield to; keep oneself back from: 不屈服於;忍住: *~ temptation.* 抗拒誘惑。*She can't ~ chocolates.* 她一看見巧克力糖就忍不住要吃。*She couldn't ~ making jokes about his baldness.* 她忍不住拿他的禿頭開玩笑。~**er** *n* person who ~s: 抵抗者;不屈服者: *passive ~ers.* 消極抵抗者。~**less** *adj* that cannot be ~ed; inevitable: 不可抵抗的;不可避免的: *a ~less impulse.* 不可抗拒的衝動。

re·sis·tance /rɪˈzɪstəns; rɪˈzɪstəns/ *n* ***~ (to),*** **1** [U] (power of) resisting: 抵抗;抵抗力: *break* *down the enemy's ~;* 粉碎敵人的抵抗; *make/offer no/not much ~ to the enemy's advance;* 對於敵人的前進未作(未作)多少抵抗; *drug ~;* 抗藥性; *passive ~,* ⇨ passive. 消極抵抗。'~ **movement,** (in an enemy-occupied country) effort made by groups of unconquered people to resist the invaders. (在敵人佔領的國家中的)反抗侵略者運動。**2** [U] opposing force: 阻力: *An aircraft has to overcome the ~ of the air.* 飛機須克服空氣的阻力。***line of least ~,*** direction in which a force meets least opposition; (fig) easiest way or method. 阻力最小的方向;最弱的抵抗力;(喻)最容易的方法。**3** [C, U] antagonism; desire to oppose: 敵對;反對;反抗之意志: *'sales/con'sumer ~,* unwillingness of the public to buy goods offered for sale. 抵制購買。*A good advertisement should not arouse ~ in the public.* 好的廣告應該不會招致公衆的反感。

re·sis·tant /rɪ'zɪstənt ; rɪ'zɪstənt/ *adj* ***~ (to),*** offering resistance. 抵抗的;反對的: *insects that have become ~ to DDT;* 對 DDT 已有抵抗力的昆蟲; *~ strains of mosquitoes.* 有抵抗力之若干種蚊蟲。

re·sis·tor /rɪ'zɪstə(r) ; rɪ'zɪstɚ/ *n* device to provide resistance in an electric circuit. 電阻器。

re·sole /ˌriː'səʊl ; ri'sol/ *vt* [VP6A] put a new sole on (a shoe). 裝新鞋底於(鞋)。

res·ol·ute /'rezəluːt ; 'rɛzəˌlut/ *adj* fixed in determination or purpose; firm: 堅決的;剛毅的: *a ~ man;* 有決心的人; *~ for peace.* 貫徹和平的。**~·ly** *adv* **~·ness** *n*

res·ol·ution /ˌrezə'luːʃn ; ˌrɛzə'luʃən/ *n* **1** [U] quality of being resolute; fixity or boldness of determination: 堅決;剛毅: *show great/not much ~;* 表現得很(不够)果斷; *a man who lacks ~.* 缺乏毅力的人。 **2** [C] sth that is resolved(1); formal expression of opinion by a legislative body or a public meeting; proposal for this: 已決定之事物;決議;提案: *pass/carry/adopt/reject a ~ (for/against/in favour of/that...).* 通過(獲得通過、採納、駁回)(有關、反對、贊成、某…的)提案。 **3** [C] resolve; sth one makes up one's mind to do: 決心;決心要做之事: *make good ~s;* 下定決心做好的事情; *her ~ never to marry;* 她永遠不嫁的決心; *a New Year ~* (sth one resolves to do in a new year, eg to give up smoking). 在新年下決心要做的事(例如戒煙)。 **4** [U] resolving, solution (of a doubt, question, discord, etc). (疑惑、問題、不和等的)解決。⇨ resolve(3). **5** process of separating into constituents: 分解: *the ~ of white light into the colours of the spectrum.* 將白色的光分解成光譜的各種顏色。

re·solve /rɪ'zɒlv ; rɪ'zɑlv/ *vt, vi* **1** [VP7A, 9, 3A] ***~ to do sth; ~ that...; ~ on/upon (doing) sth,*** decide; determine: 決定;決心: *He ~d that nothing should hold him back/~d to be held back by nothing.* 他決心不爲任何阻礙所挫。*He ~d on making an early start.* 他決定早日着手。*He ~d to succeed.* 他決心要成功。 **2** [VP9] (of a committee, public meeting, legislative body) pass by formal vote the decision (*that*): (指委員會、集會、議會)議決(與that連用): *The House of Commons ~d that....* 下議院決議…。*R~d, that this meeting is in favour of.../opposed to.../views with alarm..., etc.* 兹決議,本會贊成…(反對…、看到…極感震驚等)。**3** [VP6A] put an end to (doubts, difficulties, etc) by supplying an answer. 解決(疑問、困難等)。 **4** [VP6A, 14] ***~ sth (into sth),*** break up, separate (into parts); convert, be converted: 分析;分解(爲部分);轉變;化成: *~ a problem into its elements.* 分析一個問題之因素。*The House of Commons ~d itself into a committee.* 下議院改組爲一全院委員會。 *A powerful telescope can ~ a nebula into stars.* 一架高性能的望遠鏡能從星雲中分辨出星球來。□ *n* **1** [C] sth that has been determined on; mental resolution(3): 已決定的事物;決心: *make a ~ to do sth;* 決心做某事; *keep one's ~.* 保持決心;不改變決心。 **2** (liter) resolution(1): (文)堅決;剛毅: *deeds of high ~.* 極爲堅決的行爲。**re·solv·able** /-əbl ; -əbḷ/ *adj* that may be ~d. 可決定的;可議決的;可分解的;可溶解的;可解決的;可改變的。

res·on·ant /'rezənənt ; 'rɛzənənt/ *adj* **1** (of sound) resounding; continuing to resound: (指聲音)反響的;共鳴的: *~ notes;* 反響的音調; *a deep, ~ voice.* 深沉而宏亮的聲音。 **2** (of rooms, etc) tending to prolong sounds by vibration: (指房間等)起共鳴的: *~ walls which echo and re-echo sound;* 起共鳴的牆壁; *a ~ hall.* 起共鳴的大廳。 **3** (of places) resounding: (指地方)回響的;共振的: *Alpine valleys ~ with the sound of church bells.* 回響着教堂鐘聲的阿爾卑斯山谷。**res·on·ance** /-əns ; -əns/ *n* [U] quality of being ~. 反響;回響;共鳴;共振。**res·on·ate** /'rezəneɪt ; 'rɛzəˌnet/ *vt, vi* produce or show resonance. 造成或產生共鳴;反響。**res·ona·tor** /-tə(r) ; -tɚ/ *n* appliance or system for increasing sound by resonance. 共鳴器;共振器。

re·sort /rɪ'zɔːt ; rɪ'zɔrt/ *vi* [VP3A] ***~ to,*** **1** make use of for help or to gain one's purpose, etc: 憑藉;求助;依賴;訴諸: *If other means fail, we shall ~ to force.* 如果其他手段均失敗,我們將訴諸武力。*I'm sorry you have ~ed to deception.* 我很遺憾你竟會用欺騙手段。 **2** frequently visit: 常去: *The police watched the cafés where the wanted man was known to ~.* 警察監視着那通緝犯常去的各咖啡館。□ *n* **1** [U] recourse; ~ing(1): 憑藉: *Can we do it without ~ to compulsion/force?* 我們能够不靠强制(武力)做那件事嗎? ***in the last ~; as a last ~,*** when all else has failed, as a last means of finding help or relief. (一切均失敗後)作爲最後的憑藉;作爲最後的依靠。 **2** sb or sth that is ~ed(1) to: 所憑藉的人或物: *An old taxi was the only ~ left.* 一部舊計程車是唯一留下的可資利用之物。 **3** [C] place ~ed(2) to: 常去之處: *'seaside/'summer/'health ~s.* 海濱(避暑、休養)勝地。

re·sound /rɪ'zaʊnd ; rɪ'zaʊnd/ *vi, vt* **1** [VP2A, 3A] ***~ (with),*** (of a voice, instrument, sound) echo and re-echo; fill a place with sound; send back sound; (of a place) ring or echo: (指人聲、樂器、聲音)反響;回蕩;鳴響;使一地方充滿聲音;使聲音回響;(指地方)回響: *The organ ~ed.* 風琴的聲音回蕩著。*The hall ~ed with cries of dissent.* 大廳裡充滿反對的叫聲。 **2** [VP2C] (fig, of fame, an event) be much talked of; spread far and wide: (喻,指名譽、事件)被稱頌;轟傳;馳名: *His success ~ed through all Asia.* 他的成功傳遍整個亞洲。*The film was a ~ing success.* 那影片是馳名的成功之作。**~·ing·ly** *adv*

re·source /rɪ'sɔːs *US:* 'riːsɔːrs ; rɪ'sors/ *n* **1** (*pl*) wealth, supplies of goods, raw materials, etc which a person, country, etc has or can use: (複)資源;富源: *Our ~s in men and ammunition were inadequate for the defence of the town.* 我們在人力和彈藥方面的來源都不够保衞這城市。*We must exploit the natural ~s of our country,* its mineral wealth, potential water power, the productivity of the soil, etc. 我們必須開發本國的天然資源。*I am at the end of my ~s,* have nothing left to use. 我已到了山窮水盡(羅掘俱窮)的地步。*We must make the most of our ~s,* use what we have to the best advantage. 我們必須善加利用我們的富源。 **2** [C] sth which helps in doing sth, that can be turned to for support, help, consolation: 有助於做某事的辦法;給予支持、幫助、安慰的憑藉: *He has no inner ~s of character/no inner ~s to fall back on.* 他沒有內在的精神憑藉。*Leave him to his own ~s,* Leave him to amuse himself, find his own way of passing the time. 讓他獨自找消遣打發時間吧! **3** [U] skill in finding ~s(2); quick wit: 應變的能力;機智: *a man of ~.* 有機智的人。**~·ful** /-fl ; -fəl/ *adj* good or quick at finding ~s(2). 善於隨機應變的;機智的。**~·fully** /-fəlɪ ; -fəlɪ/ *adv*

re·spect¹ /rɪ'spekt ; rɪ'spɛkt/ *n* **1** [U] ***~ (for),*** honour; high opinion or regard; esteem for a person or quality: 尊敬;敬重;尊重: *The prime minister* *is held in the greatest* ~. 首相備受擁戴。*Children should show* ~ *for their teachers.* 學童對老師應表示尊敬。*He has no* ~ *for his promises,* does not think it necessary to keep them. 他不重視他的諾言。 **2** [U] ~ ***(for),*** consideration; attention: 顧慮;關心: *We must have* ~ *for the needs of the general reader,* think about his requirements or preferences. 我們須顧慮到一般讀者之需要。***pay*** ~ ***to,*** **(a)** consider. 考慮。 **(b)** honour. 尊敬。 ~ ***for persons,*** unfair discrimination, on the basis of wealth, social position, etc. (基於財富、社會地位等而產生之)歧視。 **3** [U] reference; relation. 關係;有關。***with*** ~ ***to,*** concerning. 關於。***without*** ~ ***to,*** paying no attention to, leaving out of the question. 不管;不顧慮。 **4** [C] detail; particular aspect. 細節;方面。***in*** ~ ***of,*** as regards: 涉及;關於;在…方面: *Your essay is admirable in* ~ *of style but unsatisfactory in other* ~*s.* 你的文章在文體方面非常好,但在其他方面不够好。***in some/any/no, etc*** ~***s,*** with regard to some aspect(s), detail(s): 在有些方面(在任何方面;絕不等): *They resemble one another in some/all/no/a few* ~*s.* 他們在某些(在所有、沒有、有些)地方彼此相像。**5** (*pl*) regards; polite greetings: (複)敬意;問候: *Give him my* ~*s.* 請代我向他致候。*My father sends you his* ~*s.* 家父問候你。***pay one's*** ~***s to sb,*** visit, etc sb as a sign of ~ for him. 拜訪某人以示敬意。

re·spect² /rɪ'spekt ; rɪ'spɛkt/ *vt* [VP6A] have ~ for; treat with consideration: 尊敬;敬重;顧慮: *He is* ~*ed by everyone.* 他受到每個人的尊敬。*We must* ~ *his wishes.* 我們必須尊重他的意願。*I* ~ *your opinions.* 我尊重你的意見。*I wish people would* ~ *my (desire for) privacy.* 我希望人們尊重我的私生活(保有私生活的意願)。*Do you* ~ *the laws of your country?* 你們尊重貴國的法律嗎？~ ***oneself,*** have proper ~ for one's own character and conduct: 自重;尊重自己: *If you don't* ~ *yourself, how can you expect others to* ~ *you?* 如果你不尊重自己,怎能期望別人尊重你？~**er** *n* (only in) (僅用在) ***no*** ~***er of persons,*** person or thing paying little or no attention to wealth, social rank, etc: 不分財富、社會地位等的人或事物;一視同仁者: *Death is no* ~*er of persons.* 死亡是不分貧富貴賤的。~**·ing** *prep* relating to; concerned with: 關於;說到: *legislation* ~*ing property.* 關於財產的立法。

re·spect·able /rɪ'spektəbl ; rɪ'spɛktəbl/ *adj* **1** (of persons) of good character and good social position; having the qualities associated with such social position; (of clothes, appearance, behaviour, etc) suitable for such persons: (指人)品格高尙而有社會地位的;品行端正的;有身份的;(指衣服、外表、行爲等) 適於高尙人士的; 文雅的; 體面的: *Are these clothes* ~ *enough for Mrs Whitehouse's party?* 穿這種衣服參加懷特豪斯太太家的宴會够體面嗎？ *It is not considered* ~ *in this country to spit in public.* 當衆吐痰在這個國家被認爲是不雅的。 **2** (ironic use) (of behaviour, appearances, etc) conventional; likely to satisfy conventional people: (反語用法)(指舉止、外表等)合乎習俗的; 保守的; 拘泥形式的;可能使保守人士感到滿意的: *Need we worry quite so much about being* ~*?* 我們需要如此拘泥形式嗎？ **3** of some size, merit, importance, etc; deserving respect: 相當大的;相當優秀的;相當重要的;值得尊敬的: *do sth from* ~ *motives.* 出於值得尊敬的動機做某事。*He has quite* ~ *talents.* 他很有才幹。*There was a* ~ *attendance at the meeting this morning.* 今天上午去開會的人相當多。*He earns a* ~ *income.* 他的收入可觀。**re·spect·ably** /-əblɪ ; -əblɪ/ *adv* in a ~ manner: 可尊重地;端莊地;適當地;體面地: *Go and get respectably dressed.* 去好好地打扮一下。**re·spect·abil·ity** /rɪˌspektə'bɪlətɪ ; rɪˌspɛktə'bɪlətɪ/ *n* [U] quality of being socially ~(1, 2). 品格高尙;有社會地位;體面。

re·spect·ful /rɪ'spektfl ; rɪ'spɛktfəl/ *adj* ~ ***(to),*** showing respect: 表示尊敬的;有禮貌的: *They stood at a* ~ *distance from the President.* 他們有禮貌地離開總統一些距離站著。~**ly** /-fəlɪ ; -fəlɪ/ *adv*

re·spect·ive /rɪ'spektɪv ; rɪ'spɛktɪv/ *adj* for, belonging to, each of those in question: 個別的;各個的: *The three men were given work according to their* ~ *abilities.* 那三人各按其才能被分派了工作。*The party ended and we all went off to our* ~ *rooms,* each of us went to his or her own room. 聚會結束了,我們各自回到自己的房間。~**·ly** *adv* separately or in turn, and in the order mentioned: 分別地;各自地: *Training colleges for miners and fishermen are to be built at Leeds and Hull* ~*ly,* ie for miners at Leeds and for fishermen at Hull. 礦工訓練學院和漁夫訓練學院將分別設在里玆和赫爾。

res·pir·ation /ˌrespə'reɪʃn ; ˌrɛspə'reʃən/ *n* [U] breathing; [C] single act of breathing, ie breathing in and breathing out. 呼吸;一次呼吸。

res·pir·ator /'respəreɪtə(r) ; 'rɛspəˌretɚ/ *n* [C] apparatus for breathing through, eg by aviators at high altitudes to warm the air inhaled, by firemen, to filter the air of smoke and fumes. 呼吸保護器; 防毒罩; 呼吸器(如飛行員在高空用以提高所吸入空氣之溫度者,救火員用以過濾空氣中之煙氣者)。

re·spire /rɪ'spaɪə(r) ; rɪ'spaɪr/ *vi* [VP2A] (formal) breathe; breathe in and out. (正式用語) 呼吸; 吸入和呼出。**re·spir·atory** /rɪ'spaɪərətrɪ *US:* 'respɪrətɔːrɪ ; rɪ'spaɪrəˌtorɪ/ *adj* of breathing: 呼吸的: *the respiratory organs/system;* 呼吸器官(系統); *respiratory diseases,* eg bronchitis, asthma. 呼吸器官疾病(如支氣管炎、哮喘)。

res·pite /'respaɪt *US:* 'respɪt ; 'rɛspɪt/ *n* **1** [C, U]

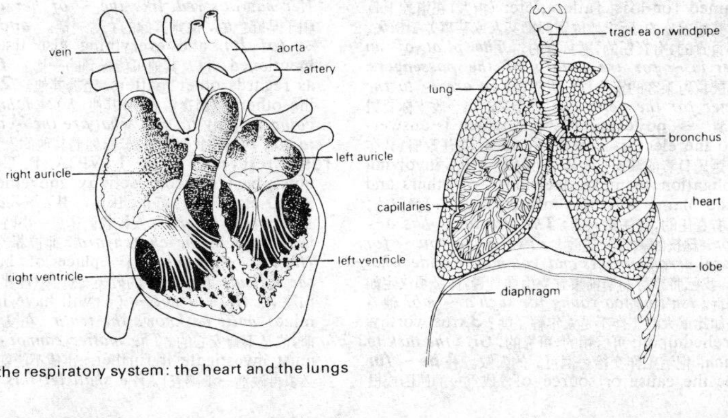

the respiratory system: the heart and the lungs

~ ***(from)***, time of relief or rest (from toil, suffering, anything unpleasant): 暫止；休息(與from 連用，後接勞苦、痛苦、任何不愉快之事物): *work without (a) ~.* 不斷地工作。**2** [C] postponement or delay permitted in the suffering of a penalty or the discharge of an obligation; reprieve. (刑罰或義務之)展延；暫緩；暫緩行刑。□ *vt* [VP6A] give a ~ to: 給予展延；緩期處決: *~ a murderer.* 暫緩處決一殺人犯。

re·splen·dent /rɪˈsplendənt ; rɪˈsplɛndənt/ *adj* very bright; splendid: 燦麗的；輝煌的: *~ in coronation robes.* 穿著燦麗奪目的加冕禮服。**~·ly** *adv* **re·splen·dence** /-əns ; -əns/, **re·splen·dency** /-ənsɪ ; -ənsɪ/ *nn* [U].

re·spond /rɪˈspɒnd ; rɪˈspɑnd/ *vi* **1** [VP2A, 3A, B] ~ ***(to)***, (of people at a church service) make the usual answers or responses to the priest. (指做禮拜的人) 對牧師作例行應答。**2** [VP2C] act in answer to, or because of, the action of another: 回報: *When Jack insulted Jill, she ~ed with a kick.* 當傑克侮辱姬兒時，她踢他一脚以爲回報。**3** [VP 3A] ~ ***to***, react to; be affected by: 有反應；有效果；有影響: *~ to kindness.* 感恩。*The illness quickly ~ed to treatment.* 病經過治療後很快就有起色。*The plane ~s well to the controls.* 這飛機對一切操縱反應良好。

re·spon·dent /rɪˈspɒndənt ; rɪˈspɑndənt/ *n* (legal) defendant (esp in a divorce case). (法律)被告(尤指離婚案件中者)。

re·sponse /rɪˈspɒns ; rɪˈspɑns/ *n* **1** [C] answer: 回答: *My letter of inquiry brought no ~.* 我的詢問信始終未得回音。*She made no ~.* 她沒有回答。*In ~ to your inquiry....* 謹覆閣下詢問…。**2** [C] (in a church service) part of the liturgy said or sung by the congregation alternately with the priest. (禮拜儀式中) 會衆同牧師交互應答或吟唱之祈禱文。**3** [C, U] reaction: 反應: *My appeal to her pity met with no／little／some ~.* 我向她求情，她沒有(很少，有些)反應。

re·spon·si·bil·ity /rɪˌspɒnsəˈbɪlətɪ ; rɪˌspɑnsəˈbɪlətɪ/ *n* (*pl* -ties) **1** [U] being responsible; being accountable: 責任；負責: *You did it on your own ~,* without being told or ordered to do it. 你那麼做是出於自己的責任感。*You have a post of great ~.* 你擔任的職位責任很大。*I will lend you my camera if you will assume full ~ for it,* pay me the cost of any damage or loss. 如果你能負全責(即任何損壞或遺失均要負責賠償)，我就把我的照相機借給你。**2** [C] sth for which a person is responsible; duty: 職責；任務: *the heavy responsibilities of the President.* 總統的繁重職責。

re·spon·sible /rɪˈspɒnsəbl ; rɪˈspɑnsəbl/ *adj* **1** ~ ***(to sb) (for sb／sth)***, (of a person) legally or morally liable for carrying out a duty, for the care of sth or sb, in a position where one may be blamed for loss, failure, etc: (指人)在道義上負有施行某種義務的；所處地位需照顧某人或某事並對損失、失敗等負責的；有責任的；應負責的: *The pilot of an airliner is ~ for the safety of the passengers.* 飛機駕駛員對乘客的安全負有責任。*You are ~ to the Manager for the petty cash.* 小宗的現金收支你要對經理負責。~ **government**, one which is answerable to the electors for its actions. 責任政府(其作爲能對選民負責的政府)。**2** ~ ***(for sth)***, involving the obligation to make decisions for others and bear the blame for their mistakes: (對…)負責的；(對…)有責任的；責任重大的: *The President has a ~ position.* 總統的職責非常重大。*I've made you ~ for the travel arrangements and you must decide what to do.* 我已將旅行的準備事宜交由你負責，你必須決定如何去進行。*Isn't he too young for such a ~ job?* 他擔任責任如此重大的工作不是太年輕了嗎？**3** trustworthy; to be relied upon: 可信賴的；可靠的: *Give the task to a ~ man.* 把這工作交給一個可靠的人做。**4** ***be ~ for sth***, be the cause or source of: 成爲…的原因或根源；對…有責任: *Bad workmanship was ~ for the collapse of the block of flats.* 這排公寓倒塌歸咎於施工拙劣。*Who's ~ for this mess in the kitchen?* 是誰把廚房裡的東西弄得一團糟的？**re·spon·sibly** /-əblɪ ; -əblɪ/ *adv*

re·spon·sive /rɪˈspɒnsɪv ; rɪˈspɑnsɪv/ *adj* **1** answering: 回答的；應答的: *a ~ gesture;* 應答的手勢; *~ sympathy.* 回報的同情。**2** ~ ***(to)***, answering easily or quickly: (對…) 易於或迅速反應的: *a ~ nature;* 反應靈敏的天性; *~ to affection／treatment.* 易爲情愛所動的(對治療易起反應的)。

rest[1] /rest ; rɛst/ *n* **1** [U] condition of being free from activity, movement, disturbance; quiet; sleep: 休息；寧靜；睡眠: *R~ is necessary after hard work.* 勞苦工作後，休息是必要的。*She had a good night's ~,* sleep. 她好好地睡了一夜。*We had several ~s／stops for ~ on the way up the mountain.* 我們在上山途中休息了幾次。*Sunday is a day of ~ for many people.* 星期日是許多人的休息日。*Let's stop and take／have a ~.* 讓我們停下來休息一下。***at ~***, **(a)** still; not troubled; free from movement or agitation. 安靜的；寧靜的；靜止的。**(b)** dead. 死的。***be laid to ~***, be buried. 被埋葬。***come to ~***, (of a moving body) stop moving. (指活動體)停止移動。***set sb's mind／fears at ~***, calm him; relieve him of doubt, anxiety, etc. 使某人平靜；使某人免除懷疑、焦慮等；使某人安心。**ˈ~-cure** *n* course of treatment for persons suffering from nervous disorders. (精神錯亂者的)寧靜治療法；靜養法。**ˈ~-day** *n* day spent in ~. 休息日；安息日。**ˈ~-home** *n* place where old or convalescent people are cared for. 養老院；療養院。**ˈ~-house** *n* house or bungalow for the use of travellers (esp in areas where there are no hotels). 供旅客休息之房舍(尤指在沒有旅館的地區)。**ˈ~ room**, (US) public lavatory; cloak-room. (美)公用盥洗室；衣帽間。**2** [C] that on which sth is supported: 支撐物；支持物: *a ~ for a billiard cue／a telescope;* 撞球球桿(望遠鏡)的支架; *an ˈarm-~;* 扶手; *a ˈneck-~.* 枕頭。**3** [C] (music) (sign marking an) interval of silence. (音樂)休止；休止符。**~·ful** /-fl ; -fəl/ *adj* quiet; peaceful; giving ~ or a feeling of ~: 寧靜的；平靜的；給予平靜的；予人以平靜感的: *a ~ful scene;* 寧靜的景色; *colours that are ~ful to the eyes.* 使眼睛感到舒適的顏色。**~·fully** /-fəlɪ ; -fəlɪ/ *adv* **~·ful·ness** *n* **~·less** *adj* never still or quiet; unable to rest: 永不安靜或寧靜的；不能安靜的: *the ~less waves;* 洶湧的波浪; *spend a ~less night.* 一夜未眠。*The audience was growing ~less,* showing signs of impatience, wishing to leave, etc. 觀衆漸漸不安起來(表現出不耐煩，欲離去的樣子等)。**~·less·ly** *adv* **~·less·ness** *n*

rest[2] /rest ; rɛst/ *n* **the ~**, **1** what remains; the remainder: 餘留者；其餘: *Take what you want and throw the ~ away.* 把你所要的拿去，把剩下的丢掉。*Her hat was red, like the ~ of her clothes.* 她的帽子是紅色的，像她其餘的衣著一樣。***and (all) the ~ (of it)***, and everything else that might be mentioned. 以及其他可能提到的一切。***for the ~***, as regards other matters. 至於其他。**2** (with *pl v*) the others: (用複數動詞)其他(人): *John and I are going to play tennis; what are the ~ of you going to do?* 約翰和我要去打網球；你們其他的人要做甚麼呢？

rest[3] /rest ; rɛst/ *vi, vt* **1** [VP2A, B, C] be still or quiet; be free from activity, movement, disturbance, etc: 平靜；靜止；休息: *We ~ed (for) an hour after lunch.* 午飯後我們休息一小時。*He ~s* (= is buried) *in the churchyard.* 他被葬於教堂墓地中。*His last ~ing-place* (= place of burial) *is on the hillside there.* 他的最後安息處 (埋葬處) 在那邊的山坡上。*He will not ~* (= will have no peace of mind) *until he knows the truth.* 在沒有獲得眞相之前，他是不會安心的。*The matter cannot ~ here,* We must investigate it further. 事情不能就此罷了(我們必須再做進一步調查)。*We shall let this field ~ for* *a year*, let it lie fallow. 我們要讓這塊地休耕一年。**2** [VP6A] give rest or relief to: 使休息;使寧靜;使減緩: *He stopped to ~ his horse.* 他停下來讓馬休息。*These dark glasses ~ my eyes.* 這副墨鏡使我的眼睛感覺舒適。*May God ~ his soul*, give repose to his soul. 願上帝使其靈魂安息。**3** [VP14, 3A] ~ ***(sth) on/upon/against***, (cause to) be supported (on or against sth): (使)被支撐;(使)倚靠;安放: *She ~ed her elbows/Her elbows were ~ing on the table.* 她將肘靠在桌上。*R~ the ladder against the wall.* 把梯子靠在牆上。*The roof ~s upon eight columns.* 這屋頂由八根圓柱支撐。**~ on one's oars**, **(a)** stop rowing for a time. 暫停划船。**(b)** (fig) have a period of rest after any kind of work or effort. (喻)在工作或努力之後小做休息。**4** [VP14, 3A] ~ ***(sth) on/upon***, lie, spread out, depend or rely (on); (of sight, etc) fall (on), be steadily directed (on): 停臥(於);伸展(於);依賴;凝視: *Look at those clouds ~ing upon the mountain top.* 請看那些籠罩山頂上的雲。*Her eyes/gaze ~ed on me.* 她的眼睛凝視着我。*She let her glance ~ on me.* 她注視着我。

rest[4] /rest ; rɛst/ *vi* **1** [VP2D] continue to be in a specified state: 繼續保持某種狀態;依然是: *You may ~ assured that everything possible will be done.* 你儘可放心,所有能做到的事均將做到。*The affair ~s* (= remains, the usu word) *a mystery.* 那件事仍然是一個謎(remain 較常用)。**2** [VP3A] ~ ***with***, be left in the hands or charge of: 在於;取決於: *It ~s with you to decide*, It is your responsibility. 全由你來決定(那是你的責任)。**3** [VP3A] ~ ***on/upon***, depend, rely: 依賴;依靠: *His fame ~s upon his plays more than upon his novels.* 他的名聲主要是建立在他的戲劇上,不是在他的小說上。

re·state /ˌriːˈsteɪt ; riˈstet/ *vt* [VP6A] state again or in a different way. 再陳述或聲明;以不同方式陳述或聲明。**~·ment** *n*

res·taur·ant /ˈrestrɒnt *US:* -tərənt ; ˈrɛstərənt/ *n* place where meals can be bought and eaten. 飯店;餐館。**res·taura·teur** /ˌrestərəˈtɜː(r) ; ˌrɛstərəˈtɝ/, **res·taur·an·teur** /ˌrestrɒnˈtɜː(r) *US:* -tərən- ; ˌrɛstərɑnˈtɝ/ *n* manager of a ~. 飯店或餐館的經理。

res·ti·tu·tion /ˌrestɪˈtjuːʃn *US:* -ˈtuː- ; ˌrɛstəˈtjuʃən/ *n* [U] **1** restoring (of sth stolen, etc) to its owner: (贓物等之)歸還原主: *make ~ of sth to sb*; 將某物歸還某人; *~ of property.* 財產之歸還。**2** = reparation.

res·tive /ˈrestɪv ; ˈrɛstɪv/ *adj* **1** (of a horse or other animal) refusing to move forward; moving backwards or sideways. (指馬或其他動物)不肯前進的;向後或向側移動的。**2** (of a person) reluctant to be controlled or disciplined. (指人)不願受控制或管束的;不安寧的;不受羈束的。**~·ly** *adv* **~·ness** *n*

re·stock /ˌriːˈstɒk ; riˈstɑk/ *vt* [VP6A] put fresh stock into: 再儲存;再補充;將新物品置於;重新進貨: *~ a lake with trout.* 在湖中補充鱒魚。

res·to·ra·tion /ˌrestəˈreɪʃn ; ˌrɛstəˈreʃən/ *n* **1** [U] restoring or being restored: 恢復;復元;歸還: *~ to health and strength;* 健康與體力之復元; *~ of stolen property.* 贓物之歸還。**2 the R~**, (the period of) the reestablishment of the monarchy in England in 1660, when Charles II became king: 1660年的英國王權復興; 英王查理二世的復辟; 復辟時代: *R~ poetry/comedy.* 復辟時代的詩(喜劇)。**3** [C] model representing the supposed original form of an extinct animal, ruined building, etc; building formerly ruined and now rebuilt: 模擬已滅絕動物,已毀建築物等之模型; 原先已毀而今重建之建築物: *The castle is a mere ~*, ie there is very little of the original left. 這座城堡只不過是重建之物(原有建築物的遺跡所留很少)。*Closed during ~s*, ie while rebuilding is in progress. 重建期間暫予關閉。

re·stora·tive /rɪˈstɔːrətɪv ; rɪˈstorətɪv/ *adj* tending to restore health and strength. 有恢復健康與體力之傾向的; 有助於恢復健康與體力的。□ *n* [C, U] ~ food, medicine, etc. 有益於恢復健康與體力的食物,藥物等;恢復劑。

re·store /rɪˈstɔː(r) ; rɪˈstor/ *vt* [VP6A, 14] ~ ***(to)***, **1** give back: 歸還;交還: *~ stolen property/borrowed books.* 歸還贓物(借的書)。**2** bring back into use; reintroduce: 再使用;再採用: *~ old customs.* 恢復古老風俗。**3** make well or normal again; bring back (to a former condition): 使恢復健康或正常;使恢復(以前的情況): *quite ~d to health;* 健康完全恢復; *feel completely ~d.* 感覺已完全復元。*Law and order were quickly ~d after the attempted revolution.* 那次革命未成之後,法律與秩序迅即恢復了。**4** repair; rebuild as before; reconstruct (sth) so that it is like the original: 修復;重建;重製(某物)使像原形: *~ a ruined abbey;* 修復一座毀壞之寺院; *~ a text*, try to make it as it was originally by supplying missing words and phrases, getting rid of errors made by copyists, etc. 校勘原文(設法補上遺漏字詞,改正抄寫者之筆誤等,使之同原文一樣)。**5** place in or bring back to the former position, etc: 使復職;使復位: *~ an employee to his old post/an officer to his command.* 使一職員復職(使一軍官恢復原指揮權)。**~r** *n* one who, that which, ~s, eg an expert who cleans old oil paintings: 使恢復原狀之人或物 (例如使舊油畫恢復原有清新之專家): ˈ*hair-~r*, preparation that, it is claimed, will ~ hair to a bald head. 生髮油;生髮劑。

re·strain /rɪˈstreɪn ; rɪˈstren/ *vt* [VP6A, 14] ~ ***(from)***, hold back; keep under control; prevent (sb or sth from doing sth): 克制; 管制; 抑制; 阻止(某人或某物做某事): *~ a child from (doing) mischief;* 阻止孩子惡作劇; *~ one's anger/laughter.* 克制一個人的憤怒(忍住不笑)。**~ed** *adj* (esp) not emotional or wild; kept under control. (尤指)不激動的;不粗野的;抑制的;受控制的。**~t** /rɪˈstreɪnt ; rɪˈstrent/ *n* **1** [U] ~ing or being ~ed: 克制;遏制;抑制;約束;阻止: *submit to ~t;* 遵守約束; *break loose from all ~t.* 掙脫或打破一切束縛。***be put under ~t***, (esp of a mentally ill person) be placed in a mental home. (尤指精神病患者)被置於精神病院。***without ~t***, freely; without control. 自由地;無拘無束地;放縱地。**2** [U] (in art, literature, etc) avoidance of excess or exaggeration. (在藝術,文學等方面)適中;適度(避免過度或誇張)。**3** [C] that which ~s; check; controlling influence: 遏制的東西;制止者;約束力: *the ~ts of poverty.* 貧窮帶來的種種束縛。

re·strict /rɪˈstrɪkt ; rɪˈstrɪkt/ *vt* [VP6A, 14] ~ ***(to)***, limit; keep within limits: 限制; 約束; 使在限度內: *Discussion at the meeting was ~ed to the agenda.* 這次會議上的討論只限於議程上的項目。*We are ~ed to a speed of 30 miles an hour in built-up areas.* 在房屋林立的地區車速限制爲每小時三十哩。*The trees ~ our vision.* 樹木限制了我們的視野。*Is the consumption of alcohol ~ed by law in your country?* 在貴國酒的消耗量是否受法律限制? **re·stric·tion** /rɪˈstrɪkʃn ; rɪˈstrɪkʃən/ *n* **1** [U] ~ing or being ~ed: 限制;被限制: *~ion of expenditure.* 經費開支之限制。**2** [C] instance of this; sth that ~s: 限制之實例; 有限制作用之事物;限制者: *place ~ions on foreign trade/on the sale of alcohol;* 管制對外貿易(酒之售賣); *currency ~ions*, eg on the sums that a person may use for foreign travel. 貨幣管制。**~·ive** /rɪˈstrɪktɪv ; rɪˈstrɪktɪv/ *adj* ~ing; tending to ~. 限制的;限制性的。**~ive practices**, (in industry) practices that hinder the most effective use of labour, technical resources, etc and tend to damage productive efficiency. (工業方面的)限制性常例(妨礙勞力、技術資源等的最有效使用,因之損及生產效率者)。**~·ive·ly** *adv*

re·struc·ture /ˌriːˈstrʌktʃə(r) ; ˌriˈstrʌktʃɚ/ *vt* [VP 6A] give new structure or arrangement to: 改組; 調整;重新安排: *~ an organization/a proposal/the plot of a novel.* 改組一機構(調整一計畫;重新安排一部小說的情節)。

re·sult /rɪ'zʌlt ; rɪ'zʌlt/ *vi* **1** [VP2A, 3A] ~ ***(from),*** come about, happen, as a natural consequence: (作爲自然結果而)發生;因…引起;起因於: *Any damage ~ing from negligence must be paid for by the borrower.* 因疏忽引起的任何損壞應由借用者負責賠償。 **2** [VP3A] ~ ***in,*** bring about; have as a consequence: 致使;造成…結果;導致: *Their dispute ~ed in war.* 他們的爭論終於造成戰爭。 **3** end in a specified manner: 終歸…;結果: *Their efforts ~ed badly.* 他們的努力結果不佳。 □ *n* **1** [C, U] that which is produced by an activity or cause; outcome; effect: 結果;效果;成績: *work without (much) ~;* 沒有(多大)效果的工作; *obtain good ~s;* 得到好的結果; *announce the ~s of a competition,* the names of prize-winners, etc; 宣佈競賽之結果(卽宣佈優勝者之姓名等); *'football ~s,* the scores. 足球賽之結果(積分)。 *His limp is the ~ of a car accident last year.* 他的跛行是去年一次車禍的不幸結果。 **2** [C] sth found by calculation; answer (to a mathematical problem, etc). 由計算得到的某項結果;(數學問題等的)答案。**~·ant** /-ənt ; -ənt/ *adj* coming as a ~, esp as the total outcome of forces or tendencies from different directions. 結果的;(尤指來自不同方面的力量或趨勢而成的) 總結果的;合成的。□ *n* [C] product or outcome (*of* sth). (某種事物的)結果。

re·sume /rɪ'zju:m *US:* -'zu:m ; rɪ'zum/ *vt* **1** [VP 6A, D] go on after stopping for a time: 停頓一段時間後再繼續; 重新開始; 恢復: ~ *one's work/a story;* 恢復工作(繼續一故事); ~ *the thread of one's discourse,* take up an interrupted discourse. 重續被打斷的談話。 **2** [VP6A] take or occupy again: 再取得;再佔有: ~ *one's seat.* 重回原位。

résumé /'rezju:meɪ *US:* ˌrezʊ'meɪ ; ˌrɛzʊ'me/ *n* [C] summary; abstract(3); (US) = *curriculum vitae,* ⇨ curriculum. 摘要;概略;(美)履歷。

re·sump·tion /rɪ'zʌmpʃn ; rɪ'zʌmpʃən/ *n* [U] resuming; [C] instance of this. 重新開始; 恢復; 再取得;再佔有。

re·sur·face /ˌri:'sɜ:fɪs ; ri'sɝfɪs/ *vt, vi* **1** [VP6A] put a new surface on (a road, etc). 再鋪(路等)之表面;換裝新面。 **2** [VP2A] (of a submarine) come to the surface again. (指潛水艇)重新露出水面。

re·sur·gent /rɪ'sɜ:dʒənt ; rɪ'sɝdʒənt/ *adj* reviving; coming back to activity, vigour, etc (after defeat, destruction, etc): 復活的;復蘇的;恢復活動的;恢復活力的: ~ *nationalism;* 復活的民族主義; ~ *hopes.* 復蘇的希望。 **re·sur·gence** /-əns ; -əns/ *n*

res·ur·rect /ˌrezə'rekt ; ˌrɛzə'rɛkt/ *vt, vi* **1** [VP6A] bring back into use; revive the practice of: 恢復使用;恢復…之實行;再流行;復興: ~ *an old word/custom.* 恢復使用一個古字(風俗)。 **2** [VP6A] take from the grave; (colloq) dig up: 從墳墓中掘出;(俗)掘起: *My dog ~ed an old bone in the garden.* 我的狗在花園中挖出一根老骨頭。 **3** [VP6A, 2A] (rare) bring or come back to life again. (罕)(使)復蘇;(使)復活。

res·ur·rec·tion /ˌrezə'rekʃn ; ˌrɛzə'rɛkʃən/ *n* [U] **1** **the R~, (a)** the rising of Jesus from the tomb; anniversary of this. 耶穌復活;耶穌復活的周年紀念日;復活節。**(b)** the rising of all the dead on the Last Day. 最後審判日所有死者之復活。 **2** revival from disuse, inactivity, etc: 復興;恢復使用;恢復活力等: *the ~ of hope.* 希望之復蘇。

re·sus·ci·tate /rɪ'sʌsɪteɪt ; rɪ'sʌsəˌtet/ *vt, vi* [VP6A, 2A] bring or come back to consciousness: 使恢復知覺;恢復知覺: ~ *a person who has been nearly drowned.* 使一個快淹死的人復蘇。 **re·sus·ci·ta·tion** /rɪˌsʌsɪ'teɪʃn ; rɪˌsʌsə'teʃən/ *n* [U].

ret /ret ; rɛt/ *vt* (-tt-) [VP6A] soften (flax, hemp, etc) by soaking or exposing to moisture: 將(亞麻、大麻等)浸水或暴露在濕氣中使之變軟: *Coconut shells are buried in wet sea-sand to ret the coir fibre.* 椰子殼被埋在潮濕的海沙中以使其纖維變軟。

re·tail /'ri:teɪl ; 'ritel/ *n* [C] sale of goods (usu in small quantities) to the general public, not for resale: 貨物(通常係少量)之直接售給用戶; 零售: *sell goods (by) ~;* 零售貨物; (attrib) (形容用法) ~ *dealers/prices;* 零售商(價格); *the '~ department.* 零售部。 ⇨ wholesale. □ *adv* by ~: 零售地: *Do you buy wholesale or ~?* 你是整批買還是零買? □ *vt, vi* **1** [VP6A, 3A] ~ ***(at),*** sell (goods) by ~; (of goods) be sold ~: 零售(貨物);(指貨物)被零售: *an article that is ~ed at/that ~s at seventy pence.* 一件零售價格七十辨士的物品。 **2** [VP6A] repeat (what one has heard, esp gossip) bit by bit or to several persons in turn: 一點一點地或一個接一個地向一些人重述;轉述(所聽到的話,尤指閒言): ~ *a slander.* 轉述誹謗之言。**~er** *n* tradesman who sells by ~. 零售商。

re·tain /rɪ'teɪn ; rɪ'ten/ *vt* [VP6A] **1** keep; continue to have or hold; keep in place: 保持;保有;保留;擋住: *This vessel won't ~ water.* 這個容器不能盛水。 *This dyke was built to ~ the flood waters.* 這堤是建來擋洪水的。 *The ~ing wall* (ie one built to support and confine a mass of earth or water) *collapsed.* 擋土牆(或擁壁)倒塌了。 *He is 90 but still ~s the use of all his faculties.* 他已九十高齡,但各種官能仍未衰退。 *She ~s a clear memory of her schooldays.* 她對求學時代仍舊記得很清楚。 **2** get the services of (esp a barrister) by payment (*a ~ing fee*). 僱用;聘請(尤指律師)(聘請費用稱作 a retaining fee)。**~er** *n* **1** (legal) fee paid to ~ the services of, eg a barrister. (法律)(律師等之)聘請費。**2** (old use) servant. (舊用法)僕人。

re·take /ˌri:'teɪk ; ri'tek/ *vt* (*pt* -took /-'tʊk ; -'tʊk/, *pp* -taken /-'teɪkn ; -'tekən/) [VP6A] take, capture, photograph, again. 再拿取;再擄獲; 再拍攝。□ *n* /'ri:teɪk ; 'riˌtek/ (esp, cinema, TV) rephotographed scene. (尤指電影、電視)重拍之景;補拍之鏡頭。

re·tali·ate /rɪ'tælɪeɪt ; rɪ'tælɪˌet/ *vi* [VP2A, 3A] ~ ***(against/on/upon),*** return the same sort of ill treatment that one has received: 報復;報仇: ~ *upon one's enemy.* 向敵人報仇。*He ~d by kicking the other boy on the ankle.* 他踢另一個男孩的脚踝骨以爲報復。 *If we raise our import duties on their goods, they may ~ against us.* 如果我們提高他們貨物的進口稅,他們可能向我們報復。 **re·tali·ation** /rɪˌtælɪ'eɪʃn ; rɪˌtælɪ'eʃən/ *n* [U] retaliating: 報復;報仇: *in retaliation for.* 爲…而報復。 **re·tali·at·ive** /rɪ'tælɪətɪv *US:* -lɪeɪt- ; rɪ'tælɪˌetɪv/, **re·tali·at·ory** /rɪ'tælɪətrɪ *US:* -tɔ:rɪ ; rɪ'tælɪəˌtorɪ/ *adjj* returning ill treatment for ill treatment; of or for retaliation: 報復的; 回報的; 爲報復的: *retaliatory measures.* 報復的手段。

re·tard /rɪ'tɑ:d ; rɪ'tɑrd/ *vt* [VP6A] check; hinder: 阻止;妨礙: ~ *progress/development;* 阻礙進步(發展); *a mentally ~ed child,* one whose mental or emotional development has been checked. 一個在智能或情緒方面有障礙的孩子。 **re·tar·da·tion** /ˌri:tɑ:'deɪʃn ; ˌritɑr'deʃən/ *n*

retch /retʃ ; rɛtʃ/ *vi* [VP2A] make (involuntarily) the sound and physical movements of vomiting but without bringing up anything from the stomach. 乾嘔 (不自覺地作嘔吐之聲音及動作,但並未吐出胃中任何東西)。

re·tell /ˌri:'tel ; ri'tɛl/ *vt* (*pt, pp* -told /-'təʊld ; -'told/) [VP6A] tell again; tell in a different way or in a different language: 再講;(以不同的方式或不同的語言)重述;改寫: *old Greek tales retold for children.* 爲孩子們改寫的古希臘故事。

re·ten·tion /rɪ'tenʃn ; rɪ'tɛnʃən/ *n* [U] retaining or being retained: 保持;保留;被保持;被保留: *suffering from ~ of urine,* inability to pass it out from the bladder. 患閉尿症。

re·ten·tive /rɪ'tentɪv ; rɪ'tɛntɪv/ *adj* ~ ***(of),*** having the power of retaining(1) things: 有保持之能力的: *a memory that is ~ of details;* 能記得詳情細節的記憶力; *a ~ soil,* one that retains water, does not dry out quickly. 能保持住水份的土壤。**~·ly** *adv*

~**·ness** *n*

re·think /ˌriːˈθɪŋk ; riˈθɪŋk/ *vt, vi* (*pt, pp* -thought /-ˈθɔːt ; -ˈθɔt/) [VP6A, 2A] think about again; reconsider: 再想;重予考慮: *They will have to ~ their policy towards China.* 他們必須重新考慮對華政策。*A good deal of ~ing is needed on this question.* 這個問題需要多加考慮。□ *n* /ˈriːθɪŋk ; ˈriθɪŋk/ (colloq) thinking again: (俗)再想;再考慮: *If that's your decision, you'd better have a ~.* 如果那是你的決定,你最好再考慮一下。

reti·cent /ˈretɪsnt ; ˈrɛtəsnt/ *adj* in the habit of saying little; not saying all that is known or felt; reserved: 沉默寡言的;言不盡意的;保留的: *She was ~ about/on what Tom had said to her.* 她對湯姆告訴她的話保持沉默。~**·ly** *adv* **reti·cence** /-sns ; -sns/ *n* [U] being ~; [C] instance of this: 沉默寡言;保留: *His reticences are often more revealing than what he says.* 他的沉默常比他所說的話顯示更多的意思。

re·ticu·late /rɪˈtɪkjʊleɪt ; rɪˈtɪkjəˌlet/ *vt, vi* [VP6A, 2A] divide, be divided, in fact or in appearance into a network of small squares or intersecting lines. 使呈網狀;呈網狀。□ *adj* /rɪˈtɪkjʊlət ; rɪˈtɪkjəlɪt/ covered with such a network. 覆以網狀物的。**re·ticu·la·tion** /rɪˌtɪkjʊˈleɪʃn ; rɪˌtɪkjəˈleʃən/ *n* (often *pl*) net-like mark or structure. (常用複數) 網狀圖案;網狀物;網狀結構。

reti·cule /ˈretɪkjuːl ; ˈrɛtɪˌkjul/ *n* (archaic) woman's small handbag. (古)女用小手提包。

ret·ina /ˈretɪnə *US:* ˈretənə ; ˈrɛtn̩ə/ *n* (*pl* ~s or -nae /-niː ; -n̩ˌi/) [C] layer of membrane at the back of the eyeball, sensitive to light. 視網膜(在眼球後部之網膜,對光甚敏感)。⇨ the illus at eye. 參看 eye 之插圖。

reti·nue /ˈretɪnjuː *US:* ˈretənuː ; ˈrɛtn̩ˌju/ *n* [C] number of persons (servants, officers, etc) travelling with a person of high rank. 隨員(與高級官員等同行的侍從,官員等)。

re·tire /rɪˈtaɪə(r) ; rɪˈtaɪr/ *vi, vt* **1** [VP2A, 3A] ~ ***(from) (to),*** withdraw; go away: 退下;離開: *He ~d to his bedroom.* 他回到他的臥室。*The batsman ~d hurt,* left the pitch and went back to the pavilion, because hurt. 擊球員因受傷退場。**2** ~ ***(to bed)*** (formal for) go to bed: (正式用語) 就寢: *My wife usually ~s at 10 o'clock.* 內人通常十時就寢。**3** [VP2A, C] (of an army) withdraw; go back: (指軍隊)撤退;退却: *Our forces ~d to prepared positions.* 我們的部隊撤回到既設陣地。Cf 參較 *The enemy retreated.* 敵人敗退。**4** [VP2A, C] give up one's work, position, business, etc: 退休;退職;退役: *reach retiring age;* 屆退休年齡; *a retiring allowance,* one given to a person when he ~s. 退休金。*He will ~ on a pension at 65.* 他將在65歲領養老金退休。**5** [VP6A] cause (sb) to ~(3,4): 使(某人)撤退或退休: *~ the head clerk.* 使主任秘書退休。**6** ~ ***from the world,*** enter a monastery or become a hermit; become a recluse. 遁世隱居(如進修道院或成爲隱居者);成爲隱士。~ ***into oneself,*** become unsociable because one is wrapped up in one's own thoughts. (因沉緬於自己的思想而)不和人交際;苦思不語。□ *n* signal to troops to ~: 撤退號: *sound the ~,* ie on the bugle. 吹撤退號。~**d** *adj* **1** having ~d(4): 退職的;退休的;退役的: *a ~d civil servant;* 一個退休的公務員; *the '~d list,* of officers (of the Army, etc) who have ~d; 退役軍官名冊; *'~d pay,* pension. 退休金。**2** secluded; quiet: 隱居的;寧靜的: *a ~d valley;* 寧靜的山谷; *live a ~d life in a small village.* 在小村中過隱居生活。**re·tir·ing** *adj* (of persons, their way of life, etc) inclined to avoid society; reserved: (指人,其生活方式等)有隱居傾向的;孤獨緘默的: *a girl of a retiring disposition.* 一個性情孤獨的女孩。~**·ment** *n* **1** [U] retiring or being ~d; seclusion: 隱退;退休;隱居: *~ment from the world,* eg in a convent. 遁世隱居(如遁入女修道院)。**2** [U] condition of being ~d: 隱退之狀況: *be/live in ~ment.* 過隱居生活。***go into ~ment,*** retire (esp 4 and 6 above). 退休;退職;退役;隱退;隱居。**3** [C] instance of retiring or being ~d: 退隱或退休之實例: *There have been several ~ments in my office recently.* 最近我那辦公室有幾個人退休了。**'~ment pension,** = old-age pension. 養老金。⇨ pension.

re·tool /ˌriːˈtuːl ; riˈtul/ *vt* [VP6A] equip (a factory, etc) with new machine tools. 給(工廠等)裝備新的工作母機。

re·tort[1] /rɪˈtɔːt ; rɪˈtɔrt/ *n* [C] **1** vessel with a long narrow neck turned downwards, used for distilling liquids. 曲頸甑;曲頸瓶(頸部細長而朝下,用於蒸餾液體者)。**2** receptacle used in the purification of mercury, and in the making of gas. 蒸餾器 (用於淨化水銀,及製造氣體的容器)。

re·tort[2] /rɪˈtɔːt ; rɪˈtɔrt/ *vt, vi* **1** [VP6A, 9, 2A] answer back quickly, wittily or angrily (esp to an accusation or challenge): (尤指對控訴或挑戰)立即機智地或憤怒地反駁: *'It's entirely your fault,' he ~ed.* '那全是你的錯,'他反駁說。**2** [VP14] (formal, rare) get equal with sb by returning (what has been received) in kind: (正式用語,罕)反擊;回報: *~ insult for insult;* 以牙還牙; *~ an argument/affront.* 反駁一論據(回報一侮辱)。□ *n* [U] ~ing: 反駁;反擊: *say sth in ~;* 反唇相譏; [C] ~ing answer: 反駁的回答: *make an insolent ~.* 作侮慢的反擊。

re·touch /ˌriːˈtʌtʃ ; riˈtʌtʃ/ *vt* [VP6A] improve (a photograph, painting, etc) by a few touches of a brush, etc. 修描(照片,畫等)。

re·trace /riːˈtreɪs ; rɪˈtres/ *vt* [VP6A] **1** go back over or along: 順…折回;折返: *~ one's steps.* 順原路返回。**2** go over (past actions, etc) in the mind. 回想;回顧(過去的活動等)。

re·tract /rɪˈtrækt ; rɪˈtrækt/ *vt, vi* **1** [VP6A, 2A] take back or withdraw (a statement, offer, opinion, etc); take back a statement: 收回;撤回(聲明,提議,意見等);撤回聲明: *The prisoner of war ~ed his parole.* 該戰俘違誓脫逃。*Even when confronted with proof the accused man refused to ~,* would not acknowledge the error of what he had said. 甚至在面對證據的時候,被告仍拒絕改正其供述。**2** [VP6A, 2A] draw in or back; move back or in; be capable of doing this: 縮進;縮回;移回;移進;能縮回或移進: *A cat can ~ its claws and a snail its horns.* 猫能縮進其爪,蝸牛能縮回其觸角。*A cat's claws can ~.* 猫的爪能縮回。~**·able** /-əbl ; -əbl/ *adj* that can be ~ed: 能收回或撤回的;能縮進或縮回的: *a ~able undercarriage,* (in an aircraft) wheels, etc which can be drawn up into the body of the aircraft during flight. 伸縮式起落架(飛機的輪等,在飛行時能够拉進機身中)。**re·trac·tile** /rɪˈtræktaɪl *US:* -tl ; rɪˈtræktl̩/ *adj* that can be drawn in: 能縮回的;能縮進的: *the retractile claws of a cat.* 能縮進的猫爪子。**re·trac·tion** /rɪˈtrækʃn ; rɪˈtrækʃən/ *n* [U] ~ing; [C] instance of this. 撤回;撤消;縮進;移回;撤回,縮進等之實例。

re·tread /ˌriːˈtred ; riˈtrɛd/ *vt* (*pt, pp* ~ed) furnish (an old tyre) with a new tread. 供(舊輪胎)以新的胎面;翻新(舊輪胎)。⇨ tread, *n*(3). □ *n* /ˈriːtred ; ˈriˌtrɛd/ tyre that has been ~ed (US 美 = *recap*). 經過翻新的輪胎。

re·treat /rɪˈtriːt ; rɪˈtrit/ *vi* **1** [VP2A, C, 3A] ~ ***(from) (to),*** (esp of an army) go back; withdraw: (尤指軍隊)撤退;退却: *force the enemy to ~;* 迫使敵人退却; *~ on (ie towards) the capital.* 向首都撤退。**2** recede (which is more usu): 向後傾(recede 較常用): *a ~ing forehead.* 向後傾斜的額頭。□ *n* **1** [U] act of ~ing: 撤退或後退的行動: *The army was in full ~.* 全軍在總撤退。*We made good our ~,* ~ed safely. 我們安全撤退。**2** [U] signal for ~ing: 退軍號;撤退號: *sound the ~,* eg on a drum or bugle. 鳴金收軍 (例如擊軍鼓或吹退軍號)。**3** [C] instance of ~ing: 撤退或後退之實例: *after many advances and ~s.* 經過許多次推進與撤退。

beat a (hasty) ~, (fig) withdraw from, abandon, an undertaking. (喻)放棄一事業；打退堂鼓。**4** [C, U] (place for a) period of quiet and rest: 一段安靜和休息期間；寧靜的休息處所：*a quiet country ~.* 鄉間寧靜處。*go into ~,* eg temporary retirement for religious exercises. 避靜(如爲宗教活動所作之暫時性隱居)。

re·trench /rɪ'trentʃ ; rɪ'trɛntʃ/ *vt, vi* [VP6A, 2A] cut down (expenses); make economies: 節省 (開支)；縮減支出；節省：*We must ~ this year in order to have a good holiday next year.* 爲了明年有個愉快的假日，我們今年必須節省。**~·ment** *n* [U] ~ing; [C] instance of this. 節省；節省之實例。

re·trial /ˌriː'traɪəl ; ri'traɪəl/ *n* act of trying again in a law court; new trial. (法院的)再審；覆審。

ret·ri·bu·tion /ˌretrɪ'bjuːʃn ; ˌrɛtrə'bjuʃən/ *n* [U] deserved punishment: 應得的懲罰；報應：*R~ for evil does not always come in this life.* 邪惡不一定在今生得到報應。*There will be a day of ~.* 總有一天會遭到報應的。**re·tri·bu·tive** /rɪ'trɪbjʊtɪv ; rɪ'trɪbjətɪv/ *adj* coming as ~; inflicted or coming as a penalty for wrongdoing. 報應的；懲罰的。

re·trieve /rɪ'triːv ; rɪ'triv/ *vt, vi* **1** [VP6A] get possession of again: 再獲得；找回：*~ a lost piece of luggage.* 找回一件遺失的行李。**2** [VP6A] put or set right; make amends for: 修整；修理；補償：*~ an error/a loss/ disaster/defeat.* 補救一錯誤(損失，災難，失敗)。**3** [VP6A, 14] *~ (from),* rescue from; restore to a flourishing state: 解救；使恢復繁盛情況：*~ sb from ruin;* 拯救某人免於沉淪；*~ one's honour/fortunes;* 挽回榮譽(財產)；*~ oneself.* 拯救自己。**4** [VP6A, 2A] (of specially trained dogs) find and bring in (killed or wounded birds, etc). (指經過特殊訓練的狗)找到並帶回(被殺死或受傷的鳥等)。**re·triev·able** /-əbl ; -əbḷ/ *adj* **re·trieval** /-vl ; -vḷ/ *n* [U] **1** act of retrieving: 尋回，補償，挽救之行動：*the retrieval of one's fortunes.* 個人的財產的恢復。**2** possibility of recovery: 恢復之可能：*beyond/past retrieval.* 不可恢復的；不可挽救的。**re·triever** *n* breed of dog used for retrieving(4). 一種用以尋回獵物之獵犬。⇨ the illus at dog. 參看 dog 之插圖。

retro·ac·tive /ˌretrəʊ'æktɪv ; ˌrɛtro'æktɪv/ *adj* (of laws, etc) (指法律等) = retrospective(2). **~·ly** *adv*

retro·grade /'retrəgreɪd;'rɛtrəˌgred/ *adj* **1** directed backwards: 向後的；後退的：*~ motion.* 逆行；後退的動作。**2** deteriorating; likely to cause worse conditions: 退化的；敗壞的；可能使情況變壞的：*a ~ policy.* 一種可能使情況變壞的政策。□ *vi* [VP2A] decline; revert; grow worse. 衰落；退步；變壞。

retro·gress /ˌretrə'gres ; 'rɛtrəˌgrɛs/ *vi* [VP2A] go or move backwards. 倒退；退步；衰退。

retro·gression /ˌretrə'greʃn ; ˌrɛtrə'grɛʃən/ *n* return to a less advanced state; decline. 退步；退化；衰微。**retro·gres·sive** /ˌretrə'gresɪv ; ˌrɛtrə'grɛsɪv/ *adj* returning, tending to return, to a less advanced state; becoming worse. 退步的；退化的；變壞的。

retro·rocket /'retrəʊrɒkɪt ; 'rɛtroˌrɑkɪt/ *n* jet engine fired to slow down or alter the course of a missile, spacecraft, etc. (使飛彈、太空船等減慢或改變航程而發射的)減速火箭；推後火箭。

retro·spect /'retrəspekt ; 'rɛtrəˌspɛkt/ *n* [U] view of past events. 回顧；回溯。*in ~,* looking back at past events, etc. 回顧。**retro·spec·tion** /ˌretrə'spekʃn ; ˌrɛtrə'spɛkʃən/ *n* [U] action of looking back at past events, scenes, etc; [C] instance of this. 回顧；回顧之實例。**ret·ro·spec·tive** /ˌretrə'spektɪv ; ˌrɛtrə'spɛktɪv/ *adj* **1** relating to retrospection; looking back on past events, etc: 回顧的；回溯往事的：*a ~ive exhibition of a painter's work,* one that traces his development from his early to his latest work. 一畫家作品的回顧展(展示其早期作品至後期的演變)。**2** (of laws, payments, etc) applying to the past; not restricted to the future: (指法律，付款等) 溯及既往的；非僅限於未來的：*~ive legislation;* 追溯既往的法律；溯及法；*a ~ive* (= backdated) *wage increase.* 從過去某一天開始計算的增加薪資。**retro·spec·tive·ly** *adv*

re·troussé /rə'truːseɪ *US:* ˌretrʊ'seɪ ; ˌrɛtrʊ'se/ *adj* (of a nose) turned up at the end. (指鼻子)上翻的；朝上的。

ret·ro·ver·sion /ˌretrəʊ'vɜːʃn *US:* -ʒn ; ˌrɛtrə'vɜʒən/ *n* state of being turned backwards; turning or tilting backward. 退轉；後轉；後傾；後屈。

ret·sina /ret'siːnə *US:* 'retsɪnə ; 'rɛtsɪnə/ *n* [U] resinated Greek wine. 瑞星娜(一種有松香味的希臘葡萄酒)。

re·turn¹ /rɪ'tɜːn ; rɪ'tɜn/ *n* **1** [C, U] ~ing or being ~ed; coming, going, giving, sending, putting, back: 回來；歸去；歸還；送回；放回：*a ~ home;* 歸家；*on my ~,* when I got/get back; 在我歸來時；*a poor ~ for kindness,* (eg) ungrateful behaviour; 對於仁慈的一個卑劣的報答 (如忘恩負義的行爲)；*the ~ of spring;* 春之歸來；*have a ~ of the symptoms* (of an illness). (疾病的)徵候復發。*by ~,* by the next post out: 由原(下)班郵遞：*Please send a reply by ~.* 請卽回示(由原班郵遞惠覆)。*in ~ (for),* as repayment (for). 以爲報答；回報；回禮。*Many happy ~s (of the day),* phrase used as a greeting on sb's birthday. (生日賀辭)祝你長命百歲。*on sale or ~,* (of goods in commerce) supplied (to retailers) on the understanding that they may be ~ed to the wholesaler or manufacturer if not sold. 賣不掉時可退貨的(指供給零售商之貨物，經雙方協議，未售出之貨物可退給批發商或廠商)。*a/the point of no ~,* (on a long voyage, flight across an ocean, etc) point at which fuel supplies, etc are insufficient for a ~ to the starting-point, so that continuation of the voyage, etc is essential; (fig) stage of negotiations at which no further progress seems possible. 不能回轉點(在橫越海洋等的長途航行或飛行中，屆臨燃料等供應不足以維持返回原地故必須繼續前行之地點)；(喻)談判時無任何進展之階段。**2** (attrib) involving going back or coming back, etc: (形容用法)歸去的；回來的：*the ~ voyage.* 回航。**~ fare,** needed for the journey both there and back. (車、船等之)來回費用。**~ half,** the half of a ~ ticket for the journey back. 回程票。**~ match,** one played between teams which have already played one match. (已經比賽過一次的兩隊間的)再次比賽。**'~ ticket,** one giving a traveller the right to go to a place and back to his starting-point (US 美 = *two-way ticket*). 來回票。**ˌday-'~,** ~ ticket available only for the day of issue: 當天來回票：*Two day-~s to London, please.* 請賣給我兩張去倫敦的當天來回票。**3** (often *pl*) profit on an investment or undertaking: (常用複數)利潤；贏利：*get a good ~ on an investment;* 在一投資上獲得優厚的利潤；*small profits and quick ~s,* motto for shops that rely on large sales and quick turnover. 薄利多銷。**4** [C] official report or statement, esp one that is compiled by order: 正式的報告或陳述 (尤指受命而爲者)：*make one's ~ of income* (to the Inspector of Taxes for purposes of income tax); (爲納所得稅向稅務稽查)申報所得；*the e'lection ~s,* figures of the voting at an election. 選舉報告(選票數字之報告)。

re·turn² /rɪ'tɜːn ; rɪ'tɜn/ *vi, vt* **1** [VP2A, C, 3A, 4A] *~ (to)(from),* come or go back: 回來；歸去：*~ home;* 回家；*~ to London;* 回倫敦；*~ from a journey;* 旅行回來；*~ to Paris from London.* 從倫敦回巴黎。*He ~ed to collect his money.* 他回來收取他的錢。*I shall ~ to this point later in my lecture.* 我稍後將在講演中回頭討論這一點。**2** [VP3A] *~ to,* pass or go back to a former state: 回復到以前狀態：*He has ~ed to his old habits.* 他又恢復了他的舊習慣。*After death animal bodies ~ (= change) to dust.* 動物死後屍體又化爲塵土。**3** [VP 6A] (rare) reply; retort: (罕)回答；反駁：*'Not this time', he ~ed.* '這次不行'，他回答說。**4** [VP6A, 12A, 13A] give, put, send, pay, carry, back: 歸還；放回；送回；償還；帶回：*When will you ~ (me) the* *book I lent you?* 你甚麼時候把我借給你的那本書還我呢？ *In case of non-delivery, ~ to (the) sender,* often written on letters sent by post. 無法投遞時，退回原處。*All books are to be ~ed to the library before Friday.* 星期五前所有借閱書籍必須歸還圖書館。*He ~ed the blow* (ie hit back) *smartly.* 他狠狠地還擊一拳。*She ~ed the compliment,* said sth pleasant after a compliment had been paid to her. 她答謝別人對她表示的敬意。**~ thanks,** express thanks, esp by saying grace before a meal, or in response to a toast. 致謝；感謝（尤用於飯前禱告或回答舉杯祝賀）。**~ed empties,** empty bottles, crates, etc ~ed to the sender for re-use. 歸還送來者（以便再使用）的空瓶、空籃等。 **5** [VP6A, 16A] (of a constituency) send (sb) as representative to Parliament. （指一選區之選民）選出（某人）爲國會議員。**'~·ing officer** *n* official in charge of a Parliamentary election and announcing the name of the person elected. 負責國會議員選舉及公佈當選人名單之官員。**6** [VP6A, 15A] state or describe officially, esp in answer to a demand: 正式宣佈或說明（尤指應一項要求而做出者）：*~ the details of one's income* (for taxation purposes); 申報個人綜合所得（爲了納稅）；*liabilities ~ed at £2000.* 宣佈爲兩千鎊之債務。*The prisoner was ~ed guilty.* 該囚犯被宣告有罪。*The jury ~ed a verdict of guilty.* 陪審團宣判有罪。 **7** [VP6A] give as a profit: 生（利）：*an investment that ~s a good interest.* 有很好利潤的投資。**~·able** /-əbl; -əbl/ *adj* that can be, or is to be, ~ed. 可退還的；必須送還的。

re·un·ion /ˌriːˈjuːnɪən; riˈjunjən/ *n* [U] reuniting or being reunited; [C] (esp) meeting of old friends, former colleagues, etc after separation: 再結合；重行結合；（尤指老友，舊日同僚等濶別後之）重聚：*a family ~ at Christmas.* 聖誕節的合家團聚。

re·unite /ˌriːjuːˈnaɪt; ˌrijʊˈnaɪt/ *vt, vi* [VP6A, 2A] bring or come together again: 使再結合；再結合；使重聚；重聚：*~d after long years of separation.* 多年別離後重聚。

rev /rev; rɛv/ *vt, vi* (-vv-) [VP2A, 6A, 2C, 15B] **rev (up),** (colloq) increase the speed of revolutions in (an internal-combustion engine): （俗）增加（內燃機）的旋轉速度：*Don't rev (up) (the engine) so hard.* 別讓（引擎）轉動得太快。□ *n* revolution: （發動機的）旋轉：*You're driving at maximum revs.* 你在全速行駛。

re·value /riːˈvæljuː; riˈvælju/ *vt* [VP6A] value again or anew; (esp) increase the value of a currency. 再估價；重新估價；（尤指）增加（貨幣）的價值。**re·valu·ation** /ˌriːvæljuːˈeɪʃn; ˌrivæljʊˈeʃən/ *n* revaluing: 再估價；重新估價；（貨幣的）升值：*revaluation of the German mark.* 德國馬克的升值。

re·vamp /ˌriːˈvæmp; riˈvæmp/ *vt* [VP6A] (colloq) patch up; reconstruct; renew: （俗）修補；重建；修改：*~ an old comedy;* 修改一個舊喜劇；*~ agriculture in a backward country,* try to improve it. 改良一落後國家之農業。

re·veal /rɪˈviːl; rɪˈvil/ *vt* [VP6A, 14, 9, 25] **~ (to), 1** allow or cause to be seen; display: 顯示；顯出：*His worn jacket ~ed his elbows.* 他的破短上衣使他露出了肘部。 **2** make known: 洩露；透露：*~ a secret.* 洩露一秘密。*One day the truth about these events will be ~ed.* 這些事件總有一天會眞相大白的。*The doctor did not ~ to him his hopeless condition.* 醫生未向他透露他那已無希望的病況。*Research has ~ed him to be/~ed that he was the father of twelve children.* 調查結果顯示了他是一個有十二個孩子的父親。**~ed religion,** religion believed to be taught to mankind directly by God. 默示教；天啓教（被認爲係直接由上帝啓示於人類的宗教）。

re·veille /rɪˈvælɪ US: ˈrevəlɪ; ˈrɛvl̩ˌi/ *n* (in the armed forces) bugle signal to men to get up in the morning: （部隊中的）起床號：*sound the ~.* 吹起床號。

revel /ˈrevl; ˈrɛvl̩/ *vi, vt* (-ll-; US -l-) **1** [VP2A, B, C, 15B] make merry; have a gay, lively time: 作樂；狂歡享樂：*They ~led until dawn.* 他們通宵作樂。*They ~led away the time.* 他們狂歡作樂虛擲光陰。 **2** [VP3A] **~ in,** take great delight in: 深愛；酷愛；以…爲樂：*~ in one's freedom;* 深愛自由；*people who ~ in gossip.* 好講閒話的人。□ *n* [C, U] (occasion of) lively, happy festivity: 作樂；作樂的時際；作樂的飲宴：*Our ~s now are ended.* 我們的歡宴現在結束了。**~·ler,** (US = **~er**) /ˈrevələ(r); ˈrɛvlɚ/ *n* person who ~s. 縱情享樂的人。

rev·el·ation /ˌrevəˈleɪʃn; ˌrɛvl̩ˈeʃən/ *n* **1** [U] revealing; making known of sth secret or hidden; [C] that which is revealed, esp sth that causes surprise: 顯示；洩露；顯示或洩露的東西（尤指引起驚愕者）：*truths which man knows only by ~,* ie from God. 唯有經神的啓示人纔能知道的眞理。*It was a ~ to John when Mary said she had married him only for his money.* 當瑪莉向約翰說她只是爲了他的錢才嫁他時，使他大爲吃驚。 **2 R~,** the last book of the New Testament, called *The R~ of St John the Divine,* or (less correctly) *R~s.* 聖約翰啓示錄；（較不正確的說法）啓示錄（爲新約最後一書）。

rev·elry /ˈrevlrɪ; ˈrɛvl̩rɪ/ *n* [U] (or *pl;* -ries) noisy, joyous festivity and merrymaking: 吵鬧作樂的飲宴；狂歡作樂：*when the ~/revelries ended.* 當狂歡作樂結束時。

re·venge /rɪˈvendʒ; rɪˈvɛndʒ/ *vt* **1** [VP6A] do sth to get satisfaction for (an offence, etc to oneself or another): 報仇；報復：*~ an injustice/insult;* 對不公（侮辱）採取報復；*~ one's friend,* inflict injury (deliberately) on the person who injured one's friend. 爲朋友報仇。 **2 *be ~d on sb; ~ oneself on sb,*** get satisfaction by deliberately inflicting injury in return for injury inflicted on oneself. 向某人報仇。⇨ avenge. □ *n* [U] **1** deliberate infliction of injury upon the person(s) from whom injury has been received: 報仇；報復：*thirsting for ~;* 渴望報仇雪恨；*nurse thoughts of ~.* 蓄意報仇。***get/take one's ~;*** 報仇；***take ~ on sb (for sth); have/get one's ~ (on sb) (for sth);*** （爲某事）向（某人）報仇；***do sth in/out of ~ (for sth).*** （爲…）報復地做某事（出於報復而做某事）。**2** [U] vindictiveness. 報復心；報仇之欲望。 **3** (in sport) opportunity given for reversing an earlier result by a return match, etc. （運動中）由再次比賽等而獲得轉敗爲勝的機會；雪恥的機會。***give sb his ~;*** 給某人雪恥的機會；***get/take one's ~.*** 盡雪前恥。**~·ful** /-fl; -fl̩/ *adj* feeling or showing a desire for ~. 復仇心的；表現復仇心的。**~·fully** /-fəlɪ; -fəlɪ/ *adv*

rev·enue /ˈrevənjuː US: -ənuː; ˈrɛvəˌnju/ *n* **1** [U] income, esp the total annual income of the State; government department which collects money for public funds: 收入；（尤指）國家的歲入；稅務署；國稅局：*a '~ officer,* a customs and excise officer; 稅務官員；*a '~ cutter,* boat used to detect and prevent smuggling. 緝私船。**Inland R~,** income from taxation, etc. 國內稅收。**'~ tax,** one designed to produce ~ (contrasted with taxes designed to protect a country's trade and commerce). 財政稅（爲謀政府歲入所課之稅，別於以保護一國工商業所課者）。**2** (*pl*) separate items of ~ put together: （複）收入之總額：*the ~s of the City Council.* 市議會的總收入。

re·ver·ber·ate /rɪˈvɜːbəreɪt; rɪˈvɝbəˌret/ *vt, vi* [VP 6A, 2A] (esp of sound) send or throw back, be sent back, again and again: （尤指聲音）反覆送或擲回；被反覆送回；回響；屈折；反射：*The roar of the train ~d/was ~d in the tunnel.* 隧道中回響着火車鳴聲。*His voice ~d from the walls of the cave.* 他的聲音從洞穴的牆壁上反折回來。 **re·ver·ber·ant** /-ənt; -ənt/ *adj* resounding. 反響的；回響的。**re·ver·ber·ation** /rɪˌvɜːbəˈreɪʃn; rɪˌvɝbəˈreʃən/ *n* [U] reverberating or being ~d; (*pl*) echoes; repercussions. 回響；反射；（複）回聲；反響。

re·vere /rɪˈvɪə(r); rɪˈvɪr/ *vt* [VP6A] have deep respect for; regard as sacred, with great respect: 崇敬；敬畏；視爲神聖：*~ virtue;* 崇敬美德；*my ~d* *grandfather.* 我所崇敬的祖父。

rev·er·ence /ˈrevərəns ; ˈrɛvrəns/ *n* [U] deep respect; feeling of wonder and awe: 尊敬;敬畏之情: *hold sb/sth in ~;* 尊敬某人或某物; *have/show ~ for sb/sth.* 對某人或某事物懷有(表示)敬仰。□ *vt* [VP6A] treat with ~. 尊敬;崇敬。

rev·er·end /ˈrevərənd ; ˈrɛvrənd/ *adj* **1** deserving to be treated with respect (because of age, character, etc). (因年齡、品德等)應受尊敬的。**2 the R~,** (usu shortened in writing to *the Rev* or *Revd*), used as a title of a clergyman: (通常縮寫爲 the Rev 或 Revd)牧師之尊稱: *the Rev John Smith* or 或寫作 *the Rev J Smith* (but not *the Rev Smith*); 約翰·史密斯牧師(注意不可寫作 the Rev Smith); *the Very R~* (of a dean); 住持或主持牧師; *the Right R~* (of a bishop); 主教; *the Most R~* (of an archbishop); 大主教; *the R~ Father* (of a R C priest). 神父。**R~ Mother,** Mother Superior of a convent. 女修道院院長。□ *n* (usu *pl*) clergyman: (通常用複數)牧師: *a crowd of ~s and right ~s at the Lambeth Conference.* 出席蘭貝斯會議的一羣牧師和主教。

rev·er·ent /ˈrevərənt ; ˈrɛvrənt/ *adj* feeling or showing reverence. 感覺或表現尊敬的;虔敬的。**~·ly** *adv*

rev·er·en·tial /ˌrevəˈrenʃl ; ˌrɛvəˈrɛnʃəl/ *adj* caused or marked by reverence. 出於尊敬的;尊敬的。**~ly** /-ʃəlɪ ; -ʃəlɪ/ *adv*

rev·erie /ˈrevərɪ ; ˈrɛvərɪ/ *n* **1** [C, U] (instance/occasion of a) condition of being lost in dreamy, pleasant thoughts: 沉緬於夢幻或快樂的思想的情況;幻想;幻想的實例;幻想的時機: *lost in ~;* 陷入幻想中; *indulge in ~s about the future.* 沉醉於對未來的幻想中。**2** [C] piece of dreamy music. 幻想曲。

re·vers /rɪˈvɪə(r) ; rəˈvɪr/ *n* (*pl* ~ /-ɪəz ; -ɪrz/) turned-back edge of a coat, etc showing the reverse side, as on a lapel. 外衣等衣裏翻折在外面的邊(如西服上衣的翻領)。

re·ver·sal /rɪˈvɜːsl ; rɪˈvɝsl/ *n* **1** [U] reversing or being reversed: 反轉;倒退;廢棄;被反轉;被倒退;被廢棄: *the ~ of the seasons in the two hemispheres.* 南北半球季節的顛倒。**2** [C] instance of this: 反轉等的實例: *a ~ of procedure.* 程序的顛倒。

re·verse[1] /rɪˈvɜːs ; rɪˈvɝs/ *adj* **~ (to/of),** contrary or opposite in character or order; inverted: 在性質上或順序上相反的;相對的;顛倒的: *this is the ~ direction to that;* 這是同那個相反的方向; *the ~ side of a length of cloth;* 一段布的反面; *the ~ side of a coin or disc.* 錢幣或唱片的反面。**in ~ order,** from the end to the start, or in the opposite order; in the ~ direction. 以顛倒的次序;方向相反的。**~·ly** *adv*

re·verse[2] /rɪˈvɜːs ; rɪˈvɝs/ *n* **1** [U] **the ~ (of),** opposite; contrary: 相對;相反: *do the ~ of what one is expected to do.* 做違背旁人期望的事。*Your remarks were the ~ of polite,* were impolite. 你的評論是不禮貌的。**2** [C] **the ~ (of),** (sth on the) reverse side (of a coin, medal, disc, etc): (錢幣、徽章、唱片等的)反面;反面上的東西: *On the ~ of this 50p coin there is a design showing a lion wearing a crown.* 這枚五十辨士硬幣的反面有個戴皇冠的獅子的圖案。⇨ reverse[1]. **3** [U, C] mechanism or device that reverses: 倒退或換向的裝置: *Most typewriters have an automatic ribbon ~.* 大部分打字機有一個自動的色帶換向裝置。*Most cars have three forward gears and (a) ~.* 大多數的汽車都有三個前進檔和(一個)倒檔。*Put the car into ~.* 把車子放在倒檔上。**4** [C] defeat; change to bad fortune: 失敗;挫折;不幸;逆運: *Our forces have suffered a slight ~.* 我們的軍隊遭到輕微失敗。*These financial ~s will prevent my taking a holiday.* 這些經濟上的挫折使我不能去度假了。

re·verse[3] /rɪˈvɜːs ; rɪˈvɝs/ *vt, vi* **1** [VP6A] turn (sth) the other way round or up or inside out: 反轉;顛倒;翻轉: *~ a procedure;* 顛倒一程序; *~ one's policy.* 完全改變自己的政策;採取與原定政策完全相反之政策。**a ~d charge,** charge for a telephone call (to be) paid by the person to whom the call is made instead of by the person who makes it. 由受話人繳納之電話費。**~ arms,** (mil) hold the rifle with the muzzle pointing down (as at military funerals). (軍)倒槍(如在軍人葬禮中槍口向下致敬)。**2** [VP6A, 2A] (cause to) go in the opposite direction: (使)向相反方向行進;(使)倒退: *~ one's car into the garage* (*back* is the more usu word). 把車倒進車庫(back 爲較常用的字)。**3** [VP6A] change the order, position, etc of: 改變…的次序或地位等: *Their conditions are now ~d: A is poor and B is rich.* 他們的狀況現在改變了: A 窮, B 富有。**4** [VP6A] revoke, annul: 廢除;取消: *~ the decision of a lower court;* 撤消下級法院的判決; *~ a decree.* 撤消一法令。**re·vers·ible** /-əbl ; -əbl/ *adj* that can be ~d, eg of cloth, either side of which can be used on the outside. 可反轉、倒退、廢棄的;兩面都可用的(例如布)。**re·versi·bil·ity** /rɪˌvɜːsəˈbɪlətɪ ; rɪˌvɝsəˈbɪlətɪ/ *n*

re·ver·sion /rɪˈvɜːʃn *US:* -ʒn ; rɪˈvɝʒən/ *n* ⇨ revert.

re·vert /rɪˈvɜːt ; rɪˈvɝt/ *vi* [VP2A, 3A] **~ (to),** **1** return (to a former state, condition, topic, etc): 恢復(至以前的狀態、情況、話題等): *The fields have ~ed to moorland,* have gone out of cultivation, etc. 這些田地又恢復成荒地。*R~ing to your original statement, I think....* 重回到你原來的敍述,我認爲…。*Garden plants sometimes ~ to type,* go back to the wild kind from which they were developed. 園藝植物有時會恢復其原來的野生形態。*Mental patients sometimes ~,* ie to their condition before treatment started. 治療中的精神病患有時會回復到治療前的狀態。**2** (legal) (of property, rights, etc) return at some named time or under certain conditions (to the original owner, the State, etc): (法律)(指財產、權利等)在某指定時間或在某些情況下復歸(原主,國家等): *If he dies without an heir, his property will ~ to the state.* 如果他死後無繼承人,他的財產卽歸屬國家。**~·ible** /-əbl ; -əbl/ *adj* that may ~. 可恢復原狀的;可復舊觀的;可復歸的。**re·ver·sion** /rɪˈvɜːʃn *US:* -ʒn ; rɪˈvɝʒən/ *n* **1** [U] ~ing (of property, etc). (財產等之)歸屬;復歸原主。⇨ 2 above. 參看上列第 2 義。**2** [C] right to possess property in certain circumstances; land, property, etc to which one has such a right. 在某些情況下具有的財產權;將來享有權;繼承權;對之有此等權利的土地、財產等。**3** [U] ~ing(1): 恢復;倒轉;返祖: *reversion of plants, etc* (ie to ancestral types). 植物等之返祖(卽恢復野生形態)。**re·ver·sion·ary** /rɪˈvɜːʃənərɪ *US:* -ʒənerɪ ; rɪˈvɝʒənˌɛrɪ/ *adj* of reversion(2). 將來可享有的;繼承的。

re·vet·ment /rɪˈvetmənt ; rɪˈvɛtmənt/ *n* retaining wall; facing of masonry, concrete, etc on an embankment, etc. 護土牆;護堤壁;擁壁;護岸;土堡。

re·view /rɪˈvjuː ; rɪˈvju/ *vt, vi* **1** [VP6A] consider or examine again; go over again in the mind: 再考慮;再檢查;檢討;回顧;復習: *~ the past;* 回顧過去; *~ last week's lesson.* 溫習上禮拜的功課。**2** [VP6A] inspect formally (troops, a fleet, etc). 正式檢閱;校閱(部隊、艦隊等)。**3** [VP6A, 2A, C] write an account of (new books, etc) for newspapers and other periodicals: (爲報紙或期刊)寫(新書等)之評論: *His new novel has been favourably ~ed.* 他新寫的小說已得到有利的批評。*Mr Hay ~s for 'The Spectator'.* 黑伊先生爲'觀察報'寫書評。□ *n* **1** [U] act of ~ing(1). 檢討;回顧;溫習。**come under ~,** be considered or examined. 被考慮或受檢查。[C] instance of such ~ing: 檢討、回顧、溫習的實例: *a ~ of the year's sporting events.* 檢討一年中的運動項目。**2** [C] inspection of military, naval, etc forces: 軍事檢閱: *hold a ~.* 舉行軍事檢閱。**3** [C] article that critically examines a new book, etc: 書評文章;評論: *write ~s for the monthly magazines;* 爲月刊寫書評; *a ~ copy of a book,* one presented by the publishers to the editor of a periodical for ~. 出版商送給雜誌編輯以供寫書評之用的書。**4** [C] periodical with articles on current events, ~s of new books, etc. 評論性雜誌(刊載時事、新書等之評論文章的雜誌)。**~er** *n* person who writes ~s (of books, etc). 評論家;書評家。

re·vile /rɪ'vaɪl ; rɪ'vaɪl/ *vt, vi* [VP6A, 3A] **~ at/against,** swear at; abuse: 向…咒罵;辱罵;謾罵: *~ at/against corruption;* 痛斥貪污舞弊; *~ one's persecutors.* 辱罵虐待者。

re·vise /rɪ'vaɪz ; rɪ'vaɪz/ *vt* [VP6A] reconsider; read carefully through, esp in order to correct and improve: 再考慮;(尤指)為改正或修訂而仔細閱讀;校訂;修訂: *~ one's estimates;* 修訂自己的估計; *~ one's opinion of sb.* 改正對某人的看法。*She's revising her notes for the exams,* going through them in preparation for them. 她為了準備考試而仔細閱讀她的筆記。**the R~d Version,** the Version of the Bible made in 1870–84 as a Revision of the translation published in 1611, known as *the Authorized Version.* 聖經修訂本(在 1870–84 年間,由修訂1611年出版的聖經欽定英譯本而成)。□ *n* [C] (printing) proof-sheet in which errors marked in an earlier proof have been corrected. (印刷)再校樣;再校稿。**re·viser** *n* person who ~s. 校訂者;修訂者;再校者。**re·vi·sion** /rɪ'vɪʒn ; rɪ'vɪʒən/ *n* [U] revising or being ~d; [C] instance of this: 修訂;校訂;被修訂;被校訂: *after two revisions;* 經兩次修訂或改正; [C] that which has been ~d; corrected version. 業經修訂或改正之物;改正之校樣或版本;修訂本。**re·vi·sion·ist** /rɪ'vɪʒənɪst ; rɪ'vɪʒənɪst/ *n* person who supports a review of the fundamental tenets of a political ideology. 修正主義者。**re·vi·sion·ism** /-ɪzəm ; -ˌɪzəm/ *n*

re·vital·ize /riː'vaɪtəlaɪz ; ri'vaɪtḷˌaɪz/ *vt* put new life into; restore vitality. 使新生;使恢復活力。**re·vital·iz·ation** /ˌriːˌvaɪtəlaɪ'zeɪʃn *US:* -lɪ'z- ; ˌrivaɪtḷɪ'zeʃən/ *n*

re·vival /rɪ'vaɪvl ; rɪ'vaɪvḷ/ *n* **1** [U] reviving or being revived; bringing or coming back into use or knowledge; [C] instance of this: 復活;復蘇;復興;再興;復活等的實例: *the ~ of an old custom;* 一個古老風俗的再興; *a ~ of a play by Maugham;* 毛姆的一個劇的重新演出; *a ~ of trade.* 貿易之振興。**the R~ of Learning,** the Renaissance. 文藝復興。**2** [C] (series of meetings intended to produce an) increase of interest in religion: 宗教的奮興;信仰恢復;(用以提高大衆信教興趣的)奮興大會: *a religious ~;* 宗教的奮興; *~ meetings.* 宗教的奮興大會。**~·ist** /-vəlɪst ; -vḷɪst/ *n* person who organizes or conducts religious ~ meetings. 組織或領導宗教奮興大會者;信仰復興運動(論)者。

re·vive /rɪ'vaɪv ; rɪ'vaɪv/ *vi, vt* [VP6A, 2A] **1** come or bring back to consciousness, strength, health or an earlier state: 恢復或使恢復知覺、力量、健康或較早的情況;(使)復活;(使)復蘇;(使)復興: *~ a person who has fainted;* 使一個暈厥的人復蘇; *~ an old play,* produce it for the theatre after many years. 重演一個老劇本。*The flowers will ~ in water.* 這些花在水中會再活。*Our hopes ~d.* 我們的希望復活了。**2** come or bring into use again: 復用;再興;使復用;使再興: *customs which ~/are ~d.* 再興的風俗。

re·viv·ify /riː'vɪvɪfaɪ ; ri'vɪvəˌfaɪ/ *vt* (*pt, pp* -fied) restore to animation; give new life or liveliness to. 使蘇醒;使復活;使有生氣、活力。

revo·cable /'revəkəbl ; 'rɛvəkəbḷ/ *adj* that can be revoked. 可廢止的;可撤銷的。**revo·ca·tion** /ˌrevə'keɪʃn ; ˌrɛvə'keʃən/ *n* [U] revoking or being revoked; [C] instance of this. 廢止;撤銷;取消;宣告無效等及其實例。

re·voke /rɪ'vəʊk ; rɪ'vok/ *vt, vi* **1** [VP6A] repeal; cancel; withdraw (a decree, consent, permission, etc): 廢止;撤銷;取消;宣告(命令、同意、允許等)無效: *~ an order/a driving licence.* 撤銷一命令(吊銷一駕駛執照)。**2** [VP2A] (of a player at such card games as whist and bridge) fail to follow suit (ie not play a card of the same suit as that led by another player although he could do so). (指玩惠斯特和橋牌者)有牌不跟。□ *n* failure of this kind. 有牌不跟。

re·volt /rɪ'vəʊlt ; rɪ'volt/ *vi, vt* **1** [VP2A, 3A] **~ (against),** rise in rebellion: 反叛;背叛: *The people ~ed against their oppressors.* 人民反叛其壓迫者。**2** [VP3A] **~ against/at/from,** be filled with disgust or horror: 嫌惡;厭惡: *Human nature ~s at/from/against such a crime.* 人性厭惡這樣的罪行。*This is a doctrine from which sensitive persons must ~.* 這是一種必為敏感的人所厭惡的教條。**3** [VP6A] fill with disgust or horror: 使充滿厭惡: *scenes that ~ed all who saw them.* 見者無不厭惡的景象。□ *n* [U] act of ~ing; state of having ~ed (1): 反叛的行為;已反叛的情況: *a period of ~;* 叛亂時期; *break out in ~;* 暴發叛亂; *stir the people to ~;* 煽動人民叛變; [C] instance of this; rebellion or rising: 反叛的實例;背叛;暴動: *~s against oppression.* 對壓迫的反抗。

re·volt·ing /rɪ'vəʊltɪŋ ; rɪ'voltɪŋ/ *adj* disgusting: 令人厭惡的: *~ behaviour;* 令人厭惡的行為; *~ to our ideas of morality.* 違反我們的道德觀念。**~·ly** *adv* in a way that disgusts: 令人厭惡地: *a ~ly dirty room.* 一個髒得令人討厭的房間。

rev·ol·ution /ˌrevə'luːʃn ; ˌrɛvə'luʃən/ *n* **1** [C] act of revolving or journeying round: 旋轉;環繞: *the ~ of the earth round the sun;* 地球繞太陽的公轉; [C] complete turn of a wheel, etc: (輪等的)旋轉一周: *sixty-five ~s* (or, colloq 俗 *revs*) *a minute.* 每分鐘旋轉六十五次。**2** [C, U] (instance of) complete change (in conditions, ways of doing things, esp in methods of government when caused by the overthrow of one system by force): (情況、做事之方式,尤指武力推翻一種制度引起的統治方法的)澈底改變;革命: *the French R~* (in 1789); (1789 年的)法國大革命; *prefer evolution to ~ in politics;* 在政治上取漸進而不取革命; *~s in our ideas of time and space;* 我們對時空觀念的大改變; *~s in our ways of travelling,* eg as the result of travel by air. 我們旅行方式的大改變(例如坐飛機旅行)。**~·ary** /-ʃənərɪ *US:* -nerɪ ; -ʃənˌɛrɪ/ *adj* of a ~(2); bringing, causing, favouring, great (and perhaps violent) changes: 革命的;帶來、造成、贊成大(並可能是狂暴的)改變的: *~ary ideas;* 革命的思想; *a ~ary society;* 革命性的社會; *imprisoned for advocating ~ary principles.* 為贊成革命的主義被監禁。□ *n* supporter of a (political) ~. (政治)革命的支持者;革命份子。**~·ize** /-naɪz ; -nˌaɪz/ *vt* [VP6A] **1** fill with ~ary principles. 使有革命信仰。**2** make a complete change in; cause to be entirely different: 對…造成澈底改革;使完全不同: *The use of atomic energy will ~ize the lives of coming generations.* 原子能的使用將使未來人類的生活有巨大改變。

re·volve /rɪ'vɒlv ; rɪ'vɑlv/ *vt, vi* **1** [VP6A, 2A, 3A] **~ (about/around),** (cause to) go round in a circle: (使)旋轉: *A wheel ~s about/round its axis.* 輪子繞軸旋轉。*The earth ~s round/about the sun.* 地球繞太陽旋轉。*This theatre has a revolving stage.* 這家戲院有個旋轉式舞臺。**2** [VP6A] turn over in the mind; think about all sides of (a problem, etc): 考慮;熟思(一問題等): *~ a problem in one's mind.* 熟思一個問題。

re·volver /rɪ'vɒlvə(r) ; rɪ'vɑlvɚ/ *n* pistol with a revolving mechanism that makes it possible to fire it a number of times without reloading. 轉輪手槍;左輪。

re·vue /rɪ'vjuː ; rɪ'vju/ *n* [C] theatrical entertainment which consists of a medley of dialogue, dance and song, usu holding up current events, fashions, etc, to satire; [U] this form of entertainment: 時事諷刺劇(包括對話、舞蹈、歌唱,通常多對時事、風尚等加以諷刺);此種形式之表演: *to appear/perform in ~.* 演出(表演)時事諷刺劇。

re·vul·sion /rɪ'vʌlʃn ; rɪ'vʌlʃən/ *n* [U] (no *pl*) (無複數) **1** sudden and complete change of feeling:

心情的突然改變: *There was a ~ of public feeling in favour of the accused woman.* 輿論突然轉而同情被控的婦人了。 **2** ~ ***(against/from),*** feeling of reaction. 厭惡;嫌棄。

re·ward /rɪˈwɔːd; rɪˈwɔrd/ *n* **1** [U] recompense for service or merit: 報酬;報答: *work without hope of ~;* 沒有希望得到報酬的工作; *the ~ of virtue;* 美德的報酬; *get very little in ~ for one's hard work.* 雖辛苦工作,得到的報酬却很少。 **2** [C] that which is offered, given or obtained in return for work or services, or the restoration of lost or stolen property, the capture of a criminal, etc: (爲工作或服務,或尋回遺失或被偸的財物,或捉住一罪犯等而給予或得到的)酬勞金;賞金: *offer a ~ of £100 for information about a stolen painting.* 懸賞一百鎊尋找失竊的畫。□ *vt* [VP6A, 14] ~ ***sb (for sth),*** give a ~ to (sb for sth): (爲某事)給(某人)報酬或獎賞: *Is that how you ~ me for my help?* 那就是你爲了我的幫忙而給予我的報酬嗎?

re·wire /ˌriːˈwaɪə(r); riˈwaɪr/ *vt* provide, eg a building, with new wiring (for electric current). 裝設新電線;改裝(電)線路。

re·word /ˌriːˈwɜːd; riˈwɝd/ *vt* [VP6A] express again in different words: 再以不同的字或話表示;改寫;改說: *If we ~ the telegram we can save one-third of the cost.* 我們如果把這電報改寫一下,就能省下三分之一的費用。

re·write /ˌriːˈraɪt; riˈraɪt/ *vt* [VP6A] write again in a different style, etc. 重寫;再寫;改寫。□ /ˈriː-raɪt; ˈriˌraɪt/ *n* (colloq) sth rewritten: (俗)改寫的作品: (attrib) (形容用法) *a ˈ~ man,* one employed to ~ articles, books, etc in a form suitable for publication. 受雇從事改寫文章、書籍等的作家。

Rex /reks; rɛks/ *n* (abbr 略作 **R**) reigning king (used as **Regina** is used). 君;王(用法如 Regina)。

rhap·sody /ˈræpsədɪ; ˈræpsədɪ/ *n* [C] (*pl* -dies) **1** enthusiastic expression of delight (in speech, poetry, etc): (在言論或詩等中)狂熱欣喜的表現: *Everyone went into rhapsodies over Helen's wedding dress.* 大家熱烈讚揚海倫的結婚禮服。 **2** (music) composition in irregular form: (音樂)狂想曲: *Liszt's Hungarian Rhapsodies.* 李斯特的匈牙利狂想曲。 **rhap·so·dize** /ˈræpsədaɪz; ˈræpsəˌdaɪz/ *vi* [VP 2A, 3A] ***rhapsodize (about/over/on),*** talk or write with great enthusiasm. 極熱烈地說或寫。

rhea /rɪə; ˈriə/ *n* three-toed ostrich of S America. 鶆鶓;美洲鴕(南美洲產三趾鴕鳥)。

Rhen·ish /ˈrenɪʃ; ˈrɛnɪʃ/ *adj* of the River Rhine and the districts on its banks: 萊茵河及其流域的: ~ *wine,* hock. 萊茵酒。

rheo·stat /ˈriːəstæt; ˈriəˌstæt/ *n* instrument for regulating the strength of an electric current by means of different resistances in the circuit, eg as in the volume control of a radio receiver. 變阻器(在電路中以不同的電阻控制電流强度的器具,如無線電接收機的音量控制器內所用者)。

rhe·sus /ˈriːsəs; ˈrisəs/ *n* small monkey with a short tail, common in N India, often used in biological experiments. 印度北部常見的一種短尾小猴;恆河猴(常被用來做生物學方面的試驗)。⇨ the illus at ape. 參看 ape 之插圖。

rhet·oric /ˈretərɪk; ˈrɛtərɪk/ *n* [U] **1** (art of) using words impressively in speech and writing. 修辭;修辭學。 **2** language with much display and ornamentation (often with the implication of insincerity and exaggeration): 辭藻華麗的語言(常含浮誇的意味): *the ~ of the politicians.* 政客的花言巧語。

rhe·tori·cal /rɪˈtɒrɪkl *US:* -ˈtɔːr-; rɪˈtɔrɪkl/ *adj* in, using, a style designed to impress or persuade; artificial or exaggerated in language: 修辭的;辭藻華麗或誇張的: *a ~ speech.* 誇張的演說。 ***a ~ question,*** one asked for the sake of effect, to impress people, no answer being needed or expected. 反問;反詰(爲獲取效果或加强別人印象,而非需要或預期有答案的問題)。 **~ly** /-klɪ; -klɪ/ *adv*

rhet·or·ician /ˌretəˈrɪʃn; ˌrɛtəˈrɪʃən/ *n* person skilled in rhetoric or fond of rhetorical language. 修辭學家;雄辯家;喜用華麗詞藻的人。

rheum /ruːm; rum/ *n* [U] watery discharge from the nose or eyes. 鼻或眼所分泌之稀黏液;鼻涕;眼淚。

rheu·matic /ruːˈmætɪk; ruˈmætɪk/ *adj* relating to, causing, caused by, rheumatism; suffering from, liable to have, rheumatism: 風濕症的;引起風濕症的;由風濕症引起的;患風濕症的;易罹風濕症的: ~ *joints.* 患風濕症的關節。 ~ **fever,** serious fever with inflammation of joints, chiefly in children. 風濕性熱。□ *n* **1** person who suffers from rheumatism. 風濕症患者。 **2** (*pl* colloq) ~ pains. (複,俗)風濕痛。

rheu·ma·tism /ˈruːmətɪzəm; ˈruməˌtɪzəm/ *n* [U] (kinds of) painful disease with stiffness and inflammation of the muscles and joints. 風濕症。

rheu·ma·toid /ˈruːmətɔɪd; ˈruməˌtɔɪd/ *adj* of rheumatism. 風濕樣的;風濕症的。 ~ **arthritis,** chronic form of arthritis. 風濕樣關節炎;風濕性關節炎。

rhinal /ˈraɪnl; ˈraɪnl̩/ *adj* (anat) of the nose or nostrils. (解剖)鼻的;鼻腔的。

Rhine /raɪn; raɪn/ *n* German river: (德國之)萊茵河: ~ *wine,* = hock. ˈ**~·stone** *n* kind of rock-crystal; paste gem made in imitation of a diamond. 萊茵石(一種水晶);假金鋼鑽。

rhino /ˈraɪnəʊ; ˈraɪno/ *n* (*pl* ~s /-nəʊz; -noz/) (colloq abbr of) rhinoceros. (俗)爲 rhinoceros 之略。

rhi·noc·eros /raɪˈnɒsərəs; raɪˈnɑsərəs/ *n* (*pl* ~es /-əsɪz; -əsɪz/ or, collectively, ~) thick-skinned, heavily built animal of Africa and Asia with one or two horns on the snout. 犀牛(非洲與亞洲產的一種動物,皮厚體重,鼻上有一角或兩角)。⇨ the illus at large. 參看 large 之插圖。

rhi·zome /ˈraɪzəʊm; ˈraɪzom/ *n* [C] (bot) thick, horizontal stem of some plants, eg iris, on or just below the ground, from which new roots grow. (植物)(鳶尾等植物長於地面上或剛好在地面下的)地下莖;根莖。

rho·do·den·dron /ˌrəʊdəˈdendrən; ˌrodəˈdɛndrən/ *n* [C] kinds of evergreen shrub with large flowers growing in clusters. 杜鵑花屬;山杜鵑。

rhomb /rɒm; rɑmb/, **rhom·bus** /ˈrɒmbəs; ˈrɑmbəs/ *nn* four-sided figure with equal sides, and angles which are not right angles (eg diamond or lozenge shape). 菱形。⇨ the illus at quadrilateral. 參看 quadrilateral 之插圖。 **rhom·boid** /ˈrɒmbɔɪd; ˈrɑmbɔɪd/ *adj* of the shape of a ~. 菱形的。□ *n* rhombus with only its opposite sides equal. 平行四邊形。⇨ the illus at quadrilateral. 參看 quadrilateral 之插圖。

rhu·barb /ˈruːbɑːb; ˈrubɑrb/ *n* [U] **1** (garden plant with) thick, juicy stalks which are cooked and eaten like fruit. 大黃;大黃莖(粗大而多汁,可如水果般煮食之)。 **2** (colloq) nonsense; (US) angry disagreement. (俗)胡說;(美)爭吵。

rhyme (US also **rime**) /raɪm; raɪm/ *n* **1** [U] sameness of sound of the endings of two or more words at the ends of lines of verse, eg *say, day, play; measure, pleasure; puff, rough.* 韻;韻腳(詩行末尾兩字以上之尾音彼此相同,如 say, day, play 同韻; measure, pleasure 同韻; puff, rough 同韻)。 ***without ~ or reason,*** without meaning; nonsensical(ly). 無意義的(地)。 **2** [C] ~ ***(for/to),*** word which provides a ~: 押韻的字: *Is there a ~ to/for 'hiccups'?* 有什麼字和 hiccups 押韻嗎? **3** [C] verse or verses with ~. 有韻的詩。 ˈ**nursery ~,** verse for small children. 搖籃歌;兒歌;童謠。 **4** [U] the employment of ~: 押韻;用韻: *The story should be told in ~,* in verse with ~s. 這個故事應該用韻文講。□ *vt, vi* **1** [VP6A] put together to form a ~: 使押韻: *Can we ~ 'hiccups' and 'pick-ups'?* hiccups 和 pick-ups 押韻嗎? **2** [VP 2A, 3A] ~ ***(with),*** (of words or lines of verse) be in ~: (指字或詩行)押韻: *'Piebald' doesn't ~ with 'ribald'.* Piebald 與 ribald 不押韻。 **rhyming**

slang, eg 'trouble and strife' for 'wife'. 押韻的俚語(如用 trouble and strife 表示 wife)。**3** [VP2A] write verse(s) with ~. 寫押韻的詩。~**d** *adj* having ~s: 有韻的: *~d verse.* 有韻的詩。~**·ster** /ˈraɪmstə(r); ˈraɪmstɚ/ *n* (usu contemptuous) person who writes ~s or verses. (通常有輕蔑之意)寫詩的人;打油詩人。

rhythm /ˈrɪðəm; ˈrɪðəm/ *n* **1** [U] regular succession of weak and strong stresses, accents, sounds or movements (in speech, music, dancing, etc); regular recurrence of events, processes, etc: (說話、音樂、舞蹈等的)韻律;節奏;(事件、過程等的)有規律的重覆: *the ~ of the tides,* their regular rise and fall. 潮汐的漲落。 **2** [C] particular kind of such regular succession or recurrence. 某種有規律的連續或重現。**rhyth·mic** /ˈrɪðmɪk; ˈrɪðmɪk/, **rhyth·mi·cal** /ˈrɪðmɪkl; ˈrɪðmɪkḷ/ *adjj* marked by ~; having ~: 有節奏的;有韻律的: *the ~ical tread of marching soldiers.* 行進中之士兵有節奏的步伐。

rib /rɪb; rɪb/ *n* [C] **1** any one of the 12 pairs of curved bones extending from the backbone round the chest to the front of the body in man, ⇨ the illus at skeleton; corresponding bone in an animal. 肋骨(參看 skeleton 之插圖);動物之肋骨。***dig/poke sb in the ribs,*** poke him to draw his attention (good-naturedly) to sth or to show enjoyment of a joke. (善意地)觸某人之肋骨(使其注意某事物,或表示欣賞一個笑話的妙處)。**2** (of various things like ribs) vein of a leaf; mark left on sand on the sea-shore by waves; (in a wooden boat) one of the curved pieces of timber to which planks are secured; raised line in a piece of knitting; long, narrow, raised ridge on cloth; hinged rod of an umbrella-frame. (指許多類似肋骨的東西)葉脈;波浪留於海岸沙灘上的痕跡;(船的)肋材;織物的稜線;布上狹長高起的稜條;傘架之骨。□ *vt* (-bb-) [VP6A] **1** supply with, mark off in, ribs: 供以肋骨狀物;以肋骨狀物標開: *ribbed cloth,* having rib-like marks. 有稜條的布。 **2** (US, colloq or sl) tease. (美,俗或俚)戲弄;嘲笑。

rib·ald /ˈrɪbld; ˈrɪbḷd/ *adj* (of a person) using indecent or irreverent language or humour; (of language, laughter, etc) coarse; mocking: (指人)使用猥褻或不敬的言語的;說髒話的;(指言語、笑聲等)粗野的;嘲弄的: *~ jests/songs.* 下流的戲謔(歌)。□ *n* person who uses ~ language. 說髒話的人。~**ry** /-drɪ; -drɪ/ *n* [U] ~ language; coarse jesting. 猥褻的言語;髒話;粗鄙的戲弄。

rib·and /ˈrɪbənd; ˈrɪbənd/ *n* (old use) ribbon. (舊用法)絲帶。

rib·bon /ˈrɪbən; ˈrɪbən/ *n* **1** [C, U] (piece or length of) silk or other material woven in a long, narrow strip or band, used for ornamenting, for tying things, etc: 絲質或其他質料的狹長帶子(用以作裝飾或綁東西等): *Her hair was tied up with a ~.* 她的頭髮用一條絲帶紮著。*Typewriter ~s may be all black or black and red.* 打字帶可以是全部黑色或黑紅兩色。**2** [C] piece of ~ of a special design, colour, etc worn to indicate membership of an order, as a symbol of a military decoration (when medals are not worn). (表示勳位,或作爲軍事勳章之象徵的)勳表;獎表。 **3** [C] long, narrow strip: 狹長之條: *His clothes were hanging in ~s,* were torn or worn to strips. 他的衣服襤褸不堪(破成一條一條的)。*The shirts were torn to ~s in the washing machine.* 這些襯衣在洗衣機中被絞成了許多長條。 **4** ˌ**~-deˈvelopment** *n* (the building of) long lines of houses along main roads leading out of a large town (considered to spoil the countryside). 帶狀發展(大城市通往郊區的大路旁的建築,被認爲會破壞鄉村)。

ri·bo·fla·vin /ˌraɪbəʊˈfleɪvɪn; ˌraɪbəˈflevɪn/ *n* [U] growth-producing factor in the vitamin B_2 complex, found in meat, milk, some vegetables, and produced synthetically. 核黃素(複合維他命B_2中促進生長之要素,肉類、牛奶和某些蔬菜均含有此種成分,並可由人工合成)。

rice /raɪs; raɪs/ *n* [U] (plant with) pearl-white grain used as a staple food everywhere: 稻;米;大米: *polished ~,* with the husks removed; 精米; *brown ~,* unpolished ~; 糙米; *ground ~,* ~ ground to a fine powder. 米磨成之粉。⇨ the illus at cereal. 參看 cereal 之插圖。ˈ**~-paper** *n* kind of thin paper used by Chinese artists for painting on; edible kind used in cooking and for packing cakes, sweets, etc. 宣紙(中國畫家繪畫所用者);糯米紙(一種可食之紙,用於烹飪及包裝糖果等)。

rich /rɪtʃ; rɪtʃ/ *adj* (-er, -est) **1** having much money or property: 富有的: *the ~ and the poor,* ~ people and poor people. 富人和窮人。**2** costly; splendid; luxurious: 昂貴的;華麗的;豪華的: *~ clothes/jewels/furniture.* 華麗的衣服(昂貴的珠寶;豪華的傢具)。**3** ~ ***in,*** producing or having much or many; abundant: 多的;富於…的;豐饒的: *~ in minerals;* 礦藏豐饒的; *an art gallery ~ in paintings by the Dutch masters.* 一個收藏了很多荷蘭大師的畫的畫廊。 **4** (of food) containing a large proportion of fat, oil, butter, eggs, etc: (指食物)含大量脂肪、油、牛油、蛋類等的;油膩的: *a ~ fruit cake;* 含大量油脂的水果餅; *a ~ diet.* 油膩的食物。 **5** (of colours, sounds, etc) full; deep; mellow; strong: (指顏色、聲音等)宏亮清晰的;深沉的;柔和的;濃厚的: *the ~ colours of the begonias;* 秋海棠的鮮麗顏色; *~ tones;* 宏亮的聲調; *the ~ voice of the baritone.* 男中音宏亮的聲音。 **6** (colloq) highly entertaining; giving opportunities for humour: (俗)非常有趣的;很好笑的: *a ~ joke;* 一個非常有趣的笑話; *a ~ incident.* 一件很好笑的事。*That's ~!* (often ironic). 眞好笑!眞有趣!(通常含有諷刺意味)。~**·ly** *adv* **1** in a ~ manner: 富裕地;華麗地;富麗地;豐饒地;濃郁地: *~ly dressed.* 衣著富麗。**2** (esp) (尤用於) ***~ly deserved,*** thoroughly; fully: 徹底地;充分地: *He ~ly deserved the punishment he received.* 他所受到的處罰實在是罪有應得。~**·ness** *n* [U] quality or state of being ~ (but not usu in sense of 1 above). 富麗、肥沃、豐饒、柔和、低沉、濃郁等的性質或狀況。

riches /ˈrɪtʃɪz; ˈrɪtʃɪz/ *n pl* wealth; being rich: 財富;財寶;富有: *the enjoyment of ~;* 財富之享受; *amass great ~.* 積聚大財富。

rick[1] /rɪk; rɪk/ *n* [C] mass of hay, straw, corn, etc regularly built up (and usu thatched or otherwise covered to protect it from the rain). 乾草堆;禾堆。□ *vt* [VP6A] make (hay, etc) into a ~. 堆(乾草等)成禾堆。

rick[2] /rɪk; rɪk/ = wrick.

rick·ets /ˈrɪkɪts; ˈrɪkɪts/ *n* (with *sing* or *pl v*) disease of childhood, marked by softening and malformation of the bones, caused by deficiency of vitamin D as found in fresh food, eg milk, butter. (與單數或複數動詞連用)佝僂病;軟骨病(小兒因缺乏新鮮食物如奶、牛油中的維他命D所致)。

rick·ety /ˈrɪkətɪ; ˈrɪkətɪ/ *adj* weak, esp in the joints; likely to break and collapse: 連接處不堅牢的;易於破碎或倒塌的;搖晃的: *~ furniture;* 搖動不牢的傢具; *a ~ old car.* 一輛搖搖晃晃的舊汽車。

rick·shaw /ˈrɪkʃɔː; ˈrɪkʃɔ/ *n* two-wheeled covered vehicle for one or two passengers, pulled by a man. 人力車;黃包車。ˈ**cycle ~,** three-wheeled bicycle with ~ seating attached behind the driver. 三輪車。

rico·chet /ˈrɪkəʃeɪ US: ˌrɪkəˈʃeɪ; ˌrɪkəˈʃe/ *n* [U] jumping or skipping movement (of a stone, bullet, etc) after hitting the ground, a solid substance or the surface of water; [C] hit made by sth after such a jumping or skipping movement. (石頭、子彈等擊中地面、堅固物體或水面後的)跳飛;回躍;漂掠;跳飛、回躍或漂掠後的一擊。□ *vi, vt* (-t- or -tt-) (*pt, pp* -che(t)ted /-ʃeɪd; -ˈʃed/) [VP6A, 2A] (of a shot, etc) (cause to) rebound, skip or bound off: (指彈丸等)(使)跳飛;回躍;漂掠: *The* *bullet ~ed off the wall.* 子彈自牆上跳飛。

rid /rɪd ; rɪd/ *vt* (*pt, pp* rid) [VP14] ***rid of,*** make free: 使獲自由;解除;免除: *rid oneself of debt/lice;* 還清債務(清除蝨子); *rid a country of terrorists/a house of mice.* 清除一個國家內的恐怖份子(一屋內的老鼠)。***be/get rid of,*** be/become free of: 擺脫;解脫;除去: *We were glad to be rid of our overcoats.* 我們很高興脫掉了外套。*These shoes are difficult to get rid of,* (eg of articles in a shop) difficult to sell. 這些鞋子很難賣掉。*How can we get rid of this unwelcome visitor,* How can we manage to make him leave? 我們怎樣才能擺脫這位不受歡迎的客人？

rid·dance /ˈrɪdns ; ˈrɪdn̩s/ *n* [U] (usu 通常作 ***good ~***) welcome clearing away; state of being rid of sth unwanted or undesirable: 清除;解除;擺脫不需要或討厭的事物的狀態: *Their departure was a good ~,* it brought satisfaction because we wanted to be rid of them. 他們的離去眞是一大快事。

rid·den /ˈrɪdn ; ˈrɪdn̩/ (*pp* of ride²) (esp in compounds) oppressed or dominated by: (尤用於複合字中)受…壓迫的;受…控制的: *ˈpriest-~;* 教士囂張的;被教士壓迫或控制的; *poˈlice-~.* 警察暴橫擾人的;受警察壓迫或控制的。

riddle¹ /ˈrɪdl ; ˈrɪdl̩/ *n* [C] **1** puzzling question, statement or description, intended to make a person use his wits: 謎(難解的問題、陳述或敍述,目的在使一個人運用他的機智): *ask sb a ~;* 出一個謎給某人猜; *know the answer to a ~.* 知道一個謎的解答。**2** puzzling person, thing, situation, etc: 難理解的人、事物、情況等: *the ~ of the universe/of existence.* 宇宙(存在)之謎。□ *vt* ***~ me this,*** solve this ~ (as a challenge). 爲我解決這個問題;請你猜這個謎(作爲一項挑戰)。

riddle² /ˈrɪdl ; ˈrɪdl̩/ *n* [C] coarse sieve (for stones, earth, gravel, cinders etc). (篩石、土、砂、煤渣等用的)粗篩。□ *vt* **1** [VP6A] pass (soil, ashes, corn etc) through a ~; agitate (a grate, eg in a stove) in order to force ashes, small cinders, etc, through. 篩(土、灰、穀物等);搜通(火爐等的鐵架)以使灰、小煤渣落下。**2** [VP6A, 14] ***~ (with),*** make many holes in (sth), eg by firing bullets into it: 打許多洞在(某物)上(如向之發射子彈): *~ a ship with shot;* 用砲彈把一條船打許多洞; *~ a man with bullets;* 用子彈把一人打得滿是窟窿; *~ an argument,* refute it by bringing many facts, etc against it. 列舉事實等反駁一議論。***be ~d with,*** be filled or permeated with: 充滿;瀰漫: *a murder ~d with puzzles.* 迷離不解的兇殺案。

ride¹ /raɪd ; raɪd/ *n* [C] **1** period of riding; journey on horseback, on a bicycle, etc or in a public conveyance 騎乘的一段時間;騎馬、騎脚踏車或乘坐公共交通工具旅行(cf 參較 *go for a drive* in a privately owned car, etc 駕自用汽車等出遊): *go for a ~ before breakfast.* 早飯前騎一會兒馬(或脚踏車)。*'Give me a ~ on your shoulders, Daddy.'* '爹爹,讓我在你肩上騎一會兒。' *It's a fivepenny ~ on a bus.* 乘公共汽車去要五辨士。***take sb for a ~,*** (colloq) deceive, swindle or humiliate him. (俗)欺騙或羞辱某人。**2** road or track (usu unpaved), esp one through a wood or forest for the use of persons on horseback and not normally used by vehicles. 供騎馬用而在正常情形下不能行車的林間道路(通常爲未鋪路面者);騎徑。

ride² /raɪd ; raɪd/ *vi, vt* (*pt* rode /rəʊd ; rod/, *pp* ridden /ˈrɪdn ; ˈrɪdn̩/) **1** [VP2A, B, C, 4A] sit on a horse, etc and be carried along; sit on a bicycle, etc and cause it to go forward: 騎馬(等);騎脚踏車(等): *He jumped on his horse and rode off/away.* 他躍上馬背馳騁而去。*He was riding fast.* 他騎馬急馳(或騎脚踏車等飛奔)。***~ for a fall,*** ride recklessly; (fig) act in such a way that failure or disaster is probable. 騎馬橫衝直撞;(喩)鹵莽行事。**2** [VP6A] sit on and control: 騎(馬等);乘(車等): *~ a horse/pony/bicycle.* 騎馬(小馬,脚踏車)。**3** [VP2A, C, 4A] be in, and be carried in, a cart, bus or other vehicle: 乘坐車輛或其他陸上交通工具: *~ in a bus;* 乘公共汽車; *~ in/on a cart.* 乘二輪馬車。**4** [VP6A] compete in, on horseback, etc: 比賽騎馬或駕車: *~ a race.* 賽馬;賽車。**5** [VP2C, 3A] *~* ***on,*** sit or go or be on sth, esp astride, as if on a horse: 如騎馬般跨坐或行進: *The boy was riding on his father's shoulders.* 那男孩正跨坐在他父親的肩上。**6** [VP15A] allow (sb) to ~(5): 讓(某人)騎坐: *Shall I ~ you on my shoulders/knees?* 你跨坐在我的肩(膝)上好嗎？ **7** [VP2A] go out regularly on horseback (as a pastime, for exercise, etc): 經常騎馬外出(作爲娛樂或運動等): *I've given up riding.* 我已放棄騎馬。***~ to hounds,*** go fox-hunting. 去獵狐。**8** [VP6A] go through or over on horseback, etc: 騎馬等穿越或躍過: *~ the prairies/the desert.* 騎馬穿過大草原(大沙漠)。**9** [VP2B] (of a jockey or other person) weigh when ready for riding: (指騎師或其他人)出賽前量體重: *He ~s 9 stone, 6 pounds.* 他出賽前重九呫六磅。**10** [VP2D] (of ground, etc) be in a specified condition for riding on (usu on horseback): (指地面等)成某種供騎乘(通常指騎馬)的特殊情況: *The heavy rain made the course ~ soft.* 大雨使那跑馬場變成鬆軟(騎起馬來覺得地面很鬆軟)。*The ground rode hard after the frost.* 降霜後的地面騎起馬來很堅硬。**11** [VP6A, 2C] float on: 漂浮於;漂行;航行: *a ship riding the waves;* 一艘乘風破浪的船; float on water: 停泊水上: *a ship riding at anchor;* 一艘拋錨停泊的船; be supported by: 被…所支撐: *an albatross riding (on) the wind.* 一隻御風飛行的信天翁。*The moon was riding high,* appeared high as if floating. 月亮高懸天空。***~ out a storm,*** (of a ship) come safely through it; (fig) come safely through trouble, attack, controversy, etc. (指船)安然度過狂風暴雨;(喩)平安度過困難、攻擊、爭辯等。***let sth ~,*** (colloq) take no action on it; leave things to take their natural course. (俗)聽其自然。**12** ***~ sb down,*** **(a)** chase (on horseback) and catch up with. 騎馬追上。**(b)** direct one's horse at sb so as to let the horse knock him down: 策馬撞倒: *~ down a fugitive.* 策馬撞倒一逃犯。**13** [VP2C] ***~ up,*** eg of an article of clothing, shift or move upwards, out of place. (如衣服等)往上滑而離開了原來的位置。**14** **ridden** *pp* tyrannized, dominated: 受…壓迫的;受…控制的: *ridden by fears/prejudices;* 充滿恐懼(偏見)的; *ˈpest-ridden.* 滿是害蟲的。

rider /ˈraɪdə(r) ; ˈraɪdɚ/ *n* **1** person who rides, esp one who rides a horse: 騎乘者;(尤指)騎馬者: *Miss White is no ~.* 懷特小姐不善騎馬。⇨ also *diˈspatch-~* at dispatch¹(2). **2** additional observation following a statement, verdict, etc: 供述、判決文等後面附加的評論;附文: *The jury added a ~ to their verdict recommending mercy.* 陪審團在他們的判決文後面添加了一段建議,請求從輕量刑。**~·less** *adj* without a ~: 無騎乘者的: *a ~less horse careering round the race-course.* 一匹無人騎坐的馬在賽馬場上急馳。

ridge /rɪdʒ ; rɪdʒ/ *n* [C] **1** raised line where two sloping surfaces meet: 脊: *the ~ of a roof.* 屋脊。**ˈ~-pole** *n* horizontal pole of a long tent; strong horizontal main beam at the apex of a roof. (長形帳篷的)横樑;(屋脊之)樑木。**ˈ~-tile** *n* tile for the ~ of a roof. 屋脊瓦。**2** long, narrow stretch of high land along the tops of a line of hills; long mountain range or watershed. 沿一列小山頂上的狹長高地;山脊;山脈;分水嶺。**3** (in ploughed land) raised part between two furrows. (耕地之)兩畦間隆起部份;畦背。□ *vt* [VP6A] make into, cover with, ~s. 使成脊狀。

ridi·cule /ˈrɪdɪkjuːl ; ˈrɪdɪkjul/ *n* [U] making or being made fun of; derision; mockery: 嘲笑;被戲弄;嘲弄: *pour ~ on a scheme;* 對一計畫加以譏笑; *an object of ~.* 被嘲弄之目標。***hold a man up to ~,*** make fun of him. 嘲弄某人。***lay oneself open to ~,*** behave so that people are likely to make fun of one. 使自己易受嘲笑。□ *vt* [VP6A] make fun of; cause (sb or sth) to appear foolish: 嘲弄;使(某人或某事物)顯出蠢相: *Why do you ~ my proposal?* 你爲甚麼嘲笑我的提議?

ri·dicu·lous /rɪˈdɪkjʊləs ; rɪˈdɪkjələs/ *adj* deserving to be laughed at; absurd: 可笑的;荒謬的: *You look ~ in those tight jeans.* 你穿上那緊身牛仔褲樣子很可笑。*What a ~ idea!* 一個多麼荒謬的想法!**~·ly** *adv*

rid·ing[1] /ˈraɪdɪŋ ; ˈraɪdɪŋ/ *n* [U] (from ride[2]) (由ride[2] 變來) **ˈ~-breeches** *n pl* used for riding on horseback. 馬褲。**ˈ~-habit** *n* woman's long skirt and tight-fitting coat (worn when riding a horse). 女用騎裝(長裙和緊身外衣)。 **ˈ~-light/-lamp** *n* light in the rigging of a ship which is at anchor. (船拋錨時纜索上掛的)碇泊燈。**ˈ~ master** *n* man who teaches horse-~. 騎術師。**ˈ~-school** *n* one for teaching and practising horse-~. 騎術學校。

rid·ing[2] /ˈraɪdɪŋ ; ˈraɪdɪŋ/ *n* (GB until 1974) one of the three administrative divisions of Yorkshire: (英,1974年以前)約克郡的三個行政區之一: *the North/East/West R~* (since 1974 replaced by *Humberside* and *North/South/West Yorkshire*). 約克郡的北(東,西)行政區(自 1974 年起改爲韓柏塞郡及北(南,西)約克郡)。

Ries·ling /ˈriːslɪŋ ; ˈrislɪŋ/ *n* dry, white wine. 一種無甜味的白葡萄酒。

rife /raɪf ; raɪf/ *adj* (*pred* only) (僅作敍述用法) **1** widespread; common: 流行的;普遍的: *Is superstition still ~ in the country?* 迷信仍盛行於鄉間嗎? **2** ~ *with*, full of: 充滿的;充斥的: *The country was ~ with rumours of war.* 這個國家充斥着戰爭的謠言。

riff /rɪf ; rɪf/ *n* repeated phrase in jazz or pop music. (爵士樂或流行音樂中之)重疊句。

riffle /ˈrɪfl ; ˈrɪfl̩/ *vt, vi* **1** [VP6A] shuffle playing cards by holding part of the pack in each hand and releasing the edges so that they fall haphazardly into one pack again. 洗紙牌(兩手各拿一些紙牌,並將牌的一端鬆開,使牌交錯混在一堆)。**2** [VP6A] turn over (the pages of a book, periodical, etc) quickly. 迅速翻動(書頁)。[VP3A] *~ through sth*, shuffle (a pack of cards); turn over quickly or casually (the pages of a newspaper, a periodical, etc). 洗(牌);迅速或隨意地翻動(報紙、雜誌書頁等)。

riff-raff /ˈrɪf ræf ; ˈrɪfˌræf/ *n the ~*, ill-behaved people of the lowest class; the rabble; disreputable persons: 下層社會;暴民;賤民;聲名狼藉的人: *Is it only the ~ who leave litter about in the parks?* 只是那些下層社會的人才在公園裡亂丟東西嗎?

rifle[1] /ˈraɪfl ; ˈraɪfl̩/ *vt* [VP6A] cut spiral grooves in (a gun, its barrel or bore). 在(槍,槍管或槍膛)中刻出螺旋形凹線;加膛線或來復線於。□ *n* gun with a long ~d barrel, to be fired from the shoulder; large gun with such spiral grooves; (*pl*) troops armed with ~s: 長槍管刻有螺旋形凹線的槍;來復槍;步槍;(複)步槍隊: *the Royal Irish R~s.* 英國愛爾蘭皇家步槍隊。**ˈ~-range** *n* **(a)** place where men practise shooting with ~s. 步槍射擊場。**(b)** distance that a ~-bullet will carry: 步槍射程: *within/out of ~-range.* 在步槍的射程內(外)。**ˈ~-shot** *n* **(a)** = ~-range(b). **(b)** good marksman with a ~. 優秀的步槍射擊手。**ˈ~·man** /-mən ; -mən/ *n* (*pl* -men) soldier of a ~ regiment. (步兵團之)步槍兵。

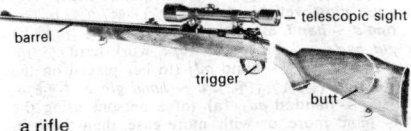

a rifle

rifle[2] /ˈraɪfl ; ˈraɪfl̩/ *vt* [VP6A] search thoroughly in order to steal from: 爲偸竊而仔細搜查: *The thief ~d every drawer in the room/~d the drawers of their contents.* 那賊把屋裏每個抽屜都搜徧了(搜尋抽屜裏的東西)。

rift /rɪft ; rɪft/ *n* [C] **1** split or crack: 裂縫;裂隙: *a ~ in the clouds.* 雲間之縫;雲縫。**ˈ~-valley** *n* steep-sided valley caused by subsidence of the earth's crust. 因地殼下沉而成的險峻之谷。 **2** (fig) dissension (eg between two friends, friendly groups, parties, etc). (喻)(兩個朋友、友好團體等之間的)失和。

rig[1] /rɪg ; rɪg/ *vt, vi* (-gg-) **1** [VP6A, 14, 2A, C] *rig (with)*, supply (a ship) with masts, spars, rigging, sails, etc; (of a ship) be supplied with these things; prepare for sea in this way: 將檣桅、帆桅、索具、帆等裝備(一船);(指船)裝備有此等物件;準備出航: *rig a ship with new sails.* 給一船裝新帆。*The schooner is rigging for another voyage.* 這艘縱帆式帆船正準備另一次航行。**2** [VP14, 15B] *rig sb (out) (in/with sth)*, **(a)** provide with necessary clothes, equipment, etc. 供以必需之衣物、裝備等。**(b)** (colloq) dress up: (俗)裝束: *She was rigged out in her best clothes.* 她穿上她最漂亮的衣裳。 *He rigged himself out as a sailor/tramp.* 他把自己裝扮得像個水手(流浪漢)。**ˈrig-out** *n* (colloq) person's clothes, etc: (俗)一個人的衣物等: *What a queer rig-out!* 一套多麼奇怪的衣服! *rig sth up*, **(a)** assemble or adjust parts of. 裝配或校準各部分。**(b)** make, put together, quickly or with any materials that may be available: 匆匆地或用任何可用的材料拼湊: *The climbers rigged up a shelter for the night on a narrow ledge.* 爬山者在一個突出的狹窄岩石上,匆匆地架起一個帳篷過夜。*They rigged up some scaffolding for the workmen.* 他們爲工人們搭了個鷹架。**(c)** = rig sth out. □ *n* [C] **1** way in which a ship's masts, sails, etc, are arranged: 船具裝置方法: *the fore-and-aft rig of a schooner.* 大帆船的縱帆裝置法。 **2** equipment put together for a special purpose: 有特殊用途的一套器材或裝置: *an ˈoil-rig/ˈdrilling-rig*, ⇨ oil; *a ˈtest-rig*, on which motor-vehicles are tested for fitness. 試車裝置。 **3** (colloq) style of dress: (俗)衣服的式樣: *a bizarre rig.* 奇異的衣服式樣。**rig·ging** *n* [U] all the ropes, etc which support a ship's masts and sails. 支撐船桅和帆的全部繩索;索具。**rig·ger** *n* person who rigs ships, etc; (esp) one whose work is to assemble and adjust the parts of aircraft. 裝置(船等之)索具者;索具工;塢工;(尤指)裝配飛機之人。

rig[2] /rɪg ; rɪg/ *vt* (-gg-) [VP6A] manage or control fraudulently, eg for private profit: 以欺詐手段爲私利而管理或控制: *rig the market*, cause prices (of stocks, shares, etc) to go up (or down) by trickery; 壟斷市場(以欺詐手段使股票等之價格上漲或下跌); *a rigged election.* 有舞弊的選舉。

right[1] /raɪt ; raɪt/ *adj* (contrasted with *wrong*) (與 wrong 相對) **1** (of conduct, etc) morally good; required by law or duty: (指行爲等)正當的;合法的;應該的: *Always do what is ~ and honourable.* 永遠做光明正大的事。*It seems only ~ to tell you that....* 似乎應該告訴你…。*You were quite ~ to refuse.* 你拒絕是很對的。*You were ~ in deciding not to go/were ~ in your decision.* 你決定不去(你的決定)是很正當的。 **2** true; correct; satisfactory: 正確的;對的;令人滿意的: *What's the ~ time?* 現在正確的時間是幾點? *Your account of what happened is not quite ~.* 你對於發生的事情所作的敍述不太正確。*Have you got the ~ (= exact) fare?* 你有恰好的錢付車資嗎? *get sth ~*, understand sth clearly, so that there is no error or misunderstanding: 確實了解某事,不致有錯誤或誤解: *Now let's get this ~ before we pass on to the next point.* 我們在討論下一點之前,先把這一點徹底搞清楚。*put/set sth ~*, restore to order, good health, a good condition, etc: 恢復秩序,健康,良好情況等: *put a watch ~*, ie to the correct time. 把錶校對準確。*It is not your business to put me ~*, to correct my errors. 犯不著你來糾正我的錯誤。*This medicine will soon put you ~.* 這藥不久就會使你恢復健康。*ˌR~ you ˈare!/ˌR~-ˈo!/R~!* *int* (colloq) used to indicate agreement to an order, request, proposal, etc. (俗)對極了！好極了！(用以表示同意一項命令，請求，建議等)。ˌ**All** ˈ**~!/Alright!** /ˌɔːlˈraɪt ; ɔlˈraɪt/ *int* used to indicate agreement, approval, etc. 對！好！(用以表示同意，贊同等)。ˌ**~-ˈminded** *adj* having opinions or principles based on what is ~: 見解正確的；公正的: *All ~-minded people will agree with me when I say....* 當我說…時,所有見解正確的人都會同意我的看法。 **3** most suitable; best in view of the circumstances, etc; preferable: 最合適的；就情況等而言最好的；可取的: *Are we on the ~ road?* 我們走的路對嗎？ *Which is the ~ way to Exeter?* 到愛塞特去走哪條路？ *He is the ~ man for the job.* 他是擔任這份工作最適當的人選。 *Which is the ~ side* (ie the side meant to be seen or used) *of this cloth?* 這塊布的正面是那一邊？ *Have you got it the ~ side up?* 你是否使正面朝上了呢？ *He's still on the ~ side of fifty,* is still under 50 years old. 他還不到五十歲。 ***get on the ~ side of sb,*** win his favour. 獲某人賞識；受某人器重。 **4** ***(all) ~,*** in good or normal condition; sound; sane: 健康的；健全的；神智清楚的: *Do you feel all ~?* 你沒什麼地方不對勁吧？ ***not (quite) ~ in the/one's head,*** (colloq) not sane; foolish. (俗)神智不(太)健全；愚笨。 ***not in one's ~ mind,*** in an abnormal mental state. 心理不正常。 ***~ as rain/as a trivet,*** (colloq) perfectly sound or healthy. (俗)十分健全；十分健康。 **5** (of an angle) of 90° (ie neither acute nor obtuse). (指角)九十度的；直角的。 ***at ˈ~ angles/at a ~ angle (to),*** at an angle of 90° (to). (與…)成直角。⇨ the illus at angle. 參看 angle 之插圖。 ˈ**~-angled** *adj* having a ~ angle: 成直角的: *a ~-angled triangle.* 一個直角三角形。 **~·ly** *adv* justly; justifiably; correctly; truly: 公正地；有理由地；正確地；確實地: *act ~ly.* 行爲正當。 *R~ly or wrongly, I think the man should not be punished.* 對也好，錯也好，我認爲這個人不應該受處罰。 *She has been sacked, and ~ly so.* 她被解雇了，一點也不冤枉。 *Am I ~ly informed?* 我所知道的消息正確嗎？ **~·ness** *n*

right[2] /raɪt ; raɪt/ *adv* **1** straight; directly: 一直地；直接地: *Put it ~ in the middle.* 把它放在正中間。 *The wind was ~ in our faces.* 風迎面吹來。 ***~ away/off,*** at once, without any delay. 立刻。 ***~ now,*** at this very moment. 在此刻；在此時。 ***~ on!*** *int* (colloq) used to indicate approval or encouragement. (俗)好！(表示同意或鼓勵)。 **2** all the way (*to/round, etc*); completely (*off/out, etc*): 全程地(與 to, round 等連用)；完全地；徹底地(與 off, out 等連用): *Go ~ to the end of this winding road, and then turn left.* 走完這條彎彎曲曲的路，再向左轉。 *He slipped ~ to the bottom of the icy slope.* 他一直滑落到蓋着冰的斜坡脚下。 *There's a veranda ~ round the building.* 這座建築物的四周有個陽台。 *The pear was rotten ~ through.* 這個梨爛透了。 *The prisoner got ~ away.* 囚犯逃得無影無踪。 *He turned ~ round.* 他轉過身來。 **3** justly; correctly; satisfactorily; properly: 公正地；正確地；令人滿意地；適當地: *if I remember ~* 如果我記得不錯 (cf 參較 *if I am ~ly informed* 如果我知道的消息不錯). *Have I guessed ~ or wrong?* 我猜得對還是錯？ *Nothing seems to go ~ with him,* Everything he does is a failure. 他似乎沒有一件事是順遂的。 ***It serves sb ~,*** It is what he deserves, he has been ~ly punished, etc. 某人罪有應得；某人受罰不冤枉。 **4** (old or dial use) to the full; very: (舊用法或方言用法)極度地；很: *We were ~ glad to hear that....* 我們非常高興聽到…。 *He knew ~ well that....* 他十分了解…。 ˈ**~-down** *adj, adv* (dial; more usu 較常用 *downright*) thorough(ly). (方)徹底的(地)。 **5 R~ Honourable,** ⇨ honourable. **R~ Reverend,** ⇨ reverend.

right[3] /raɪt ; raɪt/ *n* **1** [U] that which is right[1](1), good, just, honourable, true, etc: 正；公正；正義；公義；道理: *know the difference between ~ and wrong.* 明辨是非。 *May God defend the ~.* 願上帝維護正義。 ***be in the ~,*** have justice and truth on one's side. 站在正義與眞理的一邊。 **2** [U] proper authority or claim; the state of being justly entitled to sth; [C] sth to which one has a just claim; sth one may do or have by law: 權利；對某物有正當權利之狀態；有權利要求的東西；可依法去做或具有的東西: *He has a ~/no ~/not much ~ to do that.* 他有權利(沒有權利，不大有權利)做那件事。 *What gives you the ~ to say that?* 你有什麼權利說這話？ ***by ~(s),*** if justice were done; justly; correctly: 公正地；正當地: *The property is not mine by ~(s).* 公正地說，這財產不是我的。 ***by ~ of,*** because of: 因爲；由於: *The Normans ruled England by ~ of conquest.* 諾曼第人統治英格蘭，因爲他們征服了英格蘭。 ***in one's own ~,*** because of a personal claim, qualification, etc not depending upon another person: 憑本人的權利、資格等，而非依賴他人: *She's a peeress in her own ~,* ie not only by marriage. 她出身貴族(並非靠婚姻關係)。 ***~ of way,*** **(a)** ~ of the general public to use a path, road, etc esp a ~ which has existed from ancient times through land that is privately owned: 道路的公衆通行權(尤指自古即已存在之通過私有土地間之道路的權利): *Is there a ~ of way across these fields?* 公衆有權通過這些田地嗎？ **(b)** (in road traffic) ~ to use the carriageway before others; precedence: (在交通中)優先使用車道之權；優先通行權: *It's my ~ of way, so that lorry must stop or slow down until I've passed it.* 我有優先通行權，所以那卡車必須停駛或減慢車速直到我走過去爲止。 ***human ~s,*** those ~s that all people are or should be entitled to, eg a fair trial in a court of law, access to medical care and education, freedom of religion. 人權(人民有權享受的權利，例如公平審判，接受醫療及教育，宗教自由)。⇨ *the four freedoms* at freedom. ***women's ~s,*** (esp) of equality with men (in political, economic, social, etc affairs). 女權(尤指在政治、經濟、社會等事務上同男人平等之權)。⇨ lib. ***stand on/assert one's ~s,*** say what one's ~s are and declare that they will not be surrendered. 堅持自己的權利。 **3** (*pl*) true state. (複)眞實的狀態；眞相。 ***put/set things to ~s,*** put them in order. 使一切就緒。 ***~s and wrongs,*** true facts: 事實；眞相: *What are the ~s and wrongs of the case?* 這案件的眞相爲何？ ⇨ right[1](2).

right[4] /raɪt ; raɪt/ *vt* [VP6A] put, bring or come back, into the right or an upright condition; make sth right again: 改正；糾正；使恢復正常: *The ship ~ed herself after the big wave had passed.* 大浪過去後，船就平穩下來了。 *That fault will ~ itself,* will be corrected without help. 那錯誤會自行改正。 *The driver quickly ~ed the car after it skidded.* 汽車滑向一側，司機迅速加以控制。 ***~ the helm,*** put it amidships, ie neither to port nor to starboard. 把舵撥正(使不偏左舷，也不偏右舷)。

right[5] /raɪt ; raɪt/ *adj* (contrasted with *left*) of the side of the body which is toward the east when a person faces north: (與 left 相對)右面的；右方的: *my ~ hand/leg.* 我的右手(腿)。 *In Great Britain traffic keeps to the left, not the ~, side of the road.* 在英國，車輛行人靠路的左邊而非右邊走。 *The ~ bank of a river is on the ~ side as you look in the direction it is flowing.* 當你朝著順流方向看去時，河的右岸就在你的右邊。 ***one's ~ hand/arm,*** (fig) one's most reliable helper. (喻)一個人的得力助手。 ***one's ~ hand,*** all one's energy: 一個人所有的精力: *put one's ~ hand to the work,* work hard. 努力工作(全力以赴)。 ˈ**~-hand** *adj* (to be) placed on the ~ hand: (要)放於右手的: *a ~-hand glove.* 右手的手套。 ˌ**~-ˈhanded** *adj* **(a)** (of a person) using the ~ hand more, or with more ease, than the left. (指人)用右手較多或較靈敏的。 **(b)** (of a blow, etc) given with the ~ hand. (指打擊等)用右手擊出的。 ˌ**~-ˈhander** *n* **(a)** ~-handed person. 慣用右手的人。 **(b)** ~-handed blow. 用右手擊出之拳。 ˌ**~-ˈturn** *n* turn to the ~ into a position at ~ angles (90°)

with the original one. 向右轉。ˌ~-about ˈturn/ˈface, ~ turn continued until one is faced in the opposite direction. 向後轉。□ *adv* to the ~ hand or side: 向右方地;向右手邊地: *He looked neither ~ nor left.* 他既不向右看也不向左看。*Eyes ~!* as a military command. (軍隊口令)向右看! *The crowd divided ~ and left.* 羣衆向左右兩邊分開。**~ and left,** everywhere: 到處;四處: *He owes money ~ and left,* owes money everywhere. 他到處欠債。□ *n* [U] **1** side or direction on one's ~ hand: 右邊;右方;右面: *Take the first turning to the ~.* 在第一個轉彎處向右轉。*Our troops attacked the enemy's ~,* ~ wing or flank. 我們的軍隊攻擊敵人右翼。**2** (politics; usu **R~**) conservative or reactionary party or parties: (政治;通常大寫)保守的或反動的黨派;右翼;右派: *members of the R~.* 保守份子;右翼份子。**~·ist** /-ɪst; -ɪst/ *n* member of a ~ wing political party. 右翼份子;保守份子。□ *adj* of such a party: 保守黨的;右派的: *~ist sympathizers.* 保守黨的同情者;保守黨的支持者。

right·eous /ˈraɪtʃəs; ˈraɪtʃəs/ *adj* **1** doing what is morally right; obeying the law: 正直的;守法的: *the ~ and the wicked,* good and bad people. 正直的人和邪惡的人。**2** morally justifiable: 正當的;正義的: *~ anger.* 義憤。**~·ly** *adv* **~·ness** *n*

right·ful /ˈraɪtfl; ˈraɪtfəl/ *adj* **1** according to law and justice: 依據法律和正義的;合法的: *the ~ king;* 合法的國王; *the ~ owner of the land.* 土地的合法所有人。**2** (of actions, etc) fair; justifiable. (指行動等)公正的;有理由的。**~ly** /-fəlɪ; -fəlɪ/ *adv* **~·ness** *n*

rigid /ˈrɪdʒɪd; ˈrɪdʒɪd/ *adj* **1** stiff; unbending; that cannot be bent: 僵硬的;堅挺的;不能彎曲的: *a ~ support for a tent.* 一個帳篷的堅挺的支柱。**2** firm; strict; not changing; not to be changed: 堅强的;嚴厲的;嚴格的;不變的;不能改變的: *a ~ disciplinarian;* 一個嚴格維持紀律的人; *practise ~ economy.* 厲行節約。**~·ly** *adv* **ri·gid·ity** /rɪˈdʒɪdətɪ; rɪˈdʒɪdətɪ/ *n* [U] **1** stiffness; inflexibility: 僵硬;不變;剛性;剛度: *the ~ity of his religious beliefs.* 他的宗教信仰堅定不移。**2** strictness; sternness. 嚴格;嚴厲。

rig·ma·role /ˈrɪgmərəʊl; ˈrɪgməˌrol/ *n* [C] **1** long, wandering story or statement that does not mean much; incoherent account or description. 冗長、散漫而無多大意義的故事或陳述;散漫無章的說明或描述。**2** confusing and tiring procedure. 紛亂煩雜的手續。

rigor mor·tis /ˌrɪgə ˈmɔːtɪs; ˈraɪgɔrˈmɔrtɪs/ *n* (Lat) the stiffening of the muscles after death. (拉)死後肌肉之僵硬;屍僵。

rig·or·ous /ˈrɪgərəs; ˈrɪgərəs/ *adj* **1** stern; strict; severe: 嚴格的;嚴厲的: *~ discipline;* 嚴格的訓練; *a ~ search for dutiable goods.* 嚴格搜查應納稅貨物。**2** harsh; severe: 嚴酷的;劇烈的: *a ~ climate.* 嚴寒或酷熱的氣候。**~·ly** *adv*

rig·our (US = **rigor**) /ˈrɪgə(r); ˈrɪgə/ *n* **1** [U] sternness; strictness; strict enforcement (of rules, etc): 嚴格;嚴厲;(規則等的)嚴厲執行: *punish sb with the utmost ~ of the law.* 以最嚴厲的法律處罰某人。**2** (often *pl*) severe conditions: (常用複數)嚴酷;艱苦: *the ~s of prison life;* 監獄生活的艱苦; *the ~(s) of the winter in Canada,* the severe climatic conditions. 加拿大冬季的酷寒。

rile /raɪl; raɪl/ *vt* [VP6A] (colloq) annoy; rouse anger in: (俗)惹惱;激怒: *It ~d him that no one would believe his story.* 沒有人相信他的故事使他很惱火。

rill /rɪl; rɪl/ *n* small stream; rivulet. 小溪;小川。

rim /rɪm; rɪm/ *n* [C] circular edge of the framework of a wheel, on which the tyre is fitted, ⇨ the illus at bicycle; border (of steel, gold, etc) round the lenses of spectacles (hence *rimless spectacles,* having lenses without rims); edge, border or margin of sth circular: 輪緣;輞(參看 bicycle 之插圖);(鋼、金等的)眼鏡框(由此產生 rimless spectacles, '無框眼鏡'一詞); 任何圓形物體的緣、周或邊: *the rim of a cup/bowl;* 杯(碗)之邊緣; frame of a sieve. 篩框。ˌ**red-ˈrimmed** *adj* (of eyes) having red rims, eg from weeping. (指眼)(因哭泣等而)眼圈紅紅的。□ *vt* (-mm-) [VP6A] provide with a rim; be a rim for. 鑲以邊;爲…之邊。

rime¹ /raɪm; raɪm/ *n* (liter) hoarfrost. (文)白霜。⇨ hoar. □ *vt* [VP6A] cover with or as with ~. 覆以霜或似霜之物。

rime² /raɪm; raɪm/ *n* = rhyme.

rind /raɪnd; raɪnd/ *n* [U] hard, outside skin or covering (of some fruits, eg melons, or of bacon and cheese); [C] piece or strip of this skin; tough covering of one fruit. (某些水果,如瓜類或醃肉與奶酪的)外皮;此等外皮的一片或一條;一個水果的堅硬外皮。

rin·der·pest /ˈrɪndəpest; ˈrɪndəˌpɛst/ *n* [U] contagious virus disease of cattle. 牛瘟。

ring¹ /rɪŋ; rɪŋ/ *n* [C] **1** circular band (often of gold or platinum, and set with a gem or gems) worn round a finger as an ornament, or as a token: 戴於指上作裝飾物或信物的金屬環(常用金或鉑製成,並常鑲有珠寶);指環: *an enˈgagement ~;* 訂婚戒指; *a ˈwedding ~;* 結婚戒指; similar band for other parts of the body: 身體其他部份所戴的類似之環: *an ˈear~, a ˈnose-~.* 耳環,鼻環。**ˈ~-finger** *n* third of the left hand. 左手的無名指。**2** circular band of any kind of material, eg metal, wood, ivory: 任何材料(如金屬,木,象牙)製的環狀物: *a ˈnapkin ~;* 束餐巾用的小環; *a ˈkey-~,* one of split metal, for carrying keys on. 鑰匙環。**ˈ~-mail/-armour** *nn* = chain-armour. 鎖子鎧。⇨ chain(4). **3** circle: 圓圈;圓環: *a ~ of light round the moon;* 月亮的暈輪; *the ~s of a tree,* seen in concentric circles of wood when the trunk is cut across, showing the tree's age; 樹的年輪(橫切樹幹時所見到的許多同心圓,可顯示樹木之年齡); *puff out ˈsmoke-~s* (of cigarette smoke). (抽香煙時)噴出煙圈兒。*The men were standing in a ~.* 那些人站成一個圓圈。***make/run ˈ~s round sb,*** move, do things, much faster than he does. 行動或做事比某人快得多。**4** combination of persons working together for their own advantage: (爲私利而結合在一起的)集團: *a ~ of revolutionaries/smugglers.* 一羣革命份子(一幫走私者)。**5 (ˈcircus-)~,** circular enclosure or space for circus-riding. 馬戲場。**ˈ~-master** *n* man who directs performances in a circus-~. 馬戲團演出指導。**6** space for the showing of cattle, dogs, etc (at farming exhibitions, etc). (農業展覽會等中)家畜展覽場。**7** betting at race meetings. 賭賽馬。**the ~,** book-makers collectively. (集合用法)以賭賽馬爲業者。⇨ book¹(8). **8 the ˈprize-~,** ⇨ prize¹(3). **9** (compounds) (複合字) **ˈ~-leader** *n* person who leads others in a rising against authority. (叛黨之)首領;頭目。**ˈ~-road** *n* road round and through the outskirts of a town, for the use of through traffic and designed to avoid congestion in the centre. 環城公路(圍繞城市並穿過市郊的環狀道路,爲捷運及避免市區擁塞而設)。Cf *by-pass,* a new road specially constructed. (參較 by-pass, 係特別鋪築之新道路)。**ˈ~·side** *n* place near to the ring of a circus, prize-fight, etc: 貼近馬戲場,拳擊場等之處: *have a ~side seat,* be favourably placed for seeing an event, etc. 獲一場邊座位;位於可以看清楚的地方。**ˈ~·worm** *n* [U] contagious disease of the skin, esp of children, causing round, red patches. 癬;錢癬。□ *vt, vi* (*pt, pp* ~ed) **1** [VP6A, 15B] surround: 圍繞;環繞: *~ed about with enemies;* 爲敵人所包圍; *~ cattle,* hem them into one place. 把牲口圍於一處。**2** [VP6A] put a ~ in the nose of (a bull, etc) or on the leg of (a bird, eg a homing pigeon). 給(牛等)帶鼻圈;給(鳥,如傳信鴿)腿上繫一金屬環。**3** [VP6A] (in games) toss or throw a ring or a horseshoe round, eg a mark, peg, etc; make a ring round (sth), eg with a pencil, or by shooting holes round a target.

(遊戲中)擲環或蹄形鐵於(標的或樁)上;繞(某物)形成一圓圈(例如用鉛筆畫,或圍繞一靶子用子彈射成一圈)。 **4** [VP2A] (of a hunted fox) take a circular course. (指被獵之狐)繞圈跑。

ring² /rɪŋ; rɪŋ/ *vt, vi* (*pt* rang /ræŋ; ræŋ/, *pp* rung /rʌŋ; rʌŋ/) **1** [VP2A, B, C] give out a clear, musical sound as when metal vibrates: 發出如金屬震動時清晰悅耳之聲音;鳴;響: *How long has that telephone (bell) been ~ing?* 電話(鈴)響了多久啦? *Start work when the bell ~s.* 鈴響時就開始工作。 *A shot rang out,* The noise of a shot was heard. 聽到一聲槍響。 **2** [VP2D] produce a certain effect when heard: 聽起來…: *His words rang hollow,* What he said seemed insincere. 他的話聽起來似乎不誠懇。 *His words rang true.* 他的話聽起來似乎是眞的。 *The coin rang true/false,* seemed, when tested by being thrown down, to be genuine/counterfeit. 這硬幣聽聲音是眞的(假的)。 **3** [VP2A, 3A] ~ ***(for sb/sth),*** cause a bell to sound, as a summons, warning, etc: 鳴鈴召喚,警告等: *She rang for the porter.* 她按鈴叫門房。 *Did you ~, sir?* 是你按鈴叫我嗎,先生? *Someone is ~ing at the door,* ~ing for admittance or attention. 有人在按門鈴。 *The cyclist didn't ~.* 那個騎脚踏車的人沒有按鈴。 **4** [VP6A] cause sth, esp a bell, to ~: 使鳴;使響;(尤指)使鐘、鈴響: *~ the bells;* 鳴鐘; *~ the bell for the steward;* 按鈴叫侍者; *~ a coin,* test its genuineness by throwing it down on sth and listening to the sound. 擲硬幣於某物之上,以聽其聲音,辨其眞僞。 ***~ a bell,*** (colloq) bring sth vaguely back to mind: (俗)模糊憶起某事物: *Ah! That ~s a bell!* 啊!我好像記起來了! ***~ the bell,*** (colloq) be successful in sth. (俗)做某事成功。 **5** [VP3A] ~ ***(with sth),*** resound; re-echo: 回響;回聲: *The children's playground rang with happy shouts.* 孩子們的遊戲場上回響着快樂的呼喊聲。 *The village rang with the praises of the brave girl.* 村子裏人人皆稱道那個勇敢的女孩子。 **6** [VP2C] linger in one's hearing or memory: 縈繞於耳際或記憶中: *His last words are still ~ing in my ears.* 他的遺言仍留在我耳際。 **7** [VP2A, 3A] ~ ***(with),*** (of the ears) be filled with a ringing or humming sound: (指耳)充滿着鳴聲或嗡嗡聲: *My ears are still ~ing.* 我的耳中仍有鳴聲(我仍耳鳴)。 **8** ~ ***sb (up),*** get into communication with sb by telephone: 打電話給某人: *I'll ~ you (up) this evening.* 我今晚將給你電話。(US 美 = *call sb (up)*.) ***~ off,*** end a telephone conversation. 掛斷電話。 **9** [VP6A] (of a chime of bells) announce (the hour, etc); strike the hours: (指一套鐘)報(鐘點等);敲出鐘點: *The bell ~s the hours, but not the quarters.* 那鐘是每小時響,不是每刻鐘響。 **10** [VP6A, 15B] give a signal by ~ing a bell, etc: 鳴鐘鈴等作信號: *~ the knell of sth,* announce its end or downfall; 宣佈某事之結束或崩潰; *~ an alarm,* give one by ~ing bells. 鳴鐘示警。 ***~ the curtain up/down,*** (in a theatre) give the signal for it to be raised/lowered. (劇院中)鳴鈴以示升幕(落幕)。 **11** [VP6A] sound (a peal, etc with a bell or bells). (以鐘)鳴響(鐘樂等)。 ***~ the changes (on),*** (of church bells) ring the bells in the different orders which are possible; (fig) put or arrange things, do things, in as many different ways as possible. (指教堂的鐘)以各種不同次序鳴鐘; (喻)以各種不同方式安排或做事物。 **12** [VP15B] announce or celebrate the beginning or end of sth by ~ing bells. 以鳴鐘宣告或慶祝某事之開始或結束。 ***~ out the Old (Year) and ~ in the New.*** 鳴鐘送舊歲迎新年。□ *n* **1** (*sing* only) resonant sound produced by a bell or piece of metal when it is struck: (僅用單數)鐘或金屬片被敲擊時發出之共鳴音: *This coin has a good ~.* 這硬幣聲音很悅耳。 **2** (*sing* only) loud and clear sound: (僅用單數)宏亮而清晰的聲音: *the ~ of happy voices.* 歡聲響亮。 *There was a ~ of sincerity in his promise.* 他的允諾聽起來頗爲眞誠。 **3** [C] act of ~ing; sound of a bell: 按鈴;鳴鐘;打電話;鳴響;鐘(鈴)聲: *There was a ~ at the door.* 有人按門鈴。 *I'll give you a ~ this evening,* will ~ you up (by telephone). 我今晚給你電話。 **~er** *n* bell-ringer. 搖鈴者;鳴鐘(鈴)者。

ring·let /ˈrɪŋlɪt; ˈrɪŋlɪt/ *n* [C] small curl of hair: 小髮鬈: *Her hair hung down in ~s.* 她的頭髮呈許多小髮鬈下垂着。

rink /rɪŋk; rɪŋk/ *n* [C] specially prepared sheet of ice for skating or hockey, or floor for roller-skating. 溜冰場;冰上曲棍球場;輪式溜冰場。

rinse /rɪns; rɪns/ *vt* [VP6A, 15A, B] **1** ~ ***sth (out); ~ sth out of sth,*** wash with clean water in order to remove unwanted substances, etc: 以清水沖洗(以除去不要之物): *~ soap out of the clothes;* 以清水沖去衣服上的肥皂; *~ the clothes,* to get soapy water out; 以清水沖去衣服上的肥皂水; *~ (out) the teapot;* 以清水沖洗茶壺; *~ the tea-leaves out of the pot;* 以清水沖去茶壺裏的茶葉; *~ (out) the mouth,* eg while being treated by a dentist. 漱口(如在牙醫處接受治療時)。 **2** ~ ***sth down,*** help (food) down with a drink: 以水或其他液體吞下(食物): *R~ it down with a glass of beer.* 用一杯啤酒把它吞下。□ *n* **1** act of rinsing: 沖洗之動作;洗滌;清洗: *Give your hair a good ~ after you've shampooed it.* 頭髮用過洗髮劑後,要用清水沖洗乾淨。 **2** solution for tinting the hair: 染髮液: *the blue ~ used by some elderly women.* 某些年長的婦女所用的藍色染髮液。

riot /ˈraɪət; ˈraɪət/ *n* **1** [C] violent outburst of lawlessness by the people in a district: 暴動;騷動: *put down a ~ by force.* 以武力鎮壓一場暴動。 *R~s during the election were dealt with by the police.* 選舉時之騷動被警察制止了。 **the ˈR~ Act,** act dealing with the prevention of ~s and the breaking up of disorderly crowds. 暴亂取締法。 ***read the ˈR~ Act,*** (a) read part of this Act officially to disorderly persons after which, if they do not disperse, they can be arrested for felony. 宣讀暴亂取締法(向騷擾份子宣讀本法案之一部份條文,如羣衆不自動散去,即以重罪予以逮捕);下令禁止騷動。 (b) (joc, eg of parents) give a warning that noisy and unruly behaviour must stop. (謔,指父母等)警告吵鬧和搗亂行爲必須停止。 **2** [U] noisy, uncontrolled behaviour (not lawless). 歡鬧,放肆(但並不違法)的行爲。 ***run ~,*** throw off all discipline; (of plants) be out of control by growing fast and luxuriantly. 放肆;滋鬧;(指植物)蔓延滋長。 **3** ***a riot (of),*** profusion; luxuriance: 繁多;茂盛;豐盛: *The flower-beds were a ~ of colour.* 花壇裏一片彩色繽紛。 **4** ***a ~ (of),*** unrestrained indulgence in or display of sth: 無節制的放縱或展示: *a ~ of emotion.* 感情泛濫。 **5** ***a ~,*** (colloq) occasion of wild enthusiasm (as indicating great success): (俗)轟動之場合(如指大的成功): *His latest play was a ~ when it was produced in New York.* 他最近寫的劇本在紐約演出時極爲轟動。□ *vi* **1** [VP2A, B, C] take part in a ~(1, 2): 參與騷擾或歡鬧: *The voters were ~ing all night after the election.* 選民們於選舉之後終宵歡鬧。 **2** [VP3A] ~ ***in,*** indulge or revel in: 放縱;恣情: *The tyrant ~ed in cruelty.* 那暴君殘暴無度。 **~er** *n* person who ~s. 騷動者;歡鬧者;放縱者。 **~·ous** /-əs; -əs/ *adj* likely to cause a ~; unruly; disorderly; running wild: 可能引起暴動的;騷擾的;暴亂的;放蕩的: *a ~ous assembly;* 一個可能引起騷動的集會; *charged with ~ous behaviour.* 被控有騷擾之行爲。 **~·ous·ly** *adv*

rip /rɪp; rɪp/ *vt, vi* (-pp-) **1** [VP6A, 15A, B, 22] pull, tear or cut (sth) quickly and with force (to get it off, out, open, etc): 迅速而用力地將(某物)拉開;撕開;割開: *rip open a letter;* 撕開一信; *rip the cover off;* 把蓋子扯開; *rip the seams of a garment;* 拆開衣縫; *rip a piece of cloth in two;* 把一塊布撕爲兩段; make a long cut or tear in: 割裂;撕裂: *rip a tyre,* eg on a rocky road. 使一輪胎爆裂(如在多石的路上)。 *My poor cat had its ear ripped* *open by a dog.* 我那可憐的貓的耳朵被一隻狗撕裂了。***rip sth／sb off,*** (sl) steal (it); defraud (him). (俚)偷竊(某物)；詐騙(某人)。Hence, 由此產生，**'rip-off** *n* sth stolen; instance of stealing or defrauding. 被竊之物；偷竊；詐騙。**'rip-cord** *n* cord which, when pulled during a descent, releases a parachute from its pack; cord pulled to release gas from a balloon. 開傘索(拉動後使降落傘脫離傘包之繩索)；放氣索(拉動後使氣球放氣之繩索)。**2** [VP6A] saw (wood, etc) with the grain. 沿紋理鋸(木材等)；縱鋸。**'rip-saw** *n* saw used for this. 縱割鋸；粗齒大鋸。**3** [VP2A] (of material) tear; be ripped. (指料子)被撕開；裂開。**4** [VP2A, C] go forward, rush along. 向前行；向前闖。***Let her／it rip,*** (colloq) (of a boat, car, machine, etc) allow it to go at its maximum speed. (俗)讓它去吧(指船，車，機器等，勿限制其速度)。***let things rip,*** cease to exercise control; let things take their natural course. 任其自由發展而不予任何控制。□ *n* [C] torn place; long cut: 裂開之處；長裂痕: *The rips in my tent were made by the horns of that angry bull.* 我帳篷上的裂縫是被那隻憤怒的公牛的角撕破的。

ri·par·ian /raɪ'peərɪən ; rɪ'pɛrɪən/ *adj* of, on, the bank(s) of a river or lake: 河岸或湖岸的；在河岸或湖岸上的: ~ *rights,* eg to catch fish in the river; 河岸權(例如在該河中捕魚之權)；~ *property.* 河岸財產。

ripe /raɪp ; raɪp/ *adj* **1** (of fruit, grain, etc) ready to be gathered and used: (指水果，穀物等)成熟的: ~ *fruit;* 成熟的水果；*cherries not ~ enough to eat;* 還未熟得能吃的櫻桃；~ *corn;* 已熟的穀物；~ *lips,* red and soft like ~ fruit. 紅潤的唇。**2** matured and ready to be eaten or drunk: 已做成而可食或可飲的: ~ *cheese／wine.* 已製成的乾酪(釀好的酒)。**3** fully developed: 發展完成的: ~ *judgement／scholarship;* 成熟的判斷力(豐富的學識)；*a person of ~ age,* a mature and experienced person; 成熟而富經驗的人；*a person of ~(r) years,* past the stage of youth. 成年之人。**4** ~ ***for,*** ready, fit, prepared: 準備就緒；時機成熟的；適於…的: ~ *for mischief／revolt;* 惡作劇(叛變)的時機已成熟的; *land that is ~ for development,* eg for building houses or factories. 已適於發展(如建住宅或工廠)的土地。~**·ly** *adv* ~**·ness** *n*

ripen /'raɪpən ; 'raɪpən/ *vt, vi* [VP6A, 2A] make or become ripe. 使成熟；成熟。

ri·poste /rɪ'pɒst ; rɪ'post/ *n* **1** quick return thrust in fencing (after parrying). (劍術中在躲開後之)迅速還刺。**2** quick, sharp reply or retort. 迅速犀利的回答或反駁。□ *vi* deliver a ~. 迅速還刺；機敏的答辯或反駁。

ripple /'rɪpl ; 'rɪpl̩/ *n* [C] (sound of) small movement(s) on the surface of water, etc, eg made by a gentle wind; (sound of) the rise and fall of voices or laughter: 水面上如被微風吹起的微波；漣漪；微波激盪之聲音；起伏之聲音或笑聲；聲浪: *A long ~ of laughter passed through the audience.* 聽衆間響起長長一陣笑聲。□ *vt, vi* [VP6A, 2A] (cause to) move in ~s; (cause to) rise and fall gently: (使)起微波；(使)輕輕起伏: *The wheat ~d in the breeze.* 在微風輕拂中小麥起伏如波。*The breeze ~d the cornfields.* 微風使麥田起浪。*The tide ~d the sand,* caused a wavy surface on the sand. 潮在沙上留下波狀沙紋。

rip-tide /'rɪp taɪd ; 'rɪp,taɪd/ *n* tide causing strong currents and rough water. 巨潮(引起巨浪的潮水)。

rise¹ /raɪz ; raɪz/ *n* **1** small hill; upward slope: 小山；向上的斜坡: *a ~ in the ground;* 一個向上的斜坡；*a cottage situated on a ~.* 在小山上的一座茅屋。**2** upward progress; increase (in value, temperature, etc): 向上的進展；(價值，溫度等之)增高: *a ~ in prices／social position, etc;* 物價(社會地位等)之升高；*have a ~ in wages* (US 美 = *raise*); 工資提高；*the ~ and fall of the tide.* 潮之漲落。**3** (liter) coming up (of the sun, etc): (文)(太陽等之)升起: *at ~ of sun／day,* (more usu *sunrise*). 在日出之時(sunrise 較常用)。**4** movement of fish to the surface of water: 魚之游到水面: *not a sign of a ~.* 沒有魚上來的跡象。*I fished two hours without getting a ~.* 我垂釣兩小時，沒有一條魚上來吃餌。***get／take a／the ~ out of sb,*** cause him to show petulance or weakness (often by good-natured teasing). (常指以善意的戲弄)使某人變得暴躁或暴露弱點；招惹某人。**5** origin; start: 起源: *The river has／takes its ~ among the hills.* 這條河發源於那些小山中。***give ~ to,*** cause; suggest: 引起；招致: *Such conduct might give ~ to misunderstandings.* 這種行爲可能導致誤解。~**r** *n* **1** ***early／late ~r,*** person who gets up early／late. 早(晏)起之人。**2** vertical part of a step, connecting two treads of a staircase. 梯級間之豎板。

rise² /raɪz ; raɪz/ *vi* (*pt* rose /rəʊz ; roz/, *pp* risen /'rɪzn ; 'rɪzn̩/) [VP2A, B, C, 3A, 4A] ~ ***(up),*** **1** (of the sun, moon, stars) appear above the horizon: (指日，月，星)升起: *The sun ~s in the East.* 太陽在東方升起。*Has the moon ~n yet?* 月已升起否？ ⇨ set²(1). **2** get up from a lying, sitting or kneeling position: 從躺、坐、跪之姿勢起身: *He rose to welcome me.* 他起身歡迎我。*The wounded man fell and was too weak to ~.* 那受傷的人跌倒，無力爬起。*The horse rose on its hind legs.* 那馬用後腿站起。*On rising from table...,* leaving the table at the end of the meal.... 餐後離桌時…。*Parliament will ~ on Thursday next,* cease to sit for business, start the recess. 國會下星期四休會。*The House rose at 10pm,* ended its discussions, etc. 議院下午十時停止議事。**3** get out of bed; get up (which is commoner): 起床 (get up 較常用): *He ~s very early.* 他起床甚早。**4** come to life (*again, from the dead*): 復活；復蘇: *Jesus Christ rose (again) from the dead.* 耶穌基督死後復活。*Christ is ~n* (as an Easter greeting). 基督復活了(用作復活節之祝賀語)。*He looks as though he had ~n from the grave.* 他的樣子好像是剛從墳墓中爬出來。**5** go, come, up or higher; reach a high(er) level or position: 上升；上漲: *The smoke from our fire rose straight up in the still air.* 我們所生的火冒出的煙在無風的空氣中裊裊上升。*The river／flood, etc has ~n two feet.* 河水(洪水等)上漲兩呎。*His voice rose in anger／excitement, etc,* became high, shrill. 在憤怒(興奮等)中他的聲音提高了。*Sugar has ~n a penny a pound.* 糖價每磅漲了一辨士。*Prices continue to ~.* 物價繼續上漲。*The mercury in the barometer is rising.* 氣壓計的水銀柱正在上升。*The bread won't ~,* The dough will not swell with the yeast. 麵包不會膨鬆起來(麵發不起來)。*New office blocks are rising in our town.* 新的辦公大樓在我們鎮上建造起來了。**'high-~** *attrib adj* having many storeys: 有許多層的: *high-~ flats／office-blocks.* 有許多層的公寓(辦公大樓)。⇨ *skyscraper* at sky(1). ***the rising generation,*** young people who are growing up. (正在成長的)年輕的一代。***rising twelve, etc,*** (of a person) nearing the age of twelve, etc. (指人)近十二歲等。**6** develop greater intensity or energy: 發展成較大的強度或能力: *The wind is rising.* 風勢正增強。*His colour rose,* He became flushed. 他臉紅了。**7** come to the surface: 升到表面: *The fish were rising,* coming to the surface for food. 魚正游上水面覓食。*They say a drowning man ~s three times.* 據說一個將淹死的人會浮上水面三次。*Bubbles rose from the bottom of the lake.* 水泡從湖底冒到湖面來。**8** become or be visible above the surroundings: 因高出周圍環境而變得可見或能看見；突出: *A range of hills rose on our left.* 一列小山在我們左方出現。**9** reach a higher position in society; make progress (in one's profession, etc): 社會地位提高；升級；晉陞；(在事業等中)進步: ~ *in the world;* 發跡；出頭；~ *to greatness;* 成爲偉大人物；~ *from the ranks,* ie to be an officer; 從行伍升爲軍官；*a rising young politician／lawyer.* 一位事業蒸蒸日上的年輕從政者(律師)。**10** ~ ***to,*** develop powers equal to. 有應付…之能力。~ ***to the occasion/challenge/task, etc,*** prove oneself able to deal with an unexpected problem, a difficult task, etc. 有隨機應變(接受挑戰,完成艱難任務等)之能力。 **11** slope upwards: 漸漸高起: *rising ground.* 漸漸高起之地。**12** have as a starting-point: 以…爲起源;源於: *Where does the Nile ~?* 尼羅河發源何處? *The quarrel rose from a mere trifle.* 爭吵起於瑣事。 **13** ~ ***against,*** rebel (against the government, etc). 反叛(政府等)。**ris·ing** *n* (esp) armed outbreak; rebellion. (尤指)武裝暴動;叛變。

ris·ible /ˈrɪzəbl ; ˈrɪzəbl̩/ *adj* of laughing and laughter; inclined to laugh; causing laughter, ludicrous. 笑的; 欲笑的; 愛笑的; 引人笑的; 可笑的。**risi·bil·ity** /ˌrɪzəˈbɪlətɪ ; ˌrɪzəˈbɪlətɪ/ *n* [U] disposition to laugh. 會笑;愛笑。

risk /rɪsk ; rɪsk/ *n* **1** [C, U] (instance of) possibility or chance of meeting danger, suffering loss, injury, etc: 遭遇危難,受損失或傷害等之可能或機會;危險;風險: *There's no/not much ~ of your catching cold if you wrap up well.* 你如果把衣服穿妥當,就不會有傷風的危險。***run/take ~s/a ~,*** put oneself in a position where there is ~: 冒險: *She's too sensible to take a ~ when she's driving.* 她在開車時很有判斷力而不致冒險。*To succeed in business one must be prepared to run ~s.* 一個人想在商業上成功,必須做冒險的打算。***run/take the ~ of doing sth,*** do sth which may involve ~: 冒險做某事;冒…之險: *We'll take the ~ of being late.* 我們將冒遲到之險。*He was ready to run the ~ of being taken prisoner by the enemy.* 他願意冒被敵人俘虜的危險。***at the ~ of/at ~ to,*** with the possibility of (loss, etc): 冒…之險;不顧…之危險: *He was determined to get there even at the ~ of his life.* 他決心到那裏,雖冒生命危險在所不惜。***at ~,*** threatened by uncertainties (such as failure, loss, etc): 可能遭到失敗,損失等: *Is the Government's income policy seriously at ~?* 政府的稅收政策可能遭到嚴重失敗嗎? ***at one's own ~,*** accepting responsibility, agreeing to make no claims, for loss, injury, etc. 自己負責,同意對損失或傷害等不要求賠償。***at owner's ~,*** (of goods sent by rail, etc) the owner to bear any loss there may be. (指由火車等所運之貨物)由物主負擔一切損失。 **2** [C] (insurance) amount for which sb or sth is insured; the person or thing insured. (保險)保險金額;保險對象(被保險之人或物)。*He's a good/poor ~.* 他是個條件很好(風險很大)的保險對象。 ⇨ also *security ~* at security. □ *vt* **1** [VP6A] expose to ~: 暴露於危險;使冒危險: *~ one's health/fortune/neck* (ie life), *etc.* 冒健康(財富,生命等)之險。 **2** [VP6A, C] take the chances of: 冒…之險: *~ failure.* 冒失敗之險。*We must ~ getting caught in a storm.* 我們必須冒爲暴風雨所阻之險。 **risky** *adj* (-ier, -iest) **1** full of ~: 多危險的;多風險的: *a ~y undertaking.* 一件多風險的事業。 **2** = risqué. **~·ily** /-ɪlɪ ; -ɪlɪ/ *adv* **~i·ness** *n*

ri·sotto /rɪˈzɒtəʊ ; rɪˈsɔtto/ *n* [C] dish of rice cooked with butter, cheese, onions, etc. 一種加奶油,乾酪,洋葱等做成的燴飯。

ris·qué /ˈriːskeɪ *US:* rɪˈskeɪ ; rɪsˈke/ *adj* (of a story, remark, situation in a drama, etc) likely to offend against propriety; on the borderline of indecency. (指故事,談話,劇中場面等)很可能違反禮儀的;近乎猥褻的。

ris·sole /ˈrɪsəʊl ; ˈrɪsol/ *n* [C] small ball of minced meat, fish, etc mixed with potato, eggs, breadcrumbs, etc and fried. 碎肉或碎魚肉同馬鈴薯,蛋,麵包屑等混合以油炸成的丸子。

rite /raɪt ; raɪt/ *n* [C] act or ceremony (esp in religious services): 典禮;儀式;(尤指)宗教儀式: *ˈburial ~s;* 葬儀; *~s of baptism;* 洗禮式; *iˌnitiˈation ~s.* 入會儀式。*He died after receiving the ~s of the church,* eg the sacraments of Penance, the Eucharist, and Extreme Unction. 他行過宗教儀式(如臨終懺悔,領聖餐及臨終塗油禮等)之後就去世了。

rit·ual /ˈrɪtʃʊəl ; ˈrɪtʃʊəl/ *n* [U] all the rites or forms connected with a ceremony; way of conducting a religious service: (典禮之)儀式;宗教儀式: *the ~ of the Catholic Church;* 天主教之儀式; [C] particular form of ~; any procedure regularly followed, as if it were a ~: 特別的方式;固定的程序: *He went through the ~ of rolling his own cigarette slowly and carefully.* 他按照固定的程序緩慢而小心地捲他自己的香煙。(*pl*) ceremonial observances: (複)正式的禮儀: *initiation ~s.* 入會儀式。□ *adj* of religious rites; done as a rite: 宗教儀式的;按照儀式的: *~ laws;* 儀式法典; *the ~ dances of an African tribe.* 非洲某部落的祭神舞蹈。 **~·ism** /-ɪzəm ; -ˌɪzəm/ *n* [U] fondness for, insistence upon, ~; study of ~. 喜歡儀式;拘泥儀式;儀式主義;儀式研究。 **~·ist** /-ɪst ; -ɪst/ *n* person who has expert knowledge of ~ practices and religious rites; person who supports strict observance of ~. 對禮儀及宗教儀式有專門知識者;儀式專家;支持嚴格遵行儀式的人;拘泥儀式者;儀式主義者。 **~·is·tic** /ˌrɪtʃʊəˈlɪstɪk ; ˌrɪtʃʊəlˈɪstɪk/ *adj* relating to ~ism and ~ists. 喜歡儀式的;拘泥儀式的;儀式研究的;儀式專家的;拘泥儀式者的。

ritzy /ˈrɪtsɪ ; ˈrɪtsɪ/ *adj* (sl) luxurious; elegant. (俚)豪華的;優美的。

ri·val /ˈraɪvl ; ˈraɪvl̩/ *n* person who competes with another (because he wants the same thing, or to be or do better than the other): 競爭者;對手: *ˈbusiness ~s;* 商業上的競爭者; *~s in love;* 情敵; (attrib) (形容用法) *~ business firms.* 互相競爭的商行。□ *vt* (-ll-, US also -l-) [VP6A, 14] ~ ***(in),*** be a ~ of; seem or claim to be (almost) as good as: 爲…之競爭者;像是或聲言(幾乎)與…同樣好: *Cricket cannot ~ football in excitement.* 板球遠不如足球够刺激。 **~ry** /ˈraɪvlrɪ ; ˈraɪvl̩rɪ/ *n* [C, U] (*pl* -ries) (instance of) being ~s; competition: 敵對(之實例);競爭: *enter into ~ry with other shops;* 與其他商店競爭; *~ry between two schools,* eg in sport; 兩學校間之競爭(例如在運動方面); *the rivalries between political parties.* 兩政黨間的相互競爭。

rive /raɪv ; raɪv/ *vt, vi* (*pt* ~d, *pp* riven /ˈrɪvn ; ˈrɪvən/) [VP6A, 15A, B] (archaic or poet) break or tear away violently; split: (古或詩)猛烈地劈開或撕開;分裂: *trees riven by lightning;* 被閃電劈開的樹; (fig) (喻) *a heart riven by grief.* 因憂傷而破碎的心。

river /ˈrɪvə(r) ; ˈrɪvɚ/ *n* [C] **1** natural stream of water flowing in a channel to the sea or to a lake, etc or joining another ~: 河;江: *the R~ Thames.* (英國的)泰晤士河。***sell sb down the ~,*** (fig) betray him. (喻)出賣某人。 **2** (attrib) (形容用法) **ˈ~-basin** *n* area drained by a ~ and its tributaries. 江河流域。**ˈ~-bed** *n* ground over which a ~ flows in its channel. 河床。**ˈ~·side** *n* ground along a ~ bank: 河岸: *a ~side villa.* 河邊別墅。 **3** great flow: 巨流: *a ~ of lava;* 滾滾的熔岩; *~s of blood,* great bloodshed (in war). (戰爭中之)血流成渠。

rivet /ˈrɪvɪt ; ˈrɪvɪt/ *n* [C] metal pin or bolt for fastening metal plates (eg in a ship's sides), the plain end being hammered flat to prevent slipping. 鉚釘;包頭釘。□ *vt* [VP6A, 15A, B] **1** fasten with a ~ or ~s; flatten (the end of a bolt) to make it secure. 以鉚釘固結;打平(螺釘之一端)使牢。 **2** fix or concentrate (one's eyes, attention) on: 固定或集中(眼睛,注意力)於: *He ~ed his eyes on the scene.* 他的眼睛凝視那風景。 **3** take up, secure (attention, etc): 獲得;吸引(注意等): *The scene ~ed our attention.* 那風景吸引了我們的注意。

Rivi·era /ˌrɪvɪˈeərə ; ˌrɪvɪˈɛrə/ *n* ***the ~,*** stretch of the Mediterranean coast (of SE France and NW Italy), used as a holiday resort. 里維耶拉(法國東南與義大利西北境內地中海沿岸的一帶地方,爲度假勝地)。

rivu·let /ˈrɪvjʊlɪt ; ˈrivjəlɪt/ *n* small stream. 小溪;小川。

roach[1] /rəʊtʃ; rotʃ/ *n* (*pl* unchanged) fresh-water fish of the carp family. (複數不變)斜齒鯿(一種鯉科淡水魚)。

roach[2] /rəʊtʃ; rotʃ/ *n* (*pl* ~es) (colloq) (俗) = cockroach.

road /rəʊd; rod/ *n* [C] **1** specially prepared way, publicly or privately owned, between places for the use of pedestrians, riders, vehicles, etc: 公路; 道路: *main and minor ~s;* 主要道路和輔助道路; (attrib) (形容用法) '~ *junctions;* 道路交叉處; *a '~-map of Great Britain* (Cf a *street*-map of London); 大不列顛道路交通圖(參較: 倫敦街道圖); '~ *accidents;* 交通事件; 車禍; ~ *works in progress,* ~s under construction or repair. 修築中之道路。 ***on the ~,*** travelling: 在途中; 旅行中: *How long were you on the road?* How long did your journey take? 你在路上走了多久? ***rule of the ~,*** custom which regulates the side to be taken by vehicles, ships, etc when meeting or passing each other. 交通規則。 ***take the ~,*** start a journey. 出發; 啓程。 ***take to the ~,*** become a tramp. 成爲流浪者。 **'~ safety,** safety from traffic dangers: 交通安全: *a campaign for ~ safety,* for preventing ~ accidents. 交通安全運動。 **2** (compounds) (複合字) **'~-bed** *n* foundation of rock, stones, etc on which the surface of a ~ is laid. (以石頭等鋪築之)路基。 **'~-block** *n* barricade built across a ~ to stop or slow down traffic (eg by police to catch an escaped prisoner or by military authorities during a period of political disturbances). 路障(例如警方爲逮捕逃犯或在政治騷動期間軍事當局在道路上攔起之障礙物, 以攔截車輛或使之減低車速)。 **'~-book** *n* book describing the ~s of a country, with itineraries (for tourists, etc). 道路指南(簡介一個國家內的道路的書籍, 有爲觀光者等列出的旅行路線)。 **'~-hog** *n* (colloq) motorist who is reckless and inconsiderate of others. (俗)魯莽而不顧他人的汽車駕駛者。 **'~-house** *n* building(s) on a main ~, often one with facilities for meals, dancing, etc used by people who travel by car. 公路上供開汽車旅行者休息之客棧(通常供餐飲、跳舞等)。 **'~·man** /-mæn; -mən/, **'~-mender** *nn* man who repairs ~s. 修路工人。 **'~-metal** *n* stone used for making and repairing ~s. 鋪路碎石。 **'~-sense** *n* capacity for intelligent behaviour on ~s, eg the avoidance of accidents: 在路上安全開車之能力; 避免在路上發生意外之能力: *Harry/Harry's dog has no ~ sense.* 哈利(哈利的狗)沒有在道路上避免發生意外的能力。 **'~ show** *n* (US) theatrical performance by a touring company. (美)旅行劇團之演出。 **'~·side** *n* bordering of a ~: 路邊; 路旁: (attrib) (形容用法) *~side flowers/inns.* 路旁的花(客店)。 **'~·way** *n* (usu with *def art*) central part used by wheeled traffic (contrasted with the footpath, etc): (通常與定冠詞連用)車道 (與 footpath 等相對): *Dogs should be kept off the ~way.* 狗應該遠離車道。 **'~·worthy** *adj* (of a motor-vehicle, etc) fit for use on the ~s. (指車輛等)適合在道路上行駛的。 **3** one's way or route: 途徑; 路線: *You're in the/my ~,* in my way, obstructing me. 你擋住了我的路(你妨礙了我)。 **4** ~ ***to,*** (fig) way of getting to: (喻)(導致…之)途徑: *Is excessive drinking the ~ to ruin?* 過度飲酒會使人趨於墮落嗎? *There's no royal ~ to wisdom,* no easy way, ⇨ royal. 學識無捷徑。 **5** (in proper names) (用於專有名詞中) **(a) the ... R~,** name of a ~ leading to the town, etc named: 通往所指出名稱之城市等的路名: *the Oxford R~,* leading to Oxford; 牛津大道(通往牛津之路); *the Great West R~,* from London to the West of England. 西部大道(從倫敦通往英格蘭西部的公路)。 **(b) ... R~/Rd,** street of buildings: 街; 路: *35 York Rd, London, SW16.* 倫敦西南十六區約克路三十五號。 **6** (usu *pl*) stretch of water near the shore in which ships can ride at anchor: (通常用複數)近岸可供船隻停泊的水域; 錨地; 停泊區域: *anchored in the ~s.* 在停泊處下錨。 **7** (US) (美) = railway. **'~·less** *adj* having no ~s. 沒有路的。 **'~·stead** /-sted; -,stɛd/ *n* = road(6).

road·ster /'rəʊdstə(r); 'rodstɚ/ *n* [C] open motorcar, usu for two persons. (通常供兩人乘坐的)敞篷汽車。

roam /rəʊm; rom/ *vi, vt* [VP2A, C, 6A] walk or travel without any definite aim or destination over or through (a country, etc): 無目標或目的地漫遊; 閒逛: *go ~ing;* 出去閒逛; ~ *about the world;* 漫遊世界; ~ *the seas;* 漫遊海上; *settle down after years of ~ing.* 漂泊數年後定居下來。

roan[1] /rəʊn; ron/ *adj* (of animals) with a coat of a mixed colour, esp brown with white or grey hairs in it. (指動物)雜色的; 雜毛的; (尤指)雜有白色或灰色褐色毛皮的。□ *n* ~ horse or cow. 雜色馬或牛。

roan[2] /rəʊn; ron/ *n* [U] soft sheepskin leather sometimes used for binding books. 柔軟羊皮(有時用來裝訂書)。

roar /rɔː(r); ror/ *n* [C] loud, deep sound as of a lion, of thunder, of a person in pain, etc: (獅、雷、痛苦之人等的)吼叫; 咆哮; 隆隆聲; 哀號聲: *the ~s of a tiger;* 虎嘯; *the ~ of the sea/of waves breaking on the rocks;* 海浪(大浪沖擊岩石)之轟轟聲; *the ~ of London's traffic;* 倫敦車輛之隆隆聲; *with a ~ of rage;* 怒吼地; *~s of laughter;* 狂笑聲; *set the table/room in a ~,* cause everyone to laugh loudly. 使全桌(房間)的人捧腹大笑。□ *vt, vi* **1** [VP 2A, C, 3A] make such loud, deep sounds: 發出此等大而深沉的聲音; 吼叫; 咆哮: *lions ~ing in the distance;* 在遠處吼叫的獅子; ~ *with laughter/pain/rage;* 高聲大笑(痛苦地吼叫; 怒吼); ~ *for mercy.* 高喊請發慈悲。 *Several lorries ~ed past.* 數輛載貨卡車隆隆而過。 **2** [VP6A, 15B] ~ ***sth out,*** say, sing, loudly: 大聲地說、唱: ~ *out an order;* 高聲發出命令; ~ *out a drinking song.* 大聲唱出飲酒歌。 **3** [VP22, 15B] ~ ***oneself hoarse, etc,*** make oneself hoarse, etc by ~ing. 喊得聲音發啞等。~ ***sb down,*** ~ in order to drown the words of a speaker so that he has to give up. 大聲喊叫得使某人停止說話。 **~·ing** *adj* **1** noisy; rough. 喧囂的; 粗魯的。 **2** stormy: 有暴風雨的: *a ~ing night;* 狂風暴雨之夜; *the ~ing forties,* part of the Atlantic between 40° and 50° N latitude, often very stormy. (北緯四十度至五十度間) 大西洋之風暴帶。 **3** brisk; healthy: 活潑的; 健康的: *do a ~ing trade;* 經營一門興隆的生意; *be in ~ing health.* 甚爲健康。▭ *adv* extremely: 極端地; 十分地; 非常地: *~ing drunk.* 酩酊大醉。

roast /rəʊst; rost/ *vt, vi* [VP6A, 2A] **1** (of meat, potatoes, etc) cook, be cooked, in a hot oven, or over or in front of a hot fire, eg on a spit, the meat, etc being basted periodically with the fat and juices that come out: (指肉, 馬鈴薯等)烤; 炙: ~ *a joint.* 烤一大塊肉。 *The meat was ~ing in the oven.* 肉在烤爐裏烤着。 *You've made a fire fit to ~ an ox,* a very large, hot fire. 你生的火足以烤一隻牛。 **2** heat, be heated: 加熱; 烘; 焙; 被烘或焙: ~ *coffee-beans.* 焙咖啡豆。 **3** expose for warmth to heat of some kind: 暴露於某種熱力下以得溫暖; 取暖: ~ *oneself in front of the fire;* 爐前取暖; *lie in the sun and ~.* 躺在太陽下取暖。□ *attrib adj* that has been ~ed: 烤炙過的; 烘焙過的: ~ *beef/pork.* 烤牛肉(豬肉)。□ *n* **1** [C] joint of ~ed meat; [U] slices from such a joint: 烤好的一大塊肉; 從烤好的肉塊切成之肉片: *cold ~ on Monday.* 星期一吃冷凍烤肉。 **2** operation of ~ing: 烤; 炙; 烘; 焙: *give sth a good ~.* 好好烘烤某物。 **~er** *n* kind of oven for ~ing; apparatus for ~ing coffee-beans; article of food, eg a chicken, sucking pig, suitable for ~ing. 烘烤爐; 焙咖啡豆之器具; 適於烤食之食物(如鷄, 乳豬)。 **~·ing** *n* (from the dated use of ~ meaning criticize harshly). (沿自~的過時用法, 指嚴厲地批評)。 ***give sb a good ~ing,*** (fig) scold or ridicule him harshly. (喻)嚴厲地責罵或嘲

弄某人。

rob /rɒb；rɑb/ *vt* (-bb-) [VP6A, 14] ***rob sb／sth (of sth),*** **1** deprive (sb) of his property; take property from (a place) unlawfully (and often by force): 搶奪(某人)之財物；(常以暴力)非法地從(某地)刼去財物: *I was robbed of my watch.* 我的手錶被搶走了。Cf 參較 I had my watch *stolen.* 我的手錶被偷了。*The bank was robbed last night.* 昨晚那銀行被刼。*The village boys rob my orchard.* 村中的男孩子們強摘我的果園中的果子。Cf 參較 They *steal* apples from my orchard. 他們偷去我果園中的蘋果。 **2** deprive a person of (what is due to him, etc): 剝奪某人(有權享有的東西等): *be robbed of the rewards of one's labour.* 被剝奪其勞力應得之報酬。**rob·ber** *n* person who robs; thief. 强盜；賊。**rob·bery** /ˈrɒbərɪ；ˈrɑbərɪ/ *n* [C, U] (*pl* -ries) (instance of) robbing: 搶奪；剝奪；搶奪或剝奪的實例: *robbery with violence;* 暴力搶奪； *three robberies in one week.* 一週之內三次搶案。ˌ***daylight ˈrobbery,*** (colloq) charging of excessive prices: (俗)開價過高；漫天要價: *50p for a cup of coffee is daylight robbery!* 一杯咖啡要五十辨士眞是敲竹槓！

robe /rəub；rob/ *n* [C] **1** long, loose outer garment. 寬鬆長袍。**ˈbath-～** (US) dressing-gown. (美)浴衣；晨衣。 **2** (often *pl*) long, loose garment worn as a sign of rank or office: (常用複數)表示階級或職位的長袍: *the* ˌ*Coroˈnation ～s,* of a king or queen; (國王或女王的)登極時所著之禮服； *magistrates／judges in their black ～s.* 穿黑袍之法官。□ *vt, vi* [VP6A, 14, 2A] ～ ***(in),*** put a ～ or ～s on: (使)穿著長袍: *professors ～d in their bright-coloured gowns;* 穿着鮮麗長袍的教授們； *～d in the scarlet of a cardinal.* 穿着樞機主教所穿那種紅袍。

robin /ˈrɒbɪn；ˈrɑbɪn/ *n* **1** small, brownish bird with red breast-feathers (also called 亦稱作 ˌ**～ˈredbreast**). 紅襟鳥；知更鳥；歐鴝。 ⇨ the illus at bird. 參看 bird 之插圖。 **2** (name given to kinds of) small bird outside the British Isles (eg the American ～, a redbreasted thrush). 不列顚群島外某些種小鳥(之名稱)(如 American robin, 一種紅襟的畫眉鳥)。ˌ**R～ ˈGoodfellow** *n* type of mischievous but good-natured goblin or elf in English folklore (also called 亦稱作 *Puck*). 英國民間故事中好惡作劇但善良的鬼怪或精靈。

ro·bot /ˈrəubɒt；ˈrobət/ *n* [C] machine made to act like a man; machine-like person. 機器人；行動像機械般的人。

ro·bust /rəuˈbʌst；roˈbʌst/ *adj* vigorous; healthy: 有活力的；健康的: *a ～ young man;* 一個精力旺盛的青年； *a ～ appetite.* 好胃口。**～·ly** *adv* **～·ness** *n*

roc /rɒk；rɑk/ *n* gigantic bird of Eastern tales. (東方故事中之)巨鳥；大鵬。

rock[1] /rɒk；rɑk/ *n* **1** [U] solid stony part of the earth's crust: 地殼之堅硬石質部分；岩層；岩: *a house built upon ～.* 建築於岩石上的一座房屋。 ⇨ *bedrock* at bed[1](4). ⇨ the illus at stratify. 參看 stratify 之插圖。 **2** [C, U] mass of ～ standing out from the earth's surface or from the sea. (從地球表面或海中突出之)岩石；礁石。***as firm／solid as a ～,*** immovable; (fig) (of persons) sound; dependable. 安如磐石；(喻)(指人)穩健的；可靠的。***on the ～s,*** (of a ship) wrecked on ～s; (fig, of a person) very short of money; (of a marriage) likely to end in divorce or separation. (指船)毁於石上；觸礁而破；(喻，指人)極缺錢；(指婚姻)可能離婚或分居。***see ～s ahead,*** see danger of shipwreck (or fig, any kind of danger). 看到前面的岩礁；看到船將觸礁的危險；(喻)看到任何危險。**the R～ of Ages,** Jesus Christ. 萬世磐石(耶穌基督)。**3** [C] large, detached stone or boulder: 大石塊或大圓石: *～s rolling down the side of a mountain;* 從一山坡滾下之巨石； (US)(美) = stone[1](2). **4** [U] (GB) kind of hard, sticky sweet, usu made in long cylindrical pieces: (英)一種硬而黏之糖果(通常製成長圓柱形)；硬糖: *a stick of ～;* 一條硬糖； *almond ～.* 杏仁硬糖。 **5** ***on the ～s,*** (US) (of whisky) served on ice-cubes without water. (美)(指威士忌酒)加冰塊飲用。 **6** (compounds) (複合字) ˌ**～-ˈbottom** *n* [U] lowest point: 最低點；最低限度: *Prices have reached ～-bottom;* 價錢已到最低限度；(attrib)(形容用法) *～-bottom prices.* 最低的價錢。**ˈ～-cake** *n* [C] small cake or bun with a hard, rough surface. 表面硬粗的小甜餅。**ˈ～-climbing** *n* the climbing of masses of ～ on mountain-sides (with the help of ropes, etc). (藉繩索等之助)攀登岩壁。**ˈ～-crystal** *n* pure natural transparent quartz. 天然的透明石英石。**ˈ～-garden** *n* artificial or natural bank or mound with ～s and stones and ～-plants growing among them. 岩石庭園(人工築造之假山或自然之石坵，並有植物生長於岩石之間)。**ˈ～-plant** *n* kinds of plant found growing among ～s, esp on mountains and cultivated in ～-gardens, etc. 岩間植物(尤指長於山石間，及栽植於岩石庭園等中者)。 ˌ**～-ˈsalmon** *n* (trade name for) dogfish. (商用名稱)角鯊。**ˈ～-salt** *n* common salt as found in mines in crystal form. 岩鹽；石鹽(在礦中掘得之結晶形食鹽)。**ˈ～·ery** /ˈrɒkərɪ；ˈrɑkərɪ/ *n* [C] (*pl* -ies) = ～-garden.

rock[2] /rɒk；rɑk/ *vt, vi* [VP6A, 15A, 2A] (cause to) sway or swing backwards and forwards, or from side to side: (使)擺動；搖動: *～ a baby to sleep;* 搖一嬰兒入睡； *～ a baby in its cradle.* 搖動搖籃中之嬰兒。*The town was ～ed by an earthquake.* 該鎭爲地震所搖動。*He sat ～ing (himself) in his chair.* 他坐在椅中前後擺動着。*Our boat was ～ed by／was ～ed on the waves.* 我們的船被浪所搖動(在浪上顚簸搖動)。 ～ ***the boat,*** (fig) do sth that upsets the smooth progress of an undertaking, etc. (喩)擾亂事件等的順利進行。**ˈ～·ing-chair** *n* one fitted with rockers on which it rests. 搖椅。**ˈ～·ing-horse** *n* wooden horse with rockers for a child to ride on. (小孩騎乘的)搖動木馬。**～er** *n* **1** one of the curved pieces of wood on which a ～ing-chair or ～ing-horse rests. (搖椅或搖動木馬下面的)搖板。 **2** (US) ～ing-chair. (美)搖椅。 **3** **R～er,** (GB, 1960's) member of a teenage gang, wearing leather jackets and riding motor-bikes. (英，1960 年代)一種喜歡穿皮夾克，騎摩托車的少年幫派的一份子。 **4** ***off one's ～er,*** (sl) crazy; out of one's mind. (俚)發瘋。

rock[3] /rɒk；rɑk/ *n* (also 亦作 **～-ˈn-roll** /ˌrɒk ən ˈrəul；ˌrɑkənˈrol/) [U] highly rhythmic popular music for dancing, played on electric guitars, etc. 搖滾樂(極富節奏，適於跳舞之流行音樂，用電吉他等演奏)。□ *vi* dance to this music. 跳搖滾舞。

rocket /ˈrɒkɪt；ˈrɑkɪt/ *n* **1** [C] tube-shaped case filled with fast-burning material, which launches itself into the air (as a firework, as a signal of distress, or as a self-propelled projectile or missile; also used to launch an aircraft or spacecraft or, attached to an aircraft, to give it higher speed and range): (用作煙火、緊急信號等之)冲天炮；(用以發射飛機或太空船，或用以增加飛機速度及航程之)火箭: ～ *propulsion;* 火箭推進； *～-propelled.* 火箭推動的。⇨ also retro～. **ˈ～-base** *n* military base for ～ missiles. 火箭基地；飛彈基地。**ˈ～-range** *n* area used for experiments with missiles propelled by ～s. 飛彈試驗場。**2** (colloq) severe scolding: (俗)嚴厲的責罵: *get／give sb a ～.* 受到嚴厲的責罵(嚴厲地責罵某人)。 □ *vi* [VP2A] go up fast like a ～: 如火箭般迅速上升: (colloq) (俗) *Prices ～ed after the war.* 戰後物價飛漲。 **～ry** /-trɪ；-trɪ/ *n* [U] (art or science of) using ～s for projectiles, space missiles, etc. 利用火箭推送拋射體及太空飛彈等；火箭術；火箭學。

rock-ˈn-roll /ˌrɒk ən ˈrəul；ˌrɑkənˈrol/ *n* ⇨ rock.[3]

rocky /ˈrɒkɪ；ˈrɑkɪ/ *adj* (-ier, -iest) **1** of rock, full of or abounding in rocks; hard like rock: 岩石的；充滿或多石的；硬如石的: *a ～ road;* 一條多石子之路； *～ soil.* 多石之土壤。 **2** (colloq) shaky; unsteady: (俗)動搖的；不穩的: *The table is rather ～.*

桌子有點不穩。*His business is very ~.* 他的生意很不穩定(時賺時賠)。

ro·coco /rəˈkəʊkəʊ ; rəˈkoko/ *adj* (of furniture, architecture, etc) with much elaborate ornament (with scrolls, foliage, etc) as in Europe in the late 18th c. (指傢具,建築等)洛可可式的(有很多精美漩渦形,葉形等裝飾,如十八世紀末歐洲所用者)。

rod /rɒd ; rɑd/ *n* **1** thin, straight piece of wood or metal: 木質或金屬的細而直之桿;竿: *ˈcurtain-rods;* 吊掛帳幕之桿; *a ˈfishing-rod;* 釣魚竿; *fishing with rod and line.* 用釣竿和釣絲釣魚。 **2** stick used for punishing. 笞鞭;教鞭。 ***make a rod for one's own back,*** prepare trouble for oneself. 給自己的背做笞鞭;自討苦吃;自找麻煩。***ˌspare the ˈrod and ˌspoil the ˈchild,*** (prov) A child who is not punished will become undisciplined and unruly. (諺)孩子不打不成器。***have a rod in ˈpickle for sb,*** be saving up severe punishment for him when the opportunity comes. 等有機會再嚴懲某人。 **3** (US, sl) revolver. (美,俚)手槍。 **4** measure of length equal to 5½ yds or 5·03 metres (also called 亦稱作 *pole* or 或 *perch*). 竿(長度單位,等於 5½ 碼或 5·03 公尺)。 **5** metal bar; shaft, etc: 金屬條;軸等: *ˈpiston-rods.* 活塞桿。

rode /rəʊd ; rod/ *pt* of ride².

ro·dent /ˈrəʊdnt ; ˈrodn̩t/ *n* animal, eg *a rat, rabbit, squirrel* or *beaver,* which gnaws things with its strong teeth specially adapted for this purpose. 齧齒類動物(如鼠、兎、松鼠或海狸等)。

ro·deo /rəʊˈdeɪəʊ *US:* ˈrəʊdɪəʊ ; ˈrodɪˌo/ *n* (*pl* ~s /-əʊz ; -oz/) [C] **1** (on the plains of Western US) rounding up of cattle. (在美國西部平原)將牛馬等驅集一起。 **2** contest of skill in lassoing cattle, riding untamed horses, etc. 擲索套牛,騎野馬等之競技。

rodo·mon·tade /ˌrɒdəmɒnˈteɪd ; ˌrɑdəmɑnˈted/ *n* [U] (formal) boastful, bragging talk. (正式用語)狂言;大話;吹噓。

roe¹ /rəʊ ; ro/ *n* [C, U] (mass of) eggs or sperm in a fish: 魚子;魚精: *salted cod's-roe for Friday's supper.* 爲星期五晚餐準備的醃鱈魚子。

roe² /rəʊ ; ro/ *n* (*pl* roes or, collectively, roe) small kind of European and Asiatic deer. 歐洲和亞洲產的一種小鹿。**ˈroe·buck** *n* male roe. 雄鹿。

Roent·gen /ˈrɒntjən *US:* ˈrentgən ; ˈrɛntgən/ = Röntgen.

ro·ga·tion /rəʊˈgeɪʃn ; roˈgeʃən/ *n* (usu *pl*) litany of the saints chanted on the three days before Ascension Day: (通常用複數)(耶穌昇天節前三天所唱之)聖徒祈禱文: *R~ week,* the week including these days; (包括耶穌昇天節前三天在內之) 祈禱週; *R~ Sunday,* the Sunday before Ascension Day. 耶穌昇天節之前的星期日。

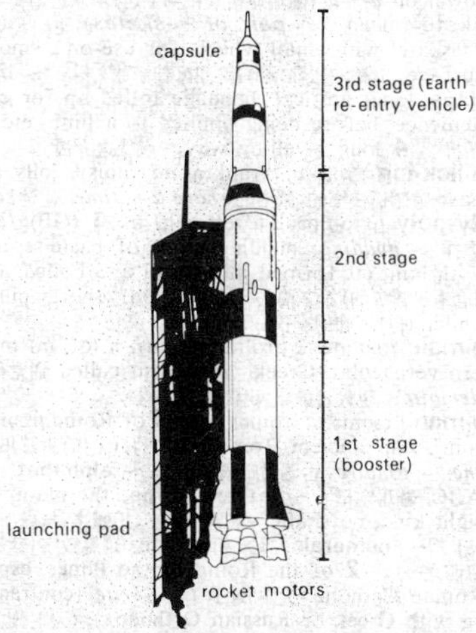

a rocket launching a spacecraft

roger /ˈrɒdʒə(r) ; ˈrɑdʒɚ/ *int* (in radio communication) message heard and understood. (用於無線電通訊)收到了!聽懂了!

Rog·er /ˈrɒdʒə(r) ; ˈrɑdʒɚ/ *n* **the Jolly ~,** pirates' black flag. 海盜用的黑旗。 **Sir ~ de Coverley** /sə ˌrɒdʒə də ˈkʌvəlɪ ; sɝˈrɑdʒɚdəˈkʌvɚlɪ/, country-dance and tune. 一種鄉村舞蹈及其舞曲。

rogue /rəʊg ; rog/ *n* [C] **1** scoundrel; rascal. 惡徒;流氓。 **~s' gallery,** collection of photographs of known criminals. 罪犯像片陳列室。 **2** (playfully or humorously) person fond of playing tricks, teasing people. (戲謔或詼諧用法)愛好捉弄人者。 **3** wild animal (esp **ˌ~-ˈelephant**) driven or living apart from the herd and of a savage temper. 離群之猛獸;(尤指)離羣之猛象。**ro·guery** /ˈrəʊgərɪ ; ˈrogərɪ/ *n* (*pl* -ries) **1** [C, U] (instance or example of the) conduct of a ~. 流氓行爲(之實例或例子)。 **2** [U] playful mischief; (*pl*) mischievous acts. 嬉戲之惡作劇;(複)惡作劇之行爲。

ro·guish /ˈrəʊgɪʃ ; ˈrogɪʃ/ *adj* **1** dishonest; of the nature of a rogue. 不誠實的;有流氓習性的。 **2** mischievous: 嬉戲的;惡作劇的: *~ eyes.* 一雙調皮的眼睛。 **~·ly** *adv* **~·ness** *n*

roist·erer /ˈrɔɪstərə(r) ; ˈrɔɪstərɚ/ *n* rough, noisy merry-maker. 粗魯喧鬧的作樂者。

role, rôle /rəʊl ; rol/ *n* [C] actor's part in a play; person's task or duty in an undertaking: (劇中演員之)角色;(一個人在某事業中之)職分;責任: *play the ˈtitle-~ in 'Hamlet',* play the part of Hamlet. 在'哈姆雷特'一劇中演主角哈姆雷特。

roll¹ /rəʊl ; rol/ *n* **1** sth made into the shape of a cylinder by being rolled: 被做成捲形之物;一捲: *a ~ of cloth/newsprint/carpet/photographic film, etc;* 一捲布(白報紙,地毯,膠捲等); sth in this shape, made by rolling or otherwise: 呈捲形之物: *a man with ~s of fat on his neck;* 脖子上有層層肥肉的人; *a bread ~,* a small quantity of bread baked in the shape of a ball; 小圓麵包; *~s of butter;* 奶油團; *a sausage ~,* a sausage rolled in pastry and then baked. 捲在麵皮中再烤的香腸;香腸捲。 **ˌ~-top ˈdesk** *n* desk with a flexible cover that slides back into a compartment at the top. 有活動頂蓋可以推入頂部隔層中的書桌;附有滑動式頂蓋的寫字檯。 **2** turned-back edge: 摺回之邊: *a ˌ~-ˈcollar,* large collar made by turning back the edge of the material. 大翻領。 **3** rolling movement: 滾轉;搖晃;擺動: *The slow, steady ~ of the ship made us sick.* 船緩慢持續的搖晃使我們暈眩。 *He walks with a nautical ~,* like a sailor. 他走起路來像海員一樣搖搖晃晃。*The young foal was enjoying a ~ on the grass.* 小馬正在草地上盡情地打滾。 **4** official list or record, esp of names. 正式的表册或記錄;(尤指)名單;名簿。 ***call the ~,*** read the names (to check who is present and who absent). 點名。Hence, 由此產生, **ˈ~-call** *n* calling of names. 點名。**ˌ~ of ˈhonour,** list of those who have died for their country in war. 陣亡將士名册。 ***strike off the ~s,*** take (a solicitor's name) off the list of those who eg have the right to practise, eg when a solicitor has been proved guilty of dishonesty. 從開業律師名册上除去(例如被證明有欺詐等罪之律師的名字)。 **5** rolling sound: 隆隆之聲: *the distant ~ of thunder/drums.* 遠方隆隆的雷(鼓)聲。

roll² /rəʊl ; rol/ *vt, vi* (For special uses with *adverbial particles* and *preps,* ⇨ 11 below.) (與副詞接語及介詞連用的特殊用法,參看下列第11義。) **1** [VP6A, 15A, B, 2A, C] (cause to) move along on wheels or by turning over and over: (使)滾動;轉動: *The man ~ed the barrel into the yard.* 那個人把圓桶

滾進院中。*Rocks and stones were ~ing down the hillside.* 岩石與碎石正從山坡滾下。*The coin fell and ~ed under the table.* 銅錢掉落,滾往桌下。*The bicycle hit me and sent me ~ing/~ed me over.* 脚踏車撞到我,使我翻落在地上。*The child was ~ing a hoop.* 孩子正在滾鐵環。***heads will roll,*** (colloq) some people will be dismissed or disgraced. (俗)某些人將要被解職或失寵。 **2** [VP6A, 12B, 13B, 15B] ***~ (up),*** cause to revolve between two surfaces; make (sth) by doing this; make into the shape of a ball or a cylinder: 搓;捲;搓或捲製(某物);將…繞成球形或圓柱形: *Please ~ me a cigarette/~ a cigarette for me.* 請替我捲一支香煙。*R~ the string/wool (up) into a ball.* 把細繩(毛線)繞成線球。*R~ up the carpet/that map on the wall.* 把地毯(掛在牆上的地圖)捲起來。*He ~ed up* (= furled) *his umbrella.* 他把傘收攏。*He ~ed* (= wrapped by turning over) *himself (up) in the blanket.* 他把自己裹在毛毯裡。⇨ sleeve. **3** [VP2C] come or go in some direction: 自某方向來;向某方向去: *The clouds ~ed away as the sun rose higher.* 太陽升高時,雲散去了。*The years ~ed on/by,* passed. 歲月匆匆逝去。*The tears were ~ing* (=flowing) *down her cheeks.* 眼淚自她雙頰流下。 **4** [VP2A, C] turn about in various directions: 向不同方向旋轉:*a porpoise ~ing in the water.* 在水中翻滾的海豚。 **5** [VP6A, 22] make or become flat, level or smooth by pressing with a ~ing cylinder of wood, metal, etc or by passing between two such cylinders: 以木質或金屬等滾筒或在兩個此種滾筒間將(某物)壓平,輾平,輾光;被壓平,輾平,輾光: *~ a lawn/a road surface;* 將草地(路面)壓平; *~ sth flat.* 把某物輾平。*This dough ~s well,* is of the sort that one can ~ easily. 這種麵團容易輾壓。 **~ed gold,** thin coating of gold on the surface of another metal, applied by ~ing. (砑貼於另一金屬上的)金箔。 **6** [VP2A, B, C] (cause to) sway or move from side to side; walk with a side-to-side movement: (使)搖晃或擺動;搖晃而行: *The ship was ~ing heavily.* 船搖晃得很厲害。*We ~ed and pitched for two days after leaving Lisbon.* 離開里斯本後,我們的船在海上搖晃顛簸了兩天。*Some sailors have a ~ing gait.* 有些水手走起路來搖搖晃晃。*The drunken man ~ed up to me.* 那醉漢向我蹣跚走來。 **7** [VP2A] (of surfaces) have long slopes that rise and fall: (指表面)綿延起伏: *miles and miles of ~ing country;* 連綿很多哩的起伏地區; *a ~ing plain.* 綿延起伏的平原。 **8** [VP2A, C] move with a rise and fall; be carried with rise-and-fall motion: 起伏地移動;被起伏的動作所帶: *The waves ~ed in to the beach.* 海浪起伏地湧向海灘。 **9** [VP2A, C, 6A, 15A, B] make, utter, be uttered with, long, deep, vibrating or echoing sounds: 發出長長的、深沉的、顫動的或廻響的聲音;發隆隆聲;以隆隆聲說出: *The thunder ~ed in the distance.* 遠處雷聲隆隆。*The drums ~ed.* 鼓聲隆隆。*He ~ed out his words/song, etc.* 他以低沉的聲音說話(唱歌等)。 *~* ***one's r's,*** utter them with the tongue making a rapid succession of taps against the palate. 把 r 發成舌尖顫音。 **10** [VP2A, C, 14] ***~ (at),*** (of the eyes) (cause to) move from side to side, change direction: (指眼睛)(使)左右轉動;溜轉: *His eyes ~ed strangely at me.* 他的眼睛奇怪地對着我打轉。*Don't ~ your eyes at me!* 你的眼睛別朝着我打轉! **~·ing** *n* (compounds) (複合字) **'~ing-mill** *n* mill where metal is ~ed out into sheets, bars, etc. 輾壓機; 輾壓工廠(把金屬輾壓成薄片,條塊等)。 **'~ing-pin** *n* cylinder of wood, glass, etc usu about a foot long, for ~ing out dough, etc. 麵棍;擀麵杖。 **'~ing-stock** *n* railway's coaches, wagons, etc; all the stock that is on wheels. 鐵路之客車,貨車等;全部車輛。 **11** [VP2C, 15B] (special uses with *adverbial particles* and *preps*): (與副詞接語及介詞連用的特殊用法):

roll sth back, turn or force back, eg enemy forces. 把(敵軍等)逼回去;把(敵軍等)趕回去。

roll in, come, arrive, in large numbers or quantities: 蜂擁而至;大量湧進: *Offers of help are ~ing in.* 大量的援助源源而來。 ***be '~ing in sth,*** have a large quantity of it: 擁有大量的: *He's ~ing in money/property.* 他擁有大量的錢(財產)。

roll on, **(a)** be capable of being put on by ~ing. (指衣物)能捲過肢體而穿上。 **(b)** (of time) pass steadily: (指時間)不斷地消逝;流逝: *Time ~ed on.* 光陰荏苒。 **(c)** (of time, chiefly *imper*) come soon: (指時間,主要用於祈使句)快點到來: *R~ on the day when I retire from this dull work!* 但願我退休的日子早日到來,以脫離這種枯燥的工作! ***~ sth on,*** put on by ~ing, eg over a part of the body: 捲過肢體而穿上(衣物): *She ~ed her stockings on.* 她穿上她的長襪。 **'~-on** *n* (woman's) elastic foundation garment ~ed on to the hips. (婦女)束腹(穿著於臀部之一種有彈性的緊身衣)。

roll sth out, **(a)** cause it (ie sth that is ~ed up) to become flat, level or smooth, by opening it out: 展開(捲起之物): *~ out a map/carpet.* 展開一地圖(地毯)。 ***~ out the red carpet,*** (fig) give an important visitor a special welcome. (喻)隆重地歡迎嘉賓。⇨ *red carpet* at red(1). **(b)** flatten it by ~ing: 搓平;擀平: *~ out pastry.* 擀餡餅皮。⇨ *~ing-pin* at 10 above. 參看上列第 10 義之 ~ing-pin。

roll up, (of a vehicle) arrive and stop; (of a person) arrive: (指車輛)到達並停下;(指人)到達: *Raymond always ~s up late.* 雷孟德老是遲到。 ***R~ up! R~ up!,*** used as an invitation to join others, eg possible customers at a street stall. 來加入!來加入!(如街上之貨攤請人光顧時所用)。 ***~ sth up,*** **(a)** ⇨ 2 above. 參看上列第 2 義。 **(b)** (mil) drive the flank of (an enemy line) back and round. (軍)迫使(敵軍陣線)之側翼向後彎退;席捲;合捲。

roller /ˈrəʊlə(r); ˈrolɚ/ *n* [C] **1** cylinder-shaped object of wood, metal, rubber, etc, usu part of a machine, for pressing, smoothing, crushing, printing, etc: 滾子;滾軸;滾輪;滾轉機: *a 'garden-~,* for use on a lawn; 輾草坪機; *the ~s of a mangle,* (between which articles are passed to press out water); 軋乾機的滾筒; *a 'road-~,* used for making roads level, by crushing rock, etc. 軋路機。 **2** cylinder of wood, metal, etc placed beneath an object to make movement easy, or round which sth may be rolled easily: 置於物下使移動容易,或用以捲物之木質或金屬等之圓柱;滾柱;捲軸: *a 'blind-~,* on which a window blind (US 美 = *shade*) is rolled; 窗戶遮陽上的捲軸; *a '~-towel,* an endless towel on a ~. (兩端連結套在軸上之)環狀毛巾。 **'~-skate** (often 常作 ***pair of ~-skates***), *n, vi* (use a) skate¹ with small wheels for use on a smooth surface. 有輪溜冰鞋;用有輪溜冰鞋溜冰。 **3** **'~ bandage,** long surgical bandage rolled up for convenience before being applied to a limb, etc. 綳帶捲。 **4** long, swelling wave. 起伏之大浪。

rol·lick·ing /ˈrɒlɪkɪŋ; ˈrɑlɪkɪŋ/ *adj* noisy, jolly and gay: 喧鬧而快樂的;歡樂的: *have a ~ time.* 盡情歡樂。

roly-poly /ˌrəʊlɪˈpəʊlɪ; ˈrolɪˌpolɪ/ *n* **1** (GB) (also 亦作 *~ pudding*) pudding made of paste spread with jam, etc formed into a roll and boiled. (英)(含有果醬等的)布丁捲。 **2** (colloq) short, plump child. (俗)矮胖的小孩。

Ro·maic /rəʊˈmeɪɪk; roˈme·ɪk/ *adj, n* (of, in) modern vernacular Greek (more usu called 通常稱作 *demotic*). 現代希臘語;現代希臘語的。

Ro·man /ˈrəʊmən; ˈromən/ *adj* **1** of Rome /rəʊm; rom/, esp ancient Rome: 羅馬的;(尤指)古羅馬的: *the ~ Empire.* 古羅馬帝國。 **the ~ alphabet,** the ABC. 羅馬字母。 **~ letters/type,** the plain, upright kind, not italic. 羅馬體鉛字;正體字(無虛飾,直體)。 **~ numerals,** ⇨ App 4(1). 羅馬數字(參看附錄四之一)。 **2** of the Rome of the Popes, esp = Roman Catholic: 天主教的: *the ~ rite* (contrasted eg with Greek or Russian Orthodox). 天主教之儀式(與希臘或俄國正教之儀式相對)。⇨ catholic(2); pope;

Protestant. □ *n* **1** citizen of ancient Rome; (*pl*) Christians of ancient Rome: 古羅馬市民;(複)古羅馬之基督教徒: *the Epistle to the ~s* (in the NT). (新約中的)羅馬書。 **2** Roman Catholic. 天主教徒。

ro·mance /rəʊˈmæns ; roˈmæns/ *n* **1** [C] story or novel of adventure; love story, esp one in which the events are quite unlike real life; [U] class of literature consisting of such stories. 冒險故事;愛情故事(尤指所述事件與現實生活頗爲不同的傳奇故事);傳奇文學。 **2** [C] **R~**, medieval story, usu in verse, relating the adventures of some hero of chivalry. 中世紀的騎士故事(通常用韻文寫成,敍述騎士的冒險事蹟)。 **3** [C] real experience, esp a love-affair, considered to be remarkable or worth description; (colloq) any love-affair. 被認爲不平凡或值得敍述的眞實經驗(尤指風流韻事);羅曼史;(俗)戀愛。 **4** [U] state of mind which welcomes stories of the marvellous, etc; the qualities characteristic of stories of love and adventure: 喜歡不平凡故事的心理傾向;愛情與冒險故事具有之特質: *travel abroad in search of ~.* 旅行外國以尋找不平凡的經驗。 *There was an air of ~ about the old castle.* 這座古堡頗富浪漫氣氛。 **5** [C, U] exaggerated description; picturesque falsehood. 誇大的描述;生動的虛構。 □ *vi* [VP2A] (more usu 較常用 *romanticize*) exaggerate by adding interesting or attractive details when telling a story, recounting events, etc. (講故事,重述發生的事件等時)增加有趣味或迷人的細節而誇張說出。

Ro·mance /rəʊˈmæns ; roˈmæns/ *adj* **~ languages**, French, Italian, Spanish, Portuguese, Rumanian and others developed from Latin. 羅曼斯語(由拉丁語演變而成之法語,義大利語,西班牙語,葡萄牙語,羅馬尼亞語及其他語言);拉丁語系諸語言。

Ro·man·esque /ˌrəʊməˈnesk ; ˌromənˈɛsk/ *n* [U] style of architecture, with round arches and thick walls (in Europe between the ancient classical and the Gothic periods). 羅馬式建築(在古典時期與哥德式時期間流行歐洲的一種建築式,以使用圓拱及厚牆爲其特色)。

ro·man·tic /rəʊˈmæntɪk ; roˈmæntɪk/ *adj* **1** (of persons) having ideas, feelings, etc remote from experience and real life; given to romance(4); visionary. (指人)有浪漫思想,感情等的;喜歡傳奇故事及不平凡經驗的; 幻想的。 **2** of, like, suggesting, romance: 傳奇故事的;像傳奇故事的;使人聯想到浪漫故事的;浪漫的: *~ scenes/adventures/tales/situations;* 富有浪漫氣氛的景色(冒險,故事,情勢); *a ~ old castle.* 一個具有傳奇性的古堡。 **3** (in art, literature and music) marked by feeling rather than by intellect; preferring grandeur, passion, informal beauty, to order and proportion (opp of *classic* and *classical*): (藝術,文學和音樂)浪漫主義的(爲 classic 及 classical 之相反字): *the ~ poets*, eg Shelley, Keats. 浪漫詩人(如雪萊,濟慈)。 □ *n* **1** person with ~(3) ideals. (文學,音樂,藝術之)浪漫主義者。 **2** (*pl*) ~ ideas; extravagantly visionary feelings, expressions, etc. (複)浪漫的思想;過於幻想的感情,言詞等。 **ro·man·ti·cally** /-klɪ ; -klɪ/ *adv* **ro·man·ti·cism** /-tɪsɪzəm ; -təˌsɪzəm/ *n* [U] ~ tendency in literature, art and music (contrasted with *realism* and *classicism*); ~ spirit; quality of allowing full play to the imagination. (文學,藝術,音樂上之)浪漫主義(與 realism 及 classicism 相對);浪漫精神;充分發揮想像之特質。 **ro·man·ti·cist** /-tɪsɪst ; -təsɪst/ *n* follower of romanticism in literature or art, eg Wordsworth. 文學或藝術方面的浪漫主義者(如華滋華斯)。 **ro·man·ti·cize** /-tɪsaɪz ; -təˌsaɪz/ *vt, vi* [VP6A, 2A] treat in a ~ way; make ~; use a ~ style in writing, etc; be ~. 以浪漫的方式處理;使浪漫化;以浪漫的風格寫作;有浪漫的思想或感情。

Rom·any /ˈrɒmənɪ ; ˈrɑmənɪ/ *n* (*pl* -nies) **1** [C] Gypsy. 吉卜賽人。 **2** [U] language of the Gypsies. 吉卜賽語。□ *adj* Gypsy. 吉卜賽人的;吉卜賽語的。

Rom·ish /ˈrəʊmɪʃ ; ˈromɪʃ/ *adj* (usu disparaging) of the Roman Catholic Church. (通常有輕蔑之意)天主教的。

romp /rɒmp ; rɑmp/ *vi* [VP2A, C] **1** (esp of children) play about, esp running, jumping and being rather rough. (尤指兒童)嬉鬧玩耍;(尤指)跑,跳且相當粗魯地玩。 **2** win, succeed, quickly or without apparent effort: 迅速或輕易地獲勝,成功: (in a horse-race) (在賽馬中) *The favourite ~ed home*, won easily. 這匹熱門馬輕而易舉地獲勝。 *John just ~s through his examinations*, passes them easily. 約翰輕而易舉地通過考試。□ *n* [C] child fond of ~ing; period of ~ing: 喜歡喧鬧嬉戲的孩子;喧鬧嬉戲的一段時間: *have a ~;* 喧鬧嬉戲; *a game of ~s.* 喧嚣的遊戲。 **~er** *n* (*sing* or *pl*) loose-fitting garment worn by a child: (單數或複數)寬鬆的連褲童裝: *a pair of ~ers;* 一套連褲童裝; *a ˈ~er suit.* 一套連褲童裝。

ron·deau /ˈrɒndəʊ ; ˈrɑndo/, **ron·del** /ˈrɒndl ; ˈrɑndl/ *nn* poem of thirteen or ten lines with two rhymes throughout and the opening words used twice as a refrain. 一種十三行或十行詩(全詩押兩韻,以首行開始的字用在兩處做爲疊句)。

rondo /ˈrɒndəʊ ; ˈrɑndo/ *n* (*pl* ~s /-dəʊz ; -doz/) piece of music in which the principal theme returns from time to time. (音樂)輪旋曲(主題時時重覆)。

Ro·neo /ˈrəʊnɪəʊ ; ˈronɪo/ *n* (P) machine that duplicates letters, circulars, etc. (商標)一種油印機。□ *vt* duplicate on a ~ machine. 以此種油印機複印。

Rönt·gen /ˈrɒntjən *US:* ˈrentgən ; ˈrɛntgən/ **~ rays** *n pl* = X-rays.

rood /ruːd ; rud/ *n* **1** (old use) (舊用法) **ˈ~(-tree)** cross on which Jesus was put to death. 耶穌被處死之十字架。 **2** crucifix, esp one raised on the middle of a wooden or stone carved screen (*a ˈ~-screen*) separating the nave and choir of a church. 苦像(十字架上的耶穌像,尤指教堂內隔開本堂和唱詩班席位的木質或石頭屏風上面突起的影像)。 **3** (GB) measure of land, one-fourth of an acre. (英)路得(丈量土地之單位,爲 1/4 英畝)。

roof /ruːf ; ruf/ *n* **1** top covering of a building, tent, bus, car, etc: (建築物,帳篷,公共汽車,車輛等之)頂: *How can you live under the same ~ as that woman*, in the same building? 你怎麼能够同那個女人住在一起? ***raise the ~***, (colloq) create an uproar; make a great noise (indoors). (俗)喧嚣不休;(在室內) 吵翻了天。 **ˈ~-garden** *n* garden on the flat ~ of a building. 屋頂花園。 **ˈ~-tree** *n* strong horizontal main beam at the apex of a ~. 屋頂之棟樑;屋脊樑。 **2** highest part: 最高點: *the ~ of heaven*, the sky; 天頂;天空; *the ~ of the world*, a high mountain range; 世界屋脊;高的山脈; *the ~ of the mouth*, the palate. 上顎。□ *vt* (*pt, pp* ~ed /ruːft ; ruft/) [VP6A, 15A, B] supply with a ~; be a ~ for: 給…蓋頂;爲…之頂: *a shed ~ed over with strips of bark.* 以一片一片狹長的樹皮爲頂的小屋。 **~·less** *adj* having no ~; (fig, of persons) homeless; lacking shelter. 沒有屋頂的;(喻,指人)無家可歸的;沒有住處的。 **~·ing** *n* (also 亦作 *ˈ~ing material*) material used for ~s (eg slates, shingles). 做屋頂的材料(如石板瓦,木瓦等)。

rook[1] /rʊk ; rʊk/ *n* large black bird like a crow. 一種類似烏鴉的大黑鳥;白嘴鴉;山烏。 **~·ery** /-ərɪ ; -ərɪ/ *n* (*pl* -ries) **1** place (a group of trees) where many ~s have their nests; colony of ~s. 白嘴鴉結巢之處(叢林);白嘴鴉之羣。 **2** colony of penguins or seals. 企鵝或海豹之羣。

rook[2] /rʊk ; rʊk/ *n* person who makes money by cheating at dice and cards, playing with inexperienced gamblers. 以賭博騙取金錢的騙子。□ *vt* [VP 6A] win money from (sb) at cards, etc by cheating; swindle; charge (a customer) a ridiculously high price. 以賭博騙取(某人)金錢;詐取;向(顧客)索過高之價錢;敲詐。

rook[3] /rʊk ; rʊk/ *n* chess piece (also called a

亦稱作 *castle*). (西洋象棋中之)城形棋子。⇨ the illus at chess. 參看 chess 之插圖。

rookie /ˈrʊkɪ ; ˈrʊkɪ/ *n* (army sl) inexperienced recruit. (軍俚)新兵。

room /ruːm ; rum/ *n* **1** [C] part of a house or other building enclosed by walls or partitions, floor and ceiling. 室;房間。**-roomed** /ruːmd ; rumd/ *adj*: *a ten-~ed house,* one having ten ~s. 一棟有十個房間的房子。 **2** (*pl*) set of ~s occupied by a person or family; apartments; (複)一個人或一家人住的一組房間;套房: *Come and see me in my ~s one evening.* 那天晚上請到我家來看我。 **ˈ~-mate** *n* one of two or more persons sharing a ~. 同住一室者;室友。 **3** [U] ~ ***(for sb/sth); ~ (to do sth),*** space that is or might be occupied, or that is enough for a purpose: 被佔或可能被佔之空間;足够某一目的所需之空間: *Is there ~ for me in the car?* 車裏還有我坐的空位嗎? *This table takes up too much ~.* 這張桌子佔的地方太多。*There was ~ in the bus to stand but not to sit.* 公共汽車上仍有站立的地方,但沒有座位了。*Standing ~ only!* eg in a bus, theatre. (公共汽車或劇院中,座位票已賣完)僅有站位!. *Can you make ~ on that shelf for some more books?* 你能在那個架子上騰出些地方再放些書嗎? ***There's no ~ for doubt,*** We can be quite certain about it. 沒有懷疑之餘地。 **4** [U] scope; opportunity: 範圍;機會: *There's ~ for improvement in your work,* It is not as good as it could be. 你的工作還有改進之餘地。 □ *vi* [VP2C] (US) lodge; occupy a ~ or ~s: (美)居住;佔一房間或一套房間: *He's ~ing with my friend Rodney.* 他和我的朋友羅德奈同住。**ˈ~·ing house,** (US) building where a number of independent ~s can be rented (usu without service). (美)公寓(有單獨房間可出租之建築,通常沒有人服務)。**~er** *n* (US) person who lives in a rented ~ in sb else's house; lodger. (美)房客;寄宿者。 **~·ful** /-fʊl ; -ˌfʊl/ *n* amount (of furniture, etc), number of persons, that fills a ~. 一室所能容納之(傢具等之)量或人數。 **~y** *adj* (-ier, -iest) having plenty of space: 有很多空間的: *a ~y cabin;* 寬敞的客艙; *a ~y raincoat,* one that is loose-fitting. 寬鬆的雨衣。**~·ily** /-ɪlɪ ; -əlɪ/ *adv*

roost /ruːst ; rust/ *n* [C] branch, pole, etc on which a bird rests, esp one for hens to sleep or rest on; hen-house, or that part of it, where fowls rest at night: 供鳥棲居的樹枝,竿等(尤指供鷄睡眠或棲止者);鷄舍;鷄舍內家禽過夜棲息之部分: *at ~,* on a ~. 棲息。***come home to ~,*** (of words) take effect upon the one who utters them. (指言語)對說出者產生效果。***rule the ~,*** be the leader or master. 做首領;做主人。 □ *vi* [VP2A] (of birds) settle down for the night's sleep. (指鳥)棲息。

rooster /ˈruːstə(r) ; ˈrustɚ/ *n* domestic cock. 公鷄。

root¹ /ruːt ; rut/ *n* [C] **1** that part of a plant, tree, etc which is normally in the soil and which takes water and food from it: (植物之)根: *pull up a plant by the ~s.* 將一植物連根拔起。*He has no ~s in society,* (fig) is not settled, does not belong to any particular group or place. (喻)他在社會上沒有根基。***pull up one's ~s,*** (fig) move from a settled home, job, etc to start a new life elsewhere. (喻)離開固定的居所、工作等而在別處開始新的生活。***put down new ~s,*** (fig) establish oneself in another place after leaving a place where one has been established. (喻)建立新的生活、居所等;另起爐竈。***take/strike ~,*** **(a)** (eg of a cutting) send out a ~ or ~s; begin to grow. (指插枝等)生根;紮根;開始生長。**(b)** (fig) become established. (喻)固定;確立。***~ and branch,*** (fig) thoroughly; completely: (喻)徹底地;完全地: *This tyrant and his henchmen must be destroyed ~ and branch.* 這暴君及其親信必須徹底剷除。 **2 ~s, ˈ~-crop,** plant with a ~ that is used as food, eg *carrots, turnips, parsnips.* 根菜作物(例如胡蘿蔔,蘿蔔,防風草根等)。**~ beer,** (US) non-alcoholic drink made from the ~s of various plants. (美)菜根汽水(一種由多種菜根製成,不含酒精,味道像沙士的飲料)。 **3** that part of a hair, tooth, the tongue, a fingernail, etc that is like a ~ in position, function, etc. 髮根,齒根,舌根,指甲根等;位置,作用等似根之部分。 **4** (fig) that from which sth grows; basis; source; essential substance: (喻)根源;基礎;泉源;主要實質: *the ~ of the trouble.* 苦惱的根源。*Is money the ~ of all evil?* 金錢果眞爲萬惡之源? ***get at/to the ~ of sth,*** tackle it at its source. 深究一事之根源。***the ~ cause,*** the fundamental cause. 基本原因。 **5** (gram) (also 亦作 *base form*) form of a word on which other forms of that word are said to be based: (文法)字根: *'Walk' is the ~ of 'walks', 'walked', 'walking', and 'walker'.* walk 爲 walks, walked, walking 及 walker 的字根。 **6** (arith) quantity which, when multiplied by itself a certain number of times, produces another quantity: (算術)根: *4 is the square* (= second) *~ of 16* ($\sqrt{16} = 4$), *the cube* (= third) *~ of 64* ($\sqrt[3]{64} = 4$), *the fourth ~ of 256* ($\sqrt[4]{256} = 4$). 4爲16之平方根,64之立方根,256之四次方根。

root² /ruːt ; rut/ *vt, vi* **1** [VP6A, 2A] (of plants, cuttings, etc) (cause to) send out ~s and begin to grow: (指植物,插枝等)(使)生根並開始生長: *~ chrysanthemum cuttings in sand and peat.* 使菊花的插枝在沙與泥煤中生根。*Some cuttings ~ easily.* 有些插枝易於生根。 **2** [VP6A, 15A] cause to stand fixed and unmoving: 使立定不動;使確立;使固定: *Fear ~ed him to the ground.* 恐懼使他呆在那裏不動。*He stood there ~ed to the spot.* 他站在該處不動。 **3** (of ideas, principles, etc) establish firmly (chiefly in *pp*): (指觀念,原則等)使根深蒂固;使堅定不移(主要用過去分詞形式): *She has a ~ed objection to cold baths.* 她堅決反對冷水浴。*Her affection for him is deeply ~ed.* 她對他的愛是堅定不移的。 **4** [VP15B] ***~ sth out,*** get rid of, exterminate (an evil, etc). 根絕;根除(禍害等)。***~ sth up,*** dig or pull up with the ~s. 連根拔起。**~·less** *adj* having no ~s; (of a person) without ~s in society. 無根的;(指人)無社會基礎的;沒有生根的。⇨ root¹ (1).

root³ /ruːt ; rut/ *vi, vt* **1** [VP2C, 15B] ***~ about (for),*** (of pigs) turn up the ground with the snout in search of food; (of persons) search for; turn things over when searching: (指豬)以鼻掘土覓食;(指人)尋覓;翻搜: *~ing about among piles of papers for a missing document.* 在一堆堆文件中找一件失掉的文件。***~ sth out,*** find by searching: 搜出;找到: *I managed to ~ out a copy of the document.* 我設法找到該文件的一份副本。 **2** [VP2A, 3A] ***~ (for),*** (US sl) cheer: (美俚)鼓舞: *~ing for the college baseball team.* 爲大學棒球隊加油。

rootle /ˈruːtl ; ˈrutl/ *vi* [VP2C] ***~ about for,*** (of pigs, etc) dig about (with the snout) for food, etc. (指豬等)(以鼻)掘土覓食等。

rope /rəʊp ; rop/ *n* **1** [C, U] (piece or length of) thick strong cord or wire cable made by twisting finer cords or wires together: (一根或一段)堅牢的粗繩;金屬纜;索: *tie sb's arms behind his back with (a) ~.* 用繩將某人的雙臂反綁在背後。*The climbers were on the ~,* fastened together with a ~ (while climbing on a difficult and dangerous surface). 攀登者(在爬一困難而危險之表面時)用繩聯繫在一起。**the ~,** noose for hanging a condemned person. (絞首用的)索套。**the ~s,** those that enclose the prize-ring or other place used for sport or games. (圍在拳擊場或其他競賽場地四周之)欄索;圈繩。***show sb/know/learn the ~s,*** the conditions, the rules, the procedure (in some sphere of action). 向某人指出(知道,學知)某行業的情況、規則、手續等。***give sb (plenty of) ~,*** freedom of action. 給某人(充分)行動自由。***Give sb enough ~ and he'll hang himself,*** (prov) Let a fool follow his own devices and he will come to ruin. (諺)任由愚人爲所欲爲,彼將自取滅亡。 **2** (compounds) (複

合字) ˈ~-dancer *n* performer on a tight-~. 走繩索者。ˌ~-ˈladder *n* ladder made of two long ~s connected by rungs of ~. 繩梯。ˈ~-walk/-yard *n* long piece of ground or long, low shed where ~ is made. 做繩索之狹長走道(狹長低矮小屋)。ˈ~-walker *n* = ~-dancer. ˈ~-way *n* means of carrying goods in buckets, etc suspended from overhead steel cables: (運送裝於桶等內的貨物之)纜路;索道: (attrib) (形容用法) ˈ~*way buckets*. 索道運輸桶。ˈ~-yarn *n* [U] material (esp when unpicked) of which ~s are made. 用以製繩索之股線(尤指未拆開者)。 **3** [C] number of things twisted, strung or threaded together: 被扭在､穿在或串在一起的東西: *a ~ of onions*. 一串洋葱。□ *vt* [VP15A, B] **1** fasten or bind with ~: 以繩縛繫: *~ a man to a tree;* 把一個人綑在一棵樹上; *~ climbers together*, connect them at intervals with a ~ for safety. 把爬山者繫聯於一根索上。 **2** *~ sth off*, enclose or mark off with a ~: 以繩圍起或界出: *Part of the field was ~d off*. 一部分土地用繩隔開了。 **3** *~ sb in*, persuade him to help in some activity. 說服某人參與一項活動。 **~y** /ˈrəupɪ ; ˈropɪ/ *adj* (sl) very inferior in quality. (俚)品質極差的。

Roque·fort /ˈrɒkfɔː(r) *US:* ˈrəukfərt ; ˈrokfɚt/ *n* [U] kind of French cheese made of goats' and ewes' milk. 一種法國製的羊乳酪。

ro·sary /ˈrəuzərɪ ; ˈrozərɪ/ *n* (*pl* -ries) **1** form of prayer used in the RC Church; book containing this. 念珠祈禱(天主教奉行的一種祈禱式);玫瑰經。 **2** string of beads for keeping count of these prayers, which are said while meditating; such beads used by a person of another religion. (此種祈禱用之)念珠;其他宗教用之念珠。 **3** rose-garden. 玫瑰園。

rose[1] /rəuz ; roz/ *pt* ⇨ rise[2].

rose[2] /rəuz ; roz/ *n* **1** (shrub or bush with prickles or thorns on its stems and bearing a) beautiful and usu sweet-smelling flower (red, pink, white, cream, yellow), ⇨ the illus at flower; one of various flowering plants: 薔薇科植物;薔薇花;玫瑰花(參看 flower 之插圖): *the* ˈ*rock-~;* 岩薔薇; ˈ*Christmas ~*. 聖誕薔薇(歐洲產的一種草本植物,開白色或紫色花,開花期在冬天)。 ***a bed of ~s***, a pleasant, easy condition of life. 愉快舒適的生活狀況。 ***not all ~s***, not perfect; having some discomfort and disadvantages. 不完美; 有某種困苦和不利。 ***no ~ without a thorn***, complete, pure happiness cannot be found. 沒有盡美盡善的快樂。 ***gather life's ~s***, seek the pleasures of life. 尋歡作樂。 **2** [U] pinkish-red colour. 粉紅色。 ***see things through ~-coloured/-tinted spectacles***, take an optimistic view of them (perhaps without good reason). 以樂觀態度(或許並無充分的理由)看事物。 **3** (of various things thought to resemble a ~ in shape) (指在形狀上被認爲像玫瑰花的各種東西) **(a)** sprinkling nozzle of a watering can or hose: 噴水壺或水管的灑水嘴: *Use a fine-~d can* (one fitted with such a nozzle) *for watering seedlings*. 用細孔噴水壺澆幼苗。 **(b)** bunch of ribbons; rosette. 絲帶束;薔薇花形絲帶結。 **(c)** ~-shaped conventional design, the national emblem of England (as the shamrock is used for Ireland). 英國的玫瑰花形國徽(愛爾蘭用酢漿草)。 **4** (compounds) (複合字) ˈ~-bed *n* bed in which ~ bushes are grown. 玫瑰花壇。 ˈ~bud *n* bud of a ~; 玫瑰花苞; (attrib) (形容用法) *a ~bud mouth*, having this shape. 如玫瑰花苞樣的小嘴。 ˈ~-leaf *n* petal from a ~ flower. 玫瑰花瓣。 ˌ~-ˈred *adj* red as a ~. 玫瑰紅的。 ˈ~-water *n* perfume made from ~s. 玫瑰香水。 ˌ~ ˈwindow *n* ornamental circular window (usu in a church, esp one with a pattern of small sections radiating from the centre). 薔薇形窗;圓花窗(裝飾性的圓形窗,通常教堂建築物上用之,尤指一種具有從中心向外輻射之小瓣型式者)。 ⇨ the illus at window. 參看 window 之插圖。 ˈ~-wood *n* [U] hard, dark red wood obtained from several varieties of tropical tree (so named for their fragrance): 花梨木(木質有玫瑰香味,因而得名): *a ~-wood piano*. 一架花梨木鋼琴。

ro·seate /ˈrəuzɪət ; ˈrozɪɪt/ *adj* rose-coloured; pinkish-red. 玫瑰色的;粉紅色的。

rose·mary /ˈrəuzmərɪ *US:* -merɪ ; ˈrozˌmɛrɪ/ *n* [U] evergreen shrub with fragrant leaves used in making perfumes. 迷迭香(一種常青灌木,其葉有香味,可製香水)。

ro·sette /rəuˈzet ; roˈzɛt/ *n* [C] small rose-shaped badge or ornament, eg of silk or ribbon; carved rose on stonework. 小的玫瑰形徽章或飾物;薔薇形緞帶結;石上刻的玫瑰花飾。

rosin /ˈrɒzɪn *US:* ˈrɒzn ; ˈrɑzn̩/ *n* [U] resin, esp in solid form, as used on the strings of violins, etc and on the bow with which violins are played. 松香(尤指固體,如小提琴等之絃及弓上所用者)。 □ *vt* [VP6A] rub with ~. 以松香塗擦。

ros·ter /ˈrɒstə(r) ; ˈrɑstɚ/ *n* list of names of persons showing duties to be performed by each in turn. 名册;名單;值勤簿。

ros·trum /ˈrɒstrəm ; ˈrɑstrəm/ *n* (*pl* ~s or -tra /-trə ; -trə/) platform or pulpit for public speaking. 講臺;講壇。

rosy /ˈrəuzɪ ; ˈrozɪ/ *adj* (-ier, -iest) **1** of the colour of red roses: 玫瑰紅的;淡紅色的: *~ cheeks*, indicating good health. 紅潤的臉頰。 **2** (fig) causing optimism; encouraging: (喩)令人樂觀的;鼓勵的: *~ prospects*. 光明的前途。

rot /rɒt ; rɑt/ *vi, vt* (-tt-) **1** [VP2A, C] decay by processes of nature: 腐爛;腐朽: *A fallen tree soon rots*. 倒在地上的樹不久就會腐爛。*The shed had fallen in, and the wood was rotting away*. 小屋塌陷,木料腐爛了。 *One of the branches had rotted off*, decayed and broken off. 其中一根樹枝已經枯朽而斷落。 **2** [VP2A, C] (fig, of a society, etc) gradually perish from lack of vigour or activity; (of prisoners, etc) waste away: (喩,指一社團等)因缺乏活力或活動而逐漸衰敗;(指囚犯等)消瘦;衰弱: *left to rot in a deep dungeon*. 被棄於深深的地牢中日趨衰弱。 **3** [VP6A] cause to decay or become useless: 使腐爛;使變爲無用: *Oil and grease will rot the rubber of your tyres*. 汽油和滑油會腐蝕你的輪胎。 ˈ**rot-gut** *n* [U] strong alcoholic liquor, esp inferior spirit, that is harmful to the stomach. 傷胃的烈酒;(尤指)劣質烈酒。□ *n* [U] **1** decay; rotting; condition of being bad: 腐爛;腐朽;腐敗;墮落: *a tree affected by rot*. 已經枯朽的樹。 *Rot has set in*, decay has begun. 開始腐爛了。 *We have dry rot in the floor*. 我們的地板有朽壞的現象。⇨ dry[1](13). **2** (usu 通常用 **the rot**) liver disease of sheep. 羊肝蛭病。 ˈ**foot-rot**, foot disease of sheep. 羊之足病。 **3** (ˌ**tommy-**)ˈ**rot**, (sl) nonsense; foolishness; rubbish: (俚)無意義的話;愚蠢;胡說: *Don't talk rot!* 不要胡謅! *His speech was all rot*. 他的講演全是胡扯。 **4** succession of failures: 一連串的失敗: *A rot set in*. 開始節節挫敗。 *How can we stop the rot?* 我們如何才能止住這一連串的失敗?

rota /ˈrəutə ; ˈrotə/ *n* (*pl* ~s) (GB) list of persons who are to do things in turn; list of duties to be performed in turn. (英)輪流執行職務者的名單;須輪流執行之任務的表册;勤務輪值表。

ro·tary /ˈrəutərɪ ; ˈrotərɪ/ *adj* **1** (of motion) moving round a central point. (指運動)旋轉的。 **2** (of an engine) worked by ~ motion: (指機器)由旋轉而工作的;轉動的: *a ~ printing machine/press*, that prints from curved metal plates on to a continuous roll of paper. 輪轉印刷機。 **3** ˈ**R~ Club**, (branch of an) international association of professional and business men in a town. 扶輪社(各地專業人員及商人所組織之國際性團體);國際扶輪社。 **Ro·tarian** /rəuˈteərɪən ; roˈtɛrɪən/ *n* member of a R~ Club. 扶輪社社員。□ *n* (US) (美) = roundabout(2).

ro·tate /rəuˈteɪt *US:* ˈrəuteɪt ; ˈrotet/ *vi, vt* [VP6A,

2A] (cause to) move round a central point; (cause to) take turns or come in succession: (使)旋轉;(使)輪流;更迭: ~ *crops,* ⇨ rotation(2). 輪植農作物。*The office of Chairman ~s.* 主席一職是輪流擔任的。

ro·ta·tion /rəʊˈteɪʃn ; roˈteʃən/ *n* **1** [U] rotating or being rotated: 旋轉;轉動: *the ~ of the earth;* 地球之自轉; [C] complete turning: 一次完全的旋轉: *five ~s an hour.* 每小時轉五次。 **2** [C, U] the regular coming round of things or events in succession: 輪流: *ˈcrop-~, ~ of crops,* varying the crops grown each year on the same land to avoid exhausting the soil. 農作物之輪植(在同一塊地上每一年換種農作物，以免耗盡土壤的生產力)。 ***in ~,*** in turn; in regular succession. 輪流地;交替地。

ro·ta·tory /ˈrəʊtətərɪ *US:* -tɔ:rɪ ; ˈrotə,torɪ/ *adj* relating to, causing, moving in, rotation: 旋轉的;輪流的;使旋轉或輪流的;在旋轉中移動的: ~ *movement.* 旋轉運動。

rote /rəʊt ; rot/ *n* (only in) (僅用於) ***by ~,*** by heart, from memory without thinking: 熟記地;由記憶而不必想地;死記地: *do/say/know/learn sth by ~.* 由熟記而做(說,知道,學)某事物。

ro·tis·se·rie /rəʊˈti:sərɪ ; roˈtɪsərɪ/ *n* cooking device with a rotating spit on which meat, etc is roasted; shop or restaurant providing food cooked in this way. 轉動的烤肉鐵叉;賣此種烤肉的商店或飯店。

roto·gra·vure /ˌrəʊtəʊgrəˈvjʊə(r) ; ˌrotəgrəˈvjʊr/ *n* **1** [U] process of printing from an engraved copper cylinder on which illustrations, etc have been etched. 凹版印刷術。 **2** [C] illustration, etc printed by this process. 以凹版印刷之圖畫等。

ro·tor /ˈrəʊtə(r) ; ˈrotɚ/ *n* [C] rotary part of a machine; (esp) assembly of horizontally rotating blades of a helicopter propellor. 機器之旋轉部分;(尤指直昇飛機的水平的)旋翼。

rot·ten /ˈrɒtn ; ˈrɑtn̩/ *adj* **1** decayed; having gone bad: 腐爛的;已變壞的: ~ *eggs.* 已壞的蛋。*The sails were ~ and so were the ropes.* 帆爛了,繩索也爛了。 **2** (sl) disagreeable; very unpleasant or undesirable: (俚)討厭的;極令人不快或嫌惡的: *What ~ luck!* 眞倒霉! *I'm feeling ~ today,* unwell, tired. 我今天覺得不適(疲倦)。 **~·ly** *adv* **~·ness** *n*

rot·ter /ˈrɒtə(r) ; ˈrɑtɚ/ *n* (dated sl) worthless, objectionable person. (過時俚語)無用的、討厭的人。

ro·tund /rəʊˈtʌnd ; roˈtʌnd/ *adj* **1** (of a person, his face) round and plump; (of the voice) full-sounding; rich and deep. (指人,其臉)圓而胖的;(指聲音)洪亮的;圓潤而深沉的。 **2** (of speech, liter style) grandiloquent. (指言辭,文體)華麗的;浮誇的。 **~·ly** *adv* **~·ity** /-ətɪ ; -ətɪ/ *n* [U] state of being ~. 圓胖;洪亮;華麗。

ro·tunda /rəʊˈtʌndə ; roˈtʌndə/ *n* round building, esp one with a domed roof. 圓形建築物(尤指有圓屋頂者)。

rouble /ˈru:bl ; ˈrubl̩/ *n* unit of currency in the USSR (100 kopecks). 盧布(蘇聯貨幣單位)。

roué /ˈru:eɪ *US:* ru:ˈeɪ ; ruˈe/ *n* (esp elderly) dissolute man; rake². 放蕩的人;浪子;(尤指)放蕩的老人;老不羞。

rouge /ru:ʒ ; ruʒ/ *n* [U] fine red powder or other cosmetic substance for colouring the cheeks; powder for cleaning silver plate. 紅粉;胭脂;擦銀器的粉末。□ *vt, vi* [VP6A, 2A] use ~ on (the face); use ~. 在(臉)上擦胭脂;用紅粉化妝;用粉末擦銀器。

rough¹ /rʌf ; rʌf/ *adj* (-er, -est) **1** (of surfaces) not level, smooth or polished; (of roads) of irregular surface, not easy to walk or ride on: (指表面)不平的;不光的;未擦亮的; (指路) 崎嶇不平的;難行的: ~ *paper;* 糙紙; *a fruit with a ~ skin;* 有粗皮的水果; *cloth that is ~ to the touch.* 摸起來很粗的布。 **2** not calm or gentle; moving or acting violently: 粗暴的;粗魯的;粗野的;劇烈的: ~ *children;* 舉止粗野的孩子; ~ *behaviour;* 粗魯的行爲; *a ~* (= stormy) *sea;* 風大浪急的海; *have a ~ crossing from Dover to Calais.* 從多佛港到加萊港間一次艱辛的橫渡。*Keep away from the ~ quarter of the town,* the part where disorderly and violent people live. 遠離城市中暴亂之徒聚居的地區。*This suitcase has had some ~ handling,* has been treated violently, thrown about, etc. 這隻小提箱曾被亂拋亂丟。*He has a ~ tongue,* a habit of speaking rudely or sharply. 他講話粗野(尖刻)。***be ~ on sb,*** be unpleasant or unlucky for: 使某人不愉快或倒霉: *It's rather ~ on her, having to live in a caravan.* 她很倒霉,不得不住在篷車裡。 ***give sb the ~ side of one's tongue,*** speak to sb rudely and/or severely. 粗魯無禮地(嚴厲地)對人講話。***give sb/have a ~ time,*** (cause sb to) experience hardship, be treated severely, etc (according to context). (使某人)受苦(受到嚴苛的待遇)。 **ˈ~ house,** (colloq) noisy quarrelling with exchange of blows, etc. (俗)大吵大鬧;大打出手。**ˈ~-house** *vt, vi* [VP6A, 2A] handle (sb) violently; act violently. 粗魯地對待(某人);行爲粗暴。**~ luck,** worse luck than is deserved. 壞運氣。 **3** made or done without attention to detail, esp as a first attempt: 約略的;概略的: *a ~ sketch/translation;* 草圖(概略的翻譯); lacking refinement, delicacy or finish: 草率的;簡陋的;未經潤飾的: *a ~ draft,* eg of a letter; 草稿; ~ *accommodation at a small country inn;* 鄉村小客棧的簡陋設備; *lead a ~ life away from civilization.* 過一種遠離文明的簡陋生活。***a ~ diamond,*** (fig) an uneducated or uncouth person, lacking social graces, but good-hearted and good-natured. (喻)未受教育,舉止粗魯,但心地善良之人。 ***~ and ready,*** good enough for ordinary purposes, occasions, etc; not particularly efficient, etc: 粗略而尙能用的: ~ *and ready methods.* 粗略而尙能用的方法。 **4** (of sounds) harsh; discordant: (指聲音)粗厲的;沙啞的;不悅耳的: *a ~ voice.* 粗厲的聲音。 **5** (compounds) (複合字) **ˌ~-and-ˈtumble** *adj, n* disorderly and violent (fight or struggle). 騷亂激烈的(打鬥)。 **ˈ~-neck** *n* (US colloq) rowdy person; hooligan. (美俗)粗暴的人;流氓。 **ˈ~-rider** *n* person who is expert at breaking in untamed horses. 馴馬師;善騎野馬者。 **~·ly** *adv* **1** in a ~ manner: 粗糙地;粗暴地;粗魯地;草率地;簡陋地;粗嗄地: *treat sb ~ly;* 粗暴地對待某人; *a ~ly made table,* not finely finished. 草草做成的桌子; **2** approximately: 約略地;大約: *at a cost of ~ly £5;* 約值五鎊; *~ly speaking,* with no claim to accuracy. 約略地說。 **~·ness** *n* quality or state of being ~. 粗糙;粗暴;粗魯;約略;草率;簡陋;粗嗄。

rough² /rʌf ; rʌf/ *adv* **1** in a rough manner: 粗魯地;嚴厲地: *play ~,* be (rather) violent (in games, etc); 玩得相當粗野; *treat sb ~.* 嚴厲地對待某人。***cut up ~,*** (colloq) become angry. (俗)發怒。***live ~,*** live in the open (as a vagrant may do). 餐風宿露(如流浪者之生活)。***sleep ~,*** (of homeless persons) sleep out of doors or wherever there is some shelter, eg under a bridge, in the open air. (指無家可歸之人)在戶外露宿;隨處棲身。 **2** (compounds) (複合字) **ˈ~-cast** *n* coarse plaster containing gravel or pebbles for the surfaces of outside walls. (含有沙石及卵石的)粗灰泥。□ *vt* coat (a wall) with this mixture. 以粗灰泥塗(牆)。**ˈ~-dry** *vt* dry (laundered clothes) without ironing them. 晒乾(洗過的衣服)而不燙。**ˈ~-hewn** *adj* shaped or carved ~ly: 粗粗地形成或彫成的: *a ~-hewn statue.* 粗粗彫成的彫像。**ˈ~·shod** *adj* (of a horse) having shoes with the heads of the nails projecting to prevent slipping. (指馬)釘有防滑釘之鐵蹄的。 ***ride ˈ~shod over sb,*** treat him harshly, inconsiderately or contemptuously. 欺凌某人;粗暴而輕蔑地對待某人。 **ˌ~-ˈspoken** *adj* addicted to, using, unrefined or harsh language. 言語粗魯的。

rough³ /rʌf ; rʌf/ *n* **1** [U] rough state; rough ground; rough surface; unpleasantness; hardship. 粗劣的狀況;崎嶇的土地;粗糙的表面;不愉快;艱辛。***take***

the ~ with the smooth, (fig) accept what is unpleasant with what is pleasant. (喻)不快意的和快意的事一起接受;逆來順受。 **2** [U] **the ~,** unfinished state: 未加工或未完成之情況: *I've seen his new statue only in the ~.* 我曾看到過他的新彫像的粗坯。 ***in ~,*** (eg of sth written) as a rough draft. (如文稿)草擬的。 **3** [U] **the ~,** (golf) part of a course (not the fairway or a green) where the ground is uneven and the grass uncut: (高爾夫)(崎嶇不平而且草長得很高的)障礙區域: *lose one's ball in the ~.* 在障礙區失落一球。 **4** man or boy ready for lawless violence; hooligan: 粗暴而不守法紀的男人或男孩;流氓;阿飛;不良少年: *He was set on by a gang of ~s who knocked him down and took all his money.* 他被一羣流氓攻擊,他們把他擊倒並且拿走他所有的錢。

rough[4] /rʌf ; rʌf/ *vt* **1** [VP6A, 15B] ***~ sth (up),*** make untidy or uneven: 使粗糙;使不平;弄亂: *Don't ~ (up) my hair!* 不要弄亂我的頭髮! ***~ sb up,*** (sl) treat him roughly, with physical violence: (俚)以暴力對付某人;向某人動粗: *He was ~ed up by hooligans.* 他被流氓毆打。 ~ (more usu 較常用 *rub*) ***sb up the wrong way,*** ⇨ rub(3). **2** [VP15B] ***~ sth in,*** make a first rough sketch of; sketch in outline. 起草;草擬;粗略地寫或畫。 **3** ***~ it,*** live without the usual comforts and conveniences of life: 過簡陋的生活: *The explorers had to ~ it when they got into the jungle.* 那些探險家進入叢林後,不得不過簡陋的生活。

rough·age /ˈrʌfɪdʒ ; ˈrʌfɪdʒ/ *n* [U] coarse, rough foodstuff, esp bran of cereals, supplying bulk, not nourishment, and taken to stimulate bowel movements. 粗糙食物(尤指穀物的糠皮,無營養,食之可通便)。

roughen /ˈrʌfn ; ˈrʌfən/ *vt, vi* make or become rough. 使粗糙;變粗糙;使成崎嶇不平;變得崎嶇不平。

rou·lette /ruːˈlet ; ruˈlɛt/ *n* [U] gambling game in which a small ball falls by chance into one of the compartments of a revolving wheel or disc. 輪盤賭。**Russian ~,** stunt in which a person holds to his head a revolver, of which only one (unknown) chamber contains a bullet, and then pulls the trigger. 一種驚險的技藝表演(一人持著不知道那一個彈膛中裝有一顆子彈的左輪手槍對準自己的頭部開槍)。

round[1] /raʊnd ; raʊnd/ *adj* **1** shaped like a circle or a ball: 圓的;球形的: *a ~ plate/window/table;* 圓盤(窗,桌); *a ~-table conference,* at which there is no position of importance at the head of the table, everyone being apparently of equal importance; 圓桌會議(參與會議的人是平等的,議席無主次要之分); *~ cheeks/arms/limbs,* plump and curved. 圓胖的臉(臂,肢)。**a ˈ~ game,** one in which there are no teams or partners and in which the number of players is not fixed. 不分隊或邊,人數亦不固定的遊戲。 **the R~ Table,** the order of knighthood founded by King Arthur. 由亞瑟王創設的武士職位;圓桌武士。 **2** done with, involving, a circular motion. 旋轉的;廻旋的。 ~ **brackets,** parentheses. 圓括弧。 **ˈ~ dance,** one in which the dancers form a circle, with revolving movements. 圓舞(跳舞者形成圓圈轉動)。~ **robin,** petition with signatures in a circle to conceal the order in which they were written. 圓形簽名陳情書(簽署者之簽字列爲圓形,使無法看出簽字的前後次序)。~ **trip,** (GB) circular trip or tour; (US) journey to a place and back again over the same route. (英)環行;環遊;(美)雙程旅行;來回旅行。 **3** entire; continuous; full: 整個的;繼續的;完全的: *a ~ dozen/score,* that number and not less; 整整一打(整整二十個); *a good, ~ sum,* a considerable sum. 相當大的數目。 ***in ~ figures/numbers,*** given in 10's, 100's, 1000's, etc; not troubling about smaller denominations; (hence) roughly correct. 以十、百、千等整數表示的;不計較較小單位的; (由此產生) 約略正確的。 **4** full; plain: 充滿的;明白的: *at a ~ pace/trot,* vigorous; 以快速的步伐; *a ~ oath,* unmistakably an oath; 確實無疑的誓言; *a ~ voice,* full-toned and mellow; 宏亮圓潤的聲音; *scold sb in good, ~ terms,* outspokenly; 直率無隱地責備某人; *a ~ unvarnished tale,* the plain truth. 實話。 **5** (compounds) (複合字) **ˈ~-arm** *adj, adv* (cricket) with the arm swung ~ at the height of the shoulder: (板球)臂搖到齊肩高度的 (地); 水平揮臂而爲的 (地): *~-arm bowling;* 手臂齊肩的投球; *bowl ~-arm.* 手臂齊肩地投球。**ˌ~-ˈbacked** *adj* having the back curved or humped. 駝背的。**ˌ~-ˈeyed** *adj* with the eyes wide open: 睜圓眼睛的: *staring/listening in ~-eyed wonder.* 睜大着眼睛驚奇地凝視(聆聽)。 **ˈ~-hand** *n* [U] **(a)** style of handwriting with the letters well rounded and clearly written. 圓而清楚的書寫字體。 **(b)** = ~-arm (bowling). 手臂齊肩的投球。**ˈR~·head** *n* member of the Parliament side in the Civil War in the 17th c in England, so called from his close-cut hair. 圓顱黨人(十七世紀英格蘭內戰時期的國會派份子,因髮齊頭剪短,故稱)。 **ˈ~-house** *n* **(a)** cabin or set of cabins on the after part of the quarter deck (of old sailing ships). (舊式帆船之)後甲板後部的房艙;後甲板室。 **(b)** building (with a turn-table in the middle) where locomotives are stored and repaired. 圓形機車庫(儲放及修理機車之建築物,內有轉車臺)。**(c)** (in former times) place where people were locked up as prisoners. (昔時)囚禁犯人的地方。 **ˈ~-shot** *n* cannon ball (contrasted with a shell). 砲彈;彈丸(與 shell 相對)。 **ˌ~-ˈshouldered** *adj* having the shoulders bent forward. 圓肩的;傴肩的。**~·ish** /-ɪʃ ; -ɪʃ/ *adj* rather ~. 略圓的。 **~·ly** *adv* in a thorough-going way; pointedly: 徹底地;率直地: *tell sb ~ly that he is not wanted;* 率直地告訴某人說不需要他; *be ~ly cursed.* 被痛罵。**~·ness** *n*

round[2] /raʊnd ; raʊnd/ *adv part* (may be replaced by *around,* except in special idiomatic uses; for special uses with *vv,* ⇨ the *v* entries; specimens only are given here) (除特殊習慣用法外,可由 around 代替; 與動詞連用之特殊用法,請參看各動詞;此處僅提供少數例子) **1** in a circle or curve to face the opposite way: 成圓形或曲線地;周轉地: *Turn your chair ~ and face me.* 把你的椅子轉過來對着我。 **2** with a return to the starting-point: 週而復始地;循環地: *The hour hand of a clock goes right ~ in twelve hours.* 鐘的時針十二小時轉一圈。 *Christmas will soon be ~ again.* 聖誕節又快到了。 *I shall be glad when spring comes ~ again.* 春天再來我將很高興。**~ and ~,** with repeated revolutions. 旋轉不息地。***all ~; right ~,*** completely ~: 從頭到尾循環一周地;處處;各處: *We walked right ~ the lake.* 我們環湖走了一周。 ***all (the) year ~,*** at all seasons of the year. 整年。 **3** in circumference: 周圍: *Her waist is only twenty-four inches ~.* 她的腰圍只有二十四吋。 **4** (so as to be) in a circle: (形成)圓形地: *A crowd soon gathered ~.* 不久就聚集了一羣人。 *The garden has a high wall all ~.* 花園有一高牆圍起。 **5** from one (place, point, person, etc) to another: 從一(地,點,人等)到另一;逐一地: *Please hand these papers ~,* ie distribute them. 請把這些文件分發給大家。*The news was soon passed ~.* 消息不久卽傳開了。*Tea was served/handed ~.* 每個人都奉了茶。 ***go ~,*** supply everybody: 供給每個人: *Have we enough food to go ~?* 我們有足夠的食物供給大家嗎?*Will the meat go ~,* ie be enough for everybody? 肉夠大家吃嗎?***look ~,*** visit and look at: 參觀遊覽: *Let's go into the town and look ~/have a look ~,* ie see the places of interest, etc. 讓我們進城去遊覽一番。***taking it all ~,*** considering the matter from all points of view. 從各方面考慮之。 **6** by a longer way or route; not by the direct route: 繞道地;迂迴地;非由近路地: *If you can't jump over the stream, you'll have to go ~ by the bridge.* 你如果不能跳過這條小河,就必須繞道由橋過河。 *The taxi-driver brought us a long way ~.* 計程車司機帶我們繞遠路走。 **7** to a place where sb is or will be: 到某人所在或將在的地方: *Come ~ and see me this evening.* 今天晚上來看我。*The Whites have asked me to go ~ this evening,* ie to visit them. 懷特夫婦約我今天晚上去看他們。 **8 ~ (about),** in the neighbourhood: 在附近地;近處地: *all the country ~;* 在附近一帶的鄉間; *everybody for a mile ~;* 一哩之內的每個人; *in all the villages ~ about.* 在附近所有的村莊內。

round[3] /raʊnd ; raʊnd/ *n* **1** sth round; a slice made by a complete cut across the end of a loaf: 圓的東西;麵包片: *two ~s* (= sandwiches) *of ham and one of beef;* 兩片火腿三明治和一片牛肉三明治; *a ~ of toast.* 一片吐司。 **2** [U] (sculpture) solid form, enabling an object to be viewed from all sides (contrasted with *relief*). (彫刻)圓彫(能從各面觀看的立體形式,與 relief 相對);立體彫刻。 ***in the ~,*** (arts) made so that it can be viewed from all sides: (藝術)立體的(能從各面觀看的): *a statue in the ~.* 一個立體彫像。***theatre in the ~,*** with the audience on (nearly) all sides of the stage. 觀衆圍繞在舞臺四周觀賞的劇院;立體劇場。 **3** regular series or succession or distribution: 規則性的系列或連續或分配: *the daily ~,* the ordinary occupations of the day; 日常的例行工作; *the earth's yearly ~,* the cycle of the four seasons; 地球每年四季的循環; *the doctor's ~ of visits* (to the homes of his patients); 醫生的巡迴探視病人(到病人家裏); *a ~ of pleasures／gaiety,* a succession of parties, gay events, etc; 一連串的宴會,遊樂節目等; *the postman's ~,* the route he takes to deliver letters. 郵差的送信路線。***go the ~s; make one's ~s,*** make one's usual visits, esp of inspection: 例行巡視或檢查: *The night watchman makes his ~s every hour.* 守夜者每小時巡迴一次。***go the ~ of,*** be passed on (to): 傳遍: *The news quickly went the ~ of the village.* 這消息很快傳遍全村。 **4** (in games, contests, etc) one stage: (在遊戲,比賽等中)一局;一回合: *a boxing-match of ten ~s;* 十回合的一場拳擊比賽; *knocked out in the third ~;* 在第三回合中被擊倒; *the semi-final ~ of the League Championship;* 棒球聯盟錦標賽的準決賽; *the sixth ~ of the FA Cup,* the quarter-finals of this soccer contest; 英國足球協會杯複賽。*have a ~ of cards;* 玩一局牌; *a ~ of golf,* to all the 9 or 18 holes of the course. 一局高爾夫球(把球打進高爾夫球場中所有的九或十八個洞)。 **5** allowance of sth distributed or measured out; one of a set or series: (分配或量出的某種東西的)一份;(一套或一組中的)一個: *pay for a ~ of drinks,* drinks for every member of the company; 付出每一同伴喝酒的錢; *another ~ of wage claims,* by trade unions for higher wages for their members; 再次要求提高工資; *~ after ~ of cheers,* successive bursts of cheering; 一次連一次的歡呼; *have only three ~s of ammunition left,* enough to fire three times. 只剩下三發彈藥。 **6** song for several persons or groups, the second singing the first line while the first is singing the second line, etc. 輪唱曲。 **7** dance in which the dancers move in a circle. 圓舞。

round[4] /raʊnd ; raʊnd/ *prep* (may be replaced by *around,* except in special idiomatic uses) (除特殊習慣用法外,可由 around 代替) **1** (expressing movement) in a path that passes on all sides of and comes back to the starting-point: (表示動作)環;繞: *The earth moves ~ the sun.* 地球環繞太陽運行。*Drake sailed ~ the world.* 杜雷克駕船航行世界一周。***(sleep／work) ~ the clock,*** all day and all night. (睡覺,工作)一晝夜。 **~-the-clock** *attrib adj* kept up continuously for 24 hours: 持續二十四小時的: *~-the-clock dancing.* 晝夜不停的跳舞。 **2** (expressing movement) in a path changing direction, from one side to another side of: (表示動作) 圍繞而進;從…之一邊至他邊: *follow sb／walk ~ a corner.* 隨某人(步行)繞過轉彎處。***~ the bend,*** (sl) mad. (俚)瘋狂的。 **3** (expressing position) so as to be on all sides of: (表示位置)圍繞: *They were sitting ~ the table.* 他們正環桌而坐。*He had a scarf ~ his neck.* 他的脖子上圍着一條圍巾。 **4** in various or all directions: 在各處或到處: *He looked ~ the room.* 他在室內四處環顧。 *Shall I show you ~ the house,* ie take you to the various rooms, etc? 要我領你參觀這座房子嗎？ **5** to or at various points away from the centre: 至或在離開中心之各點: *The captain stationed his fielders ~ the pitch.* 隊長把他的外場員配置在三柱門四周之各點。*We haven't time to go ~* (= to visit) *the museums and art galleries.* 我們沒有時間去參觀博物館和美術陳列館了。 **6** ***~ (about),*** (fig) approximate(ly): (喻)大約(地): *Come ~ about 2 o'clock.* 在兩點鐘左右來。 *He's ready to pay somewhere ~ £1000 for a car.* 他準備以一千鎊左右買一部車。

round[5] /raʊnd ; raʊnd/ *vt, vi* **1** [VP6A, 2A] make or become round: (使)成爲圓形: *~ the lips,* eg when making the sound /uː ; u/; 使嘴唇成圓形(如發 /uː ; u/ 音時); *stones ~ed by the action of water.* 被水冲成圓形的石塊。 **2** [VP6A] go round: 繞行: *~ a corner.* 繞拐角而行。 **3** [VP15B, 2C, 3A] ***~ sth off,*** bring it to a satisfactory conclusion, add a suitable finish: 使圓滿結束;使更爲完美: *~ off a sentence;* 修飾一個句子使其完美; *~ off one's career by being made a Minister.* 由於被任命爲部長而使事業達於顛峯。 ***~ out,*** (cause to) become round: (使)成爲圓的: *Her figure is beginning to ~ out.* 她的身材正開始發胖。 ***~ sb／sth up,*** drive, bring or collect, together: 使聚攏一起;圍捕: *The courier ~ed up the tourists and hurried them back into the coach.* 旅行服務員使觀光客集合一起,催他們回到車中。*The cowboy ~ed up the cattle.* 牧人把牛羣驅集一起。Hence, 由此產生, **'~-up** *n* a driving or bringing together: 驅集;聚攏: *a ~-up of criminals* (by police); 圍捕罪犯; *a ~-up of cattle.* 把牛羣驅集一起。***~ up (a figure／price),*** bring it to a whole number: 將(數目、價格)調整爲整數: *The price had been ~ed up from £647.50 to £650.* 該價格從 647.50 鎊調整爲 650 鎊整。***~ upon sb,*** turn on him and attack him (in words or action). (以言詞或行動)攻擊某人。

round·about /'raʊndəbaʊt ; 'raʊndəˌbaʊt/ *attrib adj* not going or coming by, or using, the shortest or most direct route: 繞遠道的;間接的: *I heard the news in a ~ way.* 我間接聽到這個消息。*We came by a ~ route.* 我們繞遠路而來。*What a ~ way of doing things!* 這眞是一種繞圈子的做法！ □ *n* [C] **1** (= *merry-go-round*) revolving circular platform with wooden horses, etc on which children ride for fun (at fairs, etc). 旋轉木馬(一種裝有木馬等的圓形臺供兒童乘坐玩樂)。 ***You lose on the swings what you make on the ~s,*** (prov) have losses and profits which are about equal. (諺)失之東隅,收之桑榆。 **2** circular road junction causing traffic to go round instead of directly across (US 美 = *traffic circle* or *rotary*). 道路交叉處之圓環(使交通車輛繞行而不直接駛過)。

roun·del /'raʊndl ; 'raʊndḷ/ *n* small disc, esp a decorative medallion; small circular panel (eg as used on military aircraft to indicate the country they belong to). 小圓形物;(尤指)裝飾用的圓牌;小圓形標幟(如用於軍用飛機以示國別者)。

roun·de·lay /'raʊndɪleɪ ; 'raʊndəˌle/ *n* short, simple song with a refrain. 一種有疊句的簡短民歌。

roun·ders /'raʊndəz ; 'raʊndɚz/ *n pl* game for two teams, played with bat and ball, the players running through a number of bases arranged in a square, similar to baseball. 圓場棒球(一種由兩隊參與的遊戲,用棒及球玩之,擊球員跑過方形球場邊上的幾個壘,與棒球相似)。

Round·head /'raʊndhed ; 'raʊndˌhɛd/ ⇨ round[1](5).

rounds·man /'raʊndzmən ; 'raʊndzmən/ *n* (*pl* -men) tradesman or his employee going round to ask for orders and deliver goods. 巡行各處請人訂

貨或送貨之商人或其夥計;外務員;送貨員。

rouse /raʊz ; raʊz/ *vt, vi* **1** [VP6A] wake up: 喚醒: *I was ~ed by the ringing of a bell.* 鈴聲將我吵醒。 **2** [VP6A, 15A] ***~ sb (from sth/to sth),*** cause (sb) to be more active, interested, etc (from inactivity, lack of confidence, etc): 激勵; 激動: *~ sb/oneself to action;* 激勵某人(自己)行動; *~ sb from indolence;* 激勵某人從怠惰中奮起; *~d to anger by insults;* 被侮辱所激怒; *rousing cheers.* 令人鼓舞的歡呼。 *He's terrifying when he's ~d,* when his passions have been stirred. 他激動的時候很可怕。 **3** [VP2A] (= ~ oneself) wake; become active. 醒來;變得活躍。

rout¹ /raʊt ; raʊt/ *n* **1** utter defeat and disorderly retreat: 徹底失敗與潰退: *The defeat became a ~.* 那次失敗變成潰退。 ***put to ~,*** defeat completely. 徹底擊潰。 **2** (old use) large festive gathering of people; large evening party or reception. (舊用法)一大羣歡樂的羣集者;大規模之晚會或招待會。 **3** (old use, or legal) disorderly, noisy crowd. (舊用法，或法律)烏合之衆; 騷動。 □ *vt* [VP6A] defeat completely; put to ~: 徹底擊敗: *~ the enemy.* 擊潰敵人。

rout² /raʊt ; raʊt/ *vt* [VP15A, B] ***~ sb out (of),*** get or fetch him up, out of bed, etc: 找出,喚出,强使起床等: *We were ~ed out of our cabins before breakfast for passport examination.* 我們在吃早飯前被喚出房艙以檢查護照。

route /ruːt ; rut/ *n* **1** way taken or planned from one place to another: 路途;路線;路程;航線: *The climbers tried to find a new ~ to the top of the mountain.* 攀登者試圖尋出一條通到山頂的新路。 *He flew from Europe to Tokyo by the ~ across the Pole.* 他從歐洲經北極的航線飛到東京。 ***en ~*** /ˌɒn ˈruːt ; ɑnˈrut/, on the way. 在途中。 **2** [U] (mil) ***column of ~,*** marching formation. (軍)路上縱隊。 **ˈ~-march,** long march made by soldiers in training. (部隊在訓練中所作之)長途行軍。 □ *vt* plan a ~ for; send by a specified ~: 爲…設計路線;經由某特定路線將…送達: *We were ~d to France by way of Dover.* 我們被安排經過多佛港到法國。

rou·tine /ruːˈtiːn ; ruˈtin/ *n* [C, U] fixed and regular way of doing things: 例行公事;例行手續;常規: *business ~;* 業務的例行手續; *a question of ~.* 例行手續的問題。 □ *adj* usual; ordinary: 通常的;普通的: *the ~ procedure;* 普通程序; *my ~ duties,* those performed regularly, as if by rule. 例行職責。

rove /rəʊv ; rov/ *vi, vt* **1** [VP2C, 6A] roam (the more usu word); wander: 漫遊(roam 較常用);漂泊;流浪: *~ over sea and land;* 在海上陸上漂泊; *~ the moors.* 在荒野間漫遊。 ***a roving commission,*** duties that take one from one place to another frequently. 巡迴性之任務。 **2** [VP2A] (of the eyes, one's affections) be directed first one way, then another. (指眼睛，一個人的感情)轉來轉去; 飄忽不定。 **~r** *n* **1** wanderer. 漂泊者;流浪者。**2** (old use) (舊用法) **ˈsea -~r,** pirate. 海盜。 **3** (formerly) Venture Scout. (昔時)羅浮童子軍。

row¹ /rəʊ ; ro/ *n* [C] number of persons or things in a line: 一行;一列;一排: *a row of books/houses/desks;* 一排書(房子,書桌); *plant a row of cabbages;* 栽種一排甘藍菜; *sitting in a row/in rows;* 坐成一排(數排); *a front-row seat,* eg in a theatre. (戲院等中之)前排座位。 ***a hard row to hoe,*** a difficult task. 一件困難的工作。

row² /rəʊ ; ro/ *vt, vi* [VP6A, 2A, B, C, 15A, B] propel (a boat) by using oars; carry or take (sb or sth) in a boat with oars; be an oarsman in a boat: 以槳划(船);以划艇載(人或物);在船上爲划槳者: *Can you row (a boat)?* 你會划(船)嗎? *Shall I row you up/down/across the river?* 要我划你到河的上游(下游,對岸)去嗎? *They rowed forty (strokes) to the minute.* 他們整整划了四十下。 *He rows No 5* (= has this position) *in the Oxford crew.* 他是牛津大學划船隊第五槳槳手。 *Let's row a race.* 讓我們比賽划船。 *The crew were rowed out* (= exhausted by rowing) *at the end of the race.* 比賽終了時划船隊隊員都划累了。 **ˈrow-boat** *n* (US) rowing boat. (美)划艇。 □ *n* journey or outing in a boat moved by oars; period of this; distance rowed: 以划艇所作的旅行或小遊;此種旅行或小遊的期間;划行的路程: *go for a row;* 去划船; *a long and tiring row.* 一段漫長而累人的划船旅行。 **row·ing** *n* (compounds) (複合字) **ˈrowing-boat** *n* one moved by the use of oars. 以槳划動的船;划艇。 **ˈrowing-club** *n* one for persons who row. 划船俱樂部。 **~er** *n* person who rows a boat. 划船者。

a rowing-boat

row³ /raʊ ; raʊ/ *n* **1** [U] uproar; noisy disturbance: 吼叫;吵鬧: *How can I study with all this row going on outside my windows?* 窗外這樣的吵鬧,我怎能讀書呢？ **2** [C] noisy or violent argument or quarrel: 喧鬧或激烈的爭論或吵架: *have a row with the neighbours.* 同鄰居吵架。*That man is always ready for a row,* he has a quarrelsome nature. 那人性好爭吵。 ***kick up/make a row,*** start a noisy quarrel or scene. 製造吵鬧的場面;爭吵。 **3** [C] instance of being in trouble, scolded, etc: 受責備;挨罵: *get into a row for being late at the office.* 因爲上班遲到而挨罵。□ *vt, vi* **1** [VP6A] scold; reprimand. 責備;斥責。 **2** [VP2A, 3A] ***row (with),*** quarrel noisily (with): 大聲爭吵: *He's always rowing with his neighbours.* 他總是同鄰居爭吵。

rowan /ˈrəʊən *US:* ˈraʊən ; ˈroən/ *n* **ˈ~(-tree),** small tree of the rose family, also called 亦稱作 *mountain ash.* 山梨樹; 花楸樹(一種薔薇科的小樹)。 **ˈ~(-berry),** one of the scarlet berries of this tree. 這種樹的深紅色漿果;山梨。

rowdy /ˈraʊdɪ ; ˈraʊdɪ/ *adj* (-ier, -iest) rough and noisy: 粗暴且吵鬧的: *The ~ element in the audience continually interrupted the speaker.* 聽衆間的吵鬧份子連續地打斷講演者。*There were ~ scenes at the elections.* 選舉中有爭吵情事。□ *n* (*pl* -dies) ~ person. 粗暴而愛吵鬧的人。 **row·dily** /-ɪlɪ ; -əlɪ/ *adv* **row·di·ness, ~·ism** /-ɪzəm ; -ˌɪzəm/ *nn* [U] ~ behaviour. 粗暴而喧鬧的行爲。

rowel /ˈraʊəl ; ˈraʊəl/ *n* [C] revolving disc with sharp teeth at the end of a spur. 馬刺上的小齒輪; 距輪。

row·lock /ˈrɒlək *US:* ˈrəʊlɒk ; ˈroˌlɑk/ *n* [C] pivot for an oar or scull on the side (gunwale) of a boat (US 美 =*oarlock*). 槳架;槳架。⇨ the illus at row. 參看 row 之插圖。

royal /ˈrɔɪəl ; ˈrɔɪəl/ *adj* of, like, suitable for, supported by, belonging to the family of, a king or queen: (女)王的; 像王的; 適於王的; 由王支持的;王室的;屬於王室的;威嚴的;高貴的;盛大的: *His R~ Highness;* 殿下; *the ~ family;* 王室;王族; *the R~ Society;* (英國)皇家學會; *the R~ Navy/Air Force;* 皇家海軍(空軍); *a ~ welcome,* one fit for a king, etc; splendid. 盛大的歡迎。 ***~ road to,*** (fig) easiest way of getting (to): (喻)捷徑: *Practice is the ~ road to success when learning a language.* 練習是學習語言的捷徑。**R~ Commission,** one officially appointed to hold an enquiry and issue a report. (由英國皇室正式指派的) 調查委員會。 **~ly** /ˈrɔɪəlɪ ; ˈrɔɪəlɪ/ *adv* in a ~ or splendid manner: 威嚴地;高貴地;盛大地: *We were ~ly entertained.*

我們受到盛大地招待。 ~·**ist** /ˈrɔɪəlɪst; ˈrɔɪəlɪst/ *n* supporter of a king or queen or of ~ government; supporter of the ~ side in a civil war. 保皇者;保皇黨員。

roy·alty /ˈrɔɪəltɪ; ˈrɔɪəltɪ/ *n* (*pl* -ties) **1** [U] royal persons: 皇室;王族: *The play was performed in the presence of ~.* 這個戲曾在御前演出。*The hotel has been patronized by ~.* 這家旅館曾有皇族光顧過。 **2** [U] position, rank, dignity, power, etc of a royal person. 皇室之人的地位、階級、尊嚴、權力等。 **3** [C] sum paid by a mining or oil company to the owner of the land: (開礦或石油公司付給土地所有者的)礦區使用費: *oil royalties;* 石油產地使用費; sum paid to the owner of a copyright or patent: 版稅;專利權使用費: *a ~ of 10 per cent of the price of the book on all copies sold.* 實售册數每本抽百分之十的版稅。

rub[1] /rʌb; rʌb/ *n* **1** period of rubbing: 摩擦的時間: *give the spoons/table, etc a good rub.* 把羹匙(桌子等)好好擦一擦。 **2** (esp in the phrase 尤用於片語 ***There's the rub***) difficulty; point at which doubt or difficulty arises. 困難;引起疑慮或困難之點。

rub[2] /rʌb; rʌb/ *vt, vi* (-bb-) (For special uses with *adverbial particles* and *preps*, ⇨ 3 below.) (與副詞接語及介詞連用的特殊用法,參看下列第3義。) **1** [VP 6A, 15A, 22] move (one thing) backwards and forwards on the surface of (another); make (sth *clean, dry*, etc) by doing this: 擦;搓;擦淨;擦乾: *He was rubbing his hands together.* 他搓著兩手。*Rub this oil on your skin.* 把這油擦在你的皮膚上。*He rubbed his hands with the soap.* 他在雙手上塗擦肥皂。*You've rubbed your coat against some wet paint.* 你的外套擦到未乾的油漆了。*Rub the surface dry.* 把表面擦乾。 ***rub shoulders with***, meet and mix with (people). 同(人們)來往。 **2** [VP2A, C] come into, or be in, contact with, by a sliding or up and down movement: 由滑動或上下之動作而接觸;摩擦: *What is the wheel rubbing on/against?* 這輪子擦到甚麼了? **3** [VP2C, 15B] (special uses with *adverbial particles* and *preps*): (與副詞接語及介詞連用的特殊用法):

rub along, (colloq) (of a person) manage to exist, pass one's time, without too much difficulty. (俗,指人)無太大困難地過活,消磨時間。 ***rub along with sb/together***, (of two or more persons) live without quarrelling, etc: (指兩個或兩個以上的人)和諧相處: *I manage to rub along with her.* 我和她相處得很不錯。*We manage to rub along together.* 我們相處得很不錯。 **rubber** *n* ⇨ rubber[1](4).

rub sb/oneself/a horse down, rub thoroughly, vigorously, eg with a towel, to make dry and clean: (用毛巾等)用力搓乾擦淨: *He rubbed himself down after his bath.* 他洗澡之後用力擦乾身子。 ***rub sth down***, make sth smooth or level by rubbing: 磨平: *Rub the walls down well before applying new paint.* 在塗上新油漆之前先將牆磨平。Hence, 由此產生, ˈ**rub-down** *n*: *Give the horse/the walls a good rub-down.* 把這匹馬好好擦洗一番(把這些牆好好磨平)。

rub sth in; rub sth into sth, **(a)** force (ointment, etc) into sth, eg the skin, by rubbing: 用力擦(藥膏等)使滲進某物(如皮膚): *Rub the ointment well in/into the skin.* 把這藥膏用力擦,使滲入皮膚。 **(b)** force (a lesson, a humiliating or unpleasant fact) into sb's mind: 强使接受(教訓、屈辱或不愉快事件等): *The moral needs to be well rubbed in.* 這個教訓需要好好記住。 ***rub it in***, (esp) remind sb repeatedly of a fault, failure, etc: (尤指)不斷地提起某人的錯誤、失敗等: *I know I behaved foolishly but you needn't rub it in.* 我知道我的行爲很愚蠢,但你不必老提這件事。

rub sth off, remove sth (from a surface) by rubbing: 擦掉: *How did you rub the skin off your knees?* 你怎麼把膝蓋上的皮擦破了? *The nap of this cloth has been rubbed off.* 這布上的細毛被磨掉了。

rub sth out, remove (marks, writing, etc) by rubbing: 把(記號、筆跡等)擦掉: *rub out a word/pencil marks/mistakes.* 擦掉一個字(鉛筆記號,錯誤)。*The stains won't rub out*, can't be rubbed out. 這些污點擦不掉。 ***rub sb out***, (US sl) murder him. (美俚)謀殺某人。

rub sth up, polish by rubbing: 擦光亮: *rub up the silver spoons.* 把銀匙擦亮。Hence, 由此產生, ˈ**rub-up** *n*. ***rub sb (up) the right/wrong way***, placate/irritate him. 安撫(激怒)某人。

rub-a-dub /ˌrʌb ə ˈdʌb; ˈrʌbəˌdʌb/ *n* [U] sound made by beating a drum. 鼓之咚咚聲。

rub·ber[1] /ˈrʌbə(r); ˈrʌbɚ/ *n* **1** [U] tough elastic substance made from the milky liquid that flows from certain trees when the bark is cut, used for making tyres, tennis balls, etc: 橡皮: (attrib) (形容用法) *ˈ~ trees;* 橡膠樹; *the ˈ~ plantations of Malaysia;* 馬來西亞的橡膠園; *~ bands*, elastic bands for keeping things together; 橡皮筋;橡皮圈; *a ~ stamp.* 橡皮圖章。ˌ~-ˈ**stamp** *vt* (colloq) approve or endorse (a proposal, etc) without giving it proper consideration. (俗)不加適當考慮即贊同或認可(一建議等)。 ˈ~-**neck** *n* (US colloq) tourist or sightseer of the kind who constantly turns his head to see as much as possible. (美俗)頻頻轉頭想盡量多看一些的觀光客或遊客。□ *vi* look at sights in this way. 頻頻轉頭觀看景色。 **2** [C] piece of ~ material for rubbing out pencil marks, etc: (擦鉛筆痕跡等的)橡皮: *a pencil with a ~ at one end.* 一端帶橡皮的鉛筆。 **3** (*pl*) overshoes (galoshes) made of ~. (複)橡皮套鞋。 **4** [C] person or thing that rubs, eg a part of a machine that applies friction. 擦者;搓者;摩擦之人或物;摩擦器。□ *vt* [VP6A] cover or coat with ~. 覆以橡皮;包以橡皮。 ~·**ize** /-aɪz; -ˌaɪz/ *vt* [VP6A] cover or treat with ~. 覆以橡皮;以橡皮處理。 ~**y** *adj* made of ~. 橡皮製的。

rub·ber[2] /ˈrʌbə(r); ˈrʌbɚ/ *n* [C] (in such card games as whist and bridge) (在惠斯特和橋牌類的牌戲中) **1** three successive games between the same sides or persons: (相同的組或人之間的)連續三盤比賽: *Let's play another ~.* 讓我們再連賽三盤。 **2** the winning of two games out of three; the third game when each side has won one: 三盤比賽中的連勝兩盤; 雙方各勝一盤後以決定勝負的第三盤比賽: *game and ~*, (We have won) the third game and (therefore) the ~. (我們贏了)第三盤和這一局。

rub·bing /ˈrʌbɪŋ; ˈrʌbɪŋ/ *n* impression of sth, eg a brass over a grave, by rubbing paper laid over it with wax, chalk or charcoal. 摹拓;搨印(碑文等)。

rub·bish /ˈrʌbɪʃ; ˈrʌbɪʃ/ *n* [U] **1** waste material; that which is, or is to be, thrown away as worthless; refuse. 廢物;垃圾。 **2** nonsense; worthless ideas: 無意義的話;無意義的思想: *This book is all ~.* 這本書全是一派胡言亂語。 **3** (as an exclamation) Nonsense! (用做驚嘆詞)胡說! ~**y** *adj* worthless. 無價值的。

rubble /ˈrʌbl; ˈrʌbl/ *n* [U] bits of broken stone, rock or brickwork: 碎石;碎磚瓦礫: *buildings reduced to ~ by bombing;* 因轟炸而毀成碎磚瓦礫的建築物; *build roads with a foundation of ~.* 修築以碎石爲路基的道路。

Ru·bi·con /ˈruːbɪkən *US:* -kɒn; ˈrubɪˌkɑn/ *n* ***cross the ~***, commit oneself to an enterprise from which one cannot turn back. 破釜沉舟;採斷然手段。

ru·bi·cund /ˈruːbɪkənd; ˈrubəˌkʌnd/ *adj* (of a person's face or complexion) ruddy; high-coloured. (指人的臉或面色)紅潤的;有血色的。

ru·bric /ˈruːbrɪk; ˈrubrɪk/ *n* [C] **1** title or heading printed in red or special type. 紅字標題;以特殊字體印的標題。 **2** rule; direction; explanation. 規則;指示;說明。

ruby /ˈruːbɪ; ˈrubɪ/ *n* [C] (*pl* -bies) red jewel. 紅寶石;紅玉。□ *adj, n* deep red (colour). 深紅色(的)。

ruck[1] /rʌk; rʌk/ *n* **the ~, the common ~**, ordinary commonplace things or persons: 普通的事物

或人: *He was ambitious to get out of the ~,* to escape from being thought of as ordinary, commonplace, etc. 他野心勃勃想出人頭地。

ruck² /rʌk ; rʌk/ *n* [C] irregular fold or crease (esp in cloth). 皺摺(尤指布上者)。□ *vi, vt* [VP2A, C, 6A, 15B] **~ *(up)*,** be pulled into ~s; make into ~s: 扯成皺摺;使成皺摺: *The sheets on my bed have ~ed up.* 我床上的床單已經皺起來了。

ruck·sack /ˈrʌksæk ; ˈrʌkˌsæk/ *n* [C] canvas bag strapped on the back from the shoulders, used by people on a walking holiday, etc; haversack, knapsack. 一種帆布背囊(步行度假者等用之)。

ruc·tions /ˈrʌkʃnz ; ˈrʌkʃənz/ *n pl* angry words or protests; noisy argument: 憤怒的話或抗議;吵鬧的爭辯: *There'll be ~ if you don't do what you're told.* 你如果不照吩咐去做,一定會挨罵。

rud·der /ˈrʌdə(r) ; ˈrʌdɚ/ *n* [C] **1** flat, broad piece of wood or metal hinged vertically at the stern of a boat or ship for steering. (船上的)舵。**2** similar structure on an aircraft. (飛機上的)方向舵。⇨ the illus at air.參看 air 之插圖。

ruddle /ˈrʌdl ; ˈrʌdl/ *n* [U] red ochre, esp the kind used for marking ownership of sheep. 紅土;代赭石(尤指在羊身上做記號所用者)。□ *vt* put ~ on (sheep). 在(羊身)上塗紅土。

ruddy /ˈrʌdɪ ; ˈrʌdɪ/ *adj* (-ier, -iest) **1** (of the face) red, as showing good health: (指臉)紅潤的(表示很健康): *~ cheeks;* 紅潤的臉頰; *in ~ health,* having ~ cheeks indicating good health. 有着表示健康的紅潤臉色的。 **2** red or reddish: 紅色的;淡紅色的: *a ~ glow in the sky.* 天空中紅色的光輝。 **3** (sl; euphem for) bloody(3): (俚; bloody 第3義之委婉語)用於表示强烈感情的無意義的話: *What the ~ hell are you doing?* 你在搞什麼鬼呀?

rude /ruːd ; rud/ *adj* (-r, -st) **1** (of a person, his speech, behaviour) impolite; not showing respect or consideration: (指人、其語言、行爲) 粗魯無禮的;不表示尊敬或體恤的: *It's ~ to interrupt／to point at people.* 插嘴(用手指人)是不禮貌的。 *What a ~ reply!* 多麼粗魯無禮的答覆! *Would it be ~ to ask when you are likely to leave?* eg to a guest who stays too long. 對不起,請問你大概甚麼時候告辭?(如問一位逗留過久的客人)。**2** startling; violent; rough: 駭人聽聞的;狂暴的;粗野的: *get a ~ shock.* 受到劇烈的震驚。***a ~ awakening,*** a sudden realization of sth unpleasant. 突然的覺醒。 **3** primitive; without refinement: 原始的;粗鄙的: *our ~ forefathers.* 我們未開化的祖先。 **4** roughly made; simple: 粗製的;簡單的: *a ~ wooden plough.* 一具簡陋的木犂; **5** vigorous: 有活力的: *in ~ health.* 十分健壯的。 **6** in the natural state; crude, raw (the more usu words): 天然狀態的;原質的;粗陋的;生的(crude, raw 等字較常用): *~ ore／produce;* 原礦(天然產品); *cotton in its ~ state.* 原棉。**~·ly** *adv* in a ~ manner: 無禮地;粗暴地;突然地;原始地;簡單地;有力地: *a ~ly* (ie in a primitive manner) *fashioned craft;* 原始風格的手藝; *be ~ly awakened.* 突然覺醒。⇨ 2 above. 參看上列第二義。**~·ness** *n* [U].

ru·di·ment /ˈruːdɪmənt ; ˈrudəmənt/ *n* **1** *(pl)* first steps or stages (of an art or science): (複)(藝術或科學的)初步;初階;基礎: *learn the ~s of chemistry／grammar.* 學習化學(文法)的初階。 **2** earliest form on which a later development is or might have developed; imperfectly developed part: 可進一步發展的最初的形式;發育不完全的部分;雛型: *Certain fossils reveal the ~ of a thumb.* 某些化石顯示出拇指的雛型。*A new-born chicken has only the ~s of wings.* 一隻新孵出的小鷄只有翅膀的雛型。 **ru·di·men·tary** /ˌruːdɪˈmentrɪ ; ˌrudəˈmɛntərɪ/ *adj* **1** elementary: 初步的;基礎的: *a ~ary knowledge of mechanics.* 力學的初步知識。 **2** undeveloped; existing in an imperfect or undeveloped form. 發育未完全的;以不完全或未發展成熟的形式存在的。

rue¹ /ruː ; ru/ *n* [U] small evergreen plant with bitter-tasting leaves formerly used in medicine. 芸香(一種長綠小灌木,葉味苦,以前用以製藥)。

rue² /ruː ; ru/ *vt* [VP6A] (dated or liter) repent of; think of with sadness or regret: (過時用語或文)懊悔;後悔;悔恨: *You'll live to rue it,* will one day regret it. 總有一天你會後悔的。*You'll rue the day when....* 你會後悔那一天曾…。**rue·ful** /ˈruːfl ; ˈrufəl/ *adj* showing, feeling, expressing regret: 表現、感覺、表示懊悔的: *a rueful smile.* (充滿懊悔的)苦笑。 **rue·fully** /ˈruːfəlɪ ; ˈrufəlɪ/ *adv*

ruff¹ /rʌf ; rʌf/ *n* **1** ring of differently coloured or marked feathers round a bird's neck, or of hair round an animal's neck. 鳥頸的彩羽;獸頸之毛;頸毛。 **2** wide, stiff frill worn as a collar in the 16th c. 十六世紀時所帶的寬而硬的縐領。⇨ the illus at doublet. 參看 doublet 之插圖。

ruff² /rʌf ; rʌf/ *vi, vt* trump (in a card game). (在牌戲中)出王牌以取勝;切牌。□ *n* act of trumping. 出王牌以取勝;切牌。

ruf·fian /ˈrʌfɪən ; ˈrʌfɪən/ *n* violent, cruel man. 殘暴的人;惡棍;兇徒。**~·ly** *adj* like a ~; lawless. 像惡棍的; 殘暴的; 無法紀的。 **~·ism** /-ɪzəm ; -ˌɪzəm/ *n* [U] rough, brutal conduct. 粗野殘酷的行爲。

ruffle /ˈrʌfl ; ˈrʌfl/ *vt, vi* **1** [VP6A, 15B] **~ *(up)*,** disturb the peace, calm or smoothness of: 擾亂…之和平、寧靜或平滑;弄縐;弄亂: *The bird ~d up its feathers.* 那鳥豎起了羽毛。*A sudden breeze ~d the surface of the lake.* 一陣突然的微風吹縐了湖水。*Who's been ruffling your hair?* 誰弄亂了你的頭髮? *Anne is easily ~d,* easily annoyed, put out of temper. 安容易生氣。 **2** [VP2A] become ~d: 生氣;起縐: *You ~ too easily.* 你太容易發脾氣了。□ *n* [C] **1** strip of material gathered into folds; frill used to ornament a garment at the wrist, neck or breast. 縐摺;衣裳等上做飾物用的縐邊。**2** ruffling or being ~d(1). 擾亂;被擾亂。

rug /rʌg ; rʌg/ *n* **1** floor mat of thick material (usu smaller than a carpet): 地毯(通常指較 carpet 小者): = *a ˈhearth-rug.* **2** thick, usu woollen, covering or wrap: 厚(毛)毯: *a ˈtravelling-rug* (for putting round one's knees in a car, etc). 旅行毯(坐汽車等時圍着膝部者)。

Rugby /ˈrʌgbɪ ; ˈrʌgbɪ/ *n* **~ (football),** (GB) kind of football using an oval-shaped ball which may be handled: (英)橄欖球戲(球爲橢圓形,可使用手): *~ League,* form of ~ with thirteen players and allowing professionalism; 聯盟制橄欖球(每隊十三名球員,准許職業球隊參加); *~ Union,* with fifteen players and having amateur teams only. 同盟制橄欖球(每隊十五名球員,限業餘球隊參加)。

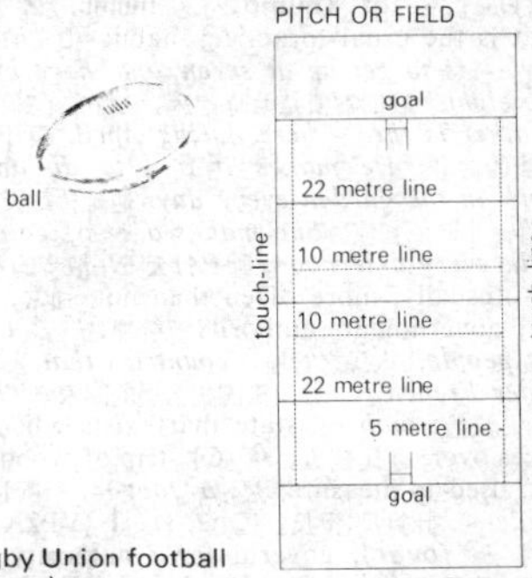

Rugby Union football (rugger)

rug·ged /ˈrʌgɪd ; ˈrʌgɪd/ *adj* **1** rough; uneven; rocky: 粗的;不平的;崎嶇的;多岩石的: *a ~ coast;* 多岩石的海岸; *~ country.* 地勢起伏的地區。 **2** having furrows or wrinkles: 有皺紋的;多皺紋的: *a ~ face;* 多皺紋的臉; *~ features.* 不平整的面貌。 **3** not refined or gentle: 粗野的;不雅的: *a ~ character;* 粗魯的人; *~ manners.* 粗野的態度。**~·ly** *adv* **~·ness** *n*

rug·ger /ˈrʌgə(r) ; ˈrʌgɚ/ *n* [U] (colloq) Rugby football. (俗)橄欖球戲。

ruin /ˈru:ɪn ; ˈruɪn/ *n* **1** [U] destruction; overthrow; serious damage: 毀滅;瓦解;推翻;嚴重的損壞: *the ~ of her hopes;* 她的希望的幻滅; *the impulse that led to my ~;* 使我身敗名裂的衝動; *brought to ~ by gambling and drink.* 因賭博與酗酒而墮落。 **2** [U] state of being decayed, destroyed, collapsed: 敗壞、毀壞、崩潰的狀態: *The castle has fallen into ~.* 那城堡已破敗不堪。***go to rack and ~,*** ⇨ rack⁴. [C] sth which has decayed, been destroyed, etc: 已敗壞、被毀壞等之物: *The building is in ~s.* 那建築物已成斷壁殘垣。*The abbey is now a ~.* 該修道院現已成廢墟。 **3** [U] cause of ~: 毀滅、敗壞等的原因: *Gambling was his ~* (= was the ~ of him). 賭博是使他墮落的原因。□ *vt* [VP6A] cause the ~ of: 使毀滅;使敗壞: *You will ~ your prospects if you continue to be so foolish.* 如果你繼續此種愚行,你將自毀前程。*The storm ~ed the crops.* 暴風雨摧毀了農作物。*He's bankrupt and ~ed,* has lost all his money, property, etc. 他完全破產了。**~·ation** /ˌru:ɪˈneɪʃn ; ˌruɪnˈeʃən/ *n* [U] being ~ed; bringing to ~: 毀滅;敗壞;導致毀滅或敗壞: *These late frosts mean ~ation to the fruit farmers.* 春寒意味着對果農之重大破壞。**~·ous** /-əs ; -əs/ *adj* **1** causing ~: 招致毀滅的: *~ous expenditure/folly.* 使人破產的花費(毀人的愚行)。 **2** in ~s: 毀壞的;破落不堪的: *live in a ~ous old house.* 住在一個破敗不堪的老屋中。**~·ous·ly** *adv*

rule /ru:l ; rul/ *n* **1** [C] law or custom which guides or controls behaviour or action; decision made by an organization, etc about what must or must not be done: 指導或控制行爲或行動的條規或慣例;一組織等對何者必須做或絕不能做所做之決定;規則;法規: *obey the ~s of the game.* 遵守遊戲(比賽)規則。*There is a ~ that....* 有一條規定…。*It's against the ~s to handle the ball in soccer.* 在足球賽中以手觸球即犯規。***~(s) of the road,*** ⇨ road(1). ***by/according to ~,*** according to ~s and regulations: 依照規則: *He does everything by ~,* never uses his own judgement. 他事事墨守成規(從不用自己的判斷力)。***work to ~,*** pay exaggerated attention (deliberately) to ~s and regulations and so slow down output: (故意地)過於遵守規則而減低生產;怠工: *Instead of coming out on strike, the men decided to work to ~.* 工人們決定不罷工而怠工。ˈ**~ book,** book (issued to workers) containing such ~s and regulations. (發給工人的)手册;須知;規章。**~ of thumb,** ⇨ thumb. **2** [C] sth that is the usual practice; habit: 慣常的事;習慣: *My ~ is to get up at seven and have breakfast at eight.* 我的習慣是七時起床,八時吃早餐。 *Rainy weather is the ~ here during April.* 四月多雨乃是這裏的常事。*He makes it a ~ to do an hour's work in the garden every day.* 他維持每天在花園中工作一小時的習慣。*She makes a ~ of going for a walk every afternoon.* 她有每天下午散步的習慣。***as a ~,*** usually; more often than not. 通常;多半。 **3** [U] government; authority: 管理;統治: *the ~ of the people;* 人民之管理; *countries that were once under French ~.* 曾由法國統治過的國家。*The ~ of law;* 法治; *mob ~,* state that exists when a mob takes over. 暴民統治。**4** [C] strip of wood, metal, etc, used to measure: 尺: *a ˈfoot-~;* 一呎長之尺; *a ˈslide-~.* 計算尺;滑尺。□ *vi, vt* **1** [VP2A, B, 6A, 3A] ***~ (over),*** govern; have authority (over): 統治;管理: *King Charles I ~d (England) for eleven years without a parliament.* 英王查理一世統治(英國)十一年不曾召開國會。*An emperor is a monarch who ~s over an empire.* 皇帝就是統治一個帝國的君主。 **2** (usu in the *passive*) be guided or influenced by; have power or influence over: (通常用被動語態)被引導或被影響;對…有控制或影響力: *Don't be ~d by your passions/by hatred.* 不要被强烈的感情(仇恨)所支配。 **3** [VP6A, 9, 15A, B, 25] give as a decision: 裁決: *The chairman ~d the motion out of order/that the motion was out of order.* 主席裁決該動議不合程序。 ***~ sth out,*** declare that it cannot be considered, that it is out of the question: 拒絕考慮某事;宣佈某事不可能: *That's a possibility that can't be ~d out,* It is something we must bear in mind. 那種可能性我們不能不加以考慮。 **4** [VP6A, 15A, B] make (a line or lines) on paper (with a ruler); make parallel lines on (paper): (用尺)在紙上畫(線);畫平行線於(紙)上: *~d notepaper;* 畫格的信紙; *~ a line across the sheet.* 畫一條橫過全紙的線。***~ sth off,*** separate it by ruling a line: 畫一線而隔開: *~ off a column of figures.* 畫一線把一欄數字隔開。 **5** [VP2C] (comm, of prices) have a certain general level: (商,指價格)保持某一水準: *Prices ~d high,* were, for the most part, high. 一般物價偏高。

ruler /ˈru:lə(r) ; ˈrulɚ/ *n* **1** person who rules or governs. 統治者。 **2** straight length of wood, plastic, metal, etc usu flat, used in drawing straight lines, or, if graduated, for measuring. 尺;直尺。

rul·ing /ˈru:lɪŋ ; ˈrulɪŋ/ *adj* that rules; predominating; prevalent: 統治的;支配的;流行的: *his ruling passion,* that which governs his actions. 支配着他的行動的激情。□ *n* [C] (esp) decision made by sb in authority, eg a judge. (尤指)裁決;判決。

rum¹ /rʌm ; rʌm/ *n* [U] alcoholic drink made from sugar-cane juice; (US) (any kind of) alcoholic liquor. 甘蔗汁製的糖酒;蘭酒;(美)(任何種類的)酒。ˈ**rum-runner** *n* (US) person or ship engaged in the illegal importation of alcoholic liquor. (美)輸入私酒之人或船。

rum² /rʌm ; rʌm/ *adj* (rummer, rummest) (colloq) queer; odd: (俗)古怪的;奇特的: *What a rum fellow he is!* 他是個多麼古怪的傢伙! **rummy** *adj* = rum².

rumba /ˈrʌmbə ; ˈrʌmbə/ *n* [C] (music for a) ballroom dance that originated in Cuba. 倫巴舞(源於古巴的一種交際舞);倫巴舞曲。

rumble /ˈrʌmbl ; ˈrʌmbḷ/ *vi, vt* **1** [VP2A, C] make a deep, heavy, continuous sound: 發出隆隆聲或轆轆聲: *thunder/gun-fire rumbling in the distance;* 遠方發出的隆隆雷(砲火)聲; move with such a sound: 隆隆地行進;轆轆地行進: *heavy carts rumbling along the street;* 在街上轆轆前行的重馬車; (of the bowels) make sounds as gas moves through them. (指腸子)發咕咕聲。 **2** [VP15B] ***~ out,*** utter, say, in a deep voice: 以低沈聲音說出: *~ out a few remarks.* 以低沈的聲音說出幾句話。□ *n* **1** [U] deep, heavy, continuous sound: 隆隆聲;轆轆聲: *the ~ of thunder.* 雷聲隆隆。 **2** [C] (old use) place at the back of a carriage for a person or for luggage, etc; (= dickey-seat; US, also 美亦作 ˈ*~-seat*) extra, open seat at the back of an (old-fashioned) automobile. (舊用法)馬車尾部供人乘坐或載行李之部位;(舊式)汽車後邊外加之無篷座位;車後座。

rum·bus·tious /rʌmˈbʌstɪəs ; rʌmˈbʌstʃəs/ *adj* boisterous. 吵鬧的;喧嚷的。

ru·mi·nant /ˈru:mɪnənt ; ˈrumənənt/ *n, adj* (animal) which chews the cud, eg cows, deer. 反芻的;反芻動物(如牛、鹿)。

ru·mi·nate /ˈru:mɪneɪt ; ˈruməˌnet/ *vi* [VP2A, B, C] meditate; turn over in the mind: 沈思;反覆思索: *~ over/about/on recent events;* 反覆思索最近發生的事; (of animals) chew the cud. (指動物)反芻。 **ru·mi·na·tive** /ˈru:mɪnətɪv *US:* -neɪtɪv ; ˈruməˌnetɪv/ *adj* inclined to meditate. 愛沈思的。**ru·mi·na·tion** /ˌru:mɪˈneɪʃn ; ˌruməˈneʃən/ *n* [U].

rum·mage /ˈrʌmɪdʒ ; ˈrʌmɪdʒ/ *vi, vt* **1** [VP2A, B, C, 3A] ***~ (among/in/through),*** turn things over, move things about, while looking for sth: 翻尋;翻找: *~ in/through a desk drawer;* 在書桌抽屜裏翻尋東西; *~ about among old papers.* 在舊

報紙中翻找東西。 **2** [VP6A, 15B] ~ ***(through)***, search thoroughly: 徹底搜查: *~ a ship*, eg by Customs officers who suspect that there is contraband. 徹底搜查一船(如因懷疑走私而由海關官員檢查)。 □ *n* [U] **1** search (esp of a ship by Customs officers). 搜尋(尤指海關官員對一船之搜查)。**2** things found by rummaging; miscellaneous old clothes, old stock, etc. 搜尋出來的東西; 雜亂的舊衣物等。**'~ sale**, = jumble (the more usu word) sale. 舊衣物拍賣(jumble sale 較常用)。

rummy¹ /ˈrʌmɪ; ˈrʌmɪ/ *adj* ⇨ rum².

rummy² /ˈrʌmɪ; ˈrʌmɪ/ *n* [U] card game for two or more players, using one or two packs of cards. 用一副或兩副紙牌供二人或多人玩的一種牌戲。

ru·mour (US = **ru·mor**) /ˈruːmə(r); ˈrumɚ/ *n* [U] general talk, gossip, hearsay, [C] (statement, report, story) which cannot be verified and is of doubtful accuracy: (不能證實且正確性可疑的)一般性談話;閒談;傳聞;謠言;傳說: *R~ has it/There is a ~ that there will be a General Election in the autumn.* 據傳聞今秋將舉行普選。*All sorts of ~s are going round.* 各種謠言正四處流傳。*There is a ~ of the Loch Ness monster having been seen/a ~ that the ... has been seen.* 據說奈斯湖中的怪物曾被人看見過。**'~-monger** *n* person who spreads ~s. 散佈謠言者;造謠者。□ *vt* (usu passive) report by way of ~: (通常用被動語態)謠傳: *It is ~ed that ....* 據謠傳⋯。*He is ~ed to have escaped to Dublin.* 據傳他已逃往都柏林。

rump /rʌmp; rʌmp/ *n* [C] **1** animal's buttocks; tail-end of a bird; (joc, of a human being) bottom. (動物的)臀部;(鳥的)尾梢;(謔,人的)臀部。 **ˌ~-'steak** *n* beefsteak cut from near the ~. 後腿部的牛排。 **2** contemptible remnant of a larger group. 可鄙的殘餘份子;餘黨。

rumple /ˈrʌmpl; ˈrʌmpḷ/ *vt* [VP6A] crease; crumple; make rough: 弄縐;壓縐;使亂: *Don't play too violently or you'll ~ your dresses.* 不要玩得太野,否則你會弄縐衣裳的。*I've just done my hair, so please don't ~ it.* 我剛做好頭髮,請不要把它弄亂。

rum·pus /ˈrʌmpəs; ˈrʌmpəs/ *n* (*sing* only; colloq) disturbance; noise; uproar: (僅用單數;俗)騷亂;喧嘩;喧囂: *have a ~ with sb.* 同某人亂吵一陣。*What's all this ~ about?* 甚麼事情亂鬨鬨的? ***kick up/make a ~***, cause a ~. 引起一場騷亂(掀起一陣喧嘩)。

run¹ /rʌn; rʌn/ *n* **1** act of running on foot: 跑: *go for a short run across the fields;* 橫過田野做一次短跑; (in fox-hunting) period of chasing a fox. (在獵狐中)追趕狐狸的一段時間。***at a run***, running: 跑: *He started off at a run but soon tired and began to walk.* 他跑步出發,但不久便累了,於是改成步行。***on the run***, **(a)** in flight: 奔逃: *He's on the run from the police.* 他正在逃避警察的追緝。*We have the enemy on the run*, We have caused them to run away. 我們迫使敵人逃竄。**(b)** continuously active and moving about: 繼續活動;一直忙個不停: *I've been on the run ever since I got up.* 我起床後一直忙個不停。***give sb/get a (good) run for his/one's money***, **(a)** obtain (sth) in return for his efforts, expenditure. 給與某人(獲得)應得的報酬或享受。**(b)** provide him with strong competition: 使某人做激烈的競爭: *We must give him a good run for his money.* 我們必須和他做激烈的競爭。**2** [C] excursion or visit: 遠足;遊覽: *a run to Paris;* 到巴黎去遊覽; *have a run in the country*, eg by car; 到鄉間一遊(如乘車遊覽); outing or journey in a car, train, etc: 乘汽車、火車等的出遊或旅行: *How many hours' run is Leeds from London by train?* 從倫敦到里茲乘火車有幾小時行程? *Can we have a trial run in the new car?* 我們可以試乘這部新汽車嗎? **3** [C] distance travelled by a ship in a specified time: (船的)航程: *make bets on the day's run*, on the distance travelled in 24 hours. 打賭一天的航程。 **4** route taken by vehicles, ships, etc: 車、船等走的路線: *The boat was taken off its usual run.* 該船不再航行原有航線。**5** quick fall: 急劇下跌: *Prices/The temperature came down in/with a run.* 物價(溫度)急劇下降。**6** series of performances: 連續的演出: *The play had a long run/a run of six months.* 這個戲已連演甚久(連演六個月)。 **7** period; succession: 一段時間;連續: *a run of bad luck*, a series of misfortunes. 一連串的不幸。***a run on sth***, sudden demand by many people for it: 許多人之突然需求某物: *a run on the bank*, a demand by many customers together for immediate repayment. 紛紛到銀行提款;擠兌。***in the 'long run***, ultimately: 最終地;終極地: *It pays in the long run to buy goods of high quality.* 買質料好的東西終究是上算的。 **8** (usu large, enclosed) space for domestic animals, fowls, etc: 家畜或家禽的(大)圈場: *a 'chicken-run;* 雞場; *a 'sheep-run*, area of pasture for sheep. 牧羊場。 **9** (cricket and baseball) unit of scoring, made by running over a certain course. (板球及棒球)分數單位;一分。 **10** common, average or ordinary type or class: 普通的型式或種類: *the common run of mankind*, ordinary, average people; 普通人; *an hotel out of the common run*, different from, and better than, the kind one usually finds. 與衆不同的旅館。 **ˌrun-of-the-'mill**, ordinary; average. 普通的;一般的。 **11** (colloq) permission to make free use (of). (俗)准許自由使用。***give sb/get the run of sth***, the permission to use it: 允許某人自由使用某物: *I have the run of his library.* 我可以自由使用他的書房。 **12** way in which things tend to move; general direction or trend: 事物進展的方式;趨勢;趨向: *The run of events is rather puzzling.* 事情發展之趨勢令人費解。*The run of the cards* (= The cards that were dealt to me during the evening) *favoured me.* (那晚)我的牌風很順。 **13** (music) series of notes sung or played quickly and in the order of the scale. (音樂)急唱;急奏。 **14** shoal of fish in motion: 一羣游動中的魚: *a run of salmon*, eg on their way upstream. 一羣鮭魚(如正逆流而上者)。**15** (US) ladder(2). (美)襪子脫針處;抽絲。

run² /rʌn; rʌn/ *vi, vt* (*pt* ran /ræn; ræn/, *pp* run; -nn-) (For special uses with *adverbial particles* and *preps*, ⇨ 26 below; for special uses of *running, part adj*, ⇨ running.) (與副詞接語及介詞連用的特殊用法,參看下列第 26 義; running 用作形容詞,參看 running。) **1** [VP2A, B, C, E, 4A] (of men and animals) move with quick steps, faster than when walking: (指人及動物)跑: *run three miles;* 跑三哩; *run fast;* 跑得快; *run (out) to see what's happening;* 跑(出)去看發生了甚麼事; *run upstairs.* 跑上樓。 *She came running to meet me.* 她跑着來接我。*She ran to meet us.* 她跑着來接我們。*We ran to his aid/ran to help him.* 我們跑去協助他。*The dog was running behind its master.* 這隻狗在牠主人後面跑着。⇨ run after in 26 below. 參看下列第 26 義的 run after。 *Don't run across the road until you're sure it's safe.* 在確定是安全之前,不要跑過街。***take a running jump***, run up to the point where one starts a jump; (sl, imper) go away, you are being foolish, etc. 跑至起跳點起跳;作急行跳;(俚,祈使)滾開,你這個笨蛋⋯。 **2** [VP2A, B, C] escape or avoid by going away; take to flight: 逃;逃走: *As soon as we appeared the boys ran off.* 我們一出現,孩子們便逃走了。*Run for your lives!* ie run if you want to save your life. 快逃命! ***run for it***, avoid sth, eg getting wet in a storm, by running. 趕快躲避(如避免在暴風雨中淋濕而快跑)。***cut and run***, (sl) escape by taking to flight. (俚)奔逃;逃脫。 ***a running fight***, a fight between a retreating ship/fleet, etc and those in pursuit. 一場(海上的)追逐戰。 **3** [VP2A, B, C] practice running for exercise or as a sport; compete in races on foot: 練習跑步;賽跑: *He used to run when he was at college.* 他在大學時常參加賽跑。*Is he running in the 100 metres?* 他將參加一百米賽跑嗎? *Is your horse* *likely to run in the Derby?* 你的馬可能參加大賽馬嗎？ **'also ran,** used of a horse not among the first three past the winning post: (用以指賽馬中)非前三名的馬；落選的馬： *Hyperion also ran.* 亥伯龍神號馬未得前三名。 Hence, 由此產生， **'also-ran** *n* [C] person or animal unsuccessful in a race or other form of competition. 在賽跑或其他競賽中未成功的人或動物。 **4** [VP3A] ～ ***for,*** (esp US) compete for (an elected office). (尤美)競選。 Cf 參較 *stand for,* the more usu GB usage: stand for 爲英國比較通行的用法： *run for President/for mayor.* 競選總統(市長)。 **5** [VP6A, 15A] cause to compete (in a race); present or nominate (for an office): 使參加賽跑；使參加競選(公職)： *run two horses in the Derby.* 讓兩匹馬參加大賽馬。 *How many candidates is the Liberal Party running in the General Election?* 在這次普選中自由黨有多少候選人競選？ **6** [VP2D, 15A] (cause to) reach a certain condition or place as the result of running: (使)達到某一地位或得到某一名次： *He ran second in the race.* 他賽跑得到第二名。 ***run oneself out (of breath),*** ⇨ run out in 26 below. 參看下列第 26 義之 run out。 ***run sb (clean) off his feet/legs,*** (colloq) keep him going until he is exhausted. (俗)使人走得筋疲力竭。 ***run oneself/sb into the ground,*** exhaust oneself/sb by hard work or exercise. 因辛苦工作或運動而(使某人)筋疲力竭。 **7** [VP6A] make one's way quickly to the end of, or through or over (sth). 匆匆跑過或通過。 ***run its course,*** develop in the usual or normal way: 依其通常或正常的情形發展下去： *The disease ran its course.* 這病依其通常的情形發展下去。 ***run a race,*** take part in one. 參加賽跑。 ***run the rapids,*** (of a boat, men in a boat) move rapidly over or through them. (指船、船上的人)迅速通過急流。 ⇨ shoot²(4), the more usu word. ***run the streets,*** (of children) spend time playing (esp without supervision) in the streets. (指兒童)在街頭嬉戲。 **8** [VP6A] expose oneself to; be open to. 使遭受；招惹；易受；易接受。 ***run the chance/danger of sth:*** 有…之可能；有…之危險： *You run the chance of being suspected of theft.* 你可能被懷疑偷竊。 ***run risks/a risk/the risk of sth,*** ⇨ risk. **9** [VP15A] chase; compete with. 追逐；與…賽跑。 ***run sb/sth to earth,*** pursue until caught or found: 追逐某人(某物)直到捉到或找到爲止；追踪到底： *run a fox to earth,* chase it until it goes to its earth(4); 追蹤一狐至其洞穴； (fig) (喻) *run a quotation to earth,* find, after searching, where it occurs. 追查到一引用句的出處。 ***run sb/sth close/hard,*** be almost equal to, as good as, in merit, etc: 與某人(某事物)不相上下；平分秋色： *We run our competitors close for price and quality.* 在價格和品質上，我們和競爭者不相上下。 *It was a close run thing,* (of competition, etc) The result was very close. (指競爭等)結果不相上下。 **10** [VP2A, C] (of ships, etc) sail or steer; (of fish) swim: (指船等)行駛；(指魚)游水： *The ship was running before the wind.* 該船正順風航行。 *Our ship ran aground/on the rocks/ashore.* 我們的船擱淺(觸礁，擱淺)。 *We ran into port for supplies.* 我們駛進港口裝補給品。 *The two ships ran foul of each other,* collided. 兩船彼此相撞。 *The salmon are running,* swimming upstream from the sea. 鮭魚從海中逆流游到河裏。 **11** [VP2C] go forward with a sliding, smooth or continuous motion; advance on, or as if on, wheels: 以一種滑動、平穩或繼續的行動前行；(在輪上等)滾動： *Trams run on rails; buses don't run on rails.* 電車在軌道上行駛；公共汽車不在鐵軌上行駛。 *Sledges run well over frozen snow.* 雪橇適於在冰凍的雪上滑行。 *The train ran past the signal.* 那火車已從信號旁邊行駛過去了。 **12** [VP2A, C] be in action; work freely; be in working order: 在活動中；自由地轉動；處於正常之運行狀態： *Don't leave the engine of your car running.* 不要讓你汽車的引擎空轉。 *The sewing-machine doesn't run properly.* 這縫衣機操作不靈。 *The works have ceased running,* The factory has closed, is no longer producing goods. 該工廠已停工。 *His life has run smoothly up to now.* 他的生活一直過得平靜無事。 **13** [VP2A, C] (of public conveyances, eg buses, ferry-boats) ply; journey to and fro: (指公共運輸工具，如公共汽車、渡船)經常來回；往來行駛： *The buses run every ten minutes.* 這些公共汽車每隔十分鐘開一班。 *The 9.05 train is not running today.* 九點零五分的火車今天不開。 *There are frequent trains running between London and Brighton.* 倫敦與布萊頓間火車行駛班次頻繁。 **14** [VP6A] organize; manage; cause to be in operation: 組織；管理；使運轉： *run a business/a theatre/a bus company;* 經營一商店(劇院，公共汽車公司)； *run extra trains during the rush hours.* 在擁擠時刻增開加班火車。 *Can I run* (= operate) *my electric sewing-machine off the light circuit?* 我能在電燈電路上接電使用電動縫紉機嗎？ *I can't afford to run a car* (= own and use one) *on my small salary.* 以我微薄的薪俸不足以擁有一部自用汽車。 *Mr Green is run by his secretary,* She is the dominant personality and tells him what to do, etc. 格林先生受他的秘書控制。 ***run the show,*** (colloq) be boss in an undertaking; have control. (俗)當家；負責指揮。 **15** [VP6A, 15A, B] convey; transport: 運送；運輸： *I'll run you up to town/run you back home,* drive you there in my car. 我用車子送你進城(回家)。 ***run errands/messages (for sb),*** make journeys to do things, carry messages, etc. (爲某人)跑腿(送信)。 ***run arms/guns,*** convey them into a country unlawfully. 私運軍火。 Hence, 由此產生， **'arms-～ner** *n* person who does this. 私運軍火者。 ***run liquor/contraband,*** smuggle it into a country; get it past the coastguards secretly. 偷運私酒(私貨)。 **16** [VP14, 15A] cause to move quickly (in a certain direction or into a certain place): 使快速移動或伸展(沿某方向或至某地方)： *run a car into a garage;* 將汽車開進汽車間； *run one's fingers/a comb through one's hair;* 以手指(梳子)攏頭髮； *run one's eyes over a page;* 瀏覽一頁； *run one's fingers over the keys of a piano.* 以手指在鋼琴的鍵上彈。 **17** [VP2C] (of thoughts, feelings, eyes, exciting news, etc) pass or move briefly or quickly: (指意念、感情、眼睛、好消息等)匆匆而過；掠過： *The thought kept running through my head.* 這意念一再掠過我的腦海。 *Mary's eyes ran critically over her friend's new dress.* 瑪莉以批評的眼光打量她朋友的新衣服。 *The pain ran up my arm.* 疼痛已經遍及我的胳臂。 *A shiver ran down his spine.* 他不禁全身戰慄。 *The news ran like wildfire.* 那消息如野火般傳佈。 *A whisper ran through the crowd.* 耳語傳遍了人群。 **18** [VP15A] cause (sth) to penetrate (intentionally or by accident) or come into contact with; penetrate or pierce (sb/sth) with sth: (故意地或偶然地)使穿透；使與…接觸；刺穿： *run a sword through a man/run a man through with a sword;* 以劍刺穿一人； *run a splinter into one's finger;* 手指扎了一根刺； *run one's head against a glass door in a dark corridor.* 在黑暗的走廊上一頭撞在玻璃門上。 *The drunken driver ran his car into a tree.* 喝醉酒的駕駛員開車撞到樹上。 **19** [VP2A, B, C] (of liquids, grain, sand, etc) flow, drip; (of surfaces) be wet (with); (of colours, eg dyes) flow and spread: (指液體，穀粒，砂等)流；滴；(指表面)弄濕；(指顏色，如染料)擴散： *Rivers run into the sea.* 河水流入海中。 *The tears ran down my cheeks.* 淚從我的臉頰流下。 *Who has left the tap/water running?* 誰忘了關水龍頭？ *The tide was running strong.* 潮漲甚急。 *The beggar's legs were covered with running sores.* 那乞丐的腿上全是流膿的瘡。 *Your nose is running—use your hanky,* ie wipe your nose clean. 你流鼻涕了——快用手帕擦擦。 *Water was running all over the bathroom floor.* 洗澡間地上全是水。 *The floor was* *running with water.* 地板上全是水。*Will the colours run if the dress is washed?* 這衣服洗起來會不會掉顏色？ **20** [VP6A, 15A, B] cause (a liquid, molten metal, etc) to flow: 使(液體、熔化的金屬等)流動: *Run some hot water into the bowl.* 倒些熱水到這碗裏。*Run the water off,* (= let it flow out) *when you've had your bath.* 洗過澡後要把水放掉。*The molten metal was run into a mould.* 熔化的金屬被倒進模內。 **21** [VP2D] become; pass into (a specified condition): 變成;進入(某指明的情況): *The rivers are running dry,* ceasing to flow. 河流乾涸了。*Supplies are running short/low.* 供應品快用完了。*I have run short of money.* 我正缺錢用。*Feelings/Passions ran high,* became stormy or violent. 群情激昂。*My blood ran cold,* I was filled with horror. 嚇得我血都涼了。***run riot,*** **(a)** behave in a wild and lawless way. 滋鬧。**(b)** (of plants, etc) grow unchecked. (指植物等)蔓延。***run wild,*** be without control, restraint, discipline, etc: 毫無控制,限制,紀律等: *The garden is running wild.* 園中野草叢生。*She lets her children run wild.* 她縱容孩子,不加管教。***run a temperature,*** (colloq) become feverish. (俗)發燒;發熱。 **22** [VP2A, B, C] extend; have a certain course or order; be continued or continuous: 擴延;有某種途徑或次序;連續: *shelves running round the walls;* 繞牆的架子; *a scar that runs across his left cheek;* 橫過他左頰的疤痕; *a road that runs across the plain;* 穿越那平原的一條路; *a fence running round the property.* 環繞那塊地產的一道籬。*It happened several days running,* several days in succession. 那事連續發生了好幾天。*He hit the target seven times running.* 他連續七次射中目標。*The play ran (for) six months,* was kept on the stage, was performed, during this period of time. 這個劇連演了六個月。*The lease of my house has only a year to run.* 我的房子的租約期限只有一年了。 **a running commentary,** account of an event as it occurs by a broadcaster: 實況轉播;現場報導: *a running commentary of a football match.* 足球比賽的實況轉播。**'running costs,** continuous costs for producing goods, etc (as opposed to costs of original manufacture). 繼續成本。 **23** [VP2C, D] have a tendency or common characteristic; have as an average price or level: 有某種傾向或共同特色;有某種之平均價格或水準: *This author runs to sentiment.* 這位作家流於傷感。*Blue eyes run in the family.* 這一家人均是藍眼睛。*Our apples run rather small this year.* 今年我們的蘋果結得很小。*Prices for fruit are running high this season.* 這個季節水果的價格偏高。 **24** [VP2A] be told or written: 被說;被寫: *So the story ran,* That is what was told or said. 傳說如此。*The story runs that...,* It is said that.... 據說…。*The agreement runs in these words.* 協議上的文字就是這樣寫的。*I forget how the next verse runs,* how the words or notes follow one another. 我忘記下一節詩了。 **25** [VP2A] (of woven or knitted material) become unwoven or unravelled; drop stitches through several rows: (指編織物)脫線;脫針: *Nylon tights sometimes run.* 尼龍緊身衣有時會脫線。 ⇨ ladder, the more usu word with reference to stockings. (指襪子時 ladder 較常用)。 **26** [VP2C, 3A, 15B] (special uses with *adverbial particles* and *preps*): (與副詞接語及介詞連用的特殊用法):

run across, pay a short informal visit: 作短暫非正式拜訪: *run across to a neighbour's flat to borrow some sugar.* 到隣居公寓去借些糖。 ***run across sb/sth,*** meet or find by chance: 不期而遇(某人或某物): *I ran across my old friend Jean in Paris last week.* 上星期我在巴黎遇見老友琴。

run after sb/sth, **(a)** try to catch: 追逐: *The dog was running after a rabbit.* 狗正在追逐一隻兎子。 **(b)** seek the society of; go after in order to get the attention of: 設法和…交際;追求: *She runs after every good-looking man in the village.* 她追求村中每個漂亮男人。

run against sb, compete with him by running in a race; (esp US) compete with him (for an elected office). 和某人賽跑;(尤美)和某人競選。

run along, (colloq) go away; be off: (俗)走開;離開: *Now, children, run along!* 孩子們,走開!

run away, leave rapidly; flee; escape: 迅速離開;逃走;逃避: *Don't run away—I want your advice.* 請不要走——我需要你的意見。*The boy ran away and went to sea,* left home and became a sailor. 那孩子離家出走,當海員去了。Hence, 由此產生, **run-away** /ˈrʌnəweɪ; ˈrʌnəˌwe/ *n* person who has run away. 逃走者;出走者。 ▭ *adj* ***runaway success, etc,*** great, immediate success, etc. 卽時獲得的大成功等。 ***run away with sb,*** **(a)** elope with: 私奔: *The butler ran away with the duke's daughter.* 僕役長和公爵的女兒私奔了。 **(b)** go at a speed too high for control: 行進速度過快而不易控制: *Don't let your horse/car run away with you.* 不要讓你的馬(汽車)跑得太快而不易控制。 **(c)** destroy the self-control of: 失去自我控制;無法自抑: *Don't let your temper run away with you.* 別讓你的脾氣失去控制。 ***run away with sth,*** **(a)** use up: 用盡: *This new scheme will run away with a lot of the ratepayers' money.* 這項新計畫將用去納稅人的許多錢。**(b)** carry off; steal: 拐走;捲逃;偷: *The maid ran away with the duchess's jewels.* 女僕帶了公爵夫人的珠寶潛逃。**(c)** get a clear win over: 獲全勝: *The girl from Peru ran away with the first set,* eg in a tennis tournament. 來自秘魯的那個女孩第一局(例如在網球聯賽中)獲得全勝。***run away with the idea/notion that,*** assume too hastily that sth is the case: 貿然假定;貿然接受;輕易相信: *Don't run away with the idea that I can lend you money every time you need help.* 不要認爲每當你需要幫助時我就能借錢給你。

run back over sth, review past events, etc: 回憶過去;重溫舊事: *run back over the past.* 回憶往事。*I'll run back over the procedure again.* 我將再查看一下這程序。 ***run sth back,*** rewind (film, tape, etc) (after it has been looked at, listened to). (在看過或聽過之後)倒回(影片、錄音帶等)。

run down, **(a)** (of a clock or other mechanism worked by weights) stop because it needs winding up. (指鐘或其他藉錘擺而工作之機械裝置)因未上絃而停擺。 **(b)** (of a battery) become weak or exhausted: (指電池)變弱;耗盡: *The battery is/has run down; it needs recharging.* 這電池已變弱;需要再充電。***(be/feel/look) run down,*** (of a person, his health) exhausted or weak from overwork, mental strain, etc. (指人、其健康)因過度工作,精神緊張等而疲憊或虛弱。***run sb/sth down,*** knock down or collide with: 撞倒;相撞: *The liner ran down a fishing-boat during the dense fog.* 那郵輪在濃霧中撞及一漁船。*The cyclist was run down by a big lorry.* 那騎脚踏車者被一輛大卡車撞倒。***run sb down,*** **(a)** say unkind things about; disparage: 誹謗;詆毀: *That man doesn't like me; he's always running me down.* 那個人不喜歡我;他總是講我的壞話。**(b)** pursue and overtake: 追獲: *run down an escaped prisoner.* 追獲一越獄的逃犯。 ***run sth down,*** allow to become less active or occupied: 容許變得較不活動或忙碌: *run down the ship's boilers;* 減少船上鍋爐的負荷; *run down a naval dockyard,* do less work and employ fewer workers. 裁減海軍造船所的工作和人員。Hence, **'run-down** *n* **(a)** reduction: 減少;減縮: *the run-down of the coal industry.* 煤礦工業的萎縮。**(b)** (colloq) detailed explanation or listing. (俗)詳細說明或列舉。▭ *adj* (of a place) decayed; dilapidated; not cared for. (指地方)破爛的;殘破的;未照料的。

run for sth, **(a)** ⇨ 2 above. 參看上列第 2 義。**(b)** ⇨ 4 above. 參看上列第 4 義。

run in, = *run across.* ***run sb in,*** (colloq, of the police) arrest and take to a police station: (俗,指

警察)逮捕並帶往派出所: *The drunken man was run in for creating a public disturbance.* 那醉漢因擾亂公共秩序被拘於派出所。***run sth in,*** bring (new machinery, esp the engine of a car) into good condition by running it carefully for a time or distance:小心使用一段時間或行駛一段距離而使(新機器,尤指汽車引擎)達於良好狀況: *He's still running in his new car and doesn't exceed fifty miles an hour.* 他仍在小心試開他的新車,車速每小時不超過五十哩。

run into sb, meet unexpectedly: 偶遇: *run into an old friend in a pub.* 在酒館偶遇一老友。***run into sth,*** **(a)** collide with: 撞及: *The bus got out of control and ran into a wall.* 公共汽車失去控制而撞到牆。**(b)** fall into: 陷入: *run into debt/danger/difficulties.* 陷於債務(危險,困難)中。**(c)** reach (a level or figure): 到達(某一標準或數目): *a book that has run into six editions.* 一本已經銷六版的書。*His income runs into five figures,* is now ten thousand (pounds, dollars, etc) or more. 他的收入已達五位數字。***run sb into sth,*** cause (sb) to fall into (a certain state): 使(某人)陷於(某種情況): *My wife has run me into despair.* 我的太太使我絕望。***run sth into sth,*** cause sth to collide or connect with sth: 使某物與另一物碰撞或銜接: *run one's car into a wall.* 開車撞及一牆。

run off with sb/sth, **(a)** steal and take away: 帶着…潛逃;竊走: *The treasurer has run off with all the club's funds.* 會計帶著俱樂部的全部款子潛逃了。**(b)** elope with: 與…私奔: *My mother has run off with her bank manager.* 我母親與她的銀行經理私奔了。***run sth off,*** **(a)** cause to flow away: 使流走: *run off the water from a tank,* empty the tank. 使桶中的水流盡。**(b)** write or recite fluently, eg a list of names: 流利地寫或背出(名單等): *run off an article for the local (news)paper.* 爲地方報紙寫一篇文章。**(c)** print; produce: 印刷;生產: *run off a hundred copies on the duplicating machine.* 在複印機上印出一百份。**(d)** decide (a race) after a tie, or trial heats; cause to be run or played: 在得分相同或初賽後再作(比賽)以定勝負;舉行比賽: *run off a heat.* 進行決賽。*When will the race be run off?* 該項比賽何時舉行? Hence, 由此產生, **'run-off** *n* deciding race, etc after a dead heat or tie. 決賽。⇨ dead. ***run off sb (like water off a duck's back),*** have no effect on him: 對(某人)毫無影響(如水流過鴨背): *Her warnings ran off him like water off a duck's back.* 她的警告對他毫無影響,如同水流過鴨背。

run on, **(a)** talk continuously: 繼續談: *He will run on for an hour if you don't stop him.* 你如不阻止他,他會一連說上一個小時。**(b)** elapse: 流逝: *Time ran on.* 時光流逝。**(c)** (of a disease) continue its course. (指疾病)繼續發展。***run (sth) on,*** **(a)** (of written letters of the alphabet) join, be joined, together: (指書寫之字母)連綴起來: *When children are learning to write, they should let the letters run on, not write them separately.* 小孩學習寫字的時候,應該把字母連著寫,不能分開寫。*They should run the letters on.* 他們應該把字母連起來寫。***run on/upon sth,*** **(a)** (of thoughts, etc) be concerned with: (指思想等)涉及;關於: *That boy's thoughts are always running on food.* 那孩子腦子裏總是想着食物。*His thoughts were running upon the past/on recent events in India.* 他在回想過去(最近發生在印度的事)。**(b)** (of ship) strike: (指船)撞及: *The ship ran upon the rocks.* 該船撞到礁石上。

run out, **(a)** go out: 消退: *The tide is running out.* 潮正退去。**(b)** (of a period of time) come to an end: (指一段時間)到期限: *When does the lease of the house run out?* 房子的租約什麼時候到期? **(c)** (of stocks, supplies) come to an end, be exhausted; (of persons) become short of (supplies, etc): (指貯存物、供應品)用盡; (指人)缺乏(供應品等): *Our provisions are running out.* 我們的糧食快吃完了。*Her patience is running out.* 她漸漸失去耐心。*The sands are running out,* (with reference to the sand in an hour-glass) the time allowed to us (before something unwelcome comes) is coming to an end. (指更漏中之沙將流盡)期限將屆。**(d)** jut out; project: 伸出;突伸: *a pier running out into the sea.* 突伸到海中的碼頭。***run (rope/string) out,*** pass (it) out; be passed out: 抽出(繩);被拉出: *The rope ran out smoothly.* 繩子很順利地拉出來了。*The sailor ran the rope out neatly.* 水手利落地把繩子拉出。***run out of sth,*** reach an end of (stocks, supplies): 用盡(貯物、供應品): *We're fast running out of beer/cigarettes.* 我們的啤酒(香煙)很快就用完了。***be run out,*** (cricket, of a batsman) have his innings ended because, while trying to make a run, he fails to reach his crease before the wicket-keeper or one of the fielders returns the ball and removes the bails or stump(s): (板球擊球員) 被殺出局 (擊球員未能在守門員或外場員將球投回和移走門柱之前得分而被殺出局): *Smith was run out before he had scored.* 史密斯未能得分就被殺出局。***run oneself out (of breath),*** exhaust oneself: 筋疲力竭: *He's completely run out.* 他已疲憊不堪。***run out on sb,*** (sl) abandon, desert: (俚)放棄;遺棄: *Poor Jane! Her husband has run out on her.* 可憐的珍!她的丈夫遺棄了她。

run over, **(a)** (of a vessel or its contents) overflow. (指容器或容器內盛的東西)流出;溢出。**(b)** = *run across.* ***run over sth,*** **(a)** review; recapitulate: 溫習;簡述要旨: *Let's run over our parts again,* eg when learning and rehearsing parts in a play. 讓我們再把我們的臺詞溫習一遍。**(b)** read through quickly: 匆匆讀一遍: *He ran over his notes before starting his lecture.* 在開始講演前他把大綱匆匆看一遍。***run over sb; run sb over,*** (of a vehicle) (knock down and) pass over (sb or sth lying on the ground): (指車輛) (撞倒並)輾過(在地上的某人或某物): *The bus ran over his legs.* 公共汽車輾過他的腿。*He was run over and had to be taken to hospital.* 他被車輾傷,必須送往醫院。

run round, = *run across.*

run sth through sth, draw a line, one's pen, through sth. 畫掉。***run sb through,*** pierce with a sword, bayonet, etc. 刺穿。***run through sth,*** **(a)** use up (a fortune, etc) esp by foolish or reckless spending: 耗盡;浪費(財產等): *He soon ran through the money he had won at poker.* 不久他就把從賭撲克牌贏來的錢花光了。**(b)** examine quickly; deal with in rapid succession: 匆匆檢查;連續很快地處理: *run through one's mail during breakfast.* 吃早飯時匆匆把信件看過。Hence, 由此產生, **'run-through** *n* quick examination or discussion: 迅速檢查或討論: *give sth a quick run-through.* 迅速檢查或討論某事物。**(c)** rehearse. 預演;排演。Hence, 由此產生, **'run-through** *n* rehearsal. 排演。

run to sth, **(a)** reach (an amount, number, etc): 達及(某量、數等): *That will run to a pretty penny,* will cost a lot of money. 那要花很多錢的。**(b)** have money for; (of money) be enough for: 有用於…之錢; (指錢) 數目足够做…: *We can't/Our funds won't run to a holiday abroad this year.* 今年我們沒有足够的錢(我們的錢不够)到外國去度假。*I can't run to that,* can't afford it. 我沒有錢做那個。**(c)** extend to: 擴展到: *His new novel runs for 900 pages/has already run to three impressions.* 他的新小說已經寫了九百頁了(出了三版了)。***run to fat,*** (of persons) tend to put on too much fat. (指人)有長胖的趨勢。***run to ruin,*** fall into ruin. 成爲廢墟。***run to seed,*** (of plants) tend to develop chiefly seed instead of new growth of leaves, etc. (指植物)有只結子而不長新葉等之傾向。***run to waste,*** (eg of water) be wasted. (指水等)被浪費。

run up, (cricket; of a bowler) gather speed by running, before releasing the ball; (of athletes in some field events) gather speed before jumping, throwing a javelin, etc. (板球;指投球手)在投

球前跑步以增加速度；(其他運動項目中)在跳或擲標槍等前跑步以增加速度。Hence, 由此產生，**'run-up** *n* **(a)** (length or manner of a) bowler's or athlete's approach: 投球員或運動員在投球或運動前跑步(的長度或方式)：*a long／short run-up.* 長程(短程)加速跑步。**(b)** period leading up (to sth): (某事物的)前導時期：*the run-up to the General Election,* the period when candidates are busy seeking support, etc. 普選前的競選時期。***run sth up,*** **(a)** raise; hoist: 提高；升起：*run up a flag on the mast.* 在旗桿上升起一面旗。**(b)** erect, make or construct quickly or in an unsubstantial way: 匆匆或不堅實地豎起，製成或建造：*run up a dress／a garden shed.* 草草做套女服(蓋一花園小棚)。**(c)** add up (a column of figures). 加起(一欄數字)。**(d)** cause to grow quickly in amount: 使疾速增加：*run up a big bill at a hotel;* 迅速積欠一大筆旅館的帳；*run up the bidding at an auction,* force others to bid higher, force up prices. 在公開拍賣中抬價。***run up against sth,*** meet by chance or unexpectedly: 偶遇：*run up against difficulties.* 遭遇困難。***run up to,*** amount, extend to (a figure): 達及(某數)：*Prices ran up to £5 a ton.* 價格達五鎊一噸。

run·away /'rʌnəweɪ；'rʌnə,we/ *n, adj* ⇨ *run away* at run(26).

rune /ru:n；run/ *n* any letter of an old alphabet used in N Europe, esp of the Scandinavians and Anglo-Saxons (from AD 200); similar mark of a mysterious or magic sort. 古代北歐人用的字母(尤指斯堪的那維亞人和盎格魯撒克遜人從第二世紀起所用者)；相似的神秘符號。**runic** /'ru:nɪk；'runɪk/ *adj* of ~s; written in, inscribed with, ~s. 北歐古文字的；以北歐古文字寫或刻的。

rung[1] /rʌŋ；rʌŋ/ *n* [C] **1** crosspiece forming a step in a ladder: 梯子橫木；梯級：*start on the lowest／reach the highest ~ (of the ladder),* (fig) a particular level in society, one's employment, etc. 從(梯子的)最低一級開始(達到最高一級)；(喻)(在社會或職務上等)從某一階層開始(達到某一階層)。**2** crosspiece joining the legs of a chair to strengthen it. 椅子腿間之橫撐。

rung[2] /rʌŋ；rʌŋ/ *pp* of ring[2].

run·nel /'rʌnl；'rʌnl/ *n* **1** brook. 小河；小溪。**2** open gutter (for rainwater) at a roadside, etc. (路邊等的)明溝。

run·ner /'rʌnə(r)；'rʌnɚ/ *n* **1** person, animal, etc that runs: 奔跑之人，獸等：*How many ~s were there in the Derby?* 賽馬大會中有多少馬出賽呀？**,~-'up** *n* person or team taking the second place in a competition. 競賽中之第二名；亞軍。**2** messenger, scout, collector, etc: 信差，偵察兵，收稅員等：*Bow Street ~,* (hist) police-officer. (史)警官。**3** (in compounds) smuggler: (用於複合字中)私運者：*'gun-~s;* 私運軍火者；*'rum-~s.* 偸運私酒者。**blo'ckade-~,** person who tries to get through the forces that are blockading a port, etc. 試圖突破港口等之封鎖線者。**4** part on which sth slides or moves along: 滑行或移動的部分：*the ~s of a sledge.* 雪橇的滑行板。**5** long piece of cloth (for a table, etc); long piece of carpet, eg for stairs. (鋪在桌子等上的)長條飾布；(鋪在樓梯等上的)長地毯。**6** stem coming from a strawberry plant and taking root; kinds of twining bean-plant: 匐枝；匍匐莖；盤繞而生的豆類植物：*scarlet ~s; ~ beans.* 紅花菜豆。⇨ the illus at vegetable. 參看 vegetable 之插圖。

run·ning /'rʌnɪŋ；'rʌnɪŋ/ *n* [U] **1** act of a person or animal that runs, esp in racing. 跑；賽跑。***make the ~,*** set the pace (lit or fig). 領跑；領先；領頭(字面或喻)。***take up the ~,*** take the lead. 領先；領導。***in／out of the ~,*** (of competitors) having some／no chance of winning. (指競賽者)有(無)獲勝機會。**2** **'~-board** *n* (now old-fashioned) footboard on either side of a car. (舊式汽車兩旁的)踏脚板。**'~ mate, (a)** horse used to set the pace for another horse in a race. (賽馬中)領跑的馬。**(b)** candidate for the lesser of two associated political offices, eg for the Vice-Presidency of the US. 競選夥伴(如美國的副總統)。□ *adj* **1** done, made, carried on, while or immediately after running: 跑時或剛剛跑過後所爲，所做，所進行的：*a ~ kick／jump／fight.* 跑着踢(急行跳；追逐戰)。⇨ run[2](1, 2). **2** continuous; uninterrupted: 連續的；不斷的：*a ~ fire of questions,* coming in a continuous stream; 一連串的問題；*a ~ hand,* (of handwriting) with the letters joined. 連寫字體；草書。***a ~ commentary,*** ⇨ run[2](22). **3** (after a *pl n*) in succession: (在複數名詞後)接連的：*win three times ~.* 連勝三次。**4** (of water) flowing; coming from a mains supply: (指水)流動的；來自總管的：*All bedrooms in this hotel have hot and cold ~ water,* coming when taps are turned. 這家旅館中每間臥房都有熱的和冷的自來水。**5** (of sores, etc) with liquid or pus coming out. (指傷口等)有膿水流出的。**6** *a '~ knot,* one that slips along a rope and so makes the noose larger or smaller. (隨繩滑動使結環可大可小的)活結。⇨ the illus at knot. 參看 knot 之插圖。

runny /'rʌnɪ；'rʌnɪ/ *adj* (colloq) semi-liquid; tending to run(19) or flow: (俗)半液體的；有流動傾向的：*a ~ nose.* 流鼻涕的鼻子。*The jam is rather ~; you'd better boil it again.* 這果醬很稀；你最好再煮一次。

runt /rʌnt；rʌnt/ *n* (colloq) undersized or stunted plant, animal (esp the smallest of a litter); or (derog) person. (俗)矮小或發育受阻的植物，動物(尤指一窩中之最小者)；(貶)矮小之人。

run·way /'rʌnweɪ；'rʌn,we/ *n* **1** specially prepared surface along which aircraft take off and land. 飛機跑道。**2** way made for rolling felled trees and logs down a hillside. (供砍伐之樹木沿山坡滾下的)滑路。

ru·pee /ru:'pi:；ru'pi/ *n* [C] monetary unit of India, Pakistan, Sri Lanka, Nepal, Mauritius, etc. 盧比(印度、巴基斯坦、斯里蘭卡、尼泊爾、模里西斯等地的貨幣單位)。

ru·piah /ru:'pi:ə；ru'piə/ *n* monetary unit of Indonesia. 盧比亞(印尼的貨幣單位)。

rup·ture /'rʌptʃə(r)；'rʌptʃɚ/ *n* **1** [U] breaking apart or bursting; [C] instance of this. 破裂；破裂之實例。**2** [C, U] (instance of) ending of friendly relations. 絕交(之實例)。**3** [C] swelling in the abdomen caused by the breaking of some organ or tissue through the wall of its retaining cavity. 脫腸；腹突逸。⇨ hernia. □ *vt, vi* [VP6A, 2A] break or burst, eg a blood-vessel or membrane; end (a connection, etc). 破裂(如血管或薄膜)；斷絕(關係等)。

ru·ral /'rʊərəl；'rʊrəl/ *adj* in, of, characteristic of, suitable for, the countryside (opp of *urban*): 在鄉村的；鄉村的；有鄉村之特色的；適於鄉村的(爲 urban 之相反字)：*~ scenery;* 鄉村風光；*live in ~ seclūsion.* 過着鄉村隱居生活。

Ru·ri·tan·ian /ˌrʊərɪ'teɪnɪən；ˌrʊrə'tenɪən/ *adj* (of a State, its politics) full of plots and intrigues (as in a melodramatic story about an imaginary country called Ruritania). (指一個國家、其政治)充滿了陰謀詭計的(如通俗鬧劇中假想國 Ruritania 內所發生的情形)。

ruse /ru:z；ruz/ *n* [C] deceitful way of doing sth, getting sth, etc; trick; stratagem. 欺詐；詐術；計謀。

rush[1] /rʌʃ；rʌʃ/ *n* **1** [U] rapid, headlong movement; sudden swift advance; [C] instance of this: 急促的動作；突進；衝進；此等動作的實例；急流：*I don't like the ~ of city life.* 我不喜歡終日紛忙的都市生活。*He was swept away by the ~ of the current and drowned.* 他被激流冲走而淹死了。*Why all this ~,* this hurry and excitement? 爲什麼這樣忙亂呢？*There were several ~es to the refreshment tent during the afternoon.* 下午點心攤上有幾陣生意很忙的時候。*There was the usual Easter ~,* ie of traffic to the holiday resorts, etc. 像往常一樣復活節時又是人車洶湧。**'gold ~,** ⇨ gold. **2** [C] sudden demand: 急需: *a ~ for raincoats,* eg when there is heavy rain; 急需大量的雨衣(如下大雨時); sudden or intense activity: 突然或緊張的活動: *the Christmas ~,* the period before Christmas when crowds of people go shopping. 聖誕節前的搶購。 **the '~-hour,** when crowds of people are travelling to or from work in a large town; (大城市上下班時的)擁擠時刻;高峰時刻: (attrib) (形容用法) *We were caught in the ~-hour traffic.* 我們碰上了交通的擁擠時刻。 **3** (cinema, often *pl*) first print of a film before cutting and editing. (電影,通常用複數)毛片(未經剪接者)。

rush² /rʌʃ; rʌʃ/ *n* [C] (tall stem of one of numerous varieties of) marsh plant with slender leafless stems containing pith, often dried and used for making seats or chairs, for weaving into baskets, etc, and, in olden times, for strewing floors. 燈心草;燈心草之莖。 **'~·light** *n* kind of candle made by dipping the pith of a ~ into tallow. 燈心草蠟燭。 **rushy** *adj* full of, abounding with, ~es: 多燈心草的: *a ~y ditch.* 一條長滿燈心草的溝。

rush³ /rʌʃ; rʌʃ/ *vi, vt* **1** [VP6A, 15A, B, 2A, C, 3A, 4A] ~ ***(away/off/out),*** (cause to) go or come, do sth, with violence or speed: (使)猛烈或匆匆地去,來,做某事: *The children ~ed out of the school gates.* 孩子們爭先恐後地跑出學校大門。 *They ~ed (away/off/out) to see the procession.* 他們衝出去看遊行的行列。 *The bull ~ed at me.* 那牛向我衝來。 *They ~ed more troops to the front.* 他們趕調更多部隊到前線去。 **~ *to conclusions,*** form them hastily. 倉促下結論。 **~ *into print,*** publish sth without proper care, consideration, etc. 急急忙忙付印。 **~ *sth through,*** do sth at high speed: 匆忙處理: *The order for furniture was ~ed through* (= The goods were packed and sent off) *in two days.* 所訂傢具已於兩天之內送出。 *The new Bill was ~ed through Parliament.* 新的議案很快地在國會中通過。 **2** [VP6A] capture by a sudden attack; get through, over, into, etc by pressing eagerly or violently forward: 突擊攻佔;突破;攻進;衝過;衝進: *~ the enemy's trenches;* 突破敵人的戰壕; *~ the gates of the football ground.* 擠進足球場的大門。 *The panic-stricken passengers tried to ~ the life-boats,* force their way into them quickly. 驚慌的旅客爭先恐後,想擠進救生艇。 **3** [VP 6A, 15A] force into hasty action: 使倉促行動: *I must think things over, so don't ~ me.* 我必須把事情考慮一下,不要催我。 **~ *sb off his feet,*** succeed in forcing him into hasty action with no time for thought; exhaust him. 迫使某人無時間思索而急速行動;使某人疲於奔命。 **4 ~ *(for sth),*** (sl) charge an exorbitant price: (俚)索高價;敲詐: *How much did they ~ you for this?* 這個東西他們敲了你多少錢?

rusk /rʌsk; rʌsk/ *n* [C] piece of bread baked hard and crisp; kind of crisp biscuit: 焙得硬而脆的麵包片;麵包乾;脆餅乾: *'teething ~s.* (嬰兒出牙期)磨牙的餅乾。

rus·set /'rʌsɪt; 'rʌsɪt/ *n* **1** [U] yellowish or reddish brown. 黃褐色;赤褐色。 **2** [C] kind of rough-skinned ~-coloured apple. 一種粗皮的赤褐色蘋果。 □ *adj* of the colour of ~. 黃褐色的;赤褐色的。

Rus·sian /'rʌʃn; 'rʌʃən/ *adj* of or from Russia. (來自)俄國的。 **R~ roulette,** ⇨ roulette. □ *n* **1** native of Russia. 俄國人。 **2** the principal language of the Soviet Union. 俄語(蘇聯的主要語言)。

rust /rʌst; rʌst/ *n* [U] **1** reddish-brown coating formed on iron by the action of water and air; similar coating on other metals: (鐵或其他金屬表面因潮濕與空氣作用而生的)鏽: *~-covered machinery;* 生了鏽的機器; *rub the ~ off sth.* 從某物表面把鏽擦去。 **2** (plant-disease with ~-coloured spots caused by) kinds of fungus; mildew; blight. (植物之)鏽病;(使植物發生鏽病之)各種黴菌;霉;鏽菌。 □ *vt, vi* [VP6A, 2A, C] (cause to) become covered with ~; (fig) become poor in quality because not used: (使)覆有鏽;生鏽;(喻)因不用而變壞: *Don't leave the lawn-mower out in the garden to ~.* 不要把剪草機丟在花園裏生鏽。 *It's better to wear out than to ~ out,* to become worn through use than to lose value by ~ing. 用壞總比不用而放着生鏽好。 **~·less** *adj* that does not ~: 不生鏽的: *~less steel,* used for stainless cutlery, etc. 不鏽鋼。 **~y** *adj* (-ier, -iest) **1** covered with ~: 生鏽的: *~y needles.* 生鏽的針。 **2** in need of practice; out-of-date: 需要練習的;過時的: *My German is rather ~y,* hasn't been used for a long time and needs to be practised. 我的德文(因經年不用)需要多加練習了。 **3** (of black cloth) discoloured by age; dingy or shabby. (指黑布)因太久而褪色的;髒舊的;破舊的。 **~i·ness** *n* [U].

rus·tic /'rʌstɪk; 'rʌstɪk/ *adj* **1** (in a good sense) characteristic of country people; simple; unaffected: (在好的意義方面)有鄉村居民特色的;純樸的;樸素的: *~ simplicity.* 質樸。 **2** rough; unrefined: 粗野的;不雅的: *~ speech/manners,* contrasted with the speech, etc of smart, city people. 粗俗的語言(態度)。 **3** of rough workmanship: 手工粗糙的: *a ~ bench/bridge,* made of rough, unplaned timber and untrimmed branches. 粗木製的長板凳(橋)。 □ *n* countryman; peasant. 村夫;農民。 **~·ity** /rʌ'stɪsətɪ; rʌs'tɪsətɪ/ *n* [U] being ~ in appearance or character. (外表或性格的)純樸;樸實;粗野;不雅。

rus·ti·cate /'rʌstɪkeɪt; 'rʌstɪˌket/ *vi, vt* **1** [VP2A] lead a rural life. 過鄉間生活。 **2** [VP6A] (GB) send (a student) temporarily away from the university as a punishment. (英)勒令(大學生)暫時停學以爲處罰。

rustle /'rʌsl; 'rʌsḷ/ *vi, vt* **1** [VP2A, C] make a gentle, light sound (like dry leaves blown by the wind, or of silk clothes in motion); move along making such a sound: 發出瑟瑟聲(如風吹枯葉,或綢衣動時相擦);瑟瑟移動: *Did you hear something rustling through the undergrowth?* 你聽見有東西在矮樹叢中瑟瑟移動嗎? **2** [VP6A] cause to make this sound: 使發出瑟瑟聲: *I wish people wouldn't ~ their programmes while the orchestra is playing.* 我希望樂隊在演奏時人們不要沙沙地翻弄他們的節目單。 **3** [VP6A] (US, colloq) steal (cattle or horses). (美,俗)偷(牛馬)。 **4** [VP15B] **~ *sth up,*** get together, provide: 湊集;供應: *~ up some food for an unexpected guest.* 給一位不速之客弄點吃的東西。 □ *n* [U] gentle light sound as of dry leaves blown by the wind, of silk clothes, etc: 瑟瑟聲;沙沙聲: *the ~ of paper.* 紙張的瑟瑟聲。 **rust·ler** /'rʌslə(r); 'rʌslɚ/ *n* (US, colloq) cattle thief. (美,俗)偷牛賊。 **rust·ling** /'rʌslɪŋ; 'rʌslɪŋ/ *n* [U] sound made by sth that ~s: 瑟瑟聲;沙沙聲: *the rustling of dry leaves/of sweet wrappings;* 枯葉(糖果紙)的沙沙聲; (*pl*) repetitions of such sounds: (複)連續不斷的瑟瑟聲: *mysterious rustlings at night.* 夜晚的神秘瑟瑟聲。

rut¹ /rʌt; rʌt/ *n* [C] **1** line or track made by wheel(s) in soft ground. 轍跡;車印。 **2** (fig) way of doing sth, behaving, living, etc that has become established. (喻)常規;常習。 ***be in/get into a rut,*** a fixed (and boring) way of living so that it becomes difficult to change. 陷入固定(而又乏味)的生活方式;墨守成規。 □ *vt* (usu in *pp*) mark with ruts: (通常用過去分詞)使留有轍跡: *a deeply rutted road.* 留有很深轍跡的路。

rut² /rʌt; rʌt/ *n* [U] periodic sexual excitement of male animals, esp deer. 雄性動物(尤指鹿)之周期性的春情發動;發淫。 □ *vi* [VP2A] be affected with this: 春情發動;發淫: *the rutting season.* 發淫期。

ruth·less /'ru:θlɪs; 'ruθlɪs/ *adj* cruel; without pity; showing no mercy. 殘忍的;無情的;無憐憫心的。 **~·ly** *adv* **~·ness** *n*

rye /raɪ; raɪ/ *n* [U] **1** (plant with) grain used for making flour, and as a food for cattle. 裸

麥;黑麥;裸麥粒。⇨ the illus at cereal. 參看 cereal 之插圖。 ˈ**rye-bread** *n* bread made with flour from rye. 黑麵包。 **2** kind of whisky made from rye. 裸麥酒。

Ss

S, s /es ; ɛs/ (*pl* S's, s's /ˈesɪz ; ˈɛsɪz/) the nineteenth letter of the English alphabet. 英文字母的第十九個字母。

sab·ba·tarian /ˌsæbəˈteərɪən ; ˌsæbəˈtɛrɪən/ *n* Christian who advocates strict observance of Sunday (eg by opposing the opening of places of entertainment, the playing of games, etc on Sundays). 主張嚴守星期日爲安息日的基督徒(例如反對在星期日開放娛樂場所,舉行比賽等); 嚴守安息日的基督徒。 ⇨ Sabbath. □ *adj* of the principles of ~s. 此派基督徒之教義的;嚴守星期日爲安息日的。

Sab·bath /ˈsæbəθ ; ˈsæbəθ/ *n* day of rest, Saturday for Jews, Sunday for Christians: 安息日(猶太教徒是星期六,基督徒是星期日): *break the ~*, work or play on the ~; 不守安息日(在安息日工作或遊樂); *keep the ~*, spend it in worship of God and in rest. 守安息日(在安息日崇拜神和休息)。

sab·bati·cal /səˈbætɪkl ; səˈbætɪkl/ *adj* of or like the Sabbath: 安息日的;似安息日的: *After this uproar there came a ~ calm.* 這陣喧囂之後,一切變得非常安靜。 **~ (year)**, year of freedom from routine duties given to some university teachers to enable them to travel or undertake special studies. 休假年(給予大學教師,使能旅行或從事專門研究)。

sa·ber /ˈseɪbə(r) ; ˈsebɚ/ ⇨ sabre.

sable /ˈseɪbl ; ˈsebl/ *n* [C] **1** small animal valued for its beautiful dark fur; [U] fur of this animal: 黑貂;黑貂皮: *a ~ coat/stole.* 黑貂皮大衣(披肩)。 **2** **~ antelope**, large, horned, dark African antelope. 非洲產的一種羚羊(大而有角,毛皮爲淺黑色)。 □ *adj* (liter) black; gloomy. (文)黑色的;陰慘的。

sa·bot /ˈsæbəʊ *US:* sæˈbəʊ ; ˈsæbo/ *n* [C] shoe hollowed out of a single piece of wood; wooden-soled shoe with a band of leather across the instep. 木鞋(由整塊木頭挖空而成);(有一條皮革橫過足背的)木底鞋;木屐。

sab·otage /ˈsæbətɑːʒ ; ˈsæbəˌtɑʒ/ *n* [U] the wilful damaging of machinery, materials, etc or the hindering of an opponent's activity, during an industrial or political dispute, or during war. 陰謀破壞(在產業或政治糾紛中,或在戰爭中,故意損壞機器、原料等,或阻礙對方之活動)。 □ *vt* [VP6A] perform an act of ~ against. 對…採取破壞行動。**sab·oteur** /ˌsæbəˈtɜː(r) ; ˌsæbəˈtɝ/ *n* person who commits ~. 陰謀破壞者。

sabre (US = **sa·ber**) /ˈseɪbə(r) ; ˈsebɚ/ *n* heavy cavalry sword with a curved blade. (騎兵所用之彎刄)軍刀;馬刀。 ˈ**~-rattling** *n* aggressive display of military strength. 炫耀軍力; 以武力威脅。 ˈ**~-toothed** *adj* having (usu two) ~-like teeth: 長有(通常爲兩顆)尖長犬齒的: *a ~-toothed tiger* (now extinct). 劍齒虎(現已絕種)。□ *vt* strike with a ~. 以軍刀斬或砍。

sac /sæk ; sæk/ *n* bag-like membrane enclosing a cavity in an animal or plant. (動植物組織中的)囊;液囊。⇨ the illus at flower. 參看 flower 之插圖。

sac·char·in /ˈsækərɪn ; ˈsækərɪn/ *n* [U] very sweet substance made from coal-tar, used in place of sugar. 糖精(由煤焦油提取之極甜物質,爲糖的代用品)。 **sac·char·ine** /-riːn ; -ˌraɪn/ *adj* resembling sugar; very sweet; too sweet. 似糖的;極甜的;太甜的。

sac·er·do·tal /ˌsæsəˈdəʊtl ; ˌsæsɚˈdotl/ *adj* connected with priests. 僧侶的;祭司的。**~·ism** /-ɪzəm ; -ˌɪzəm/ *n* [U] system of government in which priests (claiming to be mediators between God and mankind) have a great part or exercise great power. 祭司制度;僧侶當權制度;僧侶政治。

sachet /ˈsæʃeɪ *US:* sæˈʃeɪ ; sæˈʃe/ *n* **1** small perfumed bag. 香囊;小香袋。 **2** [C, U] (packet of) sweet-smelling dried lavender or other substance for laying among clothes, etc. (放置於衣服等之間的)香粉;香包。 **3** small packet, containing eg shampoo. 小封袋(例如裝洗髮粉者)。

sack[1] /sæk ; sæk/ *n* **1** (quantity held by a) large bag of strong material (eg coarse flax, hemp, stiffened paper) for storing and carrying heavy goods, eg cement, coal, flour, potatoes: 大袋(用粗麻、硬紙等做成,以放置和運輸水泥、煤、麵粉、馬鈴薯等重物);大袋之量: *coal £3 a ~;* 煤三鎊一包; *two ~s of potatoes.* 二袋馬鈴薯。 ˈ**~-race** *n* one between competitors each of whom has his legs tied into a sack and moves by short jumps. 袋鼠競走(參加者把兩腿套入袋內之競走)。 ˈ**~·cloth** *n* [U] coarse material made of flax or hemp. 麻袋布;粗麻布。 ***~cloth and ashes,*** **(a)** regret for wrongdoing; penitence. 懊悔;懺悔。**(b)** mourning. 悲悼;悲苦。 **2** short loose dress. (女用)短而鬆的袍裝;布袋裝。 **~·ing** *n* = ~cloth.

sack[2] /sæk ; sæk/ *n* ***give sb/get the ~,*** (colloq) dismiss sb/be dismissed from employment: (俗)解雇;被解雇: *He got the ~ for petty thieving.* 他因輕竊盜罪而被解雇。□ *vt* [VP6A] dismiss from employment. 解雇。

sack[3] /sæk ; sæk/ *vt* [VP6A] (of a victorious army) plunder violently (a captured city, etc). (指得勝的軍隊)刼掠;掠奪(被攻陷之城市等)。□ *n* **the ~,** ~ing of a captured town, etc. 被攻陷之城市等的刼掠;掠奪。

sack[4] /sæk ; sæk/ *n* (sl) bed. (俚)床。***hit the ~,*** go to bed. 就寢。

sack[5] /sæk ; sæk/ *n* [U] (hist) kinds of white wine imported from Spain and the Canary Islands. (史)從西班牙和加那利羣島輸入的白葡萄酒。

sack·but /ˈsækbʌt ; ˈsækˌbʌt/ *n* medieval musical wind instrument with a slide like that of a trombone. 中古時代似伸縮喇叭的一種管樂器;賽克布特。

sac·ra·ment /ˈsækrəmənt ; ˈsækrəmənt/ *n* [C] solemn religious ceremony in the Christian Church, eg Baptism, Confirmation, Matrimony, believed to be accompanied by great spiritual benefits; (基督教會之) 聖禮; 聖事 (如洗禮,堅信禮,婚禮); (esp) (尤指) **the Blessed/Holy S~,** Holy Communion, the Eucharist. 聖餐式;聖餐。**sac·ra·men·tal** /ˌsækrəˈmentl ; ˌsækrəˈmɛntl/ *adj* of, connected with, ~s: 聖禮的;聖餐的: *~al wine.* 聖餐中用的葡萄酒。

sacred /ˈseɪkrɪd ; ˈsekrɪd/ *adj* **1** of God; connected with religion: 神聖的;宗教上的: *a ~ building,* eg a church, mosque, synagogue or temple; 宗教建築物(如教堂,回教寺,猶太教會堂或寺廟); *~ music,* for use in religious services; 聖樂;宗教儀式中所用的音樂; *~ writings,* eg the Koran, the Bible; 宗教經典(如可蘭經、聖經); *~ to the memory of...,* phrase seen on tombstones and memorials to the dead. 獻給…(用於死者的墓碑及紀念碑上)。**2** solemn: 嚴肅的;鄭重的: *a ~ promise;* 鄭重的諾言; *hold a promise ~;* 信守諾言; *regard sth as a ~ duty.* 視某事爲神聖的職責。 **3** (to be) treated with great respect or reverence: (須)敬謹處理的;不可冒犯的: *In India the cow is a ~ animal.* 在印度,牛是神聖的動物。*Nothing is ~ to these wild youths,* They respect nothing. 這些狂野的年輕人什麼都不尊敬。 **~ cow,** (colloq) sth to be regarded with reverence, and as immune from reasonable criticism. (俗)神聖之事物;不容批評之事物。 **~·ly** *adv* **~·ness** *n*

sac·ri·fice /ˈsækrɪfaɪs ; ˈsækrəˌfaɪs/ *n* **1** [U] the offering of sth precious to a god; [C] instance of this; [C] the thing offered: 供奉;獻祭;祭祀;祭品;犧牲: *the ~ of an ox to Jupiter;* 以牛祭祀古羅馬主神; *kill a sheep as a ~.* 宰羊作爲犧牲。**2** [C, U] the giving up of sth of great value to oneself for a special purpose, or to benefit sb else; [C] sth given up in this way: 犧牲(自己利益);獻身;所犧牲之物: *He gave his life as a ~ for his country,* eg of a soldier killed in war. 他爲國犧牲了。*Parents often make ~s* (eg go without things) *in order to educate their children.* 父母爲了教育子女常自我犧牲(例如省吃儉用)。*Is the ~ of one's health to money-making worth while?* 犧牲健康去賺錢值得嗎? □ *vt, vi* [VP6A, 14, 3A, 16A] ~ ***(sth) (to),*** **1** make a ~(1): 供奉;獻祭;祭祀: *~ a lamb to the gods;* 以羔羊祭祀衆神; *~ to idols.* 祀奉偶像。**2** give up as a ~(2): 犧牲利益,生命或享樂: *He ~d his life to save the drowning child.* 他犧牲性命去拯救快要溺死的孩子。*Do you approve of sacrificing comfort to appearance,* eg by wearing formal clothes during hot weather? 你贊成犧牲舒適以講求儀表嗎(例如熱天穿正式服裝)? *She has ~d herself/her life/her pleasures and pastimes to her husband's interests and welfare.* 她爲了丈夫的利益和幸福,犧牲了她自己(她的生命,她的娛樂和消遣)。**sac·ri·fi·cial** /ˌsækrɪˈfɪʃl ; ˌsækrəˈfɪʃəl/ *adj* of or like a ~. 供奉的;祭祀的;犧牲的;奉獻的。

S

sac·ri·lege /ˈsækrɪlɪdʒ ; ˈsækrəlɪdʒ/ *n* [U] disrespectful treatment of, injury to, what should be sacred: 褻瀆神聖;破壞聖物: *It would be ~ to steal a crucifix from a church altar.* 從教堂的聖壇竊取耶穌受難像便是褻瀆神聖。**sac·ri·legious** /ˌsækrɪˈlɪdʒəs ; ˌsækrɪˈlɪdʒəs/ *adj*

sac·ris·tan /ˈsækrɪstən ; ˈsækrɪstən/ *n* (RC Church) sexton. (天主教)教堂司事。

sac·risty /ˈsækrɪstɪ ; ˈsækrɪstɪ/ *n* (*pl* -ties) (RC Church) room in a church where vestments and articles used in church worship are kept; vestry. (天主教)(教堂裏)聖器收藏室。

sac·ro·sanct /ˈsækrəʊsæŋkt ; ˈsækroˌsæŋkt/ *adj* (to be) protected from all harm, because sacred or holy; (fig, often ironic) not to be violated: 神聖不可侵犯的; (喻,常有諷諷之意)不可冒犯的: *He regards his privileges as ~.* 他認爲他的特權是不可侵犯的。

sad /sæd ; sæd/ *adj* (-der, -dest) **1** unhappy; causing unhappy feelings: 悲哀的;憂愁的;悽慘的;使人悲哀的: *John is sad because his dog has died.* 約翰因他的狗死了而悲傷。*It was a sad day for Mary when her mother died.* 瑪莉母親死的那一天,她悲哀極了。*Why is he looking so sad?* 爲什麼他愁容滿面呢? **2** shameful; deplorably bad: 可耻的;非常壞的: *a sad case of total callousness.* 一個十分無情的可耻事例。**sad·ly** *adv* **sad·ness** *n* **sad·den** /ˈsædn ; ˈsædn̩/ *vt, vi* [VP6A, 2A] make or become sad. (使)悲哀;(使)憂愁。

saddle /ˈsædl ; ˈsædl̩/ *n* **1** leather seat for a rider on a horse, donkey or bicycle; part of a horse's back on which the seat is placed. 鞍;鞍座;(脚踏車的)車座;(馬背的)鞍部。⇨ the illus at bicycle, harness. 參看 bicycle, harness 之插圖。***in the ~,*** on horseback; (fig) in a position of control or power. 騎着馬; (喻)處於統轄或當權的地位。**ˈ~-bag** *n* **(a)** one of a pair of bags laid over the back of a horse or donkey. 鞍囊。**(b)** small bag hung behind a bicycle ~. (掛於脚踏車車座後面的)小袋。**ˈ~-sore** *adj* (of a rider) having sores caused by chafing from the ~. (騎馬者因馬鞍之磨擦所產生之)鞍瘡。**~ of mutton/venison,** joint of meat from the back of the animal, together with part of the backbone and ribs. 帶脊骨與肋骨的羊肉(鹿肉)。**2** line or ridge of high land rising at each end to a high point. 兩峯間的凹下部分;鞍狀山脊。⇨ the illus at mountain. 參看 mountain 之插圖。□ *vt* **1** [VP6A] put a ~ on (a horse). 裝鞍於(馬)。**2** [VP14] ~ ***sb with sth,*** put a heavy responsibility on him; put a burden, etc, on him: 使負重責;加重擔等於: *be ~d with a wife and ten children;* 擔負一妻和十個子女的重擔; *~ sb with heavy tasks.* 使某人做吃重工作。**sad·dler** /ˈsædlə(r); ˈsædlɚ/ *n* maker of ~s and leather goods for horses. 鞍工;馬具師。**sad·dlery** /ˈsædlərɪ ; ˈsædlərɪ/ *n* [U] goods made by a saddler; [C] (*pl* -ries) saddler's business. 馬具;馬具業。

sadhu /ˈsɑːduː ; ˈsɑdu/ *n* Hindu holy man who leads an ascetic life. (印度)聖人。

sa·dism /ˈseɪdɪzəm ; ˈsædɪzəm/ *n* [C] **1** getting sexual pleasure from cruelty to one's partner. 性虐待狂;施虐淫。**2** (loosely) (delight in) excessive cruelty. (泛指)虐待狂;極端殘酷。**sa·dist** /-ɪst ; -ɪst/ *n* person displaying ~. 性虐待狂者;虐待狂者。**sa·dis·tic** /səˈdɪstɪk ; sæˈdɪstɪk/ *adj* of ~. 性虐待狂的;淫虐狂的;虐待狂的。

sado·maso·chism /ˌseɪdəʊˈmæsəkɪzəm ; ˌsedoˈmæsəkɪzm̩/ *n* [U] sadism and masochism found or treated together. 施虐受虐狂(性虐待狂與受虐狂混合者)。**ˌsado·ˈmasochist** /-kɪst ; -kɪst/ *n* person displaying ~. 施虐受虐狂者。

sa·fari /səˈfɑːrɪ ; səˈfɑrɪ/ *n* [C, U] hunting expedition, overland journey, esp in E and Central Africa: (尤指在東非和中非所作的)狩獵遠征;陸地旅行: *on ~;* 在狩獵旅行中; *return from ~;* 狩獵遠征歸來; (by extension) organized tour (for people on holiday) to game reserves, etc. (引伸)(假日赴獵物保護區等之)旅行團。

safe¹ /seɪf ; sef/ *adj* (-r, -st) **1** ~ ***(from),*** free from, protected from, danger: 安全的;無危險的: ~ *from attack.* 免受攻擊。**2** unhurt and undamaged. 未受傷害的;平安的。~ ***and sound,*** secure and unharmed: 平安無恙: *return ~ and sound from a dangerous expedition.* 從危險的遠征平安無恙地回來。**3** not causing or likely to cause harm or danger: 不致引起危險的;穩妥的: *Is 120 kilometres an hour ~ on this wide road?* 在這條寬路上一小時 120 公里的速度安全嗎? *Is your dog ~?* 你的狗不會咬人吧? *Are these toys ~ for small children?* 這些玩具對於小孩是安全的嗎? **4** (of a place, etc) giving security: (指地方等)給予安全的; 不會有危險的: *Keep it in a ~ place.* 把它放在一個安全的地方。*Is this beach ~ for bathing?* 這海灘是個安全的游泳地方嗎? *Is the bathing ~ here?* 在這裡游泳安全嗎? *Is this a ~ seat for the Tories,* Is it certain that the Tory candidate will be elected? 這是保守黨穩得的席次嗎? **5** cautious; not taking risks: 小心的;不冒險的: *a ~ statesman.* 穩健的政治家。*They appointed a ~ man as Headmaster.* 他們派一個穩健的人做校長。***be on the ˈ~ side,*** take more precautions than may be necessary: 妥加準備以防萬一: *Although the sun was shining he took his raincoat and umbrella to be on the ~ side.* 雖然出太陽,他仍帶雨衣和雨傘以防萬一。**6** certain (to do, be, become): 必定(做,是,變爲…)的: *Mr Hill is ~ to win the seat,* will certainly be elected. 希爾先生必定會當選爲議員。**7** (compounds) (複合字) **ˌ~-ˈconduct** *n* (document giving the) right to visit or pass through a district without the risk of being arrested or harmed (esp in time of war). (尤指戰時之)安全通行權;安全通行證。**ˈ~-deposit** (US = **ˌ~-deˈposit**) *n* building containing strong-rooms and safes which persons may rent separately for storing valuables. 保險倉庫;貴重物品保管處(其保險室與保險箱櫃可由私人租用)。**ˈ~·guard** *n* object, condition, circumstance, etc that tends to prevent harm, give protection (*against*): 有保護作用的物品,狀況,環境等;安全設備或措施: *smear one's skin with sun-tan lotion as a ~guard against sun-burn.* 將皮膚搽上防晒劑以免晒黑。□ *vt* [VP6A, 14] ***~guard (against),*** protect, guard: 保護;防衛: *~guard one's house against* *burglars,* eg with a burglar-alarm. 在家裝置防盜警鈴等以防竊賊。ˌ~-ˈ**keeping** *n* [U] care; custody: 保護;保管: *Leave your jewels in the bank for ~-keeping while you are on holiday.* 度假時把你的珠寶交給銀行保管。 **~·ly** *adv* **~·ness** *n*: *a feeling of ~ness.* 安全感。

safe² /seɪf ; sef/ *n* **1** fireproof and burglar-proof box in which money and other valuables are kept. 保險箱。 **2** cool, airy cupboard in which food is kept to protect it from flies, etc: (能防蒼蠅等之)飯櫥;菜櫥;紗櫥;冷藏櫃: *a ˈmeat-~.* 肉類冷藏櫃。

safety /ˈseɪftɪ ; ˈseftɪ/ *n* [U] **1** being safe; freedom from danger: 安全;平安;穩妥: *do nothing that might endanger the ~ of other people;* 不做可能危及他人安全的事; *seek ~ in flight;* 溜之大吉;避難; *ensure sb's ~;* 確保某人的安全; *play for ~,* avoid taking risks in a game (or fig). (在比賽中或喻)穩紮穩打;不冒險。 ***S~ First,*** motto used to warn that ~ is important. 安全第一(箴言,以示安全之重要)。 **road ~,** ~ from traffic dangers. 道路安全(不會發生交通事故)。 **2** (compounds) (複合字) ˈ**~-belt,** = seatbelt. 安全帶。 ˈ**~-bolt／-catch／-lock,** device that gives ~ against a possible danger (eg to prevent a gun from being fired by accident or a door being opened without the proper key). 保險銷(掣子,鎖)(防止槍砲走火或門戶被人開啓等)。ˈ**~-curtain** *n* fireproof curtain that can be lowered between the stage and auditorium of a theatre. (可在戲院之舞臺及觀衆席之間降落的)防火幕。 ˈ**~ glass** *n* glass that does not shatter or splinter. 安全玻璃;不碎玻璃。 ˈ**~-lamp** *n* miner's lamp in which the flame is protected so as not to ignite dangerous gases. (礦坑用的)安全燈。 ˈ**~-match** *n* one that lights only when rubbed on a special surface (on the side of the box). 安全火柴。ˈ**~-pin** *n* one with a guard for the point. 安全別針。 ˈ**~-razor** *n* razor with a guard to prevent the blade from cutting the skin. 安全剃刀;保險剃刀。 ˈ**~-valve** *n* **(a)** valve which releases pressure (in a steam boiler, etc) when it becomes too great. 安全閥(使鍋爐等過大之壓力洩出的活門)。**(b)** (fig) way of releasing feelings of anger, excitement, etc harmlessly. (喻)以無害的方式發洩怒氣,激動等的方法。 ***sit on the ~-valve,*** follow a policy of repression. 採取鎮壓手段;竭力抑制激動的情感等。

a safety-pin

saf·fron /ˈsæfrən ; ˈsæfrən/ *n* orange powder obtained from flowers of the autumn crocus, used as a dye and for flavouring; colour of this (bright orange-yellow). 一種取自番紅花的橘黃色粉(用於着色及調味);橘黃色;鮮黃色。

sag /sæg ; sæg/ *vi* (-gg-) [VP2A] **1** sink or curve down in the middle under weight or pressure: 中間下墜;壓陷: *a sagging roof.* 下陷的屋頂。*Prices are sagging,* falling. 物價在下跌。 **2** hang down unevenly; hang sideways: 不整齊地下垂;鬆垂: *His cheeks are beginning to sag.* 他的双頰開始鬆垂。 □ *n* [C] (degree of) sagging: 壓陷;鬆垂;弛垂;弛度;垂度: *There is a bad sag in the seat of this chair.* 這椅子的座部有很深的陷坑。

saga /ˈsɑːgə ; ˈsɑgə/ *n* [C] **1** mediaeval story of heroic deeds of Icelandic or Norwegian heroes. 英勇故事;(有關中世紀冰島或挪威的)北歐英勇傳說。 **2** long narrative, eg a number of connected books (esp novels) about a family, social group, etc: (有關某家族,社會團體等的)長篇故事;(尤指)家世小說: *the Forsyte S~.* 敍述福塞特家族歷代事蹟的長篇小說。 **3** (colloq) long description of an eventful experience: (俗)(有關重要經歷的)長篇記敍: *the ~ of Caroline's trip up the Amazon.* 加羅琳的亞馬遜河行記。

sa·gacious /səˈgeɪʃəs ; səˈgeʃəs/ *adj* showing good judgement, common sense or (of animals) intelligence. 睿智的;精明的;有判斷力的;(指動物)伶俐的;有靈性的。 **~·ly** *adv*

sa·gac·ity /səˈgæsətɪ ; səˈgæsətɪ/ *n* [U] sound judgement; wisdom of a practical kind: 睿智;精明: *S~, unlike cleverness, may increase with age.* 與聰明不同的是,睿智可能隨年齡俱增。

sage¹ /seɪdʒ ; sedʒ/ *n* wise man; man who is believed to be wise. 智者;哲人;賢人。□ *adj* wise; having the wisdom of experience; (often ironic) wise-looking. 明智的;賢明的;(常用作反語)貌似聰明的。 **~·ly** *adv*

sage² /seɪdʒ ; sedʒ/ *n* [U] herb with dull greyish-green leaves, used to flavour food: 鼠尾草(草本植物,所生灰綠色葉子用於調味): *~ and onions,* stuffing used for a goose, duck, etc. 鼠尾草和洋葱(用做烹調鵝,鴨等的填料)。ˌ**~-ˈgreen** *n, adj* the colour of ~ leaves. 灰綠色(的);鼠尾草色(的)。

Sag·it·tarius /ˌsædʒɪˈteərɪəs ; ˌsædʒɪˈtɛrɪəs/ *n* ninth sign of the zodiac. 人馬宮;射手座(黃道帶之第九宮)。 ⇨ the illus at zodiac. 參看 zodiac 之插圖。

sago /ˈseɪgəʊ ; ˈsego/ *n* [U] starchy food, in the form of hard, white grains, from the pith of certain palm-trees (ˈ~ *palms*). 西米;西穀米(由棕櫚之木髓製成的一種白色硬粒狀的澱粉質食物)。

Sa·hib /sɑːb *US:* ˈsɑːɪb ; ˈsɑ·ɪb/ *n* (old use, in India and Pakistan, used *after* a title or name) sir: (舊用法,印度及巴基斯坦,用於稱號或名字之後)先生: *Colonel ~;* 上校先生; *Churchill ~.* 邱吉爾先生。

said /sed ; sɛd/ **1** *pt, pp* of say. **2** = *aforesaid,* ⇨ afore.

sail¹ /seɪl ; sel/ *n* **1** [C, U] sheet of canvas spread to catch the wind and move a boat or ship forward: 帆: *hoist／lower the ~s;* 揚(下)帆; ***in full ~,*** with all the ~s spread or set. 張滿帆。 ***under ~,*** (moving) with ~s spread. 張帆地;在航行中。 ***set ~ (from／to／for),*** begin a voyage. 啓航;開船。 ***take in ~,*** reduce the area of sails spread; (fig) become less ambitious or active. 減少船帆張開之面積;減帆;(喻)減低雄心;減少活動。 ***take the wind out of sb's ~s,*** ⇨ wind¹(1). ˈ**~-cloth** *n* [U] canvas for ~s. 帆布。 **2** [C] set of boards attached to the arm of a windmill to catch the wind. 風車的翼。 **3** (*pl* unchanged) ship: (複數不變)船: *a fleet of twenty ~.* 二十艘船的艦(船)隊。 *There wasn't a ~ in sight.* 一隻船也沒有看見。 *S~ ho!* (cry announcing that a ship is in sight). 看見船了!(宣佈看見船的喊聲)。 **4** (rarely *pl*) voyage or excursion on water for pleasure: (罕用複數)航行;水上遊覽: *go for a ~;* 去坐船玩; voyage of a specified duration: 航程;持航時間: *How many days' ~ is it from Hull to Oslo?* 從赫爾到奧斯陸有幾天的航程?

sail² /seɪl ; sel/ *vi, vt* **1** [VP2A, B, C] move forward across the sea, a lake, etc by using ~s or engine-power; move forward (in sport) across ice or a sandy beach by means of a sail or sails: 張帆或藉引擎動力橫渡海、湖等;(運動)張帆滑行於冰或沙灘上: *~ up／along the coast;* 張帆沿海岸行駛; *~ into harbour;* 駛入海港; *go ~ing.* 坐帆船去。 ***~ close／near to the wind,*** **(a)** (naut) sail near to the direction in which the wind is blowing. (航海)頂風航行。**(b)** (fig) nearly, but not quite, break a law or offend against a moral principle. (喻)幾乎犯法或違反道德律。ˈ**~·ing-boat／-ship／-vessel,** *n* boat, etc moved by sails. 帆船。 **2** [VP2A, C, 3A] ~ ***(for／from／to),*** (of a ship or persons on board) begin a voyage; travel on water by use of sails or engines: (指船或乘客)啓航;坐船旅行: *When does the ship ~?* 船何時啓航? *He has ~ed for New York.* 他已乘船去紐約了。*Here is a list of ~ings* (= ships that ~, with dates) *from London.* 這是自倫敦開出的船期表。*The captain* *has received his ~ing orders*, instructions concerning the voyage. 船長已收到有關航行的訓令(開船命令)。 **3** [VP6A] voyage across or on: 航行越過；航行於: ~ *the sea / the Pacific.* 航行於海洋(太平洋)。 **4** [VP6A, 2A] (be able to) control (a boat): (會)駕駛(船): *He ~s his own yacht.* 他駕駛自用遊艇。 *Do you ~?* 你會駕駛船嗎? **'~ing-master** *n* officer who navigates a yacht. 遊艇駕駛員。 **5** [VP2C] move smoothly like a ship with sails: 平穩似帆船地行動: *The moon / clouds ~ed across the sky.* 月亮(雲)平穩地穿(飄)過天空。*The duchess ~ed into the room,* entered in a stately manner. 公爵夫人雍容華貴地步入房間。 **6** ~ ***in***, begin sth with energy and confidence. 賣力而有信心地開始做某事。~ ***into sb,*** scold; attack. 斥責;攻擊(某人)。

a sailing-boat

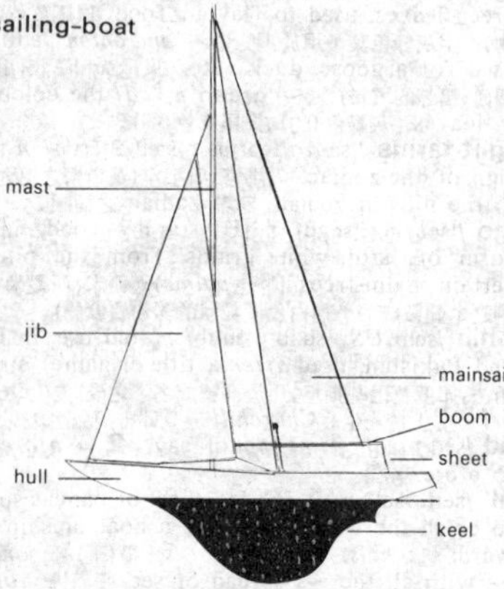

sailor /ˈseɪlə(r) ; ˈselɚ/ *n* **1** seaman; member of a ship's crew. 海員;水手。 **'~ hat / blouse / suit,** hat, etc eg to be worn by a child, made in imitation of the kind worn by a ~. 水手帽(衫,裝)(如仿照水手所穿戴之衣帽等所製的童裝)。 **2 good / bad ~,** person seldom / often seasick in rough weather. (風浪大時)不大(常會)暈船的人。

saint /seɪnt ; sent; *GB weak form immediately before names:* 英國讀音在人名前讀輕音: snt/ *n* **1** holy person. 聖人;道德崇高的人。 **2** person who, having died, is among the blessed in Heaven. 已進天國之人;死者。 **3** (abbr 略作 **St**) person who has been declared by the Church to have won by holy living on earth a place in Heaven and veneration on earth. 聖者;聖徒。 **4** unselfish or patient person. 無私心而能容忍之人。 **5 '~'s-day** *n* Church festival in memory of a ~. 聖徒紀念日。 **St 'Andrew's Day,** 30th November (patron ~ of Scotland). 聖安德魯日(十一月卅日,聖安德魯爲蘇格蘭之守護聖徒)。 **St 'David's Day,** 1st March (patron ~ of Wales). 聖大衛日(三月一日,聖大衛爲威爾斯之守護聖徒)。**St 'George's Day,** 23rd April (patron ~ of England). 聖喬治日(四月廿三日,聖喬治爲英格蘭之守護聖徒)。**St 'Patrick's Day,** 17th March (patron ~ of Ireland). 聖派屈克日(三月十七日,聖派屈克爲愛爾蘭之守護聖徒)。 **St 'Valentine's Day,** ⇨ Valentine. **6 St Bernard** /snt ˈbɜːnəd *US:* ˌseɪnt bərˈnɑːrd ; sent bɚˈnɑrd/ *n* large, powerful breed of dog, originally bred by monks in the Swiss Alps, trained to rescue travellers lost in snowstorms. 聖伯納狗(一種大而強壯的狗,最初由瑞士境內阿爾卑斯山的僧人所飼養,訓練後用以尋救在暴風雪中迷失的旅客)。 **St ˌVitus's** /ˌvaɪtəsɪz ; ˈvaɪtəsɪz/ **'dance** *n* nervous disorder with convulsive, involuntary movements. 舞蹈病(帶有抽搐,不隨意之動作的神經錯亂)。**~ed** *adj* declared to be, regarded as, a ~. 宣爲聖者的;被視爲聖人的;神聖的。 **'~·hood** /-hʊd ; -hʊd/ *n* [U] **~·like, ~·ly** *adjj* very holy or good; like a ~; of a ~: 神聖的;崇高的;似聖者或聖人的;聖者的;聖人的: *a ~ly expression on his face.* 他臉上神聖的表情。 **~·li·ness** *n* [U] holiness of life; condition of being ~ly. 生活神聖;道德崇高。

saith /seθ ; sɛθ/ old form of *says,* ⇨ say. says 的古體。

sake /seɪk ; sek/ *n* ***for the ~ of sb / sth; for sb's / sth's ~,*** for the welfare or benefit of; because of an interest in or desire for: 爲了…之好處;因爲對…之興趣: *do sth for the ~ of one's family.* 爲家庭做某事。*I'll help you for your sister's ~,* because I want to save your sister trouble, help her, etc. 爲了你姐姐(妹妹)我將幫助你。*We must be patient for the ~ of peace.* 爲了和平我們必須有耐心。 *He argues for the ~ of arguing,* only because he likes arguing. 他因爲好辯而與人爭辯。 ***for God's / goodness' / pity's / mercy's, etc ~,*** used to make an imperative request emphatic. (用來加强祈求的語氣)看在上帝面上(看在老天爺的面上; 請可憐可憐;請發發慈悲等)。

saké /ˈsɑːkɪ ; ˈsɑkɪ/ *n* [U] Japanese fermented liquor made from rice. 日本米酒。

sa·laam /səˈlɑːm ; səˈlɑm/ *n* **1** [C] Muslim greeting (from an Arabic word) meaning 'Peace'. 回教問候語(源自阿拉伯字)意指'平安'。 **2** [C] low bow. 深深的鞠躬;額手禮。 □ *vi* make a low bow (to sb). (向某人)深深地鞠躬;行額手禮。

sal·able, sale·able /ˈseɪləbl ; ˈseləbḷ/ *adj* fit for sale; likely to find buyers. 適於銷售的;可找到買主的。

sa·lacious /səˈleɪʃəs ; səˈleʃəs/ *adj* (of speech, books, pictures, etc) obscene; indecent; likely to arouse sexual excitement. (指言詞,書籍,圖畫等)猥褻的;淫穢的;會使人想入非非的。 **~·ly** *adv* **~·ness** *n* **sa·lac·ity** /səˈlæsətɪ ; səˈlæsətɪ/ *n*

salad /ˈsæləd ; ˈsæləd/ *n* **1** [C, U] (cold dish of) sliced (and usu uncooked) vegetables such as lettuce, endive, cucumber, tomatoes, seasoned with oil, vinegar, etc eaten with, or including, cheese, cold meat, fish, etc: 生菜;(一道)涼拌食品;沙拉: *prepare / mix a ~;* 調配(拌)沙拉; *a chicken / lobster ~;* 一道涼拌鷄肉(龍蝦); *cold beef and ~.* 牛肉和生菜冷盤。 **'~-days** *n pl* period of inexperienced youth. 少不更事的時期。 **'~-dressing** *n* mixture of oil, vinegar, herbs, etc used with ~. 生菜之調味醬汁(油,醋,奶油等的混合物)。 **'~-oil** *n* oil used for ~-dressing. 生菜油。 **2 fruit ~,** mixture of fruits, sliced or cut up, eaten cold. 什錦水果。 **3** [U] lettuce, endive or other green vegetable suitable for eating raw. 適於生吃的萵苣,菊苣或其他蔬菜。

sala·man·der /ˈsæləmændə(r) ; ˈsæləˌmændɚ/ *n* lizard-like animal once supposed to be capable of living in fire. 昔時被認爲生活於火中的似蜥蜴的動物;火龍。

sa·lami /səˈlɑːmɪ ; səˈlɑmɪ/ *n* [U] Italian sausage salted and flavoured with garlic. 義大利臘腸(經醃製並以大蒜調味)。

sal·ary /ˈsælərɪ ; ˈsælərɪ/ *n* [C] (*pl* -ries) (usu monthly) payment for regular employment on a yearly basis: 薪水;俸給 (通常爲年俸按月發給): *a ~ of £2000 per annum.* 年薪兩千鎊。Cf 參較 *a weekly wage.* **sal·ar·ied** *adj* receiving a ~; (of employment) paid for by means of a ~: 領薪水的;(指職業)支薪水的: *the salaried classes;* 薪水階級; *salaried posts.* 有薪職務。

sale /seɪl ; sel/ *n* **1** [U] exchange of goods or property for money; act of selling sth: 出售;賣: *The ~ of his old home made him sad.* 出售老宅使他很難過。 ***(up) for ~,*** intended to be sold (usu by or on behalf of the owners): 待售(通常由物主或代理人經手): *Is the house for ~?* 此屋出售否? *I shall put these goods up for ~,* announce that they mayb be ought. 我將把這些貨物公開出售。 ***on ~,*** (of goods in shops, etc) offered for purchase. (指商店的貨物等)出售的。 ***on ~ or return,*** (of goods sent to a retailer) either to be sold or, if unsold or unsatisfactory, to be returned. (指批給零售商的貨物)可售出或(賣不掉或有瑕疵時)退還。ˌ**bill of** ˈ**~,** (comm) document which transfers the title(3) of personal chattels, etc to another person although the goods remain with the person making the transfer (used as a method of borrowing money). (商)賣據;抵押證券。**2** [C] instance of selling sth: 賣物之實例: *I haven't made a ~ all week.* 我整個星期沒有賣出貨品。*He finds a ready ~ for the strawberries he grows.* 他所種植的草莓很有銷路。*His strawberries find a ready ~,* are quickly sold. 他的草莓很快就賣掉了。*S~s are up/down this month,* more/fewer goods have been sold. 本月銷售量增加(減少)。ˈ**~s clerk,** (US) shop assistant. (美)售貨員;店員。ˈ**~s department,** that part of a business company that is concerned with selling goods (contrasted with manufacture, dispatch, etc). 營業部(與公司之生產,發貨等部門相對)。ˈ**~s resistance,** reluctance of the public to buy goods. 公衆之不願購物;銷貨阻力。ˈ**~s talk,** (colloq 俗 ˈ**~s chat**), talk (to a prospective customer) to boost the ~s of goods. 向顧客推銷貨品時吹噓的話。ˈ**~s tax,** tax payable on the sum received for articles sold by retail. 營業稅;銷售稅。**3** [C] the offering of goods at low prices for a period (to get rid of old stock, etc): 廉售;賤賣(以清除舊貨等): *the winter/summer ~s;* 冬季(夏季)大賤賣; *buy goods at the ~s;* 廉價期間購物; ˈ*~ price,* low price at a ~. 廉售價。**4** [C] occasion when goods, property, etc are put up for ~ by auction: 拍賣: *get bargains by attending ~s.* 參加拍賣會獲得廉價品。ˈ**~•room,** room where goods, etc are sold by public auction. 售賣處;拍賣處。**5 ~ of work,** ~ of articles (eg clothing) made by members of a church, etc for charity. 教友等爲慈善事業所做物品(如衣服)的拍賣。⇨ jumble. ˈ**~s•man** /-zmən; -zmən/, ˈ**~s•woman** /-zwʊmən; -zˌwʊmən/ *nn* person selling goods in a shop or (on behalf of wholesalers) to shopkeepers. 店員(女店員);售貨員(女售貨員)。ˈ**~s•man•ship** /-zmənʃɪp; -zmənˌʃɪp/ *n* [U] skill in selling goods. 銷貨術;推銷術。**~•able** /-əbl; -əbl̩/ *adj* = salable.

sa•li•ent /ˈseɪlɪənt; ˈselɪənt/ *adj* **1** outstanding; prominent; easily noticed: 顯著的;突出的;易見的: *the ~ points of a speech.* 一篇演講之要點。*Honesty is his most ~ characteristic.* 誠實是他最顯著的特點。**2** (of an angle) pointing outwards. (指角)凸出的。□ *n* ~ angle; forward wedge driven into the enemy's battle front. 凸角;(深入敵陣之)突出部。

sa•line /ˈseɪlaɪn *US:* -liːn; ˈselaɪn/ *adj* containing salt; salty: 含鹽的;鹹的: *a ~ solution,* eg as used for gargling; 食鹽水(如用於漱喉等); *~ springs.* 鹽泉。□ *n* **1** [U] solution of salt and water. 鹽水。**2** [C] ~ lake, marsh, well, spring, etc. 鹽湖;鹽沼;鹽井;鹽泉等。**sa•lin•ity** /səˈlɪnətɪ; səˈlɪnətɪ/ *n* [U] quality of being ~. 鹹;鹽性;鹹度;鹽度。

sal•iva /səˈlaɪvə; səˈlaɪvə/ *n* [U] the natural liquid present in the mouth; spittle. 口水;唾液。**sali•vary** /ˈsælɪvərɪ *US:* -verɪ; ˈsæləˌvɛrɪ/ *adj* of or producing ~: 唾液的;分泌唾液的: *the* ˈ*~ry glands.* 唾液腺。⇨ the illus at alimentary. 參看 alimentary 之挿圖。**sali•vate** /ˈsælɪveɪt; ˈsæləˌvet/ *vi* secrete too much ~. 分泌過多唾液;大量流口水。

sal•low /ˈsæləʊ; ˈsælo/ *adj* (-er, -est) (of the human skin or complexion) of an unhealthy yellow colour. (指人的皮膚或面色)病黃色的。□ *vt, vi* make or become ~: (使)發病黃色: *a face ~ed by years of residence in the tropics.* 多年住在熱帶所致之蠟黃色的面孔。

sally /ˈsælɪ; ˈsælɪ/ *n* (*pl* -lies) [C] **1** sudden breaking out by soldiers who are surrounded by the enemy: (被敵人包圍之兵士的)突圍;出擊: *make a successful ~.* 做一次成功的突圍。**2** lively, witty remark, esp one that is a good-humoured attack on sb or sth. 俏皮話(尤指善意地批評某人或某事所說者)。□ *vi* [VP2A, C] **1** make a ~(1): 突圍;出擊: *~ out against the besiegers.* 出擊圍攻者。**2** *~ out/forth,* go out on a journey or for a walk. 出發旅行;出外散步。

salmon /ˈsæmən; ˈsæmən/ *n* [C] (*pl* unchanged) large fish, valued for food and the sport of catching it with rod and line; [U] its flesh as food; the colour of its flesh, orange-pink. (複數不變)鮭;鮭肉;橙紅色。**~ trout,** (kinds of) fish like ~, esp (kinds of) trout. 類似鮭魚的魚;(尤指)(各種)鱒魚。

salon /ˈsælɒn *US:* səˈlɑːn; saˈlõ/ *n* **1** assembly, as a regular event, of notable persons at the house of a lady of fashion (esp in Paris); reception room used for this purpose. (尤指巴黎之)名流在上流婦女家中之例行聚會;名流聚會的客廳;沙龍。**2 the S~,** annual exhibition of pictures by living artists in a French town. (在法國城市舉行的)當代畫家作品年展;沙龍畫展。**3** establishment offering services connected with fashion, etc: 提供時裝或美容服務等的公司行號: *a* ˈ*beauty-~.* 美容院。

sa•loon /səˈluːn; səˈlun/ *n* **1** room for social use in a ship, hotel, etc: (輪船,旅館等之)交誼廳;大廳: *the ship's* ˈ*dining-~.* 輪船的餐廳。ˈ**~ bar,** most comfortable bar in a public house or inn. 酒店或客棧中最舒適之酒吧;高級酒吧。⇨ *public bar* at public. **2** public room or rooms for a specified purpose: 供特殊用途的公共大廳或場所: *a* ˈ*billiards/*ˈ*hairdressing ~.* 撞球場(美容院)。**3** (US) place where alcoholic drinks may be bought and drunk (GB 英 = *pub*); bar. (美)酒店;酒吧。**4 (**ˈ**~)-car,** (GB) motor-car with wholly enclosed seating space for 4—7 passengers (US 美 = *sedan*). (英)(可供四至七人乘坐之)大轎車。

sal•sify /ˈsælsɪfaɪ; ˈsælsəfɪ/ *n* [U] (plant with a) long, fleshy root cooked as a vegetable. 婆羅門參;婆羅門參根(長而多肉,可作蔬菜)。

salt /sɔːlt; sɔlt/ *n* **1** [U] (often 常作 *common ~*) white substance obtained from mines, present in sea-water and obtained from it by evaporation, used to flavour and preserve food; sodium chloride **(NaCl)**: 鹽;食鹽;氯化鈉: *too much ~ in the soup;* 湯裡鹽太多; ˈ*table ~,* powdered for convenient use at table. 餐桌上用的精鹽。***not/hardly worth one's ~,*** not deserving one's pay. 不稱職。***take (a statement, etc) with a grain/pinch of ~,*** feel some doubt whether it is altogether true. 對(某一陳述等)有所懷疑或採取保留態度。***the ~ of the earth,*** the finest citizens; persons with very high qualities. 社會中堅份子。**2** (chem) chemical compound of a metal and an acid. (化學)金屬和酸的化合物;鹽。**3 a ~, an old ~,** an experienced sailor. 有經驗的水手。**4** (*pl*) medicine used to empty the bowels: (複)瀉鹽: *take a dose of (Epsom) ~s.* 服一劑瀉鹽。***like a dose of ~s,*** (sl) very fast. (俚)很快。⇨ also *smelling ~s* at smell[2](4). **5** (fig) sth that gives flavour or zest: (喩)增加風味或妙趣之物;刺激物: *Adventure is the ~ of life to some men.* 對於某些人而言,冒險是生活中的刺激。**6** (compounds) (複合字) ˈ**~-cellar** *n* small container (open, or with a hole or holes at the top) for ~ at table. (餐桌上開着或頂端有孔的)鹽瓶。ˈ**~-lick** *n* place where animals come to lick earth with ~ in it. 動物來舐食鹹味的含鹽地。ˈ**~-pan** *n* hollow place (natural or artificial) near the sea where ~ is obtained by evaporation of sea-water. (近海處由蒸發海水而得鹽之天然或人工)鹽田。ˈ**~-shaker** *n* (US) small container (with a hole or holes at the top for sprinkling) for ~ at table. (美)(餐桌上用的)鹽瓶。ˈ**~-water** *adj* of the sea. 海水的;鹹水的。ˈ**~-works** *n* (*sing* or *pl*) place where ~ is manufactured. (單或複)製鹽場;鹽廠。□ *vt* [VP6A] put ~ on or in (food) to season it; [VP6A, 15B] **~ sth (down),** preserve (food) with ~: 加鹽於(食物)以調味;用鹽醃(食物): *~ (down) cod;* 醃鱈魚; *~ed meat.* 醃肉。**~ sth away,** (colloq) put money away for the future: (俗)積蓄錢:

S

He's got quite a bit ~ed away. 他積蓄了不少錢。 □ *adj* **1** containing, tasting of, preserved with, ~: 含鹽的;鹹的;醃的: *~ beef;* 醃牛肉; *~ water.* 鹹水。 **2** (of land) impregnated with ~: (指土地)含有鹽份的;多鹽的: *~ marshes;* 鹽澤;鹽沼; *the '~ flats of Utah.* 猶他州的鹽地。 **~y** *adj* (-ier, -iest) containing, tasting of, ~. 含鹽的;有鹽味的;鹹的。 **~i·ness** *n*

salt·petre (US = **-peter**) /sɔːlt'piːtə(r); 'sɔlt'pitɚ/ *n* salty white powder (potassium nitrate, nitre) used in making gunpowder, for preserving food and as medicine. 硝酸鉀;硝石(有鹹味的白色粉末,用於製火藥,醃藏食物並用作藥物)。

sa·lu·bri·ous /sə'luːbrɪəs; sə'lubrɪəs/ *adj* (esp of climate) health-giving: (尤指氣候)有益健康的: *the ~ mountain air of Switzerland.* 瑞士之有益於健康的山間空氣。 **sa·lu·brity** /sə'luːbrətɪ; sə'lubrətɪ/ *n*

salu·tary /'sæljʊtrɪ *US:* -terɪ; 'sæljəˌtɛrɪ/ *adj* having a good effect (on body or mind): (對身心)有益的: *~ exercise / advice.* 有益的運動(忠告)。

salu·ta·tion /ˌsæljuː'teɪʃn; ˌsæljə'teʃən/ *n* [C, U] (act or expression of) greeting or goodwill (eg a bow or a kiss): 問候;歡迎;敬禮;招呼;致意: *He raised his hat in ~;* 他舉帽致意; (in a letter, etc) introductory phrase, eg *Dear Sir.* (信函開頭之)稱呼(如'敬啓者')。

sa·lute /sə'luːt; sə'lut/ *n* **1** sth done to welcome sb or to show respect or honour, esp (eg in the armed forces) the raising of the hand to the forehead, the firing of guns, the lowering and raising of a flag: 歡迎或致敬所行之事; (尤指軍隊等之)舉手禮;鳴禮砲;升降旗致敬: *give a ~;* 敬禮; *fire a ~ of ten guns;* 鳴禮砲十響; *stand at the ~,* stand with the right hand raised to the forehead. 立正敬禮。 ***take the ~,*** acknowledge the ~s of a body of soldiers who march past and give ~s. (整隊士兵通過並敬禮時) 接受敬禮; 還禮。 **2** friendly greeting such as a bow, raising of the hat (by a man). 致意;招呼(如鞠躬,男子舉帽)。 □ *vt, vi* [VP 6A, 2A] greet; give a ~ (to): 行禮;(向…)致敬或致意: *The soldier ~d smartly.* 那兵士行禮很有精神。

sal·vage /'sælvɪdʒ; 'sælvɪdʒ/ *n* [U] **1** the saving of property from loss (by fire or other disaster, eg a wrecked ship): (從火災或其他災難,如船難等中)搶救財貨: *a '~ company,* one whose business is to bring wrecked ships to port, raise valuables from a ship that has sunk, etc; 海難救援公司;沉船打撈公司; *a '~ tug,* for towing a disabled ship to port. 拖船;救難船。 **2** property so saved. 獲救的財貨。 **3** payment given to those who save property. (付予搶救財貨者的)救難獎金。 **4** (saving of) waste material that can be used again after being processed: (加工後可再用的)廢物;廢物收藏: *collect old newspapers and magazines for ~.* 收藏舊報紙雜誌以便利用。 □ *vt* [VP6A] save from loss, fire, wreck, etc. (在損失,火災,船難等中)搶救;援救。

sal·va·tion /sæl'veɪʃn; sæl'veʃən/ *n* [U] **1** the act of saving, the state of having been saved, from sin and its consequences. (赦免原罪及其後果之)超度;拯救;救世;得救。 **ˌS~ 'Army,** religious and missionary Christian organization on a semi-military model. 救世軍(半軍事形式之基督教傳教組織)。 **2** that which saves sb from loss, disaster, etc: 救助;救助者: *Government loans have been the ~ of several shaky business companies.* 政府的貸款挽救了幾家瀕臨倒閉的公司。 ***work out one's own ~,*** find, by one's own efforts, how to save oneself. 謀求自救之道。

salve /sælv *US:* sæv; sæv/ *n* **1** [C, U] (kinds of) oily medicinal substance used on wounds, sores or burns: 藥膏;軟膏: *'lip-~.* 口唇裂痛時所用之藥膏。 **2** (fig) sth that comforts wounded feelings or soothes an uneasy conscience. (喻)安慰情感受傷及良心不安之物;緩和物;慰藉。 □ *vt* [VP6A] soothe; put a ~ on; be a ~ to: 安慰; 敷以藥膏;緩和: *~ one's conscience by giving stolen money to charity.* 把偷來的錢用於慈善救濟以減輕良心之不安。

sal·ver /'sælvə(r); 'sælvɚ/ *n* metal household tray. (金屬的)托盤;盤子。

salvo /'sælvəʊ; 'sælvo/ *n* (*pl* ~s, ~es /-vəʊz; -voz/) **1** the firing of a number of guns together as a salute. 齊發禮砲。 **2** round of applause. 一陣喝采;齊聲歡呼。

a samovar

sal vol·atile /ˌsæl və'lætəlɪ; 'sælvo'lætḷˌi/ *n* [U] solution of ammonium carbonate (smelling salts) used medically when a person feels faint or becomes unconscious. 碳酸銨水;揮發鹽 (用作提神藥)。

Sa·mari·tan /sə'mærɪtən; sə'mærətṇ/ *n* **Good ~,** person who pities and gives practical help to persons in trouble. 同情並援助苦難者的善人。 ⇨ Luke 10: 33. 參看新約聖經路加福音第 10 章第 33 節。

samba /'sæmbə; 'sæmbə/ *n* (music for a) ballroom dance that originated in Brazil. 森巴舞(一種始自巴西的交際舞);森巴舞曲。

same /seɪm; sem/ *adj, pron* (always **the ~**, except as noted in 6 below) (除了下列第 6 義所說明的情形外,總是與定冠詞連用) **1** not different; unchanged: 同一的;相同的;無變化的: *He is the ~ age as his wife.* 他與妻同年。 *We have lived in the ~ house for fifty years.* 我們五十年來一直住在這幢房子裡。 *We are all going the ~ way.* 我們將走同一條路。 **2 *the ~ ... that; the ~ ... as:*** *She uses the ~ scent that you do / the ~ scent as you.* 她用的香水和你的一樣。 ⇨ as² (13). **3** (with a relative clause introduced by *that, where, who,* etc. *As* replaces *that* if the *v* is omitted): (後接用 that, where, who 等所引導的關係子句;如關係子句中之動詞省略,則以 as 代替 that): *Put the book back in the ~ place where you found it.* 把書放回原位。 *Our eggs are sold the ~ day that / as they come in.* 我們的鷄蛋在進貨的當天就賣掉了。 *The price is the ~ as last year.* 這價格與去年相同。 *Are these the ~ people (whom) we saw here last week?* 這些就是我們上週在此地看到的那些人嗎? **4** (as *pron*) the same thing: (用作代名詞)同樣之事物: *We must all say the ~.* 我們大家必須說相同的話。 *I would do the ~ again.* 我願重做一次。 ***be all / just the ~ to,*** make no difference to; be a matter of indifference to: 對…一樣;對…無關緊要: *You can do it now or leave it till later; it's all the ~ to me.* 你現在做或留待以後做,對我都一樣。 **5** (in phrases) (用於片語中) ***come / amount to the ~ thing,*** have the ~ result, meaning, etc: 具有相同的結果、意義等: *You may pay in cash or cheque; it comes to the ~ thing.* 你付現款或支票,結果是一樣的。 ***the very ~,*** (emph): (強勢語): *You've made the very ~ mistake again!* 你又犯了一模一樣的錯誤! ***one and the ~,*** absolutely the ~: 完全相同的: *Dr Jekyll and Mr Hyde were one and the ~ person.* 吉柯醫生和海德先生是同一人。 ***at the ~ time,*** **(a)** together: 共同地;同時: *Don't all speak at the ~ time.* 不要同時說話。 *She was laughing and crying at the ~ time.* 她一面笑一面哭。 **(b)** (introducing a fact, etc that is to be borne in mind) yet; still; nevertheless: (引導一項須予記住的事實等)然而;可是: *At the ~ time you must not forget that....* 可是,你切不可忘記…。 **6** (with *this, that, these, those*) already thought of, mentioned or referred to: (與 this, that, these, those 連用)已想到、談到或提到的;上述的: *I stayed at home on Monday, and on that ~ day, the office was wrecked by a bomb.* 星期一我在家裡,就在那天,辦公室被一枚炸彈毀壞了。 **7** (as *pron*, often without the *def art*; comm use only): (用作代名詞,常無定冠詞,僅作商業用語): *To dry-cleaning suit, £3; to repairing ~, £2.* 乾洗一套衣服,三鎊;修補一套衣服,二鎊。 □ *adv* in the ~ way: 同樣地;相同地: *Old people do not feel the ~ about these things as the younger generation.* 對於這些事情,老年人和年輕的一代持不同的看法。 ***all the ~,*** nevertheless: 仍然;然而: *He's not very reliable, but I like him all the ~.* 他不很可靠,但我仍然喜歡他。 **~·ness** *n* [U] the condition of being the ~, of being uninteresting through lack of variety. 同一;相同;單調乏味。

samo·var /ˈsæməvɑː(r) ; ˈsæmə,vɑr/ *n* metal urn with an interior tube, used in Russia for boiling water for tea. 俄國之開水壺(有一內管,用以煮開水沏茶)。

sam·pan /ˈsæmpæn ; ˈsæmpæn/ *n* small, flat-bottomed boat used along the coasts and rivers of China. (中國沿海及內河用的)舢板。

a sampan

sample /ˈsɑːmpl *US:* ˈsæmpl ; ˈsæmpl/ *n* [C] specimen; one of a number, part of a whole, taken to show what the rest is like (esp as offered by a dealer in goods sold by weight or measure). 標本;樣品;(尤指按重量或大小售物時商人提出的)貨樣。 ***up to ~,*** (comm) (of goods) equal in quality to the ~ offered. (商)(指貨物)和樣品相符。 □ *vt* [VP6A] take a ~ or ~s of; test a part of: 取…的樣品;試驗…的一部分: *spend an hour at the wine-shop, sampling* (= making a random sampling of) *the wines.* 在酒店內花費一小時抽驗各種酒。

sam·pler/ ˈsɑːmplə(r) *US:* ˈsæm- ; ˈsæmplɚ/ *n* piece of cloth embroidered to show skill in needlework, often displayed on a wall. 刺繡樣品(用以表示刺繡技藝,常貼於牆上)。

sam·urai /ˈsæmʊraɪ ; ˈsæmʊ,raɪ/ *n* **1** ***the ~,*** the military caste in feudal Japan. (日本封建時代之)武士階級。 **2** member of this caste. (日本封建時代之)武士。

sana·tor·ium /ˌsænəˈtɔːrɪəm ; ˌsænəˈtorɪəm/ (US also **sana·tar·ium** /ˌsænəˈteərɪəm ; ˌsænəˈtærɪəm/) *n* establishment for the treatment of invalid or convalescent people. 療養院;休養地。

sanc·tify /ˈsæŋktɪfaɪ ; ˈsæŋktə,faɪ/ *vt* (*pt, pp* -fied) [VP6A] make holy; set apart as sacred. 使神聖;尊崇。 **sanc·ti·fi·ca·tion** /ˌsæŋktɪfɪˈkeɪʃn ; ˌsæŋktəfəˈkeʃən/ *n*

sanc·ti·moni·ous /ˌsæŋktɪˈməʊnɪəs ; ˌsæŋktəˈmonɪəs/ *adj* making a show of being devout. 僞裝虔誠的。 **~·ly** *adv*

sanc·tion /ˈsæŋkʃn ; ˈsæŋkʃən/ *n* **1** [U] right or permission given by authority to do sth: (做某事的)權利或許可;批准: *a book that was translated without the ~ of the author and publisher.* 未經作者及出版商認可而逐譯的一本書。 **2** [U] approval, encouragement (of behaviour, etc), by general custom or tradition. 一般習俗或傳統(對行爲等)的贊許,支持。 **3** [C] penalty intended to maintain or restore respect for law or authority, esp as adopted by several States together against a country violating international law: (爲維持或恢復法律或權威的尊嚴所作的) 處罰;制裁 (尤指幾國聯合對某一違反國際法的國家之制裁): *apply arms / economic ~s against an aggressor country:* 對侵略國禁供武器(作經濟制裁)。 **4** [C] reason for obeying a rule, etc: 遵守規則等的原因;維護道德的約束力: *The best moral ~ is that of conscience; the worst ~ is the fear of punishment.* 最好的道德拘束力是良心的約束力;最壞的約束力是對懲罰的恐懼。 □ *vt* [VP6A] give a ~ to; agree to: 批准;認可: *Would you ~ flogging as a punishment for crimes of violence?* 你同意以鞭打作爲對暴行的一種處罰嗎?

sanc·tity /ˈsæŋktətɪ ; ˈsæŋktətɪ/ *n* (*pl* -ties) **1** [U] holiness; sacredness; saintliness: 神聖;莊嚴;聖潔: *violate the ~ of an oath.* 違背誓言的神聖。 **2** (*pl*) sacred obligations, feelings, etc: (複)神聖的義務,感情等: *the sanctities of the home.* 對家庭的神聖義務。

sanc·tu·ary /ˈsæŋktʃʊərɪ *US:* -ʊerɪ ; ˈsæŋktʃʊ,ɛrɪ/ *n* (*pl* -ries) **1** holy or sacred place, esp a church, temple or mosque. 聖所;聖地;(尤指)教堂;廟;回教寺院。 **2** chancel of a church. 聖壇。 **3** sacred place (eg the altar of a church) where, in former times, a person running away from the law or his creditors was secure, by Church law, against arrest or violence. 至聖所(如教堂內之祭壇、內殿,按昔時之教會法,逃犯或逃債者至此處可獲安全)。 **4** [U] (right of offering) freedom from arrest: 不受拘捕之權;庇護;庇護權: *to seek / take / be offered ~.* 尋求(受到)庇護。 **5** place of refuge: 庇護所;避難所: *Great Britain has always been a ~ of political refugees from many parts of the world.* 英國一直是世界各地政治犯的庇護所。 **6** area where by law it is forbidden to kill birds, rob their nests, etc, or to shoot animals, etc: 禁獵區: *a ˈbird-~.* 鳥類禁獵區。

sanc·tum /ˈsæŋktəm ; ˈsæŋktəm/ *n* **1** holy place. 聖地;聖所。 **2** (colloq) person's private room or study. (俗)私室;書房。

sand /sænd ; sænd/ *n* **1** [U] (mass of) finely crushed rock as seen on the seashore, in river-beds, deserts, etc: 沙: *mix ~ and cement to make concrete.* 將沙和水泥混合造成混凝土。 **2** (often *pl*) expanse of ~ (on the seashore or a desert): (常用複數)(海灘上或沙漠中的)沙地: *children playing on the ~(s).* 在沙地玩耍的小孩們。 **3** (*pl*) (複) ***The ~s are running out,*** (with reference to the ~ running through an hour-glass, etc) There is not much time left; time is passing. (源自沙漏等中流下的沙)餘時不多了。 **4** (compounds) (複合字) **ˈ~·bag** *n* bag filled with ~ used as a defence (in war, against rising flood-water, etc). 沙袋;沙包(用於作戰,防洪等)。 **ˈ~·bank** *n* bank or shoal of ~ in a river or the sea. (河或海的)沙洲;沙灘;淺灘。 **ˈ~-bar** *n* bank of ~ at the mouth of a river or harbour. (河口或港口的)沙洲。 **ˈ~-blast** *vt* [VP6A] send a jet of ~ against sth, eg stonework, to clean it, or against metal or glass to cut or make a design on it. (用壓縮空氣等噴出以清洗石造物,或割切金屬、玻璃等之)噴沙。 **ˈ~·boy** *n* (now used only in) (現僅用於) ***as happy as a ~boy,*** very happy. 極快樂。 **ˈ~ dune** *n* mound of ~, formed by the wind. 沙丘。 **ˈ~-fly** *n* (*pl* -flies) kind of midge common on seashores. 沙蠅;蚋。 **ˈ~-glass** *n* glass with two connected bulbs containing enough ~ to take a definite time, eg five minutes, one hour, in passing from one bulb to the other. 沙漏;沙鐘。 **ˈ~-paper** *n* [U] strong paper with ~ glued to it, used for rubbing rough surfaces smooth. 沙紙。 □ *vt* [VP6A] make smooth with ~paper. 用沙紙磨光。 **ˈ~·piper** *n* small bird living in wet, sandy places near streams. 磯鷸 (棲於溪流附近之濕沙地的一種小鳥)。 ⇨ the illus at water. 參看 water 之插圖。 **ˈ~-pit** *n* unroofed enclosure filled with ~, for children to play in. 沙坑(供兒童遊戲用)。'~-**shoes** *n pl* canvas shoes with rubber or hemp soles for wearing on sandy seashores. (沙灘上穿之)橡皮或大麻底的帆布鞋。'~-**stone** *n* rock formed of compressed ~. 砂岩。'~-**storm** *n* storm in a sandy desert with clouds of ~ raised by the wind. 大風沙;沙暴。□ *vt* [VP6A] cover, sprinkle or scrub with ~. 覆以沙;撒以沙;用沙或沙紙磨擦。**sandy** *adj* (-ier, -iest) **1** covered with or consisting of ~: 覆有沙的;沙質的: *a ~y bottom*, eg of part of the sea. 沙質的(海)底。 **2** (of hair, etc) yellowish-red. (指毛髮等)沙色的; 淺茶色的。 □ *n* (colloq) nickname given to a person with yellowish-red hair. (俗)髮呈沙色之人的綽號。

san·dal /'sændl ; 'sændḷ/ *n* kind of open shoe made of a sole and heel with straps to hold it on the foot. (繫以條帶的)草鞋;涼鞋;便鞋。~**led** /'sændld ; 'sændḷd/ *adj* wearing ~s. 穿草鞋、涼鞋或便鞋的。

san·dal·wood /'sændlwʊd ; 'sændḷ,wʊd/ *n* [U] hard, sweet-smelling wood used for making fans, caskets, etc. 檀香木(堅硬味香的木材,用於製扇,盒子等)。

sand·wich /'sænwɪdʒ *US:* -wɪtʃ ; 'sændwɪtʃ/ *n* [C] two slices of buttered bread with meat, etc between: 中間夾肉等並塗有牛油的兩片麵包; 三明治: *ham / chicken / cheese, etc ~es.* 火腿(鷄肉,乳酪等)三明治。'~-**man** /-mæn ; -,mæn/ *n* (*pl* -men) man who walks about the streets with two advertisement boards, one hanging over his chest and the other over his back. 胸前及背後均掛一廣告板遊街的人;夾板廣告員。'~-**board** *n* one of such boards. 夾板廣告員背後或胸前所掛的廣告牌。'~ **course**, course of training with alternating periods of theoretical and practical study. 理論與實習交替配合之課程。□ *vt* [VP6A, 14] ~ ***(between)***, put (one thing or person) between two others, esp when there is little space: 將(一物或一人)夾在(兩物或兩人)中間;插入: *I was ~ed between two very fat men on the bus.* 我在公共汽車上被夾在兩個非常肥胖的人之間。

sane /seɪn ; sen/ *adj* (-r, -st) **1** healthy in mind; not mad. 心智健全的;神志清楚的。 **2** sensible; balanced: 明智的;穩健的: *a ~ policy;* 穩健的政策; *~ views / judgement.* 明智的看法(判斷)。~**·ly** *adv*

sang /sæŋ ; sæŋ/ *pt* of sing.

sang froid /,sɑːŋ 'frwɑː ; sɑ̃'frwɑ/ *n* [U] (F) calmness in face of danger or in an emergency; composure. (法)(面臨危險或危急時之)鎮定;冷靜;從容。

san·gui·nary /'sæŋgwɪnərɪ *US:* -nerɪ ; 'sæŋgwɪn,ɛrɪ/ *adj* (formal, old use) (正式用語,舊用法) **1** with much bloodshed: 血腥的;殺傷甚多的: *a ~ battle.* 血戰。 **2** fond of bloodshed; delighting in cruel acts: 嗜殺的;殘暴的: *a ~ ruler.* 殘暴的統治者。

san·guine /'sæŋgwɪn ; 'sæŋgwɪn/ *adj* (formal) (正式用語) **1** hopeful; optimistic: 有望的;樂天的: *~ of success;* 對成功抱樂觀; *~ that we shall succeed.* 自信我們將成功。 **2** having a red complexion. 面色紅潤的。

sani·tarium /,sænɪ'teərɪəm ; ,sænə'tɛrɪəm/ *n* (US) sanatorium; health resort. (美)療養院;休養地。

sani·tary /'sænɪtrɪ *US:* -terɪ ; 'sænə,tɛrɪ/ *adj* **1** clean; free from dirt which might cause disease: 清潔的;無致病之汚垢的: *poor ~ conditions in a camp.* 露營地的環境不清潔。 **2** of, concerned with, the protection of health: 保健的;有關保健的;衞生的: *a '~ inspector,* official whose duty it is to see that regulations for the protection of health are obeyed. 衞生檢查員。'~ **towel / napkin**, absorbent pad used during menstruation. 月經帶;衞生棉。

sani·ta·tion /,sænɪ'teɪʃn ; ,sænə'teʃən/ *n* [U] arrangements to protect public health, esp for the efficient disposal of sewage. 衞生;衞生設備(尤指下水道設備)。

san·ity /'sænətɪ ; 'sænətɪ/ *n* [U] **1** health of mind. 心智健全; 神智清明。 **2** soundness of judgement. 判斷正確;明達。

sank /sæŋk ; sæŋk/ *pt* of sink².

sans /sænz ; sænz/ *prep* (colloq) without: (俗)無;缺乏: *S~ teeth, ~ eyes, ~ taste, ~ everything.* 無齒,無眼,無味,無一切。

San·skrit /'sænskrɪt ; 'sænskrɪt/ *n* the ancient language of India; the literary language of Hinduism. 梵語;梵文(印度古語)。

Santa Claus /'sæntə klɔːz ; 'sæntɪ,klɔz/ *n* (also 亦稱 *Father Christmas*) person who, small children are told, puts toys in their stockings by night at Christmas. 聖誕老人(兒童們常聽說,他會在聖誕夜放置玩具於他們的長統襪中)。

sap¹ /sæp ; sæp/ *vt* (-pp-) [VP6A] weaken; drain away the life and strength of: 削弱;使逐漸損壞;耗竭…的生命和力量: *sapped by disease / an unhealthy climate.* 因疾病(有害健康之氣候)而體力逐漸衰弱的。

sap² /sæp ; sæp/ *n* [C] tunnel or covered trench made to get nearer to the enemy (eg in a military strong-point or, formerly, a beseiged town). (接近敵人之軍事據點或昔時被圍之城池的) 地道; 對壕。'**sap-head** *n* end of a sap nearest to the enemy. 地道之最接近敵人的一端。□ *vt, vi* (-pp-) [VP6A, 2A] make a sap or saps; weaken (a wall, etc) by digging under it; (fig) destroy or weaken (sb's faith, confidence, etc). 挖地道;在(牆等)下面挖掘而損壞之;(喻)打擊或削弱(某人的信心,自信等)。**sap·per** *n* soldier engaged in making saps or (mod use) in engineering, eg road and bridge building. 挖地道之士兵;(現代用法)工兵(如從事築路造橋者)。

sap³ /sæp ; sæp/ *n* (dated sl) silly person. (過時俚語)笨人;傻子。

sap⁴ /sæp ; sæp/ *n* [U] **1** liquid in a plant, carrying food to all its parts: 樹液(將養料輸至各部分者): *The sap is beginning to rise in the maple-trees.* 樹液開始在楓樹中上升了(楓樹開始復甦了)。**sap·wood** /'sæpwʊd ; 'sæp,wʊd/ *n* soft, outer layers of wood. 邊材 (木之柔軟的外層)。 **2** (fig) (anything that provides) vigour or energy. (喻)元氣;精力;供給元氣或精力之任何事物。**sap·less** *adj* without sap; dry; lacking vigour. 無樹液的; 枯萎的; 無精力的。**sap·ling** /'sæplɪŋ ; 'sæplɪŋ/ *n* young tree; (fig) young man. 樹苗; (喻) 青年人。**sappy** *adj* (-ier, -iest) full of sap; young and vigorous. 多樹液的;年富力强的。

sa·pi·ent /'seɪpɪənt ; 'sepɪənt/ *adj* (liter) wise. (文)有智慧的。 ~**·ly** *adv* **sa·pi·ence** /-əns ; -əns/ *n* (often ironic) wisdom. (常爲反語)智慧。

Sap·phic /'sæfɪk ; 'sæfɪk/ *adj* of the Greek lesbian poetess Sappho. (希臘女詩人)莎孚的;莎孚式的。~ **verse / stanza / ode**, (prosody) with three lines that rhyme and one short line. (韻律學)莎孚式詩(詩節,賦)(三行押韻及一短行)。

sap·phire /'sæfaɪə(r) ; 'sæfaɪr/ *n* **1** [C] clear, bright blue jewel. 青玉;藍寶石。**2** [U] bright blue colour. 青玉色;蔚藍色。

sara·band /'særəbænd ; 'særə,bænd/ *n* [C] (piece of music for a) stately old Spanish dance. 莎拉邦舞(一種莊重的舊式西班牙舞);莎拉邦舞曲。

Sara·cen /'særəsn ; 'særəsṇ/ *n* (name used by later Greeks and Romans for) Arab or Muslim of the time of the Crusades. 撒拉遜人;(後世希臘人和羅馬人用以指十字軍東征時之)阿拉伯人或回教徒。

sar·casm /'sɑːkæzəm ; 'sɑrkæzəm/ *n* [U] (use of) bitter remarks intended to wound the feelings; [C] such a remark; taunt that is ironically worded. 有意傷人感情的惡言;譏諷;譏諷之使用;譏諷話;語含諷刺的嘲弄。**sar·cas·tic** /sɑː'kæstɪk ; sɑr'kæstɪk/ *adj* of, using, ~. 譏諷的;使用譏諷的。 **sar·cas·ti·cally** /-klɪ ; -klɪ/ *adv*

sar·copha·gus /sɑː'kɒfəgəs ; sɑr'kɑfəgəs/ *n* (*pl* -gi /-gaɪ ; -dʒaɪ/, ~es /-gəsɪz ; -gəsɪz/) stone coffin (esp as used in ancient times). 石棺(尤指古代所用者)。⇨ the illus at mummy. 參看 mummy 之插圖。

sar·dine /sɑː'diːn ; sɑr'din/ *n* small fish (a young pilchard), usu preserved and tinned in oil or tomato sauce. 沙丁魚(通常浸於油中或蕃茄醬裝罐保藏之)。***packed like ~s,*** closely crowded together. 擁擠不堪。

sar·donic /sɑːˈdɒnɪk ; sɑrˈdɑnɪk/ *adj* mocking; scornful: 諷刺的;譏誚的: *a ~ smile/laugh/expression.* 嘲弄的微笑(大笑，表情)。 **sar·doni·cally** /-klɪ ; -klɪ/ *adv*

sari /ˈsɑːrɪ ; ˈsari/ *n* (*pl* ~s) length of cotton or silk cloth draped round the body, worn by Hindu women. 印度女人披裹身上的一段棉布或綢布。

sa·rong /səˈrɒŋ *US:* -ˈrɔːŋ ; səˈrɔŋ/ *n* long strip of cotton or silk material worn as a skirt round the middle of the body, tucked round the waist, the national garment of Malays and Indonesians (men and women). 沙籠(裹於身體中部之長條棉布或綢布,在腰際摺入,是馬來人和印尼人的民族服裝);馬來圍裙。

sar·sa·pa·rilla /ˌsɑːspəˈrɪlə ; ˌsɑrspəˈrɪlə/ *n* [U] (tonic drink made from the roots of a) tropical American plant. 撒爾沙(一種熱帶美洲產的植物);(用撒爾沙根做成之)撒爾沙汽水;沙士。

sar·tor·ial /sɑːˈtɔːrɪəl ; sɑrˈtorɪəl/ *adj* concerned with (the making of) men's clothes: 男裝的;縫製男裝的: *~ elegance.* 男性服裝的優雅。

sash[1] /sæʃ ; sæʃ/ *n* [C] long strip of cloth worn round the waist or over one shoulder for ornament or as part of a uniform. 腰帶;肩帶(用作裝飾或作爲制服的一部分)。

sash[2] /sæʃ ; sæʃ/ *n* ~ **window,** one that slides up and down (instead of opening outwards like a casement). 上下拉動的窗子(非如一般開闔窗戶之向外推開)。⇨ the illus at window. 參看 window 之插圖。 **'~-cord/-line** *n* strong cord (with a weight at one end) running over a pulley to keep the window balanced in any desired position. 曳窗繩(用以上下拉動窗戶,一端有墜子的結實的繩子,滾動滑車以使該窗戶在任何所希望的位置保持平衡)。

Sas·sen·ach /ˈsæsənæk ; ˈsæsnˌæk/ *n* (derog or hum) (name used by the Scots for an) English person. (貶或諧)英格蘭人(爲蘇格蘭人對英格蘭人之稱呼)。

sassy /ˈsæsɪ ; ˈsæsɪ/ *adj* (US colloq) lively; stylish. (美俗)有生氣的;漂亮的。

sat /sæt ; sæt/ *pt, pp* of sit.

Satan /ˈseɪtn ; ˈsetn/ *n* the Evil One, the Devil. 撒旦;惡魔。 **~ic** /səˈtænɪk *US:* seɪ- ; seˈtænɪk/ *adj* **1** of ~: 撒旦的;惡魔的: *His ~ic Majesty,* (hum) Satan. (諧)撒旦。 **2** (small **s**) wicked; evil. (小寫 s)邪惡的;如惡魔的。

satchel /ˈsætʃl ; ˈsætʃəl/ *n* small bag for carrying light articles, esp school books. 皮包;小帆布袋(用於携帶輕便東西,尤用於上下學携帶書籍);書包。

sate /seɪt ; set/ *vt* [VP6A] = satiate.

sat·el·lite /ˈsætəlaɪt ; ˈsætlˌaɪt/ *n* **1** comparatively small body moving in orbit round a planet; moon; artificial object, eg a spacecraft, put in orbit round a celestial body: 衛星;人造衛星: *comˌmuniˈcations ~,* for relaying back to the earth telephone messages, radio and TV signals. 通信衛星。 **2** (fig, often attrib) person, state, depending upon and taking the lead from another. (喻,常作形容用法)追隨者;附庸國。 **'~ town,** one built to take the excess population of another. 衛星城鎮(用以疏散大城市之人口者)。

sati·able /ˈseɪʃəbl ; ˈseʃɪəbl/ *adj* (formal) that can be fully satisfied. (正式用語)可使滿足的;可使飽的。

sati·ate /ˈseɪʃɪeɪt ; ˈseʃɪˌet/ *vt* [VP6A] (formal) satisfy fully; cloy; weary (oneself) with too much: (正式用語)使滿足;使飽;(因過多而)使(自己)厭膩: *be ~d with food/pleasure.* 因過多食物(享樂)而厭膩。

sat·iety /səˈtaɪətɪ ; səˈtaɪətɪ/ *n* [U] (formal) condition or feeling of being satiated: (正式用語)滿足;飽足;厭膩: *indulge in pleasure to the point of ~.* 耽於享樂而達厭膩的程度。

satin /ˈsætɪn *US:* ˈsætn ; ˈsætɪn/ *n* [U] silk material smooth and shiny on one side: 緞(一面光滑的絲織品): (attrib) (形容用法) *~ dresses/ribbons.* 緞子衣服(緞帶)。□ *adj* smooth like ~. 光澤如緞的。

a sari　a sarong　a kimono

sat·in·wood /ˈsætɪnwʊd *US:* ˈsætn- ; ˈsætnˌwʊd/ *n* [U] smooth, hard wood of a tropical tree, used for furniture. 緞木(一種熱帶樹的光滑硬木材,用以做傢具)。

sat·ire /ˈsætaɪə(r) ; ˈsætaɪr/ *n* **1** [U] form of writing holding up a person or society to ridicule, or showing the foolishness or wickedness of an idea, customs, etc. 諷刺文體(譏笑個人或社會,或揭露觀念,習俗等的愚昧)。 **2** [C] piece of writing that does this; sth that exposes false pretensions: 諷刺作品;諷刺文;諷刺詩;諷刺: *Are our lives sometimes a ~ upon our religious beliefs?* 我們的生命有時是我們宗教信仰的一種諷刺嗎? **sa·tiri·cal** /səˈtɪrɪkl ; səˈtɪrɪkl/ *adj* containing, fond of using, ~; mocking. 含有諷刺的;喜好諷刺的;嘲弄的。**sa·tiri·cally** /-klɪ ; -klɪ/ *adv* **sat·ir·ist** /ˈsætərɪst ; ˈsætərɪst/ *n* person who writes ~s. 諷刺作家。 **sat·ir·ize** /ˈsætəraɪz ; ˈsætəˌraɪz/ *vt* [VP6A] attack with ~(s); describe satirically. 以諷刺文或作品攻擊;諷刺地描寫。

sat·is·fac·tion /ˌsætɪsˈfækʃn ; ˌsætɪsˈfækʃən/ *n* **1** [U] the state of being satisfied, pleased or contented; act of satisfying: 滿意;滿足;令人滿意的舉動: *feel ~ at having one's ability recognized;* 由於自己的才能得到賞識而覺得滿足; *have the ~ of being successful in life;* 一生成功覺得心滿意足; *pass an examination to one's own ~ and to the ~ of one's friends;* 通過考試使自己和友人都感到滿意; *the ~ of one's hopes/desires/ambitions.* 希望(欲望,野心)的實現。 **2** (with *indef art,* but rarely *pl*) sth that satisfies: (與不定冠詞連用,但罕用複數)令人滿意之事物: *Your success will be a great ~ to your parents.* 你的成功將使你的父母極感滿意。 *It is a ~ to know that he is well again.* 得悉他已痊愈,深感欣慰。 **3** [U] (opportunity of getting) revenge or compensation for an injury or insult: 報復;補償;報復或補償的機會: *give sb/demand/obtain ~.* 給予某人(要求,獲得)補償。 *The angry man demanded ~ but the other refused it,* would neither apologize nor fight. 那憤怒的人要求決鬥,但對方拒絕了(既不肯道歉也不肯決鬥)。

sat·is·fac·tory /ˌsætɪsˈfæktərɪ ; ˌsætɪsˈfæktrɪ/ *adj* giving pleasure or satisfaction; satisfying a need or desire; good enough for a purpose: 令人滿意的;滿足需要或欲望的;圓滿的;良好的: *The result of the experiment was ~.* 實驗的結果令人滿意。 *We want ~ reasons for your failure to help.* 我們要知道你未能協助的充分理由。 **sat·is·fac·tor·ily** /-tərəlɪ ; -trəlɪ/ *adv* in a ~ manner: 令人滿意地;圓滿地: *The patient is getting on satisfactorily.* 病人康復令人滿意。

sat·isfy /ˈsætɪsfaɪ ; ˈsætɪsˌfaɪ/ *vt, vi* (*pt, pp* -fied) **1** [VP6A, 2A] make contented; give (sb) what he wants or needs: 使滿意;使滿足;滿足(某人)的需求: *Nothing satisfies him; he's always complaining.* 任何事物都不能使他滿足;他總是抱怨。 *Riches do not* *always* ~. 財富並不能永遠使人滿足。 ~ ***the examiners,*** just reach the lowest standard needed for passing an examination. 剛好達到及格的最低標準；考及格。 **2** [VP6A, 2A] be enough for (one's needs); be equal to (what one hopes for or desires): 足够(自己的需要)；達到(所期望或欲求者)： ~ *one's hunger.* 充飢。 **3** [VP6A, 11, 14] ~ ***sb (that... / of sth),*** convince; make free from doubt: 使確信；使消除疑慮： *He satisfied me that he could do the work well.* 他使我確信他能把工作做好。 *Have you satisfied yourself of the truth of the report?* 你確信那報告的眞實性嗎？ **~·ing** *adj* giving satisfaction: 使滿意的；令人滿足的： *a ~ing meal.* 令人滿意的一頓飯。 **~·ing·ly** *adv*

sa·trap /ˈsætræp *US:* ˈseɪtræp ; ˈsetræp/ *n* governor of a province in the ancient Persian empire. (古波斯帝國的)省長。

sat·suma /ˌsætˈsuːmə ; ˌsætˈsumə/ *n* tangerine. 小蜜柑；紅橘。

satu·rate /ˈsætʃəreɪt ; ˈsætʃəˌret/ *vt* [VP6A, 14] ~ ***(with / in),*** **1** make thoroughly wet; soak with moisture; cause to take in as much as possible of sth: 浸；浸透；浸濕；使儘量吸收某物： *We were caught in the rain and came home ~d.* 我們途中遇雨，回到家全身都濕透了。 *They lay on the beach and were ~d with sunshine.* 他們躺在沙灘上，沐浴在陽光裡。 *He is ~d with Greek history.* 他精通希臘史。 **2** be unable to take any more: 飽和；飽和狀態： *The market for used cars is ~d.* 舊車買賣的市場已趨飽和。 **3** (chem) cause (one substance) to absorb the greatest possible amount of another: (化學)使(一物質)吸收他物達於飽和： *a ~d solution of salt.* 飽和的食鹽溶液。 **satu·ra·tion** /ˌsætʃəˈreɪʃn ; ˌsætʃəˈreʃən/ *n* [U] state of being ~d. 浸透，飽和的狀態。 **saturation bombing,** bombing so that everything in the target area is totally destroyed. 飽和轟炸(完全炸毀)。 **ˌsatuˈration point,** (chem) the stage at which, if more of one substance is added to another, they will not unite completely: (化學)飽和點(過此階段時，再加某一物質於另一物質，這兩種物質就不能完全混合)： *The saturation point of a hot liquid is higher than that of a cold one,* eg more sugar can be dissolved in hot tea than in cold tea; (fig) stage at which no more can be absorbed or accepted. 熱液的飽和點高於冷液(例如熱茶比冷茶能溶解更多的糖)；(喻)飽和階段。

Sat·ur·day /ˈsætədɪ ; ˈsætɚdɪ/ *n* the seventh and last day of the week. 星期六；土曜日。

Sat·urn /ˈsætən ; ˈsætɚn/ *n* **1** (astron) large planet encircled by rings. (天文)土星。 ⇨ the illus at planet. 參看 planet 之插圖。 **2** (myth) ancient Roman god of agriculture. (神話)(古羅馬之)農神。

sat·ur·na·lia /ˌsætəˈneɪlɪə ; ˌsætɚˈnelɪə/ *n pl* **1 S~,** yearly festival of the god Saturn, held in ancient Rome in December, a time of wild merry-making. (大寫 S)農神節(古羅馬於十二月慶祝者，爲一年一度之狂歡期)。 **2** [C] time of wild revelry or disorder. 狂歡或喧囂之時節。

sat·ur·nine /ˈsætənaɪn ; ˈsætɚˌnaɪn/ *adj* (liter) gloomy. (文)憂鬱的；陰沉的。

satyr /ˈsætə(r) ; ˈsætɚ/ *n* **1** (Gk and Roman myth) god of the woods, half man and half animal. (希臘及羅馬神話)半人半獸的森林之神。 **2** man with uncontrolled sexual desires. 色情狂者；性慾無度之男人。 **sa·tyric** /səˈtɪrɪk ; səˈtɪrɪk/ *adj* of or like ~s. 色情狂的；淫慾的。

sauce /sɔːs ; sɔs/ *n* **1** [C, U] (kind of) liquid or semi-liquid preparation served with some kinds of food to give a relish or flavour: (一種)調味汁；醬汁： *spaghetti and tomato ~;* 義大利麵條和蕃茄醬； *fruit pudding and brandy ~.* 水果布丁和白蘭地調味汁。 ***What is ~ for the goose is ~ for the gander,*** (prov) what applies in one case must apply in an identical or similar case. (諺)適用於某種情況者，亦必適用於類似情況。 **ˈ~-boat** *n* vessel in which ~ is served at table. 餐桌上盛調味汁的器皿。 **2** [U] (colloq) impudence (usu amusing rather than annoying): (俗)無禮；莽撞(通常爲有趣而非令人惱怒者)： *None of your ~!* Don't be impertinent. 不可莽撞！放規矩點！ *What ~!* How impudent! 多麼無禮！眞沒規矩！ □ *vt* [VP6A] (colloq) be impudent to: (俗)對…無禮或莽撞： *How dare you ~ your mother?* 你怎敢對令堂無禮？ **saucy** *adj* (-ier, -iest) **1** impudent. 無禮的；莽撞的。 **2** (colloq) smart-looking: (俗)時髦的；漂亮的；俊俏的： *a saucy little hat.* 一頂漂亮的小帽。 **sauc·ily** *adv* **sauci·ness** *n*

sauce·pan /ˈsɔːspən *US:* -pæn ; ˈsɔsˌpæn/ *n* deep metal cooking pot, usu round and with a lid and a handle. 深金屬鍋(通常爲圓形，有蓋及柄)。

saucer /ˈsɔːsə(r) ; ˈsɔsɚ/ *n* **1** small curved dish on which a cup stands. 茶杯碟；茶托。 **ˈ~-eyed** *adj* with large, round, wide-opened eyes, eg as the result of surprise. 眼睛睜得大而圓的(例如由於驚訝的緣故)。 **ˌflying ˈ~,** ⇨ flying. **2** ~-shaped disc (also called a *dish*) of a radio telescope. (無線電望遠鏡之)碟形盤。 **3** depression in the ground. 凹窪；窪地。

sauer·kraut /ˈsaʊəkraʊt ; ˈsaʊrˌkraʊt/ *n* [U] (G) cabbage cut up, salted and allowed to ferment until sour. (德)泡菜(包心菜切細，加鹽使發酵變酸)。

sauna /ˈsaʊnə ; ˈsaʊnə/ *n* steam bath or bath-house as in Finland. (芬蘭等地之)蒸氣浴；蒸氣浴室；三溫暖。

saun·ter /ˈsɔːntə(r) ; ˈsɔntɚ/ *vi* [VP2A, C] walk in a leisurely way: 閒逛；漫步： ~ *along Oxford Street window-shopping.* 沿牛津街漫步瀏覽商店櫥窗。 □ *n* quiet, unhurried walk or pace: 漫步；閒逛： *come at a ~.* 漫步走來。 **~er** *n* person who ~s. 漫步者；閒逛者。

saur·ian /ˈsɔːrɪən ; ˈsɔrɪən/ *n, adj* (one) of the order of lizards including crocodiles, lizards and some extinct kinds. 蜥蜴類動物(包括鱷魚，蜥蜴及若干已絕種的爬蟲動物)；蜥蜴類動物的。

saus·age /ˈsɒsɪdʒ *US:* ˈsɔːs- ; ˈsɔsɪdʒ/ *n* [U] chopped up meat, etc flavoured and stuffed into a casing or tube of thin skin; some kinds sliced and eaten raw, others cooked and eaten hot; [C] one section of such a tube. 臘腸；香腸；一段臘腸或香腸。 **ˈ~-dog,** (GB colloq) dachshund. (英俗)臘腸狗(一種短腿長身的小狗)；獵獾狗。 **ˈ~-meat** *n* meat for making ~s. 用來做臘腸的碎肉。 **ˌ~-ˈroll** *n* ~ in minced a covering of pastry. 臘腸捲(一種用麵皮包臘腸餡做成的點心)。

sauté /ˈsəʊteɪ *US:* səʊˈteɪ ; soˈte/ *adj* (F) (of food) quickly fried in a little fat: (法)(指食物，用少量的油)炒的；嫩煎的： ~ *potatoes.* 煎馬鈴薯。 □ *vt* fry food in this way. 炒；嫩煎。

sav·age /ˈsævɪdʒ ; ˈsævɪdʒ/ *adj* **1** in a primitive or uncivilized state: 野蠻的；未開化的： ~ *customs.* 野蠻的風俗。 **2** fierce; cruel: 兇猛的；殘酷的： *a ~ dog;* 惡犬； *make a ~ attack on sb;* 猛烈攻擊某人； ~ *criticism.* 猛烈的批評。 **3** (colloq) very angry. (俗)憤怒的。 □ *n* ~ person, esp a member of a primitive tribe living by hunting and fishing. 野人；野蠻人(尤指靠漁獵爲生之蠻族)。 □ *vt* [VP6A] attack, bite, trample on: 襲擊；亂咬；亂踏： *The man was badly ~d by his mare.* 那人被他的母馬傷得很嚴重。 **~·ly** *adv* **~·ness** *n* **~ry** /ˈsævɪdʒrɪ ; ˈsævɪdʒrɪ/ *n* [U] the state of being ~; ~ behaviour: 野蠻狀態；未開化；兇猛；殘酷；野蠻或殘酷的行爲： *living in ~ry;* 生活在野蠻狀態中； *treat conquered enemies with great ~ry.* 非常殘酷地對待被征服的敵人。

sa·van·na(h) /səˈvænə ; səˈvænə/ *n* [C] treeless, grassy plain, in tropical and subtropical America and E and W Africa. (熱帶和亞熱帶美洲及東西非洲地區之)無樹的平原；熱帶草原。 ⇨ pampas, prairie, steppe, veld.

sa·vant /ˈsævənt *US:* sæˈvɑːnt ; səˈvɑnt/ *n* person of great learning. 博學之士；學者；專家。

save[1] /seɪv ; sev/ *vt, vi* **1** [VP6A, 14] ~ ***(from),*** make or keep safe (from loss, injury, etc): 援救；

拯救;保全(以免損失,傷害等): ~ *sb from drowning;* 救人於溺; ~ *sb's life;* 救某人的性命; ~ *a person from himself,* from the results of his own foolishness. 使某人免於自食惡果。 **~ *one's bacon,*** ⇨ bacon. **~ *one's face,*** ⇨ face[1](4). **~ *one's skin,*** avoid, often by cowardice, the risk of loss, injury, etc. 避免損失,傷害等之危險(常出於膽怯)。 **~ *the situation,*** deal successfully with a situation which seems hopeless. 挽回頹勢;度過難關。 **2** [VP 2A, C, 3A, 6A, 12B, 13B, 14, 15B] **~ *(up) (for sth); ~ sth (up) (for sth),*** keep for future use: 儲存;貯蓄: ~ *(up) money for a holiday;* 儲錢度假; ~ *part of one's salary each month;* 貯蓄每月薪水的一部分; ~ *some of the meat for tomorrow;* 留下一些肉明天吃; ~ *me some ice-cream/~ some ice-cream for me;* 給我留點冰淇淋; ~ *for one's old age.* 存錢防老。 *He has never ~d,* never put money by for the future. 他從不儲蓄。 *He is saving himself/saving his strength for the heavy work he'll have to do this afternoon.* 他在養精蓄銳以應付今日下午他必須做的繁重工作。 **~ *for a rainy day,*** ⇨ rainy. **3** [VP6A, D, 12C] make unnecessary; relieve (sb) from the need of using: 省去;節省: *If you walk to the office every morning, you'll ~ spending money on bus fares.* 每天早上步行上班,可省去公共汽車費。 *That will ~ you 50 pence a week.* 那將可使你每星期節省五十辨士。 *That will ~ us a lot of trouble.* 那將可免除我們許多麻煩。 *We've been ~d a lot of expense by doing the work ourselves.* 我們自己做那工作,節省了一大筆開消。 *Do you use modern labour-saving devices in your home?* ie machines that make work (eg cleaning, cooking) in the home quicker and easier. 貴府使用節省勞力的現代化設備嗎? **4** [VP6A, 14, 2A] **~ *sb (from sth),*** (in the Christian religion) set free from the power of (or the eternal punishment for) sin: (基督教)拯救;赦罪: *Jesus Christ came into the world to ~ sinners from their sins.* 耶穌基督來到這世界拯救罪人。 **5** [VP6A] make a reservation concerning (sth): 作有關(某事物)之保留: *a saving clause,* one that stipulates an exemption, etc. 保留條款(規定免除事項等)。 □ *n* (in football, etc) act of preventing the scoring of a goal: (足球等)阻礙對方得分之動作;救球: *Banks made a brilliant ~.* 班克斯漂亮地救了一球。 **~r** *n* person who ~s: 救助者;拯救者;儉省之人: *a ~r of souls,* eg a priest; 靈魂的拯救者(例如牧師); means of saving: 節省…的器具: *This device is a useful 'time-~r.* 這是個有用的省時裝置。 *Some machines are ~rs of labour.* 有些機器是節省勞力的工具。 **sav·ing** *adj* (esp) that redeems or compensates. (尤指)彌補的;補償的。 **saving grace,** good quality that redeems a person whose other qualities are not all good: 可彌補個人缺點的優良天性: *He has the saving grace of humour.* 他有幽默的長處。 □ *n* **1** way of saving; amount ~d: 節省;儲存;節省或儲存之量: *a useful saving of time and money.* 一種有益的節省時間和金錢。 **2** *(pl)* money ~d up: (複)儲金;儲蓄: *keep one's savings in the Post Office.* 把儲蓄的錢存在郵政局。 **'savings account** *n* (with a bank) on which interest is paid. 儲蓄存款;儲蓄帳戶。 **'savings-bank** *n* bank which holds, and gives interest on, small savings. 儲蓄銀行。

save[2] /seɪv ; sev/ (also **sav·ing** /'seɪvɪŋ ; 'sevɪŋ/) *preps* except: 除…外: *all save him.* 除他以外全體。 *We know nothing about him save that he was in the army during the war.* 我們除了知道他在戰時曾在陸軍服務以外,其他一無所知。

sav·eloy /'sævəlɔɪ ; 'sævə,lɔɪ/ *n* [C] kind of highly-seasoned pork sausage. 一種味道很濃的豬肉臘腸。

sav·ing /'seɪvɪŋ ; 'sevɪŋ/ *prep* = save[2].

sav·iour (US = **-ior**) /'seɪvɪə(r) ; 'sevjɚ/ *n* person who rescues or saves sb from danger. 拯救者;救助者。 **The S~, Our S~,** Jesus Christ. 救世主(耶穌基督)。

savoir-faire /,sævwɑ: 'feə(r) ; 'sævwɑr'fɛr/ *n* [U] (F) social tact; knowledge of how to behave in any situation. (法)社交手腕;機敏;圓滑。

sa·vory /'seɪvərɪ ; 'sevərɪ/ *n* [U] herb of the mint family used in cooking; (US) (美) = savoury. (一種用於烹飪的)香薄荷。

sa·vour (US = **-vor**) /'seɪvə(r) ; 'sevɚ/ *n* [C, U] **~ *of,*** taste or flavour (of sth); suggestion (of a quality): (某物的)味道;滋味;風味;(某種性質的)跡象;意味: *soup with a ~ of garlic.* 有大蒜味道的湯。 *His political views have a ~ of fanaticism.* 他的政治見解帶有狂熱的意味。 □ *vt, vi* **1** [VP6A] (lit or fig) appreciate the taste or flavour or character of: (字面或喻) 欣賞…的味道或風味: *He ~ed the wine/the joke.* 他品嚐酒的味道(咀嚼一笑話的妙處)。 **2** [VP3A] **~ *of,*** suggest the presence: 具有…的意味: *Such a proposal ~s of impertinence.* 這樣的建議帶有莽撞的意味。

sa·voury (US = **-vory**) /'seɪvərɪ ; 'sevərɪ/ *adj* having an appetizing taste or smell; (of food dishes) having a salt or sharp, not a sweet, taste: 開胃的;可口的;香噴噴的;(指菜肴)鹹的;辛辣的: *a ~ omelette.* 可口的的蛋捲。 □ *n* [C] *(pl* -ries) ~ dish, esp one taken at the start or end of a meal. 開胃或助消化的菜(尤指餐前或餐後所吃者)。

sa·voy /sə'vɔɪ ; sə'vɔɪ/ *n* [C, U] (kind of) winter cabbage with wrinkled leaves. (一種)皺葉甘藍;皺葉捲心菜。

savvy /'sævɪ ; 'sævɪ/ *vi* (sl) know, understand. (俚)知道;了解。 **no ~,** I do not know/understand. 我不知道;不懂。 □ *n* [U] (sl) wits; understanding: (俚)機智;頭腦;理解: *Where's your ~?* 你的頭腦到那裡去了?

saw[1] /sɔ: ; sɔ/ *pt* of see[1].

saw[2] /sɔ: ; sɔ/ *n* [C] (kinds of) tool with a sharp-toothed edge, for cutting wood, metal, stone, etc worked by hand or mechanically. 鋸。 **'saw-dust** *n* [U] tiny bits of wood falling off when wood is being sawn. 鋸屑;木屑。 **'saw-horse** *n* frame of wood for supporting wood that is being sawn. 鋸木架。 **'saw-mill** *n* mill with power-operated saws. 鋸木廠;製材廠。 **'saw-pit** *n* pit in which a man stands guiding the lower part of a large hand-saw (= *pit-saw*) for sawing logs, the upper part being guided by another man at an upper level. 鋸木坑(人立其中操作一大鋸較低之一端,較高之另一端由另外一人操作)。 □ *vt, vi* (*pt* sawed, *pp* sawn /sɔ:n ; sɔn/ and (US) sawed) **1** [VP6A, 15A, B, 2A] cut with a saw; make (boards, etc) with a saw; use a saw: 鋸;鋸成(木板等);用鋸: *saw wood;* 鋸木材; *saw a log into planks;* 把圓木鋸成厚板; *saw a log in two.* 把一根木頭鋸成兩截。 ***saw sth off,*** cut off with a saw: 鋸掉(某物): *saw a branch off a tree;* 鋸掉樹枝; *a sawn-off shotgun,* one with (most of) the barrel sawn off (as used by criminals for ease of concealment and carrying). 槍管鋸短的槍(例如罪犯為便於隱藏或攜帶所用者)。 ***saw sth up,*** cut into pieces with a saw: 把某物鋸成小塊: *sawn-up timber,* timber that has been sawn into planks (contrasted with logs). 已鋸成厚板的木材(與圓木相對)。 **2** [VP2A, C, 6A] move backward and forward: 往復移動: *sawing at his fiddle,* using his bow as if it were a saw. 往復地拉提琴。 **3** [VP 2A] capable of being sawn: 可被鋸開: *This wood saws easily.* 此木材容易鋸開。 **saw·yer** /'sɔ:jə(r) ; 'sɔjɚ/ *n* man whose work is sawing wood. 鋸木匠。

saw[3] /sɔ: ; sɔ/ *n* [C] proverbial saying. 格言;諺語。

sax /sæks ; sæks/ *n* (abbr of) saxophone. 為 saxophone 之略。

sax·horn /'sækshɔ:n ; 'sæks,hɔrn/ *n* musical instrument made of brass, like a bugle, made in various sizes. 薩克號(銅製的喇叭,有多種尺寸)。

saxi·frage /'sæksɪfrɪdʒ ; 'sæksəfrɪdʒ/ *n* [U] kinds of Alpine or rock plant with white, yellow or red flowers. 虎耳草(生於高山或岩石間,開白、黃或紅花)。

Saxon /ˈsæksn; ˈsæksn̩/ *n, adj* (member, language) of a people once living in NW Germany, some of whom conquered and settled in Britain in the 5th and 6th cc. (昔時居住於德國西北部,其中部分人於五至六世紀時征服並定居英國)薩克遜人(的);薩克遜語(的)。

saxo·phone /ˈsæksəfəʊn; ˈsæksəˌfon/ *n* (colloq abbr 俗略作 *sax*) musical wind instrument with a reed in the mouthpiece and keys for the fingers, made of brass. 薩克管(一種銅管樂器)。⇨ the illus at brass. 參看 brass 之挿圖。**sax·ophon·ist** /sækˈsɒfənɪst *US:* ˈsæksəfəʊnɪst; ˈsæksəˌfonɪst/ *n* ~ player. 薩克管手;薩克管吹奏者。

say /seɪ; se/ *vt, vi* (*3rd pers, pres t* says /sez; sɛz/, *pt, pp* said /sed; sɛd/) [VP6A, 14, 9, 10] **1** ***say sth (to sb),*** utter; make (a specified word or remark); use one's voice to produce (words, sentences): 言;說(某字或話);講(辭,句): *Be polite and say 'Please' and 'Thank you'.* 要有禮貌,並且要說'請'和'謝謝你'。*Did you say anything?* 你說了什麼話嗎?*He said that his friend's name was Sam.* 他說他朋友的名字叫山姆。*Everyone was saying what a handsome couple they made.* 大家都說他們是郎才女貌的一對。*Everyone said how well I was looking.* 人人都說我氣色非常好。*I've something to say to you,* to tell you. 我有話要對你說。*I wouldn't say no to a glass of beer,* would accept one willingly. 我願意喝杯啤酒。*You may well say so,* you are right. 你那樣說很對(你說得對)。*So you say* (implying that the speaker may be mistaken). 你是那麼說的(含示對方可能有錯)。***go without saying,*** be obvious: 不用說;不待言: *It goes without saying that country life is healthier than town life.* 鄉村生活比城市生活更有益於健康,自不待言。***have nothing/anything to say for oneself,*** ie in one's own defence: 無可辯白(需要辯白): *Well, what have you to say for yourself,* What can you say to explain or defend your conduct? 你還有何話說? ***say the word,*** express agreement: 表示同意: *You've only to say the word* (eg say 'Yes') *and the money's yours,* ie I will let you have it. 只要你說聲同意,那筆錢就是你的了。***say a good word for sb/sth,*** commend; praise: 推薦;誇獎某人或某事物: *He hasn't a good word to say for anybody.* 他從不稱讚任何人。***say one's say,*** finish what one has to say: 說完所要說的話: *Have you said your say yet?* 你要說的話說完了嗎? ***that is to say,*** in other words: 換言之;即是: *three weeks tomorrow, that's to say, the 10th of May.* 三個星期後的明天,也就是說,五月十日。***What do you say (to sth/doing sth)?*** What do you think (about...): 你想不想…;你認爲…如何: *What do you say to a walk/to going round to my mother's?* 你想不想去散散步(到我母親那裡去走走)? ***I say,*** exclamation used to draw attention, open a conversation or express surprise. 我說;哎呀(用於引起注意,開始談話或表示驚訝的感嘆語)。***They say; It's said,*** forms used to introduce reports, rumours, etc: 據說(用以引述傳聞謠言等的語辭): *They say/It's said that he's a miser.* 據說他是小氣鬼。**2** (also [VP10] esp neg and interr) suppose; estimate; form and give an opinion concerning: (亦用作 VP10, 尤用於否定及疑問句中)假定;估計;姑且說;形成並說出有關…的意見: *There is no saying when this war will end.* 天曉得這場戰爭何時會結束。*And so say all of us,* that is the opinion of all of us. 我們全抱那種看法。*You may learn to play the violin in, let's say, three years.* 你大概要三年才可以學會拉小提琴。□ *n* (only in the following) (僅用於下列各片語中) ***have/say one's say,*** express one's opinion; state one's views: 表達意見;陳述觀點: *Let him have his say.* 讓他表達他的意見吧。***have a/no/not much, etc 'say in the matter,*** have some/no/not much right or opportunity to share in a discussion, decision, express one's opinions, etc: 在該事件中有若干(沒有,不大有)權利或機會參加討論、決定、表示自己的意見等: *He didn't have much say in deciding where they should spend their holidays.* 對於他們去那裡度假,他沒多少決定的權利。**say·ing** /ˈseɪɪŋ; ˈseɪŋ/ *n* remark commonly made; well-known phrase, proverb, etc: 諺語;格言;名言: *'More haste, less speed', as the saying goes.* 諺云,'欲速則不達'。

scab /skæb; skæb/ *n* **1** [C] dry crust formed over a wound or sore. (創口上結的)疤;痂。**2** [U] (= *scabies*) skin disease (esp of sheep). 癬;(尤指羊的)疥癬。**3** [C] (colloq) workman who refuses to join a strike, or his trade union, or who takes a striker's place; blackleg. (俗)不參加罷工的工人;不加入工會的工人;取代罷工者之職位的工人;破壞罷工者。**scabby** *adj* covered with scabs(1). 結痂的。

scab·bard /ˈskæbəd; ˈskæbəd/ *n* sheath for the blade of a sword, dagger or bayonet. (劍,匕首或刺刀的)鞘。⇨ the illus at sword. 參看 sword 之挿圖。

sca·bies /ˈskeɪbiːz; ˈskebɪˌiz/ *n* [U] kind of skin disease causing itching. 疥瘡(發癢的一種皮膚病)。

sca·bi·ous /ˈskeɪbɪəs; ˈskebɪəs/ *n* kinds of wild and cultivated plant with delicately coloured flowers. 山蘿蔔;輪峯菊(花色優美的多種野生和栽培植物)。

scab·rous /ˈskeɪbrəs *US:* ˈskæb-; ˈskebrəs/ *adj* **1** (of animals, plants, etc) having a rough surface. (指動植物等)表面粗糙的;不平滑的。**2** (of subjects) difficult to write delicately about. (指題目)難以寫得委婉的。**3** indelicate; salacious: 粗鄙的;猥褻的: *a ~ novel.* 一本猥褻的小說。

scads /skædz; skædz/ *n* (*sing* or *pl*) (單或複) ***~ (of),*** (US colloq) large quantity (of): (美俗)大量;許多: *~ of money/people.* 許多錢(人)。

scaf·fold /ˈskæfəʊld; ˈskæfl̩d/ *n* [C] **1** structure put up for workmen and materials around a building which is being erected or repaired. (建築或修繕房屋時四周所搭的)施工架;鷹架。**2** platform on which criminals are executed: 斷頭臺;絞臺: *go to the ~,* be executed. 上絞臺;被處死。**~·ing** /ˈskæfəldɪŋ; ˈskæfl̩dɪŋ/ *n* [U] (materials for a) ~(1) (eg poles and planks, or, *tubular ~ing,* metal tubes to be bolted together). 施工架;鷹架;搭施工架或鷹架用的材料(例如長竿和厚板,或用螺栓結合在一起的金屬管)。

scal·awag /ˈskæləwæg; ˈskæləˌwæg/ *n* (US) (美) = scallywag.

scald /skɔːld; skɔld/ *vt* [VP6A] **1** burn with hot liquid or steam: 燙傷: *~ one's hand with hot fat.* 被熱油燙傷手。*He was ~ed to death when the boiler exploded.* 汽鍋爆炸時,他被燙死了。 **~ing tears,** tears of deep and bitter grief. 熱淚;血淚。**2** clean (dishes, etc) with boiling water or steam. 以沸水或蒸氣清洗(碟子等)。**3** heat (milk) almost to boiling-point. 煮熱(牛奶)幾達沸點。□ *n* injury to the skin from hot liquid or steam: 燙傷: *an ointment for burns and ~s.* 治火傷和燙傷的油膏。

scale[1] /skeɪl; skel/ *n* **1** [C] one of the thin overlapping plates of hard material that cover the skin of many fish and reptiles: (魚及爬蟲的)鱗: *scrape the ~s off a herring.* 刮去一條青魚的鱗。⇨ the illus at fish. 參看 fish 之挿圖。**2** [C] scale-like outer piece on an organic or other object, eg a flake of skin that loosens and comes off the body in some diseases; a flake of rust on iron. 鱗狀物(例如在某些疾病中自身體脫下的皮屑);鱗屑;鐵銹屑。***remove the ~s from sb's eyes,*** (fig) enable sb who has been deceived to realize the true state of affairs. (喻)使已受騙者認清眞相。**3** [U] chalky deposit inside boilers, kettles, waterpipes, etc (from the lime in hard water); deposit of tartar on teeth. 水垢;銹皮;水銹(爲硬水中之石灰積存於鍋,壺,水管等的內壁上的白堊質沉澱物);齒垢。□ *vt, vi* **1** [VP6A, 15A, B] cut or scrape ~s from (eg fish) (but *de~* a boiler or kettle). 刮除(魚等)之鱗(但除去鍋或壺之水垢則用 descale)。**2** [VP2C] ***~ off,*** come off in flakes: 一片片剝落: *paint/plaster scaling off a wall.* 自牆上剝落的油漆(灰泥)。**scaly**

adj covered with ~ or ~s; coming off in ~s: 覆有鱗,鱗狀物的;剝落如鱗的: *a kettle scaly with rust.* 生有銹皮的水壺。

scale² /skeɪl ; skel/ *n* [C] **1** series of marks at regular intervals for the purpose of measuring (as on a ruler or a thermometer): 尺度;分度;刻度(例如尺或溫度計上者): *This ruler has one ~ in centimetres and another in inches.* 這尺上有公分的刻度和英寸的刻度。 **2** ruler or other tool or instrument marked in this way. 有刻度之尺或度量器。 **3** system of units for measuring: 度量制;記數法: *the ˈdecimal ~.* 十進度量制。 **4** arrangement in steps or degrees: 階段;等級: *a ~ of wages;* 工資之等級; *a person who is high in the social ~;* 一位社會地位高的人; *sink in the ~,* fall to a lower level. 降至下級。 **sliding ~,** ⇨ slide²(4). **5** proportion between the size of sth and the map, diagram, etc which represents it: (實物與地圖,圖解等代表物間的)比例;比例尺;縮尺: *a map on the ~ of ten kilometres to the centimetre;* 按照一公分代表十公里之比例縮成的一張地圖; *drawn to ~,* with a uniform reduction or enlargement. 按比例縮小或放大的。 **6** relative size, extent, etc. 規模;相對的大小、程度等。 ***on a large/small, etc ~,*** to a large, etc extent/degree: 大(小等)規模地: *They are preparing for war on a large ~.* 他們正在大規模地準備戰爭。 **7** (music) series of tones arranged in order of pitch, esp a series of eight starting on a keynote: (音樂) 音階 (按照音調之高低度所組成之一系列的聲音,尤指以某主音起始的一連串八個音): *the ~ of F,* beginning with F as the keynote; F 音階(以 F 作爲主音而開始者); *practise ~s on the piano.* 在鋼琴上練習音階。 ⇨ octave. □ *vt* **1** [VP6A] make a copy or representation of, according to a certain ~: 按照某種比例繪或製: *~ a map/building.* 按照比例而繪製地圖 (建築物)。 **2** [VP15B] *~ up/down,* increase/decrease by a certain proportion: 按比例增加(減少): *All wages/marks were ~d up to 10 per cent.* 所有工資(分數)都按照百分之十增加。

scale³ /skeɪl ; skel/ *n* [C] **1** one of the two pans on a balance; 天平盤; **(pair of) ~s,** simple balance or instrument for weighing. 天平;秤。⇨ the illus at balance. 參看 balance 之插圖。 ***hold the ~s even,*** judge fairly (between). (在…之間)公平裁判。 ***turn the ~(s),*** decide the result of sth which is in doubt: 決定一項尚未確定的事情的結果;改變情勢: *The arrival of reinforcements turned the ~(s) in our favour.* 援兵的到達改變了情勢而對我們有利。 ***turn the ~(s) at,*** (colloq) weigh: (俗)重(若干): *The jockey turned the ~(s) at 80 lb.* 那騎師重八十磅。 **2** any machine for weighing: 任何稱重量的機器: *bathroom ~s,* for measuring one's weight. 家用量體重機;家用磅秤。□ *vi* [VP2B] weigh: 重(若干): *~ 10 lb.* 重十磅。

scale⁴ /skeɪl ; skel/ *vt* [VP6A] climb up (a wall, cliff, etc). 攀登(牆,懸崖等)。**ˈscaling-ladder** *n* one used for scaling high walls, eg of a fortified town in former times. (古代攻城用之)雲梯;爬城梯。

scal·lop /ˈskɒləp ; ˈskɑləp/ *n* **1** kind of bivalve mollusc with a shell divided into grooves. 海扇(雙殼貝類,其貝殼分裂爲許多細槽);干貝。⇨ the illus at bivalve. 參看 bivalve 之插圖。 **ˈ~-shell** *n* one half of this shell, used as a utensil in which a savoury dish is cooked and served. 海扇殼之一扇;貝皿(用以烹煮及裝盛一道可口的菜肴)。 **2** (*pl*) ornamental edging of ~-shaped projections cut in pastry, cloth, etc. (複)(糕餅、布料等之)扇形飾邊。□ *vt* [VP6A] **1** cook (eg oysters) in a ~-shell. 在海扇殼中烹煮(蠔等)。 **2** decorate the edge of (sth) with ~s. 以扇形皺褶裝飾(某物之)邊緣。

scally·wag /ˈskælɪwæg ; ˈskælɪˌwæg/, (US = **scalawag** /ˈskæləwæg ; ˈskæləˌwæg/) *n* (hum) scamp; rascal. (諧)無賴;惡棍。

scalp /skælp ; skælp/ *n* [C] skin and hair of the head, excluding the face; this skin, etc from an enemy's head as a trophy of victory (a former practice of some American Indians). 頭皮及頭髮(面部不包括在內);(昔時北美印第安人取來)作爲戰利品之敵人的頭皮等。***out for ~s,*** (fig) making efforts to win trophies of victory over opponents. (喻)決心擊敗對手。□ *vt* [VP6A] cut the ~ off. 剝去…的頭皮。

scal·pel /ˈskælpəl ; ˈskælpəl/ *n* small, light knife used by surgeons. (外科醫生用的)輕便小刀;解剖刀。

scamp¹ /skæmp ; skæmp/ *n* (often used playfully) rascal; worthless person. (常用作戲謔語)惡漢;無用之人。

scamp² /skæmp ; skæmp/ *vt* [VP6A] do (work, etc), make sth, carelessly, hastily or without interest. 粗心,急速或無心地做(工作等);草率從事。

scam·per /ˈskæmpə(r) ; ˈskæmpɚ/ *vi* [VP2A, C] (esp of small animals, eg mice, rabbits, when frightened, or of children and dogs at play) run quickly. (尤指受驚之小動物,如鼠、兎等,或指在玩耍的小孩和狗)疾走;奔竄。□ *n* short, quick run: 疾走;奔竄: *take the dog for a ~.* 領着狗快走一陣。

scampi /ˈskæmpɪ ; ˈskæmpɪ/ *n pl* large prawns. 大蝦。

scan /skæn ; skæn/ *vt, vi* (-nn-) **1** [VP6A] look at attentively; run the eyes over every part of: 細察;審視: *The shipwrecked sailor ~ned the horizon anxiously every morning.* 這位遭船難的水手每晨焦急地審視着海天相接之處。 **2** [VP6A] glance at quickly but not very thoroughly: 匆促地略看;掃視: *He ~ned the newspaper while having his breakfast.* 他在吃早餐的時候把報紙大略地翻閱了一下。 **3** [VP6A] test the metre of (a line of verse) by noting the division into feet, as in: 藉分劃音步以測定(詩句)之韻律;按節奏吟誦,例如:

ˈNever/ˈseek to/ˈtell thy/ˈlove
ˈLove that/ˈnever/ˈtold can/ˈbe.
切勿試圖說出你的愛
愛是無法明言的。

4 [VP2A] (of verse) fit a metrical pattern; be composed so that it can be ~ned: (指詩)合韻律;可吟誦: *This line does not/will not ~.* 這詩行不合韻律。 *The verses ~ well.* 這些詩很合韻律。 **5** [VP6A] (TV) resolve (a picture) into its elements of light and shade for transmission; (radar) traverse an area with electronic beams in search of sth. (電視)分解(圖像)爲明暗單元以便播出;掃描;(雷達)以電子(波)束掃描一區域以搜尋某物。**~·sion** /ˈskænʃn; ˈskænʃən/ *n* [U] the ~ning of verse; the way verse ~s. 詩的節奏分析;詩的韻律法。

scan·dal /ˈskændl ; ˈskændl̩/ *n* **1** [C, U] (action, piece of behaviour, etc that causes a) general feeling of indignation; [C] shameful or disgraceful action: 公憤;一般人的反感;引起公憤或反感的行動、行爲等;醜行;物議;可恥的行動: *cause (a) ~.* 引起公憤。 *A series of ~s caused the Government to fall.* 一連串引起公憤的行動使得政府垮台。 *It is a ~ that the accused man was declared innocent.* 那被告被宣告無罪實在叫人憤憤不平。 *If she leaves her husband she will certainly create (a) ~ in the village.* 她如果拋棄丈夫,一定會招村人物議。 **2** [U] harmful gossip; careless or unkind talk which damages sb's reputation: 有害的閒話;(無心或惡意的)誹謗;詆毀: *Don't talk/listen to ~.* 不要誹謗人(聽誹謗話)。 *Most of us enjoy a bit of ~.* 我們大多數人都喜歡聽一點閒話。 **ˈ~·monger** /-mʌŋgə(r) ; -ˌmʌŋgɚ/ *n* person who spreads ~s(2). 誹謗者。 **~·monger·ing** /-mʌŋgərɪŋ ; -ˌmʌŋgərɪŋ/ *n* [U] the spreading of ~s(2). 散佈誹謗。 **~·ize** /ˈskændəlaɪz ; ˈskændl̩ˌaɪz/ *vt* [VP6A] shock; offend the moral feelings or the ideas of etiquette of: 使驚駭;使起反感;誹謗: *~ize the neighbours by sunbathing on the lawn in the nude.* 在草地上作裸體日光浴使鄰居們駭異。 **~·ous** /ˈskændələs ; ˈskændl̩əs/ *adj* **1** disgraceful; shocking. 可恥的;令人驚駭的。 **2** (of reports, rumours) containing ~. (指傳聞,謠

言)含有誹謗性的。**3** (of persons) fond of spreading ~. (指人)喜歡誹謗的。**~·ous·ly** *adv*

Scan·di·na·vian /ˌskændɪˈneɪvɪən ; ˌskændəˈnevɪən/ *n, adj* (native) of Scandinavia (Denmark, Norway, Sweden, Iceland). 斯堪的那維亞(包括丹麥、挪威、瑞典、冰島)的;北歐的;斯堪的那維亞人;北歐人。

scan·sion /ˈskænʃn ; ˈskænʃən/ ⇨ scan.

scant /skænt ; skænt/ *adj* **~ (of),** (having) hardly enough: 不足的;欠缺的: *~ of breath;* 上氣不接下氣; *pay ~ attention to sb's advice.* 忽略某人的忠言。□ *vt* [VP6A] skimp; make ~; cut down: 吝嗇;使不足;減少: *Don't ~ the butter when you make a cake.* 做糕餅時不要吝惜奶油。**~y** *adj* (-ier, -iest) (opp of *ample*) small in size or amount; barely large enough: (爲 ample 之相反字)(大小或數量)不足的;剛剛够大的;恰好够的: *a ~y rice crop;* 歉收的稻子; *a ~y bikini.* 剛剛够大的比基尼泳裝。**~·ily** /-ɪlɪ ; -ɪlɪ/ *adv* in a ~y manner: 不足地;剛剛够地: *~ily dressed.* 衣著單薄。**~i·ness** *n*

scant·ling /ˈskæntlɪŋ ; ˈskæntlɪŋ/ *n* small beam or piece of timber; board not more than 5 inches wide. 小木材;不超過五吋寬的木材;製材。

scape·goat /ˈskeɪpgəʊt ; ˈskepˌgot/ *n* person blamed or punished for the mistake(s) or wrongdoing of another or others. 代人受過者;替罪羊。

scape·grace /ˈskeɪpgreɪs ; ˈskepˌgres/ *n* (often used playfully) person who constantly gets into trouble. (常用作戲謔語)經常惹是非的人。

scap·ula /ˈskæpjʊlə ; ˈskæpjələ/ *n* (anat) shoulder-blade. (解剖)肩胛骨。⇨ the illus at skeleton. 參看 skeleton 之插圖。

scar /skɑ:(r) ; skɑr/ *n* mark remaining on the surface (of skin, furniture, etc) as the result of injury or damage: (皮膚,傢具等的)傷痕;痕跡;疤: *a long ~ across his cheek;* 橫過他面頰的長疤; (fig) (喩) *grief that left a ~ (on the heart).* (在心頭)留下創傷的悲哀。□ *vt, vi* (-rr-) **1** [VP6A] mark with a ~ or ~s: 使有傷痕或痕跡: *a face ~red by smallpox;* 麻臉(有天花疤痕的臉); *war-~red towns.* 受戰爭損害的城鎮。**2** [VP2C] heal over (with a ~); form ~s: 痊愈(留下疤痕);結疤: *The cut on his forehead ~red over.* 他的額上的刀傷已結疤痊愈了。

scarab /ˈskærəb ; ˈskærəb/ *n* kinds of beetle, esp one regarded as sacred in ancient Egypt; carving in the shape of a ~ (as an ornament or charm). 甲蟲;(尤指古埃及人奉爲神聖的)蜣螂;蜣螂的雕像(作爲裝飾或護符)。

scarce /skeəs ; skɛrs/ *adj* **1** (opp of *plentiful*) not available in sufficient quantity; not equal to the demand: (爲 plentiful 之相反字)不充足的;缺乏的;供不應求的: *Eggs are ~ and expensive this month.* 本月蛋缺貨且價昂。**2** rare; seldom met with: 稀罕的;難得的: *a ~ book.* 珍本;難得之書。***make oneself ~,*** (colloq) keep out of the way, go away. (俗)隱退;離去。**scarc·ity** /ˈskeəsətɪ ; ˈskɛrsətɪ/ *n* [U] state of being ~; smallness of supply compared with demand: 不充足;缺乏;供不應求: *The scarcity of fruit was caused by the drought.* 水果的供不應求係由乾旱所致。[C] (*pl* -ties) instance or occasion of scarcity. 不充足,缺乏,供不應求之實例。

scarce·ly /ˈskeəslɪ ; ˈskɛrslɪ/ *adv* barely; not quite; almost not: 僅僅;剛剛;不充分地;殆不;幾乎沒有: *There were ~ a hundred people present.* 到場的不足一百人。*I ~ know him.* 我不大認識他。*S~ had he entered the room when the phone rang.* 他一進房間電話就響了。

scare /skeə(r) ; skɛr/ *vt, vi* [VP6A, 15A, B, 2A] frighten; become frightened: 恐嚇;驚嚇: *He was ~d by the thunder.* 他爲雷聲所驚嚇。*They were ~d at the strange noise.* 他們聽到奇怪的聲音覺得害怕。*The dogs ~d the thief away.* 那些狗把賊嚇跑了。*He ~s easily/is easily ~d.* 他容易受驚。***~ sb stiff,*** (colloq) alarm sb, make sb nervous: (俗)使某人害怕或神經緊張: *He's ~d stiff of women.* 女人使他害怕或神經緊張。***~ sb out of his wits,*** make him extremely frightened: 使某人嚇得不知所措;使某人嚇呆: *The sound of footsteps outside ~d her out of her wits.* 外面的脚步聲把她嚇昏了。□ *n* [C] feeling of alarm; state of widespread fear: 驚恐;恐慌: *The news caused a war ~,* a fear that war might break out. 這消息引起了戰爭可能會爆發的恐慌。*You did give me a ~,* did frighten me. 你眞嚇了我一跳。**ˈ~·crow** *n* figure of a man dressed in old clothes, set up to ~ birds away from crops. (置於農作物中用來嚇走鳥類的)著破衣的人形;稻草人。**ˈ~ headline** *n* sensational newspaper headline in heavy black print. 聳人聽聞的報紙大標題。**ˈ~monger** /-mʌŋgə(r) ; -ˌmʌŋgɚ/ *n* person who spreads alarming news and starts a ~. 散佈駭人新聞以引起恐慌的人。**scary** /ˈskeərɪ ; ˈskɛrɪ/ *adj* (colloq) causing alarm. (俗)令人驚慌的;可怕的。

scarf /skɑ:f ; skɑrf/ *n* (*pl* ~s /skɑ:fs ; skɑrfs/ or scarves /skɑ:vz ; skɑrvz/) long strip of material (silk, wool, etc) worn over the shoulders, round the neck or (by women) over the hair. (絲,毛等的)圍巾;披肩;肩巾;頸巾;(女人之)頭巾。**ˈ~-pin** *n* ornamental pin worn on a ~. 圍巾上的裝飾別針。

scar·ify /ˈskærɪfaɪ ; ˈskærəˌfaɪ/ *vt* (*pt, pp* -fied) [VP6A] **1** (in surgery) make small cuts in, cut off skin from. (外科)在…上劃痕;自…割去皮膚。**2** (fig) hurt by severe criticism. (喩)藉嚴厲批評以傷害。**3** loosen (the surface of the soil or a road) by using an agricultural tool or a machine with prongs. 用叉具或耙機弄鬆(土壤或道路的表面);鬆(土)。

scar·let /ˈskɑ:lət ; ˈskɑrlɪt/ *n, adj* bright red: 鮮紅;猩紅: *the ~ pillarboxes in Great Britain.* 英國的鮮紅色郵筒。**ˌ~ ˈfever,** infectious disease with ~ marks on the skin. 猩紅熱(一種在皮膚上生猩紅斑點的傳染病)。**ˌ~ ˈhat,** cardinal's hat. 紅衣主教的帽子。**ˌ~ ˈrunner,** ~-flowered kind of bean plant. 紅花菜豆(一種開紅花的豆類植物)。**ˌ~ ˈwoman,** (old use) prostitute. (舊用法)娼妓。

scarp /skɑ:p ; skɑrp/ *n* steep slope; escarpment. 陡坡;急斜面。

scat /skæt ; skæt/ *int* (sl) Go away! (俚)走開!

scath·ing /ˈskeɪðɪŋ ; ˈskeðɪŋ/ *adj* (of criticism, ridicule, etc) severe; harsh: (指批評,嘲笑等)嚴苛的: *a ~ retort;* 尖刻的反駁; *a ~ review of a new book.* 對一本新書的苛刻評論。**~·ly** *adv*

scat·ter /ˈskætə(r) ; ˈskætɚ/ *vt, vi* **1** [VP6A, 15A, B, 2A, C] send, go, in different directions: 驅散;離散: *The police ~ed the crowd.* 警察驅走羣衆。*The crowd ~ed.* 羣衆散去了。**2** [VP6A, 15A] throw or put in various directions, or here and there: 散播;撒布: *~ seed;* 播種; *~ gravel on an icy road.* 撒布砂石於結冰的路面。**ˈ~-brain** *n* person who cannot keep his thoughts on one subject for long. 注意力不持久的人;浮躁的人。Hence, 由此產生, **ˈ~-brained** *adj.* □ *n* that which is ~ed; sprinkling: 散布著的東西;稀疏的少量或少數: *a ~ of hailstones.* 一陣稀疏的冰雹。**~ed** (*pp* as an) *adj* lying in different directions; not situated together; wide apart: (過去分詞用作形容詞)散布各方的;離散的;分散的: *a few ~ed fishing villages;* 一些疏疏落落的漁村; *a thinly ~ed population.* 稀疏的人口。

scatty /ˈskætɪ ; ˈskætɪ/ *adj* (-ier, -iest) (colloq) (俗) **1** mad; feeble-minded: 瘋狂的;低能的: *That man would drive any woman ~!* 那男子會使任何女人爲之瘋狂! **2** scatter-brained; absent-minded. 思想不集中的;心不在焉的。

scav·en·ger /ˈskævɪndʒə(r) ; ˈskævɪndʒɚ/ *n* **1** animal or bird, eg a vulture, that lives on decaying flesh. 以腐屍爲食之禽獸(如兀鷹)。**2** person who searches among discarded or refuse material. 在廢物或垃圾堆中搜尋有用之物者;拾荒者。**scav·enge** /ˈskævɪndʒ ; ˈskævɪndʒ/ *vi* [VP2A, 3A] **~ (for),** act as a ~. 吃腐肉;在廢物或垃圾堆中搜尋。

scen·ario /sɪˈnɑ:rɪəʊ *US:* -ˈnær- ; sɪˈnɛrɪˌo/ *n* (*pl* ~s /-rɪəʊz ; -rɪˌoz/) written outline of a play, an opera, a film, with details of the scenes, etc; imagined sequence of future events. 電影脚本；劇情概要；歌劇概要；想像中未來事件的順序。**scen·arist** /sɪˈnɑːrɪst *US:* -ˈnær- ; sɪˈnɛrɪst/ *n* writer of ~s. 電影脚本作者。

scene /siːn ; sin/ *n* [C] **1** place of an actual or imagined event: (實際或想像中的)出事地點；場景：*the ~ of a great battle.* 大戰場。*The ~ of the novel is laid/set in Scotland.* 該小說的故事發生在蘇格蘭。**2** description of an incident, or of part of a person's life; incident in real life suitable for such a description: 事件或生活片段的描述；現實生活中適於描述的事件；情景；實況：*'S~s of Clerical Life'*, tales by George Eliot. '教士生活記實'(英國小說家 George Eliot 所著的一本小說集)。*There were distressing ~s when the earthquake occurred.* 地震發生時有很多悲慘的情景。**3** (incident characterized by an) emotional outburst: 發脾氣；吵鬧；吵鬧的事件：*She made a ~/We had a ~ when I criticized her.* 當我批評她的時候，她大吵大鬧(我們吵鬧了一陣)。**4** view; sth seen; sth spread out to view (indoors or outdoors, in a town or in the country, with or without action; cf *scenery*, which is used of natural features on land): 風景；所見之物；景象(戶內的或戶外的，城市的或鄉村的，活動的或靜態的；參較指地面上自然景色之 scenery)：*The boats in the harbour make a beautiful ~.* 港中的船隻構成美麗的景色。*They went abroad for a change of ~.* 他們出國換換環境。**5** (abbr 略作 **Sc**) one of the parts, shorter than an act, into which some plays and operas are divided; episode within such a part. (戲劇及歌劇之短於一幕的)一場；一景；一場或一景中的一段情節：*'Macbeth', Act II, Sc 1;* '馬克白'，第二幕第一場；*the ˈduel ~ in 'Hamlet'.* '哈姆雷特'中決鬭的一場。**6** place represented on the stage of a theatre; the painted background, woodwork, canvas, etc representing such a place: (舞臺上的)景；佈景；道具佈置：*The first ~ of 'Lotus Blossom' is a tropical garden.* '荷花'的第一景是一熱帶花園。*The ~s are changed during the intervals.* 休息時間換景。***behind the ~s***, **(a)** out of sight of the audience; behind the stage. 觀衆看不見地；在幕後；秘密地；暗中。**(b)** (fig, of a person) influencing events secretly; (of an event) in secret, not known to the public. (喻，指人)秘密左右事件的；(指事件)未公開的。***be/come on the ~***, (fig) be present/appear. (喻)在場；到場；出現。**ˈ~-painter** *n* (theatre) person who paints scenery(2). (戲劇)繪製佈景者。**ˈ~-shifter** *n* (theatre) person who changes the ~s. (戲劇)更換佈景者。**7** (colloq) area of what is currently fashionable or notable: (俗)時髦或著名的地區：*the ˌenterˈtainment ~ in the West End of London;* 倫敦西區的娛樂場所；*the ˈdrug ~ in our big cities.* 我們大城市中著名的毒窟。***be on/make the ~***, (colloq) be part of/present in such a ~. (俗)參與時髦地區的活動(出現在時髦地區的活動中)。

scen·ery /ˈsiːnərɪ ; ˈsinərɪ/ *n* [U] **1** general natural features of a district, eg mountains, plains, valleys, forests: 一地區之天然景色；風景；景緻(例如高山，平原，谿谷，森林)：*mountain ~;* 山景；*stop to admire the ~.* 停下來欣賞風景。Cf 參較 *town scenes.* **2** the furnishings, painted canvas, woodwork, etc used on the stage of a theatre. (舞臺上之)佈景；道具佈置。

scenic /ˈsiːnɪk ; ˈsinɪk/ *adj* having fine natural scenery: 天然景色的；風景優美的：*the ~ splendours of the Rocky Mountains;* 落磯山脈壯麗的風景；*a ~ highway across the Alps.* 越過阿爾卑斯山脈的景色優美的公路。**sceni·cally** /-klɪ ; -klɪ/ *adv*

scent /sent ; sɛnt/ *n* **1** [U] smell, esp of sth pleasant coming from or belonging to sth: 氣味；(尤指)香味：*the ~ of new-mown hay;* 新刈乾草的氣味；*a rose that has no ~;* 無香味的玫瑰；[C] particular kind of smell: 某種氣味：*~s of lavender and rosemary.* 薰衣草和迷迭香的氣味。**2** [U] (usu liquid) preparation distilled from flowers, etc; perfume: (通常爲液體)香精；香水：*a bottle of ~;* 一瓶香水；*a ˈ~-bottle.* 香水瓶。*She uses too much ~.* 她用了過多的香水。**3** (usu *sing*) smell left by an animal; the track of an animal: (通常用單數)野獸的遺臭；獸跡：*follow up/lose/recover the ~.* 追踪(失去，重新發現)獸跡。*The ~ was strong/poor/hot/cold*, easy/difficult, etc for the hounds to follow. 那野獸的遺臭是强烈的(微弱的，新鮮而强烈的，微弱的)。***on the ~***, having, following, a clue. 獲得或追尋…的線索。***off the ~***, having, following, no clue or the wrong clue. 無線索或追尋錯誤的線索。***put/throw sb off the ~***, (fig) mislead him by giving false information. (喻)(以不實的情報或資料)使某人失去線索。**4** [U] sense of smell (in dogs): (犬的)嗅覺：*hunt by ~.* 藉嗅覺行獵；循臭跡獵物。□ *vt* [VP6A] **1** learn the presence of by smell: 嗅出…的存在；聞到：*The dog ~ed a rat.* 那狗嗅出有一隻老鼠。**2** begin to suspect the presence or existence of: 開始發覺到…的在場或存在；覺察；看破；疑有：*~ a crime;* 識破一項罪行；*~ treachery/trouble.* 疑有詭詐(麻煩)。**3** put ~ on; make fragrant: 灑香水；使香：*~ a handkerchief;* 灑香水在手帕上；*roses that ~ the air.* 使空氣變香的玫瑰。**~·less** *adj* having no ~: 無氣味的；無香味的；無嗅覺的：*~less flowers.* 無香味的花。

scep·ter /ˈseptə(r) ; ˈsɛptɚ/ *n* = sceptre.

scep·tic (US = **skep·tik**) /ˈskeptɪk ; ˈskɛptɪk/ *n* person who doubts the truth of a particular claim, theory, etc; person who doubts the truth of the Christian religion or of all religions. 懷疑者；懷疑論者；懷疑某主張、學說等之眞實性者；懷疑基督教或一切宗教之眞理者。**scep·ti·cal** (US = **skep-**) /-kl ; -kl̩/ *adj* inclined not to believe; in the habit of questioning the truth of claims, statements, etc. 懷疑的；慣於懷疑主張、陳述等之眞實性的。**scep·ti·cally** (US = **skep-**) /-klɪ ; -klɪ/ *adv* **scep·ti·cism** (US = **skep-**) /ˈskeptɪsɪzəm ; ˈskɛptəˌsɪzəm/ *n* [U] doubting state of mind; ~al attitude of mind. 懷疑；懷疑態度；懷疑主義。

sceptre (US = **scep·ter**) /ˈseptə(r) ; ˈsɛptɚ/ *n* rod or staff carried by a ruler as a sign of power or authority. 王節；王權。**scep·tred** (US = **-tered**) *adj* having a ~. 有王權的。⇨ the illus at regalia. 參看 regalia 之插圖。

sched·ule /ˈʃedjuːl *US:* ˈskedʒʊl ; ˈskɛdʒʊl/ *n* [C] list or statement of details, esp of times for doing things; programme or timetable for work: 表；目錄；(尤指)時間表；進度表；預定計畫表：*a production ~*, eg in a factory; (工廠等中之)生產進度表；生產計畫表；*a full ~*, a busy programme. 排得很滿的日程表。***on/behind ~***, on/not on time: 準時(遲延)；照進度進行(進度落後)：*The train arrived on ~*, on time, punctually. 火車準時到達。***(according) to ~***, as planned. 按照計畫的。□ *vt* [VP6A, 7A, 14] ~ ***(for)***, make a ~ of; put in a ~; (esp US) enter in a list of arrangements: 作…之表或目錄；列入時間表或進度表；(尤美)排定；安排：*~d services,* (eg of aircraft) flying according to announced timetables. 固定的班機。(Cf 參較 *charter flights.*) *The President is ~d to make a speech tomorrow.* 總統定於明日發表演說。*His arrival is ~d for Thursday.* 他預定於星期四到達。

sche·matic /skɪˈmætɪk ; skiˈmætɪk/ *adj* of the nature of a scheme or plan; (shown) in a diagram or chart. 綱要的；圖解(式)的。**sche·mati·cally** /-klɪ ; -klɪ/ *adv*

scheme /skiːm ; skim/ *n* [C] **1** arrangement; ordered system: 安排；配置；系統；體制：*a ˈcolour ~*, eg for a room, so that colours of walls, rugs, curtains, etc are in harmony. 色彩之調配(如爲房間所設計者，俾使牆壁、地毯、窗帘等之色彩調和)。**2** plan or design (for work or activity): (工作或活動的)計畫；設計：*a ~ for manufacturing paper from straw;* 用稻草造紙的計畫；*a ~* (= syllabus) *for the* *term's work.* 該學期之課程進度表。**3** secret and dishonest plan: 陰謀；詭計：*a ~ to defraud a widow.* 意圖欺騙一寡婦的陰謀。□ *vi, vt* **1** [VP2A, 3A, 4A] ***~ for sth／to do sth,*** make a (esp dishonest) ~ or ~s: 設計；策畫；圖謀(尤指不軌之事)：*He ~d to keep his rivals in ignorance of his plans.* 他圖謀不讓他的對手們知道他的計畫。*They ~d for the overthrow of the government.* 他們陰謀推翻政府。**2** [VP6A] make plans for (esp sth dishonest): 設計；策畫；圖謀(尤指不軌之事)：*a scheming* (= crafty) *thief.* 詭詐的竊賊。**~r** *n* person who ~s or intrigues. 設計者；陰謀者。

scherzo /ˈskeətsəʊ；ˈskɛrtso/ *n* (*pl* ~s /-səʊz；-soz/) (I) lively, vigorous passage in music. (義)輕快有力的樂節；詼諧曲。

schism /ˈsɪzəm；ˈsɪzəm/ *n* [U] (offence of causing the) division of an organization (esp a Church) into two or more groups, usu through difference of opinion; [C] instance of such separation. 組織分裂(通常由於意見不同而分爲兩個或更多的小派系)；(尤指)教會分裂；導致組織或教會分裂的冒犯行爲；分裂之實例。**schis·matic** /sɪzˈmætɪk；sɪzˈmætɪk/ *adj* tending to or inclined to ~; guilty of ~. 分裂的；有分立趨向的；有使組織或教會分裂(之冒犯行爲)的。

schist /ʃɪst；ʃɪst/ *n* kinds of rock which splits easily into thin plates. 結晶片岩；片麻岩。

schizo·phrenia /ˌskɪtsəʊˈfriːnɪə；ˌskɪzəˈfrinɪə/ *n* type of mental disorder (colloq 俗 *split personality*) marked by lack of connection between thoughts, feelings, and actions. 精神分裂症；早老性癡呆。**schizo·phrenic** /ˌskɪtsəʊˈfrenɪk；ˌskɪzəˈfrɛnɪk/ *adj* of ~. 精神分裂症的。□ *n* (colloq abbr 俗語略作 *schizo*) person suffering from ~. 精神分裂症患者。

schmal(t)z /ʃmɔːlts；ʃmɑlts/ *n* (colloq) sickly sentimentality. (俗) 過份的多愁善感；過份的傷感。**schmal(t)zy** *adj*

schnapps /ʃnæps；ʃnæps/ *n* [U] strong alcoholic spirit distilled from grain. 榖類釀製的烈酒。

schnit·zel /ˈʃnɪtsl；ˈʃnɪtsl/ *n* veal cutlet covered with breadcrumbs and fried in butter. (覆以麵包屑，再用牛油炸的)炸牛肉片。

schnor·kel /ˈsnɔːkl；ˈʃnɔrkəl/ *n* = snorkel.

scholar /ˈskɒlə(r)；ˈskɑlɚ/ *n* **1** (dated use) boy or girl at school. (過時用語)學生。**2** student who, after a competitive examination or other means of selection, is awarded money or other help so that he may attend school or college, or pursue further education: 領獎學金或津貼的學生：*British Council ~s.* 領英國文化協會獎學金的學生。**3** person with much knowledge (usu of a particular subject, and esp one who gives careful attention to evidence, method, etc). 學者(通常指某一學科的，尤指注重證據和方法的)。**schol·ar·ly** *adj* having or showing much learning; of, suitable, or right for a ~(3); fond of learning: 有學問的；博學的；學者派頭的；適於做學者的；好學的：*a ~ly translation;* 博學的翻譯；*a ~ly young woman.* 好學的女青年。

schol·ar·ship /ˈskɒləʃɪp；ˈskɑlɚˌʃɪp/ *n* **1** [U] learning or knowledge obtained by study; proper concern for scholarly methods. 學識；學問；學術上的成就；做學問的方法。**2** [C] payment of money, eg a yearly grant to a scholar(2) so that he may continue his studies: 獎學金：*win a ~ to the university.* 獲得該大學的獎學金。

schol·as·tic /skəˈlæstɪk；skoˈlæstɪk/ *adj* **1** of schools and education: 學校的；教育的：*the ˈ~ profession,* that of teaching; 教書的職業；*a ˈ~ post,* a position as a teacher; 教書的職位；*a ˈ~ agency,* private one that finds positions for teachers and teachers for schools. 教員職業介紹所。**2** connected with the learning of the Middle Ages, esp when men argued over small points of dogma. 中世紀之學術研究的；煩瑣學派的；學究的。**schol·as·ti·cism** /skəˈlæstɪsɪzəm；skoˈlæstəˌsɪzəm/ *n* [U] the system of philosophy taught in the universities in the Middle Ages. 中世紀之經院哲學；煩瑣哲學。

school[1] /skuːl；skul/ *n* **1** [C] institution for educating children: 學校：*ˈprimary and ˈsecondary ~s;* 小學和中學；*ˈevening ~s;* 夜校；*ˈSunday ~s;* 主日學校；*~ doctors,* medical officers responsible for the health of school children; 校醫；(US) college, university. (美)學院，大學。**ˈ~-board** *n* (US) local education authority. (美)(地方上的)教育委員會；學務委員會。**ˈ~-book** *n* book used in ~s; textbook. 課本；教科書。**ˈ~·boy** *n* boy at ~: 學童；男學生：(attrib) (形容用法) *~boy slang.* 學生俚語。**ˈ~-days** *n pl* time of being at ~: 求學時代：*look back upon one's ~-days.* 回顧求學時代。**ˈ~·fellow** *n* member, past or present, of the same ~. 同學；校友。**ˈ~·girl** *n* girl at ~. 女學生。**ˈ~·house** *n* building of a ~ esp a small one in a village. 校舍(尤指鄉間之小校舍)。**ˈ~·man** /-mən；-mən/ *n* (*pl* -men) teacher in a European university in the Middle Ages; theologian dealing with religious teachings by the use of Aristotle's logic. (中世紀歐洲大學的)教授；煩瑣派之神學家(用亞里斯多德之邏輯研究神學者)。**ˈ~·master／·mistress** *n* school teacher. 男(女)教師。**ˈ~·mate** *n* = ~fellow. **ˈ~-time** *n* lesson time at ~. 上課時間。**2** [U] (not with *def art*) process of being educated in a ~: (不用定冠詞)在學校受教育的過程；上學：*ˈ~ age,* between the ages of starting and finishing ~; 學齡；*~-ˈleaving age,* age at which children leave ~. 學童結束義務教育的年齡。*The ~-leaving age has been raised to 16.* 國民義務教育的年限已經提高到十六歲。*Is he old enough for ~／to go to ~?* 他的年齡大得可以上學了嗎？*He left ~ when he was fifteen.* 他十五歲時離開學校。*My boys are still at ~.* 我的孩子們仍在上學。**3** [U] (not with *def art*) time when teaching is given; lessons: (不用定冠詞)上課時間；上課：*S~ begins at 9am.* 上午九時開始上課。*There will be no ~* (= no lessons) *tomorrow.* 明天學校放假。*Will you come for a walk after ~?* 放學後你願來散散步嗎？**4** (with *def art*) all the pupils in a ~: (與定冠詞連用)全校學生：*The whole ~ hopes that its football team will win the match.* 全校學生都希望該校的足球隊贏得那場比賽。**5** department or division of a university for the study of a particular subject: 大學的院、系、研究所：*The S~ of Oriental and African Studies,* in the University of London; (倫敦大學的)東方學與非洲學學院；*the ˈLaw／ˈMedical S~;* 法(醫)學院；*the S~ of Dentistry;* 牙醫學系；(GB) branch of study for which separate examinations are given in a university: (英)大學的學位考試科目：*the ˈHistory ~;* 歷史科；hall in which these examinations are held; 舉行學位考試的試場；(*pl*) these examinations. (複)學位考試。**6** [C] (fig) circumstances or occupation that provides discipline or instruction: (喻)提供訓練或教導的環境或工作：*the hard ~ of experience／adversity.* 經驗(逆境)的磨練。**7** (*pl*) **the ~s,** medieval universities, their professors, teaching, and arguments. (複)中世紀之大學，其教授，教學，及論據。⇨ also *~man* in 1 above. 亦參看上列第 1 義之 ~man。**8** [C] group of persons who are followers or imitators of an artist, a philosopher, etc, or of persons having the same principles or characteristics: (藝術家，哲學家等的)門生；弟子；學派；門派：*the Dutch／Venetian, etc ~ of painting;* 荷蘭(威尼斯等)畫派；*the Hegelian ~,* of philosophers; 黑格爾學派；*a gentleman of the old ~,* who retains the traditions, manners, etc of older times. 舊派的紳士。***~ of thought,*** way of thinking shared by a group of persons. 學派。□ *vt* [VP6A, 15B, 16A] ***~ sb (in sth／to do sth),*** train; control; discipline: 訓練；控制；教導：*~ a horse;* 訓練馬；*~ oneself in patience／to be patient.* 養成自己的耐性。**~·ing** *n* [U] education: 教育：*He had very little ~ing.* 他受的教育很少。*Who's paying for her*

~*ing?* 誰在付她的教育費用?

school² /sku:l; skul/ *n* [C] large number (*of* fish) swimming together; shoal. 魚羣。

schoo·ner /ˈsku:nə(r); ˈskunɚ/ *n* **1** kind of sailing-ship with two or more masts and fore and aft sails. (有二或更多桅杆的) 縱帆式帆船; 斯庫納船。 **2** tall drinking-glass. 大酒杯。

schot·tische /ʃɒˈti:ʃ; ʃɑˈtiʃ/ *n* (music for a) kind of polka. 一種波爾卡類的旋舞; 此種舞曲。

schwa /ʃwɑ:; ʃwɑ/ *n* the symbol /ə; ə/ used in phonetic notation for central vowels or diphthong elements as in /əˈgəʊ; əˈgo/ for *ago*. 輕聲母音之發音符號(在國際音標中用 /ə/ 表示); 中性元音。

sci·atic /saɪˈætɪk; saɪˈætɪk/ *adj* of the hip: 臀的; 坐骨的: *the ~ nerve*, nerve extending through the hip and thigh. 坐骨神經。**sci·atica** /saɪˈætɪkə; saɪˈætɪkə/ *n* [U] neuralgia of the ~ nerve. 坐骨神經痛。

science /ˈsaɪəns; ˈsaɪəns/ *n* **1** [U] knowledge arranged in an orderly manner, esp knowledge obtained by observation and testing of facts; pursuit of such knowledge. 科學; 科學研究。*S~ is an exact discipline.* 科學是一種精確的學科。**2** [C, U] branch of such knowledge. 某門科學。⇨ art¹(2). **the natural ~s**, eg botany, zoology. 自然科學(如植物學,動物學)。**the physical ~s**, eg physics, chemistry. 自然科學(如物理,化學)。**social ~(s)**, eg psychology, politics. 社會科學(如心理學,政治學)。**the applied ~s**, eg engineering. 應用科學(如工程學)。**ˌ~ ˈfic·tion**, fiction dealing with recent or imagined scientific discoveries and advances (usu fantasies). 科幻小說(以最近或想像中的科學發現及進展爲主題者,通常爲怪異的幻想)。**3** [U] expert's skill (opp of strength): 專門技術或技巧(與'力氣'相反): *In judo ~ is more important than strength.* 在柔道中,技巧比力氣更爲重要。 **scien·tist** /ˈsaɪəntɪst; ˈsaɪəntɪst/ *n* person expert in one or more of the natural or physical ~s. 科學家; 自然科學家。

scien·tific /ˌsaɪənˈtɪfɪk; ˌsaɪənˈtɪfɪk/ *adj* **1** of, for, connected with, used in, science; guided by the rules of science: 科學的; 適於科學的; 關於科學的; 用於科學的; 合乎科學原則的: *~ methods;* 科學方法; *~ farming;* 科學耕作; *~ instruments.* 科學儀器。 **2** having, using, needing, skill or expert knowledge: 有技術或專門知識的; 利用技術或專門知識的; 需要技術或專門知識的: *a ~ boxer.* 有技術的拳擊手。**scien·tifi·cally** /-klɪ; -klɪ/ *adv*

scimi·tar /ˈsɪmɪtə(r); ˈsɪmətɚ/ *n* short, curved, single-edged sword, formerly used by Arabs, Persians, Turks. (阿拉伯人,波斯人,土耳其人昔時用的) 短彎刀; 偃月刀。

a scimitar

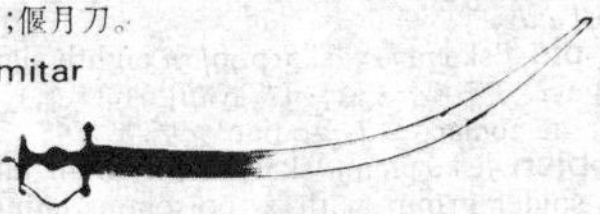

scin·tilla /sɪnˈtɪlə; sɪnˈtɪlə/ *n* [C] spark; atom; shred; iota: 火花; 微量; 碎片; 一點: *not a ~ of truth in the story;* 故事中沒有一點眞實性; *not a ~ of evidence*, none at all. 一點證據也沒有。

scin·til·late /ˈsɪntɪleɪt *US:* -təleɪt; ˈsɪntlˌet/ *vi* [VP 2A] sparkle; be brilliant: 放出火花; 閃鑠: *scintillating with wit.* 才智橫溢的。**scin·til·la·tion** /ˌsɪntɪˈleɪʃn *US:* -tlˈeɪʃn; ˌsɪntlˈeʃən/ *n*

scion /ˈsaɪən; ˈsaɪən/ *n* **1** young member of a (esp old or noble) family. (尤指世家或貴族的)年幼後裔; 子孫。 **2** shoot of a plant, esp one cut for grafting or planting. 幼枝(尤指爲接枝或栽植而剪下者); 接穗。

scis·sors /ˈsɪzəz; ˈsɪzɚz/ *n pl* ***(pair of)~***, cutting instrument with two blades which cut as they come together: 剪刀; 剪子: *Where are my ~?* 我的剪刀在那裡? ***~ and paste***, (of articles, books, etc) compiled from parts of others: (指文章、書籍等)自其他文章或書籍剪輯拼湊而成的: *This article's a ~ and paste job.* 這篇文章是剪輯拼湊而成。

scler·osis /skləˈrəʊsɪs; sklɪˈrosɪs/ *n* [U] diseased condition in which soft tissue (eg walls of the arteries) hardens. 硬化症(如血管硬化)。

scoff¹ /skɒf *US:* skɔ:f; skɑf/ *vi* [VP2A,3A] ***~ (at)***, speak contemptuously, mock (at): 輕蔑地說; 嘲弄; 嘲笑: *~ at dangers;* 蔑視危險; *~ at religion.* 嘲弄宗教。□ *n* **1** taunt; ~ing remark. 嘲笑; 嘲弄的話。 **2** object of ridicule. 嘲弄的對象; 笑柄。 **~er** *n* person who ~s. 嘲弄者; 嘲笑者。**~·ing·ly** *adv*

scoff² /skɒf *US:* skɔ:f; skɑf/ *vt* (sl) eat greedily: (俚)狼吞虎嚥地吃: *Who has ~ed all the pastries?* 是誰把糕餅全部吃掉了? □ *n* **1** act of ~ing: 狼吞虎嚥: *have a good ~.* 大吃一頓。**2** [U] (sl) food: (俚)食物; 食品: *Where's all the ~ gone?* 全部的食物到那裡去了?

scold /skəʊld; skold/ *vt, vi* [VP2A, 6A, 14] ***~ (sb) (for sth)***, blame with angry words; find fault noisily: 罵; 叱責; 責備: *~ a child for being lazy.* 責備孩子懶惰。□ *n* person who ~s. 好叱責或罵人的人。**~·ing** *n* [C] severe rebuke: 罵; 叱責: *give sb/get a ~ing for being late.* 責備某人遲到(因遲到而挨罵)。

scol·lop /ˈskɒləp; ˈskɑləp/ *n, vt* = scallop.

sconce /skɒns; skɑns/ *n* bracket fixed to a wall for a candle (or, today, any other form of light). 裝於牆上的蠟燭臺或燈臺。

scone /skɒn *US:* skəʊn; skon/ *n* [C] soft, flat cake of barley meal or wheat flour baked quickly. 一種快烤的扁平軟麵餅。

scoop /sku:p; skup/ *n* [C] **1** (sorts of) deep, shovel-like, short-handled tool for taking up and moving quantities of grain, flour, sugar, etc; long-handled, ladle-shaped tool for dipping out liquid. (挖穀粒、麵粉、糖等用的深邊短柄的)鏟子; (舀水等用的長柄)杓子; 戽斗。 **2** motion of, or as of, using a ~: 剷; 舀: *at one ~*, in one single movement of a ~: 一剷或一舀地: (fig) (喻) *He won £50 at one ~.* 他一下子賺了五十鎊。 **3** (colloq) piece of news obtained and published by one newspaper before its competitors; (comm) large profit made by anticipating competitors. (俗)獨家新聞; (商)搶先賺得的暴利。□ *vt* **1** [VP15B] ***~ sth out/up***, lift with, or as with, a ~. 剷起; 汲取; 舀出。**2** [VP6A, 15B] ***~ (out)***, make (a hole, groove, etc) with, or as with, a ~: 掘; 挖; 用或似用剷挖成(洞,溝等): *~ out a hole in the sand.* 在沙中挖洞。**3** [VP6A] (colloq) get (news, a profit, etc) as a ~(3). (俗)搶先獲得(新聞,利潤等)。**~·ful** /-fʊl; -fʊl/ *n* as much as a ~ holds. 一鏟的量; 一杓的量。

scoot /sku:t; skut/ *vi* (either imper or inf) (colloq, hum) run away quickly: (用於祈使句或不定詞)(俗,諧)趕快跑: *S~!* 趕快跑! *Tell him to ~.* 叫他趕快跑。⇨ scram.

scooter /ˈsku:tə(r); ˈskutɚ/ *n* **1** (**ˈmotor-)~**, light motor-cycle with small wheels and a low seat. 速克達機車(一種低座小輪輕型摩托車)。 **2** child's toy an L-shaped vehicle with small wheels, one for being used to move it by pushing against the ground. 滑行車; 踏板車(供小孩遊戲用)。

scooters

scope /skəʊp; skop/ *n* [U] **1** opportunity; outlet: 機會: *work that gives ~ for one's abilities.* 有機會發揮個人才能的工作。 **2** range of action or observation: 活動或觀察的範圍; 眼界; 見識: *Ought poli-*

tics to be within the ~ of a trade union's activities? 工會的活動應當包括政治嗎？ *Economics is a subject beyond the ~ of my mind.* 經濟學不是我所能了解的學科。

scor·bu·tic /skɔːˈbjuːtɪk ; skɔrˈbjutɪk/ *adj* of, affected with, scurvy. 壞血症的；患壞血症的。

scorch /skɔːtʃ ; skɔrtʃ/ *vt, vi* **1** [VP6A] burn or discolour the surface of (sth) by dry heat; cause to dry up or wither: 烘焦；燒焦(某物)之表面；使萎；使枯：*The long, hot summer ~ed the grass.* 炎熱的長夏晒枯了青草。*You ~ed my shirt when you ironed it.* 你燙我的襯衫時把它燙焦了。ˌ**~ed ˈearth policy,** policy of burning crops, and destroying buildings, etc that might be useful to enemy forces occupying a district. 焦土政策(燒毀或破壞可能對於佔領某一地區之敵軍有用的農作物及建築物等的政策)。 **2** [VP2A] become discoloured, etc with heat. 焦；萎；枯。 **3** [VP2A, C] (colloq, of cyclists, motorists, etc) travel at very high speed. (俗，指騎單車，開汽車等者)高速行駛。□ *n* [C] mark on the surface of sth (esp cloth) made by dry heat. 焦痕(尤指布上者)。**~er** *n* sth or sb that ~es: 灼熱之物；高速駕車之人：*Yesterday was a ~er,* a very hot day. 昨天熱極了。 **~·ing** *adj* very hot. 灼熱的。□ *adv*: *~ing hot,* extremely hot. 極熱的。

score¹ /skɔː(r) ; skor/ *n* [C] **1** cut, scratch or notch made on a surface: 劃痕；截痕；刻痕；記號：*~s on rock,* eg made during the Ice Age; 巖石上的痕跡(如冰河時期所留下的蝕痕)；*~s on a slave's back* (made by whipping). 奴隸背上的鞭痕。 **2** (from the old custom of chalking lines on a board in inns, to record what a customer owed for drinks, etc) account or record of money owing: (沿自舊時旅店習俗，用粉筆在木板上畫線以記錄顧客所欠之酒帳等)帳；帳目：*run up a ~,* get into debt. 負債。***pay/settle/wipe off old ~s,*** (fig) get even with sb for past offences; have one's revenge: (喻)算老帳；報仇雪恨：*I have some old ~s to settle with that fellow.* 我要跟那傢伙算一些老帳。 **3** (record of) points, goals, runs, etc made by a player or team in sport: (競技之)得分；分數；得分記錄：*The ~ in the tennis final was 6—4, 3—6, 7—5.* 網球決賽的得分記錄是六比四，三比六，七比五。*The half-time ~* (eg football) *was 2—1.* 上半場(如足球比賽)的記錄爲二比一。***keep the ~,*** keep a record of the ~ as it is made. (比賽時)記分數；記錄。 ˈ**~-board/-book/-card,** one on which the ~ (eg in cricket) is recorded (during play). (如板球賽之)記分板(簿，卡片)。 **4** reason; account. 理由；原因。***on the ~ of,*** on account of, in consideration of: 爲了；鑒於：*rejected on the ~* (*grounds* is more usu) *of ill health.* 因健康不佳而被拒絕(on the grounds 較常用)。***on more ~s than one,*** for more than one reason. 爲了種種理由。***on ˈthat ~,*** as far as that point is concerned: 在那一點上；因那理由；就那一點而言：*You need have no anxiety on that ~.* 你無需爲那個擔憂。 **5** copy of orchestral, etc music showing what each instrument is to play, each voice to sing: 總譜(表明每一樂器所該演奏，每一聲部所該演唱的管絃樂譜等)。*follow the ~ while listening to music.* 照譜聆聽音樂。 **6** twenty; set of twenty: 二十；二十之組：*a ~ of people;* 二十人；*three ~ and ten,* 70, the normal length of human life according to the Bible. 七十(根據聖經是人類的正常壽命)。*I've been there ~s of times,* very often. 我常去該處。 **7** (sl) remark or act by which a person gains an advantage for himself in an argument, etc: (俚)在辯論等中使自己佔便宜的話或動作：*a politician who is clever at making ~s off hecklers at public meetings,* clever at making them appear foolish. 擅於在公共集會中使詰問者鬧笑話的政客。⇨ score²(4).

score² /skɔː(r) ; skor/ *vt, vi* **1** [VP6A, 15A, B] mark with cuts, scratches, lines, etc: 加劃痕，截痕，刻痕，記號，線等：*The mountain side is ~d by torrents,* shows where torrents of water have washed away soil, etc. 山坡留有被急流沖刷的痕跡。*Don't ~ the floor by pushing heavy furniture about.* 不要推移笨重傢具以免損壞地板。*The composition was ~d with corrections in red ink.* 這篇作文用紅筆批改過。 **~ out,** draw a line or lines through: 畫掉；刪去：*Three words had been ~d out.* 三個字已被畫掉了。⇨ score¹(1). **2** [VP6A, 2A, 15B] **~ (up),** make or keep a record (esp for games): 記錄；(尤指)記錄比賽分數：*~ up runs,* in cricket. (板球賽)記分。*Who's going to ~?* 誰擔任記分？ **3** [VP6A, 2A] make as points in a game: 得分；獲分：*~ a goal;* 進一球；*~ a century,* 100 runs at cricket; (板球賽)得一百分；*a batsman who failed to ~,* who made no runs; 未得分的擊球員；*~ no tricks,* ie whist or bridge. (如惠斯特或橋牌戲中)未贏得一磴牌。 ***~ an advantage/a success,*** win one; have good fortune. 獲得利益(成功)。 ***~ a point (against/off/over sb),*** = ~ off sb. **4** [VP3A] ***~ off sb,*** (colloq) humiliate him; defeat him in an argument; make a clever retort to sth he says. (俗)羞辱某人；在辯論中擊敗之；駁倒其議論。 **5** [VP 15B] ***~ sth up (against sb),*** enter as a record: 記下；記住；計算：*That remark will be ~d up against you,* will be remembered (and, perhaps, be revenged). 我會記住那句話，將來再跟你算帳。 **6** [VP6A] orchestrate; write instrumental or vocal parts for a musical composition: 作成管絃樂；寫下一樂曲之樂器或歌唱部分；記入總譜：*~d for violin, viola and cello.* 爲小提琴，中提琴及大提琴配譜。⇨ score¹(5). **~r** *n* **1** person who keeps a record of points, goals, runs, etc ~d in a game. (競賽之)記分員。 **2** player who ~s runs, goals, etc. 得分之運動員。

scorn /skɔːn ; skɔrn/ *n* [U] **1** contempt; feeling that sb or sth deserves no respect: 輕蔑；蔑視：*be filled with ~ for a proposal;* 對一提議深表蔑視；*dismiss a suggestion with ~.* 輕蔑地駁回一建議。***laugh sb/sth to ~,*** treat with contemptuous laughter. 嘲笑某人(某事)。 **2** object of contempt: 輕蔑的對象：*He was the ~ of the village.* 他是全村嘲笑的對象。□ *vt* [VP6A, D, 7A] feel or show contempt for; refuse (to do sth as being unworthy): 輕蔑；蔑視；不屑(做某事)：*We ~ a liar.* 我們瞧不起說謊者。*He ~ed my advice.* 他蔑視我的忠言。*She ~s lying/telling lies/to tell a lie.* 她不屑說謊。 **~·ful** /-fl ; -fəl/ *adj* showing or feeling ~: 輕蔑的；蔑視的：*a ~ful smile;* 輕蔑的笑；*~ful of material things.* 蔑視物質方面的享受。 **~·fully** /-fəlɪ ; -fəlɪ/ *adv*

Scor·pio /ˈskɔːpɪəʊ ; ˈskɔrpɪˌo/ *n* eighth sign of the zodiac. 天蠍座；天蠍宮(黃道帶中的第八宮)。⇨ the illus at zodiac. 參看 zodiac 之插圖。

scor·pion /ˈskɔːpɪən ; ˈskɔrpɪən/ *n* small animal of the spider group with a poisonous sting in its long, jointed tail. 蠍。⇨ the illus at arachnid. 參看 arachnid 之插圖。

scot /skɒt ; skɑt/ *n* (only in) (僅用於) ***pay ~ and lot,*** share financial burdens. 分攤財政負擔。 ***get off/escape ˌ~-ˈfree,*** unharmed, unpunished. 安然逃脫；未受害；未受罰。

Scot /skɒt ; skɑt/ *n* native of Scotland. 蘇格蘭人。

Scotch /skɒtʃ ; skɑtʃ/ *adj* of Scotland or its people: 蘇格蘭的；蘇格蘭人的：*~ whisky,* the kind distilled in Scotland. 蘇格蘭威士忌酒。ˌ**~ ˈterrier,** small, rough-haired, short-legged kind of terrier. 蘇格蘭㹴(一種粗毛腿短的小狗)。□ *n* **1** **the ~,** *n pl* natives of Scotland. 蘇格蘭人。 **2** [U] ~ whisky. 蘇格蘭威士忌酒。ˈ**~·man** /-mən ; -mən/, ˈ**~·woman** *nn* = Scotsman, Scotswoman (which are the preferred terms). 蘇格蘭男人，蘇格蘭女人 (Scotsman 和 Scotswoman 較常用)。

scotch /skɒtʃ ; skɑtʃ/ *vt* [VP6A] **1** (archaic) wound without killing: (古)使受傷；傷害：*~ a snake.* 把一條蛇弄得半死。 **2** put an end to; frustrate (a plan, idea, etc). 阻止;破壞(計畫,計策等)。

Scot·land Yard /ˌskɒtlənd ˈjɑːd ; ˈskɑtləndˈjɑrd/ *n* (now *New S~ Y~*) (used for) the London police; headquarters of the Criminal Investigation Department: (現稱 New Scotland Yard) (用以指)倫敦警察廳;倫敦警察廳刑事部: *They called in ~*, asked for the help of this Department. 他們向倫敦警察廳刑事部報警。

Scots /skɒts ; skɑts/ *adj* = Scotch. **the ~** *n pl* natives of Scotland. 蘇格蘭人。**ˈ~·man** /-mən ; -mən/, **ˈ~·woman** /-wʊmən ; -wʊmən/ *nn* natives of Scotland. 蘇格蘭男人,蘇格蘭女人。

Scot·tish /ˈskɒtɪʃ ; ˈskɑtɪʃ/ *adj* = Scotch.

scoun·drel /ˈskaʊndrəl ; ˈskaʊndrəl/ *n* wicked person with no principles or scruples; villain; rascal. 寡廉鮮恥的壞人;無賴;惡棍。**~ly** /-rəlɪ ; -rəlɪ/ *adj* of or like a ~. 無賴的;似惡棍的。

scour¹ /ˈskaʊə(r) ; skaʊr/ *vt, vi* **1** [VP6A, 15A, B] make (a dirty surface) clean or bright by friction: 刷淨;擦亮(骯髒的外表): *~ the pots and pans;* 刷淨鍋和盤; *~ out a saucepan*, clean the inside (with a ~er). (用鍋刷)刷淨煮鍋的內部。**2** [VP6A, 15B] **~ sth (away/off)**, get rid of (rust, marks, etc) by rubbing or with a strong jet of water: 刷掉;沖掉(銹、汚點等): *~ the rust off.* 刷掉銹跡。**3** [VP6A, 15A] clear out (a channel, etc) by flowing over or through it: 冲刷成;冲出(河床等): *The torrent ~ed a channel down the hillside.* 急流沿著山坡冲成了一條溝。□ *n* act of ~ing: 刷;擦;冲: *give a dirty saucepan a good ~.* 把骯髒的煮鍋好好地刷洗一下。**~er** *n* (esp) pad of stiff nylon or wire for ~ing pots and pans. (尤指)刷鍋用之尼龍或金屬網墊。

scour² /ˈskaʊə(r) ; skaʊr/ *vt, vi* **1** [VP6A] go rapidly into every part of (a place) looking for: 急速走遍(一地方)而搜尋: *~ the woods.* 急速地在樹林中搜尋。*The police ~ed London for the thief.* 警察當局在倫敦搜捕那賊。**2** [VP2C] **~ about after/for sb/sth,** go quickly in search or pursuit of. 搜索;追尋。

scourge /skɜːdʒ ; skɝdʒ/ *n* **1** (old use) whip for flogging persons. (舊用法)鞭;笞。**2** cause of suffering; person regarded as an instrument of vengeance or punishment: 痛苦的原因;被視爲報復或懲罰之工具的人: *After the ~ of war came the ~ of disease.* 戰亂之後瘟疫接踵而至。□ *vt* [VP6A] **1** (old use) use a ~ on. (舊用法)鞭笞。**2** (fig) cause suffering to. (喻)使受痛苦。

scout¹ /skaʊt ; skaʊt/ *n* **1** person (not a spy), ship or small, fast aircraft, sent out to get information of the enemy's movements, strength, etc. 斥候;偵察艦;偵察機。**2 (Boy) S~,** member of an organization **(the S~ Association)** intended to develop character and teach self-reliance, discipline and public spirit. 童子軍。Cf 參較 *Girl Guides* (US 美 = *Girl S~*). **ˈ~·master** *n* officer who leads a troop of Boy S~s. 童子軍團團長或教練。**3** patrol-man on the roads, helping motorists who are members of the Automobile Association or Royal Automobile Club. (幫助身爲汽車協會或皇家汽車俱樂部會員之駕車者的)公路巡邏人員。**4** person employed to look out for talented performers (in sport, the theatre, etc) and recruit them for his employer(s): 受僱物色運動員或演員之人;球探;星探: *a ˈtalent ~.* 物色人才之人。**5** (at Oxford) college servant. (牛津大學的)校工。□ *vi* [VP2C] **~ about/around (for sb/sth),** go about as a ~(1, 4): 偵察;到處尋找: *~ about/around for...*, go about looking for.... 往各處尋找…。

scout² /skaʊt ; skaʊt/ *vt* [VP6A] dismiss (an idea, suggestion, etc) as worthless or ridiculous. 認爲無用或可笑而駁斥(意見,提議等)。

scow /skaʊ ; skaʊ/ *n* large flat-bottomed boat used for carrying sand, rock, rubbish, etc. (用於裝運沙、石、垃圾等的)平底船。

scowl /skaʊl ; skaʊl/ *n* [C] bad-tempered look (on the face). (臉上的)不豫之色;怒容。□ *vi* [VP2A, 3A] **~ (at),** look in a bad-tempered way: (對…)作不豫之色;怒目而視: *The prisoner ~ed at the judge.* 那囚犯滿面怒容地看著法官。

scrabble¹ /ˈskræbl ; ˈskræbḷ/ *n* [U] (P) game in which words are built up on a board (marked with squares) from letters printed on counters or blocks. (商標)一種拼字遊戲。

scrabble² /ˈskræbl ; ˈskræbḷ/ *vi* **1** [VP2A] scrawl, scribble. 亂寫;亂塗。**2** [VP2C] **~ about (for sth),** grope about to find or collect sth: 摸索着找;爬尋;抓攏: *~ about for sth dropped under the table.* 爬尋掉在桌下的某物。□ *n* act of scrabbling. 亂寫;亂塗;摸索着找;爬尋。

scrag /skræg ; skræg/ *n* **1** lean, skinny person or animal. 瘦瘠的人或動物。**2 ˌ~(-ˈend),** bony part of a sheep's neck, used for making soup and stews. 羊頸部的多骨部分 (用於做湯和燉菜)。□ *vt* (-gg-) put to death by strangling; twist the neck of. 招死;勒死;扼殺;絞…之頸。**scraggy** *adj* (-ier, -iest) thin and bony: 瘦瘠的: *a long, ~gy neck.* 瘦長的頸子。

scram /skræm ; skræm/ *vi* (either *imper* or *inf*) (sl) go away: (用於祈使句或不定詞)(俚)走開;滾開: *I told him to ~.* 我叫他走開。

scramble /ˈskræmbl ; ˈskræmbḷ/ *vi, vt* **1** [VP2A, C, 4A] climb, clamber or crawl (over steep or rough ground): 爬;攀緣;爬行(於陡峭或不平之地): *~ up the side of a cliff/over a rocky hillside.* 爬上峭壁(攀緣多石的山坡)。**2** [VP3A, 4A] **~ (for),** struggle with others to get sth, or as much or as many as possible of sth, from competitors: 爭取;爭奪: *The players ~d for/~d to get possession of the ball.* 球員們搶球。*The children ~d for the coins that were thrown to them.* 孩子們爭奪扔給他們的硬幣。**3** [VP6A] cook (eggs) by beating them and then heating them in a saucepan with butter and milk. (用奶油和牛奶)炒(蛋)。**4** [VP6A] make a message sent by telephone, etc unintelligible (by changing the wave frequency) without a special receiver. 改變頻率使電訊不致被竊聽。□ *n* [C] **1** climb, walk, motor-bike competition or trial, over or through obstacles, rough ground, etc. 爬過障碍或崎嶇之地等;攀緣;爬行;(摩托車之)越野比賽;越野試車。**2** rough struggle: 搶;爭取;爭奪: *There was a ~ for the best seats.* 大家都在搶最好的座位。**scram·bler** /ˈskræmblə(r) ; ˈskræmblɚ/ *n* device for scrambling telephone messages. 改變電訊頻率之裝置;擾頻器;倒頻器。⇨ 4 above.

scrap¹ /skræp ; skræp/ *n* **1** [C] small (usu unwanted) piece: 小片;碎屑(通常爲不需要者): *~s of paper/broken porcelain;* 紙(破瓷)片; (fig) small amount: (喻)小量: *not a ~ of evidence to support the charge;* 沒有一點證據可以支持該控訴; *not even a ~ of comfort in the news.* 該消息毫無令人安慰之處。**2** [U] waste or unwanted articles, esp those of value only for the material they contain: 廢料;報廢之物件 (尤指僅因其所含之物質而有價值者): *A man comes round regularly collecting ~.* 有個男人定時前來收破爛。**ˈ~-heap** *n* pile of waste or unwanted material or articles. 廢料堆;廢物堆。**ˈ~-iron** *n* [U] articles made of iron, to be melted down for re-use. 廢鐵。***throw sth/sb on the ~-heap,*** discard sth, dismiss sb, as no longer wanted. 丟棄無用之物(淘汰不再需要之人)。**3** (*pl*) odds and ends; bits of uneaten food: (複)零碎物;殘食: *Give the ~s to the dog.* 把殘食餵狗。**4** [C] picture or paragraph cut out from a periodical, etc for a collection. (從刊物等剪下以供收集的)圖片;文章;殘篇。**ˈ~-book** *n* book of blank pages on which to paste these. 剪貼簿。□ *vt* (-pp-) [VP6A] throw away as useless or worn-out: 廢棄: *You ought to ~ that old bicycle and buy a* *new one.* 你應該丢掉那輛舊自行車，再買一輛新的。 **~py** *adj* (-ier, -iest) made up of bits or ~s; not complete or properly arranged. 由零碎物件做成的；不連貫的；片斷的。 **~·ily** /-ɪlɪ ; -ɪlɪ/ *adv* **~i·ness** *n*

scrap² /skræp ; skræp/ *n* (colloq) fight, quarrel, esp one that is not planned or premeditated: (俗)打架；口角(尤指非出於預謀者)：*He had a bit of a ~ with his brother.* 他和他哥哥(弟弟)發生過一次小小的爭執。□ *vi* (-pp-) fight; quarrel: 打架；口角：*Tell those boys to stop ~ping.* 叫那些男孩子不要再打架。

scrape /skreɪp ; skrep/ *vt, vi* **1** [VP6A, 14, 15A, B, 22] **~ sth (from/off sth); ~ sth (away/off),** make clean, smooth or level by drawing or pushing the hard edge of a tool, or sth rough, along the surface; remove (mud, grease, paint, etc) in this way: (用工具)刮，削，擦；刮落；擦去(泥，油脂，油漆等)：*~ out a sticky saucepan;* 擦淨黏糊糊的煮鍋；*~ the rust off sth;* 擦掉某物上的銹；*~ paint from a door;* 刮去門上的油漆；*~ a dish clean.* 把盤子擦淨。*The ship's bottom needs to be ~d,* eg in order to remove barnacles. 船底需要刮了(如除去藤壺)。 **2** [VP6A, 14] **~ sth (from/off sth),** injure or damage by harsh rubbing, etc: 刮壞；擦傷：*The boy fell and ~d his knee/~d the skin off his knee.* 那男孩跌倒，擦傷了膝蓋(擦破了膝蓋的皮)。*He ~d the side of his car/~d the paintwork of his car.* 他刮壞了他的汽車的側邊(油漆)。 **3** [VP6A, 15B] **~ sth (out),** make by scraping: 刮成；挖空：*~ (out) a hole.* 挖洞。 **4** [VP2C, 3A] go, get, pass along, touching or almost touching: 擦過；勉強通過：*~ along a wall;* 擦牆而過；*branches that ~ against the window panes.* 擦到窗玻璃的樹枝。**~ along,** (fig) manage to live in spite of difficulties. (喻)勉强維持生活。**~ through (sth),** only just pass: 勉强通過：*The boy just ~d through (his exams).* 那男孩勉强通過了考試。**bow and ~,** bow awkwardly while drawing one foot along the floor; (fig) behave with exaggerated respect. (將一隻脚往後退)笨拙地打躬作揖；(喻)過分奉承；巴結。 **5** [VP6A, 15B] **~ sth/sb together,** obtain by being careful, or with effort: 設法得到；盡量聚積：*We managed to ~ together an audience of fifty people/enough money for a short holiday.* 我們設法聚集了五十名聽衆(足够的錢做短期度假)。**~ (up) an acquaintance with sb,** force one's acquaintance upon sb; push oneself into a person's company in order to get acquainted with him. 硬要與某人結交；極力與某人接近以結識之。**~ a living,** with difficulty make enough money for a living. 勉强够維持生活。□ *n* **1** act or sound of scraping: 刮；削；擦；刮削聲；磨擦聲：*the ~ of sb's pen on paper/of the teacher's fingernail on the blackboard.* 筆在紙上的沙沙聲(教師的指甲在黑板上的磨擦聲)。 **2** place that is ~d: 被刮削之處；擦傷：*a bad ~ on the elbow,* eg as the result of a fall. 肘上的嚴重擦傷。 **3** awkward situation resulting from foolish or thoughtless behaviour: (由於愚笨或欠考慮之行爲所造成的)困境；困難：*That boy is always getting into ~s.* 那男孩老是陷入困境。*Don't expect me to get you out of your ~s.* 不要指望我能幫助你脫離困境。**~r** *n* tool used for scraping, eg for scraping mud from one's shoes at the entrance to a building, or for scraping paint from woodwork. 刮具；擦器(例如進門處之除去鞋泥的刮具，或擦掉木器之油漆的刮刀)。**scrap·ing** *n* (esp *pl*) small bits produced by scraping: (尤用複數)被刮削下的碎屑：*scrapings from the bottom of the barrel.* 從桶底刮下來的碎屑。

scrappy /ˈskræpɪ ; ˈskræpɪ/ *adj* ⇨ scrap¹.

scratch¹ /skrætʃ ; skrætʃ/ *vt, vi* **1** [VP6A, 2A] make lines on or in a surface with sth pointed or sharp, eg fingernails, claws: (用指甲、爪等)抓；搔：*The cat ~ed me.* 猫抓了我。*Does your cat ~?* 你的猫會抓人嗎？*Who has ~ed the paint?* 誰抓壞了油漆？**~ the surface,** (fig) deal with a subject without being thorough, without getting deeply into it: (喻)討論一題目未能徹底深入：*The lecturer merely ~ed the surface of the subject.* 那演講者僅抓到該題目的皮毛。 **2** [VP6A] get (oneself, a part of the body) ~ed by accident: 意外地使(自己，身體的一部分)刮傷：*He ~ed his hands badly while pruning the rose-bushes.* 他修剪玫瑰時雙手刮傷得很厲害。 **3** [VP15B] **~ sth out,** draw a line or lines through a word or words, a name, etc: 勾掉；畫去(字，名字等)：*~ out Smith/his name from the list.* 把史密斯(他的名字)從名單上畫去。*The essay contained a lot of scratched-out words/ˌ~ings-ˈout.* 這篇論文有許多畫掉的字。 **4** [VP6A, 2A] withdraw (a horse, a candidate, oneself) from a competition; take out (the name of a horse, a candidate) from a list of entries for a race or competition: 使(馬，候選人，自己)退出比賽；自比賽的名單中畫去(馬，候選人的名字)：*The horse was ~ed,* Its name was withdrawn. 那馬退出比賽了。*I hope you're not going to ~* (= withdraw, decline) *at the last moment.* 我希望你不會在最後一刻退出比賽。 **5** [VP6A, 2A] scrape or rub (the skin), esp to relieve itching: (尤指爲止癢而)搔(皮膚)：*~ mosquito bites.* 搔蚊子咬過的地方。*Stop ~ing (yourself).* 停止搔抓皮膚。**~ one's head,** show signs of being perplexed. 搔頭(顯出困惑的樣子)。***If you'll ~ ˌmy back, I'll ~ ˈyours,*** (fig) If you'll help, flatter, etc me, I'll do the same for you. (喻)如果你幫我的忙(奉承我)，我也會幫助你(奉承你)；投桃報李。 **6** [VP6A, 15B] **~ sth (out),** make by ~ing: (用指甲，爪等)挖：*~ (out) a hole.* 挖出一個洞。 **7** [VP6A] write hurriedly; scribble: 匆促地寫；亂寫：*~ a few lines to a friend.* 潦草地寫幾句話給一位朋友。**ˈ~-pad** *n* scribbling pad. 拍紙簿；便箋簿。 **8** [VP2A] make a scraping noise: 發刮擦聲：*This pen ~es.* 這鋼筆寫字時發刮擦聲。 **9** [VP2C, 15B] **~ about (for sth); ~ sth up,** tear or dig with the claws, fingernails, etc in search of sth: (以爪，指甲等)挖尋；搜尋：*The chickens were ~ing about in the yard.* 鷄正在院子裏四處覓食。*The dog ~ed up a bone.* 那狗挖到一根骨頭。 **10** [VP15B] scrape(5): 積攢；湊攏：*~ up/together a few pounds.* 積攢數鎊錢。

scratch² /skrætʃ ; skrætʃ/ *n* **1** [C] mark, cut, injury, sound, made by scratching(1): 抓痕；搔痕；抓傷；搔傷；抓搔聲：*Her hands were covered with ~es after she had pruned her rose-bushes.* 她修剪過玫瑰叢以後，雙手盡是刺痕。*It's only a ~,* a very slight injury. (它)不過是微傷罷了。*He escaped without a ~,* quite unhurt. 他安然逃脫。***a ~ of the pen,*** a few words quickly and easily written; a signature. 匆促而隨便寫的幾個字；簽名。 **2** (*sing* only) act or period of scratching(5): (僅用單數)抓；搔；抓搔的期間：*The dog enjoys having a good ~.* 那狗喜歡搔癢。 **3** (*sing* only; no article) starting line for a race. (僅用單數；無冠詞)(競賽之)起跑線。***start from ~,*** start from this line; (fig) start without being allowed any advantage(s); (fig) begin (sth) without preparation. 從起跑線出發；(喻)從頭做起；白手起家；(喻)未經準備而開始(某事)。***be/come/bring sb up to ~,*** (fig) be ready/get sb ready to do what is expected or required: (喻)準備好(使某人準備好)做所期望或要求之事：*Will your teachers manage to bring you up to ~ before you take the examination,* get you ready for it? 你們的老師能使你們在參加考試之前有充分準備嗎？ **4** (attrib) (sport) without a handicap: (形容用法)(運動)對條件優者無限制的；無讓分優待的：*~ player.* 在同樣條件下比賽的運動員。**ˈ~-race** *n* one in which all competitors start from ~, on equal terms. 在同樣的條件下的比賽；無讓分優待的比賽。 **5** (attrib) collected by chance; brought together, done, made, with whatever is available: (形容用法)偶然湊成的；東拼西湊的；利用手頭材料做成或製成的：*a ~ crew/team;* 臨時湊成的一船水手(一個球隊)；*a ~ dinner,* prepared from what happens to be in the house. (就家中現有食物湊成的)便飯。**~y** *adj* **1** (of writing, drawings) done carelessly or unskilfully. (指寫作,圖畫)草率的;拙劣的。 **2** (of a pen) making a scratching noise. (指鋼筆)發沙沙聲的。

scrawl /skrɔ:l ; skrɔl/ *vi, vt* [VP6A, 2A, C] write or draw quickly or carelessly; make meaningless or illegible marks: 潦草地寫或畫; 亂塗: *Who has ~ed all over this wall?* 誰在這牆上亂塗? *He ~ed a few words on a postcard to his wife.* 他潦草地在一張明信片上寫了幾句話給他的妻子。□ *n* **1** [C] piece of bad writing; hurried note of letter. 拙劣的寫作; 潦草寫成的便條或信。 **2** (*sing* only) shapeless, untidy handwriting: (僅用單數)潦草的筆跡;塗鴉: *What a ~!* 多潦草的字跡! *His signature was an illegible ~.* 他的簽名是難以辨認的塗鴉。

scrawny /ˈskrɔ:nɪ ; ˈskrɔnɪ/ *adj* (-ier, -iest) bony, scraggy: 瘦瘠的: *the ~ neck of a turkey.* 火鷄細而瘦的頸子。

scream /skri:m ; skrim/ *vi, vt* **1** [VP2A, C, 6A, 15A, B, 22] **~ *(out)*,** (of human beings, birds, animals) give a loud, sharp cry or cries of, or as of, fear or pain; cry (sth) in a loud shrill voice: (指人、鳥、獸)發出(宛如)恐懼或痛苦的尖叫聲;尖叫著說(某事物): *She ~ed in anger.* 她憤怒地尖聲叫喊。*The baby has been ~ing for an hour.* 那嬰兒已經號叫了一小時。*This parrot ~s but does not talk.* 這鸚鵡會尖叫,但不會說話。*The child ~ed itself red in the face.* 這孩子尖叫得臉都紅了。 *She ~ed out that there was a burglar under the bed.* 她尖叫說床下有賊。 *We all ~ed with laughter,* laughed noisily. 我們都縱聲大笑。**~ *one's* ˈhead off,** ~ very loudly (and for a long time). 大聲喊叫;拚命喊叫。 **2** [VP2A, C] (of the wind, machines, etc) make a loud, shrill noise: (指風,機器等)呼嘯;發尖銳聲: *The wind ~ed through the trees.* 風從林間呼嘯而過。□ *n* [C] **1** loud, shrill, piercing cry or noise: 尖叫聲: *the ~ of a peacock;* 孔雀的尖叫聲; *~s of pain/laughter.* 痛苦的尖叫(縱聲大笑)。 **2** (colloq) sb or sth that causes ~s of laughter: (俗)非常可笑的滑稽人物或事件: *He/It was a perfect ~.* 他(它)是極其可笑的。 **~·ing·ly** *adv* (esp): (尤用於): *~ingly funny,* so funny as to cause ~s of laughter. 非常可笑的;非常有趣的。

scree /skri: ; skri/ *n* [C, U] (part of a mountainside covered with) small loose stones which slide down when trodden on. 山坡上的碎石;覆有碎石的山坡。⇨ the illus at mountain. 參看 mountain 之插圖。

screech /skri:tʃ ; skritʃ/ *vi, vt* [VP2A, C, 6A, 15A, B] **~ *(out)*, 1** make a harsh, piercing sound: 發尖聲;發出尖銳刺耳的聲音: *jet planes ~ing over the house-tops.* 噴射機在屋頂上呼嘯而過。 *The brakes ~ed as the car stopped.* 汽車停下時煞車發尖嘎聲。 **2** scream in anger or pain; cry out in high tones: 憤怒或痛苦地尖叫;高聲喊出: *monkeys ~ing in the trees.* 在樹上尖叫的猴子。*She ~es out her top notes instead of singing them.* 她尖聲叫出高音符,並非唱出它們。□ *n* [C] ~ing cry or noise: 尖叫;尖銳聲: *the ~ of tyres,* eg when a car is cornering fast. (汽車急轉彎等之時)輪胎磨擦的尖銳聲。**ˈ~-owl** *n* kind of owl that ~es instead of hooting. 叫梟 (一種叫聲很尖而非喨喨地叫的梟)。

screed /skri:d ; skrid/ *n* [C] long (and usu uninteresting) piece of writing; long monotonous speech. 冗長(且通常枯燥乏味)的文章;冗長乏味的演講。

screen /skri:n ; skrin/ *n* [C] **1** (often movable) upright framework (some made so as to fold), used to hide sb or sth from view, or to protect from draughts or from too much heat, light, etc. 屏;幕;簾;帳;隔板 (常爲可移動的直立構架,有的並可折疊,用於遮蔽某人或某物,或使不受風吹,過度受熱,受光等)。**2** (in a church) structure of wood or stone separating (but not completely) the main part of the church and the altar, or the nave of a cathedral and the choir. 祭壇屏飾(使教堂的中部與祭壇,或大教堂的正廳與唱詩班席位部分隔開的木造或石造建築物)。 **3** anything that is or can be used to give shelter or protection from observation, the weather, etc: 可用以防止觀察,躲避風雨等之遮蔽物: *a ~ of trees,* hiding a house from the road; 一列樹籬(使房子與大路隔開); *a ˈsmoke-~,* used in war to hide ships, etc from the enemy; 煙幕(戰時用以掩護船隻等,以免被敵人發現); *a ~ of indifference,* an appearance of indifference that hides interest. (掩飾關心之)故示冷淡的外表。 **4** white or silver surface on to which slides, film transparencies, cinema films, TV pictures, etc are projected; surface upon which an image is seen on a cathode ray tube. (電影、幻燈、透明片的)銀幕;(電視的)螢光幕。Hence, 由此產生, (attrib, = *cinema*) (形容用法) *a ~ play,* the script of a film; 電影或電視脚本; *~ actors/stars;* 電影或電視演員(明星); *a ˈ~ test,* test of a person's suitability for acting in films. 試鏡(測驗一個人是否適於演電影)。 **5** frame with fine wire netting (*ˈwindow ~, ˈdoor ~*) to keep out flies, mosquitoes, etc. 紗窗;紗門(用以阻擋蒼蠅、蚊蟲等)。 **6** large sieve or riddle used for separating coal, gravel, etc into different sizes. 大篩;粗篩(用以按顆粒大小區分煤、砂石等)。 **7** (cricket) one of two large movable erections of white wood or canvas placed near the boundary line to help batsmen to see the ball. (板球)白色木材或帆布活動大屏風(置於球場兩端,使擊球員能看得見球)。□ *vt, vi* **1** [VP6A, 14, 15A, B] **~ *(off)* *(from)*,** shelter, hide, protect from view, with a ~: (用屏、幕等)遮蔽;隱藏;掩護: *The trees ~ our house from public view.* 這些樹遮蔽了我們的房屋,使別人看不見。 *One corner of the room was ~ed off.* 房間的一角被隔開了。*You should ~ the lens of your camera from direct sunlight.* 你應該使照相機的鏡頭不直接受到陽光的照射。*We have ~ed our house* (ie doors and windows) *against mosquitoes.* 我們的房子已裝了紗門紗窗以避蚊蟲。 **2** [VP6A, 14] **~ *(from)*,** (fig) protect from blame, discovery, punishment: (喻)包庇;庇護: *I'm not willing to ~ your faults/~ you from blame.* 我不願包庇你。 **3** [VP6A] separate (coal, etc) into different sizes by passing through a ~(6): 用大篩或粗篩分(煤等);篩選: *~ed coal,* from which dust has been removed. 已篩去沙土的煤。 **4** [VP6A] investigate (sb's) past history, eg the political antecedents of a refugee or displaced person, sb applying for a position in government service, in order to judge his loyalty, dependability, etc; examine (sb) to judge his qualifications for a post, etc. 調查(某人的)過去歷史(例如難民或尋求政治庇護者,或申請公職者的政治背景)以判斷其忠誠、可靠性等; 考查(某人)以判斷其任職等的資格; 甄別。 **5** [VP 6A] show (an object, a scene) on a ~(4); make a cinema film of. 放映(物體,場景)於銀幕或屏幕上; 攝製…的電影。 [VP2C] **~ *well/badly,*** (of a stage play, an actor, etc) be suitable/unsuitable for filming. (指舞臺劇、演員等)適於(不適於)拍電影。

screws

screw /skru: ; skru/ *n* **1** metal peg with slotted head and a spiral groove cut round its length, driven into wood, metal, etc by twisting under pressure, for fastening and holding things together. 螺絲;螺絲釘;螺旋釘。 ***a* ˈ~ *loose*,** (fig) sth wrong or out of order: (喻)毛病;故障: *There's a ~ loose somewhere.* 某個地方發生故障了。*He has a ~ loose,* is a little stupid. 他有點笨。 **ˈ~-driver** *n* tool for turning ~s. 螺絲刀; 起子 (旋轉螺絲釘的工具)。⇨ the illus at tool. 參看 tool 之插圖。 **ˌ~-ˈtopped** *adj* (of jars, etc) having a top or lid with a spiral groove, put on or taken off by twisting. (指瓶等) 有螺線之口或蓋的 (由擰轉以蓋上或取下)。'~-**ball** *n, adj* (US, sl) crazy (person). (美,俚)瘋狂的(人)。 **2** sth that is turned like a screw and is used for exerting pressure, tightening, etc. 螺旋狀物;功用似螺絲之物。 ***put the ~(s) on sb; give (sb) another turn of the ~,*** use one's power, a threat of force, etc to force him to do sth. 施壓力逼迫某人做某事。 '**thumb**~ *n* ⇨ thumb. **3** action of turning; turn: 螺旋式的轉動;擰轉: *This isn't tight enough yet; give it another ~.* 這個還不够牢,把它再轉一下。 **4** '~**(-propeller)** propeller of a ship: 船的螺旋槳或推進器;暗輪: *a twin-~ ship.* 雙螺旋槳的船。 **('air)~,** propeller of an aircraft. 飛機的螺旋槳或推進器。⇨ the illus at air. 參看 air 之插圖。 **5** [C, U] (in games, eg billiards) spin given to a ball to make it curve or change direction. (撞球等遊戲) 轉球;擰 (使球作曲線運動或使之改變方向者)。 **6** small, twisted piece of paper and its contents: 小捲之紙及捲在紙中之物;紙包: *a ~ of tea/tobacco.* 一包茶葉(煙草)。 **7** (colloq) miser. (俗) 吝嗇鬼;守財奴。 **8** (GB, sl) amount of salary or wages: (英,俚)薪水或工資的數額: *He's paid a good ~.* 他拿的薪水不少。 **9** (GB, sl) (= *turnkey*) prison warder. (英,俚)典獄官;獄吏。 **10** ⚠ act of or partner in sexual intercourse. (諱)性交;與人性交者。 □ *vt, vi* **1** [VP6A, 15A, B] fasten or tighten with a ~ or ~s: 用螺旋釘釘住;用螺絲擰緊: *~ a lock on a door;* 用螺旋釘把鎖釘在門上; *~ down the lid of a coffin;* 用螺絲擰緊棺材蓋; *~ up a door,* so that it cannot be opened. 將門釘死。 ***have one's head ~ed on (the right way),*** be sensible, have good judgement. 通達事理;有良好判斷。 **2** [VP6A, 15A, B] twist round; make tight, tense or more efficient: 擰轉;使緊;使更有效率: *~ a lid on/off a jar;* 擰上(開)瓶蓋; *~ one's head round,* in order to look over one's shoulder; (為了回顧)轉頭; *~ up one's face/features/eyes,* contract the muscles, eg when going out into bright sunshine from a dark room. 皺著臉(皺起面孔;瞇著眼睛)(如剛從黑暗的房間走入强烈的陽光時)。 ***~ up one's courage,*** overcome one's fears. 鼓起勇氣。 **3** [VP6A, 15A, B] exert pressure on; force (out of): 加壓力於;壓榨;强迫;擠出: *~ water out of a sponge/more taxes out of the people.* 自海綿中將水擠出 (向人民榨取更多的稅)。 **4** (sl) ***be ~ed,*** be drunk. (俚)喝醉的。 **5** [VP6A, 2A] ⚠ have sexual intercourse with. (諱)與…性交。 **~y** *adj* (GB colloq) eccentric; crazy; (US colloq) ludicrously odd; absurd. (英俗)怪癖的;瘋癲的;(美俗)荒謬的;可笑的。

scribble /'skrɪbl ; 'skrɪbl/ *vt, vi* [VP6A, 2A] write hastily or carelessly; make meaningless marks on paper, etc. 潦草書寫;胡寫;亂畫。 '**scribbling-block** *n* pad of cheap paper making notes. 拍紙簿;便條紙。 □ *n* [U] hasty, careless handwriting; [C] sth ~d. 潦草書寫;潦草之字跡;胡亂寫成之物。 **scrib·bler** /'skrɪblə(r) ; 'skrɪblɚ/ *n* person who ~s; (colloq) inferior author. 潦草書寫的人;(俗)濫寫的作家;拙劣之作家。

scribe /skraɪb ; skraɪb/ *n* **1** professional letter-writer; person who, before the invention of printing, made copies of writings, eg in monasteries. 書記;抄寫者(例如印刷術發明前在寺院中抄寫書籍者)。 **2** (Jewish hist) maker and keeper of records; teacher of Jewish law (at the time of Jesus Christ). (猶太史)文牘;書記;(耶穌基督時代的)猶太法學者;律法師。

scrim·mage /'skrɪmɪdʒ ; 'skrɪmɪdʒ/ *n* **1** [C] confused struggle or fight. 扭打;混戰。 **2** (US football) the play that takes place when two teams are lined up for the players to begin or resume play. (美式足球) 並列爭球 (開賽或繼續比賽時兩隊球員排成橫隊,對面而立,爭取控球)。 **3** = scrum(mage). □ *vi, vt* engage in a ~(1); put (the ball) in a ~. 參與混戰;置(球)於並列爭奪的位置;並列爭(球)。

scrimp /skrɪmp ; skrɪmp/ *vt, vi* = skimp (which is more usu). (skimp 較常用)。

scrip /skrɪp ; skrɪp/ *n* [C] document, the possession of which entitles the holder to a formal certificate for ownership of stock in a business company, etc on completion of formalities; [U] such documents collectively. 臨時憑單;股票臨時收據(持有者在完成手續後有權獲得公司之正式股票等);代價券(總稱語)。

script /skrɪpt ; skrɪpt/ *n* **1** [U] (opp of *print*) handwriting; printed cursive characters in imitation of handwriting. (為 print之相反字)手跡;筆跡;草書體鉛字。 **2** [C] (short for) manuscript or typescript (esp of an actor's part in a play, a talk, discussion, drama, etc to be broadcast, etc). (為 manuscript 或 typescript 之略)手稿;打字原稿;(尤指)戲劇脚本原稿;廣播原稿。 '~·**writer** *n* person who writes ~s for films or broadcast programmes. 電影或廣播節目之撰稿人。 **~ed** *adj* read from a ~: 照原稿唸出的: *Un~ed discussions are usually livelier than ~ed discussions,* eg in a broadcast programme. (在廣播節目等中)不用稿的討論通常比讀稿的討論更為生動。

scrip·ture /'skrɪptʃə(r) ; 'skrɪptʃɚ/ *n* **1 (Holy) S~, The (Holy) S~s,** the Bible; (attrib) taken from, relating to, the Bible: 聖經;(形容用法)引自或有關聖經的: *a '~ lesson.* 聖經課。 **2** sacred book of a religion other than Christianity. (其他宗教的)經典;經文。 **scrip·tural** /'skrɪptʃərəl ; 'skrɪptʃərəl/ *adj* based on the Bible. 根據聖經的。

scrof·ula /'skrɒfjʊlə ; 'skrɔfjələ/ *n* [U] tuberculous disease in which there are swellings of the lymphatic glands. 斯科夫拉;瘰癧;淋巴腺結核病。 **scrofu·lous** /'skrɒfjʊləs ; 'skrɔfjələs/ *adj*

scroll /skrəʊl ; skrol/ *n* **1** roll of paper or parchment for writing on; ancient book written on a ~. 紙卷;卷軸;成卷軸的古書。 **2** ornamental design cut in stone; flourish in writing, suggesting by its curves a ~ of parchment. 石刻上的渦卷形裝飾圖案;渦卷形字體。

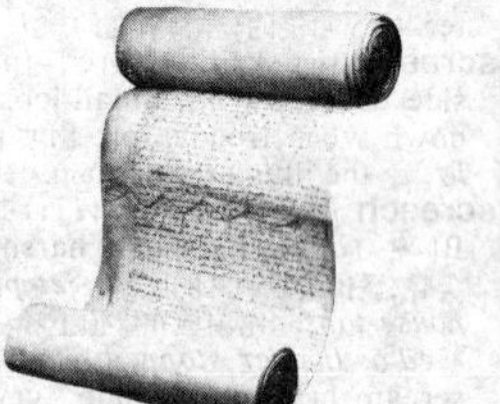

a scroll

Scrooge /skruːdʒ ; skrudʒ/ *n* mean-spirited miser. 度量狹小的吝嗇鬼。

scro·tum /'skrəʊtəm ; 'skrotəm/ *n* pouch of skin enclosing the testicles in mammals. 陰囊。

scrounge /skraʊndʒ ; skraʊndʒ/ *vi, vt* [VP2A, 6A] (colloq) get what one wants by taking it without permission or by trickery. (俗)偷;擅取;騙取。 **~r** *n* person who ~s. 偷者;擅取者;騙取者。

scrub¹ /skrʌb ; skrʌb/ *n* **1** [U] (land covered with) trees and bushes of poor quality; stunted forest growth: 拙劣的雜樹叢;長有雜樹叢之地;矮樹: (attrib) (形容用法) '*~-pine,* '*~-oak,* dwarf or stunted kinds. 矮松,矮橡樹。 **2** [C] anything below the usual size. 任何矮小之物。 **~by** /'skrʌbɪ ; 'skrʌbɪ/ *adj* (-ier, -iest) **1** small, stunted; mean. 小的;矮的;卑劣的。 **2** rough and bristly: 粗糙而有刺毛的: *a ~by chin.* 粗糙而刺人的下巴。

scrub² /skrʌb ; skrʌb/ *vt, vi* (-bb-) [VP6A, 15B, 22, 2A, C] ***~ (out),*** clean by rubbing hard, esp with a stiff brush, soap and water: 用力擦洗;擦淨(尤指用硬刷、肥皂和水): *~ the floor;* 擦洗地板; *~ out a pan;* 擦淨平鍋; *~ the walls clean;* 把牆刷洗乾淨;

cancel; ignore: 取消;不理會: ~ (*out*) *an order*. 取消命令。 **'~bing-brush** *n* stiff brush for ~bing floors, etc. 硬毛刷子(刷洗地板等所用者)。⇨ the illus at brush. 參看 brush 之插圖。□ *n* act of ~bing: 擦洗;擦淨: *The floor needs a good* ~. 這地板需要好好刷洗一番。

scruff /skrʌf ; skrʌf/ *n* (only in) (僅用於) ***the ~ of the neck,*** the back of the neck, the nape, when used for grasping or lifting: 頸背(攫握或提起時用之): *seize/take an animal by the ~ of the neck*. 抓住一動物的頸背。

scruffy /ˈskrʌfɪ ; ˈskrʌfɪ/ *adj* (-ier, -iest) (colloq) dirty, untended and untidy looking. (俗)骯髒的;不整潔的;樣子邋遢的。

scrum /skrʌm ; skrʌm/ *n* (abbr of) scrummage. 爲 scrummage 之略。 **scrum half,** the half-back who puts the ball into the ~. 拿球放在並列爭球位置的前衞。

scrum·mage /ˈskrʌmɪdʒ ; ˈskrʌmɪdʒ/ *n* the play in Rugby football when the forwards of both sides pack together with their heads down while the ball is thrown into the middle of them and they then try to kick the ball back to their own team; all those forwards when such play occurs. 並列爭球(橄欖球賽中雙方前鋒低著頭密集排列,搶奪拋入兩隊之間的球);參加並列爭球的前鋒。

scrump·tious /ˈskrʌmpʃəs ; ˈskrʌmpʃəs/ *adj* (colloq, chiefly of food) delightful: (俗,主要指食物)極好的: ~ *food*. 美食。

scrunch /skrʌntʃ ; skrʌntʃ/ *n, vt* = crunch(2).

scruple /ˈskru:pl ; ˈskrupḷ/ *n* **1** [C] weight-unit of 20 grains. 衡量單位(等於二十喱)。⇨ App 5. 參看附錄五。 **2** [C, U] (hesitation caused by) uneasiness of conscience: 良心不安;自責;(由於良心不安引起的)躊躇;猶豫;顧忌: *Have you no ~s about borrowing things without permission?* 你對於不經允許而借用旁人東西無所顧忌嗎? *He will tell lies without* ~. 他會毫無忌憚地說謊。□ *vi* [VP4C] ***~ to do sth,*** hesitate owing to ~s: 躊躇;有所顧忌: (usu neg) (通常爲否定句) *He doesn't ~ to tell a lie if he thinks it useful*. 如果他認爲說謊有用,他會無所顧忌地說謊。

scru·pu·lous /ˈskru:pjʊləs ; ˈskrupjələs/ *adj* careful to do nothing morally wrong; paying great attention to small points (esp of conscience): 多顧慮的; 小心翼翼的; (尤指對良心之所安) 審愼的: *He is not ~ in his business dealings*. 他做生意不够審愼。 *A solicitor must act with ~ honesty*. 一個律師必須審愼正直。 **~·ly** *adv* in a ~ manner: 多顧慮地;審愼地: *~ly exact/careful*. 十分精確(小心)的。

scru·ti·neer /ˌskru:tɪˈnɪə(r) *US:* -tnˈɪər ; ˌskrutəˈnɪr/ *n* official who examines ballot papers to see that they are not filled in irregularly. 選票檢查員;監票官。

scru·ti·nize /ˈskru:tɪnaɪz *US:* -tənaɪz ; ˈskrutn̩ˌaɪz/ *vt* [VP6A] make a detailed examination of. 細察;詳審。

scru·tiny /ˈskru:tɪnɪ *US:* -tənɪ ; ˈskrutn̩ɪ/ *n* (*pl* -nies) **1** [U] thorough and detailed examination; [C] instance of this. 細察; 詳審; 細察或詳審的實例。 **2** [C] official examination of votes, esp a recount of votes at an election when the result of the first count is very close: 核算選票;(尤指第一次計算後結果非常接近之)選票再計算: *demand a* ~. 要求再計算選票。

scud /skʌd ; skʌd/ *vi* (-dd-) [VP2A, C] go straight and fast, with smooth motion: (平穩地)疾行;飛馳: *The clouds ~ded across the sky*. 雲從天空飛過。 *The yacht was ~ding along before the wind*. 那遊艇正乘風向前疾行。□ *n* [C] act of ~ding; [U] vapoury clouds driven by the wind. 疾行;飛馳;飛雲;碎雨雲。

scuff /skʌf ; skʌf/ *vi, vt* **1** [VP2A, C] walk without properly lifting the feet from the ground; shuffle. 拖足而行;曳足而行。 **2** [VP6A, 15A, B] wear out or injure (shoes, etc) by walking in this way: 曳足而磨損(鞋等): ~ *one's shoes*. 把鞋磨壞。

scuffle /ˈskʌfl ; ˈskʌfḷ/ *vi* [VP2A, C], *n* (take part in a) rough, confused fight or struggle: 混戰;亂打;參加混戰或亂打: *There was a ~ between the police and some demonstrators*. 警察和一些示威的人發生了一場混戰。

scull /skʌl ; skʌl/ *n* **1** one of a pair of oars used together by a single rower, one in each hand. (每手各執其一由單人操作的) 雙槳中之一葉; 短槳。 **2** oar worked at the stern of a boat with twisting strokes. 船之尾櫓;舳楫。□ *vt, vi* [VP6A, 2A] propel (a boat) with a ~; row (a boat) with ~s; use a ~ or ~s. 以尾櫓推進(船); 以短槳划(船); 用尾櫓或短槳。 **~er** *n* person who ~s. 用短槳或尾櫓操舟者。

scul·lery /ˈskʌlərɪ ; ˈskʌlərɪ/ *n* (*pl* -ries) room usu in a large house next to the kitchen, where dishes, pots, etc are washed up. 碗碟洗滌室(通常在廚房旁)。

scul·lion /ˈskʌlɪən ; ˈskʌljən/ *n* (hist) boy or man who did rough work in the kitchen of a large house, etc. (史)在巨宅之廚房操粗重工作的用人。

sculpt /skʌlpt ; skʌlpt/ *vt, vi* = sculpture.

sculp·tor /ˈskʌlptə(r) ; ˈskʌlptɚ/ *n* artist who sculptures. 雕刻家;雕刻師。 **sculp·tress** /ˈskʌlptrɪs ; ˈskʌlptrɪs/ *n* woman ~. 女雕刻師。

sculp·ture /ˈskʌlptʃə(r) ; ˈskʌlptʃɚ/ *n* **1** [U] art of making representations in stone, wood, metal, etc by carving or modelling. 雕刻術; 雕塑術;雕刻;雕塑。 **2** [C, U] (piece of) such work. (一件)雕刻品;雕塑品。□ *vt, vi* **1** [VP6A] represent in ~; decorate with ~: 雕刻(塑);用雕刻(塑)物裝飾: ~ *a statue out of stone;* 從石塊雕出一座塑像; *~d columns*. 雕刻的柱子。 **2** [VP2A] be a sculptor; do ~. 做雕刻(塑)師;幹雕刻(塑)行業。 **sculp·tural** /ˈskʌlptʃərəl ; ˈskʌlptʃərəl/ *adj* of, like, connected with, ~: 雕刻或雕塑(術)的; 似雕刻(塑)的; 有關雕刻(塑)的: *the sculptural arts*. 雕刻(塑)技藝。

scum /skʌm ; skʌm/ *n* [U] **1** froth which forms on the surface of some boiling liquids; dirt on the surface of a pond or other area of still water. (某些煮沸液體之表面的)泡沫;(池塘或其他靜水上的)浮垢;浮渣。 **2** ***the ~ (of),*** (fig) worthless person(s) (of a place). (喻)(某地的)無用之人;渣滓。 ***the ~ of the earth,*** worthless person(s). 無價值之人。 **~my** *adj* of, like, having or containing, ~. 泡沫的;浮渣的;渣滓的;似浮渣的;有浮渣的。

scup·per /ˈskʌpə(r) ; ˈskʌpɚ/ *n* opening in a ship's side to allow water to run off the deck. 船舷上之排水孔(排除甲板上的水)。□ *vt* sink a ship deliberately; (colloq, usu passive) ruin; disable: 故意使(船)沉没; (俗,通常用被動語態)摧毁; 使殘廢: *We're ~ed!* 我們完蛋了!

scurf /skɜ:f ; skɜf/ *n* [U] small bits of dead skin, esp on the scalp, loosened as new skin grows; dandruff: 皮屑;皮垢;頭皮屑;頭垢: *monkeys searching each other's fur for* ~. 猴子們彼此搜找皮毛中的皮屑。 **~y** *adj* having, covered with, ~. 有皮屑的;有頭垢的。

scur·ri·lous /ˈskʌrɪləs ; ˈskɝələs/ *adj* using, full of, violent and taunting words of abuse: 用罵人的話; 多罵人話的; 謾罵的; 下流的: ~ *attacks upon the Prime Minister*. 對首相作謾罵的攻擊。 **scur·ril·ity** /skəˈrɪlətɪ ; skəˈrɪlətɪ/ *n* [U] ~ language; (*pl;* -ties) ~ remarks: 謾罵;下流;(複)罵人話: *indulge in scurrilities*. 肆意謾罵。

scurry /ˈskʌrɪ ; ˈskɝɪ/ *vi* (*pt, pp* -ried) [VP2A, C, 3A] ***~ (about) (for/through),*** run with short, quick steps; hurry: 急忙奔跑;疾行;趕急: *The rain sent everyone ~ing for shelter*. 雨使大家急忙找地方躲避。 *Don't ~ through your work*. 不要趕急做你的工作。□ *n* **1** [U] act or sound of ~ing; anxious or excited bustle and movement: 急忙奔跑;疾行;疾行聲;趕急;奔忙: *the ~ and scramble of town life*. 城市生活的匆促急忙。 *There was a ~ towards* *the refreshments.* 大家一窩蜂湧去吃點心。**2** [C] ~ ***(of),*** windy shower (of snow); cloud (of dust). (雪片的)飛散;一陣風雪;(灰沙的)瀰漫;飛揚的塵土。

scurvy /ˈskɜːvɪ ; ˈskɝvɪ/ *n* [U] diseased state of the blood caused (esp among sailors in former times) by eating too much salt meat and not enough fresh vegetables and fruit. 壞血症(由食鹹肉過多,食新鮮蔬菜及水果不足所致,從前患此症者尤以水手居多)。□ *adj* (sl) dishonourable, contemptuous: (俚)卑鄙的;可鄙的: *That was a ~ trick to play on an old lady.* 對一位老婦人施這樣的詭計是太卑鄙了。**scurv·ily** /-ɪlɪ ; -əlɪ/ *adv*

scut /skʌt ; skʌt/ *n* [C] short, erect tail, esp of a rabbit, hare or deer. (尤指家兔、野兔或鹿之)短尾。

scutch·eon /ˈskʌtʃən ; ˈskʌtʃən/ *n* = escutcheon.

scuttle¹ /ˈskʌtl ; ˈskʌtl̩/ *n* **(ˈcoal-)~,** container for a supply of coal at the fireside. 煤斗;煤桶(在火爐旁貯放煤者)。

scuttle² /ˈskʌtl ; ˈskʌtl̩/ *vi* [VP2A, C] ~ ***(off/away),*** scurry. 急促地跑;趕急。□ *n* hurried flight or departure; cowardly avoidance of, or running away from, difficulties and dangers: 急速的逃走或離去;膽怯的避開困難和危險: *The Opposition leader accused the Government of a policy of ~.* 反對黨領袖指責政府採取逃避政策。

scuttle³ /ˈskʌtl ; ˈskʌtl̩/ *n* small opening with a lid, in a ship's side or on deck, or in a building's roof or wall. 舷窗;艙室小孔;天窗;氣窗。□ *vt* [VP6A] cut holes in, open valves in, a ship's sides or bottom to sink it: 沉(船);鑿沉: *The captain ~d his ship to avoid its being captured by the enemy.* 船長把船鑿沉以避免被敵人俘獲。

Scylla /ˈsɪlə ; ˈsɪlə/ *n* (myth) (six-headed monster living on) a dangerous rock opposite a whirlpool (called *Charybdis* /kəˈrɪbdɪs ; kəˈrɪbdɪs/) (in the Strait of Messina, S Italy). (神話) Charybdis 渦流對面的一塊危險的岩石(位於義大利南方的墨西拿海峽);居於此石上的六頭妖怪。***between ~ and Charybdis,*** between two great dangers. 在兩大危險中;腹背受敵。

scythe /saɪð ; saɪð/ *n* tool with a slightly curved blade on a long wooden pole with two short handles, for cutting long grass, grain, etc. 大鐮刀(刃微彎,裝於有二把手之長木柄上,用於割長草,穀類等)。□ *vt* [VP6A, 15A] cut with a ~. 用大鐮刀割。

scything

sea /siː ; si/ *n* **1 the sea,** expanse of salt water that covers most of the earth's surface and encloses its continents and islands; any part of this (in contrast to areas of fresh water and dry land): 海洋(遮覆地球表面大部分地方,圍繞諸大陸及島嶼等之鹹水區域);海洋的任何部分: *Ships sail on the sea.* 船隻在海上航行。*Fish swim in the sea.* 魚在海中游。*The sea covers nearly three-fourths of the world's surface.* 海洋約佔地球表面的四分之三。*Let's go for a swim in the sea.* 我們去海邊游水吧! ***follow the sea,*** be a sailor. 當海員;做水手。***on the sea,*** (of a place) on the coast: 在海邊;臨海: *Brighton is on the sea.* 布來頓城瀕海。**2 seas,** same sense as 1 above. 海洋(與上列第1義同)。***beyond/over the sea(s),*** abroad; to or in countries separated by the sea (note that *overseas* is more usu). 在海外;往或在被海洋所隔開的國家 (overseas 較常用)。***the high seas,*** parts which are not near the land, esp outside the territorial limits over which the nearest country has or claims jurisdiction. 外海;遠洋(海洋不臨近陸地的部分);(尤指)公海(領海以外之海洋)。***the freedom of the seas,*** the right to carry on sea-trade without interference. 海上貿易權;商船在海上之自由航行權。**3** (in proper names) particular area of sea which is smaller than an ocean: (用於專有名詞中)海(海洋之某一特定區域,較洋為小者): *the Mediterranean Sea;* 地中海; *the Caribbean Sea;* 加勒比海; *the South China Sea;* 南海; inland body of water; lake: 內海;湖: *the Caspian Sea;* 裏海; *the Sea of Galilee.* 加利利海。***the Seven Seas,*** (liter or poet) the Arctic, the Antarctic, the N and S Pacific, the N and S Atlantic and the Indian Oceans: (文或詩)七大洋(指北冰洋,南冰洋,北太平洋,南太平洋,北大西洋,南大西洋及印度洋): *He has sailed the Seven Seas.* 他曾航行七大洋。**4** (in various phrases without articles) (用於無冠詞的各片語中) ***at sea,*** away from, out of sight of, the land: 離開陸地;不見陸地;在海上: *He was buried at sea.* 他葬身海中。***all/completely at sea,*** (fig) puzzled; at a loss: (喻) 茫然;迷惑;不知所措: *He was all at sea when he began his new job.* 他開始新工作時,茫然不知所措。***by sea,*** in a ship: 乘船;由海路: *travel by sea and land.* 經海路及陸路旅行。***go to sea,*** become a sailor. 做水手。***put to sea,*** leave port or land. 出港;出海。 **5** [C] local state of the sea; swell of the ocean; big wave or billow: 海洋之局部狀態;海洋之洶湧波浪;大浪: *There was a heavy sea,* large waves. 海上波濤洶湧。*The ship was struck by a heavy sea,* a large wave. 該船被巨浪沖擊。*The seas were mountains high.* 海浪高如山。***half seas over,*** having drunk too much; intoxicated. 喝酒太多;醉了。**6** [C] large quantity or expanse (*of*): 大量;廣濶(與 of 連用): *a sea of up-turned faces,* eg crowds of people looking upwards; 無數朝上看的臉; *a sea of flame.* 巨大火焰;一片火海。**7** (attrib and in compounds): (形容用法,用於複合字中): **ˌsea ˈair** *n* air at the seaside, considered to be good for health: 海邊的空氣(被認為有益於健康): *enjoy the sea air.* 享受海邊的空氣。 **ˈsea-anemone** *n* ⇨ the illus at anemone. 海葵(參看 anemone 之插圖)。**ˈsea-animal** *n* animal inhabiting the sea, eg fish, mammals, molluscs, etc. 海生動物(居於海中的動物,如魚類、哺乳動物、軟體動物等)。 **ˈsea-bathing** *n* bathing in the sea. 海水浴。**ˈsea·bed** *n* floor of the sea. 海床;海底。**ˈsea-bird** *n* any of several species of bird which live close to the sea, ie on cliffs, islands, etc. 海鳥。⇨ the illus at water. 參看 water 之插圖。**ˈsea·board** *n* coast region; line of coast. 沿海地區;海濱;海岸;海岸線。**ˈsea-boat** *n* ship with the sea-going qualities specified: 具備航行海洋之條件的船;遠洋船;海船: *a good/bad sea-boat,* one that sails well/badly. 適於(不適於)航行海洋的船隻。**ˈsea-borne** *adj* (of trade) carried in ships: (指貿易) 以船裝運的; 海運的: *sea-borne commerce/goods.* 海運的貿易 (舶來的貨物)。**ˈsea-breeze** *n* breeze blowing landward from the sea, esp during the day in alternation with a land-breeze at night. 海風(尤指白天由海洋吹向陸地的和風,與夜晚由陸地吹向海洋的風相互交替)。Cf 參較 *a ˌsea ˈbreeze,* any kind of breeze at sea. 指任何海上的微風。 **ˈsea-coal** *n* (hist) coal brought from Newcastle to London by sea (opp of *charcoal*). (史)煤; 海煤(由紐加塞耳海運至倫敦的煤) (為 charcoal 之相反字)。**ˈsea-cow** *n* kind of warm-blooded creature living in the sea and feeding its young with milk. 海牛;海象(一種海生溫血哺乳動物)。**ˈsea-dog** *n* **(a)** old sailor, esp the captains of English ships during the reign of Elizabeth I. 老練水手;(尤指)伊利莎白一世時代英國船的船長。**(b)** dogfish. 角鮫;小鯊。**(c)** seal. 海豹。**ˈsea·faring** /-feərɪŋ ; -ˌfɛrɪŋ/ *adj* of work or voyages on the sea: 海上工作的;航海的: *a 'seafaring man*, a sailor. 海員;水手。**'sea-fish** *n* fish living in the sea (opp to *freshwater-fish*). 海魚(爲 freshwater-fish 之相反字)。**'sea fog** *n* fog along the coast, caused by difference between land and sea temperatures. 海霧(沿海岸所起之霧,因陸地及海洋氣溫不同所致)。**'sea·food** *n* edible fish or shellfish from the sea: 海鮮(可食用的海產魚類或貝類): *a 'seafood restaurant;* 海鮮店; *a seafood cocktail.* 海鮮鷄尾酒。**'sea·front** *n* part of a town facing the sea: 城鎮之面海部分;濱海區: *The best hotels are on the sea-front.* 最好的旅館在濱海地區。**'sea-girt** *adj* (poet) surrounded by the sea. (詩)爲海所環繞的。**'sea-god** *n* god living in or having power over the sea, eg *Neptune*. 海神。**'sea-going** *adj* (of ships) built for crossing the sea, not for coastal voyages only; (of a person) seafaring. (指船)適於越洋的(不僅用作沿海岸航行者);(指人)在海上工作的;航海的。**ˌsea-'green** *adj, n* bluish-green as of the sea. 海綠色(的)。**'sea·gull** *n* = gull. **'sea-horse** *n* kind of small fish. 龍落子(一名海馬,亦名馬頭魚,爲一種似馬的小魚)。**ˌsea-island 'cotton** *n* fine quality of long-stapled cotton. 海島棉(有長纖維而質地優良之一種棉花)。**'sea·kale** *n* plant whose young white shoots are used as a vegetable. 宿根草(其白色幼芽用作蔬菜)。**'sea-legs** *n pl* ability to walk on the deck of a rolling ship: 能在顛簸之海船甲板上行走而且不會暈船的能力: *get/find one's sea-legs.* 不暈船;有適應船上生活的能力。**'sea level** *n* level of sea half-way between high and low tide as the basis for measuring height of land and depth of sea: 海(平)面(高低潮間之平均海面,用作測量地高及海深的基準者): *100 metres above/below sea level.* 海拔(低於海平面)一百公尺。**'sea-lion** *n* large seal of the N Pacific Ocean. (北太平洋所產之)海獅。**'Sea Lord** *n* one of four naval members of the Board of Admiralty (London). (倫敦)海軍本部四位海軍首長之一。**'sea·man** /-mən; -mən/ *n* (*pl* -men) **(a)** (in the Navy) sailor who is not an officer. (海軍)水兵。**(b)** person expert in nautical matters. 精於航海事務之人;水手;海員。Hence, 由此產生, **'sea·man-like** /-mənlaɪk; -mənˌlaɪk/ *adj* **'sea·man·ship** /-mənʃɪp; -mənˌʃɪp/ *n* skill in managing a boat or ship. 駕船術;航海技術。**'sea mile** *n* nautical mile. 海里;浬。**'sea·plane** *n* aircraft constructed so that it can come down on and rise from water. 水上飛機(可在水上升降者)。**'sea·port** *n* town with a harbour used by sea-going ships. 海埠;海港(具有可供海船使用之港口的城鎮)。**'sea-power** *n* ability to control and use the seas (by means of naval strength). (憑藉海軍力量之)制海權。**'sea-rover** *n* pirate; pirate's ship. 海盜;海盜船。**'sea·scape** *n* picture of a scene at sea. 海景;海景畫。⇨ landscape. **'sea-shell** *n* shell of any mollusc inhabiting the sea. 貝殼;螺殼。**'sea·shore** *n* land bordering on the sea; beach: 海濱;海岸;海邊: *children playing on the seashore;* 在海邊遊戲的兒童; (legal) between high and low-water marks. (法律)前灘(高潮線與低潮線之間的地方)。**'sea·sick** *adj* sick, inclined to vomit, from the motion of a ship. 因船之顛簸而感不適或想嘔吐的;暈船的。**'sea·sick·ness** *n* **'sea·side** *n* (often attrib) place, town, etc by the sea, esp a holiday resort: (常作形容用法)海邊的地區,城鎮等(尤指假日遊憩勝地): *go to the*

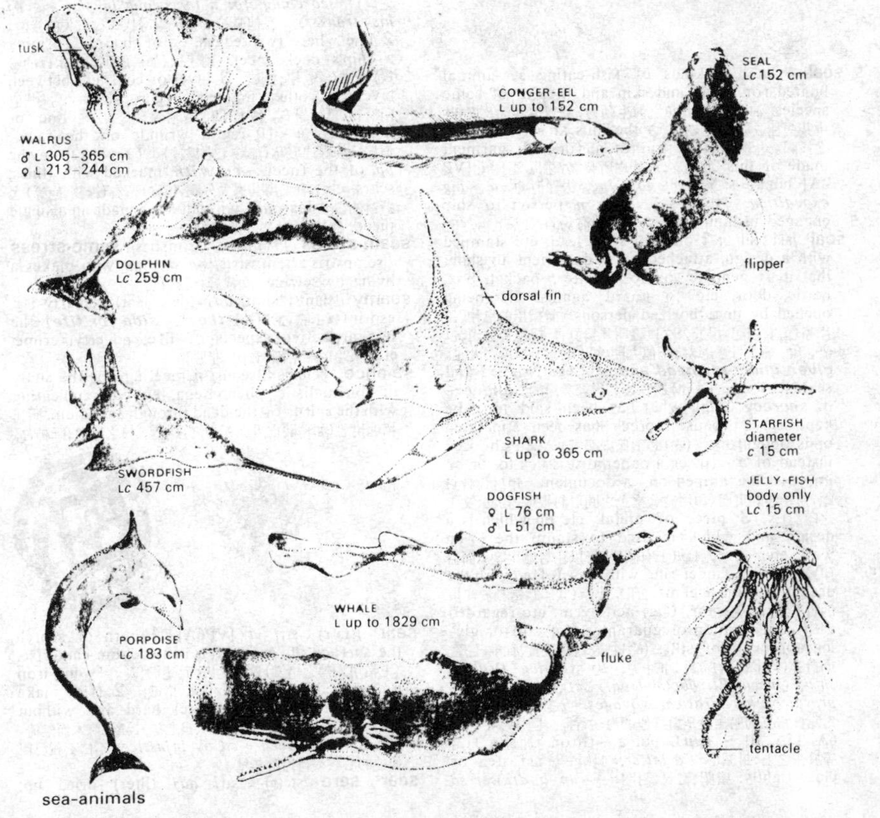

sea-animals

seaside for one's summer holidays; 去海濱度暑假；*own a house by the seaside;* 在海濱有一棟房子；*a seaside town.* 海邊的市鎮。**'sea-snake** *n* (kinds of) (usu venomous) snake living in the sea. (各種)海蛇(通常有毒)。**'sea-urchin** *n* small sea-animal with a shell covered with sharp points. 海膽 (外殼覆有尖刺的細小海生動物)。 **,sea-'wall** *n* wall built to check the encroachment of the sea on the land. 防波堤；海堤(用以阻止海水侵入陸地者)。**'sea·ward** /-wəd ; -wɚd/ *adj* towards the sea; in the direction of the sea. 向海的；朝海的。**'sea·wards** /-wədz ; -wɚdz/ *adv* **'sea-water** *n* water from the sea. 海水。**'sea·way** *n* **(a)** progress of a ship through the water. 船舶之航行。**(b)** inland waterway, eg a river, series of lakes, joined by canals and locks, used by sea-going ships: 海船之內陸航路(如以運河及水閘所連接之河，湖等)：*the St Lawrence S~way* (connecting the Atlantic and the Great Lakes between Canada and the US). 聖羅倫斯內陸航路(連接大西洋與美加間的大湖區者)。**'sea·weed** *n* [C, U] kinds of plant growing in the sea, esp on rocks washed by the sea. 海草；海藻(生長於海中，尤指生長於被海水冲刷之岩石上的植物)。**'sea·worthy** *adj* (of a ship) fit for a voyage; well built and in good repair. (指船)適於航海的；建造與保養良好的。

a sea-horse

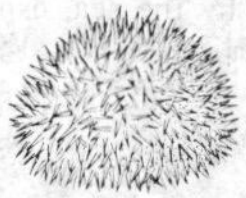

a sea-urchin

seal[1] /si:l ; sil/ *n* kinds of fish-eating sea-animal hunted for its oil and skin and the fur of some species. 海豹(數種食魚之海生動物，獵以取其油及皮，其中某些種並取其毛皮)。⇨ the illus at sea. 參看 sea 之插圖。**'~·skin** *n* skin of a fur-seal; garment made of this. 海豹皮；海豹皮所製之衣服。□ *vi* [VP 2A] hunt ~s: 獵海豹：*go ~ing;* 去獵海豹；*a ~ing expedition.* 海豹狩獵隊。**~er** *n* person to ship engaged in hunting ~s. 從事獵海豹的人或船。

seal[2] /si:l ; sil/ *n* **1** piece of wax, lead, etc stamped with a design, attached to a document to show that it is genuine, or to a letter, packet, box, bottle, door, etc to guard against its being opened by unauthorized persons. 封緘用的蠟片、鉛片等(蓋有圖記，用於公文以證明其爲眞實，或用於信函、包裹、盒、瓶、門等，以防止他人開啓)；封蠟；封鉛；火漆。***given under my hand and ~,*** (legal) signed and sealed by me. (法律)經我簽名封緘發出的。***under ~ of secrecy,*** (fig) what has been said must be kept secret because secrecy has been stipulated or is obligatory. (喩)必須保守祕密。 **2** sth used instead of a ~(1), eg a paper disc stuck to, or an impression stamped on, a document. 用以代替封蠟，封鉛等的東西(如用於公文上之圓形封籤或蓋於公文上之印記)。 **3** piece of metal, etc on which is a design and which is used to stamp the ~ on wax, etc. 印章；圖章(上有圖樣，用以在封蠟片等上面蓋印)。**'~-ring,** finger-ring with a ~ (often with the design cut on a gem). 印章戒指(其印章常刻於戒指的寶石上)。 **4** ***~ of,*** (fig) act, event, etc regarded as a confirmation or guarantee (of sth) or giving approval (of sth): (喩)被認爲是證實、批准、保證或讚許(某事物)的行爲，事件等：*By visiting Drake's ship, Queen Elizabeth I put/set the ~ of approval on his piratical voyages.* 女王伊利莎白一世駕臨杜雷克的船無異是讚許他的海盜行徑。□ *vt* **1** [VP 6A, 15A, B] **~ *(up),*** put a ~(1) on: 加封蠟，封鉛等於…之上；封緘：*~ a letter;* 封緘一信；fasten or close tightly: 密閉；密封；封閉：*~ up a drawer so that it cannot be opened;* 封閉抽屜使無法打開；*~ a jar of fruit,* make it air-tight so that the fruit will keep; 密封果罐(使不透氣，水果方能久藏)；*~ up a window,* eg by pasting paper over all the crevices. 密閉窗戶(如以紙糊起所有的縫隙)。**~ *sth in,*** keep it in by ~ing: 密封使不外洩：*Our special canning process ~s the flavour in.* 我們的特殊裝罐方法能保存味道。**~ *sth off,*** block it: 封閉：*~ off an area of land,* block all means of entering it, eg one where, after ,military use, there may be unexploded shells, etc. 封閉某地區(如經軍事使用後，可能留有未爆炸之炮彈等之地區)。***One's lips are ~ed,*** One must not speak; the matter must be kept secret. 不能講；必須保守秘密。***~ed orders,*** instructions given to a ship's captain (or other person in authority), esp in wartime, in a ~ed envelope to be opened only at a certain time or place. 密令(尤指戰時給予船長或其他當權人士的指令，密封著，只可在某時或某地拆開)。**'~ing-wax** *n* kind of wax that melts quickly when heated and quickly hardens when cooled, used to ~ letters, etc. 封蠟；火漆(加熱易溶，冷却後甚快變硬的一種蠟，用於密封信函等)。 **2** [VP6A] settle; decide: 解決；決定：*~ a bargain;* 決定某項買賣；成交；*His fate is ~ed.* 他的命運已經決定。

seal·skin /'si:lskɪn ; 'sil,skɪn/ ⇨ seal[1].

Sealy·ham /'si:lɪəm *US:* -lɪhæm ; 'silɪ,hæm/ *n* kind of terrier with a long body and short legs. 㹴之一種(體長腿短)。

seam /si:m ; sim/ *n* [C] **1** line where two edges, esp of cloth or leather, are turned back and sewn together: 縫；接縫(尤指布或皮革兩邊緣反轉縫合之處)：*searching for a lost coin in the ~s of his trousers.* 在他長褲的接縫處尋找一枚遺失的錢幣。 **2** line where two edges, eg of boards forming a ship's deck, meet. 兩邊緣(如構成甲板之木板的邊緣)之接合線；綴合處。 **3** layer of coal, etc between layers of other materials, eg rock, clay. 在其他兩層物質(如岩石，黏土)間的煤層等；層。 **4** line or mark like a ~(1) (eg a wrinkle on the face). 似接縫的線或痕跡(如臉上之皺紋)。□ *vt* (esp in the *pp*, of the face) ***~ed with,*** marked with (lines, scars, etc). (尤用其過去分詞，指臉)留有(線紋，疤等)之痕跡的。**~·less** *adj* without a ~; made in a single piece. 無縫的；整幅布做成的。

seam·stress /'si:mstrɪs ; 'simstrɪs/, **semp·stress** /'sempstrɪs ; 'sɛmpstrɪs/ *nn* woman who makes a living by sewing. 女裁縫；縫紉女。

seamy /'si:mɪ ; 'simɪ/ *adj* (-ier, -iest) (chiefly fig, esp in) (主喩，尤用於) ***the '~ side (of life),*** the less attractive aspects of life; poverty, crime, etc. 人生的黑暗面；貧困、罪惡等。

sé·ance /'seɪɑ:ns ; 'seans/ *n* meeting for the study of spiritualistic phenomena, eg communicating with the spirits of the dead through a medium. 研究招魂現象(如藉關亡人與死者之靈魂交談)之集會；降神會。

seals

sear[1] /sɪə(r) ; sɪr/ *vt* [VP6A] **1** burn or scorch the surface of, esp with a heated iron; cauterize. (尤指用灼熱之烙鐵)燒…之表面；燒灼；炙。**'~·ing-iron** *n* one used for cauterizing. 烙鐵。 **2** (fig) make (sb's heart, conscience, etc) hard and without feeling: (喩)使(某人的心腸、良心等)冷酷、麻木而無情：*His soul had been ~ed by injustice.* 不仁不義已經使他的心靈變得冷酷無情。

sear[2], **sere** /sɪə(r) ; sɪr/ *adj* (liter) dried up;

withered (esp of flowers, leaves). (文)枯乾的;枯萎的(尤指花、葉)。

search /sɜːtʃ; sɝtʃ/ *vt, vi* **1** [VP6A, 14, 15A, B, 2A, 3A] **~ (sb／sth) (for sb／sth); ~ sb／sth out,** examine, look carefully at, through, or into (in order to find sth or sb): 搜尋;查究;搜查;探查: *~ a criminal to see what he has in his pockets.* 搜查犯人,看他口袋中有何物。*He ~ed and ~ed through all the drawers for the missing papers.* 他將所有的抽屜搜了又搜,尋找遺失的文件。*I've ~ed my memory but can't remember that man's name.* 我苦思良久,仍舊記不起那人的名字。*Do you spend much time ~ing through dictionaries for words to use?* 你花費許多時間在各字典中尋找要用的字嗎? **~ out,** look for: 尋找: *~ out an old friend.* 尋找一位故友。**~ one's heart／conscience,** examine carefully one's own beliefs and conduct. 仔細檢討自己的信仰與行爲;自我反省。**ˌS~ ˈme!** (colloq) I have no idea, no knowledge (of what you are asking about)! (俗) 我不知道(你所問的事)! **2** [VP6A] (liter) go deeply into; go into every part of: (文)深入;進入…之每一部分: *The cold wind ~ed the streets.* 寒風吹遍各街道。□ *n* [C, U] **1** act of ~ing: 搜尋;查究;搜查;探查;深入: *go in ~ of a missing child;* 尋找失蹤的小孩; *a ~ for a missing aircraft;* 搜尋失蹤的飛機;*make a ~ for contraband.* 搜查違禁品。**right of ~,** right of the warships of a country at war to stop and examine a neutral ship (for contraband, etc). 搜索權(交戰國之軍艦檢查中立國的船隻是否有違禁品的權利)。**ˈ~·light** *n* powerful light with a beam that can be turned in any direction, as used for discovering enemy movements, etc in war. 探照燈(可照向任何方向的强烈光柱,戰時用以發現敵人的活動等)。**ˈ~-party** *n* number of persons looking for sb or sth that is lost. 搜索隊(找尋迷失之人或遺失之物者)。**ˈ~-warrant** *n* official authority to enter and ~ a building (eg for stolen property). 搜索票(准許搜查住宅,以尋找贓物等的令狀)。**2** (legal) investigation (eg by lawyers, from local authorities) into possible reasons (eg planned demolition) why one should not buy land or property. (法律)調查不宜置產的原因(如屬於拆除計畫等)。**~er** *n* person who ~es. 搜尋者;探究者;調查者。**~·ing** *adj* (of a look) taking in all details; (of a test, etc) thorough. (指目光)看到所有細節的;銳利的;(指考驗等)徹底的。**~·ing·ly** *adv*

sea·son /ˈsiːzn; ˈsizn̩/ *n* [C] **1** one of the divisions of the year according to the weather, eg spring, summer, etc: 季(依天氣將年所作之畫分,如春、夏等): *the ˈdry ~,* 旱季, *the ˈrainy ~.* 雨季。**2** period suitable or normal for sth, or closely associated with sth: 適於某種事物的時期;某事物慣常發生或與其有密切關聯的時期;季節;時節: *the ˈfootball ~;* 足球季節; *the ˈnesting ~,* when birds build nests and lay eggs; 鳥類築巢產卵之季節; *the ˈdead ~, the ˈoff ~,* (in hotels at holiday resorts, etc) the time when there are very few guests; (度假勝地之旅館等)遊客稀少時期;淡季; *the ˈholiday／ˈtourist ~;* 度假的季節(觀光的季節); *Christmas, the ~ of goodwill.* 聖誕節,互示親善的時節。**the ~'s greetings,** (as written on a Christmas card). 節日的祝福(如書於聖誕卡上者)。**in／out of ~, (a)** (of food) normally available／not available: (指食物)正當盛產(已過盛產)季節;正當時令(不當令): *Oysters／Strawberries are out of ~ now.* 蠔(草莓)的盛產季節已過。**(b)** at the time when most people take／do not take their holidays: (大多數人出外度假的)旺季;(大多數人不出外度假的)淡季: *Hotel charges are lower out of ~.* 在淡季旅館收費較低。**ˌin (~) and ˈout of ~,** at all times. 在所有的時候;不拘任何時間。**a word in ~,** advice at a time when it is likely to be useful. 適時的忠言。**ˈclose／the ˈopen ~,** ⇨ close¹(11), open¹(11). **ˈ~(-ticket)** *n* **(a)** one that gives the owner the right to travel between places over a specified route as often as he wishes during a stated period of time: (持有者於一定時期可隨意旅行於兩地間之) 季票; 定期車票: *a three-month ~(-ticket).* 三個月的定期車票。Cf 參較 US 美 *commutation ticket.* **(b)** ticket that gives the owner the right to attend a place of amusement, etc, eg a concert hall, as often as he wishes (for the concerts, etc specified on the ticket) during a certain period. (在一定時期內持有者可隨意進入某娛樂場所,如音樂廳等之)長期票;定期票。□ *vt, vi* **1** [VP6A, 2A] make or become suitable for use; cause to be acclimatized, etc: 使適用;使適應;變爲適用;使服水土等: *Has this wood been well ~ed,* dried and hardened? 這木材已乾燥可用嗎? *The soldiers were not yet ~ed to the rigorous climate.* 兵士們尚未能適應此種酷寒的氣候。**2** [VP6A, 14] **~ (with),** flavour (food) (with salt, pepper, etc): 調味;爲(食物)加味道(用鹽,胡椒等): *mutton ~ed with garlic;* 用大蒜調味的羊肉; *highly ~ed dishes;* 調味甚濃的菜; (fig) (喻) *conversation ~ed with wit.* 風趣(逸趣橫生)的談話。**3** [VP6A] (liter) soften; moderate: (文)使溫和;緩和: *'when mercy ~s justice',* ⇨ Mer of Ven, Act IV, Sc 1. '以仁慈調劑峻法的時候' (參看莎士比亞戲劇'威尼斯商人'第四幕第一場)。**~·ing** *n* [C, U] sth used to ~ food: 調味品;佐料: *There's not enough ~ing in the sausage.* 臘腸中放的佐料不够。*Salt and pepper are ~ings.* 鹽和胡椒是調味品。

sea·son·able /ˈsiːznəbl; ˈsiznəbl̩/ *adj* **1** (of the weather) of the kind to be expected at the time of year. (指天氣) 合時的。**2** (of help, advice, gifts, etc) coming at the right time; opportune. (指幫助,忠告,禮物等)適合時機的;及時的。

sea·sonal /ˈsiːzənl; ˈsiznəl/ *adj* dependent upon a particular season; changing with the seasons: 依賴季節而存在的;隨季節而變化的;季節性的: *~ occupations,* eg fruit-picking; 季節性的職業(例如採果); *a ~ trade,* eg the selling of Christmas cards. 季節性的生意(如銷售聖誕卡)。**~ly** /-nəlɪ; -n̩əlɪ/ *adv*

seat /siːt; sit/ *n* **1** sth used or made for sitting on, eg a chair, box, bench, the floor: 用以坐着的東西(如椅子,箱子,長櫈,地板等);座;座位: *There are no more chairs; you'll have to use that box for a ~.* 椅子都有人坐了,你只好以那個箱子代替座椅。*The back ~ of the car is wide enough for three people.* 車子的後座足够三個人坐。**keep one's ~,** remain in one's ~: 坐在自己的座位上不動: *There's no danger—keep your ~s, please,* ie don't panic. 沒有危險——請坐在自己的座位上不要動。**lose one's ~,** have one's ~ taken by someone else. 座位被別人佔去。⇨ 4 below. 參看下列第4義。**take a ~,** sit down: 坐下: *Won't you take a ~?* 請坐。**take one's ~,** sit down in one's place, eg in a hall or theatre. 就座(如在會場或劇院中)。**take a back ~,** ⇨ back⁴(3). **ˈ~-belt** *n* safety strap (worn as a belt) fastened to the sides of a ~ in a passenger vehicle or aircraft. 安全帶;保險帶(車輛或飛機上繫於座位兩側的帶子)。⇨ the illus at motor. 參看 motor 之插圖。**2** that part of a chair, stool, bench, etc on which one sits (contrasted with the back, legs, etc): (椅,櫈等之)座部(與背,腿等相對): *a ˈchair-~.* 椅子的座部。**3** part of the body (the buttocks) on which one sits; part of a garment covering this: (人體或衣服之)臀部: *a hole in the ~ of one's trousers.* 褲子後襠上的一個洞。**4** place in which one has a right to sit: 某人有權就座之席位;席次: *I have four ~s* (ie tickets for them) *for 'Swan Lake' at Covent Garden.* 卡文園(英國皇家歌劇院)上演的'天鵝湖',我已訂下四個座位。*Mr Smith has a ~ in the House of Commons,* is a member. 史密斯先生是下議院的議員。**take one's ~,** assume one's membership (in the House of Commons). 擔任下議院議員。**win a ~; lose one's ~,** win／be defeated in a Parliamentary election. 當選(未當選)國會議員。**5** place where sth is, or where sth is carried on: 所在地;中心;場所: *In the US, Washington is the ~ of government* *and New York City is the chief ~ of commerce.* 在美國,華盛頓是政治中心,紐約是主要商業中心。*A university is a ~ of learning.* 大學乃求學研究之地。 **6** (ˌ**country-**)ˈ~, large house in the country, usu the centre of a large estate: 鄉間之邸宅;別莊(通常爲大片地產的中心): *He is rich enough to have a country-~/a ~ in the country as well as a large house in London.* 他的財富,使他在鄉間擁有一座別墅,並且在倫敦擁有一座大房子。 **7** manner of sitting, esp on a horse: 坐姿;(尤指)騎馬的姿勢或方式: *That rider has a good ~,* rides his horse well. 那位騎馬者坐姿良好。□ *vt* [VP6A] **1** ~ ***oneself, be ~ed,*** (formal) sit down: (正式用語) 坐下: *Please be ~ed, ladies and gentlemen.* 請坐下,各位女士和先生。 **2** have ~s for: 有…座位;可容納…的座位: *a hall that ~s 500.* 有五百座位的會場。*Are the ~ing arrangements* (= the arrangements for providing and placing ~s) *in the hall satisfactory?* 大廳裡座位的安排還滿意嗎? ˈ**~·ing-room** *n* [U] seats: 座位: *We have ~ing-room for thirty pupils in this classroom.* 在這教室中,我們有容納卅位學生的座位。 **3** (usu 通常用 **re~**) repair the ~ or bottom of: 修理…之座部或底部: *~ a chair/an old pair of trousers.* 修理椅子的座部(修補舊褲子的後襠)。

sec /sek; sɛk/ *n* (sl abbr of) second³(2). ⇨ mo. (俚)爲 second³ 第 2 義之略。

seca·teurs /ˈsekətɜ:z; ˌsɛkəˈtɝz/ *n pl* pair of clippers used by gardeners for pruning bushes, etc. 剪枝刀;修枝鋏。

se·cede /sɪˈsi:d; sɪˈsid/ *vi* [VP2A, 3A] ~ ***(from),*** (of a group) withdraw (from membership of a state, federation, organization, etc). (指團體) 脫離;退出(聯盟、組織等之會籍)。

se·cession /sɪˈseʃn; sɪˈsɛʃən/ *n* [U] seceding; [C] instance of this (as in the US when eleven Southern States withdrew from the Federal Union in 1860–61). 脫離; 退出; 其實例(如 1860–61 年美國南部十一個州之脫離聯邦)。 **~·ist** /-ʃənɪst; -ʃənɪst/ *n* supporter of ~. 脫離論者;主張退盟者。

se·clude /sɪˈklu:d; sɪˈklud/ *vt* [VP6A, 14, 15A] ~ ***sb/oneself (from),*** keep (a person, oneself) apart from the company of others: 使(人,自己)與他人隔離;使隱居: *~ oneself from society;* 與世隔離; *keep women ~d in the harem.* 使婦女們深居於閨閣中。**~d** *adj* (esp of a place) quiet; solitary. (尤指地方) 安靜的; 幽僻的。 **se·clu·sion** /sɪˈklu:ʒn; sɪˈkluʒən/ *n* [U] secluding or being ~d; ~d place; retirement: 隔離;隱居;幽僻之地;隱退: *live in seclusion;* 隱居; *in the seclusion of one's own home.* 深居簡出。

sec·ond¹ /ˈsekənd; ˈsɛkənd/ *adj* **1** (abbr 略作 **2nd**) next after the first (in place, time, order, importance, etc): 第二的(在地位,時間,次序,重要性等方面): *February is the ~ month of the year.* 二月是一年中的第二個月。*Tom is the ~ son—he has an elder brother.* 湯姆是次男 — 他有一位長兄。*Osaka is the ~ city/the ~ largest city in Japan.* 大阪是日本的第二大城市。 ˌ**~-ˈbest** *adj* next after the best: 次好的;第二好的: *my ~-best suit.* 我的次好的衣服。□ *n, adv: I won't accept/put up with ~-best.* 我不願接受(不能忍受)次好的東西。***come off ~-best,*** get the worst of sth. 輸了;被擊敗。 ˌ**~-ˈclass** *adj, n* **(a)** (of the) class next after the first: 二等(的);次等(的): *a ~-class hotel;* 二等旅館; *~-class compartments,* in a railway carriage, etc; 二等車廂; *~-class mail,* sent at a cheaper rate. (英)平信;(美)印刷品郵件。**(b)** class below the first in examination results: (考試結果)第二等: *take a ~-class (degree) in law.* 法律科考試獲得第二等優良成績。**(c)** (regarded or treated as) inferior: 平庸的;低劣的;社會地位低的: *~-class citizens.* 社會地位低的市民;次等公民。□ *adv: go/travel ~-class.* 乘二等車旅行。**~ floor** *n* the one above the first (in GB two floors, in US one floor, above the ground): (英)三樓; (美)二樓: (attrib) (形容用法) *a ~-floor apartment.* 三(二)樓的公寓。ˌ**~-ˈhand** *adj* **(a)** previously owned by someone else: 用過的;舊的;曾屬於他人的: *~-hand furniture/books;* 舊傢具(書); *a ~-hand bookshop,* shop for ~-hand books. 舊書店。Cf 參較 *used* cars. **(b)** (of news, knowledge) obtained from others, not based on personal observation, etc: (指新聞,知識)得自他人的;非根據親身觀察所得的: *get news ~-hand.* 獲得轉述的消息。**~ lieutenant** *n* lowest commissioned rank in the Army. 陸軍少尉。ˌ**~-ˈrate** *adj* not of the best quality; inferior: 較次的;平庸的: *a man with ~-rate brains.* 頭腦平庸的人。 Hence, 由此產生, ˌ**~-ˈrater** *n* person with ~-rate intelligence or abilities: 中智之人;平庸之士: *a Cabinet made up mainly of ~-raters.* 大部分由平庸之士組成的內閣。ˌ**~ ˈsight** *n* power to see future events, or events happening at a distance, as if present. 預見力;千里眼。Hence, 由此產生, ˌ**~-ˈsighted** *adj* having this power. 有預見力的;千里眼的。ˌ**~ ˈteeth** *n* those which grow after a child's first teeth are out. 永久齒。ˌ**~ ˈwind,** ⇨ wind¹(3). ***~ to none,*** surpassed by no other. 不次於任何人(事物)。 **2** additional; extra: 補助的;額外的: *You will need a ~ pair of shoes.* 你需要額外一雙鞋。 **3** ˌ**S~ ˈAdvent/ˈComing,** the return of Jesus Christ at the Last Judgement. (最後審判時)基督的再臨。ˌ**~ ˈballot,** a method used in some elections by which, if the winner of the first ballot receives less than half the votes cast, a new ballot is taken, in which only he and the next candidate are voted for. 決選投票;第二次投票(第一次投票之獲勝者不能獲得過半數票時,就渠與得票數次多者間,再舉行第二次投票)。ˌ**~ ˈchamber** *n* upper house in a legislature: 議會之上議院: *The House of Lords is the ~ chamber of Parliament in Great Britain.* 貴族院是英國國會之上議院。ˌ**~ ˈnature** *n* acquired tendency that has become instinctive: 第二天性: *Habit is ~ nature.* 習慣成自然。ˌ**~ ˈthoughts,** opinion or resolution reached after reconsideration: 再思;重新考慮;重新考慮後的意見或決定: *On ~ thoughts I will accept the offer.* 重新考慮的結果,我願意接受那提議(價錢等)。*I'm having ~ thoughts* (= am not so sure) *about buying that house.* 關於買那棟房子的事我正重新考慮中。 **4** of the same kind as one that has gone before; subordinate: 類似的;附屬的: *This fellow seems to think he's a ~ Napoleon!* 這傢伙似乎認爲他是拿破崙第二! ˌ**~ ˈchildhood** *n* old age when accompanied by weakening of the mental powers. 老耄期 (伴以心智之衰退)。 ˌ**~ ˈcousin** *n* child of a first cousin of either of one's parents. 堂(表)伯,叔,姑,姨,舅等之小孩。 ***play ˌ~ ˈfiddle (to sb),*** be of only secondary importance (to sb else). 做(某人)之副手;居於次要地位。□ *adv* in the ~ place; ~ in order or in importance: 第二(地);次要地: *The English swimmer came (in) ~.* 那位英國游泳選手得第二。 **~·ly** *adv* in the next place; furthermore. 第二;其次。

sec·ond² /ˈsekənd; ˈsɛkənd/ *n* **1** person or thing that comes next to the first: (人,事物,日期等之)第二: *the ~ of May;* 五月二日; *George the S~,* King George II. 國王喬治二世。***get a ~,*** get a ~ class in an examination. 獲得第二等優良成績。**2** another person or thing besides the person or thing previously mentioned: (前述者以外的) 另一人; 另一物: *You are the ~ to ask me that question.* 你是另一位向我提出那問題的人。 **3** (*pl*) goods below the best in quality. (複)次等貨。 **4** (*pl*) second helping of food. (複)第二份食物。**5** person chosen by the principal in a duel to support him; supporter of a boxer in a boxing-match. 決鬪者之助手;拳擊者之幫手。

sec·ond³ /ˈsekənd; ˈsɛkənd/ *n* **1** (indicated by the mark ″) 60th part of a minute (of time or of an angle, ⇨ App 5): 秒(時間或角度的一分鐘或一分的六十分之一,以 ″ 符號表示之;參看附錄五): *winning* *time 1 minute, 5 ~s;* 優勝者的時間是一分五秒。*1° 6′ 10″ = one degree, six minutes, and ten ~s.* 1° 6′ 10″ 卽一度六分十秒。**'~-hand** *n* extra hand in some watches and clocks recording ~s. 鐘錶之秒針。⇨ also *second-hand* at second¹(1). **2** moment; short time: 片刻;短時: *I shall be ready in a ~ or two/in a few ~s.* 幾秒鐘內我卽將準備妥當。

se·cond⁴ /ˈsekənd ; ˈsɛkənd/ *vt* [VP6A] **1** support (esp in a duel or a boxing-match). 支持;輔助(尤指在決鬪或拳賽中)。**2** (of a member of a debating body) rise or speak formally in support of a motion to show that the proposer is not the only person in favour of it: (指辯論團體的一分子)贊成某提案;附議: *Mr Smith proposed, and Mr Green ~ed, a vote of thanks to the lecturer.* 史密斯先生提議向演說者致謝,格林先生附議之。**~er** *n* person who ~s a proposal at a meeting. 開會時贊成某動議的人;附議者。

se·cond⁵ /sɪˈkɒnd *US:* ˈsekənd ; ˈsɛkənd/ *vt* [VP6A, 15A] (official GB use, esp mil) take (sb) from his ordinary duty and give him special duty: (英,官方用語,尤用於軍中)調動(某人)離開其平常的職守而派以特殊任務: *Captain Smith was ~ed for service on the General's staff.* 史密斯上尉奉調擔任將軍的幕僚。**~·ment** *n* ~ing or being ~ed. 調或被調任特殊任務。

sec·ond·ary /ˈsekəndrɪ *US:* -derɪ ; ˈsɛkənˌdɛrɪ/ *adj* coming after, less important than, what is first or chief: 第二的;從屬的;次要的: *~ education/schools,* for children over eleven; 中等教育(學校); *a ~ stress,* eg on the first syllable of 'sacrificial' /ˌsækrɪˈfɪʃl ; ˌsækrəˈfɪʃəl/. 次重音(如 sacrificial 之第一音節上的)。**sec·ond·ar·ily** /-drəlɪ *US:* -derəlɪ ; -ˌdɛrəlɪ/ *adv*

se·crecy /ˈsiːkrəsɪ ; ˈsikrəsɪ/ *n* [U] keeping of secrets; ability to keep secrets; habit of keeping secrets; state of being kept secret: 守祕密;守祕密的能力;守祕密的習慣;被保守祕密的狀態;隱瞞: *rely on sb's ~;* 相信某人不會洩密; *prepare sth in ~,* secretly; 暗中準備某事; *do sth with great ~.* 極祕密地做某事。***swear/bind sb to ~,*** make him promise to keep sth secret. 使某人應允對某事守密。

se·cret /ˈsiːkrɪt ; ˈsikrɪt/ *adj* **1** (to be) kept from the knowledge or view of others; of which others have no knowledge: 防止他人知悉的;他人不知的;祕密的: *a ~ marriage;* 祕密結婚; *keep sth ~ from one's family.* 不把某事告訴家人。*He escaped through a ~ door.* 他從暗門逃走。**the ˌ~ ˈservice,** government department concerned with espionage and counter-espionage. 政府的情報機構。**ˌ~ ˈagent** *n* member of this department (called a 'spy' if he works for a foreign government and 'secret agent' if he works for one's own government). 情報人員(如爲外國政府工作稱爲'間諜',如爲本國政府工作則稱爲'情報人員')。**2** (of places) secluded; quiet. (指地方)幽僻的;寧靜的。**3** (of persons) secretive (the more usu word). (指人)有守密之習慣的;好遮掩的(secretive 較常用)。□ *n* **1** [C] sth ~. 祕密。***keep a ~,*** not tell anyone else: 保守機密: *Can you keep a ~?* 你能保守祕密嗎? ***in the ~,*** among those who are allowed to know it: 參與祕密: *Is your brother in the ~?* 你的兄弟知道這項祕密嗎? ***let sb into a/the ~,*** share it. 使某人與聞(或參與)某項祕密。***(be) an open ~,*** (of sth which is said to be ~) be (in fact) widely known. 公開的祕密。**2** [C] hidden cause; explanation, way of doing or getting sth, that is not known to some or most people: 祕訣;祕傳;訣竅: *What is the ~ of his success?* 他成功的祕訣是什麼? **3** [U] secrecy: 祕密: *I was told about it in ~.* 我被暗中告以此事。**4** [C] mystery; sth hard to learn about or understand: 神祕;奧妙;難以理解之事: *the ~s of nature.* 自然的奧祕。**~·ly** *adv*

sec·re·tariat /ˌsekrəˈteərɪət ; ˌsɛkrəˈtɛrɪət/ *n* staff or office of the Secretary-General of a large organization: 秘書處;秘書處之全體職員: *get a position on the ~ of UNO in New York.* 在紐約聯合國組織的秘書處獲得一職位。

sec·re·tary /ˈsekrətrɪ *US:* -rəterɪ ; ˈsɛkrəˌtɛrɪ/ *n* (*pl* -ries) **1** employee in an office, who deals with correspondence, keeps records, makes arrangements and appointments for a particular member of the staff (and often called *private ~*). 書記;祕書(辦公室中僱來爲某一職員處理信函,保管檔案,安排業務及約會之人員;常稱作'私人祕書')。**2** official who has charge of the correspondence, records, and other business affairs of a society, club or other organization: (會社,俱樂部或其他組織中)主管信函,通訊,記錄及其他事務的職員;幹事: *honorary ~,* (abbr 略作 *hon sec*) unpaid ~ of a society, etc which is not conducted for profit. (非以營利爲目的之會社等不支薪水的)名譽幹事。**3** (GB) (英) **S~ of State,** minister in charge of a Government office: (主管政府一部門的)國務大臣;部長: *the S~ of State for Foreign and Commonwealth Affairs/Home Affairs/Scotland/Defence, etc.* 外相(內政大臣;蘇格蘭事務大臣;國防大臣等)。(US) (美) *S~ of State,* head of the Foreign Affairs Department; 國務卿; *S~ of the Treasury,* head of the Treasury Departmemt. 財政部長。**Permanent S~,** senior official in the Civil Service. 高級文官。**ˌS~-ˈGeneral,** principal executive office of a large organization (eg of UNO). (聯合國等龐大構機之)秘書長。**sec·re·tar·ial** /ˌsekrəˈteərɪəl ; ˌsɛkrəˈtɛrɪəl/ *adj* of (the work of) secretaries: 書記(之工作)的;祕書的: *secretarial duties/training/colleges.* 書記工作(訓練,專科學校)。

se·crete /sɪˈkriːt ; sɪˈkrit/ *vt* [VP6A] **1** produce by secretion(1). 分泌。**2** put or keep in a secret place. 隱匿;隱藏。**se·cre·tion** /sɪˈkriːʃn ; sɪˈkriʃən/ *n* **1** [U] process by which certain substances in a plant or animal body are separated (from sap, blood, etc) for use, or as waste matter; [C] substance so produced, eg *saliva, bile.* 動植物體內從汁液、血液等處析出有用物或廢物之程序;分泌;分泌物(如唾液、膽汁)。**2** act of secreting: 隱匿;隱藏: *the secretion of stolen goods.* 贓物的隱藏。

se·cret·ive /ˈsiːkrətɪv ; sɪˈkritɪv/ *adj* having the habit of keeping things secret; tending to hide one's thoughts, feelings, intentions, etc. 有保守祕密之習慣的;有掩飾自已之思想,感情,意欲等之傾向的;祕而不宣的;含蓄的。**~·ly** *adv* **~·ness** *n*

sect /sekt ; sɛkt/ *n* [C] group of people united by (esp religious) beliefs or opinions that differ from those more generally accepted. (信仰或意見異於多數人所接受者的)派;宗派;(尤指)敎派。

sec·tarian /sekˈteərɪən ; sɛkˈtɛrɪən/ *n, adj* (member, supporter) of a sect or sects: 某(些)宗派的(份子,支持者): *~ jealousies,* eg between one sect and another; 派系猜忌; *~ politics,* in which the advantage of a sect is considered more important than the public welfare. 派系政治(某一派系之利益較公共福祉受到重視者)。**~·ism** /-ɪzəm ; -ɪzəm/ *n* [U] tendency to split up into sects, work in the interest of sects, etc. 門戶之見;宗派意識。

sec·tion /ˈsekʃn ; ˈsɛkʃən/ *n* [C] **1** part cut off; slice; one of the parts into which sth may be divided: 斷片;切片;部分;片段: *the ~s of an orange.* 橙的各瓣。**2** one of a number of parts which can be put together to make a structure: (可拼攏成整體的)零件;各部分: *fit together the ~s of a complete prefabricated building.* 把預製房屋的各部分拼起來。**3** subdivision of an organized body of persons (*the ˈPostal S~*), or of a piece of writing (often indicated by the *ˈ~-mark* §, as § 21), or of a town, county, country or community: 機構之次一區分(如 the Postal Section 郵務處);處;科;組(等);(文章等的)節;項(常以節號 § 標明之,如 § 21);(城鎭,國家或社會的)地區;區域;區畫;階層: *ˌresiˈdential/ˈshopping ~s* (*area* is more usu). 住宅(商業)區 (area 較常用)。**4** view or representation of sth seen as if cut straight through; thin slice of sth, eg tissue, suitable for examination under a microscope. 截面；剖面；斷面；(適合於顯微鏡下觀察之)切片。 **~al** /-ʃənl ; -ʃənl/ *adj* **1** made or supplied in ~s(2): 由各部分組合而成的；由零件拼攏的: *a ~al fishing-rod;* 可拆卸拼攏的釣魚竿； *~al furniture.* 可拆卸拼攏的傢具。 **2** of a ~ of ~s of a community, etc: 地域的；區域的；區畫的；社會之一部分或數部分的；階層的: *~al interests,* the different and often conflicting interests of various ~s of a community; 社會各階層間不同的且常爲相互衝突的利益； *~al jealousies.* 區域或階層間的猜忌。 **~·al·ism** /-ʃənəlɪzəm ; -ʃən‚ɪzəm/ *n* [U] devotion to ~al interests instead of to those of the community as a whole. 地域或偏狹觀念；地方主義；小社羣意識。

sec·tor /ˈsektə(r) ; ˈsɛktɚ/ *n* [C] **1** part of a circle lying between two straight lines drawn from the centre to the circumference. (數學) 扇形。 ⇨ the illus at circle. 參看 circle 之插圖。 **2** one of the areas into which a battle area is divided for the purpose of controlling operations. (爲了指揮作戰而劃分之)戰區；防區。 **3** branch (of industry, etc): (工業等的)部門: *the public and private ~s of industry,* those parts publicly owned and those privately owned. 國有工業和私有工業。

secu·lar /ˈsekjʊlə(r) ; ˈsɛkjəlɚ/ *adj* **1** worldly or material, not religious or spiritual: 現世的；塵世的；世俗的；物質的；非宗教的；非精神的: *~ education;* 世俗教育； *~ art / music;* 非宗教藝術(音樂)； *the ~ power,* the State contrasted with the Church. 政府(與教會相對)。 ⇨ sacred. **2** living outside monasteries: 居住於修道院以外的: *the ~ clergy,* parish priests, etc. 教區僧侶。 **~·ism** /-ɪzəm ; -‚ɪzəm/ *n* [U] the view that morality and education should not be based on religion. 現世主義；世俗主義(主張倫理與教育不應以宗教爲基礎)。 **~·ist** /-ɪst ; -ɪst/ *n* believer in, supporter of, ~ism. 現世主義者；世俗主義者。 **~·ize** /-aɪz ; -‚aɪz/ *vt* [VP6A] make ~: 使現世化；使世俗化: *~ize church property / courts;* 使教會財產作俗用(使法院不受教會之支配)； *a ~ized Sunday,* eg when professional sporting events are permitted. 世俗化的星期天(如允許職業性運動項目)。

se·cure /sɪˈkjʊə(r) ; sɪˈkjʊr/ *adj* **1** free from anxiety: 無慮的；安心的: *feel ~ about one's future.* 對於自己的前途覺得安心。 **2** certain; guaranteed: 確定的；可靠的: *Our victory is ~.* 我們的勝利是有把握的。 *He has a ~ position in the Civil Service.* 他有穩當的公務員職位。 **3** unlikely to involve risk; firm: 無危險性的；牢固的: *Don't go higher up the cliff unless you find ~ footholds.* 除非你找到穩固的踏脚處，不要再往懸崖的高處爬了。 *Are you sure the doors and windows are ~?* 你確知門窗是關牢的嗎？ *Is that ladder ~?* 那梯子牢靠嗎？ **4** ~ ***(from, against),*** safe: 安全的: *Are we ~ from interruption / attack, etc?* 我們無受打擾(攻擊等)之虞嗎？ □ *vt* **1** make fast: 使牢固；緊閉: *~ all the doors and windows before leaving the house.* 離家前關好所有門窗。 **2** [VP6A, 14] ~ ***sth (against / from),*** make certain, firm or safe: 使安全；使可靠: *By strengthening the embankments they ~d the village against / from floods.* 他們藉加强堤防使該村莊免去洪水之患。 **3** [VP6A, 12B, 13B] succeed in getting (sth for which there is a great demand): 獲得(衆所需要之物): *Can you ~ me two good seats for the concert?* 你能爲我弄到音樂會的兩個好座位嗎？ *She has ~d a good job.* 她已獲得一個好工作。 **~·ly** *adv*

Se·curi·cor /sɪˈkjʊərɪkɔ:(r); sɪˈkjʊrəkɔr/ *n* (P) commercial organization for the secure transportation of money and other valuables (eg to and from banks, offices), for guarding property, etc: (商標) 受僱護送金錢或貴重物品(如往返銀行或辦公場所)，保護財產等的商業組織: **ˈ~** ***van,*** one used for this purpose. 護送財物的貨車。

se·cur·ity /sɪˈkjʊərətɪ ; sɪˈkjʊrətɪ/ *n* (*pl* -ties) **1** [C, U] (sth that provides) safety, freedom from danger or anxiety: 安全；無危險；無憂慮；提供安全之物；使免除危險或憂慮之物: *children who lack the ~ of parental care;* 缺乏父母照顧的孩子們； *cross the street in ~ at a pedestrian crossing.* 在行人穿越道上安全地過馬路。 *Is there any ~ from / against H-bombs?* 有防禦或抵抗氫彈之物嗎？ **the Seˈcurity Council,** the permanent peace-keeping organ of the United Nations (with five permanent and ten elected members). 聯合國安全理事會。 **ˈ~ police / forces,** those policemen or soldiers whose duty it is to protect important people or places, and to see that secret agents of foreign powers do not operate successfully. 安全警察；安全部隊(其職責爲保護重要人物或場所，不讓外國之間諜得逞)。 **ˈ~ risk,** a person who, because of his political affiliations, etc may be a danger to the security of the State. 因其政治背景等而可能危害政府的人。 **2** [C, U] sth valuable, eg a life-insurance policy, given as a pledge for the repayment of a loan or the fulfilment of a promise or undertaking: 抵押品；擔保品(如壽險單等): *lend money on ~;* 抵押貸款； *give sth as (a) ~.* 以某物作擔保。 **3** [C] document, certificate, etc showing ownership of property (esp bonds, stocks and shares): 產權證明；證券；(尤指)債券；股票: *government securities,* for money lent to a government. 公債券。

se·dan /sɪˈdæn ; sɪˈdæn/ *n* **1** **‚~(-ˈchair),** enclosed seat for one person, carried on poles by two men, used in the 17th and 18th cc. 轎(通用於十七、十八世紀)。 **2** saloon car for four or more persons. 轎車。

a sedan-chair

se·date /sɪˈdeɪt ; sɪˈdet/ *adj* (of a person, his behaviour) not lively or agitated; composed. (指人，其行爲)安靜的；肅穆的；莊重的。 **~·ly** *adv* **~·ness** *n*

se·da·tion /sɪˈdeɪʃn ; sɪˈdeʃən/ *n* [U] treatment by sedatives; condition resulting from this: 施以鎮靜劑；鎮靜狀態: *The patient is under ~.* 那病人已服用鎮靜劑。

seda·tive /ˈsedətɪv ; ˈsɛdətɪv/ *n, adj* (medicine, drug) tending to calm the nerves and reduce stress: 定神的；鎮定的；鎮靜劑: *After taking a ~ she was able to get to sleep.* 服過鎮靜劑之後，她就睡着了。 *Tobacco has a ~ effect on some people.* 烟對於某些人有定神的效果。 ⇨ *tranquillizer* at tranquil.

sed·en·tary /ˈsedntrɪ *US:* -terɪ ; ˈsɛdn‚tɛrɪ/ *adj* (of work) done sitting down (at a desk, etc); (of persons) spending much of their time seated: (指工作)坐着做的；(指人)慣坐的；久坐的: *lead a ~ life.* 過着案牘生活(其工作需要久坐的或勞心的)。

sedge /sedʒ ; sɛdʒ/ *n* [U] forms of grasslike plant growing in marshes or near wet places. 蘆葦；菅茅。 **sedgy** *adj* covered or bordered with ~. 生有蘆葦的；以蘆葦爲界的；多菅茅的。

sedi·ment /ˈsedɪmənt ; ˈsɛdəmənt/ *n* [U] matter (eg sand, dirt, gravel) that settles to the bottom of a liquid, eg mud left on fields after a river has been in flood over them. 渣；沈澱物(沙，垢，礫等之沉於液體底部者，如河流泛濫後留於田野之泥土)。 **sedi·men·tary** /‚sedɪˈmentrɪ ; ‚sɛdəˈmɛntərɪ/ *adj* of the nature of ~; formed from ~: 沈澱性的；由渣形成的: *~ary rocks,* eg slate, sandstone, limestone. 水成岩(如板石,沙石,石灰石)。

se·di·tion /sɪˈdɪʃn ; sɪˈdɪʃən/ *n* [U] words or actions intended to make people rebel against authority, disobey the government, etc: 煽動叛亂的言論或行動: *incitement to ~.* 唆使從事叛亂。**se·di·tious** /sɪˈdɪʃəs ; sɪˈdɪʃəs/ *adj* of the nature of ~: 煽動性的;叛亂性的: *seditious speeches/writings.* 煽動性的演說(著作)。

se·duce /sɪˈdju:s *US:* -ˈdu:s ; sɪˈdjus/ *vt* [VP6A, 14] *~ sb (from/into sth),* **1** persuade (sb) to do wrong; tempt (sb) into crime or sin: 引誘(某人)做壞事;誘使(某人)犯罪: *~ a man from his duty;* 誘使人捨棄職守; *~d by the offer of money into betraying one's country.* 因受金錢誘惑而叛國。**2** by charm, knowledge of the world, etc persuade sb less experienced to have sexual intercourse: 勾引;誘姦: *How many women did Don Juan ~?* 唐璜勾引過多少婦女? *Potiphar's wife tried to ~ young Joseph.* 波提乏的妻子試圖勾引年輕的約瑟。**se·ducer** *n* person who ~s, esp(2). 引誘者;(尤指)誘姦者;好色者。

se·duc·tion /sɪˈdʌkʃn ; sɪˈdʌkʃən/ *n* **1** [U] seducing or being seduced; [C] instance of this. 誘惑;勾引;誘姦。**2** sth very attractive and charming; sth likely to lead a person astray (but often with no implication of immorality): 極有誘惑力之物;易使人誤入歧途之物(但通常不含不道德之意): *surrender to the ~s of country life.* 屈服於田園生活的誘惑。**se·duc·tive** /sɪˈdʌktɪv ; sɪˈdʌktɪv/ *adj* alluring; captivating: 引誘的;有魅力的: *seductive smiles;* 誘人的微笑; *a seductive offer.* 令人心動的提議。**se·duc·tive·ly** *adv*

sedu·lous /ˈsedjʊləs *US:* ˈsedʒʊləs ; ˈsɛdʒələs/ *adj* persevering; done with perseverance: 勤勉的;不屈不撓的;堅毅地做成的: *He paid her ~ attention,* was persevering in his attempt to please her. 他一心一意想討好她(一直向她獻慇懃)。**~·ly** *adv*

see¹ /si: ; si/ *vi, vt* (*pt* saw /sɔ: ; sɔ/, *pp* seen /si:n ; sin/) (For special uses with *adverbial particles* and *preps,* ⇨ 11 below.) (與副詞接語及介詞連用的特殊用法參看下列第11義。) **1** [VP2A,B,C,4A] (often with *can, could;* not usu in the progressive tenses) have or use the power of sight: 看;見;視(常與 can, could 連用;通常不用進行式): *If you shut your eyes you can't see.* 閉上眼睛,你便看不見。*It was getting dark and I couldn't see to read.* 天漸黑了,我看不見,不能閱讀。*On a clear day we can see (for) miles and miles from this hill-top.* 在晴朗的日子,我們能從這小山頂看得很遠很遠。*Move aside, please: I can't see through you!* 請讓開——你擋住了我的視線! *He'll never be able to see again,* He has gone blind. 他再也看不見了(他的眼睛已經瞎了)。***seeing is believing,*** (prov) What one sees oneself is the most satisfactory evidence. (諺)眼見是實(百聞不如一見)。 **2** [VP6A, 8, 9, 10, 18A, 19A, 24A] (often with *can, could,* esp when an effort of perception is needed; not in the progressive tenses) be aware of by using the power of sight: 藉視力發覺;看見;看到(常與 can, could 連用,尤其在需要作視覺上的努力時;不用進行式): *Can/Do you see that ship on the horizon?* 你能看到(你看到)地平線上那條船嗎? *I looked out but saw nothing.* 我向外張望,什麼也沒看到。 *I saw him put the key in the lock, turn it and open the door.* 我看到他把鑰匙插入鎖眼,轉動鑰匙,把門打開。*The suspected man was seen to enter the building.* 疑犯被人看到進入那房屋。 *I saw two men struggling for the knife.* 我看到兩個人在搶那把刀。 *He was seen running away from the scene of the crime.* 他被人看見從犯罪現場跑開。*Have you ever seen a man hanged?* 你見過將人處絞刑嗎? *I saw that the box was empty.* 我看見那盒子是空的。*If you watch carefully you will see how to do it/how I do it/how it is done.* 如果你仔細觀察,你就會看出如何做此事(我如何做此事,此事是怎樣完成的)。***be 'seeing things,*** have hallucinations, ie see things that are not there or that do not exist, as a drunken man may: 生幻覺(卽看見不在或不存在之物,如醉漢可能發生者): *You're seeing things—there's nobody there!* 你有幻覺——那裡根本沒有人! ***see the back of sb,*** get rid of him; see him for the last time: 擺脫某人;見最後一次: *That fellow's a nuisance; I shall be glad to see the back of him.* 那傢伙是個討厭鬼;我樂於擺脫他。***see the last of sb/sth,*** have done with; see for the last time: 做完;和…斷絕關係;見最後一次: *I shall be glad to see the last of this job,* get to the end of it. 我眞願這件工作趕快做完。***see the sights,*** visit notable places, etc as a sightseer. 遊覽名勝;觀光。***see stars,*** have dancing lights before the eyes, eg as the result of a blow on the head. 眼前冒金星(如頭部受打擊的結果)。***see visions,*** be a seer. 做先知;做卜者。***see one's way (clear) to doing sth,*** see how to manage to do it, feel disposed to doing it: 有把握或有意做某事: *He didn't see his way to lending me the money I needed.* 他沒有把握借給我我所需要的錢。 **3** [VP6A, 2A] (in the *imper*) look (at): (用於祈使句中)看;瞧: *See, here he comes!* 看,他來了! *See page 4.* 請看第四頁。 **4** [VP6A, 9, 10, 2A] (not in the progressive tenses) understand; learn by search or inquiry or reflection: (不用進行式)(藉研究、詢問、反省等而)了解;領會;明白;懂: *He didn't see the joke/the point of the story.* 他不明白那笑話的可笑處(故事的寓意)。 *We saw that the plan was unwise.* 我們看出那計畫是不智的。*Do you see what I mean?* 你懂得我的意思嗎? *As far as I can see...,* To the best of my understanding.... 就我所能瞭解的…。*I think I'll be able to help, but I'll have to see,* wait until I know more. 我想我能幫得上忙,但要等我把事情弄清楚再說。*Go and see if/whether the postman has been yet.* 去看看郵差來過沒有。 ***see for oneself,*** find out in order to be convinced or satisfied: 親自求證;親眼去看: *If you don't believe me, go and see for yourself!* 如果你不相信我,你親自去察看吧! ***not see the use/good/fun/advantage etc of doing sth,*** feel doubt about whether it is useful, etc to do it. 懷疑做某事的益處(好處,樂趣,利益等)。***you see,*** (used parenthetically) (作插語用) **(a)** as you no doubt know or understand. 你無疑地明白。**(b)** as I must now tell you or explain to you. 我必須現在告訴你;我必須現在向你解釋。***seeing that,*** in view of the fact that; considering. 鑒於…的事實;照…看來。**5** [VP9] learn from the newspaper or other printed sources: (從報紙或其他印刷物中)閱悉: *I see that the Prime Minister has been in Wales.* 我在報上看到首相已前往威爾斯。 **6** [VP6A, 22, 24A] have knowledge or experience of; have (sth) presented to one's attention: 經歷;閱歷(某事): *This coat of mine has seen hard wear,* ie has been worn for a long time. 我這件外套已穿過很多年了。 *He has seen a good deal in his long life.* 他在漫長的一生中閱歷甚豐。*I never saw such grief.* 我從未經歷過如此的悲傷。*I want to see you happy/settled before I leave,* I don't want to leave until I know that you are happy/settled. 我要確知你快樂(安頓好)才離開。 ***will never see thirty/forty, etc again,*** is already past that age. 年齡已逾三十(四十等)。 ***have seen the day/time when...,*** used to call attention to a past state of affairs: 曾經歷…的日子(用以引起對過去情境的注意): *He had seen the day when there were no cars on the roads,* was living before there were cars. 他經歷過沒有汽車的時代。 ***have seen better days,*** have now declined, lost former prosperity, etc. 現已式微;已失去昔日的繁榮等。***see sb damned/in hell first,*** used to express an absolute refusal to do what one is asked, etc. 堅決拒絕;絕不答應。 ***see service in sth; see (good) service,*** ⇨ service. **7** [VP15A, 6A] give an interview to; visit; receive a call from: 會見;訪問;接見: *Can I see you on business?* 我可以和你洽談公務嗎? *You ought to see a doctor about that cough.* 你

在咳嗽,該去看看醫生。 *She's too ill to see anyone at present.* 她目前病重,不能會客。*The manager can see you for five minutes.* 經理可以接見你五分鐘。Note: The progressive tenses are used for this sense: 注意:本定義可用進行式: *I'm seeing my solicitor this afternoon.* 今日下午我將與我的律師會面。*I shall be seeing them tomorrow.* 我將於明天和他們見面。**Be 'seeing you / ˌSee you 'soon,** (colloq) used as an equivalent for 'Goodbye!'. (俗)再見;再會。**8** [VP18A, 15A, 24A] allow to; look on without protest or action: 聽任;坐視: *You can't see people starve without trying to help them, can you?* 你不會坐視人們挨餓而不想法子去幫助他們吧? *You wouldn't see me left here all alone?* 你不會把我一個人留在此地吧? **9** [VP9] attend to; take care; make provision: 留神;注意;預備: *See that the windows and doors are fastened.* 務必要把門窗關牢。**10** [VP16B, 19A] call up a picture of; imagine: 想起…之情景;想像: *He saw himself as the saviour of his country.* 他幻想自己爲國家的救星。*I can't see myself allowing people to cheat me.* 我無法想像會讓人欺騙。 **11** (special uses with *adverbial particles* and *preps*): (與副詞接語及介詞連用的特殊用法):

see about sth, deal with: 處理(某事);照料(某事): *He promised to see about the matter.* 他答應處理此事。***see sb about sth,*** consult sb, take advice (on sth): 和某人商量(某事);向某人請教(某事): *I must see a builder about these tiles that have fallen from the roof.* 我必須找個建築商談談從屋頂掉下來的這些瓦。

see sb across sth, guide, conduct, help sb across (a road, etc): 指導或協助某人穿越(道路等): *That man's blind—I'd better see him across the street.* 那人是個瞎子 —— 我應該幫助他穿越這條街。

see (sb) around (sth), = see (sb) over (sth). ***See you around!*** (sl) Goodbye! (俚)再見!

see sb back / home, accompany sb: 護送或陪伴某人回家: *May I see you home?* 我可以送你回家嗎? *Tom's had too much to drink—we'd better see him back / home.* 湯姆喝了太多酒 —— 我們最好送他回家。

see sb off, go to a railway station, an airport, the docks, etc with sb about to start on a journey: (至火車站、機場、碼頭等處)送(某人): *I was seen off by many of my friends.* 許多朋友來送我。***see sb off sth,*** go with him until he is at the door, outside, etc: 送某人到門口或屋外等: *I don't want this fellow here; please see him off the premises,* get rid of him. 我不願這傢伙待在這裡;請把他趕出屋外。

see sb out (of sth), accompany sb until he is out of a building: 送某人到(…的)外面: *My secretary will see you out.* 我的秘書將送你出去。***see sth out,*** = see sth through.

see over sth, visit and examine or inspect carefully: 查視;調查: *see over a house that one wishes to buy or rent.* 查看想要購買或租賃的房子。

see (sb) over (sth), show him around (a place). 帶(某人)參觀(一地方)。

see (sb) round (sth), = see (sb) over (sth).

see through sb / sth, not be deceived by: 看透(某人或某事);不爲…所蒙蔽: *I see through your little game,* am aware of the trick you are trying to play on me. 我看穿了你玩的那套把戲(我知道你要向我耍什麼花樣)。*We all saw through him,* knew what kind of man he really was. 我們全看透他(是什麼樣的人)了。**'see-through** *adj* (esp of clothing) that can be seen through; transparent. (尤指衣服)透明的。***see sb through (sth),*** give him support, encouragement, until the end: 幫助(某人)到底: *You'll have a difficult time, but I'll see you safely through.* 你將會遭遇到困難,但我將幫助你平安度過。***see sth through,*** not give up an undertaking until the end is reached: 貫徹(某事);堅持到最後: *He said that whatever happened he would see the struggle through.* 他說不論發生什麼事,他決心奮鬪到底。

see to sth, attend to sth: 注意;留心;照料: *This machine is out of order; get a mechanic to see to it.* 這部機器壞了;找位技工來檢修一下。*Will you see to the arrangements for the next meeting of the committee?* 請你負責安排委員會的下一次會議好嗎?

see² /siː; si/ *n* district under a bishop; bishop's position, office, jurisdiction: 主教的轄區;主教的地位、職位、管轄權: *the See of Canterbury;* 坎特布里主教的轄區; *the Holy See / the See of Rome,* the Papacy. 教皇之職位及權威;羅馬教廷。

seed /siːd; sid/ *n* (*pl* ~s or ~, unchanged) (複數加s或不變) **1** flowering plant's unit of reproduction, from which another plant can grow: 種;種子(有花植物的繁殖單位): *a packet of ~(s).* 一包種子。⇨ the illus at flower, fruit. 參看 flower, fruit 之插圖。*Sow the ~ in May or June.* 在五月或六月播種。*Its ~s are / Its ~ is very small.* 它的種子很小。***run / go to ~,*** stop flowering as ~ is produced; (fig) become careless of one's appearance and clothes. 花謝結子;(喻)變爲不留心儀表和衣着;不修邊幅。**'~-bed** *n* bed of fine soil in which to sow ~. 播種床。**'~-cake** *n* cake containing ~s, eg caraway, as a flavouring. 含有芳香子實(如葛縷子等)的糕餅。**'~-corn** *n* grain kept for ~. 作種用的穀物;穀種。**'~s·man** /-mən; -mən/ *n* (*pl* -men) dealer in ~s. 種子商。**'~·time** *n* sowing season. 播種期。**2** [U] (old use) offspring: (舊用法)後裔;子嗣: *the ~ of Abraham,* the Hebrews. 亞伯拉罕的後裔(即希伯來人)。 **3** cause, origin (*of* a tendency, development, etc): (趨勢,發展等的)原由;根據(與 of 連用): *sow the ~s of virtue in young children.* 在兒童的心田播下美德的種子。 **4** [U] semen. 精液;胚種。 **5** **'~-potato** *n* potato kept and allowed to sprout before being planted. 留待發芽以供種植的馬鈴薯;馬鈴薯種。**'~-pearls** *n pl* small pearls. 小粒珍珠。**6** (sport) ~ed player: (運動)種子選手: *England's No. 1 ~* (in a championship). (在錦標賽中之)英國第一號種子選手。⇨ 4 below. 參看下列動詞第4義。□ *vi, vt* **1** [VP2A] (of a plant) produce ~ when full grown; let ~ fall. (指植物)結實;生子;自然播種。 **2** [VP6A] sow with ~: 播種於: *~ a field with wheat;* 在田裡種下小麥的種子; *a newly-~ed lawn.* 剛播種過的草地。**3** [VP6A] remove ~ from: 除去…之種子: *~ raisins.* 除去葡萄乾之子。 **4** [VP6A] (esp in tennis) separate those players well tested and known to be stronger from the weaker players (in order to have good matches later in a tournament): (尤指在網球賽中)抽出種子選手(以使精采比賽排在後頭): *~ed players.* 種子選手。**~·less** *adj* having no ~: 無子的;無核的: *~less raisins.* 無籽葡萄乾。**~·ling** /'siːdlɪŋ; 'sidlɪŋ/ *n* young plant newly grown from a ~. 剛從種子長出的幼小植物;幼苗。

seedy /'siːdɪ; 'sidɪ/ *adj* (-ier, -iest) **1** full of seed: 多(種)子的: *as ~ as a dried fig.* 像乾無花果一般地多子。 **2** shabby-looking; in worn clothes: 破舊的;襤褸的: *a ~ boarding-house;* 破舊的寄宿舍; *a ~-looking person.* 衣着襤褸的人。 **3** (colloq) unwell: (俗)不適的: *feel ~.* 覺得不舒服。**seed·ily** /-ɪlɪ; -əlɪ/ *adv* **seedi·ness** *n*

seek /siːk; sik/ *vt, vi* (*pt, pp* sought /sɔːt; sɔt/) (formal) (正式用語) **1** [VP6A, 15A] look for; try to find: 尋覓;找: *~ shelter from the rain;* 尋找避雨之所; *~ safety in flight.* 逃難;避難。*The reason is not far to ~,* is found near at hand, quickly found. 道理很顯然。*Are you ~ing a quarrel,* trying to start one? 你在尋釁爭吵嗎? *He is going to Canada to ~ his fortune,* to try to become rich. 他去加拿大想賺大錢。 **2** [VP6A] ask for: 請求;求: *I will ~ my doctor's advice.* 我將請教醫生的意見。 **3** [VP7A] try; attempt: 試圖;企圖: *They sought to kill him.* 他們企圖殺他。 **4** [VP3A] ~ ***for,*** try to win: 試圖獲得: *unsought-for fame,* fame which came without being looked for. 不謀而得的名聲。 ***(much) sought after,*** (much) in demand. 供不應求;極受歡迎。

seem /siːm ; sim/ *vi* [VP4D, E, 2A] have or give the impression or appearance of being or doing; appear to be: 似乎是;看似;好像;似覺;彷彿: *Things far off ~ (to be) small.* 遠處之物看上去小些。*What ~s easy to some people ~s difficult to others.* 某些人覺得容易的事，別的人可能覺得困難。*There ~ to be no objections to the proposal.* 對這提議似乎沒有反對意見。*He ~s to think so.* 他似乎認爲如此。*I shall act as ~s best (= as it ~s best to me).* 我將盡力而爲。*The book ~s (to be) quite interesting.* 這本書好像很有趣。*The child ~s to be asleep.* 這孩子好像是睡着了。*It ~s that no one knew what had happened.* 似乎沒有人知道發生過什麼事。*I can't ~* (= I ~ unable) *to get out of that bad habit.* 我似乎無法戒除那壞習慣。*It would ~ that...,* (a cautious way of saying 'It ~s that...'). 似乎…(爲 'It seems that' 的謹愼說法)。*'I've been out in the rain'—'So it ~s',* ie from your wet clothes it appears that you've been out in the rain. '我剛才淋過雨'—'果然有淋過雨的樣子。' **~·ing** *adj* apparent but perhaps not real or genuine: 表面上的;似乎的;彷彿的(也許不是實在的或眞正的): *In spite of his ~ing friendship he gave me no help.* 儘管他維持表面上的友誼，他未曾幫助過我。 **~·ing·ly** *adv* in appearance; apparently. 表面上;外觀上。

seem·ly /'siːmlɪ ; 'simlɪ/ *adj* (-ier, -iest) (formal) (正式用語) **1** (of behaviour) proper or correct (for the occasion or circumstances): (指行爲,在某種場合或環境)適宜的: *It isn't ~ to praise oneself.* 自誇是不適宜的。 **2** decent; decorous: 正當的;體面的: *Strip-tease is not a ~ occupation for any girl.* 脫衣舞對於任何女孩子而言，都不是正當的職業。 **seem·li·ness** *n*

seen /siːn ; sin/ *pp* of see¹.

seep /siːp ; sip/ *vi* [VP2C] (of liquids) ooze out or through; trickle: (指液體)漏出;滲出: *water ~-ing through the roof of the tunnel.* 從隧道頂部滲出的水。 **~·age** /'siːpɪdʒ ; 'sipɪdʒ/ *n* [U] slow leaking through. 漏出;滲出;滲流。

seer /sɪə(r) ; sɪr/ *n* person claiming to see into the future; prophet. 自稱能透視未來者;預言家;先知。

seer·sucker /'sɪəsʌkə(r) ; 'sɪrˌsʌkɚ/ *n* [U] thin fabric with a striped pattern and a crinkled surface: 皺面條紋薄織物: *a ~ tablecloth.* 一條皺面條紋薄織物桌布。

see·saw /'siːsɔː ; 'siˌsɔ/ *n* [C, U] (game played on a) long plank with a person astride each end which can rise and fall alternately; up-and-down or to-and-fro motion: 蹺蹺板;軒輊戲;上下或往復之運動: *play at ~.* 玩蹺蹺板。□ *vi* play at ~; move up and down or to and fro; (fig) vacillate: 玩蹺蹺板;上下或往復運動;(喩)猶疑;躊躇: *~ between two opinions.* 猶疑於兩種意見之間。

seethe /siːð ; sið/ *vi, vt* **1** [VP2A, 3A] ***~ (with),*** boil, bubble over; be crowded, agitated (esp fig): 沸騰;起泡;騷動;激昂(尤用於比喩中): *~ with anger;* 大發雷霆; *a country seething with discontent;* 激盪着不滿情緒的國家; *streets seething with people.* 擠滿人而鬧哄哄的街道。 **2** [VP6A, 2A] (old use) cook by boiling. (舊用法)煮沸;滾。

seg·ment /'segmənt ; 'sɛgmənt/ *n* [C] **1** part cut off or marked off by a line: 切開的部分;以線畫開的部分: *a ~ of a circle.* 弓形。 **2** division or section: 區分;節;段;片: *a ~ of an orange.* 一瓣橘子。 ⇨ the illus at fruit. 參看 fruit 之插圖。□ *vt, vi* /seg'ment ; sɛg'mɛnt/ divide, become divided, into ~s. 分開爲若干部分;變爲若不部分。 **seg·men·ta·tion** /ˌsegmən'teɪʃn ; ˌsɛgmən'teʃən/ *n* division into ~s. 分割;切斷。

seg·re·gate /'segrɪgeɪt ; 'sɛgrɪˌget/ *vt* [VP6A] put apart from the rest; isolate: 隔離;分開: *~ the sexes;* 將男女分開; *~ people with infectious diseases.* 隔離傳染病患者。**seg·re·ga·tion** /ˌsegrɪ'geɪʃn; ˌsɛgrɪ'geʃən/ *n* segregating or being ~d: 隔離;分開: *a policy of racial segregation.* 種族隔離政策。 ⇨ *integration* at integrate.

seign·ior /'seɪnjə(r) *US:* 'siːnjər ; 'sinjɚ/ *n* feudal lord; landowner in feudal times. 領主;諸侯;(封建時代之)地主。

seine /seɪn ; sen/ *n* [C] large fishing-net which hangs like a curtain, with floats along the top edge and sinkers (weights) along the bottom edge, used to encircle fish, and usu hauled ashore. 拉網;大捕魚網;拖地大圍網(張起時似幕;上緣有浮子,下緣有墜子,用以兜圍魚類,通常拖拉上岸)。□ *vt, vi* fish, catch (fish), with a ~. 以拉網捕(魚)。

seis·mic /'saɪzmɪk ; 'saɪzmɪk/ *adj* of earthquakes. 地震的。 **seis·mo·graph** /'saɪzməgrɑːf *US:* -græf ; 'saɪzməˌgræf/ *n* instrument which records the strength, duration and distance away of earthquakes. 地震儀(記錄地震之強度,持續時間及距離者)。 **seis·mol·ogy** /saɪz'mɒlədʒɪ ; saɪz'mɑlədʒɪ/ *n* [U] science of earthquakes. 地震學。 **seis·mol·ogist** /saɪz'mɒlədʒɪst ; saɪz'mɑlədʒɪst/ *n*

seize /siːz ; siz/ *vt, vi* **1** [VP6A, 15A] take possession of (property, etc) by law: 依法律佔有或取得(財產等);扣押;沒收;查封: *~ sb's goods for payment of debt.* 扣押某人之貨物以償付債務。 **2** [VP 6A, 15A] take hold of, suddenly and violently: 攫取;强取;抓住: *~ a thief by the collar.* 抓住賊的衣領。 **3** [VP6A, 3A] ***~ (on/upon),*** see clearly and use: 利用;採用: *~ (upon) an idea/a chance/an opportunity.* 採納意見(抓住機會;把握良機)。 **4** [VP2A, C] ***~ (up),*** (of moving parts of machinery) become stuck or jammed, eg because of too much heat or friction. (指機器)陷於停頓;停止轉動(如因爲過熱或摩擦太大等)。 **seiz·ure** /'siːʒə(r) ; 'siʒɚ/ *n* **1** [U] act of seizing or taking possession of by force or the authority of the law; [C] instance of this: 依法律佔有;强佔;沒收;查封;其實例: *seizure of contraband by Customs officers.* 海關官員沒收違禁品。 **2** [C] sudden attack of apoplexy; heart attack. 中風驟發;心臟病發作。

sel·dom /'seldəm ; 'sɛldəm/ *adv* (usu placed with the *v*) not often; rarely: (通常置於動詞之旁)很少;不常;罕: *I have ~ seen such large apples.* 我很少見到這麼大的蘋果。*She ~ goes out.* 她不常外出。*She goes out very ~.* 她極少外出。*His wife ~, if ever, has a holiday.* 他的妻子難得有一天休息。*He ~ or never gives his wife a present.* 他可以說從未送過禮物給妻子。

se·lect /sɪ'lekt ; sə'lɛkt/ *vt* [VP6A, 15A, 16A] choose (as being the most suitable, etc): 選擇;挑選: *~ a book/a Christmas present for a child.* 選擇一本書(給孩子的聖誕禮物)。*Who has been ~ed to lead the delegation?* 誰被選爲代表團的領隊?□ *adj* **1** carefully chosen: 精選的: *~ passages from Milton.* 密爾頓選粹。 **2** (of a school, society, etc) of or for carefully chosen persons, not for all: (指學校,會社等)選擇份子嚴格的;苛擇的;挑剔的: *a ~ club;* 選擇會員嚴格的俱樂部; *shown to a ~ audience.* 向經過挑選的觀衆公開的。 **~ committee,** (in the House of Commons) small committee appointed for a special investigation. (下議院中之)特別委員會(受命作某項特別調查者)。 **se·lec·tor** /-tə(r) ; -tɚ/ *n* one who, that which, ~s, eg a member of a committee ~ing a national sports team, etc. 選擇者(如挑選國家代表隊之選拔委員等);挑選器械;選擇器。

se·lec·tion /sɪ'lekʃn ; sə'lɛkʃən/ *n* **1** [U] choosing. 選擇;挑選;淘汰。 **'~ committee,** one appointed to select, eg new members for a sports team. 選拔委員會(如設立以挑選運動員者)。 **natural ~,** (Darwin's theory of) the process in nature by which certain plants and animals flourish and multiply while others are less suited to their surroundings and die out. 自然淘汰;天擇(依照達爾文的理論,某些動植物能夠興旺與繁殖,而其他較不能適應其環境者滅絕)。

2 [C] collection or group of selected things or examples; number of things from which to select: 精選品集;供選擇之物: *~s from 18th-century English poetry.* 十八世紀英國詩選。*That shop has a good ~ of denim jeans.* 那商店有很多牛仔褲可供挑選。

se·lec·tive /sɪˈlektɪv ; səˈlɛktɪv/ *adj* having the power to select; characterized by selection. 有選擇力的;淘汰的。~ **service**, (US) selection, for compulsory military service, of men with certain requirements, abilities, etc. (美)選募某些有特殊條件或能力的人服義務兵役。**~·ly** *adv* **sel·ec·tiv·ity** /sɪˌlekˈtɪvətɪ ; səˌlɛkˈtɪvətɪ/ *n* [U] (esp) power (of a radio) to receive broadcasts from one station without interference from other stations. (尤指收音機之)選擇性(卽收聽一電臺時不受其他電臺之干擾)。

se·le·nium /sɪˈliːnɪəm ; səˈlinɪəm/ *n* non-metallic element (symbol **Se**) whose power to conduct electric current increases with the intensity of the light reaching it. 硒(非金屬化學元素,符號爲 Se)。~ **cell**, one containing a strip of ~, used in photo-electric devices, eg the exposure meter of a camera. 硒(質)光電管。

self /self ; sɛlf/ *n* (*pl* selves /selvz ; sɛlvz/) **1** [U] person's nature, special qualities; one's own personality: 本性;本質;自身;自己;自我: *one's better / worse ~*, one's nobler nature / base nature; 某人較高尚(低劣)的本質; *one's former ~*, oneself as one formerly was; 本來面目;從前的樣子; *analysis of the ~;* 自我分析; *the conscious ~*. 自覺。**2** [U] one's own interests or pleasure: 私利;私慾;利己心: *She has no thought of ~*, thinks only of the interests, welfare, etc of others. 她未想到私利。**3** (comm, dated style, or joc) myself, yourself, etc: (商,過時文體或謔)我自己;你自己等: *pay to ~*, (on a cheque) pay to the person whose signature appears on it; (支票用語)認票不認人; *a room for ~ and wife.* 一個我和我太太住的房間。*Let us drink a toast to our noble selves.* 讓我們爲(高貴的)自己乾一杯。

self- /self ; sɛlf/ *pref* short for *itself, myself, himself, oneself*, etc: 爲 itself, myself, himself, oneself 等之畧: ˌ*~-ˈtaught*, taught by oneself; 自學的; ˌ*~-ˈgoverning colonies*, colonies that govern themselves. 自治殖民地。ˌ**~-aˈbasement** *n* [U] humiliation of oneself. 自卑。ˌ**~-abˈsorbed** *adj* having one's attention taken up by one's own interests, thoughts, etc; unaware of other person. 專心於自身利益的;只顧自己的。ˌ**~-ˈacting** *adj* automatic. 自動的。ˌ**~-ˈactivating** *adj* (eg of an explosive device) made so as to activate itself without external control. (指爆炸裝置等)自動引發的。ˌ**~-adˈdressed** *adj* addressed to oneself: 寫有回信地址的: *I enclose a stamped ~-addressed envelope.* 我附了一個貼好郵票寫有回信地址的信封。ˌ**~-apˈpointed** *adj* chosen or declared by oneself; unsanctioned (and perhaps unqualified): 自命的;自封的: *a ~-appointed arbiter / expert.* 一位自命的調停人(專家)。ˌ**~-asˈsertion** *n* [U] the putting forward of one's own claims in a determined manner; the putting forward of oneself in an effort to be noticed by everyone. 堅持己見;專斷;自作主張;愛出風頭。ˌ**~-asˈsertive** *adj* ˌ**~-asˈsurance** *n* [U] confidence in oneself. 自信。ˌ**~-asˈsured** *adj* ˌ**~-ˈcentred** *adj* interested chiefly in oneself and one's own affairs. 自私自利的;自我中心的。ˌ**~-colˈlected** *adj* (of persons) having or showing presence of mind and composure; calm. (指人)心平氣和的;沉靜的。ˌ**~-ˈcoloured** *adj* of the same colour all over. 單色的;純色的。ˌ**~-comˈmand** *n* [U] power of controlling one's feelings. 自制;克己。ˌ**~-comˈplacency** *n* [U] state of being too easily pleased with oneself. 自滿;自得。ˌ**~-conˈfessed** *adj* on one's own confession: 自己承認的;坦供的: *a ~-confessed thief.* 一個坦供行竊的賊。ˌ**~-ˈconfidence** *n* [U] belief in one's own abilities. 自信。ˌ**~-ˈconfident** *adj* ˌ**~-ˈconscious** *adj* aware of one's own existence, thoughts and actions; (colloq) shy; embarrassed. 意識到本身之存在,思想和行爲的;自覺的;(俗)害羞的;忸怩的;怕難爲情的。ˌ**~-ˈconsciousness** *n* [U]. ˌ**~-conˈtained** *adj* **(a)** (of a person) not impulsive or communicative. (指人)不易衝動的;沉默寡言的。**(b)** (esp of a flat) complete in itself (not sharing the kitchen, bathroom, etc with occupants of other flats) and (usu) with its own private entrance. (尤指公寓)獨立門戶的(不與其他住戶共用廚房、浴室等,且通常有自用的房門)。ˌ**~-conˈtrol** *n* [U] control of one's own feelings, behaviour, etc: 自制;克己: *exercise ~-control;* 運用自制力; *lose one's ~-control.* 失去自制力。ˌ**~-deˈfence** *n* [U] defence of one's own body, property, rights, etc: 自衞: *kill sb in ~-defence*, while defending oneself against attack; 因自衞殺死某人; *the art of ~-defence*, boxing. 拳術。ˌ**~-deˈnial** *n* [U] going without things one would like to have in order to help others: 自我克制;自我犧牲: *practise ~-denial to help the children.* 作自我犧牲以幫助孩子們。ˌ**~-deˈnying** *adj* ˌ**~-deˌtermiˈnation** *n* [U] **(a)** (in politics) decision, made by a people having the characteristics of a nation, whether they shall be independent or (continue to) be part of another state: (政治)民族自決(一民族就其自身應成爲獨立國家,或繼續爲其他國家一部分所做之決定): *the right of all peoples to ~-determination.* 所有民族自決的權利。**(b)** the making of one's own decisions; the guidance, by the individual, of his own conduct. 自己決定;自己作主。ˌ**~-ˈeducated** *adj* educated without (much) help from schools or teachers. 自修的;自學的。ˌ**~-efˈfacing** *adj* keeping oneself in the background; not trying to get attention. 謙退的;避免出頭的。ˌ**~-emˈployed** *adj* working, eg as a shopkeeper, a jobbing gardener, without an employer. 非爲僱主或不專爲某一僱主而工作的(如店主,作零工的園丁等)。ˌ**~-eˈsteem** *n* [U] good opinion of oneself; (sometimes) conceit: 自尊;(有時用作)自負;自大: *injure one's ~-esteem*, lower one's opinion of oneself. 傷害某人的自尊。ˌ**~-ˈevident** *adj* clear without proof or more evidence. 毋待證明的;自明的。ˌ**~-exˌamiˈnation** *n* [U, C] examining one's own behaviour, motives, moods, etc. 自省;自我檢討。ˌ**~-exˈplanatory** *adj* clear without (further) explanation. 毋須解釋的;不解自明的。ˌ**~-ˈhelp** *n* [U] use of one's own powers to achieve success, etc. 自助;自立。ˌ**~-imˈportant** *adj* pompous; having too high an opinion of oneself. 自誇的;自大的;自視過高的。ˌ**~-imˈportance** *n* [U]. ˌ**~-imˈposed** *adj* (of a duty, task, etc) imposed on oneself. (任務、工作等)自願負責的;自願承擔的。ˌ**~-inˈdulgent** *adj* giving way too easily to desires for one's own comfort, pleasures, etc. 縱慾的;放縱自己的。ˌ**~-inˈdulgence** *n* [U]. ˌ**~-ˈinterest** *n* [U] one's own interests and personal advantage. 私利;利己。ˌ**~-ˈlocking** *adj* locking automatically when closed. 關閉時自動鎖上的。ˌ**~-ˈmade** *adj* having succeeded by one's own efforts, esp after beginning life without money, education or influence. 自力成功的;白手起家的。ˌ**~-oˈpinionated** *adj* over-certain that one's own opinions are correct; having strong opinions not firmly based. 固執己見的;執迷不悟的;剛愎自用的。ˌ**~-ˈpity** *n* [U] (exaggerated) pity for oneself. (誇張的)自憐;自憫。ˌ**~-posˈsessed** *adj* calm, cool, confident. 沉着的;冷靜的;有信心的。ˌ**~-posˈsession** *n* [U] coolness; composure: 冷靜;沉着: *lose / regain one's ~-possession.* 失去(恢復)冷靜。ˌ**~-ˌpreserˈvation** *n* [U] keeping oneself from harm or destruction: 自保;自衞: *the instinct of ~-preservation.* 自衞的本能。ˌ**~-ˈraising** *adj* (of flour) not needing the addition of baking-powder (when bread, etc is being made). (指麵粉)自行發酵的。ˌ**~-reˈliant** *adj* having or showing confidence in one's own powers, judgement, etc. 依靠自己的；信賴自己的。ˌ~-re'liance *n* [U] ˌ~-re'spect *n* [U] feeling that one is behaving and thinking in ways that will not cause one to be ashamed of oneself: 自尊；自重；自豪: *lose all ~-respect.* 失去一切自尊。ˌ~-re'specting *adj* having ~-respect: 自尊的；自重的: *No ~-respecting man could agree to do such a thing.* 凡是有自尊心的人都不會做這樣的事。ˌ~-'righteous *adj* convinced of one's own goodness and that one is better than others. 自以爲正直(較他人公正善良)的。ˌ~-'rule *n* = ~-government. ˌ~-'sacrifice *n* [U, C] the giving up of one's own interests and wishes for the sake of other people. 自我犧牲。ˌ~-'sacrificing *adj* ˌ~-'same *adj* very same; identical: 同一的；同樣的: *Tom and I reached Paris on the ~-same day.* 湯姆和我在同一天抵達巴黎。ˌ~-'sealing *adj* (of a fuel tank, pneumatic tyre, etc) having a substance (eg soft rubber) that automatically seals a puncture made in it. (指油箱，氣胎等)有自動封閉孔眼之物質(如軟橡膠)的；自動封閉的。ˌ~-'seeker *n* person who is too much concerned with gaining advantages for himself. 唯利是圖者；自私自利者。ˌ~-'seeking *n, adj* ˌ~-'service *adj* **(a)** (of a canteen, restaurant) one at which persons collect their own food and drink from counters and carry it to tables. (指餐館，飯店)自助的。**(b)** (of a shop) one at which customers collect what they want from counters or shelves and pay as they leave. (指商店)自助的。**(c)** (of a garage) one at which customers fill their cars with petrol and then go and pay the charge at a counter. (指加油站)顧客自行加油的。ˌ~-'sown *adj* (of plants) coming from seed that has dropped from the plant (not sown by a gardener). (指植物)自然播種的；自然生長的。ˌ~-'starter *n* device (usu electric) for starting an engine. 自行起動機(通常爲電動的)；自行開動器。ˌ~-'styled *adj* using a name, title, etc which one has given oneself and to which one has no right: 自稱的；自任的；自封的(自行使用某名字，頭銜等): *The ~-styled 'Dr' Smith had never been awarded a degree of any kind.* 那位自稱爲'博士'的史密斯先生從未得過任何學位。ˌ~-suf'ficient *adj* **(a)** needing no help from others: 自給自足的: *The country has now become ~-sufficient in woollen goods,* no longer has to import them. 這個國家在毛織品方面現在已能自給自足了。**(b)** over-confident. 過於自信的；傲慢的。ˌ~-suf'ficiency *n* [U]. ˌ~-suf'ficing *adj* = ~-sufficient: *a ~-sufficing economic unit.* 自給自足的經濟單位。ˌ~-sup'porting *adj* (of a person) earning enough money to keep oneself: (指人)自謀生活的；自立的: *now that my children are ~-supporting;* 既然我的孩子們都能自立；(of a business, etc) paying its way; not needing a subsidy. (指商業等)能維持自己的；不須補助的。ˌ~-'will *n* [U] wilfulness; determined to do as one wishes and not be guided by others. 執拗；固執己見。ˌ~-'willed *adj* obstinate; refusing advice or guidance. 執拗的；固執己見的。ˌ~-'winding *adj* (of a watch) winding itself automatically (from movements of the wrist, etc). (指錶)自動上發條的。

self·ish /'selfɪʃ; 'sɛlfɪʃ/ *adj* chiefly thinking of and interested in one's own needs and welfare; without care for others: 自私的；自利的；不顧他人的: *act from ~ motives.* 出於自私的動機而行事。**~·ly** *adv* **~·ness** *n*

sell /sel; sɛl/ *vt, vi* (*pt, pp* sold /səʊld; sold/) **1** [VP6A, 12A, 13A, 15B] ~ ***sth (to sb); ~ sb sth,*** give in exchange for money: 賣；售；銷: *~ fruit;* 賣水果；*~ sth by auction;* 拍賣某物；*~ sth at a good price;* 按高價賣某物；*~ oranges at five-pence each;* 橘子每個賣五辨士；*~ a man into slavery.* 把一個人賣掉做奴隸。*I'll ~ it to you for £5.* 我願以五鎊價格把它賣給你。*Will you ~ me your bicycle?* 你願把你的脚踏車賣給我嗎？ ***~ sth off,*** ~ (a stock of goods) cheaply. 廉售(存貨)。***~ sth out,*** **(a)** ~ part or all of one's share in a business: 脫售(在某企業中之一部分或全部股份): *He sold out his share of the business and retired.* 他脫售他在公司中的股份並且退休了。**(b)** ~ all of one's stock of sth: 售出全部存貨: *We are sold out of small sizes.* 我們小號的貨品完全賣光了。*The book you ask for is sold out,* There are no copies left. 你要的書賣完了。***~ (sb) out,*** (colloq) be treacherous; betray sb. (俗)不忠；出賣某人。'**~-out** *n* **(a)** event, eg a concert, for which all tickets are sold. 入場劵全部售完的音樂會等；客滿的演出。**(b)** (colloq) betrayal. (俗)出賣；背叛。***~ sb up,*** ~ (a person's goods and property) for payment of debt: 爲償債而出賣(某人之貨物及財產): *I went bankrupt and was sold up.* 我宣告破產，財產被賣掉償債。***~ (sb) short,*** ⇨ short²(3). **2** [VP6A] keep stocks for sale; be a dealer in: 備貨出售；做…之買賣: *Do you ~ needles?* 你賣針嗎？*This little shop ~s a wide variety of goods.* 這家小店備有各色貨物。'**~·ing price,** price to be paid by the customer; cash price. 零售價格；售價。Cf 參較 *cost* price. **3** [VP 2A, C] (of goods) be sold; find buyers: (指貨物)被賣出；出售；有買主: *Ice-cream sells best in summer.* 冰淇淋在夏天銷路最好。*His new novel is ~ing well.* 他的新小說銷售良好。*These articles ~ at 20p apiece.* 這些物品按每件二十辨士出售。*Your house ought to ~ for at least £20000.* 你的房子至少要賣二萬鎊。**4** [VP6A] cause to be sold: 使賣出: *It is not the low prices but their quality which ~s our goods.* 我們的貨物能銷出，非因價廉而因質好。**5** (fig uses): (比喻用法): *~ one's life dearly,* kill or wound a number of one's attackers before being killed. 予攻擊者巨大傷亡後才被殺死。'***~ oneself,*** **(a)** present oneself to others in a convincing way (eg when applying for a job). 自我推銷；自我吹噓(如申請工作時)。**(b)** do sth dishonourable for money or reward. 出賣自己(爲金錢或報酬而做不名譽的事)。***~ the pass,*** (prov) do sth that weakens one's country or side; be a traitor. (諺)做削弱本國或己方之事；做叛徒。**6** (usu passive) cheat; disappoint by failure to keep an agreement, etc: (通常用被動語態)欺騙；因未能守約等而使失望: *I've been sold!* 我被欺騙了！*Sold again!* I've been tricked, let down, etc! 又被騙了！又上當了！ **7** ***be sold on sth,*** (colloq) accept it, believe that it is good, etc: (俗)接受某事物；相信某事物是好的等: *Are the workers sold on the idea of profit-sharing?* 工人們接受分紅的主意嗎？ □ *n* (colloq, from 6 above) disappointment: (俗，出自上列第6義)失望: *What a ~!* 多令人失望！ **hard／soft ~,** aggressive／persuasive ~ing technique. 積極的(說服式的)推銷法。**~er** *n* **1** person who ~s: 售賣人: *a 'book~er.* 書商。**a ~ers, market,** (comm) situation when goods are scarce and money plentiful, so that ~ers are favoured. (商)銷售者市場；求過於供(貨物少而貨幣多，故賣方獲利厚)。**2** sth that is sold. 出售之物。ˌ**best-'~er** *n* ⇨ best²(2).

sel·vage, sel·vedge /'selvɪdʒ; 'sɛlvɪdʒ/ *n* edge of cloth woven so that threads do not unravel. 布的織邊。

selves /selvz; sɛlvz/ *pl* of self.

sem·an·tic /sɪ'mæntɪk; sə'mæntɪk/ *adj* relating to meaning in language; of ~s. 關於語意的；語意學的。**se·man·tics** *n* (with *sing v*) branch of linguistics concerned with studying the meanings of words and sentences. (用單數動詞)語意學(語言學之一部門，討論字和句之含意)。

sema·phore /'seməfɔ:(r); 'sɛmə,for/ *n* [U] **1** system for sending signals by using arms on a post or flags held in the hands, with various positions for the letters of the alphabet: 信號；旗語(利用桿上的支臂或握於手中的旗幟傳送信號的方法，以不同的位置代表不同的字母): *send a message by ~.*

semaphore
(thin line = left arm; thick line = right arm)

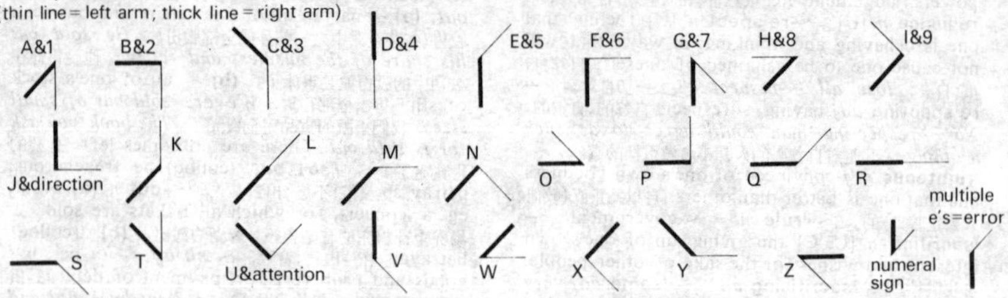

以旗語傳送信息。 **2** mechanical device with red and green lights on mechanically moved arms, used for signalling on railways. (鐵路之)信號裝置(紅綠燈)。□ *vt, vi* [VP6A, 2A] send (messages) by ~(1). 以信號或旗語發送(消息)。

sem·blance /ˈsembləns ; ˈsɛmbləns/ *n* [C] likeness; appearance: 相似;外觀: *put on a ~ of gaiety.* 佯裝快樂的樣子。

se·men /ˈsiːmən ; ˈsimən/ *n* [U] fertilizing sperm-bearing fluid of male animals. 精液。 **seminal** /ˈsemɪnl ; ˈsɛmənḷ/ *adj* of seed or semen or reproduction; embryonic; (fig) providing a basis for development: 種子的;精液的;生殖的;發生的;胚胎的;(喻)能够引發的;啓發性的: *seminal ideas.* 啓發性的念頭。

sem·es·ter /sɪˈmestə(r) ; səˈmɛstɚ/ *n* (esp in Germany and US) each of the two divisions of an academic year. (尤用於德,美)一學期;半學年。 Cf 參較 *term* in GB. 英國用 term。

semi- /ˈsemɪ- ; ˈsɛmə-/ *prep* **1** half of. …之半。 ˈ**~-circle** *n* half a circle. 半圓。 ⇨ the illus at circle. 參看 circle 之插圖。 ˌ**~·ˈcircular** *adj* having the shape of a half a circle. 半圓的。 ˈ**~·breve** (US 美 = *whole note*), the longest written musical note in common use. 全音符。 ˈ**~·quaver**, half a quaver. 十六分音符。 ⇨ the illus at notation. 參看 notation 之插圖。 ˈ**~·tone** *n* half a tone in a musical scale, the smallest interval in normal Western music. (音樂)半音;半音程(西方正規音樂中之最小音程)。 **2** on one of two sides. 在兩邊中之一邊。 ˌ**~-deˈtached** *adj* (of a house) joined to another on one side only (by one wall in common). (指房屋)一側與他屋相連的;共一牆的。 **3** little better than: 比…稍好: ˌ*~-barˈbarian;* 半野蠻的(人); ˌ*~-ˈbarbarism.* 半野蠻。 **4** (various) (用於下列各複合字中) ˌ**~-ˈcolon** (US = ˈ**semi·colon**) the punctuation mark (;) used in writing and printing, between a comma and a full stop in value. 半支點;分號(卽';',用於寫作及印刷中,其功能介於逗點與句點之間)。 ⇨ App 9. 參看附錄九。 ˌ**~-ˈconscious** *adj* partly conscious. 半清醒的;半知覺的。 ˌ**~-ˈfinal** *n* match or round that precedes the final (eg in football matches). 半決賽;準決賽。 ˌ**~-ˈfinalist** *n* player, team, in the ~-finals. 參加準決賽之選手或隊。 ˌ**~-ofˈficial** *adj* (esp of announcements, etc made to newspaper reporters by officials, with the stipulation that they must not be considered as coming from an official source). 半官方的(尤指官員對新聞記者所發表的聲明等,約定不能視爲來自官方者)。 ˌ**~-ˈrigid** *adj* (esp of airships) having a rigid keel attached to a flexible gas-bag. (尤指飛艇)半硬式的。 ˌ**~-ˈtropical** *adj* of regions near but not in the tropics. 亞熱帶的。 ˈ**~-vowel** *n* (letter representing a) sound with a vowel quality but a consonant function (eg /w/, /j/). 半母音(有母音的性質而有子音作用的音,如英語的 /w/, /j/ 等);半母音字母。 **5** occurring, published, etc twice in (a year, etc) (*bi-* is more usu): (一年等中)出現,出版等二次的(bi- 較常用): ˌ*~-ˈannual;* 半年刊的; *a* ˌ*~-ˈweekly.* 半週刊的。

semi·nal /ˈsemɪnl ; ˈsɛmənḷ/ ⇨ semen.

sem·inar /ˈsemɪnɑː(r) ; ˈsɛməˌnɑr/ *n* class of students, etc studying a problem and meeting for discussion with a tutor or professor. 學生爲研究某問題而與教師共同討論之班級;研習班。

sem·inary /ˈsemɪnərɪ *US:* -nerɪ ; ˈsɛməˌnɛrɪ/ *n* (*pl* -ries) **1** Roman Catholic training college for priests. (天主教之)神學院。 **2** (formerly used as a pretentious name for a) place of education: 養成所;學校(昔時用做矯飾之名稱): *a ~ for young ladies.* 女子專門學校。 **semin·ar·ist** /ˈsemɪnərɪst ; ˈsɛməˌnɛrɪst/ *n* man trained in a ~(1). 神學院之學生。

Sem·ite /ˈsiːmaɪt ; ˈsɛmaɪt/ *n, adj* (member) of any of the group of peoples that includes the Hebrews and Arabs and formerly the Phoenicians and Assyrians. 閃族人(包括希伯來人,阿拉伯人,腓尼基人及亞述人);閃族的;閃族人的。 **Se·mitic** /sɪˈmɪtɪk ; səˈmɪtɪk/ *adj* of the ~s or their languages: 閃族的;閃族語的: *a Semitic people.* 閃族之一支。

semo·lina /ˌseməˈliːnə ; ˌsɛməˈlinə/ *n* [U] hard grains of wheat meal, used for pasta, and in milk puddings, etc. 粗粒小麥粉(用於麵食,牛奶布丁等中)。

semp·stress /ˈsempstrɪs ; ˈsɛmpstrɪs/ ⇨ seamstress.

sen·ate /ˈsenɪt ; ˈsɛnɪt/ *n* [C] **1** (in ancient Rome) highest council of state. (古羅馬之)元老院。 **2** (in modern times) Upper House (usu the smaller) of the legislative assembly in various countries, eg France, US. (現代之)上議院;參議院(如法、美等國者,通常在國會中較下議院爲小)。 **3** governing council of some universities. (若干大學之)評議會。 **senator** /ˈsenətə(r) ; ˈsɛnətɚ/ *n* member of ~(1, 2). (古羅馬之)元老院議員;(現代之)上議員;參議員。 **senatorial** /ˌsenəˈtɔːrɪəl ; ˌsɛnəˈtorɪəl/ *adj* of a ~ or senator: 元老院的;上議院的;參議院的;元老院議員的;上議員的;參議員的: *senatorial rank / powers;* 上議員之地位(權力); *a senatorial district,* (US) one entitled to elect a senator. (美)參議員選舉區。

send /send ; sɛnd/ *vt, vi* (*pt, pp* sent) (For special uses with *adverbial particles* and *preps,* ⇨ 5 below.) (與副詞接語及介詞連用之特殊用法,參看下列第5義。) **1** [VP12A, 13A, 6A, 15A] *~ sb / sth; ~ sth to sb,* cause sb or sth to go or be carried without going oneself: 送;寄;遣;派;召: *~ a telegram;* 發送電報; *~ a message to sb / ~ sb a message.* 送消息予某人。 *The children were sent to bed.* 小孩們都被打發睡覺去了。 *John was sent to school with an older child.* 約翰跟一個較大的孩子一起去上學。 ⇨ take¹(4). **2** [VP19B] use force to cause sb / sth to move sharply or rapidly: 使某人(某物)急遽地移動: *The earthquake sent the crockery and cutlery crashing to the ground.* 地震將杯盤和刀叉震落在地上。 *Mind how you go—you nearly sent me flying,* ie you nearly knocked me over. 小心點,你差點把我撞倒。 *~ sb packing / about his business,* (colloq) dismiss him at once, without formality: (俗)解雇某人;要某人立刻捲鋪蓋: *His incompetent typist was sent packing.* 他那不稱職的打字員被解雇了。 *S~ that fellow about his business—he's* *no use to anybody!* 叫那傢伙滾蛋—他對任何人都沒有用處！⇨ bring. **3** [VP22, 6A] cause to become: 促使；使變爲: *This noise is ~ing me crazy.* 這吵聲快使我發瘋。*This music/This gorgeous girl really ~s me,* (sl) excites me intensely, rouses me to ecstasy. (俚)這音樂(這可愛的女郎)使我覺得飄飄然。**4** (old use, of God, Providence): (舊用法，指上帝、天意): *Heaven ~ that he arrives safely,* may God grant this. 天佑他安全到達。'*S~ her victorious*' (in the British national anthem) May God grant that the Sovereign may be victorious. (英國國歌中)天佑我王勝利。**5** [VP15B, 2C, 3A] (special use with *adverbial particles* and *preps*): (與副詞接語及介詞連用的特殊用法):

send sb away, dismiss. 解雇。**~ *away for sth,*** order (goods) from a distance, to be delivered by rail, post, etc: 從遠處訂(貨): *When we lived in the country, we had to ~ away for many things we needed.* 我們住在鄉下時，必須向遠處訂購我們所需要的許多東西。

send sb down, (esp) expel a student from a university (for misconduct, etc). (尤指)勒令大學生退學(因行爲不檢等)；開除。**~ *sth down,*** cause to fall: 使下降: *The good harvest sent the prices down.* 豐收使價格下跌。*The storm sent the temperature down.* 暴風雨使氣溫下降。

send for sb/sth (to do sth), ask or order sb/sth to come, for sth to be delivered: 派人去叫(某人)；遣人去拿(某物)；召；請；叫: *~ for a doctor/taxi.* 延請醫生(叫計程車)。*We must ~ for a man to repair the TV.* 我們必須叫人來修理電視機。*Please keep these things until I ~ for them.* 請替我保管這些東西，等我派人來取。

send sth forth, (formal) produce, issue: (正式用語)生出；發出: *~ forth leaves.* 生葉。

send sth in (for sth, eg a competition, exhibition): 登記或提出(以參加比賽或展覽等): *~ in one's name for a contest;* 登記參加比賽; *~ in two oil paintings;* 送兩幅油畫參加展覽; *~ in a report for consideration.* 提出一份報告作參考。**~ *one's name in,*** cause one's name to be made known. 通報某人的名字。

send sb off, (more usu *see sb off*) go with sb to the place from which he will start a journey: (see sb off 較常用)送別: *Many of his friends went to the airport to ~ him off.* 很多朋友前往機場爲他送行。Hence, 由此產生，'**~-off** *n*: *He was given a good ~-off.* 他受到熱烈的送別。**~ *sth off,*** dispatch: 發送: *Please see that these parcels are sent off at once.* 請留意把這些包裹立即送出去。

send sth on, **(a)** ~ it in advance. 預送(某物)。**(b)** (of letters) readdress and repost: (指信件)轉寄: *I asked my wife to ~ all my letters on while I was away from home.* 在我離家時，我請我太太轉寄我所有的信件。

send sth out, **(a)** distribute; give out: 分發；發出: *The sun ~s out light and warmth.* 太陽發出光和熱。**(b)** produce: 生出: *The trees ~ out new leaves in spring.* 樹在春天長新葉。

send sb/sth up, tease; parody; show that sb/sth is ridiculous or false. 取笑某人(某事物)；滑稽地模倣詩文；暴露某人(某事物)的可笑或不實之處。Hence, 由此產生，'**~-up** *n* mocking imitation or parody. 譏諷性的模仿或歪改(他人詩文)。**~ *sth up,*** cause to rise: 使上昇: *The heavy demand for beef sent the price up.* 大量的需要使牛肉價格上升。

sender /ˈsendə(r) ; ˈsɛndɚ/ *n* person or thing that sends: 送者；發送之人或物: *If lost, return to ~* (eg on a letter). (信件等上之說明)如無法投遞，請退還原寄人。

se·nes·cent /sɪˈnesnt ; səˈnɛsn̩t/ *adj* showing signs of old age: 顯老的: *I may be ~, but I'm not yet senile.* 我可能顯老，但我尚未衰老。**se·nes·cence** /-sns ; -sn̩s/ *n* [U].

sen·eschal /ˈsenɪʃl ; ˈsɛnəʃəl/ *n* (in the Middle Ages) important official (steward or major-domo) in the castle of a noble. (中世紀貴族城堡中的)管家。

se·nile /ˈsiːnaɪl ; ˈsinaɪl/ *adj* suffering from bodily or mental weakness because of old age; caused by old age: 因年老而身心衰弱的；由年老引起的；衰老的；老耄的: *~ decay.* 年老體衰。**sen·il·ity** /sɪˈnɪlətɪ ; səˈnɪlətɪ/ *n* [U] weakness (of body or mind) in old age. 衰老；老耄；龍鍾；老糊塗。

sen·ior /ˈsiːnɪə(r) ; ˈsinjɚ/ *adj* (opp of *junior*) (爲 junior 之相反字) **1 ~ *(to),*** older in years; higher in rank, authority, etc: 年長的；權位等較高的；資深的: *He is ten years ~ to me.* 他比我年長十歲。*Smith is the ~ partner in* (= the head of) *the firm.* 史密斯是公司的老板。ˌ**~ ˈcitizen,** (euphem for) person over the age of retirement; old age pensioner. (委婉語)超過退休年齡之人；領養老金者。**2** (after a person's name, esp when a father and his son have the same first name; abbr 略作 **Sen**): (置於人名之後，尤其當父子名字相同時): *John Brown (Sen).* (老)約翰·布朗。⇨ major. □ *n* **1** ~ person: 年長者；資深者: *He is my ~ by ten years.* 他比我大十歲。*The ~s* (= members of the ~ class) *defeated the juniors by 3—1.* 高班同學以三比一擊敗了低班同學。**2** (US) student in his/her fourth year at high school or college. (美)高中、學院或大學最高年級的學生；大學四年級的學生。**~·ity** /ˌsiːnɪˈɒrətɪ *US:* -ˈɔːr- ; sinˈjɔrətɪ/ *n* [U] condition of being ~ (in age, rank, etc): 年長；資深: *Should promotion be through merit or through ~ity?* 升級應該根據功績還是根據年資？*Remember the precedence due to ~ity.* 記住，優先權應該讓給長輩。

senna /ˈsenə ; ˈsɛnə/ *n* [U] dried leaves of the cassia plant, used as a laxative. 番瀉葉(山扁豆之乾葉，用作通便劑)。

se·ñor /seˈnjɔː(r) ; senˈjɔr/ *n* (*pl* señores /seˈnjɔːreɪz ; seˈnjɔrez/) used of or to a Spanish-speaking man; Mr; sir. (**S~** when prefixed to a name.) 先生；君(西班牙語系對男子之稱呼；置於人名之前用大寫 S)。**se·ñora** /seˈnjɔːrə ; senˈjorə/ *n* used of or to a Spanish-speaking woman; Mrs; Madam. 太太；夫人；女士(西班牙語系對婦女之稱呼)。**se·ñorita** /ˌsenjɔːˈriːtə ; ˌsenjəˈritə/ *n* used of or to an unmarried woman or girl; Miss. 小姐(用於未婚女子)。

sen·sa·tion /senˈseɪʃn ; sɛnˈseʃən/ *n* **1** [C, U] ability to feel; feeling: 感覺: *lose all ~ in one's legs;* 失去腿部的一切感覺; *have a ~ of warmth/dizziness/falling.* 感到溫暖(暈眩，下落)。**2** [C, U] (instance of, sth that causes, a) quick and excited reaction: 感動；激動；轟動；引起激動或轟動之實例: *Our popular newspapers deal largely in ~.* 我們那些受歡迎的報紙多報導聳人聽聞的新聞。*The news created a great ~.* 這消息造成了很大的轟動。**~al** /-ʃənl ; -ʃənl/ *adj* **1** causing a ~(2): 令人激動的；激起感情的；轟動的: *a ~al murder.* 轟動一時的謀殺案。**2** (of newspapers, etc) presenting news in a manner designed to cause ~(2): (指報紙等)聳人聽聞的: *a ~al writer/newspaper.* 聳人聽聞的作家(報紙)。**~·ally** /-ʃənəlɪ ; -ʃənl̩ɪ/ *adv* **~·al·ism** /-ʃənəlɪzəm ; -ʃənl̩ˌɪzəm/ *n* [U] the deliberate rousing of ~(2): 故意聳人聽聞；故意危言聳聽: *the ~alism of the cinema;* 那部電影的故意聳人聽聞; *avoid ~alism during an election campaign.* 在競選時避免故意危言聳聽。**~·al·ist** /-ʃənəlɪst ; -ʃənl̩ɪst/ *n*

sense /sens ; sɛns/ *n* **1** any one of the special powers of the body by which a person is conscious of things (ie sight, hearing, smell, taste and touch): 官能；感覺；知覺(如視覺，聽覺，嗅覺，味覺及觸覺): *be in the enjoyment of all one's ~s;* 享有一切知覺；五官健全; *have a keen ~ of hearing.* 聽覺銳敏。ˈ**~-organ** *n* part of the body, eg the ear or eye, concerned in producing sensation. 感覺器官；感官(如耳朵或眼睛)。ˌ**sixth** ˈ**~,** ⇨ six. **2** (*pl*) normal state of mind (as when a person has the five ~s of 1 above): (複)心智健全: *in one's* (*right*) ~*s*, sane; 心智健全的; *out of one's ~s*, insane; 心智不健全的;瘋狂的; *frighten sb out of his ~s*, frighten him so that he behaves in an excited way. 把某人嚇得驚慌失措。***bring sb to his ~s***, cause him to give up behaving foolishly or wildly. 使醒悟;使心智恢復健全。 ***come to one's ~s***, stop behaving like a fool or madman. 醒悟;心智恢復健全。 ***take leave of one's ~s***, become mad; start behaving irrationally. 發瘋;失常。 **3** ***(a/the) ~ of***, appreciation or understanding of the value or worth (of): 辨識;賞識;領悟: *a ~ of humour;* 幽默感; *my ~ of duty;* 我的責任感; *the moral ~;* 是非感; *a ~ of locality/direction*, ie recognition of places, landmarks, directions, etc. 對於方位(方向)的辨識力。 **4** ***(a/the) ~ of***, consciousness (of): 意識;自覺: *have no ~ of shame;* 無羞恥心; *a ~ of one's own importance/responsibility.* 對自己重要性(職責)的覺察。 **5** [U] power of judging; judgement; practical wisdom: 判斷力;判斷;見識: *Haven't you ~ enough to come in out of the rain?* 你怎麼不進來避一避雨呢? *There's a lot of ~ in what he says.* 他說話頗有見識。*There's no ~ in doing that*, It's pointless. 做那件事情沒有道理。*What's the ~ of doing that?* 做那件事究竟有何道理? *Now you're talking ~.* 你的話頗有道理。⇨ also *common ~* at common¹(2). **6** [C] meaning: 意義;意味: *a word with several ~s.* 具有數義的一個字。*In what ~ are you using the word?* 你用這個字所指的是那一個意義? *The ~ of the word is not clear.* 該字的意義不明確。***in a ~***, if the statement, etc is taken in a particular way: 在某種意義上: *What you say is true in a ~.* 就某種意義而言,你說的是實話。***make ~***, have a meaning that can be understood: 有意義: *What you say doesn't make ~/makes no ~*, means nothing. 你的話毫無意義。***make ~ of sth***, find a meaning in it: 懂;了解其含意: *Can you make ~ of this poem?* 你懂得這首詩的含意嗎? ***in the strict/literal/figurative/full/best*** (= most favourable) ***/proper, etc ~***, interpreting (the statement, etc) strictly/literally, etc. 就精確(字面,比喻,全般,最好,適當)的意義而言。 **7** [U] general feeling or opinion among a number of people: 一般的意見;輿論: *take the ~ of a public meeting*, ask questions in order to learn the general sentiment or opinion. 提出問題以求了解與會者的一般意見。 □ *vt* [VP6A, 9] feel; be vaguely aware of; realize: 覺得;感知;理會;了解;明白: *He ~d that his proposals were unwelcome.* 他覺得他的建議不受歡迎。

sense·less /ˈsenslɪs; ˈsɛnslɪs/ *adj* **1** foolish: 愚蠢的: *a ~ idea.* 愚蠢的觀念。 *What a ~ fellow he is!* 他是多麼愚蠢的傢伙! **2** unconscious: 無感覺的;不省人事的: *fall ~ to the ground.* 失去知覺倒在地上。**~·ly** *adv* **~·ness** *n*

sen·si·bil·ity /ˌsensəˈbɪlətɪ; ˌsɛnsəˈbɪlətɪ/ *n* (*pl* -ties) [U, C] power of feeling; (esp) power of receiving or feeling delicate emotional impressions; such feeling(s): 感覺能力;感性;(尤指)敏感性;情緒上的善感性: *the ~ of a poet.* 詩人之敏感性。*Her sensibilities are easily wounded.* 她的情感容易受到傷害。

sen·sible /ˈsensəbl; ˈsɛnsəbl̩/ *adj* **1** having or showing good sense(5); reasonable; practical: 有判斷力的;明智的;明理的;切實的: *a ~ woman;* 明理的女子; *~ shoes for mountain climbing;* 適合爬山的鞋子; *~ clothing*, functional, not merely for appearance or ornament; 實用的衣服; *~ ideas.* 明智的觀念。*That was ~ of you.* 你那樣做很明智。 **2** ***~ of***, (old use) aware of: (舊用法)知道的;覺察的: *He is ~ of the danger of his position.* 他發覺他處境的危險。 **3** (old use) that can be perceived by the senses(1); perceptible (the usu word now): (舊用法)感覺得到的;顯著的(現常用 perceptible): *a ~ fall in the temperature;* 溫度顯著的下降;*~ phenomena.* 感覺得到的現象。 **sen·sibly** /-əblɪ; -əblɪ/ *adv* in a ~ way: 有判斷力地;明智地;切實地;感知地;可感覺地: *sensibly dressed for hot weather.* 穿著適合炎熱氣候的。

sen·si·tive /ˈsensətɪv; ˈsɛnsətɪv/ *adj* ***~ (to)***, **1** quickly or easily receiving impressions: 敏感的;容易感受的: *The eyes are ~ to light.* 眼睛對光敏感。*A ~ skin is easily hurt by too much sunshine.* 敏感的皮膚晒太陽過多易受傷害。*A ~ nerve in a tooth can cause great pain.* 牙齒中敏感的神經能引起巨痛。 **2** easily hurt in the spirit; easily offended: 易受傷害的;易被冒犯的: *Children are usually ~ to blame.* 小孩子們通常容易因爲責備而受到傷害。 *An author must not be too ~ to criticism.* 作家不宜對批評太敏感。*He is very ~ about his ugly appearance.* 他對自己的醜陋外表十分敏感。**3** (of instruments, and institutions thought of as measuring things) able to record small changes: (指儀器及可作測量物之機構)能紀錄小變化的;靈敏的: *~ thermometers/scales.* 靈敏的溫度計(天平)。*The Stock Exchange is ~ to political disturbances.* 證券交易所對於政治上的不安很敏感。 **4** (of photographic film, paper, etc) affected by light. (指攝影軟片,感光紙等)易感光的。**~·ly** *adv* **sen·si·tiv·ity** /ˌsensəˈtɪvətɪ; ˌsɛnsəˈtɪvətɪ/ *n* [U] quality, degree, of being ~: 敏感;敏感性;敏感度;靈敏性;靈敏度: *The dentist gave her an injection to reduce the sensitivity of the nerves.* 牙醫師爲她注射以減少神經的敏感度。 **sen·si·tize** /ˈsensɪtaɪz; ˈsɛnsəˌtaɪz/ *vt* [VP6A] make sensitive; (photo) make (film, paper, etc) ~ to light (for use in photography). 使敏感;使(軟片,感光紙等)易於感光(以供攝影使用)。

sen·sory /ˈsensərɪ; ˈsɛnsərɪ/ *adj* of the senses(1) or sensation: 感覺的;感官的: *~ organs/nerves.* 感覺器官(神經)。

sen·sual /ˈsenʃʊəl; ˈsɛnʃʊəl/ *adj* of, given up to, the pleasures of the senses; self-indulgent in regard to food and drink and sexual enjoyment: 肉慾的;聲色之樂的;耽於聲色飲食的;淫蕩的: *~ enjoyment;* 聲色的享受; *a ~ life;* 耽於聲色的生活; *~ lips*, giving the impression that a person is ~. 性感的嘴唇。 **~·ism** /-ɪzəm; -ˌɪzəm/ *n* = ~ity. **~·ist** /-ɪst; -ɪst/ *n* ~ person. 耽於聲色之人。**~·ity** /ˌsenʃʊˈælətɪ; ˌsɛnʃʊˈælətɪ/ *n* [U] love of, indulgence in, ~ pleasures, esp of the body. 耽於聲色;耽於肉慾;淫蕩。

sen·su·ous /ˈsenʃʊəs; ˈsɛnʃʊəs/ *adj* affecting, noticed by, appealing to, the senses(1): 影響感覺的;敏感的;爲感覺所認知的;訴諸感覺的: *~ music/painting.* 引起美感的音樂(畫)。(Note that ~ is free of the sense of 'self-indulgence' in *sensual*). (注意:sensuous 沒有 sensual 一詞所含示的'放縱自己'的意味)。**~·ly** *adv* **~·ness** *n*

sent /sent; sɛnt/ *pt, pp* of send.

sen·tence /ˈsentəns; ˈsɛntəns/ *n* [C] **1** (statement by a judge, etc, of) punishment: (法官等之)判決;宣判;刑罰: *pass ~ (on sb)*, declare what the punishment is to be; 判(某人的)刑; *under ~ of death.* 被判處死刑。*The ~ of the court was three years' imprisonment.* 法院的判決是三年徒刑。**2** (gram) the largest grammatical unit, consisting of phrases and/or clauses, used to express a statement, question, command, etc. (文法)句;文句。□ *vt* [VP 6A, 14, 17] state that (sb) is to have a certain punishment: 判決;宣判: *~ a thief to six months' imprisonment.* 宣判竊賊六個月徒刑。*He had been ~d to pay a fine of £10.* 他被判罰款十鎊。

sen·ten·tious /senˈtenʃəs; sɛnˈtɛnʃəs/ *adj* **1** (old use) in the habit of saying or writing things in a short and witty manner. (舊用法)言簡意賅的;簡潔精闢的。 **2** (mod use) having, putting on, an air of wisdom; dull and moralizing: (現代用法)佯裝有智慧的;沉悶而說教的: *a ~ speaker/speech.* 沈悶而說教的演說者(演講)。**~·ly** *adv*

sen·ti·ent /ˈsenʃnt; ˈsɛnʃənt/ *adj* having, able to have, feeling; experiencing sensation. 有知覺的;有感覺的;感覺到的。

sen·ti·ment /ˈsentɪmənt ; ˈsɛntəmənt/ *n* **1** [C] mental feeling, the total of what one thinks and feels on a subject; [U] such feelings collectively as an influence: 感情;情緒;情操: *The ~ of pity is made up of the feeling of sympathy and of a desire to help and protect.* 憐憫的情緒是由同情心以及給予幫助和保護的願望所構成。*A true statesman is animated by lofty ~s.* 眞正的政治家是受到高尙情操的激勵。*Should reason be guided by ~?* 理智應受感情的支配嗎？*What are your ~s towards my sister*, Do you love her or is it sth less than love? 你對我姐姐(妹妹)的感情如何？ **2** [U] (tendency to be moved by) (display of) tender feeling (contrasted with reason): 傷感;軟弱之感情(與理智相對): *There's no place for ~ in business.* 做生意不可感情用事。 **3** expression of feeling; opinions or point of view: 意見;觀點: *The ambassador explained the ~s of his government on the question.* 大使解釋其政府對該問題的觀點。

sen·ti·men·tal /ˌsentɪˈmentl ; ˌsɛntəˈmɛntḷ/ *adj* **1** having to do with the feelings; emotional: 感情的;情緒的: *do sth for ~ reasons;* 由於感情上的緣故而做某事; *have a ~ attachment to one's birthplace.* 對某人的誕生地有深厚的情感。 *The bracelet had only ~ value*, eg because it belonged to one's mother. 那隻手鐲僅有情感上的價值。 **2** (of things) tending to arouse, expressing (often excessive, inappropriate or false) feelings: (指事物)有引起或表達情感之傾向的;感傷的;過於感傷的: *~ music;* 感傷的音樂; *~ novelettes;* 過於感傷的中篇小說; (of persons) having such excessive feelings: (指人)多愁善感的;感情過於豐富的: *She's far too ~ about her cats.* 她對她的貓過份關愛。**~ly** /-təlɪ ; -tḷɪ/ *adv* **~ist** *n* person who is ~. 多愁善感者;傷感者。**~·ity** /ˌsentɪmenˈtælətɪ ; ˌsɛntəmɛnˈtælətɪ/ *n* [U] the quality of being weakly or foolishly ~. 多愁善感;感傷。**~·ize** /-təlaɪz ; -tḷˌaɪz/ *vt, vi* [VP6A, 2A] (cause to) become ~(2). (使)溺於感情;(使)感傷。

sen·ti·nel /ˈsentɪnl ; ˈsɛntənḷ/ *n* = sentry (now the usu word): (現常用 sentry): *stand ~ (over)*, (liter) keep guard (over). (文)守衞;放哨。

sen·try /ˈsentrɪ ; ˈsɛntrɪ/ *n* (*pl* -ries) soldier posted to keep watch and guard. 哨兵;步哨。 **ˈ~-box** *n* hut or cabin for a ~. 哨崗;哨亭。 **ˈ~-go** *n* duty of pacing up and down as a ~: 步哨勤務;站崗: *be on ~-go.* 放哨。

se·pal /ˈsepl ; ˈsipḷ/ *n* (bot) one of the divisions of the calyx of a flower. (植)(花之)萼片。⇨ the illus at flower. 參看 flower 之插圖。

sep·ar·able /ˈsepərəbl ; ˈsɛpərəbḷ/ *adj* that can be separated. 可分開的;能區分的。**sep·ar·ably** /-əblɪ ; -əblɪ/ *adv* **sep·ar·abil·ity** /ˌseprəˈbɪlətɪ ; ˌsɛpərəˈbɪlətɪ/ *n*

sep·ar·ate¹ /ˈseprət ; ˈsɛprɪt/ *adj* **1** divided; not joined or united: 分離的;分開的: *Cut it into three ~ parts.* 把它切成三分。 **2** forming a unit which is distinct and which exists apart: 各別的;單獨的: *The children sleep in ~ beds*, Each of them has his own bed. 孩子們各別地睡在自己的床上。*Mr Green and his wife are living ~ (= apart) now.* 格林先生和他的妻子現在分居。 *Keep these ~ from those.* 把這些和那些分開放。 □ *n* (trade use, *pl*) ~ garments which may be worn in a variety of combinations, eg jerseys, blouses and skirts. (商業用語,複)不是成套的女裝(如緊身毛衣,襯衫,裙子等)。**~·ly** *adv* in a ~ manner: 分離地;各別地: *Tie them up ~ly.* 把它們各別地綁起來。

sep·ar·ate² /ˈsepəreɪt ; ˈsɛpəˌret/ *vt, vi* **1** [VP6A, 14, 15B] **~ *(from)***, make, be, ~ from: 使分離;分開;隔開: *S~ the good ones from the bad.* 使好的和壞的分開。*England is ~d from France by the Channel.* 英國和法國被英吉利海峽隔開。 **~ *sth (up) into***, divide into: 分開爲(幾分);分割成(幾段): *The land was ~d (up) into small fields.* 那塊地被分割爲小塊的田地。**2** [VP2A] (of a number of people) go in different ways: (指一羣人)分手;解散: *We talked until midnight and then ~d.* 我們談到午夜才分手。**sep·ar·at·ist** /ˈsepərətɪst ; ˈsɛpəˌretɪst/ *n* (opp of *unionist*) member of a group which wants (esp political or ecclesiastical) separation. (爲 unionist 之相反字)(尤指政治或宗教上之)分離主義者;要求獨立者。 **sep·ar·ator** /ˈsepəreɪtə(r) ; ˈsɛpəˌretɚ/ *n* (esp) device for separating cream from milk.分離者;分離器;(尤指)脫脂器(使奶油與奶分離者)。

sep·ar·ation /ˌsepəˈreɪʃn ; ˌsɛpəˈreʃən/ *n* **1** [U] (state of) being separated or separate; act of separating: 分離;分開: *S~ from his friends made him sad.* 與朋友們分離使他傷心。**judicial ~,** (commonly called 通常稱作 *legal ~*) arrangement (ordered by a court of law) which does not end a marriage, but which requires married persons no longer to live together. 經法庭判定的夫妻分居。⇨ divorce¹(1). **2** [C] instance of, period of, separation: 分離之實例;分離之期間: *after a ~ of five years;* 在分離五年以後; *~s of husbands and wives in time of war.* 戰時丈夫和妻子的分離。

se·pia /ˈsiːpɪə ; ˈsipɪə/ *n* [U] dark brown (ink or paint): 深褐色; 深褐色油墨或顏料: *a ˈ~-drawing*, one done in ~. 深褐色的圖畫。

sep·sis /ˈsepsɪs ; ˈsɛpsɪs/ *n* [U] contamination from a festering wound. 敗血;膿毒病。

Sep·tem·ber /sepˈtembə(r) ; sɛpˈtɛmbɚ/ *n* the ninth month of the year. 九月。

sep·tet /sepˈtet ; sɛpˈtɛt/ *n* (musical composition for a) group of seven voices or instruments. (音樂)七重奏;七重唱;七部合奏曲;七部合唱曲。

sep·tic /ˈseptɪk ; ˈsɛptɪk/ *adj* of sepsis; causing, caused by, infection (with disease germs): 腐敗的;使腐敗的;致使敗血的: *~ poisoning.* 敗血症。*A dirty wound may become ~*, affected by bacteria. 髒的傷口可能變爲膿毒。**~ tank,** one in which sewage is disposed of by bacterial activity. (藉細菌作用之)陰溝淨化槽;化糞池。

sep·ti·cemia /ˌseptɪˈsiːmɪə ; ˌsɛptəˈsimɪə/ *n* blood-poisoning. 敗血症;血毒症。

sep·tua·gen·arian /ˌseptjuədʒɪˈneərɪən *US:* -tʃudʒə-; ˌsɛptʃuədʒəˈnɛrɪən/ *n* person 70 to 79 years old. 七十歲至七十九歲之間的人。

Sep·tua·gint /ˈseptjuədʒɪnt *US:* -tu- ; ˈsɛptuəˌdʒɪnt/ *n* Greek version of the Old Testament and the Apocrypha made about 270 BC. 舊約和僞經之希臘文本(約於紀元前270年譯成)。

sep·ulchre (US = **sep·ul·cher** /ˈseplkə(r) ; ˈsɛpḷkɚ/ *n* [C] tomb, esp one cut in rock or built of stone. 墳墓;塚(尤指鑿空岩石而成或以石塊砌成者): **the Holy S~,** that in which Jesus Christ was laid. 聖墓(耶穌之墓)。**whited ~** *n* hypocrite. 僞君子;假冒爲善的人。⇨ Matt. 23:27. 參看馬太福音23章27節。 **sep·ulchral** /sɪˈpʌlkrəl ; səˈpʌlkrəl/ *adj* **1** of a ~; of burial. 墓的;埋葬的。 **2** deep and gloomy; suggestive of burial: 深而幽暗的;陰森森的;令人想到埋葬的: *sepulchral looks;* 陰森森的面貌; *in a sepulchral voice.* 陰沉的聲音。

sep·ul·ture /ˈsepltʃuə(r) ; ˈsɛpḷtʃɚ/ *n* [U] burying; putting in the tomb or grave. 埋葬;埋入墓中。

se·quel /ˈsiːkwəl ; ˈsikwəl/ *n* [C] **1** that which follows or arises out of (an earlier happening): (早先事件之)繼續;後續;後果;結局: *Famine has often been the ~ of war.* 饑饉常是戰爭的後果。*Her action had an unfortunate ~.* 她的行爲帶來不幸的結局。***in the ~,*** later on; as things developed afterwards. 後來;結果。 **2** story, film, etc with the same character of an earlier one. (故事,影片等的)續集;續篇。

se·quence /ˈsiːkwəns ; ˈsikwəns/ *n* [U] succession; [C] connected line of events, ideas, etc: 繼續;連續;(事件,觀念等之)系列;一連串;次第;順序;關聯: *deal with events in historical ~;* 按歷史的次序討論事件; *the ~ of events*, the order in which they occur; 事件發生之順序; *a ~ of bad harvests;* 接連的歉

收; *a ~ of clubs* (in playing cards), three or more next to each other in value, eg Ace, King, Queen, or 10, 9, 8. (牌戲)梅花順子(三張以上的連牌,如么點,王,后,或十點,九點,八點)。 *~ of tenses,* (gram) principles according to which the tenses of subordinate clauses are suited to the tenses of principal clauses. (文法)時態的一致(附屬子句中的動詞時態,配合主要子句中的動詞時態之原則)。 **se·quent** /-ənt ; -ənt/ *adj* (formal) following in order or time; resulting. (正式用語) 繼續的; 連續的; 結果的。 **se·quen·tial** /sɪˈkwenʃl ; sɪˈkwɛnʃəl/ *adj* following in order of time or place; following as a result. 按時間或順序而來的;連續的;繼起的;結果的。

se·ques·ter /sɪˈkwestə(r) ; sɪˈkwɛstɚ/ *vt* [VP6A] **1** keep (sb) away or apart from other people; withdraw to a quiet place: 使(某人)與他人分離;退隱;隱遁: *~ oneself from the world;* 隱居; *lead a ~ed life.* 過退隱的生活。 **2** (legal) (法律) = sequestrate. **~ed** *adj* (of places) quiet; secluded. (指地方)幽靜的;隱僻的。

se·ques·trate /sɪˈkwestreɪt ; sɪˈkwɛstret/ *vt* [VP6A] **1** (legal) take temporary possession of (a debtor's property, estate, etc) until debts are paid or other claims met. (法律)假扣押(債務人之財產,地產等)。 **2** confiscate. 查封;沒收。 **se·ques·tra·tion** /ˌsiːkweˈstreɪʃn ; sɪˌkwɛsˈtreʃən/ *n*

se·quin /ˈsiːkwɪn ; ˈsikwɪn/ *n* **1** tiny metal disc of silver, jet, etc sewn on to a dress, etc as an ornament. (衣服等上作飾物用之)小金屬圓片。 **2** (hist) gold coin once used in Venice. (史)(昔時威尼斯所用之)金幣。

se·quoia /sɪˈkwɔɪə ; sɪˈkwɔɪə/ *n* large evergreen coniferous tree of California (the *redwood*) of great height. 美洲杉(紅杉,產於美國加州之高大常青樹)。

se·ra·glio /seˈrɑːlɪəʊ ; sɪˈræljo/ *n* (*pl* ~s /-lɪəʊz ; -ljoz/) harem; (hist) Turkish ruler's walled palace with government offices, etc. 閨房;(史)(土耳其之)皇宮;皇城(包括政府機關等)。

ser·aph /ˈserəf ; ˈsɛrəf/ *n* (*pl* ~s or ~im /-fɪm ; -fɪm/) (biblical) one of the highest order of angels. (聖經)六翼天使(等級最高的天使)。 ⇨ cherub. **~ic** /sɪˈræfɪk ; səˈræfɪk/ *adj* angelic; happy and beautiful as a ~. 天使的;似天使般快樂而美麗的。

sere /sɪə(r) ; sɪr/ = sear².

ser·en·ade /ˌserəˈneɪd ; ˌsɛrəˈned/ *n* (piece of) music (to be) sung or played outdoors at night. 夜曲;小夜曲。 □ *vt* [VP6A] sing or play a ~ to (sb). 爲(某人)唱或奏夜曲。

ser·en·dip·ity /ˌserənˈdɪpətɪ ; ˌsɛrənˈdɪpətɪ/ *n* (talent for) making fortunate and unexpected discoveries by chance. 偶然發現珍寶(之才能)。

ser·ene /sɪˈriːn ; səˈrin/ *adj* clear and calm; tranquil: 晴朗的;寧靜的: *a ~ sky;* 晴朗的天空; *a ~ look;* 安祥的神情; *a ~ smile.* 安祥的微笑。 **~·ly** *adv* **ser·en·ity** /sɪˈrenətɪ ; səˈrɛnətɪ/ *n* [U].

serf /sɜːf ; sɝf/ *n* (hist) person who was not allowed to leave the land on which he worked; (fig) person treated almost like a slave; drudge. (史)農奴;(喻)被虐待如奴隸的人;苦役。 **~·dom** /-dəm ; -dəm/ *n* [U] **1** social and economic system in which land was cultivated by ~s. 農奴制(土地由農奴耕種之社會經濟制度)。 **2** ~'s condition of life. 農奴之境遇。

serge /sɜːdʒ ; sɝdʒ/ *n* [U] hard-wearing woollen cloth: (一種耐穿的)毛嗶嘰: (attrib) (形容用法) *a blue ~ suit.* 一套藍色毛嗶嘰的衣服。

ser·geant /ˈsɑːdʒənt ; ˈsɑrdʒənt/ *n* **1** non-commissioned army officer above a corporal and below a ~-major. 士官;軍士;中士。 **ˌ~-ˈmajor** *n* highest grade of non-commissioned army officer. 准尉;士官長。 **2** police-officer with rank below that of an inspector. 警官;警佐;巡佐(階級低於巡官者)。

serial /ˈsɪərɪəl ; ˈsɪrɪəl/ *adj* **1** of, in or forming a series: 連續的;一串的;排成一系列的: *the ~ number of a banknote or cheque.* 一張紙幣或支票的序號碼。 **2** (of a story, etc) appearing in parts (in a periodical, on radio, TV, etc): (指故事等)連續的;(在雜誌、廣播、電視等中)連續刊登或播出的: *An exciting new ~ story will begin in our next week's issue.* 一個刺激而新穎的連載故事,將於下週開始在本刊登出。 □ *n* ~ play, story, etc. 連續劇,連載小說等。 **~·ly** /-ɪəlɪ ; -ɪəlɪ/ *adv* **~·ize** /-laɪz ; -lˌaɪz/ *vt* [VP6A] publish or produce in ~ form. 以連續方式出版或製作。

seri·atim /ˌsɪərɪˈeɪtɪm ; ˌsɪrɪˈetɪm/ *adv* (Lat) point by point; taking subjects, etc after one another in order: (拉)逐一地;按順序地;連續地: *deal with arguments ~.* 逐一進行辯論。

seri·cul·ture /ˈserɪkʌltʃə(r) ; ˈsɛrɪˌkʌltʃɚ/ *n* (breeding of silkworms for) the production of silk. 養蠶;蠶絲業。 **seri·cul·tural** /ˌserɪˈkʌltʃərəl ; ˌsɛrɪˈkʌltʃərəl/ *adj* **ser·i·cul·tur·ist** /-tʃərɪst ; -tʃərɪst/ *n*

series /ˈsɪəriːz ; ˈsiriz/ *n* (*pl* unchanged) number of things, events, etc each of which is related in some way to the others, esp to the one before it: (複數不變)連貫的東西,事件等;連續;系列: *a ~ of stamps / coins,* eg of different values, but issued at one time; 一套郵票(錢幣)(例如一次發行之各種不同價值者); *a ~ of brilliant statesmen;* 連續出現的一批卓越政治家; *a ~ of good harvests;* 連年的豐收; *a 'Television ~,* a number of programmes, each complete in itself, linked by cast, theme, etc. 電視影集(每輯爲一完整之單元,但演員和主題則前後連貫)。 *in ~,* in an orderly arrangement; (of the components of an electrical circuit) with the supply of current fed directly through each component. 串聯電路的;成串聯的。 ⇨ *in parallel* at parallel.

serio·comic /ˌsɪərɪəʊˈkɒmɪk ; ˌsɪrɪoˈkɑmɪk/ *adj* serious in intention but appearing to be comic (or vice versa); having both serious and comic elements. 表面滑稽而實質嚴肅的;表面嚴肅而實質滑稽的;亦諧亦莊的。

seri·ous /ˈsɪərɪəs ; ˈsɪrɪəs/ *adj* **1** solemn; thoughtful; not given to pleasure-seeking: 嚴肅的;莊重的;深思的;不喜尋歡作樂的: *a ~ mind / appearance / face;* 嚴肅的心情(外表,臉); *look ~.* 表情嚴肅的。 **2** important because of possible danger: 嚴重的;重大的: *a ~ illness / mistake.* 重病(大錯)。 *The international situation looks ~.* 國際情勢看來相當嚴重。 **3** in earnest; sincere: 認眞的;眞誠的: *a ~ worker / lover.* 工作認眞者(眞誠的愛人)。 *Please be ~ about your work.* 請用心工作。 **~·ly** *adv* in a ~ manner: 嚴肅地;莊重地;嚴重地;重大地;認眞地;眞誠地: *speak ~ly to sb;* 嚴肅地對某人說話; *be ~ly ill.* 害大病。 **~·ness** *n* state of being ~: 嚴肅;莊重;嚴重;重大;認眞;眞誠: *the ~ness of the country's financial situation.* 該國財政情況嚴重。 *in all ~ness,* very ~ly; not at all in a light-hearted way: 非常嚴肅地;莊重地: *I tell you this in all ~ness.* 我十分鄭重地告訴你這件事。

ser·jeant /ˈsɑːdʒənt ; ˈsɑrdʒənt/ *n* **ˌS~-at-ˈarms,** official with ceremonial duties or who keeps order in a court, legislature, etc. (擔任禮儀勤務或維持法庭,議會等處之秩序的)衛士;警衛官。

ser·mon /ˈsɜːmən ; ˈsɝmən/ *n* [C] spoken or written address on a religious or moral subject, esp one given from a pulpit in a church; serious talk reproving a person for his faults, etc. (宗教或道德方面,說出或寫出的) 說教;(立於教堂之講壇上所作之)講道;(因某人犯錯等,對其所作之)訓誡。 **~·ize** /-aɪz ; -aɪz/ *vt, vi* [VP6A, 2A] preach or talk seriously to: (對…)說教或訓誡: *Stop ~izing,* lecturing to me on my faults, etc! 別教訓我了!

serous /ˈsɪərəs ; ˈsɪrəs/ *adj* of or like serum. 血漿的;血清的;如血漿的;如血清的;漿液性的。

ser·pent /ˈsɜːpənt ; ˈsɝpənt/ *n* snake (which is the more usu word); (fig) sly, treacherous person: 蛇(snake 較常用); (喻)狡猾的人: *the old S~,* the Devil. 魔王;魔鬼;惡魔。

ser·pen·tine /ˈsɜːpəntaɪn *US:* -tiːn ; ˈsɝpənˌtin/ *adj* twisting and curving like a snake: 似蛇般繞曲的; 蜿蜒的: *the ~ course of the river.* 蜿蜒的河道。

ser·rated /sɪˈreɪtɪd *US:* ˈsereɪtɪd ; ˈsɛretɪd/ *adj* having notches on the edge like a saw; having a toothed edge: 邊上呈鋸齒狀的;有鋸齒形邊的: *~ leaves.* 有鋸齒狀邊緣的葉子。

ser·ried /ˈserɪd ; ˈsɛrɪd/ *adj* (of lines or ranks of persons) close together, shoulder to shoulder: (指人的行列)密集的;林立的: *in ~ ranks.* 密集排列的。

serum /ˈsɪərəm ; ˈsɪrəm/ *n* **1** [U] watery fluid in animal bodies; thin, transparent part of blood. 漿液;血漿。**2** (dose of) such a fluid taken from the blood of an animal which has been made immune to a disease, used for inoculations. 血清;一劑血清。

ser·vant /ˈsɜːvənt ; ˈsɝvənt/ *n* **1 (domestic) ~,** person who works in a household for wages, food and lodging: 僕人;用人: *have a large staff of ~s;* 僕從衆多; *engage/dismiss a ~.* 僱請(開革)用人。 **2 public ~,** person who works for the public, eg a police officer, member of the Fire Service. 官吏;公僕(如警官,救火隊員等)。 **civil ~,** government employee, member of the civil service. 公務員。 ***your humble ~,*** form sometimes used preceding the signature in an official letter. 在公務信件中有時冠於簽名前之敬稱。 **3** person devoted to sb or sth: 忠於某人或某事者: *a ~ of Jesus Christ,* eg a Christian priest. 耶穌基督的僕人(如基督教教士)。 **4** sth useful that should be treated as a means but not as an end: 有用之工具: *Fire is a good ~ but a bad master.* 火可造福人類,也能成爲禍首。

serve /sɜːv ; sɝv/ *vt, vi* **1** [VP6A, 15A, 2A, C] be a servant to (sb); work for (sb): 做(某人)的僕人;爲(某人)工作;服務: *She ~d the Ambassador for ten years.* 她爲這大使工作了十年之久。 *He ~s as gardener and also as chauffeur.* 他兼爲園丁和車夫。 **2** [VP6A, 15A, 2A, B, 3A] perform duties (for): (爲…)盡責: *~ one's country,* eg in Parliament; 爲人民服務(如在國會等中); *~ a year in the Army.* 在陸軍服役一年。 *Can I ~ you in any way,* Is there anything I can do for you? 我能幫你忙嗎? ***~ on sth,*** be a member of: 爲…之一員: *~ on a committee.* 擔任委員。 ***~ under sb,*** be in the armed forces under the command of: (在軍中)爲某人的部下;在某人麾下: *My grandfather ~d under Montgomery.* 我祖父是蒙哥馬利的部下。 ***~ two masters,*** (fig) be divided in one's loyalty, or between two opposite principles. (喻)不忠;左右爲難。 **3** [VP6A, 2A, 14, 15B] ***~ sth (to sb); ~ sb (with sth); ~ sth (out),*** attend to (customers in a shop, etc); supply (with goods and services); place (food, etc) on the table for a meal; give (food, etc) to people at a meal: 侍候(顧客);供以(貨物及服務);上(菜等);開(飯等): *There was no one in the shop to ~ me.* 店鋪裡沒有人來招呼我。 *We are well ~d with gas/electricity, etc in this town.* 在這城鎮中我們有足够的煤氣(電等)。 *Rations were ~d (out) to the troops.* 口糧已發給各部隊。 *Roast pork is often ~d with apple sauce.* 烤肉常和蘋果醬一起上。 *Dinner is ~d,* is ready. 飯已備好(或已開出)。 *S~ the coffee in the next room, please.* 請在隔壁房間上咖啡。 **4** [VP6A, 2A, C, 4A] ***~ sb (for/as sth),*** be satisfactory for a need or purpose: 適合某需要或目的: *This box will ~ for a seat.* 這箱子可用做座椅。 *It isn't very good but it will ~ me.* 它並不很好,但我正用得着。 *That excuse will not ~ you/That will not ~ you as an excuse,* will not be accepted. 你的那個藉口不太合適。 *This accident ~s to show the foolishness of not being prepared.* 這次意外事件足以證明事先不作準備是多麼的愚蠢。 ***~ sb's needs/purpose(s),*** meet his requirements: 滿足某人的需要;符合某人的要求: *The house will ~ his needs admirably.* 這房子將十分符合他的需要。 ***as occasion ~s,*** when there is a suitable or convenient occasion or opportunity. 一有適當的時機或機會。 **5** [VP15A, B] act towards, treat (sb in a certain way): 對付;對待: *They have ~d me shamefully,* behaved very badly towards me. 他們待我很壞。 *I hope I shall never be ~d such a trick again,* have such a trick played on me. 我希望以後別再向我要這一套了。 ***It ~s him right,*** His failure, misfortune, etc is deserved; he does not merit sympathy. 他活該。 **6** [VP6A] pass the usual or normal number of years (learning a trade, etc); go through one's term of office: 度過通常或一般的年限(如習藝等); (在任期內)供職: *~ one's time;* 供職; *~ one's apprenticeship.* 做學徒。 **7** [VP6A] ***~ a sentence; ~ time,*** undergo a period of imprisonment. 服刑。 *He has ~d five years of his sentence.* 他已服刑五年。 **8** [VP14] ***~ a summons/writ/warrant on sb; ~ sb with a summons/writ/warrant,*** (legal) deliver (a summons, etc) to the person named in it. (法律)送達(傳票等)給某人。 **9** [VP6A, 2A] (tennis, etc) put the ball into play by striking it to an opponent: (網球等)發球: *~ a ball;* 發球; *~ well/badly.* 球發得好(壞)。 **10** [VP6A] of a male animal, eg a bull, ram or boar, copulate with. (指雄性動物,如公牛,公羊,公猪等)與…交配。 **11** [VP2A, 6A] help a priest at Mass: 在彌撒儀式中充當助祭者: *~ Mass.* 在彌撒儀式中充當助祭者。□ *n* (tennis, etc) first stroke; turn for striking and putting the ball into play: (網球等)發球;輪到發球: *Whose ~ is it?* 該誰發球? **~r** *n* **1** person who ~s, eg one who helps a priest at Mass or ~s at tennis. 服務者;服役者;侍者;送達員;(尤指)彌撒時助祭者;(網球)發球者。 **2** tray for dishes; salver. 菜盤;托盤。 **3** utensil used in serving out food: 上菜用的器皿: *ˈsalad-~rs.* 上生菜所用之叉和匙。 **serv·ing** *n* quantity of food (to be) served to one person: 一人份的食物: *This recipe will be enough for four servings.* 這食譜足够四人吃的份量。

ser·vice /ˈsɜːvɪs ; ˈsɝvɪs/ *n* **1** [U] being a servant; position as a servant. 幫傭;僕人的職位。 ***be in/go into/go out to ~,*** be employed as a domestic servant. 做用人;當僕役。 **2** [C] department or branch of public work, government employment, etc: 公務部門;政府機構: *the ˌCivil ˈS~;* 文職部門;文官之總稱; *the ˌDiploˈmatic S~;* 外交部門; *the fighting ~s,* the Navy, Army, Air Force; 海陸空軍;戰鬥軍種; *~ men and women,* members of the fighting ~s. 戰鬥人員。 ***on active ~,*** performing duties required by membership of the fighting ~s in time of war. 服現役。 ***see ~ in sth,*** serve (in the armed forces): (在軍中)服役: *He saw ~ in both World Wars.* 他在兩次世界大戰中都服過役。 *He has seen ~ in many parts of the world.* 他在世界許多地方服過役。 ***have seen (good) ~,*** have served one well: 有(大的)用途;幫(大)忙: *These old climbing-boots have seen good ~ on my numerous holidays in the Alps.* 我屢次去阿爾卑斯山度假這雙舊登山靴都有很大的用處。 **3** [C] sth done to help or benefit another or others: 服務;貢獻;幫助: *His ~s to the State have been immense.* 他對政府的貢獻很大。 *Do you need the ~s of a doctor/lawyer?* 你需要醫生(律師)(的服務)嗎? ***do sb a ~,*** help him: 協助某人;幫助某人: *She did me a great ~ by driving me to the airport.* 她駕車送我到機場,幫了我一個大忙。 **4** [U] benefit, use, advantage: 利益;有用;好處: *Can I be of ~ to you,* help you in any way? 我能幫得上忙嗎? *I am at your ~,* ready to help you. 我隨時都可以爲你效勞。 *My car is at your ~,* ready for you to use when you want to. 你隨時可用我的汽車。 **5** [C] system or arrangement that supplies public needs, esp for communications: 公共需要物之供應系統;公共設施;(尤指)交通設施: *a ˈbus/ˈtrain ~;* 公共汽車(火車)之交通服務; *the ˈtelephone ~;* 電話

設施; *a good 'postal ~.* 良好的郵政。'~ **road** *n* minor road, off a main road, giving access to houses, etc. (主要道路旁之)輔助道路;支道;支線。 **6** [C] form of worship and prayer to God: 禮拜式;崇拜儀式: *three ~s every Sunday;* 每星期日三次禮拜; *attend morning/evening ~;* 參加早(晚)禮拜; *'marriage/'burial/com'munion ~.* 結婚(葬禮,聖餐)儀式。 **7** [C] complete set of plates, dishes, etc for use at table: 盤、碟等之全套: *a 'tea/'dinner ~ of 30 pieces.* 三十人份的茶具(餐具)。 **8** [U] serving of food and drink (in hotels, etc); work done by domestic servants, hotel staff, etc: (旅館等中之)上菜;上飲料;僕役等之服務: *The food is good at this hotel, but the ~ is poor.* 這家旅館的食物不錯,但侍者的服務很差。 *The waiter added 10 per cent to the bill for ~,* eg to a bill at a restaurant, instead of getting a tip. 那侍者另加了一成服務費。 *Do you make a '~ charge at this hotel,* eg add 10%? 你們這家旅館要收服務費嗎(如另加一成)? '~ **flat** *n* one (usu furnished) of which the rent includes a charge for ~. 房租中包括服務費用之公寓(通常備有傢具)。 **9** [U] expert help or advice given by manufacturers or their agents after the sale of an article: 廠商之售後服務: *send the car in for ~ every 3000 miles,* eg for greasing, checking of brakes, etc: 每行駛三千哩把汽車送廠檢修(如加潤滑油、檢查煞車等): (attrib) (形容用法) '~ *department.* 服務部。 '~ **station** *n* petrol station which also offers general servicing facilities. 加油站(附設一般性修護設備者)。 **10** (legal) serving of a writ, summons, etc. (法律)傳票等之送達。 **11** (tennis, etc) act of serving the ball; manner of doing this; person's turn to serve: (網球等之)發球;發球之方式;輪到發球: *Her ~ is weak.* 她發球沒有力。 *Whose ~ is it?* 該誰發球? □ *vt* [VP6A] maintain or repair (a car, radio, machine, etc) after sale (⇨ 9 above): 售後保養或檢修(汽車、收音機、機器等)(參看上列第9義): *have the car ~d regularly.* 定期將汽車送廠檢修。 ~**·able** /-əbl; -əbl/ *adj* **1** suited for ordinary wear and use; strong and durable: 適於一般用途的;耐用的: *~able clothes for school-children.* 適於學童的耐穿衣服。 **2** of use; capable of giving good service. 有用的;能有助益的。

ser·vi·ette /ˌsɜːvɪ'et; ˌsɝvɪ'ɛt/ *n* [C] table napkin: 餐巾: *I prefer a linen napkin to a paper ~.* 我喜歡亞麻布餐巾而不愛用紙餐巾。

ser·vile /'sɜːvaɪl *US:* -vl; 'sɝvl/ *adj* **1** (archaic) of or like a slave. (古)奴隸的;似奴隸的。 **2** lacking in the spirit of independence; obsequious: 缺乏獨立精神的;卑躬的: *~ flattery;* 奴顏婢膝的諂媚; *~ to public opinion,* paying excessive attention to it. 過份順從輿論。 **~ly** /-aɪllɪ; -lɪ/ *adv* **ser·vil·ity** /sɜː'vɪlətɪ; sɝ'vɪlətɪ/ *n* [U] ~ behaviour or attitude. 卑躬的行爲或態度。

ser·vi·tor /'sɜːvɪtə(r); 'sɝvətɚ/ *n* (old use) servant; attendant. (舊用法)僕從;隨員。

ser·vi·tude /'sɜːvɪtjuːd *US:* -tuːd; 'sɝvəˌtjud/ *n* [U] condition of being forced to work for others and having no freedom. 苦役;奴役,勞役。⇨ penal.

servo- /'sɜːvəʊ; 'sɝvə/ *pref* (of machinery) using a system that automatically controls a larger system: (指機器)有自動控制系統的;用較小系統自動控制較大系統的: *'~-motor,* controlling motor in such a system; 伺服電動機; *ˌ~-as'sisted brakes,* eg in a large car; 副掣;輔力煞車(如大汽車中者); *ˌ~-'mechanism,* general name for the controlling system. 伺服機構。

ses·ame /'sesəmɪ; 'sɛsəmɪ/ *n* **1** plant with seeds used in various ways as food and giving an oil used in salads. 芝蔴;胡蔴。 **2** ***Open ~!*** magic words used, in one of the Arabian Nights stories, to cause a door to open; hence, easy way of securing access to what is usu inaccessible: (天方夜譚一故事中的)開門咒; (由此產生)通過難關之簡易方法: *an open ~ to high society.* 進入上流社會之捷徑。

sesqui·ped·alian /ˌseskwɪpɪ'deɪlɪən; ˌsɛskwɪpə'deljən/ *adj* (of a word) having many syllables; (fig) tedious; long-winded. (指字)多音節的;(喻)令人厭倦的;冗長的。

session /'seʃn; 'sɛʃən/ *n* [C] **1** meeting of a law court, law-making body, etc; time occupied by discussions at such a meeting: (法庭之)開庭; (議會等之)開會; 開庭期;開會期: *the autumn ~* (= sitting) *of Parliament;* (英國國會之)秋季會期; *have a long ~;* 開庭(會)期甚長; *go into secret ~.* 開秘密會議。 **Court of S~,** supreme civil court of Scotland. 蘇格蘭高等民事法庭。 **petty ~s,** courts held by magistrates to hear certain offences without a jury. 即決法庭(案件由地方法官審理,而無須成立陪審團即可開庭者)。 **2** (Scot and US) university term. (蘇,美)大學之學期。 **3** single, uninterrupted meeting for other purposes: (爲其他目的所舉行之)單獨而無中斷之集會;從事某項活動的時間: *a re'cording ~,* period of time during which material is recorded (on discs or tapes, eg for broadcasts). 錄音時間。

set¹ /set; sɛt/ *n* **1** [C] number of things of the same kind, that belong together because they are similar or complementary to each other: 套;組;副: *a set of golfclubs/the novels of Dickens/Albanian stamps;* 一套高爾夫球球桿(狄更斯的小說,阿爾巴尼亞的郵票); *a 'tea-set and 'dinner-set,* (= *service*(7), the more usu word); 一套茶具和餐具(與service 第7義相同,較常用 service); *a new set of false teeth.* 一副新的假牙。 **2** [C] number of persons who associate, or who have similar or identical tastes and interests: 一羣同伴;一群志趣相投者: *the 'racing/'literary/'golfing set;* 愛好賽馬(文學,高爾夫球)的人士; *the 'smart set,* those who consider themselves leaders in society; 自認爲領導社會的一群人; *the 'fast set,* those who gamble, etc; 不務正業之流; *the 'jet set,* rich pleasure-loving people, flying from one holiday resort to another. 喜愛遊樂的有錢人(乘飛機去各處度假)。 **3** radio or television receiving apparatus: 無線電或電視接收機: *an ˌall-'mains set;* 可適用各種電壓的收音機; *a transistor set.* 一架晶體收音機。 **4** (not *pl*) direction (of current, wind, etc); tendency (of opinion): (不用複數)(潮流,風等的)方向;(意見的)趨向: *the set of the tide.* 潮水的流向。 **5** (not *pl*) position or angle; posture: (不用複數)位置;角度;姿勢: *I recognize him by the set of his head/shoulders.* 我從他的頭(肩)的姿態認出是他。 **6** way in which a garment conforms to the shape of the body: 衣服穿在身上的樣子;款式: *I don't like the set of this coat,* the way it fits (or doesn't fit). 我不喜歡這上裝的款式。⇨ set²(14). **7** [U] (poet) sunset: (詩)日落: *at set of sun.* 在日落之際。 **8** (tennis, etc) group of games counting as a unit to the side that wins more than half the games in it. (網球等)盤(由數局組成之單位,獲勝半數以上者即算獲勝全盤)。 **9** the act of pointing at game (birds, animals) by a setter. 獵犬之以鼻指示獵物(鳥獸)。⇨ set²(15). ***make a dead set at,*** **(a)** combine to attack vigorously, by argument or ridicule. (以言詞等)協力猛烈攻擊。 **(b)** (of a person) try to win the attention and affection of (another person to whom one is attracted). (指人)設法獲得(所愛慕者)之注意和感情。 **10** [C] granite paving stone (as used for road surfaces). (用以鋪路面等的)花崗石板。 **11** [C] built-up scenery on the stage of a theatre, or in a studio or outdoors for a film: (戲劇、電影中的)佈景;場景;外景: *everyone to be on the set by 7am.* 所有的人在上午七時以前到達拍外景的地方。 **12** [C] young plant, cutting, bulb, etc ready to be planted: 幼苗;樹秧: *get the onion sets in.* 栽種洋蔥的幼苗。 **13** badger's burrow. 貛所掘之地洞。 **14** setting of the hair: 做頭髮: *shampoo and set, £4.* 洗頭做髮,定價四鎊。⇨ set²(9).

set² /set; sɛt/ *vt, vi* (-tt-, *pt, pp* set) (For special uses with *adverbial particles* and *preps*, ⇨ 19 below.) (與副詞接語及介詞連用之特殊用法，參看下列第19義。) **1** [VP2A] (of the sun, moon, stars) go down below the horizon: (指太陽、月亮、星星)降落於地平線下；沈入: *It will be cooler when the sun has/is set.* 日落之後，天就會涼爽些。*His star has set,* (fig) The time of his power, greatness, etc is over. (喻)他的好運已過。**2** [VP14] ***set sth to sth,*** move or place sth so that it is near to or touching sth else: 移動或放置(某物)致使與他物接近或接觸: *set a glass to one's lips/one's lips to a glass.* 將玻璃杯貼近嘴唇(將嘴唇貼近玻璃杯)。***set the axe to,*** cut down (a tree); (fig) start to destroy (sth). 砍倒(樹)；(喻)着手摧毁(某物)。***set fire/a match/(a) light to sth,*** cause it to begin burning. 使某物開始燃燒。***set pen to paper,*** begin to write. 開始寫。***set one's seal to sth; set the seal on sth,*** authorize or confirm it. 批准；認可。***set one's shoulder to the wheel,*** ⇨ shoulder. **3** [VP22, 16A] cause (sb/sth) to be in, or reach, a specified state or relation. 使(某人或某物)處於或達到某種特殊的狀態或關係。***set sb/sth at defiance/naught/nought,*** ⇨ defiance; nought. ***set sb at his ease,*** make him feel free from embarrassment, feel comfortable, etc. 使某人安逸；使某人心情放鬆；使某人舒坦。***set sb/sth on his/its feet,*** **(a)** help him to get to his feet after a fall. 扶某人站起(如跌倒後)。**(b)** help sb/sth to gain strength, financial stability, etc: 使某人(某事物)獲得力量、經濟安定等: *Foreign aid set the country on its feet after the war.* 外援使該國戰後經濟穩定。***set sth on fire,*** (= set fire to sth) cause it to begin burning. 點火燃某物。***ˌnot/ˌnever ˌset the ˈThames on fire,*** not/never do/be anything wonderful, extraordinary. 不會(決不會)做出驚人之事；不會(決不會)成爲傑出的人物；不會(決不會)有很大的出息。***set sb free/at liberty,*** free (prisoners, etc). 釋放(囚犯等)。***set people at loggerheads/variance,*** cause them to argue and dispute. 唆使人們爭辯；使人們不和。***set sth in order,*** arrange, organize (one's papers, affairs, etc) properly. 整理(個人的文件、事物等)。***ˌset one's (ˈown) ˈhouse in order,*** (fig) order one's own affairs, one's own life (before criticizing others). 管好自己的事；自身先站得穩(再批評別人)。***set sb's mind at ease/rest; set sb's doubts/fears/mind at rest,*** help him to be free from worry, free him from anxiety. 使某人安心；使某人放心。***set sb's teeth on edge,*** jar his nerves: 使某人心神不安: *That noise sets my teeth on edge.* 那吵聲使我不安。***set sb right,*** **(a)** correct his errors; put him on the right road. 改正某人的錯誤；引導某人走向正確的方向。**(b)** cause him to feel well and fit again. 使某人康復。***set sth right/to rights,*** correct, remedy (faults, grievances). 改正或彌補錯誤。***set sb on his way,*** (old use) go part of the way with him (when he starts out on foot). (舊用法)陪某人走一段路；送某人一程(當其徒步出發時)。***be all set (for sth/to do sth),*** be quite ready (for the start of a race, etc). 準備妥當(開始賽跑、賽馬等)。***be set on doing sth,*** be determined to do it: 決心做某事: *My Uncle Ernest is set on swimming the English Channel.* 我叔叔歐尼斯特決心游過英吉利海峽。**4** [VP19B] cause sb/sth to begin to do sth: 使某人(某物)開始做某事(發生作用): *It's time we set the machinery going,* start operations. 是我們發動機器的時候了。*What has set the dog barking?* 什麼東西使那隻狗叫起來？ *The news set me thinking.* 那消息使我陷入沉思。*My jokes set everyone laughing.* 我的笑話使每個人大笑。*'Blow, bugles, blow, set the wild echoes flying!'* '響起來，號角，響起來，讓激昂的回聲在空中震盪！' **5** [VP6A, 15A] (usu with an *adv* or *adv phrase;* ⇨ 19 below for combinations of *set* and *adverbial particles* with special meanings) put, place, lay, stand: (通常與副詞或副詞片語連用；參看下列第19義，set 與副詞接語連用而形成具有特殊意義的片語)置；放；擱；豎: *She set the dishes on the table.* 她把碟子放在桌上。*We set food and drink before the travellers.* 我們把食物和飲料放在旅客面前。*He set the stake in the ground.* 他豎樁於地上。 **6** [VP6A, 14, 12C] ***set (for),*** put forward as (material to be dealt with as a task, a pattern, etc): 提出；規定(工作，作業等)；出(題目等): *The teacher set the children a difficult problem,* gave them one to be solved. 教師給孩子們出了一個難題。*I have set myself a difficult task.* 我爲自己安排了一件困難的工作。*Who will set the papers for the examination,* draw up the examination questions? 這次考試誰命題？ *What books have been set for the Cambridge Certificate next year,* What books are to be studied? 下一年劍橋大學檢定考試規定唸那些書？ Hence, 由此產生，**ˌset ˈbook,** book on which examinations are to be given. 考試用書。***set (sb) a (good) example,*** offer a good standard for others to follow: 爲(某人)樹立(好)榜樣: *You should set the younger boys a good example.* 你應該爲較年幼的男孩子樹立好的榜樣。***set the fashion,*** start a fashion to be copied by others. 開風氣之先。***set the pace,*** fix it by leading (in a race, etc); (fig) fix a standard for an activity, style of living, etc: 領先定步調(在賽跑等中)；(喻)立下活動、生活方式等之榜樣: *The Joneses set the pace and their neighbours try to keep up with them.* 瓊斯一家人立下榜樣，他們的鄰居都想向他們看齊。***set the stroke,*** (rowing) fix the number of strokes per minute. (划船)定下每分鐘划槳的次數。 **7** [VP17A] ***set (sb/oneself) to do sth,*** give sth (to sb/oneself) as a task: 支使、派遣、規定(某人或自己)做某事: *He set the farm labourer to chop wood.* 他派遣農場工人去砍木材。*I set myself to study the problem.* 我決定研究這問題。*I've set myself* (= have resolved) *to finish the job by the end of May.* 我決心於五月底以前完成那工作。***ˌSet a ˌthief to ˈcatch a thief,*** (prov) Use illegal methods to uncover illegal actions. (諺)以毒攻毒；令賊捉賊。 **8** [VP6A, 15A] (with various grammatical objects, the *nn* in alphabetical order) (與各種文法上的受詞連用，其中名詞係按字母次序排列) ***set one's cap at sb,*** ⇨ cap. ***set eyes on sb,*** see him: 看見某人: *I hope I never set eyes on that fellow again.* 我希望再也不要看到那傢伙。***set one's face against sth,*** steadfastly oppose sth. 堅決反對。***set one's heart/hopes/mind on sth,*** be filled with strong desire for, determination to get; direct one's hopes towards: 亟欲；決心要得到；希冀: *The boy has set his heart on becoming an engineer.* 這男孩下定決心要當工程師。***set a price on sth,*** declare what it will be sold for. 給某物定價格。***set a price on sb's head,*** offer a specified reward to anyone who kills him. 懸賞殺死某人。***set much/great/little/no store by sth,*** value sth highly/little/not at all. 非常(極，不太，根本不)重視某物。**9** [VP6A, 15A] put in a certain state or condition for a particular purpose: 爲了某一目的而置於某種狀態之下: *set a (broken) bone,* bring the parts together so that they may unite. 接(碎)骨。***set a butterfly,*** arrange it with wings outspread (in a glass case) as a specimen. 擺蝴蝶(使兩翼張開，置於玻璃盒中，以作爲標本)。***set a clock/watch,*** put the hands to the correct time (or, for an alarm clock, to sound at the desired time): 對鐘；對錶；將鬧鐘等定時: *set one's watch by the time-signal on the radio.* 按收音機之報時信號對錶。***set eggs,*** place them (to be hatched) under a hen, etc in a nest. 置卵於母鷄等的下面(使孵之)。***set one's hair,*** arrange it (when damp) so that when it is dry, it is in the required style: (趁濕)做頭髮: *She's having her hair set for this evening's party.* 她爲了今晚的宴會正在

做頭髮。 ***set a hen,*** place it over eggs (to hatch them). 使母鷄孵卵。 ***set a saw,*** sharpen the teeth with a file and put them (alternately) at the right outward angle. 磨銳鋸齒並調整其傾角。 ***set the scene,*** describe a place and the people taking part in an activity, eg in a play, novel or sporting event: 描述戲劇、小說或運動項目中的地點及參與活動的人;形成…的背景或形式: *Our commentator will now set the scene in the stadium.* 我們的播報員現在將描述運動場的情形。*The scene is now set for the tragedy,* Events leading up to the tragedy have taken place and the tragedy will follow. 這齣悲劇的背景業已形成。*The scene is now set for a direct confrontation between the major powers.* 列强正面對抗的形勢已經形成。 ***set sail (from / to / for),*** begin a voyage. 啓航;開航。 ***set the table,*** lay it ready with plates, cutlery, etc: 將餐具擺在餐桌上: *She set the table for five people.* 她擺設五人的食具於餐桌上。 ***set one's teeth,*** clench them; (fig) become determined and inflexible (against some course of action, etc). 咬緊牙關;(喩)決心堅持到底。 ***set a trap (for sth / sb),*** **(a)** adjust one to catch a mouse, rat, etc. 設置捕捉機(捕鼠等)。**(b)** do sth to discover a dishonest person, etc: 設陷阱,設圈套(以揭發行爲不軌之人等): *set a trap to catch a thief / for a boy who cheats.* 設下圈套捉小偸(拆穿作弊的男孩)。 ***set (up) type,*** arrange it ready for printing sth. 排鉛字。 **10** [VP6A, 14] ***set sth in sth; set sth with sth,*** put, fix, one thing firmly in another: 使(一物)固定於(他物)之中;鑲;嵌: *set a diamond in gold;* 鑲鑽石於黃金之中; *a crown set with jewels;* 鑲有珠寶的皇冠; *a gold ring set with gems;* 鑲有寶石的金戒指; *a heavy lathe set* (= embedded) *in concrete;* 固定在混凝土中的大車床; *glass panes set in lead,* ie strips of lead, as in old lattice windows. 嵌於鉛格框中的窗玻璃。*The tops of the walls were set with broken glass,* ie to discourage persons from climbing over them. 牆頂嵌有碎玻璃(以阻人攀越)。*The sky seemed to be set with diamonds,* the stars looked like diamonds. 天空似乎鑲嵌了鑽石(星星看起來像鑽石)。 **11** [VP2A, C] (of tides, currents) move or flow along; gather force; (fig) show or feel a tendency: (指潮水,潮流,氣流,思潮)流動;增加力量;(喩)顯出或感到某種傾向:*A strong current sets through the channel.* 一股强大的潮流流過海峽。*The current sets in towards the shore.* 潮水上漲,流向岸邊。*The wind sets from the west.* 風自西方吹來。*The tide has set in his favour,* (fig) He is winning public support and approval. (喩)他逐漸赢得公衆的支持和讚許。*Public opinion is setting against the proposal.* 輿論反對那提議。 **12** [VP6A, 14] ***set sth (to sth),*** provide with music, usu composed for the purpose: 爲…配曲:*set a poem to music;* 爲詩歌配曲; *set new words to an old tune.* 爲舊曲作新詞。 **13** [VP6A, 2A] (of plants, fruit trees, their blossom) form or develop fruit as the result of fertilization: (指植物,果樹,其花)結果實: *The apple-blossom hasn't / The apples haven't set well this year.* 蘋果花(樹)今年沒有結多少果實。*This liquid, if sprayed on the flowers, helps to set the tomatoes.* 這液體灑在花上,能幫助蕃茄結實。 **14** [VP2C] (of a garment) adapt itself to the shape of the body; sit (which is the more usu word): (指衣服)適合身材;合身(sit 較常用): *A well-tailored jacket ought to set well.* 裁製良好的上衣應該很合身。*That dress sets rather badly.* 那衣服不甚合身。 **15** [VP2A, C] (of a sporting dog) stop and stand with the muzzle pointing, to indicate presence of game; (of dancers) take positions facing partners: (指獵犬)站着以口鼻指示獵物所在;(指舞者)面向舞伴: *set to partners.* 面向舞伴。 **16** [VP6A, 2A] (cause to) become firm, solid, rigid (from a liquid or soft state): (使)凝固;(使)凝結: *Some kinds of concrete set more quickly than others.* 某些種混凝土比其他混凝土凝固得快。*The jelly is / has not set yet.* 凍子尙未結好。*Heat sets eggs and cold sets jellies.* 熱使蛋凝結,冷使凍子凝結。 **17** [VP6A, 2A] (rare) (cause to) develop into definite lines and shapes, become mature: (罕)(使)發育成形;(使)變成熟: *His body has / is set,* is fully developed. 他的體型已完全發育。*Too much exercise may set a boy's muscles prematurely.* 運動過多可能使男孩子的肌肉過早僵化。*His character has / is set,* is no longer pliant, is already formed. 他的性格已經定型(不會再變)。 **18** (*pp*) **(a)** unmoving, fixed: 不動的;固定的: *a set smile / look / purpose.* 呆板的微笑(呆滯的表情;確定的目標)。 **(b)** pre-arranged: 預定的;事先安排的: *at a set time;* 在預定的時間; *set lunches £2.50,* (eg at a restaurant, there being no choice of dishes); 二鎊半的午餐客飯; *a set piece,* a large and elaborate firework set on a platform or scaffold; 固定於平臺上或臺架上的大型煙火; (attrib) (形容用法) *a set-piece attack,* ie carefully planned in advance. 預先經過周詳策畫的攻擊。**(c)** unchanging: 不變的;固執的: *set in one's ways,* having fixed habits; 有固定生活習慣的; *a man of set opinions,* unable or unwilling to change them. 固執己見的人。 **(d)** regular; fixed or planned in advance: 循規的;預先準備好的;預先計畫好的: *set phrases;* 現成的詞句;套語; *a set speech;* 預先準備好的演說; *set forms of prayers.* 規定的禱告方式。 **(e)** ***set fair,*** (of the weather) fine and with no signs of change. (指天氣)穩定的晴天。 **19** [VP15A, 2C, 3A] (special uses with *adverbial particles* and *preps*): (與副詞接語及介詞連用的特殊用法):

set about sth, start; take steps towards: 開始;着手: *I must set about my packing,* begin to pack my clothes, etc. 我必須開始收拾行裝。*I don't know how to set about this job,* how to make a start on it. 我不知怎樣着手這項工作。 ***set about sb,*** (colloq) attack: (俗)攻擊: *They set about each other fiercely,* began to exchange blows. 他們兇猛地互毆。 ***set sth about,*** spread (rumours, etc): 散佈(謠言等): *Who set* (*put* is more usu) *it about that he is resigning?* 誰說他要辭職(put 較常用)? ***set sb against sb,*** cause him to compete with, struggle against, sb. 使某人和某人競爭、對抗。 ***set one thing against another,*** regard it as compensating for, balancing, another. 使某事物和另一事物相抵補、平衡或牽制。

set sth apart / aside, **(a)** put on one side for future use. 撥出;留下將來使用。**(b)** disregard: 不注意;忽視: *Let's set aside my personal feelings.* 讓我們撇開個人的情感。**(c)** (legal) reject: (法律)拒絕;駁回;宣告無效: *set a claim aside.* 駁回一項要求。

set sth back, **(a)** move back: 將…往後移;撥回: *set back the hands of a clock.* 把鐘撥慢。*The horse set back its ears.* 這馬將其耳朵後仰放平(俗謂馬耳向後刷)。 **(b)** be placed away, at a distance, from: 置於遠處;分開放置: *The house is well set back from the road.* 這幢房子和大街有相當的距離。 ***set sb / sth back,*** **(a)** hinder or reverse the progress of: 阻礙;阻止: *All our efforts at reform have been set back.* 我們對改革所做的一切努力受到了挫折。Hence, 由此產生, **ˈset-back** *n* (*pl* set-backs) check to progress or development: 阻礙;挫折: *meet with many set-backs;* 遇到許多挫折; *have a set-back in one's career / business.* 在事業(業務)上受到一次挫折。 **(b)** (sl) cost: (俚)花費: *That haircut set me back £5.* 理那次髮花了我五鎊。

set sth down, **(a)** put down: 放下;卸下: *set down a load.* 卸下背負之物。 **(b)** write down on paper. 記載;登記。 ***set sb down,*** (of a vehicle, its driver) allow (a passenger) to get down or out: (指車輛,其駕駛者)讓(乘客)下車: *The bus stopped to set down an old lady.* 公共汽車停下讓一位老婦人下車。*I'll set you down at the corner of your street.* 我讓你在你所住街道的轉角處下車。 ***set sb / oneself***

down as, (*put* is more usu) explain or describe as: (put 較常用)把某人(自己)說成或視爲: *How should I set myself down in the hotel register—as a journalist or as an author?* 在旅館的登記簿上,我應如何寫下自己的身份 — 寫成記者還是作家呢？ *We must set him down as either a criminal or a fool.* 我們該把他視爲犯人或傻子。***set sth down to sth,*** (*put* is more usu), attribute sth to, say that sth is the result of. (put 較常用)把…歸於;認某事物由…造成: *set one's success down to hard work.* 將成功歸於努力工作。

set forth, begin a journey (*set out* is more usu). 啓程;動身(set out 較常用)。***set sth forth,*** (formal) make known; declare: (正式用語)宣佈;發表: *set forth one's political views.* 發表政見。*Is this condition set forth* (= included) *in the agreement?* 這條件載於合約中嗎？

set in, **(a)** start and seem likely to continue: 開始: *The rainy season has set in.* 雨季已開始了。*It set in to rain.* 開始下雨了。*Go to your dentist before decay of the teeth sets in.* 在牙齒開始腐蝕以前去看牙醫師。**(b)** (of tides, winds; ➪ 11 above) begin to flow: (指潮汐,風;參看上列第11義)開始流動: *The tide is setting in,* flowing towards the shore. 潮水正在上漲。

set off, start (a journey, race, etc): 開始(旅程、賽跑等);出發: *They've set off on a journey round the world.* 他們已出發環球旅行。***set sth off,*** **(a)** explode a mine, firework, etc. 使(地雷,煙火等)爆發;引爆。**(b)** make more striking by comparison: (用比較的方法)使更明顯;襯托: *Use blue eye-shadow to set off your green eyes.* 用藍色眼影襯托你的綠眼睛。*This gold frame sets off the painting very well.* 這個金框把畫襯托得很美。**(c)** balance; compensate: 平衡;抵銷: *set off gains against losses.* 以利得抵銷損失。**(d)** mark off: 分開;劃分: *set off a clause by a comma.* 用逗點把子句分開。***set sb off (doing sth),*** cause to start (doing sth): 使開始(做某事): *Don't set him off talking politics or he'll go on all evening.* 別讓他開始談政治,否則他會談上整整一個夜晚。

ˌset ˈon, (formal) go forward; advance to the attack. (正式用語)前進;迎擊。***ˈset on/upon sb,*** attack: 攻擊某人: *She was set on by a savage dog.* 她被兇犬襲擊。***be ˈset on/upon doing sth,*** be determined to do it: 決心做某事: *My daughter is set on becoming an airline pilot.* 我女兒決心做客機駕駛員。

set out, begin (a journey, venture): 出發;啓程: *They set out at dawn.* 他們在拂曉出發。*He set out with the best intentions.* 他懷着最大的希望出發。***set out to do sth,*** have sth as an aim or intention: 朝某個目標進行;爲了某個目的而努力: *He set out to break the record for the Channel swim/to make his first million in five years.* 他決心打破游過英倫海峽的記錄 (在五年內賺到第一個一百萬)。***set sth out,*** **(a)** declare; make known: 宣佈;發表: *set out one's reasons* (*for sth*). 宣佈(某事的)理由。**(b)** show; put on display: 展示;陳列: *The women set out their chickens and ducks on the market stalls.* 婦女們把雞鴨陳列在市場的攤子上。*He sets out his ideas clearly in this essay.* 他在這篇文章中明確地列出他的觀點。**(c)** plant out: 散栽;移植: *Set the young plants out one foot apart.* 把幼苗每隔一呎栽種一棵。

set sb over sb, put sb in control/command of sb. 使某人控制(指揮)某人。

ˌset ˈto, **(a)** begin doing sth: 開始做某事: *The engineers set to and repaired the bridge.* 工程師們開始修橋。*They were all hungry and at once set to,* began eating. 他們都很餓,立刻狼吞虎嚥地吃起來了。**(b)** (usu with *pl* subject) begin to fight, struggle, quarrel, etc. (通常用複數主詞)開始打鬥、爭執、吵鬧等。Hence, 由此產生, **ˌset-ˈto** *n* struggle; quarrel. 鬥爭;爭吵。

set sth up, **(a)** place sth in position: 設立;建立: *set up a post/statue/memorial.* 設置哨崗(雕像,紀念碑)。**(b)** establish (an institution, business, argument, etc): 建立(機構,商店);提出(辯護): *set up a tribunal.* 設立法庭。*What defence did his counsel set up in the trial?* 在審判時他的律師提出什麼辯護？ Hence, 由此產生, **ˈset-up** *n* (colloq) arrangement of an organization, group of people, etc: (俗)組織;結構: *What's the set-up here?* How's your business, etc organized? 你的商店(等)的組織如何？ **(c)** cause: 造成;促成: *I wonder what has set up this irritation in my throat/this rash on my face?* 我不知道是什麼東西使得我的喉頭發炎(臉部出疹)？ **(d)** utter loudly: 高聲喊出: *set up a yell.* 大聲喊叫。**(e)** make ready for printing: 排版: *set up type/a book.* 排字(排一本書)。***set sb up,*** restore after illness: 使康復: *Her holiday in the country has set her up again.* 在鄉間度假使她恢復了健康。***set (oneself) up as,*** **(a)** go into business as: 從事或經營某種行業;成爲某種行業的人: *He has set (himself) up as a bookseller.* 他已成爲書商。**(b)** have pretensions to being: 自稱爲: *I've never set myself up as a scholar.* 我從未自稱爲學者。***set sb up (as sth),*** get sb started or established, eg by supplying capital: 資助某人創業: *set up one's son in business.* 資助自己的兒子做生意。*His father set him up as a bookseller.* 他的父親資助他成爲書商。***set up house,*** start living in one, eg after being in lodgings. 開始住在自己的房子裡。***set up house with sb/together,*** (of two persons) begin living together. (指兩人)一起生活;同居。***be well set up,*** **(a)** have a body well developed by exercises, etc: 健壯的;健美的: *He has a well set up figure.* 他有健美的身材。*What a well set up young woman!* 多麼健美的女郎啊！ **(b)** be well provided with: 充分供應: *be well set up with clothes/reading matter.* 有充足的衣服(讀物)。

set-square /ˈset skweə(r) ; ˈsɛtskwɛr/ *n* [C] triangular plate of wood, plastic, metal, etc with angles of 90°, 60° and 30° (or 90°, 45°, 45°), used for drawing lines at these angles. 三角板。

sett /set ; sɛt/ *n* = set[1](10).

set·tee /seˈtiː ; sɛˈti/ *n* [C] long, soft seat like a sofa, with sides and back, for two or more persons. 有靠背及扶手之長椅(類似沙發,可坐兩人或更多的人)。

set·ter /ˈsetə(r) ; ˈsɛtɚ/ *n* **1** (breeds of) long-haired dog trained to stand motionless on scenting game. 一種長毛獵狗。➪ set[1](9). **2** (in compounds) person who, thing which, sets (various meanings): (用於複合字中)從事 set (包括各義)之人或物: *a ˈbone-~;* 接骨者; *a ˈtype-~.* 排字工人;排字機。

set·ting /ˈsetɪŋ ; ˈsɛtɪŋ/ *n* [C] **1** framework in which sth is fixed or fastened: 安置或固定東西之框、架等: *the ~ of a jewel;* 鑲嵌珠寶的底座; (by extension) (引伸) surroundings, environment: 背景;環境: *a beautiful natural ~ for a play,* eg the grounds of an old castle. 適於演出戲劇之美麗的天然背景(如一古堡之庭園)。 **2** music composed for a poem, etc. 爲一首詩等所配之音樂。➪ set[2](12). **3** descent (of the sun, moon, etc) below the horizon. (指太陽、月亮等)落下(地平線)。

settle[1] /ˈsetl ; ˈsɛtl̩/ *n* [C] long, wooden seat with a high back and arms, the seat often being the lid of a chest. 高背長靠椅(座板常爲箱蓋)。

settle[2] /ˈsetl ; ˈsɛtl̩/ *vt, vi* (For special uses with *adverbial particles* and *preps,* ➪ 10 below.) (與副詞接語及介詞連用之特殊用法參看下列第10義。) **1** [VP 2C, 6A] make one's home in (permanently, as a colonist); establish colonists in: 殖民;殖民於: *The Dutch ~d in South Africa.* 荷蘭人在南非殖民。*By whom was Canada ~d?* 加拿大是由誰殖民的？ **2** [VP2C] make one's home in; live in (not as a colonist): 安家;定居: *~ in London/in Canada/in the country.* 定居於倫敦(加拿大,鄉下)。 **3** [VP

2A, 3A] ~ ***(on sth)***, come to rest (on); stay for some time (on): 停留;暫時棲息: *The bird ~d on a branch.* 鳥棲止於枝上。*The dust ~d on everything.* 塵土落在每樣東西上。*The cold has ~d on my chest.* 感冒使我胸口難受。**4** [VP6A, 15A] cause (sb) to become used to, or comfortable in, a new position or posture (after a period of restless movement or activity): (經過一段不停的運動或活動後)使適應於或安適於新的位置或姿勢;使安身;使安定;使安息: *The nurse ~d her patient for the night,* made him/her comfortable, gave him/her medicine, etc. 那護士使她的病人安靜過夜。*Then the nurse ~d herself in an armchair in the next room.* 然後那護士自己在隔壁房間的扶手椅上坐下來休息。**5** [VP6A, 2C] make or become calm, untroubled, composed: (使)鎮定;(使)穩定;(使)平靜: *The thunderstorm will perhaps ~ the weather.* 大雷雨可能使天氣穩定下來。*We want a period of ~d weather for the harvest.* 我們收穫時需要一段穩定的天氣。*Wait until the excitement has ~d.* 等興奮的情緒平靜下來(再說或做某事)。*Things are settling into shape,* becoming orderly, normal. 事情逐漸上軌道了。*Have a brandy—it will ~ your nerves.* 喝一點白蘭地吧——它會使你鎮靜下來。**6** [VP6A, 7A, 8, 10] make an agreement about; decide; determine: 了結;決定: *That ~s the matter.* 事情就這樣決定了。*It's time you ~d the dispute/argument.* 該是你們結束爭論的時候了。*Nothing is ~d yet.* 諸事未定。*You ought to ~ your affairs* (eg by making your will) *before you go into hospital for that lung operation.* 在你住院接受肺部手術以前,你應該把諸事料理妥當(寫遺囑等)。*The lawsuit was ~d amicably/out of court/between the parties,* a decision was reached by the parties themselves (and their lawyers) instead of by the court. 該訴訟案已在庭外和解。*What have you ~d to do about it?* 你決定怎樣處理該事? *Have they ~d where to go/where they'll spend their holiday?* 他們已決定去什麼地方嗎(去什麼地方度假嗎)? **7** [VP6A, 2A, C] pay: 付;償付: ~ *a bill.* 付帳。*Will you ~ for all of us,* pay what is owing for all of us, eg at a restaurant? 你會爲我們大家付帳嗎(如在餐館)? **8** [VP6A, 2A] (of dust, etc in the air, particles of solid substances in a liquid, etc) (cause to) sink; (of a liquid) become clear as solid particles sink. (指空氣中之塵埃等,液體中之顆粒)(使)沉澱;(使)降落;(指液體)澄清: *We need a shower to ~ the dust.* 我們需要陣雨來清除塵埃。*Stir the coffee to ~ the grounds.* 攪動咖啡使其澄清。*The grounds ~d and the coffee was clear.* 渣滓沉澱,咖啡變清。**9** [VP2A, C] (of the ground, the foundation of a building, etc) sink gradually to a lower level: (指地面,地基等)下陷: *The road-bed ~d.* 路基下陷了。*The ship was settling down by the stern,* tending to sink. 船正由尾部逐漸下沉。**10** [VP2C, 14, 15B, 2A] (special uses with *adverbial particles* and *preps*): (與副詞接語及介詞連用之特殊用法):

settle down, sit or lie comfortably (after a period of movement or activity): (在活動過後)安適地坐下或躺下: *He ~d down in his armchair to read a new novel.* 他安閒地坐在扶手椅上閱讀一本新的小說。~ ***(sb) down,*** make or become calm and peaceful: (使)鎮定;(使)平靜: *Wait until the children have ~d down before you start your lesson.* 等孩子們安靜下來你再開始上課。*The chairman tried to ~ the audience down,* get them to stop talking, etc. 主席設法使聽衆安靜。~ ***(down) to sth,*** overcome distractions, etc and give one's attention to one's work: 避免分心;專心工作: *It's terrible—I can't ~ (down) to anything today,* am too restless to do my work, etc. 眞糟糕——我今天無法專心做任何事。~ ***down (to sth),*** become established (in a new way of life, new work, etc): 立身;安頓(於新的生活方式,新行業等): ~ *down well in a new career/job.* 在新的事業(工作)中安頓下來。~ ***down to married life; marry and ~ down,*** live the regular routine life said to be typical of married persons. 過規律的婚姻生活;結婚而安定下來。

settle for sth, accept, although not altogether satisfactory: 勉强接受(條件而解決某事): *I had hoped to get £1000 for my old car but had to ~ for £650.* 我原希望我的舊車子能賣一千鎊,結果只賣了六百五十鎊。

settle (sb) in, (help sb to) move into a new house, flat, job, etc and put things in order: (幫某人)遷入新居,從事新的工作: *We haven't ~d in yet.* 我們尚未遷入新居。*You must come and see our new house when we're/we've ~d in.* 我們遷入新居後,你務必要來看我們的新房子。

settle sth on/upon sb, (legal) give sb (property, etc) for use during his/her lifetime: (法律)授與(某人財產): ~ *part of one's estate on one's son;* 把部分財產授給兒子; ~ *an annuity on a nephew.* 贈予姪兒年金。⇨ settlement(2). ~ ***on/upon sth,*** decide to take; choose: 選定;決定;選擇: *Which of the recordings have you ~d on?* 你已選定那一段錄音? *We must ~ on a place to meet.* 我們須選定一個見面的地點。

settle (up) (with sb), pay what one owes to sb: 清償: *I shall ~ (up) with you at the end of the month.* 我將在月底和你清帳。*I've already settled up with the waiter,* paid for our meal. 我已向侍應生付清飯錢。*Now to ~ with you!* Now I'll deal with you (according to context, pay, fight with you, get rid of you, etc). 現在跟你算帳!(可指我將付你錢,和你打架或將你除掉等,視上下文而定)。ˌ***have an acˈcount to ~ with sb,*** (colloq) have some unpleasant business, a quarrel, etc to discuss. (俗)與某人有不歡之事,爭吵等待解決;跟某人算帳。

settled /ˈsetld; ˈsɛtḷd/ *adj* **1** fixed; unchanging; permanent: 固定的;不變的;永久的: ~ *weather;* 穩定的天氣; *a man of ~ convictions;* 信念堅定之人; ~ *melancholy.* 深深的憂鬱。**2** (written on a paid bill) payment is acknowledged. (寫於帳單上)付訖;結訖。

settle·ment /ˈsetlmənt; ˈsɛtḷmənt/ *n* **1** [U] the act of settling (a dispute, debt, etc); [C] instance of this: 解決;和解;清償;其實例: *The terms of ~ seem just.* 和解的條件似乎還公道。*We hope for a lasting ~ of all these troubles.* 我們希望這些糾紛能獲得永久的解決。*The strikers have reached a ~ with the employers.* 罷工者與雇主已達成協議。*I enclose a cheque in ~ of your account.* 我寄上支票一張以清償你的帳目。**2** [C] (statement of) property settled(10) on sb: 財產授與文書;所授與的財產: *a ˈmarriage ~,* one made by a man in favour of his wife. 授與妻子的財產。**3** [U] process of settling people in a colony; [C] new colony; group of colonists: 殖民;新殖民地;殖民團體;殖民人羣: *empty lands awaiting ~;* 尙待殖民的空曠之地; *Dutch and English ~s in North America;* 荷蘭人和英國人在北美洲的殖民地; *penal ~s in Australia.* 澳洲的罪犯殖民地。**4** [C] group of persons engaged in social welfare work, eg in a slum district. 從事社會福利工作的團體(如在貧民區等處)。

set·tler /ˈsetlə(r); ˈsɛtlɚ/ *n* colonist; person who has come to live in a newly developing country: 殖民者;僑居新興國家者: *Welsh ~s in Argentina.* 在阿根廷的威爾斯僑民。

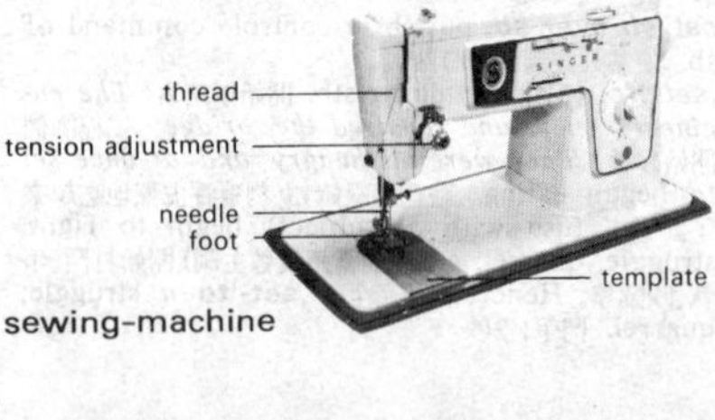

a sewing-machine

seven /ˈsevn; ˈsɛvən/ *n, adj* the number 7. 七(的); 七個(的)。 ⇨ App 4. 參看附錄四。 **ˈ~·fold** /-fəuld; -fold/ *adj, adv* ~ times as much or as many; ~ times as great. 七倍的(地)。 **sev·enth** /ˈsevnθ; ˈsɛvənθ/ *n, adj* 第七 (的) ***in the/one's ~th heaven,*** extremely happy. 極端快樂的。 **the S~th Day,** Saturday, the Sabbath of the Jews. 一週的第七天(即星期六,爲猶太人之安息日)。 **sev·enth·ly** *adv* in the 7th place. 第七。 **~·teen** /ˌsevnˈtiːn; ˌsɛvənˈtin/ *n, adj* the number 17. 十七(的);十七個(的)。**~·teenth** /ˌsevnˈtiːnθ; ˌsɛvənˈtinθ/ *n, adj* 17th; next after 16, one of ~teen parts. 第十七(的);十七分之一(的)。 **~ty** /ˈsevntɪ; ˈsɛvəntɪ/ *n, adj* the number 70. 七十(的);七十個(的)。 **the ~ties** *n pl* 70-79. 七十至七十九。 **~·ti·eth** /ˈsevntɪəθ; ˈsɛvəntɪɪθ/ *n, adj*

sever /ˈsevə(r); ˈsɛvɚ/ *vt, vi* **1** [VP6A, 15A] cut: 切斷;割開: ~ *a rope;* 割斷繩子; ~ *the head of a sheep from the body;* 割下羊頭; (fig) break off: (喻)斷絕;終止: ~ *one's connections with sb.* 與某人斷絕關係。 **2** [VP2A] break: 分裂;斷: *The rope ~ed under the strain.* 繩子拉得太緊,綳斷了。 **~·ance** /ˈsevərəns; ˈsɛvərəns/ *n* [U] severing or being ~ed: 切斷;斷絕;分裂;斷: *the severance of diplomatic relations/of communications.* 外交關係(交通)的斷絕。

sev·eral /ˈsevrəl; ˈsɛvərəl/ *adj* **1** three or more; some but not many: 三個或更多的;幾個的;數個的: *You will need ~ more.* 你還需要幾個。 *I've read it ~ times.* 我已經讀過好幾遍了。 **2** (formal) (with *pl nn* only) separate; individual: (正式用語)(僅與複數名詞連用)各自的;個別的: *They went their ~ ways,* Each went his own way. 他們各走各的路。□ *pron* a few; some: 幾個;數個: *S~ of us decided to walk home.* 我們之中有幾個人決定步行回家。 **~ly** /ˈsevrəlɪ; ˈsɛvərəlɪ/ *adv* separately. 各自地;個別地。

se·vere /sɪˈvɪə(r); səˈvɪr/ *adj* **1** stern; strict: 嚴厲的;嚴格的: ~ *looks;* 嚴厲的面容; *be ~ with one's children;* 對孩子嚴厲; *be too ~ on a pupil.* 對學生太嚴格。 **2** (of the weather, attacks of disease, etc) rigorous; violent: (指天氣,疾病之發作等)嚴重的;劇烈的: *a ~ storm;* 强烈的暴風雨; ~ *pain;* 劇痛; *a ~ attack of toothache.* 牙痛的劇烈發作。 **3** making great demands on skill, ability, patience and other qualities: 非常需要技術、能力、耐心和其他條件的;艱難的;激烈的: ~ *competition.* 激烈的競爭。 *The pace was too ~ to be kept up for long.* 速度太快,無法持久。 **4** (of style, etc) simple; without ornament. (指文體等)簡樸的;不事修飾的。 **~·ly** *adv* **se·ver·ity** /sɪˈverətɪ; səˈvɛrətɪ/ *n* (*pl* -ties) **1** [U] quality of being ~: 嚴厲;嚴格;劇烈;艱難;激烈: *punish sb with severity;* 嚴厲地責罰某人; *acts of severity;* 激烈的行爲; *the severity* (= extreme cold) *of the winter in Canada.* 加拿大冬天的嚴寒。 **2** (*pl*) ~ treatment or experiences: (複)嚴苛的待遇或艱苦的經驗: *the severities of the winter campaign.* 冬令出征的艱苦。

sew /səu; so/ *vt, vi* (*pt* sewed, *pp* sewn /səun; son/ or sewed) [VP6A, 15B, 2A, B, C] work with a needle and thread; fasten with stitches; make (a garment) by stitching: 縫紉;縫合;縫(衣服): *sew a button on;* 釘扣子; *sew a dress.* 縫製衣服。 *The garment is ˌhand-ˈsewn/sewn by hand.* 這件衣服是手縫的。 *She has been sewing all evening.* 她整個晚上都在縫紉。 ***sew sth up,*** **(a)** join (at the edges) with stitches: 縫攏;縫接: *The corpse was sewn up in a sack and thrown into the river.* 屍體被裝在布袋中縫好後拋入河裡。 **(b)** (colloq) arrange; complete: (俗)安排;完成: *All the details of the project are sewn up.* 這計畫的所有細節均有妥善安排。 *The deal is sewn up.* 交易談妥了。 **sewer** /ˈsəuə(r); ˈsoɚ/ *n* **sew·ing** *n* [U] work (clothes, etc) being sewn. 縫製物(衣服等)。 **ˈsewing-machine** *n* machine for sewing. 縫紉機。

sew·age /ˈsjuːɪdʒ *US:* suː-; ˈsjuɪdʒ/ *n* [U] foul liquid material, waste organic matter, etc carried off in sewers; the disposal of ~. (下水道中之)污水;污物;污水之處理。 **ˈ~-farm/works** *nn* place where ~ is treated and disposed of. 污水處理場(廠)。

sewer¹ /ˈsjuːə(r) *US:* suː-; ˈsjuɚ/ *n* [C] underground channel (pipeline, or construction of brick, concrete, etc) to carry off sewage and rain water to centres (sewage-farms) for treatment, or to a natural waterway for disposal. 下水道;陰溝(地下之管路或磚、混凝土等砌成的水道,用以將污水及雨水送至污水處理場處理或排至河川)。 **ˈ~-gas** *n* bad-smelling gas formed in ~s. 下水道發出的臭氣。 **ˈ~-rat** *n* brown rat commonly found in ~s. (常見於陰溝的)褐色老鼠。 **~·age** /-ɪdʒ; -ɪdʒ/ *n* system of ~s; drains. 污水排除系統;下水道系統。

sewer² /ˈsəuə(r); ˈsoɚ/ *n* ⇨ sew.

sewn /səun; son/ *pp* of sew.

sex /seks; sɛks/ *n* **1** being male or female: 性;性別: *What is its sex?* 它的性別是什麼? *Help them all, without distinction of race, age or sex.* 幫助他們全體,不分種族、年齡或性別。 **2** males or females as a group. (集合用法)男;女。 **3** [U] differences between males and females; consciousness of these differences: 兩性差別;兩性差別意識: *ˈsex antagonisms.* 異性間的敵對。 **4** [U] the activities surrounding, centring on and leading to coitus: 色情: *a film/novel with lots of sex in it;* 充滿色情的電影(小說); *the ˈsex instinct;* 性的本能; *ˈsex appeal,* sexual attractiveness. 性感。 **5** [U] sexual intercourse: 性交: *have sex with sb.* 與某人性交。□ *vt* [VP6A] determine the sex of. 決定…之性別。 **sexed** *part adj* having a (specified) sexual nature: 有某種性慾的: *highly/weakly ~ed.* 性慾很强(很弱)的。 **sex·less** *adj* neither male nor female; displaying neither masculine nor feminine characteristics. 無性的;無性別的;不具性特徵的。 **ˈsex-starved** *adj* (colloq) deprived of sexual gratification. (俗)性饑渴的;性得不到滿足的。 **sexy** *adj* (-ier, -iest) (colloq) of or about sex; sexually attractive. (俗)性的;有關性的;性感的。

sexa·gen·ar·ian /ˌseksədʒɪˈneərɪən; ˌsɛksədʒəˈnɛrɪən/ *n, adj* (person) between 59 and 70 years of age. 五十九歲至七十歲間的(人)。

sex·ism /ˈseksɪzəm; ˈsɛksɪzəm/ *n* [U] unfair or unreasonable discrimination between the sexes; unreasonable maintaining of traditional sexual roles (eg that men are strong and women are weak). 性別歧視;男性主義。 **sex·ist** /ˈseksɪst; ˈsɛksɪst/ *adj* of ~: 性別歧視的;男性主義的: *sexist attitudes;* 性別歧視的態度; ~ *words,* eg *baby, bird, chick, doll,* used to mean a girl or woman. 用以指女孩或女人的字(如 baby, bird, chick, doll 等)。□ *n* person who displays or approves of ~. 性別歧視者;男性主義者。 ⇨ *male chauvinist* at chauvinism.

using a sextant

sex·tant /ˈsekstənt; ˈsɛkstənt/ *n* instrument used for measuring the altitude of the sun, etc (in order to determine a ship's position, etc). 六分儀(用以測量太陽等之高度以決定船的位置等的儀器)。

sex·tet, sex·tette /seksˈtet; sɛksˈtɛt/ *n* [C] (piece of music for) six voices, instruments or players in combination. 六重唱(曲);六重奏(曲)。

sex·ton /ˈsekstən ; ˈsɛkstən/ *n* man who takes care of a church buildings, digs graves in the churchyard, rings the church bell, etc. 教堂司事(管理教堂,挖掘墓地,敲鐘等)。

sex·ual /ˈsekʃʊəl ; ˈsɛkʃʊəl/ *adj* of sex or the sexes: 性的;兩性的: *~ intercourse* = coitus. 性交。 **~·ity** /ˌsekʃʊˈælətɪ ; ˌsɛkʃʊˈælətɪ/ *n* [U] ~ nature or characteristics. 性的特徵;性別。

sh (also **ssh, shh**) /ʃ ; ʃ/ *int* be quiet! be silent! 噓!別作聲!別講話!

shabby /ˈʃæbɪ ; ˈʃæbɪ/ *adj* (-ier, -iest) **1** in bad repair or condition; much worn; poorly dressed: 破舊的;襤褸的;衣著寒酸的: *wearing a ~ overcoat.* 穿着破舊的大衣。*You look rather ~ in those clothes.* 你的衣著使你顯得有點寒酸。ˌ**~-genˈteel** *adj* having evidence of former gentility but now ~; trying to keep up appearances. 從前很闊而現在窮酸的;窮要面子的。 **2** (of behaviour) mean; unfair: (指行爲)卑鄙的;不正當的: *a ~ excuse;* 不正當的藉口; *play a ~ trick on sb.* 對某人耍卑鄙的手段。 **shab·bily** /ˈʃæbɪlɪ ; ˈʃæbḷɪ/ *adv* **shab·bi·ness** *n*

shack /ʃæk ; ʃæk/ *n* [C] small, roughly built shed, hut or house (usu of wood). 簡陋之小屋(通常爲木材架成)。□ *vi* [VP2C] ***~ up (with sb/together),*** (sl) live together. (俚)(與某人)同居。

shackle /ˈʃækl ; ˈʃækḷ/ *n* [C] one of a pair of iron rings joined by a chain for fastening a prisoner's wrists or ankles; (*pl*) fetters; (fig) sth that prevents freedom of action: (一隻)手銬;脚鐐;(複)(整副的)鐐銬;(喻)束縛物;羈絆物: *the ~s of convention.* 習俗的桎梏。 □ *vt* [VP6A] put ~s on; prevent from acting freely. 加鐐銬於;束縛;羈絆。

shad /ʃæd ; ʃæd/ *n* (*pl* unchanged) large edible fish of the N Atlantic coast of N America. (複數不變)鰣魚(北美北大西洋海岸所產之大食用魚)。

shad·dock /ˈʃædək ; ˈʃædək/ *n* (tropical tree with a) large edible fruit related to the grapefruit; pomelo. 柚子(樹);朱欒(樹)。

shade /ʃeɪd ; ʃed/ *n* **1** [U] (with *adj, v* and *indef art*) comparative darkness caused by the cutting off of direct rays of light; (fig) comparative obscurity: 蔭;蔭涼;(喻)幽暗;陰暗: *a temperature of 35°C in the ~.* 在蔭涼處溫度爲攝氏三十五度。 *Keep in the ~; it's cooler.* 你就待在蔭涼處吧;那兒比較涼爽。*The trees give a pleasant ~.* 樹木供給舒暢的蔭涼。***put sb/sth in/into the ~,*** cause to appear small, unimportant, etc, by contrast: 使(某人或某物)黯然無光;使相形見絀: *You are so clever and brilliant that my poor efforts are put into the ~.* 你是如此的聰明而且才華橫溢, 以致我的小小成就顯得黯然無光。 ˈ**~-tree** *n* (esp US) tree planted to give ~. (尤美)遮蔭之樹。 **2** [U] darker part(s) of a picture, etc; reproduction of the darker part of a picture: (圖畫等之)陰暗部分;陰影部分;暗影: *There is not enough light and ~ in your drawing.* 你的圖畫中明暗不够顯明。 **3** [C] degree or depth of colour: 色度;顏色之深淺: *dress materials in several ~s of blue.* 數種不同深淺之藍色的衣料。 **4** [C] degree of difference: 差異的程度;細微的差別: *a word with many ~s of meaning.* 其意義有許多差度的一個字。*She is a ~ better today.* 她今天好了一些。 **5** sth that shuts out light or lessens its brilliance: 遮光物: *an ˈeye-~;* 遮眼物;眼罩; *a ˈlamp-~;* 燈罩; *a ˈwindow-~.* 窗簾。⇨ blind[3]. (*pl*) (US colloq) sunglasses. (複) (美俗)太陽眼鏡。 **6** (*pl; liter*) darkness: (複;文)黑暗: *the ~s of evening.* 夜晚之黑暗。 **7** [C] unreal or unsubstantial thing; soul after death. 不實在之物;無實質之物;死後之靈魂。**the ~s,** the abode of spirits; the Greek underworld. 亡魂之居所;(希臘神話之)陰間; 冥府。 □ *vt, vi* **1** [VP6A, 15A] keep direct rays of light from: 遮蔽: *He ~d his eyes with his hands.* 他用手遮眼睛。 **2** [VP6A] screen (a light, lamp, etc) to reduce brightness. 遮(光,燈等)。 **3** [VP6A] darken with parallel pencil lines, etc (parts of a drawing, etc), to give the appearance of light and ~. 繪(圖畫等)之陰影;加線條等於(圖畫等)。 **4** [VP2C] change by degrees: 漸變: *scarlet shading off into pink;* 漸變爲淡紅之深紅; *a colour that ~s from blue into green.* 由藍漸變爲綠的顏色。**shad·ing** *n* **1** [U] use of black, etc to give light and shade to a drawing. (繪畫之)描影法;皴法。 **2** [C] slight difference or variation. 細微的差別。

shadow /ˈʃædəʊ ; ˈʃædo/ *n* **1** [C] area of shade, dark shape, thrown on the ground, a wall, floor, etc by sth which cuts off the direct rays of light: 影;陰影: *The earth's ~ sometimes falls on the moon.* 地球的陰影有時投落在月球上面。***be afraid of one's own ~,*** be very timid. 怕自己的影子(非常膽怯)。***Coming events cast their ~s before them,*** give warning of their coming. 未來的事件先有預兆發生。**2** [U] area of shade of indefinite shape or extent: 大小或形狀不定的陰影: *Her face was in deep ~.* 她的臉佈滿陰影。 **3** [C] sth unsubstantial or unreal: 無實質之物;不實在之物;幽靈;鬼: *catch at ~s, run after a ~,* try to get hold of sth unreal. 捕捉不實在之物,追逐不實在之物。*He is only the ~ of his former self,* is very thin and weak. 他瘦得不成樣子。 ***worn to a ~,*** (of a person) weakened, exhausted. (指人)虛弱得不成人形。 ˈ**~-boxing,** sparring against an imaginary opponent (for practice). 與假想對手鬥拳;太極拳。 **4** (*pl*) partial darkness: (複)部分黑暗;半暗: *the ~s of evening.* 暮色。 **5** [C] dark patch or area: 黑斑;烏黑之處: *have ~s under/round the eyes,* such areas thought to be caused by lack of sleep, illness, etc. 有黑眼圈(爲缺乏睡眠,疾病等所造成)。 **6** (*sing* only) slightest trace: (僅用單數)微痕: *without/beyond a ~ of (a) doubt.* 無絲毫的懷疑。 **7** person's constant attendant or companion. 形影相隨的人。 ~ **cabinet,** (GB) group formed from the leaders of the Parliamentary Opposition, ie those who might form a new cabinet if there is a change of government after a general election. (英)影子內閣(由國會中反對黨的領袖們所組成,一旦該黨大選獲勝,即可組成新閣)。□ *vt* [VP6A] **1** darken; overspread with ~. 使暗;遮蔽;覆以陰影。 **2** keep a secret watch on; follow closely and watch all the movements of: 秘密尾隨;跟梢: *The suspected spy was ~ed by detectives.* 那個有間諜嫌疑的人被偵探們秘密跟蹤。 **shad·owy** *adj* **1** having ~ or shade; shady(1): 有陰影的;陰涼的: *cool, ~y woods.* 蔭涼的樹林。 **2** like a ~; indistinct: 似陰影的;模糊的: *a ~y outline.* 模糊的輪廓。

shady /ˈʃeɪdɪ ; ˈʃedɪ/ *adj* (-ier, -iest) **1** giving shade from sunlight; situated in shade: 遮蔭的;在蔭處的: *the ~ side of the street.* 街道背陽的一邊。 **2** of doubtful honesty: 可疑的;有問題的;靠不住的: *a ~ transaction/financier;* 可疑的交易(靠不住的資本家); *a ~-looking customer,* (colloq) person who appears to be a rogue. (俗)形跡可疑的傢伙。 *Politics has its ~ side.* 政治有其黑暗面。

shaft /ʃɑːft *US:* ʃæft ; ʃæft/ *n* [C] **1** (long, slender stem of an) arrow or spear: 箭(桿);矛(柄): (fig) (喻) *~s of envy/ridicule,* expressions of envy, etc. 嫉妒(揶揄)之表情。**2** long handle of an axe or other tool. 斧柄;其他器具之長柄。**3** one of the pair of bars (wooden poles) between which a horse is harnessed to pull a cart, etc. 車轅;車杠。 **4** main part of a column (between the base and the capital). 柱幹;柱身(柱基與柱頭之間的部分)。⇨ the illus at column. 參看 column 之插圖。**5** long, narrow space, usu vertical, eg for descending into a coalmine, for a lift in a building, or for ventilation. 狹長而通常垂直之空間(如煤礦之豎坑,建築物內之升降機井或通風井)。 **6** bar or rod joining parts of a machine, or transmitting power. 機械之軸(用以連接機器之各部分,或用以傳

迸動力者)。 **7** ray (of light); bolt (of lightning). 光線;(閃電之)閃光。

shag /ʃæg ; ʃæg/ *n* [U] coarse kind of cut tobacco. 粗煙絲。

shagged /ʃægd ; ʃægd/ *pred adj* ~ ***(out)***, (GB sl) very tired. (英俚)筋疲力盡。

shaggy /ˈʃægɪ ; ˈʃægɪ/ *adj* (-ier, -iest) **1** (of hair) rough, coarse and untidy. (指毛髮)粗濃雜亂的。 **2** covered with rough, coarse hair: 覆有粗濃之毛髮的: ~ *eyebrows;* 粗眉; *a* ~ *dog.* 粗毛犬。 ˌ**~-ˈdog story,** long joke that is funny because it is so boring and its punch-line is so weak. 枯燥平淡的冗長笑話。 **shag·gily** /-ɪlɪ ; -ɪlɪ/ *adv* **shag·gi·ness** *n*

shah /ʃɑː ; ʃɑ/ *n* (title of a) former ruler of Iran. (昔時)伊朗國王(之稱號)。

shake¹ /ʃeɪk ; ʃek/ *vt, vi* (*pt* shook /ʃʊk ; ʃuk/, *pp* shaken /ˈʃeɪkən ; ˈʃekən/) **1** [VP6A, 15A, B, 2A, C] (cause to) move from side to side, up and down etc: (使)搖動;搖撼;揮動;震動;抖動: ~ *a rug;* 抖動地毯; ~ *a man by the shoulder;* 搖動某人的肩膀; ~ *the dice* (in a box, etc before throwing them on to a table); (在擲出之前)搖動盒子等中的骰子; ~ *one's head* (*at sb*), to indicate 'No', or doubt, disapproval, etc; (對某人)搖頭(表示'不'或懷疑、不贊同等); ~ *one's finger at sb,* to indicate disapproval or as a warning; 以食指指點着某人(表示不贊同或警告); ~ *one's fist at sb,* to show defiance. 對某人揮拳(表示挑戰)。*His sides were shaking with laughter.* 他捧腹大笑。*He was shaking with cold.* 他冷得打顫。*He was shaking in his shoes,* trembling with fear. 他嚇得直發抖。*The earth shook under us,* eg in an earthquake. 地在我們脚下震動。~ ***hands (with sb),*** ⇨ hand¹(1). **2** [VP6A] shock; trouble; weaken: 使震驚;動搖;減弱: ~ *sb's faith/courage.* 動搖某人的信心(勇氣)。*They were badly* ~*n by the news.* 那消息令他們大爲震驚。*The firm's credit has been badly* ~*n.* 公司的信譽已大大受損。 **3** [VP2A, C] (of sb's voice) tremble; become weak or faltering: (指人的聲音)顫抖;變弱或結結巴巴:*Her voice shook with emotion.* 她的聲音因激動而顫抖。 **shak·ing** *n* = shake: *give sth a good shaking,* shake it well; 使勁地搖動某物; *get a shaking,* be ~n. 被搖動;受驚。 **shaker** *n* one who, that which, ~s; container in which or from which sth is ~n: 搖動者;搖盪器;震盪器: *a* ˈ*cocktail-*~*r;* 鷄尾酒調酒器; *a* ˈ*flour-*~*r.* 麵粉攪拌器; **4** [VP 14, 15B] (special uses with *adverbial particles* and *preps*): (與副詞接語及介詞連用之特殊用法):

shake down, (colloq) (俗) **(a)** get into harmony, become adjusted to new conditions: 和諧相處;能適應新的狀況: *The new staff are shaking down well.* 新來人員適應良好。**(b)** lie down for sleep: 躺下睡覺: ~ *down on the beach/floor.* 躺在海灘上(地板上)睡覺。~ ***sb down,*** (US) get money from him by threats, violence, etc. (美)以威脅、暴力等索取金錢;敲詐;勒索。~ ***sb/sth down,*** (US) search him/it thoroughly. (美)徹底搜查。 ~ ***sth down,*** give it a ~-down(d). 試航;試飛。 ˈ**~-down** *n* (colloq) (俗) **(a)** temporary or makeshift bed. 臨時搭的床鋪;地鋪。**(b)** (US) extortion of money. (美)敲詐;勒索。**(c)** (US) thorough search. (美)徹底搜查。**(d)** final test (eg of a new ship, aircraft): (新船,新飛機等的)試航;試飛: *a* ~*-down voyage/flight.* 試航(試飛)。

shake sth from/out of sth, get from/out of by shaking: 把…自…中搖出(下): ~ *a leaf from a tree/out of one's shoe.* 從樹上搖下(從鞋裡抖出)一片葉子。

shake sb off, free oneself from: 擺脫;避開: *The thief ran fast and soon shook off his pursuers.* 那賊跑得很快,很快就把追逐者擺脫了。~ ***sth off,*** get rid of: 除去: ~ *off a cold/a fit of depression.* 除去風寒(沮喪)。

shake out, (mil) spread; disperse: (軍)散開: *The troops were ordered to* ~ *out when crossing open country.* 軍隊在穿越曠野時奉命散開。 ~ ***sth out,*** spread so as to be out by shaking: 抖開;展開;攤開: ~ *out a sail/tablecloth.* 揚帆(鋪桌布)。 ˈ**~-out** *n* process or act of making workers redundant: 使勞工過剩的過程或行動;汰工: *a new* ~*-out in the shipbuilding industry.* 造船業再度汰工。

shake sth up, **(a)** mix well by shaking: 搖動使均勻: ~ *up a bottle of medicine.* 搖勻一瓶藥。**(b)** restore sth to shape by shaking: 抖動使恢復原狀: ~ *up a cushion.* 抖鬆坐墊。~ ***sb up,*** restore from apathy or lethargy: 使振作;激勵;鞭策(使某人脫離淡漠、倦怠而無生氣的狀態): *Some of these managers need shaking up—they're asleep on the job.* 這些經理中有些人需要鞭策——他們在工作時睡着了。Hence, 由此產生, ˈ**~-up** *n*: *We need a good* ~*-up in our firm—the management are completely out of touch with the facts of modern life.* 我們的公司需要大事整頓——管理方面與現代生活實況完全脫了節。

shake² /ʃeɪk ; ʃek/ *n* [C] **1** shaking or being shaken: 搖動;震驚;顫抖: *a* ~ *of the head,* to indicate 'No'; 搖頭(以表示不同意); *give sth a good* ~. 猛搖某物。 **2** (colloq) moment: (俗)片刻: *in two* ~*s;* 一會兒; *in half a* ~, almost at once. 幾乎立刻地。 **3** (*pl*) (複) ***no great*** ~***s,*** (sl) not very good or efficient. (俚)平凡之物。 **4** ˈ**egg-~,** ˈ**milk-~,** etc, glass of milk and egg or milk alone, flavoured and shaken up. 蛋和牛奶之飲料(加香料攪勻);泡沫奶。

Shake·spear·ian /ʃeɪkˈspɪərɪən ; ʃekˈspɪrɪən/ *adj* (in the style) of Shakespeare. 莎士比亞的;莎士比亞風格的。⇨ App 8. 參看附錄八。

shaky /ˈʃeɪkɪ ; ˈʃekɪ/ *adj* (-ier, -iest) **1** (of a person, his movements, etc) weak; unsteady: (指人,其動作等)虛弱的;不穩的;顫抖的: ~ *hands;* 顫抖的手; *speak in a* ~ *voice;* 以顫抖的聲音說; *be* ~ *on one's legs;* 兩腿站不穩; *feel very* ~. 感到非常虛弱。 **2** unsafe; unreliable: 不安全的;不可靠的: *a* ~ *table.* 搖晃的桌子。*My French is rather* ~. 我的法文不甚流利。 **shak·ily** /-ɪlɪ ; -ɪlɪ/ *adv* **shaki·ness** *n*

shale /ʃeɪl ; ʃel/ *n* [U] soft rock that splits easily into layers. 頁岩;泥板岩(易於裂成板片的軟岩石)。ˈ**~-oil** *n* oil obtained from bituminous ~. 頁岩油(由瀝青質頁岩所提煉之油)。

shall /*weak form* ʃl ; ʃl; *strong form* ʃæl ; ʃæl/ *anom fin* (*shall not* is often shortened to shan't /ʃɑːnt *US:* ʃænt ; ʃænt/; with *thou* the old form shalt /ʃælt ; ˈʃælt/ occurred; *pt* form should /ʃʊd ; ˈʃud, *weak form* ʃəd ; ʃəd/; *should not* is often shortened to shouldn't /ˈʃʊdnt ; ˈʃudn̩t/) (shall not 常簡略爲 shan't; 與 thou 連用時,則用古體 shalt; 過去式作should; should not 常簡略爲 shouldn't) **1** (used as an *aux v* to express the future tense, used with the first person, affirm and interr, and second person, interr only. Note that *will* is often used for *shall* in colloq style. *I'll* and *We'll* are used for *I/We shall.*): (用作助動詞以表示未來時,用於第一人稱之肯定式及疑問式,及第二人稱之疑問式。在口語體中, will 常用來代替 shall): *We* ~ *arrive tomorrow.* 我們將於明日到達。*S*~ *we be back in time?* 我們將及時回來嗎? *He said I was not to go, but I certainly* ~. 他說我不會去,但我一定前往。(The use of *should* in place of ~ indicates either future in the past, or a conditional statement, with an *if*-clause expressed or understood): (以 should 代替 shall 時,或表示過去未來時態,或用於條件敍述句中,其條件子句或寫出或省略): *I told him that I should see him the next day.* 我對他說過我將於翌日去看他。*I should have bought it if I had had enough money.* 如果我有足够的錢,我早已買下它了。 **2** (used with the second and third persons to form a future or conditional statement expressing the speaker's will or intention; with stress on ~, *should,* this expresses obligation or compulsion; without special stress on ~, *should,* it expresses a promise or a threat):(用於第二及第三人稱以構成表示說話者之意志或意願的未來

式或條件式; shall, should 重讀時,表示義務或强制; shall, should 不重讀時,表示允諾或威脅): *You say you will not do it, but I say you ~ do it.* 你說你不做(它),但我說你必須做。*He says he won't go, but I say he ~.* 他說他不去,但我說他必須去。*You ~ not catch me so easily next time.* 你下次不會那樣容易抓到我了。*If you work well, you ~ have higher wages.* 如果你工作良好,你可得較高的工資。 **3** (used with all persons to form statements or questions expressing the ideas of duty, command, obligation, conditional duty, and (in the *neg*) prohibition): (用於所有人稱以構成敍述句或疑問句,表示責任、命令、義務、假定的責任及(否定式中)禁止等觀念): *S~ I* (= Do you want me to) *open the window?* 要不要我把窗子打開呀? *S~ the boy* (= Do you want the boy to) *wait?* 要讓那個男孩子等嗎? (Note that *Will I/he* is not used here, but that '*Would you like us/him to*', is the usu equivalent.) (此處不用 Will I (he), 但通常可用 Would you like us (him) to 代替。) *I asked the man whether the boy should wait.* 我問那人是否要那個男孩子等待。*You shan't have it; it's mine!* 你不可拿它;那是我的! *You should* (= ought to) *have been more careful.* 你不應該如此粗心大意。*He should't* (= oughtn't to) *do things like that.* 他不該做那種事。 **4** (used with all persons in clauses expressing purpose, equivalent to *may* or *might*, thus forming a subjunctive equivalent): (與所有人稱合用,用於表示目的的子句中,相當於 may 或 might, 而構成相當於假設語氣之說法): *I lent him the book so that he should study the subject.* 我借給他那本書,使他可以研究該問題。 **5** (used with all persons as a subjunctive equivalent): (與所有人稱合用,用作假設語氣之同等語): *I'm anxious that it ~/should be done at once.* 我急欲使這事立即做好。*It is surprising that he should be so foolish.* 他竟是那麼愚笨,實在令人驚訝。 **6** (in reported speech) ~, *should* are used when reporting the first person to other persons (eg *He said: 'I ~ do it'—he said he should do it,* but *will, would* are now commoner), or when reporting from other persons to the first person (eg *He said to me: 'You will succeed'—he told me that I should succeed*). (在間接叙述中) shall, should 用於將第一人稱引述爲其他人稱(如 He said: 'I ~ do it'—he said he should do it, 但目前 will, would 比較通用),或將其他人稱引述爲第一人稱(如 He said to me: 'You will succeed'—he told me that I should succeed)。 **7** (*should* is used after *how, why,* and (occasionally) other interrogative words): (should 用於 how, why, 及 (有時) 其他疑問詞的後面): *How should I know?* 我怎麼知道? *Why should you/he think that?* 你(他)爲什麼那麼想? **8** (*should* is used to express probability or expectation): (should 用於表示可能或期望): *They should be there by now, I think,* ie I expect they are there; they are probably there. 我想他們現在可能已經到那裏了。 **9** (*should* is used to express what is advisable or desirable): (should用以表示應該或合理): *You should drink your coffee while it's hot.* 你應該趁熱把咖啡喝掉。*You should see the new film that's on at the Odeon.* 你該去看在奥狄昂上演的新影片。(also ⇨ ought).

shal·lot /ʃə'lɒt ; ʃə'lɑt/ *n* sort of small onion with cloves like, but not so strong-tasting as, those of garlic. 多葱(一種小洋葱,有似蒜之鱗莖,不如蒜之辛辣)。

shal·low /'ʃæləʊ ; 'ʃælo/ *adj* of little depth: 淺的;不深的: *~ water;* 淺水; *a ~ saucer/dish;* 淺的茶杯碟(盤子); (fig) not earnest, sound or serious: (喻)不認眞的;膚淺的;淺薄的: *a ~ argument;* 淺薄的議論; *~ talk.* 膚淺的談話。□ *n* (often *pl*) ~ place in a river or in the sea; shoal. (常用複數)河流或海洋中的淺水處;淺灘。□ *vi* become ~. 變淺。

sha·lom /ʃæ'lɒm ; ʃɑ'lom/ *int* (Hebrew word) (used as a greeting and on parting) Peace! (希伯來字)(用於問候及道別時)平安!

shalt /ʃælt ; ʃælt/ ⇨ shall.

sham /ʃæm ; ʃæm/ *vi, vt* (-mm-) [VP2A, D, 6A] pretend to be; simulate: 假裝;佯爲: *He ~med dead/death.* 他裝死。*He's only ~ming.* 他祇是假裝罷了。□ *n* **1** person who ~s; sth intended to deceive: 假裝者;佯爲者;騙人之物;贋品: *His love was a mere ~; what he really wanted was her money.* 他的愛情是虛假的;他眞正要的是她的錢。*He's a ~,* an impostor. 他是個騙子。 **2** [U] pretence: 虛假;藉口: *What he says is all ~.* 他所說的全是托辭。□ *adj* false; pretended: 虛假的;假裝的: *~ piety;* 假虔敬; *a ~ battle* (as in military training); 演習戰;模擬戰; ,*~-'Tudor,* imitating the Tudor style of architecture. 模倣都德王朝之建築風格的。

shamble /'ʃæmbl ; 'ʃæmbḷ/ *vi* [VP2A, C] walk unsteadily as if unable to lift the feet properly: 蹣跚而行;踉蹌而行: *The old man ~d up to me.* 老人蹣跚地向我走來。□ *n* shambling walk. 蹣跚的步子;踉蹌的步子。

shambles /'ʃæmblz ; 'ʃæmbḷz/ *n sing* (作單數用) **1** (archaic) scene of bloodshed: (古)屠場;殺人流血之所;修羅場: *The place became a ~.* 那地方變成了一個屠場。 **2** (colloq) (scene of) muddle or confusion: (俗)紊亂(之處);混亂(的場面): *His flat is a complete ~.* 他的公寓非常凌亂。*He made a ~ of the job.* 他把那工作弄得一塌糊塗。

shame /ʃeɪm ; ʃem/ *n* [U] **1** distressed feeling, loss of self-respect, caused by wrong, dishonourable or foolish behaviour, failure, etc (of oneself, one's family, etc): 羞愧;羞恥;恥辱;慚愧: *feel ~ at having told a lie/at failing in an examination;* 因說謊(考試失敗)而感到羞愧; *hang one's head in/for ~.* 因羞愧而垂頭。*To my ~, I must confess that....* 我很慚愧地承認…。 **'~-faced** *adj* showing ~; looking distressed through ~. 慚愧的;羞愧的;羞怯的。 Hence, 由此產生, **'~-faced·ly** /'ʃeɪmfeɪstlɪ ; 'ʃem,festlɪ/ *adv* **'~-making** *adj* (colloq) causing a feeling of ~. (俗)引起羞恥感的。 **2** capacity for experiencing ~: 羞恥心;羞恥感: *He has no ~/is quite without ~/is lost to ~.* 他毫無羞恥心。***(For) ~!*** an appeal to sb not to disregard this feeling (used as a reproof to sb who does wrong and does not show ~). 眞丟臉! 眞可恥! (對做錯事而不表示慚愧者之譴責語)。 **3** [U] dishonour. 不名譽。***bring ~ on sb/oneself,*** dishonour sb/oneself. 使某人(自己)蒙羞。***cry ~ on sb,*** say that he is disgraceful, ought to be ashamed of himself. 說某人應該自覺可恥。***put sb to ~,*** disgrace him (eg by showing superior qualities). 羞辱某人;使某人相形見絀;使某人黯然失色。***S~ on you!*** You should be ashamed of yourself! 眞可恥! 眞丟臉! 眞不要臉! **4 a ~,** sth unworthy; sth that causes ~; sth or sb that is wrong or regrettable: 不足取之事;可恥之事;令人惋惜或遺憾之事或人: *What a ~ to deceive the girl!* 欺騙那女孩是多麼羞恥的事啊! *It's a ~ to take the money for doing such easy work.* 做那麼容易的工作而拿那麼多的錢眞難爲情。*He's a ~ to his family.* 他是他家的敗類。□ *vt* **1** [VP6A] cause ~ to; cause sb to feel ~; bring disgrace on: 使蒙羞;使慚愧;使不名譽: *~ one's family.* 玷辱門楣。 **2** [VP14] **~ *sb into/out of doing sth,*** frighten or force (sb to do/not to do sth) by ~: 使(某人)因羞愧而做某事(不做某事): *~ a man into apologizing.* 使一個人因羞愧而道歉。 **~·ful** /-fl ; -fʊl/ *adj* causing or bringing ~: 導致羞恥的;可恥的: *~ful conduct.* 可恥的行爲。 **~·fully** /-fəlɪ ; -fḷɪ/ *adv* **~·less** *adj* without ~; immodest. 無恥的;厚顏的。 **~·less·ly** *adv* **~·lessness** *n*

shammy /'ʃæmɪ;'ʃæmɪ/ *n* **'~ (leather),** ⇨ chamois.

sham·poo /ʃæm'puː ; ʃæm'pu/ *n* [C, U] (special soap, liquid, powder, etc for a) washing of the hair: 洗髮;洗髮用的肥皂、水劑、粉等;洗髮精: *give sb a ~;* 給某人洗頭; *a ~ and set.* 洗頭做髮。□ *vt* [VP6A] wash (the hair of the head). 洗(頭髮)。

sham·rock /'ʃæmrɒk ; 'ʃæmrɑk/ *n* clover-like

plant with (usu) three leaves on each stem (serving as the national emblem of Ireland). 酢漿草(爲愛爾蘭的國花)。

shandy /ˈʃændɪ ; ˈʃændɪ/ *n* [U] mixed drink of beer and ginger-beer or lemonade. 啤酒和薑汁啤酒或檸檬水混合的飲料。

shang·hai /ʃæŋˈhaɪ ; ˈʃæŋhaɪ/ *vt* (sl) make (a man) unconscious (with drink or drugs) and then carry him off to be a seaman on an outgoing ship; trick (a person) into an awkward situation. (俚)(以酒或麻醉劑)使(某人)失去知覺然後拐帶至出航的船上做水手;騙(某人)入困境。

shank /ʃæŋk ; ʃæŋk/ *n* **1** leg, esp the part between the knee and the ankle; shin-bone. 脛(膝與踝間的部分);脛骨。***go on ~'s mare/pony,*** on one's own legs (not riding a horse, etc). 步行(未騎馬等)。 **2** straight, slender part of an anchor, key, spoon, etc; smooth part of the stem of a screw. 錨、鑰、匙等之直而細長的部分;螺釘體。

shan't /ʃɑːnt *US:* ʃænt ; ʃænt/ = shall not.

shan·tung /ʃænˈtʌŋ ; ʃænˈtʌŋ/ *n* [U] kind of heavy silk, usu undyed. 山東綢;繭綢(通常未染色)。

shanty[1] /ˈʃæntɪ ; ˈʃæntɪ/ *n* [C] (*pl* -ties) poorly made hut, shed or cabin. 簡陋的小屋。**ˈ~-town** *n* slum area of a town, or on the outskirts of a town, consisting of huts or shanties. 城鎮中之簡陋房舍區,貧民區;有簡陋房舍之城郊地區。

shanty[2] (US = **chant(e)y**) /ˈʃæntɪ ; ˈʃæntɪ/ *n* (*pl* -ties) (often 常作 **ˈsea ~**) song sung by sailors in rhythm with their movements while working. 水手們隨工作的節律所唱的歌;船歌。

shape[1] /ʃeɪp ; ʃep/ *n* **1** [C, U] outer form; total effect produced by the outlines of sth: 外形;形狀;樣子: *There were clouds of different ~s in the sky.* 天空有各種形狀的雲。*The garden is in the ~ of a square/oblong/crescent.* 那園子是方(長方、弦月)形的。*What's the ~ of his nose?* 他的鼻子是什麼形狀? *That hat hasn't much ~/has a queer ~.* 那頂帽子的式樣不佳(樣子很怪)。 ***get/put sth into ~,*** give definite form to; arrange in an orderly way: 定形;有條理地安排;整理: *get/put one's ideas into ~.* 整理思緒。***give ~ to,*** express (clearly): (清晰地)表達: *He has some difficulty in giving ~ to his ideas.* 他很難清晰地表達他的意見。 ***knock sth into/out of ~,*** put sth into/out of the right ~. 使成形(使變形或走樣)。***take ~,*** become definite in form or outline: 具體化;成形: *The new building is beginning to take ~,* One begins to see what the final ~ will be. 這座新的建築物開始成形了。***take ~ in,*** find expression in: 具體化;成形;體現: *His intentions took ~ in action,* were realized in action. 他的意向已付諸行動。***in ~ ,*** in form, outline or appearance: 在形式上;在外形上: *What a fat fellow! He's like a barrel in ~!* 多胖的傢伙!他的體型像隻木桶! *He looks like a devil/monster in human ~.* 他看起來像徒具人形的魔鬼(怪物)。 **2** sort, description: 種;類: *I've had no proposals from him in any ~ or form,* none of any sort. 我未得到他任何種類的建議。**3** condition: 情況;狀況: *Her affairs are in good ~,* are satisfactory. 她的事情令人滿意。*Ali is in good ~ for his forthcoming fight,* is physically fit. 阿里的身體狀況甚佳,足以應付即將來臨的比賽。 **4** [C] sth indistinctly seen; vague form; apparition: 看來模糊之物;模糊的形影;幽靈: *Two ~s could be discerned in the darkness.* 在黑暗中可以看到兩個模糊的形影。*A huge ~ loomed up through the fog.* 一個巨大的影像在霧中隱隱出現。 **5** [C] pattern or mould on which sth is given ~, eg a block on which hats are made. 底樣;模;模型(如帽型等)。

shape[2] /ʃeɪp ; ʃep/ *vt, vi* **1** [VP6A, 15A] give a shape or form to: 使具…形狀;塑造;製作;籌畫: *~ a pot on a wheel;* 在拉坏轉輪上製作瓦罐; *~ clay into an urn,* on a potter's wheel or lathe; (在拉坏轉輪或旋盤上)將泥土製成甕; ~ (= direct) *one's course for home;* 計畫回家的路線; (*pp*) (過去分詞) *~d like a pear,* having the shape of a pear. 形狀似梨的。 **2** [VP2A, C] take shape; give signs of future shape or development: 成形;形成;發育;發展: *Our plans are shaping well,* giving promise of success. 我們的計畫進展順利。*The students are shaping satisfactorily,* making good progress. 學生們發育得很好。**~·less** *adj* **~·less·ly** *adv* **~·less·ness** *n*

shape·ly /ˈʃeɪplɪ ; ˈʃeplɪ/ *adj* (-ier, -iest) (esp of a person's form, or of limbs) well-formed; having a pleasing shape: (尤指人的體型或肢體)美好的;勻稱的;有悅人之模樣的: *a ~ pair of legs.* 一雙勻稱的腿。

shard /ʃɑːd ; ʃard/ *n* (old use, but still used by gardeners and archaeologists for a) piece of broken earthenware, eg one placed over the hole in a flower-pot. (舊用法,但園藝家及考古學家仍習用之)陶器碎片(如覆於花盆洞上者)。

share[1] /ʃeə(r) ; ʃɛr/ *n* **1** [C] part or division which sb has in, receives from, or gives to, a stock held by several or many persons, or which he contributes to a fund, expenses, etc: (共有、分得、給付或貢獻出的)一份;部份: *Please let me take a ~ in the expenses,* pay sth towards them. 這些費用請讓我出一份。*We shall all have a ~ in the profits.* 我們都可以分得一份利潤。***go ~s (with sb) (in sth),*** divide (profits, costs, etc) with others; become part owner (with others); pay (a part of an expense): 與他人分攤(利潤、費用等);(與他人)成爲共有者;付(費用之一份): *Let me go ~s with you in the taxi fare.* 讓我和你分攤計程車車費。**ˈ~-cropper** *n* (in some countries, not in GB) tenant farmer who pays a ~ of his crop as rent to the owner of the land. (在英國以外之若干國家中,以作物之一部分付與地主作爲田租的)佃農。 **2** [U] part taken or received by sb in an action, undertaking, etc, eg of responsibility, blame: (參與或分擔責任、過失等的)份: *What ~ did he have in their success?* 在他們的成功中他有何貢獻? *You must take your ~ of the blame.* 你必須承受你那一份過失。*You're not taking much ~ in the conversation,* are saying little. 你未積極參與談話。 **3** [C] one of the equal parts into which the capital of a company is divided, entitling the holder of the ~ to a proportion of the profits: 股份;股(公司資本諸等分之一,持有者得按一定比率分享紅利): *hold 500 ~s in a shipping company;* 在某一航運公司中持有五百股; *£1 ~s are now worth £1.75.* 一鎊的股份現值 1.75 鎊。**ˈordinary ~,** on which dividends are paid according to profits after payments on preference ~s. 普通股(於優先股分紅後才能分到紅利)。 **ˈpreference ~,** one on which a fixed dividend is guaranteed before payments are made on others. 優先股(較普通股優先享有定額紅利)。 **ˈ~ certificate,** document proving ownership of ~s. 股票。**ˈ~·holder** *n* owner of (business) ~s. 股東。**ˈ~ index** *n* number used to show how ~ prices have fluctuated, based on prices of ~s selected for this purpose: 股票指數: *The Financial Times ~ index went up/down five points yesterday.* 經濟時報的股票指數昨天上升了(下降了)五點。□ *vt, vi* **1** [VP 6A, 14, 15B] **~ *sth (out) (among/between),*** give a ~ of to others; divide and distribute: 分給;分配;分派: *~ (out) £100 among five men,* eg by giving them £20 each; 將一百鎊分與五人(如每人給二十鎊); *~ the sweets between you.* 你們兩人分這些糖果。Hence, 由此產生, **ˈ~-out** *n* distribution. 分配;分派。**~ *sth with sb,*** give part of it to him: 分給別人;和別人分享;和別人合用: *He would ~ his last pound with me.* 他到了只剩最後一鎊的時候,也會分給我用。 **2** [VP6A, 14] **~ *sth (with sb),*** have or use (with); have in common: 共有;共用: *He hated having to ~ the hotel bedroom with a stranger.* 他討厭與陌生人共住這個旅館房間。 **3** [VP6A, 3A] **~ *(in) sth,*** have a ~: 分攤;分享;共同負擔: *I will ~ (in) the cost with you.* 我將與你

分攤費用。*She ~s (in) my troubles as well as (in) my joys.* 她和我苦樂與共。 **~ and ~ alike,** have equal ~s with others in the use, enjoyment, expense, etc of sth. 均分;均享;均攤。

share[2] /ʃeə(r) ; ʃɛr/ *n* blade of a plough. 犂頭;犂刃。

shark /ʃɑ:k ; ʃɑrk/ *n* **1** sea-fish, some kinds of which are large and dangerous to bathers, etc. 鯊。⇨ the illus at sea. 參看 sea 之插圖。 **'~-skin** *n* textile fabric with a smooth and shiny surface, used for outer clothing: 鯊皮布(表面光滑發亮的一種織物,用製外衣): *a ~-skin jacket/suit.* 鯊皮布做的短上衣(套裝)。 **2** swindler; usurer. 騙子;放高利貸者。

sharp /ʃɑ:p ; ʃɑrp/ *adj* (-er, -est) **1** with a fine cutting edge; not blunt: 有利刃的;鋒利的: *a ~ knife;* 快刀; with a fine point, able to make holes: 尖銳的: *a ~ pin/needle.* 尖銳的大頭針(縫衣針)。 **2** well-defined; clear-cut; distinct: 輪廓明顯的;周邊清楚的;明晰的: *a ~ outline;* 明晰的輪廓; *a ~ image,* (in photography) one with clear contrasts between light and shade. 明暗對比明顯的影像。 **3** (of curves, slopes, bends) abrupt; changing direction quickly: (指曲線、斜坡、彎)陡峭的;急轉的: *a ~ bend in the road;* 路上的一處急轉彎; *a ~ turn to the left;* 向左的急轉; **,~-'featured,** (of a person) having angular features. (指人)面部輪廓分明的。 **4** (of sounds) shrill; piercing: (指聲音)尖銳的;刺耳的: *a ~ cry of distress.* 痛苦的尖叫聲。 **5** quickly aware of things; acute: 敏銳的;伶俐的;機警的: *~ eyes/ears;* 靈敏的眼(耳); *a ~ intelligence;* 聰慧; *a ~ sense of smell;* 敏銳的嗅覺; *keep a ~ look-out,* 注意地守望着; *a ~ child;* 伶俐的小孩; *~ at arithmetic.* 精於算術。 **'~-shooter** *n* man skilled at shooting with a rifle, placed where accurate shooting (in war) is required. 神槍手;狙擊手。Hence, 由此產生, **,~-'eyed/-'sighted/-'witted** *adjj* **6** (of feelings, taste) producing a physical sensation like cutting or pricking: (指感覺、味道)强烈的;辛辣的;刺骨的;刺耳的: *a ~ pain;* 劇痛; *a ~ flavour;* 辛辣的味道; *a ~ frost.* 嚴寒。 **7** harsh; severe; 尖刻的;苛刻的;厲害的;嚴厲的: *~ words;* 尖刻的話; *a ~ rebuke;* 嚴厲的指責; *a ~ tongue,* of a person who speaks sarcastically, bitterly. 利舌。 **8** quick; brisk; lively: 敏捷的;輕快的;活潑的;生氣勃勃的: *go for a ~ walk;* 去做一次輕快的散步; *a ~ struggle/contest.* 有生氣的奮鬥(競賽)。 *That was ~ work,* was finished or done quickly and energetically. 那是一鼓作氣完成的工作。 **9** quick to take advantage; unscrupulous: 精明的;狡猾的;不擇手段的: *a ~ lawyer.* 狡猾的律師。 *He was too ~ for me,* He got the better of me by being unscrupulous. 他太不擇手段,我對付不了他。 **~ practice,** business dealings that are not altogether honest. 詐騙的手段。 **10** (music) above the normal pitch; (of a note) raised half a tone in pitch: (音樂)高調的;(指音符)升半音的;嬰音的: *C ~* (= C♯), ⇨ flat²(4). ⇨ the illus at notation. 參看 notation 之插圖。 □ *n* (music) ~ note; the symbol ♯ used to indicate a ~ note. (音樂)升半音音符;升半音記號(♯)。 □ *adv* **1** punctually: 準時地: *at seven (o'clock) ~.* 七時整。 **2** suddenly; abruptly: 突然地;急劇地: *turn ~ to the left.* 向左急轉。 **3** (music) above the true pitch: (音樂)升半音地: *sing ~.* 以升半音唱。 **4** *look ~,* waste no time; hurry. 不要浪費時間;趕快。 **5** **'~-set** *adj* hungry. 饑餓的。 **~en** /'ʃɑ:pən ; 'ʃɑrpən/ *vt, vi* [VP6A, 2A] make or become ~: 使尖銳;使急劇;變尖銳;變急劇: *~en a pencil.* 削鉛筆。 *This knife needs ~ening.* 這把刀子需要磨了。 *The walk has ~ened my appetite.* 散步增進了我的食慾。 **~·ener** /'ʃɑ:pnə(r) ; 'ʃɑrpənɚ/ *n* sth that ~ens: 使尖銳或急劇之物;磨具;削具: *a 'pencil-~ener;* 鉛筆刀(鉋); *a 'knife-~ener* 磨刀石(器)。 **~er** *n* swindler, esp **('card-~er)** person who makes a living by cheating at cards. 騙子;(尤指)賭紙牌的郎中(card-sharper)。 **~·ly** *adv* in a ~ manner: 鋒利地;尖地;明晰地;苛刻地: *a ~ly pointed pencil;* 筆尖尖的鉛筆; *a ~ly defined image;* 輪廓分明的像; *to answer ~ly.* 嚴厲地回答。 **~·ness** *n*

shat /ʃæt ; ʃæt/ *pt, pp* of shit.

shat·ter /'ʃætə(r) ; 'ʃætɚ/ *vt, vi* [VP6A, 2A] break suddenly and violently into small pieces: 突然而劇烈地破成碎片;使粉碎;使破滅;損毀: *The explosion ~ed every window in the building.* 那次爆炸把該建築物所有的窗戶都震碎了。 *Our hopes were ~ed.* 我們的希望破滅了。 *What a nerve-~ing noise!* eg that of pneumatic drills or jet engines. 這種噪音眞會使人神經崩潰!(如氣壓鑽孔機或噴射引擎的聲音)。 **'~·proof,** ⇨ proof².

shave /ʃeɪv ; ʃev/ *vt, vi* (*pt, pp* ~d or, chiefly as *adj,* 主要用作形容詞 ~n /'ʃeɪvn ; 'ʃevən/) **1** [VP6A, 2A, 15B] **~ (off),** cut (hair) off the chin, etc with a razor: 剃去下顎等處之(毛髮);刮(鬍子);薙面;修面: *Do you ~ yourself or go to the barber's?* 你自己修面還是去理髮店修面? *He has ~d off his beard.* 他已剃去鬍子。 *He doesn't ~ every day.* 他並不每天刮臉。 **'shaving-brush** *n* brush for spreading lather over the face before shaving. 修面刷(刮臉前用以塗肥皂沫於臉上)。 **2** [VP15B] **~ sth off,** pare off (a thin layer, etc). 鉋;削;刮去薄薄一層等。 **3** [VP6A, 15A] pass very close to, almost but not touching: 掠過;(幾乎觸及而)擦過: *The bus just ~d me by an inch.* 公共汽車從我身邊一吋左右擦過。 **4** **~n** (*pp* as *adj*) **,clean-'~n, ,well-'~n,** having been ~d clean, well. 已剃(刮)乾淨的;已剃(刮)好的。 □ *n* [C] **1** shaving (of the face): 修(面);薙;剃: *A sharp razor gives a close ~.* 鋒利的剃刀刮得很乾淨。 *How much does a ~ cost?* 修面要多少錢? **2** close approach without touching. 掠過;擦過。(only in) (僅用於) ***a close/narrow ~,*** a narrow escape from injury, danger, etc. 間不容髮(逃脫傷害、危險等)。 **~r** *n* **1 (electric) ~r,** razor with an electric motor, operated from the mains or by a battery. 電動刮鬍刀。⇨ the illus at razor. 參看 razor 之揷圖。 **2** (joc, 諧, usu 通常作 *young ~r*) lad, youngster. 少年;年輕人。 **shav·ings** *n pl* thin parings of wood ~d off (esp with a plane): 薄木片;薄木屑;(尤指)刨花: *The floor of the carpenter's shop was covered with shavings.* 木匠店的地板上滿是木屑刨花。

Shav·ian /'ʃeɪvɪən ; 'ʃevɪən/ *adj, n* (in the manner) (devotee) of G B Shaw, Irish dramatist and critic. 戲劇家蕭伯納的;蕭伯納風格的;蕭伯納之崇拜者;致力於研究蕭伯納者。

shawl /ʃɔ:l ; ʃɔl/ *n* [C] large (usu square or oblong) piece of material worn about the shoulders or head of a woman, or wrapped round a baby. (婦女或嬰兒用之)披肩;圍巾(通常爲方形或長方形)。

she /ʃi: ; ʃi/ *pron* (⇨ her) **1** female person, etc already referred to or implied: 她: *My sister says she is going for a walk.* 我姐姐(妹妹)說她要出去散步。 *This cat's a she, not a he.* 這隻猫是雌的,不是雄的。 **2** (pref) (字首) female: 女性;雌性: *a 'she-goat/-ass, etc.* 雌山羊(母驢等)。

sheaf /ʃi:f ; ʃif/ *n* (*pl* sheaves /ʃi:vz ; ʃivz/) **1** bundle of corn, barley, etc stalks tied together after reaping. (收割後之小麥、大麥等之)束;捆。 **2** bundle of papers, arrows, etc laid lengthwise and tied together. (文件等之)束;扎。

shear /ʃɪə(r) ; ʃɪr/ *vt* (*pt* ~ed, *pp* shorn /ʃɔ:n ; ʃorn/ or ~ed) [VP6A] cut the wool off (a sheep) with shears; (fig) strip bare of; deprive of: 剪(羊)毛;(喻)剝奪: *They'll be ~ing (the sheep) next week.* 他們將在下星期剪羊毛。 ***shorn of,*** having lost completely: 完全失去: *The gambler came home shorn of his money.* 那賭徒回家,錢已輸光。

shears /ʃɪəz ; ʃɪrz/ *n pl* **(pair of) ~,** large cutting instrument shaped like scissors, used for shearing sheep, cutting cloth, etc. (用於剪羊毛、裁布等之)大剪刀;剪切機。⇨ the illus at tool. 參看 tool 之插圖。

sheath /ʃi:θ ; ʃiθ/ *n* (*pl* ~s /ʃi:ðz ; ʃiðz/) **1** cover for the blade of a weapon or tool: 鞘;套: *Put the dagger back in its ~.* 把匕首放回鞘中。 **'~-knife** *n* knife with a fixed blade, that fits into a ~. 刀身固定而裝於鞘內的刀子。 **2** ~-like cover (of tissue, skin, etc) fitting over part of an animal or plant (eg the *'wing-~* of some insects). 動植物之鞘狀包覆物;鞘(如某些昆蟲之翅鞘)。 **(protective) ~,** contraceptive device used on the penis. (避孕用的)保險套。 **3** (attrib; dressmaking) close-fitting: (形容用法;女服裁製)緊身的: *a ~ corset/gown.* 緊身的束腹(長服)。

sheathe /ʃiːð ; ʃið/ *vt* [VP6A] **1** put into a sheath: 插入鞘: *~ the sword,* stop fighting. 休戰。 **2** protect with a casing or covering: 以包覆物保護: *~ a ship's bottom with copper.* 以銅板包覆船底。 **sheathing** *n* protective layer of boards, metal plates, etc eg on parts of a building, the underpart of a ship's hull. 屋頂(或牆壁)的內層板;覆板;覆套;船底包板。

sheaves /ʃiːvz ; ʃivz/ ⇨ sheaf.

she·bang /ʃɪ'bæŋ ; ʃə'bæŋ/ *n* ***the whole ~,*** the whole collection of facts or things; the whole situation, organization. 整個的事物;情況,組織。

she·been /ʃɪ'biːn ; ʃɪ'bin/ *n* unlicensed public house (esp in Ireland and S Africa). 無執照的酒館、客棧(尤指在愛爾蘭與南非者)。

shed[1] /ʃed ; ʃɛd/ *n* building, roughly made structure, used for storing things (*'tool-~, 'wood-~, 'coal-~, etc*), for sheltering animals (*'cattle-~*), vehicles, etc (*'engine-~, 'bicycle-~*). 棚;小屋(用於儲物者如tool-shed工具房,wood-shed柴房,coal-shed煤庫;用於安頓牲畜者如 cattle-shed 畜棚,停放車輛等者如 engine-shed 機車車庫,bicycle-shed 脚踏車棚)。

shed[2] /ʃed ; ʃɛd/ *vt* (*pt, pp* ~; -dd-) [VP6A] **1** let (leaves, etc) fall; let come off: 脫落(葉等);蛻;褪;流出: *Trees ~ their leaves and flowers ~ their petals.* 樹落葉,花掉瓣。 *Some kinds of deer ~ their horns.* 有些種鹿脫換犄角。 ***~ (one's) blood,*** **(a)** be wounded or killed: 受傷或被殺死;流血: *~ one's blood for one's country.* 爲國家流血。 **(b)** cause the blood of others to flow. 使他人流血。 Hence, 由此產生, **'blood·~** *n* ***~ tears,*** weep. 流淚;哭泣。 **2** throw or take off; get rid of: 脫去;擺脫: *People in the park began to ~ their clothes as it got hotter and hotter.* 天氣愈來愈熱了,公園裡的人們開始脫去衣服。 **3** spread or send out: 散開;放射: *a fire that ~s warmth;* 發散溫暖的爐火; *a woman who ~s happiness around her;* 向周遭散播快樂的女人; *a lamp that ~s a soft light.* 發射柔光的燈。 ***~ light on,*** (fig) make clear to the mind. (喻)闡明;弄明白。 **4** **'load-~ding,** ⇨ load[1](3).

she'd /ʃiːd ; ʃid/ = she had; she would.

sheen /ʃiːn ; ʃin/ *n* [U] brightness; shiny quality: 光輝;光彩;光澤: *the ~ of silk.* 絲綢的光澤。 *That girl's hair has a ~ like gold.* 那女孩的頭髮有金色的光澤。

sheep /ʃiːp ; ʃip/ *n* (*pl* unchanged) (複數不變) grass-eating animal kept for its flesh as food (mutton) and its wool. 羊;綿羊。 ⇨ the illus at domestic. 參看 domestic 之插圖。 ⇨ ewe, lamb and ram. ***separate the ~ from the goats,*** separate good from bad persons. 分辨善人與惡人。 ⇨ Matt 25: 33. 參看馬太福音第 25 章第 33 節。 ***cast / make ~'s eyes at,*** look at in an amorous but foolish way. 向…眉目傳情;向…愚蠢地送秋波。 ***a wolf in ~'s clothing,*** a wicked man who pretends to be good. 假裝善良的壞人。 ***as well be hanged for a ~ as a lamb,*** commit a big crime rather than a small one if the punishment is the same. 如果所得處罰相同,則寧願犯大罪而捨小惡;一不做二不休。 **,black '~,** ⇨ black(4). **'~-dog** *n* dog trained to help a shepherd to look after ~. 牧羊犬。 ⇨ the illus at domestic. 參看 domestic 之插圖。 **'~-fold** *n* enclosure for ~. 羊欄;羊舍。 **'~-run** *n* tract of land (esp in Australia) on which ~ are pastured. (尤指澳洲之)大牧羊場。 **'~·skin** *n* **(a)** rug of a ~'s skin with the wool on it; garment made of two or more such skins. 帶毛之羊皮;羊皮所製之衣服;皮襖。 **(b)** leather of ~'s skin used in book-binding, etc. (用於裝訂書籍等之)羊革。 **(c)** parchment made from such skin; (esp US) diploma written on such parchment. 羊皮紙;(尤美)用羊皮紙書寫的文憑;證書。 **'~·ish** /-ɪʃ ; -ɪʃ/ *adj* **1** awkwardly self-conscious: 靦腆的;不自在的;侷促不安的: *a ~ish-looking boy.* 侷促不安的男孩。 **2** (feeling) foolish or embarrassed by consciousness of a fault. (因意識到犯錯而覺得)羞愧的;困窘的。 **~·ish·ly** *adv* **~·ish·ness** *n*

sheer[1] /ʃɪə(r) ; ʃɪr/ *adj* **1** complete; thorough; absolute: 全然的;純粹的;絕對的: *~ nonsense;* 毫無意義;一派胡言; *a ~ waste of time;* 簡直是浪費時間; *by ~ chance.* 完全出於偶然地。 **2** (of textiles, etc) finely woven and almost transparent: (指織物等)細織而幾乎透明的: *stockings of ~ nylon.* 透明尼龍絲襪。 **3** without a slope; (almost) perpendicular: 無斜坡的;陡峭的;(近乎)垂直的: *a ~ drop of 50 feet;* 五十呎的垂直降落; *a ~ rock.* 陡峭的山巖。 □ *adv* straight up or down: 陡峭地;垂直地: *a cliff that rises ~ from the beach.* 矗立於海灘上之懸崖。 *He fell 500 feet ~.* 他垂直地落下五百呎。

sheer[2] /ʃɪə(r) ; ʃɪr/ *vi* [VP2C] **1** ***~ away / off,*** (esp of a ship) deviate from course. (尤指船)逸出路線;偏航。 **2** ***~ off,*** (colloq) go away (from sb one dislikes, sb by whom one had been offended). (俗)避開(不喜歡之人、曾被其冒犯者)。

sheet[1] /ʃiːt ; ʃit/ *n* [C] **1** large rectangular piece of linen or cotton cloth, as used in pairs for sleeping between: 被單;褥單: *put clean ~s on the bed.* 鋪乾淨的床單在床上。 **2** broad, flat piece (of some thin material): 平板;薄片: *a ~ of glass/tin/wrapping-paper/note-paper, etc;* 一片玻璃(一片馬口鐵;一張包裝紙;一張信紙等); *~ copper/iron, etc,* rolled or hammered into thin ~s; 銅片(鐵片等); *'~ music,* published in ~s, not in book form. 散頁樂譜。 *The book is in ~s,* ie in ~s of paper ready for binding. 這本書尚未裝訂(準備裝訂)。 **3** wide expanse (of water, ice, snow, flame, etc): (水、冰、雪、火等的)一片: *The rain came down in ~s,* very heavily. 大雨滂沱。 **'~-lightning** *n* lightning that comes in sheet-like flashes of diffused brightness (not in zigzags, etc). 片狀閃電(漫射或散光形式之閃電,非呈鋸齒形者)。 **~·ing** *n* [U] material used for making ~s(1). 被單布;床單布。

sheet[2] /ʃiːt ; ʃit/ *n* cord fastened at the lower corner of a sail to hold it and control the angle at which it is set. 帆脚索。 ⇨ the illus at sail. 參看 sail 之插圖。 **'~-anchor** *n* (usu fig) sth on which one depends for security as a final resort when other things have failed. 副錨;(通常作喻)緊急時賴以獲得安全之事物;最後之依恃。

sheik(h) /ʃeɪk *US:* ʃiːk ; ʃik/ *n* Arab chieftain; head of an Arab village, tribe, etc. (阿拉伯的)酋長;族長。 **~·dom** /-dəm ; -dəm/ *n*

shekel /'ʃekl ; 'ʃɛkḷ/ *n* ancient silver coin used by the Jews; (*pl*) money, riches. (古猶太人使用之)銀幣;(複)錢;財富。

shel·drake /'ʃeldreɪk ; 'ʃɛl,drek/ *n* (kinds of) fish-eating wild duck with brightly coloured feathers. 潦鳧;冠鴨(數種羽色鮮艷捕食魚類的野鴨)。

shelf /ʃelf ; ʃɛlf/ *n* (*pl* shelves /ʃelvz ; ʃɛlvz/) **1** flat, rectangular piece of wood, metal, glass or other material, fastened at right angles to a wall or in a cupboard, bookcase, cabinet, etc. 架子;擱板。 ***on the ~,*** **(a)** put aside as done with, eg of a person too old to continue working. (指年老不能繼續工作之人等)投閒置散的;擱在一旁的。 **(b)** (colloq, of a woman) unmarried and considered as being unlikely to be asked to marry. (俗,指女人)無結婚希望的。 **2** ~-like projection of rock on a cliff face, etc (as used by rock-climbers). 懸崖等上突出的岩石;崖路;岩棚(如爬岩之人使用者)。

shell /ʃel ; ʃɛl/ *n* [C] **1** hard outer covering of

bird's eggs, nuts (eg walnuts, coconuts), some seeds (eg peas) and fruits, and of some animals (eg oysters, lobsters, snails) or parts of them. (鳥卵或胡桃、椰子等堅果之)殼；(豌豆等之)莢；(蠔、龍蝦、蝸牛等動物之)介殼；貝殼。⇨ the illus at mollusc. 參看 mollusc 之插圖。**go/retire into one's ~; come out of one's ~,** become/cease to be shy, reserved, uncommunicative. 變爲(不再)羞怯沈默。'~-**fish** *n* kinds of molluscs (oysters, etc) and crustaceans (crabs, shrimps, etc) having ~s. 貝(如蠔等)；介殼類(如蟹、蝦等)。**2** walls, outer structure, of an unfinished building, ship, etc or of one of which the contents have been destroyed (eg by fire): (尚未完工之房屋、船等或內部被大火等毀壞後之)框架；骨架；船體: *Only the ~ of the factory was left when the fire had been extinguished.* 火撲滅以後這工廠祇剩下屋架了。**3** (US 美 = *cartridge*) metal case filled with explosive, to be fired from a large gun. 砲彈。Cf 參較 *cartridge* for rifles, shot-guns. 用於步槍，獵槍之 cartridge。⇨ the illus at cartridge. 參看 cartridge 之插圖。'~-**proof** *adj* so thickly or strongly built that a ~ cannot pierce it. 防砲彈的。'~-**shock** *n* nervous or mental disorder caused by the noise and blast of bursting ~s. 砲彈休克；彈震症(由砲彈之爆炸和震聲所引起之精神病)。**4** light racing-boat propelled by oarsmen. (競賽用之)輕舟。□ *vt, vi* **1** [VP6A] take out of a ~(1) (cf 參較 US 美 *shuck*): 去殼；剝殼: *It's as easy as ~ing peas,* is very easy. 那就像剝豌豆一般的容易；極其容易。*These peas ~ easily,* are easily ~ed. 這些豌豆容易剝。**2** [VP6A] fire ~s(3) at: 砲擊: *~ the enemy's trenches.* 砲擊敵人之戰壕。**3 ~ out,** [VP15B, 2C] (colloq) pay up (money, a required sum): (俗)付(款，所需之數): *I shall be expected to ~ out (the money) for the party.* 我將要付出這個集會的費用。

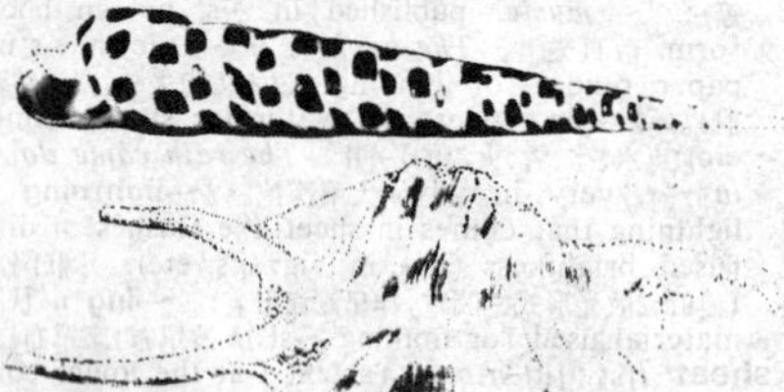

shells

she'll /ʃiːl; ʃil/ = she will; she shall.

shel·lac /ʃəˈlæk; ʃəˈlæk/ *n* [U] resinous substance in the form of thin sheets used in making varnish and (formerly) gramophone records. 蟲膠片(用以製造充漆，昔時並用以製唱片)；蟲膠；充漆；假漆。□ *vt* varnish with ~. 塗以充漆。

shel·ter /ˈʃeltə(r); ˈʃɛltɚ/ *n* **1** [U] condition of being kept safe, eg from rain, danger: 庇護；保護；遮蔽(如使不受雨、危險等之侵害): *take ~ from the rain,* eg under a tree; 躲雨(如在樹下等); *get under ~,* eg when bombs are dropping during an air raid. 獲得掩蔽(如空襲投彈時)。**2** [C] sth that gives safety or protection, esp a hut, etc built to keep off wind and rain: 庇護物；遮蔽物；(尤指)躲避風雨之處；庇護所；避難所: *a 'bus ~,* (in which people wait for buses); 公共汽車候車亭; *a taxi-drivers' ~,* one where they wait until called by phone, etc; 計程車行；計程車候客站; *an 'air-raid ~.* 防空洞(壕)。□ *vt, vi* **1** [VP6A, 14] **~ (from),** give ~ to; protect: 庇護；保護；掩護: *trees that ~ a house from cold winds;* 遮蔽房屋使不受寒風侵襲之樹木; ~ (= hide, protect) *an escaped prisoner;* 窩藏逃犯; *dig trenches to ~ the men from gunfire;* 挖戰壕使兵士免受砲火的攻擊; *~ sb from blame;* 庇護某人不受責罵; *~ed trades,* those which (like building and inland transport) are not exposed to foreign competition. 受保護的貿易。**2** [VP2A, C] take ~: 托庇；隱匿: *~ from the rain;* 躲雨; *~ under the trees.* 避在樹下。

shelve[1] /ʃelv; ʃɛlv/ *vt* [VP6A] **1** put (books, etc) on a shelf. 置(書等)於架上。**2** (fig, of problems, plans, etc) postpone dealing with; defer consideration of. (喻，指問題、計畫等)擱置；緩議。**3** cease to employ (a person). 解僱；辭退。

shelve[2] /ʃelv; ʃɛlv/ *vi* [VP2A, C] (of land) slope gently: (指土地)漸次傾斜: *The shore ~s down to the sea.* 海岸向海漸次傾斜。

shelves /ʃelvz; ʃɛlvz/ *pl* of shelf.

shep·herd /ˈʃepəd; ˈʃɛpɚd/ *n* man who takes care of sheep. 牧羊人。**the Good S~,** Jesus Christ. 好牧人(耶穌基督)。**~'s pie,** [U] minced meat baked under mashed potatoes. (以搗爛之馬鈴薯焙成之)肉餡馬鈴薯餅。**~'s plaid,** small black and white check pattern in cloth. 黑白色棋盤圖案花布。□ *vt* [VP6A, 15A] take care of; guide or direct (people) like sheep: 照看；似牧羊般引領或指導(人群): *The passengers were ~ed across the tarmac to the airliner.* 旅客們被引導走過柏油碎石跑道上飛機。**~·ess** /ˌʃepəˈdes *US:* ˈʃepərdəs; ˈʃɛpɚdɪs/ *n* woman ~ (esp as idealized in pastoral poetry). 女牧羊人(尤指牧歌中理想化者)。

Shera·ton /ˈʃerətən; ˈʃɛrətn̩/ *n* [U] 18th-century style of furniture (in GB): (英國)十八世紀之雪里頓式傢具: (attrib) (形容用法) *~ chairs.* 雪里頓式椅子。

sher·bet /ˈʃɜːbət; ˈʃɝbɪt/ *n* [C, U] (glass of) cooling drink of sweetened fruit juices, sometimes effervescent (made from powder); (US) water-ice. (一杯)加糖之清涼果汁飲料；(美)冰糕。

sher·iff /ˈʃerɪf; ˈʃɛrɪf/ *n* **1** (usu 通常作 **High S~**) chief officer of the Crown in counties and certain cities, with legal and ceremonial duties. (郡或若干城市之)擔任法律及禮儀職務的主要政府官吏；行政司法長官。**2** (US) chief law-enforcing officer of a county. (美)一郡執行法律的主要官員；郡長；郡警察局長。

sherry /ˈʃerɪ; ˈʃɛrɪ/ *n* [U] yellow or brown fortified wine of S Spain; similar kinds of wine from S Africa, Cyprus, etc. 雪利酒(西班牙南部所產加有烈酒之黃色或褐色葡萄酒)；(南非，塞浦路斯等地所產類似的)葡萄酒。

she's /ʃiːz; ʃiz/ = she is; she has.

Shet·land /ˈʃetlənd; ˈʃɛtlənd/ *n* (also 亦作 **the ~s**) group of islands NNE of Scotland. 謝德蘭羣島(蘇格蘭北北東方之羣島)。**~ pony,** small, hardy breed. 謝德蘭駒(該地所產之耐勞的小馬)。**~ wool,** soft, fine kind spun in the S~s. 謝德蘭羊毛或毛線。

shew /ʃəʊ; ʃo/ ⇨ show.

shib·bol·eth /ˈʃɪbəleθ; ˈʃɪbəlɪθ/ *n* [C] **1** custom whose use is regarded as a criterion for distinguishing membership of a group. 作爲辨別某一團體份子之標準的習慣。**2** old-fashioned and now generally abandoned custom which was at one time considered to be essential: 過去認爲必要而現在一般已拋棄的陳舊習俗: *the outworn ~s of the past.* 不合時宜的舊習俗。

shied /ʃaɪd; ʃaɪd/ ⇨ shy[2], shy[3].

shield /ʃiːld; ʃild/ *n* [C] **1** piece of armour (metal, leather, wood) carried on the arm, to protect the body when fighting; representation of a ~, eg carved on a stone gateway, showing a person's coat of arms. 盾(甲冑之一件，金屬質、皮質或木質，佩於臂，打仗時用以保護身體)；盾形紋徽(如刻於石門框上，顯示某人紋章之盾形物)。⇨ arms. ⇨ the illus at armour. 參看 armour 之插圖。**2** (fig) person or thing that protects. (喻)保護之人或物。**3** (in machinery, etc) protective plate or screen; sth designed to keep out dust, wind, etc. (US 美 *wind~* = GB 英 *windscreen.*) (機器等中之)護板；護幕；防塵板；擋風板；遮泥板。□ *vt* [VP6A, 15A] protect; keep safe; save (sb) from punishment or suffering: 保護；防禦；使(某人)免於懲罰或痛苦： ~ *one's eyes with one's hand;* 用手保護眼睛； ~ *a friend from censure.* 使朋友不受責難。

shift[1] /ʃɪft ; ʃɪft/ *n* **1** change of place or character; substitution of one thing for another: 位置或性格的改變；變換；更易： *a ~ in emphasis,* placing the emphasis differently. 重點的改變。 **2** [C] group of workmen who start work as another group finishes; period for which such a group works: 輪值之一班(在另一班下工時開始工作者)；換班；輪值之時間： *on the day/night ~;* 日(夜)班輪值； *an eight-hour ~;* 八小時的輪值時間； *working in ~s.* 輪值工作。 **3** dodge, trick, scheme, way of evading a difficulty, of getting sth: (逃避困難，獲得某物之)計謀；方策；手段： *resort to dubious ~s in order to get some money.* 使用有問題的手段以期獲得一些錢。 *As a last desperate ~, he pawned his wife's wedding ring.* 他最後迫不得已只好把妻子的結婚戒指當掉。 ***make ~ (with sth/to do sth),*** manage or contrive, be able somehow or other: 設法；盡量想辦法： *We must make ~ with the money we have.* 我們必須就我們所有的錢設法(維持生活等)。 *He must make ~ without help.* 他必須自己想辦法。 ⇨ make~ at make[1](29). **4** woman's narrow dress without a waistline; (old use) chemise. 布袋裝；(舊用法)連身襯裙。 **5 ('gear-) ~,** (motoring) mechanism for gear change: (駕車)排檔；排檔桿： *Do you prefer a manual to an automatic gear-~?* 你是不是比較喜歡手排檔而不大喜歡自動排檔呀？ **~·less** *adj* without ability to find ways of doing things; unable to get on in life. 沒有辦事能力的；沒有謀生能力的。

shift[2] /ʃɪft ; ʃɪft/ *vt, vi* [VP6A, 14, 15A, 2A, C] **1** *~ sth (from/to),* change position or direction; transfer: 改變位置或方向；移動；更易： *~ a burden from one shoulder to the other;* 將負擔自一肩移至另一肩上； *~ the blame (on) to sb else.* 諉過於他人。 *Will you help me to ~ the furniture about/round, please?* 請你幫助我移動傢具，好嗎？ *The wind has ~ed to the north.* 風轉向北吹。 *The cargo has ~ed,* has been shaken out of place by the movement of the ship. 船貨已因船身的顛簸而移動了位置。 *Don't try to ~ the responsibility on to me.* 不要企圖把責任推給我。 ***~ one's ground,*** take up a new position, approach the subject in a different way, during an argument. 採取新的立場；(辯論中)改變論據。 **2** (motoring) change (gears): (駕車)變換(排檔)： *~ into second/third gear.* 換成二(三)檔。 **3** ***~ for oneself,*** manage as best one can (to make a livelihood, get sth done) without help: 自謀生計；自行設法完成某事： *When their father died the children had to ~ for themselves.* 爸爸死後，孩子們只好自謀生活。 **shifty** *adj* (-ier, -iest) untrustworthy; deceitful; not straightforward: 不可靠的；詭詐的；不正直的： *a ~y customer;* 不可靠的傢伙； *~y behaviour;* 不正直的行爲； *~y eyes.* 詭詐的眼睛。 **~·ily** /-ɪlɪ ; -ɪlɪ/ *adv* **~i·ness** *n*

shil·ling /ˈʃɪlɪŋ ; ˈʃɪlɪŋ/ *n* **1** (until 1971) British coin with the value of twelve pennies, one-twentieth of a pound. (到1971年止)先令(英國錢幣，值十二便士，爲一鎊的二十分之一)。⇨ App 4. 參看附錄四。 **2** basic monetary unit of Kenya, Uganda and Tanzania, equal to 100 cents. 肯亞、烏干達、坦尙尼亞的基本貨幣單位，相當於100分。

shilly-shally /ˈʃɪlɪ ʃælɪ ; ˈʃɪlɪˌʃælɪ/ *vi* [VP2A] be unable to make up one's mind; be undecided. 猶豫不決；躊躇；逡巡。□ *n* [U] indecision. 猶豫不決；躊躇；逡巡。

shim·mer /ˈʃɪmə(r) ; ˈʃɪmɚ/ *vi* [VP2A, C], *n* [U] (shine with a) wavering soft or faint light: 發閃光；閃光： *moonlight ~ing on the lake;* 湖上月光閃爍； *the ~ of pearls.* 珍珠的閃光。

shin /ʃɪn ; ʃɪn/ *n* front part of the leg below the knee. 外脛。⇨ the illus at leg. 參看 leg 之插圖。 **'~-bone** *n* tibia. 脛骨。⇨ the illus at skeleton. 參看 skeleton 之插圖。 **'~-guard** *n* pad worn on the ~ at football. (踢足球用的)護脛。□ *vi* (-nn-) [VP3A] *~ up,* climb up (using arms and legs to grip sth): (用手臂和腿攀着某物)往上爬： *~ up a tree.* 爬上一棵樹。

shin·dig /ˈʃɪndɪg ; ˈʃɪndɪg/ *n* (sl) (俚) **1** lively and noisy party. 狂歡會；舞會；慶祝會。 **2** (= *shindy*) brawl. 吵鬧；喧囂；騷動。

shindy /ˈʃɪndɪ ; ˈʃɪndɪ/ *n* [C] (*pl* -dies) (colloq) brawl; noisy disturbance: (俗)吵鬧；喧囂；騷動： *kick up a ~.* 引起一陣騷動。

shine /ʃaɪn ; ʃaɪn/ *vi, vt* (*pt, pp* shone /ʃɒn *US:* ʃəun; ʃon/ but ⇨ 2 below) **1** [VP2A, C] give out or reflect light; be bright (lit or fig); excel in some way: 發光；反射光；照耀(字面或喻)；卓越；出衆： *The moon is shining.* 月光在照耀。 *The sun shone out,* suddenly began to ~ (as clouds moved). 太陽(穿雲而出)重新照耀大地。 *His face shone with excitement.* 他臉上露出興奮的神色。 *He does not ~ in conversation,* is not a good talker. 他不健談。 *I don't ~ at tennis.* 我不擅長網球。 **2** [VP6A] (colloq, and with *pp* ~d) polish (which is more usu); make bright: (俗，過去分詞作 ~d)磨光；擦亮(polish 較常用)；使發亮；使照耀： *~ shoes.* 擦鞋。 *Have you ~d your shoes/the brass?* 你把你的鞋子(那銅器)擦亮了嗎？ □ *n* **1** (*sing* only) polish; brightness: (僅用單數)刷擦；光亮；光輝： *Give your shoes a good ~.* 把你的鞋好好擦一下。 *How can I take the ~ out of the seat of my trousers?* 我怎樣才能把褲臀上的亮光去掉？ **2** [U] ***come rain or ~,*** whatever the weather may be; (fig) whatever may happen. 不論晴雨；(喻)無論如何。 **shiny** *adj* (-ier, -iest) polished; rubbed bright: 擦亮的；磨光的： *a shiny coat,* one with the nap rubbed off (so that the surface ~s). 磨去布毛而發光的外衣。

shingle[1] /ˈʃɪŋgl ; ˈʃɪŋgl̩/ *n* [U] small, rounded pebbles on the seashore. 海濱之小圓石。 **shin·gly** /ˈʃɪŋglɪ ; ˈʃɪŋglɪ/ *adj* of ~: 海濱小圓石的： *I prefer a sandy beach to a shingly beach.* 我寧愛沙灘而不喜歡有小圓石的海灘。

shingle[2] /ˈʃɪŋgl ; ˈʃɪŋgl̩/ *n* [C] **1** small, flat square or oblong piece of wood used (like tiles and slates) on roofs, spires and walls. 蓋板；屋頂板；木瓦；牆面板。 **2** (US colloq) small, wooden signboard (used by lawyers, dentists, etc): (美俗)木質小招牌(律師、牙醫等用之)： *put up one's ~,* set up for the first time, eg as a doctor. 掛牌；開業(如醫師等)。 □ *vt* cover (a roof, etc) with ~s: 以屋頂板蓋(屋頂等)： *a ~d church spire.* 以屋頂板覆蓋之教堂尖頂。

shingle[3] /ˈʃɪŋgl ; ˈʃɪŋgl̩/ *vt* [VP6A] cut (a woman's hair) so that it is short at the back but longer at the sides. 將(女髮)剪成後短側長的髮式。□ *n* this kind of haircut. 後短側長的女髮式。

shingles /ˈʃɪŋglz ; ˈʃɪŋgl̩z/ *n* (with *sing v*) skin disease forming a band of inflamed spots (often round the waist). (用單數動詞)帶狀疱疹(常生於腰際)。

ship[1] /ʃɪp ; ʃɪp/ *n* **1** sea-going vessel of considerable size: 海船；艦： *a 'sailing-~;* 帆船； *a 'merchant-~;* 商船； *a 'war~,* etc; 戰艦(等)； *take ~,* go on board a ~; 上船； *the ~'s company,* the entire crew; 全體船員； *the ~'s articles,* the terms on which seamen are engaged; 雇用船員合同； *the ~'s papers,* the documents showing ownership, nationality, nature of the cargo, etc. 船證；船照(記有船主、國籍、船貨之性質等)。⇨ the illus at barque. 參看 barque 之插圖。 ***when my '~ comes in/home,*** when I have made my fortune. 等我有錢的時候。 ***on '~·board,*** on board ~. 在船上。 **2** (colloq) spacecraft; (US colloq) aircraft. (俗)太空船；(美俗)飛機。 **3** (compounds) (複合字) **'~('s) biscuit,** hard, coarse biscuit used, in former times, during long voyage. 一種粗硬的餅乾(昔日遠航時所備用者)。 **'~·breaker** *n* contractor who buys and breaks up old ~s (for scrap). 收購並拆散廢船之承包人(以獲取廢鐵)。 **'~·broker** *n* agent of a

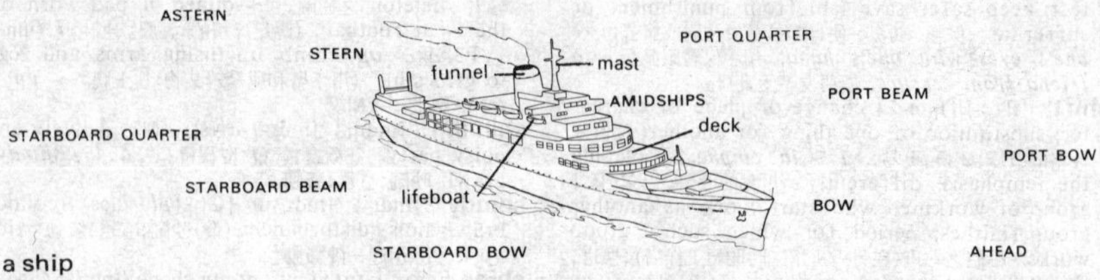

a ship

shipping company who does a ~'s business in port; one who buys, sells and charters ~s; agent for marine insurance. 船舶經紀人;買、賣和租雇船舶者;水險掮客。 ˈ~·**builder** *n* one whose business is building ~s. 造船者。Hence, 由此產生, ˈ~·**building** *n* [U]: ˈ~*building yard*, = ~yard. 船塢;造船所。 ˈ~-**canal** *n* canal large enough for sea-going vessels. (可供海船航行的)運河。ˈ~'**s-chandler** *n* one who deals in equipment for ~s. 船具商。ˈ~·**load** *n* as much cargo, or as many passengers, as a ~ can carry. 船載量。ˈ~·**mate** *n* fellow sailor; person belonging to the same ~ as another: 同船水手;同船同事: *Harry and I were ~mates in 1962.* 1962 年哈利和我是同船同事。ˈ~·**owner** *n* person who owns a ~ or ~s, or shares in a shipping company. 船主;船公司股東。ˈ~·**shape** *adj* tidy; in good order. 整齊的;井然有序的。□ *adv* in a ~shape manner. 整齊地;井然有序地。ˈ~-**way** *n* sloping structure on which a ~ is built and down which it slides into the water. 造船臺;下水台。ˈ~·**wreck** *n* [U] loss or destruction of a ~ at sea by storm, collision, etc:船舶之損失或失事;船難: *suffer ~wreck;* 遭受船難; [C] instance of this. 船難之實例。□ *vt* cause to suffer ~wreck; destroy by ~wreck. 使遭船難;使毀於船難。ˈ~·**wright** *n* ~ builder. 造船者。ˈ~·**yard** *n* place where ~s are built. 船塢;造船所。

ship² /ʃɪp ; ʃɪp/ *vt, vi* (-pp-) **1** [VP6A, 15A, B] put, take, send, in a ship: 裝上船;用船運: ~ *gold to India;* 用船運黃金前往印度; (comm) take, send, by train, road, etc: (商)以火車,公路等裝運: ~ *goods by express train.* 以特快火車運送貨物。~ ***off,*** send: 送往;遣去: ~ *off young men to the war.* 送年輕人赴戰場。 **2** [VP6A] ~ ***oars,*** take them out of the water into the boat. 把槳自水中取出置於船上。~ ***water;*** ~ ***a sea,*** be flooded by water breaking over the side. 水自舷側進入船艙。 **3** [VP6A, 15A, 2C] engage for service on a ship: 在船上服務;雇用(船員): ~ *a crew for a voyage round the world.* 雇用環航世界的一批水手。*He ~ped* (= took service) *as a steward on an Atlantic liner.* 他在航行大西洋的一艘郵輪上擔任服務員。 ~·**ment** *n* [U] putting of goods, etc on a ship; [C] quantity of goods ~ped. 裝船;裝運;所裝運之貨量。 ~·**per** *n* person who arranges for goods to be ~ped. 安排裝運貨物之人。 ~·**ping** *n* [U] all the ships of a country, port, etc. (一國,一海港等的)船舶總數。 ˈ~·**ping-agent** *n* shipowner's representative at a port. 船主在港口之代理人;水路運輸業者。 ˈ~·**ping-office** *n* ~ping-agent's office; office where seamen are engaged. 水路運輸業者之事務所;海員雇用所。

shire /ʃaɪə(r) ; ʃaɪr/ *n* [C] county (now chiefly used as a suffix in the names of certain counties, and usu pronounced /-ʃə(r) ; -ʃɚ/): (英國的)郡(現在主要用作某些郡名的字尾,通常讀作 /-ʃə(r) ; -ʃɚ/): *Hampshire,* 漢普郡(在英格蘭南部), *Yorkshire.* 約克郡(在英格蘭北部)。**the ~s,** certain midland counties of England and parts of these well known for foxhunting. 英國中部以 shire 爲字尾之各郡;這些郡以獵狐出名的各地方。 ˈ~ **horse,** powerful breed of horse used for pulling carts and wagons. (用於拖車之)大種馬。

shirk /ʃɜːk ; ʃɝk/ *vt, vi* [VP6A, D, 2A] avoid, try to escape (doing sth, responsibility, duty, etc): 規避;躲避 (做某事,盡責任,義務等): ~ *going to the dentist;* 規避去看牙醫; ~ *work/school.* 規避工作(逃學)。*He's ~ing.* 他在躲避。~**er** *n*

shirt /ʃɜːt ; ʃɝt/ *n* man's loose-fitting garment for the upper part of the body (of cotton, linen, silk, etc) usu worn under a jacket, with long sleeves or (ˈ*sports* ~) half sleeves. 男襯衣;襯衫(短袖襯衫稱作 sports ~)。 ***in one's*** ˈ~-***sleeves,*** not wearing a jacket or coat. 未穿外衣。***keep one's ~ on,*** (sl) keep one's temper. (俚)不發脾氣;保持冷靜。***put one's ~ on*** (a horse, etc), bet all one has on. 以所有的錢下注(某馬等)。 ˈ~-**front** *n* usu stiffened and starched breast of a white ~. 白襯衣的前胸(通常漿硬)。 ˈ~-**waister** (US 美 ˈ~-**waist**) woman's blouse or dress that buttons down the front. 寬鬆的女上衣(由正面扣鈕扣)。~·**ing** *n* material for making ~s. 襯衣布;襯衣料。~**y** *adj* (-ier, -iest) (sl) ill-tempered. (俚)壞脾氣的;發怒的。

shish kebab /ˌʃɪʃ kəˈbæb *US:* ˈʃɪʃ kəbæb ; ˈʃɪʃkəˌbɑb/ *n* dish of pieces of meat roasted and served on skewers. 烤肉;叉燒肉。

shit /ʃɪt ; ʃɪt/ (⚠, not in polite use) (諱,非文雅用法) *n* [U] **1** excrement. 排泄物;糞便。 **2** (sl) hashish. (俚)大麻煙。 **3** (contemptuous for a) person: (蔑)人: *You big ~!* 你這個大笨蛋! □ *vi* (-tt-) (*pt, pp* ~ted or shat /ʃæt ; ʃæt/) [VP2A, 3A] empty the bowels of excrement. 排泄糞便;大便。 ~ ***on sb,*** (vulg sl) (鄙,俚) **(a)** severely scold or find fault with him. 嚴厲責罵某人;找某人的碴。**(b)** report on him, esp to the police. (尤指向警方)密告某人。□ *int* ⚠ (vulg) (as an expression of irritation or objection) Bother! Rubbish! (諱)(鄙)(表示惱怒或反對)討厭!胡說!

shiver¹ /ˈʃɪvə(r) ; ˈʃɪvɚ/ *vi* [VP2A, C] tremble, esp from cold or fear: 顫抖(尤指因寒冷或恐懼): *~ing all over with cold;* 冷得全身顫抖; *~ing like a leaf.* 像樹葉一般地顫抖。□ *n* **1** trembling that cannot be controlled: (無法控制的)顫抖。*The sight sent cold ~s down my back.* 那景象使我的背脊打冷顫。*A ~ ran down her back.* 她的背脊打了一股冷顫。 **2** (*pl*) (複) ***get/have/give sb the ~s,*** (colloq) get/give sb ~ing movements, a feeling of fear or horror. (俗)發抖(使某人顫慄)。~**y** *adj* inclined to ~; having or causing a feeling of cold, fear, horror. 易顫抖的;感到或引起寒冷,害怕,恐懼的。

shiver² /ˈʃɪvə(r) ; ˈʃɪvɚ/ *n* (usu *pl*) one of the many small pieces into which sth is broken: (通常用複數)碎片;破片: *break sth to ~s;* 把某物打碎; *burst into ~s.* 變粉碎。□ *vt, vi* [VP15A, 2C] break into ~s. 打碎;碎裂。

shoal¹ /ʃəʊl ; ʃol/ *n* [C] great number of fish swimming together; great number (of people, things): 魚羣;(人,物之)大羣;大量: *a ~ of herring;* 一羣鯡魚; *swimming in ~s.* 成羣地游。□ *vi* (of fish) form ~s. (指魚)成羣;羣聚。

shoal² /ʃəʊl ; ʃol/ *n* [C] shallow place in the sea, esp where there are sandbanks; (*pl;* fig) hidden dangers. 海洋之水淺處(尤指有沙洲的地方);淺灘;(複;喻)隱伏的危險。□ *vi* [VP2A] become shallow(er). 變淺或更淺。

shock¹ /ʃɒk ; ʃɑk/ *n* **1** [C] violent blow or shaking (eg as caused by a collision or explosion): 衝擊;

震動(例如因相撞或爆炸所引起): *the ~ of a fall;* 落地的衝擊; *earthquake ~s.* 地震引起的顫動。'~ **absorber** *n* kinds of device fitted to motor-vehicles, aircraft, etc to lessen ~s and add to the cushioning effects of tyres, springs, etc. (汽車,飛機等之)減震器(減少震動並增加輪胎、彈簧等緩衝效果的器械)。'~ **tactics,** use of massed forces to attack (in war). (作戰中)密集襲擊法;突襲戰術。'~ **troops,** troops specially trained for violent assaults. 突擊部隊。'~-**brigade,** '~-**workers,** (esp in USSR) body of workers engaged in specially arduous work. (尤指蘇俄之)擔任特別困難工作的工人組織;工人突擊隊。'~ **wave,** region of intensely high air pressure caused by an atomic explosion or an aircraft moving at supersonic speed. (由原子爆炸或超音速飛機所引起的)空氣激流;冲擊波;激波。**2** [C] effect caused by the passage of an electric current through the body: 電震;電擊(電流通過身體所引起者): *If you touch that live wire you'll get a ~.* 如果你接觸那條已經通電的電線,你就會遭電擊。**3** [C] sudden and violent disturbance of the feelings or the nervous system (caused by bad news, severe injury, etc); [U] condition caused by such a disturbance: 休克(因壞消息,重傷等引起的情緒或神經系統之突然而激烈的障害);休克所引起的狀況;震驚;激動: *The news of her mother's death was a terrible ~ to her.* 她母親死亡的消息使她極爲震驚。*The stock market quickly recovered from the ~ of the election results.* 證券市場迅速地由選舉結果所引起的震動中恢復了常態。*It gave me quite a ~ to learn that he had married again.* 聽說他再婚,我感到很震驚。*She died of ~ following an operation on the brain.* 她死於大腦手術後所發生的休克。⇨ *shell-~* at shell(3). '~ **treatment/therapy,** treatment of (esp mental) disorder by using electric ~s or drugs on the nervous system. (電擊神經系統或給予神經系統藥物以治療精神病之)休克療法。□ *vt* [VP 6A] cause ~(3) to; fill with surprised disgust, horror, etc: 使休克;使震驚;使憤慨;使駭異: *I was ~ed at the news of her death.* 她死去的消息使我震驚。*He was ~ed to hear his daughter swearing.* 聽到女兒賭咒他甚爲震駭。*I'm not easily ~ed, but that book really is obscene.* 我不容易感到震驚,但那本書實在太猥褻。**~er** *n* **1** person who ~s: 令人震驚的人: *He's a ~er,* a ~ingly bad person. 他是個大壞蛋。**2** sth that ~s, eg a sensational novel; bad specimen of sth. 令人震驚之事物(如黃色或恐怖小說);某物的壞品;壞的事例。**~·ing** *adj* **1** very bad or wrong: 極壞的;大錯的: *~ing behaviour.* 極壞的行爲。**2** causing ~(3): 令人震驚的;可怕的: *~ing news,* eg of a flood that causes great loss of life. 令人震驚的消息(如導致重大死傷之水災等)。**3** (colloq) bad: (俗)壞的;不好的: *a ~ing dinner;* 不好的餐食; *~ing handwriting.* 不好的書法。□ *adv* (colloq, as an intensive) very: (俗,用作强勢語)甚;極: *a ~ing bad cold.* 極爲嚴重的感冒。**~·ing·ly** *adv* **1** badly: 惡劣地: *You're playing ~ingly.* 你玩得極不高明。**2** extremely: 極端地: *How ~ingly expensive!* 太貴了!

shock[2] /ʃɒk; ʃɑk/ *n* number of sheaves of grain placed together and supporting each other in a field to dry during harvest. (在收穫季,若干綑禾穀成堆放置田裡,彼此支撐,以便晒乾之)禾束堆。

shock[3] /ʃɒk; ʃɑk/ *n* (usu 通常作 **~ *of hair***) rough, untidy mass of hair (on sb's head). (某人頭上之)蓬亂的頭髮。ˌ~-'**headed** *adj* having such hair. 頭髮蓬亂的。

shod /ʃɒd; ʃɑd/ ⇨ shoe *v.*

shoddy /'ʃɒdɪ; 'ʃɑdɪ/ *n* [U] (cloth of poor quality, made from) fibre from old cloth, etc. 舊布等之纖維;用舊布等之纖維再織成的布。□ *adj* (-ier, -iest) of poor quality; made to seem better than it is: 質劣的;冒充好貨的: *~ cloth;* 用舊料之纖維再織成的布; *a ~ piece of work.* 劣貨。

shoe /ʃuː; ʃu/ *n* **1** (often 常作 ***pair of ~s***) outer covering for the foot, esp one which does not reach above the ankle (⇨ boot): 鞋(尤指鞋面未及足踝者): *put on/take off one's ~s.* 穿鞋(脫鞋)。***be in/put oneself in 'sb's ~s,*** occupy, imagine oneself to be in, his position; be in his plight: 處於他人之地位;居於他人之處境: *I wouldn't be in your ~s for a thousand pounds.* 給我一千鎊我也不願處於你那種地位。***know where the ~ pinches,*** understand from one's own experience all about hardships, etc. 知道困苦等之所在。**2** (compounds) (複合字) '~·**black** *n* boy or man who polishes ~s of passers-by. 擦鞋童;擦鞋匠。'~·**horn** *n* device with a curved blade for getting the heel easily into a ~. 鞋拔。'~·**lace** *n* cord for fastening the edges of a shoe's uppers. 鞋帶。'~-**leather** *n* leather suitable for making ~s. 製鞋用的皮革。'~·**maker** *n* person who makes and/or repairs ~s and boots. 鞋匠。'~·**making** *n* [U] trade of a ~maker. 製鞋;製鞋業。'~·**string** *n* (US) (美) = ~lace. ***do sth on a ~string,*** do sth (eg start a business) on a very small amount of capital. 以極少的資本做某事(如創業等)。'~-**tree** *n* thin, flexible, shaped block for inserting in a shoe to keep its shape. 鞋楦。**3** **(horse-)~** /'hɔːʃʃuː; 'hɔrʃ,ʃu/, metal band nailed to the hoof of a horse: 蹄鐵: *His horse cast/threw a ~,* lost one. 他的馬掉了一塊蹄鐵。**4** part of a brake that presses against the wheel or drum (of a bicycle, motor-vehicle, etc); any object like a ~ in appearance or use. 車輛的煞車皮;形狀或用途似鞋之物。□ *vt* (*pt, pp* shod /ʃɒd; ʃɑd/) [VP6A] fit with ~s: 穿以鞋;釘以蹄鐵;配以鞋狀物: *well shod for wet weather,* having good ~s able to keep out the wet; 穿着防雨良好之鞋; *an iron-shod stick,* one with an iron ferrule at the end. 裝有鐵包頭的手杖。

sho·gun /'ʃəʊguːn *US:* -gʌn; 'ʃo,gʌn/ *n* (until 1867) hereditary commander-in-chief of the Japanese army. (1867年以前之)日本陸軍世襲統帥;幕府將軍。

shone /ʃɒn *US:* ʃəʊn; ʃon/ *pt, pp* of shine.

shoo /ʃuː; ʃu/ *int* cry used for driving away birds, etc. (驅趕鳥等的)噓聲。□ *vt* (*pt, pp* ~ed) [VP15B] ***~ sth/sb away/off,*** drive away by making this cry. 以噓聲驅趕某物(某人)。

shook /ʃʊk; ʃuk/ *pt* of shake.

shoot[1] /ʃuːt; ʃut/ *n* [C] **1** new, young growth on a plant or bush: (植物或灌木之)芽;苗;嫩枝: *train the new ~s of a vine.* 整理藤蔓的新枝。**2** = chute(1, 2). **3** party of people shooting for sport; area of land over which birds, etc are shot: 狩獵隊;狩獵地: *rent a ~ for the season.* 租狩獵地以供狩獵季節之用。

shoot[2] /ʃuːt; ʃut/ *vi, vt* (*pt, pp* shot /ʃɒt; ʃɑt/) **1** [VP2C, 15A, B] move, come, go, send, suddenly or quickly (*out, in, up, forth,* etc): 突然或迅速地動,來,去,送: *The snake's tongue shot out.* 蛇舌突然伸出。*The snake shot its tongue out.* 蛇突然伸舌。*Flames were ~ing up from the burning house.* 火焰自燃燒着的房子冒出。*The meteor shot across the sky.* 隕星快速地掠過天空。*The horse stumbled and the rider was shot over its head.* 馬絆脚,騎者由馬頭上面跌了下來。*As the car hit the tree the occupants were shot out.* 汽車撞在樹上的時候,車內的人被摔了出來。*At the half-way mark, Hill shot ahead,* (in a race) came on quickly and passed his competitors. 在賽跑的半途,希爾突然衝前領先。*They shot angry glances at us.* 他們對我們投以憤怒的眼色。*Rents have shot up,* (= risen suddenly) *in the last few months.* 在過去幾個月之中,租金突然上漲了。*Tom is ~ing up fast,* quickly growing tall. 湯姆長高得很快。*She shot an angry look at him/shot him an angry look.* 她對他投以憤怒的眼色。***~ a bolt,*** send a bolt (of a door, etc) into (or out of) its fastening. 關上或打開(門等的)插梢。***~ one's bolt,*** make one's last effort. 做最後的努力。***~ dice,*** throw dice. 擲骰子。***~ rubbish,*** let it slide from a cart, etc (on to a heap or dump). 從車上等處傾倒垃圾。ˌ~ing

ˈ**star**, meteor which burns up as it passes into and through the earth's atmosphere. 流星(進入並穿過大氣層時燃燒的隕石)。 **2** [VP2A, C] (of plants, bushes) sprout; send out new twigs or branches from a stem: (指花草,灌木)發芽;生枝: *Rose bushes ~ again after being cut back.* 玫瑰叢修剪後會再發新枝。 **3** [VP2A, C] (of pain) pass with a stabbing sensation suddenly and swiftly: (指疼痛)刺痛;劇痛: *The pain shot up his arm.* 他的臂刺痛。*I have a ~ing pain in my left leg.* 我的左腿劇痛。 **4** [VP6A] (of boats) move, be moved, rapidly over, through, etc: (指船)迅速經過: *~ the rapids;* 迅速通過急流; *~ the bridge*, pass under it rapidly with the current. 隨着水流迅速穿過橋下。 **5** [VP6A, 15A, B, 2A, C, 4A] aim and fire with a gun or revolver; aim with a bow and send an arrow at; hit with a shell, bullet, arrow, etc; wound or kill (a person, animal, etc) by doing this: 放(砲);打(槍);射(箭);以砲彈,子彈,箭等打擊;射傷;射殺(人,動物等): *They were ~ing at a target.* 他們在向目標射擊。*He ~s well.* 他善於射擊。*He shot an arrow from his bow.* 他射出弓上的箭。*Can you/Does your gun ~ straight?* 你(你的槍)能命中嗎? *The soldier was shot* (= executed by ~ing) *for desertion.* 那兵士因逃亡而被槍決。*The police did not ~ to kill*, They used their weapons only to frighten the people (eg by firing over their heads). 警察鳴槍鎮壓(非爲射殺人而開槍)。 *He's in Africa ~ing lions.* 他在非洲獵獅。 *He neither rides, ~s nor fishes*, does not take part in these sports. 他不騎馬,不射擊,也不釣魚。*He fell like a shot rabbit*, like a rabbit that had been shot. 他像被射中的兎子那樣摔在地上。 *~* ***away***, (more usu 較常用 *fire away*) **(a)** begin and continue ~ing. 開始不停地射擊。 **(b)** (fig) go ahead; begin. (喩)開始。 *~* ***sth away***, (more usu 較常用 *fire sth away*) get rid of by ~ing: 射完: *~ away all one's ammunition.* 射完所有的彈藥。*~* ***sth down***, bring to the ground by ~ing: 射落;擊落: *The bomber was shot down in flames.* 那轟炸機被擊落而燃燒起來。 *~* ***sth off***, sever by ~ing: 擊掉,擊斷,射斷某物: *He had his arm shot off.* 他的臂被(砲彈)擊斷。 *~* ***a covert/an estate, etc***, ~ the game in it. 在森林(所有地等)打獵。 *~* ***a line***, (sl) exaggerate; lie; deceive. (俚)誇大;說謊;欺騙。 *~* ***one's ˈmouth off***, (US sl) talk indiscreetly or wildly. (美俚)輕率地談話;瞎吹胡扯。 *~* ***a place up***, (US sl) terrorize (a town, district, etc) by going through it and shooting at random, firing at houses, etc. (美俚)盲目放槍使(城鎮,地區等)驚恐。 ˈ**~·ing-box** *n* house used by sportsmen in the ~ing season (eg one on moorlands). 獵舍;狩獵小屋。 ˈ**~·ing-brake** *n* (former times) large horse-drawn open carriage used by sportsmen (for carrying equipment, game that was shot, etc); (in modern times, occasionally used for) estate car. (昔時)獵人所用之敞篷大馬車;(現時偶而用作)旅行車。 ˈ**~·ing-gallery** *n* place where ~ing at targets is practised with pistols or airguns. 手槍或氣槍射擊場。 ˈ**~-ing-range** *n* ground with butts for rifle practice. 射擊場;靶場。 ˈ**~ing-stick**, stick with a spiked end (to be pushed into the ground) and a handle which unfolds to form a seat. (一端插在地上,另一端可爲座墊的)獨脚支棍座椅。 **6** [VP6A, 2A] (cinema) photograph (a scene): (電影)拍攝(一景);攝影: *a ~ing script*, one to be used while a film is being shot (giving the order in which scenes are photographed, etc). 拍攝劇本(拍電影時所用之劇本,指示各景如何拍攝等者)。 **7** [VP2A] (football, hockey, etc) (chiefly imper) make a shot at scoring a goal. (足球,曲棍球等)(主用於祈使)射門。 **~·ing** *n* [U] (esp) (right of) ~ing (game) over an area of land: (尤指)狩獵;狩獵權: *sell the ~ing on an estate.* 出售所有地之狩獵權。⇨ also 6 above. 亦參看上列第 6 義。

shooter /ˈʃuːtə(r); ˈʃutə/ *n* (in compounds) shooting implement: (用於複合字中)射具;槍: *a ˈpea-~;* 豆子槍(一種玩具); *a ˌsix-ˈ~*, revolver firing six shots without reloading. 裝六發子彈之左輪手槍。

shop /ʃɒp; ʃɑp/ *n* **1** (US 美 = *store*) building or part of a building where goods are shown and sold retail: 店鋪;商店: *a butcher's/chemist's ~;* 肉(西藥)店; *a ˈfruit-~.* 水果店。 ***come/go to the wrong ~***, (colloq) to the wrong place/person (for help, information, etc). (俗)找錯地方或人(求助,打聽消息等)。 ***keep ~***, be on duty (eg in a small ~): 照顧着店: *Mr Green got a friend to keep ~ for him while he went to his wife's funeral.* 格林先生爲妻子出殯時,找到一位朋友爲他看店。 ***keep a ~***, be a shopkeeper, own and manage a ~. 做店主;開店。 ***set up ~***, set up in business as a retail trader. 開店;開業。 ˈ**~-assistant** *n* employee in a ~. 店夥計;店員。 ˈ**~-bell** *n* bell (on the door of a small ~) which rings when a customer enters, warning the ~-keeper. 店鈴(在小商店門上之鈴,顧客進入時鳴響以通知店主)。 ˈ**~-girl/-boy** *n* young ~-assistant. 年輕的女店員(男店員)。 ˈ**~-front** *n* frontage of a ~ with its window display, etc. (商店的) 店面 (包括櫥窗等部分)。 **~ hours** *n pl* hours during which a ~ is, or may legally be, open for business. 營業時間。 ˈ**~·keeper** *n* owner of (usu a small) ~. (通常爲小店之)店主。 ˈ**~-lift** *vi, vt* [VP2A, 6A] steal (sth) from a shop while pretending to be a customer. 佯爲顧客而偸竊(貨品)。 Hence, 由此產生, ˈ**~-lifter** *n* person who does this; 佯爲顧客而偸竊貨品之人; ˈ**~-lifting** *n* [U] doing this. 佯爲顧客而偸竊。 ˈ**~-soiled/-worn** *adjj* damaged or dirty as the result of being put on view or handled in a ~. 店中擺舊的。 ˈ**~-walker** *n* person who directs customers (in a large ~ or department store) to the right counters, departments, etc. (大商店或百貨公司之)接待顧客者;巡視員。 ˌ**~-ˈwindow** *n* window used for the display of wares, etc. 商店櫥窗。 ***put all one's goods in the ~window***, (fig) make a display of all one's knowledge, ability, etc and have nothing in reserve (used of a superficial person). (喩)毫不保留地賣弄才學(指膚淺之人)。 **2** [U] one's profession, trade, business, things connected with it. 職業;本行;工作;與職業有關之事。 ***talk ~***, talk about one's work, profession, etc with other people who do the same work. 與同行談論本行。 ***shut up ~***, (colloq) stop doing sth (not necessarily connected with buying and selling). (俗)停止做某事(並非一定指停止營業)。 **3** ***all ˈover the ~***, (sl) (俚) **(a)** in disorder, scattered in confusion: 零亂地;紛亂地散置: *My belongings are all over the ~.* 我的東西零亂地散置着。 **(b)** in every direction: 在各處;在每一方向: *I've looked for it all over the ~.* 我已在各處尋找過(它)。 **4** (= *work~*) place where manufacturing or repairing is done: 工廠;修理廠: *an ˌengiˈneering-~;* 工程廠; *a maˈchine-~;* 機器廠; *the men on the ~ floor*, the workers (contrasted with the management). 工人(與經理部門相對)。 ˌ**~-ˈsteward** *n* member of a local branch committee of a trade union, chosen by his fellow workers to represent them. (代表工會地方分會之工人的)工會代表。 ˌ***closed*** ˈ***~***, system of compulsory membership of trade unions or other professional associations. 必須雇用工會或其他公會會員的制度;實施此種制度的工廠或公司行號。 □ *vi* (-pp-) [VP2A, C] **1** go to ~s to buy things (usu 通常用 *go ~ping*). 購物。 *~* ***around***, (colloq) visit various ~s, markets, etc to obtain the best value for one's money, etc. (俗)逛商店(尋找物美價廉的東西)。 **2** *~* ***on sb***, (sl) inform against, esp to the police. (俚)(尤指向警方)密告某人。 **~·ping** *n* [U] *do one's ~ping;* 購物; *a ˈ~ping street*, one with many ~s; 商店衆多的街道;鬧市; *a ˈ~ping bag/basket*, in which to carry purchases. 購物袋(籃)。 ˈ**~ping centre**, part of a town where there are ~s, markets, etc close together and often where cars are not allowed. 購物中心;(城市中的)商業區。 **'window-~ping** *n* [U] visiting a ~ping centre, street, etc to look at the displays in the ~windows. 遊覽商店櫥窗。 **~·per** *n* person who is ~ping: 購物的人: *crowds of Christmas ~pers.* 聖誕節大羣購物的人。

shore[1] /ʃɔː(r) ; ʃor/ *n* [U, C] stretch of land bordering on the sea or a large body of water: (海或湖的)岸;濱: *a house on the ~(s) of Lake Geneva;* 在日內瓦湖濱的房子; *go on ~* (from a ship). (從船)上岸。

shore[2] /ʃɔː(r) ; ʃor/ *n* [C] wooden support set against a wall, tree, etc to keep it up; prop set against the side of a ship while it is being built or repaired out of the water. (支撐牆、樹等使之直立,支撐建造或修理中之船的)支柱;撐柱。□ *vt* [VP15B] **~ sth up,** support, prop up (with a wooden beam, etc). 以支柱支撐。

shore[3] /ʃɔː(r) ; ʃor/, **shorn** /ʃɔːn ; ʃorn/ ⇨ shear.

short[1] /ʃɔːt ; ʃɔrt/ *adj* (-er, -est) **1** (opp of *long*) measuring little from end to end in space or time; (opp of *tall*) below the average height: (爲 long 之相反字)短的; 短暫的;(爲 tall 之相反字)矮的: *a ~ stick;* 短棍; *a ~ way off,* not far away; 不遠; *a ~ man;* 矮人; *~ grass;* 短草; *a ~ holiday;* 短暫的假期; *a ~ time ago.* 不久以前。*You've cut my hair very ~.* 你把我的頭髮剪得太短了。 *She walked with ~, quick steps.* 她以小而快的步子走路。*The coat is a little ~ in the sleeves.* 那外衣的袖子略短。*The days are getting ~er now that autumn is here.* 秋天到了,白晝漸短。**a ~ ball,** (cricket) not bowled on a correct length. (板球)投球的距離不够長;短球。 **ˌ~ 'circuit** *n* accidental fault in wiring enabling an electric current to flow without going through the resistance of the complete circuit. (電流)短路(電路之意外故障,電流未能通過全部電路之電阻而流動)。 **ˌ~-'circuit** *vt, vi* cause, make or take a ~ circuit in; cut off current from (sth) in this way; (fig) shorten or simplify (a procedure, etc): (使)發生短路;以短路切斷(某物)之電流;(喻)縮短;簡化(手續等): *The system has ~-circuited.* 這個電路系統發生短路了。 **'~ cut** *n* way of getting somewhere, doing sth, etc (thought to be) quicker than the usual or ordinary way: (至某地,做某事等的)近路;捷徑: *They took a ~ cut across the fields instead of going by the road.* 他們穿越田野抄近路而不走大路。**'~ list,** *n* list of candidates (for a position, etc) that has been reduced to a small number from which a final selection is to be made. 決選名單(候選人已淘汰至少數, 以待作最後決定所列出的名單)。Hence, 由此產生, **'~-list** *vt*: *the candidates who have been ~-listed,* whose names have been put on a ~ list (perhaps for interviews). 已列入決選名單的候選人。 **ˌ~-'lived** /'lɪvd *US:* 'laɪvd ; 'laɪvd/ *adj* lasting for a ~ time; brief: 持續不久的;短命的;短暫的: *a ~-lived triumph.* 曇花一現的勝利。**ˌ~-'range,** *adj* **(a)** (of plans, etc) designed for a limited period of time. (指計畫等) 短程的; 短時間的。**(b)** (of missiles, etc) with a comparatively limited range[1](3). (指飛彈等)短程的;射程有限的。***have a ~ temper,*** be lacking in self-control, so that one quickly or easily becomes angry; 易怒;脾氣急躁; hence, 由此產生, **ˌ~-'tempered** *adj* **ˌ~-'term** *attrib adj* limited to, due to be repaid in, a ~ period of time: 限於短期的;須短期內清償的: *~-term loans.* 短期貸款。 **2** not reaching the usual, stated or required (amount, distance, weight, etc): (總數,距離,重量等)不足的;短少的;缺少的: *The shopkeeper was fined for giving ~ weight/measure.* 那店主因賣東西重量(分量)不足而受罰。*The factory is/The workmen are on ~ time,* working fewer hours per day, or days per week, than usual. 這工廠(工人們)縮短工作時間。*These goods are in ~ supply,* The supply is not equal to the demand (*are scarce* is more usu.) ⇨ also commons(2). 這些貨物來源不充裕(are scarce 較常用)。*You've given me ~ change,* less than the correct change. 你少找給我零錢了。Hence, 由此產生, **ˌ~-'change** *vt* cheat (sb) by giving less than the correct change. 少找零錢以欺騙(某人)。***be ~ of,*** **(a)** not have enough of: 短少;無足够之量: *~ of money/time.* 短少錢(時間)。**(b)** be distant from: 有一段距離;未達到: *The car broke down when we were still five miles ~ of our destination.* 我們距目的地尚有五哩的時候,車子拋錨了。***little/nothing ~ of,*** little/nothing less than: (幾乎不,完全不)少於或亞於: *Our escape was little ~ of miraculous,* was almost a miracle. 我們的逃亡幾乎是一項奇蹟。***make ~ work of,*** deal with, dispose of, eat or drink, quickly. 迅速處理、支配、吃或喝。***~ of breath,*** panting, eg after running fast. 喘氣;氣促(如快跑後)。**'~-coming** *n* (usu *pl*) failure (to reach a required standard, to develop properly, to do one's duty). (通常用複數)缺點;短處(未能達到所要求的標準,未充分發展或未盡責)。**ˌ~ 'drink** *n* [C] (or, colloq 俗 **a ~**) whisky, gin, etc in comparatively small glasses or small portions at a time (contrasted with a long drink such as a glass of beer). 以小杯飲用的酒(如威士忌、杜松子酒等,與大杯飲用的酒如啤酒等相對)。 **ˌ~-'handed** *adj* having not enough workmen or helpers. 人手不足的;人手短少的。 **ˌ~ 'sight** *n* [U] inability to see clearly things that are distant, or (fig) to see into the future. 近視;(喻)無眼光。Hence, 由此產生, **ˌ~-'sighted** *adj*: *The Government's policy is ~-sighted,* does not take into account future needs, developments, etc. 政府的政策是短視的。 **ˌ~-'winded** *adj* easily and quickly becoming breathless after exertion; unable to run for long. 用力後易喘氣的;不能久跑的。 **3** (in comm) maturing early; to be paid or met soon: (商)短期的;即將兌現的: *a ~ bill/paper;* 短期滙票(票據); *~ date,* early date for maturing of a bill, bond, etc. (兌現票據等的)短期。 Hence, 由此產生, **ˌ~-'dated** *adj.* **ˌ~ 'bond** *n* one which matures within a period of five years. (五年期滿的)短期債券。 **ˌ~-term 'capital,** capital raised for short periods. 短期資本;短期資金。 **4** (of a person) saying very little, or saying much in few words; (of what he says, his manner of speaking) expressed in few words; curt; abrupt: (指人)說話少的; 長話短說的; 說話扼要的; (指其所說之話、說話的態度)言簡意賅的; 簡潔的; 唐突的;簡慢的: *He/His answer was ~ and to the point.* 他說話(他的回答)扼要中肯。 *He was very ~ with me.* 他對我甚爲無禮。 ***for ~,*** as a ~er form; for brevity's sake: 簡稱; 爲簡短起見: *Benjamin, called 'Ben' for ~.* 本傑明,簡稱爲'本'。 ***in ~,*** in a few words; to sum up briefly (after a long description, etc). 簡言之;總結(在冗長的敍述之後等)。 ***the long and the ~ of it,*** all that can or need be said. 一切所能說或所需要說的話;總而言之。 **5** (of cake, pastry) easily breaking or crumbling. (指餅,麵點)易碎的;鬆脆的。 **ˌ~ 'pastry** *n* [U] made with much butter or fat. 油酥麵點。 **'~·bread/cake** *nn* easily crumbled dry cake made with flour, sugar and much butter. (用麵粉、糖和大量奶油做成的)脆餅;酥餅。 **6** (of vowels or syllables) taking the less of two usual durations: (指母音或音節)短音的;非長音的: *the ~ vowel in 'pull' and the long vowel in 'pool'.* pull 之短母音和 pool 之長母音。 **7** (other compounds and special uses). (其他複合字及特殊用法)。 **'~·fall** *n* deficit. 不足之額。 **'~·hand** *n* [U] system of rapid writing using special signs; stenography. 速記;速記術。 ***by a ~ head,*** **(a)** (racing) by a distance of less than the length of a horse's head: (賽馬)以短於馬首長度之距離: *Fly-by-Night won by a ~ head.* '夜翔'以不到一頭之差險勝。 **(b)** (fig) by only a little. (喻)藉少量(越過)。 **'~·horn** *n* [C] name of a breed of cattle with ~ curved horns. 一種短角牛。 **~ leg**

slip *n* (cricket) (板球) ⇨ the illus at cricket. 參看 cricket 之插圖。'**~ wave** *n* (radio telegraphy) one having a wave-length of from 10 to 100 metres. (無線電報)短波(波長在 10 至 100 公尺之間)。**~·ly** *adv* **1** soon; in a ~ time: 卽刻;不久: *~ly after(wards);* 不久之後; *~ly before noon.* 中午前不久。*He is ~ly to leave for Mexico.* 他卽將前往墨西哥。 **2** briefly; in a few words. 簡略地;簡言之。**3** sharply; curtly: 唐突地;簡慢地: *answer rather ~ly.* 頗爲無禮地回答。**~·ness** *n*

short² /ʃɔːt ; ʃɔrt/ *adv* **1** abruptly; suddenly: 唐突地;突然: *stop ~.* 突然停止。***bring/pull/take sb up ~,*** interrupt or check him abruptly. 唐突地打斷某人(所說的話或所做的事)。***~ of,*** leaving out of question; except: 除…外;除去: *They would commit every crime ~ of murder.* 除謀殺外,他們無惡不作。**2** before the natural or expected time. 未到自然的或預定的時間地;不足地;缺乏地。***come/fall ~ of,*** be insufficient, inadequate, disappointing (expectations, etc): 不足;不及;未達到(期望等): *The box-office receipts fell ~ of the manager's expectations.* 票房收入未達到經理的期望。***cut sth/sb ~,*** **(a)** interrupt; bring to an end before the usual or natural time: 阻止;使提早結束: *The chairman had to cut ~ the proceedings.* 主席必須提早結束議程。**(b)** make ~(er). 使短;使簡短。***go ~ (of),*** do without; deprive oneself (of): 無需;使自己不能有: *I don't want you to go ~* (of money, etc) *in order to lend me what I need.* 我不要你爲了借給我所需要的(如錢等),而自己感到短缺。***run ~ (of),*** reach the end: 用罄: *Our supplies ran ~.* 我們的給養用罄了。*We're running ~ of paraffin.* 我們的石蠟快用完了。***be taken ~,*** (colloq) have a sudden motion of the bowels necessitating a hurried visit to the lavatory. (俗)突然便急。 **3** ***sell ~,*** (comm) sell for future delivery (stocks, shares, commodities, etc that one does not own) in the expectation of being able to buy more cheaply before the date agreed upon for delivery. (商)賣空(約定將來交貨而賣出證券、股票、商品等,希望交貨前以低價買進)。***sell sb ~,*** betray, cheat, belittle him. 背叛、欺騙、貶抑某人。

short³ /ʃɔːt ; ʃɔrt/ *n* (colloq) short circuit, ⇨ short¹(1); short drink. (俗)(電)短路;用小杯飲用的酒。□ *vi, vt* short-circuit. (使)短路;簡化。

short·age /ˈʃɔːtɪdʒ ; ˈʃɔrtɪdʒ/ *n* [C, U] (amount of) deficiency; condition of not having enough: 不足;不足之量;缺乏;缺少: *'food ~s;* 食物缺乏; *a ~ of rice;* 米的缺乏; *owing to ~ of staff;* 由於人員的缺乏; *a ~ of 50 tons.* 缺少五十噸。⇨ glut, *n*

shorten /ˈʃɔːtn ; ˈʃɔrtn̩/ *vt, vi* [VP6A, 2A] make or become shorter: 使短;變短;使不足;變不足;使鬆脆;變鬆脆: *The days are beginning to ~,* eg in autumn. 白晝開始變短了(如在秋天)。 *The captain ordered his men to ~ sail,* reduce the area of sail spread to the wind. 船長命令船員縮帆。**~·ing** /ˈʃɔːtnɪŋ ; ˈʃɔrtn̩ɪŋ/ *n* [U] fat used for making pastry light and flaky. 用以使麵點鬆脆的油脂。⇨ short¹(5).

shorts /ʃɔːts ; ʃɔrts/ *n pl* ***(pair of) ~,*** short trousers extending to or above the knees, as worn by children, by adults for games, informal wear (on the beach, etc). (孩童或成人在戶外活動時穿着的)短褲。

shot¹ /ʃɒt ; ʃɑt/ *n* **1** [C] (sound of the) firing of a gun, etc: (槍,砲等的)發射;射擊;槍聲;砲聲: *hear ~s in the distance;* 聽到遠處的槍聲; *the first ~s in the campaign,* the start of the attack. 此一戰役攻擊的開始。*At each ~ he got nearer to the centre of the target.* 他每射擊一發便更接近靶心。***(do sth) like a ~,*** at once; without hesitation. 立刻;毫不遲疑地(做某事)。***off like a ~,*** off at great speed. 似彈矢般離去;飛快地離去。 **2** [C] attempt to hit sth, hitting of sth; attempt to do sth, answer a question, etc; throw, stroke, hit, etc in certain games: (擊中某物之)試圖;擊中某物;試爲;試猜;試答;(某些遊戲之)打擊;投射: *Good ~, Sir!* 先生,您射得眞準! *That remark was a ~ at me,* was aimed at me. 那話是針對我說的。***a ~ in the dark,*** a wild or random guess. 瞎猜;亂猜。***have a ~ (at sth),*** try to do sth: 嘗試;試試看;設法: *Have a ~ at solving the problem.* 設法解決問題。*The striker had a ~ at goal,* tried to score. 擊球者試圖射門得分。*Let me have a ~ at it.* 讓我試試看。*He made several lucky ~s at the examination questions.* 他幸運地猜中了數個試題。***a 'long ~,*** an attempt to solve a problem, etc with little evidence, few facts to go on: 猜測;大膽的企圖: *It's a long ~ but I think John must have known about the murder.* 雖然這只是個猜測,但我認爲約翰對這件謀殺案一定知情。***ˌnot by a 'long ~,*** not even if circumstances were most favourable. 卽使在最有利的條件下亦不可。 **3** [C] that which is fired from a gun, esp (formerly stone, later metal) nonexplosive projectile for old-fashioned cannon. 彈;彈丸;砲彈;(尤指)舊式砲所用之非爆炸性彈丸(從前爲石塊,以後爲金屬物)。⇨ shell(3); heavy iron ball thrown in athletic competition (called the '*~-put*): (運動競賽用的)鉛球: *putting the ~.* 推鉛球。 **4** **lead ~,** [U] quantity of tiny balls (or pellets) of lead contained in the cartridge of a sporting gun (instead of a single bullet), used against birds and small animals. (獵槍所用之)散彈。⇨ the illus at cartridge. 參看 cartridge 之插圖。'**~-gun** *n* sporting gun with a smooth bore firing cartridges containing ~. 散彈槍;獵槍。'**~-tower** *n* tower in which ~ is made from molten lead poured through a sieve at the top and falling into water. 製彈塔(熔化之鉛經由頂部細篩落入水中以製鉛丸)。 **5** [C] person who shoots, with reference to his skill: 射手;槍手;砲手(就其技術而言者): *He's a first-class/good/poor, etc ~.* 他是第一流(好,壞等)的射手。 **6** [C] photograph, or one of a series of photographs, taken with a cinecamera: (電影攝影機所拍的)鏡頭;景: *The exterior ~s were taken in Bermuda.* 外景係在百慕達島拍攝的。 **'long ~,** (opp of *close-up*) taken with a long distance between the camera and the subject. (爲 close-up 之相反字)遠景;遠鏡頭。 **7** (esp US) injection from a hypodermic needle (of a drug): (尤美)皮下注射(藥物): *have a ~ in the arm.* 在臂上注射。***have/get/give sb a ~ in the arm,*** **(a)** have/give sb an injection. 在(某人)臂上注射一針。**(b)** have/give sb/sth that revives or restores, eg the economy. (爲某人)注射一劑强心針(使在經濟方面復甦)。 **8** **a 'big ~,** (sl) an important person, esp a conceited one. (俚)要人;大人物;名人(尤指自負之人)。

shot² /ʃɒt ; ʃɑt/ *n* share of a reckoning or of expense: 應付的費用;該付的帳: *pay one's ~.* 付帳。

should /ʃʊd ; ʃud; *weak form* ʃəd ; ʃəd/ *v* ⇨ shall.

shoul·der /ˈʃəʊldə(r) ; ˈʃoldɚ/ *n* **1** that part of the body of a human being or animal where an arm or foreleg is joined to the trunk (⇨ the illus at trunk), or where the wing of a bird joins its neck; curve from this point to the neck: 肩(人之臂與軀幹相連處,獸之前肢與軀體相連處,參看 trunk 之插圖,鳥之翅膀與頸部相連處);肩部;肩膀(肩頸間之彎曲部): *This coat is narrow across the ~s.* 這外衣的肩部狹窄。*He has one ~ a little higher than the other.* 他的一肩比另一肩略高。**~ to ~,** side by side and touching; (fig) united. 併肩;(喻)協力;團結。***give sb the cold ~,*** ⇨ cold¹(1). ***put one's ~ to the wheel,*** work energetically at a task. 努力工作。***stand head and ~s above*** (others), be considerably taller (or, fig, mentally or morally better) than. 遠高於(他人);(喻,在智力或道德上)遠勝過。***straight from the ~,*** (fig, of criticism, rebukes, etc) frankly put. (喻,指批評、責難等)率直的;直陳的。'**~-blade** *n* either of the flat bones of the upper back, behind and below the neck.

肩胛骨。 ⇨ the illus at skeleton. 參看 skeleton 之插圖。 '~-**strap** *n* **(a)** narrow strap on the ~ of a military uniform (with badges of rank, etc). 軍人的肩章;肩徽(附有階級標誌)。 **(b)** ribbon which passes over a woman's ~ and supports a garment. (掛在女人肩上用以吊住衣服的)肩帶。 '~-**flash** *n* strip of material on the ~ of a military uniform, with a coloured patch as the distinguishing emblem of a division, etc. 軍服之肩飾(有彩色之小片用作識別某師等之標幟)。 **2** (*pl*) part of the back between the two ~s(1): (複)背的上部: *give a child a ride on one's ~s;* 讓小孩騎在肩膀上; *shift the blame to other ~s,* let others take the blame. 把責任推給別人承擔。 ***have broad ~s,*** be able to bear much weight or (fig) responsibility. 能肩負重擔;(喻)可負重任。 **3** ~-like part of a bottle, tool, mountain, etc. (瓶,器具,山等的) 肩狀部分。 **hard ~,** hard surface at the side of a roadway (esp a motorway). (高速公路等靠邊的)硬路面。 □ *vt* **1** [VP6A] take on the ~(s) (lit and fig): 肩負(字面及喻): *~ a burden/a task/the responsibility for sth.* 負擔重物(工作,某事之責任)。 *~* ***arms,*** (mil) move the rifle to an upright position in front of the right ~. (軍)使槍口朝上垂直地托於右肩前;托槍。 **2** [VP15A] push with the ~; make (one's way) thus: 以肩衝;擠(路): *~ people aside;* 用肩膀把人們推開; *be ~ed to one side;* 被擠在一旁; *~ one's way through a crowd.* 從人叢中擠過。

shout /ʃaut ; ʃaʊt/ *n* [C] loud call or cry: 大叫;呼喊: *~s of joy;* 歡樂的呼聲; *a ~ of alarm.* 驚恐的喊叫。 *They greeted him with ~s of 'Long live the President'.* 他們高呼着'總統萬歲'迎接他。 □ *vi, vt* ***~ (out),*** **1** [VP2A, B, C, 4B, 22] speak or cry out in a loud voice: 大聲喊;呼;叫: *Don't ~ at me!* 不要對我叫喊! *He ~ed to attract attention.* 他大聲叫喊以吸引注意。 *He ~ed with pain.* 他痛得大叫。 *He ~ed himself hoarse.* 他叫得嗓子都啞了。 **2** [VP6A, 15A, B, 3A] say in a loud voice: 大聲說: *~ (out) one's orders.* 高聲發出命令。 *They ~ed their disapproval,* expressed it by ~ing. 他們喊叫表示反對。 *He ~ed to me/~ed for me to come.* 他大聲喊我來。 *'Go back!' he ~ed.* '回去!'他大喊着說。 ***~ sb down,*** ~ to prevent sb from being heard: 大聲喊叫而使對方的聲音聽不見;大聲喝倒某人: *The crowd ~ed the speaker down.* 羣衆大聲喝倒采以壓制那位演說者的聲音。 **~·ing** *n* [U] ~s. 叫;喊。 ***It's all over but/bar the ~ing,*** The struggle, fight, etc is over and the praise, cheers, etc will follow. 競賽(等)已完畢,歡呼聲不絕。

shove /ʃʌv ; ʃʌv/ *vt, vi* [VP6A, 15A, B, 2A, C] (colloq) push (usu heavily): (俗)推;擠;撞: *~ a boat into the water.* 把船推進水中。 *Stop shoving!* 別推了! ***~ off,*** **(a)** start from the shore in a boat (by pushing the shore, etc). (藉推撑岸等而)開船離岸。 **(b)** (sl) leave (a place): (俚)離開(一地方): *I'm sick of this place; let's ~ off.* 我討厭這地方,我們離開吧。 □ *n* [C] vigorous push: 用力推;推開: *Give it a ~.* 推它一下。 ,~-'**ha'penny** /,ʃʌv 'heɪpnɪ ; 'ʃʌv'hepənɪ/ *n* = shovel-board.

shovel /'ʃʌvl ; 'ʃʌvl̩/ *n* spade-like tool, used for moving coal, sand, snow, etc, ⇨ the illus at tool; large device used for the same purpose, mechanically operated from a crane in a vehicle. 鏟;鍬(用以鏟煤、沙、雪等)(參看 tool 之插圖);(挖土機之)鏟頭。 □ *vt* (-ll-, US -l-) **1** [VP6A, 15A, B] lift, move, with a ~: 鏟起;鏟動: *~ up coal;* 鏟煤; *~ the snow away from the garden path.* 自園徑上鏟去雪。 **2** [VP6A, 15A] clear or clean with a ~: 鏟乾淨: *~ a path through the snow.* 在雪中鏟開一條小路。 **~·ful** /-fʊl ; -fʊl/ *n* as much as a ~ will hold. 一鏟或一鍬之量。

shovel-board /'ʃʌvl bɔːd ; 'ʃʌvl̩,bord/ *n* [U] game in which discs or coins are pushed along a board to a mark. (在板上推小圓片或硬幣的)推移板遊戲。

show¹ /ʃəʊ ; ʃo/ *n* **1** [U, C] showing (chiefly in): 表示(主要用於): *by (a) ~ of hands,* (voting) by the raising of hands for or against (a proposal). (投票)藉舉手以贊成或反對(提案)。 **2** [C] collection of things publicly displayed, esp for competition, or as a public entertainment: 展覽;展覽物;展覽會;競賽會: *a 'flower/'horse/'cattle ~;* 花(馬,牛)的展覽(競賽會); *the 'motor ~,* = exhibition; 汽車展覽會; *the Lord Mayor's ~,* a procession through the City of London when a new Lord Mayor is installed; 倫敦市長的就任遊行; *a travelling ~,* eg of circus animals. 巡廻展(如馬戲團之動物等)。 ***on ~,*** exhibited. 被陳列着;展覽中。 **3** [C] (colloq) natural display; sth to be seen: (俗)自然景觀;景物: *a fine ~ of blossom in the Kent orchards.* 肯特果園內百花盛開的景觀。 **4** [C] (colloq) kind of public entertainment, eg circus, theatre, radio, TV, etc: (俗)公衆娛樂;表演(如馬戲、戲劇、無線電、電視等): *Have you seen any good ~s lately?* 你最近看過什麼好的表演嗎? '~-**business,** (colloq) (俗) '~-**biz** /-bɪz ; -bɪz/ *n* the public entertainment business. 表演業;娛樂界。 **5** [C] (colloq) performance (not theatrical, etc): (俗)表現: *put up a good ~,* do sth creditably; 表現很好; *a poor ~,* sth done badly. 表現不佳。 ***steal the ~,*** attract all the attention: 吸引全部注意力;搶鏡頭: *Good ~!* used to express approval of sth done well. 精彩!做得好! **6** [C] (colloq) organization; undertaking; business; something that is happening: (俗)組織;事業;企業;(正在發生的)事情: *Who's running this ~,* Who controls or manages it? 誰在主持這業務? ***give the (whole) '~ away,*** let people know what is being done or planned: 把整個事情洩漏;走漏消息: *I wish she wouldn't talk and give the ~ away.* 我希望她不會多話而走漏消息。 **7** (*sing* only; dated colloq use) opportunity of doing sth, defending oneself, etc: (僅用單數;過時俗語用法) (做某事,爲自己辯護等之)機會: *Give the man a fair ~.* 給那人一個公平的機會。 *He had no ~ at all.* 他簡直沒有機會。 **8** outward appearance; impression: 外觀;印象: *a claim with some ~ of justice;* 看起來相當合理的要求; *with a ~ of reason.* 似乎有理地。 *He didn't offer even a ~ of resistance.* 他甚至未作出抵抗的樣子。 **9** [U] pomp; display; ostentation: 炫耀;誇示;鋪張;虛飾: *a house furnished for ~, not comfort.* 不爲舒適,只爲虛飾而裝璜的房子。 *They're fond of ~.* 他們好賣弄。 **10** (compounds) (複合字) '~-**boat** *n* river steam-boat on which theatrical performances were given (esp on the Mississippi, US). 演藝船(尤指在美國密西西比河上者)。 '~-**case** *n* case with glass sides and (or) top, for showing and protecting articles in a shop, museum, etc; (fig) special exhibition of sth, esp sth new. (店鋪,博物館等之)玻璃櫃櫥;陳列櫥;(喻)特展(尤指新產品或新作品)。 '~-**down** *n* (colloq) full and frank declaration of one's strength, intentions, etc: (俗)明白表示自己的力量,意向等;攤牌: *call for a ~-down,* ask (opponents, rivals, etc) for such a declaration; 要求(對方,敵人等)攤牌; *if it comes to a ~-down,* if such a declaration is (or has to be) made. 如果到了攤牌的階段。 '~-**girl** *n* girl who sings or dances (or is merely decorative) in a musical play, revue, etc. (在音樂喜劇,時事諷刺劇等中之)歌舞女郎。 '~-**jumping** *n* display of skill in riding horses over fences, barriers, etc. 騎馬跳越圍牆、障礙物等之表演。 '~·**man** /-mən ; -mən/ *n* (*pl* -men) **(a)** organizer of public entertainments (esp circuses). 大衆娛樂(尤指馬戲團)之主持人。 **(b)** person (esp in public life) who uses publicity, etc to attract attention to himself: 自我宣傳之人(尤指從事公務者): *Some politicians are great ~men and very little else.* 有些政客別無所長,只會做自我宣傳。 '~·**man·ship** /-mənʃɪp ; -mənʃɪp/ *n* art of attracting, ability to attract, public attention, eg to what one is trying to sell. 吸引大衆注意之技術或能力(如使注意所售賣之物)。 '~-**place** *n* one that tourists go to see: 可遊覽之處;勝地: *old palaces, castles and other ~-places.* 故宮,古堡及其他勝地。 **'~-room/-window** *n* one in which goods are kept for display, inspection, etc. 貨品陳列室(商店之櫥窗)。 **~y** *adj* (-ier, -iest) likely to attract attention; (often contemptuous) (too) decorated or ornamented; (too) brightly coloured: 可能吸引注意的;(常含輕蔑意味)(過分)裝飾的;(太)華麗的: *~y flowers,* eg some kinds of dahlia; 豔麗的花(如某些大麗花); *a ~y dress;* 華服; *the ~y patriotism of persons hoping for titles.* 希冀獲得勳位的人所誇示的愛國心。 **~·ily** /-ɪlɪ; -əlɪ/ *adv* **~i·ness** *n*

show² (archaic **shew**) /ʃəʊ; ʃo/ *vt, vi* (*pt* ~ed, *pp* ~n /ʃəʊn; ʃon/, rarely ~ed) **1** [VP6A, 12A, 13A, 15A, 19B, 24A] ***~ sth (to sb); ~ sb sth,*** bring before the sight: 出示;展示;上演;放映: *You must ~ your ticket at the barrier.* 你在入口處必須出示門票。*What films are they ~ing at the local cinema this week?* 本地的電影院本週放映什麼影片? *He won several prizes for the roses he ~ed,* exhibited. 他展出的玫瑰獲得好幾個獎。*He ~ed me his pictures.* 他把他的照片給我看。 *He has ~n them to all his friends.* 他把它們給所有的朋友看。*The photograph ~s him sitting/seated at his desk.* 在這張照片裡,他坐在書桌旁邊。 **2** [VP6A] allow to be seen: 使顯露: *That frock ~s your petticoat,* is too short to cover it. 那件洋裝太短,讓你的襯裙露出來了。*A dark suit will not ~ the dirt.* 黑色的套裝不顯髒。*My shoes are ~ing signs of wear.* 我的鞋子已穿舊了。 **3** [VP2A, C] be visible or noticeable: 可看出;顯露: *Your petticoat is ~ing, Jane.* 你的襯裙露出來了,珍。*Does the mark of the wound still ~?* 傷痕還看得見嗎? *The pink of the apple-blossom is beginning to ~.* 蘋果花的淡紅色已開始出現。*His fear ~ed in his eyes.* 他的眼中露出恐懼。 **4** [VP6A] ***~ itself,*** be visible: 呈現;可看出: *His annoyance ~ed itself in his looks.* 他的煩惱在他的表情上可以看出。**~ *oneself,*** be present (at a meeting, etc): 出席;出現(在會議等中): *Ought we to ~ ourselves at the Evans's party tonight?* 我們應出席今晚伊凡家的宴會嗎? **~ *one's face,*** appear before people: 露臉;出面: *He's ashamed to ~ his face in the street.* 他羞於在街上露面。 **~ *fight,*** give signs of being ready to fight. 顯出願戰的樣子;表示不妥協。 **~ *one's hand/cards,*** (fig) make known one's intentions or plans. (喻)表明意圖或計畫;攤牌。**~ *a leg,*** (colloq) get out of bed. (俗)起床。**~ *one's teeth,*** (fig) look angry. (喻)發怒。***have nothing to ~ for it/sth,*** have nothing that is evidence of what one has achieved or tried to achieve. 毫無成就可言;無表現。 **5** [VP6A, 14, 12A, 13A] give; grant: 給;施與: *~ mercy on sb.* 寬恕某人。 *He ~ed me great kindness.* 他對我極爲親切或幫忙。 **6** [VP6A, 25] give evidence or proof of having or being: 表現;顯示: *He ~s no sign of intelligence.* 他表現得一點也不聰明。 *She ~ed great courage.* 她表現得很有勇氣。*His new book ~s him to be a first-rate novelist.* 他的新書顯示他是第一流的小說家。 **7** [VP15A, B] direct; conduct. 引導;引領。 ***~ sb in; ~ sb into sth; ~ sb out; ~ sb out of sth,*** direct or conduct sb into/out of a place: 引領某人進入(離開)一地方: *Please ~ this gentleman out.* 請送這位先生出去。 *We were ~n into the living-room.* 我們被引入起居室。 ***~ sb over/around/round sth,*** take sb round a place: 帶某人參觀某處: *The guide ~ed us over the old castle.* 嚮導帶我們去參觀那古堡。**~ *sb the door,*** require him to leave and go with him to the door to see that he does so. 要某人離開,並且陪他走到門口看著他離去。 **~ *sb the way,*** explain which way to go; (fig) set an example. 指示走那一條路;(喻)示範。 **8** [VP6A, 9, 10, 20, 21, 25] make clear; cause (sb) to understand; prove: 說明;表明;證明;顯出: *He ~ed me how to do it/how he had done it.* 他向我說明如何做這事(他如何做這事)。 *He ~ed his annoyance/that he was annoyed/how annoyed he was.* 他顯得很懊惱。*That ~s how little you know.* 那證明你所知極少。*We have ~n the falsity of the story/that the story is false/the story to be false.* 我們已證明那個報導不眞實。 **9** [VP2C, 15B] ***~ sb/sth off,*** display (sth) to advantage: 顯示(某物)的優點;使顯眼: *a swim-suit that ~s off her figure well;* 能充分顯示她美好身材的泳裝; *mothers who like to ~ off their daughters,* display their daughter's good looks, abilities, accomplishments, etc. 喜歡宣揚女兒長處的母親們。 **~ *off,*** make a display of one's wealth, learning, abilities, etc in order to impress people: 炫耀自己的財富,學識,能力等;賣弄: *a man who is always ~ing off.* 老是賣弄的人。 Hence, 由此產生, **'~-off** *n* person who ~s off: 喜愛炫耀、賣弄之人: *He's an irritating ~-off,* is always trying to show his abilities, etc. 他是個討人嫌的喜歡賣弄之人。 ***~ sb/sth up,*** make the truth about (sb or sth dishonest, disreputable, etc) known: 揭露(不誠實,不名譽等的人或事物)之眞相;拆穿: *~ up a fraud/a rogue/an impostor.* 揭發騙局(惡徒,騙子)。 **~ *up,*** **(a)** be conspicuous, easily visible: 顯眼;易見: *Her wrinkles ~ed up in the strong sunlight.* 她的皺紋在强烈的陽光下很顯眼。 **(b)** [VP2A] (colloq) put in an appearance; be present (*at* sth): (俗)出現;出席: *Only three of the people we invited to the party didn't ~ up.* 我們邀請來參加宴會的人只有三人未出席。 **~·ing** *n* (usu *sing*) (act of) displaying or pointing out; appearance; evidence: (通常用單數)表現;陳述;外觀;外表;形跡: *a firm with a poor financial ~ing,* whose financial accounts do not appear to be good; 財政狀況不佳的公司; *on present/past ~ing,* on present/past evidence. 就現在(過去)的跡象。 ***on one's own ~ing,*** by one's own admission. 如某人自己所承認的。

shower /ˈʃaʊə(r); ˈʃaʊɚ/ *n* [C] **1** brief fall of rain, sleet or hail; sudden sprinkle of water: 一陣雨,霰或雹;一陣噴灑: *be caught in a ~;* 被陣雨淋濕; *a ~ of spray.* 一陣噴霧。 **'~(-bath)** *n* (washing one's body by using a) device by which water comes down in a ~ through a plate with numerous small holes: 淋浴設備;淋浴: *have a ~(-bath) every morning.* 每天早上淋浴一次。 **2** large number of things arriving together: 大量湧到之事物;接踵而來之事物: *a ~ of blows/stones/blessings/insults;* 一陣打擊(石塊,祝福,侮辱); *sparks falling in a ~/in ~s.* 陣雨似的火花。 **3** (US) party at which presents are given to a woman about to become a bride. (美)送禮給卽將做新娘者的聚會。□ *vt, vi* **1** [VP14] ***~ sth upon sb; ~ sb with sth,*** send or give it to him in a ~: 大量地給與: *They ~ed honours upon the hero/~ed the hero with honours.* 他們紛紛向那英雄致敬。 *Questions were ~ed upon the new arrival.* 大家紛紛向那位新到達者提出問題。 **2** [VP2C] fall in a ~: 似陣雨般降落: *Good wishes ~ed (down) upon the bridegroom.* 大家紛紛向新郎祝福。 **~y** *adj* (of the weather) with frequent ~s. (指天氣)多陣雨的。

shown /ʃəʊn; ʃon/ *pp* of show².

shrank /ʃræŋk; ʃræŋk/ *pt* of shrink.

shrap·nel /ˈʃræpnəl; ˈʃræpnəl/ *n* [U] fragments of shell or bullets packed inside a shell which is designed to explode and scatter these contents over a wide area: 榴霰彈(含有使彈片及彈頭散佈於廣濶地區之炸藥的砲彈或炸彈): *hit by (a piece of) ~.* 被榴霰彈(彈片)擊中。

shred /ʃred; ʃrɛd/ *n* [C] strip or piece scraped, torn or broken off sth; fragment: 碎片;裂片;細條: (fig) (喻) *not a ~ of truth in what she says;* 她所說的話無一絲眞實性; *not a ~ of evidence against me.* 沒有絲毫對我不利的證據。 ***tear to ~s,*** (lit and fig) destroy: (字面和喻)毀滅;破壞: *They have torn her reputation to ~s.* 他們已使她身敗名裂。□ *vt* (-dd-) [VP6A] tear or scrape into ~s. 撕成碎片;裂爲細條。

shrew /ʃruː ; ʃru/ *n* **1** bad-tempered, scolding woman. 壞脾氣而好罵人的婦女；潑婦；悍婦。 **2** '**~(-mouse)**, small mouse-like animal that feeds on insects. 鼩鼱(似鼠小動物，以昆蟲為食)。 **~·ish** /-ɪʃ ; -ɪʃ/ *adj* scolding; sharp-tongued. 好罵人的；利舌的；悍潑的。 **~·ish·ly** *adv* **~·ish·ness** *n*

shrewd /ʃruːd ; ʃrud/ *adj* (-er, -est) **1** having, showing, sound judgement and common sense: 有可靠的判斷力和常識的；明智的；精明的： *~ business-men;* 精明的商人； *~ arguments.* 明智的辯論。 **2** astute; discriminating: 狡獪的；明辨的；有眼光的： *make a ~ guess,* one likely to be correct; 準確的猜測； *a ~ blow／thrust,* one carefully made and likely to be effective. 有效的一擊。 **~·ly** *adv* **~·ness** *n*

shriek /ʃriːk ; ʃrik/ *vi, vt* **~ *(out),*** **1** [VP2A, C] scream shrilly. 尖叫。 **2** [VP6A, 15B] utter in a shrill, screaming voice: 以尖叫聲說出： *~ out a warning;* 尖聲警告； *~ with laughter.* 尖聲大笑。□ *n* [C] shrill scream: 尖叫： *~s of girlish laughter;* 女孩的尖銳笑聲； *the ~* (= whistle) *of a railway engine.* 火車頭的尖鳴聲。

shrift /ʃrɪft ; ʃrɪft/ *n* [U] (archaic) confession (of sins) to a priest; confession and absolution. (古)對教士之懺悔；告解。 ***give sb／get short ~,*** give him／get curt treatment, brief and unwilling attention. 怠慢某人(受到怠慢)。

shrike /ʃraɪk ; ʃraɪk/ *n* (kinds of) bird (also called 亦稱作 '*butcher-bird*) with a strong, hooked bill and the habit of fastening its prey (small birds and insects) on thorns. 伯勞；百舌鳥(喙彎而堅，慣於將其捕獲之小鳥與昆蟲固牢於荊棘上)。

shrill /ʃrɪl ; ʃrɪl/ *adj* (of sounds, voices, etc) sharp; piercing; high-pitched: (指聲音，語音等)尖銳的；刺耳的；高頻率的： *~ cries;* 尖銳的喊叫； *a ~ voice／whistle.* 尖銳的聲音(汽笛)。 **~y** /'ʃrɪlɪ ; 'ʃrɪlɪ/ *adv* **~·ness** *n*

shrimp /ʃrɪmp ; ʃrɪmp/ *n* [C] small marine shellfish used for food, ⇨ the illus at crustacean; (hum) very small person. 小蝦(參看 crustacean 之插圖)；(謔)短小之人。□ *vi* catch ~s: 捕蝦： (usu) (通常作) *go ~ing.* 去捕蝦。

shrine /ʃraɪn ; ʃraɪn/ *n* [C] **1** tomb or casket containing holy relics; altar or chapel of special associations or hallowed by some memory. 藏置聖徒遺骨之墓或小箱；神龕；聖祠；殿堂。 **2** building or place associated with sth or sb deeply respected or venerated: 與深受敬重之某物或某人有關係的建築物或地方： *a Shinto ~,* in Japan. (日本之)神道廟。 ***worship at the ~ of Mammon,*** give excessive devotion to wealth and money-making. 崇拜財神之廟堂(卽過份追求財富)。□ *vt* = enshrine (the usu word). (enshrine 為常用字)。

shrink /ʃrɪŋk ; ʃrɪŋk/ *vi, vt* (*pt* shrank /ʃræŋk ; ʃræŋk/, or shrunk /ʃrʌŋk ; ʃrʌŋk/, *pp* shrunk, or, as *adj* shrunken /'ʃrʌŋkən ; 'ʃrʌŋkən/) **1** [VP6A, 2A] make or become less, smaller (esp of cloth through wetting): (使)收縮；(使)縐縮(尤指布浸濕後之收縮)： *Will this soap ~ woollen clothes?* 這種肥皂會使毛織品收縮嗎？ *Those jeans will ~ in the wash.* 那些牛仔褲洗過以後會縮水。 *How your gums have shrunk since your teeth were extracted!* 你的牙齒拔去後，你的齒齦萎縮了不少啊！ **2** [VP2A, C, 3A] **~ *(back) (from),*** move back, show unwillingness to do sth (from shame, dislike, etc): 退縮；畏縮(由於羞恥，厭惡等)： *A shy man ~s from meeting strangers.* 羞怯的人怕見生人。 *She shrank back from the horrifying spectacle.* 她看到那可怖的景象就往後退。 '**~·age** /-ɪdʒ ; -ɪdʒ/ *n* [U] process of ~ing; degree of ~ing: 收縮；縐縮；收縮的過程或程度： *Make the pullover a little longer, and allow for ~age.* 把這套頭毛衣織長一些，以防縮水。 *The ~-age in our export trade／in the value of our currency is serious.* 我們的出口貿易(幣值)嚴重萎縮。

shrive /ʃraɪv ; ʃraɪv/ *vt* (*pt* ~d or shrove /ʃrəʊv ; ʃrov/, *pp* ~d or shriven /'ʃrɪvn ; 'ʃrɪvən/) [VP6A] (archaic, of a priest) hear the confession of a penitent sinner and absolve him from the spiritual consequences of his sin(s). (古，指教士)聽懺悔者懺悔而赦其罪。

shrivel /'ʃrɪvl ; 'ʃrɪvl/ *vt, vi* (-ll-, US also -l-) [VP 6A, 15B, 2A, C] **~ *(up),*** (cause to) become dried or curled (through heat, frost, dryness or old age): (使)枯萎；(使)捲縮： *The heat ~led up the leaves／the leather.* 炎熱使樹葉枯萎(皮革捲縮)。 *He has a ~led face,* with the skin wrinkled. 他有一張滿是皺紋的臉。

shriven /'ʃrɪvn ; 'ʃrɪvən/ ⇨ shrive.

shroud /ʃraʊd ; ʃraud/ *n* [C] **1** (also called 亦稱 '*winding-sheet*) cloth or sheet (to be) wrapped round a corpse: 屍布；壽衣： *You'll have no pockets in your ~.* 你死後帶不走財產。 **2** sth which covers and hides: 覆蓋物；遮蔽物： *a ~ of mist.* 一片濃霧。 **3** (*pl*) ropes supporting a ship's masts, ⇨ the illus at barque; ropes linking a parachute and the harness which is strapped to the parachutist. (複)護桅索；橫桅索(參看 barque 之插圖)；(降落傘的)吊傘索。□ *vt* [VP6A, 15A] **1** wrap (a corpse) in a ~. 以屍布包裹(屍體)。 **2** cover; hide: 覆蓋；遮蔽： *~ed in darkness／mist;* 籠罩在黑暗(霧)中； *a crime ~ed in mystery.* 一件離奇的罪案。

shrove /ʃrəʊv ; ʃrov/ ⇨ shrive.

Shrove Tues·day /ˌʃrəʊv 'tjuːzdɪ *US:* 'tuːz- ; 'ʃrov-'tjuzdɪ/ *n* day before the beginning of Lent, on which, and on preceding days **(Shrove·tide)**, it was formerly the custom to be shriven. 四旬齋開始之前一日(舊俗於是日及前數日 (Shrovetide) 向神父告解可獲赦罪)。

shrub /ʃrʌb ; ʃrʌb/ *n* [C] plant with woody stem, lower than a tree, and (usu) with several separate stems from the root. 灌木(較喬木矮，通常自根部叢生數幹)。 **~·bery** /'ʃrʌbərɪ ; 'ʃrʌbərɪ/ *n* (*pl* -ries) place, eg part of a garden, planted with ~s. 灌木栽植地；灌木叢。

shrug /ʃrʌg ; ʃrʌg/ *vt* (-gg-) [VP6A, 15B] lift (the shoulders) slightly (to show indifference, doubt, etc). 聳(肩)(以表示冷淡，懷疑等)。 **~ *sth off,*** dismiss it as not deserving attention, as sth trivial. 對某事物不屑一顧。□ *n* [C] such a movement: 聳肩： *with a ~ of the shoulders／a ~ of despair.* 聳聳肩(失望地聳聳肩)。

shrunk(en) /ʃrʌŋk, 'ʃrʌŋkən ; ʃrʌŋk, 'ʃrʌŋkən/ ⇨ shrink.

shuck /ʃʌk ; ʃʌk/ *n* (US) husk; pod; outer covering; (fig) sth of little value. (美)殼；莢；外皮；(喻)無價值之物。 **S~s!** *int* (US) (exclamation of disbelief, regret, or irritation). (美)胡說！唉！眞無聊！(表示不信，懊悔或氣惱之感歎詞)。□ *vt* [VP6A] remove the ~s from: 剝…之殼，莢或外皮： *~ pea-nuts／maize.* 剝花生殼(玉米之外皮)。

shud·der /'ʃʌdə(r) ; 'ʃʌdɚ/ *vi* [VP2A, C, 4C] shake convulsively; tremble with fear or disgust: 抽動；戰慄；因恐懼或厭惡而發抖： *~ with cold／horror;* 寒冷(恐怖)得發抖； *~ at the sight of blood.* 看見流血便戰慄。 *The ship ~ed as she struck the rocks.* 船因撞着礁石而搖動。 *He ~ed to think of it.* 他一想到它就發抖。□ *n* [C] uncontrollable shaking: 戰慄；發抖： *a ~ passed over her.* 她不由自主地發抖。 *It gives me the ~s,* (colloq) terrifies me. (俗)它使我害怕極了。

shuffle /'ʃʌfl ; 'ʃʌfl/ *vi, vt* **1** [VP2A, C, 6A] walk without raising the feet properly. 曳(足)而行。 **~ *one's feet,*** slide or drag them on the ground when walking, or when standing or sitting. 曳足(走、站或坐時，雙足在地上滑或拖)。 **2** [VP6A, 15A, B, 2A] slide or move (playing-cards, etc) one over the other to change their relative positions: 洗(紙牌等)；弄混；亂堆： *~ the dominoes.* 洗骨牌。 *He ~d the papers together in a drawer.* 他把文件胡亂地放置在抽屜裡。 **3** [VP2C, 15B] do sth in a careless way; slip (sth *off, on*) casually: 馬虎地做某事;隨便地脫下或穿上(某物,與 off, on 連用): ~ *through one's work;* 敷衍了事; ~ *one's clothes on / off;* 隨便地穿衣(脫衣); (fig) (喻) ~ *off responsibility upon others,* get rid of it by passing it to others. 把責任推諉給他人。 **4** [VP2A] keep shifting one's position; be unstraightforward; try to avoid giving a certain answer, etc: 閃避;蒙混;支吾;閃爍其辭: *Don't ~; give a clear answer.* 不要閃爍其辭,給一個明確的答覆。 □ *n* [C] **1** shuffling movement; shuffling dance: 曳足而行;曳足跳舞: ˌ*soft-shoe* ˈ*~;* 滑步舞; shuffling of cards: 洗牌: *Give the cards a good ~.* 把這副紙牌好好洗一下。 **2** general change of relative position: 改組;混合: *a ~ of the Cabinet; a Cabinet ~,* giving members different portfolios. 內閣改組。 **3** piece of dishonesty; misleading statement or action. 欺騙之行爲;支吾之辭;閃避之行爲。 **shuf·fler** *n* one who ~s. 曳足而行者;洗牌者;做事馬虎者;蒙混者。

shufty /ˈʃʌftɪ; ˈʃʌftɪ/ *n* (GB sl) ***take / have a ~ (at sth / sb),*** have a (quick) look (at it / him). (英俚) (很快地)瞄…一眼。

shun /ʃʌn; ʃʌn/ *vt* (-nn-) [VP6A, D] keep away from; avoid: 規避;避免: ~ *temptation / publicity / society.* 避開誘惑(避免出風頭;避免交際)。

'shun /ʃʌn; ʃʌn/ *int* (abbr of) attention(3) (as a word of command). (口令)立正!(爲 attention(3) 之略)。

shunt /ʃʌnt; ʃʌnt/ *vt, vi* **1** [VP6A, 15B] send (railway wagons, coaches, etc) from one track to another, esp to keep a track clear for important traffic: 使(鐵路之貨車,客車等)調到另一軌道上以讓更重要車輛通過;使轉軌: ~ *a train on to a siding.* 將一列火車調至旁軌。 **2** [VP2A] (of a train) be ~ed to a siding. (指火車)被轉至旁軌。 **3** [VP6A, 15A] (fig, colloq) divert; postpone or evade discussion of (sth): (喻,俗)轉移;拖延或迴避討論(某事): *She ~ed the conversation on to less morbid topics.* 她把話轉向比較不可怕的話題上。 **4** [VP6A, 15A] (fig) lay aside (a project); leave (sb) unoccupied, or inactive. (喻)擱置(計畫);使(某人)閑散或無事可做。 **~er** *n* (esp) railway employee who ~s wagons, etc. (尤指)調動貨車等於旁軌之鐵路工人;轉轍手。

shush /ʃʊʃ; ʃʌʃ/ *vi, vt* **1** = hush. **2** = sh.

shut /ʃʌt; ʃʌt/ *vt, vi* (*pt, pp* shut; -tt-) (For special uses with *adverbial particles* and *preps,* ⇨ 5 below.) (與副詞接語及介詞連用之特殊用法,參看下列第5義。) **1** [VP6A, 15A] move (a door, one's lips, etc) into position to stop an opening: 關;閉(門,唇等): ~ *the doors and windows;* 關閉門窗; ~ *a drawer;* 關抽屜; ~ *one's mouth.* 閉嘴。 *He ~ his ears to all appeals for help,* refused to listen to them. 他對於一切求助的呼聲都充耳不聞。 *He ~ his eyes to* (= deliberately refused to notice) *her faults.* 他對她的過失裝做沒看見。 *Why have you ~ the door upon further negotiations,* refused to consider them? 你爲什麼要拒絕進一步的談判呢? *They ~ the door against her / on her / in her face,* refused to receive or admit her. 他們不准她進去(對她享以閉門羹)。 ˈ**~-eye** *n* (colloq) nap; sleep: (俗)午睡;睡覺: *It's time for half an hour's ~-eye.* 到了午睡半小時的時候了。 **2** [VP2A] become closed; be able to be closed: 關上;閉起;能關閉: *The window ~s easily.* 這窗子容易關閉。 *The door won't ~.* 這門關不上。 **3** [VP6A] bring the folding parts of (sth) together: 摺起;合攏: ~ (= *close,* the more usu word) *a book / a clasp-knife.* 合攏 (close 較常用) 書 (摺刀)。 **4** [VP15A] catch or pinch by shutting sth: (因關閉某物而)夾住: ~ *one's fingers / dress, etc in the door,* ie between the door and the door-post. 把手指(衣服等)夾在門與門柱之間。 **5** [VP2C, 15B] (special uses with *adverbial particles* and *preps*): (與副詞接語及介詞連用之特殊用法):

shut (sth) down, (of a factory, etc) stop working; end activity; close: (指工廠等)停工;關閉: *The workshop has ~ down and the workers are unemployed.* 那工場已關閉,工人失業了。 *They've ~ down their factory.* 他們關閉了他們的工廠。 Hence, 由此產生, ˈ**~-down** *n* (temporary or permanent) closing of a factory, etc. (工廠等暫時或永久之)關閉。

shut sb in, confine or enclose: 監禁;圍住: *We're ~ in by hills here,* surrounded by hills which make access difficult and which prevent us from seeing far. 我們這裡被山丘環繞着(交通閉塞,視野有限)。 *They ~ the boy in the cellar,* kept him there as a prisoner. 他們把那男孩囚禁在地窖中。

shut sth off, stop the supply or flow of, eg gas, steam, water. 停止供應(煤氣,蒸氣,水等)。

shut sb / sth out, keep out; exclude; block: 將…關在外面;排除;遮住: ~ *out immigrants / competitive goods.* 拒絕移民(競爭性的貨物)。 *Don't ~ me out,* Don't close the door(s) so that I must stay out. 不要把我關在門外。 *These trees ~ out the view.* 這些樹遮住了那邊的景色。

shut sth up, **(a)** close and secure all the doors and windows of: 關閉…所有門窗: ~ *up a house before going away for a holiday.* 去度假之前關閉房屋所有的門窗。 *It's time to ~ up shop,* close the shop and stop doing business. 是打烊(或停業)的時候了。 **(b)** put away for safety: 妥藏: ~ *up one's jewels in the safe.* 將珠寶妥藏在保險箱中。 ~ ***(sb) up,*** (colloq) (cause sb to) stop talking: (俗)(使)停止談話;(使)住口: *Tell him to ~ up.* 叫他住口。 *Can't you ~ him up?* 你不能叫他住口嗎?

shut·ter /ˈʃʌtə(r); ˈʃʌtɚ/ *n* [C] **1** movable cover (wooden panel or iron plate, hinged or separate and detachable) for a window, to keep out light or thieves: 窗板;窗扇;鎧窗(窗戶之木質或金屬質之活動遮板,或以鉸鏈相連,或可自由裝卸,用以遮光或防賊): *The shop-front is fitted with rolling ~s.* 那商店的店面裝有捲門。 ***put up the ~s,*** stop doing business (for the day, or permanently). 打烊;歇業。 **2** device that opens to admit light through the lens of a camera. (照相機鏡頭的)光閘;快門。 □ *vt* [VP6A] provide with ~s; put up the ~s of. 爲…裝窗板或快門;關閉…之窗板或快門。

shuttle /ˈʃʌtl; ˈʃʌtl̩/ *n* **1** (in a loom) cigar-shaped instrument with two pointed ends by which thread of weft is carried between threads of warp; (in a sewing-machine) sliding holder which carries the lower thread to meet the upper thread to make a stitch. (織布機之)梭(形似雪茄,兩端尖,用以使緯線穿織於經線間者);(縫紉機之) 滑梭 (使底線與面線相合而構成一針脚)。 **2** (compounds) (複合字) ˈ**~-cock** *n* round-based cork with feathers in it, struck to and fro across a net in the games of battledore and ~cock and badminton. 羽毛球;毽球。 ⇨ the illus at badminton. 參看 badminton 之插圖。 **~ diplomacy,** diplomatic negotiation requiring the diplomat(s) to travel to and fro between the groups involved. 穿梭外交活動(外交人員需往返於有關團體間以磋商事務者)。 ˈ**~ service,** service (of trains, buses, etc) to and fro between places not far apart. (火車,公共汽車等之)短距離的區間車。 □ *vt, vi* [VP6A, 15A, 2C] (cause to) move backwards and forwards, to and fro, like a ~. (使)穿梭般前後活動;(使)往返移動。

shy[1] /ʃaɪ; ʃaɪ/ *adj* (-er, -est) **1** (of persons) self-conscious and uncomfortable in the presence of others; (of behaviour, etc) showing this: (指人) 在別人面前難爲情或不自在的;怕羞的;害臊的; (指行爲等)表現怕羞的: *He's not at all shy with women.* 他與女人們在一起一點也不害臊。 *She gave him a shy look / smile.* 她對他做羞怯的一瞥(笑)。 **2** (of animals, birds, fish, etc) easily frightened; unwilling to be seen. (指動物,鳥,魚等)易被驚走的;不願被看見的。 **3** ***shy of,*** chary of; hesitating about: 慎於;對…躊躇: *They're shy of speaking to one another.* 他們彼此之間很少談話。 *Don't be shy of tell-*

ing me what you want. 你需要什麼，儘管告訴我好了。 ***fight shy of,*** ⇨ fight²(1). **shy·ly** *adv* **shy·ness** *n*

shy² /ʃaɪ ; ʃaɪ/ *vi* (*pt, pp* shied /ʃaɪd ; ʃaɪd/) [VP2A, 3A] ***shy (at sth),*** (of a horse) turn aside from in fear or alarm: (指馬)驚退；驚逸: *The horse was shying at a white object in the hedge.* 那馬看到樹籬中有個白色東西就嚇得往後退。

shy³ /ʃaɪ ; ʃaɪ/ *vt* (*pt, pp* shied /ʃaɪd ; ʃaɪd/) (colloq) [VP6A, 15A] throw: (俗)投；擲: *shying stones at a bottle.* 對着瓶子擲石頭。□ *n* (*pl* shies /ʃaɪz ; ʃaɪz/) throw: 投；擲: *fivepence a shy,* eg throwing balls at coconuts at a fair; 五辨士擲一次(如在義賣會中以球擲椰子); (colloq) any kind of attempt: (俗)嘗試: *have a shy at a task／an examination.* 嘗試做某工作(參加考試)。

shy·ster /ˈʃaɪstə(r) ; ˈʃaɪstɚ/ *n* (US colloq) person without professional honour, esp an unscrupulous lawyer. (美俗)無職業道德之人；(尤指)奸猾的律師。

Sia·mese /ˌsaɪəˈmiːz ; ˌsaɪəˈmiz/ *adj* of Siam (now 現稱作 *Thailand*). 暹羅的；泰國的。 ～ **twins,** two persons joined together from birth. 連體雙胞胎。 ～ **(cat),** oriental breed of cat with blue eyes and short-haired coat of cream, fawn or light grey hair. 暹羅貓。□ *n* (now 現稱作 *Thai*) native of Siam; language of Siam. 暹羅人；泰國人；暹羅語；泰國語。⇨ App 6. 參看附錄六。

Si·berian /saɪˈbɪərɪən ; saɪˈbɪrɪən/ *adj* of, coming from, Siberia. 西伯利亞的；來自西伯利亞的。

sibi·lant /ˈsɪbɪlənt ; ˈsɪbl̩ənt/ *adj* having, making, a whistling kind of sound. 有嘶嘶聲的；發嘶嘶聲的。□ *n* sound such as one of the six English sounds /s, z, ʃ, ʒ, tʃ, dʒ/. 有嘶聲的子音；嘶音(如英語中之 /s, z, ʃ, ʒ, tʃ, dʒ/)。

sib·ling /ˈsɪblɪŋ ; ˈsɪblɪŋ/ *n* one of two or more persons having the same parents; brother or sister. 兄弟(或姐妹)。

sibyl /ˈsɪbl ; ˈsɪbl̩/ *n* one of several women in ancient times who, it was believed, could see the future and give out messages from the gods; (hence, contemptuous or hum) fortune-teller; prophetess. 古代女預言家；(由此產生，蔑或諧)算命者；女先知。 **～·line** /ˈsɪbəlaɪn ; ˈsɪbl̩ˌin/ *adj* uttered by, characteristic of, a ～; mysteriously prophetic. 女預言家或算命者所言的；女預言家的；神祕預言的。

sic /sɪk ; sɪk/ *adv* (Lat) thus (placed in brackets to indicate that the preceding word, statement, etc is correctly quoted even though this seems unlikely or is clearly incorrect). (拉)原文如此(置放於括號內，表示前面的字或敍述等，縱有不妥當處，但係照原文引用)。

Si·cil·ian /sɪˈsɪlɪən ; sɪˈsɪlɪən/ *n, adj* (native) of Sicily. 西西里島的；西西里島人。

sick /sɪk ; sɪk/ *adj* **1** (*pred* only) (僅作敍述用法) ***be ～,*** throw up food from the stomach. 翻胃；反胃；作嘔。***feel ～,*** feel that one is about to do this. 覺得要嘔；欲嘔。 **ˈair-／ˈcar-／ˈsea-～** *adj* vomiting or inclined to vomit because of the motion of a plane／car／ship. 暈機(車，船)的。Hence, 由此產生， **ˈair-／ˈcar-／ˈsea-～ness** *n: I was sea-～ on the first day of the voyage.* 我在航海的第一天暈船。 **2** unwell; ill (in GB *ill* and *unwell* are polite usage, in US *sick* is normal usage): 不適的；患病的(在英國用 ill 及 unwell 二字較雅；在美國 sick 爲通用字): *He's been ～ for six weeks.* 他已經病了六週。*He's a ～ man.* 他是病人。***be off ～ (with sth),*** be away from one's work because of bad health or disease: 因健康不佳或生病而不上班: *Kate's off ～ with flu／a bad back.* 凱蒂因流行性感冒(背痛)而未上班。 ***fall ～,*** become ill. 生病。***go／report ～,*** (mil use) report to the doctor for medical treatment. (軍事用語)到醫生處去看病；掛病號。**the ～,** (*pl*) those who are ill. (複)患者。 **ˈ～-bay** *n* **(a)** (Navy) part of a ship for those who are ill. (海軍)(船上之)醫務室。 **(b)** medical centre on a university campus, etc. (大學等的)醫療中心。 **ˈ～·bed** *n* bed of a sick person. 病床。 **ˈ～-benefit** *n* ⇨ sickness. **ˈ～-berth** *n* = *～-bay*(a). **ˌ～-ˈheadache** *n* bilious headache. 偏頭痛。 **ˈ～-leave** *n* [U] permission to be away from duty or work because of illness: 病假: *on ～-leave.* 在病假中。 **ˈ～-list** *n* list of those who are ill (eg in a regiment, on a warship, etc). (團，軍艦等中之)病患名簿。 **ˈ～-parade** *n* (mil) parade of those who are reporting ～. (軍)患病士兵排隊請假或接受診療之行列。 **ˈ～-pay** *n* [U] pay to an employee who is absent from work because he is ill. 付給生病員工的薪資；生病補助費。 **ˈ～-room** *n* room occupied by, or kept ready for, sb who is ill. 病房。 **3** ***～ (and tired／to death) of,*** (colloq) tired of, disgusted with: (俗)厭倦；厭惡: *I'm ～ to death, of being blamed for everything that goes wrong.* 每件差錯都推在我頭上，眞把我煩死了。 **4** ***～ at heart,*** deeply sad. 深爲悲傷。 ***～ at／about sth,*** (colloq) unhappy, filled with regret about it: (俗)對…感到不快，遺憾: *～ at failing to pass the examination.* 對考試不及格感到遺憾。 **5** ***～ for,*** filled with a longing for: 渴望；戀慕: *～ for home／old happy times.* 懷念家鄉(舊時歡樂時光)。 **6** (sl) morbid; perverted: (俚)病態的；不健全的；反常的: *～ humour／jokes;* 下流的詼諧(笑話); *a ～ mind.* 精神不健全。□ *vt* ***～ sth up,*** (colloq) vomit; throw up from the stomach. (俗)嘔吐。

sicken /ˈsɪkən ; ˈsɪkən/ *vi, vt* **1** [VP2A, 3A] ***～ (for sth),*** be in the first stages of (an illness): 染上初期之(病疾)；生病: *The child is ～ing for something.* 這孩子像是生病了。 **2** [VP6A] cause to feel disgusted: 使感到厭惡: *Cruelty ～s most of us.* 殘酷使我們大多數人感到厭惡。*Their business methods ～ me.* 他們做生意的方法使我感到厭惡。 **3** [VP3A, 4C] ***～ at sth／to see sth,*** feel sick to see: 對(看到)…感到厭惡或難過: *They ～ed at the sight of so much slaughter／～ed to see so many people slaughtered.* 看到那麼多人遭受屠殺他們感到很難過。 **4** ***～ of sth,*** become tired of, disgusted with: 厭倦；厭惡: *He ～ed of trying to bring about reforms.* 他對試圖改革感到厭惡。 **～·ing** /ˈsɪkənɪŋ ; ˈsɪkənɪŋ/ *adj* disgusting: 使人厭惡的: *～ing smells／cruelty.* 使人厭惡的氣味(殘忍)。 **～·ing·ly** *adv*

sick·ish /ˈsɪkɪʃ ; ˈsɪkɪʃ/ *adj* somewhat sick or sickening: 有點要嘔吐的；令人作嘔或厭惡的；像是生病的；有些生病的: *feel ～;* 覺得有些生病似的; *a ～ smell.* 令人作嘔的氣味。

sickle /ˈsɪkl ; ˈsɪkl̩/ *n* [C] short-handled tool with a curved blade for cutting grass, grain, etc. 鐮刀。⇨ the illus at tool. 參看 tool 之插圖。

sick·ly /ˈsɪklɪ ; ˈsɪklɪ/ *adj* (-ier, -iest) **1** frequently ill; often in poor health: 多病的；不健康的: *a ～ child.* 多病的小孩。 **2** having the appearance of sickness or ill health; pale: 有病容的；不健康的；蒼白的: *These plants are／look rather ～.* 這些植物看來長得不大好。 **3** weak; faint; suggesting unhappiness: 虛弱的；無力的；顯示不快的: *a ～ smile.* 苦笑。 **4** causing, or likely to cause, a feeling of sickness or distaste: 使人作嘔的；易令人生厭的: *a ～ smell／taste;* 令人作嘔的氣味(味道); *～ sentiments.* 令人生厭的傷感。

sick·ness /ˈsɪknɪs ; ˈsɪknɪs/ *n* **1** [U] illness; ill health: 患病；不健康: *Is there much ～ in the village now?* 這村莊現在有許多疾病嗎？ *They were absent because of ～.* 他們因病缺席。 **ˈ～ benefit,** insurance payment to sb absent from work through illness. 疾病保險給付。 **2** [C, U] (an) illness or disease: 病；疾病: *suffering from ˈmountain ～／ˈsea-～／ˈair-～.* 患高山病(暈船；暈機)。 **3** [U] inclination to vomit; vomiting. 作嘔；嘔吐。

side¹ /saɪd ; saɪd/ *n* [C] (except 13 below) (下列第13義爲不可數名詞) **1** one of the flat or fairly flat surfaces of a solid object: (物體之平或相當平的)面: *the six ～s of a cube.* 立方體的六面。 **2** one of the surfaces which is not the top or the bottom: 側面(物體之面不屬於頂或底者): *A box has a* *top, a bottom, and four ~s.* 匣子有一頂,一底和四個側面。 **3** one of the surfaces which is not the top, bottom, front or back: 側(物體之面不屬於頂,底,前面或後面者): (attrib) (形容用法) *the ~ entrance of the house* (contrasted with the *front* or *back* entrance). 房子的側門(與前門或後門相對)。 **4** (maths) one of the lines bounding a plane figure such as a rectangle or triangle. (數學)邊。 **5** either of the two surfaces of a thin, flat object or of material such as paper, cloth, anything manufactured in sheets: (紙,布等平而薄的製品的)面: *Write on one ~ of the paper only.* 祇在紙的一面書寫。 *Which is the right ~ of the cloth,* the ~ intended to be seen? 那一面是這塊布的正面? **6** inner or outer surface of sth vertical, sloping, round or curved: (垂直物,傾斜物,圓形物或彎曲物的)內面;外面: *the ~ of a mountain;* 山坡; *put one's socks on the wrong ~ out* (= inside out, the usu phrase); 反穿襪子(inside out 較常用); *prehistoric paintings on the ~s* (= walls) *of a cave.* 穴壁上的史前圖畫。 **7** one of the two halves of a person on his left or right, esp from armpit to hip: (身體的)側邊(尤指腋至股之部分);脇: *wounded in the left ~.* 左脇受傷。 *Come and sit by/at my ~.* 來坐在我的旁邊。 *~ by ~,* close together, for mutual support. 並肩地;互相支持地。 ***split/burst one's ~s (laughing/with laughter),*** laugh heartily. 捧腹大笑。Hence, 由此產生, **'~-splitting** *adj* causing hearty laughter. 令人捧腹大笑的。 ***by the ~ of; by one's ~,*** close to and compared with: 與…在一起比較: *She looks small by the ~ of her companion.* 她與她的同伴站在一起,顯得嬌小。 **8** one of the two halves of an animal from foreleg to hindleg, esp as part of a carcass: (尤指宰後之動物由前腿至後腿分開的)半邊軀體;肋肉: *a ~ of beef/bacon.* 牛的肋肉(醃薰的豬肋肉)。 **9** part of an object, area, space, etc away from, at a distance from, a real or imaginary central line: 物體,地區,空間等與(眞實的或想像的)中心線離開的部分;面;方;邊: *the left/right/shady/sunny ~ of the street;* 街道的左面(右面,背陽面,向陽面); *the east ~ of the town;* 城鎮的東區; *the debit/credit ~ of an account.* 帳簿中的借(貸)方。 *He crossed to the far/the other ~ of the room.* 他走向房間的另一邊。 ***on/from all ~s; on/from every ~,*** in/from all directions; everywhere. 在(從)各方面;到處。 ***take sb on one ~,*** take him aside, apart, eg to speak to him in confidence. 帶某人到一邊(如單獨和他講話)。 ***on the right/wrong ~ of (fifty, etc),*** below/above (50 years of age, etc). 不足(已過)(五十歲等)。 ***(do sth) on the ~,*** **(a)** as a ~line. 作爲兼差或副業。 ⇨ sideline below. 參看下列之sideline。 **(b)** secretly, discreetly: 秘密地;謹愼地: *He lived with his wife but regularly saw Julia on the ~.* 他和妻子住在一起,但暗地裡經常會見茱麗。 ***put sth on one ~,*** **(a)** put it aside, apart. 將某物置於一邊。 **(b)** postpone dealing with it. 延緩處置;擱置。 **10** one of two groups or parties of people who are opposed (in games, politics, war, etc) or who uphold beliefs, opinions, etc against the other: (比賽的)隊;(政治的)黨;(敵對的)一方;集團;派系: *be on the winning/losing ~;* 屬於勝(敗)方; *faults on both ~s;* 咎在雙方; *to pick* (= choose) *~s.* 選擇立場。 *Austria has a strong ~,* eg a good football team. 奧國有一支强勁的代表隊(如足球隊)。 ***be on sb's ~,*** be a supporter of him: 支持某人: *Whose ~ are you on, anyway?* Aren't you supposed to be supporting me? 你到底在支持誰? *Both countries claimed that God was on their ~,* eg in a war. 兩國均稱上帝站在他們的一方(如在交戰時)。 ***let the '~ down,*** give an inferior performance and disappoint one's colleagues, team-mates, etc. 表現不佳而使其他同事(隊友)失望。 ***take ~s (with),*** support (sb, a party) in a dispute. (爭論中)袒護(某人,某團體)。 ⇨ side². ***off/on ~,*** (football, hockey) in a position (for receiving or playing the ball) that is/is not contrary to the rules. (足球,曲棍球)在不合(合)於規則的位置。 **11** aspect or view that is not complete; aspect different from or opposed to other aspects: 不完全的方面或觀點; 與其他方面不同或相對的一方面: *look on the dark/bright/gloomy, etc ~ of things/life, etc;* 看事物(生命等)的黑暗面(光明面,暗澹面等); *study all ~s of a question;* 研究一問題的各方面; *a man with many ~s to his character.* 有多種性格的人。 *There are two ~s to the story,* two aspects. 這故事有兩個說法。 ***on the 'high/'low, etc ~,*** rather high/low, etc: 相當高(低等): *Prices offered for fat cattle were on the high ~.* 購買肥牛所出的價錢相當高。 **12** line of descent through a parent: 家系;血統: *a cousin on my father's ~.* 父系的堂親。 **13** [U] (colloq) behaviour suggesting that one is better than other people; arrogance. (俗)妄自尊大;自負。 ***have no/be without ~,*** make no pretence, assumption, of being superior or important. 不擺架子;不自負。 ***put on ~,*** claim to be, behave as if one is, superior. 擺架子;自負。 **14** (compounds, etc) (複合字等) **'~-arms** *n pl* swords or bayonets, worn at the left ~ by soldiers. (軍人佩於左側的)佩劍;刺刀;隨身武器。 **'~-board** *n* table, usu with drawers and cupboards, placed against the wall of a dining-room. 餐具桌(通常有抽屜和食櫃,置於餐室之牆邊);餐具架。 **'~-burns/-boards** *n pl* ~-whiskers. (蓄於兩頰的)側鬢。 **'~-car** *n* small one-wheeled car fastened to the ~ of a motorcycle. (附於機器腳踏車旁之)獨輪側車。 **'~-chapel** *n* one in the aisle or at one ~ of a church. (教堂走廊或其一側之)附屬禮拜堂。 ⇨ the illus at church. 參看 church 之插圖。 **'~-dish** *n* extra dish or course at a meal. (正菜外加的)附加菜;小菜。 **'~-drum** *n* small, double-sided drum, (originally hung at the drummer's ~) in a jazz or military band. (爵士樂隊或軍樂隊中早先掛在鼓手身邊之)小鼓。 **'~ effect** *n* secondary or indirect effect, eg an undesirable effect of a drug used for a specific purpose. (藥物等之)副作用。 **'~-face** *adv* in profile: 側面地: *photograph sb ~-face.* 拍攝某人之側面照片。 **'~-glance** *n* look to or from one ~. 斜視;側視。 **'~ issue** *n* question of less importance (in relation to the main one). (與主題有關的)次要問題。 **'~-light** *n* light from or at the ~; (fig) incidental illumination, eg of a person's character, of a problem, etc. 側光;側燈;(喻)(對某人性格或某一問題等的)偶然啓示;間接說明。 **'~-line** *n* class of goods sold in addition to the chief class of goods; occupation which is not one's main work. 附帶售賣之貨品;副業;兼職。 **'~-lines** *n pl* (space immediately outside) lines bounding a football pitch, tennis-court, etc at the ~s. (球場等之)界線;界線以外之地。 ***on the ~-lines,*** (fig) merely as a spectator, not taking part. (喻)做旁觀者;不參與。 **'~-long** *adj, adv* (directed) to or from one ~: 橫向的(地);斜向的(地);側面的(地): *look ~long at sb;* 斜視某人; *a ~long glance.* 斜視。 **'~-road** *n* minor road branching off a main road. 叉路;小道。 **'~-saddle** *n* woman's saddle, made so that both feet may be on the same ~ of the horse. 偏座鞍;橫鞍;女鞍。 □ *adv* on a ~-saddle: 偏座地;在女鞍上: *In former times most women used to ride ~-saddle.* 從前大多數女子用偏座鞍騎馬。 **'~-show** *n* **(a)** small show at a fair or exhibition. 附屬之表演;雜耍。 **(b)** activity of small importance in relation to the main activity. 小活動;附屬事件。 **'~-slip** *n* **(a)** (motoring) skid. (駕車)橫滑;滑向一邊。 **(b)** (flying) movement to one ~ instead of forward. (飛行)側滑。 □ *vi* (-pp-) make a ~-slip. 橫滑;側滑。 **'~-s-man** /-zmən; -zmən/ *n* (*pl* -men) church helper who shows people to their seats, takes up the collection, etc. (教堂之)助手(帶領禮拜者就座,收集捐款等)。 **'~-step** *n* step taken to one ~

(eg to avoid a blow in boxing). 側步;橫步(如在拳擊中躲開打擊等)。▭ *vt, vi* (-pp-) [VP6A] avoid (a blow, etc) by stepping to one ~; evade (a question); [VP2A] step to one ~. 走側步以避免(打擊等);規避(問題等);走側步。**'~-stroke** *n* (kinds of) stroke used in swimming in which one ~ is above and the other below the water. 側泳。**'~-track** *n* railway siding; branch road. (鐵路之)側線;旁軌。▭ *vt* [VP6A] turn (a train) into a siding; (fig) turn (a person) from his purpose; postpone consideration of (a proposal, etc). 將(火車)轉入側線;(喻)轉移(某人)的目標;緩議(提案等)。**'~-view** *n* view obtained from the ~. 側景;側面圖。**'~·walk** *n* (chiefly US; GB 英 = *pavement*) path at the ~ of a street for persons on foot. (主美)人行道。**~·wards** /-wədz; -wərdz/, **~·ways** /-weɪz; -ˌwez/ *advv* to, towards, from, the ~; with the ~ or edge first: 斜着;斜向一邊地;自一邊地;一邊向前地: *look ~ways at sb;* 斜視某人; *walk/carry sth ~ways through a narrow opening;* 側着身子走過(攜物經過)狹窄的通道; (attrib) directed to one ~. (形容用法)向旁邊的;橫斜的。**'~-whiskers** *n pl* hair on the ~s of the face down to, but excluding, the chin. (蓄於兩頰之)側鬢;絡腮鬍子。⇨ beard. **-sided** /-'saɪdɪd; -'saɪdɪd/ *suff* having a specified number of ~s: 有(若干)邊的: *a 'five-~d figure.* 五邊形。

side² /saɪd; saɪd/ *vi* [VP3A] **~ with,** take part, be on the same side (as sb in an argument or quarrel): (在辯論或爭論中) 參與;袒護;支持 (某人): *It is safer to ~ with the stronger party.* 參與實力較强的一邊比較穩妥。

sid·ereal /saɪ'dɪərɪəl; saɪ'dɪrɪəl/ *adj* of the stars and their measurements: 星的;恒星的;以恒星爲衡量標準的: ~ *time,* measured by the stars; 恒星時(以恒星的位置作衡量標準的時間); *the ~ year,* 365 days, 6 hours, 10 minutes. 恒星年(卽365天,6小時,10分)。

sid·ing /'saɪdɪŋ; 'saɪdɪŋ/ *n* [C] short railway track to and from which trains may be shunted. (鐵路之)側線;旁軌(轉軌之用)。

sidle /'saɪdl; 'saɪdl/ *vi* [VP2C] **~ along/off; ~ away from/up to sb,** move in a shy or nervous way: 羞怯或不安地走過來(走開);羞怯或不安地離開(走向)某人: *The little girl ~d up to me.* 那小女孩羞怯地走向我。

siege /si:dʒ; sidʒ/ *n* [C, U] (period of) operations of armed forces who surround and blockade a town or fortress in order to capture it: 圍困;圍攻;圍城;圍攻期間: *a ~ of 50 days.* 圍困五十天。*Before the ~ ended, the citizens were almost starving.* 在圍困結束以前,市民已瀕臨飢餓邊緣。**lay ~ to (a town, etc),** surround and blockade it. 圍攻(一城等)。**raise a ~,** end it by forcing the enemy's forces to withdraw. 解圍;强迫敵人撤圍。**'~ artillery/guns,** big guns used in ~s (too heavy, in former times, for use in the field). 攻城砲。

si·en·na /sɪ'enə; sɪ'ɛnə/ *n* [U] kind of earth used as a colouring matter: 濃黃土;赭土 (用作顏料): *burnt ~,* reddish-brown; (經過鍛製之)紅褐色顏料;鍛赭土; *raw ~,* brownish-yellow. 赭黃顏料。

si·er·ra /sɪ'erə; sɪ'ɛrə/ *n* [C] long mountain chain with sharp slopes and edges (esp in Spain and Spanish America). 峯巒起伏之山嶺(尤指在西班牙及西班牙語系的美洲國家)。

si·es·ta /sɪ'estə; sɪ'ɛstə/ *n* [C] period of rest or sleep taken in the early afternoons, as is customary in hot countries. 午睡(氣候炎熱國家的習慣)。

sieve /sɪv; sɪv/ *n* [C] utensil with wire network or gauze for separating finer grains, etc from coarse grains, etc or solids from liquids. 篩;漏杓;濾器。**have a head/memory like a ~,** be incapable of remembering anything. 健忘。□ *vt* [VP 6A] put through, sift with, a ~. 以篩或漏杓篩;濾。

sift /sɪft; sɪft/ *vt, vi* **1** [VP6A, 14, 15A, B] **~ (out) (from),** put, separate by putting, through a sieve: 篩;篩分;過濾: ~ *the cinders;* 篩煤渣; ~ *(out) ashes from the cinders/the wheat from the chaff.* 自煤渣中篩出灰(將小麥的殼子篩掉)。**2** [VP6A, 15A] shake through a sieve: 篩撒: ~ *flour;* 篩撒麵粉; ~ *sugar on to a cake.* 篩糖在糕餅上。**3** [VP6A] (fig) examine carefully: (喻)詳審;細審: ~ *the evidence.* 細審證據。**4** [VP2C] fall, pass, come through, as from a sieve. 篩下;紛落。**~er** *n* small sieve-like utensil, chiefly used in cooking: 小篩(主要用於烹飪): *a 'flour-~er.* 麵粉篩。

sigh /saɪ; saɪ/ *vi, vt* **1** [VP2A] take and exhale a deep breath that can be heard (indicating sadness, tiredness, relief, etc); (of the wind) make a sound like ~ing. 歎息;嘆氣(表示悲哀,疲倦,慰藉等);(指風)發出似嘆息之聲;哀鳴。**2** [VP3A] **~ for sth,** feel a longing for: 熱望;渴念: *~ for the good old days to return.* 渴望昔日美好的時光再度出現。**3** [VP6A, 15B] **~ (out),** express, utter, with ~s: 以歎息表示;歎息地說出: *~ out a prayer.* 歎息著說出禱告詞。□ *n* [C] act of ~ing; sound of ~ing: 歎息;歎息聲;哀鳴聲: *utter/heave a ~;* 發出一聲歎息; *with a ~ of relief.* 帶着慰藉的嘆息。

sight¹ /saɪt; saɪt/ *n* **1** [U] power of seeing: 視力;視覺: *lose one's ~,* become blind; 失明;變盲; *have long/short* or *far/near ~,* be able to see things well only at long/short range; 患遠(近)視; *have good/poor ~* (= eyesight). 目力良好(不好)。**know sb by ~,** know him by appearance only, not as an acquaintance. 和某人面熟(並不相識)。**second ~,** ⇨ second¹(1). **2** [U, but sometimes with *indef art* 但有時用不定冠詞] seeing or being seen: 見;被見;觀覽: *Their first ~ of land came after three days at sea.* 他們在海上三天之後才首次看見陸地。**catch ~ of; have/get a ~ of,** begin to see; succeed in seeing: 發現;看到: *If you ever catch ~ of Ted Clark anywhere, call the police.* 如果你在任何地方看見泰德·克拉克,就去報警。**keep ~ of; keep sb/sth in ~,** remain near enough to see or watch. 將…保持在視線之內;照看;監視。**lose ~ of,** see no longer; fail to pay further attention to; forget about: 再也看不見;忽略;忘記: *I've lost ~ of that bird.* 我不知那鳥的去向。*We must not lose ~ of the fact that....* 我們切不可忽略…之事實。**at/on ~,** as soon as (sb or sth) is seen: 一見到(某人,某物)立卽: *play music at ~,* from printed music without previous study or practice; 看譜演奏(未先行研究或練習); *a draft payable at ~/a '~ draft,* to be paid at once when presented. 卽期滙票。*The sentry had orders to shoot at/on ~,* as soon as he saw any suspicious person, etc. 哨兵奉令見到可疑的人立卽射殺。**at first ~,** when first seen; without study, examination, etc: 初見;乍看;未加研究,細察等: *At first ~ the problem seemed insoluble.* 乍看之下這問題似乎無法解決。*He fell in love with her at first ~.* 他對她一見鍾情。**at (the) ~ of,** on seeing: 一看見…就: *At ~ of the police officers the men ran off.* 那些人一看到警官們就跑開了。*They all laughed at the ~ of old Percy dancing with a girl of sixteen.* 他們看到老勃西與一位十六歲的女郎跳舞,全都大笑。**3** [U] range of seeing; distance within which seeing is possible: 視域;眼界: *in/within/out of (one's) ~,* (of objects, etc) visible / invisible. (指物體等)看得見(看不見)。*The train was still in ~/was not yet out of ~.* 那火車尙看得見(尙未消失)。*Victory was not yet in ~.* 勝利尙不可預料。**in/within/out of ~ of sth,** (of the viewer) where sth can/cannot be seen: (指觀看者)能看見(看不見): *We are not yet out of ~ of land,* can still see it. 我們仍可看見陸地。*We are now within ~ of the end of this boring task,* can look forward to reaching the end. 這件令人厭煩的工作不久可望結束。**come into/go out of ~,** come near enough/go too far away to be visible. 進入(走出)視界。**keep out of ~,** stay where one cannot be seen. 待在不會被人

看見的地方。***keep out of sb's ~,*** stay where he cannot see you. 不要讓某人看見。 **4** [U] opinion; way of looking at sth: 意見: *Do what is right in your own ~.* 做你認爲對的事。*All men are equal in the ~ of God.* 上帝對所有的人同等看待。 **5** [C] sth seen or to be seen, esp sth remarkable; (*pl*) noteworthy buildings, places, features, etc of a place or district: 情景;景象;(尤指)奇觀;(複)一地方或地區之值得看的建築物,勝地,特色等;名勝;風景: *The Grand Canyon is one of the ~s of the world.* 大峽谷是世界名勝之一。*Our tulips are a wonderful ~ this year/are a ~ to see.* 我們的鬱金香(今年)至爲可觀。*Come and see the ~s of London.* 來看看倫敦的名勝。Hence, 由此產生, **'~·seeing** *n* going about to see places, etc. 觀光; 遊覽。 **'~·seer** /-siːə(r); -,siɚ/ *n* person who goes to see the ~s. 觀光者。***a ~ for sore eyes,*** person or thing one enjoys seeing; sb or sth very welcome. 樂於看見的人或物;極受歡迎的人或物。 **6 a ~,** (colloq) person or thing that excites ridicule or unfavourable comment: (俗)惹起嘲弄或物議的人或事物: *What a ~ she looks in that old dress!* 她穿那件舊衣服看起來怪裡怪氣! *What a ~ you are!* 瞧你這副德性! *She 'does look a ~!* 她的樣子眞怪! **7** [C] (often *pl*) device that helps to aim or observe when using a rifle, telescope, etc: (常用複數)(步槍,望遠鏡等幫助瞄準或觀察的)瞄準器; 照準具; 準星;準頭;照門: *the ~s of a rifle;* 步槍之準星與照門; aim or observation taken with such a device: (以瞄準器所作的)瞄準: *take a careful ~ before firing;* 發射前仔細瞄準; *take a ~ with a compass/quadrant;* 以羅盤(象限儀)瞄看; *take a ~ at the sun,* eg to determine a ship's position. 觀測太陽(以推定船的位置等)。 **8 a ~,** (sl) great quantity: (俚)大量;很多: *It cost him a ~ of money/trouble.* 那花了他一大筆錢(爲他招來一大堆麻煩)。 *He's a ~* (adverbial, 作副詞用, = very much) *too clever to be caught by the police.* 他非常聰明,警察抓不到他。***not by a 'long ~,*** not nearly. 差得遠;遠不如。 **-~ed** *suff* (with *adjj*) having the kind of ~(1) indicated: (與形容詞連用)有某種之視力的: *'weak-/'long-/'far-~ed.* 視力弱的(眼光遠大的;遠視的)。

sight² /saɪt; saɪt/ *vt* [VP6A] **1** get sight of, esp by coming near: 看見(尤指因接近而看見): *After many months at sea, Columbus ~ed land.* 在海上航行多月以後,哥倫布終於看見陸地。 **2** observe (a star, etc) by using sights(7); adjust the sights(7) of (a gun); furnish (a gun, etc) with sights: 觀測(星等);調整(槍砲)的瞄準器;將瞄準器裝於(槍,砲等): *a '~ing shot,* one to get the range. (爲測距及調整瞄準器所作之)試射。 **~·ing** *n* occasion on which sth is ~ed: 某物被看到之時機;出現: *new ~ings of the Loch Ness monster.* 涅斯湖水怪新近的出現。

sight·less /'saɪtlɪs; 'saɪtlɪs/ *adj* blind. 盲的;無視力的。

sign¹ /saɪn; saɪn/ *n* [C] **1** mark, object, symbol, used to represent sth: 記號;符號: *mathematical ~s,* eg +, −, ×, ÷. 數學符號(如 +, −, ×, ÷)。 **2** word or words, design, etc, on a board or plate to give a warning, or to direct sb towards sth: 告示;牌示: *'traffic ~s,* eg for a speed limit, a bend in the road. 交通牌示(如說明速度限制,路彎等)。 **'~·post** *n* post at or near crossroads with names of places on each road (and often distances). 路標(置於十字路口,標示地名、距離等)。 □ *vt* provide with ~posts: 爲…設置路標: *The road is well ~posted.* 這條路設有明確的路標。 **3** sth that gives evidence, points to the existence or likelihood of sth: 跡象;徵兆;痕跡: *the ~s of suffering on his face.* 他臉上的痛苦的痕跡。*Are dark clouds a ~ of rain?* 烏雲是天雨的徵兆嗎? *Violence is a ~ of weakness or fear, not a ~ of strength or confidence.* 暴力是懦弱或恐懼的跡象,不是力量或信心的表徵。 **~ and counter~,** secret sentences, etc by which friends can be distinguished from enemies or from those who do not share a secret. 口令;隱語;黑話。 **4** movement of the hand, head, etc used with or instead of words; signal: 手、頭等的示意動作;手勢;信號: *a '~-language,* eg one used by deaf and dumb persons; 手語(聾啞者等所用之語言); *the ~ of the cross,* a movement with the hand outlining a cross, as a blessing, or with a prayer. (祝福或祈禱時)用手畫十字。 **5 '~(-board),** device (often painted on a board) displayed by traders and shopkeepers (*'shop-~*), and by inns (*'inn-~*), to advertise their business: 招牌;店招(商店,旅社等用以招攬生意者,如: 'shop-~, 'inn-~): *at the ~ of the Red Lion,* at the inn of this name. 在紅獅旅社。 **'~-painter** *n* person who paints ~boards. 製作招牌者。

sign² /saɪn; saɪn/ *vt, vi* **1** [VP6A, 15B, 2A, 2C] write one's name on (a letter, document, etc) to show that one is the writer or that one accepts or agrees with the contents: 簽字於(信,文件等): *~ a letter/a Will and Testament/a cheque;* 簽字於信件(遺囑,支票); *~ one's name,* write it for this purpose. 簽名。*Please ~ on the dotted line.* 請在虛線上簽名。***~ sth away,*** give up (rights, property, etc) by ~ing one's name. 簽字讓渡(權利,財產等)。***~ (sb) in/out,*** write one's/sb's name as a record of arrival/departure. 登記(自己或某人的)姓名以示到達(離去)。 ⇨ *clock in/out* at clock¹(2). ***~ on,*** (colloq) (of an unemployed worker) become formally registered for money on social security, ⇨ social(2). (俗)(指失業工人)正式登記領社會救濟金。***~ on/up,*** (of a worker, etc), ~ an agreement about employment: (指工人等)簽約受雇: *The seaman ~ed on for a voyage to Valparaiso and back.* 那水手簽約受雇作一次來往法耳巴拉索之航行。***~ sb on/up,*** (of an employer, etc) ~ an agreement about employment: (指雇主等)簽約雇用: *The firm ~ed on fifty more workers last week.* 該公司上週簽約增雇了五十名工人。*The manager,* ie of a football team, *has ~ed up some new players.* (足球隊之)經理已簽約雇用幾名新的球員。***~ sth over (to sb),*** confirm the sale of sth (to sb) by ~ing legal papers. 簽字轉讓某物(與某人)。 **2** [VP3A, 6A, 16A] ***~ (to/for) sb (to do sth),*** make known (to sb) an order or request by making signs(4): 做手勢;做信號: *The policeman ~ed (for) them to stop.* 警察做手勢叫他們停住。*He ~ed to me to be quiet.* 他做手勢要我安靜。 **3** [VP2C] ***~ on/off,*** (radio) indicate the beginning/end of a broadcast, eg by means of a few bars of a tune or by other sound effects. (無線電)以曲調或音響表示廣播開始(結束)。 ⇨ signature(2).

sig·nal¹ /'sɪgnəl; 'sɪgnḷ/ *n* [C] **1** (making of a) movement, (showing of a) light, (sending of a) message, device used, to give a warning, an order or information, esp to sb at a distance; order, warning, etc, conveyed in this way: 信號;暗號;打信號等;藉信號所發出的命令,警告等: *'traffic ~s,* for cars, etc in the streets; 交通信號; *'hand ~s,* made with the hand by the driver of a motor-vehicle to show which way it will turn, etc; 汽車駕駛者的手勢(如表示轉彎等); *give the ~ for an attack.* 發出進攻的信號。*A red light is usually a ~ of danger.* 紅燈通常是危險的信號。*A train must not pass a ~ that is at danger.* 火車切不可闖危險號誌。 **'~-box** *n* building on a railway from which ~s and movements of trains are controlled. (鐵路上之)信號所。 **'~·man** /-mən; -,mæn/ *n* (*pl* -men) person who operates ~s on a railway; man who sends and receives ~s (in the army and navy). (鐵路之)信號手;(陸海軍之)信號兵。 **'~-gun** *n* one fired as a ~ in case of distress, eg on a wrecked ship. (危難時,如遭船難,所用之)信號槍; 號砲。 **2** event which is the immediate cause of general activity, etc: (一般活動等之)直接原因;導火線: *The arrival of the President was the ~ for an outburst of cheering.* 總統的到達

引起一陣歡呼。 **3** electronic impulse in radio, TV, etc; sound or TV image, transmitted or received: 訊號；電台、電視發送或接收之聲音或影像： *an area with a poor/excellent TV signal.* 影像不清(極佳)之地區。□ *vt, vi* (-ll-, US, -l-) [VP6A, 9, 17, 2A, C] make a ~ or ~s to; send by ~; make use of ~(s): 向…發信號；以信號報知；用信號： *~ a message;* 以信號發送消息； *~ (to) the commanding officer (that...);* 向指揮官發信號(報告…)； *~ (to) the waiter to bring the menu;* 作手勢要侍者拿菜單； *~ that one is about to turn left.* 作手勢表示將向左轉。 *Sailors ~ with flags by day and with lights at night.* 水手們白日用旗，夜晚用燈，發信號。**~·ler** (US= **~er**) /ˈsɪgnələ(r) ; ˈsɪgnələ˞/ *n* person who ~s, esp a soldier (cf Navy, 參較海軍用語，**ˈ~·man**) specially trained in sending and receiving messages. 信號員；(尤指)信號兵。

sig·nal[2] /ˈsɪgnəl ; ˈsɪgnl/ *attrib adj* remarkable; outstanding: 顯著的；非常的： *a ~ victory/success/achievement.* 重大的勝利(成功，成就)。**~·ly** /-nəlɪ;-nlɪ/ *adv* in a ~ manner: 顯著地；非常地： *fail ~ly.* 大敗。

sig·nal·ize /ˈsɪgnəlaɪz ; ˈsɪgnəˌlaɪz/ *vt* [VP6A] make (an event) noteworthy or conspicuous. 使(事件)著名；使顯著。

sig·na·tory /ˈsɪgnətrɪ *US:* -tɔːrɪ ; ˈsɪgnəˌtorɪ/ *n* [C] (*pl* -ries) (person, country, etc) that has signed an agreement: 簽約者；簽約國： *the signatories to the Treaty;* 簽約之各國； (attrib) (形容用法) *the ~ powers.* 簽約諸强國。

sig·na·ture /ˈsɪgnətʃə(r) ; ˈsɪgnətʃə˞/ *n* [C] **1** person's name signed by himself: 簽字： *put one's ~ to a letter;* 簽名於信件； *send letters in to the manager for ~,* for him to sign. 把信送給經理簽字。**2** **ˈ~ tune,** tune (a few bars of a piece of music) identifying a broadcasting station or a particular programme or performer. 信號調；信號曲(某一廣播節目或表演者啓播前的數小節音樂)。**ˈkey ~,** (music) indication of a (change of) key. (音樂)調號。

sig·net /ˈsɪgnɪt ; ˈsɪgnɪt/ *n* [C] private seal used with or instead of a signature. 私章；圖章。**ˈ~-ring,** finger ring with a ~ set in it. 圖章戒指。**Writer to the S~,** Scottish law officer. (蘇格蘭之)律師；(蘇格蘭最高法院的)狀師。

sig·nifi·cance /sɪgˈnɪfɪkəns ; sɪgˈnɪfəkəns/ *n* [U] meaning; importance: 意義；意味；重要；重大： *understand the ~ of a remark;* 了解某句話的意義； *a matter/speech of great/little ~;* 重大的(無關緊要的)事(演講)； *a look of deep ~.* 含意深刻的一瞥。

sig·nifi·cant /sɪgˈnɪfɪkənt ; sɪgˈnɪfəkənt/ *adj* ~ ***(of),*** having a special or suggestive meaning; important: 有特殊意義的；有含義的；重要的；重大的： *a ~ speech.* 意味深長的演說。 *Few things are more ~ of a man's interests than the books on his shelves.* 一個人書架上的書籍最能顯示這個人的興趣。 **~·ly** *adv*

sig·nifi·ca·tion /ˌsɪgnɪfɪˈkeɪʃn ; sɪgˌnɪfəˈkeʃən/ *n* [C] (intended) meaning (of a word, etc). (字等的)意義；含意。

sig·nifi·cat·ive /sɪgˈnɪfɪkətɪv *US:* -keɪtɪv ; sɪgˈnɪfəˌketɪv/ *adj* ~ ***(of),*** offering evidence (of). 提供證據的；有意義的。

sig·nify /ˈsɪgnɪfaɪ ; ˈsɪgnəˌfaɪ/ *vt, vi* (*pt, pp* -fied) **1** [VP6A, 9, 15A] make known (one's views, intentions, purpose, etc); be a sign of; mean: 表示(個人的見解，意向，目的等)；爲…之表徵；意味： *He signified his agreement/that he agreed by nodding.* 他點頭表示同意。 *His wife signified her approval.* 他的妻子表示贊成。 *Do dark clouds ~ rain?* 烏雲表示有雨嗎？ *What does this phrase ~?* 這片語的意義是什麼？ **2** [VP2A, C] matter; be of importance: 有關係；有重要性： *It doesn't ~.* 那無關重要。 *It signifies much/little.* 那甚爲重要(不大重要)。

si·gnor /ˈsiːnjɔː(r) ; ˈsinjor/, **si·gnora** /sɪˈnjɔːrə ; sinˈjorə/, **si·gnor·ina** /ˌsɪnjɔːˈriːnə ; ˌsinjəˈrinə/ *nn* **S~,** titles used of or to Italians corresponding to Mr, Mrs and Miss or (with a small *s*) Sir, Madam and young lady. (大寫 S，義大利人稱呼)先生；太太；小姐；(小寫 s)大人；夫人；少女。

Sikh /siːk ; sik/ *n* member of a monotheistic Hindu sect founded in the 16th c in the Punjab. (印度北方的)西克教徒。

si·lage /ˈsaɪlɪdʒ ; ˈsaɪlɪdʒ/ *n* [U] green fodder stored in a silo or pit without drying (to feed cattle in winter). 保藏於糧秣庫或坑中之新鮮飼料(以備冬季飼牛用)。

si·lence /ˈsaɪləns ; ˈsaɪləns/ *n* [U] **1** condition of being quiet or silent; absence of sound: 寂靜；無聲： *the ~ of night/of the grave.* 夜(墓地)的寂靜。**2** condition of not speaking, answering (questions, spoken or written), or making comments, etc; (with *indef art*) period (of saying nothing): 沈默；(與不定冠詞連用)沈默的一段時間： *Your ~ on recent events surprises me.* 你對於近來發生的事情保持沈默令我驚奇。 *There was a short ~ and then uproar broke out.* 沈默片刻之後又喧囂起來了。***S~ gives consent,*** (prov) If nothing is said in answer to a proposal or suggestion we may suppose that it is agreed to. (諺)沉默即表示同意。***reduce sb to ~,*** (esp) refute his arguments so that he has to stop talking. (尤指)(反駁其論點)使無話可說。***in ~,*** silently: 沈默地；無聲地： *listen to sb in ~.* 默默地聽某人說話。 *We should not pass over this disgraceful affair in ~,* We ought to protest, etc. 我們不應對這件可恥的事保持緘默。 □ *vt* [VP6A] make (sb or sth) silent; cause to be quiet(er): 使(某人或某物)沈默；使啞口無言；使(較)安靜： *~ a baby's crying;* 使嬰兒停止哭叫； *~ one's critics/the enemy's guns.* 使批評者啞口無言(壓制敵人砲火)。**si·lencer** *n* device that reduces the noise made by the exhaust of a petrol engine, the report of a gun, etc. (汽油引擎，槍，砲等之)消音器；滅音器；遏聲器。

si·lent /ˈsaɪlənt ; ˈsaɪlənt/ *adj* **1** making no or little sound; still; not accompanied by any sound: 聲音極小的；寂靜的；無聲的： *a ~ prayer;* 默禱； *with ~ footsteps;* 脚步輕悄地； *the ~ running of a Rolls Royce car;* 勞斯萊斯汽車跑起來聲音非常小； *a ~ film,* without a sound track. 無聲電影；默片。**2** saying little or nothing; giving no answer, views, etc: 沈默的；寡言的： *Do you know when to keep ~,* say nothing, keep a secret? 你知道在什麼時候該保持沈默嗎？ *You'd better be ~ about what happened.* 你對於所發生的事最好不開口。 *Her husband is the strong, ~ type.* 她丈夫是個堅定、沉默型的人。**ˈ~ partner,** (US) (美) = sleeping partner. ⇨ sleep[2](1). **3** written but not pronounced: 寫出而不發音的： *a ~ letter,* eg *b* in *doubt, w* in *wrong.* 不發音的字母(如 doubt 中之 b, wrong 中之 w)。**~·ly** *adv*

sil·hou·ette /ˌsɪluːˈet ; ˌsɪluˈɛt/ *n* picture in solid black showing only the outline; outline of sb or sth seen against a light background: 黑色輪廓像；黑色半面畫像；側影；輪廓；剪影： *see sth in ~.* 看見某物的輪廓。□ *vt* (usu passive) show, exhibit, in ~: (通常用被動語態)現出…之輪廓： *~d against the eastern sky at dawn.* 破曉時東方天際映出的輪廓。⇨ the illus at hansom. 參看 hansom 之挿圖。

sil·ica /ˈsɪlɪkə ; ˈsɪlɪkə/ *n* [U] silicon dioxide (**SiO_2**), occurring as ~ sand (used in glass-making) and in quartz, and as the principal constituent of sandstone and other rocks. 矽石；二氧化矽(SiO_2，天然者爲矽沙，用以製玻璃，存於石英中，並爲沙岩及其他岩石之主要成分)。

sili·cate /ˈsɪlɪkeɪt ; ˈsɪlɪˌket/ *n* [U] one of a great number of compounds containing silica: 矽酸鹽： *~ of soda.* 矽酸蘇打。

sili·con /ˈsɪlɪkən ; ˈsɪlɪkən/ *n* [U] non-metallic element (symbol **Si**) found combined with oxygen in quartz, sandstone, etc. 矽(Si)(非金屬元素，以氧化物之形式見於石英、沙岩等中)。**ˌ~ ˈchip** *n* chip made of ~, used to make an integrated circuit. (用以製造積體電路之)矽片。⇨ integrate(1).

sili·cone /ˈsɪlɪkəʊn ; ˈsɪlɪkon/ *n* [U] (kinds of) complex organic compounds of silicon used in paints, varnish and lubricants. 矽酮(用於油漆,假漆及滑潤劑中的(數種)複合有機化合物)。

sili·co·sis /ˌsɪlɪˈkəʊsɪs ; ˌsɪlɪˈkosɪs/ *n* [U disease caused by breathing in quartz dust (eg in a coal-mine). 石末沉着病(因吸進石英塵所產生之病,如在煤礦中者)。

silk /sɪlk ; sɪlk/ *n* **1** [U] fine, soft thread from the cocoons of certain insects; material made from this; (attrib) made of this: 絲;絲織品;綢;(形容用法)絲製的;綢做的: *raw ~;* 生絲; *~ stockings;* 絲襪; *a ~ shirt.* 絲製襯衫。**ˈ~·screen (printing),** method of printing by forcing the colour(s) through a stencil of ~ or other finely woven material. 絹印(印製法)。**ˈ~·worm** *n* caterpillar that spins ~ to form a cocoon. 蠶。**2** (*pl*) garments of ~: (複)綢衣: *dressed in ~s and satins,* wearing rich clothes. 穿著錦衣華服。**3** [C] (in England) Queen's/King's Counsel (abbr 略作 **QC, KC**). (英)勅選律師; 高等律師。⇨ counsel¹(3). ***take ~,*** become a QC/KC. 做勅選律師。

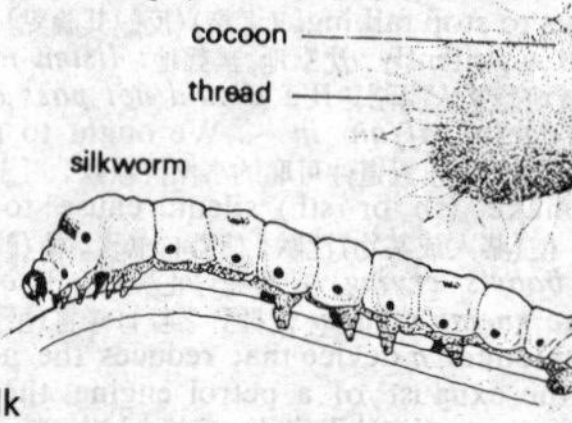

silk

silken /ˈsɪlkən ; ˈsɪlkən/ *adj* **1** soft and smooth; soft and shining: 柔軟光滑的;柔和而有光澤的: *a ~ voice;* 柔和的聲音; *~ hair.* 柔軟光滑的頭髮。**2** (old use, or liter) made of silk: (舊用法,文)絲織的;綢製的: *~ dresses.* 綢衣。

silky /ˈsɪlkɪ ; ˈsɪlkɪ/ *adj* (-ier, -iest) soft, shiny, smooth, like silk: 像絲一般柔軟,光亮,光滑的: *a ~* (= suave) *manner;* 溫和的態度; *a ~ voice.* 柔和的聲音。**silki·ness** *n*

sill /sɪl ; sɪl/ *n* [C] flat shelf or block of wood or stone at the base of a window (=ˈ**window-sill**) or (rarely) of a doorway. 窗臺;(罕)門檻。⇨ the illus at window. 參看 window 之插圖。

sil·la·bub (US = **syll-**) /ˈsɪləbʌb ; ˈsɪləˌbʌb/ *n* [C, U] soft, sweet dish of food made of cream or milk mixed with wine into curd, etc. 乳酒凍(一種用奶油或牛奶加葡萄酒製成之凍狀甜食)。

silly /ˈsɪlɪ ; ˈsɪlɪ/ *adj* (-ier, -iest) foolish; weak-minded: 愚蠢的;低能的;無智慧的: *say ~ things;* 說蠢話; *a ~ little boy.* 傻小男孩。*Don't be ~!* 別傻! *How ~ of you to do that!* 你做那事多笨啊! □ *n* (*pl* -lies) (chiefly used to or by children) ~ person. (主要用於指小孩或由小孩所用)傻人;笨伯。**sil·li·ness** *n*

silo /ˈsaɪləʊ ; ˈsaɪlo/ *n* (*pl* ~s /-ləʊz ; -loz/) [C] air-tight structure (either a tall cylindrical tower or a pit) in which green food (*silage*) is stored for farm animals. 貯藏新鮮飼料之密室(圓柱型高塔或地下坑);糧秣室。

silt /sɪlt ; sɪlt/ *n* [U] sand, mud, etc carried by moving water (and left at the mouth of a river, in a harbour, etc). 淤沙;淤泥;泥滓(由流動之水帶至河口,港中等處者)。□ *vt, vi* [VP2C, 15B] *~ (sth) up,* (cause to) become stopped with ~: (使)爲淤泥充塞: *The harbour has ~ed up.* 這海港已爲淤泥充塞。*The sand has ~ed up the mouth of the river.* 泥沙充塞了河口。

sil·van /ˈsɪlvən ; ˈsɪlvən/ = sylvan.

sil·ver /ˈsɪlvə(r) ; ˈsɪlvɚ/ *n* [U] **1** shining white precious metal (symbol **Ag**) used for ornaments, coins, utensils, etc: 銀(Ag)(光亮之白色貴重金屬,用於製裝飾品、硬幣、器皿等): *ˈtable ~,* spoons, forks, etc. 銀餐具。**~ plate,** metal articles coated with ~. 鍍銀之金屬器具。***be born with a ~ ˈspoon in one's mouth,*** be born into a wealthy family. 生來有錢;生於有錢人家。**2** ~ coins: 銀幣: *£20 in notes and £5 in ~;* 二十鎊紙幣和五鎊銀幣; *a handful of ~;* 一把銀幣; *a ~ collection,* to which ~ coins are to be given. 銀幣募捐。*Have you any ~ on you?* 你身上帶有銀幣(錢)嗎? **3** ~ vessels, dishes, articles, eg candlesticks, trays: 銀器;銀皿;銀具(如燭臺,盤等): *have all one's ~ taken by burglars;* 所有銀器全被竊賊偷走; *sell one's ~ to pay the mortgage interest.* 出售銀器以償付抵押貸款之利息。**4** (attrib) the colour of ~: (形容用法)銀色: *the ~ moon;* 銀色的月亮; (of sounds) soft and clear: (指聲音)清越的;清亮的: *He has a ~ tongue/is ˌ~-ˈtongued,* is eloquent. 他能言善辯。**~ grey,** lustrous grey. 銀灰色(的)。**the ~ screen,** cinema; cinema screen. 電影;銀幕。**5** (in art and literature) second best: (藝術及文學之)第二等;次好的: *the ~ age,* ⇨ golden(2). 白銀時代。**6** (compounds) (複合字) ˌ~ ˈ**birch** *n* common white birch with ~-coloured bark. 白樺樹(其皮爲銀白色)。ˈ**~-fish** *n* (kinds of) small wingless insect that damages book bindings, clothes, etc. 蠹魚(蛀蝕書籍、衣物之無翼小蟲)。**~ paper,** (colloq) thin, light foil made of tin or aluminium (as used for packing chocolates, cigarettes, etc). (俗)錫(鋁)箔紙(用來包裝巧克力,香煙等)。ˈ**~·side** *n* best side of a round of beef. 最上頭之牛腿肉。ˈ**~·smith** *n* manufacturer of ~ articles; merchant who sells these. 銀匠;銀器商。ˌ**~ ˈwedding** *n* 25th anniversary. 銀婚(二十五週年)。□ *vt, vi* **1** [VP6A] coat with ~ or with sth that looks like ~; make (sth) bright like ~: 鍍以銀;敷以似銀之物;使(某物)光亮如銀: *The years have ~ed her hair.* 歲月使她的頭髮變白了。**2** [VP 2A] become white or ~ colour: 變白;變銀色: *Her hair had ~ed.* 她的頭髮白了。**~y** *adj* like ~: 似銀的: *the ~y notes of a temple bell.* 清越的寺院鐘聲。

sil·vern /ˈsɪlvən ; ˈsɪlvɚn/ *adj* (archaic) silver: (古)銀的;似銀的: *Speech is ~ but silence is golden,* it is better to be silent than to speak. 說話爲銀,沉默是金。

sim·ian /ˈsɪmɪən ; ˈsɪmɪən/ *adj, n* (of, like, a) monkey or ape. 猴或猿(的);似猴或猿的。

simi·lar /ˈsɪmələ(r) ; ˈsɪmələ/ *adj ~ (to),* like; of the same sort: 類似的;同樣的: *My wife and I have ~ tastes in music.* 我的妻子和我在音樂方面有相似的愛好。*Gold is ~ in colour to brass.* 金和黃銅的顏色相似。**~·ly** *adv* **~·ity** /ˌsɪməˈlærətɪ ; ˌsɪməˈlærətɪ/ *n* (*pl* -ties) [U] likeness; state of being ~; [C] point or respect in which there is likeness: 類似;相似;相似之點: *points of ~ity between the two men.* 二人相似之點。*Are there any ~ities between China and Japan?* 中國和日本有任何相似之點嗎?

sim·ile /ˈsɪmɪlɪ ; ˈsɪməˌli/ *n* [C, U] (use of) comparison of one thing to another, eg 'He is as brave as a lion,' 'Childhood is like a swiftly passing dream': 直喻;明喻;直喻或明喻之使用(例如:'他勇猛如獅,' '童年像一場疾逝的夢'): *He uses interesting ~s.* 他慣用有趣的直喻。*His style is rich in ~.* 他的文體頗多明喻。

sim·ili·tude /sɪˈmɪlɪtjuːd US: -tuːd ; səˈmɪləˌtjud/ *n* **1** [U] (formal) resemblance (in general details but not in everything). (正式用語)類似;相似。**2** [C] comparison; simile: 比喻;直喻: *talk in ~s.* 說話引用比喻。

sim·mer /ˈsɪmə(r) ; ˈsɪmɚ/ *vi, vt* **1** [VP2A, B, 6A, 15A] be, keep (sth), almost at boiling-point: 燉;煨;慢煮: *Let the soup ~ for a few minutes.* 讓那湯再煨幾分鐘。*S~ the stew for an hour.* 把那菜用慢火燉一小時。**2** [VP2C] be filled with (anger, etc), which is only just kept under control: 內心充滿;按捺著(怒氣等): *~ with rage/laughter/*

annoyance. 按捺著怒氣(很想笑;心裡感到很厭煩)。~ ***down,*** (fig) become calm (after being angry or excited). (喻)變冷靜;安靜下來(在發怒或激動之後)。□ *n* (*sing* only) (僅用單數) ***keep sth at a ~/on the ~,*** ~ing. 使某物保持在將沸未沸的狀態。

sim·ony /ˈsɪmənɪ ; ˈsaɪmənɪ/ *n* [U] (hist) offence of accepting or offering money for a position in the Church. (史)買賣聖職罪。

si·moom /sɪˈmu:m ; sɪˈmum/, **si·moon** /sɪˈmu:n ; sɪˈmun/ *n* hot, dry, dust-laden wind blowing in a straight track in the Sahara and the deserts of Arabia. 撒哈拉及阿拉伯沙漠地區所颳的乾燥而帶有塵沙的熱風;西蒙風。

sim·per /ˈsɪmpə(r) ; ˈsɪmpɚ/ *vi* [VP2A], *n* (give a) silly, self-conscious smile. (作)癡笑;假笑。**~·ing·ly** /ˈsɪmprɪŋlɪ ; ˈsɪmpərɪŋlɪ/ *adv*

simple /ˈsɪmpl ; ˈsɪmpl̩/ *adj* (-r, -st) **1** unmixed; not divided into parts; having only a small number of parts: 單純的;單一的;簡單的;簡易的: *a ~ substance;* 單純的物質; *a ~ machine;* 簡單的機器; *a ~ sentence,* one without subordinate clauses. 簡單句。**~ interest,** on capital only, not on accumulated interest. 單利(祇對本金而不對其累積之利息所生者)。⇨ compound¹(3). **2** plain; not much decorated or ornamented: 樸實的;無甚裝飾的: *~ food/cooking;* 簡單的食物(烹飪); *a ~ style of architecture;* 樸實的建築風格; *the ~ life,* a way of living without luxuries, servants or artificial pastimes, or in the country, contrasted with cities. 簡樸的生活(如鄉居生活等)。 **3** not highly developed: 未充分發展的: *~ forms of life.* 未充分發展的生命形態。 **4** easily done or understood; not causing trouble: 易做的;易懂的;不會引起困難的: *written in ~ English;* 以簡單英文寫出; *a ~ task.* 易做的工作。 **5** innocent; straight-forward: 天眞的;率直的;老實的: *behave in a pleasant and ~ way;* 舉止可愛而率眞; *as ~ as a child;* 像小孩一樣天眞的; *~ folk.* 老實人。**ˌ~-ˈhearted** *adj* frank. 坦白的;率直的。**ˌ~-ˈminded** *adj* **(a)** frank; unsophisticated. 率直的;不世故的。 **(b)** feeble-minded. 低能的。 **6** inexperienced; easily deceived: 無經驗的;易受欺的: *Are you ~ enough to believe everything your newspapers tell you?* 你會蠢到相信報紙告訴你的每一件事嗎? *I'm not so ~ as to suppose you like me.* 我不致於笨到以爲你喜歡我。*She's a ~ soul,* innocent of guile. 她是個沒有心眼的人。 **7** with nothing added; absolute: 純然的;絕對的: *a ~ fact.* 純粹的事實。***pure and ~,*** (colloq) absolute(ly), unquestionably: (俗)絕對地;無疑地: *It's a case of kill or be killed, pure and ~.* 這無疑是個殺人或被殺的情況。□ *n* [C] (old use) herb used medicinally. (舊用法)草藥。**sim·ply** /ˈsɪmplɪ ; ˈsɪmplɪ/ *adv* **1** in a ~(2) manner: 樸素地;樸實地;無甚裝飾地: *live simply;* 過樸實的生活; *dress simply;* 衣著樸素; *simply dressed.* 衣著樸素。 **2** completely; absolutely: 完全地;絕對地: *His pronunciation is simply terrible,* is very bad indeed. 他的發音實在糟透了。*She looks simply lovely.* 她看起來十分可愛。 **3** only; merely; nothing more nor less than: 僅;祇;恰好地: *This drink consists simply of fresh oranges.* 這飲料僅含新鮮柑汁。*You must believe me simply on my word,* with nothing more than my assertion, without proof or evidence. 你必須完全相信我的話。*It is simply a matter of working hard.* 此事祇須努力做去。

simple·ton /ˈsɪmpltən ; ˈsɪmpl̩tən/ *n* foolish, weak-minded person, esp one who is easily deceived. 傻瓜;笨蛋;(尤指)容易受騙的人。

sim·plic·ity /sɪmˈplɪsətɪ ; sɪmˈplɪsətɪ/ *n* [U] the state of being simple: 簡單;簡易;樸素;樸實;率眞: *the ~ of the problem;* 該問題的單純性; *speak with ~.* 平實地說話。***be ~ itself,*** (colloq) be extremely easy. (俗)極爲容易。

sim·plify /ˈsɪmplɪfaɪ ; ˈsɪmpləˌfaɪ/ *vt* (*pt, pp* -fied) [VP6A] make simple; make easy to do or understand: 使單純;使易做;使易懂;簡化: *a simplified reader/text.* 簡易讀本(教本)。*That will ~ my task.* 那將簡化我的工作。 **sim·pli·fi·ca·tion** /ˌsɪmplɪfɪˈkeɪʃn ; ˌsɪmpləfəˈkeʃən/ *n* [U] act or process of ~ing; [C] instance of ~ing; sth simplified. 單純化;簡化;簡化之實例;簡化之物。

simu·lac·rum /ˌsɪmjʊˈleɪkrəm ; ˌsɪmjəˈlekrəm/ *n* (*pl* -cra /-krə ; -krə/) sth made in the likeness of a person or object; shadowy likeness that deceives. 像;類像;僞物;幻影。

simu·late /ˈsɪmjʊleɪt ; ˈsɪmjəˌlet/ *vt* [VP6A] **1** pretend to be; pretend to have or feel: 假裝;僞裝;佯爲: *~d innocence/enthusiasm.* 假裝的天眞(熱心)。 **2** counterfeit: 僞造;倣造;模倣: *insects that ~ dead leaves.* 僞裝枯葉的昆蟲。**simu·la·tion** /ˌsɪmjʊˈleɪʃn ; ˌsɪmjəˈleʃən/ *n* [U] pretence; imitation. 假裝;佯爲;模倣;擬態。**simu·la·tor** /-tə(r) ; -tɚ/ *n* (esp) apparatus designed to provide (for testing purposes) conditions (eg non-gravity, for simulating weightlessness) like those which are encountered in real operations. (尤指做試驗用的)摹擬儀器(如摹擬失重之試驗)。

sim·ul·ta·neous /ˌsɪmlˈteɪnɪəs *US:* ˌsaɪm- ; ˌsaɪml̩ˈtenɪəs/ *adj* ***~ (with),*** happening or done at the same time as: 同時發生的;同時做出的;同時的。**~·ly** *adv* **~·ness, sim·ul·ta·ne·ity** /ˌsɪmltəˈni:ətɪ *US:* ˌsaɪm- ; ˌsaɪml̩təˈniətɪ/ *nn*

sin /sɪn ; sɪn/ *n* **1** [U] breaking of God's laws; behaviour that is against the principles of morality, ⇨ crime; [C] instance of this; immoral act such as telling a lie, stealing, murder: 對上帝律法之違背;(宗教上的)罪;違背道德原則之行爲;此種罪行之實例;不道德行爲(如說謊,偷竊,謀殺): *confess one's sins to a priest;* 向教士告解; *ask for one's sins to be forgiven.* 請求赦罪。***live in sin,*** (dated or hum use) live together as if married. (過時或詼諧用語)過同居生活。**original sin,** proneness to commit sin which, some Christians believe, is part of mankind's nature. 原罪(犯罪之傾向,某些基督教徒認爲此乃人類本性的一部分)。**deadly/mortal sin,** one that is fatal to salvation of the soul. 嚴重的罪惡;使靈魂不得超度的罪。***the seven deadly sins,*** pride, covetousness, lust, anger, gluttony, envy, sloth. 七大罪(驕傲,貪婪,色慾,憤怒,貪食,妬嫉,怠惰)。 **2** [C] (colloq) offence against convention; sth considered contrary to common sense: (俗)違背習俗;不合情理之事;過失: *It's a sin to give the children so much homework.* 給小孩如此多的家庭作業有悖情理。*It's a sin to stay indoors on such a fine day.* 這樣好的天氣留在屋裡實在罪過。□ *vi* (-nn-) [VP2A, 3A] ***sin (against),*** commit sin; do wrong: 犯罪;違過: *We are all liable to sin.* 我們都易於犯罪。*Is it sinning against society to have a very large family?* 生很多孩子是違反社會的嗎? **sin·ful** /-fl ; -fəl/ *adj* wrong; wicked. 有過的;有罪的;邪惡的。**sin·ful·ness** *n* **sin·less** *adj* free from sin; innocent. 無罪的;無辜的。 **sin·less·ness** *n* **sin·ner** /ˈsɪnə(r) ; ˈsɪnɚ/ *n* person who sins/has sinned. 犯罪者;犯過者。

since /sɪns ; sɪns/ *adv* **1** (with the perfect tenses) after a date, event, etc in the past; before the present time; between some time in the past and the present time, or the time referred to: (與完成式連用)在過去的某日期,事件等以後;在現在以前;在過去的某一時間與現在或所提及的時間之間: *The town was/had been destroyed by an earthquake ten years ago/earlier and has/had ~ been rebuilt.* 這小城在十年前爲地震所毀,後來曾予以重建。*He left home in 1970 and has not been heard of ~.* 他在一九七〇年離家,以後卽無音訊。***ever ~,*** throughout the whole of a period of time referred to and up to the present: 從那時到現在;此後一直: *He went to Turkey in 1956 and has lived there ever ~.* 他在一九五六年前往土耳其,此後一直住在那裡。 **2** (with the simple tenses) ago (which is the usu word): (與簡單式連用)以前 (ago 較常用): *He did it many years* ~. 他在許多年以前做該事。*How long ~ is/was it?* 那是多久以前的事? □ *prep* (with the perfect tenses in the main clause) after; during a period of time after: (與主要子句中的完成式連用)自…以後;自從: *S~ last seeing you I have been ill.* 上次看到你以後我就病了。*She hasn't/hadn't been home ~ her marriage.* 她自結婚後未曾回過家。□ *conj* **1** (with the perfect tenses in the main clause) from the past time when: (與主要子句中的完成式連用)自…以後;從…以來: *Where have you been ~ I last saw you?* 自上次見面以後,你到那裡去了? (with the simple present tense in the main clause): (與主要子句中之簡單現在式連用): *How long is it ~ you were in London?* 你在倫敦多久了? *It is just a week ~ we arrived here.* 我們到達此地剛好一星期。**2** seeing that; as: 既然;因爲: *S~ we've no money, we can't buy it.* 因爲我們沒錢,我們買不起(它)。

sin·cere /sɪn'sɪə(r) ; sɪn'sɪr/ *adj* **1** (of feelings, behaviour) genuine; not pretended: (指感情,行爲)眞實的;誠摯的: *It is my ~ belief that....* 我確信…。*Are they ~ in their wish to disarm?* 他們眞的想裁軍麼? **2** (of persons) straightforward; not in the habit of expressing feelings that are pretended. (指人)直率的;不矯情的。**~·ly** *adv* in a ~ manner: 眞實地: ***Yours ~ly,*** commonly used before a signature at the end of a letter to a friend or acquaintance. 一般用於致友人信札末尾簽名前的套語。**sin·cer·ity** /sɪn'serətɪ ; sɪn'sɛrətɪ/ *n* [U] the quality of being ~; honesty: 眞實;誠摯;誠實: *speaking in all sincerity,* very ~ly and honestly. 極其誠懇地談話。

sin·ecure /'saɪnɪkjʊə(r) ; 'saɪnɪˌkjʊr/ *n* [C] position for which one receives credit or payment but which does not entail work or responsibility. 領乾俸的職位;閒差事。

sine die /ˌsaɪnɪ 'daɪiː ; 'saɪnɪ'daɪ·i/ *adv* (Lat) without a date fixed: (拉)無確定日期地;無限期地: *adjourn a meeting ~*, indefinitely. 無限期休會。

sine qua non /ˌsɪneɪ kwɑː 'nəʊn ; 'saɪnɪkwe'nɑn/ *n* (Lat) condition or qualification that cannot be done without; essential condition. (拉)必須條件(或資格)。

sinew /'sɪnjuː ; 'sɪnju/ *n* [C] **1** tendon (strong cord) joining a muscle to a bone. 腱(連接骨與肉的强韌索狀組織)。**2** (*pl*) muscles; energy; physical strength; (fig) means of acquiring strength: (複)肌肉;精力;體力;(喻)獲得力量的方法: ***the ~s of war,*** money (with which to buy supplies). 軍費。**sin·ewy** *adj* tough; having strong ~s: 堅韌的;强壯的: *~y arms;* 强壯的手臂; (fig) vigorous; having or showing nervous strength. (喻)精力充沛的;强有力的。

sing /sɪŋ ; sɪŋ/ *vi, vt* (*pt* sang /sæŋ ; sæŋ/, *pp* sung /sʌŋ ; sʌŋ/) **1** [VP2A, C, 3A, 6A, 12B, 13B, 15A] make musical sounds with the voice, utter words one after the other to a tune: 唱;歌唱: *She ~s well.* 她很會唱歌。*He was ~ing a Malay song.* 他在唱一首馬來亞歌。*He was ~ing to the guitar/to a piano accompaniment.* 他正和着吉他(由鋼琴伴奏)唱歌。*She sang the baby to sleep.* 她唱歌使小兒入睡。*You're not ~ing in tune.* 你唱得不合調子。*You're ~ing out of tune.* 你唱走調了。*Will you ~ me a song/~ a song for me?* 唱一支歌給我聽好嗎? ***~ another tune,*** behave or speak in a different way, eg with less confidence or presumption. 改變態度;變謙恭。***~ small,*** (colloq) speak or behave humbly (after being reproved, etc). (俗)(在受責等後)言行變謙遜。**2** [VP2A, C] make a humming, buzzing or ringing sound: 發嗡嗡聲;發嚶嚶聲;發鳴叫聲: *The kettle was ~ing (away) on the cooker.* 水壺在爐子上發鳴鳴的叫聲。*My ears are ~ing,* are affected with buzzing sounds. 我的耳朶在鳴響。**3** [VP6A, 3A] ***~ (of) sth,*** (liter) celebrate in verse: (文)歌頌;吟詠: *~ (of) sb's exploits.* 歌頌某人的勳業。***~ sb's praises,*** praise him with enthusiasm. 衷心讚美某人;歌頌某人。**4** ***~ out (for),*** shout (for). 大聲叫;喊叫。***~ sth out,*** shout sth: 大聲喊;大叫: *~ out an order.* 喊出命令。***~ up,*** ~ with more force, ~ more loudly: 更用力唱;更大聲唱: *S~ up, girls, and let's hear you.* 唱大聲一點,女孩子們,讓我們聽清楚。**~er** *n* person who ~s, esp one who does this in public. 歌者;歌手。**~·ing** *n* (esp) art of the ~er: 歌唱;(尤指)歌唱者的技巧: *teach ~ing;* 教唱歌; *my '~ing-master;* 我的歌唱老師; *take '~ing lessons.* 上歌唱的課程;學歌唱。**~·able** /-əbl ; -əbḷ/ *adj* that can be sung: 可歌唱的;可吟詠的: *Some of this modern music is not ~able.* 這種現代音樂有的不能歌唱。

singe /sɪndʒ ; sɪndʒ/ *vt, vi* (*pres part* singeing) **1** [VP6A] burn off the tips or ends (esp of hair, as may be done at the hair-dresser's): 燒焦尖端(尤指頭髮,如在理髮店中所做者);燙: *have one's hair cut and ~d.* 剪燙頭髮。**2** [VP6A] blacken the surface of by burning; burn slightly: 燒黑…之表面;微燒: *If the iron is too hot you'll ~ that nightdress.* 如果熨斗過熱,你會把睡衣燙焦。*She was busy ~ing the poultry,* burning the downy feathers off the birds (after they had been killed). 她正忙於燒去(殺死之)家禽的細毛。**3** [VP2A] become ~d or scorched. 燒焦;燙焦。□ *n* slight burn or scorch (on cloth, etc). (布等上面的)輕微的燒灼。

single /'sɪŋgl ; 'sɪŋgḷ/ *adj* **1** one only; one and no more: 唯一的;單一的;一個的: *a ~ cherry hanging from the tree.* 樹上唯一的一顆櫻桃。***in ~ file,*** (moving, standing) one behind the other in a line. (行進,站立)一路縱隊。**ˌ~-'breasted** *adj* (of a coat) having only one row of buttons down the front. (指外衣)單排鈕的。**ˌ~ 'combat,** fight with weapons, one man against another man. 一人對一人的作戰。**ˌ~-'handed** *adj, adv* done by one person without help from others. 獨自的(地);獨力的(地)。**ˌ~-'minded** *adj* having, intent on, only one purpose. 一心一意的;赤誠的。**'~·stick** *n* [C, U] (fencing with a) stick about the length of a sword. 劍狀木棍;木劍;使用木劍之劍術。**~ ticket** *n* ticket for a journey to a place, not there and back. 單程票。Cf 參較 US 美 *one-way* ticket. **~ track** *n* (on a railway) one line only, with traffic in one direction only at one time. (鐵路)單線。**2** not married: 未婚的;獨身的: *~ men and women;* 未婚男女; *remain ~;* 仍然單身; *the ~ state/life,* that of an unmarried person. 獨身狀態(生活)。**3** for the use of, used for, done by, one person: 適於一人的;一人用的;一人做的: *a ~ bed;* 單人床; *reserve* (at a hotel) *two ~ rooms and one double room.* (在旅社)預定兩間單人房和一間雙人房。**4** (bot) having only one set of petals. ⇨ double¹(5): (植物)單瓣的: *a ~ tulip.* 單瓣之鬱金香。□ *n* [C] **1** (tennis and golf) game with one person on each side: (網球,高爾夫球)單打: *play a ~;* 玩單打球戲; *the men's/women's ~s at Wimbledon;* 溫布頓網球錦標賽之男子(女子)單打; (cricket) hit for which one run is scored: (板球)一分打: *run a quick ~;* 打擊後快跑得一分; (baseball) base hit. (棒球)一壘打。**2** (short for a) ~ ticket: 單程票(爲 single ticket 之略): *two second-class ~s to Leeds.* 兩張前往里玆之二等單程票。□ *vt* [VP15B] ***~ sb/sth out,*** select from others (for special attention, etc): 挑選;揀選: *Why have you ~d out this incident for criticism?* 你爲什麼單挑這件事批評呀? **sing·ly** /'sɪŋglɪ ; 'sɪŋglɪ/ *adv* one by one; by oneself. 一個個地;個別地;獨自地;單獨地。**~·ness** *n* [U] quality of being ~. 單一;獨身;獨自;專一。***~ness of purpose,*** complete devotion to one purpose only. 一心一意;專心致志。

sin·glet /'sɪŋglɪt ; 'sɪŋglɪt/ *n* (GB) sleeveless garment worn for games or under a shirt; vest. (英)無袖之運動衫或汗衫;背心。

single·ton /'sɪŋgltən ; 'sɪŋgḷtən/ *n* [C] (in card

games) single card of any suit held in one hand (of 13 cards): (紙牌戲)一手牌中某一花色獨有的一張牌: *a ~ in hearts.* 一張紅心孤牌。

sing·song /ˈsɪŋsɒŋ ; ˈsɪŋˌsɔŋ/ *n* **1** meeting of friends to sing songs together; impromptu vocal concert: (朋友們聚在一起的)歌唱會;即席歌唱會: *have a ~ round the camp fire.* 圍繞着營火舉行歌唱會。**2** ***in a ~,*** (of a voice) in a rising and falling way; in a monotonous rhythm: (指聲音)忽高忽低地;節奏單調地: (attrib) (形容用法) ***in a ~ voice/manner.*** 聲音單調地(態度呆板地)。

sin·gu·lar /ˈsɪŋgjʊlə(r) ; ˈsɪŋgjələ/ *adj* **1** (liter) uncommon; strange: (文)殊異的;奇特的: *Isn't it unwise to make yourself so ~ in your dress,* to be so unconventional? 你這樣奇裝異服不是不明智嗎? **2** (formal) outstanding: (正式用語)非凡的;卓越的: *a man of ~ courage and honesty.* 異常勇敢和誠實的人。 **3** (gram) of the form used in speaking or writing of one person or thing. (文法)單數的。□ *n* the ~ number: (文法)單數;單數式: *What is the ~ of children?* 'children' 的單數是什麼? **~·ly** *adv* outstandingly; strangely; peculiarly. 非凡地;奇特地;特殊地。**~·ity** /ˌsɪŋgjʊˈlærətɪ ; ˌsɪŋgjəˈlærətɪ/ *n* (*pl* -ties) [U] strangeness; [C] sth unusual or strange. 奇異;特異;非凡或奇特之事物。 **ˈ~·ize** /-aɪz ; -aɪz/ *vt* make ~(1). 使殊異;使奇特。

Sin·ha·lese, Sin·gha·lese /ˌsɪnhəˈliːz, ˌsɪŋhəˈliːz ; ˌsɪnhəˈliz, ˌsɪŋgəˈliz/ *adj* of the larger of the communities in Sri Lanka and their language. 錫蘭族的;錫蘭語的。⇨ Tamil. □ *n* member, language, of this community. 錫蘭族人;錫蘭語。

sin·is·ter /ˈsɪnɪstə(r) ; ˈsɪnɪstə/ *adj* **1** suggesting evil or the likelihood of coming misfortune: 不吉祥的;凶兆的: *a ~ beginning.* 不吉祥的開始。 **2** showing ill will: 顯示惡意的;兇惡的;陰險的: *a ~ face;* 兇惡的臉; *~ looks.* 陰險的神情。 **3** (in heraldry) on the left side of the shield (regarded from the bearer's point of view). (紋章)在盾之左方的(由持者之觀點認定之)。***bar ~,*** mark on a shield showing illegitimate descent. 盾牌上表示庶出之記號。

sink¹ /sɪŋk ; sɪŋk/ *n* [C] **1** fixed basin (of stone, porcelain, steel, etc) with a drain for taking off water, usu under water taps in a kitchen or scullery, used for washing dishes, cleaning vegetables, etc: 洗滌槽(爲石,瓷,鋼等做成之固定盆槽,有排水管,通常在廚房之水龍頭下面,用於洗滌碗碟,蔬菜等): *She complains that she spends half her life at the kitchen ~,* seldom gets away from dull domestic work. 她埋怨做了半輩子的家事。**2** cesspool. 污水池;污水坑;糞坑。 **3** (fig) place where evil people and evil practices collect: (喻)壞人惡事滋生之地;藏污納垢之所: *That part of the town is a ~ of iniquity.* 小城的那一區是罪惡的淵藪。

sink² /sɪŋk ; sɪŋk/ *vi, vt* (*pt* sank /sæŋk ; sæŋk/, *pp* sunk /sʌŋk ; sʌŋk/, and, as *adj,* sunken /ˈsʌŋkən ; ˈsʌŋkən/) **1** [VP2A, C] go down, esp below the horizon or the surface of water or other liquid or a soft substance, eg mud: 沈下;沈落(尤指低於地平面或水等之面): *The sun was ~ing in the west.* 太陽正在西方沈落。 *Wood does not ~ in water, it floats.* 木在水中不沈,它漂浮着。*The ship sank,* went to the bottom. 那船沈了。***~ or swim,*** phrase used of running great risks when the alternatives are complete loss or failure and safety or success. 成敗全憑自己;無論成敗;不管好歹。**2** [VP2A, C] slope downwards; become lower or weaker: 傾斜;下陷;變低;變弱: *The foundations have sunk.* 地基已下陷。*The ground ~s to the sea.* 陸地向海傾斜。*The soldier sank to the ground badly wounded.* 這兵士重傷倒地。(fig) (喻) *His heart sank at the thought of failure.* 他一想到失敗就覺得沮喪。**3** [VP6A, 15A] make by digging: 掘;挖;鑿: *~ a well;* 掘井; place (sth) in a hole made by digging: 掘洞插入(某物);埋入: *~ a post one foot deep in the ground.* 將一根柱子埋在地裡一呎深。 **4** [VP2C, 3A] ***~ in; ~ into sth,*** (of liquids, and fig) go down deep: (指液體,喻)沁進;滲入: *The rain sank into the dry ground.* 雨水沁進乾地。*Let this warning ~ into your mind.* 把這個警告銘記於心。*The lesson hasn't sunk in,* (fig) has not been learnt or fully understood. 這一課還不十分了解。**5** [VP2C, 3A] ***~ in; ~ into/to sth,*** come to a lower level or state (physical or moral): 陷入;降低(物質的或精神的): *~ into a deep sleep;* 陷入沉睡中; *~ into vice;* 墮入惡習; *~ into insignificance;* 降爲微不足道; *~ in the estimation of one's friends.* 朋友們對他的評價降低。*He was sunk in thought/despair.* 他陷入沉思(失望)。*He is ~ing fast,* will soon die. 他快要死了。*The old man has sunken cheeks.* 這老人臉頰凹陷。*His cheeks have sunk in.* 他的臉頰凹陷。 *His voice sank to a whisper.* 他的聲音降低成耳語。 **6** [VP6A, 15A] cause or allow to ~: 使沉;使低落: *~ a ship.* 沉船。*He sank* (= lowered) *his voice to a whisper.* 他把聲音降低爲耳語。*Let us ~ our differences* (= put them out of our thoughts, forget them), *and work together.* 讓我們摒棄歧見,一起工作罷。 **7** [VP6A, 14] ***~ (in),*** invest (money), esp so that it is not easy to withdraw it: 投(資)(尤指不易收回者): *He has sunk half his fortune in a new business undertaking.* 他已把一半財產投資於一新的企業中。**ˈ~·able** /-əbl ; -əbl̩/ *adj* that can be sunk. 可沉的;會低落的。

sinker /ˈsɪŋkə(r) ; ˈsɪŋkə/ *n* [C] (esp) lead weight attached to a fishing line or net to keep it under the water. (尤指裝於釣絲或網使之沉入水中之)鉛錘。***hook, line and ~,*** ⇨ hook(1).

sink·ing /ˈsɪŋkɪŋ ; ˈsɪŋkɪŋ/ *n* (*gerund*) (esp) (動名詞)(尤用於) ***a ˈ~ feeling,*** feeling in the stomach caused by fear or hunger. 由恐懼或飢餓在胃中造成的感覺;無力氣;虛弱。**ˈ~-fund** *n* money from revenue put aside by a government, business company, etc for gradual repayment of a debt. (政府,公司等撥出的)償債基金。

Sinn Fein /ˌʃɪn ˈfeɪn ; ˈʃɪnˈfen/ *n* political movement and organization founded in Ireland in 1905 for independent republican government. (以爭取獨立爲目的於1905年成立的)愛爾蘭新芬黨。

Si·nol·ogy /saɪˈnɒlədʒɪ ; saɪˈnɑlədʒɪ/ *n* [U] knowledge, study, of the Chinese language and culture. 漢學(關於中國語言,文化等之知識與研究)。**Si·nol·ogist** /-dʒɪst ; -dʒɪst/ *n* expert in ~. 漢學家。

sinu·ous /ˈsɪnjʊəs ; ˈsɪnjʊəs/ *adj* winding; full of curves and twists. 彎曲的;蜿蜒的。 **sinu·os·ity** /ˌsɪnjʊˈɒsətɪ ; ˌsɪnjʊˈɑsətɪ/ *n* (*pl* -ties) [U] being ~; [C] curve or twist. 彎曲;蜿蜒;彎曲處;曲折。

sinus /ˈsaɪnəs ; ˈsaɪnəs/ *n* (*pl* ~es) [C] hollow in a bone, esp one of several air-filled cavities in the bones of the skull, communicating with the nostrils. 竇(骨骼中之孔穴,尤指腦骨中充有空氣的數穴之一,而與鼻相通者)。 **~·itis** /ˌsaɪnəˈsaɪtɪs ; ˌsaɪnəˈsaɪtɪs/ *n* [U] inflammation of a ~. 竇炎。⇨ the illus at skeleton. 參看 skeleton 之插圖。

Sioux /suː ; su/ *n* member of a N American Indian tribe. 蘇族(北美印地安人的一族);蘇族印第安人。

sip /sɪp ; sɪp/ *vt, vi* (-pp-) [VP6A, 15B, 2A] drink, taking a very small quantity at a time: 啜;呷;細飲: *sip* (*up*) *one's coffee.* 啜飲咖啡。□ *n* [C] (quantity taken in a) sipping: 啜;一啜之量: *drink brandy in sips, not gulps.* 細品白蘭地酒,不是牛飲。

si·phon /ˈsaɪfən ; ˈsaɪfən/ *n* [C] **1** bent or curved tube, pipe, etc so arranged (like an inverted U) that liquid will flow up through it and then down. 彎管;虹吸管。 **2** bottle from which soda-water can be forced out by the pressure of gas in it. 虹吸瓶;壓力瓶。□ *vt, vi* [VP15B] ***~ sth off/out,*** draw (liquid) out or off through or as if through a ~: 用虹吸管或類似裝置抽出(液體): *Who has ~ed off all the petrol from the tank of my car?* 誰把我汽車油箱的汽油抽光了?

sir /sɜː(r) ; sɜ/ *n* **1** polite form used in addressing a man to whom one wishes to show respect: 先生；君；閣下；足下（對人表示敬意的禮貌稱呼）: *Yes, sir.* 是的，先生。*Dinner is served, sir.* 先生，飯已備好。*Sir, it is my duty to inform you that....* 先生，我必須通知你…。 **2 Sir,** used at the beginning of a formal letter: 用於正式信函之開頭: *Dear Sir/Sirs.* 先生台鑒（執事諸君台鑒）。 **3 Sir** /sə(r); sɚ/, title used before the first name of a knight or baronet: 冠於爵士或准男爵的名之前: *Sir 'Edward;* 愛德華爵士; *Sir ˌJohn 'Jackson.* 約翰·傑克遜爵士。

sir·dar /'sɜːdɑː(r); sɚ'dɑr/ *n* (in some Asian countries) officer or leader of high, esp military, rank. (某些亞洲國家中的)首領；司令官。

sire /saɪə(r); saɪr/ *n* **1** (old use) father or male ancestor. (舊用法)父；男性祖先。 **2** (old use) title of respect used when addressing a king or emperor. (舊用法)陛下（對國王或皇帝的敬稱）。 **3** male parent of an animal: 動物之雄親；父獸: *race-horses with pedigree ~s.* 有雄親血統記錄之比賽用的馬。□ *vt* [VP6A] (esp of horses) be the ~ of: (尤指馬)爲…之雄親: *a Derby winner ~d by Pegasus.* 屬於'裴佳沙斯'種的賽馬會優勝馬。

si·ren /'saɪərən; 'saɪrən/ *n* **1** (Gk myth) one of a number of winged women whose songs charmed sailors and caused their destruction; (hence) woman who attracts and is dangerous to men. (希神)海妖（爲有翅膀的女人，其曼妙歌聲蠱惑水手而使彼等毀滅）；(由此產生) 引誘男人而對其有害的女子。 **2** ship's whistle for sending warnings and signals; device for producing a loud shrill noise (as a warning, etc): 船上的號笛（用以發出警報及信號）；警報器（用作警號等）: *an 'air-raid ~;* 空襲警報器; *an ambulance/a fire-engine racing along with its ~s wailing.* 一輛救護車（救火車）響着警報器急馳而過。

sir·loin /'sɜːlɔɪn; 'sɚlɔɪn/ *n* [C, U] best part of loin of beef. 最好的牛腰肉。

sir·occo /sɪ'rɒkəʊ; sə'rɑko/ *n* (*pl* ~s /-kəʊz; -koz/) [C] hot, moist wind reaching Italy from Africa. (由非洲吹到義大利之)潮濕熱風。

sir·rah /'sɪrə; 'sɪrə/ *n* (contemptuous; archaic) sir. (蔑；古)先生。

sirup /'sɪrəp; 'sɪrəp/ = syrup.

si·sal /'saɪsl; 'saɪsl/ *n* [U] plant (⇨ agave) with fleshy leaves which provide strong fibre used for making rope: 西沙爾蔴（適於製繩用）: (attrib) (形容用法) ~ *grass/fibre/rope.* 西沙爾蔴草（纖維，繩）。

sissy /'sɪsɪ; 'sɪsɪ/ *n* (colloq; derog) effeminate or cowardly person. (俗；貶)柔弱或怯懦的人。 **sis·si·fied** /'sɪsɪfaɪd; 'sɪsɪˌfaɪd/ *adj* effeminate or cowardly. 女人似的；女人氣的；柔弱的；怯懦的。

sis·ter /'sɪstə(r); 'sɪstɚ/ *n* **1** daughter of the same parents as oneself or another person: 姐；妹；姐妹: *my/your/his ~.* 我(你，他)的姐姐(妹妹)。 **'half-~** *n* related by one parent only. 異父姐妹；異母姐妹。 ⇨ also *step-~* at step-. **'~-in-law** *n* (*pl* ~s-in-law) ~ of one's wife or husband; wife of one's brother. 夫或妻之姐妹；姑；姨；兄或弟之妻；嫂；弟婦。 **2** person who behaves towards one as a ~ does: 親如姐妹之人: *She was like a ~ to him.* 她對他親如姐妹。 **3** (GB) senior hospital nurse. (英)(醫院裡的)資深護士。 **4** member of certain religious orders; nun: 修女；尼姑: *S~s of Mercy,* a nursing sisterhood. 慈光修女會。 **5** (attrib) of the same design or type: (形容用法)同樣款式的；同型的: ~ *ships/organisations.* 姐妹艦（團體）。 **~·ly** *adj* of or like a ~: 姐妹的；姐妹般的: *~ly love;* 姐妹般的愛; *a ~ly kiss.* 姐妹般的親吻。 **~·hood** /-hʊd; -ˌhʊd/ *n* [C] society of women who devote themselves to charitable works, nursing, etc or live together in a religious order. 婦女團體（從事慈善事業，護理等）；修女會。

sit /sɪt; sɪt/ *vi, vt* (*pt, pp* sat /sæt; sæt/, -tt-) (For special uses with *adverbial particles* and *preps,* ⇨ 8 below.) (與副詞接語及介詞連用的特殊用法，參看下列第8義。) **1** [VP2A, C] take or be in a position in which the body is upright and supported by the buttocks (resting on the ground or on a seat): 坐(在地上或座位上): *sit on a chair/on the floor/in an armchair/at a table or desk/on a horse, etc.* 坐在椅子上(地板上，扶手椅中，桌子或書桌前，馬上等)。*The child is not big enough to sit at table yet.* 那孩子尚小，不能上桌進食。 ***sit to an artist,*** have one's portrait painted by him (while sitting). 坐着由畫家畫像。 ***sit (for) an examination,*** take one. 參加考試。 ***sit for one's portrait,*** have one's portrait painted while sitting before an artist. 坐着由人畫像。 ***sit tight,*** **(a)** remain firmly in one's place, esp in the saddle. 坐穩；(尤指)坐穩在馬鞍上。 **(b)** (colloq) stick firmly to one's purpose, opinions, etc. (俗)堅持目標，意見等。 ***sit for (a borough, etc),*** represent it in Parliament. 在國會代表(某自治市鎮等)。Hence, 由此產生, ***sitting member,*** the candidate (at a general election) who held the seat before the dissolution of Parliament. 競選連任的國會議員。 **2** [VP6A] cause to sit; place in a sitting position: 使坐；安置於坐着的姿勢: *He lifted the child and sat* (= seated) *her at a little table;* 他抱起小孩，把她安置在小桌前; (*reflex*): (反身式): *Sit yourself down,* be seated. 請坐。 **3** [VP2A] (of Parliament, a law court, a committee, etc) hold meetings: (指國會，法庭，委員會等)開會；開庭: *The House of Commons was still sitting at 3am.* 下議院在清晨三點鐘仍在開會。 **4** [VP6A] keep one's seat on (a horse, etc): 騎；乘(馬等): *She sits her horse well.* 她善於騎馬。*He couldn't sit his mule.* 他不會騎自己的騾子。 **5** [VP2A, C] (of birds) perch: (指鳥)棲: *sitting on a branch.* 棲息於枝上。 **ˌsitting 'duck,** an easy target or victim. 容易擊中之目標；容易受騙之人。 **ˌsitting 'tenant,** one who is actually in occupation (of a house, flat, etc, contrasted with a prospective tenant): (房舍、公寓等之)現住租用人 (與未來租用人相對): *greedy owners who want to get rid of sitting tenants and then charge higher rates to new tenants.* 想趕走現住租用人而以較高的租金把房子租給新租戶之貪婪房東。 **6** [VP2A] (of domestic fowls) remain on the nest in order to hatch eggs: (指家禽)孵卵: *That hen wants to sit.* 那母鷄要孵卵。 **7** [VP2C] (of clothes) suit, fit, hang: (指衣服)合身；適合；穿起來: *That dress sits well/loosely, etc on her.* 那衣服她穿起來很合適(寬鬆等)。*The coat sits badly across the shoulders.* 那外衣肩部不合適。*His new dignity sits well on him,* (fig) suits him well. (喻)他的新的顯赫地位很適合他。 **8** [VP2C, 3A, 15B] (special uses with *adverbial particles* and *preps*): (與副詞接語及介詞連用的特殊用法):

sit back, **(a)** settle oneself comfortably back, eg in a chair. 舒適地倚坐在椅子上等。 **(b)** (fig) take one's ease (after strenuous activity, etc); take no action. (喻)寬舒地休息(在緊張活動等之後)；不採取行動；觀望。

sit down, take a seat: 坐下: *Please sit down, all of you.* 請大家都坐下。 **ˌsit-down 'strike,** strike by workers who refuse to leave the factory, etc until their demands are considered or satisfied. 靜坐罷工；怠留罷工(工人拒絕離開廠房等，直到要求被接受或獲得滿意答覆爲止)。 ***sit down under (insults, etc),*** suffer without protest or complaint. 未抗議或無怨言地忍受(凌辱等)。

sit in, (of workers, students, etc) demonstrate by occupying a building (or part of it) and staying there until their grievances are considered or until they themselves are ejected: (指工人、學生等)靜坐示威 (佔據一建築物或建築物之一部分，直到他們的抱怨被重視或直到他們被趕走爲止): *There are reports of students sitting in at several universities.* 據報導有學生在幾所大學裡靜坐示威。Hence, 由此產生, **'sit-in** *n* such a demonstration. 靜坐示威。 ***sit in on sth,*** attend (a discussion, etc) as an observer, not as a participant. 列席(討論會等)。

sit on/upon sth, **(a)** (of a person) be a member of (a jury, committee, etc). (指人)做陪審員，委員等。**(b)** (colloq) neglect to deal with: (俗)疏於處理;忽畧: *They've been sitting on my application for a month.* 他們把我的申請擱置一個月了。***sit on/upon sth,*** (of a jury, etc) inquire into, investigate (a case). (指陪審團等)調查;審查。***sit on/upon sb,*** (colloq) repress; snub: (俗)壓制;冷落: *That impudent fellow needs to be sat on.* 那厚臉皮的傢伙需要壓制一下。
sit out, sit outdoors: 坐在戶外: *It's hot indoors—let's sit out in the garden, shall we?* 室內很熱，我們到外面花園坐坐，好嗎？ ***sit sth out,*** **(a)** stay to the end of (a performance, etc): 留在(表演等)現場直到結束的時候: *sit out a boring play.* 看完一場乏味的戲。**(b)** take no part in (esp a particular dance): 不參加(尤指某一支舞): *I think I'll sit out the next dance.* 我不想跳下一支舞。
sit up, not go to bed (until later than the usual time): (超過通常的就寢時間)不睡: *I shall be late getting back, so please don't sit up for me.* 我將晚歸，請不要不睡覺等我。*The nurse sat up with her patient all night.* 那護士整夜不睡照顧她的病人。*Ought children to sit up late looking at TV programmes?* 孩子們看電視而晚睡應該嗎？***sit (sb) up,*** (cause to) take an upright position after lying flat or sitting badly: (使)在躺平或坐姿不正以後坐起;坐正: *The patient is well enough to sit up in bed now.* 那病人現在已能在床上坐起來了。*Just sit me up a little,* help me to sit up. 幫我坐直一些。***sit up straight!*** Don't lean back! Don't sprawl! 坐直！不要向後倚！不要伸開著手脚坐！ ***make sb sit up (and take notice),*** (colloq) alarm or frighten him; rouse him from lethargy to activity. (俗)驚嚇某人;促使活動。

si·tar /sɪˈtɑː(r) ; sɪˈtar/ *n* Hindu stringed musical instrument. 一種印度弦樂器。⇨ the illus at string. 參看 string 之插圖。

site /saɪt ; saɪt/ *n* [C] place where sth was, is, or is to be: 位置;場所: *built on the ~ of an old fort;* 建築於古堡的舊址上; *a ~ for a new school;* 建一新學校的地點; *deliver materials to a ˈbuilding ~.* 把建築材料送至工地。 □ *vt* [VP6A] locate; place: 設置;定場所: *Where have they decided to ~ the new factory?* 他們決定把新工廠設置在何處？

sit·ter /ˈsɪtə(r) ; ˈsɪtɚ/ *n* **1** person who is sitting for a portrait. 坐供畫像者。**2** hen that sits(6): 孵卵的母鷄: *a good/poor ~.* 善(不善)於孵卵的母鷄。**3** bird or animal that is sitting and therefore easy to shoot; (hence) easy shot; sth easily done. 棲息的禽獸(易於獵殺);(由此產生)容易的一擊;易做的事。**4** ⇨ *baby-~* at baby.

sit·ting /ˈsɪtɪŋ ; ˈsɪtɪŋ/ *n* **1** time during which a court of law, Parliament, etc is ~ continuously: 開庭，開會等的期間;庭期;會期: *during a long ~.* 在冗長的庭(會)期中。**2** period of time during which one is engaged continuously in a particular occupation: 連續從事某一工作的期間: *finish reading a book at one ~.* 一口氣把書讀完。**3** act of ~ for a portrait: 坐着供人畫像: *The artist wants you to give him six ~s,* sit for him six times. 那畫家要你坐着供他畫像六次。**4** occasion of ~ (for a meal, etc): 就座(進食等): *In the dining-room of this hotel 100 people can be served at one ~,* ie at the same time, together. 這旅館的餐廳，可供一百人同時進餐。**5** collection of eggs on which a hen sits. 孵卵數。**6** ˈ**~-room** *n* room for general use (contrasted with a dining-room, bedroom, etc). 起居室(別於飯廳，寢室等)。

situ·ated /ˈsɪtʃʊeɪtɪd ; ˈsɪtʃʊˌetɪd/ *pred adj* **1** (of a town, building, etc) placed: (指城鎮，建築物等)位於…的;坐落在…的: *The village is ~ in a valley.* 這村莊位於一山谷中。**2** (of a person) in (certain) circumstances: (指人)處於(某種)境地的: *Having six children and no income, the widow was badly ~.* 這寡婦有六個孩子又沒有收入，處境不好。*I'm awkwardly ~ just now,* in difficult circumstances. 我目前處境困難。

situ·ation /ˌsɪtʃʊˈeɪʃn ; ˌsɪtʃʊˈeʃən/ *n* [C] **1** position (of a town, building, etc). (城鎮，建築物等之)位置;場所。**2** condition, state of affairs, esp at a certain time: 狀況;事態;情勢(尤指在某一時間者): *be in an embarrassing ~.* 處於尷尬的境地。**3** work, employment: 工作;職業: *S~s vacant, S~s wanted,* headings of newspaper notices of employment offered and asked for; 事求人，人求事(報紙之人事廣告欄標題); *be in/out of a ~,* be employed/unemployed. 有工作(失業)。

six /sɪks ; sɪks/ *n, adj* the number 6, ⇨ App 4. 六;六個;六的;六個的(參看附錄四)。***(It is) six of one and half a dozen of the other,*** There is very little difference between the one and the other. 半斤八兩;差不多。***in sixes,*** in groups of six at a time. 六個六個地。***at sixes and sevens,*** in confusion. 亂七八糟;雜亂地。ˌ**six-ˈfooter** *n* (colloq) person six feet in height; thing six feet long. (俗)身高六呎之人;六呎長的東西。ˈ**six·pence** *n* **(a)** former GB coin worth (formerly) six pennies (*6d*), or (since 1971) $2\frac{1}{2}$p. (英國昔時之)六辨士硬幣(原值六辨士，自 1971 年後值 $2\frac{1}{2}$ 辨士)。**(b)** the sum of six pennies, either *6p* or *6d.* 六辨士之額(畧作 6p 或 6d)。⇨ App 5. 參看附錄五. ˈ**six·penny** *adj* costing *6d* or *6p.* 值六辨士的。**six-shooter** *n* revolver with six chambers. 六發左輪手槍。ˈ**six·fold** /-fəʊld ; -ˈfold/ *adj, adv* six times as much or as many; six times as great. 六倍的(地);六重的(地)。**six·teen** /sɪkˈstiːn ; sɪksˈtin/ *n, adj* the number 16. 十六; 十六個; 十六的; 十六個的。 **six·teenth** /sɪkˈstiːnθ ; sɪksˈtinθ/ *n, adj* **sixth** /sɪksθ ; sɪksθ/ *n, adj* ˈ**sixth form,** *n* (in secondary schools, GB) form (= class) for pupils being prepared for A-level examinations. (英國的中等學校)六年級(爲參加A級考試之學生的級次)。⇨ level²(3). ˈ**sixth-former** *n* pupil in this form. (英國中等學校之)六年級學生。ˌ**sixth ˈsense,** power to be aware of things independently of the five senses; intuition. 第六感;直覺。**sixthly** *adv* **six·ti·eth** /ˈsɪkstɪəθ ; ˈsɪkstɪɪθ/ *n, adj* **sixty** /ˈsɪkstɪ ; ˈsɪkstɪ/ *n, adj* the number 60. 六十;六十的。**the sixties** *n pl* 60-69. 六十至六十九。

size¹ /saɪz ; saɪz/ *n* **1** [U] degree of largeness or smallness: 大小;尺寸: *a building of vast ~;* 甚大的建築物; *about the ~ of* (= about as large as) *a duck's egg;* 大小約如鴨蛋; *of some ~,* fairly large. 相當大的。*They're both of a ~,* are the same ~. 它們大小一樣。***That's about the ~ of it,*** (colloq) That's a fair account of the affair, situation, etc. (俗)其眞相大致如此。 **2** [C] one of the standard and (usu) numbered classes in which articles of clothing, etc are made: (衣着等之)號;碼: *a ~ fifteen collar;* 十五號領; *trousers three ~s too large;* 大了三號的褲子; *all ~s of gloves* 各種號碼的手套。*I take ~ nine shoes.* 我穿九號的鞋子。□ *vt* **1** [VP6A] arrange in ~s or according to ~. 按大小排列。 **2** [VP15B] ***~ sb/sth up,*** (colloq) form a judgement or opinion of. (俗)判斷;品評。**-sized** /-saɪzd ; -saɪzd/ *suff* (in compounds) having a certain ~: (用於複合字中)有…大小的;…號的: *medium-sized.* 中號的。 ˈ**siz(e)·able** /-əbl ; -əbl̩/ *adj* fairly large. 頗大的;相當大的。

size² /saɪz ; saɪz/ *n* [U] sticky substance used to glaze textiles, paper, plaster, etc. 膠水;漿糊(用以使紡織品，紙，灰泥，石膏等變光滑)。 □ *vt* [VP6A] stiffen or treat with ~. 以膠水或漿糊使挺實;上膠於;上漿於。

sizzle /ˈsɪzl ; ˈsɪzl̩/ *vi* [VP2A], *n* (colloq) (make the) hissing sound as of sth cooking in fat: (俗)發嘶嘶聲; 嘶嘶聲 (如油炸食物時之聲音): *sausages sizzling in the pan;* 在鍋中發嘶嘶聲的香腸; (fig)(喻) *a sizzling hot day.* 灼熱的一天。

skate¹ /skeɪt ; sket/ *n* (ˈ**ice-**)**~,** one of a pair of sharp-edged steel blades to be fastened to a boot for moving smoothly over ice. 溜冰鞋。⇨ the illus at hockey. 參看 hockey 之插圖。⇨ also *roller-~s* at roller(2). □ *vi* [VP2A, C] move on ~s: 溜冰: ~ *over/round a difficulty/a delicate problem*, make only passing and cautious reference to it. 謹慎而約略地提及某困難(微妙的問題)。~ ***on thin ice,*** talk about a subject that needs great tact. 談論一個必須謹慎處理的題目。 **ˈ~·board** *n* narrow board for standing on, about 50cm long, mounted front and back on two pairs of roller-skate wheels, used in sport over a smooth surface (eg for racing, demonstrating skill). 滑板(約五十公分長之窄板,板下前後端各裝有一對滑輪,於平滑表面上做溜滑競賽、表演等)。**ˈ~·boarder** *n* person using a ~board. 溜滑板者。 **ˈ~·boarding** *n* [U] sport of using a ~board. 溜滑板運動。**ˈskat·ing** *n* sport of using ~s. 溜冰;滑冰。**ˈskat·ing-rink** *n* specially prepared surface for skating. 溜冰場。~**r** *n* person who ~s. 溜冰者。

ice-skating

skate² /skeɪt ; sket/ *n* large, flat, long-tailed sea-fish, valued as food. 鰩魚;魟魚(大而扁平之長尾海魚,爲珍貴食品)。

ske·daddle /skɪˈdædl ; skɪˈdædḷ/ *vi* [VP2A] (GB, colloq, usu imper) run away. (英,俗,通常用於祈使句中)跑開;逃竄。

skeet /ski:t ; skit/ *n* (kind of) clay-pigeon shooting. 陶土盤飛靶射擊(之一種)。⇨ pigeon(2).

skein /skeɪn ; sken/ *n* [C] length of silk or wool yarn or thread coiled loosely into a bundle. (絲,毛線或線之)一束;一絞。

skel·eton /ˈskelɪtn ; ˈskɛlətn̩/ *n* [C] **1** bony framework of an animal body; bones of an animal body in the same relative positions as in life; hard framework of woody fibre containing a vegetable body: (動物之)骨骼;骨架;(植物之)木質纖維結構: *He looks like a living ~.* 他看來像具活骨架。 ***reduced to a ~,*** (of an animal, a human being) very thin as the result of hunger, illness, etc. (指動物,人)因飢餓,疾病等而皮包骨。 ***the ~ in the cupboard, the family ~,*** sth of which a family is ashamed and which it tries to keep secret. 家醜。 **2** framework of a building, organization, plan, theory, etc; outline to which details are to be added: (建築物,組織,計畫,理論等之)骨架;基幹;綱要: *the steel ~ of a new building.* 新建築物之鋼架。 **3** (attrib) (形容用法) **ˈ~ key,** one that will open a number of different locks. 萬能鑰匙。 **a ~ staff/crew/service, etc,** one reduced to the smallest possible number needed for maintenance. 基幹作業人員(照料或處理業務所需之最少人數)。

skep /skep ; skɛp/ *n* (kinds of) wicker basket; straw or wicker bee-hive. 柳條籃子;稻草或柳條做成的蜂房。

skep·tic /ˈskeptɪk ; ˈskɛptɪk/ ⇨ sceptic.

sketch /sketʃ ; skɛtʃ/ *n* [C] **1** rough, quickly made drawing: 略圖;素描;速寫: *make a ~ of a face/place.* 作一面孔(一地方)之速寫。**ˈ~-book/-block** *nn* book or pad of sheets of drawing-paper for making ~es on. 素描簿。**ˈ~-map** *n* one with outlines but little detail. 略圖。 **2** short account or description; rough draft or general outline, without details: 簡短的記載或描述;概略;大綱: *He gave me a ~ of his plans for the expedition.* 他對我略述其遠征的計畫。 **3** short, humorous play or piece of writing. 詼諧之短劇或短文。□ *vt, vi* **1** [VP6A] make a ~ of; [VP15B] ~ ***sth out,*** give a rough plan of; indicate without detail: 草繪;草擬: ~ *out proposals for a new road.* 草擬開闢新路的計畫。 **2**

the human skeleton

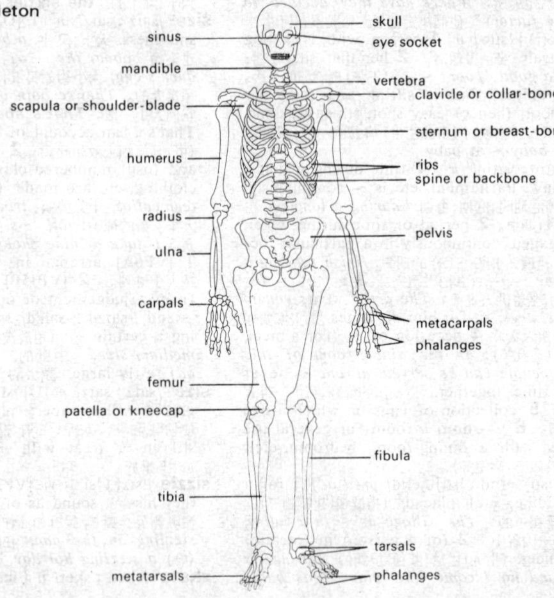

[VP2A] practise the art of making ~es: 繪略圖;作素描: *My sister often goes into the country to* ~. 我的姐姐(妹妹)常去鄉下寫生。 **~er** *n* person who ~es(2). 繪略圖者;作素描者 。**sketchy** *adj* (-ier, -iest) **1** done roughly and without detail or care. 簡略的;概要的;隨便的。 **2** incomplete: 不完全的;不足的: *He has a rather ~y knowledge of geography.* 他對於地理僅有些概略的知識。 **~·ily** /-ɪlɪ; -əlɪ/ *adv* **~i·ness** *n*

skew /skjuː; skju/ *adj* twisted or turned to one side; not straight. 歪的;斜的;不直的。 **'~-eyed** *adj* (colloq) squinting. (俗)斜視的。 ***on the ~,*** (colloq) ~. (俗)歪斜着。

skewer /'skjuə(r); 'skjuɚ/ *n* pointed stick of wood or metal for holding meat together while cooking. (烤肉時串肉用的)串肉籤;烤肉籤。□ *vt* [VP6A] fasten with, or as with, a ~. (用串肉籤等)串起。

ski /skiː; ski/ *n* (*pl* skis) one of a pair of long, narrow strips of wood, strapped under the feet for moving over snow: 滑雪屐: *a pair of skis;* 一副滑雪屐; *bind on one's skis.* 縛在滑雪屐上。**'ski-bob** *n* bicycle frame fitted with skis in place of wheels. 滑雪脚踏車。**'ski-jump** *n* jump made after getting up speed on a downward slope. 滑雪跳躍(下坡高速時所作之跳躍)。 **'ski-lift** *n* ropeway for carrying skiers up a mountain side. 運送滑雪者上山坡之吊索設備。 **'ski-plane** *n* aircraft fitted with skis instead of wheels, to enable it to land on an expanse of snow. 雪屐飛機(以滑雪屐代替起降輪之飛機,適於雪地降落)。□ *vi* (*pt, pp* ski'd, *pres part* ski-ing) move over snow on ski(s): 滑雪: *go skiing in Switzerland;* 到瑞士去滑雪; *go in for skiing.* 喜好滑雪。 **skier** /'skiːə(r); 'skiɚ/ *n* person using ski(s). 滑雪者。

skiing

skid /skɪd; skɪd/ *n* [C] **1** piece of wood or metal fixed under the wheel of a cart, etc to prevent it from turning, and in this way check the speed when going downhill. 制輪器;煞車。 **2** log, plank, etc used to make a track over which heavy objects may be dragged or rolled. (使重物等在上面容易滑動的)滑材;枕木。 ~ **row** /rəʊ; ro/ *n* (US) slum area where vagrants live. (美)流浪者駐脚之貧民區。 **3** slipping movement, often sideways, of the wheels of a car, etc on a slippery or icy road, or caused by excessive speed while turning a corner: (在光滑或結凍之道路上,或因速度過高在轉彎時所引起的)車輪之打滑: *How would you get out of/correct a ~?* 車輪打滑時你如何控制你的車子? **'~·pan** *n* surface specially prepared to cause ~s, used for practice in controlling vehicles which ~. 練習控制車輛打滑的特製路面。 ***put the ~s under sb,*** (sl) do sth to make him hurry. (俚)催促某人。□ *vi* (-dd-) [VP2A] (of a car, etc) move or slip sideways, etc; have a ~(3). (指汽車等)滑向一側;打滑。

skies /skaɪz; skaɪz/ *pl* of sky.

skiff /skɪf; skɪf/ *n* small, light boat, esp one rowed or sculled by a single person. 小艇;輕舟(尤指單人所划者)。

skiffle /'skɪfl; 'skɪfəl/ *n* [U] (1950's) mixture of jazz and folksong, with improvised instruments and a singer who usu has a guitar or a banjo. (一九五〇年代)爵士民謠。 **'~-group,** group of such players. 爵士民謠團。

skil·ful (US = **skill·ful**) /'skɪlfl; 'skɪlfəl/ *adj* having or showing skill: 有技巧的;巧妙的;熟練的: *He's not very ~ with his chopsticks/at using chopsticks.* 他用筷子不大熟練。 **~ly** /-fəlɪ; -fəlɪ/ *adv*

skill /skɪl; skɪl/ *n* [U] ability to do sth expertly and well; [C] particular kind of ~: 技能;熟練;某種技能;技藝: *Is learning a foreign language a question of learning new ~s, or a question of acquiring new knowledge?* 學習外國語是學習一種技能,還是獲取新知呢? **~ed** *adj* **1** trained; experienced; having ~: 有訓練的;有經驗的;熟練的: *~ed workmen;* 有經驗的工人; *~ed in doing sth.* 做某事熟練。 **2** needing ~: 需要技能的: *~ed work.* 需要技能的工作。

skil·let /'skɪlɪt; 'skɪlɪt/ *n* **1** small metal cooking-pot with a long handle and (usu) feet. 長柄煮鍋(通常有支脚)。 **2** (US) frying-pan. (美)平底鍋;煎鍋。

skilly /'skɪlɪ; 'skɪlɪ/ *n* [U] thin broth or soup (usu oatmeal and water flavoured with meat). 薄羹(通常爲燕麥加羹湯);稀粥。

skim /skɪm; skɪm/ *vt, vi* (-mm-) **1** [VP6A, 15B, 14] ~ ***(off) (from),*** remove floating matter from (the surface of a liquid): 撇去(液體表面)之飄浮物: *~ milk;* 撇去牛乳之乳皮; remove (cream, scum, etc) from the surface of a liquid: 自液體表面撇取(油脂、浮渣等): *~ the cream from the milk;* 自牛奶中撇取奶油; *~ off the fat from the soup.* 把菜湯的油脂撇去。 **'~med-milk** *n* milk from which the cream has been ~med. 脫脂牛奶。 **2** [VP2C, 3A, 6A, 15A] move lightly over (a surface), not touching, or only lightly or occasionally touching (it): (使)輕輕掠過(某表面);輕輕擦過: *The swallows were ~ming (over) the water/~med along the ground.* 燕子掠過水面(地面)。 **3** [VP6A, 3A] ~ ***(through) sth,*** read quickly, noting only the chief points: 略讀;快讀: *~ (through) a newspaper/catalogue, etc.* 略讀報紙(目錄等)。 **~·mer** *n* **1** utensil with a perforated bowl for ~ming liquids. 撇取浮面的用具;撇清器。 **2** long-winged water-bird. 撇水鳥(一種長翼海鳥)。

skimp /skɪmp; skɪmp/ *vt, vi* [VP6A, 2A] supply, use, less than enough of what is needed: 吝於供給或使用;吝嗇;節儉: *~ the butter when making cakes/the material when making a dress.* 做餅時省牛油(做衣服時省布料)。*They are so poor that they have to ~.* 他們很窮所以必須撙節。**skimpy** *adj* (-ier, -iest) **1** giving, using, less than enough. 不充分給予的;吝於使用的;節儉的。 **2** (of a dress, etc) made with insufficient material; too small; too tight. (指衣服等)材料不足做成的;太小的;太窄的。**~·ily** /-ɪlɪ; -əlɪ/ *adv: a ~ily made dress.* 做得太小的衣服。

skin /skɪn; skɪn/ *n* **1** [U] elastic substance forming the outer covering of the body of a person or animal: (人或動物之)皮;皮膚: *We all got wet to the ~,* thoroughly wet (eg in heavy rain). 我們全都渾身淋濕了。 ***~ and bone,*** very thin: 瘦成皮包骨: *He's only ~ and bone.* 他瘦成皮包骨。 ***by the ~ of one's teeth,*** by a narrow margin; narrowly. 好不容易;僥倖。 ***get under one's ~,*** (fig) annoy, irritate, anger one; infatuate one. (喻)激怒;使迷戀。 ***get sb under one's skin,*** be infatuated with him. 迷戀某人。 ***have a thin/thick ~,*** (fig) be sensitive/insensitive; be easily/not easily hurt by unkindness, criticism, rebuke, etc. (喻)臉皮薄(厚);敏感(不敏感);容易因冷待、批評、責罵等而受傷害(不易受傷害)。Hence, 因此產生, **,thin-/,thick-'~ned** *adjj* ***save one's ~,*** avoid being hurt, etc; escape safely. 免受損傷;安然逃脫。 **'~-diving** *n* form of sport in which a person dives into and swims under the water without a diving-suit, with goggles to protect the eyes and a snorkel or aqualung to help breathing. 赤身潛水(不穿潛水衣，以潛水面罩保護眼睛，以呼吸管或水肺幫助呼吸)。ˌ~-ˈ**deep** *adj* (of beauty, feelings, etc) only on the surface; not deep or lasting. (指美、感情等)膚淺的;皮相的;不深刻的;不持久的。ˈ~-**flint** *n* miser. 吝嗇者。ˈ~ **game** *n* fraudulent gambling game; swindle. 欺騙;詐賭。ˈ~-**graft** *n* surgical process of grafting ~ from one part of a person's body (or from another person's body) on to a part which has been damaged, eg by burning. 皮膚移植(把自身某處或他人之皮膚移植於傷患之處的外科手術)。ˈ**skin·head** *n* (GB, early 1970's) young gangster with closely-cut hair. (英，1970年代早期)留平頭的不良少年。ˌ~-ˈ**tight**, (of a garment) fitting closely to the body. (指服裝)貼身的;合身的。**2** [C] animal ~ with or without the hair or fur; hide; pelt: 獸皮;毛皮;皮革;生皮: ˈ*rabbit-~s.* 兔皮。**3** [C] vessel for storing or carrying liquid, made of the whole ~ of an animal: 裝液體用之皮囊(用整塊之獸皮製成者): ˈ*wine-~s.* 酒囊。**4** [C, U] outer covering of a fruit, or plant: 果皮;植物之外皮: *slip on a baˈnana ~;* 踩上香蕉皮而滑倒; ˈ*grape ~s.* 葡萄皮。⇨ the illus at fruit. 參看 fruit 之插圖。Cf 參較 *peel* for potatoes, apples, etc; the *bark* of a tree. 馬鈴薯、蘋果等之皮用 peel; 樹皮用 bark。**5** thin layer that forms on boiled milk: 結於煮沸牛奶上之薄層;乳皮: *the ~ on a milk pudding.* 牛奶布丁上之乳皮。□ *vt, vi* (-nn-) **1** [VP 6A] take the ~ off: 剝皮;去皮;去殼: *~ a rabbit.* 剝兔皮。***keep one's ˈeyes ~ned,*** (colloq) be alert, watchful. (俗)留心;警戒。**2** [VP6A, 14] (colloq) swindle; fleece: (俗)欺騙;訛詐: *He was ~ned of all his money by confidence tricksters.* 他所有的錢都被專騙老實人的騙子騙去了。**3** [VP2C] ~ ***over,*** become covered with ~: 爲皮所覆蓋;生皮;長皮: *The wound ~ned over.* 傷處長皮了。~**ny** *adj* (-ier, -iest) with little flesh; (colloq) mean; miserly. 無肉的;瘦削的;(俗)小氣的;吝嗇的。⇨ skinflint above. 參看上列之 skinflint。

skint /skɪnt ; skɪnt/ *adj* (GB sl) without money; penniless. (英俚)一文不名的;囊空如洗的。

skip¹ /skɪp ; skɪp/ *vi, vt* (-pp-) **1** [VP2A, C] jump lightly and quickly: 輕快地跳;跳躍: *~ over an obstacle / over a brook / out of the way of a bus.* 跳過障礙物(跳過小河;閃開公共汽車)。*The lambs were ~ping about in the fields,* jumping about, gambolling. 小羊在田裡跳來跳去。**2** [VP2A] jump over a rope which is turned over the head and under the feet as one jumps. 跳繩。ˈ~·**ping-rope** *n* length of rope (usu with two wooden handles) used in the children's game of ~ping. 跳繩遊戲所用之繩。**3** [VP2C] go from one place (or, fig, subject) to another quickly or casually: 匆匆地或隨興所至地由一地到另一地;(喻)隨興所至東談西談: *~ over / across to Paris for the weekend.* 匆匆前往巴黎度週末。*He ~ped off* (= left) *without saying anything to any of us.* 他匆匆離開，未對我們任何人說什麼。*He ~ped from one subject to another.* 他隨便地從一個話題跳到另一個話題。**4** [VP6A, 2A] make omissions, go from one part (of a book, etc) to another without reading, paying attention, etc: 漏看(書等之)某部分;略過;遺漏: *He ~ped the dull parts of the book.* 他把這書的枯燥部分略過不讀。*We'll ~ the next chapter.* 我們將略過下一章。*Do you read without ~ping?* 你讀書不跳着讀吧? □ *n* [C] ~ping movement: 跳;跳躍;漏讀;略過;遺漏: *a hop, a ~ and a jump.* 三級跳遠。

skip² /skɪp ; skɪp/ *n* cage or bucket in which men or materials are raised and lowered in mines and quarries; large metal container for carrying away builders' refuse, etc. (礦坑及採石場中載人或物上下之籠形或桶形)吊箱;(用以運走工地廢料等之)大鐵箱。

skip·per /ˈskɪpə(r) ; ˈskɪpɚ/ *n* captain, esp of a small merchant ship or fishing-boat; (colloq) captain of a team in games such as football and cricket. 船長(尤指小商船或漁船者);(俗)(足球、板球等之)球隊隊長。

skirl /skɜːl ; skɝl/ *n* shrill, piercing sound: 尖銳聲: *the ~ of the bagpipes.* 風笛之尖銳聲。

skir·mish /ˈskɜːmɪʃ ; ˈskɝmɪʃ/ *n* [C] (often unpremeditated) fight between small parts of armies or fleets; (hence) short argument or contest of wit, etc. 陸上或海上之小戰;小衝突(通常爲遭遇戰);(由此產生)小爭論;短暫的鬥智。□ *vi* [VP2A, C] engage in a ~. 小戰;小爭論。~**er** *n* one who ~es, esp a member of a force sent out from the main body of troops to hide its movements, or to learn about the movement of the enemy. 參與小戰者;(尤指)散兵;斥候(派出以掩護本隊或探知敵情者)。

skirt /skɜːt ; skɝt/ *n* **1** woman's garment that hangs from the waist. 女裙。**2** part of a dress or other garment (eg a long coat or shirt) that hangs below the waist. 衣服之下身(如長外套或襯衣的下部);下襬。**3** (*pl*) (= outskirts) border; extreme parts: (複)邊界;邊緣;極端的部分: *on the ~s of the town.* 在城郊。□ *vt, vi* [VP6A, 2C] be on, pass along, the edge of: 位於…之邊緣;沿…之邊緣而行: *Our road ~ed the forest.* 我們的路位於森林的邊緣。*Our path ~ed along the moor.* 我們的小徑沿松鷄獵場蜿蜒。~ ***round sth,*** be indirect about it; avoid direct reference to it: 不直接處理某事;避免提及某事: *He ~ed round the subject of his family.* 他避免談論有關他家庭的問題。ˈ~·**ing-board** *n* strip or line of boards fixed round the walls of a room close to the floor. 踢脚板;壁脚板。

skit /skɪt ; skɪt/ *n* [C] short piece of humorous writing, short play, mimicking and making fun of sth or sb: (模擬而取笑某人或某事物之)幽默之短文或短劇: *a ~ on Wagner / on 'Macbeth'.* 諷刺華格納('馬克白'劇本)的短文。

skit·tish /ˈskɪtɪʃ ; ˈskɪtɪʃ/ *adj* (of horses) excitable; lively; difficult to control; (of a person) lively and coquettish, fond of flirting, etc. (指馬)易驚恐的;活潑的;難控制的;(指人)輕浮的;喜調情的。~·**ly** *adv* ~·**ness** *n*

skittle /ˈskɪtl ; ˈskɪtl/ *n* (*pl* ~s, with *sing v*) (複數 skittles 用單數動詞) game in which a ball is bowled along an alley **(ˈ~-alley)** with the purpose of knocking down a number of bottle-shaped pieces of wood (called **~s** or **ˈ~-pins**). 九柱戲;擲柱戲(以球沿球道 ~-alley 撞擊數個瓶狀木柱 ~s 或 ~-pins 的遊戲)。⇨ ninepins, tenpins. ***(all) beer and ~s,*** amusement; fun: 娛樂;嬉戲: *Life is not all beer and ~s.* 人生非僅遊樂而已。□ *vt* [VP15B] ~ ***out,*** (cricket) dismiss easily: (板球)輕易地使遭封殺出局: *The whole side was ~d out for 100 runs.* 滿100分時，全隊出局。

skivvy /ˈskɪvɪ ; ˈskɪvɪ/ *n* (*pl* -vies) (GB sl) (pej) servant who is required to do all sorts of work. (英俚，蔑)僕人;佣人。

skua /ˈskjuːə ; ˈskjuə/ *n* large kind of seagull. 一種大海鷗。

skulk /skʌlk ; skʌlk/ *vi* [VP2A, C] hide, move secretly, through cowardice, or to avoid work or duty, or with an evil purpose. 藏匿;潛伏;潛行(因膽小，或逃避工作責任，或心懷不軌)。~**er** *n* 隱藏的人;潛行者;潛伏者。

skull /skʌl ; skʌl/ *n* bony framework of the head. 腦殼;頭蓋骨。⇨ the illus at skeleton. 參看 skeleton 之插圖。***have a thick ~,*** be stupid. 笨頭笨腦。ˌ~ **and ˈcross-bones,** picture of a ~ and two thigh-bones crossed below it (as an emblem of death or danger, and formerly used on a flag by pirates). 骷髏畫;骷髏旗(爲死亡或危險之象徵，昔時海盜用作旗幟)。ˈ~-**cap** *n* close-fitting (often velvet) cap worn indoors by old or bald men, by Popes and cardinals. 室內便帽(常用天鵝絨製成，老人、禿頭者、教宗及紅衣主教等戴之)。-**skulled** *suff* (with *adj* prefixed): (用形容詞作字首): ˌ*thick-ˈ~ed,* having a thick ~. 笨頭笨腦的。

skull·dug·gery /skʌlˈdʌgərɪ ; skʌlˈdʌgərɪ/ *n* (colloq) clever deception; trickery. (俗)詐騙；詭計；奸計。

skunk /skʌŋk ; skʌŋk/ *n* **1** small, bush-tailed N American animal able to send out a strong, unpleasant smell as a defence when attacked; [U] its fur. 臭鼬(北美洲產，體小，尾毛厚，遇敵放出惡臭以自衛)；臭鼬毛皮。**2** detestable or contemptible person. 可惡的人；卑鄙的人。

sky /skaɪ ; skaɪ/ *n* (*pl* skies /skaɪz ; skaɪz/) **1** (usu **the sky**; **a sky** when modified by an *adj*, often *pl* in the same sense) the space we look up to from the earth, where we see the sun, moon and stars: (通常以形容詞修飾時，可與定冠詞或不定冠詞連用；複數意義同)天；天空： *under the open sky*, out of doors; 在戶外； *a clear, blue sky;* 晴朗蔚藍的天空； *a starry sky／(the) starry skies.* 多星辰的天空。***praise／extol／laud sb to the skies,*** praise him very highly. 極力稱讚某人。ˌ**sky-ˈblue** *adj, n* (of) the bright blue colour of the sky on a cloudless day. 天藍色的；天藍色。ˌ**sky-ˈhigh** *adv* so as to reach the sky; as high as the sky: 高入雲霄地；極高地： *When the bomb exploded, the bridge was blown sky-high.* 炸彈爆炸時，那橋被炸裂飛散得極高。ˈ**sky·lark** *n* small bird that sings as it flies up into the sky. 雲雀(高飛時鳴唱之小鳥)。□ *vi* = lark². ˈ**sky·light** *n* window in a sloping roof. 天窗。ˈ**sky·line** *n* outline of hills, buildings, etc, defined against the sky: 山，建築物等以天空爲背景所映出的輪廓： *the skyline of New York.* 紐約市高大建築物的空中輪廓。ˈ**sky pilot** *n* (sl) parson (esp, among sailors, a chaplain on a warship). (俚)牧師(尤指軍艦上的隨軍牧師)。ˈ**sky-rocket** *vi* (of prices) soar; go up steeply. (指物價)上升；猛漲。ˈ**sky-scraper** *n* very tall building. 摩天樓。ˈ**sky-writing** *n* [U] (making of) smoke-trails forming legible words in the sky (by aircraft for advertising purposes). (飛機放煙書寫的)空中文字；(做)空中廣告。**2** (often *pl*) climate: (常用複數)天氣；氣候： *the sunny skies of southern Italy.* 義大利南部之晴朗的氣候。□ *vt* hit (eg a ball) high up. 將(球等)擊向空中。**sky·ward(s)** /ˈskaɪwəd(z) ; ˈskaɪwɚd(z)/ *adj, adv* toward(s) the sky; upward(s). 向天空；向上。

skyscrapers

slab /slæb ; slæb/ *n* thick flat (usu square or rectangular) piece of stone, wood or other solid substance: 板；片(石、木或其他硬物的厚塊，通常爲方形或矩形)： *paved with ～s of stone;* 以石板鋪成的； *a ～ of cheese／cooking chocolate;* 一塊乾酪(烹調用的巧克力)； *a mortuary ～.* 停屍板。

slack¹ /slæk ; slæk/ *adj* **1** giving little care or attention to one's work; having or showing little energy: 疏忽職守的；懈怠的；無氣力的： *Don't get ～ at your work.* 不要懈怠你的工作。 *She feels ～* (= lacking in energy) *this morning.* 她今晨感覺沒有氣力。**2** dull; inactive; with not much work to be done or business being done: 呆鈍的；蕭條的；不景氣的： *Trade／Business is ～ this week.* 這週的貿易(營業)不景氣。*There is only a ～ demand for S African mining shares.* 南非的礦業股票滯銷。**3** loose, not tight: 鬆弛的；不緊的： *a ～ rope.* 鬆弛的繩。***keep a ～ rein on sth,*** control sth negligently, (fig) govern carelessly. 粗心大意地管理；(喻)懶散地治理。**4** slow-moving; sluggish: 緩慢的；遲滯的： *periods of ～ water,* when the tide is neither ebbing nor flowing. 平潮的期間(潮水不漲不退之時)。□ *vi* [VP2A, C] **1** *～ (off),* be lazy or careless in one's work: 懈怠；疏忽職守： *Don't ～ off in your studies.* 不要荒廢你的學業。**2** *～ up,* reduce speed: 減速： *S～ up before you reach the cross-roads.* 到交叉路以前減速。**3** *～ off／away,* make loose (a rope, etc). 放鬆(繩等)。**～er** *n* (colloq) lazy person; person who avoids his proper share of work. (俗)懶惰者；規避職責者。**～·ly** *adv* **～·ness** *n*

slack² /slæk ; slæk/ *n* **1** *the ～,* that part of a rope, etc that hangs loosely. 繩等鬆弛的部分。***take up the ～,*** pull a rope so that it is taut; (fig) regulate industry so that it is active and productive. 拉緊繩子；(喻)整頓工業(使其增產)。**2** (*pl*) loose-fitting trousers, not part of a suit, eg as informal wear for men or women. (複)寬鬆的褲子(如男女平時所穿者)。**3** [U] coal dust. 煤屑；煤渣。

slacken /ˈslækən ; ˈslækən/ *vt, vi* [VP6A, 2A] **1** make or become slower, less active, etc: 使緩慢；變緩慢；使遲滯；變爲不景氣： *～ speed.* 減緩速度。*The ship's speed ～ed.* 船速減緩。*The gale is ～ing a little.* 暴風減弱了一點。**2** make or become loose(r): 使鬆弛；變鬆弛： *～ the reins.* 放鬆韁繩。***S～ away／off!*** eg as an order to loosen ropes. 放開！放鬆！(如吩咐放鬆繩等)。

slag /slæg ; slæg/ *n* [U] waste matter remaining when metal has been extracted from ore. 礦渣；熔渣。ˈ**～-heap** *n* hill of ～ (dumped from a mine). 熔渣堆(礦坑倒出者)。

slain /sleɪn ; slen/ *pp* of slay.

slake /sleɪk ; slek/ *vt* [VP6A] **1** satisfy or make less strong (thirst, desire for revenge). 滿足或緩和(口渴、報復之心)。**2** change the chemical nature of (lime) by adding water. (加水)使(生石灰)熟化；消和(生石灰)。⇨ calcium.

sla·lom /ˈslɑːləm ; ˈslɑləm/ *n* ski-race along a zig-zag course marked out by poles with flags. 彎道滑雪比賽。

slam /slæm ; slæm/ *vt, vi* (-mm-) **1** [VP6A, 15A, B, 22] *～ (to),* shut violently and noisily: 使勁關；砰然關閉： *～ the door (to);* 砰然關門； *～ the window shut;* 使勁關上窗子； *～ the door in sb's face.* 當某人之面將門砰然關閉。**2** [VP2A, C] *～ (to),* be shut violently: 砰然關起： *The door ～med (to).* 門砰然關起來。**3** [VP15A, B] put, throw or knock with force: 砰然放下；猛力投擲或敲擊： *She ～med the box down on the table.* 她將匣子砰然摔在桌上。*The batsman ～med the ball into the grand-stand.* 擊球員把球擊入了大看臺。□ *n* **1** noise of sth being ～med: 砰然聲： *the ～ of a car door.* 關車門時的砰然聲。**2** (in whist, bridge) **a grand ～,** taking of 13 tricks. (惠斯特紙牌戲，橋牌戲)大滿貫(贏十三磴牌)。**a small ～,** taking of 12 tricks. 小滿貫(贏十二磴牌)。

slan·der /ˈslɑːndə(r) *US:* ˈslæn- ; ˈslændɚ/ *n* [C, U] (offence of making a) false statement that damages a person's reputation: 誹謗；詆毀；誹謗罪： *bring a ～ action against sb,* charge him with ～ in a court of law. 以誹謗罪控告某人。□ *vt* [VP6A] utter ～ about (sb). 誹謗；詆毀(某人)。**～er** *n* **～·ous** /-əs ; -əs/ *adj* uttering or containing ～. 誹謗的；造謠中傷的。

slang /slæŋ ; slæŋ/ *n* [U] (abbr *sl* used in this dictionary) words, phrases, meanings of words, etc commonly used in talk among friends or colleagues, but not suitable for good writing or formal occasions, esp the kind used by and typical of only one class of persons: (本辭典用 sl 爲其略語)俚語(一般用於朋友或同事間之談話，但不適於好的寫作或正式場合的字辭)；(尤指)某一階層人士的慣用語： *army ～;* 軍隊俚語； *prison ～;* 獄中俚語；(attrib)(形容用法) *～ words and expressions.* 俚語的字和語法。*The use of out-of-date ～ is sometimes a* *feature of foreigners' English.* 使用過時的俚語是外國人所用英文的特色。⇨ colloquial. □ *vt* [VP6A] use violent language to; abuse: 對…講粗話;謾罵: *Stop ~ing me.* 別罵我。***a '~ing match,*** a long exchange of insults and accusations. 長期的彼此攻訐或辱罵。**~y** *adj* (-ier, -iest) using, in the nature of, ~. 用俚語的;俚語性的。**~·ily** /-ɪlɪ; -əlɪ/ *adv* **~i·ness** *n*

slant /slɑːnt *US:* slænt; slænt/ *vi, vt* **1** [VP2A, C, 6A] slope: (使)傾斜;歪向: *His handwriting ~s from right to left.* 他寫的字從右往左斜。 **2** [VP 6A] ***~ the news,*** present it so that it is seen from, and supports, a particular point of view, eg of the writer's newspaper or government. 由某一觀點或立場(如報社或政府)發佈或報導新聞。□ *n* **1** [C] slope. 傾斜;斜面。***on a/the ~,*** in a sloping position. 傾斜着。**2** (colloq) point of view (sometimes prejudiced or biased) when considering sth: (俗)考慮某事時的觀點(有時是偏見或成見);意見;看法: *get a new ~ on the political situation.* 獲知對政治形勢的新觀點。**~·ing·ly, ~·wise** /-waɪz; -waɪz/ *advv* in a ~ing position or direction. 傾斜地;歪斜地。

slap /slæp; slæp/ *vt* (-pp-) **1** [VP6A, 15A] strike with the palm of the hand; smack: 掌擊;摑;拍: *She ~ped his face/~ped him on the face.* 她打他一個耳光。*I don't like being ~ped on the back as a greeting.* 我不喜歡在背上被拍一下當做招呼。**2** [VP15B] ***~ sth down,*** put sth down with a ~ping noise: 拍的一聲放下某物: *He ~ped the book down on the table.* 他拍的一聲把書擲在桌上。□ *n* [C] quick blow with the palm of the hand or with sth flat. 以手掌或扁平物快速的擊;摑;拍。***get/give sb a ~ in the face,*** (fig) a rebuff or snub. (喻)嚴拒;奚落。□ *adv* straight; directly; full: 一直地;直接地;充分地: *The car ran ~ into the wall.* 那汽車與牆撞個正着。ˌ**~-'bang** *adv* violently; headlong. 猛烈地;鹵莽地。**'~·dash** *adj, adv* careless(ly); impetuous(ly): 粗心的(地);鹵莽的(地);猛烈的(地);草率的(地): *a ~dash worker;* 粗心的工人; *do one's work ~dash/in a ~dash manner.* 草率地做工作。**'~-happy** *adj* (colloq) impetuous, carefree. (俗)魯莽的;無憂無慮的。**'~·stick** *n* [U] low comedy of the roughest kind; fun arising from violence: 打打鬧鬧的滑稽劇;動作激烈的笑鬧: (attrib) (形容用法) *~stick comedy.* 粗俗喜劇;鬧劇。**'~-up** *adj* (sl) first-class; extremely good: (俚)第一流的;極好的;上等的: *be treated to a ~-up dinner at a ~-up restaurant.* 在上等的餐館接受款待吃了一頓上等的大餐。

slash /slæʃ; slæʃ/ *vt, vi* **1** [VP6A, 2C] make a cut or cuts in or at sth with sweeping strokes; strike with a whip: 揮砍;揮擊;揮斬;切傷;鞭打: *His face had been ~ed with a razor-blade.* 他的臉被刀片割傷了。*Don't ~ your horse in that cruel way.* 不要那麼殘忍地鞭打你的馬。*He ~ed at the tall weeds with his stick.* 他用手杖揮擊高高的野草。**2** [VP6A] condemn vigorously and outspokenly: 嚴苛而直言地譴責;酷評: *a ~ing attack on the government's policy;* 對政府政策之猛烈的攻擊; *~ a new book/play,* criticize it adversely. 嚴苛地批評新書(劇本)。 **3** [VP6A] (colloq) cut, reduce drastically: (俗)削減;大幅減少: *~ prices/taxes/salaries.* 大大地減低價格(稅金,薪水)。**4** (usu passive) make long, narrow gashes in (for ornament, etc): (通常用被動語態)開長縫;開叉(以爲裝飾等): *~ed sleeves,* the lining or other material being seen through the ~es. 開叉的衣袖。□ *n* **1** act of ~ing; long cut or gash. 揮砍;鞭打;譴責;削減;傷痕;長縫;叉。**2** (vulg sl) act of urinating. (鄙俚)小便;排尿。

slat /slæt; slæt/ *n* long, thin narrow piece of wood, metal or plastic material, eg as in Venetian blinds or louvred doors. (木、金屬或塑膠等之)薄的細狹長條;條板(如百葉板或羽板)。**~·ted** *adj* made with, having, ~s. 裝有條板的;有條板的。

slate /sleɪt; slet/ *n* **1** [U] kind of blue-grey stone that splits easily into thin, flat layers; [C] one of these layers, square or oblong, used for roofs: 板石;粘板岩;石板;石板瓦: *hit on the head by a falling ~;* 被落下的一塊石片打在頭上; *a ~-covered roof;* 石板瓦覆蓋的房頂; **'~-coloured,** blue-grey; 灰藍色的; *a '~ quarry.* 採板石場。**2** [C] sheet of ~ in a wooden frame for writing on (as formerly used by school-children). 石板(昔時學童書寫用)。***a clean ~,*** (fig) a good record: (喻)好的記錄: *start with a clean ~,* (fig) make a new start with past errors, enmities, etc, forgotten. (喻)改過自新;重新開始;棄嫌言好。**'~-club** *n* (GB) club collecting small weekly contributions of money, usu saved until Christmas, when the total is distributed to members. (英)每週繳出少數錢的互助會(通常儲存到聖誕節,全部用以分配於會員)。ˌ**~-'pencil** *n* thin rod of soft ~, used for writing on ~s(2). 石筆(細而軟之板石,用於書寫石板者)。□ *vt* **1** [VP 6A] cover (a roof, etc) with ~s. 以石板瓦蓋(屋頂等)。 **2** (US, colloq) propose (sb) for an office, a position, etc: (美俗)提名(某人)擔任公職、職務等: (newspaper headline) (報紙標題) *Green ~d for the Presidency.* 格林被提名爲總統候選人。 **3** [VP 6A] (colloq) criticize severely (esp in a newspaper notice of a book, play, etc). (俗)酷評(尤指在報紙中的書籍、戲劇等的評述)。**slaty** *adj* of or like ~; containing ~: 板石的;似板石的;含板石的: *slaty coal.* 含板石成分的煤。**slat·ing** *n* adverse criticism: 批評;酷評: *give sb a sound slating.* 痛責某人。

slat·tern /ˈslætən; ˈslætɚn/ *n* dirty, untidily dressed woman. 衣著不整潔的女人。**~·ly** *adj* (of women) dirty and untidy. (指女人)不整潔的。**~·li·ness** *n*

slaugh·ter /ˈslɔːtə(r); ˈslɔtɚ/ *n* [U] **1** killing of animals (esp for food). 屠宰(尤指爲食物)。**'~-house** *n* place where animals are butchered for food. 屠宰場。 **2** killing of many people at once; massacre: 屠殺;殺戮: *the ~ on the roads,* the killing of people in road accidents. 道路車禍造成的死亡。□ *vt* [VP6A] kill (animals, people) in large numbers. 屠殺(動物、人);殺戮;屠宰。**~er** *n*

Slav /slɑːv; slɑv/ *n* member of a race spread over most of Eastern Europe, including Russians, Czechs, Poles, Bulgarians, etc. 斯拉夫族人(包括俄人、捷克人、波蘭人、保加利亞人等)。□ *adj* of the ~s. 斯拉夫人的。

slave /sleɪv; slev/ *n* **1** person who is the property of another and bound to serve him. 奴隸。**'~-driver** *n* overseer of ~s at work; person who makes those who are under him work very hard. 奴工監督;迫使下屬工作過度的人。**'~ ship** *n* ship used in the ~-trade. 奴隸貿易船。**'~ States** *n pl* southern States of N America in which there was slavery before the Civil War. 南北戰爭以前美國南方蓄奴各州。**'~-trade/-traffic** *n* capturing, transportation, buying and selling, of ~s. 奴隸買賣。 **2** person compelled to work very hard for someone else: 被奴役之人;苦工;奴工: *You mustn't make a ~ of your au pair girl.* 你不可把那個以工作交換食宿的女孩當做你的奴隸。**3** sb completely in the power of, under the control of, an impulse, habit, etc: 完全受衝動、習慣等控制之人: *~s of fashion,* eg persons who feel compelled to dress in the latest fashions; 拚命趕時髦的人們; *a ~ to duty/passion/convention/drink.* 被職務(熱情,習俗,杯中物)所控制的人。□ *vi* [VP2A, B, C, 3A] ***~ (away) (at sth),*** work hard: 努力工作;作苦工: *Poor Jane! She's been slaving away (= cooking) over a hot stove for three hours!* 可憐的珍!她已在熱火爐旁邊辛苦工作(烹飪)三個小時了! **~r** *n* '~-trader; '~ ship. 販賣奴隸者;奴隸貿易船。

slav·ery /ˈsleɪvərɪ; ˈslevərɪ/ *n* [U] **1** condition of being a ~: 奴隸狀態;奴役: *sold into ~ry.* 被賣爲奴。 **2** custom of having ~s: 奴隸制度: *men who worked for the abolition of ~ry.* 爲廢除奴隸制度奮鬥的人們。 **3** hard or badly paid work. 苦役;低酬工作。**slav·ish** /ˈsleɪvɪʃ; ˈslevɪʃ/ *adj* lacking in independence or originality; abject(2): 奴隸性的;缺乏獨立或創作性的;卑鄙的;可鄙的: *a slavish imitation,* an exact copy showing no originality. 抄襲;毫無創造性的傚品。**slav·ish·ly** *adv*

slaver /ˈslævə(r); ˈslævɚ/ *vi* [VP2A, 3A] *~ (over),* let spit run from the mouth (because of hunger): (因飢餓而)流涎;垂涎: *~ing over a plate of spaghetti;* 垂涎於一盤義大利麵條; (fig) (喻) *~ing over a travel brochure.* 興奮或渴望地看着旅遊手册。□ *n* [U] spit; saliva. 吐沫;口水。also ⇨ *slaver* at slave.

slavey /ˈsleɪvɪ; ˈslevɪ/ *n* (*pl* -veys) (sl) young servant. (俚)年輕的僕人。

Slav·onic /sləˈvɒnɪk; sləˈvɑnɪk/ *adj* of the Slavs or their languages. 斯拉夫族的;斯拉夫語的。

slaw /slɔː; slɔ/ *n* [U] (often 通常作 **ˈcole·~**) sliced cabbage, raw or cooked, served with a dressing. (生或熟的)甘藍菜絲(菜餚之一,食時加醬汁等佐料)。

slay /sleɪ; sle/ *vt* (*pt* slew /sluː; slu/, *pp* slain /sleɪn; slen/) [VP6A] (liter, or rhet) kill, murder. (文,修辭)殺;謀殺。**~er** *n* (journalism) murderer. (新聞)謀殺者;兇手。

sleazy /ˈsliːzɪ; ˈslezɪ/ *adj* (-ier, -iest) (colloq) uncared-for, dirty, untidy: (俗)沒人照顧的;骯髒的;不整齊的: *a ~ hotel/appearance.* 骯髒的旅社(外貌)。

sled /sled; slɛd/ *n* = sledge.

sledge[1] /sledʒ; slɛdʒ/ *n* vehicle with runners (long, narrow strips of wood or metal) instead of wheels, used on snow, larger types being pulled by horses or dogs and smaller types used in sport for travelling downhill at speed. 雪橇;雪車(以木質或金屬質長條代輪之交通工具,用於雪地,大型者以馬或狗曳之,小型者用於沿斜坡迅速滑行以爲遊戲)。□ *vi, vt* (-dd-) travel or carry by ~: 乘雪橇旅行;以雪橇運送: *go sledging.* 乘雪橇去。

sledge[2] /sledʒ; slɛdʒ/ *n* **ˈ~(-hammer),** heavy hammer with a long handle, used for driving posts into the ground, and by blacksmiths. (鐵匠用的)大鍾。

sleek /sliːk; slik/ *adj* (of hair, an animal's fur, etc) soft, smooth and glossy; (of a person) having such hair. (指毛髮、動物之毛皮等)柔滑而發亮的;(指人)有柔軟而發亮之毛髮的。***as ~ as a cat,*** (fig) having smooth manners (perhaps over-anxious to please). (喻)像貓一般地圓滑諂媚。□ *vt* [VP6A] make ~: 使柔軟發亮;使光滑: *~ a cat's fur.* 使貓的毛皮光滑。**~·ly** *adv* **~·ness** *n*

sleep[1] /sliːp; slip/ *n* **1** [U] condition of the body and mind such as recurs regularly every night, in which the eyes are closed and the muscles, nervous system, etc are relaxed: 睡眠: *How many hours' ~ do you need?* 你需要幾小時的睡眠? *He didn't get much ~.* 他睡得不多。*Do you ever talk in your ~?* 你睡覺時說夢話嗎? ***get to ~,*** manage to fall asleep, succeed in passing into the condition of ~: 睡着;入眠: *I couldn't get to ~ last night.* 我昨夜睡不着。***go to ~,*** fall asleep. 睡着。***have one's ˈ~ out,*** continue ~ing until one wakes up naturally: 睡足而自行醒來: *Don't wake her up—let her have her ~ out.* 别叫醒她—讓她睡足而自己醒。***put sb to ~,*** cause him to fall asleep. 使某人入睡。***put (a pet animal) to ~,*** (euphem) deliberately kill it (because of illness, etc). (委婉語)故意殺死(生病等的心愛動物)。**2** ***a ~,*** period of ~: 睡眠時間: *have a short/good/restful, etc ~;* 有一個短時間(良好,安靜等)的睡眠; *a ~ of three hours.* 三小時的睡眠。**ˈ~-walker** *n* person who walks while asleep. 夢遊者;患夢遊症者。**~·less** *adj* without ~: 缺乏睡眠的;失眠的: *pass a ~less night.* 一夜無眠。**~·less·ly** *adv* **~·less·ness** *n*

sleep[2] /sliːp; slip/ *vi, vt* (*pp, pt* slept /slept; slɛpt/) **1** [VP2A, B, C] rest in the condition of ~, be or fall asleep: 睡;睡着: *We go to bed to ~.* 我們上床睡覺。*He ~s well/badly.* 他睡得好(不好)。*She slept (for) eight hours.* 她睡了八小時。***~ like a top/log,*** ~ very soundly. 熟睡。***~ round the clock; ~ the clock round,*** ~ for twelve hours continuously. 連續睡十二小時。**2** [VP6A] provide beds for: 供給床位;供給住宿: *This hotel ~s 300 guests.* 這旅館可供三百客人住宿。**~·ing** *n* (in compounds) (複合字) **ˈ~·ing-bag** *n* warmly lined and water proof bag in which to ~ when out of doors (eg on holiday) or in a tent. 睡袋(在戶外或露營時用之,有暖和的襯墊物,並防水)。**ˈ~·ing-car** *n* railway coach fitted with beds or berths. (鐵路的)臥車。**ˈ~·ing-draught/-pill** *n* one that contains a drug to help sb to ~. 安眠劑(藥丸)。**~·ing partner** *n* (US 美 = *silent partner*) person who provides a share of the capital of a business but does not share in the management. 不參與實際業務的股東;隱名合夥人。**ˈ~·ing-sickness** *n* [U] disease caused by the tsetse-fly; it results in weakening of the mental powers and (usu) death. 睡眠症;昏睡病(采采蠅所引起之一種疾病;會導致患者心智減弱,而且通常會造死成亡)。**~er** *n* **1** person who ~s: 睡眠者: (with *adjj*) (與形容詞連用) *a heavy/light ~er,* one whom it is hard/easy to wake up; 沉(淺)睡者; *a good/bad ~er.* 易熟睡(不能熟睡)者。**2** (US 美 = *tie*) heavy beam of wood (or similarly shaped piece of other material) on a railway track, etc supporting the rails. (鐵路軌道之)枕木。**3** (bed or berth in a) ~ing-car on a train. (火車之)臥車;臥舖。**3** [VP2C, 15B, 3A] (with *adverbial particles* and *preps*): (與副詞接語及介詞連用):

sleep around, (colloq) be promiscuous. (俗)亂交;雜交。

sleep in/out, ~ at/outside one's place of employment: 在(不在)工作場所住宿: *Does the housekeeper ~ in?* 管家在他的僱主處住宿嗎?

sleep sth off, recover from sth by ~ing: 藉睡眠而消除: *~ off a bad headache/a hangover.* 藉睡眠消除頭痛(宿醒)。

sleep on, continue to sleep: 繼續睡: *Don't wake him up—let him ~ on for another hour.* 别叫醒他—讓他再繼續睡一小時。***~ on sth,*** (often 常作 ***~ on it***), leave the answer, solution, to a problem, etc to the next day. 把(問題等)留待第二天解決。

sleep through sth, not be woken up by (a noise, the alarm-clock, etc). 不被(噪音、鬧鐘等)吵醒。

sleep with sb, (euphem for) have sexual intercourse with. (委婉語)與某人性交。

sleepy /ˈsliːpɪ; ˈslipɪ/ *adj* (-ier, -iest) **1** needing, ready for, sleep: 要睡的;欲睡的;睏的: *feel/look ~.* 覺得(看來)欲睡。**ˈ~-head** *n* (esp as a form of address to a) ~ or inattentive person. 貪眠者;玩忽者(尤用於稱呼某人)。**2** (of places, etc) quiet; inactive: (指地方等)靜寂的;不活動的: *a ~ little village.* 靜寂的小村。**3** (of some kinds of fruit) over-ripe: (指某些水果)太熟的: *~ pears/bananas,* soft and brown inside. 過熟的梨子(香蕉)。**sleep·ily** /-ɪlɪ; -əlɪ/ *adv* **sleepi·ness** *n*

sleet /sliːt; slit/ *n* [U] falling snow or hail mixed with rain: 雨雪;霙;冰珠;雨雹;霰: *squalls of ~.* 帶雨雪冰雹的狂風。□ *vi* [VP2A] *It was ~ing,* S~ was falling. 下雨雪;降霰。**sleety** *adj*

sleeve /sliːv; sliv/ *n* **1** part of a garment that covers all or part of the arm: 袖;衣袖: *roll up the ~s of one's shirt/one's ˈshirt-~s.* 捲起襯衫的袖子。***have sth up one's ~,*** have an idea, plan, etc which one keeps secret for future use. 懷藏應付的計策等。***laugh up one's ~,*** be secretly amused. 竊喜。***roll up one's ~s,*** prepare to work or fight. 準備工作或打架。***wear one's heart on one's ~,*** allow one's feelings (of love for sb) to be seen; fail to show proper reserve. 流露眞情;表示愛慕;未能作適當之保留。**2** stiff envelope for a disc of recorded sound, often with notes on the composer, player(s), etc. 唱片之封套(常印有作曲者,演奏者等之說明)。**3** wind-sock. 風向袋;套筒風標。⇨ wind[1](8). **-sleeved** *suff*: *ˈshort/ˈloose-~d.* 短(寬)袖的。**~·less** *adj* without ~s. 無袖的。

sleigh /sleɪ ; sle/ *n* sledge, esp one drawn by a horse: 雪車；雪橇(尤指馬拖者)：*go for a* '～*-ride／a ride in a* ～. 乘雪車(橇)。'～**-bell** *n* one of several small tinkling bells commonly attached to a ～ or to the harness of the horse pulling the ～. 雪橇鈴（繫於雪橇或拖雪橇之馬上的小鈴）。□ *vi, vt* [VP2A, 6A] travel in a ～; carry (goods) by ～. 乘雪車旅行；以雪車搬運(貨物)。

sleight /slaɪt ; slaɪt/ *n* (usu in) (通常用於) ～ ***of hand,*** great skill in using the hand(s) in performing tricks, juggling, etc. 手法巧妙；精於手上把戲。

slen·der /'slendə(r) ; 'slɛndɚ/ *adj* **1** small in width or circumference compared with height or length: 細長的；纖細的：～ *fingers;* 修長的手指；*a* ～ *waist;* 纖腰；細腰；*a wineglass with a* ～ *stem.* 細腰酒杯；高脚杯。**2** (of persons) slim; not stout: (指人)纖巧的；輕盈的：*a* ～ *girl,* slight and graceful; 纖巧的女郎；*a woman with a* ～ *figure.* 身材細挑的女子。**3** slight; scanty; inadequate: 微薄的；不足的；不充分的：*a* ～ *income;* 微薄的收入；～ *means／hopes.* 微少的資產(渺茫的希望)。～**·ly** *adv* ～**·ness** *n* '～**·ize** /-aɪz ; -aɪz/ *vt, vi* [VP6A, 2A] (US) make, cause to appear, become, ～(2). (美)使，使顯得，變得苗條。

slept /slept ; slɛpt/ *pt, pp* of sleep.

sleuth /slu:θ ; sluθ/ *n* (colloq) detective. (俗)偵探。'～**-hound** *n* bloodhound; dog that follows a scent. 警犬；探犬；嗅跡獵犬。

slew[1] /slu: ; slu/ *pt* of slay.

slew[2] (US = **slue**) /slu: ; slu/ *vi, vt* [VP2C, 15B] ～ ***(sth) round,*** force or turn round in a new direction: 使或迫使(某物)轉向新方向；轉向：*The crane* ～*ed round.* 吊車轉向了。*The driver* ～*ed his crane round.* 駕駛員轉動吊車。

slice /slaɪs ; slaɪs/ *n* [C] **1** thin, wide, flat piece cut off sth, esp bread or meat: 薄片(尤指麵包或肉類)：*S*～*s of cold beef between* ～*s of bread make good sandwiches.* 冷牛肉片夾在麵包片間卽爲上好的三明治。**2** part, share: 部分；份兒：*a* ～ *of good luck.* 一份好運氣。*Smith took too large a* ～ *of the credit for our success.* 對於我們的成功，史密斯所獲得的稱讚超過了他的貢獻。**3** utensil with a wide, flat blade for cutting, serving or lifting (eg cooked fish, fried eggs). (切片、上菜或挑起用的)切刀；餐刀；菜鏟。**4** (in games such as golf) bad stroke that causes the ball to go spinning off in a direction different from that desired, ie to the right of a right-handed player. (高爾夫球等)右曲球；斜擊。□ *vt, vi* **1** [VP6A, 15A, B, 22, 3A] cut into ～s: 切成片：～ *into／through a cake;* 切蛋糕；～ *(up) a loaf.* 把一條麵包切片。*S*～ *the beef thin.* 把牛肉切成薄片。*The butcher* ～*d off a thick steak.* 屠夫切下厚厚的一片肉。**2** [VP6A] (golf): (高爾夫球)：～ *the ball,* strike with a ～(4). 曲打球；斜擊球；擊成右曲球。

slick /slɪk ; slɪk/ *adj* (colloq) (俗) **1** smooth; slippery: 平滑的；滑溜的：*The roads were* ～ *with wet mud.* (那些)道路泥濘滑溜。**2** carried through smoothly and efficiently, perhaps with some trickery: 圓滑而有效完成的；巧妙完成的；做得漂亮而有技巧的：*a* ～ *business deal;* 一筆漂亮的生意；(of a person) doing things in a ～ way: (指人)有手段的；有技巧的；熟練的；伶俐的：*a* ～ *salesman.* 一個伶俐的推銷員或售貨員。□ *n* [C] '**oil** ～**,** film of thick oil covering an area of the sea, etc (eg from an oil-tanker after a collision). 水上浮油(如從撞毀的油船流出浮於海面等者)。□ *adv* directly, completely: 直接地；完全地：*hit a man* ～ *on the jaw.* 正好打在一個人的下顎上。～**er** *n* (US colloq) (美俗) **1** long, loose, waterproof coat. (長而寬鬆的)雨衣。**2** ～ person, ⇨ 2 above: 騙子；(大都市的)老滑頭；老油條(參看上列第2義)：*city* ～*ers.* 都市裡的老油條、騙徒等。

slide[1] /slaɪd ; slaɪd/ *n* **1** act of sliding(1); smooth stretch of ice, hard snow, etc on which to slide: 滑；滑行；(冰、硬雪等的)滑面：*have a* ～ *on the ice.* 在冰上滑行。**2** smooth slope down which persons or things can slide (eg for felled timber down a mountain slope, or a wooden or metal slope made for children to play on). 滑道；滑坡；滑梯(如運送木材下山或兒童遊戲所用者)。**3** picture, diagram, etc on photographic film (and usu mounted in a frame); (formerly) such a picture on a glass plate, to be slid into a projector and shown on a screen. 幻燈片。**4** glass plate on which is placed sth to be examined under a microscope. (顯微鏡的)承物玻璃片。**5** part of a machine, etc that slides (eg the U-shaped part of a trombone). (機器等的)滑動機件(如大喇叭上的U型部分)。**6** **('land)**～**,** ⇨ land[1](6). **7** **('hair)-**～**,** ⇨ hair(2).

slide[2] /slaɪd ; slaɪd/ *vi, vt* (*pt, pp* slid /slɪd ; slɪd/) **1** [VP2A, C, 6A, 15A] (cause to) move smoothly over, slip along, a polished surface: (使)在光滑表面上滑動或滑行：*children sliding on the ice.* 溜冰的孩子們。*The book slid* (= slipped, which is more usu) *off my knee.* 書從我膝蓋上滑落了(slipped比slid常用)。*Let's* ～ *down this grassy slope.* 咱們順着這草坡滑下去吧。*The drawers of this desk* ～ *in and out easily.* 這張書桌的抽屜拉出推進都很容易。*S*～ *the drawer into its place.* 把抽屜推進去。～ ***over sth,*** pass over (a delicate subject, etc) quickly; barely touch upon it. 輕輕帶過某事；輕觸(某一棘手問題等)卽過；點到爲止。***let things*** ～**,** not trouble about them, be negligent. 聽其自然。**2** [VP3A] ～ ***into,*** pass gradually, without being fully aware, into (a condition, etc): 不知不覺地逐漸陷入(某種情況等)：～ *into dishonesty／bad habits.* 逐漸變得不誠實(慢慢染上壞習慣)。**3** [VP2C, 15A] (cause to) move quickly, or so as to avoid observation: (使)快速行動；溜進；潛行：*The thief slid behind the curtains.* 竊賊溜到帷幕後面。*She slid a coin into his hand.* 她很快把一枚硬幣塞進他的手裡。**4** (compounds) (複合字) '～**-rule** *n* device of two rulers with logarithmic scales, one of which ～s in a groove, used for rapid calculations. 計算尺；滑尺。**slid·ing door** *n* one that is pulled across an opening (instead of turning on hinges). 拉門。**slid·ing scale** *n* scale by which one thing, eg wages, goes up or down in relation to changes in sth else, eg the cost of living. 滑準法(某一事項之高低計算隨另一事項而改變的計算法，如薪金隨生活費用之變化而決定其升降)。**slid·ing seat** *n* seat on runners, esp in a racing boat, to lengthen the stroke of the rower or sculler. 滑座(裝在滑板上的座位，尤指賽艇上可藉以延伸槳手之划動者)。

slight[1] /slaɪt ; slaɪt/ *adj* (-er, -est) **1** slim; slender; frail-looking: 細長的；苗條的；瘦小的；脆弱的：*a* ～ *figure;* 苗條的身材；*supported by a* ～ *framework.* 由脆弱的骨架支撐的。**2** small; not serious or important: 微小的；輕微的；不重要的：*a* ～ *error;* 小錯；小差誤；*a* ～ *headache;* 輕微的頭痛；*do sth without the* ～*est difficulty,* with no difficulty at all. 毫無困難地做某事。*She takes offence at the* ～*est thing,* is very easily offended. 她動不動就生氣。***not in the*** ～***est,*** not at all: 毫不；一點也不：*You didn't embarrass me in the* ～*est.* 你一點也沒有使我爲難。～**·ly** *adv* **1** slenderly: 細長地；苗條地：*a* ～*ly built boy.* 瘦長的男孩。**2** to a ～ degree; somewhat: 些許；稍稍：*The patient is* ～*ly better today.* 病人今天稍稍好一點。*I know her* ～*ly.* 我略略知道她。～**·ness** *n*

slight[2] /slaɪt ; slaɪt/ *vt* [VP6A] treat without proper respect or courtesy; neglect in a marked manner: 慢待；輕視；藐視；不禮遇：*She felt* ～*ed because no one spoke to her.* 她感到受輕視，因爲沒有人跟她談話。□ *n* [C] marked failure to show respect or courtesy: 慢待；輕視；藐視：*put a* ～ *on sb;* 慢待某人；*suffer* ～*s.* 受到慢待。～**·ing·ly** *adv*

slim /slɪm ; slɪm/ *adj* (-mer, -mest) **1** slender: 苗條的；細長的；纖細的：*a* ～*-waisted girl.* 細腰女郎。**2** (colloq) small; insufficient: (俗)細小的；微少的；不足的：～ *hopes／chances of success;* 成功的希望

(機會)不大; *condemned upon the ~mest (of) evidence.* 根據微不足道的證據被判罪。□ *vi* (-mm-) eat less, diet, take exercise, etc with the object of reducing one's weight and becoming ~(1): 藉少吃、節食、運動等以減輕體重而變苗條: *~ming exercises.* 減肥運動;健美運動。**~·ly** *adv* **~·ness** *n*

slime /slaɪm; slaɪm/ *n* [U] **1** soft, nasty, thick, sticky mud. 爛泥;泥濘。**2** sticky substance from snails, etc: (蝸牛等的)黏液: *a trail of ~.* 一道(蝸牛等的)黏液痕。**slimy** /ˈslaɪmɪ; ˈslaɪmɪ/ *adj* (-ier, -iest) of, like, covered with, ~; hard to hold because slippery with ~; (fig) disgustingly dishonest, meek, flattering, obsequious, etc: 泥濘(般)的; 黏滑而難以捉握的;(喻)奸詐的;過於溫順的;諂媚的;卑躬屈節的: *a slimy(-tongued) coward.* 油腔滑調的懦夫。

sling[1] /slɪŋ; slɪŋ/ *n* [C] **1** band of material, length of rope, chain, etc looped round an object, eg a barrel, a broken arm, to support or lift it. (用以固定斷臂的)吊帶;(用以懸提圓桶等物件的)吊索。**2** strip of leather used (held in the hand in a loop) to throw stones to a distance. 投石器;投石環索; 擲石環帶。**3** act of throwing. 投擲;拋;投。□ *vt* (*pt, pp* slung /slʌŋ; slʌŋ/) **1** [VP6A, 15A, B] throw with force: 用力投擲: *naughty boys ~ing stones at street lamps.* 向路燈投擲石塊的頑皮男孩們。**~ one's hook,** (sl) go away: (俚)走開;滾蛋: *Tell him to ~ his hook.* 叫他滾蛋。**~ mud at sb,** (fig) abuse him. (喻)詆毀某人。**~ sb out,** throw sb out; expel him by force. 攆走某人;驅逐某人。**2** [VP6A, 15A, B] support (sth) so that it can swing, be lifted, etc: 懸吊: *~ a hammock between two tree-trunks;* 在兩樹幹間懸一吊床; *~ (up) a barrel;* 懸吊(起)一隻大桶; *with his rifle slung over his shoulder.* 他的步槍掛在肩上。**~er** /ˈslɪŋə(r); ˈslɪŋɚ/ *n* person armed with a ~(2). 攜帶或使用投石器的人。

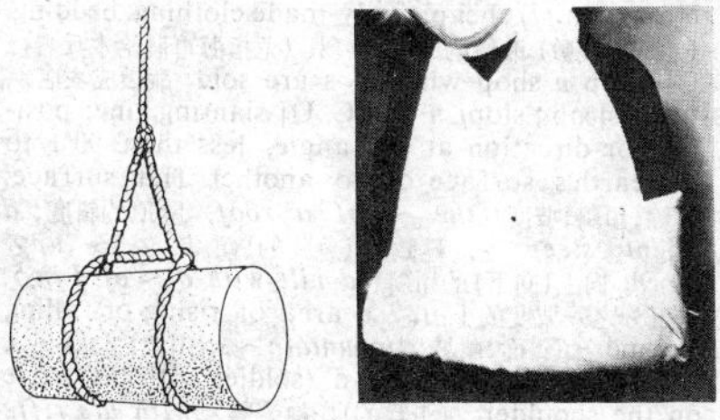

slings

sling[2] /slɪŋ; slɪŋ/ *n* drink made of gin, rum, etc sweetened with fruit juices (esp lime). 用杜松子酒,蘭酒等加酸橙或其他果汁調製而成的一種飲料。

slink /slɪŋk; slɪŋk/ *vi* (*pt, pp* slunk /slʌŋk; slʌŋk/) [VP2C] go or move (*off, away, in, out, by*) in a secret, guilty or sneaking manner. 潛行;溜走; 潛逃(與 off, away, in, out, by 等連用)。

slip[1] /slɪp; slɪp/ *n* [C] **1** act of slipping; false step; slight error caused by carelessness or inattention: 滑;溜;失足;失誤;小疏忽: *make a ~.* 失誤; 犯小錯。***a ~ of the tongue/pen,*** error in speaking/writing. 口(筆)誤。***give sb the ~; give the ~ to sb,*** escape from, get away from (one's pursuers, etc). 躲開、避開或逃離(追踪者等)。***There's many a ~ 'twixt (the) cup and (the) lip,*** (prov) Something may easily go wrong before a plan is fully carried out. (諺)事情往往會功敗垂成。**2** (**'pillow-~**) loose cover for a pillow; loose sleeveless garment worn under a dress; (**'gym-~**) girl's garment for gymnastic exercises. 枕套;女用襯裙;女子運動裝。**3** narrow strip of paper; printer's proof on such a strip. 紙條;(印刷)校樣條。**4** cutting (short length of stem) taken from a plant for planting or grafting (to grow a new plant, etc). (種植用的)接枝;插枝。**5** young, slender person: 瘦弱的年輕人: *a (mere) ~ of a boy/girl,* a slim boy/girl. 瘦削的男孩(女孩)。**6** (usu *pl;* 通常用複數; also 亦作 **'~·way**) sloping way (of stone or timber) down to the water, on which ships are built, or pulled up out of the water for repairs: 修造船隻的坡道;船台: *The ship is still on the ~s.* 該船仍在建造(或修理)中。**7** (*pl*) (more usu 較常用 *wings*) parts of the stage of a theatre from which the scenery is pushed on, and where actors stand before going on to the stage: (複)舞台側翼(上佈景或演員出場前停留處): *watch a performance from the ~s.* 從舞台側翼看表演。**8** (cricket) one of the fielders: (板球)三柱門守球員背後的守球員: *first/second/leg ~;* 第一(第二,左後)守球員; (*pl*) part of the ground where these fielders stand. (複)上述守球員的守球區。⇨ the illus at cricket. 參看 cricket 之插圖。**9** [U] semi-fluid clay for coating earthenware or making patterns on it. (塗於陶器外表或用以塗繪圖樣的)泥釉。

slip[2] /slɪp; slɪp/ *vi, vt* (-pp-) **1** [VP2A, C] lose one's balance; fall or almost fall as the result of this: 失足;滑;滑倒: *He ~ped on the icy road and broke his leg.* 他在結冰的路面上滑倒而跌斷了腿。**2** [VP2A, C] go or move quietly or quickly, esp without attracting attention: 匆匆行動或悄悄移動;潛行: *She ~ped away/out/past without being seen.* 她悄悄溜走(溜出去,溜過去),沒人看見。*The years ~ped by.* 歲月在不知不覺中逝去。**3** [VP2A, C] move, get away, escape, fall, by being difficult to hold, or by not being held firmly: (由於很難抓住或未抓緊而)滑落;滑脫;掉: *The fish ~ped out of my hand.* 魚從我手中滑落。*The blanket ~ped off the bed.* 毯子從床上滑落。*The knife ~ped and cut my hand.* 刀子滑動割破了我的手。***let sth ~,*** **(a)** allow sth to fall from one's hands, escape, or be neglected: 放手;放開;放過;錯過: *Don't let the opportunity ~.* 不要坐失良機。**(b)** accidentally reveal (a secret, etc): 無意中洩露(秘密等): *let ~ a secret.* 無意中洩露秘密。**~ *through one's fingers,*** (lit or fig) fail to grasp, keep a hold on. (字面或喻)未掌握住;未抓住。**4** [VP15A, B, 2C] put, pull on or push off, with a quick, easy movement: 迅速俐落地放置、穿上或脫去: *~ a coat on/off;* 迅速穿上(脫下)上裝; *~ into/out of a dress;* 迅速穿起(脫去)衣服; *~ a coin into the waiter's hand.* 把一枚硬幣很快地塞進侍者的手中。**5** [VP2C] (of small mistakes, etc) be allowed to enter, esp by carelessness: (指小錯誤等,由於粗心而)發生: *errors that have ~ped into the text;* 發生在原文裡的錯誤; make a small error. 犯小錯。**~ up,** (colloq) make a mistake. (俗)犯錯。Hence, 由此產生, **'~-up** *n* [C] mistake. 錯誤。**6** [VP2C] move smoothly and effortlessly; go with a gliding motion: 滑動; 滑行: *The ship ~ped through the water.* 那條船在水上滑行。**7** [VP6A] get free from; let go from restraint: 放開;釋放: *~ greyhounds from the leash;* 鬆開皮帶釋放靈猩; *~ anchor,* detach a ship from the anchor; 起錨;開航; (of a cow) (指母牛) *~ her calf,* give birth to it prematurely; 早產小牛; *~ a stitch,* (knitting) move a stitch from one needle to the other without knitting it. (針織)滑漏一針。*The dog ~ped its collar,* got out of it. 那狗滑脫了頸圈。*The point ~ped my attention.* 那一點我疏忽了。***~ one's mind,*** (of a name, address, message, etc) be forgotten (because one is in a hurry, busy, etc). (指姓名、住址、信息等)被忘記(因匆忙、忙碌等)。**8** (compounds) (複合字) **'~-carriage/-coach** *nn* one at the end of a train which can be detached without stopping the train. (火車的)末節車廂(不必停車即可將之與列車分離)。**'~-cover** *n* detachable cover for a piece of furniture. 家具套。⇨ 2 above. 參看上列第2義。**'~-knot** *n* **(a)** knot which slips along the cord round which it is made to tighten or loosen the loop. (繩索的)滑結。**(b)** knot which can be undone by a pull. 活結。⇨ the illus at knot. 參看 knot 之插圖。 ˈ**~·on／·over** *n* shoe or garment to be slipped easily on or over sth. (便於穿脫的)套頭外衣;套鞋。ˈ**~-road** *n* road for joining or leaving a motorway (US 美 = *access-road*); minor or local by-pass road.(與快車道相接的)側道;叉道。ˈ**~-stream** *n* stream of air from the propeller or jet engine of an aircraft. (由飛機的螺旋槳或噴射引擎造成的)後向氣流;滑流。

slip·per /ˈslɪpə(r) ; ˈslɪpɚ/ *n* (often 常作 ***pair of ~s***) loose-fitting light shoe worn in the house. 拖鞋;便鞋。**~ed** *adj* wearing ~s. 穿着拖鞋的。

slip·pery /ˈslɪpərɪ ; ˈslɪpərɪ/ *adj* (-ier, -iest) **1** (of a surface) smooth, wet, polished, etc so that it is difficult to hold, to stand on, or to move on: (指表面)光滑的;濕滑的: *~ roads;* 濕滑的路; *~ under foot;* 脚下滑溜的; (fig) (of a subject) needing care: (喻)(指問題)需要小心的: *We're on ~ ground when dealing with this subject.* 我們處理這個問題時需要小心。***be on a ~ slope,*** (fig) on a course of action which may lead to failure or disgrace. (喻)採取可能招致失敗或恥辱的行動。**2** (fig, of persons) unreliable; unscrupulous: (喻,指人)不可靠的;滑頭的;無恥的: *a ~ customer,* a rogue. 無賴。*He's as ~ as an eel,* is untrustworthy, difficult to manage. 他非常狡滑。**slip·peri·ness** *n*

slippy /ˈslɪpɪ ; ˈslɪpɪ/ *adj* (colloq) (俗) **1** slippery. 滑的;不可靠的;狡滑的。**2** (dated) quick: (過時用語)快: *Be ~ about it!* 快點(做)! *Look ~!* 趕快!

slip·shod /ˈslɪpʃɒd ; ˈslɪp,ʃɑd/ *adj* slovenly; careless: 懶散的;隨便的;散漫的;粗心的: *a ~ piece of work;* 潦草的作品; *a ~ style.* 散漫的風格。

slit /slɪt ; slɪt/ *n* [C] long, narrow cut, tear or opening: 狹長的切口;裂縫;裂口: *the ~ of a letter-box* (through which letters are put); 信箱的投信口; *eyes like ~s.* 細長的眼睛;瞇瞇眼。□ *vt, vi* (*pt, pp* slit; -tt-) **1** [VP6A, 15A, 22] make a ~ in; open (by ~ting): 切開;撕裂;在…開豁口: *~ a man's throat;* 切割一男人的喉嚨(殺死一男人); *~ an envelope open;* 拆開信封; *~ cloth into strips／a sheet of leather into thongs.* 把布撕成細條(把一張皮革分割成條)。 **2** [VP2A, C] be cut or torn lengthwise: 被縱切(割或撕): *The shirt has ~ down the back.* 那襯衣的背部被由上而下撕破了。

slither /ˈslɪðə(r) ; ˈslɪðɚ/ *vi* [VP2A, C] slide or slip unsteadily: 顛簸地滑動或滑行: *~ down an ice-covered slope.* 顛簸地滑下結冰的斜坡。**~y** *adj* slippery. 滑的;滑溜的。

sliver /ˈslɪvə(r) ; ˈslɪvɚ/ *n* [C] small, thin strip of wood; splinter; thin piece pared off a large piece: 小而薄的木條;小木片;(大塊上削下來的)薄片;碎片: *a ~ of cheese.* 一片乾酪。□ *vt, vi* [VP6A, 2A] break off as a ~; break into ~s; splinter. 把…切成薄片;把…裂成碎片;碎裂;分裂。

slob /slɒb ; slɑb/ *n* (sl) unpleasantly dirty or rude person. (俚)骯髒或粗魯的人。

slob·ber /ˈslɒbə(r) ; ˈslɑbɚ/ *vi, vt* **1** [VP2A, 3A] let saliva run from the mouth (as a baby does). 淌口水;(如嬰兒般)流涎。***~ over sb,*** show excessive and maudlin love or admiration for (eg by giving wet kisses). 露骨或粗俗地向某人表達戀情或仰慕(如吮吻愛戀或仰慕的對象)。**2** [VP6A] make wet with saliva: 以口涎弄濕: *The baby has ~ed its bib.* 那嬰兒的口水弄濕了自己的圍兜。□ *n* [U] saliva running from the mouth; maudlin talk, etc. 口水;涎;涕泗縱橫的談話等。

sloe /sləʊ ; slo/ *n* [C] small, bluish-black, very bitter wild plum, fruit of the blackthorn; the blackthorn bush. 野李;野李樹。ˌ**~-ˈgin** *n* liqueur made from ~s steeped in gin. (用野李泡在杜松子酒中製成的)野李酒。

slog /slɒg ; slɑg/ *vi, vt* (-gg-) [VP6A, 2C, 3A] ***~ (at),*** hit hard and wildly, esp in boxing and cricket; walk or work hard and steadily: 猛擊(尤指拳擊及板球賽時);辛苦而堅定地工作或步行: *~ (at) the ball;* 猛擊球; *~ing away at one's work;* 孜孜地工作; *~ing along the road.* 沿途跋涉前進。**~·ger** *n* person who ~s, eg at cricket; hard worker. 猛擊者(如板球賽時);孜孜工作者。

slo·gan /ˈsləʊgən ; ˈslogən/ *n* [C] striking and easily remembered phrase used to advertise sth, or to make clear the aim(s) of a group, organization, campaign, etc: 標語;口號(顯明易記的辭句,用以宣傳某物或明示某一組織或運動等之目標者): *political ~s.* 政治口號。

sloop /slu:p ; slup/ *n* small one-masted sailing-ship with fore-and-aft rig. (縱帆裝置的)單桅帆船。

slop[1] /slɒp ; slɑp/ *vi, vt* (-pp-) **1** [VP2A, C] (of liquids) spill over the edge: (指液體)溢出;潑出: *The tea ~ped (over) into the saucer.* 茶溢出流入茶托中。 **2** ***~ over sb,*** = slobber over sb. **3** [VP6A, 15A] cause to spill: 使溢出或潑出: *~ beer over the counter of a pub;* 使啤酒溢出流到酒吧的櫃臺上; splash. 潑出;濺出。**4** ***~ out,*** empty ~s(1). 倒汚水;倒馬桶。**5** [VP6A, 15A] make a mess with: 以…弄汚;濺汚: *~ paint all over the floor.* 使地板上到處濺了油漆。 **6** [VP2C] splash: 濺着水行進: *Why do some children love ~ping about in puddles?* 爲什麼有些孩子喜歡在水坑裡濺着水走來走去呢? □ *n* **~s,** **1** dirty waste water from the kitchen or from bedrooms (where there are no basins with running water and drains); urine, excrement (in pails, as in a prison cell). (厨房或臥房的)汚水;(馬桶裡的)糞便(如牢房中者)。ˈ**~-basin** *n* basin into which dregs from teacups are emptied at table. 殘茶盆(盛茶杯中的殘渣者)。ˈ**~-pail** *n* one in which bedroom ~s are removed. 汚水桶;馬桶。 **2** liquid food, eg milk, soup, esp for people who are ill; swill (for pigs). 流質食物(如牛奶、湯等,尤指供病人食用者);(餵豬的)殘食。

slop[2] /slɒp ; slɑp/ *n* (esp as supplied to sailors in the Navy, usu *pl*) cheap, ready-made clothing; bedding. (通常用複數) 廉價的成衣; 寢具 (尤指海軍發給水兵者)。ˈ**~-shop** *n* shop where ~s are sold. 廉價成衣店。

slope /sləʊp ; slop/ *n* **1** [C, U] slanting line; position or direction at an angle, less than 90°, to the earth's surface or to another flat surface: 斜線;傾斜;坡度: *the ~ of a roof;* 屋頂的斜度; *a slight／steep ~;* 輕微的(急陡的)傾斜; *a ~ up／down;* 向上(向下)的傾斜; *a hill with a ~ of 1 in 5.* 有五分之一坡度的小山。 **2** area of rising or falling ground: 傾斜面;斜坡: *ˈmountain ~s;* 山坡; *ˈski ~s.* 滑雪斜坡。**3** position of a (soldier with his) rifle on the shoulder: (士兵的)托槍姿勢: *with his rifle at the ~.* 托着槍。□ *vi, vt* **1** [VP2A, C] have a ~; slant: 有斜度;傾斜: *Our garden ~s (down) to the river.* 我們的花園向河傾斜。*Does your handwriting ~ forward or backward?* 你的書法是向前斜還是向後斜? **2** [VP6A] cause to ~. 使傾斜;使有斜度。***~ arms,*** (mil) place and hold the rifle in a sloping position on the left shoulder. (軍)托槍。**3** [VP2C] (colloq) (俗) ***~ off,*** (also 亦作 *do a ~*), go off or away (to evade sb, or escape doing sth). 走開;避開(避開某人或逃避做某事)。**slop·ing·ly** *adv*

sloppy /ˈslɒpɪ ; ˈslɑpɪ/ *adj* (-ier, -iest) **1** wet or dirty with rain, etc; full of puddles; (of a table, etc) wet with slops: 爲雨水等弄濕或沾汚的;泥濘的;多水坑的;(指桌子等)汚濕的: *The melting snow made the roads ~.* 融雪使道路泥濘。 **2** (of food) consisting of slops. (指食物)流質的。 ⇨ slop[1] *n*(2). **3** (colloq) unsystematic; not done with care and thoroughness: (俗)無系統的;做得馬虎而不徹底的;草率的: *a ~ piece of work.* 一件草率的製品。 **4** (colloq) foolishly sentimental; weakly emotional: (俗)過分多情的;感情脆弱的;容易感傷的: *~ sentiment;* 多愁善感; *~ talk about girlfriends and boyfriends.* 有關交女友和交男友的傷心話。**slop·pily** /-ɪlɪ ; -ɪlɪ/ *adv* in a ~ manner: 汚濕地;泥濘地;無系統地;草率地;感傷地: *sloppily* (= carelessly) *dressed.* 衣着隨便的。**slop·pi·ness** *n*

slosh /slɒʃ; slaʃ/ *vt, vi* **1** [VP6A, 15A] (sl) hit: (俚)打;擊: ~ *sb on the chin.* 打某人的下顎。 **2** [VP2C] ~ ***about,*** flounder about in slush or mud. 在泥雪中或爛泥中掙扎著前行或移動。 **3** [VP15B] ~ ***sth about,*** throw water or other liquid or semi-liquid substance about. 濺潑水或其他液體或半液體。 **~ed** *adj* (sl) drunk. (俚)酒醉的。

slot /slɒt; slat/ *n* [C] **1** narrow opening through which sth is to be put; slit for a coin in a machine (**'~-machine** or *vending-machine*) that automatically delivers sth, eg tickets, cigarettes, packets of sweets. (容物出入的)狹縫;長孔;口;(自動售貨機上的)投幣孔(自動售貨機稱爲 '~-machine 或 vending-machine)。 **2** slit, groove or channel into which sth fits or along which sth slides. 溝;槽;槽溝。 **3** (colloq) right or suitable place for sth (in a broadcast programme, scheme, etc): (俗)(廣播節目、設計、計畫等中)某項目的正確或適當位置: *find a ~ for a talk on bee-keeping.* 設法安排一個以養蜂爲題的演講。 □ *vt* (-tt-) [VP6A, 15A] provide with ~s; make a ~ or ~s in: 在…上開長孔;開槽於;安排;安插: ~ *a song recital into a radio programme;* 在廣播節目中安排一個獨唱項目; ~ *30000 graduates a year into jobs,* find jobs for them. 爲一年三萬大學畢業生安排工作。

sloth /sləʊθ; sloθ/ *n* **1** [U] laziness; idleness. 懶散;怠惰。 **2** [C] S American mammal which lives in the branches of trees and moves very slowly. 樹懶(南美洲的哺乳動物,棲於樹枝,行動緩慢)。 **~·ful** /-fl; -fəl/ *adj* inactive; lazy. 不活潑的;怠惰的。

slouch /slaʊtʃ; slautʃ/ *vi* [VP2A, C] stand, sit or move, in a lazy, tired way: 沒精打彩地站、坐或行動: *louts who ~ about at street corners all day.* 整天在街角閒蕩的粗漢。 □ *n* ~ing attitude or way of walking: 沒精打彩的態度或步態: *walk with a ~.* 沒精打彩地走。 **,~-'hat** *n* soft hat with a turned-down brim. 垂邊帽。 **~·ing·ly** *adv*

slough[1] /slaʊ; slaʊ; *in US topography:* slu:; slu/ *n* [C] swamp; marsh. 沼地;沼澤。

slough[2] /slʌf; slʌf/ *n* [C] cast-off skin of a snake; any dead part of an animal dropped off at regular periods. 蛇的蛻皮;脫殼;動物體上按時脫落的部分。 □ *vt, vi* [VP6A, 15B, 2A] ~ ***(off),*** put, come or throw off: 蛻去;脫除;棄去: ~ *(off) bad habits;* 拋棄壞習慣; *a snake that has ~ed its skin.* 已蛻皮的蛇。

sloven /'slʌvn; 'slʌvən/ *n* person who is untidy, dirty, careless or slipshod in his appearance, dress, habits, etc. 邋遢的人;不修邊幅的人;儀表、穿著、習慣等方面不整潔、草率、懶散的人。 **~·ly** *adj* of or like a ~: 邋遢的;不修邊幅的;不整潔的;潦草的: *a ~ly appearance;* 不整潔的儀容; ~ *in his dress.* 衣著邋遢的。 **~-li·ness** *n*

slow[1] /sləʊ; slo/ *adj* (-er, -est) **1** not quick; taking a long time: 慢;緩慢的;遲緩的;費時的: *a ~ runner;* 跑得慢的人; *a ~ train,* eg one that stops at all or almost all stations, contrasted with an express train; 慢車(如每站或幾乎每站都停的火車,與快車相對); *a ~ journey.* 費時的旅程。 **2** at less than the usual rate or speed. 未達常速的;速度緩慢的。 ***a ~ march,*** eg at a military funeral. 緩慢行進(如軍隊的送葬行列)。 ***in ~ motion,*** (of a cinema film) with the number of exposures per second greatly increased (so that when the film is shown at normal rate the action appears to be ~); (指電影片高速拍攝後,以常速播放所映出之)慢動作的; Hence, 由此產生, *a ~-motion film.* 慢動作電影。 **3** not quick to learn; dull: 遲鈍的;笨的: *a ~ child;* 遲鈍的小孩; not acting immediately; acting only after a time: 不立刻起作用的;反應慢的: ~ *poison.* 慢性毒藥。 *He is ~ to anger/~ to make up his mind/~ of speech/~ at accounts/not ~ to defend himself.* 他不輕易發怒(不容易下決心,嘴鈍,不精於算帳,敏於自衛)。 **'~·coach** *n* person who is ~ in action, or who is dull, or who has out-of-date ideas. 行動遲鈍的人;笨伯;思想陳腐的人。 **4** (usu *pred;* of watches and clocks) showing a time behind the correct time (eg 1.55 when it is 2.00): (通常作敍述用法;指鐘錶)慢的;較正確時刻落後的(如正確時間爲兩點,而鐘面上爲一點五十五分): *That clock is five minutes ~.* 那(座)鐘慢五分鐘。 **5** not sufficiently interesting or lively: 不太有趣味的;不太精采的;不太有生氣的: *We thought the party was rather ~.* 我們覺得那次舞會不太精采。 **6** (of a surface) of such a nature that what moves over it (esp a ball) tends to do so at a reduced speed: (指表面)能減低(尤指球的)速度的: *a ~ running track/cricket pitch/billiard table.* 減低速度的跑道(板球兩三柱門間的球道,撞球臺)。 **~·ly** *adv* in a ~ manner: 緩慢地: *walk/speak/learn ~ly.* 緩慢地走(說話,學習)。 *He ~ly opened the door.* 他慢慢地打開門。 *S~ly the door opened.* 那門慢慢地開了。 ⇨ slow[2] below. 參看下列 slow[2]。 **~·ness** *n*

slow[2] /sləʊ; slo/ *adv* (-er, -est) (Note that *slowly* may precede the finite *v* as in 'He slowly walked up the path', or follow, as in 'He walked slowly up the path', or have front position, as in 'Slowly he walked up the path', whereas ~ follows the *v,* except when used with *how,* or in participial compounds as in 2 below.) (注意: slowly 可用於限定動詞之前,如 'He slowly walked up the path', 或用於限定動詞之後,如 'He walked slowly up the path', 或置於句首,如 'Slowly he walked up the path', 而 slow 除與 how 連用外,祇可用於動詞之後,或用於如第 2 義中所舉的分詞複合字中。) **1** at a low speed; slowly: 低速地;緩慢地: *Tell the driver to go ~er.* 告訴司機開慢一點。 *How ~/How slowly the time passes!* 時間過得多麼慢啊! *S~ astern!* (a command to go astern slowly). 緩慢退後!(口令或命令)。 ***go ~,*** **(a)** (of workers in a factory, etc) work slowly as a protest, or in order to get attention to demands, etc. (指工廠裡的工人等)怠工(以示抗議或使提出之要求等受到注意)。 Hence, 由此產生, **,go-'slow** *n* 怠工。 **(b)** be less active: 減少活動: *You ought to go ~ until you feel really well again.* 你在完全康復以前應該減少活動。 **2** (compounds) (複合字) *,~-'going/-'moving/-'spoken,* going/moving/speaking slowly. 進行緩慢的(活動緩慢的;說話緩慢的)。

slow[3] /sləʊ; slo/ *vi, vt* [VP2C, 15B] ~ ***(sth) up/down,*** (cause to) go at a slower speed: (使)緩行;(使)減速: *S~ up/down before you reach the crossroads.* 到達十字路口前你要減速。 *You should ~ up a bit* (= stop working so hard) *if you want to avoid a breakdown.* 如果你不想把身體累病了,你應該減少一點工作。 *All this conversation ~s down the action of the play.* 所有這些對話使劇情緩慢。 **'~-down** *n* (esp) intentional decrease of industrial production by labour or management. 降低生產(尤指勞工或資方特意安排者)。

slow-worm /'sləʊ wɜ:m; 'slo,wɝm/ *n* small, limbless nonpoisonous reptile. 蛇蜥蜴(一種無腿、無毒的小爬行動物)。

sludge /slʌdʒ; slʌdʒ/ *n* [U] **1** thick, greasy mud; slush. 爛泥;泥濘的雪。 **2** sewage. 污水;下水道中的污物。 **3** thick, dirty oil or grease. 濃厚的污油或油垢。

slue /slu:; slu/ ⇨ slew[2].

slug[1] /slʌg; slʌg/ *n* slow-moving creature like a snail but without a shell, a garden pest destructive to seedlings and plants. 黑蛞蝓(一種行動緩慢,似蝸牛而無殼的園藝害蟲,危害幼苗及植物)。 ⇨ the illus at mollusc. 參看 mollusc 之插圖。

slug[2] /slʌg; slʌg/ *n* **1** bullet of irregular shape. 形狀不規則的子彈。 **2** strip of metal with a line of type along one edge. (印刷用的)嵌條。

slug[3] /slʌg; slʌg/ *vt, vi* (-gg-) (US) (美) = slog.

slug·gard /'slʌgəd; 'slʌgəd/ *n* lazy, slow-moving person. 懶散而行動遲緩的人;懶人。

slug·gish /'slʌgɪʃ; 'slʌgɪʃ/ *adj* inactive; slow-moving: 不活潑的;行動緩慢的: *a ~ river/pulse/*

liver. 流動緩慢的河(跳動緩慢的脈搏;功能減弱的肝臟)。 **~·ly** *adv* **~·ness** *n*

sluice /slu:s ; slus/ *n* [C] **1** **'~(-gate/-valve),** apparatus, contrivance, for regulating the level of water by controlling the flow into or out of (a canal, lake, etc): 水門;水閘: *open the ~-gates of the reservoir.* 放開水庫的水閘。 **2** **'~(-way),** artificial water channel, eg one made by gold-miners for rinsing gold from sand and dirt. 人工水道;水槽;洗礦槽(如金礦工人沖洗金砂者)。 **3** flow of water above, through or below a floodgate. 經閘門上面,下面或閘門的水流;堰水。□ *vt, vi* **1** [VP 6A] send a stream of water over; wash with a stream of water: 放水流過;沖洗: ~ *ore,* to separate it from gravel, etc. 沖洗礦砂(使之與砂礫等分開)。 **2** [VP6A, 15B] ~ ***(out),*** wash or flood with water from a ~. 引水道或水槽的水沖洗或灌溉。 **3** [VP3A] ~ ***out,*** (of water) rush out as from a ~. (指水)流出;奔流。

slum /slʌm ; slʌm/ *n* **1** court, alley or street of small, badly-built, dirty, crowded houses: 房屋骯髒而擁擠的巷弄或街道;陋巷: *live in a ~.* 居於陋巷。 **2 the ~s,** part(s) of a town where there are such houses. 貧民區;貧民窟。 ~ **clearance,** the demolishing of ~s and the rehousing of the people living in them. 消除貧民窟運動(重新安置貧民窟住戶的努力)。□ *vi* (-mm-) **1** visit the ~s to give charitable aid to the people in them. 訪問貧民窟而給予慈善救濟。 **2** (colloq) live very cheaply. (俗)過貧民窟般的生活;過貧苦生活。 **~my** *adj* of ~s: 貧民窟的: *a ~my part of the town.* 城市裡的貧民窟。

slum·ber /'slʌmbə(r) ; 'slʌmbɚ/ *vi, vt* (liter and rhet) (文學及修辭) **1** [VP2A] sleep, esp sleep peacefully or comfortably. 睡眠;(尤指)安祥而舒服地睡。 **2** [VP15B] pass (time) in ~: 以睡眠度過(時間): ~ *away a hot afternoon.* 以睡覺打發掉一個炎熱的下午。□ *n* (often *pl*) sleep: (常作複數)睡眠: *fall into a troubled ~;* 進入不安寧的睡眠; *disturb sb's ~(s).* 打擾某人的睡眠;擾人清夢。 **~er** *n* one who ~s. 睡眠者。 **~·ous** /-əs ; -əs/ *adj* sleepy. 想睡的;不活潑的。

slump /slʌmp ; slʌmp/ *vi* **1** [VP2A, C] drop or fall heavily: 沉重地落下或倒下;重陷: *Tired from his walk, he ~ed into a chair.* 他走累了,一屁股坐在一張椅子上。 *The bullet entered his chest and he ~ed down to the floor.* 子彈打進他的胸膛,於是他重重地倒在地板上。 **2** [VP2A] (of prices, trade, business activity) fall steeply or suddenly. (指價格、貿易、商業活動)突然下落,下跌或下降;暴跌。□ *n* [C] general drop in prices, trade activity, etc; business depression. (物價、商業活動等的) 普遍下降或跌落;商業蕭條;不景氣。

slung /slʌŋ ; slʌŋ/ *pt, pp* of sling.

slunk /slʌŋk ; slʌŋk/ *pt, pp* of slink.

slur /slɜ:(r) ; slɝ/ *vt, vi* (-rr-) **1** [VP6A] join (sounds, letters, words) so that they are indistinct; (music) sing or play legato. 連接(聲音、字母、字)使之不清楚;含糊地讀或寫;(音樂)圓滑唱;圓滑奏。 **2** [VP 3A] ~ ***over sth,*** deal quickly with in an attempt to conceal: 意圖掩飾或隱匿而匆匆處理; 略過; 忽視: *He ~red over the dead man's faults and spoke chiefly of his virtues.* 他對死者的過失輕輕帶過,主要講述他的美德。□ *n* **1** [U, C] reproach; suggestion of wrongdoing: 責備;微詞;對過失的諷示: *cast a ~ on sb's reputation;* 損毀某人的名譽; *keep one's reputation free from ~.* 保持美譽(使不受責備)。 **2** [C] act of ~ring sounds. 發含糊音。 **3** [C] (music) the mark ⌒ or ⌣ used to show that two or more notes are to be sung to one syllable or performed legato. (音樂)連結線;圓滑線(表示兩個以上的音符唱做一個音節或圓滑演奏的符號,即⌒或⌣。記於同度音符者稱連結線,記於不同度音符者稱圓滑線)。⇨ the illus at notation. 參看 notation 之挿圖。

slurry /'slʌrɪ ; 'slɝɪ/ *n* [U] thin semi-liquid mixture of cement, clay, mud, etc. 水泥、黏土、泥漿等的半流體稀薄混合物。

slush /slʌʃ ; slʌʃ/ *n* [U] soft, melting snow; soft mud; (fig) foolish sentiment. 半融之雪;爛泥;(喻)痴情;愚痴情懷。 **'~ fund** *n* (comm) fund of money used by a business company for the purpose of bribing public officials, etc. (商)用以行賄官員等的錢。 **~y** *adj*

slut /slʌt ; slʌt/ *n* slovenly woman; slattern. 邋遢女子;懶女人。 **~·tish** /-ɪʃ ; -ɪʃ/ *adj*

sly /slaɪ ; slaɪ/ *adj* (-er, -est) **1** deceitful; keeping or doing things secretly; seeming to have, suggesting, secret knowledge: 狡詐的;詭譎的;暗中進行的;似有或含示有祕聞的: *a sly look.* 詭譎的神情。 ***a sly dog,*** secretive person. 做事隱祕的人。 ***on the sly,*** secretly. 祕密地;暗中地。 **2** playful, mischievous. 好玩的;頑皮的;淘氣的。 **sly·ly** *adv* **sly·ness** *n*

smack[1] /smæk ; smæk/ *n* [C] **1** (sound of a) blow given with the open hand on sth with a flat surface; sound of the lips parted suddenly or of a whip: 掌摑;掌摑聲;咂唇聲;拍擊聲: *with a ~ of the lips,* with this sound (suggesting enjoyment of food or drink); 咂着嘴唇(表示對食物或飲料的欣賞); *give sb a ~ on the lips,* a loud kiss. 給某人一個響吻。 *I heard the ~* (= crack) *of a whip.* 我聽到鞭子的噼啪聲。 **2** slap, blow: 拍擊;打擊: *give the ball a hard ~,* hit it hard (eg in cricket). 用力擊球(如板球)。 ***get a ~ in the eye,*** (colloq) experience a setback; suffer a sharp disappointment. (俗)遭受挫折;感到很大的失望。 ***have a ~ at sth,*** (colloq) have a try to do it. (俗)試做某事。□ *vt* [VP6A] **1** strike with the open hand: 掌摑;拍擊: ~ *a naughty child.* 掌摑淘氣的孩子。 **2** ~ ***one's lips,*** part the lips with a ~ing sound to show pleasure (at food or drink, or in anticipation of other sensual pleasures). 咂唇作響(表示對飲食感到滿意,或預期其他肉體上的樂趣)。□ *adv* in a sudden and violent way: 急劇而猛烈地: *run ~ into a brick wall;* 猛然撞在磚牆上; *hit sb ~ in the eye.* 猛然打在某人的眼部。 **~er** *n* (colloq) (俗) **1** loud kiss. 響吻。 **2** pound (£) or dollar. 英鎊或美元。 **~·ing** *n* act or occasion of hitting with the palm of the hand: 用巴掌打;掌摑: *The child needs a good ~ing.* 這孩子該好好打一頓。

smack[2] /smæk ; smæk/ *n* small sailing-boat for fishing. 小漁舟;捕魚小帆船。

smack[3] /smæk ; smæk/ *vi* [VP3A], *n* ~ ***of,*** (have a) slight flavour or suggestion (of): 微帶某味;微含某意;滋味;氣味;意味: *opinions that ~ of heresy;* 帶有異端意味的意見; *medicine that ~s of sulphur;* 微帶硫磺氣味的藥; *have a ~ of obstinacy in one's character.* 某人性格有點頑强。

small /smɔ:l ; smɔl/ *adj* (-er, -est) (opp of *big* or *large;* also ⇨ little) (爲 big 或 large 之相反字) **1** not large in degree, size, etc: 小的;少的: *a ~ town/room/audience/sum of money, etc;* 小鎮(小房間;人數少的聽衆;小額的錢等); *a ~ pony,* 小馬, Cf 參較 *a nice little pony,* 漂亮的小馬, 'little' being preferred when there are emotive implications; 有感情成分時,宜用 'little'; ~ *children,* 小孩們, Cf 參較 *charming/nice/naughty, etc little children.* 可愛的(漂亮的,頑皮的等)小孩們。 **2** not doing things on a large scale: 小規模的: ~ *farmers/business men/shopkeepers.* 小農(小本商人;小店東)。 **3** unimportant, trifling. 不重要的;瑣細的。 ***be thankful for ~ mercies,*** for trifling pieces of good fortune. 對小的恩惠或幸運要表示感激。 **'~ talk,** conversation about everyday and unimportant social matters. 閒談;閒聊。 **4** (attrib only) (僅作形容用法) *a ~ eater,* person who eats ~ quantities of food. 食量小的人。 **5** morally mean; ungenerous: 卑鄙的;卑劣的;氣量狹小的;吝嗇的: *Only a ~ man/a man with a ~ mind would behave so badly.* 祇有卑鄙的(小心眼的)人行爲才會這樣惡劣。 Hence, 由此產生, **,~-'minded** *adj* 氣量小的;心地狹小的。 **6** of low social position; humble:

社會地位低的;卑微的: *great and* ~, all classes of people. 社會各階層。 **7** ***in a ~ way,*** modestly, unpretentiously: 適度地;謙恭地;小範圍地: *He has contributed to scientific progress in a ~ way.* 他對於科學的進展小有貢獻。*They live in quite a ~ way,* simply and without social ambitions. 他們過着樸實的生活。 **8** little or no: 些微的;幾無的: *have ~ cause for gratitude.* 幾無可感激的原因。*He failed, and ~ wonder,* It is not surprising. 他失敗了,如衆所料。 **9** (compounds and special uses) (複合字及特殊用法) **'~-arms** *n pl* weapons light enough to be carried in the hand by a single soldier, eg rifles, revolvers. 輕武器(可由一士兵單獨携帶者,如步槍、左輪等)。 **~ change** *n* **(a)** coins of ~ denominations: 小額硬幣: *Can you give me ~ change for this note?* 你能不能把這張鈔票兌成小額的硬幣? **(b)** (fig) trivial remarks; light conversation. (喻)無關重要的話;輕鬆的談話。 **'~ fry** *n* ⇨ fry². **'~-holding** *n* (in GB) piece of land under fifty acres in extent let or sold to sb for cultivation. (英)小片耕地(五十英畝以下者)。 **'~·holder** *n* person owning or renting a ~holding. (擁有或租有小片耕地的)小農。 **the ~ hours** *n pl* ⇨ hour(1). **~ letters** *n pl* not capitals. 小寫字母。 **'~·pox** *n* [U] serious contagious disease which leaves permanent scars on the skin. 天花(傳染病的一種)。 **'~·time** *adj* (colloq) of minor importance; third-rate. (俗)不重要的;三等的;劣等的。 ***the still, ~ voice,*** the voice of conscience. 良心的低呼。 ***on the '~ side,*** somewhat too small. 略嫌小;太小了一點。 ***look/feel ~,*** be humiliated. 自慚形穢;感到羞愧。 □ *adv* ***sing ~,*** ⇨ sing(1). □ *n* ***the ~ of,*** the slenderest part of: 最纖細部分: *the ~ of the back.* 後腰(背部的最細處)。 **~s,** (colloq) ~ articles of clothing (for laundering). (俗)內衣褲。 **~·ness** *n*

smarmy /'smɑːmɪ; 'smɑrmɪ/ *adj* (GB, colloq) ingratiating; trying to win favour by flattery, etc. (英,俗)迎合的;逢迎的;巴結的。

smart¹ /smɑːt; smɑrt/ *adj* (-er, -est) **1** bright; new-looking; clean; well-dressed: 鮮明的;新奇的;整潔的;衣冠楚楚的: *a ~ hat/suit/car.* 別緻的帽子(套裝,汽車)。*You look very ~.* 你看起來很帥。*Go and make yourself ~ before we call on the Joneses.* 我們去拜訪瓊斯家以前,你先去打扮整齊。 **2** fashionable; conspicuous in society: 時髦的;社會上特出的;有名氣的: *the '~ set;* 時髦的一群; *~ people.* 社會名流。 **3** clever; skilful; having a good, quick brain; showing ingenuity: 聰敏的;有技巧的;機靈的;精明的;有創造力的: *a ~ student/officer;* 一個聰敏的學生(幹練的軍官); *a ~ retort/saying;* 巧妙的反駁(說法); *~ dealing,* clever and intelligent, but perhaps dishonest. 巧妙的手段(但可能是狡滑的)。 **4** quick; brisk: 輕快的;敏捷的: *go for a ~ walk;* 做一次輕快的散步; *start out at a ~ pace.* 以輕快的步子起程。 ***Look ~!*** Hurry! 趕快!趕緊! **5** severe: 厲害的;劇烈的: *~ punishment;* 嚴厲的處罰; *a ~ rebuke;* 嚴厲的呵斥; *a ~ box on the ear.* 重重的一記耳光。 **~·ly** *adv* **~·ness** *n* **~en** /'smɑːtn; 'smɑrtn/ *vt, vi* [VP6A, 15B, 2C] ***~en (oneself) (up),*** make or become ~(1, 4): 使或變得漂亮、整潔等;使或變得活潑、敏捷等: *~en oneself up to receive visitors.* 打扮整潔以便迎客。*She has ~ened up since*

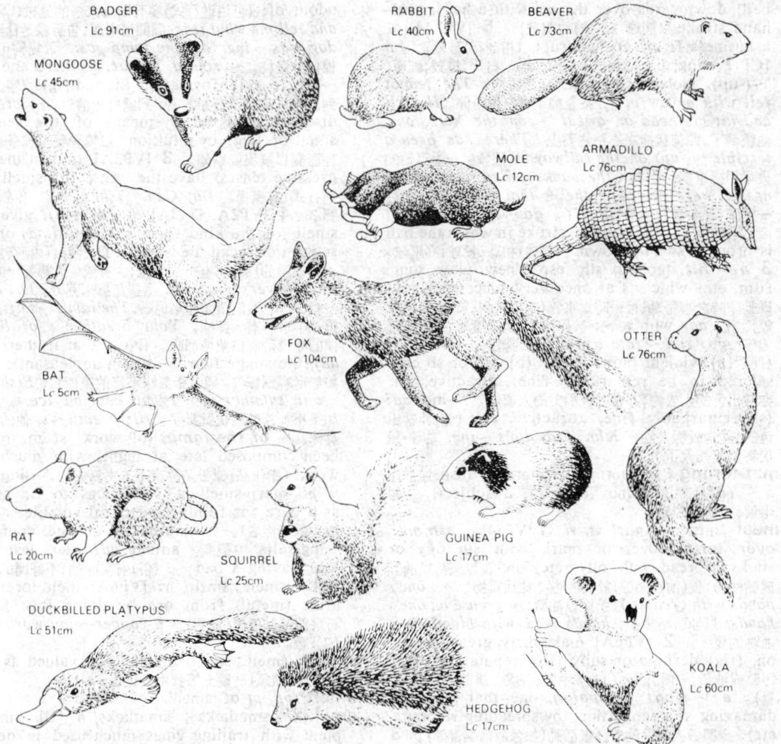

small wild animals

I met her last. 我上次見到她以後，她變得活潑了。

smart² /smɑːt ; smɑrt/ *vt* [VP2A, C, 3A] feel or cause a sharp pain (of body or mind): 感到或引起(身體或心靈方面的)劇痛: *The smoke made my eyes ~.* 烟使我的眼睛感到劇痛。*He was ~ing under an injustice／under his father's rebukes.* 他因受冤屈(挨父親斥責)而深感痛苦: *She was ~ing with vexation.* 她因有事煩惱而痛苦。 **~ for,** suffer the consequences of, be paid out for: 因…而吃苦頭，受罪等；因…而付出代價: *He will make you ~ for this impudence.* 你這次對他的失禮他必將給你顏色看。□ *n* [U] sharp pain, bodily or mental: (身體或心靈方面的)劇痛: *The ~ of his wound kept him awake.* 他傷口的劇痛使他無法入睡。

smash /smæʃ ; smæʃ/ *vt, vi* **1** [VP6A, 15A, B, 22, 2A, C] break, be broken, violently into small pieces: (被)打破；(被)打碎；(被)搗爛: *~ a window.* 打破一扇窗戶。*The drunken man ~ed up all the furniture.* 那醉漢搗毀了所有的家具。*The firemen ~ed in／down the doors.* 消防人員破門而入。*Don't ~ the door open; I have a key!* 不要把門撞開；我有鑰匙！ ˌ**~-and-ˈgrab raid,** one in which a thief ~es a shop-window, eg a jeweller's, and grabs valuables from behind it. 破窗行竊(竊賊打破珠寶店等之櫥窗，竊走貴重物品)。 **2** [VP2A, C] rush, force a way, violently (*into, through, etc*): 猛衝；猛然撞入；猛然碰撞: *The car ~ed into a wall.* 汽車撞到牆。 **3** [VP6A] deal a heavy blow to; defeat: 痛擊；重擊；打敗: *give sb a ~ing blow;* 重擊某人；*~ the enemy;* 擊敗敵人；*~ a record,* (in sport, etc) set up a far better record. (運動等)大破記錄；遠勝舊記錄；創造新記錄。 **4** [VP6A] (tennis) hit (a ball) downwards over the net with a hard, overhand stroke. (網球)殺(球)；扣(球)。 **5** [VP2A] (of a business firm) go bankrupt. (指商行)破產。□ *n* [C] **1** ~ing; breaking to pieces. 打碎；搗毀；破產。 **ˈ~(-up),** violent collision: 猛烈碰撞: *The teapot fell with an awful ~.* 茶壺掉下來打得粉碎。*He fell and hit his head an awful ~ on the kerbstone.* 他跌倒了，頭部猛撞在馬路邊石上。*There has been a terrible ~(-up) on the railway.* 曾經發生一次可怕的火車相撞車禍。*When the banks failed, many businesses were ruined in the ~ that followed.* 銀行一倒閉，許多商行連帶地破產了。 ***go ~,*** be ruined. 破產；毀滅；垮臺。 **2** (tennis) stroke in which the ball is brought swiftly down. (網球)扣球；殺球；高壓球。 **3** ***a ~ hit,*** (colloq) sth (esp a new play, song, film, etc) which is at once very successful. (俗)轟動一時之事物；風行一時之事物(尤指新劇、新歌、新影片等)。□ *adv* with a ~: 破碎地；猛烈碰撞地；打得粉碎地等: *go／run ~ into a wall.* 撞到牆上。 **~er** *n* (sl) (俚) **(a)** violent blow. 重擊。 **(b)** sth or sb considered to be remarkably fine, attractive, etc. 非常出色的人或物；非常有吸引力的人或物。 **~·ing** *adj* (sl) remarkably fine, attractive, etc: (俚)非常出色的；非常吸引人的: *John Travolta's ~ing!* 約翰•屈伏塔眞迷死人了！

smat·ter·ing /ˈsmætərɪŋ ; ˈsmætərɪŋ/ *n* (usu 通常作 ***a ~ (of)***) slight knowledge (*of* a subject). 一知半解；淺薄的知識。

smear /smɪə(r) ; smɪr/ *vt, vi* **1** [VP14] ***~ sth on／over／with,*** cover or mark with sth oily or sticky; spread (sth oily, etc) on: 覆以或沾以油質或黏性物；敷(油質物等)於；塗、搽、抹油質物: *~ one's hands with grease;* 雙手塗以油脂；*~ grease on one's hands;* 以油脂塗雙手；*hands ~ed with blood.* 染有血跡的雙手。 **2** [VP6A] make dirty, greasy marks on; (fig) defame or sully (sb's reputation). 沾以汚跡或油漬；弄髒；使汚；(喻)中傷、玷辱、誹謗(某人的名譽)。 ***a ˈ~(ing) campaign,*** one that aims at damaging sb's reputation (by spreading rumours, etc). 企圖毀人名譽的有計畫活動(如藉散佈謠言等)。 **3** [VP6A] blot; obscure the outline of: 抹掉；塗去；使模糊: *~ a word.* 塗掉一個字。 **4** [VP2A] become ~ed. 弄髒；塗汚；染汚。□ *n* [C] stain; mark made by ~ing: 汚點；汚跡；塗抹痕跡: *a ~ of paint;* 油漆的汚跡；*~s of blood on the wall.* 牆上的血跡。 **ˈ~-word** *n* word (eg *communist* in US) suitable for ~ing (sb's reputation). 足以中傷或毀人名譽的字眼(如在美國稱人'共產黨員')。

smell¹ /smel ; smɛl/ *n* **1** [U] that one of the five senses which is special to the nose: 嗅覺: *Taste and ~ are closely connected.* 味覺和嗅覺關係密切。*S~ is more acute in dogs than in men.* 狗的嗅覺比人靈敏。 **2** [C, U] that which is noticed by means of the nose; quality that affects this sense: 氣味；引起嗅覺的特質: *What a nice／horrible／unusual ~!* 多麼好聞(難聞，不尋常)的氣味！ *There's a ~ of cooking.* 有一股食物的香味。*I like the ~ of thyme.* 我喜歡麝香草的氣味。 **3** [C] (without an *adj*) bad or unpleasant quality that affects the nose: (不加形容詞)臭味；難聞的氣味: *What a ~!* 多難聞的氣味！ **4** [C] (usu 通常作 **a ~**) act of breathing in through the nose to get the ~(2) of sth: 嗅；聞: *Have／Take a ~ of this egg and tell me whether it's bad.* 聞一聞這個蛋，告訴我是不是壞的。

smell² /smel ; smɛl/ *vt, vi* (*pt, pp* smelt /smelt ; smɛlt/) **1** [VP6A, 19A] (not in the progressive tenses; often with *can, could*) be aware of through the sense of smell: (不用進行式；常與 can, could 連用)嗅出；聞到；經由嗅覺察覺: *Can／Do you ~ anything unusual?* 你有沒有聞到(一股)特別的氣味？ *The camels smelt the water a mile off.* 駱駝嗅出一哩外有水。*I can ~ something burning.* 我聞到有燒焦的氣味。 ***~ a rat,*** ⇨ rat. **2** [VP6A, 15B, 2A, C] (with progressive tenses possible) use one's sense of smell in order to learn sth; inhale the odour of: (可用進行式)嗅；聞；吸入…的氣味: *S~ this and tell me what it is.* 聞聞這東西，告訴我是什麼。*The dog was ~ing (at) the lamp-post.* 那隻狗正在聞那根(路)燈柱。 ***~ round／about,*** go here and there ~ing, to get information (lit and fig). (字面及喻)到處用鼻子聞以察知某事；到處打聽消息。 ***~ sth out,*** discover, hunt out, by means of the sense of smell or (fig) by intuition. 以嗅覺發現或察知；(喻)藉直覺以發現或察知。 **3** [VP2A] (not in the progressive tenses) have the sense of smell: (不用進行式)有嗅覺: *Do／Can fishes ~?* 魚類有嗅覺嗎？ **4** [VP2A, D, 3A] ***~ (of sth),*** give out a smell (of the kind specified by an *adj* or *adv*); suggest or recall the smell (of): 發出(由形容詞或副詞所顯示的)氣味；有…的氣味；含有或令人想起…的氣味: *The flowers ~ sweet.* 這些花氣味芬芳。*The dinner ~s good.* 這飯菜聞起來眞香。*The lamb ~s of garlic.* 這羔羊(肉)有大蒜味。*Your breath ~s of brandy.* 你的呼吸帶有白蘭地酒味。(Note that if there is no *adj*, the suggestion is usu sth unpleasant): (注意：如無形容詞修飾，通常指氣味不好的東西): *Fish soon ~s in summer if it is not kept on ice.* 魚在夏天如果不加冷凍很快就臭了。*His breath ~s.* 他的呼吸有臭味。 ***~ of the lamp,*** (of work) seem to have been composed late at night, with much hard work. (指作品)似乎是熬夜下工夫寫成的。 **ˈ~·ing-salts** *n pl* sharp-smelling substances to be sniffed as a cure for faintness, etc; sal volatile. 嗅鹽(治療昏暈等症者)。 **ˈ~·ing-bottle** *n* one containing ~ing-salts. 嗅鹽瓶。 **smelly** *adj* (-ier, -iest) (colloq) having a bad ~. (俗)有臭味的；不好聞的。

smelt¹ /smelt ; smɛlt/ *vt* [VP6A] melt (ore); separate (metal) from ore by doing this: 鎔解(礦石)；鎔礦以提煉(金屬): *a copper-~ing works.* 煉銅(工)廠。

smelt² /smelt ; smɛlt/ *n* small fish valued as food. 香魚；沙鑽魚(一種上等食用小魚)。

smelt³ *pp, pt* of smell².

smi·lax /ˈsmaɪlæks ; ˈsmaɪlæks/ *n* [U] kind of plant with trailing vines much used in decoration. 牛尾菜(其蔓藤多用於裝飾)。

smile /smaɪl ; smaɪl/ *n* [C] pleased, happy, amused or other expression on the face, with (usu a parting of the lips and) loosening of the face muscles: 微笑;笑臉(愉快、高興、歡喜等的面部表情): *There was a pleasant/ironical/amused, etc ~ on her face.* 她露出了悅人的(諷刺的,高興的等)微笑。*He was all ~s,* looked very happy. 他滿臉笑容(看起來非常高興)。*His face was wreathed in ~s.* 他面帶笑容。□ *vi, vt* **1** [VP2A, B, 4B, 3A] **~ (at/on/upon),** give a ~ or ~s; show pleasure, amusement, sympathy, contempt, irony, etc by this means: 微笑;以微笑表現愉快、興趣、同情、輕視、諷刺等: *He never ~s.* 他從不露笑臉。*What/who are you smiling at?* 你在笑什麼(誰)? *Fortune has not always ~d upon* (= favoured) *me.* 幸運之神並不一直向我微笑(垂青於我)。*He ~d to see her so happy.* 看到她這麼高興,他笑了。 **2** [VP6B] express by means of a ~: 以微笑表示: *Father ~d his approval.* 父親以微笑表示讚許。*She ~d her thanks.* 她以微笑表示感謝。 **3** [VP6B] give the kind of ~ indicated: 發出某種微笑: *~ a bitter ~.* 苦笑。**smil·ing·ly** *adv* with a ~ or ~s. 帶微笑地;微笑着。

smirch /smɜːtʃ; smɝtʃ/ *vt* [VP6A] make dirty; (fig) dishonour. 使汚;弄髒;(喻)汚辱;玷汚。□ *n* [C] (fig) blot or stain. (喻)汚點;瑕疵。

smirk /smɜːk; smɝk/ *vi* [VP2A], *n* (give a) silly, self-satisfied smile. 傻笑;得意地笑。

smite /smaɪt; smaɪt/ *vt, vi* (*pt* smote /sməʊt; smot/, *pp* smitten /ˈsmɪtn; ˈsmɪtn̩/) (archaic, or, in mod use, hum or liter) (古;或現代用法中,諧或文) **1** [VP6A] strike; hit hard: 打;痛擊;重擊: *He smote the ball into the grandstand.* 他把球打進了看臺。*His conscience smote him,* he was conscience-stricken. 他的良心受到譴責。*He was smitten with remorse/smitten with that pretty girl.* 他悔恨交加(那個漂亮女孩子令他神魂顛倒)。 **2** [VP6A] defeat utterly: 徹底擊敗: *God will ~ our enemies.* 上帝將擊潰我們的敵人。**3** [VP2A, C] strike; come forcibly: 打;擊;侵襲: *A strange sound smote upon our ears.* 一怪聲震耳欲聾。

smith /smɪθ; smɪθ/ *n* worker in iron or other metals: 鐵匠;冶工;鍛工: *ˈblack~.* 鐵匠。⇨ black, gold, silver, tin. **smithy** /ˈsmɪðɪ; ˈsmɪθɪ/ *n* black~'s workshop. 鐵匠店。

smith·er·eens /ˌsmɪðəˈriːnz; ˌsmɪðəˈrinz/ *n pl* small fragments: 碎片;碎屑: *smash sth to/into ~.* 將某物打得粉碎。

smit·ten /ˈsmɪtn; ˈsmɪtn̩/ *pp* of smite.

smock /smɒk; smɑk/ *n* loose garment (with smocking on it) like an overall. (有蜂窩形褶飾,式樣類似工作服的)罩衫;罩衣。**~·ing** *n* [U] kind of ornamentation on a garment made by gathering the cloth tightly with stitches. (衣服上)蜂窩形褶飾。

smog /smɒg; smɑg/ *n* [U] mixture of fog and smoke. 烟霧(烟與霧的混合物)。

smoke[1] /sməʊk; smok/ *n* **1** [U] visible vapour with particles of carbon, etc coming from a burning substance: 烟(燃物所生的含炭粒霧氣): *~ pouring from factory chimneys;* 工廠烟囱冒出的烟; *ˌcigaˈrette/ciˈgar ~.* 香烟(雪茄)的烟。***end up in ~,*** come to, end in, nothing. 烟消雲散;轉眼成空;化爲烏有。***go up in ~,*** be burnt up; (fig) be without result, leave nothing solid or worth while behind. 被燒光;(喻)無結果;未留下實在或有價值之物。***There is no ~ without fire,*** (prov) ⇨ fire[1](1). **ˈ~-bomb** *n* one that sends out clouds of ~ (used to conceal military operations, etc). 烟幕彈(用以掩護軍事行動等者)。 **ˈ~-cured/-dried** *adj* (of ham, certain kinds of fish, etc) dried and cured in wood ~. (指火腿,某些種類的魚等)烟燻的。**ˈ~-screen** *n* clouds of ~ made to hide military or naval operations; (fig) explanation, etc designed to mislead people about one's real intentions, etc. 烟幕(掩護軍事行動者);(喻)掩飾作用的解釋等(使人發生錯覺以掩飾眞正意圖)。**ˈ~-stack** *n* **(a)** outlet for ~ and steam from a steamship (and, US, from a steam locomotive). 輪船的烟囱;(美國又指)火車的烟囱。**(b)** tall chimney. 高大的烟囱。 **2** [C] act of smoking tobacco: 吸烟: *stop working and have a ~;* 停止工作吸一口烟; (colloq) cigar or cigarette: (俗)雪茄;香煙: *pass the ~s round.* 傳遞香煙。**~·less** *adj* **1** that burns without ~: 燃燒而無烟的: *~less fuel.* 無烟燃料。 **2** free from ~: 不發烟的;無烟的: *a ~less zone,* where ~ is prohibited; 無烟帶;禁烟區; *the ~less atmosphere of the countryside.* 鄉間不含烟的清新空氣。**smoky** *adj* (-ier, -iest) **1** giving out much ~; full of ~: 發烟多的;充滿烟的: *smoky chimneys/fires;* 冒烟的烟囱(火); *the smoky atmosphere of an industrial town.* 工業城市多烟的空氣。 **2** like ~ in smell, taste or appearance. 氣息、味道或外表似烟的。

smoke[2] /sməʊk; smok/ *vi, vt* **1** [VP2A] give out smoke, or sth thought to resemble smoke, eg visible vapour or steam: 冒烟;冒氣;起烟霧: *a smoking volcano.* 冒烟的火山。*That oil-lamp ~s badly.* 那盞油燈烟冒得很厲害。 **2** [VP2A] (of a fire or fireplace) send out smoke into the room (instead of up the chimney): (指火或壁爐)烟燻入屋內(未由烟囱冒出): *This fireplace ~s badly.* 這壁爐烟燻得厲害。**3** [VP2A, 6A] draw in and let out the smoke of burning tobacco or other substance: 抽烟: *~ a pipe/cigar, etc.* 抽烟斗(雪茄等)。*Do you ~?* 你抽不抽煙? *If you ~ opium, give it up.* 如果你吸鴉片,就戒掉吧。 **4** [VP22] bring (*oneself*) into a specific state by smoking tobacco, etc: 因抽烟而(使自己)入於某種狀態: *He ~d himself sick.* 他因吸烟而致病。 **5** [VP2A, C] (of pipes, cigars, etc, with passive force): (指烟斗、雪茄等,含被動意義): *This pipe ~s well,* is satisfactory when ~d. 這烟斗抽起來很够味。*A good cigar will ~* (= can be ~d) *for at least half an hour.* 一根好的雪茄至少可抽半小時。**6** [VP6A] dry and preserve (meat, fish) with smoke (from wood fires): 用烟燻製(肉,魚): *~d ham/salmon.* 燻製的火腿(鮭)。**7** [VP6A] stain, darken, dry, with smoke: 燻汚;燻黃;燻黑;燻乾: *a ~d ceiling;* 燻黃的天花板; *a sheet of ~d glass,* eg through which to look at the sun. 一片燻黑的玻璃片(可用以觀看太陽等)。 **8** [VP6A, 15B] send smoke on to (plants, insects): 以烟燻(植物,昆虫): *~ the plants in a greenhouse,* to kill insects. 以烟燻溫室植物(以殺死害虫)。***~ sth out,*** force to leave by smoking: 因烟燻出: *~ out snakes from a hole.* 燻出洞中的蛇。**smok·ing** *n* [U] (*gerund,* in compounds) (動名詞,用於複合字中) **ˈsmoking-carriage/-car/-compartment** *nn* one for smokers on a railway train. (火車上的)吸烟車廂。**ˈsmoking-mixture** *n* blend of tobaccos for smoking in pipes. (烟斗用的)混合烟草。**ˈsmoking-room** *n* room (in a hotel, etc) where smoking is permitted. (旅館等處的)吸烟室。**smoker** *n* **1** person who habitually ~s tobacco. 吸烟者;癮君子。 **2** smoking-carriage on a train. (火車上的)吸烟車廂。

smol·der /ˈsməʊldə(r); ˈsmoldɚ/ ⇨ smoulder.

smooth[1] /smuːð; smuð/ *adj* (-er, -est) **1** having a surface like that of glass; free from roughness or (fig) difficulty: 平滑的;平靜的;光滑如鏡的;(喻)無困難的;順利的: *~ paper/skin;* 光滑的紙(皮膚); *a ~ road;* 平坦的路; *a ~ sheet of ice;* 一片光滑的冰; *~ to the touch;* 摸起來光滑的; *a ~ sea,* calm, free from waves; 平靜的海; *make things ~ for sb,* (fig) remove difficulties for him. (喻)爲某人除去困難。*The way is now ~,* is no longer difficult. 前路現在已無阻碍;困難清除了。***take the rough with the ~,*** take things (both the good and the bad things of life) as they come. 逆來順受。**ˈ~-bore** *adj* (of a gun) having no rifling in the barrel. (指槍砲)滑膛的;無膛線(或來復線)的。**ˌ~-ˈfaced** *adj* (fig) friendly but hypocritical. (喻)假友善的;作友善狀的;虛僞的。 **2** (of movement) free from shaking, bumping, etc: (指運動)不搖晃的;不顚簸的;平穩的: *a ~ ride in a good car;* 坐一部好汽車所作的一次平穩行駛; *a ~ flight in a* *jet airliner;* 乘噴射客機所作的一次平穩航行; *a ~ crossing,* eg by sea from England to France. 一次平穩的橫渡(如從英國渡海到法國)。 **3** (of a liquid mixture) free from lumps; well beaten or mixed: (指液體混合物)無顆粒的; 勻和的; 攪拌得好的: *a ~ paste.* 沒有疙瘩的糊。 **4** free from harshness of sound or taste; flowing easily: 無刺耳聲音的;無澀味的;悅耳的;柔和的;醇美的;圓潤的;流暢的: *~ verse;* 流暢的詩句; *a ~ voice;* 悅耳的聲音; *~ claret/whisky.* 味醇的紅葡萄酒(威士忌)。 **5** (of a person, his manner) flattering, polite, unruffled, conciliatory: (指人,舉止及儀態)奉承的;有禮貌的;溫和的;願修好的: *a ~ temper;* 溫和的脾氣; *~ manners;* 奉承的態度; *a ~ face,* often used to suggest hypocrisy. 溫和有禮的面孔(常暗示虛僞); Hence, 由此產生, ˌ**~-ˈfaced/-ˈspoken/-ˈtongued** *adjj* (all having a suggestion of insincerity). (均含示不誠實)。 **~·ly** *adv* in a ~ manner: 平滑地;光滑地;平靜地: *a ~ly running engine.* 運轉平穩的引擎。 *Things are not going very ~ly,* There are troubles, obstacles, interruptions, etc. 事情進行得不太順利。 **~·ness** *n*

smooth² /smuːð ; smuð/ *vt, vi* **1** [VP6A, 15B] ~ ***sth (down/out/away/over),*** make smooth: 使光滑;使平滑;使順利;使平靜等: *~ down one's dress;* 拉平衣服; *~ away/over obstacles/difficulties/perplexities, etc,* get rid of them. 清除障碍(困難,困惑等)。 *~* ***sb's path,*** (fig) make progress easier. (喻)清除或鋪平某人的道路;掃除前途的障碍。 **2** [VP2C] become smooth or quiet: 變光滑;變平滑;變平靜: *The sea has ~ed down.* 海上已風平浪靜。 **3** (compounds) (複合字) ˈ**~·ing-iron** *n* (*iron* is the usu word) flat-iron used (heated) to ~ linen, clothes, etc. (通常用 iron)熨斗;熨斗。 ˈ**~·ing-plane** *n* small plane for finishing the planing of wood. 小鉋子(用以修整鉋平木料者)。 □ *n* act of ~ing: 使光滑、平滑、平靜等: ***give one's hair a ~.*** 梳理一下頭髮。

smor·gas·bord /ˈsmɔːgəsbɔːd ; ˈsmɔrgəsˌbɔrd/ *n* [U] (Swedish) meal with a variety of dishes served from a buffet. (瑞典式)精美自助餐(備有各式精美菜肴)。

smote /sməʊt ; smot/ *pt* of smite.

smother /ˈsmʌðə(r) ; ˈsmʌðɚ/ *vt* **1** [VP6A] cause the death of, by stopping the breath of or by keeping air from; kill by suffocation. 使窒息; 悶死。 **2** [VP6A] put out (a fire); keep (a fire) down (so that it burns slowly) by covering *with* ashes, sand, etc. 熄(火);覆以灰、沙等而使(火)慢燃。 **3** [VP14] ~ ***sth/sb with sth,*** cover, wrap up, overwhelm with: 覆蓋;掩蔽;掩沒;壓止: *~ a grave with flowers/a child with kisses/one's wife with kindness;* 以花覆蓋墳墓(接二連三地吻小孩;體貼得叫妻子不知所措); *be ~ed with/in dust by passing cars.* 全身沾滿來往汽車所揚起的塵土。 **4** [VP6A, 15B] suppress; hold back: 遏止;壓制: *~ a yawn/one's anger/feelings of resentment;* 抑制呵欠(憤怒,憎恨); *~ up a scandal,* try to conceal it. 掩飾醜聞。 □ *n* (usu **a ~**) cloud of dust, smoke, steam, spray, etc. 塵、烟、水氣等造成的煙霧。

smoul·der (US = **smol-**) /ˈsməʊldə(r) ; ˈsmoldɚ/ *vi* [VP2A, C] burn slowly without flame; (fig, of feelings, etc) exist or operate unseen, undetected, suppressed, etc: 無火焰地悶燒;(喻,指感情等)潛伏;醞釀: *~ing discontent/hatred/rebellion.* 醞釀着的不滿(憎恨,反叛)。 □ *n* [U] ~ing burning: 悶燒;不發火焰的燃燒: *The ~ became a blaze.* 悶火變成了烈焰。

smudge /smʌdʒ ; smʌdʒ/ *n* [C] **1** dirty mark; blotted or blurred mark: 污點;污跡;斑痕: *You've got a ~ on your cheek.* 你的臉頰上有一塊污跡。 *Wash your hands or you'll make ~s on the writing-paper.* 把手洗乾淨,否則你會弄髒寫字紙。 **2** (chiefly US) outdoor fire with thick smoke made to keep away insects. (主美)戶外燻虫用的濃烟。 □ *vt, vi* **1** [VP6A] make a ~ or ~s on; make a ~ on (when writing a letter or word). 弄污;(書寫時)弄髒。 **2** [VP2A] (of ink, paint, etc) become blurred or smeared. (指墨水,油漆等)變模糊或污成一片: *Ink ~s easily.* 墨水很容易污濡。

smug /smʌg ; smʌg/ *adj* (-gg-) self-satisfied; having, showing, a character that is satisfied although without ambition, imagination, broad-mindedness: 自滿的;自鳴得意的;沾沾自喜的: *a ~ smile;* 自鳴得意的微笑; *a life of ~ respectability;* 沾沾自喜的體面生活; *~ optimism;* 自鳴得意的樂觀; *~ rich men.* 自滿的有錢人。 **~·ly** *adv* **~·ness** *n*

smuggle /ˈsmʌgl ; ˈsmʌgl̩/ *vt* [VP6A, 14, 15A, B] **1** get (goods) secretly and illegally (*into, out of,* a country, *through* the customs, *across* a frontier): 走私;偸運(貨物進出某國,通過海關,越過邊界等): *~ Swiss watches into England.* 偸運瑞士錶進入英國。 **2** take (sth or sb) secretly and in defiance of rules and regulations: 偸帶(某物或某人): *~ a letter into a prison.* 偸帶信件到監獄。 **smug·gler** /ˈsmʌglə(r) ; ˈsmʌgl̩ɚ/ *n*

smut /smʌt ; smʌt/ *n* **1** [C] (mark or stain made by a) bit of soot, dirt, etc. 一點點煤烟、煤灰、油烟、塵垢等;污物;積烟;污處;污點;污跡。 **2** [U] disease of corn (wheat, etc) that causes the ears to turn black. (穀物的)黑穗病。 **3** [U] (colloq) indecent or obscene words, stories: (俗)淫詞;穢語;淫穢的故事: *Don't talk ~.* 不要說髒話。 □ *vt* (-tt-) [VP6A] mark with ~s(1). 弄污;弄髒;污染。 **~ty** *adj* (-ier, -iest) **1** dirty with ~s. 給烟灰等弄髒的;燻黑的。 **2** containing ~(3): 含淫詞的;猥褻的: *~ty stories.* 猥褻的故事。 **~·tily** /-ɪlɪ ; -ɪlɪ/ *adv* **~·ti·ness** *n*

snack /snæk ; snæk/ *n* light usu hurriedly eaten meal. 小吃;點心。 ˈ**~-bar/-counter** *nn* bar/counter where ~s may be eaten. 小吃店;小吃檯。

snaffle¹ /ˈsnæfl ; ˈsnæfl̩/ *n* ˈ**~(-bit)** horse's bit without a curb. 輕勒(無勒索的輕馬銜)。

snaffle² /ˈsnæfl ; ˈsnæfl̩/ *vt* [VP6A] (GB sl) take without permission; pinch(4). (英俚)偸;竊;不告而取。

snag /snæg ; snæg/ *n* [C] **1** rough or sharp object, root of a tree, hidden rock, which may be a source of danger. (可造成危險的)不平、尖銳、粗糙等之物;樹根;暗礁。 **2** (colloq) hidden, unknown or unexpected difficulty or obstacle: (俗)隱伏或突發的困難或障碍: *strike/come upon a ~.* 遭遇阻碍或困難。 *There's a ~ in it somewhere.* 其中某處有障碍。

snail /sneɪl ; snel/ *n* kinds of small, soft animal, most of them with a spiral shell. 蝸牛。 ⇨ the illus at mollusc. 參看 mollusc 之插圖。 ***at a ˈ~'s pace,*** very slowly. 非常緩慢;像蝸牛般行進。

snake /sneɪk ; snek/ *n* kinds of long, legless, crawling reptile, some of which are poisonous; (fig) (often ~ ***in the grass***) treacherous person who pretends to be a friend. 蛇;(喻)(常作~ in the grass) 陰險而佯爲友善的人。 ***see ~s,*** have hallucinations. 發生錯覺或幻覺。 ˈ**~-charmer** *n* person who can control ~s with music. 弄蛇者(可藉音樂控制蛇者)。 □ *vi* [VP2C] move in twists and glides: 蜿蜒;蛇行;曲折滑行: *The road ~s through the mountains.* 那條路蜿蜒穿越羣山。 **snaky** *adj* of or like a ~; (fig) venomous, ungrateful, treacherous. 蛇的;像蛇的;(喻)惡毒的;狡詐的;陰險的。

snap /snæp ; snæp/ *vt, vi* (-pp-) **1** [VP6A, 15B, 2A, 3A] ~ ***(at) (sth),*** (try to) snatch with the teeth: 咬;猛然咬;猛地咬住: *The dog ~ped at my leg.* 那條狗咬我的腿。 *The fish ~ped at the bait.* 魚咬餌。 *They ~ped at the offer,* (fig) offered eagerly to accept it. (喻)他們迫不及待地接受該提議。 *~* ***sth up,*** buy eagerly: 急切地買;搶購: *The cheapest articles were quickly ~ped up.* 最便宜的東西很快地被搶購一空。 **2** [VP6A, 14, 15A, B, 22, 2A, C] break with a sharp crack; open or close with, make, a sudden, sharp sound; say (sth), speak, sharply: 發破裂聲而折斷;啪的一聲關閉或打開;

發啪聲；厲聲地說話或說出(某事)：*He stretched the rubber band till it ~ped.* 他拉長橡皮筋，啪的一聲拉斷了。*The rope ~ped.* 繩子突然斷了。*He ~ped down the lid of the box.* 他啪噠一聲關上箱子的蓋。*He ~ped his whip.* 他揮鞭作響。*Her whip ~ped down on the pony's back.* 她的鞭子抽在小馬背上發出清脆的聲音。*The sergeant ~ped out his orders.* 那士官厲聲地發佈命令。~ ***at sb,*** speak to sb sharply: 向某人厲聲說：*I'm sorry I ~ped at you just now.* 我很抱歉剛才對你厲聲說話。~ ***one's finger at sb/in sb's face,*** make a cracking noise by flicking a finger audibly against the thumb (usu to show contempt). 向某人或當某人面彈指(通常表示輕視)。~ ***sb's 'nose/'head off,*** speak angrily to; interrupt rudely or impatiently. 向某人憤怒地說話；無禮或不耐煩地打斷某人的話。**3** [VP6A] take a ~shot (⇨ 8 below) of. 拍…的快照(參看下列第8義)。**4** (sl) ~ ***'to it,*** start moving, get going, quickly. (俚)快速地開動、移動或進行。~ ***'out of it,*** get out of a mood, habit, etc. 突然改變心情、習慣等。□ *n* **1** [C] act or sound of ~ping: 咬；猛咬；折斷；折斷聲；脆裂聲：*The dog made an unsuccessful ~ at the meat.* 那條狗企圖咬而未咬到那塊肉。*The lid shut with a ~.* 蓋子啪噠一聲關上了。*The oar broke with a ~.* 槳啪噠一聲折斷了。*S~ went the oar,* (adverbial use) It broke with a ~ping noise. (作副詞用)槳啪噠一聲斷了。**2** [C] **cold ~,** sudden, short period of cold weather. 突然而短暫的寒冷天氣。**3** [U] (colloq) energy, dash, vigour, liveliness: (俗)精力；衝力；活力；生氣：*Put some ~ into it.* 用一點勁。⇨ snappy below. 參看下列之 snappy. **4** [C] kinds of small, crisp cake: 小脆餅：(usu in compounds) (通常用於複合字中) *'ginger-~s.* 薑脆餅。**5** [C] (usu in compounds) (通常用於複合字中) catch, device for fastening things, closed by pressing. 鈎；扣(藉壓力而關閉者)。**'~-fasteners** (also 亦作 *press-stud*) fastening device used on dresses, gloves, etc. 暗扣；按扣。**6** = ~shot ⇨ 8 below. 參看下列第8義。**7** (attrib) done quickly and with little or no warning: (形容用法)急就的；突然的；倉卒的：*a ~ election;* 倉卒的選舉；*take a ~ vote;* 舉行臨時表決；*a ~ division,* in the House of Commons. (在下議院)匆匆分組表決。**8** (compounds, etc) (複合字等) **'~-dragon** *n* [C] (= antirrhinum) kinds of plant with flowers that are like bags and can be made to open (like lips) when pressed. 金魚草(開袋狀花，可壓之使開，形似嘴唇)。**'~-shot** *n* quickly taken photograph with a hand camera (and usu by an amateur). 快照；快相(通常爲業餘攝影師用手提照相機所拍攝)。**~py** *adj* (-ier, -iest) bright; lively: 聰明的；活潑的；生動的：***Make it ~py! Look ~py!*** (sl) Be quick about it! (俚)爽快一點！乾脆一點！**~·pish** /-ɪʃ; -ɪʃ/ *adj* inclined to ~, to be ill-tempered or irritable. 愛咬人的；脾氣大的；急躁的。**~·pish·ly** *adv* **~·pish·ness** *n*

snare /sneə(r); snɛr/ *n* [C] **1** trap, esp one with a noose, for catching small animals and birds. 羅網；陷阱(尤指有索套，用以捕捉小動物及鳥類者)。**2** (fig) sth that tempts one to expose oneself to defeat, disgrace, loss, etc: (喻)(誘人失敗、丟臉、損失等之)圈套：*His promises are a ~ and a delusion.* 他的諾言是一種圈套，也是欺騙。**3** string of gut stretched across the bottom of side-drum to produce a sharp, rattling sound. 邊鼓之響弦。**'~-drum** *n* side-drum with ~s attached. 響弦鼓。□ *vt* [VP6A] catch in a ~: 用羅網或陷阱捕捉：*~ a rabbit.* 用陷阱捕捉兔子。

snarl[1] /snɑ:l; snɑrl/ *vi, vt* [VP2A, 3A, 6A] ~ ***(at),*** (of dogs) show the teeth and growl (at); (of persons) speak in a harsh voice. (指狗)嗥叫；狺狺；(指人)咆哮；厲聲地說。□ *n* act or sound of ~ing: 嗥叫；咆哮；嗥叫聲；咆哮聲：*answer with a ~.* 咆哮着回答。

snarl[2] /snɑ:l; snɑrl/ *n* tangle; cofused state: 纏結；糾結；混亂：*the traffic ~s in a big town.* 大城市交通混亂的情形。□ *vt, vi* [VP6A, 15B, 2A, C, 3A] ~ ***(up),*** (cause to) become jammed: (使)變得擁塞或擠在一起：*The traffic (was) ~ed up.* 交通擁塞了。Hence, 由此產生，**'~-up** *n* = traffic jam. ⇨ traffic.

snatch /snætʃ; snætʃ/ *vt, vi* [VP6A, 2A, 15A, B] **1** put out the hand suddenly and take: 突然伸手拿取；搶；奪；攫取：*He ~ed the letter from me/~ed the letter out of my hand.* 他從我這裡(從我手上)搶去了那封信。*It's rude to ~.* 搶取是魯莽行爲。*He ~ed at* (ie tried to seize) *the letter but was not quick enough.* 他想搶走那封信，但動作不够快。*He ~ed up his gun and fired.* 他突然拿起槍來射擊。**2** get quickly or when a chance occurs: 迅速獲得；趁機獲取：*~ an hour's sleep/a meal;* 抓住機會睡一小時覺(吃一頓飯)；*~ a kiss.* 偷吻。□ *n* [C] **1** act of ~ing; sudden attempt to get sth by stretching out the hand: 搶；攫；奪；突然伸手拿取：*make a ~ at sth;* 攫取某物；(attrib) (形容用法) *a ~ decision,* one that is ~ed(2). 迅速決定；突下決心；趁勢決定。**2** short outburst or period: 片刻；短暫；片段；一陣：*short ~es of music;* 片段的音樂；*overhear ~es of conversation;* 偶然聽到片段的談話；*work in ~es,* not continuously. 斷斷續續地工作。**~er** *n*

snaz·zy /'snæzɪ; 'snæzɪ/ *adj* (sl) smart; fine. (俚)漂亮的；美好的。

sneak /sni:k; snik/ *vi, vt* **1** [VP2A, 3A] go quietly and furtively *(in, out, away, back, past,* etc). 潛行；偷偷走(與 in, out, away, back, past 等連用)。**2** [VP2A] ~ ***(on sb),*** (school sl) go to the teacher and tell him about the faults, wrongdoing,

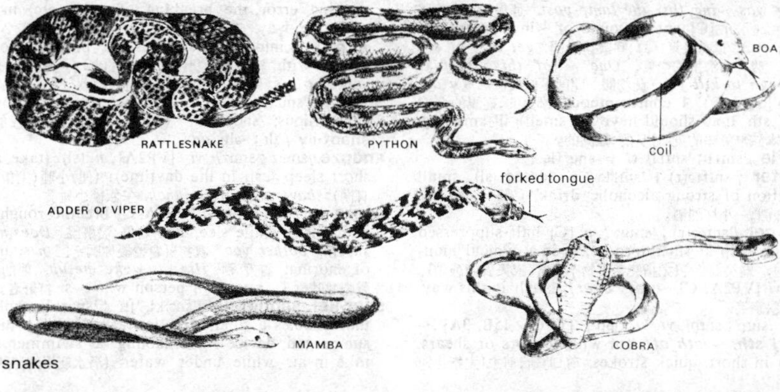

snakes

etc of another. (學校俚語)(向老師)告密;打小報告。**3** [VP6A] (sl) steal. (俚)偷竊。□ *n* **1** (sl) cowardly, treacherous person. (俚)怯懦鬼祟的人。'**~-thief** *n* petty thief; person who steals things from open doors and windows. (順手牽羊的)小偷;從開着的門窗偷東西的人。 **2** (school sl) boy or girl who ~s(2). (學校俚語)向老師告密的男生或女生。**~·ing** *adj* furtive: 鬼鬼祟祟的; 偷偷摸摸的; 詭秘的: *have a ~ing respect/sympathy, etc for sb,* respect, etc which is not shown openly; 私下(非公開地)對某人懷有敬意(表示同情等); *a ~ing suspicion,* a vague, puzzling one. 令人困擾而扯不清的嫌疑。**~·ing·ly** *adv* **sneaky** *adj* = ~ing. **~·ers** *n pl* (chiefly US) (also 亦作 ***a pair of ~ers***) rubber-soled canvas shoes; plimsolls. (主美)膠底帆布鞋;軟底鞋。

sneer /snɪə(r) ; snɪr/ *vi* [VP2A, 3A] ~ ***(at),*** show contempt by means of a derisive smile; utter contemptuous words: 嘲笑;譏誚;說輕蔑話: *~ at religion.* 嘲笑宗教。□ *n* ~ing look, smile, word or utterance: 譏誚的表情、微笑、字或言詞: *You should ignore their ~s at your efforts.* 你應當不理會他們對你努力的成果所作的嘲笑。**~·ing·ly** *adv*

sneeze /sni:z ; sniz/ *n* [C] sudden, uncontrollable outburst of air through the nose and mouth: 噴嚏: *Coughs and ~s spread diseases.* 咳嗽和噴嚏會傳播疾病。□ *vi* [VP2A] make a ~: 打噴嚏: *Use a handkerchief when you ~.* 打噴嚏的時候,用手帕遮住。***not to be ~d at,*** (colloq) not to be despised; passable: (俗)不可輕視;過得去;還可以: *A prize of £50 in the lottery is not to be ~d at.* 五十鎊的彩券獎金不可小看。

snick /snɪk ; snɪk/ *vt, vi, n* **1** (make a) small cut in sth. 細刻痕;細割痕;作細刻痕或割痕(於某物)。 **2** (cricket) (make a) slight deflection of the ball with the bat: (板球)削(球)(以球棒擦觸投出之球,使之略微偏向);削球: *~ a ball through the slips.* 削球使滾過左後或右後防區。

snicker /'snɪkə(r) ; 'snɪkɚ/ *vi, n* whinny; snigger. (指馬)嘶叫;嘶叫聲;暗笑;竊笑。

snide /snaɪd ; snaɪd/ *adj* sneering; slyly critical: 輕視的;嘲笑的;譏誚的: *~ remarks.* 譏誚話。

sniff /snɪf ; snɪf/ *vi, vt* **1** [VP2A] draw air in through the nose so that there is a sound: 以鼻吸氣而帶聲音: *They all had colds and were ~ing and sneezing.* 他們都傷風了,呼吸有聲音而且打噴嚏。 **2** [VP2A, 3A] ~ ***(at),*** ~(1) to show disapproval or contempt: 嗤之以鼻(表示輕視或不贊成): *The offer* (eg to buy a good car for £4000) *is not to be ~ed at.* 出價還算過得去(如出價四千鎊買一輛好的轎車)。 **3** [VP2A, 3A, 6A, 15B] ~ ***(at) sth;*** ~ ***sth up,*** draw in through the nose as one breathes: 用鼻子吸入;用鼻子聞;嗅: *~ the sea-air;* 吸入海上的空氣; *~ (at) a rose;* 聞玫瑰花; *a preparation* (eg for catarrh) *to be ~ed up through the nostrils.* 由鼻孔吸入的一種藥物(如治療鼻黏膜炎的藥物)。 *The dog was ~ing (at) the lamp-post.* 那隻狗正在嗅路燈柱。□ *n* [C] act or sound of ~ing; breath (of air, etc): 以鼻吸氣(聲);呼吸;嗅;聞: *get a ~ of sea air.* 吸一口海上的空氣。 *One ~ of this stuff is enough to kill you.* 此物聞一聞即足以致命。**~y** *adj* (colloq) (俗) **1** contemptuous. 鄙夷的;輕視的。 **2** (of sth that should have no smell) ill smelling. (指本該無氣味的東西)臭的;難聞的。

sniffle /'snɪfl ; 'snɪfl/ *vi* = snuffle.

snif·ter /'snɪftə(r) ; 'snɪftɚ/ *n* (dated sl) small portion of strong alcoholic drink. (過時俚語)一小份烈酒;一小杯烈酒。

snig·ger /'snɪgə(r) ; 'snɪgɚ/ *n* [C] half-suppressed laugh (esp at sth improper, or in a cynical manner). 竊笑;暗笑(尤指笑某事物不適當,或笑裏帶譏誚)。□ *vi* [VP2A, C] ~ ***(at/over),*** laugh in this way. 暗笑;竊笑。

snip /snɪp ; snɪp/ *vt, vi* (-pp-) [VP6A, 15B, 3A] ~ ***(at) sth;*** ~ ***sth off,*** cut with scissors or shears, esp in short, quick strokes: 剪;剪斷;剪去(尤指快速而張開角度小地剪動): *~ off the ends of sth;* 剪去某物的末端; *~ a hole in sth;* 在某物上剪一個洞; *~ cloth/paper.* 剪布(紙)。□ *n* **1** cut made by ~ping; sth ~ped off. 剪;剪下之物。 **2** (colloq) profitable bargain: (俗)獲利的交易;賺錢的交易;合算的交易: *Only 50p! It's a ~!* 才五十辨士!眞合算! **~·ping** *n* small piece of material ~ped off a larger piece. 從大片物料剪下來的小片。

snipe[1] /snaɪp ; snaɪp/ *n* (*pl* unchanged) (複數不變) bird which frequents marshes with a long bill. 鷸;沙雖鳥。 ⇨ the illus at water. 參看 water 之插圖。

snipe[2] /snaɪp ; snaɪp/ *vi, vt* [VP2A, 3A] ~ ***(at),*** fire shots (at) from a hiding-place, usu at long range; [VP6A] kill or hit thus. 伏擊;狙擊(通常指長距離);藉伏擊或狙擊射殺或命中。 **sniper** *n* person who ~s. 狙擊手;狙擊兵。

snip·pet /'snɪpɪt ; 'snɪpɪt/ *n* small piece cut off; (*pl*) bits (of information, news, etc). 切下的小片;斷片;碎片;(複)(消息、新聞等的)片段。

snitch /snɪtʃ ; snɪtʃ/ *vt, vi* **1** [VP6A] (sl) steal (usu sth of little or no value). (俚)偷(通常指價值很小或無價值之物)。 **2** [VP2A, 3A] ~ ***(on sb),*** sneak, inform (on sb). 告密;告發(某人)。

snivel /'snɪvl ; 'snɪvl̩/ *vi* (GB -ll-; US -l-) [VP2A] cry from pretended grief, sorrow or fear; complain in a miserable, whining way: 假哭;啜泣;哭訴;抽泣着抱怨: *a harassed woman with six ~ling children.* 帶着六個哭哭啼啼的孩子的苦命女人。**~·ler** (US = **~er**) *n* person who ~s. 假哭者;哭訴者。

snob /snɒb ; snɑb/ *n* person who pays too much respect to social position or wealth, or who despises persons who are of lower social position: 諂上欺下之人;勢利之人: '*~ appeal,* power to attract the interest of ~s. 財勢(引起勢利之人興趣的力量)。 **~·bish** /-ɪʃ ; -ɪʃ/ *adj* of or like a ~. 諂上欺下的;勢利的。**~·bish·ly** *adv* **~·bish·ness, ~·bery** /'snɒbərɪ ; 'snɑbərɪ/ *nn* [U] state, quality, of being ~bish; (*pl*) ~bish acts or utterances. 諂上欺下;勢利;(複)勢利的言行。

snood /snu:d ; snud/ *n* ornamental net worn by a woman to keep her hair in position. (女子的)束髮網。

snook /snu:k ; snuk/ *n* (only in) (僅用於) ***cock a ~ (at sb),*** (lit or fig) show impudent contempt by placing the thumb to the nose and spreading out the fingers towards him. (字面或喻)以拇指指着鼻尖並以其餘四指向對方張搖以表示輕蔑。

snooker /'snu:kə(r) ; 'snukɚ/ *n* game (a variety of *pool*) played with 15 red balls and six balls of other colours on a billiard-table. 落袋撞球遊戲(爲 pool 之一種,使用15個紅色球,及 6 個他色球)。***be ~ed,*** (colloq) be placed in a difficult position. (俗)處困境。

snoop /snu:p ; snup/ *vi* [VP2A, C, 3A] (colloq) (俗) ~ ***(about/around),*** search, examine (eg to find error, the breaking of rules, etc) in a secretive way. 窺察(以找出過失,違規等);窺探。 ~ ***into,*** pry into matters one is not properly concerned with. 窺視或探聽(與己無關的事)。**~er** *n* person who ~s. 窺察者;管閒事者;包打聽。

snooty /'snu:tɪ ; 'snutɪ/ *adj* (-ier, -iest) (colloq) supercilious; snobbish. (俗)自大的; 目中無人的。 **snoot·ily** /-ɪlɪ ; -əlɪ/ *adv*

snooze /snu:z ; snuz/ *vi* [VP2A], *n* (sl) (take a) short sleep (esp in the daytime): (俚)小睡(尤指在日間): *have a ~ after lunch.* 午飯後小睡。

snore /snɔ:(r) ; snor/ *vi* [VP2A, C] breathe roughly and noisily while sleeping: 打鼾;發鼾聲: *Does my snoring bother you?* 我打鼾會攪擾你嗎?□ *n* sound of snoring: 打鼾聲: *His ~s woke me up.* 他的鼾聲把我吵醒了。**snorer** *n* person who ~s. 打鼾者。

snor·kel, schnor·kel /'snɔ:kl, 'ʃn- ; 'snɔrkl̩/ *n* tube that enables a submarine to take in air while submerged; device for enabling a swimmer to take in air while under water. (潛水艇用的)呼吸

管;通氣管;(潛水者用的)通氣裝置或呼吸裝置。 ⇨ the illus at frog. 參看 frog 之插圖。

snort /snɔːt; snɔrt/ *vi, vt* **1** [VP2A, C] force air violently out through the nose; do this to show impatience, contempt, etc: 自鼻噴氣作聲;嗤之以鼻;噴鼻息以表示不耐煩、輕視等: ~ *with rage* (*at* sb or sth); (對某人或某事)憤怒地嗤之以鼻; (colloq) indicate amusement with a burst of loud laughter. (俗)突然大笑表示歡娛。 **2** [VP6A, 15B] express by ~ing: 噴鼻息以表示;哼然表示: ~ *defiance at sb;* 對某人噴鼻息以表示不服; ~ *out a reply.* 哼鼻作答(噴鼻息作答)。 *'Never!' he ~ed.* 他哼了一聲說,'決不!' □ *n* **1** act or sound of ~ing: 哼鼻或噴鼻息的動作或聲音;哼鼻;哼鼻聲: *give a ~ of contempt.* 作輕蔑的哼鼻聲。 **2** snorkel (of a submarine). (潛水艇的)通氣管。 **~y** *adj* (colloq) ill-tempered. (俗)壞脾氣的;脾氣大的。 **~er** *n* (colloq) (俗) **1** sb or sth that is violent or outstanding in some way: (在某方面)特別激烈或突出的人或事物: *This problem is a real ~er,* very difficult. 這問題確是非常棘手。 **2** strong gale. 强風;暴風。

snot /snɒt; snɑt/ *n* [U] (vulg) mucus of the nose. (鄙)鼻涕。 **~ty** *adj* (vulg) (鄙) **1** running with, wet with, ~. 流鼻涕的;鼻涕弄濕的。 **2** **'~(-nosed),** (sl) superior; snooty: (俚)高傲的;目中無人的: *You ~-nosed little bastard!* 你這個目中無人的小雜種!

snout /snaʊt; snaut/ *n* nose (and sometimes the mouth or jaws) of an animal (esp a pig); pointed front of sth, thought to be like a ~. 動物(尤指猪)的鼻子或鼻口部;猪嘴;(某物之)猪嘴形前端;狀似猪嘴的裝置。 ⇨ the illus at domestic, fish. 參看 domestic, fish 之插圖。

snow¹ /snəʊ; sno/ *n* **1** [U] frozen vapour falling from the sky in soft, white flakes; mass of such flakes on the ground, etc: 雪;雪片;雪花;(地面上等處的)積雪: *a heavy fall of ~;* 下大雪; *roads deep in ~;* 積雪深的道路; (*pl*) falls or accumulation of ~. (複)積雪;降雪。 **2** (compounds) (複合字) **'~·ball** *n* **(a)** mass of ~ pressed into a hard ball for throwing in play. (團雪而成的)雪球(用以投擲以爲遊戲)。 **(b)** sth that increases quickly in size as it moves forward. 像滾雪球般快速增大的事物。 □ *vt, vi* **(a)** throw ~balls (at). (向…)擲雪球。 **(b)** grow quickly in size, importance, etc: (在體積、重要性等方面)快速增加: *Opposition to the war ~balled.* 反戰的情緒迅速增長。 **'~·berry** *n* garden shrub with white berries. 一種結白色漿果的園藝灌木。 **'~·blind** *adj* (temporarily) unable to see because the eyes are tired by the glare of the sun on ~. 雪盲(眼睛受雪地反射的陽光刺激而暫時失明)的。 Hence, 由此產生, **'~·blind·ness** *n* **'~·bound** *adj* unable to travel because of heavy falls of ~. 被大雪困阻的; 被大雪封閉的。 **'~-capped / -clad / -covered** *adjj* covered with ~: 爲雪所覆蓋的: *~-capped mountains;* 覆蓋着雪的山; *~-covered roofs.* 覆蓋着雪的屋頂。 **'~·drift** *n* bank of ~ heaped up by the wind: (爲風吹成的)雪堆: *The train ran into a ~drift.* 火車開進了雪堆。 **'~·drop** *n* bulb plant with small white flowers at the end of winter or in early spring. 雪花(一種球莖植物,殘冬或初春時開小白花)。 ⇨ the illus at flower. 參看 flower 之插圖。 **'~·fall** *n* [C] amount of ~ that falls on one occasion or in a period of time, eg one winter, one year. 降雪;(一次或某一時期的)降雪量。 **'~-field** *n* permanent wide expanse of ~, eg on high mountains. 雪原;雪野(面積廣大的常年積雪,如高山上者)。 **'~·flake** *n* one of the feather-like collections of small crystals in which ~ falls. 雪花;雪片。 **'~-line** *n* level (in feet or metres) above which ~ lies permanently at any place: 雪線(以呎或公尺丈量,在此一水平線之上積雪終年不溶): *climb above the ~-line.* 攀越雪線。 **'~-man** /-mæn; -ˌmən/ *n* (*pl* -men) figure of a man made of ~ by children for amusement. (兒童以雪堆成的)雪人。 **'~-plough** (US 美 **'~-plow**) *n* device for pushing ~ from roads and railways. 除雪機; 雪犂 (用以清除道路及鐵軌上之積雪者)。 **'~-shoes** *n pl* frames with leather straps for walking on deep ~ without sinking in. 雪鞋(以革條穿在木框等上製成,可在積雪處行走而不致下陷)。 **'~·storm** *n* heavy fall of ~, esp when accompanied by strong wind. 大雪;(尤指)暴風雪。 **ˌ~-'white** *adj* pure, bright white in colour. 雪白的;純白的。 **~y** *adj* (-ier, -iest) **1** covered with ~: 被雪所覆蓋的: *~y roofs.* 被雪覆蓋的屋頂。 **2** characterized by ~: 下雪的;雪花紛飛的: *~y weather.* 下雪的天氣。 **3** as white or fresh as newly fallen ~: (像剛下的雪那樣)潔白清新的: *a ~y tablecloth.* 潔白的桌布。

snow² /snəʊ; sno/ *vi, vt* **1** [VP2A, B] (of snow) come down from the sky: (指雪)降雪;落下: *It ~ed all day.* 整天下雪。 **2** [VP2C] **~ in,** come in large numbers or quantities: 大量擁到;似雪片般飛來: *Gifts and messages ~ed in on her birthday.* 她生日那天,禮物和函電像雪片般湧來。 **3** ***be ~ed 'in/'up,*** be prevented by heavy snow from going out. 被大雪困阻。 ***be ~ed 'under (with),*** (fig) be overwhelmed: (喩)被壓倒;累倒: *~ed under with work/with invitations to dinner parties.* 爲工作(宴會的邀請)累倒。

snub¹ /snʌb; snʌb/ *vt* (-bb-) [VP6A] treat (esp a younger or less senior person) with cold behaviour or contempt; reject (an offer) in this way: 慢待或冷落(尤指年齡較幼或地位較低者);冷冷地或輕蔑地拒絕(建議、要求等): *be/get ~bed by a civil servant.* 被一位公務員所慢待。 □ *n* [C] ~bing words or behaviour: 慢待;冷落;慢待或冷落的言辭: *suffer a ~.* 受冷落。

snub² /snʌb; snʌb/ *adj* (only in) (僅用於) **a ~ nose,** short, stumpy, turned up; 獅鼻(短粗而上翻者); hence, 由此產生, **'~-nosed** *adj*

snuff¹ /snʌf; snʌf/ *n* [U] powdered tobacco to be taken up into the nose by sniffing: 鼻烟(粉末狀烟草,俾從鼻孔吸入者): *take a pinch of ~.* 吸一撮鼻烟。 ***up to ~,*** (colloq) (俗) **(a)** shrewd; not childishly innocent. 精明的;老練的。 **(b)** in normal health. 健康正常的。 **'~-box** *n* box for ~. 鼻烟盒。 **'~-colour(ed)** *adj, n* (of) dark yellowish-brown. 鼻烟色(的);黃褐色(的)。

snuff² /snʌf; snʌf/ *vi, vt, n* = sniff.

snuff³ /snʌf; snʌf/ *vt, vi* **1** [VP6A, 15B] cut or pinch off the burnt black end of the wick of (a candle). 剪(燭)花。 **~ *sth out,*** (lit or fig) put out, extinguish (the light of a candle): (字面或喩)熄滅(燭光);消滅: *His hopes were nearly ~ed out.* 他的希望幾乎破滅了。 **2** [VP2C] **~ *out,*** (sl) die. (俚)死亡。 **~·ers** *n pl* scissors with a kind of box to catch the burnt wick of candles when they are ~ed. 剪燭花用的剪刀。

snuffle /'snʌfl; 'snʌfl/ *vi* [VP2A] make sniffing sounds; breathe noisily (as when the nose is partly stopped up while one has catarrh). 抽鼻子;發聲地呼吸(如鼻子半塞時)。 □ *n* act or sound of snuffling: 抽鼻子;發聲呼吸;鼻塞聲;鼻音: *speak in/with a ~,* nasally. 講話帶鼻音。

snug /snʌg; snʌg/ *adj* (-gg-) **1** sheltered from wind and cold; warm and comfortable: 不受風寒侵襲的;溫暖而舒適的: *~ and cosy by the fireside;* 在火爐旁邊溫暖而舒適; *~ in bed;* 舒適的在床上; *a ~ woollen vest.* 溫暖的毛背心。 **2** neat and tidy; rightly or conveniently placed or arranged: 整潔的;安排適當的: *a ~ cabin,* on a ship. 整潔的船艙。 **3** good enough for modest needs: 可滿足適度需要的: *a ~ little income.* 可維持適度生活的微薄收入。 **4** closely fitting: 緊貼的;緊身的: *a ~ jacket;* 緊身的上衣; (as an *adv*) (作副詞用) *a ~-fitting coat.* 合身的上裝。 □ *n* = snuggery. **~·ly** *adv* **~·ness** *n*

snug·gery /'snʌgərɪ; 'snʌgərɪ/ *n* (*pl* -ries) snug place, esp a private room planned for comfort. 溫暖而舒適的地方;(尤指)舒適的私人房間。

snuggle /'snʌgl; 'snʌgl/ *vi, vt* **1** [VP2C] **~ *(up)***

(to sb), lie or get (close to sb) for warmth, comfort or affection: 挨近;貼近;靠近(某人)(俾獲得溫暖或溫情): *The child ~d up to its mother/~d into its mother's arms.* 那孩子貼在母親身邊(貼在母親懷裡)。*The children ~d up (together) in bed.* 孩子們在床上擠做一團。*She ~d down in bed,* made herself comfortable. 她舒舒服服地蜷在被窩裡。**2** [VP14] ~ ***sb to sb,*** draw close (to one): 拉近;緊抱;擁近: *She ~d the child close to her.* 她把孩子拉近自己。

so[1] /səʊ; so/ *adv of degree* 程度副詞 to such an extent. 至某種程度。 **1** (in the pattern: 用於句型: ***not*** + ***so*** + *adj/adv* + ***as***): *It is not so big as I thought it would be.* 那東西不如我想像的大。*We didn't expect him to stay so long,* (as, in fact, he did stay). 我們未料到他會停留那麼久。*He was not so much angry as disappointed.* 他的失望甚於惱怒。**2** (in the pattern: 用於句型: ***so*** + *adj* + ***as*** + ***to*** + *inf*): *Would you be so kind as to help me,* ie will you please help me? 請幫幫忙好嗎? *He is not so stupid as to do that.* 他不至於蠢到做那種事。**3** (in the pattern: 用於句型: ***so*** + *adj/adv* + ***that***): *He was so ill that we had to send for a doctor.* 他病得不輕,我們必須爲他請醫生。*There were so many that we didn't know where to put them all.* 數量太多了,我們不知道什麼地方才放得下。*He was so angry that he couldn't speak.* (Colloq: 俗: *He couldn't speak, he was so angry*). 他非常憤怒,竟至說不出話來。**4** (If the *adj modifies a sing n,* the *indef art* is placed between the *adj* and the *n.* It is often better to use *such*):(形容詞修飾單數名詞時,不定冠詞應放在形容詞與名詞之間。such 常較 so 佳): *He is not so clever a boy* (= such a clever boy) *as his brother.* 他不如他哥哥(弟弟)聰明。 **5** (used, colloq style, with exclamatory emphasis for *very.* ˈ*Ever so* is colloq): (在口語用法中代替 very, 具有感嘆和加强語氣的作用。ˈEver so 爲口語): *I'm ˈso glad to see you!* 我眞高興見到你!*It was ˈso kind of you!* 你眞好!*There was ˈso much to do!* 有這麼多事情要做!*That's ˈever so much better!* 那再好也沒有了! **6** (in phrases) (用於片語中) ***ˈso far,*** up to this/that time, point or extent: 至此(那)時;至此(那)點;到此(那)程度或範圍: *Now that we've come so far, we may as well go all the way.* 我們既然已經走到這裡,乾脆就走完全程。*Everything is in order so far.* 迄今諸事順遂。***so ˈfar as,*** to the extent or degree that: 至某種限度或程度: *So far as I know/as I'm concerned....* 就我所知(就我而言)…。***ˌSo far, so ˈgood,*** Up to this point all is satisfactory. 到現在爲止,一切都很好。***so ˈfar from,*** instead of; quite contrary to: 決不是;絕非: *So far from being a help, he was a hindrance.* 他不但幫不上忙,反而礙事。 ***so ˈlong as,*** on condition that; provided that: 設或;假如;祇要: *You may borrow the book so long as you keep it clean.* 你可以借這本書,祇要你將它保持乾淨。 ***ˈso much/many,*** an unspecified quantity/number: 這麼多(表示未明確指出的分量或數目): *So much butter, so much sugar, so many eggs,....* 這麼多的奶油,這麼多的糖,這麼多的雞蛋,…。*Twelve dinners, at so much a head.* 來十二個客飯,每客這個價錢。***not so ˈmuch as:*** 甚至不;與其…不如: *He didn't so much as* (= didn't even) *ask me to sit down.* 他甚至沒有請我坐。*He is not so much unintelligent as uneducated,* ie he lacks education, not intelligence. 他缺乏的是教育,並非聰明才智。⇨ much[1]. ***ˈso much*** (nonsense, etc), all, merely: 不過;全是(無稽之談等): *What you have written is so much nonsense.* 你寫的這些全是無稽之談。***ˈso much for,*** that is all that need be said, done, etc, about: 有關…要說的或要做的等盡在於此: *So much for the first stage of our journey.* 我們旅行的第一個階段到此爲止。***ˌso much ˈso that,*** to such an extent that: 到這種程度以致: *He is rich—so much so that he does not know what he is worth.* 他很富有──富有到連自己都不知道究竟有多少錢。

so[2] /səʊ; so/ *adv of manner* 表方式的副詞 **1** in this/that way; thus: 這樣;那樣;以這(那)種方式: *So, and so only, can it be done.* 這樣做,並且祇有這樣做,才做得成。*Stand just so.* 就這樣站着。*So it was* (= That is how) *I became a sailor.* 那就是我變成水手的來由。*As X is to Y, so Y is to Z.* Y跟Z的關係猶如X跟Y的關係。*As you treat me, so I shall treat you.* 你怎麼對待我,我就怎麼對待你。 **2** (in phrases) (用於片語中) ***ˈso-called,*** called or named thus but perhaps wrongly or doubtfully: 所謂的;號稱的: *Your so-called friends won't help you in your troubles.* 你那些所謂的朋友在你遇到困難時不會幫助你。***ˈso that,*** **(a)** in order that: 爲的是;以便: *Speak clearly, so that they may understand you.* 講清楚一點,好讓他們聽懂。**(b)** with the result that: 因此;結果是;以致: *Nothing more was heard of him, so that people thought that he was dead.* 未再聽到他的消息,因此人們以爲他死了。***ˈso...that,*** **(a)** with the intent that: 意圖;有意要: *We have so arranged matters that one of us is always on duty.* 我們已經安排好,我們之間總有一個人當班。 **(b)** with the result that; in a way that: 因此;結果是;以致: *It so happened that I couldn't attend the meeting.* 事情就發生的那樣巧,以致我無法參加那次會議。***ˈso as to do sth,*** in order to; in such a way that: 爲了;以便;以致: *Don't let your television blare so as to disturb your neighbours.* 不要把你的電視機的聲音開得太大,以致打擾鄰居。*I will have everything ready so as not to keep you waiting.* 我會把一切準備就緒,使你不用等候。 ⇨ as[2](15). **3** (used as a substitute for a word, phrase or situation): (用以代替單字、片語或某種情況): *I told you so!* That is what I told you! 我告訴過你會這樣的! *I could scarcely believe it, but it was so,* ie that was the state of affairs, etc. 我簡直無法相信,但的確是這樣。*So I believe/hope/suppose, etc.* 我相信(希望,以爲等)如此。 **4** (used to express agreement, in the pattern: 用以表示同意,其句型爲: *so + pron + aux v*): *A: 'It was cold yesterday.' B: 'So it was.'* 甲:'昨天很冷。' 乙:'的確很冷。' *A: 'Tomorrow will be Friday.' B: 'So it will.'* 甲:'明天是禮拜五。' 乙:'不錯,是禮拜五。' *A: 'We have all worked hard.' B: 'So we have.'* 甲:'我們大家都很辛苦。' 乙:'的確都很辛苦。' **5** (used meaning 'also' in the pattern: 作 also 解,其句型爲: *so + aux v + (pro)n*): *You are young and so am I,* ie I also am young. 你(們)年輕,我也年輕。*Tom speaks French and so does his brother.* 湯姆會講法語,他哥哥(弟弟)也會。*A: 'I went to the cinema yesterday.' B: 'Oh, did you? So did I.'* 甲:'昨天我去看電影了。' 乙:'噢,是嗎?我也去了。' **6** (various uses) (其他用法) ***or so*** (unstressed), about: (不重讀)大約: *He must be forty or so,* about forty years old. 他一定有四十來歲了。*It will be warmer in another month or so,* in about a month from now. 大約再過一個月(天)就會暖和一點了。***and ˈso on (and ˈso forth),*** and other things of the same kind; et cetera. 等等;諸如此類。***just ˈso,*** **(a)** used to express agreement. (用以表示同意)正是如此;一點不錯。**(b)** neat and tidy: 整齊清潔: *Eric likes everything to be just so.* 艾立克喜歡每樣東西都整齊清潔。 ***ˈso to say/speak,*** used as an apology for an unusual use of a word or phrase, an exaggeration, etc. 可以說;打個比方說(表示勉强將某一字,片語,誇張語等作不尋常用法)。**ˈso-so,** ⇨ this entry below. 參看下列 so-so 條。**ˈso-and-so** /ˈsəʊənsəʊ; ˈsoənˌso/ (*pl* so-and-so's) (colloq) (俗) **(a)** person or thing not needing to be named: 某某;某人;某事物(指無須說出姓名或名稱者): *Don't worry about what old so-and-so says.* 某某老先生說的話不要放在心上。**(b)** (derog) unpleasant person. (貶)討厭的人。

so[3] /səʊ; so/ *conj* **1** therefore; that is why: 因此;所以: *The shops were closed so I couldn't buy anything.* 商店都打烊了,所以我什麼也買不到。 *She asked me to go, so I went.* 她要我去,所以我去了。

They cost a lot of money, so use them carefully. 這些東西花不少錢,所以要小心使用。**2** (exclamatory) (驚嘆用法) *So you're back again!* 你又回來了! *So you've lost your job, have you?* 那麼你失業了,是不是? *So you're not coming!* 這麼說,你不來了! *So there you are!* 情況就是如此!

so⁴, soh /səʊ; so/, **sol** /sɒl; sɑl/ *n* fifth note in the musical octave. 任何大音階之第五音。

soak /səʊk; sok/ *vt, vi* **1** [VP2A] become wet through by being in liquid or by absorbing liquid: 浸濕;泡: *The clothes are ~ing in soapy water.* 衣服在肥皂水裡泡着。 **2** [VP6A, 14] **~ sth (in sth),** cause sth to absorb as much liquid as possible: 使某物盡量吸收液體;使浸透;使濡濕: *~ dirty clothes in water/bread in milk.* 把髒衣服泡在水裡(把麵包泡在牛奶裡)。 *S~ the cloth in the dye for one hour.* 把布放進顏料裡泡一個鐘頭。 **3** [VP 15A, B] **~ sth up,** absorb; take in (liquid): 吸收;吸入(液體): *Blotting-paper ~s up ink.* 吸墨紙吸收墨水。**~ oneself in sth,** (fig) absorb: (喻)沈醉;沈湎: *~ oneself in the atmosphere of a place.* 沉湎於某一個地方的氣氛中。 **4** [VP6A, 15B] (of rain, etc) (指雨等) **~ sb (through),** make him very wet: 淋濕;使濕透: *We all got ~ed (through).* 我們都淋得濕透了。**be ~ed to the skin,** get wet right through one's clothes. 全身濕透。 **5** [VP3A] **~ through sth,** penetrate; enter and pass through: 浸入;透過;滲透: *The rain had ~ed through the roof/his overcoat.* 雨水已經透過屋頂(透過他的大衣)。 **6** [VP6A] (sl) extract money from by charging or taxing very heavily: (俚)向…榨取金錢或徵收重稅: *Are you in favour of ~ing the rich?* 你贊成向富人課重稅嗎? **7** [VP2A] (colloq) drink alcohol excessively (and habitually). (俗)狂飲;酗酒。□ *n* **1** act of ~ing: 浸;泡;漬: *Give the sheets a good ~.* 把被單好好泡一泡。**in ~,** being ~ed: 在浸泡中;泡着: *The sheets are in ~.* 被單在浸泡中。**2** (sl, 俚, usu 通常作 **old ~**) person greatly addicted to alcoholic drink. 酗酒者;酒徒。**~er** *n* **1** (colloq) heavy fall of rain: (俗)大雨: *What a ~er!* 好大的雨! **2** drunkard. 醉漢;酒徒。

soap /səʊp; sop/ *n* [U] substance made of fat or oil and an alkali, used for washing and cleaning: 肥皂: *a bar/cake of ~;* 一條(一塊)肥皂; *'~-flakes;* 肥皂片; *'~-powder;* 肥皂粉; *use plenty of ~ and water.* 用大量的肥皂和水。**'soft ~,** ⇨ soft(15). **'~-box** *n* improvised stand for an orator (in a street, park, etc): (街頭、公園等處的)臨時演說臺;肥皂箱演說臺: *~-box oratory,* of the kind heard from demagogues. 肥皂箱演說(政客們的煽動性演說)。 **'~-bubble** *n* filmy ball of ~y water with changing colours, full of air. 肥皂泡。**'~-opera** *n* (US) radio or TV serial drama dealing with domestic problems, etc in a sentimental or melodramatic way. (美)(無線電廣播或電視)連續劇(以傷感或鬧劇的方式處理家庭問題等)。**'~-suds** *n pl* frothy lather of ~ and water. (含肥皂和水的)肥皂泡沫。□ *vt* **1** [VP6A, 15B] apply ~ to; rub with ~: 塗肥皂於;用肥皂擦: *~ oneself down.* 用肥皂擦洗身子。**2** [VP 6A] (colloq) flatter; try to please. (俗)討好;諂媚。**~y** *adj* (-ier, -iest) **1** of or like ~: 肥皂的;似肥皂的: *This bread has a ~y taste.* 這麵包有肥皂味。**2** (fig) over-anxious to please: (喻)過分想討好的;諂媚的;圓滑的: *He has a ~y voice/manner.* 他有一種諂媚的聲音(態度)。

soar /sɔː(r); sor/ *vi* [VP2A, C] fly or go up high in the air; hover in the air without flapping of wings; rise: 高飛;翱翔;高聳;升高: *~ like an eagle;* 像老鷹一般翱翔; *a ~ing flight,* eg in a sailplane; 翱翔飛行(如乘翱翔機); *a cathedral nave that ~s up to the vaulted roof;* 高聳至拱頂的大教堂正廳; *the ~ing spire of Salisbury cathedral.* 薩利斯伯萊大教堂的高聳尖頂。*Prices ~ed when war broke out.* 戰爭爆發時,物價飛漲。

sob /sɒb; sɑb/ *vi, vt* (-bb-) **1** [VP2A, C] draw in the breath sharply and irregulary from sorrow or pain, esp while crying; [VP15A, B]: 嗚咽;啜泣;欷歔: *She sobbed her heart out,* sobbed bitterly. 她哭得死去活來。*She sobbed herself to sleep.* 她啜泣着入睡了。 **2** [VP15B] **sob sth out,** tell while doing this: 嗚咽地說;哭訴: *She sobbed out the story of her son's death in a traffic accident.* 她哽咽着敍說她兒子死於車禍的經過。□ *n* [C] act or sound of sobbing: 嗚咽(聲);啜泣(聲);欷歔(聲): *The child's sobs gradually died down.* 那孩子的啜泣漸趨沉寂。**'sob-stuff** *n* [U] (colloq) the sort of writing, film, etc which is full of pathos and sentiment. (俗)充滿傷感情緒的文章、電影等。**sob-bing·ly** *adv*

so·ber /'səʊbə(r); 'sobɚ/ *adj* **1** self-controlled; temperate; serious in thought, etc; calm: 自制的;適度的;冷靜的;鎮定的;認眞的;嚴肅的: *be in ~ earnest;* 嚴肅認眞的; *make a ~ estimate of what is possible;* 對可能的情況作冷靜的估計; *exercise a ~ judgement;* 作冷靜的判斷; *be ~-minded,* serious; 認眞的;嚴肅的; *~ colours,* not bright; 素色; *in ~ fact,* in fact (contrasted with what is fancied or imagined). 事實上(與空想或想像相對)。**'~-sides** *n* (dated colloq) serious and sedate person. (過時俗語)嚴肅而正經的人。 **2** avoiding drunkenness; not drunk: 未醉的;清醒的: *Does he ever go to bed ~?* 他有清醒着就寢的時候嗎? □ *vt, vi* [VP6A, 15B, 2C] **1 ~ (sb) down,** make or become ~(1): 使或變自制、嚴肅、鎮定: *The bad news ~ed all of us.* 那壞消息使我們全都變嚴肅了。*I wish those noisy children would ~ down,* become less excited, etc. 我希望那些鬧鬨鬨的孩子們靜下來。**2 ~ (sb) up,** make or become ~(2): 使或變清醒;使不醉: *Put him to bed until he ~s up.* 送他上床等他清醒過來。*Throw a pail of water over him—that'll ~ him up.* 澆他一桶水 — 這會使他清醒過來。**~·ly** *adv*

so·bri·ety /sə'braɪətɪ; sə'braɪətɪ/ *n* [U] quality or condition of being sober(1, 2). 清醒;自制;嚴肅;鎮定。

so·bri·quet /'səʊbrɪkeɪ; 'sobrɪ,ke/ *n* [C] nickname. 綽號;渾名。

soc·cer /'sɒkə(r); 'sɑkɚ/ *n* [U] (colloq) (as used by those who play Rugby football for) association football. (俗)(Rugby football 球員所指的)英式足球。

so·ciable /'səʊʃəbl; 'soʃəbl/ *adj* fond of the company of others; friendly; showing friendliness. 好與人交往的;好交際的;友善的;表示友善的。**so·ciably** /-əblɪ; -əblɪ/ *adv* **so·cia·bil·ity** /ˌsəʊʃə'bɪlətɪ; ˌsoʃə'bɪlətɪ/ *n* [U].

so·cial /'səʊʃl; 'soʃəl/ *adj* **1** (of animals, etc) living in groups, not separately: (指動物等)群居的;營社會生活的: *~ ants/wasps.* 群居的螞蟻(黃蜂)。*Man is a ~ animal.* 人是羣居的動物。 **2** of people living in communities; of relations between persons and communities: 群居之人的;社區的;人與社區間之關係的: *~ customs/reforms/welfare.* 社會的習俗(改革,福利)。**ˌS~ 'Democrat,** (in politics) person who wishes society to move, by peaceful, democratic changes, to a system of socialism. (政治)社會民主主義者;社會民主黨員。**ˌ~ se'curity,** government provisions for helping people who are unemployed, ill, disabled, etc: 社會救濟;社會福利(政府對失業、生病、殘障等的人所作的救濟): *The family is on ~ security,* receiving such help. 這個家庭領社會救濟金。**(the) ˌ~ 'services** *n pl* organized government service providing help and advice (eg in matters of health, housing, mental illness, law-breaking) to people who are in need or trouble. 社會服務(政府對人民之協助,如解決健康、房屋、精神病、違法等問題)。**'~-work** *n* [U] the profession of those who work in the ~ services. 社會服務。**'~ worker** *n* person who works in the ~ services. 社會服務者。 **3** of or in society: 社會的;社會上的: *one's ~ equals,* persons of the same class as oneself in society; 同一階層者;社會地位相當的人; *~ advancement,* improvement of one's position in society; 個人社會地位的提高; ~ *climbers,* persons trying to obtain ~ advancement. 謀求提高社會地位者。 **4** for companionship: 社交的;交誼的: *a* '~ *club;* 聯誼會; *spend a* ~ *evening,* in the company of friends. 與友人度過一個晚上。 **5** = sociable. □ *n* ~ gathering, party, organized by a club. (某團體的)交誼會;聯歡會。**~ly** /-ʃəlɪ ; -ʃəlɪ/ *adv*

so·cial·ism /'səʊʃəlɪzəm ; 'soʃəl,ɪzəm/ *n* [U] philosophical, political and economic theory that land, transport, the chief industries, natural resources, eg coal, waterpower, etc, should be owned and managed by the State or by public bodies, and wealth equally distributed. 社會主義(主張土地,運輸工具,主要工業,天然資源如煤、水力等應歸國家或公共團體所有及經營,並且財富應平均分配的學說)。**so·cial·ist** *n* supporter of, believer in ~. 社會主義者。□ *adj* of, tending towards, ~: 社會主義的; 趨向社會主義的: *a Socialist Party,* political party which advocates and works for ~. 社會黨。**so·cial·ize** /-aɪz ; -aɪz/ *vt* [VP6A] make social(1) or socialist; govern on socialist principles. 使社會主義化;以社會主義的原則治理。**socialized medicine,** (US) the provision of free medical services by the Government. (美)社會醫療(政府提供的免費醫療)。**so·cial·iz·ation** /,səʊʃəlaɪ'zeɪʃn *US:* -lɪ'z- ; ,soʃəlɪ'zeʃən/ *n*

so·cial·ite /'səʊʃəlaɪt ; 'soʃə,laɪt/ *n* (colloq) person prominent in fashionable society. (俗)上流社會人士;名流;聞人。

so·ciety /sə'saɪətɪ ; sə'saɪətɪ/ *n* (*pl* -ties) **1** [U] social way of living; customs, etc of a civilized community; system whereby people live together in organized communities: 群體生活;文明社會的習俗;社會體制: *a danger to* ~, person, idea, etc that endangers the bodily or moral welfare of the members of a community; 社會之患(危害社會人群身心福祉的人、觀念等); *pests of* ~, persons who prey on the community and contribute nothing to its welfare. 社會的害蟲。 **2** [C] social community: 社會: *modern industrial societies;* 近代工業社會; certain grouping of humanity, eg Western Christendom, the people of Islam. 人類集團(如西方基督教世界,回教教徒)。 **3** [U] company; companionship: 友伴;友誼;交際: *spend an evening in the* ~ *of one's friends.* 和朋友們聚會度過一個晚上。 **4** [U] people of fashion or distinction in a place, district, country, etc; the upper classes: (一個地方、地區、國家等的)社會名流;上流社會(人士): *leaders of* ~; 上流社會的領袖; *high* (ie the most wealthy, influential, etc) ~; 上流社會人士(有錢有勢者); *the customs of polite* ~; 上流社會的習俗; (attrib) (形容用法) *a* '~ *man/woman;* 上流社會的男子(女士); ~ *weddings,* of fashionable persons; 名流們的婚禮; ~ *gossip/news,* as printed in newspapers, etc. 上流社會間的瑣聞(新聞)。 **5** [C] organization of persons formed with a purpose; club; association: (爲某種目的組成的)會;社;團體;協會: *the school de'bating* ~; 學校裡的辯論社; *a co-'operative* ~; 合作社; *the S~ of Friends.* 教友會(基督教一支派)。

socio- /,səʊsɪəʊ- ; ,sosɪo-/ *pref* of society or sociology. 表示 '社會' 或 '社會學'。

so·ci·ol·ogy /,səʊsɪ'ɒlədʒɪ ; ,soʃɪ'ɑlədʒɪ/ *n* [U] science of the nature and growth of society and social behaviour. 社會學(研究社會本質,社會成長及社會行爲之學科)。 **so·ci·ol·ogist** /-dʒɪst ; -dʒɪst/ *n* student of, expert in ~. 社會學家;社會學者。**so·cio·logi·cal** /,səʊsɪə'lɒdʒɪkl ; ,soʃɪə'lɑdʒɪkl/ *adj* of ~. 社會學的。**so·cio·logi·cally** /-klɪ ; -klɪ/ *adv*

sock[1] /sɒk ; sɑk/ *n* **1** (often 常作 **pair of ~s**) short stocking not reaching the knee. 短襪。***pull one's ~s up,*** (colloq) improve oneself, one's performance. (俗)改進自己;改進自己的成績。***put a ~ in it,*** (sl) be quiet; stop speaking. (俚)安靜;停止說話。 **2** loose sole used inside a shoe. (鞋子裡面的)活動襯底。⇨ *wind-~* at wind[1](8).

sock[2] /sɒk ; sɑk/ *n* (sl) blow given with the fist or sth thrown: (俚)用拳頭或投擲物的打擊;拳擊;擲擊: *Give him a ~ on the jaw!* Hit him hard! 在(他)下顎上給他一拳!(用力揍他!) □ *vt* [VP6A, 15A] (sl) give (sb) such a blow: (俚)用拳頭或投擲物打(某人);拳打;擲擊: *S~ him on the jaw!* 在下顎上給他一拳! *S~ a brick at him!* 丟磚頭砸他! *S~ it to him!* 丟(那東西)過去打他!□ *adv* (sl) squarely: (俚)正對地;不偏不倚地: (*hit sb*) ~ *in the eye.* 正(打)在(某人的)眼睛上。

socket /'sɒkɪt ; 'sɑkɪt/ *n* natural or artificial hollow into which sth fits or in which sth turns: 承物凹處;承口;插座;窩;孔: *the 'eye-~s;* 眼窩; *a ~ for an electric light bulb/a candle.* 電燈燈座(蠟燭承座)。

So·cratic /sə'krætɪk *US:* səʊ- ; so'krætɪk/ *adj* characteristic of Socrates, the Greek philosopher. (希臘哲學家)蘇格拉底的;有蘇格拉底特色的。***the ~ method,*** examining an idea, theory, etc, by question and answer between two or more people. 蘇格拉底法;問答法;對話法。

sod[1] /sɒd ; sɑd/ *n* [U] upper layer of grassland including the grass with its roots and earth; [C] square or oblong piece of this pared off; turf. 草地;草皮;草泥。

sod[2] /sɒd ; sɑd/ *n* ⚠ (vulgar term of abuse, used in annoyance and sudden anger): (諱)(厭煩或突然發怒時之粗鄙的罵人語)畜生: *You sod!* 你這畜生!□ *vi* ⚠ ***Sod it!*** Damn (it)! (諱)畜生!他媽的! ***Sod off!*** Go away! 滾開! **sod·ding** *attrib adj* ⚠ (used as an intensive) (諱)(用以加强語氣) *What a sodding mess!* 眞他媽的亂七八糟!

soda /'səʊdə ; 'sodə/ *n* [U] common chemical substance used in soap-making, glass manufacture, etc: 蘇打;碳酸鈉(用以製肥皂、玻璃等): *'washing-~* (sodium carbonate, **Na_2CO_3**), used for softening water, etc; 洗滌用蘇打(用以使水軟化等); *'baking-~* (sodium bicarbonate, **$NaHCO_3$**), used in cooking. 烹調用蘇打;小蘇打。'**~-biscuit/-cracker** *n* biscuit from dough containing baking-~ and sour milk. 蘇打餅乾(含烹調用蘇打及酸奶者)。 '**~-fountain** *n* counter, bar, from which ~-water, ices, etc are served. 蘇打泉(供應汽水、冰等的櫃臺)。'**~ pop** (US colloq) soft drink of ~-water, flavoured sometimes with ice-cream. (美俗)蘇打冷飲(一種汽水,有時加冰淇淋以增味)。'**~-water** *n* water charged with carbon dioxide gas to make it bubble. 蘇打水;汽水。

sod·den /'sɒdn ; 'sɑdn̩/ *adj* **1** soaked through: 浸透的;泡透的;水漬的: *clothes ~ with rain.* 爲雨水浸透的衣服。 **2** (of bread, etc) heavy and dough-like; moist or sticky because undercooked. (指麵包等)沒發好而似麵團的;(因未烘熟而)黏濕的。 **3** (often 常作 *'drink-~*) stupid through too much drinking of alcoholic liquor. (因嗜酒而變成)遲鈍的;痴呆的。

so·dium /'səʊdɪəm ; 'sodɪəm/ *n* [U] silver-white metal (symbol **Na**) occurring naturally only in compounds: 鈉(銀白色金屬,符號爲 Na, 自然界僅存其化合物): ~ *chloride,* **(NaCl)** common salt. 氯化鈉;食鹽(分子式爲 NaCl)。⇨ soda.

sod·omy /'sɒdəmɪ ; 'sɑdəmɪ/ *n* [U] anal sexual intercourse, esp between males. (尤指男性)雞姦;獸姦;同性戀。 **sod·om·ite** /'sɒdəmaɪt ; 'sɑdəm,aɪt/ *n* person practising ~. 雞姦者;獸姦者;同性戀者。

so·ever /səʊ'evə(r) ; so'ɛvɚ/ *suff* (formal, used with *relative pronouns, advv* and *adjj*) any kind or extent of: (正式用語,與關係代名詞,副詞及形容詞連用)任何種類;任何程度;無論: *'how ~,* 無論如何, *'who ~,* 無論是誰, etc.

sofa /'səʊfə ; 'sofə/ *n* long seat with raised ends and back, on which several persons can sit or one person can lie. 沙發。

soft /sɒft *US:* sɔːft ; sɔft/ *adj* **1** (opp of *hard*) (爲 hard 之相反字) changing shape easily when pressed; not resisting pressure: 軟的; 柔軟的: ~ *soil/*

ground/mud. 軟土(地,泥)。*Warm butter is* ~. 溫熱的奶油是軟的。*She likes a ~ pillow and a hard mattress.* 她喜歡軟的枕頭,硬的床墊。***a ~ landing,*** (eg of a spacecraft on the moon) one that avoids damage or destruction. 徐緩的着陸(如太空船降落月球表面的著陸,以避免損壞或破壞)。Hence, 由此產生,ˌ**~-ˈland** *vi* land in this way. 徐緩(或緩慢)着陸。 **2** (of surfaces) smooth and delicate: (指表面)軟滑的;細嫩的;細軟的: *as ~ as velvet;* 像天鵝絨一般細軟的; *~ fur;* 軟滑的毛皮; *~ furnishings,* curtains, hangings, etc; 軟滑的室內陳設(帷幔、簾幕等); *~ goods,* textiles. 紡織品。 **3** (of light, colours) opp of glaring; restful to the eyes: (指光、顏色)不刺目的;柔和的: *lampshades that give a ~ light.* 使光線柔和的燈罩。 **4** (of sounds) subdued; not loud: (指聲音)輕柔的;放低的: *~ music;* 輕柔的音樂; *~ murmurs/whispers;* 低聲的呢喃(耳語); *in a ~ voice.* 輕聲地。 **5** (of outlines) indistinct. (指輪廓)不明顯的。 **6** (of answers, words, etc) mild; gentle; intended to please: (指答語,話等)溫和的;文雅的;悅人的: *a ~ answer;* 溫和的回答; *have a ~ tongue.* 講話溫文的。 **7** (of the air, weather) mild: (指空氣,氣候)溫和的;宜人的: *a ~ breeze/wind;* 和風; *~ weather.* 溫和的氣候。 **8** (of water) free from mineral salts and therefore good for washing: (指水)軟性的;不含礦鹽的(宜於洗滌): *as ~ as rainwater.* 像雨水一般不含礦鹽的。 **9** (of certain sounds) not a plosive: (指某些語音)軟音的: *C is ~ in 'city' and hard in 'cat'.* 在 city 中, C 爲軟音;在 cat 中, C 爲硬音。 *G is ~ in 'gin' and hard in 'get'.* 在 gin 中, G 爲軟音;在 get 中, G 爲硬音。 **10** easy: 容易的;輕鬆的: *have a ~ job,* (sl) an easy, well-paid job; business deal with easily earned money. (俚)擔任輕鬆而待遇優厚的工作(好差使);做一筆容易賺錢的買賣。 **11** feeble; lacking in strength and determination: 軟弱的;意志不堅的: *muscles that have got ~ through lack of exercise;* 因缺乏運動而變得鬆軟的肌肉; *a ~ generation,* eg of young people. 柔弱的一代(例如年輕人)。 **12** sympathetic; considerate: 有同情心的;心軟的;體諒的: *have a ~ heart.* 有一副軟心腸。 ***have a ~ spot for sb,*** a liking or fondness for him. 偏愛某人。 **13** (colloq) feeble-minded: (俗)癡愚的;瘋癲的: *He's not as ~ as he looks.* 他並不像他的外貌那樣癡愚。 *He's gone ~.* 他變得瘋瘋癲癲了。 *Jack is ~* (= sentimentally silly) *about Anne.* 傑克癡戀着安。 **14** (various uses; compounds) (其他用法;複合字) ˌ**~-ˈboiled** *adj* (of eggs) boiled so that the egg is ~. (指蛋)煮得半熟的。ˌ**~ ˈcoal** *n* coal that burns with yellow, smoky flames. 煙煤;軟煤。ˌ**~ ˈcurrency** *n* one that is not convertible to gold, or into certain other currencies which are more in demand. 軟性貨幣(不能兌換爲黃金或某些其他更爲人所需要之貨幣者)。 ˌ**~ ˈdrink** *n* [C] cold, sweet and non-alcoholic drink, eg fruit juice (often charged with gas). 軟飲料(不含酒精的冷飲,如果汁或帶果汁味的汽水等)。ˈ**~ drug** *n* [C] drug (eg marijuana) that is mildly habit-forming (as opposed to a *hard drug,* eg heroin, which is addictive). 軟性毒品;軟性痲醉藥(如大痲烟,毒癮較緩和,與毒癮劇烈的海洛英等硬性毒品相對)。ˌ**~-ˈfooted** *adj* (of a person) moving with quiet, gentle steps. (指人)步履輕盈的。ˌ**~-ˈheaded** *adj* idiotic; foolish. 笨的;愚蠢的。ˌ**~-ˈhearted** *adj* sympathetic; kind. 軟心腸的;有同情心的;仁慈的。**~ option** *n* alternative which is thought to involve little work. 比較輕鬆的選擇;比較省事的選擇。 ˌ**~ ˈpalate** *n* back part of the roof of the mouth. 軟顎(口腔的後上部)。ˌ**~-ˈpedal** *vi, vt* play (music, the piano) with the ~ pedal down; (fig) make (a statement, etc) less definite or confident. 減弱音量演奏(音樂,鋼琴);(喻)使(陳述等)變得較不肯定或較不明確。ˈ**~ soap** *n* semi-liquid soap made with potash; (fig) flattery. 軟皂(含鉀鹼的半流質肥皂);(喻)諂媚。ˌ**~-ˈsoap** *vt* flatter. 諂媚。ˌ**~-ˈsolder** *n* kinds of solder used for easily fusible metal. 軟銲料;軟銲錫。ˌ**~-ˈsolder** *vt* solder with these soft kinds. 以軟銲料銲接。ˌ**~-ˈspoken** *adj* having a gentle voice; saying pleasant, friendly things. 聲音柔和的;講話中聽的。ˈ**~·ware** *n* data, programmes, etc not forming parts of a computer but used for its operation. 軟體;軟品(電腦作業系統,包括資料,計算程式等,不含計算機之機件)。 ⇨ *hardware* at hard¹(9). ˌ**~-ˈwitted** *adj* foolish. 愚蠢的。 ˈ**~-wood** *n* [C, U] (kinds of) easily sawn wood such as pine and other coniferous trees. 軟木料;軟材(如針葉樹材)。ˈ**~·ish** /-ɪʃ; -ɪʃ/ *adj* somewhat ~. 略軟的。**~·ly** *adv* in a ~ manner: 軟地;柔軟地;輕輕地: *tread/speak ~ly.* 輕輕地走(溫和地說話)。 *She ~ly pressed his hand.* 她輕握他的手。 **~·ness** *n* ˈ**~y** *n* stupid person; feeble person. 愚蠢的人;軟弱的人。

sof·ten /ˈsɒfn *US:* ˈsɔːfn; ˈsɔfən/ *vt, vi* [VP6A, 2A] make or become soft: (使)變軟;(使)變溫和、柔和、軟弱: *curtains that ~ the light;* 使光線柔和的窗簾; *people who are ~ed by luxurious living.* 由於生活奢侈而變得意志消沈的人們。 ***~ sb up,*** weaken (enemy positions) by shelling, bombing, etc; make (persons) unable or less able to resist (attack, salesmanship, etc). 藉砲擊、轟炸等減弱敵人的防衞力;說服某人或使某人不再頑强抗拒(批評、推銷等)。 **~er** *n* [C] sth used to ~, esp a chemical substance (or apparatus using this) for ~ing hard water. 軟化劑;軟水劑;硬水軟化器。

soggy /ˈsɒgɪ; ˈsagɪ/ *adj* (-ier, -iest) (esp of ground) heavy with water. (尤指地面)濕潤的;濕透的。**sog·gi·ness** *n*

soh /səʊ; so/ *n* ⇨ so⁴.

Soho /ˈsəʊhəʊ; ˈsoho/ *n* district in the West End of London noted for its foreign restaurants, food shops and night clubs. 蘇和區(倫敦西區之一地區,以其外國餐館,食品店及夜總會出名)。

soi·gné /ˈswɑːnjeɪ *US:* swɑːˈnjeɪ; ˌswaˈnje/ *adj* (F) (fem 陰性作 **-née**) (of a person's way of dressing, etc) carefully finished or arranged, with attention to detail. (法)(指衣著等)非常考究的。

soil /sɔɪl; sɔɪl/ *n* [C, U] **1** ground; earth, esp the upper layer of earth in which plants, trees, etc grow: 土地;土壤;地表層(植物、樹木等生長之處): *good/poor/alluvial/sandy, etc ~;* 沃(瘠,冲積,砂質等)土; *clay ~s.* 黏土。ˈ**~-pipe** *n* pipe from a water-closet pan to the drains. 排糞管(自抽水馬桶至下水道的管道)。 **2** *one's native ~,* one's native country; 故國;故土; *a man of the ~,* one who works on the land (and is devoted to it). 農夫;熱愛農作的人。□ *vt, vi* **1** [VP6A] make dirty: 弄髒;弄污: *~ed linen/underwear, etc,* that has been used and is to be laundered. (用過待洗的)衣物(內衣等)。*He refused to ~ his hands,* refused to do dirty work. 他不肯弄髒手(不肯做骯髒工作)。 **2** [VP2A, C] admit of being ~ed: 可被弄髒;容易弄髒;易於變污: *material that ~s easily,* is easily ~ed. 容易髒的料子。

soi·rée /ˈswɑːreɪ *US:* swɑːˈreɪ; swɑˈre/ *n* social gathering in the evening, esp for music, conversation, etc, and often to help the aims of a society(5). (音樂,聊天等)晚會(往往用以促成社團預定的目標)。

so·journ /ˈsɒdʒən *US:* səʊˈdʒɜːrn; soˈdʒɝn/ *vi* [VP2C], *n* (liter) (make a) stay (*with* sb, *at* or *in*) for a time. (文)逗留;寄居(與 with sb, at 或 in 連用)。**~er** *n*

sol /sɒl; sal/ *n* ⇨ so⁴.

Sol /sɒl; sal/ *n* (hum) (often 常作 *old Sol*) the sun. (諧)太陽。

sol·ace /ˈsɒlɪs; ˈsalɪs/ *n* [C, U] (that which gives) comfort or relief (when one is in trouble or pain): (困難或痛苦時的)慰藉;安慰;安慰物;慰藉物: *The invalid found ~ in music.* 那病人從音樂中獲得安慰。□ *vt* [VP6A, 15A] give ~ to: 安慰;慰藉: *The unhappy man ~d himself with whisky.* 那憂傷的人以威士忌

酒澆愁。

so·lar /ˈsəʊlə(r); ˈsoləʳ/ *adj* of the sun. 太陽的;與太陽有關的。**a ~ cell,** device (as used in satellites) which converts the energy of sunlight into electric energy. 太陽電池(轉太陽光爲電能的設計,如用於人造衛星者)。**the ˈ~ system,** the sun and the planets which revolve round it. 太陽系(太陽與繞行的諸行星)。**ˌ~ ˈplexus** /ˈpleksəs; ˈplɛksəs/ *n* complex of nerves at the pit of the stomach. 腹腔叢(在心窩處)。**the ~ year,** time occupied by the earth to complete one revolution round the sun, about 365 days, 5 hours, 48 minutes and 46 seconds. 太陽年(地球繞太陽一周所需的時間,爲 365 天 5 時 48 分 46 秒)。

so·larium /səʊˈleərɪəm; soˈlɛrɪəm/ *n* (*pl* -ria /-rɪə; -rɪə/) place enclosed with glass for enjoyment of the sun's rays, esp one for the medical use of sunlight. 日光浴室(享受日光的玻璃房間,尤指供醫療用者)。

sold /səʊld; sold/ *pt, pp* of sell.

sol·der /ˈsɒldə(r) *US*· ˈsɒdər; ˈsɑdəʳ/ *n* [U] easily melted alloy used, when melted, to join harder metals, wires, etc. 銲料(銲接較堅硬金屬、金屬線等的易熔合金)。□ *vt* [VP6A, 15A, B] join with ~. 銲接。**ˈ~·ing-iron** *n* tool used for this work. 銲鐵(銲接用的工具)。

sol·dier /ˈsəʊldʒə(r); ˈsoldʒəʳ/ *n* member of an army: (陸軍)軍人;士兵: *three ~s, two sailors and one civilian.* 三個(陸軍)士兵,兩個海員及一個平民。*The children were playing at ~s.* 孩子們在扮演軍人。**private ~,** one who is not a commissioned or non-commissioned officer. 士兵;兵。**~ *of fortune,*** man who will take service under any State or person who will hire him; mercenary. 傭兵(論價替任何國家或個人作戰的軍人)。□ *vi* [VP2A] serve as a ~: 當兵: (chiefly in) (主要用於) *go／enjoy ~ing;* 從軍; *be tired of ~ing.* 厭倦戎馬生涯。**~ *on,*** continue bravely with one's work, etc in the face of difficulties. (遭遇困難而)勇敢地繼續工作等。**~·ly, ˈ~-like** *adjj* like a ~; smart; brave. 似軍人的;英俊的;帥的;勇敢的。**~y** *n* (*sing* only, *collective n*) ~s of a specified character: (僅用單數形,爲集合名詞)某種軍人;軍隊: *the undisciplined ~y;* 不守紀律的軍隊; *brutal, licentious ~y.* 殘暴放肆的軍隊。

sole[1] /səʊl; sol/ *n* flat sea-fish with a delicate flavour. 鰈(一種扁平的海水魚,味美)。

sole[2] /səʊl; sol/ *n* under surface of a human foot, or of a sock, shoe, etc, other than the heel. (人足、鞋、襪等的)底部;脚掌;鞋底;襪底。□ *vt* [VP6A] put a ~ on (a shoe, etc): 上(鞋等的)底;配底於(鞋等): *send a pair of shoes to be ~d and heeled.* 送一双鞋去換底和補後跟。**-soled** *suff* (with *n* or *adj* prefixed) (加於名詞或形容詞之後) *ˈrubber-~d boots;* 橡皮底的靴子; *ˈthin-~d shoes.* 薄底鞋。

sole[3] /səʊl; sol/ *adj* **1** one and only; single: 唯一的;獨一的;僅有的: *the ~ cause of the accident.* 失事的唯一原因。**2** restricted to one person, company, etc: (某人或某公司等)專用的;獨佔的: *We have the ~ right of selling the article.* 我們有獨家出售該物的權利。**~·ly** *adv* alone; only: 單獨;僅僅;唯一: *~ly responsible;* 單獨負責的; *~ly because of you.* 僅僅爲了你。

sol·ecism /ˈsɒlɪsɪzəm; ˈsɑləˌsɪzəm/ *n* [C] error in the use of language; offence against good manners; mistake in etiquette. 使用語言錯誤;語法錯誤;舉止不當;失禮。

sol·emn /ˈsɒləm; ˈsɑləm/ *adj* **1** performed with religious or other ceremony; causing deep thought or respect: 以宗教或其他儀式舉行的;令人深思或崇敬的;神聖的;合儀式的;莊嚴的: *a ~ silence as the coffin was carried out of the church;* 棺材抬出教堂時一陣肅穆的沉寂; *a ~ duty;* 莊嚴的職責; *~ music;* 肅穆的音樂; *a ~ oath,* grave and important. 莊嚴的誓言。**2** serious-looking; grave: 表情嚴肅的;沈重的: *~ faces;* 陰沈的面孔; *look as ~ as a judge.* 顯得像法官般的嚴肅。**~·ly** *adv* **~·ness** *n*

sol·em·nity /səˈlemnətɪ; səˈlɛmnətɪ/ *n* (*pl* -ties) **1** [U] seriousness; gravity. 莊重;嚴肅。**2** [U] (but also *pl*) solemn ceremony: (但可用複數形)莊嚴的儀式: *The Queen was crowned with all ~／with all the proper solemnities.* 女王在極爲莊嚴的儀式中加冕(女王在適當的儀式中加冕)。

sol·em·nize /ˈsɒləmnaɪz; ˈsɑləmˌnaɪz/ *vt* [VP6A] perform (a religious ceremony, esp a wedding) with the usual rites; make solemn. 舉行(宗教儀式);(尤指)舉行(宗教婚禮);使莊重;使嚴肅。**sol·em·niz·ation** /ˌsɒləmnaɪˈzeɪʃn *US:* -nɪˈz-; ˌsɑləmnəˈzeʃən/ *n* [U].

sol-fa /ˌsɒlˈfɑ: *US:* ˌsəʊl; ˌsolˈfɑ/ *n* = *tonic ~,* ⇨ tonic.

sol·icit /səˈlɪsɪt; səˈlɪsɪt/ *vt, vi* **1** [VP6A, 14] ~ ***sb (for sth),*** ask (for) earnestly; make requests (for): 懇求;請求;乞求: *Both the candidates ~ed (me for) my vote.* 兩位候選人都向我拉票。*The tradesmen are all ~ing us for our custom,* asking us to deal with them. 那些商人都向我們拉生意。**2** [VP6A, 2A] (of a prostitute) make an immoral sexual offer (to), esp in a public place: (指妓女)在公開場所拉客: *I was openly ~ed at Piccadilly Circus.* 我在皮卡底里廣場遇到妓女公開向我兜攬生意。**sol·ici·ta·tion** /səˌlɪsɪˈteɪʃn; səˌlɪsəˈteʃən/ *n* [U] ~ing; [C] instance or occasion of this. 懇求;懇請;(妓女之)拉客。

sol·ici·tor /səˈlɪsɪtə(r); səˈlɪsətəʳ/ *n* **1** (GB) lawyer who prepares legal documents, eg wills, sale of land or buildings, advises clients on legal matters, and speaks on their behalf in lower courts. (英)律師。⇨ advocate, attorney, barrister. **SoˌlicitorˈGeneral,** one of the principal law officers in the British Government, advising on legal matters. 英國政府中之主要法律官員之一(爲法律事務的顧問);副檢察長。**2** (US) person who solicits trade, support, etc; canvasser (eg for votes). (美)招攬生意,懇求支持等的人;遊說者(如拉票者)。

sol·ici·tous /səˈlɪsɪtəs; səˈlɪsɪtəs/ *adj* ~ ***(for／about sth／sb);*** ~ ***(to do sth),*** anxious, concerned about (sb's welfare, etc) or to help／serve sb: 焦慮的;懸慮的;熱心的;切望(助人等)的;關心(某人福利等)的: *~ to please;* 渴望討人喜歡; *~ for her comfort.* 關心她的安適。**~·ly** *adv* **sol·ici·tude** /səˈlɪsɪtjuːd *US:* -tuːd; səˈlɪsəˌtjud/ *n* [U] being ~; concern or anxiety: 焦慮;懸慮;切望;關心: *my deep solicitude for your welfare.* 我深深關心你的福祉。

solid /ˈsɒlɪd; ˈsɑlɪd/ *adj* **1** not in the form of a liquid or gas: 固體的;非液體或氣體的: *~ fuels,* eg coal, wood; 固體燃料; *~-fuelled rockets.* 固體燃料火箭。*When water freezes and becomes ~, we call it ice.* 水凍結變成固體時,我們稱之爲冰。**ˌ~-ˈstate** *adj* (of electronic devices) totally transistorized, ie without valves: (指電子裝置)全晶體的: *a ~-state amplifier.* 全晶體擴大器。**2** compact; substantial; heavy: 緻密的;結實的;豐富的;難消化的: *a man with good ~ flesh on him;* 一個肌肉結實的男人; *~ food,* not slops. 固體食物(不是流質的)。**3** without holes or spaces; not hollow: 實心的;無孔的;無空隙的: *a ~ sphere.* 實心球。**4** of strong or firm material or construction; able to support weight or resist pressure: 堅固的;可支持重物的;可抵抗壓力的: *~ buildings／furniture;* 堅固的建築物(家具); *build on ~ foundations;* 在堅實的地基上建築; *a man of ~ build;* 體格結實的人; *on ~ ground;* 在堅實的地面上; *steps cut in the ~ rock.* 在堅石上鑿出的台階。**5** that can be depended on: 可靠的;可依賴的: *~ arguments;* 理由充分的論點; *a ~ (= financially sound) business firm;* 信用可靠的商家; *a man of ~ character.* 性格穩定的人。**6** alike all through; of the same substance throughout: 純的;全部爲同一物質的;全部一樣的: *made of ~ gold.* 純金製成。**7** unanimous; undivided: 一致的;不分歧的: *We are ~ for peace.* 我們一致擁護和平。*The miners are ~ on this issue.* 礦工們對此一爭端立場

一致。*There was a ~ vote in favour of the proposal.* 該提案獲全體一致通過。 **8** continuous; without a break: 繼續不斷的;無間斷的: *wait for a ~ hour;* 整整等了一個小時; *sleep ten ~ hours/ten hours ~.* 連續睡了十小時。 **9** (maths) having length, breadth and thickness: (數學)立體的;立方體的: *a ~ figure*, eg a cube; 立體圖形(如立方體); *~ geometry*, of ~, not plane, figure. 立體幾何。 □ *n* [C] **1** body or substance which is ~, not a liquid or a gas. 固體。 **2** (geom) figure of three dimensions. (幾何)立體(圖)形。 **~·ly** *adv* **sol·id·ity** /səˈlɪdətɪ ; səˈlɪdətɪ/, **~·ness** *nn* [U] quality of being ~: 固體性;可靠性;堅固;緻密: *the ~ity of a building/argument, etc.* 建築物的堅固(論點之可靠性)。

soli·dar·ity /ˌsɒlɪˈdærətɪ ; ˌsɑləˈdærətɪ/ *n* [U] unity resulting from common interests or feelings: (因共同利益或感情所產生的)團結;一致: *national ~ in the face of danger.* 面臨危難時全國之團結一致。

sol·id·ify /səˈlɪdɪfaɪ ; səˈlɪdəˌfaɪ/ *vt, vi* (*pt, pp* -fied) [VP6A, 2A] make or become solid, hard or firm. (使)變堅固;(使)變凝結;(使)變一致。**sol·idi·fi·ca·tion** /səˌlɪdɪfɪˈkeɪʃn ; səˌlɪdəfəˈkeʃən/ *n*

sol·il·oquy /səˈlɪləkwɪ ; səˈlɪləkwɪ/ *n* (*pl* -quies) [C, U] (instance of) speaking one's thoughts aloud; (in drama) speech in which a character speaks his thoughts without addressing a listener. 自言自語;(戲劇)獨白。**sol·il·oquize** /səˈlɪləkwaɪz ; səˈlɪləˌkwaɪz/ *vi* [VP2A] talk to oneself; think aloud. 自言自語;獨語;獨白。

sol·ip·sism /ˈsɒlɪpsɪzəm ; ˈsɑlɪpsɪzm̩/ *n* (metaphysics) theory that one can have knowledge only of the self. (形而上學)唯我論(人的知識止於認識自己的理論)。

soli·taire /ˌsɒlɪˈteə(r) *US:* ˈsɒlɪteə(r) ; ˌsɑləˈtɛr/ *n* **1** (ornament such as an earring having a) single gem or jewel. 獨粒寶石;鑲嵌獨粒寶石的飾物(如耳環)。 **2** (also called 亦稱 *patience*) kinds of card-game for one player. 單人紙牌戲。

soli·tary /ˈsɒlɪtrɪ *US:* -terɪ ; ˈsɑləˌtɛrɪ/ *adj* **1** (living) alone; without companions; lonely: 獨居的;無伴的;孤獨的: *a ~ life;* 獨居的生活; *a ~ walk.* 獨自散步。**~ confinement**, prison punishment by which a person is isolated in a separate cell. 隔離拘禁(監獄的一種懲罰)。***in ~***, in ~ confinement. 受隔離拘禁。 **2** only one: 祇有一個的;唯一的: *not a ~ instance of sth*, not even one instance of it. 一個例子都沒有。 **3** seldom visited: 人跡罕到的;偏僻的: *a ~ valley.* 人跡罕到的山谷。 **soli·tar·ily** /ˈsɒlɪtrəlɪ *US:* ˌsɒlɪˈteəlɪ ; ˈsɑləˌtɛrəlɪ/ *adv*

soli·tude /ˈsɒlɪtjuːd *US:* -tuːd ; ˈsɑləˌtjud/ *n* **1** [U] being without companions; solitary state: 獨居;孤獨;單獨: *live in ~;* 獨居; *not fond of ~.* 不喜孤獨。 **2** [C] lonely place: 人跡罕到之處;荒僻的地方: *spend six months in the ~s of the Antarctic.* 在人跡罕到的南極待了六個月。

solo /ˈsəʊləʊ ; ˈsolo/ *n* (*pl* ~s /-ləʊz ; -loz/) **1** piece of music (to be) performed by one person: 獨奏曲;獨唱曲: *a violin/piano ~.* 小提琴(鋼琴)獨奏曲。 **2** any performance by one person: 任何單獨表演;單獨作業;單獨執行任務: (as *adv*) (作副詞用) *fly ~;* 單獨飛行; (attrib) (形容用法) *his first ~ flight.* 他的首次單獨飛行。 **3** [U] kind of whist in which one player opposes others. 一種惠斯特紙牌戲(由一人對抗其餘的人)。 **ˈ~·ist** /-ɪst ; -ɪst/ *n* person who gives a ~(1). 獨唱者;獨奏者。

So·lon /ˈsəʊlɒn ; ˈsolən/ *n* (the name of an Athenian lawgiver, hence) wise legislator. (梭倫,古雅典立法者之名,由此產生)賢明的立法者。

sol·stice /ˈsɒlstɪs ; ˈsɑlstɪs/ *n* [C] either time (*summer ~*, about 21 June; winter ~, about 22 Dec) at which the sun is farthest N or S of the equator. 至;冬至或夏至(太陽離赤道南北最遠之時,北半球夏至約在六月廿一日;冬至約在十二月廿二日)。

sol·uble /ˈsɒljʊbl ; ˈsɑljəbl̩/ *adj* **1** ~ ***(in)***, that can be dissolved. 可溶解的。 **2** (= solvable) that can be solved or explained. 可解決的;可解釋的。 **solu·bil·ity** /ˌsɒljʊˈbɪlətɪ ; ˌsɑljəˈbɪlətɪ/ *n*

sol·ution /səˈluːʃn ; səˈljuʃən/ *n* **1** [C] ~ ***(to/for/of)***, answer (to a question, etc); way of dealing with a difficulty: (問題的)解答;(困難的)解決方法或方式: *Recourse to arms is not the best ~ to a quarrel between two countries.* 訴諸武力不是兩國間解決爭端的最好辦法。 *Might economy be the ~ to/for/of your financial troubles?* 節約能解決你財務方面的困難嗎? **2** [U] process of finding an answer or explanation: 尋求解答或解釋的過程或途徑: *problems that defy ~*, cannot be solved. 無法解決的問題。 **3** [U] process of dissolving a solid or a gas in liquid: 溶解;溶解過程: *the ~ of sugar in tea.* 糖在茶中溶解。 **4** [C, U] liquid that results from this process: 溶液: *a ~ of salt in water.* 鹽水;鹽的水溶液。

solve /sɒlv ; sɑlv/ *vt* [VP6A] find the answer to (a problem, etc): 解答(問題等): *~ a crossword puzzle/an equation;* 解答縱橫字謎(方程式); find a way out of a difficulty, etc: 解決(困難等): *Help me to ~ my financial troubles.* 幫助我解決我的經濟困難。**solv·able** /-əbl ; -əbl̩/ *adj* that can be ~d or explained. 可解決的;可解釋的。

sol·vent /ˈsɒlvənt ; ˈsɑlvənt/ *adj* **1** of the power of dissolving or forming a solution: 溶解力的: *the ~ action of water.* 水的溶解作用。 **2** having money enough to meet one's debts. 能償還債務的。 □ *n* [C] substance (usu a liquid) able to dissolve another substance (usu specified): 溶劑;溶媒(通常為一種液體): *grease ~*, eg petrol. 油脂溶劑(如汽油)。**sol·vency** /-nsɪ ; -nsɪ/ *n* [U] being ~(2). 有償債力。

so·matic /səʊˈmætɪk ; soˈmætɪk/ *adj* of the body. 身體的。

sombre (US = **som·ber**) /ˈsɒmbə(r) ; ˈsɑmbɚ/ *adj* dark-coloured; gloomy; dismal: 暗色的;憂鬱的;陰沉的;慘淡的: *a ~ January day;* 正月某一個陰沈的日子; *~ clothes;* 暗色的衣服; *a ~ picture of the future of mankind.* 人類未來的慘淡寫照(或遠景)。 **~·ly** *adv* **~·ness** *n*

som·brero /sɒmˈbreərəʊ ; sɑmˈbrɛro/ *n* (*pl* ~s /-rəʊz ; -roz/) broad-brimmed hat (as worn in Latin American countries). (拉丁美洲等國人所戴的)濶邊帽。

some[1] /sʌm ; sʌm; *weak form* səm ; səm, *used only in the adjectival sense of* 'consisting of an undefined amount or number of' 祇用於作形容詞,表示某一不確定的數量/ *adj* **1** (used in affirm sentences; usually replaced by *any* in interr and neg sentences, in conditional clauses, and in sentences where doubt or negation is implied. *S~* and *any* are used with material *nn* to indicate an amount or quantity that is either unknown or not given, with abstract *nn* to indicate a certain degree, and with *pl* common *nn* to indicate a certain number (three or more). *S~* and *any* are *pl* equivalents of the numeral article *a/an* (⇨ a²), of numeral *one*, and the *indef pron 'one'*): (用於肯定句中;在問句與否定句中,條件子句中,及含示懷疑或否定的句中,通常用 any 代替。Some 及 any 與物質名詞連用時,表示未知或未指明的總額或分量,與抽象名詞連用時,表示某種程度,與複數普通名詞連用時,表示某一數目(三個或三個以上)。 Some 及 any 係數字冠詞 a/an, 數字 one, 以及不定代名詞 one 的複數用語): *Please give me ~ milk.* 請給我一些牛奶。 Cf 參較 *Have you any sugar?* 你有沒有糖? *We haven't any tea.* 我們沒有茶了。*There are ~ children outside.* 外面有幾個小孩。Cf 參較 *There is a child outside.* 外面有一個小孩。 *They haven't any children.* 他們沒有小孩。*Are there any stamps in that drawer?* 那個抽屜裡有郵票嗎? *I wonder whether Mr Black has any flowers in his garden.* 我不知道布來克先生的花園裡有沒有種花。 *I doubt whether there are any* *flowers in Mr Green's garden.* 我懷疑格林先生的花園裡有沒有花。*I don't like a garden without any flowers in it.* 我不喜歡沒有花的花園。*There are scarcely/hardly any flowers in this garden.* 這個花園裡很少(簡直沒有)花。 *S~* (= S~ people) *say that....* 有些人說…。 **2** (*S~* is used in sentences that are interr in form if the speaker expects, or wishes to suggest, an affirm answer): (如果問話者期待或希望對方作肯定答覆時，some 亦用於問句中): *Aren't there ~ stamps in that drawer?* 那抽屜裡不是有幾張郵票嗎？ Cf 參較 *There are ~ stamps in that drawer, aren't there?* 那抽屜裡有幾張郵票,不是嗎？ *Didn't he give you ~ money?* 他不是給了你一些錢嗎？ Cf 參較 *He gave you ~ money, didn't he?* 他給了你一些錢,不是嗎？ (*S~* is used in sentences that are interr in form if these sentences are really invitations or requests: 如果問句實際上表示邀請或請求時，some 亦用於問句中: *Will you have ~ cake?* 請用一點糕餅好嗎？Cf 參較 *Please have ~ cake.* 請用一點糕餅。*Will you please buy me ~ stamps when you go out?* 你出去的時候請替我買幾張郵票好不好？Cf 參較 *Please buy me ~ stamps.* 請替我買幾張郵票)。 **3** (After *if*, introducing a supposition, either *some* or *any* may be used): (在 If 引導的假設子句之後，some 及 any 皆可用): *If we had ~/any money, we could buy it.* 如果我們有錢，我們就能買(它)了。*If we find ~/any, we'll share them with you.* 如果我們找得到一些,我們會分給你。**4** (*S~* and *any* are used with *more*): (Some 與 any 可與 more 連用): *Give me ~ more* /sə ˈmɔː(r); səˈmɔr/. 再給我一些。*Do you want any more?* 你還要(一些)嗎？ *I haven't any more.* 我再沒有了。*Won't you have ~ more?* 你不再要一些嗎？ (不再來一點嗎？) **5** (*S~* (always 總是讀作 /sʌm; sʌm/) is often contrasted with *the rest*, *other(s)*, and *all*): (Some 常與 the rest, other(s) 及 all 相對): *S~ children learn languages easily (and others with difficulty).* 有些小孩學習語言很容易 (不過有些則很困難)。*All work is not dull; ~ work is pleasant.* 工作不全是枯燥的;有些工作滿有趣的。 **6** (*S~* (always 總是讀作 /sʌm; sʌm/) is used before *sing* common *nn* to indicate that the person, place, object, etc is unknown, or when the speaker does not wish to be specific. The words *or other* are often added): (Some 用於單數普通名詞前，表示該人、地、物等不詳或不欲指明。作此用時，後常接 or other 兩字): *He's living at ~ place in East Africa.* 他(目前)住在東非某地。*I've read that story before in ~ book or other.* 我在一本書中讀過那個故事。*S~ man at the door is asking to see you.* 門口有一個人要見你。 **7** (*S~* (always stressed) is used with *nn* meaning 'a considerable quantity or number of'): (Some 可與名詞連用表示 '相當大的數量', 唯須重讀): *I shall be away for ˌ~ ˈtime,* a fairly long time. 我將離開相當長的一段時間。 *Mr Green spoke at ~* (= considerable) *length.* 格林先生滔滔不絕地說了好一陣子。*We went ~* (= several) *miles out of our way.* 我們叉出正路好幾哩。*The railway station is at ~ distance* (= quite a long way) *from the village.* 火車站離村子相當遠。 **8** (*S~* (always stressed) is also used with *nn* meaning 'to a certain extent or degree'): (Some 亦可與名詞連用,表示 '到達某種範圍或程度',須重讀): *That is ~ help* (ie It helps to a certain extent) *towards understanding the problem.* 那對於瞭解該問題確有一些幫助。□ *adv* (*S~* (always 總是讀作 /sʌm; sʌm/) is used adverbially, meaning *about* or *approximately*, before numbers): (Some 可作副詞用,作 '大約或相近' 解,用在數字之前): *That was ~ twenty years ago.* 那大約是二十年前的事。*There were ~ fifteen people there.* 那裡大約有十五個人。 **~ few**, ⇨ few(3).

some² /sʌm; sʌm/ *pron* (*S~* as a *pron* is used in the same ways as ~, *adj*, (1, 2 and 3). *S~ of* and *any of* are equivalent to *a few of*, *a little of*, *part of*): (some 作代名詞用時,與作形容詞用的 1, 2, 3 義的用法相同。Some of 及 any of 與 a few of, a little of, part of 相等): *S~ of these books are quite useful.* 這些書中有幾本頗為有用。*I don't want any of these (books).* 這些(書)我一本也不需要。 *I don't want any of this (paper).* 這東西(這種紙)我不要。*I agree with ~* (= part) *of what you say.* 你說的話我部分同意。*Scotland has ~ of the finest scenery in the world.* 蘇格蘭有幾處全世界最美麗的風景。

some·body /ˈsʌmbədɪ; ˈsʌmˌbɑdɪ/, **some·one** /ˈsʌmwʌn; ˈsʌmˌwʌn/ *pron* **1** (replaced by *anybody* in *interr*, *neg*, etc sentences) some person: 某人(在否定句,問句等中用 anybody 代替): *There's ~ at the door.* 門口有一個人。*Is there anyone at home?* 家裡有人嗎？ *That must be ~ from the Department of Education.* 那一定是教育部某人士。 **2** (often with the *indef art;* also in the *pl*) a person of some importance: (常與不定冠詞連用;並有複數形)重要人物;有分量的人: *If you had studied harder at college you might have become (a) ~.* 你當初上大學時如果多用點功，說不定已經變成重要人物了。*He's nobody here in town but I suppose he's a ~ in his own village.* 他在這城裡默默無聞,不過我想在他村子裡他是一位頗有分量的人物。

some·how /ˈsʌmhaʊ; ˈsʌmˌhaʊ/ *adv* **1** in some way (or other); by one means or another: 以某種方法或方式; 藉某種手段; 設法地: *We must find money for the rent ~ (or other).* 我們總得設法找錢付房租。*We shall get there ~.* 我們總會有辦法到那裡的。 **2** for some (vague) reason (or other): 為某種理由;說不上什麼理由;反正: *She never liked me, ~.* 她反正從未喜歡過我。*S~ I don't trust that man.* 說不出什麼道理,我就是不相信那個人。

some·one /ˈsʌmwʌn; ˈsʌmˌwʌn/ *n* = somebody.

some·place /ˈsʌmpleɪs; ˈsʌmples/ *adv* (US colloq) somewhere: (美俗)某處: *I've left my bag ~.* 我把我的提袋忘在某處了。*He lives ~ between Baltimore and Washington.* 他住在巴的摩爾與華盛頓之間的某個地方。*Let's go ~ else.* 我們到別處去吧。

som·er·sault /ˈsʌməsɔːlt; ˈsʌmɚˌsɔlt/ *n* [C] leap or fall in which one turns heels over head before landing on one's feet: 觔斗: *turn/throw a ~.* 翻觔斗。□ *vi* [VP2A] turn a ~. 翻觔斗。

some·thing /ˈsʌmθɪŋ; ˈsʌmθɪŋ/ *pron* **1** (replaced by *anything* in *interr*, *neg*, etc sentences) some thing, object, event, etc (of an indefinite nature): (未明的)某事;某物 (在否定句與問句中,用 anything 代替): *There's ~ on the floor.* 地板上有一樣東西。*Is there anything in that box?* 那盒子裡有東西嗎？ *I want ~ to eat.* 我想吃東西。*There's ~* (= some truth, some point) *in what he says.* 他說的有點道理。*It's ~* (= some satisfaction, some comfort) *to be home again without an accident.* 平平安安地回到家裡頗值得安慰。*He is ~* (= has some position or other) *in the Department of the Environment.* 他在環境衛生部頗有地位。 **2** ***or ~***, (colloq) indicates absence of precise information: (俗)表示不十分肯定: *Mr Green is a shopkeeper or ~,* is engaged in trade of some kind. 格林先生大概是商店老闆之類的人物。*I hear he has broken an arm or ~,* met with some sort of accident and has broken a limb, etc. 我聽說他折斷了手臂什麼的。*He struck a match too near the petrol tank or ~,* or did something equally foolish and dangerous. 他在太靠近汽油桶的地方擦火柴或做出同等愚蠢及危險的事情。 **3** ***~ of***, used to indicate an indefinite degree: 用以表示不確定的程度: *The soldier found himself ~ of a hero* (= was greeted as a hero to some extent) *when he returned to his village.* 那士兵回到家鄉,發現人們把他當英雄般看待。 *He's ~ of a liar,* (= is not wholly truthful), *don't you think?* 他說話不大靠得住,你不覺得嗎？ *I'm ~ of a carpenter,* I have some ability as a carpenter. 我懂一點木工。□ *adv* ***~ like***, **(a)** rather like; having some resemblance to: 頗似;有一點像: *The* *airship was shaped* ~ *like a cigar.* 那飛船的外型有點像一支雪茄。**(b)** approximately: 近乎;大約;約: *He left* ~ *like ten thousand,* ie died leaving about £10 000. 他遺留下大約一萬鎊(的財產)。**(c)** (colloq) *Now that's* ~ *like it,* (used to denote satisfaction). (俗)那倒滿好(用以表示滿意)。

some·time /ˈsʌmtaɪm; ˈsʌm,taɪm/ *adv* **1** at some time: 於某時;在某一時間: *I saw him* ~ *in May.* 我在五月裏見過他。*It was* ~ *last summer.* 去年夏天的某個時候。*I will speak to him about it* ~. 我將找個時間同他談此事。*I hope you will come* ~ *soon.* 我希望你不久能撥空前來。(Do not confuse with *some time* meaning 'for some period of time', as in: 不要與意爲 '一段時間' 的 some time 混淆,如: I have been waiting some time 我已等了一些時候了)。**2** (also as *adj*) (亦用作形容詞) former(ly): 以前;從前: *The Rev Thomas Atkins,* ~ *priest of this parish;* 湯瑪斯·阿特金斯牧師,本教區從前的牧師; *Mr Snuffle,* ~ *fellow of Trinity College.* 斯諾佛先生,三一學院的前校務委員。

some·times /ˈsʌmtaɪmz; ˈsʌm,taɪmz/ *adv* at some times; now and then; from time to time: 有時;不時;往往;間或: *I* ~ *have letters from him.* 我有時會接到他的信。*I have* ~ *had letters from him.* 我不時接到他的來信。*S*~ *we go to the cinema and at other times we go for a walk.* 我們有時去看電影,有時去散步。(When ~ is used in a contrasting statement, or when it is repeated, it may follow the *v*): (用於對照的句子中,或重覆使用時,可接在動詞後): *She likes* ~ *the one and* ~ *the other.* 她有時喜歡這個,有時喜歡那個。*He says* ~ *the one thing and at other times the exact opposite.* 他有時這麼說,有時卻說的完全相反。

some·way /ˈsʌmweɪ; ˈsʌm,we/ *adv* (US colloq) (美俗) = somehow.

some·what /ˈsʌmwɒt *US:* -hwɒt; ˈsʌm,hwɑt/ *adv* **1** rather; in some degree: 頗爲;稍稍;有幾分: *I was* ~ *surprised/disappointed, etc.* 我略感吃驚(失望等)。*He answered* ~ *hastily.* 他回答得略嫌草率。*We've arrived* ~ *late, I'm afraid.* 恐怕我們到得晚了一點。**2** ~ **of,** rather: 頗爲;稍稍;有一點: *He was* ~ *of a liar.* 他講話有點不誠實。*I found it* ~ *of a difficulty.* 我發現這事有些困難。

some·where /ˈsʌmweə(r); *US:* -hweər; ˈsʌm,hwɛr/ *adv* (in *interr, neg,* etc sentences replaced by *anywhere*) in, at, to, some place: (在問句,否定句等中用 anywhere 代替) 在某處;到某處: *It must be* ~ *near here.* (它)一定在附近某處。*Is it anywhere near here?* (它)就在附近嗎?*I didn't go anywhere yesterday.* 昨天我那裡都沒有去。*He lost it* ~ *between his office and the station.* 他在辦公室與車站之間的路上遺失了那件東西。*You will find the text* ~ *in the Bible.* 你可以在聖經裡(某處)找到該原文。

som·nam·bu·lism /sɒmˈnæmbjʊlɪzəm; sɑmˈnæmbjə,lɪzəm/ *n* [U] sleep-walking. 夢遊;夢行;夢遊症。**som·nam·bu·list** /-ɪst; -ɪst/ *n* sleep-walker. 夢遊者;患夢遊症者。

som·nol·ent /ˈsɒmnələnt; ˈsɑmnələnt/ *adj* sleepy; almost asleep; causing sleep. 思睡的;欲睡的;快睡著的;催眠的;致睡的。**~·ly** *adv* **som·nol·ence** /-əns; -əns/ *n* [U] sleepiness. 欲睡;瞌睡;思睡。

son /sʌn; sʌn/ *n* **1** male child of a parent. 兒子。***the Son of God; the Son of Man,*** Jesus Christ. 耶穌基督。***the sons of men,*** mankind. 人類。**ˈson-in-law** *n* (*pl* sons-in-law) husband of one's daughter. 女婿。**2** (used as a form of address, eg by an older man to a young man, a priest to a penitent): (用作稱呼語,如年長者對年幼者,神父對告解者): *my son.* 我的孩子。**3** ***son of,*** person having the qualities, etc indicated: 具有指明之性質等的人: *sons of freedom,* those who have inherited freedom from their ancestors; 自由的兒女(由其祖先繼承自由的人們); *a son of the soil,* one whose father worked on the land and who follows his father's occupation. (繼承父業的)農夫。

so·nar /ˈsəʊnɑː(r); ˈsonɑr/ *n* device or system for detecting and locating objects submerged in water by means of reflected sound waves. 聲納(藉聲波反射作用,探知水面下物體位置的儀器)。

so·nata /səˈnɑːtə; səˈnɑtə/ *n* (*pl* ~s /-təz; -təz/) musical composition for one instrument (eg the piano), or two (eg piano and violin), normally with three or four movements. 奏鳴曲(供一種樂器如鋼琴,或兩種樂器,如鋼琴及小提琴,演奏的樂曲,通常有三或四個樂章)。

song /sɒŋ *US:* sɔːŋ; sɔŋ/ *n* **1** [U] singing; music for the voice: 歌唱;聲樂: *burst into* ~; (突然)歌唱;唱; *the* ~ (= musical cry) *of the birds.* 鳥的鳴囀。**ˈ~·bird** *n* bird (eg blackbird, thrush) noted for its ~. 鳴禽;鳴鳥(如山烏、畫眉等)。**2** [U] poetry; verse: 詩;韻文: *renowned in* ~. 以詩着稱。**3** [C] short poem or number of verses set to music and intended to be sung: 歌詞;歌曲: *a marching* ~; 進行曲; *popular* ~*s.* 流行歌曲。**ˈ~-book** *n* collection of ~s (with both words and music). 歌集;歌本。***buy sth for a*** ~***/an old*** ~***; go for a*** ~**,** buy sth/be sold for a small amount. 賤價買入;賤價賣出。***nothing to make a*** ~ ***and dance about,*** (colloq) of little or no importance. (俗)區區的;不重要的。***a*** ~ ***and dance,*** (colloq) fuss. (俗)無謂的紛擾。**~·ster** /-stə(r); -stɚ/ *n* singer; ~bird. 歌唱者;歌手;鳴禽。**~·stress** /-strɪs; -strɪs/ *n* female singer. 女歌唱者;女歌手。

sonic /ˈsɒnɪk; ˈsɑnɪk/ *adj* relating to sound, sound-waves or the speed of sound: 聲音的;音波的;音速的: *a* ~ *bang/boom,* noise made when an aircraft exceeds the speed of sound; 音爆(飛機超過音速時所發的響聲); *the* ~ *barrier,* ⇨ *sound barrier* at sound²(3). 音障。⇨ super~, ultra~.

son·net /ˈsɒnɪt; ˈsɑnɪt/ *n* kind of poem containing 14 lines, each of 10 syllables, and with a formal pattern of rhymes. 十四行詩(每行十個音節,具嚴整的押韻格式)。**~·eer** /ˌsɒnɪˈtɪə(r); ˌsɑnəˈtɪr/ *n* (usu derog) writer of ~s. (通常含貶義)十四行詩作者。

sonny /ˈsʌnɪ; ˈsʌnɪ/ *n* (*pl* -nies) familiar form of address to a young boy. 孩子;寶寶(對小男孩的親密稱呼)。

son·or·ous /səˈnɔːrəs; səˈnorəs/ *adj* **1** having a full, deep sound: 發宏亮聲音的;響亮的: *a* ~ *voice;* 宏亮的聲音; *the* ~ *note of the temple bell.* 寺廟的宏亮鐘聲。**2** (of language, words, etc) impressive; imposing: (指語言、文字等)造成深刻印象的;醒目的;堂皇的: ~ *titles;* 醒目的標題; *a* ~ *style of writing.* 莊嚴的文體。**~·ly** *adv* **son·or·ity** /səˈnɒrətɪ *US:* -ˈnɔːr-; səˈnɔrətɪ/ *n*

sonsy /ˈsɒnsɪ; ˈsɑnsɪ/ *adj* (Scot) (蘇) *a* ~ *lass,* a plump, merry, cheerful girl. 一個豐滿、愉快、高興的女孩子。

soon /suːn; sun/ *adv* **1** not long after the present time or the time in question; in a short time. (*S*~ may occupy mid-position with the *v*, or, esp if modified by *too, very* or *quite,* end position): 不久;卽刻。(soon 可置於動詞前後,如爲 too, very 或 quite 修飾時,多置於句末): *We shall* ~ *be home.* 我們不久就到家了。*We shall be home quite* ~ *now.* 現在我們很快就會到家。*He'll be here very* ~. 他很快就會到達(此地)。*It will* ~ *be five years since we came to live in London.* 自從我們搬到倫敦來住,轉瞬就快五年了。~ ***after,*** a short time after: 在…之後不久: *He arrived* ~ *after three.* 三點鐘過後不久他就到了。(The opposite of ~ *after* is *a little before.*) (soon after 的相對語是 a little before。) **2** early: 早;快: *How* ~ *can you be ready?* 你最快在什麼時候可以準備好?*Must you leave so* ~*?* 你一定要這麼早就離去嗎?*We reached the station half an hour too* ~. 我們早半小時到達車站。*He will be here* ~*er than you expect.* 他會比你所期待的時間早到。**3** ***as/so*** ~ ***as,*** at the moment that; when; not later than: 一…就;當;不遲於;於某一時刻: *He started as* ~ *as he received the news.* 他一聽到消

息就立刻動身了。*I'll tell him the news as ~ as I see him.* 我一見到他就會告訴他這個消息。*We didn't arrive so / as ~ as we had hoped.* 我們未能像我們所希望的那麼早到達。***no ~er... than,*** immediately when or after: 一…就;剛…就: *He had no ~er / No ~er had he arrived home than he was asked to start on another journey.* 他剛到家就被要求作另一次旅行。*No ~er said than done,* ie done immediately. 說了就做。**4** (in double comparative constructions): (用於複式比較結構中): *The ~er you begin the ~er you'll finish.* 你愈早開始,就會愈早結束。*The ~er the better.* 愈快愈好。***~er or later,*** one day whether ~ or (much) later. 遲早;早晚。**5** (suggesting comparison) (含示比較意) ***(just) as ~... (as),*** with equal readiness or willingness ... (as): 同樣願意;無軒輊之分: *I would (just) as ~ stay at home as go for a walk.* 我待在家裡也好,出去散步也好。***~er than,*** rather than: 寧可…而不: *He would ~er resign than take part in such dishonest business deals.* 他寧可辭職,也不願意參與這種不誠實的買賣。*S~er than marry that man, she would earn her living as a waitress.* 她不肯嫁給那人,寧願做女侍維持生活。***as ~ as not,*** (most) willingly: (很)願意;再樂意不過: *I'd go there as ~ as not.* 我很樂意去彼處。

soot /sʊt ; sut/ *n* [U] black powder in smoke, or left by smoke on surfaces: 黑烟灰;煤烟;煤灰;油烟: *sweep the ~ out of the chimney.* 掃除烟囪的烟灰。**~y** *adj* black with ~; black like ~. 因有煤灰、烟灰等而黑的;黑如烟灰的。□ *vt* cover with ~. 覆以黑烟灰等。

sooth /suːθ ; suθ/ *n* (archaic) truth. (古)事實;眞相。*in ~,* truly. 事實上。**'~·sayer** /-seɪə(r) ; -seɚ/ *n* fortune-teller. 算命先生;占卜者。

soothe /suːð ; suð/ *vt* [VP6A] **1** make (a person, his nerves, passions) quiet or calm: 使(某人,其神經,其激情)平靜;安慰;撫慰;使鎮靜: *~ a crying baby;* 撫慰哭叫的嬰兒; *~ sb's anger;* 使人息怒; *a soothing voice.* 安撫的語氣。**2** make (pains, aches) less sharp or severe: 使(痛苦,疼痛)緩和或減輕: *~ an aching tooth;* 減輕牙疼; *a soothing lotion for the skin,* eg against sunburn. 潤膚劑(如防日晒者)。**sooth·ing·ly** *adv*

sop /sɒp ; sɑp/ *n* [C] **1** piece of bread, etc soaked in milk, soup, etc. (泡在牛奶、湯等中的)麵包片等。**2** ***a sop to sb,*** sth offered to prevent trouble or to give temporary satisfaction: 賄賂: *(throw) a sop to Cerberus,* (do) sth to pacify or bribe a troublesome person. 賄賂;收買某人;向某人行賄。□ *vt* (-pp-) [VP6A, 15B] soak (bread, etc in broth, etc). 浸泡(麵包等於湯等中)。***sop sth up,*** take up liquid, etc: 吸取液體等: *Sop up the water with this towel.* 用這條毛巾把水吸乾。**sop·ping** *adj* soaking (wet): 浸濕的;泡透的: *sopping (wet) clothes.* 濕淋淋的衣服。

soph·ism /'sɒfɪzəm ; 'sɑfɪzəm/ *n* [C, U] false reasoning or argument, intended to deceive. 詭辯;詭辯之辭。

soph·ist /'sɒfɪst ; 'sɑfɪst/ *n* person who uses clever but misleading arguments. 詭辯者。

soph·is·ti·cated /sə'fɪstɪkeɪtɪd ; sə'fɪstɪˌketɪd/ *adj* **1** having learnt the ways of the world and having lost natural simplicity; showing this: 世故的;老練的;失去天眞的: *a ~ girl;* 世故的女孩子; *a girl with ~ tastes.* 趣味及愛好顯得很世故的女孩子。**2** complex; with the latest improvements and refinements: 複雜的;最新式而且最進步的: *~ modern weapons;* 複雜的近代武器; *~ devices used in spacecraft.* 太空船的最新設備。**3** (of mental activity) refined; complex; subtle: (指心靈活動)精細的;複雜的;高深的;奥妙的: *a ~ discussion / argument.* 高深的討論(議論)。**soph·is·ti·ca·tion** /səˌfɪstɪ'keɪʃn ; səˌfɪstɪ'keʃən/ *n*

soph·is·try /'sɒfɪstrɪ ; 'sɑfɪstrɪ/ *n* (*pl* -tries) [U] use of sophisms; [C] instance of this. 詭辯(的使用);詭辯法;詭辯事例。

sopho·more /'sɒfəmɔː(r) ; 'sɑfṃˌor/ *n* (US) person in his second year at a four-year college. (美)大學二年級學生。

sop·or·ific /ˌsɒpə'rɪfɪk ; ˌsopə'rɪfɪk/ *n, adj* (substance, drink, etc) producing sleep. 催眠的;催眠劑。

sop·ping /'sɒpɪŋ ; 'sɑpɪŋ/ *adj* ⇨ sop.

soppy /'sɒpɪ ; 'sɑpɪ/ *adj* (-ier, -iest) **1** very wet. 非常濕的;浸透的。**2** (colloq) foolishly sentimental. (俗)過於感情用事的;過於傷感的。

so·prano /sə'prɑːnəʊ *US:* -'præn- ; sə'præno/ *n* (*pl* ~s /-nəʊz ; -noz/), *adj* (person having the) highest singing voice of women and girls and boys. (女子、女孩及男孩聲樂的)最高音(的);女高音(的);唱女高音或最高音者;能唱女高音或最高音者。

sorbet /'sɔːbət ; 'sɔbət/ *n* = sherbet.

sor·cerer /'sɔːsərə(r) ; 'sɔrsərɚ/ *n* man who practises magic with the help of evil spirits. 男巫;術士;魔法師。**sor·cer·ess** /'sɔːsərɪs ; 'sɔrsərɪs/ *n* woman ~. 女巫;女術士;女魔法師。**sor·cery** /'sɔːsərɪ ; 'sɔrsərɪ/ *n* (*pl* -ries) [U] witchcraft; (*pl*) evil acts done by a ~. 巫術;(複)術士行的法術或魔法。

sor·did /'sɔːdɪd ; 'sɔrdɪd/ *adj* **1** (of conditions) wretched; shabby; comfortless: (指狀況)破爛的;汚穢的;骯髒的;不舒服的: *a ~ slum;* 破爛骯髒的貧民窟; *living in ~ poverty.* 生活於貧苦中。**2** (of persons, behaviour, etc) contemptible; prompted by self-interest or meanness: (指人、行爲等)卑鄙的;自私的;下賤的: *~ motives.* 卑鄙的動機。**~·ly** *adv* **~·ness** *n*

sore /sɔː(r) ; sor/ *adj* **1** (of a part of the body) tender and painful; hurting when touched or used: (指身體的某部)敏感而疼的;碰到或用到就痛的;疼痛的: *a ~ knee / throat.* 膝(喉嚨)痛。***like a bear with a ~ head,*** ill tempered, grumpy. 脾氣大的;拗性的。***a sight for ~ eyes,*** sb or sth welcome, pleasant. 受歡迎的、令人愉快的人或物。**2** filled with sorrow; sad: 充滿哀傷的;傷心的: *a ~ heart.* 哀傷的心。**3** causing sorrow or annoyance. 使人或引起哀傷或煩惱的。***a ~ point / subject,*** one that hurts the feelings when talked about. 使人傷心之處(話題)。**4** irritated; aggrieved: 惱怒的;受冤抑的: *feel ~ about not being invited to the party.* 因未被邀請參加舞會而惱怒。**5** (old use; also adverbial) grievous(ly); severe(ly): (舊用法;亦作副詞用)嚴重的(地);劇烈的(地): *in ~ distress;* 極爲悲痛的; *in ~ need of help;* 極端需要幫助; *~ oppressed.* 深受壓迫的。□ *n* [C] **1** ~ place on the body (where the skin or flesh is injured): (身上的)痛處;傷處;瘡;潰瘍: *treat / bandage / heal a ~.* 治療(用繃帶包紮,治癒)一傷處。**2** (fig) ~ subject; painful memory: (喻)傷心的話題;痛苦的回憶: *Let's not recall old ~s.* 我們不要再提那些傷心的往事了。**~·ly** *adv* **1** severely: 嚴重地;劇烈地: *~ly tempted / afflicted.* 深受誘惑(折磨)。**2** greatly: 非常;很: *More financial help is ~ly needed.* 迫切需要更多的經濟支援。**~·ness** *n*

sor·ghum /'sɔːgəm ; 'sɔrgəm/ *n* [U] kinds of millet. 蜀黍;高粱。

sor·or·ity /sə'rɒrətɪ *US:* -'rɔːr- ; sə'rɔrətɪ/ *n* (*pl* -ties) (US) women's social club in a college or university. (美)(大學中的)女生聯誼會。

sor·rel[1] /'sɒrəl *US:* 'sɔːrəl ; 'sɔrəl/ *n* kinds of herb with sour-tasting leaves used in cooking. (植)酸模(葉含酸液的植物,用於烹調)。

sor·rel[2] /'sɒrəl *US:* 'sɔːrəl ; 'sɔrəl/ *adj, n* (of a) reddish-brown colour; horse of this colour. 紅褐色(的);栗色(的);栗色馬。

sor·row /'sɒrəʊ ; 'sɑro/ *n* [C, U] (cause of) grief or sadness; regret: 悲哀;悲傷;悔恨;其原由: *express ~ for having done wrong;* 因做錯事而悔恨; *to my great ~;* 使我感到非常悲哀; *to the ~ of all who were present;* 使所有在場的人感到悲哀; *in ~ and in joy,* when we are sad and also when we are happy. 在悲哀時及喜悅時。*His ~s had turned his hair white.* 哀傷使他的頭髮變白。***more in ~ than in anger,*** with more regret than anger for what was done, etc. (對做過的事等)懊悔多於憤怒。***the***

Man of S~s, Jesus. 耶穌。□ *vi* [VP2A, 3A] ~ ***(at/for/over),*** feel ~ (*at/for/over* sth): (爲…)感到悲哀、悲傷、悔恨等: *~ing over her child's death.* 爲她孩子的死感到悲傷。**~·ful** /-fl ; -fəl/ *adj* feeling, showing, causing, ~. 感到、顯示、引起悲哀(悲傷、悔恨等)的;可悲的;悔恨的。**~·fully** /-fəlɪ ; -fəlɪ/ *adv*

sorry /ˈsɒrɪ ; ˈsɔrɪ/ *adj* **1** (*pred* only) feeling regret or sadness: (僅作敍述用法)感到遺憾或悲傷的;惋惜的;抱歉的: *We're ~ to hear of your father's death.* 聽到令尊逝世,我們甚爲難過。*I should be ~ for you to think/if you were to think that I dislike you.* 如果你認爲我不喜歡你,我會感到遺憾。*I was ~ to hear that you thought I disliked you.* 我聽說你認爲我不喜歡你,我實在感到遺憾。***be/feel ~ (about/for sth),*** feel regret or repentance: 感到遺憾或懊悔: *Aren't you ~ for/about what you've done?* 你對你做的事情不感到遺憾嗎? *If you'll say you're ~* (= that you repent), *we'll forget the incident.* 如果你說你懊悔,我們就不再計較這件事。***be/feel ~ for sb,*** **(a)** feel sympathy: (對某人)表同情: *I feel ~ for anyone who has to drive in weather like this.* 我對於在這種天氣還必須駕車的(任何)人表示同情。**(b)** feel pity or mild contempt: 表憐憫或輕微的輕視: *I'm ~ for you, but you've been rather foolish, haven't you?* 我很替你難過,不過你頗爲不智,不是嗎? *If he doesn't realize that he must make sacrifices, I'm ~ for him.* 如果他不明白他必須有所犧牲,那我覺得他實在可憐。**2** (used to express mild regret or an apology): (用以表示適度的遺憾或道歉): *'Can you lend me a pound?'—'(I'm) S~, but I can't.'* '你能借給我一鎊錢嗎?'—'抱歉,我無能爲力。' ⇨ excuse[2](3), pardon(2). **3** (attrib) (形容用法) (-ier, -iest) pitiful: 可憐的: *in a ~ state;* 處於可憐的狀況; worthless; shabby: 無價值的;不體面的: *a ~ excuse.* 理由不充足的藉口。

sort[1] /sɔːt ; sɔrt/ *n* [C] **1** group or class of persons or things which are alike in some way: (人或物的)類;輩;品等: *Pop music is the ~ she likes most.* 流行音樂是她最喜歡的音樂。*What ~ of people does he think we are?* 他認爲我們是哪一類的人? *We can't approve of this ~ of thing/these ~ of things/things of this ~.* 我們不能贊同這類的事。***of a ~; of ~s,*** used (colloq) to suggest that what is referred to does not fully deserve the name: (俗)用以暗示名實不全相符的事物: *They served coffee of a ~/coffee of ~s/a ~ of coffee.* 他們供應勉强稱得上是咖啡的飲料。***~ of,*** (colloq) rather; to some extent: (俗)頗爲;有幾分;到某種程度: *I sort of thought* (= had a vague idea) *this would happen.* 我總有點覺得這事會發生。⇨ *kind of* at kind[2](2). **2** ***after a ~; in a ~,*** to a certain extent. 到達某種程度;有幾分;有些。**3** ***a good ~,*** (esp) a person who is likable, who has good qualities. (尤指)可愛的人;有良好品質的人。**4** ***out of ~s,*** (colloq) feeling unwell, out of spirits. (俗)不適;精神不佳。

sort[2] /sɔːt ; sɔrt/ *vt, vi* **1** [VP6A, 15B] ***~ sth (out),*** arrange in groups; separate things of one sort from things of other sorts: 分類;整理;歸類;畫分: *The boy was ~ing/~ing out/over the foreign stamps he had collected.* 那男孩在整理他所搜集的外國郵票。*We must ~ out the good apples from the bad.* 我們必須把好的蘋果與壞的分開。***~ sth out,*** (colloq) put in good order; solve: (俗)整理好;解決: *I'll leave you to ~ that out,* find a solution. 我將把該問題交給你解決。*Let's leave that pair to ~ themselves out,* clear up their problems, misunderstandings, etc. 我們讓那一對(夫婦等)自行解決他們之間的問題吧。**2** ***~ well/ill with,*** (liter) be in/out of harmony with: (文)配得上(配不上);與…相符(不相符): *His heroic death ~ed well with his character.* 他那種英雄式的死法正合他的個性。**~er** *n* (esp) post-office worker who ~s letters. 分類者;整理者;(尤指)郵局中的信件歸類者。

sor·tie /ˈsɔːtiː ; ˈsɔrti/ *n* [C] **1** attack made by besieged soldiers on their besiegers. (被圍攻之士兵對圍攻者的)出擊;突擊;反擊。**2** flight made by one aircraft during military operations: (作戰時一架飛機的)出勤;架次: *The four planes each made two ~s yesterday.* 那四架飛機昨天各出動兩架次。

SOS /ˌes əʊ ˈes ; ˈɛs,oˈɛs/ *n* [C] **1** message for help (sent by radio, etc) from a ship, aircraft, etc when in danger. Cf 參較 *mayday call.* (船、飛機等遇險時經由無線電等發出的)求救信號;求救電碼。**2** urgent call for help, eg a broadcast to find relatives of a person seriously ill. 緊急求救呼籲(如廣播找尋重病者的親屬等)。

so-so /ˌsəʊˈsəʊ ; ˈso,so/ *pred adj, adv* (colloq) not very good: (俗)還好;馬馬虎虎;勉勉强强: *'How are you feeling today?'—'Oh, only so-so.'* '你今天覺得如何?'—'哦,馬馬虎虎。'

sot /sɒt ; sɑt/ *n* habitual drunkard, esp one whose mind has become dulled. 經常喝醉酒的人;酒鬼(尤指心智已變遲鈍者)。**sot·tish** /ˈsɒtɪʃ ; ˈsɑtɪʃ/ *adj* habitually drinking too much and, for this reason, dull or stupid. 經常飲酒過多(因而變愚鈍)的;濫飲酒的。**sot·tish·ly** *adv* **sot·tish·ness** *n*

sotto voce /ˌsɒtəʊ ˈvəʊtʃɪ ; ˈsɑtoˈvotʃɪ/ *adv* (I) in a low voice, aside. (義)低聲地;輕聲地;旁白地。

sou /suː ; su/ *n* former French coin of low value; (fig) very small amount of money: 蘇(法國昔時一種低值硬幣);(喻)極少量金錢: *He hasn't a sou,* is penniless. 他一文不名。

sou·brette /suːˈbret ; suˈbrɛt/ *n* maidservant (usu pert, coquettish, fond of intrigue) in a comedy for the theatre; actress taking such a part. (舞臺劇中)喜劇裡的女傭(通常孟浪、賣俏而喜弄詭謀);扮此角色的女演員。

sou·bri·quet /ˈsuːbrɪkeɪ ; ˈsubrɪ,ke/ *n* = sobriquet.

souf·flé /ˈsuːfleɪ *US:* suːˈfleɪ ; suˈfle/ *n* [C] (F) dish of eggs, milk, etc beaten to a froth, flavoured (with cheese, etc) and baked. (法)蛋奶酥(蛋、奶等攪成泡沫狀,以乳酪等調味,焙製而成的食品)。

sough /sʌf *US:* saʊ ; sʌf/ *vi* [VP2A], *n* (make a) murmuring or whispering sound (as of wind in trees). (發)颯颯聲;(發)颼颼聲(如樹間風聲)。

sought /sɔːt ; sɔt/ *pt, pp* of seek.

soul /səʊl ; sol/ *n* [C] **1** non-material part of a person, believed to exist for ever: 靈魂(人之非物質部分,被相信永遠存在者): *believe in the immortality of the ~;* 相信靈魂不朽; *commend one's ~ to God,* (when at the point of death). (彌留時)把靈魂付託給上帝。*He eats hardly enough to keep body and ~ together,* to keep him alive. 他吃的份量簡直不够維持其生命。*She has a ~ above material pleasures.* 她有一個超越物質享受的靈魂。**2** (often without *indef art*) emotional, moral and intellectual energy: (常不加不定冠詞)感情、精神及智力;心力;精神;魄力: *This music has no soul.* 這音樂缺乏力量。*He is a man without a soul,* is unfeeling, selfish. 他是個寡情自私的人。*He put his heart and ~ into the work.* 他把精神心力全部貫注在工作上。**3** ***the life and ~ of the party, etc,*** (person looked upon as the) liveliest person present at the party, etc. (某團體等中的)核心人物;主腦。**4** person regarded as the pattern or personification of some virtue or quality: 典型;化身: *He is the ~ of honour/discretion.* 他是榮譽(謹愼)的典型。**5** spirit of a dead person: 幽靈;死者的靈魂: *ˌAll 'S~s' Day,* 2 Nov. 萬靈節(十一月二日)。**6** person: 人: *There wasn't a ~ to be seen,* No one was in sight. 連一個人也看不見。*The ship sank with 200 ~s.* 那船載着二百人沉沒了。**7** (expressing familiarity, pity, etc according to context): (依上下文,表示熟悉、親密、憐憫等): *He's a cheery ~,* a cheerful man. 他是一個活潑愉快的人。*Be a good ~ and lend me a dollar.* 做做好事借給我一塊錢吧。*She's lost all her money, poor ~.* 她損失了全部的錢,可憐的人。**8** (US colloq) all those qualities that enable a person to be in harmony with himself and others, used esp by Afro-Americans and expressed through their music and dancing. (美俗)諧和力(使自己保持諧和以及與他人保持諧和的一切特質，尤指美國黑人所使用，並表現在他們的音樂及舞蹈中者)。 ~ **brother/sister,** fellow Afro-American; person who thinks and feels in the same way as oneself. 美國黑人;與自己想法和感覺相同的人。 '~ **music,** modern Afro-American popular blues music with strong rhythm for dancing. 美國黑人音樂(指其近代流行的布魯斯舞曲)。 **9** (compounds) (複合字) '~**-destroying** *adj* killing the ~ or spirit: 毀滅靈魂的: *~-destroying work.* 損人神志的作品。 '~**-stirring** *adj* exciting, etc. 振奮的;鼓舞的;提神的。 **~ful** /-fl ; -fl/ *adj* having, affecting, showing, deep feeling: 熱情的;深情的: *~ful eyes/music/glances.* 熱情的眼睛(音樂，瞥視)。 **~·fully** /-fəlɪ ; -flɪ/ *adv* **~·less** *adj* without higher or deeper feelings. 無靈魂的;無情的;膚淺的。 **~·less·ly** *adv*

sound[1] /saund ; saund/ *adj* **1** healthy; in good condition; not hurt, injured or decayed: 健全的;完好的;未受損傷的;未腐敗的: *~ fruit/teeth;* 完好的水果(牙齒); *have a ~ constitution.* 有健全的體格。 ***a ~ mind in a ~ body,*** good mental and physical health. 身心健康。 ***~ in wind and limb,*** (colloq) physically fit. (俗)體格健全的。 **2** dependable; based on reason; prudent: 可靠的;有理由的;愼重的: *a ~ argument/policy;* 可靠的論據(政策); *~ advice;* 睿智的忠告; *a ~ business firm.* 信譽昭著的商家。 *Is he ~ on national defence?* Are his views, etc reasonable, well-founded? 他的國防見解正確嗎？ **3** capable, careful: 有能力的;小心的;穩健的: *a ~ tennis player.* 穩健的網球員。 **4** thorough; complete: 徹底的;完全的: *have a ~ sleep,* a deep and peaceful sleep; 酣睡; *be a ~ sleeper;* 是酣睡者; *give sb a ~ thrashing.* 痛毆某人。 □ *adv* ***be/fall ~ asleep,*** be/become deeply and peacefully asleep. 酣睡。 **~·ly** *adv* in a ~ manner; thoroughly: 健全地;完好地;可靠地;愼重地;穩健地;徹底地: *a ~ly based argument;* 基礎健全的論據; *sleep ~ly;* 酣睡; *be ~ly beaten at tennis.* 在網球賽中被徹底擊敗。 **~·ness** *n*

sound[2] /saund ; saund/ *n* [C, U] **1** that which is or can be heard: 聲音;音響: *within ~ of the guns,* near enough to hear them; 在可聞槍砲聲範圍內; *'vowel ~s,* eg /uː, ʌ, ə/ *and 'consonant ~s,* eg /p, b, ʃ, ʒ/. 母音(如 /uː, ʌ, ə/)和子音(如 /p, b, ʃ, ʒ/)。 *We heard the ~ of voices.* 我們聽到人聲。 **2** (*sing* only) mental impression produced by sth stated (or read): (僅用單數)敍述或閱讀的事物所產生的印象: *The news has a sinister ~,* seems to be sinister. 這新聞似乎不吉祥。 *I don't like the ~ of it.* 這東西聽起來叫我不喜歡。 **3** (compounds, etc) (複合字等) ˌ~ '**archives** *n pl* recordings on disc or magnetic tape of broadcasts considered to deserve being kept for future use: 錄音檔案;音響檔案(廣播錄音帶等，被認爲有保存價值者): *the BBC ~ archives.* 英國廣播公司的音響檔案。 '~ **barrier** *n* point at which an aircraft's speed equals that of ~-waves, causing sonic booms: 音障(飛機達到音速產生音爆的分際)。 *break the ~ barrier,* exceed the speed of sound. 超越音速。 '~**-box** *n* part of an old-fashioned gramophone containing a diaphragm and into which the needle that moves over a record is fixed (corresponding to the pick-up of an electrical reproducer). (舊式留聲機的)唱頭(相當於電唱機的 pick-up). '~ **effects** *n pl* sounds (recorded on discs, magnetic tape, film, etc) for use in broadcasts, in making films, etc or produced when needed (in a studio, etc). 音響效果(錄於唱片、錄音帶、軟片等上的聲音，用於廣播、電影製作等中)。 '~**-film** *n* cinema film with dialogue, music, etc recorded on it. 有聲影片。 '~**-proof** *adj* constructed so that ~(s) cannot pass through or into: 隔音的;防音的: *a ~proof studio.* 有隔音設備的工作室。 Hence, 由此產生， '~**·proof,** *vt* [VP6A] make ~proof. 使隔音;給…隔音。 '~**-recording,** (contrasted with *video-recording*) sth recorded in ~ only. 錄音(與 video-recording 相對)。 '~**-track** *n* (music, etc on a) track or band at the side of a cinema film which has the recording ~. 音帶;音道(有聲電影片邊上的錄音部分);音帶上所錄之音樂等。 '~**-wave** *n* vibrations made in the air or other medium by which ~ is carried. 音波;聲波。 **~·less** *adj* **~·less·ly** *adv*

sound[3] /saund ; saund/ *vt, vi* **1** [VP6A] produce sound from; make (sth) produce sound: 使響;使(某物)發聲: *~ a trumpet.* 吹喇叭。 **2** [VP6A] utter: 發出: *~ a note of alarm/danger.* 放警報(發出危險訊號)。 **3** [VP6A] pronounce: 發…的音;讀…的音: *Don't ~ the 'h' in 'hour' or the 'b' in 'dumb'.* hour 中的 h 或 dumb 中的 b 不要發音。 **4** [VP6A] give notice of: 通知;發布: *~ the alarm,* eg by ringing a bell; 發布警號(如藉敲鐘); *~ the retreat,* by blowing a bugle. 吹撤退號。 **5** [VP2A] give forth sound: 發聲;作響: *The trumpet ~ed.* 喇叭響了。 *This black key* (eg on the piano) *won't ~,* No sound is produced when the key is struck. 這黑鍵(如鋼琴上者)按下去不會響。 **6** [VP6A] test, examine (the wheels of a railway carriage, etc by striking them; a person's lungs by tapping the chest). 聽驗(火車之輪等);擊驗;聽診(人之肺);敲診。 **7** [VP2C, D] give an impression when heard (often fig): 聽起來;似乎(常作比喻用法): *How sweet the music ~s!* 這音樂聽起來多悅耳！ *It ~s to me as if there's a tap running somewhere,* I think I can hear water running from a tap. 我好像聽到某處水龍頭的流水聲。 *His explanation ~s all right,* seems reasonable enough. 他的解釋聽起來似乎有道理。 *Her excuse ~s very hollow,* is unconvincing. 她的藉口難以令人心服。 **8** '~**·ing-board** *n* canopy placed over a platform to direct the ~ of the speaker's voice towards his listeners; thin plate of wood on a musical instrument, for magnifying its ~; (fig) way of causing an opinion, plan, etc to be widely heard. (裝在講臺等上面，使聲音送至聽者的)響板;共鳴板;樂器上擴大音響的薄板;(喻)宣揚意見，計畫等的方法。

sound[4] /saund ; saund/ *vt, vi* **1** [VP6A, 2A] test the depth of (the sea, etc) by letting down a weighted line (called a *'~ing-line* or *~ing apparatus);* find the depth of water in a ship's hold (with a *'~ing-rod*); get records of temperature, pressure, etc in (the upper atmosphere) (by sending up instruments in a *'~ing-balloon*). 以測深索(sounding-line 或 sounding apparatus) 測量(海等)的深度; 以測深桿 (sounding-rod) 探測船艙內的水深;藉升空探測氣球中的儀器以獲得(上層大氣層)之溫度、壓力等的記錄。 **2** [VP6A, 15A, B] ***~ sb (out) (about/on sth),*** try (esp cautiously or in a reserved manner) to learn sb's views, sentiments, etc: (尤指小心或含蓄地)試探他人的觀點、意見等: *I will ~ the manager about/on the question of holidays.* 我將就假日問題試探經理的意見。 *Have you ~ed him out yet,* tried to learn his views? 你已探聽出他的看法嗎？ **~·ings** *n pl* **1** measurements obtained by ~ing(1). (以測深索等測出的)水之深度;(藉升空氣球記錄下來的) 上層氣流的溫度、壓力等。 **2** reactions obtained by ~ing(2). 試探或調查他人意見等所得的反應。 **3** place or area near enough to the shore to make it possible to ~(1): 近岸可測出水深之處或區域: *We are in ~ings/have come into ~ings.* 我們在淺水處(接近海岸了)。

sound[5] /saund ; saund/ *n* [C] narrow passage of water joining two larger areas of water; strait. 海峽;水峽。

soup[1] /suːp ; sup/ *n* [U] liquid food made by cooking meat, vegetables, etc in water: 湯;羹: *chicken/pea/tomato ~.* 雞(豌豆,蕃茄)湯。 ***in the ~,*** (colloq) in trouble. (俗)在困難中。 '~**-kitchen** *n* public establishment for supplying ~ to persons who are poor, or after a calamity such as an earthquake or flood. (救濟貧苦者,或在災後所設立的)施湯所;施粥場。

soup² /suːp ; sup/ *vt* [VP15B] ～ ***sth up,*** (sl) fit (a motor-vehicle, its engine) with a supercharger (to increase the power output, and so its speed): (俚)以增壓器裝在(機動車,其引擎)上(俾加大其馬力,增加其速度): *a ～ed-up car.* 裝有增壓器的轎車。

soup·çon /ˈsuːpsɒn *US:* suːpˈsɒn ; supˈsɔ̃/ *n* (F) (usu 通常作 ***a*** ～ ***of***) small amount; trace: (法)少量;少許: *a ～ of garlic in the salad／of malice in his remarks.* 沙拉中的蒜味(他的言詞中的惡意)。

sour /saʊə(r) ; saʊr/ *adj* **1** having a sharp taste (like that of vinegar, a lemon or an unripe plum, apple, etc). 酸的;有酸味的。～ ***grapes*** ⇨ grape. **2** having a taste of fermentation: 有發酵味道的; 酸腐的: ～ *milk;* 酸奶; *a ～ smell,* ie of sth that has fermented. 酸腐氣味。 **3** (fig) bad-tempered; sharp-tongued: (喻)壞脾氣的; 乖戾的; 說話尖刻的: *made ～ by disappointments.* 因失望而變得乖戾。 *What a ～ face she has!* 她的臉色多難看！□ *vt, vi* [VP6A, 2A] turn or become ～ (lit, fig): (使)變酸;(使)變乖戾(字面,喻): *The hot weather has ～ed the milk.* 炎熱的天氣使牛奶變酸了。*Her personality has ～ed.* 她的性情變得乖戾了。*The old man has been ～ed by poverty.* 那老人因貧困而變得乖戾了。 **～·ly** *adv* **～·ness** *n*

source /sɔːs ; sors/ *n* [C] **1** starting-point of a river: 河的源頭;水源: *the ～s of the Nile.* 尼羅河的發源地。*Where does the Rhine have its ～?* 萊茵河發源於何處？ **2** place from which sth comes or is got: 來源;出處: *The news comes from a reliable ～.* 這項消息出自可靠的來源。*Is that well the ～ of infection for these cases of typhoid?* 那口井是傳染這些傷寒病例的來源嗎？ **3** (*pl*) original documents, etc serving as material for a study, eg of sb's life, a period of history: (複)原始資料; 原始文件等: (attrib) (形容用法) ～ *materials.* 原始資料。

souse /saʊs ; saʊs/ *vt* [VP6A] **1** throw into water; throw water on. 投入水中;潑水於…上。**2** put (fish, etc) into salted water, vinegar, etc to preserve it: 把(魚等)放進鹽水、醋等中以醃藏;醃漬: *～d herrings.* 醃青魚。 **3** **～d** (*pp*) (sl) drunk. (俚)酒醉的。

sou·tane /suːˈtɑːn ; suˈtɑn/ *n* (F) (in the RC Church) priest's cassock. (法)(天主教)祭師的法衣。

south /saʊθ ; saʊθ/ *n* **1** ⇨ the illus at compass. (參看 compass 之插圖) one of the four cardinal points of the compass, on the right of a person facing the sunrise; part of any place, country, etc lying farther in this direction than other parts: 南;南方;南部: *the ～ of London／England.* 倫敦(英格蘭)南部。*Mexico is to the ～ of the US.* 墨西哥在美國南方。 **2** (attrib) situated in, living in, pertaining to, coming from, the ～: (形容用法) 位於、住在、有關、來自南方的: *S～ Wales;* 南威爾斯; *S～ America;* 南美洲; *the S～ Pacific;* 南太平洋; *a room with a ～ aspect,* with windows facing ～; 南面有窗的房間; *grow roses on a ～ wall;* 在南面的牆上種薔薇; *the S～ Pole.* 南極。□ *adv* to or towards the ～: 在或向南方: *The ship was sailing due ～.* 那船向正南方航行。 **ˌ～-ˈeast, ˌ～-ˈwest** (abbr 略作 **SE, SW**), *nn, adjj, advv* (sometimes, esp naut, 有時作,尤用於航海, **sou'-east** /ˌsaʊˈiːst ; ˌsaʊˈist/, **sou'-west** /ˌsaʊ ˈwest ; ˌsaʊˈwɛst/) (regions) midway between ～ and east, ～ and west. (向)東南方(的); (向)西南方(的)。 **ˌ～-～-ˈeast, ˌ～-～-ˈwest** (abbr 略作 **SSE, SSW**) *nn, adjj, advv* (sometimes, esp naut, 有時作,尤用於航海, **ˌsou'-sou'-ˈeast, ˌsou'-sou'-ˈwest**) (regions) midway between ～ and ～east, ～west. (向)南南東方(的); (向)南南西方(的)。 **ˌ～-ˈeaster** *n* [C] strong wind blowing from the ～east. 東南(强)風。 **ˌ～-ˈeaster·ly** *adj* (of wind) from the ～east; (of direction) towards the ～east. (指風)來自東南的; (指方向)向東南方的。 **ˌ～-ˈwester, sou'-wester** /ˌsaʊ ˈwestə(r) ; ˌsaʊˈwɛstɚ/ *n* **(a)** strong ～west wind. 西南(强)風。 **(b)** (always 總是作 *sou'wester*) waterproof (usu oilskin) hat with a wide flap at the back to protect the neck. 護頸防水帽(通常爲油布製成,後沿寬平,可護頸)。 **ˌ～-ˈwester·ly** *adj* (of wind) from the ～west; (of direction) towards the ～west. (指風)來自西南方的; (指方向)向西南方的。 **ˌ～·ˈeastern** /-ˈiːstən ; -ˈistɚn/ *adj* of, from, situated in, the ～east. 來自、位於、有關東南方的。 **ˌ～·ˈwestern** /-ˈwestən ; -ˈwɛstɚn/ *adj* of, from, situated in the ～west. 來自、位於、有關西南方的。 **～·ward(s)** /ˈsaʊθwədz ; ˈsaʊθwɚdz/ *adv* towards the ～. 向南方。

south·er·ly /ˈsʌðəlɪ ; ˈsʌðɚlɪ/ *adj, adv* **1** (of winds) blowing from the south. (指風)吹自南方: **2** towards the south: 朝向南方: *The plane flew off in a ～ direction.* 那飛機向南方飛去。

south·ern /ˈsʌðən ; ˈsʌðɚn/ *adj* in or of the south: 南方的;在南方的;有關南方的: ～ *Europe;* 南歐; *the S～ States of the USA.* 美國南方各州。 **～er** *n* person from the ～ part of the country, esp from the S～ States (US). 南方人;南部人;(尤指)美國南方各州的人。 **ˈ～·most** /-məʊst ; -ˌmost/ *adj* farthest south. 極南的。

sou·venir /ˌsuːvəˈnɪə(r) *US:* ˈsuːvənɪər ; ˌsuvəˈnɪr/ *n* [C] sth taken, bought or received as a gift, and kept as a reminder of a person, place or event. 紀念物;紀念品;有紀念意義的禮物。

sou'·wester /ˌsaʊˈwestə(r);ˌsaʊˈwɛstɚ/ ⇨ south(2).

sov·er·eign /ˈsɒvrɪn ; ˈsɑvrɪn/ *adj* **1** (of power) highest; without limit; (of a nation, state, ruler) having ～ power: (指權力)最高的;無上的;無限的;(指國家、政府、統治者)有至高無上權力的; 有主權的: *become a ～ state,* fully self-governing and independent in foreign affairs. 變爲主權國(獨立自主的國家)。 **2** excellent; effective: 極好的;有效的: *Is there a ～ remedy for cancer?* 治療癌症有好的方法嗎？□ *n* **1** ～ ruler, eg a king, queen or emperor. 最高統治者(如國王、女王、皇帝)。 **2** British gold coin not now in circulation (face value one pound). 英國金幣(面值一鎊,現已不通用)。 **～ty** /ˈsɒvrəntɪ ; ˈsɑvrɪntɪ/ *n* [U] ～ power. 主權;君權;統治權;至高無上的權力。

so·viet /ˈsəʊvɪət ; ˈsovɪɪt/ *n* [C] one of the councils of workers, etc in any part of the USSR (the Union of S～ Socialist Republics); any of the higher groups to which these councils give authority, forming part of the system of government (*the Supreme S～*) of the whole of the USSR: (蘇聯各地區或各部分的) 工人代表會; 評議會; (經由代表會授權,成爲政府體制一部分的)蘇維埃: *S～ Russia;* 蘇俄; *the S～ Union.* 蘇聯。 **ˈ～·ize** /-aɪz ; -ˌaɪz/ *vt* convert to the ～ system of government. 蘇維埃化(使變爲蘇維埃體制的政府)。

sow¹ /saʊ ; saʊ/ *n* fully grown female pig. (發育成熟的)母豬;牝豬。⇨ boar, hog, swine.

sow² /səʊ ; so/ *vt, vi* (*pt* sowed, *pp* sown /səʊn ; son/ or sowed) [VP6A, 15A, 2A] put (seed) on or in the ground or in soil (in pots, seed-boxes, etc); plant (land *with* seed): 播(種子)於地面或土壤中,或花盆中,或種子箱中等;以種子播種於(土地): *sow grass;* 種草; *sow a plot of land with grass;* 播青草種子於一片土地; (fig) (喻) *sow the seeds of hatred.* 散佈仇恨種子。*It's too soon to sow yet.* 現在還不到播種的時候。 **～er** *n* one who sows. 播種者。

sox /sɒks ; sɑks/ *n pl* (trade use) (商業用法) *pl* of *sock.*

soy /sɔɪ ; sɔɪ/, **soya** /ˈsɔɪə ; ˈsɔɪə/ *n* **ˈsoy(a) bean,** bean grown as food and for the oil obtained from its seeds. 黃豆(作物);大豆(作物)。 **ˌsoy ˈsauce,** sauce made by fermenting soy beans in brine. (用黃豆製造的)醬油。

soz·zled /ˈsɒzld ; ˈsɑzəld/ *adj* (GB, sl) very drunk. (英,俚)爛醉的。

spa /spɑː ; spɑ/ *n* (place where there is a) spring

of mineral water having medicinal properties. 有治療功效的礦泉；溫泉；有礦泉或溫泉之處。

space /speɪs ; spes/ *n* **1** [U] that in which all objects exist and move: 空間；太空: *The universe exists in ~.* 宇宙存在於太空。*Travel through ~ to other planets interests many people today.* 現在很多人對去太空其他行星旅行感到興趣。**'~-capsule, '~-craft, '~-helmet, '~-rocket, '~-ship, '~-suit, '~-vehicle** *nn* of the kind needed for travel beyond the earth's atmosphere. (太空旅行所需要的各種裝備) 太空艙；太空船；太空帽；太空火箭；太空船；太空衣；太空車。⇨ the illus at capsule, rocket. 參看 capsule, rocket 之插圖。**,~-'time** *n* (also known as 'the fourth dimension') fusion of time and the three dimensions of ~, as a concept much used in modern physics and philosophy. 第四度空間(時間與三度空間的隔合，近代物理及哲學用到甚多的概念)。 **2** [C, U] interval or distance between two or more objects: (二物或多物之間的)間隔；距離: *the ~s between printed words;* 印刷文字間的間隔; *separated by a ~ of ten feet;* 隔以十呎距離; *put as much ~ as possible between the lines;* 盡量拉開各行間的距離; *leave a blank ~ for sth to be added.* 留出空白以便加添某物。**'~-bar** *n* bar in a typewriter, tapped to make ~s between words. (打字機上的)空間棒(按之即可在字間留出空格)。**3** [C, U] area or volume: 面積；體積: *open ~s,* (esp) land, in or near a town, not built on. 空曠處；(尤指市內或市郊的)空地。*Clear a ~ on the platform for the speakers.* 給演說的人們在台上騰出一塊地方。**'~-heater** *n* heating apparatus (electric, or oil-burning) designed to warm a room by radiation or convection. 空間加熱器(用電力或燃油，藉輻射或對流作用，使房間溫暖)。 **4** [U] limited or unoccupied place or area; room(3): 有限的或未佔用的地方或區域；空位；空處；餘地: *There isn't enough ~ in this classroom for thirty desks.* 這教室容納不下三十張書桌。*Have you enough ~ to work in?* 你有够你做事的空間嗎？ **5** (*sing* only) period of time: (僅用單數)一段時間；時期: *a ~ of three years.* 三年的時間。□ *vt* [VP6A, 15B] **~ *sth (out)*,** set out with regular ~s between: (依一定的距離)分隔某物；隔開: *~ out the posts three feet apart;* 按三呎的間隔栽放柱子; *~ out the type more;* 字間多留些空白；(打字或鉛印)字母與字母間隔開一點；~ (= spread) *out payments* (eg for a house) *over twenty years;* 二十年分期付款(如購屋)；*a well-~d family,* one in which children are born at planned intervals of time. 計畫生育的家庭(子女生育相隔的時間依照計畫者)。**,~ed 'out** *adj* (US sl) drugged; drunk. (美俚)服過麻醉藥的；服過迷幻藥的；喝醉了的。 **,single-/,double-'spacing** *n* [U] the arrangement of typed material with single/double ~s between the lines. (打字時行與行間的)單行(雙行)空距。

spacious /'speɪʃəs ; 'speʃəs/ *adj* having much space; roomy. 空間多的；廣大的；寬敞的。**~·ly** *adv* **~·ness** *n*

spade /speɪd ; sped/ *n* **1** tool for digging. 鏟；鍬。⇨ the illus at tool. 參看 tool 之插圖。**'~-work** *n* (fig) hard work (to bed) one at the start of an undertaking. (喻)事業等起始的艱苦工作；起步工作。***call a ~ a ~*,** speak plainly. 直言無諱；坦白地說。**2** (one of a) suit of playing-cards: (一張)黑桃牌: *the five of ~s.* 黑桃五(點)(牌面上有五個黑桃圖形者)。⇨ the illus at card. 參看 card 之插圖。□ *vt* [VP6A, 15B] **~ *sth (up)*,** dig (up) with a ~. 以鏟或鍬挖掘；鏟起。**'~·ful** /-fʊl ; -,fʊl/ *n* amount that is taken up by a ~. 一鏟或一鍬(之量)。

spa·ghetti /spə'getɪ ; spə'gɛtɪ/ *n* [U] Italian pasta of narrow long rods, cooked by boiling. 義大利麵條。

spake /speɪk ; spek/ (old or poet) (舊或詩) *pt* of speak.

spam /spæm ; spæm/ *n* [U] (P) chopped or minced ham, spiced, cooked, sold tinned in the form of a loaf, and usu eaten cold. 斯般(剁碎的火腿，加香料烹製而成，以長條形罐頭包裝，通常冷食)。

span /spæn ; spæn/ *n* [C] **1** distance between the tips of a person's thumb and little finger when stretched out (esp as a measure, = 9 inches). 指距；一扠(拇指與小指伸開時的距離，尤用作量度單位，合九吋)。 **2** distance or part between the supports of an arch: 拱架二支柱間的距離或部分；跡距；跨度；架徑；孔；支點距: *The bridge crosses the river in a single ~.* 這橋祇用一個架徑跨河。*The arch has a ~ of 60 metres.* 這拱門內寬六十公尺。 **3** length in time, from beginning to end: 自始至終的一段時間；期間: *the ~ of life;* 一生的時間; *for a short ~ of time.* 短短的一段時間。 **4** (S Africa) pair of horses or mules; yoke of oxen. (南非)雙馬；雙騾；共軛牛。 **5 ~ roof** *n* one with two inclined roofs (contrasted with a lean-to roof): 等斜屋頂；雙斜屋頂(與單向傾斜之屋頂相對): *a ~-roof greenhouse.* 等斜(屋)頂溫室。□ *vt* (-nn-) [VP6A] **1** extend across (from side to side): 跨過；架(從一邊至另一邊): *The Thames is ~ned by many bridges.* 泰晤士河上架設有許多橋。*His life ~ned almost the whole of the 19th c.* 他的一生幾乎跨過整個十九世紀。**2** measure by ~s(1). 以指距量；以扠量。

spangle /'spæŋgl ; 'spæŋgl/ *n* [C] tiny disc of shining metal, esp one of many, as used for ornament on a dress, etc. 發光的小金屬片(尤指衣着等上裝飾用者)。□ *vt* (esp in *pp*) (尤用過去分詞) cover with, or as with, ~s. 覆以或似覆以發光的小金屬片。**the Star-S~d Banner,** ⇨ star(2).

Span·iard /'spænɪəd ; 'spænjəd/ *n* native of Spain. 西班牙人。

span·iel /'spænɪəl ; 'spænjəl/ *n* sorts of dog with short legs, long, silky hair and large, drooping ears. 獚(一種毛長耳垂之犬)。

Span·ish /'spænɪʃ ; 'spænɪʃ/ *adj* of Spain; of the Spaniards, or their language. 西班牙的；西班牙人的；西班牙語的。**~ onion,** mild flavoured, yellow-skinned variety. 西班牙洋蔥(皮黃，味較淡)。**the S~ Main,** (hist) the NE coast of S America and the Caribbean Sea, near this coast. (史)南美洲之東北岸及靠近此海岸的加勒比海。□ *n* the ~ language. 西班牙語。

spank /spæŋk ; spæŋk/ *vt, vi* **1** [VP6A] punish (a child) by slapping on the buttocks with the open hand or a slipper, etc. 用巴掌或拖鞋等打(小孩)屁股以爲懲罰；拍打；拍擊。 **2** [VP2C] **~ *(along)*,** (esp of a horse or a ship) move along at a good pace. (尤指馬或船)急行；快行。**~·ing** *n* slapping on the buttocks: 打屁股: *give a child a ~ing.* 打小孩一頓屁股。□ *adj* (dated colloq) first-rate; excellent: (過時俗語)第一流的；極好的: *have a ~ing time;* 玩得很開心; *a ~ing* (= strong) *breeze.* 疾風。

span·ner /'spænə(r) ; 'spænɚ/ *n* (US 美 = *wrench*) tool for gripping and turning nuts on screws, bolts, etc. 扳手；扳鉗；螺旋鉗。⇨ the illus at tool. 參看 tool 之插圖。***throw a '~ in/into the works*,** sabotage a scheme, etc. 破壞一項計畫等。

spar¹ /spɑː(r) ; spɑr/ *n* strong wooden or metal, pole used as a mast, yard, boom, etc. 檣；桁；帆桅。⇨ the illus at barque. 參看 barque 之插圖。

spar² /spɑː(r) ; spɑr/ *vi* (-rr-) [VP2A, C] make the motions of attack and defence with the fists (as in boxing); (fig) dispute or argue. 用拳攻擊及防禦(如拳賽中)；拳鬪；(喻)爭論；爭辯；對駁。**'~·ring-match** *n* demonstration boxing match; (fig) dispute or argument. 示範或練習性拳賽；(喻)爭論；爭辯；對駁。**'~·ring-partner** *n* man with whom a boxer ~s as part of his training. 拳擊者訓練時的對手；練拳伴。

spar³ /spɑː(r) ; spɑr/ *n* kinds of non-metallic mineral, easily cleavable. 晶石(各種易劈裂的非金屬礦石)。

spare¹ /speə(r) ; spɛr/ *adj* **1** additional to what is usually needed or used; in reserve for use when needed; (of time) for leisure; unoccupied; 多餘的；剩餘的；備用的；(指時間)空暇的；未佔用的: *I have* *no/very little ~ time/money*, no time/money that I cannot use. 我沒有(很少有)空暇(餘錢)。*Surely you carry a ~ wheel in the back of your car?* 你一定在車子後面帶着一個備用輪胎罷？ *We have no ~ room/We don't have a ~ room* (= extra bedroom, eg for a guest) *in our house.* 我們家裡沒有多餘的房間(如供客人住者)。**~ part,** part to replace a broken or worn-out part of a machine, etc. (機器等的)備用零件。 **2** (of persons) thin; lean: (指人)瘦的: *a tall, ~ man;* 高而瘦的人; *a ~ figure;* 瘦身材; *~ of build.* 體態清瘦的。 **3** (attrib only) small in quantity: (僅作形容用法)少量的;貧乏的: *a ~ meal;* 不豐富的一餐; *on a ~ diet.* 在節食。 **ˌ~-'rib,** rib of pork with most of the meat cut off. (豬肉)小排。□ *n* [C] ~ part (for a machine, etc). (機器等的)備件。**~·ly** *adv* in a ~(2, 3) manner: 瘦瘠的;清瘦地;不豐富地: *~ly built.* 體態清瘦的。**~·ness** *n*

spare² /speə(r) ; spɛr/ *vt, vi* **1** [VP6A, 12A, 13A] refrain from hurting, damaging or destroying; show mercy to: 不傷害;赦免;寬宥: *~ sb's life, ~ sb his life,* not kill him or have him killed. 饒某人的命; *We may meet again if we are ~d,* if our lives are ~d by Providence. 如果我們不死,還會見面的。*He doesn't ~ himself,* is severe with himself, does not refrain from making great demands upon himself (his energies, time, etc). 他律己甚嚴。**~ *sb's feelings,*** avoid hurting his feelings. 避免傷某人的感情。***S~ the rod and spoil the child,*** (prov) If you refrain from punishing the child, you will spoil its character. (諺)孩子不打不成器。 **2** [VP12B, 13B, 6A] ***~ sth (for sb/sth); ~ sb sth,*** afford to give (time, money, etc) to sb, or for a purpose: 提供(時間、金錢等)給某人或爲某種目的;勻出;分出;分讓: *Can you ~ me a few litres of petrol?* 你能勻給我幾公升汽油嗎？*Can you ~ one of them for me?* 你能讓(其中的)一個給我嗎？*Can you ~ me a few minutes (of your time)?* 我能躭擱你幾分鐘嗎？ *I can't ~ the time for a holiday at present.* 目前我抽不出時間來度假。*We have enough and to ~,* more than we need. 我們不但足够而且有多。**3** [VP6A] use in small quantities, rarely or in a saving manner. 小量使用;愛惜;節省。***no expense(s)/pains ~ed,*** with no economy in money or effort: 不惜工本(不遺餘力);全力以赴: *I'm going to redecorate the house, no expense ~d.* 我將不惜工本重新把房子裝修一番。**spar·ing** *adj* ***sparing of,*** economical, frugal, careful (of): 節約的;儉省的;小心的;謹慎的: *You should be more sparing of your energy.* 你應該多多節省你的精力。**spar·ing·ly** *adv*

spark¹ /spɑːk ; spɑrk/ *n* [C] tiny glowing bit thrown off from a burning substance or still present in ashes, etc or produced by striking flint or hard metal and stone together; flash of light produced by the breaking of an electric current; (fig) sign of life, energy, etc; flash of wit: 火星;火花;(電流切斷時產生的)電花;(喩)生命、精力等的標誌;智慧的閃動: *The firework burst into a shower of ~s.* 那烟火爆散爲一陣火花。*He hasn't a ~ of generosity in him.* 他一點也不慷慨。□ *vt, vi* [VP 2A, 15B] give out ~s. 發出火花;放散火星。***~ sth off,*** (fig) lead to; be the immediate cause of: (喩)導致;爲…的直接原因: *His statement ~ed off a quarrel between them.* 他的話引起他們之間一場爭吵。**'~(·ing)-plug** *n* device for firing the gas in a petrol engine by means of an electric ~. (內燃機的)火星塞;火花塞。⇨ the illus at motor. 參看 motor 之插圖。

spark² /spɑːk ; spɑrk/ *n* (colloq) gay and elegant person. (俗)風度翩翩之人;愉快而風雅的人。

sparkle /'spɑːkl ; 'spɑrkl/ *vi* [VP2A, C] send out flashes of light: 閃閃發光;閃耀;閃鑠: *Her diamonds ~d in the bright light.* 她的鑽石在亮光下閃閃發光。*Her eyes ~d with excitement.* 她的眼睛由於興奮而發亮。□ *n* spark; glitter. 火花;火星;閃光;閃耀。**spark·ler** /'spɑːklə(r) ; 'spɑrklə/ *n* sth that ~s, eg a kind of firework; (sl, esp among criminals, often *pl*) diamond. 發閃光物(如某種的烟火);(俚,尤用於盜賊間,常作複數)鑽石;金剛鑽。 **spark·ling** /'spɑːklɪŋ ; 'spɑrklɪŋ/ *adj* (esp) (of wines) giving out tiny bubbles of carbonic acid gas when the bottle is opened. (尤指酒類)起泡沫的;開瓶時冒出碳酸氣泡的。⇨ still¹(2).

spar·row /'spærəʊ ; 'spæro/ *n* small brownish-grey bird common in many parts of the world, esp *the 'house~,* European kind found around buildings. 麻雀(尤指家雀,稱 the house~). ⇨ the illus at bird. 參看 bird 之插圖。

sparse /spɑːs ; spɑrs/ *adj* **1** thinly scattered: 稀少的: *a ~ population.* 稀少的人口。 **2** not dense, thick or crowded: 稀落的;稀疏的;不濃密的: *a ~ beard.* 稀疏的鬍鬚。**~·ly** *adv*: *a ~ly furnished room,* one with little furniture. 陳設簡陋的房間。**~·ness, spar·sity** /'spɑːsətɪ ; 'spɑrsətɪ/ *nn* [U].

Spar·tan /'spɑːtn ; 'spɑrtn̩/ *n, adj* (person) caring little for the ordinary comforts of life, unafraid of pain and hardship; (of living conditions) hard because very simple: 刻苦的(人);不畏痛苦和艱辛的(人);(指生活狀況)簡樸而刻苦的: *live a ~ life;* 過簡單刻苦的生活; *in ~ simplicity.* 簡樸地。

spasm /'spæzəm ; 'spæzəm/ *n* [C] **1** sudden and involuntary tightening of a muscle or muscles: 痙攣;抽筋: *asthma ~s.* 喘哮性痙攣。 **2** sudden, convulsive movement: 突然顫動的動作;突發的一陣;痙攣性動作: *in a ~ of pain/excitement/grief;* 在一陣痛苦(興奮,憂傷)中; *a ~ of coughing.* 一陣咳嗽。**3** sudden burst (of energy). (精力或能量的)一陣發作或突然爆發。

spas·modic /spæz'mɒdɪk ; spæz'mɑdɪk/ *adj* **1** taking place, done, at irregular intervals. 時作時停的;斷斷續續的。 **2** caused by, affected by, spasms: 由痙攣引起的;受痙攣影響的;陣發性的: *~ asthma.* 痙攣性氣喘。**spas·modi·cally** /-klɪ ; -klɪ/ *adv*

spas·tic /'spæstɪk ; 'spæstɪk/ *n, adj* (person) suffering from cerebral palsy, physically disabled because of faulty links between the brain and motor nerves, causing spasmodic movements through difficulty in controlling voluntary muscles. 患腦痲痺的(人);痙攣的(人)。

spat¹ /spæt ; spæt/ *n* **(a pair of) ~s,** cloth cover worn over the upper part of a shoe and round the ankle. 鞋罩(著於鞋面及踝部的覆蓋物)。

spat² /spæt ; spæt/ *pt, pp* of spit.

spat³ /spæt ; spæt/ *vi, vt* (-tt-), *n* (US) (have a) slight quarrel; (give a) light slap (to). (美)口角;小爭吵;輕拍;輕擊。

spat⁴ /spæt ; spæt/ *n* spawn of oysters. 蠔卵;牡蠣卵。□ *vi* (-tt-) (of oysters) spawn. (指蠔)產卵。

spatch·cock /'spætʃkɒk ; 'spætʃˌkɑk/ *n* fowl killed and cooked at once. 殺後立予烹調的雞。□ *vt* [VP 6A, 14] ~ ***(in/into),*** (colloq) insert (words): (俗)插入(文字): *He ~ed into his speech a curious passage about....* 他在演說中加入一段有關…的奇特的話。

spate /speɪt ; spet/ *n* **1** strong current of water at abnormally high level (in a river): (河中之)洪流;洪水: *After the storm the rivers were all in ~.* 暴風雨過後各河流河水暴漲。 **2** sudden rush of business, etc: 營業等突然湧到: *a ~ of orders;* 訂單大量湧到; *a ~ of new cars on the market.* 市場大量的新車。

spa·tial /'speɪʃl ; 'speʃəl/ *adj* of, in relation to, existing in, space. 空間的;有關空間的;存在於空間的。**~ly** /-ʃəlɪ ; -ʃəlɪ/ *adv*

spat·ter /'spætə(r) ; 'spætə/ *vt, vi* **1** [VP6A, 14] ***~ sth (on/over sth); ~ sth (with sth),*** splash, scatter, in drips: 濺;灑;潑: *~ grease on one's clothes/~ one's clothes with grease.* 油脂濺到衣服上。*As the bus went by it ~ed us with mud.* 公共汽車開過時,濺了我們一身泥。 **2** [VP2C] fall or spread out in drops: 呈點滴降落或散開;滴落;紛落;濺開;濺散: *We heard the rain ~ing down on the tin roof of the hut.* 我們聽到雨滴落在小屋的鐵皮屋頂上。□ *n* [C] sprinkling; shower: 濺;灑;潑;滴落;紛落;灑落: *a ~ of rain/bullets.* 一陣雨(槍彈)。

spat·ula /ˈspætjʊlə *US:* ˈspætʃʊlə ; ˈspætʃələ/ *n* tool with a wide, flat, flexible blade used for mixing or spreading various substances. (混合或塗敷用的)濶扁而有彈性的抹刀;刮鏟。

spavin /ˈspævɪn ; ˈspævɪn/ *n* [U] disease of horses in which a bony swelling forms at the hock, causing lameness. 馬的後脚踝關節內腫; 飛節內腫。**spav·ined** *adj* affected with ~. 患飛節內腫的。

spawn /spɔːn ; spɔn/ *n* [U] **1** eggs of fish and certain water animals, eg frogs. 魚卵;魚子;(蛙等水生動物的)卵;子。⇨ the illus at amphibian. 參看 amphibian 之插圖。 **2** threadlike matter from which mushrooms and other fungi grow. 菌絲(眞菌類植物卽由此生長)。□ *vt, vi* [VP6A, 2A] lay or produce in great numbers: 大量產生: *departments which ~ committees and sub-committees.* 委員會及附屬委員會衆多的政府機構。

spay /speɪ ; spe/ *vt* [VP6A] remove the ovaries of (a female animal). 割除(雌性動物)的卵巢。

speak /spiːk ; spik/ *vi, vt* (*pt* spoke /spəʊk ; spok/, archaic (古) spake /speɪk ; spek/, *pp* spoken /ˈspəʊkən ; ˈspokən/) **1** [VP2A, C] make use of language in an ordinary, not a singing, voice: 說;說話: *Please ~ more slowly.* 請說慢一點。 **2** [VP2B, C, 3A] ~ ***(to/with sb) (about sth):*** 與某人談論某事: *I was ~ing to him about plans for the holidays.* 我在同他談論度假的計畫。 ~ ***for sb,*** **(a)** state the views, wishes, etc of; act as spokesman for. 作某人的發言人; 陳述某人的意見、願望等。**(b)** give evidence on behalf of. 代表…證明某事;證實。~ ***for oneself,*** **(a)** express one's views, etc in one's own way. 以自己的方式說明自己的見解等。**(b)** (usu 通常作 ***S~ for yourself!***) not presume to ~ for others. 說說你自己的意見(不要代表旁人發言)。~ ***to sb,*** admonish: 訓誡;訓斥;告誡;規勸;說: *Your secretary was late again this morning—you'd better ~ to her about it.* 你的秘書今天早晨又遲到了——你最好說說她。~ ***to sth,*** ~ in confirmation of or in reference to: 說到;提到;證明: *Is there anyone here who can ~ to his having been at the scene of the crime,* who can say that he was there? 這裡有人能够證明他曾在犯罪的現場嗎? *You must ~ to the subject,* not wander away from it. 你(講話)不可離題。~ ***of the devil!*** said when, just after being spoken about, sb is seen, heard, etc. 剛談到某人,某人就來了; 說曹操,曹操就到。 ***nothing to ~ of,*** nothing worth mentioning; not much. 無可稱述;乏善可陳;不值一談。 ~ ***out/up,*** **(a)** ~ loud(er). 大(更大)聲說。**(b)** give one's opinions, etc without hesitation or fear. 毫不遲疑或恐懼地說出自己的意見等。***be not on*** ˈ~***ing terms with sb,*** **(a)** not know him well enough to ~ to him. 與某人認識的程度還不到可以談話的地步。**(b)** no longer ~ to him because one has quarrelled with him. 因與人交惡而不再與之談話。***so to ~,*** as one might say; if I may use this expression, etc. 可以說;可謂。ˈ**~·ing-trumpet** *n* (now replaced by *hearing-aids*) trumpet-shaped device held to the ear by a deaf person to help him to hear. (現已爲 hearing-aids 所取代)喇叭形助聽器。ˈ**~·ing-tube** *n* tube that carries the voice from one place to another, eg from a ship's bridge to the engine-room. 通話管 (如從艦橋通至引擎室者)。 **3** [VP2C, 15A] give evidence (of), convey ideas (not necessarily in words): 說明; 證實; 傳達概念 (不一定用語言): *Actions ~ louder than words.* 行動勝於空言。*The portrait ~s/is a ~ing likeness,* is excellent, tells us well what the sitter was like. 這人像畫得非常好(很像本人)。~ ***volumes for,*** be strong evidence of: 極足以證明;爲有力證據: *This evidence ~s volumes for his honesty.* 這證據足以證明他的誠實。~ ***well for,*** be evidence in favour of. 對…爲有利證據。 **4** [VP6A] know and be able to use (a language): 懂或通(某種語言); 會使用或會說(某種語言): *He ~s several languages.* 他通數種語言。*Is English spoken here?* 此地通用英語嗎? **5** [VP2A, B] address an audience; make a speech: 演說;演講: *He spoke for forty minutes.* 他(演)講了四十分鐘。*Are you good at ~ing in public?* 你擅長當衆演說嗎? **6** [VP6A] make known; utter: 說明;說出: *~ the truth.* 說實話。~ ***one's mind,*** express one's views frankly or bluntly. 坦率表明自己的見解及意見。 **7** (in the pattern, *adv* (in *-ly*) and *pres part*): (用於副詞 (以 -ly 結尾) 加現在分詞的句型中): *strictly/roughly/generally, etc ~ing,* using the word(s) in a strict/rough/general, etc sense. 嚴格地(約略地,一般地等)說來。 **8** [VP6A] (naut) hail and exchange information with (by flag signals, etc): (航海)(藉旗語等)聯絡;招呼;交換情報: *~ a passing ship.* 與經過的船聯絡。 **9** [VP2A] (of a gun, musical instrument, etc) make sounds. (指槍砲、樂器等)發響聲。 **10** ˈ**~-easy** *n* illicit liquor shop (esp in the US during the period of prohibition). 非法賣酒的商店(尤指美國禁酒時期)。**~er** *n* **1** person who makes speeches (in the manner indicated): 說話者;演說者(與形容詞連用): *He's a good/poor, etc ~er.* 他是一個好的(差勁的等)演說者。 **2** (short for) *loud-~er.* 爲 loud-~er 之略。 **3** ***the S~er,*** presiding officer of the House of Commons and other legislative assemblies. (英國下議院及其他議會的)議長。ˈ**~er·ship** /-ʃɪp ; -ˌʃɪp/ *n* office of the S~er; period of office of a S~er. 議長的職位;議長的任期。

spear /spɪə(r) ; spɪr/ *n* weapon with a metal point on a long shaft, used in hunting, or (formerly) by men fighting on foot. 矛;槍。□ *vt* [VP6A] pierce, wound, make (a hole) in, with a ~. 用矛刺、戳或傷;用矛戳(洞)於。ˈ**~-head** *n* (usu fig) individual or group chosen to lead an attack. (通常爲喩)前鋒;先鋒;領導攻擊的個人或部隊。□ *vt* act as ~-head for: 爲…的先鋒: *armoured vehicles that ~-head the offensive.* 作爲攻擊前鋒的裝甲車輛。

spear·mint /ˈspɪəmɪnt ; ˈspɪrˌmɪnt/ *n* aromatic variety of mint used for flavouring; chewing-gum flavoured with this. 荷蘭薄荷(用於調味);薄荷口香糖。

spec /spek ; spɛk/ *n* (colloq abbr of) speculation: (俗)爲 speculation 之略: *Those mining shares turned out a good ~,* proved profitable. 那些礦產股票結果賺了錢。***on ~,*** as a speculation; as a guess. 推測;臆測。

special /ˈspeʃl ; ˈspɛʃəl/ *adj* **1** of a particular or certain sort; not common, usual or general; of or for a certain person, thing or purpose: 特別的;特殊的;專用的;特設的: *He did it for her as a ~ favour.* 他爲她做那件事以示特別待遇。*What are your ~ interests?* 你的特殊興趣是什麼? *Newspapers send ~ correspondents to places where important events take place.* 報館派遣特派員至發生重要事件的地方。*On holidays the railways put on ~ trains,* run extra trains for ~ purposes. 假日各線鐵路增開加班火車。~ **constable,** man enrolled to help the ordinary police in time of need. 臨時警察。~ **delivery,** delivery of mail (a letter, package, etc) by a ~ messenger instead of by the usual postal services. 快遞;快信。 ~ **licence,** licence which allows a marriage to take place at a time or place other than those legally authorized. 特別結婚許可證(准予在非規定的時間或地方擧行婚禮)。 **2** exceptional in amount, degree, etc: 在數量、程度等上例外的;格外的: *Why should we give you ~ treatment?* 我們爲什麼要給你特殊待遇呢? *You've taken no ~ trouble with your work for us.* 你爲我們工作,並不特別賣力。□ *n* ~ constable, ~ train, ~ edition of a newspaper, etc. 臨時警察;加班火車;

(報紙等的)特刊。~ly /-ʃəlɪ; -ʃəlɪ/ *adv* particularly: 特別的;專門的: *I came here ~ly* (= on purpose) *to see you.* 我是特意來看你的。~·ist /-ʃəlɪst; -ʃəlɪst/ *n* person who is an expert in a ~ branch of work or study, esp medicine: 專家(尤指醫科): *an 'eye ~ist;* 眼科專家; *a ~ist in plastic surgery.* 整形外科專家。

spe·ci·al·ity /ˌspeʃɪˈælətɪ; ˌspɛʃɪˈælətɪ/ *n* [C] (*pl* -ties) **1** special quality or characteristic of sb or sth. 特質;特性。 **2** (also 亦作 **spe·cialty** /ˈspeʃəltɪ; ˈspɛʃəltɪ/ (*pl* -ties)) special pursuit, activity, product, operation, etc; thing to which a person (firm, etc) gives special attention or for which a place is well known: 專門研究;專業;專長;特製品;特產品: *Embroidery is her ~.* 刺繡是她的專長。*Wood-carvings are a ~ of this village.* 木器雕刻品是這個村子的特產。

spe·cial·ize /ˈspeʃəlaɪz; ˈspɛʃəlˌaɪz/ *vi, vt* **1** [VP2A, 3A] **~ *(in sth)*,** be or become a specialist; give special or particular attention to: 成爲或變爲專家;專攻;專門研究: *~ in oriental history.* 專攻東方史。*After his first degree he wishes to ~.* 獲得學士學位以後,他希望專攻某科。 **2** (usu *pp*) (通常用過去分詞) adapt for a particular purpose: 使適應特殊目的;使專用於: *a hospital with ~d wards,* (cf 參較 *general wards*); 有專科病房的醫院; *~d knowledge,* (cf 參較 *general knowledge*). 專門知識。**spe·cial·iz·ation** /ˌspeʃəlaɪˈzeɪʃn *US:* -lɪˈz-; ˌspɛʃəlɪˈzeʃən/ *n*

spe·cialty /ˈspeʃəltɪ; ˈspɛʃəltɪ/ *n* (*pl* -ties) ⇨ speciality(2).

specie /ˈspi:ʃi:; ˈspiʃɪ/ *n* [U] (store of, consignment of) money in the form of coins: 硬幣;錢幣;錢幣的儲備或支付: *~ payments;* 硬幣支付; *payment in ~.* 硬幣支付。

spe·cies /ˈspi:ʃi:z; ˈspiʃɪz/ *n* (*pl* unchanged) (複數不變) **1** (biol) group having some common characteristics (division of a genus) able to breed with each other but not with other groups: (生物)種(屬以下的分類法);具有共同特質可相互繁殖的類群: *the human ~,* mankind. 人類。 **2** sort: 種類: *Blackmail is a ~ of crime hated by all decent folk.* 恫嚇勒索是所有正人君子所憎恨的一種罪行。

spe·ci·fic /spəˈsɪfɪk; spɪˈsɪfɪk/ *adj* **1** detailed and precise: 詳細而精確的;明確的: *~ orders.* 明確的命令。*What are your ~ aims?* 你的明確目標是什麼? **2** relating to one particular thing, etc, not general: 特種的;特殊的;涉及某特定一個的: *The money is to be used for a ~ purpose.* 該款將用於特定的用途。 **~ gravity,** mass of any substance relative to that of an equal volume of water. 比重(任何物質的重量與同體積水的重量之比)。 **~ name,** (biol) distinguishing name of the species. (生物)種名。 **~ remedy,** one for a particular disease. 特效藥。 □ *n* [C] ~ remedy: 特效藥: *Quinine is a ~ for malaria.* 奎寧是治瘧疾的特效藥。 **spe·cifi·cally** /-klɪ; -klɪ/ *adv* in a ~ manner: 明確地;特種地;特殊地: *You were ~ally warned by your doctor not to eat lobster.* 醫生曾特別警告你不可吃龍蝦。

spec·ifi·ca·tion /ˌspesɪfɪˈkeɪʃn; ˌspɛsəfəˈkeʃən/ *n* **1** [U] specifying. 指定;載明;詳述。 **2** (often *pl*) details, instructions, etc for the design, materials, of sth to be made or done: (常用複數)做某事物的詳細說明;計畫書;清單;規格: *~s for (building) a garage;* (建造)車房的詳細規格; *the technical ~s of a new car.* 一輛新汽車的技術說明。

spec·ify /ˈspesɪfaɪ; ˈspɛsəˌfaɪ/ *vt* (*pt, pp* -fied) [VP6A, 9] state or name definitely; include in the specifications: 指定;載明;詳述;逐一登記: *The contract specifies red tiles, not slates, for the roof.* 合約載明屋頂用紅瓦,而非石板。 *The regulations ~ that you may use a dictionary in the examination.* 規則指明考試時可用字典。

speci·men /ˈspesɪmɪn; ˈspɛsəmən/ *n* [C] **1** one as an example of a class: 標本;範例: *~s of rocks and ores.* 岩石及礦石的標本。 **2** part taken to represent the whole: 樣品: *a publisher's catalogue with ~ pages of books.* 有書籍樣張的出版物目錄。 **3** sth to be tested, etc for definite or special purposes: (爲特定目的而取的)待試驗物;抽樣;取樣: *supply a ~ of one's urine.* 檢送某人的小便取樣。 **4** (colloq) unusual thing or person regarded with contempt or amusement: (俗)(含輕視意或出以戲言)怪人;怪物: *What a queer ~ (of humanity) he is!* 他是一個多麼古怪的人啊!

spe·cious /ˈspi:ʃəs; ˈspiʃəs/ *adj* seeming right or true, but not really so: 似是而非的;華而不實的;表裏不一致的: *a ~ argument/person.* 似是而非的論點(表裏不一致的人)。 **~·ly** *adv* **~·ness** *n*

speck /spek; spɛk/ *n* [C] small spot or particle (of dirt, etc); stain; discoloured spot on fruit (showing rottenness); dot: (泥土等的)微粒;污點;斑點;(水果上表示腐爛的)疵傷;瑕疵: *Do you ever seem to see ~s in front of your eyes?* 你曾否感覺眼睛前面似可看見許多小點? *The ship was a mere ~ on the horizon.* 那條船在水平線僅是一個小黑點。 **~ed** *adj* marked with ~s: 有微粒的;有斑點的;有疵痕的: *~ed apples.* 有疵痕的蘋果。 **~·less** *adj*

speckle /ˈspekl; ˈspɛkḷ/ *n* [C] small mark or spot, esp one of many, distinct in colour, on the skin, feathers, etc. 小點;斑點(尤指皮膚、羽毛等上顏色不同者)。 **~d** *adj* marked with ~s: 有斑點的;有小點的: *a ~d hen;* 有斑點的母雞; *~d plumage.* 帶斑點的羽毛。

specs /speks; spɛks/ *n pl* (colloq) spectacles(3). (俗)眼鏡。

spec·tacle /ˈspektəkl; ˈspɛktəkḷ/ *n* [C] **1** public display, procession, etc, esp one with ceremony: 公開展示、行列等(尤指有儀式者);觀覽(物);展覽(物): *The ceremonial opening of Parliament was a fine ~.* 英國國會的開幕式是一個很壯麗的場面。 **2** sth seen; sth taking place before the eyes, esp sth fine, remarkable or noteworthy: 景象;光景;奇觀;壯觀: *The sunrise as seen from the top of the mountain was a tremendous ~.* 從山頂所見的日出景象,蔚爲奇觀。 *The poor drunken man was a sad ~.* 那可憐的醉漢樣子令人悲痛。 *Don't make a ~ of yourself,* don't draw attention to yourself by dressing, behaving, etc ridiculously. 不要現眼(衣着及舉止等,不可荒唐可笑而引人注意)。 **3** ***~s; a pair of ~s,*** pair of lenses in a frame, resting on the nose and ears, to help the eyesight (or to protect the eyes from bright sunlight) (*glasses* is the more usu name). 眼鏡;護目鏡(glasses 較常用)。 ***see everything through rose-coloured ~s,*** take a cheerful, optimistic view of things. 對事持樂觀看法。 **~d** *adj* wearing ~s. 戴眼鏡的。

spec·tacu·lar /spekˈtækjʊlə(r); spɛkˈtækjələ/ *adj* making a fine spectacle (1, 2); attracting public attention: 造成引人場面的;蔚爲奇觀的;壯觀的;引人入勝的;吸引人的: *a ~ display of fireworks.* 施放烟火的壯觀景象。 □ *n* [C] spectacle; ~ show: 奇觀;壯觀;引人入勝的表演: *a Christmas TV ~.* 聖誕節引人入勝的電視演出。 **~·ly** *adv*

spec·ta·tor /spekˈteɪtə(r) *US:* ˈspekteɪtər; ˈspɛkteta/ *n* onlooker (esp at a show or game): 旁觀者;(尤指表演或比賽的)觀衆: (attrib) (形容用法) *~ sports,* those which draw crowds of ~s, eg football. 觀衆多的體育活動(如足球)。

spectre (US = **spec·ter**) /ˈspektə(r); ˈspɛktə/ *n* [C] ghost; haunting fear of future trouble. 鬼;幽靈;對未來困難的憂懼。 **spec·tral** /ˈspektrəl; ˈspɛktrəl/ *adj* **1** of or like a ~. 鬼的;幽靈的;似鬼或幽靈的。 **2** of spectra or the spectrum: 光譜的: *spectral colours.* 譜色。

spec·tro·scope /ˈspektrəskəʊp; ˈspɛktrəˌskop/ *n* instrument for producing and examining the spectra of a ray of light. 分光鏡;分光器。 **spec·tro·scopic** /ˌspektrəˈskɒpɪk; ˌspɛktroˈskɑpɪk/ *adj* of, by means of, a ~: 分光鏡(器)的;藉分光鏡(器)的: *spectroscopic analysis.* 藉分光鏡所作的分析;分光分析。

spec·trum /ˈspektrəm ; ˈspɛktrəm/ *n* (*pl* -tra /-trə, -trə/) image of a band of colours (as seen in a rainbow and usu described as red, orange, yellow, green, blue, indigo and violet) formed by a ray of light which has passed through a prism; (fig) wide range or sequence: 光譜(光線通過三稜鏡所產生的色帶)；(喻)廣濶的範圍、領域或系列: *the whole ~ of recent philosophical enquiry.* 新近哲學研究的整個範圍。

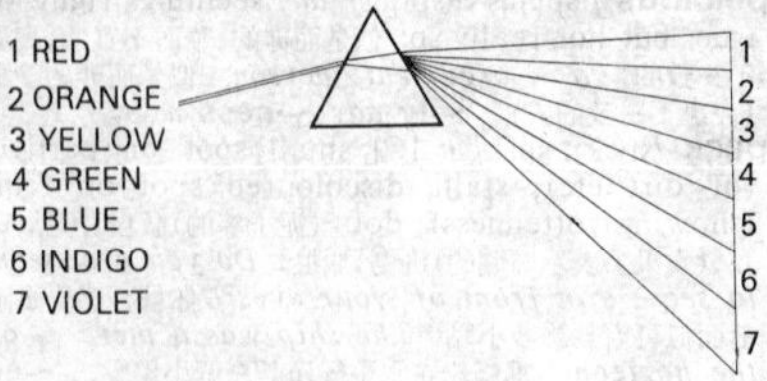

the colours of the spectrum

specu·late /ˈspekjʊleɪt ; ˈspɛkjəˌlet/ *vi* [VP2A, C] **1** consider, form opinions (without having complete knowledge); guess: (無充分知識而)思考並形成意見；思索；玄想；臆測；推測: *~ about/upon the future of the human race;* 推測人類的未來；*~ as to what sort of man one will marry.* 思索何類男子可爲結婚對象。 **2** buy and sell goods, stocks and shares, etc with risk of loss and hope of profit through changes in their market value: 做投機買賣: *~ in oil shares/wheat.* 做石油股票(小麥)投機買賣。 **specu·la·tor** /-tə(r) ; -tɚ/ *n* person who ~s(2). 做投機買賣者；投機商人。

specu·la·tion /ˌspekjʊˈleɪʃn ; ˌspɛkjəˈleʃən/ *n* **1** [U] speculating(1); meditation; [C] opinion reached by this means; guess. 思索；沉思；默想；玄思；推測；臆測。 **2** [U] speculating(2): 做投機買賣: *~ in rice;* 做稻米投機生意；[C] transaction, business deal, of this kind: 投機買賣；投機生意: *make some bad ~s;* 做數次虧本的投機生意；*buy mining shares as a ~.* 投機買進礦業股票。

specu·lat·ive /ˈspekjʊlətɪv *US* -leɪtɪv ; ˈspɛkjəˌletɪv/ *adj* **1** concerned with speculation(1): 玄想的；思索的；推測的: *~ philosophy.* 思辨哲學。 **2** concerned with speculation(2). 投機的；投機生意的: *~ purchase of grain;* 投機性購買穀物；*~ housing,* the building of houses as a speculation(2). 投機性營造房屋。 **~·ly** *adv*

sped /sped ; spɛd/ *pt, pp* of speed.

speech /spiːtʃ ; spitʃ/ *n* **1** [U] power, act, manner, of speaking: 語言；說話；講話的能力、方式等: *Man is the only animal that has the faculty of ~.* 人是唯一有語言能力的動物。*Our thoughts are expressed by ~.* 我們的思想是用語言表達的。*They say that ~ is silver but silence is golden.* 人們說言語是銀，沉默是金。*His indistinct ~ made it impossible to understand him.* 他口齒不清使人無法聽懂他的話。**~ therapy,** remedial treatment for defective speech, eg for stuttering. 語言醫療(矯治語言缺失，如口吃的醫療)。 **2** [C] talk or address given in public: 演說；當衆講話: *make a ~ on/about the Common Market to a receptive audience.* 就歐洲共同市場問題向能接受該政策的聽衆發表演說。 **ˈ~-day** *n* annual school celebration with ~es and distribution of certificates and prizes. 學校每年的畢業典禮授獎日(發表演說，並分發證書及獎品)。 **~·less** *adj* **1** unable to speak, esp because of deep feeling: 說不出話來的(尤指由於情緒激動): *~less with surprise.* 因驚訝而說不出話的。*Anger left him ~less.* 憤怒使他說不出話來。 **2** that causes a person to be unable to speak: 使人說不出話來的: *~less rage.* 使人說不出話來的盛怒。 **~·less·ly** *adv* **~·ify** /ˈspiːtʃɪfaɪ ; ˈspitʃəˌfaɪ/ *vi* (*pt, pp* -fied) make ~es; talk as if making ~es (usu implying that this is done unnecessarily or badly): 演說；長篇大論(通常含示無必要或很差勁): *town councillors ~ifying at the unveiling of a statue/at a welcome to the Queen.* 在雕像揭幕(歡迎女王)時市議員們發表演說。

speed /spiːd ; spid/ *n* **1** [U] swiftness; rapidity of movement. 迅速；(行動)快捷。***More haste, less ~,*** (prov) Too much haste may result in delay. (諺)欲速則不達。 **2** [C, U] rate of motion or moving: 速度；速率: *travelling at full/top ~;* 以全(高)速行進；*at a ~ of thirty miles an hour.* 以每小時三十英里的速度。*It's dangerous to corner at ~,* to go round corners (in a vehicle) at a high ~. 高速轉彎是危險的。 **3** (sl) amphetamine used as a drug to produce euphoria. (俚)(使人產生舒適感的藥物)安非太明；苯齊特林。 **4** (compounds) (複合字) **ˈ~-boat** *n* motor-boat designed for high ~s. 快艇。 **ˈ~-cop** *n* (sl) police motor-cyclist who checks the ~ of motorists. (俚)取締汽車超速的騎摩托車的警察；驗速警察。 **ˈ~-indicator** *n* = ~ometer. ⇨ below. 參看下列之 ~ometer。 **ˈ~-limit** *n* ~ which must not be exceeded, eg in a built-up area. 速度上限。 **ˈ~ merchant,** (sl) person who drives a car or motor-bike extremely fast. (俚)速度販子(以極高速度駕駛汽車或機車者)。 **ˈ~·way** *n* **(a)** track, for fast driving and racing, esp by motor-bikes. 高速道；(尤指)機車賽車道。 **(b)** (US) road for fast traffic; expressway. (美)高速公路。 □ *vt, vi* (*pt, pp* sped) **1** [VP2A, C] move along, go, quickly: 速進；急行: *cars ~ing past the school.* 快速經過學校的車輛。*He sped down the street.* 他沿街急行。 **2** [VP6A, 14] cause to move or go quickly: 使速進；使急行: *~ an arrow from the bow.* 拉弓射箭。 **3** (archaic) give success to: (古)使成功: *God ~ you,* May God make you prosper. 祝你成功(願上帝使你成功)。 **4** [VP15B, 2C] (*pt, pp* ~ed) ***~ (sth) up,*** increase the ~ (of): 增加…的速度或速率: *They have ~ed up production/the train service.* 他們業已加速生產(增加火車班次)。*He ~ed the engine up.* 他加快引擎的速率。*The train soon ~ed up.* 火車不久就加速前進。 Hence, 由此產生, **ˈ~-up** *n* ~ing up the rate of production, etc. 加快；加速(生產等)。 **~·ing** *n* (of motorists) travelling at an illegal or dangerous ~: (指駕車者)超速: *fined £30 for ~ing.* 因超速而罰款三十鎊。 **~·om·eter** /spiːˈdɒmɪtə(r) ; spiˈdɑmətɚ/ *n* instrument showing the ~ of a motor-vehicle, etc. (汽車等的)計速表。⇨ the illus at motor. 參看 motor 之插圖。 **~y** *adj* (-ier, -iest) quick; coming, done, without delay: 快速的；迅速來臨或完成的: *wish sb a ~y recovery from illness.* 希望某人迅速康復。

a speed-boat

speed·well /ˈspiːdwel ; ˈspidwɛl/ *n* kinds of small, wild plant with bright blue flowers. 草本威靈仙屬植物(開鮮艷的藍花)。

spelae·ol·ogy (also **spele-**) /ˌspiːlɪˈɒlədʒɪ ; spilɪˈɑlədʒɪ/ *n* [U] the scientific study and exploration of caves. 洞窟學(巖洞的探測及其科學研究)。 **spelae·ol·ogist** (also **spele-**) /-dʒɪst ; -dʒɪst/ *n* expert in, student of, ~. 洞窟學家。

spell[1] /spel ; spɛl/ *n* [C] **1** words used as a charm, supposed to have magic power: 符咒；咒語: *cast* *a ~ over sb;* 以符咒鎮某人; *put a ~ on sb;* 以符咒鎮某人; *be under/lay sb under a ~.* 被符咒鎮住(以符咒鎮住某人)。 **'~·bound** /-baʊnd ; -,baʊnd/ *adj* with the attention held by, or as by, a ~: 被符咒鎮住的; 入迷的: *The speaker held his audience ~bound.* 那演說者使聽衆入迷。 **'~·binder** /-baɪndə(r) ; -,baɪndɚ/ *n* speaker who can hold audiences ~bound. 能使聽衆入迷的演說者。 **2** attraction, fascination, exercised by a person, occupation, etc: 吸引力;迷惑力;魔力;魅力: *under the ~ of her beauty;* 爲她的美色所吸引; *the mysterious ~ of the music of Delius.* 狄里雅斯音樂的神秘魅力。

spell[2] /spel ; spɛl/ *n* **1** period of time: 一段時間;時期: *a long ~ of warm weather;* 一段長時間的暖和天氣; *a cold ~ in January;* 正月裡一段寒冷的時期; *rest for a (short) ~.* 休息一段(短)時間。 **2** period of activity or duty, esp one at which two or more persons take turns: 活動時間;工作時間;(尤指)輪值時間: *take ~s at the wheel,* eg of two persons making a long journey by car. 輪流開車。 □ *vt* **~ sb (at sth),** take turns with sb: 與某人輪值;輪替;輪流: *Will you ~ me at rowing the boat?* 你願意同我輪流划船嗎?

spell[3] /spel ; spɛl/ *vt, vi* (*pt, pp* ~ed /speld ; spɛld/ or spelt /spelt ; spɛlt/) **1** [VP6A] name or write the letters of (a word): 拼或寫出(某字)的字母;拼字;拼寫: *How do you ~ your name?* 你的名字怎麼拼? **'~·ing pronunciation,** one suggested by the written form of the word (eg /'nefju: ; 'nɛfju/ instead of /'nevju: ; 'nɛvju/ for nephew). 照拼法發音(如 nephew 一字讀成 /'nefju: ; 'nɛfju/ 而不讀成 /'nevju: ; 'nɛvju/)。 **2** [VP6A] (of letters) form when put together in a particular order: (指字母)拼作;拼綴;拼成: *C-A-T ~s cat.* C-A-T 拼成 cat (貓)。 **3** [VP15B] **~ sth out, (a)** make out (words, writing) laboriously, slowly: 費力而緩慢地瞭解(字或文): *It took the boy an hour to ~ out a page of German.* 那男孩花了一小時才吃力地讀懂一頁德文。 **(b)** make clear and easy to understand; explain in detail: 使清楚易懂;詳細解釋: *My request seems simple enough—do you want me to ~ it out for you?* 我的要求很簡單——你要不要我爲你詳細解釋? **4** [VP6A] have as a consequence: 招致;帶來: *Does laziness always ~ failure?* 怠惰必會招致失敗嗎? **5** [VP2A, 6A] place the letters of words in the correct or accepted order: 拼字;綴字: *These children can't ~.* 這些孩子不會拼字。 *Why don't you learn to ~ my name (correctly)?* 你爲什麼不學習我的名字的(正確)拼法呢? **~er** *n* person who ~s: 拼字者;綴字者: *a good/poor ~er.* 長於(不長於)拼字者。 **~·ing** *n* [C] way a word is spelt: (字的)拼法;綴字法: *Which is the better ~ing: Tokio or Tokyo?* 那一種拼法較佳: Tokio 還是 Tokyo? *Do you use English or American ~ing(s)?* 你使用英國拼法還是美國拼法?

spelt[1] ⇨ spell[3].

spelt[2] /spelt ; spɛlt/ *n* [U] kind of wheat giving very fine flour. 一種小麥(可製上好的麵粉)。

spend /spend ; spɛnd/ *vt, vi* (*pt, pp* spent /spent ; spɛnt/) **1** [VP6A, 14, 2A] **~ money (on sth),** pay out (money) for goods, services, etc: 用(錢);花(錢): *~ all one's money;* 用光所有的錢; *~ too much money on clothes;* 花在服裝上的錢太多; *~ £30 a week.* 每週花費三十鎊。*He's always ~ing.* 他揮霍成性。 **'~·thrift** *n* person who ~s money extravagantly. 揮霍者;浪費者;揮金如土的人。 **2** [VP 6A, 14, 19B] **~ sth (on sth/(in) doing sth),** use up; consume: 用盡;耗盡;消耗;使竭盡: *~ a lot of time on a project / (in) explaining a plan;* 花費許多時間於一計畫(說明一計畫); *~ all one's energies.* 耗盡所有的精力。 *They went on firing until all their ammunition was spent.* 他們繼續射擊,直到耗盡所有的彈藥。 **3** [VP6A, 19B] pass: 度過;消磨: *~ a weekend in London/one's spare time in gardening.* 在倫敦度過週末(把空閒消磨在園藝上)。 *How do you ~ your leisure?* 你如何消磨空暇時間? **~er** *n* person who ~s money (usu in the way indicated by the *adj*): 用錢者;花錢者(通常用形容詞以示其花錢方式): *an extravagant ~er.* 揮金如土者。 **spent** (*pp* as *adj*) exhausted; used up: (過去分詞作形容詞用)筋疲力竭的;耗盡的: *a spent runner/swimmer/horse;* 筋疲力竭的跑者(游泳者,馬); *a spent cartridge/bullet,* one that has been fired and is now useless. 打過的子彈(彈頭)。

sperm /spɜ:m ; spɝm/ *n* [U] fertilizing fluid of a male animal. (雄性動物的)精液。 **'~-whale** *n* whale producing spermaceti. 抹香鯨(產鯨腦者)。

sper·ma·ceti /ˌspɜ:mə'setɪ ; ˌspɝmə'sɛtɪ/ *n* [U] white, waxy, fatty substance contained in solution in the heads of sperm-whales, used for ointments, candles, etc. 鯨腦油(抹香鯨腦部的白色蠟狀油脂,呈溶液狀態,用製油膏、蠟燭等)。

sper·mato·zoon /ˌspɜ:mətə'zəʊən ; ˌspɝmətə'zoən/ *n* (*pl* **-zoa** /-'zəʊə ; -'zoə/) male fertilizing element contained in sperm (fusing with an ovum to produce new offspring). 精蟲;精子(與卵結合,產生新生的後代)。

spew /spju: ; spju/ *vt, vi* [VP6A, 15B, 2A] vomit. 嘔吐;吐;嘔。

sphag·num /'sfægnəm ; 'sfægnəm/ *n* (*pl* ~s) kinds of moss growing in peat and bogs, used in packing and medicinally. 水苔;水蘚(生長於泥炭地及沼澤的苔蘚,用作填料及藥用)。

sphere /sfɪə(r) ; sfɪr/ *n* **1** solid figure that is entirely round; form of a ball or globe. 球體;球形。 ***music of the ~s,*** (myth) music produced by the movement of heavenly bodies, inaudible to mortals. (神話)星球樂(天體運動發出的樂聲,一般凡人聽不到)。 **2** globe representing the earth or the sky. 地球儀;渾天儀。 **3** person's interests, activities, surroundings, etc: 個人的興趣、活動、環境等;活動範圍;圈子;方面: *a woman who is distinguished in many ~s,* eg in literary and artistic circles, in the political world. 一位在多方面傑出的婦女(如在文藝界、政界等)。 *Skiing lies outside the ~ of my activities.* 滑雪超出了我的活動範圍(非我所長)。 **4** range, extent: 領域;範圍: *a ~ of influence,* area over which a country claims certain rights or is recognized as having them. (一國的)勢力範圍。 **spheri·cal** /'sferɪkl ; 'sfɛrɪkl̩/ *adj* shaped like a ~. 球形的。 **sphe·roid** /'sfɪərɔɪd ; 'sfɪrɔɪd/ *n* body that is almost spherical. 球狀體;橙形體(幾乎呈球狀)。

sphinx /sfɪŋks ; sfɪŋks/ *n* stone statue (esp 尤作 **the S~**) in Egypt with a lion's body and a woman's head; person who keeps his thoughts and intentions secret; enigmatic person. (埃及的)斯芬克斯(獅身人首雕像); 不露出自己的思想及意願的人; 神秘人物;謎樣的人。

a pyramid and the Sphinx

spice /spaɪs ; spaɪs/ *n* **1** [C, U] sorts of substance, eg ginger, nutmeg, cinnamon, cloves, used to flavour food: 香料;調味品(如薑、肉荳蔻、肉桂、丁香等): *a dealer in ~* (collective) (集合用法);香料經銷商; *mixed ~(s);* 混合的香料; *too much ~ in the cake.* 糕餅中香料太多。 ⇨ herb. **2** [U] (and with *indef art*) (fig) interesting flavour, suggestion, or trace (of): (可與不定冠詞連用)(喻)趣味;意味;風味: *a story that lacks ~.* 缺乏趣味的故事。*She has* *a ~ of wildness in her character.* 她的性格有點放蕩不羈。□ *vt* [VP6A] add flavour to (sth) with ~, or as with ~: 藉香料以增(某物)之味;為…增添趣味: *~d with humour.* 因幽默而趣味增加的。**spicy** *adj* (-ier, -iest) of, flavoured with, ~; (fig) exciting or interesting because somewhat improper: 香料的;用香料調味的;加有香料的;(喻)跡近猥褻而富於低級趣味的: *spicy details of the film star's love life.* 該電影明星愛情生活跡近猥褻而富於低級趣味的細節。**spic·ily** /-ɪlɪ ; -ɪlɪ/ *adv* **spici·ness** *n*

spick /spɪk ; spɪk/ *adj* (only in) (僅用於) ~ ***and span,*** bright, clean and tidy. 整齊清潔的;一塵不染的。

spi·der /ˈspaɪdə(r) ; ˈspaɪdɚ/ *n* sorts of creature with eight legs, many species of which spin webs for the capture of insects as food. 蜘蛛。⇨ the illus at arachnid. 參看 arachnid 之插圖。**~y** *adj* (esp of handwriting) with long, thin strokes. (尤指書法)筆畫細長的。

spied /spaɪd ; spaɪd/ *pt, pp* of spy.

spiel /ʃpiːl *US:* spiːl ; spil/ *vi, vt* (sl) talk, say (sth) glibly and at length. (俚)流利而冗長地講話或講述(某事);滔滔不絕地說;口若懸河地講述。□ *n* long voluble talk (usu intended to persuade sb). 滔滔不絕的談話(通常意圖說服或勸阻某人)。

spigot /ˈspɪgət ; ˈspɪgət/ *n* **1** (usu wooden) plug or peg which can be used to stop the hole of a cask or barrel. (通常為木質)(桶口用的)栓;塞子。**2** valve for controlling the flow of water or other liquid from a tank, barrel, etc. (控制槽、桶等之水流或其他液體的)活門;龍頭。

spike /spaɪk ; spaɪk/ *n* **1** sharp point; pointed piece of metal, eg on iron railings or on running-shoes. 尖端;金屬尖頭或尖釘(如鐵欄杆或跑鞋上者)。~ **heel,** (also 亦作 *stiletto heel*) thin, pointed heel on a (woman's) shoe. (女鞋上)尖而細的鞋後跟。**2** ear of grain, eg barley; long, pointed cluster of flowers on a single stem: 穗(如大麥穗);穗狀花: *~s of lavender.* 薰衣草的穗狀花。□ *vt* [VP6A] **1** put ~s (on shoes, etc): 加尖釘於(鞋等)上: *~d running-shoes.* 釘鞋(帶尖釘的跑鞋)。**2** pierce or injure with a ~; (of cannon in former times) make useless by driving a ~ into the opening where the powder was fired. 以尖釘刺穿或傷害;(指昔日大砲)把尖釘打入火門使無用。Hence, 由此產生, ~ ***sb's guns,*** spoil his plans. 破壞某人的計畫。**spiky** *adj* (-ier, -iest) having ~s or sharp points; (fig, of persons) difficult to manage because unwilling to yield. 有尖釘或尖端的;(喻,指人)(因不肯屈服而)難駕馭的。

spike·nard /ˈspaɪknɑːd ; ˈspaɪknɚd/ *n* [U] (costly ointment formerly made from a) tall, perennial, sweet-smelling plant. 甘松香(一種高大,有香味的多年生植物);甘松油(從前用甘松香製的一種高貴油膏)。

spill[1] /spɪl ; spɪl/ *vt, vi* (*pt, pp* spilt /spɪlt ; spɪlt/ or ~ed) **1** [VP6A, 2A, C] (of liquid or powder) (allow to) run over the side of the container: (指液體或粉末)(使)溢出;灑出;潑出: *Who has spilt / ~ed the milk?* 誰把牛奶潑出來了? *The ink has spilt on the desk.* 墨水灑在桌子上了。~ ***the beans,*** ⇨ bean. ~ ***blood,*** be guilty of wounding or killing sb. 傷害某人;殺死某人;使某人流血。**2** [VP6A] (of a horse, cart, etc) upset; cause (the rider, passenger, etc) to fall: (指馬,馬車等)弄翻使(騎者、乘客等)摔下;使跌落: *His horse spilt him.* 他的馬把他摔下來了。*The horse shied and we were all spilt* (= thrown out of the cart, etc) *into the ditch.* 那馬驚跳了起來,把我們全都摔入溝中。□ *n* fall from a horse, out of a cart, etc: (從馬,馬車等上)跌落;摔下: *have a nasty ~.* 摔得很重。**ˈ~·over** *n* (often attrib) (of population) excess: (常作形容用法)(指人口)過剩: *new towns for London's ~over (population).* 容納倫敦過剩人口的新市鎮。**ˈ~·way** *n* passage for surplus water from a reservoir, river, etc. (堰,河等的)放水道;溢洪道。

spill[2] /spɪl ; spɪl/ *n* [C] thin strip of wood, rolled or twisted strip of paper, used to light candles, tobacco in a pipe, etc. (點燃蠟燭,烟斗等用的)木片;紙捻。

spilt /spɪlt ; spɪlt/ ⇨ spill[1].

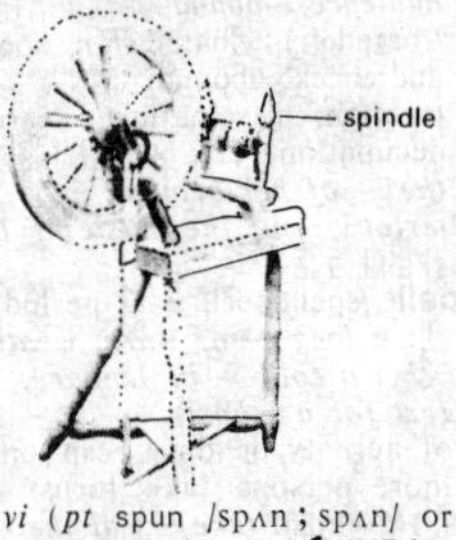

a spinning-wheel

spin /spɪn ; spɪn/ *vt, vi* (*pt* spun /spʌn ; spʌn/ or span /spæn ; spæn/, *pp* spun) (-nn-) **1** [VP6A, 14, 2A] ~ ***(into / from),*** form (thread) by twisting wool, cotton, silk, etc; draw out and twist (wool, cotton, etc) *into* threads; make (yarn) *from* wool etc in this way; engage in the occupation of ~ning thread: 紡(紗);抽績(毛,棉等)成紗;紗績;從事紡績工作: *~ning wool / thread / yarn.* 紡績毛(線,紡)。**~·ning jenny** *n* early kind of machine for ~ning more than one thread at a time. (早期的)多軸紡紗機。**ˈ~·ning-wheel** *n* simple household machine for ~ning thread continuously on a spindle turned by a large wheel, usu worked by a treadle. (家庭用的)紡車。**2** [VP6A] form by means of threads: 以絲或線做成: *spiders ~ning their webs;* 結網的蜘蛛; *silkworms ~ning cocoons.* 做繭的蠶。**3** [VP6A, 15B] (fig) produce, compose (a narrative). (喻)編製;杜撰;講述;撰述(故事)。~ ***a yarn,*** tell a story: 講故事: *The old sailor loves to ~ yarns about his life at sea.* 那老水手喜歡講述他的航海生涯。~ ***sth out,*** make it last as long as possible: 盡量使某物持續;延長: *~ out the time by talking;* 以談話拖延時間; *economize in order to make one's money ~ out until next pay-day.* 節省用費以期維持到下一次發薪日。**4** [VP6A] cause (sth) to go round and round: 使(某物)旋轉: ~ *a top,* ⇨ top[3]; 抽陀螺; ~ *a coin,* send it up in the air, revolving as it goes up, to decide sth (by 'heads or tails'); 拋轉錢幣(以落下後呈現正面或背面以決定某事); ~ *the ball,* (in cricket, tennis). 抽球;旋球(在板球或網球中)。**ˌ~-ˈdrier** *n* device that uses centrifugal force to dry what is placed in it (eg laundered clothes). 脫水機(利用離心力旋乾洗過之衣服等)。**ˌ~-ˈdry** *vt* (*pt, pp* dried) dry in a ~-drier. 在脫水機中脫除…的水分;在脫水機中旋乾。**ˈ~-off** *n* incidental benefit or product (from a larger enterprise, or from research for such an enterprise). (從較大企業,或從其研究工作產生的)附帶利益;副產品。**5** [VP2A, C] move round rapidly: 迅速旋轉: *The top was ~ning merrily.* 陀螺在輕快地旋轉。*The collision sent the car ~ning across the roadway.* 那輛汽車被撞得轉向而橫在道路上。*The blow sent him ~ning to the wall.* 他被重擊而暈轉到牆邊。*The bicycle was ~ning along* (= moving along) *at a good speed.* 那輛腳踏車快速疾馳。**6 spun glass,** glass made into threads (by being spun when heated). 玻璃絲(玻璃加熱後抽成絲狀者)。**spun silk,** cheap material of short-fibred and waste silk, often mixed with cotton. 紡綢(由短而零碎的絲織成的便宜料子,常混有棉紡)。□ *n* **1** [U] turning or ~ning motion, esp as given to the ball in some games, eg cricket, baseball: 旋轉(尤指給予板球,網球等者): *The pitcher gave (a) ~ to the ball.* 投手使球旋轉。**2** short ride for pleasure in a motor-car, on a bicycle, etc: 乘汽車,腳踏車等短途的旅行;乘車兜風:

go for/have a ~. 坐(乘,騎等)車溜溜。 **3** fast ~ning movement of an aircraft during a diving descent: 飛機快速螺旋下降: *get into/out of a* ~. 開始(停止)螺旋下降。 ***in a flat*** **~,** in a panic. 驚慌地。

spin·ach /ˈspɪnɪdʒ *US:* -ɪtʃ ; ˈspɪnɪdʒ/ *n* [U] common garden plant with green leaves, cooked and eaten as a vegetable. 菠菜。

spi·nal /ˈspaɪnl ; ˈspaɪnḷ/ *adj* of or to the spine: 脊椎骨的;脊柱的: *the ~ column,* the backbone; 脊椎骨; *the ~ cord,* nerve-fibres in the spine; 脊髓; *a* ˈ*~ injury.* 脊椎受傷。

spindle /ˈspɪndl ; ˈspɪndḷ/ *n* **1** (in spinning) thin rod for twisting and winding thread by hand. (紡績)紡錘;錠子。 ⇨ the illus at spin. 參看 spin 之插圖。 **2** bar or pin which turns round, or on which sth turns (eg an axle or a shaft). 指軸; 心軸。 **ˈ~-legged/-shanked** *adjj* having long, thin legs. 有細長之腿的。 **ˈ~-shanks** *n* person with such legs. 腿細長的人。 **ˈ~-berry/-tree** *n* small tree with deep-pink berries and hard wood, used for ~s. 衞矛(一種小樹,木質堅硬,結深桃紅色漿果,用製紡錘)。 **spin·dly** /ˈspɪndlɪ ; ˈspɪndlɪ/ *adj* long and thin; too tall and thin. 細長的;過於高而細的。

spin·drift /ˈspɪndrɪft ; ˈspɪn,drɪft/ *n* [U] foam or spray blown along the surface of the sea. (海面激起的)浪花。

spine /spaɪn ; spaɪn/ *n* **1** backbone. 脊椎骨。⇨ the illus at skeleton. 參看 skeleton 之插圖。 **2** one of the sharp needle-like parts on some plants, eg a cactus, and animals, eg a porcupine. (植物如仙人掌,動物如豪猪等的)棘狀突起;刺;針。 **3** part of a book's cover that is visible when it is in a row on a shelf, usu with the book's title on it. 書背;書脊。 **~·less** *adj* having no ~(1); (fig) cowardly; timid. 無脊椎骨的; (喻)怯懦的;優柔寡斷的。 **spiny** *adj* (-ier, -iest) having ~s(2). 有棘狀突起的;多針的;多刺的。

spinet /spɪˈnet *US:* ˈspɪnɪt ; ˈspɪnɪt/ *n* old type of keyboard instrument like a harpsichord. 古鋼琴(早期的一種有鍵樂器,似大鍵琴)。⇨ the illus at keyboard. 參看 keyboard 之插圖。

spin·na·ker /ˈspɪnəkə(r) ; ˈspɪnəkɚ/ *n* large triangular sail carried on the main-mast of a racing yacht on the side opposite the mainsail when runnig before the wind. (賽艇主桅上的)大三角帆。

spin·ney /ˈspɪnɪ ; ˈspɪnɪ/ *n* (*pl* ~s) thicket; small wood with thick undergrowth, esp (in England) one used for sheltering gameˈ(6). 雜樹林;小叢(尤指在英國供獵物棲身者)。

spin·ster /ˈspɪnstə(r) ; ˈspɪnstɚ/ *n* (usu official or legal use) unmarried woman; woman who remains single after the conventional age for marrying. (通常爲正式或法律用語)未婚女人;老處女。 **ˈ~·hood** /-hʊd ; -,hʊd/ *n* the state of being a ~. (女子的)獨身;未婚。

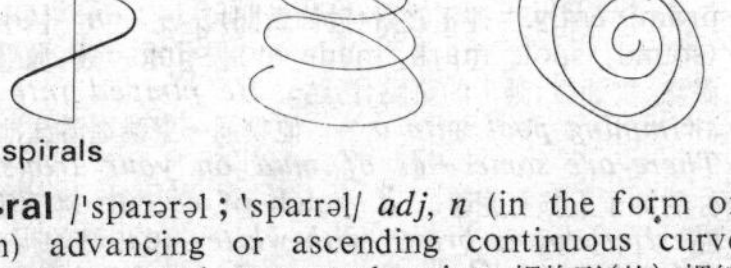

spirals

spi·ral /ˈspaɪərəl ; ˈspaɪrəl/ *adj, n* (in the form of an) advancing or ascending continuous curve winding round a central point: 螺旋形(的);螺線(的): *A snail's shell is ~.* 蝸牛殼是螺旋形的。*The rocket went up in a ~.* 火箭盤旋着上升。*A ~ nebula is a group of stars that has the appearance of a ~.* 螺旋星雲是成螺旋形狀的星羣。⇨ also *inflationary ~* at inflate. ⇨ the illus at whorl. 參看 whorl 之插圖。□ *vi* (-ll-, US also -l-) [VP2A, C] move in a ~: 呈螺旋狀移動;盤旋移動: *The smoke ~led up.* 煙盤旋上升。*Prices are still ~ling.* 物價仍在盤旋上漲。

spire /ˈspaɪə(r) ; spaɪr/ *n* pointed structure like a tall cone or pyramid rising above a tower (esp of a church). (尤指教堂的)塔尖;尖頂。⇨ the illus at church. 參看 church 之插圖。

spirit /ˈspɪrɪt ; ˈspɪrɪt/ *n* **1** [C, U] soul; immaterial, intellectual or moral part of man: 心靈;精神(指個人之心智,道德或其他超物質的層面): *He was vexed in ~,* inwardly. 他內心氣惱。*I shall be with you in (the) ~,* My thoughts will be with you even though I am not with you in the flesh. 我的心思將與你同在(雖然我不和你在一起)。*The ~ is willing but the flesh is weak,* One is willing to do sth, but physically unable to do it. 心有餘而力不足;力不從心。 **the Holy S~,** the Third Person of the Trinity. 聖靈(和天父,耶穌成三位一體)。 **2** the soul thought of as separate from the body; disembodied soul: 靈魂;亡魂: *the abode of ~s,* where the ~s of the dead are; 靈魂安息處; *believe in ~s;* 相信靈魂; *raise a ~.* 招魂。**ˈ~-rapper** *n* person who claims to receive messages from the dead by means of raps on a table. 招魂巫師(宣稱可藉敲桌子而通亡魂)。 **3** [C] sprite; elf; goblin. 幽靈;妖精;鬼怪。 **4** [U] life and consciousness not associated with a body; supernatural being: (不與肉體結合的)生命與意識;神靈: *God is pure ~.* 上帝是純靈。 **5** [C] (always with an *adj*) person considered from the intellectual, moral or emotional point of view: (恆與形容詞連用)人(從智力、道德或情緒的觀點而論);具有某種特質的人: *What a noble/generous, etc ~ he is!* 他是一位多麼高貴(慷慨等)的人啊! *He was one of the leading ~s of the Reform Movement.* 他是革新運動領導人物之一。 **moving ~,** person who is the originator and sustainer of an idea, project, etc. 倡導者。 **6** [U] quality of courage, vigour, liveliness: 勇氣;銳氣;元氣;生氣: *Put a little more ~ into your work.* 工作要多賣點力。*You haven't the ~ of a mouse.* 你的膽子還不如老鼠。 **7** (*sing* only) mental or moral attitude: (僅用單數)心理或道德方面的態度;氣度: *in a ~ of mischief.* 以戲謔的態度。*Whether it was unwise or not depends upon the ~ in which it was done.* 這事之是否不智,端視做此事所持的態度而定。 **8** [U] real meaning or purpose underlying a law, etc (contrasted with the apparent meaning of the words, etc): 法律等的眞諦;本旨;精神(與文字的表面含義相對): *obey the ~, not the letter, of the law.* 遵從法律的眞諦,非拘泥條文字句。*Have you followed out the ~ of his instructions?* 你已貫徹執行他的指示的本意了嗎? **9** (*pl*) state of mind (as being happy, hopeful, etc or the opposite): (複)心境;心情(如愉快、充滿希望或痛苦、失望等): *in high ~s,* cheerful; 高興的; *in poor/low ~s, out of ~s,* depressed, unhappy. 不高興的。*Have a glass of brandy to keep up your ~s.* 喝一杯白蘭地提提神。 **10** (*sing* only) influence or tendency that rouses or causes development: (僅用單數)引起進展的影響或趨勢: *The wind of change is blowing and we cannot resist the ~ of the times.* 要求改變現狀的風氣正在流行,我們無法抗拒時代的潮流。 **11** [U] industrial alcohol. 火酒;酒精。 **ˈ~-lamp/-stove** *n* one in which ~ is burned. 酒精燈(爐)。**ˈ~-level** *n* glass tube partly filled with water or alcohol, with a bubble of air which, when centred, shows that a surface is horizontal. 酒精水平器。 **12** (*pl*) solution in alcohol: (複)酒精溶液: *~s of camphor/turpentine;* 樟腦油(松節油); *~(s) of salt,* hydrochloric acid. 氫氯酸;鹽酸。 **13** (usu *pl*) strong alcoholic drink (eg whisky, brandy, gin, rum): (通常用複數)烈酒(如威士忌、白蘭地、杜松子酒與蘭酒): *a glass of ~s and water.* 一杯和水的烈酒。 *She drinks no ~ but vodka.* 除伏特加酒外,她不飲其他烈酒。□ *vt* [VP 15B] **~** ***sb/sth away/off,*** take sb/sth rapidly, secretly or mysteriously: 迅速、秘密或神秘地帶走(某人或某物);誘拐;拐帶: *She has disappeared as completely as if she had been ~ed away to another* *planet.* 她一直沒有踪影,像是被人拐到另外一個星球上去了。**~ed** /ˈspɪrɪtɪd; ˈspɪrɪtɪd/ *adj* **1** full of ~(6); lively; courageous: 有銳氣的; 有生氣的;活潑的;勇敢的: *a ~ed attack/defence/reply;* 猛烈的攻擊(英勇的防禦;有力的答覆); *a ~ed horse;* 有生氣的馬; *a ~ed conversation.* 活潑的談話。**2** (in compounds) (用於複合字中) having the kind of spirits(9) indicated: 有…心境的: ˌ*high-*/ˌ*low-*/ˌ*poor-*ˈ*~ed*, etc. 高興的(沮喪的,不高興的等)。**~·less** *adj* without ~(6); not having or showing energy or courage; depressed. 無精神的;無生命力的;沒有勇氣的;委靡的。

spiri·tual /ˈspɪrɪtʃʊəl; ˈspɪrɪtʃʊəl/ *adj* **1** of the spirit(1) or soul(1); of religion, not of material things; of, from, God: 精神的;心靈的;宗教上的;上帝的;神聖的;屬靈的: *concerned about sb's ~ welfare.* 關心某人精神上的福祉。**2** of spirits(2); supernatural. 神靈的;超自然的。**3** caring much for things of the spirit(1). 愛好精神方面的事物的;脫俗的;崇高的。**4** of the church: 教會的: *lords ~,* (GB) bishops and archbishops in the House of Lords. (英)上議院中有主教及大主教身份的議員。□ *n* **(Negro) ~,** religious song as sung by Negroes in the US. (美國黑人等所唱的)黑人聖歌。**~ly** /-tʃʊlɪ; -tʃʊəlɪ/ *adv* **~·ity** /ˌspɪrɪtʃʊˈælətɪ; ˌspɪrɪtʃʊˈælətɪ/ *n* [U] ~ quality; devotion to ~ things. 屬於心靈或精神方面的特質;靈性;有關宗教信仰、教會、教堂、教士等的事物。

spiri·tu·al·ism /ˈspɪrɪtʃʊəlɪzəm; ˈspɪrɪtʃʊəlˌɪzəm/ *n* [U] belief in the possibility of receiving messages from the spirits of the dead; practice of attempting to do this. 靈魂論;招魂術。**spiri·tu·al·ist** /-ɪst; -ɪst/ *n* believer in ~. 靈魂論者。**spiri·tu·al·is·tic** /ˌspɪrɪtʃʊəˈlɪstɪk; ˌspɪrɪtʃʊəˈlɪstɪk/ *adj* of ~ or spiritualists. 靈魂論的;靈魂論者的。

spiri·tu·al·ize /ˈspɪrɪtʃʊəlaɪz; ˈspɪrɪtʃʊəlˌaɪz/ *vt* [VP 6A] make pure or spiritual. 使純淨;使精神化;靈化。**spiri·tu·al·iz·ation** /ˌspɪrɪtʃʊəlaɪˈzeɪʃn *US:* -lɪˈz-; ˌspɪrɪtʃʊəlɪˈzeʃən/ *n* [U].

spiri·tu·ous /ˈspɪrɪtjʊəs *US:* -tʃʊəs; ˈspɪrɪtʃʊəs/ *adj* (of liquids) containing alcohol: (指液體)含酒精的: *~ liquors,* distilled liquors such as whisky, not (usu) fermented liquors such as beer. 蒸餾酒(如威士忌,非如啤酒之釀造者)。

spirt /spɜːt; spɝt/ *vi* [VP2C, 2A], *n* = spurt.

spit[1] /spɪt; spɪt/ *n* **1** long thin metal spike to which meat, etc is secured for roasting. 烤肉叉;炙叉。**2** small, narrow point of land running out into a body of water. (伸入水域中的)狹長地峽;岬。□ *vt* (-pp-) put a ~ through (a chicken, piece of meat, etc); pierce with the point of a sword, spear, etc. 以炙叉穿過(雞、肉片等);(以刀、矛等)刺;戳。

spit[2] /spɪt; spɪt/ *vt, vi* (*pt, pp* spat /spæt; spæt/) (-tt-) **1** [VP2A, C, 3A] ~ ***(at/on/upon sb/sth),*** send liquid (saliva) out from the mouth; do this as a sign of contempt or hatred: 吐口水;吐痰;吐口水以示藐視或憎恨: *If you ~ in a London bus you may be fined £5.* 如果你在倫敦的公共汽車上吐痰,你可能被罰五鎊。*He spat in the man's face/spat at him.* 他吐口水在那人的臉上(向他吐口水)。*The cat spat* (= made an angry or hostile ~ting noise) *at the dog.* 那隻猫向那條狗發出憤怒或表示敵意的呼嚕呼嚕聲。**2** [VP6A, 15B] ~ ***sth (out),*** send out from the mouth; (fig) utter angrily or sharply: 吐出;(喻)憤怒地或尖刻地說: *The baby spat out the nasty pill.* 那嬰兒吐出了那難吃的藥丸。*After the tooth had been extracted the boy spat a lot of blood.* 牙齒拔掉後,那男孩吐出了許多血。*She spat (out) curses at me.* 她尖刻地咒詛我。~ ***it out,*** (colloq) say what you have to say, quickly. (俗)爽爽快快地說出來。**3** [VP2A, 6A] (of a fire, candle, gun, etc) throw out; make the noise of ~ting: (指火、燭、槍等)發出;發吐物聲;發突突聲: *The engine was ~ting.* 引擎在突突地作響。*The guns were ~ting fire.* 槍砲在不斷地發射。ˈ**~·fire** *n* hot-tempered person. 急躁的人;急性子的人。**4** [VP2A] (of rain or snow) fall lightly: (指雨或雪)微降: *It's not raining heavily, only ~ting.* 雨下得不大,祇是小雨而已。□ *n* **1** [U] saliva. 唾液;口水。**2** act of ~ting. 唾吐。~ ***and polish,*** the cleaning and polishing of equipment (by soldiers, etc). (兵士等)裝備的擦洗。**3** ***the dead ~ of; the ~ and image of*** /ˌspɪt n ˈɪmɪdʒ; ˈspɪtn̩ˈɪmɪdʒ/; ***the ~ting image of,*** exact counterpart or likeness of: 與…完全相同或相似的人或物: *He's the dead ~/the ~ting image of his father.* 他像極了他的父親。**4** frothy secretion of some insects (seen on plants, etc). (見於植物等上的)某些昆蟲之泡沫狀分泌物。

spit[3] /spɪt; spɪt/ *n* (*pl* ~ or ~s) spade's depth: 一鏟之深度;一鍬之深度: *Dig the patch two ~(s) deep.* 把這塊地挖兩鏟深。

spite /spaɪt; spaɪt/ *n* **1** [U] ill will; desire to cause pain or damage: 惡毒;惡意;使遭受痛苦或損害的意願: *do sth out of/from ~.* 出於惡意做某事。**2** (with *indef art*) grudge: (與不定冠詞連用)怨恨: *have a ~ against sb;* 怨恨某人; *do sth to satisfy a private ~.* 做某事洩私怨。**3** (*prep* phrase) (介詞片語) ***in ~ of,*** not to be prevented by; notwithstanding: 雖然;不顧;儘管…仍: *They went out in ~ of the rain.* 儘管下雨,他們仍然外出。*In ~ of all his efforts he failed.* 他雖然做了各種努力,仍然失敗了。□ *vt* [VP6A] injure or annoy because of ~: 因怨恨而傷害或攪擾;向…洩憤;刁難: *The neighbours let their radio blare every afternoon just to ~ us.* 隣居每天下午故意把收音機的聲音開得很大,以向我們洩憤。**~·ful** /-fl; -fəl/ *adj* having, showing, ~. 有惡意的;懷恨的。**~·fully** /-fəlɪ; -fəlɪ/ *adv* **~·ful·ness** *n*

spittle /ˈspɪtl; ˈspɪtl/ *n* [U] liquid of the mouth; saliva. 口水;唾液;痰。

spit·toon /spɪˈtuːn; spɪˈtun/ *n* container to spit into. 痰盂。

spiv /spɪv; spɪv/ *n* (GB sl) person not in regular employment but who makes money by dubious business methods, and who goes about smartly dressed and having a good time. (英俚)靠不正當行業賺錢,並且講究衣著經常遊手好閒的人。

splash /splæʃ; splæʃ/ *vt, vi* **1** [VP6A, 15B, 14] ~ ***sth (about) (on/over sth); ~ sth/sb (with sth),*** cause (a liquid) to fly about in drops; make (sb or sth) wet: 濺(水等);潑濕(某人或某物): *~ water on/over the floor;* 潑水在地板上; *~ the floor with water;* 以水潑在地板上; *~ water about.* 四處濺水。*The children love to ~ water over one another.* 孩子們喜歡彼此往身上潑水。**2** [VP2A] (of a liquid) fly about and fall in drops: (指液體)飛濺;激濺: *fountains ~ing in the park.* 公園中飛濺的噴泉。*This tap is a bad one—it ~es.* 這龍頭不好——會濺水。**3** [VP2C] move, fall, so that there is ~ing: 濺著水行進;濺著水落下: *We ~ed (our way) across the stream/into the lake, etc.* 我們濺著水走過溪流(跳入湖中等)。*Look at that hippo ~ing about in the river.* 看那隻在河裡濺水的河馬。*The spacecraft ~ed down in the Pacific.* 太空船降落在太平洋中。Hence, 由此產生, ˈ**~-down** *n* landing of a spacecraft in the sea. (太空船之)海上降落。**4** [VP15B] ~ ***money/news about,*** spend/display it freely, prominently. 揮霍錢財(散佈新聞)。□ *n* [C] **1** (sound, spot, mark, made by) ~ing: 濺;飛濺;飛濺聲;噗通聲;濺污的斑點;污跡: *He jumped into the swimming pool with a ~.* 他噗通一聲跳進游泳池中。*There are some ~es of mud on your trousers.* 你的褲子上濺有泥漿。**2** patch of colour: 有顏色斑點: *Her dog is brown with white ~es.* 她的褐毛狗帶有白色斑點。**3** (colloq) small quantity of soda-water etc: (俗)少量汽水等: *a whisky and ~.* 摻有少量汽水的威士忌酒。**4** ***make a ~,*** (colloq, fig) attract attention by making a display of (esp) one's wealth. (俗,喻)炫耀(尤指)財富;擺闊;擺排場。

splay /spleɪ; sple/ *vt, vi* make opposite sides (of an opening) diverge; cause to slant or slope; (of an opening) be constructed in this way: 使(開口、缺口等)相對兩邊斜出;使成斜面;使傾斜;(指開口)呈斜

面;傾斜: *a ~ed window*, eg one in a very thick wall, so that the opening in the wall is wider on one side than the other. 側斜窗(兩側斜出,如開在厚牆上者,兩面的開口,一面較另一面寬)。*The plumber ~ed the end of the pipe before fitting it over the next section.* 水管工人先把管口弄斜,再接合在下一段管子上。□ *n* sloping side of a window opening, etc. (窗等)開口的傾面。□ *adj* (esp of feet) broad, flat and turned outwards. (尤指脚)平蹠外翻的;成外八字形的。Hence, 由此產生, **'~-foot** *n*. **'~-footed** *adj* having ~ feet. 外八字脚的。

spleen /spli:n ; splin/ *n* **1** [C] bodily organ in the abdomen which causes changes in the blood. 脾;脾臟。⇨ the illus at alimentary. 參看 alimentary 之插圖。 **2** [U] lowness of spirits; bad temper: 抑鬱;意氣消沉;壞脾氣;憤怒: *in a fit of ~;* 在發怒; *vent one's ~ on sb.* 對某人發脾氣。

splen·did /ˈsplendɪd ; ˈsplɛndɪd/ *adj* **1** magnificent: 華麗的;壯麗的;堂皇的;輝煌的: *a ~ sunset/house/victory;* 燦麗的夕陽(堂皇的房屋;輝煌的勝利); *~ jewellery.* 燦爛的珠寶。 **2** (colloq) very satisfactory; excellent: (俗)極令人滿意的;絕妙的;極佳的: *a ~ dinner/idea.* 極好的餐食(意見)。**~·ly** *adv*

splen·dif·er·ous /splenˈdɪfərəs ; splɛnˈdɪfərəs/ *adj* (colloq, often hum or ironic) splendid. (俗,常用作諧或反語)華麗的;壯麗的;堂皇的;絕妙的;極佳的。

splen·dour (US = **-dor**) /ˈsplendə(r) ; ˈsplɛndɚ/ *n* **1** [U] magnificence; brightness: 華麗;壯麗;光亮: *the ~ of stained glass windows.* 彩色玻璃窗之燦麗。 **2** (sometimes *pl*) grandeur, glory. (有時用複數)堂皇;威嚴;榮耀。

sple·netic /splɪˈnetɪk ; splɪˈnɛtɪk/ *adj* ill-tempered; peevish. 壞脾氣的;乖戾的;易怒的。

splice /splaɪs ; splaɪs/ *vt* [VP6A] **1** join (two ends of rope) by weaving the strands of one into the strands of the other; join (two pieces of wood, magnetic tape, film) by fastening them at the ends. 編接(繩頭);疊接(木材、錄音帶、影片)。 **2** ***get ~d,*** (sl) get married. (俚)結婚。□ *n* joint made by splicing. 編接或疊接的接合處;連接點;接頭。**~r** *n* device for joining two pieces of paper or magnetic tape, film, etc. 編接器;疊接器。

splint /splɪnt ; splɪnt/ *n* strip of wood, etc bound to an arm, leg, etc to keep a broken bone in the right position: (綁在臂,腿等上用以固定骨折之)夾板: *put an arm/a limb in ~s.* 以夾板夾住臂(肢)。

splin·ter /ˈsplɪntə(r) ; ˈsplɪntɚ/ *n* sharp-pointed or sharp-edged bit of hard material (wood, metal, glass, etc) split, torn or broken off a larger piece: (木、金屬、玻璃等的)尖片;碎片;裂片: *get a ~ into one's finger.* 指頭上扎了根刺。**a '~ group/party,** (in politics) group of persons who have broken off from their party. (政治)自原來政黨分裂出來的團體。**'~-proof** *adj* (eg of glass) that will not ~; giving protection against ~s, eg of broken glass, or from a bomb. 不會碎裂的;防裂片的(如防碎玻璃片或彈片)。□ *vt, vi* [VP2A, C, 6A, 15B] ***~ (off),*** break into ~s; come off as a ~. 碎裂;成碎片;分裂。**~y** *adj* apt to ~; full of ~s; like ~s. 易碎裂的;多碎片的;似碎片的。

split /splɪt ; splɪt/ *vt, vi* (*pt, pp* split; -tt-) **1** [VP 6A, 14, 2A, C] ***~ (into),*** break, cause to break, be broken, into two or more parts, esp from end to end along the line of natural division: 裂開;劈開;破裂(尤指沿自然紋理從一端至另一端裂開者): *~ting logs.* 劈木。*Some kinds of wood ~ easily.* 有些木頭易劈開。*Only a skilled workman can ~ slate into layers.* 惟有巧匠才能把板岩劈成石片。 **2** [VP2D, 22] ***~ (open),*** break open by bursting 爆裂;撐破;綳裂;綻裂: *His coat has ~ at the seams.* 他的上衣綻線了。 **3** [VP6A, 15A, B, 2A, C] ***~ (up) (into),*** (cause to) break into parts; divide: (使)分裂;分開: *~ the atom;* 分裂原子; *~ (up) a compound into its parts.* 分裂某種化合物爲諸元素。*The party ~ up into small groups.* 該黨分爲若干小派系。*Let's ~,* (mod colloq) leave (a party, etc). (現代俗語)咱們走吧(離開一聚會等)。*Let's ~ the cost of the meal,* share it. 我們來分攤餐費。*Joe and Jenny have ~ up,* (of a couple) separated from each other. 喬和珍妮已離異了。**~ *the difference,*** (when making a bargain) compromise (on the price, cost, etc). (講價錢時)(在價錢、價格等方面)讓步;妥協。**a ~ting *headache,*** so severe that it feels that one's head may crack. 劇烈或嚴重頭痛。**~ *hairs,*** make very fine distinctions (in an argument, etc). (在論辯等中)剖析毫髮;吹毛求疵。Hence, 由此產生, **'hair-~ting** *adj* **~ *an infinitive,*** place an adverb between *to* and the infinitive, (as in *'to quickly read a book'*). 分離一不定詞(在 to 與動詞之間加入一副詞,如 to quickly read a book)。**~ level** *adj* (of houses, housing) in which adjoining rooms are in a level midway between successive storeys of other parts. 錯層式的(指一房屋或一住處,其中各鄰接房間的地高錯落不一)。**a ~ mind/personality,** person who behaves sometimes with one set of actions, emotions, etc, and sometimes with another set; 有雙重人格之人;患人格分裂症者。also ⇨ schizophrenia; Jekyll and Hyde. **~ peas,** dried peas ~ into halves. 豌豆瓣。**a ~ ring,** one split along its length, as used for keeping keys on. 鑰匙圈。**a ~ second,** a brief instant of time. 刹那;頃刻。**~ *one's sides (with laughter),*** laugh with movements of the sides. 捧腹(大笑)。Hence, 由此產生, **'side-~ting** *adj* **4** [VP2A, 3A] ***~ (on sb),*** (sl) give away the secret of (usu an accomplice); give information about him (to his disadvantage). (俚)洩露(通常爲同犯)的秘密;告密;告發。 **5** [VP2A] (US sl) leave (a place). (美俚)離開(某地)。□ *n* [C] **1** splitting; crack or tear made by splitting: 裂開;劈開;分裂;分開: *sew up a ~ in a seam.* 把裂開的縫縫起來。 **2** separation or division resulting from splitting: 分歧;不和;內訌: *a ~ in the Labour Party.* 勞工黨之內訌。 **3** (colloq) half-bottle of soda water, etc. (俗)半瓶汽水(等)。 **4 the ~s,** acrobat's feat of sinking to the floor by extending the legs laterally with the trunk upright: 兩腿劈開坐落地上的技藝;劈叉;劈八字: *do the ~s.* 表演劈叉把式。

splosh /splɒʃ ; splɑʃ/ *vt* = splash(4).

splotch /splɒtʃ ; splɑtʃ/, **splodge** /splɒdʒ ; splɑdʒ/ *nn* [C] daub or smear (of ink, dirt, etc); irregular patch (of colour, light, etc). (墨水、泥污等的)污痕;污漬;(顏色、光等的)不規則形的一片。

splurge /splɜ:dʒ ; splɝdʒ/ *vi, n* (colloq) (make a) noisy display or effort (intended to attract attention); show off. (俗)大聲誇示;炫耀;賣弄。

splut·ter /ˈsplʌtə(r) ; ˈsplʌtɚ/ *vi, vt* **1** [VP2A, C] speak quickly and confusedly (from excitement, etc). (因激動等)急促而雜亂地說。 **2** [VP6A, 15B] ***~ sth (out),*** say quickly, confusedly, indistinctly: 急促、雜亂、含糊地說出某事: *~ out a few words/a threat.* 急促含糊地說出幾個字(威脅)。 **3** [VP2A] make a series of spitting sounds; sputter(1): 發爆裂聲;作拍拍聲: *The swimmers dived and came ~ing to the surface.* 游泳的人們跳入水中,拍擊着水浮出水面。□ *n* [U] ~ing sound. 劈拍聲;爆裂聲。

Spode /spəʊd ; spod/ *n* [U] type of English porcelain. 斯潑德(英國的一種瓷器)。

spoil /spɔɪl ; spɔɪl/ *vt, vi* (*pt, pp* ~t or ~ed) **1** [VP6A] make useless or unsatisfactory: 使無用或不令人滿意;損壞;破壞: *fruit ~t by insects;* 被昆蟲損壞的水果; *holidays ~t by bad weather;* 爲壞天氣破壞的假日; *~t ballot papers,* made invalid because the voters have not marked them as required by regulations. 廢票(未按規定圈選的無效選票)。*Don't ~ your appetite by eating sweets just before dinner.* 不要在飯前吃糖果以免吃不下飯。**'~-sport** *n* person who does things that interfere with the enjoyment of other people. 掃人興的人;煞風景的人。 **2** [VP6A] harm the character or temperament of by wrong upbringing or lack of discipline: 寵壞;溺愛;姑息: *parents who ~ their children.* 溺愛孩子的父母親。 **3** [VP6A] pay great attention to the comfort and wishes of: 非常注意照應…的安適和願望;寵愛: *He likes having a wife who ~s him.* 他喜歡有一位對他非常關心的太太。 **4** [VP2A] (of food, etc) become bad, unfit for use: (指食物等)變壞;腐敗: *Some kinds of food soon ~.* 有些食物很容易變壞。 **5** *be ~ing for (a fight, etc)*, be eager for. 渴望;切望(打鬥等)。 **6** [VP6A, 14] ~ *sb (of sth)*, (old use, or liter; *pt, pp* always ~ed, never ~t) plunder, rob by force or stealth: (舊用法或文;過去式及過去分詞總是作 ~ed, 不作 ~t) 掠奪;搶刼;偸竊: *financiers who ~ed* (= despoiled) *widows of their money.* 掠奪寡婦們錢財的金融家。 □ *n* **1** (either [U] or *pl*, not with numerals) stolen goods; plunder: (用單數或複數皆可,但不與數字連用)掠奪物;偸來的東西;贓物: *The thieves divided up the ~(s).* 賊分贓。 **2** (*pl*) profits, profitable positions, gained from political power: (複)(用政治力量獲得的)利益;肥缺: *the ~s of office;* 肥缺; *the '~s system,* (in some countries) system by which positions in the public service (their salaries and other advantages) are given to supporters of the political party which wins power. (某些國家的)政黨分贓制(公職委派給獲勝政黨之支持者的制度)。 **3** [U] earth, unwanted material, etc thrown or brought up in excavating, draining, etc. 挖出的泥土等;棄土。

spoke[1] /spəʊk ; spok/ *n* **1** any one of the bars or wire rods connecting the hub (centre) of a wheel with the rim (outer edge). 輪輻;輻條。⇨ the illus at bicycle. 參看 bicycle 之挿圖。 *put a '~ in sb's wheel,* hinder him; prevent him from carrying out his plans. 阻礙某人;使某人計不得逞。 **2** rung of a ladder. 梯級;梯磴。

spoke[2], **spoken** /spəʊk, 'spəʊkən ; spok, 'spokən/ *pt* and *pp* of speak.

spokes·man /'spəʊksmən ; 'spoksmən/ *n* (*pl* -men) person speaking, chosen to speak, on behalf of a group. 發言人;代言人。

spo·li·ation /ˌspəʊlɪ'eɪʃn ; ˌspolɪ'eʃən/ *n* [U] plunder, esp of neutral merchant ships by countries at war. (尤指交戰國對中立國商船所作的)掠奪;搶刼。

spon·dee /'spɒndiː ; 'spɑndi/ *n* (prosody) metrical foot of two long or stressed syllables, used in poetry to vary other metres. (韻律學)揚揚格(二長音節或重音節之音步,在詩歌中用以使其他韻律有變化)。 **spon·daic** /spɒn'deɪɪk ; spɑn'de·ɪk/ *adj*

sponge /spʌndʒ ; spʌndʒ/ *n* **1** [C] kinds of simple sea animal with light structures of elastic material full of holes and able to absorb water easily; one of these, or sth of similar texture (eg porous rubber), used for washing, cleaning, etc. 海綿;海綿體;(用於洗濯、清潔等用的)海綿或似海綿物。 *pass the ~ over,* wipe out, agree to forget (an offence, etc). 抹消;同意忘記(嫌隙等);不念(舊惡)。 *throw up/in the ~,* admit defeat or failure. 承認失敗;認輸。 **2** piece of absorbent material, eg gauze, used in surgery; mop used in cleaning the bore of a gun, etc. (外科用的)棉球;(清潔砲膛等用的)洗桿;擦膛刷。 **3** *'~-cake* *n* soft, light yellow cake made of eggs, sugar and flour. 軟蛋糕;海綿蛋糕。□ *vt, vi* **1** [VP6A, 15B] ~ *sth (out),* wash, wipe or clean with a ~: 用海綿等洗滌、擦拭或清除: *~ a wound/a child's face;* 用棉球洗擦傷口(孩子的臉); *~ out a memory,* wipe it out, end it. 抹除記憶。 **2** [VP15B] ~ *sth up,* take up (liquid) with a ~: 用海綿吸收(液體): *~ up the mess.* 用海綿吸去汚水(等)。 **3** [VP3A] ~ *on/upon sb,* (colloq) live at his expense, get money from him, without giving, or intending to give, anything in return: (俗)依賴某人生活;詐取某人錢財: *~ (up) on one's friends;* 依賴朋友爲生; [VP6A, 14] *~ sth (from sb),* get by sponging: 詐得;騙取: *~ a dinner;* 騙得一餐飯; *~ a fiver* (= £5) *from an old acquaintance.* 從老友處騙得五鎊。 *~r* *n* person who ~s(3). 依賴他人生活者;詐騙者。 **spongy** *adj* (-ier, -iest) soft, porous and elastic like a ~: 像海綿的;柔軟、多孔而有彈性的: *spongy, moss-covered land.* 生滿苔蘚的柔軟土地。 **spongi·ness** *n*

spon·sor /'spɒnsə(r) ; 'spɑnsɚ/ *n* **1** person (eg a godfather) making himself responsible for another. 負責人(如教父等)。 **2** person who first puts forward or guarantees a proposal; person, firm, etc paying for a commercial radio or TV programme (usu in return for advertising of products). 發起人;保證人;資助人;贊助人;贊助廣播或電視節目的人或公司行號(通常爲其產品做宣傳);廣告客戶。□ *vt* [VP6A] act as a ~ for. 資助;贊助。

spon·ta·neous /spɒn'teɪnɪəs ; spɑn'tenɪəs/ *adj* done, happening, from natural impulse, not caused or suggested by sth or sb outside: 自然產生的;自發的;自動的: *He made a ~ offer of help.* 他自動提供幫助。 *Nothing he says is ~—he always thinks carefully before he speaks.* 他從不貿然發言——他總是謹愼思考後才講話。 *~ combustion,* burning caused by chemical changes, etc inside the material, not by the application of fire from outside. 自燃(藉自身的化學變化等而燃燒)。 *~·ly* *adv* *~·ness,* **spon·ta·neity** /ˌspɒntə'niːətɪ ; ˌspɑntə'niətɪ/ *nn*

spoof /spuːf ; spuf/ *vt, n* (sl) hoax; trick; swindle: (俚)愚弄;欺騙: *You've been ~ed,* You've been hoaxed. 你上當了。

spook /spuːk ; spuk/ *n* (hum) ghost. (諧)鬼。 *~y* *adj* (-ier, -iest) of, suggesting, ~s: 鬼的;使人想到鬼的: *a ~y* (= haunted) *house.* 鬼屋。

spool /spuːl ; spul/ *n* reel (for thread, wire, photographic film, typewriter ribbon, paper or magnetic tape, etc). (纏繞線、鐵絲、照相軟片、打字機色帶、紙、錄音帶等的)捲軸;捲盤。⇨ the illus at tape. 參看 tape 之挿圖。

spoon[1] /spuːn ; spun/ *n* utensil with a shallow bowl on a handle, used for stirring, serving and taking up food; named according to use, as: 匙;調羹;按其用途分爲: *des'sert-/'soup-/'table/'tea/'egg-~.* 甜食匙(湯匙,桌匙,茶匙,蛋匙)。 *be ˌborn with a ˌsilver '~ in one's mouth,* ⇨ silver(1). *'~-feed* *vt* **(a)** feed (a baby, etc) from a ~. 用羹匙餵(嬰兒等)。 **(b)** (fig) give (sb) excessive help or teaching: (喩)給予(某人)過分的幫助或教導;塡鴨式地教(不給學生獨立思考的機會): *Some teachers ~-feed their pupils.* 有些老師用塡鴨式的方法教學生。□ *vt* [VP15B] *~ sth up/out,* take with a ~: 以匙取: *~ up one's soup;* 以匙舀湯; *~ out the peas,* serve them. 以匙取食豌豆。 *'~·ful* /-fʊl ; -ˌfʊl/ *n* (*pl* ~-fuls) as much as a ~ can hold. 一匙之量。

spoon[2] /spuːn ; spun/ *vi* [VP2A] (dated colloq) behave in a way that shows that one is in love. (過時俗語)做出在戀愛中的舉動。

spoon·er·ism /'spuːnərɪzəm ; 'spunəˌrɪzəm/ *n* [C] confusion of two or more words by wrong placing of the initial sounds, eg *well-boiled icicle* for *well-oiled bicycle.* 混淆(字的)始音;首音誤置(如把 well-oiled bicycle 說成 well-boiled icicle)。

spoor /spʊə(r) ; spʊr/ *n* [C] track or trail of a wild animal, enabling it to be followed. (野獸的)足跡;嗅跡。

spor·adic /spə'rædɪk ; spo'rædɪk/ *adj* occurring, seen, only here and there or occasionally: 偶然見到的;時有時無的;散見於各處的: *~ raids/firing.* 偶發性的襲擊(零星的射擊)。 **spor·adi·cally** /-klɪ ; -kl̩ɪ/ *adv*

spore /spɔː(r) ; spor/ *n* [C] germ, single cell, by which a flowerless plant (eg moss, a fern) reproduces itself. (無花植物如苔蘚、羊齒等藉以繁殖的)孢子;芽胞。

spor·ran /'spɒrən ; 'spɑrən/ *n* pouch, usu fur-covered, worn by Scottish Highlanders in front of the kilt. 蘇格蘭高地人佩於短裙前的囊袋(通常以毛皮包覆)。⇨ the illus at kilt. 參看 kilt 之挿圖。

sport /spɔːt ; sport/ *n* **1** [U] amusement, fun: 有

趣;娛樂;玩笑;戲謔: *say sth in* ～, not seriously; 戲言; *make* ～ *of sb*, make him seem ridiculous. 開某人玩笑。 **2** [U] ⇨ the illus at base, cricket, football, hockey, rugby, tennis. activity engaged in, esp outdoors, for amusement and exercise; [C] particular form of such activity: (參看 base, cricket, football, hockey, rugby, tennis 之插圖)活動;運動;遊戲(尤指戶外者);某種形式的戶外活動或運動: *fond of／devoted to* ～; 喜愛(熱心於)戶外運動; *country* ～*s*, eg hunting, fishing, shooting, horse-racing; 鄉間戶外活動(如打獵、釣魚、射擊、賽馬); *athletic* ～*s*, eg running, jumping; 體育活動(如賽跑、跳高、跳遠); ˈ～*s coverage／reporting on TV*. 電視之體育新聞報導。 **3** (*pl*) meeting for athletic contests: (複)運動會: *the school* ～*s*; 學校(舉行的)運動會; *inter-university* ～*s*. 大學校際運動會。 **4** (compounds, etc) (複合字等) **ˈ～s-car** *n* small motor-car designed for high speeds. 跑車。 **ˈ～s-coat／-jacket,** informal jacket. 運動衣。 **ˈ～s-editor** *n* newspaper editor responsible for reports of ～s and games. 報紙的體育版編輯。 **ˈ～s•man** /-mən; -mən/ *n* (*pl* -men) **(a)** person who takes part in, is fond of, ～. 運動員;愛好運動者。 **(b)** (also 亦作 ～) person who plays fairly, who is willing to take risks, and is not downhearted if he loses. 有運動精神的人;失敗而不氣餒的人;輸得起的人。 Hence, 由此產生, **ˈ～s•man•ship** /-ʃɪp; -ˌʃɪp/ *n* **ˈ～s-man•like** *adj*. **5** (colloq) (俗) = ～sman; agreeable, easy-going person: 有運動精神的人;討人喜歡的人;平易近人的人: *Come on, be a* ～*!* 好了,不要再彆扭了! **6** [C] plant or animal that deviates in a striking way from the normal type. 變態的植物或動物。 □ *vi, vt* **1** [VP2C] play about, amuse oneself: 自娛;遊戲;嬉戲;玩耍: *seals* ～*ing about in the water.* 在水中嬉戲的海豹。 **2** [VP6A] (colloq) have or wear for proud display: (俗)誇示地保有、穿、戴等;炫耀: ～ *a moustache／a diamond ring／a flower in the buttonhole of one's jacket.* 炫耀鬍髭(鑽石戒指,上衣鈕孔中佩戴的花)。 **～•ing** *adj* **1** connected with ～, interested in ～. 娛樂的;運動的;對運動有興趣的。 **2** willing to take a risk of losing; involving a risk of losing: 願冒失敗危險的;輸得起的;有輸贏的;有風險的: *make sb a* ～*ing offer;* 提供某人一具冒險性的建議; *give sb a* ～*ing chance.* 給予某人一賭輸贏的機會。 **3** ～smanlike: 有運動家風度的: *It's very* ～*ing of you to give me such an advantage.* 你讓我佔這樣的便宜,很有運動員的風度。 **～•ing•ly** *adv*

sport•ive /ˈspɔːtɪv; ˈsportɪv/ *adj* playful; merry. 嬉戲的;愉快的;開心的。 **～•ly** *adv* **～•ness** *n*

spot /spɒt; spɑt/ *n* **1** small (esp round) mark different in colour from what it is on: 小點;(尤指)圓形斑點: *white dress material with red* ～*s.* 帶紅色斑點的白色衣料。 *Which has* ～*s, the leopard or the tiger?* 豹與虎,哪一個有斑點? **2** dirty mark or stain: 污點;污跡: ～*s of mud on your boots.* 你長靴上的泥污。 **3** small, red mark, blemish, on the skin; pimple: (皮膚上的)紅斑,丘疹: *This ointment won't clear your face of* ～*s.* 這種油膏不會去除你臉上的紅斑。 **4** (fig) moral blemish: (喻)道德上的污點或瑕疵: *There isn't a* ～ *on her reputation.* 她的名譽上沒有污點。 **5** drop: 滴;點: *Did you feel a few* ～*s of rain?* 你有沒有感覺到下了幾滴雨? **6** particular place or area: 地點;場所: *the (very)* ～ *where he was murdered.* 他被謀殺的(確實)地點。 **TV／radio** ～, place in a TV／radio programme for an item or a commercial advertisement. 電視(無線電廣播)節目中某一項目或廣告出現的位置。⇨ slot(3). **7** (phrases) (片語) **a** ～ **check,** a quickly-made investigation, esp one made suddenly and without warning. 臨時檢查;突擊檢查。 **a tender** ～, (fig) a subject on which a person's feelings are easily hurt. (喻)易傷某人感情的話題;痛處。 ***in a*** ～, (colloq) in a difficult situation. (俗)處困難境遇;在困境中。 ***knock*** ～***s off sb,*** easily surpass, do better than, him. 輕易超越或勝過某人。 ***on the*** ～, **(a)** at the place where one is needed: 在現場;臨現場: *The police were on the* ～ *within a few minutes of hearing about the crime.* 獲悉該項犯罪後幾分鐘,警察卽趕到現場。 **(b)** then and there; immediately: 當時當地;卽刻;立卽;當場: *He fell dead on the* ～. 他當場就死了。 *The bullet struck his head and he was killed on the* ～. 子彈打中他的頭部,他當時卽被打死。 **(c)** (sl) in trouble. (俚)在困難中。Cf 參較 'on the carpet'. ***the person on the*** ～, the man at the place in question (who, presumably, is acquainted with local conditions, happenings, etc and able to deal with them): 熟悉當地情況並能應付事情的人;當地有辦法的人;當地有力人士: *Let's leave the decision to the man／the men／the people on the* ～. 讓我們留給當地有辦法的人(們)去決定好了。 ***put sb on the*** ～, **(a)** place sb in danger or difficulty: 置某人於危境或困境: *You've put me on the* ～ *here: I can't answer your question.* 這你可把我難住了:我無法回答你的問題。 **(b)** (of gangsters) decide to kill (eg a rival gangster). (指歹徒)決定殺死(如敵對的歹徒)。 ***put one's finger on／find sb's weak*** ～, find the point (of character, etc) where he is most open to attack. 找出某人的弱點。 **8** (comm) ～ **cash,** payment on delivery of goods. (商)交貨付款;現金。 ～ **prices,** prices quoted for such payment. 現金價格。 **9** (GB colloq) small quantity of anything: (英俗)小量;少許: *I need a* ～ *of brandy.* 我需要一點白蘭地。 *What about doing a* ～ *of work?* 做一點事怎麼樣? *He's having a* ～ *of bother with his brother,* a quarrel. 他同他的哥哥(弟弟)在吵架。 □ *vt, vi* (-tt-) **1** [VP6A, 2A] mark, become marked, with ～s: 加斑點於;弄污;變得有斑點;變污: *a table* ～*ted with ink;* 被墨水弄污的桌子; *material that* ～*s easily,* easily becomes ～ted. 易被弄污的料子。 **2** [VP6A] pick out, recognize, see (one person or thing out of many): (從很多人或物中)察出;認出;看出;看見(某一個人或物): ～ *a friend in a crowd;* 在人群中認出一位朋友; ～ *the winner in a race*, pick out the winner before the start. 預先指出賽跑的獲勝者(看好某人)。 **3** [VP2A] (colloq) rain slightly: (俗)下小雨: *It's beginning to* ～*／is* ～*ting with rain.* 天開始下起小雨來了。 **～•ted** *adj* marked with ～s, eg of such animals as the leopard and panther, and of birds with ～s of different colour on their plumage, of textile material with ～s. 有斑點的(如指豹、美洲豹等動物,羽毛有不同顏色斑點的鳥,以及有斑點的布料等)。 **ˌ～•ted ˈfever** *n* form of meningitis; form of typhus. 斑疹熱;流行性腦脊髓膜炎;斑疹傷寒。 **～•less** *adj* free from ～s; clean: 乾淨的;清潔的;無污點的;無瑕疵的: *a* ～*less kitchen／reputation.* 清潔的厨房(無瑕疵的名譽)。 **～•less•ly** *adv*: ～*lessly clean.* 極爲清潔的;一塵不染的。 **～ty** *adj* (-ier, -iest) **1** marked with ～s (esp on the skin): (尤指皮膚上)有斑點的: *a* ～*ty complexion;* 多雀斑的臉; *windows that are* ～*ty with fly marks.* 有蒼蠅污痕的窗戶。 **2** of varying quality: 品質不一的;不規則的: *a* ～*ty piece of work*, done unevenly. 做得不均勻的工作(有的地方做得好,有的地方做得壞)。 **～•ter** *n* person who ～s(2), eg ˈ*aircraft-*～*ter*, person who, eg during a war, looks for and identifies different types of aircraft; ˈ*train-*～*ter*, (usu) schoolboy who looks for and notes different types of railway-engines. 觀察員;偵察員(例如飛機偵察員,如在戰時搜尋及辨認敵機機種的人員;火車觀察員,通常指注意火車機車之不同類型的學童)。

spot•light /ˈspɒtlaɪt; ˈspɑtˌlaɪt/ *n* [C] (projector or lamp used for sending a) strong light directed on to a particular place or person, eg on the stage of a theatre: 注光;射光圈(投射於舞台等上某處或某人的强光);聚光燈(射出注光者): *He likes to be in the／to hold the* ～, (fig) be the centre of attention. (喻)他喜歡出風頭。□ *vt* [VP6A] direct a ～ on to. 投射注光於;把光線集中於;使顯著。

spouse /spaʊz *US:* spaʊs ; spaʊs/ *n* (legal or archaic) husband or wife. (法律或古)配偶;夫;妻。

spout /spaʊt ; spaʊt/ *n* [C] **1** pipe or lip through or from which liquid pours, eg for carrying rain-water from a roof, or tea from a teapot. (液體流出或經過的)管道;管口;嘴;噴水孔;水筧(如茶壺嘴或屋簷下的導水管槽)。 **2** stream of liquid coming out with great force. 噴水;水柱;液柱;湧流。⇨ *water-~* at water¹(7). **3** ***up the ~,*** (sl) (俚) **(a)** in pawn. 在典當中。**(b)** in difficulties, broken, etc according to context. 處困境;破產等。**(c)** pregnant. 懷孕的。□ *vt, vi* **1** [VP2A, C, 6A] ~ ***(out),*** (of liquid) come or send out with great force: (指液體)噴;湧;噴出;湧出: *water ~ing (out) from a broken water-main;* 從破裂的自來水主管噴出的水; *blood ~ing from a severed artery;* 從切斷的動脈湧出的血; *a broken pipe ~ing water.* 噴水的破裂水管。*The whales were ~ing,* sending up jets of water. 那些鯨魚正在噴水。 **2** [VP2A, 6A] (colloq) speak, recite (verses, etc) pompously: (俗)裝腔作勢地說、朗誦(詩等): *~ing unwanted advice.* 裝腔作勢地說出多餘的忠告。

sprain /spreɪn ; spren/ *vt* [VP6A] injure (a joint, eg in the wrist or ankle) by twisting violently so that there is pain and swelling: 扭傷(關節): *~ one's wrist;* 扭傷腕關節; *suffering from a ~ed ankle.* 因踝部扭傷而感到痛苦。□ *n* [C] injury so caused. 扭傷。

sprang /spræŋ ; spræŋ/ *pt* of spring³.

sprat /spræt ; spræt/ *n* small European sea-fish used as food. 小鰛(歐洲產的食用小海魚)。

sprawl /sprɔːl ; sprɔl/ *vi* [VP2A, C] **1** sit or lie with the arms and legs loosely spread out; fall so that one lies in this way: 伸展手足坐或臥;手足攤開地倒下: *~ing on the sofa;* 伸開四肢躺在沙發上; *be sent ~ing in the mud.* 被擊倒而仰臥在污泥中。 **2** (of plants, handwriting, fig of large towns) spread out loosely and irregularly over much space: (指植物、筆跡,並喻指大城市)蔓生;蔓延;塗鴉;散亂地延伸: *suburbs that ~ out into the country-side.* 向鄉間散亂延展的市郊。□ *n* [U, C] ~ing position or movement; widespread untidy area, esp of buildings: 四肢伸開躺臥的姿勢或動作;大片雜亂的地區;(尤指)建築物散亂的大片地區: *London's sub-urban ~.* 倫敦近郊建築物散亂的大片地區。

spray¹ /spreɪ ; spre/ *n* small branch of a tree or plant, esp a graceful one with leaves and flowers as an ornament; artificial ornament in a similar form: 小枝(尤指有花帶葉優美而作裝飾者);(人工做的)小枝花飾: *a ~ of diamonds.* 鑲有鑽石的枝狀飾物。

spray² /spreɪ ; spre/ *n* **1** [U] liquid sent through the air in tiny drops (by the wind, or through an apparatus): (藉風力或噴霧器形成的)水霧;水花;浪花: *'sea-~,* ~ blown from waves; 海水的浪花; *the ~ of a water-fall.* 瀑布的水花。 **2** [C, U] kinds of liquid preparation, eg a perfume, disinfectant or insecticide, to be applied in the form of ~ through an atomizer or other apparatus. (用噴霧器或其他器具噴射的)液體製劑(如香水、消毒劑、殺虫劑等)。 **3** [C] atomizer, etc used for applying such a liquid. 噴霧器。 **'~-gun** *n* apparatus using pressure to spread cellulose, paint, varnish, etc over surfaces. 噴(漆)槍。□ *vt* [VP6A, 14] ~ ***sth/sb (with sth); ~ sth (on sth/sb),*** scatter ~ on: 噴液體製劑於;似噴霧般發射: *~ mosquitoes/fruit-trees;* 噴殺虫劑於蚊蟲(果樹); *~ the enemy with bullets.* 向敵人掃射。**~er** *n* **1** person who ~s. 噴霧者;噴漆者。 **2** apparatus for ~ing. 噴霧器;噴漆槍;噴灑器。

spread /spred ; sprɛd/ *vt, vi* (*pt, pp* ~) **1** [VP6A, 14, 15B] ~ ***sth on/over sth; ~ sth with sth; ~ sth (out),*** extend the surface or width of sth by unfolding or unrolling it; cover (sth) by doing this: 展開;鋪開;攤開;鋪遮(某物): *~ a cloth on a table/a table with a cloth;* 把桌布鋪在桌面上; *~ out a map;* 展開地圖; *~ (out) one's arms.* 張開兩臂。*The bird ~ its wings.* 鳥展翅。 **2** [VP14] ~ ***sth on sth; ~ sth with sth,*** put (a substance) on a surface and extend its area by flattening, etc; cover (a surface) by doing this: 塗敷;塗佈: *~ butter on bread/a slice of bread with butter.* 塗奶油在(一片)麵包上。 **3** [VP6A, 15A, B, 2A, C] (cause to) become more widely extended or distributed: (使)傳佈;(使)廣佈;(使)散開;(使)流傳: *~ knowledge.* 傳播知識。*Flies ~ disease.* 蒼蠅傳佈疾病。*The water ~ over the floor.* 水漫佈在地板上。*The rumour quickly ~ through the village.* 這謠言很快就在村子裡傳開了。*The fire ~ from the factory to the houses near by.* 火勢從工廠延燒至附近的房舍。~ ***oneself,*** **(a)** occupy much space, eg by lying with the limbs extended. 伸開四肢躺臥等而佔去很多地方。**(b)** talk or write at length (on a subject). (就某一問題)滔滔不絕地說或寫。**(c)** let oneself go, eg by being generous in hospitality. 盡力而爲;十分盡力(如慇懃待客)。 **4** [VP2A, B, C] show an extended surface: 伸展;擴展: *a desert ~ing for hundreds of miles.* 綿延數百英里的沙漠。 **5** [VP6A, 15B] extend in time: (時間)延長;延伸: *a course of studies ~ over three years;* 爲時三年的課程; *instalments/payments ~ over twelve months.* 分十二個月償付的分期付款。 **6** ˌ~-**'eagle** *n* figure of an eagle with the legs and wings extended (as seen on coins). 張足展翼的鷹像(如硬幣上者)。□ *vt* (reflex) take up a lying position with arms and legs extended to form a cross: (反身)伸展四肢躺臥: *sunbathers ~eagled on the grass/sands.* 在草地(沙灘)上四肢張開躺臥的日光浴者。 **'~-over** *n* arrangement in an industry by which hours of work are adjusted to special needs. 工作時間按工作需要調整的制度。□ *n* (rarely *pl*) (罕用複數) **1** extent; breadth: 範圍;廣袤: *the ~ of a bird's wings.* 鳥的翼展。 **2** extension; spreading(3): 傳播;散佈;蔓延: *the ~ of disease/knowledge/education.* 疾病的蔓延(知識的傳播;教育的普及)。 **3** (colloq) table ~ with good things to eat and drink: (俗)擺美酒佳肴的桌子;豐盛的酒席: *What a ~!* 多豐盛的酒席呀! **4** sth that is ~(1) (usu in compounds): 鋪開之物(通常用於複合字中): *a 'bed~,* a cover ~ over the bed-clothes. 床單;被單;墊單。*He's developing (a) middle-age ~,* (colloq) is getting big round the waist (as some persons do in middle age). (俗)他逐漸發福了(腰圍逐漸增大,像有些中年人那樣)。 **5** name used for various kinds of paste (to be) ~ on bread, etc. 塗敷於麵包等上的某些醬的名稱。 **~er** *n* one who, that which, ~s, eg a *'flame-~er* in an oil-stove; an implement used for ~ing paste, etc on bread. 展開、塗敷、傳佈、伸展、延長等的人或物(如 flame-~er 油爐上的火焰擴散裝置);塗敷器(塗醬等於麵包上者)。

spree /spriː ; spri/ *n* lively frolic: 歡鬧;遊樂: *have a ~,* have a lively, merry time. 作樂;興高采烈。***be on the ~; go out on a ~,*** be having, go out to enjoy, a ~. 在作樂、狂歡;外出尋樂或狂歡。**a 'spending/'buying ~,** an occasion of (extravagant or unusual) spending of money. 瘋狂揮霍(狂購亂買)。

sprig /sprɪg ; sprɪg/ *n* **1** small twig (*of* a plant or bush) with leaves, etc: 有葉的小枝;嫩枝: *a ~ of mistletoe for Christmas.* 用作聖誕節裝飾用的槲寄生的小枝。 **2** (usu contemptuous) young person. (通常爲輕蔑語)少年;青年。 **~·ged** *adj* ornamented with designs of ~s: 用小枝或嫩枝圖案裝飾的: *~ged muslin.* 有小枝圖案的薄棉布。

spright·ly /'spraɪtlɪ ; 'spraɪtlɪ/ *adj* (-ier, -iest) lively; brisk. 活潑的;輕快的。**spright·li·ness** *n*

spring¹ /sprɪŋ ; sprɪŋ/ *n* **1** act of springing or jumping up. 跳;跳躍。 **2** (place where there is) water coming up from the ground: 泉;泉水;有泉水處: *'hot-~;* 溫泉; *'mineral-~;* 礦泉; *a hot-'~ resort;* 有溫泉的勝地; (attrib) (形容用法) *~ water.* 泉水。

3 device of twisted, bent or coiled metal or wire which tends to return to its shape or position when pulled or pushed or pressed: 發條;彈簧;板彈簧: *the ~s of a motor-car;* 汽車的板彈簧(俗稱鋼板); *the ~ of a watch.* 錶的發條。ˌ**~-'balance** *n* device that measures weight by the tension of a ~. 彈簧秤。'**~-board** *n* board to give a ~ing motion to sb jumping from it. 跳板;彈板。'**~-gun** *n* one that goes off when a trespasser comes against a wire which is attached to the trigger. 伏擊槍 (扳機與一金屬線相連,線被觸及即引發)。ˌ**~-'mattress** *n* one containing spiral ~s in a rigid frame. 彈簧床墊。**~ tide** *n* (two words; 此處須分開寫; ⇨ *~tide, ~time* at spring²) tide with the greatest rise or fall, occurring shortly after new and full moon in each month; ⇨ *neap-tide* at neap. 每個月新月及滿月後的大潮;子午潮。 **4** [U] elastic quality: 彈性;彈力: *rubber bands that have lost their ~.* 失去彈性的橡皮圈。*The old man's muscles have lost their ~.* 這老人的肌肉已失去了彈性。 **5** (often *pl*) cause or origin: (常用複數)起源;本源;原由;動機: *the ~s of human conduct.* 人類行爲的動機。**~·less** *adj* without ~s(3): 無發條、彈簧(板)等的: *a ~less cart.* 無彈簧的馬車。**~y** *adj* (-ier, -iest) (of movement or substances) elastic; that springs: (指動作或物質)有彈性的;有彈力的: *walk with a youthful, ~y step.* 以富有青春活力、有彈性的脚步行走。

spring² /sprɪŋ ; sprɪŋ/ *n* [U, C] season of the year in which vegetation begins; season between winter and summer (in GB from about 21 March to 22 June): 春;春季(在英國約自三月廿一日至六月廿二日): *in (the) ~;* 在春天; (attrib) (形容用法) *~ flowers/weather.* 春季的花(天氣)。ˌ**~-'clean** *vt* clean (a house, a room) thoroughly. 徹底打掃(房子,房間);大掃除。Hence, 由此產生, ˌ**~-'cleaning** *n.* '**~·like** *adj*: *~like weather.* 和煦如春的天氣。'**~·time** (also, poet 詩中亦作 '**~·tide**) *nn* season of ~. 春季。

spring³ /sprɪŋ ; sprɪŋ/ *vi, vt* (*pt* sprang /spræŋ ; spræŋ/, *pp* sprung /sprʌŋ ; sprʌŋ/) **1** [VP2C] jump suddenly from the ground; move suddenly (*up, down, out,* etc) from rest, concealment, etc: 跳;跳躍;躍出;突然活動(與 up, down, out 等連用): *He sprang to his feet/sprang out of bed/sprang forward to help me/sprang up from his seat.* 他跳了起來(從床上跳下來,跳過來幫助我,從座位上突然站起來)。*The branch sprang back and hit me in the face.* 那樹枝彈回來打在我臉上。 **2** [VP2C] *~ (up),* appear; grow up quickly from the ground or from a stem: 出現;發生;萌芽;迅速長出: *A breeze has sprung up.* 吹起了微風。*Weeds were ~ing up everywhere.* 雜草到處叢生。*The wheat is beginning to ~ up.* 小麥正開始茁長。(fig) (喻) *A suspicion/doubt sprang up in her mind.* 她心中起了懷疑。 **3** [VP3A] *~ from,* arise or come from: 崛起;來自: *He is sprung from royal blood,* is of royal ancestry. 他是皇室胄裔。*Where have you sprung from,* suddenly and unexpectedly appeared from? 你從哪裡跳出來(突然出現)的? **4** [VP14] *~ sth on sb,* bring forward suddenly: 突然提出;突然帶來: *~ a surprise on sb;* 使某人吃一驚; *~ a new theory/proposal on sb.* 突然向某人提出新理論(建議)。 **5** [VP6A] cause to operate by means of a mechanism: (藉機械作用)使發動;開動: *~ a mine,* cause it to explode; 使地雷爆炸; *~ a trap,* cause it to go off. 觸引(拉動)陷阱(或捕機等)。 **6** [VP6A, 2A] (of wood) (cause to) warp, split, crack: (指木材)(使)彎曲;(使)裂開;(使)分裂: *My cricket bat has sprung.* 我的板球拍彎曲了。*I have sprung my tennis racket.* 我把我的網球拍弄彎了。 *~ a leak,* (of a ship) crack or burst so that water enters. (指船)漏裂;生漏縫。

spring·bok /'sprɪŋbɒk ; 'sprɪŋˌbɑk/ *n* small S African gazelle. 南非洲產的一種小瞪羚。

sprinkle /'sprɪŋkl ; 'sprɪŋkḷ/ *vt* [VP6A, 14] *~ sth (on/with sth),* direct, throw, a shower of (sth) on to (a surface): 撒(某物)於(某物之表面);灑: *~ water on a dusty path;* 灑水於多塵土的路上; *~ a dusty path with water;* 以水灑於多塵土的路上; *~ the floor with sand.* 把沙撒在地板上。**sprink·ler** /'sprɪŋklə(r) ; 'sprɪŋklɚ/ *n* (esp) apparatus or device for sprinkling water (eg on to a lawn) or (permanently installed in buildings) for fighting fire. (尤指)灑水器;灑水車;灑水裝置;(固定在建築物上的)消防裝置。**sprink·ling** *n* small quantity or number here and there: (散布在各處的)微量或少數: *There was a sprinkling of hooligans in the crowd.* 群衆之中夾雜有少數的不良少年。

sprint /sprɪnt ; sprɪnt/ *vi* [VP2A, C] run a short distance at full speed: 以全速跑短距離: *He ~ed past his competitors just before reaching the tape.* 剛好在到達終點之前,他全速衝刺而超越了他的對手們。□ *n* such a run; (esp) burst of speed at the end of a race. 短距離快跑;短跑;(尤指)賽跑到達終點前的衝刺。**~er** *n*

sprit /sprɪt ; sprɪt/ *n* small spar reaching from a mast to the upper outer corner of a sail. (自桅伸至帆上外角以撑帆的)斜杠。⇨ the illus at barque. 參看 barque 之插圖。'**~·sail** *n* sail extended by a ~. 斜杠帆。

sprite /spraɪt ; spraɪt/ *n* fairy; elf. 妖精;鬼怪;精靈。

sprocket /'sprɒkɪt ; 'sprɑkɪt/ *n* each of several teeth on a wheel connecting with the links of a chain or holes in a movie film, paper or magnetic tape. 扣連齒(鏈輪上與鏈條結合之齒,或與影片、紙帶、磁帶旁邊小洞結合之齒)。'**~-wheel** *n* such a wheel, eg as on a bicycle. 扣連輪(如脚踏車上者)。

sprout /spraʊt ; spraʊt/ *vi, vt* **1** [VP2A, C] *~ (up),* put out leaves; begin to grow: 發芽;萌芽;開始生長: *Peter has really ~ed up in the past year.* 彼得過去這一年長高了不少。 **2** [VP6A] cause to grow: 使生長;使發芽: *The continuous wet weather has ~ed the barley,* eg after it has been cut and left in the field. 連續下雨的天氣已使大麥發芽了(如收割後仍置於田中者)。 **3** [VP6A] develop, produce: 發展;產生: *When do deer first ~ horns?* 鹿在多大的時候開始生角? *Tom has ~ed a moustache.* 湯姆長鬍子了。□ *n* [C] shoot, newly ~ed part, of a plant. 植物的苗、芽等新生部分。⇨ Brussels ~s.

spruce¹ /spru:s ; sprus/ *adj* neat and smart in dress and appearance. 衣著及外表整潔漂亮的。□ *vt, vi* [VP6A, 15B, 2C] *~ (sb/oneself) (up),* make oneself ~: 打扮;修飾: *Go and ~ yourself up.* 去打扮打扮。*They were all ~d up for the party.* 他們爲參加舞會都打扮得漂漂亮亮。**~·ly** *adv* **~·ness** *n*

spruce² /spru:s ; sprus/ *n* **~ (fir),** kinds of fir-tree grown in plantations for its wood, used for making paper. 針樅;雲杉。

sprung /sprʌŋ ; sprʌŋ/ *pp* of spring³.

spry /spraɪ ; spraɪ/ *adj* (-er, -est) lively; nimble: 活潑的;輕快的;敏捷的: *still ~ at eighty.* 八十歲仍很矯健。*look ~,* be quick. 輕快;敏捷。

spud /spʌd ; spʌd/ *n* [C] **1** (colloq) potato. (俗)馬鈴薯。 **2** short spade with a narrow blade for digging or cutting up weeds. 草鏟;小鏟。

spue /spju: ; spju/ *vt, vi* = spew.

spume /spju:m ; spjum/ *n* [U] foam; froth. 泡沫。

spun /spʌn ; spʌn/ *pp* of spin.

spunk /spʌŋk ; spʌŋk/ *n* [U] (colloq) courage; mettle; spirit: (俗)勇氣;膽量;精神: *have no ~;* 沒有膽子; *a boy with plenty of ~;* 膽量大的男孩; (sl) semen. (俚)精液。**~y** *adj* having ~. 有勇氣的;有膽量的。

spur /spɜ:(r) ; spɝ/ *n* **1** one of a pair of sharp-toothed wheels, worn on the heels of a rider's boots and used to make the horse go faster. 馬刺;馬扎子;馬靴刺。*win one's ~s,* (hist) gain knighthood; (fig) win honour and reputation. (史)獲得爵位;(喻)獲得榮譽及聲名。 **2** (fig) sth that urges a person on to greater activity: (喻)激勵物;刺激

物;驅策: *the ~ of poverty.* 貧困的驅策。***act on the ~ of the moment,*** on a sudden impulse. 憑一時的衝動做事。 **3** sharp, hard projection on a cock's leg. 公雞腿上的肉距。 ⇨ the illus at bird. 參看 bird 之插圖。 **4** ridge extending from a mountain or hill. 山的支脈;橫嶺。 □ *vt, vi* (-rr-) **1** [VP 6A, 15B] ***~ sb/sth (on),*** urge on with, or as with, ~s: 以馬刺刺激;驅策;激勵: *It's foolish to ~ on a willing horse.* 驅策溫馴的馬是愚蠢的。*He was ~red on by ambition.* 他爲野心所驅使。 **2** [VP2C] ride fast or hard: 疾馳;疾驅: *The rider ~red on/forward to his destination.* 騎者向目的地疾馳而去。

spu·ri·ous /ˈspjʊərɪəs; ˈspjʊrɪəs/ *adj* false; not genuine: 錯誤的;假的;僞造的: *~ coins / credentials / arguments.* 假硬幣(僞造的證件;錯誤的論據)。 **~·ly** *adv* **~·ness** *n*

spurn /spɜːn; spɝn/ *vt* [VP6A] reject or refuse contemptuously; have nothing to do with (an offer, a person or his advances). 輕蔑地拒絕;棄絕;擯斥(提議,某人,某人的親近)。

spurt /spɜːt; spɝt/ *vi* **1** [VP2C, 3A] ***~ (out) (from),*** (of liquids, flame, etc) come out in a sudden burst: (指液體,火焰等)噴出;迸出;湧出: *Blood ~ed (out) from the wound.* 血從傷口湧出。 **2** [VP2A] make a sudden, short and violent effort, esp in a race or other contest: 作突然、短暫而劇烈的努力(尤指在賽跑或其他比賽時);衝刺: *The runner ~ed as he approached the winning-post.* 那賽跑者在接近終點時全力衝刺。□ *n* [C] sudden bursting forth; sudden burst of energy: 噴出;湧出;精力的奮發: *~s of water / flame / energy;* 水的湧出(火焰的噴出;精力的奮發); *a ~ of anger;* 一股怒氣; *put on a ~* (= increase speed) *towards the end of a race.* 賽跑接近終點時加快速度。

sput·nik /ˈspʊtnɪk; ˈspʊtnɪk/ *n* artificial unmanned satellite put into space by means of rocket propulsion (esp the first, launched from the Soviet Union in 1957). (火箭射入太空無人駕駛的)人造衛星(尤指 1957 年蘇聯發射的第一顆人造衛星)。

sput·ter /ˈspʌtə(r); ˈspʌtɚ/ *vi, vt* **1** [VP2A, C] make a series of spitting sounds: 發連續吐唾液聲;作拍拍聲: *The sausages were ~ing in the frying-pan.* 臘腸在煎鍋中拍拍作響。 ***~ out,*** stop burning after making spitting sounds: 發拍拍聲後熄滅: *The candle ~ed out.* 那支蠟燭發出拍拍聲後熄滅了。 **2** = splutter(1, 2).

spu·tum /ˈspjuːtəm; ˈspjutəm/ *n* [U] saliva; matter coughed up from the throat (esp as indicating the nature of an illness). 唾液;口涎;痰(尤指顯示某種疾病性質者)。

spy /spaɪ; spaɪ/ *n* (*pl* spies) **1** person who tries to get secret information, esp about the military affairs of other countries (called a 'secret agent' if he is employed by one's own government and a 'spy' if he is working for other countries). 間諜(受雇於本國政府者,稱爲'特工人員',爲其他國家工作者,稱爲'間諜')。 **2** person who keeps a secret watch on the movements of others: 偵探;探員;秘密偵察他人行動者: *police spies,* persons employed by the police to watch suspected criminals; 警探(警察雇用以偵察嫌疑犯者); *industrial spies,* employed to learn trade secrets, etc. 工業間諜(受雇刺探商業秘密等者)。 □ *vi, vt* **1** [VP2A, 3A, 15B] ***~ (into/on/upon sth); ~ sth out,*** act as a spy on, watch secretly: 作偵探;偵察;窺探: *spy on the enemy's movements;* 偵察敵方行動; *spy out the land;* 秘密偵察該地; *spy into other people's affairs.* 窺探他人事物。 **2** [VP6A, 19A] observe; see; discover: 觀察;看見;發現: *I spy someone coming up the garden path.* 我看到有人從花園小徑走過來。*You are quick at spying her faults.* 你很容易看出她的缺點。 **ˈspy-glass** *n* small telescope. 小望遠鏡。 **ˈspy-hole** *n* peep-hole. 窺視孔。

squab /skwɒb; skwɑb/ *n* **1** young bird, esp an unfledged pigeon: 雛鳥;(尤指)羽毛未豐的雛鴿: *~ pie,* pigeon pie. 鴿肉餡餅。 **2** (comm) soft seat or cushion, esp as a seat in a car. (商)軟座;軟坐墊(尤指用於轎車中者)。

squabble /ˈskwɒbl; ˈskwɑbl/ *vi* [VP2C] engage in a petty or noisy quarrel: 口角;爭吵;爭論: *Tom was squabbling with his sister about who should use the bicycle.* 湯姆正同他姐姐(妹妹)爭論誰該使用那輛腳踏車。□ *n* [C] noisy quarrel about sth trivial. (因小事而)大聲的口角;無謂的爭吵或爭論。

squad /skwɒd; skwɑd/ *n* small group of persons, eg of soldiers, working or being trained together: 一小羣一起工作或受訓的人;小隊;小組;班: *Scotland Yard's flying ~,* number of special police cars and men always ready for prompt action, eg on reports of burglaries, etc. 英國倫敦警察廳的機動小組(隨時待命行動的人車編組)。 **ˈ~ car,** (US) police patrol car. (美)警察巡邏車。

squad·ron /ˈskwɒdrən; ˈskwɑdrən/ *n* **1** sub-unit of a cavalry, armoured or engineer regiment (120-200 men). (由 120 人至 200 人組成的)騎兵隊;裝甲連;工兵連。 **2** number of warships or military aircraft forming a unit. (海軍)戰隊;中隊;(空軍)中隊。 **ˈS~ Leader** *n* RAF rank, next below Wing Commander. 英國皇家空軍少校。

squalid /ˈskwɒlɪd; ˈskwɑlɪd/ *adj* dirty, mean, uncared for: 污穢的;卑劣的;無人照顧的: *living in ~ conditions / houses.* 住在污穢的環境(房屋)中。 **~·ly** *adv*

squall /skwɔːl; skwɔl/ *n* [C] **1** loud cry of pain or fear (esp from a baby or child). 痛苦或恐懼的高聲喊叫(尤指嬰兒或孩童所發出者);大聲尖叫。 **2** sudden violent wind, often with rain or snow: 狂風;暴風(常夾有雨或雪者): *look out for ~s,* (often fig) be on one's guard against danger or trouble. (常作喻)防備危險或困厄。□ *vi* [VP2A] utter ~s(1): 大聲喊叫;尖叫: *~ing babies.* 大聲喊叫的嬰兒。*The boy ~s as soon as he sees the dentist.* 那男孩一見到牙醫就大聲尖叫。 **~y** *adj* having, marked by, ~s(2): 有狂風的;有暴風的: *a ~y February day.* 二月裡颳狂風的一天。

squalor /ˈskwɒlə(r); ˈskwɑlɚ/ *n* [U] squalid state: 污穢;卑劣: *born in ~;* 出身卑下的; *the ~ of the slums.* 貧民窟的污穢狀況。

squan·der /ˈskwɒndə(r); ˈskwɑndɚ/ *vt* [VP6A] waste (time, money). 浪費(時間,金錢)。 **ˈ~·mania** /-meɪnɪə; -ˈmenɪə/ *n* [U] (craze for) extravagant spending of money. 浪費金錢(狂)。

square[1] /skweə(r); skwɛr/ *adj* **1** having the shape of a square[2](1): 正方形的;方的: *a ~ table.* 方桌。***a ~ peg in a round hole,*** ⇨ peg[1](1). **ˈ~ dance / game,** one in which the dancers/players face inwards from four sides. 方塊舞(遊戲)。 **2** having or forming (exactly or approx) a right angle: 成直角或近似直角的;方的: *~ corners;* 方隅; *a ~ jaw / chin,* with angular, not curved, outlines. 方形下顎(下巴)。 **ˌ~ ˈbrackets** *n pl* the marks [ ]. 方括弧 ⇨ bracket(2). **ˌ~-ˈbuilt** *adj* (of a person) of comparatively broad shape. (指人)體型寬闊的。 **ˌ~-ˈrigged** *adj* (of a sailing ship) having the principal sails set at right angles to the mast. (指帆船)有橫帆裝置的。 Cf 參較 *fore-and-aft.* **ˌ~-ˈshouldered** *adj* with the shoulders at right angles to the neck, not sloping. 方肩的;肩膀平(不傾斜)的。 **ˈ~-toed** *adj* (of shoes) having a ~ toe-cap; (fig, of persons) formal; prim. (指鞋)平頭的;方頭的;(喻,指人)方方正正的;拘謹的;古板的。 **ˈ~-toes** *n* formal or prim person. 拘謹的人;老古板。 **3** level or parallel (*with*); balanced; settled: 水平的;平行的(與 with 連用);平衡的;結清的: *get one's accounts ~,* settled. 把帳結清。 ***be (all) ~,*** **(a)** (golf) have equal scores: (高爾夫)積分相等: *all ~ at the ninth hole.* 在第九洞積分相等。 **(b)** with neither person in debt to the other: 兩不欠帳;兩不虧欠: *Let's call it all ~, shall we?* 我們從此兩不虧欠,行嗎? ***get ~ with sb,*** settle accounts;

(fig) have one's revenge on him. 和某人結帳;(喻)找某人算帳;找某人報仇。 **4** of a number multiplied by itself: 平方的;自乘的: *a ~ metre,* surface area of a ~ which has sides of one metre in length; 一平方公尺; *nine ~ cm.* 九平方公分。*The ~ root of* x^4 *is* x^2*/of 9 is 3.* x^4 的平方根是 x^2 (9 的平方根是 3)。*A carpet 6 metres ~ has an area of 36 ~ metres.* 六公尺見方的地毯面積是三十六平方公尺。**~ measure,** expressed in ~ feet, metres, etc. 平方積;面積(用平方英尺、公尺等表示者)。**5** thorough; uncompromising: 澈底的;不妥協的;堅決的: *meet with a ~ refusal.* 遭到斷然拒絕。**a ~ meal,** one that is satisfactory because there is plenty of good food. 豐盛的餐食。 **6** fair, honest: 公正的;誠實的: *~ dealings,* in business; (生意)公平交易; *play a ~ game,* in sport. (運動)公平競賽。***(get/give sb) a ~ deal,*** a fair bargain, fair treatment, equality of opportunity. (獲得,給予某人)公平的交易,公平的待遇,公平的機會等。 **7 ~ leg,** ⇨ the illus at cricket. 參看 cricket 之插圖。□ *adv* **1** in a ~(2) manner: 成直角地;直地: *stand/sit ~;* 直立(坐); *hit a man ~ on the jaw.* 正好打在一個人的下顎上。**2** ***fair and ~,*** in a ~(6) manner. 正大光明地;公平地;正直地。**~·ly** *adv* **1** so as to form a right angle. 成直角地;成方形地。**2** fairly; honestly: 公正地;誠實地: *act ~ly.* 行爲正直。 **3** directly opposite: 正對面地: *He faced me ~ly across the table.* 他在桌子那邊正對着我。**~·ness** *n*

square² /skweə(r); skwɛr/ *n* [C] **1** plane figure with four equal sides and four right angles, ie □. 正方形。⇨ the illus at quadrilateral. 參看 quadrilateral 之挿圖。***back to ~ one,*** (from the use of ~s on board games, played by throwing dice, and with penalties for certain numbered ~s) back to the starting-point and forced to start again. 回到出發點;被迫重新開始(起源於擲骰子玩的方塊戲,方塊上帶號碼,遇到某些號碼時須受罰)。 **2** anything having the shape of a ~. 方形物。**3** four-sided open area, eg in a town, used as a garden or for recreation, or one enclosed by streets and buildings: (城市等中的)廣場;方場: *listening to the band playing in the ~.* 聆聽廣場上樂隊的演奏。**'barrack ~** *n* such an open space in a military barracks. 營房中的廣場或操場。**'~-bashing** (sl) military drill (esp marching, etc). (俚)軍事訓練(尤指行軍等)。**4** buildings and streets surrounding a ~(3): 廣場四週的建築及街道: *He lives at No 95 Russell S~.* 他住在羅素廣場九十五號。 **5** block of buildings bounded by four streets; distance along one side of such a block (the word *block* being more usu, esp US). (四週有街道的)街區;街區一面的距離(block 較常用,尤其在美國)。 **6** result when a number or quantity is multiplied by itself: 平方;自乘;二次冪: *The ~ of 7 is 49.* 7 的平方是 49。*What is the ~ of* x^2*?* x^2的自乘是什麼? **7** L-shaped or **('T-~)** T-shaped instrument for drawing or testing right angles. 曲尺;丁字尺;矩尺;直角規。***out of ~,*** not at right angles. 不成直角的(地);不正的(地)。**8** ***on the ~,*** fair(ly), honest(ly): 正直的(地);公平的(地);誠實的(地): *Can we trust them to act on the ~?* 我們能信賴他們處事公正嗎? *Is their business on the ~?* 他們做生意規矩嗎? **9** body of infantry drawn up in a ~ form. 步兵的方陣。 **10 'word ~,** number of words arranged so that they read alike forwards and downwards. 縱橫字謎;字陣遊戲(方格內塡入字母,縱橫方向可組合成相同之字)。**11** (sl) person (considered to be) out of touch with new ideas, styles, etc: (俚)與新的觀念、風尚等脫節的人;老古板;舊派人物: *I'm not even a ~, I'm a cube!* I'm rigidly conventional and old-fashioned. 說我是舊派人物還嫌不够,我是舊派中的舊派人物。

square³ /skweə(r); skwɛr/ *vt, vi* **1** [VP6A] make square; give a square shape to. 使成方形。***~ the circle,*** attempt sth that is impossible. 嘗試做不可能的事;變圓爲方。 **2** [VP6A] cause one line or side to make a right angle with another: 使成直角;使垂直: *~ timber,* give it rectangular edges. 使木材各邊成直角。 **3** [VP6A] make straight or level: 使直;使平: *~ one's shoulders.* 把肩膀放平;挺胸。**4** [VP6A] multiply a number by itself; get the square²(6) of a number: 自乘;得出某數的平方: *Three ~d is nine.* 3 自乘得 9。$x^2 = x$ *~d.* x自乘得x平方。 **5** [VP6A, 15B] ***~ sth off,*** mark (off) in squares. 劃分爲方形。**6** [VP2C, 14, 15B] ***~ (sth) (up) (with sb),*** settle, balance: 結算: *~ accounts with sb,* settle one's debts; (fig) have one's revenge on him. 與某人結帳;(喻)找某人算帳;找某人報仇。*It's time I ~d up with you/time we ~d up,* settled our accounts. 我該同你結帳了(我們該結帳了)。 **7** [VP6A] bribe; get the (dishonest) co-operation of: 賄賂;自…處獲得非法合作: *All the officials had to be ~d before they would do anything for us.* 所有的官吏須先行賄賂才能爲我們作事。*He has been ~d to hold his tongue.* 他已被收買而保持緘默。 **8** [VP14, 3A] ***~ (sth) with,*** make or be consistent: (使)與…相符;(使)與…一致: *You should ~ your practice with your principles.* 你應該言行一致(使你的行爲符合你的主張)。*It would be convenient if the facts ~d with the theory, but they do not.* 如果事實與理論相符,那就好了,不過並非如此。 **9** [VP2C] ***~ up to sb,*** take up the attitude of a boxer (ready to begin fighting). 對某人擺起拳擊手的姿勢(準備格鬥);對某人摩拳擦掌。

squash¹ /skwɒʃ; skwɑʃ/ *vt, vi* **1** [VP6A, 15A, B, 22] crush; press flat or into a small space: 壓壞;壓爛;壓扁;壓擠;壓縮: *~ too many people into a bus.* 把太多的人擠進一輛公共汽車。*Don't sit on my hat; you'll ~ it flat.* 不要坐在我的帽子上;你會把它壓扁。**2** [VP2A] become ~ed or pressed out of shape: 被壓壞;被壓爛;被壓扁: *Soft fruits ~ easily.* 柔軟的水果容易壓爛。 **3** [VP2C] squeeze or crowd: 擠;擠進去: *Don't all try to ~ into the lift together.* 不要統統擠進電梯裡去。*They ~ed through the gate into the football ground.* 他們擠過大門進入足球場。**4** [VP6A] (colloq) silence (sb) with a crushing retort; snub: (俗)以壓服性的反駁使(某人)緘默;斥止;反駁(某人)使啞口無言;完全駁倒(某人): *He was/felt completely ~ed.* 他被(他感覺被)完全駁倒了。 **5** [VP6A] (colloq) subdue (a rebellion). (俗)鎮壓(反叛)。□ *n* (rarely *pl*) (罕用複數) **1** crowd of persons ~ed together: 擠在一起的人羣;雜沓的人羣: *There was a violent ~ at the gate.* 大門口擠滿了一群暴民。**2** (sound of) sth ~ing or being ~ed: (被)壓壞之物;(被)壓爛之物;壓壞或壓爛的聲音: *The ripe tomato hit the speaker in the face with a ~.* 那個熟蕃茄趴躂一聲打中了演說者的臉。**3** [C, U] drink (cold, usu bottled) made from fruit juice: 果汁(冰的,通常瓶裝)飲料;果汁冷飲: *orange/lemon ~.* 橘子(檸檬)水。 **4** **'~(-rackets),** game played with rackets and a rubber ball in a walled, roofed court. 軟式網球(用球拍及橡皮球在四周圍起並且有頂的場地上玩的一種球戲)。**~y** *adj* easily ~ed; soft and wet. 易壓爛的;軟而濕的。

squash² /skwɒʃ; skwɑʃ/ *n* (*pl* unchanged) kinds of gourd, like a pumpkin, eaten as a vegetable. (複數不變)南瓜;葫蘆。

squat /skwɒt; skwɑt/ *vi, vt* (-tt-) **1** [VP2A, C] sit on one's heels, or on the ground with the legs drawn up under or close to the body; [VP6A, 15B] put (oneself) in this position: 蹲踞;跪坐;盤坐;使(自己)蹲踞、跪坐或盤坐: *The old man ~ted in front of the fire.* 那老人蹲在火(爐)前面。*He ~ted (himself) down.* 他蹲了下來。 **2** [VP2A, C] (of animals) crouch with the body close to the ground. (指動物)蹲伏。**3** [VP2A, C] (colloq) sit: (俗)坐: *Find somewhere to ~.* 找個地方坐下。**4** [VP2A] settle on land without permission, esp publicly owned and unoccupied land (in order to acquire ownership); occupy empty (usu deserted, derelict) buildings without authority. 擅自定居於未佔用的公地(以期獲得所有權);擅自搬進(通常係爲人遺棄或無人居住的)空屋。□ *adj* short and thick: 矮胖的: *a ~ man;* 矮胖的人; dumpy: 粗短的;粗矮的: *a ~ teapot.* 粗矮的茶壺。 **~·ter** *n* **1** person who ~s(4); (in Australia) sheep-farmer. 擅自定居於未佔用的公地者;(在澳洲)牧羊農場主。 **2** person who takes unauthorized possession of unoccupied premises. 擅自佔有無人居住的房屋者。

squaw /skwɔː; skwɔ/ *n* N American Indian woman or wife. 北美印第安人的婦女或妻子。

squawk /skwɔːk; skwɔk/ *vi* [VP2A, C], *n* (chiefly of birds) (utter a) loud, harsh cry, as when hurt or frightened; (colloq) (make a) loud complaint; (sl) betray: (主要指鳥)(發)粗厲的叫聲(如受傷或受驚嚇時);(俗)高聲抱怨;訴苦;(俚)洩露秘密: *The old man ~ed (to the police).* 那老人(向警察)高聲抱怨。 **~er** *n*

squeak /skwiːk; skwik/ *n* [C] **1** short, shrill cry, eg made by a mouse, or similar sound, eg from an unoiled hinge. 吱吱聲(如鼠叫);軋軋聲(如未塗油的鉸鏈所發者);短而尖的聲音。 **2** ***a narrow ~,*** a narrow escape from danger or failure. 險遭不測;幸免於難;險勝。□ *vi, vt* **1** [VP2A] make a ~: 發吱吱聲或軋軋聲;發短而尖銳的聲音: *These new shoes ~.* 這雙新鞋吱吱作響。 **2** [VP6A, 15B] ~ ***sth (out)***, utter in a ~ing voice: 以尖銳聲音說出: *~ out a few frightened words.* 尖銳地說出幾個充滿恐懼的字。 **3** [VP2A, C] (colloq) become an informer. (俗)告密。 **~er** *n* (colloq) informer. (俗)告密者。 **~y** *adj* (-ier, -iest) ~ing: 發短而尖銳之聲的;吱吱叫的;作軋軋聲的: *a ~y floor;* (走上去)發吱吱聲的地板; *in a ~y voice.* 尖聲地;吱吱地。

squeal /skwiːl; skwil/ *n* [C] shrill cry or sound, longer and louder than a squeak, often indicating terror or pain: 吱嘎聲;長而尖銳的叫聲(常表示恐懼或痛苦);號叫: *the ~ of brakes,* eg on lorries. 煞車發出的吱嘎聲。□ *vi, vt* **1** [VP2A, C] make a ~: 發吱嘎聲;發長而尖銳的叫聲: *The pigs were ~ing.* 猪在號叫。 *He ~ed like a pig.* 他像猪一樣地號叫。 **2** [VP6A, 15B] utter with a ~; say in a ~ing voice. 尖聲地說;號叫着說。 **3** [VP2A, C] (colloq) become an informer. (俗)告密;揭露。 **~er** *n* **1** animal that ~s. 號叫的動物;尖聲喊叫的動物。 **2** informer. 告密者。

squeam·ish /ˈskwiːmɪʃ; ˈskwimɪʃ/ *adj* **1** having a delicate stomach and easily made sick; feeling sick. 胃敏感而易嘔吐的;想嘔吐的;惡心的。 **2** easily disgusted or offended; too modest, scrupulous or proper. 易感厭惡或易生氣的;太講究規矩的;太拘謹、謙遜等的。 **~·ly** *adv* **~·ness** *n*

squee·gee /ˌskwiːˈdʒiː *US:* ˈskwiːdʒiː; ˈskwidʒi/ *n* implement with a rubber edge, fastened to a long handle, used for pushing water, etc off a smooth surface; similar implement with a short rubber roller for pressing water from photographic prints. (掃去光滑表面上的水等的)橡皮拖把;(壓去相片上水分的)橡皮滾子。□ *vt* [VP6A] use a ~ on. 用此等工具拖擦或輾滾。

squeeze /skwiːz; skwiz/ *vt, vi* **1** [VP6A, 15A, 22] press on from the opposite side or from all sides; change the shape, size, etc of sth by doing this: 壓;擠;榨;緊握;把…壓成;把…擠成: *~ sb's hand;* 緊握某人的手; *~ a sponge;* 擠壓海綿; *~ a lemon dry;* 將檸檬榨乾; *~ one's fingers,* eg by catching them in a doorway; 手指給夾住了(如夾在門縫); *~ paste into a ball.* 把麵團捏成球形。 **2** [VP6A, 14, 15A, B] ~ ***sth (from/out of sth);*** ~ ***sth out,*** get (water, juice, etc) out of sth by pressing hard: 壓出;榨出(水,汁等): *~ (the juice out of) a lemon;* 榨檸檬(汁); *~ the water out.* 壓出水分。 **3** [VP15A, B, 2C] force (sb, oneself) into or through a narrow passage or small space: 推擠(某人,自己)進入或通過狹窄的過道或狹小的空間;擠入;擠過: *~ (one's way) into a crowded bus;* 擠進擁擠的公共汽車; *~ (oneself) through a gap in a hedge;* 由籬笆的缺口擠過去; *~ (one's way) through a crowd.* 從人叢中擠過去。 *Can you ~ in?* eg into a crowded lift. 你能擠進去(如擁擠的電梯)嗎? **4** [VP 15B] ~ ***sth out of sth/sb,*** get by extortion, entreaty, etc: 榨取;勒索;敲詐: *~ more money out of the public,* eg by increasing taxes; 榨取大衆的金錢(如加稅); *blackmailers who ~ the last penny out of their victims.* 榨取受害者最後一分錢的勒索者。 **5** [VP2A] yield to pressure: 壓縮;受壓變形: *Sponges ~ easily.* 海綿容易壓縮。□ *n* [C] **1** act of squeezing; condition of being ~d; sth obtained by squeezing: 壓榨;緊握;擠;被壓擠等的狀態;壓榨出之物: *give sb a hug and a ~;* 緊抱某人; *a ˈ~ bottle,* plastic container that ejects the contents, eg scent, liquid detergent, when ~d. 壓擠瓶(受壓時卽排出所盛裝之物,如香水、液體清潔劑等的塑膠瓶)。 *It was a tight ~,* we were ~d tightly, eg in a crowd. 太擁擠了。 *Add a ~ of lemon to your drink.* 在你的飲料中加一點檸檬汁吧。 ⇨ also credit[1](3). **2** ***close/narrow/tight ~,*** narrow escape. 幸免;勉强逃過。 **3** [U] (colloq) policy of high taxation, high interest rates, etc aimed at deflation; [U] money obtained by squeezing(4). (俗)(爲防止通貨膨脹所採取的)高稅政策;高利率政策;榨取來的錢;回扣。 **~r** *n* one who, that which, ~s, eg a device for squeezing out juice: 壓榨者;壓榨器;壓榨等的人或物: *a ˈlemon-~r.* 檸檬壓汁器。

squelch /skweltʃ; skwɛltʃ/ *vi, vt* **1** [VP2A, C] make a sucking sound as when feet are lifted from stiff, sticky mud: 發格喳聲;發吮吸聲(如脚從黏泥中拔出時): *cows ~ing through the mud.* 格喳着走過泥地的母牛羣。 *The water ~ed in my boots.* 我靴子裡的水發出格喳聲。 **2** [VP6A] crush; put an end to; force to be silent. 壓碎;壓制;使終止;使緘默。□ *n* ~ing sound; act of ~ing. 格喳聲;吮吸聲;壓碎;壓制;使緘默。

squib /skwɪb; skwɪb/ *n* **1** small firework of the kind thrown by hand, one that first hisses and then explodes. 水鴛鴦(一種用手投出的小爆竹,先發嘶嘶聲,然後再爆炸)。 ***damp ~,*** unsuccessful attempt to do sth impressive. 未成功的引人注意之擧;未達預期效果之事。 **2** short satirical attack on sb, spoken or (more usu) written. 簡短的諷刺(文)。

squid /skwɪd; skwɪd/ *n* kind of cuttle-fish with ten arms round the mouth (smaller kinds used as bait). 烏賊;墨魚;魷魚。 ⇨ the illus at mollusc. 參看 mollusc 之插圖。

squiffy /ˈskwɪfɪ; ˈskwɪfɪ/ *adj* (sl) slightly drunk. (俚)微醉的。

squiggle /ˈskwɪgl; ˈskwɪgl/ *n* small twisty line or scrawl: 小的彎曲線或潦草筆畫: *Is this ~ supposed to be his signature?* 這個彎彎曲曲的筆畫就視爲他的簽名嗎? **squig·gly** /ˈskwɪglɪ; ˈskwɪglɪ/ *adj*

squint /skwɪnt; skwɪnt/ *vi* **1** [VP2A] have eyes that do not turn together but look in different directions at once; be cross-eyed. 斜視。 **2** [VP 3A] ~ ***at/through,*** look at sideways or with half-shut eyes or through a narrow opening. 瞟;瞇着眼看;由小孔窺視。□ *n* **1** ~ing position of the eyeballs: 眼球的斜視位置;斜視;瞟: *a man with a ~.* 斜視的人。 **ˈ~-eyed** *adj* having a ~; cross-eyed; (fig) malignant; disapproving. 眼睛斜視的;(喻)惡意的;不讚許的。 **2** (colloq) look or glance: (俗)瞥;看: *Let me have a ~ at it.* 讓我看一看。

squire /ˈskwaɪə(r); skwaɪr/ *n* **1** (in England) chief landowner in a country parish. (在英國)鄉紳(英國鄉區的大地主)。 **2** (hist) young man who was a knight's attendant until he himself became a knight. (史)武士或騎士的年輕扈從(至他自己變爲騎士爲止)。 **3** (often hum) man who escorts a woman; man who is attentive to women and frequents their company. (常爲諧語)婦女的護衛;護花者;對婦女慇懃而常與婦女廝混的人。 **4** (US) justice of the peace or local judge. (美)治安推事;地方法官。 **5** (GB sl) fellow. (英俚)人;傢伙。□ *vt* [VP6A,

15A] (of a man) attend upon, escort (a woman). (指男子)隨侍,護衞(婦女)。 **'~·ar·chy** /-ɑːkɪ ; -ˌɑrkɪ/ *n* (*pl* -chies) (in England) great landowners (before 1832); these men as a class. (在英國) (1832年以前的)大地主;大地主階級。

squirm /skwɜːm ; skwɝm/ *vi* [VP2A, C] twist the body, wriggle (from discomfort, shame or embarrassment). 蠕動;扭曲身體;侷促不安(由於不舒服、羞恥或困窘)。□ *n* ~ing movement. 蠕動;扭曲。

squir·rel /'skwɪrəl ; 'skwɝəl/ *n* (kinds of) small, tree-climbing, bushy-tailed animal with red or grey fur. 松鼠。⇨ the illus at small. 參看 small 之插圖。

squirt /skwɜːt ; skwɝt/ *vt, vi* [VP6A, 15A, B, 2A, C] (of liquid, powder) force out, be forced out, in a thin stream or jet: (指液體,粉末)迸出;噴出: ~ *soda-water into a glass.* 把汽水倒在玻璃杯中。*The water ~ed all over me.* 水噴了我一身。□ *n* **1** thin stream or jet (of liquid, powder, etc). (液體、粉末等的)噴射;噴射的液體或粉末。 **2** sth from which liquid, etc can be ~ed, eg a syringe, as a child's toy. 噴射液體等的器具;注射器;噴射器;(兒童玩的)水槍。 **3** (colloq, as a term of abuse) insignificant but self-assertive person. (俗,用作駡人話)夜郎自大的人。

stab /stæb ; stæb/ *vt, vi* (-bb-) **1** [VP6A, 15A, 3A] ~ ***(at),*** pierce or wound with a sharp-pointed weapon or instrument; push (a knife, etc) into (sb); aim a blow (at sb) with such a weapon: 以尖器刺或刺傷;用(刀等)刺入(某人身體);用尖銳武器刺向(某人);戳;扎: ~ *a man in the back;* 刺某人之背;背後中傷某人; ~ *sb to the heart.* 刺某人之心臟;使某人極爲傷心。*His conscience ~bed (at) him,* (fig) caused him to feel regret. (喻)良心刺痛(使他感到懊悔)。 **2** [VP2A] produce a sensation of being ~bed: 產生刺痛: *~bing pains in the back.* 背部刺痛。□ *n* [C] **1** ~bing blow; pain inflicted by this. 刺;戳;扎;刺痛;傷痛;劇痛。***a ~ in the back,*** (fig) a treacherous attack, eg on sb's reputation. (喻)背後中傷;暗箭傷人。 **2** (colloq) try, attempt (= colloq 'go' or 'shot'): (俗)試作;試圖(與俗語中的 go 或 shot 同): *Let me have a ~ at it,* try to do it. 讓我試試(試做此事)。**~·ber** *n*

stable¹ /'steɪbl ; 'stebl/ *adj* firm; not likely to move or change: 堅固的;穩定的;安定的;不動搖的: *What we need is a ~ Government.* 我們所需要的是一個穩定的政府。*He needs a ~ job.* 他需要一份安定的工作。 **sta·bil·ity** /stə'bɪlətɪ ; stə'bɪlətɪ/ *n* [U] quality of being ~. 堅固性;穩定性;安定;不動搖。 **sta·bil·ize** /'steɪbəlaɪz ; 'stebḷˌaɪz/ *vt* [VP6A] make ~: 使堅固、穩定、不動搖等: *stabilize prices and wages.* 穩定物價與工資。**sta·bi·lizer** *n* person or thing that stabilizes; (esp) device to keep a ship or aircraft steady, free from rolling or pitching. 有穩定力的人或物;安定劑;(尤指)(使船或飛機穩定的)穩定裝置;平衡器;安定面。 **sta·bil·iz·ation** /ˌsteɪbəlaɪ'zeɪʃn *US:* -lɪ'z- ; ˌstebḷə'zeʃən/ *n* making or becoming ~. 使或變穩定、安定等。

stable² /'steɪbl ; 'stebḷ/ *n* building in which horses are lodged and fed; number of horses (esp race-horses) belonging to one particular owner and kept in one set of ~s. 廐;馬房;(尤指賽馬用的馬)一位主人所擁有並養在一列馬房中的馬群。**'~-boy/-man** *nn* boy/man employed in a ~. 馬童;馬伕。 **'~-companion/-mate** *n* horse of the same ~; (fig) member of same group. 廐伴(同廐中的馬);(喻)伙伴;同伙。□ *vt* put, keep, in a ~: 置於馬房;養於馬房: *Where did you ~ your horse?* 你的馬養在哪個馬房裡? **stab·ling** /'steɪblɪŋ ; 'steblɪŋ/ *n* [U] accommodation for horses: 馬房設備: *The house has stabling for 20 horses.* 這幢房子有容納二十匹馬的馬房設備。

stac·cato /stə'kɑːtəʊ ; stə'kɑto/ *adj, adv* (musical direction) (to be played) with each successive note clear and detached. (樂譜說明)(應奏成)斷音的(地);以斷奏;以斷唱。

stack /stæk ; stæk/ *n* [C] **1** circular or rectangular pile of hay, straw, grain, etc usu with a sloping, thatched top, for storage in the open. 堆(乾草、麥稭、穀物等的圓形或長方形堆,通常有覆蓋的斜頂,以便於戶外貯存)。 **2** group of rifles arranged in the form of a pyramid; pile or heap (of books, papers, wood, etc); (colloq) large amount: 架起的槍;堆置的書、報、木材等;(俗)大量: *I have ~s of work waiting to be done.* 我有很多工作要做。 **3** (brickwork or stonework enclosing a) number of chimneys. 烟囪群(結在一起的數烟囪);烟囪群的磚、石圍砌。⇨ *smoke-~* at smoke¹(1). **4** rack with shelves for books (in a library or bookshop). (圖書館或書店中的)書架;書庫。 **5** number of aircraft circling at different heights while waiting for instructions to land. 在不同高度盤旋等待指示降落的諸飛機。□ *vt* **1** [VP6A, 15B] ~ ***(up),*** make into a ~ or ~s; pile up: 使成堆;堆起: ~ *hay/wood;* 堆置乾草(木材); ~ *up the dishes on the draining-board.* 把碗盤放在滴水板上。 **2** (US) arrange (playing-cards) unfairly. (美)洗牌作弊。***have the cards ~ed a'gainst one,*** be at a great disadvantage. 洗牌作弊使對某人大不利。 **3** [VP6A] arrange aircraft in a ~(5). 指示(諸飛機)在不同高度盤旋等待降落。

sta·dium /'steɪdɪəm ; 'stedɪəm/ *n* (*pl* ~s) enclosed area of land for games, athletic competitions, etc, usu with stands for spectators: (通常有看臺的)體育場;運動場: *build a new ~ for the Olympic Games.* 爲世界運動會建造新的運動場。

an Olympic stadium

staff /stɑːf *US:* stæf ; stæf/ *n* **1** strong stick used as a support when walking or climbing, or as a weapon; (now usu fig): (用作身體支持物,或用作武器的)棍;杖;棒;(現通常作比喻用法): *the ~ of life,* bread. 麵包。*He is the ~ of my old age,* eg a son who supports his old father. 他是我老年的依恃(如奉養老父的兒子)。 **2** such a ~ as a sign of office or authority: 權杖;權標: *a pastoral ~,* eg an ornamental one carried by or before a bishop, etc. 牧杖(主教等所携或持於主教之前的飾杖)。 **3** pole serving as a support: 竿;支柱: *a 'flag~.* 旗竿。 **4** group of assistants working together under a manager or head: (輔佐首長的)全體職員;(某一首腦下面的)全體工作人員: *the headmaster and his ~,* ie the teachers; 校長及全體教師; *'office-~;* 辦公人員; *be on the ~.* 爲正式職員。*A large ~* (collective *n, sing v*) *of advisers has been employed for the President.* 總統已任用許多顧問 (staff 爲集合名詞,用單數動詞)。*The school ~* (= Members of the ~, *pl v*) *are expected to supervise school meals.* 學校的教職員應監督學校的膳食 (staff 視爲複數,用複數動詞)。**'~-office,** personnel office. 人事室。⇨ personnel. **5** group of senior army officers engaged in planning and organization: (軍)參謀;幕僚;參謀部: *the General S~;* 參謀本部; (attrib) (形容用法) *'~ officers.* 參謀;參謀軍官。 **6** (music) (*pl* staves /'steɪvz ; stevz/) set of five parallel lines on or between which notes are placed to indicate their pitch. (音樂)五線譜。⇨ the illus at notation. 參看 notation 之插圖。□ *vt* [VP6A] provide with, act as, a ~(4): 供以人員;

預備職員或幕僚；充當職員或幕僚: ~ *a new school;* 預備一個新學校的人員; *a well-~ed hotel/hospital;* 人員充足的旅館(醫院); *an under-~ed office.* 人員不足的機關。

stag /stæg; stæg/ *n* **1** male deer. 牡鹿。 **'~-party** *n* (colloq) party for men only (eg one for a man about to get married). (俗)雄鹿會(祇有男子參加的聚會,如爲某一郎將結婚的男子所舉行者)。 **2** person who buys newly issued stocks and shares hoping that prices will rise and enable him to sell at a profit. 購買新發行的股票及證券,希望漲價後賣出獲利者。

stage /steɪdʒ; stedʒ/ *n* **1** (in a theatre) raised platform or structure of boards on which the actors appear. (戲院的)舞臺。 **2 the ~,** theatrical work; the profession of acting in theatres. 戲劇工作;劇業;劇壇。 ***be/go on the ~,*** be/become an actor or actress. 當演員。 **'~-craft** *n* [U] skill or experience in writing or directing plays. 編劇及導演的技巧或經驗。 **'~ direction** *n* printed direction in a play to actors about their positions, movements, etc. 舞臺指導(劇本中有關演員位置、動作等的說明)。 **ˌ~ 'door** *n* entrance at the back of a theatre, used by actors and workmen. 舞台後門(戲院的後門,供演員及工作人員使用)。 **'~ fright** *n* [U] nervousness felt when facing an audience. 怯場(面對觀衆或聽衆時所感到的緊張)。 **ˌ~ 'manager** *n* person who superintends the production of a play, supervises the rehearsals, etc. 舞臺監督。 **'~-struck** *adj* having a strong desire to become an actor or actress. 渴望做演員的。 **ˌ~-'whisper** *n* whisper that is meant to be overheard. 存心叫人聽見的私語;舞臺低語。 **3** (fig) scene of action; place where events occur. (喻)(活動的)場所;(事件發生的)現場。 **4** point, period or step in development: 發展的程度、時期、階段、步驟等: *at an early ~ in our history.* 在我們歷史發展的早期。 *The baby has reached the 'talking ~,* is learning to talk. 這嬰兒已到達學話的階段。 **5** any of two or more successive periods on the journey of a rocket vehicle when one part has been jettisoned: 火箭的節;火箭飛行途中依次脫離其環節的步驟: *a multi-~ rocket.* 多節火箭;要經過數次脫離步驟的火箭。 **6** journey, distance, between two stopping-places along a road or route; such a stopping-place: 一程;一段路;站;驛: *travel by easy ~s,* for only a short distance at a time. 分段從容旅行。 **'~(-coach)** *n* (hist) horse-drawn public vehicle carrying passengers (and often mail) along a regular route. (史)驛(馬)車。 **'fare-~** *n* section along the route of a bus or tram for which there is a fixed fare. (公車或電車)車資固定的路段。 **7** structure with tiers or shelves, eg for plants. 臺架(如花架等)。 ⇨ also staging below, and *landing-~* at landing. □ *vt, vi* **1** [VP6A] put on the ~(1); put before the public: 搬上舞臺;上演: ~ *'Hamlet';* 上演'哈姆雷特'; (fig) arrange to take place dramatically. (喻)使(某事)戲劇性地發生。 **~ a 'come-back,** come back (to a sport, eg to the boxing ring) from retirement or after having failed. 安排或準備東山再起(如已退休或被擊敗的拳擊手重返拳壇)。 **2** [VP2C] ~ *well/badly,* (of a drama) be well/badly suited for the theatre. (指劇本)適於(不適於)上演。

stager /'steɪdʒə(r); 'stedʒɚ/ *n* (only in) (僅用於) **an old ~,** a person of long experience; an old hand. 經驗豐富的人;老手。 ⇨ hand¹(6).

stag·fla·tion /ˌstæg'fleɪʃn; ˌstæg'fleʃən/ *n* [U] (fin) (word formed from *stag*nation + in*flation*) monetary inflation without growth of industrial production. (財政)(爲 *stag*nation 和 in*flation* 二字所形成)停滯性通貨膨脹。

stag·ger /'stægə(r); 'stægɚ/ *vi, vt* **1** [VP2A, C] walk or move unsteadily (from weakness, a heavy burden, drunkenness, etc): 蹣跚;搖擺(因衰弱、負重、酒醉等): *The man ~ed along/to his feet/across the room/from side to side of the road.* 那人搖搖晃晃地走(搖擺地站起來,蹣跚地走過房間,搖晃着橫過道路)。 **2** [VP6A] (of a blow or shock) cause to walk or move unsteadily; (of news, etc) shock deeply; cause worry or confusion to: (指打擊或震驚)使蹣跚;使搖擺;(指新聞等)使驚愕;使對…擔心或不知所措: *receive a ~ing blow.* 受到使人搖搖晃晃的打擊。 *I was ~ed to hear/on hearing/when I heard who the group's leader was.* 聽到誰是那個團體的領導人時,我感到十分震驚。 **3** [VP6A] arrange (times of events) so that they do not all occur together: 錯開(事情的時間): ~ *office hours,* so that employees are not all using buses, trains, etc, at the same time; 錯開辦公時間; ~ *the annual holidays.* 錯開年假。 □ *n* **1** (*sing*) ~ing movement. (單數)蹣跚;搖擺。 **2 the ~s,** giddiness; nervous disease of cattle and horses, marked by ~ing. 家畜暈倒病;蹣跚病。 **~er** *n*

stag·ing /'steɪdʒɪŋ; 'stedʒɪŋ/ *n* **1** [C, U] stage(6); (platform or working area on) scaffolding for men on constructional work, eg building. 台架;鷹架;構架;工作架。 **2** [U] (method of) presenting a play on the stage of a theatre. (戲劇的)演出;導演術。

stag·nant /'stægnənt; 'stægnənt/ *adj* **1** (of water) without current or tide; still and stale: (指水)不流動的;停滯的;靜止的: *water lying ~ in ponds and ditches.* 池塘和溝渠中的死水。 **2** (fig) unchanging; inactive: (喻)不變化的;不活潑的;不景氣的: *Business was ~ last week.* 上週生意蕭條。 **stag·nancy** /-nənsɪ; -nənsɪ/ *n*

stag·nate /stæg'neɪt *US:* 'stægneɪt; 'stægnet/ *vi* [VP2A] be stagnant; (fig) be or become dull or sluggish through disuse, inactivity, etc. 不流動;靜止;(喻)變呆鈍;不活潑;不景氣。 **stag·na·tion** /stæg'neɪʃn; stæg'neʃən/ *n* [U].

stagy /'steɪdʒɪ; 'stedʒɪ/ *adj* theatrical in style, manner or appearance. 戲劇性的;具戲劇效果的;誇大做作的。 **stag·ily** /-ɪlɪ; -əlɪ/ *adv* **stagi·ness** *n*

staid /steɪd; sted/ *adj* (of persons, their appearance, behaviour, etc) conservative, quiet and serious. (指人,其外表、行爲等)保守的;沉靜而嚴肅的。 **~·ly** *adv* **~·ness** *n*

stain /steɪn; sten/ *vt, vi* **1** [VP6A] (of liquids, other substances) change the colour of; make coloured patches or dirty marks on: (指液體,其他物質)改變…的顏色;染汚;沾汚: *fingers ~ed with nicotine;* 爲尼古丁染黃的手指; *blood-~ed hands;* 血汚的手; *a tablecloth ~ed with gravy;* 沾有肉汁的桌布; (fig) (喻) *a guilt-~ed reputation.* 爲罪名沾汚的聲譽。 **2** [VP6A, 22] colour (wood, fabrics, etc) with a substance that penetrates the material: 着色於(木材、布等);染色: *He ~ed the wood brown.* 他把木材染爲褐色。 *The scientist ~ed his specimen before examining it under the microscope.* 那位科學家先把抽樣染色,再置於顯微鏡下檢視。 **~ed glass,** glass made by mixing into it transparent colours during the process of manufacture: 着色玻璃;彩色玻璃: *~ed glass windows in a church.* 教堂裡的彩色玻璃窗。 **3** [VP2A] (of material) become discoloured or soiled: (指布料等)褪色;變色;變汚: *Does this material ~ easily?* 這料子容易褪色(弄髒)嗎? □ *n* **1** [U] liquid used for ~ing wood, etc. (染木材等的)着色劑;染料。 **2** [C] ~ed place; dirty mark or patch of colour: 染汚之處;汚點: *'ink-/'blood-~s;* 墨水(血)的汚漬; (fig) (喻) *a ~ on one's reputation;* 名譽上的汚點; *without a ~ on your character.* 你品格上沒有瑕疵。 **~·less** *adj* **1** without a ~: 無汚點的;無瑕疵的;清白的: *a ~less reputation.* 清白的名譽。 **2** (esp of a kind of steel alloy) that resists rust and corrosion: (尤指一種合金鋼)不銹的;抗銹的: *~less steel cutlery.* 不銹鋼刀。

stair /steə(r); stɛr/ *n* [C] (any one of a) series of fixed steps leading from one floor of a building to another. 樓梯;梯級。⇨ downstairs, upstairs. *The child was sitting on the bottom ~.* 那孩子正坐在樓梯最下面的一級上。*She always runs up/down the ~s.* 她總跑着上(下)樓。*I passed her on the ~s.* 我在樓梯上遇見她。***below ~s,*** in the basement of a house (in large houses, formerly the part used by servants): 在一幢房屋的地下室 (昔爲僕人住處): *Their affairs were being discussed below ~s,* by the servants. 他們的事情正在僕人之間談論著。***a flight of ~s,*** a set of ~s in a continuous line, or from one landing, eg halfway between two floors, to another. (兩樓間或兩拐彎高度間,成一直行的)一段樓梯。***at the foot/head of the ~s,*** at the bottom/top of a flight of ~s. 在一段樓梯的底部(頂端)。**'~-carpet** *n* strip of carpet for laying on ~s. 梯毯(條狀地毯,鋪於梯階上)。**'~-rod** *n* rod for keeping a ~-carpet in the angle between two steps. 梯毯夾條(壓在二梯級轉角處,以固定梯毯)。**'~-case** *n* series of ~s (often with banisters) inside a building: 樓梯(指室內者,常有扶欄): *Many old Edinburgh houses have spiral ~cases,* ie winding round a central pillar. 愛丁堡的許多古老房屋有螺旋梯。**'~·way** *n* = ~case.

stake /steɪk ; stek/ *n* [C] **1** strong, pointed length of wood or metal (to be) driven into the ground as a post (eg for a fence) or as a support for sth, eg plants, young trees. 樁;杙;柱。**2** post, as used in olden times, to which a person was tied before being burnt to death as a punishment (for heresy): (昔時的)火刑柱(處死宗教異端者): *condemned to the ~;* 被判處火刑; *suffer at the ~.* 在火刑柱上受苦。***go to the ~,*** be burned at the ~; (fig) suffer the consequences of an ill-advised action. 被處以火刑; (喻)因行爲鹵莽而受苦。**3** sum of money risked on the unknown result of a future event, eg a horse-race; interest or concern (*in* sth); sum of money invested in an enterprise: 賭注;賭金;利害關係;關心;投於某一企業的金額;投資: *He has a ~ in the country,* is concerned in its welfare, is interested in its prosperity, etc (eg because he is a landowner). 他關心農村的情形(例如因爲他是地主)。***at ~,*** to be won or lost; risked, depending, upon the result of sth: 得失攸關;瀕勝敗關頭;處危險境地: (fig) (喻) *His reputation/His life itself was at ~.* 他面臨身敗名裂的危險(他有生命危險)。**'~-holder** *n* person with whom ~s are deposited until the result is known. 賭金保管者。**4** (*pl*) money to be contended for, esp in a horse-race; such a race: (複)(尤指賽馬的)獎金;(有獎金的)賽馬: *the trial ~s at Newmarket.* 新市賽馬的預賽。□ *vt* **1** [VP6A] support with a ~: 以樁或杙支撐: *~ newly planted trees.* 以樁支撐新栽的樹。**2** [VP6A, 15B] ***~ sth (out/off),*** mark (an area) with ~s: 以樁區分或界分(地區): *~ out a claim* (to land in a new country, etc; also fig). 用樁標出地權界限(亦作比喻用法)。**3** [VP6A, 14] ***~ sth on sth,*** risk (money, one's hopes, etc): 賭;以(金錢,希望等)下注: *~ £5 on the favourite,* eg in a horse-race. 以五鎊下注於被看好的馬。*I'd ~ my all/my life on it,* am very confident about it. 我願意拿我的一切(生命)打賭(我極有把握)。

stal·ac·tite /ˈstæləktaɪt *US:* stəˈlæk- ; stəˈlæktaɪt/ *n* [C] pencil-shaped or cone-shaped formation of lime hanging from the roof of a cave as water drips from it. 鐘乳石(洞穴頂部因滴水作用所形成的鉛筆形或圓錐狀的石灰石)。**stal·ag·mite** /ˈstæləgmaɪt *US:* stəˈlæg- ; stəˈlægmaɪt/ *n* [C] similarly shaped growth mounting upwards from the floor of a cave as water containing lime drips from the roof. 石筍(含石灰質的水,自洞穴頂部滴下時,在地面上所形成的筍狀直立物)。

stale /steɪl ; stel/ *adj* **1** (of food) dry and unappetizing because not fresh: (指食物)因不新鮮而乾癟無味的;陳舊的: *~ bread.* 陳麵包。**2** uninteresting because heard before: 因以前曾聽到過而感到無趣味的;老的;陳舊的;陳腐的;拾人牙慧的: *~ news/jokes.* 舊新聞(老笑話)。**3** (of athletes, pianists, etc) no longer able to perform really well because of too much playing, training, practice, etc: (指運動員、鋼琴家等)因過勞而表現不佳的;疲憊的: *become ~.* 變爲疲憊。□ *vi* [VP2A] become ~: 變陳舊;變疲憊: *Are there any kinds of pleasure that never ~?* 有沒有永不會讓人感到乏味的娛樂呢? **~·ness** *n*

stale·mate /ˈsteɪlmeɪt ; ˈstel,met/ *n* [C, U] **1** position of the pieces in chess from which no further move is possible. (西洋棋)無法繼續;僵棋;和棋。**2** (fig) any stage of a dispute at which further action by either side seems to be impossible. (喻)(爭執的)僵持;僵局。□ *vt* [VP6A] (chess) reduce a player to a ~; (fig) bring to a standstill. (西洋棋)使棋手受困;(喻)使停頓。

stalk¹ /stɔːk ; stɔk/ *n* [C] non-woody part of a plant that supports a flower or flowers, a leaf or leaves, or a fruit or fruits; stem. (植物的)柄;梗;稈(支持花、葉、果實的非木質部分)。

stalk² /stɔːk ; stɔk/ *vt, vi* **1** [VP2C, 6A] walk with slow, stiff strides, esp in a proud, self-important or grim way: 高視闊步;大踏步走: *~ out of the room;* 大踏步走出房間; *~ along (the road).* 高視闊步(地沿路前進)。*Famine ~ed (through) the land.* 饑饉遍及全境。**2** [VP6A] move quietly and cautiously towards (wild animals, etc) in order to get near: 潛近;偷偷接近(動物等): *~ deer.* 潛近鹿。**'~·ing-horse** *n* horse behind which a hunter hides; (more usu, fig) pretext; means of hiding one's real intentions. 其後有獵人掩藏的馬;(較常用作喻)託詞;口實;烟幕。**~er** *n* person who ~s animals: 用潛近法獵動物的人: *a 'deer-~er.* 用潛近法捕鹿者。

stall /stɔːl ; stɔl/ *n* **1** compartment for one animal in a stable or cattle shed. 畜舍中的一間或一欄;廐。**'~-fed** *adj* kept and fattened in a ~, not in the fields. 在廐中飼養的。**2** small, open-fronted shop; table, etc used by a trader in a market, on a street, in a railway-station, etc: 攤;售貨臺;貨品陳列臺: *a 'book-/'flower-/'coffee-~.* 書(花,咖啡)攤。**3** (usu *pl*) (not US) seat in the part of a theatre nearest to the stage. (通常用複數)(不用於美國)戲院中的正廳前排座位;最近舞臺的座位。**4** fixed seat in a church (usu enclosed at sides and back, often in carved wood) for the special use of a clergyman (usu in the choir or chancel): (教堂中)聖職或牧師的座位(常以雕花的木材製成,兩側及背後皆圍起,通常置於合唱團席位或高壇上): *canon's/dean's ~.* 牧師(地方主教)的座位。**5 ('finger-)~,** ⇨ finger. **6** condition of an aircraft when its speed has decreased to the point at which it no longer answers to the controls. (飛機之)失速(飛機速度減低到無法控制的程度)。□ *vt, vi* **1** [VP6A] place or keep (an animal) in a ~(1), esp for fattening: 置(動物)於畜舍中飼肥;關(動物)於廐中: *~ed oxen.* 關着養肥的牛。**2** [VP2A] (eg of an internal combustion engine) fail to keep going through insufficient power or speed; [VP

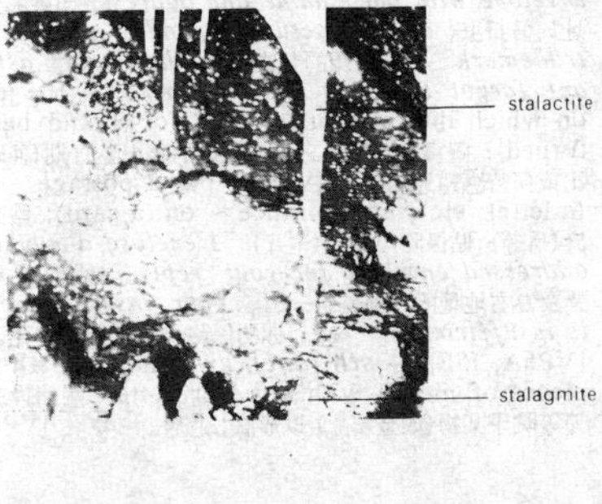

2A, 6A] (of a driver) cause an engine to stop from such a cause. (指內燃機等)力量或速度不够而停止轉動；發生故障；(指司機)減低引擎速力而停止轉動。 **3** [VP6A, 2A] (of an aircraft) cause to be, become, out of control through loss of speed. (指飛機)(使)失速而無法控制。 **4** [VP2A] avoid giving a clear answer to a question (in order to get more time): 避免給予明確的答覆(以拖延時間)；不作正面答覆：~ *for time;* 避免正面答覆以拖延時間；~ *off creditors.* 敷衍債主。*Quit ~ing!* 不要規避！(不要拖延時間！)

stal·lion /ˈstælɪən ; ˈstæljən/ *n* uncastrated fully grown male horse, esp one used for breeding. 長成的(未閹)公馬；(尤指)種馬。

stal·wart /ˈstɔːlwət ; ˈstɔlwɚt/ *adj* tall and muscular; solidly built; firm and resolved: 高大而結實的；强壯的；堅決的：~ *supporters.* 堅決的支持者。□ *n* loyal supporter of a political party, etc. (政黨等的)忠實擁護者。

sta·men /ˈsteɪmən ; ˈstemən/ *n* male part of a flower, bearing pollen. (花的)雄蕊(產生花粉部分)。⇨ the illus at flower. 參看 flower 之插圖。

stam·ina /ˈstæmɪnə ; ˈstæmənə/ *n* [U] vigour, energy, enabling a person or animal to work hard for a long time, to survive a serious illness, exposure, etc; (fig) mental toughness; moral strength. (使人或動物能做長久辛苦工作，挨過重病等的)體力；精力；活力；道德力；(喻) 精神上的耐力；心理上的堅忍力。

stam·mer /ˈstæmə(r) ; ˈstæmɚ/ *vi, vt* **1** [VP2A] speak haltingly with a tendency to repeat rapidly the same sound or syllable, as in 'G-g-give me that b-b-book'. 口吃；結結巴巴地說。 **2** [VP6A, 15B] ~ ***sth (out),*** say sth in this confused or halting way: 結結巴巴地說出某事：~ *out a request.* 結結巴巴地請求某事。□ *n* (tendency to) ~ing talk. 口吃；結巴說話；口吃的傾向。**~er** *n* person who ~s. 口吃者。**~·ing·ly** *adv*

stamp[1] /stæmp ; stæmp/ *vt, vi* **1** [VP6A, 3A, 2C, 22, 15B] put (one's foot) down with force (on sth): 跺(脚)；頓足；用力踏或踩：~ *one's foot;* 跺脚；~ *the ground;* 用力踏地；~ *on a spider;* 踩一隻蜘蛛；move (about, etc) doing this: 來回地跺脚；重步走：~ *about/out of the room;* 在屋裡來回跺脚(跺着脚走出屋子)；~ *upstairs;* 在樓上跺脚；flatten by doing this: 踏平；踩扁：~ *the soil flat.* 把土地踏平。~ ***sth out,*** crush, destroy, end: 撲滅；踏滅；毀掉；鎭服：~ *out a fire in the grass/a rebellion/an epidemic disease.* 撲滅草地上的火(叛變，傳染病)。 **ˈ~·ing-ground** *n* **(a)** place where specified animals, eg elephants, may usually be found. 踐踏地；某些獸類(如象)常出沒之地。**(b)** place where specified people often gather: 某類人士常聚集之地：*Soho, the ~ing-ground in London of those who enjoy exotic food and entertainment.* 蘇和區，倫敦喜愛外國食物及娛樂人士聚集之處。 **2** [VP6A, 14] ~ ***sth (on/with sth),*** print (a design, lettering, the date, etc) on paper, cloth or other surface: 印(圖案、字、日期等)於紙、布或其他表面上；壓印：~ *one's name and address on an envelope/~ an envelope with one's name and address;* 印姓名及地址於信封上；*a manufacturer's goods ~ed with his trademark.* 印有商標的製成品。*The library assistant forgot to ~ my library books,* ~ the date on which they were taken out (or should be returned). 圖書館助理員忘了在我借的書上蓋日期(何時借出或何時應歸還)。 **3** [VP6A] put a postage ~ on (a letter, etc), an insurance ~ on (a card): 貼郵票於(信等)；貼保險印花於(卡片)：*I enclose a ~ed and addressed envelope for your reply.* 玆附上貼有郵票及寫有地址的回郵信封一個。*Your insurance card is insufficiently ~ed.* 你的保險卡片未貼足印花。**4** [VP6A, 15B] ~ ***sth (out),*** give shape to sth (eg pieces of metal) with a die or cutter. 用鑄模或刻刀等賦予某物(如金屬片) 以形狀；造形。 **5** [VP6A, 15A] (fig uses) impress: (比喩用法)給予印象；銘刻；刻記：*He ~ed his authority/personality on the game,* eg of a great footballer. 他的權威(人格)已經銘刻在這項運動上了(如指一位偉大的足球員)。 [VP 16B] mark out: 標出；顯示出；表示出：*These actions ~ him as a man of high principles.* 這些行爲顯示出他是個很有節操的人。

stamp[2] /stæmp ; stæmp/ *n* **1** act of stamping with the foot: 踏；跺；踩；頓足：*a ~ of impatience.* 因不耐煩而跺脚。 **2** that with which a mark or design is made on a surface: 印章；圖章：*a rubber ~,* one on which a design, words, etc are cut (used for printing dates, signatures, addresses, etc). 橡皮圖章。 **3** design, word(s), etc made by stamping on a surface. 印記；圖記。**4 (ˈpostage-) ~,** piece of printed paper (usu with perforated edges) stuck on letters, etc to show the postage, insurance dues, etc paid, or the duty paid on legal documents. 郵票；印花。 **ˈ~-album** *n* one in which a collector of postage-~s keeps his specimens. 郵票簿；集郵簿。**ˈ~-collector** *n* person who collects ~s. 集郵者；集郵家。 **ˈ~-dealer** *n* person who buys and sells ~s for collectors. 郵票商(爲集郵者買賣郵票者)。**ˈ~-duty** *n* tax imposed on certain kinds of legal documents. 印花稅。 **5** (usu *sing*) characteristic mark or quality: (通常用單數)表徵；標記；特點；特質：*He bears the ~ of genius.* 他具有天才的特質。*Her face bears the ~ of suffering.* 她面露痛苦。 **6** (usu *sing*) kind; class: (通常用單數)種；類：*men of that ~.* 那類的人(們)。

stam·pede /stæmˈpiːd ; stæmˈpid/ *n* [C] sudden rush of frightened people or animals. (受驚嚇的人或動物的)驚逃；奔逃；奔竄；潰散。□ *vi, vt* **1** [VP 2A, 6A] take part in a ~; cause to do this. (使)驚逃；(使)奔逃；(使)奔竄；(使)潰散。 **2** [VP14] ~ ***sb into sth/doing sth,*** hustle or frighten sb into rash action: 慫恿、催促或恐嚇某人致輕率做某事：*Don't be ~d into buying the house.* 不要受慫恿而輕率買那幢房子。

stance /stæns ; stæns/ *n* (golf, cricket) position taken for a stroke; pose; person's (intellectual, moral, etc) attitude. (高爾夫，板球)擊球(時的)姿勢；看法；(一個人所持的)觀點。

stanch /stɑːntʃ *US:* stæntʃ ; stæntʃ/ = staunch[1].

stan·chion /ˈstænʃən *US:* ˈstæntʃ- ; ˈstænʃən/ *n* upright post for supporting sth (eg bars for confining cattle in stalls). 直立的支柱(如關牛於廐中的柵等)。

stand[1] /stænd ; stænd/ *n* **1** stopping of motion or progress: 停止；停頓：*come/be brought to a ~* (or, more usu 或，較常用 *~still*), stop, be stopped. 陷於停頓。 **2 *make a ~,*** be ready to resist or fight: 準備抵抗或格鬥；準備奮鬥：*make a ~ against the enemy;* 抵抗敵人；*make a ~ for one's principles.* 爲某人的原則奮鬥。**3** position taken up: 立場；立腳地；位置：*He took his ~ near the window.* 他站在窗旁。***take one's ~,*** declare one's position, opinion, etc. 宣布立場、意見等；表明態度。*I take my ~ upon sound precedents,* use these to support my claim, etc. 我採取的立場係基於有力的先例。 **4** small article of furniture, support, etc on or in which things may be placed: 置物臺；架：*a ˈmusic-/ˈhat-/umˈbrella-~.* 樂譜(帽，傘)架。⇨ also *hand~* at hand[1](16), *ink~* at ink, *wash-~* at wash-. **5** structure from which things are sold: 售貨臺；攤：*a ˈnews~;* 報攤；area, structure(s), for the exhibition of goods, etc: 陳列貨物的區域或構築；攤位：*the British ~ at the Hanover Fair.* 漢諾威博覽會中的英國攤位。 **6** place where vehicles may stand in line in a street, etc while waiting for passengers: (車輛等的)停留地；候客站：*a ˈcab-~;* 出租馬車站；出租汽車站；*a ~ for six taxis.* 容六輛計程車的候客站。 **7** structure, usu sloping, where people may stand or sit to watch races, sports-meetings, etc: 看臺：*open ~s;* 露天看臺；*the ˈgrand~.* 大看

臺;級級升高或有頂蓋的看台。 **8** halt made by a theatrical company when touring the country. (旅行劇團所作的)停留;上演站;演出地。**ˌone-night ˈ~,** theatrical performance on one evening only; (fig) an (esp sexual) encounter that will not be repeated. 祇演出一晚的戲劇等;(喻)(不會重複發生的)短暫聚會;(尤指)一夜夫妻。 **9** (US) witness-box (in a law court): (美)(法庭上的)證人席: *take the ~.* 做證。 **10** growing crop in a certain area: (一地區之)正在成長的作物: *a good ~ of wheat/timber.* 生長茂盛的小麥(林木)。 **11** (compounds) (複合字) **ˈ~-pipe** *n* vertical pipe (connected with a water-main and used as a hydrant). (供消防用的)直立水管(與總管連接,供救火車等取水者)。**ˈ~-point** *n* point of view: 立場;見解;觀點: *from the ~point of the consumer.* 從顧客的立場言。 **ˈ~•still** *n* stop; halt: 停頓;停止: *be at/come to/bring sth to a ~still;* 陷於停頓; (attrib) (形容用法) *a ~still agreement,* one that agrees to no change, eg in wage rates or hours of work. 不變動的協議(如維持原來的工資或工作時間,不加變動)。

stand² /stænd; stænd/ *vi, vt* (*pt, pp* stood /stʊd; stʊd/) (For special uses with *adverbial particles* and *preps*, ⇨ 10 below.) (與副詞接語及介詞連用的特殊用法,參看下列第 10 義。) **1** [VP2A, B, C, 4A] have, take, keep, an upright position; balance, support, the body on the feet: 站;立;站住;站定;站穩;起立: *He was too weak to ~.* 他太虛弱,不能站立。 *A chair will not ~ on two legs.* 一把椅子祇用兩條腿着地是站不穩的。*We had to ~ all the way back in the bus.* 我們在回程的公車上不得不站着。*S~ing room only,* all seats are occupied, eg in a bus or cinema. 僅有站位了(座位賣光了,如公車或電影院裡)。 *His hair stood on end,* ie with terror. 他的毛髮豎立(感到恐怖)。*He ~s six foot two,* is of this height when ~ing. 他站着時身高六呎二吋。*Don't ~ there arguing about it.* 不要站在那兒爭論此事。*He stood looking over my shoulder.* 他站起來從我的肩頭望過去。*S~ still while I take your photograph.* 我爲你拍照的時候,站着不要動。*S~ and deliver!* (command given by a highwayman) Stop and give me your valuables, etc! 站住,把值錢的東西交出來! (剪徑者所發的口令)。 **2** [VP2A, C, 4A] **~ (up),** rise to the feet: 站立;站起來: *S~ up, please.* 請站起來。*Everyone stood (up) when the Queen entered.* 女王進來時大家都站起來。*We stood (up) to see better.* 我們站了起來,以便看得清楚些。**3** [VP2A, C] remain without change: 持續;維持不變;原樣繼續: *Let the words ~,* don't alter them or take them out. 不要改動這些字。*The agreement must ~,* cannot be altered or cancelled. 這合約必須維持原狀。*The house has stood two hundred years and will ~ another century.* 這房子已有兩百年之久,還可以再維持一百年。**~ firm/fast,** not give way, retreat, change one's views, etc. 堅定;不退讓;不撤退;不改變意見等。 **4** [VP2C] be in a certain condition or situation: 處於某種狀況或情形: *The emergency services ~ (= are) ready to help if called on.* 緊急救難處一獲得通知隨時可以馳援。*The matter ~s thus,* this is the state of affairs. 事情就是這樣的;事實就是這樣。*As affairs now ~...,* As they are at present.... 其現況是…。*He ~s (= is) in need of help.* 他正處於需要幫助的情況。*Who ~s (= is) first on the list?* 名單上誰的名字列在首位? *Will you ~ (= be) godmother to the child?* 你願意做那孩子的教母嗎? *He stood convicted of treachery.* 他被判犯有叛逆罪。*I ~ corrected,* accept the correction of my views, etc. 我願接受指正。*He ~s alone among his colleagues,* None of them equals him in ability, etc. 他在同儕間鶴立雞群。 **~ clear (of sth),** move away: 站開;避開;移開: *S~ clear of the gates,* eg as a warning when they are about to be closed. 離開大門(如將關閉時的警語)。**~ easy/at ease,** ⇨ easy, ease. **5** [VP2C] have a certain place; be situated: 位於;在某處: *These dishes ~ on the top shelf.* 這些碗盤是放在頂架上的。*A tall poplar tree once stood there.* 該處曾有一棵高大的白楊樹。*The house ~s on the hill.* 那幢房子位於小山上。*Where does Tom ~ in class,* What is his position (in order of ability, etc)? 湯姆在班上的名次如何? **6** [VP15A] cause to be placed in an upright position: 使直立;豎起: *S~ the ladder against the wall.* 把梯子靠着牆放。*S~ the bottle on the table.* 把瓶子豎立在桌子上。*S~ the empty barrels on the floor.* 把空桶豎着放在地板上。 *Don't ~ this tin of petrol near the fire.* 不要把這罐汽油放在火旁邊。*The traitor was stood up against the wall and shot.* 那叛逆犯奉令靠牆站立接受槍決。 **7** [VP6A, C] endure; bear: 忍耐;忍受: *He can't ~ hot weather.* 他不能忍受炎熱的天氣。*She says she will ~ no nonsense,* not put up with foolish behaviour. 她說她不能容忍愚蠢的行爲。*I can't ~ that woman,* strongly dislike her. 我不能忍受那女人(深惡她)。*She can't ~ being kept waiting.* 她不能忍受久等。**~ one's ground,** maintain one's position, eg in battle; (fig) not give way in an argument. 堅守陣地(如作戰時); 堅持立場;(喻)固執己見。**~ (one's) trial,** be tried (in a court of law). (在法庭上)受審。 **8** [VP6A, 12A] **~ sb sth,** provide at one's expense: 付帳; 供給;供應: *~ sb a good dinner;* 供應某人一頓好飯; *~ drinks all round,* pay for drinks for everyone. 爲每個人喝的飲料付帳。*Will he ~ us champagne?* 他會供應我們香檳酒嗎? **~ treat,** pay the costs of entertaining sb or others. 請客;作東。**9** (phrases) (片語) **~ a (good/poor, etc) chance,** (of success, etc) have a (good/poor, etc) prospect (of success, etc). (指成功等)有(很大,很小等)成功等的機會。**~ sb in good stead,** ⇨ stead. **~ on ceremony,** ⇨ ceremony. **It ~s to reason that,** ⇨ reason¹(3). **~ to win/gain/lose sth,** be in a position where one is likely to win, etc: 很可能會贏(獲利,輸或虧損): *What do we ~ to gain by the agreement?* 依照合約我們可能得到何種利益? **10** [VP 2C, 3A, 15B] (special uses with *adverbial particles* and *preps*): (與副詞接語及介詞連用的特殊用法):

stand aside, **(a)** be inactive, do nothing: 不活躍; 不活動;不做事: *He's a man who never ~s aside when there's something that needs doing.* 有事需要做時,他從不會避開不做。**(b)** move to one side: 站開;站在一邊: *~ aside to let someone pass.* 站開讓人通過。**(c)** withdraw one's name (as a candidate): 撤消名字(如候選人); 退出競選: *~ aside in favour of a better man.* 讓賢。

stand at, be at a certain level (on a scale, etc): (在尺度、等級、程度等上) 處於某一程度、位置、水準、階段等: *The appeal fund ~s at £10 000.* 救助基金爲數一萬英鎊。*The temperature stood at 30°C.* 氣溫爲攝氏 30 度。

stand back, **(a)** move back: 退後;向後站: *The policeman ordered us to ~ back.* 警察命令我們向後退。**(b)** be situated away from: 離開;隔開;隔有距離: *The house ~s back from the road.* 那房子不在路邊。

stand by, **(a)** be a bystander; look on without doing anything: 袖手旁觀: *How can you ~ by and see such cruelty?* 你怎能對這樣殘酷的行爲袖手旁觀呢? **(b)** be ready for action: 準備行動;待機: *The troops are ~ing by.* 部隊隨時待命行動。**~ by sb,** support, side with, sb; show oneself to be a good friend: 援助、支持某人;向某人表示友好: *I'll ~ by you whatever happens.* 無論發生什麼事,我都會支持你。**~ by sth,** be faithful to (a promise, one's word, etc). 信守(承諾、話等);遵守。 Hence, 由此產生, **ˈ~-by** *n* **(a)** state of readiness: 待機;準備就緒: *The troops are on 24-hour ~by,* ready to move at 24 hours' notice. 部隊處於二十四小時待命狀態。**(b)** sb or sth that one may depend upon: 可信賴或依靠的人或物;備用的人或物: (attrib) (形容用法) *a ~by generator,* one for use in an emergency, eg for use when electric current from the mains is cut off.

備用發電機。*Aspirin is a good ~by for headaches.* 阿斯匹林是必備的頭痛良藥。

stand down, retire from a witness-box or similar position; (of a candidate) withdraw (in favour of sb else). 離開證人席;(指候選人)退出競選(以支持他人)。

stand for sth, **(a)** represent: 代表;代替: *PO ~s for Post Office or postal order.* PO 兩個字母代表 Post Office (郵局) 或 postal order (郵政滙票)。*I condemn fascism and all it ~s for.* 我譴責法西斯主義及其所代表的一切。 **(b)** support, contend for: 贊同;支持;擁護: *~ for racial tolerance.* 支持種族平等自由。**(c)** (GB) be a candidate for: (英)爲候選人: *~ for Parliament.* 爲國會議員候選人。**(d)** (colloq; ⇨ 8 above) tolerate: (俗;參看上列第 8 義)容忍: *She says she's not going to ~ for her own children disobeying her.* 她說她不容許自己的孩子不服從她。

stand in (with sb), take a share in: 參加;分擔;分攤一份: *Let me ~ in with you if it's expensive.* 如果花錢很多,讓我爲你分攤一份。*~ in (for sb),* take the place of, eg a principal actor or actress until filming begins. 代替(某人)(如影片開拍前代替男女主角)。Hence, 由此產生, **'~-in** *n* person who does this. 替身。

stand off, remain at a distance; move away. 遠離;離開;避開。*~ **sb off,*** dispense with the services of, eg workers, temporarily. 暫時解雇(如工人)。**ˌ~-'off·ish** *adj* reserved; cold and distant in behaviour. 冷淡的;矜持的。Hence, 由此產生, **ˌ~-'off·ish·ly** *adv* **ˌ~-'off·ish·ness** *n*

stand out, **(a)** be easily seen above or among others: 顯着;傑出: *Does your work ~ out from that of others,* Is it obviously better? 你的工作比別人的突出嗎? ⇨ outstanding. *~ **out a mile,*** be extremely obvious. 極爲明顯。 **(b)** continue to resist: 繼續抵抗: *The troops stood out against the enemy until their ammunition was exhausted.* 這支軍隊繼續抵抗敵人,直至彈藥用盡。

stand over, be postponed: 延緩;延後;展期: *Let the matter ~ over until the next meeting.* 這件事等下次開會再討論吧。*~ **over sb,*** supervise, watch closely: 監督;監視: *Unless I ~ over him he makes all sorts of foolish mistakes.* 如果我不監督他,他就會犯各種錯誤。

stand to, (mil) take up positions to resist possible attack: (軍)各就崗位以戒備敵患;警戒: *The company (was) stood to for half an hour.* 該連(奉命)警戒防守半小時。Hence, 由此產生, **'~-to** *n* army signal to be on the alert. 軍隊警戒訊號。

stand up, ⇨ 2 above. 參看上列第 2 義。**'~-up** *adj* **(a)** (of collars) upright (opp of *turn-down*). (指衣領) 直立的 (爲 turn-down 之相反字)。 **(b)** (of a meal) eaten while ~ing: (指餐食)站着吃的: *a ~-up buffet.* 立食餐館。 **(c)** (of a fight) violent and hard-hitting. (指打鬥)猛烈狠毒的。*~ **sb up,*** (colloq) not keep a rendezvous with him: (俗)爽約;不守約;不赴約: *First she agreed to come out with me, then she stood me up.* 起初她答應同我一起出去,後來她爽約了。*~ **up for sb,*** support; take the part of; defend. 支持某人;維護某人;袒護某人。 *~ **up to sb,*** defend oneself with courage against him. 勇敢地對抗某人。*~ **up to sth,*** (of materials) remain in good condition after long or hard use, etc: (指物料)耐久;耐用;經得起: *metals that ~ up well to high temperatures.* 耐高熱金屬。

stand (well) with sb, be on (good) terms with, be (well) thought of: 與某人相處(甚佳);得某人(好)評: *How do you ~ with your boss?* 你同你的上司相處如何? *He ~s well with his bank manager* (and may, therefore, get an overdraft without difficulty). 他在他的銀行經理那裡信用很好 (因此,透支一點錢,可能不會有困難)。

stan·dard /ˈstændəd ; ˈstændɚd/ *n* **1** distinctive flag, esp one to which loyalty is given or asked: 旗;旗幟;旗標(尤指擁有或要求効忠的標誌): *the royal ~,* eg as flown to show that the Queen is in residence. 王室旗標(如懸出以示女王駐蹕處)。***raise the ~ of revolt,*** (fig) begin a struggle and call for support. (喻)揭竿而起。**'~-bearer** *n* person who carries a ~; (fig) prominent leader in a cause. 掌旗者;(喻)卓越的領導者。**2** (often attrib) sth used as a test or measure for weights, lengths, qualities or for the required degree of excellence: (常作形容用法)標準;基準;模範;水準;規範: *the ~ yard/pound, etc;* 標準碼(磅等); *~ weights and measures;* 標準度量衡; *the ~ of height required for recruits to the police force;* 招募警察人員所需要的身高標準; *set a high ~ for candidates in an examination;* 爲參加考試人員規定一項高的錄取標準; *conform to the ~s of society,* live and behave as society expects; (生活)合於社會的規範; *a high ~ of living,* one with plenty of material comforts, etc; 高的生活水準; *a high moral ~;* 崇高的道德標準; *~ authors,* accepted as good. 够水準的作家。***be up to/below ~,*** be equal to/not so good as, what is normal, required, etc: 達(未達)到標準: *Their work is not up to ~.* 他們的工作未達到標準。*~ **time,*** time officially adopted for a country or part of it. 標準時間。**3** (former) grade of classification in primary schools (now usu *class*): (昔)小學的年級(現通常用 class): *boys in S~ One.* 小學一年級的男生。 **4 monetary ~,** proportion of weight of fine metal and alloy in gold and silver coin. 金銀硬幣中之純金銀與合金的比例; (貨幣的)法定純分; 純度基準。**the 'gold ~,** system by which the value of money is based on that of gold. 金本位制。***abandon/go off the gold ~,*** abandon such a system. 放棄金本位制。**5** (often attrib) upright support; pole or column; vertical water- or gas-pipe. (常作形容用法)直立的支持物;支柱;垂直的水管或煤氣管。**'~ lamp,** lamp on a tall support with its base on the floor. 落地燈。 **6** tree or shrub that has been grafted on an upright stem (contrasted with a bush or climbing plant): 接枝於直幹上的樹或灌木(與矮叢或攀緣植物相對): *~ roses.* 接枝在直立樹幹上的玫瑰。

stan·dard·ize /ˈstændədaɪz ; ˈstændɚdˌaɪz/ *vt* [VP 6A] make of one size, shape, quality, etc according to fixed standards: 使合乎規格; 使標準化: *The parts of motor-vehicles are usually ~d.* 機動車輛的零件通常都是標準化的。*S~d products are usually cheaper than hand-made articles.* 標準化的產品通常比手工製品便宜。**stan·dard·iz·ation** /ˌstændədaɪˈzeɪʃn *US:* -dɪˈz- ; ˌstændɚdəˈzeʃən/ *n* [U] standardizing; making regular: 標準化: *the problem of the standardization of the use of hyphens in compounds.* 統一複合字中連字號使用法的問題。

stand·ing /ˈstændɪŋ ; ˈstændɪŋ/ *n* **1** [U] duration: 持續;期間: *a debt/dispute of long ~.* 長期債務(糾紛)。 **2** [C, U] position or reputation; (if there is no *adj*) established position: 身份;地位;名譽; (不加形容詞)美名;令譽;好名譽: *men of (high) ~;* 地位高的人;名望高的人; *a member in full ~.* 正式會員。□ *adj* **1** established and permanent; ready for use: 永久的;固定的;持續的;備用的;常備的: *a ~ army;* 常備軍; *a ~ committee,* a permanent one that meets regularly; 常務(常設)委員會; *a ~ order for newspapers and periodicals,* to be delivered regularly; 長期訂閱報紙及雜誌; *a ~ order to a bank,* customer's order for payments that recur regularly, eg rent, rates; 客戶對銀行之長期委託(由銀行從存款代爲支付固定開銷,如房租,水電等); *a ~ joke,* sth that regularly causes amusement. 經常引人發笑的笑料;笑柄。*~ **orders,*** (*pl*) rules and regulations which remain in force until repealed by the proper authorities. (複)常規;常法。**2 ~ corn,** not yet cut (harvested). 尚未收割之穀物。**~ jump,** made without a preliminary run. 立定跳高或跳遠。

stank /stæŋk ; stæŋk/ *pt* of stink.

stanza /ˈstænzə ; ˈstænzə/ *n* (*pl* ~s) [C] group of rhymed lines forming a division in some forms of poem. (詩的)節;段。

staple[1] /ˈsteɪpl ; ˈstepl/ *n* U-shaped metal bar with pointed ends hammered or pressed into a surface, to hold sth, eg flexible wire for electric current, in position; hoop-shaped bar hammered into wood, etc to take the point of a hook, or the hasp of a padlock, ⇨ the illus at padlock; piece of wire for fastening sheets of paper together (as in some periodicals). U 形釘(固定某物於表面所使用者,如固定電線);鎖扣環(參看 padlock 之插圖);U 形環;訂書針。□ *vt* [VP6A] fasten or fit with a ~. 以 U 形釘或訂書針固定或釘住;以U形環或鎖扣環套住。**ˈsta·pling-machine** *n* one used for fastening sheets of paper together with ~s. 訂書機。**sta·pler** /ˈsteɪplə(r) ; ˈsteplɚ/ *n* small hand-operated device for fastening papers together. (用手操作的)小訂書機。

staple[2] /ˈsteɪpl ; ˈstepl/ *n* **1** [C] chief sort of article or goods produced or traded in: 主要產品或商品;土產;名產: *Cotton is one of the ~s of Egypt.* 棉花是埃及主要產品之一。 **2** chief material or element (*of* sth): (事物的)主要原料;主要成分;主要因素: *The weather forms the ~ of their conversation.* 天氣是他們的主要話題。**3** [U] fibre of cotton, wool, etc (as determining its quality): (棉、羊毛等的)纖維(可藉以決定其質地者): *cotton of short/fine, etc ~;* 短(細等)纖維棉花; *long-~ cotton.* 長纖維棉花。**4** (attrib) forming the ~(2): (形容用法)構成主要原料、成分、因素等的;主要的: *Is coffee still the ~ product of Brazil?* 咖啡仍舊是巴西主要產物嗎?*Rice is the ~ food in many Asian countries.* 米是許多亞洲國家的主食。

star /stɑː(r) ; stɑr/ *n* **1** any one of the bodies seen in the sky at night as distant points of light. (晚上天空中見到的)星。**fixed ~** *n* one which is not a planet. 恆星。**shooting ~** *n* ⇨ shoot[2](1). **ˈ~·fish** *n* ~-shaped sea-animal. 海星;海盤車(星狀海生動物)。⇨ the illus at sea. 參看 sea 之插圖。**ˈ~·light** *n* [U] light from the ~s: 星光: *walk home by ~light;* 在星光下步行回家; (attrib) (形容用法) *a ~light night.* 星光照耀之夜。**ˈ~·lit** *adj* lighted by the ~s: 星光照耀的: *a ~lit scene.* 星光照耀的景色。**2** figure or design with points round it, suggesting a ~ by its shape; an asterick (*): 星標;星符;星狀物: *a five-~ hotel,* given five ~s (in guide-books, etc) to show its grading; 五星(標)旅館(旅行指南等上賦以五個星標,以示其等級); badge of rank (worn by officers on the shoulder-strap). (軍官肩帶上表示階級的)星標;階級標誌。***see ~s,*** seem to see flashes of lights, eg as the result of a blow in the eye(s). (眼睛)冒金星;目眩(如眼睛被擊後所感覺者)。**the ˌS~-Spangled ˈBanner, (a)** the national flag of the US. 美國國旗。**(b)** the national anthem of the US. 美國國歌。**the S~s and Stripes** *n sing* the national flag of the US. 美國國旗。**3** planet or heavenly body regarded as influencing a person's fortune, etc: (被視爲影響個人命運等的)星宿: *born under a lucky ~.* 生有福星照命。*What do the ~s foretell?* 星象預示什麼?*You may thank your lucky ~s you were not killed in that accident.* 你多虧有福星高照,在那次意外事故中沒有喪生。**ˈ~·gazer** *n* (hum) astrologer or astronomer. (諧)占星家;天文家。 **4** person famous as a singer, actor, actress, etc: (歌唱,演戲等的)明星;高手;名家: *the ~s of stage and screen;* 舞臺及影視明星; *ˈfilm ~s;* 電影明星; *an all-~ cast,* in which leading players are all ~s; 主角均爲大明星的演員陣容; *the ~ turn,* the principal item in an entertainment or performance. 餘興或表演中的主要節目。□ *vi, vt* (-rr-) **1** [VP6A] mark or decorate with, or as with, a ~ or ~s, eg an asterisk to direct attention to sth: 以星標或星狀物標示或裝飾;點綴;加星號以引起注意: *a lawn ~red with daisies.* 點綴着雛菊的草坪。**2** [VP3A, 14] ~ ***(sb) in,*** be a ~(4) (*in* a play, film, etc); present (sb) as a ~(4): (在一部戲劇,電影等中)演出;主演;使(某人)擔任主角或主演: *She is to ~/to be ~red in a new film.* 她將主演一部新片(在一部新片中擔任主角)。**ˈ~·dom** /-dəm ; -dəm/ *n* status of being a ~(4). 明星或主角的身份、地位等。**~·let** /-lɪt ; -lɪt/ *n* young actress on the way to ~dom. 未成名的年輕女演員;準明星。**~·less** *adj* with no ~s to be seen: 看不見星的;無星的: *a ~less sky/night.* 無星的天空(夜晚)。**~ry** /ˈstɑːrɪ ; ˈstɑrɪ/ *adj* lighted by, shining like, ~s: 星光照耀的;閃爍如星的: *a ~ry night;* 星空之夜; *~ry eyes.* 閃閃發光的眼睛;明眸。**ˌ~ry-ˈeyed** *adj* (colloq) visionary but impractical: (俗)不切實際的;幻想的: *~ry-eyed reformers.* 不切實際的改革者。

star·board /ˈstɑːbəd ; ˈstɑrˌbord/ *n* right side of a ship or aircraft from the point of view of a person looking forward. ⇨ port: (船的)右舷;(飛機的)右側(邊): *alter course to ~;* 轉向右(舷)航; *on the ~ bow.* 在船首右舷。⇨ the illus at ship. 參看 ship 之插圖。□ *vt* turn to ~: 把…轉向右舷: *~ the helm,* turn the helm to ~. 將舵轉向右邊。

starch /stɑːtʃ ; stɑrtʃ/ *n* [U] **1** white, tasteless, carbohydrate food substance, plentiful in potatoes, grain, etc. 澱粉。**2** this substance prepared in powdered form and used for stiffening cotton clothes, etc; (fig) stiffness of manner; formality. (漿硬棉布等用的)漿粉;(喻)拘謹;古板;生硬。□ *vt* [VP6A] make, eg shirt collars, stiff with ~: 漿(襯衫領等): (fig, in *pp*) (喻,用過去分詞) *a ~ed manner.* 古板的態度。**~y** *adj* of or like ~; containing ~: 澱粉的;似澱粉的;含澱粉的: *~y foods.* 含澱粉的食物。

stare /steə(r) ; stɛr/ *vi, vt* **1** [VP2A, B, C, 3A] ~ ***(at),*** look fixedly; (of eyes) be wide open: 凝視;盯着看;瞪;(指眼)睜大;張大: *Do you like being ~d at?* 你喜歡被人注視嗎?*She was staring into the distance.* 她凝視着遠方。*They all ~d with astonishment.* 他們都驚異地張大眼睛。*He gazed at the scene with staring eyes.* 他張大眼睛注視那景象。***make sb ~,*** surprise him. 使某人驚愕。**2** [VP 15B] ~ ***sb out (of countenance),*** ~ until he becomes nervous, etc. 盯得某人難爲情;把某人盯得侷促不安。~ ***sb out/down,*** ~ at him longer than he is able to ~ at you. (在互盯的場合)把某人盯下去(你盯他的時間長於他盯你的時間);盯勝某人。~ ***one in the face,*** **(a)** ~ at sb's face. 注視某人的面孔。**(b)** be right in front of one: 就在面前;就在眼前: *The book I was looking for was staring me in the face.* 我找的書就在我的面前。*Defeat was staring them in the face,* was clearly inevitable. 他們的失敗就在眼前。□ *n* [C] staring look: 凝視;注視;瞪;盯: *give sb a rude ~;* 魯莽地盯某人一眼; *with a ~ of horror/astonishment;* 心懷恐怖(驚愕)的凝視; *with a vacant ~,* suggesting an empty mind; 茫然凝視着; *with a glassy ~,* suggesting indifference. 帶着漠不關心的眼神。**star·ing** *adj* (of colours, etc) too bright or conspicuous: (指色彩等)過於鮮艷的;太顯眼的: *His tie was a staring red.* 他的領帶是大紅色的。▭ *adv* (only in) (僅用於) ***stark staring mad,*** completely mad. 完全瘋狂的。

stark /stɑːk ; stɑrk/ *adj* **1** stiff, esp in death. (尤指死亡後)僵硬的。**2** complete; downright: 完全的;純然的: *~ madness/folly.* 簡直瘋狂(愚蠢)。□ *adv* completely: 完全地: *~ naked.* 全裸的。**~ers** /ˈstɑːkəz ; ˈstɑrkɚz/ *pred adj* (GB sl) completely naked. (英俚)完全赤裸的。

star·ling /ˈstɑːlɪŋ ; ˈstɑrlɪŋ/ *n* common bird (with black, brown-spotted plumage) which nests near buildings and is a good mimic. 歐椋鳥;燕八哥(一種常見之鳥,羽毛黑色而有褐色斑點,築巢於建築物附近,善模倣)。

starry /ˈstɑːrɪ ; ˈstɑrɪ/ ⇨ star.

start[1] /stɑːt ; stɑrt/ *n* **1** [C] beginning of a journey, activity, etc: 啓程;動身;開始;着手: *make an* *early ~;* 動身(開始)早; *the ~ of a race;* 賽跑的起始; *after several false ~s;* 數次錯誤的起步以後; *from ~ to finish.* 自始至終。 **2** [U, C] (no *pl*) amount of time or distance by which one person starts in front of competitors; advantageous position: (無複數形)先跑權; 先跑的時間或距離; 優勢地位: *The small boys were given a ~ of ten yards.* 小男孩們獲得先跑十碼的優先權。*They didn't give me much/any ~.* 他們未給我很多(任何)優先。*He got the ~ of* (= gained an advantage over) *his rivals.* 他較他的對手們佔優勢。*He got a good ~* (= a position of advantage) *in life/business.* 他在人生(商業)中得天獨厚。**a ˌhead ˈ~** *n* (lit or fig) advantageous position: (字面或喻)優勢: *give sb/have/get a head ~ (over sb).* 讓某人(比某人)佔優勢。 **3** [C] sudden movement of surprise, fear, etc: (驚愕、恐懼等的)驚起;突動: *He sat up with a ~.* 他一驚而坐起。*The news gave me a ~,* surprised me. 這消息使我吃驚。***by fits and ~s,*** ⇨ fit³(3)

start² /stɑːt; stɑrt/ *vi, vt* (Note: *begin* may replace *start* only as in 2 below) (注意: begin 僅在第2義中可代替 start) **1** [PV2A, C] ~ ***(out),*** leave; set out: 出發;啓程;動身: *We must ~ (out) early.* 我們必須早些動身。*We ~ed at six.* 我們在六時出發。*At last the bus ~ed.* 公共汽車終於啓程了。 **2** [VP6A, D, 7A] begin: 開始;着手: *~ work.* 着手工作。*It ~ed raining.* 開始下雨了。*It's ~ing to rain.* 開始下雨了。*Have you ~ed working yet?* 你開始工作了嗎? **3** [VP6A, 3A] ~ ***(on) sth,*** make a beginning: 創始;啓始: *~(on) one's journey home.* 啓程回家。*Have you ~ed on your next book yet,* begun to read (or write) it? 你已經開始(讀或寫)下一本書了嗎? **4** [VP2A, C] ~ ***(up),*** make a sudden movement (from pain, surprise, fear, etc) or change of position; jump: (因痛苦、驚訝、恐懼等)驚起;驚跳: *He ~ed up from his seat.* 他從座位上驚跳起來。*He ~ed at the sound of my voice.* 他聽到我的聲音嚇了一跳。**5** [VP2C] move, rise, spring, suddenly: 突然活動、升起、跳起、躍起: *Tears ~ed to her eyes,* suddenly came to her eyes. 她的眼睛裡突然湧出了淚水。*His eyes nearly ~ed out of his head,* suddenly opened wide (in surprise, etc). 他的眼睛突然睜得很大(因驚愕等)。**6** [VP2A,C,6A] (of timbers) (cause to) spring out of position; make or become loose: (指梁木或棟木)(使)歪;(使)彎翹;(使)脫離定位;(使)變鬆: *The ship has ~ed at the seams.* 船的接縫處已經鬆了。*The planks have ~ed.* 厚板已經彎翹了。*The damp has ~ed the timbers.* 潮濕已使梁木彎翹了。**7** [VP6A, 15A, 19B] set going; originate, bring into existence; cause or enable to begin: 發動;引起;使產生;使開始: *This news ~ed me thinking.* 這消息引起我的思緒。*The smoke ~ed her coughing.* 那烟使她咳嗽。*He decided to ~ a newspaper.* 他決定創辦一份報紙。*A rich uncle ~ed him in business,* helped him, eg by supplying capital. 一位有錢的叔父幫助他創辦事業(如提供資金)。*She has ~ed a baby,* (colloq) become pregnant. (俗)她懷孕了。 **8** [VP2C, 15B] (with *adverbial particles*) (與副詞接語連用) ~ ***back,*** begin to return: 開始回程;賦歸: *It's time we ~ed back.* 我們該回去了。~ ***in (on sth/to do sth),*** (colloq) begin to do it: (俗)開始做某事;着手: *Poor Jane! She's ~ed in on a huge pile of ironing.* 可憐的珍!她着手燙那一大堆衣服了。~ ***off,*** begin to move: 開始活動: *The horse ~ed off at a steady trot.* 那馬以穩健的快步出發。~ ***out (to do sth),*** (colloq) begin; take the first steps: (俗)開始;起始;動工: *~ out to write a novel.* 開始寫一部小說。~ ***up,*** **(a)** rise suddenly; jump. 驚起;驚跳。⇨ 4 above. 參看上列第4義。**(b)** come into existence suddenly or unexpectedly: 突然出現;崛起: *Many difficulties have ~ed up.* 突然出現了很多困難。~ ***sth up,*** put (an engine, etc) in motion: 發動(引擎等): *We couldn't ~ up the car.* 我們無法發動那部汽車。 **9** ***to ~ with,*** **(a)** in the first place: 第一;首先: *To ~ with, we haven't enough money, and secondly we haven't enough time.* 第一,我們沒有足够的錢;第二,我們也沒有足够的時間。**(b)** at the beginning: 起初;起始: *We had only six members to ~ with.* 開始的時候我們祇有六個會員。 **10** **ˈ~·ing-gate** *n* barrier where horses ~ a race, raised when the time comes for them to ~. (賽馬時的)起跑門;起賽柵門。**ˈ~·ing-point** *n* place at which a start is made. 起點。**ˈ~·ing-post** *n* place from which competitors ~ in a race. (賽跑的)起跑點;起賽點。**ˈ~·ing-prices** *n pl* (in horse-racing) the odds just before the start of a race. (賽馬)臨賽賭價;起賽價(開賽前一刻的勝算比例)。 **~er** *n* **1** person, horse, etc that takes part in a race: 參加賽跑的人、馬等: *There were only five ~ers in the last race.* 上次的賽跑僅有五人參加。 **2** person who gives the signal for a race to ~. 賽跑中的起賽發令員。***under ~er's orders,*** (of horses, athletes, etc lined up for a race) awaiting the starter's order or signal to ~ the race. (指參加賽跑排成一列的馬、運動員等)等待起賽的口令或訊號。**3** device for causing an engine to ~ working; ignition. (引擎中的)啓動裝置;引燃物或裝置。⇨ *self-~er* at self-. **4** (colloq) first course of a meal. (俗)餐食的第一道食物或菜。***for ~ers,*** (sl) = to ~ with, ⇨ 9 above. (俚)第一;首先;起初(參看上列第9義)。

startle /ˈstɑːtl; ˈstɑrtl̩/ *vt* [VP6A, 15A] give a shock of surprise to; cause to move or jump: 使驚愕;使吃驚;驚嚇;驚動;驚跳: *~d out of one's sleep;* 從睡夢中驚起; *~d out of one's wits,* suffered a sudden great shock. 驚呆了。*She was ~d to see him looking so ill.* 看到他病到這種程度,使她大爲吃驚。*What startling news!* 多令人震驚的消息!

starve /stɑːv; stɑrv/ *vi, vt* **1** [VP6A, 15A, 2A, C, 3A] (cause to) suffer or die from hunger: (使)餓;(使)餓死: *~ to death.* 餓死。*The proud man said he would ~ rather than beg for food.* 那個驕傲的人說他寧願挨餓也不願討飯。*They tried to ~ the army into surrender/~ them out,* force them to surrender by preventing them from getting supplies of food. 他們試圖使守軍因饑餓而投降。***be ~d of/~ for,*** (fig) long for, be in great need of: (喻)渴望;急需;迫切需要: *The motherless children were ~d of/were starving for affection.* 這些沒有母親的孩子們渴望親情。 **2** (colloq) feel very hungry: (俗)感覺很餓: *What's for dinner?—I'm starving!* 晚餐吃什麼?——肚子餓死了! **star·va·tion** /stɑːˈveɪʃn; stɑrˈveʃən/ *n* [U] suffering or death caused by lack of food: 饑餓;餓死: *die of starvation;* 餓死; *starvation wages,* too low to buy adequate supplies of food; 饑餓工資(低到不能維持生活者); *be on a starvation diet,* a diet that is inadequate for health. 吃不足維持健康的飲食。 **~·ling** /ˈstɑːvlɪŋ; ˈstɑrvlɪŋ/ *n* starving or ill-fed person or animal. 挨餓或營養不足的人或動物。

stash /stæʃ; stæʃ/ *vt* [VP15B] ~ ***sth away,*** (sl) put it safely; hide it. (俚)存放;藏起。

state¹ /steɪt; stet/ *n* **1** (*sing* only) condition in which sth or sb is (in circumstances, appearance, mind, health, etc): (僅用單數)(人或物在環境、外觀、心情、健康等方面的)狀態;情況;情形: *The house was in a dirty ~.* 那房子很髒。*These buildings are in a bad ~ of repair,* need to be repaired. 這些房屋極須修葺。*She's in a poor ~ of health.* 她的健康欠佳。*What a ~ he's in!* How anxious, dirty, untidy, etc he is, according to context. 他竟然成了這個樣子!(不安、骯髒、不修邊幅等,根據上下文決定。) *Now don't get into a ~,* (colloq) Don't get excited or anxious! (俗)不要激動或擔心! ~ ***of play,*** **(a)** (cricket) score. (板球)分數。**(b)** (fig) how parties in dispute stand in relation to one another (as likely to win or lose). (喻)爭論雙方的相對處境(如可能獲勝或失敗)。 **2** (often 常作 **S~**) organized political community with its apparatus of government; territory in which this exists; such a community forming part of a federal republic: 國家;領土;(構成聯邦共和國的)州;邦: *Railways in Great Britain belong to the S~.* 大不列顛的鐵路是屬於國家的。*How many S~s are there in the United States of America?* 美國有多少州? *The President's 'Message to the Union' is not addressed to individual S~s but to the Union as a whole/to the nation.* 總統的'國情咨文'不是向各別的州,而是向整個聯邦(國家)發表的。**the (United) S~s** (also 亦作 **the US**), (colloq) the United States of America (the USA). (俗)美國。**Head of S~,** ⇨ head¹(12). ⇨ also *police ~, totalitarian ~* at police, totalitarian. **3** (attrib) of, for, concerned with, the S~(2): (形容用法)國家的;領土的;州的;有關國家的;國務的;公的: *S~ documents/records/archives;* 公文(官方記錄,檔案); *S~ forests,* belonging to the S~, not privately owned; 國有森林; *bring industries under S~ control;* 使工業由國家管制; *S~ socialism,* policy of ~ control of industry etc. 國家社會主義。**the 'S~ Department,** (US) Government Ministry of Foreign Affairs. (美)國務院。**,~'s 'evidence,** (US) evidence for the state in criminal cases. (美)(刑事案件中的)政府(檢查官)提出的證據。Cf 參較 *King's/Queen's evidence* in GB. **'S~·house,** building in which a S~ Legislature sits. 州(邦)議事廳或議會大廈。**,S~ 'Legislature,** representative law-making assembly of a ~ within a federation, eg that of the S~ of Madras in India. 州或邦議會(如印度 Madras 邦議會)。Cf 參較 *the National Assembly* for the whole of India. (印度全國的)國民大會。**,S~(s') 'rights,** (US) all rights which are not delegated to the 'Federal Government in Washington. (美)州權(各州保有而未交付聯邦政府的權利)。**4** [U] civil government: 政府;民治政府: *Church and S~;* 教會與政府;政教; *S~ schools,* contrasted with Church schools. 政府辦的學校(與教會學校相對)。**5** [U] rank; dignity: 階級;地位;尊嚴;榮耀: *persons in every ~ of life.* 各階層人士。*He lived in a style befitting his* (high or low) *~.* 他過着適合他身分的生活方式。**6** [U] pomp; ceremonial formality: 盛觀;隆重的儀禮: *The Queen was in her robes of ~.* 女王著御禮服。***in ~,*** with ceremonial formality: 以隆重的儀禮: *The President was driven in ~ through the streets of Washington.* 總統在隆重的儀禮下乘車穿過華府市街。**7** (attrib) of or for ceremony and formality: (形容用法)儀禮的;儀式的;禮儀用的: *the ~ coach,* eg as used by the Queen on ceremonial occasions; 禮車;貴賓車;御輦; *the ~ apartments at the palace;* 王宮中的大廳; *a ~ call,* (colloq) formal visit. (俗)正式的訪問;官式拜會。**8** ***lie in ~,*** (of a dead person) be placed on view in a public place before burial. (指死人埋葬前)置於公共場所供人憑弔。**9** **'~·room** *n* private cabin (or sleeping-compartment) on a ship (and, in US, in a railway-carriage). (輪船的)特別房艙;睡艙;(美國火車上的)特別包廂;臥室。**~·ly** *adj* (-ier, -iest) impressive; dignified: 威嚴的;莊嚴的;堂皇的;高貴的: *a ~ly dowager;* 儀態高貴的富孀; *the ~ly homes of England,* those of the nobility, etc; 英國貴族等的富麗堂皇的家庭; *with ~ly grace.* 莊重文雅地。**~·li·ness** *n* **'~·craft** *n* [U] = ~smanship. ⇨ below. 參看下列之 statesmanship。**~·less** *adj* (of a person) not recognized as a citizen or national of any country: (指人)無國籍的: *~less persons,* eg some political refugees. 無國籍的人(如某些政治難民)。

state² /steɪt; stet/ *vt* [VP6A, 9] express in words, esp carefully, fully and clearly: 説;陳述(尤指仔細、詳盡而明確地): *~ one's views.* 陳述見解。*I have seen it ~d that....* 我曾經見過有人這麼説…。*He ~d positively that he had never seen the accused man.* 他肯定地說他從未見過被告。**~d** *adj* made known; announced: 説出的;宣佈的;陳述的: *at ~d times/intervals.* 在明示的時間(間隔)。**~·ment** *n* **1** [U] expression in words: 陳述;叙述;藉語言表達: *Clearness of ~ment is more important than beauty of language.* 叙述清楚較用辭優美更重要。**2** [C] stating of facts, views, a problem, etc; report: (事實、見解、問題等的)供述;説明;聲明;報告: *issue a ~ment;* 發表聲明; *a 'bank ~ment;* 銀行報告;銀行結單; *make a ~ment (in court),* give a formal account in a law court setting out the cause of a legal action or its defence. (在法庭上)供述。*My bank sends me monthly ~ments of the state of my bank account.* 銀行按月寄給我存款帳目。

states·man /'steɪtsmən; 'stetsmən/ *n* (*pl* -men) person taking an important part in the management of State affairs; disinterested political leader. 政府高級要員;政治家。**'~·like** *adj* gifted with, showing, wisdom and a broad-minded outlook in public affairs. 有政治家風範的(在政治上具有睿智和遠見的)。**'~·ship** /-ʃɪp; -ʃɪp/ *n* [U] skill and wisdom in managing public affairs. 治國之才;政治家的才能、智慧、技巧等。

static /'stætɪk; 'stætɪk/ *adj* at rest; in a state of balance: 靜止的;靜態的;平衡狀態的: *~ water,* not flowing (eg water in a tank, needing to be pumped); 靜止的水(如儲水池中需要抽掉的水); *~ electricity,* as accumulated on an insulated body. 靜電。**statics** *n* [U] (*pl* with *sing v*) (複數形式作單數用) **1** branch of knowledge dealing with bodies remaining at rest or with forces which balance one another. 靜力學(研究靜態物體或平衡力)。⇨ dynamic. **2** (radio, TV) atmospherics. (無線電,電視)靜電干擾;天電。

sta·tion /'steɪʃn; 'steʃən/ *n* [C] **1** place, building, etc where a service is organized and provided: (提供某種服務的)站,所,台等: *a 'bus/po'lice/'broadcasting/'radar/'fire-~.* 公車站(警察派出所;廣播電台;雷達站;消防隊)。**2** [U] position, or relative position, to be taken up or maintained by sb/sth: (人或物所採取、佔據或保持的)地位;位置;相對或相關的位置: *One of the cruisers was out of ~,* not in its correct position relative to other ships. 有一艘巡洋艦未在其編隊位置。**3** stopping-place for railway trains; the buildings, offices, etc, connected with it: 火車站;火車站的建築物、辦公室等: *a 'goods ~,* one for merchandise. 貨物站。**'~·master** *n* man in charge of a railway ~. (鐵路的)站長。**4** social position, rank: 社會地位、身份等;職分: *people in all ~s of life.* 社會各階層人士。**5** (Australia) (usu extensive) sheep or cattle ranch. (澳州)(通常指大的)牧場;牧羊(或牛)場。**6** military or naval base; those living there. 陸(海)軍基地;駐紮基地人員。**7** **S~s of the Cross,** fourteen crosses, usu with images telling the story of the sufferings and death of Jesus, for religious devotions, set up in a church or along a path. (置於教堂中或道路旁供人膜拜之)十四幅耶穌受難像。**8** **'~-wagon** *n* (US) estate car. (美)旅行轎車。⇨ estate(5). □ *vt* [VP6A, 15A] put (sb, oneself, a military or naval force, etc) at or in a certain place: 安置;配置;置(某人、自己、一支軍隊等)於某處: *The detective ~ed himself among the bushes,* hid there. 那偵探藏身於矮叢中。*HMS Tiger has been ~ed at Hong Kong for the last two years.* 英國皇家軍艦「老虎號」派駐香港已有兩年。

sta·tion·ary /'steɪʃənrɪ *US:* -nerɪ; 'steʃən,ɛrɪ/ *adj* **1** not intended to be moved from place to place: 固定的;定置的;非移動的: *a ~ crane/engine.* 固定式起重機(發動機)。⇨ mobile(1). **2** not moving or changing: 不活動的;不變動的: *remain ~;* 保持不變動; *collide with a ~ van.* 與一停着的貨車相撞。

sta·tioner /'steɪʃnə(r); 'steʃənɚ/ *n* dealer in ~y. 文具商。**~y** /'steɪʃənrɪ *US:* -nerɪ; 'steʃən,ɛrɪ/ *n* [U] writing materials, etc. 文具。**Her Majesty's/the 'S~y Office** (abbr 略作 **HMSO**), government department which publishes and distributes government papers, books, etc. (英)政府文書部(出版及發行政府文件及書籍等的部門)。

stat·is·tics /stəˈtɪstɪks ; stəˈtɪstɪks/ *n* **1** (with *pl v*) collection of information shown in numbers: (用複數動詞)統計;統計數字: *S～ suggest that the population of this country will be doubled in ten years' time.* 統計顯示本國人口十年後將增加一倍。**vital ～**, ⇨ vital. **2** (with *sing v*) the science of ～. (用單數動詞)統計學。**stat·is·ti·cal** /stəˈtɪstɪkl ; stəˈtɪstɪkl̩/ *adj* of ～: 統計的;統計學的: *statistical tables／experts.* 統計圖表(專家)。**stat·is·ti·cally** /-klɪ ; -klɪ/ *adv* **stat·is·ti·cian** /ˌstætɪˈstɪʃn ; ˌstætəsˈtɪʃən/ *n* person who is expert in ～. 統計專家;統計學家。

statu·ary /ˈstætʃʊərɪ *US:* -ʊerɪ ; ˈstætʃʊˌɛrɪ/ *adj* of or for statues: 雕像的;雕塑的;雕塑用的:～*marble.* 雕塑用的大理石。□ *n* [U] sculpture; statues. 雕塑;雕像。

statue /ˈstætʃuː ; ˈstætʃu/ *n* figure of a person, animal, etc in wood, stone, bronze, etc, usu of life size or more than life size. 雕像;塑像;鑄像(木、石、銅等製成，通常與活物體積相等，或大於活物)。 ⇨ the illus at discus. 參看 discus 之挿圖。**statu·ette** /ˌstætʃʊˈet ; ˌstætʃʊˈɛt/ *n* small ～. 小雕像;小塑像。**statu·esque** /ˌstætʃʊˈesk ; ˌstætʃʊˈɛsk/ *adj* like a ～ in having clear-cut outlines, in being motionless, etc. 宛若雕像的;似雕像的。

stat·ure /ˈstætʃə(r) ; ˈstætʃɚ/ *n* [U] (person's) natural bodily height: (人的)身高;身長;身材: *short of ～;* 身材短的; (fig) mental or moral quality; calibre. (喻)氣質;器量;才幹。

status /ˈsteɪtəs ; ˈstetəs/ *n* [U] person's legal, social or professional position in relation to others: (人的)地位;身分: *have no official ～*, no official rank, eg in the Civil Service. 未任公職;無公職身分。*Many young people desire ～* (= an established social position) *and security.* 許多年輕人希冀社會地位與生活保障。ˈ**～ symbol,** sth which the ownership of is thought to be evidence of social rank, wealth, etc, eg a better car than one's neighbours, a yacht, a colour TV. 身分標誌;身分表徵(被視爲可代表其社會地位、財富等者，如華麗轎車、遊艇、彩色電視機等)。

status quo /ˌsteɪtəs ˈkwəʊ ; ˈstetəsˈkwo/ (Lat) social situation as it is now: (拉)社會現狀: *conservatives who defend the ～.* 爲社會現狀辯護的保守人士。 ～ ˈ**ante** /ˈæntɪ ; ˈæntɪ/, social situation as it was before a recent change. 社會原狀; 新近變動之前的社會狀況。

stat·ute /ˈstætʃuːt ; ˈstætʃʊt/ *n* [C] (written) law passed by Parliament or other law-making body. 成文法;法規;條例。ˈ**～ law** *n* all the ～s (contrasted with *case-law* and *common law*). 成文法 (與case-law 及 common law 相對)。 ⇨ case¹(2) ˌcommon¹(1). ˈ**～-book** *n* book(s) containing the ～ law. 成文法典; 法規全書。 **statu·tory** /ˈstætʃʊtrɪ *US:* -tɔːrɪ ; ˈstætʃʊˌtorɪ/ *adj* fixed, done, required, by ～: 法定的;依法完成的;依照法規的: *statutory control of prices and incomes.* 物價與工資的法定管制。

staunch¹ /stɔːntʃ ; stɔntʃ/ (US also **stanch** /stɑːntʃ *US:* stæntʃ ; stɑntʃ/) *vt* [VP6A] stop the flow of (esp blood); check the flow of blood from (a wound): 制止(尤指血)的流動; 止住(傷口) 出血: *～ blood／a wound.* 止血(止住一傷口流血)。

staunch² /stɔːntʃ ; stɔntʃ/ *adj* (of a friend, supporter, etc) trustworthy; loyal; firm. (指朋友、支持者等)可信賴的;可靠的;忠實的;堅定的。**～·ly** *adv* **～·ness** *n*

stave¹ /steɪv ; stev/ *n* **1** one of the curved pieces of wood used for the side of a barrel or tub. 桶板;桶材(用作桶邊的弧形木材)。 **2** (music) (音樂) = staff(6). 譜表。 **3** stanza; verse. 詩節;詩句。

stave² /steɪv ; stev/ *vt, vi* (*pt, pp* ～d or stove /stəʊv ; stov/) **1** [VP15B] *～ sth in,* break, smash, make a hole in: 打破;砸破;擊穿;鑿孔於: *The side of the yacht was ～d in by the collision.* 該遊艇的舷側被撞穿了。[VP3A] *～ in,* become or get broken or smashed: 被打破;被砸破;被擊穿: *The boat stove in when it struck the rocks.* 該船觸礁時被撞穿了。 **2** [VP15B] *～ sth off,* keep off, delay (danger, disaster, bankruptcy, etc). 避開;延緩(危險,災難,破產等)。

stay¹ /steɪ ; ste/ *vi, vt* **1** [VP2A, B, C, 4A] be, remain, continuously in a place or condition (for a long or short time, permanently or temporarily, as specified by the context): 停留;逗留;待在或保持某種情況或位置 (長期或短期，永久或暫時，由上下文指明) : *～ in the house／at home／in bed;* 待在房子裡(家裡,床上) ; ～ (= be a guest) *at a hotel／with friends.* 住在旅館裡(朋友家裡)。*I'm too busy to ～／I can't ～,* I must leave now. 我太忙,不能再待了(我必須走了)。*I can only ～ a few minutes.* 我祇能待幾分鐘。*I ～ed to see what would happen.* 我留下來看進一步的發展。*Why don't you ～ with us* (as a guest) *when you next visit Oxford?* 你下次到牛津來,住在我們這裡好嗎？ *Jenny's ～ing in Dublin* (eg at a hotel, or with friends) *for a few weeks, but she now lives／is living* (= has her home) *in Belfast.* 珍妮目前在都柏林暫住幾個星期,但她的家是在貝爾發斯特。*～ for (an event／meal); ～ to (a meal),* remain for it: 爲(某件事或一餐飯)而留下;留下來(吃飯): *Won't you ～ for／to supper?* 你不留下來吃晚飯嗎？ *～ in,* **(a)** not go outdoors: 不出門;待在家裡: *The doctor advised me to ～ in for a few days.* 醫生勸我在家裡待幾天。**(b)** remain in school after hours: 放學後留在學校: *The teacher made the boy ～ in and do his exercises again.* 老師命該男生留在學校重做他的練習。 *～ out,* **(a)** remain outdoors: 待在外面;待在戶外: *Tell the children they mustn't ～ out after dark.* 告訴孩子們天黑以後不可待在外面。**(b)** remain on strike: 繼續罷工: *The miners ～ed out for several weeks.* 礦工們罷工達數週之久。*～ up,* not go to bed: 不就寢;熬夜: *I ～ed up reading until midnight.* 我讀書一直讀到午夜才睡。*I'll be late home, but please don't ～ up for me.* 我要晚一點才能回家,請不用等門。 *be ˌhere to ˈ～; have ˌcome to ˈ～,* (colloq) be permanent: (俗)持久;繼續流行;變成根深蒂固: *I hope that the principle of equality of opportunity for men and women has come to ～／is here to ～.* 我希望男女機會平等的原則能持久。*come to ～ (with sb),* (of a person) visit sb (ie temporarily); start to live with sb (ie permanently): 到某人處小住;開始與某人長住: *Sue is coming to ～ for a week next month.* 蘇下月來住一個星期。 *Since my wife's mother came to ～ with us last year, the TV has been on more or less continuously.* 自從去年我的岳母來與我們同住,電視幾乎沒有停過。ˈ**～-at-home** *n* person who seldom goes anywhere; unadventurous person. 甚少離家外出的人; 不喜出遠門的人。**2** [VP2C] continue in a certain state: 繼續保持某種狀態;維持;保持: ～ *single,* not marry. 不結婚;保持單身。*That fellow never ～s sober for long,* frequently gets drunk. 那傢伙經常爛醉(難得清醒)。 *～ put,* (colloq) remain where placed: (俗)待在原處;停留在原處: *I wish this earring would ～ put instead of falling out every time.* 我希望這個耳環攏緊，不要老是掉下來。 **3** [VP6A] stop, delay, postpone, check: 停止; 延緩; 延後; 制止: ～ *the progress of a disease;* 防止疾病惡化; ～ *one's hand,* refrain from doing sth; 住手(抑制不做某事) ; ～ (= delay) *judgement／proceedings.* 遲遲不作評斷(拖延訴訟程序)。 **4** [VP2A, 6A] be able to continue (work, etc); show endurance: 能够繼續(工作等);顯示耐力: *The horse lacks ˈ～ing power.* 這馬缺乏耐力。*～ the course,* be able to continue to the end of the race, (fig) the struggle, etc. 跑完全程;(喻)堅持到底。 **5** (usu in imper; archaic or lit) pause: (通常用於祈使句中;古或文)停止;停下: *S～!* (= Stop!) *You've forgotten your overcoat!* 等一下！你忘了你的大衣！ **6** [VP6A] satisfy for a time: 暫時滿足;滿足一時: *have a sandwich to ～ one's hunger.* 吃一塊三明治壓饑。□ *n* **1** period of ～ing; visit: 停留;逗留;做客: *make a short ～ in*

Karachi; 在喀拉蚩作短暫停留; *a fortnight's ~ with my rich uncle.* 到我那有錢的叔父家做客兩星期。**2** (legal) delay; postponement. (法律) 延遲; 延緩; 延後; 中止。~ ***of execution,*** order that a court judgement need not be carried out for the time being. 延緩執行(某一法庭裁決)。 **~er** *n* person or animal able to ~(4): 有耐力的人或動物: *The horse that won the race is a good ~er.* 獲勝的那匹馬是一匹很有耐力的馬。

stay² /steɪ ; ste/ *n* [C] **1** rope or wire supporting a mast, pole, etc. (支持桅,杆等的)繩索或鋼絲。⇨ the illus at barque. 參看 barque 之插圖。 **2** (fig) support: (喻)支持物; 倚靠: *the ~ of his old age,* person who helped him, eg by giving him a home, looking after him. 他老年時的倚靠(如供他住處、照顧他等之人)。 **3** (*pl*) (old-fashioned name for) kind of corset reinforced with strips of stiff material (bone or plastic). (複)(舊稱)有硬物支撐的束腹。□ *vt* [VP6A, 15B] ~ ***(up),*** support by means of a wire, rope or prop. (以繩索,鋼絲或支撐物)支撐; 支持。

stead /sted ; stɛd/ *n* [U] ***in sb's ~,*** in his place; instead of him. 代替某人。 ***stand sb in good ~,*** be useful or helpful to him in time of need: 在需要時對某人有助益: *My anorak has stood me in good ~ this winter.* 我這件帶兜帽的夾克今年冬天對我很有用。

stead·fast /ˈstedfɑːst *US:* -fæst ; ˈstɛd,fæst/ *adj* firm and unchanging; keeping firm (*to*): 堅定的; 不變的; 不移的: *a ~ gaze;* 凝視; *~ in adversity;* 處變不驚; *be ~ to one's principles.* 堅守自己的原則。 **~·ly** *adv* **~·ness** *n*

steady /ˈstedɪ ; ˈstɛdɪ/ *adj* (-ier, -iest) **1** firmly fixed or supported; balanced; not likely to fall over: 堅固的; 牢靠的; 平衡的; 不動搖的: *make a table ~,* eg by repairing a leg; 使桌子站穩(如修復一隻桌腿); *on a ~ foundation;* 在穩固的基礎上; *not very ~ on one's legs,* eg of sb after a long illness. 步履不太穩(如長期病後)。 **2** regular in movement, speed, direction, etc: (動作,速度,方向等)規律的; 穩定的: *a ~ wind/speed/rate of progress/improvement.* 穩定的風(速度,進度,進步)。 **3** regular in behaviour, habits, etc: (行爲、習慣等)規則的; 穩健的; 可靠的: *a ~ young man;* 穩健的年輕人; *a ~ worker.* 可靠的工作者。 **4** constant, unchanging: 持續的; 不變的: *a ~ faith/purpose.* 不變的信仰(目標)。 **5** (in exclamations) (用於驚嘆句中) *Keep her ~!* (naut) Keep the ship on her course unchanged. (航海)航向不變! ***S~ (on)!*** (colloq, used as a warning) Control yourself! (俗)(用作警告)鎮定! 別急! 留心! □ *adv* = steadily. ***go ~,*** (colloq) go about regularly with sb of the opposite sex, though not being engaged to marry: (俗)與異性固定交往(雖尚未論婚嫁): *Are Tony and Jane going ~?* 湯尼同珍已經是情侶了嗎? □ *n* (sl) regular boy-friend or girl-friend. (俚)固定的異性朋友; 固定的情人。□ *vt, vi* [VP6A, 2A] make or become ~; keep ~: 使或變得牢靠、穩固等; 保持堅固、穩定等: *~ a boat/table-leg;* 使船(桌子腿)穩定; *~ oneself by holding on to the rail,* eg on the deck of a ship that is rolling. 扶住欄杆使自己站穩(如在顚簸的船甲板上)。 *Prices are ~ing.* 物價漸趨穩定。 **stead·ily** /ˈstedɪlɪ ; ˈstɛdəlɪ/ *adv* in a ~ manner: 堅固地; 穩定地; 不變地; 穩健地: *work steadily.* 規律地工作。 *His health is getting steadily worse.* 他的健康每況愈下。 **steadi·ness** *n*

steak /steɪk ; stek/ *n* [U, C] (thick slice of) meat or fish for (usu) frying or grilling: (供煎,烤等的)肉; 魚; 肉片; 魚片; 肉排: *fillet/rump ~;* 菲力牛排(大腿部肉排); *two tuna ~s.* 兩片鮪排。

steal /stiːl ; stil/ *vt, vi* (*pt* stole /stəʊl ; stol/, *pp* stolen /ˈstəʊlən ; ˈstolən/) **1** [VP6A, 14, 2A] ~ ***sth (from sb),*** take (sb else's property) secretly, without right, unlawfully: 偷; 竊取(他人財物): *Someone has stolen my watch.* 有人把我的錶偷走了。 *I have had my watch stolen.* 我的錶被人偷走了。 Cf 參較 I have been *robbed of* my watch. 我的錶被人搶走了。 *It is wrong to ~.* 偷東西是不法的行爲。 **2** [VP6A, 15A] obtain by surprise or a trick: 出其不意地取得; 以詭計獲得: *~ a kiss from sb;* 偷吻某人; *~ a glance at sb in the mirror.* 在鏡中偷瞥某人。 ***~ a march on sb,*** do sth before him and so gain an advantage. 占先; (偷偷地)搶先某人。 **3** [VP2C] move, come, go (*in, out, away, etc*) secretly and quietly: 偷偷地移動; 潛行; 隱祕而悄悄地移動: *He stole into the room.* 他潛入房間。 *A tear stole down her cheek.* 一顆淚珠在她的面頰上悄悄地滾下。 *The morning light was ~ing through the shutters.* 晨光悄悄地穿過了百葉窗。

stealth /stelθ ; stɛlθ/ *n* [U] (only used in) (僅用於) ***by ~,*** secretly and quietly: 偷偷地; 祕密地: *enter a house by ~.* 潛入一房屋。 **~y** *adj* (-ier, -iest) doing things, done, quietly and secretly: 偷偷進行的; 祕密做成的: *~y footsteps.* 潛行的脚步。 **~·ily** /-ɪlɪ ; -əlɪ/ *adv*

steam /stiːm ; stim/ *n* [U] **1** gas or vapour into which boiling water changes; power obtained from ~: 蒸汽; 水氣; 蒸汽產生的動力: *~-covered windows;* 佈滿水氣的窗子; *a building heated by ~.* 藉蒸汽取暖的建築物。 *The ship was able to proceed under her own ~,* using her own engines and not needing to be towed. 那條船可藉其本身的蒸汽動力前進(無須拖船曳進)。 ***Full ~ ahead!*** order to go forward at full speed. (命令)全速前進! ***get up/raise ~,*** provide ~ at a higher pressure in the boilers, etc: 提高或增加(鍋爐等裡的)蒸汽壓力: *The stokers got up ~.* 火伕增加了蒸汽的壓力。 **2** (fig uses; colloq) energy. (比喻用法; 俗)能力; 精力。 ***get up ~,*** collect one's energy; become excited or angry. 振作; 奮發; 激動; 發怒。 ***let off ~,*** release surplus energy or emotion; become less excited. 發洩過剩的精力或激動的情緒; 變得不太激動。 ***run out of ~,*** become exhausted: 變得筋疲力竭; 耗盡: *Is there a danger of the housing programme running out of ~,* losing its impetus? 住宅興建計畫有半途而廢的危險嗎? ***under one's own ~,*** without help from others. 憑一己之力; 不靠別人之幫助。 **3** (compounds) (複合字) **ˈ~·boat** *n* vessel propelled by ~. 汽船。 **ˌ~-ˈboiler** *n* vessel in which ~ is generated (to work an engine). 蒸汽鍋爐。 **~ brake/hammer/whistle/winch, etc** *nn* worked by ~. 蒸汽煞車(汽鎚,汽笛,汽絞盤等)。 **ˌ~-ˈcoal** *n* coal used for heating in ~-boilers. 汽鍋用煤。 **ˈ~-engine** *n* locomotive or stationary engine worked or driven by pressure of ~. 蒸汽機。 **ˌ~-ˈheat** *n* heat given out by ~ from radiators, pipes, etc. 汽熱。□ *vt: ~-heated buildings,* kept warm by ~-heat. 藉蒸汽取暖的建築物。 **ˌ~ ˈradio** *n* (sl) sound broadcasting (contrasted with TV). (英俚)聲音廣播; 無線電廣播(爲電視之對)。 **ˈ~-roller** *n* heavy, slow-moving locomotive with wide wheels used in road-making. 蒸汽壓路機; 汽輾。 □ *vt* [VP6A] crush as with a ~-roller: (似用蒸汽壓路機般)壓平; 粉碎: *~-roller all opposition.* 粉碎一切反對(力量)。 **ˈ~·ship** *n* ship driven by ~. 汽船; 輪船。□ *vi, vt* **1** [VP2A, C] give out ~ or vapour: 蒸發; 冒蒸汽: *~ing hot coffee.* 冒汽的熱咖啡。 *The kettle was ~ing (away) on the stove.* 水壺在爐子上冒汽。 **2** [VP2C] move, work, etc under (or as if under) the power of ~: 藉(或似藉)蒸汽力量行駛, 運轉等: *a ship ~ing up the Red Sea;* 航行於紅海的船; *~ at ten knots.* 以每小時十浬的速度航行。 *The train ~ed into the station.* 火車駛入車站。 **3** [VP6A, 22] cook, soften, clean, by the use of ~: 蒸; 蒸軟; 用蒸汽清除或清洗: *~ fish;* 蒸魚; *~ open an envelope,* use steam to soften the gum on the flap. 用蒸汽(軟化封口的膠而)開啓信封。 **4** ~ ***up,*** become misty with condensed ~: 因凝結的蒸汽而變模糊不清: *The windows ~ed up.* 窗戶蒙上一層蒸汽。 ***be/get (all) ~ed up,*** (colloq) become excited and perhaps violent:

(俗)變得激動、興奮、憤怒等: *Now don't get all ~ed up over nothing!* 不要無緣無故地發脾氣嘛！ **~er** *n* **1** ~ship. 輪船;汽船。 **2** vessel in which food is cooked by being ~ed. 蒸煮器;蒸籠。 **~y** *adj* of, like, full of, ~: 蒸汽的;像蒸汽的;充滿蒸汽的: *~y windows;* 水氣朦朧的窗子; *the ~y heat of the rainy season in the tropics.* 熱帶雨季潮濕的悶熱。

steed /sti:d ; stid/ *n* (liter or hum) horse. (文或諧)馬。

steel /sti:l ; stil/ *n* [U] **1** strong, hard alloy of iron and carbon, used for knives, tools, machinery, etc. 鋼(鐵與碳結合成的合金)。 **~ band** *n* (as, orig, in Trinidad) band of musicians who use empty oil drums as percussion instruments. (起源於千里達島)鋼鐵樂隊(利用空油桶作打擊樂器所組成的樂隊)。 **'~-clad** *adj* covered with ~ armour. 裝甲的;穿着甲冑的。 **,~-'plated** *adj* covered with ~ plates; armoured. 裝甲的;覆以鋼板的。 **~ wool,** fine ~ shavings (used for scouring and polishing). 鋼絲絨(用以擦亮或磨光物件)。 **'~-works** *n pl* (often with *sing v*) factory where ~ is made. (常用單數動詞)煉鋼廠。 **2** ~ weapon, eg a sword, contrasted with a firearm: 鋼製武器(如刀劍,與 firearm 相對): *an enemy worthy of one's ~,* (rhet or fig) one who will fight well. (修辭或喻)勁敵;强敵。 **cold ~,** ⇨ cold¹(1). □ *vt* [VP6A, 15A, 16A] harden: 使堅硬: *~ oneself/one's heart (against pity/to do sth).* 硬起心腸(狠起心來)(不寄以同情,做某事)。 **~y** *adj* like ~ in hardness, polish, brightness, etc. 堅硬、光亮等如鋼的。

a steel band

steel·yard /'sti:ljɑ:d ; 'stɪljəd/ *n* balance(1) with an arm in two parts, the longer side being graduated for a weight which slides along it. 秤;提秤。

steen·bok /'sti:nbɒk ; 'stin,bɑk/ *n* kind of small S African antelope. (南非洲產的)小羚羊。

steep¹ /sti:p ; stip/ *adj* (-er, -est) **1** (of a slope) rising or falling sharply: (指斜坡)陡峭的;險峻的: *a ~ gradient/path/descent;* 陡峭的傾斜度(小徑,下坡); *a ~ roof,* with a ~ pitch. 陡峭的屋頂。 **2** (colloq, of a demand) unreasonable; excessive: (俗,指一項要求)不合理的;過分的: *It's a bit ~ that I should pay for all of you!* 要我爲你們全體付帳,有點過分吧! *£10 for this dictionary—isn't that a bit ~?* 這本字典索價十鎊—是不是貴了一點? *That story's rather ~,* difficult to believe, exaggerated. 那故事不甚合情理。 **~·ly** *adv* **~·ness** *n* **~en** /'sti:pən ; 'stipən/ *vt, vi* [VP6A, 2A] make or become ~ or ~er. (使)變爲陡峭或更陡峭; (使)變得險峻或更險峻。 **'~·ish** /-ɪʃ ; -ɪʃ/ *adj* rather ~. 頗爲陡峭的;有點險峻的。

steep² /sti:p ; stip/ *vt, vi* [VP6A, 14, 2A] **~ sth (in sth), 1** soak or bathe in liquid: 浸;漬;濡濕: *~ onions in vinegar,* to pickle them. 醃泡洋葱於醋中。 **2** (fig) pervade with; get a thorough knowledge of: (喻)沉緬;充滿;精通: *~ed in ignorance/prejudice;* 充滿無知(偏見); *a scholar ~ed in the literature of ancient Greece and Rome.* 精通古希臘羅馬文學的學者。

steeple /'sti:pl ; 'stipl̩/ *n* high tower with a spire, rising above the roof of a church. (教堂的)尖閣或尖塔。 ⇨ the illus at church. 參看 church 之插圖。 **'~·chase** *n* cross-country horse-race or race on foot with obstacles such as fences, hedges and ditches. 越野障礙賽馬;越野障礙賽跑。 ⇨ *flat racing* at flat²(1). **'~·jack** *n* man who climbs ~s, tall chimney-stacks, etc to do repairs. 高空作業工人(如裝修教堂尖塔,高煙囪等之人)。

steer¹ /stɪə(r) ; stɪr/ *n* young (usu castrated) male of an animal of the ox family, raised for beef. 牡犢(通常閹過,飼供食用)。 ⇨ bull¹(1), bullock, heifer, ox.

steer² /stɪə(r) ; stɪr/ *vt, vi* [VP6A, 2A, C] direct the course of (a boat, ship, car, etc): 駕駛(舟、船、汽車等): *~ north;* 向北行駛; *~ by the stars;* 藉星(的位置)辨別方向行駛; (with passive force): (含被動意): *a ship that ~s (= is ~ed) well/easily/badly.* 好(容易,不好)駕駛的船。 **~ clear of,** (fig) avoid. (喻)避開。 **'~·ing-gear** *n* [U] (of a ship) rudder and the mechanism controlling it. (指船)舵及操舵裝置。 **'~·ing-wheel** *n* **(a)** (on a ship) wheel turned to control for rudder. (船上的)舵輪。 **(b)** (on a motor-vehicle) wheel for ~ing (mounted on the *'~ing-column*). (汽車上的)方向盤;駕駛盤。 ⇨ the illus at motor. 參看 motor 之插圖。 **~s·man** /-zmən ; -zmən/ *n* (*pl* -men) person who ~s a vessel. (掌)舵手。

steer·age /'stɪərɪdʒ ; 'stɪrɪdʒ/ *n* [U, C] (*sing* only, or attrib) (僅用單數形,或作形容用法) **1** act or effect of steering. 駕駛;操舵。 **2** that part of a ship nearest the rudder; this section formerly used for providing for passengers travelling at the lowest fares. 船靠近舵的部分;統艙(票價最低的客艙)。 **'~·way** *n* forward progress needed by a vessel to enable her to be controlled by the helm. 舵效速率(使舵發生功效的最低速度)。

stele /'sti:lɪ ; 'stili/ *n* (also 亦作 **stela** /'sti:lə ; 'stilə/ *pl* stelae /-li: ; -li/) (Gk archaeology) upright slab or pillar, usu with a sculptured design or inscription. (希臘考古學)石碑;石柱(通常刻有題字或圖案)。

stel·lar /'stelə(r) ; 'stelɚ/ *adj* of stars: 星的: *~ light.* 星光。

stem¹ /stem ; stɛm/ *n* **1** part of a plant coming up from the roots; part of a leaf, flower or fruit that joins it to the main stalk or twig. (植物的)莖;幹;葉柄;花梗;果柄。 ⇨ the illus at flower. 參看 flower 之插圖。 **~med** *suff* (with *adjj*) (與形容詞連用) *,long-'~med, ,short-'~med, ,thick-'~med,* having long, short, thick, ~s. 長莖(幹,柄,梗等)的,短莖(幹,柄,梗等)的,粗莖(幹,柄,梗等)的。 **2** ~-shaped part, eg the slender part of a wineglass, between the base and the bowl, the part of a tobacco pipe between the mouthpiece and the bowl. 莖狀部分;杯(子的)脚;烟斗桿等。 **3** root or main part of a noun or verb from which other words are made by additions (esp inflectional endings). (名詞或動詞的)語幹(可衍生其他字的主體部分)。 **4** main upright timber at the bow of a ship. 船首;船頭;船首材;船首柱。 ***from ~ to stern,*** throughout the whole length of a ship. 從船首到船尾。 □ *vi* (-mm-) [VP3A] **~ from,** arise from; have as origin. 發生;源於;來自。

stem² /stem ; stɛm/ *vt* (-mm-) [VP6A] **1** check,

stems

stop, dam up (a stream, a flow of liquid, etc). 阻止;遏制;堵住(河流,水流等)。 **2** make headway against the resistance of: 逆…而行;逆…而上;對抗;抗拒: ~ *the tide/current;* 逆潮(流)而上; (fig) (喻) ~ *the tide of popular indignation.* 不顧公憤。

stench /stentʃ; stɛntʃ/ *n* [C] horrid smell. 惡臭;臭氣。

sten·cil /ˈstensl ; ˈstɛnsḷ/ *n* [C] thin sheet of metal, cardboard, waxed paper, etc with letters or designs cut through it; lettering, design, etc printed by inking paper, etc through a stencil: 模板; 型板(有雕空之文字或圖案的金屬板,厚紙板,蠟紙等);(在鋼板上書寫的)蠟紙;(模板、用蠟紙等印出的)文字或圖案等: *cut a* ~, eg by typing without the ribbon on a waxed sheet. 寫蠟紙;打字於蠟紙上。□ *vt* (-ll-, US also -l-) [VP6A] produce (a pattern, wording, etc) by using a ~. 用模板,蠟紙等印刷(文字,花樣等)。

Sten gun /ˈsten gʌn ; ˈstɛn gʌn/ *n* small kind of machine-gun, usu fired from the hip. 斯頓機槍(一種衝鋒槍)。

sten·ogra·phy /stəˈnɒgrəfɪ ; stəˈnagrəfɪ/ *n* (US) shorthand. (美) 速記; 速記法。 **sten·ogra·pher** /-fə(r) ; -fɚ/ *n* (US) writer of shorthand (GB 英 = ˌ*shorthand-*ˈ*typist*). (美)速記員。

sten·torian /stenˈtɔːrɪən ; stɛnˈtorɪən/ *adj* (of a voice) loud and strong. (指人聲)宏亮的;響亮的。

step[1] /step ; stɛp/ *vi, vt* (-pp-) **1** [VP2C] move the foot, or one foot after the other (forward, or in the direction indicated): 走;舉步;踏步;行走: ~ *across a stream;* 走過小溪; ~ *into a boat;* 踏進船中; ~ *on to/off the platform;* 走上(下)講臺; ~ *across to a neighbour's,* cross (the road) to his house. 越過馬路到隣居家去。~ ***this way,*** (polite invitation to) follow sb somewhere, eg into a room. (客套話)請往這邊走;請隨我來(如進入某房間)。~ ***on the gas;*** ~ ***on it,*** **(a)** (gas = gasoline) press down the accelerator pedal of a motor vehicle to increase speed. 踏汽車等的加速器加快速度;踩油門。**(b)** (sl) hurry. (俚)趕緊;趕快。ˈ~**·ping-stone** *n* **(a)** one of a number of flat stones placed in a shallow stream, so that it can be crossed with dry feet. (淺河中的)踏脚石。**(b)** (fig) means of attaining sth: (喻)達成目標的手段;進身之階: *a first* ~*ping-stone to success.* 成功的第一步。ˈ~**-ins** *n pl* (colloq) woman's undergarment or shoes, put on by being ~ped into. (俗)由脚部套上的女用襯裙、襯褲等;不繫帶的鞋子。 **2** [VP2C, 15B] (uses with *adverbial particles*): (與副詞接語連用的用法):

step aside, **(a)** move to one side. 走到一邊;站開。**(b)** (fig) allow sb else to take one's place. (喻)讓位子給別人。

step down, (fig) resign (to make way for sb else). (喻)辭職;讓賢。

step in, (fig) intervene (either to help or hinder): (喻)(爲幫助或阻止而)介入;干預;干涉: *If the police hadn't* ~*ped in during the demonstration there would have been a violent struggle.* 示威時若不是警察介入,早就引起激烈的打鬥了。

step sth off/out, measure by taking steps: (以脚)步測(量): ~ *out a distance of ten metres.* 步測十公尺距離。

step out, **(a)** walk faster, walk briskly. 快步行進;輕快地走。**(b)** (colloq) have a gay time, a busy social life. (俗)過歡樂而繁忙的社交生活;尋歡作樂。

step sth up, **(a)** (naut) fix (the foot of a mast) in its socket. (航海)插(桅脚)於桅座中。**(b)** increase: 增加;促進: ~ *up production;* 促進生產; ~ *up the doses (of medicine);* 增加(藥的)劑量; ~ *up the campaign,* put more effort into it. 加强該運動。

step[2] /step ; stɛp/ *n* **1** act of stepping once; distance covered by doing this: 步;舉步;一步的距離: *He was walking with slow* ~*s.* 他慢步行走。*The water was deeper at every* ~. 每走一步水就更深。*We must retrace our* ~*s,* go back. 我們必須折回(循原路回去)。*It's only a few* ~*s farther.* 祇有幾步遠了。*We have made a long* ~ (fig, much progress) *towards success.* (喻)我們已向成功邁進一大步。***watch one's*** ~, be careful or cautious. 謹慎;小心。~ ***by*** ~, gradually; by degrees. 逐漸地;一步一步地。ˈ**one-**~, ˈ**two-**~ *nn* names of dances. (舞名)單步舞,双步舞。 **2** (ˈ**foot·**)~, sound made by somebody walking; way of walking (as seen or heard): 脚步聲;步態;步調: *We heard (foot)*~*s outside.* 我們聽到外面有脚步聲。*That's Lucy—I recognize her* ~. 那是露西──我聽得出她的脚步聲。 **3** ***be/get in/out of*** ~ ***(with),*** **(a)** put/not put the right foot to the ground at the same time as others (in walking, marching, dancing). (走路、齊步行進、跳舞等)(與…)合(不合)步調;(與…)步調一致(不一致)。**(b)** conform/not conform with other members of a group: 與(一團體中的其他分子)諧調(不諧調): *He's out of* ~ *with the rest of us.* 他同我們大家不諧調。***keep*** ~ ***(with),*** walk or march in ~ (with). (與…)步調一致地行走或行進。***break*** ~, get out of ~. 走亂步伐。 **4** one action in a series of actions with a view to effecting a purpose: 步驟;措施: *take* ~*s to prevent the spread of influenza;* 採取步驟阻止流行性感冒蔓延; *a false* ~, a mistaken action. 錯誤的步驟(或措施)。*What's the next* ~, What are we to do next? 下一步該怎麼辦? *That would be a rash* ~ *to take.* 那會是輕率的措施。 **5** place for the foot when going from one level to another: 臺階;梯級;踏脚處: *Mind the* ~*s when you go down into the cellar.* 走下地下室時當心梯級。*They had to cut* ~*s in the ice as they climbed.* 他們往上爬時,必須在冰上鑿出踏脚處。*The child was sitting on the bottom* ~. 那孩子坐在最底下的臺階上。 ~***s, a pair of*** ~***s, a*** ˈ~**-ladder** *nn* portable folding ladder with ~s, not rungs and usu a small platform at the top. 摺梯;四脚梯。 **6** grade, rank; promotion: 官階的一級;階級;升遷: *When do you get your next* ~ *up?* When will you be promoted? 你何時晉級(升遷)?

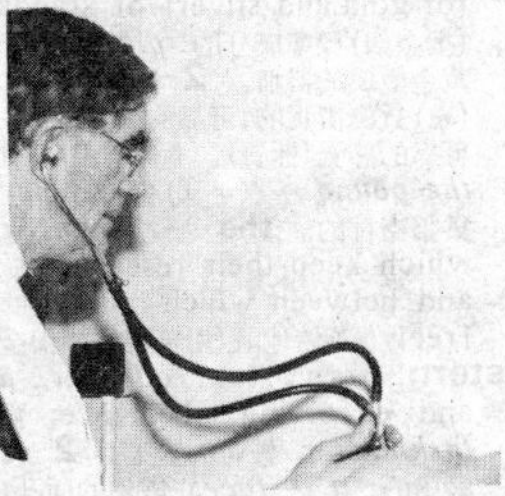

a step-ladder a stethoscope

step- /step ; stɛp/ *pref* (used to show a relationship not by blood but by a later marriage) (用以表示非血親關係,而係由再婚產生的家庭關係) ˈ~**-child/·son/·daughter** *nn* child of an earlier marriage of one's wife or husband. 與前妻或前夫所生的孩子(兒子,女兒);晚子;晚女。ˈ~**·brother/·sister** *nn* child of an earlier marriage of one's stepfather or stepmother. 異父(母)兄弟(姊妹);隔山兄弟(姊妹)。 ˈ~**·father/·mother/·parent** *nn* one's parent's later husband or wife. 繼父(繼母;繼父母)。

steppe /step ; stɛp/ *n* [C] level, grassy treeless plain, esp in SE Europe and central Asia. (尤指東南歐及中亞的)無樹大平原;大草原。⇨ pampas, prairie, savanna, veld.

stereo /ˈsterɪəʊ ; ˈstɛrɪo/ *n* (abbr of ~*phonic*) ~phonic record-player, apparatus, sound, etc. (爲 ~phonic 之略)立體電唱機,音響裝置,音響等。

stereo·phonic /ˌsterɪəˈfɒnɪk ; ˌstɛrɪəˈfanɪk/ *adj* (of broadcast and recorded sound, using two separately placed loudspeakers) giving the effect of naturally distributed sound; (of apparatus) designed for recording or reproducing sound in this way: (指用兩個分開放置的擴音器放出的廣播及錄音)立體音響的;(指儀器)錄製或發出立體音響的: *a ~ recording.* 立體音響錄音。

stereo·scope /ˈsterɪəskəup ; ˈstɛrɪəˌskop/ *n* [C] apparatus by which two photographs of sth, taken from slightly different angles, are seen as if united and with the effect of depth and solidity. 立體鏡(以此鏡觀看兩張角度稍異的照片可產生立體感)。 **stereo·scopic** /ˌsterɪəˈskɒpɪk ; ˌstɛrɪəˈskɑpɪk/ *adj* of, by means of, a ~. 立體鏡的;藉立體鏡的。

stereo·type /ˈsterɪətaɪp ; ˈstɛrɪəˌtaɪp/ *n* [C, U] **1** (process of printing from a) printing-plate cast from a mould of a piece of printing set in movable type. 鉛版印刷術;(澆製而成的印刷用)鉛版。 **2** fixed, formalized or standardized (and therefore perhaps false) phrase, idea, belief. 定型的語句、觀念或信仰。□ *vt* [VP6A] **1** make ~s of; print by the use of ~s. 澆製…的鉛版;用鉛版印刷。 **2** (fig) (of phrases, ideas, etc) fix in form; use and repeat without thought or change: (喻)(指語句,觀念等)使成固定形式;反覆因襲: *~d greetings,* eg 'Good morning', 'How d'you do'? 已成固定形式的問候語(如'早安,''你好'!)。

ster·ile /ˈsteraɪl *US:* ˈsterəl ; ˈstɛrɪl/ *adj* **1** not producing, not able to produce, seeds or offspring. 不結果實的;不能生育的。 **2** (of land) barren. (指土地)不毛的;貧瘠的。 **3** (fig) having no result; producing nothing: (喻)無結果的;無效果的: *a ~ discussion.* 無結果的討論。 **4** free from living germs. 無細菌的。 **ste·ril·ity** /stəˈrɪlətɪ ; stəˈrɪlətɪ/ *n* [U] being ~. 不結果實;不能生育;不毛;無結果;無細菌。 **ster·il·ize** /ˈsterəlaɪz ; ˈstɛrəˌlaɪz/ *vt* [VP6A] make ~: 使不生產;使無結果;消毒;殺菌: *The surgeon carefully sterilized his instruments.* 外科醫生小心消毒他的器械。 **ster·il·iz·ation** /ˌsterəlaɪˈzeɪʃn *US:* -lɪˈz-; ˌstɛrələˈzeʃən/ *n* [U].

ster·ling /ˈstɜːlɪŋ ; ˈstɝlɪŋ/ *adj* **1** (abbr 略作 **stg**) (of gold and silver) of standard value or purity: (指金銀)標準成分的: *plates of ~ gold.* 由標準成分之黃金製成的器皿。 **2** (fig) of solid worth; genuine: (喻)貨眞價實的;可靠的;眞正的: *~ sense/qualities.* 可靠的感覺(性質)。□ *n* British money: 英國貨幣: *the pound ~* (= £);英鎊; *payable in ~.* 可按英國貨幣支付的。 **the ˈ~ area,** group of countries which keep their reserves in British ~ currency and between which money can be transferred freely. 英鎊地區(用英鎊作準備金的各國)。

stern¹ /stɜːn ; stɝn/ *adj* (-er, -est) **1** demanding and enforcing obedience: 嚴苛的;嚴格的: *a ~ taskmaster.* 嚴苛的監工。 **2** severe; strict: 嚴厲的;嚴肅的: *a ~ face;* 嚴肅的面孔; *~ looks;* 嚴厲的表情; *~ treatment/rebukes.* 嚴厲的對待(叱責)。 **~·ly** *adv* **~·ness** *n*

stern² /stɜːn ; stɝn/ *n* [C] rear end of a ship or boat: 船尾: *move out of dock ~ foremost.* 船尾向前倒退出船塢。⇨ the illus at ship. 參看 ship 之插圖。 **~-ˈwheeler** *n* steamer with a larger paddle-wheel at the ~ (instead of paddle-wheels at the sides). 船尾裝蹼輪的船。

ster·num /ˈstɜːnəm ; ˈstɝnəm/ *n* (anat) narrow bone in the front of the chest (also called 亦稱作 *ˈbreast-bone*) connecting the collar-bone and the top seven pairs of ribs. (解剖)胸骨(胸前的狹骨,連接鎖骨與最上面的七對肋骨)。⇨ the illus at skeleton. 參看 skeleton 之插圖。

ster·tor·ous /ˈstɜːtərəs ; ˈstɝtərəs/ *adj* (of breathing or a person breathing) making a loud snoring sound. (指呼吸或呼吸的人)發鼾聲的;打鼾的。 **~·ly** *adv*

stet /stet ; stɛt/ *vi* (Lat) direction to a printer, etc to disregard a correction in a MS or proof. (拉)(校對用語,給予印刷工人等之指示)不改;不刪;保持原樣。

stetho·scope /ˈsteθəskəup ; ˈstɛθəˌskop/ *n* instrument used by doctors for listening to the beating of the heart, sounds of breathing, etc. (醫生用的)聽診器。⇨ the illus at step². 參看 step² 之插圖。

stet·son /ˈstetsn ; ˈstɛtsn̩/ *n* man's hat with a high crown and a wide brim. (男用)高頂闊邊帽。

steve·dore /ˈstiːvədɔː(r) ; ˈstivəˌdor/ *n* man whose work is loading and unloading ships. (碼頭的)裝卸工人。

stew /stjuː *US:* stuː ; stju/ *vt, vi* [VP6A, 15A, 2A, C] cook, be cooked, in water or juice, slowly in a closed dish, pan, etc: 用文火煮;燉;燜: *~ed chicken/fruit;* 燉鷄(水果); *ˈ~ing pears,* suitable for ~ing but not for eating uncooked. 煮食梨(祇宜燉食,不宜生食者)。 ***let sb ˌ~ in his own ˈjuice,*** do nothing to help him (when he is in trouble for which he is himself responsible). 讓某人自食其果或自作自受。 ***ˌ~ in one's own ˈjuice,*** suffer from trouble of one's own making. 自食其果;自作自受。 ***let sb ~,*** let him continue suffering from the consequences of his own stupidity without offering help or sympathy. 讓某人自食其果。□ *n* **1** [C, U] (dish of) ~ed meat, etc: 燉肉;燉煮的菜餚: *have mutton ~ for supper;* 晚餐吃燉羊肉; *prepare a ~.* 做一道燉的菜。 **2** ***be in/get into a ~ (about sth),*** (colloq) a nervous, excited condition. (俗)(對某事)憂慮、敏感、激動等。 **stewed** *adj* (sl) intoxicated. (俚)醉的;酒醉的。

stew·ard /stjuəd *US:* ˈstuː- ; ˈstjuwɚd/ *n* **1** man who arranges for the supply of food, etc in a club, college, etc. (俱樂部、大學等處的)膳務員。 **2** man who attends to the needs of passengers in a ship or airliner: (輪船或飛機上的)服務員: *the ˈbaggage/ˈcabin/ˈdeck, etc ~.* 負責行李(客艙,甲板等上)的侍者。 **3** man responsible for organizing details of a dance, race-meeting, public meeting, show, etc: (舞會,賽馬會,公共集會,表演等的)籌備人: *~s of the Jockey Club.* 賽馬俱樂部的籌備人。 *The hecklers were thrown out by the ~s.* 詰難者被籌備人攆出去了。 **4** man who manages another's property (esp a large house or estate). (管理他人財產,尤指大厦或大地產的) 管家;管理人。 **5** ***shop ~,*** ⇨ shop(3). **~·ess** /ˌstjuəˈdes *US:* ˈstuːərdɪs ; ˈstjuwɚdɪs/ *n* woman ~ (esp 2 above). 女管家;(尤指)輪船或飛機上的女招待員;女侍者;空中小姐。 **~·ship** /-ʃɪp ; -ʃɪp/ *n* rank and duties of a ~(4); period of office. 管家的職位及其職責;管家的任期。

stick¹ /stɪk ; stɪk/ *n* **1** thin branch broken, cut or fallen, from a bush, tree, etc: (折斷,砍下或落下的)小樹枝;柴枝: *gather dry ~s to make a fire;* 拾乾柴枝生火; *cut ~s to support the peas in the garden.* 砍些小樹枝以支撐園中的豌豆。 **2** such a branch cut to a convenient length, piece of cane cut, shaped, etc for a special purpose: (爲某種用途砍成大小、長短適用的)杖;棍;棒: *The old man cannot walk without a ~.* 那老年人沒有手杖不能走路。 *We have only a few ~s of furniture,* only a few very roughly made articles of furniture of the simplest kind. 我們祇有幾件極簡陋的傢具。 ***give sb the ~,*** beat him with a cane, as punishment; (fig) punish him. 用杖打某人;(喻)懲罰某人。 ***get hold of the ˌwrong end of the ˈ~,*** be confused; misunderstand things completely. 弄混;迷惘;困惑;完全弄錯。 **the big ~,** (fig) threat of the use of force, eg in relationships between countries: (喻)巨棒(政策)(如兩國之間以武力爲要脅): *a policy of the big ~.* 巨棒政策。 **hockey ~,** ⇨ hockey. **3** slender, rod-shaped piece (of chalk, sealing-wax, charcoal, dynamite, celery, etc). 棒狀物(如粉筆、封蠟、木炭、炸藥、芹菜等)。 **4** (colloq) person, esp one who is dull, stiff and reserved: (俗)呆板、固執、拘謹的人;呆頭呆腦的人;木頭人: *He's a dull/dry old ~.* 他是個乏味的老傢伙。 **5** ***the ~s,*** (colloq) the backwoods; rural areas far from cities. (俗)森林地帶;遠離城市的鄉村地區。 ***out in the ~s,*** away from the centre of things. 遠離熱鬧、紛擾或繁華之地。□ *vt* (*pt, pp* ~ed) [VP6A] support with ~s(1): 以樹枝支持: *Have you ~ed your peas yet?*

你已用樹枝把豌豆撐好了嗎？

stick[2] /stɪk ; stɪk/ *vt, vi* (*pt, pp* stuck /stʌk ; stʌk/) (For special uses with *adverbial particles* and *preps*, ⇨ 7 below.) (與副詞接語及介詞連用的特殊用法，參看下列第7義。) **1** [VP6A, 15A, B] **~ sth (in)**, push (sth pointed) (into, through, etc): 以(尖物)插入，刺，戳，貫穿等: *S~ the fork into the potato/S~ it in.* 把叉子插入馬鈴薯(把它挿進去)。*The cushion was stuck full of pins.* 針墊上插滿了針。**~ a pig**, (in sport) kill one with a spear. (打獵)用矛刺殺野豬。**2** [VP2C] (of sth pointed) be, remain, in a position by the point: (指尖物)扎在某處；尖端停在某處；刺入: *The needle stuck in my finger.* 針扎進我的手指。*I found a nail ~ing in the tyre.* 我發現一根釘子刺進車胎裡。**3** [VP15A, B, 2A, C] (cause to) be or become joined or fastened with, or as with, paste, glue or other substance: (用或似用黏性物質)使或變得黏附；黏合；附着: *~ a stamp on a letter/a placard on a hoarding.* 貼郵票於信上(在柵牆上張貼佈告)。*These stamps have stuck (together).* 這些郵票黏在一起了。**be/get stuck with sb/sth**, (colloq) be/become permanently involved with him/it; be/become unable to escape from him/it: (俗)與某人(某事物)糾纏不清；無法擺脫某人(某事物): *It looks as if I'm stuck with the job of clearing up this mess.* 我好像非要收拾這個爛攤子不可了。**'~·ing-plaster** *n* [U] plaster for ~ing on and protecting a cut, injury, etc. (保護傷口等用的)橡皮膏；膠布。**4** [VP15A] (colloq) put (in some position or place), esp quickly or carelessly: (俗)插；放置；(尤指)亂塞: *He stuck his pen behind his ear/his hands in his pockets/the papers in a drawer.* 他把筆隨手塞在耳後(把手插進口袋，把文件胡亂塞進抽屜)。**5** [VP2A, C] (also in the passive) (亦用被動語態) **~ (in)**, be or become fixed (in); fail to work properly: 陷住；卡住；不能轉動；動彈不得: *The key stuck in the lock,* could not be turned or withdrawn. 鑰匙在鎖中卡住(不能轉動)了。*The bus (was) stuck in the mud.* 公車陷在泥裡開不動了。*Don't get stuck in the bog.* 不要陷進泥沼中。*The door has stuck,* eg as the result of being newly painted. 門打不開了(關不上了)(如由於剛油漆過)。**~ in one's throat**, (of a proposal, etc) be difficult to accept; (of words) be difficult to utter (because of unwillingness, etc). (指建議等)難以接受；(指言辭)難以啓齒(由於不願意等)。**'~-in-the-mud** *attrib adj* resistant to change: 遲滯的；不進步的；守舊的: *~-in-the-mud ideas.* 守舊的觀念。□ *n* person of this kind: 守舊分子；頑固分子: *My grandfather is an old ~-in-the-mud.* 我的祖父是一個老頑固。**6** [VP6A] (colloq) bear; endure: (俗)忍耐；忍受: *How can you ~ that fellow?* 你怎麼忍受得了那個傢伙？*I can't ~ it any longer.* 我無法再忍受了。⇨ 7, *~ it out,* below. 參看下列第7義中的 ~ it out。*S~ to it!* (used as a cry of encouragement meaning 'Bear the conditions bravely', etc.) (用作鼓勵語)勇敢地堅持下去！**7** [VP2C, 3A, 15B] (special uses with *adverbial particles* and *preps*): (與副詞接語及介詞連用的特殊用法):

stick around, (sl) (of a person) stay in or near a place: (俚)(指人)(在某處或附近)徘徊；逗留: *S~ around; we may need you.* 不要走遠；我們可能需要你。

stick at sth, **(a)** stop short of, hesitate at: 遲疑；猶豫；顧慮: *Don't ~ at trifles.* 不要爲小事傷腦筋。*He ~s at nothing,* allows no feelings of doubt, no scruples, to stop him. 他毫無顧忌。**(b)** keep on with sth: 繼續做某事: *He ~s at his work ten hours a day.* 他繼續每天工作十小時。

stick sth down, **(a)** (colloq) put down: (俗)放下: *S~ it down anywhere you like.* 把它放在你認爲合適的地方。**(b)** (colloq) write down. (俗)寫下。**(c)** fasten with paste, etc: 黏住: *~ down (the flap of) an envelope.* 把信封(的口蓋)黏起。

stick on sth, remain on: 停留在: *Can you ~ on a horse?* 你能騎在馬背上嗎？**~ sth on**, fasten to with paste, etc: 把某物黏上: *~ on a label.* 黏上標籤。Hence, 由此產生，**'~-on** *attrib adj*: *~-on labels* (as contrasted with *tie-on* labels). 黏貼上的標籤(以別於繫上的標籤)。**~ it on**, (sl) make very high charges: (俚)索高價: *The hotel keepers ~ it on during the (busy) season.* 旅館老闆在旺季索取高價。

stick (sth) out, (cause to) project, stand out: (使)突出；伸出；顯眼: *with his chest stuck out;* 他的胸部挺出；*a rude boy ~ing his tongue out at his sister.* 一個向他姊姊(妹妹)伸舌頭的粗魯的男孩。*Don't ~ your head out of the car window.* 不要把頭伸出車窗。**~ it/sth out**, (colloq) endure hardship, etc until the end. (俗)忍耐到底。⇨ 6 above. 參看上列第6義。**~ one's neck out**, ⇨ neck(1). **~ out for sth**, refuse to give way until one gets (sth demanded): 堅索某物；堅持要求某事(不達目的不罷休): *They're ~ing out for higher wages.* 他們堅持要求較高的工資。

stick to sb/sth, **(a)** be faithful to (one's ideals, a friend, etc); remain determined: 忠於(自己的理想，朋友等)；堅持；堅守: *~ to a resolution.* 堅持決議。**(b)** continue at: 繼續；維持: *~ to a task until it is finished;* 繼續一項任務直到完成爲止；*~ to a timetable,* make no changes in what has been agreed. 不改動原時間表。**~ to one's guns**, ⇨ gun(1).

stick together, (colloq) (of persons) remain loyal or friendly to one another. (俗)(指人)彼此忠誠友善；共患難；同甘苦。

stick up, be upright, project upwards: 直立；豎立: *The branch was ~ing up out of the water.* 樹枝直直地伸出水面。**~ sb/sth up**, (sl) threaten to shoot sb in order to rob him/it: (俚)威嚇要開槍以便搶刼；威逼刼掠；持槍搶刼: *~ up a bank.* 持槍搶刼銀行。Hence, 由此產生，**'~-up** *n.* **~ your 'hands up; ~ 'em 'up**, raise your hands (so that resistance is not intended). 把手舉起來(以示不抵抗)。**~ up for sb/oneself/sth**, defend, support: 維護；支持；辯護: *~ up for one's friends.* 爲朋友辯護。

stick with sb/sth, remain loyal to, continue to support: 忠於；繼續支持: *~ with a friend/an ideal.* 忠於朋友(理想)。

sticker /'stɪkə(r) ; 'stɪkɚ/ *n* **1** one who, or that which, sticks, eg a persevering person. 堅持者；固守者；黏貼者；尖物；芒刺。⇨ stick[2](7). **2** adhesive label to be stuck on sth. 黏貼的標籤。

stick·ler /'stɪklə(r) ; 'stɪklɚ/ *n* **~ for sth**, person who insists upon the importance of sth (eg accuracy, discipline, formality, etc). 堅持某事(如精確、紀律、形式等)重要的人；拘泥某事的人；不能權變的人。

sticky /'stɪkɪ ; 'stɪkɪ/ *adj* (-ier, -iest) **1** that sticks or tends to stick to anything that touches it: 黏的；黏性的: *~ fingers/toffee;* 黏糊糊的手指(太妃糖)；*a ~ road,* eg deep in wet mud. 泥濘的路。**a ~ wicket**, (cricket) soft wet area which makes batting difficult. (板球)濕軟三柱門區(擊球困難)。**be on a ~ wicket**, (fig) in a situation that is difficult to deal with. (喻)處困境；遇到難以應付的情況。**2** (sl) unpleasant; difficult: (俚)不愉快的；困難的: *have a ~ time.* 遭遇困難。**come to a ~ end**, die in an unpleasant and painful way. 悽慘而痛苦地死去。**3** (colloq) making, likely to make, objections, be unhelpful, etc: (俗)持異議的；很可能反對的；不肯幫忙的；難同意的: *The bank manager was ~ about letting her have an overdraft.* 那銀行的經理不同意她透支。**stick·ily** /-ɪlɪ ; -əlɪ/ *adv* **sticki·ness** *n*

stiff /stɪf ; stɪf/ *adj* **1** not easily bent or changed in shape: 不易彎曲的；堅硬的；僵直的；硬的: *a ~ (ie starched) collar;* (漿過的)硬領；*a sheet of ~ cardboard;* 一塊硬紙板；*have a ~ leg/back,* not easily bent; 腿(背)僵直的；*feel ~ after a long walk,* have ~ muscles and joints; 走長路後感覺肢體發僵；*lying ~ in death.* 死後僵硬地躺着。**keep a ~ upper lip**, show firmness of character (by not complaining when in pain or trouble). 咬緊牙根(遇痛苦或困難

而不抱怨以示剛毅堅强)。ˌ~-ˈ**necked** *adj* obstinate. 頑固的;倔强的。 **2** hard to stir, work, move, etc: 不靈活的;不易移動的: *stir the flour and milk to a ~ paste;* 把麵粉及牛奶攪成濃糊; hard to do; difficult: 難做的;困難的: *a ~ climb／examination.* 困難的攀登(考試)。 *The book is ~ reading.* 這書很不容易懂。 **3** (of manners, behaviour) formal, unfriendly, haughty: (指態度、行爲)拘謹的;呆板的;不友善的;冷淡的;傲慢的: *get a ~ reception;* 受到冷淡的接待; *be rather ~ with one's neighbours;* 對隣居相當冷淡; *give sb a ~ bow.* 向某人生硬地一鞠躬。 **4** great in degree: 强烈的;强勁的;高昂的: *a ~* (= strong) *breeze;* 强勁的風; *a ~* (= high) *price;* 高昂的價格; *a ~ glass of rum／a ~ drink,* strong in alcoholic content. 一杯强烈的蘭酒(含酒精成分高的酒)。□ *adv* thoroughly; to the point of exhaustion: 徹底地;極度地: *It bored me ~,* bored me very much. 煩死我了。 *She was scared ~,* very badly scared. 她嚇呆了。□ *n* (sl) (俚) **1** corpse. 屍體。 **2** (sl) fool. (俚)傻瓜。 **~·ly** *adv* **~·ness** *n* **~en** /ˈstɪfn ; ˈstɪfən/ *vt, vi* [VP6A, 2A] make or become ~. 使或變得堅硬、呆板、强烈等。 **~·en·ing** /ˈstɪfnɪŋ ; ˈstɪfənɪŋ/ *n* [U] material used to ~en a substance or object. 加勁材料(使某一物質或物體變硬的材料)。 **~·ener** /ˈstɪfnə(r) ; ˈstɪfənə/ *n* sth used to ~en. 使堅硬之物;使强烈之物。

stifle /ˈstaɪfl ; ˈstaɪfḷ/ *vt, vi* **1** [VP6A, 2A] give or have the feeling that breathing is difficult: 使或感到窒息;使或感到呼吸困難: *They were ~d by the heat.* 他們熱得透不過氣來。 *The heat was stifling.* 熱得令人透不過氣來。 *The smoke filled the building and almost ~d the firemen.* 建築物裡滿是烟,幾乎使救火員窒息。 **2** [VP6A] suppress; put down; keep back: 鎮壓;敉平;阻遏;抑止: *~ a rebellion;* 敉平叛亂; *~ a yawn／a cry／one's laughter.* 抑止呵欠(哭叫,笑)。

stigma /ˈstɪgmə ; ˈstɪgmə/ *n* [C] **1** (*pl* -mas /-məz ; -məz/) (fig) mark of shame or disgrace: (喩)汚名;恥辱;瑕疵: *the ~ of illegitimacy.* 私生子的恥辱。 **2** (*pl* ~ta /-tə ; -tə/) marks resembling those made by the nails on the body of Jesus at his crucifixion, said to have appeared on the body of St Francis of Assisi and others. 與耶穌受難的釘痕相似的記號 (據說曾在聖法蘭西斯及其他人身上出現過)。 **3** (*pl* ~s) that part of the pistil of a flower which receives the pollen. 花的柱頭(接受花粉部分)。 ⇨ the illus at flower. 參看 flower 之挿圖。

stig·ma·tize /ˈstɪgmətaɪz ; ˈstɪgməˌtaɪz/ *vt* [VP16B] describe (sb) scornfully (*as*): 輕蔑地把(某人)描繪爲;誣衊;非難: *be ~d as a coward and a liar.* 被指爲懦夫及說謊者。

stile /staɪl ; staɪl/ *n* arrangement of steps or rungs to enable persons on foot to get over or through a fence, hedge, wall, etc but keeping cattle out. (能讓行人爬越籬笆、圍欄、圍牆等,但能阻止畜類進入的)踏級;階梯。⇨ *turnstile* at turn²(6). ***help a lame dog over a ~,*** ⇨ dog¹(2).

sti·letto /stɪˈletəʊ ; stɪˈleto/ *n* (*pl* ~s, ~es /-təʊz ; -toz/) small dagger with a narrow tapering blade. 小劍;匕首。 ~ **heel,** (on a woman's shoes) high, thin and (usu) made of metal. (女鞋的)高而細的後跟(通常爲金屬製成)。

still¹ /stɪl ; stɪl/ *adj, adv* **1** without movement or sound; quiet: 不動的(地);靜止的(地);寂靜的(地);無聲的(地): *Please keep／stay ~ while I take your photograph.* 我爲你拍照的時候請不要動。 *How ~ everything is!* (一切)多麼寂靜啊! ***the ~ small voice,*** the voice of conscience. 良心的呼喚。 ˌ~-ˈ**life** *n* [U] representation of non-living things (eg fruit, flowers, etc) in painting; [C] (*pl* ~-lifes) painting of this kind. (繪畫中的)靜物(如水果、花等);靜物畫。 ˈ~-**birth** *n* child or foetus dead at birth. 死胎;死產。⇨ *live-birth* at live¹(4). ˈ~-**born** *adj* (of a child) dead at birth. (指小孩)死產的。 **2** (of wines) not sparkling; not containing gas. (指酒)不起泡的;不含氣體的。□ *n* **1** [U] (poet) deep silence: (詩)寂靜;萬籟俱寂: *in the ~ of the night.* 在萬籟俱寂的深夜。 **2** [C] ordinary photograph selected from, and contrasted with, a cinema film: (自電影片中選出而與活動影片相對而言的)劇照: *~s from a new film,* eg as used for advertising in the press. 新影片的劇照(如用以登在報上做廣告者)。□ *vt* [VP6A] cause to be ~ or at rest; make calm. 使靜止;使安靜;使平靜。 **~y** *adj* (poet) calm; quiet. (詩)平靜的;安靜的;寂靜的。 **~·ness** *n*

still² /stɪl ; stɪl/ *adv* **1** (usu mid position, but may occur after a direct object) even to this or that time: (通常置於動詞前後,但可置於直接受詞之後) 仍;尙;還: *He is ~ busy.* 他仍然很忙。 *He ~ hopes／is ~ hoping for a letter from her.* 他仍希望收到她的信。 *Will he ~ be here when I get back?* 我回來的時候,他還會在這裡嗎? *In spite of his faults she ~ loved him／loved him ~.* 儘管他有缺點,她仍舊愛他。 Cf *still* and *yet*: 比較 still 與 yet 的用法: *Is your brother here yet,* Has he arrived? 你哥哥(弟弟)到了嗎? *Is your brother ~ here,* Hasn't he left? 你哥哥(弟弟)還在這裡嗎? **2** (with a comp) even; yet; in a greater degree: (與比較級連用)更;愈: *Tom is tall but Mary is ~ taller／taller ~.* 湯姆很高,但是瑪莉更高。 *That would be better ~／be ~ better.* 那就更好了。 **3** nevertheless; admitting that: 然而;可是;依然: *He has treated you badly: ~, he's your brother and you ought to help him.* 他待你不好;但他總是你的兄弟,你仍舊應該幫助他。

still³ /stɪl ; stɪl/ *n* [C] apparatus for making liquors (brandy, whisky, etc) by distilling. (蒸餾酒類,如白蘭地、威士忌等,用的)蒸餾器。 ˈ~-**room** *n* house-keeper's storeroom in a large house. 大宅中管家的儲藏室。

stilt /stɪlt ; stɪlt/ *n* (often 常作 **(pair of) ~s**) one of a pair of poles, each with a support for the foot at some distance from the bottom, used to raise the user from the ground: 高蹺: *walk on ~s.* 踩高蹺。

stilted /ˈstɪltɪd ; ˈstɪltɪd/ *adj* (of liter style, talk, behaviour, etc) stiff and unnatural; too formal. (指文體、談話、擧止等)生硬的;不自然的;太呆板的。 **~·ly** *adv*

Stil·ton /ˈstɪltən ; ˈstɪltṇ/ *n* rich, white, creamy cheese with a green-blue mould in it. 斯提爾頓乾酪(一種有墨綠色霉紋之白色多脂膏狀乾酪)。

stimu·lant /ˈstɪmjʊlənt ; ˈstɪmjələnt/ *n* [C] drink (eg coffee, brandy), drug, etc that increases bodily or mental activity; sth that spurs one on (eg praise, hope of gain). 興奮劑;刺激物(如咖啡、白蘭地、藥物等);激勵;鼓舞(如稱讚、獲利的希望等)。

stimu·late /ˈstɪmjʊleɪt ; ˈstɪmjəˌlet/ *vt* [VP6A, 14, 17] ~ ***sb (to sth／to do sth),*** excite; rouse; quicken thought or feeling: 刺激;激勵;鼓舞;促進思想或感覺: *~ sb to further efforts;* 鼓勵某人進一步努力; *~ sb to make greater efforts.* 激勵某人作更大的努力。 **stimu·lat·ing** *adj*

stimu·lus /ˈstɪmjʊləs ; ˈstɪmjələs/ *n* (*pl* -li /-laɪ ; -laɪ /) [C] sth that stimulates: 刺激物;激勵(物);鼓勵(物): *work harder under the ~ of praise;* 受到稱讚後更加努力工作; *a ~ to further exertions.* 促使進一步努力的激勵。

sting¹ /stɪŋ ; stɪŋ/ *n* **1** [C] sharp, often poisonous, pointed organ of some insects (eg bees, wasps, gnats): (蜜蜂、黃蜂、蚋等的)尖而常帶毒性的器官;刺;螫;針: *The ~ of a scorpion is in its tail.* 蠍子的毒刺在其尾部。 ˈ~-**ray** *n* broad, flat, tropical fish which can cause severe wounds with its sharp spines. 黃貂魚(一種扁而寬的熱帶魚,其尖銳的棘狀突起可致重創)。 **2** hairs projecting from the surface of the leaf of a plant (esp a ˈ*~ing-nettle*), which causes pain to the fingers, etc when touched. (植物,尤指蕁蔴,葉上突起的)刺毛(能刺痛手指等)。 **3** [C] sharp pain caused by the ~ of an insect or by nettles, etc; place of a wound made by a ~: (昆

蟲的刺、蕁蔴的刺毛等造成的)刺痛;刺傷;刺傷之處: *Her face was covered with ~s.* 她的臉上佈滿被刺的傷痕。*Have you any ointment to put on these ~s?* 你有什麼塗擦這些刺傷的藥膏嗎? **4** [C, U] any sharp pain of body or mind: (身心方面的)劇痛;刺痛: *the ~ of a whip/the northeast wind/hunger/remorse.* 鞭打(東北風,饑餓,懊悔)的刺痛。*His service* (in tennis) *has no ~ in it,* is weak. 他(打網球時)發的球沒有勁。

sting² /stɪŋ ; stɪŋ/ *vt, vi* (*pt, pp* stung /stʌŋ ; stʌŋ/) **1** [VP6A, 2A] prick or wound with a sting or as with a sting; have the power to ~: 刺;螫;刺傷;螫傷;有刺痛或刺傷力: *A hornet stung me on the cheek.* 一隻大黃蜂在我臉上螫了一下。*The blows of the cane stung the boy's fingers.* 籐條的鞭打使那男孩的手指感到刺痛。*Not all nettles ~.* 並非所有的蕁蔴都會刺人。 **2** [VP6A, 14, 15A] **~ sb (to/into sth/doing sth),** cause sharp pain to; anger: 造成劇痛;刺痛;刺傷;激怒: *He was stung by his enemy's insults.* 他被敵人的侮辱激怒了。*Anger stung* (= roused) *him to action/into fighting.* 憤怒使他採取行動(跟人打起來)。 **3** [VP2A] (of parts of the body) feel sharp pain: (指身體器官)感到劇痛: *His fingers were still ~ing from the caning he had had.* 他的手指挨過鞭打後仍舊感到刺痛。 **4 ~ sb (for sth),** (colloq) charge him an excessive price (for sth); swindle sb: (俗)向某人索過高價錢;敲某人竹槓;騙某人錢: *He was stung for £5,* had to pay this sum. 他被敲了五鎊。*How much did they ~ you for?* 他們敲了你多少錢? **~er** *n* (esp) smart, painful blow. (尤指)刺痛的打擊。**~·less** *adj* having no ~. 無刺、螫、刺毛等的。

stingy /ˈstɪndʒɪ ; ˈstɪndʒɪ/ *adj* (-ier, -iest) spending, using or giving unwillingly; niggardly; miserly: 吝嗇的;小氣的;不大方的: *Don't be so ~ with the sugar!* 不要那麼吝惜糖! **stin·gily** /-dʒɪlɪ ; -dʒəlɪ/ *adv* **stin·gi·ness** *n*

stink /stɪŋk ; stɪŋk/ *vi, vt* (*pt* stank /stæŋk ; stæŋk/ or 或 stunk /stʌŋk ; stʌŋk/, *pp* stunk) **1** [VP2A, 3A] **~ (of sth),** have a horrid and offensive smell: 有臭味;發臭: *That fish ~s.* 那魚發臭了。*Her breath stank of garlic.* 她的呼吸帶有大蒜味。**cry ~ing fish,** condemn one's own goods, etc. 非難自己的貨物等;自敗己事。 **2** [VP15B] **~ sb/sth out,** (a) drive out by means of sth evil-smelling: 以臭物驅逐;以難聞之物逐出: *~ out a fox,* eg by sending smoke into its hole. 逐出狐狸(如將烟送入狐狸洞中)。(b) fill a place with ~s: 以難聞的氣味充塞某處: *You'll ~ the place out with your cheap cigars!* 這地方會被你的劣質雪茄烟味所熏臭! □ *n* [C] horrid smell. 臭味;難聞的氣味。**raise/kick up a ~ (about sth),** (colloq) cause trouble or annoyance, eg by complaining. (俗)惹麻煩;惹煩惱(如發牢騷而引起)。**~er** *n* (sl) (俚) **1** letter intended to convey strong disapproval, reproach, etc. 表達强烈反對、譴責等的信函;惹人討厭的信。 **2** person who arouses strong dislike. 令人討厭的人。 **3** (colloq) sth difficult: (俗)困難之事;難題: *The biology paper* (ie in an examination) *was a ~er.* 生物考卷很難答。

stint /stɪnt ; stɪnt/ *vt, vi* [VP6A, 14] **~ sb (of sth),** restrict (sb) to a small allowance: 限制(某人)的花費;緊縮;吝惜: *She ~ed herself of food in order to let the children have enough.* 她節省自己的食物好讓孩子們吃飽。*Don't ~ the food.* 不要捨不得吃。□ *n* **1** (usu) (通常作) **without ~,** without limit, without sparing any effort. 不加限制地;不遺餘力地。 **2** [C] fixed or allotted amount (of work): 定量(的工作);指定的分量: *do one's daily ~.* 做某人每天指定(或定量)的工作。

sti·pend /ˈstaɪpend ; ˈstaɪpɛnd/ *n* [C] (esp clergyman's) salary. (尤指神職人員的)薪水;薪給。**sti·pen·di·ary** /staɪˈpendɪərɪ *US:* -dɪerɪ ; staɪˈpɛndɪˌɛrɪ/ *adj* receiving a ~, not working without pay: 受薪的;支取薪金的;非義務工作的: *a ~iary magistrate,* paid magistrate in a large town (appointed by the Home Secretary) dealing with police court cases. (大城市的)受薪治安推事(內政部長委派,受理違警案件者)。□ *n* (*pl* -ries) ~iary magistrate. (大城市的)受薪治安推事。

stipple /ˈstɪpl ; ˈstɪpl̩/ *vt* [VP6A] draw or paint with dots instead of lines. 點畫;點描(不用線條)。

stipu·late /ˈstɪpjʊleɪt ; ˈstɪpjəˌlet/ *vt, vi* **1** [VP6A, 9] state, put forward, as a necessary condition: 規定;約定: *It was ~d that the goods should be delivered within three days.* 經約定該項貨物須在三日內送交。 **2** [VP3A] **~ for sth,** insist upon (as part of an agreement): 堅持(作爲協議的條件): *~ for the best materials to be used.* 堅持以使用最好的材料爲條件。**stipu·la·tion** /ˌstɪpjʊˈleɪʃn ; ˌstɪpjəˈleʃən/ *n* [C] sth ~d; condition: 規定;約定;條件;條款: *on the stipulation that....* 按規定…。

stir /stɜː(r) ; stɝ/ *vi, vt* (-rr-) **1** [VP6A, 2A, C] be moving; cause to move: 動;移動;使動: *Not a leaf was ~ring,* There was no wind to move the leaves. 沒有一片樹葉在動(一點兒風都沒有)。*A breeze ~red the leaves.* 微風吹動樹葉。*Nobody was ~ring in the house,* Everyone was resting. 屋子裡沒有人在走動(都在休息)。*She is not ~ring yet/has not ~red yet,* is still in bed. 她尚未起床。*You had better ~ yourself,* get busy, be active. 你最好找點事做(活動活動)。*I haven't ~red out all morning,* haven't left the house. 我整個上午未出過門。**not ~ an eyelid,** remain unmoved, showing no alarm or concern. 不動聲色(未顯示驚慌或關心)。**not ~ a finger,** make no effort to do things; give no help. 一事不做;一點都不幫忙;袖手旁觀。**~ one's stumps,** (colloq) make haste, walk faster. (俗)趕忙;趕緊;快走。 **2** [VP6A, 15B] **~ sth (up),** move a spoon, etc round and round in liquid, etc in order to mix it thoroughly: 攪和;拌勻: *~ one's tea;* 攪動茶; *~ the porridge;* 攪動麥片粥; *~ milk into a cake mixture.* 把牛奶和做蛋糕的混合原料攪和。**~ the fire,** use the poker in it. 撥火(使旺)。 **3** [VP6A, 14, 15B] **~ sb to sth; ~ sth (up),** excite: 使激動;惹起: *The story ~red the boy's imagination.* 那故事引起那男孩的幻想。*Discontented men ~red the crew to mutiny/~ed up trouble among the crew.* 心懷不滿的人鼓動船員叛變(在船員間製造糾紛)。*He wants ~ring up,* needs to be roused from lethargy. 他需要激勵。**~ the blood,** rouse to excitement or enthusiasm. 激起興奮或熱忱。 **4** [VP2A, C] be roused: 被激動;奮起;被激起: *Pity ~red in his heart.* 他的憐憫心被激起了。□ *n* (usu 通常作 **a ~**) commotion; excitement: 騷動;激動: *The news caused quite a ~ in the village.* 這項消息在村子裡引起相當大的騷動。**~·ring** *adj* exciting: 激動的;刺激的;令人興奮的: *~ring tales of adventure;* 刺激的冒險故事; *live in ~ring times.* 生活於轟轟烈烈的時代。**~·ring·ly** *adv*

stir·rup¹ /ˈstɪrəp ; ˈstɝəp/ *n* [C] foot-rest, hanging down from a saddle, for the rider of a horse. (馬鞍上垂下的)馬鐙。⇨ the illus at harness. 參看 harness 之插圖。**ˈ~-cup** *n* drink (of wine, etc) offered to sb mounted on a horse ready for departure. 獻給上馬欲行者的酒;餞別酒。

stir·rup² /ˈstɪrəp ; ˈstɝəp/ *n* (anat) bone in the ear. (解剖)鐙骨。⇨ the illus at ear. 參看 ear 之插圖。

stitch /stɪtʃ ; stɪtʃ/ *n* **1** [C] (in sewing) the passing of a needle and thread in and out of cloth, etc; (in knitting) one complete turn of the wool, etc over the needle. (縫紉)縫;一縫;一針;(編織)一針。 **2** the thread, etc seen between two consecutive holes made by a needle; result of a single movement with a threaded needle, knitting-needle, etc: 縫線(連續的兩個針孔間的可見部分);針脚: *make long/neat, etc ~es;* 縫長(平整等)針脚; *put a few ~es in a garment;* 在一件衣服縫幾針; *drop a ~,* allow a loop to slip off the end of a knitting-needle; (編織時)漏織一針;漏脫一針; *put ~es into/*

take ~es out of a wound. 縫合傷口(拆去傷口的縫線)。***have not a ~ on,*** (colloq) be naked. (俗)一絲不掛;赤裸。***A ~ in time saves nine,*** (prov) A small piece of work done now may save a lot of work later. (諺)及時一針省九針(及時行事,則事半功倍)。 **3** (in compounds) particular kind of ~: (用於複合字中)某種針法或編織法: *a 'button-hole ~;* 鈕孔的縫法; *a 'chain-~,* etc. 鏈形縫法等。 **4** (*sing* only) sharp pain in the side (as caused sometimes by running too soon after a meal). (僅用單數)脅部劇痛(如有時飯後立刻跑步所引起者)。□ *vt, vi* [VP6A, 15A, B, 2A, C] sew; put ~es in or on. 縫;縫合;縫紉。

stoat /stəut ; stot/ *n* small furry animal larger than a rat; weasel; ermine (in its summer coat of brown). 白鼬;銀鼠(尤指夏季毛爲棕褐色者)。

stock¹ /stɒk ; stɑk/ *n* **1** [C, U] store or goods available for sale, distribution or use, esp goods kept by a trader or shopkeeper. (尤指商人所保有的)儲積品;存貨;現貨。***(be) in/out of ~,*** be available/not available: 有(無)現貨或存貨: *The book is in/out of ~.* 該書有(無)存貨。*Have you any linen sheets in ~?* 你有沒有亞麻布被單存貨? **'~-list** *n* list of goods, etc available. 存(現)貨清單。 **'~-room** *n* room in which ~ is kept. 貯藏室。 ***take ~,*** examine and make a list of goods in ~; 盤點存貨;清點存貨; Hence, 由此產生, **'~-taking** *n*: 盤(點)存(貨): *The annual ~-taking starts to-morrow,* eg in a draper's shop. 每年一度的盤存明天開始(如布店)。***take ~ of sth/sb,*** (fig) review (a situation); estimate (sb's abilities, etc). (喻)檢討(情勢);估計(某人的能力等);鑑定。 **ˌ~-in-'trade** *n* [U] everything needed for a trade or occupation. 生財;營業或職業需要的全部用具。**2** (attrib use, from 1 above) usually kept in ~ (and therefore usually obtainable): (形容用法,來自上面第1義)通常備有的;通常可獲得的: *~ sizes in hats;* 常備的帽子尺碼; commonly or regularly used; hackneyed: 通常或經常使用的;平常的;陳腐的: *~ arguments/comparisons;* 陳腐的論點(比較); *~ questions/answers.* 常遇見的問題(回答)。*She's tired of her husband's ~ jokes.* 她已聽厭了她丈夫所說的那些陳腐的俏皮話。 **~ company,** company of actors who have a ~ (or *repertoire*) of plays which they perform. 備妥若干隨時可上演的劇目的劇團。 **3** [C, U] supply of anything: 貯存備用的任何事物;貯積;儲蓄: *a good ~ of information;* 見聞豐富; *get in ~s of coal and coke for the winter.* 購進煤炭和焦炭以備過冬。**'~-piling** *n* purchase (esp by a Government) of ~s of raw materials or goods not easily available from local sources (eg tin, rubber, needed in war). 物資貯備(尤指政府購進原料或當地不易獲得之物資,如戰時所需之錫、橡膠等)。**4** [U] **('live-) ~,** farm animals. 家畜。**'*fat* ~,** ~ fit for slaughter as food: (適於屠宰供食用的)肥家畜: *fat-~ prices.* 肥家畜的價格。**'~-breeder/farmer** *n* farmer who breeds or raises cattle. 牧畜業者。 **'~·car** *n* (US) railway truck for carrying cattle. (美)運輸家畜的火車車廂。 **'~·car racing** *n* racing of ordinary models of motor-cars as sold generally. 普通型式(非跑車)的汽車競賽。 **'~·yard** *n* enclosure where cattle are kept temporarily, eg at a market, or before being slaughtered. 臨時關家畜的圍欄(如市場上或屠宰場上者)。 **5** [C, U] money lent to a government in return for interest; shares in the capital of a business company: 公債;股票: *have £5000 in the ~s;* 有五千鎊公債券; *invest one's money in (a) safe ~.* 投資於可靠的股票。**'~·broker** *n* man whose business is the buying and selling of ~(s). 證券經紀人。**'~ exchange** *n* place where ~s and shares are publicly bought and sold. 證券交易所。 **'~·holder** *n* (chiefly US) shareholder. (主美)股東。 **'~-jobber** *n* member of a ~ exchange from whom a ~broker buys and to whom he sells. 股票批發商(與股票經紀人做買賣者)。 **'~-list** *n* publication with current prices of ~s(5) and shares. 證券行情表。 **6** [U] line of ancestry: 家系;世系;血統;祖先: *a woman of Irish ~/of Puritan/farming, etc ~.* 一位有愛爾蘭血統(有清教徒世系,祖先務農等)的女子。 **7** ***~s and stones,*** lifeless things. 木石;無生命之物。**ˌ~-'still** *adv* motionless. 靜止的;不動的。 **'laughing-~,** target or object of ridicule. 笑柄;嘲笑的對象。 **8** [U] raw material ready for manufacture: 原料;材料: *'paper ~,* eg rags, etc to be made into paper. 造紙原料。 **9** [U] liquid in which bones, etc have been stewed; juices of meat and vegetables, used for making soup, gravy, etc. (骨頭等燉成的)原湯;(做湯等用之)肉汁;菜汁;湯料。 **'~-cube** *n* cube of dehydrated ~. (經過脫水之)粒狀湯料。 **'~·fish** *n* fish (esp cod) split open and dried in the air without salt, a staple food in some countries. (鱈)魚乾(剖開除去內臟,風乾,不加鹽,爲某些國家之主要食物)。 **'~·pot** *n* one in which ~(9) is made or stored. 湯鍋。 **10** [C] base, support, or handle of an instrument, tool, etc: (儀器、器具等的)基部;支撐;把手: *the ~ of a rifle/plough/whip;* 步槍槍托(犂柄;鞭子的把手); *the ~ of an anchor,* the crossbar. 錨桿。***lock, ~ and barrel,*** (fig) completely. (喻)完全地;整個地。 **11** [C] lower part of a tree trunk. 樹幹的下部;根莖。 **12** [C] growing plant into which a graft is inserted. (插入接木的)臺木;本幹。 **13** (*pl*) framework supporting a ship while it is being built or repaired. (複)造船臺;修船架。***on the ~s,*** under construction; in preparation. 在建造中;在準備中;在籌畫中。 **14** (*pl*) wooden framework with holes for the feet in which wrongdoers were formerly locked in a sitting position. (複)足枷;足械(昔日的刑具)。 **15** [C] wide band of stiff linen worn around the neck by men in former times (like the modern tie). (昔日男子頸間圍的)硬領(如同現代男人結領帶)。 **16** sort of garden plant with single or double brightly coloured sweet-smelling flowers. 紫羅蘭花(園藝植物之一種)。

stock² /stɒk ; stɑk/ *vt* [VP6A, 14] ~ ***(with),*** supply or equip with; have a stock of; keep in stock: 供應;備置;採辦;貯存: *~ a shop with goods;* 供應商店貨物; *well ~ed with the latest fashions.* 充分備有最新式樣。*Do you ~ raincoats?* 你有雨衣存貨嗎? *He has a memory well ~ed with facts.* 他記得許多事實。 **~·ist** /-ɪst ; -ɪst/ *n* one who ~s (certain goods) for sale. 採辦貨物的商人。

stock·ade /stɒ'keɪd ; stɑk'ed/ *n* [C] line or wall of upright stakes, built as a defence. (作防禦工事用的)圍柵;圍樁。□ *vt* (usu *pp*) defend with a ~. (通常用過去分詞)用圍樁防禦。

stock·in·ette /ˌstɒkɪ'net ; ˌstɑkɪn'ɛt/ *n* [U] elastic machine-made knitted fabric (esp as used for underclothing). (一種機器織成的)鬆緊內衣料。

stock·ing /'stɒkɪŋ ; 'stɑkɪŋ/ *n* [C] (often 常作 **(pair of) ~s**) tight-fitting covering of nylon, silk, cotton, wool, etc for the foot and leg, reaching to or above the knee. 長(統)襪。***in one's ~ feet,*** wearing ~s or socks but not shoes. 穿襪而未穿鞋的。⇨ tights.

stocky /'stɒkɪ ; 'stɑkɪ/ *adj* (-ier, -iest) (of persons, animals, plants) short, strong and stout. (指人、動植物)短粗而結實的;矮而壯的。**stock·ily** *adv* in a ~ manner: 短粗而結實地;矮而壯地: *a stockily built man.* 身材矮而結實的人。

stodge /stɒdʒ ; stɑdʒ/ *n* [U] (sl) heavy and solid food. (俚)油膩而且難消化的食物。**stodgy** /'stɒdʒɪ ; 'stɑdʒɪ/ *adj* **1** (of food) heavy and solid: (指食物)油膩而且難消化的: *a stodgy meal.* 一頓油膩而且難消化的餐食。 **2** (of books, etc) written in a heavy, uninteresting way (overweighted with facts, details, etc); (of persons) having a heavy personality; dull and unenterprising. (指書等)冗長無趣的(如事實、細節等過多的);(指人)又胖又笨的;遲鈍

的;無事業心的。

stoep /stʊp ; stʊp/ *n* (S Africa) terraced veranda; porch or steps outside the front entrance of a house. (南非)臺式的走廊;房屋正門外的門廊或臺階。

stoic /ˈstəʊɪk ; ˈsto·ɪk/ *n* person who has great self-control, who bears pain and discomfort without complaint. 高度自制者;忍受痛苦和不適而不抱怨者;堅忍不拔者。 **sto·ical** /-kl ; -kl/ *adj* of or like a ~. 高度自制的;堅忍的。 **sto·ically** /-klɪ ; -klɪ/ *adv* **sto·icism** /ˈstəʊɪsɪzəm ; ˈsto·ɪ,sɪzəm/ *n* [U] patient and uncomplaining endurance of suffering, etc. 堅忍的精神或操守。

stoke /stəʊk ; stok/ *vt, vi* [VP6A, 15B, 2A, C] ~ ***(sth) (up)***, put (coal, etc) on the fire of (an engine, furnace, etc); attend to a furnace: 加(煤炭等)於(火車頭、火爐等)的火上;司爐: ~ *(up) the furnace;* 加煤炭於爐; ~ *(up) twice a day.* 一天加煤二次。 **ˈ~-hole/-hold** *nn* place where a ship's furnaces are ~d. (輪船上的)火艙; 鍋爐室。 **~r** *n* workman who ~s a furnace, etc; mechanical device for feeding a furnace with fuel. 司爐;照管火爐的工人;加煤機;加燃料機。

stole¹ /stəʊl ; stol/ *n* **1** strip of silk or other material worn (round the neck with the ends hanging down in front) by priests of some Christian Churches during services. (某些基督教會之教士在宗教儀式中所佩的)聖帶。⇨ the illus at vestment. 參看 vestment 之插圖。 **2** woman's wrap worn over the shoulders. 婦女的披肩。

stole², stolen *pt, pp* of steal.

stolid /ˈstɒlɪd ; ˈstɑlɪd/ *adj* not easily excited; slow to show the feelings. 不易激動的;不動聲色的;神經麻木的;獃頭獃腦的。 **~·ly** *adv* **~·ness, sto·lid·ity** /stəˈlɪdətɪ ; stəˈlɪdətɪ/ *nn* [U].

stom·ach /ˈstʌmək ; ˈstʌmək/ *n* **1** [C] bag-like part of the alimentary canal into which food passes to be digested: 胃(消化管之消化食物部分): *It is unwise to swim on a full ~/to work on an empty ~.* 吃飽了游泳(枵腹工作)是不智的。⇨ the illus at alimentary. 參看 alimentary 之插圖。 **ˈ~-ache** *n* pain in the ~ or the bowels. 胃痛;肚子痛;腹痛。 **ˈ~-pump** *n* pump with a flexible tube, inserted into the ~ through the mouth (for use, eg in a case of poisoning). 胃唧筒(經口腔伸入胃中,爲醫療用具)。 **2** [U] appetite. 胃口;食慾;愛好;興趣。 ***have no ~ for sth,*** be disinclined to do or agree with sth, (because one disapproves of it): 對某事沒有胃口(不感興趣);對某事不表贊同: *have no ~ for bull-fighting.* 對鬥牛不感興趣(不表贊同)。 □ *vt* [VP6A] (usu neg or interr) endure; put up with: (通常用於否定句與問句中)忍受;容忍: *How could you ~ the violence in that film?* 你怎麼能够忍受那部電影裡的暴力呢?

stomp /stɒmp ; stɑmp/ *vi* [VP2C] ~ ***about,*** stamp, tread, heavily. 用力地踏、踩、跺。 □ *n* (jazz music for a) dance with a heavy beat. 重步舞;重步舞(爵士)樂。

stone /stəʊn ; ston/ *n* **1** [U] (often attrib) solid mineral matter which is not metallic; rock (often with a defining word as prefix, as *ˈsand~, ˈlime~*): (常作形容用法)石; 岩石(常以一界說性質之字作爲字首,如 sand~, lime~): *a wall made of ~;* 石砌的牆; *~ walls/buildings;* 石牆(石屋); *~ jars,* made of *ˈ~ware,* ⇨ below; 粗陶罐(參看下列之 ~ware); *have a heart of ~,* (fig) be hard-hearted. (喻) 鐵石心腸; 硬心腸。 ***the ˈS~ Age,*** period of culture when weapons and tools were made of ~ (before the use of metals was known). 石器時代 (人類使用金屬以前的時期)。 **,~-ˈblind/-ˈcold/-ˈdead/-ˈdeaf/-ˈsober** *adjj* completely blind, etc. 全盲的(冷透的;完全死的;完全聾的;完全清醒的)。 **ˈ~-breaker** *n* person who breaks up ~, esp for road-making; machine for crushing ~. 打碎石塊的人或機器;碎石工人;碎石機。 **ˈ~·mason** *n* man who cuts, prepares and builds with ~. 石匠;石工。 **ˈ~-pit** *n* quarry for ~. 採石場;石坑。 **,~-ˈwall** *vt* (cricket) be excessively cautious when batting so that runs come slowly; (fig) (in Parliament) obstruct progress by making long speeches, etc. (板球)過度小心地打 (故得分緩慢); (喻) (英國國會) 藉冗長演說等延宕議事。 Hence, 由此產生, **,~-ˈwalling** *n* **,~-ˈwaller** *n* person given to this. 過度小心的擊球員;(藉演說等)阻礙議事者。 **ˈ~·ware** *n* [U] pottery made from clay and flint. 粗陶器;石器。 **ˈ~·work** *n* [U] masonry; part(s) of a building made of ~. 石砌工;石造物;建築物的石造部分。 **2** [C] piece of ~(1) of any shape, usu broken off: 石塊;碎石: *a road covered with ~s;* 碎石路; *a fall of ~s down a hillside.* 石塊從山坡落下。 ***leave no ~ unturned (to do sth),*** try every possible means (to do it). 千方百計;想盡辦法(做某事)。 ***throw ~s at,*** (fig) attack the character of: (喻)攻擊…的品格: *Those who live in glass houses should not throw ~s,* (prov) If your own character is not beyond reproach you should not attack the character of others. (諺)自己有缺點不應挑剔別人。 ***within a ˈ~'s throw (of),*** very close (to). 很接近;一擲之遙;在短距離內。 **3** [C] **(precious) ~,** jewel. 寶石;玉。 **4** [C] piece of ~ of a definite shape, for a special purpose (usu in compounds): 有確定形狀,作特殊用途的石塊(通常用於複合字中): *a ˈgrave~,* ⇨ grave²; 墓碑; *ˈstepping-~s,* ⇨ step¹; 踏脚石; *ˈtomb~s,* ⇨ tomb; 墓碑; *ˈmill~s,* ⇨ mill¹. 磨石。 **5** [C] sth round and hard like a ~, esp 圓硬似石之物,尤指 **(a)** the hard shell and nut or seed of such fruits as the apricot, peach, plum and cherry. (杏、桃、李及櫻桃等的)硬殼;核。⇨ the illus at fruit. 參看 fruit 之插圖。 **ˈ~-fruit** *n* fruits of this kind. 核果。 **(b)** (usu 通常作 **ˈhail·~**) small frozen drop of rain: 雹;霰: *hail with ~s as big as peas.* 降雹大如豌豆。 **(c)** small hard object that has formed in the bladder or kidney: 結石;膽結石;腎結石;膀胱結石: *have an operation for ~.* 開刀取出結石。 **ˈgall·~,** ⇨ gall¹(1). **6** (not US; *pl* unchanged) unit of weight, 14 lb: (不用於美國;複數不變)呫(重量單位,等於十四磅): *two ~ of flour.* 麵粉二呫。 □ *vt* **1** [VP6A, 15A] throw ~s at: 向…投石頭;以石擲向: *Christian martyrs who were ~d to death.* 被石塊擊斃的基督教殉道者。 **2** [VP6A] take the ~s(5a) out of (fruit): 去(水果)之硬核: *~d dates.* 去核的棗。 **~·less** *adj* (esp of ~-fruit, ⇨ 5(a) above) without ~s. (尤指) 無核的 (參看上列第 5 義 (a))。 **stoned** *adj* (colloq) under the influence of (usu) soft drugs; very drunk. (俗)在(通常爲)軟性毒品支配之下的;吸食大麻等後身不由己的;爛醉的。

stony /ˈstəʊnɪ ; ˈstonɪ/ *adj* (-ier, -iest) **1** having many stones: 多石的: *~ soil/ground;* 石質土壤(多石之地); covered with stones: 覆有石塊或碎石的: *a ~ path/road.* 碎石小徑(道路)。 **2** hard, cold and unsympathetic: 鐵石心腸的;冷酷無情的: *a ~ heart;* 鐵石心腸; *,~-ˈhearted;* 鐵石心腸的; *a ~ stare;* 冷冷的凝視; *~ politeness.* 冷淡的禮貌。 **3** (sl) (俚) **,~(-ˈbroke),** completely without money; penniless. 一文不名的;手無分文的。 **ston·ily** /-tɪlɪ ; -əlɪ/ *adv* in a ~(2) manner: 冷酷無情地;鐵石心腸地: *stonily polite.* 冷淡有禮的。

stood /stʊd ; stʊd/ *pt, pp* of stand².

stooge /stuːdʒ ; studʒ/ *n* person who, in variety entertainment, is made fun of by a comedian; (colloq) person used as an assistant (to perform unpleasant jobs or duties that may incur blame, punishment, etc). 在雜耍中爲滑稽演員取笑的人;笑把兒;丑角助手;(俗)替身;替罪者(執行不愉快或可能受到懲罰、指責等之任務者)。 □ *vi* ~ ***for sb,*** act as a ~. 做丑角助手;做替罪者;做替身。

stool /stuːl ; stul/ *n* **1** seat without a back or arms, usu for one person: 凳子(通常供一人坐): *sitting on ~s at the bar drinking beer;* 坐在酒館凳子上喝啤酒; *a piˈano-~.* 鋼琴凳。 ***fall between***

two ~s, lose an opportunity through hesitating between two courses of action. 兩頭落空(在兩種行動間猶豫不決而失去機會)。 **2** **('foot)~,** low support on which to rest the feet. 脚凳(放脚的矮凳)。 **3** [U] (med) solid excrement: (醫)糞便: *send a specimen of one's ~s to the doctor,* eg to be tested for amoebic infection. 送糞便抽樣給醫生檢查。 **4** **'~-pigeon** *n* pigeon used as a decoy; (fig) person acting as a decoy, eg one employed by the police to trap a criminal. 媒鴿;囮鴿; (喻)囮子(如警察雇用誘捕罪犯之人)。

stoop[1] /stu:p; stup/ *vi, vt* **1** [VP2A, C, 4A, 6A] bend the body forwards and downwards; bend the neck so that the head is forward and down: 屈身;彎腰;俯首;低頭: *~ing with old age;* 因年老而彎腰; *~ to pick sth up;* 俯身拾物; *~ one's head to get into a car.* 俯首進入轎車。 **2** [VP3A] *~ to sth,* (fig) lower oneself morally: (喻)降格;卑屈;墮落而做出某事: *~ to folly/cheating.* 自甘墮落而做出愚蠢行爲(而行詐欺)。 *He's a man who would ~ to anything,* who has no moral scruples. 他是一個沒原則(沒節操)的人。 □ *n* (usu *sing*) ~ing position of the body: (通常作單數)屈身;傴僂: *walk with a ~,* as when very old or ill. 傴僂而行(如年老或生病時)。

stoop[2] /stu:p; stup/ *n* (in N America) porch or unroofed platform or set of steps at the entrance to a house. (北美)房屋入口處的門階;無頂之平臺;門廊;臺階。 ⇨ stoep.

stop[1] /stɒp; stɑp/ *n* [C] **1** stopping or being stopped: 停止;中止: *The train came to a sudden ~.* 火車突然停了下來。 *This train goes from London to Leeds with only two ~s.* 這列火車從倫敦至里玆僅停兩站。 ***put a ~ to sth; bring sth to a ~,*** cause it to ~ or end: 停止某事;結束某事;制止某事: *I'll put a ~ to this nonsense.* 我要制止這種胡鬧的事情。 *Traffic was brought to a complete ~.* 交通完全停頓了。 **2** place at which buses, trams, etc stop regularly or (*re'quest ~*) when requested to do so: 公共汽車、電車等的車站;招呼站(有人招呼時停車,稱 request ~): *Where's the nearest 'bus-~?* 離此最近的公車站在哪裡? **3** (music) key or lever (eg in a flute) for regulating pitch; row of pipes (in an organ) providing tones of one quality; knob or lever working such a row of pipes. (音樂)音栓。 ⇨ the illus at church, key. 參看 church, key 之插圖。 ***pull out all the ~s,*** (fig) appeal to all the emotions; make a great effort. (喻)竭盡所能;全力以赴。 **4** mark of punctuation, esp *full ~*(.). 標點符號;(尤指)句點(.)。 ⇨ App 9. 參看附錄九。 **5** (in a camera) device for regulating the size of the aperture through which light reaches the lens. (照相機的)光圈快門。 **6** (in phonetics) consonant produced by the sudden release of air which has been held back (eg /p, b, k, g, t, d/). (語音學) 塞音 (如 /p, b, k, g, t, d/)。 **7** device that stops the movement of sth at a fixed point, eg a peg of wood to prevent an ill-fitting window from rattling. 塞子;制子;阻塞物(如防止窗戶被風吹動時發出聲響的木栓等)。 **8** (compounds) (複合字) **'~·cock** *n* valve inserted in a pipe by which the flow of liquid or gas through the pipe can be regulated: (水管或瓦斯管上的)管閘;管制閥;制栓;停止旋塞: *A water-pipe has burst—where's the ~cock?* 一條水管爆裂了——制水栓在哪裡? **'~·gap** *n* temporary substitute. 臨時代替的人或物。 **'~ press** *n* [U] (not US) latest news inserted in a newspaper already on the printing machines. (不用於美國)報紙付印中臨時加挿的最新消息。 **'~-watch** *n* watch with a hand that can be started and stopped when desired, used to time events such as races to a fraction of a second. (賽跑等用的)跑錶;停錶;計秒錶。 **~·page** /'stɒpɪdʒ; 'stɑpɪdʒ/ *n* [C] **1** condition of being stopped up, ⇨ stop[2](6); obstruction. 被阻塞的狀況;阻礙。 **2** stopping(7): 停止;扣留;截斷;拒絕給予: *~page of leave/pay,* (esp in the armed forces, eg as a form of punishment). 假期(薪餉)的停止(尤指軍中作爲一種懲罰等者)。 **3** interruption of work (in a factory, etc as the result of strike action). (工廠等因罷工等而造成的)停工。 **~·per** *n* object which fits into and closes an opening, esp the mouth of a bottle or pipe; (US) plug(1). 阻塞物;(尤指)瓶塞;管塞。 ⇨ the illus at decanter. 參看 decanter 之挿圖。 ***put a ~per/the ~pers on (sth),*** (fig) bring it to an end; suppress it. (喻)停止或結束(某物);阻止或壓制(某事物)。

stop[2] /stɒp; stɑp/ *vt, vi* (-pp-) **1** [VP6A] put an end to the movement or progress of (a person, thing, activity, etc): 停止(人、物、活動等)的動作或進展: *~ a car/a train/a runaway horse.* 停住汽車(火車,脫韁之馬)。 *The earthquake ~ped all the clocks.* 地震使所有的鐘都停了。 **2** [VP6A, C, 14] ***~ sb (from) (doing sth),*** prevent; hinder: 阻止某人(做某事);妨碍;制止: *What can ~ our going/~ us from going if we want to go?* 如果我們要去,什麼能阻止我們(使我們不能成行)呢? *Can't you ~ the child (from) getting into mischief?* 你不能制止那孩子惡作劇嗎? *He will certainly go—there's no one to ~ him.* 他一定會去——沒有人能阻止他。 **3** [VP6A, C] leave off; discontinue (doing sth): 中止(做某事);停止: *~ work.* 停止工作。 *We ~ped talking.* 我們中止談話。 *Why doesn't he ~ beating his wife?* 他爲什麼不停止毆打他的妻子? ***S~ it!*** (imper) ~ doing that (sth disliked or disapproved of). (祈使)停止!不要做了! **4** [VP2A, 3A, 4A] ***~ (at),*** break off; discontinue: 停;中斷;停下來: *The rain has ~ped.* 雨已停了。 *The clock/His heart has ~ped.* 鐘已停了(他的心臟不再跳動了)。 *It has ~ped raining.* 雨已停止。 *We ~ped to have a rest.* 我們停下來休息一下。 *We ~ped (in order) to talk.* 我們停下來以便談話。 Cf 參較 *We ~ped talking.* 我們停止了談話。 **5** [VP 2A, 3A, 4A] ***~ (at),*** come to rest; halt: 停下;停住;止住: *The train ~ped.* 火車停下了。 *Does this train ~ at Crewe?* 這列火車在克魯停嗎? ***~ dead,*** ~ suddenly. 突然停止。 ***~ short at sth,*** limit one's actions, etc: 限制在某方面的行動等;停做某事: *Will our neighbours ~ short at war?* 我們的隣國會停止戰爭嗎? **6** [VP6A, 15A, B] ***~ sth (up),*** fill or close (a hole, opening, etc): 堵塞;塡塞;阻塞(洞,口等): *~ a leak in a pipe;* 塞住管子的漏洞; *~ up a mouse-hole;* 堵塞老鼠洞; *have a tooth ~ped,* have a cavity filled; 塡補牙洞; *~ one's ears,* (fig) refuse to listen; (喻)不聽; *~ the way,* prevent progress. 阻碍發展。 **7** [VP 6A, 14] cut off; keep back or refuse to give (sth normally supplied): 截斷;扣留;拒絕給予(通常供給之物): *~ (payment of) a cheque,* order the bank not to cash it; 止付支票(通知銀行不予兌現); *~ sb's wages.* 扣發某人薪水。 *The bank has ~ped payment,* is unable to meet its obligations. 該銀行已無力支付。 ***~ sth out of sth,*** deduct sth from (wages, salary, etc). 從(工資,薪金等)中扣除某款項。 **8** [VP2A, B, C] (colloq) stay: (俗)停留;待在;逗留;住: *~ at home.* 待在家裡。 *Are you ~ping at this hotel?* 你住在這家旅社嗎? ***~ off (at/in),*** break a journey for a short period: 中途稍作停留: *~ off at a store to buy sth.* 半路上在一家商店購物。 ***~ off/over (at/in),*** break a journey for a stay: 中途在某處停留或小住: *~ off overnight in Edinburgh.* 中途在愛丁堡停留過夜。 **'~-over** *n* [C] break in a journey; place where one does this; (attrib): 中途停留;中途停留之處;(形容用法): *'~-over ticket,* one that permits a journey to be broken in this way. 准許中途下車(下機、下船等)的票。 ***~ up (late),*** stay up, not go to bed until late. 熬夜;遲睡。 **9** (music) produce desired note(s) by pressing fingers on strings (eg of a violin), or over holes (eg in a flute). (音樂)按弦;按孔(以發出所要的聲音)。 **~·ping** *n* filling for a dental cavity. 補牙洞之塡補物。⇨ 6 above. 參看上列第 6 義。

stor·age /ˈstɔːrɪdʒ; ˈstorɪdʒ/ *n* [U] (space used for, money paid for) the storing of goods: (貨物的)貯存;貯藏;貯藏所;倉庫;倉庫費;貯藏費用;棧租;棧費: *put one's furniture in ~;* 把傢具存放起來; *keep fish in cold ~;* 冷藏魚; (attrib) (形容用法) *'~ tanks,* eg for oil; 貯存槽(如貯油槽); *'~ heater,* electric radiator which stores heat (accumulated during off-peak periods). 儲熱電暖爐(可在非尖峯用電時貯存熱能者)。

store /stɔː(r); stor/ *n* **1** [C] quantity or supply of sth kept for use as needed: 貯藏;貯積;儲備;儲蓄: *lay in ~s of coal for the winter;* 貯藏煤以備過冬; *have a good ~ of provisions in the house.* 家裡貯存有豐富的食物。**2** [U] *in ~,* **(a)** kept ready for use; for future use: 準備着;備用的;供將來用的: *That's a treat in ~,* a pleasure still to come. 那是往後還會再有的樂事。**(b)** destined (*for*); coming to: 必將發生的;就要來到的;注定的: *Who knows what the future has in ~ for us?* 誰知道我們將來注定會如何? **3** (*pl*) goods, etc of a particular kind, or for a special purpose: (複)(某一種類或作特殊用途的)貨物;物品: *naval and military ~s;* 海陸軍的軍需品; *marine ~s* (but note: *ˌmarine-'~ dealer*). 船舶用品(但是注意: ˌmarine-'~ dealer 船舶用品商)。**4** [C] **'~(-house),** place where goods are kept; warehouse: 倉庫;棧房: *The book is a ~-house of information.* 那本書是知識的寶庫。**'~·room** *n* one in which household supplies are kept. 貯藏室。**5** [C] (chiefly US but ⇨ 6 below) shop: (主美,但參看下列第 6 義)商店: *a 'clothing ~;* 服裝店; *~ clothes,* bought from a ~, ready to wear, not tailor-made. 成衣(非定做或量身裁製者)。**6** (*pl*) shop selling many varieties of goods: (複)百貨店: *the big department ~s of London;* 倫敦的大百貨公司; *the ˌArmy and 'Navy S~s;* 陸軍及海軍的百貨店; *a general ~s,* (esp) village shop selling a variety of goods. (尤指)鄉村的百貨店;雜貨店。⇨ also *chain-~* at chain(4). **7** [U] ***set great/little/no/not much ~ by,*** consider of great/little, etc value or importance. 重視(忽視;不重視;不太重視)。□ *vt* [VP6A, 15B] ***~ sth (up),*** **1** collect and keep for future use: *Do all squirrels ~ up food for the winter?* 是不是所有的松鼠都爲冬季儲備食物? **2** put (furniture, etc) in a warehouse, etc, for safe keeping. 把(傢俱等)寄存某貨棧等以妥善保存。**3** furnish, equip, supply: 供給;供應;裝備: *a mind well ~d with facts.* 見聞廣博的人。

storey (US = **story**) /ˈstɔːrɪ; ˈstorɪ/ *n* (*pl* ~s, (US) -ries) floor or level in a building: 建築物的一層: *a house of two ~s,* ie with rooms on the ground floor and one floor upstairs. 二層樓的房屋。**-storeyed** (US = **stor·ied**) /-ˈstɔːrɪd; -ˈstorɪd/ *adj* having the number of ~s indicated by the prefixed number: 有若干層樓的(數字加於其前): *a six-~ed building.* 六層樓的建築。

stor·ied /ˈstɔːrɪd; ˈstorɪd/ *adj* (liter) made famous in legend or stories: (文)在傳說中或故事中有名的: *the ~ Rhine.* 歷史上有名的萊茵河。

stork /stɔːk; stork/ *n* large, long-legged, usu white wading-bird (some of which build their nests on the tops of high buildings). 鸛(長腿大涉禽,通常爲白色,有些築巢於高樓頂部)。⇨ the illus at water. 參看 water 之插圖。

storm /stɔːm; storm/ *n* **1** [C] occasion of violent weather conditions: 風暴;暴風雨;暴風雪;狂風暴雨;狂暴天氣: *a 'thunder-/'wind-/'rain-/'dust-/'sand-~;* 雷雨(風暴;暴雨;塵暴;大風沙); *cross the Channel in a ~.* 在暴風雨中渡過英吉利海峽。*The forecast says there will be ~s.* 氣象報告說將有暴風雨。***a ~ in a teacup,*** much excitement about sth trivial. 大驚小怪。**'~-beaten** *adj* damaged by ~s. 被暴風雨摧毀的。**'~-bound** *adj* unable to continue a journey, voyage, etc, unable to go out, because of ~s. 旅途,行程等爲暴風雨所阻的。**'~-centre** *n* centre of a ~ or (fig) of a disturbance or trouble. 風暴中心;(喻)紛擾或騷亂的中心。**'~-cloud** *n* heavy rain-cloud accompanying, or showing the likelihood of, a ~. 暴風雲(伴隨或預示暴風雨的密雲)。**'~-cone/-signal** *n* one hoisted as a warning of high wind. 風暴球(風暴信號)。**'~-lantern** *n* one for use outdoors, made so that the light is well protected from wind. 防風燈。**'~-proof** *adj* able to resist ~s. 防風暴的;抗風暴的。**'~-tossed** *adj* damaged or blown about by ~s. 被暴風雨損壞的;在暴風雨中飄搖的。**2** violent outburst of feeling: 情感的猛烈發作: *a ~ of protests/cheering/applause/abuse.* 激烈的抗議(熱烈的歡呼;熱烈的喝采;嚴厲的斥責)。***bring a '~ about one's ears,*** do or say sth that rouses strong opposition, indignation, etc. 做或說某事而引起强烈反對、憤懣等。**3** ***take by ~,*** capture by a violent and sudden attack. 襲取;强奪;攻佔。**'~-troops** *n pl* troops trained for violent attacks. 突擊隊。**'~-trooper** *n* one of these. 突擊隊員。□ *vi, vt* **1** [VP2A, 3A] ***~ (at),*** give violent expression to anger; shout angrily. 狂怒;咆哮。**2** [VP15A, B, 2C] force (a way) into a building, etc; [VP6A] capture (a place) by sudden and violent attack: 强入建築物等;闖入;突擊(某地);襲取;攻佔: *The men ~ed (their way) into the fort/~ed the fort.* 士兵們猛攻後進入(襲取了)那座堡壘。**~y** *adj* (-ier, -iest) **1** marked by strong wind, heavy rain or snow or hail: 有暴風雨的;有暴風雪(雹)的: *~y weather;* 暴風雨的天氣; *a ~y night/crossing.* 暴風雨之夜(暴風雨中橫渡)。**2** marked by strong feelings of indignation, anger, etc: 感情激烈的;狂怒的;憤懣的: *a ~y discussion/meeting;* 激烈的討論(會議); *~y scenes during the debate.* 辯論時的激烈情景。**~·ily** /-ɪlɪ; -əlɪ/ *adv*

story[1] /ˈstɔːrɪ; ˈstorɪ/ *n* [C] (*pl* -ries) **1** account of past events: 事蹟;軼事;史話: *the ~ of Columbus;* 哥倫布的事蹟; *stories of ancient Greece.* 古希臘史話。**2** account of imaginary events: 小說;故事;傳奇: *a 'ghost ~;* 鬼故事; *a children's '~-book;* 一本兒童故事書; *a ~-book ending,* a happy one (as in most stories for children). 愉快的結局。*The ~ goes that ...,* People are saying that.... 傳說…;據聞…。**'~-teller** *n* person who tells stories. 講故事者。**3** (journalism) any descriptive article in a newspaper; an event, situation, etc suitable for such an article. (新聞)(報紙上的)報導;記事;記述;適合報導的事件、情況等。**4** untrue statement: 謊言;假話: *Don't tell stories, Tom.* 湯姆,不要扯謊。

story[2] /ˈstɔːrɪ; ˈstorɪ/ *n* ⇨ storey.

stoup /stuːp; stup/ *n* **1** (old use) drinking-vessel; flagon. (舊用法)酒杯;(有把手的)酒瓶。**2** stone basin for holy water on the wall of a church or near the porch. (宗教)聖水鉢。

stout /staʊt; staut/ *adj* **1** strong, thick, not easily broken or worn out: 粗壯的;堅固的;結實的: *~ shoes for mountain-climbing.* 爬山用的堅固的鞋子。**2** determined and brave: 堅決的;勇敢的;剛毅的: *offer a ~ resistance to the enemy;* 對敵人作頑强的抵抗; *a ~ fellow;* 剛毅的人; *a ~ heart.* 勇敢。Hence, 由此產生, **ˌ~-'hearted** *adj* courageous. 勇敢的;有勇氣的。**3** (of a person) rather fat; tending to fatness: (指人)相當胖的;要發胖的;有發胖趨勢的: *She's growing too ~ to walk far.* 她胖起來了,不能走遠路。□ *n* [U] strongest kind of dark beer. 最烈的黑啤酒。**~·ly** *adv* **~·ness** *n*

stove[1] /stəʊv; stov/ *n* [C] closed apparatus burning wood, coal, gas, oil or other fuel, used for warming rooms, cooking, etc. 爐;火爐;暖爐。**'~-pipe** *n* pipe for carrying off smoke from a ~. 烟囪;烟筒。

stove[2] /stəʊv; stov/ ⇨ stave[2].

stow /stəʊ; sto/ *vt* [VP6A, 15A, B] ***~ sth (away); ~ sth into/with sth,*** pack, esp carefully and closely: 裝;載;堆置;包裝(尤指小心而緊密地): *~ cargo in a ship's holds;* 裝貨物於船艙中; *~ things* *away in the attic;* 把東西堆置在閣樓上； ~ *clothes into a trunk/~ a trunk with clothes.* 把衣服裝在衣箱中。 **'~·away** *n* person who hides himself in a ship or aircraft (at least until after it starts) in order to make a journey without paying. 偷乘者；藏匿於輪船或飛機中以期免費搭乘者。

straddle /'strædl ; 'strædl̩/ *vt, vi* **1** [VP6A] sit or stand across (sth) with the legs widely separated: 跨；騎；叉腿坐或站於(某物)上： ~ *a ditch/a seat/a horse/a fence.* 跨在溝(座位，馬，柵欄)上。 **2** [VP 2A] stand with the legs wide apart. 叉腿站立；跨立。

strafe /strɑːf *US:* streɪf ; stref/ *vt* [VP6A] (colloq) (俗) **1** bombard. 轟擊；砲轟。 **2** punish; scold. 處罰；斥責。

straggle /'strægl ; 'strægl̩/ *vi* [VP2A, C] **1** grow, spread, in an irregular or untidy manner: 蔓延；蔓生；散漫： *a straggling village;* 房舍散漫的村落； *vines straggling over the fences.* 蔓生於籬笆上的蔓藤。 **2** drop behind while on the march; stray from the main body. 落伍；落後；掉隊。 **strag·gler** /'strægla(r) ; 'strægla/ *n* person who ~s(2). 落伍者；掉隊者。 **strag·gly** /'stræglɪ ; 'stræglɪ/ *adj* straggling. 蔓延的；散漫的；落伍的。

straight[1] /streɪt ; stret/ *adj* **1** without a bend or curve; extending in one direction only: 直的；呈直線的；向一個方向延伸的： *a ~ line/road;* 直線(直路)； ~ *hair,* with no curls in it. 直直的頭髮。 **2** parallel to (sth else, esp the horizon); level: 與(他物，尤指地平線)平行的；水平的： *Put the picture ~.* 把這幅畫放正。 *Is my hat on ~?* 我的帽子(戴得)正不正？ **3** in good order; tidy: 井然有序的；整齊的： *put a room ~.* 把房間收拾整齊。 ***put sth ~,*** make it tidy: 把某物弄整齊： *Please put your desk ~ before you leave the office.* 離開辦公室前，請把你的辦公桌整理好。 ***put the record ~,*** give an accurate account of events, etc. 正確記載事件等。 **4** (of a person, his behaviour, etc) honest, frank, upright: (指人，其行為等)誠實的；坦白的；正直的： *give a ~ answer to a question,* answer frankly; 坦白回答某問題； *keep ~,* avoid wrongdoing, live as a good citizen. 安分守己；奉公守法。 *He is perfectly ~ in all his dealings.* 他在所有的交易中絕對誠實。 *His wife will keep him ~* (= help him to live honestly) *when he is released from prison.* 他出獄後，他的妻子將幫助他改過自新。 ⇨ straight[2](4). **5** (colloq) (of a person) conventional; heterosexual. (俗)(指人)守習俗的；異性戀的。 **6** (phrases) (片語) **a ~ fight,** (in politics) one in which there are only two candidates. (政治)祇有兩人參加的競選。 **a ~ play,** an ordinary drama (contrasted with variety). 普通的戲劇(與'雜耍'相對)。 **a ~ tip,** (eg about the likely winner of a race, an investment in shares), one (said to come) from a direct and reliable source. 可靠情報(如有關可能獲勝的馬，對股票的投資等)。 ***keep a ~ face,*** refrain from smiling or laughing. 忍住不笑；板起面孔。 ***vote the ~ ticket,*** ⇨ ticket(3). **7** (of alcoholic drinks) neat, ie without added (soda-)water, etc: (指酒類)純的；未加水或汽水等的： *Two ~ whiskies, please.* 請來兩杯不加水威士忌。 □ *n* [C] (colloq) conventional or heterosexual person. (俗)守習俗或異性戀的人。 **~en** /'streɪtn ; 'stretn̩/ *vt, vi* ***~en (out/up),*** [VP6A, 15B, 2A, C] make or become ~: (使)變直；(使)變平正；(使)變整潔： *~en a piece of wire/one's tie/one's skirt.* 把鐵絲(領帶，裙子)拉直。 **~·ness** *n*

straight[2] /streɪt ; stret/ *adv* **1** directly; not in a curve or at an angle: 直地；筆直地： *The smoke rose ~ up.* 烟筆直地上升。 *Keep ~ on.* 一直往前走。 *Look ~ ahead.* 向前直視。 *The drunken man couldn't walk ~.* 那醉漢無法向前直走。 *Can you shoot ~,* aim accurately? 你能瞄準射擊嗎？ **2** by a direct route; without turning aside; without delay: 由直路；不拐彎；不延誤；直接地： *Come ~ home.* 直接回家去。 *He went ~ to Rome without staying in Paris.* 他直接前往羅馬，未在巴黎停留。 *He went ~ from school into the navy.* 他一畢業就加入海軍。 ***come ~ to the point,*** make a prompt and clear statement of what is meant, wanted, etc. 直截了當地說；開門見山地說。 **3** ***~ away/off,*** immediately. 立即；馬上。 ***~ out,*** without hesitation or deliberation: 未猶豫地；直言地： *I told him ~ out that I thought he was mistaken.* 我老實告訴他，我認為他錯了。 **4** ***go ~,*** (fig) live an honest life (esp after having been dishonest). (喻)正直地生活；(尤指)改過自新；棄邪歸正。

straight[3] /streɪt ; stret/ *n* (usu 通常作 **the ~**) condition of being straight; straight part of sth, esp the final part of a track or race-course, near the winning-post: 直；平直；(事物的)平直部分；(尤指)(跑道接近終點的)直線跑道： *The two horses were together as they entered the final ~.* 這兩匹馬同時進入最後的直線跑道。

straight·for·ward /ˌstreɪt'fɔːwəd ; ˌstret'fɔrwəd/ *adj* **1** honest; without evasion: 誠實的；坦白的： *a ~ explanation.* 坦率的解釋。 **2** easy to understand or do: 易懂的；易做的： *written in ~ language;* 用淺易文字寫成的； *a ~ problem in algebra.* 一道容易的代數題。 **~·ly** *adv*

straight·way /ˌstreɪt'weɪ ; 'stretˌwe/ *adv* (archaic) at once; immediately. (古)立即；馬上。

strain[1] /streɪn ; stren/ *n* **1** [C, U] condition of being stretched; force exerted: 拉緊；扯緊；緊張；加力；拉力；應變： *The rope broke under the ~.* 繩子被拉斷了。 *Engineers calculate the ~s and stresses of a bridge.* 工程師們計算橋樑的應變和應力。 *What is the breaking ~ of this cable,* the ~ that will break it? 這鐵纜的斷裂應變如何？ **2** [C, U] sth that tests and strains one's powers; severe demand on one's strength, etc: 考驗能力之事物；需要用勁、使力、費神等之事物： *the ~ of sleepless nights.* 連夜不眠的辛勞。 *The payment of the lawyer's bills was a great ~ on my resources.* 支付律師費是我經濟上一項很大的負擔。 *Do you suffer from the ~ of modern life?* 現代生活使你感到緊張嗎？ *He has been under severe ~.* 他一直處於極度緊張的狀態。 **3** [U] exhaustion; fatigue: 勞累；竭盡；疲憊： *suffering from mental/nervous ~.* 精神(神經)疲勞過度。 **4** [C] sprain; injury caused by twisting a joint, etc. 扭筋；脫臼；扭傷關節等。 **5** (poet; usu *pl*) music, song, verse (of the kind indicated): (詩；通常用複數)(某種指明的)音樂；歌；詩： *the ~s of an organ;* 風琴奏出的音樂； *the martial ~s of the band of the Royal Marines.* 皇家海軍陸戰隊樂隊奏出的軍樂。 **6** [C] manner of speaking or writing: 談話或寫作的方式；語調；筆調；風格： *in a lofty/cheerful/dismal ~;* 以高傲(愉快，憂鬱)的語調； *and much more in the same ~,* the same general tendency. 並以相同語氣說了許多其他的事。 **7** tendency in a person's character: 性格的傾向；氣質；性情： *There is a ~ of insanity in the family/of mysticism in her.* 那一家人都有瘋癲的傾向(她有神祕的氣質)。 **8** breed (of animals, insects, etc); line of descent: (動物、昆蟲等的)種；血統： *~s of mosquitoes that are resistant to DDT;* 對 DDT 有抗力的各種蚊蟲； *a spaniel of good ~.* 一隻有優良血統的長毛垂耳小狗。

strain[2] /streɪn ; stren/ *vt, vi* **1** [VP6A, 15A, 3A] stretch tightly by pulling (*at*): 拉緊；扯緊；張緊： *~ a rope to breaking-point;* 把繩子拉緊到快斷的地步； *a dog ~ing at its lead.* 一條使勁拖拽皮帶的狗。 **2** [VP6A, 16A] make the greatest possible use of; exert one's powers: 盡量利用；盡全力： *~ every nerve (to do sth),* do one's utmost; 竭盡全力(做某事)； *~ one's eyes/ears/voice,* look/listen/speak to the best of one's power. 全神貫注地看(聚精會神地聽；聲嘶力竭地說)。 ⇨ 3 below. 參看下列第 3 義。 **3** [VP6A] injure or weaken by ~ing(2): 因過分用力而損傷；耗損；耗弱： *~ a muscle;* 因過分用力而使肌肉受損傷； *~ one's heart,* injure it by over-exertion; 因過勞而損傷心臟； *~ one's eyes,* by using them too much, or on small print, in poor light, etc; 耗損目力(因過度使用、看小字、光線不佳等); ~ *one's voice,* by speaking or singing too long or too loudly. 嗓子變啞(因說話太多,或唱得太久或太大聲等)。 **4** [VP 2A, 3A] ~ ***(at/on),*** make an intense effort: 努力;奮力: *The wrestlers ~ed and struggled.* 摔角者奮力扭鬥。*We ~ed at the oars.* 我們用力划槳。~ ***after effects,*** make exaggerated efforts to get effects: 爲求效果而矯揉造作: *There is no ~ing after effects in this writer's work.* 這位作家的作品不矯揉造作。 **5** [VP6A] (fig) stretch the meaning of; force beyond a limit or what is right: (喻)曲解;歪曲;濫用: ~ *the belief/credulity of one's listeners,* ask too much of it; 過分利用聽衆的信心(輕信); ~ *one's authority/rights,* apply them in a way that is beyond what is allowable or reasonable; 濫用權威(權利); ~ *the meaning of a word.* 曲解一字的意義。 **6** [VP15A] (liter) hold tightly; squeeze: (文)緊握;緊抱: *She ~ed the boy to her bosom.* 她把那男孩緊摟在懷中。 **7** [VP6A, 15B] ~ ***(off/out),*** pass (liquid) through a cloth, or a network of fine wire, etc; separate solid matter in this way: 濾(某種液體); 過濾: ~ *the soup;* 濾湯; ~ *off the water from the vegetables.* 濾去青菜中的水。 **8** ~ ***at sth,*** be too scrupulous or hesitant about accepting sth. 對某事過度顧慮或遲疑。 **9** **~ed** (*pp*) (esp of feelings and behaviour) forced; unnatural; as if forced: (尤指感情及行爲)勉强的;不自然的;似出於被迫的: *~ed cordiality;* 不自然的熱誠; *a ~ed laugh.* 勉强的笑。 **~ed relations,** marked by loss of patience, irritability, risk of quarrelling. (彼此間)緊張的關係(彼此失去耐心,易怒,隱伏爭吵危機等)。**~er** *n* sieve or other device by means of which solid matter is separated from liquid: 濾器;濾網: *a 'tea-~er,* for keeping back tea-leaves when tea is poured out from a teapot. 濾茶具;濾茶器。

strait[1] /streɪt; stret/ *adj* (old use) narrow (舊用法)狹窄的 (rare except in: 罕用,僅見於: ~ *gate,* 窄門, ⇨ Matt 7: 14. 參看新約馬太福音第 7 章第 14 節)。 **'~-jacket,** long-sleeved jacket used to bind the arms of a mentally ill person to the body and prevent him from struggling; (fig) sth that prevents growth or development. (用以拘束瘋人的)拘束衣(袖特長,可將其手臂與身體縛起,以防其掙扎); (喻)阻止生長或發展之事物;約束;束縛。 **,~-'laced** *adj* severely virtuous; having a strict attitude towards moral questions; puritanical. (在道德和行爲方面)極端拘謹的。 **~en** /'streɪtn; 'stretn̩/ *vt* (usu in *pp*) (通常用過去分詞) ***in ~ed circumstances,*** in poverty. 在窮困中。

strait[2] /streɪt; stret/ *n* **1** narrow passage of water connecting two seas or two large bodies of water (*pl* or *sing* with proper names): 海峽;峽 (與專有名詞連用時,用複數或單數皆可): *the S~s of Gibraltar;* 直布羅陀海峽; *the Magellan S~.* 麥哲倫海峽。 **2** (usu *pl*) trouble; difficulty: (通常用複數) 困難; 窘迫: *be in financial ~s;* 經濟困難; *in great ~s.* 在極度困難中。

strand[1] /strænd; strænd/ *n* (poet or rhet) sandy shore of a lake, sea or river. (詩或修辭)湖,海或河的沙岸;濱;礁。 □ *vi, vt* **1** [VP6A, 2A] (of a ship) (cause to) run aground. (指船)(使)擱淺。 **2** ***be (left) ~ed,*** (of a person) be left without means of transport, in a difficult position, without money or friends: (指人)陷於無交通工具的情況; 難以行動; 陷入困境; 處於無錢或無友的境地; 束手無策: *be ~ed in a foreign country.* 在異國陷入困境。

strand[2] /strænd; strænd/ *n* [C] **1** any of the threads, hairs, wires, etc twisted together into a rope or cable, or in a textile material; tress of hiar. (線、毛髮、鐵絲等絞成繩或纜等的)一股;縷;條;一束髮。 **2** (fig) line of development (in a story, etc): (喻)(故事等)發展的線索;情節: *May I pick out one ~ in that narrative?* 我可以光談該故事的某一情節嗎?

strange /streɪndʒ; strendʒ/ *adj* (-r, -st) **1** not previously known, seen, felt or heard of; (for this reason) surprising: 前所未知、未見、未覺察或未聽說過的;奇怪的;奇異的;奇妙的;奇特的: *hear a ~ noise;* 聽到一奇異的聲音; *in a ~ land.* 在陌生之地。 *What ~* (= unusual) *clothes you're wearing!* 你穿的衣服眞新奇啊! *Truth is ~r than fiction.* 事實比想像的事物還奇怪。 *She says she feels ~,* not in her usual condition, perhaps rather dizzy, etc. 她說她覺得不大舒服。 **~ to say...,** It is surprising that.... 說來奇怪…。 **2** (*pred*) (敍述用法) **~ to sth,** fresh or unaccustomed to: 對…感到陌生或不習慣的: *The village boy was ~ to city life.* 那村童不慣於城市生活。 *He is still ~ to the work,* has not yet learnt his new job. 他對這項工作仍很生疏。 **~·ly** *adv* **~·ness** *n*

stran·ger /'streɪndʒə(r); 'strendʒɚ/ *n* person one does not know; person in a place or in company that he does not know: 陌生人;異國人;異鄉人;外地人: *The dog always barks at ~s.* 這隻狗總向陌生人吠叫。*You're quite a ~,* (colloq) It's a long time since we met. (俗)你眞是稀客(很久不見了;久違)。*I am a ~ in this town,* do not know my way about. 這城市我很陌生(我不認得此地的路)。 *He is no ~ to misfortune,* (fig) has had experience of it. (喻)他飽經不幸。

strangle /'stræŋgl; 'stræŋgl̩/ *vt* [VP6A] kill by squeezing the throat of; hinder the breathing of: 扼殺;勒死;絞死;使窒息;阻塞…的呼吸: *This stiff collar is strangling me,* is so tight that it squeezes my neck. 這硬領扼住了我的頸子。 **'~·hold** *n* (usu fig) deadly grip: (通常作喻)致命的緊扼;壓制;束縛: *The new tariffs have put a ~hold on our trade with them.* 這項新關稅增加了我們同他們貿易上的束縛。 **stran·gu·la·tion** /,stræŋgjʊ'leɪʃn; ,stræŋgjə'leʃən/ *n* [U] strangling or being ~d. 扼殺;勒死;絞死;窒息。

strap /stræp; stræp/ *n* strip of leather or other flexible material (often with a buckle) to fasten things together or to keep sth (eg a wrist-watch) in place. 帶;皮帶;吊帶(通常有釦,用於束縛或使某物位置固定)。 **'~-hanger** *n* standing passenger in a bus, train, etc who holds on to a ~ with a loop (hanging from the roof) when all the seats are occupied. (公車、火車等上拉着吊帶的)站客。□ *vt* (-pp-) **1** [VP6A, 15B] ~ ***sth (on/up),*** fasten or hold in place with a ~: 用帶捆紮;用帶束起或固定: ~ *on a wrist-watch;* 帶上手錶; ~ *up a suitcase,* using ~s and buckles. 扣緊手提箱(扣上皮帶的扣環)。 **2** [VP6A] beat with a ~. 用帶抽打。**~·ping** *adj* big, tall, healthy-looking: 高大健壯的;魁偉的: *a ~ping girl.* 高大健壯的女孩。

strata /'strɑːtə *US:* 'streɪtə; 'stretə/ *pl* of stratum. stratum 之複數。

strat·agem /'strætədʒəm; 'strætədʒəm/ *n* [C, U] (use of a) trick or device to deceive sb (esp the enemy in war). 計謀;詭計(尤指戰時用以誘騙敵人者)。

stra·tegic /strə'tiːdʒɪk; strə'tidʒɪk/, **stra·tegi·cal** /-kl; -kl/ *adj* of, by, serving the purpose of, strategy: 戰略的;藉戰略的;合於戰略的: *a ~ retreat;* 戰略性撤退; *a ~ link in a line of defence;* 防線上的一個戰略環節; ~ *bombing,* eg of industrial areas and communications; 戰略性轟炸(如轟炸工業區或通訊設施); ~ *materials,* those essential for war. 戰略物資。 **stra·tegi·cally** /-klɪ; -kl̩ɪ/ *adv* **stra·tegics** *n* [U] science or art of strategy. 兵學;兵法;軍事學。

strat·egy /'strætədʒɪ; 'strætədʒɪ/ *n* [U] the art of planning operations in war, esp of the movements of armies and navies into favourable positions for fighting; skill in managing any affair. 戰略;軍略;策略;謀略。⇨ tactic(2). **strat·egist** /-dʒɪst; -dʒɪst/ *n* person skilled in ~. 戰略家;謀略家。

strat·ify /'strætɪfaɪ; 'strætə,faɪ/ *vt, vi* (*pt, pp* -fied) **1** [VP6A] arrange in strata: 使成層;層疊;按層排列:

stratified rock. 成層岩。*English society is highly stratified.* 英國社會層次分明。**2** [VP2A] form into strata. 形成層次。**strat·ifi·ca·tion** /ˌstrætɪfɪˈkeɪʃn ; ˌstrætəfɪˈkeʃən/ *n* arrangement in strata. 成層;層疊;層化。

stratified rock

strato·sphere /ˈstrætəsfɪə(r) ; ˈstrætəˌsfɪr/ *n* layer of atmospheric air between about 10 and 60 km above the earth's surface. 平流層;同溫層(距地球表面約 10 至 60 公里之間的大氣層)。

stra·tum /ˈstrɑːtəm *US:* ˈstreɪtəm ; ˈstretəm/ *n* (*pl* -ta /-tə ; -tə/) horizontal layer of rock, etc in the earth's crust; social class or division: (地殼的)岩層;地層;(社會的)階層;階級: *Students in Britain come from various strata in society.* 英國的學生來自社會各階層。

straw /strɔː ; strɔ/ *n* **1** [U] dry cut stalks of wheat, barley, rice and other grains, as material for making hats, mats, etc or bedding for cattle, or thatching roofs, etc: 稻草;麥稭(用以製帽、蓆等,或用以做家畜的墊草,或用來蓋屋頂等): *a ~ mattress,* one stuffed with ~. 草墊。***make bricks without ~,*** make sth without all the necessary materials. 作無米之炊。⇨ Exod 5 : 7. 參看舊約'出埃及記'第 5 章第 7 節。***a man of ~,*** imaginary person, easily overcome, set up as an opponent. 稻草人(容易擊敗的假想對手)。**'~·board** *n* [U] coarse cardboard made of ~ pulp. 馬糞紙;草紙板。**'~-coloured** *adj* pale yellow. 淡黃色的;草黃色的。**2** [C] single stalk or piece of ~; thin tube of other material for sucking up liquid: (稻草或麥稭的)莖管;(吸取液體的)吸管: *suck lemonade through a ~.* 用吸管吸檸檬水。***catch at a ~; clutch at ~s,*** try any expedient, however useless (like a drowning man clutching at a ~). 嘗試最沒有用的方法(正如溺水的人連一根草都要抓)。***not care a ~,*** not at all. 毫不介意。***not worth a ~,*** worth nothing. 一文不值;毫無價值。***a ~ in the wind,*** a slight hint that shows which way things may develop; 事態動向的徵兆; hence, 由此產生, **a ~ vote,** attempt to discover public opinion on a topic of current interest by an unofficial poll (eg as made by a newspaper). 民意調查(報館等就當前重要問題所作的非正式投票)。**the last ~,** an addition to a task, burden, etc, that makes it intolerable. 突破容忍(耐力等)極限的一樁事、工作、壓力等。□ *vt* spread ~ on; cover with ~. 鋪草於…之上;覆以草。

straw·berry /ˈstrɔːbrɪ *US:* -berɪ ; ˈstrɔˌbɛrɪ/ *n* (*pl* -ries) [C] (perennial, low-growing plant having) juicy red fruit with tiny yellow seeds on its surface, eaten raw and in jam. 草莓樹;草莓(多年生矮小植物,結紅色漿果,生食或製果醬)。⇨ the illus at fruit. 參看 fruit 之插圖。**'~ mark,** reddish birthmark on the skin. (皮膚上的)紅色胎記;莓狀痣(一種先天性血管瘤)。

stray /streɪ ; stre/ *vi* (*pt, pp* ~ed) [VP2A, C] wander (from the right path, from one's companions, etc); lose one's way: 走失;迷路;離題: *Don't ~ from the point.* 不要離題。□ *n* **1** animal or person (esp a child) that has ~ed. 迷失的動物或人;(尤指)迷失的小孩。***waifs and ~s,*** homeless children. 無家可歸的孩童。**2** (attrib) having ~ed: (形容用法)迷失了的: *~ cats and dogs;* 迷失的貓和狗; *killed by a ~ bullet,* killed by chance, not purposely; 被流彈射殺; occasional; seen or happening occasionally: 偶然的;偶見的;偶爾發生的: *The streets were empty except for a few ~ taxis.* 除了偶爾可以看到幾輛計程車外,街上沒有人跡。

streak /striːk ; strik/ *n* [C] **1** long, thin, usu irregular line or band: 線條;條紋;條痕;脈;層(通常呈不規則形): *~s of lean and fat,* eg in meat; 瘦肉和肥肉相間的肉層; *like a ~ of lightning,* very fast. 似一道閃電般(快速)地。**2** trace or touch (*of*): 些微;少許: *There's a ~ of vanity/cruelty in his character.* 他的性格有點虛浮(殘酷)。**3** brief period: 短時間;一陣: *The gambler had a ~ of good luck,* won for a time. 那賭徒有過一陣好運(贏過一陣)。***hit a winning ~,*** have a series of successes (in gambling, etc). 接連獲勝或成功(如在賭博中)。□ *vt, vi* **1** [VP6A, 15A] mark with ~s: 加線條或條紋於: *white marble ~ed with brown.* 有褐色條紋的白色大理石。**2** [VP2C] (colloq) move very fast (like a ~ of lightning): (俗)疾動;飛跑(似閃電般): *The children ~ed off as fast as they could.* 孩子們拔腿飛跑。**~y** *adj* (-ier, -iest) marked with, having, ~s: 有條紋的;有線條的;有層脈的: *~y bacon,* with ~s of fat and lean in it. 五花醃肉(肥瘦相間者)。

stream /striːm ; strim/ *n* **1** river or brook; current. 河;川;溪;水流。***go up/down ~,*** move up/down the river. 逆流而上(順流而下)。***go with the ~,*** (fig) do or think as the majority of people do, be carried along by the course of events. (喻)順應潮流;跟着大多數人去做或去想。**2** steady flow (of liquid, persons, things, etc): (液體、人、物等的)不斷流出: *a ~ of blood/curses.* 一股血(一連串的咒詛)。*S~s of people were coming out of the railway station.* 人潮從火車站湧出。**~ of consciousness,** continuous conscious experience of an individual; (in literature) technique of writing novels to indicate this, eg as in James Joyce's *Ulysses.* 意識流(個人連續的意識經驗);(文學)意識流小說寫作技巧(如喬伊斯所寫的'尤利西斯')。**3** (education) (division of a) class of children in age groups according to ability and intelligence: (教育)(英)同一年級學生根據能力及智力編成的小組;能力分組: *bright boys and girls in the 'A-stream.* A組的聰慧男孩和女孩。□ *vi, vt* **1** [VP2A, C] flow freely; move continuously and smoothly in one direction: 未受阻礙地流動;任意地流;連續而流暢地向一個方向移動: *Sweat was ~ing down his face.* 他臉上汗水直流。*His face was ~ing with sweat.* 他滿臉都是汗水。**2** [VP2C] float or wave (in the wind): (在風中)飄揚;招展: *The flag/Her long hair ~ed in the wind.* 旗幟(她的長髮)在風中飄動。**3** [VP6A] place (children) in ~s(3). 按能力及智慧將(孩童)分組。**~er** *n* **1** long narrow flag; long narrow ribbon of paper. 狹而長的旗;旗旛;狹長的紙帶。**~er headline,** (US) (美) = banner headline. ⇨ banner. **2** column of light shooting out in the aurora. 從極光射出的光柱;流光。**'~·let** /-lɪt ; -lɪt/ *n* small ~ or brook. 小溪;小河。

stream·line /ˈstriːmlaɪn ; ˈstrimˌlaɪn/ *vt* make more efficient (by simplifying, getting rid of, wasteful methods, etc): 使更爲有效(藉簡化或廢除不經濟的方法等);提高效率: *~ production,* eg in a factory. 提高生產效率(如工廠中)。**'~d** *adj* **1** having a shape that offers least resistance to the flow of air, water, etc: 流線型的: *~d cars.* 流線型轎車。**2** having nothing likely to impede progress: 無阻礙的;有效率的: *~d controls/methods.* 高效率管理(方法)。

street /striːt ; strit/ *n* town or village road with houses on one side or both: 街;街道: *meet a friend in the ~;* 在街上遇見一位朋友; *cross the ~;* 穿越街道; *a '~-map/-plan of York.* 約克城的市街圖(計畫)。Cf 參較 *a road-map of Yorkshire.* 約克

郡的道路圖。'~•car *n* (esp US) tram-car. (尤美)電車;街車。~ door *n* door which opens (usu directly) on to the ~. (If there is a garden *front door* is preferred). 臨街大門。(前有庭園時,以稱front door 爲宜。) ***the man in the ~,*** typical citizen. 典型公民;一般人。***not in the same ~ (as),*** not nearly so good (as). 難以和… 相比;不如… 那樣好。***~s ahead of,*** (colloq) far ahead of. (俗)遠在前面。***(right) up one's ~,*** (colloq) within one's area of knowledge, interests, etc. (俗)在自己的知識、興趣等範圍內。***go on the ~s,*** earn one's living by prostitution. 以賣淫爲生;當妓女。'**~-girl,** '**~-walker** *nn* prostitute. 妓女;阻街女郎。

strength /streŋθ ; strɛŋθ/ *n* [U] **1** quality of being strong: 强壯;强度;强壯的性質;力量;力氣: *a man/horse of great ~;* 强壯的人(馬); *the ~ of a rope,* its ability to resist strain; 繩子的强度(耐拉力); *the ~ of our army;* 我們軍隊的力量; *get back one's health and ~ after an illness.* 病後恢復健康及體力。*She hasn't the ~/hasn't ~ enough to walk upstairs.* 她沒有力氣走上樓。*How is the ~ of alcoholic liquors measured?* 烈酒的濃度是怎樣測定的? ***on the ~ of,*** encouraged by, relying upon: 受…的鼓勵;依恃;憑藉: *I employed the boy on the ~ of your recommendation.* 由於你的推薦我雇用那男孩。**2** that which helps to make sb or sth strong: 使某人或某物堅强之事物;支持物;依恃物: *God is our ~.* 我們依賴上帝。**3** power measured by numbers of persons present or persons who can be used: 實力;兵力;人力;可供使用的人員: *The enemy were in (great) ~,* Their numbers were great. 敵人的人馬衆多。*The police force is 500 below ~,* needs 500 more men. 警察的人數尙需五百。***bring sth/be up to ~,*** reach/be the required number: 使達到(達到)所需數字: *We must bring the police force up to ~.* 我們必需使警察達到所需員額。**~en** /'streŋθn ; 'strɛŋθən/ *vt, vi* [VP 6A, 2A] make or become strong(er). 使或變得强壯、堅强、更强壯、更堅强等;加强;强化。

strenu·ous /'strenjʊəs ; 'strɛnjʊəs/ *adj* using or needing great effort; energetic: 費力的;須全力以赴的;奮發的;精力充沛的: *~ work;* 吃力的工作; *~ workers;* 辛苦的工作者; *make ~ efforts;* 大大地努力; *lead a ~ life.* 過奮鬥的生活。**~·ly** *adv* **~·ness** *n*

strep·to·coc·cus /ˌstreptə'kɒkəs ; ˌstrɛptə'kɑkəs/ *n* (*pl* -cocci /-'kɒkaɪ ; -'kɑksaɪ/) any of a group of bacteria which causes serious infections and illnesses. (導致多種嚴重疾病的)鏈球菌屬。

strep·to·my·cin /ˌstreptəʊ'maɪsɪn ; ˌstrɛptə'maɪsɪn/ *n* antibiotic medical preparation. 鏈黴素(一種抗生素)。

stress /stres ; strɛs/ *n* **1** [U] pressure; condition causing hardship, disquiet, etc: 壓力;壓迫;引起困難、憂慮、不寧等的情況: *times of ~,* of trouble and danger; 危難之際;非常時期; *driven into harbour by ~ of weather;* 因惡劣天氣而進入港內; *under the ~ of poverty/fear/excitement.* 在貧困(恐懼,激動)的壓力下。**2** [U] (also with *indef art*) weight or force: (亦可與不定冠詞連用)重要: *a school that lays (a) ~ on foreign languages.* 著重外國語的學校。**3** [C, U] (result of) extra force, used in speaking, on a particular word or syllable: 重讀;重音: *In 'strategic' the ~ is on the second syllable.* 'strategic' 一字的重音在第二個音節。*S~ and rhythm are important in speaking English.* 講英語時重音及節奏都很重要。*You must learn where to place the ~es.* 你必須學習何處須重讀。'**~-mark** *n* mark (eg ' (principal or main ~) and ˌ (secondary ~) as used in this dictionary) that indicates the ~ on a syllable. 重音符號(表示某一音節須重讀的符號,如本字典用的 ' 及 ˌ 兩個符號)。**4** [C, U] (in mechanics) tension; force exerted between two bodies that touch, or between two parts of one body. (機械)拉力;應力。□ *vt* [VP6A] put ~ or emphasis on: 重讀;着重;强調: *He ~ed the point that...* 他强調這一點…。

stretch /stretʃ ; strɛtʃ/ *vt, vi* **1** [VP6A, 15A, B, 16A, 22] make wider, longer or tighter, by pulling; be or become wider, etc when pulled: 伸展;張開;拉長;拉緊;擴大: *~ a rope tight;* 把繩子拉緊; *~ a rope across a path;* 拉繩橫越道路; *~ a pair of gloves/shoes,* eg to make them fit better; 撐開手套(鞋子); *~ one's neck,* eg to see over the heads of people in a crowd; 伸長脖子(如在人叢中從旁人頭上看過去); *~ one's arms/legs/oneself/one's muscles,* extend the limbs, etc and thus tighten the muscles; 伸臂(伸腿;伸展身體;伸展肌肉); *~ out one's arm for a book.* 伸出手臂去拿一本書。***~ one's legs,*** exercise oneself by walking as a relief from sitting or lying. 散步;走動以舒展身體。**2** ***~ (oneself) out (on),*** lie on at full length: 直躺: *They were ~ed out on the lawn.* 他們(被打倒)直躺在草地上。*He ~ed himself out on the beach.* 他直躺在海灘上。**3** [VP6A] make (a word, law, etc) include or cover more than is strictly right; exert beyond what is right: 不當地引伸(字義、法律等);濫用;曲解: *~ the law/one's principles/a point in sb's favour,* ⇨ point¹(9); 曲解法律(原則,某一點等以利某人); strain to the utmost: 盡力地使用、努力、拉扯等: *~ one's powers,* work very hard or too hard. 非常或過度努力地工作。***be fully ~ed,*** working to the utmost of one's powers. 竭盡所能;全力以赴。**4** [VP2A, B, C] extend: 延伸;綿亙: *forests ~ing for hundreds of miles;* 綿亙數百哩的森林; *a road ~ing away across the desert.* 穿越沙漠的道路。□ *n* [C] **1** act of ~ing or being ~ed: 伸展;張開;拉長;拉緊;擴大;濫用;曲解: *by a ~ of language/the law/one's principles.* 濫用語言(法律,某人的原則)。⇨ 3 above. 參看上列第3義。*The cat woke and gave a ~.* 那隻貓醒過來伸伸懶腰。*He got up with a ~ and a yawn.* 他站起來伸伸懶腰,打個呵欠。***by 'any/'no ~ of the imagination,*** however much one may try to imagine sth. 無論怎麽推想。***at full ~,*** fully ~ed(3): 盡力而爲: *The factory was/The workers were at full ~.* 工廠全力生產(工人們全力工作)。**2** unbroken or continuous period of time or extent of country, etc: 連續的期間;綿亙的鄉野;伸延的空間: *a beautiful ~ of wooded country;* 一大片美麗而有林木的鄉野; (sl) (俚) *do a two-year ~ in prison.* 坐牢兩年。***at a ~,*** continuously: 連續不斷地: *Can you work for six hours at a ~?* 你能連續工作六小時嗎? **3** straight side of a track or course (for racing). (跑道的)直線部分;直邊。**~er** *n* **1** framework of poles, canvas, etc for carrying a sick, injured or wounded person. (抬傷患用的)擔架;舁床。'**~er-bearer** *n* person who helps to carry a ~er. 抬擔架者。'**~er-party** *n* number of persons with ~ers (to carry an injured or wounded person). 擔架隊。**2** device for ~ing things (eg gloves, shoes). (撐物用的)撐具;撐架;伸張器。

strew /struː ; stru/ *vt* (*pt* ~ed, *pp* ~ed or strewn /struːn ; strun/) [VP6A, 14] ***~ sth (on/over sth);*** ***~ sth with sth,*** scatter (sth) over a surface; (partly) cover (a surface) (with sth scattered): 撒(某物)於表面上; (以撒布之物)遮蔽(某一表面)的全部或一部;散播;點綴: *~ flowers over a path;* 散花於路上; *~ a path with flowers.* 以花撒在路上。

strewth /struːθ ; struθ/ = struth.

stri·ated /straɪ'eɪtɪd *US:* 'straɪeɪtɪd ; 'straɪetɪd/ *adj* striped; furrowed. 有條紋的;有溝痕的。

stricken /'strɪkən ; 'strɪkən/ *adj* (*pp* of strike; used pred) (strike 的過去分詞;叙述用法) affected or overcome: 受害的; 染患的; 被壓服的: *'grief-/'panic-/'terror-~,* overcome by grief/panic/terror; 非常悲傷的(非常驚慌的; 嚇壞了的); *~ with fever/malaria/cancer;* 發燒(染瘧疾;得癌症); *'cancer-~.* 患癌症的。***~ in years,*** (archaic) old and feeble. (古)老而衰弱的。

strict /strɪkt ; strɪkt/ *adj* (-er, -est) **1** stern; demanding obedience or exact observance: 嚴厲的;嚴格的: *a ~ father;* 嚴父; *~ discipline;* 嚴格的紀律; *be ~ with one's children;* 對子女嚴格; *keep a ~ hand over the children;* 嚴格管教子女; *a ~ rule against smoking,* eg at a petrol station. 禁止吸烟的嚴格規定(如在加油站)。 **2** clearly and exactly defined; precisely limited: 明確的;嚴密的;精確的: *tell sb sth in ~est confidence;* 極秘密地將某事告訴某人; *in the ~ sense of the word;* 就某字精確的意義而言; *the ~ truth.* 千眞萬確的事。**~·ly** *adv* in a ~ manner: 嚴厲地;嚴格地;明確地;嚴密地: *Smoking is ~ly prohibited.* 嚴禁吸烟。**~·ness** *n*

stric·ture /ˈstrɪktʃə(r); ˈstrɪktʃɚ/ *n* [C] **1** (often *pl*) severe criticism or blame: (常用複數)嚴厲的批評或責難: *pass ~s on sb.* 嚴厲地批評某人。**2** (med) contraction of a tube-like part of the body, causing a diseased condition. (醫)狹窄(身體上管道收縮,造成生理異常)。

stride /straɪd; straɪd/ *vi, vt* (*pt* strode /strəʊd; strod/, *pp* (rare) (罕) stridden /ˈstrɪdn; ˈstrɪdn̩/) **1** [VP2C] walk with long steps: 大步行走: *~ along the road;* 沿路大步行走; *~ off/away.* 大步走開。 **2** *~ over/across sth,* pass over in one step: 跨過或跨越某物: *~ over a ditch.* 跨過小溝。 **3** [VP6A] = bestride. □ *n* [C] (distance covered in) one long step: 大步;濶步;一大步的距離;跨幅: *walk with vigorous ~s.* 有力地大步行走。 ***make great ~s,*** make good and rapid progress. 大有進步;突飛猛進。 ***take sth in one's ~,*** do it without special effort. 輕易地做某事。

stri·dent /ˈstraɪdnt; ˈstraɪdn̩t/ *adj* (of sound) loud and harsh; shrill: (指聲音)粗嗄的;尖銳的: *the ~ notes of the cicadas.* 蟬的尖銳鳴聲。**~·ly** *adv*

stridu·late /ˈstrɪdjʊleɪt *US:* ˈstrɪdʒʊleɪt; ˈstrɪdʒəˌlet/ *vi* [VP2A] make shrill grating sounds (esp of insects such as crickets). 發尖銳的磨擦聲(尤指昆蟲如蟋蟀所發)。**stridu·la·tion** /ˌstrɪdjʊˈleɪʃn *US:* -dʒ-; ˌstrɪdʒəˈleʃən/ *n*

strife /straɪf; straɪf/ *n* [U] quarrelling; state of conflict: 爭吵;傾軋;敵對;衝突: *industrial ~* (between workers and employers). 工人與雇主間的衝突。

strike[1] /straɪk; straɪk/ *n* **1** act of striking(5): 罷工: *the numerous ~s in the coalmines;* 煤礦區的無數次罷工; *a ~ of bus-drivers;* 公共汽車司機的罷工; (attrib) (形容用法) *take ~ action.* 採取罷工行動。 ***be/go on ~; be/come/go out on ~,*** be engaged in, start, a ~. 從事罷工;開始罷工。**a general ~,** by workers in all or most trades, etc; (各行業)總罷工;全面罷工; also ⇨ hunger, lightning, sympathetic, unofficial. **ˈ~-bound** *adj* unable to function because of a ~: 因罷工而停頓的: *The docks were ~-bound for a week.* 碼頭因罷工而癱瘓一週。 **ˈ~-breaker** *n* worker brought in or coming in to take the place of a striker. 代替罷工者工作的人;破壞罷工者。**ˈ~ fund** *n* special fund to supplement ~-pay. 罷工準備金;罷工基金。 **ˈ~-leader** *n* worker or official who leads a ~. 罷工領袖。**ˈ~-pay** *n* money paid to strikers from trade-union funds (during a ~ officially recognized by a union). (工會給予罷工者的)罷工津貼。 **2** act of striking (oil, etc) in the earth. (油田等的)發現。 **lucky ~,** fortunate discovery. 幸運的發現。**3** sudden attack by aircraft. 飛機的出擊。

strike[2] /straɪk; straɪk/ *vt, vi* (*pt, pp* struck /strʌk; strʌk/) (also ⇨ stricken, above) (亦參看上列之 stricken) (For special uses with *adverbial particles* and *preps,* ⇨ 17 below.) (與副詞接語及介詞連用的特殊用法,參看下列第 17 義。) **1** [VP6A, 12C, 14, 2A, C, 3A] hit; give a blow or blows to; aim a blow *at:* 打;擊;敲;向…打擊: *He struck me on the chin* (note use of *def art*). 他打在我的下巴上(注意須加定冠詞)。 *He struck the table with a heavy blow.* 他重重地拍了一下桌子。 *He struck his knee with his hand/struck his hand on his knee.* 他以手拍擊膝頭。*He seized a stick and struck at me.* 他抓起一根棍子向我打來。 *Who struck the first blow,* started the fight? 誰先出手打人? *The ship struck a rock.* 該船觸礁了。*That tree was struck by lightning.* 那棵樹被閃電擊中了。 ***~ at the root of sth,*** attack trouble, evil, etc at its source. 斬草除根;除惡務盡;徹底根絕。***S~ while the iron is hot,*** (prov) Act promptly while action is likely to get results. (諺)打鐵趁熱。***a ˈ~/ˈstriking force,*** military force ready to attack at short notice. 打擊部隊(可隨時待命出擊者)。 ***within ˈstriking distance,*** near enough to reach or attack easily. 在易達到或攻擊範圍內。 **2** [VP6A, 2A] produce (a light) by striking or scraping: 藉打或擦而產生(光亮): *~ sparks from a flint;* 自燧石打出火花; *~ a match,* cause it to burst into flame by scraping it on a surface; 擦燃火柴; *~ a light,* produce one in this way. 擦(打)出亮光。*These matches are damp—they won't ~.* 這些火柴潮濕了,擦不燃。 **3** [VP6A] come upon, discover (by mining, drilling, etc): (藉開礦、鑽探等而)發現;找到: *to ~ gold.* 發現黃金。***~ oil,*** **(a)** discover oil by drilling. 藉鑽探而發現石油。**(b)** (fig) have good fortune; find a means of getting rich. (喻)交到好運;發橫財;發現致富的方法。***~ it rich,*** win wealth suddenly. 突然致富。 **4** [VP6A, 2A] (cause to) sound: (使)發聲;(使)鳴;(使)響: *~ a chord on the piano.* 彈一下鋼琴。*This clock ~s the hours.* 這鐘每小時報時一次。*The clock has just struck (four).* 這鐘剛敲過(四下)。*The/His hour has struck,* (fig) the critical moment has come or gone. (喻)(他的)緊要關頭已到(已過)。 ***~ a note of,*** give an impression (of the kind indicated): 給予某種(指明的)感覺;造成某種效果: *The President struck a note of warning against over-optimism.* 總統的話有警惕大家勿過分樂觀的作用。 **5** [VP2A, 3A] ***~ (for/against),*** (of workers, etc) stop working for an employer (in order to get more pay, shorter hours, better conditions, etc or as a protest against sth): (指工人等)(爲要求增加工資,縮短工時,改善環境等而)罷工: *~ for higher pay/against bad working conditions.* 爲要求增加工資(抗議惡劣工作環境)而罷工。 ⇨ strike[1](1). **6** [VP6A, 16A] impress; have an effect upon the mind: 給予…感覺;在心靈上產生某種效果;造成某種印象: *How does the idea/suggestion ~ you?* 你對於那個主意(建議)看法如何? *The plan ~s me as ridiculous.* 我覺得那項計畫很可笑。*What struck me* (= The impression I had) *was that he was not telling the truth.* 就我的看法,他講的不是眞話。*An idea suddenly struck me,* came to me, with an immediate response. 我突然想到一個主意(忽然心生一計)。 **7** [VP 16B, or 2D with object and *as* omitted 或 2D 省略受詞及 as] have an effect on the body or mind: 對身體或心靈產生某種效果;使身體或心靈感覺到: *The room ~s you as warm and comfortable when you enter.* 那房間你一進去就會感到溫暖與舒適。*The prison cell struck cold and damp,* was felt as cold and damp by anyone entering it. 那牢房使人覺得陰冷而潮濕。 **8** [VP6A] produce by stamping or punching: 鑄造;壓製: *~ a coin/medal/medallion.* 鑄造錢幣(紀念章,獎章)。 **9** [VP6A] achieve, arrive at, by reckoning or weighing: 藉計算或衡量而達到;計算出;衡量出: *~ an average;* 算出平均數值; *~ a balance between anarchy and authoritarian rule/between licence and repression.* 在無政府主義與獨裁統治之間(放縱與壓抑之間)找出中道。***~ a bargain (with sb),*** reach one by agreement; conclude one. (與某人)達成交易;訂定買賣合同。 **10** [VP6A] come upon; find: 偶遇;遇見;發現: *~ the track/the right path.* 發現踪跡(正確的路徑)。 **11** [VP2A, C] ***~ (off/out),*** set out, go (in a certain direction): 出發;行進;(向某一方向)走: *We struck (off)* (= turned and went) *into the woods.* 我們轉入林中。 *The boys struck (out) across the fields.* 那些男孩走過田野。 *The explorers struck out* (= started, set out) *at dawn.* 那些探險的人天

一亮就出發了。 **12** [VP22] cause (sb) to be, suddenly and as if by a single stroke: 使(某人)突然成爲;使(某人)突然變作: *be struck blind/dumb/silent.* 突然瞎了(啞了,沉默下來)。**13** [VP14] ～ ***fear/terror/alarm into sb,*** fill, afflict, with fear, etc: 使某人心起恐懼(畏懼,警戒): *Attila struck terror into the people of eastern Europe.* 匈奴王阿提拉曾令東歐人民膽寒。*The bombing attack struck fear into their hearts.* 轟炸使他們心驚肉跳。 **14** [VP6A] lower or take down (sails, tents). 落下;取下;扯下(帆);撤除(帳篷)。～ ***one's flag,*** lower it (as a signal that one surrenders a ship, fortress, etc to the enemy). 下旗(交出船、堡壘等,向敵人投降的表徵)。～ ***tents/camp,*** pack up tents, etc. 捆紮帳篷等;拔營。 **15** [VP6A] ～ ***a cutting,*** take a cutting from a plant and insert it in soil to ～ root. 插枝(把插條種在泥土裡)。 ～ ***root,*** put out roots. 扎根;生根。 **16** [VP6A] hold or put the body in a certain way to indicate sth: 把身體擺成某種姿態;採取;裝出;擺出: ～ *an attitude of defiance;* 擺出一付藐視人的態度; ～ *a pose.* 採取某種姿勢。 **17** [VP 2C, 3A, 15B] (special uses with *adverbial particles* and *preps*): (與副詞接語及介詞連用的特殊用法):

strike sb down, (formal) hit him so that he falls to the ground; (of a disease, etc) attack him: (正式用語)把某人打倒在地上;(指疾病等)侵襲某人: *He was struck down in the prime of life,* eg of sb who was assassinated. 他正值盛年卽被打倒(如遭暗殺)。

strike sth off, **(a)** cut off with a blow, eg of an axe. 將某物砍掉或切除等(如用斧頭)。**(b)** print: 印刷: ～ *off 1000 copies of a book.* 將一本書印一千本。 ～ ***sth off (sth),*** remove: 刪除: ～ *sb's name off a list.* 將某人的名字從名單上刪除。 *The doctor's name was struck off the Medical Register,* was cancelled, eg because of professional misconduct. 那醫師的名字已從醫師錄上刪除(如因職業上的過失)。

strike on/upon sth, get or find suddenly or unexpectedly: 突然得到或發現: ～ *on an idea/a plan.* 突然想起一個主意(計畫)。

strike out, **(a)** use the arms and legs vigorously in swimming: (以手臂和腿)用力游: ～ *out for the shore.* 用力游向岸邊。 **(b)** aim vigorous blows: 用力打擊: *He lost his temper and struck out wildly.* 他大發脾氣,瘋狂地出手打人。 **(c)** follow a new or independent path, a new form of activity: 走一條新的或獨立的路線;採取新的行爲方式;獨樹一幟;創新格局: ～ *out on one's own/in a new direction.* 自謀生計(另求發展)。～ ***sth out/through,*** cross out, put a line or lines through: 刪除;劃去;塗去: ～ *out a word/name/item.* 刪掉一字(一個名字,一個項目)。

strike (sth) up, begin to play: 開始演奏等: *The band struck up (a tune).* 樂隊開始演奏(一曲)。～ ***up sth (with sb),*** begin (perhaps casually) a friendship or acquaintance: 開始(也許是偶然地)(與某人)結交或認識: *The two boys quickly struck up a friendship.* 這兩個男孩子很快就熟悉起來了。 *She struck up an acquaintance with a fellow passenger during the cruise.* 那次(乘船)旅行她結交了一位同船的旅客。

striker /ˈstraɪkə(r); ˈstraɪkɚ/ *n* **1** worker who strikes(5). 罷工者。 **2** (football) player in an attacking position. (足球)前鋒(在攻擊位置的球員)。

strik·ing /ˈstraɪkɪŋ; ˈstraɪkɪŋ/ *adj* **1** attracting attention; arousing great interest. 引人注意的;引起很大興趣的。 **2** that strikes(4): 鳴響的: *a* ～ *clock.* 自鳴鐘。～**·ly** *adv* in a ～ manner: 顯著地;引人注意地: *a ～ly beautiful woman.* 美貌驚人的女子。

string¹ /strɪŋ; strɪŋ/ *n* **1** [C, U] (piece or length of) fine cord for tying things, keeping things in place, etc; narrow strip of other material used for the same purposes: 細繩;帶子;一段帶子或細繩;一根細繩或帶子: *a ball of* ～; 一團細繩; *a piece of* ～; 一根細繩; ～ *and brown paper for a parcel.* 包裹用的細繩和牛皮紙。 ***tied to one's mother's/wife's apron-～s,*** ⇨ apron. 繫在母親(太太)圍裙的帶子上;受母親(太太)操縱而不能獨立。 (US) **ˈshoe ～s,** ⇨ lace(2). (美)鞋帶。 **2** [C] = *bow*～, ⇨ bow¹(1). 弓弦。***have two ～s to one's bow,*** have an alternative means of achieving one's purpose. 某人的弓有兩根弓弦;有兩套達到目標的方法。 ***the first/second ～,*** the first/the alternative person or thing relied upon for achieving one's purpose. 第一(第二)弦;賴以完成某項任務的第一(第二)個人或物。 **3** [C] tightly stretched length of cord, gut or wire, eg in a violin or guitar, for producing musical sounds. (緊繃在小提琴、吉他等上,用以發出樂音的)琴弦。 ***keep harping on one ～/on the same ～,*** keep talking or writing on one subject. 繼續不斷彈一根(同一根)弦;繼續談或寫同一個題目。**the ～s,** the instruments of the violin family in an orchestra. (管弦樂隊中的)弦樂器。 **ˌ～ ˈorchestra/ˈband** *n* one composed of ～ed instruments only. 弦樂隊(團)。**ˌ～ quarˈtet** *n* (music for a) quartet of four ～ed instruments. 弦樂四重奏;弦樂四重奏曲。**4** [C] ～ used for causing puppets to move. 木偶上的線。 ⇨ the illus at puppet. 參看 puppet 之插圖。 ***have sb on a ～,*** have him under one's control. 置某人於控制之下。 ***pull ～s,*** exert a (hidden) influence: 運用(暗中的)影響力: *pull ～s to get sb a job/to have sb dismissed.* 運用影響力給某人找一工作(讓某人被解職)。***pull the ～s,*** control events, or the actions of other people (as if they were puppets on ～s). 操縱事件或他人行動。***no ～s (attached); without ～s,*** (colloq; of help, esp of money, eg given by one country to another) without conditions about how the help is to be used. (俗;指一國對他國等的援助,尤指金錢)不附帶條件的;受援者不受限制的。 **5** [C] series of things threaded on a ～: 穿在細繩上的一串東西;一串: *a ～ of beads/pearls/onions;* 一串珠子(珍珠,洋葱); number of things in, or as in, a line: 一系列之物;連續的事物: *a ～ of abuses/curses/lies;* 一連串的咒罵(咒詛,謊言); *a ～ of horses,* number of horses kept for racing. (屬於同一主人或馬房的)一列準備要參加比賽的馬。⇨ stud². **6** tough fibre or ～-like substance. 韌纖維;似細繩物質;筋。 ～ **bean,** kind of bean of which the pod is used as a vegetable. 菜豆(豆莢可作蔬菜)。**ˈheart～s,** ⇨ heart(7). 深摯的情愛。～**y** *adj* (-ier, -iest) like ～; having tough fibres: 似帶、繩等的;有韌纖維的: *～y meat,* tough. 多筋的肉。

string² /strɪŋ; strɪŋ/ *vt, vi* (*pt, pp* strung /strʌŋ; strʌŋ/) **1** [VP6A] put a string or strings on (a bow, violin, tennis racket, etc). 裝弦於(弓,小提琴,網球拍等);上弦。～**ed instrument** *n* musical instrument with ～s(3). 弦樂器。 **2** (*pp*) ***strung (up),*** (of a person, his senses, nerves) made tense, ready, excited, etc: (指人,其感覺,神經)緊張的;警覺的;準備好了的;興奮的;抖擻的: *The athlete was strung up before the important race.* 那運動員在重要賽跑前緊張而振奮。***highly strung,*** very nervous or tense. 很緊張的。 **3** [VP6A] put (pearls, etc) on a string. 串(珍珠)等於細繩上。 **4** [VP15A, B] ～ ***(up),*** tie or hang on a string, etc: 綁或懸於繩等上: ～ *up lanterns among the trees/lamps across a street.* 在林木間懸掛燈籠(橫越街道掛燈)。**5** [VP2C, 15B] (special uses with *adverbial particles*): (與副詞接語連用的特殊用法):

string sb along, deliberately mislead him into the belief that he will benefit, etc: 騙人;故意使人誤信將獲得利益等;吊胃口: *He doesn't intend to marry the girl—he's just ～ing her along.* 他並不想同那女孩子結婚 — 吊吊她罷了。～ ***along with sb,*** maintain a relationship with sb for as long as it suits one, without making genuine commitments. 與某人虛與委蛇(以達利用的目的)。

string out, be, become, spread out at intervals in a line. 成串地相繼展開;間隔着散開;間歇地呈現。～

sth out, cause this to happen: 使成串地或間歇性地發生;使間隔着散開: *horses strung out towards the end of a long race.* 長途賽馬接近終點時間隔着散開的馬。

string sb up, (sl) put him to death by hanging. (俚)吊死或絞死某人。~ ***sth up,*** 把某物綁在或懸在繩等上，⇨ 4 above. 參看上列第 4 義。

strin·gent /ˈstrɪndʒənt ; ˈstrɪndʒənt/ *adj* **1** (of rules) strict, severe; that must be obeyed: (指規則)嚴格的;必須遵守的;嚴峻的: *a ~ rule against smoking.* 禁止吸烟的嚴格規定。 **2** (of the money-market) tight; difficult to operate because of scarcity of money. (指金融市場)銀根緊的;週轉困難的。**~·ly** *adv* **strin·gency** /-nsɪ ; -nsɪ/ *n*

strip /strɪp ; strɪp/ *vt, vi* (-pp-) **1** [VP2A, C, 6A, 14, 15B, 22] ~ ***(off);*** ~ ***sth/sb (off);*** ~ ***sth (from/off sth);*** ~ ***sth/sb (of sth),*** take off (coverings, clothes, parts, etc): 脫去;剝去;除去(遮蔽物、衣服、某部分等): ~ *a machine,* dismantle it; 拆卸(拆開)一機器; ~ *paint from a surface/~ a surface of paint,* remove the paint; 除去漆面; ~ *the bark off a tree/~ a tree of its bark.* 剝去樹皮。*The bandits ~ped him naked/~ped him of his clothes.* 强盗們剝光了他的衣服。*They ~ped the house of all its furnishings.* 他們搬走了房子裡的一切設備。*They ~ped,/~ped off,/~ped off their clothes, and jumped into the lake.* 他們脫下衣服跳入湖中。~ ***sth down,*** (eg of an engine) remove detachable parts (for overhaul, etc). (如指引擎)分解或拆開(以便仔細檢查等)。 **ˈ~-tease, ˈ~-show** *nn* dance, cabaret or theatrical entertainment in which a woman takes off her garments one by one. 脫衣舞。Hence, 由此產生，**ˈ~per** *n* woman who does this. 脫衣舞孃。**ˌ~-ˈpoker** *n* game of poker in which the loser of each hand must take off one garment. 脫衣撲克戲(每輸一局就得脫下一件衣服的遊戲)。 **2** [VP14] ~ ***sb of sth,*** deprive him of property, etc: 剝奪某人之財產等: ~ *a man of his possessions/titles, etc.* 剝奪某人之財產(頭銜等)。 **3** [VP6A] tear parts from: 拆散;拆開: ~ *a gear/screw,* tear the cogs/thread from it (by misuse, etc). (因使用不當而)損壞齒輪的齒(螺釘之螺線)。**4** [VP6A] squeeze out the last milk from (a cow's udder); obtain (milk) in this way. 擠乾(母牛乳頭)的乳;盡量擠出(牛奶)。□ *n* [C] **1** long narrow piece (of material, land, etc): 狹長的一塊或一片(材料、土地等): *a ~ of garden behind the house;* 屋後一塊狹長的園子; *a ~ of paper;* 一條紙片; *an ˈair~,* ⇨ air¹(7). 臨時機場。**ˈ~-lighting** *n* method of lighting, using long tubes instead of bulbs. 光管照明法(利用長管代替燈泡)。~ **cartoon** *n* sequence of small drawings in a row, telling a story. 連環圖畫;連環漫畫。⇨ *comic* ~ at comic. **2** (colloq) clothes worn by players in a team: (俗)(球隊等穿的)隊服: *the colourful ~ of many football teams.* 許多足球隊所穿的彩色隊服。

stripe /straɪp ; straɪp/ *n* [C] **1** long, narrow band (usu of the same breadth throughout) on a surface different in colour, material, texture, etc: 條紋;條帶(通常寬度從頭至尾保持一致，其顏色、質料、織地等與底面不同): *a white table-cloth with red ~s;* 有紅色條紋的白桌布; *the tiger's ~s.* 老虎的斑紋。**the Stars and S~s,** the national flag of the US. 星條旗;美國國旗。**2** (often a V-shaped) badge worn on a uniform, showing rank, eg of a soldier: 士兵等的階級臂章;袖章(通常作V形): *How many ~s are there on the sleeve of a sergeant?* 陸軍中士的袖子上有多少V字條紋? **3** (old use) blow with a whip (*stroke* is now the usu word). (舊用法)鞭打(現通常用 stroke)。**~d** /straɪpt ; ˈstraɪpɪd/ *adj* marked with ~s(1): 帶有條紋的;帶條的: *~d material,* eg for clothing. 有條紋的料子(如衣料)。**stripy** *adj* having ~s: 有條紋的;有條子的: *a stripy tie.* 有條子(圖案)的領帶。

strip·ling /ˈstrɪplɪŋ ; ˈstrɪplɪŋ/ *n* youth. 青年;年輕小伙子。

strive /straɪv ; straɪv/ *vi* (*pt* strove /strəʊv ; strov/, *pp* striven /ˈstrɪvn ; ˈstrɪvən/) **1** [VP2A, 3A] ~ ***(with/against sth/sb),*** struggle. 與某事或某人奮鬪;抗爭;搏鬪。**2** [VP3A, 4A] ~ ***for sth/to do sth,*** make great efforts. 奮力;奮勉;努力。**~r** *n* person who tries hard. 努力者;奮勉者。

strobe /strəʊb ; strob/ *n, adj* **ˈ~ (light),** (light) that goes on and off very fast. 急速閃動的(光)。

strode /strəʊd ; strod/ *pt* of stride.

stroke¹ /strəʊk ; strok/ *n* [C] **1** (act of striking

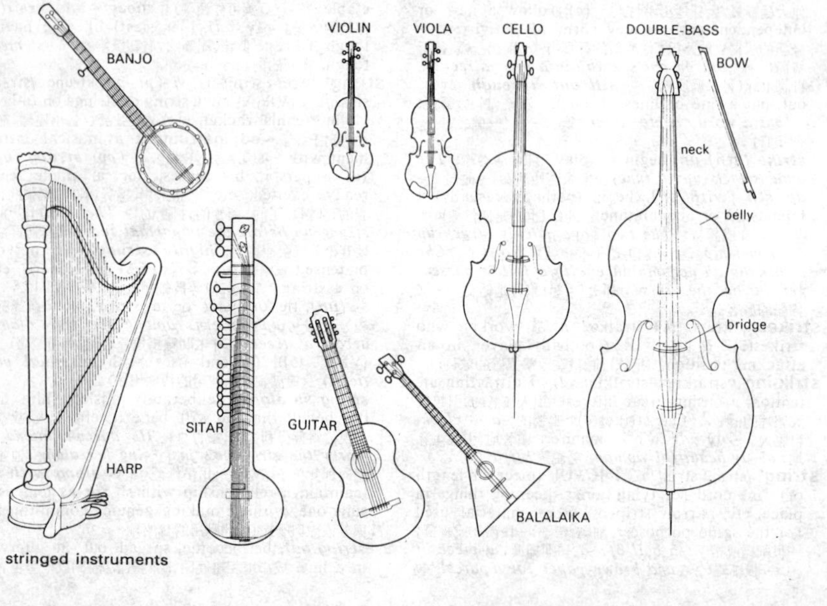

stringed instruments

or dealing a) blow: 打擊;一擊: *kill a man with one ~ of a sword;* 揮劍一擊而殺死某人; *the ~ of a hammer;* 鎚的敲擊; *20 ~s of the lash.* 鞭打二十下。 **2** one of a series of regularly repeated movements, esp as a way of swimming or rowing: 一連串有規律的反覆動作之一;(尤指)(游泳或划船時的)一划;一動: *swimming with a slow ~;* 慢划著游泳; *'breast-/'back-~;* 俯泳(仰泳);*a fast/slow ~* (in rowing). (划船)快划(慢划)。**3** (in a rowing crew) oarsman nearest the boat's stern who sets the rate of striking the oars. (划船諸槳手中的)尾槳手(最近船尾者,爲主要划手,指揮並決定划船的速度)。⇨ the illus at eight; 參看 eight 之插圖; ⇨ bow³(2). **4** single movement of the upper part of the body and arm(s), esp in games, eg cricket, golf. 身體上部及手臂的活動;(尤指)(板球、高爾夫等的)一擊;一揮。**5** single effort; result of this: 一次努力;一次努力的結果: *That was a good ~ of business.* 那是一筆好買賣。*I haven't done a ~ of work today.* 今天我還未動手工作。*What a ~ of luck!* What a piece of good fortune! 多幸運啊!眞走運!眞是運氣! ***at a/one ~,*** with one effort and immediately. 一舉;一氣;一鼓作氣。***put sb off his ~,*** ⇨ *put off* at put²(11). **6** (mark made by a) single movement of a pen or brush: 一筆;筆畫: *with one ~ of the pen;* 用筆一揮; *thin/thick ~s.* 細(粗)筆畫。**7** sound made by a bell striking the hours: (報時的)鐘聲;鳴(鐘)聲;敲擊聲: *on the ~ of three,* at three o'clock. 鐘鳴三響;三時正。*He was here on the ~,* punctually at the time appointed. 他準時到此。**8** sudden attack of illness in the brain, with loss of feeling, power to move, etc: 中風: *a paralytic ~.* 癱瘓性中風。⇨ also *sun~* at sun(4). □ *vt* (*pt, pp* ~d) [VP6A] act as ~(3) to. 充當…的尾槳手。

stroke² /strəʊk; strok/ *vt* [VP6A, 15B] pass the hand along a surface, usu again and again: 撫摸(通常爲反覆地): *~ a cat/one's beard.* 撫摸貓(鬍鬚)。***~ sb the wrong way,*** irritate him instead of soothing him. 激怒某人。***~ sb down,*** mollify him, cause him to be no longer irritated. 安撫某人;勸人息怒;哄人。□ *n* act of stroking; stroking movement. 撫摸;撫摸的動作。

stroll /strəʊl; strol/ *n* [C] quiet, unhurried walk: 漫步;閒逛;遨遊: *have/go for a ~.* 去散步。□ *vi* [VP2A, C] go for a ~. 散步;漫步;閒逛;遨遊。**~·er** *n*

strong /strɒŋ *US:* strɔːŋ; strɔŋ/ *adj* (-nger /-ŋgə(r); -ŋgɚ/, -ngest /-ŋgɪst; -ŋgɪst/) **1** (opp of *weak*) having power to resist; not easily hurt, injured, broken, captured, etc; having great power of body or mind: (爲 weak 之相反字)有抵抗力的;不易受傷、折斷、被捕獲等的;身心方面强有力的;强壯的;强大的;堅固的: *a ~ stick,* not easily broken; 堅固的手杖; *a ~ fort,* not easily captured; 堅固的堡壘; *a ~ wind;* 强風; *a ~ will/imagination/determination;* 堅强的意志(豐富的想像力;堅定的決心); *have ~ nerves,* be not easily frightened, worried, etc; 沉着;勇敢; *~ eyes;* 犀利的目光; *feel quite ~ again,* in good health after an illness; 感到身體康復; *a ~ army;* 强大的軍隊; *an army 500000 ~,* numbering 500000; 爲數五十萬的軍隊; *a ~ candidate,* one likely to be well supported, etc; 有實力的候選人; *~ (= deeply held or rooted) beliefs/convictions.* 堅定的信念(信仰)。***as ~ as a horse,*** physically powerful. 身體壯如馬。***one's ~ point,*** that which one does well. 某人的特長(長處)。**'~-arm,** (of methods, tactics, etc) violent; bullying. (指方法、策略等)暴烈的;用暴力的;蠻横的;威嚇的。**'~-box** *n* one that is ~ly built for keeping valuables. 保險箱;鐵櫃。**'~·hold** /-həʊld; -ˌhold/ *n* **(a)** fort. 要塞;堡壘。**(b)** (fig) place where a cause or idea has ~ support: (喻)某種運動或觀念被强力支持的地方;根據地;大本營: *a ~hold of Protestantism.* 新教的大本營。**ˌ~-'minded** /-ˈmaɪndɪd; -ˈmaɪndɪd/ *adj* having a mind that is capable and vigorous. 心智堅强的;有雄心的;果斷的。**'~-room** *n* one built with thick walls and (usu) a thick steel door (eg in a bank) for storing valuables. (保藏珍貴物品的)保險庫。**2** having a large proportion of the flavouring element, etc: 濃烈的: *~ tea/coffee;* 濃茶(咖啡); *a ~ whisky,* whisky with very little water, etc. 猛烈的威士忌酒。**3** having a considerable effect on the mind or the senses: (對心靈或感覺)有强烈效果的: *the ~ light of the tropics;* 熱帶的强光; *a ~ smell of gas;* 瓦斯的强烈氣味; *~ bacon/butter/cheese/onions.* 味厚的燻肉(奶油、乳酪、洋葱)。*His breath is rather ~,* is ill-smelling. 他的呼吸帶臭味。**~ language** *n* forcible expressions, esp words that are blasphemous or abusive. 激烈話;(尤指)罵人話。**4 ~ drink,** containing alcohol, eg gin, rum. 烈性飲料(含酒精者,如杜松子酒及蘭酒)。⇨ *soft drink* at soft(9). **5** (*adverbial* use) (作副詞用) ***going ~,*** (colloq) continuing (the race, activity, etc) vigorously; continuing in good health: (俗)使勁地繼續(賽跑、活動等); 保持健康: *aged 90 and still going ~.* 年屆九十而仍身强體壯。***come/go it (rather/a bit) ~,*** (colloq) go to greater lengths than is right; exaggerate somewhat. (俗)做得過分;有幾分誇張。**6 ~ verb,** one that forms the past tense by a vowel change (eg *sing, sang*), not by adding *-d, -ed* or *-t.* 以母音變化構成過去式的動詞(如 sing, sang, 而非加 -d, -ed 或 -t 者)。**7** (comm; of prices) rising steadily: (商;指物價)堅挺的;穩定上升的: *Prices/Markets are ~.* 價格(行情)堅挺。**8 '~ form,** (of the pronunciation of some words) form occurring in a prominent (and therefore stressed) position: (指某些單字的發音)强式(處於須重讀的位置): *The ~ form of 'and' is /ænd/.* and 的强式發音是 /ænd/。⇨ weak(5). **~·ly** *adv* in a ~ manner: 堅持地;堅決地;强烈地;極力地: *I ~ly advise you to go.* 我極力勸你去。*I ~ly feel/I feel ~ly that you've made the wrong decision,* I am ~ly convinced that.... 我深信你所做的決定是錯誤的。

stron·tium /ˈstrɒntɪəm *US:* -nʃɪəm; ˈstrɑnʃɪəm/ *n* [U] soft silver-white metallic element (symbol **Sr**). 鍶(一種柔軟的銀白色金屬元素,符號Sr)。**~ 90** *n* [U] variety of ~ that is a component of the fall-out from nuclear explosions. 鍶九十(爲核子爆炸後輻射塵中的成分之一)。

strop /strɒp; strɑp/ *n* leather strap for sharpening razors, eg as used by barbers. 磨剃刀用的皮條;革砥(理髮師等使用者)。□ *vt* (-pp-) [VP6A] sharpen on a ~. 在革砥上磨利。

strophe /ˈstrəʊfɪ; ˈstrofɪ/ *n* [C] (lines of verse recited during a) movement of the chorus in ancient Greek drama; one section of a lyric poem. 古希臘戲劇中唱歌隊的舞動; 舞動時所吟唱的詩句;(合唱歌的)一節;(抒情詩的)一段。

stroppy /ˈstrɒpɪ; ˈstrɑpɪ/ *adj* (GB sl) (of a person) bad-tempered; difficult to deal with. (英俚)(指人)脾氣壞的;難對付的。

strove /strəʊv; strov/ *pt* of strive.

struck /strʌk; strʌk/ *pt, pp* of strike².

struc·ture /ˈstrʌktʃə(r); ˈstrʌktʃɚ/ *n* **1** [U] way in which sth is put together, organized, etc: 結構;構造;建造法: *the ~ of the human body;* 人體的構造; *molecular ~;* 分子的結構; *sentence ~.* 句子的結構。**2** [C] building; any complex whole; framework or essential parts of a building: 建築物;構造物;建築物的構架或主要部分: *The Parthenon was a magnificent marble ~.* 巴特農神殿是雄偉的大理石建築物。**struc·tural** /ˈstrʌktʃərəl; ˈstrʌktʃərəl/ *adj* of a ~, esp the framework: 構造的;結構的;(尤指)構架的: *structural alterations to a building,* eg combining two rooms into one; 房屋結構上的改變(如把兩房併爲一房); *structural steel,* ie bars, beams, girders, for use in building. 建築用鋼材。**struc·tur·ally** /-ərəlɪ; -ərəlɪ/ *adv*: *The building is* *structurally sound.* 這建築物在結構上很牢固。

stru·del /ˈstruːdl ; ˈstrudl̩/ *n* kind of tart made of fruit, etc rolled up in puff pastry and baked: 水果捲 (水果餡餅的一種，捲起後烘焙而成)： *a slice of apple* ～. 一片蘋果捲。

struggle /ˈstrʌgl ; ˈstrʌgl̩/ *vi* [VP2A, B, 3A, 4A] ***～(against／with),*** fight, make great efforts: 抗爭;奮鬪;努力;掙扎;搏鬪: ～ *against difficulties;* 與困難搏鬪; ～*for influence／power.* 爭奪權勢(權力)。*The thief ～d in the policeman's arms／～d to get free.* 那賊在警察的手臂中掙扎(掙扎着要脫逃)。□ *n* [C] struggling; contest: 抗爭;奮鬪;努力;掙扎;搏鬪: *the ～ for freedom;* 爲自由奮鬪; *not surrender without a ～.* 未經奮戰不投降。

strum /strʌm ; strʌm/ *vi, vt* (-mm-) [VP2A, B, C, 3A, 6A] ～ ***(on),*** play music, play (on a musical instrument) carelessly or monotonously (and esp without skill): 胡亂地彈奏音樂;漫不經心(尤指無技巧)地彈奏(樂器)：～ (*on*) *the banjo;* 亂彈五絃琴; ～ *a tune on the piano.* 在鋼琴上胡亂彈奏一曲。□ *n* sound of ～ming: 胡亂彈奏的聲音: *the ～ of a guitar.* 一陣錯落的吉他聲。

strum·pet /ˈstrʌmpɪt ; ˈstrʌmpɪt/ *n* (archaic) prostitute. (古)娼妓。

strung /strʌŋ ; strʌŋ/ *pt, pp* of string².

strut¹ /strʌt ; strʌt/ *n* [C] piece of wood or metal inserted in a framework and intended to strengthen it by bearing weight or resisting pressure in the direction of its length. (構架的)支柱;支桿;撐子;抗壓構件。

strut² /strʌt ; strʌt/ *vi* (-tt-) [VP2A, C] walk (*about, along, in, out, into a room, etc*) in a stiff, self-satisfied way. 趾高氣揚地走;高視闊步。□ *n* such a way of walking. 高視闊步;趾高氣揚的行走。

strych·nine /ˈstrɪkniːn ; ˈstrɪknɪn/ *n* [U] strong poison (used in very small doses to stimulate the nerves). 馬錢子鹼;番木鼈鹼(一種烈性毒劑，以極微之量，可用作刺激神經)。

stub /stʌb ; stʌb/ *n* [C] **1** short remaining end of a pencil, cigarette or similar object: (鉛筆、香烟或類似物的)殘餘部分;殘段;鉛筆頭;烟蒂;殘根: *The dog has only a ～ of a tail,* a very short one. 那隻狗祇有一小截短尾巴。**2** counterfoil: 票根;存根: *the ～s of a cheque-book.* 支票簿的存根。□ *vt* (-bb-) **1** [VP6A] ～ *one's toe,* strike it against sth. 碰到脚趾。 **2** [VP15B] ～ ***sth out,*** extinguish (esp a cigarette) by pressing it against sth hard. 捻熄某物(尤指香烟)。

stubble /ˈstʌbl ; ˈstʌbl̩/ *n* [U] ends of grain plants left in the ground after harvest; sth suggesting this, eg a short stiff growth of beard: (稻等割下後遺留的)殘株;殘梗;似此之物(如短鬚)：*three days' ～ on his chin.* 他的下巴上三天未刮的短鬚。 **stubbly** /ˈstʌblɪ ; ˈstʌblɪ/ *adj* of or like ～: (似)殘株的;(似)殘梗的: *a stubbly beard.* 短鬚。

stub·born /ˈstʌbən ; ˈstʌbən/ *adj* obstinate; determined; difficult to deal with: 頑固的;固執的;堅定的;堅決的;難應付的;難處理的: ～ *soil,* difficult to plough, etc; 堅硬的土壤(難犂等); *a ～ illness.* 難治的病。***as ～ as a mule,*** extremely obstinate. 非常頑强的;像騾子般倔强的。 **～·ly** *adv* **～·ness** *n*

stubby /ˈstʌbɪ ; ˈstʌbɪ/ *adj* (-ier, -iest) short and thick: 短而粗的: ～ *fingers.* 短而粗的手指。

stucco /ˈstʌkəʊ ; ˈstʌko/ *n* (*pl* ～s, ～es /-kəʊz ; -koz/) [C, U] (kinds of) plaster or cement used for covering and decorating ceilings or wall surfaces. (塗天花板或牆壁用的)灰泥。□ *vt* (*pt, pp* ～ed; ～ing) coat with ～. 用灰泥塗。

stuck /stʌk ; stʌk/ *pt, pp* of stick².

stuck-up /ˌstʌk ˈʌp ; ˈstʌkˈʌp/ *adj* (colloq) conceited; insolently refusing to be companionable. (俗)自大的;傲慢的;倨傲不群的;自以爲了不起的。

stud¹ /stʌd ; stʌd/ *n* **1** small two-headed button-like device put through button-holes to fasten a collar, shirt-front, etc. (穿過鈕孔以固定衣領、胸口等的)飾鈕;袖釦;領釦。 **2** large-headed nail or knob, usu one of many, on the surface of sth (eg a gate or shield), as ornament or protection. (釘於門、盾等上，作爲裝飾或保護用的)飾釘;大頭釘。**reˈflector ～,** (colloq 俗 *cat's eye*) used on roads to mark out lanes (and reflecting light from headlamps at night). 反光釘(釘在路面上標示車道，且能在夜間反射車輛前燈的燈光)。□ *vt* (-dd-) (usu *pp*) (通常用過去分詞) ***～ded with,*** having (sth) set in or scattered on the surface: 滿佈;散佈: *a crown ～ded with jewels;* 飾滿珠寶的王冠; *a sea ～ded with islands／the sails of yachts.* 散佈着小島(遊艇之帆)的海面。

stud² /stʌd ; stʌd/ *n* number of horses kept by one owner for a special purpose (esp breeding or racing). (屬於同一主人的)馬群; (尤指爲繁殖或賽馬而飼養的一群)種馬;賽馬。 **ˈ～-book** *n* register of the pedigrees of horses. 馬種系譜;馬的血統記錄簿。**ˈ～-farm** *n* place where horses are bred. 種馬農場。 **ˈ～-mare** *n* mare kept for breeding purposes. 母種馬;雌性種馬。

stu·dent /ˈstjuːdnt *US:* ˈstuː- ; ˈstjudn̩t/ *n* **1** (GB) (undergraduate or postgraduate) person who is studying at a college, polytechnic or university: (英)大學生;工藝學院的學生;研究生: ˈ*medical ～s;* 醫科學生; (US also) boy or girl attending school. (美亦指)中學生; 小學生。 **2** anyone who studies or who is devoted to the acquisition of knowledge: 學者;從事研究工作者: *a ～ of bird-life／nature／theology.* 研究鳥類生活(大自然，神學)的學者。

stu·dio /ˈstjuːdɪəʊ *US:* ˈstuː- ; ˈstjudɪˌo/ *n* (*pl* ～s /-dɪəʊz ; -dɪˌoz/) **1** well-lit workroom of a painter, sculptor, photographer, etc. 畫室; 雕塑室; 照相室;工作室;技術室。 ～ **couch,** couch that can be used as a bed. 沙發床;可作床用的躺椅。 **2** room or hall where cinema films are acted and photographed; (*pl*) all the ～s of a cinema company, with the office buildings, etc. (製作電影的)攝影棚; (複)(電影公司的)攝影場; 製片廠。 **3** room from which radio or TV programmes are regularly broadcast or in which recordings are made. (無線電或電視節目的)播放室; 廣播室; 錄製室; 工作室。 ～ **audience,** audience in a ～, to provide applause, laughter, etc. 現場觀(聽)衆(提供掌聲、笑聲等效果者)。

stu·di·ous /ˈstjuːdɪəs *US:* ˈstuː- ; ˈstjudɪəs/ *adj* **1** having or showing the habit of learning. 好學的;用功的;勤學的。 **2** painstaking; deliberate: 費力的;用心的;小心的;故意的: *with ～ politeness.* 謹愼有禮地。**～·ly** *adv* **～·ness** *n*

study¹ /ˈstʌdɪ ; ˈstʌdɪ/ *n* (*pl* -dies) **1** [U and in *pl* 並可用複數] devotion of time and thought to getting knowledge of, or to a close examination of, a subject, esp from books: 研究;研讀;讀書: *fond of ～;* 喜讀書; *give all one's leisure time to ～;* 空暇時間全部用來讀書; *make a ～ of the country's foreign trade.* 研究該國的對外貿易。*My studies show that....* 我的研究顯示…。**2** [C] sth that attracts investigation; that which is (to be) investigated: 學科;研究或待研究的對象或課題: *scientific studies.* 科學方面的學科。*The proper ～ of mankind is man.* 研究人類的適當課題就是人。*His face was a ～,* was well worth observing closely. 他的臉孔很值得去仔細觀察。 **3** ***be in a brown ～,*** musing, unaware of people, happenings, etc near one. 出神;沉思;冥想。 **4** room used by sb (eg in his home) for reading, writing, etc: 書房: *You will find Mr Green in the／his ～.* 你在(他)書房裡可找到格林先生的。 **5** sketch etc made for practice or experiment; piece of music played as a technical exercise. (爲練習或實驗而作的)習作;試作;(音樂的)練習曲。 **6** [U] (old use) earnest effort. (舊用法)認眞的努力。

study² /ˈstʌdɪ ; ˈstʌdɪ/ *vt, vi* (*pt, pp* -died) **1** [VP 6A, 8, 15A, 2A, B, 4A] give time and attention to learning or discovering sth: 學習;研究;求學: ～ *medicine.* 研究醫學。*He was ～ing for the medical* *profession/~ing to be a doctor.* 他在讀醫科。 **2** [VP6A] examine carefully: 仔細察看、核閱、檢查等: *~ the map.* 細閱地圖。 **3** [VP6A, 4A] give care and consideration to: 留心;顧及;考慮到: *~ the wishes of one's friends/only one's own interests.* 考慮到朋友們的願望(祇顧到自己的利益)。 **4** (*pp*) **studied,** intentional, deliberate: 有意的;故意的: *a studied insult.* 故意的侮辱。

stuff[1] /stʌf ; stʌf/ *n* **1** [C, U] material or substance of which sth is made or which may be used for some purpose (often fig); [U] material of which the name is uncertain, unknown or unimportant; material of (a certain) quality: 材料;原料;質料;資料;素材(常作喻);名稱不知道、不確定或不重要的物質;有某種性質的物質: *We're short of 'green/'garden ~,* vegetables. 我們缺乏蔬菜。*He is not the ~ heroes are made of,* is not likely to be a hero, to act heroically. 他不是做英雄的材料(不太可能成爲英雄)。*Do you call this ~ beer?* 你把這東西叫做啤酒嗎? *We must find out what ~ he is made of,* what sort of man he is, what his character is. 我們必須弄清楚他是個什麼樣的人。***S~ and nonsense!*** That's foolish talk! 胡扯!胡說八道! **2** (sl uses) (俚語用法) *That's the ~ to give 'em,* That's how to treat them, etc. 對待他們就要這樣。***Do your ~,*** Show what you can do, etc. 顯顯你的本領;露一手。***know one's ~,*** be expert in what one claims to be able to do, etc. 精通本行。 **3** [U] (old use) woollen cloth: (舊用法)毛織品;毛料: *a ~ gown.* 毛料長袍。

stuff[2] /stʌf ; stʌf/ *vt* **1** [VP6A, 14, 15B] ***~ sth with/into sth; ~ sth up,*** fill tightly with; press tightly into: 以某物塞滿、塞緊或填塞某物;以某物塞入或裝進某物: *~ a bag with feathers;* 將一隻袋子裝滿羽毛; *~ feathers into a bag;* 把羽毛塞入袋中; *~ oneself with food,* overeat; 暴食;吃得太飽; *a head ~ed with facts/silly romantic ideas;* 滿腦子事實(天眞的想法); *~ (up) one's ears with cotton-wool;* 以脫脂棉塞住耳朵; *~ up a hole.* 塞洞。 *My nose is ~ed up,* full of mucus (as when one has a cold). 我的鼻子塞住了(如感冒時)。 ***a ~ed shirt,*** (colloq) a pretentious or pompous person. (俗)擺架子的人;神氣十足的人。 **2** [VP6A, 14] ***~ (with),*** (colloq) make (sb) believe what is not true: (俗)使(某人)誤信;誆騙(某人): *He's ~ing you with silly ideas.* 他想用鬼主意欺騙你。 **3** [VP6A, 14] put chopped up and specially flavoured food into (a bird, etc) before cooking it: 烹煮前用剁碎的或加味的食物填入(禽等): *a ~ed turkey;* 加塡料的火雞; *~ed veal.* 加塡料的小牛肉。 **4** [VP6A] fill the empty carcass of (a bird, an animal, etc) with enough material to restore it to its original shape, eg for exhibition in a museum: 塡塞除却內臟的(鳥、獸等)的軀骸以做成標本: *a ~ed tiger/owl.* 製成標本的老虎(梟)。 **5** [VP2A, 6A] overeat: 暴食;過食: *When will that boy stop ~ing (himself)?* 那男孩何時才會不暴食呢? **6** ***~ it/sth,*** (sl) do what one likes with it: (俚)隨意處理: *If you don't like it you can ~ it,* will just have to put up with it/do what you like with it. 你如果不喜歡(它),你祇有忍耐(隨意處理)。 **7** ⚠ (vulg sl) have sexual intercourse (with a woman). (諱)(鄙俚)與(女人)性交。 **~·ing** *n* [U] material for ~ing, eg cushions, birds, 塡料;塡塞物, ⇨ 3, 4 above. 參看上列第 3, 4 義。 ***knock the '~ing out of sb,*** **(a)** take away his conceit or self-confidence. 挫某人的傲氣或銳氣。 **(b)** (of an illness, etc) weaken; make tired. (指疾病等)使弱;使疲憊;使疲倦。

stuffy /'stʌfɪ ; 'stʌfɪ/ *adj* (-ier, -iest) **1** (of a room) badly ventilated. (指房間)氣悶的;通風不良的。 **2** (colloq) sulky; ill-tempered. (俗)不高興的;慍怒的。 **3** (colloq, of a person) easily shocked or offended. (俗,指人)易吃驚的;易怒的;易得罪的。 **4** dull; formal. 不活潑的;拘謹的;呆板的。 **stuff·ily** /-ɪlɪ ; -əlɪ/ *adv* **stuffi·ness** *n*

stul·tify /'stʌltɪfaɪ ; 'stʌltə,faɪ/ *vt* (*pt, pp* -fied) [VP6A] cause to seem foolish or to be useless; reduce to absurdity: 使顯得愚蠢或無用;使…變成荒謬: *~ efforts to reach agreement.* 使達成協議的努力枉費心機。 **stul·ti·fi·ca·tion** /ˌstʌltɪfɪ'keɪʃn ; ˏstʌltəfə'keʃən/ *n*

stumble /'stʌmbl ; 'stʌmbl/ *vi* [VP2A, C, 3A] **1** strike the foot against sth and almost fall: 脚碰撞某物而幾乎跌倒;絆跌: *~ over the root of a tree.* 爲樹根絆倒。*The child ~d and fell.* 那孩子絆倒了。 ***~ across/upon sth,*** find unexpectedly or by accident. 偶然發現某物。 **'stumbling-block** *n* obstacle; sth that causes difficulty or hesitation. 阻碍;造成困難或引起遲疑之物。 **2** ***~ about/along/around,*** move or walk in an unsteady way. 蹒跚而行;行動不穩。 **3** speak in a hesitating way, with pauses and mistakes: 斷續而有錯誤地說話;結結巴巴地說: *~ over one's words;* 結結巴巴地說話; *~ through a recitation.* 斷續而有錯誤地背誦。 □ *n* act of stumbling. 絆跌;結巴。

stump /stʌmp ; stʌmp/ *n* [C] **1** part of a tree remaining in the ground when the trunk has fallen or has been cut down. (樹倒下或被砍斷後留下的)樹樁;殘幹;殘株;根株。 **~ oratory/speeches,** political speeches to persuade or rouse the audience. (爲說服或爭取選票所做的)政治演說。 ***on the ~,*** (colloq) engaged in political speech-making, agitation, etc. (俗)從事政治演說、煽動等。 **2** anything remaining after the main part has been cut or broken off or has worn off, eg an amputated limb, a worn-down tooth, the useless end of a pencil, cigar, etc; (hum) leg. 殘餘部分(如割斷的肢體,磨損的牙齒,鉛筆頭,烟蒂等);(諧)腿;脚。 ***stir one's ~s,*** (colloq) move quickly. (俗)急行;快速行動。 **3** (cricket) one of the three upright pieces of wood at which the ball is bowled: (板球)三柱門的柱: *send the middle ~ flying.* 撞倒三柱門的中柱。 ***draw ~s,*** end play. 結束比賽。 ⇨ the illus at cricket. 參看 cricket 之插圖。 □ *vi, vt* **1** [VP2C] walk (*along, about, etc*) with stiff, heavy movements. 以僵直而沉重的步伐行走(與 along, about 等連用)。 **2** [VP6A] (colloq) be too hard for; leave at a loss: (俗)難倒;使困惑: *All the examination candidates were ~ed by the second question.* 全體考生都被第二個問題難倒了。 **3** [VP6A] go about (a district, the country) making ~ speeches. 在(某地區,全國各處)作巡廻政治演說。 ⇨ the *n,* 1 above. 參看上列名詞第1義。 **4** [VP6A] (cricket) end the innings of (a batsman) by touching the ~s with the ball while he is out of his crease. (板球)以球觸三柱門之柱而封殺跑分的擊球員。 ⇨ crease(2). **5** [VP15B, 2C] ***~ money up,*** (sl) pay or give a sum of money; produce (a sum of money): (俚)付出所需要之款;拿出(一筆錢): *Mr Green has had to ~ up (£50) for his son's debts.* 格林先生必須爲其子償還(五十鎊)債務。 **~er** *n* (colloq) question that ~s(2); difficult or embarrassing question. (俗)難題;令人困惑的問題。

stumpy /'stʌmpɪ ; 'stʌmpɪ/ *adj* (-ier, -iest) short and thick: 短而粗的: *a ~ little man;* 矮胖的人; *a ~ umbrella.* 短而粗的傘。

stun /stʌn ; stʌn/ *vt* (-nn-) [VP6A] **1** make unconscious by a blow, esp one on the head; knock senseless: 打擊而使失知覺;(尤指)打擊頭部使失知覺;擊暈: *The blow ~ned me.* 那一擊把我擊暈了。 **2** shock; confuse the mind of: 使震驚;使發楞;使目瞪口呆: *He was ~ned by the news of his father's death.* 獲悉父親逝世的消息他目瞪口呆。 **~·ning** *adj* (colloq) splendid; ravishing: (俗)出色的;令人喜悅的;銷魂的: *What a ~ning figure!* 多美的身段呀! **~·ning·ly** *adv* **~·ner** *n* (colloq) delightful, attractive person, object, etc. (俗)漂亮的人、物等。

stung /stʌŋ ; stʌŋ/ *pt, pp* of sting[2].

stunk /stʌŋk ; stʌŋk/ *pp* of stink.

stunt[1] /stʌnt ; stʌnt/ *n* [C] (colloq) sth done to

attract attention: (俗)做來引起人注意之事;噱頭;特技表演: *advertising ~s,* eg sky-writing by an aircraft; 廣告噱頭(如飛機在天空作烟幕文字等); *~ flying,* aerobatics. 特技飛行。*That's a good ~,* a clever idea (for getting publicity, etc). 那是(打知名度的)好主意。'~ **man,** person employed to perform ~s (involving risk, etc) as a stand-in for an actor in films, etc. (電影等中臨時雇用代替演員表演特技之)替身。

stunt² /stʌnt ; stʌnt/ *vt* [VP6A] check the growth or development of: 阻碍…的生長或發展: *~ed trees;* 做盆景的矮小樹; *a ~ed mind.* 未獲充分發展的心智。

stu·pefy /'stju:pɪfaɪ *US:* 'stu:- ; 'stjupə,faɪ/ *vt* (*pt, pp* -fied) [VP6A] make clear thought impossible: 使昏亂;使茫然;使錯亂;使糊塗: *stupefied with drink/amazement.* 醉得迷迷糊糊(驚得目瞪口呆)。*He was stupefied by what happened.* 他爲所發生之事弄糊塗了。**stu·pe·fac·tion** /ˌstju:pɪ'fækʃn *US:* ˌstu:- ; ˌstjupə'fækʃən/ *n* [U] state of being stupefied. 昏迷;昏亂;茫然;錯亂;糊塗。

stu·pen·dous /stju:'pendəs *US:* stu:- ; stju'pɛndəs/ *adj* tremendous; amazing (in size, degree): (在體積、程度方面)巨大的;驚人的: *a ~ error/achievement.* 大錯(驚人的成就)。*What ~ folly!* 實在荒唐到極點! **~·ly** *adv*

stu·pid /'stju:pɪd *US:* 'stu:- ; 'stjupɪd/ *adj* **1** slow-thinking; foolish: 魯鈍的;愚蠢的: *Don't be ~ enough to believe that.* 不要傻到相信那種事。 **2** in a state of stupor. 昏迷的;昏亂的;不省人事的。□ *n* (colloq) ~ person: (俗)蠢材;愚人;笨伯: *I was only teasing, ~!* 我祇不過是開開玩笑,傻瓜! **~·ly** *adv* **~·ity** /stju:'pɪdətɪ *US:* stu:- ; stju'pɪdətɪ/ *n* [U] being ~; [C] (*pl* -ties) ~ act, utterance, etc. 魯鈍;愚行;傻話等。

stu·por /'stju:pə(r) *US:* 'stu:- ; 'stjupɚ/ *n* [C, U] almost unconscious condition caused by shock, drugs, alcohol, etc: (震驚、藥物、酒等所造成的)昏迷;恍惚;不省人事: *in a drunken ~.* 爛醉如泥。

sturdy /'stɜ:dɪ ; 'stɝdɪ/ *adj* (-ier, -iest) strong and solid; vigorous: 堅實的;強健的;有力的;不屈的: *~ children;* 健壯的孩子們; *offer a ~ resistance;* 作堅强抵抗; *~ common sense.* 豐富的常識。**stur·dily** /-ɪlɪ ; -ɪlɪ/ *adv: a sturdily built bicycle.* 構造結實的脚踏車。**stur·di·ness** *adv*

stur·geon /'stɜ:dʒən ; 'stɝdʒən/ *n* kinds of large fish valued as food, from which caviare is obtained. 鱣魚;鱘魚;鰈鮫(其卵可製魚子醬)。

stut·ter /'stʌtə(r) ; 'stʌtɚ/ *vi, vt n* = stammer. 結巴;口吃而言。**~er** *n* person who ~s. 口吃者;結巴者。**~·ing·ly** *adv*

sty¹ /staɪ ; staɪ/ *n* (*pl* sties) pigsty. 猪圈;猪欄。⇨ pig(1).

sty² (also **stye**) /staɪ ; staɪ/ *n* (*pl* sties, styes) inflamed swelling on the edge of the eyelid. (醫)瞼腺炎;麥粒腫。

Styg·ian /'stɪdʒɪən ; 'stɪdʒɪən/ *adj* (as) of the River Styx or Hades (the lower world in Gk myth); 希臘神話中之冥府的;陰間之Styx河的;如冥府的;如Styx河的; hence, 由此產生, dark; gloomy. 黑暗的;陰幽的。

style /staɪl ; staɪl/ *n* **1** [C, U] manner of writing or speaking (contrasted with the subject matter); manner of doing anything, esp when it is characteristic of an artist or of a period of art: 寫作或說話的方式(與題材相對); 做某事的方式; 文體; (尤指)某一藝術家或某一時期藝術的特殊風格: *written in an irritating ~.* 以令人不快的文體寫成。*The ~ in this book is more attractive than the matter.* 此書的文體勝過其內容。*What do you know about the Norman/decorated/perpendicular, etc ~s of English architecture?* 你對英國諾曼式(十三至十四世紀英國哥德式,十四至十六世紀英國哥德式)的建築知道多少? **2** [C, U] quality that marks out sth done or made as superior, fashionable or distinctive: 卓越;時髦;氣派;特異;格調: *living in a ~ beyond his means,* in a way that he cannot afford. 過著打腫臉充胖子的生活。*Did they live in European ~ when they were in Japan?* 他們在日本的時候是過歐洲式的生活嗎? ***in ~,*** in a grand or elegant way: 富麗堂皇;高雅脫俗: *do things in ~,* not in a commonplace way; 做事不落俗套; *live in (grand) ~,* with servants, luxuries, etc; 生活闊綽(擁有大批僕役、奢侈品等); *drive up in ~,* eg in a very fine car, not a taxi. 開著豪華轎車來。 **3** [C, U] fashion in dress, etc: 衣服等的時式;樣式;款式;時尚: *the latest ~s in trousers/in hair-dressing.* 最新的褲子式樣(髮式)。 **4** [C] general appearance, form or design; kind or sort: 一般的外表、形式、圖案或設計;種;類: *made in all sizes and ~s;* 照各種尺碼及種類製造的; *this ~, £18.50.* 這種的,18 鎊半。 **5** [C] right title (to be) used when addressing sb: 稱呼;稱謂;尊稱: *Has he any right to assume the ~ of Colonel?* 他有資格稱上校嗎? **6** [C] implement used in ancient times for scratching letters on wax-covered surfaces. (古代在蠟板上書寫所用的)尖筆;鐵筆。 **7** [C] (bot) part of the seed-producing part of a flower. (植)植物的花柱(產種子的部分)。⇨ the illus at flower. 參看flower之插圖。□ *vt* [VP6A] **1** describe by a specified ~(5): 稱呼;命名: *Should he be ~d 'Right Honourable' or 'Mister'?* 應該稱他爲'閣下'還是'先生'? **2** design: 設計: *new cars ~d by the Italian experts;* 義大利專家設計的新型汽車; *an electric cooker brilliantly re-~d,* re-designed. 重新設計的精美電鍋。**styl·ish** /-ɪʃ ; -ɪʃ/ *adj* having ~(2, 3); fashionable: 有氣派的;時髦的;漂亮的: *stylish clothes.* 時髦的衣服。**sty·lish·ly** *adv: stylishly dressed.* 穿著入時的。**styl·ish·ness** *n*

sty·list /'staɪlɪst ; 'staɪlɪst/ *n* **1** person, esp a writer, who achieves a good or original literary style. (尤指)文體漂亮或獨具一格的作家;講究文體者;文體家。 **2** (comm, etc) person who is concerned with the styles of decorating, clothes, etc: (商等)設計新款式、花樣等的人: *a 'hair-~,* a hairdresser. 髮式(髮型)家;美容師。**sty·lis·tic** /staɪ'lɪstɪk ; staɪ'lɪstɪk/ *adj* of style in writing. 文體的。**sty·lis·ti·cally** /-klɪ ; -klɪ/ *adv*

sty·lize /'staɪəlaɪz ; 'staɪlaɪz/ *vt* represent or treat (art forms, etc) in a particular style. 以某種特殊的式樣處理或代表(藝術形式等);使因襲某派風格;使合於某種風格。

sty·lus /'staɪləs ; 'staɪləs/ *n* (*pl* ~es /-ləsɪz ; -ləsɪz/) sharp point (made of diamond or sapphire) used to cut the groove of a gramophone record, or to reproduce sound by following this groove. (金鋼鑽或剛石製成的)電唱機的唱針。

sty·mie /'staɪmɪ ; 'staɪmɪ/ *n* (in golf) situation on the green when an opponent's ball is between one's own ball and the hole; (fig, colloq) check; obstruction. (高爾夫球)果嶺上對手的球介於自己的球與球洞之間的位置;自己的球在果嶺上處於困境; (喻,俗)阻礙;妨礙。□ *vt* [VP6A] put (one's opponent or his ball, or oneself) in this difficulty; (fig) check; obstruct. 使(對手,對手的球或自己)處此困境; (喻)阻礙;妨礙。

styp·tic /'stɪptɪk ; 'stɪptɪk/ *n, adj* (substance) checking the flow of blood: 止血的;止血劑;止血藥: *a ~ pencil,* stick of this (eg as used on a cut made while shaving). 止血(藥)筆(止血劑製成的藥筆,如用於刮臉時刮破之處)。

Styx /stɪks ; stɪks/ *n* (Gk myth) river that encircles Hades, where the spirits of the dead exist. (希神)冥河(圍繞於死者靈魂生存之冥府)。***cross the ~,*** die. 過冥河;死。

sua·sion /'sweɪʒn ; 'sweʒən/ *n* [U] (formal) persuasion. (正式用語)勸說;勸告。***moral ~,*** persuasion based on moral grounds, not force. 道義上的勸告(曉以義理而非藉武力者)。

suave /swɑ:v ; swɑv/ *adj* smooth and gracious (but possibly insincere) in manner. 態度嫻雅(但可能是不真誠)的;和藹的。**~·ly** *adv* **suav·ity** /-ətɪ ; -ətɪ/ *n* [U] quality of being ~; (*pl*) instances of being ~; ~ utterances, etc. 嫺雅;和藹;嫺雅和藹的實例、言談、舉止等。

sub[1] /sʌb; sʌb/ *n* (colloq, abbr of) (俗,爲下列各字之略) **1** submarine. 潛水艇。**2** subscription. 訂閱。**3** sub-lieutenant. 海軍中尉。**4** sub-editor. 副編輯;副主筆。

sub[2] /sʌb; sʌb/ *vi, vt* **1** [VP2A, 3A] ~ ***(for sb)***, (colloq) act as a substitute (for him). (俗)代理;代替。**2** [VP6A] (colloq abbr of) subedit. (俗)爲 subedit 之略。

sub- /sʌb; sʌb/ *pref* ⇨ App 3. 參看附錄三。

sub·al·tern /ˈsʌbltən *US:* səˈbɔːltərn; səbˈɔltɚn/ *n* (GB) (formerly) commissioned army officer of lower rank than a captain. (英)(昔時)陸軍中少尉。

sub·atomic /ˌsʌbəˈtɒmɪk; ˌsʌbəˈtɑmɪk/ *adj* of, relating to, any of the particles smaller than an atom. 小於原子之質點的;與小於原子之質點有關的。

sub·com·mit·tee /ˈsʌb kəmɪtɪ; ˈsʌbkəˌmɪtɪ/ *n* committee formed from members of a main committee. (由大委員會中的委員組成的) 小組委員會;附屬委員會。

sub·con·scious /ˌsʌbˈkɒnʃəs; sʌbˈkɑnʃəs/ *adj* of one's mental activities of which one is not (wholly) aware: 潛意識的;下意識的: *the ~ self.* 潛意識的自我。□ *n* **the ~,** ~ thoughts, desires, impulses, etc collectively. 潛意識;下意識 (潛意識的思想、欲望、衝動等的集合用法)。**~·ly** *adv* **~·ness** *n*

sub·con·ti·nent /ˌsʌbˈkɒntɪnənt; sʌbˈkɑntənənt/ *n* mass of land large enough to be regarded as a separate continent but forming part of a larger mass: 次大陸;次洲: *India is often called the S~.* 印度常被稱爲次大陸。

sub·con·tract /ˌsʌbˈkɒntrækt; sʌbˈkɑntrækt/ *n* contract which is for carrying out a previous contract or a part of it. 附屬契約;分契;轉訂的契約 (爲執行先前訂立之契約或其一部分所訂的契約)。□ *vt, vi* /ˌsʌbkənˈtrækt *US:* -ˈkɒntrækt; ˌsʌbkənˈtrækt/ [VP6A, 2A] give or accept a ~. 訂立附屬契約、分契或轉包契約。**~or** /ˌsʌbkənˈtræktə(r) *US:* ˈkɒntræk-; ˌsʌbkənˈtræktɚ/ *n* person who accepts a ~. 接受此種契約者;承約人。

sub·cu·taneous /ˌsʌbkjuːˈteɪnɪəs; ˌsʌbkjuˈtenɪəs/ *adj* under the skin: 皮下的: *~ parasites,* living under the skin; 皮下寄生蟲; *a ~ injection.* 皮下注射。

sub·di·vide /ˌsʌbdɪˈvaɪd; ˌsʌbdəˈvaɪd/ *vt, vi* [VP 6A, 2A] divide into further divisions. 再分;細分。**sub·di·vi·sion** /ˌsʌbdɪˈvɪʒn; ˌsʌbdəˈvɪʒən/ *n* [U] subdividing; [C] sth produced by subdividing. 再分;細分;再分成的部分或事物。

sub·due /səbˈdjuː *US:* -ˈduː; səbˈdju/ *vt* [VP6A] **1** overcome; bring under control: 征服;克服;壓制: *~ the tropical jungle/one's passions.* 征服熱帶森林(壓制激情)。**2** make quieter, softer, gentler: 使較爲安靜、柔和、溫順;緩和;減弱: (esp *pp*) (尤用其過去分詞) *~d voices/lights;* 降低的聲音(減弱的光線); *a tone of ~d satisfaction in his voice.* 他聲音中略帶滿足的語氣。

sub·edit /sʌbˈedɪt; sʌbˈɛdɪt/ *vt* act as an assistant editor of (a newspaper, etc). 作(報紙等)的助理編輯或副編輯。**sub·edi·tor** /-tə(r); -tɚ/ *n* 助理編輯;副編輯。

sub·fusc /ˈsʌbfʌsk; sʌbˈfʌsk/ *adj* rather dark in colour; (fig colloq) unimpressive. 黑黝黝的;帶黑色的;(喻)不顯眼的;予人印象不深的。

sub·head·ing /ˈsʌbhedɪŋ; ˈsʌbˌhɛdɪŋ/ *n* [C] words showing the contents of part of an article, etc eg in a newspaper. (報紙等上的)小標題;副標題;細目。

sub·hu·man /ˌsʌbˈhjuːmən; sʌbˈhjumən/ *adj* less than human; more like an animal than a human being. 低於人類的;更像動物的。

sub·ject[1] /ˈsʌbdʒɪkt; ˈsʌbdʒɪkt/ *adj* **1** under foreign government, not independent: 由他國統治的;未獨立的;藩屬的: *a ~ province;* 屬地; *~ peoples.* 屬民。**2** ***be ~ to,*** owe obedience (to): 應服從的;受制於…的: *We are ~ to the law of the land.* 我們受當地法律的約束。**3** ***~ to,*** having a tendency (to); prone to: 有…傾向的;易罹;易受;常有: *Are you ~ to colds?* 你易患感冒嗎? *The trains are ~ to delays when there is fog.* 有霧的天氣火車常會誤點。**4** ***~ to,*** (*adj, adv*) conditional(ly) upon: 以…爲條件;聽候…;須經…: *The plan is ~ to confirmation.* 本計畫須經批准。*The arrangement is made ~ to your approval.* 這項安排須經你贊同方能成立。***~ to contract,*** (legal) conditional upon the signing of a contract. (法律)有待合約之簽訂;須經簽約。***~ to prior sale,*** conditional upon no sale having been made before a further offer is made, before the date of the auction, etc. 依照先售原則(如果在更高出價出現之前,或拍賣限期前未售出)。

sub·ject[2] /ˈsʌbdʒɪkt; ˈsʌbdʒɪkt/ *n* **1** any member of a State except the supreme ruler: 人民;庶民;臣民: *British ~s;* 英國臣民; *French by birth and a British ~ by marriage.* 出生是法國人,因結婚而成爲英國臣民。⇨ citizen, (usu preferred in republics). (共和國多用 citizen)。**2** sth (to be) talked or written about or studied: 題目;主題;科目;學科: *an interesting ~ of conversation;* 有趣的話題; *a ~ for an essay;* 文章的題目; *the ~ of a poem/picture.* 詩(畫)的主題。***change the ~,*** talk about sth different. 改變話題。***on the ~ of,*** concerning, dealing with: 關於;論及: *While we are on the ~ of money, may I ask when you will repay that loan?* 我們既談到錢,我可不可以問一問你何時償還那筆貸款? **'~ matter** *n* [U] the content of a book, speech, etc (contrasted with style). (書或演講的)主題;主旨;題材(與 style 相對)。**3** person, animal or thing (to be) treated or dealt with, to be made to undergo or experience sth: (待)處理或討論的對象(指人、動物或事物);被實驗者: *a ~ for experiment/dissection.* 實驗(解剖)的對象。**4** ***~ for sth,*** circumstance, etc that gives cause for it: 做…的理由、場合或情況: *a ~ for pity/ridicule/congratulation.* 叫人同情(受人揶揄,值得恭賀)的原因。**5** person with the tendencies (usu undesirable) specified: 有某種(疾病或其他不正常)傾向的人: *a hysterical ~.* 有歇斯底里傾向的人。**6** (gram) (contrasted with predicate[1]) word(s) in a sentence about which sth is predicated; (contrasted with object[1](4)) *n* or *n* equivalent which carries out the action of a *v*, and which must agree(6) with the *v*, *eg book* in There was a book lying on the table' and *they* in Did they come early? (文法)主語(與 predicate 相對);主詞(與 object 相對) (如 There was a book lying on the table 中之 book, 及 Did they come early? 中之 they)。**7** (music) theme on which a composition (or one of its movements) is based. (音樂)主題;主旨;主旋律。

sub·ject[3] /səbˈdʒekt; səbˈdʒɛkt/ *vt* [VP14] ~ ***to,*** **1** bring, get (a country, nation, person) under control: 征服(國家,民族,人);使隸屬;使服從: *Ancient Rome ~ed most of Europe to her rule.* 古羅馬征服了大半個歐洲。**2** cause to undergo or experience; expose: 使遭受;使經歷;使蒙受;使有…之險: *~ oneself/one's friends to criticism/ridicule;* 使自己(朋友)遭受批評(嘲笑); *~ a man to torture.* 使人受折磨。*As a test the metal was ~ed to great heat.* 該金屬曾置於高溫下試驗。**sub·jec·tion** /səbˈdʒekʃn; səbˈdʒɛkʃən/ *n* [U] ~ing or being ~ed: 征服;隸屬;服從: *The ~ion of the rebels took several months.* 該項叛亂歷時數月始敉平。*The people lived in a state of ~ion/were kept/held in ~ion for half a century.* 那個民族被統治達半世紀之久。

sub·jec·tive /səbˈdʒektɪv; səbˈdʒɛktɪv/ *adj* **1** (of ideas, feelings, etc) existing in the mind, not produced by things outside the mind; not objective: (指觀念、感情等)主觀的;存在於心中而非由外在事物產生的;非客觀的: *Did he really see a ghost or was it only a ~ impression?* 他眞的見到了鬼,抑或僅僅是主觀的感覺? **2** (of art and artists, writing, etc) giving the personal or individual point of view or feeling (opp to realistic art, writing, etc). (指藝術及藝術家，寫作等) 表現個人的觀點或感覺的；主觀的(與寫實藝術、作品等相反)。 **3** (gram) of the subject. (文法)主詞的。**~·ly** *adv* in a ~ manner: 主觀上；主觀地: *An examination paper in arithmetic can be marked objectively, but a literary essay can be marked only ~ly,* ie on the personal impression of the examiner. 算術試卷可以客觀評分，但是一篇文章卻祇能憑閱卷者的主觀印象評分。 **sub·jec·tiv·ity** /ˌsʌbdʒekˈtɪvətɪ ; ˌsʌbdʒɛkˈtɪvətɪ/ *n* [U].

sub·join /ˌsʌbˈdʒɔɪn ; səbˈdʒɔɪn/ *vt* [VP6A] (formal) add at the end: (正式用語) 補述；增補；添加: *~ a postscript to a letter.* 信後加一附記。

sub judice /ˌsʌbˈdʒuːdɪsɪ ; sʌbˈdʒudɪsi/ (Lat) under judicial consideration, not yet decided (and for this reason, in GB, not (by law) to be commented upon). (拉丁) 在審理中；尚未判決(因此，在英國，(依法)不得置評)。

sub·ju·gate /ˈsʌbdʒʊgeɪt ; ˈsʌbdʒəˌget/ *vt* [VP6A] subdue, conquer. 壓服；征服；抑制。**sub·ju·ga·tion** /ˌsʌbdʒʊˈgeɪʃn ; ˌsʌbdʒəˈgeʃən/ *n* [U].

sub·junc·tive /səbˈdʒʌŋktɪv ; səbˈdʒʌŋktɪv/ *adj* (gram) expressing a condition, hypothesis, possibility, etc. (文法) 假設(虛擬)語氣的。□ *n* [U, C] the ~ mood; form of a verb in this mood. 假設(虛擬)語氣；假設(虛擬)語氣的動詞形式。

sub·lease /ˌsʌbˈliːs ; ˈsʌbˌlis/ *vt, vi* [VP6A, 2A] lease to another person (a house, land, etc which one has oneself leased); sublet. 轉租；分租(房屋、土地等)。□ *n* lease of this kind. 轉租；分租。

sub·let /ˌsʌbˈlet ; sʌbˈlɛt/ *vt, vi* (-tt-) [VP6A, 2A] **1** rent to sb else (a room, house, etc of which one is a tenant). 轉租或分租(房間、房屋等)給他人。 **2** give part of (a contract, eg for building a factory) to sb else. 轉包或分包(建工廠等的合約)給他人。

sub-lieu·ten·ant /ˌsʌbləˈtenənt *US:* -luːˈt- ; ˌsʌbluˈtɛnənt/ *n* naval officer with rank next below that of a lieutenant. 海軍中尉。

sub·li·mate /ˈsʌblɪmeɪt ; ˈsʌbləˌmet/ *vt* [VP6A] **1** (chem) convert from a solid state to vapour by heat and allow to solidify again (in order to purify it). (化學) 使昇華(加熱使由固體變爲氣體，再凝爲固體，俾使之淨化)。 **2** (psych) unconsciously change (emotions and activities arising from the instincts) into higher or more desirable channels. (心理學) 不自覺地將(本能的情緒及活動)導入比較高尚或理想的途徑；使(本能)昇華；使高尚。□ *n, adj* (substance) refined by being ~d. 昇華的(物質)；淨化的(物質)；精華。**sub·li·ma·tion** /ˌsʌblɪˈmeɪʃn ; ˌsʌbləˈmeʃən/ *n*

sub·lime /səˈblaɪm ; səˈblaɪm/ *adj* **1** of the greatest and highest sort; causing wonder or reverence: 至大至高的；莊嚴的；偉大的；令人驚異或崇敬的；卓越的: *~ scenery/heroism/self-sacrifice.* 壯麗的景色(令人崇敬的英勇行爲；偉大的自我犧牲)。 **2** extreme; astounding (as of a person who does not fear the consequences): 極；最；令人震驚的(如指不顧後果的人): *What ~ conceit/impudence/indifference!* 多麼令人吃驚的自負(厚顏，冷漠)！□ *n* **the ~,** that which fills one with awe or reverence. 令人敬畏或崇敬的事物；卓絕。 ***(go) from the ~ to the ridiculous,*** (pass) from what is beautiful, noble, etc to what is trivial, inferior, absurd, etc: 煞風景(從原本美好、高貴等的事物變成平凡、低劣、荒謬等的事物): *To find a snack bar at the top of Mount Olympus would be to go from the ~ to the ridiculous.* 在奧林帕斯山頂發現一個小吃店，眞是煞風景。**~·ly** *adv* in a ~ manner: 偉大地；崇高地；卓越地；令人驚異地；異常地: *He was ~ly unconscious* (= completely ignorant) *of how foolish he looked.* 他根本不知道他的樣子有多愚蠢。**sub·lim·ity** /səˈblɪmətɪ ; səˈblɪmətɪ/ *n* [U and in *pl* 並用複數; -ties] ~ quality or qualities: 偉大性；崇高性；卓越性；異常性: *the sublimity of the Alps;* 阿爾卑斯山的壯麗; *the sublimities of great art.* 偉大藝術的崇高性。

sub·lim·inal /ˌsʌbˈlɪmɪnl ; sʌbˈlɪmənl̩/ *adj* below the threshold of consciousness; of which one is not consciously aware: 下意識的；潛意識的；*~ advertising,* as when an advertisement is projected on to a cinema or TV screen for a fraction of a second and is noted only by the subconscious mind. 潛意識廣告(如電影院的銀幕或電視上放映的瞬間廣告，觀衆祇在潛意識中留下印象)。

sub·mar·ine /ˌsʌbməˈriːn *US:* ˈsʌbməriːn ; ˈsʌbməˌrin/ *adj* existing, designed for use, under the surface of the sea: 海生的；海中的；存在於海面下的；爲海面下使用而設計的: *~ plant life;* 海生植物; *a ~ cable.* 海底電纜。□ *n* ship which can be submerged to operate under water. 潛水艇；潛水艦。**sub·mari·ner** /sʌbˈmærɪnə(r) ; ˌsʌbməˈrinɚ/ *n* member of a ~'s crew. 潛水艇上的工作人員。

a submarine

sub·merge /səbˈmɜːdʒ ; səbˈmɝdʒ/ *vt, vi* **1** [VP6A] put under water; cover with a liquid. 置於水中；置於液體中；浸於水或液體；淹沒。 **2** [VP2A] sink out of sight; (of a submarine) go down under the surface. 沉沒；(指潛水艇) 潛入水中；潛航。**sub·merged** *adj* under the surface of the sea, etc: 在海面等下的；在水面下的；被水等淹沒的: *~d rocks;* 暗礁；水面下的岩石; *a wreck that is ~d at high tide.* 高潮時被水淹沒的難船。**sub·merg·ence** /səbˈmɜːdʒəns ; səbˈmɝdʒəns/, **sub·mer·sion** /səbˈmɜːʃn *US:* -ʒn ; səbˈmɝʃən/ *nn* [U] submerging or being ~d. (被)浸沒；(被)沒入液體中。**sub·mers·ible** /səbˈmɜːsəbl ; səbˈmɝsəbl̩/ *adj* capable of submerging. 有潛入水中能力的；可潛的。

sub·mission /səbˈmɪʃn ; səbˈmɪʃən/ *n* **1** [U] act of submitting; acceptance of another's power or authority: 歸順；投降；降服: *The rebels made their ~ to the army.* 叛徒們向軍隊投降。*The enemy were starved into ~,* compelled to submit by hunger. 敵人因饑餓而被迫投降。 **2** [U] obedience; humility: 服從；忠順；謙遜: *with all due ~,* with profound respect. 必恭必敬地。 **3** [C, U] (legal) theory, opinion, etc submitted to a judge or jury: (法律) 向法官或陪審團提出的意見、理論等: *My ~ is that.../In my ~, ...* I submit(3) that .... 我認爲…；據我的看法…；玆提出意見如下…。

sub·miss·ive /səbˈmɪsɪv ; səbˈmɪsɪv/ *adj* yielding to the control or authority of another: 歸順的；降服的；服從的: *~ to advice.* 順從忠告。*Marian is not a ~ wife.* 瑪麗安不是一位順服的妻子。**~·ly** *adv* **~·ness** *n*

sub·mit /səbˈmɪt ; səbˈmɪt/ *vt, vi* (-tt-) **1** [VP6A, 14] ***~ oneself to sb/sth,*** put (oneself) under the control of another: 使(自己)受他人控制；服從；屈服於: *~ oneself to discipline.* 服從紀律。*Should a wife ~ herself to her husband?* 妻子應順從她的丈夫嗎？ **2** [VP14] ***~ sb to sth,*** cause him to endure it: 使某人忍受某事: *~ a prisoner to torture/interrogation.* 使一囚犯受刑(受審訊)。 **3** [VP6A, 14] ***~ sth (to sb/sth),*** put forward for opinion, discussion, decision, etc: 提出某事物(供評斷，討論，決定等): *~ plans/proposals, etc to a city council;* 向市議會提出計畫(建議等); *~ proofs of identity.* 提出鑑定證明。 **4** [VP9] (legal) suggest, argue: (法律) 建議；主張；聲辯: *Counsel ~ted that there was no case against his client.* 辯護人辯稱沒有一條指控可加罪於他的當事人。 **5** [VP3A] ***~ to sb/sth,*** surrender; give in; abstain from resistance: 投降；順

從;屈服: ~ *to the enemy/ill treatment/separation from one's family.* 屈服於敵人(甘受虐待;忍痛與家庭分離)。

sub·nor·mal /ˌsʌbˈnɔːml ; sʌbˈnɔrml̩/ *adj* below normal: 正常以下的;低於正常的: ~ *temperatures;* 低於正常的溫度; less than normal: 未達正常的;遜常的: *a child of ~ intelligence.* 智力低於常人的兒童。□ *n* person of ~ intelligence. 智力低於常人之人。

sub·or·bital /ˌsʌbˈɔːbɪtl ; sʌbˈɔrbɪtl̩/ *adj* of less duration or distance than one orbit. 少於繞軌道一圈的距離或時間的。

sub·or·di·nate /səˈbɔːdɪnət *US:* -dənət ; səˈbɔrdn̩ɪt/ *adj* **1** ~ ***(to)***, junior in rank or position; less important: 下級的;次要的;附屬的: *in a ~ position.* 居次要地位。 **2** ~ **clause**, (gram) dependent clause; clause which, introduced by a conjunction, serves as a *noun, adj* or *adv.* (文法)從屬子句;附屬子句(以連接詞引導而用作名詞、形容詞或副詞者)。⇨ co-ordinate. □ *n* person in a ~ position; person working under another. 居次位者;屬下;屬僚。□ *vt* /səˈbɔːdɪneɪt *US:* -dəneɪt ; səˈbɔrdn̩ˌet/ [VP6A, 14] ~ ***sth (to)***, treat as ~; make ~ (to). 當作屬下對待; 輕視; 使居下位或次要地位。 **subordinating conjunction**, (gram) one that introduces a ~ clause, eg *because, if, as.* (文法)從屬連接詞(如 because, if, as)。**sub·or·di·na·tion** /səˌbɔːdɪˈneɪʃn *US:* -dənˈeɪʃn ; səˌbɔrdn̩ˈeʃən/ *n* subordinating or being ~d. 下位;次要;附屬。**sub·or·di·na·tive** /səˈbɔːdɪnətɪv *US:* -dəneɪtɪv ; səˈbɔrdəˌnetɪv/ *adj* subordinating. 附屬的;從屬的。

sub·orn /səˈbɔːn ; səˈbɔrn/ *vt* [VP6A] induce (a person) by bribery or other means to commit perjury or other unlawful act. 以賄賂或其他方法使(人)僞證或爲其他不法行爲;買通(某人)。**sub·or·na·tion** /ˌsʌbɔːˈneɪʃn ; ˌsʌbɔrˈneʃən/ *n* [U].

sub·poena /səˈpiːnə ; səˈpinə/ *n* (*pl* ~s) [C] (legal) written order requiring a person to appear in a law court. (法律)傳票。□ *vt* (*pt, pp* -naed) [VP 6A] summon with a ~: 以傳票傳喚;傳審;票傳: *be ~ed as a witness.* 被傳喚作證人。

sub rosa /ˌsʌbˈrəʊzə ; sʌbˈrozə/ (Lat) (of communications, etc) in strict confidence. (拉丁)(指聯絡、通信等)極端秘密地。

sub·scribe /səbˈskraɪb ; səbˈskraɪb/ *vi, vt* **1** [VP 2A, 3A, 6A, 14] ~ ***(sth) (to/for)***, (agree to) pay (a sum of money) in common with other persons (to a cause, for sth): 認捐;捐助;應募;認股(與 to 連用,後接緣由;與 for 連用,後接某事物): *He ~s liberally to charities.* 他慷慨地捐助慈善事業。*He ~ed £5 to the flood relief fund.* 他認捐五鎊作爲水災救濟基金。*How many shares did you ~ for in the new company?* 那新公司你認了多少股份? **2** [VP3A] ~ ***to sth***, **(a)** agree to take (a newspaper, periodical, etc) regularly for a specified time. 訂閱(報紙、雜誌)等。**(b)** agree with, share (an opinion, view, etc). 同意或贊成(某項意見、觀點等)。~ ***for a book***, agree before it is published to buy a copy or copies. 預約某書。 **3** [VP6A] (formal) write (one's name, etc) at the foot of a document: (正式用語)簽(名等)於文件後;簽署: ~ *one's name to a petition.* 簽名於請願書。**~r** *n* person who ~s (esp to funds, newspapers). 捐助者;訂購者;贊同者;簽署者;(尤指)捐助基金或訂閱報紙者。 **sub·scrip·tion** /səbˈskrɪpʃn ; səbˈskrɪpʃən/ *n* **1** [U] subscribing or being ~d: 捐助;訂閱;簽署: *The monument was erected by public subscription.* 該紀念碑是由各界捐款建立的。**2** [C] sum of money ~d (for charity, for receiving a newspaper, magazine, etc), or paid for membership of a club. 慈善捐款;捐助金;(報紙雜誌等的)訂閱費;預約金;(俱樂部會員的)會費。 **subˈscription concert**, one whose seats are all paid for in advance. (座位全部預先訂好的)預約式音樂會。

sub·se·quent /ˈsʌbsɪkwənt ; ˈsʌbsɪˌkwɛnt/ *adj* ~ ***(to)***, later; following: 後來的;隨後的;繼起的: ~ *events;* 接着發生的事件; ~ *to this event.* 在此事以後。**~·ly** *adv* afterwards. 此後;接着。

sub·serve /səbˈsɜːv ; səbˈsɝv/ *vt* [VP6A] serve as a means in helping or promoting (an end, a purpose). 有助於(某一目標或目的);促進(某一目標或目的)。

sub·ser·vi·ent /səbˈsɜːvɪənt ; səbˈsɝvɪənt/ *adj* ~ ***to***, **1** giving too much respect to: 過分恭順的;阿諛的;卑屈的;奉承的: ~ *shopkeepers.* 奉承顧客的店主。 **2** useful as a means to a purpose; subordinate or subject to. 有助於某項目的的;有用的;輔助的;隸屬的。**~·ly** *adv* **sub·ser·vi·ence** /-əns ; -əns/ *n* [U].

sub·side /səbˈsaɪd ; səbˈsaɪd/ *vi* [VP2A] **1** (of flood water) sink to a lower or to the normal level. (指洪水)降落;退去。 **2** (of land) sink, eg because of mining operations. (指土地)下沉;凹陷(如因採礦等)。 **3** (of buildings) settle lower down in the ground, eg because of a clay subsoil that shrinks in a dry season. (指建築物)下陷(如因下層的黏土在乾旱季節時收縮所致)。 **4** (of winds, passions, etc) become quiet(er) after being violent: (指風,激情等)(暴烈後)歸於平靜;平息;減弱: *The storm began to ~.* 暴風雨漸漸平息了。**5** (hum) (of a person) go down slowly: (諧)(指人)慢慢降下: ~ *into a chair.* 在一張椅子上慢慢地坐下來。**sub·sid·ence** /səbˈsaɪdns ; səbˈsaɪdns/ *n* [C, U] act or process of subsiding (2, 3); instance of this. 降落;下沉;凹陷。

sub·sidi·ary /səbˈsɪdɪərɪ *US:* -dɪerɪ ; səbˈsɪdɪˌɛrɪ/ *adj* ~ ***(to)***, serving as a help or support but not of first importance: 輔助的;幫助的;次要的;附屬的: *a ~ company,* one that is controlled by a larger one. 附屬公司。□ *n* (*pl* -ries) ~ company; ~ thing or person. 附屬公司;輔助物;協助者;助手。

sub·sidy /ˈsʌbsədɪ ; ˈsʌbsədɪ/ *n* [C] (*pl* -dies) money granted, esp by a government or society, to an industry or other cause needing help, or to an ally in war, or (eg *food subsidies*) to keep prices at a desired level. 補助金(尤指政府或社團補助某項工業或某項運動,補助戰時盟國,協助穩定物價等者);資助金;獎助金。**sub·si·dize** /ˈsʌbsɪdaɪz ; ˈsʌbsəˌdaɪz/ *vt* [VP6A] give a ~ to: 給予補助金;資助;獎助: *subsidized industries.* 受資助的工業。**sub·si·diz·ation** /ˌsʌbsɪdaɪˈzeɪʃn *US:* -dɪˈz- ; ˌsʌbsədəˈzeʃən/ *n* [U].

sub·sist /səbˈsɪst ; səbˈsɪst/ *vi* [VP2A, 3A] ~ ***(on)***, exist; be kept in existence on: 生存;存在;維持生活;賴(…)爲生: ~ *on a vegetable diet/on charity.* 靠素食(施捨)維持生活。**sub·sis·tence** /-təns ; -təns/ *n* [U] existence; means of existing: 生存;存在;生計;維生之道: *a ~ence wage,* one that is only just enough to enable a worker to exist; 維持生活的工資; *my means of ~ence,* how I make a living; 我的生計; *ˈ~ence crops,* those grown for consumption (contrasted with *ˈcash crops,* those sold for money); 消費作物(爲自用種植者,與種來賣錢的 cash crops 相對); *on a ˈ~ence ˈlevel,* on a standard of living only just adequate for remaining alive. 過僅足以餬口的生活。

sub·soil /ˈsʌbsɔɪl ; ˈsʌbˌsɔɪl/ *n* [U] layer of soil that lies immediately beneath the surface layer. (表層之下的)亞壤土;下層土;底土。

sub·sonic /ˌsʌbˈsɒnɪk ; ˌsʌbˈsɑnɪk/ *adj* (of speed) less than that of sound; (of aircraft) flying at ~ speed. (指速度)低於音速的;(指飛機)以低於音速飛行的。⇨ supersonic.

sub·stance /ˈsʌbstəns ; ˈsʌbstəns/ *n* **1** [C, U] (particular kind of) matter: 物質;物;特殊種類的物質: *Water, ice and snow are not different ~s; they are the same ~ in different forms.* 水,冰及雪並非不同種類的物質;它們係不同形式的同一物質。 **2** [U] most important part, chief or real meaning, of sth: 實質;實體;要義;主旨;眞義: *an argument of little ~;* 內容貧乏的議論; *the ~ of a speech.* 講辭的主旨。*I agree in ~ with what you say, but differ on some small points.* 我大體上同意你所說的

話，不過某些小地方，我不同意你的意見。 **3** [U] firmness; solidity: 牢固；堅實: *This material has some ~*, is fairly solid or strong. 這種料子相當結實。 **4** [U] money; property: 錢；財產；資產: *a man of ~*, eg a property owner; 有資產者; *waste one's ~*, spend one's money unwisely. 浪費金錢。

sub·stan·dard /ˌsʌbˈstændəd ; sʌbˈstændɚd/ *adj* below average standard. 低於標準的；不够標準的；一般標準之下的。

sub·stan·tial /səbˈstænʃl ; səbˈstænʃəl/ *adj* **1** solidly or strongly built or made. 構造牢固的；堅實的。 **2** large; considerable: 大的；相當可觀的: *a ~ meal / improvement / loan*. 豐盛的餐食(相當大的進步；大筆貸款)。 **3** possessing considerable property; well-to-do: 擁有相當財產的；富有的: *a ~ business firm;* 股實的商號; *~ farmers*. 富有的農人。 **4** essential; virtual: 實際上的；大體上的；實質的: *We are in ~ agreement*. 我們大體上意見相同。 **5** real; having physical existence: 眞實的；實在的；有實體的；眞實存在的: *Was what you saw something ~ or only a ghost?* 你見到的是實實在在的東西，或僅僅是鬼影？ **~ly** /-ʃəlɪ ; -ʃəlɪ/ *adv*: *Your efforts contributed ~ly* (= considerably) *to our success*. 你的努力對於我們的成功有重大貢獻。

sub·stan·ti·ate /səbˈstænʃɪeɪt ; səbˈstænʃɪˌet/ *vt* [VP6A] give facts to support (a claim, statement, charge, etc). 列舉事實以支持(某一主張、陳述、指控等)。 **sub·stan·ti·ation** /səbˌstænʃɪˈeɪʃn ; səbˌstænʃɪˈeʃən/ *n*

sub·stan·ti·val /ˌsʌbstənˈtaɪvl ; ˌsʌbstənˈtaɪvḷ/ *adj* (gram) of the nature of a substantive: (文法)實體詞的；名詞的；有名詞之性質的: *a ~ clause*, a clause functioning as a noun. 名詞子句。

sub·stan·tive /ˈsʌbstəntɪv ; ˈsʌbstəntɪv/ *adj* having an independent existence; real; actual: 獨立存在的；眞正的；實際的: *Almost all of Great Britain's colonies now have the status of ~ nations*. 幾乎所有英國的殖民地現在都變成了獨立的國家。 **a ~ motion**, (in a debate) an amendment which, having been carried, becomes the subject of further discussion. (在國會等辯論中的)正式動議(修正意見經採納後成爲進一步之討論主題者)。 **~** /səbˈstæntɪv ; ˈsʌbstəntɪv/ **rank**, (GB) permanent rank (in the army, etc). (英)(陸軍等的)永久軍階。 □ *n* (gram) noun. (文法)名詞。

sub·sta·tion /ˈsʌbsteɪʃn ; ˈsʌbˌsteʃən/ *n* branch or subordinate station, eg for the distribution of electric current. 支局；分局；分所；分站；變電所。

sub·sti·tute /ˈsʌbstɪtjuːt *US:* -tuːt ; ˈsʌbstəˌtjut/ *n* person or thing taking the place of, acting for or serving for another: 代理人；代替者；代用品；代用物: *Is chicory a satisfactory ~ for coffee?* 菊苣是一種令人滿意的咖啡代用品嗎？ *S~s for rubber can be made from petroleum*. 石油中可製出橡膠的代用品。 □ *vt, vi* [VP6A, 14, 3A] **~ (sth / sb) (for)**, put, use or serve as a ~: 代替；替換；代用: *~ margarine for butter*. 以人造奶油代替奶油。 *Mr X ~d for the teacher who was in hospital*. 某先生代替生病住院的那位老師。 **sub·sti·tu·tion** /ˌsʌbstɪˈtjuːʃn *US:* -ˈtuːʃn ; ˌsʌbstəˈtjuʃən/ *n* [U]

sub·stra·tum /ˌsʌbˈstrɑːtəm *US:* -ˈstreɪt- ; sʌbˈstretəm/ *n* (*pl* -ta /-tə ; -tə/) **1** level lying below another: 下面的一層；下層: *a ~ of rock*. 下層岩石。 **2** foundation: 基礎；根基: *The story has a ~ of truth*, is based upon facts (though perhaps at first sight seeming false). 這故事有事實爲根據(雖然乍看或似荒誕不經)。

sub·struc·ture /ˈsʌbstrʌktʃə(r) ; sʌbˈstrʌktʃɚ/ *n* foundation; supporting part. 基礎；根柢；根基；支撐結構；下層結構。 ⇨ superstructure.

sub·sume /səbˈsjuːm *US:* -ˈsuːm ; səbˈsum/ *vt* [VP6A, 14] **~ (under)**, include (an example, etc) under a rule or in a particular class. 把(某一事例等)納入某一規則或歸入某一種類。

sub·tend /səbˈtend ; səbˈtɛnd/ *vt* (geom) (of a chord, the side of a triangle) be exactly opposite to (an arc or angle). (幾何)(指弦，三角形之邊)正對(弧或角)。

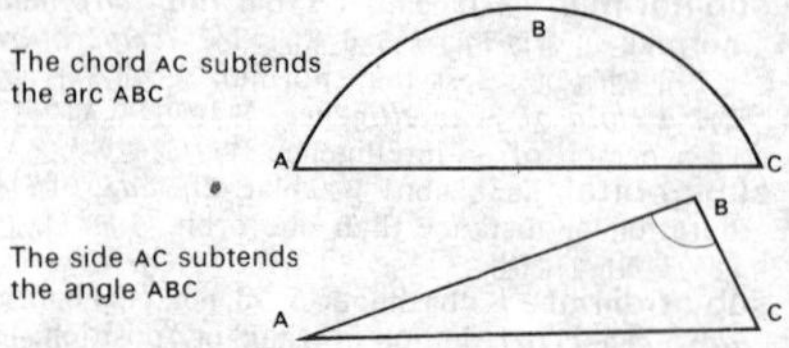
The chord AC subtends
the arc ABC
A
B
C
The side AC subtends
the angle ABC
A
B
C

sub·ter·fuge /ˈsʌbtəfjuːdʒ ; ˈsʌbtɚˌfjudʒ/ *n* [C] trick, excuse, esp one used to evade trouble or sth unpleasant; [U] trickery. 詭計；遁辭(尤指用以逃避困難或不愉快之事者)；詭詐；欺騙。

sub·ter·ranean /ˌsʌbtəˈreɪnɪən ; ˌsʌbtəˈrenɪən/ *adj* underground: 地下的: *a ~ passage;* 地下通道; *~ fires*. 地下火。

sub·title /ˈsʌbtaɪtl ; ˈsʌbˌtaɪtl/ *n* secondary title (of a book); translation of the dialogue of a foreign language film, printed on the film. (書的)副標題；小標題；(印在外國語發音電影片上的)對話譯文；對白翻譯。

subtle /ˈsʌtl ; ˈsʌtl/ *adj* **1** difficult to perceive or describe because fine or delicate: 因細微、精巧或微妙而難於覺察或描述的；精巧的；巧妙的: *a ~ charm / flavour;* 難以形容的魅力(味道); *~ humour;* 巧妙的幽默; *a ~ distinction*. 細微的差別。 **2** ingenious; complex: 機敏的；靈巧的；錯綜複雜的: *a ~ argument / design*. 巧妙的議論(設計)。 **3** quick and clever at seeing or making delicate differences; sensitive: 精明的；敏銳的；明察秋毫的；敏感的: *a ~ observer / critic*. 敏銳的觀察者(批評家)。 **sub·tly** /ˈsʌtlɪ ; ˈsʌtlɪ/ *adv* **~ty** /ˈsʌtltɪ ; ˈsʌtltɪ/ *n* (*pl* -ties) [U] the quality of being ~; [C] ~ distinction, etc. 微妙；靈巧；錯綜；明敏；細微的差別等。

sub·topia /ˌsʌbˈtəʊpɪə ; sʌbˈtopɪə/ *n* [U] (part of the country where there is a) monotonous urban sprawl of standardized buildings, etc; (result of such a) tendency to urbanize the country. 鄉村都市化；都市化的鄉村(如採取單調一致的都市建築等)；鄉村都市化的趨勢；此一趨勢所產生的結果。

sub·tract /səbˈtrækt ; səbˈtrækt/ *vt* [VP6A, 14] **~ (from)**, take (a number, quantity) away from (another number, etc): 自(他數等中)減除(某數或量)；減去；扣除: *~ 6 from 9;* 九減六; *6 ~ed from 9 gives 3*, ie 9 - 6 = 3. 九減六得三。 **sub·trac·tion** /səbˈtrækʃn ; səbˈtrækʃən/ *n* [U] the process of ~ing; [C] instance of this: 減法；減去；扣除；減除的實例: *Two from five is a simple ~ion*. 五減二是簡單的減法。

sub·tropi·cal /ˌsʌbˈtrɒpɪkl ; sʌbˈtrɑpɪkḷ/ *adj* bordering on the tropics; nearly tropical; of ~ areas: 亞熱帶的；近熱帶的；亞熱帶地區的: *a ~ climate;* 亞熱帶氣候; *~ plants*. 亞熱帶植物。

sub·urb /ˈsʌbɜːb ; ˈsʌbɝb/ *n* [C] outlying residential district of a town or city. 市郊；城郊；郊區。 **the ~s**, all these districts collectively. 郊區總稱；郊外。 **sub·ur·ban** /səˈbɜːbən ; səˈbɝbən/ *adj* **1** of or in a ~: 市郊的；城郊的；(在)郊區的: *~an shops*. 郊區的商店。 **2** (derog) having the good qualities of neither town nor country people; narrow in interests and outlook. (貶)既無城市人又無鄉下人之優點的；偏狹的；偏見的；井底之蛙的。 **sub·ur·bia** /səˈbɜːbɪə ; səˈbɝbɪə/ *n* [U] (usu derog) (kind of life lived by, characteristic outlook of, people in) ~s (collectively). (通常作貶)郊外；郊區居民的生活及其見識；興趣及見識偏狹。

sub·ven·tion /səbˈvenʃn ; səbˈvɛnʃən/ *n* subsidy; grant of money in aid. 補助金；津貼。

sub·vers·ive /səbˈvɜːsɪv ; səbˈvɝsɪv/ *adj* tending to subvert: 顚覆的；促使滅亡的；有推翻之傾向的；破壞性的: *speeches that are ~ of peace and order;* 破壞治安的演說; *~ propaganda*. 顚覆性的宣傳。

sub·vert /sʌbˈvɜːt ; səbˈvɝt/ *vt* [VP6A] destroy, overthrow (religion, a government) by weakening people's trust, confidence, belief: 推翻(政府);破壞(宗教);顛覆;使滅亡: *~ the monarchy.* 推翻君主政體。**sub·ver·sion** /səbˈvɜːʃn *US:* -ʒn ; səˈbvɝʃən/ *n* [U].

sub·way /ˈsʌbweɪ ; ˈsʌbˌwe/ *n* **1** [C] underground passage or tunnel, eg one to enable people to get from one side of a busy street to another: 地面下通道;(尤指穿越馬路的)地下道;隧道: *Cross by the ~.* 走地下道過馬路。**2 (the) ~,** (US) underground railway in a town (GB = *the Underground* or, colloq, *the tube*): (美)(城市中的)地下火車(英國稱為 the Underground, 俗語稱為 the tube): *take the ~;* 乘地下火車; *travel by ~.* 乘地下火車旅行。

suc·ceed /səkˈsiːd ; səkˈsid/ *vi, vt* **1** [VP2A, 3A] **~ (in),** do what one is trying to do; gain one's purpose: 成功;完成;遂行: *~ in life;* 發跡; *~ in (passing) an examination.* 考試及格(通過考試)。*The attack ~ed.* 這次襲擊成功了。**2** [VP6A, 16B] come next after and take the place of: 繼任;繼續: *Who ~ed Churchill as Prime Minister?* 繼邱吉爾出任首相的是誰? **3** [VP2A, 3A] **~ (to),** inherit; have (a title, position, etc) on the death of sb: 繼承;承襲(爵位,地位等): *~ to an estate.* 繼承產業。*On George VI's death, Elizabeth II ~ed (to the throne).* 喬治六世死後,伊利莎白二世繼位(繼承王位)。

suc·cess /səkˈses ; səkˈsɛs/ *n* **1** [U] succeeding; the gaining of what is aimed at: 成功;成就: *meet with ~.* 獲得成功。***Nothing succeeds like ~,*** (prov) S~ in one case is likely to be followed by ~ in other cases. (諺)一事如意,事事順利。**2** [U] good fortune; prosperity: 好運;發達;興旺: *have great ~ in life.* 交大運;獲得大成功。**3** [C] sb or sth that succeeds; example of succeeding: 成功的人或事物;成功的例子: *The plan was a great ~.* 這項計畫極為成功。*He has had three ~es and one failure,* eg of a dramatist. 他曾獲得三次成功,一次失敗(如指劇作家)。*The army has had several ~es* (= victories) *recently.* 軍隊最近曾獲得數次勝利。**~·ful** /-fl ; -fəl/ *adj* having ~: 成功的;得到成功的: *~ful candidates;* 成功的候選人; *~ in everything.* 事事成功。**~·fully** /-fəlɪ ; -fəlɪ/ *adv*

suc·cession /səkˈseʃn ; səkˈsɛʃən/ *n* **1** [U] the coming of one thing after another in time or order: 繼續;連續: *the ~ of the seasons.* 四季的接續。***in ~,*** one after the other: 連續地;接續地: *five wet days in ~.* 連續五個雨天。**2** [C] number of things in ~: 連續的若干事物: *a ~ of wet days/defeats.* 連續的雨天(失敗)。**3** [U] (right of) succeeding to a title, the throne, property, etc; person having this right: 繼承;繼承權;有繼承權的人: *Who is first in ~ to the throne?* 誰是王位第一繼承人? **the Apostolic S~,** the unbroken passing of spiritual authority through the bishops from the Apostles of Jesus, and through the Popes from St Peter. 使徒大統(自耶穌十二門徒歷經主教,以及由聖彼得經諸教皇傳繼的信仰大統)。**ˈ~ duty,** tax on inherited property. 遺產稅;繼承稅。

suc·cess·ive /səkˈsesɪv ; səkˈsɛsɪv/ *adj* coming one after the other in an uninterrupted sequence: 繼續的;連續的: *The school team won five ~ games.* 校隊連續獲得五場比賽的勝利。Cf 參較 *five games in succession,* and *five games running.* 連續的五場比賽。**~·ly** *adv*

suc·cessor /səkˈsesə(r) ; səkˈsɛsɚ/ *n* person or thing that succeeds another: (指人或物)後繼者;繼承者;繼任者: *the ~ to the throne;* 王位繼承人; *appoint a ~ to a headmaster.* 任命校長繼任人。

suc·cinct /səkˈsɪŋkt ; səkˈsɪŋkt/ *adj* expressed briefly and clearly; terse. 簡明的;扼要的;簡潔的。**~·ly** *adv* **~·ness** *n*

suc·cour (US = **-cor**) /ˈsʌkə(r) ; ˈsʌkɚ/ *n* [U] (liter) help given in time of need. (文)及時的援助;需要時的救助;援助。□ *vt* [VP6A] give help to (sb in danger or difficulty). 援助(處於危險或困難中的人);救助。

suc·cu·bus /ˈsʌkjʊbəs ; ˈsʌkjəbəs/ *n* female demon supposed to have sexual intercourse with a sleeping man. 妖精(傳說中和熟睡的男子性交的女妖)。⇨ incubus.

suc·cu·lent /ˈsʌkjʊlənt ; ˈsʌkjələnt/ *adj* **1** (of fruit and meat) juicy; tasting good: (指水果及肉類)多汁液的;味道好的;好吃的: *a ~ steak.* 好吃的牛排。**2** (of stems, leaves) thick and fleshy; (of plants) having ~ stems and leaves. (指莖,葉)厚而肥的;多肉質的;(指植物)有肥厚之莖和葉的。□ *n* [C] ~ plant, eg a cactus. 莖葉肥厚的植物(如仙人掌)。**suc·cu·lence** /-əns ; -əns/ *n* [U].

suc·cumb /səˈkʌm ; səˈkʌm/ *vi* [VP2A, 3A] **~ (to),** yield (to temptation, flattery, etc); die: 屈服於(誘惑、諂媚等);死: *~ to one's injuries.* 受傷而死。

such /sʌtʃ ; sʌtʃ/ *adj* (no comp or superl; not placed between the *indef art* and its *n;* note, in the examples, the place of *such* after *no, some, many, all*). (無比較級和最高級;不置於不定冠詞與名詞之間;注意例句中的 such 置於 no, some, many, all 之後)。**1** of the same kind or degree (as): 同類的;同等的;這樣的;如此的: *~ a word (as that);* (像那樣的)這樣一個字; *~ words (as those);* (像那些)同類的字; *no ~ words (as those);* 沒有(像那些)同類的字;無此類字; *poets ~ as Keats and Shelley;* 像濟慈和雪萊這樣的詩人; *~ poets as Keats and Shelley;* 像濟慈和雪萊這樣的詩人; *~ people as these;* 像這一類的人們; *people ~ as these;* 像這一類的人們; *on ~ an occasion as this; on an occasion ~ as this;* 在這樣的場合; *Harrison, or some ~ name.* 哈利生,或和這個差不多的名字。*Some ~ plan was in his mind.* 他心裡有過這樣的計畫。*All ~ possibilities must be considered.* 所有這樣的可能性都須加以考慮。*I have met many ~ people.* 我曾遇到過許多這樣的人。*I've never heard of ~ a thing!* 我從未聽說過這樣的事! *I hope I never have ~ an experience again.* 我希望(我)永遠不再有這種經驗了。**2 ~ *as it is,*** used to suggest that sth is of poor quality, of little value, etc: 用於表示某物品質不佳,無甚價值等: *You can use my bicycle, ~ as it is.* 你可以用我的腳踏車,只是不太好騎。**~ *as to*** + *inf,* of a degree or kind that would or might: 至…的程度或種類;竟致: *Your stupidity is ~ as to fill me with despair.* 你愚蠢得叫我十分失望。*His illness is not ~ as to cause anxiety.* 他的病況尚不足憂慮。**3 ~ *that;* ~... *that:*** 如此(…)竟致: *His behaviour was ~ that everyone disliked him.* 他的行為使人人都嫌惡他。*S~ was the force of the explosion/The force of the explosion was ~ that all the windows were broken.* 爆炸的力量大到把全部的窗子都震破了。**4** (Cf the positions of ~ and *so* in these examples): (參較以下諸例中 such 及 so 的位置): *Don't be in ~ a hurry,* in so much of a hurry, in so great a hurry. 不要這樣匆忙。*I haven't had ~ an enjoyable evening* (= so enjoyable an evening) *for months.* 數月來我從未度過像這樣愉快的一晚。**5** (intensive, esp in exclamatory sentences): (用作強意語,尤用於感嘆句中): *It was ~ a long time ago!* 那是很久以前的事了! *You gave me ~ a fright!* 你嚇死我了! *We've had ~ a good time!* 我們這一段時間過得多愉快啊! Cf 參較 What a fright you gave me! What a good time we've had! **6** (pred use) this, that, these, those (as already stated, etc): (敘述用法)這(些);那(些)(表示已陳述者等): *S~ is not my intention.* 我的意圖不是這樣。*S~ were his words.* 他是這麼說的。*S~ was her reward.* 這就是她的報酬。*S~ is life!* Life is like that, life is as these circumstances show it to be! 人生就是這樣!(人生就像那樣,像這些情況所顯示者!) □ *pron* ~ person(s) or thing(s); that/those: 像這樣的人(們)或(諸)事物;那(些): *I may have hurt her feelings but ~* (= that) *was certainly not my intention.* 我可能已傷害了她的感情,但是我的確不是故意的。*He is a brilliant scholar and is everywhere* *recognized as* ~, as a brilliant scholar. 他是一位有才華的學者，而且是各地的人都有這樣的看法。*Down with anarchists and all* ~, all persons of that kind! 打倒無政府主義者及其所有的同路人！ ***as*** ~, properly so called; in every way: 確切而言；完全地: *I didn't have a nervous breakdown as* ~, *it was more a reaction to overwork.* 我不是眞的得了精神崩潰，那祇是工作過度的反應。~ ***as***, those that: 諸如: *I haven't many specimens but I will send you* ~ *as I have.* 我沒多少樣本，但我將全部送給你。 **'~·like** *adj* (colloq) of the same kind; similar: (俗)同類的；同樣的；相似的: *I have no time for concerts, theatres, cinemas and* ~*like.* 我沒有時間赴音樂會，看戲，看電影及諸如此類的消遣。

suck /sʌk ; sʌk/ *vt, vi* **1** [VP6A, 15A, B] ~ ***sth (in/out/up/through, etc) (from/out of, etc)***, draw (liquid) into the mouth by the use of the lip muscles: 用嘴吸(液體)；啜: ~ *the juice from an orange;* 吸橘子的汁; ~ *poison out of a wound;* 吸出傷口的毒液; (fig) (喩) ~ *in knowledge.* 吸收知識。 **2** [VP6A, 22] draw liquid or (fig) knowledge, information, etc from: 自…吸取液體; (喩)自…吸取知識、消息等: *a baby* ~*ing its mother's breast.* 正在吸食母乳的嬰兒。 Cf 參較 The mother was nursing her baby at the breast. 母親把她的嬰兒抱在懷裡哺乳。*She* ~*ed the orange dry.* 她把橘子吸乾了。~ ***sb's brains***, = *pick* (now the usu word) sb's brains. 剽竊或抄襲某人的思想 (pick sb's brains 較常用)。 **'~·ing-pig** *n* young pig still taking its mother's milk. 乳豬；小豬。 **3** [VP6A] hold (sth) in the mouth and lick, roll about, squeeze, etc with the tongue: 含(物)在口中以舌舐之、轉動、壓擠等; 吮；舐: ~ *a toffee.* 吮食太妃糖。*The child still* ~*s its thumb.* 這孩子還會吮吸拇指。 **4** [VP2C] perform the action of ~ing: 吸；啜；吮；舐；咂: *The baby was* ~*ing away at the empty feeding-bottle.* 那嬰兒繼續吮吸那隻空奶瓶。*The old man was* ~*ing at his pipe.* 那老人在吸他的烟斗。 **5** [VP6A, 15B] ~ ***sth (up)***, absorb: 吸收: *plants that* ~ *up moisture from the soil.* 從土壤中吸收水份的植物。 **6** [VP 15A, B] (of a whirlpool, etc) engulf, pull in: (指漩渦等)吞噬；拉進；捲入: *The canoe was* ~*ed (down) into the whirlpool.* 那獨木舟被捲進了漩渦。 **7** [VP 2C] ~ ***up (to)***, (sl) try to please by flattery, offers of service, etc. (俚)諂媚；拍馬屁；巴結。□ *n* act or process of ~ing: 吸；吮；咂；舐；捲入: *have/take a* ~ *at a lollipop.* 吮食棒棒糖。 ***give*** ~ ***to***, allow (a baby) to ~ at the breast (but *nurse* and *suckle* are more usu). 讓(嬰兒)吸奶(但 nurse 及 suckle 較常用)。

sucker /'sʌkə(r) ; 'sʌkɚ/ *n* [C] **1** one who, that which, sucks. 吸吮者(指人或物)。 **2** organ in some animals enabling them to rest on a surface by suction. (動物的)吸盤；吸管。 **3** rubber device, eg a concave rubber disc, that adheres by suction to a surface (and can be used to cause articles to adhere in this way). 橡皮吸子(如凹入的橡皮圓盤，可藉吸力附着於平面上，並可藉此固着物件)。 **4** unwanted shoot (new growth) coming up from the roots of a tree, shrub, etc. (植物的)吸枝；吸根(從樹或灌木等的根部生出者)。 **5** (colloq) person foolish enough to be deceived by unscrupulous tricksters, advertisements, etc. (俗)被無恥騙徒、廣告等所欺騙的人。

suckle /'sʌkl ; 'sʌkl̩/ *vt* [VP6A] feed with milk from the breast or udder. 哺乳；餵奶。 **suck·ling** /'sʌklɪŋ ; 'sʌklɪŋ/ *n* baby or young animal still being ~d. (仍在哺乳的)嬰兒或幼獸。 ***babes and sucklings***, innocent children. 無知的孩子。⇨ mouth¹.

suc·tion /'sʌkʃn ; 'sʌkʃən/ *n* [U] **1** action of sucking; removal of air, liquid, etc from a vessel or cavity so as to produce a partial vacuum and enable air-pressure from outside to force in liquid or dust: 吸；吸收；吸力；吸入；吸除: *Some pumps and all vacuum-cleaners work by* ~. 有些唧筒和所有的眞空吸塵器都是藉吸力發生作用的。 **2** similar process, eg in a rubber disc with a concave surface, a fly's foot, causing two surfaces to be held together. 吸；吸引；相吸(如橡皮吸子、蒼蠅脚等，藉吸力使兩平面相結合)。

sud·den /'sʌdn ; 'sʌdn̩/ *adj* happening, coming, done, unexpectedly, quickly, without warning: 忽然；突然；出乎意料的；快速的；急速的: *a* ~ *shower;* 驟雨; *a* ~ *turn in the road.* 路上的急轉彎。□ *n* (only in) (僅用於) ***all of a*** ~, unexpectedly. 忽然地；突然地；出乎意料地。 **~·ly** *adv* **~·ness** *n*

suds /sʌdz ; sʌdz/ *n pl* froth, mass of tiny bubbles, on soapy water. 肥皂水上的泡沫。

sue /sju: ; su/ *vt, vi* ***sue (for)***, **1** [VP6A, 14] make a legal claim against: 起訴；控告: *sue a person for damages,* for money in compensation for loss or injury. 控告某人要求損害賠償。 **2** [VP14, 3A] beg; ask: 乞；請求: *sue (the enemy) for peace;* (向敵人)謀求和平; *suing for mercy;* 求饒; *sue for a divorce,* in a law court. (在法庭)要求離婚。

suede /sweɪd ; swed/ *n* [U] kind of soft leather made from the skin of goats, with the flesh surface rubbed into a soft nap: 小山羊皮；軟羔皮(帶肉的一面磨擦成細軟的絨毛): (attrib) (形容用法) ~ *shoes/gloves.* 軟羔皮鞋(手套)。

suet /'su:ɪt ; 'suɪt/ *n* [U] hard fat round the kidneys of sheep and oxen, used in cooking. (牛羊腰子上的)硬脂肪；板油(烹調用)。 **~y** *adj* like, containing, ~. 似板油的；含有板油的。

suf·fer /'sʌfə(r) ; 'sʌfɚ/ *vi, vt* **1** [VP2A, 3A] ~ ***(from)***, feel or have pain, loss, etc: 受苦；受害；受罰；受損失；患病等: ~ *from* (= often have) *headaches;* 時常頭痛; ~*ing from loss of memory.* 患遺忘症。*His business* ~*ed while he was ill,* His business did not do well. 在他患病期間他的生意不大好。*You will* ~ (= be punished) *one day for your insolence!* 你總有一天會因爲你的無禮而受到懲罰！ **2** [VP6A] experience, undergo (sth unpleasant). 經歷，遭受(不愉快之事): ~ *pain/defeat/adversity;* 遭受痛苦(失敗，不幸); ~ *death,* lose one's life, eg as a condemned criminal or as a martyr. 喪生(如被處死或殉道)。 **3** [VP17] allow, permit (which are the more usu words). 容許；准許 (allow, permit 較常用)。 **4** [VP6A] tolerate; put up with: 忍受；忍耐；忍住: *How can you* ~ *such insolence?* 你怎能忍受這樣的侮辱呢？ ~ ***fools gladly***, be patient with foolish people. 忍耐地與笨人相處。 **~er** /'sʌfərə(r) ; 'sʌfərɚ/ *n* person who ~s. 受苦者；受害者；患病者。 **~·able** /'sʌfərəbl ; 'sʌfrəbl̩/ *adj* bearable. 可忍受的；可容許的；可堪的。 **~·ing** *n* **1** [U] pain of body or mind: 身體或心靈的痛苦；苦難: *How much* ~*ing is there in the world?* 世界上有多少苦難？ **2** (*pl*) feelings of pain, unhappiness, etc: (複)痛苦、不幸等的感覺；苦惱；折磨: *They laughed at the prisoner's* ~*ings.* 他們嘲笑這囚犯所受的折磨。

suf·fer·ance /'sʌfərəns ; 'sʌfrəns/ *n* [U] ***on*** ~, with permissions implied by the absence of objection: 默許；寬許；容許；容忍: *He's here on* ~, allowed to be here but not wanted. 他是被容許留在此地(並非人家需要他)。

suf·fice /sə'faɪs ; sə'faɪs/ *vi, vt* **1** [VP2A, 3A] ~ ***(for)***, be enough (which is more usu): 足够(enough 較常用): *Will £10* ~ *for the trip?* 這趟旅行十鎊够用嗎？ *Your word will* ~, I am content to accept your promise. 有你的承諾就够了。 *S~ it to say that...* (= It ~s to say), I will content myself by saying that.... 祇須說…就够了。 **2** [VP6A] meet the needs of: 足敷…之需用；使滿足: *One meal a day won't* ~ *a growing boy.* 一天一頓飯不够一個正在發育中的男孩子的需要。

suf·fi·cient /sə'fɪʃnt ; sə'fɪʃənt/ *adj* enough: 足够的；充分的: *Is £10* ~ *for the expenses of your journey?* 十鎊够你在路上花費嗎？ *Have we* ~ *food for ten people?* 我們有够十個人吃的食物嗎？ **~·ly**

adv **suf·fi·ciency** /-nsɪ; -nsɪ/ *n* (usu 通常作 ***a sufficiency of sth***) ~ quantity: 足够的分量;充足: *a sufficiency of fuel for the winter.* 足够過多的燃料。

suf·fix /ˈsʌfɪks; ˈsʌfɪks/ *n* (abbr *suff* used in this dictionary) letter(s), sound(s) or syllable(s) added at the end of a word to make another word, eg *y* added to *rust* to make *rusty*, or as an inflexion, eg *-en* in *oxen*. (本辭典略作 suff)字尾;接尾語(卽加於一字之後的字母、聲音或音節,以構成另一字,如 y 加於 rust 後構成 rusty; 或構成語尾變化,如 oxen 中的 -en)。⇨ prefix and App 3. 參看 prefix 及附錄三。

suf·fo·cate /ˈsʌfəkeɪt; ˈsʌfəˌket/ *vt, vi* **1** [VP6A, 2A, C] cause or have difficulty in breathing: (使)窒息;(使)呼吸困難: *The fumes almost ~d me.* 濃烟幾乎使我窒息。*He was suffocating with rage.* 他因發怒而呼吸困難。 **2** [VP6A] kill, choke, by making breathing impossible. 把…悶死。**suf·fo·ca·tion** /ˌsʌfəˈkeɪʃn; ˌsʌfəˈkeʃən/ *n*

suf·fra·gan /ˈsʌfrəgən; ˈsʌfrəgən/ *n* ~ **bishop, bishop ~,** bishop who is consecrated to help the bishop of a see by managing part of the diocese. (宗教的)副主教;副監督。

suf·frage /ˈsʌfrɪdʒ; ˈsʌfrɪdʒ/ *n* **1** [C] (formal) vote; consent expressed by voting. (正式用語)投票;投票同意。**2** [U] franchise; right of voting in political elections: 選舉權;投票權: *When was the ~ extended to all women in Great Britain?* 英國何時選舉權擴及全體婦女? *Is there universal ~ in your country,* Have all adults the right to vote? 貴國有普遍的選舉權嗎(所有的成人都有投票權嗎)? **suf·fra·gette** /ˌsʌfrəˈdʒet; ˌsʌfrəˈdʒɛt/ *n* woman who, in the early part of the 20th c, agitated for women's ~ in GB. 女權運動者(特指廿世紀初,爲英國婦女爭取選舉權的女子)。

suf·fuse /səˈfjuːz; səˈfjuz/ *vt* [VP6A] (esp of colours, tears) spread slowly over the surface of: (尤指顏色、眼淚)漸漸佈滿;充盈: *eyes ~d with tears;* 淚汪汪的眼睛; *the evening sky ~d with crimson.* 映滿深紅色的傍晚天空。**suf·fu·sion** /səˈfjuːʒn; səˈfjuʒən/ *n* [U].

sugar /ˈʃʊgə(r); ˈʃʊgɚ/ *n* [U] sweet substance obtained from the juices of various plants, esp **(ˈcane-~)** from **ˈ~-cane** and **(ˈbeet-~)** from **ˈ~-beet,** used in cooking and for sweetening tea, coffee, etc. 糖(尤指用甘蔗製成的蔗糖以及用甜菜製成的甜菜糖)。**ˌ~-ˈcoated** *adj* coated with ~: 塗有糖的;有糖衣的: *~-coated pills;* 糖衣藥丸; (fig) superficially attractive: (喩)表面可愛動人的: *~-coated promises.* 聽起來動人的諾言。**ˈ~-daddy** *n* (colloq) rich, usu elderly, man who is generous to a young woman in return for sexual favours or friendship. (俗)糖老爹;老瘟生(通常指有錢的老漢,肯在年輕女子身上花大錢,以換取性方面的享受或友情)。**ˈ~-loaf** *n* hard lump of ~ in the form of a cone, as sold in former times. (昔時售賣的)圓椎形硬糖塊。**ˈ~-lump** *n* small cube of ~, used to sweeten a cup of tea, coffee, etc. 方糖。**ˈ~-refinery** *n* establishment where raw ~ is refined. 煉糖廠;製糖廠。**ˈ~-tongs** *n pl* small tongs for taking lumps (cubes) of ~ at table. (桌上用的)方糖鉗子;夾糖鉗。□ *vt* [VP6A] sweeten or mix with ~. 加糖使甜;混以糖。⇨ pill(1). **sugary** *adj* tasting of ~; (fig) too sweet: 甜的;(喩)甜美的;太甜的;阿諛的: *~y compliments/music.* 阿諛的恭維(甜美的音樂)。

sug·gest /səˈdʒest *US:* səgˈdʒ-; səgˈdʒɛst/ *vt* **1** [VP6A, C, 9, 10, 14] ***~ sth (to sb); ~ (to sb) that...; ~ doing sth,*** propose; put forward for consideration, as a possibility: 提出;提議;建議: *I ~ed a visit.* 我提議去參觀。*I ~ed going home/that we should go home.* 我提議(我們)回家。*I ~ we go to the theatre.* 我建議我們去看戲。*What did you ~ to the manager?* 你向經理作何建議? *Can you ~ where I could park my car?* 你能建議我在何處停車嗎? **2** [VP6A] bring (an idea, possibility, etc) into the mind: 使想起(主意、念頭、可能性等);使聯想;提醒;暗示;諷示: *Your wheezing breathing ~s asthma or bronchitis,* causes me to think that these are what you may be suffering from. 你的哮喘顯示你可能患氣喘病或支氣管炎。 **3** [VP14] (reflex) come into the mind: (反身)想起;浮現心頭: *An idea ~s itself to me,* has occurred to me. 我想到一個主意。**~·ible** /-əbl; -əbḷ/ *adj* that can be influenced by ~ion; that can be ~ed. 能被暗示影響的;可暗示的;可提議的。 **sug·ges·tion** /səˈdʒestʃən *US:* səgˈdʒ-; səgˈdʒɛstʃən/ *n* **1** [U] ~ing: 提議;建議: *at the ~ion of my brother;* 由於我哥哥(弟弟)的建議; *on your ~ion.* 照你的建議。*S~ion is often more effective than persuasion.* 建議常比勸說有效。 **2** [C] idea, plan, etc that is ~ed: 所提出或建議的主意、觀念、計畫等: *These ~ions didn't appeal to me.* 我對這些計畫毫無興趣。 **3** [C] slight indication: 微示;意味;略含;稍帶有: *He speaks English with a ~ion of a French accent.* 他講起英語來稍稍帶有法國口音。 **4** [U] process of bringing an idea into the mind through association with other ideas. 聯想;聯想作用;暗示。**hypnotic ~ion,** putting ideas or impulses into the mind of a person who is hypnotized. 催眠暗示(把觀念或衝動灌輸於受催眠者的心中)。 **sug·ges·tive** /səˈdʒestɪv *US:* səgˈdʒ-; səgˈdʒɛstɪv/ *adj* **1** tending to bring ideas, etc into the mind: 提醒的;暗示的;引起聯想的: *~ive remarks.* 暗示的話。**2** tending to ~ sth improper or indecent: 猥褻的: *~ive jokes.* 猥褻的笑話。**sug·ges·tive·ly** *adv*

sui·cide /ˈsjuːɪsaɪd; ˈsjuəˌsaɪd/ *n* **1** [U] self-murder: 自殺: *commit ~;* 自殺; [C] instance of this: 自殺實例: *three ~s last week;* 上週的三起自殺事件; [C] person who commits ~. 自殺者。**2** [U] action destructive to one's interests or welfare: 自毀;給自己帶來傷害或損失的行爲: *political ~,* that makes continuance in office, etc, impossible; 政治自殺;自毀政治前程; *economic ~,* eg adoption of policies that ruin the country's economy. 經濟自殺(如施行導致國家經濟破產的政策)。**sui·cidal** /ˌsjuːɪˈsaɪdl; ˌsuəˈsaɪdḷ/ *adj* of ~; very harmful to one's own interests: 自殺的;自毀的;自取滅亡的: *a man with suicidal tendencies;* 有自殺傾向的人; *a suicidal policy.* 自殺政策。

suit¹ /suːt; sjut/ *n* **1** [C] set of articles of outer clothing of the same material: (外着衣服等的)一套;一副: *a ~ of armour;* 一副甲冑; *a man's ~,* jacket (waistcoat) and trousers; 男子的成套衣服(包括外套、(背心)和褲子); *a woman's ~,* coat and skirt; 女子套裝(包括上衣和裙子); *a ˈtrouser-~,* woman's ~ of jacket and trousers; 長褲套裝(包括外套及褲子的女裝); *a two-/three-piece ~,* of two/three garments; 二(三)件式套裝; *a ˈdress ~,* a man's formal evening ~. 男子的晚禮服。**ˈ~-case** *n* portable flat-sided case for clothes, used when travelling. 手提衣箱;小提箱。**2** [C] (formal) request made to a superior, esp to a ruler: (正式用語)(對上級,尤指對統治者的)請求;懇求: *grant sb's ~;* 接受某人的請求; *press one's ~,* beg persistently. 堅決懇求。**3** [C] (liter or old use) asking a woman's hand in marriage: (文或舊用法)求婚: *plead/press one's ~ with a young woman.* 向年輕女子求婚。 **4** **(ˈlaw·)~,** case in a law court; prosecution of a claim: 訴訟;控告;法律案件: *bring a ~ against sb;* 控告某人; *be a party in a ~;* 爲訴訟當事人; *a criminal/civil ~.* 刑事(民事)案件。 **5** [C] any of the four sets of cards (*spades, hearts, diamonds, clubs*) used in many card games. (若干紙牌戲中)同花色(黑桃,紅心,方塊,梅花)的一組牌。⇨ the illus at card. 參看 card 之插圖。***a long ~,*** many cards of one ~, eg ace, king, 10, 8, 6; one player's hand. 一手同花牌(多張同花色的牌,如么點,老K,十,八,六等); 一位玩牌者手中所有的牌。***follow ~,*** **(a)** play a card of the ~ that has been led. 跟牌。**(b)** (fig) do what sb else has done. (喩)學樣;蕭規曹隨。**~·ing**

n (shop term for) material for clothing: (商店用語)衣料;套裝料: *gentlemen's ~ings,* material for men's suits. 男子套裝衣料。

suit² /su:t ; sjut/ *vt, vi* **1** [VP6A, 2A] satisfy; meet the needs of; be convenient to or right for: 使滿意;適合…的要求;適應;對…方便: *The seven o'clock train will ~ us very well.* 七點鐘那一班火車對我們很合適。*Does the climate ~ you/your health?* 這氣候對你(你的健康)適合嗎?*Will Thursday ~ (you),* be convenient? 星期四(對你)方便嗎? **~ oneself,** do what one chooses to do; act according to one's own wishes. 由自己作主;我行我素。**~ sb down to the ground,** ~ him very well. 非常適合某人。 **2** [VP6B] (esp of articles of dress, styles of dressing the hair, etc) look well; be appropriate for: (尤指衣服,髮式等)相配;合式;適合;恰當: *Does this skirt ~ me?* 這裙子我穿起來好看嗎? *That colour does not ~ your complexion.* 那顏色不適合你的膚色。*It doesn't ~ you to have your hair cut short.* 你不適合剪短髮。 **3 ~ sth to,** make fit or appropriate: 使相配;使適合: *~ the punishment to the crime;* 使懲罰與罪相稱; *~ one's style to one's audience.* 使演講方式適合聽衆。**~ the action to the word,** carry out the promise (threat, etc) at once. 言行合一;實踐諾言(威脅等);隨說隨做。 **4** (*pp*) ***be ~ed (to/for),*** be fitted, have the right qualities: 適合於;有資格: *Is Western democracy ~ed to/for the nations of Asia and Africa?* 西方的民主政治適合亞洲與非洲的國家嗎? *That man is not ~ed for teaching/to be a teacher.* 那人不適於教書(當老師)。*Jack and his wife seem well ~ed to one another,* likely to be and remain on good terms. 傑克和他的妻子似乎很相配。

suit·able /ˈsu:təbl ; ˈsjutəbl̩/ *adj* right for the purpose or occasion: 適合的;適宜的;恰當的: *clothes ~ for cold weather;* 適於寒冷天氣穿的衣服; *a ~ place for a picnic;* 適合於野餐的地方; *a ~ case for* (medical, psychiatric, etc) *treatment.* 適於(藥物,心理等)治療的病例。 **suit·ably** /-əblɪ ; -əblɪ/ *adv* **suit·abil·ity** /ˌsu:təˈbɪlətɪ ; ˌsutəˈbɪlətɪ/ *n* **~·ness** *n*

suite /swi:t ; swit/ *n* [C] **1** group of personal attendants of an important person (eg a ruler). (要人,如統治者的)一羣隨員;一班扈從。 **2** complete set of matching articles of furniture: 一套傢俱: *a dining-room ~,* ie a table, chairs, a sideboard; 一套飯廳用的傢俱; *a lounge/bedroom ~.* 一套客廳(臥房)用的傢俱。 **3** complete set of rooms (eg in a hotel, a bedroom, a sitting-room and a bathroom). 套房(如旅館中,包括一間臥房,一間起居室及一間浴室)。 **4** complete set of objects that belong together: 一套東西;一組物品: *a computer suite,* all the machinery needed to run a computer. 一套電腦用具。 **5** (music) orchestral composition made up of three or more related parts. (音樂)組曲(多部管絃樂曲)。

suitor /ˈsu:tə(r) ; ˈsjutɚ/ *n* **1** person bringing a lawsuit. 起訴者;控告者;原告。⇨ suit¹(4). **2** man courting a woman. 向女子求婚者。⇨ suit¹(3).

sulfa (US) = sulpha. ⇨ sulphonamides.

sul·fate (US) = sulphate.

sul·fide (US) = sulphide.

sul·fona·mides (US) = sulphonamides.

sul·fur, sul·fur·ic, sul·fur·ous, etc (US) = sulphur, sulphuric, sulphurous, etc.

sulk /sʌlk ; sʌlk/ *vi* [VP2A, C] be in a bad temper and show this by refusing to talk. 慍怒;生氣而不講話;生悶氣。**the ~s** *n pl* condition of ~ing: 慍怒;生悶氣: *be in the ~s;* 在生悶氣;在發脾氣; *have (a fit of) the ~s.* 發(一陣)脾氣;生(一陣)悶氣。**~y** *adj* (-ier, -iest) having a tendency to ~; unsociable: 慍怒的;鬱鬱不樂的;不高興的;不友善的: *as ~y as a bear;* 很不高興的;像熊一般慍怒的; *be/get ~y with sb about a trifle.* 與某人有小爭執而鬱鬱不樂。 **~·ily** /-ɪlɪ ; -ɪlɪ/ *adv* **~i·ness** *n*

sulky /ˈsʌlkɪ ; ˈsʌlkɪ/ *n* (*pl* -kies) light two-wheeled carriage for one person, drawn by one horse. 蘇克馬車(單人乘坐的兩輪輕便馬車,由一匹馬拖曳)。

sul·len /ˈsʌlən ; ˈsʌlɪn/ *adj* **1** silently bad-tempered; unforgiving: 慍怒的;鬱鬱不樂的;愁眉不展的;不寬恕的: *~ looks.* 怒容。 **2** dark and gloomy; dismal: 陰鬱的;陰沉的;悲哀的: *a ~ sky.* 陰沉的天空。**~·ly** *adv* **~·ness** *n*

sully /ˈsʌlɪ ; ˈsʌlɪ/ *vt* (*pt, pp* -lied) [VP6A] (usu fig) stain or discredit: (通常作喻)染汚;玷汚;毀損: *~ sb's reputation.* 毀損某人名譽。

sulpha (US = **sulfa**) /ˈsʌlfə ; ˈsʌlfə/ *n* ⇨ sulphonamides.

sul·phate (US = **sulfate**) /ˈsʌlfeɪt ; ˈsʌlfet/ *n* [C, U] salt of sulphuric acid: 硫酸鹽;硫酸化合物: *~ of copper/copper ~,* chemical **($CuSO_4$)** used in water to kill algae and fungi; 硫酸銅;膽礬; *~ of magnesium,* Epsom salts. 硫酸鎂;瀉鹽。

sul·phide (US = **sulfide**) /ˈsʌlfaɪd ; ˈsʌlfaɪd/ *n* [C, U] compound of sulphur and another element: 硫化物: *hydrogen ~,* **(H_2S)** sulphuretted hydrogen, a gas with a smell like that of rotten eggs. 硫化氫。

sul·phona·mides (US = **sul·fo-**) /sʌlˈfɒnəmaɪdz ; sʌlˈfɑnəmaɪdz/ *n pl* group of drugs (synthetic chemical compounds, also called *the ˈsulpha drugs*) acting as anti-bacterial agents. 磺胺類藥劑(有抗菌功效,亦稱 the sulpha drugs)。

sul·phur (US = **sul·fur**) /ˈsʌlfə(r) ; ˈsʌlfɚ/ *n* light-yellow non-metallic element (symbol **S**) that burns with a bright flame and a strong smell, used in medicine and industry. 硫;硫磺(淡黃色非金屬元素,符號爲S,燃之發强光及惡臭,用於醫藥及工業)。**~·etted** /ˈsʌlfjʊretɪd ; ˈsʌlfjʊrɛtɪd/ *adj* having ~ in combination: 含硫的;硫化的: *~etted hydrogen,* **(H_2S)**. 硫化氫。**sul·phu·reous** (US = **sul·fu-**) /sʌlˈfjʊərɪəs; sʌlˈfjʊrɪəs/ *adj* of, like, containing ~. 硫(磺)的;似硫(磺)的;含硫(磺)的。**sul·phu·ric** (US = **sul·fu-**) /sʌlˈfjʊərɪk ; sʌlˈfjʊrɪk/ *adj* **~ic acid,** oily, colourless, very strong acid **(H_2SO_4)** important in many industries. 硫酸。**~·ous** /-əs ; -əs/ *adj* of, containing, ~. 硫(磺)的;含硫(磺)的。

sul·tan /ˈsʌltən ; ˈsʌltn̩/ *n* Muslim ruler, esp of the former Ottoman Empire. 蘇丹;回教國的君主;(尤指昔日的)奧圖曼帝國的皇帝。**~·ate** /ˈsʌltəneɪt ; ˈsʌltn̩ɪt/ *n* position, period of rule of, a ~; territory ruled by a ~. 回教國君主的地位,統治期;其所統治的領土。**sul·tana** /sʌlˈtɑ:nə *US:* -ænə ; sʌlˈtænə/ *n* wife, mother, sister or daughter of a ~. 蘇丹的妻子、母親、姐妹或女兒;回教國王室女眷。

sul·tana /sʌlˈtɑ:nə *US:* -ænə ; sʌlˈtænə/ *n* [C] kind of small seedless raisin used in puddings and cakes. 一種無籽的小葡萄乾(用於布丁及糕餅中)。

sul·try /ˈsʌltrɪ ; ˈsʌltrɪ/ *adj* (-ier, -iest) (of the atmosphere, the weather) hot and oppressive; (of a person's temper) passionate. (指大氣,天氣)悶熱的;酷熱的;(指人的性情)熱情的;急躁的。 **sul·trily** /-trəlɪ ; -trɪlɪ/ *adv* **sul·tri·ness** *n*

sum /sʌm ; sʌm/ *n* **1** (also 亦作 **sum total**) total obtained by adding together items, numbers or amounts. 總數;總計;和。 **2** problem in arithmetic: 算術題目: *good at sums;* 長於算術; *do a sum in one's head.* 心算。 **3** amount of money: 金額;錢數: *win a large sum at the Casino;* 在賭場贏一大筆錢; *save a nice little sum out of one's wages each week.* 從每週工資中節省一筆可觀的數目。 **4 *in sum,*** in a few words. 簡言之。□ *vt, vi* (-mm-) [VP 15B, 2C] ***sum (sb/sth) up,*** **(a)** give the total of. 總計;合計。**(b)** express briefly (the chief points of what has been said): 總結;概括前言;總括起來;歸納: *The judge summed up (the evidence).* 法官做一總結(歸納證詞)。**(c)** form a judgement or opinion of: 對…形成判斷或意見: *He summed up the situation at a glance,* realized it at once. 他一眼就認清了當時的情況。*She quickly summed him up,* judged his character, etc. 她很快就對他的人品

下評論。ˌ**summing-ˈup** *n* (*pl* summings-up) judge's review of evidence, arguments, etc, in a law-case. (訟案中法官對證據、辯論等的)總結;扼要敍述。

su·mac(h) /ˈʃuːmæk ; ˈʃumæk/ *n* (kinds of) shrub or small tree, the dried leaves being used in tanning and dyeing. 鹽膚木(其葉乾後可用於製革或作染料)。

sum·mary /ˈsʌmərɪ ; ˈsʌmərɪ/ *adj* **1** brief; giving the chief points only: 簡短的;簡明的;扼要的: *a ~ account.* 簡要的說明。 **2** done or given without delay or attention to small matters: 卽決的;卽時的;當場的; 立刻的: *~ justice/punishment/methods.* 卽時裁決(當場的懲罰; 直接快速的方法)。 □ *n* (*pl* -ries) brief account giving the chief points. 摘要;概略。 **sum·mar·ily** /ˈsʌmərəlɪ *US:* səˈmerəlɪ ; ˈsʌmərəlɪ/ *adv* **sum·mar·ize** /ˈsʌməraɪz ; ˈsʌməˌraɪz/ *vt* [VP6A] be or make a ~ of. 摘要;概述。

sum·mat /ˈsʌmət ; ˈsʌmət/ *n* (sl and dial) something. (俚及方)某事(物)。

sum·ma·tion /səˈmeɪʃn ; sʌmˈeʃən/ *n* **1** addition. 加;加法。 **2** summing up. 總計;總和;總結。

sum·mer /ˈsʌmə(r) ; ˈsʌmə/ *n* [U, C] (in countries outside the tropics) the warmest season of the year, May or June to August in the northern hemisphere: (在熱帶地區以外的國家)夏;夏季(在北半球指五或六月至八月): *in (the) ~;* 在夏季; *in the ~ of 1999;* 在1999年的夏天; *this/next/last ~;* 今(明,去)夏; (attrib) (形容用法) *~ weather;* 夏季的天氣; *the ~ holidays;* 暑假; *a ~ cottage/house,* for use during the ~; 夏季別墅; *a girl of ten ~s,* (liter) ten years of age. (文)一個十歲的女孩子。 *It's been an unusually hot ~.* 那是個特別酷熱的夏天。 ˈ**~-house** *n* shelter with seats in a garden, park, etc. 涼亭。 ˈ**~ school** *n* course of lectures, often at a university, during the ~ vacation. 暑期班;暑期學校(通常指大學暑假期間所開的課程)。 ˈ**~·time** *n* the season of ~. 夏季。 ˈ**~ time** *n* time as recognized in some countries where clocks are put forward one hour so that darkness falls an hour later, giving long light evenings during the ~ months. 夏令時間; 日光節約時間。 ⇨ *daylight saving* at daylight. **Indian ~,** ⇨ Indian(3). □ *vi* [VP2C] spend the ~: 過夏天;避暑;度暑天: *~ at the seaside/in the mountains.* 在海邊(山中)避暑。 **~y** *adj* characteristic of, suitable for, ~: 夏天的;有夏天特徵的;適於夏季的: *a ~y dress.* 夏天的衣服。

sum·mit /ˈsʌmɪt ; ˈsʌmɪt/ *n* [C] highest point; top: 最高點;頂點;絕頂: *reach the ~,* of a mountain; 到達山頂; (fig) (喻) *the ~ of his ambition/power;* 他的野心(權力)的極致; *talks at the ~.* 高峯會談。ˈ**~ talk/meeting,** discussion between heads of States. (各國政府首長間的)高峯會談(會議)。

sum·mon /ˈsʌmən ; ˈsʌmən/ *vt* **1** [VP6A, 14, 17] *~ sb (to sth/to do sth),* demand the presence of; call or send for: 召喚;傳喚;召集: *~ shareholders to a general meeting;* 召集股東大會; *~ sb to appear as a witness,* eg in a law court. 傳喚某人出席作證(如法庭上)。 *The debtor was ~ed,* ie to appear in a law court. 債務人被傳(出庭)。 *The Queen has ~ed Parliament,* ordered members to assemble. 女王召集國會。 **2** [VP15B] *~ sth up,* gather together; call up: 集攏;聚集;徵集: *~ up one's courage/energy/nerve for a task/to do sth.* 鼓起勇氣(精力)做一件工作(做某事)。

sum·mons /ˈsʌmənz ; ˈsʌmənz/ *n* (*pl* ~es) [C] **1** order to appear before a judge or magistrate; document with such an order: 傳喚;傳票: *issue a ~.* 發出傳票。 *The ~ was served by a bailiff.* 該傳票由執達吏遞送。 **2** command to do sth or appear somewhere: 召喚;命令。 □ *vt* [VP6A] serve a ~(1) on. 以傳票送達。

sump /sʌmp ; sʌmp/ *n* **1** inner casing of a petrol engine containing lubricating oil. (汽油內燃機中裝有潤滑油的)潤滑油槽。 **2** hole or low area into which waste liquid drains. 汚水坑;排水坑。

sump·ter /ˈsʌmptə(r) ; ˈsʌmptə/ *n* (old use) (often 常作 *ˈ~-horse, ˈ~-mule*) horse or mule for carrying burdens; pack-animal. (舊用法)馱馬;馱騾;馱獸。

sump·tu·ary /ˈsʌmptjʊərɪ *US:* -tʃʊerɪ ; ˈsʌmptʃʊˌɛrɪ/ *adj* (attrib only) (of laws) controlling or limiting private expenditure of money (on what is considered extravagant, etc). (祇作形容用法)(指法律) 規定或限制私人花費的;控制私人費用的 (對於奢侈等項的花費予以限制)。

sump·tu·ous /ˈsʌmptʃʊəs ; ˈsʌmptʃʊəs/ *adj* magnificent; costly-looking: 華麗的;奢侈的;豪華的: *a ~ feast;* 豪華的宴會; *~ clothes.* 華服。 **~·ly** *adv* **~·ness** *n*

sun /sʌn ; sʌn/ *n* **1 (the) sun,** the heavenly body from which the earth gets warmth and light. 日;太陽。 ⇨ the illus at planet. 參看 planet 之插圖。 ***rise with the sun,*** get up at dawn. 黎明卽起;早起。 ***the midnight sun,*** the sun as seen in the arctic and antarctic regions. 午夜太陽(在兩極地區所見者)。 **2 (the) sun,** light and warmth from the sun: 陽光;日光: *sit in the sun;* 坐在陽光下; *have the sun in one's eyes;* 陽光照在眼中; *draw the curtains to shut out/let in the sun.* 拉窗簾遮蔽(放進)陽光。 ***under the sun,*** (anywhere) in the world: 太陽之下;在世界上(任何地方): *the best wine under the sun.* 世界上最好的酒。 ***give sb/have a place in the sun,*** (fig) space and conditions favourable to development. (喻)處順境(給予某人有利的發展空間及環境)。 **3** [C] any fixed star: 任何恆星: *There are many suns larger than ours.* (宇宙間)有許多恆星比我們的太陽還要大。 **4** (compounds) (複合字) ˈ**sun·baked** *adj* made hard by the heat of the sun: 太陽晒乾的: *sunbaked fields.* 太陽晒乾的田地。 ˈ**sun·bathe** *vi* expose one's body to sunlight, eg to give a pale skin a tan. 作日光浴。 ⇨ *sunburn* below. 參看下列之 sunburn。 ˈ**sun·beam** *n* ray of sunshine; (colloq) cheerful and happy person (esp a child). 日光;陽光;(俗)愉快的人(尤指小孩)。 ˈ**sun·blind** *n* window shade, esp an awning outside a window. 遮陽;(尤指窗外的)遮篷;篷蓋。 ˈ**sun-bonnet/-hat** *nn* hat or (usu linen) bonnet made so as to shade the face and neck from the sun. 遮陽帽;太陽帽。 ˈ**sun·burn** *n* [C, U] (place where there is a) darkening of the skin caused by the sun, or reddening and blistering caused by too much exposure to the sun. 曬黑;曬黑處;曬斑;日炙;曬紅或曬痛(處)。 ˈ**sun·burnt,** ˈ**sun·burned** *adjj* having sunburn. 曬黑的;日炙的;有晒斑的。 ˈ**sun·burst** *n* sudden burst of sunlight (through broken clouds). (雲縫中)突現的陽光。 ˈ**sun·dial** *n* device that shows the time by the shadow of a rod or plate on a scaled dial. 日規;日晷(儀)。 ˈ**sun·down** *n* [U] sunset. 日落;日沒。 ˈ**sun·downer** *n* **(a)** (in Australia) tramp who habitually arrives (at a sheep farm, etc) at nightfall. (澳洲)常到牧場等處借宿的徒步旅客。 **(b)** (colloq) drink (usu of sth alcoholic) at sundown. (俗)傍晚的飲料(通常爲酒類)。 ˈ**sun-drenched** *adj* exposed to great light and heat from the sun: 飽受陽光照射的;晒透了的: *sun-drenched beaches along the Riviera.* 里維耶拉陽光普照的海灘。 ˈ**sun-dried** *adj* (of fruit, etc) dried naturally, by the sun, not by artificial heat. (指水果等)太陽晒乾的。 ˈ**sun·fish** *n* large fish almost spherical in shape. 翻車魚(一種幾乎呈球形的大魚)。 ˈ**sun·flower** *n* tall garden plant with large

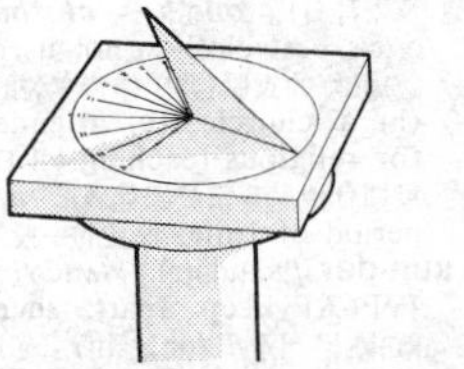

a sundial

golden-rayed flowers. 向日葵。 ⇨ the illus at flower. 參看 flower 之插圖。**'sun-glasses** *n pl* glasses of dark-coloured glass to protect the eyes from bright sunshine. 太陽眼鏡。**'sun-god** *n* sun worshipped as a god. 日神;太陽神。**'sun-helmet** *n* hat specially made to protect the head from the sun in the tropics. (熱帶用的)太陽盔;遮陽盔。**'sun-lamp** *n* lamp that gives out ultra-violet rays with effects like those of the sun, used for artificial sun-bathing. 太陽燈(可產生紫外線,用於人工日光浴)。**'sun·light** *n* [U] the light of the sun. 日光;太陽光。**'sun·lit** *adj* lighted by the sun: 陽光照耀的;被陽光照射的: *a sunlit landscape.* 陽光照耀下的景色。**'sun-lounge**, or, less usu 或,較不常用, **'sun-parlour/-porch** *nn* made with glass sides and so situated as to admit much sunlight. 日光浴室(廊)(四面以玻璃爲屏,以容大量陽光)。**'sun-ray** *n* ultra-violet ray used on the body: (用於人體的)紫外光線;太陽光線: (attrib) (形容用法) *'sun-ray treatment.* 日光療法;紫外線療法。**'sun·rise** *n* [U] (time of) the sun's rising: 日出;日出的時刻;黎明: *start at sunrise.* 拂曉動身。**'sun-roof** (or, less usu 或,較不常用 **'sunshine-roof**) *n* panel on the roof of a saloon car which slides back to admit sunshine. (某種轎車的)活動頂(可拉開讓陽光射入者)。**'sunset** /-set; -sɛt/ *n* [U] (time of) the sun's setting. 日落;日落時刻;傍晚。**'sun·shade** *n* parasol (like an umbrella) to keep off the sun; awning of a shop window. 遮陽傘;商店櫥窗的遮陽篷。**'sun·shine** *n* [U] light of the sun. 日光;陽光。**'sun·spot** *n* (astron) dark patch on the sun at times, often causing electrical disturbances and interfering with radio communications; (colloq) place that has a sunny climate (eg for holidays). (天文)太陽黑子;日斑(不時出現在太陽上的黑斑,常引起電的擾亂,並干擾無線電通訊);(俗)多陽光的地方(如假日去處)。**'sun·stroke** *n* [U] illness caused by too much exposure to the sun, esp on the head. 日射病;中暍;中暑。**'sun·tan** *n* [U, C] browning of the skin from exposure to sunlight: (因晒太陽而)皮膚變黑;晒黑;晒紅: *'suntan lotion/oil.* 防晒劑(油)。**'sun-trap** *n* warm sunny place (sheltered from wind). 日光窩(避風而多陽光的暖和處)。**'sun-up** *n* [U] (colloq) sunrise. (俗)日出;日出時刻;黎明。**'sun-worship** *n* [U] worship of the sun as a deity; (colloq) fondness for sun-bathing. 太陽崇拜(把太陽看作神);(俗)愛好日光浴。□ *vt* (-nn-) [VP6A] put in, expose (*oneself*) to, the rays of the sun: 曝;曬: *The cat was sunning itself on the path.* 那隻貓在小徑上晒太陽。**sun·less** *adj* receiving little or no sunlight; without sun; dark: 晒不到太陽的;無太陽的;黑暗的: *a sunless day/room.* 陰天(陰暗的房間)。**sunny** *adj* (-ier, -iest) **1** bright with sunlight: 向陽的;陽光充足的;晴朗的: *a sunny room;* 向陽的房間; *sunny days.* 晴朗的日子。***ˌsunny-side 'up,*** (US) (of an egg) fried on one side only. (美)(指蛋)只煎一面的。**2** cheerful: 歡樂的;愉快的: *a sunny smile/disposition/welcome.* 愉快的微笑(性情,歡迎)。**sun·nily** /-ɪlɪ; -ɪlɪ/ *adv*

sun·dae /'sʌndeɪ *US:* -di:; 'sʌndɪ/ *n* portion of ice-cream with crushed fruit, fruit-juice, nuts, etc. 聖代(加有壓碎的水果、果汁、堅果等的冰淇淋)。

Sun·day /'sʌndɪ; 'sʌndɪ/ *n* the first day of the week, a day of rest and worship among Christians. 星期日;禮拜日;日曜日(一週的首日,基督徒的休息及崇拜日)。***one's ~ clothes/best,*** (colloq, joc) one's best clothes, not used for working in. (俗,諧)最好的衣服(非工作時穿著的衣服)。**'~ school,** one (in a church, etc) attended by children on ~s for religious teaching. 主日學(校)(教堂等中所設,於星期日授兒童宗教課程者)。***a month of ~s,*** a long period of time. 很長的一段時間;長久。

sun·der /'sʌndə(r); 'sʌndɚ/ *vt* (old use, or liter) [VP6A] keep apart; sever. (舊用法或文)分開;隔離;斷絕。□ *n* (only in) (僅用於) ***in ~,*** = asunder. 分開;離開;隔離;折斷。

sun·dries /'sʌndrɪz; 'sʌndrɪz/ *n pl* various small items not separately named. 雜物;雜貨;雜項;雜事。

sun·dry /'sʌndrɪ; 'sʌndrɪ/ *adj* various: 不同的;各種的;多方面的: *on ~ occasions.* 在各種不同的時機。***all and ~,*** (colloq) everyone; everything. (俗)人人;每人;所有的人;一切事物。

sung /sʌŋ; sʌŋ/ *pp* of sing.

sunk /sʌŋk; sʌŋk/ *pp* of sink².

sunk·en /'sʌŋkən; 'sʌŋkən/ *pp* of sink² esp(5).

sunny /'sʌnɪ; 'sʌnɪ/ *adj* ⇨ sun.

sup¹ /sʌp; sʌp/ *vi, vt* (-pp-) [VP2A, C, 6A, 15B] ***sup (up),*** (esp Scot and N Eng) drink in small amounts; take (liquid) into the mouth a little at a time: (尤用於蘇格蘭及英格蘭北部)啜飲;啜;每次一點點地飲(液體): *Sup (up) your broth.* 喝(你的)肉湯。□ *n* small quantity (of liquid): (液體的)少量;一飲;一啜: *a sup of ale.* 少量的麥酒(或淡啤酒)。*I've had neither bite nor sup* (= neither food nor drink) *for six hours.* 我已六小時未進飲食。

sup² /sʌp; sʌp/ *vi* (-pp-) [VP3A] ***sup on/off,*** (rare) eat (on, off): (罕)吃: *sup on bread and cheese.* 吃麵包及乳酪。***He that sups with the devil must have a long spoon,*** (prov) Caution is needed in dealings with someone of doubtful character. (諺)與惡人打交道須特別提防。

super /'su:pə(r); 'supɚ/ *n* (colloq) (俗) = supernumerary; superintendent (of police). 冗員;額外人員;(警察)局長。□ *adj* (colloq) excellent; splendid. (俗)傑出的;特佳的;上等的。

super·abun·dant /ˌsu:pərə'bʌndənt; ˌsupərə'bʌndənt/ *adj* very abundant; more than enough. 極多的;過剩的;多餘的。**super·abun·dance** /-əns; -əns/ *n*

super·an·nu·ate /ˌsu:pər'ænjʊeɪt; ˌsupɚ'ænjʊˌet/ *vt* **1** [VP6A] give a pension to (an employee) when he is old or unable to work; dismiss (an employee) because of age or weakness. 發給(老弱員工)退休金;令(老弱員工)退休。**2** (*pp*, **~d,** as *adj*) too old for work or use; (colloq) old-fashioned or out of date. (過去分詞,作形容詞用)老朽的;老而無用的;(俗)老式的;陳舊的;過時的。**super·an·nu·ation** /ˌsu:pərˌænjʊ'eɪʃn; ˌsupɚˌænjʊ'eʃən/ *n*

su·perb /su:'pɜ:b; sə'pɝb/ *adj* magnificent; first-class. 宏偉的;壯麗的;華美的;頭等的。**~·ly** *adv*

super·cargo /'su:pəkɑ:gəʊ; ˌsupɚ'kɑrgo/ *n* (*pl* ~es /-gəʊz; -goz/) person on a merchant ship who manages the sale of the cargo, etc. (商船上的)營運主管。

super·charger /'su:pətʃɑ:dʒə(r); 'supɚˌtʃɑrdʒɚ/ *n* device used in an internal-combustion engine to force extra oxygen into the cylinders. (內燃機的)增壓器(將額外的氧氣壓入氣缸中者)。**'super·charged** *adj* fitted with a ~. 裝有增壓器的。

super·cili·ous /ˌsu:pə'sɪlɪəs; ˌsupɚ'sɪlɪəs/ *adj* showing contemptuous indifference: 傲慢的;目空一切的;自大的;不屑一顧的: *nose high in the air, looking like a ~ camel.* 仰臉朝天,活像一隻傲慢的駱駝。**~·ly** *adv* **~·ness** *n*

super·ego /'su:pəregəʊ *US:* -i:gəʊ; ˌsupɚ'igo/ *n* [U] **(the) ~,** (psych) the part of the mind that responds to conscience and morality. (心理)超我(個人自我架構中反應良心和道德規範的部分)。⇨ ego, id.

super·ero·gation /ˌsu:pərˌerə'geɪʃn; ˌsupɚˌɛrə'geʃən/ *n* [U] the doing of more than is required or expected: 額外工作;職務以外的工作: *a work of ~.* 一件功德;餘功。

super·fat·ted /ˌsu:pə'fætɪd; ˌsupɚ'fætɪd/ *adj* (chiefly of soap) containing a larger than usual proportion of fat. (主要指肥皂)含脂肪過多的。

super·fi·cial /ˌsu:pə'fɪʃl; ˌsjupɚ'fɪʃəl/ *adj* **1** of or on the surface only: 表面的;表皮的;在表面上的;在表皮上的: *a ~ wound;* 表皮的傷; *~ area.* 面積。**2** not thorough or profound: 膚淺的;淺薄的: *a ~ book;* 立論膚淺的書; *have only a ~ knowledge of a subject;* 對某一學科僅略知皮毛; *a ~ mind.*

淺薄的心智。~**ly** /-ʃəlɪ ; -ʃəlɪ/ *adv* ~**·ity** /ˌsuːpəˌfɪʃɪˈælətɪ ; ˌsupɚˌfɪʃɪˈælətɪ/ *n* [U].

super·fi·cies /ˌsuːpəˈfɪʃiːz ; ˌsupɚˈfɪʃɪˌiz/ *n* (*pl* unchanged) (複數不變) **1** surface; surface area. 表面;表面積。 **2** outward appearance. 外表;外觀。

super·fine /ˈsuːpəfaɪn ; ˌsupɚˈfaɪn/ *adj* **1** unusually fine in quality. 極精緻的;最佳品質的;最上品的。 **2** unnecessarily refined or subtle: 過分精細的;過於微妙的: *a ~ distinction.* 過細的區別。

super·flu·ous /suːˈpɜːfluəs ; suˈpɝfluəs/ *adj* more than is needed or wanted. 累贅的;過多的;多餘的;不必要的。 ~**·ly** *adv* **super·flu·ity** /ˌsuːpəˈfluːətɪ ; ˌsupɚˈfluətɪ/ *n* (*pl* -ties) [C, U] (an amount that is) more than is needed: 累贅;多餘;過剩;過量: *have a superfluity of good things.* 擁有過多的好東西。

super·hu·man /ˌsuːpəˈhjuːmən ; ˌsupɚˈhjumən/ *adj* exceeding ordinary human power, size, knowledge, etc: 超乎常人之力量、體積、尺寸、智識等的; 超人的: *by a ~ effort;* 藉一種超乎常人的努力; *an apparition of ~ size.* 超乎常人體積的鬼魂。

super·im·pose /ˌsuːpərɪmˈpəʊz ; ˌsupərɪmˈpoz/ *vt* [VP6A, 14] put (one thing) on top of sth else: 置(一物)於他物之上;添加;附加;重疊: *a map of Great Britain ~d on a map of Texas,* eg to show comparative size. 疊在德克薩斯州地圖上的大不列顛地圖(以示相對大小)。

super·in·tend /ˌsuːpərɪnˈtend ; ˌsjupərɪnˈtɛnd/ *vt, vi* [VP6A, 2A] manage; watch and direct (work, etc). 管理;監督(工作等)。 ~**·ence** /-əns ; -əns/ *n* [U] ~ing: 管理;監督: *under the personal ~ence of the manager.* 在經理的親自監督之下。 ~**·ent** /-ənt ; -ənt/ *n* person who ~s; manager; police officer above a chief inspector in rank. 管理者;監督者;經理;警察局長。

su·perior /suːˈpɪərɪə(r) ; səˈpɪrɪɚ/ *adj* **1** better than the average: 優良的; 卓越的; 超過一般水準的: *~ cloth;* 上等布; *a girl of ~ intelligence;* 智力高的女孩子; *~ grades of coffee.* 上等咖啡。 **2** greater in number: 數目較大的;較多的: *The enemy attacked with ~ forces/were ~ in numbers.* 敵人以優勢兵力進攻(敵人在人數上佔優勢)。 **3** *~ to,* **(a)** better than: 優於;勝過: *This cloth is ~ to that.* 這一種布比那一種好。 **(b)** higher in rank or position than. 階級或地位高於。 **(c)** not influenced by; not giving way to: 不受…的影響;不屈服於: *~ to flattery;* 不爲諂媚所動; *rise* (= be) *~ to temptation.* 不爲誘惑所影響。 **4** priggish; supercilious: 傲慢的;自負的;自大的: *'I never apologize,' he said, with a ~ air.* '我從不向人道歉,'他傲慢地說。 □ *n* **1** person of higher rank, authority, etc than another, or who is better, etc than another (in sth): 長官;上司;長者;長輩;在某方向優於他人者: *my ~s in rank/in expertise.* 階級高於我的人(專門技術或知識優 我的人)。 *Napoleon had no ~ as a general.* 拿破崙之爲將,無出其右者。 **2** (in titles) head of a religious community: (用於稱號中)修道院院長: *the Father S~,* eg an abbot; 男修道院院長; *the Mother S~,* eg an abbess. 女修道院院長。 ~**·ity** /suːˌpɪərɪˈɒrətɪ *US:* -ˈɔːr- ; səˌpɪrɪˈɔrətɪ/ *n* [U] state of being ~: 優秀;卓越;優越: *the ~ity of one thing to another;* 一物之優於他物; *his ~ity in talent.* 他才能方面的卓越。 **ˈ~ity complex,** (pop use) aggressive or domineering attitude as a defence against a feeling of inferiority. (流行用法)自傲情結(以侵犯性或高控式的作爲掩飾自卑的一種行爲模式)。

su·per·la·tive /suːˈpɜːlətɪv ; səˈpɝlətɪv/ *adj* **1** of the highest degree or quality: 最高的;無上的: *a wine of ~ bouquet and flavour.* 無比香醇的酒。 **2** (gram) (文法) *the ~ degree,* the form of an *adj* or *adv* expressing the highest degree, eg *best, worst, slowest, most foolish(ly).* 最高級(表示最高程度的形容詞或副詞形式,如 best, worst, slowest, most foolish(ly) 等)。 □ *n* ~ form of an *adj* or *adv.* 形容詞或副詞的最高級形式。 ***speak in ~s,*** use language expressing extreme opinions and feelings; exaggerate. 誇大;誇張;講話不離 '最' 字。

super·man /ˈsuːpəmæn ; ˈsupɚˌmæn/ *n* (*pl* -men) man having more than ordinary human powers and abilities, eg as imagined by sb writing about the future of mankind. 具有超乎常人力量及能力的人;超人(如描寫人類未來的作家所想像者)。

super·mar·ket /ˈsuːpəmɑːkɪt ; ˈsupɚˌmɑrkɪt/ *n* large self-service store selling food, household goods, etc. 超級市場。

su·per·nal /suːˈpɜːnl ; suˈpɝnl/ *adj* (liter) heavenly; divine: (文)天上的;超凡的;神聖的: *~ loveliness.* 超凡的美妙。

super·natu·ral /ˌsuːpəˈnætʃrəl ; ˌsupɚˈnætʃrəl/ *adj* spiritual; of that which is not controlled or explained by physical laws: 神奇的;不可思議的;超自然的: *~ beings,* eg angels and devils. 超自然的生物(如天使及魔鬼)。 **the ~,** ~ agencies, phenomena, etc. 超自然的作用、現象等。 ~**·ly** /-ˈnætʃrəlɪ ; -ˈnætʃrəlɪ/ *adv*

super·nor·mal /ˌsuːpəˈnɔːml ; ˌsupɚˈnɔrməl/ *adj* beyond what is normal. 異常的;非凡的;超出正常的。

super·nu·mer·ary /ˌsuːpəˈnjuːmərərɪ *US:* -ˈnuːməreri ; ˌsupɚˈnjuməˌrɛrɪ/ *n* (*pl* -ries), *adj* (person or thing) in excess of the normal number; (esp) person engaged for odd jobs; actor who has only a small part, eg in crowd scenes. 額外的;多餘的;額外或多餘的人或物;(尤指)雜工;小工;小配角;臨時演員。

super·scrip·tion /ˌsuːpəˈskrɪpʃn ; ˌsupɚˈskrɪpʃən/ *n* [C] word(s) written at the top of or outside sth, eg the address on the envelope of a letter. 寫於某物頂端或外面的文字(如寫在信封上的地址)。

super·sede /ˌsuːpəˈsiːd ; ˌsupɚˈsid/ *vt* [VP6A] take the place of; put or use sb or sth in the place of: 代替;取代: *Motorways have ~d ordinary roads for long-distance travel.* 在長途旅行方面,高速公路已取代了一般的道路。 **super·session** /ˌsuːpəˈseʃn ; ˌsupɚˈsɛʃən/ *n*

super·sonic /ˌsuːpəˈsɒnɪk ; ˌsupɚˈsɑnɪk/ *adj* (of speeds) greater than that of sound; (of aircraft) able to fly at ~ speed. (指速度)超音速的;超聲速的;(指飛機)能够作超音速飛行的。

super·sti·tion /ˌsuːpəˈstɪʃn ; ˌsupɚˈstɪʃən/ *n* [C, U] (idea, practice, etc founded on) unreasoning belief in magic, witchcraft, etc; irrational fear of what is unknown or mysterious: 迷信;迷信的觀念;迷信的習俗(盲從魔術、巫術等所形成的觀念或作爲);對未知、陌生或神秘事物的本能恐懼: *sunk in ignorance and ~.* 沉溺於無知與迷信中。 **super·sti·tious** /ˌsuːpəˈstɪʃəs ; ˌsjupɚˈstɪʃəs/ *adj* of, showing, resulting from, ~; believing in ~s: 迷信的;顯示或來自迷信的;相信迷信事物的: *superstitious beliefs/ideas/people.* 迷信的說法(觀念,人們)。 **super·sti·tious·ly** *adv*

super·struc·ture /ˈsuːpəstrʌktʃə(r) ; ˈsupɚˌstrʌktʃɚ/ *n* structure built on the top of sth else; parts of a ship above the main deck. 上層構造;上層建築物;船隻主甲板上面的部分。

super·tax /ˈsuːpətæks ; ˈsupɚˌtæks/ *n* [C, U] tax on, or the taxation of, incomes (additional to income tax) above a certain level. 附加所得稅;特別附加稅。

super·vene /ˌsuːpəˈviːn ; ˌsupɚˈvin/ *vi* [VP2A] (formal) come or happen as a change from or interruption of (a condition or process). (正式用語)附帶發生;併發;橫生枝節;節外生枝。

super·vise /ˈsuːpəvaɪz ; ˌsjupɚˈvaɪz/ *vt, vi* [VP6A, 2A] watch and direct (work, workers, an organization). 監督(工作、工人、組織);管理; 指導。 **super·vi·sor** /-zə(r) ; -zɚ/ *n* person who ~s. 監督者;管理者; 指導者。 **super·vi·sion** /ˌsuːpəˈvɪʒn ; ˌsjupɚˈvɪʒən/ *n* supervising: 監督;管理;指導: *under the supervision of,* ~d by. 在…監督(指導)之下。 **super·vis·ory** /ˌsuːpəˈvaɪzərɪ ; ˌsupɚˈvaɪzərɪ/ *adj* supervising: 監督的;管理的;指導的: *supervisory duties.* 監督的職責。

su·pine /ˈsuːpaɪn *US:* suˈpaɪn ; suˈpaɪn/ *adj* **1** lying flat on the back, face upwards. 仰臥的;仰着的。 ⇨ prone(1). **2** inactive; slow to act; indolent. 不活潑的;怠惰的;遲緩的;因循的;沒精打采的。 **~·ly** *adv*

sup·per /ˈsʌpə(r) ; ˈsʌpɚ/ *n* [C, U] last meal of the day, when this is less large or less formal than a dinner: 晚餐: *have cold meat for ~;* 晚餐吃冷肉; *eat very little ~;* 晚飯吃得很少; *have a good ~;* 吃一頓好吃的晚飯; *late ~s after the theatre.* 看戲後才吃的延遲的晚餐。 **~·less** *adj* without ~: 無晚餐的;未吃晚餐的: *go to bed ~less.* 未吃晚餐就上床。

sup·plant /səˈplɑːnt *US:* -ˈplænt ; səˈplænt/ *vt* [VP 6A] **1** take the place of (sth): 代替;取代: *Trams in London have been ~ed by buses.* 倫敦的公共汽車已經取代了電車。 **2** take the place of (sb), esp after getting him out of office: 取代(某人);(尤指) 排擠而取代(某人); 使某人去職而代替(某人): *The Prime Minister was ~ed by his rival.* 首相已被其對手用計排擠掉。 *She has been ~ed in his affections by another woman.* 另外一個女人奪走了他對她的愛。 **~er** *n* person who ~s another. 取代者;排擠他人者。

supple /ˈsʌpl ; ˈsʌpl̩/ *adj* easily bent or bending; not stiff: 易彎曲的;柔軟的;靈活的: *the ~ limbs of a child;* 小孩子的柔軟四肢; *a ~ mind,* quick to respond to ideas. 反應靈敏的心智。 **~·ness** *n*

supple·ment /ˈsʌplɪmənt ; ˈsʌpləmənt/ *n* [C] **1** sth added later to improve or complete, eg a dictionary. 補遺;(字典等的)補編。**2** extra and separate addition to a newspaper or other periodical: (報紙或雜誌的)增刊;附刊: *The Times Literary S~;* 泰晤士報的書評週刊; *the Observer colour ~.* 觀察報的彩色增刊。 □ *vt* /ˈsʌplɪment ; ˈsʌpləˌmɛnt/ [VP6A, 15A] make an addition or additions to: 增補;補充: *~ one's ordinary income by writing books.* 著書以增加平常的收入。

supple·men·tary /ˌsʌplɪˈmentrɪ ; ˌsʌpləˈmɛntrɪ/ *adj* **1** additional; extra: 增補的;補充的;附加的: *~ estimates,* eg for additional expenditure; 追加預算; *~ benefit,* (in GB) extra money granted by the State to people in need. (在英國)(政府對困厄人民的)額外津貼。 **2** (of an angle) making with another a total of 180°. (指角度)補角的。

sup·pli·ant /ˈsʌplɪənt ; ˈsʌplɪənt/ *n, adj* (formal) (person) asking humbly for sth: (正式用法)哀求者;懇求者;懇求的;哀求的: *kneel as a ~ at the altar,* ie praying to God; 跪在神壇前懇求(向上帝祈禱); *in a ~ attitude.* 態度懇切地。

sup·pli·cate /ˈsʌplɪkeɪt ; ˈsʌplɪˌket/ *vt, vi* [VP6A, 14, 17, 2C] (formal and liter) make a humble petition to sb: (正式用語及文)懇求;籲請: *~ sb to help;* 懇求某人幫助; *~ sb's protection;* 懇請某人保護; *~ for pardon.* 懇求原諒。 **sup·pli·cant** /ˈsʌplɪkənt ; ˈsʌplɪkənt/ *n* person who ~s; suppliant. 懇求者;籲請者。**sup·pli·ca·tion**/ˌsʌplɪˈkeɪʃn ; ˌsʌplɪˈkeʃən/ *n* [C, U] humble prayer. 祈求;祈禱。

supply /səˈplaɪ ; səˈplaɪ/ *vt* (*pt, pp* -lied) [VP6A, 14] ***~ sth to sb; ~ sb with sth,*** **1** give or provide (sth needed or asked for): 供給;供應(所需要或所要求之物): *~ gas/electricity to domestic consumers;* 供應瓦斯(電)給住戶; *~ consumers with gas, etc.* 以瓦斯等供應消費者。 **2** meet (a need): 滿足(需要): *Should the government ~ the need for more houses,* (help to) provide them (eg by building them, or giving subsidies or making loans)? 政府應該滿足(人們)對更多房屋的需要嗎? □ *n* **1** [U] ~ing; [C] (*pl* -lies) that which is supplied; stock or amount of sth which is obtainable: 供給;供應;供給之物;現貨;現貨貯存量: *Have you a good ~ of reading matter for the train journey,* plenty of books, magazines, etc? 你有供火車旅行的許多讀物嗎? *We shall be receiving new supplies of shoes next week,* (eg of a shop) new stocks. (如指商店)我們將於下週收到鞋子的新貨。 ***~ and demand,*** quantities available and quantities asked for (thought of as regulating prices). 供給和需要;供與求(被認爲係決定物價的因素)。 ***in short ~,*** scarce (which is the more usu word). 稀少的;缺乏的 (scarce 一字較常用)。 **2 supplies,** (esp) stores necessary for some public need, eg the armed forces: (尤指) 公衆必需品 (如軍需品); 生活必需品: *ˈmedical supplies.* 醫療用品。 **3** ***be/go on ~,*** work as a temporary substitute, eg for a teacher or clergyman: 臨時代人工作;作臨時替工: (attrib) (形容用法) *a ˈ~ teacher.* 代課教員。 **4 supplies,** (GB) grant of money by Parliament for the cost of government. (英)國會對政府的開支所做之撥款。 **S~ Day,** (in the House of Commons) day on which approval of the Estimates (of expenditure) is asked for. (下議院中)請求批准預算日。 **5 supplies,** allowance of money to a person: 個人的津貼;零用金: *Tom's father cut off the supplies.* 湯姆的父親停發零用金。**sup·plier** *n* person or firm ~ing goods, etc. 供應貨物等的人或商店;供應商。

sup·port /səˈpɔːt ; səˈport/ *vt* [VP6A] **1** bear the weight of; hold up or keep in place: 支持;支撐;扶持: *Is this bridge strong enough to ~ heavy lorries?* 這座橋禁得起重卡車通行嗎? *He hurt his ankle, so he had to be ~ed home,* someone had to help him to walk home. 他傷了足踝,因此不得不讓人攙着回家。 **2** strengthen; help (sb or sth) to continue: 加强;使有力;擁護;支援;幫助(某人或某事物)持續: *~ a claim/a political party;* 支持一項要求(某一政黨); *~ a football team,* eg by regularly watching it play; 支持一足球隊(例如經常觀其賽球); *~ing troops,* held in reserve to help those who are fighting; 支援部隊; *a hospital ~ed by voluntary contributions;* 由捐款維持開支的醫院; *a theory that is not ~ed by the facts;* 無事實爲根據的理論; *an accusation not ~ed by proofs;* 無證據的指控; *a ˈ~ing actor,* one who takes a part secondary to that of the leading actor; 配角; *a ˈ~ing film,* secondary to the main feature film. (電影的)副片;短片。 **3** provide for (financially, etc): 維持;贍養: *He has a large family to ~.* 他要養一大家人。 **4** endure: 忍受;忍耐: *I can't ~ your jealousy any longer.* 我無法再忍受你的嫉妒了。□ *n* **1** [U] ~ing or being ~ed: 支持;支撐;扶持;擁護;幫助;維持;贍養: *This bridge needs more ~.* 這座橋需要加强支承。 *I hope to have your ~ in the election.* 我希望在選舉中得到你的支持。 *The proposal obtained no/little/not much ~.* 這項建議未獲得(鮮獲,略獲)支持。 *Mr X spoke in ~ of the motion.* 某先生發言支持該項動議。 *The divorced wife claimed ~* (ie a regular financial contribution) *for her children from her ex-husband, but he was found to be without visible means of ~,* with no apparent resources (money, work) on which to live. 那離婚的妻子爲其子女向前夫索取贍養費,但他被發現並無可察見的資財或收入。 ***in ~,*** (of troops) in reserve, ready to give ~. (指部隊)預備的;支援的。 ***(be) in ~ of sb/sth,*** (be) ~ing him/it. 支援某人(某事物)。 **2** [C] sb or sth that ~s: 支持的人或物;支援者;支撐物;贊助者;贍養者;贊助金;贍養金: *Dick is the chief ~ of the family,* earns the money for the family. 狄克是這一家的主要贍養者。 **ˈprice ~s,** (US) subsidies, eg paid by the government to farmers. (美)價格補助金;價格津貼(如政府給予農民者)。 **~·able** /-əbl ; -əbl̩/ *adj* that can be ~ed; endurable. 可維持的;可贍養的;可忍受的。**~er** *n* person or device that ~s. 支持者;支援者;支持器械或設備。 **~·ive** *adj* ~ing; giving help, encouragement. 支持的;支援的;擁護的;幫助的;鼓勵的。

sup·pose /səˈpəʊz ; səˈpoz/ *vt* **1** [VP9, 6A, 25] let it be thought that; take it as a fact that: 認定;假定: *Let us ~ (that) the news is true.* 讓我們假定這消息是眞確的。 *S~ the world were flat.* 假定地球是扁平的。 *Everyone is ~d to know the rules,* It is assumed, taken for granted, that we all know the rules. 大家都該知道這些規則。*I don't ~ for one／a minute that...*, I don't believe that.... 我壓根兒不相信…。 **2** [VP9, 6A, 25] guess; think: 推測;猜想;想像: *What do you ~ he wanted?* 你想他需要什麼？*All her neighbours ~d her to be／~d that she was a widow.* 她的鄰人們都以爲她是一個寡婦。*You'll be there, I ~.* 我想你會去的。*'Will he come?'—'Yes, I ~ so'／'No, I ~ not'／'No, I don't ~ so'.* '他會來嗎？'—'是的，我想他會'('不,我想他不會';'不,我認爲他不會來')。*I ~ you want to borrow money again!* 我猜你又要借錢了！ **3** [VP6A] (forming an imper, or used to make a suggestion or proposal): (構成祈使句，或用以做成一項建議或提議): *S~ we go* (= Let's go) *for a swim.* (我提議)我們去游泳吧。 **4** [VP6A] require as a condition; imply: 須以…爲條件;必須有;意味着: *Creation ~s a creator.* 創造必須先有創造者。 **5** ***be ~d to,*** **(a)** be expected or required to (by customs, duty, etc): 被期望或要求;應該: *Is he ~d to clean the outside of the windows or only the inside?* 他應該把窗戶外面也擦乾淨呢，還是擦窗戶裡面就可以？ **(b)** (colloq) (in the neg) not be allowed to: (俗)(用於否定句中)不被許可: *We're not ~d to play football on Sundays.* 我們在禮拜天不許踢足球。**sup·pos·ing** *conj* if: 假如;倘若: *Supposing it rains, what shall you do?* 如果下起雨來,你怎麼辦呢？ **~d** *adj* accepted as being so: 被信以爲眞的;假定的;推測的;咸信的: *his ~d generosity.* 他那種被信以爲眞的慷慨。*The ~d beggar was really a police officer in disguise.* 那個大家認爲是乞丐的人,原來是喬裝的警官。**sup·pos·ed·ly** /-ɪdlɪ ; -ɪdlɪ/ *adv* according to what is／was ~d. 臆測上;想像上;恐怕;大概。

sup·po·si·tion /ˌsʌpəˈzɪʃn ; ˌsʌpəˈzɪʃən/ *n* **1** [U] supposing: 想像;臆測;推斷;假設: *This newspaper article is based on ~*, on what the writer supposes to be the case, not on fact. 報上這篇文章是根據想像寫的,並非事實。*We mustn't condemn him on mere ~.* 我們不可全憑臆測指責他。 **2** [C] sth supposed; guess: 被假定之事物;臆測;推想: *Our ~s were fully confirmed.* 我們所假定的全都證實了。***on this ~; on the ~ that...***, supposing that this is the case. 假如這樣;假使。

sup·posi·tory /səˈpɒzɪtrɪ *US:* -tɔːrɪ ; səˈpɑzəˌtorɪ/ *n* (*pl* -ries) medical preparation (in a soluble capsule) inserted into the rectum or vagina and left to dissolve. 塞藥;坐藥;栓劑(如裝於可溶膠囊中的藥劑,插入直腸或陰道中,讓其溶解)。

sup·press /səˈpres ; səˈprɛs/ *vt* [VP6A] **1** put an end to the activity or existence of: 鎭壓;平定;制止: *~ a rising／the slave trade.* 鎭壓叛亂(制止奴隸販賣)。**2** prevent from being known or seen: 抑制;扣留;查禁;隱瞞: *~ the truth／a yawn／one's feelings;* 隱匿眞相(抑制呵欠;壓抑感情); *~ a newspaper*, prevent its publication. 查禁一家報紙。**~ion** /səˈpreʃn ; səˈprɛʃən/ *n* ~ing: 鎭壓;平定;壓止;抑制;扣留;查禁;隱瞞: *a policy of ~ion*, eg of ~ing movements for independence or for freedom. 高壓政策。**~ive** *adj* tending to ~; designed to ~. 鎭壓性的; 爲鎭壓而設計的; 平定的; 抑制的; 隱瞞的。**~or** /-sə(r) ; -sɚ/ *n* sth that ~es; (esp) a device fitted to electric apparatus to prevent interference with radio and television reception: 鎭壓等的事物;(尤指)干擾遏止器(裝於電器上,以防止干擾無線電及電視之接收的裝置): *fit a ~ to an electric motor.* 在電動機(馬達)上裝置一干擾遏止器。

sup·pu·rate /ˈsʌpjʊreɪt ; ˈsʌpjəˌret/ *vi* [VP2A] (formal) form pus, fester. (正式用語)生膿;化膿;醸膿。**sup·pu·ra·tion** /ˌsʌpjʊˈreɪʃn ; ˌsʌpjəˈreʃən/ *n*

supra /ˈsuːprə ; ˈsuprə/ *adv* (Lat; formal) above; earlier on (in a book, etc): (拉;正式用語)在上;(書等中)在前: *See ~, p 21*, See p 21 earlier on in this book. 請參閱本書前文第二十一頁。

supra·na·tional /ˌsuːprəˈnæʃnəl ; ˌsuprəˈnæʃənl/ *adj* above nations or states: 超國家的;在國家之上的: *a ~ authority*, one that might be created for world government. 一個超國家的政權。

su·preme /suːˈpriːm ; səˈprim/ *adj* **1** highest in degree or rank or authority: 階級、地位或權力最高的;至高的;無上的: *the S~ Commander;* 最高統帥; *the S~ Court*, highest in one of the States of the US or in the whole of the US; (美國各州的或全美國的)最高法院; *the S~ Soviet*, the legislature of the USSR; 最高蘇維埃(蘇聯的立法機構); *the S~ Being*, God. 上帝。 **2** most important; greatest: 最重要的;最大的: *make the ~ sacrifice*, lay down one's life (eg in war). 作最大的犧牲(如戰爭中捐軀)。**~·ly** *adv* in a ~ manner: 至高地;無上地;最重要地;最大地: *~ly happy.* 極快樂的。**su·prem·acy** /sʊˈpreməsɪ ; səˈprɛməsɪ/ *n* [U] ***supremacy over,*** being ~ over; highest authority: 至高;無上;最高的權威: *His supremacy was unchallenged.* 他那種至高無上的權威無人置疑。

sur·charge /ˈsɜːtʃɑːdʒ ; ˈsɝˌtʃɑrdʒ/ *n* **1** payment demanded in addition to the usual charge, eg as a penalty for a letter with insufficient postage paid on it. 額外的索價;額外的償付(如郵資不足的罰款)。 **2** excessive or additional load. 過大的負擔;額外負荷;超載。**3** mark overprinted on a postage-stamp changing its value. 郵票上的變值印記。□ *vt* **1** [VP6A] overload. 使負擔過重;使裝載過多。 **2** [VP6A, 15A] demand a ~(1) on or in. 向…額外索價;對…處以附加罰款。

surd /sɜːd ; sɝd/ *n* (math) quantity, esp a root (√), that cannot be expressed in finite terms of ordinary numbers or quantities. (數學)不盡根數。

sure /ʃʊə(r) ; ʃʊr/ *adj* (-r, -st) **1** (pred only) (僅作敘述用法) free from doubt; having confidence; knowing and believing; having, seeming to have, good reason for belief: 一定的;必定的;有信心的;無疑的;確知的;確信的;有理由相信的: *I think he's coming, but I'm not quite ~.* 我想他會來的,但我不太敢確定。*You're ~ of* (= certain to receive) *a welcome.* 你一定會受到歡迎。*I'm not ~ whether I have a copy／where I left my copy／when I lost it.* 我不能確定我是不是有一本(我把我那一本遺留在什麼地方,我何時遺失了它)。*I'm not ~ why he wants it.* 我不太知道他何以需要它。***be／feel ~ (about sth),*** have no doubts (about): 有把握;確信: *I think the answer's right, but I'm not ~ (about it).* 我想這答案是對的,但是我(對它)沒有把握。*Smith's a good man for the job, but I'm not so ~ about Robinson.* 史密斯是這項工作的恰當人選,但是羅賓遜能不能勝任,我就沒有這麼大把握了。***be／feel ~ of sth／that...***, have confidence: 確信某事(確定…): *Are you ~ of your facts?* 你確信你所說的都是眞的嗎？ *Can we be ~ of his honesty／that he's honest?* 我們能確定他是誠實的嗎？***be／feel ~ of oneself,*** have self-confidence. 有自信心。***be ~ to do sth;*** (colloq) (俗) ***be ~ and do sth,*** don't fail to: 務必;一定要: *Be ~ to write and give me all the news.* 務必寫信告訴我所有的消息。***to be ~,*** it is admitted, granted: 誠然;確然;的確: *She's not pretty, to be ~, but she's very intelligent.* 誠然,她並不漂亮,但是她却非常聰明。*Well, to be ~!* 唉呀,眞的呀！***make ~ that.../of sth,*** **(a)** feel ~: 確信;感到確定無疑: *I made ~ he would be here.* 我確信他會來這裡。**(b)** satisfy oneself; do what is necessary in order to feel ~ to get sth, etc: 使自己滿足或弄明白;查明;做必要之事以證實、得到某物等: *I think there's a train at 5.15, but you'd better make ~*, eg by looking up trains in a timetable. 我想五點一刻有一班火車,但是你最好去查一查。*There aren't many seats left for this concert; you'd better make ~ of one／make ~ that you get one today.* 這音樂會剩下的座位不多了;你最好今天訂妥一個位子。**2** (attrib and pred) proved or tested; reliable; trustworthy: (形容用法及敘述用法)經過證實有效、妥當、無害、無誤等;可靠的;穩妥的;靠得住的: *no ~ remedy for colds;* 沒有一定能治好傷風的藥物; *~ proof;* 確切無疑的證據; *send a letter by a ~ hand／a ~*

messenger. 經由可靠的人(專差)送信。 ˌ~-ˈ**footed** *adj* not likely to stumble or slip. 脚步穩的;踏實的;無失誤之虞的。□ *adv* **1** ~ ***enough,*** certainly, in fact: 確實地;事實上: *I said it would happen, and ~ enough it did happen.* 我說(它)會發生,而確實發生了。 ***for ~,*** (usu colloq) certainly. (通常爲俗語用法)的確;確實地。 **2** ***as ~ as,*** as certain as: 如…一樣確切: *as ~ as fate;* 千眞萬確; *as ~ as my name's Bob.* 的確。 **3** (colloq, esp US) certainly: (俗,尤美)確實地;的確: *It ~ was cold.* 確實很冷。 **~·ness** *n*

sure·ly /ˈʃʊəlɪ ; ˈʃʊrlɪ/ *adv* **1** (usu placed with the *v*) with certainty: (通常與動詞連用)確實地;無誤地;必然地: *He will ~ fail.* 他必然會失敗。*He was working slowly but ~.* 他(那時)工作得很慢,但很確實。 **2** (placed either with the subject, usu preceding it, or at the end of the sentence, often indicating either confidence or incredulity) if experience or probability can be trusted. (或與主詞連用,通常置於主詞前,或放在一句的末尾,常用以表示信心或懷疑)如果照經驗或常理推斷(進展): *S~ this wet weather won't last much longer!* 這種下雨的天氣必定不會再繼續很久! *You didn't want to hurt his feelings, ~!* 不用說,你無意傷他的感情! *S~ I've met you before somewhere.* 我一定在什麼地方遇見過你。 **3** (esp US) (in answers) certainly; undoubtedly: (尤美)(在答話中)當然;無疑地: *'Would you be willing to help?'—'S~!'* (*Certainly* is more usu in GB usage.) '你願意幫忙嗎?'—'當然(願意)!'(英國多用 certainly。)

surety /ˈʃʊərətɪ *US:* ˈʃʊərtɪ ; ˈʃʊrətɪ/ *n* (*pl* -ties) [C, U] (sth given as a) guarantee; person who makes himself responsible for the conduct or debt(s) of another person: 擔保;擔保品;保證人: *stand ~ for sb.* 做某人的保證人。

surf /sɜːf ; sɝf/ *n* [U] waves breaking in white foam on the seashore, on sand-banks or reefs. 拍岸之浪;擊岸碎浪;海濱的激浪;海邊澎湃之浪。 ˈ**~·ing,** ˈ**~-riding** *nn* sport in which one balances oneself on a long narrow board while being carried along by heavy ~. 衝浪遊戲;衝浪。 ˈ**~-board** *n* board used for this sport. (衝浪遊戲用的)衝浪板。 ˈ**~-boat** *n* boat specially built for use in ~. 碎浪艇(能衝過海濱碎浪的特別建造的小艇)。

surfing

sur·face /ˈsɜːfɪs ; ˈsɝfɪs/ *n* [C] **1** the outside of any object, etc; any of the sides of an object: (任何物體的)表面; 物體的任何一面: *Glass has a smooth ~.* 玻璃有光滑的表面。 *A cube has six ~s.* 立方體有六面。 **2** top of a liquid, esp of a body of water, eg the sea: 液面;(尤指海等之)水面: *The submarine rose to the ~.* 那艘潛艇升至水面上來了。*Most people consider ~ vessels* (= ordinary ships) *to be more vulnerable than submarines.* 大多數人認爲水面上的船隻較潛水艇易遭受攻擊。 **3** ˈ**~ mail,** mail sent by vehicles or ships moving on the earth's ~: 水陸郵件(由車或船等運送者): *S~ mail is cheaper than airmail.* 水陸郵件比航空郵件便宜。 ˌ**~-to-ˈair,** (of missiles, etc) fired or launched from the ground or from ships, and aimed at aircraft. (指飛彈等)地對空的。 **4** outward appearance; what is seen or learnt from a quick view or consideration: 外表;外觀;皮相;皮毛: *You must not look only at the ~ of things.* 你不可祇看事物的皮相。 *His faults are all on the ~. When you get below the ~, you find that he is warm-hearted and considerate.* 他的缺點都是表面上的。當你深一層觀察時,你就會發現他是既熱心而又體諒旁人。 **5** (attrib) of the ~ only: (形容用法)表面的;膚淺的: *~ politeness;* 表面上的禮貌; *~ impressions,* received quickly or casually, with no depth of thought, observation, etc; 膚淺的印象; ˈ*~ noise,* eg from a gramophone record, made by the stylus. 表面雜音(如唱片由唱針磨擦而生者)。□ *vt, vi* **1** [VP 6A] give a ~ to: 裝以面;使成平面: *~ a road with gravel/tarmac.* 以砂礫(柏油和砂礫)加鋪路面。 **2** [VP 6A, 2A] (of a submarine, skin-diver, etc) (cause to) come to the ~. (指潛水艇,潛水者等)(使)升至水面。

sur·feit /ˈsɜːfɪt ; ˈsɝfɪt/ *n* (usu 通常作 ***a ~ (of)***) too much of anything, esp food and drink: 過量;過度;(尤指)過食;過飲: *have a ~ of curry while in Madras;* 在馬德拉斯的時候吃了太多咖哩; feeling of discomfort resulting from a ~. 飲食過量帶來的不適感;食傷;食滯。□ *vt* [VP6A, 14] ~ ***sb/oneself (with),*** (cause to) take too much of anything: (使)取用過度;(使)飲食過度: *~ oneself with fruit;* 吃過多的水果; *be ~ed with pleasure.* 作樂過度。

surge /sɜːdʒ ; sɝdʒ/ *vi* [VP2C] move forward, roll on, in or like waves: (在波浪中或像波浪般)滾流;起伏;洶湧;澎湃: *The floods ~d over the valley.* 洪水在山谷中滾滾流動。*The crowds ~d out of the sports stadium.* 觀衆從運動場湧出。*Anger ~d (up) within him.* 怒氣在他內心洶湧澎湃。□ *n* [C] forward or upward movement; onrush: 滾流;起伏;洶湧;澎湃;奔流: *the ~ of the sea;* 海浪洶湧; *a ~ of anger/pity.* 一陣怒氣(憐憫)。

sur·geon /ˈsɜːdʒən ; ˈsɝdʒən/ *n* **1** doctor who performs operations. 外科醫生。 **dental ~** *n* dentist qualified in surgery. 口腔外科醫生。 ˈ**house ~** *n* one of the staff of a hospital. 駐院外科醫生。 **2** medical officer in the navy: 海軍軍醫: ˌ*~-comˈmander.* (海軍)軍醫中校。

sur·gery /ˈsɜːdʒərɪ ; ˈsɝdʒərɪ/ *n* (*pl* -ries) **1** [U] the science and practice of treating injuries and disease by manual and instrumental operations: 外科;外科手術: *qualified in both ~ and medicine.* 內外科皆合格的。 **2** [C] (GB) doctor's or dentist's room where patients come to consult him: (英)(醫師或牙醫的)診療室;應診室: *~ hours, 4pm to 6pm;* 應診時間,下午四時至六時; *political ~,* (colloq) where constituents can consult their member of Parliament. (俗)政治應診室(國會議員接見其選民處)。

sur·gi·cal /ˈsɜːdʒɪkl ; ˈsɝdʒɪkḷ/ *adj* of, by, for, surgery: 外科的;外科手術的;外科用的: *~ treatment;* 外科治療; *~ instruments;* 外科器具; *a ~ boot,* one specially designed to fit a deformed foot. 爲治療畸形足所設計的鞋子。 **~·ly** /-klɪ ; -klɪ/ *adv*

sur·ly /ˈsɜːlɪ ; ˈsɝlɪ/ *adj* (-ier, -iest) bad-tempered and unfriendly. 乖戾的;粗暴的;不友善的。 **sur·lily** /-ɪlɪ ; -ɪlɪ/ *adv* **sur·li·ness** *n*

sur·mise /səˈmaɪz ; sɚˈmaɪz/ *vt, vi* [VP6A, 9, 2A] (formal) guess, conjecture: (正式用語)猜測;臆度: *She ~d as much.* 她如此猜測。□ /ˈsɜːmaɪz ; sɚˈmaɪz/ *n* [C] guess: 猜測;臆度: *You were right in your ~.* 你猜對了。

sur·mount /səˈmaʊnt ; sɚˈmaʊnt/ *vt* **1** [VP6A] overcome (difficulties); get over (obstacles). 克服(困難);越過(障碍)。 **2** (passive) (被動語態) ***be ~ed by/with,*** have on or over the top: 在頂上有: *a spire ~ed by a weather-vane.* 頂上裝有風標的尖塔。 **~·able** /-əbl ; -əbḷ/ *adj* that can be overcome or conquered. 可克服的;可超過的。

sur·name /ˈsɜːneɪm ; ˈsɝˌnem/ *n* [C] person's hereditary family name: 姓;氏: *Smith is a very common English ~.* 史密斯是一個很普通的英國姓。 ⇨ *given name* at give¹(11), *Christian name* at Christian, and forename.

sur·pass /səˈpɑːs *US:* -ˈpæs ; sɚˈpæs/ *vt* [VP6A,

15A] do or be better than; exceed; excel: 超越;凌駕;勝過: ~ *sb in strength/speed/skill.* 在氣力(速度,技術)方面勝過某人。*The beauty of the scenery ~ed my expectations.* 該處風景之秀麗超出我的預料。**~·ing** *adj* matchless: 卓越的;無與倫比的: *of ~ing beauty.* 美貌超羣的。**~·ing·ly** *adv* in a way that is not ~ed: 卓越地;超絕地;無與倫比地: *~ingly ugly.* 極醜的。

sur·plice /ˈsɜːplɪs; ˈsɝplɪs/ *n* loose-fitting (usu white) gown with wide sleeves worn by (some) priests (over a cassock) during church services. (某些教士於教堂禮拜時所著的) 白法衣 (罩於袈裟外的長袍)。⇨ the illus at vestment. 參看 vestment 之插圖。**sur·pliced** *adj* wearing a ~. 著白法衣的。

sur·plus /ˈsɜːpləs; ˈsɝplʌs/ *n* **1** [C] amount (of money) that remains after needs have been supplied; excess of receipts over expenditure, ⇨ deficit; amount (of anything) in excess of requirements: 餘款; 盈餘; (指任何事物) 剩餘; 過剩: *Brazil had a ~ of coffee last year.* 巴西去年咖啡供過於求。**2** (attrib) exceeding what is needed or used: (形容用法) 剩餘的; 過剩的: ~ *labour,* workers for whom there are no jobs; 剩餘勞力(過剩勞工); *a sale of ~ stock;* 出售剩餘的存貨; *~ population,* in excess of what is thought desirable, or for which there is not enough food, employment, etc; 過剩人口; ˈ~ *store,* (GB) shop where ~ items (eg military clothing) are sold. (英)(出售軍服等之)剩餘物品店。

sur·prise /səˈpraɪz; sɚˈpraɪz/ *n* **1** [C, U] (feeling caused by) sth sudden or unexpected: 驚駭;驚愕;驚奇;突然或意外之事物: *His failure did not cause much ~/was not a great ~.* 他的失敗未引起很大的驚奇(並非很意外之事)。*What a ~!* 多令人吃驚的事! *To my ~/To the ~ of everyone, his plan succeeded.* 使我(大家)驚奇的是他的計畫竟然成功了。*We have some ~s in store for you.* 我們還有一些出乎你意料的話(禮物)奉告(奉贈)。*He looked up in ~.* 他吃驚地向上看。***take sb by ~,*** catch him unprepared, at a time when he is not expecting to be seen, etc. 冷不防地使某人嚇一跳;(出乎某人意料地)撞見、捉到某人等。***take a fort/town, etc by ~,*** capture it by making an unexpected attack. 奇襲攻佔某堡壘(城鎮等)。**2** (attrib) unexpected; made, done, etc, without warning: (形容用法) 出乎意料的; 出其不意的;突然的;奇襲的: *a ~ visit/attack.* 突然的訪問(奇襲)。□ *vt* **1** [VP6A] give a feeling of ~ to: 使驚駭;使驚愕;使驚奇: *You ~ me!* 你嚇了我一跳! *She was more ~d than frightened.* 她驚訝的程度超過了害怕。**2** ***be ~d,*** experience ~: 感到吃驚、驚奇、驚愕等: *We were ~d at the news/~d to hear the news.* 我們聽到那項消息感到震驚。*I'm ~d (to learn that) he didn't come.* 他居然沒有來,我感到很意外。*We were ~d at finding the house empty.* 我們發現房子是空的,感到很意外。*It's nothing to be ~d about/at.* 這事不值得大驚小怪。*I shouldn't be ~d if it rained this afternoon,* It seems to me likely that it will rain. 如果今天下午下雨,我不會感到意外。**3** [VP6A] come upon suddenly, without previous warning; take by ~: 不期而遇;撞見;奇襲: *~ the enemy,* attack them when they are off their guard; 奇襲敵人; *~ a burglar in the act of breaking into a house.* 撞見正要潛入某住宅的夜賊。**4** ***~ sb into doing sth,*** hurry him into doing sth, eg by making a sudden challenge. 冷不防地促使某人做某事(如突然向某人挑戰)。**sur·pris·ing** *adj* causing ~. 令人吃驚的;奇異的。**sur·pris·ing·ly** *adv* **sur·prised** *adj* showing or feeling ~. 驚愕的;驚奇的;吃驚的。**sur·pris·ed·ly** /-ɪdlɪ; -ɪdlɪ/ *adv* in a ~d manner. 驚愕地;驚奇地;吃驚地。

sur·real·ism /səˈrɪəlɪzəm; səˈriəlˌɪzm/ *n* [U] 20th-century movement in art and literature that aims at expressing what there is in the subconscious mind (so that a painting may depict a number of unrelated objects as seen in a dream). 超寫實主義;超現實主義(廿世紀的文學及藝術潮流,其目的在呈現潛意識中的事物,比如,一張畫所呈現的可能是如夢中所見,許多互不關連的景像)。**sur·real·ist** /-ɪst; -ɪst/ *n* artist, writer, etc of this movement. 超寫實或現實主義者(指藝術家,作家等)。**sur·real·is·tic** /səˌrɪəˈlɪstɪk; səˌriəlˈɪstɪk/ *adj* of ~; fantastic. 超寫實或現實主義的;幻想的。

sur·ren·der /səˈrendə(r); səˈrɛndɚ/ *vt, vi* **1** [VP 6A, 14, 2A] ~ ***(to),*** give up (oneself, a ship, a town, etc) (to the enemy, the police, etc): 放棄(船,城市等);(向敵人,警察等)投降;投案;自首: *We shall never ~.* 我們永不投降。*We advised the hijackers to ~ (themselves) to the police.* 我們勸那些劫持者向警察投案。**2** [VP6A] yield up under pressure or from necessity; abandon possession of: 拋棄;捨棄;讓與: *We shall never ~ our liberty.* 我們永不會捨棄自由。*He ~ed his insurance policy,* gave up his rights under the policy in return for a lump sum of money (called the ~ *value* of the policy). 他退出保險,獲得一筆退保金(surrender value)。**3** [VP14] ~ ***(oneself) to,*** yield or give way to (a habit, emotion, influence, etc): 屈服於(習慣、感情、影響等);任由(習慣等)擺佈: *He ~ed (himself) to despair and committed suicide.* 他感到絕望而自殺了。□ *n* ~ing or being ~ed: 屈服;投降;放棄;讓與: *demand the ~ of a town/of all firearms;* 要求一個城市投降(交出所有武器); *~ value,* ⇨ 2 above. (保險)解約退款;退保金額(參看上列第2義)。*No ~!* Let us not ~! 絕不投降!

sur·rep·ti·tious /ˌsʌrəpˈtɪʃəs; ˌsɝəpˈtɪʃəs/ *adj* (of actions) done secretly or stealthily. (指動作) 偷偷摸摸的;暗中進行的。**~ly** *adv*

sur·ro·gate /ˈsʌrəgeɪt; ˈsɝəˌget/ *n* deputy, esp of a bishop. (尤指主教的)代理者;替身。⇨ suffragan.

sur·round /səˈraʊnd; səˈraʊnd/ *vt* [VP6A] be, go, all round, shut in on all sides: 包圍;環繞: *a house ~ed with trees.* 四周爲樹木所環繞的房子。*We are ~ed with/by dangers.* 我們(現在)的處境危機四伏。*The troops were ~ed,* had enemy forces all round them. 部隊被(敵人)包圍了。□ *n* floor between the walls and the carpet; its covering: 地毯四周與牆之間的地板;其覆蓋物: *a linoleum ~.* 鋪在地毯四周的油布。**~·ing** *adj* which is around about: 周圍的;環繞的: *York and the ~ing countryside.* 約克城及其近郊。**~·ings** *n pl* everything around and about a place; conditions that may affect a person: 周圍的事物;環境: *living in pleasant ~ings.* 生活於舒適的環境中。*You don't see animals in their natural ~ings at a zoo.* 你在動物園裡看不到生活在自然環境中的動物。

sur·tax /ˈsɜːtæks; ˈsɝˌtæks/ *n* [C, U] (levying of) additional tax on personal incomes beyond a certain level. 附加稅(對超過某一標準之個人收入所課者);附加稅的徵收。□ *vt* impose ~ on. 課以附加稅。

sur·veil·lance /sɜːˈveɪləns; sɚˈveləns/ *n* [U] close watch kept on persons suspected of wrongdoing, etc: (對嫌疑犯等的)監視;盯梢: *under police ~.* 受警察監視。

sur·vey /səˈveɪ; sɚˈve/ *vt* [VP6A] **1** take a general view of: 眺望;縱覽: *~ the countryside from the top of a hill.* 從山頂眺望鄉區。**2** examine the general condition of: 通盤考慮; 審度; 衡量一般情況: *The Prime Minister, in his speech at the Guildhall, ~ed the international situation.* 首相在倫敦市政廳大會堂所作的演說中,檢討了國際情勢。**3** measure and map out the position, size, boundaries, etc of (an area of land, a country, coast, etc): 測量;查勘(地區、國家、海岸等): *~ a parish/a railway.* 測量某一教區(一條鐵路)。**4** examine the condition of (a building, etc): 檢查(房屋等)的狀況;鑑定: *Have the house ~ed before you offer to buy it.* 在你出價買那房子之前,先找人鑑定一下。**~·ing** *n* [U] the work of ~ing (3, 4): 測量;查勘;檢查;鑑定: ˈ*land-~ing;* 土地查勘; *a* ˈ*~ing ship,* used for ~ing coasts; 海岸測量船; instruction in the principles of making surveys(3). 測量術;測量學。□ *n* /ˈsɜːveɪ; ˈsɝve/ [C] **1** general view: 概觀;審視;考察: *make a general ~ of the situation/subject.* 對情勢(問題)作通盤考慮。**2** piece of land-surveying; map or record of this: 土地測量;測量圖;測量記錄: *an aerial ~ of East Africa,* made by photography from aircraft; 東非的空中測量(圖); *the ordnance ~ of Great Britain,* ⇨ ordnance. 英國官方土地測量;其所製的地圖。**~or** /səˈveɪə(r); səˈveə/ *n* **1** person who ~s(3) land, etc. 測量員(測量土地等者)。 **2** person who ~s and values buildings, etc. 房屋等的鑑定人。**3** official inspector: 檢查人員或官員;視查人員或官員: *~or of weights and measures;* 度量衡的檢查官員; *the ~or of highways.* 公路視查員。**quantity ~or,** ⇨ quantity. (建築)估料師;積算師。

sur·vival /səˈvaɪvl; sәˈvaɪvḷ/ *n* **1** [U] state of continuing to live or exist; surviving: 繼續生存或存在;殘存;生存: *~ after death,* of the spirit after the death of the body; 死後靈魂的存在; *the ~ of the fittest,* the continuing existence of those animals and plants which are best adapted to their surroundings, etc; 適者生存(指動植物之最能適應其環境者得以繼續生存,否則淘汰); (attrib) (形容用法) *a* ˈ*~ kit,* package of necessities for a person after a disaster, etc (eg at sea). 救生背囊(裝有維持生命的必需品,供遭逢災變者,如遭海難者,使用)。 **2** [C] person, custom, belief, etc that has survived but is looked upon as belonging to past times. 殘存的人、風俗、信仰等;遺風;殘存物;過時代的人。

sur·vive /səˈvaɪv; sәˈvaɪv/ *vt, vi* [VP6A, 2A] continue to live or exist; live or exist longer than; remain alive after: 殘存;繼續生存;經歷…後仍然活着;生命較…長久: *~ an earthquake/shipwreck;* 遭地震(沉船)後幸存; *those who ~d.* 殘存者。*The old lady has ~d all her children.* 那位老婦人的子女都先她而去世了。*I hope I shall never ~ my usefulness,* continue to live (or to hold a position) after I have ceased to be useful. 我希望在我有生之年永遠不要變成廢物。**sur·vivor** /-və(r); -vә/ *n* person who has ~d: 殘存者;生還者;生存者: *send help to the survivors of the earthquake.* 對地震生還者予以救助。

sus·cep·tible /səˈseptəbl; sәˈsɛptәbḷ/ *adj* **1** easily influenced by feelings; impressionable: 易受感情影響的;易動感情的;多情的: *a girl with a ~ nature;* 易動感情的女郎; *a ~ young man,* one who easily falls in love. 多情的年輕人。**2** *~ to,* sensitive to; easily affected by: 易感的;敏感的;易受…感動的: *~ to flattery/kind treatment;* 易為諂媚(禮遇)所動的; *~ to pain.* 對痛苦敏感的。 **3** *~ of,* (formal) capable of, that can receive or be given: (正式用語)能…的;容許…的: *Is your statement ~ of proof?* 你的陳述可加以證明嗎? **sus·cep·ti·bil·ity** /səˌseptəˈbɪlətɪ; sәˌsɛptәˈbɪlәtɪ/ *n* (*pl* -ties) **1** [U] sensitiveness: 易感性;敏感性;感受性: *~ to hay fever/hypnotic influences.* 對花粉熱(催眠)的敏感性。 **2** (*pl*) sensitive points of a person's nature: (複)(一個人性格上的)敏感處;感情: *We must avoid wounding their susceptibilities,* not say or do anything that might hurt their feelings. 我們必須避免傷害他們的感情。

sus·pect /səˈspekt; sәˈspɛkt/ *vt* **1** [VP6A, 9, 25] have an idea or feeling (concerning the possibility or likelihood of sth): 猜想;疑有;覺得會;有點感覺到: *He ~ed an ambush.* 他疑有伏兵。*She has more intelligence than we ~ed her to possess.* 她的智慧比我們所猜想的要多。*I ~ (that) he's a liar* (less usu 較不常用 *~ him to be a liar*). 我料想他是一個說謊者。 **2** [VP6A] feel doubt about: 懷疑;覺得可疑: *~ the truth of an account.* 懷疑一項報告的眞實性。 **3** [VP6A, 14] *~ sb (of sth),* have a feeling that sb may be guilty (of): 懷疑某人有…罪: *He is ~ed of telling lies.* 別人懷疑他說謊。□ *n* /ˈsʌspekt; ˈsʌspɛkt/ person ~ed of wrongdoing, disloyalty, etc: 有嫌疑的人;嫌疑犯: *Are political ~s kept under police observation in your country?* 貴國的政治嫌疑犯受警察監視嗎? □ *pred adj* /ˈsʌspekt; ˈsʌspɛkt/ of doubtful character; possibly false; ~ed: 具有可疑性質的;可疑的;被懷疑的: *His statements are ~.* 他的陳述可疑。

sus·pend /səˈspend; sәˈspɛnd/ *vt* **1** [VP6A, 14] *~ sth (from),* hang up (from): 懸掛;吊起: *lamps ~ed from the ceiling.* 懸掛在天花板上的燈。 **2** (passive) (被動語態) (of solid particles, in the air or other fluid medium) be or remain in place: (指空氣中或其他流體中的固體微粒)懸浮: *dust/smoke ~ed in the still air.* 懸浮在靜止空氣中的塵埃(烟)。 **3** [VP6A] stop for a time; delay; keep in an undecided state for a time: 暫停;延緩;懸而不決: *~ payment,* stop payment (eg when bankrupt); 暫停支付(如破產時); *~ a rule;* 中止一項規則; *~ judgement,* postpone giving one; 延緩判決; (of a person) *in a state of ~ed animation,* alive but unconscious, (fig, joc; of institutions, committees, etc) temporarily inactive. (指人)不省人事;(喻、諧;指制度、委員會等)暫時停止活動的。 *He was fined £50 with a ~ed sentence/~ed execution of sentence,* the payment of the fine being not required for a time, ie while he continues to observe the law. 他被判罰款50鎊,暫緩繳納(只要他繼續守法,可暫時不繳罰款)。 **4** [VP6A] announce that (sb) cannot be allowed to perform his duties, enjoy privileges, etc for a time: 使停職;暫停權利: *~ a (professional) football player,* eg because of repeated breaches of the rules. 暫停一位(職業)足球員的比賽權。

sus·pender /səˈspendə(r); sәˈspɛndә/ *n (pair of) ~s,* **1** (GB) garter. (英)束襪帶。ˈ*~* **belt,** light garment worn round the waist, with clasps for keeping up women's stockings. 吊襪帶(婦女繫於腰際,附有吊襪子的鈕鉤)。 **2** (US) pair of straps (*braces* in GB) worn over the shoulders to keep up trousers. (美)吊褲帶;背帶(英國稱作 braces)。

sus·pense /səˈspens; sәˈspɛns/ *n* [U] uncertainty, anxiety (about news, events, decisions, etc): (有關新聞、事件、決定等)懸而未決;不確定;懸疑;焦慮: *We waited in great ~ for the doctor's opinion.* 我們非常焦慮地等候醫生的意見。 ***keep sb in ~,*** delay telling him what he is eager to know: 使某人懸念或掛慮: *They've kept me in ~ for five days already.* 他們已使我掛慮五天了。

sus·pen·sion /səˈspenʃn; sәˈspɛnʃәn/ *n* [U] suspending or being suspended: 懸掛;懸浮;暫停;延緩;停職;懸而未決: *the ~ of a member of Parliament,* eg for abuse of Parliamentary privileges; 暫停某一國會議員的職權(如因濫用國會特權等); ⇨ suspend(4); *the ~ of a motor-vehicle,* the means by which it is supported on its axles (springs, shock absorbers, etc). 汽車等的緩衝裝置(彈簧,避震器等)。ˈ~ **bridge** *n* bridge suspended on or by means of steel cables supported from towers. 吊橋。⇨ the illus at bridge. 參看 bridge 之插圖。

sus·pi·cion /səˈspɪʃn; sәˈspɪʃәn/ *n* **1** [C, U] feeling that a person has when he suspects; suspecting or being suspected; feeling that sth is wrong: 猜疑;懷疑;嫌疑;疑心: *I have a ~ that he is dishonest.* 我懷疑他不誠實。*I resent your ~s about my motives.* 我討厭你懷疑我的動機。*He was looked upon with ~.* 他被人猜疑。 *He was arrested on (the) ~ of having stolen the money.* 他因有偷那筆錢的嫌疑而被捕。 *His behaviour aroused no ~.* 他的行為未引起懷疑。*Don't lay yourself open to ~.* 不要招惹嫌疑。*Don't let ~ fall on you/Don't fall under ~.* 不要使自己受到懷疑。 ***above ~,*** of such good reputation that ~ is out of the question. (名譽極好而)無可懷疑。 **2** *a ~ (of),* slight taste or suggestion: 些微;一點點;稍含某意味: *There was a ~ of sadness in her voice/of garlic in the stew.* 她的聲音有一點悲愴意味(那道燉菜有一點大蒜味道)。

sus·pi·cious /səˈspɪʃəs ; səˈspɪʃəs/ *adj* having, showing or causing suspicion: 懷疑的;表示懷疑的;引起懷疑的;可疑的: *The affair looks ~ to me.* 這事在我看來可疑。*He's a ~ character,* There is reason to suspect that he is dishonest, etc. 他是一個品性不太可靠的人物(不誠實等)。***(be/become/feel) ~ about/of sb/sth,*** have suspicions about: 對某人(某物)感到懷疑: *The policeman became increasingly ~ of his movements.* 那警察對他的行動日益懷疑。**~·ly** *adv*

suss /sʌs ; sʌs/ *vt* [VP15B] **~ *sth out,*** (colloq) (俗) **1** discover. 發現。 **2** reconnoitre. 偵察。

sus·tain /səˈsteɪn ; səˈsten/ *vt* [VP6A] **1** keep from falling or sinking: 支撐;承住;承受得起: *Will this light shelf ~ (the weight of) all these books?* 這個輕便的書架承受得住所有這些書(的重量)嗎? **2** (enable to) keep up, maintain: (使能)維持;支持: *~ing food,* that gives strength; 維持體力的食物; *~ an argument/attempt;* 支持一項議論(一項嘗試); *~ a note,* continue to sing or play the note without faltering; 繼續(唱或奏)某一音符; *make a ~ed effort.* 作不斷的努力。 **3** suffer; undergo: 蒙受;遭受: *~ a defeat.* 遭受失敗。*The pilot ~ed severe injuries when his plane crashed.* 飛機墜毀時駕駛員受到重傷。 **4** (legal) uphold; give a decision in favour of: (法律)確認;准許: *The court ~ed his claim/~ed him in his claim.* 法庭准許他的要求。

sus·ten·ance /ˈsʌstɪnəns ; ˈsʌstənəns/ *n* [U] (nourishing quality of) food or drink; nourishment: 食物;飲料;營養: *There's more ~ in cocoa than in tea.* 可可比茶富有營養。

sut·tee /ˈsʌtiː ; sʌˈti/ *n* Hindu widow who cremated herself on the funeral pyre of her husband; practice (now illegal) of doing this. 印度昔時隨同丈夫火葬的寡婦;寡婦殉夫的習俗(現已非法)。

su·ture /ˈsuːtʃə(r) ; ˈsutʃɚ/ *n* seam formed in sewing up a wound; thread used for this. (傷口的)縫合;(縫合傷口所用的)縫線。

su·ze·rain /ˈsuːzəreɪn *US:* -rɪn ; ˈsuzərɪn/ *n* State or ruler in relation to a country over which it or he has some control or authority; (formerly) feudal overlord. 宗主國;宗主;(昔日的)封建大君主。**~ty** /ˈsuːzərəntɪ ; ˈsuzərɪntɪ/ *n*: 宗主權: *under the ~ty of.* 在…保護之下;在…宗主權下。

svelte /svelt ; svɛlt/ *adj* (F) (of a person) slender and graceful. (法)(指人)苗條而優雅的;婷婷裊裊的。

swab /swɒb ; swɑb/ *n* **1** mop or pad for cleaning, eg floors, decks. (擦地板、甲板等的)拖把;擦帚。 **2** sponge, bit of absorbent material, etc for medical use, eg taking a specimen from the throat for testing infection; specimen (eg of mucus) so taken: 醫療用的海綿、具吸收性物質等;拭子;藥籤(用拭子取供檢驗的)拭樣(如喉黏膜等): *take ~s from children suspected of having diphtheria.* 從疑似患有白喉的小孩(喉中)取拭樣供檢驗。□ *vt* (-bb-) [VP6A, 15B] clean with a ~: (以拖把等)擦淨;擦洗: *~ down the decks;* 用拖把擦洗甲板; *~ up water that has been upset on the floor.* 用擦帚把打翻在地板上的水拖乾。

swaddle /ˈswɒdl ; ˈswɑdl̩/ *vt* [VP6A] bind (a baby) with long narrow strips of cloth (as was formerly the custom). 以襁褓包裹(嬰兒)(如昔日風俗所為);縛裹。 **ˈswaddling-clothes,** the strips of cloth used: 襁褓: *still in his swaddling-clothes,* (fig) still not free from restraining influences. (喻)仍在襁褓中;仍受束縛或支配。

swag /swæg ; swæg/ *n* [U] **1** (sl) stolen goods; things obtained dishonestly. (俚)贓物;不正當所得物。**2** (Australia) bundle of personal belongings carried by a vagrant. (澳洲)流浪漢隨身攜帶的捆紮物。

swag·ger /ˈswægə(r) ; ˈswægɚ/ *vi* [VP2A, C] walk or behave in a self-important or self-satisfied manner. 自大地或自我滿足地行走或舉止;裝模作樣;擺架子。□ *n* ~ing walk or way of behaving: 裝模作樣;擺架子: *with a ~.* 裝模作樣地。□ *adj* (sl) very chic. (俚)非常時髦的;非常別緻的。**~er** *n*

swain /sweɪn ; swen/ *n* (poet or archaic) young rustic man (esp regarded as a lover): (詩或古)年輕的鄉下人(尤指被當作情郎者): *lasses and their ~s;* 女孩子和她們的情郎; (joc) lover. (謔)愛人。

swal·low¹ /ˈswɒləʊ ; ˈswɑlo/ *n* kinds of small, swift-flying insect-eating bird with a forked tail, which migrates to warm countries, eg to England every summer, and is associated with the beginning of summer. 燕子(體小、飛行迅速、食昆蟲的小鳥,尾部分叉,徙棲溫暖處,如夏季遷徙至英格蘭,故在英國燕子使人聯想到初夏)。⇨ the illus at bird. 參看 bird 之插圖。***One ~ doesn't make a summer,*** (prov) It is unwise to form a judgement on the basis of a single instance. (諺)一燕不成夏(僅憑一個事例卽下判斷是不智的)。 **ˈ~ dive** *n* dive with the arms outspread till close to the water. 燕子式跳水(跳起時兩手分開,近水時合攏)。 **ˈ~-tailed** *adj* (of butterflies, birds) with a deeply forked tail; (of a man's coat) with long tails (as of an evening dress coat). (指蝴蝶,鳥類)尾巴分叉長的;(指男服)燕尾形式的(如晚禮服)。

swal·low² /ˈswɒləʊ ; ˈswɑlo/ *vt, vi* [VP6A, 15B, 2C] **1 ~ *(up),*** cause or allow to go down the throat: 吞;嚥: *~ one's food,* eat it quickly; 吞嚥食物(很快地吃); work the muscles of the throat as when ~ing sth (to give relief to some kind of emotion): 吞嚥般活動喉部肌肉;忍氣吞聲: *He ~ed hard,* eg as if ~ing an insult; 他強忍下去(如似將侮辱吞下); ⇨ 3 below. 參看下列第3義。 **2 ~ *(up),*** take in; exhaust; cause to disappear; use up: 吞沒;耗盡;使消失;用罄: *earnings that were ~ed up by lawyers' bills.* 被律師費用耗盡的收入。*The earth seemed to ~ them up,* They suddenly disappeared. 地球好像把他們吞沒了(他們突然不見了)。*The aircraft was ~ed (up) in the clouds.* 飛機沒入雲中。 **3** (fig uses) (比喻用法) *~ an insult/affront,* accept it meekly; 忍受侮辱(無禮); *~ sth whole,* believe it without argument, doubt; 囫圇吞棗(輕易相信某事物); *~ one's words,* take them back, express regret for them; 取消前言; *~ a story,* believe it too easily; 輕信一個故事; *~ the bait,* (of a person) accept a proposal, an offer, etc made to tempt one to do sth. (指人)上當;上鉤。□ *n* act of ~ing; amount ~ed at one time. 吞;嚥;一吞之量。

swam /swæm ; swæm/ *pt* of swim.

swami /ˈswɑːmɪ ; ˈswɑmɪ/ *n* Hindu religious teacher; (loosely) mystic, yogi. 印度教的教師;(非嚴格用法)神秘主義者;瑜伽信徒。

swamp /swɒmp ; swɑmp/ *n* [C, U] (area of) soft wet land; marsh. 濕地;沼地;沼澤;沼澤區。□ *vt* **1** [VP6A] flood, soak, with water: 淹水;淹沒;浸在水中;使覆水而沉沒: *A big wave ~ed the boat.* 一個巨浪淹沒了那隻小舟。*Everything in the boat was ~ed.* 船上的東西都浸水了。 **2** [VP14] **~ *with,*** (fig) overwhelm: (喻)使困窘;使應接不暇;使忙得不可開交: *We are ~ed with work.* 我們被工作壓得透不過氣來。*The firm is ~ed with orders,* ie for their goods. 大量訂單使那家商行應接不暇。**~y** *adj* (-ier, -iest).

swan /swɒn ; swɑn/ *n* large, graceful, long-necked (usu white) water-bird. 天鵝(通常為白色)。⇨ the illus at water. 參看 water 之插圖。**ˈ~ dive,** (US) (美) = swallow-dive. **ˈ~-song** *n* (from the old belief that a swan sang sweetly when about to die) last performance, appearance, work before death of a poet, musician, etc. 天鵝之歌;(卽)詩人、音樂家等的最後演出、出現或其最後的作品等(此典來自古老的傳說,謂天鵝將死時,發悅耳的鳴聲);絕筆;臨終作品等。**ˈ~'s-down** *n* [U] **(a)** soft underfeathers of ~s. 天鵝的軟絨毛。 **(b)** kind of thick cotton cloth with a soft nap on one side. 一種單面有絨毛的厚棉布;棉法蘭絨;天鵝絨布。□ *vi* (-nn-) [VP2C] (colloq) (俗) ~ ***off/around, etc,*** move, go in a leisured, often aimless manner, esp of a privileged person or one who need not work: 優閒地走動;優哉游哉地閒逛;優游度日(尤指擁有特權者,或無須工作者): *I suppose you're ~ning off to Paris for the weekend.* 我想你週末要到巴黎去優游一番。*The boys are ~ning around Austria on a mountaineering holiday.* 在登山假日裡那些男孩在奧地利四處漫遊。

swank /swæŋk ; swæŋk/ *vi* [VP2A, C] (colloq) swagger; behave or talk in a boastful way; show off. (俗)裝模作樣;擺架子;炫耀。□ *n* [U] ~ing behaviour: 裝模作樣;擺架子;炫耀: *wear a gold wristwatch just for ~;* 僅為炫耀而戴金手錶; [C] person who ~s. 裝模作樣的人;炫耀者。 **~y** *adj* smart; characteristic of a person who ~s: 時髦的;炫耀的;裝模作樣的: *a ~y sports car;* 時髦的跑車; *Jill and her ~y friends.* 姬兒和她那些時髦的朋友們。

swap /swɒp ; swɑp/ *vt, vi* (-pp-) = swop.

sward /swɔːd ; swɔrd/ *n* [U] (liter) turf. (文)草土;草地。

swarm¹ /swɔːm ; swɔrm/ *n* [C] colony, large number, of insects, birds, etc moving about together: (昆蟲,鳥等的)大羣: *a ~ of ants/locusts;* 一大羣螞蟻(蝗蟲); *a ~ of bees,* cluster of honeybees when migrating with a queen bee to establish a new colony; 分封中的蜂羣(隨一蜂王遷徙建立新巢者); *~s of children in the parks.* 在公園裏的一羣羣的孩子們。□ *vi* **1** [VP2A] (of bees) move or go in large numbers round a queen bee for emigration to a new colony. (指蜜蜂)隨蜂王遷徙建立新巢;分封。 **2** [VP3A] ***be ~ing with; ~ with,*** (of places) be overrun or crowded: (指地方)充滿;擁擠: *The beaches were ~ing with bathers.* 海灘上擠滿了作海水浴的人們。*The stables ~ed with flies.* 馬廐裏到處都是蒼蠅。 **3** [VP2C] be present in large numbers; move in a ~: 羣集;蜂擁而進: *When the rain started the crowd ~ed back into the hotel.* 雨一開始下,人羣即擁回旅社。*Beggars ~ed round the rich tourists.* 乞丐成羣地圍在有錢的觀光客的四周。

swarm² /swɔːm ; swɔrm/ *vt* [VP6A, 15B] ***~ (up),*** climb by clinging with the arms and legs. 抱着…往上爬;用手臂及腿攀住…往上爬。

swarthy /ˈswɔːðɪ ; ˈswɔrðɪ/ *adj* having a dark complexion. 黑皮膚的;黝黑的。

swash·buck·ler /ˈswɒʃbʌklə(r) ; ˈswɑʃˌbʌklɚ/ *n* bully; boastful fellow who behaves recklessly. 暴漢;欺凌弱小者;輕率而浮誇之徒。 **swash·buck·ling** /ˈswɒʃbʌklɪŋ ; ˈswɑʃˌbʌklɪŋ/ *adj* reckless and boastful. 輕率而浮誇的。□ *n* [U] behaviour of a ~. 虛張聲勢;輕率而浮誇。

swas·tika /ˈswɒstɪkə ; ˈswɑstɪkə/ *n* [C] kind of cross emblematic of the sun, good fortune or Nazism. (象徵太陽、好運或納粹主義的)卍字;万字形。⇨ the illus at cross. 參看 cross 之插圖。

swat /swɒt ; swɑt/ *vt* (-tt-) slap with a flat object: (用平物)拍打: *~ a fly.* 拍蒼蠅。□ *n* **1** slap of this kind: 拍打;拍擊: *Give that fly a ~.* 給那隻蒼蠅一拍。 **2** flexible device on a handle for ~ting (flies, etc): 用來拍打之物;蒼蠅拍: *a ˈfly-~* (also 亦作 *ˈfly-swatter*). 蒼蠅拍。

swath /swɔːθ ; swɑθ/, **swathe** /sweɪð ; sweð/ *n* **1** ridge of grass, wheat, barley, etc lying after being cut. 刈下的一行草、小麥、大麥等。 **2** space left clear after one passage of a mower. 一刈的面積;刈幅。

swathe¹ /sweɪð ; sweð/ *vt* [VP6A, 15A] wrap or bind up: 包裹;捲;綁: *He came out of hospital with his leg still ~d in bandages.* 他離開了醫院,腿仍裹在繃帶中。□ *n* bandage; wrapping. 繃帶;包布。

swathe² /sweɪð ; sweð/ *n* ⇨ swath.

sway /sweɪ ; swe/ *vi, vt* **1** [VP2A, C, 6A, 15A] (cause to) move, first to one side and then to the other; swing: (使)搖擺;(使)擺動: *The branches of the trees were ~ing in the wind.* 樹枝在風中搖曳。*Do you sway your hips when you walk?* 你走路時擺動臀部嗎? **2** [VP6A] control or influence; govern the direction of: 控制;影響;支配: *~ed by his feelings;* 受他感情的支配; *a speech that ~ed the voters.* 一篇影響選民決定的演說。□ *n* [U] **1** ~ing movement. 搖擺;擺動。 **2** rule or control: 統治;支配: *the peoples who were under the ~ of Rome,* were ruled by Rome (in ancient times). (古代)被羅馬帝國統治的諸民族。

swear /sweə(r) ; swɛr/ *vt, vi* (*pt* swore /swɔː(r) ; swor/, *pp* sworn /swɔːn ; sworn/) **1** [VP6A, 7A, 9] say solemnly or emphatically: 鄭重地說;強調;發誓: *He swore to tell the truth/swore that he would tell the truth.* 他發誓要說實話。 *I could have sworn that there was somebody in the next room,* I felt certain of this. 我敢說(當時)隔壁房間裏有人。 **2** [VP6A, 15A, B] take an oath; cause (sb) to take an oath. 宣誓;使(某人)宣誓或立誓。***~ sb in,*** cause him to take the oath of office. 使某人宣誓就職。***~ sb to secrecy,*** make him ~ to keep sth secret. 使某人誓守秘密。 ***~ a witness,*** administer the oath to him. 使證人宣誓。***sworn enemies,*** enemies who can never be reconciled. 不共戴天的仇敵。***sworn friends/brothers,*** very close friends. 莫逆之交(結拜兄弟)。 **3** [VP 3A] ***~ by sth,*** **(a)** appeal to as a witness or witnesses: 對…發誓: *~ by all the gods that...;* 對諸神發誓(請諸神證明); *~ by all that one holds dear.* 在所有親人面前發誓。 **(b)** (colloq) use and have great confidence in: (俗)使用並深信;極其信賴: *He ~s by quinine for malaria.* 他深信奎寧可以治好瘧疾。***~ off sth,*** (colloq) declare that one will give up, stop using: (俗)立誓棄絕或停止用: *He swore off smoking when the doctors said it caused lung cancer.* 醫生們說吸烟能引起肺癌時,他立誓戒烟。***~ to sth,*** say emphatically: 強調地說;斷然地說: *He swore to having paid for the goods,* said emphatically that he had done so (when accused of not having done so). 他斷然地說已經付清該貨款。*I think I've met that man somewhere but I wouldn't ~ to it,* am not very confident of having met him. 我想我曾在什麼地方見過那個人,但是我不太敢確定。 **4** [VP6A, 14] make an affirmation after having taken an oath: 立誓後確定;起誓證實: *~ an accusation/a charge against sb;* 立誓指控某人; *sworn evidence/statements.* 立誓指證(陳述)。 **5** [VP2A, B, C, 3A, 22] ***~ (at sb),*** use obscene etc words to insult, or for emphasis (⇨ section on *stylistic values* in introduction): 咒罵;詬罵(參看序文中的'文體標準'): *The foreman swore at his workers.* 工頭咒罵工人。*He gave vent to his anger by ~ing loudly.* 他高聲咒罵以發洩他的憤怒。*He swore himself hoarse,* continued ~ing until he was hoarse. 他一直到嗓子嘶啞才停止了咒罵。 **ˈ~-word** *n* word used in ~ing. 詛咒;罵人話;褻瀆之語。 **~er** *n* person who ~s(5). 咒罵者;詬罵者。

sweat /swet ; swɛt/ *n* **1** [U] moisture that is given off by the body through the skin: 汗: *wipe the ~ off one's brow.* 揩去額上的汗。 **ˈ~-band** *n* **(a)** band of absorbent material inside a hat. (帽子裏的)吸汗箍;汗圈。 **(b)** cloth tied round the forehead, wrist, etc to absorb ~. (繞在前額、手腕等處的)吸汗帶。 **ˈ~ shirt** *n* cotton sweater with sleeves, worn esp by athletes before and after exercise. 長袖棉線衫(尤指運動員所穿者)。 **2** **a ~,** condition of a person or animal (esp a horse) when covered with ~: 發汗;出汗;滿身汗: *be in a ~.* 滿身大汗。*They say that a good ~ will cure a cold.* 人們說好好發一身汗可以治愈感冒。 ***be in a cold ~,*** in a state of fear or anxiety. 發冷汗;冒冷汗;處於恐懼或焦慮狀態。 ***all of a ~,*** (colloq) wet with ~; (fig) anxious or frightened. (俗)汗濕的;(喻)焦慮的;害怕的。 **3** (colloq, *sing* only) hard work: (俗,僅用單數)苦工;辛苦工作: *This job is a frightful ~.* 這工作極為辛苦。 **4** [C] ***an old ~,***

(sl) soldier with many years' service; (by extension) person with many years' experience of his job. (俚)老兵;(引伸義)老手;有多年經驗的工作者。**5** [U] moisture on the surface of anything, eg condensation on an inner wall. (任何東西表面上的)水氣、水珠或濕氣(如內壁上凝聚者)。□ *vt, vi* **1** [VP 2A] give out ~(1, 5): 出汗;結成水珠;發出水氣或濕氣: *The long hot climb made him ~.* 長距離的激烈攀登使他出汗。 **2** [VP6A, 15B] give out (sth that comes out of a surface). 使發出;使滲出;使從表面發出。**~ *blood,*** (fig) work like a slave. (喩)像奴隸般地工作。**~ *out a cold,*** get rid of it by ~ing. 發汗醫治感冒。 **3** [VP6A] (cause to) ~: (使)出汗;(使)流汗: *The doctor ~ed his patient.* 醫生使他的病人出汗。*Don't ~ your horse.* 不要使馬流汗。 **4** [VP6A, 2A, C] (cause to) work hard: (使)辛苦工作;(使)努力工作: *~ one's workers.* 使工人們辛苦工作。**~ed goods,** produced by ~ed labour. 廉價勞工的產品。**~ed labour,** the labour of underpaid workers. 工資低微的勞工;廉價勞工。**'~-shop** *n* workshop where ~ed labour is used. 雇用廉價勞工的工廠。**~y** *adj* (-ier, -iest) **1** damp with ~: 汗濕的;多汗的: *~y underwear.* 汗濕的內衣。**2** causing one to ~: 使出汗的;費力的: *~y work.* 費力的工作。

sweater /'swetə(r); 'swɛtɚ/ *n* knitted garment usu of thick wool with long sleeves, worn by athletes before or after exercise; similar woolly garment (not necessarily thick or heavy) worn for warmth. 厚運動衫;毛線衫;衞生衣。⇨ jersey, jumper, pullover.

swede /swi:d; swid/ *n* kind of turnip. 蕪菁;瑞典蕪菁。

sweep¹ /swi:p; swip/ *n* **1 '~ *(-up/-out),*** act of sweeping with, or as with, a broom, etc: 掃;掃除;打掃: *Give the room a good ~.* 把這房間好好打掃一下。*Let's have a thorough ~-up/out.* 讓我們來一次大掃除。***make a clean ~ (of sth),*** get rid of (what is unwanted) completely: 清除;清掃;全部去掉: *They made a clean ~ of their old furniture and replaced it with brand new pieces.* 他們把舊傢俱全部丟掉,換成全新的。*In forming his new Cabinet the Prime Minister has made a clean ~.* 首相組織新內閣時,除掉全部舊閣員。**2** sweeping movement: 掃動;揮動;打掃的動作: *with a ~ of his arm/scythe.* 他的手臂(鐮刀)揮了一揮。 **3** space covered by a sweeping movement; range of such a movement: 一揮所及的空間;一揮的距離或範圍:*The knight killed everyone who came within the ~ of his sword.* 那武士殺死了他的刀刃所及的每一個人。**4** long unbroken stretch, esp curved, on a road, river, coast, etc or of sloping land: (路、河、海岸等的)彎曲部分;綿亙的區域;一片地區: *a fine ~ of country.* 一片美麗的鄉野。**5** steady uninterrupted flow: 穩定不斷的流動: *the ~ of the tide.* 潮的流動。**6 ('chimney-)~,** man whose work is sweeping soot from chimneys. 清掃烟囱者;烟囱清掃夫。 **7** long oar worked by a rower who stands, for steering or moving a boat, eg a sailing-boat when there is no wind. (立划槳手所操作的)長槳;大橈。**8** long pole mounted as a lever for raising a bucket from a well. 自井中提起水桶用的長槓桿。 **9 '~ (-stake),** form of gambling on horse-races, the money staked by all those who take part being divided among those who have drawn numbered tickets for the winners (usu the first three). 賽馬的賭金獨得制 (通常由押注前三名賽馬的勝利者分之)。

sweep² /swi:p; swip/ *vt, vi* (*pt, pp* swept /swept; swɛpt/) **1** [VP6A, 15A, B, 22, 2A] **~ *sth (from sth); ~ sth (free) of sth; ~ sth up/away, etc,*** clear (dust, dirt, etc) away with, or as with, a brush or broom; clean by doing this: 掃除(塵、土等);清掃;清除;打掃: *~ the dust from the carpets;* 清除地毯上的塵土;*~ the carpets/the floor/the yard;* 打掃(地毯,地板,院子); *~ the chimney (free of soot);* 掃除烟囱(的煤灰); *~ up dead leaves from the garden paths;* 掃除園中小徑的枯葉; *~ up the crumbs;* 清掃碎屑; *~ the crumbs under the carpet/into a corner/into a dustpan.* 清掃地毯下面的碎屑(把碎屑掃到角落裏,掃進畚箕)。 **2** [VP6A, 15A, B] clean or clear away as with a broom; push away: 似用掃帚清掃; 掃蕩; 清理; 推開; 冲掉: *~ the seas of pirates.* 掃蕩海盜。*The current swept the logs along.* 水流冲走了木材。*The wind swept my hat off/the clouds away.* 風吹掉了我的帽子(吹散了雲)。*Many bridges were swept away by the floods.* 很多橋梁被洪水冲斷了。*We were almost swept off our feet by the waves.* 我們幾乎被浪冲倒了。**~ *all before one,*** have complete uninterrupted success. 所向披靡;大獲全勝。**~ *the board,*** **(a)** win all the money on the table when gambling. 横掃臺面;(賭博時)贏去臺面上所有的錢。**(b)** win all the prizes; have every possible success. 囊括所有獎品;大獲全勝。***be swept off one's feet,*** (fig) be overcome by feeling, filled with enthusiasm, eg an audience by a great singer. (喩)被弄得神魂顚倒;變得如醉如癡(如聽衆之被某一偉大歌唱家所感動)。**,swept-'back** *adj* **(a)** (of aircraft wings) attached so that they are at an acute angle to the axis of the aircraft. (指飛機機翼)與飛機軸線呈銳角安裝的;後斜的。 **(b)** (of hair) arranged so that it is combed or brushed away from the face. (指頭髮)梳向後方的。 **3** [VP2C, 6A] pass over or along, esp so as to overcome obstacles; move quickly over or with a rush: 冲過;掃過;掠過;疾馳;馳過: *A huge wave swept over the deck.* 巨浪掠過甲板。 *A blizzard swept the country.* 大風雪横掃全國。*The big tanks swept over the enemy's trenches.* 大型戰車衝過敵人的戰壕。*The wind swept along the street.* 風吹過街道。**4** [VP2C] move in a dignified or stately manner; go majestically: 威風凜凜地行走;昂然地走: *She swept out of the room.* 她昂然地走出房間。*The big car swept up the drive to the entrance of the palace.* 那輛大型轎車威風凜凜地駛過車道抵達皇宮大門。**5** [VP2C] extend in an unbroken line, curve or expanse: 綿亘;伸展;延展: *The road ~s round the lake.* 這條路環湖延伸。*The coast ~s northwards in a wide curve.* 海岸向北方呈大弧形展開。 **6** [VP6A] pass over (as if) to examine or survey: (似)掃視;環視;周覽: *The searchlights swept the sky.* 探照燈掃索天空。*Her eyes swept the room.* 她的眼睛掃視那房間。 **7** [VP6A] move along lightly and quickly: 輕快地移動;拂;輕掠過: *His fingers swept the keys of the piano.* 他的手指在鋼琴鍵盤上輕快地移動。*Her dress swept the ground.* 她的衣服在地面拖曳。 **8** [VP12A] make (a bow, curtsey) with a ~ing movement: 匆匆或草草地鞠(躬)或行(禮): *She swept him a curtsey.* 她走過時對他匆匆行一屈膝禮。**~er** *n* **1** person or thing that ~s: 掃除之人或物: *'street ~ers;* 清道夫; *a 'carpet-~er.* 地毯掃除器。**2** (football) defender who covers the backs, tackling any opponent who passes them. (橄欖球)後衞(防守球門附近區域、阻止對方球員帶球進入該區者)。**~ing** *adj* far-reaching; taking in very much: 範圍廣大的;包括很廣的;概括的: *~ing changes/reforms;* 澈底的改變(改革); *a ~ing statement/generalization,* with no limitations or exceptions; 概括的敍述(歸納); *a ~ing* (= complete) *victory;* 全勝; *~ing* (= very great) *reductions in prices,* eg at a sale. 大減價。**~ing·ly** *adv* **~ings** *n pl* dust, rubbish, scraps, etc, collected by ~ing: 掃集物;掃攏的塵屑;垃圾;廢物堆: *a heap of 'street ~ings.* 一堆街頭垃圾。

sweet /swi:t; swit/ *adj* **1** (opp of *sour*) tasting like sugar or honey: (爲 sour 之相反字)甜的;甘的: *Do you like your tea ~?* 你喜歡你的茶加糖嗎? *It tastes ~,* has a ~ taste. 這東西味道是甜的。***have a ~ tooth,*** like things that taste ~. 愛吃甜食。**~ *wine,*** wine with a ~ or fruity flavour (contrasted with *dry* wine). 甜酒(帶甜味或水果味道者,

與 dry wine 相對)。 **2** fresh and pure: 新鮮而純淨的: *~ milk;* 鮮奶; *keep a room clean and ~;* 保持房間的清新; *~ breath;* 清新的呼吸; *~ water,* fit to drink (contrasted with brackish water, etc). 淨水;清水;飲用水(與帶鹹味的水等相對)。**3** having a fragrant smell, like roses: 芬芳的;芳香的: *The garden is ~ with thyme.* 園子裏有麝香草的芬芳氣味。*Don't the roses smell ~!* 多芳香的玫瑰花! ˌ**~-'scented** *adj* having a ~ smell. 芳香的;芬芳的。 **4** pleasant or attractive: 可愛的;漂亮的;有吸引力的: *a ~ face;* 討人喜歡的臉; *a ~ voice;* 悅耳的聲音; *a ~ singer,* sb having a ~ voice; 聲音悅耳的歌唱家; *a ~ little girl;* 漂亮的小女孩; *a ~ temper;* 溫和的性情; ˌ*~-'tempered.* 性情溫和的。*It was ~ to hear people praise me so much.* 眞高興聽到人們這樣稱讚我。*What a ~ little poodle you have!* 你這隻小獅子狗眞可愛! *Isn't the baby ~!* 多可愛的娃娃! **5** (phrases) (片語) ***at one's own ~ will,*** as and when one pleases, with no one to give orders or advice. 隨自己喜歡;任某人自便。***be ~ on (sb),*** (colloq) very fond of, in love with. (俗)非常喜歡或愛上(某人)。 **6** (compounds) (複合字) **'~·bread** *n* pancreas of a calf or lamb used as food. (小牛或小羊的)膵;胰臟(供食用者)。 ˌ**~-'briar/-'brier** *n* wild rose with ~-scented leaves and single pink flowers. 野薔薇(葉芳香,開淡紅色單瓣花)。**'~·heart** *n* either of a pair of lovers: 愛人;情人;戀人: *David and his ~heart.* 大衞和他的愛人。**'~·meat** *n* piece of ~-tasting food (usu made of sugar or chocolate); fruit preserved in sugar. 糖果(通常用糖或巧克力做成);甜品;蜜餞。 ˌ**~ 'pea** *n* garden plant (an annual) with brightly-coloured, ~-scented flowers. 麝香豌豆;香黎豆(一年生園藝植物,花芳香而色艷)。**'~ potato** *n* tropical climbing plant with thick edible roots, cooked as a vegetable. 紅薯;甘薯。 ˌ**~ 'william** *n* garden plant with flowers in close clusters, often parti-coloured. 美洲石竹(園藝植物,花叢集,色常斑駁)。□ *n* [C] **1** (US 美 = *candy*) small piece of ~-tasting food (eg boiled flavoured sugar, chocolate, etc). 糖果;甜食(糖,巧克力等)。 **2** (US 美 = *dessert*) dish of ~ food (eg a pudding, tart, jelly, trifle, etc) as one of the courses of a meal. (In GB *dessert* usu means a course of fresh fruit, nuts, etc.) 飯後甜食(布丁、餡餅、凍子、蛋糕等,包括於正餐的一道食品)。(在英國, dessert 通常指餐末上的新鮮水果,堅果等)。**3** (*pl*) delights; pleasures: (複)快樂;歡樂: *taste the ~s of success;* 嘗到成功的樂趣; *enjoy the ~s of life while one is young.* 年輕時享受人生的歡樂。 **4** (as a form of address) darling: (稱呼語)親愛的;愛人: *Yes, my ~.* 是的,我親愛的。**~·ly** *adv* **~·ness** *n* **~·ish** /-ɪʃ ; -ɪʃ/ *adv* rather ~. 略甜的;有點可愛的。**~en** /'swi:tn ; 'switn/ *vt, vi* [VP6A, 2A] make or become ~. 使或變甜;使或變香;使或變可愛等。➪ pill(1). **~·en·ing** /'swi:tnɪŋ ; 'switn̩ɪŋ/ *n* [C, U] that which ~ens; sth ~ used in cooking, etc. 使甜之物;用於烹調等的甜東西。

swell /swel ; swɛl/ *vi, vt* (*pt* ~ed /sweld ; swɛld/, *pp* swollen /'swəʊlən ; 'swolən/, rarely ~ed) **1** [VP6A, 14, 15B, 2A, C] ~ ***(up) (with),*** (cause to) become greater in volume, thickness or force: (使)增大,增厚或增强; 膨脹; 腫起: *Wood often ~s when wet.* 木材浸濕後常會膨脹。*The river was swollen with melted snow.* 河水因融雪而上漲。 *His face began to ~ up,* eg from toothache. 他的臉孔開始腫起(如因牙痛)。*He/His heart was ~ing with pride.* 他驕傲自大。*The boy's eyes were swollen up with tears.* 那男孩的眼裏充滿了淚水。*These small items help to ~ the total.* 這些小項目使總額增加了。***have/suffer from a swollen head,*** be conceited. 自負;自大。Hence, 由此產生, ˌ**swollen-'headed** *adj* **2** [VP2A, C, 6A, 15B] ~ ***(out),*** have, cause to have, a curved surface: (使)隆起;鼓脹; (使)有弧形表面: *The sails ~ed out in the wind.* 船帆迎風鼓起。*The wind ~ed the sails.* 風使船帆鼓脹。□ *n* **1** gradual increase in the volume of sound: 音量逐漸增加: *the ~ of an organ.* 風琴聲音漸響。 **2** (*sing* only) slow rise and fall of the sea's surface after a storm (with large but unbroken waves): (僅用單數) 暴風雨後海上的滾滾大浪; 潮湧: *There was a heavy ~ after the storm.* 暴風雨後有滾滾的大浪。 **3** (US colloq) smartly dressed person; person of distinction or ability: (美俗) 衣著入時的人;優秀人士;有才能的人: *What a ~ you look in that new suit!* 你穿起那套新衣多帥! ***come the heavy ~ over sb,*** (sl) try to appear great and important and in this way impress him. (俚)圖示顯貴以打動某人。□ *adj* (US colloq) (美俗) **1** smart, fashionable: 漂亮的;時髦的: *Who are your ~ friends?* 你那些時髦的朋友是誰? *He took her to a ~ dinner party.* 他帶了她去參加一個講究的餐會。 **2** excellent; first-rate: 極好的;第一流的: *He's a ~ tennis player.* 他是第一流的網球手。**~·ing** *n* [U, C] **1** swollen place on the body, eg the result of a knock or blow or toothache. 身體上的腫處(如因碰撞、打擊或因牙痛所致)。 **2** increase in size. 增大;加大;脹大;膨脹。

swel·ter /'sweltə(r) ; 'swɛltɚ/ *vi* [VP2A] be uncomfortably warm; suffer from the heat: 酷熱;熱得發昏;中暑: *a ~ing hot day.* 酷熱的一天。

swept /swept ; swɛpt/ *pt, pp* of sweep[2].

swerve /swɜ:v ; swɝv/ *vi, vt* [VP2A, C, 4A, 6A] (cause to) change direction suddenly: (使)突然轉向: *The car ~d to avoid knocking the boy down.* 那轎車突然轉向,以免撞着那男孩。*Don't ~ from your purpose.* 不要突然改變你的目標。□ *n* [C] swerving movement; (esp) turn or curve of a ball in the air. 突然轉向;逸出常軌;(尤指)球在空中的轉動或弧線。

swift[1] /swɪft ; swɪft/ *adj* (-er, -est) quick; fast; prompt: 快的;迅速的;敏捷的: *~ of foot;* (liter) able to run fast; (文)能跑得快的; *a ~ revenge;* 迅速的報復; *~ to anger,* (formal) quickly becoming angry. (正式用語)易於發怒的。**~·ly** *adv* **~·ness** *n*

swift[2] /swɪft ; swɪft/ *n* sorts of small insect-eating bird with long wings, similar to a swallow. (褐)雨燕(食蟲小鳥,翼長,似燕)。➪ the illus at bird. 參看 bird 之插圖。

swig /swɪg ; swɪg/ *vt, vi* (-gg-) [VP6A, 15B, 2A, C] ~ ***(down/off),*** (colloq) take drinks of: (俗)飲;大口喝: *~ging beer;* 飲啤酒; *~ off a glass of rum.* 飲完一杯蘭酒。□ *n* long drink: 長飲;痛飲;牛飲: *take a ~ at a bottle of beer,* have a drink direct from the bottle. 拿著整瓶啤酒猛喝。

swill /swɪl ; swɪl/ *vt, vi* **1** [VP6A, 15B] ~ ***sth (out),*** rinse; wash by pouring liquid into, over or through: 涮;冲洗;冲涮: *~ out a dirty tub.* 冲洗髒盆子。 **2** [VP6A] (colloq) drink greedily: (俗)暴飲;大喝: *The workmen were ~ing tea when they ought to have been working.* 工人們在應該工作的時候大喝其茶。□ *n* **1** [C] rinsing: 涮;冲洗;冲涮: *Give the bucket a good ~ out.* 把那隻桶好好冲洗一下。 **2** [U] waste food, mostly liquid, eg as given to pigs. 殘食;泔脚;潲水(如用以餵猪者)。

swim /swɪm ; swɪm/ *vi, vt* (*pt* swam /swæm ; swæm/, *pp* swum /swʌm ; swʌm/) (-mm-) **1** [VP 2A, B, C] move the body through water by using arms, legs, fins, the tail, etc: 游泳; 游水: *Fishes ~.* 魚游水。*We swam all afternoon.* 我們游泳游了一個下午。*Let's go ~ming.* 咱們去游泳吧。*He swam across the river.* 他游過了那條河。*When the boat sank they had to ~ for it,* save themselves by ~ming. 小船下沉的時候,他們必須游水逃生。 ***~ with the tide/the stream,*** do as the majority do (taking the easiest course). 順應潮流。 **'~-ming-bath/-pool** *n* indoor or outdoor, large or small, pool for ~ming in. (室內或室外的,大的或小的)游泳池。**'~·ming costume,** **'~-suit** *nn* garment worn for ~ming. 游泳衣;泳裝。**'~·ming-trunks** *n pl* garment worn by boys and men for ~ming. (男用)游泳褲。 **2** [VP6A] cross by

~ming: 游過;游泳橫渡;從一邊游至另一邊: *~ the English Channel;* 游過英吉利海峽; take part in (a race) in this way; compete with (sb) in this way: 參加(游泳比賽);與(某人)作游泳比賽: *~ a race;* 參加游泳比賽; *~ two lengths of the pool;* 在游泳池中來回游了一趟; cause (an animal) to ~: 使(動物)游泳: *~ one's horse across a river.* 使馬游過河。 **3** [VP3A] *~ **with**; ~ **in/on**,* be covered or overflowing (with); be (as if) floating (in or on): 覆滿;盈溢;漂浮;浸;泡: *eyes ~ming with tears;* 淚珠盈眶的眼睛; *meat ~ming in gravy;* 浸泡在濃汁中的肉; *strawberries ~ming in cream.* 浸泡在乳脂中的草莓。 **4** [VP2A] seem to be moving round and round; have a dizzy feeling: 似在轉動;暈眩;眼花: *The room swam before his eyes.* 他感覺房子在他眼前轉動。 *His head swam.* 他的頭感到暈眩。□ *n* **1** act or period of ~ming: 游泳;游泳的期間: *have/go for a ~.* 去游泳。 **2 the ~,** main current of affairs. 潮流;時勢。***be in/out of the ~,*** be/not be taking part in, aware of, current affairs. 合乎(不合)時代潮流。**~·mer** *n* person who ~s. 游泳者。**~·ming·ly** *adv* easily and without trouble: 容易地;順利地: *We're getting along ~mingly.* 我們進展順利。*Everything went ~mingly,* without obstruction or delay of any kind. 一切進行順利。

swindle /ˈswɪndl; ˈswɪndḷ/ *vt, vi* [VP6A, 14] *~ **sth out of sb; ~ sb out of sth,*** cheat; get (money, etc out of sb) by cheating: 行騙;欺騙;詐取(錢財等): *~ money out of sb;* 詐取某人錢財; *~ sb out of his money.* 詐取某人錢財。*Some people are easily ~d.* 有些人容易受詐欺。□ *n* [C] piece of swindling; sth sold, etc that is less valuable than it is described to be: 行騙;欺騙;騙人的假貨;名實不符的貨色: *This new radio set is a ~,* the quality of the sound is bad. 這種新的收音機是騙人的玩藝兒。**swin·dler** /ˈswɪndlə(r); ˈswɪndlɚ/ *n* person who ~s. 行騙者;欺騙者;詐欺者。

swine /swaɪn; swaɪn/ *n* (*pl* unchanged) (複數不變) **1** (old use, or liter) pig. (舊用法或文)豬。**ˈ~·herd** *n* man who (formerly) looked after ~ (when they were out in the woods, etc). (昔時的)牧豬人。 **2** ⚠ (abusive, derog) disgusting person. (諱)(罵人話,貶)豬玀;下流胚子;賤人。**swin·ish** /-ɪʃ; -ɪʃ/ *adj* beastly and disgusting. 像豬一樣的;討厭的;鄙賤的。

swing /swɪŋ; swɪŋ/ *vi, vt* (*pt, pp* swung /swʌŋ; swʌŋ/) **1** [VP2A, B, C, 6A, 15A, B, 22] (of sth having one end or one side fixed and the other free) move, cause to move, forwards and backwards or in a curve: (指一端固定,他端活動之物)(使)搖擺;(使)擺動: *His arms swung as he walked.* 他走路的時候擺動手臂。*He was ~ing his arms.* 他在擺動手臂。*The door swung shut/swung to.* 門關上了。*The big ape swung (itself) from branch to branch.* 那隻大猿猴在樹枝間盪來盪去。*~ **for sb/sth,*** (colloq) be hanged (for murder). (俗)(因謀殺而)被處絞刑。***no room to ~ a cat in,*** (of an enclosure) very small; having very little space for movement. (指範圍)非常狹小;很少活動餘地。*~ **the lead,*** ⇨ lead¹(3). **2** [VP6A, C] walk or run with a free easy movement (the arms ~ing freely): (手臂自由擺動而)輕快地走或跑: *The soldiers advanced at a ~ing trot.* 士兵們以輕快的步伐前進。 **3** [VP2A] dance to or play ~ music; (sl) be lively, gay and up-to-date. 演奏搖擺樂;(配合此樂而)跳搖擺舞;(俚)顯得活潑,快活和時髦。 **4** [VP2C, 15A, B] turn, cause to turn, in a curve: (使)旋轉;(使)廻轉;廻旋: *He swung* (= turned quickly) *round and faced his accusers.* 他迅速地轉身,面對指控他的人們。*The car swung round the corner.* 那輛轎車在街角轉彎。□ *n* **1** ~ing movement: 搖擺;擺動;旋轉;廻旋: *the ~ of the pendulum.* 鐘擺的擺動。 **2** strong rhythm. 强烈的節奏;韻律;旋律。***in full ~,*** active; in full operation. 活躍的;全力進行中。***go with a ~,*** **(a)** (of music, poetry) have a good rhythm. (指音樂,詩歌)有節奏地;節奏分明地。**(b)** (fig) (of an entertainment, event, etc) proceed smoothly, without delays, etc. (喻)(指表演,事件等)順利進行(未延緩等)。**~ (music),** (1930's) orchestral jazz, usu played by big bands. 搖擺樂(一種二十世紀三十年代的爵士樂,通常由大樂隊演奏)。 **3** [C] seat held by ropes or chains for ~ing on; act, period, of ~ing on such a seat. 鞦韆;打鞦韆;打鞦韆的時間。**~·ing** *adj* (sl) lively; gay; up-to-date; enjoyable. (俚)活潑的;歡樂的;時髦的;令人快樂的。

swinge /swɪndʒ; swɪndʒ/ *vt* (archaic) strike hard. (古)猛打;猛擊。**~·ing** *part adj* huge; very forcible: 巨大的;非常有力的: *~ing damages,* eg awarded by a judge in a law suit; 巨額的損害賠償金(如訴訟中經法官判與者); *~ing taxation.* 巨額的課稅。

swipe /swaɪp; swaɪp/ *vt* (colloq) (俗) **1** [VP6A, 15A, 3A] hit hard: 重擊;猛打: *The batsman ~d the ball into the grandstand.* 擊球員把球打進了大看臺。*He ~d at the ball and missed it.* 他向球猛擊,但未打中。 **2** [VP6A] (colloq, usu hum) steal. (俗,通常作詼諧語)偷;竊。□ *n* swinging blow: 重打;猛擊: *have/take a ~ at the ball.* 向球猛擊。

swirl /swɜːl; swɝl/ *vi, vt* [VP2C, 15B] (of water, air, etc) (cause to) move or flow at varying speeds, with twists and turns: (指水、空氣等)(使)渦旋而動;(使)起漩流: *dust ~ing about the streets;* 在街道上渦旋的塵土; carry (sth) *off, away,* in this way. 使(某物)渦旋而去;把(某物)打着旋帶走。□ *n* **1** ~ing movement; eddy: 渦旋的動作;旋渦;渦流: *a ~ of dust.* 一陣渦旋的塵土。 **2** (US) twist or curl: (美)扭曲;捲曲: *a hat with a ~ of lace round it.* 有一匝花邊圍繞的帽子。

swish /swɪʃ; swɪʃ/ *vt, vi* **1** [VP6A, 15B] *~ **sth (off),*** move (sth) through the air with a hissing or brushing sound; cut (sth off) in this way: 發瑟瑟聲地揮動(某物); 颼颼地揮動; 瑟瑟地或颼颼地弄斷(某物): *The horse ~ed its tail.* 那匹馬瑟瑟地揮動尾巴。*He ~ed his whip/~ed off the tops of the thistles with his whip.* 他颼颼地揮動鞭子(用鞭子抽斷薊叢的頂部)。 **2** [VP2A] make, move with, a sound like that of sth moving through the air: 作瑟瑟聲;颼颼地響;瑟瑟地動: *Her long silk dress ~ed as she came in.* 她進來的時候,她穿的絲質長服瑟瑟作響。□ *n* sound of, sound suggesting, sth being ~ed: (揮動某物時的) 瑟瑟聲; 颼颼聲; 咻咻聲: *We heard the ~ of a cane.* 我們聽到籐杖的抽打聲。□ *adj* (colloq) smart; expensive and fashionable: (俗)豪華的;時髦的;價錢很貴的: *a ~ restaurant.* 豪華而氣派的餐廳。

switch /swɪtʃ; swɪtʃ/ *n* [C] **1** device for making and breaking a connection at railway points (to allow trains to go from one track to another). (鐵路的)轉轍器;閘。**ˈ~·man** /-mən; -mən/ *n* (*pl* -men) man in charge of railway ~es. (鐵路的)轉轍手;搬閘夫。 **2** device for making and breaking an electric circuit: (電路的)開關: *a two-way ~,* one of a pair that can be used for turning electric current on or off from two points (eg at the bottom and the top of a staircase). 兩線開關; 雙路開關 (可在兩處接通或關閉電流的裝置,如樓梯上下皆可開關者)。**ˈ~·board** *n* panel with nu-

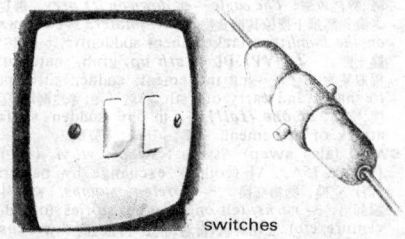

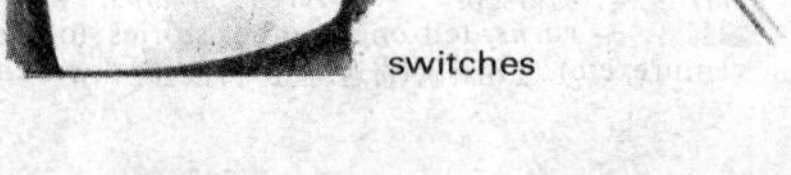

switches

merous ~es, esp for making connections by telephone or operating electric circuits. 電鍵板;交換機;(尤指)電話總機;配電板(或盤)。 **3** thin twig or easily bent shoot cut from a tree, eg as used for urging a horse on. (從樹上砍下的)枝條;軟枝;嫩枝(如用於策馬)。 **4** bunch of false hair used by a woman to make her hair appear thicker or longer. (女人的)假髮。 **5** **'~·back** *n* **(a)** *~back (railway)*, one that twists and turns up and down steep slopes, esp the kind seen in amusement parks (US 美 = *roller-coaster*). 在陡斜坡上迴旋升降的鐵道(尤指遊樂場之雲霄飛車)。 **(b)** *~back (road)*, road with numerous ups and downs. 多斜坡的道路; S形斜坡路。 **6** transfer; change-over: 調換;調職;改變: *a ~ from glass bottles to plastic cartons.* 把玻璃瓶換成塑膠盒。□ *vt, vi* **1** [VP15B] *~ **sth on/off**,* use a ~(2) to turn (electric current) on/off: 接通或切斷(電流);打開或關閉: *~ the light/radio, etc on.* 打開電燈(收音機等)。 *Don't ~ off yet, please.* 請暫且不要關。 **2** *~ **sb on**,* (sl, esp *pp*) cause sb to feel happy, excited: (俚,尤用過去分詞形式)使某人感到快樂或興奮: *That music really ~es me on!* 那音樂的確使我入迷! *He's really ~ed on!* 他真的被迷住了! **3** [VP 6A, 15B] move (a train, tram, etc) on to another track: 使(火車,電車等)轉轍: *~ a train into a siding.* 使火車轉轍至傍軌。 **4** [VP6A, 15A] *~ **(to)**; ~ **(over to)**,* shift; change: 轉變;改變: *~ the conversation (to a less embarrassing subject)*; 改變談話內容(談論較不尷尬的話題)。 *~ over to modern methods.* 改採現代方法。 **5** [VP6A] whip or flick with a ~(3). 以枝條鞭打。 **6** [VP6A, 15A] swing (sth) round suddenly; snatch suddenly: 突然擺動(某物); 甩動; 突然搶奪: *The cow ~ed (more usu swished) her tail.* 那隻母牛擺動尾巴(較常用 swished)。 *He ~ed it out of my hand.* 他一下子從我手中(把它)搶了過去。

swivel /ˈswɪvl; ˈswɪvl̩/ *n* ring and pivot or ring with a linked hook to a chain joining two parts so that one can turn round without turning the other: 轉鐶; 轉臂;旋轉軸承;鉸丁鐶: *a '~-chain/-hook*, provided with a ~; (裝有轉鐶的)轉動鏈(轉動鈎); *a '~-chair/-gun*, one that can rotate on a pivot. (裝有轉動軸承的)轉椅(轉動槍砲)。□ *vt, vi* (-ll-, US also -l-) [VP6A, 15B, 2A, C] turn on or as on a ~: (在或似在旋軸上)轉動;迴旋: *He ~led round in his chair/~led his chair round to see who had come in.* 他把所坐椅子轉過來看看進來的是誰。

swiz /swɪz; swɪz/ *n* (sl) bitter disappointment; fraud. (俚)深切的失望;欺騙。

swizzle /ˈswɪzl; ˈswɪzl̩/ *n* (colloq) (kinds of) mixed alcoholic drink served in a tall glass. (俗)用高腳杯盛的雞尾酒;瑞落雞尾酒。 **'~-stick** *n* glass rod for stirring such a drink. 瑞落雞尾酒棒。

swob /swɒb; swɑb/ *n, vt* (-bb-) = swab.

swol·len /ˈswəʊlən; ˈswolən/ *pp* of swell, esp as *adj*: 爲 swell 的過去分詞,尤用作形容詞: *a ~ ankle.* 腫踝。

swoon /swuːn; swun/ (archaic) (古) *vi* [VP2A] faint. 昏暈;暈倒;暈過去。□ *n* fainting fit. 暈厥;暈倒。

swoop /swuːp; swup/ *vi, vt* **1** [VP2A, C] *~ **(down) (on)**,* come down on with a rush: 猝然下降;猝然攻擊: *The eagle ~ed down on its prey.* 那隻老鷹猝然飛下攫掠其捕食物。 *The soldiers ~ed down on the bandits,* attacked them suddenly. 兵士們突襲土匪。 **2** [VP15B] *~ **sth up**,* grab, snatch it. 攫取某物。□ *n* ~ing movement; sudden attempt to snatch and carry off sth. 猝然下降;猝然攫取;猛撲;突襲。 ***at one (fell) ~,*** in one sudden swift attack or movement. 一舉;一下子;突襲地。

swop (also **swap**) /swɒp; swɑp/ *vt, vi* (-pp-) [VP6A, 15A, 2A] (colloq) exchange by barter: (俗) 交換; 物物交換: *~ foreign stamps;* 交換外國郵票; *~ yarns*, tell one another stories (of adventure, etc). 互相訴說(奇遇、歷險等)故事。 ***~ places with sb,*** exchange seats. 與某人交換座位。 ***Don't ~ horses in mid-stream,*** (prov) If changes are needed, make them before the crisis is reached. (諺) 過河中途莫換馬(莫在危急時作更易)。 □ *n* exchange by barter: 交換;物物交換: *I think your hat would suit me—shall we try a ~?* 我想你的帽子我戴很合適 — 我們交換一下好嗎?

sword /sɔːd; sord/ *n* long steel blade fixed in a hilt, used as a weapon, or worn by army officers, etc as part of a uniform or as court dress. 劍;刀。 ***cross ~s with sb,*** (fig) dispute with him. (喻)與…爭論。 ***draw/sheathe the ~,*** (rhet) begin/end a war. (修辭)開戰(停戰)。 ***put to the ~,*** (rhet) kill. (修辭)殺死。 ***at the point of the ~,*** under threat of violence. 在暴力威脅下。 **'~-cane/-stick** *n* ~-blade enclosed in a hollow walking-stick. 內藏刀劍的手杖。 **'~-cut** *n* (scar left by a) wound given with a ~-edge. 刀(劍)傷;刀(劍)傷疤。 **'~-dance** *n* dance over ~s laid on the ground, or one in which ~s are waved or clashed. 刀劍舞(穿行刀劍之間,或揮動刀劍); (揮)劍舞。 **'~·fish** *n* large sea-fish with a long ~-like upper jaw. 旗魚(爲一種大海魚,有劍狀長上顎)。 ⇨ the illus at sea. 參看 sea 之插圖。 **'~-play** *n* [U] fencing; (fig) repartee; lively arguing. 劍術;舞劍;(喻)巧答;激辯。 **'~sman** /-zmən; -zmən/ *n* (*pl* -men) man skilled in the use of a ~ (usu with *adjj*): 精於劍術者;擊劍家;劍客(通常與形容詞連用): *a good ~sman.* 優秀的擊劍家。 **'~s·man·ship** /-mənʃɪp; -mən,ʃɪp/ *n*

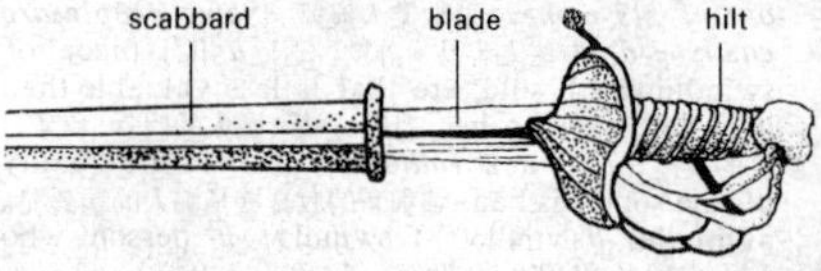

a sword

swore, sworn ⇨ swear.

swot /swɒt; swɑt/ *vi, vt* (-tt-) [VP2A, C, 3A, 15B] (not US) (不用於美國) *~ **(for sth)**,* study hard (for an examination, etc). 苦讀;用功(爲應付考試等);臨陣磨槍地研讀。 *~ **sth up**,* work hard at; revise: 辛苦工作;用功;溫習: *~ up one's geometry.* 用功溫習幾何。□ *n* **1** person who ~s. 苦讀者;用功者;臨陣磨槍的學生。 **2** hard work: 辛苦的工作: *What a ~!* 多吃力的工作!

swum /swʌm; swʌm/ *pp* of swim.

swung /swʌŋ; swʌŋ/ *pt, pp* of swing.

syb·ar·ite /ˈsɪbəraɪt; ˈsɪbə,raɪt/ *n* person who is devoted to comfort and luxury. 耽於奢侈逸樂的人;淫逸之徒。 **syb·ar·itic** /ˌsɪbəˈrɪtɪk; ˌsɪbəˈrɪtɪk/ *adj* luxurious; characteristic of a ~. 愛奢侈的;好享樂的。

syca·more /ˈsɪkəmɔː(r); ˈsɪkə,mor/ *n* **1** [C] large tree valued for its wood (in GB a kind of maple-tree; in US a kind of plane-tree, also called a 'buttonwood'; in Egypt and Syria a kind of fig-tree). 木材貴重的大樹(在英國爲一種大楓樹; 在美國爲篠懸木;在埃及和敍利亞,爲無花果樹)。 **2** [U] valuable hard wood of the ~. 上述大樹的珍貴木材。

syco·phant /ˈsɪkəfænt; ˈsɪkəfənt/ *n* person who tries to win favour by flattering rich or powerful people. 阿諛者;奉承有錢有勢者;趨炎附勢者。**~ic** /ˌsɪkəˈfæntɪk; ˌsɪkəˈfæntɪk/ *adj*

syl·lable /ˈsɪləbl; ˈsɪləbl̩/ *n* minimum rhythmic unit of spoken language, consisting of a vowel or sustained consonant, often preceded or followed by unsustained consonant(s); similar unit of written language: 音節(由一個母音或持續子音構成,常伴以非持續子音): *'Arithmetic' is a word of four ~s.* arithmetic 一字有四個音節。 **-syl·labled** *adj* having a stated number of ~s: 有…個音節的: *'Sycophant' is a three-~d word.* sycophant 是一個三音節字。 **syl·la·bary** /ˈsɪləbərɪ *US:* -berɪ; ˈsɪlə,bɛrɪ/

n [C] (*pl* -ries) list of characters (eg in Japanese) representing ~s. 音節表;字音表;(日文的)假名表。 **syl·labic** /sɪˈlæbɪk ; sɪˈlæbɪk/ *adj* **(a)** of or in ~s. 音節的;拼音的。**(b)** (of consonant) making a ~. (指子音)自成音節的。**syl·labi·cate** /sɪˈlæbɪkeɪt ; sɪˈlæbɪˌket/, **syl·labify** /sɪˈlæbɪfaɪ ; sɪˈlæbəˌfaɪ/ (*pt, pp* -fied), **syl·la·bize** /ˈsɪləbaɪz ; ˈsɪləˌbaɪz/ *vvt* divide into ~s. 分成音節。**syl·labi·ca·tion** /sɪˌlæbɪˈkeɪʃn ; sɪˌlæbɪˈkeʃən/, **syl·labi·fi·ca·tion** /sɪˌlæbɪfɪˈkeɪʃn ; sɪˌlæbəfəˈkeʃən/ *nn* (system of) division into ~s. 分成音節;音節劃分法。

syl·la·bus /ˈsɪləbəs ; ˈsɪləbəs/ *n* (*pl* ~es /-bəsɪz ; -bəsɪz/ or 或 -bi /-baɪ ; -ˌbaɪ/) outline or summary of a course of studies; programme of school studies. 課程摘要;教學大綱;課程進度表。

syl·lo·gism /ˈsɪlədʒɪzəm ; ˈsɪləˌdʒɪzəm/ *n* [C] reaching a conclusion from two statements, eg: 三段論法(從兩個前提得出結論的推理方式),如: *All men must die; I am a man; therefore I must die.* 凡人必定會死;我是人;所以我必定會死。⇨ premise(2). **syl·lo·gis·tic** /ˌsɪləˈdʒɪstɪk ; ˌsɪləˈdʒɪstɪk/ *adj* in the form or nature of a ~. 三段論法的;推論式的;演繹的。

sylph /sɪlf ; sɪlf/ *n* one of a class of female nature spirits believed to inhabit the air (cf *nymph*, spirit of the woods, etc); (hence) slender, graceful girl or woman. 風精(據說住在空中的女精靈)(參較nymph,山林等的精靈);(由此產生)優雅苗條的女郎或婦女。**ˈ~-like** *adj* slender and graceful. 苗條而優雅的;窈窕的。

syl·van, sil·van /ˈsɪlvən ; ˈsɪlvən/ *adj* (liter) of trees and woodland: (文)森林的;林木的;林地的: *~ scenes;* 森林景色; *a ~ retreat,* eg a cottage in a forest. 林中隱居處(如林中小屋)。

sym·bio·sis /ˌsɪmbɪˈəʊsɪs ; ˌsɪmbaɪˈosɪs/ *n* [U] (biol) harmonic association of different organisms, etc: (生物)共生;共棲: *the tall Dingas of the southern Sudan, living in ~ with their magnificent cattle.* 蘇丹南部高大的丁加人,與其壯觀的牛馬住在一起。

sym·bol /ˈsɪmbl ; ˈsɪmbl̩/ *n* [C] sign, mark, object, etc looked upon as representing sth: 符號;象徵;代表物: *mathematical ~s,* eg ×, ÷, +, −; 數學符號(如×, ÷, +, −); *phonetic ~s.* 注音符號;音標。*Red is a symbol of danger.* 紅色是危險的象徵。*The Cross is the ~ of Christianity.* 十字架是基督教的象徵。**~ic** /sɪmˈbɒlɪk ; sɪmˈbɑlɪk/, **~i·cal** /-kl ; -kl̩/ *adjj* of, using, used as, a ~. 符號的;象徵的;用符號的;用作符號的。**~i·cally** /-klɪ ; -klɪ/ *adv* **~·ize** /ˈsɪmbəlaɪz ; ˈsɪmbl̩ˌaɪz/ *vt* [VP6A] be a ~ of; make use of a ~ or ~s for. 象徵;爲…的符號;以符號表示。**~·iz·ation** /ˌsɪmbəlaɪˈzeɪʃn *US*: -lɪˈz- ; ˌsɪmbl̩əˈzeʃən/ *n* **~·ism** /ˈsɪmbəlɪzəm ; ˈsɪmbl̩ˌɪzəm/ *n* **1** [U] representation of ideas by the use of ~s; literary and artistic movement (late 19th c) that used artistic invention to express sensually ideas, emotions, abstractions in place of realism. 用符號代表概念;象徵主義(十九世紀晚期興起的文學及藝術潮流,提倡藉巧構的具體意象,表達思想、感情、意念等,以取代先前流行的寫實風格)。**2** [C] system of ~s used to represent a particular group of ideas. (代表某系列概念的)符號系統;意象體系。

sym·me·try /ˈsɪmətrɪ ; ˈsɪmɪtrɪ/ *n* [U] (beauty resulting from the) right correspondence of parts; quality of harmony or balance (in size, design, etc) between parts: 對稱;勻稱;調和;對稱美: *The bump on the left side of her forehead spoilt the ~ of her face.* 她前額左方腫起的一塊,破壞了她臉部的對稱美。**sym·met·ric** /sɪˈmetrɪk ; sɪˈmɛtrɪk/, **sym·met·ri·cal** /-kl ; -kl̩/ *adjj* having ~; (of a design) having (usu two) exactly similar parts on either side of a dividing line. 有對稱美的;對稱的;勻稱的;調和的;(指圖案)對稱的。**sym·met·ri·cally** /-klɪ ; -klɪ/ *adv*

sym·path·etic /ˌsɪmpəˈθetɪk ; ˌsɪmpəˈθɛtɪk/ *adj* having or showing sympathy; caused by sympathy: 有同情心的;表示同情的;由同情心引起的;同感的: *~ looks / words;* 顯示同情的表情(話); *a ~ face / heart;* 顯示同情的面孔(心); *a ~ audience;* 起共鳴的觀衆(聽衆); *be / feel ~ to / towards sb.* 對某人表同情。**~ strike** *n* strike¹(1) by workers purely to show support for other workers who are on strike. 同情罷工(爲表示支持其他罷工之工人所作的罷工)。**sym·path·eti·cally** /-klɪ ; -klɪ/ *adv*

sym·path·ize /ˈsɪmpəθaɪz ; ˈsɪmpəˌθaɪz/ *vi* [VP 2A, 3A] ~ ***(with),*** feel or express sympathy (with): 同情;同意: *~ with sb in his afflictions.* 同情某人的困苦。*Tom's parents do not ~ with his ambition to become an actor,* do not give him their approval and encouragement. 湯姆的雙親不贊同他當演員的志願。**sym·path·izer** *n* person who ~s, eg one who supports a cause or political party. 同情者;贊同者(如支持某種主義或政黨者)。

sym·pathy /ˈsɪmpəθɪ ; ˈsɪmpəθɪ/ *n* (*pl* -thies) **1** [U] (capacity for) sharing the feelings of others, feeling pity and tenderness: 同情;憐憫;同感;贊同;同情心: *send sb a letter of ~;* 寄給某人一封慰問信; *feel ~ for sb;* 對某人表同情; *have no ~ with sb's foolish opinions.* 不贊同某人愚蠢的意見。*I have some ~ with their views,* share them to some extent. 我對於他們的意見略有同感。***in ~ with,*** agreeing with, approving of: 同意;贊同: *We are all in ~ with your proposals.* 我們全都贊同你的提議。*Will the bus workers strike in ~ with* (= to show their ~ for) *the railway workers?* 公共汽車工人會同情鐵路工人而罷工嗎? **2** (*pl* in a few usages): (若干用法中用複數): *a man of wide sympathies,* with a great capacity for fellow-feeling. 極富同情心的人。*You have my sympathies,* my feelings of ~. 我非常同情你。*My sympathies are with the miners in this dispute,* I'm on their side. 在這項爭議中,我同情礦工(的立場)。

sym·phony /ˈsɪmfənɪ ; ˈsɪmfənɪ/ *n* [C] (*pl* -nies) (long and large-scale) musical composition in (usu) three or four parts (called *movements*) for (usu a large) orchestra. 交響樂;交響曲(通常有三或四個樂章,由管絃樂團演奏)。**sym·phonic** /sɪmˈfɒnɪk ; sɪmˈfɑnɪk/ *adj* of, having the character of, a ~. 交響樂的;有交響樂特點的。

sym·po·sium /sɪmˈpəʊzɪəm ; sɪmˈpozɪəm/ *n* (*pl* ~s or 或 -sia /-zɪə ; -zɪə/) collection of essays, etc (eg forming a book) by several persons on a problem or subject; conference for discussion of a subject. (對某一問題的)諸家論叢;專題論文集;(爲某一問題所召開的)專題研討會。

symp·tom /ˈsɪmptəm ; ˈsɪmptəm/ *n* **1** change in the body's condition that indicates illness: 症候;症狀: *A persistent cough may be a ~ of tuberculosis.* 持續的咳嗽可能是肺結核的症候。 **2** sign of the existence of sth: (事物存在的)表徵;徵兆;徵候: *The Government must not ignore these ~s of discontent among their own supporters.* 政府切不可忽視其支持者間所表現出的這些不滿徵候。**symp·to·matic** /ˌsɪmptəˈmætɪk ; ˌsɪmptəˈmætɪk/ *adj* serving as a ~: 症狀的;徵兆的;表徵的: *A headache may be ~atic of brain fever.* 頭痛可能是腦膜炎的症狀。**symp·to·mati·cally** /-klɪ ; -klɪ/ *adv*

syna·gogue /ˈsɪnəgɒg ; ˈsɪnəˌgɔg/ *n* [C] (building used for an) assembly of Jews for religious teaching and worship. 猶太教教堂;猶太教徒的聚會。

syn·chro·flash /ˌsɪŋkrəʊˈflæʃ ; ˈsɪŋkrəˌflæʃ/ *n* (usu attrib) device for simultaneous flashlight and opening of the shutter of a camera: (通常作形容用法) 同閃裝置 (使閃光燈與照相機快門同時起作用的裝置): *~ photography / attachments for a camera.* 同閃照相術(照相機上的同閃裝備)。

syn·chro·mesh /ˌsɪŋkrəʊˈmeʃ ; ˈsɪŋkrəˌmɛʃ/ *n* system of gear-changing (esp in motor-vehicles) so that the parts revolve at the same speed and so change smoothly. 同步齒輪系(尤指汽車中的齒輪變速

inside a synagogue

裝置,可使變速平穩順利)。

syn·chron·ize /ˈsɪŋkrənaɪz ; ˈsɪŋkrəˌnaɪz/ *vt, vi* [VP6A, 2A] (cause to) happen at the same time, agree in time, speeds, etc: (使)同時發生;時間一致;同速進行: ~ *the sound-track of a film with the movements seen;* 使電影的音帶配合動作; ~ *all the clocks in a building.* 把一座建築物內所有時鐘校準。 **syn·chron·iz·ation** /ˌsɪŋkrənaɪˈzeɪʃn *US:* -nɪˈz- ; ˌsɪŋkrənɪˈzeʃən/ *n*

syn·chro·tron /ˈsɪŋkrəʊtrɒn ; ˈsɪŋkrəˌtrɑn/ *n* apparatus for accelerating electrons. 同步加速器(使電子加速的器械)。

syn·co·pate /ˈsɪŋkəpeɪt ; ˈsɪŋkəˌpet/ *vt* [VP6A] (music) change the rhythm of; displace the normal beats or accents of, eg as in some jazz. (音樂)改變…的韻律;不守或改置…的正常節奏或重拍子;切分(如某些爵士樂中)。 **syn·co·pa·tion** /ˌsɪŋkəˈpeɪʃn ; ˌsɪŋkəˈpeʃən/ *n*

syn·cope /ˈsɪŋkəpɪ ; ˈsɪŋkəpɪ/ *n* (med term for) fainting; brief loss of consciousness from fall of blood-pressure.(醫學名稱)暈厥;因血壓降低而失去知覺。

syn·dic /ˈsɪndɪk ; ˈsɪndɪk/ *n* member of a committee (for business purposes) of a university or other organization. (大學或其他機構的)委員會的委員。

syn·di·cal·ism /ˈsɪndɪkəlɪzəm ; ˈsɪndɪkl̩ˌɪzəm/ *n* [U] theory that political power should be in the hands of trade unions and that these unions should own and manage the industries in which their members work. 工團主義(認爲政權應操在工會手中,而此等工會應擁有並管理其會員所從事的工業)。 **syn·di·cal·ist** /-ɪst ; -ɪst/ *n* supporter of ~. 工團主義者。

syn·di·cate /ˈsɪndɪkət ; ˈsɪndɪkɪt/ *n* **1** business association that supplies articles, cartoons, etc to periodicals. 資料供應社(以稿件、文章、漫畫等供給報章雜誌的機構);報業辛廸加。 **2** combination of commercial firms associated to forward a common interest. 企業的聯合組織;辛廸加。 □ *vt* /ˈsɪndɪkeɪt ; ˈsɪndɪˌket/ [VP6A] publish (articles, strip-cartoons, etc) in numerous periodicals through a ~(1). 經由報業辛廸加在多個刊物發表(文章、連環漫畫等)。 **syn·di·ca·tion** /ˌsɪndɪˈkeɪʃn ; ˌsɪndɪˈkeʃən/ *n*

syn·drome /ˈsɪndrəʊm ; ˈsɪndrom/ *n* (med) number of symptoms which collectively indicate an often abnormal condition of the body or mind; (fig) particular combination of a person's actions, opinions, etc that can be expected to occur together. (醫)症候簇;症狀羣;綜合病徵;複徵;(喻)(個人)經常同時出現的行動,言論等。

synod /ˈsɪnəd ; ˈsɪnəd/ *n* [C] meeting of church officers to discuss and decide questions of policy, government, teaching, etc. (討論和決定政策、管理、教義等問題的)宗教會議。

syn·onym /ˈsɪnənɪm ; ˈsɪnəˌnɪm / *n* word with the same meaning as another in the same language but often with different implications and associations. 同義字。 **syn·ony·mous** /sɪˈnɒnɪməs ; sɪˈnɑnəməs/ *adj*

syn·op·sis /sɪˈnɒpsɪs ; sɪˈnɑpsɪs/ *n* (*pl* -opses /-siːz ; -siz/) summary or outline (of a book, play, etc). (書、劇本等的)大綱;要略。 **syn·op·tic** /sɪˈnɒptɪk ; sɪˈnɑptɪk/ *adj* giving a ~: 提示大綱的;要略的: *the synoptic Gospels,* those of Matthew, Mark and Luke (similar in contents, order, etc). 對觀福音書(指馬太,馬可及路加三福音書)。 **syn·op·ti·cally** /-klɪ ; -klɪ/ *adv*

syn·tax /ˈsɪntæks ; ˈsɪntæks/ *n* [U] (gram) (rules for) sentence-building. (文法)造句;造句法。 **syn·tac·tic** /sɪnˈtæktɪk ; sɪnˈtæktɪk/ *adj* of ~. 造句(法)的。 **syn·tac·ti·cally** /-klɪ ; -klɪ/ *adv*

syn·thesis /ˈsɪnθəsɪs ; ˈsɪnθəsɪs/ *n* (*pl* -theses /-siːz ; -ˌsiz/) [C, U] combination of separate parts, elements, substances, etc into a whole or into a system; that which results from this process: 綜合;合成;由合成法製成之物: *produce rubber from petroleum by* ~. 藉合成法從石油製造橡皮。 **syn·thesize** /ˈsɪnθəsaɪz ; ˈsɪnθəˌsaɪz/ *vt* [VP6A] produce a whole by this process: 由合成法製成: *synthesize diamonds / rubber.* 用合成法製鑽石(橡皮)。 **syn·thetic** /sɪnˈθetɪk ; sɪnˈθɛtɪk/ *adj* **1** produced by ~: 藉合成法產生的;人工製造的: *synthetic rubber,* artificially made. 人造橡皮。 **2** pertaining to ~: 綜合的;合成的: *synthetic chemistry.* 合成化學。 **3** (of a language) containing, tending to form, many compound words: (指語言)含有許多複合字的;有形成許多複合字之趨勢的;綜合性的: *German is a synthetic language.* 德語是一種複合式的語言。 **syn·theti·cally** /-klɪ ; -klɪ/ *adv.* ⇨ analysis.

syph·ilis /ˈsɪfɪlɪs ; ˈsɪfl̩ɪs/ *n* [U] infectious venereal disease. 梅毒 (一種傳染的性病)。 **syphi·litic** /ˌsɪfɪˈlɪtɪk ; ˌsɪfəˈlɪtɪk/ *adj* pertaining to, suffering from, ~. 梅毒的;患梅毒的。 □ *n* person affected with ~. 梅毒患者。

syphon *n* = siphon.

syr·inga /sɪˈrɪŋgə ; səˈrɪŋgə/ *n* shrub with strong-scented white flowers (popularly called the mock-orange); botanical name of the lilac genus. 山梅花;紫丁香花(開白花,香味濃郁,一般通稱爲 mock-orange); 紫丁香屬。

syr·inge /sɪˈrɪndʒ ; ˈsɪrɪndʒ/ *n* kinds of device for drawing in liquid by suction and forcing it out again in a fine stream, used for washing out wounds, injecting liquids into the body, in spraying plants, etc: 注射器;注水器;洗滌器;灌腸器;噴水器: *a hypodermic* ~; 皮下注射器; *a garden* ~. 澆花木用的噴水器。 □ *vt* [VP6A, 15B] clean, inject liquid into, with a ~; apply (liquid) with a ~. 灌洗;注射。

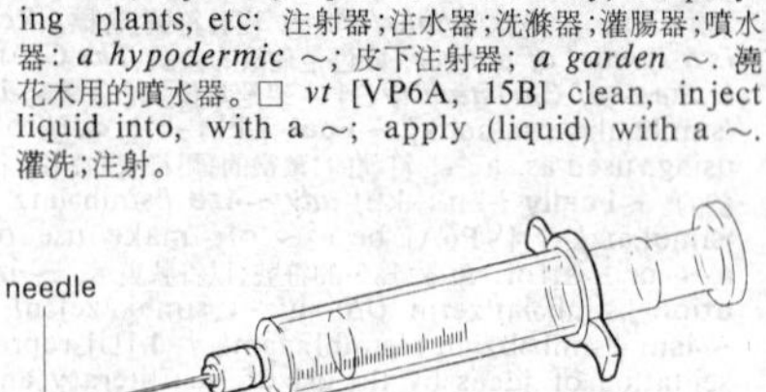

a hypodermic syringe

syrup /ˈsɪrəp ; ˈsɪrəp/ *n* [U] thick sweet liquid made from sugar-cane juice or by boiling sugar with water: 糖漿: *pineapple tinned in* ~; 浸於糖漿的罐裝鳳梨; ˈ*cough* ~, ~ with medicine in it to relieve a cough; 治咳糖漿(摻和咳嗽藥水製成者); *fruit* ~, ~ flavoured with fruit juices. 果汁糖漿(以果汁增味者)。 **~y** *adj* of or like ~; (fig, eg of music) too sweet. 糖漿的; 似糖漿的; (喻,指音樂等)太甜蜜的。

sys·tem /ˈsɪstəm ; ˈsɪstəm/ *n* **1** group of things or parts working together in a regular relation: 系統: *the* ˈ*nervous* ~; 神經系統; *the di*ˈ*gestive* ~; 消化系統; *a* ˈ*railway* ~. 鐵路系統。 *The poison has passed into his* ~, his body as a whole. 毒藥已進入他的體內。 *Too much alcohol is bad for the* ~. 喝酒太多有害身體。 **2** ordered set of ideas, theories, principles, etc: (思想、理論、原則等的)體系;體制;制度;方式;方法: *a* ~ *of philosophy;* 哲學體系;

a ~ of government; 政府體制;政體; *a good ~ of teaching languages;* 教授語言的良好方法; '~-*building*/'~-*built houses,* built of prefabricated sections, put together on the site. 系統建築(系統建築的房屋);預築(預築房屋)。 **3** [U] orderliness: 秩序;規律: *You mustn't expect good results if you work without ~.* 如果你工作不講究先後秩序,你休想有好的結果。 **~·atic** /ˌsɪstəˈmætɪk ; ˌsɪstəˈmætɪk/ *adj* methodical; based on a ~: 有方法的;有系統的;有體系的;基於制度、系統等的;按照法式的: *a ~atic attempt.* 有計畫的行爲。 **~·ati·cally** /-klɪ ; -klɪ/ *adv* **~·atize** /ˈsɪstəmətaɪz ; ˈsɪstəməˌtaɪz/ *vt* [VP6A] arrange according to a ~; make into a ~. 系統化;體系化;做成制度。 **~·ati·za·tion** /ˌsɪstəmətaɪˈzeɪʃn *US:* -tɪˈz- ; ˌsɪstəmətɪˈzeʃən/ *n*

Tt

T, t /tiː ; ti/ (*pl* T's, t's /tiːz ; tiz/) the twentieth letter of the English alphabet; used before names of various objects shaped like the letter T: 英文字母的第二十個字母; T 形(物);丁字形(物): *a 'T-bandage;* 丁字形繃帶; *a 'T-shirt,* short-sleeved, close-fitting, collarless and buttonless usu cotton shirt worn informally; 短袖汗衫;圓領衫;運動衫(短袖,緊身,無領,無扣,通常爲棉質,非正式場合着用); *a 'T-square,* ⇨ square²(7). ***to a T,*** ⇨ tee.

ta /tɑː ; tɑ/ *int* (colloq) thank you. (俗)謝謝你。

tab /tæb ; tæb/ *n* **1** small piece or strip of cloth, etc fixed to a garment, etc as a badge or distinguishing mark or (as a loop) for hanging up a coat, etc; binding at the end of a shoelace, etc. (釘於衣服等上,用作記號、標誌或掛環的)垂片;飄帶;垂圈;懸垂牌;鞋帶等的護頭。**2** (colloq) account; check. (俗)帳目;查核。 ***keep a tab/tabs on sth/sb,*** keep an account of, keep under observation: 記錄…的帳目;看顧;監視: *keep a tab on the expenses.* 記錄各筆費用的帳目。

tab·ard /ˈtæbəd ; ˈtæbɚd/ *n* (hist) short, sleeveless outer garment (worn eg by a knight over his armour, or by a herald). (史)(武士穿在鎧甲外面的)無袖短外套;傳令官制服。

tabby /ˈtæbɪ ; ˈtæbɪ/ *n* (*pl* -bies) **'~(-cat),** cat with grey or brown stripes. 虎斑貓。

tab·er·nacle /ˈtæbənækl ; ˈtæbɚˌnækl̩/ *n* **1** (in the Bible) **the T~,** the portable structure used by the Israelites as a sanctuary during their wanderings before they settled in Palestine. (聖經)聖幕(以色列人定居巴勒斯坦以前所使用的移動式神殿)。 **2** (eccles) receptacle for a pyx. (教會)聖體容器。 **3** place of worship, eg a Baptist Church or Mormon temple. 教堂;禮拜堂;會堂(如浸信會或摩門教者)。

table /ˈteɪbl ; ˈtebl̩/ *n* [C] **1** piece of furniture consisting of a flat top with (usu four) supports (called legs): 桌;檯;几: *a 'dining-~;* 餐桌; *a 'kitchen-~;* 厨房用桌; *a 'billiard-~.* 撞球檯。 ***at ~,*** having a meal: 用餐;用飯: *They were at ~ when we called.* 我們往訪時,他們正在吃飯。 **'~-cloth** *n* one (to be) spread on a ~. 桌布;檯布。 **'~-knife** *n* steel knife for use at ~. 餐刀。**'~-lifting/-rapping/-turning** *nn* lifting/rapping, etc of a ~, apparently without physical exertion, occurring while people sit at a ~ during a spiritualistic seance. (行降神術時)桌子的靈動(桌子升起、敲擊、轉動等,似未加外力者)。**'~-linen** *n*[U] ~-cloths, napkins, etc. 桌布,餐巾等。**'~-mat** *n* one to be placed under a hot dish on a ~. 碗盤墊。**'~·spoon** *n* large spoon for serving food at ~ from a dish, etc. 餐匙;大調羹。**'~·spoon·ful** *n* as much as a ~spoon holds. 一餐匙(之量)。 **'~-talk** *n* conversation during a meal. 餐敍;進餐時的談話。 **'~ tennis** *n* game (sometimes called *ping-pong*) played with bats and balls, similar to tennis, on a ~. 桌球;乒乓球。 **'~-ware** *n* [U] dishes, silver, cutlery, etc used for meals. 餐具。 **2** (*sing* only) people seated at a ~: (僅用單數)同席的人;坐在一桌的人: *a ~ of card-players;* 一桌玩牌的人; *King Arthur and his Round T~,* his knights; 亞瑟王及其圓桌武士; *jokes that amused the whole ~.* 使舉座歡悅的笑話。 **3** (*sing* only) food provided at ~: (僅用單數)餐食;伙食: *He keeps a good ~,* provides good meals. 他講究餐食。 **4** **'~(-land),** plateau; extensive area of high, level land. 高原;臺地。**5** [C] list, orderly arrangement, of facts, information, etc (usu in columns): 表;一覽表;目錄: *a ~ of contents,* summary of what a book contains; 目次;目錄; *multiplication ~s;* 乘法表;九九表; *a railway 'time~.* 火車時刻表。 **6** (phrases) (片語) ***lay sth on the ~,*** (in Parliament) postpone (a measure, report, etc) indefinitely. (國會中)擱置一項法案、報告等。 ***turn the ~s on sb,*** gain a position of superiority after having been defeated or in a position of inferiority. 從劣勢轉爲優勢;扭轉形勢。 **7** [C] (in the Bible) flat slab of stone, wood, etc; tablet(1); what is written or inscribed on such a ~: (聖經)石板;木板;平板;刻寫於此種平板上的文字: *the ~s of the law,* the ten commandments given to Moses by God. 摩西十誡。 □ *vt* [VP6A] **1** submit for discussion: 提出討論: *~ a motion/Bill/amendment.* 提出動議(議案,修正案)。⇨ 6 above. 參看上列第6義。 **2** (esp US) postpone (a proposal, etc) indefinitely. (尤美)擱置(提議等)。 **3** put in the form of a ~(5). 列表。

tab·leau /ˈtæbləʊ ; ˈtæblo/ *n* (*pl* ~x /-ləʊz ; -loz/) (often 常作 **~ vivant** /ˈviːvɑːn *US:* viːˈvɑːn ; viˈvɑn/) representation by living persons of a picture or scene, without words or action, esp on a stage or platform; dramatic situation suddenly brought about. 活人造景(以活人扮演的靜態畫面,尤指在舞臺或講臺上者);(突然發生的)戲劇性場面。

table d'hôte /ˌtɑːblˈdəʊt ; ˈtæbl̩ˈdot/ *adj, adv* (F) (of a restaurant meal) at an inclusive fixed price: (法)(指餐館飲食)客飯式的;和菜方式: *a ~ lunch.* 一頓客飯式的午餐。⇨ à la carte.

tab·let /ˈtæblɪt ; ˈtæblɪt/ *n* **1** flat surface with words cut or written on it, eg one fixed to a wall in memory of sth or sb. 碑;牌;匾額(如固定於牆壁以紀念某事或某人者)。 **2** number of sheets of writing-paper fastened together along one edge. 拍紙簿。 **3** lump of hard soap; small flattened pellet of compressed medicine: 硬肥皂塊;藥片;錠劑: *two ~s of aspirin;* 兩片阿斯匹林; flat, hard sweet: 硬糖片: *throat ~s,* to be sucked to relieve a cough, sore throat, etc. (治咳嗽、喉痛等的)喉片。 **4** (hist) flat sheet of wood, stone, etc for cutting words on (eg as used in ancient Rome). (史)書板(供刻字的木板、石板等,如古羅馬所使用者)。

tab·loid /ˈtæblɔɪd ; ˈtæblɔɪd/ *n* small size newspaper with many pictures, strip cartoons, etc and with its news presented in simplified form: 小(型)報(有大量圖片、連環圖畫等,並以簡明扼要的方式報導新聞者): (attrib) (形容用法) *~ journalism.* 小型報紙;小報業。

ta·boo /təˈbuː *US:* tæˈbuː ; təˈbu/ *n* **1** [C, U] (among some peoples) something which religion or custom regards as forbidden, not to be touched, spoken of, etc: (某些民族的)禁忌: *That tree is under (a) ~.* 那棵樹禁止接近(不可褻瀆等)。 **2** [C] general agreement not to discuss sth, do sth. 避諱;忌諱。 □ *adj* under ~: 禁忌的;避諱的:

T

Questions and problems that were once ~ are now discussed openly. 過去曾經列爲禁忌的許多問題現在可以公開討論了。*Unkind gossip ought to be ~.* 不厚道的閒話應該避諱。'~ **words**, those which convention avoids or prohibits (eg most of those marked ⚠ in this dictionary). 忌諱語(爲社會習俗所避免或禁止者,如本辭典標有⚠者大多屬此類語)。□ *vt* [VP6A] forbid, esp on moral or religious grounds. 禁止;禁用(尤指基於道德或宗教立場)。

ta·bor /'teɪbə(r); 'tebɚ/ *n* small drum, esp one used to accompany a pipe or fife. 小鼓(尤指用以伴奏無鍵短笛者)。

tabu·lar /'tæbjʊlə(r); 'tæbjələ/ *adj* arranged or displayed in tables(5): 列成表的: *a report in ~ form.* 列表式報告。

tabu·late /'tæbjʊleɪt; 'tæbjə,let/ *vt* [VP6A] arrange (facts, figures, etc) in tables(5), in lists or columns. 將(事實、數字等)列成表。**tabu·la·tor** /-tə(r); -tɚ/ *n* machine, device, that ~s. 製表機(儀)。**tabu·la·tion** /,tæbjʊ'leɪʃn; ,tæbjʊ'leʃən/ *n*

tacho·graph /'tækəʊgrɑːf; 'tækə,græf/ *n* device that records the speed and duration of a journey in a motor-vehicle. (汽車之)速度計。

tacit /'tæsɪt; 'tæsɪt/ *adj* unspoken; understood without being put into words: 沉默的;心照不宣的: *~ consent/agreement.* 默許(默契)。**~·ly** *adv*

taci·turn /'tæsɪtɜːn; 'tæsə,tɝn/ *adj* (in the habit of) saying very little. 沉默寡言的;不好說話的。**~·ly** *adv* **taci·tur·nity** /,tæsɪ'tɜːnətɪ; ,tæsə'tɝnətɪ/ *n* [U].

tack /tæk; tæk/ *n* **1** small, flat-headed nail (eg as used for securing some kinds of carpet or linoleum to a floor): 大頭釘;平頭釘(如用於將地毯或油布等釘於地板上者): '*tin-~*, of iron coated with tin; 鍍錫平頭釘; '*thumb-~* (US) (美) = drawing-pin. **2** long, loose stitch used in fastening pieces of cloth together loosely or temporarily. 假縫;粗縫。**3** sailing-ship's direction as fixed by the direction of the wind and the position of the sails: (依風向及帆的位置而定的) 航行方向: *on the port/starboard ~*, with the wind on the port/starboard side. 風在船的左(右)方。***on the right/wrong ~***, (fig) following a wise/unwise course of action. (喻)方針正確(錯誤)。**4** [U] **(hard) ~**, hard ship's biscuits. 硬餅乾。□ *vt, vi* **1** [VP 6A, 15A, B] fasten with ~s(1): 以平頭釘固定: *~ down the carpet.* 把地毯釘起來。**2** [VP6A, 15A, B] fasten with ~s(2): 假縫;粗縫: *~ a ribbon on to a hat;* 在帽子上加縫一條飾帶; *~ aown a fold;* 粗縫衣摺; (fig) (喻) *~ an appeal for money on to a speech,* add one. 在說話中加添要錢的請求。**3** [VP2A, C] sail in a zigzag course; make a ~ or ~s(3): 作Z字形航行;蛇航;迎風;搶風轉向: *~ing about;* 搶風轉向; *~ to port.* 左舷搶風。

tackle /'tækl; 'tækḷ/ *n* **1** [C, U] set of ropes and pulleys for working a ship's sails, or for lifting weights, etc. (操縱船帆,或吊起重物等用的)滑車;滑車轆轤;複滑車。⇨ the illus at pulley. 參看 pulley 之插圖。**2** [U] equipment, apparatus, for doing sth: 用具;器械: '*fishing ~*, a rod, line, hooks, etc. 釣(魚)具。**3** [C] act of seizing and bringing down an opponent with the ball (in Rugby and American-style football). (橄欖球及美式足球中的)擒抱(即抱住帶球跑的對方球員)。□ *vt, vi* **1** [VP6A, 14] deal with, attack (a problem, a piece of work): 處理; 解決; 應付(問題,工作): *I don't know how to ~ this problem,* how to start on it. 我不知道如何着手處理此一問題。***~ sb about/over sth***, speak to sb frankly (about a matter). 坦白地向某人談(某事)。**2** [VP6A, 2A] seize, lay hold of, sb, eg a thief, a player who, in Rugby, has the ball: 捉住(賊等); 擒抱(橄欖球中帶球跑的對方球員): *He ~s fearlessly.* 他無所畏懼地緊抱住對方。

tacky /'tækɪ; 'tækɪ/ *adj* **1** sticky; not yet dry: 黏的;未乾的: *The paint/varnish is still ~.* 油漆(亮光漆)還沒有乾。**2** (US) (美) = tatty.

tact /tækt; tækt/ *n* [U] (use of) skill and understanding shown by sb who handles people and situations successfully and without causing offence: (運用) 機智;老練;圓通;圓滑: *show ~/have great ~ in dealing with people.* 在與人交往上顯得圓滑(極爲圓滑)。**~·ful** /-fl; -fəl/ *adj* having or showing ~. 機智的;老練的;圓通的;圓滑的。**~·fully** /-fəlɪ; -fəlɪ/ *adv* **~·less** *adj* lacking ~. 缺乏機智的;不圓滑的。**~·less·ly** *adv* **~·less·ness** *n*

tac·tic /'tæktɪk; 'tæktɪk/ *n* **1** expedient; means of achieving an object. 權謀;權變;達成目標的方法。**2** (*pl* often with *sing v*) art of placing or moving fighting forces for or during battle. (複數,常與單數動詞連用)戰術;兵法。⇨ strategy; (fig) plan(s) or method(s) for carrying out a policy: (喻)實現政策的計畫或方法; 策略: *win by surprise ~s;* 出奇制勝; *These ~s are unlikely to help you.* 這些方法對你未必有幫助。**tac·ti·cal** /-kl; -kḷ/ *adj* of ~s: 戰術的;兵法的;策略的: *~al exercises;* 戰術演習; *a ~al error.* 戰術上的錯誤。⇨ strategic. **tac·ti·cally** /-klɪ; -klɪ/ *adv* **tac·ti·cian** /tæk'tɪʃn; tæk'tɪʃən/ *n* expert in ~s. 戰術家;兵法家。

tac·tile /'tæktaɪl *US:* -təl; 'tæktḷ/, **tac·tual** /'tæktʃʊəl; 'tæktʃʊəl/ *adjj* of, experienced by, the sense of touch: 觸覺的;觸知的;可感觸到的: *a ~ organ/reflex.* 觸覺器官(反射)。

tad·pole /'tædpəʊl; 'tæd,pol/ *n* form of a frog or toad from the time it leaves the egg to the time when it takes its adult form. 蝌蚪。⇨ the illus at amphibian. 參看 amphibian 之挿圖。

taf·feta /'tæfɪtə; 'tæfɪtə/ *n* [U] thin, shiny, rather stiff silk material; similar material of linen, rayon, etc. 一種光亮而質硬的薄綢;波紋綢;與波紋綢相似的亞麻布、人造絲等。

taff·rail /'tæfreɪl; 'tæf,rel/ *n* rail round a ship's stern. 船尾欄杆。

Taffy /'tæfɪ; 'tæfɪ/ *n* (colloq) Welshman. (俗)威爾斯人。

taffy /'tæfɪ; 'tæfɪ/ *n* **1** (US) toffee. (美)太妃糖。**2** insincere flattery. 諂媚。

tag /tæg; tæg/ *n* **1** metal or plastic point at the end of a shoe-lace, string, etc. 鞋帶、繩子等末端的金屬或塑膠頭。**2** label (eg for showing prices, addresses) fastened to or stuck into sth. 附籤;標籤(如標示價格、地址者)。**3** phrase or sentence often quoted: 常被引用的片語或句子: *Latin tags.* 常被引用的拉丁文句。**4** any loose or ragged end. 任何鬆散或不完整的末端。'**question tags**, (gram) phrases such as *isn't it? won't you? are there?* added to statements. (文法) 附加問句 (附加於敘述句後的短問句)。**5** [U] game in which one child chases and tries to touch another. 小孩子玩的捉人遊戲。□ *vt, vi* (-gg-) **1** [VP6A] fasten a tag(2) to. 附以籤條;加標籤於。**2** [VP14] ***tag sth on (to)***, fasten, attach. 附加某物於…上; 繫某物於…上。**3** [VP2C] ***tag along/behind/after***, follow closely: 尾隨;緊隨: *children tagging after their mother.* 緊跟在母親後面的孩子們。*Tag along with us* (= Come with us) *if you like.* 你如果喜歡,就跟着我們走吧。**4** [VP15A, B] join: 連接;結合: *tag old articles together to make a book.* 把舊文章湊成一本書。

tail /teɪl; tel/ *n* **1** movable part (from the end of the backbone) at the end of the body of a bird, animal, fish or reptile: (鳥、獸、魚或爬蟲的)尾;尾巴: *Dogs wag their ~s when they are pleased.* 狗在高興時會擺動尾巴。***turn ~***, run away. 逃走。***~s up***, (of persons) in good spirits. (指人)心情好;興致勃勃。**2** ⇨ the illus at aircraft. 參看 aircraft 之挿圖。sth like a ~ in position: 尾狀物;似尾之部;尾部: *the ~ of a kite/comet/aircraft/cart/procession;* 紙鳶(彗星,飛機,馬車,行列)的尾部; (attrib) (形容用法) *a ~* (= following) *wind.* 順風;後面吹來的風。'**~-board** *n* board, usu on hinges, forming the back part of a cart or truck. (馬車或汽車的)尾板(通常用鉸鏈相連接)。ˌ~-**ˈcoat, ~s** *n* man's evening coat, long, divided and tapered at the back. 燕尾服。ˌ~-**ˈend** *n* (usu 通常作 ***the ~-end (of)***) final part: 末端;尾端;結尾;後部: *at the ~-end of the procession.* 在行列的末尾。**ˈ~-gate** *n* door or flap at the rear of a motor-vehicle which can be opened for loading and unloading. (汽車的)尾門(可供上下或裝卸用者)。**ˈ~-light** *n* light at the end of a train, tram or other vehicle. 尾燈(裝於火車、電車等之尾部者)。**ˈ~-piece** *n* **(a)** (in a book, etc) decoration printed in the blank space at the end of a chapter, etc. (印在書等章節後的空白處的)補白圖案。**(b)** sth added at the end of sth. 附加之物。**ˈ~-spin** *n* spiral dive of an aircraft in which the ~ makes wider circles than the front. (飛機的)尾旋下降(尾部較頭部旋轉的圓形大)。***the ~ of the eye,*** the outer corner: 眼角: *watching me from the ~ of his eye.* 他從眼角斜視我。 **3** **~s,** side of a coin opposite to that in which there is the head of sb. 硬幣的背面或反面(與人頭相對的一面)。⇨ head¹(3). **4** **~s,** (colloq) ~-coat: (俗)燕尾服: *Am I to wear a dinner-jacket or ~s?* 我該穿常禮服還是燕尾服? **5** (colloq) sb employed to follow and watch sb, eg a suspected criminal: (俗)尾隨的偵探: *put a ~ on sb.* 派偵探尾隨某人。□ *vt, vi* **1** [VP3A] ***~ after sb,*** follow close behind. 尾隨某人。 **2** [VP6A] ***~ a person,*** follow him closely, eg because he is suspected to be a criminal. 跟踪某人(例如因他有罪嫌)。 **3** [VP2C] ***~ off/away,*** **(a)** become smaller in number, size, etc. 變小;變少。**(b)** (of remarks, etc) end in a hesitating or inconclusive way. (指談話等)遲疑或不得要領地結束。**(c)** fall behind or away in a scattered line. 落伍;零零落落地掉在後面。 **-tailed** /-teɪld ; -teld/ *adj* (in compounds) (用於複合字) ˌ*long-ˈ~ed,* ˌ*short-ˈ~ed,* having a long/short ~. 長尾的;短尾的。 **~·less** *adj* having no ~: 無尾的: *a ~less cat.* 一隻無尾貓。

tailor /ˈteɪlə(r) ; ˈtelɚ/ *n* maker of (esp outer) garments: 成衣匠;裁縫(尤指縫製外衣者): *go to the ~'s to be measured for a suit/an overcoat.* 去裁縫店量身做一套衣服(一件大衣)。ˌ~-**ˈmade** *adj* made by a ~, with special attention to exact fit; (fig) appropriate, well-suited: 定製的;定做的;合身的;(喻)適當的;合適的: *He seems ~-made for the job.* 他好像很適合這項工作。□ *vt* **1** [VP6A] cut out and sew: 裁製;縫製: *a well-~ed suit.* 裁製得好的一套衣服。 **2** [VP15A] adapt: 適應;適合: *~ed for a special purpose/to a particular audience.* 適合一項特殊目的(特定的聽衆)。

taint /teɪnt ; tent/ *n* [C, U] trace of some bad quality, decay or infection: 品質惡劣、腐敗或感染的跡象;污點;恥辱: *There was a ~ of insanity in the family.* 這個家族(的成員)有癲狂的跡象。*Is the meat free from ~?* 這肉是好的(新鮮的)嗎? □ *vt, vi* [VP6A, 2A] make or become infected: 使感染;受感染;使腐敗;變汚;變壞: *~ed meat.* 腐肉。**~·less** *adj* without ~; pure. 未感染的;未腐敗的;純潔的;無汚的。

take¹ /teɪk ; tek/ *vt, vi* (*pt* took /tʊk ; tʊk/, *pp* taken /ˈteɪkən ; ˈtekən/) (For uses with a large number of *nn,* ⇨ 15 below. For special uses with *adverbial particles* and *preps* ⇨ 16 below.) (與諸多名詞的連用法,參看下列第15義。與副詞接語及介詞連用的特殊用法,參看下列第16義。) **1** [VP6A, 15A] get or lay hold of with the hand(s) or any other part of the body, eg the arms, teeth or with an instrument (Cf *let go of* or *release,* as opposite in meaning): 握;攫;執;抱(參較反義字 let go of 或 release): *~ sb's hand;* 握住某人的手; *~ sth on one's back;* 背負某物; *~ a man by the throat;* 扼住某人的咽喉; *~ sb in one's arms,* put one's arms round him, embrace him; 擁抱某人; *~ sth up* (= pick it up) *with one's fingers/with a pair of tongs;* 用手指(鉗子)拾起或夾起某物; *~ a person's arm,* put, rest, one's hand on his arm, eg to support him or be supported by him. 挽住某人的臂(例如扶着他,或被他扶着)。***~ hold of sth,*** grasp or seize it. 抓住或捉住某物。**2** [VP6A, 15A, 2A] capture; catch (sb or sth) by surprise or pursuit; win (in a contest, etc): 捕捉;襲取;佔領;獲得;(競賽等中)獲勝: *~ a town/a fortress,* in war; (作戰中)攻佔一城市(堡壘); *~ 500 prisoners;* 俘獲五百名俘虜; *be ~n prisoner/captive,* be caught and be made a prisoner. 被俘。*The rabbit was ~n in a trap.* 那兔子被捕兔機捉住了。*The major's bull took* (= was awarded) *the first prize at the agricultural show.* 少校的公牛在農業展覽會上獲得首獎。*How many tricks did you ~,* ie win, eg at a card game such as whist or bridge? 你們得了多少磴牌(如在惠斯特或橋牌戲中)? *Be careful not to ~ cold,* become ill with a cold (*catch cold* is more usu). 小心不要着涼(catch cold 較常用)。***~ sb's fancy,*** please, delight: 使高興;使愉快: *The new dance has really taken the public's fancy.* 這種新的舞蹈深爲大家所喜愛。***~ sb at a disadvantage,*** be approached, attacked, etc when unready, in an unfavourable situation, etc. 乘人不備;乘人之危。***be ~n ill,*** (passive only) become ill, catch an illness. (祇用被動語態)患病;罹疾。***~ sb unawares/by surprise,*** approach or discover sb doing sth when he is unaware of one's presence, that one sees him, etc. 在某人不知有人在場,不知有人看到等時接近某人或發現某人做某事;冷不防出現;突然接近;撞見某人做某事。**3** [VP6A] use; use or borrow without permission; steal; avail oneself of: 使用;不經同意擅自利用或借用;偷竊;自取;擅自利用: *Someone has ~n my hat,* ie by mistake. 有人把我的帽子拿走了(無意中拿錯了)。*Who has ~n my bicycle,* borrowed or stolen it? 誰把我的脚踏車拿走了(借用或偷去)? *He ~s whatever he can lay his hands on.* 他取用他能拿到手的東西。 **4** [VP6A, 15A, B, 12A, 13A, 19B] carry (sth), accompany (sb), away from a place: 携帶;拿走某物;伴隨某人: *~ letters to the post;* 把信付郵; *~ the luggage upstairs;* 把行李搬上樓; *~ a friend home in one's car;* 用汽車送朋友回家; *~ the dog out for a walk;* 帶狗出去散步; *~ one's wife to the cinema;* 帶太太去看電影; *~ the children swimming/for a swim.* 帶孩子們去游泳。*Please ~ these things in/out/away/back/home, etc.* 請把這些東西拿進去(拿出去,拿開,拿回來,拿回家等)。*Shall I ~ your message to her/~ her your message?* 要我把你的信帶給她嗎? *T~ her some flowers.* 帶一些花給她。*He took me a new way to the coast,* by a route that was new to me. 他帶我走一條新路去海濱。**ˈ~-home wages/pay,** (colloq) net sum after deduction of national insurance contribution, income tax, etc. (俗)(扣除各項捐稅後的)淨薪;實領工資。 **5** [VP6A, 15A] get, have; eat or drink; allow oneself: 得到;享有;吃;喝;享受: *~ a holiday/a walk/a bath/a quick look round/a deep breath;* 休假(散步;沐浴;迅速向四周望一眼;作深呼吸); *~ a chair/a seat,* sit down; 坐下;就座; *~ medical/legal advice,* get the advice of a doctor/lawyer; 聽取醫生(律師)的意見; *~ driving lessons;* 學習駕駛; ~ (= hire) *a taxi;* 雇計程車; ~ (= rent) *a cottage at the seaside for the holidays.* 在海邊租一幢別墅度假; *Let's go into the garden and ~ the air,* have some fresh air. 咱們到園子裏去透透氣。*Will you ~ tea or coffee?* 你要喝茶還是要喝咖啡? *I'll ~* (= buy) *2 lb of your Kenya coffee.* 我要向你買兩磅肯亞咖啡。*Why don't you ~ a wife,* (old use) marry? (舊用法)你爲什麼不娶妻? *You should ~ a partner into the business/~ your brother into the business.* 你應該找一個人合夥經營這生意(找你兄弟合夥經營)。 **6** [VP6A, 15A, 16A, B] accept; receive: 接受;領受;收到: *Will you ~ £1500 for the car,* sell it for this sum? 你願意以一千五百鎊的價錢出售該車嗎?

T

This small café ~s £500 a week, This is the total of the receipts. 這家小飲食店每週做五百鎊的生意。⇨ takings below. 參看下列之 takings。(From the C of E marriage service) (來自英國教會婚禮儀式) *Do you ~ this man to be your lawful wedded husband?* 你接受此人爲你合法婚姻的丈夫嗎？*You must ~ us as you find us,* not expect exceptional treatment, consideration, etc (while you are with us). 你不可對我們另有期望(我們對你的態度或待遇,就是你見到的這樣)。*He will ~ no nonsense,* will not allow any. 他不允許胡鬧。*I'm not taking any more of your insults,* I refuse to listen to them. 我不再聽你這些無禮的話了。**~ one's chance,** **(a)** trust to one's luck; accept whatever may come or happen: 碰運氣;接受可能發生或來臨之事: *She'll have to ~ her chance with the other applicants for the job.* 她必須碰自己的運氣與其他的求職者競爭那份工作。**(b)** attempt sth though aware of the possibility of failing. 明知可能失敗而從事某事。**~ a chance (on sth),** accept the possibility of not getting sth: 做做看;冒險試做(某事);接受失敗的可能性: *I'm ready to ~ a chance on finding him at home,* will call hoping to find him there. 我準備到他家去看看他,希望他在家。**~ it from me; ~ my word for it,** believe me when I say: 當我說…時相信我;我保證;我這話你可以相信: *T~ it from me, there'll be some big changes made in the coming year.* 我保證未來這一年會發生若干重大的變化。**be able to ~ it; can ~ it,** be able to endure suffering, punishment, attack, etc without showing weakness, readiness to admit defeat, etc. 能忍受痛苦、懲罰、攻擊等;挺得住;挨得過;受得了。**7** [VP6A] subscribe to; receive and pay for regularly: 訂閱;訂購;定: *Which newspapers do you ~?* 你訂閱那些報紙？ **8** [VP6A, 15A, B] **~ (down),** make a record of: 記錄;記下: *~ notes of a lecture;* 作聽講筆記; *~ sth down in shorthand;* 用速記記下某事; *~ a letter,* from dictation; (根據口述)寫下一封信; *~ (down) a broadcast on tape,* ie using a tape-recorder; 用錄音機錄下一段廣播; *~ a photograph.* 拍照片。[VP2A] *He does not ~ well,* It is difficult to ~ good photographs of him. 他不上照(不容易拍到他的好看的照片)。 **9** [VP2B, 6B, 15A] need, require: 需要;花費: *The work took four hours.* 這項工作花了四小時。*These things ~ time.* 這些事情需要花時間去做。*How long will this job ~ you/How long will you ~ over this job?* 你做這事要花多久的時間？*The wound took a long time to heal.* 這傷口過了很久才痊愈。 **~ one's time (over sth),** **(a)** not hurry; use as much time as one needs: 不匆忙;不急;慢慢來;用時不限制: *Take your time over the job, and do it well.* 這工作慢慢做,把它做好。**(b)** (ironic) use more time than is reasonable: (反語)浪費時間;拖延;磨洋工: *The workmen are certainly taking their time over the job.* 工人們顯然在那裏拖延工作的時間。**It ~s 'two to make a quarrel,** (prov) suggesting that both parties to a quarrel are at fault. (諺)一個巴掌拍不響;兩個人才吵得起來(含示雙方皆有錯)。**~ a lot of doing,** need much effort, skill, etc. 費事;費力;需要努力、技巧等。 **10** [VP14, 25] **~ sb/sth for...; ~ sb/sth to be...,** suppose; conclude; infer; consider: 假定;推斷;推定;以爲: *I took you to be an honest man.* 我(過去)認爲你很誠實。*Do you ~ me for a fool?* 你以爲我是傻瓜嗎？*Even the experts took the painting for a genuine Rembrandt.* 甚至專家們也把那幅畫認定是倫布蘭特的眞品。**~ it (from sb) that...,** assume: 認爲;假定;想像: *I ~ it that we are to come early.* 我認爲我們應該早點來。*You may ~ it from me that...,* be confident because I tell you.... 你可以相信我所說的…。**~ sb/sth for granted,** ⇨ grant *v*(2). **11** [VP 6A] find out (by inquiry, measurement, etc): (藉詢問、測量等) 找出;量出;測出: *The doctor took my temperature.* 醫生量我的體溫。*Has the tailor ~n your measurements for that new suit?* 裁縫已爲你量身做那套新衣嗎？ *Did the police ~ your name and address?* 警察問過了你的姓名及住址嗎？ **12** [VP22, 16B] treat or regard in a specified way: (用某種指明的方式) 處理;對待: *~ it/things easy,* not work too hard or too fast; 不趕做;不趕工;不過勞或過快; *~ things coolly/calmly,* not get excited; 處之泰然;不激動; *~ sth ill/amiss,* resent it. 對某事表示不高興。*I should ~ it kindly* (= be grateful to you) *if....* 我應該感謝你,如果…。*Don't ~ it so seriously,* Don't treat the matter with such seriousness. 不要把這事看得如此嚴重。**~ sth as+pp,** assume it to be: 認爲某事業經…: *~ an apology as given/an objection as answered.* 認爲已經道歉(答覆一異議)。**~ sth as read,** agree that it is unnecessary to read it, eg the minutes of the previous meeting. 認爲不必讀(上次會議記錄等)。**~ (it) as read (that...),** assume it, assume that...: 認爲…;以爲…: *We can ~ (it) as read that an apology was given.* 我們可認爲業已道歉。 **13** [VP6A] accept responsibility for: 負起…的責任;履行: *~ evening service,* (at church) conduct it; (在教堂)主持晚間禮拜; *~ a class,* be in charge, give the class its lesson, etc. 授課;督導某班級。**14** [VP2A] be successful: 成功;成就: *George Green's second novel did not ~,* did not become popular; 喬治•格林的第二部小說不暢銷。have the required effect: 奏效;起所要的反應;生預期效果: *That smallpox injection did not ~.* 那次種的牛痘沒有效果。*The dye doesn't ~ in cold water,* is ineffective. 那染料在冷水中不起作用。 **15** (with *nn*) (For other examples, ⇨ the *n* entries). (與名詞連用) (其他例句參看各名詞) **~ account of sth,** (= ~ sth into account), ⇨ account[1](7). **~ advantage of sb/sth,** ⇨ advantage. **~ aim,** ⇨ aim[1] (2). **~ the biscuit/the cake,** ⇨ biscuit, cake. **~ care,** ⇨ care[1](2). **~ a chair,** ⇨ 5 above. 參看上列第 5 義。**~ a/one's chance,** ⇨ 6 above. 參看上列第 6 義。**~ charge (of),** ⇨ charge[1](5). **~ courage,** ⇨ courage. **~ a degree,** obtain a degree(5). 獲得學位。**~ (a) delight/an interest/(a) pleasure/(a) pride in sth,** be, show that one is, delighted/interested, etc in it. 對某事感到高興(興趣,愉快,驕傲)。**~ a dislike to sb,** ⇨ dislike. **~ effect,** ⇨ effect(1). **~ an examination,** be tested on one's knowledge or ability. 應試;參加考試。**~ exception to,** ⇨ exception(3). **not/never take one's eyes off,** ⇨ 16 below. 參看下列第 16 義。**~ a fancy to; ~ the fancy of,** ⇨ fancy[1](3). **~ fright (at sth),** become frightened. (對某事)感到驚懼。**~ a gamble (on sth),** do sth knowing it is risky. 冒險做(某事)。**~ a hand at,** ⇨ hand[1](13). **~ sb in hand,** accept responsibility for him (esp to improve his behaviour). 負責照顧某人(尤指改進其行爲)。**~ (fresh) heart; ~ sth to heart,** ⇨ heart(2). **~ heed,** pay attention. 注意。**~ a/the hint,** ⇨ hint. **~ (one's) leave (of sb),** ⇨ leave[2](3). **~ the liberty of; ~ liberties with,** ⇨ liberty(2). **~ a liking to,** become fond of. 喜歡。**~ the measure of sb,** ⇨ measure[1](1). **~ one's/sb's mind off (sth),** ⇨ mind[1](2). **~ no notice (of),** ⇨ notice(3). **~ an oath,** ⇨ oath(1). **~ objection to,** ⇨ objection(1). **~ offence (at sth),** ⇨ offence(2). **~ the opportunity of doing/to do sth,** recognize a favourable moment and act. 趁機或抓住機會做某事。**~ (holy) orders,** become a priest, etc. 出任聖職(當僧侶等)。**~ (great) pains (over sth/to do sth),** ⇨ pains. **~ part (in),** ⇨ part[1](4). **~ place; ~ the place of,** ⇨ place[1](10). **~ the risk of; ~ risks,** ⇨ risk(1). **~ a seat,** ⇨ 5 above. 參看上列第 5 義。**~ silk,** ⇨ silk(3). **~ stock,** ⇨ stock[1](1). **~ one's time (over sth),** ⇨ 9 above. 參看上列第 9 義。 **~ trouble (over sth); ~ the trouble to do sth,** ⇨ trouble, *n*(3). **~ umbrage (at),** ⇨ umbrage. **~ my word for** *it*, ⇨ 6 above. 參看上列第 6 義。 **16** [VP3A, 2C, 15B, 14] (special uses with *adverbial particles* and *preps*): (與副詞接語及介詞連用的特殊用法):

be taken aback, ⇨ aback.

take after sb, resemble (esp a parent or relation) in features or character: (在長相或性格方面)像某人 (尤指像父母親或某一親屬): *Your daughter does not ~ after you in any way.* 你的女兒沒有一個地方像你。

take sth apart, separate sth (machinery, etc) into its (component) parts. 把某物(機器等)分解爲其組成部分;拆散;拆開。

take (away) from, lessen, weaken, diminish: 減少;減弱;減小;降低: *That foolish indiscretion took away from his public image.* 那次愚蠢的輕率行爲損壞了他的形象。 *These faults to some extent ~ (away) from his credit as a biographer.* 身爲傳記作家,這些缺點多少會降低他的信譽。 ***~ sth/sb away (from sb/sth)***, remove: 拿去;消除;移動;使離開;使退出: *Not to be ~n away*, eg books from a library. 不可取走(如圖書館裏的書)。 *The child was ~n away from school*, not allowed to attend. 那孩子被勒令退學。 *What ~s you away so early*, Why are you leaving so early? 你爲什麼這麼早就要走? *'Sandwiches to ~ away'* (eg as a sign outside a shop, = '... to be ~n away'), Sandwiches may be bought here and eaten elsewhere. '可攜走食用的三明治'; '三明治外賣' (例如商店外面之標示)。 Hence, 由此產生, **'~-away** *attrib* to be ~n away: 可帶走的;外賣的: *~-away hamburgers;* 外賣牛肉餅; *a ~-away restaurant*, one that sells food that may be ~n away. 外賣餐館。

take sth back, **(a)** retreat or withdraw (what one has said) as an admission of error, as an apology, etc: 撤銷;收回(所說的話,以承認錯誤或道歉等): *I ~ back what I said.* 我收回我所說的話。 **(b)** agree to receive back: 同意拿回;取回: *Shopkeepers will not usually ~ back goods after they have been paid for.* 店主人通常不收回已付過錢的貨物。 ***~ sb back (to)***, carry or conduct to an earlier period: 使某人回想或追憶: *These stories took him back to his childhood days*, (fig) brought them back to his mind. (喻)這些故事使他回想到童年時代。

take sth down, **(a)** write down: 記錄: *The reporters took down the speech.* 記者們記錄演講詞。 **(b)** lower; get by lifting down from (a shelf, etc): 降下;降低;從(架上等)取下: *~ down a book from the top shelf;* 從最上面的架上取下一本書; *~ down the curtains/pictures from the walls;* 落幕(從牆上取下圖畫); *~ down a mast.* 降下桅杆。 **(c)** dismantle; pull down; get into separate parts: 拆毀;拆除;拆開: *~ down a crane/the scaffolding round a building;* 拆除起重機(房屋四周的鷹架); *~ down a partition.* 拆掉隔板。 ***~ sb 'down a peg (or two)***, humble; lower the pride of: 挫某人的傲氣;貶抑: *That fellow needs to be ~n down a peg.* 那傢伙需要挫挫他的傲氣。

take from, ⇨ *take (away) from* above. 參看上列之 take (away) from。

take sth in, **(a)** receive (work) to be done in one's own house for payment: 承攬(工作)在自己家中做: *The poor widow earns money by taking in washing/sewing.* 那貧苦的寡婦靠在家裏替人洗(縫)衣服度日。 **(b)** (⇨ 7 above) pay for and receive regularly: (參看上列第 7 義)訂閱;訂購: *~ in journals/periodicals.* 訂閱雜誌(期刊)。 **(c)** reduce the size, area, length or width of (a garment, sail, etc): 減小(衣服、帆等)的尺碼、面積、長度或寬度;改小;縮小;捲起;叠起: *This dress needs to be ~n in* (= made smaller) *at the waist.* 這件女裝腰部需要改小。 *Orders were given to ~ in sail.* 已發布了收帆的命令。 ⇨ *~ up the slack* at slack²(1). **(d)** comprise; include, eg in one's journey or route: 包含;包括(如包括在某人的行程中): *a motor-coach tour that ~s in six European capitals.* 行程包括歐洲六個國家首都在內的乘坐遊覽車的觀光旅行。 **(e)** take (territory, common land, etc) into one's possession; (re)claim: 取得(領土,公有地等);開墾;填築: *A good deal of Romney Marsh was ~n in from the sea by monks.* 洛木尼沼地有很大一部分係由僧侶們填海而成。 **(f)** understand; absorb; digest mentally: 瞭解;吸收;領會: *They listened to my lecture, but how much did they ~ in, I wonder?* 他們聽了我的課,但是我不知道他們領會了多少? *We need more time to ~ in the situation*, form a correct idea of it. 我們需要多一點時間來瞭解當前的情況。 **(g)** see at a glance; see at once: 一眼看清;同時看到: *She took in every detail of the other woman's clothes.* 她一眼就看到了另一位女士衣服的每一個細微處。 *He took in the scene at a glance.* 他看了一眼那(地方的)景色。 **(h)** listen to, watch, with excitement: 激動地聽或看: *The children took in the whole spectacle open-mouthed.* 孩子們張着嘴驚奇地注視整個的精采表演。 ***~ sb in***, **(a)** receive, admit: 接待;收容: *make a living by taking in guests/lodgers;* 靠接待客人(寄宿者)維持生活。 *~ a traveller in for the night.* 接待旅客住夜。 **(b)** deceive; get the better of by a trick: 欺騙;詐騙: *Don't let yourself be ~n in by these politicians.* 不要(使你自己)受這些政客的欺騙。 *He was badly ~n in when he bought that second-hand car.* 他購買那輛舊汽車時,大大地受騙了。

take sth into account, ⇨ account(7). ***~ a person into one's confidence***, ⇨ confidence(1). ***~ sth into one's head***, ⇨ head¹(19).

take off, **(a)** make a start in jumping. 起跳。 **(b)** (of an aircraft) leave the ground and rise: (指飛機)起飛: *The plane took off despite the fog.* 那架飛機不顧大霧而起飛。 Hence, 由此產生, **'~-off** *n* **(a)** (also *jump-off*, esp in show jumping) place at which the feet leave the ground in jumping. (亦作 jump-off, 尤指超越障礙騎術表演中) (脚離地面的)起跳處;起跳點。 **(b)** (of aircraft) leaving the ground and rising: (指飛機)起飛: *a smooth ~-off.* 平穩的起飛。 ⇨ *touch-down* at touch²(11). ***~ sth off***, **(a)** remove: 除去;脫掉: *~ off one's shirt.* 脫掉襯衫。 *Why don't you ~* (= shave) *off that silly little moustache?* 你爲什麼不剃掉那無聊的小鬍子呢? *The surgeon took off* (= amputated) *his leg.* 外科醫生切去了他的腿。 ***~ one's hat off to sb***, ⇨ hat. **(b)** withdraw (from service): 撤消(…的服務): *The 7am express to Bristol will be ~n off next month*, will not run. 上午七時開往布里斯托的快車將於下月停駛。 ***~ sth off (sth)***, **(a)** lift and move to another position: 移動;搬位: *T~ your hand off my shoulder.* 把你的手從我肩膀上拿開。 **(b)** deduct: 減去;減少: *~ 50p off the price.* 減價五十辨士。 ***~ sb off***, **(a)** conduct; lead away somewhere: 引導;帶走;引開: *He was ~n off to prison.* 他被送進監獄。 *She took me off to see her garden.* 她引導我去看她的花園。 ***~ sb off sth***, remove him from it: 使某人離開某物: *The crew were ~n off* (rescued from) *the wrecked ship by the lifeboat.* 船員們被救生艇救離了難船。 **(b)** ridicule by imitation; mimic; burlesque: 藉學樣取笑: *Alice is clever at taking off the headmistress.* 愛麗絲善於模倣女校長的樣子以取笑她。 Hence, 由此產生, **'~-off** *n* caricature; burlesque imitation of sb's behaviour: (對某人行爲等的)滑稽的模倣: *a good ~off of the Prime Minister.* 學首相的樣子而模倣得維妙維肖的動作。 ***not/never ~ one's eyes off sth/sb***, look at constantly: 不停地注視某物或某人;釘着看: *He never took his eyes off his small daughter while she was swimming in the sea.* 當他的小女兒在海裏游泳時,他一直注視着她。 ***~ one's mind off (sth)***, ⇨ mind¹(2).

take on, **(a)** (colloq) become excited or agitated; make a fuss: (俗)激動;激昂;作無謂紛擾: *She took on something dreadful when I said she'd told a pack of lies.* 當我告訴她她撒了很多謊時,她激動得可怕。 **(b)** (colloq) become popular; have a vogue: (俗)受歡迎;流行: *We introduced a new sports car last year but it never took on.* 去年我們引進一種新型跑車，但未受歡迎。 **~ sth on, (a)** undertake; charge oneself with: 從事;擔任;承當: *~ on extra work/heavy responsibilities.* 承擔額外工作(重責)。*You've ~n on too much.* 你承擔的工作太多了。**(b)** assume; put on (a quality, appearance): 裝出;表現(某種性質,外表): *The chameleon can ~ on the colours of its background.* 變色蜥蜴可現出與其背景相同的顏色。 **~ sb on, (a)** accept as an opponent: 接受某人作爲對手;接受挑戰: *~ sb on at golf/billiards;* 與某人比賽高爾夫球(撞球); *ready to ~ on all comers,* play against, fight, anyone who accepts a challenge. 準備迎戰所有接受挑戰者。 **(b)** engage: 雇用: *~ on twenty more workers.* 再雇用二十名工人。 **(c)** (of a train, etc) allow to enter: (指火車等)許可進入: *The bus stopped to ~ on some children.* 公共汽車停下來載一些小孩子。 **(d)** (of trains, etc) carry too far, past the destination: (指火車等)使過站;運送過遠: *I fell asleep in the train and was ~n on to York.* 我在火車上睡着了,一直坐到了約克。

***take sth out,* (a)** extract; remove: 除去;拔去;剪除: *have one's appendix/a tooth ~n out.* 切除盲腸(拔牙)。*How can I ~ out* (= remove) *these inkstains from my blouse?* 我怎樣才能把我罩衫上這些墨水污跡除去呢？**(b)** obtain; procure (sth issued): 獲得;領得(頒發之文件等): *~ out an insurance policy/a driving licence/a summons/a patent.* 領到保險單(駕駛執照,傳票,專利證書)。 **~ sb out, (a)** conduct; accompany: 帶某人外出;引領;伴隨: *~ the children out for a walk;* 帶孩子們出去散步; *~ one's wife out for dinner,* ie at a restaurant. 帶太太出去(在館子裏)吃飯。 **(b)** (in bridge): (橋牌戲中): *~ one's partner out,* make a higher bid (than that which he has made). 叫牌高於搭檔。**~ it out in sth,** accept as recompense or compensation: 接受某物作爲賠償或補償: *The innkeeper couldn't pay me the £10 he owed me but let me ~ it out in drinks and cigars.* 小旅店老闆無力償還欠我的十鎊,但是他讓我拿酒及雪茄作爲抵償。**~ it out of sb,** leave him weak and exhausted: 使某人衰弱;使某人筋疲力竭: *His recent illness/All that hard work has ~n it out of him.* 他最近的一場病(所有那些繁重的工作)已耗盡他的體力。 **~ it out on sb,** vent one's anger, disappointment, etc on (usu) sb else: 向某人發洩怒氣、失望等: *He came home angry at losing his job and took it out on his wife.* 他回到家裡因爲失去工作而生氣,並把一肚子的怒氣發洩到他太太身上。

take sb over (to), carry from one place to another: 從一地送某人至另一地: *Mr White took me over to the island in his launch.* 懷特先生用他的汽艇載我至該島。 **~ sth over (from sb),** assume control of; succeed to the management or ownership of (a business, etc): 接管;接收(商店等): *Was it in 1948 that the Government took over the railways in Great Britain,* nationalized them? 英國政府接管鐵路(將鐵路收爲國有)是在 1948 年嗎？ *When Mr Green retired his son took over the business from him.* 格林先生退休後,由他兒子接管他的生意。Hence, 由此產生, **'~-over** *n* change of control of a firm or company, eg after another has made a successful bid to buy its stock: (公司或商店的)接收;接管;改變控制權(如因他人購得其股票): *a '~over bid.* 取得控制權的出價。 **~ over (from sb),** accept duties, responsibilities, etc: (從某人) 接收職務、責任等;接任: *The new Chancellor took over* (ie *from* his predecessor) *yesterday.* 新校長昨天(從他的前任)接事。

***take to sth,* (a)** adopt as a practice or hobby, as a means of livelihood; get into a habit: 採納某事(作爲習慣或嗜好,或作爲謀生的方法);從事;養成;耽於: *~ to gardening when one retires;* 退休後從事園藝; *~ to drink(ing),* get into the habit of taking alcoholic liquor; 嗜酒;耽酒; *~ to the road,* become a tramp (or, in former times a highwayman); (of a circus, etc) go on tour from town to town giving shows. 淪爲流浪漢;(指昔時)淪爲强盜;(指馬戲班等)到各處巡廻演出。 **(b)** take refuge in; use as a means of escape: 逃入;利用…作爲逃亡工具: *~ to flight,* run away; 逃走; *~ to the woods/the jungle/the heather,* go to the woods, etc, to avoid capture. 逃入林中(叢林,石南林)。*The crew took to the boats when the torpedo struck the ship.* 魚雷擊中那船時,船員們乘救生艇逃生。**~ to one's heels,** ⇨ heel¹(1). **~ to sth/sb,** conceive a liking for: 對某事物或某人懷有好感;喜歡: *Has the baby ~n to its new nursemaid?* 那嬰兒喜歡新來的保姆嗎？*That boy will never ~ to cricket.* 那個男孩子永遠不會喜歡板球。

***take sth up,* (a)** lift up; raise: 拿起;舉起;抬起;收起: *~ up one's pen/book/gun;* 拿起筆(書,槍); *~ up a carpet.* 收起地毯。**(b)** (of trains, taxis, etc; more usu 較常用 *~ on*) stop to allow (passengers) to enter. (指火車,計程車等)停下來接納(旅客)。 **(c)** absorb (a liquid): 吸收(液體): *Blotting-paper ~s up ink.* 吸墨紙吸收墨水。**(d)** dissolve (solids): 溶解(固體): *How much water is needed to ~ up a pound of salt?* 溶解一磅食鹽需要多少水？ **(e)** interest oneself in; engage in (sth) (as a hobby, business, etc): 對…有興趣; 從事(某事)(作爲嗜好,事業等): *~ up photography/market gardening.* 從事攝影(蔬菜種植)。 **(f)** pursue further; begin afresh (sth left off, sth begun by sb else): 繼續;重新開始(停頓之事,他人所開始之事): *Harry took up the tale at the point where John had left off.* 哈利接着約翰停止的地方繼續講那個故事。**(g)** occupy (time, space): 佔據(時間,空間);佔用: *This table ~s up too much space.* 這張桌子佔地方太大。*My time is fully ~n up with writing.* 我的時間全都花在寫作上了。**(h)** (comm) advance money (on a mortgage); accept (a Bill of Exchange); subscribe for (shares, etc) at the time of issue. (商)(按抵押) 墊款;承兌(滙票);(發行時)認購(股份等)。 **(i)** catch the end of and make secure: 抓住…的末端並使牢固;使穩定: *~ up a dropped stitch.* 繫牢一處脫線的針脚。**'~-up spool** *n* (on a ciné projector, tape-recorder, etc) spool on to which film, tape, etc is wound from the spool having the film, tape, etc that is being used. (電影放映機,錄音機等上的)收片捲軸;收帶捲軸 (從另一捲軸收捲使用中之影片或錄音帶者)。 **~ sth up (with sb),** speak or write (to him) about it: (口頭或書面向某人)提出某事: *I will ~ the matter up with the Ministry,* eg by asking for information, or by making a protest. 我將向政府提出此事(如要求說明或提出抗議)。 **~ sb up,** make a protégé of; help: 保護;幫助: *The young soprano was ~n up by the famous conductor,* He encouraged and helped her in her career. 那位年輕的女高音得到那位名指揮家的照顧。 **~ sb 'up on sth,** accept from him his offer, challenge, bet, etc: 接受某人的提議,挑戰,打賭等: *Why don't you take Jim up on his offer to lend you £50?* 吉姆要借給你五十鎊,你爲何不接受？ **be ~n up with sb/sth,** be much interested in: 對某人或某事物深感興趣: *He seems to be very much ~n up with that tall Swedish girl.* 他似乎對那位高個子瑞典女郎特別感興趣。 **~ sb up sharp/short,** interrupt and correct (a speaker): 打斷並改正(說話者): *He took me up short when I suggested that....* 當我建議…時,他打斷了我的話。 **~ up one's residence at,** (formal) proceed to occupy: (正式用語)定居於;遷入: *The new ambassador has ~n up his residence* (in the Embassy). 新任大使已經遷入(大使館)定居。

take sth upon/on oneself, assume responsibility; undertake: 承擔責任;攬事;從事: *You mustn't ~ upon yourself the right to make decisions.* 你不可以擅權而自做主張。

take² /teɪk; tek/ *n* **1** amount (of money) taken.

取得或獲得的金錢數額。 **2** (film industry) scene that has been or is to be photographed. (電影製片)已拍攝或待拍攝的景;鏡頭。 **3** act of taking. 拿取的動作;取;拿。

taker /ˈteɪkə(r); ˈtekɚ/ *n* one who, that which, takes, esp one who takes a bet: 拿取的人或物;接受者;(尤指)接受打賭者: *There were no ~s,* no one willing to take bets. 沒有人願意接受打賭。

tak·ing /ˈteɪkɪŋ; ˈtekɪŋ/ *adj* attractive; captivating. 動人的;迷人的。□ *n* (*pl*) money taken in business; receipts. (複)營業所得;收入。

talc /tælk; tælk/ *n* [U] soft, smooth mineral that can be split into thin transparent plates. 雲母;滑石。 **ˈ~ powder** *n* perfumed powder to rub on the body, made from ~. (滑石製成的)撲粉;滑石粉;爽身粉。

tal·cum /ˈtælkəm; ˈtælkəm/ *n* **ˈ~ powder,** = talc powder.

tale /teɪl; tel/ *n* [C] **1** story: 故事: *ˈfairy-~s;* 神仙故事;童話; *~s of adventure.* 冒險故事。 *It tells its own ~,* explains itself, requires no comment or explanation. 顯而易見;無須說明。 **2** report; account. 報告;記述;傳聞。 ***tell ~s,*** tell sth about another person that he wishes to be kept secret, eg his wrongdoing. 搬弄是非;講壞話;揭人短處。 Hence, 由此產生, **ˈ~-bearer/-teller** *nn* person who tells ~s. 搬弄是非者。

tal·ent /ˈtælənt; ˈtælənt/ *n* **1** [C, U] (particular kind of) natural power to do sth well: (某種的)天才;才幹;才能;智能: *a man of great ~;* 有大才幹的人; *local ~,* (usu amateur) musicians, actors, etc of a district; 地方上的人才(通常指當地業餘的音樂家、演員等); *a ˈ~ scout,* (colloq) person who watches out for persons of ~ for films, the theatre, sports, etc; (俗)星探;球探(發掘適於做演員、球員等的人); *have a ~ for music/not much ~ for painting;* 有音樂天才(不大有繪畫天才); *an exhibition of local ~,* of works, eg paintings, by people of a district or locality. 當地人士作品展(如畫展等)。 **2** [C] measure of weight, unit of money, used in ancient times among the Greeks, Romans, Assyrians, etc. (古希臘、羅馬、亞述等國的)一種重量及貨幣單位;泰倫。 **~ed** *adj* having ~; gifted: 有才能的;有才幹的;有天才的: *a ~ed musician.* 天才音樂家。

tal·is·man /ˈtælɪzmən *US:* -ɪsm-; ˈtælɪsmən/ *n* [C] (*pl* ~s) sth that is thought to bring good luck, eg a trinket or ring. 被認爲可帶來好運之物(如小裝飾物或戒指);辟邪物。

talk¹ /tɔːk; tɔk/ *n* **1** [C, U] talking; conversation; discussion: 談話;商議;討論: *I've had several ~s with the headmaster about my boy.* 我已與校長就我的男孩作過數次談話。 *There's too much ~ (= ~ing) and not enough work being done.* 說得太多而做得太少。 **2** [C] informal speech: 非正式的演講: *give a ~ to the Women's Institute on one's travels in Asia.* 就個人的亞洲旅行對婦女會發表非正式的演講。 **3** (phrases) (片語) ***the ~ of the town,*** sth or sb everyone is ~ing about. 爲大家談論的人或事物;街頭巷尾的話題。 ***be all ~,*** said of sb who ~s a lot but does not get results. 祇會說空話(指某人會說不會做)。 **ˈsmall ~,** conversation on everyday but not important topics. 閒話;閒談;雜談。

talk² /tɔːk; tɔk/ *vi, vt* (*pt, pp* ~ed) **1** [VP2A, B, C, 3A, 15B] ~ ***(to/with sb) (about/of sth),*** say things; speak to give information; discuss sth, etc: 說話;談話;討論: *He was ~ing to* (less often 較少用 *with*) *a friend.* 他在和一個朋友談話。 *What are they ~ing about* (less often 較少用 *of*)*?* 他們在談什麼? *We ~ed all afternoon/for two hours.* 我們整整談了一個下午(兩個鐘頭)。 *Were they ~ing in Spanish or in Portuguese?* 他們談話用的是西班牙語還是葡萄牙語? ***be/get oneself ~ed about,*** (in some contexts) be made the subject of gossip: (在某些上下文中)成爲閒談的話題;成爲話柄: *You'll get yourself ~ed about if you go on being so foolish.* 如果你繼續這種愚行,你會成爲旁人的話柄。 ***~ at sb,*** speak to sb without paying attention to his replies: 影射某人;指桑罵槐: *I don't like people who ~ at me instead of with me.* 我不喜歡人們含沙射影地對我講話,而不直接跟我講話。 ***~ away,*** continue ~ing: 繼續談話: *They were still ~ing away at midnight.* 他們談到半夜還沒有停止。 ***~ back (to sb),*** (often 常作 *answer back*) reply defiantly. (對某人)反脣相譏;回嘴。 ***~ big,*** brag; boast. 吹牛;說大話。 ***~ sb down,*** silence him by talking loudly at him. 高聲壓倒某人。 ***~ down an aircraft,*** ~ by radio to the pilot while he is about to make a landing, giving him instructions, etc. (藉無線電)指示飛機降落。 ***~ down to sb,*** ~ in a way that suggests that the speaker is superior, eg by using condescendingly simple words, etc: 自覺高人一等地對某人談話;以含示優於對方的方式說話: *It's unwise for a lecturer to ~ down to his audience.* 演說者自覺高人一等地向聽衆發表演講是不智的。 ***~ing of,*** while on the subject of: 說到;講到;談到: *T~ing of travel, have you been to Munich yet?* 談到旅行,你去過慕尼黑嗎? ***~ sth over,*** discuss it. 討論某事。 ***~ round sth,*** ~ about a subject without reaching the point or a conclusion. 不得要領地或無結論地談論某事;兜圈子地談論某事。 ***~ to sb,*** (colloq) scold; reprove. (俗)訓誡;斥責;數說。Hence, 由此產生, **ˈ~·ing-to** *n* scolding: 斥責;訓誡: *The teacher gave the lazy boy a good ~ing-to.* 老師把那個懶惰的男孩好好訓斥了一頓。 **2** [VP2A] have the power of speech: 有說話的能力: *Can the baby ~ yet?* 這娃娃會說話了嗎? **3** [VP6A] be able to use (a language): 會使用(一種語言);會講(某種語言): *~ English/Spanish.* 說英語(西班牙語)。 **4** [VP6A] discuss: 討論;磋商: *~ business, ~ shop,* 談正經事,講本行的話, ⇨ shop(2). *We ~ed music all evening.* 我們整晚都在談論音樂。 **ˈ~·ing-point,** topic likely to cause discussion; argument likely to persuade or convince sb. 話題;有說服力的論據。 **5** [VP6A] express in words: 用話表達;藉語言表示: *~ sense/nonsense/treason.* 講得有道理(講得無道理;言談中有叛國之意)。 **6** [VP14, 22] bring into a certain condition by ~ing: 藉講話而使陷入某一狀況;以言語使: *~ oneself hoarse,* ~ until one is hoarse. 講話講到聲音嘶啞。 ***~ sb into/out of doing sth,*** persuade sb to do/not to do sth: 說服某人做(不做)某事: *She ~ed her husband into having a holiday in France.* 她說服她丈夫去法國度假。 *He ~ed his wife out of buying a new car.* 他說服他太太不要買部新車。 ***~ sb over/round,*** persuade sb to agree to or to accept sth: 說服某人同意或接受某事物: *We ~ed them over to our way of thinking.* 我們說服他們接受我們的想法。 **7** [VP2A] (various uses): (各種用法): *Don't do anything indiscreet—you know how people ~,* gossip. 行爲不要太隨便──你知道,別人會說閒話的。*Has the accused man ~ed yet,* given information, eg under coercion or threats? 被告招供了嗎? *Some parrots can ~,* imitate the sounds of human speech. 有些鸚鵡會學人語。 **~a·tive** /ˈtɔːkətɪv; ˈtɔkətɪv/ *adj* fond of ~ing. 多話的;喜歡談話的;多嘴的。 **~·er** *n* **1** (esp with an *adj*) person who ~s: 談話者;說話者(尤與形容詞連用): *a good/poor, etc ~er.* 健談(不善於講話等)的人。*What a ~er that woman is!* How fond she is of ~ing! 那女人眞喜歡講話! **2** person who ~s a lot but does not get results: 空談者: *He's a mere ~er.* 他祇會講空話。

talkie /ˈtɔːkɪ; ˈtɔkɪ/ *n* [C] (dated colloq term for a) cinema film with spoken dialogue (used when these were a novelty). (過時俗語)有聲影片(初期尚感新奇時之用語)。 ***the ~s,*** (colloq) cinema films with spoken dialogue. (俗)有聲電影。

tall /tɔːl; tɔl/ *adj* (-er, -est) **1** (of persons) of more than average height; (of objects such as a ship's mast, a flagpole, a church spire, a tree whose height is greater than its width, but not

T

of mountains) higher than the average or than surrounding objects: (指人)高的;(指桅杆、旗杆、教堂尖塔、樹等高而細之物,但不指山)超過一般高度的;高於周圍事物的: *She is ~er than her sister.* 她比她姊姊(妹妹)高。*She wears high heels to make herself look ~er.* 她穿高跟鞋使自己看起來高一些。*That yacht has a very ~ mast.* 那遊艇有一根非常高的桅杆。'~-**boy** (GB; US 美 = *highboy*) *n* bedroom chest of drawers 5 or 6 ft high. (英)(臥室用的)高衣櫃(約五、六呎高)。**2** of a specified height: 有某種(指明的)高度的: *Tom is six foot ~.* 湯姆身高六呎。**3** (colloq) excessive, exorbitant. (俗)過分的;逾恆的。**a ~ order,** an unreasonable request; a task difficult to perform. 過分的要求;難完成的任務。**a ~ story,** one that it is difficult to believe. 荒誕不經的故事。**~·ish** /-ɪʃ ; -ɪʃ/ *adj* rather ~. 頗高的;高高的;略高的。

tal·low /'tæləʊ ; 'tælo/ *n* [U] hard (esp animal) fat used for making candles, etc. (用於製蠟燭等的)硬脂肪;脂;(尤指)獸脂。

tally /'tælɪ ; 'tælɪ/ *n* [C] (*pl* -lies) **1** score; reckoning: 分數;計算: *keep the ~.* 記分數。**2** ticket, label, etc used for identification. 用以核對的票據、標籤等。'~-**clerk** *n* clerk who checks cargo, etc eg at the docks. 貨物核對員(如碼頭等處者)。'~·**man** /-mæn ; -mən/ *n* (*pl* -men) person who sells goods and collects weekly payments. 賒賣人;賒賣者(每週收款一次)。□ *vi* (*pt, pp* -lied) [VP2A, 3A] ~ ***(with),*** (of stories, amounts, etc) correspond; agree: (指敍事、故事、數量等)符合;脗合: *The two lists do not ~.* 這兩張單子不相符。*Does your list ~ with mine?* 你的單子與我的符合嗎? *The stories of the two men tallied.* 這兩個人說的話一致。

tally-ho /ˌtælɪ 'həʊ ; ˌtælɪ'ho/ *int* huntsman's cry on catching sight of the fox. 嗬(獵人發現狐狸時的喊聲)。

Tal·mud /'tælmʊd *US:* 'tɑ:l- ; 'tælmʌd/ *n* compendium of Jewish law and teaching. 猶太法典。

talon /'tælən ; 'tælən/ *n* claw of a bird of prey, eg an eagle. 猛禽(如鷹)的爪。

talus /'teɪləs ; 'teləs/ *n* (geol) sloping mass of fragments at the foot of a cliff or precipice. (地質)崖錐(懸崖脚下的斜坡狀碎石堆)。

ta·male /tə'mɑ:lɪ ; tə'mɑlɪ/ *n* Mexican dish of chopped meat, red peppers, etc steamed in corn (= maize) husks. 特馬利(一種墨西哥食物,將碎肉、辣椒等包在玉蜀黍外殼中蒸熟而成)。

tam·ar·ind /'tæmərɪnd ; 'tæməˌrɪnd/ *n* (edible fruit of a) tropical tree. 羅望子(一種熱帶植物);羅望子的果實(可食)。

tam·ar·isk /'tæmərɪsk ; 'tæməˌrɪsk/ *n* [C] evergreen shrub with feathery branches, often planted in sandy soil near the sea. 檉柳(一種枝條輕柔的常綠灌木,常栽於近海沙土中,又名赤楊、三春柳等)。

tam·bour /'tæmbʊə(r) ; 'tæmbʊr/ *n* rolling front for a TV set or the top of a writing-desk, made of narrow strips of wood glued to canvas. (多根細木條黏在帆布上製成的)電視機的拉門;書桌的活動桌面。

tam·bour·ine /ˌtæmbə'ri:n ; ˌtæmbə'rin/ *n* small, shallow drum with metal discs in the rim, played by striking with the knuckles and shaking it at the same time. 鈴鼓(四周有金屬圓片,邊擊邊搖,使發鼓聲及鈴鈴聲)。⇨ the illus at percussion. 參看 percussion 之插圖。

tame /teɪm ; tem/ *adj* (-r, -st) **1** (of animals) brought under control and/or accustomed to living with human beings; not wild or fierce: (指動物)馴服的;養乖了的;不野的: *a ~ monkey.* 馴服的猴子。*The deer in the park are very ~.* 公園裏的鹿非常馴服。**2** (of a person) spiritless; submissive; docile: (指人)無精打采的;順從的;溫順的: *Her husband is a ~ little man.* 她的丈夫是一位個子矮小的好好先生。**3** dull: 沉悶的;乏味的: *a ~ baseball match.* 不精采的棒球賽。*The story/film, etc has a ~ ending.* 這故事(電影等)結尾很沈悶。□ *vt* [VP6A] make ~: 使馴服;使順從: *~ a lion.* 馴獅。**tamer** *n* (usu in compounds) person who ~s: (通常用於複合字中)馴養者;馴獸師: *a 'lion-~r.* 馴獅者。**tam·able** /-əbl ; -əbl̩/ *adj* that can be ~d, converted from a savage state. 可馴服的;可改變其野性的。**~·ly** *adv* **~·ness** *n*

Tam·many /'tæmənɪ ; 'tæmənɪ/ *n* ~ **(Hall),** central organization of the Democratic Party in New York City; (attrib) of its politics, members, etc. 坦慕尼協會(美國民主黨在紐約市的中心組織);(形容用法)其政策、會員等的。

tam-o'-shan·ter /ˌtæm ə 'ʃæntə(r) ; ˌtæmə'ʃæntɚ/, **tammy** /'tæmɪ ; 'tæmɪ/ *nn* round, woollen or cloth cap fitting closely to the forehead. 一種圓帽(用呢或布製成,緊覆於前額)。

tamp /tæmp ; tæmp/ *vt* [VP15B] **~ *sth down,*** tap or drive down by repeated light blows: 藉連續的輕擊而敲下;搗固;舂牢: *He ~ed down the tobacco in his pipe.* 他把烟絲輕按幾下使緊塞在烟斗裏。

tam·per /'tæmpə(r) ; 'tæmpɚ/ *vi* [VP3A] **~ *with,*** meddle or interfere with; make unauthorized changes in: 干預;干涉;亂弄;擅自改變;未經授權而改動: *Someone has been ~ing with the lock/the seal of this letter.* 有人亂動了這把鎖(這信上的封蠟)。

tan /tæn ; tæn/ *n, adj* yellowish brown; brown colour of sunburnt skin: 黃褐色(的);曬黑的皮膚顏色(的): *tan leather shoes/gloves;* 黃褐色的皮鞋(手套); *get a good tan* (on one's skin). (皮膚)曬得很黑。□ *vt, vi* (-nn-) [VP6A, 2A] **1** (of an animal's skin) make, be made, into leather (by treatment with tannic acid, etc). (指動物皮)製成革;被製成革;硝皮;鞣。***tan sb's hide,*** (sl) give him a good beating. (俚)痛打某人。**2** make or become brown with sunburn: 曬成褐色: *return from the holidays with a tanned face.* 休假回來面孔曬得很黑。*Some people tan quickly.* 有些人易於曬黑。**tan·ner** *n* workman who tans skins. 製革工人;硝皮匠。**tan·nery** /'tænərɪ ; 'tænərɪ/ *n* (*pl* -ries) place where skins are tanned. 製革廠;硝皮廠。

tan·dem /'tændəm ; 'tændəm/ *n* bicycle made for two persons to ride on, one behind the other, with pedals for both. 前後雙座脚踏車(有兩副踏板者)。□ *adv* ***(in) ~,*** (of horses in harness or two persons on a ~ bicycle) one behind the other: (指上了軛具的馬,或騎在雙座脚踏車上的兩人)一前一後地;縱列地: *drive/ride in ~.* 縱列地駕車(騎車)。

tang /tæŋ ; tæŋ/ *n* sharp taste or flavour, esp one that is characteristic of sth: 强烈的味道或氣味;(尤指)某物的特有氣味或風味: *the salt ~ of the sea air.* 海上空氣中的强烈鹽味。**tangy** *adj: a ~y aroma/sauce.* 味道濃烈的香味(醬油)。

tan·gent /'tændʒənt ; 'tændʒənt/ *n* straight line touching but not cutting a curve. 切線;正切;正切線。⇨ the illus at circle. 參看 circle 之插圖。***go/fly off at a ~,*** (fig) change suddenly from one line of thought, action, etc to another. (喻)突然改變思想、行動等。

tan·ger·ine /ˌtændʒə'ri:n *US:* 'tændʒəri:n ; 'tændʒəˌrin/ *n* [C] small, sweet-scented, loose-skinned orange. 紅橘。

tan·gible /'tændʒəbl ; 'tændʒəbl̩/ *adj* **1** that can be perceived by touch. 可觸知的。**2** clear and definite; real: 確切的;眞實的;明確的: *~ proof;* 明確的證據; *the ~ assets,* eg of a business company, its buildings, machinery, etc but not its goodwill. 有形資產(如指公司的建築物、機器等,但不包括商譽)。**tan·gibly** /-əblɪ ; -əblɪ/ *adv* **tan·gi·bil·ity** /ˌtændʒə'bɪlətɪ ; ˌtændʒə'bɪlətɪ/ *n*

tangle[1] /'tæŋgl ; 'tæŋgl̩/ *n* [C] **1** confused mass (of string, hair, etc): (繩子、毛髮等的)糾結;纏結;亂糟糟的一團: *brush the ~s out of a dog's hair.* 把狗毛的糾結刷除;刷順狗毛。*The kitten has made a ~ of my ball of wool.* 那小貓把我的毛線球弄得一團糟。**2** confused state: 混亂的狀態: *The traffic was in a frightful ~.* 交通亂得可怕。□ *vt, vi* **1** [VP6A, 15B, 2A, C] make or become confused, disordered: 使或變得混亂;使或變得糾結: *~d* *hair*. 蓬亂的頭髮。**2** [VP3A] ~ ***with sb,*** (colloq) be/become involved in a fight or quarrel with: (俗)與某人吵嘴或打架;與某人糾纏: *I shouldn't ~ with Peter — he's bigger than you.* 我不該與彼得糾纏——他比你塊頭大。

tangle² /ˈtæŋgl; ˈtæŋgl/ *n* [U] (kinds of) seaweed with long leathery fronds. (數種)長葉海草;昆布;海帶。

tango /ˈtæŋgəʊ; ˈtæŋgo/ *n* (*pl* ~s /-gəʊz; -goz/) (music for a) S American dance with strongly marked rhythm. (南美的)探戈舞;探戈舞曲。

tank /tæŋk; tæŋk/ *n* **1** (usu large) container for liquid or gas: (通常指大型的)液體或氣體的大容器;大桶、箱、槽等: *the ˈpetrol-~ of a car;* 汽車的油箱; *a ˈrain-water ~,* eg for storing rain-water from roofs; 雨水槽(如儲存屋頂雨水者); *a ship's ~s,* the compartments into which the double hull is divided, to contain fuel-oil, fresh water, etc. 船的儲油(水)艙。**ˈ~-car,** large (usu cylindrical) ~ for carrying petroleum, etc by rail. (鐵路運送石油等的)油(槽)車。**2** (in India, Pakistan, etc) large, artificial (usu rectangular) pool for storing water. (印度、巴基斯坦等處的)人工大水池(通常為長方形)。**3** armoured fighting vehicle with guns, moving on caterpillar tracks. 坦克車;戰車。**ˈ~ trap,** deep ditch or other obstruction built to hinder or stop the advance of ~s. 戰車陷穽。□ *vt* ~ ***sth up,*** fill up the ~ of a vehicle, etc. 把車輛等的油箱加滿。***be/get ~ed up,*** (sl) be/get drunk. (俚)喝醉。**~er** *n* ship or aircraft with ~s for carrying petroleum as freight; heavy road vehicle with a large cylindrical ~ for carrying oil, milk or other liquid in bulk. (運送石油的)油輪;運油機;(陸上運送油、奶或其他液體的)水車;油車等。

a tank

tank·ard /ˈtæŋkəd; ˈtæŋkəd/ *n* large drinking mug, esp one for beer. 大杯;(尤指)大啤酒杯。

tan·ner¹ /ˈtænə(r); ˈtænə/ *n* (sl) former British silver coin, value sixpence (6d, = 2½p). (俚)英國昔時銀幣名(面值為六辨士,改制後合 2½ 辨士)。

tan·ner² /ˈtænə(r); ˈtænə/ **tan·nery,** ⇨ tan.

tan·nic /ˈtænɪk; ˈtænɪk/ *adj* ~ **acid,** = tannin.

tan·nin /ˈtænɪn; ˈtænɪn/ *n* [U] acid obtained chiefly from the bark of oak and other trees, and used in preparing leather, dyeing, the manufacture of ink, etc. 鞣酸;單寧酸(由橡樹等樹皮提取的一種酸,用於硝皮,染物,製造墨水等)。

tan·noy /ˈtænɔɪ; ˈtænɔɪ/ *n* (P) type of loudspeaker or loudspeaker system, eg as used for public-address systems. (商標) 坦諾擴音器; 坦諾擴音器系統(如用於公衆演說)。

tansy /ˈtænzɪ; ˈtænzɪ/ *n* herb with yellow flowers and bitter leaves, used in medicine and cooking. 艾菊(草本植物,開黃花,葉味苦,用於醫藥及烹調)。

tan·ta·lize /ˈtæntəlaɪz; ˈtæntḷˌaɪz/ *vt* [VP6A] raise hopes that cannot (yet) be realized; keep just out of reach sth that sb desires: 引起(尚)無法實現的希望;使某人對想獲得之事物可望而不可及;挑逗;逗惹: *a tantalizing smell of food.* 引起人食慾的食物氣味。

tan·ta·mount /ˈtæntəmaʊnt; ˈtæntəˌmaʊnt/ *adj* ~ ***to,*** equal in effect to: 效果等於;相等於: *The Queen's request was ~ to a command.* 女王的要求等於命令。

tan·trum /ˈtæntrəm; ˈtæntrəm/ *n* [C] fit of bad temper or anger: 發脾氣;陣怒: *He's in one of his ~s again.* 他又在發脾氣了。

tap¹ /tæp; tæp/ *n* **1** device for controlling the flow of liquid or gas from a pipe, barrel, etc. (Cf *valve* for controlling flow *through* a pipe; cf *faucet,* the usu word in the US): (控制液體流出的)龍頭;活嘴(參較 valve, 控制液體在管內流動的裝置;參較 faucet, 美國通用之字): *turn the tap on/off.* 打開(關閉)龍頭。*Don't leave the taps running,* ie turn them off. 把龍頭關上。***on tap,*** (of beer, etc) in a barrel with a tap, ready to be drawn off; (hence, fig) available when needed. (指啤酒等)隨時可自裝有活嘴的桶中放出;(由此產生,喻)現成的;需要時即可獲得的。**ˈtap-room** *n* (in an inn, etc) room in which barrels are stored and cheaper drinks sold. (旅館等中的)酒室; 酒吧間。**ˈtap·root** *n* chief descending root of a plant, tree, etc (going straight down for moisture). (植物的)直根;主根(向下直伸吸收水份者)。 **2** plug used to close the opening of a cask. (桶口的)栓;塞子。□ *vt* (-pp-) [VP6A, 14, 15B] ***tap (off) sth (from sth),*** **1** draw out liquid through the tap of a (barrel): 從(桶)的龍頭或開口取出液體: *tap a cask of cider;* 打開桶的活塞取蘋果酒; *tap (off) cider from a cask;* 打開活塞從桶裏汲取蘋果酒; cut (the bark of a tree) and get (the sap, etc): 切開(樹皮)並汲取(樹液等): *tap rubber-trees;* 切開橡膠樹(的樹皮)汲取樹液; *tap sugar-maples,* eg in Canada. 在糖楓樹上鑿孔以汲取樹液(如在加拿大)。**2** extract or obtain (sth from sb or sth): 引出;獲取(自某人或某物得到某物): *tap a man for money/information;* 圖自某人獲得金錢(消息); *tap a telephone/wire/line,* make a connection so as to intercept messages. 私接電話線以竊聽消息。*My phone is being tapped.* 我的電話現在有人竊聽。**3** furnish (a cask, etc) with a tap. 在(桶等)上裝龍頭或塞子。

tap² /tæp; tæp/ *n* [C] **1** quick, light blow: 輕快的敲擊;輕拍;輕踏: *a ~ on the window/at the door.* 敲窗 (門)。**ˈtap-dancing** *n* stage-dancing with rhythmical tapping of the foot, toe or heel. 踢躂舞。**2 taps,** (US armed forces) last signal of the day (by drum or bugle) for lights to be put out. (美軍)熄燈鼓;熄燈號。□ *vt, vi* (-pp-) [VP6A, 15A, 2A, C] give a tap or taps (to): 輕敲;輕拍;輕踏;輕擊: *tap a man on the shoulder;* 輕拍一個人的肩膀; *tap at/on the door;* 敲門; *tap one's foot on the floor impatiently.* 不耐煩地用腳敲擊地板。

tape /teɪp; tep/ *n* [C, U] **1** (piece, length of) narrow strip of material used for tying up parcels, etc or in dressmaking: (用以捆紮包裹等,或用於製作女服的)帶子;線帶: *three yards of linen ~;* 三碼亞麻帶; *do up the ~s of an apron into neat bows.* 把圍裙上的帶子打成漂亮的蝴蝶結。**ˈ~-measure** *n* length of ~ or strip of thin, flexible metal or of strengthened cloth graduated for measuring things with. 卷尺;皮尺。**ˈ~·worm** *n* kinds of many-jointed, long, flat worm that lives during its adult stage as a parasite in the intestines of man and other animals. 絛蟲。**2 (ˈticker-)~,** narrow strip of paper on which telegraph instruments automatically print news, etc. 電報的收報紙帶。**ˈinsulating ~,** strip of sticky cloth used for insulating electrical connections, etc. (使電線接頭絕緣的)絕緣包帶;膠帶。**magnetic ~,** strip of a plastic material magnetized to record sound or vision. 錄音帶;錄影帶。**red ~,** ⇨ red, *adj*(3). **ˈ~ deck,** ~ recorder (without amplifiers or speakers) as a component in a hi-fi system. (高度傳真系統中的) 錄音座 (但無揚聲器)。 **ˈ~-recorder** *n* apparatus for recording sound on, and playing sound back from, this kind of ~. 錄音機。**3** length of ~ stretched between the winning-posts on a race-track: (拉在跑道終點的)終點線:

breast the ~, reach and pass this ~. 抵達終點;衝過終點。□ *vt* [VP6A] **1** fasten, tie together, with ~. 以帶繫、捆、紮。**2** record (sound) on magnetic ~. 錄(音)。 **3** (colloq) ***have sth / sb ~d,*** understand it / him thoroughly. (俗)徹底瞭解某事物(某人)。

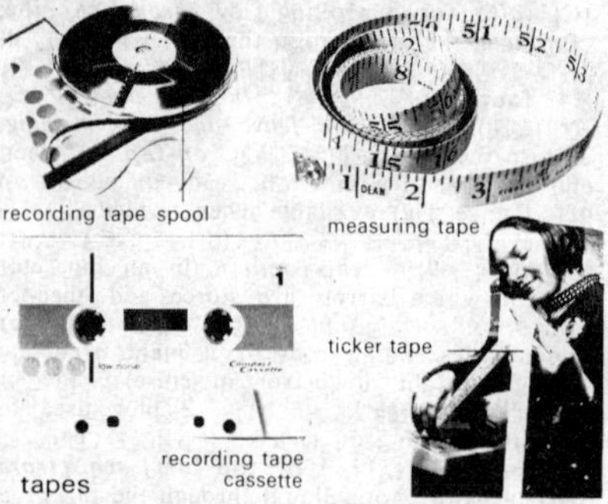

taper[1] /ˈteɪpə(r) ; ˈtepɚ/ *n* [C] length of thread with a covering of wax, burnt to give a light; very slender candle. 蠟(燭)心;小蠟燭。

taper[2] /ˈteɪpə(r) ; ˈtepɚ/ *vt, vi* [VP6A, 15B, 2A, C] make or become gradually narrower towards one end: (使)逐漸向一端尖細;漸尖: *One end ~s / is ~ed off to a point.* 一端逐漸變細成一尖頭。

tap·es·try /ˈtæpɪstrɪ ; ˈtæpɪstrɪ/ *n* (*pl* -ries) [C, U] (piece of) cloth into which threads of coloured wool are woven by hand to make designs and pictures, used for covering walls and furniture. (一塊)繡帷;綴錦;掛帷;掛毯。**tap·es·tried** *adj* hung, decorated, with ~: 掛有繡帷或掛毯的;以繡帷或掛毯裝飾的: *tapestried walls.* 掛有繡帷的牆。

tapi·oca /ˌtæpɪˈəʊkə ; ˌtæpɪˈokə/ *n* [U] starchy food (in the form of hard, white grains) from the root of the cassava plant. 參茨澱粉;樹葛粉;珍粉(一種澱粉質食料,自參茨根中提取,呈堅硬白粒狀)。

ta·pir /ˈteɪpə(r) ; ˈtepɚ/ *n* pig-like animal of Central and S America with a long, flexible nose. (產於中南美洲的)貘。

taps /tæps ; tæps/ ⇨ tap[2](2).

tap·ster /ˈtæpstə(r) ; ˈtæpstɚ/ *n* person employed to draw and serve beer, spirits, etc. 酒保。⇨ *taproom* at tap[1](1).

tar[1] /tɑː(r) ; tɑr/ *n* [U] black substance, hard when cold, thick and sticky when warm, obtained from coal, etc used to preserve timber (eg in fences and posts), in making roads, etc. 瀝; 柏油; 木焦油; 瀝青(用於保護木材,築路等)。 **tar·macadam** = tarmac. □ *vt* (-rr-) [VP6A] cover with tar. 鋪以柏油;以柏油覆蓋。***tar and feather sb,*** put tar on him and then cover with feathers as a punishment. 將某人塗以柏油然後覆以羽毛(作爲一種處罰)。***tarred with the same brush,*** having the same faults. 具有相同的缺點。

tar[2] /tɑː(r) ; tɑr/ *n* **(Jack) tar,** (dated colloq) sailor. (過時俗語)水手;水兵。

tara·diddle /ˈtærədɪdl *US:* ˌtærəˈdɪdl ; ˈtærəˌdɪdl/ *n* (colloq) untruth; fib. (俗)虛言;謊話。

tar·an·tella /ˌtærənˈtelə ; ˌtærənˈtɛlə/, **tar·an·telle** /-ˈtel ; -ˈtɛl/ *nn* [C] (music for a) rapid, whirling Italian dance for two persons. 塔朗泰拉舞(義大利的一種快速旋動的二人舞);塔朗泰拉舞曲。

ta·ran·tula /təˈræntjʊlə *US:* -tʃʊlə ; təˈræntʃələ/ *n* large, hairy, poisonous spider of S Europe; other kinds of spider. (南歐產的)一種大而帶毛的毒蜘蛛;袋蜘蛛類。

tar·boosh /tɑːˈbuːʃ ; tɑrˈbuʃ/ *n* brimless felt cap like a fez, worn by some Muslim men. (有些回教徒戴的)無沿氈帽。

tardy /ˈtɑːdɪ ; ˈtɑrdɪ/ *adj* (-ier, -iest) **1** slow; slow-moving; coming or done late: 緩慢的;緩緩移動的;遲來的;遲做的: ~ *progress / repentance;* 緩慢的進步(爲時已晚的懺悔); ~ *in offering help.* 幫助提供得太慢。**2** (US) late: (美)遲的;晚的: *be ~ for school.* 上學遲到。**tar·dily** /-ɪlɪ ; -ɪlɪ/ *adv* **tar·di·ness** *n*

tare[1] /teə(r) ; tɛr/ *n* (Biblical; usu *pl*) weed growing among corn. (聖經;通常用複數)稗子;莠草。

tare[2] /teə(r) ; tɛr/ *n* allowance made to a purchaser for the weight of the vehicle carrying the commodity he has brought or for the weight of the container in which the commodity is packed, in cases where the commodity is weighed together with the vehicle or container; weight of a motor-vehicle, etc without fuel. 皮重;包裝重量(貨物與搬運工具或包裝容器同時過秤時,在商品重量上對購買者所作的折讓);(汽車等除去燃料的)車身重;淨重;空重。

tar·get /ˈtɑːgɪt ; ˈtɑrgɪt/ *n* **1** sth to be aimed at in shooting-practice; any object aimed at. 標的;靶;鵠。⇨ the illus at archery. 參看 archery 之插圖。**2** thing, plan, etc against which criticism is directed: 被批評的事物、計畫等;批評目標: *This book will be the ~ of bitter criticism.* 這本書將受到嚴厲的批評。 **3** objective (set for savings, production, etc); total which it is desired to reach. (儲蓄、生產等的)目標;欲達到的總數。

tar·iff /ˈtærɪf ; ˈtærɪf/ *n* [C] **1** list of fixed charges, esp for meals, rooms, etc at a hotel; price-list. 價目表(尤指旅館的餐食、房間等者)。 **2** list of taxes on goods imported or (less often) exported; tax on a particular class of imported goods: 進出口貨物(較少指出口貨物)課稅表;某一類貨物進口稅或關稅: *raise ~ walls against foreign goods,* (try to) exclude them by means of import taxes; 建立關稅壁壘以抵制舶來品; ~ *reform,* movement (esp in GB, 19th century) to get rid of inequalities in ~s. 關稅改革(尤指十九世紀英國所推行者)。

tar·mac /ˈtɑːmæk ; ˈtɑrmæk/ *n* [U] mixture of tar and gravel, as used for the surfaces of paths, roads, aircraft runways, etc. 柏油碎石(用以鋪道路,飛機跑道等)。

tarn /tɑːn ; tɑrn/ *n* small mountain lake. 山中的小湖。

tar·nish /ˈtɑːnɪʃ ; ˈtɑrnɪʃ/ *vi, vt* [VP6A, 2A] (esp of metal surfaces) lose, cause the loss of, brightness: (尤指金屬表面)失去或使失去光澤: *The damp atmosphere has ~ed the gilt.* 潮濕的空氣已使鍍金表面失去光澤。*Chromium does not ~ easily.* 鉻不易失去光澤。*His reputation is ~ed.* 他的名譽受到玷污了。□ *n* dullness; loss of polish. 暗晦;失去光澤。

taro /ˈtɑːrəʊ ; ˈtɑro/ *n* (*pl* ~s /-rəʊz ; -roz/) kinds of tropical plant with a starchy root used as food, esp in the Pacific islands. 芋;芋頭(熱帶植物,根富澱粉,用作食品,尤產於太平洋諸島)。

tar·pau·lin /tɑːˈpɔːlɪn ; tɑrˈpɔlɪn/ *n* [C, U] (sheet or cover of) canvas made waterproof, esp by being tarred: (一塊)防水帆布;柏油防水帆布;防水帆布罩;雨布(罩): *cover the goods on the lorry with a ~.* 用防水帆布遮蓋卡車上的貨物。

tar·pon /ˈtɑːpɒn *US:* -pən ; ˈtɑrpɑn/ *n* large fish found in the warmer parts of the Atlantic Ocean. (產於大西洋溫暖區域的)大鰽白魚。

tarra·diddle *n* = taradiddle.

tar·ra·gon /ˈtærəgən *US:* -gɒn ; ˈtærəˌgɑn/ *n* [U] herb with sharp-tasting leaves, used in salads and for flavouring vinegar (~ *vinegar*). 茵陳蒿(草本植物,葉有辛辣味,用於做沙拉,並用以增醋味,用此增味的醋稱爲 ~ vinegar)。

tarry[1] /ˈtɑːrɪ ; ˈtɑrɪ/ *adj* covered, sticky, with tar. 塗有柏油的;因塗有柏油而黏黏的。

tarry[2] /ˈtærɪ ; ˈtærɪ/ *vi* (archaic or liter) (古或文) [VP2A, B, C] **1** stay, remain, lodge: 停留;逗留;住: ~ *a few days at / in a place;* 在某處小住幾天; ~ (*behind*) *for sb.* 等待某人。**2** be slow in coming, going, appearing. 躭擱;遲延。

tar·sal /ˈtɑːsl ; ˈtɑrsl̩/ *adj* (anat) of the bones in

the ankle. (解剖)跗骨的;跗的。□ *n* (anat) bone in the ankle. (解剖)跗骨。⇨ the illus at skeleton. 參看 skeleton 之插圖。

tar·sus /ˈtɑːsəs ; ˈtɑrsəs/ *n* (*pl* tarsi /-saɪ ; -saɪ/) (anat) collection of seven small bones in the ankle. (解剖)跗;跗骨(由七塊小骨聚合而成)。

tart¹ /tɑːt ; tɑrt/ *adj* acid; sharp in taste; (fig) sharp: 酸的;辛辣的;(喻)尖酸的;尖刻的: ~ *fruit;* 酸的果子; *a ~ flavour;* 酸味; ~ *humour;* 尖酸的詼諧; *a ~ manner/disposition.* 尖刻的態度(性情)。 **~·ly** *adv* **~·ness** *n*

tart² /tɑːt ; tɑrt/ *n* **1** fruit pie. 水果餡餅。 **2** circle of pastry cooked with fruit or jam on it. (上面有水果或果醬的)小圓餅。

tart³ /tɑːt ; tɑrt/ *n* (derog sl) prostitute. (貶,俚)妓女。□ *vt* [VP15B] **~ *sth/sb up,*** (colloq) make gaudy; add superficial attractions to; smarten. (俗)使某物或某人變得俗麗;增加外表的吸引力;使漂亮。

tar·tan /ˈtɑːtn ; ˈtɑrtn̩/ *n* [U] Scottish woollen fabric woven with coloured crossing stripes; [C] particular pattern of ~, eg of a Scottish clan. 蘇格蘭格子呢; 有某種圖案的格子呢(如蘇格蘭某一氏族者)。⇨ the illus at kilt. 參看 kilt 之插圖。

tar·tar¹ /ˈtɑːtə(r) ; ˈtɑrtɚ/ *n* [U] **1** chalk-like substance deposited on the teeth. 齒垢;齒石;牙砂。 **2** substance deposited on the sides of casks from fermented wine. (由於盛發酵的酒而積附於酒桶側的)酒石。 **cream of ~,** purified form of this, used with baking soda to make baking powder. 酸性酒石;酒石酸氫鉀(與小蘇打合製發酵粉)。 **~ic** /tɑːˈtærɪk ; tɑrˈtærɪk/ **acid,** acid of ~, found in the juice of grapes, oranges, etc (used in making baking powder, etc). 酒石酸(含於葡萄汁、橘汁等中的一種酸,用製發酵粉等)。

tar·tar² /ˈtɑːtə(r) ; ˈtɑrtɚ/ *n* rough, violent, troublesome person. 粗暴而難處的人;慓悍的人。 ***catch a ~,*** have to deal with a person of this kind, esp one who is more than one's match. 遭遇頑強對手;碰到強敵。

tar·tar³ /ˈtɑːtə(r) ; ˈtɑrtɚ/ *n* **~ sauce,** cold mayonnaise with chopped onions, herbs, gherkins, pickles, etc. 塔塔(辣)醬油(冷美乃滋加碎洋蔥、香料、小黃瓜及泡菜等合製而成)。

task /tɑːsk *US:* tæsk ; tæsk/ *n* [C] piece of (esp hard) work (to be) done: 任務;工作;作業;課業等(尤指困難的): *set a boy a ~.* 分派男孩一項工作。*She finds housekeeping an irksome ~.* 她發現操持家務是一項令人厭煩的工作。 ***take sb to ~ (about/for sth),*** scold him: 斥責或責備某人: *take sb to ~ for arriving late.* 責備某人之遲到。 **ˈ~-force** *n* specially organized unit (of warships, etc) for a special purpose. 特遣部隊;特遣艦隊。 **(hard) ˈ~-master/-mistress** *nn* (strict) overseer. (嚴厲的)男(女)監工。□ *vt* [VP6A] (of a ~) put a strain on: (指工作)使費力;使辛勞: *Mathematics ~s that boy's brain.* 數學使那男孩大感吃力。

tas·sel /ˈtæsl ; ˈtæsl̩/ *n* bunch of threads, etc tied together at one end and hanging (from a flag, hat, etc) as an ornament. (旗、帽等垂下的)繸;縷;流蘇。⇨ the illus at kilt. 參看 kilt 之插圖。 **~·led** (US = **~ed**) *adj* having a ~ or ~s. 有繸的;有流蘇的。

taste¹ /teɪst ; test/ *n* **1 the ~,** sense by which flavour is known: 味覺: *sweet/sour to the ~.* 嘗起來是甜(酸)的。 **ˈ~ bud** *n* group of cells in the tongue for this sense. 味蕾(舌上的味覺細胞)。⇨ the illus at mouth. 參看 mouth 之插圖。 **2** [C, U] quality of a substance made known by this sense, eg by putting some on the tongue: (某物的)味;味道: *Sugar has a sweet ~.* 糖有甜味。*I don't like the ~ of this mixture.* 我不喜歡這混合物的味道。*This medicine has no/very little/not much/a queer ~.* 這藥沒有(很少,不大有,有一股怪)味道。 ***leave a bad/nasty ˈ~ in the mouth,*** (lit or fig) be followed by a feeling of dislike or disgust. (字面或喻)留下一種嫌惡的感覺。 **3** (usu 通常作 ***a ~ (of)***) small quantity (of sth to eat or drink, or fig): 小量; 少量; 一口(指飲食或作比喻用法): *Won't you have a ~ of this cake/wine?* 你不嘗一點這糕餅(酒)嗎? *Give him a ~ of the whip,* enough to be a sample of what it feels like to be whipped. 讓他嘗嘗鞭子的滋味。 **4** [C, U] **~ *(for),*** liking or preference for: 愛好;嗜好: *He has a ~ for French cigarettes.* 他喜歡法國香煙。*She has expensive ~s in clothes.* 她愛好貴重的衣服。*There's no accounting for ~s,* We cannot explain why different people like different things. 嗜好是無法解釋的(各人有不同的嗜好,無法解釋)。*Abstract art is not to his ~/not to the ~ of everyone.* 抽象藝術不合他的口味(並非人人喜愛)。 **5** [U] ability to enjoy beauty, esp in art and literature; ability to form judgements about these; ability to behave in the most appropriate and pleasing way: (尤指對藝術及文學的)審美力;鑑賞力; 欣賞力; 判斷力;舉止適度宜人: *She has excellent ~ in dress/dresses in perfect ~.* 她對衣着有極好的鑑賞力(她穿着極佳)。 *It would be bad ~ to refuse their invitation.* 拒絕他們的邀請是不禮貌的。 ***(be) in good/bad/poor/excellent, etc ~,*** (be, be done, etc) showing this ability well/badly, etc. 有良好的(壞的,差的,極佳的)審美力或風度。 ***(be) in the best/worst of ~,*** (be, be done, etc) showing this ability in the best/worst way. 鑑賞力或風度極佳的(極差的)。 **~·ful** /-fl ; -fəl/ *adj* showing good ~(5). 有良好審美力、鑑賞力等的;舉止高雅的。 **~·fully** /-fəlɪ ; -fəlɪ/ *adv* in a ~ful manner: 有良好審美力、鑑賞力等地;舉止高雅地: *~fully decorated with flowers.* 用花裝飾得雅緻的。 **~·less** *adj* **1** (of food) having no ~ or flavour. (指食物)無味的。 **2** without ~(5); in bad ~(5). 無鑑賞力、審美力等的;舉止庸俗的。 **~·less·ly** *adv* **tasty** *adj* (-ier, -iest) having a pleasant flavour; pleasing to the ~. 味美的;可口的。 **tast·ily** /-ɪlɪ ; -ɪlɪ/ *adv*

taste² /teɪst ; test/ *vt, vi* **1** [VP6A, 2A] (not in the progressive tenses; often with *can, could*) be aware of the taste of sth: (不用進行式;常與can, could 連用)認出或辨別出某物的味道;嘗出;品嘗: *Can you ~ anything strange in this soup?* 你嘗得出這湯裏有什麼怪味道嗎? *If you have a bad cold you cannot ~ (anything).* 如果你患重感冒,你嘗不出(任何東西的)味道。 **2** [VP3A, 2D] **~ *(of),*** have a particular taste or flavour: 有某種特殊的味道: *~ sour/bitter/sweet.* 有酸(苦,甜)味。 *It ~s too much of garlic/spice.* 這東西大蒜(香料)的味道太重。 **3** [VP6A] test the ~ of: 嘗…的味道;試…的味道: *The cook ~d the soup to see whether he had put enough salt in it.* 廚師嘗嘗湯的味道,看看鹽放的够不够。 **4** [VP6A] (fig) experience: (喻)體驗;領略: *~ happiness/the joys of freedom.* 領略幸福(自由的快樂)。 **~ *of,*** (liter) know; experience. (文)知道;經驗。 **~r** *n* person who is employed to judge teas, wines, etc by ~: 受雇品嘗茶、酒等以鑑定其品質的人;品嘗員: *A wine-~r doesn't swallow what he ~s.* 嘗酒員並不吞下他所品嘗的酒。

tat¹ /tæt ; tæt/ *vi, vt* (-tt-) do tatting; make by tatting. 梭織;用梭織法編織。

tat² /tæt ; tæt/ *n* [U] quality of being tatty; tatty person or thing. 不整潔;邋遢;不整潔的人或物。

tat³ /tæt ; tæt/ *n* ⇨ tit².

ta ta /ˌtəˈtɑː ; ˈtɑˌtɑ/ *int* (baby language) goodbye. (兒語)再會。

tat·ter /ˈtætə(r) ; ˈtætɚ/ *n* (usu *pl*) rag; piece of cloth, paper, etc torn off or hanging loosely from sth: (通常用複數) 破布;襤褸;(撕下或懸垂的)紙片、布片等: *in ~s,* in rags or torn strips; 破爛;襤褸; *tear sb's reputation to ~s,* (fig) destroy it. (喻)破壞某人名譽。 **~ed** *adj* ragged. 破爛的;襤褸的。 **~·de·ma·lion** /ˌtætədəˈmeɪlɪən ; ˌtætɚdɪˈmeljən/ *n* sb dressed in ~s. 衣衫襤褸的人。

tat·ting /ˈtætɪŋ ; ˈtætɪŋ/ *n* [U] (art or process of making a) kind of handmade knotted lace-work used for trimming. 梭織;梭織法;梭織的花邊。

T

tattle /'tætl; 'tætḷ/ *vi, vt* [VP2A] chatter, gossip, prattle. 閒談;聊天;空談。 □ *n* [U] idle talk. 閒談;聊天;空談。 **tat·tler** /'tætlə(r); 'tætlɚ/ *n* person who ~s. 閒談者;聊天者;空談者。

tat·too[1] /tə'tu: *US:* tæ'tu:; tæ'tu/ *n* (*pl* ~s) **1** (sing only) beating of drum(s) to call soldiers back to quarters; hour at which a ~ is sounded: (僅用單數)歸營鼓;擊歸營鼓的時刻: *beat/sound the ~.* 擊(鳴)歸營鼓。 **2** [C] continuous tapping: 連續的輕擊: *He was beating a ~ on the table with his fingers.* 他用手指在桌子連續輕擊。 **3** [C] public entertainment, usu at night (often 常作 *torchlight ~*) with music and marching, by soldiers. 軍隊的遊行(通常在夜晚,配以音樂行進)。

tat·too[2] /tə'tu: *US:* tæ'tu:; tæ'tu/ *vt* [VP6A] mark (sb's skin) with a permanent picture or pattern by pricking it and putting in dyes or stains; put (a picture or pattern) on the skin thus: 文刺(某人的皮膚);刺染(圖案)於皮膚上;文身: *The sailor had a ship ~ed on his arm.* 那水手在手臂上刺着一隻船。 □ *n* [C] (*pl* ~s) picture or pattern of this kind. 文身;刺花;黥墨。

tatty /'tætɪ; 'tætɪ/ *adj* (-ier, -iest) (sl) untidy and shabby looking; tawdry. (俚)樣子不整潔的;邋遢的;俗麗的。 **tat·tily** /-ɪlɪ; -ɪlɪ/ *adv*

taught /tɔ:t; tɔt/ *pt, pp* of teach.

taunt /tɔ:nt; tɔnt/ *n* [C] remark intended to hurt sb's feelings; contemptuous reproach: 辱罵;譏笑: *endure the ~s of a successful rival.* 忍受一位成功敵手的辱罵。 □ *vt* [VP6A, 14] **~ sb (with sth),** attack (sb) with ~s: 辱罵;譏笑: *They ~ed the boy with cowardice/with being a coward.* 他們譏笑那男孩膽怯(是懦夫)。 **~·ing·ly** *adv*

T

Taurus /'tɔ:rəs; 'tɔrəs/ *n* (astrol) second sign of the zodiac. (天文)黃道第二宮;金牛宮;金牛座。 ⇨ the illus at zodiac. 參看 zodiac 之插圖。

taut /tɔ:t; tɔt/ *adj* (of ropes, wires, etc) tightly stretched; (of muscles and (fig) of nerves) tense. (指繩索、金屬線等) 拉緊的; (指肌肉,(喻) 指神經) 緊張的。 **~·ly** *adv* **~·ness** *n*

taut·ology /tɔ:'tɒlədʒɪ; ˌtɔ'tɑlədʒɪ/ *n* [U] the saying of the same thing again in different ways without making one's meaning clearer or more forceful; needless repetition; [C] (*pl* -gies) instance of this. 同義反複;無謂的重複;贅言。 **tauto·logi·cal** /ˌtɔ:tə'lɒdʒɪkl; ˌtɔtə'lɑdʒɪkḷ/ *adj*

tav·ern /'tævən; 'tævɚn/ *n* (archaic or liter) inn or public house. (古或文)客棧;旅店;酒店。

taw·dry /'tɔ:drɪ; 'tɔdrɪ/ *adj* (-ier, -iest) showy; brightly coloured or decorated, but cheap or in bad taste: 俗麗的;鮮艷而廉價的;庸俗的: *~ jewellery/dresses.* 俗麗的珠寶(衣服)。 **taw·drily** /-əlɪ; -ɪlɪ/ *adv* **taw·dri·ness** *n*

tawny /'tɔ:nɪ; 'tɔnɪ/ *adj* brownish yellow. 黃褐色的;茶色的。

tawse /tɔ:z; tɔz/ *n* [C] (Scot) leather strap for punishing children. (蘇)打孩子用的皮鞭。

tax /tæks; tæks/ *n* **1** [C, U] (sum of) money (to be) paid by citizens (according to income, value of purchases, etc) to the government for public purposes: 稅;稅額: *state/local taxes;* 國(地方)稅; *levy a tax on sth;* 課某物之稅; *direct taxes,* ie on income; 直接稅(卽所得稅); *indirect taxes,* eg paid when one buys goods. 間接稅(如貨物稅)。 *How much income tax did you pay last year?* 去年你繳了多少所得稅? *He paid £50 in taxes.* 他付了稅金五十鎊。 **'tax-collector** *n* official who collects taxes. 稅務員;收稅員。 **'tax-payer** *n* person who pays taxes. 納稅人。 **ˌtax-'free** *adj* **(a)** not subject to taxation. 免稅的。 **(b)** (of dividends or interest) on which tax has been deducted before distribution. (指股利或利息)已先行扣繳稅金的。 **2** *a tax on,* sth that is a burden or strain: 負擔;重負: *a tax on one's strength/health/patience.* 對某人體力(健康,耐心)的一項負擔。 □ *vt* **1** [VP6A] put a tax(1) on; require (a person) to pay a tax: 課稅於;抽稅;征稅: *tax luxuries/incomes/rich and poor alike.* 課征奢侈品稅(課征所得稅;貧富同樣課稅)。 **2** [VP6A] be a tax(2) on: 爲…的負擔或重負;使負重荷: *tax a person's patience,* eg by asking him many silly questions. 使某人不勝其煩(如提出許多愚蠢的問題)。 **3** [VP14] ***tax sb with sth,*** accuse him of it: 指控;責備: *tax sb with neglect of/with having neglected his work.* 責備某人疏忽職守。 **4** (legal) examine and decide, eg costs of a lawsuit. (法律)判定;評定(如訴訟費用)。 **tax·able** /-əbl; -əbḷ/ *adj* capable of being taxed. 可課以稅的;應課稅的。 **tax·abil·ity** /ˌtæksə'bɪlətɪ; ˌtæksə'bɪlətɪ/ *n* **tax·ation** /tæk'seɪʃn; tæks'eʃən/ *n* [U] (system of) raising money by taxes; taxes (to be) paid: 課稅;稅制;徵稅;稅: *reduce taxation;* 減稅; *grumble at high taxation.* 抱怨重稅。

taxi /'tæksɪ; 'tæksɪ/ *n* (*pl* ~s) (also 亦作 **'~·cab,** usu abbr to 通常略作 *cab,* esp in US 尤用於美國) motor-car, esp one with a ~meter, which may be hired for journeys. 出租汽車;計程車。 **'~·meter** *n* (usu abbr to 通常略作 *meter*) device which automatically records the fare during a journey in a ~. 計程表;計程器;計價表。 **'~ rank,** place where ~s wait to be hired. 計程車候客處。 □ *vi, vt* [VP2C, 15A] (of an aircraft) (cause to) move on wheels along the ground (or on floats, etc on the surface of water): (指飛機) (使)在地面或水面滑行: *The plane ~ed/was taxiing along the runway.* 飛機在跑道上滑行。

taxi·dermy /'tæksɪdɜ:mɪ; 'tæksəˌdɝmɪ/ *n* [U] art of preparing and stuffing the skins of animals, birds and fish so that they look as they did when living. (動物標本的)剝製術。 **taxi·der·mist** /-ɪst; -ɪst/ *n* person who practises ~. 剝製動物標本的人;標本剝製家。

tax·on·omy /tæk'sɒnəmɪ; tæks'ɑnəmɪ/ *n* [U, C] (principles of) classification. 分類;分類學。

tea /ti:; ti/ *n* **1** [U] (dried leaves of an) evergreen shrub of eastern Asia, Africa, etc; drink made by pouring boiling water on these leaves: 茶葉;茶樹;(泡成的)茶: *a pound of tea;* 一磅茶葉; *Ceylon/China, etc tea;* 錫蘭(中國等)茶; *a cup of tea;* 一杯茶; *make (the) tea,* prepare it. 泡茶;沏茶。 ***not my cup of tea,*** (fig) not the sort of thing I like. (喻)不是我所喜歡的事物。 **'tea-bag** *n* small porous bag holding enough tea-leaves for use in a teacup or teapot. 茶袋(裝有少量茶葉的有孔小袋,置茶杯或茶壺中用之)。 **'tea-break** *n* (in an office, factory, etc) short period when work is stopped for tea drinking. 喝茶時間(辦公室、工廠等處,讓工作人員喝茶的短暫休息時間)。 **'tea-caddy** *n* (*pl* -dies) air-tight box in which to keep a supply of tea for daily use. 茶罐;茶筒。 **'tea-cake** *n* small, flat, sweetened cake, usu eaten hot with butter at tea. 茶餅(扁平的甜餅,通常在飲茶時趁熱加奶油食之)。 **'tea-chest** *n* large wooden box in which tea is packed for export. 茶箱(裝運茶葉出口的大木箱)。 **'tea-cloth** *n* **(a)** cloth to be spread on a tea-table or tea-tray. 茶儿布;茶盤布。 **(b)** tea-towel. 擦拭茶具用的抹布。 **'tea-cosy** *n* cover for keeping the contents of a teapot warm. 茶壺保溫罩;茶壺暖罩。 **'tea-cup** *n* cup in which tea is served. 茶杯。 ***a storm in a teacup,*** a lot of fuss about sth trivial. 因小事而引起的風波;小題大做。 **'tea-garden** *n* **(a)** garden in which tea and other refreshments are served to the public. 露天茶館。 **(b)** tea plantation. 茶圃;茶園。 **'tea·house** *n* (in Japan and China) restaurant where tea is served. (日本及中國等處的)茶館。 **'tea-kettle** *n* one in which water is boiled for making tea. (燒水沏茶的)茶壺; 開水壺。 **'tea-leaf** *n* (usu *pl;* -leaves) one of the leaves in a teapot after tea has been made, or left in a teacup: (通常用複數)(茶壺裏或茶杯中泡開的)茶葉或茶葉渣: *tell sb's fortune from the tea-leaves in her cup.* 藉察看她杯中的茶葉渣爲其算命。 **'tea-party** *n* social gathering for afternoon tea. 茶會(下午舉行的社交集會)。ˈ**tea·pot** *n* vessel in which tea is made. (沏茶的)茶壺。ˈ**tea·room** *n* restaurant in which tea and light refreshments may be obtained. 茶室(販賣茶及點心處)。ˈ**tea-service／-set** *nn* set of cups, saucers, plates, with a teapot, milk-jug, etc. 一套茶具。ˈ**tea·spoon** *n* small spoon for stirring tea. (攪茶用的)茶匙。ˈ**tea·spoon·ful** /-fʊl ; -fʊl/ *n* as much as a teaspoon can hold. 一茶匙之量。ˈ**tea-strainer** *n* device for keeping back tea-leaves when pouring tea into a cup. 濾茶網;濾茶器。ˈ**tea-table** *n* (usu small) table at which tea is served: (通常爲小的)茶几;茶桌: (attrib) (形容用法) *tea-table conversation.* 茶話。ˈ**tea-things** *n pl* (colloq) tea-set as needed for a meal: (俗)茶具: *put the tea-things on the table.* 把茶具放在桌上。ˈ**tea-time** *n* [U] time at which tea is usu taken in the afternoon. 喝(下午)茶時間。ˈ**tea-towel** *n* cloth for drying washed crockery, cutlery, etc. 擦乾陶器,餐具等的抹布。ˈ**tea-tray** *n* one on which a tea-set is used or carried. 茶盤。ˈ**tea-trolley** *n* tea-wagon. (有脚輪的)茶具檯。ˈ**tea-urn** *n* urn in which water is boiled for making tea in quantity, eg in a café. (泡大量茶用的)大型茶壺。ˈ**tea-wagon** *n* small table on wheels, used for serving tea. (有脚輪的)茶具檯。**2** [C, U] occasion (in the late afternoon) at which tea is drunk: 下午茶;午後茶點: *We have tea at／Tea is at half-past four.* 我們在四點半喝下午茶。*They were having／at tea when I called.* 我往訪時他們在喝下午茶。*The waitress has served twenty teas since four o'clock.* 這位女侍四點鐘起已供應了二十份下午茶。 **high tea,** meal taken between lunch and supper if a dinner is not taken in the evening (usu a more substantial meal than afternoon tea as taken by people who have dinner in the evening). 大下午茶(正餐不在晚上的人們,於下午五六點鐘所進食的簡便小餐,較一般下午茶豐盛)。

teach /tiːtʃ ; titʃ/ *vt, vi* (*pt, pp* taught /tɔːt ; tɔt/) [VP6A, 11, 12A, 13A, 17, 20, 21, 2A, B, C] give instruction to (sb); cause (sb) to know or be able to do sth; give to sb (knowledge, skill, etc); give lessons (at school, etc); do this for a living: 教(某人);使(某人)知道做某事;教授(知識、技能等);(在學校等)授課;教書維持生活: ~ *children;* 教小孩子們; ~ *French／history, etc;* 教授法文(歷史等); ~ *a child (how) to swim.* 教小孩(如何)游泳。*He has taught his dog to perform some clever tricks.* 他已經訓練他的狗玩幾樣靈巧的把戲。*Who taught you German?* 誰教你德文? *She is ~ing the piano to several of the village children.* 她教幾個村子裡的兒童彈鋼琴。*He ~es for a living.* 他以教書爲生。*He has been ~ing four hours already this morning.* 今天早上他已經上了四小時的課。*I'll ~ you (not) to . . .,* (colloq, used as a threat) I'll show the risk or penalty of . . . . (俗,用作威嚇語)你如果(如果不)…我可要教訓你。ˈ**~-in** *n* (colloq) discussion of a subject of topical interest (as held in a college, with students, staff and other speakers). (俗)時事問題討論(如大學中由學生,教師及其他演講者所舉行的討論)。**~·able** /-əbl ; -əbl/ *adj* that can be taught. 可教的;肯學的。**~er** *n* person who ~es. 教師;老師;教員。**~·ing** *n* **1** [U] work of a ~er: 教師的工作;教導;教授: *earn a living by ~ing.* 靠教書維持生活。**2** [U, C] that which is taught: 所教的東西;教訓;教義;訓示: *the ~ing(s) of Buddha.* 佛陀的教訓。

teak /tiːk ; tik/ *n* tall, evergreen tree of India, Burma, Malaysia, etc; [U] its hard wood, used for making furniture, in shipbuilding, etc. (印度、緬甸、馬來西亞等地的)麻栗樹;其堅硬木材;柚木(用於製造傢俱、船等)。

teal /tiːl ; til/ *n* (*pl* unchanged) kinds of small wild duck living on rivers and lakes. (複數不變)小野鴨;小鳧。

team /tiːm ; tim/ *n* [C] **1** two or more oxen, horses, etc pulling a cart, plough, etc together. (共同拉車,拉犂等的)一組牛、馬等;聯畜。**2** number of persons playing together and forming one side in some games, eg football, cricket, hockey, and in some sports, eg relay races; group of people working together: 運動比賽的隊(如足球、板球、曲棍球及接力賽跑等);在一起工作的隊、組等: *the players in my ~,* my fellow players. 我隊的選手。ˈ**~-work** *n* [U] combined effort; organized co-operation: 協力工作;同隊工作;有組織的合作: *succeed by means of good ~-work.* 藉良好的協力合作而成功。**~ spirit,** spirit in which each member of a ~ thinks of the success, etc of the ~ and not of personal advantage, glory, etc. 團隊精神;合作精神。□ *vi* [VP2C] **~ up (with sb),** (colloq) make an effort in co-operation (with); work together (with). (俗)(與…)協力從事;(與…)合作。**~·ster** /ˈtiːmstə(r) ; ˈtimstɚ/ *n* driver of a ~ of animals; (US) truck-driver. 駕馭聯畜者;(美)卡車司機。

tear[1] /tɪə(r) ; tɪr/ *n* [C] drop of salty water coming from the eye: 淚;淚水;淚珠: *Her eyes filled with ~s.* 她的眼睛裏充滿了淚水。*The sad story moved us to ~s,* made us cry. 這個悲慘故事使我們感動得流淚。*The girl burst into ~s,* ~s began to flow from her eyes. 那女孩子哭起來了。*They all laughed till ~s came.* 他們全都笑出眼淚來了。ˈ**~-drop** *n* single ~. 淚珠。ˈ**~-gas** *n* [U] gas that causes severe watering of the eyes: 催淚性毒氣;催淚瓦斯: ˈ*~-gas bombs,* as used by the police to disperse a mob of demonstrators, unruly crowds, etc. 催淚彈。**~·ful** /-fl ; fl/ *adj* crying; wet with ~s: 哭泣的;眼淚汪汪的;爲淚水所濕的: *a ~ful face;* 眼淚縱橫的臉; *~ful looks.* 含淚的表情。**~·fully** /-fəlɪ ; -flɪ/ *adv* **~·less** *adj* without ~s, not weeping: 無淚的;未哭泣的: *The mother stared at her dead baby in ~less grief,* grief that was too deep for ~s. 母親帶着欲哭無淚的深切悲哀凝視着她那死去的嬰兒。

tear[2] /teə(r) ; tɛr/ *vt, vi* (*pt* tore /tɔː(r) ; tor/, *pp* torn /tɔːn ; torn/) **1** [VP6A, 15A, B, 22, 3A] pull sharply apart or to pieces; make (a rent in sth), damage, by pulling sharply: 撕;扯;撕碎;撕裂;扯破: *~ a sheet of paper in two／~ it to pieces／to bits;* 把一張紙撕成兩半(把它撕成小片,小塊); *~ sth up, ~* it into small pieces; 把某物撕碎; *~ one's dress on a nail;* 在釘子上掛破了衣服; *~ a hole in one's jacket;* 上衣撕破一個洞; *wearing old and torn clothes;* 穿着又舊又破的衣服; ~ (= hurt, injure, cause to bleed) *one's hand on a nail.* 在釘子上戳傷了手。*He tore* (= pulled violently) *at the wrapping of the parcel.* 他用力撕包裹的包裝紙。*He tore* (= pulled at) *his hair with rage.* 他憤怒地拉扯頭髮。*He tore the parcel open.* 他把包裹撕開。**2** [VP6A, 15A, B] cause (sth) to be out of place (*down, off, away, etc*) by pulling sharply: 撕下(某物);撕掉;扯去(與 down, off, away 等連用): *~ a page out of a book／a notice down from a notice-board／a leaf from a calendar.* 撕下一頁書(布告牌上的布告,一張日曆)。**~ oneself away (from),** leave; stop doing sth: 離開;停止做某事: *She could scarcely ~ herself away from the scene,* make up her mind to leave. 她幾乎捨不得離去。*He could not ~ himself away from his book,* couldn't put it down. 他放不下他那本書。**3** [VP6A] (usu passive) destroy the peace of: (通常用被動語態)破壞…的安寧;擾亂: *a country torn by civil war;* 因內戰而動亂不安的國家; *a heart torn by grief.* 憂傷的心。***torn between,*** painfully distracted by having to choose between (conflicting demands, wishes, etc). (在相互牴觸的願望、要求等之間)作痛苦的抉擇。**4** [VP2A] become torn: 撕碎;撕裂;撕破: *This material ~s easily.* 這料子容易撕破。*As I pulled the sheet out of the typewriter it tore.* 我把那張紙從打字機上拉出來的時候拉破了。**5** [VP2C] go in excitement or at great speed: 激動地或急速

地奔跑;急奔;衝: *The children tore out of the school gates/were ~ing about in the playground.* 孩子們衝出校門(在運動場上奔跑)。*He tore down the hill.* 他奔跑下山。'~·**away** *adj, n* (colloq) impetuous (person). 衝動的(人);魯莽的(人)。□ *n* [C] torn place in sth, eg cloth, paper. 破處;裂縫(如布,紙上的)。

tease /ti:z ; tiz/ *vt* **1** [VP6A, 15A] make fun of (sb) playfully or unkindly; worry with questions, etc; annoy: 取笑;揶揄;嘲弄;逗弄;煩擾: *She ~d her father about his bald head.* 她取笑她父親的禿頭。*You must never ~ a child because he stutters.* 你切不可因爲孩子口吃而嘲弄他。*Molly was teasing the cat*, eg by pulling its tail. 摩莉在逗弄貓。 **2** [VP6A, 15B] pick into separate fibres; fluff up the surface of (cloth, etc) by doing this: 梳理;使(布等)的表面起毛: *~ flax/wool.* 梳理亞麻(羊毛)。□ *n* person who is fond of teasing others: 好揶揄他人者;嘲弄者;逗弄者: *What a ~ she is!* 她眞好揶揄別人! **~r** *n* **1** person who often ~s or who is fond of teasing. 好揶揄他人者;嘲弄者。 **2** (colloq) difficult question or task; puzzling problem. (俗)困難的問題或工作;令人困惑的難題。 **teas·ing·ly** *adv* in a teasing manner; in order to ~. 揶揄地;嘲弄地。

tea·sel, tea·zel, teazle /'ti:zl ; 'tizl̩/ *n* (kinds of plant with) large prickly flower with hooked points (used formerly for teasing cloth, etc). 起絨草;起絨草的球花(昔時用來使布等表面起絨毛)。

teat /ti:t ; tit/ *n* nipple. 奶嘴;乳頭;奶頭。⇨ the illus at domestic. 參看 domestic 之插圖。

tec /tek ; tɛk/ *n* (sl abbr for) detective. (俚)偵探(爲 detective 之略)。

T

tech /tek ; tɛk/ *n* (colloq abbr for) technical college. (俗)工(藝)學院;工藝學校(爲 technical college 之略)。

tech·ni·cal /'teknɪkl ; 'tɛknɪkl̩/ *adj* **1** of, connected with, the execution of a work of art (as contrasted with general considerations of the form of the work): 技術上的;技巧方面的: *~ difficulties;* 技術上的困難; *a pianist who has ~ skill but not much feeling.* 有專門技巧而無太多感情的鋼琴家。**2** of, connected with, a particular art, craft, science, etc: 專門的;工藝的;有關工業技術的: *~ terms/training.* 專門術語(訓練)。~ **college,** (former name for a) polytechnic. 工藝學院(爲 polytechnic 之舊稱)。**~ly** /-klɪ ; -klɪ/ *adv* **~·ity** /ˌteknɪ'kælətɪ ; ˌtɛknɪ'kælətɪ/ *n* (*pl* -ties) ~(2) word, phrase, point, etc: 專門用字、用語、細節等: *The two architects were discussing building ~ities.* 這兩位建築師在討論建築上的專門問題。*The judge explained the legal ~ities of the case to the jury.* 法官向陪審團解釋該案件涉及法律的有關各點。

tech·ni·cian /tek'nɪʃn ; tɛk'nɪʃən/ *n* expert in the technique(s) of a particular art, etc; highly skilled craftsman or mechanic. (精通某一專門技藝的) 技術人員;專門技師;巧匠。

Tech·ni·color /'teknɪkʌlə(r) ; 'tɛknɪˌkʌlɚ/ *n* (P) process of colour photography used for cinema films. (商標)電影片的彩色印片法。

tech·nique /tek'ni:k ; tɛk'nik/ *n* **1** [U] technical(1) or mechanical skill in music, painting, etc. (音樂、繪畫等的)技巧;技術。 **2** [C] method of doing sth expertly; method of artistic expression in music, painting, etc. 熟練的方法;行家手法;(音樂、繪畫等的)表現法。

tech·noc·racy /tek'nɒkrəsɪ ; tɛk'nɑkrəsɪ/ *n* [C, U] (*pl* -cies) (state where there is) organization and management of a country's industrial resources by technical experts. 技術管理(一國之工業資源由技術專家加以組織及管理);行技術管理的政府。 **tech·no·crat** /'teknəkræt ; 'tɛknəˌkræt/ *n* supporter, member, of a ~. 支持、擁護技術管理者;行技術管理的政府中的一員。

tech·nol·ogy /tek'nɒlədʒɪ ; tɛk'nɑlədʒɪ/ *n* [U] study, mastery and utilization of manufacturing and industrial methods; systematic application of knowledge to practical tasks in industry: 工藝學;工業技術;工藝: *the ~ of computers/printing/plastics, etc.* 電腦(印刷,塑膠等)的工業技術。 **tech·nol·ogist** /-dʒɪst ; -dʒɪst/ *n* expert in, student of, ~. 工藝專家; 工藝學家; 工學家。 **tech·no·logi·cal** /ˌteknə'lɒdʒɪkl ; ˌtɛknə'lɑdʒɪkl̩/ *adj* of ~: 工藝(學)的;工學的: *technological advances/problems.* 工藝的進步(問題)。

techy /'tetʃɪ ; 'tɛtʃɪ/ = tetchy.

teddy bear /'tedɪ beə(r) ; 'tɛdɪ bɛr/ *n* child's toy bear stuffed with soft material. 兒童的玩具熊。

Teddy boy /'tedɪ bɔɪ ; 'tɛdɪ bɔɪ/, (also colloq 俗亦作 **Ted** /ted ; tɛd/) *n* (GB) teenager (in the 1950's and early 1960's), who expressed opposition to authority by engaging in vicious gang fights and wore clothes like those worn during the reign of Edward VII (1901-10). (英) (1950 年代及 1960 年代早期)不良少年; 太保(穿着愛德華七世時代(1901—10)的衣服,行爲恣縱,反抗權威)。

Te Deum /ti: 'di:əm ; tɪ'diəm/ *n* (music for a) Latin hymn beginning *Te Deum laudamus* (meaning 'We praise you, God'), sung at morning service and on special occasions of thanksgiving. 感恩讚美詩(拉丁文讚美詩,開頭一句爲 Te Deum laudamus '我們讚美你,上帝',於早禱及特殊感恩場合唱之);此種讚美詩的樂曲。

tedi·ous /'ti:dɪəs ; 'tidɪəs/ *adj* tiresome; wearying; uninteresting: 沉悶的;厭煩的;乏味的: *a ~ lecture(r);* 沉悶的演說(者); *~ work.* 乏味的工作。 **~·ly** *adv* **~·ness** *n* **te·dium** /'ti:dɪəm ; 'tidɪəm/ *n* [U] ~ness; monotony; boredom. 沉悶;單調;乏味。

tee /ti: ; ti/ *n* **1** (golf) place from which a player starts in playing a hole; small pile of sand, or specially shaped piece of wood, plastic, etc, on which the ball is placed before the player drives, used instead of such a pile of sand. (高爾夫)開球處; 球座(發球時放置球的小沙堆等;用以代替此種沙堆的小塊木材或塑膠等)。'**tee-shirt** *n* = *T-shirt*, ⇨ T. **2** mark aimed at in certain games, such as quoits. 套圈或擲環遊戲的目標。 ***to a tee/T***, perfectly; exactly. 完美地;正確地。□ *vt, vi* **1** [VP 2C, 15B] ***tee (the ball) up***, put (the ball) on a tee(1). 置(高爾夫球)於球座上。 **2** [VP2A] ***tee off***, drive from a tee. 自球座擊球。

teem[1] /ti:m ; tim/ *vi* **1** [VP2C] be present in large numbers: 大量出現;有很多: *Fish ~ in this river.* 這條河中魚很多。 **2** [VP3A] ~ ***with***, have in great numbers: 有很多;充滿;富於: *The lakeside ~ed with gnats and mosquitoes.* 湖濱充滿蚊蚋。*His head is ~ing with bright ideas.* 他的腦子裏有很多聰明的主意。

teem[2] /ti:m ; tim/ *vi* [VP2A,C,3A] ~ ***(down)(with)***, (of rain, etc) fall heavily; pour: (指雨等)傾盆;暴降: *It was ~ing with rain /a ~ing wet day.* 大雨傾盆(下大雨的日子)。*The rain was ~ing down.* 大雨傾盆。

teens /ti:nz ; tinz/ *n pl* the ages of 13 to 19: 十三至十九的年齡: *girls in their ~*, between the ages of 13 and 19 inclusive. 少女;十三至十九歲的女孩子。*She's still in/not yet out of her ~*, is under 20. 她還不到二十歲。 **teen·age** /'ti:neɪdʒ ; 'tinɪdʒ/ *adj* of or for a teenager: 青少年的: *teenage fashions/problems.* 青少年的風尙(問題)。 **teen·ager** /'ti:neɪdʒə(r) ; 'tinˌedʒɚ/ *n* boy or girl in his or her ~; (loosely) young person up to 21 or 22 years of age: 青少年(十三至十九歲的少年男女); (不嚴格地指) 十三至二十一或二十二歲的年輕人: *a club for teenagers.* 青少年俱樂部。

teeny /'ti:nɪ ; 'tinɪ/ *adj* = tiny.

teeny·bop·per /'ti:nɪbɒpə(r) ; 'tinɪbɑpɚ/ *n* young, fashion-conscious teenager. 愛趕時髦的青少年。

tee·ter /'ti:tə(r) ; 'titɚ/ *vi* [VP2C] stand or walk unsteadily: 搖擺地或不穩地站立或步行: *~ing on the edge of disaster.* 在災難邊緣搖搖欲墜。

teeth /tiːθ ; tiθ/ *pl* of tooth.

teethe /tiːð ; tið/ *vi* [VP2A] (used only in progressive tenses, and as gerund and pres part) (of a baby) be getting its first teeth. (僅用於進行式中，並用作動名詞及現在分詞) (指嬰兒) 生牙；出牙齒；長牙。 **'teething troubles,** discomfort, slight illnesses, etc of a baby while its first teeth are coming through; (fig) troubles which may occur during the early stages of an enterprise. 嬰兒長牙時的不舒適；(喻)創業初期所遭遇的困難。

tee·total /tiː'təʊtl *US:* 'tiːtəʊtl ; ti'totl̩/ *adj* not drinking, opposed to the drinking of, alcoholic liquor. 不飲酒的；戒酒的；反對飲酒的。 **~·ler** (US also **~er**) /-tlə(r) ; -tl̩ɚ/ *n* person who abstains completely from alcoholic liquor. 完全不飲酒者；滴酒不沾者。

tee·totum /tiː'təʊtəm ; ti'totəm/ *n* top spun with the fingers, esp a four-sided one with letters on it. 手轉陀螺；捻轉兒(尤指四面形，其上有字母者)。

teg /teg ; tɛg/ *n* sheep in its second year. 兩歲的綿羊。

tegu·ment /'tegjʊmənt ; 'tɛgjəmənt/ *n* [C] (more usu 較常用 *integument*) natural covering of (part of) an animal body, eg a turtle's shell. (動物身上天生的)外被；覆皮；殼(如海龜的殼)。

tele·cast /'telɪkɑːst *US:* -kæst ; 'tɛlə,kæst/ *n, vt* broadcast by television. 用電視播送；電視播放。

tele·com·muni·ca·tions /ˌtelɪkəˌmjuːnɪ'keɪʃnz ; ˌtɛləkəˌmjunə'keʃənz/ *n pl* communications by cable, telegraph, telephone, radio or TV. 電訊(藉海底電纜、電報、電話、無線電或電視所作的通訊)。

tele·gram /'telɪgræm ; 'tɛlə,græm/ *n* [C] message sent by telegraphy. 電報；電信。

tele·graph /'telɪgrɑːf *US:* -græf ; 'tɛlə,græf/ *n* means of, apparatus for, sending messages by the use of electric current along wires or by wireless. 電報；電報機。 **'~-post/-pole** *nn* post supporting ~ wire(s). 電線桿。 **'~-line/-wire** *nn* wire along which messages (including telephone messages) travel. 電線；電線線路。 **bush ~** *n* sending of messages over long distances by smoke signals, beating of drums, etc. 叢林傳信術(藉烟火訊號、擂鼓等輾轉傳信至遠方的方法)。 □ *vi, vt* [VP6A, 12A, 13A, 11, 2A] send (news, etc) by ~: 以電報傳達(消息等)：*Shall I ~ or telephone?* 我該打電報還是打電話？ *He ~ed (to) his brother.* 他打電報給他的哥哥(弟弟)。(Note: *send a telegram* and *send a cable* are commoner than the use of the *v.*) (注意：send a telegram 及 send a cable 較 telegraph 的動詞用法更爲普遍。) **tel·egra·pher** /tɪ'legrəfə(r) ; tə'lɛgrəfɚ/ *n* skilled operator whose work is to send and receive messages by ~. 電報員；報務員。 **~ic** /ˌtelɪ'græfɪk ; ˌtɛlə'græfɪk/ *adj* sent by, suitable for, connected with, the ~: 電報的；由電報發送的；適於電報的；有關電報的：*a ~ic address,* abbreviated address or brief registered address, for use in telegrams. 電報掛號。 **~i·cally** /-klɪ ; -klɪ/ *adv* **tel·egra·phese** /ˌtelɪgrə'fiːz ; ˌtɛləgræ'fiz/ *n* [U] style of language used in telegrams (with unessential words omitted). (省略非必要字句的)電報文體。 **tel·egra·phist** /tɪ'legrəfɪst ; tə'lɛgrəfɪst/ *n* = ~er. **tel·egra·phy** /tɪ'legrəfɪ ; tə'lɛgrəfɪ/ *n* [U] art, science, process, of sending and receiving messages by ~, of constructing ~ic apparatus, etc. 電報術；電報學；電報收發過程；電報機裝置術、學或其過程。

te·lem·etry /tɪ'lemətrɪ ; tə'lɛmətrɪ/ *n* [U] automatic transmission and measurement of data from a distance, usu by radio. 遙測術(由無線電等自動發射及測量遠方之資料)。

tele·ol·ogy /ˌtelɪ'ɒlədʒɪ ; ˌtɛlɪ'ɑlədʒɪ/ *n* theory, teaching, belief, that events and developments are due to the purpose or design that they are serving (as opposed to the mechanistic theory of the universe, ⇨ mechanisitic). (哲學上的)宇宙目的論(認爲事件的發生及演變，都有其目的的理論、敎訓或信仰，與宇宙機械論相反)。 **teleo·logi·cal** /ˌtelɪə'lɒdʒɪkl ; ˌtɛlɪə'lɑdʒɪkl̩/ *adj* **tele·ol·ogist** /ˌtelɪ'ɒlədʒɪst ; ˌtɛlɪ'ɑlədʒɪst/ *n* believer in ~. 宇宙目的論者。

tel·epa·thy /tɪ'lepəθɪ ; tə'lɛpəθɪ/ *n* [U] **1** transference of thoughts or ideas from one mind to another without the normal use of the senses. 心靈感應；傳心術；兩心靈通(不使用一般的官能，而思想意念等可在二人心中相互傳遞)。 **2** (colloq) ability to be immediately aware of the thoughts and feelings of others. (俗)解心(能)力(對旁人的思想及感情能够立卽瞭解的能力)。 **tele·pathic** /ˌtelɪ'pæθɪk ; ˌtɛlə'pæθɪk/ *adj* **tel·epa·thist** /tɪ'lepəθɪst ; tə'lɛpəθɪst/ *n* person who studies or believes in ~ or who claims to have telepathic powers. 研究或信仰心靈感應者；自稱通傳心術者。

tele·phone /'telɪfəʊn ; 'tɛlə,fon/ (usu abbr *phone* in colloq speech) (談話中常略作 phone) *n* [U] means, system, of transmitting the human voice by electric current, through wires (usu called *telegraph wires,* not *~ wires*) supported by poles (usu called *telegraph poles,* not *~ posts*), or by radio (*radio-~*); [C] apparatus (with receiver and mouthpiece) for this purpose: 電話(通常經由電線桿 telegraph poles 所支持的電線 telegraph wires 或無線電傳達)；電話機：*You're wanted on the phone.* 你有電話(請你來接你的電話)。 *Mr Green is on the phone just now,* is using the ~. 格林先生正在打電話。 *Will you answer the phone, please,* pick up the receiver and answer. 請接電話。 **'~ booth,** (also 亦作 *'phone-booth* or 或 *'call-box*) small enclosure with a coin-operated public ~. 公用電話亭。 **'~ directory,** (also 亦作 *'phone-book*) list of names with numbers and addresses. 電話簿。 **'~ exchange,** place where ~ connections are made. 電話局；電話交換所；總機。 □ *vt, vi* [VP 6A, 9, 12A, 13A, 11, 2A, 4A] send (a message to sb) by ~: 以電話傳送(信息給某人)：*I'll phone you tomorrow.* 我明天會打電話給你。 *He phoned (through) to say that....* 他電話上說…。 *It's Mary's birthday today—we must phone her a greetings telegram,* send her a greeting ('Happy Birthday') by asking for such a telegram to be sent (and usu received by ~). 今天是瑪麗的生日——我們必須發一通電話賀電給她(要求電信局發'生日快樂'的賀電，而通常是從電話上收到該賀電)。 **tel·eph·ony** /tɪ'lefənɪ ; tə'lɛfənɪ/ *n* [U] method, process, of sending and receiving messages by ~. 電話術；電話學；電話機的收發過程。 **tel·ephon·ist** /tɪ'lefənɪst ; 'tɛlə,fonɪst/ *n* operator in a ~ exchange. (電話交換所或總機的)接線生；接線員。

tele·photo /ˌtelɪ'fəʊtəʊ ; 'tɛlə,foto/ *n* **1 ~ lens,** = telescopic lens. (攝影機的)望遠鏡頭。 **2** (colloq abbr of) ~graph. (俗)爲 telephotograph 之略。 **~·graph** /-grɑːf *US:* -græf ; -græf/ *n* **1** photograph made with a ~ lens. 用望遠鏡頭攝得的相片。 **2** picture transmitted and received by ~graphy. 傳眞相片。 **tele·pho·togra·phy** /ˌtelɪfə'tɒgrəfɪ ; ˌtɛləfo'tɑgrəfɪ/ *n* [U] **1** process of photographing distant objects, etc using a ~ lens. (用望遠鏡頭)望遠攝影術。 **2** process of transmitting and receiving charts, pictures, etc over a distance. 遠距離傳眞術。

tele·prin·ter /'telɪprɪntə(r) ; 'tɛlɪ,prɪntɚ/ *n* telegraph instrument for sending messages (typed by an operator at the sending end), which are retyped automatically and almost simultaneously by machine at the other end. 打字電報機(報務員在發報處打字發送消息，在收報處立卽自動重新打出)。

tele·promp·ter /'telɪprɒmptə(r) ; 'tɛlɪ,prɑmptɚ/ *n* TV device by which a speaker can read in front of him an enlargement of his script, so that he seems to speak spontaneously. 電視提詞器(可將講話者的原稿逐行放大顯出，故講話者雖在讀預先準備的講稿，而在觀衆看來，似在當場自由發言)。

tele·scope /'telɪskəʊp ; 'tɛlə,skop/ *n* tube-like instrument with lenses for making distant objects appear nearer and larger. 望遠鏡。 ˌ**radio** '~, ⇨ radio-. □ *vt, vi* [VP6A, 2A] make or become shorter by means of or in the manner of sections that slide one within the other: 把一部分套進、滑進或縮進另一部分而使之變短;嵌進;叠縮: *When the trains collided, the first two cars of one of the trains ~d/were ~d.* 火車相撞時,其中一列火車的前兩節車廂疊嵌在一起了。 **tele·scopic** /ˌtelɪ'skɒpɪk ; ˌtɛlə'skɑpɪk/ *adj* **1** of, containing, able to be seen with, a ~: 望遠鏡的;包括望遠鏡的;可用望遠鏡見到的: *a telescopic lens,* extra lens attached to a camera to enable distant objects and scenes to be photographed (and now often called a *telephoto lens*); (照相機的)望遠鏡頭(現常稱爲 telephoto lens); *a telescopic sight,* (on a rifle, to magnify the target); (來復槍上的)望遠照門;望遠瞄準器; *a telescopic view of the moon,* seen through a ~. 從望遠鏡中所見到的月亮。 **2** having sections which slide one within the other: 嵌進的;叠縮的;套入的: *a telescopic aerial,* eg as part of a portable radio receiver. 伸縮式天線(如手提無線電收音機上者)。

tele·type·writer /ˌtelɪ'taɪpraɪtə(r); ˌtɛlə'taɪpˌraɪtɚ/ *n* (US) (美) = teleprinter.

tele·vi·sion /'telɪvɪʒn ; 'tɛləˌvɪʒən/ *n* **1** [U] (abbr 略作 **TV**, or colloq 俗 **telly** /'telɪ ; 'tɛlɪ/) process of transmitting a view of events, plays, etc (while these are taking place, or from films or tapes on which a record has been made) by radio to a distant ~ receiving set with synchronized sound: 電視: *Did you see the boat race on (the) ~?* 你看了電視上的賽船(節目)嗎? **2** [C] '~ **(set)**, apparatus for receiving and showing this transmission. 電視機。 **tele·vise** /'telɪvaɪz ; 'tɛləˌvaɪz/ *vt* [VP6A] send views of by ~: 用電視播送或播出: *The Olympic Games were televised.* 奧林匹克運動會的實況曾由電視播出。

telex /'teleks ; 'tɛlɛks/ *n* system of communication using teleprinters. 使用打字電報機的傳送系統;打字電報;交換電報。

tel·fer /'telfə(r) ; 'tɛlfɚ/ = telpher.

tell /tel ; tɛl/ *vt, vi* (*pt, pp* told /təʊld ; told/) **1** [VP6A, 13A, 12A, 11, 20, 21] ~ ***sth (to sb),*** ~ ***sb sth,*** make known (in spoken or written words); give information concerning or a description of: (用語言或文字)告知;告訴;講述: *He told the news to everybody in the village.* 他把這項消息告訴了村子裏每一個人。 *I told him my name.* 我把我的名字告訴了他。 *T~ me where you live.* 把你的住處告訴我。 *I can't ~ you how happy I am,* can't find words that are adequate. 我無法告訴你我是多麼的快樂。 *He told me (that) he was coming.* 他告訴我他要來。 *So I've been told,* I've already been told that. 有人告訴過我了。 *If he asks, ~ him.* 如果他問起,就告訴他。 *Don't ~ me it's too late!* (used to express surprise or alarm). 不會太晚罷!(用以表驚訝或驚恐)。 *I'll ~ you what...,* used meaning 'Here's a suggestion, idea, etc that may help'. 我講給你聽(意謂'我有一項建議、主意等,可能有幫助')。 *I ~* (= assure) *you, he's thoroughly dishonest!* 我敢說,他一點也不誠實! ***I told you so,*** I warned you that this would happen, etc and now you see that I'm right: 我早跟你說過吧(我以前警告過你會如何如何,現在你知道我對了吧): *Things have gone wrong but please don't say 'I told you so!'* 事情弄糟了,但請不要講'我早跟你說過吧!' ***You're ~ing me!*** I fully agree with you. 我完全同意你! ***T~ me another!*** I don't believe you. 我才不相信哩! ***~ the world,*** (colloq) ~ everybody: (俗)告訴每一個人: *We all know you're clever, but do you have to ~ the world,* be so emphatic about it? 我們都知道你很聰明,不過你有必要告訴每一個人嗎(或:你有必要特別强調這一點嗎)? **2** [VP6A, 13A, 12A, 15A] utter; express with words: 講;述;說: *~ a lie;* 說謊; *~ the children a tale/story.* 講故事給小孩聽。 *'When in doubt, ~ the truth', said Mark Twain.* '沒有把握的時候,要照實說,' 馬克吐温說。 ***~ the tale,*** (colloq) ~ a pitiful story in order to get sympathy, etc. (俗)講述悲慘故事以爭取同情等。 ***~ tales about/on sb,*** make known sb's secrets, misconduct, etc in a malicious way. 講某人壞話;搬弄是非。 **~·tale** /'telteɪl ; 'tɛlˌtel/ *n* person who ~s about another's private affairs, makes known a secret, etc; circumstances, etc that reveal a person's thoughts, activities, etc (often attrib): 談論旁人私事者;洩露秘密者;顯露某人思想、活動等的環境、景況等(常作形容用法): *a ~tale blush;* 洩露底蘊的臉紅; *the ~tale cigarette ash on the carpet,* that made known the fact that someone had been smoking a cigarette. 地毯上的香煙灰(顯示曾有人吸過香煙)。 **3** [VP17] order; direct: 吩咐;命令: *Do what I ~ you.* 照我吩咐你的去做。 *You must do what you're told.* 你必須遵照命令做事。 *T~ him to wait.* 叫他等一等。 *He was told to start at once.* 他接到命令(或指示)立即出發。 **4** [VP6A, 14] (esp with *can/could/be able to*) ~ ***sb/sth (from sb/sth),*** know apart; distinguish: (尤與 can, could, be able to 連用)辨識;區別: *Can you ~ Tom from his twin brother?* 湯姆和他的孿生兄弟,你認得出誰是誰嗎? *They look exactly the same—how can you ~ which is which?* 他們看起來完全一樣——你怎麼認得出那個是那個呢? **5** [VP6A, 8, 10, 2A] learn by observation; make out; become aware (of sth): 藉觀察而認知;弄明白;瞭解;知道(某事物): *How do you ~ which of these buttons to press?* 你怎麼知道要按這些電鈕中的那一個? ~ ***the time,*** (be able to) read (or say) the time from a clock, etc: (能够)看鐘錶等而說出時間;(能够)看懂鐘錶等上的時間: *Can Mary ~ the time yet?* 瑪莉現在看得懂(鐘錶上的)時間了嗎? *Can you ~ me what time it is?* 你能告訴我現在的時刻嗎? ***You can never ~; You never can ~,*** you can never be sure, eg because appearances are often deceptive. 誰也不知道;誰也沒把握(譬如,因爲外表常常靠不住)。 ***there is/was, etc no ~ing,*** it is impossible or difficult to know: 不可能知道;很難知道: *There's no ~ing what may happen/where she's gone/what he's doing, etc.* 不可能(很難)知道會發生甚麼事(她到那裏去了,他在幹什麼等)。 **6** [VP6A, 15B] (old use) count. (舊用法)計算;數。 ~ ***one's beads,*** say one's prayers (counting beads on a rosary). 念經;數念珠;念禱詞。 ~ ***sb off (for sth/to do sth),*** **(a)** count one by one and give orders: 一個一個地點派工作;逐一授予命令: *Ten men were told off for special duty/to clean the latrines.* 十個人被點派從事特殊任務(去打掃厠所)。 **(b)** (colloq) give a list of sb's misdoings; scold him: (俗)數說某人的壞行爲;斥責;責罵: *That fellow needs to be told off.* 那傢伙該罵一頓。 *She told the typist off for making so many careless mistakes.* 她因爲打字員犯了很多粗心的錯誤而把她說了一頓。 **7** [VP2A, 3A] ~ ***(on/upon sb),*** have a marked effect on; influence the result of: 奏效;對…產生顯著效果;影響…的結果: *All this hard work is ~ing on him,* is affecting his health. 所有這些辛苦的工作都對他的健康有影響。 *Every blow ~s.* 每一擊都擊中了。 **~·ing** *adj* effective; impressive: 有效的;有力的;顯著的: *a ~ing speech/argument/blow.* 有力的演說(論據,打擊)。 **~·ing·ly** *adv* **8** [VP2A, 3A] ~ ***(on sb),*** (colloq) reveal a secret; inform against: (俗)洩露秘密;告發(某人): *John told on his sister.* 約翰打他姐姐(妹妹)的小報告。 ⇨ *tale-bearer* at tale(2). *You promised not to ~ and now you've done so!* 你答應過不洩露秘密,而你現在已經洩露了!

tel·ler /'telə(r) ; 'tɛlɚ/ *n* **1** person who receives, and pays out, money over a bank counter. (銀行的)出納員。 **2** man who counts votes, eg in the House of Commons. (投票時的)計票員(如下議院中者)。

telly /'telɪ ; 'tɛlɪ/ *n* (colloq abbr for) television. (俗)爲 television 之略。

tel·pher /'telfə(r) ; 'tɛlfɚ/ *n* conveyance for

goods, suspended from overhead wire cables, usu driven by electricity; transportation system of this kind, eg for rock from a quarry. 索道輸送;索道車;索道運輸工具;纜車;纜車系統。

Tel·star /ˈtelstɑ:(r); ˈtɛl,star/ *n* (P) communications satellite used (commercially) for the transmission of telephone messages and TV. (商標)通信(訊)衛星;電訊衛星。

te·mer·ity /tɪˈmerətɪ; təˈmɛrətɪ/ *n* [U] rashness. 鹵莽;孟浪。

tem·per¹ /ˈtempə(r); ˈtɛmpɚ/ *n* **1** condition of the mind and emotions: 心情;脾氣;性情;氣質: *in a good ~*, calm and pleasant; 心情好的; *in a bad ~*, angry, impatient, etc. 心情壞的(憤怒、不耐等)。 ***get/fly into a ~,*** become angry. 發怒。 ***keep/lose one's ~,*** keep/fail to keep one's ~ under control. 忍住(發)脾氣。 ***out of ~ (with),*** angry (with). (對…)發脾氣。 **-tem·pered** /ˈtempəd; ˈtɛmpɚd/ *adj* (in compounds) (用於複合字中) having or showing a certain kind of ~: 有某種心情的;顯示某種氣質的: *a ˌgood-/ˌsweet-/ˌfiery-/ˌhot-, etc ˈ~ed man.* 脾氣好(柔和,急,躁等)的人。**-tem·pered·ly** *adv* (in compounds) (用於複合字中) *good-~edly.* 好脾氣地。 **2** [U] degree of hardness, toughness, elasticity, of a substance, esp of steel. (尤指鋼等物質的)硬度、韌度、彈性;回火度。

tem·per² /ˈtempə(r); ˈtɛmpɚ/ *vt, vi* **1** [VP6A] give the required temper(2) to (eg steel) by heating and cooling; bring (eg clay) to the required condition by moistening, mixing, kneading, etc; 回火;鍛鍊(鋼等);鍊至所需要的硬度;捏和(黏土等); [VP2A] come to the required condition as the result of treatment. 經處理後成爲所需要的情況。 **2** [VP6A, 15A] soften or modify; mitigate: 使軟化;調劑;緩和: *~ justice with mercy*, be merciful when giving a just punishment. 恩威並施;執法公正而仁慈。

tem·pera /ˈtempərə; ˈtɛmpərə/ *n* [U] = distemper, esp as used in fresco painting. 色膠(尤指用於壁畫中者)。

tem·pera·ment /ˈtemprəmənt; ˈtɛmprəmənt/ *n* **1** [C, U] person's disposition or nature, esp as this affects his way of thinking, feeling and behaving: 氣質;性情(尤指影響人的思想、感情及行爲者): *a girl with a nervous/an artistic ~.* 帶有神經質(藝術家氣質)的女孩子。*The two brothers have entirely different ~s.* 這兩兄弟的性情完全不同。*Success often depends on ~.* 成功常視一個人的性情而定。 **2** [U] (without an *adj*) kind of disposition that is easily excited, passionate, not easily controlled or restrained, eg as in some actresses and opera singers. (不與形容詞連用)(某些女演員及歌劇演唱家等之)易激動;易怒;急躁。 **tem·pera·men·tal** /ˌtemprəˈmentl; ˌtɛmpərəˈmɛntl̩/ *adj* **1** caused by ~: 由氣質引起的;本質的: *a ~al dislike for study.* 本性不喜讀書。 **2** subject to quickly changing moods: 神經質的;喜怒無常的;心情變化快的: *a ~al tennis player*, one whose playing changes according to his mood. 球技不穩定的網球員(球技隨心情而改變)。 **tem·pera·men·tally** /-təlɪ; -tl̩ɪ/ *adv*

tem·per·ance /ˈtempərəns; ˈtɛmprəns/ *n* [U] **1** moderation, self-control, in speech, behaviour and (esp) in the use of alcoholic drinks. (言詞、行爲上的)節制;自制;克己;(尤指)節酒;節飲。 **2** total abstinence from alcoholic drinks: 禁酒: (attrib) (形容用法) *a ˈ~ society*, one for the restriction or abolition of the use of alcoholic drinks. 禁酒會。

tem·per·ate /ˈtempərət; ˈtɛmprɪt/ *adj* **1** showing, behaving, with temperance(1): 有節制的;適度的: *Be more ~ in your language, please.* 言詞上請節制一點。 **2** (of climate, parts of the world) free from extremes of heat and cold: (指氣候,世界上某些地區)溫和的: *the north ˈ~ zone*, between the Tropic of Cancer and the arctic zone. 北溫帶。 **~·ly** *adv* **~·ness** *n*

tem·pera·ture /ˈtemprətʃə(r) *US:* ˈtempərtʃʊər; ˈtɛmprətʃɚ/ *n* [C, U] degree of heat and cold: 溫度;冷熱;體溫: *In Hawaii there are no extremes of ~.* 在夏威夷沒有特別冷或特別熱的氣溫。 *The nurse took the ~s of all the patients*, measured their body ~s with a thermometer. 那位護士爲所有的病人量體溫。 ***have/run a ~,*** have a fever. 發燒。

tem·pest /ˈtempɪst; ˈtɛmpɪst/ *n* [C] violent storm; (fig) violent agitation: 暴風雨;風暴;(喻)騷亂;風潮;騷動;大激動: *A ~ of laughter swept through the crowd.* 羣衆爆發出一陣大笑。 **ˈ~-swept/-tossed** *adjj* (liter) swept, etc by ~s. (文)遭暴風雨襲擊的;風暴橫掃的。 **tem·pes·tu·ous** /temˈpestʃʊəs; tɛmˈpɛstʃʊəs/ *adj* (of the weather and fig) violent; stormy: (指天氣,亦作比喻用法)劇烈的;騷亂的;有暴風雨的: *in a ~uous mood;* 心情極爲激動的; *a ~uous political meeting.* 騷動的政治集會。

tem·plate, tem·plet /ˈtemplɪt; ˈtɛmplɪt/ *nn* pattern or gauge (usu a thin board or metal plate) used as a guide in cutting or drilling metal, wood, etc. (切割或鑽穿金屬、木材等用的)樣板;模板;型板。

temple¹ /ˈtempl; ˈtɛmpl̩/ *n* **1** building used for the worship of a god (esp ancient Greek, Roman, Egyptian and modern Hindu, Buddhist, etc). 廟;寺;神殿(尤指古代希臘、羅馬、埃及和近代印度教及佛教等者)。 **2** (applied occasionally to a) place of Christian worship (*church* and *chapel* being the usu words): (偶而用以指)教堂;禮拜堂(church 與 chapel 較爲通用): *a Mormon ~.* 摩門教堂。 **3** any of the three successive religious centres of the Jews in ancient Jerusalem. 古代耶路撒冷猶太人連續建立的三個宗教中心之任一。 **4 the Inner/Middle T~,** two Inns of Court in London. 倫敦的內(中)殿法學協會。⇨ inn(2).

T

a Hindu temple

temple² /ˈtempl; ˈtɛmpl̩/ *n* flat part of either side of the forehead. (前額兩側的)太陽穴;顳;顳顬。 ⇨ the illus at head. 參看 head 之插圖。

tem·plet /ˈtemplɪt; ˈtɛmplɪt/ *n* ⇨ template.

tempo /ˈtempəʊ; ˈtɛmpo/ *n* (*pl* ~s or, 或, in music, 在音樂術語中, tempi /-pi:; -pi/) (I) (義) **1** rate of movement or activity: 動作或活動的速率;進度;進行或發展的速度: *the tiring ~ of city life.* 叫人疲於奔命的都市生活。*This long strike has upset the ~ of production.* 這次的長期罷工已經破壞了生產進度。 **2** speed at which music is (to be) played. (音樂的)速度;拍子;緩急。

tem·poral /ˈtempərəl; ˈtɛmpərəl/ *adj* **1** of, existing in, time: 時(間)的;時間上的;暫時的: (gram) (文法) *~ conjunctions,* eg *when, while.* 表示時間的連接詞(如when, while)。 **2** of earthly human life; of this physical life only, not spiritual: 塵世生活的;世俗的;現世的;非精神生活的: *the ~ power of the Pope*, ie as head of the Vatican State; 教宗的世俗權力(卽作爲教廷領袖); *the lords ~* (= the peers of the realm) *and the lords spiritual* (= the bishops). 上議院中的貴族議員及主教議員。 **~·ity** /ˌtempəˈrælətɪ; ˌtɛmpəˈrælətɪ/ *n* (usu *pl;* -ties) secular possessions: (通常用複數)世俗的財產;俗利: *the temporalities of the Church.* 教會的財產。**~ty** /'tempərəltɪ; 'tɛmpərəltɪ/ *n* laity. 俗人。

tem·por·ary /'temprərɪ *US:* -pərerɪ; 'tɛmpə,rɛrɪ/ *adj* lasting for, designed to be used for, a short time only: 暫時的;臨時的;一時的: *~ employment;* 臨時工作; *a ~ bridge.* 臨時橋。**tem·por·ar·ily** /'temprərəlɪ *US:* ,tempə'rerəlɪ; 'tɛmpə,rɛrəlɪ/ *adv* **tem·por·ari·ness** *n*

tem·por·ize /'tempəraɪz; 'tɛmpə,raɪz/ *vi* [VP2A] delay making a decision, giving an answer, stating one's purpose, etc; act so as gain time: 稽延作決定、作答覆、陳述自己的目的等;敷衍;拖延以爭取時間: *a temporizing politician/answer.* 八面玲瓏的政客(敷衍的答覆)。

tempt /tempt; tɛmpt/ *vt* [VP6A, 17, 14] ~ ***(to sth/into doing sth),*** **1** (try to) persuade (sb) to do sth wrong or foolish: 勸誘(某人)做壞事或蠢事;勾引: *Nothing could ~ him to such a course of action/to take such a step.* 沒有什麼事情能够誘使他那樣做(採取這樣的步驟)。*He was ~ed into making a false step,* doing sth unwise. 他被引誘做了一件傻事。**2** attract (sb) to have or do sth: 誘使(某人)保有或做出某事;誘導;導致: *The warm weather ~ed us to go for a swim.* 暖和的天氣誘使我們去游泳。*She ~ed the child to have a little more soup.* 她誘使那孩子多喝一點湯。*What a ~ing* (= attractive) *offer!* 多吸引人的提議(出價等)! **3** (old use, biblical) test. (舊用法,聖經用法)考驗;試驗。*~ **Providence,*** take a risk. 冒險。**~·ing·ly** *adv* **~er** *n* person who ~s; 勸誘者;誘惑者; (esp) (尤指) **the T~er,** Satan, the Devil. 撒旦;魔鬼。**temp·tress** /'temptrɪs; 'tɛmptrɪs/ *n* woman who ~s. 女引誘者、誘惑者等。

T

temp·ta·tion /temp'teɪʃn; tɛmp'teʃən/ *n* **1** [U] tempting or being tempted: (被)勸誘;(被)誘惑: *the ~ of easy profits;* 賺錢容易的誘惑; *yield/give way to ~;* 屈服於誘惑; *put ~ in sb's way.* 誘惑某人。**2** [C] that which tempts or attracts: 誘惑物;有吸引力之物: *The sight of the purse on the table was a strong ~ to the poor child.* 桌上的那個錢包對那貧苦的孩子是一個很大的誘惑。*Clever advertisements are ~s to spend money.* 巧妙的廣告誘使人花錢。

ten /ten; tɛn/ *n, adj* the number 10. 十;拾。⇨ App 5. 參看附錄五。***ten to one,*** very probably: 十之八九;非常可能地: *Ten to one he will arrive late.* 十之八九他會遲到。**tenth** /tenθ; tɛnθ/ *n, adj* the next after the 9th; one of 10 equal parts. 第十(的);十分之一(的)。**tenth·ly** *adv* **'ten·fold** *adv* ten times as many or much. 十倍地。**'ten·pence** *n* (GB decimal coin with the) value of ten pennies. (英國十進制硬幣)十辨士(的價值)。

ten·able /'tenəbl; 'tɛnəbl/ *adj* **1** that can be defended successfully: 可防守的;守得住的;可維護或防護的: *His theory is hardly ~.* 他的理論很難站得住。**2** (of an office or position) that can be held (*by* sb *for* a time): (指職務或職位)可保有的;可維持的(與 *by* sb *for* a time 連用): *The lectureship is ~ for a period of three years.* 該講師的職位爲期三年。**ten·abil·ity** /,tenə'bɪlətɪ; ,tɛnə'bɪlətɪ/ *n*

ten·acious /tɪ'neɪʃəs; tɪ'neʃəs/ *adj* holding tightly, refusing to let go: 抓緊的;不放鬆的;緊握的: *a ~ memory;* 很强的記憶力; *~ of our rights.* 堅決維護我們的權利。**~·ly** *adv* **~·ness** *n* **ten·ac·ity** /tɪ'næsətɪ; tɪ'næsətɪ/ *n*

ten·ant /'tenənt; 'tɛnənt/ *n* person who pays rent for the use of land, a building, a room, etc: 佃戶;房客;租戶: *evict ~s for non-payment of rent;* 趕出未付房租的房客; *~ farmers,* who cultivate farms which they do not own. 佃農。□ *vt* (usu passive) occupy as a ~: (通常用被動語態)租賃;租佃: *houses ~ed by railway workers.* 鐵路工人租賃的房屋。**ten·ancy** /-ənsɪ; -ənsɪ/ *n* **1** [U] use of land, etc as a ~: 租賃;租用: *during his tenancy of the farm.* 在他租用該農地期間。**2** [C] length of time during which a ~ uses land, etc: 租賃或租用期間: *hold a life tenancy of a house.* 終生租用某房屋。**ten·an·try** /'tenəntrɪ; 'tɛnəntrɪ/ *n* (collective *sing*) all the ~s occupying land and houses on one estate. (集合單數)某一地產的全體佃戶及租戶。

tench /tentʃ; tɛntʃ/ *n* edible European freshwater fish; carp. 歐洲產可食淡水鯉魚。

tend¹ /tend; tɛnd/ *vt* [VP6A] watch over; attend to: 照料;照管: *shepherds ~ing their flocks;* 照料其羊羣的牧羊人; (esp US) (尤美) *~ the store,* serve customers. 招呼顧客;照看店鋪。

tend² /tend; tɛnd/ *vi* [VP2C, 4A] be inclined to move; have a direction: 傾向;有某種趨勢;向;趨於: *Prices are ~ing upwards.* 物價正在上漲。*He ~s to pitch the ball too high.* 他常把球擲得過高。*He ~s towards atheism.* 他傾向於無神論。**ten·dency** /'tendənsɪ; 'tɛndənsɪ/ *n* [C] (*pl* -cies) turning or inclination, leaning: 傾向;趨勢: *Business is showing a ~ency to improve.* 業務有改進的趨勢。*There was a strong upward ~ency in oil shares yesterday,* prices ~ed upwards. 石油股票昨天有强烈上漲的趨勢。

ten·den·tious /ten'denʃəs; tɛn'dɛnʃəs/ *adj* (of a speech, a piece of writing, etc) having an underlying purpose, aimed at helping a cause; not impartial: (指演說、文章等)有目的的;宣傳的;非持平之論的: *Countries at war often send out ~ reports,* reports designed to show their cause in a favourable light, win sympathy, etc. 交戰國常發出宣傳性的報導。**~·ly** *adv* **~·ness** *n*

ten·der¹ /'tendə(r); 'tɛndɚ/ *adj* **1** delicate; easily hurt or damaged; quickly feeling pain: 脆弱的;纖弱的;敏感的;易傷的;易損壞的;觸及卽感疼痛的: *~ blossoms,* eg easily hurt by frosts; 嬌嫩的花; *touch sb on a ~ spot,* one that hurts when touched; 碰到某人的痛處; *a ~ subject,* (fig) one that has to be dealt with carefully to avoid hurting people's feelings; (喻)敏感的問題(需要小心處理以免傷人感情者); *a person of ~ age/years,* young and immature; 年幼而未成熟的人; *have a ~ conscience;* 容易感到良心不安; *a ~ heart,* easily moved to pity, 軟心腸, hence, 由此產生, **,~-'hearted** *adj* **'~·foot** *n* (*pl* -foots) new-comer to the sort of country where there is rough living, hardship, etc. 新來到艱苦生活環境的人;生手。**2** (of meat) easily chewed; not tough: (指肉)嫩的;易咀嚼的;柔軟的: *a ~ steak.* 嫩牛排。**'~·loin** *n* [U] ~ part of the loin of beef or pork; undercut of sirloin. 牛或猪的腰部嫩肉;嫩腰肉。**3** kind, loving: 溫柔的;仁慈的;親切的: *~ looks;* 溫柔的表情; *~ care;* 悉心的照顧; *~ parents;* 仁慈的雙親; *bid sb a ~ farewell.* 與某人親切地道別。**~·ly** *adv* **~·ness** *n*

ten·der² /'tendə(r); 'tɛndɚ/ *n* **1** person who looks after, watches over, sth: 照管者;照料者;照看者: *a ma'chine-~;* 機器工人; *a 'bar~,* ⇨ bar¹(13). 酒保;酒館侍者。**2** small ship attending a larger one, to carry stores, put on or take off passengers, etc. 大船的勤務船(運送必需品,接運旅客等);供應船。**3** wagon for fuel and water behind a steam locomotive. (蒸汽火車頭後面的)煤水車。

ten·der³ /'tendə(r); 'tɛndɚ/ *vt, vi* **1** [VP6A, 12A, 13A] offer; present: 提出;提供;貢獻: *~ money in payment of a debt.* 提出金錢償還債務。*He ~ed his resignation to the Prime Minister/his services to the Government.* 他向首相提出辭呈(爲政府效力)。**2** [VP2A, 3A] ~ ***(for),*** make an offer (to carry out work, supply goods, etc) at a stated price: 投標: *~ for the construction of a new motorway.* 投標承建一條新的高速公路。□ *n* [C] **1** statement of the price at which one offers to supply goods or services, or to do sth: 投標: *invite ~s for a new bridge;* 新橋工程招標; *put in/make/send in a ~ for sth;* 參加某項投標; *accept the lowest ~.* 接受最低價格的投標。**2** **legal ~,** form of money which must, by law, be accepted in payment of a debt: 償還債務時必須接受的合法錢幣;法償;合法貨

幣: *Are copper coins legal ~ for a sum in excess of £10?* 超過十鎊的數目可以用銅幣償付嗎?

ten·don /ˈtendən ; ˈtɛndən/ *n* [C] tough, thick cord that joins muscle to bone; sinew. 腱。

ten·dril /ˈtendrəl ; ˈtɛndrɪl/ *n* [C] thread-like part of a plant, eg a vine, that twists round any near-by support. 植物的卷鬚。⇨ the illus at ivy. 參看 ivy 之插圖。

ten·ement /ˈtenəmənt ; ˈtɛnəmənt/ *n* [C] **1** **ˈ~(-house),** large building with apartments for the use of many families at low rents. 廉租公寓(多家合住,租金便宜的大房屋)。 **2** (legal) any dwelling-house; any kind of permanent property. (法律)住宅;不動產。

tenet /ˈtenɪt ; ˈtɛnɪt/ *n* [C] principle; belief; doctrine. 主義;信條;教理;教條。

ten·ner /ˈtenə(r) ; ˈtɛnɚ/ *n* (colloq) ten pounds in GB money; ten-pound note. (俗)十英鎊;十鎊的紙幣。

ten·nis /ˈtenɪs ; ˈtɛnɪs/ *n* [U] game for two or four players who hit a ball backwards and forwards across a net. 網球。**ˈ~-court** *n* marked area on which ~ is played. 網球場。**ˌ~-ˈelbow** *n* inflammation of the elbow caused by playing ~. 網球員肘病(因打網球而引起的肘部發炎)。

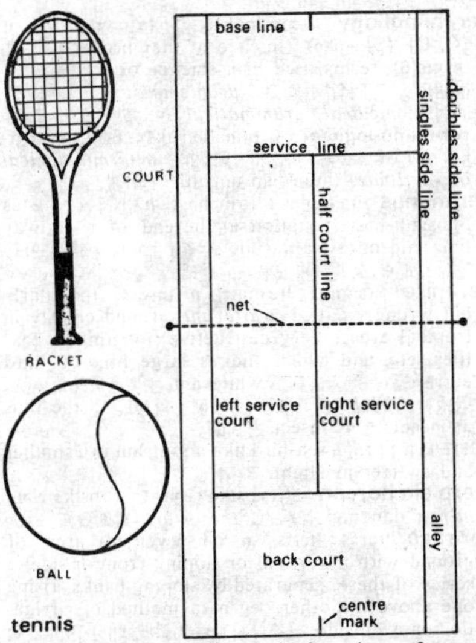

tennis

tenon /ˈtenən ; ˈtɛnən/ *n* end of a piece of wood shaped to go into a mortise to make a joint. 榫;筍頭。

tenor¹ /ˈtenə(r) ; ˈtɛnɚ/ *n* (usu 通常作 ***the ~ (of)***) general routine or direction (*of* one's life): (生活的)常規或方向: *interrupt sb's even ~;* 擾亂了某人生活的常規; general meaning, thread, drift (*of* a speech, etc): (演講等的)要旨;條理;大意(與 of 連用): *She knew enough Spanish to get the ~ of what was being said.* 她懂得的西班牙語足以瞭解對方談話的大意。

tenor² /ˈtenə(r) ; ˈtɛnɚ/ *n* **1** (music for, singer with, the) highest normal adult male voice: 男高音;次中音;適於男高音或次中音的樂曲;男高音或次中音歌手或歌唱家: (attrib) (形容用法) *~ voice;* 男高音;次中音; *the ~ part.* (樂譜中的)男高音或次中音部。 **2** (of instruments) with a range about that of the ~ voice: (指樂器)音域相當於男高音或次中音的: *a ~ horn/saxophone.* 次中音喇叭(薩克管)。

ten·pin /ˈtenpɪn ; ˈtɛnˌpɪn/ *n* **1** (*pl* with *sing v*) game like *ninepins* with ten skittles instead of nine. (複數與單數動詞連用)十柱戲(與 ninepins相似,但用十柱);十柱保齡球。 **2** pin used. 十柱戲中所用之柱。 **3** (attrib) (形容用法) *~ bowling.* 十柱保齡球。

tense¹ /tens ; tɛns/ *adj* (lit or fig) tightly stretched; strained to stiffness: (字面或喻)拉緊的; 緊張的: *~ nerves;* 緊張的神經; *faces ~ with anxiety;* 因焦急而顯得緊張的面孔; *a moment of ~ excitement.* 極度激動的一刻。 *We were ~ with expectancy,* Our nerves were ~, keyed up. 我們因期待而神經緊張起來。 *There was a ~ atmosphere,* People had a feeling of nervous strain and an attitude of expectancy. 人們緊張地期待着。 □ *vt, vi* [VP6A, 2A] make or become ~; stiffen: 拉緊;使緊張;變緊;變緊張: *He ~d his muscles for the effort.* 他緊繃着肌肉使勁。 ***be/get ~d up,*** feel nervous strain: 感到神經緊張: *He's always ~d up before a game/an exam.* 他在比賽(考試)前總會感到神經緊張。 **~·ly** *adv* **~·ness** *n*

tense² /tens ; tɛns/ *n* (gram) verb form that shows time: (文法)動詞的時態;時式: *the present/past, etc ~.* 現在(過去等)時式。

ten·sile /ˈtensaɪl *US:* ˈtensl ; ˈtɛnsl/ *adj* **1** of tension: 拉緊的;緊張的: *measure the ~ strength of wire,* eg to find the load it will support without breaking. 測量金屬線的抗張強度。 **2** capable of being stretched. 可延展的;可伸長的;可伸延的。

ten·sion /ˈtenʃn ; ˈtɛnʃən/ *n* [U] **1** state of, degree of, being tense: 拉緊;拉力;張力;緊張的狀態或程度: *If you increase the ~ of that violin string it will break.* 如果你增加小提琴那根絃緊張的程度,它就會斷。 **2** stretching or being stretched. 伸展;被伸展;延伸;被延伸。 **3** mental, emotional or nervous strain; condition when feelings are tense, when relations between persons, groups, states, etc are strained: 心理、情緒或神經方面的緊張;(人、團體、國家等間的)緊張狀態;不安: *racial ~(s) in Africa;* 非洲種族間的緊張狀態; *political ~.* 政治上的不安。 **4** voltage: 電壓: *Keep away from those high ~ wires or you'll be electrocuted.* 不要接近那些高壓電線,否則你會被電死。 **high ~ battery,** one made up of a number of small batteries connected in series. 高壓電池或電瓶(一系列小電池或電瓶連接而成者)。⇨ series. **5** expansive force of gas or vapour. 氣體或蒸氣張力;蒸氣壓;汽壓。

tens·ity /ˈtensətɪ ; ˈtɛnsətɪ/ *n* = tenseness. ⇨ tense¹.

tent /tent ; tɛnt/ *n* (usu portable) shelter made of canvas supported by poles and ropes, esp as used by campers, scouts, soldiers, etc. 帳篷;帳棚(通常可攜帶,尤指露營者、童子軍、士兵等所使用者)。**ˈoxygen ~,** airtight cover (over a bed) for a person who is being given extra oxygen. 氧氣帳;氧氣罩(密封,置床上,需額外氧氣者用之)。**ˈ~-peg** *n* wooden peg used to secure a rope to the ground. 帳篷樁(用以把帳篷繩子固定於地上)。

ten·tacle /ˈtentəkl ; ˈtɛntəkl/ *n* [C] long, slender, flexible, snake-like, boneless growth on the head or round the mouth of certain animals used for touching, feeling, holding, moving, etc. (動物的)觸鬚;觸角;觸手。⇨ the illus at mollusc. 參看 mollusc 之插圖。

ten·ta·tive /ˈtentətɪv ; ˈtɛntətɪv/ *adj* made or done as a trial, to see the effect: 試驗性質的;嘗試的;暫時的: *only a ~ suggestion;* 僅係試驗性質的建議; *come to a ~ conclusion;* 獲致暫時的結論; *make a ~ offer.* 作嘗試性的出價(建議)。 **~·ly** *adv*

ten·ter·hooks /ˈtentəhʊks ; ˈtɛntɚˌhʊks/ *n pl* (only in) (僅用於) ***on ~,*** in a state of anxious suspense. 憂慮不安;如坐針氈。

tenth /tenθ ; tɛnθ/ *n, adj* ⇨ ten.

tenu·ous /ˈtenjʊəs ; ˈtɛnjʊəs/ *adj* thin; slender: 薄的;細的: *the ~ web of a spider;* 纖細的蜘蛛網; (of distinctions) subtle. (指區別)細微的;微妙的。 **ten·uity** /tɪˈnju:ətɪ *US:* teˈnu:- ; tɛnˈjuətɪ/ *n*

ten·ure /ˈtenjʊə(r) *US:* -jə(r) ; ˈtɛnjɚ/ *n* [C, U] (period, time, condition of) holding (eg political office) or using (land): (官職,職位等的)保有;保有期間或狀態;(土地之)使用;使用期間或狀態: *The farmers want security of ~*, to be secure in their tenancies. 農夫們希望土地使用權有保障。*The ~ of office of the President is four years.* 總統的任期是四年。

tepee /ˈtiːpiː; ˈtipi/ *n* cone-shaped tent of skins or bark of the American Indians; wigwam. (美洲印第安人的)獸皮或樹皮帳篷。

tepid /ˈtepɪd; ˈtɛpɪd/ *adj* lukewarm (lit and fig). 微溫的;不大熱心的(字面及喻)。**~·ly** *adv* **~·ness** *n* **~·ity** /teˈpɪdətɪ; tɪˈpɪdətɪ/ *n*

ter·cen·ten·ary /ˌtɜːsenˈtiːnərɪ *US:* tɜːˈsentənerɪ; tɝˈsɛntəˌnɛrɪ/, **ter·cen·ten·nial** /ˌtɜːsenˈtenɪəl; ˌtɝsɛnˈtɛnɪəl/ *nn* 300th anniversary: 三百週年紀念: (attrib) (形容用法) *~ celebrations.* 三百週年慶典。

ter·gi·ver·sate /ˈtɜːdʒɪvəseɪt; ˈtɝdʒɪvɚˌset/ *vi* (formal) make a complete change in one's opinions, principles, etc; make conflicting statements. (正式用語) 完全改變自己的見解、原則等;作矛盾的陳述;支吾;搪塞;變節。**ter·gi·ver·sa·tion** /ˌtɜːdʒɪvəˈseɪʃn; ˌtɝdʒɪvɚˈseʃən/ *n*

term /tɜːm; tɝm/ *n* [C] **1** fixed or limited period of time: 期限;期間: *a long ~ of imprisonment;* 長期監禁; *during his ~ of office as President.* 在其總統任期內。**2** (of schools, universities, etc) one of the periods (usu three or four) into which the academic year is divided: (指學校,大學等)學期(通常一學年分爲三或四學期);季: *the summer ~;* 夏季學期;夏季班; *end-of-~ examinations;* 期考; *during ˈ~(-time).* 在學期當中。**3** (legal) period during which a Court holds session. (法律)法庭的開庭期。**4** (*pl*) conditions offered or agreed to: (複)(提出的或同意的)條件: *enquire about ~s* (ie prices) *for a stay at a hotel;* 詢問住旅館的價錢; *~s of surrender,* eg offered to a defeated enemy; 投降條件(如向戰敗的敵人提出者); *~s of reference,* ⇨ reference(1). ***come to ~s/make ~s (with sb),*** reach an agreement (with him). (與某人)達成協議。***come to ~s with sth,*** accept, become resigned to it: 接受或容忍某事物: *come to ~s with a difficult situation.* 逆來順受。***do sth on one's own ~s/sb else's ~s,*** on conditions that one/sb else decides: 照自己(旁人)的意思或決定做某事: *If he agrees to help, it will be on his own ~s.* 如果他答應幫忙,那是他自己的意思。**5** (*pl*) relations. (複)關係;交誼。***be on good/friendly/bad ~s (with sb),*** be friendly, etc (with him): (與某人)關係良好(友善,惡劣): *I didn't know you and she were on such good ~s,* were such good friends. 我並不知道你同她是非常要好的朋友。***on equal ~s,*** as equals. 伯仲之間;不相上下;相匹敵。***not be on ˈspeaking ~s with sb,*** ⇨ speak(2). **6** word(s) used to express an idea, esp a specialized concept: 名詞;術語;表示特殊化概念的用字: *technical/scientific/legal ~s.* 專門(科學,法律)術語。*In box-office ~s* (as expressed in financial, or box-office receipts) *the film was a failure.* 從票房記錄看,這部影片是失敗的。**7** (*pl*) mode of expression: (複)措辭;說法: *He referred to your work in ~s of high praise/in flattering ~s.* 他對你的工作大加讚揚(奉承)。*How dare you speak of her in such abusive ~s?* 你怎麼敢用這種惡言罵她? ***a contradiction in ~s,*** a statement that contradicts itself. 自相矛盾的陳述。**8** (maths) part of an expression joined to the rest by + or −: (數學)項: *The expression $a^2 + 2ab + b^2$ has three ~s.* $a^2 + 2ab + b^2$ 這一個式子有三項。□ *vt* [VP23] name; apply a ~ to: 把…稱做: *He has no right to ~ himself a professor.* 他無權自稱爲教授。

ter·ma·gant /ˈtɜːməgənt; ˈtɝməgənt/ *n* noisy, quarrelsome woman; shrew. 好爭吵的女子;潑婦;悍婦。

ter·min·able /ˈtɜːmɪnəbl; ˈtɝmɪnəbl̩/ *adj* that may be terminated. 可終止的;有期限的。

ter·minal /ˈtɜːmɪnl; ˈtɝmənl̩/ *adj* **1** of, taking place, each term (1, 2, 3): 每期的;每學期的;按期舉行的: *~ examinations/accounts.* 學期考試(按期結帳)。**2** of, forming, the point or place at the end: 末期的;末端的;終點的;盡頭的: *~ cancer,* not curable; ending in death; 末期癌症 (無法救治者,必死無疑); *the ˈ~ ward,* (in a hospital) for persons who cannot be cured and must soon die. (醫院裡的)垂死病房;彌留病房。□ *n* **1** end of a railway line, bus line, etc; centre (in a town) used by passengers departing for, or arriving from, an airport: (鐵路、公路等的)終點站;(城市中的)航空集散站(往來飛機場之旅客的集散中心): *the ˌWest ˌLondon ˈAir T~.* 倫敦西區的航空集散站。**2** point of connection in an electric circuit: (電路的)接頭: *the ~s of a battery.* 電池的接頭。**ter·min·ally** *adv*

ter·min·ate /ˈtɜːmɪneɪt; ˈtɝməˌnet/ *vt, vi* [VP6A, 2A, 15A] (formal) bring to an end; come to an end: (正式用語)終止;終結;結束: *~ sb's contract;* 終止某人的合約; *~ a pregnancy.* 墮胎。

ter·mi·na·tion /ˌtɜːmɪˈneɪʃn; ˌtɝməˈneʃən/ *n* **1** [C, U] ending: 終止;結束;結局;結尾: *the ~ of a contract;* 合約的終止; *~ of pregnancy,* abortion. 墮胎。**2** [C] final syllable or letter of a word (as in inflexion or derivation). 字的末一音節或末一字母;語尾(如見於字尾變化或衍生字中者)。

ter·mi·nol·ogy /ˌtɜːmɪˈnɒlədʒɪ; ˌtɝməˈnɑlədʒɪ/ *n* [C, U] (*pl* -gies) (science of the) proper use of terms(6); terms used in a science or art: 術語學;術語用法;專門名詞;術語: *problems of ~;* 專門術語的問題; *medical/grammatical ~.* 醫學(文法)術語。**ter·mi·no·logi·cal** /ˌtɜːmɪnəˈlɒdʒɪkl; ˌtɝmɪnəˈlɑdʒɪkl̩/ *adj* of ~: 專門名詞的;術語的: *a terminological inexactitude,* (hum) an untruth. (諧)謊話。

ter·mi·nus /ˈtɜːmɪnəs; ˈtɝmənəs/ *n* [C] (*pl* ~es /-nəsɪz; -nəsɪz/) station at the end of a railway line; end of a tram, bus or air route. (鐵路的)終點站;(電車、公共汽車或航線的)終點。

ter·mite /ˈtɜːmaɪt; ˈtɝmaɪt/ *n* insect (popularly but wrongly called *white ant*), found chiefly in tropical areas, very destructive to timber, textiles, etc and which makes large hills of hard earth. 蟻(一般人誤稱爲 white ant, 主要產於熱帶地區,對木材、紡織品等極具破壞力,以硬土營垤)。⇨ the illus at insect. 參看 insect 之插圖。

tern /tɜːn; tɝn/ *n* sea-bird like a gull, but usu smaller and swifter in flight. 燕鷗(較海鷗小,飛行較快)。

Terp·si·chorean /ˌtɜːpsɪkəˈriːən; ˌtɝpsɪkəˈriən/ *adj* of dancing: 舞蹈的: *the ~ art.* 舞蹈藝術。

ter·race /ˈterəs; ˈtɛrɪs/ *n* **1** level(led) area of ground with a vertical or sloping front or side; a series of these, separated by sloping banks, rising one above the other, eg as a method of irrigation on a hillside. (邊緣呈垂直或斜坡狀的)平坦地區;臺地;梯田;階梯狀地段。**2** flight of wide, shallow steps (eg for spectators at a sporting event such as a football match, or on the banks of the Ganges at Benares, used by bathers). 寬廣而淺的階梯(如球場上觀衆坐的梯座,或貝那拉斯印度恒河堤岸上供沐浴者使用的梯級)。**3** continuous row of houses in one block (often as part of a postal address): 一排房屋(常作爲通信地址的一部分);巷;坊;里;臺街: *6 Olympic T~, Glasgow.* 格拉斯哥市奧林匹克臺街六號。**4** (US) porch, paved area, adjacent to a house, used as an outdoor living area. (美)走廊;(連接房屋的)露台;陽台;平台(用作戶外活動場所)。□ *vt* [VP6A] (usu *pp*) form into ~s; make ~s in: (通常用過去分詞)使成梯形地;築梯形地於: *a ~d lawn;* 梯形草坪; *~d houses,* (long line of) houses joined together, sometimes with an alley in the rear for access to the backyards. 成排的房屋(有時後面有巷弄可通後院)。

terra-cotta /ˌterə ˈkɒtə; ˈtɛrəˈkɑtə/ *n* [U] hard, reddish-brown pottery (used for vases, small statues, ornamental building material, etc): 混合陶器;赤陶(用作花瓶,小雕像,建築的飾物等): (attrib)

(形容用法) *a ~ vase;* 赤陶花瓶; the colour reddish-brown. 赤褐色;土紅色。

terra firma /ˌterəˈfɜːmə ; ˈtɛrəˈfɝmə/ *n* [U] (Lat) dry land, solid land (contrasted with water): (拉) 陸地;大地(與 water 相對): *glad to be on ~ again.* 很高興又踏上陸地。

ter·rain /teˈreɪn *US:* tə- ; tɛˈren/ *n* stretch of land, esp with regard to its natural features: 地形;地貌;地勢;地帶: *difficult ~ for heavy armoured vehicles.* 重裝甲車輛難以行走的地形。

terra in·cog·nita /ˌterə ɪnˈkɒgnɪtə ; ˈtɛrəɪnˈkɑgnɪtə/ *n* (Lat) unknown territory, eg on maps of unexplored areas. (拉)未知地域(如地圖上未勘探之區域)。

ter·ra·pin /ˈterəpɪn ; ˈtɛrəpɪn/ *n* kinds of freshwater tortoise and turtle of N America: (北美產的)泥龜;鼈;甲魚: (esp) (尤指) *the diamond-back ~,* valued as food. 菱紋背泥龜(爲珍貴食品)。

ter·res·trial /tɪˈrestrɪəl ; təˈrɛstrɪəl/ *adj* **1** of, on, living on, the earth or land: 陸地的;陸棲的;長於陸上的: *the ~ parts of the world.* 地球的陸地部分。 **2** of the earth (opposed to *celestial*): 地球的;世界的;現世的(爲 celestial 之相反字): *a ~ globe,* representing the earth. 地球儀。

ter·rible /ˈterəbl ; ˈtɛrəbl/ *adj* **1** causing great fear or horror: 可怕的;可怖的;令人恐懼的: *a ~ war/accident.* 可怕的戰爭(意外災難)。 *He died in ~ agony.* 他在可怕的痛苦中死去。 **2** causing great discomfort; extreme: 使人感到極度不舒服的; 極端的: *The heat is ~ in Baghdad during the summer.* 巴格達在夏季炎熱異常。 **3** (colloq) extremely bad: (俗)極壞的: *My room was in a ~ state of disorder.* 我的房間凌亂不堪。 *What ~ food they gave us!* 他們供給我們的食物多糟啊! **ter·ribly** /-əblɪ ; -əblɪ/ *adv* (colloq) extremely: (俗)極端地;非常地: *How terribly boring he is!* 他是多麼令人討厭!

ter·rier /ˈterɪə(r) ; ˈtɛrɪɚ/ *n* kinds of small and active dog, esp the kind that digs into burrows to pursue its prey. 㹴(數種活潑的小狗,尤指進入地穴追趕其獵物者)。⇨ the illus at dog. 參看 dog 之插圖。

ter·rific /təˈrɪfɪk ; təˈrɪfɪk/ *adj* **1** causing fear; terrible. 可怕的;令人恐怖的。 **2** (colloq) very great; extreme: (俗)非常大的;極端的: *driving at a ~ pace.* 以極高的速度駕駛。 **ter·rifi·cally** /-klɪ ; -klɪ/ *adv* (colloq) extremely. (俗)極度地。

ter·rify /ˈterɪfaɪ ; ˈtɛrəˌfaɪ/ *vt* (*pt, pp* -fied) [VP 6A, 15A] fill with fear: 使恐怖;驚嚇: *The child was terrified of being left alone in the house.* 那孩子因爲一個人留在家裡而害怕。 *She was terrified out of her wits.* 她嚇得魂不附體。 *What a ~ing experience!* 多可怕的一次經驗!

ter·ri·torial /ˌterɪˈtɔːrɪəl ; ˌtɛrəˈtorɪəl/ *adj* **1** of land, esp land forming a division of a country: 領土的;土地的: *~ possessions;* 領地; *have ~ claims against a State,* claim part of its territory. 對某國提出領土要求。 **~ waters,** the sea near a country's coast, over which special rights are claimed, eg for fishing. 領海。 **2 T~,** of any of the US Territories: 美國之領地的: *T~ laws.* 美國領地的法律。 **3** (GB) (often 常作 *T~*) of the force of mostly non-professional soldiers organized for the defence of Great Britain and trained in their spare time: (英)本土防衞隊的;國防義勇軍的: *the T~ Army.* 國防義勇軍。□ *n* member of the T~ Army. 國防義勇軍兵士。

irrigation terraces

ter·ri·tory /ˈterɪtrɪ *US:* -tɔːrɪ ; ˈtɛrəˌtorɪ/ *n* (*pl* -ries) **1** [C, U] (area of) land, esp land under one ruler or Government: 領土: *Turkish ~ in Europe.* 土耳其在歐洲的領土。 **2** [C] land or district; [U] extent of such land, etc: 土地;地方;區域;此等土地的範圍;領域: *This salesman travels over a large ~.* 這位推銷員旅行推銷很大一個區域。 *How much ~ does he travel over?* 他旅行的地方有多大? *Mating blackbirds will defend their ~* (= the area which they regard as belonging to themselves) *against intruders.* 山鳥交配時不容許入侵者侵犯它們(視爲己有)的領域。 **3** (US) district not admitted as a State but having its own law-making body: (美)屬地;地方(尚未成爲一州,但有其立法機構): *Until 1959 Hawaii was a T~, not a State.* 在 1959 年之前,夏威夷是一個屬地,不是一個州。

ter·ror /ˈterə(r) ; ˈtɛrɚ/ *n* **1** [U] great fear: 恐怖;驚駭: *run away in ~;* 驚慌地跑開; *be in ~ of one's life,* fear that one will lose one's life. 恐懼自己有生命的危險。 ***strike ~ into sb,*** fill him with ~. 使某人恐懼。Hence, 由此產生, **ˈ~-struck, ˈ~-stricken** *adjj* struck, filled, with ~. 驚懼的;害怕的;恐懼的。 **2** [C] instance of great fear; sth or sb that causes great fear: 恐怖的實例;令人恐怖的人或事物: *have a ~ of fire.* 害怕火。 *This added to our ~s.* 這增加了我們的恐懼。 **3** [C] (colloq) troublesome person: (俗)討厭的人: *This child is a perfect ~,* a great nuisance. 這孩子討厭透了。 **~·ism** /-ɪzəm ; -ˌɪzəm/ *n* use of violence and intimidation, esp for political purposes. 恐怖手段;恐怖主義 (尤指爲達到政治目的者)。 **~·ist** /-ɪst ; -ɪst/ *n* supporter of, participant in, ~ism. 支持或參與恐怖主義者;恐怖份子。 **~·ize** /-aɪz ; -ˌaɪz/ *vt* [VP6A] fill with ~ by threats or acts of violence. 藉威脅或暴行使充滿恐怖;恐嚇。

terse /tɜːs ; tɝs/ *adj* (of speech, style, speakers) brief and to the point; concise. (指言詞、文體、說話者)簡明切題的;精簡的。 **~·ly** *adv* **~·ness** *n*

ter·tian /ˈtɜːʃn ; ˈtɝʃən/ *adj* (of fever) marked by paroxysms which occur every other day. (指熱病)隔日發作的;間日的。

ter·ti·ary /ˈtɜːʃərɪ *US:* -ʃɪerɪ ; ˈtɝʃɪˌɛrɪ/ *adj* third in rank, order, occurrence, importance: 第三位的;第三等的; 第三級的; 第三的: *the T~ period,* (geol) the third period in the formation of rocks; (地質)岩石形成的第三紀; *~ burns/syphilis,* a severe stage. 三級灼傷(三期梅毒)。

tery·lene /ˈterəliːn ; ˈtɛrəˌlin/ *n* [U] (GB) (P) (fabric made from) kinds of man-made fibre. (英)(商標)人造纖維;人造纖維布料;台麗龍。

tes·sel·lated /ˈtesəleɪtɪd ; ˈtɛslˌetɪd/ *adj* formed of small, flat pieces of stone of various colours (as used in mosaic): 以不同顏色的小石塊(如鑲嵌細工所用者)做成的;嵌裝圖案的: *a ~ pavement.* 嵌裝圖案的人行道。

test /test ; tɛst/ *n* [C] (often attrib) examination or trial (of sth) to find its quality, value, composition, etc; trial or examination (of sb, his powers, knowledge, skill, etc): (常作形容用法) 測驗;試驗;考驗: *methods that have stood the ~ of time;* 禁得起時間考驗的方法; *an endurance ~,* eg for a new aero-engine; 耐力試驗(如測驗新的飛機引擎); *a ˈblood ~,* eg at a hospital, for infection, etc. 驗血。 *a ~ in arithmetic;* 算術測驗; *an inˈtelligence ~.* 智力測驗。 ***put sth to the ~,*** submit it to conditions, etc, that will show its qualities, etc. 使某物接受考驗。 **a ˈ~ bore,** hole bored into the ground or sea-bed to learn whether there is mineral ore, oil, etc: (探測礦藏、石油等,在地面或海床所作的)鑽(探)孔: *~ bores in the North Sea.* 北海鑽(探)孔。 **a ˈ~ case,** (in law) one that shows the principle involved (even though it may not be important in itself). (法律)判例案件;判決先例。 **ˈ~ drive** *n* drive in a car one thinks of buying, to judge its qualities, worth, etc. 試車(駕駛欲購之車，以判定其性質、價值等)。Hence, 由此產生，'~-drive *vt.* a 'driving ~, an examination of one's ability to drive a car in the way required by law. 駕駛考試。'~ match *n* one of the matches in any of the cricket or Rugby tours arranged between certain countries. (板球或橄欖球的)國際錦標賽。'~ pilot *n* one who flies newly built aircraft to try their qualities, performance, etc. (新飛機的)試飛員。'~-tube *n* slender glass tube, closed at one end, used in chemical ~s and experiments. 試管。'~-tube baby, baby whose early development took place in a laboratory (after artificial insemination) and is later implanted in the womb. 試管嬰兒(人工受精後，先在實驗室中培育，再移入子宮者)。□ *vt* [VP6A, 15A] put to the ~; examine: 試驗;考驗;檢驗: *have one's eyesight ~ed;* 檢驗視力; *~ore for gold;* 化驗礦石中黃金的成分; *a well-~ed remedy.* 經試驗有效的醫療法。*The long climb ~ed* (= was a ~ of) *our powers of endurance.* 那次長距離的爬山考驗了我們的持久力。

tes·ta·ment /'testəmənt ; 'tɛstəmənt/ *n* **1** [C] (often 常作 ***last Will and T~***) statement in writing saying how sb wishes his property to be distributed after his death. 遺囑。**2 Old T~, New T~,** the two main divisions of the Bible. 舊約(聖經)，新約(聖經)。⇨ App 10. 參看附錄十。**tes·ta·men·tary** /ˌtestə'mentrɪ ; ˌtɛstə'mɛntərɪ/ *adj* of, connected with, given in, a ~(1). 遺囑的;關於遺囑的;遺囑中寫明的。

tes·tate /'testeɪt ; 'tɛstet/ *n, adj* (person) who has made a testament (and died leaving it in force). 立有遺囑的(人);死後留有有效遺囑的(人)。**tes·ta·tor** /te'steɪtə(r) *US:* 'testeɪtər ; 'tɛstetɚ/ *n* man who has made a testament. 立有遺囑的男子。**tes·ta·trix** /te'steɪtrɪks ; tɛs'tetrɪks/ *n* woman testator. 立有遺囑的女子。

tes·ticle /'testɪkl ; 'tɛstɪkl̩/ *n* each of the two glands of the male sex organ that secrete spermatozoa. 睪丸。

tes·tify /'testɪfaɪ ; 'tɛstəˌfaɪ/ *vt, vi* (*pt, pp* -fied) **1** [VP2A, 3A, 9] ~ ***that. . . ; ~ to sth; ~ against / in favour of sb,*** bear witness, give evidence: 作證;提供證據: *He testified under oath that he had not been at the scene of the crime.* 他發誓作證他當時並不在犯罪現場。*The teacher testified to the boy's ability.* 教師爲那男孩的能力作證。*Two witnesses will ~ against her and three will ~ on her behalf.* 兩位證人將作不利於她的證明，另三位將作有利於她的證明。**2** [VP6A] serve as evidence of: 成爲…的證據;證明: *Her tears testified her grief.* 她的眼淚證明了她的憂傷。

tes·ti·mo·nial /ˌtestɪ'məʊnɪəl ; ˌtɛstə'monɪəl/ *n* **1** written statement testifying to a person's merits, abilities, qualifications, etc eg as sent with an application for a position. (優點、能力、資格等的)推荐書;證明書。**2** sth given to sb to show appreciation of services, usu sth subscribed for by several or many colleagues. 褒揚狀;感謝狀;謝禮;紀念品(通常係同事或同僚間集資贈與某人者)。

tes·ti·mony /'testɪmənɪ *US:* -məʊnɪ ; 'tɛstəˌmonɪ/ *n* [U] **1** declaration, esp in a law court, testifying that sth is true: 證言;證詞(尤指在法庭上所作者): *The witness's ~ is false.* 那證人的證言不實。*Several men were called in to bear ~ to what the police officer said.* 數人被傳入爲警官所說的話作證。**2** declarations; statements: 宣言;陳述: *According to the ~ of the medical profession, the health of the nation is improving.* 根據醫學界的陳述，國民的健康在進步中。

tes·tis /'testɪs ; 'tɛstɪs/ *n* (*pl* -tes /-ti:z ; -tiz/) = testicle.

testy /'testɪ ; 'tɛstɪ/ *adj* (-ier, -iest) quickly or easily annoyed; impatient. 易被激怒的; 性子急的;暴躁的。**tes·tily** /-ɪlɪ ; -əlɪ/ *adv* **tes·ti·ness** *n*

teta·nus /'tetənəs ; 'tɛtn̩əs/ *n* [U] disease marked by stiffening and tightening of some or all of the muscles which are normally under conscious control: 破傷風(平時可隨意控制的肌肉，部分或全部變爲强直的疾病): ~ *of the lower jaw* (colloq called 俗稱 *lockjaw*). 下顎破傷風;咀嚼肌痙攣。

tetchy /'tetʃɪ ; 'tɛtʃɪ/ *adj* (-ier, -iest) peevish; irritable. 易怒的 ; 暴躁的。**tetch·ily** /-ɪlɪ ; -əlɪ/ *adv* **tetchi·ness** *n*

tête-à-tête /ˌteɪt ɑ: 'teɪt ; 'tetə'tet/ *n* private meeting between two persons; their talk: 兩人間的祕密聚會;兩人間的面談或密談;促膝談心: *have a ~ with sb;* 與某人密談; *have a ~ talk.* (與某人)密談。□ *adv* in a ~: 兩人在一起私下地;兩人間秘密地: *He dined ~ with the Prime Minister.* 他單獨與首相共餐。

tether /'teðə(r) ; 'tɛðɚ/ *n* rope or chain by which an animal is fastened while grazing. (拴牲畜的)繫繩;繫鏈。***at the end of one's ~,*** (fig) at the end of one's powers, resources, endurance, etc. (喻)用盡某人的體能、智能、忍耐力等; 智窮技竭; 筋疲力盡;忍無可忍。□ *vt* [VP6A, 15A] fasten with a ~: 以繫繩或繫鏈拴: *He ~ed his horse to the fence.* 他把馬拴在籬笆上。

Teu·ton /'tju:tən *US:* 'tu:tn ; 'tjutn̩/ *n* member of any of the Teutonic nations. 條頓人。~**ic** /tju:'tɒnɪk *US:* tu:- ; tju'tɑnɪk/ *adj* of the Germanic (ie Anglo-Saxon, Dutch, German and Scandinavian) peoples. (包括盎格魯撒克遜人，荷蘭人，日耳曼人及斯堪的那維亞人之)條頓民族的。

text /tekst ; tɛkst/ *n* **1** [U] main body of a book or printed page (contrasted with notes, diagrams, illustrations, etc):(書或印刷物的)正文;本文(與 notes, diagrams, illustrations等相對): *too much ~ and not enough pictures.* 正文太多而插圖不够。**2** [C] original words of an author, apart from anything else in a book: (作者的)原文: *a corrupt ~,* one that, perhaps because of mistakes in copying, is no longer in its original form. 與原作有出入的原文。**3** [C] short passage, sentence, esp of Scripture, as the subject of a sermon or discussion. (講道或討論的)主題文句;主要經文。**4** ~**(·book)** /'teksbʊk ; 'tɛkstˌbʊk/) book giving instruction in a branch of learning: 教科書: *an algebra ~book.* 代數教科書。**tex·tual** /'tekstʃʊəl ; 'tɛkstʃʊəl/ *adj* of, in, a ~: 正文的; 本文的; 原文的; 在正文、原文等中的: *~ual errors;* 原文的錯誤; *~ual criticism.* 原文校勘。

tex·tile /'tekstaɪl ; 'tɛkstl̩/ *attrib adj* of the making of cloth: 紡織的;織物的: ~ *processes;* 紡織的過程; *the ~ industry;* 紡織工業; woven; suitable for weaving: 織成的;適於紡織的: *~fabrics / materials.* 紡織品(紡織原料)。□ *n* [C] ~ material. 紡織品;織物;紡織原料。

tex·ture /'tekstʃə(r) ; 'tɛkstʃɚ/ *n* [C, U] **1** the arrangement of the threads in a textile fabric: (織物的)質地;織質: *cloth with a loose / close ~.* 質地稀鬆(緊密)的布。**2** arrangement of the parts that make up sth: 構造;結構;紋理: *the ~ of a mineral.* 礦物的構造。**3** tissue: 組織: *a skin of fine / coarse ~.* 細(粗)皮膚。~**d** *pp* (in compounds): (用於複合字中): *ˌcoarse- / ˌthin-'~d.* 質地、紋理等粗(薄)的。

thal·ido·mide /θə'lɪdəmaɪd ; θə'lɪdəˌmaɪd/ *n* [U] (P) sedative drug which caused some women to give birth to deformed babies (esp with undeveloped limbs). (商標) 撒利豆邁(一種鎮痛劑，某些婦女服用此藥會生產畸形嬰兒，特別是四肢發育不全)。

than /ðən ; ðən; *rarely heard strong form:* ðæn ; ðæn/ *conj* **1** (introducing the second part of a comparison): 比(後面接比較的第二部分): *John is taller ~ his brother.* 約翰比他哥哥(弟弟)高。*I have never met anyone more stupid ~ you.* 我從未碰到過比你更笨的人。***different than,*** ⇨ different. **2** (with a *transitive v* the form of a *pron* after *than* depends upon the sense of the complete sentence. Note the words in parenthesis in these examples): (與及物動詞連用時，than 後的代名詞形式視全句文意而定。注意下列諸例句括號內的字)：*I know you better* ~ *he* (*does*), ie ~ he knows you. 我比他更瞭解你。*I know you better* ~ *him*, ie ~ I know him. 我瞭解你勝過我瞭解他。*I like her no better* ~ *he* (*does*), ie ~ he likes her. 我和他喜歡她的程度相等。*I like her no better* ~ *him*, ie ~ I like him. 我喜歡她和他的程度相等。 **3** (with an *intransitive v* the *pron* after *than* is often in the object form, in both colloquial and written English, even though the subject form is required by formal grammar. This is esp so when the *pron* is followed by *all*): (與不及物動詞連用時，無論是在口語或是文章中，than 後面的代名詞常用受格形式，儘管正式的文法要求使用主格。而代名詞後接有 all 時，該代名詞尤其要用受格)：*He is several years older* ~ *me*/~ *I am.* 他比我大幾歲。*He can run faster* ~ *me*/~ *I can.* 他跑得比我快。*He is wiser* ~ *us all.* 他比我們都聰明。 **4** (in phrases) (用於片語中) ***no other*** **~,** (used as an equivalent to a construction with an emphatic *pron*): 就是(其用法等於含加重語氣的代名詞結構)：*It was no other* ~ *my old friend Jones*, ie it was Jones himself. 就是我的老友瓊斯。***nothing else*** **~,** only, entire(ly): 僅僅；完全的；完全地：*His failure was due to nothing else* ~ (= was entirely due to) *his own carelessness.* 他的失敗完全由於他自己的疏忽所致。*What he told you was nothing else* ~ *nonsense*, was complete nonsense. 他告訴你的全是無稽之談。***rather*** **~,** ⇨ rather(1). ***sooner*** **~,** ⇨ soon(3, 5).

thane /θeɪn; θen/ *n* (hist) man who gave military service in return for land. (史)藉服兵役而取得土地的大鄉紳。

thank /θæŋk; θæŋk/ *vt* **~ *sb* (*for sth*), 1** [VP 6A, 14] express gratitude to: 謝；感謝；道謝：~ *a person for his help.* 感謝某人幫忙。*There's no need to* ~ *me.* 無須向我道謝。 **ˈ*T~ you*,** the usual formula for 'I ~ you.' 謝謝你。**ˌ*No*, ˈ*~ you*,** formula used to decline an offer. (Note that the 'No' is essential; '*T~ you*' is used for acceptance and may mean 'Yes, please.') 不(必)了，謝謝你(用於婉拒一項提議)。(注意：'No' 字是必要的；如無 no, 即變爲接受該提議，其含義可能就是 '好的，麻煩你了。') [VP11] *T~ Heaven* (*that*) *you've come.* 感謝老天，你可來了。*T~ God she's safe.* 感謝上帝，她安然無恙。 **2** [VP14, 17] (in peremptory requests, future tense): (用於表示强制的要求，用未來式)：*I'll* ~ *you for that book*, please give it to me. 請把那本書給我。*I'll* ~ *you to be a little more polite/to mind your own business.* 請你客氣一點(請你別管閒事)。□ *n* (now only in *pl* except in *~-offering* and with suffixes as below): (現僅用複數形，唯 ~-offering 一語及下列諸例中與字尾連用的情形，仍用單數形)：(expression of) gratitude: 謝意；謝忱；感謝的表示：*give ~s to God*; 感謝上帝；***T~s/No, ~s,*** colloq formulas of gratitude/refusal. 謝謝(不必了，謝謝)。 **~*s to*,** as the result of; owing to: 由於；因爲：*T~s to your help we were successful.* 由於你的幫助，我們成功了。***small ~s to*,** used ironically: 一點也不感謝(反語用法)：*We were successful, but small ~s to you*, you gave us no help. 我們成功了，但並不感謝你(你未幫我們忙)。 **ˈ~-offering** *n* offering made, eg to a charity, a religious organization, as an expression of gratitude. 感恩捐獻。 **ˌ~s-ˈgiving** *n* **(a)** expression of gratitude, esp to God; form of prayer for this. 感謝(尤指對上帝)；感恩；感恩祈禱。 **(b)** (US) (also 亦作 **ˌT~s-ˈgiving Day**) day set apart each year for giving ~s to God (usu the fourth Thursday in November). (美)感恩節(通常爲十一月的第四個星期四)。 **~·ful** /-fl; -fəl/ *adj* grateful: 感謝的；感激的；欣慰的：*Be ~ful for small mercies.* 雖小恩亦要感激。*You should be ~ful to have/that you have escaped with minor injuries.* 你應該爲你僅受輕傷而脫險感到欣慰。 **~·fully** /-fəlɪ; -fəlɪ/ *adv* **~·ful·ness** *n* **~·less** *adj* not feeling or expressing gratitude; (of actions) not arousing gratitude or winning appreciation: 不感謝的；不領情的；忘恩的；(指行爲)徒勞的；不令人感謝的：*a ~less task*, one which brings no ~s, appreciation or reward. 徒勞的工作。

that[1] /ðæt; ðæt (*no weak form*)/ (*pl* those /ðəʊz; ðoz/) *adj, pron* (contrasted with *this, these.* ~/*those* and *this/these* are used to make a person or thing specific. *this/these* are used when the person or thing is near to the speaker.) (與 this, these 相對。that, those 與 this, these 均特指某(些)人或物，this, these 指與說話人較近者。) **1** *Look at* ~ *man/those men there.* 看那個人(那些人)。*What's* ~ *over there?* 那邊那個是什麼？*What are those?* 那些是什麼？*What was* ~ *noise?* 那是什麼響聲？*What noise was* ~? 那是什麼響聲？*Is* ~ *you, Mary?* 是你嗎，瑪莉？*Are those children yours?* 那些孩子是你(們)的嗎？*Is* ~ *what you really think?* 你眞的那樣想嗎？*T~'s what he told me.* 那就是他告訴我的(話)。*This book is much better than* ~ (*one*). 這本書比那本好得多。*These are much better than those.* 這些遠比那些好。*Life was easier in those days/at* ~ *time*, then, during that period. 那時(在那個時期)，謀生比較容易。*So ~'s ~!* (formula used to indicate finality, the end of a discussion, an argument, etc). 就這樣了！就這樣決定了！(用於表示定局，表示討論、辯論等的終結。) **2** (as antecedent to a *rel pron*, expressed or omitted): (用作關係代名詞的先行詞，明示或省略)：*All those* (*that*) *I saw were old.* 我見到的那些統統是舊的。*Those who do not wish to go need not go.* 凡是不願意去的人就不必去。*It's a different kind of car from* ~ (= kind of car) (*which*) *I am used to.* 這種汽車同我用習慣的那一種不一樣。*Throw away all those* (*which are*) *unfit for use.* 把那些不合用的統統扔掉。*Those* (= People who were) *present at the ceremony were....* 出席典禮的那些人是…。*There are those who say* (= some people who say).... 有人說…。 **3** (with a *pl n*, considered as a collective *sing*): (與複數名詞連用，視爲集合單數)：*What about* ~ *five pounds you borrowed from me last month?* 你上個月向我借的那五鎊何時歸還？*When do you intend to repay* ~ *sum of five pounds?* 你打算何時還我那五鎊？ **4** (*That* and a possessive cannot be used together. Note the construction used when ~ and a possessive are both needed): (that 不可與所有格連用。注意需要同時使用 that 與所有格時的句型結構)：*I don't like* ~ *new secretary of his.* 我不喜歡他那位新來的秘書。*Well, how's* ~ *bad leg of yours getting on?* 唔，你那條疼痛的腿復元的情況如何？ □ *adv* (colloq) to such a degree; so: (俗)達到這樣的程度；如許：*I can't walk* ~ *far*, = as far as ~. 我可走不了那麼遠。*I've done only* ~ *much*, ie as much as is shown, indicated, etc. 我就做了那麼多。*It's about* ~ *high*, ie as high as ~. 它大約有那麼高。*I was* ~ (= so) *angry I could have hit him*, ie I wanted to hit him. 我那時氣得簡直想揍他。*It isn't all* ~ *cold*, eg not so cold that a fire/overcoat, etc is needed. 還沒有冷到那種程度(如還沒有冷到生火、穿大衣等的程度)。

that[2] /*usual form:* ðət; ðət; *strong form:* ðæt; ðæt/ *conj* **1** (introducing *n* clauses, but often omitted): (引導名詞子句，但常被省略)：*She said* (~) *she would come.* 她說她要來的。*It so happens* ~ *I know the man.* 碰巧我認識那個人。*The trouble is* ~ *we are short of money.* 困難就在於我們缺錢。*I will see to it* ~ *everything is ready.* 我會注意把一切準備妥當的。 **2 *so ~; in order ~,*** (introducing clauses of purpose): 俾；以便；爲了(引導表示目的的子句)：*Bring it nearer* (*so*) ~ *I may see it better.* (把它)拿近一點，好讓我看清楚些。*I will give up my claim so ~/in order ~ you may have the property.* 我願意放棄我的要求權，俾使你獲得那份財產。 **3** (introducing clauses of result): (引導表示結果的子

句): *His behaviour was such ~/was so bad ~ we all refused to receive him in our homes.* 他行爲不檢，我們全都拒絕在家裡招待他。 **4** (introducing clauses of condition): (引導表示條件的子句): *supposing ~...;* 假使…; *on condition ~....* 設若…。 **5** (introducing clauses of reason or cause) (引導表示理由或原因的子句) ⇨ not(4), and now, *conj.* **6** (rhet) in exclamations: (修辭)用於感嘆句中: *Oh, ~ I could be with you again!* How I wish...! 我眞希望能够再同你在一起！ *Oh, ~ I should live to see my own son sent to prison as a thief!* How sad it is ~...! 我竟然(活着)親眼看到我的兒子作賊而被抓去坐牢(多令人傷心啊)！

that[3] /*usual form:* ðət ; ðət; *strong form:* ðæt ; ðæt/ *rel pron* (*pl* unchanged; used in defining or restrictive clauses; not preceded by a pause or a comma; often preferred to *which* for things; often preferred to *whom* and often used in place of *who*) (複數不變;用於限定子句中;前面不停頓亦不加逗點;指物時較 which 常用;較 whom 常用,並常代替 who) **1** (as the subject of the *v* in a clause): (在子句中作動詞的主詞): *The letter ~ came this morning is from my father.* 今天早晨收到的那封信是我父親寄來的。*Those dogs ~ attacked your sheep ought to be shot.* 攻擊你羊羣的那些狗該射殺。*The man ~* (*who* is preferred) *sold you that camera is a rogue.* 賣照相機給你的那個人是個流氓 (本句中 who 較 that 佳)。*The man ~* (*who* is preferred) *cycled past you is nearly ninety.* 騎脚踏車從你旁邊經過的那個人快要九十歲了 (本句中 who 較 that 佳)。 **2** (Although *who* is usually preferred to *that, that* is preferred to *who* after superlatives, *only, all, any,* and *it is* or *it was*): (雖然 who 通常較 that 佳,惟在最高級形容詞後,在 only, all, any 後,以及在 it is 或 it was 後時, that 較 who 爲佳): *Newton was one of the greatest men ~ ever lived.* 牛頓是世上最偉大的人物之一。*He's the cleverest man ~ I ever met.* 他是我所遇到的人當中最聰明的了。*You're the only person ~ can help me.* 你是唯一能幫我忙的人。*Anyone ~ wants to succeed must work hard.* 任何人要想獲得成功就必須勤奮工作。*It's you ~ I want to speak to, not Paul.* 我要跟你說話,不是跟保羅。 **3** (as the object of the *v* in the clause; *whom* is to be avoided; the *pron* ~ is often omitted): (在子句中作動詞的受詞; whom 避免用;代名詞 that 常省略): *The watch* (~) *you gave me is working perfectly.* 你給我的那個錶走得好極了。*Is this the best* (~) *you can do?* 你最多祇能做到這樣嗎？ *The girl* (~) *you met yesterday wants to see you again.* 你昨天遇到的那個女孩想再見你。 *All the people* (~) *I invited have agreed to come.* 所有經我邀請的人都同意來。 **4** (after an expression of time. Cf *when, rel adv*): (用於表時間的用語之後。參較關係副詞 when): *the year* (~) *my father died;* 我父親過世的那一年; *the week* (~) *we went camping.* 我們去露營的那個禮拜。 **5** (as the object of a *prep; whom* is to be avoided; *that* is often omitted, and the *prep* follows the *v*): (用作介詞的受詞; whom 避免用; that 常省略,介詞接在動詞後): *The photographs* (~) *you were looking at were taken by my brother.* 你看的那些相片是我哥哥(弟弟)拍的。*The man* (~) *I was talking to had just arrived from Canada.* 和我談話的那個人剛從加拿大來。*Where's the man* (~) *you borrowed it from?* 你向他借這東西的那個人在那裡？

thatch /θætʃ ; θætʃ/ *n* [U] (roof covering of) dried straw, reeds, etc; (colloq) thick hair of the head. 茅草(乾的稻草、蘆葦等);茅草(屋)頂;(俗)厚密的頭髮。 □ *vt* [VP6A] cover (a roof, etc) with ~. 以茅草蓋(屋頂等)。

thaw /θɔː ; θɔ/ *vi, vt* [VP6A, 15B, 2A, C] ~ ***(out),*** **1** *It is ~ing,* The temperature has risen above freezing-point (so that snow and ice begin to melt). 天解凍了(冰雪開始融化了)。 **2** (cause anything frozen to) become liquid or soft again: (使)融化;融解: *~ out the radiator,* (of a car); 使(汽車)冷却器的冰化除; *leave frozen food to ~ before cooking it.* 讓冰凍食物在烹調前先行退冰。 **3** (of persons, their behaviour) (cause to) become less formal, more friendly: (指人,其行爲)(使)變得較不拘禮,較友善: *After a good dinner he began to ~.* 吃過一餐美好的飯,他開始變得友善了。*A bottle of wine helped to ~* (*out*) *our guests.* 我們的客人喝過一瓶酒之後不再那麼拘束了。□ *n* (usu *sing*) (state of the weather causing) ~ing: (通常用單數)融化;融解;解凍的天氣: *Let's go skating before the ~/a ~ sets in.* 我們趁着還未解凍去溜冰吧。

the /*before consonants:* ðə ; ðə; *before vowels:* ðɪ ; ðɪ; *strong form:* ðiː ; ði/ *def art* **1** (used as a less specific form of *this, these, that, those,* applied to person(s), thing(s), event(s), etc already referred to or being discussed. Note the changes from the *indef art* to the *def art* in these sentences): (爲 this, these, that, those 的較不明確的形式,用以指已提過的或正在討論中的人、物、事等。注意下列諸句中從不定冠詞變爲定冠詞的用法): *An old man and an old woman once lived in a small hut by a river near a forest. One day the old man left the hut and went into the forest to gather wood. The old woman went to the river to wash clothes.* 從前有一位老人及一位老婦住在河畔靠近森林的一座小茅屋裡。有一天那位老人離開茅屋,進入森林去採薪。那位老婦到河邊去洗衣服。 **2** (used when who or what is referred to is quite obvious): (用於所指的人或物十分明顯的情況): *Please take these letters to the post office,* ie the post office near by, the post office of this district. 請把這些信拿到郵局去(指附近的或本區的郵局)。*Please close the window,* ie the window that is open. 請把窗戶關起來(指開着的那個窗戶)。*Shall we have a walk by the river?* eg in London, the River Thames. 咱們到河邊去散散步好不好？(如在倫敦,指的是泰晤士河。) **3** (used with a *n* when it stands for sth unique): (與代表獨一無二事物的名詞連用): *the sun;* 太陽; *the moon;* 月亮; *the year 1939;* 一九三九年; *the universe.* 宇宙。 **4** (used with *nn* such as *sea, sky, wind* (as in 2 above) when there is no *adj*): (與無形容詞修飾的名詞如 sea, sky, wind 等字連用,用法如上列第 2 義): *The sea was calm.* 海上風平浪靜。*There's an aeroplane in the sky.* 天上有一架飛機。*Isn't the wind strong!* 多强的風啊！ Note that the use of an *adj* to describe the sea, wind, etc may make the use of the *indef art* possible: 注意:這些字如有形容詞修飾,亦可能用不定冠詞: *There was a calm sea* (cf 參較 *The sea was calm*) *when I crossed from Dover to Calais.* 我從多佛渡海至加來時,海上風平浪靜。*What a stormy-looking sky!* 好一個陰沈的天空,像是暴風雨要來了！ *There was a cold wind* (cf 參較 *The wind was cold*)颳起了一陣冷風。 **5** (used with a *n* if it is modified by a phrase or clause that makes it unique): (如某名詞爲片語或子句所修飾因而具有獨特性質時,則與該名詞連用): *the back of the house;* 房屋的後部; *the left side of the road;* 路的左側; (In many phrases the *def art* is or may be omitted: 在許多片語中,定冠詞須省去或可以省去: *from beginning to end;* 自始至終; *from* (*the*) *top to* (*the*) *bottom;* 從頂端到底部; *in* (*the*) *future.* 在未來。) **6** (used with the superl): (與最高級連用): *the best way to get there;* 去那裡最佳的方法; *the tallest of the five men;* 五人中的最高者; *the most interesting book I have ever read.* 我讀過的最有趣的書。(The *def art* is not needed in the predicate after the *v 'be'* when the superl is used without a *n*: 接在 be 動詞後面的最高級形容詞不與名詞連用時無需定冠詞: *It is wisest* (= *The* wisest plan is) *to avoid the centre of the town.* 避開市中心是最聰明的(最聰明的計畫)。When *most* means 'very', the *def art* is not used: 作 very 解的 most 之前,不加定冠詞: *The story was most exciting.* 這故事非常動人。*This is a most useful reference book.* 這是一本極有用的參考書。) ⇨ most[2](3). **7** used before 用於下列各專

有名詞之前 **(a)** names of seas and oceans: 海洋的名稱: *the Mediterranean, the Red Sea;* 地中海,紅海; *the Atlantic (Ocean), the Indian Ocean.* 大西洋,印度洋。**(b)** names of rivers and canals: 河流及運河的名稱: *the Nile;* 尼羅河; *the river Thames;* 泰晤士河; *the Suez Canal.* 蘇伊士運河。**(c)** *pl* geographical names: 複數地理名稱: *the Alps;* 阿爾卑斯山; *the Philippines;* 菲律賓群島; *the West Indies;* 西印度群島; *the Netherlands.* 荷蘭。**(d)** in a few geographical names: 在少數幾個地名中: *the Sudan;* 蘇丹; *the Sahara.* 撒哈拉。 **8** (used with *adjj* and participles to denote all members of a class): (與形容詞及分詞連用,表示一類的全體分子): *the rich, the young, and the beautiful;* 富人、年輕人及美麗的人; *the dead, the dying, and the wounded,* eg after a battle. 死者、垂死者及傷者。 **9** ***the*** + *adj,* (equivalent to an abstract *n*): (與形容詞連用,相當於抽象名詞): *the sublime,* sublimity. 崇高。**10** (used formerly with names of diseases, now usually ommitted except with colloq or sl *pl*): (昔與病名連用,現在除口語或俚語的複數外,通常不加定冠詞): *She's got the creeps/the fidgets/the blues.* 她感到戰慄(不安,沮喪)。Survivals of the older use: 殘存的舊用法: *The child has (the) measles.* 那孩子患痲疹。 **11** Note: 注意(樂器名稱前面加 the): *to play the piano/the violin/the banjo, etc,* 彈鋼琴(拉小提琴;彈班究琴等), but (with names of games): 但是(遊戲名稱前面不加 the): *to play tennis/football/cards/chess/billiards. etc.* 打網球(踢足球;玩牌;下棋;打彈子等)。 **12** (used with a *sing common n* to denote the whole class, eg of animals or plants): (與單數普通名詞連用表示全類,如指動物或植物): *Is it true that the owl cannot see well in daylight?* 貓頭鷹白天看不清楚是眞的嗎？ (In colloq style, the use of the *pl,* without the *def art,* is more usu: 口語中,不加定冠詞的複數形式更爲通用: *Is it true that owls cannot. . .?*). **13** (used in a similar way with names of inventions. In this case the use of the *def art* with the *sing n* is usu in both liter and colloq styles): (與發明物連用,用法同上。唯定冠詞與單數名詞連用的用法,在文學及口語文體中皆通用): *We don't know who invented the wheel.* 我們不知道輪子是誰發明的。*The telephone is a most useful invention.* 電話是一項極有用的發明。 **14** (used with *nn* expressing a unit): (與名詞連用表示一單位): *This car does thirty miles to the gallon,* ie to each gallon of petrol. 這部汽車每加侖汽油跑三十英里。*These apples are small; there are seven or eight to the kilo,* ie to each kilo. 這些蘋果很小;一公斤有七、八個。*I get paid by the hour,* ie I earn so much for each hour's work. 我是按小時計酬的。□ *adv* by so much; by that amount; (used before an *adj* or *adv* in the comparative degree to indicate that two things increase or decrease in a parallel way, or that one increases in a degree equal to that by which another decreases): 達此程度; 至該數額; 愈; 更; (用於形容詞或副詞的比較級前,表示二物同樣增加或減少,或一方增加的程度相當於另一方減少的程度): *The more he gets the more he wants.* 他得到的愈多,想要的愈多。*The more he reads the less he understands.* 他愈讀愈讀不懂。

the·atre (US = **the·ater**) /ˈθɪətə(r) ; ˈθiətɚ/ *n* **1** building or arena (*open-air* ～) for the performance of plays, for dramatic spectacles, etc: 戲院;劇場;露天劇場(稱open-air ～): *go to the* ～ *to see a Shakespeare play.* 去戲院看莎士比亞的戲。**ˈ～-goer** *n* person who frequently goes to ～s. 常看戲者;戲院常客;戲迷。 **2** hall or room with seats in rows rising one behind another for lectures, scientific demonstrations, etc. (供演講、科學示範等用的)有階梯式座位的講堂或會場。**ˈoperating** ～, room (in a hospital, etc) where surgical operations are performed. (醫院等處的)手術室;手術示教室。 **3** scene of important events: 重大事件發生的場所;現場: *Belgium has often been a* ～ *of war.* 比利時常常成爲戰場。**4** [U] dramatic literature or art; the writing and acting of plays, esp when connected with one author, country, period, etc: 戲劇;戲劇文學或藝術; 劇本的寫作及演出(尤指關於某一作家、國家、時代等者): *a book about the Greek* ～. 討論希臘戲劇的書。*Do Henry James's plays make good* ～, are they satisfactory when presented on the stage? 亨利•詹姆士的劇本演出的效果好嗎？ **the·atri·cal** /θɪˈætrɪkl ; θɪˈætrɪkḷ/ *adj* **1** of or for the ～: 戲院的; 劇場的;戲劇的;適於演出的: *theatrical scenery/performances;* 舞台佈景(戲劇演出); *a theˈatrical company,* of actors. 劇團;戲班。 **2** (of behaviour, manner, way of speaking, persons, etc) designed for effect; showy, not natural. (指行爲,樣子,說話方式,人等)爲產生某種效果而設計的; 炫耀的; 誇張的;做作的;戲劇性的。▭ *n* (usu *pl*) (usu amateur) dramatic performance. (通常用複數)(通常指業餘的)戲劇演出;票戲。**the·atri·cally** /-klɪ ; -kḷɪ/ *adv*

thee /ðiː ; ði/ *pron,* ⇨ thou.

theft /θeft ; θɛft/ *n* [C, U] (the act of, an instance of) stealing. 偷;行竊;偷竊的事例。

their /ðeə(r) ; ðɛr/ *adj* of them: 他(她、它)們的: *They have lost* ～ *dog.* 他們的狗丟了。*They have a house of* ～ *own.* 他們自己有一幢房子。**～s** /ðeəz ; ðɛrz/ *pron* of them: 他們的: *That dog is* ～*s, not ours.* 那隻狗是他們的,不是我們的。*It's a habit of* ～*s,* one of ～ habits. 那是他們的習慣。

the·ism /ˈθiːɪzəm ; ˈθiɪzəm/ *n* [U] belief in the existence of a revealed God, creator and ruler of the universe. 一神論;有神論。⇨ deism. **the·ist** /ˈθiːɪst ; ˈθiɪst/ *n* believer in ～. 一神論信徒。**the·is·tic** /θiːˈɪstɪk ; θiˈɪstɪk/, **the·is·ti·cal** /-kl ; -kḷ/ *adjj*

them /ðəm ; ðəm; *strong form:* ðem ; ðɛm/ *pron,* ⇨ they.

them·atic /θɪˈmætɪk ; θiˈmætɪk/ *adj* (music) of a theme(3) or themes. (音樂)主題的;主題曲的。

theme /θiːm ; θim/ *n* [C] **1** topic; subject of a talk or a piece of writing. 題;(談話或寫作的)題目。 **2** (esp US) (subject set for a) student's essay. (尤美)學生的作文;作文題。 **3** (music) short melody which is repeated, expanded, etc eg in a sonata or symphony. (音樂)主題;主題曲;主旋律(如奏鳴曲或交響曲中者)。**ˈ～ song,** one that is often repeated in a musical play, film, etc. (音樂劇、電影等中的)主題歌。

them·selves /ðəmˈselvz ; ðəmˈsɛlvz/ *pron* **1** (reflex): (反身式): *They hurt* ～. 他們弄傷了自己。*They kept some for* ～. 他們爲自己保存了一些。*They did the work by* ～, without help. 他們靠自己做那項工作。*They were by* ～ (=alone, without company) *when I called.* 我往訪時他們沒有客人。 **2** (emphat): (加重語氣): *They* ～ *have often made that mistake.* 他們自己也常犯那項錯誤。

then /ðen ; ðɛn/ *adv* **1** at the time (past or future): (指過去或未來皆可)當時; 那時; 其時; 屆時: *We were living in Wales* ～. 那時我們住在威爾斯。*I was still unmarried* ～. 當時我還沒有結婚。***(every) now and*** ～, ⇨ now(3). ～ ***and there; there and*** ～, ⇨ there¹(5). **2** (used to modify a *n*): (用以修飾名詞): *the* ～ *Lord Mayor,* the Lord Mayor at that time. 當時的市長。 **3** (used after a *prep*): (用於介詞後): *from* ～ (= from that time) *onwards;* 自那時以後; *until* ～*;* 直至那時; *since* ～. 自那時以來。**4** next; after that; afterwards: 其後;然後;以後;繼之: *We'll have fish first, and* ～ *roast chicken.* 我們將先吃魚,然後吃烤雞。*We had a week in Rome and* ～ *went to Naples.* 我們在羅馬住了一星期,然後前往那不勒斯。**5** (usu at the beginning or end of a sentence) in that case; that being so: (通常置於句首或句尾)那麼;因此;既然這樣: *A: 'It isn't here.'—B: 'It must be in the next room,* ～.' 甲: '(它)不在這裡。'——乙: '那麼,一定在隔壁房間。' *You say you don't want to call a doctor. —T～ what do you want to do?* 你說你不想請醫生。—— 那麼你想怎麼辦？ **6** furthermore; and also: 並且;還;而且: *T～*

there's Mrs Green — she must be invited to the wedding. 還有格林太太 — 必須請她來參加婚禮。*And ~, you must remember....* 而且,你必須記得…。**7** **'Now ~,** used to call attention, or to express a warning, make a protest, etc: 用以引起注意,或表示警告、抗議等: *Now ~, who's been smoking?* 喂,誰在抽煙？

thence /ðens ; ðɛns/ *adv* (formal) from there; for that reason. (正式用語)由彼處;因爲那個緣故;因而。**~·forth** /ˌðens'fɔ:θ ; ˌðɛns'forθ/, **~·for·ward** /ˌðens'fɔ:wəd ; ˌðɛns'fɔrwəd/ *advv* from that time onwards. 從那時以後;從那時起。

the·oc·racy /θɪ'ɒkrəsɪ ; θi'ɑkrəsɪ/ *n* [C, U] (*pl* -cies) (country with a) system of government in which the laws of the State are believed to be the laws of God; (hence) government by priests or a priestly class. 神權政治;神治國;神權國家;(由此產生)僧侶政治;僧侶統治。**theo·cratic** /ˌθɪə'krætɪk ; ˌθiə'krætɪk/ *adj*

the·odo·lite /θɪ'ɒdəlaɪt ; θi'ɑdḷˌaɪt/ *n* instrument used by surveyors for measuring horizontal and vertical angles. 經緯儀(測量水平及垂直角度者)。

the·ol·ogy /θɪ'ɒlədʒɪ ; θi'ɑlədʒɪ/ *n* **1** [U] formal study of the nature of God and of the foundations of religious belief. 神學;宗教學;宗教信仰學。**2** [C] theological system or interpretation: 宗教信仰制度或解說: *rival theologies;* 敵對的宗教信仰制度或解釋; *a/the ~ of sex.* 宗教上對於性的解說。**theo·lo·gian** /ˌθɪə'ləʊdʒən ; ˌθiə'lodʒən/ *n* expert in or student of ~. 神學者;神學家。**theo·logi·cal** /ˌθɪə'lɒdʒɪkl ; ˌθiə'lɑdʒɪkḷ/ *adj* **theo·logi·cally** /-klɪ ; -klɪ/ *adv*

the·orem /'θɪərəm ; 'θiərəm/ *n* **1** statement which logical reasoning shows to be true. 定理;可藉推理證明的命題。**2** (maths) statement for which a reasoned proof is required. (數學)定理。

the·or·etic, the·or·eti·cal /θɪə'retɪk, -ɪkl ; ˌθiə'rɛtɪk, -kḷ/ *adjj* based on theory, not on practice or experience. 基於理論的;理論上的;推理的;非基於實用或經驗的。**the·or·eti·cally** /-klɪ ; -kḷɪ/ *adv*

the·ory /'θɪərɪ ; 'θiərɪ/ *n* (*pl* -ries) **1** [C, U] (explanation of the) general principles of an art or science (contrasted with practice): 學理;原理;理論(與 practice 相對): *Naval officers must understand both the ~ and practice of navigation.* 海軍軍官對於航海術的理論與實務皆須瞭解。*Your plan is excellent in ~, but would it succeed in practice?* 你的計畫在理論上甚佳,但是實行起來會成功嗎？ **2** [C] reasoned supposition put forward to explain facts or events: 學說;論說: *Darwin's ~ of evolution.* 達爾文的進化論。**3** [C] sth conjectured, not necessarily based on reasoning: 意見;推測;臆說;說法(未必基於推理): *He has a ~ that wearing hats makes men bald.* 他有一種說法,認爲戴帽子會使人禿頂。*In ~, three things could happen,* There are three possibilities. 推測起來,有三種可能性。**the·or·ist** /'θɪərɪst ; 'θiəˌrɪst/ *n* person who forms theories. 理論家。**the·or·ize** /'θɪəraɪz ; 'θiəˌraɪz/ *vi* [VP2A, 3A] ~ ***(about sth),*** form theories. 建立理論;理論化。

the·os·ophy /θi:'ɒsəfɪ ; θi'ɑsəfɪ/ *n* [U] any of several systems of philosophy which aim at a direct knowledge of God by means of spiritual ecstasy and contemplation. 通神學;通神論(認爲可藉精神上的忘我及冥想達到直接認識神的哲學體系)。**the·os·oph·ist** /-fɪst ; -fɪst/ *n* believer in ~. 通神論者;信通神論者。**theo·sophi·cal** /ˌθi:ə'sɒfɪkl ; ˌθiə'sɑfɪkḷ/ *adj*

thera·peutic, thera·peut·i·cal /ˌθerə'pju:tɪk, -ɪkl; ˌθɛrə'pjutɪk, -kḷ/ *adj* connected with the art of healing, the cure of disease: 治療學的;治療術的;關於治病的: *take ~ baths at a spa.* 在一處礦泉沐浴療病。**thera·peutic(s)** /ˌθerə'pju:tɪk(s);ˌθɛrə'pjutɪk(s)/ *n* (usu with *sing v*) branch of medicine concerned with curing disease. (通常用單數動詞)治療學。

ther·apy /'θerəpɪ ; 'θɛrəpɪ/ *n* [U] curative treatment, esp of a kind indicated by a preceding word: 治療;療法(尤用於前面有字標明的某種治療法): *radio-~,* treatment by x-rays; 放射(線)療法; *psycho~,* treatment by psychoanalytic methods; 心理療法; *occupational ~,* treatment by means of work that exercises certain muscles. 職業治療法(藉可使某些肌肉運動的工作以治療的方法)。**thera·pist** /'θerəpɪst ; 'θɛrəpɪst/ *n* specialist in ~. 精於某種療法的專家;(尤指)物理治療家;精神治療家。

there[1] /ðeə(r) ; ðɛr/ *adv of place and direction* (contrasted with *here*)表示地方及方向的副詞(與here相對) **1** in, at or to, that place: 在那裡;在彼處;往那裡;向彼處: *We shall soon be ~.* 我們很快就會到那裡。*We're nearly ~,* have nearly arrived. 我們快到了。*Put the box ~, in that corner.* 把盒子放在那裡,那個角落裡。*I've never been to Rome but I hope to go ~ next year.* 我還沒有去過羅馬,但是我希望明年去那裡。**2** (front position, in exclamatory style; always stressed, and not to be confused with *there + be/appear/seem, etc,* dealt with at there[2] below; ⇨ here(2); used with inversion of subject and *v* if the subject is a *n,* but not if the subject is a *pers pron*): (置於句首,具感嘆詞性質;總是重讀,不可與下面 there[2] 中所提到之 there+be, appear, seem 等形式混淆;主詞爲名詞時,主詞須與動詞對換位置,主詞爲人稱代名詞時,位置不對換): *T~ goes the last bus!* 最後一班公車開走了！*T~ it goes!* (它)走了！(去了！) *T~ come the rest of the party!* 該組(隊等)其餘的人到了！*T~ they come!* 他們來了！**3** (used to call attention; always stressed): (用以引起注意;總是重讀): *T~'s the bell ringing for church.* 聽,做禮拜的鐘聲響了。*T~'s a fine stroke!* (used to give praise or encouragement.) 做得好！(用於讚美或鼓勵。) *You have only to turn the switch and ~ you are,* ie you get the desired result. 你祇要轉動開關就行了(就可達到目的)。*T~'s a fine, ripe pear for you!* See what a fine, ripe pear this is! 瞧,給你這個梨多漂亮,多成熟！ *T~'s gratitude for you!* Note how grateful he, she, etc is! (used either sincerely or ironically). 你看,他(她等)對你是多麼的感激！(眞誠的或諷刺的用法皆可)。 **4** at, in connection with, that point (in an action, story, argument, etc): (行動,故事,辯論等)在那一點上;有關那一點: *Don't stop ~!* 不要停在那兒！ *T~* (ie on that point) *I disagree with you.* 在那一點上,我不同意你的意見。*T~ you are mistaken.* 這一點你錯了。*T~ comes the difficulty.* 關於這一點,困難來了。 **5** (in phrases): (用於片語中): ***all ~,*** ⇨ all[2](1). ***here and ~,*** ⇨ here(5). ***~ and back,*** to a place and back again: 往返;來回: *Can I go ~ and back in one day?* 我一天能够來回嗎？ ***over ~,*** (indicating a place farther than is indicated by ~ alone): (指較單獨用 there 爲遠的地方)在那裡: *I live here, Mr Green lives ~, and Mr Brown lives over ~, on the other side of the river.* 我住在這裡,格林先生住在那裡,布朗先生住得更遠些,在河對岸。***then and ~; ~ and then,*** at that time and place. 當場立即;當時當地。Cf 參較 *here and now.* **6** (in colloq style only, after a *n* or *pron,* for emphasis): (僅用於口語文體中,接在名詞或代名詞後,用以加重語氣): *Hi! You ~!* 嗨！喂！ *That woman ~ is eating a lot!* 那女人吃得好多！ **7** (used after *preps* and *advv*): (用於介詞及副詞之後): *Put them in/under/near, etc ~.* 把它們放在那裡面(那下面,靠近那裡等)。*Pass along ~, please!* (used to request people to move along in a crowded street, bus, etc). 請往前走！(用於請求擁擠在街道上,公車上等的人羣向前移動)。

there[2] /*usual form:* ðə(r) ; ðɚ; *strong form:* ðeə(r) ; ðɛr/ *adv* (used to introduce a sentence in which the *v* (esp *'be'*) normally precedes its subject, which is usu *indef,* ⇨ [VP1, 2A, 4E]) (用以引導一個句子,其動詞,尤其是 be 動詞,經常置於主詞前,主詞通常是不確定的) **1** (with the *v 'be'*): (與動詞 be

連用)：*T~'s a man at the door.* 門口有一個人。Cf 參較 *The man is at the door.* 那個人就在門口。*T~ can be no doubt about it.* 此事無可懷疑。*I don't want ~ to be any misunderstanding.* 我不想有任何誤會存在。*T~'s no stopping him,* It is impossible to stop him. 阻止他是不可能的。**2** (with other *vv*, esp *seem* and *appear*)：(與其他動詞連用,特別是 seem 及 appear)：*T~ seems (to be) no doubt about it.* 此事似乎無可懷疑。*T~ appeared to be no one who could answer our inquiries.* 好像沒有人能回答我們的詢問。*T~ comes a time when....* 有這麼一個時期…。

there[3] /ðeə(r)；ðɛr/ *int* (always stressed) (總是重讀) **1** (used, chiefly to children, to soothe or comfort)：(用於撫慰或安慰,主要對象爲小孩)：*T~! T~! Never mind, you'll soon feel better.* 好啦！好啦！不要緊,很快你就會感到舒服一點。**2** (used to suggest that the speaker was right in sth, or to indicate triumph, dismay, etc according to the context)：(用以暗示說話者是對的,或用以表示勝利、沮喪等,依上下文而定)：*'T~, now! What did I tell you,* You now see that I was right！你瞧！我怎麼跟你說的？(你現在知道我對了吧！) *T~! You've woken the baby!* 哎呀！你把小孩吵醒了！

there·about(s) /'ðeərəbaʊt(s)；ˌðɛrə'baʊt(s)/ *adv* (usu preceded by *or*) near that place, number, quantity, degree, etc：(通常前面加 or) (表接近某地方、數目、數量、程度等)大約;左右;附近：*in Rye or ~;* 在瑞埃附近；*£5/15 lb/3 o'clock or ~.* 五鎊(十五磅,三點鐘)左右。

there·after /ðeər'ɑːftə(r) *US:* -'æf- ; ðɛr'æftɚ/ *adv* (formal) afterwards. (正式用語)此後;其後。

there·by /ðeə'baɪ；ðɛr'baɪ/ *adv* (formal) by that means; in that connection. (正式用語)藉以;從而;由此;在那一點上;在那一方面。

there·fore /'ðeəfɔː(r)；'ðɛrˌfor/ *adv* for that reason. 爲了那種理由;爲此;因此。

there·in /ðeər'ɪn；ðɛr'ɪn/ *adv* (formal) in that place; in that respect; in that particular. (正式用語)在那地方;在那裡;在那方面;在那一點上。

there·in·after /ˌðeərɪn'ɑːftə(r) *US:* -'æf-；ˌðɛrɪn-'æftɚ/ *adv* (chiefly legal) in that part which follows. (主要爲法律用語)以下;在下文。

there·of /ðeər'ɒv；ðɛr'ɑv/ *adv* (formal) of that; from that source. (正式用語)由是;由此;從那個來源;其。

there·to /ðeə'tuː；ðɛr'tu/ *adv* (formal) to that; in addition to that. (正式用語)至彼；到那裡；其外；此外;更。

there·under /ðeər'ʌndə(r)；ðɛr'ʌndɚ/ *adv* (formal) under that. (正式用語)在其下。

there·upon /ˌðeərə'pɒn；ˌðɛrə'pɑn/ *adv* (formal) then; as the result of that. (正式用語)隨後;立即;於是;因此。

there·withal /'ðeəwɪðɔːl；ˌðɛrwɪð'ɔl/ *adv* (archaic) in addition; besides. (古)此外;除此而外。

therm /θɜːm；θɝm/ *n* [C] (100000 GB thermal units as a) unit of heat as used for measuring the consumption of gas (coal-gas or natural gas). 撒姆(熱量單位,用以計算瓦斯消耗量,相等於十萬個英國熱量單位)。

ther·mal /'θɜːml；'θɝml̩/ *adj* of heat: 熱的;熱量的：*~ springs,* of warm or hot water; 溫泉；*the '~ barrier,* barrier to the use of high speeds (in flying) caused by increased friction of the air on the surfaces of the aircraft; 熱障碍(由空氣與飛機表面的摩擦所產生的對高速飛行的障碍)；*a ˌ~ 'power station,* one using heat (from coal, oil) (contrasted with a hydro-electric power station). 火力發電廠(以煤或油爲燃料,以別於水力發電廠)。**~ capacity,** (phys) number of units of heat needed to raise the temperature of a body by one degree. (物理)熱容量。**~ unit,** (phys) unit of measure of heat. (物理)熱量單位。**British ~ unit** (abbr 略作 **BTU**), amount of heat needed to raise 1 lb of water by 1°F. 英國熱量單位(使一磅水之溫度增加華氏一度所需之熱量)。□ *n* rising current of warm air (as needed by a glider to gain height). 熱氣流(熱空氣的上升氣流,如滑翔機上升時所需要者)。

ther·mi·onic /ˌθɜːmɪ'ɒnɪk；ˌθɝmɪ'ɑnɪk/ *adj* of that branch of physics that deals with the emission of electrons at high temperatures. 熱離子學的。**~ valve** (US 美＝ **~ tube**) *n* system of electrodes arranged in a glass or metal envelope exhausted of air. 熱離子管。

thermo- /ˌθɜːməʊ；ˌθɝmo/ (in compounds) (用於複合字中) of heat. 熱的。**ˌ~-dy·'nam·ics** *n pl* [U] (usu with *sing v*) science of the relations between heat and mechanical work. (通常與單數動詞連用)熱力學。**ˌ~-'nu·clear** *adj* (eg of weapons) of, using, the high temperatures released in nuclear fission: (指武器等)熱核子的：*the ~-nuclear bomb,* the hydrogen bomb. 氫彈;熱核子彈。**ˌ~-'plastic** *n, adj* (substance) which can at any time be made plastic by the application of heat. 受熱卽變軟及可塑的;熱熔的；熱塑或熱熔物質；熱熔塑膠。**ˌ~-'setting** *adj* (of plastics) becoming permanently hard after being heated and shaped. (指塑膠)加熱成形後即硬化的。**'~·stat** /'θɜːməstæt；'θɝməˌstæt/ *n* [C] device for automatically regulating temperature by cutting off and restoring the supply of heat (eg in central heating, refrigerators, air-conditioning). 恆溫器(自動調節並可保持一定溫度者,如中央暖氣系統、電冰箱及空氣調節系統中者)。**~·statci** /ˌθɜːmə'stætɪk；ˌθɝmə'stætɪk/ *adj* of a ~stat: 恆溫器的：*~static control.* 恆溫器的控制。

ther·mom·eter /θə'mɒmɪtə(r)；θə'mɑmətɚ/ *n* instrument for measuring temperature. 溫度計;寒暑表。⇨ App 5. 參看附錄五。

ther·mos /'θɜːməs；'θɝməs/ *n* (also 亦作 **'~ flask**) (P) vacuum flask. (商標)熱水瓶。⇨ vacuum.

the·sau·rus /θɪ'sɔːrəs；θɪ'sɔrəs/ *n* (*pl* ~es /-rəsɪz；-rəsɪz/) dictionary of words and phrases grouped together according to similarities in their meanings. 同義語字彙;同義語字典。

these /ðiːz；ðiz/ ⇨ this.

the·sis /'θiːsɪs；'θisɪs/ *n* (*pl* theses /'θiːsiːz；'θisiz/) statement or theory (to be) put forward and supported by arguments, esp a lengthy written essay submitted (as part of the requirements) for a university degree. 論題;論文;(尤指)畢業論文;學位論文。

Thes·pian /'θespɪən；'θɛspɪən/ *adj* (liter) connected with the drama. (文)戲劇的;有關戲劇的。□ *n* actor or actress. 演員。

thews /θjuːz；θjuz/ *n pl* (liter) muscles: (文)肌肉：*~ and sinews,* bodily strength. 體力。

they /ðeɪ；ðe/ *pers pron* (subject form, *pl*, of *he, she, it*)：(主格形式,爲 he, she, it 的複數)：*T~* (= People in general) *say that the government will have to resign.* 據說內閣勢將辭職。*What a lot of questions ~* (= those in authority) *ask in this tax form!* 這張稅務調查表上問的問題好多啊！ **them** /ðəm；ðəm; *strong form:* ðem；ðɛm/ *pers pron* (object form of *they*)：(they 的受格形式)：*Give them to me.* 把它們給我。*It was very kind of them,* They were very kind. 他們很客氣。

they're /ðeə(r)；ðɛr/ = they are.

thick /θɪk；θɪk/ *adj* (-er, -est) **1** (opp of *thin*) of relatively great or a specified measurement in diameter, from one side to the other, or from the front to the back: (爲 thin 的相反字)厚的;粗的：*a ~ slice of bread;* 厚厚的一片麵包；*a ~ line;* 一條粗線；*ice three inches ~;* 三吋厚的冰；*~ print,* of ~ lines. 粗體字。**ˌ~-'skinned** *adj* (fig) not sensitive to reproach or insults. (喩)臉皮厚的;對責備或侮辱感覺遲鈍的。**2** having a large number of units close together: 稠密的;密集的：*~ hair;* 濃密的頭髮；*a ~ forest;* 叢林；*in the ~est part of the crowd.* 在人叢最密集的部分。*The corn was ~ in the fields.* 田裡的麥子長得很茂盛。**ˌ~-'set**

adj **(a)** having a short, stout body; solidly built. 矮而壯的；結實的。**(b)** (of a hedge) with bushes, etc closely planted. (指樹籬)密植矮樹等的；繁密的。**3** ~ ***with,*** abounding or packed with: 充滿…的；塡滿…的: *The air was ~ with dust/snow.* 空氣中充滿了塵埃(雪花)。 **4** (of liquids) semi-solid: (指液體)稠的；濃厚的: ~ *soup;* 濃湯；(of vapour, the atmosphere) not clear; dense: (指烟霧，大氣)不清明的；濃密的: *a ~ fog.* 濃霧。 **5** (of voices) obstructed, eg because one has a cold. (指聲音)阻塞的；重濁的(如因傷風所致)。 **6** (colloq) stupid; dull. (俗)愚笨的；遲鈍的。 ˌ**~-'headed** *adj* stupid. 愚笨的。 **7** (colloq) intimate: (俗)親密的: *John is very ~ with Anne now.* 約翰現在和安很親近。 ***as ~ as thieves,*** very friendly. 非常親密。 **8** (various colloq uses) (各種口語用法) ***a bit ~; rather ~,*** beyond what is reasonable or endurable: 不太合理的；令人受不了的: *Three weeks of heavy rain is a bit ~.* 一連下了三星期的大雨，眞叫人受不了。***give sb a ~ ear,*** give him a blow that causes his ear to swell. 打腫某人的耳朵。***lay it on ~,*** (sl) be profuse, esp in paying compliments. (俚)過分(尤指過分恭維)。□ *n* [U] **1** most crowded part; part where there is greatest activity: 最擁擠的部分；活動最多的部分: *in the ~ of the fight.* 在酣戰中。*We were in the ~ of it.* 我們正積極參與此事。***through ~ and thin,*** under any kind of conditions, good or bad. 在任何情況下；不計甘苦。**2** ~ part of anything: 事物的濃厚部分；事物的粗大濃密部分: *the ~ of the thumb.* 拇指最粗部分。□ *adv* ~ly: 厚地；密地；密集地；充塞地: *You spread the butter too ~.* 你塗的奶油太厚。*The snow/dust lay ~ everywhere.* 雪(塵土)到處堆積得很厚。*His blows came ~ and fast,* rapidly and in large numbers. 他出拳快而密。**~·ly** *adv* in a ~ manner: 厚地；濃密地: *cut the bread/spread the butter ~ly.* 厚厚地切麵包(抹奶油)。**~en** /ˈθɪkən ; ˈθɪkən/ *vt, vi* make or become ~: (使)變厚；(使)變濃；(使)變密集: *~en the gravy.* 使肉汁濃厚。*The plot ~ens,* becomes more complex. 情節變複雜了。**~·en·ing** /ˈθɪkənɪŋ ; ˈθɪkənɪŋ/ *n* [U] material or substance used to ~en sth; process of becoming ~(er) or making sth ~(er). 濃化劑；濃化或加厚的過程。**~·ness** *n* **1** [U] quality or degree of being ~: 厚；濃；厚度；濃度: *four centimetres in ~ness;* 厚四公分；*a ~ness of four centimetres.* 四公分的厚度。**2** [C] layer: 層；張: *one ~ness of cotton-wool and two ~nesses of felt.* 一層棉花及兩層毛氈。

thicket /ˈθɪkɪt ; ˈθɪkɪt/ *n* [C] mass of trees, shrubs, undergrowth, growing thickly together. 灌木叢。

thief /θiːf ; θif/ *n* (*pl* thieves/ θiːvz ; θivz/) person who steals, esp secretly and without violence. 賊；小偷；竊賊。⇨ bandit, burglar, *robber* at rob. **thieve** /θiːv ; θiv/ *vi, vt* [VP2A] be a ~; [VP6A] steal (sth). 做賊；當小偷；偷竊(東西)。**thiev·ery** /ˈθiːvərɪ ; ˈθivərɪ/ *n* theft. 偷竊。**thiev·ish** /-ɪʃ ; -ɪʃ/ *adj* having the habit of stealing; thief-like. 有偷竊習慣的；像賊的。**thiev·ish·ly** *adv*

thigh /θaɪ ; θaɪ/ *n* [C] **1** part of the human leg between the knee and the hip. 股；大腿(人腿自膝至臀的部分)。⇨ the illus at leg. 參看 leg 之插圖。ˈ**~-bone** *n* bone of this part of the leg; femur. 股骨；大腿骨。**2** corresponding part of the hind legs of other animals. 其他動物之後腿的相當部分；股。

thimble /ˈθɪmbl ; ˈθɪmbl/ *n* cap (of metal, etc) used to protect the end of the finger when pushing a needle through cloth, etc. 頂針；針箍；嵌環。**~·ful** /-fʊl ; -ˌfʊl/ *n* (colloq) sip, very small quantity (of a liquid). (俗)(液體的)微量；一啜。

thin /θɪn ; θɪn/ *adj* (-ner, -nest) **1** (opp of *thick*) having opposite surfaces close together; of small diameter: (爲 thick 的相反字)薄的；細的: *a ~ slice of bread;* 一片薄麵包；*a ~ sheet of paper;* 一張薄紙；*~ boards;* 薄板；*a ~ piece of string;* 一根細繩；*a ~ stroke,* of the pen, etc. (鋼筆等的)細的筆畫。ˌ**~-'skinned** *adj* (fig) sensitive to criticism; easily offended. (喻)臉皮薄的；對批評敏感的；容易得罪的。**2** lacking density: 稀薄的；*a ~ mist.* 薄霧。***~ air,*** invisibility; nothingness: 看不見；不存在；虛無: *He seemed to vanish into ~ air,* disappear mysteriously without leaving a trace. 他好像消失在虛無中了。**3** (opp of *fat*) having not much flesh: (爲 fat 的相反字)瘦的: *rather ~ in the face.* 臉孔清瘦的。*Your illness has left you very ~.* 你的病使你消瘦多了。**4** not full or closely packed: 稀疏的；寥寥的: *a ~ audience,* with more seats empty than occupied. 寥寥可數的觀衆。*'Your hair's getting rather ~ on top, sir', said the barber.* 理髮師說，'先生，您頭頂上的頭髮有點稀疏了。' **5** (of liquids) lacking substance; watery: (指液體)稀薄的；淡的: *~ beer/wine,* lacking body; weak. 淡啤酒(葡萄酒)。**6** lacking in some important ingredient; poor: 缺乏某些重要成分的；貧乏的；淺薄的；淺顯的: *~ humour;* 膚淺的詼諧；*a ~ excuse,* not very convincing; 不能令人信服的託辭；*a ~ disguise,* easily seen through; 易爲人識破的僞裝；*a ~ story,* one that contains nothing vey exciting; one that does not convince (as an excuse, etc). 乏味的故事；不能自圓其說的藉口等。 **7** (colloq) (俗) ***have a ~ time,*** an uncomfortable, distasteful one. 過得很不舒服，很不愉快。□ *adv* so as to be ~: 稀薄地；稀疏地；淡地: *You've spread the butter very thin.* 你奶油塗得太薄了。□ *vt, vi* (-nn-) [VP6A, 15B, 2A, C] make or become ~. (使)變薄；(使)變細；(使)變瘦；(使)變稀疏；(使)變貧乏。 ~ ***(down),*** make (a liquid) less dense: 使(液體)變稀: *~ down paint with turpentine.* 加松節油使油漆變稀。 ~ ***(out),*** make or become less dense, or fewer in number: (使)變爲稀薄；(使)減少: *War and disease had ~ned (out) the population.* 戰爭和疾病已使人口減少。*He ~ned out the seedlings,* pulled up some of them to allow the others to grow better. 他拔掉一些幼苗使變稀疏(好讓別的幼苗長得更好)。*We had better wait until the fog ~s out.* 我們最好等到霧變薄一點。*At last the crowd/traffic ~ned out.* 人羣(車輛)終於變得稀少了。**~·ly** *adv* in a ~ manner: 薄地；細地；瘦地；淡地；稀疏地: *Sow the seed ~ly.* 把種子撒稀一點。**~·ness** /ˈθɪnnɪs ; ˈθɪnnɪs/ *n*

thine /ðaɪn ; ðaɪn/ ⇨ thy.

thing /θɪŋ ; θɪŋ/ *n* **1** any material object: 東西；物: *What are those ~s on the table?* 桌上的那些東西是什麼？*There wasn't a ~* (=nothing) *to eat.* 沒有東西可吃。*She's too fond of sweet ~s,* sweet kinds of food. 她太愛吃甜食了。**2** (*pl*) belongings; articles of which the nature is clear (or thought to be clear) from the context: (複)所有物；物件；用品(其性質可由上下文判斷者): *Bring your swimming ~s* (= your swimming-suit, towel, etc) *with you.* 帶着你的游泳用品。*Have you packed your ~s* (= clothes, etc) *for the journey?* 你旅行用的衣物都收拾好了嗎？*Put your ~s* (= coat, hat, etc) *on and let's leave.* 把你的衣帽等穿戴起來讓我們離開這裡。**3** subject: 題目；主題: *There's another ~* (= something else) *I want to ask you about.* 還有一件事我想要問你。**4** that which is non-material: 非物質的事物: *He values ~s of the mind more than ~s of the body.* 他對於心靈方面的事物看得比肉體方面的事物重。***be 'seeing ~s,*** have hallucinations. 產生幻覺。 **5** circumstance; event; course of action: 情況；事件；行爲: *That only makes ~s* (= the situation) *worse.* 那祇會使情況更糟。*You take ~s* (= happenings) *too seriously.* 你把事情看得太嚴重了。*I must think ~s over,* consider what has happened, what has to be done, etc. 我必須把情勢考慮一下。*What's the next ~ to do,* What must be done next? 下一步該做什麼？*It's just one of those ~s,* sth that can't be helped, explained, remedied, etc (according to context). 那眞是沒有法子的事(指無可奈何，無法解釋，無法挽救的事等，根據上下文而定)。*T~s* (= The state of affairs) *are getting worse and worse.* 事態愈來愈糟了。*Well, of* '*all* ~*s!* (expressing surprise, indignation, etc, at what has been done, suggested, etc). 哼,居然如此!(對所做、所建議等的事情表示驚呀、憤慨等。) ***for 'one*** ~, used to introduce a reason: 一則;首先(用以舉出一項理由): *For one* ~, *I haven't any money; for another....* 一則,我沒有錢;再則,…。***Taking one*** ~ ***with another,*** considering various circumstances, etc. 考慮各種情況;考慮各方面的情形。**6** (used of a person or an animal, expressing an emotion of some kind): (用以指人或動物,顯露某種情緒): *She's a sweet little* ~/*a dear old* ~. 她是一個可愛的小東西(一位親切的老太太)。*Poor* ~, *he's been ill all winter.* 可憐的人,他已經病了整個冬天。 **7** ***the*** ~, just what will be best in the circumstances: 最適合的事物;最好的事物: *A holiday in the mountains will be the best* ~ *for you.* 上山去度假對你來說最好不過。*That's not the* ~ *to do,* is unsuitable, inappropriate. 那是不宜做的事。*He always says the right/wrong* ~, makes the most suitable/unsuitable remark or comment. 他說話總是很得體(不適當)。***quite the*** ~, fashionable. 時髦的。 **8** (phrases) (片語) ***the ˌ~ 'is,*** the question to be considered is: 目前的問題是;目前要考慮的是;最要緊的是: *The* ~ *is, can we get there in time?* 目前的問題是,我們能否及時趕到那裡? *The* ~ *is* (= The most important factor is) *to make your views quite clear to everyone.* 現在最要緊的是把你的觀點向每一個人解釋清楚。 ***first*** ~, before anything else; early: 第一件事;最先;早: *I'll do it first* ~ *tomorrow morning.* 明天一早我便做這件事。***first* ~*s first,*** ⇨ first²(1). ***the ˌgeneral/ˌcommon/ˌusual '***~, the common practice. 常例;慣例。***a near*** ~, a narrow escape (from an accident, missing a train, etc). 好險的事;僥倖的事(如倖免於難,險些未趕上火車等)。***an understood*** ~, sth that has been/is accepted. 已被接受或認可之事。***do one's (own)*** ~, (colloq) do sth which one does well, or which one feels an urge to do; act without inhibition. (俗)做得心應手之事;做渴望做之事;爲所欲爲。***have a*** ~ ***about,*** (colloq) be obsessed by. (俗)被…迷住;被…困擾;對…感到厭惡。 **9** (*pl* with an *adj* following) all that can be so described: (複數,後接形容詞)…的事物;文物;該形容詞所描述的事物總稱: ~*s Japanese,* Japanese customs, art, etc. 日本的文物。 **10** (legal) (法律) ~*s personal/real,* personal/real property. 動產(不動產)。

thing·ummy /'θɪŋəmɪ; 'θɪŋəmɪ/, **thing·(u)ma·bob** /'θɪŋ(ə)məbɒb; 'θɪŋ(ə)məˌbɑb/, **thing·(u)ma·jig** /'θɪŋ(ə)mədʒɪg; 'θɪŋ(ə)məˌdʒɪg/ *nn* (colloq) person or thing whose name one forgets or is not known (used in the same way as *what's-his-name, what d'you call it*). (俗)某人或某物(指其名爲人忘記或不詳的人或事物,用法與 what's-his-name, what d'you call it 相同)。

think¹ /θɪŋk; θɪŋk/ *vi, vt* (*pt, pp* thought /θɔ:t; θɔt/) (For special uses with *adverbial particles* and *preps,* ⇨ 8 below.) (與副詞接語及介詞連用的特殊用法,參看下列第8義。) **1** [VP2A, B, C, 6A, 8] (with cognate object) use, exercise, the mind in order to form opinions, come to conclusions: (與同系受詞連用)思索;考慮;想: *Are animals able to* ~*?* 動物能思考嗎? *You should* ~ (= not be hasty) *before doing that.* 做那事之前你應該考慮考慮。 *Do you* ~ *in English when you speak English, or translate mentally?* 你講英語時是用英語構思,還是經過心裏的翻譯過程? *Let me* ~ *a moment,* Give me time before I answer. 讓我先想一下。*He may not say much but he* ~*s a lot.* 他也許不大講話,但是他想得很多。~ ***aloud,*** utter one's thoughts as they occur. 自言自語。'~-***tank*** *n* group or organization that provides advice, ideas, solutions to problems, etc. 提供意見、解決問題之方法等的團體或組織;智囊團。 **2** [VP9, 25] consider; be of the opinion: 認爲;以爲: *Do you* ~ *it will rain?* 你認爲會下雨嗎? *Yes, I* ~ *so.* 是的,我認爲會。*No, I don't* ~ *so.* 不,我認爲不會。*It's going to rain, I* ~. 我看快要下雨了。*I* ~ *(that) you're very brave.* 我認爲你很勇敢。*Do you* ~ *it likely/that it is likely?* 你認爲這事可能嗎? *I thought I heard a scream.* 我認爲我聽到一聲尖叫。*They had been thought (to be) lost.* 大家都以爲他們迷路了。*It will be better, don't you* ~, *to start early.* 早一點動身比較好,你說是吧。~ ***fit.*** 認爲適當。⇨ fit¹(2). **3** [VP10] (neg with *can/could*) imagine, form a conception of: (用於否定句,與 can 或 could 連用)構想;想像;形成概念: *I can't* ~ *what you mean.* 我想像不出你的意思是什麼。 *I can't* ~ *where she has gone off to/how she did it/why she left.* 我想不出她逃往何處(她怎麼做的,她爲什麼離開)。*You can't* ~ *how glad I am to see you.* 你無法想像我是多麼高興見到你。 **4** [VP9] have a half-formed intention: 有意;打算: *I* ~ *I'll go for a swim.* 我想去游泳。 **5** [VP10] reflect: 反省;思維;細想: *She was* ~*ing (to herself) how cold the room was.* 她在想那房間眞冷。 **6** [VP7A, 9] expect, intend: 預料;企圖: *I never thought that I'd see you here!* 我從未料到會在這裏見到你! *Who would have thought to see you here!* 誰會想到在這裏看到你! ***I thought as much,*** That is what I expected or suspected. 我也這樣想。 **7** [VP22] bring into a mental condition by ~ing: 因想而導致某種心理狀態;想到某種地步: *Stop worrying or you'll* ~ *yourself sick!* 別着急,否則你會急出病來的! **8** [VP3A, 15B] (special uses with *adverbial particles* and *preps*): (與副詞接語及介詞連用的特殊用法):

think about sth, **(a)** examine, consider (esp a plan, idea, to see whether it is desirable, practicable, etc): 考慮;愼思;審查(尤指計畫、觀念,看它是否相宜、可行等): *She's* ~*ing about emigrating to Canada.* 她在考慮移居加拿大。*Please* ~ *about the proposal and let me have your views tomorrow.* 請考慮那項建議,明天把你的看法告訴我。 **(b)** recall; reflect upon: 想起;回想;回顧: *She was* ~*ing about her childhood days.* 她在回想她的童年時期。

think of sth, **(a)** consider; take into account: 考慮;計及;思索: *We have a hundred and one things to* ~ *of before we can decide.* 在我們做決定前,我們有許許多多的事情待考慮。*You* ~ *of everything!* 你全都想到了! **(b)** consider, contemplate (without reaching a decision or taking action): 有意;想;打算;盤算(未做成決定亦未採取實際行動): *We're* ~*ing of emigrating to Canada.* 我們打算移民到加拿大。*I did* ~ *of visiting him, but I've changed my mind.* 我確曾想去拜訪他,不過我已改變了主意。 **(c)** imagine: 想像: *Just* ~ *of the cost/danger!* 想想那筆費用(那危險)吧! *To* ~ *of his not knowing anything about it!* Isn't it surprising! 想想看,他對此事竟一無所知(寧非怪事)! **(d)** have, entertain, the idea of (often with *could, would, should,* and *not* or *never,* with *dream* as a possible substitute for *think*): 有…的看法;持…的念頭(常與 could, would, should, 以及 not, never 連用, dream可代替 think): *Surrender is not to be thought of.* 投降不列入考慮。*I couldn't* ~ *of such a thing.* 我不可能有這種想法。*He would never* ~ *of letting his daughter marry a fellow like you.* 他從未想到讓他的女兒嫁給像你這樣的人。 **(e)** call to mind; recall: 記憶;記起: *I can't* ~ *of his name at the moment.* 我一時想不起他的名字。 **(f)** put forward; suggest: 提出;建議: *Who first thought of the idea?* 誰先提出那個主意的? *Can you* ~ *of a good place for a weekend holiday?* 你能提出一個週末度假的好去處嗎? ~ ***highly/well/not much/little, etc of sb/sth,*** (not in the progressive tenses) have a high/good/poor, etc opinion of: (不用進行式)對某人或某事物評價甚高(評價高,評價不太高,評價甚低等): *His work is highly thought of by the critics.* 批評家對他的作品評價甚高。*He* ~*s the world of her,* ~s she's wonderful, loves her dearly. 他對她十分傾心。~ ***nothing of sth/doing sth,*** consider (doing) it to be insignificant or unremarkable: 輕視;看不

起；不把…當一回事：*Barbara ~s nothing of walking 20 miles a day.* 芭芭拉並不把每天走二十哩路當一回事。**~ nothing 'of it,** (formal) Don't mention it, ⇨ mention. (正式用語)不必客氣。**~ better of sb,** have a higher opinion of (than to...): 看重某人(不至於做…)；對某人持較…高的看法：*I had always thought better of you than to suppose you could be so unkind.* 我過去一直認爲你不至於會那樣殘忍。**~ better of sth,** reconsider and give up: 重新考慮並放棄：*What a foolish idea! I hope you'll ~ better of it.* 多麼愚蠢的想法！我希望你重新考慮一下(把它放棄)吧。

think sth out, consider carefully and make a plan for: 想出；想通；熟思：*It seems to be a well-thought out scheme.* 那似乎是一項考慮周詳的計畫。*That wants ~ing out,* needs careful consideration. 那事需要仔細考慮。

think sth over, reflect upon, consider further (before reaching a decision, etc): 仔細想；作進一步考慮；審慎思考：*Please ~ over what I've said.* 請仔細考慮我說的話。*I'd like more time to ~ things over.* 我希望多一點時間把事情做進一步的考慮。

think sth up, devise, conceive, invent (a scheme, etc): 想出；想到；設計出(一項計畫等)：*There's no knowing what he'll ~ up next.* 誰也不知道下一回他會想出什麼花樣。

think² /θɪŋk ; θɪŋk/ *n* (colloq) occasion of, need for, thinking: (俗)思索；思考；考慮：*If that's what he wants, he's got another ~ coming,* will need to think again. 如果那就是他想要的，他需要再考慮一下。

think·able /ˈθɪŋkəbl ; ˈθɪŋkəbḷ/ *adj* conceivable: 可想像的：*It's not ~* (more usu 較常用 *It's un~*) *that....* 不可想像的是…。

thinker /ˈθɪŋkə(r) ; ˈθɪŋkɚ/ *n* person who thinks (usu with an *adj*): 思考者；思想家(通常與形容詞連用)：*a great / shallow ~.* 偉大的(膚淺的)思想家。

think·ing /ˈθɪŋkɪŋ ; ˈθɪŋkɪŋ/ *adj* thoughtful; intelligent: 有思考力的；思想的：*the ~ public;* 有思想力的人們；思想界；有心人士；*all ~ people.* 凡是有思想的人們。□ *n* thought; reasoning: 思想；思考：*do some hard ~,* think deeply. 深思；沉思。*You are of my way of ~,* You think as I do. 你和我的想法一樣。*He is, to my (way of) ~* (ie in my opinion), *the best living novelist.* 依我看來，他是當代最優秀的小說家。*Can I bring you round to my way of ~,* get you to think as I do, agree with me? 我能使你同意我的想法嗎？**put one's '~-cap on,** (colloq) think about a problem, etc. (俗)好好思考；認眞思考。

third /θɜːd ; θɝd/ *adj, n* (abbr 略作 **3rd**) next after the second (in place, time, order, importance, etc); one of the three equal divisions of a whole: 第三(的)；三分之一(的)：*the ~ month of the year,* ie March; 三月；*on the ~ of April;* 四月三號；*on the ~ floor* (US 美 = fourth floor); 在四樓；*every ~ day;* 每三天；每隔兩天；*the ~ largest city in France;* 法國的第三大城；*Edward the T~,* Edward III, the ~ king of this name; 愛德華三世；*one-~ of a litre.* 三分之一升。**~ degree,** prolonged or hard questioning, use of torture (as used by the police in some countries to get confessions or information). (某些國家的警察爲獲得口供或情報所用的)疲勞訊問；刑訊；逼供。**a / the ~ party,** another person besides the two principal people. 第三者。**~-party insurance,** of a person other than the person insured, which the insurance company undertakes to meet. 第三者責任保險(對受保人以外的第三者有承諾的保險)。**~ rail,** conductor rail, carrying electric current. 帶電的第三軌。**ˌ~-ˈrate** *adj* of poor quality. 三流的；三等的；劣質的。**ˌ~-ˈrater** *n* person who is ~-rate. 三流人物；差勁的人。**the T~ World,** the developing countries not aligned with the great power blocs. 第三世界(不與大國結盟的開發中國家)。**~·ly** *adv*

thirst /θɜːst ; θɝst/ *n* [U, and with *indef art* as in examples] (不可數名詞，但如例句所示，可與不定冠詞連用) **1** feeling caused by a desire or need to drink; suffering caused by this: 渴；口渴：*The horse satisfied its ~ at the river.* 那馬在河裏飲水解渴。*This kind of work gives me a ~.* 這種工作使我感到口渴。*They lost their way in the desert and died of ~.* 他們在沙漠中迷路而渴死了。 **2** (fig) strong desire (*for,* or, liter and biblical, *after*): (喻)熱望；渴望(與 for 連用；文學及聖經，與 after 連用)：*a ~ for knowledge;* 求知慾；*satisfy one's ~ for adventure.* 滿足冒險的熱望。□ *vi* [VP2A, 3A] **~ (for),** have ~; be eager (for): 口渴；渴望；熱望：*~ for* (liter and biblical, *after*) (文學及聖經，與 after 連用) *revenge.* 渴望復仇。**~y** *adj* (-ier, -iest) having or causing ~: 渴的；使人口渴的：*be / feel ~y.* 口渴。*Some kinds of food make one ~y.* 有些種類的食物吃了使人口渴。*Tennis is a ~y game on a hot day.* 熱天打網球是一種令人口渴的運動。*The fields are ~y for rain.* 田地亢旱需要雨水。**~·ily** /-ɪlɪ ; -əlɪ/ *adv*

thir·teen /ˌθɜːˈtiːn ; θɝˈtin/ *adj, n* the number 13. 十三(的)；十三個。⇨ App 4. 參看附錄四。**thir·teenth** /ˌθɜːˈtiːnθ ; θɝˈtinθ/ *adj, n* next after the twelfth; one of ~ equal parts. 第十三(的)；十三分之一(的)。

thirty /ˈθɜːtɪ ; ˈθɝtɪ/ *adj, n* the number 30. 三十(的)；三十個。⇨ App 4. 參看附錄四。**the thirties,** 30-39. 三十至三十九之間；三十年代。**thir·ti·eth** /ˈθɜːtɪəθ ; ˈθɝtɪɪθ/ *adj, n* next after the 29th; one of ~ equal parts. 第三十(的)；三十分之一(的)。

this /ðɪs ; ðɪs/ (*pl* these /ðiːz ; ðiz/) *adj, pron* (contrasted with *that, those.* *~ / these* and *that / those* are used to make a person or thing specific. *~ / these* are used when the person or thing is near in space or time to the speaker.) (與 that, those 相對。this, these 與 that, those 均用以特指人或物。this 和 these 用來指在空間或時間上距說話者較近者。) **1** *Look at ~ box / these boxes here.* 看這裏的這個(這些)盒子。*What's ~ over here?* 這個是什麼？*What are these?* 這些是什麼？*Are these books yours?* 這些書是你的嗎？ *Are these your children?* 這些孩子是你(們)的嗎？ *Is ~ what you want?* 這就是你要的嗎？*T~ (one) is larger than that.* 這個比那個大。*These are better than those.* 這些比那些好。*Do it like ~,* ie in ~ way, as shown here, etc. 照這樣去做。*Life is difficult these days,* nowadays. 目前謀生不容易了。*He will be here ~ Thursday,* Thursday of ~ week. 他將於這個星期四來此。*What's all ~?* (colloq) What's the trouble? What's happening? (俗)這是怎麼一回事？怎麼了？(有什麼麻煩？或，發生了何事？) **2** (*T~* and a possessive cannot be used together. Note the construction used when ~ and a possessive are both needed): (this 與所有格不能連在一起用。注意下列例句中 this 與所有格同時使用的結構)：*T~ car of yours needs a thorough overhaul.* 你的這部汽車需要澈底檢修。*These new shoes of mine are painfully tight.* 我的這雙新鞋太緊，夾得脚疼。**3** (in narrative) a certain: (故事中)某一個：*Then ~ funny little man came up to me.* 然後一個有趣的小矮子向我走過來。*We all ended up at ~ pub.* 我們統統到一家酒館(痛飲)。□ *adv* (colloq) to ~ degree; so: (俗)到此程度；如此：*It's about ~ high.* (它)大約有這麼高。*Now that we have come ~ far* (= as far as ~)*....* 我們既然已經走了這麼遠…。*Can you spare me ~ much* (= as much as ~)*?* 你能不能勻給我這麼多？ *I know ~ much* (= what I am about to state), *that his story is exaggerated.* 就我所知，他的故事過分誇大。

thistle /ˈθɪsl ; ˈθɪsḷ/ *n* [C] (sorts of) wild plant with prickly leaves and yellow, white or purple flowers. 薊(野生植物，葉帶刺，開黃、白或紫色花)。**'~-down** *n* [U] fluff of ~ flowers, carrying the seed. 薊花的冠毛(帶有種子)。

thither /ˈðɪðə(r) *US:* ˈθɪðər ; ˈθɪðɚ/ *adv* (old use) to that place; in that direction. (舊用法)到彼處；向彼方。**hither and ~,** here and there; in all directions. 到處；向各方。

tho' /ðəʊ; ðo/ *adv, conj* (informal spelling of) though. 爲 though 之非正式拼法。

thole /θəʊl; θol/ *n* (also 亦作 '~-**pin**) pin or peg in the gunwale of a boat to keep an oar secure; one of two pins between which an oar is held. 橈座;槳座;槳架。⇨ rowlock.

thong /θɒŋ *US:* θɔːŋ; θɔŋ/ *n* narrow strip of leather, eg as a fastening, the lash of a whip. 狹長的皮帶(如用以繫物或用作鞭梢)。

tho·rax /'θɔːræks; 'θoræks/ *n* **1** part of an animal's body between the neck and the belly, eg in a man, the chest. 動物的胸;(人的)胸部。 **2** middle of the three main sections of an insect (bearing the legs and wings). 昆蟲身體三主節的中間一節。⇨ the illus at insect. 參看 insect 之挿圖。

thorn /θɔːn; θɔrn/ *n* **1** [C] sharp-pointed growth on the stem of a plant. (植物之)刺;棘。⇨ the illus at flower. 參看 flower 之挿圖。***a ~ in one's flesh/side,*** (fig) constant source of annoyance. (喻)經常苦惱的原因;不斷使人煩惱的事物;芒刺在背。 **2** [C, U] (usu in compounds) kinds of shrub or tree with ~s: (通常用於複合字中)荆棘;有刺的樹: '*haw~;* 山楂; '*black~*. 黑刺李。 **~y** *adj* (-ier, -iest) **1** having ~s. 有刺的;多刺的。 **2** (fig) full of trouble and difficulty; causing argument: (喻)麻煩多的;困難多的;棘手的;引起爭論的: *a ~y problem/subject.* 棘手的問題(題目)。

thor·ough /'θʌrə *US:* -rəʊ; 'θɝo/ *adj* complete in every way; not forgetting or overlooking anything; detailed: 完全的;徹底的;周到的;詳細的;充分的: *a ~ worker;* 徹底的工作者; *receive ~ instruction in English;* 接受完善的英語訓練; *give a room a ~ cleaning;* 把房間徹底打掃一番; *be ~ in one's work.* 工作認眞。 '~-**going** *adj* ~; complete; uncompromising. 徹底的;完全的;十足的;不妥協的: *a ~-going revision.* 徹底的校訂。 **~·ly** *adv* **~·ness** *n*

thor·ough·bred /'θʌrəbred; 'θɝo,brɛd/ *n, adj* (animal, esp a horse, also fig, person) of pure breed; high-spirited, thoroughly trained. 純種的;純種的動物(尤指馬);(喻)精神奕奕的(人);經過嚴格訓練的(人)。

thor·ough·fare /'θʌrəfeə(r); 'θɝo,fɛr/ *n* [C] road or street, esp one much used by traffic and open at both ends: 通衢;大道;大街: *The Strand is one of London's busiest ~s.* 斯特蘭德大街是倫敦最熱鬧的要衢之一。*No ~,* (as a sign) Not open to the public; no way through. (用作告示)禁止通行。

those /ðəʊz; ðoz/ *pl* of that.

thou /ðaʊ; ðaʊ/ *pron* (archaic) you (*sing*). (古)你。 **thee** /ðiː; ði/ *pron* object form of ~. 你(thou 的受格形式)。

though /ðəʊ; ðo/ *conj* **1** (also 亦作 **al·~** /ɔːl'ðəʊ; ɔl'ðo/) in spite of the fact that; notwithstanding the fact that: 雖然;雖則: *Al~ it was so cold, he went out without an overcoat.* 天氣雖然很冷,他沒有穿大衣就出去了。(cf 參較 *but*: It was very cold, but he.... 天很冷,但是他…。) *T~ they are so poor, they have enough to eat.* 他們雖然很窮,食物還是够吃的。 *He passed the examination al~ he had been prevented by illness from studying.* 雖然他一直生病無法念書,他還是考及格了。 **2** (also 亦作 **al·~** and **even ~**) even if: 卽使;縱然: *strange ~ it may appear/al~ it may appear strange,* even if it appears strange. 卽使看來有點奇怪(雖似奇怪)。 *He will never be dishonest even ~ he (should) be reduced to poverty.* 卽使他淪爲貧困,他也決不會不誠實。 **3** ***what ~,*** (liter) what does it matter if: (文)卽使…又有什麼關係: *What ~ the way be long,....* 卽使路途遙遠又有何妨…。 **4** ***as ~,*** ⇨ *as ~/as if* at as²(11). **5** (also 亦作 **al·~**) (introducing an independent statement) and yet; all the same: (引導獨立敍述)可是;然而;不過: *He will probably agree, ~ you never know,* and yet one can never be certain. 他很可能會同意,不過誰也不知道。 *I'll try to come, ~ I don't think I shall manage it.* 我會盡量來,不過我看我來不了。 □ *adv* (used absolutely, in the sense 5 above) however: (用於獨立敍述中,同上面第5義)可是;然而;不過: *He will probably agree; you never know, ~.* 他很可能同意;不過沒有人知道。 *He said he would come; he didn't, ~.* 他說他會來;不過他沒有來。

thought¹ /θɔːt; θɔt/ *pt, pp* of think¹.

thought² /θɔːt; θɔt/ *n* **1** [U] (power, process of) thinking: 思索;思考;思考力;思考的過程: *He spends hours in ~.* 他經常思考好幾個小時。 *He was lost/deep in ~,* thinking so deeply as to be unaware of his surroundings, etc. 他陷於沉思中。 **2** [U] way of thinking characteristic of a particular period, class, nation, etc: (某一時期、階層、國家等的)思想;思潮: *Greek/working-class/scientific/modern ~.* 希臘(工人階級,科學,現代)思想。 **3** [U] ***~ (for),*** care, consideration: 懸念;顧慮;關懷;考慮: *after serious ~.* 認眞考慮後。 *He often acts without ~.* 他常常魯莽行事。 *The nurse was full of ~ for her patient.* 那護士非常關懷她的病人。 ***take ~ for,*** be concerned about. 顧慮到;對…懸念。 **4** [C, U] idea, opinion, intention, formed by thinking: (由思考形成的)觀念;概念;意見;意向;企圖: *His speech was full of striking ~s.* 他的演講充滿了不平凡的見解。 *Please write and let me have your ~s on the matter.* 請寫信讓我知道你對此事的意見。 *That boy hasn't a ~ in his head.* 那男孩不用腦筋(自己沒有主見)。 *He keeps his ~s to himself,* does not tell anyone what he thinks. 他不對別人吐露心事。 *She says she can read my ~s.* 她說她能看出我的意向。 *He had no ~ (= intention) of hurting your feelings.* 他無意傷你的感情。 *You must give up all ~ of marrying Tom.* 你必須完全放棄與湯姆結婚的念頭。 *I had some ~ of going* (= had half intended to go) *to Spain this summer.* 今年夏天我曾經打算到西班牙去。 ***on ˌsecond '~s,*** after further consideration. 再思之後;經過進一步考慮。'~-**reader** *n* person who claims to know people's ~s. 自稱瞭解旁人思想者;讀心術者。 '~ **transference,** telepathy. 心靈感應。 **5** ***a ~,*** a little: 些微;稍稍;一點: *You should be a ~ more considerate of other people.* 你應該多體諒旁人一點。 **~·ful** /-fl; -fəl/ *adj* **1** full of ~; showing ~: 深思的;思索的: *~ful looks.* 深思的表情。 **2** considerate; thinking of, showing ~(3) for, the needs of others: 體諒的;體貼的;關切的;顧慮到旁人需要的: *a ~ful friend.* 關心旁人的朋友。 *It was ~ful of you to warn me of your arrival.* 你來之前先通知我,眞是顧慮得很周到。 **~·fully** /-fəlɪ; -fəlɪ/ *adv* **~·ful·ness** *n* **~·less** *adj* **1** careless; unthinking: 欠考慮的;粗心的;疏忽的;不注意的: *Young people are often ~less for the future.* 年輕人常常沒想到未來。 **2** selfish; inconsiderate (*of* others): 自私的;不顧及別人的(與 of 連用): *a ~less action.* 自私的行爲。 **~·less·ly** *adv* **~·less·ness** *n*

thou·sand /'θaʊznd; 'θaʊzn̩d/ *adj, n* the number 1000, ⇨ App 4; (loosely, exaggerated style) a great number: 千(的);千個(的)(參看附錄四);(非嚴格地,誇張用法)大數目;成千上萬: *A ~ thanks for your kindness.* 多謝你的盛情。 *He made a ~ and one excuses.* 他的藉口多極了。 ***a ˌ~ to 'one (chance),*** remote (possibility). 極小的(可能性);渺茫的(機會)。 ***one in a ~,*** a rare exception. 稀有的例外;千不挑一;極優秀的人物。 **~th** /'θaʊznθ; 'θaʊzn̩dθ/ *adj, n* **~·fold** /-fəʊld; -'fold/ *adj, adv* a ~ times (as much or many). 千倍的(地)。

thrall /θrɔːl; θrɔl/ *n* [C, U] (condition of being a) slave: 奴隸;爲奴的狀況: (fig) (喻) *He is (in) ~ to his passions.* 他是感情的奴隸(感情用事)。 **thral·dom** /-dəm; -dəm/ *n* [U] slavery. 奴役;奴隸的身分。

thrash /θræʃ; θræʃ/ *vt, vi* **1** [VP6A] beat with a stick, whip, etc: 鞭打;笞打;棒打: *Stop ~ing that donkey, you cruel boy!* 不要打那驢子,你這殘忍的孩子! *He ~ed the boy soundly,* gave him a thorough beating. 他痛打那男孩。 *He threatened to ~ the life out of me.* 他威嚇着要打死我。 **2** [VP6A] (colloq) defeat (a team, etc) in a contest. (俗)競賽中擊敗(一隊等);勝過。 **3** [VP15B] ~ ***sth out,*** (colloq) (俗) **(a)** clear up (a problem, etc) by discussion. 藉討論而澄清或解決(一問題等)。**(b)** arrive at (the truth, a solution, etc) by discussion. 藉討論獲致(眞相,解決等)。 **4** [VP6A, 15A, 2C] (cause to) toss, move violently: (使)顚簸;(使)劇烈移動: *The whale ~ed the water with its tail.* 那條鯨魚用尾巴猛烈地打水。*The swimmer ~ed about in the water.* 那游泳者在水中用力地游動。*The gale made the branches of the trees ~ against the windows.* 强風吹得樹枝猛擊窗戶。 **5** = thresh. **~·ing** *n* [C] (esp) beating: (尤指)鞭打;笞打: *give sb/get a good ~ing;* 痛打某人(挨痛打); defeat, eg in games. (在比賽中)被擊敗;失敗。

thread /θred ; θrɛd/ *n* **1** [C, U] (length of) spun cotton, silk, flax, wool, etc esp for use in sewing and weaving: (一段)線;細絲;纖維(尤指用於縫紉及紡織者): *a reel of silk ~;* 一捲絲線; *a needle and ~;* 針線; *gold ~,* ~ with gold wire wound round it. 金線。***hang by a ~,*** (fig) be in a dangerous or precarious state. (喻)千鈞一髮;勢如累卵;處境危殆。 **2** sth very thin, suggesting a ~: 線狀物: *A ~ of light came through the keyhole.* 從鑰匙孔射出來一線光亮。 **3** chain or line (connecting parts of a story, etc): (連接故事等各部分的)線索;脈絡: *lose the ~ of one's argument;* 失去議論的線索; *gather up the ~s of a story,* bring parts of it together and relate them to one another; 綜合一個故事的脈絡; *pick up/resume the ~s,* continue (after an interruption). (打斷後)接續下去。 **4** spiral ridge round a screw or bolt. 螺紋。⇨ the illus at bolt. 參看 bolt 之插圖。 □ *vt* **1** [VP6A] pass a ~ through the eye of (a needle); put (beads, pearls, etc) on a ~; make (a chain of beads, etc) thus: 穿線於(針)孔;以線穿起(珠子、珍珠等);以線穿成(珠鍊等): *~ a film,* put it in place (eg in a ciné-projector, ready for showing it on a screen). 裝妥影片(以待放映等)。**2** [VP15A] ***~ one's way through,*** find, pick, one's way (through a crowd, streets, etc). 擠過(人叢等);穿過(街道等)。**3** (of hair) streak: (指頭髮)雜有…的髮絲: *black hair ~ed with silver,* with streaks of silver hair in it. 雜有銀絲的黑髮。 **ˈ~·bare** /-beə(r) ; -ˌbɛr/ *adj* **1** (of cloth) worn thin; shabby: (指布)磨薄的;襤褸的: *a ~bare coat.* 襤褸的上衣。 **2** (fig) much used and therefore uninteresting or valueless; hackneyed: (喻)陳腐的;無趣的;用舊的: *~bare jokes/arguments.* 陳舊的笑話(議論)。**ˈ~·like** *adj* resembling a ~; long and slender. 像線的;細長的。

threat /θret ; θrɛt/ *n* [C] **1** statement of an intention to punish or hurt sb, esp if he does not do as one wishes: 恐嚇;威脅: *utter a ~ (against sb);* 威嚇(某人); *carry out a ~;* 採取恐嚇; *be under the ~ of expulsion,* eg from a university. 受到開除的威脅;有被開除之虞。 **2** ***a/the ~ (to sb/sth) (of sth),*** sign or warning of coming trouble, danger, etc: 惡兆;壞兆頭;不祥之兆: *the ~ to the country's economy of inflation.* 該國通貨膨脹之危機。*There was a ~ of rain in the dark sky.* 天空黑雲密佈有下雨的朕兆。

threaten /ˈθretn ; ˈθrɛtn̩/ *vt, vi* **1** [VP6A, 14, 17] ***~ sth; ~ sb (with sth); ~ to do sth,*** announce sth, using a threat; be a threat of sth to sb; use a threat (of sth) against sb: 恐嚇;威脅;威脅着要;揚言要: *~ an employee with dismissal;* 用開革威脅一位雇員; *~ an enemy;* 恐嚇敵人; *~ to murder sb.* 揚言要謀殺某人。*They ~ed revenge.* 他們揚言要報復。*The race was ~ed with extinction,* It seemed possible that all people of this race would die. 這種族有滅絕之虞。 **2** [VP6A, 2A] give warning of: 預示;有…朕兆: *The clouds ~ed rain.* 這烏雲預示有雨。*It ~s to rain.* 天有下雨之勢。 **3** [VP2A] seem likely to occur or come: 似有發生或來臨的可能;似將發生;可能來臨: *Knowing that danger ~ed, the sentry kept an extra careful watch.* 因爲知道隨時有危險發生,那崗哨特別注意戒備。**~·ing·ly** *adv*

three /θriː ; θri/ *adj, n* the number 3, ⇨ App 4: 三(的);三個(的)(參看附錄四): *a ~-act play,* one with ~ acts. 三幕劇。**ˌ~-ˈcornered** *adj* triangular: 三角形的: *a ~-cornered contest/fight,* with ~ contestants or competitors, eg in a Parliamentary election. 三角競爭(戰鬥)(有三個角逐者參加者,如競爭下議院席位)。⇨ *straight fight* at straight¹(5). **ˌ~-ˈD,** (abbr for) *~-dimensional.* 爲 ~-dimensional 之略。⇨ below. 參看下列之 ~-dimensional。**ˌ~-ˈdecker** *n* **(a)** old type of sailing-ship with ~ decks. (舊式的)三層甲板的帆船或軍艦。 **(b)** kind of sandwich with ~ layers of bread and two layers of filling. 三層三明治(有三層麵包,兩層夾物)。 **(c)** novel in ~ volumes (common in the 18th and 19th cc). 三部頭小說(十八九世紀間甚爲流行)。**ˌ~-diˈmensional** *adj* (abbr 略作 **3-D**) having, or appearing to have, ~ dimensions (length, breadth and depth); stereoscopic. 三度空間(長、寬、高)的;具有或似有三度空間的;立體的。**ˌ~-ˈfigure** *adj* (of numbers) between 100 and 999 (inclusive). (指數字)三位數字(100 與 999 之間者)的。**~·pence** /ˈθriːpens ; ˈθrɪpəns/ *n* the sum of ~ pence. 三辨士金額。**~·penny** /ˈθriːpenɪ ; ˈθriˌpɛnɪ/ *adj* costing or worth ~ pence: 價值三辨士的: *a ~penny stamp.* 三辨士的郵票。**ˌ~-ˈlane** *adj* (of a roadway) marked for ~ lanes of traffic. (指車道)三線車道的。**ˌ~-ˈlegged** /-ˈlegɪd ; -ˈlɛgɪd/ *adj* **(a)** having ~ legs: 三條腿的: *a ~-legged stool.* 三條腿的櫈子。**(b)** (of a race) one in which the competitors run in pairs, the right leg of one runner being tied to the left leg of the other. (指賽跑)兩人三脚賽跑(兩人爲一組,中間的兩腿綁在一起)。**ˌ~-ˈpiece** *adj* consisting of ~ pieces: 三件式的: *a ~-piece suit,* set of ~ garments (a man's jacket, waistcoat and trousers, or a woman's jacket, skirt/trousers and blouse); 三件頭的衣服(男服包括上下裝及背心,女服包括上裝、裙或褲、及襯衫);*a ~-piece suite,* set of ~ pieces of furniture (usu a sofa and two armchairs). 三件式的傢俱(通常爲一個長沙發,兩個小沙發)。**ˌ~-ˈply** *adj* **(a)** (of wool, thread) having ~ strands. (指毛線,線)三股的。 **(b)** (of wood) having ~ layers glued together. (指木材)三層黏合的;三層的。**~-ˈquarter** *n* (Rugby football) person who plays between the half-backs and the full-back. (橄欖球)中衞。⇨ the illus at Rugby. 參看 Rugby 之插圖。□ *adj* (of a portrait) down to the hips. (指畫像)半身像。Cf 參較 *a full-length portrait* at full(7). **ˌ~-ˈscore** *adj, n* sixty. 六十(的)。**ˈ~·some** /-səm ; -səm/ *n* group of, or game played by, ~ persons. 三人之一組;三人一組之遊戲或競技。**ˌ~-ˈstorey(ed)** *adj* (of a building) having ~ storeys. (指建築)有三層的;三層的。**ˌ~-ˈwheeled** *adj* having ~ wheels. 有三個輪子的;三輪的。

thren·ody /ˈθrenədɪ ; ˈθrɛnədɪ/ *n* (*pl* -dies) song of lamentation; funeral song. 輓歌;哀歌。

thresh /θreʃ ; θrɛʃ/ *vt, vi* [VP6A, 15A, 2A] beat the grain out of (wheat, etc); beat wheat, etc for this purpose: 打(麥等);打穀: *~ corn by hand.* 用手打穀。*Have the farmers started ~ing yet?* 農夫們已開始打穀了嗎? **ˈ~·ing-floor** *n* part on which grain is ~ed out. 打穀場。**ˈ~·ing-machine** *n* one for ~ing grain. 打穀機。**~er** *n* **1** ~ing-machine; person who ~es. 打穀機;打穀者。 **2** large shark with a long tail. 長尾鯊魚;長尾鮫。

thresh·old /ˈθreʃhəʊld ; ˈθrɛʃold/ *n* [C] **1** stone or plank under an outside doorway; part of an entrance over which one must step: 門檻;門口: *cross the ~,* enter. 跨越門檻;進入。 **2** (fig) entrance, start, beginning: (喻)入口;開端;開始: *He was on the ~ of his career.* 他的事業剛剛開始。*We are at the ~ of an era of peace.* 我們是處於和平時代的開端。 **3** (physiol, psych) limit: (生理,心理)閾: *a pain ~,* point at which a sensation is felt as pain; 痛閾; *above/below the ~ of consciousness,* above/below the limit at which we are aware of things. 在意識閾之上(下);有意識作用(下意識)的。⇨ subliminal.

threw /θruː ; θru/ *pt* of throw¹.

thrice /θraɪs ; θraɪs/ *adv* (rarely used) three times. (罕用)三倍地;三度地。

thrift /θrɪft ; θrɪft/ *n* [U] care, economy, in the use of money or goods. 節儉;儉約。**~y** *adj* (-ier, -iest) **1** economical; using ~. 節儉的;儉約的。**2** (US) thriving; prosperous. (美)旺盛的;繁榮的。**~ily** /-ɪlɪ ; -ɪlɪ/ *adv* **~less** *adj* without ~; wasteful. 不節儉的;浪費的;奢侈的。**~less·ly** *adv* **~less·ness** *n*

thrill /θrɪl ; θrɪl/ *n* [C] (experience causing an) excited feeling passing like a wave along the nerves: 激動;震顫;震顫感;令人震顫的經驗: *a ~ of joy/pleasure/horror.* 一陣高興(愉快,恐怖)。*It gave her quite a ~ to shake hands with the Princess.* 同公主握手使她至感興奮。*This film will give you the ~ of a lifetime,* excite you as you have never been excited before. 這部電影將會帶給你前所未有的刺激。□ *vt, vi* **1** [VP6A] cause a ~ or ~s in: 使震顫;使激動;使生震顫感: *The film ~ed the audience.* 那部電影帶給觀衆很大的刺激。*We were ~ed with horror/joy.* 我們恐懼(喜悅)極了。**2** [VP2A, C] feel a ~ or ~s: 感到震顫或激動: *We ~ed at the good news.* 我們聽到那項好消息感到很興奮。*She ~ed with delight when the handsome footballer kissed her.* 當那位英俊的足球員親吻她的時候,她高興得顫抖。*There was a ~ing finish to the race.* 最後一段賽程非常緊張刺激。**~er** *n* novel, play or film in which excitement and emotional appeal are the essential elements. 驚險、動人、恐怖、刺激等的小說、戲劇或電影。

thrive /θraɪv ; θraɪv/ *vi* (*pt* ~d or (archaic) 或(古) throve /θrəʊv ; θrov/, *pp* ~d or (archaic) 或(古) thriven /ˈθrɪvn ; ˈθrɪvən/) [VP2A, 3A] ~ ***(on sth),*** prosper; succeed; grow strong and healthy: 興盛;成功;長得健壯: *A business cannot ~ without good management.* 管理不善的企業不可能興盛。*Children ~ on good food.* 兒童要吃得好才能長得健壯。*He has a thriving business.* 他的生意興旺。

thro' /θruː ; θru/ (informal spelling of) through. 爲 through 的非正式拼法。

throat /θrəʊt ; θrot/ *n* **1** front part of the neck: 喉頭: *grip sb by the ~;* 抓住某人的喉頭;*cut one's ~,* eg intending to commit suicide or (fig) destroy one's own opportunities. 割喉嚨(如企圖自殺);(喻)自取滅亡;自毀前程;毀壞自己的機會。⇨ the illus at head. 參看 head 之挿圖。**'cut-~** *attrib adj* **(a)** (of a razor) having a long movable blade set into the handle, ⇨ the illus at razor. (指剃刀)有活動長刃和把手的(參看 razor 之挿圖)。**(b)** (of competition, etc) intense and ruthless. (指競爭等)劇烈而無情的;殘酷的。**2** passage in the neck through which food passes to the stomach and air to the lungs: 咽喉;喉嚨: *A bone has stuck in my ~.* 有一根骨頭梗在我的喉嚨。***force/thrust sth down sb's ~,*** (fig) try to make sb accept one's views, beliefs, etc. (喻)勉强旁人接受自己的見解、信仰等。***stick in one's ~,*** (fig) not be readily acceptable. 梗在喉頭;(喻)不能立刻接受。**-~ed** in compounds: 用於複合字中: *a red-~ed bird.* 紅脖子鳥。**~y** *adj* (-ier, -iest) uttered deep in the ~: 喉音的;發自喉嚨深處的: *a ~y voice,* guttural. 喉音;低沈重濁的聲音。

throb /θrɒb ; θrɑb/ *vi* (-bb-) [VP2A, C] (of the heart, pulse, etc) beat, esp beat more rapidly than usual: (指心臟、脈搏等)跳動;悸動(尤指跳動較平常快): *His head ~bed,* He had a bad headache. 他頭痛得很厲害。*His wound ~bed with pain.* 他的傷口陣陣地疼痛。*Her heart was ~bing with excitement.* 她的心因興奮而跳得很快。□ *n* [C] ~bing or vibration: 跳動;悸動;震顫: *~s of joy/pleasure;* 一陣陣的高興(愉快); *the ~ of distant gun-fire.* 遠處陣陣的砲聲。**~·bing** *adj* that ~s: 跳動的;悸動的;震顫的: *the ~bing (sound of) machinery.* 機器的震顫(聲)。

throe /θrəʊ ; θro/ *n* **~s,** sharp pains, esp of childbirth. 劇痛;(尤指)分娩時的陣痛。***in the ~s of sth/of doing sth,*** (colloq) struggling with the task of it/doing it: (俗)辛苦地做某事;苦幹: *in the ~s of an examination/of packing one's luggage.* 爲考試(包捆行李)而辛苦。

throm·bo·sis /θrɒmˈbəʊsɪs ; θrɑmˈbosɪs/ *n* [U] clot of blood in a blood-vessel or in the heart. (血管或心臟的)栓塞;血栓形成。

throne /θrəʊn ; θron/ *n* [C] **1** ceremonial chair or seat of a king, queen, bishop, etc. (國王、女王、主教等的)寶座;御座。**2 the ~,** royal authority: 王權;王位;帝位: *come to the ~,* become king/queen; 登王位;即位; *united in loyalty to the T~,* to the Sovereign. 團結一致效忠帝王。

throng /θrɒŋ *US:* θrɔːŋ ; θrɔŋ/ *n* crowd. 群;群衆。□ *vt, vi* [VP6A, 4A, 2C] crowd: 擠;群集: *The railway stations were ~ed with people going away for their holidays.* 火車站擠滿了外出度假的人們。*People ~ed to see the new play.* 人們蜂擁着去觀賞那齣新戲。

throstle /ˈθrɒsl ; ˈθrɑsl/ *n* song-thrush. 善鳴的畫眉鳥。

throttle /ˈθrɒtl ; ˈθrɑtl/ *vt, vi* **1** [VP6A] seize (sb) by the throat and stop his breathing; choke; strangle: 扼(某人)的喉頭;勒死;使窒息;縊死: *~ the nightwatchman and then rob the bank.* 勒死守夜者然後搶刼銀行。*The tyrant ~d freedom in his country.* 那個暴君在他的國家內壓制自由。**2** [VP6A, 15B, 2C] ~ ***(back/down),*** control the flow of steam, petrol vapour, etc in an engine; lessen the speed of (an engine) by doing this. 控制引擎或機車的蒸氣流、氣化汽油等;調整節氣閥以減低(引擎)的速度;節流。□ *n* **'~(-valve)** valve controlling the flow of steam, petrol vapour, etc in an engine: 節氣閥;節流閥: *open out the ~;* 打開節氣閥; *close the ~;* 關閉節氣閥; *with the ~ full open.* 全速地。

through¹ /θruː ; θru/ *adv* (⇨ the *v* entries; 參看各動詞; specimens only here 以下僅舉範例) **1** from end to end, beginning to end, side to side: 自一端至另一端;貫穿地;自始至終: *They wouldn't let us ~,* eg pass ~ the gate. 他們不讓我們過去(如通過大門等)。*Did your brother get ~,* eg the examination? 你的哥哥(弟弟)通過(考試等)了嗎?*He slept the whole night ~,* all night. 他睡了一個通宵。*His trousers are ~* (= have holes or rents in them) *at the knees.* 他的褲子膝頭已破了。*Read the book ~ carefully.* 把這本書仔細讀完。***all ~,*** all the time (while sth was happening, etc): (當某事發生等之際)始終;一直;老是: *I knew all ~ that he was lying.* 我完全知道他在說謊。**2** to the very end. 徹底地;到最後。***be ~ (with),*** **(a)** finish (with): 結束;做好;完成: *When will you be ~ with your work?* 你什麼時候可以做完你的工作? **(b)** (colloq) have had enough of; be tired of: (俗)對…已經厭煩: *I'm ~ with this job; I must find something more interesting.* 我厭煩這項工作;我必須找一份更有趣味的工作做。***go ~ with sth,*** continue until it is finished or completed. 貫徹某事;繼續做完某事;完成某事。***see sth ~,*** be present at, help in, a series of events, etc until the end. 將某事做到底;參與或協助貫徹某事。***~ and ~,*** in all parts; completely: 完全地;徹底地: *He's a reliable man ~ and ~.* 他是一個完全可靠的人。*You're wet ~/~ and ~,* Your clothes are thoroughly wet. 你全身濕透了。**3** all the way to: 全程地;直達地: *This train goes ~ to Paris,* There is no need to change trains. 這列火車直達巴黎(無須換車)。*Book your tickets/luggage ~ to Vienna.* 訂購直達維也納的車票(把你的行李托運至維也納)。**4** (telephoning) (電話) **(a)** (GB) connected: (英)接通: *I will put you ~ to the manager,* connect you. 我將把你的電話接到經理那裡。*You're ~,* Your telephone connection has been made. 你的電話接

通了。**(b)** (US) finished; not wishing to continue the call. (美)講完了;不打算繼續講話。 **5** (used, in the sense of 3 above, to modify *nn*): (用以修飾名詞,其意義與上面第3義同): *a ~ train to Paris;* 到巴黎的直達火車; *~ tickets/passengers/fares;* 直達車的車票(乘客,車費); *~ traffic,* road traffic which is going ~ a place (contrasted with local traffic). 直達車(與區間車相對)。 **'~·put** /-pʊt; -ˌpʊt/ *n* [U, C] output; amount of material put ~ a process. 生產量;生產總額。 **'~·way** *n* ~ express way. 高速公路。⇨ express[1](2).

through[2] (US in informal writing also 在美國非正式寫作中亦作 **thru**) /θruː; θru/ *prep* **1** (of places) from end to end or side to side of; entering at one side, on one surface, etc and coming out at the other: (指地方)從一端至另一端;從一邊至另一邊;穿過;貫穿;經過: *The River Thames flows ~ London.* 泰晤士河流經倫敦。*The burglar came in ~ the window.* 夜賊是從窗戶進來的。*The road goes ~ the forest.* 該路穿越那森林。*There is a path ~* (= across) *the fields.* 有一條小路穿過田野。*She passed a comb/her fingers ~ her hair.* 她用梳子(用她的手指)攏梳她的頭髮。*He was looking ~ a telescope.* 他從望遠鏡裏觀望。*One can see ~ glass.* 人能從玻璃看過去。 **2** (fig uses; 比喻用法; ⇨ the *v* entries; 參看各該動詞; specimens only here 下列僅係範例): *He went ~/has come ~* (= experienced) *many hardships.* 他經歷過許多艱辛。*He soon got/went ~* (= got to the end of, spent the whole of) *his fortune.* 他很快就花光了他的財產。*We must go ~* (= examine) *the accounts.* 我們必須查閱帳目。*He got ~* (= passed) *the examination.* 他通過了考試。*He saw ~* (= was not deceived by) *the trick.* 他看穿了那項詭計(未受騙)。 **3** (of time) from beginning to end of: (指時間)從頭至尾;自始至終: *He won't live ~ the night,* He will die before morning. 他活不過今晚了。*The children are too young to sit ~ a long concert.* 孩子們太小,不能坐着聽完冗長的音樂會。 **4** (US) up to and including: (美)一直到並包括: *We'll be in London from Tuesday ~ Saturday.* 從星期二至星期六,我們將在倫敦。 **5** (indicating the agency, means or cause): (表示作用、方法、工具或原因): *I learnt of the position ~ a newspaper advertisement.* 我從報上一則廣告獲知這一職位。*The accident happened ~ no fault of yours.* 這意外事件的發生,並非由於你的過失。*We lost ourselves ~ not knowing the way.* 我們因爲不認識路而迷失了。*It was all ~ you* (= It was your fault) *that we were late.* 我們之所以遲到,完全要怪你。 **6** without stopping for: 一直;繼續不斷;未停下;闖過: *Don't drive ~ a red light.* 不要駕車闖過紅燈。

through·out /θruːˈaʊt; θruˈaʊt/ *adv* right through; in every part; in all ways or respects: 一直;全部;各處;各方面: *The coat is lined with fur ~.* 那外套全部用毛皮做襯裡。*The woodwork in the house was rotten ~.* 那幢房子的木造部分整個腐爛了。□ *prep* all or right through; from end to end of: 遍及;在整個期間;從一端至另一端: *~ the country;* 遍及全國;整個國家; *~ the length and breadth of the land;* 遍及該土地; *~ the war.* 在整個戰爭期間。

throve /θrəʊv; θrov/ ⇨ thrive.

throw[1] /θrəʊ; θro/ *vt, vi* (*pt* threw /θruː; θru/, *pp* thrown /θrəʊn; θron/) (For special uses with *adverbial particles* and *preps,* ⇨ 12 below) (與副詞接語及介詞連用的特殊用法,參看下列第12義) **1** [VP 2A, 6A, 15A, B, 12A, 13A] cause (sth) to go through the air, usu with force, by a movement of the arm or by mechanical means: 投;抛;擲;扔: *He ~s well.* 他擲得很好。*He can ~ a hundred yards.* 他能擲一百碼遠。*Don't ~ stones at my dog!* 不要向我的狗投石子!*He threw the ball to his sister.* 他把球抛給他的姊姊(妹妹)。*Please ~ me that towel.* 請把那條毛巾丟給我。*He threw the ball up and caught it.* 他把球抛起再把它接住。*He seized the man and threw him to the ground.* 他抓住那人,把他摔在地上。*The drunken man was thrown out.* 那醉漢被推出門外。*He threw an angry look at me/me an angry look.* 他對我怒目而視。 **2** [VP15A, B] put (articles of clothing) (*on, off, over,* etc) quickly or carelessly: 匆忙或粗心地穿、脫、披起(衣物等): *~ off one's clothes/disguise;* 匆促脫去衣服(卸下僞裝); *~ a scarf over one's shoulders.* 匆忙把圍巾披在肩上。 **3** [VP15A, B] move (one's arms, legs, etc) (*out, up, down, about*) violently: 用力或猛烈地移動(臂、腿等): *~ one's chest out;* 用力挺起胸膛; *~ up one's arms;* 用力舉臂; *~ one's head back.* 把頭用力向後仰。*You'll never learn to swim properly while you ~ your legs and arms about so wildly.* 你這樣猛烈地划動腿和臂,永遠不會把游泳學好。 **4** [VP6A] **(a)** (of a horse) cause the rider to fall to the ground: (指馬)把騎者摔在地上: *Two of the jockeys were ~n in the second race.* 兩位騎師在第二次賽馬時被摔了下來。**(b)** (of a wrestler) force (an opponent) to the floor. (指摔角者)摔倒(對手)。**(c)** (of a snake) cast (its skin). (指蛇)蛻(皮)。**(d)** (of animals) bring forth (young). (指動物)生產(幼仔)。 **5** [VP6A] (of dice) ~ on to the table (after shaking them in sth); get by doing this: (指骰子)擲出;擲得: *~ three sixes.* 擲得三個六點。 **6** [VP6A] twist (silk) into threads. 搓(絲)成線。 **7** [VP6A] shape (pottery) on a potter's wheel. 在拉坯輪車上製成(陶器)。 **8** [VP6A] (colloq) disturb; distress; distract: (俗)驚擾;使苦惱;使分心: *The news of her death really threw me.* 她去世的消息眞使我難過。 **9** (sl) (俚) ***~ a party,*** give a party. 舉行宴會、酒會等。***~ a fit,*** have a fit. 大驚;大怒;突然發作等。⇨ fit[3](2). **10** ***~ sth open (to),*** [VP22] **(a)** make (eg a competition) open to all persons. 公開舉行(競賽等)。**(b)** allow the general public to enter (eg gardens which are usually closed). 開放(如通常關閉的花園)。 **11** [VP6A] (with *nn,* to which cross-references are given): (與名詞連用,參看各名詞): ***~ cold water on sth,*** ⇨ water[1](1). ***~ doubt upon,*** ⇨ doubt[1]. ***~ dust in sb's eyes,*** ⇨ dust[1](1). ***~ down the gauntlet,*** ⇨ gauntlet[1](1). ***~ light on,*** ⇨ light[3](5). ***~ a sop to Cerberus,*** ⇨ sop. ***~ one's weight about,*** ⇨ weight. **12** [VP15B, 14, 2C] (special uses with *adverbial particles* and *preps*): (與副詞接語及介詞連用的特殊用法):

throw sth about, scatter: 撒佈;亂抛: *Don't ~ waste paper about in the park.* 不要在公園亂抛紙屑。*He's ~ing his money about,* (fig) spending it recklessly. (喻)他在胡亂花錢。

throw oneself at, **(a)** rush violently at. 衝向;向…突進。**(b)** force one's attentions on; behave without restraint in an effort to win the love of. 全力爭取…的愛、友誼或恩寵;博取…的歡心;勾引。

throw sth away, **(a)** lose by foolishness or neglect: 因愚蠢或疏忽而失去;抛却;丢掉: *~ away an advantage.* 失去優勢。*My advice was ~n away upon him,* wasted. 我對他的忠告是白費了。 **(b)** (of words spoken by actors, broadcasters, etc) utter in a casual way, with conscious under-emphasis. (指演員、廣播員等所說的話)有意不予强調;輕輕帶過;點到卽止。Hence, 由此產生, **'~·away** *n* sth that may be ~n away (eg a printed handbill); sth of small value, discarded after use: 可予抛棄之物(如廣告單);價值小而且用過卽可丢棄之物: (attrib) (形容用法) *a ~away ballpen;* 用完卽可抛棄的原子筆; *a ~away line,* sth spoken casually, without emphasis. 可輕輕帶過的話(隨便說出,無須加重)。

throw back, show characteristics of, revert to, a remote ancestor. 顯示出遠祖的特徵;返回祖先型態;祖型重現。Hence, 由此產生, **'~-back** *n* (example of) reversion to an ancestral type. 祖型重現;返祖現象;其實例。***~ sb back on/upon sth,*** (often passive) force sb to go back to (because nothing else is available): (常用被動語態)迫使重新依靠(某事物);

迫使反求(某事): *After this failure to get help we were ~n back upon our own resources.* 經過這一次求助失敗以後,我們被迫依賴自己的力量。

throw oneself down, lie down at full length. 全身伸展地躺下;倒下。

throw sth in, **(a)** supply sth extra, without an addition to the price: 額外贈送: *You can have the piano for £60, with the stool ~n in.* 你可以用六十鎊購買那鋼琴,坐櫈奉送。 **(b)** put in (a remark, etc) casually. 偶爾挿進(話等);挿嘴說。**(c)** (football) ~ the ball in after it has gone out of play. (足球)球出界後把球扔進。Hence, 由此產生, **'~-in** *n.* ~ ***in one's hand,*** give up an attempt to do sth; confess one's inability to do sth. 放棄嘗試;承認無能爲力;坦承不能做某事。 ~ ***in one's lot with sb,*** decide to share his fortunes. 與某人同進退;與某人禍福與共。~ ***in the towel/sponge,*** (colloq) (from boxing) admit defeat. (俗)(來自拳擊)承認失敗。

throw oneself into sth, begin to work vigorously at. 投身於;開始積極從事。

throw sb/sth off, manage to get rid of; become free from: 擺脫某人或某事;除去: ~ *off a cold/a troublesome acquaintance/one's pursuers.* 傷風痊癒(擺脫一位討厭的熟人;擺脫追逐者)。 ~ ***sth off,*** produce or compose, easily, as if without effort: 輕易做成;輕易作出: ~ *off a few lines of verse.* 卽席寫成數行詩句。

throw oneself on/upon sb/sth, place one's reliance on: 仰賴於;信賴;委身於: ~ *oneself (up)on the mercy of one's captors/the court/the judge.* 任憑捕捉者(法庭,法官)的處置。

throw sth out, **(a)** utter (esp casually): 說出;(尤指無意間)吐露: ~ *out a hint/suggestion;* 作暗示(提出建議); ~ *out a challenge.* 出言挑戰。 **(b)** reject (a Bill in Parliament, etc). 否決(國會議案等)。**(c)** build as an extension: 增建;加蓋: ~ *out a new wing,* eg to a hospital or other large building. 增建一幢邊房或廂房。 ~ ***sb out,*** **(a)** (cricket, of a fielder) get (a batsman) out by ~ing the ball and hitting the wicket. (板球,指外場員)投球擊中三柱門而使(擊球員)出場。**(b)** disconcert or distract (sb whose attention is concentrated on sth) so that he makes an error, has to stop, etc: 使(某人)分心;擾亂(某人): *Keep quiet for a while or you'll ~ me out in my calculations.* 安靜一會兒,否則我就無法專心計算了。

throw sb over, desert, abandon: 放棄;捨棄: ~ *over an old friend/one's girlfriend.* 遺棄一位老朋友(女朋友)。

throw sth together, assemble hastily: 倉促地集成: *That last textbook of his seems to have been ~n together,* written or compiled carelessly and hurriedly. 他寫的最後一冊教科書似乎是倉促間編成的。 ~ ***people together,*** bring together: 集合;集攏: *Chance had ~n us together at a skiing resort.* 機緣使我們在一個滑雪勝地相遇。

throw sth up, **(a)** vomit (food). 吐出(食物);嘔。**(b)** resign from: 辭去: ~ *up one's job.* 辭職。~ ***sth up,*** bring it to notice: 使某物被人看到: *A search through his pockets threw up a very strange collection of objects.* 搜查他的口袋發現一些十分奇怪的東西。~ ***up one's hands (in horror),*** express horror by doing this. 嚇得舉起雙手。

throw[2] /θrəʊ ; θro/ *n* [C] throwing; distance to which sth is or may be thrown: 投;擲;拋;投擲的距離: *a well-aimed ~,* eg cricket, to get a batsman out; 一次準確投擲(如板球,使擊球員出局的一次投球); *a ~ of the dice;* 骰子的一擲; *a record ~ with the hammer* (as a competition in athletic sports). (運動會中)鏈球創記錄的一擲。 ***within a 'stone's ~ (of),*** quite near (to). 近在咫尺;在投石可及的距離內。

thru /θruː ; θru/ (US informal spelling for) through. (美)爲 through 的非正式拼法。

thrum /θrʌm ; θrʌm/ *vt, vi* (-mm-) [VP6A, 3A] ~ ***(on) sth,*** play monotonously or idly on (a stringed instrument): 漫彈或單調地彈(絃樂器); 彈弄: ~ *(on) a guitar,* ⇨ strum; 彈弄吉他; tap or drum idly with the fingers: 以手指輕敲或輕擊: ~ *on the table.* 以手指輕敲桌子。

thrush[1] /θrʌʃ ; θrʌʃ/ *n* [C] sorts of song-bird, esp the kind called *'song-~,* or *throstle.* 鶇;畫眉鳥(尤指善鳴的一種,稱作 song-~ 或 throstle).

thrush[2] /θrʌʃ ; θrʌʃ/ *n* internal inflammatory disease. 鵝口瘡;雪口症。

thrust /θrʌst ; θrʌst/ *vt, vi* (*pt, pp* ~) [VP6A, 15A, B, 2A, C] push suddenly or violently; make a forward stroke with a sword, etc: 力推;挿;擠;刺;戳: *He ~ his hands into his pockets/a dagger into his enemy's heart.* 他把雙手挿入衣袋內(把短劍刺入敵人的心臟中)。*We had to ~ our way through the crowd.* 我們不得不擠過人叢。 *They ~ themselves forward/past/into the bus.* 他們用力向前擠(擠過去,擠進公車)。*Some people have greatness ~ upon them,* ie obtain renown without their own effort. 有些人的成名是時勢造成的。*He has ~ himself into a well-paid position,* obtained one by ruthless methods. 他不擇手段取得一個待遇優厚的工作。□ *n* **1** [C] act of ~ing; (in war) strong attempt to push forward into the enemy's positions; (in debate, etc) attack in words; hostile remark aimed at sb. 推;擠;刺;戳;(作戰時之)挺進;突襲;(辯論等時之)口頭攻擊;抨擊;諷刺。 **2** [U] stress or pressure on a neighbouring part of a structure (eg an arch); force directed forward in a jet-engine as a reaction to the ejection rearward of gases. (拱等)向隣接部分的推壓(力量);(噴射引擎的)推進力;推力。**~er** *n* (esp) person who ~s himself forward (to win an advantage, etc). (尤指)爭先恐後(以取得某項利益等)者;鑽營者;强求名利者。

thud /θʌd ; θʌd/ *n* dull sound as of a blow on sth soft: 重擊聲;砰擊聲;重擊軟物聲: *The bullet entered his brain and he fell with a ~ to the carpet.* 子彈射進他的腦部,他砰然倒在地毯上。□ *vi* (-dd-) [VP 2C] strike, fall, with a ~: 砰然打擊或落下;重擊: *Bullets ~ded into the sandbags behind which we were sheltering.* 子彈砰砰地射進掩護我們的沙袋內。

thug /θʌg ; θʌg/ *n* violent criminal; murderous ruffian. 兇殘的罪犯;嗜殺的惡棍。**~·gery** *n* [U].

thumb /θʌm ; θʌm/ *n* short, thick finger set apart from the other four. 拇指。⇨ the illus at arm. 參看 arm 之挿圖。***(one's fingers) be all ~s; have ten ~s,*** be very clumsy. 十分笨拙;笨手笨脚。 ***rule of ~,*** method or procedure based on experience and practice. 根據經驗的作法;經驗得來的法則。***under sb's ~,*** under his influence and control. 在某人的影響或支配之下。 ***~s up/down,*** (phrase signifying success/failure). (表示成功或失敗的用語)。 **~-nail sketch,** portrait on a small scale; hasty word-picture. 小型畫像;速寫;簡略描述。 **'~·screw** *n* **(a)** (also 亦作 **'~-nut**) one that can be turned easily with the ~ and a finger. 翼形螺釘;翼形螺母。**(b)** old instrument of torture which squeezed the ~s. 拇指夾(昔時的刑具)。 **'~-stall** *n* sheath to cover an injured ~. 拇指套(保護受傷拇指者)。 **'~-tack** *n* (US) drawing-pin. (美)圖釘。□ *vt* **1** [VP 6A] turn over (pages, etc); make dirty by doing this: 翻動(書頁等);以拇指翻動而弄髒: ~ *the pages of a dictionary;* 翻動字典(的書頁); *a well-~ed book.* 常被翻動的書。 **2** ~ ***a lift,*** ask for (and get) a free ride in a motor-vehicle (by signalling to the driver). 向駕車者翹拇指要求(並獲准)搭便車。 ⇨ hitch-hike. ~ ***one's nose at sb,*** cock a snook at him. 把拇指放在鼻子上向某人張搖其餘四指以表示輕蔑。⇨ snook.

thump /θʌmp ; θʌmp/ *vt, vi* [VP6A, 15A, 22, 2A, C, 3A] strike heavily, esp with the fists; deliver heavy blows: 重擊(尤指用拳);給予重擊: *He ~ed (on) the door.* 他重擊門。 *She ~ed the cushion flat.* 她把墊子捶平。 *His heart was ~ing with excitement.* 他激動得心砰砰跳。 *The two boys began* *to ~ one another.* 那兩個男孩子開始用拳頭互毆。*He was ~ing the keys of the piano/~ing out a tune on the piano,* playing noisily. 他用力彈鋼琴(用力在鋼琴上彈奏一曲)。□ *n* [C] (noise of, or as of, a) heavy blow (esp one given with the fist): 重擊(尤指用拳者);重擊聲;砰然聲: *I dislike being given a friendly ~ on the back.* 我討厭別人友善却很重的拍打我的背。*The baby fell out of its cot with a ~.* 那娃娃砰然一聲從小床上跌落。**~·ing** *adj* (colloq) of great size. (俗)尺碼大的。□ *adv* (colloq) extremely: (俗)極度地;極端地: *What a ~ing great lie!* 好大的一個謊言!

thun·der /ˈθʌndə(r); ˈθʌndɚ/ *n* **1** [U] noise which usu follows a flash of lightning: 雷;雷聲: *a loud crash/a long roll of ~.* 雷聲大作(隆隆)。*There's ~ in the air,* T~ seems likely. 好像要打雷了。*We haven't had much ~ this summer.* 今年夏天我們未聽到很多雷聲。**'~·bolt** *n* flash of lightning with a crash of ~; (fig) unexpected and terrible event. 雷電;霹靂;(喻)突然而又可怕的事件。**'~·clap** *n* crash of ~; sth that comes like ~; sudden, terrible event, bad news, etc. 雷響;霹靂;來勢如霹靂的事物;突然、可怕的事件,壞消息等。**'~·storm** *n* storm of ~ and lightning, usu with heavy rain. (通常為大的)雷雨。**'~·struck** *adj* (pred; fig) amazed. (敍述用法;喻)驚呆的;驚愕的。**2** [U, C] loud noise like or suggesting ~: 似雷的聲響: *the ~ of the guns;* 大砲的隆隆聲; *~s of applause.* 如雷的掌聲。***steal sb's ~,*** spoil his attempt to be impressive by anticipating him. 搶先使用別人的方法或觀念;掠人之美。□ *vi, vt* **1** [VP2A, C] (impersonal): (無人稱): *It was ~ing and lightening.* 其時雷電交加。**2** [VP2C] make a noise like ~: 發出如雷之聲: *Someone was ~ing at the door,* beating at it. 有人在猛烈地敲門。*The train ~ed through the station.* 火車隆隆地駛過車站。*The juggernauts ~ed past.* 巨型運輸車隆隆而過。**3** [VP2C, 3A, 15B] ***~ (out) (against),*** speak in a loud voice, attack violently in words: 大聲地說話;以言詞猛烈攻擊: *The reformers ~ed against gambling.* 社會改革者大聲疾呼反對賭博。*How dare you ~ out your orders at me?* 你怎敢對我大聲地發號施令? **~er** *n* (esp) (尤指) *the T~er,* one of the names of the god Jupiter. 羅馬主神的名稱之一。**~·ing** *adj, adv* = thumping: *He was in a ~ing* (= violent) *rage.* 他大發雷霆。**~·ous** /-əs; -əs/ *adj* making a noise like, sounding like, ~: 喧聲如雷的;轟隆如雷的: *~ous applause.* 歡聲雷動。**~y** /-dərɪ; -dərɪ/ *adj* (of weather) giving signs of ~. (指天氣)預示要打雷的;像要打雷的。

thu·rible /ˈθjʊərəbl *US:* ˈθʊər-; ˈθjʊrəbl̩/ *n* = censer.

Thurs·day /ˈθɜːzdɪ; ˈθɝzdɪ/ *n* fifth day of the week. 星期四;禮拜四;木曜日。

thus /ðʌs; ðʌs/ *adv* in this way; so: 像這樣;如此: *~ far,* to this point. 至此;迄今。

thwack /θwæk; θwæk/ *vt, n* = whack.

thwart¹ /θwɔːt; θwɔrt/ *n* seat across a rowing-boat for an oarsman. (划艇上槳手的)坐板。

thwart² /θwɔːt; θwɔrt/ *vt* [VP6A] obstruct, frustrate: 阻撓;挫折;妨礙;反對: *~ sb's plans;* 阻撓某人的計畫; *be ~ed in one's ambitions/aims.* 自己的企圖(目標)受到挫折。

thy /ðaɪ; ðaɪ/ *adj* (archaic) your. (古)你的。**thine** /ðaɪn; ðaɪn/ *adj* (archaic) (before a vowel sound) your. (古)(用於母音前)你的。□ *pron* yours. 你的。**thy·self** /ðaɪˈself; ðaɪˈsɛlf/ *reflex, emph pron* (archaic) yourself. (古)你自己。

thyme /taɪm; taɪm/ *n* [U] kinds of herb with fragrant aromatic leaves, growing wild and in gardens, used in cookery. 百里香(葉芳香,野生或培植,用於烹飪)。

thy·roid /ˈθaɪrɔɪd; ˈθaɪrɔɪd/ *n* **~ (gland),** gland in the front part of the neck, producing a substance which affects the body's growth and activity. 甲狀腺(位於頸之前部,其分泌物能影響身體的發育及活動)。⇨ the illus at head. 參看 head 之插圖。

ti /tiː; ti/ *n* seventh note in the musical octave. 全音階的第七音。

ti·ara /tɪˈɑːrə; taɪˈerə/ *n* [C] **1** coronet for a woman. 女人的冠狀頭飾;女人的冠冕。**2** triple crown worn by the Pope. 羅馬教宗的三重冠。

tibia /ˈtɪbɪə; ˈtɪbɪə/ *n* (*pl* ~e /-bɪiː; -bɪ,i/) (anat) shin-bone; inner and thicker of the two bones between the knee and the foot. (解剖)脛骨;脛節。⇨ the illus at skeleton. 參看 skeleton 之插圖。

tic /tɪk; tɪk/ *n* involuntary, spasmodic twitching of the muscles (esp of the face). 肌肉抽搐;(尤指)面肌抽搐。

tick¹ /tɪk; tɪk/ *n* [C] **1** light, regularly repeated sound, esp of a clock or watch. 滴答聲(尤指鐘錶的)。**,~-'tock** *n* ~ing sound (of a clock, etc). (鐘等的)滴答聲。**2** (colloq) moment: (俗)片刻;刹那: *I'll be with you in two ~s.* 過一會兒我就來陪你。*Half a ~!* Just a moment! 馬上就好! **3** small mark (often ✓) put against names, figures, etc in a list or to show that sth is correct. 核對記號;勾號(通常作✓形,註於表册中的名稱、數字等旁邊,或表示某事物為正確者)。**4** **'~-tack** *n* system of signalling (a kind of hand semaphore) used by bookmakers' assistants on race-courses. (賽馬場上賭業者之助手所用的)手勢信號。□ *vi, vt* **1** [VP2A, C] (of a clock, etc) make ~s(1): (指鐘等)作滴答聲: *The child put the watch to its ear and listened to it ~ing.* 那孩子把錶放近耳邊,聽它的滴答聲。*The taxi's meter was ~ing away.* 計程車的計程表在滴答的跳動。***What makes sb/sth ~,*** (colloq) What makes him/it function, act, behave, etc in the way he/it does? (俗)什麼使得某人(某事物)成爲這個樣子呢? **2** [VP15B] ***~ away,*** (of a clock): (指鐘): *~ away the minutes,* mark their passing with ~s(1). 滴答地響,表示時間一分一分地過去。**3** [VP2C] ***~ over,*** (of an internal-combustion engine) operate slowly with gears disconnected (and the vehicle stationary). (指內燃機)(未接合聯動裝置地)空擋慢轉。**4** [VP6A, 15B] ***~ sth (off),*** put a ~(3) against: 畫勾號於…旁邊: *~ off a name/the items on a list.* 畫勾號於名字(清單上各項目)旁邊。***~ sb off,*** (colloq) rebuke, scold him: (俗)指責或叱責某人: *get ~ed off;* 受責罵; *give sb a good ,~ing-'off.* 痛責某人。

tick² /tɪk; tɪk/ *n* small spider-like parasite that fastens itself on the skin, eg of dogs, and sucks blood. 扁蝨(似蜘蛛的小寄生蟲,附於狗等的皮膚上,並吸取其血液)。⇨ the illus at arachnid. 參看 arachnid 之插圖。

tick³ /tɪk; tɪk/ *n* **1** [C] outside cover of stout striped linen for a mattress, bolster or pillow. (褥、墊或枕頭的)堅固而有條紋的亞麻布外套;套袋。**2** [U] (also 亦作 **~·ing**) material used for ~s. (用以做套袋的)堅固而有條紋的亞麻布。

tick⁴ /tɪk; tɪk/ *n* [U] (colloq) credit(1): (俗)信用;賒欠: *buy goods on ~;* 賒帳購物; *get ~.* 賒帳。

ticker /ˈtɪkə(r); ˈtɪkɚ/ *n* [C] **1** telegraphic machine which automatically prints news (esp stock market prices) on paper tape (called **'~-tape**): 自動收報機(將資訊自動印在'現字紙條'上者);(尤指)股票行情的自動指示器: *get a ~-tape reception,* eg in New York City, of a visiting celebrity in a procession through the streets, be welcomed with streamers of ~-tape thrown from office windows, etc. 受到盛大歡迎(如紐約市自辦公室窗戶等拋出彩色紙帶,以歡迎通過街道的貴賓等)。⇨ the illus at tape. 參看 tape 之插圖。**2** (colloq) watch. (俗)錶。**3** (sl) heart: (俚)心;心臟: *a dicky ~,* a weak heart. 心臟衰弱。

ticket /ˈtɪkɪt; ˈtɪkɪt/ *n* [C] **1** written or printed piece of card or paper giving the holder the right to travel in a train, bus, ship, etc or to a seat in a cinema, concert hall, etc: 票;車票;入場券: *Do you want a single or a return ~* (US 美=

one-way or *round-trip* ~)? 你要單程票還是來回票？*Admission by ~ only,* (as a notice outside a hall, etc). 憑票入場。'**~-collector** *n* person who collects ~s (esp railway ~s). 收票員(尤指火車票收票員)。**2** piece of card or paper, label, attached to sth and giving information, eg about the price, size of clothing, etc. 標籤(附於某物上,標明價格、尺碼等者)。**3** (US) list of candidates to be voted on, belonging to one political party: (美)(某一政黨提出的)候選人名單: *vote the straight ~,* cast the ballot on strict party lines. 嚴格地根據政黨路線投票；投票給本黨提名的候選人。**4** printed notice of an offence against traffic regulations (eg a parking offence): 交通違規通知單；罰款單: *get a ~.* 接到違規通知單。**5** **the ~,** (dated sl) the proper thing to do. (過時俚語)適當的事情；該做之事；對的事情。**6** **~ of leave,** (archaic) parole. (古)(犯人的)假釋許可狀。**7** certificate listing the qualifications of a pilot, a ship's mate, etc. (飛行員、船上的大副等的)資格證明書。□ *vt* [VP6A] put a ~(2) on; mark with a ~. 加標籤於；標明。

tick·ing /'tɪkɪŋ; 'tɪkɪŋ/ *n* ⇨ tick³.

tickle /'tɪkl; 'tɪkḷ/ *vt, vi* **1** [VP6A, 2A] excite the nerves of the skin by touching lightly, esp at sensitive parts, often so as to cause laughter: 輕觸以刺激表皮神經；胳肢；搔癢: *~ sb in the ribs.* 胳肢某人的肋骨。*The rough blanket ~s (me).* 粗毯使我的皮膚發癢。**2** [VP6A] please (one's sense of humour, etc): 使愉悅；滿足(某人的幽默感等): *The story ~d her fancy.* 那故事討她喜歡。*I was ~d to death/~d pink* (colloq, very amused and delighted) *at the news.* 我聽到那消息高興死了。*They ~d his vanity by praising his work to the skies.* 他們極力讚揚他的工作以滿足他的虛榮心。**3** [VP2A, 6A] have, feel, cause, an itching or tingling sensation: (使)感覺酥癢: *Pepper ~s if it gets into the nose.* 胡椒進入鼻孔會使人有酥癢的感覺。*My nose ~s.* 我的鼻子發癢。*It ~d my nose.* 那東西使我的鼻子發癢。**tick·ler** /'tɪklə(r); 'tɪklɚ/ *n* (colloq) puzzle. (俗)難題；棘手之事。**tick·lish** /'tɪklɪʃ; 'tɪklɪʃ/ *adj* **1** (of a person) easily made to laugh or wriggle when ~d. (指人)怕癢的；易癢的。**2** (of a problem, piece of work, etc) needing delicate care or attention: (指問題,工作等)需小心處理的；棘手的: *a ticklish question;* 棘手的問題；*in a ticklish situation.* 處於需要小心應付的情況中。

ti·dal /'taɪdl; 'taɪdḷ/ *adj* of a tide or tides: 潮的；潮水的；有潮的: *a ~ river/estuary/harbour,* in which the tide rises and falls. 感潮河道(感潮河口；潮港)。'**~ wave** *n* great ocean wave, often destructive of life and property, eg one that is (thought to be) caused by an earthquake; (fig) great wave of popular feeling (enthusiasm, indignation, etc). 潮波；海嘯；(喻)公衆情緒(如熱情、憤恨等)的浪潮；激動的民心。

tid·bit /'tɪdbɪt; 'tɪd,bɪt/ *n* (US) (美) = titbit.

tid·dler /'tɪdlə(r); 'tɪdḷɚ/ *n* (colloq) (俗) **1** very small fish. 非常小的魚。**2** young small child. 嬰兒。

tid·dley /'tɪdlɪ; 'tɪdḷɪ/ *adj* (colloq) (俗) **1** small; negligible. 很小的；微不足道的。**2** tipsy; slightly drunk. 有醉意的；微醉的。

tid·dly·winks /'tɪdlɪwɪŋks; 'tɪdḷɪ,wɪŋks/ *n* [U] game in which players try to make small discs or counters jump into a tray or cup in the centre of a table by pressing them on the edge with a larger disc. 提得利溫(一種以大圓片用力壓小圓片或籌碼的邊緣,使之跳入桌子中央大盤或杯中的遊戲)。

tide /taɪd; taɪd/ *n* **1** [C, U] regular rise and fall in the level of the sea, caused by the attraction of the moon: 潮；潮汐: *at high/low ~;* 在高(低)潮；*washed up by the ~(s);* 被潮水冲激的；*spring (= maximum) and neap (= minimum) ~s.* 大潮和小潮。'**~·mark** *n* highest point reached by a ~ on a beach. 高潮標(潮水達到的最高點)。'**~·way** *n* channel where ~s run; ebb or flow in such a channel. 潮路；潮流。**2** [C] flow or tendency (of public opinion, feeling, etc): (輿論、公衆情緒等的)潮流；趨勢: *We must not ignore the rising ~ of public discontent.* 我們切不可忽視大衆不滿情緒的不斷增漲。*The Socialists hoped for a turn of the ~,* that public opinion might turn in their favour. 社會黨人士希望輿論轉變爲對他們有利。**3** (old use) season (舊用法)時；季 (now only in compounds, as 現僅用於複合字中,如 '*Easter~,* 復活節季節，'*even~,* 日暮，'*Whitsun~* 聖靈降臨週). □ *vt* [VP14, 15B] **~ sb over (sth),** get over; help him to get through or survive (a period of difficulty, etc): 幫助某人度過(困難時期等): *He sold his car to ~ himself over his period of unemployment,* to provide money for his needs. 他賣掉汽車以度過失業的一段時期。*She needs more coal to ~ her over the winter.* 她需要更多的煤炭度過嚴冬。*Will £5 ~ you over until you get your wages?* 五鎊錢能幫助你維持到領薪水的時候嗎？

tid·ings /'taɪdɪŋz; 'taɪdɪŋz/ *n pl* (archaic) news: (古)消息；音信: *Have you heard the glad ~?* 你聽到了那令人愉快的消息嗎？

tidy /'taɪdɪ; 'taɪdɪ/ *adj* (-ier, -iest) **1** arranged neatly and in order; having the habit of placing and keeping everything in its right place: 安排得或排列得整齊的；整潔的；愛整齊的；有整潔習慣的: *a ~ room/desk;* 整潔的房間(書桌)；*a ~ boy;* 整潔的男孩；*~ habits.* 愛整潔的習慣。**2** (colloq) considerable; fairly large (esp of money): (俗)相當大的；可觀的(尤指錢): *a ~ sum of money;* 一筆鉅款；*cost a ~ penny,* quite a lot of money. 値相當多的錢。□ *n* (*pl* -dies) receptacle for odds and ends: 盛零星物件的容器: *a* '*hair-~,* eg on a dressing-table for hair from a hair-brush; 盛髮屑的容器；*a* '*sink-~,* for bits of kitchen waste. 廚房洗滌槽的殘渣過濾器。□ *vt, vi* [VP6A, 15B, 2A, C] **~ (up),** make ~: 使整齊；使整潔: *I must ~ myself,* make myself look ~. 我得梳理一下。*You'd better ~ up (the room) before the guests arrive.* 客人們到達前,你最好先整理一下(房間)。**ti·dily** /'taɪdɪlɪ; 'taɪdɪlɪ/ *adv* **ti·di·ness** *n*

tie¹ /taɪ; taɪ/ *n* [C] **1** sth used for fastening; rod or beam holding parts of a structure together; (US) railway sleeper, ⇨ *sleeper*(2) at sleep²; (fig) sth that holds people together: 用以繫捆之物；帶；繩；(連接結構物各部分的)繫材；繫桿；繫條；(美)鐵路枕木；軌枕；(喻)使人結合在一起的關係: *the ties of friendship;* 朋友關係；*family ties;* 家族關係；*ties of blood.* 血緣。**2** sth that takes up one's attention and limits one's freedom of action: 使某人勞神並限制其行動自由的事物；束縛: *Mothers often find their small children a tie.* 做母親的常覺得小孩子是一種束縛。**3** equal score in a game, etc: (比賽等)得分相同；不分勝負；平手: *The game ended in a tie, 2—2.* 這場比賽不分勝負,二比二。*The tie will be played off* (= will be replayed) *on Saturday.* 星期六將加賽一場以定勝負。**4** (music) curved line joining two notes of the same pitch that are to be played or sung as one. (音樂)連結線。⇨ the illus at notation. 參看 notation 之插圖。**5** = necktie.

tie² /taɪ; taɪ/ *vt, vi* (*pres p* tying, *pt, pp* tied) **1** [VP6A, 15A, B] fasten or bind (with string, rope, wire, etc): (用帶、繩、鐵絲等)繫；結；縛；綁；紮；捆；拴: *tie a man's feet together;* 將某人兩脚縛在一起；*tie up a parcel;* 捆包裹；*tie a branch down;* 將樹枝縛成垂枝；*tie a dog to the street railings.* 將狗拴在街旁的欄杆上。**tie sb down,** restrict sb's freedom: 限制某人自由；束縛某人: *He's not in a hurry to get married; he doesn't want to get tied down.* 他還不急於結婚；因爲他不想受束縛。*Young children do tie a woman down, don't they?* 小孩子的確會使一個女人受到束縛,對不對？**tie sb down to sth,** restrict sb to (the terms of a contract, etc). 置某人於(契約條款等)約束之下。**tie oneself down to sth,** accept limits to one's freedom of action. 使自己接受某事物的約束。**tie (sth) in with sth,** link, be linked, with: 連繫;與…連繫;與…關聯: *Doesn't this tie in with what we were told last week?* Aren't the two things linked, connected? 這件事與我們上週所聽到的那件事不是有關聯嗎？ ***tie sth up,*** **(a)** invest (capital) so that it is not easily available, eg because of legal restrictions. 使(資金)專作某種用途;凍結(資金)。**(b)** ensure that (property, eg land, buildings) can be used, sold, etc only under certain (usu legal) conditions. 確保(某財產,如土地或房屋)祇有在某些(通常爲法律的)條件下始得使用、出售等;凍結(財產)。***be/get tied up (with sth/sb),*** **(a)** be, get, involved (with sth/sb) so that one has no time for other things: 爲(某人或某事)纏住而無暇顧及其他事;爲…所羈絆: *I'm afraid I can't help you now—I'm too tied up with other things.* 恐怕我現在不能幫你的忙 — 旁的事情把我纏得太緊了。**(b)** be, become, linked with: 與…相連繫;與…有關聯: *Isn't this company tied up with Vickers-Armstrong?* 這家公司不是 Vickers-Armstrong 的關係企業嗎？Hence, 由此產生, **'tie-up** *n* link; merger; partnership. 連繫;合併;合夥。 **tied house,** (GB) public house controlled by a particular brewery. (英)(專銷某一酒廠產品的)特約酒店。⇨ *free house* at free¹(3). **2** [VP6A, 15B] ***tie sth (on),*** fasten by means of the strings, etc of: 繫上或繫牢: *tie an apron (on);* 繫上圍裙; *tie on a label.* 繫上標籤。Hence, 由此產生, **'tie-on,** *attrib adj*: *a tie-on label.* 繫上的標籤。 **3** [VP6A, 15A] arrange (a ribbon, etc) in the form of a bow or knot: 繫結(絲帶等): *tie one's shoelaces;* 繫鞋帶; *tie a ribbon/scarf;* 繫絲帶(圍巾); *tie the ribbon in(to) a bow.* 把絲帶打成蝴蝶結。 **4** [VP6A, 15A] make by tying: 繫作;打(結): *tie a knot in a piece of string.* 在一條細繩上打結。 **5** [VP2A] be fastened: 結起;打結: *Does this sash tie in front or at the back?* 這條腰帶是在前面還是在後面打結？ **6** [VP2A, 3A] ***tie (with) (for),*** (of players, teams, candidates in a competitive examination) make the same score (as); equal in points, marks, etc: (指選手、隊、應試者)得分(與…)相同;不分勝負: *The two teams tied.* 兩隊賽成平手。*They tied for first place (in the examination).* 他們(在考試中)同列第一名。*We tied with Arsenal in the last game.* 上一次比賽我們和阿森奈隊得分相同。

tier /tɪə(r) ; tɪr/ *n* row (esp of seats), shelf, etc esp one of a number parallel to and rising one above another, eg in a theatre or stadium: (階梯式的)一排;一層;一列;(尤指)(戲院,體育館等中的)一排座位: *a first/second ~ box,* in a theatre. (戲院中)第一(二)排的一個包廂。

tiff /tɪf ; tɪf/ *n* slight quarrel (between friends or acquaintances): (朋友或熟人間的)小爭執: *Alice has had a ~ with her boyfriend.* 愛麗絲和她的男朋友發生了小爭執。

ti·ger /'taɪgə(r) ; 'taɪgɚ/ *n* large, fierce animal of the cat family, yellow-skinned with black stripes, found in Asia. 虎;老虎(產於亞洲)。⇨ the illus at cat. 參看 cat 之插圖。 **'~-lily** *n* garden lily with orange flowers spotted with black or purple. 虎皮百合;卷丹;萱草。 **~·ish** /-ɪʃ ; -ɪʃ/ *adj* like, cruel as, a ~. 似虎的;虎一般殘忍的。 **ti·gress** /'taɪgrɪs ; 'taɪgrɪs/ *n* female ~. 母老虎;雌虎。

tight /taɪt ; taɪt/ *adj* (-er, -est) **1** fastened, fixed, fitting, held, closely: 緊的: *a ~ knot.* 繫得很緊的結。*I can't get the cork out of the bottle—It's too ~.* 我無法把瓶塞拔出來 — 太緊了。*The drawer is so ~ that I can't open it.* 這抽屜太緊了,我打不開。*These shoes are so ~ that they hurt.* 這雙鞋太緊,擠脚。 **,~-'lipped** *adj* keeping the lips firmly together; saying little or nothing; (fig) grim-looking. 緊閉嘴唇的;寡言的;沉默的;(喻)表情冷酷的;樣子殘忍的。 **2** closely or firmly put together in a small space: 緊密的;堅固的;密集的: *a ~ joint;* 緊密的接頭; (esp in compounds) made so that sth cannot get out or in: (尤用於複合字中)不漏的;不透的: *'water-/'air- ~.* 不漏水(不透氣)的。 **3** packed so as to occupy the smallest possible space or to get in as much as possible: 裝滿的;裝緊的: *Make sure that the bags are filled/packed ~.* 務必確實把那些袋子裝滿(塞滿)。 **4** (colloq) having had too much alcoholic drink: (俗)喝酒太多的;醉的: *He gets ~ every pay-day.* 他每逢發薪的日子都會喝得爛醉。 **5** fully stretched: 繃緊的;張緊的: *a ~ rope.* 繃緊的繩子。 **'~-rope** *n* one on which acrobats perform feats. (賣藝者表演特技用的)繃索。 **6** produced by pressure; causing difficulty. 由壓力或壓迫產生的;緊迫的;引起困難的。***in a ~ corner/spot,*** (usu fig) in a difficult or dangerous situation. (通常作喩)處於困境或危境。***~ schedule,*** one that it is difficult to keep to. 非常緊迫的日程。***~ squeeze,*** condition of being uncomfortably crowded: 擠得水洩不通;十分擁擠: *We got everyone into the bus, but it was a ~ squeeze.* 我們讓每一個人都搭上了那輛公車,不過擁擠得很厲害。 **7** (of money) not easily obtainable, eg on loan from banks: (指錢)難得到的;銀根緊的: *Money is ~.* 銀根很緊。*The money-market is ~,* It is possible to borrow money only by paying a high rate of interest. 金融市場銀根很緊。 **8** **,~-'fisted,** stingy; miserly. 吝嗇的;小氣的。 **,~-'laced** *adj* = strait-laced. ⇨ strait¹. **'~-wad** /-wɒd ; -,wɑd/ *n* (sl) stingy person. (俚)小氣鬼;吝嗇者。□ *adv* = ~ly: *squeeze/hold sth ~.* 緊緊地壓榨(執握)某物。***sit ~,*** ⇨ sit(1). (Note that ~ *adv* is not used before a *pp*; ~*ly* must be used in this position: *packed ~,* but *~ly packed*). (注意: 分詞之前不用 tight 做副詞,必須用 tightly, 例如 packed tight, tightly packed)。 **~·ly** *adv* in a ~ manner: 緊緊地;緊密地: *squeeze/hold sth ~ly;* 緊緊地壓榨(執握)某物; *~ly packed together;* 緊密地包裝在一起; *~ly sealed.* 密封的。 **~·ness** *n* **~en** /'taɪtn ; 'taɪtn/ *vt, vi* [VP6A, 15B, 2A, C] make or become ~(er): (使)變緊;(使)變得更緊: *~en (up) the screws;* 旋緊螺釘; *~en the ropes of the tent.* 拉緊帳篷的繩子。*It needs ~ening up.* (它)需要再拉緊一點。***~en one's belt,*** go without food (when there is little or none available); become frugal. 枵腹;束緊腰帶(食物不足或無食物時);節省。

tights /taɪts ; taɪts/ *n pl* **1** close-fitting garment covering the hips, legs and feet, as worn by girls and women. (婦女穿的)緊身下裝;褲襪(等)。 **2** skin-tight garment covering the legs and body, worn by acrobats, ballet-dancers, etc. (表演特技者,跳芭蕾舞者等穿的)緊身衣。

tike /taɪk ; taɪk/ *n* = tyke.

tilde *n* **1** /'tɪldə ; 'tɪldə/ the mark ˜ placed over Spanish *n* when it is pronounced *ny* /nj ; nj/ (as in *cañon*). 顎音符(即 ˜, 西班牙語中的 n 讀作 ny 時,加在上面的符號,如 cañon)。 **2** /tɪld ; tɪld/ the mark (~) as used in this dictionary to indicate the use of a headword in an entry. 代字號;波浪號(即 ~,在本辭典中代表每一條的首字)。

tile /taɪl ; taɪl/ *n* (usu square or oblong) plate of baked clay for covering roofs, walls, etc, often, eg Dutch, Italian and Portuguese ~s, painted with designs or pictures. 瓦;瓷磚(通常爲方形或長方形,用以蓋屋頂、貼牆壁等,荷蘭、義大利、葡萄牙等國所用者常繪有圖案或圖畫)。***be (out) on the ~s,*** (sl) be merry-making. (俚)作樂;行樂。***have a '~*** (more usu 較常用 *screw*) ***loose,*** (sl) be rather mad. (俚)有點發瘋。□ *vt* [VP6A] cover (a roof, etc) with ~s. 用瓦覆蓋(屋頂等)。

till¹ /tɪl ; tɪl/ (also 亦作 **until** /ʌn'tɪl ; ən'tɪl/) (*until* is more formal than *till*; *until* is preferred when its clause or phrase comes first) (until 較 till 正式;由其引導的片語或子句置於句首時,多用 until) *conj* up to the time when: 直到…之時;在…以前: *Go straight on until you come to the post-office and then turn left.* 一直向前走到郵局再向左轉。*Let's wait ~ the rain stops.* 讓我們等到雨停。*Until you* *told me, I had heard nothing of what happened.* 一直到你告訴我,我才知道發生了什麼事。*She won't go away ~ you promise to help her.* 在你答應幫助她之前,她不會走的。□ *prep* up to (the time when): 直到…之時;直至;迄: *I shall wait ~ ten o'clock/next Monday, etc.* 我將要等到十點鐘 (下週一等)。*Goodbye ~ tomorrow.* 明天見。*Until now I knew/Until then I had known nothing about it.* 直到現在(直到那時)我才知道這件事。*He works from morning ~ night, day after day.* 他從早到晚都在工作,日復一日。*He lived at home until soon after his father's death.* 他一直住在家裡,到他父親死後不久才離開。

till[2] /tɪl ; tɪl/ *n* money-drawer, eg in a cash-register: (店鋪中的)錢櫃;盛錢抽屜: *The boy was caught with his hand in the ~,* caught stealing. 那男孩從錢櫃裡偷錢時當場被捉到。

till[3] /tɪl ; tɪl/ *vt* [VP6A] cultivate (land). 耕(地)。**~·age** /ˈtɪlɪdʒ ; ˈtɪlɪdʒ/ *n* [U] act or process of ~ing; ~ed land. 耕種;耕作;耕作的過程;耕過的田地。**~er** *n* person who ~s. 耕者;農夫。

tiller /ˈtɪlə(r) ; ˈtɪlɚ/ *n* lever (like a long handle) used to turn the rudder of a small boat. (小船的)舵柄。⇨ the illus at sail. 參看 sail 之插圖。

tilt /tɪlt ; tɪlt/ *vt, vi* **1** [VP6A, 15A, B, 2A, C] (cause to) come into a sloping position (as by lifting one end); tip: (使)傾斜;(使)傾側: *Don't ~ the table.* . 不要使桌子傾斜。*T~ the barrel (up) to empty it.* 把大桶傾側倒空裡面的東西。*The table ~ed (over) and the plates slid off it to the floor.* 桌子傾斜了,碗盤滑落到地板上。**2** [VP2A, 3A] ~ ***(at)***, (hist, of men on horseback) ride (at another) with a lance; (fig) attack in speech or writing: (史,指騎士)騎在馬上用長矛刺(另一騎士);(喻)以言詞或文字攻擊;抨擊: *The reformer ~ed at the tax and property laws.* 該社會改革者抨擊稅法和財產法。***~ at windmills,*** fight imaginary enemies (from the story of Don Quixote). 攻擊想像中的敵人(由吉訶德先生的故事而來);無的放矢。□ *n* [C] **1** ~ing; sloping position. 傾側;傾斜;傾斜的位置。**2** act of ~ing with a lance: 馬上以長矛刺;馬上比武: *have a ~ at sb,* (fig) attack him (in a friendly way) in a debate, etc. (喻)(在辯論等中以友善的方式)攻擊某人。***(at) full ~,*** at great speed; with great force: 高速地;用力地: *The boy ran full ~ into me.* 那男孩猛然向我撞來。**'~-yard** *n* place where ~ing was practised in former times. (昔時的)馬上比武場。

tilth /tɪlθ ; tɪlθ/ *n* depth of soil affected by cultivation; tilled land: 耕作深度;耕地: *rake a seed-bed to a good ~,* until there is a depth of fine, crumbly soil. 把苗床耙成適耕的深度。

tim·ber /ˈtɪmbə(r) ; ˈtɪmbɚ/ *n* **1** [U] wood prepared for use in building, etc: (建築等用的)木材;木料: *'~-merchants;* 木材商; *a '~-yard,* place where ~ is stored, bought and sold, etc; 貯材場;木材場; *dressed ~,* sawn, shaped and planed ready for use. 修整材(可立即使用者)。**2** [U] growing trees (sometimes *standing ~*) thought of as containing wood suitable for building, carpentry, etc: 樹林;森林;木材林(被認爲含有建築、木工等用之木材者,有時作 standing ~): *cut down/fell ~;* 伐林(取材); *put a hundred acres of land under ~,* plant with trees for ~. 種植一百英畝的木材林。*The fire destroyed thousands of acres of ~.* 大火摧毀了數千英畝的木材林。**3** [C] large piece of shaped wood, beam, forming a support (eg in a roof or a ship). 棟木;梁木(如建築屋頂或船隻所用者)。**4** [U] (in fox-hunting) wooden fences and gates. (獵狐)木造障礙物;圍籬與門。**~ed** /ˈtɪmbəd ; ˈtɪmbɚd/ *adj* (of buildings) made of ~ or with a framework of ~. (指建築物)木造的;木質架構的。

timbre /ˈtæmbrə *US:* ˈtɪmbər ; ˈtɪmbɚ/ *n* characteristic quality of sound produced by a particular voice or instrument. 音色;音質;音品。

tim·brel /ˈtɪmbrəl; ˈtɪmbrəl/ *n* tambourine. 鈴鼓;手鼓。

time[1] /taɪm ; taɪm/ *n* **1** [U] all the days of the past, present and future: 時;時間(指過去、現在、未來全部的日子): *past, present and future ~.* 過去、現在及未來的時間。*The world exists in space and ~.* 世界存在於空間與時間中。**2** [U] the passing of all the days, months and years, taken as a whole (sometimes personified as *(old) Father T~*): 時間的度過;光陰的流逝;時間流逝 (有時予以擬人化,稱爲'時間老人'): *T~ will show who is right.* 時間會證明誰是對的。*T~ waits for no man,* (prov). (諺)歲月不待人;時不我與;歲月不饒人。**3** [U] (also 亦作 ***a + adj + ~***) portion or measure of ~: 一段時間;一部分時間: *Six o'clock is a point of ~; six hours is a period of ~.* 六點鐘是時間的一點;六小時是一段時間。*What a (long) ~ you've been!* 你花費相當(長)的時間了! *I had a most unpleasant ~ at the dentist's.* 我在牙醫那裡經歷了一段很不愉快的時間。*That will take ~,* cannot be done soon or quickly. 那要花費相當的時間(才能做成)。*I have no/not much ~ for sport.* 我沒有(沒有太多)時間做戶外運動。*We have no ~ to lose,* We must hurry. 我們不能躭誤時間了(必須趕緊)。*He spent a lot of ~ (in) getting ready.* 他花了很多時間做準備。*Take your ~ over it,* Don't hurry. 慢慢來,不要急。*We were pressed for ~,* had not enough ~, were forced to hurry. 我們的時間甚爲急迫。***behind ~,*** **(a)** late: 遲;晚: *The train is ten minutes behind ~.* 火車誤點十分鐘。**(b)** behindhand: 落後;拖欠: *He's always behind ~ with his payments.* 他總不能按時付款。***for the ~ being,*** ⇨ be[3](4). ***on ~,*** up to ~, not late, punctual(ly): 按時;準時: *The train is/came in on ~.* 火車準時(到達)。***in 'no ~,*** very soon; very quickly. 立卽;很快地。***(from/since) ~ immemorial; (from/since) ~ out of mind,*** for a period of ~ longer than any one can remember. (從)遠古時代(起);(從)人們不復記憶的時代(起)。***gain ~,*** obtain extra ~ by making excuses, deliberately using slow methods, etc. 拖延時間。***all the ~,*** **(a)** during the whole of the ~ in question: (在某段時間內)一直: *I looked all over the house for that letter, and it was in my pocket all the ~,* while I was searching. 我在屋裡到處找那封信,而它却一直在我口袋裏。**(b)** at all times; first and last: 始終;從頭到尾;自始至終: *He's a business man all the ~,* has no other interests in life. 自始至終他就是一個生意人。***'half the ~,*** **(a)** half of the ~ available: 一半的時間: *He did the work in four hours; I could have done it in half the ~,* in two hours. 他花了四小時才做完那工作;我花一半的時間 (兩小時)就能做好。**(b)** for long periods of ~; (loosely) very often; nearly always: 長時間地;(非嚴格用法)常常;幾乎總是: *He says he works hard, but he's day-dreaming half the ~.* 他說他工作很努力,但他大部分時間都在做白日夢。**4** [U] point of ~ stated in hours and minutes of the day: (以當日的小時和分說明的)時刻: *What ~ is it?* 幾點鐘了? *What is the ~?* 幾點鐘了? *The child can now tell the ~.* 那孩子看得懂鐘(錶)了。**5** [U] ~ measured in units (years, months, hours, etc): 以(年、月、小時等)單位量出的時間: *The winner's ~ was 11 seconds.* 獲勝者使用的時間共十一秒。*He ran the mile in record ~,* in a period of ~ shorter than that of any previous runner. 他跑一英里的時間已打破以往的記錄。***keep good/bad ~,*** (of a clock or watch) show the hour correctly/incorrectly. (指鐘錶)走得準確(不準確)。***the ~ of day,*** the hour as shown by a clock. (鐘錶上的)時刻。***pass the ~ of day (with . . .),*** exchange a greeting, say 'Good morning!', etc. 相互問候或請安(如說'早安'等)。**6** [U] point or period of ~ associated with, or available or suitable for, a certain event, purpose, etc: 時機;時限;時候;機會: *at the ~ you're speaking of;* 在你所說的時間; *by the ~ we reached home;* 在我們到家的時候; *last ~ I was there;* 我上次在那兒的時候; *every ~ I looked at her.* 每次我看她的時候。*It is* '*lunch-*~. 是午餐的時間了。*There is a ~ for everything.* 凡事必有其時。*Now's your ~* (= opportunity). (現在)你的機會來了。*It's ~ I was going/~ for me to go,* I ought to leave now. 我(現在)該走了。*It's ~ somebody taught you to behave yourself.* (現在)該有人教導你如何待人接物了。*I must bide my ~,* be patient, wait for a suitable ~. 我必須等待時機。*T~ is up,* The ~ allowed for something is ended. 時間到。***(work, etc) against ~,*** with the greatest speed (because only a limited amount of ~ is available). 以最快速度;全力(工作等);加緊(趕工等)。***at the same ~,*** **(a)** together: 同時;一齊: *to laugh and cry at the same ~.* (同時)又哭又笑。**(b)** notwithstanding; nevertheless: 可是;然而: *He's slightly mad; at the same ~, he's one of the kindest men I know.* 他有一點瘋狂;然而他是我所認識的最和善的人之一。***at ~s; from ~ to ~,*** occasionally; now and then. 間或;偶爾。***at 'all ~s,*** always. 總是;始終;經常。***at 'your/'his, etc ~ of life,*** at your/his, etc age. 在你(他等)這樣的年紀。***in ~,*** **(a)** not late; early enough: 及時;還早: *We were in ~ for the train/to catch the train.* 我們趕上了火車。*We arrived in good ~,* with ~ to spare. 我們到得很早。**(b)** sooner or later; after the passing of an indefinite period of ~: 早晚;終久;經過一段(不確定的)時間以後;將來: *You will learn how to do it in ~.* 你將來會學到怎樣來做這件事。***in the nick of ~,*** ⇨ nick[1](2). ***near her ~,*** (of a woman) soon to give birth to a child. (指婦女)臨盆;分娩期近。***do ~,*** (colloq) undergo a period of imprisonment. (俗)服刑。***serve one's ~,*** **(a)** work as an apprentice for an agreed number of years: 當學徒;做(若干年)學徒: *The boy has served half his ~.* 這男孩做學徒的期限已經過去一半。**(b)** = do ~, ⇨ above. 參看上列之 do ~。***My/His, etc ~ is drawing near,*** I am/He is, etc near a ~ of crisis, of some important happening, etc (according to the context). 我(他等)面臨危急關頭(決定性時刻等,視上下文而定)。 **7** [C] (Cf 參較 *twice*) occasion: 次數;次;回: *this/that/next/another ~;* 這(那,下一,另一)回; *the ~ before last;* 上上一次; *for the first/last ~.* 第一(最後一)回。*He failed five ~s.* 他失敗過五次。*I've told you a dozen ~s,* (= very often, repeatedly) *not to do that.* 我已經一再告訴你不要那樣做。***at 'one ~,*** during a period of past ~, known but not mentioned: 過去有一段時間: *At one ~ I used to go mountain-climbing every summer.* 過去有一段時間我每年夏天去爬山。***at other ~s,*** on other occasions. 在其他時候;又有時。***~ and again; ~s without number,*** again and again; repeatedly. 一再;屢屢。***'many a ~; 'many ~s,*** often; on many occasions. 時常;多次;屢屢。***one/two, etc at a ~,*** one/two, etc on each occasion; separately: 一次一個(兩個等)地;各別地: *Hand them to me two at a ~.* 把那些東西拿給我,一次兩個。 **8** (*pl*) used to indicate multiplication (but note that *twice* is used instead of *two ~s*): (複)倍;乘(注意: twice 用以表示二倍): *Three ~s five is/are fifteen,* 3 × 5 = 15. 三乘五得十五。*Yours is ten ~s the size of mine/ten ~s as large as mine.* 你的(那東西)比我的大十倍。 **9** [C] (often *pl*) period of ~, more or less definite, associated with certain events, circumstances, persons, etc: (常用複數)時代;時期: *in 'Stuart ~s,* when the Stuart kings ruled; 在斯圖亞特王朝時代; *in the ~(s) of the Stuarts;* 在斯圖亞特諸王治理時期; *in 'ancient/prehis'toric ~s.* 在古代(史前期)。*Mr Curtis was the manager in 'my ~,* when I was working there. 我在那裏工作時期,寇蒂斯先生是經理。*The house is old but it will last my ~,* will serve me for the rest of my life. 這房子舊了,不過在我有生之年尚可住。 **10** [C] (often *pl*) the conditions of life, the circumstances, etc of a period characterized by certain qualities, etc: (常用複數)某一時期的生活狀況、環境等(有某些特色者): *We lived through terrible ~s during the war years.* 打仗的那幾年我們過得很淒慘。*T~s are good/bad,* (often meaning that it is easy/difficult to make a living). 年頭好(壞)(常表示謀生容易,困難等)。***ahead of one's ~; born before one's ~,*** having ideas too much in advance of, too enlightened for, the period in which one lives. 超出時代前,具有不容於當世的前進或開明的思想。***(even) at the 'best of ~s,*** even when conditions are good: 卽使情況良好;在狀況最好的時候: *He's an irritating fellow even at the best of ~s.* 卽使在好的時候,他也是一個令人討厭的傢伙。***behind the ~s,*** antiquated; having out-of-date ideas, etc. 過時的;落伍的;思想等陳舊的。***have a good ~,*** enjoy oneself. 自得其樂;玩(等)得很痛快。***have the ~ of one's life,*** (colloq) experience a period of exceptional happiness or enjoyment. (俗)度過一段非常歡樂或愉快的時間。 **11** [U] **Greenwich/local/summer/standard ~,** 格林尼治(當地,夏令,標準)時間, ⇨ these words. 參看各字。 **12** [U] (music) style of rhythm depending upon the number of beats in the successive bars of a piece of music: (音樂)拍子: '*common ~,* two or four beats in a bar; 普通拍子(每一小節二拍或四拍); '*waltz ~,* three or six beats in a bar; 華爾茲拍子(一小節三或六拍); also, the rate (or *tempo*) at which a piece of music is to be played. 演奏(樂曲的)速度。***in/out of ~,*** in/not in accordance with the ~ of the music. 合(不合)節拍。***in double-quick ~,*** very quickly. 非常快。***beat ~,*** show the ~ (*tempo,* etc) by movements made with the hand or a stick (*baton*). (用手或指揮棒)打拍子。***keep ~,*** sing or dance in ~. 按節拍唱歌或跳舞。 **13** (compounds) (複合字) **'~-ball** *n* one which slides down a staff (at an observatory to show a fixed ~, usu noon or 1 pm). (升降於氣象台桿子上的)報時球(所報的時刻通常爲中午或下午一時)。 **'~-bomb** *n* designed to explode at some ~ after being dropped, placed in position, etc. 定時炸彈。 **'~-card/-sheet** *n* one for a record of workmen's hours of work. 工作時間記錄卡(紙)。 **'~-expired** *adj* (of soldiers and sailors) having completed the period of service. (指兵士和水手)已服役期滿的。 **'~-exposure** *n* exposure of a photographic film for a ~ longer than half a second. 照相底片超過半秒鐘的曝光。 **'~-fuse** *n* one that has been made to burn for a given ~, eg to explode a bomb. 定時信管。 **'~-honoured** (US = **-honored**) *adj* respected because of its antiquity. 因年代久遠而受尊敬的;由來已久的。 **'~-keeper** *n* **(a)** one who, or that which, records the ~ spent by workers at their work. 工作時間記錄員或記錄器。 **(b)** (of a watch, etc) one that keeps ~ well, etc: (走得準或不準的)時計: *a good/bad ~keeper.* 走得準(不準)的時計。 **'~-lag** *n* interval of ~ between two connected phenomena or events (eg between a flash of lightning and the thunder, or between a decision to do sth and its accomplishment). 時滯(兩個相關聯現象或事件所間隔的時間,如閃電與打雷之間或決心做某事與其完成之間者)。 **'~-limit** *n* limited period of ~; last moment of this: 時限;時限的最後片刻: *set a ~-limit for the completion of a job.* 爲某項工作的完成規定時限。 **'~·piece** *n* clock. 鐘;錶;時計。 **'~-saving** *adj* serving to save ~: 節約時間的: *a ~-saving idea.* 省時的辦法(主意)。 **'~-server** *n* one who acts, not according to principles, but according to self-interest, esp one who is always trying to please powerful people. 趨炎附勢者;以一己的利益爲行事準則者。 **'~-serving** *adj* behaving as a ~-server: 趨炎附勢的;謀私利的: *~-serving politicians.* 趨炎附勢的政客。 **'~-signal** *n* signal (eg a series of pips) indicating the ~. 報時信號。 **'~ slip** *n* = *time warp.* **'~-switch** *n* switch set to operate at a desired ~ (eg to turn a heating system on or off). 定時開關(如暖氣系統上者)。 **'~·table** *n* list showing the days or hours at which events will take place, work will be done, trains etc will depart. 時間表;時刻表。'~ **warp** *n* (in science fiction) breaking of past or future ~ into present ~. (科幻小說) 將過去或未來時間變成現在時間。'~-**work** *n* [U] work (esp manual work) paid for by the hour or day (contrasted with *piece-work*). 計時工作(尤指手工,與 piece-work 相對)。~·**less** *adj* (liter) unending; not to be thought of as having duration. (文)無限的;永久的;超時間的。

time² /taɪm ; taɪm/ *vt* **1** [VP6A, 15A] choose the time or moment for; arrange the time of: 選擇…的時機;安排…的時間;使合時宜: *He ~d his journey so that he arrived before dark.* 他把旅程的時間做了適當的安排,因此在天黑前就到了。*The remark was well/ill ~d,* made at a suitable/an unsuitable moment. 這話正合(不合)時宜。**2** [VP6A] measure the time taken by or for (a race, runner, an action or event). 記錄(賽跑、跑者、行動或事件)的時間;計算時間。**3** [VP6A] regulate: 調整;校準: *~ one's steps* (in dancing) *to the music;* 調整舞步使配合音樂; *~ the speed of a machine.* 調整機器的速度。**tim·ing** *n* [U] act of determining or regulating the (order of) occurrence of an action, event, etc to achieve the desired results: 定時;調整時間: *a 'timing device;* 定時設計; (theatre) speed of dialogue/cues, etc: (戲劇)對白(尾白,表演等)的速度: *The timing in last night's performance was excellent.* 昨晚的演出,時間控制得非常好。

time·ly /'taɪmlɪ ; 'taɪmlɪ/ *adj* (-ier, -iest) occurring at just the right time; opportune. 適時發生的;合時宜的。**time·li·ness** *n* [U].

timid /'tɪmɪd ; 'tɪmɪd/ *adj* easily frightened; shy: 膽怯的;羞怯的: *That fellow is as ~ as a rabbit.* 那傢伙膽小如兔。~·**ly** *adv* ~·**ity** /tɪ'mɪdətɪ ; tɪ'mɪdətɪ/, ~·**ness** *nn* [U].

tim·or·ous /'tɪmərəs ; 'tɪmərəs/ *adj* (liter) timid. (文)膽怯的;羞怯的。~·**ly** *adv*

tim·othy /'tɪməθɪ ; 'tɪməθɪ/ *n* [U] '~ **(grass)**, grass grown as fodder for cattle. (餵牛之)筒狀長穗牧草。

tim·pani /'tɪmpənɪ ; 'tɪmpə,ni/ *n pl* set of kettle-drums (eg of an orchestra). (音樂)一組定音鼓(如交響樂團者)。⇨ the illus at percussion. 參看 percussion 之插圖。**tim·pan·ist** /'tɪmpənɪst; 'tɪmpənɪst/ *n* player of a kettledrum. 定音鼓手。

tin /tɪn ; tɪn/ *n* **1** [U] soft, white metal (symbol **Sn**) used in alloys and for coating iron sheets. 錫(符號 Sn, 用於合金中,並用於鍍鐵皮)。'**tin·foil** *n* [U] tin in the form of foil (thin pliable sheets), used for wrapping and packing. 錫箔(用於包裝)。***(little) tin god,*** (colloq) sth or sb mistakenly given great veneration or worship. (俗)受到不應得的過份崇敬的人或物。~ **hat,** (sl) steel helmet (as worn by soldiers in modern times). (俚)鋼盔。'**tin-plate** *n* [U] sheet iron coated with tin (used in the canning industry). 洋鐵皮;馬口鐵;白鐵皮。'**tin·smith** *n* worker in tin-plate. 洋鐵匠。'**tin·tack** *n* short nail of tinned iron. 包鐵釘;鍍錫釘。**2** [C] tin-plated container for food, etc esp one made so as to be air-tight (US 美 = *can*): 洋鐵罐 (尤指作罐頭用而且可密封者); 聽: *a tin of sardines/oil.* 一罐沙丁魚(油)。(Cf 參較 *a can of beer* 一罐啤酒)。'**tin-opener** *n* device for opening tins. 開罐器。□ *vt* (-nn-) [VP6A] **1** put a coating of tin on. 鍍錫;包以錫。**2** pack (food, etc) in tins(2) (US 美 = *can*): 裝(食物等)於罐中: *tinned peaches* 罐裝桃子。**tinny** *adj* of or like tin (eg in sound): 錫的;似錫的;玎玲聲的: *a tinny piano.* 發玎玲聲的鋼琴。

tinc·ture /'tɪŋktʃə(r) ; 'tɪŋktʃɚ/ *n* **1** medical substance dissolved in alcohol: 溶解在酒精中的藥物;酊劑: *~ of iodine/quinine.* 碘酒(奎寧酊劑)。**2** ***a ~ (of),*** slight flavour or suggestion (of). 些微的味道或跡象。□ *vt* give a ~(2) of (sth) to: 使帶味道、氣息、意味等: *teachings ~d with heresy.* 微帶異端意味的教義。

tin·der /'tɪndə(r) ; 'tɪndɚ/ *n* [U] material (eg dry, scorched linen, etc) that easily catches fire from a spark. 火絨;導火線(與火花接觸即易着火之物)。'~-**box** *n* box containing ~, flint and steel (as used in former times for kindling fire). 火絨箱(內裝火絨、燧石及鋼片,昔時用以引火)。

tine /taɪn ; taɪn/ *n* point, prong (eg of a fork, harrow, etc); branch of a deer's antler. (叉、耙等的)叉齒;尖端;鹿角的分叉。⇨ the illus at large. 參看 large 之插圖。-~**d** /-taɪnd ; -taɪnd/ *suff* (in compounds) having the number or kind of ~s indicated: (用於複合字中)有若干或某種叉齒的: *a three-~d hayfork.* 三叉乾草耙。

ting /tɪŋ ; tɪŋ/ *vi, vt, n* (cause to make, make, a) clear, ringing sound. 玎玲聲;(使)發玎玲聲。

tinge /tɪndʒ ; tɪndʒ/ *vt* [VP6A, 14] ***~ sth (with),*** **1** colour slightly (with red, etc). 微染(紅色等)。**2** (esp in *pp*) affect slightly: (尤用過去分詞) 微沾;微感染;含: *admiration ~d with envy.* 含有妒意的讚美。□ *n* slight colouring or mixture (*of*): 微染;意味;些微氣息(與 of 連用): *There was a ~ of sadness in her voice/of irony in his remark.* 她的聲音中略帶哀傷(他的話中略帶譏諷)的意味。

tingle /'tɪŋgl ; 'tɪŋgl/ *vi* [VP2A, C] have a pricking or stinging feeling in the skin; (fig) be stirred: 皮膚有刺痛的感覺;(喻) 被激動;興奮: *His cheek ~d from the slap she had given him.* 他的臉上因挨了她一巴掌而有刺痛的感覺。*His fingers ~d with the cold.*他的手指凍得有刺痛感。*The children were tingling with excitement.* 孩子們大爲興奮。□ *n* tingling feeling: 刺痛之感: *have a ~ in one's finger-tips.* 指尖有刺痛感。

tin·ker /'tɪŋkə(r) ; 'tɪŋkɚ/ *n* **1** worker with metal who travels from place to place and repairs kettles, pans, etc. 補鍋匠; 修理鍋盤等的流動匠人。***not care/give a ~'s cuss/damn,*** not care in the least. 毫不介意。**2** ~ing: 笨拙的修補或修理;不內行的做: *have an hour's ~ at the radio set,* try to mend it. 笨拙地修理收音機一小時。□ *vi* [VP 2A, C, 3A] ***~ (at/with),*** work in an amateurish or inexpert way (at): 不內行地、笨拙地或不熟練地做或修理: *~ (away) at a broken machine.* 笨拙地修理一架壞機器。*Please don't ~ with my car engine.* 請不要亂弄我的汽車引擎。

tinkle /'tɪŋkl ; 'tɪŋkl/ *vi, vt* [VP2A, C, 6A] (cause to) make a succession of light, ringing sounds, eg of a small bell. (使)發玎璫聲;(使)發玎玲聲。□ *n* (*sing*) such sounds: (單)玎玲聲;玎璫聲: *the ~ of a bell/of falling glass/of ice being stirred round in a glass.* 鈴(玻璃落地,冰塊在杯中攪動)的玎璫聲。

tinny /'tɪnɪ ; 'tɪnɪ/ *adj* ⇨ tin.

tin pan alley /,tɪn pæn 'ælɪ ; ,tɪn pæn 'ælɪ/ *n* composers, players and publishers of popular music (as a group). 丁班巷;丁班胡同(原爲地名,轉用作流行音樂的作曲家、演奏者及出版商的總稱)。

tin·sel /'tɪnsl ; 'tɪnsl/ *n* [U] **1** glittering metallic substance made in sheets, strips and threads, used for ornament: 裝飾用的光亮金屬片、金屬條或金屬線: *trim a Christmas tree/a dress with ~.* 以光亮金屬片等裝飾耶誕樹(衣物)。**2** superficial, cheap, showy brilliance. 表面的光亮;庸俗而華麗的光彩。~**ly** /-səlɪ ; -slɪ/ *adj* trimmed with, suggesting, ~. 以或似以光亮金屬物裝飾的。□ *vt* (-ll-, US also -l-) trim with ~. 以光亮金屬物裝飾。

tint /tɪnt ; tɪnt/ *n* (esp pale or delicate) shade or variety of colour: 色度;顏色的濃淡;(尤指)淡色: *~s of green in the sky at dawn;* 黎明時天空中濃淡不同的綠色; *an artist who excels at 'flesh-~s.* 長於使用肉色的藝術家。□ *vt* [VP6A, 22] give a ~ to; put a ~ on; tinge. 着色於;加色度於…上;微染。

tin·tin·nabu·la·tion /,tɪntɪn,æbjʊ'leɪʃn ; ,tɪntɪ,næbjə'leʃən/ *n* [U] tinkling of bells. 鈴聲;玎玲聲。

tiny /ˈtaɪnɪ; ˈtaɪnɪ/ *adj* (-ier, -iest) very small. 甚小的;微小的。

tip¹ /tɪp; tɪp/ *n* [C] **1** pointed or thin end of sth: 尖;尖端: *the tips of one's fingers/one's ˈfinger-tips;* 手指尖端; *the tip of one's nose;* 鼻尖; *asparagus tips.* 蘆筍尖。*The bird measured 12 inches from tip to tip,* from the tip of one wing to the tip of the other. 那鳥兩翼張開時兩翼端的距離爲十二吋。***(have sth) on the tip of one's tongue,*** (be) just going to say (it). 話到嘴邊;即將要說某話。ˌ**tip-ˈtop** *adj, adv* (dated colloq) first-rate: (過時俗語)第一流的(地): *a tip-top hotel/dinner.* 第一流的旅館(餐食)。*You've done tip-top.* 你做得好極了。**2** small piece put at the end of sth: 裝在末端的小物: *cigarettes with filter-tips.* 末端裝有濾嘴的香烟。□ *vt* (-pp-) supply with a tip(2): 裝以尖頭: *filter-tipped cigarettes.* 裝有濾嘴的香烟。

tip² /tɪp; tɪp/ *vt, vi* (-pp-) **1** [VP6A, 15A, B, 2A, C] ***tip (sth) (up),*** (cause to) rise, lean or tilt on one side or at one end: (使)傾斜;(使)翻倒: *The table tipped up.* 那桌子翻倒了。*Tip the barrel up and empty it.* 把那桶倒空。***tip sth (over),*** (cause to) overbalance or overturn: (使)翻倒;顛覆: *Careful! You'll tip the canoe over.* 當心!你會把小船弄翻。***tip the scale (at),*** **(a)** be just enough to cause one scale or pan (of a balance) to go lower than the other; (fig) be the deciding factor (for or against). 剛可使天平傾斜;(喻)成爲決定因素。**(b)** weigh: 稱量;秤: *He tipped the scale at 140 lb.* 他體重一百四十磅。**tip-up seat,** seat with a hinge, eg the kind used in cinemas, etc to allow people to pass freely. (戲院等處的)翻椅(一端有絞鍊,可翻起俾便利人們通行者)。**2** [VP6A, 15A, B] ***tip sth (out); tip sth (out of sth) (into sth),*** empty (the contents of sth) out/out of/into: 把(盛裝物)倒出或倒入: *No rubbish to be tipped (out) here,* a warning put up in open spaces. 此處不准傾倒垃圾。*She tipped the slops out of the bucket into the sink.* 她把髒水從桶裡倒進洗滌槽中。*He was tipped out of the cart into the ditch.* 他從馬車上翻落到溝中。*Which is better, to incinerate the rubbish from our towns or to tip it into disused quarries?* 我們城裡的垃圾予以焚化,或是倒進廢棄的採石坑,那一種方法好? □ *n* (not US) place where rubbish may be tipped(2): (不用於美國)垃圾堆置場: *the municipal ˈrefuse tip;* 市區垃圾堆置場; hill of waste material from a coalmine, etc; (colloq) untidy place: 煤礦區等的廢物堆;(俗)不雅觀處;髒亂處: *They live in a tip.* 他們住在陋巷裡。

tip³ /tɪp; tɪp/ *vt* (-pp-) **1** [VP6A] touch or strike lightly: 輕觸;輕打;輕敲: *His bat just tipped the ball.* 他的球棒僅僅擦到球。ˌ**tip-and-ˈrun** *adj* (of a raid by robbers, etc) in which there is a brief attack followed by a quick escape. (指强盜的搶刼等)搶了就逃的;拿了就跑的。**2** [VP6A, 12C] give a tip to (1, 2 below): 賞給小費;給予勸告;供以情報: *tip the porter 50p.* 賞給脚伕五十辨士。***tip sb off,*** (colloq) give him a warning or a hint. (俗)給予某人警告或暗示。Hence, 由此產生, ˈ**tip-off** *n* hint or warning: 警告;暗示: *give the police a tip-off.* 給予警方警告或暗示。***tip sb the wink,*** (colloq) give him special information; warn him secretly. (俗)予某人特別情報;暗中警告某人。***tip the winner,*** name the winner (usu of a horse-race) before the event takes place. 事先指出(通常爲賽馬的)獲勝者。□ *n* [C] **1** gift of money to a porter, waiter, taxi-driver, etc for personal services: 小費;賞錢: *leave a 50p tip,* eg at a restaurant. 留五十辨士小費(如在餐館中)。**2** piece of advice on how to do sth, esp information about the probable winner of a horse-race, on the future value of shares (on the Stock Exchange, etc): 勸告;(尤指有關賽馬的可能獲勝者,或未來的證券價值的)情報;特別消息;秘密提示: *a tip for the Derby.* 德比大賽馬的一項情報。*If you take my tip* (= advice) *you'll make a lot of money.* 你如果採納我的意見,你會賺大錢。**3** light blow; tap. 輕擊;輕拍。

tip·pet /ˈtɪpɪt; ˈtɪpɪt/ *n* (archaic) scarf or long fur worn by a woman round the neck and shoulders with the ends hanging down to the waist in front; similar article of dress worn by judges, clergy, etc. (古)婦女的肩巾(垂至腰前者);(法官、僧侶等所著的)披肩。⇨ the illus at vestment. 參看 vestment 之插圖。

tipple /ˈtɪpl; ˈtɪpl/ *vi, vt* **1** [VP2A] be in the habit of drinking alcoholic liquor. 酗酒;慣於飲烈酒。**2** [VP6A] drink (wine, spirits, etc). 飲(葡萄酒、烈酒等)。□ *n* [U] alcoholic drink; (hum) any kind of drink: 烈酒;(諧)飲料: *John's favourite ~ is lager; mine is sherry.* 約翰喜歡淡啤酒;我喜歡雪利(酒)。**tip·pler** *n*

tip·staff /ˈtɪpstɑːf *US:* -stæf; ˈtɪpˌstæf/ *n* sheriff's officer. 法警;警吏;執達員。

tip·ster /ˈtɪpstə(r); ˈtɪpstɚ/ *n* person who gives tips about races. 提供賽馬情報者;洩露內情者。⇨ tip³(2).

tipsy /ˈtɪpsɪ; ˈtɪpsɪ/ *adj* (colloq) slightly drunk. (俗)微醉的。

tip·toe /ˈtɪptəʊ; ˈtɪpˌto/ *adv* ***on ~,*** on the tips of one's toes: 踮着脚: *be/wait on ~ with excitement.* 興奮地翹首企望(等待)。□ *vi* [VP2A, C] walk quietly on ~: 踮著脚走: *She ~d to the bedside of the sleeping child.* 她踮著脚走到酣睡孩子的床邊。

ti·rade /taɪˈreɪd; ˈtaɪred/ *n* long, angry or scolding speech. 長篇的激烈演說;冗長的指摘性演說。

tire¹ /ˈtaɪə(r); taɪr/ *n* (US) (美) = tyre.

tire² /ˈtaɪə(r); taɪr/ *vt, vi* [VP6A, 15B, 2A, 3A] ***~ (sb) (out); ~ of,*** make or become weary, or in need of rest, or uninterested: (使)疲倦;(使)厭倦: *The long walk ~d the child/~d him out/made him ~d.* 長距離的步行使那孩子(使他)疲倦了。*The long lecture ~d the audience.* 冗長的演說使聽衆厭倦了。*She never ~s of talking about her clever son.* 談到她兒子的聰明伶俐,她從不會感到厭倦。***be ~d of,*** have had enough of, be exhausted with: 對…感到厭煩;厭倦: *I'm ~d of boiled eggs,* I have had too many of them, or too often. 我吃厭了煮蛋。**~d** /ˈtaɪəd; taɪrd/ *adj* weary in body or mind: (身體或精神)疲倦的;疲乏的: *He was a ~d man when he got back from the long climb.* 長途爬山回來,他感到疲倦了。***~d out,*** completely exhausted. 筋疲力竭的。**~d·ness** *n* **~·less** *adj* **1** not easily ~d: 不易疲倦的: *a ~less worker.* 不倦的工作者。**2** ceaseless; continuing a long time: 不停的;持續長時間的: *~less energy.* 持久的精力。**~·less·ly** *adv* **~·some** /-səm; -səm/ *adj* troublesome; tedious. 令人厭倦的;討人厭的。**tir·ing** *adj* making ~d: 令人疲倦的;使人厭倦的: *a tiring journey/argument.* 令人疲倦的旅行(令人厭倦的議論)。

tiro, tyro /ˈtaɪərəʊ; ˈtaɪro/ *n* (*pl* ~s /-rəʊz; -roz/) beginner; person with little experience. 新手;缺乏經驗者。

tis·sue /ˈtɪʃuː; ˈtɪʃʊ/ *n* **1** [C, U] (any kind of) woven fabric. (任何種類的)織物。**2** [C, U] mass of cells and cell-products in an animal body: (動物的)組織: *muscular/connective ~.* 肌肉(結締)組織。**3** ˈ**~ paper,** thin, soft paper for wrapping things, protecting delicate articles, etc: (包裝、保護精緻物品等用的)薄紙;棉紙: *ˈtoilet ~,* soft paper for use in the WC; 衞生紙; *ˈface/ˈfacial ~s,* for use in wiping off lip-stick, face-cream, etc. 面紙;化粧紙(用於揩去口紅,面霜等)。**4** [C] (fig) web or network; series: (喻)網狀物;一連串: *a ~ of lies.* 一套謊言。

tit¹ /tɪt; tɪt/ *n* kinds of small bird: (數種)小鳥: *titmouse;* 小山雀; *titlark;* 雲雀類的小鳴禽; *tomtit;* 山雀類; *long-tailed tit,* etc. 長尾山雀等。⇨ the illus at bird. 參看 bird 之插圖。

tit² /tɪt; tɪt/ *n* (only in) (僅用於) ***tit for tat,*** blow in return for blow; (fig) equal retaliation. 還擊;(喻)以牙還牙;一報還一報。

tit³ /tɪt; tɪt/ *n* ⚠ (vulg sl) teat; nipple; woman's

breast. (諱)(鄙俚)奶頭;乳頭;婦女的乳房。

ti·tan /ˈtaɪtn ; ˈtaɪtən/ *n* **1** **T~,** (Gk myth) one of a family of giants who once ruled the world. (希神)泰坦(曾統治世界的巨人家族中的一員)。 **2** person of super-human size, strength, intellect, etc. 身材、體力、智慧等出衆的人;巨人;傑出之士。 **~ic** /taɪˈtænɪk ; taɪˈtænɪk/ *adj* immense. 巨大的;極有力的。

tit·bit /ˈtɪtbɪt ; ˈtɪtˌbɪt/ *n* [C] choice and attractive bit (*of* food, news, gossip, etc). 精美而有吸引力的少量(食物,消息,漫談等);珍品;珍聞。

tithe /taɪð ; taɪð/ *n* [C] **1** (hist) tenth part of farm produce given for the support of (Church of England) parish priests. (史)(用以維持英國國教的)農產品什一稅。 ˈ**~-barn** *n* barn in which ~s were stored. 儲放什一稅農產品的倉房。 **2** (rhet) tenth part. (修辭)十分之一;小部分。

tit·il·late /ˈtɪtɪleɪt ; ˈtɪtḷˌet/ *vt* [VP6A] stimulate or excite pleasantly. 刺激使感到愉快;使爽快;使高興。 **tit·il·la·tion** /ˌtɪtɪˈleɪʃn ; ˌtɪtḷˈeʃən/ *n*

titi·vate (also **tit·ti-**) /ˈtɪtɪveɪt ; ˈtɪtəˌvet/ *vt, vi* [VP6A, 2A] (colloq) adorn; make smart: (俗)裝飾;打扮;使漂亮: *She was titivating (herself) before the mirror.* 她在鏡前打扮(自己)。

tit·lark /ˈtɪtlɑːk ; ˈtɪtˌlɑrk/ *n* ⇨ tit[1].

title /ˈtaɪtl ; ˈtaɪtl/ *n* **1** [C] name of a book, poem, picture, etc. (書籍,詩歌,圖畫等的)名稱;題目;標題。 ˈ**~-page** *n* page at the front of a book giving the ~, the author's name, etc. 書名頁。 ˈ**~-role** *n* part in a play that gives the play its name: 劇名角色(以該劇中人之名爲劇名者): *a performance of 'Othello' with Olivier in the ~-role,* with Olivier as Othello. 演出奧賽羅,以奧利維爾擔任奧賽羅這一角色。 **2** [C] word used to show a person's rank, occupation, status, etc, eg Lord, Prince, Professor, Dr. 稱號;頭銜(如勛爵、王子、教授、博士等)。 **3** [C, U] ~ *to sth/to do sth,* (legal) right or claim, esp right to the possession of a position, property: (法律)權益;權利(尤指對某地位或財產所保有的權利): *What ~ has he to the throne?* 他有何種權利繼承王位? *Has he any ~ to the land?* 他有權保有該土地嗎? ˈ**~-deed** *n* document proving a ~ to property. 所有權狀;地契;房契。 **4** ˈ**credit ~s,** (or 或 *credits*), names of persons (eg scriptwriters, producers, camera men) responsible for a cinema film or TV production, shown at the beginning or end of the film, etc. 電影或電視製作者的名單(如編劇、製片人、攝影等)。**~d** /ˈtaɪtld ; ˈtaɪtḷd/ *adj* having a ~ of nobility: 有爵位的;有貴族頭銜的: *a ~d lady,* eg a duchess. 命婦(如女公爵)。

tit·mouse /ˈtɪtmaʊs ; ˈtɪtˌmaʊs/ *n* (*pl* -mice /-maɪs ; -ˌmaɪs/) ⇨ tit[1].

tit·ter /ˈtɪtə(r) ; ˈtɪtɚ/ *vi* [VP2A], *n* (give a) silly, half-suppressed little laugh. 傻笑;竊笑。

tittle /ˈtɪtl ; ˈtɪtḷ/ *n* ***not one jot or ~,*** not a particle; not even a very little bit. 沒有一點;根本沒有。

tittle-tattle /ˈtɪtl tætl ; ˈtɪtḷˌtætḷ/ *n, vi* gossip. 閒談;聊天。

titu·lar /ˈtɪtjʊlə(r) *US:* -tʃʊ- ; ˈtɪtʃəlɚ/ *adj* **1** held by virtue of a title(3): 有權持有或保有的: *~ possessions.* 有權保有的財產。 **2** existing in name but not having authority or duties: 有名無實的;名義上的: *the ~ ruler;* 名義上的統治者; *~ sovereignty.* 有名無實的統治權。

tizzy /ˈtɪzɪ ; ˈtɪzɪ/ *n* ***be in a ~,*** (colloq) in a nervous state. (俗)處於緊張狀態;處於激動狀態。

T-junction /ˈtiː dʒʌŋkʃn ; ˈti dʒʌŋkʃən/ *n* one where two roads, wires, pipes, etc meet to form a T. 丁字形結合;丁字形結合處或結合點。

TNT /ˌtiː en ˈtiː ; ˈtiˌɛnˈti/ *n* (= *t*ri*n*itro*t*oluene) powerful explosive. 黃色炸藥。

to[1] /*usual form before consonants:* tə ; tə; *before vowels:* tʊ *or* tuː ; tʊ or tu; *strong form or finally:* tuː ; tu/ *prep* **1** in the direction of; towards: 向;對;朝…方向: *walk to work;* 步行上班; *go to the pub;* 到酒館去; *fall to the ground;* 落向地面; *off to London;* 到倫敦去; *point to sth;* 指向某物; *hold sth (up) to the light;* 持物至光亮處; *on the way to the station;* 在前往車站途中; *twenty miles to Dover;* 距多佛二十哩; *sitting with his feet to the fire;* 他的腳朝着火坐着; *turn to the right;* 轉向右方; *going from town to town/place to place, etc.* 由一城走向另一城(一地走向另一地等)。*Scotland is to the north of England.* 蘇格蘭在英格蘭以北。 **2** (fig uses) towards (a condition, quality, etc); to reach the state of: (比喻用法)趨於;傾向(某種情況、性質等);至某種狀態: *a tendency to laziness/fat,* to be lazy/fat; 懶惰(發胖)的傾向; *all to no purpose,* without any, or a satisfactory, results; 毫無結果; *stir sb to action;* 鼓勵某人行動; *bring/move/reduce sb to tears.* 使某人(感動)落淚。*The mother sang her baby to sleep,* sang until the baby slept. 母親唱歌直到那嬰兒睡着。*He tore the letter to pieces,* eg in anger. 他把那封信撕碎(如在憤怒時)。 *Don't start moving until the traffic lights change from red to green.* 交通燈由紅變綠時再開始走。 **3** (introducing the *indirect object,* as in VP13A): (引導間接受詞,用法見VP13A): *To whom did you give it?* 你(把它)給誰了? *Who did you give it to?* 你(把它)給誰了? *The man I gave it to has left.* 我把它交給他的那個人已經離開了。 **4** as far as: 至;到;達;迄: *from beginning to end;* 自始至終; *from first to last;* 從頭到尾; *faithful to the end/last;* 忠實到底; *fight to the last gasp;* 戰鬥至最後一口氣; *wet to the skin;* 濕透; *frozen to the marrow;* 冷徹骨髓; *count (up) to ten;* 數到十; *shades of colour from red to violet;* 從紅到紫的各種色度; *push sb to violent action.* 迫使某人採激烈行動。 **5** before: 在…之前: *a quarter to six;* 五點三刻; *ten to two.* 一點五十。⇨ past. **6** until: 直至;到: *from Saturday to Monday;* 從禮拜六到禮拜一; *from morning to night.* 從早到晚。*I didn't stay to the end of the meeting.* 我未待到會議結束。 *He was conscious to the last.* 他到最後仍很清醒。 **7** (indicating comparison, ratio, reference): (表示比較,比率,參照): *He's quite rich now, compared to what he uesd to be.* 同他過去比起來,他現在很富有了。 *It's nothing to what it might be.* 比起可能的結局,這算不了什麼。*I prefer walking to climbing.* 我喜歡步行勝過爬山。*We won by six goals to three.* 我們以六比三獲勝。*The picture is true to life/nature.* 那幅畫畫得逼眞。*This is inferior/superior to that.* 這個不如(勝過)那個。 *Draw it to scale.* 按比例畫(它)。 **8** against; touching: 緊靠;接觸: *dance cheek to cheek;* 臉貼臉跳舞; *march shoulder to shoulder.* 肩并肩行進。**9** for; of: 爲;屬於: *the key to the door;* 這個門的鑰匙; *a secretary to the managing director;* 總經理的秘書; *the words to a tune;* 一致的言語; *be/hear/say etc sth to one's/sb's advantage/liking, etc.* (聽到,說出)對自己(某人)有利(自己(某人)愛聽等)的話。 **10** forming; making: 形成;構成: *100p to the pound/100c to the dollar,* ie £1 = 100p/$1 = 100c. 一鎊有一百辨士(一元有一百分)。 **11** in honour of: 向…表敬意: *drink (a health) to sb;* 舉杯向某人致敬(祝某人健康); *erect a monument to (the memory of) the soldiers who died in the war.* 爲陣亡將士立紀念碑。⇨ health(4); monument(1). **12** (when comparing two amounts; when quoting a rate) for each; per: (比較兩個數量或談及比率時)每一: *petrol consumption of 30 miles to the gallon;* 每加侖汽油可駛三十哩; *a tax of 10p to the pound.* 每鎊抽十辨士的稅。 ⇨ per; rate[1](1). **13** causing: 使: *To my surprise/annoyance/delight/sorrow, etc, the Liberals were defeated in the election,* Their defeat caused surprise, etc, in me. 自由黨的人在選舉中落敗使我感到驚訝(煩惱,高興,悲傷等)。 *To my shame, I completely forgot our date,* I am ashamed that I forgot it. 眞慚愧,我竟然把我們的約會忘得乾乾淨淨。 **14** (used with verbs of perception like *seem, appear, feel, look, smell, sound,* etc) in the judgement of; according to: (與 seem, appear, feel, look, smell, sound 等表示感覺的動詞連用)據…的判斷; 根據: *It feels／looks／smells／sounds, etc to me like velvet／gold／ammonia／crying, etc.* 摸起來像天鵝絨(看起來像金子;聞起來像阿摩尼亞;聽起來像是在哭等)。

to² /*usual form before consonants:* tə ; tə; *before vowels and strong form:* tuː ; tu/ *particle,* marking the infinitive, used immediately before the *v* (作不定詞的符號,直接用於動詞前) **1** (⇨ VP7A, 17; used after many *vv* but not after *can, do, may, must, shall, will* 用於許多動詞之後,但不用於 can, do, may, must, shall, will 之後): *He wants to go.* 他想要去。*He wants me to go.* 他要我去 **2** (with *adverbial* functions of purpose, result, outcome): (具有副詞功能,表示目的、結果、結局): *They came (in order) to help me.* 他們來(爲要)幫助我。*He lived to be ninety.* 他活到九十歲。*We make our goods to last,* ie so that they will last. 我們的貨物造得經久耐用。 **3** (limiting the meanings of *adjj* and *advv*): (限制形容詞及副詞的意義): *I'm ready to help.* 我願意幫忙。*The book is easy to understand.* 這本書易懂。*He's old enough to go to school.* 他已屆學齡。*She's too young to marry.* 她年紀太輕,還不能結婚。*This coffee's too hot to drink,* to be drunk. 這咖啡太熱,還不能喝。 **4** (indicating a subsequent fact; 表示後繼事實; ⇨ VP4B): *The good old days have gone never to return,* and will never return. 美好的往日已成過去,永不會再來了。*He awoke to find himself* (= and found himself) *in a strange room.* 他醒過來發現自己在一個陌生的房間中。 **5** (with an *adjectival* function): (具有形容詞的功能): *John was the first to arrive,* who arrived first. 約翰第一個到。 **6** (used with an inf as a *n*): (與不定詞結合,作名詞用): *It is wrong to steal.* 偷竊是不對的。*To err is human, to forgive divine.* 犯錯是人之常情,寬恕是超凡的。 **7** (as a substitute for the inf): (代替不定詞): *We didn't want to go but we had to.* 我們本不想去,但是不去不行。*I intended to go, but forgot to.* 我打算要去,但是忘了去。*He often does things you wouldn't expect him to.* 他常會做出你意料不到的事。

to³ /tuː ; tu (*no weak form*)/ *adv* **1** to or in the usual or required position, esp to a closed or almost closed position: 到或在通常或被要求的位置;(尤指)達到密閉或幾乎密閉的位置: *Push the door* ˈ*to.* 把門關上。*Leave the door* ˈ*to,* almost closed. 讓門就那樣虛掩着好了。 **2** ***to and fro,*** ⇨ fro. **3** ***bring*** ˈ***to; come*** ˈ***to; fall*** ˈ***to,*** ⇨ bring(6); come(15); fall²(14).

toad /təʊd ; tod/ *n* rough-skinned, frog-like animal that lives on land except when breeding. 蟾蜍;癩蝦蟆。⇨ the illus at amphibian. 參看 amphibian 之挿圖。ˌ**~-in-the-**ˈ**hole** *n* sausages baked in batter. 拖臘腸(一種將臘腸裹上麵糊烤成之食物)。ˈ**~·stool** *n* kinds of umbrella-shaped fungus, some of them poisonous. 菌蕈;毒蕈。⇨ the illus at fungi. 參看 fungi之挿圖。

toady /ˈtəʊdɪ ; ˈtodɪ/ *n* obsequious flatterer. 諂媚者;拍馬屁者。□ *vi* [VP2A, 3A] ~ ***(to sb),*** flatter in the hope of advantage or gain: 奉承;諂媚: *~ to the boss.* 對上司諂媚。

toast¹ /təʊst ; tost/ *n* [U] (slice of) bread made brown and crisp by heating at a fire, etc: 烤麵包;烤麵包片;吐司: *a poached egg on ~;* 烤麵包加一個荷包蛋; *two slices of buttered ~.* 兩片塗奶油的烤麵包。ˈ**~·rack** *n* for holding slices of ~. 吐司架;烤麵包架。□ *vt, vi* [VP6A, 2A] **1** make or become brown and crisp by heating. 烤;烘。ˈ**~·ing-fork** *n* fork with a long handle used for holding bread in front of a fire. 吐司叉;烤麵包叉。 **2** warm (oneself, one's toes, etc) before a fire. 烘暖(自己,脚趾等)。 **~er** *n* device (usu electric) for ~ing bread. 烤麵包機(通常是電動的)。

toast² /təʊst ; tost/ *vt* [VP6A] wish happiness, success, etc to (sb or sth) while raising a full drinking-glass: 敬酒;舉杯祝頌(某人或某事物)快樂、成功等: *~ the bride and bridegroom.* 舉杯祝頌新娘和新郎。□ *n* [C] act of ~ing; person, etc ~ed: 敬酒;舉杯祝頌;被敬酒的人等: *propose a ~ to the bridesmaids;* 提議向女儐相敬酒; *drink a ~;* 敬酒;乾杯; *respond／reply to the ~,* eg of the speeches made after a wedding to and by the bride and bridegroom. 答謝敬酒(例如,婚禮後向新娘新郎或由新娘新郎所作的演說)。ˈ**~-master** *n* person who announces the ~s at a banquet at which there are distinguished guests. (宴會上的)祝酒人;宴會主人。

to·bacco /təˈbækəʊ ; təˈbæko/ *n* [U] (plant having) leaves which are dried, cured and used for smoking (in pipes, cigars, cigarettes) or as snuff; (*pl,* for kinds of ~ leaf): 烟草;烟葉;(複數指各種烟葉): *This is a mixture of the best ~s.* 這是由各種最好的烟葉配製成的。 **~·nist** /təˈbækənɪst ; təˈbækənɪst/ *n* dealer in ~. 烟草商。

to·bog·gan /təˈbɒgən ; təˈbɑgən/ *n* long, narrow sledge, curved up in front, used for going downhill on snow. 長滑橇(前端向上彎曲,用以在積雪的山坡上往下滑)。□ *vi* [VP2A, C] go down a snow- or ice-covered slope on a ~. 乘滑橇滑下。

tobogganing

toby-jug /ˈtəʊbɪ dʒʌg ; ˈtobɪ dʒʌg/ *n* drinking-mug shaped like a man, wearing a three-cornered hat. 人形(酒)杯。

toc·cata /təˈkɑːtə ; təˈkɑtə/ *n* (music) composition for a keyboard instrument (organ, piano, etc) in a free style, designed to show the performer's technique. (音樂)觸技曲。

toc·sin /ˈtɒksɪn ; ˈtɑksɪn/ *n* [C] (bell rung to give a) signal of alarm (now usu fig). 警鐘;警鈴;警聲;警報(現通常作喩)。

to·day /təˈdeɪ ; təˈde/ *adv, n* [U] **1** (on) this day: 今天;本日: *T~ is Sunday.* 今天是禮拜天。*Have you seen ~'s newspaper?* 你看過今天的報紙嗎？ *We're leaving ~ week／a week ~,* in one week's time. 我們將於下週今日(七天後)離開。 **2** (at) this present age or period: 當今;現代;當世: *the writers／the young people of ~.* 現代的作家(年輕人)。

toddle /ˈtɒdl ; ˈtɑdl̩/ *vi* [VP2A, C] walk with short, uncertain steps as a baby does; (colloq) walk: 嬰兒般搖搖擺擺地走路;以短而不穩定的步伐行走;(俗)步行;走: *~ off／round to see a friend.* 走去看朋友。 **tod·dler** /ˈtɒdlə(r) ; ˈtɑdlɚ/ *n* baby who can ~. 初學走路的嬰兒。

toddy /ˈtɒdɪ ; ˈtɑdɪ/ *n* (*pl* -dies) **1** [C, U] (drink of) alcoholic spirits (esp whisky) and hot water. 加熱水的烈酒;攙水威士忌。 **2** [U] fresh or fermented sap of some kinds of palm-trees. 某些棕櫚樹的汁液(新鮮或經發酵)。

to-do /təˈduː ; tʊˈdu/ *n* ado; fuss; commotion: 騷亂;紛擾;喧鬧: *What a ~!* What a lot of excitement and talk! 多吵鬧啊！

toe /təʊ ; to/ *n* **1** each of the five divisions of the front part of the foot; similar part of an animal's foot: 脚趾;動物的足趾: *turn one's toes in／out,* ie in walking. (走路時)脚尖朝內(外)。⇨ the illus at leg. 參看 leg 之挿圖。***tread／step on sb's toes,*** (fig) offend his feelings or prejudices. 踩(踏)在某人脚趾上;(喩)傷某人感情;觸怒某人。 ***from top to toe,*** from head to foot, completely. 從頭

到脚；完全。***on one's toes,*** (fig) alert, ready for action. (喻)警覺的；準備行動的。 **'toe-cap** *n* outer covering of the toe of a shoe or boot. 鞋或靴尖的飾皮；鞋頭；靴頭。 **'toe-hold** *n* small, insecure foothold (eg when climbing a cliff). 不穩的小立足點；踏趾處(如攀爬時)。 **'toe-nail** *n* nail of the toe of a human being. 脚趾甲。 **2** part of a sock, shoe, etc covering the toes. 襪、鞋等的趾部。 □ *vt* [VP6A] touch, reach, with the toes. 以趾觸；足趾伸及。 ***toe the line,*** **(a)** stand with a toe on the starting-line ready for a race. (賽跑時)準備起跑。 **(b)** (fig) obey orders given to one as a member of a group or party. (喻)服從團體或黨的命令。

toff /tɒf ; tɔf/ *n* (dated GB sl) well-dressed or distinguished-looking person. (過時英俚)衣着講究的人；儀表出衆的人。

toffee /'tɒfɪ *US:* 'tɔːfɪ ; 'tɔfɪ/ *n* (*pl* ~s) (US = *taffy* /'tæfɪ ; 'tæfɪ/) [C, U] (piece of) hard, sticky sweet made by boiling sugar, butter, etc. (一塊)太妃糖。

tog /tɒg ; tɑg/ *vt* (-gg-) [VP15B] ***tog oneself up／out (in),*** (colloq) put on smart clothes. (俗)穿起漂亮衣服。 **togs** *n pl* (colloq) clothes: (俗)衣服: *put on one's best togs.* 穿起最漂亮的衣服。

toga /'təʊgə ; 'togə/ *n* loose flowing outer garment worn by men in ancient Rome. (古羅馬男子所著的)寬鬆外袍；托加袍。

to·gether /tə'geðə(r) ; tə'gɛðɚ/ *adv* **1** in company: 在一起；共同地: *They went for a walk ~.* 他們一起去散步。 *We are working ~.* 我們在一起工作。 ***~ with,*** as well as; in addition to; and also: 和；加之；連同: *These new facts, ~ with the evidence you have already heard, prove the prisoner's innocence.* 這些新的事實，連同你已聽到的證據，證明在押被告是無辜的。 **2** so as to be in the same place, to be in contact, to be united: 致使在同一地方，有接觸，相結合；在一起: *Tie the ends ~.* 把末端結起來。 *He nailed the boards ~ and made a crate.* 他把木板釘起來，做成一個板條箱。 *Stand the two boys ~ and see who is taller.* 讓這兩個男孩站在一起比比看誰高。 *The leader called his men ~.* 首領召集他的部屬。 ***be ~; get sth／it ~,*** (sl) (cause it to) be, become organised, under control. (俚)(使)有組織；在控制之下。 ***put your／our, etc heads ~,*** consult with each other (to find a solution to sth, make plans, etc). 你們(咱們等)商量一下(以解決某事，做成計畫等)。 **3** at the same time: 同時: *All his troubles seemed to come ~.* 他的一切麻煩似乎同時來臨。 **4** without interruption; in continuous succession: 不間斷地；連續地: *They sat talking for hours ~.* 他們坐着聊天一連好幾個鐘頭。 *He has been away from school for weeks ~ through illness.* 他因病已連續數週未去上學。 **~·ness** *n* [U] comradeship; feeling of unity. 同志關係；友誼；團結一致。

toggle /'tɒgl ; 'tɑgl/ *n* short piece of wood (like a peg) (to be) put through a loop (to fasten two things together, eg as used instead of a button on a coat). 掛索樁；套索釘(用以套索眼的短木栓，俾使兩物連繫在一起者)。

togs /tɒgz ; tɑgz/ *n pl* ⇨ tog.

toil /tɔɪl ; tɔɪl/ *vi* [VP2A, B, C, 3A, 4A] ***~ (at),*** work long or hard (at a task); move with difficulty and trouble: 辛勞；辛苦工作；艱難地行動；跋涉: *~ at one's studies;* 苦讀； *~ up a steep hill.* 吃力地爬上陡峭的山。 □ *n* [U, C] labour; hard work: 辛勞；辛苦工作: *after long ~.* 長時間辛苦工作之後。 **~er** *n* hard worker. 辛勞者；辛苦工作的人。 **~·some** /-səm ; -səm/ *adj*

toilet /'tɔɪlɪt ; 'tɔɪlɪt/ *n* **1** process of dressing, cleaning, arranging the hair, face, body, etc: 化粧；梳粧；打扮: *She spent only a few minutes on her ~.* 她祇花了幾分鐘打扮一下。 **2** (attrib) (形容用法) *a '~ set, '~ articles,* such things as a hair-brush, comb, hand-mirror, etc. 一套梳粧用具，梳粧用具(髮刷，梳子，手鏡等)。 **'~-powder** *n* [U] talc. 撲粉；爽身粉。 **'~-table** *n* dressing-table (with a mirror or mirrors). 梳粧臺。 **3** water-closet. 盥洗室；廁所。 **'~-paper** *n* for use in a water-closet. 衛生紙；手紙。 **'~-roll** *n* roll of ~-paper. 一捲衛生紙。

toils /tɔɪlz ; tɔɪlz/ *n pl* nets; snares: 羅網；陷網；圈套: (usu fig) (通常作喻) *caught in the ~ of the law.* 落入法網。

To·kay /təʊ'keɪ ; to'ke/ *n* [U] kind of sweet, rich Hungarian wine. 投咯酒(一種甜而醇的匈牙利葡萄酒)。

to·ken /'təʊkən ; 'tokən/ *n* [C] **1** sign, evidence, guarantee or mark: 表徵；表號；證據；保證；象徵；記號: *A white flag is used as a ~ of surrender.* 白旗是用作投降的信號。 *I am giving you this jewel as a ~ of my esteem／affection.* 我送給你這珠寶以表示我對你的敬意(摯情)。 ***in ~ of,*** as evidence of. 作爲…的證據；表示。 **'book／'record／'gift ~,** receipt (usu on an attractive card) for payment of money, exchangeable for a book／record, etc of the value stated. 書券(唱片券；禮券)(可換取券面所載金額同值的書，唱片等)。 **2** (attrib) serving as a preliminary or small-scale substitute: (形容用法)象徵性的；用作初期或小規模之代表的: *The enemy offered only a ~ resistance,* did not resist seriously. 敵人僅作了象徵性的抵抗。 **'~ money,** coins of low intrinsic value, but exchangeable for money of standard value. 代幣(實值較低而可兌換標準價值之錢幣者)。 **~ payment,** payment of a small part of what is owed, made to show that the debt is recognized. 象徵性的償付(償付小部分欠款，作爲承認該債務的象徵)。 **~ strike,** for a few hours only (as a warning that a long strike may follow). 象徵性罷工(僅罷工數小時，以警告對方可能發動長時間罷工)。 **~ vote,** Parliamentary vote of money for government purposes, it being understood that a larger sum may be taken without further discussion or voting. 議會象徵性的撥款(表示政府可支付較大金額的款項，不必再行討論或表決)。

told /təʊld ; told/ *pt, pp* of tell.

tol·er·ate /'tɒləreɪt ; 'tɑlə,ret/ *vt* [VP6A, C] **1** allow or endure without protest: 容許: *I won't ~ your selfishness／your doing that.* 我不能容許你那麼自私(你做那件事)。 **2** endure the society of: 容忍；忍受: *How can you ~ that pompous idiot?* 你怎麼能容忍那個自大的糊塗蟲呢？ **tol·er·able** /'tɒlərəbl ; 'tɑlərəbl/ *adj* that can be ~d; fairly good: 可容忍的；可忍受的；尙佳的: *tolerable food;* 尙佳的伙食; *in tolerable health.* 健康還好的。 **tol·er·ably** /-əblɪ ; -əblɪ/ *adv* in a tolerable manner or degree: 可容忍地；可忍受地；尙可地；相當地: *feel tolerably (= fairly) certain about sth.* 對某事覺得相當有把握。 **tol·er·ance** /'tɒlərəns ; 'tɑlərəns/ *n* [U] quality of tolerating opinions, beliefs, customs, behaviour, etc different from one's own: 容忍；寬容: *religious／racial tolerance.* 宗教(種族)上的容忍。 **tol·er·ant** /-rənt ; -rənt/ *adj* having or showing tolerance: 容忍的；寬容的: *Mr X is not very tolerant of criticism／contradiction,* does not endure it easily. 某先生不大能容忍批評(反駁)。 **tol·er·ant·ly** *adv* **tol·er·ation** /,tɒlə'reɪʃn ; ,tɑlə'reʃən/ *n* [U] tolerance. 容忍；寬容。

toll[1] /təʊl ; tol/ *n* [C] **1** payment required for the use of a road, bridge, harbour, etc. (使用道路、橋樑、海港等的)通行稅或費；過橋費；過路費；港稅。 **'~-bar／-gate** *n* bar／gate across a road at which a ~ is payable. (徵收過路費的)卡門；徵收卡；關閘。 **'~-house** *n* house for the man in charge of a ~-bar. (過路費等的)徵收所。 **2** (fig) sth paid, lost or suffered: (喻)付出、失去或損失之物；代價；犧牲: *the ~ of the roads,* deaths and injuries from traffic accidents. 交通事故的傷亡人數。 *The war took a heavy ~ of the nation's manhood.* 戰爭攫取了該國許多男子的生命。 **3** **'~ call** *n* telephone call for which the rates are higher than for local calls. 長途電話(比當地電話費高者)。

toll² /təʊl ; tol/ *vt, vi* [VP6A, 2A] (of a bell) (cause to) ring with slow, regular strokes: (指鐘)(使)緩慢而有規律地鳴響;鳴鐘;敲鐘:*The funeral bell ~ed solemnly.* 喪鐘肅穆地鳴響。*Whose death is being ~ed?* 在爲誰敲喪鐘? □ *n* (*sing* only) ~ing stroke, of a bell. (僅用單數)鳴鐘;敲鐘;鐘聲。

toma·hawk /ˈtɒməhɔːk ; ˈtɑməˌhɔk/ *n* light axe used as a tool and a weapon by N American Indians. (北美印第安人用作工具和武器的)輕斧;戰斧;鉞。□ *vt* strike with a ~. 用輕(戰)斧揮砍或殺。

tom·ato /təˈmɑːtəʊ *US:* təˈmeɪtəʊ ; təˈmeto/ *n* (*pl* **~es** /-təʊz ; -toz/) [C] (plant with) soft, juicy, red or yellow fruit usu eaten with meat, in salads, and in sauces: 番茄: (attrib) (形容用法) ˈ~ *juice.* 番茄汁。⇨ the illus at vegetable. 參看 vegetable 之插圖。

tomb /tuːm ; tum/ *n* place dug in the ground, cut out of rock, etc for a dead body, esp one with a monument over it. 墳;墓。ˈ**~·stone** *n* stone set up over a ~. 墓碑。

tom·bola /tɒmˈbəʊlə ; ˈtɑmbolə/ *n* [C] (*pl* ~s) (now usu called 現通常稱作 *bingo*) kind of lottery with sums of money or small fancy articles as prizes. 唐伯拉(以錢或小的裝飾品作爲獎品)。

tom·boy /ˈtɒmbɔɪ ; ˈtɑmˌbɔɪ/ *n* girl who likes rough, noisy games and play. 野丫頭;頑皮的女孩子。

tom·cat /ˈtɒmkæt ; ˈtɑmˌkæt/ *n* male cat. 雄貓。

tome /təʊm ; tom/ *n* large, heavy book. 大部頭書;大本書。

tom·fool /ˌtɒmˈfuːl ; ˈtɑmˈful/ *n* stupid person; (attrib) stupid: 笨伯;愚人;(形容用法)愚蠢的: *a ~ speech.* 愚蠢的談話(演說)。**~·ery** /-ərɪ ; -ərɪ/ *n* [U] senseless behaviour; [C] (*pl* -ries) stupid joke. 愚蠢的舉止;愚蠢的笑話。

tommy-gun /ˈtɒmɪ gʌn ; ˈtɑmɪ gʌn/ *n* submachine-gun (light kind that can be carried and used by one man). 湯姆遜衝鋒槍。

tommy-rot /ˌtɒmɪˈrɒt ; ˈtɑmɪˌrɑt/ *n* (colloq) utter foolishness: (俗)極愚;荒唐: *You're talking ~.* 你在胡扯。*That's all ~.* 荒唐之至。

to·mor·row /təˈmɒrəʊ ; təˈmɔro/ *adv, n* [U] (on) the day after today: 明天;在明天: *If today is Monday, ~ will be Tuesday and the day after ~ will be Wednesday.* 如果今天是星期一,明天就是星期二,後天就是星期三。*Don't wait until ~.* 不要等到明天。*Where will he be ~ morning/afternoon/evening/night?* 明天早上(下午,晚上,夜裏)他會在哪兒呢? *The announcement will appear in ~'s newspapers.* 這項宣布將刊在明天的報紙上。*What will the men and women of ~* (= of the next few years) *think of us?* 未來的男女會對我們作何看法呢? **~ week,** eight days hence. 八天後(下週明日)。

tom-tit /ˈtɒm tɪt ; ˈtɑmˌtɪt/ *n* kind of small bird. 山雀類。⇨ tit¹.

tom-tom /ˈtɒmtɒm ; ˈtɑmˌtɑm/ *n* (kind of) African or Asian drum, esp a long and narrow kind, beaten with the hands. 唐唐鼓(見於非洲及印度等處,用手擊之)。

ton /tʌn ; tʌn/ *n* **1** measure of weight (2 240 lb in GB, 2 000 lb in the US). 噸(英國爲 2 240 磅,美國爲 2 000 磅)。**metric ton,** = tonne. ⇨ App 5. 參看附錄五。**2** measure of the internal capacity (100 cu ft) or carrying capacity (40 cu ft) of a ship. 船的噸位(船的登記噸位,爲 100 立方呎;或指船的載運或容積噸位,爲 40 立方呎)。**3** (colloq) large weight, quantity or number: (俗)沉重;大量;衆多: *He has tons of money.* 他有很多錢。**4 the ton,** (sl) speed of 100 mph: (俚)一百哩時速: *Can your motor-bike do the ton?* 你的機車每小時能跑 100 哩嗎? □ *vi* [VP2C] **ton up,** drive (a motor-cycle) for sport at a high speed. 高速騎(機車)出遊;飛車兜風。

to·nal /ˈtəʊnl ; ˈtonl̩/ *adj* of tone or tones; of ~-ity. 聲音的;音調的;調性的。**~·ity** /təʊˈnælətɪ ; toˈnælətɪ/ *n* (*pl* -ties) (music) character of a melody, depending upon the scale in which it is written, the key in which it is developed, etc. (音樂)音調;調性(旋律的性質,視該曲調所用的音階、調子的演變等而定)。

tone¹ /təʊn ; ton/ *n* **1** [C] sound, esp with reference to its quality, pitch, duration, feeling, etc: 聲音;音調;音質;語調;語氣: *the sweet ~(s) of a violin;* 小提琴的優美聲音; *speak in an angry/entreating ~.* 以憤怒(懇求)的語氣說話。*The doctor's ~ was serious.* 醫生的語氣很嚴肅。ˌ**~-ˈdeaf** *adj* unable to distinguish between differences of pitch. 不能辨別不同音高的;音痴的。ˈ**~-poem** *n* musical composition for an orchestra, illustrating a poetic idea, legend, etc. 音詩(管絃樂隊演奏的樂曲,表現一種詩的意境、傳說等者)。**2** [C] the pitch aspect of a (usu stressed) syllable; rise, fall, etc of the pitch of the voice in speaking: 音節(通常指重音節)的高低或抑揚;語調的高低或抑揚: *In 'Are you ill?' there is usu a rising ~ on 'ill'; in 'He's ill', there is usu a falling ~ on 'ill'.* 在 Are you ill? 一句中, ill 一字的音調通常上揚;在 He's ill 一句中, ill 一字的音調通常下降。**3** (*sing* only) general spirit, character, morale, of a community, etc: (僅用單數)社會等的風氣、特性、風紀等: *The ~ of the country is buoyant.* 該國的風氣活潑。*The next speaker gave a serious/flippant ~ to the discussion.* 次一位發言者爲這場討論加添了一些嚴肅(不正經)的氣氛。*There was a ~ of quiet elegance in the room,* The furnishings, etc gave this impression. 房間中有一種靜謐的高雅氣氛。**4** [C] shade (of colour); degree (of light): 色調;色度;光度: *a carpet in ~s of brown;* 有深淺不同褐色之地毯; *a picture in warm ~s,* in shades suggesting warmth. 有溫暖色調的照片。**5** (music) any one of the five larger intervals between one note and the next which, together with two semi-~s, make up an octave. (音樂)全音。**6** [U] proper and normal condition of (parts of) the body: 身體(各器官)的健康狀態: *good muscular ~;* 肌肉結實; *recover mental ~.* 恢復心理健康。**-toned** *adj* having a particular kind of ~(1): 有某種聲音,音調,語氣等的: *silver-~d trumpets.* 清脆的喇叭聲。**~·less** *adj* lacking colour, spirit, etc; dull: 無風格的;單調的;沉悶的: *answer in a ~less voice.* 以單調的聲音回答。**~·less·ly** *adv*

tone² /təʊn ; ton/ *vt, vi* **1** [VP6A] give a particular tone of sound or colour to. 加以某種聲調或色調。**2** [VP15B, 2C] **~ *(sth)* down,** make or become less intense: 緩和;減輕: *The excitement ~d down.* 興奮的情緒降低了。*The artist ~d down the cruder colours in his painting.* 那位畫家使他畫中刺眼的色彩變得柔和些。*You'd better ~ down some of the offensive statements in your article.* 你最好把你文章裏的攻擊性詞句說得含蓄一點。**~ *(sth)* up,** make or become more vigorous, intenser, brighter, etc: 提高;加强;强化: *Exercise ~s up the muscles.* 運動使肌肉結實。**3 ~ *in (with),*** (esp of colours) be in harmony: (尤指顏色)(與…)調和;相配合: *These curtains ~ in well with your rugs.* 這些簾幕的色調與你的地毯配合得很好。

tongs /tɒŋz ; tɔŋz/ *n pl* ***(pair of)* ~,** one of various kinds of usu hinged tool for taking up and holding sth: 鉗;夾具: ˈ*sugar ~;* 糖夾子; ˈ*coal ~;* 火鉗;煤炭夾子; ˈ*ice ~.* 冰塊夾子。***be/go at it hammer and ~,*** ⇨ hammer(1).

tongue /tʌŋ ; tʌŋ/ *n* **1** [C] movable organ in the mouth, used in talking, tasting, licking, etc: 舌;舌頭: *The doctor asked me to put out my ~.* 醫生要我伸出舌頭。*Don't put your ~ out at me, you cheeky girl!* 不要向我伸舌頭,你這沒規矩的丫頭! ⇨ the illus at mouth, snake. 參看 mouth, snake 之插圖。***have sth on the tip of one's ~,*** ⇨ tip¹(1). ***find one's ~,*** become able to speak again (after being too shy to do so). (在羞怯得說不出話之後)開口說話;恢復說話能力。***have/say sth with/***

speak with one's ~ in one's cheek, say sth that one does not intend to be taken seriously. 無誠意地說話;非認眞地說話。 Hence, 由此產生, ˌ~-in-ˈ**cheek** *adj, adv*: *~-in-cheek remarks;* 無誠意的話; *speak ~-in-cheek.* 非認眞地說。 ***have lost one's ~,*** be too shy to speak. 羞怯得說不出話來。 ***have a ready ~,*** be fluent, quick to answer questions, etc. 口齒伶俐;能言善道;口才好。 ***hold one's ~,*** be silent, saying nothing. 緘默;不開口。 ***keep a civil ˈ~ in one's head,*** not be rude. 謹愼措辭;談吐溫雅。 ˈ**~-tied** *adj* silent; unable or unwilling to speak through shyness, fear, etc. 沉默的; (因羞怯、恐懼等而)張口結舌的; 說不出話的。 ˈ**~-twister** *n* word or succession of words difficult to utter quickly and correctly. 繞口令。 **2** [C] language: 語言: *one's mother ~*, one's native language; 本國話;母語; *the German ~.* 德國話。 **3** [C, U] animal's ~ as an article of food: (用作食物的)動物的舌頭;舌肉: *boil an ˈox-~;* 煮牛舌; *ham and ~ sandwiches.* 火腿和舌肉的三明治。 **4** sth like a ~ in shape or function, eg the clapper of a bell, the strip of leather under the laces of a shoe, a jet of flame (which licks things), a long promontory (*a ~ of land*). 舌狀物 (如鈴舌、鞋舌、火舌、狹長的海角等)。 **-~d** *adj* (in compounds) having a ~ of the kind indicated: (用於複合字中)有某種舌的;說話…的: *a sharp-~d woman.* 言詞鋒利的女人。

tonic /ˈtɒnɪk ; ˈtɑnɪk/ *n, adj* **1** (sth, eg, medicine) giving strength or energy: 滋補品(如藥物);給予力量或精力的; 滋補的; 激勵的: *the ~ quality of sea air;* 海上空氣使人振奮的特性; *get a bottle of ~ from the doctor.* 從醫生處拿到一瓶補劑。 *Praise can be a fine ~.* 稱讚可成爲一種良好的鼓勵。 *The good news acted as a ~ on us all,* cheered us up. 那好消息使我們大家感到振奮。 ˈ**~ (water),** bottled, carbonated water with quinine: (通常爲瓶裝)奎寧水: *a gin and ~* (as a drink). 奎寧杜松子酒(用作飲料)。 **2** (music) keynote. (音樂)主音。ˌ**~ ˌsol-ˈfa** /ˌsɒlˈfɑː *US:* ˌsəul ; solˈfɑ/ *n* (in teaching singing) method of showing musical notes by syllables, eg *sol, fa, do.* 首調唱法(以字音,如 sol, fa, do, 表示音符的歌曲教唱法)。 ⇨ do[5].

to·night /təˈnaɪt ; təˈnaɪt/ *adv, n* [U] (on) the night of today: (在)今晚;今夜: *last night, ~, and tomorrow night;* 昨晚,今晚和明晚; *after ~;* 今夜以後; *~'s radio news.* 今晚的新聞廣播。

ton·nage /ˈtʌnɪdʒ ; ˈtʌnɪdʒ/ *n* **1** internal cubic capacity of a ship (1 ton = 100 cu ft). 船的登記噸位(每噸爲 100 立方呎)。 **2** cargo-carrying capacity of a ship stated in tons (of 40 cu ft). 船的貨運或容積噸位(每噸爲 40 立方呎)。 **3** total ~(1) of a country's merchant shipping. (一國商船的)總噸位(指登記噸位)。 **4** charge per ton on cargo, etc for transport. 每噸貨物的運費;噸稅。

tonne /tʌn ; tʌn/ *n* metric ton, = 1 000 kilograms. 公噸(1 000 公斤)。 ⇨ App 5. 參看附錄五。

ton·sil /ˈtɒnsl ; ˈtɑnsl̩/ *n* either of two small oval masses of tissue at the sides of the throat, near the root of the tongue: 扁桃腺: *have one's ~s out,* have them removed by a surgeon. 割除扁桃腺。⇨ the illus at head. 參看 head 之挿圖。 **~·litis** /ˌtɒnsɪˈlaɪtɪs ; ˌtɑnsl̩ˈaɪtɪs/ *n* [U] inflammation of the ~s. 扁桃腺炎。

ton·sorial /tɒnˈsɔːrɪəl ; tɑnˈsorɪəl/ *adj* (often hum, 常爲詼諧語, eg 如 *the ~ art* 理髮技藝) of a hairdresser and his work. 理髮師的;理髮的。

ton·sure /ˈtɒnʃə(r) ; ˈtɑnʃɚ/ *n* shaving of the top of the head of a person about to become a monk or priest; part of the head that has been shaved in this way. 做僧侶時頭頂的剃光;削髮;(僧侶的)光禿圓頂。 □ *vt* give the ~ to. 爲…削髮。

ton·tine /ˈtɒntiːn ; ˈtɑntin/ *n* annuity shared by subscribers to a loan, the shares increasing as the subscribers die, till the last subscriber gets all that is left. 聯合養老保險法(參加者共享一筆基金,有人死亡時,生者卽增加其份額,最後僅存者,獲該基金之全部餘額)。

too /tuː ; tu/ *adv* **1** also; as well, in addition (usu in end position but placed immediately after the word it modifies if there is a risk of ambiguity): 也;又;加之(通常置於句末,若有意義含糊之虞時,則緊放在所修飾之字後): *I, too, have been to Paris,* eg I, as well as he, you, etc. 我也去過巴黎(如謂不祇他、你等去過)。 *I've been to Paris, too,* eg to Paris as well as to Rome, Milan, etc. 我還去過巴黎(如謂不祇去過羅馬、米蘭等)。 *She plays the piano, and sings, too,* plays the piano and also sings. 她會彈鋼琴,也會唱歌。 *Sally, too,* (= Sally, as well as Mary, etc) *plays the piano.* 莎莉也會彈鋼琴(意謂不祇瑪莉等會)。 (Cf the construction in negative sentences: 參較否定結構: *I know the answer, too.* 我也知道那答案。Neg: 否定: *I don't know the answer, either.* 我也不知道那答案。) **2** moreover; nevertheless: 而;此外;而且: *There was frost last night, and in May too!* 昨晚降霜了,而竟在五月! **3** (*adv of degree,* modifying *adjj* and *advv*) in a higher degree than is allowable, required, etc: (表程度的副詞,修飾形容詞及副詞)過於;太: *We've had too much rain lately.* 近來這裏的雨下得太多了。 *You're driving too fast for safety.* 你開車太快了,恐不安全。 *These shoes are much too small for me.* 這雙鞋我穿太小了。*It's too hot for work/too hot to work.* 天太熱無法工作。 *It's too difficult a task for me.* 這工作對我來說是太難了。 *That's too small a box/That box is too small to hold all these things.* 那盒子太小,裝不下所有這些東西。(Note that *too* is used to modify a participle that is adjectival, but that with a participle that is purely verbial, *too much* is preferred in formal style. 注意: too 用以修飾作形容詞用的分詞,如該分詞純爲動詞性質,正式文體中,宜用 too much。 Cf: 參較: *He was too tired to go any farther.* 他太疲倦不能再往前走了。 *I hope you were not too (much) disturbed by all the noise we made.* 我希望我們的鬧聲不致打擾你太厲害。 *I'm not too (much) bothered by his criticisms.* 我未因他的批評而感到太大的困擾。) **4** (phrases) (片語) ***carry sth/go too far,*** ⇨ far[2](2). ***all too soon/quickly, etc,*** sooner, more quickly, etc than is desired: 太早(太快等): *The holidays ended all too soon.* 假期結束得太早了。 ***none too soon, etc,*** not at all too soon, etc: 一點也不早等: *We were none too early for the train,* We caught the train with very little time to spare. 我們剛好趕上火車。 ***one too many,*** ⇨ many(1). ***have one too many,*** take more than one can drink and remain sober. 飲酒過量。 ***be too much for,*** ⇨ much[1]. ***only too*** (+ *adj*), ⇨ only[2](2).

took /tʊk ; tʊk/ *pt* of take[1].

tool /tuːl ; tul/ *n* **1** instrument held in the hand(s) and used by workmen, eg gardeners and carpenters. 工具; 用具; 器具。 **maˌchine ˈ~** *n* ⇨ machine. **2** person used by another for dishonest purposes: 受人利用做不正當活動者;爲人利用的工具;走狗;傀儡: *He was a mere ~ in the hands of the dictator.* 他祇是那獨裁者手中的工具而已。□ *vt, vi* **1** [VP6A] ornament (the edges of a book-cover) with designs pressed on with a heated ~. 壓印圖案於(書籍封面的邊緣)。 **2** [VP2C] *~ up,* provide a factory with machine-~s (eg as needed for a particular kind of work). 以工作母機裝備某一工廠。

toot /tuːt ; tut/ *n* [C] short, sharp warning sound from a horn, whistle, trumpet, etc. (號角、笛、喇叭等)短而尖銳的鳴聲;(示警之)嘟嘟聲。□ *vi, vt* [VP2A, 6A] (cause to) give out a ~ or ~s. (使)發嘟嘟聲。

tooth /tuːθ ; tuθ/ *n* (*pl* teeth /tiːθ ; tiθ/) **1** each of the hard, white, bone-like structures rooted in the gums, used for biting and chewing: 牙;齒: *have a ~ out* (US 美 = *have a ~ pulled*), ie by a dentist; 拔一顆牙; *have all one's own teeth/a* *fine set of artificial teeth.* 有一嘴好牙(一副好的假牙)。⇨ the illus at mouth. 參看 mouth 之挿圖。 ***armed to the teeth,*** completely and elaborately armed. 全副武裝。 ***cast sth in a person's teeth,*** reproach him with it. 以某事責備某人。 ***escape by the skin of one's teeth,*** have a narrow escape. 僅以身免;幸免於難。 ***fight ~ and nail,*** fiercely, with a great effort. 猛烈打鬥、作戰等。 ***get one's teeth into sth,*** attack (a job) vigorously. 奮力工作。 ***have a sweet ~,*** be fond of sweet food. 喜吃甜食。 ***lie in one's teeth/throat,*** lie shamelessly. 無恥地說謊。 ***long in the ~,*** (originally of horses, because gums recede with age) old. 上年紀;年紀大(原指馬,因馬年紀大則齒齦向後收縮)。 ***show one's teeth,*** take up a threatening attitude. 恐嚇;作威脅姿態。 ***in the teeth of,*** against the full force of; in opposition to. 抵抗…的全力;對抗。 **(a/the) '~·ache** *n* pain in a ~ or teeth. 牙痛。 **'~-brush** *n* one for cleaning the teeth. 牙刷。⇨ the illus at brush. 參看 brush 之插圖。 **'~·paste/·powder** *n* [U] for cleaning the teeth. 牙膏(牙粉)。 **'~·pick** *n* short, pointed piece of wood, etc, for removing bits of food from between the teeth. 牙籤。 **2** ~-like part, esp of a comb, saw or rake. (尤指梳子、鋸或耙的)齒狀部分。⇨ the illus at gear. 參看 gear 之挿圖。 **,fine-'~ comb,** one with fine teeth set closely together. 細齒梳;篦子。 ***go over/through sth with a ,fine-'~ comb,*** examine it closely and thoroughly. 密切而徹底地調查某事。 **3** (*pl*, colloq) effective force: (複,俗)有效的力量: *When will the new legislation be given some teeth,* be made effective? 新的立法何時生效? **~ed** /tu:θt; tuθt/ (attrib) having teeth (eg of the kind named): (形容用法) 有某種(名稱之)齒的: *a saw-~ed wheel.* 鋸齒輪。 **~·less** *adj* without teeth. 無牙的;無齒的。 **~·some** /-səm; -səm/ *adj* (liter) (of food) pleasant to the taste. (文)(指食物)美味的;可口的。

tootle /'tu:tl; 'tutl/ *vi, n* toot softly or continuously, as on a flute. (發)柔和或連續的嘟嘟聲(如橫笛所發者)。

top¹ /tɒp; tɑp/ *n* (usu 通常作 ***the top (of)***) **1** highest part or point: 頂;巔;上端;上部: *at the top of the hill;* 在山頂; *the hilltop;* 山頂; *at the top of the page;* 在書頁上端; *line 5 from the top.* 從上面數下來第五行。 ***on top,*** above: 在上邊: *The green book is at the bottom of the pile and the red one is on top.* 綠皮書在那一堆的底下,紅皮書在上邊。 ***on (the) top of,*** **(a)** over, resting on: 在…之上: *Put the red book on (the) top of the others.* 把紅皮書放在其他書的上面。 **(b)** in addition to: 加之;除…外: *He borrowed £50 from me for the*

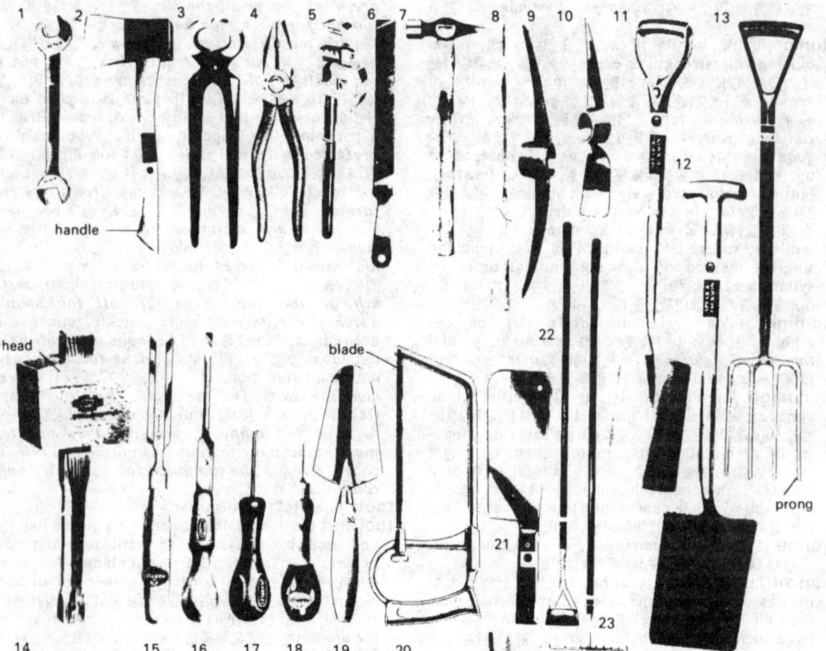

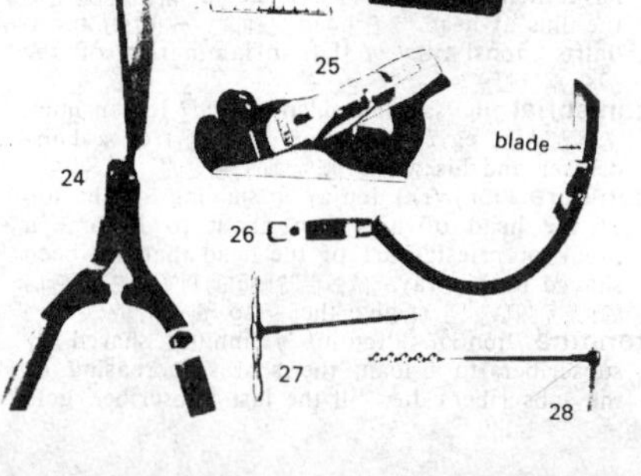

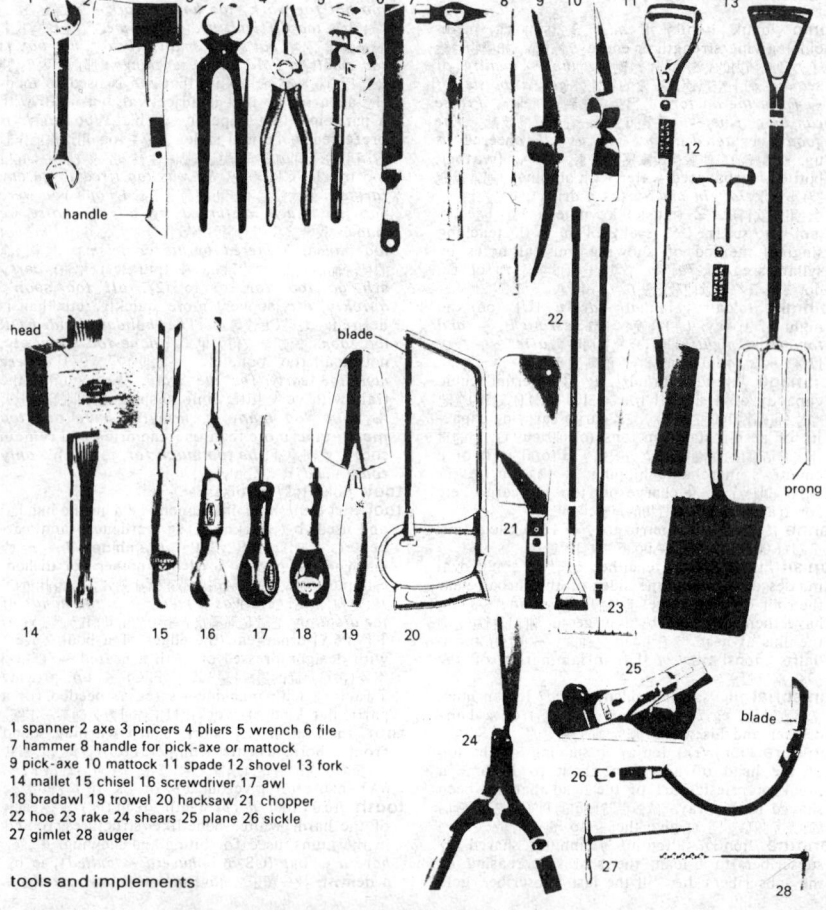

1 spanner 2 axe 3 pincers 4 pliers 5 wrench 6 file
7 hammer 8 handle for pick-axe or mattock
9 pick-axe 10 mattock 11 spade 12 shovel 13 fork
14 mallet 15 chisel 16 screwdriver 17 awl
18 bradawl 19 trowel 20 hacksaw 21 chopper
22 hoe 23 rake 24 shears 25 plane 26 sickle
27 gimlet 28 auger

tools and implements

journey and then, on top of that, asked me if he could borrow my car. 他向我借五十鎊作旅費,除此而外,還向我借汽車。***from top to bottom,*** completely. 完全地;全部地。***from top to toe,*** from head to foot. 從頭到脚。***blow one's top,*** (colloq) explode in rage. (俗)異常惱怒;氣炸了。***off the top of one's head,*** (of sth said) without careful thought or preparation. (指說出的話)未經仔細考慮或準備的。 **2** upper surface, eg of a table: (桌子等的)上表面;上邊: *polish the top of a table/the* ˈ*table top;* 擦亮桌面; *put the luggage on the top of the car.* 把行李放在汽車頂上。***go over the top,*** (mil) go over the front of a trench to attack the enemy; (fig) act quickly after a period of doubt or hesitation. (軍)爬出戰壕攻擊敵人;(喻)(經過一陣遲疑或猶豫後)迅速行動。***on top of the world,*** (colloq) extremely happy, satisfied with everything: (俗)極為愉快;萬事如意;樣樣滿足;諸事順遂: *I'm feeling on top of the world today!* 今天我眞覺得萬事如意。 **3** highest rank, foremost (or most important) place: 最高階級;最前面或最重要的位置: *He came out at the top of the list,* eg of examination results. 他名列前茅(例如指考試的結果)。 *Our host placed us at the top* (= the upper end) *of the table,* the part for honoured guests. 我們的主人安置我們坐在首席上。***come to the top,*** (fig) win fame, success, etc. (喻)成名,成功等。***reach/be at the top of the ladder/tree,*** the highest position in a profession, career, etc. 達到(居於)職業、事業等的最高地位;達到(處於)顚峯。 **4** utmost height or degree. 最高度;最高級。***shout at the top of one's voice,*** ⇨ voice, *n*(3); ***to the top of one's bent,*** ⇨ bent¹. **5** (motoring) (駕車) ***in top,*** in top (the highest) gear: 以高速擋;全速地: *What will the car do in top?* 這車高速行駛的情況如何? **6** (often *pl*) leaves, etc of a plant grown chiefly for its root: (常用複數)根菜植物的葉子等: ˈ*turnip tops.* 蕪菁的葉子。 **7** ***the big top,*** very large circus tent. 馬戲團的大帳篷。 **8** (attrib, and in compounds) highest in position or degree: (形容用法,並用於複合字中)地位或程度最高的;最大的: *on the top shelf;* 在最高一層架子上; *at top speed;* 全速地;以全速; *in top gear;* (駕車)全速;以高速擋; *the top right-hand corner;* 右上角; *charge top prices.* 討高價。**ˈtop-boot** *n* boot with a high top, usu reaching to just below the knee. 長統(及膝)馬靴。**ˈtop-coat** *n* overcoat. 大衣;外套。***be top dog,*** (sl) victor, master. (俚)優勝者;主人。⇨ underdog. **ˌtop ˈdrawer** *n* the highest social class: 社會最高階層;上流社會: *She's out of the top drawer/is very top drawer.* 她出身上流社會。**ˌtop-ˈdress** *vt* apply (manure, etc) to the surface of (ground) instead of ploughing or digging it in; 施(肥料等)於地面;施追肥;施頂肥; Hence, 由此產生, **ˌtop-ˈdressing** *n*: 追肥;頂肥: *give a field a top-dressing of lime.* 在田地上施石灰。**ˌtop-ˈflight/-ˈnotch** *attrib adjj* (colloq) first-rate; best possible: (俗)第一流的;最好的: *top-flight French authors.* 法國的第一流作家。**ˌtop-ˈgallant** *adj, n* mast, sail, etc immediately above the topmast and topsail. 上桅(帆);上桅(帆)的。⇨ the illus at barque. 參看 barque 之插圖。**ˌtop ˈhat** *n* tall silk hat. 高頂絲質禮帽。**ˌtop-ˈheavy** *adj* over-weighted at the top so as to be in danger of falling. 上部過重的;頭重脚輕的;不穩的。 **ˌtop-ˈhole** *adj* (dated sl) excellent; first-rate. (過時俚語)最優的;第一流的。 **ˈtop·knot** *n* knot of hair, bunch of feathers, etc on the top of the head. 冠毛;頂髻;頭飾。**ˈtop·mast** *n* upper mast (clamped to the mainmast). 中桅(夾於主桅上)。 **ˈtop·most** /-məʊst ; -ˌmost/ *adj* highest. 最高的;最上的。**ˌtop ˈpeople,** those at the top of their profession, holding the highest positions, etc: (某一行業的)頂尖人物;高階層人士: *Not all top people read 'The Times'.* 並非所有頂尖人物都閱讀'泰晤士報'。 **ˌtop-ˈranking** *adj* of the highest rank. 最高等級的。**ˈtop·sail** *n* square sail next above the lowest. 中桅帆。⇨ the illus at barque. 參看 barque 之挿圖。**ˌtop ˈsecret,** most secret. 絕對機密的。**top·less** *adj* (of a woman's garment) leaving the breasts bare: (指女裝)上空的;露出胸部的: *a topless dress/swimsuit;* 上空裝(上空泳裝); (of a woman) wearing such a garment: (指女子)穿著上空裝的: *topless waitresses in California.* 加州穿上空裝的女侍。

top² /tɒp ; tap/ *vt* (-pp-) [VP6A] **1** provide a top for; be a top for; be a top to: 加以頂;作為…之頂端: *a church topped by/with a steeple.* 頂部有尖閣的禮拜堂。 **2** reach the top of; be at the top of: 達於…之頂峯;居於…的最高位: *When we topped the hill we had a fine view.* 當我們爬到山頂時,看到了優美的景色。 **3** ***top (sth) up,*** fill up (a partly empty container): 裝滿(部分尙空的容器): *top up a car battery,* add distilled water to raise the level to what is normal; 把汽車電瓶裏的蒸餾水加足; *top up with oil,* add lubricating oil; 加潤滑油; *top up a drink,* refill a partly emptied glass. 加滿(原來未滿的)杯中的酒或飲料。***top (sth) out,*** mark the completion of a tall building (a tower block, etc) with drinks, speeches, etc: 藉舉杯、演講等以慶祝某一高聳建築物的落成: *a ˌtopping-ˈout ceremony.* 高大建築落成典禮。 **4** surpass, be taller or higher than: 超越;高過;勝過: *Our exports have just topped the £80 000 000 mark.* 我們的出口貿易剛剛超過八千萬鎊。 ***to ˈtop it all,*** to crown all, add the last (and surprising, etc) touch. 更妙的是;增添最後(而令人驚訝等)的一筆。 **5** cut the tops off: 截去頂端: *lift and top beets/turnips,* take them from the ground and cut off the leaves; 拔起甜菜(蕪菁)並去其葉; *top and tail gooseberries,* remove the ends from the berries. 除去醋栗的末梢。

top³ /tɒp ; tap/ *n* toy that spins and balances on a point, set in motion by hand, or by winding round it a string which is pulled away, and (in some cases) kept in motion by being whipped. 陀螺(一種玩具)。***sleep like a top,*** soundly. 睡得很熟。

to·paz /ˈtəʊpæz ; ˈtopæz/ *n* [U] transparent yellow mineral; [C] gem cut from this. 黃玉礦;黃玉;黃晶。

tope /təʊp ; top/ *vi, vt* [VP2A, 6A] (dated) drink (alcoholic liquors) to excess; drink habitually. (過時用語)飲(酒)過量;經常飲酒。 **toper** *n* person who ~s. 酒鬼;過量或經常飲酒者。

topi /ˈtəʊpɪ *US:* təʊˈpiː ; toˈpi/ *n* sun-helmet. 遮陽盔;兜帽。

topi·ary /ˈtəʊpɪərɪ *US:* -ɪerɪ ; ˈtopɪˌɛrɪ/ *n* [U], *adj* (concerned with) the clipping of shrubs, eg yew, into ornamental shapes, eg birds, animals: 修剪灌木(使成裝飾形狀,例如將紫杉修剪作鳥獸形);修剪灌木的: *the ~ art;* 灌木修剪術; *a ~ garden.* 修剪過的花園。

topic /ˈtɒpɪk ; ˈtapɪk/ *n* subject for discussion. 論題;話題;題目。 **topi·cal** /-kl ; -kl̩/ *adj* of present interest; of ~s of the day: 與目前有關的;時事問題的: *a ~al ˈnews film,* of current events. 時事影片。 **topi·cally** /-klɪ ; -klɪ/ *adv*

top·ogra·phy /təˈpɒgrəfɪ ; toˈpagrəfɪ/ *n* [U] (description of the) features, eg rivers, valleys, roads, of a place or district. 地形;地誌;地形學。 **topo·graphi·cal** /ˌtɒpəˈgræfɪkl ; ˌtapəˈgræfɪkl̩/ *adj* **topo·graphi·cally** /-klɪ ; -klɪ/ *adv*

top·per /ˈtɒpə(r) ; ˈtapɚ/ *n* (colloq) top hat. (俗)高帽;禮帽。

top·ping /ˈtɒpɪŋ ; ˈtapɪŋ/ *adj* (colloq) excellent. (俗)第一流的;最優的。**~·ly** *adv*

topple /ˈtɒpl ; ˈtapl̩/ *vi, vt* [VP2A, C, 6A, 15B] (cause to) be unsteady and overturn: (使)搖搖欲墜;(使)傾覆;倒下: *The chimney ~d and fell.* 烟囱傾倒了。*The pile of books ~d over/down.* 那一堆書倒了。*The dictator was ~d from power.* 那獨裁者被推翻了。

tops /tɒps ; taps/ *n pl* (usu 通常作 **the tops**) (colloq) the very best. (俗)最佳者;最好者。

topsy-turvy /ˌtɒpsɪ ˈtɜːvɪ ; ˈtɑpsɪˈtɝvɪ/ *adj, adv* (colloq) in confusion; upside down: (俗)混亂的(地);顛倒的(地): *The whole world is/has turned ~.* 整個世界是混亂的(已混亂)。**~·dom** /-dəm ; -dəm/ *n* condition of being ~. 混亂;顛倒。

toque /təʊk ; tok/ *n* (woman's) small, brimless, closefitting hat. (婦女的)小圓帽;無邊女帽。

tor /tɔː(r) ; tɔr/ *n* small hill, rocky peak (esp in placenames on Dartmoor, S W England): 岡;岩山(尤用於英格蘭西南部達特木的地名中): *Hay Tor.* 赫岡。

torch /tɔːtʃ ; tɔrtʃ/ *n* **1** piece of wood, twisted flax, etc treated with oil, soaked in tallow, etc for carrying or using as a flaming light; (fig) sth that gives enlightenment: 火炬;火把;(喻)啓發之物: *the ~ of learning;* 學問之光; *hand on the ~,* keep knowledge, etc alive. 使知識等繼續不衰;傳薪火。***carry a ~ for sb,*** have (esp unrequited) love for him. 愛上某人;(尤指)單戀(某人)。**ˈ~·light** *n* [U] light of a ~ or ~es: 火炬光: *a ~light procession/tattoo,* one in which lighted ~es are used. 火炬遊行。**ˈ~-race** *n* (in ancient Greece) performance of runners who handed lighted ~es to others in relays. (古希臘)火炬接力賽跑。**ˈ~-singer** *n* woman who sings sentimental love-songs. 唱感傷戀歌的女歌手。**2** (GB) electric hand-light (US 美 = *flashlight*); (US) blow-lamp (for welding, etc). (英)手電筒;(美)(焊接等用的)吹燈。

tore /tɔː(r) ; tor/ *pt* of tear².

tor·ea·dor /ˈtɒrɪədɔː(r) *US:* ˈtɔːr- ; ˈtɔrɪəˌdɔr/ *n* Spanish bullfighter (usu mounted on a horse). 西班牙的鬥牛士(通常指騎馬者)。

tor·ment /ˈtɔːment ; ˈtɔrmɛnt/ *n* [C, U] (sth that causes) severe bodily or mental pain or suffering: (身體或心靈的) 劇烈的痛苦或煩惱; 痛苦或煩惱之因: *be in ~;* 受苦;受折磨; *suffer ~(s) from an aching tooth;* 忍受牙痛折磨; *the ~s of jealousy.* 嫉妒的苦惱。*What a little ~ that child is!* (because it worries, asks constant questions, etc). 那孩子多煩人啊! □ *vt* /tɔːˈment ; tɔrˈmɛnt/ [VP6A, 15A] cause severe suffering to; annoy: 使受劇烈痛苦;使煩惱;折磨: *~ed with neuralgia/hunger/mosquitoes.* 爲神經痛(饑餓,蚊子)所苦。*Stop ~ing your father by asking silly questions.* 別再問一些愚蠢的問題折磨你父親了。**tor·men·tor** /tɔːˈmentə(r) ; tɔrˈmɛntɚ/ *n* sb or sth that ~s. 使痛苦的人或物;造成苦惱的人或物;折磨者。

torn /tɔːn ; tɔrn/ *pp* of tear².

tor·nado /tɔːˈneɪdəʊ ; tɔrˈnedo/ *n* (*pl* ~es /-dəʊz ; -doz/) violent and destructive whirlwind. 龍捲風;陸龍捲。

tor·pedo /tɔːˈpiːdəʊ ; tɔrˈpido/ *n* (*pl* ~es /-dəʊz ; -doz/) cigar-shaped self-propelling shell filled with explosives, aimed at ships (from surface ships, submarines and aircraft), and launched to travel below the surface of the sea. 魚雷。**ˈ~-boat** *n* small, fast warship from which ~es are fired. 魚雷艇。**ˈ~-tube** *n* tube from which ~es are discharged. 魚雷發射管。□ *vt* [VP6A] attack or destroy with a ~ or ~es; (fig) attack (a policy, institution, etc) and make it ineffective: 以魚雷襲擊或摧毁;(喻)破壞(某項政策,某一制度等): *Who ~ed the Disarmament Conference?* 誰破壞裁軍會議?

tor·pid /ˈtɔːpɪd ; ˈtɔrpɪd/ *adj* **1** dull and slow; inactive. 呆鈍的;不活潑的。**2** (of animals that hibernate) not moving or feeling. (指冬眠動物)蟄伏的。**~·ly** *adv* **~·ness, ~·ity** /tɔːˈpɪdətɪ ; tɔrˈpɪdətɪ/ *nn* [U] ~ condition. 呆鈍;不活潑;蟄伏。

tor·por /ˈtɔːpə(r) ; ˈtɔrpɚ/ *n* [U, C] torpid condition. 呆鈍;不活潑;蟄伏。

torque /tɔːk ; tɔrk/ *n* **1** [C] necklace, collar or armband of twisted metal, as worn by the ancient Britons and Gauls. (古不列顛人及高盧人佩用的)捻扭的金屬項圈、領圈或臂圈。**2** [U] twisting force causing rotation, eg as exerted on a ship's propeller shaft. 扭(力)矩;轉(力)矩(如施於船的螺旋槳軸者)。

tor·rent /ˈtɒrənt *US:* ˈtɔːr- ; ˈtɔrənt/ *n* [C] **1** violent, rushing stream of liquid (esp water): (尤指水的)急流;湍流: *mountain ~s;* 山洪; *~s of rain;* 雨水的急遽下降;大雨如注; *rain falling in ~s.* 傾盆大雨。**2** (fig) violent outpouring: (喻)爆發;迸發;連續不斷: *a ~ of words/abuse/insults.* 連續不斷的話(謾罵,凌辱)。**tor·ren·tial** /təˈrenʃl ; tɔˈrɛnʃəl/ *adj* of, like, caused by, a ~: 急流的;湍流的;似急流的;由急流形成的: *~ial rain.* 暴雨。

tor·rid /ˈtɒrɪd *US:* ˈtɔːr-;ˈtɔrɪd/ *adj* (of the weather, a country) very hot; tropical: (指天氣、國家)很熱的;熱帶的: *the ˈ~ zone,* part of the earth's surface between the tropics(1). 熱帶。**~·ity** *n* [U] extreme heat. 酷熱;炎熱。

tor·sion /ˈtɔːʃn ; ˈtɔrʃən/ *n* [U] act or process of twisting; state of being twisted. 扭;捻;扭轉;被扭捻的狀態。

torso /ˈtɔːsəʊ ; ˈtɔrso/ *n* (*pl* ~s) (statue of a) human body without head, arms and legs. (無頭和四肢的)軀幹雕像;人體的軀幹。

tort /tɔːt ; tɔrt/ *n* (legal) private or civil wrong for which the wronged person may get redress in a law court. (法律)民事過失;侵權行爲(受害者可在法庭上獲得損害賠償)。

tor·tilla /tɔːˈtiːjə ; tɔrˈtija/ *n* pancake omelette (Mexican style). 托提亞(墨西哥式薄玉米煎餅)。

tor·toise /ˈtɔːtəs ; ˈtɔrtəs/ *n* slow-moving, four-legged land (and fresh-water) varieties of turtle with a hard shell. 龜;陸龜。⇨ the illus at reptile. 參看 reptile 之插圖。**ˈ~-shell** *n* [U] outer shell, esp the kind with yellow and brown markings, of some sea-turtles. 海龜甲;(尤指有黃色和褐色斑點之)玳瑁殼。

tor·tu·ous /ˈtɔːtʃʊəs ; ˈtɔrtʃʊəs/ *adj* full of twists and bends: 彎曲的;多扭曲的: *a ~ path;* 彎曲的小路;(fig) not straightforward; devious: (喻)不正直的;不正當的;拐彎抹角的: *a ~ argument/policy/politician.* 拐彎抹角的議論(不正當的政策;不正直的政客)。**~·ly** *adv*

tor·ture /ˈtɔːtʃə(r) ; ˈtɔrtʃɚ/ *vt* [VP6A, 16A] cause severe suffering to: 使受劇烈痛苦; 折磨: *~ a man to make him confess sth;* 對某人施刑使招認某事;拷問;刑求; *~d with anxiety.* 爲煩惱所苦。□ *n* **1** [U] torturing; infliction of severe bodily or mental suffering: 折磨;拷問;對身心的折磨: *put a man to the ~, ~* him (esp to get a confession or to make him supply information); 折磨某人;(尤指)拷問;刑求; *instruments of ~.* 刑具。**2** [C, U] pain so inflicted or suffered; method of torturing: (折磨或刑求所造成的)痛苦;折磨或拷問的方法: *suffer ~ from toothache;* 因牙痛而受折磨; *the ~s of the damned,* ie in Hell. 地獄中永刼不復的靈魂所受的痛苦。**tor·turer** *n*

Tory /ˈtɔːrɪ ; ˈtorɪ/ *n* (*pl* -ries) = Conservative.

tosh /tɒʃ ; tɑʃ/ *n* (sl) nonsense. (俚)胡言亂語;瞎扯。

toss /tɒs *US:* tɔːs ; tɔs/ *vt, vi* **1** [VP6A, 12A, 13A, 15B] throw up into or through the air; jerk: 投;擲;拋: *~ a ball to sb;* 投球給某人; *~ sth aside/away.* 把某物丢在一邊(丢開)。*The horse ~ed its rider,* caused the rider to fall to the ground. 那馬把騎者摔落(地上)。*He ~ed the beggar a coin/~ed a coin to the beggar.* 他丢給那乞丐一個銅板。*The horse ~ed its head.* 那馬揚起頭。*She ~ed her head back,* ie with a suggestion of contempt, indifference, etc. 她把頭往上一抬(表示輕視、冷漠等)。*He was ~ed by the bull.* 他被那隻公牛牴拋在地上。***~ (up) a coin; ~ (sb) for sth; ~ up,*** send a coin spinning up in the air and guess which side will be on top when it falls; use this method to decide sth (with sb): 擲銅板(以猜其正反面);(與某人)擲銅板以作決定: *Who's to pay for the drinks? Let's ~ up/Let's ~ for it.* 誰來付飲料的錢呢?讓我們擲銅板決定吧。**ˈ~-up** *n* such ~ing of a coin; (hence) sth about which there is doubt: 擲錢幣;(由此產生)有疑問的事: *It's a ~-up whether he will get here in time.* 他是否能及時來此地,尚有疑問。**2** [VP2C, 6A, 15A, B] (cause to) move restlessly from side to side or up and down: (使)搖蕩;(使)搖擺;顛簸: *The ship (was) ~ed about on the stormy sea.* 那條船在洶湧的海上顛簸不定。*The sick child ~ed about in its sleep all night.* 病童整夜在睡眠中輾轉反側。*The branches were ~ing in the wind.* 樹枝在風中搖曳。**3 ~ sth off, (a)** drink sth straight down. 一飲而盡。**(b)** produce sth quickly and without much thought or effort: 迅速而不費力地做成某事: *~ off a newspaper article.* 迅速地寫成報紙文章。□ *n* [C] **1** ~ing movement: 投;擲;拋;搖蕩;顛簸: *a contemptuous ~ of the head;* 輕視的把頭一揚; *take a ~,* (esp) be thrown from the back of a horse. 跌下;(尤指)從馬背上摔下。**2 win/lose the ~,** guess correctly/incorrectly when a coin is ~ed up (esp at the beginning of a game). 擲錢幣猜中(猜錯);擲贏(輸)(尤指比賽開始時)。

tot[1] /tɒt ; tɑt/ *n* **1** (often 常作 **tiny tot**) very small child. 小孩;小娃娃。 **2** (colloq) small glass of liquor. (俗)小杯的酒;少量的酒。

tot[2] /tɒt ; tɑt/ *vt, vi* (-tt-) [VP15B, 2C] ***tot (sth) up,*** (colloq) add up: (俗)加;總計: *expenses totting up to £5;* 合計五鎊的費用; *tot up a column of figures.* 把一欄的數字加起來。

to·tal /ˈtəʊtl ; ˈtotl̩/ *adj* complete; entire: 完全的;全部的;全體的: *~ silence;* 寂靜無聲; *be in ~ ignorance of sth.* 全然不知某事。*What are your ~ debts?* 你的全部債務有多少? *There was a ~ eclipse of the sun.* 有一次日全蝕。**~ war,** war in which all the resources of a country (manpower, industry, etc) are involved. 總體戰。□ *n* [C] ~ amount: 總數;總額: *Our expenses reached a ~ of £20.* 我們的花費總計達廿鎊。*What does the ~ come to?* 總數若干? □ *vt, vi* (-ll-, US also -l-) [VP6A, 2C] find the ~ of; reach the ~ of; amount to: 總計;共計;總數達: *The visitors to the exhibition ~led 15 000.* 展覽會的參觀者達一萬五千人。*It ~s up to £16.* 總計十六鎊。**~ly** /ˈtəʊtəlɪ ; ˈtotl̩ɪ/ *adv* completely: 完全地;全部地: *~ly blind.* 全盲的。 **~·ity** /təʊˈtælətɪ ; toˈtælətɪ/ *n* entirety; (esp) period during which an eclipse is ~. 全體;完全;(尤指)(日、月)全蝕的時間。

to·tali·tar·ian /ˌtəʊtælɪˈteərɪən ; toˌtæləˈtɛrɪən/ *adj* of a political system in which only one political party and no rival loyalties are permitted: 極權主義的: *a ~ State,* eg Germany under Hitler. 極權國家(如希特勒統治下的德國)。**~·ism** /-ɪzəm ; -ˌɪzəm/ *n*

to·tal·iz·ator /ˈtəʊtəlaɪzeɪtə(r) *US:* -lɪz-; ˈtotl̩əˌzetɚ/ *n* machine for registering bets (eg on horses) with a view to dividing the total amount among those who bet on the winners. (賽馬等的)賭金計算機。

tote[1] /təʊt ; tot/ *n* (colloq abbr of) totalizator. (俗)爲 totalizator 之略。

tote[2] /təʊt ; tot/ *vt* [VP6A] (sl) carry (esp a gun): (俚)携帶;荷(尤指槍): *He ~s a six-shooter.* 他帶著一支六發左輪手槍。

to·tem /ˈtəʊtəm ; ˈtotəm/ *n* [C] natural object, esp an animal, considered, esp by N American Indians, to have a close connection with a family group. 圖騰(北美印第安人等原始民族認爲與其家族有密切關係的自然物,尤指動物)。 **ˈ~-pole** *n* one on which is carved or painted a series of ~s. 圖騰柱(刻有或繪有一系圖騰者)。

tot·ter /ˈtɒtə(r) ; ˈtɑtɚ/ *vi* [VP2A, C] **1** walk with weak, unsteady steps; get up unsteadily: 以軟弱而不穩定的步子走路;不穩地起立;蹣跚: *The wounded man ~ed to his feet.* 傷者不穩地站了起來。 **2** be almost falling; seem to be about to collapse: 搖搖欲墜;搖動: *The tall chimney-stack ~ed and then fell.* 那座高烟囪搖搖晃晃,然後倒了下來。**~y** *adj* unsteady; insecure. 不穩的;搖動的;蹣跚的。

tou·can /ˈtuːkæn ; ˈtukæn/ *n* kinds of tropical American bird with brightly coloured feathers and an immense beak. 鵎鵼;巨嘴鳥(產於美洲熱帶,有彩色鮮豔的羽毛及巨喙)。⇨ the illus at rare. 參看 rare 之插圖。

touch[1] /tʌtʃ ; tʌtʃ/ *n* **1** [C] act or fact of touching: 觸;接觸: *I felt a ~ on my arm.* 我覺得臂上有人摸了一下。*Even the slightest ~ will break a soap-bubble.* 卽使最輕微的一觸也會弄破一個肥皂泡。***at a ~,*** if touched, however lightly. 一觸卽;一碰就。**2** [U] (sense giving) feeling by touching: 觸覺;觸感: *soft/rough to the ~,* when touched; 摸起來柔軟(粗糙); *the cold ~ of marble.* 觸摸大理石的冰冷感覺。**ˈ~·stone** *n* sth used as a test or standard (of purity, etc); criterion. 試金石;(批評、判斷等的)標準;準則。 **3** [C] stroke made with a brush, pen, etc: (刷,筆等的)一揮;一筆;一碰;一觸;筆畫;筆法;筆致: *add a few finishing ~es* (to a drawing or any piece of work); 添加最後的幾筆; *give a horse a ~ of the spurs.* 以馬刺驅策馬。**4** [C] ***a ~ (of),*** slight quantity, trace: 少許;微量: *a ~ of frost in the air;* 空氣中少許的霜; *have a ~ of the sun,* slight sunstroke; 輕微中暑; *a ~ of irony/bitterness in his remarks;* 他話中諷刺(怨恨)的意味; *have a ~* (= a slight attack) *of rheumatism.* 害輕微的風濕症。 **5** [C] style or manner of touching the keys, strings, etc of a musical instrument, etc of workmanship (in art): 彈奏法;觸鍵法;(藝術作品的)風格;特徵: *the ~ of a master,* expert style, eg in painting; 名家手法或風格; *a sculpture with a bold ~;* 作風豪邁的雕刻作品; *have a light ~,* eg on a piano, a typewriter; 以輕觸法(彈鋼琴、打字等); *the* (eg) *ˈNelson ~,* the bold way of dealing with a situation characteristic of (eg) Nelson. 納爾遜(等)的作風;處事大膽的作風。**ˈ~-type** *vi* [VP2A] type without looking at the typewriter keyboard (because familiar with it). 觸打(不看打字機鍵盤,憑熟練的指法打字)。 **6** [U] communication. 連繫。***in/out of ~ (with),*** in/not in regular communication (with); having/not having information about: 與…有(無)連繫;有(無)…的消息: *keep in ~ with old friends;* 與老友保持連繫; *be out of ~ with the political situation.* 對政局生疏。***lose ~ (with),*** be out of ~ (with): (與…)失去聯絡: *If we correspond regularly we shan't lose ~.* 如果我們經常通信,我們就不會失去聯絡。**7** (football and Rugby) part of the pitch outside the side-lines: (足球,橄欖球)邊線區域: *The ball is in/out of ~.* 球在(已出)邊線區。**ˈ~-line** *n* side line of the field of play. (足球場,橄欖球場的)邊線。⇨ *goal-line* at goal; ⇨ the illus at football, Rugby. 參看 football, Rugby 之插圖。 **8** ***a near ~,*** a narrow escape. 九死一生;幸免於難。**ˌ~-and-ˈgo** *adj* (colloq) risky; of uncertain result: (俗)危險的;結果不定的;無把握的: *It was ~-and-go whether the doctor would arrive in time.* 醫生能否及時到達並無把握。*It was ~-and-go with the sick man,* uncertain whether he would live. 那病人情況危篤。**9 *a soft/easy ~,*** (sl) sb from whom one can beg or borrow easily. (俚)好講話的人;好好先生。⇨ *~ sb for sth,* at touch[2] (11).

touch[2] /tʌtʃ ; tʌtʃ/ *vt, vi* (For special uses with *adverbial particles* and *preps,* ⇨ 11 below.) (與副詞接語及介詞連用的特殊用法,參看下列第 11 義。) **1** [VP6A, 15A, B, 2A] (cause to) be in contact with; be separated from at one or more points by no space or object; bring a part of the body (esp the hand) into contact with: (使)接觸;碰及;觸摸: *One of the branches is ~ing the water.* 有一根樹枝碰到了水面。*The two farms ~ (each other),* have, in part, a common boundary. 這兩塊農田(彼此)相毗鄰。*Can you ~* (= reach with your hand) *the top of the door?* 你搆得到門頂嗎? *The mountains seemed to ~ the clouds.* 群山似乎觸及雲霄。*Visitors* (eg in a museum) *are requested not to ~ the exhibits.* 遊客請勿觸摸陳列品。*He ~ed me on the arm/shoulder,* eg to attract my attention. 他碰我的臂(肩)(如促我注意)。*I merely ~ed the eggs together and they cracked.* 我祇

把這些蛋放在一起，它們就破了。*The thermometer ~ed 35°C yesterday.* 昨天氣溫高達攝氏三十五度。**~ bottom, (a)** reach the bottom: 到達底部: *The water isn't deep here; I can just ~ bottom,* ie with my feet. 這裏的水不深，我觸得到底。**(b)** (fig) reach the lowest point of misfortune, depravity, etc. (喩)達到極度不幸、墮落等。**~ wood,** ~ sth made of wood in the belief that one will avert ill luck: 摸觸木製物以避開霉運或不幸; 觸木辟邪: *I've never been in a road accident—~ wood.* 我從未出過車禍——觸木辟邪(一面說一面觸摸木製物以避開霉運)。**2** [VP6A] apply a slight or gentle force to: 輕觸; 輕輕地施力於: *He ~ed the bell,* rang it by pressing the button. 他輕輕按鈴。*He ~ed the keys of the piano.* 他輕觸鋼琴鍵。**3** [VP6A] (usu in neg) compare with; be equal to: (通常用於否定句中)匹敵;及得上: *No one can ~ him as an actor of tragic roles.* 作爲一個悲劇角色的演員，沒有人及得上他。*There's nothing to ~ mountain air for giving you an appetite.* 沒有東西及得上山間清新的空氣更能促進你的食慾了。**4** [VP6A] (usu neg) take (food, drink): (通常用於否定句中)吃;喝: *He hasn't ~ed food for two days.* 他兩天未吃東西了。**5** [VP6A] affect (a person or his feelings); concern: 感動(某人或其情緒);關心: *The sad story ~ed us/our hearts.* 那悲慘的故事令我們感動。*We were all ~ed with remorse/pity when we heard what had happened.* 當我們聽到所發生的事故時，我們的內心感到懊悔(憐憫)。**6** [VP6A] have to do with: 關涉;涉及;論到;談及: *What you say does not ~ the point at issue.* 你所說的未涉及討論的主題。*The question ~es your interests closely.* 該問題與你的利益有密切關係。**7** [VP6A] injure slightly: 微傷;微損: *The apple-blossom was ~ed by the frost.* 蘋果的花微受霜害。*The valuable paintings were not ~ed by the fire.* 那些名畫未遭火災波及。**8** (*pp* **~ed**) (colloq) slightly mad or deranged: (俗)微瘋的;精神有點錯亂的: *He seems to be a bit ~ed.* 他似乎有點精神錯亂。**9** [VP6A, 15A] rouse painful or angry feeling in; wound: 引起痛苦或憤怒;傷害: *You've ~ed his self-esteem.* 你損傷了他的自尊。*You've ~ed him on a tender place* (lit or fig). 你觸及他的痛處(字面或喩)。⇨ quick(*n*). **10** [VP6A] deal with; cope with; get a result from: 對付;應付;善處;從…得到結果: *Nothing I have used will ~* (= get rid of) *these grease spots.* 我用過的東西，沒有一樣能除去這些油漬。*She couldn't ~* (= even begin to answer) *the first two questions in the biology paper,* ie in an examination. 她無法答出生物學試卷上的頭兩個問題。**11** [VP 3A, 2C, 15B] (special uses with *adverbial particles* and *preps*): (與副詞接語及介詞連用的特殊用法):

touch at, (of a ship) call at: (指船)停靠: *Our steamer ~ed at Naples.* 我們的輪船曾在那不勒斯停靠。

touch down, (a) (Rugby) ~ the ball on the ground behind the opponent's goal line. (橄欖球)底線得分; 挽球(在對方球門線後以球觸地)。**(b)** (of aircraft) come down to land; alight. (指飛機)落地;降落。Hence, 由此產生，**'~-down** *n*

touch sb for sth, (sl) get money from (by begging): (俚)(藉乞求)從…得到錢: *He ~ed me for a fiver* (ie £5). 他向我乞求五鎊錢。

touch sth off, discharge (a cannon, etc); (fig) cause to start: 發射(砲等);(喩)觸發;引起: *The arrest of the men's leaders ~ed off a riot.* 逮捕那些人的首領觸發了一場暴動。

touch on/upon sth, treat (a subject) briefly. 簡略地論述(某題目)。

touch sth up, make small changes in (a picture, a piece of writing, etc) to improve it, give the finishing touches, etc. 修飾(圖畫,文章);潤色。

touch·able /ˈtʌtʃəbl ; ˈtʌtʃəbl̩/ *adj* that may be touched. 可觸的;可觸知的;可被感動的。

touch·ing /ˈtʌtʃɪŋ ; ˈtʌtʃɪŋ/ *adj* pathetic; arousing pity or sympathy. 感傷的;悲慘的;引起憐憫或同情的。□ *prep* concerning. 關於。**~·ly** *adv*

touchy /ˈtʌtʃɪ ; ˈtʌtʃɪ/ *adj* (-ier, -iest) easily or quickly offended. 易怒的;暴躁的。**touch·ily** /-ɪlɪ ; -ɪlɪ/ *adv* **touchi·ness** *n*

tough /tʌf ; tʌf/ *adj* (-er, -est) **1** (of meat) hard to cut or get one's teeth into. (指肉)堅韌的;咬不動的。**2** not easily cut, broken or worn out: 强韌的;不易切開、打破或磨損的: *as ~ as leather.* 堅韌如皮革。*T~ rubber is needed for tyres.* 强韌橡皮爲製輪胎所需。**3** strong; able to endure hardships: 强壯的;堅强的;能耐勞苦的: *~ soldiers.* 能耐勞苦的軍人。**4** (of persons) rough and violent: (指人)粗暴的;兇惡的: *a ~ criminal.* 兇惡的罪犯。**~ customer,** (colloq) person likely to cause trouble, unlikely to submit to control or discipline. (俗)愛惹禍的人;惹是生非者; 難駕馭者。**5** stubborn; unyielding. 倔强的;固執的。***be/get ~ (with sb):*** (對某人)强硬: *The employers got ~ with/adopted a get-~ policy towards their workers.* 僱主們對他們的工人毫不讓步(採取嚴峻措施)。**6** hard to carry out; difficult: 難以執行的;困難的: *a ~ job/problem.* 棘手的工作(問題)。**7 ~ luck,** (colloq) bad luck. (俗)壞運氣;霉運。□ *n* (also 亦作 **~ie** /ˈtʌfɪ ; ˈtʌfɪ/) (colloq) ~(4) person. (俗)粗暴的人;兇惡的人。**~·ly** *adv* **~·ness** *n* **~en** /ˈtʌfn ; ˈtʌfn̩/ *vt, vi* make or become ~. (使)變堅韌;(使)變强壯;(使)變倔强。

tou·pee /ˈtu:peɪ *US:* tu:ˈpeɪ ; tuˈpe/ *n* patch of false hair worn to cover a bald spot; small wig. (遮覆禿處的)一撮假髮;小頂假髮。

tour /tʊə(r) ; tʊr/ *n* **1** journey out and home again during which several or many places are visited: 旅行;漫遊;周遊: *a round-the-world ~;* 環球旅行; *a coach ~ of France;* 乘坐長途汽車的法國旅行; *conducted ~s,* made by a group conducted by a guide. 導遊旅行(有導遊的團體旅行)。**2** brief visit to or through: 短暫訪問;參觀: *a ~ of the palace/house.* 參觀皇宮(房舍)。**3** period of duty (at a military or naval station overseas); interval between passage-paid home leaves (⇨ leave²(1)) in service abroad: (在海外陸海軍基地的)任職期間;海外服務期間: *a ~ of three years as a lecturer in the University of Ibadan.* 在伊巴丹大學擔任講席的三年海外服務期間。**4** round of (official) visits to institutions, units, etc: (至機構,單位的)視察: *The Director leaves tomorrow on a ~ of overseas branches.* 董事長明天離此視察海外分支機構。**5** number of visits to places made by a theatrical company, etc. 劇團等赴各地之一連串訪問;巡廻演出。***on ~,*** visiting in this way: 巡廻演出: *be/go on ~;* 作巡廻演出; *take a company on ~ to perform three of Shakespeare's plays.* 率領劇團巡廻演出三部莎士比亞戲劇。□ *vt, vi* [VP6A, 2A, C] make a ~ (of): (作…)旅行;遊歷;巡廻;漫遊: *~ Mexico.* 漫遊墨西哥。*They are ~ing in Spain.* 他們正在西班牙遊歷。*The play will ~ the provinces in the autumn.* 該劇將於秋天在各地巡廻演出。**~·ing** *n, adj: a '~ing car,* one suitable for ~ing; 遊覽車; *a '~ing party.* 旅行團。**~·ist** /-ɪst ; -ɪst/ *n* **1** person making a ~ for pleasure: 旅行者;遊歷者;觀光客: *London is full of ~ists in summer.* 倫敦在夏季有很多觀光客。**2** (attrib) of or for ~s: (形容用法)旅行的;觀光的: *a '~ist agency;* 旅行社; *a '~ist ticket,* one issued on special terms, eg at a lower price; 遊覽票(按特別條件,如低價,所發售者); *'~ class,* (on liners, airliners) second class. (船、機上的)二等艙(座);經濟艙(座)。**~ism** /ˈtʊərɪzəm ; ˈtʊrˌɪzəm/ *n* [U] organized ~ing: 遊覽;觀光;觀光事業: *Some countries obtain large sums of foreign exchange from ~ism,* from the money brought in by ~ists. 有些國家靠觀光事業賺取大量外滙。

tour de force /ˌtʊə də ˈfɔ:s ; ˌturdəˈfɔrs/ *n* (F) feat of strength or skill. (法)力技; 特技; 絕技。

tour·na·ment /ˈtɔ:nəmənt *US:* ˈtɜ:rn- ; ˈtɝnəmənt/ *n* [C] **1** series of contests of skill between a number of players: 聯賽;比賽;競賽: *a 'tennis/'chess ~.* 網球(西洋棋)比賽。 **2** (in the Middle Ages) contest between knights on horseback, armed with blunted weapons. (中世紀之)武士的馬上比武;馬上比武大會。

tour·ney /'tɜːnɪ ; 'tɝnɪ/ *n* = tournament (2).

tour·ni·quet /'tʊənɪkeɪ *US:* 'tɜːnɪkɪt ; 'tʊrnɪˌkɛt/ *n* device for stopping a flow of blood through an artery by twisting sth tightly around a limb. 止血帶;壓脈器。

tousle /'taʊzl ; 'taʊzl/ *vt* [VP6A] put (esp the hair) into disorder by pulling it about, rubbing it, etc; make untidy: 弄亂(尤指頭髮);使零亂: *a girl with ~d hair.* 蓬髮女孩。

tout /taʊt ; taʊt/ *n* person who worries others to buy sth, use his services, etc, esp one who sells information about race-horses: 招徠顧客者;兜售物品者;(尤指)出售賽馬情報者: *a 'ticket ~,* eg selling tickets for a major football match at a greatly inflated price. 售黃牛票者;售票黃牛。 □ *vi* [VP2A, 3A] ~ ***(for),*** act as a ~: 招徠;出售賽馬情報: *There were men outside the railway station ~ing for the hotels.* 火車站外有人爲旅館招徠顧客。

tout en·sem·ble /ˌtuːt ɒn'sɒmbl ; ˌtuˌtɑ̃'sɑ̃bl/ *n* (F) sth viewed as a whole; its general effect. (法)整體;整體觀念;整體效果;概觀。

tow¹ /təʊ ; to/ *vt* [VP6A, 15A, B] pull along by a rope or chain: 拖;曳: *tow a damaged ship into port;* 將損壞的船拖進港; *tow a broken-down car to the nearest garage.* 將拋錨汽車拖至最近的修車廠。 **'tow(ing)-line/-rope** *nn* one used in towing. 拖繩;曳纜。 **'tow(ing)-path** *n* path along the bank of a river or canal for use in towing, eg by horses pulling canal boats. (河或運河沿岸的)曳船路;縴路。 □ *n* [C, U] towing or being towed: 拖;被拖;曳;被曳: *have/take a boat in tow.* 拖一艘船。 *Can we give you a tow?* 我們能幫你拖一下嗎? *The lorry was on tow.* 那貨車被拖曳前進。 *He usually has his family in tow,* (colloq) has them with him. (俗)他通常帶着家人在一起。

tow² /təʊ ; to/ *n* [U] coarse and broken fibres of flax, hemp, etc (for making rope). 粗麻屑(用製繩索)。

to·ward(s) /tə'wɔːd(z) *US:* tɔːrd(z) ; tord(z)/ *prep* **1** approaching; in the direction of: 向;對;趨;朝…的方向: *walking ~ the sea;* 向着海走去; *sit with one's back turned ~ the window;* 背向窗子坐下; *drifting ~ war;* 盲目地走向戰爭; *first steps ~ the abolition of armaments.* 走向廢除軍備的最初步驟。 **2** as regards; in relation to: 對於;關於: *Are his feelings ~ us friendly?* 他對我們友善嗎? *What will the Government's attitude be ~ the plan?* 政府對於該項計畫持何態度? **3** for the purpose of (helping): 爲了(幫助): *We must save money ~ the children's education.* 我們必須爲了孩子們的教育而存錢。 **4** (of time) near: (指時間)接近: *~ the end of the century;* 將近該世紀的末尾; *~ evening.* 傍晚;黃昏。

towel /'taʊəl ; 'taʊəl/ *n* [C] piece of cloth or absorbent paper for drying or wiping sth wet (eg one's hands or body): 毛巾;手巾;抹布;擦拭紙;紙巾: *a 'bath-~;* 浴巾; *a 'roller-~,* an endless one on a revolving bar. 捲式毛巾;環狀毛巾(紙巾)。 **'~-rack/-horse** *nn* wooden frame for hanging ~s on. (木製)毛巾架。 **'~-rail** *n* (usu metal) rail for a ~ (eg near a wash-basin). (通常爲金屬的)毛巾桿;晾毛巾的橫桿。 ***throw in the ~,*** ➪ throw¹ (12). □ *vt* (-ll-, US -l-) dry or rub (oneself) with a ~. 以毛巾擦乾或擦搓(自己)。 **~·ling** (US = **~·ing**) *n* [U] material for ~s. 毛巾料。

tower /'taʊə(r) ; 'taʊɚ/ *n* **1** tall, usu equal-sided (esp square) or circular building, either standing alone (eg as a fort, *the T~ of London*) or forming part of a church, castle or other large building (eg a college). 塔;高樓(或爲獨立建築物,如堡壘,倫敦塔,或爲構成教堂、城堡或大建築物之一部分)。 ➪ the illus at church. 參看 church 之插圖。 **2** (fig) (喻) ***a ~ of strength,*** a person who can be relied upon for protection, strength or comfort in time of trouble. 可依賴的人;干城。 **3 'water ~,** ~ that supports a large tank for the storage and distribution of water at high pressure. 水塔。 **'~-block** *n* high block of flats or offices. 高樓區;連幢高樓。 □ *vi* [VP2C] rise to a great height, be very tall, esp in relation to the height of the surroundings: 高聳;超越(尤指與周圍的高度相比較而言): *the skyscrapers that ~ over New York.* 高聳於紐約市的摩天大樓。 ***~ above sb,*** (fig, of eminent persons) greatly exceed in ability, in intellectual or moral qualities: (喻,指傑出人士)在能力、智慧或道德方面超出或高於: *a man who ~s above his contemporaries.* 超出其同時代的人。 **~·ing** *adj* (esp): (尤指): *in a ~ing rage,* violently angry. 暴怒的。

town /taʊn ; taʊn/ *n* **1** centre of population larger than a village, smaller than, or not created, a city (and often used in contrast to *country*): 鎮;城鎮;市鎮(大於村而尚未成爲市,常用做 country 的相對字): *Would you rather live in a ~ or in the country?* 你願意住在城裏還是鄉下? (In GB the word ~ is used much more frequently than *city,* even when the place actually is a city, the word *city* being used chiefly in connection with local government affairs.) (在英國,town 遠比 city 常用,卽使該地實際上爲城市,亦用 town 字,city 一字主要用於地方政府事務方面。) ➪ city (1). ***be/go out on the ~,*** be/go out to enjoy the entertainment facilities of a ~. 去城裏享樂。 ***paint the ~ red,*** ➪ red (1). **2** (attrib) (形容用法) **~ centre,** area around which public buildings, eg the town hall, the public library, are grouped. 市鎮中心(如市政廳、圖書館等公共建築集中地)。 **~ clerk,** official who keeps ~ or city records. 鎮執事;鎮書記(掌管案卷)。 **~ council,** governing body of a ~. 鎮(議)會。 **~ councillor,** member of a ~ council. 鎮議會議員;鎮會評議員。 **'~-gas** *n* manufactured gas for domestic and industrial use. 自來瓦斯(將煤加熱而製成,供家庭及工業之用)。 **~ hall,** building with offices of local government and usu a hall for public events (meetings, concerts, etc). 市政廳;鎮公所;市鎮集會所。 **'~ house,** house in ~, belonging to sb who also has a house in the country. 市內宅邸(屬於在鄉間另有住宅者)。 **~ planning,** preparation of plans for the regulated growth and improvement of ~s. 都市計畫。 **3** (preceded by a *prep,* and without the *def* or *indef art*) the business, shopping, etc part of a ~ (contrasted with the suburbs, etc): (前加介詞,不加冠詞)市鎮商業區;鬧市;市中心區(與市郊等相對): *go to ~ to do some shopping.* 到市區購物。 *He's in ~ today.* 他今天上街去了。 *I'm going down ~ this afternoon.* 我今天下午要到市區去。 ➪ downtown. ***go to ~,*** (sl) act, behave, without inhibitions, eg by spending lavishly, having a spree. (俚)放浪形骸;舉止無節制(如揮霍無度,狂歡作樂等)。 **4** (without the *def* or *indef art*) the chief city or ~ in the neighbourhood (esp, in England, London): (不加冠詞)附近的主要城市(在英格蘭,尤指倫敦): *He is spending the week-end in ~.* 他正在倫敦度週末。 *He went up to ~ from Leeds.* 他從里茲前往倫敦。 *Mr Green is not in ~/is out of ~.* 格林先生不在城裡。 ***man about ~,*** fashionable man who spends much time amusing himself. 把很多時間花在享樂上的時髦人士;花花公子。 **5 the ~,** the people of a ~: 市民;全鎮鎮民: *The whole ~ was talking about it.* 全鎮的人都在談論此事。 ***the talk of the ~,*** ➪ talk¹ (3). **6 the ~,** ~s in general: 市鎮通稱: *Farm workers are leaving the country in order to get better paid work in the ~.* 農場工人離開鄉間,爲要在城市中獲得待遇較好的工作。 **7 '~s·folk** *n pl* **(a)** (with *def art*) the people of the ~ referred to. (與定

冠詞連用)市民;全體鎮民。 **(b)** (without *def art*) people who live in ~s. (不加定冠詞)住在城裡的人們。 **'~s·people** *n pl* =~sfolk. **'~s·man** /-zmən; -zmən/ *n* (*pl* -men) **(a)** man who lives in a ~. 住在城裡的人。**(b)** (often 常作 ˌ*fellow-'~sman*) person who lives in one's own ~. 本城居民;同城市民。

tow·nee /taʊ'niː; taʊ'ni/ *n* (derog) person who lives in a town and is ignorant of rural things. (貶)不諳農事的城市居民;五穀不分的城裡人。

town·ship /'taʊnʃɪp; 'taʊnʃɪp/ *n* **1** (US, Canada) subdivision of a county having certain powers of government; district six miles square in US surveys of land. (美國,加拿大)鎮區(爲郡下面的行政區劃,享有若干行政權);(美國土地測量)六哩見方的地區。 **2** (S Africa) area, suburb, for houses, etc, of non-Europeans. (南非)非歐洲人居住的地或郊區。 **3** (Australia) site laid out for a town. (澳洲)都市計畫地區;都市預留地。

tox·aemia (also **tox·emia**) /tɒk'siːmɪə; tɑks'imɪə/ *n* [U] blood-poisoning. 血中毒症;毒血症。

toxic /'tɒksɪk; 'tɑksɪk/ *adj* of, caused by, a toxin; poisonous. 毒的;中毒的;有毒的;毒素的。 **~·ity** /tɒk'sɪsətɪ; tɑks'ɪsətɪ/ *n* [U] quality or degree of being ~: 毒性;毒力: *study the ~ity of insecticides.* 研究殺蟲劑的毒性。 **toxi·col·ogy** /ˌtɒksɪ'kɒlədʒɪ; ˌtɑksɪ'kɑlədʒɪ/ *n* [U] branch of medical science dealing with the nature and effects of poisons. 毒理學;毒物學(醫學一部門)。**toxi·col·ogist** /-dʒɪst; -dʒɪst/ *n* student of, expert in, toxicology. 毒物學家;毒理學家。

toxin /'tɒksɪn; 'tɑksɪn/ *n* [C] poisonous substance, esp one formed by bacteria in plants and animals and causing a particular disease. 毒素(尤指細菌在動植物中所形成,而引起某種疾病者)。

toy /tɔɪ; tɔɪ/ *n* **1** child's plaything; small thing meant for amusement rather than for serious use. 玩具。 **2** (attrib) (形容用法) *toy dog/spaniel, etc,* small kinds kept as pets; (供玩賞的)小狗(長耳狗等); *toy soldier,* one made as a toy(1). 玩具士兵。 **'toy·shop** *n* shop where toys are sold. 玩具店。 □ *vi* [VP3A] ***toy with sth,*** **1** amuse oneself (with); think not very seriously about: (以…)自娛;不太認眞地考慮: *He toyed with the idea of buying a yacht.* 他考慮買一艘遊艇,但不太認眞。 **2** handle carelessly or absent-mindedly: 玩弄;不小心或心不在焉地耍弄: *toying with a pencil.* 耍弄鉛筆。

trace¹ /treɪs; tres/ *n* **1** [U, C] mark, sign, etc showing that sb or sth has been present, that sth has existed or happened: 踪跡;痕跡;形跡: *~s of an ancient civilization.* 古代文明的遺跡。*The police were unable to find any ~ of the thief.* 警察找不出那竊賊的任何踪跡。 *We've lost all ~ of them,* don't know where they are. 我們不知道他們現在何處。 **2** [C] very small amount: 微量;少許: *The post-mortem showed ~s of arsenic in the intestines.* 驗屍顯示腸內留有微量的砒霜。**'~ element,** element of which a ~ is necessary for the development of animal or plant life and without which growth is poor (eg manganese in the soil, for wheat and oats). 微量元素(此種元素之少量爲動植物生長所必須,如栽種小麥及燕麥時土壤中之錳)。

trace² /treɪs; tres/ *vt, vi* **1** [VP6A, 15B] ***~ sth (out),*** draw, sketch, the course, outline, etc, of: 畫出…的輪廓、路線、過程等;描繪出;標出: *~ out the site of an old castle;* 標出一古城堡的所在地; *~ (out) one's route on a map;* 在地圖上畫出某人行經的路線; (fig) (喻) *~ out a policy,* give its outlines. 釐訂政策大綱。 **2** [VP6A] copy (sth), eg by drawing on transparent paper the lines, etc on (a map, design, etc) placed underneath. 描摹。 **3** [VP6A] write slowly and with difficulty: 緩慢而困難地書寫: *He ~d the words laboriously.* 他很費力地寫了那幾個字。 **4** [VP6A, 15A, B, 2C] follow or discover (sb or sth) by observing marks, tracks, bits of evidence, etc: 追踪;追溯;探索: *The criminal was ~d to Glasgow.* 那罪犯被追踪至格拉斯哥。*I cannot ~* (= cannot find, do not think I received) *any letter from you dated 1st June.* 我找不到(或想不出曾收到)你六月一日寄來的信。 ***~ (sth/sb) back (to sth),*** **(a)** find the origin of by going back in time: 追究;追溯;回溯;溯自: *He ~s his descent back to an old Norman family.* 他的血統可追溯至一個古老的諾爾曼家族。 *His fear of dogs ~s back/can be ~d back to a childhood experience.* 他對狗的恐懼溯自他孩童時代的一次經驗。 **(b)** find the origin of by going back through evidence: (藉證據而)找出根源;源自;來自: *The rumour was ~d back to a journalist,* It was discovered that he had started it. 那項謠言來自一個新聞記者。 **5** [VP6A] discover the position, size, etc of (sth) from its remains: 由遺跡發現(某物)之位置、大小等;探尋出: *Archaeologists have ~d many Roman roads in Britain.* 考古學家已在英國發現許多古羅馬的道路。 **~·able** /-əbl; -əbḷ/ *adj* capable of being ~d (*to*). 可描摹的;可追踪的;可探尋的。 **~r** *n* **1** person who ~s(2). 描摹者。 **2** (often 常作 *'~r bullet/shell*) projectile whose course is made visible by a line of flame or smoke left behind it. 曳光彈。 **'~r element,** radioactive element which, when introduced into sth, can be ~d by the use of a Geiger counter. 放射追踪元素;放射顯跡劑(導入某物時,可用蓋氏計數器追踪)。 **trac·ing** *n* reproduction (of a map, design, etc) made by tracing(2). (地圖、圖案等的)複製;摹繪。**'tracing-paper** *n* [U] strong transparent paper on which tracings are made. (透明)摹圖紙。

trace³ /treɪs; tres/ *n* [C] either of the leather straps, ropes, etc by which a wagon, carriage, cart, etc is pulled by a horse. (馬車的)挽繩;挽韁。 ⇨ the illus at harness. 參看 harness 之插圖。***kick over the ~s,*** (fig) become undisciplined; refuse to accept control. (喻)變得不守紀律;不受管束。

tracery /'treɪsərɪ; 'tresərɪ/ *n* [C, U] (*pl* -ries) ornamental arrangement of designs (eg as made by frost on glass, or of stonework in a church window); decorative pattern. 裝飾的圖案;花紋(如玻璃上由霜結成者,或教堂窗子上的石細工); 裝飾花樣。 ⇨ the illus at window. 參看 window 之插圖。

tra·chea/ trə'kɪə *US:* 'treɪkɪə; 'trekɪə/ *n* (*pl* ~e /-kɪiː; -'ki·i/) (anat) windpipe. (解剖)氣管。⇨ the illus at respiratory. 參看 respiratory之插圖。

tra·choma /trə'kəʊmə; trə'komə/ *n* [U] contagious eye disease causing inflammation of the inner surfaces of the eyelids. 沙眼;顆粒性結膜炎。

track /træk; træk/ *n* [C] **1** line or series of marks left by a vehicle, person, animal, etc in passing along; path or rough road made by persons/animals: (車輛、行人、動物等經過後留下的)踪跡;足跡;痕跡;(人或動物)踏成的路或小徑: *~s in the snow,* eg footprints; 雪上的踪跡(如足印); *follow the ~s left by a bear;* 跟蹤熊的踪跡; *'sheep-~s across the moor;* 由羊群踏出的越過荒野的小徑; *a ~ through the forest.* 穿越森林的小路。***be on sb's ~/on the ~ of sb,*** be in pursuit of: 追踪: *The police are on the ~ of the thief.* 警察在追踪那竊賊。*I'm on his ~.* 我在追他。***cover up one's ~s,*** conceal one's movements or activities. 掩飾自己的行動或活動;隱藏行踪。 ***go off/keep to the beaten ~,*** ⇨ beaten. ***have a ˌone-~ 'mind,*** habitually follow the same line of thought; give all one's attention to one topic. 習慣性地循相同的思想路線;固執於某種想法;把全部注意力集中於一項問題上。***keep/lose ~ of sb/sth,*** keep in/lose touch with; follow/fail to follow the course or development of: 與…保持(失去)接觸;跟上(跟不上)…的進程或發展: *read the newspapers to keep ~ of current events.* 閱讀報紙俾熟悉時事。***make ~s,*** (colloq) depart (usu in a hurry); run away. (俗)離開(通常爲匆忙地);跑開。 ***make ~s for,*** (colloq) go towards: (俗)走向: *It's time we made ~s for home.* 是我們回家的時候了。

in one's ~s, (sl) where one stands, there and then: (俚)就在那裏;當場;立卽: *He fell dead in his ~s.* 他當場死去。***off the ~,*** (fig) away from the subject; following a wrong line of action. (喻)離題;離譜;出軌;誤入歧途。 **2** course; line taken by sth (whether marked or not): 進程;路徑;某事物所採取的路線(標明或未標明者): *the ~ of a storm/comet/spacecraft.* 風暴(彗星,太空船)的路線。 **3** set of rails for trains, etc: (火車等的)軌道;轍: *single/double ~*, one pair/two pairs of rails. 單軌(雙軌)。*The train left the ~,* was derailed. 火車出軌了。***on/from the wrong side of the ~s,*** (US) on/from the part of a town that is socially inferior, the part lived in by poor people. (美)在(來自)低層社會;出身貧寒。 **4** path prepared for racing (eg made of cinders, clinkers, etc): 跑道(如用煤渣,熔渣等鋪成者): *a 'motor-racing/'cycling/'running ~;* 汽車比賽(單車比賽,賽跑)的跑道;(*attrib*) (形容用法) *'~-racing;* 徑賽; *'~ events,* eg running races, contrasted with field events such as jumping, throwing the discus. 徑賽項目(如賽跑等,與田賽項目,如跳高、跳遠、擲鐵餅等相對)。**'~suit** *n* loose-fitting warm suit worn by an athlete while not taking part in ~ events. 田徑裝(運動員未比賽時所着的寬鬆保暖裝)。 **5** endless belt used instead of wheels on some tractors, military tanks, etc. (曳引車、戰車等的)輪帶;履帶。 □ *vt, vi* **1** [VP6A, 15A, B] follow the ~ of: 追蹤;尾隨:~ *an animal to its den.* 追蹤動物至其窩穴。 **'~·ing station** *n* one which, by radar or radio, maintains contact with space-vehicles, etc. 追蹤站(藉雷達或無線電與太空船等保持接觸者)。***~ sb/sth down,*** find by searching: 追踪、搜索等而發現: *~ down a bear/a reference.* 搜尋到一隻熊(找到一項參考資料)。***~ out,*** trace (the course or development of sth) by examining ~s. 藉研究踪跡、痕跡等而找到(某事物的進程或發展情形)。 **2** (cinema, TV) move a camera (mounted on a mobile platform) while taking a long shot (called *a '~ing shot*). (電影,電視)(攝取遠距離鏡頭 a ~ing shot 時)轉動或移動架於活動平臺上的攝影機;追踪攝影。**~ed** *adj* having ~s(5): 有輪帶的;有履帶的: *~ed vehicles.* 履帶車。**~er** *n* person, esp a hunter, who ~s wild animals. 追踪野獸者;(尤指)獵人。 **'~er dog,** dog used in pursuing persons escaping from justice. (追踪逃犯的)追踪犬;搜索犬。**~·less** *adj* having no ~s(1): 無路的;人跡未到的: *~less forests.* 人跡未到的森林。

tract¹ /trækt ; trækt/ *n* **1** stretch or area (*of* forest, farmland, etc): (森林、農地等的)廣濶的地面;區域: *the wide ~s of desert in N Africa.* 北非一片片的廣大沙漠。 **2** system of related parts in an animal body: 動物身體上相關器官的系統;道;徑;束;管;域: *the di'gestive/re'spiratory ~.* 消化(呼吸)道。

tract² /trækt ; trækt/ *n* short printed essay on sth, esp a moral or religious subject. 小册子;短文(尤指以道德或宗教爲題材者)。

tract·able /'træktəbl ; 'træktəbl/ *adj* easily controlled or guided. 易駕馭的;易於引導的。**trac·ta·bil·ity** /ˌtræktə'bɪlətɪ ; ˌtræktə'bɪlətɪ/ *n*

trac·tion /'trækʃn ; 'trækʃən/ *n* [U] (power used in) pulling or drawing sth over a surface: 拖;曳;牽引;牽(引)力: *electric/steam ~.* 電力(蒸汽力)牽輓。**'~-engine** *n* engine used for pulling heavy loads. (牽引重物的)牽引機。

trac·tor /'træktə(r) ; 'træktɚ/ *n* powerful motor-vehicle used for pulling agricultural machinery (ploughs, drills, etc), or other heavy equipment. 拖拉機;曳引機 (用於拖曳農業機械,或其他笨重裝備者)。⇨ the illus at plough. 參看 plough 之插圖。

trad /træd ; træd/ *n* [U] (colloq abbr of) traditional; (esp) jazz (of the 1920's and 1930's) played by a small group with simple rhythms and much improvisation. (俗)爲 traditional 之略;(尤指)(1920年代及1930年代的) 傳統爵士樂。

trade¹ /treɪd ; tred/ *n* **1** [U] buying and selling of goods; exchange of goods for money or other goods; [C] particular branch of this: 買賣;交易;貿易;商業;某一行業: *Great Britain does a lot of ~ with some countries and not much with others.* 大不列顛與某些國家交易甚多,與另一些國家則交易不多。*T~ was good last year.* 去年貿易良好。*He's in the 'cotton/'furniture/'book, etc ~.* 他做棉花(家具,書籍等)生意。**ˌstock-in-'~,** ⇨ stock¹(1). **the ~,** (colloq) those engaged in the manufacture and sale of a certain commodity. (俗)商人;製造商。**'~·mark** *n* design, special name, etc used to distinguish a manufacturer's goods from others; (fig) distinguishing characteristics: 商標;(喻)明顯的特徵: *He leaves his ~mark on all his undertakings.* 他做每件事情都會留下他那明顯的特徵。 **'~ name** *n* name given by manufacturers to a proprietary article. 商品名稱;專利品名稱。**'~ price** *n* the price charged by a manufacturer or wholesaler to a retailer. 同業賣價;批發價格。**ˌ~(s)-'union** *n* organized association of workers in a ~ or group of ~s, formed to protect their interests, improve their conditions, etc. 工會;職工協會。**ˌ~-'unionism** *n* [U] this system of association. 工會制度;工會主義。 **ˌ~-'unionist** *n* member of a ~-union. 工會會員。**T~s Union Congress,** (abbr 略作 **TUC**) association of British ~ unions. (英國的)工會聯合會;工會聯盟;全國總工會。**'~-wind** *n* strong wind blowing always towards the equator from the SE and NE. 信風;貿易風(由東南或東北方向赤道吹襲的强風)。**the T~s,** these winds. 東南及東北信風。 **2** occupation; way of making a living, esp a handicraft: 職業;謀生之道;(尤指)手藝: *He's a weaver/mason/carpenter/tailor by ~.* 他是織工(石匠,木匠,裁縫)。*Shoemaking is a useful ~.* 製鞋是一種有用的手藝。*The college teaches many useful ~s.* 該學院傳授許多有用的手藝。 **'~s·folk, '~s·people** *nn* persons engaged in ~; shopkeepers (and their families). 商人;開店者(及其家屬)。**'~s·man** /-zmən ; -zmən/ *n* (*pl* -men) shopkeeper. 開店者;店主。

trade² /treɪd ; tred/ *vi, vt* **1** [VP2A, C, 3A] ~ ***(in) (with),*** engage in trade(1); buy and sell: 做生意;從事貿易;買賣: *~ in furs and skins;* 做皮貨生意; *ships that ~ between London and ports in the Mediterranean.* 往來於倫敦與地中海各港口的貿易船。*Britain ~s with many European countries.* 英國與很多歐洲國家貿易。**'trad·ing estate,** (usu large) planned industrial area rented to manufacturers. 計畫工業區 (租給廠商使用,通常爲大工業區)。**'trad·ing stamp,** (= gift coupon) coupon given to customers with purchases, exchangeable for various articles or cash. (購物時附帶的)贈劵(可換取他物或現金)。 **2** [VP14] ~ ***sth for sth,*** exchange; barter: 交換;交易;互易: *The boy ~d his knife for a cricket bat.* 那男孩用他的刀子換了一個板球棒。 **3** [VP15B] ~ ***sth in,*** hand over (a used article) in part payment for a new purchase: 以(同類舊品)折價購物: *He ~d in his old car for a new model.* 他以舊車折價添錢買了一部新型汽車。Hence, 由此產生, **'~-in** *n* [C] sth sold in this way. 用作折價之舊物品。 **4** [VP3A] ~ ***on/upon,*** take a wrong advantage of, use, in order to get sth for oneself: 利用…以圖私利;濫用:~ *upon sb's sympathy;* 濫用某人的同情; ~ *upon one's past reputation.* 利用過去的名譽。 **5** (US) shop: (美)購物;買東西: *Which stores do you ~ at,* do your shopping? 你平常到那幾家商店去買東西? **~r** *n* merchant. 商人;貿易者。

tra·di·tion /trə'dɪʃn ; trə'dɪʃən/ *n* [U] (handing down from generation to generation of) opinions, beliefs, customs, etc; [C] opinion, belief, custom, etc handed down: 傳統;因襲;意見、信仰、風俗等的世代相傳;傳統的意見、信仰、風俗等;慣例;傳說: *The stories of Robin Hood are based mainly on ~(s).* 羅賓漢的故事主要是根據傳說而來的。*It is a ~ in that family for the eldest son to enter the* *army and for the second son to become a lawyer.* 那個家庭的傳統是長子從軍，次子當律師。 **~al** /-ʃənl; -ʃənl/ *adj* **~·ally** /-ʃənəlɪ; -ʃənl̩ɪ/ *adv* **~·al·ism** /-ʃənəlɪzəm; -ʃənl̩,ɪzəm/ *n* (excessive) respect for ~, esp in religious matters. 傳統主義；過分墨守傳統；過分尊重傳統(尤指對宗教事務)。 **~·al·ist** /-ʃənəlɪst; -ʃənl̩ɪst/ *n* person who attaches great importance to ~. 傳統主義者；守舊分子。

tra·duce /trəˈdju:s *US:* -ˈdu:s; trəˈdjus/ *vt* [VP6A] (formal) slander. (正式用語)詆毀；中傷。 **tra·ducer** *n* slanderer. 詆毀者；中傷者。

traf·fic /ˈtræfɪk; ˈtræfɪk/ *n* [U] **1** (movement of) people and vehicles along roads and streets, or aircraft in the sky: 交通；運輸；通行；往來於街道上的行人及車輛或天空中的飛機；交通量: *There was a lot of/not much ~ on the roads yesterday.* 昨天道路上的行人車輛很多(不多)。 *T~ in large towns is controlled by ~ lights.* 大城市的交通由交通燈管制。 *The ~ control tower at an airport uses radar screens.* 機場上的航行管制塔使用雷達幕。 **ˈ~ circle,** (US) (美) = roundabout. **ˈ~ indicator** = trafficator. ⇨ the illus at motor. 參看 motor 之插圖。 **ˈ~ jam,** condition in which many road vehicles are prevented from moving forward. 交通擁塞。 **ˈ~ light(s),** mechanical signal controlling road ~ (esp at junctions) by coloured lights (red, amber, green). 交通指揮燈；紅綠燈。 **ˈ~ warden,** ⇨ warden. **2** transport business done by road, rail, ship, air, etc. (公路、鐵路、輪船、飛機等的)運輸業。 **3** illicit trading: 違法買賣；非法行業: *the ~ in liquor;* 非法賣酒； *illegal drug ~.* 非法販毒。 □ *vi* (-ck-) [VP3A] ***~ in sth (with sb),*** trade: (與某人)做生意；從事貿易: *~ in hides (with...).* (與…)做皮貨生意。 **traf·ficker** *n* (usu in a bad sense) trader: (通常指壞的或不法的)商人；販子: *a ˈdrug ~ker.* 毒品販子；鴉片商。

traf·fi·ca·tor /ˈtræfɪkeɪtə(r); ˈtræfɪ,ketɚ/ *n* device (usu a flickering amber light) used on a motor-vehicle to indicate the direction in which the vehicle is about to turn. (汽車的)方向燈；方向指示器。

tra·gedy /ˈtrædʒədɪ; ˈtrædʒədɪ/ *n* (*pl* -dies) **1** [C] play for the theatre, cinema, TV, of a serious or solemn kind, with a sad ending; [U] branch of the drama with this kind of play. 悲劇(嚴肅而結局悲慘的舞臺劇、電影或電視劇)；悲劇(戲劇中的一部門)。 **2** [C, U] very sad event, action, experience, etc, in real life. 實際生活中的極爲悲慘的事件、行爲、經歷等；悲劇。 **tra·gedian** /trəˈdʒi:dɪən; trəˈdʒidɪən/ *n* writer of, actor in, ~. 悲劇作家或演員。 **tra·gedi·enne** /trə,dʒi:dɪˈen; trə,dʒidɪˈɛn/ *n* actress in ~. 悲劇女演員。

tra·gic /ˈtrædʒɪk; ˈtrædʒɪk/ *adj* of tragedy: 悲劇的；悲慘的: *a ~ actor/event.* 悲劇演員(悲慘事件)。 **tragi·cally** /-klɪ; -klɪ/ *adv*

tragi-com·edy /,trædʒɪˈkɒmədɪ; ,trædʒɪˈkɑmədɪ/ *n* (*pl* -dies) drama, event, that is a mixture of tragedy and comedy. 悲喜劇；悲喜事件。 **,tragi-ˈcomic** /-ˈkɒmɪk; -ˈkɑmɪk/ *adj*

trail /treɪl; trel/ *n* [C] **1** line, mark or series of marks, drawn or left behind by sb or sth that has passed by: 踪跡；痕跡: *a ~ of smoke,* (from a railway steam-engine); (火車頭冒出的)一道烟; *ˈvapour ~s,* as left in the sky by high-flying aircraft; 蒸氣尾跡(如高空飛行的飛機在天空中留下者)； *a ~ of destruction,* eg left by a violent storm. 破壞的痕跡(如暴風雨留下者)。 *The wounded tiger left a ~ of blood.* 那受傷的老虎留下了一條血跡。 **2** track or scent followed in hunting. 打獵的嗅跡；獵跡。 ***hot on the ~ (of),*** (lit or fig) close behind. (字面或喩)緊跟在後。 **3** path through rough country. 小徑；崎嶇小道。 ***blaze a ~,*** ⇨ blaze³. □ *vt, vi* **1** [VP6A, 15A, B, 2A, C] pull, be pulled, along: 拖；拉；曳: *The child was ~ing a toy cart.* 那孩子拖着一輛玩具車。 *Her long skirt was ~ing along/on the floor.* 她的長裙拖在地板上。 **2** [VP6A, 15A] follow the ~ of: 追踪；尾隨: *~ a wild animal/a criminal.* 追踪野獸(罪犯)。 **3** [VP2C] (of plants) grow over or along the ground, etc: (指植物)蔓生；蔓延；長在地面: *roses ~ing over the walls;* 蔓延於牆壁上的玫瑰; (of persons) walk wearily: (指人)沒精打采地走；慢行；拖着步子走: *The wounded soldiers ~ed past us.* 傷兵們拖着步子走過我們身邊。 *The tired children ~ed along behind their father.* 疲倦的孩子們沒精打采地跟在他們父親的後面。 **~er** *n* **1** transport-vehicle hauled by a tractor or truck; van or caravan drawn by a motor-vehicle (used for living in when parked). 拖車；掛車；(汽車拖着的)活動住宅。 **2** ~ing plant. 蔓生植物。 **3** series of short extracts from a cinema or TV film to advertise it in advance. (電影或電視的)預告片。

train¹ /treɪn; tren/ *n* **1** [C] (locomotive and) number of railway coaches, wagons, etc joined together: 火車(包括機車)；列車: *ˈpassenger/ˈgoods/ˈfreight ~s;* 客車(貨車；貨車)； *take the 1.15 am ~ to town;* 乘凌晨一點十五分的火車進城； *travel by ~;* 乘火車旅行; *get into/out of a ~;* 上(下)火車; *get on/off a ~;* 上(下)火車; *have lunch on the ~.* 在火車上進午餐。 *The ~ is in/is waiting,* is at the station. 火車現在停在車站。 *He missed/just caught his ~.* 他錯過了(剛好趕上)火車。 **ˈ~ ferry,** for carrying ~s over water (eg from England to France). 火車渡輪 (載火車渡過水面者)。 **ˈ~·man** /-mən; -mən/ *n* (*pl* -men) (US) member of the crew operating a ~. (美)列車車務員。 **2** number of persons, animals, carriages, etc, moving in a line: 成縱隊行進的若干人，動物，車輛等；隊列: *a ~ of camels;* 駱駝隊; *the ˈbaggage ~;* 輜重隊(馱輜重的一隊牲畜、車輛等)； *persons in the king's ~,* in his retinue of attendants. 國王的扈從。 **3** series or chain: 連續；連串: *A knock at the door interrupted my ~ of thought.* 敲門聲打斷了我的思緒。 *What an unlucky ~ of events!* 多麼不幸的一連串事件！ *War often brings disease in its ~.* 戰爭常帶來疾病。 **4** part of a long dress or robe that trails on the ground behind the wearer. 長袍拖曳在地上的部分；拖裾。 **ˈ~-bearer** *n* attendant who holds up, or helps to hold up, such a ~. 牽衣裙的人。 **5** line of gunpowder leading to a place where material has been placed for an explosion (eg in a mine), to be lit at a safe distance. 導火線(連於爆炸物，以便在安全距離點燃)。 ***in ~,*** in readiness; being prepared. 準備妥當。

train² /treɪn; tren/ *vt, vi* **1** [VP6A, 14, 17, 2C, 3A] ***~ (for),*** give teaching and practice to (eg a child, a soldier, an animal) in order to bring to a desired standard of behaviour, efficiency or physical condition: 教養；教育；訓練；鍛鍊: *~ children to be good citizens;* 教養小孩使成爲良好公民； *~ a horse for a race/performing seals for a circus.* 訓練馬參加比賽(海豹在馬戲團表演)。 *Very little escapes his ~ed eye.* 很少東西能逃過他那老練的眼睛。 *He was ~ed for the law/to be a lawyer.* 他受過做律師的訓練。 *There is a shortage of ~ed nurses.* 缺乏受過正規訓練的護士。 *They are ~ing for the boat-race.* 他們在接受訓練準備划船比賽。 **2** [VP6A, 15A] cause to grow in a required direction: 使朝某方向生長；整枝；修剪: *~ roses against/over a wall.* 使玫瑰靠(覆)牆生長。 **3** [VP6A, 14] ***~ sth on/upon sth,*** point, aim: 指向；瞄準: *~ a gun upon the enemy's positions.* 把大砲瞄準敵人的陣地。 **~ee** /treɪˈni:; trenˈi/ *n* person undergoing some form of (usu industrial) ~ing. 受訓者；(通常指接受工藝訓練的)練習生。 **~er** *n* **1** person who ~s (esp athletes, horses for races, animals for the circus, etc). 訓練者；(尤指)訓練運動員的教練；馴馬師；馴獸師。 **2** aircraft used for ~ing pilots. 教練機。 **~·ing** *n* [U] ~ing or being ~ed. 教養；教育；訓練。 ***in/out of ~ing,*** in/not in good physical condition (eg for athletic contests). 身體狀況良好(不好)；身體鍛鍊得好(不好)。 ***go into ~ing,*** ~ oneself.

訓練自己;開始練習。'~·ing-college *n* college for ~ing people for a trade, profession, etc. 專科學校;職業學院。'~·ing-ship *n* one for ~ing boys in seamanship. (海員)訓練船。

traipse /treɪps; treps/ *vi* [VP2A, B, C] (colloq) walk wearily: (俗)疲累地走: ~ *round the shops buying food for the family.* 在各商店疲乏地走來走去,購買家用的食物。

trait /treɪt; tret/ *n* [C] distinguishing quality or characteristic: 顯著的特質,特性或特點: *Two ~s in the American character are generosity and energy.* 美國人性格中的兩大特點是豪爽和幹勁十足。

trai·tor /'treɪtə(r); 'tretɚ/ *n* ~ ***(to),*** person who betrays a friend, is disloyal to a cause, his country, etc. 出賣朋友者;背叛主義者;賣國賊;奸逆;叛逆。***turn ~,*** become a ~. 變為奸逆。**~·ous** /-əs; -əs/ *adj* treacherous; of or like a ~: 背叛的;不忠的;奸逆的;似奸逆的: *~ous conduct.* 背叛的行為。**~·ous·ly** *adv* **trai·tress** /'treɪtrɪs; 'tretrɪs/ *n* woman ~. 女叛徒;女叛逆。

tra·jec·tory /trə'dʒektərɪ; trə'dʒɛktərɪ/ *n* (*pl* -ries) curved path of a projectile (eg a bullet, missile). 抛射物(如子彈,飛彈)的弧形行程;彈道;射道;軌線;軌道。

tram /træm; træm/ *n* **1** (also 亦作 '~·**car** or '*trolley-bus*) electric car used for public transport, running on rails along public streets (US 美 = '*street-car* or '*trolley-car*). 電車。'~·**line** *n* line of rails for ~s; route served by ~s. 電車道;電車所行駛的路線。**2** four-wheeled car used in coalmines. 煤礦坑中所用的四輪車;煤車。

tram·mel /'træml; 'træml̩/ *vt* (-ll-; US -l-) [VP6A] hamper; make progress difficult. 阻碍;妨害。□ *n pl* ~**s,** sth that ~s: 阻礙物;束縛物: *the ~s of routine/etiquette/superstition.* 例行手續(禮儀,迷信)的束縛。

tramp /træmp; træmp/ *vi, vt* **1** [VP2A, C] walk with heavy steps: 重步行走;踩;踏;践: *He ~ed up and down the platform waiting for the train.* 他脚步沉重地在月臺上走來走去,等候火車。**2** [VP2A, B, C, 6A] walk through or over (esp for a long distance): 步行;徒步行過或穿越(尤指長距離): ~ *through the mountains of Wales;* 徒步穿越威爾斯山區; ~ *over the moors.* 走過荒野。*They ~ed (for) miles and miles/~ed all day.* 他們行行重行行(整日步行)。*He enjoys ~ing the hills.* 他喜歡在山間徜徉。□ *n* **1** ***the ~ of,*** sound of heavy footsteps: 重脚步聲: *I heard the ~of marching soldiers.* 我聽到兵士們行進的重步聲。**2** long walk: 長途步行;徒步旅行: *go for a ~ in the country.* 在鄉間作徒步旅行。**3** person (usu homeless) who goes from place to place and does no regular work: (無固定工作的)飄泊者(通常為無家者);流浪漢;遊民: *There's a ~ at the door begging for food.* 有一個流浪漢在門口乞食。**4** '~**(-steamer),** cargo boat which goes to any port(s) where cargo can be picked up. 航線不定的貨船;不定期貨船。

trample /'træmpl; 'træmpl/ *vt, vi* **1** [VP6A, 15B] ~ ***sth (down),*** tread heavily on with the feet; crush under the feet: 用力踐踏;踩壞;踏碎;踩躪: *The children have ~d (down) the flowers/~d the grass down.* 孩子們把花踐踏壞(把草踐踏壞)了。*You wouldn't like to be ~d to death by elephants.* 你不會願意被象踩死。**2** [VP3A] ~ ***on,*** tread heavily on: 踐踏;重步踩過: ~ *on sb's toes/feelings.* 踩到某人的脚趾(傷害某人的情感)。**3** [VP2C] ~ ***about,*** walk about heavily. 重步行走。□ *n* sound, act, of trampling. 踐踏;踩躪;踐踏聲。

tram·po·line /'træmpəli:n; 'træmpəlin/ *n* [C] sheet of strong canvas on a spring frame, used by gymnasts for acrobatic leaps. (體操表演用的)彈簧床(彈簧框架上覆以牢固帆布,用作表演花式彈跳技巧者)。

trance /trɑ:ns *US:* træns; træns/ *n* **1** sleep-like condition: 出神;恍惚: *be in/fall/go into a ~.* 精神恍惚。**2** abnormal, dreamy state; hypnotic state: 昏睡狀態;催眠狀態: *send sb into a ~.* 使某人進入催眠狀態。

tran·quil /'træŋkwɪl; 'trænkwɪl/ *adj* calm; quiet: 安靜的;平靜的;寧靜的: *a ~ life in the country.* 鄉間寧靜的生活。~**ly** /-wɪlɪ; -wɪlɪ/ *adv* ~**·lity** (US also ~**·ity**) /træŋ'kwɪlətɪ; træn'kwɪlətɪ/ *n* [U] ~ state. 安靜;平靜;寧靜。~**·lize** (US also ~**·ize**) /-aɪz; -aɪz/ *vt* [VP6A] make ~ (esp by means of a drug). 使安靜(尤指用藥物);使平靜;鎮定。~**·li·zer** (US also ~**·izer**) *n* drug that ~lizes; sedative. 鎮靜劑。

trans·act /træn'zækt; træns'ækt/ *vt* [VP6A, 14] ~ ***sth (with sb),*** conduct, carry through (business, etc with sb). 辦理;處理;執行(事務等)。

trans·ac·tion /træn'zækʃn; træns'ækʃən/ *n* **1** [U] ***the ~ of,*** transacting: 辦理;處理;執行: *the ~ of business.* 處理事務。**2** [C] piece of business: 事務;事項;交易: *cash ~s;* 現金交易; *the bank's ~s in stocks and shares.* 銀行的股票業務。**3** (*pl*) (records of the) proceedings of (esp a learned society, eg its meetings, lectures): (複)(學術團體等的)會議;會報;議事錄;記錄: *the ~s of the Kent Archaeological Society.* 肯特考古學會的記錄。

trans·al·pine /træn'zælpaɪn; træns'ælpɪn/ *n, adj* (person living) beyond the Alps (esp as viewed from Italy). (尤指自義大利方面言)阿爾卑斯山彼方的;阿爾卑斯山彼方的居民。

trans·at·lan·tic /ˌtrænzət'læntɪk; ˌtrænsət'læntɪk/ *adj* beyond the Atlantic; crossing the Atlantic: 大西洋彼岸的;横越大西洋的: *a ~ voyage/flight;* 横渡大西洋的航行(飛行); concerning (countries on) both sides of the Atlantic: 涉及大西洋兩岸(之國家)的: *a ~ treaty/trade agreement.* 大西洋兩岸國家的條約(貿易協定)。

tran·scend /træn'send; træn'sɛnd/ *vt* [VP6A] go or be beyond or outside the range of (human experience, reason, belief, powers of description, etc). 超出;超越(人類的經驗,理性,信念,描寫力等)。

tran·scen·dent /træn'sendənt; træn'sɛndənt/ *adj* surpassing; excelling: 超出的;超越的;超凡的;卓越的: *a man of ~ genius.* 才華出衆之士。**tran·scen·dence** /-dəns; -dəns/, **tran·scen·dency** /-dənsɪ; -dənsɪ/ *nn*

tran·scen·den·tal /ˌtrænsen'dentl; ˌtrænsɛn'dɛntl̩/ *adj* **1** not based on experience or reason; going beyond human knowledge; that cannot be discovered or understood by practical experience; known by intuition. 先驗的;直覺的;超出人類知識的;不能藉實際經驗去發現或瞭解的。⇨ empirical. **2** (colloq) vague; not clear to ordinary minds. (俗)含糊的;曖昧的;一般人不懂的。~**ly** /-təlɪ; -tl̩ɪ/ *adv* ~**·ism** /-təlɪzəm; -tl̩ˌɪzəm/ *n* [U] ~ philosophy; doctrine that knowledge may be obtained by a study of the mental processes, apart from experience. 先驗哲學;認為不必依賴經驗,僅研究心智活動卽可獲得知識的學說。~**·ist** /-təlɪst; -tl̩ɪst/ *n* believer in ~ism. 先驗論者;先驗主義者;先驗哲學的信奉者。

trans·con·ti·nen·tal /ˌtrænzkɒntɪ'nentl; ˌtrænskɑntə'nɛntl̩/ *adj* crossing a continent: 横越大陸的;貫穿大陸的: *a ~ railway.* 横越大陸的鐵道。

tran·scribe /træn'skraɪb; træn'skraɪb/ *vt* [VP6A] copy in writing, esp write (sth) in full from shorthand notes. 轉錄;抄寫;謄寫;(尤指)譯寫出速記符號所代表的全文。**tran·script** /'trænskrɪpt; 'trænˌskrɪpt/ *n* [C] sth ~d. 抄本;謄本;副本。**tran·scrip·tion** /træn'skrɪpʃn; træn'skrɪpʃən/ *n* **1** [U] transcribing: 抄寫;謄寫;速記符號的翻譯: *errors in transcription.* 抄寫的錯誤。**2** [C] sth ~d, esp into a special form of writing: 抄本;謄本;(尤指)以某種特別書寫方式改寫之物: *phonetic transcriptions.* 用發音符號注出的字或句;音標。**3** (broadcast made from a) recording (on a disc or tape): 錄音;灌片;錄音廣播: *the BBC transcription service.* 英國廣播公司的錄音(廣播)業務。

tran·sept /'trænsept; 'trænsɛpt/ *n* [C] (archit) (either end of the) transverse part of a cross-shaped church: (建築) 十字形教堂的左右翼部; 袖廊: *the north / south ~ of the cathedral.* 大教堂(或主教座堂)的北(南)袖廊。⇨ the illus at church. 參看 church 之插圖。

trans·fer[1] /ˈtrænsfɜː(r) ; ˈtrænsfɝ/ *n* [C, U] (instance of) transferring; document that transfers sth or sb; drawing, plan, etc transferred from one surface to another; ticket that allows a passenger to continue his journey on another bus, etc. 遷移; 移轉; 讓渡; 轉印; 轉接; 換車; 轉業; 調任; 讓渡證書; 轉印的圖畫、圖表等; 換車票。ˈ**~ fee,** sum paid for a ~ (esp of a professional footballer to another club). 轉移費(尤指職業足球員轉移至另一俱樂部時所付者)。

trans·fer[2] /trænsˈfɜː(r) ; trænsˈfɝ/ *vt, vi* (-rr-) [VP 6A, 14, 3A] ~ ***(sb / sth) (from) (to).*** **1** change position, move: 遷移; 移動; 調動; 移轉: *The head office has been ~red from York to London.* 總部已由約克移至倫敦。*He has been ~red from the Manchester branch to the London branch.* 他已由曼徹斯特分公司(或辦事處) 調往倫敦分公司 (或辦事處)。*The dog has ~red its affection to its new master.* 那狗已把它的感情轉移給新主人。 **2** hand over the possession of (property, etc to): 讓渡(財產等): *~ rights to sb.* 讓渡權利給某人。**3** convey (a drawing, design, pattern, etc) from one surface to another (eg from a wooden surface to canvas). 轉寫; 摹寫; 轉印 (圖畫, 設計, 圖案等) (如從木質表面轉至帆布上)。 **4** change from one train, bus, etc to another; move from one occupation, position, etc to another: 換車, 換船等; 轉業, 轉學等; 調任, 調職等: *He has ~red from the warehouse to the accounts office.* 他已由倉庫調至會計室服務。**~·able** /-əbl ; -əbl̩/ *adj* that can be ~red: 可遷移的; 可轉移的; 可讓渡的; 可轉印的: *~able accounts,* of money that may be ~red from one currency to another. 可轉換爲他種貨幣的帳戶。*Railway tickets are not ~able.* 火車票不能換車使用。**~·abil·ity** /ˌtrænsˌfɜːrəˈbɪlətɪ ; ˌtrænsfɝəˈbɪlətɪ/ *n* [U]. **~·ence** /ˈtrænsfərəns *US:* trænsˈfɜːrəns ; trænsˈfɝəns/ *n* ~ing or being ~red, esp from one job to another. 遷移; 轉移; 讓渡; 轉印; 換車; 轉業; (尤指) 調任。

trans·fig·ure /trænsˈfɪgə(r) *US:* -gjər ; trænsˈfɪgjɚ/ *vt* [VP6A] change the shape and appearance of, esp so as to make glorious, exalted or idealized. 使變形; 使改觀; (尤指) 使變得壯麗、高尚或理想化。**trans·figur·ation** /ˌtrænsfɪgəˈreɪʃn *US:* -gjəˈr- ; ˌtrænsfɪgjəˈreʃən/ *n* [U, C] change of this sort, esp **the Transfiguration,** that of Jesus, as described in the Bible. 變形; 改觀; (尤指) 耶穌的改變形像。⇨ Matt 17. 參看馬太福音第 17 章。

trans·fix /trænsˈfɪks ; trænsˈfɪks/ *vt* [VP6A] **1** pierce through: 刺穿; 戳穿: *~ a leopard with a spear.* 以矛刺穿一豹。 **2** cause (sb) to be unable to move, speak, think, etc; paralyse the faculties of: 使(某人)不能活動、說話、思想等; 使麻木: *He stood ~ed with fear / horror / amazement.* 他因害怕(恐怖, 驚愕) 而站着發呆。

trans·form /trænsˈfɔːm ; trænsˈfɔrm/ *vt* [VP6A, 14] ***~ sth (into sth),*** change the shape, appearance, quality or nature of: 改變…之形狀, 外觀, 品質或性質; 轉變某事物至另一事物: *Success and wealth ~ed his character.* 成功和財富改變了他的性格。*A steam-engine ~s heat into energy.* 蒸汽機把熱變成能。*A caterpillar is ~ed into a butterfly.* 一隻毛蟲變成了蝴蝶。**~·able** /-əbl ; -əbl/ *adj* that can be ~ed. 可變形的; 可變化的。 **trans·form·ation** /ˌtrænsfəˈmeɪʃn ; ˌtrænsfɚˈmeʃən/ *n* [U] ~ing or being ~ed; [C] instance of this: 變形; 變化; 變質; 轉變; 轉變的實例: *His character has undergone a ~ation since his brain operation.* 自從他動過腦部手術以後, 他的性格已經改變了。**~er** *n* sb or sth that ~s, esp apparatus that increases or decreases the voltage of an electric power supply. 促使改變的人或物; (尤指) 變壓器。

trans·fuse /trænsˈfjuːz ; trænsˈfjuz/ *vt* [VP6A] transfer (sth, esp the blood of one person to another). 移注; 灌輸; (尤指) 輸(血)。 **trans·fusion** /trænsˈfjuːʒn ; trænsˈfjuʒən/ *n* [U] act or process of transfusing; [C] instance of this: 移注; 灌輸; 輸血; 其實例: *The injured man was given a ˈblood transfusion.* 受傷者輸過一次血。

trans·gress /trænzˈgres ; trænsˈgrɛs/ *vt, vi* **1** [VP 6A] go beyond (a limit or bound): 踰越(某一限度或範圍): *~ the bounds of decency.* 踰越軌範; 不守禮法。**2** [VP6A] break (a law, treaty, agreement). 違犯(法律, 條約, 協議)。 **3** [VP2A] sin; offend against a moral principle. 道德犯罪; 違背道德規範。 **trans·gress·ion** /trænzˈgreʃn ; trænsˈgrɛʃən/ *n* [U] ~ing; [C] instance of this; sin. 踰越; 違犯; 犯規; 其實例; 道德犯罪。**~or** /-sə(r) ; -sɚ/ *n* person who ~es; sinner. 違規者; 罪人。

tran·si·ent /ˈtrænzɪənt *US:* ˈtrænʃnt ; ˈtrænʃənt/ *adj* lasting for a short time only; brief: 短暫的; 倏忽的; 僅持續片刻的: *~ happiness;* 片刻歡樂; *a ~ success.* 一時的成功。□ *n* (US) guest (in a hotel, boarding-house, etc) who is not a permanent resident. (美) (旅館、寄宿舍等的) 暫時寄居的人; 過客。**tran·si·ence** /-əns ; -əns/, **tran·si·ency** /-nsɪ ; -nsɪ/ *nn*

tran·sis·tor /trænˈzɪstə(r) ; trænˈzɪstɚ/ *n* [C] **1** small electronic device, often used in place of a thermionic valve, used in radio sets, hearing aids and other kinds of electronic apparatus: 電晶體(小型電子裝置, 常用以代替眞空管, 用於收音機、助聽器及其他電子儀器中): (attrib) (形容用法) *a portable ~ (set).* 一架手提電晶體收音機。**2** ~ set; ~ radio. 電晶體收音機。 **~·ized** /-aɪzd ; -aɪzd/ *adj* fitted with ~s instead of valves: 裝有電晶體的: *a ~ized computer.* 電晶體計算機。

tran·sit /ˈtrænsɪt ; ˈtrænsɪt/ *n* [U] **1** conveying or being conveyed, across, over or through: 通過; 經過; 搬運; 運送: *goods lost / delayed in ~,* while being carried from one place to another. 搬運中遺失(延誤)的貨物。ˈ**~ camp,** one for the use of persons (eg refugees, soldiers) who are in ~ from one place to another. 過境者(如難民, 士兵等) 所用的營地。ˈ**~ visa,** visa allowing passage through (but not a stay in) a country. 過境簽證(允許在某一國家過境, 但不許停留)。 **2** apparent passage of a heavenly body, eg a planet, across the disc of another one, eg of Venus across the sun. 凌日; 中天(某一天體, 如一行星, 經過另一天體圓面的現象, 例如金星經過太陽圓面)。

tran·si·tion /trænˈzɪʃn ; trænˈzɪʃən/ *n* [C, U] changing, change, from one condition or set of circumstances to another: 轉移; 變化; 變遷; 過渡; 經過: *the period of ~ in Africa,* eg when colonial countries there were becoming self-governing states. 非洲國家的過渡時期(如那裡的殖民地變爲自治國的時期)。*Adolescence is the ~ period / the period of ~ between childhood and adulthood.* 青春期是童年與成年之間的過渡時期。*The frequent ~s from cold to warm weather this spring have caused much illness.* 今年春天的天氣時冷時熱, 引起了許多疾病。**~al** /-ʃənl ; -ʃənl̩/ *adj* **~·ally** /-ʃənəlɪ ; -ʃənl̩ɪ/ *adv*

tran·si·tive /ˈtrænsətɪv ; ˈtrænsətɪv/ *adj* (gram) (of a verb) taking a direct object. (文法) (指動詞) 及物的。**~·ly** *adv*

tran·si·tory /ˈtrænsɪtrɪ *US:* -tɔːrɪ ; ˈtrænsəˌtorɪ/ *adj* transient. 短暫的; 倏忽的; 片刻的。

trans·late /trænzˈleɪt ; trænsˈlet/ *vt, vi* [VP6A, 14, 2A] **1** ~ ***sth (from) (into),*** give the meaning of (sth said or written) in another language: 翻譯; 迻譯: *~ an English book into French;* 將一本英文書譯成法文; *~d from (the) Italian.* 由義大利文譯成的。*The poems don't ~ well.* 這些詩不容易翻譯得好。**2** remove (a bishop) to a different see; (in the Bible) take to heaven without death. 調動(主教)至另一教區; (聖經) 使肉身不死而昇天。**trans-**

lat·able /-əbl; -əbl̩/ *adj* **trans·la·tor** /-tə(r); -tɚ/ *n* person who ~s (esp sth written). 翻譯者(尤指筆譯者)。Cf 參較 *interpreter* for sth spoken. 指"口譯者"。 **trans·la·tion** /-ˈleɪʃn; -ˈleʃən/ *n* [U] translating: 翻譯: *errors in translation;* 翻譯的錯誤; [C] sth ~d: 翻譯品;譯文: *make/do a translation into French.* 譯成法文。

trans·lit·er·ate /trænzˈlɪtəreɪt; trænsˈlɪtəˌret/ *vt* [VP6A, 14] ~ ***sth (into...),*** write (a word, passage) in the characters of a different language or system: 將(一字,一節)改用另一種語言或系統的單字或符號寫出;字譯;音譯;拼寫: ~ *Greek into Roman letters;* 把希臘文拼寫爲羅馬字母; ~ *English words into phonetic symbols.* 把英文字以音標寫出。**trans·lit·er·ation** /ˌtrænzlɪtəˈreɪʃn; trænsˌlɪtəˈreʃən/ *n* [C, U] transliterating; sth ~d. 字譯;音譯;拼寫;字譯、音譯或拼寫成的文字。

trans·lu·cent /trænzˈluːsnt; trænsˈlusn̩t/ *adj* allowing light to pass through but not transparent (as ordinary glass is): 半透明的: *Frosted glass is ~.* 毛玻璃是半透明的。 **trans·lu·cence** /-sns; -sn̩s/, **trans·lu·cency** /-snsɪ; -sn̩sɪ/ *nn*

trans·mi·gra·tion /ˌtrænzmaɪˈgreɪʃn; ˌtrænsmaɪˈgreʃən/ *n* [U] migration; 移居;移民; (esp) (尤指) ~ ***of the soul,*** the passing of the soul at death into another body. 死後靈魂的轉生;轉世。

trans·mission /trænzˈmɪʃn; trænsˈmɪʃən/ *n* **1** [U] transmitting or being transmitted: 傳送;傳達;傳播;遺傳;傳導;傳遞: *the ~ of news/disease/a radio or TV programme.* 消息的傳達(疾病的傳播;無線電或電視節目的播送)。 **2** [C] clutch, gears and drive which transmit power from the engine to (usu) the rear axle (of a motor-vehicle). (汽車等的)傳動系統。

trans·mit /trænzˈmɪt; trænsˈmɪt/ *vt* (-tt-) [VP6A, 14] ~ ***sth (to),*** **1** pass or hand on; send on: 傳送;傳達;傳播;遺傳: ~ *a message by radio;* 由無線電傳送訊息; ~ *a disease.* 傳播疾病。*Parents ~ some of their characteristics to their children.* 父母把一些特質遺傳給子女。 **2** allow through or along: 傳導: *Iron ~s heat.* 鐵傳熱。**~·ter** *n* sb or sth that ~s, esp (part of a) telegraph or radio apparatus for sending out signals, messages, music, etc. 傳送者;傳達者;(尤指)發報機;發送器;傳達器。

trans·mog·rify /trænzˈmɒgrɪfaɪ; trænsˈmɑgrəˌfaɪ/ *vt* (*pt, pp* -fied) [VP6A] cause to change completely in appearance or character, esp in a magical or surprising way. 使形像或性質完全轉變; 使變形; 使變性(尤指藉魔法或以令人吃驚的方式)。 **trans·mog·ri·fi·ca·tion** /ˌtrænzmɒgrɪfɪˈkeɪʃn; trænsˌmɑgrəfɪˈkeʃən/ *n*

trans·mute /trænzˈmjuːt; trænsˈmjut/ *vt* [VP6A, 14] ~ ***sth (into),*** change the shape, nature or substance of: 改變…的形狀、性質或質料: *We cannot ~ base metals into gold.* 我們不能把賤金屬變爲黃金。 **trans·mut·able** /-əbl; -əbl̩/ *adj* that can be ~d. 可改變的; 可變化的。 **trans·mu·ta·tion** /ˌtrænzmjuːˈteɪʃn; ˌtrænsmjuˈteʃən/ *n*

trans·oceanic /ˌtrænzˌəʊʃɪˈænɪk; ˌtrænsoʃɪˈænɪk/ *adj* beyond or crossing an ocean: 在海洋彼岸的;橫越海洋的: *the ~ migrations of birds.* 鳥類的越洋遷徙。

tran·som /ˈtrænsəm; ˈtrænsəm/ *n* horizontal bar of wood over the top of a door or window. (門、窗上的)橫楣。 **ˈ~(-window),** hinged window over a door or other window; (US) fanlight. (門,窗上面的)頂窗;腰窗;(美)門上的扇形窗;氣窗。

trans·par·ent /trænsˈpærənt; trænsˈpɛrənt/ *adj* **1** allowing light to pass through so that objects (or at least their outlines) behind can be distinctly seen: 透明的: ~ *window-panes;* 透明的窗玻璃; ~ *silk.* 透明的綢子。⇨ translucent. **2** about which there can be no mistake or doubt: 顯明的; 顯然的;無疑的: *a ~ lie;* 顯明的謊話; *a man of ~ honesty.* 顯而易見的老實人。**3** clear; easily understood: 明晰的;易瞭解的: *a ~ style of writing.* 明晰的文體。 **~·ly** *adv* **trans·par·ence** /-rəns; -rəns/ *n* [U] state of being ~. 透明;透明性;透明度。 **trans·par·ency** /-rənsɪ; -rənsɪ/ *n* (*pl* -cies) **1** [U] = transparence. **2** [C] diagram, picture, etc (usu in a frame) on photographic film, made visible by light behind it (so that it may be projected on to a screen). 幻燈片(其上有圖表、圖畫等之透明軟片,可放映在銀幕上)。

tran·spire /trænˈspaɪə(r); trænˈspaɪr/ *vi, vt* **1** [VP 2A] (of an event, a secret) become public; come to be known: (指事件、秘密)洩露;公開;爲人所知: *It ~d that the President had spent the weekend golfing.* 據報總統打高爾夫球度過週末。 **2** [VP2A] (colloq) happen. (俗)發生。**3** [VP6A] (of the body, plants) give off, pass off (moisture, vapour). (指身體,植物)散發;排出(濕氣,蒸氣)。**tran·spi·ra·tion** /ˌtrænspəˈreɪʃn; ˌtrænspəˈreʃən/ *n* transpiring (3); loss of water vapour, eg from the surface of leaves. 散發;蒸發(如自葉表面)。

trans·plant /trænsˈplɑːnt *US:* -ˈplænt; trænsˈplænt/ *vt, vi* **1** [VP6A, 2A] take up (plants, etc) with their roots and plant in another place: 移植;移種: ~ *young cabbage plants.* 移植甘藍幼苗。*Some seedlings do not ~ well.* 有些幼苗不適於移植。 **2** transfer (tissue, or an organ, eg a heart or kidney) from one body to another. 移植(組織或器官,如心或腎)。 **3** [VP6A] (fig, of people) move from one place to another. (喻,指人)使遷徙;使遷移。 □ *n* /ˈtrænsplɑːnt *US:* -plænt; ˈtrænsˌplænt/ instance of ~ing(2): (組織或器官的)移植: *a ˈkidney ~.* 腎臟移植(換腎)。 **trans·plan·ta·tion** /ˌtrænsplɑːnˈteɪʃn *US:* -plæn-; ˌtrænsplænˈteʃən/ *n*

trans·po·lar /ˌtrænzˈpəʊlə(r); trænsˈpolɚ/ *adj* across the polar regions: 橫越極區的: ~ *flights from London to Tokyo.* 從倫敦至東京橫越(北)極區的飛行。

trans·port¹ /ˈtrænspɔːt; ˈtrænsport/ *n* **1** [U] conveying or being conveyed; means of conveyance: 輸送;運輸;運輸工具: *the ~ of troops by air;* 空運軍隊; *road ~;* 道路運輸; *water-borne ~,* by ship. 水路運輸。*My car is being repaired so I am without ~/without means of ~ at present.* 我的汽車正在修理,因此我現在沒有交通工具。 **2** (attrib) of or for carrying, conveying: (形容用法)輸送的;運輸的: *London's ~ system;* 倫敦的運輸系統; *~ charges.* 運輸費用。 **ˈ~ café,** one used by long-distance lorry drivers, etc. 運輸餐館(長途貨車司機等所用者)。 **3** [C] **(ˈtroop-)~,** ship or aircraft for carrying troops and supplies. (運送部隊及補給品的)運輸船;運輸機。 **4** (often *pl*) (常用複數) ***in a ~/in ~s of,*** (liter) filled with, carried away by, strong feelings of (delight, rage, etc). (文)滿懷(喜悅、憤怒等)强烈情緒而不能自制;(喜)不自勝;(怒)不可遏。

trans·port² /trænˈspɔːt; trænsˈport/ *vt* **1** [VP6A, 15A] carry (goods, persons) from one place to another: 運送;運輸(貨物,人): ~ *goods by lorry.* 用卡車運貨。**2** [VP6A, 15A] (hist) send (a criminal) to a distant colony as a punishment: (史)放逐(罪犯);流放;處以流刑: *~ed to Australia.* 被放逐到澳洲。 **3** ***be ~ed with,*** (liter) be overcome with, carried away by (strong emotion): (文)爲(强烈情緒)所激動;心蕩神移;失去自制力: *On hearing of the victory, the nation was ~ed with joy.* 聽到勝利的消息,舉國歡騰。 **~·able** /-əbl; -əbl̩/ *adj* that can be ~ed or conveyed. 可運輸的;應處以流刑的;應放逐的。 **trans·por·ta·tion** /ˌtrænspɔːˈteɪʃn; ˌtrænspɚˈteʃən/ *n* [U] ~ing or being ~ed: 運送;運輸;放逐;流刑: *The criminal was sentenced to ~ation for life.* 那罪犯被判終身放逐。

trans·porter /trænˈspɔːtə(r); trænsˈportɚ/ *n* person or thing that transports, eg a travelling crane, or a long vehicle for carrying motor-vehicles from a factory, or a conveyor belt. 輸送者;運送者; 運送的裝置或機械(如移動式起重機,汽車運送車或輸送帶)。 **ˈ~ bridge,** bridge with a movable deck or car used to convey passengers and goods from one end to the other. 輸送橋(以移動的平台或汽車,運送人或貨往返於兩岸)。

trans·pose /træn'spəʊz ; træns'poz/ *vt* [VP6A, 14] **1** cause (two or more things) to change places. 改換(兩件或三件以上事物)的位置;換置;換位。**2** (music) put into another key. (音樂)變調;移調。**trans·po·si·tion** /ˌtrænspə'zɪʃn ; ˌtrænspə'zɪʃən/ *n* [C, U] transposing or being ~d. 轉換;換置;換位;移調。

trans·sexual /trænz'sekʃʊəl ; trænz'sɛkʃʊəl/ *n* (psych) person who belongs physically to one sex, but who feels psychologically that he belongs to the other sex; person who has had a surgical operation, medical treatment, etc, to modify his sexual organs, etc, so that he physically resembles the other sex. (心理) 心理上認爲自己屬於異性者;(經外科手術等)變性者。

trans·ship /træn'ʃɪp ; træns'ʃɪp/ *vt* (-pp-) [VP6A] transfer from one ship or conveyance to another. 使換船;使換運輸工具。**~·ment** *n*

tran·sub·stan·ti·ation /ˌtrænsəbˌstænʃɪ'eɪʃn ; ˌtrænsəbˌstænʃɪ'eʃən/ *n* (RC Church) doctrine that the bread and wine in the Eucharist are changed into the body and blood of Christ. (天主教)化體說(領聖餐時麵包和酒卽轉變爲基督的身體和血的說法)。

trans·verse /'trænzvɜːs ; træns'vɝs/ *adj* lying or placed across: 橫亙的;橫放的;橫斷的;橫向的: *a ~ engine,* one placed parallel, instead of at right angles, to the axles of a car. 橫向引擎(與車軸平行裝置者)。**~·ly** *adv*

trans·vest·ism /trænz'vestɪzəm ; trænz'vɛstɪzəm/ *n* [U] (psych) practice of dressing in clothing of the other sex. (心理)易裝狂(喜穿着異性服裝的變態行爲)。**trans·ves·tite** /-taɪt ; -taɪt/ *n* person who practises ~. 易裝狂者。

trap /træp ; træp/ *n* **1** device for catching animals, etc: 捕捉機;陷穽: *a 'fly-~;* 捕蠅器; *a 'mouse-~;* 捕鼠機; *caught in a ~;* 掉入陷穽; (fig) plan for deceiving sb; trick or device to make sb say or do sth he does not wish to do or say: (喩)詭計;圈套: *The employer set a ~ for the man by putting marked money in the till.* 雇主把有記號的錢放入錢櫃中作爲圈套,來誘捕那個人。*Our soldiers pretended to run away and the enemy, in pursuing them, fell into a ~.* 我們的士兵假裝逃跑,敵人追趕他們,遂陷入圈套。**2** U- shaped or other section of a drain-pipe which retains liquid and so prevents return flow of sewer gas (eg under the pan of a lavatory). (排水管之盛水而能阻止下水道的臭氣倒流的)存水彎; U 形門瓣;凝氣瓣。**3** light, two-wheeled vehicle pulled by a horse or pony. 輕便二輪馬車。**4** **ˌ~('-door),** hinged door or opening in roof, ceiling, floor or the stage of a theatre. (屋頂、天花板、地板或戲院舞臺上的)活門。**5** (sl) mouth: (俚)口;嘴: *Shut your ~!* 住嘴! **6** device (eg a box) from which an animal or object can be released, eg greyhounds at the start of a race, or clay pigeons, balls, etc. 釋放器(如賽狗時放出狗的箱子,或練習射擊時,放出活靶的裝置等)。**'~-shooting,** the sport of shooting at clay pigeons or balls released by springs into the air. 活靶射擊(射擊彈入空中之活靶或球者)。□ *vt* (-pp-) [VP6A, 15A] take in a ~; capture by a trick. 以捕捉機捕捉;設陷穽捕捉;誘捕;使落入圈套。**~·per** *n* person who ~s animals, esp fur-bearing animals. (設陷穽)誘捕野獸(尤指有毛皮的獸類)者。

tra·peze /trə'piːz *US:* træ- ; træ'piz/ *n* horizontal bar or rod supported by two ropes, used by acrobats and for gymnastic exercise. (特技表演者所用,並用作健身練習的)高鞦韆。

tra·pezium /trə'piːzɪəm ; trə'pizɪəm/ *n* (*pl* ~s) (geom) (GB) four-sided figure having only two sides parallel; (US) = trapezoid. (幾何) (英)梯形; (美)不規則四邊形(= trapezoid)。⇨ the illus at quadrilateral. 參看 quadrilateral 之插圖。

trap·ezoid /'træpɪzɔɪd ; 'træpəˌzɔɪd/ *n* (geom) (GB) four-sided figure having no sides parallel; (US) = trapezium. (幾何) (英)不規則四邊形;(美)梯形 (= trapezium)。⇨ parallelogram. ⇨ the illus at quadrilateral. 參看 quadrilateral 之插圖。

trap·pings /'træpɪŋz ; 'træpɪŋz/ *n pl* (fig) ornaments or decorations, esp as a sign of public office: (喩)裝飾物;裝飾品(尤指作爲官職之標幟者): *He had all the ~ of high office but very little power.* 他有大官的一切排場,但權力却很小。

Trap·pist /'træpɪst ; 'træpɪst/ *n* member of an order of monks noted for refraining from speaking and for other austerities. 特拉比斯特會的修道士(以禁言及他種嚴肅規律著稱);苦修會修道士。

trash /træʃ ; træʃ/ *n* [U] **1** worthless material or writing. 無價值之物;無聊作品。**2** (US) rubbish; refuse: (美)垃圾;廢物;殘屑: *a '~-can* (GB 英 = *dustbin*). 垃圾箱。**~y** *adj* worthless: 無價值的;無用的: *~y novels.* 無價值的小說。

trauma /'trɔːmə *US:* 'traʊmə ; 'trɔmə/ *n* (*pl* ~s /-məz ; -məz/) (med) diseased condition of the body produced by a wound or injury; (psych) emotional shock, often leading to neurosis. (醫)(身體上的)外傷;創傷;損傷;(心理)精神創傷(常導致神經機能病)。**trau·matic** /trɔː'mætɪk *US:* traʊ- ; trɔ-'mætɪk/ *adj* of a wound or injury; of or for the treatment of a wound or injury; (of an experience) distressing and unforgettable. 外傷的;創傷的;治療外傷的;(指經驗)痛苦而難忘的。

tra·vail /'træveɪl *US:* trə'veɪl ; trə'vel/ *n* [U] **1** (liter) laborious effort. (文)辛勞;勞苦。**2** (archaic) pains of childbirth. (古)分娩的陣痛。

travel /'trævl ; 'trævḷ/ *vi, vt* (-ll-; US -l-) **1** [VP 2A, B, C, 4A, 6A] make a (esp long) journey or journeys: 旅行;遊歷;(尤指)作長途旅行: *go ~ling;* 旅行; *~ round the world;* 環球旅行; *~ (for) thousands of miles;* 旅行數千哩; *~ (for) three months;* 旅行三個月; *~ (over) the whole world.* 遊徧世界各地。**2** [VP3A] **~ *(in sth) (for sb),*** go from place to place as a salesman: 外出推銷;巡兜生意;到各處兜售: *He ~s in cotton goods.* 他到各處推銷棉織品。*He ~s* (ie as a salesman) *for a London publisher.* 他爲一家倫敦出版商巡兜生意。**3** [VP2A, B, C] move; go: 移動;行進: *Light ~s faster than sound.* 光比聲(行進的速度)快。*Cars are assembled as they ~ from one part of a workshop to another.* 汽車係移送至工廠各部門逐漸裝配完成的。**4** [VP2C] pass from point to point: 依次經過;遍歷: *The general's eyes ~led over the enemy's positions.* 將軍的眼睛掃視敵人的陣地。*Her mind ~led over recent events.* 她把新近發生的事件思索了一遍。**~·ling,** (US = **~·ing**) *n* [U] (esp attrib) (尤作形容用法): *'~ling expenses;* 旅費; *a '~ling bag/dress,* used or designed for ~ling. 旅行袋(服裝)。***~ling fellowship*** *n* grant of money for educational ~ing. (爲教育旅行所發的)旅行補助金。□ *n* **1** [U] ~ling: 旅行;遊歷: *T~ was slow and dangerous in olden days.* 從前旅行費時而且危險。*He is fond of ~.* 他喜歡遊歷。**'~ agent** *n* person who makes arrangements for ~ing, by selling tickets, reserving accommodation, etc. 旅遊代理商;旅遊掮客(代客人買票、安排膳宿等)。Hence, 由此產生, **~ agency/bureau** *n* **'~ sickness** *n* [U] nausea caused by the motion of ~ling. 暈車,暈船或暈機。**2** (in compounds) (用於複合字中) **'~-soiled/-stained/-worn,** soiled, etc, by ~. 風塵僕僕的(旅行中弄髒的;因旅行而疲倦的)。**3** (*pl*) journeys, esp abroad: (複)(尤指海外的)遊歷: *write a book about one's ~s.* 寫遊記。**4** extent of the movement of a mechanical part, eg the shuttle of a loom. (機件的)行程;衝程;活動範圍(如織布機的梭)。**~led,** (US = **~ed**) *adj* **1** having made many long journeys: 曾作多次長途旅行的;富於旅行經驗的: *a ~led man.* 富於旅行經驗的人。**2** used by people who ~: 旅客用的: *a much ~led part of the coun-*

try. 該國經常有旅客往來的地方。**~·ler**, (US = **~er**) /ˈtrævlə(r); ˈtrævlɚ/ *n* **1** person on a journey. 旅客;旅遊者;遊歷者。**ˈ~ler's cheque** (US **ˈ~er's check**), *n* one issued by a bank, tourist agency, etc, for the convenience of ~lers. 旅行支票(爲旅客方便由銀行、旅行社等所發行者)。 **2** (often 常作 *commercial ~ler*) ~ling salesman. 旅行推銷員。

trav·elogue (also 亦作 **-log**) /ˈtrævəlɒg *US:* -lɔːg; ˈtrævḷ,ɔg/ *n* film or lecture describing ~s. 描寫遊歷的演講或電影;遊記影片或演說。

tra·verse /ˈtrævɜːs *US:* trəˈvɜːs; ˈtrævɚs/ *vt* [VP6A] travel across; pass over: 走過;經過;橫過: *Searchlights ~d the sky.* 探照燈掃過天空。*The railway ~s hundreds of miles of desert.* 這條鐵路貫穿數百哩的沙漠。□ *n* [C] **1** (mountaineering) sideways movement across the face of a precipice, steep slope of ice, etc from one point where ascent or descent is possible to another; place where this is necessary. (爬山)Z字形爬登;Z字形爬登處。 **2** change of direction in a trench to prevent the enemy from firing along it. 戰壕的折曲;Z形戰壕(俾阻止敵人沿壕溝方向射擊)。

trav·esty /ˈtrævəstɪ; ˈtrævɪstɪ/ *n* [C] (*pl* -ties) parody; imitation or description (of sth) that is, often on purpose, unlike and inferior to the real thing: 拙劣的模倣或描述(常爲故意地);歪曲;曲解: *His trial was a ~ of justice.* 他的審判是對法律正義的歪曲。□ *vt* (*pt, pp* -tied) [VP6A] make or be a ~ of: 拙劣地模倣或描述;歪曲: *~ a person's style of writing.* 拙劣地模倣某人的文體。

trawl /trɔːl; trɔl/ *n* [C] **1** **ˈ~(-net)**, large wide-mouthed net to be dragged along the sea-bottom. (海上漁船用的)拖網。 **2** (US) (美) **ˈ~ line** (also 亦作 *setline*), long sea-fishing line to which are attached many short lines with hooks. 捕海魚的排鈎。□ *vi, vt* [VP2A] fish with a ~; [VP6A] drag along the sea-bottom: 用拖網或排鈎捕魚;沿海底拖: *~ a net.* 拖網。**~er** *n* boat, fisherman, that ~s. 以拖網或排鈎捕魚的船或漁夫;拖網船;拖撈船;拖撈漁夫。

a trawler

tray /treɪ; tre/ *n* flat piece of wood, metal, etc with raised edges, for holding light articles, eg *a ˈpen-~*, or carrying things, eg *a ˈtea-~*; container on a writing-desk for papers, etc. 盤;碟(裝小物件者,如 a pen-~ 筆盤,或承托東西者,如 a tea-~ 茶盤);書桌上的公文盤。**ˈin-/ˈout-tray**, for papers, letters, etc coming in/ready to go out. 收文盤(發文盤)。

treach·er·ous /ˈtretʃərəs; ˈtrɛtʃərəs/ *adj* **1** false or disloyal (to a friend, cause, etc). (對朋友、主義等)虛僞的;不忠的;叛逆的;奸詐的。 **2** deceptive; not to be relied upon: 不可恃的;靠不住的: *~ weather.* 靠不住的天氣。*The ice is ~*, appears to be strong but may break. 這冰可能會破(雖然看起來很厚實)。*My memory is ~.* 我的記憶靠不住。**~·ly** *adv*

treach·ery /ˈtretʃərɪ; ˈtrɛtʃərɪ/ *n* (*pl* -ries) [U] being ~; (*pl*) ~ acts. 不忠;叛逆;(複)奸詐行爲;叛逆行爲。

treacle /ˈtriːkl; ˈtrikl/ *n* [U] thick, sticky, dark liquid produced while sugar is being refined (US 美 = *molasses*). 糖蜜;糖漿。**treacly** /ˈtriːkəlɪ; ˈtriklɪ/ *adj* like ~; thick and sweet; (fig) excessively sweet: 似糖漿的;濃而甜的;(喻)過分親熱的: *treacly sentiments.* 過分親熱的感情。

tread /tred; trɛd/ *vi, vt* (*pt* trod /trɒd; trɑd/, *pp* trodden /ˈtrɒdn; ˈtrɑdn̩/ or trod) **1** [VP2C, 3A] **~ *(on sth)***, walk, put the foot or feet down (on): 走;踩;踐踏: *~ on sb's toes.* 踩在某人的足趾上。*Don't ~ on the flower beds.* 勿踐踏花壇。*She trod lightly so as not to wake the baby.* 她輕輕地走,以免驚醒孩子。**~ *on air***, be light-hearted and gay, transported with joy. 得意洋洋;歡天喜地。**~ *on sb's corns/toes***, (fig) offend him. (喻)觸怒某人。**~ *on sb's heels***, (lit or fig) follow closely after. (字面或喻)緊隨…之後。 **2** [VP6A, 15A, B] **~ *(out/down)***, stamp or crush; push (down, etc) with the feet: 踩碎;踩破;踩出;踩緊: *~ out a fire in the grass;* 踩滅草中的火; *~ grapes*, when making wine; (製酒時)踩碎葡萄; *~ (out) the juice from grapes;* 踩出葡萄汁; *~ (down) the earth round the roots.* 把根部四周的泥土踩緊。 **3** [VP6A] make by walking: 踏成;踩出;藉步行而做成: *The cattle had trodden a path to the pond.* 牛群踏出了一條通往池塘的小徑。 **4** [VP6A] walk along: 沿…走;行走於;步行在: (fig) (喻) *~ a dangerous path*, follow a risky course of action; 採取冒險行動; *~ the boards*, (rhet) be an actor; (修辭)作演員; *~ a measure*, (archaic) dance. (古)跳舞。**~ *water***, keep oneself afloat in deep water by moving the feet up and down (as if working the pedals of a bicycle). 踩水(在深水中使足上下動而不使身體下沉,動作像踩腳踏車般)。□ *n* **1** way or sound of walking: 踏;踩;步法;步態;足音: *with a heavy/loud ~.* 腳步沉重(大聲)地。 **2** part of a step or stair on which the foot is placed. 踏面;踏板(臺階或梯級的踏腳部分)。**ˈ~-mill** *n* appliance or apparatus for producing circular motion by the movements of a person or animal walking on the steps (or treads) of a wheel or a sloping endless belt (eg the kind formerly used in prisons as a punishment); (fig) monotonous routine. (藉人力或獸力的)踏輪;(昔時用以懲治囚犯等的)踏車;(喻)單調的例行工作。 **3** grooved part of a tyre which touches the ground: 輪胎的接地部分;胎面: *Good ~s minimize the risk of skidding.* 良好的胎面可將滑動的危險減至最低限度。⇨ retread.

treadle /ˈtredl; ˈtrɛdl/ *n* pedal or lever that drives a machine, eg a lathe or sewing-machine, worked by pressure of the foot or feet. (車床,縫級機等的)踏板。□ *vi* [VP2A] work a ~. 用腳踏機械的踏板。

trea·son /ˈtriːzn; ˈtrizn̩/ *n* [U] treachery to, betrayal of, one's country or ruler; disloyalty; betrayal of trust. 叛國;叛逆;不忠;背信。**~·ous** /ˈtriːzənəs; ˈtriznəs/, **~·able** /ˈtriːzənəbl; ˈtriznəbl̩/ *adjj* **~·ably** /-əblɪ; -əblɪ/ *adv*

treas·ure /ˈtreʒə(r); ˈtrɛʒɚ/ *n* **1** [C, U] (store of) gold and silver, jewels, etc; wealth: 金銀;珠寶;財寶;寶物;財貨;財富: *The pirates buried their ~.* 海盜埋藏他們的財寶。**ˈ~-house** *n* building where ~ is stored. 寶庫;寶藏室。**ˈ~-trove** *n* [U] ~ found hidden in the earth and of unknown ownership. 埋於地下的無主寶藏。 **2** highly valued object or person: 極受珍愛的物或人: *The National Gallery has many priceless ˈart ~s.* 國家畫廊有許多無價的藝術珍藏。*She says her new secretary is a perfect ~.* 她說她新用的秘書非常理想。 *My ~!* (as a term of endearment). 我的寶貝!(親密語)。□ *vt* **1** [VP 6A, 15B] **~ *sth (up)***, store for future use: 儲藏;珍藏: *~ memories of one's holiday in Thailand;* 珍惜在泰國度假的回憶; *~ sth up in one's memory.* 銘記某事。 **2** [VP6A] value highly: 重視;珍惜: *~ sb's friendship.* 珍惜某人的友誼。*He ~s the watch his father gave him.* 他珍愛他父親送給他的那隻錶。**~r** /ˈtreʒərə(r); ˈtrɛʒərɚ/ *n* person in charge of money, etc belonging to a club or society. 掌管

俱樂部或社團之錢財者;財務;會計;出納。

treas·ury /ˈtreʒərɪ ; ˈtrɛʒərɪ/ *n* (*pl* -ries) **1 the T~,** (in GB) department of State controlling public revenue. (英國的)財政部。**First Lord of the T~,** the Prime Minister. 首相。**the ˈT~ Board/Lords of the T~,** officers in charge of public revenue (usu the Prime Minister, the Chancellor of the Exchequer, and three others). 財政委員會(通常由首相、財政大臣及另外三人組成)。 **the ˈT~ Bench,** bench in the House of Commons occupied by members of the Cabinet. (英國下議院的)內閣閣員席。**ˈ~ bill,** (GB) bill of exchange issued by the T~ to raise money for temporary needs. (英)國庫債券(臨時需款時,由英國財政部所發行者)。**ˈ~ note,** currency note issued by the US T~; (formerly) currency note issued by the British T~ (now replaced by Bank of England notes). 國庫券(美國財政部所發行者;昔英國財政部所發行者,現爲英格蘭銀行發行之紙幣所代替)。 **2** place where funds are kept; funds of a society, organization, etc: 經費存放處;金庫;社團、機關等的經費;基金: *The ~ of our tennis club is almost empty.* 我們網球俱樂部的基金幾乎用光了。 **3** person, book, etc looked upon as containing valuable information or as a valued source: 被視爲寶庫的人、書等: *This dictionary is a ~ of information.* 這部字典是知識的寶庫。

treat /triːt ; trit/ *vt, vi* **1** [VP15A, 16B] *~ (as),* act or behave towards: 對待;看待: *He ~s his wife badly.* 他對待太太不好。*Don't ~ me as (if I were) a child.* 不要把我當作小孩子看待。*You must ~ them with more consideration.* 你必須多體諒他們一點。**2** [VP16B] *~ as,* consider: 視爲;以爲: *We had better ~ it as a joke,* instead of taking it seriously. 我們最好把它當作笑話(不必認眞)。 **3** [VP6A] discuss; deal with: 討論;探討: *The lecturer ~ed his subject thoroughly.* 那演講者對其講題闡釋得很透徹。*The problem has been ~ed by numerous experts.* 這問題已由很多專家探討過了。**4** [VP3A] *~ of,* (formal) be about: (正式用語)論述;論及: *The essay/lecture/book ~s of the progress of cancer research.* 這篇文章(這演講,這本書)論述癌症研究的進展情形。 **5** [VP6A] give medical or surgical care to: 治療: *Which doctors are ~ing her for her illness?* 哪幾位醫生在爲她診治?*How would you ~ a case of rheumatism/~ sb ill with influenza?* 你怎樣治療風濕症(治療流行性感冒患者)? **6** [VP6A] put (a substance) through a process (in manufacture, etc): (在製造等過程中)處理(某物): *~ a substance with acid/wood with creosote.* 以酸處理某物(以雜酚油處理木材)。 **7** [VP6A, 14] *~ sb/oneself (to sth),* supply (food, drink, entertainment, etc) at one's own expense (to): (以食物、飲料、娛樂等)宴饗;款待;招待: *~ one's friends to oysters and champagne.* 請朋友享用蠔及香檳酒。*I shall ~ myself to a good weekend holiday.* 我要好好地度個週末。*It's my turn to ~ us today.* 今天該我請客。 **8** [VP3A] *~ with sb,* discuss or arrange with him: 談判;磋商: *~ with the enemy for peace.* 與敵人談和。*If we are to ~ with you, it must be on equal terms.* 如果我們同你談判,必須基於平等的條件。□ *n* **1** [C] sth that gives pleasure, esp sth not often enjoyed or sth that comes unexpectedly: 予人喜悅的事物;樂事(尤指不常享用或突如其來者): *What a ~ to get into the peace and quiet of the country!* 居住在寧靜的鄉間眞是一件樂事! *It's a great ~ for her to go to the ballet.* 去欣賞芭蕾舞對她來說眞是一大樂事。 **2** act of ~ing (7): 宴饗;款待;招待: *This is to be my ~,* I'm going to pay. 這次我請客。 ***stand ~,*** (colloq) bear the expense of the entertainment. (俗)作東道。

treat·ise /ˈtriːtɪz *US:* -tɪs ; ˈtritɪs/ *n ~ (on/upon),* book, etc that deals systematically with one subject: 論文;論說: *a ~ on racial prejudice.* 一篇有關種族偏見的論文。

treat·ment /ˈtriːtmənt ; ˈtritmənt/ *n* [C, U] (particular way of) treating sb or sth; what is done to obtain a desired result: 對待;待遇;處置;處理;治療;處理或對待人或物的特別方法: *Is the ~ of political prisoners fair in your country?* 在貴國對政治犯的處置公平嗎? *He soon recovered under the doctor's ~.* 他在醫生治療下很快就康復了。 *That dog has suffered from cruel ~.* 那隻狗受到殘酷的待遇。*He has tried many ~s for skin diseases.* 他已試過許多治療皮膚病的方法。*They are trying a new ~ for cancer.* 他們正在試驗一種治療癌症的新方法。*She is still under ~ in hospital.* 她仍在住院接受治療。

treaty /ˈtriːtɪ ; ˈtritɪ/ *n* (*pl* -ties) **1** [C] formal agreement made and signed between nations: (國與國間締結的)條約: *a ˈpeace ~;* 和約; *enter into a ~ of commerce (with).* (與…)締結商約。**ˈ~ port,** one that a country is bound by ~ to keep open for foreign trade. (根據條約開放的)商港;通商口岸。 **2** [U] agreement or negotiation between persons: (人與人間的)協商;協議;談判: *be in ~ with sb for...;* 與某人談判…; *sell a house by private ~,* instead of by public auction or other method. 私下協議售賣房屋(非經由公開拍賣或其他方法)。

treble[1] /ˈtrebl ; ˈtrɛbl̩/ *adj, n* three times as much or many (as): 三倍(的);三重(的): *He earns ~ my salary.* 他賺的薪水是我的三倍。**ˌ~ ˈchance,** method of competing in football pools. 三重機會(一種賭足球比賽的方法)。 □ *vt, vi* [VP6A, 2A] make or become ~: (使)增爲三倍: *He has ~d his earnings/His earnings have ~d during the last few years.* 在過去的數年間他的收入已增爲三倍。

treble[2] /ˈtrebl ; ˈtrɛbl̩/ *n* (boy's voice with, instrument that takes, the) highest part in a piece of music. (樂曲的)最高音部;唱最高音部的童聲;演奏最高音部的樂器。**~ clef,** ⇨ clef, and the illus at notation. 參看 clef 與 notation 之插圖。

tree /triː ; tri/ *n* **1** perennial plant with a single self-supporting trunk of wood with (usu) no branches for some distance above the ground: 樹;樹木;喬木: *cut down ~s for timber.* 伐樹取材。⇨ bush, shrub. ***at the top of the ~,*** at the top of one's profession. 居某行業的最高地位。***up a (ˈgum-)~,*** (colloq) cornered; in a position from which escape is difficult. (俗)進退維谷;處於困境。**family ~,** diagram or list showing or giving family descent. 家系圖;系譜;家譜。**ˈ~-fern** *n* fern that grows to the size of a tree. 桫欏(高大如樹的蕨類植物);巨大羊齒類植物。 **2** piece of wood, metal, etc for a special purpose: (用於特殊目的的)木材;木塊;金屬塊: *a ˈboot-/ˈshoe-~,* for keeping a boot or shoe in shape while not being worn; 鞋(靴)楦;鞋(靴)型; *an ˈaxle-~,* connecting two opposite wheels. 軸料;軸木;心棒。□ *vt* [VP6A] cause to take refuge up a ~: 驅使上樹以避難: *The hunter was ~d by the bear.* 獵人被熊趕上了樹。*The dog ~d the cat.* 狗趕貓上樹。**~·less** *adj* without ~s: 無樹木的: *the ~less plains of Argentina.* 阿根廷的無樹大平原。

tre·foil /ˈtrefɔɪl ; ˈtrifɔɪl/ *n* kinds of three-leaved plant, eg clover; ornament or design like a three-fold leaf, eg as in stonework. 車軸草;三葉植物;三葉型裝飾或花樣(如石器上者)。

trek /trek ; trɛk/ *vi* (-kk-) [VP2A, B, C] make a long, hard journey. 作艱辛的長途旅行。□ *n* long, hard journey. 艱辛的長途旅行。

trel·lis /ˈtrelɪs ; ˈtrɛlɪs/ *n* light upright structure of strips of wood, etc esp as used for supporting climbing plants. 格子架;格子棚(尤指用以支撐蔓生植物者)。□ *vt* [VP6A] furnish with, support on, a ~. 爲…裝設格子架;以格子架支撐。

tremble /ˈtrembl ; ˈtrɛmbl/ *vi* [VP2A, B, C, 4B] **1** shake involuntarily (as from fear, anger, cold, physical weakness, etc): 戰慄;震顫;發抖(因恐懼、憤怒、寒冷、體弱等): *His voice ~d with anger.* 他的聲音因憤怒而發抖。 *We were trembling with cold/excitement.* 我們因寒冷(興奮)而顫抖。 **2** move to and fro: 搖動;擺動;顫動: *The bridge ~d as the heavy lorry crossed it.* 那座橋因重卡車通過而顫動。*The ground ~d under our feet.* 地面在我們脚下顫動。**3** be in a state of agitation: 擔心;擔憂;不安: *I ~ to think what has happened to him,* am deeply worried. 我一想到他的遭遇就替他擔心。*She ~d for his safety.* 她擔憂他的安全。***in fear and trembling,*** in a state of frightened anxiety. 提心吊膽地。□ *n* shudder; uncontrollable shaking: 戰慄;震顫;身不由己的發抖: *There was a ~* (more usu 較常用 *a tremor) in his voice.* 他的聲音有一點發抖。*He was all of a ~,* (colloq) was trembling all over. (俗)他全身發抖。

tre·men·dous /trɪˈmendəs ; trɪˈmɛndəs/ *adj* **1** very great; enormous; powerful: 極大的;巨大的;極有力的: *a ~ explosion;* 威力極大的爆炸; *travelling at a ~ speed.* 高速行進。**2** (colloq) extraordinary: (俗)異常的;非常的: *He's a ~ eater/talker,* eats/talks to an extraordinary degree; 他的食量驚人(他是一個非常健談的人); splendid, first-rate: 極好的;第一流的: *a ~ concert/performance/meal.* 極佳的音樂會(表演,餐食)。**~·ly** *adv*

trem·olo /ˈtreməlǝʊ ; ˈtrɛmə,lo/ *n* (*pl* ~s /-lǝʊz ; -loz/) (music) trembling or vibrating effect in singing, or in the playing of a bowed musical instrument. (音樂)(歌唱或有弓弦樂器的)顫音。

tremor /ˈtremə(r) ; ˈtrɛmɚ/ *n* [C] **1** shaking or trembling: 顫抖;戰慄;顫動: *the ~ of a leaf,* eg in a breeze; 樹葉的顫動(如在微風中); *ˈearth ~s,* as during an earthquake. 地面的顫動(如地震時)。**2** thrill: 激動;興奮: *A ~ of fear went through the audience when the assassin fired at the President.* 刺客對着總統開槍時,觀衆感到一陣驚恐。

tremu·lous /ˈtremjʊləs ; ˈtrɛmjələs/ *adj* **1** trembling: 戰慄的; 震顫的;抖動的: *in a ~ voice;* 聲音顫抖地; *with a ~ hand.* 手顫動地。**2** timid; nervous. 膽怯的;緊張的。**~·ly** *adv*

trench /trentʃ ; trɛntʃ/ *n* [C] ditch dug in the ground, eg for the draining of water, for a latrine, as a protection for soldiers against the enemy's fire: 溝;溝渠;壕溝;戰壕: *dig ~es for irrigation;* 挖掘灌溉用的溝渠; *~ warfare,* fought in and from ~es; 塹壕戰(據壕的作戰); *a ˈ~-coat,* soldier's waterproof coat. 戰壕衣(士兵穿的防水衣)。□ *vt* [VP6A] surround with a ~; fortify with a ~ or ~es; make ~es in: 以溝圍繞;築壕以防禦;挖壕溝於: *~ a field,* for draining. 在田地上挖溝(以排水)。

trench·ant /ˈtrentʃənt ; ˈtrɛntʃənt/ *adj* (of language) vigorous; incisive: (指言詞)有力的;犀利的: *~ wit;* 犀利的言詞; *a ~ speech.* 有力的演講。**~·ly** *adv* **trench·ancy** /-ənsɪ ; -ənsɪ/ *n*

trencher /ˈtrentʃə(r) ; ˈtrɛntʃɚ/ *n* (hist) large wooden plate on which food was formerly served or carved. (史)(用以端菜或切菜的)大木盤。**ˈ~·man** /-mən ; -mən/ *n* (*pl* -men) *a good/poor ~man,* person who usu eats a lot/a little. 食量大(小)的人。

trend /trend ; trɛnd/ *n* [C] general direction; tendency: 朝向;趨勢;傾向: *The ~ of the coastline is to the south.* 海岸線向南延伸。*Is the ~ of modern thought away from materialism?* 現代思潮有擺脫唯物主義的傾向嗎? *The ~ of prices is still upwards.* 物價仍有上漲趨勢。***set the ~,*** start a style, etc which others follow. 開風氣之先。Hence, 由此產生, **ˈ~-setter, ˈ~-setting** *nn.* **~y** *adj* (-ier, -iest) (sl, often derog) showing, following, the latest ~s of fashion, etc. (俚,常爲貶抑語)最時髦的;趕時髦的。□ *vi* [VP2C] have a certain ~: 向;傾向: *The road ~s towards the west.* 這條路通向西方。

tre·pan /trɪˈpæn ; trɪˈpæn/ *vt* (-nn-), *n* **1** = trephine. **2** bore for drilling a mine shaft. 鑽掘礦坑。

tre·phine /trɪˈfiːn *US:* -ˈfaɪn ; trɪˈfaɪn/ *vt* [VP6A] (med) make a small hole in (sb's skull). (醫)以環鋸在(頭蓋)上開圓洞;環鑽。□ *n* cylindrical saw used for this. (此種手術用的)環鋸。

trepi·da·tion /ˌtrepɪˈdeɪʃn ; ˌtrɛpəˈdeʃən/ *n* [U] alarm; excited state of mind. 驚恐;惶恐;激動。

tres·pass /ˈtrespəs ; ˈtrɛspəs/ *vi* **1** [VP2A, 3A] ~ ***(on/upon),*** go on to privately owned land without right or permission: 未得許可進入私地;非法侵入: *~ upon sb's (private) property.* 非法侵入某人的(私有)土地。*No ~ing!* (a sign put up on pri-

trees

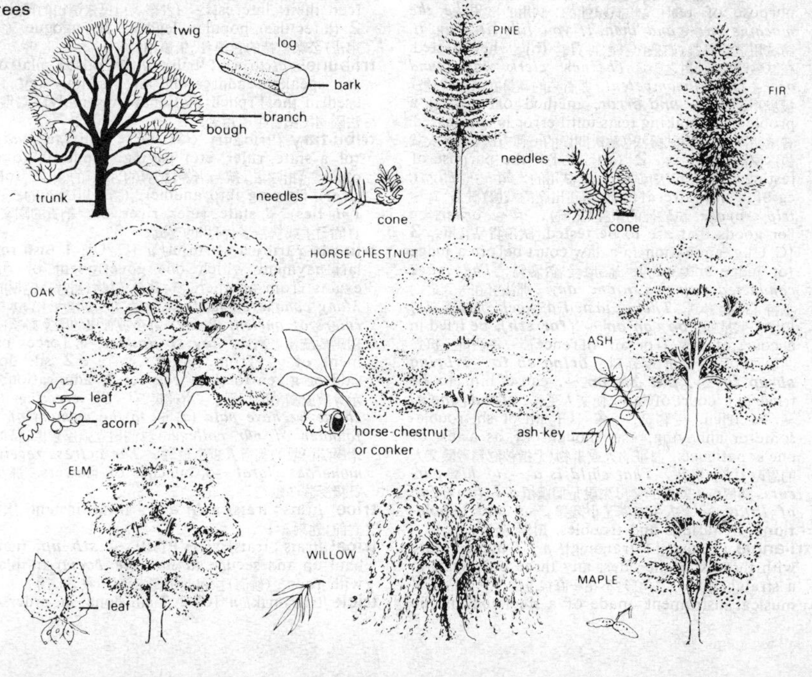

vately owned land as a warning). 不准入內！(用作告示)。 **2** [VP3A] ~ ***on/upon,*** encroach upon, make too much use of: 侵奪;侵犯: *~ upon sb's time/hospitality/privacy.* 佔用某人的時間 (叨擾某人;打擾某人的清靜)。 **3** [VP2A, 3A] ~ ***(against),*** (archaic) do wrong; sin: (古)違規;犯罪: *'as we forgive them that ~ against us.'* '如同我們原諒那些冒犯了我們的人。' . □ *n* **1** [U] ~ing(1); [C] instance of this. 非法入侵;其實例。 **2** [C] (old use, and biblical) sin; wrong: (舊用法,聖經)罪;過失;罪過: *'Forgive us our ~es.'* '赦免我們的罪。' **~er** *n* person who ~es(1): 非法入侵者: *T~ers will be prosecuted.* 非法入侵者將依法究辦。

tress /tres ; trɛs/ *n* (poet or liter) (詩或文) **1** (*pl*) hair (esp of a woman's or girl's head): (複)頭髮(尤指女人或女孩者): *her beautiful golden ~es.* 她的美麗金髮。 **2** plait or braid of hair. 辮子;髮辮。

trestle /ˈtresl ; ˈtrɛsḷ/ *n* horizontal beam of wood with two diverging legs at each end, used in pairs to support planks, a table top, a workman's bench, etc. 叉架;支架(橫木兩端支以人字支脚而成,成對使用,以支撐桌面、工作枱等)。 **ˌ~-ˈbridge** *n* bridge supported by a framework of timber or steel. 支架橋;架柱橋;構脚橋。⇨ the illus at bridge. 參看 bridge 之插圖。 **ˌ~-ˈtable** *n* one made by laying planks on ~s. 檯架,支架枱。

trews /tru:z ; truz/ *n pl* close-fitting tartan trousers. 格子花呢製成的緊身褲。

tri- /traɪ- ; traɪ-/ *pref* three. 三。⇨App 3. 參看附錄三。

triad /ˈtraɪæd ; ˈtraɪæd/ *n* group or set of three closely related persons or things. 三人或三物組成的一組;三個之一組。

trial /ˈtraɪəl ; ˈtraɪəl/ *n* **1** [U] testing, trying, proving; [C] instance of this: 試驗;考驗;證明;其實例: *give sth a ~,* use it to learn about its qualities, value, etc; 試驗某物; *give a new worker a ~,* give him a chance to show his skill; 試用新工人; *have a ~ of strength with sb,* a contest to learn who is stronger. 與某人較量氣力。*We shall put the machine to further ~,* test it further. 我們將進一步試驗這部機器。*The ship performed well during her ~s.* 那艘船在試航時情況良好。***on ~,*** **(a)** for the purpose of testing: 試驗性的;試用的: *Take the machine on ~ and then, if you like it, buy it.* 請試用這部機器,如果你喜歡再買。 **(b)** when tested: 在試驗時;被試用之際: *The new clerk was found on ~ to be incompetent.* 那新來的職員在試用時(被)發現不合格。***~ and error,*** method of solving a problem by making tests until error is eliminated. 嘗試錯誤法;反覆試驗法(解決問題的一種方法,藉多次試驗逐漸消除錯誤)。 **2** (attrib) for the purpose of testing: (形容用法)試驗性的;試用的: *a ~ flight,* eg of a new aircraft; (如指新出廠的飛機)試飛; *a ~ trip/voyage;* 試驗性的旅程(試航); *a ~ order,* eg for goods that are to be tested. 試用貨品訂單。 **3** [C, U] examination in a law court before a judge (or judge and jury): 審訊;受審;審判: *The judge conducted four ~s in one day.* 那法官在一天之內主持了四次審判。*The ~ lasted a week.* 那項審訊持續了一個星期。***be/go on ~ (for sth),*** be tried in a court of law (for an offence). (在法庭上)(爲某項罪名而)受審訊;受審判。***bring sb to ~; bring sb up for ~; put sb on ~,*** cause him to be tried in a court of law. 使某人受審。***stand (one's) ~,*** be tried. 受審訊。 **4** [C] sth or sb troublesome or annoying, esp thought of as a test of one's patience: 討厭的人或事物(尤指被認爲考驗某人的忍耐力者);磨難: *That child is a ~ to his parents.* 那個小孩對他的父母來說是個麻煩。*Life is full of little ~s.* 人生充滿了小磨難。**~s and tribulations,** irritations and troubles. 煩惱;憂患。

tri·angle /ˈtraɪæŋgl ; ˈtraɪˌæŋgḷ/ *n* **1** plane figure with three straight sides; any three points not in a straight line. 三角形;不在一直線上的任意三點。 **2** musical instrument made of a steel rod in the shape of a ~, struck with another steel rod. (音樂)三角鈴(一種由鋼條彎曲成三角形的敲擊樂器,用另一根鋼桿敲擊之)。⇨ the illus at percussion. 參看 percussion 之插圖。 **3** group of three. 三個的組或群。***the eternal ~,*** the situation existing when two persons are both in love with a third. (兩人同時愛上第三者的)三角戀愛。 **tri·angu·lar** /traɪˈæŋgjʊlə(r) ; traɪˈæŋgjələ˞/ *adj* **1** in the shape of a ~. 三角形的。 **2** in which there are three persons, etc: 三人之間的;三者的: *a triangular contest in an election,* with three candidates. 有三位候選人的競選。

tribal /ˈtraɪbl ; ˈtraɪbḷ/ *adj* of a tribe or tribes: 種族的;部落的;部族的;族類的;夥衆的: *~ loyalties;* 對部族的效忠; *~ dances.* 部族舞蹈。 **~·ism** /ˈtraɪbəlɪzəm ; ˈtraɪbḷɪzṃ/ *n*

tribe /traɪb ; traɪb/ *n* **1** racial group, esp one united by language and customs, living as a community under one or more chiefs: 種族;部落;部族: *the Indian ~s of America;* 美洲的印第安部落; *the twelve ~s of ancient Israel.* 古代以色列人的十二支族。 **2** (bot, zool) group of plants or animals, usu ranking between a genus and an order. (植物,動物)族;類。 **3** (usu contemptuous) group of persons, etc of one profession: (通常爲輕蔑語)同一行業或職業的衆人;儕輩;夥黨: *the ~ of politicians.* 政客之輩。 **ˈ~s·man** /-zmən ; -zmən/ *n* (*pl* -men) member of a ~(1). 部族的一分子;種族或部落的一員。

tribu·la·tion /ˌtrɪbjʊˈleɪʃn ; ˌtrɪbjəˈleʃən/ *n* [C, U] (cause of) trouble, grief: 苦難;憂患;苦難或憂患的原由: *The war was a time of ~ for all of us.* 那次戰爭對我們大家來說是一段苦難的時期。*He bore his ~s bravely.* 他勇敢地承受困苦。⇨ trial(4).

tri·bu·nal /traɪˈbju:nl ; trɪˈbjunḷ/ *n* [C] place of judgement; board of officials or judges appointed for special duty, eg to hear appeals against high rents, for exemption from military service: 法庭;裁判所;審理團(被派審理特殊案件的官吏或法官,如受理反對高地租、或免除兵役之訴願等): (fig) (喻) *the ~ of public opinion.* 輿論的裁決。

tri·bune[1] /ˈtrɪbju:n ; ˈtrɪbjun/ *n* **1** official chosen by the common people of ancient Rome to protect their interests. (古羅馬由民衆選出的)護民官。 **2** (later use) popular leader; demagogue. (後來用法)公衆支持的首領;民衆領袖。

tri·bune[2] /ˈtrɪbju:n ; ˈtrɪbjun/ *n* raised platform for speakers addressing an assembly (eg that used in the French National Assembly). 講壇(如法國國民議會中所用者)。

tribu·tary /ˈtrɪbjʊtrɪ *US:* -terɪ ; ˈtrɪbjəˌtɛrɪ/ *adj* **1** (of a state, ruler, etc) paying tribute(1) to another. (指國家、統治者等)納貢的;進貢的。 **2** (of a river) flowing into another. (指河川)支流的。□ *n* (*pl* -ries) ~ state, ruler, river, etc. 納貢的國家;納貢的君主或統治者;河川的支流。

trib·ute /ˈtrɪbju:t ; ˈtrɪbjut/ *n* [C, U] **1** (usu regular) payment which one government or ruler exacts from another: 貢;貢金;貢物(通常爲定期的): *Many conquered nations had to pay ~ to the rulers of ancient Rome.* 許多被征服的國家必須向古羅馬的統治者納貢。***lay sb under ~,*** force payment of ~ from. 强使某人進貢。 **2** sth done, said or given to show respect or admiration: 表示尊敬或讚美的行爲、言辭或東西: *By erecting this statue we have paid (a) ~ to the memory of the founder of our college.* 我們樹立這座雕像,藉以對本學院已故的創辦人表示敬意。*The actress received numerous floral ~s,* bunches of flowers. 那女演員接受許多獻花。

trice[1] /traɪs ; traɪs/ *n* ***in a ~,*** in an instant. 頃刻;立即;立刻。

trice[2] /traɪs ; traɪs/ *vt* [VP15B] ~ ***sth up,*** (naut) haul up and secure (*a sail, the boom*) in place with rope. (航海)拉起並用繩索縛住(帆,帆桁)。

trick /trɪk ; trɪk/ *n* [C] **1** sth done in order to

deceive, to outwit or outdo, sb; sth done to make a person appear ridiculous: 詭計;計謀;欺詐手段: *The wearing of white clothes is a common ~ of soldiers fighting in snow-covered country.* 在積雪的地區作戰時,穿著白衣服是士兵們慣用的計謀。*He got the money from me by a ~.* 他從我這裏詐取到那筆錢。***the ~s of the trade,*** ways of attracting customers, gaining advantages over rivals, etc. 生意經;商業技巧、花招等。**2** mischievous act, practical joke: 頑皮的行爲;惡作劇: *The children are always up to amusing ~s.* 孩子們總喜歡調皮搗蛋尋開心。*That was an unfair ~.* 那是個過分的惡作劇。***play a ~ on sb,*** ⇨ play²(3). ***dirty ~,*** a contemptible action. 卑劣行爲。**3** feat of skill or dexterity: 技巧;技藝;妙訣戲法;把戲: *conjuring ~s.* 變戲法。*Does your dog know any ~s?* 你的狗會耍把戲嗎? *Are you clever at card ~s?* 你擅長用紙牌變戲法嗎? ***do the ~,*** (sl) accomplish one's purpose: (俚)達到目的: *One more turn of the screwdriver should do the ~,* fasten the screw securely. 再把那(螺絲)起子轉一圈就行了(就把那螺絲轉緊了)。***a ~ worth two of that,*** (colloq) a better way of doing it (than yours). (俗)(比你的方法)更好的方法。***(soon) get/learn the ~ of it,*** learn the knack (which is the more usu word) of doing it, managing it, etc. (很快就)學會(做或處理某事等的)訣竅(較常用 knack)。**4** strange or characteristic habit, mannerism, etc: 特異的習慣、風格等;奇癖: *He has a ~ of pulling his left ear when he is thinking out a problem.* 當他思索某一問題時,他有拉左耳的習慣。**5** (cards played in) one round (of bridge, etc): (橋牌等的)一圈; 一磴; 一圈所打的牌; 一磴牌: *take/win a ~,* win one round. 得一磴牌。**6** (naut) period of duty at the helm (usu two hours): (航海)舵手的輪值時間(通常爲兩小時): *take one's ~ at the wheel.* 當值掌舵。□ *vt* **1** [VP6A, 14] ***~ sb (into/out of sth),*** deceive; swindle: 欺;騙: *You've been ~ed.* 你受騙了。*He ~ed the poor girl out of her money/~ed her into marrying him by pretending that he was rich.* 他騙去了那可憐女孩的錢(他假裝有錢而騙她與他結婚)。**2** [VP15B] ***~ sb/sth out/up,*** decorate, dress, ornament. 修飾;打扮;裝璜。**~·ery** /-ərɪ; -ərɪ/ *n* [U] deception; cheating. 欺騙;欺詐;詭計。**~·ster** /-stə(r); -stɚ/ *n* person who makes a practice of ~ing people; swindler. 有騙人習慣者;騙子。**~y** *adj* (-ier, -iest) **1** (of persons and their actions) deceptive: (指人及其行爲)奸詐的;狡猾的: *a ~y politician.* 狡猾的政客。**2** (of work, etc) requiring skill; full of hidden or unexpected difficulties: (指工作等)需要技巧的;多困難的;不易處理的: *a ~y problem/job.* 困難的問題(工作)。

trickle /ˈtrɪkl; ˈtrɪkḷ/ *vi, vt* [VP2A, C, 15A] (cause to) flow in drops or in a thin stream: (使)滴流;細流: *Blood ~d from the wound.* 血從傷口緩緩地流出。*The tears ~d down her cheeks.* 淚水從她的面頰上緩緩地滴下來。*He was trickling oil into the bearings of the machine.* 他正在把潤滑油徐徐地注入機器的軸承。*People began to ~ out of the bar as midnight approached.* 午夜時人們一個個慢慢地走出酒吧。□ *n* weak or thin flow: 滴流;細流: *The stream had shrunk to a mere ~.* 那條溪已乾涸到祇有細微的流水了。**'~ charger,** device for the slow continuous charging of an accumulator (from the mains). 涓流充電器(一種使蓄電池緩慢持續充電的裝置)。

tri·col·our (US = **-color**) /ˈtrɪkələ(r) *US:* ˈtraɪkʌlər; ˈtraɪˌkʌlɚ/ *n* flag of three colours in stripes of the same width, esp, **the T~,** the French national flag of blue, white and red stripes. 三色旗(三種顏色寬度均等者);(尤指 the T~)法國國旗。

tri·cycle /ˈtraɪsɪkl; ˈtraɪsɪkl/ *n* three-wheeled bicycle 三輪脚踏車。

tri·dent /ˈtraɪdnt; ˈtraɪdṇt/ *n* spear with three points (as carried by Neptune); this as a symbol of sea-power. 三叉戟(如海神 Neptune 所持者);海權的標幟。

tried /traɪd; traɪd/ *n* ⇨ try¹.

tri·en·nial /traɪˈenɪəl; traɪˈɛnɪəl/ *n, adj* (sth) lasting for, happening or done every, three years. 延續三年的; 每三年發生或完成的; 延續三年的事物;每三年有一次的事件;三年生植物;三週年紀念。

trier /ˈtraɪə(r); ˈtraɪɚ/ *n* ⇨ try¹.

trifle /ˈtraɪfl; ˈtraɪfḷ/ *n* **1** thing, event, etc of little value or importance: 無價值或不重要的東西、事件等;瑣事;小事;瑣物: *It's silly to quarrel over ~s.* 爲小事爭吵是愚蠢的。*The merest ~ upsets that man,* He easily gets out of temper, etc. 一點點小事就會使那人發脾氣。***not stick at ~s,*** not allow small things to interfere with one's plans; etc. 不讓小事阻擾自己的計畫等。**2** small amount of money: 少量的錢: *It cost me only a ~.* 我祇花了很少的錢。**3** ***a ~,*** (*adv*) somewhat, a little: 稍微;有點: *This dress is a ~ too short.* 這衣服稍嫌短了一點。*Isn't the meat a ~ tough?* 這肉不是稍稍硬了一點嗎? **4** [C, U] sweet dish made of cream, white of eggs, cake, jam, etc: 一種用奶油、蛋白、糕餅、果醬等製成的甜食;蛋糕;鬆糕: *make a ~;* 做蛋糕; *eat too much ~.* 吃太多的甜食。□ *vi, vt* **1** [VP 3A] **~ *with,*** play idly with, behave lightly or insincerely towards: 玩弄;戲弄;忽視: *He's not a man to be ~d with,* He must be given serious attention. 他不是一個可以輕慢的人。*It's wrong of you to ~ with the girl's affections,* make her think that you love her when you don't. 你玩弄那女孩的感情是不對的。*Don't ~ with your food: either eat it or leave it.* 不要玩你的食物:要麼就把它吃掉,要麼就把它剩下。**2** [VP15B] **~ *sth away,*** fritter away (which is more usu): 浪費;虛擲(較常用 fritter away): *~ away one's time/energies/money.* 浪費時間(精力,金錢)。**trif·ling** /ˈtraɪflɪŋ; ˈtraɪflɪŋ/ *adj* unimportant: 不重要的;微小的: *a trifling error;* 小錯誤; *of trifling value.* 價值小的。*It's no trifling matter,* is serious. 這不是無關重要的事(這事很要緊)。**tri·fler** /ˈtraɪflə(r); ˈtraɪflɚ/ *n* person who ~s. 玩弄者;戲弄者;浪費者。

trig·ger /ˈtrɪgə(r); ˈtrɪgɚ/ *n* lever for releasing a spring, esp of a firearm. (釋放彈簧的)扳柄;觸發器;(尤指槍上的)扳機。***be quick on the ~,*** quick to shoot. 射擊迅速的。***have one's finger on the ~,*** (fig) be in full control, esp of military operations. (喻)完全控制(尤指軍事行動)。**'~-happy** *adj* (sl) ready to use violence, eg by shooting, at slight provocation. (俚)動不動就動武的;動輒開槍的。□ *vt* [VP15B] **~ *sth off,*** be the immediate cause of (sth serious or violent): 爲(某嚴重或激烈事件)的直接原因;引發;引起: *Who/What ~ed off the rebellion?* 是誰(什麼原因)觸發了這次叛變?

trig·on·om·etry /ˌtrɪgəˈnɒmətrɪ; ˌtrɪgəˈnɑmətrɪ/ *n* [U] branch of mathematics that deals with the relations between the sides and angles of triangles. 三角學。

tri·lat·eral /ˌtraɪˈlætərəl; traɪˈlætərəl/ *adj* three-sided: 三邊的;三方面的: *a ~ agreement/treaty.* 三邊協定(條約)。

trilby /ˈtrɪlbɪ; ˈtrɪlbɪ/ *n* (*pl* -bies) ~ **(hat),** (man's) soft felt hat. (男子的)軟呢帽。

trill /trɪl; trɪl/ *n* [C] **1** quavering sound; shaky or vibrating sound made by the voice or as in bird song. 抖顫聲; (鳥叫般的) 顫聲。**2** (music) quick alternation of two notes a tone or a semitone apart. (音樂)顫音;震音。**3** speech sound (eg Spanish *rr*) uttered with a ~. 顫(動語)音(如西班牙語中的 rr 音)。□ *vi, vt* [VP6A, 2A, C] sing or play (a musical note) with a ~; pronounce with a ~: 以顫音唱或奏(一音符);以顫音發音: *The canary was ~ing away in its cage.* 那隻金絲雀在籠子裏(顫聲)鳴叫。*Can you ~ the sound 'rr' as in Spanish?* 你能發西班牙語 'rr' 那樣的顫音嗎?

tril·lion /ˈtrɪlɪən; ˈtrɪljən/ *n, adj* (GB) million million million; (US) million million. (英)百萬兆(卽百萬個百萬的百萬);(美)兆(卽百萬個百萬)。⇨ App 4. 參看附錄四。

tril·ogy /ˈtrɪlədʒɪ; ˈtrɪlədʒɪ/ *n* [C] (*pl* -gies) group of three plays, novels, operas, etc to be performed, read, etc in succession, each complete in itself but having a common subject. (戲劇、小說、歌劇等的)三部曲(各自獨立完整,而有共同的主題)。

trim /trɪm; trɪm/ *adj* (-mmer, -mmest) in good order; neat and tidy: 整齊的;整潔的: *a ~ ship/cabin;* 整潔的船(艙); *a ~ little garden.* 整潔的小花園。□ *n* [U] ~ state; readiness; fitness: 整齊;整潔;齊備;準備;適當: *Everything was in good/proper ~.* 一切都已準備就緒。*The crew is in/out of ~ for the boat-race.* 划船選手已經(還沒有)準備好划船比賽。*We must get into (good) ~ for the sports meeting.* 我們必須好好準備這次運動會。□ *vt, vi* (-mm-) **1** [VP6A, 15A, 22] make ~, esp by taking or cutting away uneven, irregular or unwanted parts: 使整齊;整飾(尤指藉除去或切除不整齊、不規則或不需要的部分): *~ one's beard/the wick of a lamp.* 修鬍子(剪燈心)。 **2** [VP6A, 14] **~ sth (with sth),** decorate or ornament (a hat, dress, etc): 裝飾(帽,衣等): *a hat ~med with fur;* 飾有毛皮的帽子; *~ a dress with lace.* 以花邊裝飾衣服。 **3** [VP6A] make (a boat, ship, aircraft) evenly balanced by arranging the position of the cargo, passengers, etc; set (sails) to suit the wind. 安排貨物、旅客等的位置使(船,輪船,飛機)平衡;調整(船帆)以適應風向。 **4** [VP2A] hold a middle course in politics; change one's views, policy, etc in an effort to win popular approval: 採取中間政治路線;改變見解、政策等以搏取大衆讚許;見風轉舵;騎牆: *a politician who is always ~ming.* 總是採取騎牆態度的政客。**~·mer** *n* person or thing that ~s. 整修者;整修的人或物;騎牆者;剪切器具。**~·ming** *n* [U, C] sth used for ~ming(2): 裝飾物: *lace ~ming(s).* 裝飾用的花邊。**~·ly** *adv*

tri·maran /ˈtraɪməræn; ˈtraɪməˌræn/ *n* boat with three parallel hulls. 三體船(三船身並列者)。⇨ catamaran.

tri·nitro·tolu·ene /ˌtraɪˌnaɪtrəʊˈtɒljʊiːn; traɪˌnaɪtroˈtɑljʊˌin/ *n* [U] (usu 通常作 **TNT** /ˌtiː en ˈtiː; ˌti ɛn ˈti/) powerful explosive. 黃色炸藥;三硝基甲苯(一種猛烈炸藥)。

trin·ity /ˈtrɪnətɪ; ˈtrɪnətɪ/ *n* group of three. 三個的一組或一群。**the T~,** (in Christian teaching) union of three persons, Father, Son and Holy Spirit, in one God. (基督教)三位一體(聖父,聖子,聖靈合爲一神之謂)。 **T~ House,** British institution which licenses pilots of ships, maintains lighthouses, marks wrecks, etc. (英國的)領港公會(主持領港員的考試,管理燈塔,標示船難等)。ˌ**T~ ˈSunday,** Sunday after Pentecost. 三一節(聖靈降臨節後第一個禮拜天)。

trin·ket /ˈtrɪŋkɪt; ˈtrɪŋkɪt/ *n* ornament or jewel of small value; small fancy article. 價值微小的飾物或珠寶;小裝飾品;瑣物。

trio /ˈtriːəʊ; ˈtrio/ *n* (*pl* ~s) group of three; (musical composition for) group of three singers or players. 三個之一組;(音樂)三人合唱團;三人合奏團;三重唱(奏)曲。

trip /trɪp; trɪp/ *vi, vt* (-pp-) **1** [VP2A, C] walk, run or dance with quick, light steps: 以輕快的腳步走、跑或跳舞: *She came ~ping down the garden path.* 她輕快地沿花園小徑跑過來。 **2** [VP2A, C, 3A, 15B] **~ (over) (sth),** catch one's foot, etc in an obstacle and stumble: 絆在某物上而跌跤;失足;顚躓: *He ~ped over the root of a tree.* 他被樹根絆倒。 **~ (sb) (up),** (cause to) stumble or make a false step: (使某人)絆倒或失足: *He ~ped up and nearly fell.* 他失足而幾乎跌倒。*The wrestler ~ped (up) his opponent.* 那摔角者把對手摔倒。*That lawyer is always trying to ~ the witness up,* (fig) trying to make him contradict himself, be inaccurate, etc. (喩)那律師總想使證人自相矛盾。 **3** [VP2A, C] **~ (out),** (sl) have a ~ (3 below). (俚)(因服用迷幻藥而)陷入幻覺;進入迷幻狀態。 **4** (archaic) (古) **~ a measure,** dance with quick light steps. 以輕快步子跳舞。□ *n* [C] **1** journey, esp a pleasure excursion: 旅行;(尤指)遠足: *a ~ to the seaside;* 去海濱遠足; *a weekend ~;* 週末旅行; *a holiday/honeymoon ~ to Venice.* 往威尼斯的假日(蜜月)旅行。 **2** fall or stumble; (fig) fault or error: 顚躓;絆倒;失足;(喩)錯誤;過失: *a ~ of the tongue* (*slip* is more usu). 失言(此語中較常用 slip)。 ˈ**~ wire** *n* wire stretched along the ground, working a trap when an animal, etc trips against it. 陷穽的絆索(動物觸及進入陷穽)。 **3** (sl) experience, esp one resulting from taking a hallucinatory drug. (俚)(服迷幻藥後產生的)迷幻感覺;幻覺經驗。 **~·per** *n* person making a (usu short) excursion for pleasure: (通常爲短程的)旅行者;遠足者: *weekend ~pers.* 週末的旅行者。 **~·ping** *adj* light and quick. 輕快的。**~·ping·ly** *adv*

tri·par·tite /ˌtraɪˈpɑːtaɪt; traɪˈpɑrtaɪt/ *adj* **1** in which three parties have a share: 三者間的;三方面締結的: *a ~ agreement;* 三方面締結的合約; *~ talks,* discussion(s) between three (groups of) people. 三者(三個團體)間的協談。 **2** having three parts. 有三部分的。

tripe /traɪp; traɪp/ *n* [U] **1** part of the wall of the stomach of an ox or cow used as food: (供食用的)牛肚: *a dish of stewed ~ and onions.* 一道洋蔥燉牛肚。 **2** (sl) worthless talk, writing, ideas etc: (俚)無價值的談話、寫作、主意等: *Stop talking ~!* 別胡扯了!

triple /ˈtrɪpl; ˈtrɪpl̩/ *adj* made up of three (parts or parties): 三部分合成的;三重的;三方面的: *the T~ Alliance,* one of several military alliances (in European history) between three countries; 三國聯盟 (指歐洲史的數次軍事聯盟之任一); *~ time,* (music) of 3 beats to the bar; (音樂)三拍子; *the ~ crown,* the Pope's tiara. (羅馬敎宗的)三重皇冠。□ *vt, vi* [VP6A, 2A] make, become, be, three times as much or many: (使)成爲三倍: *He ~d his income.* 他使他的收入增至三倍。*His income ~d.* 他的收入增至三倍。

trip·let /ˈtrɪplɪt; ˈtrɪplɪt/ *n* **1** (*pl*) three children born at one birth: (複)三胞胎;同胎所生的三個孩子: *One of the ~s is ill.* 三胞胎中有一個病了。 **2** set of three. 三個所組成的一組

trip·lex /ˈtrɪpleks; ˈtrɪplɛks/ *adj* triple; threefold. 三倍的;三重的。 **~ (glass),** (P) strong glass (as used in motor-cars, etc) made of a sheet of plastic material between two sheets of glass. (商標) 三夾安全玻璃 (汽車等上所用者,係兩層玻璃中間夾一層塑膠而成)。

trip·li·cate /ˈtrɪplɪkət; ˈtrɪpləkɪt/ *adj* of which three copies are made. 一式三份的。□ *n* **in ~,** consisting of three like things, esp documents: (尤指文件)一式三份的(地): *drawn up in ~,* consisting of one original and two copies. 寫成一式三份(原本一份及副本兩份)的。□ *vt* /ˈtrɪplɪkeɪt; ˈtrɪpləˌket/ [VP6A] make in ~. 將…作成一式三份。

tri·pod /ˈtraɪpɒd; ˈtraɪpɑd/ *n* three-legged support, eg for a camera; stool, table, etc, resting on three legs. (攝影機等使用的)三腳架;三腳凳;三腳桌等。

tri·pos /ˈtraɪpɒs; ˈtraɪpɑs/ *n* examination for an honours degree at Cambridge University: (劍橋大學的)榮譽學位考試: *the History/Classics, etc ~.* 歷史學(古典文學等)榮譽學位考試。

trip·per /ˈtrɪpə(r); ˈtrɪpɚ/ *n* ⇨ trip.

trip·tych /ˈtrɪptɪk; ˈtrɪptɪk/ *n* picture or carving on three (usu hinged) panels fixed side by side, eg of religious subjects in a Christian church. 三幅相聯的圖畫或雕刻(通常用鉸鏈結合,如教堂中的宗教畫)。

tri·reme /ˈtraɪriːm; ˈtraɪrim/ *n* ancient (esp Greek) warship with three tiers of oars on each side. 古代(尤指希臘)有三層槳座的戰船。

tri·sect /traɪˈsekt ; traɪˈsɛkt/ *vt* [VP6A] divide (a line, an angle, etc) into three (esp equal) parts. 分(線,角等)成三部分;(尤指)三等分。

trite /traɪt ; traɪt/ *adj* (of remarks, ideas, opinions) commonplace; not new. (指評語,觀念,意見)平凡的;陳腐的。**~·ly** *adv* **~·ness** *n*

tri·umph /ˈtraɪʌmf ; ˈtraɪəmf/ *n* **1** [C, U] (joy or satisfaction at a) success or victory: 成功;勝利;成功或勝利的喜悅;狂喜;得意揚揚: *return home in ~;* 凱旋歸來; *shouts of ~,* 一陣陣勝利的歡呼聲; *score a resounding ~ over one's enemies;* 擊敗敵人而獲得一次轟動的勝利; *recount all one's ~s.* 細述所有得意事件。 **2** [C] (in ancient Rome) procession and ceremony in honour of a victorious general. (古羅馬向打勝仗之將軍祝賀的)凱旋式。 □ *vi* [VP2A, 3A] *~ (over),* win a victory (over); show joy because of success: 獲勝;成功;擊敗;因成功而欣喜;得意: *~ over opposition/adversity,* overcome it; 克服阻碍(艱苦); *~ over a defeated enemy.* 擊敗敵人而奏凱。 **tri·um·phal** /traɪˈʌmfl ; traɪˈʌmfl̩/ *adj* of, for, a ~; expressing ~: 成功的;勝利的;凱旋的;慶祝勝利的;表現欣喜的: *erect a ~al arch,* one built to commemorate a victory. 建築一座凱旋門。 **tri·um·phant** /traɪˈʌmfnt ; traɪˈʌmfənt/ *adj* (rejoicing at) having ~ed. 成功的;獲勝的;得意揚揚的。 **tri·um·phant·ly** *adv*

tri·um·vir /traɪˈʌmvə(r) ; traɪˈʌmvɚ/ *n* (in ancient Rome) each of three men holding an office jointly. (古羅馬的)三執政之一。**tri·um·vir·ate** /traɪˈʌmvɪrət ; traɪˈʌmvərɪt/ *n* set of ~s. 三頭政治;三人政治;三人小組。

tri·une /ˈtraɪjuːn ; ˈtraɪjun/ *adj* three in one: 三位一體的;三合一的: *the ~ Godhead,* the Trinity. 三位一體的神。

trivet /ˈtrɪvɪt ; ˈtrɪvɪt/ *n* (usu three-legged or three-footed) stand or support for a pot or kettle on or by a fire; iron bracket to be hooked on to the bars of a fire-grate. (擱在火上支承烹煮器皿的)臺架;三脚架;掛於爐格的托架。 ***as right as a ~,*** in good condition or health; in satisfactory circumstances. 情況或健康良好;在令人滿意的環境。

trivia /ˈtrɪvɪə ; ˈtrɪvɪə/ *n pl* trivial, unimportant things. 瑣事;不重要的事。

triv·ial /ˈtrɪvɪəl ; ˈtrɪvɪəl/ *adj* **1** of small value or importance: 無價值的;不重要的;瑣屑的: *a ~ offence;* 小過失; *a ~ loss;* 輕微損失; *raise ~ objections against a proposal.* 對某建議提出無足輕重的反對。 **2** commonplace; humdrum: 平凡的;無聊的;沒有趣味的: *the ~ round,* the ordinary course of everyday events, duties, etc. 平凡的日常事務。 **3** (of a person) trifling; lacking seriousness; superficial: (指人)輕浮的;不嚴肅的;淺薄的: *Don't marry that ~ young man.* 切勿與那輕浮的年輕人結婚。**~ly** /-ɪəlɪ ; -ɪəlɪ/ *adv* **~·ity** /ˌtrɪvɪˈælətɪ ; ˌtrɪvɪˈælətɪ/ *n* [U] state of being ~; [C] (*pl* -ties) ~ idea, event, etc: 瑣屑;平凡;輕浮;平凡的觀念、事件等: *talk/write ~ities.* 談論(論述)瑣屑之事。**~·ize** /-aɪz ; -aɪz/ *vt* [VP6A] make ~. 使無足輕重;使平凡。

tro·chee /ˈtrəʊkiː ; ˈtroki/ *n* (prosody) metrical foot of one stressed and one unstressed syllable (—◡),(詩體)揚抑格(由一重音節及一輕音節構成的音步), as in: 如: ˈ*Life is/*ˈ*but an/*ˈ*empty/*ˈ*dream.* 人生不過一場幻夢。**tro·chaic** /trəʊˈkeɪɪk ; troˈke·ɪk/ *adj*

trod, trod·den /trɒd, ˈtrɒdn ; trɑd, ˈtrɑdn̩/ *pt, pp* of tread.

trog·lo·dyte /ˈtrɒglədaɪt ; ˈtrɑgləˌdaɪt/ *n* cave-dweller in ancient times. 古代的穴居者。

troika /ˈtrɔɪkə ; ˈtrɔɪkə/ *n* [C] **1** small Russian carriage drawn by a team of three horses abreast. 俄式三馬並曳的小馬車。 **2** group of three persons (esp political leaders). 三人集團;(尤指)三頭政治。

Tro·jan /ˈtrəʊdʒən ; ˈtrodʒən/ *n, adj* (inhabitant) of ancient Troy: 古代特洛伊城的;特洛伊人: *the ~ war,* between the Greeks and the Trojans, as described by Homer. 特洛伊戰爭(古希臘人與特洛伊人之間的戰爭,荷馬曾作詩敘述其事)。 ***work like a ~,*** work very hard. 勤奮地工作。 ***~ horse,*** (fig) sb or sth, introduced from outside, that causes the downfall of an enemy from within. (喻)滲入敵人內部而使其毀滅的人或物。

troll[1] /trəʊl ; trol/ *n* (in Scandinavian myth) supernatural being, a giant, or, in later tales, a mischievous but friendly dwarf. (北歐神話)巨神;(後期神話中的)頑皮而友善的小精靈或侏儒。

troll[2] /trəʊl ; trol/ *vt, vi* [VP2A, C] fish with rod and line by pulling bait through the water behind a boat: 在船後拉餌釣魚;拖釣: *~ for pike.* 拖釣梭子魚。

trol·ley /ˈtrɒlɪ ; ˈtrɑlɪ/ *n* (*pl* ~s) **1** two- or four-wheeled handcart. (二輪或四輪的)手推車。**2** small, low truck running on rails, eg one worked by a handlever, used by workers on a railway. 鐵軌上行駛的查道車;台車;壓車。 **3** (often 常作 **ˈtea-~**) small table on castors (small wheels) used for serving food. (裝有小脚輪,送食物用的) 活動食枱;活動茶枱。 **4** small contact-wheel between a tram and an overhead cable. (電車與架空電線接觸的)觸輪。 **5** **ˈ~-(bus),** (US) (美) **ˈ~-(-car),** = tram.

trol·lop /ˈtrɒləp ; ˈtrɑləp/ *n* (colloq) slut; prostitute. (俗)邋遢女人;妓女。

trom·bone /trɒmˈbəʊn ; ˈtrɑmbon/ *n* large brass musical instrument with a sliding tube. 伸縮喇叭;長喇叭。 ⇨ the illus at brass. 參看 brass 之插圖。 **trom·bon·ist** /trɒmˈbəʊnɪst ; ˈtrɑmbonɪst/ *n* ~ player. 吹奏伸縮喇叭者。

troop /truːp ; trup/ *n* [C] **1** company of persons or animals, esp when moving: 人或動物的羣(尤指移動中者): *a ~ of schoolchildren;* 一羣學童; *a ~ of antelope(s).* 一羣羚羊。 **2** (*pl*) soldiers: (複)軍隊;部隊: *find billets for the ~s.* 爲部隊找尋住宿地。 ⇨ trooper below. 參看下列之 trooper。 **ˈ~-carrier** *n* ship or large aircraft for transporting ~s. 運兵船;運兵機。 **ˈ~·ship** *n* ship for transporting ~s. 運兵船。 **3** unit of cavalry, armoured vehicles or artillery (under the command of a lieutenant). 騎兵隊或連;裝甲騎兵隊或連(指揮官爲中尉)。 **4** company of boy scouts. 童子軍隊。□ *vi, vt* **1** [VP2C] (with *pl* subject) come or go together in a group: (用複數主詞)結隊;羣集;成羣而行: *children ~ing out of school.* 結隊離開學校的學童。 **2** ***~ the colour,*** (GB, mil) carry the colour (flag) through the ranks of a regiment. (英,軍) 行軍旗敬禮分列式 (持軍旗穿過部隊行列)。 ***~ing the colour,*** such a ceremony (esp as on the Sovereign's birthday). 軍旗敬禮分列式(尤指君主生日所舉行者)。 **~er** *n* **1** soldier in a cavalry or armoured regiment. 騎兵;裝甲兵。 **2** (US) member of state police force (now using a motor-vehicle). (美)州警察(從前騎馬,現在駕摩托車或警車)。 ***swear like a ~er,*** swear fluently. 不住地咒詛。

trope /trəʊp ; trop/ *n* figurative use of a word (as of *tread* in 'The years like great black oxen tread the world'). 借喩;比喩;轉義(如 'The years like great black oxen tread the world' 一句中的 tread 卽爲借喩)。

trophy /ˈtrəʊfɪ ; ˈtrofɪ/ *n* [C] (*pl* -phies) **1** sth kept in memory of a victory or success (eg in hunting, sport, etc). 戰利品;勝利紀念品(如狩獵,運動等)。 **2** prize, eg for winning a tournament: 獎品(如贏得比賽者): ˈ*tennis trophies.* 網球賽的獎品。

tropic /ˈtrɒpɪk ; ˈtrɑpɪk/ *n* **1** line of latitude 23°27′ north (*T~ of Cancer*) or south (*T~ of Capricorn*) of the equator. 回歸線(北回歸線稱 T~ of Cancer, 南回歸線稱 T~ of Capricorn)。 **2** ***the ~s,*** the parts of the world between these two latitudes. 熱帶;熱帶地方。 **tropi·cal** /-kl ; -kl̩/ *adj* of, or as of, the ~s: (似)熱帶的;(似)熱帶地方的: *a ~al climate;* 熱帶氣候; *~al fruits.* 熱帶水果。 **tropi·cally** /-klɪ ; -klɪ/ *adv*

trot /trɒt ; trɑt/ *vi, vt* (-tt-) **1** [VP2A, B, C] (of horses, etc) go at a pace faster than a walk but not so fast as a gallop. (指馬等)疾走;快步走。 **2** [VP2A, C] run with short steps; (colloq, hum) go (at an ordinary speed): 小跑;(俗,諧)(以普通速度)走: *Well, I must be ~ting off home.* 唔,我必須回家了。*You ~ along!* Go away! 走開! **3** [VP 15B] **~ sth out,** (colloq) produce; bring out: (俗)提出;舉以示人: *~ out one's knowledge,* eg to get admiration. 誇示學識。 **4** [VP15A, B] cause to ~: 使疾走;使快步走;使小跑: *~ a person off his legs,* take him round, eg sight-seeing, until he is exhausted; 領人走得筋疲力盡; *~ sb round,* take him round with one (eg shopping). 帶着某人走動(如購物)。□ *n* (*sing* only) (僅用單數) **1** ~ting pace: 疾走;快步;小跑: *go at a steady ~.* 一路以快步行進。**on the ~,** (sl) one after the other: (俚)一個接一個: *five whiskies on the ~.* 一連五杯威士忌。**be on the ~; keep sb on the ~,** **(a)** (colloq) busy on one's feet, moving from one task to another: (俗)奔波;奔走;忙碌;席不暇暖: *I've been (kept) on the ~ all morning and I'm exhausted.* 我忙了一個上午,現在疲憊不堪。 **(b)** (sl) be running away (esp from prison or the police). (俚)逃脫(尤指從監獄或警方)。**be on the ~,** (US 美 = **have the ~s**), (colloq) have diarrhoea. (俗)瀉肚子。**2** period of ~ting: 疾走、快步或小跑的一段時間: *go for a ~.* 去小跑一陣。**~·ter** *n* **1** horse bred and trained to ~. 快步馬;受過疾行訓練的馬。 **2** (usu *pl*) pig's or sheep's foot as food. (通常用複數)(作食物用的)豬蹄或羊蹄。

troth /trəʊθ *US:* trɔːθ ; trɔθ/ *n* [U] (archaic) (古) **plight one's ~,** pledge one's word; (esp) promise to marry. 盟誓(尤指答應結婚)。

trou·ba·dour /ˈtruːbədɔː(r) ; ˈtrubəˌdʊr/ *n* travelling poet and singer in France and Italy, 11th to 13th cc. (十一至十三世紀在法國及義大利的)吟遊詩人;遊唱詩人。

trouble /ˈtrʌbl ; ˈtrʌbḷ/ *vt, vi* **1** [VP6A] cause worry, discomfort, anxiety or inconvenience to: 使憂慮,不適,苦惱或不方便: *be ~d by bad news;* 爲壞消息煩惱; *~d with a nasty cough.* 爲頑咳所苦。*What ~s me is that...* 使我苦惱的是…。 **2** [VP17, 14] **~ sb to do sth; ~ sb for sth,** put sb to the inconvenience of doing sth. 麻煩某人做某事。**(a)** (with *may/might,* a polite request): (與 may, might 連用,表示客氣的請求): *May I ~ you to pass the salt, please.* 麻煩您把鹽遞給我好嗎? *May I ~ you for a match?* 請給我一支火柴好嗎? **(b)** (with *I'll, I must,* a sarcastic or ironic request): (與 I'll, I must 連用,表示諷刺性質的請求): *I'll ~ you to be quiet.* 拜託拜託,安靜一點。*I must ~ you to remember your manners.* 我必須請你規矩一點。 **3** [VP2A, C, 4A] (esp in neg and interr) bother or inconvenience oneself: (尤用於否定句及問句中)麻煩自己;費神;費心: *Don't ~ to meet me at the station.* 不必勞駕來車站接我了。*Don't ~ about that.* 不必爲那事煩心。*Oh, don't ~, thanks.* 啊,不要麻煩了,謝謝。*Why should I ~ to explain?* 我爲什麼要費事解釋呢? **4** [VP6A] agitate; disturb: 激動;擾亂: (esp *pp*) (尤用過去分詞) *a ~d expression;* 憂慮的表情; *~d looks.* 苦惱的表情。**fish in ~d waters,** try to gain an advantage from a confused state of affairs. 混水摸魚。□ *n* **1** [C, U] worry; anxiety; discomfort; unhappiness; difficulty; possible punishment: 憂慮;苦惱;不適;不幸;困難;可能的處罰: *Her heart was full of ~.* 她內心充滿了煩惱。*She's always making ~ for her friends.* 她總是給她的朋友們帶來麻煩。*He has been through much ~/has had many ~s.* 他已度過許多困難(已遭遇到許多困難)。*He has a lot of family/domestic ~(s).* 他有許多家務上的麻煩。*His ~s are over now* (sometimes said of a person who dies). 他的煩惱算過去了(有時用以指死去的人)。*The ~ is that...,* The difficulty is that.... 困難的是…。*What's the ~ now?* What unfortunate thing has happened? (現在)發生了什麼不幸事件? **in ~,** suffering, or likely to suffer, misfortune, anxiety, etc, eg because one has done wrong. 處於不幸,煩惱等苦境中(如因做錯某事)。 **ˈask/ˈlook for ~,** (colloq) behave in such a way that ~ is likely: (俗)自尋煩惱;自找苦吃;自找麻煩: *It's asking for ~ to experiment with drugs.* 隨便試用藥品乃是自找麻煩。**get into ~,** do sth that will bring unhappiness, punishment, etc. 陷入困境;因做某事而將招致不幸,處罰等。**get sb into ~,** **(a)** cause sb to be in ~. 使某人陷入困境。 **(b)** (sl) make (an unmarried woman) pregnant. (俚)使(未婚女子)懷孕。 **2** [C] (*sing* only) sb or sth that causes ~(1): (僅作單數)引起憂慮、苦惱、不適、不幸、困難等的人或事物: *I don't want to be any ~* (= nuisance) *to you.* 我不想惹你討厭。*Some dishes are very enjoyable to eat but a great ~ to prepare.* 有些菜很好吃,但是做起來却很麻煩。*I find it a great ~ to get up at 6 am.* 我覺得早上六點鐘起床是一件苦事。 **3** [U] care; attention; (extra) work; inconvenience: 小心;注意;(額外的)工作;煩勞;不方便: *Did the work give you much ~?* 那工作給你添了許多麻煩嗎? *I don't like putting you to* (= causing you) *so much ~.* 我不願意爲你添那麼多麻煩。*Thank you for all the ~ you've taken to help my son.* 多謝你盡心幫助我兒子。*It will be no ~,* will not inconvenience me. 那不費事(不會給我添麻煩)。 **4** [C, U] political or social unrest: (政治或社會的)不安;紛爭;擾亂: *ˈLabour ~(s)* (eg strikes) *cost the country enormous sums last year.* 勞工糾紛(如罷工)去年使國家耗損了鉅額金錢。*They've been having a lot of ~(s) in Southern Africa recently.* 非洲南部最近一直擾攘不安。 **5** [C, U] illness: 疾病: *ˈliver ~;* 肝病; *ˈmental ~;* 精神病; *ˈchildren's ~s.* 兒童的疾病。 **6** (compounds) (複合字) **ˈ~-maker,** person who stirs up discontent (eg in industry). 是非人物;挑撥是非者;鼓動不滿情緒者(例如在工業上)。**ˈ~-shooter,** person employed in conciliating and arbitrating between parties in conflict (eg in industry), or in detecting and correcting faults (esp in machinery). 調解人;調停人(如工業上的);(機器的)修理人或矯正人。**~·some** /-səm ; -səm/ *adj* causing ~: 使人苦惱或煩勞的;困難的;麻煩的: *a ~some child/headache/problem.* 使人苦惱的孩子(頭痛,問題)。*Her cough is very ~some today.* 她今天咳嗽得很厲害。 **ˈ~ spot,** place where ~(4) often occurs. 常發生紛爭的地方;是非之地。**troub·lous** /-əs ; -əs/ *adj* (liter) disturbed; unsettled: (文)動亂不安的;紛擾的: *live in troublous times.* 生於動亂時代。

trough /trɒf *US:* trɔːf ; trɔf/ *n* **1** long, open (usu shallow) box for animals to feed or drink from. (餵動物用的)食槽;水槽。 **2** long open box in which a baker kneads dough for bread. (麵包師用的)揉麵槽;和麵槽。 **3** (in the sea, etc) long hollow between two waves. (海洋等之)波谷;兩海浪間的凹處。 **4** (met) region of lower atmospheric pressure between two regions of higher pressure. (氣象)槽(兩個高氣壓地區中間的低壓帶)。

trounce /traʊns ; traʊns/ *vt* [VP6A] beat; thrash; defeat; reprimand: 打;痛打;鞭笞;擊敗;痛懲;嚴責: *Our team was ~d on Saturday.* 我隊在禮拜六慘遭擊敗。**trounc·ing** *n* beating; reprimand: 痛打;嚴責: *give sb a good trouncing.* 痛打(責)某人。

troupe /truːp ; trup/ *n* company, esp of actors or of members of a circus. 班;隊;團(尤指伶人或馬戲團員所組成者)。**~r** *n* member of a theatrical ~: (戲團、馬戲團等的)團員;演員: *He's a good ~r,* a loyal, hard-working and uncomplaining colleague. 他是個忠心耿耿、任勞任怨的好同事。

trouser /ˈtraʊzə(r) ; ˈtraʊzə/ *n* **1** **(pair of) ~s,** two-legged outer garment, reaching from the waist to the ankles. 褲子。⇨ shorts, slack². **2** (attrib) of or for ~s: (形容用法)褲子的;爲褲子之用的;用在褲子上的: *ˈ~ buttons/pockets.* 褲釦(袋)。

trous·seau /ˈtruːsəʊ ; truˈso/ *n* (*pl* ~s or ~x /-səʊz ; -soz/) outfit of clothing, etc, for a bride. 嫁妝;

妝奩。

trout /traʊt ; traʊt/ *n* (*pl* unchanged) freshwater fish valued as food and for the sport of catching it (with rod and line). (複數不變)鱒魚。

trove /trəʊv ; trov/ *n* ⇨ treasure(1).

trowel /ˈtraʊəl ; ˈtraʊəl/ *n* **1** flat-bladed tool for spreading mortar on bricks or stone, plaster on walls, etc. (用以塗抹灰泥於磚石或牆上的)鏝刀;抹子;抹刀。 **2** hand-tool with a curved blade for lifting plants, etc. (移植樹木等用的)小鏟子。⇨ the illus at tool. 參看 tool 之插圖。

troy /trɔɪ ; trɔɪ/ *n* [U] British system of weights, used for gold and silver, in which one pound = 12 ounces: (英國的)金衡; 金衡制 (每金衡磅等於十二唡): *This spoon weighs 4 oz ~.* 此匙重四金衡唡。⇨ App 5. 參看附錄五。

tru·ant /ˈtru:ənt ; ˈtruənt/ *n* **1** child who stays away from school without good reason. 逃學的學童。 ***play ~,*** stay away thus. 逃課;逃學;曠課。 **2** (attrib) (of persons, their conduct, thoughts, etc) wandering; idle; shirking (duty, etc). (形容用法)(指人,其行爲、思想等)遊蕩的;怠惰的;規避(責任等)的。 **tru·ancy** /-ənsɪ ; -ənsɪ/ *n* (*pl* -cies) [U] playing ~; [C] instance of this. 逃學;曠課;其實例。

truce /tru:s ; trus/ *n* [C] (agreement for the) stopping of fighting for a time (eg to take away the wounded). 休戰;停戰(如俾運走傷兵等);休戰協定。

truck[1] /trʌk ; trʌk/ *n* **1** (GB) open railway wagon for heavy goods. (英)(鐵路上運笨重貨物的)敞篷貨車。 **2** (US) lorry. (美)貨車;卡車。 **3** porter's two-wheeled barrow (for moving heavy objects). (搬運伕的)兩輪手車(用以搬運重物者)。

truck[2] /trʌk ; trʌk/ *n* [U] **1** barter; exchange. 買賣;交易。 ***have no ~ with,*** have no dealings with. 不與…來往;不與…打交道。 **2** ˈ**garden-~,** (US) fresh garden produce (vegetables, fruit) grown for the markets. (美)新鮮蔬菜水果(爲出售而種植者)。 **3** **~ (system),** (hist) payment of wages in goods instead of money. (史)以實物償付工資(的制度)。

truckle[1] /ˈtrʌkl ; ˈtrʌkḷ/ *vi* [VP3A] ***~ to,*** submit in a timid or cowardly way: 屈從;膽小或懦弱地順從: *This country will never ~ to bullies.* 這個國家絕不會向恃强凌弱者低頭。

truckle[2] /ˈtrʌkl ; ˈtrʌkḷ/ *n* ˈ**~-bed,** low, wheeled bed that can be pushed under another when not in use. 有脚輪的矮床(不用時可推入另一床下)。

trucu·lent /ˈtrʌkjʊlənt ; ˈtrʌkjələnt/ *adj* looking for, desiring, a fight; aggressive. 尋釁的;找碴兒的;愛打架的;好攻擊的。**~·ly** *adv* **trucu·lence** /-ləns ; -ləns/, **trucu·lency** /-lənsɪ ; -lənsɪ/ *nn*

trudge /trʌdʒ ; trʌdʒ/ *vi* [VP2A, B, C] walk wearily or heavily: 疲累或沉重地走; 跋涉: *trudging through the deep snow.* 在深雪中跋涉。*He ~d 20 miles.* 他艱苦地走了二十哩。□ *n* long tiring walk. 跋涉;長途疲累的步行。

true /tru: ; tru/ *adj* (-r, -st) **1** in accordance or agreement with fact: 合於事實的;確實的: *Is it ~ that you are going to Rome?* 你眞的要去羅馬嗎? *Is the news ~?* 這消息確實嗎? ***come ~,*** (of a hope, dream) really happen, become fact. (指希望,夢想)實現;達到。 **2** ***~ (to),*** loyal, faithful: 忠誠的;忠實的: *be ~ to one's word/promise,* do what one has promised to do. 重然諾;守信。 ˌ**~-**ˈ**blue** *n, adj* (person who is) of uncompromising principles, firmly loyal. 堅持原則的(人);忠於主義的(人);堅貞的(人);忠心耿耿的(人)。 ˌ**~-**ˈ**hearted** *adj* loyal. 忠實的;誠實的。 ˈ**~-love** *n* one who loves truly/is truly loved. 愛人(眞正愛人或被人所愛者)。 **3** in accordance with reason or received standards; genuine; rightly so named: 合於道理或一般標準的;眞正的;名副其實的: *T~ friendship should last for ever.* 眞實的友誼(應)永恆不渝。*The frog is not a ~ reptile.* 青蛙不是眞正的爬蟲。*Who was the ~ heir to the throne?* 誰是眞正的王位繼承人? **4** ***~ to type,*** accurately conforming to its type or class: 與原型或原種完全相同的: *Plants grown from seed are not always ~ to type.* 從種子長出來的植物並不總是與原型相同。 **5** accurately fitted or placed: 安裝得確實的;裝置得妥當的: *Is the wheel/post ~?* 那輪子(柱子)裝妥了嗎? **6** exact; accurate: 精確的;切實的;正確的: *a ~ copy of a document;* 一項文件的正確抄本; *a ~ pair of scales.* 精確的天平。□ *n* (only in) (僅用於) ***out of ~,*** not in its exact or accurate position: 不在其正確或確實的位置;脫離定位: *The axle/beam/door is out of ~.* 軸(樑,門)的位置不正了。□ *adv* (with certain *vv*) truly: (與某些動詞連用)眞實地;正確地: *aim ~;* 正確地瞄準; *breed ~(4);* 育出純種; *tell me ~.* 老實告訴我。□ *vt* [VP15B] ***~ sth up,*** make, adjust so as to be ~(5): 使安裝、調整得確實;配準;校正: *~ up a wheel.* 把車輪安裝妥當。

truffle /ˈtrʌfl ; ˈtrʌfḷ/ *n* kind of fungus that grows underground, used for flavouring savoury food dishes, pâté, etc. 松露;麥蕈;塊菌(一種地下菌,用於調製美味餚饌及小麵餅等)。

tru·ism /ˈtru:ɪzəm ; ˈtruɪzəm/ *n* [C] statement that is obviously true and need not have been made: 顯然眞實而沒有必要說出的話; 自明之理; 不提自明的事實: *It's a ~ to say that your body was once much smaller than it is now.* 說你的身體過去曾比現在小得多,乃是不提自明的事實。

truly /ˈtru:lɪ ; ˈtrulɪ/ *adv* **1** truthfully: 眞實地;誠實地: *speak ~.* 說實話。 **2** sincerely: 誠懇地;篤實地: *feel ~ grateful.* 眞誠地感激。*Yours ~* (used at the close of a letter, before the signature). (用於信札末尾簽名前的套語)。 **3** genuinely; certainly: 眞正地;確定地: *a ~ beautiful picture;* 一幅眞正美麗的圖畫; *a ~ brave action.* 眞正勇敢的行爲。

trump[1] /trʌmp ; trʌmp/ *n* [C] **1** (in card games such as whist, bridge) each card of a suit that has been declared as having higher value than the other three suits: (牌戲,如惠斯特,橋牌)王牌;將牌: *Hearts are ~s.* 紅心是王牌。⇨ declare(1). ***play one's ~ card,*** (fig) make use of one's most valuable resource, means of gaining one's ends (esp after trying other means). (喻)使用最後手段;使出殺手鐧;拿出王牌;使出最厲害的一招。 ***turn up ~s,*** (colloq) (俗) **(a)** have a better result than was expected. 結果較預期爲佳。 **(b)** have a stroke of good luck. 走好運。 **2** (colloq) excellent fellow; person who is full of resource, is generous, etc. (俗)才俊;傑出之士;好人;有智謀,性情慷慨等的人。□ *vt, vi* **1** [VP6A, 2A] play a ~ card (on): 出王牌;以王牌取勝: *~ the ace of clubs.* 出王牌吃掉梅花么點牌。 **2** [VP15B] (usu passive) (通常用被動語態) ***~ sth up,*** invent (an excuse, a false story, etc) in order to deceive sb: 捏造(藉口,虛假故事等): *He was arrested on a ~ed-up charge.* 他以誣告罪被捕。

trump[2] /trʌmp ; trʌmp/ *n* (liter) (sound made by a) trumpet. (文)喇叭;喇叭聲。***the last ~; the ~ of doom,*** the trumpet call which will, some people believe, be sounded on the Last Day, the day when everyone will be judged by God. 世界末日的號聲。

trump·ery /ˈtrʌmpərɪ ; ˈtrʌmpərɪ/ *adj* showy but of little value: 華麗而無甚價值的;俗麗的: *~ ornaments.* 俗麗的飾物。

trum·pet /ˈtrʌmpɪt ; ˈtrʌmpɪt/ *n* **1** musical wind instrument of brass. 喇叭;號。⇨ the illus at brass. 參看 brass 之插圖。 ***blow one's own ~,*** (fig) praise oneself. (喻)自吹自擂。 **2** sound (as) of a ~. 喇叭聲;似喇叭聲。 **3** sth suggesting a ~ in shape or use (eg the corona of a daffodil). 形狀或功用似喇叭之物(如水仙花的花冠)。□ *vt, vi* **1** [VP 6A, 15B] proclaim, make known; celebrate: 宣佈;鼓吹;慶祝: *~ (forth) sb's heroic deeds.* 宣揚某人的英勇事蹟。 **2** [VP2A, C] (esp of an elephant) make loud sounds. (尤指象)高聲鳴叫。**~er** *n* person who plays a ~. 喇叭手;號手。

trun·cate /trʌŋ'keɪt *US:* 'trʌŋkeɪt ; 'trʌŋket/ *vt* [VP6A] shorten by cutting the tip, top or end from: 切掉…的頭或末端;截短;修短: *a ~d cone/pyramid.* 截錐(截角錐)。

trun·cheon /'trʌntʃən ; 'trʌntʃən/ *n* short thick club (esp one used by the police). 粗短之棍;(尤指)警棍。

trundle /'trʌndl ; 'trʌndl̩/ *vt, vi* [VP6A, 15A, B, 2C] (esp of sth heavy or awkward in shape) move or roll: (尤指外形笨重之物) 移動;推動;滾動: *The porter ~d his barrow along the platform.* 脚伕在月台上推動手推車。*The child was trundling a hoop along the sidewalk.* 那孩子沿人行道在滾動鐵環。'**~ bed,** (US) (美) = truckle bed. (可推至其他床下面的) 有脚輪矮床。

trunk /trʌŋk ; trʌŋk/ *n* [C] **1** main stem of a tree (contrasted with the branches). 樹幹(與樹枝相對)。⇨ the illus at tree. 參看 tree 之插圖。**2** body without head, arms or legs; main part of any structure. 軀幹(頭、臂、腿除外的部分);任何結構的主體部分。**3** large box with a hinged lid, for clothes, etc while travelling. (旅行用的) 大衣箱。**4** long nose of an elephant. 象鼻。⇨ the illus at large. 參看 large 之插圖。**5** (*pl*) (複) = shorts. **6** (US) (美) = boot(2) of a car. 汽車尾部的貯物箱;車尾箱。**7** (attrib) (形容用法) '**~-call** *n* telephone call to a distant place, with charges according to distance. (按距離計費的) 長途電話;幹線通話;長途呼叫。'**~-line** *n* **(a)** main line of a railway. 鐵路的幹線。**(b)** long-distance telephone line. 長途電話線。'**~-road** *n* main road. 幹道;幹線道路。

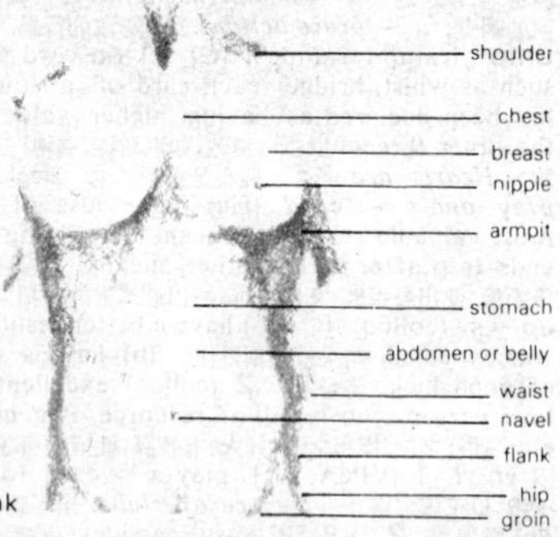

the trunk

truss /trʌs ; trʌs/ *n* [C] **1** (GB) bundle (of hay, straw). (英) (乾草,稻草的)捆;束。 **2** framework supporting a roof, bridge, etc. (支持屋頂,橋等的) 構架;桁架。 **3** padded belt worn by a person suffering from hernia. 疝帶;突逸帶(患疝氣病者所圍的有襯墊的帶子)。□ *vt* [VP6A, 15B] *~ sth (up),* **1** tie or fasten up: 捆;繫: *~ hay;* 捆乾草; *~ up a chicken,* pin the wings to the body before boiling or roasting it. (烹烤前)把鷄翅膀串緊在鷄身上。*The policemen ~ed up the struggling criminal with rope,* tied his arms to his sides. 警察用繩子把掙扎的罪犯縛起。 **2** support (a roof, bridge, etc) with a ~ or ~es(2). 以構架或桁架支持(屋頂,橋樑等)。

trust¹ /trʌst ; trʌst/ *n* **1** [U] *~ (in),* confidence, strong belief, in the goodness, strength, reliability of sth or sb: 信賴;信任;信靠: *put one's ~ in God.* 信靠上帝。*A child usually has perfect ~ in its mother.* 小孩通常完全信賴母親。*She hasn't/doesn't place much ~ in his promises.* 她不大信任他的諾言。***on ~,*** **(a)** without proof; without close examination: 不加證明地; 不作深究地; 憑信任地: *You'll have to take my statement on ~.* 你必須信任我的話。**(b)** on credit. 以賒欠方式。 **2** [U] responsibility: 責任;職責: *a position of great ~.* 責任重大的職位。**3** [C] (legal) property held and managed by one or more persons (*trustees*) for the benefit of another or others; [U] the legal relation between the trustee(s) and the property; the obligation assumed by the trustee(s): (法律)受委託保管的財產; 信託財產; 信託物(由受託人為他人利益所保管和經營的財產);信託;託管;受託人的義務: *By his will he created ~s for his children.* 他在遺囑裡為孩子們建立了信託財產。*This property is not mine; it is a ~.* 這財產不是我的,是信託財產。*I am holding the property in ~ for my nephew.* 我受託為我的姪子管理財產。'**~-money,** '**~ fund** *nn* money held in ~. 委託金;託管金。 **4** [C] association of business firms for the achievement of various objects, eg reducing competition, maintenance of prices. 企業聯合;托拉斯 (為了減少競爭,維持價格等而組成者)。**5** '**brains ~,** ⇨ brain. **~·ful** /-fl ; -fəl/, **~·ing** *adjj* ready to have ~ in others; not suspicious. 易於相信他人的; 信任的; 不疑的。 **~·fully** /-fəlɪ ; -fəlɪ/, **~·ing·ly** *advv* '**~·worthy** *adj* worthy of ~; dependable. 值得信賴的; 可信任的; 可靠的。'**~-worthi·ness** *n* **~y** *adj* (archaic or hum) ~-worthy: (古或諧)值得信賴的;可信任的;可靠的: *a ~y sword/bicycle.* 可靠的劍(脚踏車)。

trust² /trʌst ; trʌst/ *vt, vi* **1** [VP6A] have trust(1) in; believe in the honesty and reliability of: 信賴;信任;相信: *He's not the sort of man to be ~ed/not a man I would ~.* 他不是一個可靠的人(不是我可以信賴的人)。*Can you ~ his account of what happened?* 你能相信他對發生的事情所作的報告嗎? **2** [VP3A] *~ **in sb,*** have confidence in; believe that he will act for the best: 信仰;對…有信心: *~ in God.* 信上帝。*~ **to sth,*** have reliance on: 依賴;依靠: *Don't ~ to chance.* 不要依靠機會。*You ~ to your memory too much.* 你過分依賴你的記憶了。 **3** [VP14] *~ **sth to sb,*** = entrust (the more usu word). 委託;託付(entrust 較常用)。**4** [VP15A, B, 17] allow (sb) to do sth, have sth, go somewhere, etc without anxiety, knowing that he will act sensibly, etc: 對(某人)放心;信任;信得過: *Can I ~ you to get the money safely to the bank?* 我能信任你將這筆錢安全存入銀行嗎? *He may be ~ed to do the work well.* 他或許可以信得過做好那項工作。 *We can't ~ that boy out of our sight.* 那男孩一離開我們的視線,我們就不放心。*It's unwise to ~ small children out of doors in a big town,* eg because of traffic dangers. 在大城市中聽任小孩在外面玩是不智的 (例如因有交通事故的危險)。*Should boys of 16 be ~ed with high-powered motor-bikes?* 十六歲的男孩子應該聽任其騎馬力大的機車嗎? **5** [VP6A] allow credit to a customer: 賒賣: *I wonder whether the newsagent will ~ me; I need some cigarettes and I've no money on me.* 我不知道報紙經銷商會不會讓我賒帳;我需要幾支香烟,而我沒有帶錢。**6** [VP7A, 9] earnestly hope: 熱望;切望: *I ~ you're in good health.* 我希望你身體安康。*You're quite well, I ~.* 我希望你身體很好。(comm) (商) *We ~ to receive a cheque from you in settlement of this account.* 我們盼望收到你的支票以清理這筆帳。

trustee /trʌ'stiː ; trʌs'ti/ *n* person who has charge of property in trust(3) or of the business affairs of an institution. 受託人; 被信託的人; 受託管理財產或業務的人。**the Public T~,** state official who executes wills and trusts when asked to do so. 公設信託人 (得到請求時處理遺囑及信託財產的政府官員)。**~·ship** /-ʃɪp ; -ʃɪp/ *n* position of a ~; (esp) responsibility for the administration of a territory, granted to a country by the United Nations Organization: 受託人的職位; (尤指)聯合國的託管(委託某一國家管理某一領土): '*~ship territories,* eg the Cameroons from 1947 until 1960. 聯合國委託管理的領土(如 1947 至 1960 年的喀麥隆)。

truth /truːθ ; truθ/ *n* (*pl* ~s /truːðz ; truðz/) **1** [U] quality or state of being true: 確實;眞實性: *There's no ~/not a word of ~ in what he says.*

他說的話毫不確實(他說的沒有一句實話)。***moment of ~,*** time of crisis, test, or revelation. 緊要關頭;考驗時刻;頓悟之際。 **2** [U] that which is true: 眞實;眞相;事實: *tell the ~.* 說實話。***to tell the ~, ...,*** (formula used when making a confession): (作坦白陳述時所用的套語): *To tell the ~, I forgot all about your request.* 說實話,我把你要求的事情忘得乾乾淨淨。***in ~,*** (liter) truly, really. (文)實在地;實際上。 **3** [C] fact, belief, etc accepted as true: 眞理;眞義: *the ~s of religion/science.* 宗教的眞義(科學的眞理)。**~·ful** /-fl; -fəl/ *adj* **1** (of persons) in the habit of telling the ~. (指人)慣於說實話的;誠實的。 **2** (of statements) true. (指陳述)眞實的。**~·fully** /-fəlɪ; -fəlɪ/ *adv* **~·ful·ness** *n*

try[1] /traɪ; traɪ/ *vi, vt* (*pt, pp* tried) **1** [VP2A, B, 7A] (Note that, in colloq style, *try to + inf* is often replaced by *try and + inf*, esp in the imperative, and *don't try to* and *didn't try to* are often replaced by *don't try and* and *didn't try and*) make an attempt: (注意: try to + inf 這種句型在口語中常改用 try and + inf, 尤其在祈使句中更常見;否定形式 don't try to 與 didn't try to 常改作 don't try and 與 didn't try and) 試做;勉力而爲: *I don't think I can do it, but I'll try.* 我不認爲我能做該事,但是我要試試看。*I've tried till I'm tired.* 我一直做累了才停下來的。*He's trying his hardest,* using his utmost efforts. 他現在正全力而爲。*Try to get here early.* 請盡量早一點來。*Try to/Try and behave better.* 規矩一點(不要亂來)。*He didn't try to do it.* 他未做嘗試(他未試做該事)。*Don't try and swim across the river.* 不要嘗試游過那河。 **2** [VP3A] ***try for sth,*** make an attempt to get or win (esp a position): 試圖得到;爭取(尤指職位): *try for a scholarship/a position in the Civil Service.* 爭取獎學金(文官職位)。 **3** [VP6A, B, C, 10] use sth, do sth, as an experiment or test, to see whether it is satisfactory: 試驗;試用或試做以觀其結果: *Have you tried sleeping on your back as a cure for snoring?* 你試過仰睡以防止打鼾的辦法嗎? *Won't you try* (= buy and use) *this new kind of detergent?* 請試購用這種新的清潔劑吧? *Try how far you can jump/whether you can jump across this stream.* 試試看你能跳多遠(你是否跳得過這條小河)。*Try knocking at the back door if nobody hears you at the front door.* 如果前門沒有人應門,去敲後門試試看。*Please try me for the job,* let me do it as an experiment. 請讓我試試那工作。 ⇨ trial(1). [VP15B] ***try sth on,*** **(a)** put on (a garment, show, etc) to see whether it fits, looks well, etc: 試(衣服等): *I want to try the shoes on before I buy them.* 我要在購買前試穿鞋子。**(b)** (colloq) make a bold or impudent attempt to discover whether sth will be tolerated: (俗) 作大膽或厚顏的嘗試以發現某事是否被容忍; 試探: *It's no use your trying it/your games/your tricks on with me.* 你對我要這一套是沒有用的(我不吃這一套)。Hence, 由此產生, **'try-on** *n* (colloq) an attempt of this sort. (俗)試穿;試探。 [VP15B] ***try sth out,*** use it, experiment with it, in order to test it: 藉使用、實驗以考驗某事物;實際試驗某事物: *The idea seems good but it needs to be tried out.* 這構想似乎不壞,但是需要實際考驗。 **'try-out** *n* preliminary test of ability, qualification, etc, eg of an athlete. (運動員等的)預選;預賽;(能力、資格等的)初步鑑定。***try one's hand at sth,*** ⇨ hand[1](5). **4** [VP6A, 15A] inquire into (a case) in a court of law: (法庭上)審判;審問(案件): *He was tried and found guilty.* 他經過審判並被判決有罪。*He will be tried for murder.* 他將以殺人罪受審。*Which judge will try the case?* 哪一位法官將要審訊這個案子? ⇨ trial(3). **5** [VP6A] put a strain on; cause to be tired, exhausted, out of patience, etc: 考驗;過度使用而損傷;使疲勞、竭盡、失去耐性等: *Small print tries the eyes.* 小字體傷眼睛。*Don't try his patience too much.* 不要太過分而使他受不了。*His courage was severely tried.* 他的勇氣受到了嚴厲的考驗。**tried** *adj* that has been tested; reliable: 經過試驗的;可信賴的: *a tried friend/remedy.* 可靠的朋友(驗方)。 **trier** *n* person who tries hard, who always does his best. 勤勞者;努力工作者;盡力工作者。**try·ing** *adj* (⇨ 5 above) distressing; putting a strain on, eg the temper, one's patience: (參看上列第 5 義)使人痛苦的;難堪的;考驗(脾氣,耐性等)的: *a trying person to deal with;* 不易相處的人; *have a trying day,* one during which one's temper, patience, etc are tried; 經歷難挨的一天; *work that is trying to the eyes.* 費眼力的工作。

try[2] /traɪ; traɪ/ *n* **1** attempt: 嘗試;試驗;努力: *Let me have a try at it.* 這事讓我試試看。*He had three tries and failed each time.* 他嘗試了三回,每回都失敗了。 **2** (Rugby) touching down the ball behind the opponents' goal-line (with a score of three points). (橄欖球)在對方球門線後以球觸地(獲三分);三分觸地球。

tryst /trɪst; trɪst/ *n* (archaic) (time and place for, agreement to have, a) meeting, esp between lovers: (古)約會(尤指愛人間的幽會);約會的時間及地點;會晤的約定: *keep/break ~ (with* sb). 赴(不赴)(與某人的)約會。

Tsar /zɑː(r); tsɑr/, **Tsa·rina** /zɑː'riːnə; tsɑ'rinə/ *nn* = Czar, Czarina.

tsetse /'tsetsɪ; 'tsɛtsɪ/ *n* **'~(-fly)** blood-sucking fly (in tropical Africa) carrying and transmitting (often fatal) disease to men and animals. (熱帶非洲的)吸血蠅;采采蠅(引起並傳播人或動物之疾病,常可致死)。⇨ the illus at insect. 參看 insect 之插圖。

T-shirt /'tiː ʃɜːt; 'ti͵ʃɝt/ *n* ⇨ **T, t.**

T-square /'tiː skweə(r); 'ti͵skwɛr/ ⇨ square[2](7).

tub /tʌb; tʌb/ *n* **1** large open vessel, usu round, made of wood, zinc, etc used for washing clothes, holding liquids, growing plants in, etc: 桶;盆: *a rain-water tub.* 盛雨水的桶。**'tub-thumper** *n* mob orator. 煽惑群情的演說家。 **2** (also 亦作 **'tub·ful**) as much as a tub holds: 一桶或一盆之量: *a tub of water.* 一桶水。 **3** (colloq) bath-tub; (GB) bath: (俗)浴盆;(英)沐浴;洗澡: *have a cold tub before breakfast;* 早餐前洗一個冷水澡; *prefer a tub to a shower.* 喜歡盆浴勝過淋浴。 **4** (colloq) clumsy slow boat. (俗)笨重緩慢的船。

tuba /'tjuːbə *US:* 'tuː-; 'tjubə/ *n* large musical instrument of brass, of low pitch. 低音大喇叭;低音號。⇨ the illus at brass. 參看 brass 之插圖。

tubby /'tʌbɪ; 'tʌbɪ/ *adj* (-ier, -iest) shaped like a tub; fat and round: 桶或盆狀的;胖而圓的: *a tubby little man.* 矮小而圓胖的男子。

tube /tjuːb *US:* tuːb; tjub/ *n* **1** long hollow cylinder of metal, glass or rubber, esp for holding or conveying liquids, etc: (金屬,玻璃或橡皮製的)管;筒: *'boiler ~s;* 鍋爐管; *the 'inner ~ of a bicycle/car tyre,* of rubber, filled with air at pressure; 脚踏車(汽車)輪胎的內胎; *tor'pedo ~s,* from which torpedoes are launched. 魚雷發射管。**'~-well** *n* metal ~ placed in the ground to obtain water through perforations in the ~ near its end. 管井。 **2** soft metal container with a screw-cap, used for pastes, paints, etc: (裝牙膏、顏料等的)軟金屬筒管: *a ~ of toothpaste.* 一管牙膏。 **3** [U, C] (in London) underground railway: (在倫敦)地下鐵道: *travel in to work by ~ every morning;* 每天早晨乘地下火車到倫敦上班; *take a/the ~ to Oxford Circus.* 乘地下火車至牛津廣場。 **4** (US) thermionic valve as used in electronic apparatus; large ~ with a screen (*cathode ray ~,* ⇨ cathode) as used in a television set. (美)眞空管;電視機的映像管。 **5** hollow ~-shaped organ in the body: (身體內)管狀器官: *the bronchial ~s.* 支氣管。**tub·ing** *n* [U] material in the form of a ~: 管子材料;管料: *five feet of rubber/copper tubing.* 五呎橡皮(銅)管。**tu·bu·lar** /'tjuːbjʊlə(r) *US:* 'tuː-; 'tjubjələ˞/ *adj* **1** having the shape of a ~: 管狀

的: *a tubular bridge,* a bridge in the shape of a ~ through which a railway, etc passes. 函梁橋(鐵路等穿過其中的管道)。 **2** having, consisting of, ~s or tubing: 有管的;管式的;由管或管料構成的: *a tubular boiler,* in which water or steam is heated as it passes through many ~s; 管式鍋爐(水或蒸汽經過諸管時受熱); *tubular furniture,* with parts made of metal tubing; 管料家具(零件由金屬管製成者); *tubular scaffolding.* 管料鷹架。 **~·less** *adj* having no inner ~: 無內胎的;無內管的: *~less tyres.* 無內胎的輪胎。

tu·ber /ˈtjuːbə(r) *US:* ˈtuː- ; ˈtjubɚ/ *n* [C] enlarged part of an underground stem with buds from which new plants will grow, eg a potato, Jerusalem artichoke, yam, etc. 塊莖;球根(如馬鈴薯、菊芋、蕃薯等)。

tu·ber·cu·lo·sis /tjuːˌbɜːkjʊˈləʊsɪs *US:* tuː- ; tjuˌbɝkjəˈlosɪs/ *n* [U] (common abbr 通常略作 **TB** /ˌtiːˈbiː ; ˌtiˈbi/) wasting disease affecting various parts of the body's tissues, esp the lungs: 結核病;(尤指)肺結核;肺癆: *pulmonary ~,* consumption. 肺結核;肺癆。 **tu·ber·cu·lous** /tjuːˈbɜːkjʊləs *US:* tuː- ; tjəˈbɝkjələs/, **tu·ber·cu·lar** /tjuːˈbɜːkjʊlə(r) *US:* tuː- ; tjəˈbɝkjəlɚ/ *adjj* of, affected by, ~. 結核病的;肺結核的;感染結核病的。

tub·ing, tu·bu·lar ⇨ tube.

tuck /tʌk ; tʌk/ *n* **1** [C] flat, stitched fold of material in a garment, for shortening or for ornament: (衣服的)褶;襉;襞: *make / put in / take out a ~ in a dress / the sleeve of a shirt.* 在女服(襯衫袖)上打褶(加褶,去褶)。 **2** [U] (GB, sl) food, esp the cakes, pastry, etc that children enjoy. (英,俚)食物;(尤指兒童喜吃的)糕餅、點心等。 **ˈ~-shop** *n* shop (esp at a school) where ~ is sold. (尤指學校裡的)點心店;糖果店。□ *vt, vi* **1** [VP15A, B] draw together into a small space; put or push into a desired or convenient position: 縮攏;捲摺;叠起;打褶襉;塞在或放在所要的或方便的地方: *~ one's shirt in,* put the bottom of it inside one's trousers, etc. 將襯衣底部塞入褲內。 *She ~ed the ends of her hair into her bathing-cap.* 她把頭髮的末端塞進游泳帽中。 *He sat with his legs ~ed up under him.* 他跪坐著。 *The bird ~ed its head under its wing.* 那鳥把頭縮藏在翼下。 *The map is ~ed away in a pocket at the end of the book.* 那地圖藏在該書後面的小袋中。 *She ~ed the child up in bed,* pulled the bed-clothes up round the child and under the mattress. 她為那孩子蓋好被子並且把被子的邊緣塞在墊褥下面。 *She took off her shoes, ~ed up* (= rolled or turned up) *her skirt, and waded across the stream.* 她脫去鞋子,捲起裙子,涉過小河。 **2** [VP2C, 3A] *~ in,* eat heartily. 大吃;盡情地吃。 *~ into sth,* eat it heartily: 大吃;盡情地吃: *He ~ed into the cold ham.* 他大吃冷火腿。 **ˌ~-ˈin** *n* full meal: 盛饌;豐宴: *The boys had a good ~-in.* 男孩子們享受了一頓盛餐。

tucker /ˈtʌkə(r) ; ˈtʌkɚ/ *n* piece of lace, linen, etc, worn (in the 17th and 18th cc) to cover a woman's neck and shoulders. (十七,十八世紀時,女人圍於頸部及肩上的)領邊;飾紗。 ***one's best bib and ~,*** (colloq) one's best or finest clothes. (俗)個人最講究或最漂亮的衣服。

Tues·day /ˈtjuːzdɪ *US:* ˈtuː- ; ˈtjuzdɪ/ *n* third day of the week, next after Monday. 星期二;禮拜二;火曜日。

tuft /tʌft ; tʌft/ *n* bunch of feathers, hair, grass, etc growing or held together at the base. (生長或固着於底部的)一束羽毛,髮鬚,草等;一叢;一卷;一簇。 **~ed** *adj* having ~s; growing in a ~ or ~s. 有簇羽、髮等的;成簇生的。

tug /tʌg ; tʌg/ *vt, vi* (-gg-) [VP6A, 15A, B, 2A, C, 3A] ***tug (at),*** pull hard or violently; pull hard (*at*): 用力拉;拖曳: *The child was tugging her toy cart round the garden / tugging it along behind.* 那孩子繞着花園拖曳她的玩具車(拖着她的玩具車往前走)。 *We tugged so hard that the rope broke.* 我們用力拖曳,以致繩子斷了。 *The kitten was tugging at my shoe-lace.* 那小貓在拉曳我的鞋帶。□ *n* [C] **1** sudden hard pull: 突然而用力的拉;拉扯;拖曳: *The naughty boy gave his sister's hair a tug.* 那頑皮的男孩用力拉了一下他姊姊(妹妹)的頭髮。 *I felt a tug at my sleeve.* 我覺得有人拉了一下我的袖子。 *Parting from his family was a tug* (*at his heart-strings*), It was difficult to leave them. 與家人離別使他難過。 ***tug of war,*** contest in which two teams pull against each other on a rope. 拔河比賽。 **2** **ˈtug(-boat),** small powerful boat for towing ships, etc. 拖船。

a tug-boat

tu·ition /tjuːˈɪʃn *US:* tuː- ; tjuˈɪʃən/ *n* [U] (fee for) teaching: 教學;講授;學費: *have private ~ in mathematics.* 私下請人教數學。

tu·lip /ˈtjuːlɪp *US:* ˈtuː- ; ˈtjuləp/ *n* bulb plant with, in spring, a large bell-shaped or cup-shaped flower on a tall stem. 鬱金香;山慈姑。

tulle /tjuːl *US:* tuːl ; tjul/ *n* [U] soft, fine, silk net-like material for veils and dresses. 軟薄的綢紗(作婦女面紗和衣服)。

tumble /ˈtʌmbl ; ˈtʌmbḷ/ *vi, vt* **1** [VP2A, C] fall, esp quickly or violently: 跌倒;跌落(尤指快速或猛烈地): *~ down the stairs / off a horse or bicycle / out of a window / over the roots of a tree.* 從樓梯跌下(從馬或脚踏車上跌下;從窗子摔落;為樹根絆倒)。 *The baby is just learning to walk and he's always tumbling over.* 那嬰兒正在學步,常常跌倒。 **2** [VP2A, C] move up and down, to and fro, in a restless or disorderly way: 滾動;輾轉;不安地或紊亂地行動: *The puppies were tumbling about on the floor.* 小狗在地板上打滾。 *The sick man tossed and ~d in his bed.* 那病人在床上輾轉反側。 *I was so tired that I threw my clothes off and ~d into bed.* 我疲倦得把衣服一脫就上床睡覺了。 **3** [VP2C] be in a weak state (as if ready to fall): 衰弱;弱不禁風(似將隨時傾倒): *The old barn is tumbling to pieces.* 那陳舊的穀倉似將傾塌。 **ˈ~-down** *attrib adj* dilapidated; likely to collapse: 破爛的;似要坍塌的;可能倒塌的: *What a ~-down old house you live in!* 你住的房子多破舊啊! **4** [VP15A, B] cause to fall; upset: 使跌倒;使跌落;使傾覆: *The accident ~d us all out of the bus.* 那車禍把我們從公共汽車裡全摔了出來。 **5** [VP6A] put into a state of disorder: 使紊亂;弄亂;擾亂: *~ one's bed-clothes / sb's hair or clothes.* 弄亂床單被褥(某人的頭髮或衣服)。 **6** [VP3A] *~ to sth,* (colloq) grasp, realize (an idea, etc): (俗)領悟;瞭解(觀念等): *At last he ~d to what I was hinting at.* 他終於明白了我暗示給他的意思。□ *n* [C] **1** fall: 跌倒;摔落: *have a nasty ~.* 重重地跌了一跤。 **2** confused state: 混亂(狀態): *Things were all in a ~.* 局勢很混亂。 **ˈ~-weed** *n* (US) plant which grows in desert areas and, when withered, breaks off and is rolled about by the wind. (美)野莧(長於沙漠地區,枯乾後斷落,隨風滾動)。

tum·bler /ˈtʌmblə(r) ; ˈtʌmblɚ/ *n* **1** flat-bottomed drinking-glass without a handle or stem, ⇨ goblet. (無柄或脚的)平底玻璃杯。 **2** part of the mechanism of a lock which must be turned by a key before the lock will open. 鎖的制栓(用鑰匙

撥動才能使鎖開啓的部分)。 **3** kind of pigeon that turns over in flight. 翻頭鴿(飛翔時會向後翻滾)。 **4** acrobat. 特技表演者。

tum·brel, tum·bril /ˈtʌmbrəl ; ˈtʌmbrəl/ *n* (hist) cart, esp the kind that carried prisoners to the guillotine during the French Revolution. (史)車; (尤指)(法國大革命期間載運囚犯至斷頭台的)囚車。

tu·mes·cent /tjuːˈmesnt *US:* tuː- ; tjuˈmɛsn̩t/ *adj* swelling; swollen. 腫起的; 腫脹的。 **tu·mes·cence** /-sns ; -sn̩s/ *n*

tu·mid /ˈtjuːmɪd *US:* ˈtuː- ; ˈtjumɪd/ *adj* (of parts of the body) swollen; (fig, of a style of writing, etc) bombastic. (指身體的部分)腫起的; (喻,指某種文體等)浮誇的。**~·ity** /tjuːˈmɪdətɪ *US:* tuː- ; tjuˈmɪdətɪ/ *n*

tummy /ˈtʌmɪ ; ˈtʌmɪ/ *n* (*pl* -mies) (colloq) stomach; belly. (俗)胃; 肚子。

tu·mour (US = **tu·mor**) /ˈtjuːmə(r) *US:* ˈtuː- ; ˈtjumɚ/ *n* diseased growth in some part of the body. 腫; 腫塊; 瘤。

tu·mult /ˈtjuːmʌlt *US:* ˈtuː- ; ˈtjumʌlt/ *n* [C, U] **1** uproar; disturbance: 喧囂; 擾亂; 紛擾: *the ~ of battle.* 戰鬪的喧囂。 **2** confused and excited state of mind: (心境的)煩亂; 激昂; 激動: *in a ~;* 激動的(地); *when the ~ within him had subsided.* 當他內心的激動消滅的時候。

tu·mul·tu·ous /tjuːˈmʌltʃʊəs *US:* tuː- ; tjuˈmʌltʃʊəs/ *adj* disorderly; noisy and violent: 騷亂的; 紛擾的; 喧囂而猛烈的: *a ~ welcome.* 喧囂熱烈的歡迎。**~·ly** *adv*

tu·mu·lus /ˈtjuːmjʊləs *US:* ˈtuː- ; ˈtjumjələs/ *n* (*pl* -li /-laɪ ; -ˌlaɪ/) mound of earth over a (usu ancient) grave. 冢; 墓(通常爲古墓之隆起部分)。

tun /tʌn ; tʌn/ *n* large cask for beer, wine, etc; measure of capacity (252 gallons). (裝啤酒,葡萄酒等的)大酒桶; 大桶(容量單位,等於 252 加侖)。

tuna /ˈtjuːnə *US:* ˈtuːnə; ˈtunə/ *n* (*pl* ~ or ~s) = tunny.

tun·dra /ˈtʌndrə ; ˈtʌndrə/ *n* [U, C] wide, treeless plain of the arctic regions (of Russia, Siberia), marshy in summer and frozen hard in winter. (俄羅斯,西伯利亞的) 凍土地帶; 苔原 (北極地區不生樹木的遼濶地帶,夏季濕軟,冬季凍結)。

tune /tjuːn *US:* tuːn ; tjun/ *n* **1** [C] succession of notes forming a melody (of a song, hymn, etc): (歌,讚美詩等的)曲; 調子: *whistle a popular ~;* 以口哨吹流行的曲子; *~s that are easy to remember.* 容易記憶的曲子。 **2** [U] quality of having a well-marked melody: 具有某一顯明旋律的性質: *Some of this modern music has very little ~ in it.* 這種現代音樂有的旋律不太明顯。 **3** [U] ***in/out of ~,*** at/not at the correct pitch: 音高正確(不正確); 和調(不和調): *sing/play in ~.* 唱(奏)得合調。*The piano is out of ~.* 這鋼琴音調不正確。*The piano and the violin are not in ~.* 這鋼琴和小提琴的調子不諧和。 **4** [U] (fig) harmony; harmonious adjustment: (喻)和合; 調和; 諧和; 協調: *be in/out of ~ with one's surroundings/companions.* 與環境(友伴)協調(不協調)。 **5** (fig uses) (比喻用法) ***change one's ~; sing another ~,*** change one's way of speaking, behaviour, etc, or one's attitude to others (eg from insolence to respect). 改變一己的論調、行爲等,或改變對人的態度(如前倨後恭)。***to the ~ of,*** (colloq) to the amount of (usu with the suggestion that the sum is high or exorbitant): (俗) 總數高達 (通常含示總額甚大或過度): *He was fined* (eg for a motoring offence) *to the ~ of £30.* 他被罰款(例如駕車違警)高達三十鎊。 □ *vt, vi* **1** [VP6A] adjust the strings, etc (of a musical instrument) to the right pitch: 調整(樂器)的絃等使合調; 調準: *~ a guitar.* 調整吉他絃。[VP2C] ***~ up,*** (eg of a player or players in an orchestra) ~ a musical instrument: (如指管絃樂隊的演奏者)調整樂器; 調絃; 調音: *The orchestra were tuning up when we entered the concert-hall.* 當我們進入音樂廳時,管絃樂隊正在調音。**ˈtuning-fork** *n* small steel instrument, which produces a musical note of fixed pitch when struck. 音叉。 **2** [VP2C] ***~ in (to),*** **(a)** adjust the controls of a radio to a particular frequency/station: 調整收音機至某一頻率或電台; 校準頻率或波長; 撥收; 收聽: *~ in to the BBC World Service.* 收聽英國廣播公司對全球的播音。*You're not properly ~d in.* 你沒有把收音機校準。 **(b)** (fig) be aware of what other people are saying, feeling, etc; (喻)知道或發覺到他人所說的話或表現的情緒等: *He's not very well ~d in to his surroundings.* 他不太瞭解他周遭的環境。 **3** [VP6A] adjust or adapt the engine of a motor-vehicle so that it gives its best, or a special, performance. 調整汽車等的引擎使發生最佳或特定效能。**~r** *n* **1** (in compounds) person who ~s musical instruments: (用於複合字中) 調整樂器音調的人; 調音師: *a ˈpiano-tuner.* 鋼琴調音師。 **2** part of a radio etc which receives the signals. (收音機等的)調諧器。⇨ *amplifier* at amplify, *loud-speaker* at loud(1). **~·ful** /-fl ; -fʊl/ *adj* having a pleasing ~; melodious. 有悅耳音調的; 諧美的。**~·fully** /-fəlɪ ; -fʊlɪ/ *adj* **~·ful·ness** *n*

tung-oil /ˈtʌŋ ɔɪl ; ˈtʌŋ ɔɪl/ *n* [U] oil (from a tree) used chiefly in varnishing woodwork. 桐油。

tung·sten /ˈtʌŋstən ; ˈtʌŋstən/ *n* [U] grey metal (symbol **W**) used in making steel and the filaments of electric light bulbs. 鎢(符號 W,用以製合金鋼及電燈之絲)。

tu·nic /ˈtjuːnɪk *US:* ˈtuː- ; ˈtjunɪk/ *n* **1** close-fitting jacket as worn by policemen, soldiers, etc. (警察、軍人等所着的)緊身上衣。 **2** loose blouse or coat for a woman or girl, gathered at the waist with a belt, and reaching down to, or below, the hips. (婦女所著垂至臀部或低於臀部的)束腰外衣。 **3** loose, short-sleeved or sleeveless outer garment reaching to the knees, as worn by ancient Greeks and Romans. (古希臘、羅馬人所著,長及膝部的)短袖或無袖寬大外袍。

tun·nel /ˈtʌnl ; ˈtʌnl̩/ *n* underground passage (esp through a hill or mountain, for a road, railway, etc); underwater passage (eg the proposed Channel ~ between England and France). 地下通道; (尤指)(道路,鐵路等穿越山嶺或海底的)隧道(如擬議中穿過英倫海峽者)。 □ *vi, vt* (-ll-, US also -l-) [VP2A, C, 3A, 6A] ~ ***(into/through),*** dig a ~ (into/through) sth; dig a ~ or ~s through (sth). 在…掘地道; 開隧道穿過。

tunny /ˈtʌnɪ ; ˈtʌnɪ/ *n* (*pl* -nies or unchanged 或不變) large sea-fish, used as food, and valued for the sport of catching it. 鮪; 金槍魚(一種大海魚,可捕之爲食或作爲消遣)。

tup /tʌp ; tʌp/ *n* male sheep; ram. 公綿羊; (未閹過的)公羊。

tup·pence /ˈtʌpəns ; ˈtʌpəns/ *n* (colloq) two pence. (俗)兩辨士。 **tup·penny** /ˈtʌpənɪ ; ˈtʌpənɪ/ *adj* costing ~; (fig)of trifling value. 值兩辨士的; (喻)價值小的; 微不足道的。

tu quo·que /ˌtjuː ˈkwəʊkwɪ *US:* ˌtuː ˈkwəʊkweɪ ; tjuˈkwokwɪ/ *n* (Lat) (phrase used as a retort) So are you! So did you! (拉)(用於回嘴或反唇相譏)你也是! 彼此彼此!

tur·ban /ˈtɜːbən ; ˈtɝbən/ *n* **1** headdress made by winding a length of cloth round the head (as worn in some Asian and African countries). (某些亞洲及非洲國家的人民所纏的)頭巾; 包頭巾。 **2** close-fitting hat resembling a ~. (類似頭巾之)小帽。**~ed** *adj* wearing a ~: 戴頭巾的; 戴小帽的: *a ~ed Sikh.* 戴頭巾的印度塞克教徒。

tur·bid /ˈtɜːbɪd ; ˈtɝbɪd/ *adj* **1** (of liquids) thick; muddy; not clear: (指液體)濃厚的; 混濁的; 不清的: *~ waters/rivers.* 混濁的礦泉(河流)。 **2** (fig) disordered; confused: (喻)混亂的; 紊亂的: *a ~ imagination;* 紊亂的想像; *~ thoughts.* 雜亂的思緒。**~·ness, ~·ity**/ tɜːˈbɪdətɪ ; tɝˈbɪdətɪ/ *nn*

tur·bine /ˈtɜːbaɪn ; ˈtɝbaɪn/ *n* engine or motor whose driving-wheel is turned by a current of water, steam or air. 渦輪機(主動輪由水流,蒸汽或空

氣所推動的引擎);透平機;水輪機;汽輪機。⇨ the illus at air. 參看 air 之插圖。

tur·bo·jet /ˌtɜːbəʊˈdʒet ; ˈtɝboˌdʒɛt/ *n* (aircraft with a) turbine engine that delivers its power in the form of a jet of hot gases (no propellers being needed on the aircraft). 渦輪噴射引擎;渦輪噴射飛機(無需螺旋槳)。

tur·bo·prop /ˌtɜːbəʊˈprɒp ; ˈtɝboˌprɑp/ *n* (aircraft with a) turbine engine that uses its power, from hot gases, to turn a propeller. 渦輪螺旋槳引擎;渦輪螺旋槳飛機。

tur·bot /ˈtɜːbət ; ˈtɝbət/ *n* (*pl* unchanged) large, flat sea-fish valued as food. (複數不變)大比目魚(一種扁平的大海魚,可作珍貴食品)。

tur·bu·lent /ˈtɜːbjʊlənt ; ˈtɝbjələnt/ *adj* violent; disorderly; uncontrolled: 狂烈的;混亂的;無秩序的: *~ waves/passions;* 洶湧的波浪(激動的情緒); *a ~ mob.* 一羣暴徒。 **~·ly** *adv* **tur·bu·lence** /-ləns ; -ləns/ *n*

turd /tɜːd ; tɝd/ *n* [U, C] (sl) (ball or lump of) excrement: (俚)糞塊;屎球;屎: *sheep ~s.* 羊糞。

tu·reen /tjʊˈriːn *US:* tʊ- ; tuˈrin/ *n* deep dish with a lid, from which soup, vegetables, etc are served at table. (盛湯、菜等的)有蓋湯碗。

turf /tɜːf ; tɝf/ *n* **1** [U] soil-surface with grass-roots growing in it: 草泥;草皮;草根土: *strip the ~ off a field;* 除去田中的草泥; *make a lawn by laying ~* (instead of sowing grass-seed). 鋪草根土(代替撒草種)以做成草地。 **the ~,** the race-course; the occupation of profession of horse-racing. 跑馬場;賽馬業。 **ˈ~ accountant, ~ commission agent,** bookmaker, ⇨ book[1](8). 賽馬業者。 **2** (*pl* ~s or 或 turves /tɜːvz ; tɝvz/) piece of ~ cut out; (in Ireland) (piece of) peat. 草皮;草皮塊;(愛爾蘭)泥炭(塊);泥煤(塊)。□ *vt* **1** [VP6A] cover or lay (a piece of land) with ~. 以草泥覆蓋(一片土地);鋪草皮。 **2** [VP15B] *~ out,* (GB sl) throw out. (英俚)趕出;拋出。

tur·gid /ˈtɜːdʒɪd ; ˈtɝdʒɪd/ *adj* **1** swollen; bloated. 因病腫脹的;浮腫的。 **2** (of language) pompous; full of high-sounding words. (指語言)虛飾的;多浮誇用語的。 **~·ly** *adv* **~·ity** /tɜːˈdʒɪdətɪ ; tɝˈdʒɪdətɪ/ *n*

Turk /tɜːk ; tɝk/ *n* native or inhabitant of Turkey. 土耳其人或其居民。

tur·key /ˈtɜːkɪ ; ˈtɝkɪ/ *n* (*pl* ~s) **1** [C] large bird valued as food; [U] its flesh; ⇨ the illus at fowl. 吐綬鷄; 火鷄(參看 fowl 之插圖); 火鷄肉。 **2** (US sl) a flop. (美俚) 失敗的創作(戲劇、電影、作品等)。 ***cold ~,*** **(a)** sudden withdrawal from, or hangover after taking, narcotics. 突然(而完全地)戒毒;吸毒後的殘留不適。 **(b)** frank, determined statement of truth (usu about sth unpleasant). 實話實說(通常指說出令人不愉之事)。 ***talk ~,*** (US sl) talk frankly and bluntly. (美俚)直率地講;直截了當地說;開門見山地講。

Tur·kish /ˈtɜːkɪʃ ; ˈtɝkɪʃ/ *n, adj* (language) of Turkey or the Turks. 土耳其語;土耳其的;土耳其人的。 **~ bath,** of hot air or steam, followed by a shower and massage. 土耳其浴;蒸汽浴。 **~ delight,** sweetmeat of jelly-like substance covered with powdered sugar. 軟糖;橡皮糖。 **~ towel,** one made of rough absorbent cloth. (富吸水性的)粗面毛巾。

tur·meric /ˈtɜːmərɪk ; ˈtɝmərɪk/ *n* [U] (E Indian plant with a) root which is used, in powdered form, as a colouring substance and a flavouring (esp in making curries). 鬱金(東印度植物,其根磨成粉,可作染料及調味料,尤用於製咖哩粉);鬱金根(粉)。

tur·moil /ˈtɜːmɔɪl ; ˈtɝmɔɪl/ *n* [C, U] (instance of) trouble, agitation, disturbance: 騷動;混亂;擾亂;其實例: *The town was in (a) ~ during the elections.* 該城在選舉期間陷入一片混亂。

turn[1] /tɜːn ; tɝn/ *n* **1** act of turning; turning movement: 旋轉;轉動: *a few ~s of the handle;* 把手的數次轉動; *a ~ of Fortune's wheel,* a change of fortune. 機運的轉變。 ***~ of the century,*** the time when a new century (2) starts. 新世紀開始時(一世紀末與下一世紀初)。 ***on the ~,*** about to change: 即將改變;正要改變: *The milk is on the ~,* about to turn sour. 牛奶快要酸了。 *The tide is on the ~.* 潮水快要漲(退)了。 ***done to a ~,*** (from the use of a ~spit) cooked just enough, neither underdone nor overdone. (來自從前使用狗轉動烤肉叉之方法)(指食物)烹煮得恰到好處;火候到家。 **2** change of direction: 轉變方向;彎: *sudden ~s in the road.* 路上的急彎。 ***at every ~,*** (fig) very frequently: (喻)經常地;不時地: *I've been coming across old friends at every ~ during this reunion.* 在這次團聚中,我經常遇見老友。 *He was frustrated at every ~,* every time he tried to achieve his aim. 他每次都遭遇挫折。 **3** change in condition: 改變情況;轉機;變化: *The sick man/My affairs took a ~ for the better/worse.* 病人(我的事情)轉好(壞)了。 *His illness took a favourable ~.* 他的病情有了良好的轉機。 **4** occasion or opportunity for doing sth, esp in one's proper order among others: (輪流做某事的)時機;機會;次序: *It's your ~ to read now, John.* 約翰,現在輪到你讀了。 *Wait (until it is) your ~.* 等着輪到你。 *My ~ will come* (sometimes meaning 'I shall have my time of success, triumph, revenge, etc', according to context). 總會輪到我(有時意謂'我總有出頭、勝利、報復等的一天')。 ***(do sth) ~ and ~ about,*** (of two or more persons) first one and then the other(s); alternately (指兩人或多人)輪流地(做某事);交替地。 ***by ~s,*** (of persons, groups, actions) in rotation; one after the other: (指人,團體,行爲)輪流地;輪替地;依次地: *She went hot and cold by ~s.* 她一陣發熱一陣發冷。 *They laughed and cried by ~s.* 他們一會兒笑一會兒哭。 ***in ~,*** (of two persons) = ~ and ~ about; (of more than two persons) in succession: (指兩人)輪流地;(指三人以上)一個接一個地;接連地;依次: *The boys were summoned in ~ to see the examiner.* 男孩子們依次被召入會見考試官。 ***out of ~,*** before or after the permitted time: 在規定時間之前或後;不按順序地: *You mustn't speak out of (your) ~.* 未輪到你的時候,不可發言。 ***take ~s (at sth); take ~s about,*** do it in ~: 輪流做某事: *Mary and Helen took ~s at sitting up with their sick mother,* Mary sat up first, Helen next, and so on. 瑪莉和海倫輪流熬夜陪伴她們生病的母親。 **5** action regarded as affecting sb. 被認爲具有影響力的舉動或行爲。 ***One good ~ deserves another,*** (prov) Help, kind service, etc should be repaid. (諺)施惠者應受惠(好心應有好報)。 ***do sb a good/bad ~,*** be/not be helpful. (對某人)有恩惠或幫助(有損害)。 **6** natural tendency: 自然的趨勢;傾向;癖性: *a boy with a me'chanical ~,* interested in, clever at, mechanical things. 愛好機械的男孩子。 *He has a gloomy ~ of mind.* 他有憂鬱的癖性。 **7** purpose; special need. 目的;特殊需要。 ***serve one's ~,*** meet one's requirements: 適合自己的需要: *I think this book will serve my ~.* 我想這本書將可適合我的需要。 **8** short period of activity: 短時間的活動: *I'll take a few ~s* (= have a walk) *round the deck before I go to bed.* 就寢前我將在甲板上散一會兒步。 *I'll take a ~ at the oars now if you want a rest.* 如果你需要休息,我來划一會兒槳。 **9** short performance on the stage (esp of a variety theatre, or similar entertainment for sound or TV broadcasts), eg a song, dance, juggling feat, display of skill. 短時間的綜藝節目(尤指雜耍戲院,或無線電、電視廣播中出現的娛樂節目,如歌、舞、戲法、特技)。 ***star ~,*** most popular ~. 最受歡迎的綜藝節目。 **10** (colloq) nervous shock: (俗)震驚;吃驚: *The news gave me quite a ~.* 這消息使我大吃一驚。

turn[2] / tɜːn ; tɝn/ *vt, vi* (For uses with *adverbial particles* and *preps,* ⇨ 7 below.) (與副詞接語及介詞連用的用法,參看下列第 7 義。) **1** [VP6A, 15A, B, 2A, C, 4A] (cause to) move round a point; (cause to) move so as to face in a different direction: (使)旋轉;(使)轉動;翻轉: *The earth ~s round the sun.* 地球繞日運行。*The wheels of the car were ~ing slowly.* 汽車的輪子在緩緩地轉動。*What ~s the wheels?* 什麼力量使車輪轉動? *He ~ed away from me.* 他避開我。*He ~ed his back on me,* ⇨ back¹(1). 他轉過身去不理我。*He ~ed his back to the wall.* 他把背轉向牆。*He ~ed his head (round) and looked back.* 他轉頭往後看。*He ~ed to look at me.* 他轉過(身)來看着我。*He ~ed (to the) left.* 他向左邊轉。*It's time we ~ed and went back home.* 我們(現在)應該折返回家去了。*He was idly ~ing the pages of a magazine.* 他在無聊地翻(看)一本雜誌。*The car ~ed (round) the corner.* 汽車轉過街角。*Be careful how you ~ that corner.* 轉那個(街)角要格外當心。*Please ~ your eyes* (= look) *this way.* 請朝這邊看。*The mere thought of food ~ed his stomach,* upset his stomach, made him feel ill. 一想到食物就使他作嘔。*His stomach ~ed at the sight of food.* (當時)他一看到食物就覺得想吐。*When does the tide ~,* begin to flow in/out? 潮水何時漲(退)? *This tap ~s easily.* 這個水龍頭轉動起來很容易。*It's easy to ~ this tap.* 這個水龍頭容易轉動。*Nothing will ever ~ him from* (= cause him to change) *his purpose.* 什麼也不能使他改變他的目標。**~ one's mind/thoughts/attention to sth,** direct one's mind, etc to: 把自己的心智(思想,注意力)灌注在某事物上: *Please ~ your attention to something more important.* 請把注意力用在較重要的事上。**~ one's hand to sth,** (be able to) undertake (a task, etc): (能够)從事或擔任(一項工作等): *He can ~ his hand to most jobs about the house,* can deal with them. 家裡的事情大多數他都能做。**~ sth to account,** ⇨ account¹(3). **~ a deaf ear to sth,** refuse to listen to: 不聽;拒絕聽: *They ~ed a deaf ear to my request for help.* 他們對我的求助置若罔聞。**~ sb's flank; ~ the flank of sb,** pass round an enemy's position so as to attack it in the flank or rear; (fig) outwit him; defeat him in debate, etc. 由側面迂迴包抄敵人;(喻)機智上勝過某人;在辯論等中擊敗某人。**~ the corner,** (fig use) (比喻用法) ⇨ corner(1). **~ the scale(s),** ⇨ scale³(1). **2** [VP6A, 14, 15A, B, 2A, C, 3A] **~ (sth) (into sth),** (cause to) change in nature, quality, condition, etc: (使)改變性質,品質,狀況等: *Frost ~s water into ice.* 嚴寒使水結成冰。*Caterpillars ~ into* (= become) *butterflies.* 毛蟲會變成蝴蝶。*This hot weather has ~ed the milk,* made it sour. 這炎熱的天氣使牛奶變酸了。*His hair has ~ed grey.* 他的頭髮花白了。*Anxiety ~ed his hair white.* 焦慮使他的頭髮變白了(他的頭髮愁白了)。*The leaves are beginning to ~,* change colour (as in autumn). 樹上的葉子開始改變顏色了(如在秋天)。*Could you ~ this piece of prose into verse/this passage into Greek?* 你能把這篇散文改寫成韻文(把這段文字翻譯成希臘文)嗎? *He has ~ed traitor,* become a traitor. 他變成了叛逆。*He's a politician ~ed poet,* who has become a poet. 他由從政者變成了詩人。*T~ the dog loose,* let it go free, eg by releasing it from a chain. 把那隻狗放開。**~ sb's brain,** upset him mentally. 使某人精神恍惚或錯亂。**~ sb's head,** unsettle him, make him vain: 使某人狂妄;使某人自負: *The excessive praise the young actor received ~ed his head.* 那年輕(男)演員所受到的過分讚譽使他狂妄起來了。**3** [VP6A] reach and pass: 到達並超過: *He has ~ed* (= reach the age of) *fifty.* 他已屆知命之年。*It has just ~ed two,* is just after two o'clock. 現在剛過兩點鐘。**4** [VP6A] shape (sth, wood or metal) on a lathe, etc: 在車床等上車(某物,木質或金屬): *~ brass;* 在車床上車銅器; *a machine-~ed cigarette-case;* 機械彫花的香煙盒; *~ a bowl on a potter's wheel;* 在拉坯輪車上車一陶碗; (fig) give a graceful form to: (喻)賦與優美的形式: *~ an epigram/a compliment;* 作雋語(動聽的恭維話); *a well-~ed phrase/sentence;* 措辭巧妙的話(句子); *a well-~ed ankle;* 外型美好的足踝; (with passive force): (含被動意): *wood/metal that ~s* (= can be ~ed) *easily.* 容易加工的木材(金屬)。**5** [VP6A] remake (a garment) so that the inner surface becomes the outer surface: 翻面改做(衣服): *I'll have this old overcoat ~ed.* 我(將)要把這件舊大衣翻一翻。**~ one's coat,** ⇨ coat(1). **'~·coat** *n* person who deserts one party to join another, esp to win profit, advantage, safety, etc. 脫黨者;變節者(尤指為獲得利益,好處,安全等)。**6** (compounds) (複合字) **'~·cock** *n* person employed to ~ water on or off (at the mains). (總水管的)水龍頭開閉員。**'~·key** *n* keeper of the keys in a prison; jailer. (監獄的)看守;獄卒。**'~·pike** *n* (hist) gate kept closed across a road and opened on payment of a toll; (US) toll road for fast traffic. (史)收路稅關卡;(美)收費高速公路。**'~·spit** *n* (hist) dog or servant who turned the spit on which meat, etc used to be roasted. (史)(往昔烤肉時轉動肉叉的)轉叉狗;轉叉僕。**'~·stile** *n* revolving gate that admits, lets out, one person at a time. (一次祇能容許一人出入的)旋轉柵門。**'~-table** *n* flat circular platform, eg one on which gramophone discs are played, or on which a railway locomotive is turned round. 圓形轉盤(如唱機轉盤);圓形轉臺(如鐵路機車的調向臺)。**7** [VP14, 15B, 2C, 3A] (special uses with *adverbial particles* and *preps*): (與副詞接語和介詞連用的特殊用法):

turn (sb) about, (cause to) ~ to one side or in a different direction: (使)轉向;回頭;轉向一邊: *About ~!* (as a military command, in drills, etc). 向後轉!(軍隊操練等時的口令)。

turn sb adrift, send sb away without help or support: 逐出某人(使漂泊無依);使某人流浪: *He ~ed his son adrift in the world,* sent him away from home and refused to help him. 他將其子逐出家門。

turn (sb) against sb, (cause to) become hostile to: (使)對…變為敵對;採取敵對態度;反抗: *She ~ed against her old friend.* 她敵視她的老友。*He tried to ~ the children against their mother.* 他試圖使孩子們反抗他們的母親。

turn (sb) aside (from), (more usu 較常作 *~ away*) (cause to)~ to one side or in a different direction. (使)轉變方向;(使)轉向一邊;(使)避開。

turn (sb) away, (cause to) ~ in a different direction so as not to face sb/sth; refuse to look at, welcome, help, admit (to a place): (使)轉臉而不面對某人或某物;拒絕看,歡迎,幫助,讓人進入某地: *She ~ed away in disgust.* 她感到厭惡而把臉轉開。*He ~ed away a beggar.* 他逐出一名乞丐。*We had to ~ away hundreds of people,* eg from a stadium, because all seats were sold. 我們不得不謝絕數以百計的觀衆(如球場的票已全部賣光)。

turn (sb/sth) back, (cause to) return the way one has come: (使)從原路回去;折回;逐回;趕回去: *It's getting dark—we'd better ~ back.* 天快黑了——我們最好回去吧。*We were/Our car was ~ed back at the frontier.* 我們(我們的車)在邊界上被趕了回來。

turn (sth) down, (a) (cause to) fold down: (使)摺起;翻下: *~ down one's coat collar;* 把衣領翻下; *a ~-down collar;* 翻領; *~ down the bed-clothes.* 摺起床單等。**(b)** reduce (the flame or brilliance of a gas- or oil-lamp, stove, etc) by ~ing a wheel or tap: 轉小或扭小(煤氣燈或油燈,爐火等): *~ down the lamps.* 扭小燈光。**(c)** place (a playing-card) on the table face downwards. 使(紙牌)面向下;翻扣(紙牌)在桌上。**~ sb/sth down,** refuse to consider (an offer, a proposal, or the person who makes it): 拒絕;摒斥(提議,建議,作建議的人等): *He tried to join the army but was ~ed down because of poor health.* 他想從軍,但因身體不好而遭到拒絕。*He asked Jane to marry him but she ~ed him down/~ed down his proposal.* 他要珍嫁給他,但她拒絕了他(拒絕了他的求婚)。

turn in, (colloq) go to bed. (俗)就寢。**~ in on oneself/itself,** withdraw from contact with

others; become a recluse; (of a country) become isolationist. 隱居(不與他人接觸); 做隱士; (指國家)變爲孤立主義者。~ ***sb in,*** (colloq) surrender sb to the police. (俗)把某人交給警察;向警方交出某人。~ ***(sth) in,*** (cause to) fold or slant inwards: (使)向內彎: *His toes ~ in.* 他的足趾內彎。*He ~ed his toes in.* 他使足趾內曲。~ ***sth in,*** (colloq) give back to those in authority: (俗)歸還當局: *You must ~ in your equipment* (eg uniform) *before you leave.* 你離開軍隊時,必須繳回裝備(如制服)。
turn (sth) inside out, (cause to) become inside out: (使)翻轉;將裡面翻作外面: *The wind ~ed my old umbrella inside out.* 風把我的傘吹得翻過去了。*He ~ed his pockets inside out in search of his keys.* 他把口袋翻出來找他的鑰匙。
turn off, change direction; leave (one road) for another: 改變方向;離開(一條路)而走上另一條路;轉彎;分歧: *Is this where we ~ off/where our road ~s off for Hull?* 這裡就是我們要轉往赫爾(我們的路轉向赫爾)的地方嗎? ~ ***sth off,*** stop the flow of (liquid, gas, current) by ~ing a tap, switch or other control: 藉轉動龍頭、開關或其他控制器而停止(液體、瓦斯、電流等)的流動; 關上; 關閉: ~ *off the water/lights/radio/TV.* 關掉自來水(電燈,收音機,電視)。~ ***(sb) off,*** (sl) (cause sb to) lose interest, desire, etc: (俚)(使某人)失去興趣、欲望等;掃某人的興緻: *He/This music really ~s me off!* 他(這音樂)眞使我掃興! Hence, 由此產生, **'~-off** *n* sth/sb that causes this. 令人掃興的人或事物。
turn sth on, start the flow of (liquid, gas, current) by ~ing a tap, switch, etc: 藉轉動龍頭、開關等而使(液體、瓦斯、電流等)流動; 打開; 轉開; 開啓: *T~ the lights/radio on.* 打開電燈(收音機)。*She's fond of ~ing on the charm,* (fig) using her charm to influence people. (喻)她喜歡利用她的姿色去影響別人。~ ***(sb) on,*** (sl) (cause sb to) have great pleasure or excitement: (俚)(使某人)感到極大的愉快或激動; (使)高興或興奮: *Some girls ~ on easily.* 有些女孩子很容易激動。*What kind of music ~s you on?* 哪一種音樂特別使你感到興奮? *Some drugs ~ you on very quickly,* quickly change your mental or emotional state. 有些藥物很快就會使你興奮。Hence, 由此產生, **'~-on** *n* sth/sb that causes this. 使人激動與興奮的人或事物。~ ***on sth,*** depend on: 依賴;視…而定;以…爲轉移: *The success of a picnic usually ~s on the weather.* 一次野餐的成功通常要靠天氣。~ ***on sb,*** become hostile to; attack: 變爲與…敵對;攻擊: *The dog ~ed on me and bit me in the leg.* 那狗向我襲擊並且咬傷了我的腿。
turn out (well, etc), prove to be; be in the end: 證明爲;結果: *Everything ~ed out well/satisfactory.* 結果一切都很好(令人滿意)。*The day ~ed out wet.* 那天竟然下雨了。*As it ~ed out...,* As it happened in the end.... 結果(終於)…;後來演變成…。~ ***(sth) out,*** (cause to) point outwards: (使)向外: *His toes ~ out.* 他的足趾外翻。*He ~ed his toes out.* 他使足趾外曲。~ ***sth out,*** **(a)** extinguish by ~ing a tap, switch, etc: 關掉;滅掉: *Please ~ out the lights/gas-fire before you go to bed.* 請在就寢前關掉電燈(煤氣爐)。**(b)** empty (a drawer, one's pockets, a room, etc) when looking for sth, when cleaning sth: 倒空或騰空(抽屜,口袋,房間等,如尋物或清理時);徹底清除或清理: ~ *out all the drawers in one's desk;* 徹底清理書桌所有的抽屜; ~ *out the attic,* to get rid of unwanted articles, etc. 徹底清理閣樓(丟棄不需要的東西等)。~ ***sb/sth out,*** produce, eg manufactured goods: 製造;生產(如工業製品): *Our new factory is ~ing out large quantities of goods.* 我們的新工廠正在生產大量的貨物。*The school has ~ed out some first-rate scholars.* 該校已造就出若干位第一流的學者。~ ***(sb) out,*** **(a)** (cause him to) assemble for some event, or for duty: (使某人)爲某事件或某職責而集合;出動: *The whole village ~ed out to welcome the princess.* 全村的人都出來歡迎公主。*Not many men ~ed out for duty.* 沒有許多人出勤。**(b)** (colloq) (cause sb to) get out of bed. (俗)(使某人)起床。~ ***sb out (of/from sth),*** expel by force, threats, etc: (以强迫、威脅等方式)驅逐;迫使放棄: ~ *sb out of his job/chair;* 迫使某人放棄他的工作(講座); ~ *out a tenant* (= from his house) *for not paying the rent.* 因不付租金而逐出房客。**~ed out,** (of a person, equipment, etc) dressed, equipped: (指人,裝備等)穿著…的;有…裝備的: *a well-~ed out young man.* 衣著良好的年輕人。*She was beautifully ~ed out,* elegantly dressed. 她裝束得很美麗。Hence, 由此產生, **'~-out** *n* **(a)** persons who have ~ed out (assembled): 羣集的人們;一批出勤者: *There was a good ~-out at the meeting.* 出席會議者十分踴躍。**(b)** occasion when one ~s out (empties, etc) a drawer, etc: 清理;清除: *The drawers in my desk are full of old papers—it's time I had a good ~-out.* 我書桌的抽屜裡塞滿了舊文件——我該徹底整理一下了。**(c)** equipment; way in which sth is equipped; clothes and accessories worn together: 裝備;裝備的方式;裝束;穿著打扮(包括衣服及配件): *a smart/sloppy ~-out.* 漂亮(草率)的裝扮。**(d)** output (the more usu word) of manufactured goods, etc. 產額;生產量(output 較常用)。
turn (sb/sth) over, (cause to) fall over, upset; change the position of: (使)跌落;(使)打翻;翻轉;倒轉;翻身: *The car (was) ~ed right over,* completely upset. 那輛汽車來了個大翻身。*He ~ed over in bed.* 他在床上翻身。*The nurse ~ed the old man over and gave him an injection in the left buttock.* 那護士把那位老人翻過去,在他的左臀上打了一針。~ ***sth over,*** do business to the amount of: 營業額達於: *His business ~s over £500 a week.* 他的商店每週的營業額爲五百鎊。~ ***sth over in one's mind,*** think about sth (before making a decision). 思考某事;熟思;(做決定前)再三考慮。~ ***sth/sb over (to sb),*** give the control or conduct of sth/sb to: 移交;交付;讓渡;轉賣: *I've ~ed over the management of my affairs to my brother.* 我已經把我的事務交給我的哥哥(弟弟)處理。*He's ~ed over his business to his successors.* 他已經把他的事業移交給他的繼承人了。*The thief was ~ed* (=handed) *over to the police.* 那竊賊已被送交警察。Hence, 由此產生, **'~-over** *n* **(a)** amount of money ~ed over in business within a period of time or for a particular transaction: (某一期間或某一筆買賣的) 營業額;銷貨金額: *a profit of £1 000 on a ~over of £10 000;* 做一萬鎊的生意獲利一千鎊; *sell goods at low prices hoping for a quick ~over,* quick sales and quick replacement of stock. 低價售貨以期週轉迅速。**(b)** rate of renewal: 更換率;換新率: *There is a higher ~over of the labour force in unskilled trades than in skilled trades,* unskilled workers leave and are replaced more quickly. 非技術行業比技術行業的人事變動率高。**(c)** tart made by folding over half of a circular piece of pastry over the other half, with jam, meat, etc inside. 捲酥;半圓捲餅。
turn (sth/sb) round, (cause to) face another way, be in another direction: (使)面對另一方向;轉向;採取新方向: *T~ round and let me see your profile.* 轉過去,讓我看看你的側面。*T~ your chair round to the fire.* 把你的椅子轉向火。Hence, 由此產生, **'~-round** *n* (esp of a ship or aircraft) process of getting it ready for the return voyage or flight: (尤指船或飛機)回航的準備過程或手續(如進港、卸貨、裝貨、離港等);裝卸: *a ~-round of 24 hours in Southampton,* eg for an Atlantic liner. 在南安普頓作廿四小時的裝卸停留(如一艘大西洋客輪)。
turn to, get busy: 開始工作;動手做事: *The design staff ~ed to and produced a set of drawings in twenty-four hours.* 製圖人員着手工作並在廿四小時內製成了一套圖樣。~ ***to sb,*** go or apply to: 求助於: *The child ~ed to its mother for comfort.* 那孩子向母親求安慰。*She has nobody to ~ to.* 她無人可求助。

turn up, **(a)** make one's appearance; arrive: 出現;出席;到達: *He promised to come, but hasn't ~ed up yet.* 他答應來,但尚未到。*My boss hasn't ~ed up this morning — I hope she isn't ill.* 我的老板今天早晨還沒有來 — 我希望她沒有生病。**(b)** be found, esp by chance: 被發現(尤指偶然地): *The book you've lost may ~ up one of these days.* 你遺失的那本書也許這幾天會找到。**(c)** (of an opportunity, etc) happen; present itself: (指機會等) 發生;出現: *He's still waiting for something* (eg a job, a piece of good luck) *to ~ up.* 他仍在期待機會出現。***~ (sth) up***, **(a)** (cause to) slope upwards: (使)向上傾斜: ~ (= roll) *up one's shirt sleeves.* 捲起襯衣袖子。**(b)** expose; make visible: 暴露;使可見: *The share of a plough ~s up the soil.* 犁頭將土翻起。*The ploughman ~ed up some buried treasure / an old skull.* 那農夫用犁翻起了若干埋藏的財寶(一個古老的頭蓋骨)。***~ sb up***, (colloq) cause to vomit; disgust: (俗)使作嘔;使厭惡: *The stink from the slaughter-house ~ed me up.* 屠宰場的惡臭使我作嘔。***~ up one's nose at sth***, (fig) express a superior and critical attitude towards: (喻)輕視;瞧不起;對…持優越及批評態度: *She ~ed up her nose at the suggestion.* 她對這項建議顯出不屑一顧的樣子。**'~-up** *n* **(a)** turned fold at the bottom of a trouser-leg. (褲脚的)捲邊。**(b)** ***~-up (for the book)***, surprising and unexpected event: 出人意表的驚人事件;突發事件: *Fancy seeing you after all these years. What a ~-up for the book!* 沒料到過了這許多年(在這裡)見到你。眞是做夢也想不到!

turn upon, ⇨ ~ on above, (= attack). 參看上列之 ~ on。

turner /'tɜːnə(r) ; 'tɝnɚ/ *n* person who works a lathe. 車床工人;鏇匠。⇨ turn²(4).

turn·ing /'tɜːnɪŋ ; 'tɝnɪŋ/ *n* place where a road turns, esp where one road branches off from another: (路的)轉彎處;(尤指)岔路口: *Take the first ~ on / to the right.* 在第一個拐彎處向右轉。**'~-point** *n* (fig) point in place, time, development, etc which is critical: (喻)轉捩點;重大關鍵;轉機: *reach a ~-point in history / in one's life.* 到達歷史上(生命中)的重大關鍵。*There was a ~-point in the negotiations yesterday.* 昨天的商談有了轉機。

tur·nip /'tɜːnɪp ; 'tɝnɪp/ *n* [C] (plant with a) large round root used as a vegetable and as food for cattle. 蘿蔔;蕪菁。

tur·pen·tine /'tɜːpəntaɪn ; 'tɝpən,taɪn/ *n* [U] oil obtained from certain trees, used as a solvent in mixing paint and varnish, and in medicine. 粗松脂;松油;松節油(用作溶劑以調油漆,並用於藥物中)。

tur·pi·tude /'tɜːpɪtjuːd *US:* -tuːd ; 'tɝpə,tjud/ *n* [U] (formal) wickedness; depravity. (正式用語)邪惡;卑鄙。

turps /tɜːps ; tɝps/ *n* [U] (colloq abbr for) turpentine. (俗)松脂;松節油(爲 turpentine 之略)。

tur·quoise /'tɜːkwɔɪz ; 'tɝkwɔɪz/ *n* [C] (colour of a) greenish-blue precious stone. 綠松石;土耳其玉;藍綠色;青綠色。

tur·ret /'tʌrɪt ; 'tɝɪt/ *n* **1** small tower, esp at a corner of a building or defensive wall. (建築物或城牆的)小塔;角樓。**2** steel structure protecting gunners, often made so as to revolve with the gun(s): 砲塔(通常可連同砲旋轉): *a warship armed with twin-gun ~s.* 一艘裝備著雙聯砲塔砲的軍艦。

turtle¹ /'tɜːtl ; 'tɝtḷ/ *n* sea-animal with a soft body protected by a hard shell like that of a tortoise. 海龜;甲魚;海鼈。⇨ the illus at reptile. 參看 reptile 之挿圖。***turn ~***, (of a ship) turn upside down; capsize. (指船)翻覆;傾覆。**'~-neck(ed)** *adj* (of a garment, esp a sweater) having a high, circular, close-fitting collar. (指衣服,尤指毛線衫)有高而緊的圓領的;高領的。

turtle² /'tɜːtl ; 'tɝtḷ/ *n* (usu) (通常作) **'~-dove**, kinds of dove, esp a wild kind noted for its soft cooing, and its affection for its mate and young. 斑鳩;雉鳩。

turves /tɜːvz ; tɝvz/ *n pl* ⇨ turf.

tusk /tʌsk ; tʌsk/ *n* long-pointed tooth, esp one coming out from the closed mouth, as in the elephant, walrus or wild boar. (象,海象或野豬等的)長牙。⇨ the illus at large, sea. 參看 large, sea 之挿圖。

tussle /'tʌsl ; 'tʌsḷ/ *n, vi* [VP2A, 3A] ~ ***(with)***, (colloq) (have a) hard struggle or fight. (俗)劇烈的爭鬥;作劇烈的打鬥;扭打。

tus·sock /'tʌsək ; 'tʌsək/ *n* clump or hillock of growing grass. (生長中的)草叢;簇。

tut /tʌt ; tʌt/, **tut-tut** /ˌtʌt 'tʌt ; 'tʌt 'tʌt/ *int* used to express impatience, contempt, rebuke. 噓!嘖!不要講了!(用以表示不耐煩,輕蔑,責難。) □ *vt* (-tt-) [VP6A] express impatience, etc by using this word: (用此字)對…表示不耐煩等: *He tut-tutted the idea.* 他對那主意表示輕蔑。

tu·te·lage /'tjuːtɪlɪdʒ *US:* 'tuː- ; 'tutḷɪdʒ/ *n* [U] (formal) guardianship: (正式用語)保護;監護;教導: *a child in ~;* 受監護的孩子;(period of) being under ~. 受保護;受監護;受教導;保護期;監護期;教導期。

tu·te·lary /'tjuːtɪlərɪ *US:* 'tuːtələrɪ ; 'tutḷ,ɛrɪ/ *adj* (formal) serving as a guardian or protector; of a guardian: (正式用語)保護的;守護的;監護的;保護者的;守護者的;監護人的: ~ *authority.* 監護人的權威。

tu·tor /'tjuːtə(r) *US:* 'tuː- ; 'tutɚ/ *n* **1** private teacher, esp one who instructs a single pupil or a very small class, sometimes one who lives with the family of his pupil(s). 家庭教師;私人教師。**2** (GB) university teacher who guides the studies of a number of students. (英)大學的指導教師;導師。□ *vt* [VP6A, 15A, 16A] **1** teach as a ~. (以家庭教師或大學導師身份而) 個別教授; 個別指導。**2** train, exercise restraint over: 薰陶;養成;管制: ~ *one's passions;* 抑制激情; ~ *oneself to be patient.* 培養耐心。**~ial** /tjuː'tɔːrɪəl *US:* tuː- ; tu'torɪəl/ *adj* of a ~ or his duties: 家庭教師的;大學指導教師的;其職責的: *~ial classes.* (導師的)個別指導課。□ *n* period of instruction given by a college ~: 大學導師的指導期間;個別指導時間: *attend a ~ial.* 上導師指導課。

tutti-frutti /ˌtuːtɪ'fruːtɪ ; 'tutɪ'frutɪ/ *n* (portion of) ice-cream with chopped nuts and various fruits. 什錦水果冰淇淋;一份什錦水果冰淇淋。

tutu /'tuːtuː ; 'tutu/ *n* short skirt with many layers of stiffened fabric worn by women dancers in classical ballet. 突突裙(芭蕾舞女演員所穿的硬布料製的短裙)。

tux·edo /tʌk'siːdəʊ ; tʌk'sido/ *n* (*pl* ~s /-dəʊz ; -doz/) (US) dinner-jacket. (美)(男子在晚間正式場合所穿的)黑色禮服。

twaddle /'twɒdl ; 'twɑdḷ/ *n* [U] foolish talk. 愚蠢的話。□ *vi* [VP2A] talk or write ~: 說或寫愚蠢的話: *Stop twaddling!* 別再說蠢話!

twain /tweɪn ; twen/ *n* (archaic) two. (古)兩;二。

twang /twæŋ ; twæŋ/ *n* **1** sound of a tight string or wire being pulled and released: 繃緊的弦或金屬絲被拉扯及放開時發出的聲音;弦聲: *the ~ of a guitar.* 吉他的弦聲。**2** harsh, nasal tone of voice: 刺耳的鼻音或鼻聲: *speak with a ~.* 說話帶鼻音。□ *vt, vi* [VP6A, 2A] (cause to) make this kind of sound: (使)發弦聲;(使)發刺耳鼻音: *The bow ~ed and the arrow whistled through the air.* 弓噹的一聲,箭嘘嘘地破空而過。*He was ~ing a banjo.* 他在彈班究琴。

'twas /twɒz ; twɑz; *weak form:* twəz ; twəz/ (archaic or poet) (古或詩) = it was.

tweak /twiːk ; twik/ *vt* [VP6A] pinch and twist: 擰;扭: *Wouldn't you like to ~ that rude fellow's nose / ears?* 你不想擰那個無禮的傢伙的鼻子(耳朵)嗎? □ *n* act of ~ing. 扭;擰。

twee /twiː ; twi/ *adj* affectedly or inappropriately dainty or quaint. 漂亮但矯飾的;冶艷的。

tweed /twiːd ; twid/ *n* **1** [U] (often attrib) thick, soft, woollen cloth, usu woven of mixed colours:

(常作形容用法) 花呢 (厚而軟的毛呢，通常由雜色織成)：*a ~ hat/coat.* 花呢帽(上衣)。 **2** (*pl*) (suit of) clothes made of ~: (複) (一套)花呢製的衣服：*dressed in Scottish ~s.* 穿蘇格蘭花呢裝。

'tween /twi:n ; twin/ *adv, prep* (archaic or poet) between, (古或詩)在…之間；當中，esp (尤用於) **'~-decks,** between decks. 在二甲板之間。

tweet /twi:t ; twit/ *n, vi* (of a bird) chirp. (指鳥)啾啾聲；啁啾而鳴。

tweeter /'twi:tə(r) ; 'twitɚ/ *n* loudspeaker for reproducing high notes. 高頻揚聲器(用以播出高聲調者)。⇨ woofer.

tweez·ers /'twi:zəz ; 'twizɚz/ *n pl* ***(pair of) ~,*** tiny pair of tongs for picking up or pulling out very small things, eg hairs from the eyebrows. 鑷子；小鉗子(用以拾取或拔出細小物者)。

twelfth /twelfθ ; twɛlfθ/ *adj, n* next after the 11th; one of twelve equal parts. 第十二；第十二的；十二分之一；十二分之一的。~ **man,** (in cricket) reserve player. (板球)候補隊員。**'T~-night,** eve of the festival of Epiphany, celebrated with festivities. 主顯節前夕(以祝典慶祝)。

twelve /twelv ; twɛlv/ *adj, n* the number 12. 十二；十二的。⇨ App 4. 參看附錄四。**the T~,** the ~ apostles of Jesus. 耶穌的十二使徒。**'~-month** *n* (archaic) year. (古)年；十二個月。

twenty /'twentɪ ; 'twɛntɪ/ *adj, n* the number 20. 二十；二十的。⇨ App 4. 參看附錄四。**the twenties,** 20-29. 二十至二十九；二十年代。**twen·ti·eth** /'twentɪəθ ; 'twɛntɪɪθ/ *adj, n* next after the 19th; one of 20 equal parts. 第二十；第二十的；二十分之一；二十分之一的。

'twere /twɜ:(r) ; twɝ/ (archaic or poet) (古或詩) = it were (= *it would be*).

twerp /twɜ:p ; twɝp/ *n* (sl) contemptible or insignificant person. (俚)可鄙的人；無足輕重的人。

twice /twaɪs ; twaɪs/ *adv* two times: 兩倍；兩次：~ *as much/as many.* 兩倍之多。*I've been there once or ~.* 我去過那兒一兩回。*He's ~ the man he was,* ~ as well, strong, confident, capable, etc. 他現在比以前强兩倍。***think '~ about doing sth,*** hesitate, think carefully, before deciding to do it. 三思而行；仔細考慮(做)某事。***a ,~-told 'tale,*** a well-known one. 衆所皆知的故事。

twiddle /'twɪdl ; 'twɪdḷ/ *vt, vi* **1** [VP6A] twist or turn idly or aimlessly: 旋弄；捻弄：~ *one's thumbs.* 旋弄大拇指；閒着没事做。**2** [VP3A] ***~ with sth,*** play idly: 玩弄；撫弄：~ *with one's hair/a ring on one's finger.* 撫弄頭髮(手指上的戒指)。□ *n* slight twist or turn. 旋弄；捻弄；小捲；小彎。**twid·dly** /'twɪdlɪ ; 'twɪdḷɪ/ *adj* having a ~. 有小捲或小彎的。

twig[1] /twɪg ; twɪg/ *n* [C] small shoot on or at the end of a branch (bush, plant). 小枝；嫩枝。⇨ the illus at tree. 參看 tree 之挿圖。 **~gy** *adj* having many ~s: 多小枝或嫩枝的：*support plants with ~gy sticks.* 用多小枝的柴枝支撐植物。

twig[2] /twɪg ; twɪg/ *vt, vi* (-gg-) [VP6A, 2A] (GB colloq) observe; notice; understand: (英俗)觀察到；注意到；瞭解；懂：*I soon ~ged what he was up to,* saw the trick he was trying to play. 我很快就看穿了他想要什麼把戲。

twi·light /'twaɪlaɪt ; 'twaɪ,laɪt/ *n* [U] **1** faint half-light before sunrise or after sunset: (日出前或日落後的)微明；曙光；薄暮：*go for a walk in the ~.* 在黄昏散步。 **2** (fig) remote period about which little is known: (喩)遙遠而鮮爲人所知的時代：*in the ~ of history.* 在遠古時代。**twi·lit** /'twaɪlɪt ; 'twaɪ,lɪt/ *adj* dimly lit. 微明的；昏暗的。

twill /twɪl ; twɪl/ *n* [U] strong cotton cloth woven so that fine diagonal lines or ribs appear on the surface. 斜紋布。**~ed** *adj* (of cloth) woven in this way. (指布)斜紋的。

'twill /twɪl ; twɪl/ (archaic or poet) (古或詩) = it will.

twin /twɪn ; twɪn/ *n* **1** either of two children born together of the same mother: 双胞胎之一：*one of the ~s;* 双胞胎中的一個；(attrib) (形容用法) *~ brothers.* 孿生兄弟。**2** (usu attrib) completely like, closely associated with, another: (通常作形容用法)完全相似的；關係密切的：*a ship with ~ propellers,* two identical propellers; 双螺旋槳輪船；*~ beds,* two identical single beds; 兩張完全一樣的單人床；*a '~-set,* woman's jumper and long sleeved cardigan of the same colour and style. (顏色與式樣相同、配在一起穿的)女用套頭毛衣及長袖毛線外套。□ *vt* [VP6A, 14] ***~ (with),*** join closely together; couple; pair. 密切結合；匹配；成對。⇨ twinned.

twine /twaɪn ; twaɪn/ *n* [U] thin strings made by twisting two or more yarns together. 細繩；合股線。□ *vt, vi* [VP15A, B, 2A, C] twist; wind: 編結；纏繞；搓捻：~ *flowers into a garland;* 把花編成花環；*vines that ~ round a tree.* 纏繞樹的藤枝。*She ~d her arms round my neck.* 她用双臂圍繞着我的脖子。

twinge /twɪndʒ ; twɪndʒ/ *n* [C] sudden, sharp pain: 劇痛；刺痛：*a ~ of toothache/rheumatism/conscience.* 一陣牙痛(風濕痛，良心的譴責)。

twinkle /'twɪŋkl ; 'twɪŋkḷ/ *vi* [2A, C] **1** shine with a light that gleams unsteadily: 閃爍；閃耀：*stars that ~ in the sky.* 天上閃爍的星辰。 **2** (of eyes) sparkle; (of eyelids, feet in dancing, etc) move rapidly up and down, to and fro: (指眼睛)閃亮；(指眼瞼，跳舞時之双足等) 迅速移動；閃動；眨眼：*Her eyes ~d with amusement/mischief.* 她的眼睛閃耀著歡愉(淘氣)的神情。□ *n* **1** [U] twinkling light: 閃爍；閃光：*the ~ of the stars/of a distant light.* 星辰(遠處燈火)的閃光。 **2** sparkle; rapid twitching: 閃亮；閃動；抽動；急動：*There was a mischievous ~ in her eyes.* 她眼睛裡閃耀著淘氣的眼神。**twink·ling** /'twɪŋklɪŋ ; 'twɪŋklɪŋ/ *n* (*sing* only) (僅用單數) ***in the twinkling of an eye,*** in an instant. 轉瞬間；頃刻。

twinned /twɪnd ; twɪnd/ *attrib adj* ***~ (with),*** paired (with): 結成一對的：*a town in England ~ with a town in France,* (for cultural, educational, etc exchanges). 英國某城市與法國某城市結爲姊妹市(爲文化、教育等交流)。

twirl /twɜ:l ; twɝl/ *vt, vi* [VP6A,15B,16A,2A,C] **1** (cause to) turn round and round quickly: (使)迅速旋轉；快速地轉動：*She ~ed the mop to get the water out of it.* 她迅速地轉動拖把，把它擰乾。*He sat ~ing his thumbs.* 他坐着轉動他的拇指。 **2** curl: 扭轉；捲曲：*He ~ed his moustache (up).* 他捻起他的鬍子。□ *n* rapid circular motion. 快速的旋轉；扭曲。

twist /twɪst ; twɪst/ *vt, vi* **1** [VP6A, 15A, B] wind or turn (a number of threads, strands, etc) one around the other: 搓；捻；絞(若干條線，若干股等)：~ *pieces of straw into a rope.* 把稻草搓成繩子。*She ~ed the girl's hair round her fingers to make it curl.* 她把那女孩的頭髮捲在她手指上使之捲曲。**2** [VP 6A] make (a rope, a garland, etc) by doing this. 編；織(繩索，花環等)。 **3** [VP6A, 15A, B, 16A] turn, esp by the use of force; turn the two ends of (sth) in opposite directions; turn one end of (sth): 轉動(尤指用力地)；以相反的方向轉動(某物)的兩端；轉動(某物)的一端；擰；扭：~ (more usu 較常用 *wring*) *a wet cloth,* to squeeze out the water; 擰乾一塊濕布；~ *the cap off a fountain-pen/a tube of toothpaste.* 轉開鋼筆帽(牙膏蓋)。*If you use too much force, you'll ~ the key,* bend it out of shape. 如果你太用力，你會把鑰匙扭彎。*His features were ~ed* (= distorted) *with pain.* 他的面容因痛苦而扭曲。*He fell and ~ed his ankle.* 他摔下來，扭傷了足踝。*She ~ed her head round as she reversed the car into the garage.* 她轉頭向後把車倒進車房裡。~ ***sth off,*** break off by ~ing: 擰斷；扭斷：~ *off the end of a piece of wire.* 擰斷一根鐵絲的末端。~ ***sb's arm,*** **(a)** force it round to cause pain. 扭某人的臂使之痛苦。**(b)** (fig, colloq) put (friendly or unfriendly) pressure on him to do sth. (喩，俗)對某人威迫利誘；對某人施加壓力使做某事。

~ sb round one's little finger, (colloq) get him to do what one wants him to do. (俗)任意指使某人;對某人頤指氣使。 **4** [VP6A, 15A] force (sb's words) out of their true meaning: 曲解(某人的話): *The police tried to ~ his words into a confession of guilt.* 警察試圖把他的話曲解爲招供。 **5** [VP 6A, 15A, 2A, C] give a spiral form to (a rod, column, etc); receive, have, move or grow in, a spiral form: 使(桿,柱等)成螺旋形;作螺旋形;呈螺旋狀移動或生長: *~ed columns,* as in architecture. (建築物等的)螺旋形柱;捲柱。 **6** [VP2A, C] turn and curve in different directions; change position or direction: 盤旋;曲折;迂迴: *The road ~s and turns up the side of the mountain.* 這條路沿著山坡彎來彎去。 *The thief ~ed out of the policeman's grip and ran off.* 那賊掙脫警察的手逃跑了。*The injured man ~ed about in pain.* 受傷者痛苦地掙扎着。 **7** [VP 6A, 2A] (of a ball, esp in billiards) (cause to) take a curved path while spinning. (指球,尤指撞球)(使)旋轉着作曲線前進。 **8** [VP2A] dance the ~, ⇨ 6 below. 跳扭扭舞(參看下列第 6 義)。□ *n* **1** ~ing or being ~ed: 搓;捻;絞;編;織;擰;扭;彎曲;曲折: *The bully gave the little boy's arm a ~.* 那惡漢把小男孩的手臂扭了一下。 *Give the rope a few more ~s.* 把那繩子再搓幾下。 *There are numerous ~s in the road over the pass.* 那條路越過隘口處有無數彎道。 **2** sth made by ~ing: 搓捻而成之物;扭捲而成之物: *a rope full of ~s* (= kinks, coils); 一根滿是扭結的繩子; *a ~ of paper,* a paper packet with screwed-up ends. 將末端擰緊而成的紙袋。 **3** [C, U] thread, yarn, rope, etc made by ~ing together two or more strands, esp certain kinds of silk thread and cotton yarn; coarse tobacco made by ~ing dried leaves into a roll. 線;索;繩;(尤指)絲線;棉紗;烟草捲。**4** motion given to a ball to make it take a curved path. (使球成曲線前進的)擰轉;曲球。 **5** peculiar tendency of mind or character: (心境或性格的)失常;偏差;癖: *He has a criminal ~ in him.* 他有犯罪癖。 **6 the ~,** dance (popular in the 1960's) in which there is ~ing of the arms and hips. 扭扭舞(盛行於 1960 年代,跳時扭動臂部及臀部)。**~er** *n* **1** (colloq) dishonest person. (俗)不誠實的人;說謊話的人。 **2** difficult task, problem, etc: 困難的事情、問題等: *a ˈtongue-~er,* word or phrase difficult to pronounce. 繞口令。 **~y** *adj* (-ier, -iest) **1** having many ~s: 扭曲的;捲纏的;多彎曲的: *a ~y road.* 彎彎曲曲的道路。**2** not straightforward: 不正直的;歪曲事實的: *a ~y politician.* 不正直的政客。

twit[1] /twɪt; twɪt/ *vt* (-tt-) [VP6A, 14] tease sb (usu in jest) (with or about sth): 嘲笑;挖苦;揶揄(某人): *~ a man about the state he was in after a drinking bout.* 嘲笑某人狂飲後的狼狽相。

twit[2] /twɪt; twɪt/ *n* (sl) contemptible fool; idiot. (俚)傻子;白癡。

twitch /twɪtʃ; twɪtʃ/ *n* [C] **1** sudden, quick, usu uncontrollable movement of a muscle; tic. 抽搐;抽動;痙攣。 **2** sudden quick pull: 急拉;急扯: *I felt a ~ at my sleeve.* 我覺得有人拉了一下我的袖子。□ *vi, vt* **1** [VP2A, C, 6A] (cause to) move in a ~(1): (使)抽搐;抽動;痙攣: *The dog's nose ~ed as it passed the butcher's shop.* 那狗經過肉店時,鼻子在抽動。*His face ~ed with terror.* 他的面孔因恐懼而抽動。*The horse ~ed its ears.* 那馬抽動耳朵。 **2** [VP15A, B] jerk; give a ~(2) to: 急拉;急扯: *The wind ~ed the paper out of my hand.* 風吹走了我手中的紙。

twit·ter /ˈtwɪtə(r); ˈtwɪtɚ/ *vi* [VP2A, C] (of birds) chirp; make a succession of soft short sounds; (of persons) talk rapidly through excitement, nervousness, etc. (指鳥)吱吱地叫;囀;(指人)嘁嘁喳喳地說。□ *n* **1** chirping: 鳥囀: *the ~ of sparrows.* 麻雀的叫聲。 **2** (of persons) (colloq, esp in) (指人)(俗,尤用於) ***(all) of a ~,*** in an excited state. 興奮地;緊張地。

ˈtwixt /twɪkst; twɪkst/ *prep* (archaic or poet) (古或詩) = betwixt.

two /tuː; tu/ *n, adj* **1** the number 2. 二;兩個。⇨ App 4. 參看附錄四。***break/cut sth in two,*** into two parts. 分裂(切割)某物爲二。***put two and two together,*** infer sth from what one sees, hears, learns, etc. 根據所見、所聞、所知等推斷某事物。 ***by twos and threes,*** two or three at a time. 三三兩兩地;(一次)兩個三個地。***ˌTwo can play (at) ˈthat game,*** used as a threat of retaliation. 那把戲可是彼此都可玩的啊(此語係在一人吃虧後的威脅話,意謂你這樣做,我也可以照樣報復)。 **2** (compounds) (複合字) **ˌtwo-ˈedged** *adj* (of a sword) having a cutting edge on each side; (fig, of an argument, etc) having two possible (and contrary) meanings. (指刀劍)雙鋒的;有兩刃的;(喻,指論據等)有正反兩意義的。 **ˌtwo-ˈfaced** *adj* (fig) insincere. (喻)兩面的;虛僞的。**ˈtwo·fold** *adj, adv* double, doubly. 二倍;二重。 **ˌtwo-ˈhanded** *adj* (of a sword) needing two hands to use it; (of a saw, etc) to be used by two persons, one at each end. (指刀劍)需要雙手運用的;(指鋸等)需要兩人使用的。 **ˈtwo·pence** /ˈtʌpəns *US:* ˈtuːpens; ˈtʌpəns/ *n* sum of two pence. 兩辨士金額。**ˈtwo·penny** /ˈtʌpənɪ *US:* ˈtuː-penɪ; ˈtuˌpɛnɪ/ *adj* costing two pence. 值兩辨士的。 **ˌtwo·penny ˈpiece,** GB coin worth two pence. (英)兩辨士硬幣。**ˌtwo·penny-ˈhalf·penny** /ˌtʌpnɪ ˈheɪpnɪ *US:* ˌtuːpenɪ ˈhæfpenɪ; ˈtʌpənɪˈhe-pənɪ/ *adj* (colloq) almost worthless; petty. (俗)幾乎無價值的;微不足道的。**ˈtwo-a-penny** *adj* easy to obtain; cheap; almost worthless. 易得到的;便宜的;幾乎無價值的。**ˌtwo-ˈpiece** *n* set of garments of similar or matching material, eg skirt and jacket, trousers and jacket; bra and briefs (for swimming); 兩件式的成套衣服(質料等相似或相配的兩件衣服,如裙子及上衣,褲子及上裝);(女子的)兩件式泳裝(奶罩及短褲); (attrib) (形容用法) *a two-piece suit.* 二件式套裝。**ˈtwo-ply** *adj* of two strands or thicknesses: 雙股的;兩層(厚)的: *two-ply wool/wood.* 雙股毛線(雙層木料)。 **ˌtwo-ˈseater** *n* car, aircraft, etc with seats for two persons. 雙座汽車、飛機等。**ˈtwo-timing** *adj* (sl) deceitful; engaged in double-crossing. (俚)欺騙的;不忠實的;從事欺騙勾當的。**ˌtwo-ˈway** *attrib adj* **(a)** (of a switch) allowing current to be switched on or off from either of two points. (指開關)雙向的;兩路的。**(b)** (of a road or street) in which traffic may move in both directions. (指路或街)雙向的;對向交通的。Cf 參較 *one-way street.* **(c)** (of radio equipment, etc) for both sending and receiving. (指無線電裝備等)收發兩用的。

ˈtwould /twʊd; twʊd/ (archaic or poet) (古或詩) = it would.

ty·coon /taɪˈkuːn; taɪˈkun/ *n* (colloq) wealthy and powerful business man or industrialist: (俗)大實業家;大亨: *ˈoil ~s.* 石油界的大亨們。

ty·ing /ˈtaɪɪŋ; ˈtaɪɪŋ/ *pres p* of tie².

tyke, tike /taɪk; taɪk/ *n* cur; (as a term of abuse) low fellow. 劣犬;野狗;(罵人話)壞蛋;下三濫;小子。

tym·pa·num /ˈtɪmpənəm; ˈtɪmpənəm/ *n* (*pl* ~s or -na /-nə; -nə/) (anat) (解剖) **1** eardrum. 耳鼓;鼓膜。 **2** middle ear. 中耳;鼓室。⇨ middle; ⇨ the illus at ear. 參看 ear 之挿圖。

type[1] /taɪp; taɪp/ *n* **1** [C] person, thing, event, etc considered as an example of a class or group: 典型;模範;表率(被視爲可代表一類或一羣的人、物、事等): *Abraham Lincoln was a fine ~ of the American patriot.* 林肯是美國愛國者的良好典型。 **2** [C] class or group considered to have common characteristics: 型;型式;樣式;類型: *men of this ~.* 這一類型的人們。*Her beauty is of the Italian ~.* 她的美是義大利型的。*They claim to make good Burgundy ~ wine/wine of the Burgundy ~ in Australia.* 他們聲言在澳洲釀造出良好的勃艮地紅葡萄酒。***true to ~,*** representative of that ~: 代表其類型的: *A cowardly bulldog is not true to ~.* 一隻

膽小的獵牛犬不足以代表其類型。 **3** [U] letters, etc cast in blocks of (usu) metal, for use in printing; any fount of these; [C] one of these blocks: 印刷用的活字;一套字體;一個活字或鉛字: *The printers are short of ~/certain ~s.* 印刷廠缺乏鉛字(某些鉛字)。*Wooden ~ is/wooden ~s are sometimes used for printing posters.* 木刻的活字有時用來印刷海報。*The material is now in ~*, has been set ready for printing. 該項資料現正付印中。*The examples in this dictionary are in italic ~.* 本字典中的例句用斜體字排印。 **4** (compounds) (複合字) **'~·face** *n* style of type(3). 鉛字之字體。⇨ face¹(3). **'~·script** *n* typewritten copy (prepared for printing, etc). 用打字機打出的文稿或原稿;打字稿。**'~·setter** *n* worker or machine that sets ~ for printing. 排字工人;排字機。**'~·writer** *n* machine with which one prints letters on paper, using the fingers on a keyboard. 打字機。**'~·written** *adj* written using a ~writer: 用打字機打出的: *a ~-written message.* 用打字機打出的訊息。

type² /taɪp ; taɪp/ *vt, vi* **1** [VP6A, 2A] use a typewriter; write with a typewriter: 打字;用打字機打出: *~ a letter.* (用打字機)打信。*She ~s well.* 她打字打得很好。 **2** [VP6A] determine the type(2) of sth: 確定或決定某物的型式或種類: *~ a virus;* 確定一種病毒的類型; *~ a person's blood.* 確定一個人的血型。**typ·ist** /'taɪpɪst ; 'taɪpɪst/ *n* person who ~s. 打字員。

type·cast /'taɪpkɑːst *US:* -kæst ; 'taɪp,kæst/ *vt* (*pt, pp* unchanged) (過去式及過去分詞不變) [VP6A] (theatre) cast (a person) for a part which he/she has the reputation of doing well or which seems to fit his/her own personality. (戲劇)分派(某人)角色(使之擔任最拿手或是最適合其個性的角色)。

ty·phoid /'taɪfɔɪd ; 'taɪfɔɪd/ *n* [U] ~ **(fever)**, infectious disease which attacks the intestines, caused by bacteria taken into the body with food or drink. 傷寒;腸熱病。

ty·phoon /taɪ'fuːn ; taɪ'fun/ *n* [C] violent hurricane of the kind that occurs in the western Pacific. 颱風(西太平洋發生的颶風)。

ty·phus /'taɪfəs ; 'taɪfəs/ *n* [U] infectious disease marked by fever, great weakness and the appearance of purple spots on the body. 斑疹傷寒。

typi·cal /'tɪpɪkl ; 'tɪpɪkḷ/ *adj* ~ **(of)**, serving as a type; representative or characteristic. 代表性的;典型的;象徵性的。**~ly** /-klɪ ; -klɪ/ *adv*

typ·ify /'tɪpɪfaɪ ; 'tɪpə,faɪ/ *vt* (*pt, pp* -fied) [VP6A] be a symbol of; be representative of. 作爲…的象徵;代表。

typ·ist /'taɪpɪst ; 'taɪpɪst/ *n* ⇨ type².

ty·pogra·phy /taɪ'pɒgrəfɪ ; taɪ'pɑgrəfɪ/ *n* [U] art or style of printing. 印刷術;印刷式樣。**ty·pogra·pher** /taɪ'pɒgrəfə(r) ; taɪ'pɑgrəfɚ/ *n* person skilled in ~. 印刷工人;排字工人。**ty·po·graphic** /,taɪpə'græfɪk ; ,taɪpə'græfɪk/ *adj* **ty·po·graphi·cally** /-klɪ ; -klɪ/ *adv*

ty·ran·ni·cal /tɪ'rænɪkl ; tɪ'rænɪkḷ/ *adj* of or like a tyrant; acting like a tyrant; obtaining obedience by force or threats. 暴君的;似暴君的;暴虐的;專橫的;殘暴統治的。

tyr·an·nize /'tɪrənaɪz ; 'tɪrə,naɪz/ *vi, vt* [VP6A, 3A] ~ **(over)**, rule cruelly and unjustly: 暴虐統治;虐待;壓制: *~ over the weak.* 欺壓弱小。*He ~s his family.* 他虐待其家人。

tyr·anny /'tɪrənɪ ; 'tɪrənɪ/ *n* (*pl* -nies) **1** [U] cruel or unjust use of power; [C] instance of this; tyrannical act. 殘暴;專橫;暴虐;其實例;暴行。 **2** [C, U] (instance of, country with, the) kind of government existing when a ruler has complete power, esp when this power has been obtained by force and is used unjustly: 暴政;其實例;施行暴政的國家: *live under a ~.* 在暴政下生活。

tyr·an·ous /'tɪrənəs ; 'tɪrənəs/ *adj* = tyrannical.

ty·rant /'taɪərənt ; 'taɪrənt/ *n* cruel or unjust ruler, esp one who has obtained complete power by force. 暴君;暴虐統治者(尤指藉武力獲得全部權力者)。

tyre (US = tire) /'taɪə(r) ; taɪr/ *n* band of solid or inflated rubber on the rim of a wheel, esp (*pneumatic ~*) the kind on bicycle and motor-car wheels. 輪箍;輪胎;車胎;(尤指脚踏車及汽車輪上的)氣胎。⇨ the illus at bicycle, motor. 參看 bicycle, motor 之插圖。

tyro /'taɪərəʊ ; 'taɪro/ *n* = tiro.

tzar /zɑː(r) ; tsɑr/, **tza·rina** /zɑː'riːnə ; tsɑ'rinə/ *nn* = czar, czarina.

Uu

U, u /juː ; ju/ the 21st letter of the English alphabet. 英文字母的第二十一個字母。**'U-boat** *n* German submarine. 德國潛水艇。**'U-turn,** one of 180° (by a car, etc): (汽車等) 一百八十度的轉彎; 向後轉; 迴轉: *No U-turns!* (as a traffic notice in towns, on motorways). 禁止迴轉(用於城市中或高速公路上的交通牌示)。

ubi·qui·tous /juː'bɪkwɪtəs ; ju'bɪkwətəs/ *adj* (formal) present everywhere or in several places at the same time. (正式用語)無所不在的;遍在的;在數處同時出現的。**ubi·quity** /juː'bɪkwətɪ ; ju'bɪkwətɪ/ *n* [U] quality of being ~. 到處存在;遍在。

ud·der /'ʌdə(r) ; 'ʌdɚ/ *n* bag of a cow, goat or other animal, from which milk comes, esp a large one with two or more teats. 牛、羊或其他動物的乳房(尤指乳頭不祗一個者)。⇨ the illus at domestic. 參看 domestic 之插圖。

ugh /*This usu suggests a sound like* ɜː *made with the lips either spread or rounded very strongly and one's facial expression showing disgust* 此字通常含示一種類似 ɜː ; ɝ 的聲音,發此音時,或撇着嘴唇,或用力撮起嘴唇發出,同時面部現出厭惡的表情/ *int* used to indicate disgust. (用以表示厭惡)啊!呃!

ugly /'ʌglɪ ; 'ʌglɪ/ *adj* (-ier, -iest) **1** unpleasant to look at; hideous: 難看的;醜陋的: *~ children/furniture/surroundings.* 難看的兒童(家具,環境)。 **2** threatening; unpleasant: 險惡的; 陰沉的; 不祥的;令人厭惡的: *The sky looks ~*, suggests bad weather. 天色陰沉。*The news in today's newspapers is ~*, suggests unpleasant possibilities, eg of war. 今天報上的消息不妙(意味將有不祥事件發生,如戰爭)。 **~ customer,** (colloq) dangerous person; person difficult to deal with. (俗)危險人物;很難對付的人。**ug·lify** /'ʌglɪfaɪ ; 'ʌglɪ,faɪ/ *vt* (*pt, pp* -fied) make ~. 使變得醜陋;弄得難看。**ug·li·ness** *n*

ukase /juː'keɪs ; 'jukes/ *n* (hist) edict of the Czarist Russian government; arbitrary order. (史)帝俄沙皇政府的敕令;諭旨;專橫的命令。

uku·lele /,juːkə'leɪlɪ ; ,jukə'lelɪ/ *n* Hawaiian four-stringed guitar. 烏克賴里琴(一種類似吉他的夏威夷四絃琴)。

ul·cer /'ʌlsə(r) ; 'ʌlsɚ/ *n* open sore forming poisonous matter (on the outside or inside surface of the body); (fig) corrupting influence or condition. (身體內部或外部表面形成的) 潰瘍;(喻) 令人腐化的影響或情況。**~·ous** /-əs ; -əs/ *adj* **~·ate** /-eɪt ; -et/ *vt, vi* [VP6A, 2A] form, convert or be converted into, an ~. 生潰瘍;形成潰瘍;使生潰瘍;被弄成潰爛。**~·ation** /,ʌlsə'reɪʃn ; ,ʌlsə'reʃən/ *n*

ulna /'ʌlnə ; 'ʌlnə/ *n* (*pl* ~e /-niː ; -ni/) (anat) inner of the two bones of the forearm. (解剖)(前臂的)尺骨。⇨ the illus at skeleton. 參看 skeleton

之插圖。

ul·ster /ˈʌlstə(r)；ˈʌlstɚ/ *n* long, loose, belted overcoat. 阿斯特大衣（一種長而寬鬆並繫帶的大衣）。

ul·terior /ʌlˈtɪərɪə(r)；ʌlˈtɪrɪɚ/ *adj* situated beyond; beyond what is first seen or said. 在那一邊的；超出最初所見或所說之範圍的；未揭露的；隱秘的。～ **motive,** motive other than what is expressed or admitted. 隱秘或未顯露的動機。

ul·ti·mate /ˈʌltɪmət；ˈʌltəmɪt/ *adj* last, furthest, basic: 最後的；最遠的；終極的；根本的；主要的：～ *principles／truths;* 基本原理（眞理）；*the ～ cause,* beyond which no other cause is known or can be found; 終極原因；第一因；第一原理；*the ～ deterrent* (used of nuclear weapons). 終極或最後的嚇阻力量（用指核子武器）。～**·ly** *adv* finally; in the end. 最後；終極地。

ul·ti·ma·tum /ˌʌltɪˈmeɪtəm；ˌʌltəˈmetəm/ *n* (*pl* ～s, -ta /-tə；-tə/) [C] final statement of conditions to be accepted without discussion, eg one sent to a foreign government and threatening war if the conditions are not accepted. 最後通牒；哀的美敦書。

ul·timo /ˈʌltɪməʊ；ˈʌltəˌmo/ *adj* (abbr 略作 **ult**) (formerly used in business letters) of the month before the current month: （往昔用於商業信函中）上月份的：*Thank you for your letter of the 10th ult.* 謝謝你上月十日的來函。

ultra- /ˈʌltrə；ˈʌltrə/ *pref* beyond. 超過；在…那邊。⇨ App 3. 參看附錄三。

ultra·mar·ine /ˌʌltrəməˈriːn；ˌʌltrəməˈrin/ *adj, n* brilliant pure blue (colour). 紺青的；羣青的；紺青色；羣青色。

ultra·mon·tane /ˌʌltrəmɒnˈteɪn；ˌʌltrəˈmɑnten/ *adj* (RC Church) favouring the absolute authority of the Pope in matters of faith and discipline. （天主教）（在信仰及教規方面）贊成教宗有絕對權力的。

ultra·sonic /ˌʌltrəˈsɒnɪk；ˌʌltrəˈsɑnɪk/ *adj* relating to sound waves beyond the range of normal human audibility. （指聲波）超出人類正常聽力範圍的；超聲的。

ultra·vio·let /ˌʌltrəˈvaɪələt；ˌʌltrəˈvaɪəlɪt/ *adj* of the invisible part of the spectrum beyond the violet. 光譜之紫色外方看不見之部分的；紫外的；紫外線的。～ **rays,** invisible rays (in sunlight, light from mercury-vapour lamps, etc) which have an effect upon the skin, curing certain skin diseases, forming vitamins, etc. 紫外線。

ultra vires /ˌʌltrə ˈvaɪəriːz；ˌʌltrəˈvaɪriz/ *adj, adv* (Lat) beyond the powers or authority granted by law. （拉）超過法律所賦予之權力的（地）；逾越權限的（地）；越權的（地）。

ulu·late /ˈjuːljʊleɪt *US:* ˈʌl-；ˈjuljəˌlet/ *vi* [VP2A] howl; wail loudly. 嗥；吠；大聲哭。**ulu·la·tion** /ˌjuːljʊˈleɪʃn *US:* ˌʌl-；ˌjuljəˈleʃən/ *n*

um·ber /ˈʌmbə(r)；ˈʌmbɚ/ *adj, n* yellowish-green (colouring substance). 赭色的；赭土（顏料）。**burnt** ～, reddish-brown. 煆赭土（顏料）。

um·bili·cal /ʌmˈbɪlɪkl；ʌmˈbɪlɪkḷ/ *adj* ～ **cord,** cord connecting a foetus at the navel with the placenta. （連結胎兒與胎盤的）臍帶。⇨ the illus at reproduce. 參看 reproduce 之插圖。

um·brage /ˈʌmbrɪdʒ；ˈʌmbrɪdʒ/ *n* [U] ***give／take ～ (at sth),*** cause the feeling／feel that one has been treated unfairly or without proper respect. 感覺未受到公正待遇或未受尊重；憤恚；埋怨；不快。

um·brella /ʌmˈbrelə；ʌmˈbrɛlə/ *n* **1** folding frame (with a stick and handle), covered with cotton, silk, etc used to shelter the person holding it from rain; (in some countries) such a device, used as a symbol of rank. 傘；雨傘；（某些國家用以代表階級的）傘形物。⇨ parasol; ⇨ *sunshade* at sun(4). **2** (fig) screen of fighter aircraft, eg flying over bombers to protect them against enemy aircraft. （喻）由戰鬥機構成的掩護幕；傘幕。**3** protection; patronage: 庇護；保護：*under the ～ of the UNO.* 在聯合國組織的庇護下。

um·laut /ˈʊmlaʊt；ˈʊmlaʊt/ *n* (in Germanic languages) vowel change shown by two dots over the vowel (as in the German plurals *Männer,* of *Mann,* and *Füsse,* of *Fuss*). （日耳曼語系中的）母音變化（在母音上加兩點表示之，如德語 Mann 的複數形 Männer, Fuss 的複數形 Füsse）。

um·pire /ˈʌmpaɪə(r)；ˈʌmpaɪr/ *n* person chosen to act as a judge in a dispute, to see that the rules are obeyed in cricket, baseball, tennis, netball and other games. 仲裁人；公斷人；（板球、棒球、網球、落網球及他種比賽的）裁判員。Cf 參較 *referee* for football and boxing. 足球及拳擊之裁判員稱作 referee。□ *vt, vi* [VP6A, 2A] act as ～: 仲裁；裁判；擔任仲裁者或裁判員：～ *a cricket match.* 擔任板球賽裁判。

ump·teen /ˈʌmptiːn；ˈʌmpˈtin/ *adj* (sl) many. （俚）許多的。～**th** /ˈʌmptiːnθ；ˈʌmpˈtinθ/ *adj*: *for the ～th time,* for I don't know how many times. 無數次。

'un /ən；ən/ *pron* (colloq) one: （俗）（一個）人或東西：*He's a good 'un,* a good fellow. 他是一個好人。*That's a good 'un,* a good specimen, joke, etc. 那是一個好的樣品、有趣的笑話等。

un- /ʌn；ʌn/ *pref* (⇨ App 3; 參看附錄三；specimens only here 此處所舉者僅爲範例). **1** (before *adjj* and *advv*) not: （用於形容詞和副詞前）不；非；未：*uncertain(ly);* 不確定的（地）；*unwilling(ly).* 不願意的（地）。**2** (before *vv*) do the opposite of, reverse the action of, what is indicated by the *v*: （用於動詞前）做出與該動詞所表示之動作相反的行爲：*unscrew;* 扭鬆螺絲；*unroll;* 展開；*undress;* 脫去衣服；*unlock.* 開鎖。**3** (before *nn*) indicating absence of: （用於名詞前）無；不：*uncertainty;* 不確定；*unwillingness.* 不願意。

un·abashed /ˌʌnəˈbæʃt；ˌʌnəˈbæʃt/ *adj* not abashed, embarrassed or awed. 不臉紅的；不難爲情的；滿不在乎的。

un·abated /ˌʌnəˈbeɪtɪd；ˌʌnəˈbetɪd/ *adj* (of a storm, etc) (continuing) as strong, violent, etc as before. （指風暴等）未減弱的；猛烈如前的。

un·able /ʌnˈeɪbl；ʌnˈebḷ/ *adj* (*pred* only) （僅作敘述用法）～ ***to do sth,*** not able to do it. 不能做某事。

un·accom·pan·ied /ˌʌnəˈkʌmpənɪd；ˌʌnəˈkʌmpənɪd/ *adj* **1** without a companion: 無伴的：～ *luggage,* sent separately, the owner not travelling with it. 無人伴行而單獨交運的行李。**2** (music) performed without an accompaniment. （音樂）無伴奏的。

un·ac·count·able /ˌʌnəˈkaʊntəbl；ˌʌnəˈkaʊntəbḷ/ *adj* in a way that cannot be accounted for or explained. 不能說明的；無法解釋的。**un·ac·count·ably** /-əblɪ；-əblɪ/ *adv*

un·ac·cus·tomed /ˌʌnəˈkʌstəmd；ˌʌnəˈkʌstəmd/ *adj* **1** ～ **to,** not accustomed to: 不習慣的；不適應的：～ *as I am to speaking in public.* 像我這樣不慣於作公開演說的。**2** not usual; strange: 不尋常的；奇異的：*his ～ silence.* 他那罕有的沉默。

un·ad·vised /ˌʌnədˈvaɪzd；ˌʌnədˈvaɪzd/ *adj* without advice; (esp) not discreet or wise; rash. 未經磋商的；（尤指）不明智的；鹵莽的；輕率的。～**·ly** /ˌʌnədˈvaɪzɪdlɪ；ˌʌnədˈvaɪzɪdlɪ/ *adv* rashly. 鹵莽地；輕率地。

un·af·fec·ted /ˌʌnəˈfektɪd；ˌʌnəˈfɛktɪd/ *adj* **1** free from affectation; sincere. 不矯揉造作的；自然的；眞心的。**2** ～ ***by,*** not affected by. 未受…影響的；未被…感化的。

un·alien·able /ʌnˈeɪlɪənəbl；ʌnˈeljənəbḷ/ *adj* that cannot be taken away or separated: 不能轉讓的；不能讓渡的：～ *rights.* 不能轉讓的權利。

un·al·loyed /ˌʌnəˈlɔɪd；ˌʌnəˈlɔɪd/ *adj* pure; unmixed: 純粹的；完全的：～ *joy.* 眞正的快樂。

un·al·ter·ably /ʌnˈɔːltərəblɪ；ʌnˈɔltərəblɪ/ *adv* in a way that cannot be changed. 不可改變地。

unani·mous /juːˈnænɪməs；juˈnænəməs/ *adj* in, showing, complete agreement: 全體一致的；無異議

U

的: *The country is ~ in support of the Government's policy.* 舉國一致支持政府的政策。*He was elected by a ~ vote.* 他獲得全部選票而當選。*The proposal was accepted with ~ approval.* 該項建議經全體一致的同意而通過。~**·ly** *adv* **una·nim·ity** /ˌjuːnəˈnɪmətɪ ; ˌjunəˈnɪmətɪ/ *n* [U] complete agreement or unity. 全體同意或一致;無異議。

un·an·nounced /ˌʌnəˈnaʊnst ; ˌʌnəˈnaʊnst/ *adj* without having been announced: 未先通報的;未經宣佈的;未通知的: *He walked into the room ~*, no one having told the persons there who he was, that he had arrived. 他未先通報而走入房間。

un·an·swer·able /ˌʌnˈɑːnsərəbl *US:* -ˈæn- ; ʌnˈænsərəbl/ *adj* (esp) against which no good argument can possibly be brought: 無法回答的; (尤指)無可辯駁的: *His case is ~.* 他的案子無法申辯。

un·an·swered /ˌʌnˈɑːnsəd *US:* -ˈæn- ; ʌnˈænsəd/ *adj* not replied to: 無回答的;無答覆的: *~ letters;* 未回覆的信件; not returned: 無回報的: *~ love.* 單戀。

un·ap·proach·able /ˌʌnəˈprəʊtʃəbl ; ˌʌnəˈprotʃəbl/ *adj* (esp, of a person) difficult to approach (because too stiff or formal): (尤指人)(因爲太呆板或拘謹而)難接近的: *The new manager is an ~ sort of man.* 新任經理是一位不易接近的人。

un·armed /ˌʌnˈɑːmd ; ʌnˈɑrmd/ *adj* without weapons or means of defence. 未武裝的;徒手的;無武器的。

un·asked /ˌʌnˈɑːskt *US:* -ˈæs- ; ʌnˈæskt/ *adj* *~ (for)*, not asked (for), requested, or invited: 未經要求的;未經邀請的: *She's always ready to help and often does so ~.* 她總是樂於幫助旁人,而且常常是出於自動。*Many of the contributions to the relief fund were ~ for.* 救濟金的捐獻,有許多是未經要求而主動捐出的。

un·as·sum·ing /ˌʌnəˈsjuːmɪŋ *US:* -ˈsuː- ; ˌʌnəˈsumɪŋ/ *adj* not pushing oneself forward; not drawing attention to oneself; modest. 不愛出風頭的;不愛表現的;謙遜的。~**·ly** *adv*

un·at·tached /ˌʌnəˈtætʃt ; ˌʌnəˈtætʃt/ *adj* **1** not connected or associated with a particular person, group, organization, etc; independent. 不與某人、團體、組織等相關聯的;獨立的。**2** not married or engaged to be married. 未結婚的;未訂婚的。

un·at·tended /ˌʌnəˈtendɪd ; ˌʌnəˈtɛndɪd/ *adj* **1** without attendants or escort. 沒有隨員的;沒有同伴的。**2** not attended to; with no one to give care or attention to: 沒人管的;沒人照顧的: *Would you leave small children at home ~ while you went to the cinema?* 你(們)去看電影時,會把小孩子留在家裡無人照顧嗎?

un·avail·ing /ˌʌnəˈveɪlɪŋ ; ˌʌnəˈvelɪŋ/ *adj* without effort or success. 無效的;無益的;無用的。

un·avoid·able /ˌʌnəˈvɔɪdəbl ; ˌʌnəˈvɔɪdəbl/ *adj* that cannot be avoided. 不可避免的; 不得已的。**un·a·void·ably** /-əblɪ ; -əblɪ/ *adv*: *He was unavoidably absent.* 他不得已而缺課(席)。

un·aware /ˌʌnəˈweə(r) ; ˌʌnəˈwɛr/ *adj* (*pred*) (敘述用法) ~ ***of sth/that...***, not knowing; not aware: 不知道的;未覺察的: *He was ~ of my presence/that I was present.* 他不知道我在場。~**s** /-ˈweəz ; -ˈwɛrz/ *adv* **1** by surprise; unexpectedly. 意外地;突如其來地;未料到地。***take sb ~s***, surprise him. (由於突然出現而)令某人驚訝。**2** without being aware; unconsciously: 不知不覺地; 無意地: *She probably dropped the parcel ~s.* 她很可能無意間丟掉了那包裹。

un·backed /ˌʌnˈbækt ; ʌnˈbækt/ *adj* **1** (of a proposal, etc) not supported. (指提議等)不受支持的。**2** (of a horse in a race) having no bets placed on it. (指賽馬中的馬)無人下注的。

un·bal·anced /ˌʌnˈbælənst ; ʌnˈbælənst/ *adj* (esp of a person, the mind) disordered; not sane or normal. (尤指人,其心智)不正常的;不健全的;錯亂的。

un·bar /ˌʌnˈbɑː(r) ; ʌnˈbɑr/ *vt* (-rr-) remove bars from (a gate, etc); (fig) throw open: 移除(門等)上的橫木;拔去門閂;打開;(喻)開放: *~ all the professions to women.* 開放所有的職業給婦女。

un·bear·able /ʌnˈbeərəbl ; ʌnˈbɛrəbl/ *adj* that cannot be borne or tolerated: 不能忍受的;忍無可忍的;難堪的: *I find his rudeness ~.* 我覺得他的無禮難以忍受。**un·bear·ably** /-əblɪ ; -əblɪ/ *adv* in a way that cannot be endured: 不能忍受地;無法忍耐地: *unbearably hot/rude.* 熱(粗野)得叫人受不了。

un·beaten /ˌʌnˈbiːtn ; ʌnˈbitn/ *adj* (esp) not having been beaten, defeated or surpassed: (尤指)未被打破、擊敗或勝過的: *an ~ record for the 1 000 metres race;* 未被打破的一千公尺賽跑記錄; *an ~ team.* 常勝隊。

un·be·com·ing /ˌʌnbɪˈkʌmɪŋ ; ˌʌnbɪˈkʌmɪŋ/ *adj* **1** not suited (to the wearer): (對於穿戴者)不稱身的;不合身的: *an ~ dress.* 不合身的衣服。**2** ~ ***to/for***, not appropriate or befitting. 不適當的;不相配的。~**·ly** *adv*

un·be·known /ˌʌnbɪˈnəʊn ; ˌʌnbɪˈnon/, **un·be·knownst** /-nst ; -nst/ *adj, adv* (colloq) not known (*to*), without the knowledge of: (俗)爲…所不認識的(地);不爲人知的(地): *He did it ~st to me*, without my being aware of it. 他瞞着我幹那事。

un·be·lief /ˌʌnbɪˈliːf ; ˌʌnbɪˈlif/ *n* [U] (esp) lack of belief, state of not believing, in God, religion, etc. (尤指)不信上帝;不信宗教。**un·be·liev·able** *adj* **1** not believable. 難以相信的。**2** (colloq) very surprising. (俗)非常驚人的。**un·be·liev·ably** *adv* **un·be·liev·ing** *adj* not believing; doubting. 不信的;懷疑的。**un·be·liev·ing·ly** *adv*

un·bend /ʌnˈbend ; ʌnˈbɛnd/ *vi, vt* (*pt, pp* unbent /-ˈbent ; -ˈbɛnt/ or -ed) **1** [VP2A] behave in a way free from strain, formality; become relaxed: 不拘泥; 變得平易近人; 變得緩和: *In the classroom the teacher maintains discipline but after class he ~s.* 教師在課堂上很嚴厲,但下課後就變得平易近人了。**2** [VP6A] relax: 鬆弛: *~ one's mind.* 使心情鬆弛。~**·ing** *adj* (esp) firm in purpose, in not changing decisions, etc: (尤指)堅持目標的;不改變決定、主張等的: *maintain an ~ing attitude*, make no concessions, etc. 採取堅定不移的態度。

un·biassed (also **-biased**) /ˌʌnˈbaɪəst ; ʌnˈbaɪəst/ *adj* not biassed; impartial. 沒有偏見的;不偏不倚的;公正的。

un·bid·den /ˌʌnˈbɪdn ; ʌnˈbɪdn/ *adj* (formal) uninvited; not requested or ordered. (正式用語)未受邀請的;未被要求的;未受到指使或命令的。

un·bind /ˌʌnˈbaɪnd ; ʌnˈbaɪnd/ *vt* (*pt, pp* -bound /-ˈbaʊnd ; -ˈbaund/) [VP6A] free from fastenings, bindings, etc. 釋開;拆散;解開。

un·blush·ing /ʌnˈblʌʃɪŋ ; ʌnˈblʌʃɪŋ/ *adj* (esp) shameless:(尤指)無羞恥心的;不知恥的: *the ~ corruption of some politicians.* 若干政客恬不知恥的腐敗。

un·born /ˌʌnˈbɔːn ; ʌnˈbɔrn/ *adj* not yet born; future: 尚未出生的;未來的: *~ generations.* 未來的世代;後代。

un·bosom /ʌnˈbʊzəm ; ʌnˈbuzəm/ *vt* [VP6A, 14] ~ ***oneself (to sb)***, tell, reveal (one's sorrows, etc). 告知;表白;說出;傾訴(自己的憂愁等)。

un·bounded /ʌnˈbaʊndɪd ; ʌnˈbaʊndɪd/ *adj* boundless; without limits: 無限制的;無際的;極大的: *~ ambition.* 極大的野心。

un·bowed /ˌʌnˈbaʊd ; ʌnˈbaud/ *adj* not bowed or bent; not conquered or subdued: 不彎曲的;不屈服的: *His head is bloody but ~.* 他的頭是血淋淋的,但他沒有低頭。

un·bridled /ˌʌnˈbraɪdld ; ʌnˈbraɪdld/ *adj* (esp, fig) not controlled: (尤指,喻)放縱的;放肆的: *~ insolence/passions;* 放肆的侮辱(放縱的情慾); *an ~ tongue.* 饒舌。

un·bro·ken /ˌʌnˈbrəʊkən ; ʌnˈbrokən/ *adj* (esp) (尤指) **1** (eg of a horse) not tamed or subdued. (指馬等)未養馴的;不馴服的。**2** not interrupted: 不間斷的;未受阻礙的: *six hours of ~ sleep.* 六小時不間斷的睡眠。**3** (of records, etc) not beaten or surpassed. (指記錄等)未被打破的;未被超過的。

un·buckle /ˌʌnˈbʌkl ; ʌnˈbʌkl/ *vt* [VP6A] loosen, undo, the buckle(s) of. 鬆開或解開…的釦子或帶釦。

un·bur·den /ˌʌnˈbɜːdn ; ʌnˈbɝdn/ *vt* [VP6A, 15A] ~ ***oneself/sth (of sth),*** relieve of worry, anxiety, etc: 釋負;解除負擔: *~ one's heart/conscience,* eg by talking about one's troubles, making a confession; 解除心情(良心)上的負擔(如藉訴苦,告解); *~ oneself to a friend,* find relief by speaking to him about one's feelings, etc; 對朋友叙說隱衷; *~ oneself of a secret,* tell it to sb. 把秘密告知某人。

un·but·toned /ˌʌnˈbʌtnd ; ʌnˈbʌtnd/ *adj* with the buttons not fastened; (fig) relaxed; (feeling) free from formality. 解開鈕扣的;(喻)鬆弛的;不(覺得)拘束的。

un·called-for /ʌnˈkɔːld fɔː(r) ; ʌnˈkɔld,fɔr/ *adj* neither desirable nor necessary: 不必要的;沒有理由的;不應當的: *~ insults.* 沒道理的侮慢。*Such comments are ~.* 這種評論是多餘的。

un·canny /ʌnˈkænɪ ; ʌnˈkænɪ/ *adj* unnatural, mysterious; weird: 離奇的;怪異的;神秘的: *an ~ noise;* 神秘的聲響; *~ shapes in the darkness.* 黑暗中呈現的怪異形像。**un·can·nily** /-ɪlɪ ; -ɪlɪ/ *adv*

un·cared-for /ˌʌnˈkeəd fɔː(r) ; ʌnˈkɛrd,fɔr/ *adj* not looked after; neglected: 沒人照顧的;被忽略的: *~ children;* 沒有人照顧的孩子們; *an ~ garden.* 荒廢的花園。

un·ceas·ing /ʌnˈsiːsɪŋ ; ʌnˈsisɪŋ/ *adj* incessant; going on all the time. 不斷的;繼續的;始終不停的。**~·ly** *adv*

un·cer·emo·ni·ous /ˌʌnˌserɪˈməʊnɪəs ; ˌʌnsɛrəˈmonɪəs/ *adj* (esp) informal; lacking in courtesy. (尤指)隨便的;不拘禮的;沒有禮貌的;不客氣的。**~·ly** *adv* **~·ness** *n*

un·cer·tain /ʌnˈsɜːtn ; ʌnˈsɝtn/ *adj* **1** changeable; not reliable: 變化的;不可靠的: *~ weather;* 變化無常的天氣; *a man with an ~ temper.* 喜怒無常的人。**2** not certainly knowing or known: 不確知的;不明的;不爲人確知的: *be/feel ~ (about) what to do next;* 不確知下一步如何做; *~ of/about/as to one's plans for the future;* 不確知未來的計畫; *a woman of ~ age,* one whose age cannot be guessed. 無法斷定其年齡的女子。**~·ly** *adv* **~·ty** /-tntɪ ; -tntɪ/ *n* (*pl* -ties) **1** [U] state of being ~. 變化無常;不可靠;不確知。**2** [C] sth which is ~: 不確定的事物: *the uncertainties of adequate reward in the profession of an actor.* 演員這一行的報酬時高時低。

un·chari·table /ˌʌnˈtʃærɪtəbl ; ʌnˈtʃærətəbl/ *adj* (esp) severe or harsh (in making judgements of the conduct of others): (尤指)(在評判他人行爲時)嚴厲的;苛刻的: *offer an ~ explanation of/put an ~ interpretation on sb's actions.* 對某人的行爲作嚴厲的解釋。

un·charted /ˌʌnˈtʃɑːtɪd ; ʌnˈtʃɑrtɪd/ *adj* **1** not marked on a map or chart: 圖上未標明的: *an ~ island.* 地圖上沒有標明的島嶼。**2** (lit or fig) not explored and mapped: (字面或喻)未經探勘並繪製成圖的: *an ~ sea;* 未經探勘和繪圖的海; *~ emotions.* 未經探究的情緒。

un·checked /ˌʌnˈtʃekt ; ʌnˈtʃɛkt/ *adj* not checked or restrained: 未被遏止的;未受抑制的: *an ~ advance;* 未受制止的前進; *~ anger.* 未抑制的憤怒。

un·chris·tian /ˌʌnˈkrɪstʃən ; ʌnˈkrɪstʃən/ *adj* **1** not Christian; contrary to Christian principles. 不是基督徒的;非基督教的;反基督教教義的。**2** (colloq) inconvenient and unreasonable: (俗)不方便的;不合理的: *Why do you call on me at this ~ hour?* (eg at 5am). 你爲什麼在這個時候(如凌晨五時)來看我呢?

un·civil /ˌʌnˈsɪvl ; ʌnˈsɪvl/ *adj* (esp) impolite. (尤指)不禮貌的;不客氣的;失禮的。

un·claimed /ˌʌnˈkleɪmd ; ʌnˈklemd/ *adj* that has not been claimed: 無人認領的: *~ letters/parcels* (at the post-office, a lost property office, etc). 沒有人認領的信件(包裹)。

uncle /ˈʌŋkl ; ˈʌŋkl/ *n* brother of one's father or mother; husband of one's aunt: 伯父;叔父;舅父;姑丈;姨丈: *my ~ Charlie.* 我的伯父(叔父等)查理。**U~ Sam,** personification of the US. 山姆大叔(美國的擬人稱)。**U~ Tom,** ⚠ (US, derog) black person who is very friendly to white people. (諱)(美,貶)湯姆叔叔(對白人非常友善的黑人)。**Dutch U~,** ⇨ Dutch(2).

un·clean /ˌʌnˈkliːn ; ʌnˈklin/ *adj* (esp, Jewish law) ceremonially impure, eg the pig. (尤用於猶太法律)在禮儀上不潔淨的(例如豬)。

un·clouded /ˌʌnˈklaʊdɪd ; ʌnˈklaʊdɪd/ *adj* (esp fig) bright; serene: (尤用作喻)晴朗的;平靜的: *a life of ~ happiness.* 平靜幸福的生活。Cf 參較 *cloudless,* as in *a cloudless sky.*

unco /ˈʌŋkəʊ ; ˈʌŋko/(Scot)(蘇)*adj* strange; unusual: 古怪的;奇異的;不尋常的: *an ~ sight.* 奇觀。□ *adv* remarkably: 顯著地;非常地: (esp) (尤指) *the ~ good,* religious people who are rigid in their views and behaviour. 看法及行爲均極嚴謹的教徒。

un·col·oured (US=**-colored**) /ˌʌnˈkʌləd; ʌnˈkʌlɚd/ *adj* (esp fig) not exaggerated or heightened in description: (尤用作喻)未誇張的;未加渲染的: *an ~ description of events.* 對事件未加渲染的叙述。

un·come-at-able /ˌʌnkʌmˈætəbl ; ˌʌnkʌmˈætəbl/ *adj* (colloq) not easy to get to; not accessible. (俗)難達到的;難接近的。

un·com·fort·able /ʌnˈkʌmftəbl *US:* -fərt- ; ʌnˈkʌmfɚtəbl/ *adj* not comfortable; uneasy: 不舒適的;不安的: *an ~ chair/feeling.* 不舒適的椅子(不安的感覺)。

un·com·mit·ted /ˌʌnkəˈmɪtɪd ; ˌʌnkəˈmɪtɪd/ *adj* ~ ***(to),*** not committed or bound (to a course of action, etc); free, independent: 不負義務的;不受(某行動等)限制的;自由的;獨立的: *the ~ countries,* those not allied to or bound to either of the power blocs of the modern world. 不結盟國家(第三世界)。

un·com·mon /ʌnˈkɒmən ; ʌnˈkɑmən/ *adj* unusual; remarkable. 不普通的;非尋常的;不凡的;顯著的。**~·ly** *adv* (esp) remarkably: (尤指) 顯著地;極: *an ~ly intelligent child.* 極聰明的兒童。

un·com·pro·mis·ing /ʌnˈkɒmprəmaɪzɪŋ ; ʌnˈkɑmprə,maɪzɪŋ/ *adj* not ready to make any compromise; unyielding; firm: 不妥協的; 不讓步的; 堅定的: *an ~ member of the Tory party.* 一個不妥協的保守黨黨員。

un·con·cern /ˌʌnkənˈsɜːn ; ˌʌnkənˈsɝn/ *n* [U] lack of care or interest. 冷漠;不關心;不感興趣。

un·con·cerned /ˌʌnkənˈsɜːnd ; ˌʌnkənˈsɝnd/ *adj* **1** ~ ***in sth,*** not involved in. 沒有關係的;不相干的;未牽入的。~ ***with sth/sb,*** not (emotionally) concerned with. (對某事或某人)無感情牽連的。**2** free from anxiety; untroubled; uninterested. 無憂慮的;漠不關心的;不感興趣的。**un·con·cern·ed·ly** /-ˈsɜːnɪdlɪ ; -ˈsɝnɪdlɪ/ *adv*

un·con·di·tional /ˌʌnkənˈdɪʃənl ; ˌʌnkənˈdɪʃənəl/ *adj* absolute; not subject to conditions: 絕對的;無條件的: *The victors demanded ~ surrender.* 勝利者要求無條件投降。**~·ly** /-ʃənəlɪ ; -ʃənəlɪ/ *adv*

un·con·di·tioned /ˌʌnkənˈdɪʃnd ; ˌʌnkənˈdɪʃənd/ *adj* not subject to conditions; 無條件的; (esp) (尤指) *~ reflex,* instinctive response to a stimulus. 非制約反射;無條件反射(對刺激的本能反應)。

un·con·scion·able /ʌnˈkɒnʃənəbl ; ʌnˈkɑnʃənəbl/ *adj* unreasonable; not guided by conscience; excessive: 不合理的;沒良心的;過分的: *You take an ~ time dressing.* 你花在化妝上的時間太多了。

un·con·scious /ʌnˈkɒnʃəs ; ʌnˈkɑnʃəs/ *adj* not conscious (all senses): 失去知覺的;無意識的;不能察覺的;無意的: *~ humour,* not intended as humour by the speaker or writer; 無意中的幽默; *be ~ of having done wrong.* 不知道做錯。□ *n* **the ~,** (psych) that part of one's mental activity of which one is unaware, but which can be detected and un-

U

derstood through the skilled analysis of dreams, behaviour, etc. (心理)無意識(自己覺察不到的心智活動,但可從夢與行爲等的巧妙分析,探知其存在並瞭解其性質)。~·ly *adv* ~·ness *n*

un·con·sid·ered /ˌʌnkənˈsɪdəd ; ˌʌnkənˈsɪdərd/ *adj* **1** (of words, remarks) spoken, made, etc without proper consideration or reflection. (指文字,言詞)未加熟慮而說出,寫出等的。 **2** disregarded (as if of little value or worth). 未受到理會的;被忽視的。

un·con·ven·tional /ˌʌnkənˈvenʃənl ; ˌʌnkənˈvɛnʃənḷ/ *adj* not usual or ordinary; not bound by the customs of society: 不尋常的;不依慣例的;不從習俗的: *an ~ dress/person/way of life.* 不從習俗的衣服(人,生活方式)。

un·con·vinc·ing /ˌʌnkənˈvɪnsɪŋ ; ˌʌnkənˈvɪnsɪŋ/ *adj* not seeming true, right, or real: 不足以令人相信的;不令人信服的: *an ~ explanation/attempt/disguise.* 不足以令人相信的解釋(企圖,僞裝)。

un·cork /ˌʌnˈkɔːk ; ʌnˈkɔrk/ *vt* [VP6A] draw the cork from (a bottle). 拔去(瓶)上的塞子;開(瓶)口。

un·couple /ˌʌnˈkʌpl ; ʌnˈkʌpḷ/ *vt* [VP6A] unfasten: 解開: *~ hounds from the leash/a locomotive from a train.* 解開獵狗的繫帶(使火車的機車與列車分離)。

un·couth /ʌnˈkuːθ ; ʌnˈkuθ/ *adj* (of persons, their behaviour) rough, awkward, not cultured. (指人,其行爲)粗魯的;笨拙的;無教養的。~·**ly** *adv* ~·**ness** *n*

un·cover /ʌnˈkʌvə(r) ; ʌnˈkʌvɚ/ *vt, vi* **1** [VP6A] remove a cover or covering from; (fig) disclose; make known: 移去…的覆蓋物;(喻)揭露;宣佈: *The police have ~ed a plot against the President.* 警方已破獲了一件謀害總統的陰謀。 **2** [VP6A] (mil) expose to attack: (軍)使暴露;除去掩護: *By a sudden movement we ~ed the enemy's right flank.* 我們採突然的行動攻擊敵人的右翼。 **3** [VP2A] (archaic) take off one's hat or cap. (古)脫帽。

un·crossed /ˌʌnˈkrɒst *US:* -ˈkrɔːst ; ʌnˈkrɔst/ *adj* (esp, of a cheque) not crossed. (尤指支票)未劃線的。⇨ cross²(2).

U

un·crowned /ˌʌnˈkraʊnd ; ʌnˈkraʊnd/ *adj* **1** (of a king, etc) not yet crowned. (指國王等)尚未加冕的;尚未舉行加冕禮的。 **2** having the power but not the title or name of a king, etc. 有國王等的權力而無名位的;有實權而無名份的。

unc·tion /ˈʌŋkʃn ; ˈʌŋkʃən/ *n* [U] **1** act of anointing with oil, esp as a religious rite. 塗油;(尤指)宗教的塗油式。**Extreme U~,** the anointing of a dying person by a priest (of the Orthodox and Roman Catholic Churches). (東方正教及天主教)僧侶爲垂死者所行的塗油式。 **2** (pretended, insincere) earnestness, smoothness in speech or manner: 虛情假意;油腔滑調: *She related the scandal with a great deal of ~;* 她添油加醋地叙述那件醜聞; flattery. 諂媚。

unc·tu·ous /ˈʌŋktʃʊəs ; ˈʌŋktʃʊəs/ *adj* (insincerely) earnest, smooth in speech or manner; flattering: 虛情假意的;油腔滑調的;諂媚的: *~ tones/assurances.* 虛情假意的語調(承諾)。**unc·tu·ous·ly** *adv*

un·cut /ˌʌnˈkʌt ; ʌnˈkʌt/ *adj* (of a book) with the outer folds of the pages not trimmed or cut; (of a book, film, etc) not abridged or censored. (指書)邊沒切齊的;書頁未割開的;(指書,電影等)未被刪節的;未被剪掉的。

un·dated /ˌʌnˈdeɪtɪd ; ʌnˈdetɪd/ *adj* not having a date: 無日期的;未註明年月日的: *an ~ cheque;* 未註日期的支票; *~ stocks*, with no specified date for redemption. 無定期債券(未明確規定貼現日期者)。

un·daunted /ˌʌnˈdɔːntɪd ; ʌnˈdɔntɪd/ *adj* not daunted; fearless. 大無畏的;勇敢的;不懼怕的。

un·de·ceive /ˌʌndɪˈsiːv ; ˌʌndɪˈsiv/ *vt* [VP6A] cause to be no longer deceived or in error. 使不再受欺騙;使不再犯錯誤;使醒悟。

un·de·cided /ˌʌndɪˈsaɪdɪd ; ˌʌndɪˈsaɪdɪd/ *adj* not decided; not yet having made up one's mind: 未被決定的;尚未作決定的: *She was ~ whether to go to a concert or the cinema.* 她還沒有決定是去聽音樂會還是去看電影。

un·de·clared /ˌʌndɪˈkleəd ; ˌʌndɪˈklɛrd/ *adj* **1** (of goods liable to customs duty) not declared or shown to the customs officers. (指應繳納關稅的貨物)未向稅務人員申報的;未報關的。 **2** not announced or made known: 未(被)宣佈的;未公之於世的: *~ war.* 不宣而戰的戰爭。

un·de·fended /ˌʌndɪˈfendɪd ; ˌʌndɪˈfɛndɪd/ *adj* (esp of a lawsuit) in which no defence is offered. (尤指訴訟)未提答辯或抗辯的。

un·de·mon·stra·tive /ˌʌndɪˈmɒnstrətɪv ; ˌʌndɪˈmɑnstrətɪv/ *adj* reserved; not in the habit of showing feelings of affection, interest, etc. 含蓄的;不慣於表露喜怒、好惡等。

un·de·ni·able /ˌʌndɪˈnaɪəbl ; ˌʌndɪˈnaɪəbḷ/ *adj* that cannot be denied; undoubtedly true: 無可否認的;確實的: *of ~ worth/value.* 確有價值的。**un·de·ni·ably** /-əblɪ ; -əblɪ/ *adv*

un·de·nomi·na·tional /ˌʌndɪˌnɒmɪˈneɪʃənl ; ˌʌndɪˌnɑməˈneʃənḷ/ *adj* not connected with any particular religious sect: 不屬於任何宗教派系的;非教派的: *~ education/schools.* 非教會教育(學校)。

un·der¹ /ˈʌndə(r) ; ˈʌndɚ/ *adv* **1** in or to a lower place, position, etc: 在下;在下位;往下面: *The ship went ~*, sank. 那條船下沉了。 *Can you stay ~* (= ~ the water) *for two minutes?* 你能在水面下停留兩分鐘嗎? ***down ~,*** (used in GB, colloq) (in/to) Australia and New Zealand. (用於英國,俗)在(往)澳洲及紐西蘭。 **2** (used to modify *nn*) subordinate; lower in rank, etc: (用以修飾名詞)下級的;從屬的;在下面的;階級等較低的: ˌ*~ ˈsecretary.* 次長;(美)副部長;副國務卿;(尤指)政務次長。

un·der² /ˈʌndə(r) ; ˈʌndɚ/ *prep* **1** in or to a position lower than: (位置)低於;在…之下: *The cat was ~ the table.* 貓在桌子下面。 *It is shady ~ the trees.* 在樹下是蔭涼的。 *There's nothing new ~ the sun,* (prov), nothing new anywhere. (諺)太陽底下無新事。*We passed ~ several bridges.* 我們在幾座橋下面通過。*The soldiers were standing ~* (= at the foot of) *the castle wall.* 兵士們站在城堡的牆脚下。*The village nestles ~* (= at the foot of) *the hill.* 那村莊坐落在山脚下。 **2** in and covered by: 被…遮蔽着;在…的包裹中: *The part of an iceberg ~ the water is much larger than the part above the water.* 冰山在水面下的部分遠大於在水面上的部分。*He hid his face ~ the bedclothes.* 他用被單遮住臉。*Her hair came out from ~ her hat.* 她的頭髮從帽子下面露了出來。 **3** less than; lower (in rank) than: 少於;在階級或地位上低於: *children ~* (opp 相反字: *over/above*) *fourteen years of age;* 十四歲以下的兒童; *books for the* ˌ*~-ˈtens* (opp 相反字: *over-tens*), children under ten; 適於十歲以下兒童的書; *incomes ~* (opp 相反字: *over/above*) *£3000;* 不到三千鎊的收入; *run a hundred metres in ~ ten seconds;* 不到十秒鐘跑完一百公尺; *~ half an acre;* 不到半英畝; *no one ~* (opp 相反字: *above/over*) (*the rank of*) *a captain;* 沒有人低於上尉(的階級); *speak ~ one's breath,* in a whisper. 低聲說話;悄悄講。~ ***age,*** ⇨ age. **4** (indicating various conditions): (表示各種情況): *road ~ repair,* being repaired; 在修理中的道路; *~ discussion,* being discussed; 在討論中; *fifty acres ~* (= planted with) *wheat;* 五十英畝的小麥田; *~ sentence of* (= sentenced to) *death;* 被判處死刑; *living ~ an assumed name;* 隱姓埋名度日; *England ~ the Stuarts,* during the times of the Stuart kings and queens; 在斯圖亞特王朝統治下的英國; *be ~ the impression that...,* have the idea or belief that.... 以爲;相信…。*The book is listed ~ biology,* within that classification. 該書列入生物學的類別下。 **5** weighed down by (lit and fig): 被…重壓(字面及喻): *marching ~ a heavy load;* 載負着重物行進; *sink ~ a load of grief* (*taxation, etc*). 因悲傷(重稅等)的負擔而倒下去。

under- /ˈʌndə(r) ; ˈʌndɚ/ *pref* ⇨ App 3. 參看附錄三。

under·act /ˌʌndər'ækt；ˌʌndɚ'ækt/ *vt, vi* [VP6A, 2A] act with too little spirit, energy, emphasis, etc: 表演不够賣力;表演不够精彩: ～ *the part of Hamlet.* 沒演出哈姆雷特這個角色的特色。*The star overacted; the other players ～ed.* 主角演得太過火;而其他演員却不太賣力。

under·arm /'ʌndərɑːm；'ʌndɚˌɑrm/ *adj, adv* (cricket, tennis) with the hand kept below the level of the elbow: (板球,網球)低手的(地)：～ *bowling;* 低手式投球; *bowl／serve* ～. 投(發)低手球。

under·belly /'ʌndəbelɪ；'ʌndɚˌbɛlɪ/ *n* (*pl* -lies) under surface of an animal's body, eg as a cut of meat, esp pork. 動物身體的下腹部(如一塊下腹肉,尤指豬肉)。

under·bid /ˌʌndə'bɪd；ˌʌndɚ'bɪd/ *vt* (*pt, pp* unchanged) ⇨ bid¹(1). **1** make a lower bid than (sb else). 出價低於(他人);出價較低。**2** (card games, bridge) bid less on (a hand of cards) than its strength warrants. (紙牌,橋牌)叫(牌)低於手上的牌力。

under·brush /'ʌndəbrʌʃ；'ʌndɚˌbrʌʃ/ *n* [U] = undergrowth (which is more usu 此字較常用).

under·car·riage /'ʌndəkærɪdʒ；'ʌndɚˌkærɪdʒ/ *n* landing gear of an aircraft. 飛機的起落架。⇨ the illus at air. 參看 air 之挿圖。

under·charge /ˌʌndə'tʃɑːdʒ；'ʌndɚ'tʃɑrdʒ/ *vt* [VP 6A] charge too little for (sth) or to (sb). 少討(某物)的價錢;對(某人)少討某物的價錢。□ *n* /'ʌndətʃɑːdʒ；'ʌndɚˌtʃɑrdʒ/ charge that is too low or small. 太低或太少的價格。

under·clothes /'ʌndəkləʊðz；'ʌndɚˌkloðz/ *n pl* clothing worn under a shirt, dress, etc next to the skin. 內衣褲;貼身內衣。**under·cloth·ing** /'ʌndəkləʊðɪŋ；'ʌndɚˌkloðɪŋ/ *n* [U] =～.

under·cover /ˌʌndə'kʌvə(r)；ˌʌndɚ'kʌvɚ/ *adj* secret; surreptitious: 秘密的;暗中從事的: *an* ～ *agent,* person who associates with suspected criminals, etc to get evidence against them, or who acts as a spy, eg during a war; 密探;間諜; ～ *payments,* eg made in order to bribe sb. 暗中所付的款(如用以行賄)。

under·cur·rent /'ʌndəkʌrənt；'ʌndɚˌkɝənt/ *n* [U] current of water flowing beneath the surface; (fig) tendency (of thought or feeling) lying below what is apparent: 潛流;底流;暗流;(喻)(思想或感情的)暗潮;潛勢: *an* ～ *of opposition／melancholy.* 一股反對的暗潮(內心的傷感情懷)。

under·cut¹ /'ʌndəkʌt；'ʌndɚˌkʌt/ *n* [U] meat cut from the underside of sirloin. 牛腰的下側肉。

under·cut² /ˌʌndə'kʌt；ˌʌndɚ'kʌt/ *vt* (*pt, pp* unchanged; -tt-) [VP6A] (comm) offer (goods, services) at a lower price than competitors. (商)減低(貨物,服務)的價格;索價低於競爭者。

under·de·vel·oped /ˌʌndədɪ'veləpt；ˌʌndɚdɪ'vɛləpt/ *adj* not yet fully developed: 發育尙不充分的;未充分發展的;未完全開發的: ～ *muscles／countries.* 發育不充分的肌肉(低度開發國家)。

under·dog /'ʌndədɒg *US:* -dɔːg；'ʌndɚ'dɔg/ *n* (often 常作 **the** ～) poor and helpless person who usu gets the worst of an encounter, a struggle, etc: 在競賽、打鬥等中居於劣勢的人;失敗者;受壓迫者: *plead for the* ～, for sb who is oppressed. 爲受壓迫者說項。

under·done /ˌʌndə'dʌn；'ʌndɚ'dʌn/ *adj* (esp of meat) not completely cooked throughout. (尤指肉)未完全煮熟的。

under·esti·mate /ˌʌndər'estɪmeɪt；'ʌndɚ'ɛstəˌmet/ *vt* [VP6A] form too low an estimate of: 低估;對…作過低的評價: ～ *the enemy's strength.* 低估敵人的兵力。□ *n* /-mət；-mɪt/ [C] estimate which is too low. 低估;評價過低。

under·ex·pose /ˌʌndərɪk'spəʊz；'ʌndərɪk'spoz/ *vt* [VP6A] (photo) expose (a plate or film) for too short a time. (攝影)使(底片)感光不足。**under·ex·posure** /-'spəʊʒə(r)；-'spoʒɚ/ *n*

under·fed /ˌʌndə'fed；'ʌndɚ'fɛd/ *adj* having had too little food. 吃得太少的;沒吃飽的。

under·floor /ˌʌndə'flɔː(r)；ˌʌndɚ'flor/ *adj* (of systems for heating buildings) with the source of heat placed under the floor(s): (指房屋的暖氣系統)熱源裝置於地板下面的: ～ *heating.* 熱源置於地板下的暖氣系統。

under·foot /ˌʌndə'fʊt；ˌʌndɚ'fʊt/ *adv* under one's feet; on the ground: 在脚下面;在地上: *It is very hard* ～, eg when the ground is frozen hard. 地面很硬(如地面凍結時)。

under·gar·ment /'ʌndəgɑːmənt；'ʌndɚˌgɑrmənt/ *n* [C] article of underclothing. 內衣。

under·go /ˌʌndə'gəʊ；ˌʌndɚ'go/ *vt* (*pt* -went /-'went；-'wɛnt/, *pp* -gone /-'gɒn *US* -'gɔːn；-'gɔn/) [VP6A] experience; pass through: 經驗;經歷;遭受: *The explorers had to* ～ *much suffering.* 探險的人們不得不忍受很多困苦。*The new aircraft underwent its tests well.* 這架新飛機經試驗後令人滿意。

under·grad·uate /ˌʌndə'grædʒʊət；ˌʌndɚ'grædʒʊɪt/ *n* university student working for a bachelor's degree: 大學生;大學肄業生: (attrib) (形容用法) '～ *work／studies;* 大學生的課業(學業); *in his* '～ *days.* 在他的大學時代。

under·ground /'ʌndəgraʊnd；'ʌndɚ'graʊnd/ *attrib adj* **1** under the surface of the ground: 在地面下的;地下的: *London's* ～ *railways;* 倫敦的地下鐵路; ～ *passages／caves.* 地下通道(洞穴)。**2** (fig) secret, esp of a secret political movement or one for resisting enemy forces in occupation of another country: (喻)秘密的(尤指有關秘密的政治活動或反抗敵人佔領軍的秘密活動的): ～ *workers.* 地下工作者。□ *adv* (in the senses of the *adj*): (用作形容詞各義): *He went* ～ (= into hiding) *when he heard the police were after him.* 他聽到警察要抓他就躱起來了。□ *n* **(the)** ～, (in the senses of the *adj*): (用作形容詞各義): *travel in London by* ～, ie the ～ railway (US 美 = *subway*); 乘地下火車遊倫敦; *a member of the French* ～, the secret resistance movement during World War Two. (第二次世界大戰期間)法國地下抗敵組織的一名工作人員。

under·growth /'ʌndəgrəʊθ；'ʌndɚˌgroθ/ *n* [U] shrubs, bushes, low trees, growing among taller trees. 下層林叢(生長於較高大林木下的灌木、小樹叢或矮樹)。

under·hand /'ʌndəhænd；'ʌndɚˌhænd/ *adj, adv* secret(ly); deceitful(ly); sly(ly): 秘密的(地);欺瞞的(地);狡詐的(地): *play an* ～ *game;* 玩弄詭謀; ～ *methods;* 卑鄙手段; *behave in an* ～ *way.* 舉止狡詐。～**ed** *adj* = ～.

under·hung /ˌʌndə'hʌŋ；ˌʌndɚ'hʌŋ/ *adj* (attrib) (of the lower jaw) projecting beyond the upper jaw. (形容用法)(指下頜)比上頜突出的。

under·lay /'ʌndəleɪ；'ʌndɚˌle/ *n* [U] material (felt, rubber, etc) laid under a carpet or mattress (to preserve its condition). (放在地毯或床墊下面的)襯墊(如毛氈或橡皮等,以保持其良好狀態)。

under·lie /ˌʌndə'laɪ；ˌʌndɚ'laɪ/ *vt* [VP6A] **1** be or lie under. 位於…之下。**2** form the basis of (a theory, conduct, behaviour, doctrine): 成爲(理論,行爲,舉止,主義)的基礎: *the underlying reason／fault／guilt.* 根本的原因(根本的毛病;內心的愧疚)。

under·line /ˌʌndə'laɪn；ˌʌndɚ'laɪn/ *vt* [VP6A] draw a line under (a word, etc); (fig) emphasize. 畫線於(字等)的下面;(喻)强調;加强。□ *n* /'ʌndəlaɪn；'ʌndɚˌlaɪn/ line drawn under a word or words. (畫在字下面的)底線。

under·ling /'ʌndəlɪŋ；'ʌndɚlɪŋ/ *n* (usu contemptuous) person in an unimportant position under another or others. (通常含輕蔑意)職位低的人;下屬。

under·manned /ˌʌndə'mænd；'ʌndɚ'mænd/ *adj* (of a ship, factory, etc) having not enough men to do all the work that needs to be done. (指船上、工廠等)人員不足的。

under·men·tioned /ˌʌndə'menʃnd；'ʌndɚ'mɛnʃənd/ *adj* mentioned below or later (in an article, etc). (在文章等中)下面提到的;下述的;下記的。

under·mine /ˌʌndəˈmaɪn; ˌʌndɚˈmaɪn/ *vt* [VP6A] **1** make a hollow or tunnel under; weaken at the base: 在…之下掘洞或地道;使從基礎損壞: *cliffs ～d by the sea.* 被海浪冲壞底部的懸崖。 **2** weaken gradually: 逐漸削弱或損壞: *His health was ～d by drink.* 他的健康由於飲酒而逐漸損壞。*The President's enemies are spreading rumours to ～ his authority.* 總統的敵人在散佈謠言,以逐漸破壞他的威信。

under·neath /ˌʌndəˈniːθ; ˌʌndɚˈniθ/ *adv, prep* beneath; below; at or to a lower place. 在…的下面;在…之下;在下位;向下位。

under·nour·ished /ˌʌndəˈnʌrɪʃt; ˈʌndɚˈnɜɪʃt/ *adj* not provided with sufficient food for good health and normal growth. 營養不良的。 **under·nour·ish·ment** *n*

under·pants /ˈʌndəpænts; ˈʌndɚˌpænts/ *n pl* short undergarment worn by men and boys over the loins. (男人或男孩穿的)內褲。⇨ panties.

under·pass /ˈʌndəpɑːs *US:* -pæs; ˈʌndɚˌpæs/ *n* [C] section of a road that goes under another road or railway. 地下穿越道(爲某道路的一段,自另一條道路或鐵路下面穿過)。⇨ overpass, flyover.

under·pay /ˌʌndəˈpeɪ; ˌʌndɚˈpe/ *vt* (*pt, pp* -paid /-ˈpeɪd; -ˈped/) [VP6A] pay (workmen, etc) inadequately. 付給(工人等)太低的工資。 **～·ment** *n*

under·pin /ˌʌndəˈpɪn; ˌʌndɚˈpɪn/ *vt* (-nn-) place a support of masonry, etc under (a wall, etc); (fig) support, form the basis for (a case, an argument, etc). 在(牆等)下面加置基礎;(喩)支持;爲(某一立場,論據等)立基礎。

under·popu·lated /ˌʌndəˈpɒpjʊleɪtɪd; ˈʌndɚˈpɑpjəˌletɪd/ *adj* (of a country or area) having a small population in view of its size or natural resources. (指一國家或地區)人口稀少的。

under·privi·leged /ˌʌndəˈprɪvəlɪdʒd; ˈʌndɚˈprɪvəlɪdʒd/ *adj* not having had the educational and social advantages enjoyed by more fortunate people, social classes, nations, etc. 沒有地位的;下層社會的;貧困的。

under·pro·duc·tion /ˌʌndəprəˈdʌkʃn; ˈʌndɚprəˈdʌkʃən/ *n* [U] production of goods in insufficient quantity or below full capacity. 生產不足;生產能力未全部發揮。

under·quote /ˌʌndəˈkwəʊt; ˌʌndɚˈkwot/ *vt* [VP 6A] quote lower prices for goods than (others). 開價較(他人)低;開價低於。

under·rate /ˌʌndəˈreɪt; ˈʌndɚˈret/ *vt* [VP6A] place too low a value or estimate on: 低估;估計過低: *～ an opponent,* fail to realize his abilities, strength, etc. 低估對手的能力、力量等。

under·score /ˌʌndəˈskɔː(r); ˌʌndɚˈskor/ *vt* [VP6A] = underline.

under-sec·retary /ˌʌndəˈsekrətrɪ *US:* -terɪ; ˌʌndɚˈsɛkrəˌtɛrɪ/ *n* (*pl* -ries) assistant secretary, esp (*Parliamentary U～*) member of the Civil Service and head of a Government Department. 次長;(美)副部長;副國務卿;(尤指)政務次長。

under·sell /ˌʌndəˈsel; ˌʌndɚˈsɛl/ *vt* (*pt, pp* -sold /-ˈsəʊld; -ˈsold/) [VP6A] sell (goods) at a lower price than (competitors). 較(競爭者)廉價出售貨物。

under·sexed /ˌʌndəˈsekst; ˌʌndɚˈsɛkst/ *adj* having less sexual desire or potency than normal. 性慾或性機能較常人低的;性慾很弱的。

under·shoot /ˌʌndəˈʃuːt; ˌʌndɚˈʃut/ *vt* (*pt, pp* -shot /-ˈʃɒt; -ˈʃɑt/) (of an aircraft) (指飛機) *～ the runway,* land short of it. 進場太低;未抵跑道卽已着陸。⇨ overshoot.

under·side /ˈʌndəsaɪd; ˈʌndɚˌsaɪd/ *n* side that is underneath. 下側;底面。

under·sign /ˌʌndəˈsaɪn; ˌʌndɚˈsaɪn/ *vt* [VP6A] sign (a letter, etc) at the foot: 簽名於(信函等)的下方: *We, the ～ed,* We whose signatures appear below. 我們,文件下方署名者。

under·sized /ˌʌndəˈsaɪzd; ˈʌndɚˈsaɪzd/ *adj* of less than the usual size; stunted or dwarfish. 較一般尺寸小的;發育不全的;矮小的。

under·slung /ˌʌndəˈslʌŋ; ˌʌndɚˈslʌŋ/ *adj* (in a vehicle) having springs attached to the axles from below. (指車輛)彈簧與軸的下方相連接的;車身置於車軸下面之彈簧上的。

under·staffed /ˌʌndəˈstɑːft *US:* -stæft; ˌʌndɚˈstæft/ *adj* having too small a staff: 職員過少的;工作人員太少的;人手不足的: *The school／hospital is badly ～.* 這所學校(醫院)人手不足的現象很嚴重。⇨ undermanned.

under·stand /ˌʌndəˈstænd; ˌʌndɚˈstænd/ *vt, vi* (*pt, pp* -stood /-ˈstʊd; -ˈstʊd/) **1** [VP6A, C, 8, 10, 19C, 2A] know the meaning, nature, explanation, of (sth): 懂;了解;領會;知道(某事物)的意義、性質、解釋: *～ French／figures／a problem.* 懂得法語(計算,某一問題)。*He didn't ～ me／what I said.* 他不懂我的話。*You don't ～* (= realize) *what a difficult position I'm in.* 你不了解我處境是如何艱苦。*A good teacher must ～ children.* 一位優秀教師必須了解兒童。*I cannot ～ his robbing his friend／why he robbed his friend.* 我不明白他爲何搶劫他的朋友。*It is easy to ～ his anger／why he was angry.* 他發怒的原因(他何以發怒)不難了解。***make oneself understood,*** make one's meaning clear: 使自己的意思被人明白;說清楚自己的意思: *Can he make himself understood in Russian?* 他能用俄語把他的意思表達清楚嗎？***(Now), ～ me,*** phrase often used to preface a warning or threat. (喂),聽清楚;聽着(常用於警告或威脅之前)。***～ one another,*** (of two persons, parties) be clearly aware of one another's views, feelings, intentions: (指二人,兩方)互相了解;彼此了解對方的觀點、感情、意圖等: *The employers and workers have not reached an agreement yet, but at least they ～ one another,* 雇主與工人之間尚未達成協議,不過至少彼此已臻相互瞭解。 **2** [VP9, 17] learn (from information received); infer; take for granted: 聞悉;推斷;以爲;相信;視爲當然: *I ～ that you are now married.* 我聽說你現在已結婚了。*Am I to ～ that you refuse?* 我可以認爲你是拒絕嗎？*I understood him to say that he would cooperate.* 我推斷他會說他願意合作。***give sb to ～ (that...),*** cause sb to believe or have the idea (that): 告訴某人;通知;使某人相信或認爲: *We were given to ～ that free accommodation would be supplied.* 我們得到通知,住宿將免費供應。 **3** [VP6A] supply (a word or phrase) mentally: 不言而喩;能意會而無需說出(某字或片語): *In the sentence 'He is taller than I', the verb 'am' is to be understood after 'I'.* 在 He is taller than I 這句話中, I 後面省去了動詞 am。 **～·able** /-əbl; -əbl̩/ *adj* that can be understood: 可被了解的;能領會的: *His reluctance to agree is ～able.* 他之不願意同意是可以理解的。 **～·ably** /-əblɪ; -əblɪ/ *adv*: *He is ～ably furious.* 他大怒是可以理解的。 **～·ing** *adj* (good at) ～ing or realizing other persons' feelings or points of view; having or showing insight: (擅長)了解他人的情緒或觀點的;善解人意的;有理解力的;穎悟的;聰明的: *with an ～ing smile.* 帶着會心的微笑。 *Please be ～ing; do not punish the child.* 請體諒一點;不要處罰那孩子。 □ *n* **1** [U] power of clear thought. 理解力;悟性;了解。 **2** [U] capacity for sympathizing, seeing from another's point of view, etc. 同情心;同感;體諒。 **3** (often **an ～ing,** but rarely *pl*) agreement; realization of another's views or feelings towards oneself: (常作 an ～ing,但罕用複數)協議;協定;諒解: *reach／come to an ～ing with sb.* 與某人達成協議(諒解)。 ***on this ～ing,*** on this condition. 在此條件之下。 ***on the ～ing that...,*** on condition that.... 以…爲條件;如果…。

under·state /ˌʌndəˈsteɪt; ˌʌndɚˈstet/ *vt* [VP6A] fail to state fully or adequately; express in excessively restrained language: 未充分或完整地陳述;以比較謹愼或簡略的語句表達;少報;少說: *They exaggerated the enemy's losses and ～d their own.* 他們誇大敵人的損失,而把自己的損失輕描淡寫地帶過。*She*

~d her age on the census form. 她在戸口調查表上少報她的年齡。 **~·ment** /ˈʌndəsteɪtmənt ; ˈʌndɚ-ˌstetmənt/ *n* [U] understating; [C] statement that expresses an idea, etc, too weakly: 不充分的陳述; 保守或簡略的陳述;少報;少說: *To say that the boy is rather clever is an ~ment,* eg of a boy who is brilliant. 說這男孩頗爲聰明是一種保守的說法(如指一個非常聰明的男孩言)。

under·stock /ˌʌndəˈstɒk ; ˌʌndɚˈstɑk/ *vt* [VP6A] equip with less stock than is desirable: 未充分供以存貨;未充分供以牲畜: *Is the farm ~ed,* Could it support more animals, etc than it now has? 這農場還能飼養更多的牲畜嗎？

under·study /ˈʌndəstʌdɪ ; ˈʌndɚˌstʌdɪ/ *n* (*pl* -dies) person learning to, able to, take the place of another (esp an actor). 候補人員;(尤指)候補演員。□ *vt* (*pt, pp* -died) [VP6A] study (a part in a play) for this purpose; act as ~ to (an actor): 研習(劇中的角色)以爲候補演員;充當(某一演員)的候補演員: *He is ~ing Macbeth/~ing the leading actor in the play.* 他正在研習馬克白一角以備臨時做替角(目前是該劇主角的候補演員)。

under·take /ˌʌndəˈteɪk ; ˌʌndɚˈtek/ *vt* (*pt* -took /-ˈtʊk ; -ˈtʊk/, *pp* -taken /-ˈteɪkən ; -ˈtekən/) **1** [VP 6A, 7A] *~ (to do) sth,* make oneself responsible for; agree (to do sth): 擔任;承攬;答應;約定(做某事): *Gladstone undertook the premiership when he was 82 years old.* 格萊斯頓在他八十二歲時擔任首相職務。 *He undertook to finish the job by Friday.* 他答應在星期五以前完成那工作。 **2** [VP6A] start (a piece of work). 着手;開始(某項工作)。 **3** [VP7A, 9] affirm; promise: 確定;許諾;擔保: *I can't ~ that you will make a profit.* 我不能擔保你會獲利。 **under·tak·ing** /ˌʌndəˈteɪkɪŋ ; ˌʌndɚˈtekɪŋ/ *n* [C] **1** work that one has ~n to do; task or enterprise. 所承擔的工作;事業; 企業。 **2** promise; guarantee. 承諾;保證。

under·taker /ˈʌndəteɪkə(r) ; ˈʌndɚˌtekɚ/ *n* one whose business is to prepare the dead for burial or cremation and manage funerals (US 美 = *mortician*). 承辦殯葬者;殯儀員。 **under·tak·ing** /ˈʌndəteɪkɪŋ ; ˈʌndɚˌtekɪŋ/ *n* [U] the business of an ~. 殯葬事宜;喪葬事宜。

under-the-counter /ˌʌndə ðə ˈkaʊntə(r) ; ˌʌndɚðə-ˈkaʊntɚ/ *adj* ⇨ counter¹.

under·tone /ˈʌndətəʊn ; ˈʌndɚˌton/ *n* [C] **1** low, quiet, tone: 低調;低音: *talk in ~s,* with subdued voices. 低聲談話。 **2** underlying quality: 潛伏的感情或意思: *an ~ of discontent/hostility/sadness.* 潛伏的不滿(敵意,悲哀)。 **3** thin or subdued colour. 淡色;底彩。

under·took /ˌʌndəˈtʊk ; ˌʌndɚˈtʊk/ *pt* of undertake.

under·tow /ˈʌndətəʊ ; ˈʌndɚˌto/ *n* (current caused by the) backward flow of a wave breaking on a beach: (波浪冲擊岸邊後退回去的)回流;退波: *The swimmer was caught in an ~ and carried out to sea.* 那游泳者陷入回流而被捲出海。

under·value /ˌʌndəˈvæljuː ; ˈʌndɚˈvælju/ *vt* [VP 6A] value at less than the true worth. 低估…的價值。 **under·valu·ation** /ˌʌndəˌvæljʊˈeɪʃn ; ˈʌndɚ-ˌvæljʊˈeʃən/ *n*

under·water /ˈʌndəwɔːtə(r) ; ˈʌndɚˌwɔtɚ/ *adj* below the surface of the water: 水面下的;水中的: *~ swimming,* eg with a snorkel. 潛水游泳(如帶有呼吸管)。

under·wear /ˈʌndəweə(r); ˈʌndɚˌwɛr/ *n* [U] underclothing. 內衣。

under·weight /ˈʌndəweɪt ; ˈʌndɚˈwet/ *n* [U] weight less than what is usual or legal. 未達標準之重量;不足之重量。□ *adj* /ˌʌndəˈweɪt ; ˈʌndɚˌwet/ below the weight that is usual or legal: 重量未達標準的;重量不足的: *an ~ boy.* 體重未達標準的男孩。 *These onions are ~/are ten ounces ~.* 這些洋葱重量不足(重量差十盎斯)。⇨ overweight.

under·went /ˌʌndəˈwent; ˌʌndɚˈwɛnt/ *pt* of undergo.

under·whelm /ˌʌndəˈwelm *US:* -ˈhwelm ; ˌʌndɚ-ˈhwɛlm/ *vt* [VP6A] (colloq, facet) fail to cause enthusiasm, interest, excitement in: (俗,玩笑語)未能引起…之熱情,興趣或興奮: *to ~ an audience;* 未能引起觀衆的熱情,興趣或興奮; *an ~ing argument/speech/performance.* 不動人的辯論(演說,表演)。

under·world /ˈʌndəwɜːld ; ˈʌndɚˌwɝld/ *n* **1** (in Gk myths, etc) place of the departed spirits of the dead. (希神等)下界;地獄。 **2** part of society that lives by vice and crime. 下流社會;黑社會。

under·write /ˌʌndəˈraɪt ; ˌʌndɚˈraɪt/ *vt* (*pt* -wrote /-ˈrəʊt ; -ˈrot/, *pp* -written /-ˈrɪtn ; -ˈrɪtn̩/) [VP6A] undertake to bear all or part of possible loss of (by signing an agreement about insurance, esp of ships); engage to buy all the newly issued stock in (a company) not bought by the public. (藉簽名於保險船隻等的合約而)負責保險; 承保全部或部分損失; 認購(公司)尚未出售的新股票; 包銷。 **ˈunder·writer** *n* one who ~s policies of (esp marine) insurance: 保險業者;保險商;(尤指)海上保險商: *an ~r at Lloyd's.* 英國勞埃德公司的保險業者。

un·de·served /ˌʌndɪˈzɜːvd ; ˌʌndɪˈzɝvd/ *adj* not fair or just: 不公平的;不當的;不應得的: *an ~ punishment/reward.* 不公平的懲罰(報酬)。

un·de·signed /ˌʌndɪˈzaɪnd ; ˌʌndɪˈzaɪnd/ *adj* (esp) not premeditated or done on purpose; not foreseen. (尤指)非故意的;非預謀的;偶然的。

un·de·sir·able /ˌʌndɪˈzaɪərəbl ; ˌʌndɪˈzaɪrəbl̩/ *adj* objectionable; (esp of persons) of a kind not to be welcomed in society. 令人不快的;不理想的;(尤指人)不受歡迎的;討厭的。□ *n* ~ person. 討厭的人。

un·de·terred /ˌʌndɪˈtɜːd ; ˌʌndɪˈtɝd/ *adj* not deterred or discouraged: 未受阻的;未受挫折的: *~ by the weather/by failure.* 未爲天氣所阻礙的(未因失敗而氣餒的)。

un·de·vel·oped /ˌʌndɪˈveləpt ; ˌʌndɪˈvɛləpt/ *adj* not developed: 未發展的;未發達的;未開發的: *~ land,* not yet used (for agriculture, industry, building, etc). 未開發的土地(尚未用於農、工、建築等方面者)。

un·did /ʌnˈdɪd ; ʌnˈdɪd/ *pt* of undo.

un·dies /ˈʌndɪz ; ˈʌndɪz/ *n pl* (colloq) underclothes. (俗)內衣。

un·dig·nified /ʌnˈdɪgnɪfaɪd ; ʌnˈdɪgnəˌfaɪd/ *adj* not showing proper dignity; clumsy. 不莊重的;樣子不好看的。

un·dis·charged /ˌʌndɪsˈtʃɑːdʒd ; ˌʌndɪsˈtʃɑrdʒd/ *adj* (of a cargo) not unloaded; (of a debt) not paid; (esp, of a bankrupt person or firm) not relieved of a further liability to pay money still owing to creditors. (指船貨)未卸下的;未起貨的; (指債務) 未償付的;未還清的;(尤指已破產的個人或公司)所欠債務將來仍須償付的;未解除償債義務的。⇨ discharge²(5).

undo /ʌnˈduː ; ʌnˈdu/ *vt* (*pt* undid /ʌnˈdɪd ; ʌnˈdɪd/, *pp* undone /ʌnˈdʌn ; ʌnˈdʌn/) [VP6A] **1** untie, unfasten, loosen (knots, buttons, etc): 解開;鬆開(結、鈕扣等): *My shoe-lace has come undone.* 我的鞋帶鬆開了。 **2** destroy the result of; bring back the state of affairs that existed before: 破壞…的結果;恢復…的原狀: *He has undone the good work of his predecessor.* 他已毀棄了他前任者的良好成就。 *What is done cannot be undone.* 覆水難收。 **~·ing** *n* (cause of) ruin: 毀滅;毀滅的原因: *Drink was his ~ing.* 酗酒是他失敗的原因。 *He went to the money-lenders, to his complete ~ing.* 他向高利貸者借貸,以致完全毀了。 **un·done** *pred adj* **1** not done; not finished: 未做的;未做完的: *leave one's work undone.* 留下工作未做完。 *We have left undone those things which we ought to have done.* 我們沒做完那些該完成的工作。 **2** (archaic) (of a person) ruined. (古)(指人)破產的。

un·dock /ʌnˈdɒk ; ʌnˈdɑk/ *vt, vi* [VP6A, 2A] uncouple (a module, etc) from a spacecraft: 使(太空艙等)與太空船分離: *The astronauts had some difficulty in ~ing the lunar module.* 太空人在使登月小艇與太空船分離時,遭遇到一些麻煩。

U

un·dom·es·ti·cated /ˌʌndəˈmestɪkeɪtɪd ; ˌʌndəˈmɛstɪˌketɪd/ *adj* not trained or interested in household affairs. 對家務無訓練或無興趣的;不諳家事的。

un·doubted /ʌnˈdaʊtɪd ; ʌnˈdaʊtɪd/ *adj* certain; accepted as true: 確定的;無疑的: *There is an ~ improvement in the patient's condition.* 病人的情況有明顯的進步。~**·ly** *adv*

un·dreamed /ʌnˈdri:md ; ʌnˈdrimd/, **un·dreamt** /ʌnˈdremt ; ʌnˈdrɛmpt/ *adjj* (usu) (通常作) **~-of,** not thought of; not imagined: 夢想不到的;想像不到的: *earn ~-of wealth;* 賺到夢想不到的財富; *~-of beauties.* 意想不到的美女。

un·dress /ʌnˈdres ; ʌnˈdrɛs/ *vt, vi* **1** [VP6A] remove the clothes of: 除去或脫去…的衣服: *Jane ~ed her doll.* 珍脫去她那洋娃娃的衣服。 **2** [VP2A] take off one's clothes: 脫去自己的衣服;寬衣;卸裝: *~ and get into bed.* 寬衣就寢。□ *n* [U] **1** uniform for ordinary (nonceremonial) occasions. 便服;軍便服。 **2** state of being partly or not dressed. 半裸;全裸。

un·due /ˌʌnˈdju: *US:* -ˈdu: ; ʌnˈdju/ *adj* improper; more than is right: 不適當的;過度的;過分的: *with ~ haste;* 過分匆忙地; *exercise an ~ influence upon sb.* 對某人施展不當的影響力。**un·duly** /ˌʌnˈdju:li *US:* -ˈdu:lɪ ; ʌnˈdjulɪ/ *adv* in an ~ manner: 不適當地;過度地;過分地: *unduly pessimistic.* 過度悲觀的。

un·du·late /ˈʌndjʊleɪt *US:* -dʒʊ- ; ˈʌndjəˌlet/ *vi* [VP2A, C] (of surfaces) have a wave-like motion or look: (指表面)波動;起伏;呈波浪形: *a field of wheat undulating in the breeze;* 在微風中起伏的麥田; *undulating land,* that rises and falls in gentle slopes. 波狀地;起伏地。**un·du·la·tion** /ˌʌndjʊˈleɪʃn *US:* -dʒʊ- ; ˌʌndjəˈleʃən/ *n* [U] wave-like motion or form; [C] one of a number of wave-like curves or slopes. 波動;波形;起伏;波狀的彎曲或斜坡。

un·dy·ing /ˌʌnˈdaɪɪŋ ; ʌnˈdaɪɪŋ/ *adj* everlasting; never-ending: 不朽的;永恆的: *~ love / hatred / fame.* 不朽的愛(永久的恨;不朽的名譽)。

un·earned /ˌʌnˈɜ:nd ; ʌnˈɝnd/ *adj* **1** not gained by work or service: 不勞而獲的: *~ income,* eg from investments, or land or property that is inherited; 不勞而獲的收入;不勞所得; *~ increment,* increase in the value of property, eg houses, land, not due to the owner's expenditure or efforts, eg because of a rise in the value of land. 自然增值(房、地等財產非因所有者的投資或努力,而其價值有所增加之謂)。 **2** not deserved: 不應得的: *~ praise.* 不應得的讚美。

un·earth /ʌnˈɜ:θ ; ʌnˈɝθ/ *vt* [VP6A] discover and bring to light: 發掘;發現: *~ new facts about the life of Shakespeare;* 發現有關莎士比亞生平的新事實; *~ a buried treasure.* 發掘埋在地下的寶藏。*The dog has ~ed some bones.* 那狗掘出了幾根骨頭。

un·earth·ly /ʌnˈɜ:θlɪ ; ʌnˈɝθlɪ/ *adj* **1** supernatural. 超自然的; 非塵世的。 **2** mysterious; ghostly; frightening: 神秘的;鬼怪的;可怕的: *~ screams.* 可怕的尖叫。 **3** (colloq) unreasonable: (俗)不合理的: *Why do you wake me up at this ~ hour?* 你爲什麼在這個時候叫醒我?

un·easy /ʌnˈi:zɪ ; ʌnˈizɪ/ *adj* not easy in body or mind; troubled or anxious: 身體或心境不舒適的;不安的;焦慮的: *have an ~ conscience;* 良心不安; *be ~ in one's mind about the future;* 懸慮未來; *pass an ~ night,* sleep badly. 一夜未睡好。*We grew ~ at their long absence.* 他們離開甚久我們漸感不安。**un·eas·ily** /ʌnˈi:zɪlɪ ; ʌnˈizlɪ/ *adv* **un·easi·ness, un·ease** /ʌnˈi:z ; ʌnˈiz/ *nn*

un·eaten /ʌnˈi:tn ; ʌnˈitn̩/ *adj* (of food, a meal) set out but left unused. (指食物,餐食)擺出而未吃的。

un·edu·cated /ʌnˈedʒʊkeɪtɪd ; ʌnˈɛdʒəˌketɪd/ *adj* not educated; suggesting lack of education (or the kind of education or social background considered desirable): 未受教育的; 缺乏適當教育的; 缺乏教養的: *He has an ~ mind / voice.* 他的思想(說話的方式)缺乏教養。

un·em·ploy·able /ˌʌnɪmˈplɔɪəbl ; ˌʌnɪmˈplɔɪəbl̩/ *adj* that cannot be employed. 不能被雇用的;不能使用的。

un·em·ployed /ˌʌnɪmˈplɔɪd ; ˌʌnɪmˈplɔɪd/ *adj* not being used: 未在使用中的;未用的: *~ capital;* 游資; not working, not able to get work: 無工作的;失業的: *~ men.* 無工作的人們。**the ~,** those for whom there is no work or who are temporarily without work. 失業者。

un·em·ploy·ment /ˌʌnɪmˈplɔɪmənt ; ˌʌnɪmˈplɔɪmənt/ *n* [U] **1** state of being unemployed: 失業;無工作: *U~ is a serious social evil.* 失業是社會的一大弊害。 **2** amount of unused labour: 失業人數: *There is more ~ now than there was six months ago.* 現在失業的人比六個月以前多。 **3** (attrib) (形容用法): *~ insurance;* 失業保險; *~ pay / benefit,* money paid from insurance funds to a worker who cannot get employment. 失業津貼(救濟金)。

un·end·ing /ʌnˈendɪŋ ; ʌnˈɛndɪŋ/ *adj* everlasting; unceasing; (colloq) frequently repeated: 永遠的;不斷的;(俗)經常被重複的: *She's tired of your ~ grumbles.* 她厭倦了你那無休止的抱怨。~**·ly** *adv*

un·en·dur·able /ˌʌnɪnˈdjʊərəbl ; ˌʌnɪnˈdjʊrəbl̩/ *adj* not able to be endured: 不能忍受的;無法忍耐的: *~ pain / injustice.* 不能忍受的痛苦(寃枉)。

un·en·light·ened /ˌʌnɪnˈlaɪtnd ; ˌʌnɪnˈlaɪtn̩d/ *adj* uneducated; not well-informed; (in some contexts) prejudiced or superstitious. 未受或缺乏教育的;見聞不廣的;(在某些上下文中可解釋爲)偏見的;迷信的;閉塞的。

un·equal /ˌʌnˈi:kwəl ; ʌnˈikwəl/ *adj* **~ (to sth). 1** not equal. 不相等的。 **2** (esp of work such as writing) not of the same quality throughout; variable. (尤指寫作)品質不均勻的;前後不一致的;不一律的。 **3** not strong, clever, etc enough: 不勝任的;不够强壯、聰明等的: *I feel ~ to the task.* 我對這項工作感到無法勝任。~**ly** /-kwəlɪ ; -kwəlɪ/ *adv*

un·equalled /ˌʌnˈi:kwəld ; ʌnˈikwəld/ *adj* unmatched; unrivalled. 無與倫比的; 無敵手的; 無雙的; 極好的。

un·equivo·cal /ˌʌnɪˈkwɪvəkl ; ˌʌnɪˈkwɪvəkl̩/ *adj* clear; having one only possible meaning. 清楚的;不含混的;祇有一種可能之含義的。

un·err·ing /ʌnˈɜ:rɪŋ ; ʌnˈɝɪŋ/ *adj* accurate: 正確的;無錯誤的: *fire with ~ aim;* 瞄得很準地射擊; *strike an ~ blow.* 不偏不倚地一擊。~**·ly** *adv*

un·ex·ampled /ˌʌnɪgˈzɑ:mpld *US:* -ˈzæm- ; ˌʌnɪgˈzæmpl̩d/ *adj* of which there is no other expample that can be compared with it: 無可比擬的;無前例的: *the ~ heroism of our soldiers.* 我們士兵無可比擬的英勇。

un·ex·cep·tion·able /ˌʌnɪkˈsepʃənəbl ; ˌʌnɪkˈsɛpʃənəbl̩/ *adj* beyond criticism; altogether admirable. 無可非難的;極好的;完美的。

un·ex·pected /ˌʌnɪkˈspektɪd ; ˌʌnɪkˈspɛktɪd/ *adj* not expected: 意外的;未料到的: *~ guests / questions / results.* 不速之客(未料到的問題;未料到的結果)。

un·fail·ing /ʌnˈfeɪlɪŋ ; ʌnˈfelɪŋ/ *adj* never coming to an end; meeting one's expectations at all times: 無止境的; 始終符合期望的; 可靠的: *his ~ good humour / patience;* 他那始終如一的好脾氣(耐性); *an ~ (= loyal) friend.* 忠實可靠的朋友。~**·ly** *adv* at all times: 始終;永遠;永久: *~ly courteous.* 始終有禮貌的。

un·fair /ˌʌnˈfeə(r) ; ʌnˈfɛr/ *adj* not right or fair; unjust: 不正當的;不公平的;不公正的: *~ treatment / competition.* 不公平的待遇(競爭)。~**·ly** *adv* ~**·ness** *n*

un·faith·ful /ˌʌnˈfeɪθfl ; ʌnˈfeθfəl/ *adj* not true to one's duty, a promise, etc; (esp) not faithful to marriage vows: 不忠實的;不信實的;(尤指)不貞潔的;有外遇的: *Her husband is ~ to her.* 她的丈夫對她不忠實。~**ly** /-fəlɪ ; -fəlɪ/ *adv* ~**·ness** *n*

un·fal·ter·ing /ʌnˈfɔ:ltərɪŋ ; ʌnˈfɔltərɪŋ/ *adj* not wavering or hesitating: 不躊躇的;堅決的: *with ~ steps / courage.* 脚步堅定地(以堅定不移的勇氣)。~**·ly** *adv*

un·fam·il·iar /ˌʌnfəˈmɪlɪə(r) ; ˌʌnfəˈmɪljə/ *adj* **1 ~ (to),** not well known: 不深知的;生疏的: *That face is not ~ to me,* I feel that I know it, have seen it before. 那面孔我並不生疏(似曾相識)。**2** ~ ***with,*** not acquainted with: 不熟悉的;不熟識的: *He is still ~ with this district.* 這一地區他仍舊不熟悉。

un·fath·om·able /ʌnˈfæðəməbl ; ʌnˈfæðəməbl̩/ *adj* so deep that the bottom cannot be reached; (fig) too strange or difficult to be understood. 深不可測的;(喻)難以瞭解的;深奧的。 **un·fath·omed** /ʌnˈfæðəmd ; ʌnˈfæðəmd/ *adj* (of a person's character) not understood; (of a crime, etc) not solved; (of ocean depths, etc) not measured. (指人的個性)不可解的;(指一項犯罪等)未定案的;未偵破的;(指海深等)未測定的。

un·feel·ing /ʌnˈfi:lɪŋ ; ʌnˈfilɪŋ/ *adj* **1** hard-hearted; unsympathetic. 殘酷的;無情的。**2** not able to feel. 無感覺的。 **~·ly** *adv*

un·feigned /ʌnˈfeɪnd ; ʌnˈfend/ *adj* not pretended; genuine (which is more usu 較常用 genuine); sincere: 不虛僞的;眞實的;誠心的: *He showed ~ satisfaction at his son's success.* 他對他兒子的成功表現出眞正的滿足。 **~·ly** *adv* openly and sincerely. 開誠地;誠心地。

un·fit /ˌʌnˈfɪt ; ʌnˈfɪt/ *adj* ~ ***(for sth/to do sth),*** not fit or suitable: 不適當的;不勝任的;不合適的: *He is ~ for business/~ to be a doctor.* 他不適合做生意(當醫生)。*This road is ~ for heavy traffic.* 這條路不能負荷頻繁的交通。*He was rejected* (eg for military service) *as medically ~.* 他因健康不合格而遭淘汰(如服兵役)。□ *vt* (-tt) [VP14] ~ ***sb for sth,*** make ~ (which is more usu): 使不適合;使不相宜;使不能勝任(較常用 make ~): *A bad attack of lumbago ~ted him for work in the garden.* 因腰部風濕痛發作得很厲害,他無法做園子裡的工作。

un·flag·ging /ˌʌnˈflægɪŋ ; ʌnˈflægɪŋ/ *adj* not showing signs of weariness; uninterrupted: 毫無倦容的;不減弱的;不鬆懈的;未間斷的: *work with ~ energy.* 精力充沛地工作。

un·flap·pable /ˌʌnˈflæpəbl ; ʌnˈflæpəbl̩/ *adj* (colloq) unlikely to get into a flap; never upset in a crisis. (俗)不易驚慌失措的;臨危不亂的;從容不迫的。⇨ flap[1](4).

un·fledged /ˌʌnˈfledʒd ; ʌnˈflɛdʒd/ *adj* (of a bird) not yet able to fly; (fig, of a person) immature; inexperienced. (指鳥)還不會飛的;羽毛未豐的;(喻,指人)未成熟的;無經驗的。

un·flinch·ing /ʌnˈflɪntʃɪŋ ; ʌnˈflɪntʃɪŋ/ *adj* fearless; resolute. 無畏懼的;堅定的。

un·fold /ʌnˈfəʊld ; ʌnˈfold/ *vt, vi* [VP6A, 2A, C] **1** (of sth folded) open out: (指摺疊,合攏之物)展開: ~ *a newspaper/a prospectus.* 展開報紙(計畫書)。 **2** reveal, make known; become known or visible: 顯露;表露;顯現;呈現: *as the story ~s (itself).* 如故事所呈現。*She ~ed to him her plans for the future.* 她向他表露她未來的計畫。*The landscape ~ed before us.* 景色顯現在我們面前。

un·for·get·table /ˌʌnfəˈgetəbl ; ˌʌnfəˈgɛtəbl̩/ *adj* that cannot be forgotten: 不能忘記的;永遠記得的: *an ~ experience.* 永遠忘不了的一次經驗。

un·for·tu·nate /ʌnˈfɔ:tʃʊnət ; ʌnˈfɔrtʃənɪt/ *adj* unlucky: 不幸運的;倒霉的: *an ~ expedition;* 一次運氣不佳的探險; regrettable: 令人遺憾的;抱歉的;可惜的: *an ~ remark/lack of good manners.* 失言(失禮)。 **~·ly** *adv: You're wrong, ~ly.* 抱歉,你錯了。*U~ly for you, you're wrong.* 爲你遺憾的是,你錯了。

un·founded /ˌʌnˈfaʊndɪd ; ʌnˈfaʊndɪd/ *adj* without foundation: 無根據的;無稽的: *~ rumours.* 無稽的謠言。

un·fre·quented /ˌʌnfrɪˈkwentɪd ; ˌʌnfrɪˈkwɛntɪd/ *adj* seldom visited. 冷落的;罕有人訪問的;人跡罕到的。

un·friend·ly /ʌnˈfrendlɪ ; ʌnˈfrɛndlɪ/ *adj* not friendly; unfavourable. 不友善的;有敵意的;不相宜的;不利的。

un·frock /ˌʌnˈfrɒk ; ʌnˈfrɑk/ *vt* [VP6A] (of a priest guilty of bad conduct) dismiss from the priesthood. (指行爲不檢的僧侶)解除僧職。

un·fruit·ful /ʌnˈfru:tfl ; ʌnˈfrutfəl/ *adj* not bearing fruit; without results or success. 不結果實的;無結果的;不成功的;徒然的。

un·furl /ʌnˈfɜ:l ; ʌnˈfɝl/ *vt, vi* [VP6A, 2A] roll out; spread out: 展開;張開;鋪開: ~ *the sails.* 揚帆。

un·fur·nished /ˌʌnˈfɜ:nɪʃt ; ʌnˈfɝnɪʃt/ *adj* (esp) without furniture: (尤指)無家具的;無陳設的: *rooms/a house to let ~.* 無家具的房間(房屋)招租。

un·gain·ly /ʌnˈgeɪnlɪ ; ʌnˈgenlɪ/ *adj* clumsy; awkward; ungraceful. 笨拙的;難看的;不雅的。

un·gen·er·ous /ʌnˈdʒenərəs ; ʌnˈdʒɛnərəs/ *adj* not generous; unkind. 不慷慨的;氣量小的;胸襟狹窄的。

un·get-at-able /ˌʌngetˈætəbl ; ˌʌngɛtˈætəbl̩/ *adj* = un-come-at-able.

un·god·ly /ʌnˈgɒdlɪ ; ʌnˈgɑdlɪ/ *adj* **1** not religious; not giving reverence to God; sinful. 不敬神的;不虔誠的;罪孽的。 **2** (colloq) annoying; shocking. (俗)討厭的;驚人的;可怕的。 **3** (colloq) unreasonable: (俗)不合理的: *Why did you phone me at this ~ hour?* 你爲什麼在這個時候打電話給我呢?

un·gov·ern·able /ʌnˈgʌvənəbl ; ʌnˈgʌvənəbl̩/ *adj* that cannot be controlled: 不能控制的;難駕馭的: *~ passions;* 難控制的熱情; *a man with an ~ temper.* 不能控制脾氣的人。

un·grate·ful /ʌnˈgreɪtfl ; ʌnˈgretfəl/ *adj* **1** not showing gratitude. 不感謝的;不領情的;忘恩負義的。 **2** (of a task) not pleasant or agreeable. (指工作)討厭的;令人不快的。

un·guarded /ˌʌnˈgɑ:dɪd ; ʌnˈgɑrdɪd/ *adj* (esp of a person and what he says) careless; indiscreet: (尤指人及其所說的話)不小心的;不謹愼的: *In an ~ moment, he gave away most important secrets.* 一不留神,他洩露了非常重要的祕密。

un·guent /ˈʌŋgwənt ; ˈʌŋgwənt/ *n* [C, U] any soft substance used as an ointment (eg for soothing skin injuries) or for lubrication. 藥膏;軟膏;潤滑油。

un·hal·lowed /ʌnˈhæləʊd ; ʌnˈhælod/ *adj* **1** not made holy: 未奉爲神聖的;褻瀆神明的: *buried in ~ ground,* not consecrated by the Church. 葬在未經教會奉獻的土地上。 **2** wicked; impious: 邪惡的;不恭敬的: *with ~ joy.* 帶着邪惡的喜悅。

un·hand /ʌnˈhænd ; ʌnˈhænd/ *vt* [VP6A] (archaic) let go; take the hands off. (古)放開;鬆手。

un·happy /ʌnˈhæpɪ ; ʌnˈhæpɪ/ *adj* (-ier, -iest) **1** not happy. 不高興的;不愉快的。 **2** not suitable or tactful: 不適合的;不適當的: *an ~ comment.* 不適當的評論。

un·healthy /ʌnˈhelθɪ ; ʌnˈhɛlθɪ/ *adj* harmful to bodily or mental health; (colloq) dangerous. 對身心有害的;不衛生的;不利於健康的;(俗)危險的。

un·heard /ʌnˈhɜ:d ; ʌnˈhɝd/ *adj* not heard; not allowed a hearing. 未聽見的;聽不到的;未予審理的;不允審判的。***go ~,*** **(a)** not be heard. 未審理;未加審判。 **(b)** have no-one willing to listen to it: 無人願意聽;無人理會: *Her request for help went ~.* 她求助的呼籲無人理會。 **un·heard-of** /ʌnˈhɜ:d ɒv ; ʌnˈhɝdˌɑv/ *adj* extraordinary; without an earlier example. 不尋常的;空前的;前所未聞的。

un·hinge /ʌnˈhɪndʒ ; ʌnˈhɪndʒ/ *vt* [VP6A] take (a door, gate, etc) from the hinge(s); cause (sb's mind, brain) to be off its balance: 從樞紐拿下(門,門扉等);使(某人的精神,頭腦)失常: *His mind is ~d,* He is mentally ill. 他的精神失常。

un·holy /ʌnˈhəʊlɪ ; ʌnˈholɪ/ *adj* **1** wicked; sinful. 邪惡的;有罪的。 **2** (colloq) unreasonable. (俗)不合理的。

un·hook /ʌnˈhʊk ; ʌnˈhʊk/ *vt* [VP6A] undo the hooks of (a dress, etc); release from a hook. 鬆開或解開(衣服等)上的鈎釦;從鈎上取下或放下。

un·hoped-for /ʌnˈhəʊpt fɔ:(r) ; ʌnˈhoptˌfɔr/ *adj* unexpected: 未料到的;意外的: *an ~ piece of good fortune.* 意外的好運。

un·horse /ˌʌnˈhɔ:s ; ʌnˈhɔrs/ *vt* [VP6A] throw from a horse's back; cause to fall from a horse. 自馬背上拋下;使從馬背上摔下。

uni·corn /ˈju:nɪkɔ:n ; ˈjunɪˌkɔrn/ *n* (in old stories) horse-like animal with one long horn; (heraldry)

U

representation of this with a lion's tail. (古老故事中似馬的)獨角獸;(紋章)(帶有獅尾的)獨角獸標記。

un·iden·ti·fied /ˌʌnaɪˈdentɪfaɪd ; ˌʌnaɪˈdɛntɪˌfaɪd/ *adj* which cannot be identified: 不能指證的;無從辨識的;來路不明的: *The dead man is still* ~. 死者身份仍未查明。~ **flying object**, (abbr 略作 **UFO** /ˌjuː ef ˈəʊ ; ˌju ɛf ˈo/ or /ˈjuːfəʊ ; ˈjufo/) ⇨ *flying saucer* at flying.

uni·form /ˈjuːnɪfɔːm ; ˈjunəˌfɔrm/ *adj* the same; not varying in form, quality, etc: 相同的;一律的;形式、性質等無變化的: *sticks of* ~ *length;* 長度一致的棍子; *to be kept at a* ~ *temperature.* 保持於恆溫。□ *n* [C, U] (style of) dress worn by all members of an organization, eg the police, the armed forces: 制服;軍服;制服或軍服的服式: *the blue* ~*(s) of the police;* 警察的藍色制服; *the khaki* ~*(s) of the army.* 卡其布軍服。*in* ~, wearing such dress: 穿制服或軍服: *He looks handsome in* ~. 他穿制服看起來很帥。~**ed** *adj* wearing ~: 穿着制服或軍服的: *the* ~*ed branch of the police,* contrasted with those who wear plain clothes, eg detectives. 警察編制之着制服組(以別於着便衣組,如便衣警探)。~**·ly** *adv* ~**·ity** /ˌjuːnɪˈfɔːmətɪ ; ˌjunəˈfɔrmətɪ/ *n* [U] ~ condition; condition of being the same throughout. 同一;一律;一致。

unify /ˈjuːnɪfaɪ ; ˈjunəˌfaɪ/ *vt* (*pt, pp* -fied) [VP6A] **1** form into one; unite. 使合一;統一;結合。**2** make uniform. 使一致。 **uni·fi·ca·tion** /ˌjuːnɪfɪˈkeɪʃn ; ˌjunəfəˈkeʃən/ *n* [U] ~ing or being unified: 統一;一致;單一化: *work for the unification of Europe.* 致力於歐洲的統一。

uni·lat·eral /ˌjuːnɪˈlætrəl ; ˌjunɪˈlætərəl/ *adj* of, on, affecting, done by, one side or party only: 單方面的;片面的;單方面做的;僅影響一方的: *a* ~ *declaration of independence,* (abbr 略作 **UDI**); 單方面宣告獨立; ~ *repudiation of a treaty,* by one of the parties that signed it, without the consent of the other party or parties. 單方面廢除條約。~**ly** /-rəlɪ ; -rəlɪ/ *adv*

U

un·im·peach·able /ˌʌnɪmˈpiːtʃəbl ; ˌʌnɪmˈpitʃəbl̩/ *adj* that cannot be questioned or doubted: 無可指責的;無可懷疑的;可靠的: ~ *honesty;* 無可懷疑的誠實; *news from an* ~ *source.* 來源可靠的消息。

un·in·formed /ˌʌnɪnˈfɔːmd ; ˌʌnɪnˈfɔrmd/ *adj* (esp) not having, made without, adequate information: (尤指)無充分認識或情報的; 無充分知識(而做成)的: ~ *criticism.* 無知的批評。

un·in·hib·ited /ˌʌnɪnˈhɪbɪtɪd ; ˌʌnɪnˈhɪbətɪd/ *adj* without inhibitions; free from the social and moral restraints usual among conventional people. 無限制的;無拘束的;不拘形式的。

un·in·spired /ˌʌnɪnˈspaɪəd ; ˌʌnɪnˈspaɪrd/ *adj* without inspiration; dull: 無靈感的; 枯燥的; 無趣味的: *an* ~ *lecture/lecturer.* 枯燥的演講(者)。

un·in·ter·ested /ʌnˈɪntrəstɪd ; ʌnˈɪntərɪstɪd/ *adj* ~ *(in),* having, showing no interest. 無興趣的;不感興趣的;不關心的。

union /ˈjuːnɪən ; ˈjunjən/ *n* **1** [U] uniting or being united; joining or being joined; [C] instance of this: 聯合;合併;其實例: *the* ~ *of the three towns into one;* 三市鎮合而爲一; *the Universal Postal U*~, of countries for the purpose of interchanging mail services to mutual advantage; 萬國郵政協會; *the U*~ *of Soviet Socialist Republics* (abbr 略作 **USSR**). 蘇維埃社會主義共和國聯邦;蘇聯。**the U~**, **(a)** of England and Scotland (in 1707). (1707 年)英格蘭和蘇格蘭的合併。**(b)** the United States of America: 美利堅合衆國;美國: *the President's address to the U*~, to all US citizens. (美國)總統對全民的演講。**the U~ Jack**, the British flag. 英國國旗。⇨ the illus at flag. 參看 flag 之挿圖。**2** [U] state of being in agreement or harmony: 一致;和諧: *live in perfect* ~; 十分和睦地生活; [C] instance of this: 一致或和諧的實例: *a happy* ~, eg a happy marriage. 美滿的結合(如愉快的婚姻)。**3** [C] association formed by the uniting of persons, groups, etc, 同盟;協會, esp 尤指 **trade-~**, ⇨ trade¹(1). **4** (old use; GB) workhouse built by two or more parishes for administration of the poor laws. (舊用法;英)救貧院;貧民所。**5 the U~**, general society at some universities, etc. (某些大學等的)學聯會。**6** [C] coupling for connecting rods or pipes. (機械)管接;管套節。**7** ~ **suit**, (US) combinations(4). (美)連褲內衣。~**·ist** /-ɪst ; -ɪst/ *n* [C] **1** member of a trade ~; supporter of trade ~s. 工會的會員;支持工會者。**2 U~·ist**, **(a)** (GB politics) person who, before the Irish Free State was established, opposed the granting of independence to Ireland. (英國政治)(愛爾蘭自由邦成立前)反對愛爾蘭獨立者。**(b)** supporter of the Federal Government of the US during the Civil War; opponent of secession. (美國內戰期間)聯邦主義者;反對分裂者;支持聯邦政府者。

unique /juːˈniːk ; juˈnik/ *adj* having no like or equal; being the only one of its sort. 唯一的;獨特的;無與倫比的。~**·ly** *adv* ~**·ness** *n*

uni·sex /ˈjuːnɪseks ; ˈjunɪsɛks/ *adj* (of clothes, etc) of a style designed for both sexes. (指衣服等)不分性別的;男女皆可穿的。

uni·son /ˈjuːnɪsn ; ˈjunəsn̩/ *n* [U] *(in)* ~, (in) concord or agreement: 和諧;一致: *sing in* ~, all singing the same notes, not harmonizing; 齊唱;同聲合唱; *act in* ~ *(with others).* (與他人)一致行動。

unit /ˈjuːnɪt ; ˈjunɪt/ *n* [C] **1** single person, thing or group regarded as complete in itself: 一人;一物;一個;整體;組織單位;部隊單位: (mil) (軍) *an armoured* ~; 裝甲兵單位;裝甲兵部隊; ~*s of the US Sixth Fleet.* 美國第六艦隊各單位。*The family is often taken as the* ~ *of society.* 家庭常被視爲社會的基本單位。**2** quantity or amount used as a standard of measurement: 用作計算標準的數或量;單位: *The metre is a* ~ *of length.* 公尺是長度單位。*The monetary* ~ *of Great Britain is the pound.* 英國的貨幣單位是鎊。**3** smallest whole number; the number 1. 最小的整數;一。**4** (compounds) (複合字) **ˈkitchen** ~, article of kitchen equipment, eg a sink, draining board, with cupboards, that can be fitted with others of similar design and appearance along a wall. 廚房的成套用具。**ˌ~ ˈfurniture**, article of furniture of similar design, materials, etc, to be used together. 成套家具。**ˈ~ trust**, trust(3) that invests in a large number and wide variety of stocks and issues certificates (called 稱作 ~*s*) on which dividends are payable. 投資信託(受託機構將資金投資於多種股市並發行憑證,信託者憑證分紅)。

Uni·tar·ian /ˌjuːnɪˈteərɪən ; ˌjunəˈtɛrɪən/ *n* member of a Christian church which rejects the doctrine of the Trinity and believes that God is one person. 唯一神教派(基督教的一支派,反對三位一體說,認爲上帝係單一體)的教徒。□ *adj* of the ~s: 唯一神教派的: *the U*~ *Church.* 唯一神教派教會。~**·ism** /-ɪzəm ; -ˌɪzəm/ *n*

unite /juːˈnaɪt ; juˈnaɪt/ *vt, vi* **1** [VP6A, 2A] make or become one; join: (使)聯合;結合;合併;團結: ~ *one country to another;* 使一國與另一國結合; *the common interests that* ~ *our two countries,* that bring them together. 使我們兩國團結一致的共同利益。*England and Scotland* ~*d in 1707.* 英格蘭與蘇格蘭於1707年合併。**2** [VP2A, 3A, 4A] ~ *(in sth/to do sth),* act or work together: 協力;一致行動: *Let us* ~ *in fighting/*~ *to fight poverty and disease.* 讓我們協力來克服貧窮和疾病。~**d** *adj* **1** joined in spirit, by love and sympathy: (因愛和同情)在精神上結合的;和睦的: *a* ~*d family.* 和睦的家庭。**2** resulting from association for a common purpose: 爲共同目標相結合而產生的;一致的: *make a* ~*d effort;* 一致努力; *present a* ~*d front to the enemy;* 成立聯合陣線以對抗敵人; *the U*~*d Nations.* 聯合國。**3** joined politically: 在政治上聯合的: *the*

U~d Kingdom; 聯合王國; *the U~d States of Mexico.* 墨西哥合衆國。**~d·ly** *adv*

unity /ˈjuːnətɪ ; ˈjunətɪ/ *n* (*pl* -ties) **1** [C, U] the state of being united; (an) arrangement of parts to form a complete whole: 聯合;結合;單一;獨一;統一;協調: *The figure on the left spoils the ~ of the painting.* 左邊那個人像破壞了那幅畫的整體性。 ***the dramatic unities; the unities of place, time and action,*** (drama) the use of the same scene throughout, the limitation of the duration of the play to one day, or the time taken to act it, and the use of one single plot, with nothing irrelevant to that plot. (戲劇)三一律;地點,時間和情節的一致。 **2** [U] harmony, agreement (of aims, feelings, etc): (目標,感情等的)和諧;一致: *in ~ with others;* 與他人一致地; *live together in ~;* 和睦地住在一起; *political ~.* 政治上的統一。*National ~ is essential in time of war.* 舉國團結在戰時是必要的。

uni·ver·sal /ˌjuːnɪˈvɜːsl ; ˌjunəˈvɝsl/ *adj* of, belonging to, done by, all; affecting all: 普遍的;一般的;全體的;屬於全體的;全體做的;影響全體的: *War causes ~ misery.* 戰爭引起普遍的苦難。*Television provides ~ entertainment.* 電視提供了大衆化的娛樂。 ***a ~ joint,*** one that permits the turning of connected parts in all directions. 萬向接頭。***a ~ rule,*** one with no exceptions. 普遍(適用)的法則。**~ suffrage,** suffrage extending to all members of a community. 普選權;全民參政權。 **~ time,** ⇨ Greenwich. **~ly** /-səlɪ ; -sl̩ɪ/ *adv* **~·ity** /ˌjuːnɪvɜːˈsælətɪ ; ˌjunəvɝˈsælətɪ/ *n* [U].

uni·verse /ˈjuːnɪvɜːs ; ˈjunəˌvɝs/ *n* **1 the U~,** everything that exists everywhere; all the galaxies, stars, planets, their satellites, etc; the whole creation and the Creator. 天地萬物;萬有;宇宙;造物主與其所造之物;世界。 **2** [C] system of galaxies: 恆星系;星辰系: *a new telescope that may reveal new ~s.* 一座可能顯現新恆星系的新型望遠鏡。

uni·ver·sity /ˌjuːnɪˈvɜːsətɪ ; ˌjunəˈvɝsətɪ/ *n* (*pl* -ties) (colleges, buildings, etc of an) institution for the promotion and dissemination of advanced learning, conferring degrees and engaging in academic research; members of such an institution collectively; 大學;(集合用法)大學的全體組成分子; (attrib) (形容用法) *a ~ student/lecturer;* 大學生(大學講師); *the ~ chess team.* 大學西洋棋隊。

un·kempt /ˌʌnˈkempt ; ʌnˈkɛmpt/ *adj* untidy; (esp of the hair) uncombed. 不整潔的;(尤指頭髮)未梳理的;蓬亂的。

un·kind /ʌnˈkaɪnd ; ʌnˈkaɪnd/ *adj* lacking in, not showing, kindness: 不和善的;不客氣的;不禮貌的;不厚道的: *an ~ remark.* 不客氣的話。**~·ly** *adv* in an ~ manner: 不客氣地;不禮貌地: *Don't take it ~ly if...,* Don't think I intend to be ~ if .... 不要認爲我無情,如果…。

un·know·ing /ʌnˈnəʊɪŋ ; ʌnˈnoɪŋ/ *adj* not knowing; unaware. 不知道的;無知的;沒有發覺的。**~·ly** *adv* in ignorance; unawares. 無知地;未發覺地。

un·known /ˌʌnˈnəʊn ; ʌnˈnon/ *adj* not known or identified: 不爲人知道的;未認明的;不詳的;無名的: *the tomb of the ~ warrior,* of an ~ soldier (in Westminster Abbey) buried there in memory of those killed in World Wars I and II; 無名戰士墓(在西敏寺,以紀念兩次大戰中之陣亡將士); *an ~ quantity,* of which the value, etc is not known. 未知量。

un·learn /ˌʌnˈlɜːn ; ʌnˈlɝn/ *vt* [VP6A] get rid of (ideas, habits, etc); learn to give up (sth one has previously learnt). 掃除(觀念、習慣等);忘卻(從前所學者)。

un·leash /ʌnˈliːʃ ; ʌnˈliʃ/ *vt* [VP6A] let go from a leash: 解開皮帶以釋放: *~ a dog;* 放開一條狗; (fig) release; set into action: (喻)發洩;發動;實行: *~ one's fury;* 勃然大怒; *~ a new atomic weapon.* 使用一新原子武器。

un·leav·ened /ˌʌnˈlevnd ; ʌnˈlɛvənd/ *adj* (of bread) made without yeast. (指麵包)未用酵粉做成的;不經發酵的。

un·less /ənˈles ; ənˈlɛs/ *conj* if not; except when: 若不;除非;如果…不;除非在…的時候: *You will fail ~ you work harder.* 你若不更加努力,你就會失敗。*U~ bad weather stops me, I go for a walk every day.* 除非受阻於壞天氣,我每天都出去散步。

un·let·tered /ʌnˈletəd ; ʌnˈlɛtəd/ *adj* uneducated; unable to read. 未受教育的;目不識丁的;文盲的。

un·like /ˌʌnˈlaɪk ; ʌnˈlaɪk/ *pred adj, prep* not like; different from: 不同;不像;與…有別: *His new novel is ~ all his previous ones.* 他的新小說與他以前的小說不同。*My son is ~ me in every respect.* 我的兒子沒有一處像我。

un·like·ly /ʌnˈlaɪklɪ ; ʌnˈlaɪklɪ/ *adj* not likely to happen or be true: 不太可能發生的;靠不住的: *an ~ event/hypothesis.* 不太可能的事情(靠不住的假設)。

un·load /ʌnˈləʊd ; ʌnˈlod/ *vt, vi* **1** [VP6A, 2A] remove a load from: 從…卸下貨物: *~ a ship;* 卸下船上之貨; remove (cargo) from: 卸(貨): *~ cargo.* 卸貨。*The ship is ~ing.* 該船正在卸貨。 **2** [VP6A, 14] **~ *(on to),*** (colloq) get rid of (sth not wanted): (俗)除去(不需要之物);擺脫…的負擔: *She ~ed her old car/her mother-in-law on to me.* 她將舊汽車脫手(婆婆的負擔推給我)。

un·looked-for /ʌnˈlʊkt fɔː(r) ; ʌnˈlʊktˌfɔr/ *adj* unexpected; for which one is not prepared. 意外的;沒有料到的;沒有防備的。

un·loose /ʌnˈluːs ; ʌnˈlus/ *vt* [VP6A] let loose; make free. 放開;放鬆;釋放。

un·man /ˌʌnˈmæn ; ʌnˈmæn/ *vt* (-nn-) [VP6A] weaken the courage and self-control of: 削弱…的勇氣和自制: *The news of his friend's death ~ned him for a while.* 他朋友逝世的消息使他悲傷了一陣子。

un·man·ly /ʌnˈmænlɪ ; ʌnˈmænlɪ/ *adj* **1** weak; cowardly. 軟弱的;懦弱的。 **2** effeminate. 無丈夫氣概的;帶女人氣的。

un·manned /ˌʌnˈmænd ; ʌnˈmænd/ *adj* having no crew: 無人員的;缺乏人員的: *an ~ aircraft with remote control;* 一架遙控的無人飛機; *send an ~ spacecraft to Mars.* 發射無人太空船至火星。

un·man·nered /ʌnˈmænəd ; ʌnˈmænəd/, **un·man·ner·ly** /ʌnˈmænəlɪ ; ʌnˈmænəlɪ/ *adjj* discourteous; having bad manners. 不禮貌的;粗魯的;失禮的。

un·mask /ʌnˈmɑːsk *US:* -ˈmæsk ; ʌnˈmæsk/ *vt, vi* **1** [VP6A, 2A] remove a mask (from): 揭去(…的)假面具或僞裝: *The revellers ~ed at midnight,* took off their masks. 狂歡者在午夜時除下了面具。 **2** [VP6A] show the true character or intentions of: 展示…的眞正性格或意向;暴露;揭發;揭穿: *~ a traitor/hypocrite;* 揭穿賣國賊(僞君子)的假面具; *~ treachery/hypocrisy.* 揭發叛逆(虛僞)。

un·match·able /ʌnˈmætʃəbl ; ˌʌnˈmætʃəbl/ *adj* that cannot be matched or equalled. 不能匹敵的;無法相比的。**un·matched** /ʌnˈmætʃt ; ʌnˈmætʃt/ *adj* without an equal. 無匹敵的。

un·men·tion·able /ʌnˈmenʃənəbl ; ʌnˈmɛnʃənəbl̩/ *adj* so bad, shocking, etc that it may not be spoken of. 不堪出口的;不宜出口的;說出來會令人難堪的。

un·mind·ful /ʌnˈmaɪndfl ; ʌnˈmaɪndfəl/ *adj* **~ *(of),*** forgetful; oblivious; heedless: 忘記的;不留心的;不注意的;漫不經心的: *~ of the time/the need to hurry.* 未注意到時間的消逝(情況的急迫)。

un·mis·tak·able /ˌʌnmɪˈsteɪkəbl ; ˌʌnməˈstekəbl̩/ *adj* clear; about which no mistake or doubt is possible: 明顯的;不會錯的;無容置疑的: *Are black clouds an ~ sign of rain?* 烏雲是下雨的明顯徵兆嗎? **un·mis·tak·ably** /-əblɪ ; -əblɪ/ *adv*

un·miti·gated /ʌnˈmɪtɪgeɪtɪd ; ʌnˈmɪtəˌgetɪd/ *adj* complete; absolute: 完全的;純然的;絕對的: *an ~ disaster;* 十足的大災難; *an ~ evil,* sth which has no accompanying advantages whatever. 一件徹頭徹尾的歹事。

un·moved /ʌnˈmuːvd ; ʌnˈmuvd/ *adj* (esp) not moved in feelings; undisturbed; indifferent: (尤指)不動心的;不動情的;堅決的;冷淡的: *He remained ~*

by her entreaties for pity. 他未因她懇求憐憫而動心。

un·natu·ral /ʌnˈnætʃrəl ; ʌnˈnætʃərəl/ *adj* not natural or normal: 不自然的;反常的: *A mother who is cruel to her children is ~.* 對子女殘酷的母親是反常的。**~·ly** *adv*: *He expected, not ~ly, that his father would help him.* 他理所當然地期望他父親會幫助他。

un·nec·ess·ary /ʌnˈnesəsrɪ *US:* -serɪ ; ʌnˈnɛsəˌsɛrɪ/ *adj* not necessary; superfluous. 不需要的;無必要的;多餘的;累贅的。**un·nec·ess·ar·ily** /ˌʌnˈnesəsərəlɪ *US:* ˌʌnˌnesəˈserəlɪ ; ʌnˈnɛsəˌsɛrəlɪ/ *adv* in an ~ manner. 無必要地;不需要地;多餘地。

un·nerve /ˌʌnˈnɜːv ; ʌnˈnɝv/ *vt* [VP6A] cause to lose self-control, power of decision, courage. 使失去自制,決斷,勇氣。

un·not·iced /ʌnˈnəʊtɪst ; ʌnˈnotɪst/ *adj* not observed or noticed: 未被注意的;未顧及的: *The event passed ~.* 那件事被忽略過去了。*Are you going to let the insult pass ~?* 你對那番侮辱就這樣不了了之嗎?

un·num·bered /ˌʌnˈnʌmbəd ; ʌnˈnʌmbɚd/ *adj* **1** more than can be counted. 不可勝數的;數不清的。**2** having no number(s): 無數字的; 未編號的: *~ tickets/seats,* eg at a concert-hall. 不劃座的票(席次)。

un·ob·trus·ive /ˌʌnəbˈtruːsɪv ; ˌʌnəbˈtrusɪv/ *adj* not too obvious or easily noticeable; discreet. 不太顯著的;不太容易注意到的;不冒失的;謹慎的。

un·of·fi·cial /ˌʌnəˈfɪʃl ; ˌʌnəˈfɪʃəl/ *adj* not official: 非官方的;非正式的: *an ~ strike,* not authorized by the union; 非工會認可的罷工; *~ news,* not officially confirmed. 未經官方證實的消息。

un·or·tho·dox /ˌʌnˈɔːθədɒks ; ʌnˈɔrθəˌdɑks/ *adj* not in accordance with what is orthodox, conventional, traditional: 非正統的;非傳統的: *~ teaching methods.* 非正統的教學方法。

un·pack /ˌʌnˈpæk ; ʌnˈpæk/ *vt, vi* [VP6A, 2A] take out (things packed): (由某包裝)取出(東西): *~ one's clothes;* (開箱等)取出衣服; take things out of: 開啓包裹、行囊等: *~ a suitcase.* 開啓衣箱。

un·par·al·leled /ʌnˈpærəleld ; ʌnˈpærəˌlɛld/ *adj* having no parallel or equal; matchless: 無比的;無雙的;空前的: *an ~ achievement/disaster.* 空前的成就(災難)。

un·par·lia·men·tary /ˌʌnˌpɑːləˈmentrɪ ; ˌʌnpɑrləˈmɛntərɪ/ *adj* (of language, conduct) not suitable (because abusive, disorderly) for Parliament. (指語言,行爲)不適於議會的(因爲侮慢,不守秩序)。

un·placed /ˌʌnˈpleɪst ; ʌnˈplest/ *adj* (esp) not one of the first three in a race or competition. (尤指)(在比賽中)未獲得前三名的。

un·play·able /ʌnˈpleɪəbl ; ʌnˈpleəbl̩/ *adj* (of a ball, in games) that cannot be played; (of ground) not fit to be played on. (指球,在比賽等中)打不着的;很難打的;(指場地)不適於比賽的。

un·pleas·ant /ʌnˈpleznt ; ʌnˈplɛznt̩/ *adj* disagreeable. 不愉快的;不中意的。**~·ness** *n* [U] ~ or disagreeable feeling; bad feeling (between persons); [C] quarrel, disagreement: 不愉快;(人與人之間的)惡感;不和;爭執: *a slight ~ness.* 小爭執。

un·prac·tised /ʌnˈpræktɪst ; ʌnˈpræktɪst/ *adj* having little experience, inexpert; unskilled. 無經驗的;不熟練的;不內行的。

un·prece·dented /ʌnˈpresɪdentɪd ; ʌnˈprɛsəˌdɛntɪd/ *adj* without precedent; never done or known before. 無前例的;空前的。**~·ly** *adv*

un·preju·diced /ʌnˈpredʒʊdɪst ; ʌnˈprɛdʒədɪst/ *adj* free from prejudice. 無偏見的;公平的。

un·pre·ten·tious /ˌʌnprɪˈtenʃəs ; ˌʌnprɪˈtɛnʃəs/ *adj* modest; not trying to seem important. 謙虛的;不自大的;不驕傲的。

un·prin·cipled /ʌnˈprɪnsəpld ; ʌnˈprɪnsəpl̩d/ *adj* without moral principles; unscrupulous; dishonest. 無道德原則的;無節操的;無恥的;不正直的。

un·print·able /ʌnˈprɪntəbl;ʌnˈprɪntəbl̩/ *adj* too rude or indecent to be printed. 粗鄙或猥褻不宜印出的。

un·pro·fessional /ˌʌnprəˈfeʃnəl ; ˌʌnprəˈfɛʃənl̩/ *adj* (esp of conduct) contrary to the rules or customs of a profession. (尤指行爲)違反職業慣例或習俗的;不合行規的。

un·prompted /ˌʌnˈprɒmptɪd ; ʌnˈprɑmptɪd/ *adj* (of an answer, action) spontaneous; not said, done, etc as the result of a hint, suggestion, etc. (指回答、行爲)主動的;未受到提示、暗示等的。

un·pro·vided /ˌʌnprəˈvaɪdɪd ; ˌʌnprəˈvaɪdɪd/ *adj* **1** *~ for,* without provision having been made for: 未預先準備好的; 無供給的; 無所給養的: *The widow was left ~ for,* No means of support had been left for her on her husband's death. 這寡婦自丈夫死後,生活無着落。**2** *~ with,* not provided with: 無…設備的: *schools ~ with books and equipment.* 無圖書及其他設備的學校。

un·pro·voked /ˌʌnprəˈvəʊkt ; ˌʌnprəˈvokt/ *adj* without provocation: 未經挑釁的;無刺激之原因的;無端的: *~ aggression/attacks.* 無端侵犯(攻擊)。

un·put·down·able /ˌʌnpʊtˈdaʊnəbl ; ˌʌnpʊtˈdaʊnəbl̩/ *adj* (colloq) (of a book, etc) so interesting that the reader cannot put it down until he has finished it. (俗)(指書籍等)太有趣味而不忍釋手的。

un·quali·fied /ʌnˈkwɒlɪfaɪd ; ʌnˈkwɑləˌfaɪd/ *adj* **1** not limited or restricted; absolute: 無限制的;無條件的;絕對的: *~ praise;* 讚不絕口;極力稱讚; *an ~ denial.* 完全否認。**2** *~ as sth/to do sth,* not qualified: 不合格的;無資格(做某事)的: *~ to speak on the subject.* 無資格就此一題目發表意見。

un·ques·tion·able /ʌnˈkwestʃənəbl ; ʌnˈkwɛstʃənəbl̩/ *adj* beyond doubt; certain. 無疑的;確定的。**un·ques·tion·ably** /-əblɪ ; -əblɪ/ *adv*

un·ques·tioned /ʌnˈkwestʃənd ; ʌnˈkwɛstʃənd/ *adj* not questioned or disputed: 未受到質問或質疑的: *I cannot let your statement pass ~,* I must dispute its truth. 我不能毫無疑問地接受你的聲明(我必須對它的眞實性表示懷疑)。

un·ques·tion·ing /ʌnˈkwestʃənɪŋ ; ʌnˈkwɛstʃənɪŋ/ *adj* (esp) given, done, without question or protest: (尤指)不質問的;不質疑的;無異議的: *~ obedience.* 無異議的遵從。

un·quiet /ʌnˈkwaɪət ; ʌnˈkwaɪət/ *adj* (formal) restless; uneasy; disturbed: (正式用語)不安的;杌隉的;紛擾的: *live in ~ times.* 生於亂世。

un·quote /ʌnˈkwəʊt ; ʌnˈkwot/ (*v,* imper only 僅用祈使語氣) (in a telegram, a telephoned message, etc) end the quotation; close the inverted commas: (在電報,以電話發出的電文等中)結束引語;引號止於此;引號終止: *The rebel leader said (quote) 'We shall never surrender' (unquote).* 叛軍領袖說(引號開始)'我們決不投降'(引號終止)。

un·ravel /ʌnˈrævl ; ʌnˈrævl̩/ *vt, vi* (-ll-; US -l-) [VP6A, 2A] **1** separate the threads of; pull or become separate: 解開…的線;拆開: *The cuff of my jersey has ~led.* 我的毛織上裝袖口鬆線了。*The baby ~led the knitting that its mother left on the chair.* 那嬰兒弄散了她母親放在椅子上的編織物。**2** make clear; solve: 使明白;闡明;解決: *~ a mystery/plot.* 揭開一秘密(陰謀)。

un·real /ʌnˈrɪəl ; ʌnˈriəl/ *adj* imaginary; illusory. 不眞實的;空想的;虛幻的。

un·reas·on·able /ʌnˈriːznəbl ; ʌnˈriznəbl̩/ *adj* not governed by reason; immoderate; excessive: 不合理的;無理性的;無節制的;過分的: *make ~ demands.* 做過分的要求。

un·reas·on·ing /ʌnˈriːzənɪŋ ; ʌnˈriznɪŋ/ *adj* not using or guided by reason. 不使用理性或推理的;非由理性引導的;沒道理的。

un·re·lent·ing /ˌʌnrɪˈlentɪŋ ; ˌʌnrɪˈlɛntɪŋ/ *adj* not becoming less in intensity, etc: 强度等未減弱的: *~ pressure/attacks.* 未減弱的壓力(攻擊)。⇨ *relentless* at relent.

un·re·li·able /ˌʌnrɪˈlaɪəbl ; ˌʌnrɪˈlaɪəbl̩/ *adj* that cannot be relied on; untrustworthy. 不能依賴的;靠不住的;不能相信的。

un·re·lieved /ˌʌnrɪˈliːvd ; ˌʌnrɪˈlivd/ *adj* (esp) without anything to vary monotony: (尤指)單調而無變化的: *a plain black dress ~ by a touch of colour or trimming of any kind;* 沒有一點彩色或裝飾的單調黑色女裝; *~ boredom/tedium.* 單調而無變化的厭煩(沉悶)。

un·re·mit·ting /ˌʌnrɪˈmɪtɪŋ ; ˌʌnrɪˈmɪtɪŋ/ *adj* unceasing: 不停止的;不間斷的: *~ care/efforts.* 不斷的注意(努力)。*The doctor was ~ in his attention to the case.* 醫生毫不鬆懈地注意那病例。

un·re·quit·ed /ˌʌnrɪˈkwaɪtɪd ; ˌʌnrɪˈkwaɪtɪd/ *adj* not returned or rewarded: 無報答的;無報酬的: *~ love/service.* 單戀(無報酬的服務)。

un·re·serv·ed·ly /ˌʌnrɪˈzɜːvɪdlɪ ; ˌʌnrɪˈzɝvɪdlɪ/ *adv* without reservation or restriction; openly: 無保留地;無限制地;坦白地: *speak ~;* 坦白地說; *trust sb ~.* 完全信任某人。

un·rest /ʌnˈrest ; ʌnˈrɛst/ *n* [U] (esp) disturbed condition(s): (尤指)紛亂的狀態;不安;不穩: *social ~*, eg because of widespread unemployment or poverty; 社會的不安(如因普遍失業或貧窮); *political ~.* 政治的不安。

un·re·strained /ˌʌnrɪˈstreɪnd ; ˌʌnrɪˈstrend/ *adj* not checked or held in. 無節制的;無拘束的;放縱的。

un·re·strict·ed /ˌʌnrɪˈstrɪktɪd ; ˌʌnrɪˈstrɪktɪd/ *adj* without restriction(s); (esp of a road) not having a speed limit for traffic. 無限制的;(尤指道路)無速度限制的。

un·ri·valled (US = **-ri·valed**) /ʌnˈraɪvld ; ʌnˈraɪvl̩d/ *adj* having no rival (*in* courage, etc); unequalled: (在勇氣等方面)無對手的(與 in 連用);無雙的;無匹敵的;無與倫比的: *an ~ reputation.* 極佳的聲譽。

un·roll /ʌnˈrəʊl ; ʌnˈrol/ *vt, vi* [VP6A, 2A] roll out; open out by rolling: 展開;(將成捲之物)打開: *~ a carpet/map.* 展開一地毯(地圖)。*My sleeping-bag has ~ed.* 我的睡袋已經打開。

un·ruffled /ʌnˈrʌfld ; ʌnˈrʌfl̩d/ *adj* calm; not upset or agitated: 平靜的;鎮定的;從容不迫的;沉着的: *He remained ~ by all these criticisms.* 受到這些批評他仍能保持鎮靜。

un·ruly /ʌnˈruːlɪ ; ʌnˈrulɪ/ *adj* (-ier, -iest) not easily controlled; disorderly: 難控制的;難駕馭的;蠻橫的;任性的;不守規矩的: *an ~ child.* 任性的小孩。

un·said /ʌnˈsed ; ʌnˈsɛd/ *adj* not expressed: 未說明的;未講出的: *Some things are better left ~.* 有些事情還是不說出來好。

un·sa·voury (US = **-sa·vory**) /ʌnˈseɪvərɪ ; ʌnˈsevərɪ/ *adj* (esp) nasty; disgusting: (尤指)不好的;令人厭惡的: *~ stories/scandals;* 令人厭惡的故事(醜聞); *a man with an ~ reputation.* 聲名狼藉的人。

un·say /ˌʌnˈseɪ ; ʌnˈse/ *vt* (*pt, pp* -said /-ˈsed ; -ˈsɛd/) [VP6A] (liter) take back (sth that has been said); retract (which is the usu word). (文)取消(前言);撤回(retract 較常用)。

un·scathed /ʌnˈskeɪðd ; ʌnˈskeðd/ *adj* unharmed; unhurt. 未受損傷的;未遭傷害的。

un·scramble /ˌʌnˈskræmbl ; ʌnˈskræmbl̩/ *vt* (of a scrambled message) restore to a form that can be understood. (指雜亂片段的消息、情報等)修整爲可瞭解的形式。

un·scripted /ʌnˈskrɪptɪd ; ʌnˈskrɪptɪd/ *adj* (eg of a broadcast talk or discussion) not read from a prepared script. (如指廣播談話或討論)無底稿的;不是宣讀講稿的;當場講出的。

un·scru·pu·lous /ʌnˈskruːpjʊləs ; ʌnˈskrupjələs/ *adj* not guided by conscience; not held back (from doing wrong) by scruples. 無恥的;沒有操守的;不受良心節制的。**~·ly** *adv*

un·seas·oned /ˌʌnˈsiːznd ; ʌnˈsizn̩d/ *adj* (of wood) not matured; (of food) not flavoured with seasoning. (指木材)未熟的;未長成的;(指食物)沒有調味的;未加作料的。

un·seat /ˌʌnˈsiːt ; ʌnˈsit/ *vt* [VP6A] **1** remove from office: 免職;罷免;罷黜: *Mr Powell was ~ed at the General Election,* lost his seat in the House of Commons. 鮑威爾先生在大選中落選了(失去了下議院席位)。**2** throw from a horse: 使落馬;使從馬上摔下: *Several riders were ~ed at the water-jump,* eg in a steeplechase. 有幾位騎士在躍過積水障礙時摔了下來(例如在障礙賽馬中)。

un·seem·ly /ʌnˈsiːmlɪ ; ʌnˈsimlɪ/ *adj* (of behaviour, etc) not suitable or proper. (指行爲等)不相宜的;不適當的。

un·seen /ʌnˈsiːn ; ʌnˈsin/ *adj* not seen; invisible. 未被看見的;看不見的。□ *n* **1 the ~**, the spiritual world. 精神世界。**2** [C] passage to be translated, without preparation, from a foreign language into one's own language: 未經準備而要從外國語譯爲本國語的一段文字;需要即席翻譯的文字: *German ~s.* 需要即席翻譯的幾段德文。

un·settle /ˌʌnˈsetl ; ʌnˈsɛtl̩/ *vt* [VP6A] make troubled, anxious or uncertain: 使不安、擔心或不確定;擾亂: *~d weather,* uncertain, changeable weather. 不穩定而多變的天氣。

un·sex /ˌʌnˈseks ; ʌnˈsɛks/ *vt* [VP6A] deprive of the attributes of one's sex. 使失去性別的特徵。**~ed** *adj* not separated according to sex. 尚未分出性別的。

un·sight·ly /ʌnˈsaɪtlɪ ; ʌnˈsaɪtlɪ/ *adj* displeasing to the eye: 難看的;不雅觀的: *~ advertisements in the countryside.* 鄉間不雅的廣告。**un·sight·li·ness** *n*

un·skilled /ʌnˈskɪld ; ʌnˈskɪld/ *adj* (of work) not needing special skill; (of workers) not having special skill or special training. (指工作)不需特別技巧的;粗笨的;(指工人)無特別技巧的;未受特殊訓練的。

un·soph·is·ti·cat·ed /ˌʌnsəˈfɪstɪkeɪtɪd ; ˌʌnsəˈfɪstɪˌketɪd/ *adj* naive; inexperienced; simple: 天眞的;純樸的;沒心眼兒的;無經驗的;單純的: *~ children/techniques.* 天眞的兒童(簡單的技巧)。

un·sound /ˌʌnˈsaʊnd ; ʌnˈsaʊnd/ *adj* not in good condition; unsatisfactory: 不健全的;不佳的;不能令人滿意的;不堅固的: *an ~ argument.* 沒有根據的論據。*The structure/building is ~.* 那建築物(房屋)不堅固。***of ~ mind,*** unbalanced in mind; mentally disordered. 精神不健全的;精神錯亂的。

un·spar·ing /ʌnˈspeərɪŋ ; ʌnˈsperɪŋ/ *adj* liberal; holding nothing back: 慷慨的;不吝惜的: *be ~ in one's efforts;* 不遺餘力; *~ of praise.* 大加讚賞。

un·speak·able /ʌnˈspiːkəbl ; ʌnˈspikəbl/ *adj* that cannot be expressed or described in words: 不能以言語表達的;無法形容的: *~ joy/wickedness;* 無法形容的快樂(邪惡); (colloq) very unpleasant: (俗)令人很不愉快的: *~ behaviour.* 令人討厭的行爲。**un·speak·ably** *adv*

un·spot·ted /ʌnˈspɒtɪd ; ʌnˈspɑtɪd/ *adj* (of reputation) without stain; pure. (指名譽)無瑕疵的;清白的。

un·strung /ˌʌnˈstrʌŋ ; ʌnˈstrʌŋ/ *adj* (esp) with little or no control over the nerves, mind or emotions. (尤指)失去自制力的;不能抑制的。

un·stuck /ˌʌnˈstʌk ; ʌnˈstʌk/ *adj* not stuck or fastened: 未黏牢的;未繫住的;未貼緊的: *The flap of the envelope has come ~.* 這信封的封口鬆開了。***come (badly) ~,*** (colloq) be unsuccessful; fail to work according to plan: (俗)未成功的;未照計畫進行的;不靈光的: *Our plan has come ~.* 我們的計畫未成功。

un·stud·ied /ˌʌnˈstʌdɪd ; ʌnˈstʌdɪd/ *adj* (of behaviour) natural; not aimed at impressing other persons. (指行爲)自然的;非着眼於使他人有深刻印象的;不矯揉造作的。

un·sung /ˌʌnˈsʌŋ ; ʌnˈsʌŋ/ *adj* not celebrated (in poetry or song): 未(在詩或歌中)被讚頌的: *an ~ hero.* 未被人歌頌的英雄。

un·swerv·ing /ʌnˈswɜːvɪŋ ; ʌnˈswɝvɪŋ/ *adj* (esp of aims, purposes) not changing; straight: (尤指目標,目的)不改變的;堅定的: *~ loyalty/devotion;* 不變的忠誠(奉獻); *pursue an ~ course.* 採取某一堅定的方針。**~·ly** *adv*

un·syl·labic /ˌʌnsɪˈlæbɪk ; ˌʌnsɪˈlæbɪk/ *adj* **1** not syllabic. 非音節的。**2** (of a consonant) not making a syllable, eg in the word *little* /ˈlɪtl ; ˈlɪtl̩/ the first /l/ is unsyllabic and the second is syllabic. (指子音)不構成音節的（如 little 中的第一個 /l/ 不成音節,第二個 /l/ 成音節）。

un·think·able /ʌnˈθɪŋkəbl ; ʌnˈθɪŋkəbl̩/ *adj* such as one cannot have any real idea of or belief; not to be considered: 難以想像的;難以置信的;不加以考慮的;不可能的: *It's ~ that he should resign now.* 他現在要辭職令人難以想像。

un·think·ing /ʌnˈθɪŋkɪŋ ; ʌnˈθɪŋkɪŋ/ *adj* thoughtless; done, said, etc without thought of the effect: 無思想的;輕率的;未加思考的: *in an ~ moment.* 一時輕率。 **~·ly** *adv*

un·thought-of /ʌnˈθɔːt ɒv ; ʌnˈθɔt,ɑv/ *adj* quite unexpected; not imagined. 完全未料到的;出乎意外的;想像不到的。

un·tidy /ʌnˈtaɪdɪ ; ʌnˈtaɪdɪ/ *adj* (-ier, -iest) (of a room, desk, etc) in disorder; (of a person) slovenly; not neat. (指房間,書桌等)零亂的;不整齊的;(指人)邋遢的;不整潔的。 **un·tidi·ly** *adv*

un·til /ənˈtɪl ; ənˈtɪl/ *prep, conj* ⇨ till.

un·time·ly /ʌnˈtaɪmlɪ ; ʌnˈtaɪmlɪ/ *adj* occurring at a wrong or unsuitable time, or too soon: 不合時宜的;過早的: *an ~ remark.* 不合時宜的話。 *He came to an ~ end,* died before he had completed his life's work. 他齎志以歿。

un·tir·ing /ʌnˈtaɪərɪŋ ; ʌnˈtaɪrɪŋ/ *adj* **1** continuing to work without getting tired: 繼續工作而不疲倦的: *She seems to be ~.* 她似乎不知疲倦。 **2** continuing as if never causing tiredness: 堅持不懈的;不屈不撓的: *his ~ efforts.* 他那堅持不懈的努力。

unto /ˈʌntuː ; ˈʌntu/ *prep* (archaic) (古) = to (*prep*).

un·told /ˌʌnˈtəʊld ; ʌnˈtold/ *adj* (esp) too many or too much to be counted, measured, etc: (尤指)不能計數的;數不清的;無數的;太多的: *a man of ~ wealth.* 財富數不清的人。

un·touch·able /ʌnˈtʌtʃəbl ; ʌnˈtʌtʃəbl̩/ *n, adj* (member) of the lowest caste in India. 印度最低階級的(成員)。

un·to·ward /ˌʌntəˈwɔːd *US:* ʌnˈtɔːrd ; ʌnˈtord/ *adj* (formal) unfavourable; unfortunate; inconvenient: (正式用語)不利的;不幸的;困難重重的: *There were no ~ incidents.* 並無不吉利事件。

un·truth /ʌnˈtruːθ ; ʌnˈtruθ/ *n* [U] lack of truth; [C] (*pl* ~s /-ˈtruːðz ; -ˈtruðz/) untrue statement; lie. 虛僞;不眞實;虛言;謊話。 **~·ful** /-fl ; -fəl/ *adj* **~·fully** /-fəlɪ ; -fəlɪ/ *adv*

un·tu·tored /ʌnˈtjuːtəd *US:* -ˈtuː- ; ʌnˈtutɚd/ *adj* untaught; ignorant. 未受教育的;無知的。

un·used¹ /ʌnˈjuːzd ; ʌnˈjuzd/ *adj* not made use of; not put to use; never having been used. 未使用的;未利用的;從未使用過的。

un·used² /ʌnˈjuːst ; ʌnˈjust/ *adj* **~ to,** not accustomed to: 不習慣的;不慣的: *The children are ~ to city life.* 孩子們過不慣城市生活。

un·usual /ʌnˈjuːʒl ; ʌnˈjuʒʊəl/ *adj* not usual; strange; remarkable: 不尋常的;奇異的;罕有的;獨特的: *~ clothes/opinions;* 奇異的衣服(意見); *a nose of ~ size.* 罕有的大鼻子。 **~ly** /-ʒəlɪ ; -ʒʊəlɪ/ *adv*: *~ly small/large/late/early.* 非常小(大,晚,早)。

un·ut·ter·able /ʌnˈʌtərəbl ; ʌnˈʌtərəbl̩/ *adj* unspeakable. 說不出的;無法形容的;非語言所能表達的。

un·var·nished /ʌnˈvɑːnɪʃt ; ʌnˈvɑrnɪʃt/ *adj* (esp of accounts, descriptions) plain; straightforward: (尤指說明,描述)未加修飾的; 率直的; 直言無諱的: *the ~ truth;* 未加渲染的實情; *give an ~ account of what happened.* 照直記述所發生之事。

un·veil /ˌʌnˈveɪl ; ʌnˈvel/ *vt, vi* **1** [VP6A, 2A] remove a veil from; remove one's veil. 除去…的面紗或面罩;除去面罩。 **2** [VP6A] disclose; reveal; (trade use) show publicly for the first time: 揭示;揭露;(交易用語)首次公開;首次展示: *Several new models were ~ed yesterday at the Motor Show.* 昨天的汽車展示會上公開了數種新型汽車。

un·voiced /ˌʌnˈvɔɪst ; ʌnˈvɔɪst/ *adj* (of thoughts, etc) not expressed or uttered. (指思想等)未明說的;未表明的;未講出來的。

un·wieldy /ʌnˈwiːldɪ ; ʌnˈwildɪ/ *adj* awkward to move or control because of shape, size or weight. (因形狀、大小或重量等而)不易移動或控制的; 龐大的; 笨重的。 **un·wieldi·ness** *n*

un·wind /ˌʌnˈwaɪnd ; ʌnˈwaɪnd/ *vt, vi* (*pt, pp* -wound /-ˈwaʊnd ; -ˈwaʊnd/) **1** [VP6A, 2A] wind off (what has been wound up); become unwound. 解開,展開(纏或捲在一起之物);旋開;轉開。 **2** [VP2A] (colloq) relax after a period of tension, exhausting work, etc. (俗)(經過一段緊張時期、吃力的工作等之後)放鬆自己;輕鬆一下。 ⇨ wind³ (6).

un·wit·ting /ʌnˈwɪtɪŋ ; ʌnˈwɪtɪŋ/ *adj* unknowing; unaware; unintentional. 不知情的;無心的;非故意的。 **~·ly** *adv*: *If I hurt your feelings it was ~ly.* 如果我傷了你的感情,那不是故意的。

un·writ·ten /ˌʌnˈrɪtn ; ʌnˈrɪtn̩/ *adj* not written down: 未寫下的;不成文的;口傳的: *the ~ songs of the countryfolk,* folksongs not to be found in writing or print. 鄉民口傳的歌謠。 ***an ~ law,*** one based on custom or tradition, but not precisely stated anywhere. 不成文法。

un·zip /ˌʌnˈzɪp ; ʌnˈzɪp/ *vt* (-pp-) unfasten or open by pulling a zip fastener: 拉開…的拉鍊: *~ a handbag.* 拉開拉鍊以打開手提包。

up /ʌp ; ʌp/ *adv part* (contrasted with *down.* ⇨ the *v* entries for combinations with *up.* Specimen entries only here.) (與 down 相對,參看與 up 連用的動詞諸條。下面所列,僅係範例。) **1** to or in an erect or vertical position (esp as suggesting readiness for activity): 趨向於或處於直立的姿勢或位置(尤指含有準備活動的意思): *He's already up,* out of bed. 他已起床。 *I was up late* (= did not go to bed until late) *last night.* 我昨夜很晚才就寢。 *She was up all night with a sick child.* 她陪伴着生病的孩子徹夜未眠。 *It's time to get up,* out of bed. 是起床的時候了。 *He got up* (= stood up) *to ask a question.* 他站起來發問。 *He jumped up* (ie to his feet) *from his chair.* 他從椅子上跳了起來。 *Up with you!* Get up! Stand up! 起來!(起床!起立!) *Up with them!* Put, bring, etc them up! 把它們直立起來! *Parliament is up,* no longer sitting, no longer in session. 國會閉會了。 *His blood was up,* His passions were roused. 他發脾氣了。 ***What's up,*** (colloq) What's going on, happening? (俗)什麼事?發生什麼事了? *There's something up,* Sth unusual is happening, being planned, etc. 不尋常的事卽將發生。 ***up and about,*** out of bed and active (esp of a person recently ill). (尤指最近生過病的人)已起床活動。 **2** to or in a high(er) place, position, degree, etc: 往或居於高或較高的地方、位置、程度等: *Lift your head up.* 抬起頭來。 *Pull your socks up.* 振作起來。 *The tide's up,* in. 潮水上漲了。 *He lives three floors up.* 他住在往上第三樓。 *Prices are still going up,* rising. 物價仍在上漲。 *He's well up in Greek,* has made good progress. 他的希臘文大有進步。 **3** to a place of importance; (in England) to London; to a place in or to the north: 至重要之處或地方;(在英國)至倫敦;至北部或北方之地: *He has gone up to London for the day.* 他今天上倫敦去了。 *He lives up in the Lake District.* 他住在北部的大湖區。 *We're going up to Edinburgh.* 我們要去愛丁堡。 *The case was brought up before the High Court.* 那案件已呈請高等法院審理。 **4** (used vaguely, in a way similar to the use of *down, round, over, across*) to the place in question, or in which the speaker is, was, will be: (籠統用法,與 down, round, over, across 的用法相似)至所談或所指定的地方;至講話者所在之處: *He came up (to me) and asked the time.* 他走過來(走至我面前)詢問時間。 *She went straight up to the door.* 她一直走到門口。 **5** (with *vv* to indicate completeness, finality): (與動詞連用,表示完全,徹底,終結): *The stream has dried up,* has become completely dry. 溪水全乾了。 *We've eaten everything up.* 我們把每一樣食物都吃光了。 *Time's* *up*, The allowed time is ended. 時間到了。*When is your leave up?* When must you return to duty? 你的假期何時屆滿？ *Tear it up.* 把它撕碎。*Lock/Tie/Fasten/Chain/Nail it up,* Make it fast, secure, safe, etc by locking, tying, etc. 把它鎖好(綁好,固定好,用鏈子拴好,用釘子釘好)。 **6** (with *vv* to indicate an increase in intensity, etc): (與動詞連用,表示強度等的增加): *Speak/Sing up!* (ie with more force). 說(唱)大聲一些！*Her spirits went up,* rose. 她的興致提起來了。*Blow the fire up.* 把火吹大一些。 **7** (attrib uses with *nn*): (形容用法,置名詞前): *the* ˈ*up train* (to London); (開往倫敦的)上行火車; *the* ˈ*up line/platform* (used by up trains); 上行線(上行火車使用的月臺); *an* ˈ*up stroke,* eg of the pen when writing the letter l. 向上的筆劃(如寫l時)。 **8** ***up against sth,*** faced with (difficulties, obstacles, etc). 面臨(困難,阻碍等)。***be up before sb,*** appear in court (before a magistrate, etc): 上法庭(接受法官等審訊): *He was up before the magistrate for being drunk while driving a car.* 他因酒醉駕車而被法庭傳訊。***up and down,*** **(a)** backwards and forwards; to and fro: 前後地;往返地;來回地: *walking up and down the station platform.* 在車站月臺上來回地走。**(b)** so as to rise and fall: 上下地;起伏地: *The float bobbed up and down on the water.* 漂浮物在水面上下浮動。Hence, 由此產生, **ups and downs,** (usu fig) alternations of good and bad fortune. (通常作比喩用法)好運與壞運的交替;盛衰;浮沉。***on the up (and up),*** (colloq) steadily improving; becoming more successful. (俗)愈來愈好;越來越成功。***up for sth,*** **(a)** being tried for (an offence, etc): 爲(某項罪行等)受審: *up for exceeding the speed limit.* 因(駕車)超速而受審。 **(b)** being considered for; on offer: 考慮中;出賣;出售: *The contract is up for renewal.* 該合約正考慮換新。*The house is up for auction/sale.* 該房屋在拍賣(出售)。***be well up in/on sth,*** be well informed about; be expert in: 熟知;對…內行;對…有充分知識: *He's well up on electronic music.* 他對電子音樂很內行。***up to sth,*** **(a)** occupied or busy with: 忙於;從事於;正在做: *What's he up to?* 他在忙什麼呢？ *He's up to no good.* 他在做壞事。*What tricks has she been up to,* playing? 她一直在玩什麼把戲？ **(b)** equal to: 勝任;能作;及得上: *I don't feel up to going to work today.* 我今天身體不適不能去工作。*This new book of Hugh Fleetwood's isn't up to his last,* is not as good. 休•福利伍德的這本新書不及他的前一本。*He's not up to his work/to the job,* not good enough for the job. 他不能勝任他的工作(這份工作)。**(c)** as far as: 直到: *up to now/then;* 直到現在(那時); *count from one up to twenty.* 從一數到二十。***up to sb,*** required, looked upon as necessary, from him: 應由某人…;視爲某人的職責: *It's up to us* (= It is our duty) *to give them all the help we can.* 我們理應竭盡所能給予他們協助。***all up (with sb),*** ⇨ all²(1). ˌ**up-and-**ˈ**coming,** (of a person) making good progress, likely to succeed, in his profession, career, etc: (指人)在其職業、事業等方面有長足進步的;很可能成功的;進取的: *an up-and-coming young MP.* 一位有進取心的年輕國會議員。□ *prep* (in the senses of the *adv*): (具有副詞的各種意義): *climb up a mountain;* 爬山; *walk up the stairs;* 上樓梯; *sail up* (towards the source of) *a river;* 向河的上游航行; *travel up country,* away from the coast; 到內陸旅行; *walk up* (= along) *the road.* 沿大路而行。□ *vi, vt* (-pp-) [VP2A, 6A] **1** (humor or colloq use only) rouse oneself; get or jump up: (僅作詼諧或口語用法)奮起;起立;跳起: *She upped and threw the teapot at him.* 她跳起來將茶壺向他擲去。 **2** (colloq) increase: (俗)增加: *up the price;* 加價; *up an offer.* 提高出價。

up- /ʌp- ; ʌp-/ *pref* in an upward direction. 向上。

up·beat /ˈʌp biːt ; ˈʌpˌbit/ *n* (music) unaccented beat, esp at the end of a bar (eg when the conductor's hand is raised). (音樂)上拍;弱拍(尤指一小節末尾的一拍)。

up·braid /ˌʌpˈbreɪd ; ʌpˈbred/ *vt* [VP6A, 14] ~ ***sb (for doing sth/with sth),*** scold, reproach. 譴責;叱責(某人)。

up·bring·ing /ˈʌpbrɪŋɪŋ ; ˈʌpˌbrɪŋɪŋ/ *n* [U] training and education during childhood: 兒童期的訓練和教育;幼年的教養: *His ~ explains a lot about his attitude towards authority/women.* 他幼年的教養充分說明他對權威(婦女)的態度。

up·coun·try /ˌʌpˈkʌntrɪ ; ˈʌpˈkʌntrɪ/ *adj, adv* (esp in a large thinly populated country) towards the interior; inland: (尤指地廣人稀的地區) 向內地(的);在內地(的): ~ *districts;* 內陸區域; *travel ~.* 在內地旅行。

up·date /ˌʌpˈdeɪt ; ʌpˈdet/ *vt* [VP6A] bring up-to-date; modernize: 使…現代化;使…合時代: ~ *a dictionary/textbook.* 修訂字典(教科書)。

up·grade /ˌʌpˈgreɪd ; ˈʌpgred/ *vt* [VP6A] raise to a higher grade. 提高…之等級。□ *n* /ˈʌpgreɪd ; ˈʌpˌgred/ (esp) (尤用於) ***on the ~,*** improving; making progress. 有進步;有進展。

up·heaval /ˌʌpˈhiːvl ; ʌpˈhivl/ *n* [C] great and sudden change: 巨大而突然的變化;巨變;驟變: *a volcanic ~;* 火山突然爆發; *political/social ~s.* 政治(社會)的大變動。

up·held /ˌʌpˈheld ; ʌpˈhɛld/ *pt, pp* of uphold.

up·hill /ˌʌpˈhɪl ; ˈʌpˈhɪl/ *adj* sloping upward; ascending: 上坡的;向上的: *an ~ road;* 上坡路; (fig) difficult; needing effort. (喩)困難的;費力的。***an ~ task,*** very difficult one. 極艱鉅的工作。□ *adv* up a slope: 上坡: *walk ~.* 爬坡;走上坡。

up·hold /ˌʌpˈhəʊld ; ʌpˈhold/ *vt* (*pt, pp* upheld /-ˈheld ; -ˈhɛld/) [VP6A] **1** support or approve (a person, his conduct, a practice, etc): 支持;贊成(某人,其行爲,某習俗等): *I cannot ~ such conduct.* 我不能贊成這種行爲。 **2** confirm (a decision, a verdict). 證實;確定(一項決定,判決)。

up·hol·ster /ˌʌpˈhəʊlstə(r) ; ʌpˈholstɚ/ *vt* [VP6A] provide (seats, etc) with padding, springs, covering material, etc; provide (a room) with carpets, curtains, cushioned seats, etc: 爲(椅子等)加裝墊子、彈簧、面子等;爲(房間)裝設地毯、簾幕、座墊等;裝潢: ~ *a settee in tapestry;* 爲長靠椅裝上花氈的面子; *~ed in/with velvet.* 以天鵝絨裝設的。 **~er** *n* person whose trade is to ~. 室內裝潢商;室內裝潢匠。 **~y** /-stərɪ ; -stərɪ/ *n* [U] (materials used in, business of) ~ing. 室內裝潢;室內裝潢品;室內裝潢業。

up·keep /ˈʌpkiːp ; ˈʌpˌkip/ *n* [U] (cost of) keeping sth in good order and repair: 保養;維護費;保養費: *£450 for rent and ~,* eg of a house. 租金及維護費四百五十鎊(如指房屋)。*The ~ of this large garden is more than I can afford.* 這個大花園的維護費非我所能負擔。

up·land /ˈʌplənd ; ˈʌplənd/ *n* (often *pl*) higher part(s) of a region or country (not necessarily mountainous): (常用複數)高地(並不一定是山): (attrib) (形容用法) *an ~ region.* 高地區域。

up·lift /ˌʌpˈlɪft ; ʌpˈlɪft/ *vt* [VP6A] (fig) raise (spiritually or emotionally): (喩)(在精神或情緒方面)提高;振奮: *His soul was ~ed by the music.* 那種音樂使他的精神振奮起來了。□ *n* /ˈʌplɪft ; ˈʌpˌlɪft/ [U] socially or mentally elevating influence; moral inspiration. 社會或精神方面有激發或振奮作用的影響力;道德的鼓舞。

up·most /ˈʌpməʊst ; ˈʌpˌmost/ *adj* = uppermost.

upon /əˈpɒn ; əˈpɑn/ *prep* (formal) (正式用語) = on²(1-7) (which is more usual. *Upon* is the only normal form in): (通常多用 on。在下例中 upon 爲唯一正規的形式): ~ *my word;* 的確; *once ~ a time.* 從前。

up·per /ˈʌpə(r) ; ˈʌpɚ/ *adj* (contrasted with *lower*) higher in place; situated above: (與 lower相對) 位置較高的;在上的: *the ~ lip;* 上唇; *the ~ arm;* 上臂; *one of the ~ rooms.* 樓上的一個房間。~ **case,** ⇨ case²(2). ~ **class,** ⇨ class(3). **the ~ crust,** (colloq) the highest social class. (俗)社會

U

的最高階層;上流社會;貴族。 **the ~ storey,** (fig, colloq) the brain: (喻,俗)頭腦: *wrong in the ~ storey,* mentally disordered. 精神錯亂。 ***have/get the ~ hand (of),*** have/get the advantage or control (over). 勝過;(比…)佔優勢;佔(…的)上風。**the U~ House,** (in Parliament) the House of Lords. (國會的)上議院。 **'~-cut** *n* (boxing) a blow delivered upwards with the arm bent inside an opponent's guard. (拳擊)上擊拳(曲臂向上出擊對方的防禦部位)。 □ *n* part of a shoe or boot over the sole. 鞋面或靴面;鞋幫。 ***be (down) on one's ~s,*** be at the end of one's financial resources. 窮困不堪。 **'~·most** /-məʊst ; -ˌmost/ *adj* highest; predominant: 最高的; 最主要的: *Thoughts of the holidays were ~most in their minds.* 他們心中最主要的念頭就是假日。 □ *adv* on, to, at, the top or surface: 最上地;至上面;在上面;在或至表面: *It's not always wise to say whatever comes ~most,* whatever comes to the top of one's thoughts. 想到什麼就說什麼並不一定是明智的。

up·pish /'ʌpɪʃ ; 'ʌpɪʃ/ *adj* (colloq) self-assertive, conceited: (俗)盛氣凌人的; 自大的: *Don't get ~ with me!* 不要對我盛氣凌人! *Don't be too ~ about it!* 對此事不要太驕傲! **~·ly** *adv* **~·ness** *n*

up·pity /'ʌpətɪ ; 'ʌpətɪ/ *adj* (colloq) uppish. (俗)盛氣凌人的;自大的。

up·right /'ʌpraɪt ; 'ʌpˌraɪt/ *adj* **1** erect; placed vertically (at an angle of 90° to the ground): 直立的;垂直的(與地面成九十度): *an ~ post;* 直立的柱子; *stand/hold oneself ~;* 筆直地站立; *set a post ~.* 把柱子豎直。 **~ piano,** with the strings vertical, not horizontal, as in a grand piano. 豎式鋼琴(琴絃直立者)。 **2** honourable; straightforward in behaviour: 正直的;老實的;規矩的: *an ~ man/judge;* 正直的人(法官); *be ~ in one's business dealings.* 規規矩矩地做生意。 □ *n* [C] ~ support in a structure; ~ post. (結構中的)直立支撐物;直柱。 **~·ly** *adv* **~·ness** *n* [U].

up·ris·ing /'ʌpraɪzɪŋ ; 'ʌpˌraɪzɪŋ/ *n* [C] revolt; rebellion. 叛亂;叛變;起義。

up·roar /'ʌprɔː(r) ; 'ʌpˌror/ *n* [U, C] (*sing* only) (僅用單數) (outburst of) noise and excitement; tumult: 喧囂;騷動;鼓噪; 爆出喧囂聲: *The meeting ended in (an) ~.* 會議在一陣喧囂中結束。 **~i·ous** /ʌp'rɔːrɪəs ; ʌp'rorɪəs/ *adj* very noisy, esp with loud laughter and great good humour: 喧囂的;騷動的;鼓噪的;鬧哄哄的;(尤指)哄然大笑的: *We were given an ~ious welcome.* 我們受到熱烈的歡迎。 *They burst into ~ious laughter.* 他們哄然大笑。 **~i·ous·ly** *adv*

up·root /ˌʌp'ruːt ; ʌp'rut/ *vt* [VP6A] pull up by the roots: 將…連根拔起;拔根: *The gale ~ed numerous trees.* 大風將很多樹連根拔起。 *After he had lived in New York for fifteen years his firm ~ed him and sent him to Chicago.* 他在紐約住了十五年後,他的公司調派他去芝加哥。

up·set /ˌʌp'set ; ʌp'sɛt/ *vt, vi* (*pt, pp* upset) (-tt-) **1** [VP6A, 2A] tip over; overturn: 打翻;弄翻;傾覆: *Don't ~ the boat.* 不要把船弄翻了。*The boat ~.* 船傾覆了。*The cat has ~ its saucer of milk.* 那隻貓弄翻了它的牛奶碟子。 **2** [VP6A] trouble; cause (sb or sth) to be disturbed: 擾亂;使(某人或某物)不安: *~ the enemy's plans;* 破壞敵人的計畫; *~ one's stomach by eating too much rich food.* 因吃太多油膩食物而使胃不舒服。*The sight of physical suffering ~s her.* 肉體受苦的景象使她不安。 *She is easily ~ emotionally.* 她的心緒容易煩亂。□ *n* /'ʌpset ; 'ʌpˌsɛt/ [C] **1** ~ting or being ~: 翻覆;傾覆;擾亂;不安: *have a 'stomach ~.* 胃不舒服。*She's had a terrible ~,* eg an emotional shock. 她情緒上受了大震撼。 *You can imagine what an ~ we have had with the decorators and upholsterers in the house all week.* 室內設計師和裝潢工人在我們家整整忙了一個禮拜,我們受到的打擾可想而知。 **2** (sport) unexpected result. (運動)出乎意料的敗北。

up·shot /'ʌpʃɒt ; 'ʌpˌʃɑt/ *n* ***the ~ (of sth),*** outcome; result: 結果;結局: *What will be the ~ of it all?* 其結局將如何呢?

up·side-down /ˌʌpsaɪd'daʊn ; 'ʌpˌsaɪd'daʊn/ *adv* with the upper side underneath or at the bottom; (fig) in disorder: 倒轉地;倒置地;(喻)混亂地: *The boy pretended he could read, but he was holding the book ~.* 那男孩假裝會閱讀,但是他倒拿着那本書。 *The house was turned ~ by the burglars,* Everything was left in disorder.那房屋被竊賊翻得亂七八糟。

up·stage /ˌʌp'steɪdʒ ; 'ʌp'stedʒ/ *adj* (colloq) uppish; uppity. (俗)高傲的;自負的。□ *adv* (theatre) towards the back of the stage. (戲劇)向舞臺後部地。□ *vt* [VP6A] divert attention from sb else to oneself; put at a disadvantage. 把(某人)所受到的注意引向自己;搶(某人)的鋒頭;搶去(某人)的光彩;使處於不利情況。

up·stairs /ˌʌp'steəz ; ʌp'stɛrz/ *adv* **1** to or on a higher floor: 向樓上;在樓上: *go/walk ~.* 上樓。**2** (attrib) belonging to, situated on, an upper floor: (形容用法)屬於樓上的;位於樓上的: *an ~ room.* 樓上的房間。

up·stand·ing /ˌʌp'stændɪŋ ; ʌp'stændɪŋ/ *adj* standing erect; strong and healthy: 直立的; 强健的: *fine ~ children.* 健康的孩子們。

up·start /'ʌpstɑːt ; 'ʌpˌstɑrt/ *n, adj* (person) who has suddenly risen to wealth, power or higher social position, esp one whose behaviour causes resentment: 暴富者;驟貴者;暴發戶(尤指其行爲招致反感者);暴富的;驟貴的: *~ officials in government offices.* 政府機構中突然發跡的官員們。

up·stream /ˌʌp'striːm ; 'ʌp'strim/ *adv* up a river; against the stream or current. 往上游地;逆流地。

up·surge /'ʌpsɜːdʒ ; 'ʌpˌsɝdʒ/ *n* surging up (of emotion): (情緒的) 激起;洶湧: *an ~ of anger/indignation.* 勃然發怒(憤怒)。

up·take /'ʌpteɪk ; 'ʌpˌtek/ *n* ***quick/slow on the ~,*** (colloq) quick/slow to understand (sth said or hinted at). (俗)敏(鈍)於瞭解(所說或所暗示的事物);領悟很快(慢)。

up·tight /ˌʌp'taɪt ; ˌʌp'taɪt/ *adj* **~ (about),** (sl) (俚) **1** extremely tense; nervous: 極度緊張的;神經質的;情緒不自然的: *~ about an interview/examination.* 對於會見(考試)顯得神經緊張。 **2** uneasy; prejudiced; hostile; fearful. 不安的;有偏見的;敵意的;害怕的。

up-to-date /'ʌp tə deɪt ; 'ʌptə'det/ *adj* modern; fashionable: 新近的; 時髦的: *~ clothes/ideas/books.* 時髦的衣服(新思想;新書)。

up·town /ˌʌp'taʊn ; 'ʌp'taʊn/ *adj, adv* (US) to or in the upper (the residential or non-business, non-commercial) part (of a town): (美)向或在上城區(卽住宅區或非商業區): *~ New York;* 紐約的住宅區; *go ~.* 往上城區(住宅區)。

up·turn /'ʌptɜːn ; 'ʌpˌtɝn/ *n* upward turn; change for the better: 向上翻轉;向上轉;情況好轉: *an ~ in business/employment/production.* 營業(就業,生產)情況好轉。

up·ward /'ʌpwəd ; 'ʌpwɚd/ *adj* moving or directed up: 上升的;向上的: *the ~ trend of prices;* 物價上升的趨勢; *an ~ glance.* 向上的一瞥。 **~ (social) mob·il·ity,** ~ movement of sb from one class(3) to another. 社會地位之升高。□ *adv* **~(s),** towards a higher place, level, etc: 向上地;上升地: *The boat was on the beach, bottom ~s,* turned upside-down. 那船擱置在海灘上,船底朝天。 *Is our civilization moving ~?* 我們的文明還在繼續上升嗎? ***~s of,*** more than: 多於;超過: *~s of a hundred people.* 超過一百人。

ura·nium /jʊ'reɪnɪəm ; jʊ'renɪəm/ *n* [U] heavy white metal (symbol **U**) with radioactive properties, a source of atomic energy. 鈾(白色重金屬,符號作 U,具放射性,爲原子能之來源)。

Ura·nus /jʊ'reɪnəs ; 'jʊrənəs/ *n* (astron) planet seventh in order from the sun. (天文)天王星(太

陽系中的第七個行星)。 ⇨ the illus at planet. 參看 planet 之挿圖。

ur·ban /ˈɜːbən; ˈɜbən/ *adj* of or in a town: 都市的;在都市的: *the overcrowded ~ areas of England;* 英格蘭過度擁擠的都市區; *~ guerrillas,* 城市游擊隊, ⇨ guerrilla. **~·ize** /-aɪz; -ˌaɪz/ *vt* [VP6A] change from a rural to an ~ character. 使都市化。 **~·iz·ation** /ˌɜːbənaɪˈzeɪʃn *US:* -nɪˈz-; ˌɜbənɪˈzeʃən/ *n* [U].

ur·bane /ɜːˈbeɪn; ɜˈben/ *adj* polite; polished in manners; elegant. 有禮貌的; 態度溫文的; 文雅的。 **~·ly** *adv* **ur·ban·ity** /ɜːˈbænətɪ; ɜˈbænətɪ/ *n* [U] refinement; politeness; (*pl;* -ties) courteous manners. 溫文;有禮;(複)禮貌;有禮貌的態度。

ur·chin /ˈɜːtʃɪn; ˈɜtʃɪn/ *n* mischievous small child; (often 常作 **ˈstreet-~**) poor destitute child. 頑童; 惡作劇的小孩;貧苦無依的孩子。

Urdu /ˈʊəduː; ˈurdu/ *adj, n* (of) one of the official languages of Pakistan. 烏爾都語(巴基斯坦法定語言之一);烏爾都語的。

urge /ɜːdʒ; ɜdʒ/ *vt* **1** [VP6A, 15B] ~ ***sb/sth (on/onward/forward),*** push or drive on: 驅策;推進: *With whip and spur he ~d his horse onward.* 他以馬鞭及馬刺策馬前進。 *The foreman ~d his workmen on.* 工頭督促工人努力工作。 **2** [VP6A, D, 9, 14, 17, 19C] ~ ***sb (to sth),*** request earnestly; try to persuade; strongly recommend: 力請;力勸;敦促: *The salesman ~d me to buy a new car.* 那推銷商向我大力推銷一部新的汽車。 *Agitators ~d the peasants to revolt/to revolution.* 煽動者慫恿農民叛變(革命)。 *He ~d leaving/our leaving/that we should leave/us to leave.* 他極力主張離去(我們離去)。 **3** [VP6A, 14] ~ ***sth (on/upon sb),*** press it (on him) with requests and arguments: 力陳;力言: *He ~d on his pupils the importance of hard work.* 他向學生們力言用功的重要。 *He ~d his youth/the fact that he was young.* 他强調他是年輕的。 □ *n* [U, C] strong desire: 强烈的慾望: *He has/feels an ~/no ~ to travel.* 他很想(不太想)去旅行。

ur·gent /ˈɜːdʒənt; ˈɜdʒənt/ *adj* **1** needing prompt decision or action: 需要立即決定或行動的; 急迫的: *An SOS is an ~ message.* SOS 是緊急呼救信號。 *It is most ~ that the patient should get to hospital.* 那病人應該立即送醫院。 *The earthquake victims are in ~ need of medical supplies.* 地震災民迫切需要醫療品。 **2** (of a person, his voice, etc) showing that sth is ~; persistent in making a demand. (指人,其聲音等)表示某事物是急迫的;堅持某項要求的。 **~·ly** *adv* **ur·gency** /-dʒənsɪ; -dʒənsɪ/ *n* [U] need for, importance of, haste or prompt action: 緊急;急迫: *a matter of great urgency.* 極爲緊急的事件。

uric /ˈjʊərɪk; ˈjurɪk/ *adj* of urine. 尿的。

urine /ˈjʊərɪn; ˈjurɪn/ *n* [U] waste liquid which collects in the bladder and is discharged from the body. 尿。 **uri·nal** /ˈjʊərɪnl; ˈjurənl/ *n* **1** (ˈ*bed urinal*) vessel into which ~ may be discharged (by sb ill in bed). 尿壺;(病人在床上使用的)便壺。 **2** (*public* ˈ*urinal*) place for the convenience of men who need to discharge ~. 小便所;(男人用的)公共小便處。 **uri·nate** /ˈjʊərɪneɪt; ˈjurəˌnet/ *vi* discharge ~. 排尿;小便。 **uri·nary** /ˈjʊərɪnrɪ *US:* -nerɪ; ˈjurəˌnɛrɪ/ *adj* of ~: 尿的: *a urinary infection.* 尿毒。

urn /ɜːn; ɜn/ *n* **1** vase, usu with stem and base, esp as used for holding the ashes of a person whose body has been cremated. 甕;(尤指)骨灰缸。 **2** large metal container in which a drink such as tea or coffee is made or kept hot, eg in cafés and canteens. (烹煮或保溫用的金屬質的) 大茶壺;大咖啡壺。

us /*weak form:* əs; əs; *strong form:* ʌs; ʌs/ *pron* object form of *we.* 爲 we 的受格形式。

usage /ˈjuːzɪdʒ *US:* ˈjuːs-; ˈjusɪdʒ/ *n* **1** [U] way of using sth; treatment: 用法;對待: *Machines soon wear out under rough ~.* 機器如果使用不小心,很快就會用壞。 **2** [C, U] body of conventions governing the use of a language (esp those aspects not governed by grammatical rules): 語言的慣用法(尤指超出文法規則者): *a guide to English grammar and ~.* 英文文法及用法指南。 *Do you have difficulty in learning the finer points of ~?* 你在學習(語言)較爲精微細緻的用法上有困難嗎? *Such ~s are not characteristic of educated speakers.* 這種用法並非有教養人士所慣用。 **3** [C, U] agreed codes of behaviour: 習俗;慣例: *Industrialization and urbanization influence social ~(s).* 工業化及都市化影響社會習俗。

use¹ /juːs; jus/ *n* **1** [U] using or being used; condition of being used: 用;使用;利用;被使用狀況: *the use of electricity for lighting;* 利用電力照明; *learn the use of tools;* 學習使用工具; *a room for the use of women only;* 婦女專用的房間; *for use only in case of fire;* 限火警時使用;限用於消防; *bought for use, not for ornament.* 買來使用,非爲裝飾。 ***in use,*** being used. 在使用中。 ***out of use,*** not being, no longer, used. (目前)不使用;不再使用。 ***come into use,*** begin to be used: 開始被使用: *When did the word 'transistor' come into common use?* '電晶體'一詞何時開始被普遍使用? ***go/fall out of use,*** be no longer used: 被廢棄;不再被使用: *The custom has gone out of use.* 那風俗已被廢棄。 ***make (good/the best) use of,*** use (well/in the best way): (好好地,盡量地)利用: *You must make good use of any opportunities you have of practising English.* 你該好好地利用所有的機會練習英文。 **2** [C, U] purpose for which sth or sb is or may be employed; work that sth or sb is able to do: (某事物或某人的)用途;用處;效用;功能: *a tool with many uses;* 有多種用途的工具; *find a use for sth;* 設法利用某物; *put sth to (a) good use;* 善爲利用某物; *have no further use for sth.* 不再需要某物。 *I have no use for* (fig, dislike, have no patience with) *people who are always grumbling.* 我討厭那些總是發牢騷的人。 **3** [U] value; advantage: 價值;效用;益處: *Is this of any use to you?* 這東西對你有什麼益處嗎? *It's no use your pretending/no use for you to pretend that you didn't know the rules.* 假裝不懂規則對你無益。 *There isn't much use for that sort of thing nowadays.* 那種東西在當前沒有多大價值了。 **4** [U] power of using: 使用的能力: *lose the use of one's legs,* become a cripple, unable to walk. 失去使用腿的能力;變瘸;不能行走。 **5** [U] right to use: 使用權: *give a friend the use of one's bike.* 讓朋友使用自己的腳踏車。 **6** [U] usage; familiarity through continued practice: 慣用;慣例;習慣;習例: *In these cases use is the best guide.* 在這些事件中,慣例是最好的指針。 **use·ful** /ˈjuːsfl; ˈjusfəl/ *adj* **1** helpful; producing good results: 有幫助的;有助益的;有用的: *A spade is a useful tool.* 鏟子是有用的工具。 *Are you a useful member of society?* 你是社會上有用的成員嗎? **2** (colloq) capable, efficient: (俗)能幹的;有效率的: *He's a useful member of the team.* 他是該隊的一員猛將。 **use·fully** /-fəlɪ; -fəlɪ/ *adv* **use·ful·ness** *n* **use·less** *adj* **1** of no use; worthless: 無用的;無價值的: *A car is useless without petrol.* 汽車如無汽油就沒有用了。 **2** without result; inef-

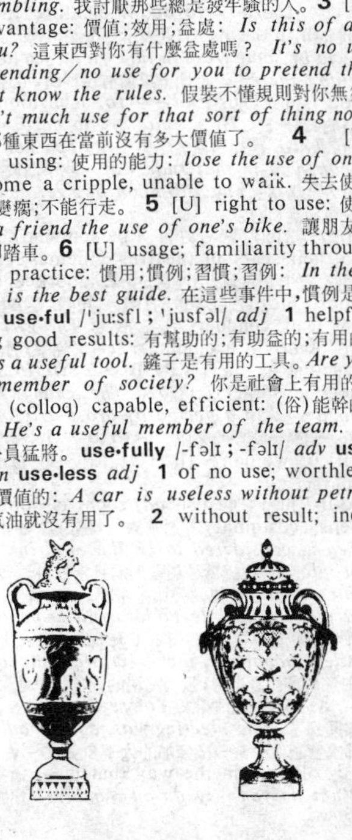

urns

fectual: 無結果的;無效的: *It's useless to argue with them.* 同他們辯論是不會有結果的。 **use·less·ly** *adv* **use·less·ness** *n*

use² /ju:z ; juz/ *vt* (*pt, pp* used /ju:zd ; juzd/) **1** [VP6A, 16A, 14] ***use (for),*** employ for a purpose: 用;使用;利用: *You use your legs when you walk.* 你走路時用腿。*You use a knife to cut bread.* 你用刀切麵包。 *A hammer is used for driving in nails.* 鎚是用來敲釘子的。 *When persuasion failed they used force.* 勸說無效時,他們就使用武力了。*May I use* (= quote) *your name as a reference,* eg in an application for a post. 我可以把你(的名字)列爲我的證明人嗎(如列在求職申請單上)? **2** [VP6A, 15B] ***use sth (up),*** consume: 消耗;用(盡): *How much coal did we use last winter?* 去年冬天我們用了多少煤? *He has ~d up all his strength.* 他已耗盡了他的體力。 **3** [VP15A] behave towards: 對待: *Use others as you would like them to use you.* 你希望別人如何對待你,你就該如何對待別人。*He thinks himself ill used,* considers that he is badly treated. 他認爲自已受到了虐待。 **used** /ju:zd ; juzd/ *adj* no longer new: 用舊了的: *used cars,* cars offered for sale after they have been used and are no longer in new condition. (出售的)舊汽車。 **us·able** /'ju:zəbl ; 'juzəbl/ *adj* that can be used, that is fit to be used. 可被使用的;堪用的;適宜使用的。 **user** *n* sb or sth that uses: 使用者(指人或物): *There are more telephone users in the USA than in any other country.* 美國使用電話的人數多於任何其他國家。

used¹ /ju:st ; just/ *anom fin* (neg 否定式爲 used not; usedn't/usen't /'ju:snt ; 'jusnt/; (colloq) (俗) didn't use /ju:s ; jus/) ~ ***to*** + *inf,* (indicating a constant or frequent practice in the past): (~ to + 不定詞表示過去經常的習慣): *That's where I ~ to live when I was a child.* 那就是我幼年的住處。*Life isn't so easy here as it ~ to be.* 如今在此地謀生已經不像往日那麼容易了。*You ~ to smoke a pipe, use(d)n't you* (or *didn't you*)*?* 你過去是抽煙斗的,是不是? *Didn't you use to smoke a pipe?* 你過去不是抽煙斗嗎? ***there ~ to be,*** (indicating the existence of sth in the past): (表示過去某事物的存在): *There ~ to be some trees in this field, use(d)n't there/didn't there?* 這片地上以前有幾棵樹,不是嗎?

used² /ju:st ; just/ *adj* ~ ***to,*** accustomed to: 習於;慣於;適應於: *He's quite ~ to hard work/working hard.* 他頗習慣於辛苦工作。*I'm not ~ to being spoken to in that rude way.* 我不慣於別人對我那樣粗魯地講話。*You will soon be/get ~ to it.* 你很快就會適應(它)。

usher /'ʌʃə(r) ; 'ʌʃɚ/ *n* **1** person who shows people to their seats in theatres, cinemas, etc. (戲院,電影院等的)招待員;引座員。 **2** doorkeeper in a law court, etc. (法院等處的)門房;司閽。□ *vt* **1** [VP15B, 14] lead, conduct: 引導;招待: *The girl ~ed me to my seat* (in a cinema). (電影院中)引座小姐引我至我的座位上。 **2** [VP15B] ~ ***sth in,*** herald, announce: 預報;預示;宣佈: *The change of government ~ed in a period of prosperity.* 政府的變動預示一個繁榮時期的來臨。 **~ette** /,ʌʃə'ret ; ,ʌʃɚ'ɛt/ *n* girl or woman ~(1). (戲院,電影院等處的)女引座員;女招待員。

usual /'ju:ʒl ; 'juʒuəl/ *adj* such as commonly happens; customary: 通常的; 尋常的; 平素的; 通例的: *Tea is considered to be the ~ drink of British people.* 茶被認爲是英國人的日常飲料。 *He arrived later than ~.* 他到得比平常晚。*As is ~ with many picnickers, they left a lot of litter behind them.* 像許多野餐者一樣,他們留下了大堆的垃圾。*When the accident happened, the ~ crowd quickly gathered.* 那意外事件發生時,照例圍觀的人群很快地聚攏來了。***as ~,*** as is ~: 如平常: *You're late, as ~.* 你像平常一樣遲到了。*The meeting was, as ~, badly attended.* 那次會議像平常一樣參加的人不多。 **~ly** /'ju:ʒəlɪ ; 'juʒuəlɪ/ *adv* in the way that is ~: 通常地;通例地: *What do you ~ly do on Sundays?* 你禮拜天通常做什麼? *He's ~ly early.* 他通常早到。

usurer /'ju:ʒərə(r) ; 'juʒərɚ/ *n* person whose business is usury. 放高利貸者。

usurp /ju:'zɜ:p ; ju'zɝp/ *vt* [VP6A] wrongfully take (sb's power, authority, position): 霸佔;篡奪;僭取(某人的權力,權威,地位): *~ the throne.* 篡奪王位。**~er** *n* person who does this. 篡奪者;僭取者;霸佔者。**usur·pa·tion** /,ju:zɜ:'peɪʃn ; ,juzɚ'peʃən/ *n* [C, U] (instance of) ~ing. 篡奪;僭取;霸佔;其實例。

usury /'ju:ʒərɪ ; 'juʒərɪ/ *n* [U] (practice of) lending money, esp at a rate of interest considered to be too high; such high interest. (放)高利貸;高利。 **usuri·ous** /ju:'zjʊərɪəs *US:* -'ʒʊ- ; ju'ʒurɪəs/ *adj* of ~: (放)高利貸的;高利的: *a usurious transaction;* 一筆高利借貸; *a usurious rate of interest.* 高利利率。

uten·sil /ju:'tensl ; ju'tɛnsl/ *n* instrument, tool, etc esp for use in the house: 器皿;器具;(尤指)家庭用具: *'household ~s,* eg pots, pans, brushes; 家庭用具(如壺,鍋,刷子); *'writing ~s,* eg paper, pens, ink. 書寫用具(如紙,筆,墨水)。

uterus /'ju:tərəs ; 'jutərəs/ *n* (anat) womb. (解剖)子宮。⇨ the illus at reproduce. 參看 reproduce 之插圖。 **uter·ine** /'ju:təraɪn ; 'jutərɪn/ *adj* of the ~. 子宮的。

utili·tar·ian /ju:,tɪlɪ'teərɪən ; ,jutɪlə'tɛrɪən/ *adj* **1** characterized by usefulness rather than by beauty, truth, goodness. 以實用爲主的;功利的;不以美、眞、善爲目的的。**2** of the U~s and their ideas. 功利主義者的;功利主義者的觀念的。□ *n* **U~,** supporter of ~ism. 功利主義者。**~·ism** /-ɪzəm ; -,ɪzəm/ *n* [U] political and moral theory that the best rule of life is to aim at 'the greatest happiness of the greatest number,' actions being considered right or wrong according as they help or hinder the achievement of this aim. (政治及道德上的)功利主義(認爲生活最好的準則旨在增進'絕大多數人最大的幸福,'並以此爲衡量行爲的標準)。

util·ity /ju:'tɪlətɪ ; ju'tɪlətɪ/ *n* (*pl* -ties) **1** [U] quality of being useful: 有用;實用;效用: (attrib) (形容用法) *'~ van/truck,* one that can be used for various purposes. 可作多種用途的篷車(貨車)。 **2** [C] **(public) ~,** public service such as the supply of water, electricity, gas, or a bus or railway service. 公共事業(指自來水,電,瓦斯,公車,鐵路等)。

util·ize /'ju:tɪlaɪz *US:* -təlaɪz ; 'jutl,aɪz/ *vt* [VP6A] make use of; find a use for. 利用;使有用;化爲有用。**util·iz·able** /-əbl ; -əbl/ *adj* that can be ~d or put to a useful purpose. 有用的;可利用的。 **util·iz·ation** /,ju:tɪlaɪ'zeɪʃn *US:* -təlɪ'z- ; ,jutlə'zeʃən/ *n* [U] utilizing or being ~d. 利用;被利用。

ut·most /'ʌtməʊst ; 'ʌt,most/ *adj* most extreme; greatest: 極度的;極端的;最大的: *in the ~ danger.* 處於極端危險中; *of the ~ importance;* 極爲重要; *with the ~ care.* 極爲當心。□ *n* **one's/the ~,** the most that is possible: 極限;竭盡所能: *do one's ~;* 竭盡全力; *exert/enjoy oneself to the ~.* 盡力而爲(盡情享受)。*That is the ~ I can do.* 那是我所能做到的極限。

Uto·pia /ju:'təʊpɪə ; ju'topɪə/ *n* [C] imaginary perfect social and political system. 烏托邦;理想國。 **Uto·pian** /-pɪən ; -pɪən/ *adj* (also 亦作 **u-**) attractive and desirable but impracticable: 烏托邦的;理想而不切合實際的;空中樓閣的: *a ~n scheme for giving all old people a pension of £100 a week.* 計畫給予所有老年人每週一百鎊養老金的一項不切實際的構想。

ut·ter¹ /'ʌtə(r) ; 'ʌtɚ/ *adj* complete; total: 完全的;全然的: *~ darkness;* 漆黑;完全黑暗; *an ~ slander.* 十足的誹謗。*She's an ~ stranger to me.* 我根本不認識她。**~·ly** *adv* **1** completely. 完全地。 **2** to the depths of one's being: 極致;徹底;透頂: *She ~ly detests him.* 她對他憎惡透頂。

ut·ter² /'ʌtə(r) ; 'ʌtɚ/ *vt* [VP6A] **1** make (a sound or sounds) with the mouth: 以口發出(聲音): *~ a sigh/a cry of pain.* 嘆息(發出痛苦的喊叫)。**2**

say: 說;講: *the last words he ~ed.* 他臨終之言。 **3** put (false money, etc) into circulation. 流通;使用(假鈔票等)。 **~·ance** /ˈʌtərəns ; ˈʌtərəns/ *n* **1** (*sing* only) way of speaking: (僅用單數)說法;語調;發音: *a clear/defective/very rapid ~ance.* 清晰(有缺陷,很快)的語調。 **2** [C] sth said; spoken word or words. 所說的話;言詞。 **3** [U] ~ing: 說;講;表達: *give ~ance to* (*one's feelings, etc*), express in words. 以言詞表達(感情等)。

ut·ter·most /ˈʌtəməust ; ˈʌtəˌmost/ *adj, n* = utmost: 最遠的;最大的;極度的;最大限度: *the ~ ends of the earth.* 天涯海角。

uvula /ˈjuːvjulə ; ˈjuvjələ/ *n* (anat) small piece of fleshy matter hanging from the back of the roof of the mouth. (解剖) 懸壅垂; 小舌。 ⇨ the illus at mouth. 參看 mouth 之插圖。 **uvu·lar** /-lə(r) ; -lɚ/ *adj* of the ~. 懸壅垂的;小舌的。

ux·ori·ous /ˌʌkˈsɔːrɪəs ; ʌkˈsorɪəs/ *adj* excessively fond of one's wife. 過度寵愛妻子的;對妻子言聽計從的。 **~·ly** *adv* **~·ness** *n*

Vv

V, v /viː ; vi/ *n* (*pl* V's, v's) **1** the 22nd letter of the English alphabet; symbol for the Roman numeral 5. 英文字母的第二十二個字母;羅馬數字的五。 ⇨ App 4. 參看附錄四。 **2** V-shaped thing: V形物: *the V sign,* sign made by the hand with the palm outwards and the first and second fingers spread to form a V (for *victory*). 勝利手勢 (以食指和中指伸出作 V 形,表示勝利)。 **V 1, 2** /ˌviːˈwʌn, ˈtuː ; ˌviˈwʌn, ˈtu/, flying bomb. V 1, 2 型飛彈。 ⇨ doodlebug.

vac /væk ; væk/ *n* (colloq, abbr of) vacation (= holidays). (俗)假日(爲 vacation 之略)。

va·cancy /ˈveɪkənsɪ ; ˈvekənsɪ/ *n* (*pl* -cies) **1** [U] condition of being empty or unoccupied. 空;未佔用。 **2** [U, C] unoccupied space; blank: 空處;空白;空間: *look over the edge of a cliff into ~.* 由懸崖邊緣望入空際。 **3** [U] lack of ideas or intelligence; lack of concentration. 頭腦空虛;茫然若失;失神。 **4** [C] position in business, etc for which sb is needed: 空缺: *good vacancies for typists and clerks.* 待遇不錯的打字員和職員的空缺。

va·cant /ˈveɪkənt ; ˈvekənt/ *adj* **1** empty: 空的: *gaze into ~ space.* 凝視浩瀚空際。 **2** not occupied by anyone: 未被佔用的: *a ~ room,* eg in a hotel; (旅館等的)空房間; *apply for a ~ position,* eg in an office. 申請(如某機構中的)空缺職位。 **~ possession,** phrase used in advertisements of houses, etc declaring that the buyer can enter into immediate occupation. 空產可立即遷入(賣房子等的廣告用語)。 **3** (of time) not filled with any activity; leisured. (指時間)未安排活動的;空檔的;空閒的。 **4** (of the mind) unoccupied with thought; (of the eyes) showing no signs of thought or interest: (指心智)空虛的;(指眼睛)茫然的: *with ~ looks;* 帶着茫然的神情; *a ~ stare/expression.* 茫然的凝視(表情)。 **~·ly** *adv*

va·cate /vəˈkeɪt *US:* ˈveɪkeɪt ; ˈveket/ *vt* [VP6A] **1** give up living in: 搬出;遷出: *~ a house/rented rooms.* 遷出房屋(所租的公寓)。 **2** leave unoccupied: 空出;騰出: *~ one's seat.* 空出自己的座位。 **3** (formal) give up possession or use of. (正式用語)放棄。

va·ca·tion /vəˈkeɪʃn *US:* veɪ- ; veˈkeʃən/ *n* **1** [U] (formal) vacating: (正式用語)放棄;空出;遷出: *His ~ of a good position in the Civil Service was unwise.* 他放棄政府機構的一個好職位誠屬不智。 **2** [C] weeks during which universities and law courts stop work: (大學的)假期;(法庭的)休庭期: *the long ~;* 長假; *the summer ~;* 暑假; *the Christmas ~.* 聖誕假期。 **3** [C] (esp US) holiday(2); any time or period of rest and freedom from work. (尤美)假日;休息日;休假。 ***on ~,*** on holiday. 度假。 □ *vi* [VP3A] ***~ at/in,*** (US) spend a holiday: (美)在…度假: *~ing in Florida.* 在佛羅里達州度假。 **~·ist** /-ʃənɪst ; -ʃənɪst/ *n* (US) person on ~(3). (美)度假者。

vac·ci·nate /ˈvæksɪneɪt *US:* -səneɪt ; ˈvæksn̩ˌet/ *vt* [VP6A, 14] **~ *sb (against sth),*** protect (sb) (against a disease) by injecting vaccine. 爲(某人)種痘,接種疫苗,打預防針(以預防某種疾病)。 **vac·ci·na·tion** /ˌvæksɪˈneɪʃn ; ˌvæksn̩ˈeʃən/ *n* [C, U] (instance of) vaccinating or being ~d. 種痘;接種疫苗;其實例。

vac·cine /ˈvæksiːn *US:* vækˈsiːn ; ˈvæksin/ *n* [C, U] substance injected into the bloodstream, used to protect persons from a disease by causing them to have a slight, but not dangerous, form of the disease. 疫苗;痘苗。

vac·il·late /ˈvæsɪleɪt ; ˈvæsl̩ˌet/ *vi* [VP2A, 3A] **~ *(between),*** waver; hesitate; be uncertain (in opinion, etc): (在意見等方面)猶豫;遲疑;躊躇: *~ between hope and fear.* 既抱着希望又感到恐懼。 **vac·il·la·tion** /ˌvæsɪˈleɪʃn ; ˌvæsl̩ˈeʃən/ *n* [C, U] (instance of) vacillating. 猶豫;遲疑;其實例。

vacu·ous /ˈvækjuəs ; ˈvækjuəs/ *adj* showing or suggesting absence of thought or intelligence: 沒有思想的;沒有頭腦的;空洞的;空虛的;愚蠢的;茫然的: *a ~ expression/stare/remark/laugh.* 茫然的表情(茫然的凝視;空洞的話;傻笑)。 **~·ly** *adv* **vacu·ity** /vəˈkjuːətɪ ; væˈkjuətɪ/ *n* (*pl* -ties) [U] state of being ~; (*pl*) ~ remarks, acts, etc. (思想或智力的)貧乏;空虛;愚蠢;茫然;(複)空洞的話;愚蠢的行爲等。

vac·uum /ˈvækjuəm ; ˈvækjuəm/ *n* (*pl* ~s or, in science, 或在科學用語中作, -ua /-juə ; -juə/) space completely empty of substance or gas(es); space in a container from which the air has been pumped out. 眞空;眞空狀態。 **ˈ~ cleaner,** apparatus which takes up dust, dirt, etc by suction. 眞空吸塵器。 **ˈ~ flask/bottle,** one having a ~ between its inner and outer walls, keeping the contents at an unchanging temperature. 熱水瓶;保溫瓶。 ⇨ thermos. **ˈ~ pump, (a)** pump to create a partial ~ in a vessel. 抽氣唧筒;眞空唧筒。 **(b)** pump in which a partial ~ is used to raise water. 眞空式抽水機。 **ˈ~ tube/valve,** sealed glass tube with an almost perfect ~ in it, for observing the passage of an electric charge. 眞空管。

vade-mecum /ˌveɪdɪˈmiːkəm ; ˈvedɪˈmikəm/ *n* [C] small handbook which can be carried about and used for reference. (隨身攜帶以供參考的)便覽;手册。

vaga·bond /ˈvægəbɒnd ; ˈvægəˌbɑnd/ *adj* having no fixed living-place; habitually wandering: 無固定住所的;漂泊的;遊蕩的: *live a ~ life;* 過遊蕩生活; *~ Gypsies.* 流浪的吉卜賽人。□ *n* ~ person; tramp. 漂泊者;流浪者。

va·gary /ˈveɪgərɪ ; vəˈgɛrɪ/ *n* [C] (*pl* -ries) strange, unusual act or idea, esp one for which there seems to be no good reason: 怪異的行爲或觀念(尤指似無良好理由者);異想天開: *the vagaries of fashion/of human emotions.* 時尚(人類感情)所表現出的怪異。

va·gina /vəˈdʒaɪnə ; vəˈdʒaɪnə/ *n* (anat) passage (in a female mammal) from the external genital organs to the womb (colloq *ˈbirth canal*). (解剖)陰道(俗稱 birth canal 產道);屄。 ⇨ the illus at reproduce. 參看 reproduce 之插圖。 **vag·inal** /vəˈdʒaɪnl; vəˈdʒaɪnl̩/ *adj*

va·grant /ˈveɪgrənt ; ˈvegrənt/ *adj* leading a wandering life: 生活無定居的;過流浪生活的: *~ tribes/musicians;* 生活無定居的部落 (各處遊蕩的音樂師); wandering: 漂泊的;遊蕩的;飄忽不定的: *lead a ~*

life; 過流浪生活; ～ *thoughts.* 飄忽不定的思想。□ *n* ～ person; vagabond or tramp. 漂泊者;流浪者遊;民。 **va·grancy** /-rənsɪ ; -rənsɪ/ *n* [U] being a ～. 漂泊;流浪;遊蕩。

vague /veɪg ; veg/ *adj* (-r, -st) **1** not clear or distinct: 不清楚的;模糊的;含混的: ～ *outlines;* 模糊的輪廓; ～ *demands.* 含混的要求。*I haven't the ～st idea what they want.* 我絲毫不知道他們需要什麼。 **2** (of persons, their looks, behaviour) uncertain, suggesting uncertainty (about needs, intentions, etc). (指人、其表情、行爲)含糊的;茫然的;(有關需要、意向等)不確知的。 **～·ly** *adv* **～·ness** *n*

vain /veɪn ; ven/ *adj* (-er, -est) **1** without use, value, meaning or result: 無益的;無效的;徒然的;無結果的: *a ～ attempt;* 徒勞的嘗試; ～ *hopes／promises.* 無結果的希望(許諾)。 **2** *in* **～, (a)** without the desired result: 無效地;無結果地;徒然: *try in ～ to do sth.* 試圖做某事而無結果。*All our work was in ～.* 我們的一切工作均歸徒然。 **(b)** without due reverence, honour or respect: 隨便地;冒瀆地;不尊敬地: *take the name of God in ～,* use the word 'God' irreverently; 妄用或濫用上帝之名; *take a person's name in ～,* use it lightly, disrespectfully. 不尊敬地使用一個人的名字。 **3** having too high an opinion of one's looks, abilities, etc; conceited: (對自己的容貌、能力等)自視過高的;自負的: *He's as ～ as a peacock.* 他極其自負。*She's ～ of her beauty.* 她自負貌美。 **ˌ～ˈglory** *n* extreme vanity or pride in oneself 極度的自負或自傲;虛榮。 **ˌ～ˈglorious** *adj* full of ～glory; conceited and boastful. 虛榮心强的;自滿而浮誇的。 **～·ly** *adv* **1** in ～. 無效地;無結果地。 **2** in a conceited manner. 自負地。

val·ance, val·ence /ˈvæləns ; ˈvæləns/ *n* short curtain or frill, round the frame or the canopy of a bedstead, above a window, or under a shelf. (床架四週,窗子上方或架子下方的)短帷幔;掛布。

vale /veɪl ; vel/ *n* (liter except in place-names) valley. (文,或用於地名)谷。

val·edic·tion /ˌvælɪˈdɪkʃn ; ˌvæləˈdɪkʃən/ *n* [C] (words used in) saying farewell. 告別;告別辭。

val·edic·tory /ˌvælɪˈdɪktərɪ ; ˌvæləˈdɪktərɪ/ *adj* relating to, in the nature of, a farewell: 告別的;辭別性的: *a ～ speech.* 告別演說。

val·ence¹ /ˈveɪləns ; ˈveləns/ *n* **1** [U] (chem) capacity of an atom to combine with, or to be replaced by, another atom. (化學)原子價(原子與其他原子相結合或由其他原子所代替的能力)。 **2** [C] (US) (美) = valency.

val·ence² /ˈvæləns ; ˈvæləns/ *n* ⇨ valance.

val·ency /ˈveɪlənsɪ ; ˈvelənsɪ/ *n* (*pl* -cies) [C] (chem) unit of valence¹: (化學)原子價之單位: *Carbon has 4 valencies.* 碳是四價。

val·en·tine /ˈvæləntaɪn ; ˈvælənˌtaɪn/ *n* (letter, card, etc, usu anonymous, sent on St V～'s Day, 14 Feb, to a) sweetheart. 在二月十四日聖華倫泰節寄給情人的信或卡片等(寄發者通常匿名);情人。

val·erian /vəˈlɪərɪən ; vəˈlɪrɪən/ *n* [U] kinds of small perennial plant with strong-smelling pink or white flowers; root of this used medically. 纈草;纈草根(作藥用)。

valet /ˈvælɪt ; ˈvælɪt/ *n* manservant who looks after his master's clothes; employee in a hotel with similar duties. 專司主人衣服的男僕;旅館中洗燙衣服的人。□ *vt* [VP6A] act as ～ to: 爲…管理衣服;替(某旅館)洗燙衣服: *The hotel has a good ～ing service.* 那旅館有良好的洗燙衣服的服務。

val·etu·di·nar·ian /ˌvælɪtjuːdɪˈneərɪən *US:* -tuːd- ; ˌvæləˌtjudn̩ˈɛrɪən/ *adj* (formal) of poor health; unduly troubled about, almost wholly occupied with, the state of one's health. (正式用語)有病的;健康不佳的;過份爲自己的健康擔憂的。□ *n* ～ person. 健康不佳者;過份爲自己健康憂慮者。

val·iant /ˈvælɪənt ; ˈvæljənt/ *adj* brave. 勇敢的;豪勇的。 **～·ly** *adv*

valid /ˈvælɪd ; ˈvælɪd/ *adj* **1** (legal) effective because made or done with the correct formalities: (法律)有效的: *a ～ claim／marriage.* 有效的要求(婚姻)。 **2** (of contracts, etc) having force in law: (指合約等)依法有效的;有法律效力的: ～ *for three months;* 三個月內有效; *a ticket ～ for one single journey between London and Dover.* 倫敦與多佛間的單程有效票。 **3** (of arguments, reasons, etc) well based; sound: (指論據、理由等)有充分根據的;正當的;健全的: *raise ～ objections to a scheme.* 對某一計畫提出有力的反對。 **～·ly** *adv* **～·ity** /vəˈlɪdətɪ ; vəˈlɪdətɪ/ *n* [U] state of being ～. 有效;效力;正確。 **vali·date** /ˈvælɪdeɪt ; ˈvæləˌdet/ *vt* [VP 6A] make ～: 使有效;使有法律效力;使有充分根據: *～ate a claim.* 使一要求生效。

va·lise /vəˈliːz *US:* vəˈliːs ; vəˈlis/ *n* small leather bag for clothes, etc during a journey; soldier's kitbag. (裝衣服等的)皮製小旅行袋;兵士的背囊。

val·ley /ˈvælɪ ; ˈvælɪ/ *n* (*pl* -leys) stretch of land between hills or mountains, often with a river flowing through it. 谷;山谷(通常有河流穿過);谿谷;河谷。⇨ the illus at mountain. 參看 mountain 之插圖。

val·our (US = **valor**) /ˈvælə(r) ; ˈvælɚ/ *n* [U] bravery, esp in war. 勇敢;(尤指在戰爭中)英勇;勇武。 **val·or·ous** /ˈvælərəs ; ˈvælərəs/ *adj* brave. 勇敢的;英勇的。

valu·able /ˈvæljʊəbl ; ˈvæljʊəbl̩/ *adj* of great value, worth or use: 有很大價值的;貴重的;很有用的: *a ～ discovery.* 有價值的發現。□ *n* (usu *pl*) sth of much value, eg articles of gold, jewels. (通常用複數)貴重物品(如黃金、珠寶等)。

valu·ation /ˌvæljʊˈeɪʃn ; ˌvæljʊˈeʃən/ *n* [U] process of deciding the value of sth or sb; [C] the value that is decided upon: 評價;估價;估定的價格;價值: *The surveyors arrived at widely different ～s.* 鑑定人作了截然不同的估價。*It is unwise to accept a person at his own ～,* the opinion which he has of himself. 相信一個人對他自己的評價是不智的。

value /ˈvæljuː ; ˈvælju/ *n* **1** [U] quality of being useful or desirable: 有用性;重要性;價值: *the ～ of walking as an exercise.* 散步的運動價值。 **2** [U] worth of sth when compared with sth else: 某物與他物比較時的價值;某物的相對價值: *This book will be of great／little／some／no ～ to him in his studies.* 這本書對於他的研究(與其他書比起來)有很大(很小,一些,沒有)價值。 **3** [C, U] worth of sth in terms of money or other goods for which it can be exchanged: 交換價值;交易價值;購買價值;價格: *Is the ～ of the American dollar likely to decline?* 美金價格可能會下降嗎? *Does this volume give you good ～ for your money?* 這本書值得你所花的錢嗎? *The property is going down in ～ all the time.* 那地產一直在落價。*Market ～s rose sharply last week.* 市場價格上週漲得很兇。 **ˌ～-ˈadded tax,** (abbr 略作 **VAT**) tax on the rise in ～ of a product at each stage of manufacture and marketing. 增價稅;增值稅。 **4** [U] what sth is considered to be worth (contrasted with the price obtainable): 價值(與該物的賣價(索價)相對): *I've been offered £500 for my old car but its ～ is much higher.* 我這舊車有人出價五百鎊,但是它的價值遠高於此數。 **5** [C, U] **(a)** (in music) full time indicated by a note: (音樂)音符所表示的音長: *Give the note its full ～.* 把這一音符的音長充分唱(奏)出。 **(b)** (in painting) relation of light and shade. (繪畫)明暗的關係。 **(c)** (in language) meaning; effect: (語言)意義;意旨;效果: *use a word with all its poetic ～.* 充分發揮一個字的詩意。 **(d)** (*pl*) standards: (複)標準: *moral／artistic ～s.* 道德(藝術)標準。 **～·less** *adj* without ～; worthless. 無價值的;無用的。□ *vt* [VP 6A, 15A, 16B] **1** estimate the money ～ of: 估…的價格;定…價: *He ～d the house for me at £20 000.* 那幢房子他替我估價兩萬鎊。 **2** regard highly; have a high opinion of: 尊重;重視: ～ *sb's advice.* 尊重某人的勸告。*Do you ～ her as a secretary?* 你重視她的秘書才幹嗎? **～r** *n* person whose profession is to estimate the money ~ of property, land, etc. 職業估價者。

valve /vælv; vælv/ *n* **1** (sorts of) mechanical device for controlling the flow of air, liquid, gas or electrons in one direction only: (控制空氣、液體、瓦斯或電子使之單向流動的)制閥; 活門; 活瓣; 汽門: *the inlet/outlet ~s of a petrol or steam engine;* 汽油發動機或蒸汽機的進氣(排氣)門; *the ~ of a bicycle tyre.* 脚踏車輪胎的氣嘴。⇨ the illus at bicycle. 參看 bicycle 之挿圖。**2** structure in the heart or in a blood-vessel allowing the blood to flow in one direction only. (心臟或血管的)瓣膜。**3 ('radio) ~,** thermionic ~ used in a radio (US 美 = *tube*). 眞空管。⇨ thermionic. **4** device in musical wind instruments, eg a cornet, for changing the pitch by changing the length of the column of air. (管樂器,如短號,用以改變音調的)栓塞。**val·vu·lar** /ˈvælvjʊlə(r); ˈvælvjələ/ *adj* of the ~s of the heart or blood-vessels: (心臟或血管的) 瓣膜的: *valvular disease of the heart.* 心臟瓣膜病。

va·moose /vəˈmuːs; væˈmus/ *vi* (US sl) go away quickly. (美俚)匆匆離去;跑開。

vamp¹ /væmp; væmp/ *n* upper front part of a boot or shoe. 靴或鞋前端的鞋面;鞋面皮。□ *vt, vi* **1** [VP6A, 15B] repair (a boot or shoe) by putting a new ~ on. 換修(靴或鞋)的鞋面。**~ *sth up,*** (fig) make sth from odds and ends: (喩)以零星材料湊成某物: *~ up some lectures out of old notes.* 利用舊稿材料拼寫成幾篇演講。**2** [VP6A, 2A] make up (a tune) for a song; improvise a musical accompaniment to a song or dance. 譜(曲);即席爲某歌或舞伴奏或作伴奏曲。

vamp² /væmp; væmp/ *n* seductive woman who uses her attractions to exploit men. 以美色利用男子或榨取男子金錢的婦人。

vam·pire /ˈvæmpaɪə(r); ˈvæmpaɪr/ *n* **1** (in stories) reanimated corpse that leaves its grave at night and sucks the blood of sleeping persons; ruthless ill-disposed person who preys on others. (故事中的) 吸血鬼 (夜間離開其墳墓並吸取睡覺者的血); 剝削他人的惡漢; 吸血者。**2 '~ (bat),** sorts of blood-sucking bat. 吸血蝙蝠。

van¹ /væn; væn/ *n* **1** covered or roofed motor-vehicle for carrying and delivering goods: (有蓋的)貨車: *the ˈbaker's van;* 裝載麵包的貨車; *a ˈfurniture van.* 搬運家具的貨車。**2** (GB) roofed railway carriage for goods: (英)有頂蓋的鐵路貨車廂: *the ˈluggage van.* 行李車。

van² /væn; væn/ *n* **1** front or leading part of an army or fleet in battle. (作戰時軍隊或艦隊的)前鋒; 前衛;先頭部隊;先驅。**2** = vanguard.

Van·dal /ˈvændl; ˈvændḷ/ *n* one of a Germanic tribe that overran Gaul, Spain and N Africa in the 4th and 5th cc and sacked Rome in 455 AD. 汪達爾人(日耳曼一部族,約第四、五世紀時,橫掃高盧、西班牙及北非,並於紀元 455 年攻掠羅馬)。⇨ Goth.

van·dal /ˈvændl; ˈvændḷ/ *n* person who wilfully destroys works of art or public and private property, spoils the beauties of nature, etc. 故意破壞藝術品、天然美景等的人;藝術品或公私財產等的破壞者。**~·ism** /-dəlɪzəm; -dḷˌɪzəm/ *n* [U] behaviour characteristic of ~s. 藝術品或公私財產等的破壞行爲。**~·ize** /-dəlaɪz; -dḷˌaɪz/ *vt* [VP6A] wilfully destroy or spoil (as above). 故意破壞藝術品或公私財產等。

vane /veɪn; ven/ *n* **1** arrow or pointer on the top of a building, turned by the wind so as to show its direction. 風向標;風信旗。**2** blade of a propeller, sail of a windmill, or other flat surface acted on by wind or water. (螺旋槳、風車、水輪等的)葉;翼。

van·guard /ˈvæŋɡɑːd; ˈvænˌɡɑrd/ *n* **1** advance party of an army, etc as a guard against surprise attack. (軍隊中以防突襲之)先鋒;先頭部隊。**2** those persons who lead a procession or (fig) a movement: (行列之)領隊;(喩)(運動之)領導人;先驅: *in the ~ of scientific progress.* 在領導科學進步的人物中。

va·nilla /vəˈnɪlə; vəˈnɪlə/ *n* **1** [C] (pods or beans of) plant with sweet-smelling flowers. 香草; 香草莢。**2** [U] flavouring substance from ~ beans or synthetic product used for it: (自香草莢中提出或由人工合成的)香精: *~ custard;* 香草乳蛋糕; *two ~ ices.* 兩份香草冰淇淋。

van·ish /ˈvænɪʃ; ˈvænɪʃ/ *vi* [VP2A] suddenly disappear; fade away gradually; go out of existence: 突然不見;逐漸消散;消失;消滅: *Your prospects of success have ~ed.* 你成功的希望已經消失了。*The thief ran into the crowd and ~ed from sight.* 那賊跑進人羣中不見了。**~ *into thin air,*** disappear suddenly and completely. 突然完全消失;突然不見。**ˈ~·ing cream,** cosmetic cream quickly absorbed into the skin. 粉底霜(一種塗後很快即爲皮膚所吸收的面霜)。**ˈ~·ing point,** (in perspective) point at which all parallel lines in the same plane appear to meet. (透視法)沒影點(同一平面上所有平行線似乎相會合的那一點)。

van·ity /ˈvænətɪ; ˈvænətɪ/ *n* (*pl* -ties) **1** [U] conceit; having too high an opinion of one's looks, abilities, etc: 自負;自大; 虛誇;虛榮心: *do sth out of ~;* 出於虛榮心而做某事; *tickle sb's ~,* do or say sth that pleases his conceit; 迎合某人的虛榮心(說或做某事以滿足其虛榮心); *injured ~,* resentment caused by some slight or humiliation. 受到傷害的虛榮心。**ˈ~ bag/case,** bag or case carried by the owner for a small mirror, cosmetics, etc. (隨身携帶的)小梳粧袋(盒)。**2** [U] worthlessness; quality of being unsatisfying, without true value: 無價值; 空虛; 無眞實價值因而不能令人滿足的性質: *the ~ of pleasure;* 歡樂的空虛; [C] vain, worthless thing or act. 空虛而無價值的東西或行爲。

van·quish /ˈvæŋkwɪʃ; ˈvænkwɪʃ/ *vt* [VP6A] (liter) conquer. (文)征服;克服。

van·tage /ˈvɑːntɪdʒ *US:* ˈvæn-; ˈvæntɪdʒ/ *n* **1** advantage: 優勢;好機會;有利之點: *ˈ~-ground;* 有利地形; *point of ~.* 有利地位。**ˈ~-point** *n* (lit or fig) place from which one has a (good) view of sth; (advantageous) position. (字面或喩)(良好的)觀望地方;有利地勢;地利。⇨ coign. **2** (in tennis) first point scored after deuce. (網球)平手後獲得的第一分。

vapid /ˈvæpɪd; ˈvæpɪd/ *adj* dull; uninteresting: 乏味的;索然的;無趣味的: *~ conversation;* 乏味的談話; *the ~ utterances of the clergy.* 敎士的索然無味的言詞。**~·ly** *adv* **~·ness** *n* **va·pid·ity** /vəˈpɪdətɪ; vəˈpɪdətɪ/ *n* [U] state of being ~; (*pl;* -ties) ~ remarks. 索然乏味;乏味的話語。

va·por·ize /ˈveɪpəraɪz; ˈvepəˌraɪz/ *vt, vi* [VP6A, 2A] convert into, become, vapour. (使)化爲蒸氣; 蒸發。**va·por·iz·ation** /ˌveɪpəraɪˈzeɪʃn *US:* -rɪˈz-; ˌvepərəˈzeʃən/ *n*

va·por·ous /ˈveɪpərəs; ˈvepərəs/ *adj* **1** full of, like, vapour. 多蒸氣的;似蒸氣的。**2** (fig) full of idle fancies; unsubstantial. (喩)多妄想的;無實質內容的。

va·pour (US = **va·por**) /ˈveɪpə(r); ˈvepə/ *n* **1** [U] steam; mist; gaseous form to which certain substances may be reduced by heat: 汽;霧;烟霧; 蒸氣: *ˈwater ~.* 水(蒸)氣。**ˈ~-bath** *n* (enclosed space or apparatus for a) bath in ~ or steam. 蒸氣浴;蒸氣浴室或設備。**ˈ~ trails,** ⇨ trail(1). **2** [C] unsubstantial thing; sth imagined: 無實質之物;空想的事物;幻想的事物: *the ~s of a disordered mind.* 精神錯亂者的幻象。**3 the ~s,** (archaic) melancholy. (古)憂鬱。

vari·able /ˈveərɪəbl; ˈvɛrɪəbḷ/ *adj* varying; changeable: 變化的;可變的;易變的: *~ winds;* 方向不定的風; *~ standards;* 可變易的標準; *~ costs,* (accounting) costs that go up or down according to the quantity of goods produced. (會計)可變成本(隨產量之多少昇降者)。*His mood/temper is ~.* 他的心情(脾氣)變化無常。□ *n* [C] ~ thing or quantity; factor which may vary, eg in an experiment. 可變物;可變量;(實驗等中之)變量;變數;變項。**vari·ably**

/-əblɪ ; -əblɪ/ *adv* ～**·ness** *n* **varia·bil·ity** /ˌveərɪəˈbɪlətɪ ; ˌvɛrɪəˈbɪlətɪ/ *n* [U] quality of being ～; tendency to vary. 變化性;變化的傾向;易變。

vari·ance /ˈveərɪəns ; ˈvɛrɪəns/ *n* [U] ***at ～ (with)***, in disagreement; having a difference of opinion: (與…)不和;意見不同;齟齬: *The two sisters have been at ～ for years.* 這兩姊妹不和睦已有若干年了。*We are at ～ among ourselves／at ～ with the others.* 我們彼此(與他人)不和。

vari·ant /ˈveərɪənt ; ˈvɛrɪənt/ *adj* different or alternative: 不同的;變異的;替換的: ～ *spellings of a word* (eg 'tire' and 'tyre'). 一字的不同拼法(如 tire 和 tyre)。□ *n* ～ form (eg of spelling). 替換的形式(如指拼字法)。

vari·ation /ˌveərɪˈeɪʃn ; ˌvɛrɪˈeʃən/ *n* **1** [C, U] (degree of) varying or being variant: 變異;異差;變異的程度: ～*(s) of pressure／temperature;* 壓力(溫度)的異差; ～*s in public opinion.* 輿論的變異。**2** [C] (music) simple melody repeated in a different (and usu more complicated) form: (音樂)變奏曲;變奏: ～*s on a theme by Mozart.* 莫扎特所作某一曲子的變奏。**3** [U] (biol) change in bodily structure or form caused by new conditions, environment, etc; [C] instance of such change. (生物)變種;變異;變種的實例。

vari·col·oured (US = **-col·ored**) /ˈveərɪkʌləd ; ˈvɛrɪˌkʌlɚd/ *adj* of various colours. 雜色的;五顏六色的。

vari·cose /ˈværɪkəʊs ; ˈværɪˌkos/ *adj* (esp in) (尤用於) ～ **vein,** vein that has become permanently swollen or enlarged. (永久性)靜脈腫大或曲張。

var·ied /ˈveərɪd ; ˈvɛrɪd/ *adj* **1** of different sorts; diverse: 各種不同的;各式各樣的: ～ *opinions;* 各種不同的意見; *the* ～ *scenes of life.* 生活中各式各樣的情景。**2** full of changes or variety: 多變化的: *a* ～ *career.* 多變化的生涯。

varie·gated /ˈveərɪgeɪtɪd ; ˈvɛrɪˌgetɪd/ *adj* marked irregularly with differently coloured patches: 雜色的;斑駁的: *The leaves of geraniums／The flowers of pansies are often* ～. 天竺葵的葉(紫羅蘭的花)常是雜色的。**varie·ga·tion** /ˌveərɪˈgeɪʃn ; ˌvɛrɪˈgeʃən/ *n*

var·iety /vəˈraɪətɪ ; vəˈraɪətɪ/ *n* (*pl* -ties) **1** [U] quality of not being the same, or not being the same at all times: 變化性;多變性;多樣性;多變: *a life full of* ～. 變化多端的生活。*We demanded more* ～ *in our food.* 我們要求我們的伙食多一點變化。**2** (*sing* only) number or range of different things: (僅用單數)若干不同的事物;種種: *for a* ～ *of reasons;* 由於種種原因; *a large* ～ *of patterns to choose from.* 可供選擇的種類繁多的花樣。**3** [C] (biol) subdivision of a species. (生物)品種;種類。**4** [C] kind or sort which differs from others of the larger group of which it is a part: 異種;異類;同類中的少數變異物: *rare varieties of early postage stamps.* 早期郵票中的珍品。*There are now several varieties of spaniel.* 長耳狗現在有好些不同種類。**5** [U] kind of entertainment consisting of singing, dancing, acrobatic feats, short plays, etc as given in music-halls (GB), some nightclubs and hotels, and for broadcasting: 雜耍;綜藝(包括歌、舞、特技表演、短劇等): *a* ˈ～ *entertainment;* 雜耍(綜藝)表演; *a* ˈ～ *theatre;* 雜耍(綜藝)劇場; ˈ～ *artists.* 雜耍(綜藝)演員。(*US* 美 = *vaudeville*).

vari·form /ˌveərɪˈfɔːm *US:* ˈvær- ; ˈvɛrɪˌfɔrm/ *adj* of various forms. 形形色色的;形式繁多的。

vari·orum /ˌveərɪˈɔːrəm ; ˌvɛrɪˈorəm/ *adj* (only in) (僅用於) ˈ～ **edition,** edition, eg of a Shakespeare play, with the notes of various commentators. 集註本(如莎士比亞劇本的集註本)。

vari·ous /ˈveərɪəs ; ˈvɛrɪəs/ *adj* (usu attrib) different; of a number of different sorts: (通常作形容用法)不同的;種種的;各式各樣的: *for* ～ *reasons;* 爲了種種的理由; *at* ～ *times;* 在不同的時代; *a criminal who is known to the police under* ～ *names.* 警方認得其許多化名的罪犯。～**·ly** *adv*

var·let /ˈvɑːlɪt ; ˈvɑrlɪt/ *n* (archaic) rascal. (古)無賴;流氓。

var·nish /ˈvɑːnɪʃ ; ˈvɑrnɪʃ/ *n* [C, U] (particular kind of) (liquid used to give a) hard, shiny, transparent coating on the surface of sth, esp woodwork or metalwork; (fig) false or deceiving appearance: 假漆;光漆;亮漆;凡立水(尤指用於木器或金屬器上者);(喻)虛飾;文飾;粉飾: *scratch the* ～ *on a table;* 刮壞桌子上的亮漆; *a* ～ *of good manners;* 虛飾的禮貌; ˈ*nail*-～, for fingernails. 指甲油。□ *vt* [VP6A] put a coating of ～ on: 塗亮漆或凡立水於…上;上光: ～ *a piece of furniture／an oil-painting.* 上光於一件家具(一幀油畫)。*Some women* ～ *their toe-nails.* 有些女人在脚趾甲上塗指甲油。

vars·ity /ˈvɑːsətɪ ; ˈvɑrsətɪ/ *n* (*pl* -ties) (colloq) university. (俗)大學。

vary /ˈveərɪ ; ˈvɛrɪ/ *vi, vt* (*pt, pp* -ried) [VP2A, 6A] be, become, cause to become, different: 不同;改變;使不同;使有變化: ～*ing prices;* 變動的物價; *prices that* ～ *with the season.* 隨季節而變動的物價。*They* ～ *in weight from 3 lb to 5 lb.* 這些東西的重量從三磅到五磅不等。*You should* ～ *your diet.* 你應該變換飲食。

vas·cu·lar /ˈvæskjʊlə(r) ; ˈvæskjəlɚ/ *adj* of, made up of, containing, vessels or ducts through which blood, lymph or sap flows: 脈管的;血管的;導管的;脈管形成的;含有脈管的: ～ *tissue.* 脈管組織。

vase /vɑːz *US:* veɪs ; ves/ *n* [C] vessel of glass, pottery, etc for holding cut flowers, or as an ornament. 花瓶;飾瓶。

vases

va·sec·tomy /vəˈsektəmɪ ; væsˈɛktəmɪ/ *n* (*pl* -mies) simple surgical operation to make a man sterile. (男性的)輸精管切除術(一種簡單的絕育手術);男性結紮術。

vas·eline /ˈvæsəliːn ; ˈvæslˌin/ *n* [U] (P) yellowish substance, petroleum jelly, almost without taste or smell, used as an ointment or lubricant. (商標)礦脂;凡士林。

vas·sal /ˈvæsl ; ˈvæsl/ *n* (hist) person who held land in return for which he vowed to give military service to the owner of the land; feudal tenant; (fig) humble dependant: (史)家臣;封臣;(喻)謙恭的從屬者;下屬: (attrib) (形容用法) *a* ～ *state,* one subject to another. 屬國。ˈ～**·age** /-səlɪdʒ ; -slɪdʒ/ *n* [U] state of being a ～; servitude. 家臣的地位;從屬;隸屬;服從;忠順。

vast /vɑːst *US:* væst ; væst/ *adj* immense; extensive: 巨大的;廣袤的: ～ *sums of money;* 巨額金錢; *a* ～ *expanse of desert.* 一片廣大的沙漠。～**·ly** *adv* ～**·ness** *n*

vat /væt ; væt/ *n* tank or great vessel for holding liquids, esp in distilling, brewing, dyeing and tanning. 大桶;大缸(尤指供蒸餾、釀造、染色及鞣皮用者)。

Vati·can /ˈvætɪkən ; ˈvætɪkən/ *n* **the** ～, the residence in Rome of the Pope; centre of Papal government. 梵蒂岡(羅馬教宗的駐在地);教廷;教廷政府所在地。

vaude·ville /ˈvɔːdəvɪl ; ˈvodəˌvɪl/ *n* [U] (US) (美) = variety(5).

vault[1] /vɔːlt ; vɔlt/ *n* **1** arched roof; series of arches forming a roof. 拱形圓屋頂;穹窿。⇨ the illus at crypt. 參看 crypt 之插圖。**2** underground room or cellar (with or without an arched roof) as a place of storage (ˈ*wine-*~*s*), or for burials (eg under a church, or in a cemetery), or for safe-keeping of valuables: 窖；地下室(用作貯存物品之處，如 wine-~s 酒窖，或作埋葬所，如教堂或墓地的地窖，或用以存放貴重物品): *keep one's jewels in the ~ at the bank.* 把珠寶存放在銀行地窖中。**3** ~-like covering: 穹窿狀覆蓋物: (poet) (詩) *the ~ of heaven,* the sky. 蒼穹；天空。**~ed** *adj* built with, having, a ~ or ~s; in the form of a ~: 有拱形圓屋頂的；穹窿狀的: *a ~ed roof/chamber.* 拱形屋頂(有拱形屋頂的會堂)。

vault² /vɔːlt ; vɔlt/ *vi, vt* [VP2A, B, C, 6A] jump in a single movement, with the hand(s) resting on sth, or with the help of a pole: 以手撐物跳躍(過)；撐竿跳躍(過): *~ (over) a fence.* 跳過籬牆。*The jockey ~ed into the saddle.* 騎士一躍而跨坐鞍上。**ˈ~·ing-horse** *n* apparatus for practice in ~ing. (練習跳躍用的)木馬。□ *n* jump made in this way. 撐物跳躍；撐竿跳。**~er** *n* person who ~s. 撐物(竿)跳者。

vaunt /vɔːnt ; vɔnt/ *vi, vt, n* (liter) boast. (文)吹牛；誇張。**~er** *n* **~·ing·ly** *adv*

veal /viːl ; vil/ *n* [U] flesh of a calf as food. (供食用的)小牛肉。

veer /vɪə(r) ; vɪr/ *vi* [VP2A, C] (esp of the wind, fig of opinion, talk) change direction: (尤指風，喻指意見或談話)改變方向；轉向；轉變: *The wind ~ed round to the north.* 風改向北吹了。

veg·etable /ˈvedʒtəbl ; ˈvɛdʒtəbl/ *adj* of, from, relating to, plants or plant life: 植物的；由植物得來的；關於植物的；蔬菜的: *the ~ kingdom;* 植物界；*~ oils.* 植物油。□ *n* [C] plant, esp of the sort used for food, eg potatoes, cabbages, beans, onions, carrots, etc. 植物；(尤指)蔬菜(如馬鈴薯、捲心菜、豆類、洋葱、胡蘿蔔等)。

veg·etar·ian /ˌvedʒɪˈteərɪən ; ˌvɛdʒəˈtɛrɪən/ *n* person who, for humane or religious reasons or for his health's sake, eats no meat: 蔬食者；素食者: (attrib) (形容用法) *a ~ diet;* 素菜；*~ principles.* 素食戒條(規則)。

veg·etate /ˈvedʒɪteɪt ; ˈvɛdʒəˌtet/ *vi* [VP2A] live as plants do, without mental effort or intellectual interests; lead a dull life with little activity or interest. 像植物般生活(不運用心智，缺乏智力方面的興趣)；過枯燥而少活動或趣味的生活。

veg·eta·tion /ˌvedʒɪˈteɪʃn ; ˌvɛdʒəˈteʃən/ *n* [U] plants generally and collectively: (泛指一般的)植物；草木: *the luxuriant ~ of the tropical forests;* 熱帶森林中茂盛的草木；*a desert landscape with no sign of ~ anywhere.* 寸草不生的沙漠景觀。

ve·he·ment /ˈviːəmənt ; ˈviəmənt/ *adj* **1** (of feelings) strong, eager; (of persons, their speech, behaviour, etc) filled with, showing, strong or eager feeling: (指感情)强烈的；熱切的；(指人、其言詞、其行爲等)充滿或顯示强烈或熱切情感的: *a man of ~ character;* 熱情的人；*~ desires/passions.* 强烈的慾望(情慾)。**2** violent: 猛烈的: *a ~ wind.* 强風。**~·ly** *adv* **ve·he·mence** /-məns ; -məns/ *n*

ve·hicle /ˈviːɪkl ; ˈviɪkl/ *n* [C] **1** any conveyance (usu wheeled, eg a cart, lorry, motor-car, but also a sledge) for goods or passengers on land. 陸上交通工具；車輛(包括雪橇)。Cf 參較 *craft* for

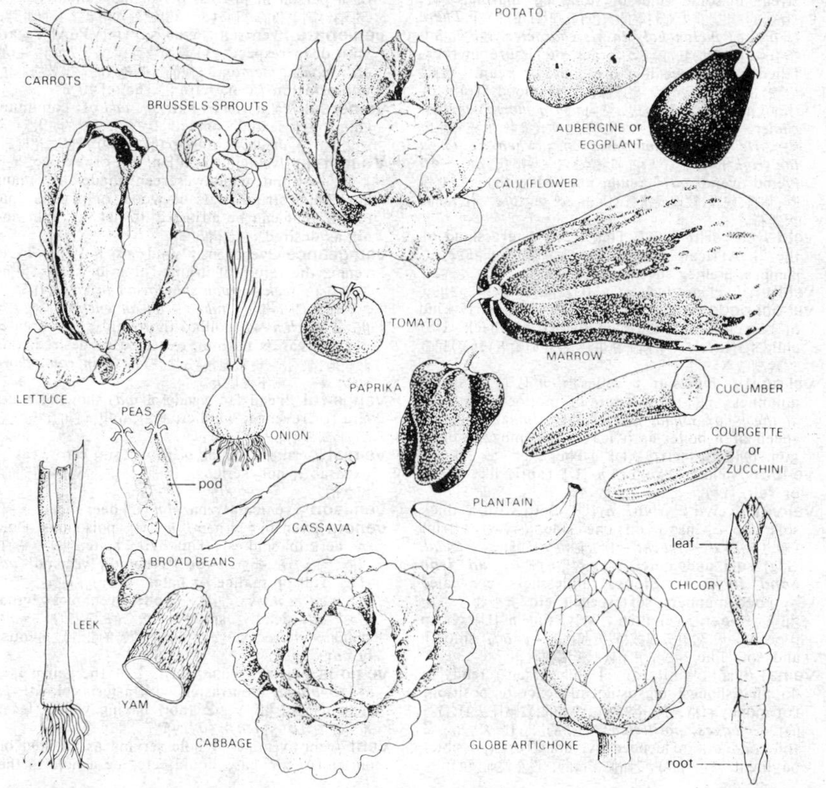

vegetables

water, space. 指水上及空中交通工具。 **2** means by which thought, feeling, etc can be conveyed: 傳達思想、情感等的工具;媒介物: *Art may be used as a ~ for/of propaganda.* 藝術可用作宣傳的工具。 **ve·hicu·lar** /viˈhɪkjʊlə(r); viˈhɪkjələ/ *adj* related to, consisting of, conveyed by, ~s: 車輛的;陸上交通工具的;媒介物的: *The road is closed to vehicular traffic.* 此路不准車輛通行。

veil /veɪl; vel/ *n* [C] **1** covering of fine net or other material to protect or hide a woman's face, or as part of a headdress: (婦女的)面紗;面罩: *She raised/dropped/lowered her ~.* 她揭起(拉下,放下)面罩。 ***take the ~,*** become a nun. 當修女。 **2** (fig) sth that hides or disguises: (喻)遮蔽物;掩飾物;假託;口實: *a ~ of mist;* 一層霧; *commit murder under the ~ of patriotism,* do so under the pretence of patriotism. 假愛國之名而謀殺。 ***draw a ~ over sth,*** be discreet or secretive about: 隱瞞或隱藏某事;對某事警覺或謹慎: *Let us draw a ~ over what followed.* 後來的事情我們不必提了。□ *vt* [VP6A] put a ~ over; (fig) conceal: 以面紗遮掩;(喻)隱蔽: *Some Muslim women are ~ed.* 有些回教婦女戴面罩。 *He could not ~ his distrust.* 他不能掩飾他的疑惑。 **~·ing** *n* [U] light material used for making ~s; such material used as a ~. (做面罩用的)薄紗;面紗。

vein /veɪn; ven/ *n* **1** blood-vessel along which blood flows from all parts of the body to the heart. 靜脈(血液從身體各部流回心臟的血管)。 ⇨ the illus at respiratory. 參看 respiratory 之插圖。 ⇨ artery(1). **2** one of the ~-like lines in some leaves or in the wings of some insects; a coloured line or streak in some kinds of stone, eg marble; 葉脈;(昆蟲的)翅脈;(大理石等的有色)紋理;(fig):(喻): *There is a ~ of melancholy in his character.* 他的性格中帶有少許憂鬱的氣質。 **3** crack or fissure in rock, filled with mineral or ore; lode or seam: 礦脈;岩脈: *a ~ of gold.* 金礦脈。 **4** mood; train of thought: 心情;心緒;心思;意向: *in a merry/melancholic/imaginative ~.* 心情愉快的(憂鬱的;充滿想像的)。 *He writes humorous songs when he is in the (right) ~.* 他心情好的時候會寫一些幽默歌曲。 **~ed** /veɪnd; vend/ *adj* having, marked with, ~s: 有靜脈、葉脈、翅脈、紋理或礦脈的: *~ed marble.* 有紋理的大理石。

veld /velt; vɛlt/ *n* [U] flat, treeless grassland of the S African plateau. (南非高原上的)草原。 ⇨ pampas, prairie, savannah, steppe.

vel·lum /ˈveləm; ˈvɛləm/ *n* [U] parchment. 皮紙。

vel·oci·pede /vɪˈlɒsɪpiːd; vəˈlɑsəˌpid/ *n* early kind of bicycle with pedals on the front wheel; (US) child's tricycle. 早期腳踏車(踏板在前輪者);(美)兒童三輪腳踏車。

vel·oc·ity /vɪˈlɒsətɪ; vəˈlɑsətɪ/ *n* [U] **1** speed; quickness. 迅速;快。 **2** rate of motion: 速率;速度: *at the ~ of sound;* 以聲音的速度; *ˈmuzzle ~,* the speed of a bullet as it leaves the muzzle of a gun. (彈丸離開槍口或砲口時的)初速。

ve·lour /vəˈlʊə(r); vəˈlʊr/ *n* [U] fabric like velvet or felt. 絲絨。

vel·vet /ˈvelvɪt; ˈvɛlvɪt/ *n* [U] cloth with a thick soft nap (⇨ nap[2]) on one side: 天鵝絨: (attrib)(形容用法) *a ~ frock;* 一件天鵝絨女長服; *a ~ tread,* (fig) soft and quiet. (喻)輕悄的腳步。 ***an iron hand in a ~ glove,*** ruthlessness concealed by good manners, soft speech, etc. 笑裡藏刀;外柔內剛。 **~·een** /ˌvelvɪˈtiːn; ˌvɛlvəˈtin/ *n* [U] cheap type of ~. 劣質天鵝絨;假天鵝絨。 **~y** *adj* smooth and soft like ~. 光滑柔軟似天鵝絨的。

ve·nal /ˈviːnl; ˈvinl/ *adj* **1** (of persons) ready to do sth dishonest (eg using influence or position) for money: (指人)爲金錢而做壞事的;貪贓枉法的;貪污的: *~ judges/politicians.* 貪污的法官(政客)。 **2** (of conduct) influenced by, done for, (possible) payment: (指行爲)受賄賂影響的;爲金錢而做的: *~ practices.* 受賄的惡習。 **~ly** /-nəlɪ; -nlɪ/ *adv* **~·ity** /vɪˈnælətɪ; viˈnælətɪ/ *n* quality of being ~. 貪贓枉法;貪污;受賄。

vend /vend; vɛnd/ *vt* [VP6A] (chiefly legal) sell; offer for sale (esp small wares). (主要爲法律用語)販賣;售賣(尤指小商品)。 **ˈ~·ing machine,** coin-operated slot machine for the sale of small articles, eg cigarettes and food. 自動販賣機(販賣香烟、食品等小物品)。 **~ee** /venˈdiː; vɛnˈdi/ *n* person to whom sth is sold. 買主;買方。 **~er, ~or** /-də(r); -də/ *nn* seller: 小販;賣主;賣方: *ˈnewsvendor,* seller of newspapers. 報販。

ven·detta /venˈdetə; vɛnˈdɛtə/ *n* hereditary feud between families in which members of each family commit murders in revenge for previous murders. 家族間的宿怨;仇殺;血仇。

ve·neer /vəˈnɪə(r); vəˈnɪr/ *n* **1** [C, U] (thin layer of) fine quality wood glued to the surface of cheaper wood (for furniture, etc). 粘在廉價木材上的上等木材;此種上等木材薄板(如家具等上者)。 **2** (fig) surface appearance (of politeness, etc) covering the true nature: (喻)遮掩真情的外表;虛飾: *a ~ of Western civilization.* 西方文明的外表。□ *vt* [VP6A] put a ~ on: 以上等木材薄板粘於…上: *~ a deal desk with walnut.* 以胡桃木薄板粘於樅木書桌的表面上。

ven·er·able /ˈvenərəbl; ˈvɛnərəbl̩/ *adj* **1** deserving respect because of age, character, associations, etc: 年歲、品格、交往關係等方面值得尊敬的;令人肅然起敬的: *a ~ scholar;* 可敬的學者; *the ~ ruins of the abbey.* 古老的大寺院的遺跡。 **2** (Church of England) title of an archdeacon; (Church of Rome) title of a person in process of being canonized. (英國國教)副主教的尊稱;(天主教)被列入聖者之人的頭銜。

ven·er·ate /ˈvenəreɪt; ˈvɛnəˌret/ *vt* [VP6A] regard with deep respect: 對…深懷敬意;崇敬: *They ~ the old man's memory.* 他們對那老人懷着崇敬的追念。 **ven·er·ation** /ˌvenəˈreɪʃn; ˌvɛnəˈreʃən/ *n*

ve·nereal /vəˈnɪərɪəl; vəˈnɪrɪəl/ *adj* of, communicated by, sexual contact: 性交的;交媾的;因性交而感染的: *~ diseases,* (abbr 略作 **VD**). 性病;花柳病。

Ve·ne·tian /vəˈniːʃn; vəˈniʃən/ *adj* of Venice. 威尼斯的。 **~ blind,** window screen made of many horizontal strips (slats of wood or plastic material) that can be adjusted to let in light and air as desired. 百葉窗。

ven·geance /ˈvendʒəns; ˈvɛndʒəns/ *n* [U] **1** revenge; the return of injury for injury: 報仇;復仇;以牙還牙: *seek ~ upon sb (for an injury);* (因遭其傷害而)向某人報復; *take ~ on an enemy.* 向敵人復仇。 **2** ***with a ~,*** (colloq) thoroughly; to a greater degree than is normal, expected or desired: (俗)澈底地;激烈地;極端地;過分地: *The rain came down with a ~.* 雨下得很大。

venge·ful /ˈvendʒfl; ˈvɛndʒfəl/ *adj* showing a desire for revenge; vindictive. 顯示復仇心的;報仇心切的;報復的。

ve·nial /ˈviːnɪəl; ˈvinɪəl/ *adj* (of a sin, error, fault) excusable; not serious. (指罪、錯誤、過失)可寬恕的;輕微的。

ven·ison /ˈvenɪzn; ˈvɛnəzn̩/ *n* [U] deer meat. 鹿肉。

venom /ˈvenəm; ˈvɛnəm/ *n* [U] poisonous fluid of certain snakes; (fig) hate; spite. (某些蛇的)毒液;(喻)怨恨;惡意: **~ed** /ˈvenəmd; ˈvɛnəmd/ *adj* (fig) full of malice or hate: (喻)充滿惡意或怨恨的: *~ed remarks.* 惡言。 **~·ous** /ˈvenəməs; ˈvɛnəməs/ *adj* deadly; spiteful: 致命的;惡毒的: *~ous snakes/criticism.* 致命的毒蛇(惡毒的批評)。 **~·ously** *adv*

ve·nous /ˈviːnəs; ˈvinəs/ *adj* **1** of the veins: 靜脈的: *~ blood,* (contrasted with arterial blood). 靜脈血(與動脈血相對)。 **2** (bot) having veins: (植物)多葉脈的: *a ~ leaf.* 有脈的葉子。

vent /vent; vɛnt/ *n* **1** hole serving as an inlet or outlet for air, gas, liquid, etc, eg a hole in the top of a barrel, for air to enter as liquid is drawn out. 孔；口；通風孔(如大桶頂上的通孔，液體抽出時，供空氣進入)。 '**~-hole** *n* hole for the escape of air, smoke, etc. 出氣口(孔)；出烟孔(口)。 **2** (trade use) slit in the back of a coat or jacket. (商業用語)上衣背部的叉口。 **3** means of escape: 逃避或逃脫的出路；漏洞: *The floods found a ~ through the dykes.* 洪水從堤上的一處漏洞溢流。 **4** (*sing* only) outlet for one's feelings. (僅用單數)感情的出口；發洩；吐露。 ***give ~ to,*** (fig) give free expression to: (喻)(無禁忌或拘束地)發出；發洩；吐露: *He gave ~ to his feelings in an impassioned speech.* 在一篇激動的演說中，他無顧忌地吐露心聲。□ *vt* [VP6A, 14] ***~ sth on sb／sth,*** find or provide an outlet for: 發洩；出氣: *He ~ed his ill-temper upon his long-suffering wife.* 他把怒氣向他長久受苦的妻子發洩。

ven·ti·late /ˈventɪleɪt *US:* -təleɪt ; ˈvɛntḷˌet/ *vt* [VP6A] **1** cause air to move freely through: 使空氣流通；使通風: *~ a room／the galleries of a coalmine.* 使房間(煤礦坑道)通風。 **2** (fig) make (a question, a grievance) widely known and cause it to be discussed. (喻)宣洩；公開；引起公開討論(某問題，苦況)。 **ven·ti·la·tor** /ˈventɪleɪtər *US:* -təl- ; ˈvɛntḷˌetɚ/ *n* device for ventilating. 通風設備。 **ven·ti·la·tion** /ˌventɪˈleɪʃn *US:* -təˈleɪʃn ; ˌvɛntḷˈeʃən/ *n* [U] ventilating or being ~d: 通風；流通空氣: *the ventilation shaft of a coalmine.* 煤礦的通風豎坑道。

ven·tricle /ˈventrɪkl ; ˈvɛntrɪkḷ/ *n* cavity in the body; hollow part of an organ, esp of the heart. (體內的)穴；腔；室；(尤指)心室。 ⇨ the illus at respiratory. 參看 respiratory 之挿圖。

ven·tril·oquism /venˈtrɪləkwɪzəm ; vɛnˈtrɪləˌkwɪzəm/ *n* [U] art of producing voice-sounds so that they seem to come from a person or place at a distance from the speaker. 腹語術(使語音聽起來非發自說話者，而似發自他人或他處的技術)。 **ven·tril·oquist** /-kwɪst ; -kwɪst/ *n* person skilled in ~. 擅長腹語者；精於腹語者。

ven·ture /ˈventʃə(r) ; ˈvɛntʃɚ/ *n* [C, U] undertaking in which there is risk. 冒險；冒險事業。□ *vt, vi* **1** [VP6A, 15A, 16A, 3A] ***~ (on),*** take the risk of, expose to, danger or loss: 冒險；使…可能遭受危險或損失: *~ one's life to save sb from drowning;* 冒生命危險拯救某人使免淹死； *~ too near the edge of a cliff;* 冒險地過分接近懸崖的邊緣； *~ on a dangerous journey.* 大膽地從事危險的旅行。 ***Nothing ~, nothing gain／win／have,*** (prov) One cannot expect to achieve anything if one risks nothing. (諺)不入虎穴，焉得虎子(不敢冒險者將一事無成)。 **2** [VP6A, 7A] go so far as, presume, dare: 敢；敢於；膽敢；竟敢: *~ (to put forward) an opinion;* 敢於陳述一項意見； *~ a guess.* 大膽地猜測。 *I ~ to disagree／to suggest that....* 我冒昧地不同意(建議)…。 '**V~ Scout,** senior Scout. 年長的童子軍。 '**~·some** /-səm ; -səm/ *adj* **1** (of persons) ready to take risks; daring. (指人)好冒險的；大膽的。 **2** (of acts, behaviour) involving danger; risky. (指動作，行爲)有危險的；危險的。 **ven·tur·ous** /ˈventʃərəs ; ˈvɛntʃərəs/ *adj* = adventurous.

venue /ˈvenjuː ; ˈvɛnju/ *n* rendezvous; meeting-place; (sport) place fixed for a contest or match. 集合地點；會場；(運動)競賽場；比賽地點。

Venus /ˈviːnəs ; ˈvinəs/ *n* **1** (Roman myth) goddess of love and beauty. (羅神)維納斯(愛和美的女神)。 **2** (astron) planet second in order from the sun. (天文)金星；太白星(環繞太陽的第二顆行星)。⇨ the illus at planet. 參看 planet 之挿圖。

ver·acious /vəˈreɪʃəs ; vəˈreʃəs/ *adj* (formal) true; truthful. (正式用語)眞實的；可靠的；誠實的。 **~·ly** *adv* **ver·ac·ity** /vəˈræsətɪ ; vəˈræsətɪ/ *n* [U] truth; truthfulness. 眞實；可靠。

ve·ran·da(h) /vəˈrændə ; vəˈrændə/ *n* roofed and floored open space along the side(s) of a house, sports pavilion, etc (US often called 美常作 *porch*). 走廊；遊廊；陽臺。

verb /vɜːb ; vɝb/ *n* word or phrase indicating what sb or sth does, what state sb or sth is in, what is becoming of sth or sb. 動詞；動詞片語。

ver·bal /ˈvɜːbl ; ˈvɝbḷ/ *adj* **1** of or in words: 言辭的；字句的: *a ~ error;* 用字的錯誤； *have a good ~ memory,* be able to remember well the exact words of a statement, etc. 對文句有好記性。 **2** spoken, not written: 口頭的: *a ~ statement／explanation.* 口頭的敍述(解釋)。 **3** word for word, literal: 逐字的；照字面的: *a ~ translation.* 直譯。 **4** of verbs: 動詞的: *a ~ noun* (eg *swimming* in the sentence 'Swimming is a good exercise'). 動名詞(如 'Swimming is a good exercise' 中的 swimming)。 **~ly** /ˈvɜːbəlɪ ; ˈvɝblɪ/ *adv* in spoken words, not in writing. 口頭上。

ver·bal·ize /ˈvɜːbəlaɪz ; ˈvɝbḷˌaɪz/ *vt* put into words. 用言辭表達。

ver·ba·tim /vɜːˈbeɪtɪm ; vɚˈbetɪm/ *adv, adj* word for word, exactly as spoken or written: 逐字地(的)；完全照字面地(的): *report a speech ~;* 逐字地報導一項演說； *a ~ report.* 逐字報告。

ver·bena /vɜːˈbiːnə ; vɚˈbinə/ *n* kinds of herbaceous plant of which garden varieties have flowers of many colours. 馬鞭草。

ver·bi·age /ˈvɜːbɪɪdʒ ; ˈvɝbɪɪdʒ/ *n* [U] (use of) unnecessary words for the expression of an idea, etc: 冗詞；贅語；使用冗詞贅語: *The speaker lost himself in ~.* 那演講者廢話連篇。

ver·bose /vɜːˈbəʊs ; vɚˈbos/ *adj* using, containing, more words than are needed: 用字過多的；冗贅的；冗長的: *a ~ speech／speaker／style.* 冗長的演講(冗贅的演講者；冗贅的文體)。 **~·ly** *adv* **~·ness, ver·bos·ity** /vɜːˈbɒsətɪ ; vɚˈbɑsətɪ/ *nn* [U] state or quality of being ~. 冗長；冗贅。

ver·dant /ˈvɜːdnt ; ˈvɝdṇt/ *adj* **1** (liter) (esp of grass, vegetation, fields) fresh and green: (文)(尤指草，植物，田野)青葱的；新綠的: *~ lawns.* 新綠的草地。 **2** (fig) inexperienced; unsophisticated. (喻)無經驗的；不老練的。 **ver·dancy** /-dnsɪ ; -dṇsɪ/ *n*

ver·dict /ˈvɜːdɪkt ; ˈvɝdɪkt/ *n* [C] **1** decision reached by a jury on a question of fact in a law case: 陪審團的裁決；判決: *The jury brought in* (= announced) *a ~ of guilty／not guilty.* 陪審團判決有(無)罪。 **open ~,** ⇨ open¹(6). **2** decision or opinion given after testing, examining, or experiencing sth: (對某事物的)決定；判斷；論斷；意見: *the ~ of the electors.* 選舉人的決定。 *The popular ~* (= The opinion of people in general) *was that it served him right.* 公衆的意見認爲他罪有應得。

ver·di·gris /ˈvɜːdɪgrɪs ; ˈvɝdɪˌgris/ *n* [U] green substance formed on copper, brass and bronze surfaces (as rust is formed on iron surfaces). 銅銹；銅綠。

ver·dure /ˈvɜːdʒə(r) ; ˈvɝdʒɚ/ *n* [U] (liter) (fresh green colour of) growing vegetation: (文)生長中的草木；新綠色；青葱色: *the ~ of (the trees in) spring.* 春天(樹木)的青葱。

Verey /ˈverɪ ; ˈvɛrɪ/ *adj* '**~ light,** ⇨ Very.

verge /vɜːdʒ ; vɝdʒ/ *n* **1** [C] edge; border (eg strip of ground at the side of a road, grass edge of a lawn). 邊；緣；邊際；外緣。 **2** ***be on the ~ of; bring (sb) to the ~ of,*** very close to, on the border of: 瀕於；使(某人)瀕臨: *The country is on the ~ of disaster.* 該國瀕於災難。 *She was brought to the ~ of bursting into tears.* 她給弄得幾乎要哭出來了。□ *vi* [VP3A] ***~ on／upon,*** approach closely, border upon: 瀕臨；接近: *verge on bankruptcy.* 瀕於破產。 *Such ideas ~ on foolhardiness.* 這種念頭近於蠻勇。

verger /ˈvɜːdʒə(r) ; ˈvɝdʒɚ/ *n* **1** (C of E) official with various duties (eg showing people to their seats). (英國國教)教堂的司事；堂守(如領人入座者)。 **2** officer who carries a staff before a bishop in a cathedral, a vice-chancellor in a university, etc. (爲主教座堂的主教，大學的副校長等)持權杖者。

ver·ify /ˈverɪfaɪ; ˈvɛrəˌfaɪ/ *vt* (*pt, pp* -fied) [VP 6A] **1** test the truth or accuracy of: 鑑定;查對;核對: *~ a report/statement;* 核對一項報告(陳述)的眞實性; *~ the figures/details of a report.* 查對一項報告中的數字(細節)。 **2** (of an event, etc) show the truth of; bear out: (指事件等)證實;證明: *Subsequent events verified my suspicions.* 接著發生的事件證實了我的猜疑。 **veri·fi·able** /ˈverɪfaɪəbl; ˈvɛrəˌfaɪəbḷ/ *adj* that can be verified. 可證實的;能鑑定的。**veri·fi·ca·tion** /ˌverɪfɪˈkeɪʃn; ˌvɛrɪfɪˈkeʃən/ *n* ~ing or being verified; proof or evidence. 鑑定;證實;證據。

ver·ily /ˈverəlɪ; ˈvɛrəlɪ/ *adv* (archaic) really; truly. (古)眞實地;眞正地;確然地。

veri·si·mili·tude /ˌverɪsɪˈmɪlɪtjuːd *US:* -tuːd; ˌvɛrəsəˈmɪləˌtjud/ *n* [U] appearance, semblance, of truth; [C] sth that seems to be true. 逼眞;逼眞的事物。

veri·table /ˈverɪtəbl; ˈvɛrətəbḷ/ *adj* real; rightly named. 眞正的;名符其實的。

ver·ity /ˈverətɪ; ˈvɛrətɪ/ *n* (*pl* -ties) **1** [U] (old use) truth (*of* a statement, etc). (舊用法)(陳述等的)眞實;確實。 **2** [C] sth that really exists; true statement: 實物;實存事物;眞實的陳述: ***the eternal verities,*** fundamental moral principles; laws of God. 基本的道德準則;上帝的律法。

ver·mi·celli /ˌvɜːmɪˈselɪ; ˌvɝməˈsɛlɪ/ *n* [U] paste of white flour made into long slender threads, like spaghetti but much thinner. 細麵條;線麵。

ver·mi·form /ˈvɜːmɪfɔːm; ˈvɝməˌfɔrm/ *adj* worm-like in shape: 蠕蟲形的: *the ~ appendix.* 蚓突;闌尾。⇨ the illus at alimentary. 參看 alimentary 之插圖。

ver·mil·ion /vəˈmɪlɪən; vɚˈmɪljən/ *adj, n* bright red (colour). 朱紅;朱紅色;朱紅的。

ver·min /ˈvɜːmɪn; ˈvɝmɪn/ *n* [U] (with *pl v*, but not with numerals) (用複數動詞,但不與數詞連用) **1** wild animals (eg rats, weasels, foxes) harmful to plants, birds and other animals. 害獸(如鼠,鼬,狐)。 **2** parasitic insects (eg lice) sometimes found on the bodies of human beings and other animals. 寄生蟲;害蟲(如虱)。**3** human beings who are harmful to society; persons who prey on others. 社會上的蟊賊;歹徒。**~·ous** /-əs; -əs/ *adj* **1** infested with fleas, lice, etc: 長有蚤、虱等的: *~ous children.* 長有虱子的孩子們。**2** caused by insect ~: 由害蟲引起的: *~ous diseases.* 由害蟲引起的疾病。

ver·mouth /ˈvɜːməθ *US:* vərˈmuːθ; ˈvɝmuθ/ *n* [U] fortified white wine flavoured with herbs, drunk as an aperitif (often in cocktails). 苦艾酒(作爲開胃酒飲用,常放於雞尾酒中)。

ver·nacu·lar /vəˈnækjʊlə(r); vɚˈnækjəlɚ/ *adj* (of a word, a language) of the country in question: (指文字,語言) 該國的;本國的;土語的: *the ~ newspapers in India,* those in the various languages (except English) of India; 印度諸語(英語除外)的報紙; *a ~ poet,* one who uses a ~ language. 方言詩人。□ *n* [C] language or dialect of a country or district: 方言;土語: *the ~s of the USA.* 美國的方言。

ver·nal /ˈvɜːnl; ˈvɝnḷ/ *adj* (liter) of, in, as in, the season of spring. (文)春季的;在春季的;如在春季的。**the ~ equinox,** about 21st March. 春分(約在三月廿一日)。

ve·ron·ica /vəˈrɒnɪkə; vəˈrɑnɪkə/ *n* kinds of herb or shrub with blue, purple, pink or white flowers. 水苦賈;葳靈仙屬。

ver·ruca /vəˈruːkə; vəˈrukə/ *n* small, hard growth on the skin (usu on the bottom of the feet); wart. 疣(通常生於足底);瘤腫。

ver·sa·tile /ˈvɜːsətaɪl *US:* -tl; ˈvɝsətḷ/ *adj* interested in and clever at many different things; having various uses: 多才多藝的;多方面的;有多種功用的: *a ~ inventor;* 多方面的發明家; *a ~ mind;* 多才多藝的人; *a ~ tool.* 多種功用的工具。**ver·sa·til·ity** /ˌvɜːsəˈtɪlətɪ; ˌvɝsəˈtɪlətɪ/ *n*

verse /vɜːs; vɝs/ *n* **1** [U] (form of) writing arranged in lines, each conforming to a pattern of accented and unaccented syllables: 詩;韻文;詩體: *prose and ~;* 散文和韻文; *written in ~;* 以詩體寫成的; *a ~ translation of Homer's 'Odyssey';* 荷馬'奧德賽'的詩體翻譯; *blank ~,* without rhymes at the end of the lines. 無韻詩。 **2** [C] group of lines of this kind forming a unit in a rhyme scheme: 詩節: *a poem/hymn of five ~s.* 一首有五節的詩(讚美詩)。 **3** [C] one line of (a) ~ with a definite number of feet or accented syllables: (有一定音步或重音節的)一行詩: *quote a few ~s from Tennyson.* 引用英國詩人但尼生的幾行詩。 **4** one of the short numbered divisions of a chapter in the Bible. (聖經的)節。***give chapter and ~ (for sth),*** supply the exact reference (for a statement, an authority one quotes, reports, etc). 註明所引用的章節;說明…的出處。

versed /vɜːst; vɝst/ *adj ~* ***in,*** skilled or experienced in: 精通的;熟練的: *well ~ in mathematics/the arts.* 精通數學(文史)。⇨ *conversant with* at conversant.

ver·sify /ˈvɜːsɪfaɪ; ˈvɝsəˌfaɪ/ *vt, vi* (*pt, pp* -fied) [VP6A] put into verse: 寫成詩;改寫爲韻文: *~ an old legend;* 將一古老的傳說用韻文寫出; [VP2A] write verses. 作詩。**ver·si·fier** *n* maker of verses. 改寫散文爲韻文的作者;詩人。**ver·si·fi·ca·tion** /ˌvɜːsɪfɪˈkeɪʃn; ˌvɝsəfəˈkeʃən/ *n* [U] art of ~ing; style in which verse is written; metre. 作詩法;詩體;韻律。

ver·sion /ˈvɜːʃn *US:* -ʒn; ˈvɝʒən/ *n* [C] **1** account of an event, etc from the point of view of one person: (由個別觀點對事件等所作的)敘述;說法;看法: *There were contradictory ~s of what happened/of what the Prime Minister said.* 對於所發生的事(首相所說的話)有相互矛盾的說法。 **2** translation into another language: 翻譯;譯本: *a new ~ of the Bible.* 聖經的新譯本。

verso /ˈvɜːsəʊ; ˈvɝso/ *n* (*pl* ~s, /-səʊz; -soz/) any left-hand page of a book (opp of *recto*); reverse side of a medal or coin. 書籍左方的書頁(爲 recto 之相反字);獎章、勳章、硬幣等的反面。

ver·sus /ˈvɜːsəs; ˈvɝsəs/ *prep* (Lat) (in law and sport; often shortened to **v** or **vs** in print) against: (拉)(法律和運動用語;印刷時常略作 v 或 vs) 對;對抗: (legal) (法律) *Robinson v Brown;* 魯賓遜對布朗案; (cricket) (板球) *Kent vs Surrey.* 肯特對薩里(的比賽)。

ver·te·bra /ˈvɜːtɪbrə; ˈvɝtəbrə/ *n* (*pl* ~e /-briː; -ˌbri/) any one of the segments of the backbone. 脊骨的一節;脊椎骨。⇨ the illus at skeleton. 參看 skeleton 之插圖。 **ver·te·brate** /ˈvɜːtɪbreɪt; ˈvɝtəˌbret/ *n, adj* (animal, bird, etc) having a backbone. (動物,鳥等)有脊椎骨的;脊椎動物。

ver·tex /ˈvɜːteks; ˈvɝtɛks/ *n* (*pl* vertices /-tɪsiːz; -təˌsiz/) highest point; top; point of a triangle, cone, etc opposite the base. 最高點;頂點;(三角形,圓錐等與底相對的)頂。

ver·ti·cal /ˈvɜːtɪkl; ˈvɝtɪkḷ/ *adj* (of a line or plane) at a right angle to the earth's surface or to another line or plane: (指線或平面)垂直的;直立的: *a ~ cliff;* 陡直的峭壁; *a ~ take-off aircraft,* one that can rise ~ly, not needing a runway. 可垂直起飛的飛機。⇨ horizontal. □ *n* ~ line: 垂直線: *out of the ~,* not ~. 不垂直的。**~ly** /-klɪ; -kḷɪ/ *adv*

ver·tices /ˈvɜːtɪsiːz; ˈvɝtəˌsiz/ *n pl* ⇨ vertex.

ver·tigo /ˈvɜːtɪɡəʊ; ˈvɝtɪˌɡo/ *n* [U] (formal) dizziness. (正式用語)眩暈;頭暈。 **ver·tigin·ous** /vɜːˈtɪdʒɪnəs; vɝˈtɪdʒənəs/ *adj* of, causing, ~. 眩暈的;令人眩暈的。

verve /vɜːv; vɝv/ *n* [U] enthusiasm, spirit, vigour. 熱情;精神;活力。

very[1] /ˈverɪ; ˈvɛrɪ/ *attrib adj* **1** itself and no other; truly such: 同一的;眞正的;恰好的: *This is the ~ thing I want!* 這正是我所需要的東西! *At that ~ moment the phone rang.* 恰在那個時候電話鈴響了。 *You're the ~ man I want to see.* 你就是我想要見的人。 **2** extreme: 極端的: *at the ~ end/begin-*

ning. 在結束(開始)之際。 **3** (equivalent to an emphatic or intensive *pron* ending in *-self* or *-selves*): (相當於以 -self 或 -selves 爲字尾的加强語氣的代名詞): *He knows our ~ thoughts,* ie our thoughts themselves, even our innermost thoughts. 他深知我們的想法。*The ~ idea of being sent abroad* (ie the idea alone, quite apart from the reality) *delighted him.* 單是想到可能被派往國外就使他覺得高興。

very² /ˈverɪ ; ˈvɛrɪ/ *adv* **1** (used intensively with *advv, adjj* and *part adjj*): (與副詞、形容詞及分詞形容詞連用,以加强語氣): *~ quickly／carefully／soon, etc;* 十分快速(當心,早等); *~ much／little;* 很多(少); *~ amusing／interesting, etc;* 很好玩(有趣等); *~ small／cold／useful, etc.* 很小(冷,有用等)。(Note that when the *pp* is part of a passive *v* phrase, *much,* or *very much* is preferred; when the *pp* is the complement of *be, seem, feel, ~* is used): (注意:過去分詞爲被動語態動詞片語的一部分時,宜用 much 或 very much; 過去分詞爲 be, seem, feel 的補語時,用 very): *I wasn't much surprised at the news.* 我對那消息不太驚訝。*He wasn't much interested in the news.* 他對那消息並不太感興趣。Cf 參較 *He was／seemed ~ interested.* 他(似乎)很感興趣。**~ well,** often used to indicate agreement or assent (often after persuasion or argument, or in obedience to a command, request, etc): 好;很好(常用來表示同意或贊成,多用於勸告或辯論之後,或對命令、請求等的服從): *V~ well, doctor, I'll give up smoking.* 好的,醫生,我就戒烟好了。*Oh, ~ well, if you insist.* 哦,好罷,如果你堅持的話。 **2** (with a superl, or *own*) in the highest possible degree: (與最高級的字或 own 連用)極度地;極點地;完全地: *the ~ best quality;* 最好的品質; *the ~ first to arrive;* 最先到達者; *six o'clock at the ~ latest.* 最遲六點鐘。*You can keep this for your ~ own.* 你可以保有這個東西做爲你自己的。

Very, Verey /ˈverɪ ; ˈvɛrɪ/ *adj* **ˈ~ light,** (P) coloured signal flare fired from a *ˈ~ pistol,* eg as a signal of distress from a ship. (商標)威利信號閃光彈(從'威利槍'中射出的彩色曳光彈,如用作船的遇難信號)。

ves·icle /ˈvesɪkl ; ˈvɛsɪkḷ/ *n* (anat) small cavity, cyst or swelling. (解剖)泡;胞;囊。**ves·icu·lar** /vəˈsɪkjʊlə(r) ; vəˈsɪkjələ/ *adj* of ~s: 胞的;胞狀的;囊狀的: *vesicular disease.* 胞狀疾病。

ves·pers /ˈvespəz ; ˈvɛspəz/ *n pl* church service in the evening; evensong. (英國國教之)晚間禮拜;晚間聚會。

vessel /ˈvesl ; ˈvɛsḷ/ *n* [C] **1** hollow receptacle, esp for a liquid, eg a cask, tub, bucket, bowl, bottle, cup. 容器;器皿(尤指盛液體者,如桶,盆,吊桶,碗,瓶,杯)。 **2** ship or large boat. 船;艦。 **3** ⇨ *blood-~* at blood¹(7).

vest¹ /vest ; vɛst/ *n* [C] **1** (GB) garment worn under a shirt, blouse, etc next to the skin. (英)汗衫(貼身穿者)。 **2** (trade use in GB; ordinary use in US) short, sleeveless garment worn by men under a jacket (*waistcoat* being the usual name in GB): (英國爲商業用法;美國爲一般用法)馬甲;背心(英國一般用語爲 waistcoat): *coat, ~ and trousers;* 上裝,背心和褲子; *a ~-pocket* (ie very small) *camera.* 超小型攝影機(可放在背心口袋中者)。

vest² /vest ; vɛst/ *vt, vi* **1** [VP14] **~ *sth in sb;* ~ *sb with sth,*** furnish or give as a fixed right: 給與;授與某人某種權利: *~ a man with authority／rights in an estate.* 授與某人權力(產權)。*In some countries authority is said to be ~ed in the people,* ie the people possess final authority on matters of government, etc. 在某些國家,最高決定權是歸於人民的。*In the United States, Congress is ~ed with the power to declare war.* 在美國,國會有宣戰的權力。 ***have a ~ed interest in sth,*** be likely to gain or lose from it, or be affected in some way by it. 對某事物保有既得的利益。**~ed interests／rights,** (eg in trade or manufacture) which are by law securely in the possession of a person or a group of persons. (貿易或製造業等依法保有之)既得利益(權利)。 **2** [VP3A] **~ *in,*** (of property, etc) be ~ed in: (指財產等)歸屬: *power／authority that ~s in the Crown.* 屬於王室的權力(職權)。 **3** [VP6A] (poet or eccles) clothe. (詩或教會)使穿衣服。

ves·tal /ˈvestl ; ˈvɛstḷ/ *n* **~ (virgin),** one of the maidens dedicated to the service of the goddess Vesta in ancient Rome, vowed to chastity. 古羅馬終身侍奉女竈神的女尼之一(須誓守貞潔)。 □ *adj* (liter) pure; chaste. (文)純潔的;貞潔的。

ves·ti·bule /ˈvestɪbju:l ; ˈvɛstə,bjul/ *n* **1** lobby or entrance hall to a building (eg where hats and coats may be left). 前廳;門廳;玄關(可置放衣帽等的地方)。**2** porch of a church. 教堂的門廊。**3** (US) enclosed space at the end of a railway coach. (美)(火車車廂末端的)連廊。

ves·tige /ˈvestɪdʒ ; ˈvɛstɪdʒ/ *n* [C] **1** trace or sign; small remaining bit of evidence of what once existed: 痕跡;形跡;遺跡: *Not a ~ of the abbey remains.* 那修道院的遺跡蕩然無存了。*There is not a ~ of truth in the report.* 這項報導沒有一點眞實性。 **2** (anat) organ, or part of one, which is a survival of sth that once existed: (解剖)退化器官;已退化器官的遺跡: *A human being has the ~ of a tail.* 人類仍有尾巴的痕跡。 **ves·tigial** /veˈstɪdʒɪəl ; vɛsˈtɪdʒɪəl/ *adj* remaining as a ~. 尚留有痕跡的;退化的。

vest·ment /ˈvestmənt ; ˈvɛstmənt/ *n* garment, esp one worn by a priest in church; ceremonial robe. 衣服;(尤指)法衣;聖衣;禮服。

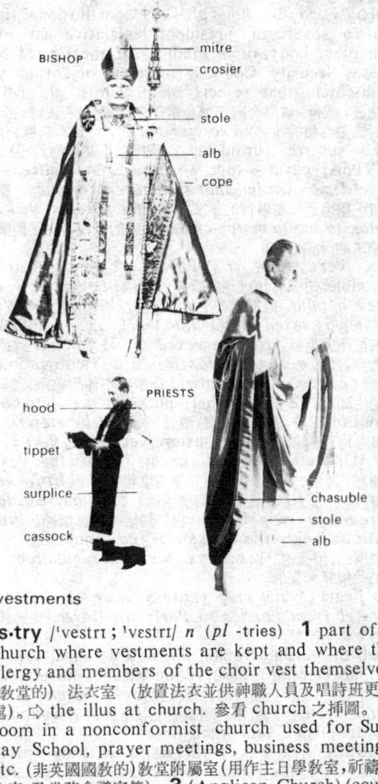

vestments

ves·try /ˈvestrɪ ; ˈvɛstrɪ/ *n* (*pl* -tries) **1** part of a church where vestments are kept and where the clergy and members of the choir vest themselves. (教堂的) 法衣室 (放置法衣並供神職人員及唱詩班更衣處)。⇨ the illus at church. 參看 church 之插圖。 **2** room in a nonconformist church used for Sunday School, prayer meetings, business meetings, etc. (非英國國教的)教堂附屬室(用作主日學教室,祈禱聚會室,及堂務會議室等)。**3** (Anglican Church) (council of) ratepayers of a parish, or their representatives, assembled to discuss parish business. (英國國教) 教區會 (教區納稅人或其代表集會以討論教區事務者); 教區委員會(由教區納稅人或其代表組成)。 **'~-man** /-mən ; -mən/ *n* (*pl* -men) member of a ~. 教區會會員; 教區委員。

ves·ture /'vestʃə(r) ; 'vɛstʃɚ/ *n* (poet) clothing. (詩)衣服; 衣著。□ *vt* clothe. 使穿衣服; 覆蓋。

vet /vet ; vɛt/ *n* (colloq abbr for) veterinary surgeon. (俗)獸醫(爲 veterinary surgeon 之略)。□ *vt* (-tt-) [VP6A] (colloq) (俗) **1** give (sb) a medical examination. 診療(某人)。 **2** (GB) examine closely and critically, eg sb's past record, qualifications, etc: (英)嚴格審查(如某人過去的記錄, 資格等): *He must be thoroughly vetted before he's given the job.* 他必須經過嚴格審查才能得到該項工作。

vetch /vetʃ ; vɛtʃ/ *n* kinds of plant of the bean family used, wild or cultivated, as fodder for cattle. 大巢菜; 野豌豆(用作牲畜飼料)。

vet·eran /'vetərən ; 'vɛtərən/ *n* **1** person who has had much or long experience, esp as a soldier: 老手; 老練者; (尤指)老兵: *~s of two World Wars;* 經歷兩次大戰的老兵; (attrib) (形容用法) *a ~ teacher;* 資深的教師; (of cars) of the years before 1916: (指汽車)1916年前的: *a ~ Rolls Royce.* 一部1916年前的勞斯萊斯車。 **2** (US) any ex-service man. (美)退伍軍人。 **'V~s Day,** 11th November, commemorating the armistice (1918) in World War I. 退伍軍人節(十一月十一日, 爲第一次大戰停戰日)。

vet·erin·ary /'vetrɪnrɪ *US:* 'vetərɪnerɪ ; 'vɛtrə,nɛrɪ/ *adj* (abbr 略作 **vet** /vet ; vɛt/) of or concerned with the diseases of (esp farm and domestic) animals: 獸疾的; 有關家畜之疾病的: *a ~ surgeon/college.* 獸醫(獸醫學院)。

veto /'vi:təʊ ; 'vito/ *n* (*pl* ~es) constitutional right of a sovereign, president, legislative assembly or other body, or a member of the United Nations Security Council, to reject or forbid sth; statement that rejects or prohibits sth: (國王, 總統, 議會, 或聯合國安理會常任理事國的)否決權; 否決; 否決某事物的陳述: *exercise the ~;* 行使否決權; *put a ~ on sth,* forbid it. 否決或禁止某事物。□ *vt* [VP6A] put a ~ on: 否決; 禁止: *The police ~ed the demonstration that the students wanted.* 警察禁止學生們所要舉行的示威。*John's parents ~ed his plan to buy a motor-cycle.* 約翰的雙親否決了他購買機車的計畫。

vex /veks ; vɛks/ *vt* [VP6A] **1** annoy; distress; trouble: 使惱怒; 使苦惱; 煩擾: *His silly chatter would vex a saint.* 他那喋喋不休的無聊話連聖人也會被惹惱。*She was vexed that I didn't help her.* 她因爲我未幫忙她而生氣。*He was vexed at his failure.* 他因失敗而苦惱。***a vexed question,*** a difficult problem that causes much discussion. 爭論不休的難題; 議論紛紛的問題。 **2** (poet, rhet) put (the sea) into commotion: (詩, 修辭)使(海)激盪: *vexed by storms.* 因風暴而洶湧澎湃的。 **vex·ation** /vek'seɪʃn ; vɛks'eʃən/ *n* [U] state of being vexed; [C] sth that vexes: 惱怒; 苦惱; 煩擾; 令人惱怒等的事物: *the little vexations of life;* 生活中的小煩惱; *constant vexations from our neighbours.* 我們隣居的經常煩擾。 **vex·atious** /vek'seɪʃəs ; vɛks'eʃəs/ *adj* annoying: 令人煩惱的; 困擾的: *vexatious rules and regulations.* 苛細的規章和條例。

via /'vaɪə ; 'vaɪə/ *prep* (Lat) by way of: (拉)經由: *travel from London to Paris via Dover.* 從倫敦經由多佛至巴黎。

vi·able /'vaɪəbl ; 'vaɪəbl/ *adj* able to exist; capable of developing and surviving without outside help: 能生存的; 能生長發育的; 行得通的: *Is the newly created State ~?* 這個新國家能生存下去嗎? **vi·abil·ity** /,vaɪə'bɪlətɪ ; ,vaɪə'bɪlətɪ/ *n*

vi·aduct /'vaɪədʌkt ; 'vaɪə,dʌkt/ *n* long bridge (usu with many spans or arches) carrying a road or railway across a valley or dip in the ground. (跨越山谷或下傾地段的)高架橋(通常爲多孔橋)。

vial /'vaɪəl ; 'vaɪəl/ *n* small bottle, esp for liquid medicine. 小瓶; 小藥水瓶。

via media /,vaɪə 'mi:dɪə ; ,vaɪə 'midɪə/ (Lat) middle course between extremes. (拉)(介於兩極端的)中間路線; 中庸之道。

vibes /vaɪbz ; vaɪbz/ *n pl* **1** (colloq abbr for) vibraphone. (俗)鐘琴; 外布拉風(爲 vibraphone 之略)。 **2** (sl) atmosphere(3). (俚)氣氛。

vi·brant /'vaɪbrənt ; 'vaɪbrənt/ *adj* thrilling; vibrating: 震動的; 震顫的: *the ~ notes of a cello/an electric guitar.* 低音提琴(電吉他)的震顫音調。

vi·bra·phone /'vaɪbrəfəʊn ; 'vaɪbrə,fon/ *n* (music) instrument like a xylophone but with metal bars and tone sustained by electronic resonators. (音樂)鐘琴; 外布拉風。

vi·brate /vaɪ'breɪt *US:* 'vaɪbreɪt ; 'vaɪbret/ *vi, vt* **1** [VP2A, 6A] (cause to) move rapidly and continuously backwards and forwards: (使)快速擺動; 搖動; 震動; 顫動: *The house ~s whenever a heavy lorry passes.* 每有大貨車經過時, 該屋都會顫動。 **2** [VP2A, C] (of stretched strings, the voice) throb; quiver: (指繃緊的絃, 聲音)震顫; 顫動; 顫抖: *The strings of a piano ~ when the keys are struck.* 鋼琴的琴鍵受擊時, 琴絃就會震顫。*His voice ~d with passion.* 他的聲音因激動而顫抖。 **vi·brator** /-tə(r) ; -tɚ/ *n* device that ~s. 震動器。

vi·bra·tion /vaɪ'breɪʃn ; vaɪ'breʃən/ *n* **1** [U] vibrating movement: 擺動; 搖動; 震動; 顫動: *The ship's engines even at full speed cause very little ~.* 這條船的引擎即使是在全速時引起的震動也甚微。 **2** [C] single movement to and fro when equilibrium has been disturbed: 來回一次振動: *20 ~s per second.* 每秒鐘振動二十次。

vi·brato /vɪ'brɑ:təʊ ; vɪ'brɑto/ *n* (music) throbbing or tremulous effect in singing and the playing of stringed and wind instruments with minute and rapid variations in pitch. (音樂)振音(唱出或管絃樂器所奏出的快速顫動聲音)。

vicar /'vɪkə(r) ; 'vɪkɚ/ *n* **1** (C of E) clergyman in charge of a parish, the tithes of which were partly or wholly payable to another person or body (eg a college) for whom or for which the ~ acts. (英國國教)教區牧師(教區的什一收入, 部分或全部交付其所代表的人或團體)。⇨ rector. **2** (RC Church) deputy; representative: (天主教)代理; 代表: *the ~ of Christ,* (sometimes used of) the Pope; (有時指)教宗; *cardinal ~,* Pope's delegate acting as the bishop of the diocese of Rome. 羅馬教區主教。 **~·age** /'vɪkərɪdʒ ; 'vɪkərɪdʒ/ *n* ~'s residence. 教區牧師的住宅。

vi·cari·ous /vɪ'keərɪəs *US:* vaɪ'k- ; vaɪ'kɛrɪəs/ *adj* **1** done, undergone, by one person for another or others: 爲別人所做的; 代別人遭受的: *the ~ sufferings of Jesus;* 耶穌代人類所受的苦; *a ~ ruler;* 代理的統治者; *feel a ~ pleasure/satisfaction,* eg when sth is done for you or which is sth you would like to do. 感到一種替代性的愉快(滿足)(如當他人完成一件爲你而做或你願意做的事情時)。 **2** deputed; delegated: 代理的; 受託的: *~ authority.* 代理權; 受託而獲得的職權。 **~·ly** *adv*

vice[1] /vaɪs ; vaɪs/ *n* [C, U] **1** (any particular kind of) evil conduct or indulgence in depraving practices: 惡; 邪惡; 惡行; 不道德的行爲: *Gluttony is just as much a ~ as drunkenness.* 饕餮之爲惡, 不亞於酗酒。 **2** (in a horse) bad habit (eg kicking) which makes control difficult: (馬)使人難駕馭的壞習慣(如踢人); 壞毛病: *He said the horse was free from ~/had no ~s.* 他說那匹馬沒有壞毛病。

vice[2] (US = **vise**) /vaɪs ; vaɪs/ *n* [C] apparatus with strong jaws in which things can be held tightly while being worked upon: 虎頭鉗; 鉗砧: *as firm as a ~,* immovable. 無法移動的; 像虎頭鉗般夾得很緊的。

vice[3] /vaɪs ; vaɪs/ *n* (colloq abbr for) vice-president, vice-captain, etc. (俗)副總統; 副隊長等(爲 vice-president, vice-captain 等之略)。

vice⁴ /vaɪs ; vaɪs/ *prep* (Lat) (formal) in place of: (拉)(正式用語)代替;取代: *Mr Smith has been appointed chief accountant ~ Mr Brown, who has retired.* 史密斯先生被任命爲會計主任,以接替已退休的布朗先生。

vice- *pref* ⇨ App 3. 參看附錄三。

viceroy /ˈvaɪsrɔɪ ; ˈvaɪsrɔɪ/ *n* (eg formerly in India) person governing as the deputy of a sovereign. (如昔時印度的)副王;總督。**vice·reine** /vaɪsˈreɪn *US:* ˈvaɪsreɪn ; ˈvaɪsren/ *n* ~'s wife. 副王妃;總督夫人。**vice·regal** /vaɪsˈriːgl ; vaɪsˈrigl/ *adj* of a ~. 副王的;總督的。

vice versa /ˌvaɪsɪ ˈvɜːsə ; ˈvaɪsɪˈvɝsə/ *adv* (Lat) the other way round; with the terms or conditions reversed: (拉)反過來;反之亦然;逆之亦眞: *We gossip about them and ~,* they gossip about us. 我們談論他們,他們也談論我們。

vi·cin·ity /vɪˈsɪnətɪ ; vəˈsɪnətɪ/ *n* (*pl* -ties) **1** [U] nearness; closeness of relationship: 近;接近;密切的關係: *in close ~ to the church.* 與教會有密切的關係。**2** [C] neighbourhood: 附近;近處;隣近地區: *the northern vicinities of the capital.* 首都北方的隣近地區。*There isn't a good school in the ~.* 附近沒有好學校。

vi·cious /ˈvɪʃəs ; ˈvɪʃəs/ *adj* **1** of vice¹; given up to vice¹: 惡的;邪惡的;惡行的;爲惡的: *~ practices/habits;* 惡習; *a ~ life.* 墮落的生活。 **2** spiteful; given or done with evil intent: 刻毒的;有惡意的: *a ~ kick/look.* 含有惡意的一踢(一看)。 **3** (of a horse) having bad habits such as biting, kicking, bolting. (指馬)有惡習(如咬人、踢人、逃脫)的;壞癖的。**4** having faults, corrupt: 有缺點的;有錯誤的;不正確的;謬誤的: *a ~ argument.* 謬誤的論據。**,~ ˈcircle,** state of affairs in which a cause produces an effect which itself produces the original cause, eg War breeds hate, and hate leads to war again. 惡性循環(如戰爭產生仇恨,仇恨又導致戰爭)。**,~ˈspiral,** continuous rise in one thing (eg prices) caused by a continuous rise in sth else (eg wages). 循環盤旋上昇(如工資不斷的增加,造成物價不斷的上昇)。**~·ly** *adv* **~·ness** *n*

vi·ciss·itude /vɪˈsɪsɪtjuːd *US:* -tuːd ; vəˈsɪsəˌtjud/ *n* [C] change, esp in sb's fortunes: 變遷;變化;(尤指個人的)盛衰;榮枯;成敗: *His life was marked by ~s,* eg changes from wealth to poverty, success to failure. 他的一生飽經滄桑。

vic·tim /ˈvɪktɪm ; ˈvɪktɪm/ *n* **1** living creature killed and offered as a religious sacrifice. 犧牲(爲祭神而宰殺的動物)。 **2** person, animal, etc suffering injury, pain, loss, etc because of circumstances, an event, the ill-will of sb, etc: 犧牲者;受害或遇難的人、動物等: *He is the ~ of his brother's anger/of his own foolishness.* 他爲他哥哥(弟弟)發怒的對象(他因自己的愚昧而自食其果)。*A fund was opened to help the ~s of the earthquake.* 設立一筆專款救助地震的災民。*Thousands were ~s of the plague in the Middle Ages.* 中世紀時無數的人死於瘟疫。**~·ize** /-aɪz ; -ˌaɪz/ *vt* [VP6A] make a ~ of; single out for ill treatment because of real or alleged misconduct, etc: 使犧牲;使受害;選定(某人)受過、抵罪等: *Trade union leaders claimed that some of their members had been ~ized,* eg by being dismissed. 工會領袖們宣稱他們的部份會員被犧牲了(如遭解雇等)。**~·iz·ation** /ˌvɪktɪmaɪˈzeɪʃn *US:* -mɪˈz- ; ˌvɪktɪməˈzeʃən/ *n*: *The strikers said they would return to work if they were promised that there should be no ~ization,* that none of their leaders (or ringleaders) should be ~ized. 罷工者說他們將恢復工作,如果當局保證他們之中無人成爲代罪羔羊。

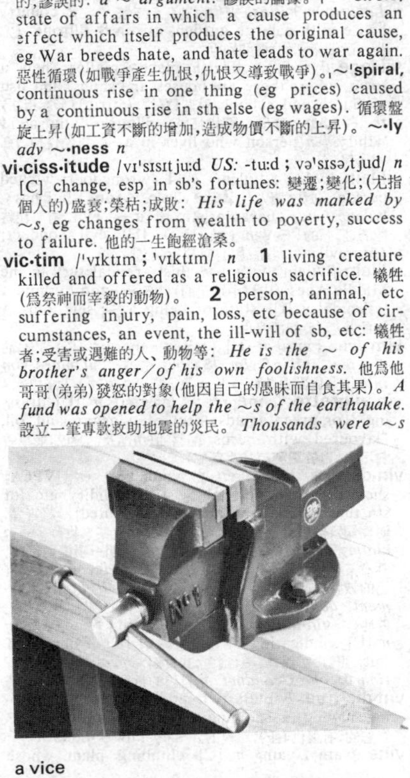

a vice

vic·tor /ˈvɪktə(r) ; ˈvɪktɚ/ *n* person who conquers or wins. 勝利者;征服者。

vic·toria /vɪkˈtɔːrɪə ; vɪkˈtorɪə/ *n* **~ plum,** juicy, sweet-flavoured plum, changing from green to yellow and red. 維多利亞李子(甜而多汁,由綠色轉爲黃色和紅色)。

Vic·tor·ian /vɪkˈtɔːrɪən ; vɪkˈtorɪən/ *n, adj* (person) of, living in, the reign of Queen Victoria (1837–1901): 維多利亞女王時代(1837–1901)的;生活於此時代的;此時代的人: *~ authors/manners/dress.* 維多利亞女王時代的作家(禮儀,服飾)。

vic·tory /ˈvɪktərɪ ; ˈvɪktərɪ/ *n* [C, U] (*pl* -ries) (instance, occasion, of) success (in war, a contest, game, etc): (戰爭、競爭、遊戲等中的)勝利;成功;勝利的實例;勝利的時際: *gain/win a ~ over the enemy;* 戰勝敵人; *lead the troops to ~.* 率領軍隊邁向勝利。**vic·tori·ous** /vɪkˈtɔːrɪəs ; vɪkˈtorɪəs/ *adj* having gained the ~; triumphant. 獲得勝利的;戰勝的;凱旋的。**vic·tori·ous·ly** *adv*

vict·ual /ˈvɪtl ; ˈvɪtl̩/ *vt, vi* (-ll-; US also -l-) **1** [VP6A] supply with provisions (of food): 供以食物;儲備食物: *~ a ship.* 供給一艘船食物。 **2** [VP2A] take in provisions: 取得食物;裝貯食物: *The ship ~led at Colombo.* 那艘船在可倫坡裝貯食物。□ *n* (usu *pl*) food and drink; provisions. (通常用複數)食料和飲料;食物。**~·ler** (US also **~er**) /ˈvɪtlə(r) ; ˈvɪtl̩ɚ/ *n* trader in ~s. 食物供應商。**licensed ~ler,** (GB) public house keeper who is licensed to sell food, spirits, beer, etc to be consumed on the premises. (英)領有執照的酒店店主(持照可販賣飲食、烈酒、啤酒等供顧客在店內食用)。

vi·cuña /vɪˈkjuːnə *US:* -ˈkuːnə ; vɪˈkjunə/ *n* animal of the central Andes somewhat like, but much smaller than, a camel, with soft, delicate wool. (產於南美安地斯山中部的)駱馬。

vide /ˈvaɪdɪ ; ˈvaɪdɪ/ *v* (Lat) (imperative form used in references). (拉) (表示參考時所用的祈使形式)見;參看。**,~ ˈinfra,** see below. 見下。**,~ ˈsupra,** see above. 見上。

vide·licet /vɪˈdiːlɪset *US:* -ˈdel- ; vɪˈdɛləsɪt/ *adv* (common abbr 通常略作 **viz**, pronounced 讀作/vɪz ; vɪz/ or spoken as 或說作 *namely*) that is to say; namely. 就是說;即是。

video /ˈvɪdɪəʊ ; ˈvɪdɪˌo/ *adj* **1** of television broadcasting (cf 參較 *audio*). 電視播送的。 **2** of ~tape recording. 電視錄影的。□ *n* **1** (colloq) ~tape recording machine. (俗)錄影機。**2** (US) television. (美)電視。**ˈ~·tape** *n* [U] magnetic tape used to record television pictures and sound. 錄影帶。□ *vt* [VP6A] make a recording on ~tape. 錄影。

vie /vaɪ ; vaɪ/ *vi* [VP3A] ***vie (with sb) (for sth),*** rival or compete: 競爭;爭勝: *The two boys vied with one another for the first place.* 那兩個男孩子爭第一名。

view¹ /vjuː ; vju/ *n* **1** [U] state of seeing or being seen; field of vision: 看或被看;觀察;視野;視域;眼界: *Clouds came down and the hill tops passed from our ~,* could no longer be seen. 雲層籠罩了下來,我們看不見山頂了。***in ~ of,*** considering, taking into account: 鑒於;由於: *In ~ of the facts, it seems useless to continue.* 由這些事實看來,繼續

下去似乎是無效果的。***in full ~ of***, fully seen by: 完全被看到: *The speaker stood in full ~ of the crowd*, could see them and could be seen by them. 那演說者站在羣衆可以完全看得見的地方。***on ~***, being shown or exhibited: 陳列着; 展覽着: *The latest summer fashions are now on ~ in the big shops.* 最新的夏裝款式現在正在大的商店中展示著。***come into ~***, become visible: (就外界事物言)進入視野;被看見;被看到: *As we rounded the bend the lake came into ~*. 我們轉過彎,那湖泊就呈現在我們的眼前。***come in ~ of***, be able to see: (就本身言)能够看見: *As we rounded the bend, we came in ~ of the lake.* 我們轉過彎,就看見了那湖泊。**2** [C] (picture, photograph, etc of) natural scenery, landscape, etc: 天然景色; 風景;風景畫;風景相片等: *a house with fine ~s over valleys and mountains;* 面山臨谷風景優美的房子; *an album of ~s*, eg photographs. 風景照片(畫片)簿。**3** [C] opportunity to see or inspect sth; occasion when there is such an opportunity: 看到或考察某事物的機會;此種場合或時際: *a private ~*, eg of paintings, before public exhibition. (正式展覽前的)預展。**4** [C] personal opinion; mental attitude; thought or observation (on a subject): 個人的意見; 對某事的態度; 對某一問題的想法或見解: *She had/expressed strong ~s on the subject of equal pay for men and women.* 在男女同酬這一問題上,她具有(表現出)堅強的態度。*Your ~s on the situation are not helpful.* 你對於這一情勢的見解於事無補。*He holds extreme ~s*, eg in politics. 他持極端的態度(如在政治上)。*He took a poor ~ of my conduct*, regarded it unfavourably. 他對於我的行爲不以爲然。***fall in with/meet sb's ~s***, agree with, accept, his ideas, opinions, etc. 同意(接受)某人的觀念,意見等。**5** aim; intention; purpose. 目標;意圖;目的。***with a/the ~ to/of***, with the intention or hope: 打算要;有意要;希望;爲了: *with a ~ to facilitating research;* 爲了便利研究; *with the ~ of saving trouble.* 爲了省却麻煩。**6** (compounds) (複合字) **'~·point, point of ~**, ⇨point¹(4). **'~-finder** *n* device in a camera showing the area, etc that will be photographed through the lens. (照相機上的)取景器(顯示攝入鏡頭之範圍者)。

view² /vjuː; vju/ *vt* [VP6A] look at; examine; consider: 看;觀察;檢視;考慮;認爲: *The subject may be ~ed in various ways.* 這問題可從各方面考慮。*Has the matter been ~ed from the taxpayers' standpoint?* 這件事可曾以納稅人的立場考慮過? ***an order to ~***, written authority to look over a house, etc with the idea of buying it: 允許看想買之物(如房屋)的書面許可: *The house agents gave me an order to ~.* 房屋經紀人給了我一張看房子的書面許可。**~er** /ˈvjuːə(r); ˈvjuɚ/ *n* (esp) (尤指) **1** person watching a television programme. 電視觀衆。**2** device for looking at photographic transparencies. 幻燈機。**~·less** *adj* **1** (rhet or poet) invisible. (修辭或詩)看不見的。**2** (US) without ~s (= opinions). (美)無意見的;無見解的。

V

vigil /ˈvɪdʒɪl; ˈvɪdʒəl/ *n* **1** [U] staying awake to keep watch or to pray: 守夜;徹夜清醒(以守望或祈禱): *keep ~ over a sick child;* 徹夜不眠看顧一病童; (*pl*) instances of this: (複)守夜或徹夜不眠的實例: *tired out by her long ~s.* 她由於長時間的熬夜而疲憊不堪。**2** eve of a religious festival, esp when observed with prayer and fasting. 宗教節日的前夕(尤指須祈禱及齋戒者)。

vigi·lance /ˈvɪdʒɪləns; ˈvɪdʒələns/ *n* [U] watchfulness; keeping watch: 警備;警戒;守夜: *exercise ~.* 警戒;守夜。**'~ committee**, (chiefly US) self-appointed group of persons who maintain order in a community where organization is imperfect or has broken down. (主美)保安委員會(一種在組織不健全的地方自行設立的民間治安團體)。

vigi·lant /ˈvɪdʒɪlənt; ˈvɪdʒələnt/ *adj* watchful; on the look-out for danger of any kind. 警戒的;警惕的。**~·ly** *adv*

vigi·lante /ˌvɪdʒɪˈlæntɪ; ˌvɪdʒəˈlæntɪ/ *n* member of a vigilance committee. (主美)保安委員會的委員。

vi·gnette /viːˈnjet; vɪnˈjɛt/ *n* [C] **1** ornamental design, esp on the title-page of a book, or at the beginning or end of a chapter. 裝飾圖案;(尤指)(書籍的書名頁上或章節的開始或結束處的)小插圖。**2** picture of a person's head and shoulders with the background gradually shaded off. 半身暈映照片或畫像(頭與肩的背景漸漸變淡)。**3** short sketch of a person's character. (描寫某人性格的)簡介;短文。

vig·our (US = **vigor**) /ˈvɪgə(r); ˈvɪgɚ/ *n* [U] mental or physical strength; energy; forcefulness (of language). 智力; 體力; 精力; 活力; (語言中的)力量。**vig·or·ous** /ˈvɪgərəs; ˈvɪgərəs/ *adj* strong; energetic. 强壯的;有力的;精力充沛的。**vig·or·ous·ly** *adv*

Vik·ing /ˈvaɪkɪŋ; ˈvaɪkɪŋ/ *n* any of the Scandinavian sea-rovers who raided the coasts of Europe during the 8th, 9th and 10th cc. (八至十世紀間掠奪歐洲海岸的)北歐海盜;威金人。

vile /vaɪl; vaɪl/ *adj* (-r, -st) **1** shameful and disgusting: 可恥的;卑鄙的;令人厭惡的: *~ habits/language;* 令人厭惡的習慣(語言); *the ~ practice of bribery.* 可恥的賄賂惡習。**2** (colloq) bad: (俗)壞的: *~ weather.* 壞天氣。**3** (old use) valueless: (舊用法)無價值的: *this ~ body*, ie contrasted with the soul or spirit. 這不足道的軀體(與靈魂或精神相對而言)。**~·ly** /ˈvaɪllɪ; ˈvaɪllɪ/ *adj* **~·ness** *n*

vil·ify /ˈvɪlɪfaɪ; ˈvɪləˌfaɪ/ *vt* (*pt, pp* -fied) [VP6A] slander; say evil things about (sb). 誣毀;中傷(某人)。**vil·ifi·ca·tion** /ˌvɪlɪfɪˈkeɪʃn; ˌvɪləfəˈkeʃən/ *n*

villa /ˈvɪlə; ˈvɪlə/ *n* **1** (in GB) (usu as part of the address) detached or semi-detached house or esp one on the outskirts of a town: (在英國)(通常寫作住址的一部分)別莊;莊宅;別業(尤指在城郊者): *No 13 Laburnum Villas.* 來伯南別莊十三號。**2** country house with a large garden, esp in S Europe. (尤指在歐洲南部的)鄉間別墅。

vil·lage /ˈvɪlɪdʒ; ˈvɪlɪdʒ/ *n* place smaller than a town, where there are houses and shops, and usu a church and school: 村莊;鄉村: (attrib) (形容用法) *the ~ post-office.* 鄉村郵局。**villager** /ˈvɪlɪdʒə(r); ˈvɪlɪdʒɚ/ *n* person who lives in a ~. 村民;村人;鄉村居民。

vil·lain /ˈvɪlən; ˈvɪlən/ *n* **1** wrongdoer; wicked person. 惡徒;壞人。**2** = villein. **~·ous** /ˈvɪlənəs; ˈvɪlənəs/ *adj* characteristic of a ~; evil. 有惡徒特性的;邪惡的。**~y** *n* (*pl* -nies) [U] evil conduct; (*pl*) evil acts. 邪惡;(複)惡行;邪惡行爲。

vil·lein /ˈvɪleɪn; ˈvɪlɪn/ *n* (hist) feudal serf in the Middle Ages. (史)(中世紀的)農奴。**~·age** /ˈvɪlɪnɪdʒ; ˈvɪlənɪdʒ/ *n* [U] state of being a ~; serfdom. 農奴的狀態;農奴的身份。

vim /vɪm; vɪm/ *n* [U] (colloq) energy: (俗)精力;活力: *feel full of vim.* 感到活力充沛。*Put more vim into it!* 賣點力做(它)!

vin·ai·grette /ˌvɪnɪˈgret; ˌvɪnəˈgrɛt/ *n* [U] dressing (for green salads, etc) of vinegar and oil, flavoured with herbs. 醋醬油(由醋及油製成,並以香料增味,用於調製涼拌生菜等)。

vin·di·cate /ˈvɪndɪkeɪt; ˈvɪndəˌket/ *vt* [VP6A] show or prove the truth, justice, validity, etc (of sth that has been attacked or disputed): 證實;辯明;辯護;剖白 (已受攻擊或曾引起爭辯之某事物): *~ a claim/one's title to a privilege;* 辯明一項權利(自己具有某種特權); *~ one's veracity/judgement.* 爲自己的誠實(判斷)辯護。*Events have ~d his judgement/actions.* 事情本身已經證實了他的判斷(行爲的正確性)。**vin·di·ca·tion** /ˌvɪndɪˈkeɪʃn; ˌvɪndəˈkeʃən/ *n* [U] vindicating or being ~d; [C] instance of this: 證實;辯明;辯護;剖白;其實例: *speak in vindication of one's conduct.* 爲自己的行爲辯護。

vin·dic·tive /vɪnˈdɪktɪv; vɪnˈdɪktɪv/ *adj* unforgiving; having or showing a desire for revenge. 不寬恕的;有復仇心的;報復的。**~·ly** *adv* **~·ness** *n*

vine /vaɪn; vaɪn/ *n* [C] climbing plant whose

fruit is the grape; any plant with slender stems that trails, eg melons, or climbs (eg peas, hops). 葡萄樹；蔓生植物(如甜瓜)；攀緣植物(如豌豆、蛇麻草)；藤；蔓。**~·yard** /ˈvɪnjəd ; ˈvɪnjɚd/ *n* [C] area of land planted with grape-~s. 葡萄園。**vin·ery** /ˈvaɪnərɪ ; ˈvaɪnərɪ/ *n* (*pl* -ries) greenhouse for ~s. 栽植葡萄的暖房。

vin·egar /ˈvɪnɪgə(r) ; ˈvɪnɪgɚ/ *n* [U] acid liquor (made from malt, wine, cider, etc) used in flavouring food and for pickling. 醋。**~y** /ˈvɪnɪgərɪ ; ˈvɪnɪgərɪ/ *adj* like ~; (fig) sour-tempered. 似醋的；(喻)尖酸刻薄的。

vino /ˈviːnəʊ ; ˈvino/ *n* (*pl* ~es /-nəʊz ; -noz/) [U] (colloq) wine. (俗)葡萄酒；酒。

vi·nous /ˈvaɪnəs ; ˈvaɪnəs/ *adj* of, like or due to wine. 葡萄酒的；似葡萄酒的；由葡萄酒產生的。

vin·tage /ˈvɪntɪdʒ ; ˈvɪntɪdʒ/ *n* **1** (rarely *pl*) (period or season of) grape harvesting: (罕用複數)葡萄收穫；葡萄收穫期或季節：*The ~ was later than usual last year.* 去年葡萄收穫季節較平常晚。**2** [C, U] (wine from) grapes of a particular year: 某一年所產的葡萄；該年葡萄所釀的葡萄酒：*of the ~ of 1959;* 1959 年所產的葡萄(酒)的；*rare old ~s;* 名貴的陳年葡萄酒；*a ~ year,* one in which good wine was made; 釀製好葡萄酒的年份；*~ wines,* from ~ years. 上等葡萄酒。**3** (by extension; attrib) of a period in the past and having a reputation for high quality: (引伸用法；形容用法)屬於過去某一時期而且以品質優良著名的：*a ~ car,* one built between 1916 and 1930, ⇨ veteran; 老式的名貴汽車(造於 1916 至 1930 年者)；sports car more than 30 years old. 車齡超過三十年的跑車。

vint·ner /ˈvɪntnə(r) ; ˈvɪntnɚ/ *n* wine-merchant. 葡萄酒商。

vi·nyl /ˈvaɪnɪl ; ˈvaɪnɪl/ *n* (kinds of) tough, flexible plastic, used for clothing, coverings and binding books. 維尼龍(數種柔軟而强韌的塑膠產品，用作衣料，覆蓋物及裝訂書籍)。

viol /ˈvaɪəl ; ˈvaɪəl/ *n* (usu six-)stringed instrument of the Middle Ages from which the modern violin was developed. 維奧爾(一種中世紀的絃樂器，通常爲六絃，現代小提琴卽由此發展而來)。

vi·ola[1] /vɪˈəʊlə ; vɪˈolə/ *n* tenor violin, of larger size than the ordinary violin. 中提琴(較小提琴大)。⇨ the illus at string. 參看 string 之插圖。

vi·ola[2] /ˈvaɪələ ; ˈvaɪələ/ *n* kinds of plant including pansies of one colour only (not variegated) and violets. 菫菜科植物(包括紫羅蘭)。

vi·ol·ate /ˈvaɪəleɪt ; ˈvaɪəˌlet/ *vt* [VP6A] **1** break (an oath, a treaty, etc); act contrary to (what one's conscience tells one to do, etc). 違犯(誓言，條約等)；違背(良心要一個人所做的事等)。**2** act towards (a sacred place, sb's seclusion, etc) without proper respect: 褻瀆；冒犯；侵害(神聖的地方，某人的獨處等)：*~ sb's privacy.* 侵犯某人的私生活。**3** rape. 强姦。**vi·ol·ation** /ˌvaɪəˈleɪʃn ; ˌvaɪəˈleʃən/ *n* [U] violating or being ~d: 違犯；違背；褻瀆；冒犯；侵害：*act in violation of a treaty;* 行事違犯某條約；[C] instance of this: 其實例：*violations of the rights of the citizens／the right of free speech, etc.* 侵犯公民權(言論自由權等)。

vi·ol·ent /ˈvaɪələnt ; ˈvaɪələnt/ *adj* **1** using, showing, accompanied by, great force: 使用暴力的；顯示暴力的；伴以暴力的；猛烈的；强烈的；激烈的；兇暴的：*a ~ wind／attack;* 暴風(猛攻)；*~ blows;* 猛烈的打擊；*~ passions;* 强烈的情慾；*in a ~ temper;* 在盛怒之下；*~ abuse;* 謾罵；*a ~* (=extreme) *contrast.* 極端的對比。**2** caused by ~ attack: 由猛烈攻擊、打擊等造成的：*meet a ~ death.* 橫死。**3** severe: 厲害的；劇烈的：*~ toothache.* 劇烈的牙痛。**~·ly** *adv* **vi·olence** /-əns ; -əns/ *n* [U] state of being ~; ~ conduct: 猛烈；强烈；兇暴；暴力；暴行：*crimes／acts of violence;* 暴力罪行(兇暴的行爲)；*robbery with violence;* 暴力搶劫；*an outbreak of violence,* rioting, etc. 暴動。**do violence to,** (fig) be a breach of: (喻)違背；破壞：*It would do violence to his principles to eat meat.* 吃肉會違背他的原則。

vi·olet /ˈvaɪələt ; ˈvaɪəlɪt/ *n* **1** [C] small wild or garden plant with sweet-smelling flowers. 紫羅蘭(野生或栽培)。**2** [U] bluish-purple colour of wild ~s. 紫羅蘭色；藍紫色(野生紫羅蘭之色)。

vi·olin /ˌvaɪəˈlɪn ; ˌvaɪəˈlɪn/ *n* four-stringed musical instrument played with a bow, ⇨ the illus at string. 小提琴(一種四絃樂器，參看 string 之插圖)。**~·ist** /-ɪst ; -ɪst/ *n* player of a ~. 小提琴手。

vi·per /ˈvaɪpə(r) ; ˈvaɪpɚ/ *n* kinds of poisonous snake of Africa, Asia, and Europe; (fig) spiteful and treacherous person. 蝰(產於非洲、亞洲和歐洲之數種毒蛇)；(喻)惡毒之人；奸詐之人。**the common ~,** the adder (the only poisonous snake in GB). 蝮蛇(英國唯一之毒蛇)。

vir·ago /vɪˈrɑːgəʊ ; vəˈrego/ *n* (*pl* ~s or ~es /-gəʊz ; -goz/) violent and bad-tempered woman who scolds and shouts. 潑婦；悍婦。

vir·gin /ˈvɜːdʒɪn ; ˈvɝdʒɪn/ *n* girl or woman (and in recent use, man) who has not experienced sexual union. 處女；(晚近用法)處男。**the (Blessed) V~ (Mary),** (abbr 略作 **BVM**), the mother of Jesus Christ. 聖母馬利亞。□ *adj* **1** pure and chaste: 處女的；童貞的：*the V~ Queen,* Elizabeth I of England. 處子女王(卽英國伊利莎白女王一世)。**the ~ birth,** the doctrine that Jesus was miraculously conceived by the V~ Mary. 童身胎(認爲耶穌係由童貞女馬利亞神奇地懷孕的說法)。**2** pure and untouched: 純潔的；潔白無瑕疵的；未被玷汚的：*~ snow.* 白雪。**3** in the original condition; unused: 原始的；處於原來狀態的；未經使用的：*a ~ forest,* one in its natural state, no trees having been felled, planted, etc; 原始森林；未採伐過的森林；*~ soil,* soil never before used for crops; (fig) a mind open to receive new ideas. 處女地；未種植過作物的土地；(喻)易接受新觀念的心靈。**~·ity** /vəˈdʒɪnətɪ ; vɚˈdʒɪnətɪ/ *n* [U] state of being a ~; ~ condition. 處女的狀態；童貞的或原始的狀況。

vir·ginal[1] /ˈvɜːdʒɪnl ; ˈvɝdʒɪnl/ *adj* of, suitable for, a virgin. 處女的；童貞的；適於處女的。

vir·ginal[2] /ˈvɜːdʒɪnl ; ˈvɝdʒɪnl/ *n* (often *pl*) square spinet without legs used in the 16th and 17th cc (and also called 亦稱作 *the ~s／a pair of ~s*). (常用複數)古鋼琴(十六、十七世紀時所用的方形無腿小鍵一名維琴娜爾)。

Vir·ginia /vəˈdʒɪnɪə ; vɚˈdʒɪnjə/ *n* [U] kinds of tobacco produced in the State of V~, US: (美國維吉尼亞州所產的)維吉尼亞烟葉：*~ cigarettes.* 維吉尼亞烟葉製成的香烟。**~ creeper,** ornamental vine often grown on walls, with large leaves which turn scarlet in the autumn. 美國籐(一名蛇葡萄，常蔓生於牆上以爲裝飾，葉大，秋天變爲猩紅色)。

Virgo /ˈvɜːgəʊ ; ˈvɝgo/ *n* sixth sign of the zodiac. 處女座；處女宮(黃道十二宮之第六宮)。⇨ the illus at zodiac. 參看 zodiac 之插圖。

vir·gule /ˈvɜːgjuːl ; ˈvɝgjul/ *n* diagonal mark (／), used to separate alternatives (as in *and／or*). 短斜線(用以表示二者中可任擇其一，如 and／or 表示 and 與 or 可任擇其一)。

vir·ile /ˈvɪraɪl *US:* ˈvɪrəl ; ˈvɪrəl/ *adj* **1** having or showing strength, energy, manly qualities: 具有或顯示力氣、活力、男子氣概的；剛健的；雄糾糾的：*~ eloquence;* 雄辯；*a ~ style (of writing);* 有力的文體；*live to a ~ old age.* 活到老年身體仍然很硬朗。**2** (of men) sexually potent. (指男人)性機能强的。**vir·il·ity** /vɪˈrɪlətɪ ; vəˈrɪlətɪ/ *n* [U] masculine strength and vigour; sexual power. 男子氣概；男性的精力；生殖力；性能力。

vi·rol·ogy /vaɪəˈrɒlədʒɪ ; vaɪˈrɑlədʒɪ/ *n* [U] the study of viruses and virus diseases. 濾體學；濾毒學(研究病毒及病毒疾病者)。

virtu /vɜːˈtuː ; vɝˈtu/ *n* (only in) (僅用於) ***articles／objects of ~,*** art objects interesting because of fine workmanship, antiquity, rarity, etc. 奇珍；古

玩;骨董。

vir·tual /ˈvɜːtʃʊəl ; ˈvɝtʃʊəl/ *adj* being in fact, acting as, what is described, but not accepted openly or in name as such: 事實上的;實際上的;實質上的(但未公開或在名義上爲人接受): *the ~ head of the business;* 商店的實際上的老闆; *a ~ defeat/confession.* 實際上的失敗(懺悔)。 **~·ly** /-tʃʊəlɪ ; -tʃʊəlɪ/ *adv*

vir·tue /ˈvɜːtʃuː ; ˈvɝtʃʊ/ *n* **1** [C, U] (any particular kind of) goodness or excellence: 善;德行;美德;好處;優點: *Patience is a ~.* 忍耐是一種美德。*Is patriotism always a ~?* 愛國永遠是一種美德嗎? *Our climate has the ~s of never being too hot or too cold.* 我們這裡的氣候有不太熱亦不太冷的好處。 ***make a ~ of necessity,*** do sth pretending it to be an act of ~ when one really does it under compulsion. 以逆來順受的心情去做迫不得已的事。***V~ is its own reward,*** (prov) One should not expect a reward for doing sth that is truly virtuous. (諺)爲善不望報;爲善最樂。 **the cardinal ~s,** prudence, fortitude, temperance, justice. (四種)基本美德(審愼、堅毅、克制、公正)。 **the theological ~s,** faith, hope, charity. (基督敎的)三德(信、望、愛)。 **2** [U] chastity. 貞節;純潔。 **3** [U] efficacy; ability to produce a definite result: 效力;效能: *Have you any faith in the ~ of herbs to heal sickness?* 你對於草藥治病的效力有信心嗎? **4** [U, C] excellence; advantage: 優點;長處;有利處: *The great ~ of the scheme is that it costs very little.* 該項計畫的一大優點就是花費很少。 **5** ***by/in ~ of,*** by reason of; because of: 由於;因爲: *He claimed a pension in ~ of his long military service.* 他以在軍中服役多年爲由要求發給養老金。 **vir·tu·ous** /ˈvɜːtʃʊəs ; ˈvɝtʃʊəs/ *adj* having or showing ~. 有品德的;善良的。 **vir·tu·ous·ly** *adv*

vir·tu·oso /ˌvɜːtʃʊˈəʊzəʊ *US:* -ˈəʊsəʊ ; ˌvɝtʃʊˈoso/ *n* (*pl* ~s or 或 -si /-ziː *US:* -siː ; -si/) person with special knowledge of, or taste for, works of art; person skilled in the methods of an art, esp one who plays a musical instrument with great skill: 藝術品專家或愛好者; (藝術界的)名家; (尤指)大演奏家: (attrib) (形容用法) *a ~ performer.* 名演奏家。 **vir·tu·os·ity** /ˌvɜːtʃʊˈɒsətɪ ; ˌvɝtʃʊˈɑsətɪ/ *n* [U] skill of a ~. 藝術品鑑賞力;(演奏等的)精湛技巧。

V

viru·lent /ˈvɪrʊlənt ; ˈvɪrjələnt/ *adj* (of poison) strong; deadly; (of ill feeling, hatred) bitter; (of words, etc) full of ill feeling; (of diseases, sores) poisonous. (指毒物)劇烈的;致命的;(指惡感,仇恨)厲害的; 深刻的; (指言詞等)惡毒的;刻毒的;(指疾病,瘡)有毒的;惡性的。 **~·ly** *adv* **viru·lence** /-ləns ; -ləns/ *n*

vi·rus /ˈvaɪərəs ; ˈvaɪrəs/ *n* [C] any of various poisonous elements, smaller than bacteria, causing the spread of infectious disease: (造成傳染病蔓延的)病毒;濾過性病原體;毒素: *the ~ of rabies;* 狂犬病的病毒; *~ diseases.* 濾過性疾病。

visa /ˈviːzə ; ˈvizə/ *n* [C] stamp or signature put on a passport to show that it has been examined and approved by the officials of a foreign country which the owner intends to visit (ˈ*entrance* or ˈ*entry ~*) or leave (ˈ*exit ~*). 簽證 (entrance visa 入境簽證, exit visa 出境簽證)。 □ *vt* [VP6A] put a ~ on: 簽證: *get one's passport ~ed* /ˈviːzəd ; ˈvizəd/ *before going to Poland.* 去波蘭前先在護照上辦妥簽證。

vis·age /ˈvɪzɪdʒ ; ˈvɪzɪdʒ/ *n* [C] (liter) face (of a human being). (文) (人的) 面貌; 面容。 **-vis·aged** /ˈvɪzɪdʒd ; ˈvɪzɪdʒd/ *suff* (in compounds) having the kind of ~ indicated: (用於複合字中)有某種面貌的: *gloomy-~d funeral directors.* 面容悲戚的喪葬承辦人。

vis-à-vis /ˌviːz ɑː ˈviː *US:* ˌviːz ə ˈviː ; ˌvizəˈvi/ *adv, prep* **1** facing (one another): 和…面對面;相對: *sit ~ in a train.* 在火車上相對而坐。 **2** (fig) in relation to; compared with. (喻)關於;與…相較。

vis·cera /ˈvɪsərə ; ˈvɪsərə/ *n pl* internal organs of the body, esp the intestines. 內臟;(尤指)腸。 **vis·ceral** /ˈvɪsərəl ; ˈvɪsərəl/ *adj* of the ~. 內臟的;腸子的。

vis·cid /ˈvɪsɪd ; ˈvɪsɪd/, **vis·cous** /ˈvɪskəs ; ˈvɪskəs/ *adjj* sticky; semi-fluid. 黏的;黏性的;半流體的。 **vis·cos·ity** /vɪsˈkɒsətɪ ; vɪsˈkɑsətɪ/ *n* [U] being viscous. 黏;黏性。

vis·count /ˈvaɪkaʊnt ; ˈvaɪkaʊnt/ *n* nobleman higher in rank than a baron, lower than an earl. 子爵(高於男爵而低於伯爵)。 **~·ess** /-ɪs ; -ɪs/ *n* wife of a ~; woman who is a ~ in her own right. 子爵夫人;女子爵。 **~cy** /-tsɪ ; -tsɪ/ *n* (*pl* -cies) title, rank, dignity, of a ~. 子爵的頭銜、地位、尊榮。

vise /vaɪs ; vaɪs/ *n* (US) = vice².

vis·ible /ˈvɪzəbl ; ˈvɪzəbl̩/ *adj* that can be seen; that is in sight: 可見的;看得見的: *The eclipse will be ~ to observers in western Europe.* 這次的日(月)蝕西歐的觀測者可以見到。 **vis·ibly** /-əblɪ ; -əblɪ/ *adv* in a ~ manner: 可見地;看得見地;顯而易見地: *She was visibly annoyed.* 她顯然被惹惱了。 **vis·ibil·ity** /ˌvɪzəˈbɪlətɪ ; ˌvɪzəˈbɪlətɪ/ *n* [U] being ~; (esp) condition of the atmosphere for seeing things at a distance: 可見性;(尤指)明視度;能見度: *The aircraft turned back because of poor visibility.* 由於能見度太低,飛機折返了。

vi·sion /ˈvɪʒn ; ˈvɪʒən/ *n* **1** [U] power of seeing or imagining, looking ahead, grasping the truth that underlies facts: 視力;視覺;想像力;遠見;洞察力;觀察力: *the field of ~,* all that can be seen from a certain point; 視野; *the ~ of a poet/prophet;* 詩人的想像力(預言家的先見之明); *a man of ~.* 有眼光的人。 **2** [C] sth seen, esp by the mind's eye or the power of imagination, or sth seen during sleep or in a trance-like state: 視見之物;景象;(尤指)幻想;夢幻;幻像;幻影: *the romantic ~s of youth.* 青年人浪漫的幻想。*Have you ever had ~s of great wealth and success?* 你曾有過發大財成大功的幻想嗎?

vi·sion·ary /ˈvɪʒənrɪ *US:* -ʒənerɪ ; ˈvɪʒənˌɛrɪ/ *adj* **1** existing only in a vision or the imagination; unpractical; fanciful: 僅存在於幻想或想像中的;不切實際的;空幻的: *~ schemes/scenes/plans.* 幻想中的策略(景象,計畫)。 **2** (of persons) having ~ ideas; dreamy. (指人)愛幻想的;愛空想的。 □ *n* ~ person. 幻想者;空想者。

visit /ˈvɪzɪt ; ˈvɪzɪt/ *vt, vi* **1** [VP6A] go to see (sb); go to (a place) for a time: 訪問;拜訪(某人);遊覽;參觀(某地): *~ a friend;* 訪友; *~ Rome.* 遊羅馬。*His rich relatives seldom ~ him.* 他那些有錢的親戚很少去拜訪他。 [VP2C] (US) stay: (美)停留;下榻: *~ing in Paris;* 在巴黎停留; *~ing at a new hotel.* 在一家新旅館下榻。 **2** [VP6A] (chiefly US) go to in order to inspect or examine officially: (主美) 正式的視察或檢查: *Restaurant and hotel kitchens are ~ed regularly by public health inspectors.* 餐館及旅館的厨房定期由公共衞生官員檢查。 **3** [VP3A] (chiefly US) (主美) ***~ with,*** pay a ~ to; talk with: 過訪;與…談話: *She loves ~ing with her neighbours and having a good gossip.* 她喜歡去隣居家開心地閒話家常。 **4** [VP14] ***~ sth on sb,*** (biblical use) punish. (聖經用語)懲罰。 ***~ the sins of the fathers upon the children,*** make the children suffer for their parent's failings. 使兒子因父親的罪孽而受懲罰。 □ *n* act of ~ing; time of ~ing: 訪問;遊覽;訪問或遊覽的時間: *pay a ~ to a friend/a patient/a prospective customer;* 訪友(探望病人,訪問可望成爲顧客者); *go on a ~ to the seaside;* 去海濱遊玩; *a ~ of several hours;* 一次數小時的訪問; *during her first ~ to her husband's parents.* 在她第一次探望其翁姑的時候。 **~·ing** *n* [U] paying ~s; making calls (on people): 訪問;訪晤(人): ˈ*~ing hours at a hospital;* 醫院裡的探病時間; *We are not on ~ing terms,* not sufficiently well acquainted to ~ one another. 我們尚不熟悉,彼此無往來。 **visi·tor** /ˈvɪzɪtə(r) ; ˈvɪzɪtɚ/ *n* person who ~s; person who stays at a place: 訪問者;參觀者;賓客: *summer ~ors,* eg at a holiday resort; 夏季的遊客(如在度假勝地者); *the ~ors' book,* one in which ~ors sign their names, eg at a hotel or a place of public interest. 來賓簽名簿;旅客或遊客登記簿。

visi·tant /ˈvɪzɪtənt ; ˈvɪzətənt/ *n* **1** (liter) visitor, esp an important or supernatural one. (文)訪問者;(尤指)貴賓;(來到人世的)鬼神。**2** migratory bird: 候鳥: *a rare ~ to these shores.* 到這一帶海邊的罕見候鳥。

visi·ta·tion /ˌvɪzɪˈteɪʃn ; ˌvɪzəˈteʃən/ *n* **1** [C] visit, esp one of an official nature or one made by a bishop or priest: 訪問;(尤指)巡視;視察;(主教或教士所作的)訪晤: *a ~ of the sick,* made by a clergyman as part of his duties. (教士的)探視病人。 **2** [C] trouble, disaster, looked upon as punishment from God: (視為上帝懲罰的)災禍;苦難: *The famine was a ~ of God for their sins.* 那次饑饉被視爲上帝對他們犯罪的懲罰。

vi·sor /ˈvaɪzə(r) ; ˈvaɪzɚ/ *n* **1** (hist) movable part of a helmet, covering the face. (史)盔的面甲。⇨ the illus at armour. 參看 armour 之挿圖。 **2** peak of a cap. 帽舌;帽簷。 **3** **(ˈsun-)~,** oblong sheet of dark-tinted glass hinged at the top of a windscreen in a car to lessen the glare of bright sunshine. (汽車擋風玻璃上方的)遮陽板。

vista /ˈvɪstə ; ˈvɪstə/ *n* [C] **1** long, narrow view: 狹長的景色;遠景: *a ~ of the church spire at the end of an avenue of trees.* 林蔭道末端教堂塔尖的景色。 **2** (fig) long series of scenes, events, etc which one can look back on or forward to: (喻)(對一連串情景、事件等之)回顧;展望: *the ~s of bygone times;* 昔日的一連串追憶; *a discovery that opens up new ~s.* 開拓新的遠景的一項發現。

vis·ual /ˈvɪʒuəl ; ˈvɪʒuəl/ *adj* concerned with, used in, seeing: 看的;視覺的;用於看的: *~ images.* 視覺像。*She has a ~ memory,* is able to remember well things she sees. 她對看過的事物能記得很清楚。 **~ aids,** (eg in teaching) eg pictures, film-strips, cinema films. 直觀教具(如教學上用的圖片、幻燈片及電影片)。**~ly** /ˈvɪʒuəlɪ ; ˈvɪʒuəlɪ/ *adv* **~·ize** /-aɪz ; -ˌaɪz/ *vt* [VP6A] bring (sth) as a picture before the mind: 想像;設想: *I remember meeting the man two years ago but can't ~ize him,* recall what he looked like. 我記得兩年前遇見過那個人,但是他的樣子我想不起來了。**vis·ual·iz·ation** /ˌvɪʒuəlaɪˈzeɪʃn *US:* -lɪˈz- ; ˌvɪʒuəlɪˈzeʃən/ *n*

vi·tal /ˈvaɪtl ; ˈvaɪtl/ *adj* **1** of, connected with, necessary for, living: 生命的;與生命有關的;維持生命所必需的: *wounded in a ~ part.* 在要害處受傷。**the ~ force/principle,** that which is assumed to account for organic life. 生命力;生機;活力。**~ statistics,** **(a)** relating to the duration of life, and to births, marriages and deaths. 生命統計;人口動態統計(卽有關壽命、出生、婚姻及死亡的統計)。 **(b)** (colloq) woman's measurements at bust, waist and hips. (俗)婦女的三圍(胸、腰、臀)數字。 **2** supreme; indispensable: 極度的;非常的;不可缺少的: *of ~ importance;* 非常重要的; *a ~ necessity.* 極端需要。**~s** *n pl* ~ parts of the body, esp the lungs, heart and brain. 身體的重要器官(尤指肺、心和腦);要害。**~ly** /ˈvaɪtəlɪ ; ˈvaɪtl̩ɪ/ *adv* **~·ism** -ɪzəm ; -ˌɪzəm/ *n* [U] belief that there is a controlling force in living things which is distinct from chemical and physical forces (opp of *mechanism*). 生機論(認爲生物中之控制力不同於化學力和物理力) (爲 mechanism 之相反字)。**~·ist** /-ɪst ; -ɪst/ *n* person who believes in ~ism. 生機論者;持生機說者。

vi·tal·ity /vaɪˈtælətɪ ; vaɪˈtælətɪ/ *n* [U] vital power; capacity to endure and perform functions: 活力;生命力;持續力: *Can an artificial language have any ~?* 人造的語言能持久嗎?

vi·tal·ize /ˈvaɪtəlaɪz ; ˈvaɪtl̩ˌaɪz/ *vt* [VP6A] fill with vitality; put vigour into. 賦予生命力;給予活力。

vit·amin /ˈvɪtəmɪn *US:* ˈvaɪt- ; ˈvaɪtəmɪn/ *n* [C] any of a number of organic substances which are present in certain food-stuffs and are essential to the health of man and other animals: 維他命;維生素: *illnesses* (eg scurvy, rickets) *caused by ~ deficiency;* 因缺乏維生素而引起的疾病(如壞血病,佝僂病); *ˈ~ tablets.* 維他命片。

vi·ti·ate /ˈvɪʃɪeɪt ; ˈvɪʃɪˌet/ *vt* [VP6A] lower the quality of; weaken or destroy the force of: 降低…的品質;削弱或破壞…的力量;汚損;敗壞:*~d blood;* 汚血; *the ~d air of an overcrowded room.* 過分擁擠之房間內的混濁空氣。*This admission ~s your argument/cliam.* 這項供認減弱了你的論據(權利要求)的力量。

vit·reous /ˈvɪtrɪəs ; ˈvɪtrɪəs/ *adj* of or like glass: 玻璃的;似玻璃的: *~ rocks,* hard and brittle; 堅硬而脆的岩石; *~ enamel,* used instead of porcelain. 搪瓷。

vit·rify /ˈvɪtrɪfaɪ ; ˈvɪtrəˌfaɪ/ *vt, vi* (*pt, pp* -fied) [VP6A, 2A] change, be changed, into a glass-like substance. (使)變成玻璃狀物質。

vit·riol /ˈvɪtrɪəl ; ˈvɪtrɪəl/ *n* [U] sulphuric acid; any of the salts of sulphuric acid: 硫酸;硫酸鹽;礬: *blue ~,* copper sulphate; 硫酸銅;膽礬; (fig) sarcasm. (喩)尖酸的諷刺;尖刻的話;譏刺。 **~ic** /ˌvɪtrɪˈɒlɪk ; ˌvɪtrɪˈɑlɪk/ *adj* (fig, of words, feelings) biting; full of invective: (喩,指言詞、感情)尖刻的;謾罵的: *a ~ic attack on the President;* 對總統的犀利攻擊; *~ic remarks.* 尖刻的批評。

vit·uper·ate /vɪˈtjuːpəreɪt *US:* vaɪˈtuː ; vaɪˈtupəˌret/ *vt* [VP6A] abuse in words; curse; revile. 罵;責罵;咒罵;辱罵。**vit·uper·at·ive** /vɪˈtjuːpərətɪv *US:* vaɪˈtuːpəreɪtɪv ; vaɪˈtjupəˌretɪv/ *adj* abusive. 責罵的;辱罵的。**vit·uper·ation** /vɪˌtjuːpəˈreɪʃn *US:* vaɪˌtuː- ; vaɪˌtupəˈreʃən/ *n* [U] abusive language; severe scolding. 罵人的話;辱罵。

viva /ˈvaɪvə ; ˈvaɪvə/ *n* (colloq) (俗) = viva voce.

vi·vace /vɪˈvɑːtʃeɪ ; vɪˈvɑtʃɪ/ *adv* (music) briskly. (音樂)輕快地;活潑地。

vi·va·cious /vɪˈveɪʃəs ; vaɪˈveʃəs/ *adj* lively; high-spirited; gay: 活潑的;快活的;愉快的: *a ~ girl.* 活潑的女郎。**~·ly** *adv* **vi·vac·ity** /vɪˈvæsətɪ ; vaɪˈvæsətɪ/ *n* [U].

viva voce /ˌvaɪvə ˈvəʊsɪ ; ˈvaɪvəˈvosɪ/ *adj, adv* oral(ly): 口頭的(地): *a ~ examination.* 口試。□ *n* ~ examination or test. 口試。

vivid /ˈvɪvɪd ; ˈvɪvɪd/ *adj* **1** (of colours, etc) intense; bright: (指顏色等)强烈的;鮮明的: *a ~ flash of lightning;* 一道耀眼的閃電; *~ green trousers.* 翠綠色的長褲。 **2** lively; active: 有生氣的;活潑的: *a ~ imagination.* 活潑的想像。 **3** clear and distinct: 清晰的;生動的: *a ~ description of an event;* 對一事件的生動描述; *have ~ recollections of a holiday in Italy.* 對在義大利度假的情景保有清晰的記憶。**~·ly** *adv* **~·ness** *n*

vi·vipar·ous /vɪˈvɪpərəs *US:* vaɪ- ; vaɪˈvɪpərəs/ *adj* having offspring which develop within the mother's body (not from eggs). 胎生的。

vivi·sect /ˌvɪvɪˈsekt ; ˈvɪvəˌsɛkt/ *vt* [VP6A] operate or experiment on (living animals) for scientific research. 活體解剖; (爲科學研究而)解剖或實驗(活動物)。 **vivi·sec·tion** /ˌvɪvɪˈsekʃn ; ˌvɪvəˈsɛkʃən/ *n* [U]~ing; [C] instance of this. 活體解剖;其實例。 **vivi·sec·tion·ist** /-ʃənɪst ; -ʃənɪst/ *n* person who ~s; person who considers vivisection justifiable. 作活體解剖者;活體解剖論者;爲活體解剖辯護者。

vixen /ˈvɪksn ; ˈvɪksn̩/ *n* female fox; bad-tempered quarrelsome woman. 雌狐; 牝狐; 悍婦; 潑婦; 刁婦。 **~·ish** /ˈvɪksənɪʃ ; ˈvɪksn̩ɪʃ/ *adj* scolding; bad-tempered. 責罵的;潑辣的;壞脾氣的。

viz /vɪz ; vɪz/ (Lat 拉丁 *videlicet,* usu spoken as 通常說作 *namely*) that is to say; namely. 卽是說;就是。

vi·zier /vɪˈzɪə(r) ; vɪˈzɪr/ *n* official of high rank in some Muslim countries, esp the old Turkish empire. (若干回教國家的,尤其是鄂圖曼帝國的)高級官

吏;大官;大員;大臣。

vo·cabu·lary /vəˈkæbjʊlərɪ *US:* -lerɪ ; vəˈkæbjə-ˌlerɪ/ *n* (*pl* -ries) **1** total number of words which (with rules for combining them) make up a language: 某一語言所含的全部語詞;語詞總數: *No dictionary could list the whole ~ of a language.* 沒有一本字典能够盡列一種語言的全部語詞。 **2** [C, U] (range of) words known to, or used by, a person, in a trade, profession, etc: (某人或某行業或某職業等的)用語;詞彙;語彙: *a writer with a large ~.* 詞彙很廣的作家。 **3** [C] book containing a list of words; list of words used in a book, etc, usu with definitions or translations. 單字集;(書等的)字彙表(通常列有定義或翻譯)。

vo·cal /ˈvəʊkl ; ˈvokl̩/ *adj* of, for, with or using, the voice: 嗓音的;聲音的;適於嗓音的;有嗓音的;使用嗓音的: *the ~ chords,* ⇨ cord(2); *the ~ organs,* the tongue, lips, etc; 發聲器官(舌、唇等); *~ music,* to be sung; 聲樂;歌樂; *a ~ score,* musical score, eg of an opera, giving the vocal parts in full. 歌樂總譜。*Anger made the shy girl ~,* helped her to express her feelings by speaking. 憤怒使那害羞的女孩子開口了。 **~ly** /ˈvəʊkəlɪ ; ˈvoklɪ/ *adv* **~·ist** /ˈvəʊkəlɪst ; ˈvokl̩ɪst/ *n* singer. 聲樂家;歌唱家。 ⇨ *instrumentalist* at instrumental. **~·ize** /-aɪz ; -ˌaɪz/ *vt* say or sing; voice(2). 說;唱;將(某音)發成濁音。

vo·ca·tion /vəʊˈkeɪʃn ; voˈkeʃən/ *n* **1** (*sing* only) feeling that one is called to (and qualified for) a certain kind of work (esp social or religious): (僅用單數)(覺得自己受到召示而且適於做某種工作的)使命感;(尤指)天職;天命;神召: *The nursing of the sick, said Florence Nightingale, is a ~ as well as a profession.* 南丁格爾說,看護病患不僅是一種職業,更是天職。 **2** [U] special aptitude (*for*): 特殊的才能;異禀(與 for 連用): *He has little or no ~ for teaching.* 他不適於教書。 **3** [C] person's trade or profession. 行業;職業。 **~al** /-ʃənl ; -ʃənl̩/ *adj* of or for a ~(3): 職業的;適於職業的: *~al guidance,* advice on the choice of a ~. 就業指導;職業輔導。

voca·tive /ˈvɒkətɪv ; ˈvɑkətɪv/ *adj, n* (of the) form of a word used when addressing sb: 呼格;呼格語;呼格的;呼格語的: *the ~ case.* 呼格。⇨ case¹(3).

vo·cif·er·ate /vəˈsɪfəreɪt *US:* vəʊ- ; voˈsɪfəˌret/ *vt, vi* [VP6A, 2A] say loudly or noisily; shout. 大聲說;呼喊。 **vo·cif·er·ation** /vəˌsɪfəˈreɪʃn *US:* vəʊ- ; ˌvosɪfəˈreʃən/ *n* [U] shouting; yelling. 呼喊;大叫。 **vo·cif·er·ous** /vəˈsɪfərəs *US:* vəʊ- ; voˈsɪfərəs/ *adj* noisy; yelling: 嘈雜的;呼喊的;大叫的: *a vociferous crowd.* 嘈雜的羣衆。

vodka /ˈvɒdkə ; ˈvɑdkə/ *n* [U] strong Russian alcoholic drink distilled from rye and also other vegetable products. 伏特加酒(俄國產的一種烈酒)。

vogue /vəʊg ; vog/ *n* **1** current fashion; sth currently being done or used: 時髦;流行之物: *Are blue jeans still the ~?* 藍色牛仔褲還流行嗎? *The ~s of the 18th century seem amusing today.* 十八世紀流行的東西現在看起來很好笑。 **2** popularity; popular use or acceptance: 風行;普遍;普遍的使用或接受: *Georgette Wheatley's novels had a great ~ ten years ago, but are not read today.* 喬治特•惠特勒的小說十年前風行一時,但是現在已無人閱讀了。 ***be in/come into ~; be/go out of ~,*** be/become (un)fashionable, (un)popular: 正在(開始)流行;不再流行: *When did pointed shoes come into/go out of ~?* 尖頭鞋是何時開始(才不)流行的? ***all the ~,*** popular everywhere; the latest fashion. 到處受歡迎的;最新流行品;最新式樣。

voice /vɔɪs ; vɔɪs/ *n* **1** [U] sounds made when speaking or singing: 說話聲;歌唱聲;嗓音: *He is not in good ~,* not speaking or singing as well as usual. 他現在嗓子不好。 **2** [C] power of making such sounds: 發聲力: *He has lost his ~,* cannot speak or sing properly, eg because of a bad cold. 他的嗓子啞了。 **3** [C, U] sounds uttered by a person, esp considered in relation to their quality: 人聲;聲音(尤指就其音質方面言): *in a loud/soft/shrill/rough, etc ~.* 大(柔,尖,粗等)聲地。 *I did not recognize her ~.* 我聽不出她的聲音。 *The choir boys have sweet ~s.* 唱詩班的男孩聲音很美。 *They gave ~ to their indignation.* 他們大聲說出他們的憤慨。 ***lift up one's ~,*** (old use) sing, speak. (舊用法)唱;說。 ***shout at the top of one's ~,*** shout as loudly as one can. 提高嗓門大聲喊叫。 ***with one ~,*** (liter) unanimously. (文)一致地;異口同聲地。 **4** ***a/some/no, etc ~ in sth,*** a/some/no, etc right to express an opinion on: 具有(要求)對某事有(有一些,沒有)發言權: *I have no ~ in the matter.* 我對此事無發言權。 **5** [C] anything which may be compared or likened to the human ~ as expressing ideas, feelings, etc: (在表現意念、情感等上)類似或可比擬人類聲音之事物: *the ~ of Nature;* 天籟; *the ~s of the night;* 夜之聲; *the ~ of God,* conscience. 良知。 **6** [U] (in phonetics) sound produced by vibration of the vocal cords, not with breath only, as for vowel sounds and the consonants /b, d, ð, z/, etc. (語音)有聲音;濁音(由聲帶顫震而發出的聲音,非僅由氣息發出者,如母音及子音 /b, d, ð, z/ 等)。 **7** (gram) the contrast between *active* and *passive* as shown in the sentences: (文法)動詞的(主動及被動)語態: *The dog ate the meat* and *The meat was eaten by the dog.* '狗吃肉'爲主動語態而'肉被狗吃'則爲被動語態。 □ *vt* [VP6A] **1** put into words: 用話說出來;道出;宣述: *The spokesman ~d the feelings of the crowd.* 那發言人說出了羣衆的心聲。 **2** utter (a sound) with ~(6): 把(某音)發成濁音: *~d sounds* (eg /d, v, ŋ/). 濁音(如 /d, v, ŋ/)。 **-~d** *adj* (in compounds) having the kind of ~ indicated: (用於複合字中)有某種聲音的: *rough-~d.* 粗聲的。 **~·less** *adj* **1** having no ~; unable to utter words. 無聲的;沉寂的;啞的。 **2** (of consonants) uttered without ~(6): (指子音)清(音)的;不帶聲的: *The sounds/p, tʃ, f/are ~less.* /p, tʃ, f/ 諸音是清音的。

void /vɔɪd ; vɔɪd/ *adj* **1** empty; vacant. 空的;空虛的。 **2** ***~ of,*** without: 沒有;缺乏: *a subject ~ of interest;* 沒有趣味的題目; *a proposal ~ of reason.* 沒有道理的建議。 **3** ***null and ~,*** (legal) without force; invalid: (法律)無效的: *The agreement, not having been signed, was null and ~.* 那項合約因未經簽字故無效。□ *n* [C] space: 空處;空虛;太空: *There was an aching ~ in his heart,* (fig) a feeling of sadness caused by the loss of someone he had loved. (喻)他心中有悲痛的空虛感(因親人死亡而引起者)。 □ *vt* [VP6A] (legal) make ~(3). (法律)使無效。

voile /vɔɪl ; vɔɪl/ *n* [U] thin, light dress material. 輕而薄的衣料。

vol·atile /ˈvɒlətaɪl *US:* -tl ; ˈvɑlətl̩/ *adj* **1** (of a liquid) that easily changes into gas or vapour. (指液體)易發散的;易揮發的。 **2** (of a person, his disposition) lively; changing quickly or easily from one mood or interest to another. (指人,其性情)快活的;易變的;心境或興趣轉變快速的;反覆無常的。 **vola·til·ity** /ˌvɒləˈtɪlətɪ ; ˌvɑləˈtɪlətɪ/ *n*

vol·cano /vɒlˈkeɪnəʊ ; vɑlˈkeno/ *n* (*pl* ~es or ~s /-nəʊz ; -noz/) hill or mountain with opening(s) (⇨ crater) through which gases, lava, ashes, etc, come up from below the earth's crust (in *an active ~*), or may come up after an interval (in *a dormant ~*), or have long ceased to come up (in *an extinct ~*). 火山(地殼下的氣體、熔岩、灰燼等由火山口 crater 噴出,如活火山 active ~; 或間歇地噴出,如休火山 dormant ~; 或久已停止噴出,如死火山 extinct ~)。 **vol·canic** /vɒlˈkænɪk ; vɑlˈkænɪk/ *adj* of, from, like, a ~. 火山的;來自火山的;似火山的。

vole /vəʊl ; vol/ *n* rat-like animal: 野鼠類動物: *a ˈfield-~,* one like a mouse; 田鼠; *a ˈwater-~,* large water-rat. 大河鼠。

vo·li·tion /vəˈlɪʃn *US:* vəʊ- ; voˈlɪʃən/ *n* [U] act, power, of using one's own will, of choosing, making a decision, etc: 意志;決意;取捨;意志力: *do sth of one's own ~.* 出於自願而做某事。 **~al** /-ʃənl ;

-fənl/ *adj*

vol·ley /ˈvɒlɪ; ˈvalɪ/ *n* [C] **1** hurling or shooting of a number of missiles (stones, arrows, bullets, etc) together. (石,箭,彈丸等的)齊射;羣射;齊發。 **2** number of oaths, curses, questions, directed together, or in quick succession, at sb. (咒詛,咒罵,質問等的)齊發;連發。 **3** (tennis) stroke which returns the ball to the sender before it touches the ground. (網球)飛擊;截擊(把對方擊來的球在落地之前擊回對方)。 ˌ**half-**ˈ~, return of the ball as soon as it touches the ground. 半飛擊;半截擊;觸地擊(在球與地接觸的瞬間擊回對方)。 ˈ~**·ball** *n* game in which players on each side of a high net try to keep a ball in motion by hitting it with their hands back and forth over the net without letting it touch the ground. 排球。□ *vt, vi* **1** [VP2A, C] (of guns) sound together: (指槍砲)齊響;齊發: *The guns ~ed on all sides.* 大砲從各方面齊發。 **2** [VP6A, 2A] return a tennis-ball across the net before it touches the ground. 飛擊;截擊(網球);在球落地前擊回對方。

volt /vəʊlt; volt/ *n* [C] (abbr 略作 **v**) unit of electrical force; force that would carry one ampere of current against one ohm resistance. (電壓單位)伏特。 ~**·age** /ˈvəʊltɪdʒ; ˈvoltɪdʒ/ *n* electrical force measured in ~s. 電壓;伏特數。

volte-face /ˌvɒlt ˈfɑːs; ˈvalt,fas/ *n* complete change; act of turning round to the opposite way of standing or to the opposite way of thinking: 完全改變;(位置、立場或思想等的)徹底轉變;轉向: *make a complete ~.* 徹底轉變。

vol·uble /ˈvɒljʊbl; ˈvaljəbl/ *adj* talking, able to talk, very quickly and easily; (of speech) fluent. 健談的;口若懸河的;(指言辭)流利的。 **vol·ubly** /-jʊblɪ; -jəblɪ/ *adv* **volu·bil·ity** /ˌvɒljʊˈbɪlətɪ; ˌvaljəˈbɪlətɪ/ *n*

vol·ume /ˈvɒljuːm *US:* -jəm; ˈvaljəm/ *n* **1** [C] book, esp one of a set of books; number of sheets, papers, periodicals, etc bound together: 書本;(尤指一套書中的)一部;一卷;一册;(紙頁、報紙、雜誌等的)合訂本: *an encyclopedia in 20 ~s.* 一部有二十册的百科全書。 ***speak ~s for,*** supply strong evidence of: 充分地證明或顯示: *His donations to charity speak ~s for his generosity.* 他對慈善事業的捐助充分地表明他的慷慨。 **2** [U] amount of space (expressed in cubic metres, etc) occupied by a substance, liquid or gas; cubic contents of a container, etc: 體積(以立方公尺等表示者);(容器等的)容量;容積: *the ~ of a cask;* 大桶的容量; *the ~ of wine in a cask.* 大桶裡的酒的體積。 **3** [C] large mass, amount or quantity: 大量;多量;大宗: *the ~ of business/work, etc;* 大宗交易(大量的工作等);(esp *pl*) rounded masses of steam or smoke: (尤用複數)大團的蒸氣或烟霧: *V~s of black smoke belched out from the chimneys.* 大量的黑烟從烟囱裡冒出。 **4** [U] (of sound) power; sonority: (指聲音)響度;音量: *a voice of great ~.* 音量大的聲音。 *Your radio has a ~ control.* 你的收音機有音量控制的裝置。

vol·umi·nous /vəˈljuːmɪnəs; vəˈlumənəs/ *adj* **1** (of writing) great in quantity: (指著作)大量的;長篇的;大部頭的: *a ~ work/history;* 大部頭的作品(歷史書); (of an author) producing many books. (指作家)多產的;著作多的。 **2** occupying much space: 體積大的;寬大的: *a ~ correspondence;* 大堆信函; *~ skirts.* 寬大的裙子。

vol·un·tary /ˈvɒləntrɪ *US:* -terɪ; ˈvalən,terɪ/ *adj* **1** doing or ready to do things, willingly, without being compelled; (sth) done thus: 自願的;自動的;自動或自願做成的: *~ work/service;* 志願的工作(服務); *a ~ statement/confession;* 自動的陳述(自白); *~ workers/helpers.* 志願工人(幫助者)。 **2** carried on, supported by, ~ work and gifts: 靠自由捐助或志願工作維持的: *a* ˈ*~ school,* one supported by ~ contributions, not by the State, etc. 靠捐助維持的學校。 **3** (of bodily, muscular, movements) controlled by the will (opp of *involuntary*). (指身體的或肌肉的運動)爲意志所控制的; 隨意的(爲 involuntary 之相反字)。□ *n* [C] (*pl* -ries) organ solo, esp one played not as part of a church service. (尤指不屬禮拜儀式的)風琴獨奏。 **vol·un·tar·ily** /ˈvɒləntrəlɪ *US:* ˌvɒlənˈterəlɪ; ˈvalən,tɛrəlɪ/ *adv*

vol·un·teer /ˌvɒlənˈtɪə(r); ˌvalənˈtɪr/ *n* **1** person who offers to do sth, esp sth unpleasant or dangerous. 志願者(尤指自願從事厭煩或危險工作者)。 **2** soldier who is not conscripted: 志願兵;義勇兵: (attrib) (形容用法) *a ~ corps.* 義勇軍。□ *vt, vi* [VP6A, 7A, 2A, 3A] ~ ***sth/to do sth/for sth,*** offer voluntarily; come forward as a ~: 自動提供;自動貢獻; 自願效勞: *He ~ed some information/~ed to get some information.* 他自動提供一些消息(自願去獲取某些資料)。 *How many of them ~ed?* 他們之中有多少人自願效勞? *He ~ed for the campaign.* 他自願參加這次戰役。

vo·lup·tu·ary /vəˈlʌptʃʊərɪ *US:* -ʊerɪ; vəˈlʌptʃʊ,ɛrɪ/ *n* person who gives himself up to luxury and sensual pleasures. 耽於奢華及逸樂的人;酒色之徒。

vo·lup·tu·ous /vəˈlʌptʃʊəs; vəˈlʌptʃʊəs/ *adj* of, for, arousing, given up to, sensuous or sensual pleasures: 耽於聲色享受的; 富於聲色的; 激起聲色之慾或快感的;肉感的: *~ music/beauty/thoughts/sensations.* 華麗的音樂(冶艷;慾念;聲色的刺激)。 ~**·ly** *adv* ~**·ness** *n*

vo·lute /vəˈljuːt *US:* vəˈluːt; vəˈlut/ *n* spiral scroll, esp as on Ionic and Corinthian capitals. (尤指愛奧尼亞式及科林斯式石柱柱頭的)渦卷式雕飾;螺旋形裝飾。 ⇨ the illus at column. 參看 column 之插圖。 ~**d** *adj* decorated with, having, ~s: 渦卷飾的;有螺旋形飾的: *a ~d sea-shell.* 螺旋形的海貝。

vomit /ˈvɒmɪt; ˈvamɪt/ *vt, vi* **1** [VP6A, 15B, 2A] bring back from the stomach through the mouth; throw up from the mouth: 嘔吐; 吐出: *He ~ed everything he had eaten.* 他吐出了所吃的全部食物。 *He was ~ing blood.* 他在吐血。 *He began to ~.* 他開始嘔吐。 **2** [VP6A] send out in large quantities: 大量傾出: *factory chimneys ~ing smoke.* 大量噴烟的工廠烟囱。□ *n* [U] food that has been ~ed. 嘔出的食物。

voo·doo /ˈvuːduː; ˈvudu/ *n* [U] debased form of religion, made up of sorcery and witchcraft, practised by some people in the West Indies, esp Haiti. 巫毒教(西印度羣島,尤指海地,某些人所崇奉的一種巫蠱術)。

vo·racious /vəˈreɪʃəs; voˈreʃəs/ *adj* very hungry or greedy; desiring much: 非常饑餓的;極爲貪心的;貪婪的: *a ~ appetite;* 極大的胃口; *a ~ reader,* one who reads many books. 求知欲强烈的讀者。 ~**·ly** *adv* in a ~ manner: 貪婪地;貪得無厭地: *He ate his food ~ly.* 他狼吞虎嚥地吃東西。 **vo·racity** /vəˈræsətɪ; vəˈræsətɪ/ *n*

vor·tex /ˈvɔːteks; ˈvɔrtɛks/ *n* (*pl* ~es or vortices /-tɪsiːz; -tɪ,siz/) **1** mass of whirling fluid or wind, esp a whirlpool. 水漩;旋風;(尤指)漩渦。 **2** (fig) whirl of activity; system, pursuit, viewed as sth that tends to absorb things, engross those who engage in it: (喻)忙碌紛亂;被認爲會把事物和參加者捲入的制度或活動: *be drawn into the ~ of politics/war;* 被捲入政治(戰爭)的漩渦; *the ~ of social life/pleasure.* 忙碌紛亂的社交活動(遊樂)。

vo·tary /ˈvəʊtərɪ; ˈvotərɪ/ *n* (*pl* -ries) person who gives up his time and energy to sth, esp to religious work and service: 熱心者;愛好者;支持(尤指宗教工作)者: *a ~ of peace/liberation.* 倡導和平(解放運動)者。

vote /vəʊt; vot/ *n* **1** (right to give an) expression of opinion or will by persons for or against sb or sth, esp by ballot or by putting up of hands: 投票(權);表決(權);選舉(權): *give one's ~ to the more handsome candidate.* 投票給容貌比較好看的候選人。 *Do women have the ~* (ie the franchise) *in your country?* 貴國的婦女有選舉權嗎? *I'm going to the polling-booth to record/cast my ~.* 我現在去

投票所投票。*Mr X proposed a ~ of thanks to the principal speaker*, asked the audience to show, by clapping their hands, that they thanked him. 某先生提議向主講人鼓掌致謝。*The Government received a ~ of confidence*, a majority of ~s was in its favour, to show confidence in its policies, etc. 政府獲得一次信任投票。***put sth to the ~***, decide it by asking for ~s. 提付表決;交付表決。**2** total numbers of ~s (to be) given (eg at a political election): 選票數;總投票數;獲票總數: *Will the Labour ~ increase or decrease at the next election?* 下屆選舉工黨的票數將增加還是減少? **3** money granted, by ~s, for a certain purpose: (爲某項用途經投票決定的)撥款;議決撥款額: *the Army ~*. 給陸軍的撥款。□ *vi, vt* **1** [VP3A] ~ ***for/against sb/sth***, support/oppose by voting. 投票贊成(反對)某人(某事物)。~ ***on sth***, express an opinion on sth by voting. 表決某問題;就某事進行表決。**2** [VP 6A, 12A, 13A] ~ ***sb/sth (for sth)***, grant money (to sb): 撥款(給某人);爲某事而撥款: *~ a sum of money for Education*. 通過一筆教育經費。*Parliament ~d Charles I £100 000 for the Army*. 國會撥給查理一世十萬鎊陸軍經費。**3** [VP15B] ~ ***sth down***, defeat by ~s: 投票否決;投票拒絕: *~ down* (= reject) *a proposal*. 投票否決一項提議。~ ***sth through***, support, approve: 表決通過;投票同意: *~ a Bill through*. 投票通過一項法案。**4** [VP 25] (colloq) declare, by general opinion: (俗)憑大家意見而宣佈;公認: *The new teacher was ~d a pompous bore*, The children gave this as their opinion. 那位新老師被公認是個自大和令人討厭的傢伙。**5** [VP9] suggest, propose: 提議;建議: *I ~ (that) we avoid him in future*. 我建議我們今後躲開他。**~r** *n* person who ~s; person who has the right to ~. 投票者;表決者;選舉者;有投票、表決、選舉權的人。**~·less** *adj* having no ~; not having the right to ~. 未得選票的;無投票權的;無表決權的;無選舉權的。

vo·tive /ˈvəʊtɪv ; ˈvotɪv/ *adj* offered or consecrated in connection with the fulfilment of a vow: 還願的;因誓約而奉獻的: *There were numerous ~ tablets on the walls of the church*. 教堂的牆壁上有無數的還願名牌。

vouch /vaʊtʃ ; vaʊtʃ/ *vi* ~ ***for sb/sth***, be responsible for, express one's confidence in (a person, his honesty, the truth of a statement, etc): 保證;擔保(某人,其誠實,某項記述等的眞實性等): *I am ready to ~ for him/for the truth of his story/for his ability to pay*. 我願替他擔保 (擔保他所言眞實,擔保他有能力付款)。

voucher /ˈvaʊtʃə(r) ; ˈvaʊtʃɚ/ *n* receipt or document showing payment of money, correctness of accounts, etc: 收據;傳票;憑單: *hotel/meal ~s*, (eg as bought from travel agencies) showing that payment has been made in advance. 預付旅館(餐食)費用的憑單。**ˈgift ~**, supplied with some articles (eg petrol, cigarettes), to be exchanged for gifts. (商品,如汽油、香烟等的) 附帶贈券(可換取贈品者)。**ˈluncheon ~**, one supplied by some employers, exchangeable for all or part of a meal (at restaurants which have agreed to accept them). 午餐券(某些雇主發給員工在指定的餐廳用膳者,全部或部分費用已付)。

vouch·safe /vaʊtʃˈseɪf ; vaʊtʃˈsef/ *vt* [VP6A, 7A, 12C] (formal) be kind enough to give (sth), *to do* (sth): (正式用語)惠予(某物);給;賜: *He ~d (me) no reply*. 他不給(我)回話。*He ~d to help*. 他惠予協助。

vow /vaʊ ; vaʊ/ *n* solemn promise or undertaking: 誓;誓約;許願: *ˈmarriage vows;* 婚誓; *a vow of chastity;* 守貞的誓約; *under a vow of celibacy/silence*, having solemnly undertaken not to marry/speak about sth; 發過誓要獨身(保密); *break a vow;* 違反誓約; *perform a vow*, do what one promised. 履行誓言。□ *vt* **1** [VP6A, 7A, 9] make a vow; promise or declare solemnly: 立誓;發誓;許願: *He vowed to avenge the insult/that he would avenge the insult*. 他發誓要報復那次侮辱。*She vowed never to speak to him again*. 她發誓永不再同他講話。*They were forced to vow obedience*. 他們被迫宣誓服從。**2** [VP9] (old use) = avow. (舊用法)宣佈;宣稱;說出。

vowel /ˈvaʊəl ; ˈvaʊəl/ *n* sustainable vocal sound made without audible stopping of the breath, or friction in its passage out through the mouth; letter or symbol used to represent such a sound (eg the letters *a, e, i, o, u*; the symbols /iː, ɪ, e, æ, ɑː, ɒ, ɔː, ʊ, uː, ʌ, ɜː, ə/). 元音;母音;元音或母音的字母或符號(如字母 a, e, i, o, u, 及音標 /iː, ɪ, e, æ, ɑː, ɒ, ɔː, ʊ, uː, ʌ, ɜː, ə/)。⇨ diphthong.

vox /vɒks ; vɑks/ *n* (Lat) voice. (拉丁)聲音。**vox populi** /ˌvɒks ˈpɒpjʊlaɪ ; ˌvɑksˈpɑpjəlaɪ/, the voice of the people; public opinion. 民衆的聲音;輿論。

voy·age /ˈvɔɪɪdʒ ; ˈvɔɪ·ɪdʒ/ *n* journey by water, esp a long one in a ship: 航海;航行(尤指長途者): *a ~ from Mombasa to Colombo;* 由蒙巴薩島至可倫坡的航行; *go on a ~;* 航海去; *on the ~ out/home;* 在出(回)航途中; *on the outward/homeward ~*. 在出(回)航途中。□ *vi* [VP2A, C] go on a ~: 航行;航海: *~ through the South Seas*. 航行穿越南太平洋。**~r** /ˈvɔɪədʒə(r) ; ˈvɔɪ·ɪdʒɚ/ *n* person who makes a ~ (esp of those who, in former times, explored unknown seas). 航行者;航海者(尤指昔時探測未知的海洋者)。

vo·yeur /vwɑːˈjɜː(r) ; ˌvwɑˈjɚ/ *n* person who gets pleasure from looking at sexual objects or the sexual activities of others, esp in secret. 窺淫狂;觀看(尤指秘密地)色情物或他人性行爲獲得樂趣和滿足者。

vul·can·ite /ˈvʌlkənaɪt ; ˈvʌlkənˌaɪt/ *n* [U] hard plastic made from rubber and sulphur. 硬橡皮;硫化橡皮。**vul·can·ize** /ˈvʌlkənaɪz ; ˈvʌlkənˌaɪz/ *vt* [VP6A] treat (rubber) with sulphur at great heat to harden it. 以高溫加硫磺使(橡皮)硬化;使(橡皮)硫化。**vul·can·iz·ation** /ˌvʌlkənaɪˈzeɪʃn *US:* -nɪˈz- ; ˌvʌlkənəˈzeʃən/ *n*

vul·gar /ˈvʌlgə(r) ; ˈvʌlgɚ/ *adj* **1** ill mannered; in bad taste: 粗鄙的;粗俗的: *~ language/behaviour/ideas;* 粗鄙的語言(行爲,觀念); *a ~ person;* 粗俗的人; *a ~ display of wealth*. 一番庸俗的財富誇耀。**2** in common use; generally prevalent: 通俗的;一般流行的: *~ errors/superstitions*. 一般的錯誤 (迷信)。~ **fraction**, one written in the usual way (eg ¾), contrasted with a decimal fraction (eg 0·75). 普通分數(用普通寫法,如 ¾;與小數,如 0·75, 相對)。**the ~ herd**, (contemptuous) the masses of ordinary people. (蔑) 庶民;一般民衆。**the ~ tongue**, the language commonly spoken by the people (formerly, in England, English contrasted with Latin). 本地語;當地語;土語(昔時在英國指英語,與拉丁語相對)。**~·ly** *adv* **vul·garian** /vʌlˈgeərɪən ; vʌlˈgɛrɪən/ *n* ~ person, esp a rich person whose manners and tastes are bad. 粗俗的人;(尤指)粗俗的有錢人。**~·ism** /ˈvʌlgərɪzəm ; ˈvʌlgɚˌɪzəm/ *n* [C] word, phrase, expression, etc used only by ignorant persons; [U] ~ behaviour. 粗俗的語辭;粗鄙的話;粗鄙的行爲。**~·ity** /vʌlˈgærətɪ ; vʌlˈgærətɪ/ *n* (*pl* -ties) [U] ~ behaviour; (*pl*) ~ acts, utterances, etc. 粗俗的行爲;粗鄙;(複)粗俗的動作,言詞等。**~·ize** /ˈvʌlgəraɪz ; ˈvʌlgəˌraɪz/ *vt* [VP6A] make ~. 使粗俗;使通俗化。**~·iz·ation** /ˌvʌlgəraɪˈzeɪʃn *US:* -rɪˈz- ; ˌvʌlgərəˈzeʃən/ *n* [U].

Vul·gate /ˈvʌlgeɪt ; ˈvʌlget/ *n* **the V~**, Latin version of the Bible made in the 4th c. (第四世紀譯成的)拉丁文聖經。

vul·ner·able /ˈvʌlnərəbl ; ˈvʌlnərəbl/ *adj* that is liable to be damaged; not protected against attack: 易受傷害的;易受攻擊的;脆弱的: *find sb's ~ spot;* 發現某人的弱點; *a position ~ to attack;* 易受攻擊的地位; *people who are ~ to criticism*. 易受抨擊的人們。**vul·ner·abil·ity** /ˌvʌlnərəˈbɪlətɪ ; ˌvʌlnərəˈbɪlətɪ/ *n*

vul·pine /ˈvʌlpaɪn ; ˈvʌlpaɪn/ *adj* of, like, a fox; crafty. 狐狸的;似狐狸的;狡猾的。

vul·ture /ˈvʌltʃə(r) ; ˈvʌltʃɚ/ *n* **1** large bird, usu with head and neck almost bare of feathers, that lives on the flesh of dead animals. 兀鷹。⇨ the illus at prey. 參看 prey 之插圖。 **2** greedy person who profits from the misfortunes of others. (利用他人的不幸而謀取利益的)貪婪者。

vulva /ˈvʌlvə ; ˈvʌlvə/ *n* opening of the female genitals. 陰戶;陰門。⇨ the illus at reproduce. 參看 reproduce 之插圖。

vy·ing /ˈvaɪɪŋ ; ˈvaɪɪŋ/ *pres p* of vie.

Ww

W, w /ˈdʌbljuː ; ˈdʌbljʊ/ (*pl* W's, w's) the 23rd letter of the English alphabet. 英文字母的第二十三個字母。

wad /wɒd ; wɑd/ *n* **1** lump of soft material for keeping things apart or in place, or to stop up a hole. 塊狀軟物;塡料(用以使東西隔離,固定,或用以塡洞)。 **2** collection of documents or banknotes folded or rolled together. 一捲或一疊(文件或鈔票)。□ *vt* (-dd-) stuff with a wad; hold in place with a wad; line (a garment, etc) with soft material (usu cotton or wool): (以塡料)塡塞;固定;以軟物(棉、毛等)襯塡(衣服等): *a wadded jacket/dressing-gown/quilt.* 塡有棉或毛的短外套(晨衣,棉被)。**wad·ding** /ˈwɒdɪŋ ; ˈwɑdɪŋ/ *n* [U] soft material, esp raw cotton or felt, used for packing, lining things, etc. 軟物;塡料(尤指用於包裝、襯物等的生棉或毛氈)。

waddle /ˈwɒdl ; ˈwɑdl̩/ *vi* [VP2A, C] walk with slow steps and a sideways roll, as a duck does: 蹣跚而行;搖擺而行(腳步緩慢而橫擺如鴨子般走路): *The stout old man ~d across the road.* 那肥胖的老人搖擺地橫過馬路。□ *n* (*sing* only) this kind of walk. (僅用單數)蹣跚;搖擺的步態。

wade /weɪd ; wed/ *vi, vt* [VP2A, C, 6A] **1** walk with an effort (through water, mud or anything that makes progress difficult); walk across (sth) in this way: (從水、泥濘或其他阻碍物中)費力行走;涉過: *He ~d through the weeds on the bank and then into and across the stream.* 他費力地穿過岸上的雜草,然後涉過小河。 *Can we ~ the brook,* cross it by wading? 我們能涉水走過這小河嗎? *The boy ~d* (= read slowly and without interest) *through the dull book.* 那男孩費力地閱讀這本枯燥的書。 **ˈwading bird,** long-legged water-bird that ~s (opp to web-footed birds that swim). 涉禽(涉水的長腿水鳥,與游水的蹼足鳥相對而言)。 **2** *~ in,* make a vigorous attack. 作猛烈攻擊。 *~ into sth,* attack sth vigorously. 猛烈攻擊(某物)。 **~r** *n* **1** wading bird (⇨ above). 涉禽(參看上列之 wading bird)。 **2** (*pl*) waterproof boots reaching the hips, used by anglers when wading in streams. (複)(釣魚者涉水時穿著的)高統防水靴。

wadi /ˈwɒdɪ ; ˈwɑdɪ/ *n* (*pl* ~s) (in the Middle East, Arabia, northern Africa) rocky water-course dry except after a heavy fall of rain. (中東,阿拉伯,北非等處的)多岩石的乾涸河床(下大雨後才有水);河道;谷。

wa·fer /ˈweɪfə(r) ; ˈwefɚ/ *n* **1** thin flat biscuit (eg as eaten with ice-cream). 薄餅乾(如連同冰淇淋吃者)。 **2** small round piece of bread used in Holy Communion. (領聖體所用的)小圓餅;聖餅。

waffle¹ /ˈwɒfl ; ˈwɑfl̩/ *n* small cake made of batter baked in a special kind of griddle (*a ˈ~-iron*) with two parts hinged together. (用麵粉、蛋、牛奶等混合製成的)雞蛋餅(烘此餅的鐵模,稱爲 ~-iron)。

waffle² /ˈwɒfl ; ˈwɑfl̩/ *vi* [VP2A, C] (GB colloq) talk vaguely, unnecessarily, and without much result: (英俗)作模糊、不必要、而無結果的談話;含糊而言;說無聊話: *How that man does ~ on!* 那個人怎麼那樣喋喋不休盡講一些無聊的話? *What's she waffling abou tnow?* 她現在在瞎說些什麼? □ *n* [U] utterance which (even when it sounds impressive) means little or nothing. 動聽而無內容的話;無聊話。

waft /wɒft *US:* wæft ; wæft/ *vt* [VP6A] carry lightly and smoothly through the air or over water: 使飄浮;使飄蕩;使飄流: *The scent of the flowers was ~ed to us by the breeze.* 微風送來了花香。□ *n* [C] **1** breath of air, scent, etc. 一陣風;一陣香氣等。 **2** waving movement. 搖動;飄動;浮動。

wag¹ /wæg ; wæg/ *vt, vi* (-gg-) [VP6A, 2A, C] (cause to) move from side to side or up and down: (使)搖擺;搖動;上下移動: *The dog wagged its tail.* 狗搖尾。*The dog's tail wagged.* 狗尾擺動。*Don't wag your finger at me,* show disapproval in this way. 不要指責我。*The news set tongues/chins/beards wagging,* caused people to talk (esp of sth scandalous). 那則新聞引起人們議論紛紛(尤指關於某項醜聞)。 **ˈwag·tail** *n* kinds of small bird with a long tail that wags constantly when the bird is standing. 鶺鴒(站立時其長尾搖動不停的小鳥)。□ *n* wagging movement: 搖擺;搖動: *with a wag of the tail.* 搖擺着尾巴。

wag² /wæg ; wæg/ *n* merry person, full of amusing sayings and fond of practical jokes. (好說笑及惡作劇的)詼諧者。**wag·gery** /ˈwægərɪ ; ˈwægərɪ/ *n* (*pl* -ries) [U] behaviour or talk of a wag; (*pl*) acts, remarks, etc of a wag. 詼諧;惡作劇;(複)詼諧話;詼諧的動作。**wag·gish** /ˈwægɪʃ ; ˈwægɪʃ/ *adj* of or like a wag; done in a joking way. 詼諧的;滑稽的;惡作劇的;諧謔地做出的: *waggish tricks/remarks.* 惡作劇的詭計(滑稽的話)。 **wag·gish·ly** *adv* **wag·gish·ness** *n*

wage¹ /weɪdʒ ; wedʒ/ *n* **1** (now usu *pl* except in certain phrases and when attrib) payment made or received (usu weekly) for work or services: (除用於某些片語中及作形容用法外,現在通常用複數形)工資;薪給(通常按週計算): *His ~s are £50 a week.* 他的工資每週五十鎊。 *We expect a fair day's ~ for a fair day's work.* 我們做好一天的工作,希望能拿到一天應得的工資。 *He takes his ~s/his ˈ~-packet home to his wife every Friday.* 每星期五他把薪水(薪水袋)帶回家交給妻子。 *The postal workers have asked for a ˈ~ increase/rise of £5 a week.* 郵務人員要求週薪提高五鎊。 ⇨ fee(1), pay¹, salary. **living ~,** one which allows a man to live without fear of hunger and hardship. 够維持生活的薪資。 **minimum ~,** guaranteed basic level for ~s in an industry or country. 最低工資(某項工業或某一國家所保障的工資最低基準)。 **ˈ~-claim** *n* ~ demanded from the management for workers by their trade union. (工會爲工人向經理部門所作的)工資要求。 **ˈ~-earner** *n* person who works for ~s (contrasted with the salaried classes). 工資勞動者(與薪水階級相對)。 **ˈ~-freeze,** ⇨ freeze, *n*(2). **2** (old use; *pl* in form with *sing v*) reward or requital: (舊用法;用複數時接單數動詞)報酬;報償;代價: *The ~s of sin is death.* 罪惡的代價是死。

wage² /weɪdʒ ; wedʒ/ *vt* [VP6A] carry on, engage in (*war, a campaign*). 進行;從事(戰爭、戰役、運動)。

wa·ger /ˈweɪdʒə(r) ; ˈwedʒɚ/ *vt, vi* [VP6A, 11, 14, 12C, 2A] bet: 打賭: *~ £5 on a horse.* 對某一匹馬下注五鎊。 *I'm ready to ~ you a pound that....* 我願爲…同你打賭一鎊。□ *n* bet: 賭注: *lay/make a ~;* 下注; *take up* (= accept) *a ~.* 接受打賭。

waggle /ˈwægl ; ˈwægl̩/ *vt, vi* = wag¹.

wag·gon (US usu **wagon**) /ˈwægən ; ˈwægən/ *n* **1** four-wheeled vehicle for carrying goods, pulled by horses or oxen. 四輪運貨馬(牛)車。⇨ cart. *on* *the ('water) ~*, (colloq) not drinking alcoholic liquors. (俗)不飲酒的。 **2** (US 美 = *freight car*) open railway truck (eg for coal). 鐵路敞篷貨車(如運煤車)。**'station-~** *n* (US) (美) = estate-car. **~er** *n* man in charge of a ~ and its horses. 運貨馬車伕。

wa·gon-lit /ˌvæɡɒn ˈliː ; ˌvagōˈli/ *n* (*pl* wagons-lit pronunciation unchanged) (複數發音不變) sleeping-car (as on European railways). (歐洲鐵路上行駛的)臥車。

wag·tail /ˈwæɡteɪl ; ˈwæɡˌtel/ ⇨ wag[1].

waif /weɪf ; wef/ *n* homeless person, esp a child: 無家可歸者;(尤指)流浪兒童: *~s and strays,* homeless and abandoned children. 流浪兒童們。

wail /weɪl ; wel/ *vi, vt* [VP2A, B, C, 6A] **1** cry or complain in a loud, usu shrill, voice: (大而通常尖聲地)哭;哭泣;哭號;哀泣: ~ (*over*) *one's misfortunes;* 爲不幸而哀泣; *an ambulance racing through the streets with sirens ~ing.* 救護車穿過街道,發出尖銳的嗚嗚聲。*She was ~ing for her lost child.* 她爲她死去的孩子哀號。 **2** (of the wind) make sounds like a person ~ing. (指風)發哀號聲;發呼嘯聲。□ *n* ~ing cry; lament: 哭;哭泣;哀悼: *the ~s of a new-born child.* 初生嬰兒的哭叫聲。

wain /weɪn ; wen/ *n* (old use, or poet) large farm wagon.(舊用法或詩)(農場上使用的)大馬車。**Charles's W~**, the constellation of stars also called the Plough and the Great Bear. 北斗七星。

wain·scot /ˈweɪnskət ; ˈwenskət/ *n* wooden panelling (usu on the lower half of the walls of a room). 壁板(通常指室內牆壁下半截的木板)。**~ed** *adj* lined with ~: 裝以壁板的: *a ~ed room.* 裝有壁板的房間。

waist /weɪst ; west/ *n* **1** part of the body between the ribs and the hips: 腰;腰部: *wear a sash round the ~;* 在腰際圍飾帶; *measure 30 inches round the ~.* 腰圍(量起來有)三十吋; *The workmen were stripped to the ~,* were wearing nothing above the ~. 工人們赤裸着上身。*That man has no ~,* is so stout that he has no narrowing at the ~ as in a normal figure. 那人胖得看不出腰來。 ⇨ the illus at trunk. 參看 trunk 之插圖。**'~-band** *n* band on a garment (eg a skirt) fitting round the ~. 衣服(如裙)的腰帶;束腰帶。**ˌ~-'deep** *adj, adv* up to the ~: 深及腰部的(地): *~-deep in the water;* 在深及腰部的水中; *wade ~-deep into a stream.* 涉水走入深及腰部的小河。**ˌ~-'high** *adj, adv* high enough to reach the ~: 高達腰部的(地): *The wheat was ~-high.* 小麥長得高達腰部。**'~-line** *n* line round the body at the smallest part of the ~: 腰線;腰圍: *a girl with a neat ~-line.* 腰圍纖美的女郎。**2** that part of a garment that goes round the ~; (US 美 *'shirt-~*) garment, or part of a garment, covering the body from the shoulders to the ~. 衣服的腰部;胸衣(遮覆肩至腰部者);衣服的上身部分。**3** middle and narrow part: 中間的細狹部分: *the ~ of a ship,* between the forecastle and quarter-deck; 船的中間部分(前後甲板之間者); *the ~ of a violin/an hour-glass.* 小提琴(沙漏時計)的腰部。**~-coat** /ˈweɪskəʊt *US:* ˈweskət ; ˈwestˌkot/ *n* close-fitting sleeveless garment worn under a coat or jacket, buttoned down the front (called *vest* by tailors, and in the US). 背心;馬甲(英國的裁縫及美國稱之爲 vest)。

wait[1] /weɪt ; wet/ *n* **1** act or time of waiting: 等;等待;等候的時間: *We had a long ~ for the bus.* 我們等候公車很久。*I don't like these long ~s.* 我不喜歡這種長時間的等候。**2** [U] **lie in ~ for;** (less usu) (較不常作) **lay ~ for,** be in hiding in order to attack, etc: 埋伏以待;伏擊: *The highwayman lay in ~ for the stage-coach.* 那强盜等候伏擊驛馬車。 **3** (*pl*) **the ~s,** persons who go from house to house singing carols at Christmas. (複)聖誕節沿門唱讚美詩者;報佳音者。

wait[2] /weɪt ; wet/ *vi, vt* **1** [VP2A, B, C, 3A, 4A] **~ (for),** stay where one is, delay acting, until sb or sth comes or until sth happens: 等;等候;期待: *Please ~ a minute.* 請等一會兒。*W~ for me, please.* 請等一等我。*How long have you been ~ing?* 你已經等候多久了? *We are ~ing for the rain to stop.* 我們在等待雨停。 *We are ~ing for better weather.* 我們在期待較好的天氣。*We ~ed* (in order) *to see what would happen.* 我們等着看會發生什麼事情。*They say that everything comes to those who ~.* 人們說能耐心等候的人自有良機。**keep sb ~ing,** fail to meet him or be ready at the appointed time: 叫人等;讓人等候;在約定的時間不能見某人或未準備妥當: *His wife never keeps him ~ing.* 他的妻子從不讓他等候。**~ up (for sb),** stay up, not go to bed. (爲等某人而)熬夜;(爲某人)等着不睡。**No ~ing,** warning (indicated by the sign ⊘) that motor-vehicles must not stop at the side of the roadway. 禁止停車(警告機動車輛不得在路邊停車,以⊘表示之)。**2** [VP6A] (= *await*) ~ for; ~ and watch for: 等候;等待;守候: *He is ~ing his opportunity.* 他在等候機會。*He always expects me to ~ his convenience,* until it is convenient for him (to do sth). 他總是希望我等到他方便的時候(做某事)。*You must ~ your turn,* ~ until it is your turn. 你必須等到輪到你的時候。 **3** [VP6A, 14] **~ (for),** defer, postpone (a meal): 耽擱;延緩(餐食): *Don't ~ dinner for me.* 不要爲我而延緩開飯。 **4** [VP3A] **~ on/upon sb, (a)** act as a servant to, fetch and carry things for. 服侍;伺候。**~ on sb hand and foot,** attend to his every need: 伺候某人無微不至: *A Japanese wife was formerly expected to ~ upon her husband hand and foot.* 從前日本太太被認爲應該無微不至地伺候丈夫。**(b)** (old use) pay a visit to: (舊用法)訪問;拜訪: *Our commercial agent will ~ upon you next Monday.* 我們的商務代理將於下週一拜訪你。 **5** [VP3A] **~ at/on,** act as a servant at table, serving food, clearing away dishes, etc: 伺候開飯(端菜、清理碗盤等): *~ at table* (US 美 = *~ on table*). 伺候開飯。 **6** **'~·ing-list,** list of persons who cannot be served, treated, etc now, but who will be served, etc later, if possible: 等候者名單(等待機會接受服務、診療等之人的名單): *put sb on a ~ing-list for theatre tickets/an appointment, etc.* 把某人列入申請戲票(某項約會等)的等候名單中。**'~·ing-room** *n* room in a railway-station, etc used by people who are ~ing for trains; room (eg in a doctor's or dentist's house or office) where people ~ until they can be attended to. 候車室;候診室;等候室。**~er** *n* man who ~s at table in a restaurant, hotel dining-room, etc. (餐廳,旅館餐室等的)侍者;侍應生;跑堂的。**~·ress** /ˈweɪtrɪs ; ˈwetrɪs/ *n* woman ~er. 女侍者;女侍應生。

waive /weɪv ; wev/ *vt* [VP6A] (say that one will) not insist on (a right or claim): 放棄;不堅持;聲明放棄(權利或要求): *~ a privilege/the age-limit.* 放棄特權(摒棄年齡的限制)。 **~r** /ˈweɪvə(r) ; ˈwevɚ/ *n* (legal) (written statement) waiving (a right, etc): (法律)放棄;棄權;棄權書: *sign a waiver of claims against sb.* 簽字於放棄對某人作要求的文件。

wake[1] /weɪk ; wek/ *vi, vt* (*pt* woke /wəʊk ; wok/ or ~d, *pp* woken /ˈwəʊkən ; ˈwokən/ or ~d) **1** [VP2A, C, 4B] **~ (up),** stop sleeping: 醒;不再睡: *What time do you usually ~* (*up*) ? 你通常什麼時候醒來? *I woke early.* 我醒得很早。*Has the baby ~d/woken yet?* 那嬰兒已醒了嗎?*He woke up with a start.* 他一驚而醒。 *He woke to find himself in prison.* 他醒來發現自己在監獄中。 **2** [VP6A, 15B] **~ sb (up),** cause to stop sleeping: 打斷睡眠;喚醒;吵醒: *Don't ~ the baby.* 不要弄醒嬰兒。*The noise woke me* (*up*). 那鬧聲把我吵醒了。*They were making enough noise to ~ the dead.* 他們吵鬧聲大得能把死人吵醒。 **3** [VP6A, 15B] **~ sb (up),** stir up; rouse from inactivity, inattention, etc: 激發;使奮起;喚起注意: *He needs someone to ~ him up,* stir him from his sloth, stir him to activity. 他需要人激勵。*The incident ~d memories of his school-days.*

那件事喚起他對學生時代的記憶。 **4** [VP6A] disturb with noise; cause to re-echo: 以鬧聲擾亂;使再反響;引起再回聲: *~ echoes in a mountain valley.* 在山谷中引起反覆回響。**wak·ing** *adj* being awake: 醒的: *in his waking hours,* while awake; 在他醒着的時候; *waking or sleeping,* while awake or asleep. 醒時或睡時。 **waken** /ˈweɪkən ; ˈwekən/ *vt, vi* [VP6A, 2A] (cause to) ~. (使)醒;喚醒。 **~·ful** /-fl ; -fəl/ *adj* unable to sleep; with little sleep: 不能入睡的;睡眠少的: *pass a ~ful night.* 一夜未眠。

wake[2] /weɪk ; wek/ *n* **1** (usu *pl;* 通常用複數; often 常作 **ˈW~s Week**) annual holiday in N England, esp in the manufacturing towns of Lancashire. (英格蘭北部,尤指蘭開郡工業都市的)每年一度的假日。 **2** (in Ireland) all-night watch by a corpse before burial, with lamentations and drinking of alcoholic liquor. (在愛爾蘭)葬禮前的守屍;守喪(徹夜伴守屍旁,並時作哀歌與飲酒)。

wake[3] /weɪk ; wek/ *n* track left by a ship on smooth water, eg as made by propellers. 航跡;船跡(如推進器在靜水上留下者)。 ***in the ~ of,*** after; following: 在…之後; 追隨;隨着: *Traders came in the ~ of the explorers.* 商人們在探險隊後接踵而至。

wale /weɪl ; wel/ *n* alternative spelling (esp US) of weal[2] or welt. (尤美)爲 weal[2] 或 welt 的另一種拼法。

walk[1] /wɔːk ; wɔk/ *n* [C] **1** journey on foot, esp for pleasure or exercise: 步行;(尤指爲遊樂或運動所作的)散步: *go for a ~;* 去散步; *have a pleasant ~ across the fields.* 做一次越過田野的愉快散步。*The station is a short ~/ten minutes' ~ from my house.* 車站離我家衹有幾步路(步行十分鐘可到)。 **2** manner or style of walking: 步態;步法: *His horse slowed to a ~,* ie after trotting or galloping. 他的馬(跑過一陣以後)慢下來改以慢步行進。 *After running for two miles he dropped into a ~,* began to walk. 他跑了兩哩以後,開始步行。 *I recognized him at once by his ~,* his way of walking. 從走路的樣子我立刻認出是他。 **3** path or route for walking: 步道;人行道;散步之處:*my favourite ~s in the neighbourhood.* 附近我喜歡去散步的地方。 **4** ***~ of life,*** calling, profession, occupation: 行業; 職業;身分: *They interviewed people from all ~s of life.* 他們會晤了各行各業的人。

walk[2] /wɔːk ; wɔk/ *vi, vt* **1** [VP2A, B, C] (of persons) move by putting forward each foot in turn, not having both feet off the ground at once, ⇨ run; (of animals) move at the slowest pace, ⇨ trot, gallop: (指人)行走;步行;(指動物)慢步走: *We ~ed five miles.* 我們走了五哩路。*Shall we ride or ~?* 我們是騎馬還是步行? *How old are babies when they learn to ~?* 嬰兒多大開始學步? *He was ~ing up and down the station platform.* 他在火車站的月臺上走來走去。**ˈ~-about** *n* **(a)** (Australian sl, of aborigines in the desert) journey. (澳洲俚,指沙漠中的土著)旅行; 遊蕩。 **(b)** (colloq) occasion when a celebrity ~s round meeting people informally. (俗)名人或重要人物非正式地在人羣中周旋的場合。 ***~ away from,*** beat easily in a contest: 在比賽中輕易勝過: *Smith ~ed away from all his competitors,* beat them easily. 史密斯輕易地擊敗了他所有的對手。 Hence, 由此產生, **ˈ~·away** *n* easily won contest. 輕易獲勝的比賽。(⇨ ~-over below). (參看下列的 ~-over)。 ***~ away with sth,*** win sth easily: 輕易地贏得某物;輕易地獲勝: *Newcombe ~ed away with the match.* 紐康姆輕易地贏了那場比賽。 ***~ off with sth,*** (colloq) carry off; take (either on purpose or unintentionally): (俗)(故意或無意地)携走;拿走;偸走: *Someone has ~ed off with my umbrella.* 有人把我的傘拿走了。 ***~ into,*** (sl) (俚) **(a)** eat heartily of: 開懷地吃; 大吃: *~ into a meat-pie.* 大吃肉餡餅。 **(b)** abuse; scold. 譴責;斥責。 **(c)** (colloq) meet with through inattention: (俗)因疏忽或不留心而遭遇: *He just ~ed into the ambush.* 他恰好中了埋伏。 ***~ on,*** play a non-speaking part on the stage: 在舞臺上扮演不講話的角色: (attrib) (形容用法) *a ˌ~-ˈon part.* 無臺詞的角色。 ***~ out,*** (colloq) go on strike: (俗)罷工: *The men in this factory ~ed out yesterday.* 這工廠的工人昨天罷工。 Hence, 由此產生, **ˈ~-out** *n* (workers') strike. (工人的)罷工。 ***~ out on sb,*** (sl) abandon or desert him. (俚)遺棄某人。 ***~ out with sb,*** (dated colloq) court; have as a sweetheart. (過時俗語)追求某人;以某人做情人。 ***~ over sb,*** defeat him easily. 輕易擊敗某人。Hence, 由此產生, **ˈ~-over** *n* easy victory; contest in which there is little or no opposition: 輕易獲得的勝利;對手不强的競賽: *The race was a ~over for Jones.* 瓊斯輕而易舉地贏了這場賽跑。 ***~ up,*** **(a)** invitation to enter (eg as given by men outside a circus). 請進(如請人進去看馬戲等)。 **(b)** ~ along: 沿…行走: *as I was ~ing up Oxford Street.* 當我沿牛津街走的時候。**(c)** ~ upstairs. 走上樓。 Hence, 由此產生, *a ˈ~-up flat,* one in a building without a lift. 沒有電梯的公寓。 **(d)** ***~ up (to sb/sth),*** approach: 走近;趨近: *A stranger ~ed up to me and asked me the time.* 一位陌生人走近我,問我(當時的)時間。 **2** [VP6A, 15A, B] cause to ~: 使步行;使行走;使慢步: *Horses should be ~ed for a while after a race.* 馬在比賽後應讓它作緩步行走。*He ~ed his horse up the hill.* 他驅馬走上小山。*He put his arm round me and ~ed me away/off.* 他用一隻臂摟着我,帶我走開。 ***~ sb off his feet/legs,*** tire him out by making him ~ far. 使某人走得筋疲力竭。 **3** [VP6A] go over on foot: 步行於;走過: *I have ~ed this district for miles round.* 我走遍了這附近好幾哩內的地區。 **4** (with various *nn*): (與名詞連用): *~ the boards,* be an actor; 作演員; *~ the wards,* be a medical student; 習醫;作醫學院學生; *~ the plank,* (of a person captured by pirates in former times) be compelled to ~ blindfolded into the sea along a plank laid over the ship's side; (指昔時被海盜虜獲的人)蒙着眼睛被迫走上突出於舷外的木板而終落入海中; *~ the streets,* be a prostitute (*a ˈstreet-~er*). 做妓女;爲娼。**~er** *n* person who ~s, esp for exercise or enjoyment. 行走者;步行者;(尤指)散步者。 **~·ing** *n* (in compounds) (用於複合字中) *ˈ~ing-shoes,* strong ones for ~ing in; 走路穿的結實鞋子; *ˈ~ing-stick,* stick used in, or carried while, ~ing; 手杖; *ˈ~ing-tour,* holiday spent ~ing from place to place. 假日徒步旅行。

walkie-talkie /ˌwɔːkɪ ˈtɔːkɪ ; ˈwɔkɪˈtɔkɪ/ *n* (colloq) portable two-way radio set. (俗)手提式無線電對話機;步話機。

wall /wɔːl ; wɔl/ *n* **1** continuous, usu vertical, solid structure of stone, brick, concrete, wood, etc forming one of the sides of a building or room, or used to enclose, divide or protect sth (including land): 牆;壁;垣: *The castle ~s are very thick.* 那城堡的牆很厚。 *Hang the picture on that ~.* 把這幅畫掛在那邊的牆上。*Some old towns have ~s right round them.* 有些古老的城市周圍有城牆。 *Dry-stone ~s* (ie of stones not fixed in mortar) *extend across the moors in some parts of England.* 祇用石塊堆成 (無灰泥黏合) 的牆, 散見於英格蘭某些地方的曠野中。 *Fruit trees are often trained against garden ~s for protection and warmth.* 果樹常經修整,使靠近果園的圍牆生長,以利保護和保暖。 ***with one's back to the ~,*** in a position where retreat or escape is impossible; at bay. 處於無法撤退或逃走的境地;作困獸鬪。 ***be/go up the ~,*** (sl) be/become furious, distracted. (俚) (變得)狂怒或發狂。 ***bang/run one's head against a (brick) ~,*** attempt to do sth that is clearly impossible. 試圖做顯然不可能的事情。 ***see through a brick ~,*** have wonderful vision or insight. 有眼光;有深刻的領悟力。 **2** (fig) sth suggesting or resembling a ~: (喩)似牆之物: *a ~ of fire;* 一道似牆的火;火牆; *a mountain ~;* 山壁; *the ~s of the chest,* the enclosing tissue and ribs; 胸壁; *the abdominal ~.* 腹壁。 **3** side (contrasted with the centre) of the street: 街道的靠牆部分;路側(與路中心相對): (chiefly fig) (主要爲比喻用法) ***go to the ~,*** be pushed aside as weak or helpless, get the worst of it in competition. 失敗;敗北;被推在一旁。***push / drive sb to the ~,*** defeat him. 使某人陷入困境;使某人束手無策;擊敗某人。**4** (compounds) (複合字) **'~-flower** *n* **(a)** common garden plant with (usu) brownish-red or orange sweet-smelling flowers. 香羅蘭;牆花(園藝植物,通常開褐紅色或橘紅色而有香味的花)。**(b)** person who sits out dances because of a lack of partners. 壁花;因無舞伴僅在一旁作壁上觀的人。**'~-painting** *n* [C] painting on a ~, esp a fresco. 牆上的畫;(尤指)壁畫。**'~-paper** *n* [U] paper, usu with a coloured design, for covering the ~s of rooms. 糊牆紙;壁紙。□ *vt* **1** (usu *pp*) surround with a ~ or ~s: (通常用過去分詞)圍以牆: *~ed cities;* 有城牆的城市; *a ~ed garden.* 有圍牆的花園。 **2** [VP15B] ~ ***sth up / off,*** fill or close up with bricks, etc: 以磚等堵塞;填塞;隔開: *~ up a window / opening;* 堵塞窗子(開口); *~ off part of a room.* 隔開房間的一部分。

wal·laby /ˈwɒləbɪ ; ˈwaləbi/ *n* (*pl* -bies) sorts of small kangaroo. 小袋鼠。

wal·lah /ˈwɒlə ; ˈwalə/ *n* (sl, in India) person employed about or concerned with sth. (俚,在印度)受僱做某事的人;從事某事的人。

wal·let /ˈwɒlɪt ; ˈwalɪt/ *n* folding pocket-case, usu leather, for papers, banknotes, etc (US 美 = *pocket-book*). 小夾子;錢夾;皮夾。

wall-eyed /ˌwɔːl ˈaɪd ; ˈwɔlˌaɪd/ *adj* having eyes that show an abnormal amount of white (eg as caused by a squint). 露出的眼白較一般爲多的(如由斜眼所致者);白星眼的。

wal·lop /ˈwɒləp ; ˈwaləp/ *vt* (sl or hum) beat severely; hit hard. (俚或諧)痛毆;重擊。□ *n* heavy blow; crash: 重擊;擊潰;轟隆聲: *Down he went with a ~!* 他轟隆一聲摔倒了! **~·ing** *adj* big; thumping: 大的;極大的: *What a ~ing lie!* 多大的謊言啊! □ *n* defeat: 擊潰;失敗: *Our football team got a ~ing.* 我們的足球隊大敗。

wal·low /ˈwɒləʊ ; ˈwalo/ *vi* [VP2A, C] roll about (in mud, dirty water, etc): (在泥,髒水等中)打滾: *pigs ~ing in the mire;* 在泥沼中打滾的豬; (fig) take gross delight in (sth sensual): (喻)沉迷於(聲色的享樂): *~ing in sensual pleasures.* 沉迷於聲色的享樂。***be '~ing in money,*** (colloq) be very rich. (俗)很富有。□ *n* place to which animals (eg buffaloes) go regularly to ~. (水牛等動物經常前往打滾的)泥沼;水坑。

Wall Street /ˈwɔːl striːt ; ˈwɔlˌstrit/ *n* (used for) the American money-market: 華爾街;(指)美國金融市場: *Shares rose sharply on ~ yesterday.* 昨天美國金融市場的股票暴漲。

wal·nut /ˈwɔːlnʌt ; ˈwɔlnət/ *n* [C] (tree producing a) nut with an edible in a hard shell; [U] the wood of this tree, used (esp as a veneer) for making furniture. 胡桃;核桃;胡桃樹;胡桃木(用於製家具,尤用作鑲飾家具的薄板)。

wal·rus /ˈwɔːlrəs; ˈwɔlrəs/ *n* large sea-animal of the arctic regions with two long tusks, ⇨ the illus at sea: 海象(參看 sea 之插圖): *a ~ moustache,* (colloq) one of which the ends come downwards like the tusks of a ~. (俗)(末端下垂如海象牙似的)海象鬍鬚。

waltz /wɔːls *US:* wɔːlts ; wɔlts/ *n* [C] (music in ¾ time for a) ballroom dance. 華爾茲舞;華爾茲舞曲。□ *vi, vt* **1** [VP2A, C] dance a ~: 跳華爾茲舞: *She ~es divinely.* 她的華爾茲舞跳得好極了。~ ***in / out / into / out of,*** dance, run or walk (in, out, etc) gaily: 愉快地舞動;愉快地跑或走: *She ~ed into the room and out again.* 她愉快地走進房間,又愉快地走了出來。 **2** [VP15A] cause to ~: 使跳華爾茲舞: *He ~ed her round the room.* 他引導她在屋裡跳華爾茲舞。

wam·pum /ˈwɒmpəm ; ˈwampəm/ *n* [U] shells threaded like beads and used as ornaments by N American Indians (and formerly used as money). 貝殼串珠(北美印第安人用作裝飾品,昔時並用作錢幣)。

wan /wɒn ; wan/ *adj* (-nn-) **1** (of a person, his looks, etc) looking ill, sad, tired, anxious: (指人,其容貌等)有病容,愁容,倦容,憂容等的;蒼白的;無力的: *a wan smile.* 微弱的一笑。 **2** (of light, the sky) pale; not bright. (指光,天空)淡弱的;陰暗的。**wan·ly** *adv* **wan·ness** /ˈwɒnnɪs ; ˈwannɪs/ *n*

wand /wɒnd ; wand/ *n* **1** slender stick or rod as used by a conjurer, fairy or magician; baton(2). (咒法家,仙子,或魔術師用的)杖;棍;棒;魔杖。 **2** rod or staff carried as a symbol of authority (eg by an usher, steward or sheriff on ceremonial occasions). 權標(表示職權的官杖,如儀禮中的引座員、招待員或執法官所用者)。

wan·der /ˈwɒndə(r) ; ˈwandɚ/ *vi, vt* **1** [VP2A, B, C, 6A] go from place to place without any special purpose or destination: 漫遊;漫步;漂泊;徘徊: *~ over the countryside;* 在鄉間漫步; *~ up and down the road aimlessly;* 無目的地在路上徘徊; *~ (through / over) the world.* 漫遊世界。*Kevin ~ed in to see me this morning,* paid me a casual visit. 克文今晨順便來看我。**2** [VP2A, C] leave the right path or direction: 離開正途或正確的方向;迷失: *Some of the sheep have ~ed away,* are lost. 有些羊走失了。*We ~ed (for) miles and miles in the mist.* 我們在霧中迷失了很多哩路。 **3** [VP2A, C] be absent-minded; allow the thoughts to go from subject to subject: 心不在焉;胡思亂想: *Don't ~ from the subject / point.* 不要岔離本題(主旨)。*His mind is ~ing.* 他心不在焉。*Don't let your thoughts ~.* 不要胡思亂想。*His mind / thoughts ~ed back to his college days.* 他回想到他的大學時代。**~er** *n* person or animal that ~s. 漫遊者;徘徊者;迷失的人;走失的動物。**~·ings** *n pl* **1** long travels; journeys: 長途旅行;漫遊: *tell the story of one's ~ings.* 敘述自己的漫遊經歷。 **2** confused speech during illness (esp high fever). (病中,尤指發高燒時,的)胡言亂語;囈語。

wan·der·lust /ˈwɒndəlʌst ; ˈwandɚˌlʌst/ *n* [U] strong desire to travel. 強烈的旅行慾;旅行癖;流浪癖。

wane /weɪn ; wen/ *vi* [VP2A] **1** (of the moon) show a decreasing bright area after full moon. (指月亮)虧;缺;呈下弦(月)。⇨ wax² (1). **2** become less or weaker: 減少;減弱;減小;衰弱: *His strength / influence / reputation is waning.* 他的力量(勢力,名聲)漸弱了。□ *n* esp 尤用於 ***on the ~,*** process of waning. 減小;變弱;衰微。

wangle /ˈwæŋgl ; ˈwæŋgl/ *vt* [VP6A] (sl) get, arrange sth, by using improper influence, by trickery, plausible persuasion, etc: (俚)以不正當的影響力、欺詐、巧言等取得或處理某事物: *~ an extra week's holiday.* 不正當地取得一週的額外假期。□ *n* act of wangling: 狡詐行爲;不正當手段: *get sth by a ~.* 藉不正當手段獲得某物。

wank /wæŋk ; wæŋk/ *vi* [VP2A] (GB vulg sl) masturbate. (英鄙俚)手淫。□ *n* [C] instance of masturbation. 手淫。

wanna /ˈwanə ; ˈwanə/ (US sl) (美俚) = want to. ⇨ want² (2).

want¹ /wɒnt *US:* wɔːnt ; want/ *n* **1** [U] lack; scarcity; state of being absent: 缺乏;稀少;缺少的狀態: *The earthquake victims are suffering for ~ of food and medical supplies.* 地震的災民缺乏食物及藥物。*The plants died from ~ of water.* 這些植物因缺水而死。*Your work shows ~ of thought / care.* 你的工作顯示你缺乏思想(不够細心)。 **2** [U] need; absence of some necessary thing: 需要;匱乏: *The house is in ~ of repair.* 這房子需要修理了。*We may one day be in ~,* very poor. 我們也許有一天會很窮。 **3** [C] (usu *pl*) desire for sth as necessary to life, happiness, etc; thing to be desired: (通常用複數)欲望;欲獲得之物: *He is a man of few ~s.* 他是一個欲望很少的人。*We can supply all your ~s.* 我們可以供應你所需要的一切東西。 *The book* *meets a long-felt ~*, sth that has been needed for a long time. 這本書滿足了人們久已感到的需要。

want² /wɒnt; wɑnt/ *vt, vi* **1** [VP6A,17,19B,24A] require; be in need of; lack: 要;需要;缺乏: *You won't be ~ed* (=Your services will not be required) *this afternoon.* 今天下午不需要你做什麼了。*These plants are drooping—they ~ water.* 這些植物枯萎了— 它們需要水。*That man ~s a woman to look after him.* 那位男士需要一位女子照顧他。*I don't ~* (= I object to having) *anyone meddling in my affairs.* 我不要任何人干涉我的事。*Do you ~* (= Would you like to have) *this box opened?* 你要讓這個匣子打開嗎? **'~-ad** *n* (colloq) (usu short) advertisement (in a newspaper, etc) for sth ~ed, eg a job. (俗) (報紙等上通常較短的)徵求廣告。 **2** [VP6A, 7A, 17] wish for; have a desire for (⇨ wish *vi, vt* (6); *want* is used for sth which it is possible to obtain; *wish for* is used for sth unlikely to be obtained, or obtainable only in exceptional circumstances): 希望;願望;欲得(參看 wish 條動詞第6義; want 用於可能獲得的事物, wish for 用於不大可能獲得,或僅在例外情況下才能獲得的事物): *She ~s a holiday.* 她想獲得一個假日。*She ~s to go to Italy.* 她想去義大利。*She ~s me to go with her.* 她希望我同她一道兒去。*He is ~ed by the police*, ie because he is suspected of wrongdoing. 警察在通緝他。*I don't ~ there to be any misunderstanding.* 我不想發生任何誤會。 **3** [VP6A, E, 7A] need, ought (as in the notes to the examples): 需要;應該(用法見例句的說明): *Your hair ~s cutting*, needs to be cut. 你的頭髮該理了。*You ~* (= ought) *to see your solicitors about that problem.* 那問題你該去請教你的律師。*What that naughty boy ~s* (= needs to be given) *is a good beating.* 那頑皮的男孩子該好好的揍一頓。*That sort of thing ~s some doing*, (colloq) needs effort, skill, etc (because it is not an easy matter). (俗)那種事情需要相當的努力與技巧等。 **4** [VP2A] (progressive tenses only) (with non-human subject) (僅用於進行式中) (主詞須爲事物,而非人) ***be ~ing***, be missing or lacking: 缺失;缺少: *A few pages of this book are ~ing.* 這本書少了幾頁。*The infinitive of the verb 'must' is ~ing.* 動詞 must 無不定詞形式。***be ~ing (in sth)***, (with human subject): (主詞須爲人,而非物)缺乏;沒有: *He's ~ing in courtesy*, is impolite. 他缺乏禮貌。***be found ~ing:*** 被發現不合格: *He was put to the test and found ~ing*, inadequate. 他經過考試後被發現不合格。*He/It was tried and found (to be) ~ing*, unequal to a standard or to a need. 他(它)經過試驗後被發現不合格。 **5** [VP6A] (impers) fall short by: (無人稱) 缺少;不够;差: *It ~s one inch of the regulation length.* (它)較規定的長度短一吋。*It ~s half an hour to the appointed time.* 距約定的時間還有半小時。 **6** [VP2A, 3A] be in want (⇨ want¹(3)): 貧乏;缺少: *We mustn't let our soldiers ~* (= suffer poverty or hardship) *in their old age.* 我們不可使我們的軍人在老年時受貧困之苦。 ***~ for nothing,*** have all one needs. 不匱乏;具所需要的一切。 **~·ing** *prep* without; in the absence of: 沒有;無: *W~ing mutual trust, friendship is impossible.* 沒有互信便無友誼可言。

wan·ton /'wɒntən *US:* 'wɔːn-; 'wɑntən/ *adj* **1** (liter) playful; irresponsible; capricious: (文)嬉戲的;頑皮的;不負責的;反覆無常的: *a ~ breeze;* 變化無常的微風; *in a ~ mood.* 嬉笑地。 **2** unchecked; luxuriant; wild: 未被遏止的; 繁茂的; 野生的: *a ~ growth* (of weeds, etc); (野草等的)繁茂;叢生;茂密; *in ~ profusion.* 過分豐富地;浪費地。**3** wilful; serving no useful purpose: 任性的;胡亂的;無謂的: *~ destruction/damage;* 胡亂的破壞(損壞); *a ~ insult.* 沒道理的侮辱。**4** (archaic) immoral; unchaste: (古)不道德的;不貞潔的; *a ~ woman;* 蕩婦; lewd, licentious: 放肆的;放蕩的;淫蕩的: *~ thoughts.* 淫念。□ *n* (archaic) unchaste person. (古)不貞潔的人。□ *vi* [VP2A, C] (liter) be ~ in behaviour: (文)嬉戲;閒蕩;變化無常;放肆;淫蕩;漫無目的地行事: *the wind ~ing with the leaves.* 風舞樹葉。 **~·ly** *adv* **~·ness** *n*

war /wɔː(r); wɔr/ *n* **1** [C, U] (state created by) the use of armed forces between countries or (*civil war*) rival groups in a nation: 戰爭;戰爭狀態;內戰: *We have had two world wars in this century.* 本世紀我們已經歷了兩次世界大戰。***at war,*** in a state of war: 處於戰爭或交戰狀態: *Ruritania and Utopia are at war again.* 假想國與烏托邦又交戰了。***carry the war into the enemy's camp,*** attack (instead of being satisfied to defend). 向敵人進攻(不以防禦爲滿足)。 ***declare war (on),*** announce that a state of war exists (with another state). (向某一國)宣戰。***go to war (against),*** start fighting. 啓戰端;和…開戰。 ***have been in the wars,*** (used colloq or hum) have suffered injury (eg as the result of an accident). (俗或諧)受到創傷(如遇到車禍等)。***make/wage war on,*** engage in fighting against. 和…開戰; 從事戰爭。 **2** (compounds) (複合字) **'war-baby** *n* (*pl* -babies) illegitimate child with a soldier as father and attributable to conditions during a war. 戰時私生子(父爲軍人,係由戰時狀態所致)。**'war-bride** *n* bride of a soldier during a war. 戰時新娘(新郎爲戰時軍人)。 **'war-cloud(s)** *n* state of affairs that seems to threaten war. 戰雲;似將引起戰爭的局勢。**'war-cry** *n* (*pl* -cries) word or cry shouted as a signal in battle; catch-word (eg used by a political party) in any kind of contest. 作戰時的吶喊;(政黨競選等時所用的)口號;標語。**'war-dance** *n* one by tribal warriors before going into battle, to celebrate a victory, or (in peace) to represent fighting. (蠻族戰士於出發作戰前,慶祝勝利,或在平時扮演打仗的)戰舞。**'war-god** *n* god (eg Mars) worshipped as giving victory in war. 戰神(如 Mars)。 **'war·head** *n* (of a torpedo, shell, etc) explosive head (contrasted with a dummy charge as used in practice, etc). (指魚雷、砲彈等的)彈頭; 實彈彈頭(與演習時用的空包彈相對而言)。 **'war-horse** *n* (rhet) horse used in battle; charger; (fig) veteran soldier, politician, etc. (修辭)戰馬; 軍馬; (喩)老兵; 資深政客等。 **'war-lord** *n* (rhet) great military leader, esp a Chinese general in the period of civil wars, early 20th c. (修辭)大將軍;(尤指)(廿世紀初中國內戰時期的)軍閥。 **'war·monger** *n* person who advocates or stirs up war. 戰時販子(鼓動戰爭者)。**'War Office,** (formerly in GB) State department in charge of the Army, under the Secretary of State of War. (昔英國的)陸軍部。(Now named 現稱做 *Ministry of Defence*). **'war-paint** *n* [U] **(a)** paint put on the body before battle by some primitive people; (fig) full, ceremonial dress: 蠻人出戰前塗於身上的顏料;(喩)盛裝;禮服: *The General was in full war-paint.* 那位將軍穿著大禮服。**(b)** (sl) make-up (cosmetics). (俚)化粧品。**'war-path** *n* (only in) (僅用於) ***on the war-path,*** ready for, engaged in, a fight or quarrel. 準備作戰或爭吵;正在作戰或爭吵。 **'war·ship** *n* ship for use in war. 戰艦;軍艦。 **'war-torn** *adj* exhausted by, worn out in, war. 疲於戰爭的;爲戰爭所耗盡的;飽經戰禍的。**'war-widow** *n* woman whose husband has been killed in war. 戰時寡婦(丈夫死於戰爭中)。 **3** [U] science or art of fighting, using weapons, etc: 軍事學;兵學;兵法: *trained for war;* 受過作戰訓練的; *the art of war*, strategy and tactics. 戰略及戰術。 **4** (fig) any kind of struggle or conflict: (喩)任何種類的鬪爭;衝突;不和: *the war against disease;* 對疾病的作戰; *the wars of the elements*, storms, natural calamities; 天災(暴風雨等); *a war of nerves/words.* 神經戰(筆戰)。□ *vi* (-rr-) fight; make war: 戰鬪;作戰: *warring for supremacy;* 爲爭奪霸權而戰; *warring* (= rival) *creeds/ideologies.* 對立的信念(意識)。 **'war·fare** /'wɔːfeə(r); 'wɔr,fɛr/ *n* [U] making war; condition of being at war;

fighting: 作戰;戰爭狀態;交戰: *the horrors of modern warfare.* 近代戰爭的恐怖。 **war·like** /ˈwɔːlaɪk ; ˈwɔrˌlaɪk/ *adj* ready for, suggesting, war: 準備作戰的;表示戰爭的: *warlike preparations;* 軍備;戰備; fond of war: 好戰的: *a cruel, warlike people.* 殘忍好戰的民族。 **war·time** /ˈwɔːtaɪm ; ˈwɔrˌtaɪm/ *n* [U] time when there is war: 戰時: *in wartime;* 在戰時; (attrib) (形容用法) *wartime regulations／rationing.* 戰時條例(配給)。

warble /ˈwɔːbl ; ˈwɔrbl̩/ *vi, vt* [VP2A, C, 6A] (esp of birds) sing, esp with a gentle trilling note: (尤指鳥類)鳴;唱;(尤指) 柔和顫動地叫: *larks warbling high up in the sky;* 在高空鳴叫的雲雀; *a blackbird warbling from a branch.* 在枝頭歌唱的畫眉鳥。 □ *n* warbling; bird's song. 啁啾;鳴囀;鳥叫。 **war·bler** /ˈwɔːblə(r) ; ˈwɔrblɚ/ *n* (kinds of) bird that ～s. (各種的)鳴禽。

ward /wɔːd ; wɔrd/ *n* **1** ***keep watch and ～,*** guard and protect. 守衛;監護。 **2** [U] state of being in custody or under the control of a guardian: 受監護的狀態: *a child in ～;* 在監護下的孩子; [C] person under the guardianship of an older person or of law authorities. 被監護人;受監護人。 **3** division of a local government area, each division being represented by one Councillor. 地方政府的區劃;(由一議員代表的)選擧區。 **4** division of, separate room in, a building, esp a prison or a hospital: 建築物內的分區或房間; (尤指)監房; 病房: *the fever／isolation／children's ～.* 熱病(隔離,兒童)病房; **5** notch in a key; corresponding part in a lock. 鑰匙的缺刻;鎖中相對鑰匙的部分。 □ *vt* [VP15B] ***～ sth off,*** keep away, avoid: 躲開;避免: *～ off a blow／danger.* 躲開打擊(危險)。

war·den /ˈwɔːdn ; ˈwɔrdn̩/ *n* **1** person having control or authority: 有管轄權或控制權的人;看守人;監護人: *the ～ of a youth hostel.* 青年招待所的管理人。 **ˈair-raid ～,** (during World War II in GB) member of a civilian organization with various duties during air-raids. (二次大戰時英國的)民防隊員。 **ˈtraffic ～,** (eg in London) person responsible for controlling the parking of cars in streets, squares, etc at parking meters. (倫敦等地的)計時停車處的管理人。 **2** (old use except in a few cases) title of certain governors or presidents: (除少數用法外,爲舊用法)某些總督、州長、校長等的稱謂: *the W～ of Merton College, Oxford.* 牛津大學懋頓學院的院長。 **3** (US) (美) = warder.

war·der /ˈwɔːdə(r) ; ˈwɔrdɚ/ *n* (GB) man acting as guard in a prison; jailer. (英)典獄官; 獄吏。 **war·dress** /ˈwɔːdrɪs ; ˈwɔrdrɪs/ *n* woman ～. 女獄吏;女看守。

ward·robe /ˈwɔːdrəʊb ; ˈwɔrdˌrob/ *n* **1** cupboard (*built-in-～*) or movable cupboard-like piece of furniture with pegs, shelves, etc for a person's clothes. 衣櫃;衣櫥;衣室。 **2** stock of clothes: 衣服;行頭(總稱): *My ～ needs to be renewed,* I must buy some new clothes. 我需要添購一些新衣服了。 **3** stock of costumes of a theatrical company. (某一劇團的)劇裝。

ward·room /ˈwɔːdrʊm *US:* -ruːm ; ˈwɔrdˌrum/ *n* living and eating quarters for commissioned officers in a warship except the commanding officer. (軍艦上)艦長以外的軍官的起居室及餐廳;官廳。

ware[1] /weə(r) ; wɛr/ *n* **1** (in compounds) manufactured goods: (用於複合字中) 製造品;加工品: *ˈsilver-～;* 銀器; *ˈiron～;* 鐵器; *ˈhard～;* 金屬器皿。 **2** (*pl*) articles offered for sale: (複)貨物;商品: *advertise one's ～s.* 推銷某人的貨物。 **～·house** /ˈweəhaʊs ; ˈwɛrˌhaʊs/ *n* building for storing goods before distribution to retailers; storehouse for furniture (on behalf of owners). 倉庫;貨棧;家具寄存的棧房。 □ *vt* [VP6A] store in a ～house. 儲存於倉庫中。

ware[2] /weə(r) ; wɛr/ *vt* [VP6A] (in imper) look out for; be cautious about; beware of: (用於祈使句中)留心;小心;注意: *W～ wire!* (warning to riders in a fox-hunt that there is barbed wire on a fence, etc). 留心鐵絲網!(獵狐時向騎者警告籬笆等上有倒鈎鐵絲)。

war·fare /ˈwɔːfeə(r) ; ˈwɔrˌfɛr/ ⇨ war.

war·ily, wari·ness ⇨ wary.

warm[1] /wɔːm ; wɔrm/ *adj* (-er, -est) **1** having a fairly high degree of heat (between *cool* and *hot*); (of clothing) serving to keep the body ～: 暖的;溫暖的(介於冷與熱之間);(指衣服)保暖的: *Come and get ～ by the fire.* 來爐火旁取暖。 *It was ～, but not hot, yesterday.* 昨天暖和而不炎熱。 *Put your ～est clothes on before you go out in the snow.* 下雪天外出前要穿起你最暖和的衣服。 *Red, yellow and orange are called ～ colours.* 紅、黃、橙三色被稱爲暖色。 ***～ work,*** **(a)** work or activity that makes one ～. 使人暖和的工作或活動。 **(b)** strenuous or dangerous activity or occupation. 吃力或危險的活動或職業。 ***make things ～ for sb,*** make things unpleasant, make trouble for him; punish him. 困擾某人;爲某人找麻煩;懲罰某人。 ***～ blood,*** that of mammals and birds (ranging from 36°C—42°C). 溫血(哺乳類及鳥類的體溫,自攝氏 36°至 42°)。 Hence, 由此產生, **ˌ～-ˈblooded** *adj* **(a)** having ～ blood; not cold-blooded like snakes, etc. 溫血的;非冷血(如蛇等)的。 **(b)** having feelings and passions that are easily roused. 熱情的;易激動的。 **～ front,** ⇨ front(7). **2** enthusiastic, hearty: 熱心的;熱誠的: *give sb a ～ welcome;* 熱烈歡迎某人; *a ～ friend／supporter.* 熱心的朋友(支持者)。 **3** sympathetic; affectionate: 同情的;熱情的: *He has a ～ heart.* 他具有同情心。 Hence, 由此產生, **ˌ～-ˈhearted** *adj* kind and sympathetic. 親切而有同情心的。 **4** (of scent in hunting) fresh; recently made and easily followed by the hounds; (in children's games, when an object is hidden and searched for) close to the object: (指獵物的氣味)新鮮的;新近發出而易被獵犬跟蹤的;(在兒童遊戲中,尋找某隱藏物時)接近目標的: *You're getting ～,* near to what is being sought. 你快找到了。 **～·ly** *adv* in a ～ manner: 溫暖地;親切地;熱烈地: *～ly dressed;* 穿得暖和的; *thank sb ～ly.* 熱烈地感謝某人。 **warmth** /wɔːmθ ; wɔrmθ/ *n* [U] state of being ～: 溫暖;親切;熱烈: *He was pleased with the ～th of his welcome.* 他因受到熱烈歡迎而高興。 *He answered with ～th,* with some emotion (of pleasure, resentment, etc, according to context). 他激動地(愉快、憎恨等,視上下文而定)回答。

warm[2] /wɔːm ; wɔrm/ *vt, vi* [VP6A, 15B, 2A, C] ***～ (sth) (up),*** make or become warm or warmer: 使暖; 變暖; (使)感到親切或激動: *～ oneself／one's hands by the fire.* 烤火取暖(使手溫暖)。 *Please ～ (up) this milk.* 請把這牛奶熱一熱。 *The milk is ～ing (up) on the stove.* 牛奶正在爐子上熱着。 *He ～ed up* (= became more animated, enthusiastic) *as he went on with his speech.* 他愈講愈起勁。 ***～ to one's work／task, etc,*** become more interested; like it more. 對工作等開始發生興趣;對工作等更爲喜歡。 **ˈ～·ing-pan** *n* (hist) round metal pan with a lid and a long handle, holding hot coals and used for ～ing the inside of a bed before it was occupied. (史)長柄暖床器。 **～·er** *n* (usu in compounds) sth which ～s. (通常用於複合字中)溫暖器;保暖裝置。

warn /wɔːn ; wɔrn/ *vt* [VP6A, 14, 11, 15, 17] give (sb) notice of possible danger or unpleasant consequences; inform in advance of what may happen: 警告;警戒;預告;預先通知: *He was ～ed of the danger.* 他已得到危險的警告。 *We ～ed them not to go skating on such thin ice.* 我們警告他們不要在這樣薄的冰上溜冰。 *You've been ～ed.* 你已受到警告了。 *He ～ed me that there were pickpockets in the crowd／～ed me against pickpockets.* 他提醒我人叢中有扒手(謹防扒手)。 ***～ sb off,*** give him notice that he must go or stay away, eg from private property. 通知某人離開或勿歸。 **～·ing** *adj* that ～s: 警告的;預告的: *He gave me a ～ing look.* 他向我使

了一個警告的眼色。 *They fired some ~ing shots.* 他們發射了幾槍示警。 □ *n* **1** [C] that which ~s or serves to ~: 警告或用以警告之物;警號;警戒;預兆;殷鑑: *He paid no attention to my ~ings.* 他不重視我的警告。 *Let this be a ~ing to you,* Let this accident, misfortune, etc teach you to be careful in future. 讓此事做爲你的殷鑑。 *There were gale ~ings to shipping along the coast.* 有强風警報要沿海航行船隻注意。 **2** [U] action of ~-ing; state of being ~ed: 警告或預告;受警告的狀態: *You should take ~ing* (= be ~ed) *from what happened to me.* 你應該把我的遭遇作爲殷鑑。 *The speaker sounded a note of ~ing,* spoke of possible danger. 講話的人透露出警告之意(提到可能的危險)。 *The enemy attacked without ~ing.* 敵人突然來襲。

warp¹ /wɔ:p ; wɔrp/ *vt, vi* [VP6A, 2A] (cause to) become bent or twisted from the usual or natural shape: (使)彎翹;變彎;歪曲: *The hot sun ~ed the boards.* 灼熱的太陽把木板晒得彎翹了。 *His judgement/disposition is ~ed,* biased because of possible advantage for himself. 他的判斷(處置)不公平(可能與其切身利益有關而產生偏見)。□ *n* [C] twisted or bent condition in timber, etc, caused by uneven shrinking or expansion. (木材等的)彎翹;翹曲(由不均勻的脹縮所致)。

warp² /wɔ:p ; wɔrp/ *n* **the ~,** the threads over and under which other threads (the *weft* or *woof*) are passed when cloth is woven on a loom. (布的)經;經紗;經線。

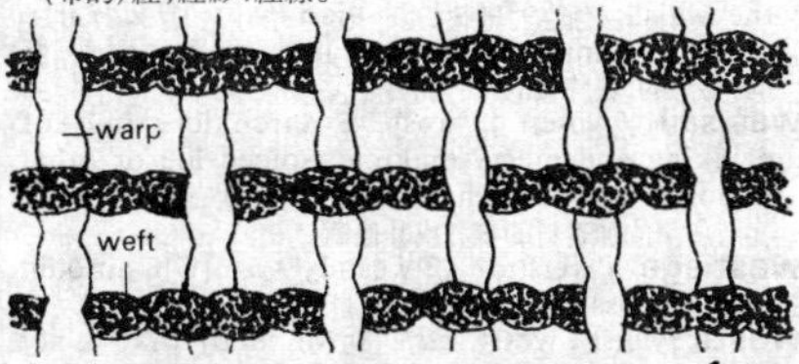

war·rant /ˈwɒrənt *US:* ˈwɔ:r- ; ˈwɑrənt/ *n* **1** [U] justification or authority: 正當;正當的理由;根據;權威: *He had no ~ for saying so/for what he did.* 他那樣說(做)毫無理由。 **2** [C] written order giving official authority for sth: 令狀;授權狀;委任狀: *a ~ to arrest a suspected criminal.* 逮捕嫌疑犯的令狀或拘票。 *The ˈdeath-~ has been signed.* 死刑執行令已簽字了。 *A ~ is out for his arrest/against him.* 逮捕他的拘票已發出了。 *Here are the ~s for your dividends,* ie on shares. 這是你的股利券。 **3** [C] certificate appointing a man as a ~ officer. 准尉委任狀。 ˈ**~ officer** *n* highest grade of non-commissioned officer in the army, air force, (GB) marines, (US) navy. (陸軍,空軍,英國海軍陸戰隊,美國海軍之)准尉。□ *vt* **1** [VP6A] be a ~(1) for: 證明…爲正當;有理由;有權力: *Nothing can ~ such insolence.* 這等無禮毫無道理。 *His interference was certainly not ~ed.* 他顯然無權干預。 **2** [VP6A, 9, 25] guarantee (the more usu word); (colloq) assure: 保證 (guarantee 較常用); 擔保;(俗)確定;包準: *This material is ~ed (to be) pure silk.* 這料子保證是純絲的。 *I'll ~ him an honest and reliable man.* 我保證他是一個誠實可靠的人。 *I can't ~ it to be/~ that it is genuine.* 我不能擔保那是眞貨。 *He'll be back, I ~* (= assure) *you, when the money's paid out.* 這筆錢一付,我保證他會回來。 **war·ran·tee** /ˌwɒrənˈti: *US:* ˌwɔ:r- ; ˌwɔrənˈti/ *n* person to whom a warranty is made. 被保證人。 **war·ran·tor** /ˈwɒrəntɔ:(r) *US:* ˈwɔ:r- ; ˈwɔrənˌtɔr/ *n* person who makes a warranty. 保證人。 **war·ranty** /ˈwɒrəntɪ *US:* ˈwɔ:r- ; ˈwɔrəntɪ/ *n* [C] (*pl* -ties) authority; (written or printed) guarantee (eg to repair or replace defective goods): 權威;根據;(寫出或印出的)擔保;保證(如修理或掉換有缺點的貨物);保單: *What ~y have you for doing this?* 你憑什麼做這件事? *Can you give me a ~y of quality for these goods?* 你能給我一張這些貨物的品質保單嗎? *The car is still under ~y.* 這部車仍在保用期間。

war·ren /ˈwɒrən *US:* ˈwɔ:rən ; ˈwɑrən/ *n* [C] area of land in which there are many burrows in which rabbits live and breed; (fig) (usu over-populated) building or district in which it is difficult to find one's way about: 養兎場;(喩)(通常指)過分擁擠而易迷路的建築或地區: *lose oneself in a ~ of narrow streets.* 在縱橫交錯的狹窄街道間迷了路。

war·rior /ˈwɒrɪə(r) *US:* ˈwɔ:r- ; ˈwɔrɪɚ/ *n* (liter, rhet) soldier; fighter: (文,修辭)兵士;戰士;勇士: (attrib) (形容用法) *a ~ race.* 驍勇的民族。

wart /wɔ:t ; wɔrt/ *n* small, hard, dry growth on the skin; similar growth on a plant. 疣;瘊;瘤腫;樹疣;樹癭。 ˈ**~·hog** *n* kinds of African pig with two large tusks and ~-like growths on the face. (非洲產的)疣豬。

wary /ˈweərɪ ; ˈwɛrɪ/ *adj* (-ier, -iest) cautious; in the habit of looking out for possible danger or trouble: 小心的;警惕的;慣於留神可能的危險或困難的: *be ~ of giving offence/of strangers;* 提防冒犯他人(當心陌生人); *keep a ~ eye on sb;* 密切注意某人; *a ~ old fox.* 機警的老狐。 **war·ily** /-əlɪ ; -əlɪ/ *adv* **wari·ness** *n*

was /*weak form:* wəz ; wəz; *strong form:* wɒz *US:* wʌz ; wɑz, wʌz/ ⇨ be¹

wash¹ /wɒʃ *US:* wɔ:ʃ ; wɑʃ/ *n* **1** (*sing* only, usu with *indef art*) act of washing; being washed: (僅用單數,通常與不定冠詞連用)洗;洗滌: *Will you give the car a ~/a ˌ~-ˈdown, please.* 請把車子洗(沖洗)一下。 ***have a ~ and brush up,*** wash oneself and make oneself tidy. 盥洗;梳洗;整容。 **2** (*sing* only) clothing, sheets, etc to be washed or being washed; place (laundry) where they are being washed: (僅用單數)洗濯物;洗濯處;洗衣店: *She has a large ~ this week.* 這星期她有很多衣物要洗。 *She was hanging out the ~.* 她正在晾衣服。 *All my shirts are at the ~.* 我所有的襯衣都在洗衣店。 *When does the ~ come back from the laundry?* 送洗的衣服何時取回? **3** ***the ~ (of),*** movement or flow of water; sound made by moving water: 水的流動;水流聲;沖擊;沖擊聲: *the ~ of the waves;* 浪的沖擊; *the ~ made by a steamer's propeller(s).* 汽船的推進器發出的擊水聲。 **4** [U] thin, weak or inferior liquid: 稀薄或濃度不足的液體: *This soup is a mere ~,* is too watery, has no flavour or substance. 這湯實在太稀了。 **5** [U] kitchen liquid with waste food (eg vegetable peelings and scraps) to be given to pigs. 厨房的殘汁;餿水。 **6** (usu in compounds, ⇨ under the first part) liquid prepared for a special purpose: (通常用於複合字中,參看各該字的第一部分)特別調製的液體: ˈ*white~,* for putting on walls; (刷牆的)石灰水; ˈ*mouth-~,* for disinfecting the mouth; (消毒用的)漱口劑; ˈ*eye~.* 洗眼水。

wash² /wɒʃ *US:* wɔ:ʃ ; wɑʃ/ *vt, vi* **1** [VP6A, 15B, 22, 2A] make clean with or in water or other liquid: 洗;清洗;洗去: *~ one's hands/clothes.* 洗手(衣)。 *W~ them clean.* 把它們洗乾淨。 *Go and ~ yourself.* 去洗澡。 *I must ~ before dinner.* 飯前我必須洗手。 *He never ~es* (ie ~es himself) *in cold water.* 他從不用冷水洗澡。 ***~ one's hands of sth/sb,*** say one is no longer responsible for. 宣佈對某事(某人)不再負責;從…撒手;斷絕…的關係。 ***~ one's dirty linen in public,*** ⇨ linen. ***~ sth down,*** clean by ~ing, esp by using a stream or jet of water (eg from a hose): 洗淸;(尤指)沖洗;沖淨: *~ down a car/the decks of a ship.* 沖洗汽車(船上的甲板)。 ***~ sth away/off/out,*** remove by ~ing: 洗去;洗掉: *~ dirty marks off a wall;* 把牆上的汚跡洗掉; *~ out blood stains.* 洗去血跡。 ***be/look/feel ~ed out,*** (fig, colloq) pale and tired; exhausted. (喩,俗)蒼白而疲倦的;筋疲力竭的。 ***~ up,*** **(a)** (GB) ~ dishes, cutlery, etc, after a meal. (英)餐後洗碗盤、刀叉等。**(b)** (US) ~ one's face and hands. (美)洗臉洗手。~ ***sth up,*** (GB) ~ dishes, cutlery, etc after a meal: (英)餐後洗碗碟、刀叉等: ~ *up the dinner things.* 洗餐具。Hence, 由此產生, ˌ**~·ing-ˈup** *n* [U]. (Note: *up* indicates that a number of dishes, etc are to be ~ed. For a single article *up* is not used: *Please ~ this plate.*) (注意:up意謂要洗的碗盤有若干件,如祇有一件,不用 up, 如: Please ~ this plate. 請把這盤子洗一洗。) ***(all) ~ed up,*** (colloq) ruined; failed. (俗)(全部)毀滅;失敗;完蛋。 **2** [VP2A] (of materials) be capable of being ~ed without damage or loss of colour: (指物料或布料)耐洗;不褪色: *Does this material ~ well?* 這料子耐洗嗎？ *That argument/excuse will not ~,* (fig) will not bear examination, is weak. (喻)那項論據(藉口)站不住腳。 **3** [VP6A] (of the sea or a river) flow past or against: (指海或河)流過;冲擊;拍打: *The sea ~es the base of the cliffs.* 海水冲擊懸崖的底部。 **4** [VP15B] (of moving liquid) carry away, or in a specified direction: (指流動的液體)冲去;捲走: *He was ~ed overboard by a huge wave.* 他被一個巨浪從船上捲入海中。 *All this timber has been ~ed up* (ie carried up on to the beach) *by the waves.* 這些木料都是被浪冲到岸上來的。*The cliffs are being gradually ~ed away by the sea.* 懸崖正逐漸被海水冲損。 ~ ***sth down (with),*** swallow (liquid) with: 連同…吞下(某種液體): *My lunch was bread and cheese ~ed down with beer.* 我的中餐是麵包和乳酪,用啤酒幫助嚥下去。**~ed out, (a)** (of games such as cricket, of horse-races, etc) made impossible, cancelled, by heavy rain or flooding. (指遊戲如板球,指賽馬等)因大雨或淹水而停止或取消。 **(b)** (of roads, etc) made impassable by heavy rain, floods, etc. (指路等)因大雨、淹水等而不通。 **5** [VP 6A, 15A] scoop out: 挖;冲出: *The water had ~ed a channel in the sand.* 水在沙中冲出了一條溝。 **6** [VP2C] go flowing, sweeping or splashing (*along, out, in, into, over,* etc): 流過;冲擊;冲刷;濺潑(與 along, out, in, into, over 等連用): *We heard the waves ~ing against the sides of our boat.* 我們聽到波浪冲擊我們的船舷。*Huge waves ~ed over the deck.* 巨浪濺潑在甲板上。 **~·able** /-əbl; -əbl/ *adj* that can be ~ed without being spoiled. 可洗的;耐洗的。

wash- /wɒʃ *US:* wɔːʃ; wɑʃ/ (in compounds; often used as a substitute for *washing*). (用於複合字中;常用以代替 washing)。 **ˈ~-basin** *n* basin for holding water in which to wash one's face and hands. 洗面盆;洗臉盆。 **ˈ~-board** *n* board with ridges on it, on which clothes are washed (at home). 洗衣板;搓板。 **ˈ~-bowl** *n* (US) (美) = ~-basin. **ˈ~-cloth** *n* (US) (美) = face-cloth. **ˈ~-day** *n* day on which clothes were washed (at home). 洗濯日;洗衣日。 **ˈ~-hand-basin** *n* = ~-basin. **ˈ~-drawing** *n* one made with a brush in a black or neutral water-colour. 淡彩畫。 **ˈ~-hand-stand** *n* = ~-stand. **ˈ~-house** *n* room or out-building equipped for washing. 洗衣間;洗衣房。 **ˈ~-leather** *n* [C, U] (piece of) chamois leather, used for cleaning and polishing windows and other surfaces. 擦拭皮(擦拭窗子及其他表面的小羊皮)。 **ˈ~-out** *n* **(a)** place in a railway or road where a flood or heavy rain has carried away earth, rock, etc and interrupted communications. (因洪水或大雨冲去泥土、碎石等,而阻礙交通的)鐵路或道路的冲蝕處;冲蝕缺口。 **(b)** (colloq) useless or unsuccessful person; complete failure or fiasco. (俗)無用或失敗的人;大敗。 **ˈ~·room** *n* (US) lavatory (esp in a public building, etc). (美)廁所(尤指公共場所者)。 **ˈ~-stand** *n* (now old-fashioned, except in houses where there is no piped supply of water to bathrooms or bedrooms) piece of furniture with a basin, jug, etc for washing in a bedroom. (除尚無自來水接入浴室或臥房的建築外,現爲舊用法) (臥室用的) 面盆架;盥洗台。 **ˈ~-tub** *n* large wooden tub in which to wash clothes. 洗濯盆;洗衣盆。

washer /ˈwɒʃə(r) *US:* ˈwɔː-; ˈwɑʃɚ/ *n* **1** machine for washing clothes, or (ˈ*dish-~*) dishes. 洗衣機; 洗碗機;洗濯機。 **2** **ˈ~-woman,** laundress. 洗衣婦。 **3** small flat ring of metal, plastic, rubber or leather for making a joint or screw tight. (使接頭或螺絲密合的)墊圈;皮圈。⇨ the illus at bolt. 參看 bolt 之插圖。

wash·ing /ˈwɒʃɪŋ *US:* ˈwɔː-; ˈwɑʃɪŋ/ *n* [U] **1** washing or being washed. 洗;洗滌;洗濯。 **2** clothes being washed or to be washed: (正在洗或待洗的)衣物: *hang out the ~ on the line to dry.* 把洗好的衣服晾在繩子上。 **ˈ~-day** *n* = wash-day, ⇨ wash-. **ˈ~-machine** *n* power driven machine for washing clothes. 洗衣機。 **ˈ~ soda** *n* sodium carbonate, used, dissolved in water, for washing clothes or dishes. 洗滌用的碳酸鈉;洗滌鹼。 ˌ**~-ˈup** *n* ⇨ *wash up* at wash²(1).

washy /ˈwɒʃɪ *US:* ˈwɔː-; ˈwɑʃɪ/ *adj* (of liquids) thin, watery; (of colours) faded-looking; pale; (of feeling, style) lacking in vigour. (指液體)稀薄的;水多的;(指色彩)淺的;淡的;(指感情,文體)軟弱的;無活力的;無生氣的。

wasp /wɒsp *US:* wɔːsp; wɑsp/ *n* kinds of flying insect of which the common kind has a narrow waist, black and yellow stripes and a powerful sting in the tail. 黃蜂;胡蜂。⇨ the illus at insect. 參看 insect 之插圖。 ˌ**~-ˈwaisted** *adj* slender at the waist. 蜂腰的;細腰的。 **~·ish** /-ɪʃ; -ɪʃ/ *adj* irritable; ill tempered; sharp in making retorts. 暴躁的;易怒的;壞脾氣的;尖刻的。

was·sail /ˈwɒseɪl; ˈwɑsl/ *n* (archaic) time of drinking and merry-making; spiced ale or other liquor drunk at such a time. (古)飲宴取樂之時;飲宴時所用的加香料的麥酒或其他酒。

wast·age /ˈweɪstɪdʒ; ˈwestɪdʒ/ *n* [U] amount wasted; loss by waste. 消耗量;損耗。

waste /weɪst; west/ *adj* **1** (of land) that is not or cannot be used; no longer of use; barren: (指土地)未或無法利用的; 廢棄的; 荒蕪的: ~ *land,* not occupied or used for any purpose. (未作任何利用的)荒蕪地;未利用地。 **ˈ~·land** /-lænd; -ˌlænd/ *n* **(a)** barren, desolate or unused land. 荒蕪、人跡罕至或未利用的土地;荒地。**(b)** land ravaged by war, etc: 爲戰爭等所破壞之地;瘡痍之地: *Vietnam reduced to ~-land by bombing and shelling.* 越南因轟炸及砲擊而變成瘡痍之地。**(c)** (fig) life, society, looked upon as culturally and spiritually barren. (喻)文化和精神上貧乏的生活或社會。***lay ~,*** destroy the crops in, ravage (eg territory occupied in war). 損毀…上面的作物;蹂躪(戰時佔領的土地等)。 **2** useless; thrown away because not wanted: 無用的;拋棄的;廢棄的: *~-paper;* 廢紙; ~ *products,* unwanted after a manufacturing process. 製造過程剩下的無用副產品;廢物。□ *vt, vi* **1** [VP6A, 14, 2A] ~ ***sth (on sth),*** make no use of; use without a good purpose; use more of (sth) than is necessary: 未用;浪費;徒耗: ~ *one's time and money on paying bribes;* 將時間和金錢浪費於賄賂; ~ *one's words/breath,* talk without making any impression (on sb). 徒費唇舌。*All his efforts were ~d,* had no result. 他的全部努力都白費了。***W~ not, want not,*** (prov) If you do not ~ your money, etc you are unlikely to be in need. (諺)不浪費則不虞匱乏。 **2** [VP6A] make (land) waste; ravage. 使(土地)荒蕪;損毀;蹂躪。 **3** [VP6A, 2A, C] (cause to) lose strength by degrees: (使)逐漸失去力量;耗損;衰弱: *He's wasting away.* 他漸漸消瘦了。*Consumption is a wasting disease.* 肺癆是一種耗損體力的疾病。 *His body was ~d by long illness.* 他的身體因久病而衰弱了。 **4** [VP2A] be ~d: 被浪費或耗損: *Turn that tap off—the water is wasting.* 把那水龍頭關起來,水給浪費了。□ *n* **1** [U] wasting or being ~d: 浪費;徒耗: *There's too much ~ in this house.* 這一

家人太浪費了。*It's a ~ of time to wait any longer.* 再等下去是白費時間。*What a ~ of energy!* 這多麼浪費精力！***go/run to ~,*** be ~d: 被浪費；未被利用: *What a pity to see all that water running to ~!* eg instead of being used for generating electric current. 眼看着那些水白白浪費掉，多可惜呀！(如未用來發電等。) **2** [U] ~ material; refuse. 廢物；殘物。 **'~-basket/-bin** (US) (美)， **,~-'paper-basket** (GB) (英) *nn* basket or other container for scraps of paper, etc. 字紙簍。 **'~-pipe** *n* pipe for carrying off used or superfluous water. 排水管。 **3** [U] area of ~ land: 荒地；原野；沙漠: *the ~s of the Sahara;* 撒哈拉沙漠; dreary scene: 淒涼的景色: *a ~ of waters.* 一片汪洋的淒涼景色。 **~r** *n* (colloq) wastrel. (俗)無用的人；飯桶；浪子；浪費者。 **~·ful** /-fl; -fəl/ *adj* causing ~; using more than is needed: 使無用的；浪費的: *~ful habits/processes;* 浪費的習慣(方法)； *~ful expenditure.* 浪費的開支。 **~·fully** /-fəlɪ; -fəlɪ/ *adv*

wast·rel /ˈweɪstrəl; ˈwestrəl/ *n* good-for-nothing person; wasteful person. 廢人；飯桶；浪費者。

watch¹ /wɒtʃ; wɑtʃ/ *n* **1** [U] act of watching, esp to see that all is well. 看；注意；警戒；監視；守望。 ***be on the ~ (for),*** be watching for (sth or sb, or esp possible danger). 看守着；提防着；監視着(某人或某物，尤指可能的危險)。 ***keep ~ (on/over),*** look out for danger, etc. 注意危險等。 **'~-dog** *n* dog kept to protect property, esp a house; (fig) sb or sth that protects. 警犬；守望犬；(尤指)看家狗；(喻)保護的人或物。 **'~-tower** *n* high tower from which to keep ~, eg in a forest, to look for forest fires, or a fortified observation post. 守望台；瞭望台；更樓。 **2 the ~,** (hist) body of men employed to go through the streets and protect people and their property, esp at night: (史)看守者；守夜者；更夫: *the constables of the ~;* 守夜的警官; *call out the ~.* 召喊守夜者。 **3** (in ships) period of duty (4 or 2 hours) for part of the crew (船上的)輪值；輪班時間(四或二小時) (**the first ~,** 8pm to midnight; 頭班；首班(夜晚八時至午夜)； **the middle ~,** midnight to 4 am; 中班(午夜至凌晨四時)； **the 'dog-~es,** 4 pm to 6 pm or 6pm to 8pm 暮更(下午四至六時或六至八時的輪班))； either of the halves into which a ship's crew is divided for purposes of duty (called **the starboard** and **port ~es** from the positions of the men's bunks in former times). (船員輪值分爲兩班)二輪班船員之任何一班(昔時依船員之床位而分，稱右舷班及左舷班)。 ***on ~,*** on duty in this way. 當班；值班；輪值。 ***keep ~,*** be on ~. 值班；守望。 **4** (old use) period of wakefulness in the night: (舊用法)夜裡睡不着的時刻: *in the ~es of the night,* while one lies awake. 躺在床上睡不著的時候。 **'~ night service,** church service at midnight, New Year's Eve. (教堂在除夕舉行的)守歲禮拜；除夕午夜禮拜。 **~·ful** /-fl; -fəl/ *adj* on the ~; wide-awake. 注意的；警戒的；警醒的。 **~·fully** /-fəlɪ; -fəlɪ/ *adv* **~·ful·ness** *n* **~·man** /-mən; -mən/ *n* (*pl* -men) **1** (hist) member of the ~(2). (史)守夜者；更夫。 **2** man employed to guard a building (eg a bank, block of offices, factory) against thieves, esp at night. (尤指雇來在夜間看守銀行、辦公廳、工廠等建築物，以防盜竊的)警衛。 **~·word** /-wɜːd; -,wɝd/ *n* **1** password. 口令。 **2** slogan. 口號；標語。

watch² /wɒtʃ; wɑtʃ/ *vt, vi* **1** [VP2A, B, C, 3A, 4A, 6A, 8, 10, 15A, 18A, 19A] look at; keep the eyes on: 看；注視；注意；警戒: *W~ me carefully.* 仔細看看我。 *W~ what I do and how I do it.* 注意看我做什麼及如何做。 *We sat there ~ing the cricket.* 我們坐在那裡看板球賽。 *Are you going to play or only ~?* 你將參加(比賽)或祇當觀衆？ *He ~ed to see* (= ~ed in order to see) *what would happen.* 他注意看會發生什麼事情。 *I ~ed her cross the street,* looked at and saw this action from start to finish. 我看着她走過街道(指留意其過街的整個過程和其間一舉一動)。 *I sat ~ing the shadows creep across the floor,* looked at and saw this happening (but not necessarily from start to finish). 我坐着，觀看陰影在地板上緩緩移動(不一定從開始看到結束)。 *My solicitor is ~ing the case for me/holds a ~ing brief for me,* is present in court during the case to protect my interests. 我的律師正替我照料這個案子(爲我到法庭旁聽，留意案情發展)。 ***~ one's step,*** **(a)** be careful not to fall or stumble. 小心走路；留意不跌倒或摔跤。 **(b)** be careful not to make an error, let sb win an advantage, etc, eg in negotiations. 留意不犯錯；不讓旁人佔便宜(如在談判中)。 ***~ one's time,*** (more usu *bide*) wait for the right time. (bide 較常用)等待時機。 ***~ the time,*** keep your eye on the time (eg to avoid being late for sth). 注意時間(俾不致耽誤某事等)。 ***~ (out) (for sth),*** look out for: 注意；監視；當心(某事): *There's a policeman ~ing outside,* ie for anything suspicious. 有一位警察在外面監視。 *The doctor told her to ~ out* (= be on the look-out) *for symptoms of measles.* 醫生告訴她當心痲疹的病徵。 ***~ out,*** be on one's guard. 警戒；提防；警惕。 ***~ (over) sth,*** guard; protect: 照顧；照看；保護: *Will you ~ (over) my clothes while I have a swim?* 我去游泳時，你替我照看衣服好嗎？ **2** [VP2A] (old use) remain awake: (舊用法)不睡；守夜: *~ all night at the bedside of a sick child.* 徹夜在病童床邊看護。 **~er** *n* person who ~es. 看者；注視者；守望者；監視者。

watch³ /wɒtʃ; wɑtʃ/ *n* small timepiece that can be carried in the pocket or worn on the wrist (cf 參較 *clock*): 錶；掛錶；手錶: *What time is it by your ~?* 你的錶幾點鐘了？ *What does your ~ say?* 你的錶幾點鐘了？ **'~-glass** *n* disc covering the face of a ~. 錶面玻璃。 **'~-guard/-chain** *n* strap or chain for securing a ~ to the clothing. 掛錶帶；掛錶鍊。 **'~-key** *n* separate key for winding a ~. 上錶的鑰匙。 **'~-maker** *n* person who makes or repairs ~es. 鐘錶製造人；修錶匠。

water¹ /ˈwɔːtə(r); ˈwɔtɚ/ *n* **1** [U] liquid **(H_2O)** as in rivers, lakes, seas and oceans: 水 (H_2O): *W~ is changed into steam by heat and into ice by cold.* 水加熱則變爲蒸氣，冷却則結爲冰。 *Fish live in (the) ~.* 魚生活在水中。 ***by ~,*** by boat, ship, barge, etc. 由水路；乘船。 ***in deep ~(s),*** experiencing or undergoing difficulty or misfortune. 遭遇困難或不幸。 ***in smooth ~,*** making smooth or easy progress. 進展順利地。 ***on the ~,*** in a boat, etc. 在船(等)上。 ***under ~,*** flooded: 被水淹的: *The fields were under ~ after the heavy rain.* 大雨後田地爲水所淹。 ***be in/get into hot ~,*** have/get into trouble (esp because of foolish behaviour, etc). 陷於困境(尤指因愚蠢行爲等所致)。 ***cast/throw one's bread upon the ~(s),*** do a good action without requiring reward, although later some unexpected return may come. 不求報酬做善事；積陰德。 ***drink the ~s,*** go to a spa where there are mineral ~s and drink them for one's health. 至礦泉處飲礦泉水(以維護健康)。 ***go through fire and ~ (for sb/sth),*** undergo severe hardship and trials. (爲某人或某事)赴湯蹈火；歷經千辛萬苦。 ***hold ~,*** (of a theory, etc) be sound when tested. (指理論等)有道理；站得住脚；說得通。 ***keep one's head above ~,*** avoid (esp financial) troubles or misfortunes. 盡力避免(尤指財務上的)虧欠或損失；不舉債。 ***make ~,*** **(a)** pass urine from the bladder. 小便；撒尿。 **(b)** (of a ship) have a leak. (指船)漏水。 ***spend money, etc like ~,*** extravagantly. 揮霍無度；揮金如土。 ***throw cold ~ on*** (a plan, etc), discourage (it). (爲一項計畫等)澆冷水。 ***tread ~,*** ⇨ tread, *vi, vt*(4). ***like a fish out of ~,*** feeling uncomfortable, behaving awkwardly, because of unaccustomed surroundings, an unfamiliar situation, etc. 如出水之魚；因處生疏環境而感覺不自在或尷尬。 ***Still ~s run deep,*** (prov) Beneath a quiet manner there may be depths of emotion, knowledge, cunning, etc. (諺)靜水流深;沉着的舉止可能蘊函深厚的感情、知識、謀略等。 ***written in ~,*** (of a name, reputation, etc) soon forgotten; transient. (指聲名等)曇花一現的;轉瞬卽逝的。 ***~ on the brain/knee, etc,*** morbid accumulation of fluid. 水腦(膝關節等水腫)。 ***the ~s of forgetfulness,*** oblivion. 忘却;湮滅。 **'table/'mineral ~s,** with a mineral ingredient, bottled for use at table. (餐桌上用的瓶裝)礦泉水。 **'back~,** ⇨ back[4](3). **2** [U] the state of the tide: 潮位;潮: *at high/low ~;* 在高(低)潮; *high/low '~ mark.* 高(低)水位標。 ***in low ~,*** (fig) short of money. (喻)缺錢。 **3** (*pl*) seas as indicated by a preceding word: (複)(由前面的字說明之)海;海域: *in Korean ~s,* on the seas near Korea; 在韓國附近的海面; *a ship for service in Home ~s,* on the seas near the country to which the ship belongs. 航行近海的船。 **4** (usu *pl*) mass of ~: (通常用複數)河;湖;澤;大片的水;洪水: *the ('head-)~s of the Nile,* the lake from which it flows. 尼羅河的河源。 *The ~s of the lake flow out over a large waterfall.* 湖水流經一處大瀑布直瀉而下。 **5** [U] solution of a substance in ~: 溶液: *'lavender-~;* 薰衣草香水; *'rose-~, etc.* 玫瑰香水等。 **6** ***of the first ~,*** of the finest quality: 最佳品質的;第一等貨色的: *a diamond of the first ~.* 最佳品質的鑽石。 **7** (in compounds) (用於複合字中) **'~-bird** *n* kinds of bird that swim or wade in (esp fresh) ~. 水鳥;水禽(尤指棲於淡水中者)。 **'~-biscuit** *n* thin, hard biscuit made of flour and ~, usu eaten with butter and cheese. 一種薄而硬的餅乾(以麵粉和水製成,通常加奶油及乾酪食用)。 **'~-blister** *n* blister on the skin containing a colourless liquid, not blood. (皮膚上的)水疱。 **'~-borne** *adj* **(a)** (of goods) carried by ~. (指貨物)由水路運送的。 **(b)** (of diseases) passed on by the use of contaminated drinking-~. (指疾病)由飲水傳染的。 **'~-bottle** *n* **(a)** glass container for ~ at table or in a bedroom. 玻璃水瓶。 **(b)** metal flask (US 美 = *canteen*) for use by a soldier, scout, etc. (兵士、童軍等使用的)水壺。 **'~-buffalo** *n* the common domestic buffalo of India, Indonesia, etc. 水牛。⇨ the illus at domestic. 參看 domestic 之插圖。 **'~-butt,** ⇨ butt[1](2). **'~-cannon,** high-pressure hose, for forcing a jet of ~, eg to disperse rioters. 水砲(噴射高壓水流的管道,如用以驅散暴亂人羣者)。 **'~-cart** *n* cart with a tank for ~, either for sale or for sprinkling on dusty roads, etc. 運水車。 **'~-chute** *n* sloping channel leading to ~, down which boats, toboggans, etc slide, eg at a fun fair. (樂園等中供人駕小舟、長橇等自高處滑到水面之)滑槽。 **'~-closet** *n* (common abbr 通常略作 **WC**) small room with a pan in which matter evacuated from the bowels may be flushed down a drain-pipe by ~ from a cistern. (有抽水設備的)厠所。 **'~-colour** (US = **-color**) *n* **(a)** (*pl*) paints (to be) mixed with ~, not oil. (複)水彩;水彩顏料。 **(b)** picture painted with ~-colours. 水彩畫。 **(c)** (*pl* or *sing*) the art of painting such pictures. (複數或單數)水彩畫法。 **'~-course** *n* (channel of a) brook or stream. 河;溪;水道;河床。 **'~-cress** *n* [U] creeping plant that grows in running ~, with hot-tasting leaves

waterbirds and seabirds

used in salads. 水芥子(生於流動水中的攀爬植物,葉有辣味,用於生菜食品)。'~ **diviner,** ⇨ diviner. '~**·fall** *n* [C] fall of ~, esp where a river falls over rocks or a cliff. 瀑布。'~**-finder** *n* dowser, ⇨ dowsing. 探尋地下水脈或礦脈者。'~**·fowl** *n* (collective *pl*) ~birds, esp those that swim, considered as suitable for shooting by sportsmen. (集合複數)水鳥;水禽(尤指能游泳,被認爲適於獵殺者)。'~**-front** *n* land at the ~'s edge, esp the part of a town facing the sea, the harbour, a lake, etc. (尤指都市靠近海、海港、湖等的)濱水區;海邊;江邊;湖濱(等)。'~**-glass** *n* [U] thick liquid used for coating eggs to keep them in good condition. 水玻璃(用以塗在蛋上以保持其新鮮)。'~**·hen** *n* = *moorhen,* ⇨ moor'. '~**-hole** *n* shallow depression in which ~ collects (esp in the bed of a river otherwise dry, and to which animals go to drink). 水洞(尤指河床乾涸時之低窪積水部分,爲動物飲水處)。'~**-ice** *n* [C] frozen ~ with sugar and fruit-juices or other flavouring. 冰糕(由糖、果汁或其他調味品凝凍而成)。'~**-jacket** *n* case filled with ~ and fitted over part of a machine which is to be kept cool. (附裝於機器某部分而有散熱作用的)水套;冷却筒管。'~**-jump** *n* obstacle (in show-jumping, steeplechases) of a ditch or water, usu with a fence, over which horses jump. (障碍賽馬等中,馬需要躍過的)水障碍(溝渠或水灘等)。'~**-level** *n* surface of ~ in a reservoir or other body of ~, esp as a datum for measurement. 水平面;水準。'~**-lily** *n* kinds of plant with broad, flat leaves floating on the surface of the ~, and white, blue or yellow flowers. 睡蓮。'~**-line** *n* line along which the surface of the ~ touches a ship's side: 船的吃水線;水線: *the load ~-line,* when the ship is loaded; 船裝載後的水線;載貨水線; *the light ~-line,* when the ship is empty of cargo. 船未載貨時的水線;未載貨水線。'~**-logged** /-lɒgd *US:* -lɔ:gd ; -ˌlɑgd/ *adj* **(a)** (of wood) so saturated with ~ that it will barely float. (指木材)吸飽水的(幾乎浮不起)。 **(b)** (of a ship) so full of ~ that it will barely float. (指船) 漏水嚴重的; 進水太多幾乎浮不起的。 **(c)** (of land) thoroughly soaked with ~. (指土地)被水浸透了的;泥濘的。'~**-main** *n* main pipe in a system of ~-supply. 自來水的主管。'~**·man** /-mən ; -mən/ *n* (*pl* -men) boatman; man who manages a boat for hire; ferryman. 船夫;舟子;渡船夫。'~**·mark** *n* **1** manufacturer's design in some kinds of paper, seen when the paper is held against light. 紙上的水印;透明花紋(迎光時可見)。 **2** mark which shows how high ~ (eg the tide, a river) has risen or how low it has fallen. (潮水,河道等處的)水位標;水量標。'~**·melon** *n* large, smooth-skinned melon with juicy pink or red flesh; trailing plant bearing such melons. 西瓜;西瓜籐。'~**·mill** *n* mill whose machinery is turned by ~-power. 水車;水磨。'~**-nymph** *n* nymph associated with a river, lake, etc. 水中女仙;水精;水仙。'~**-polo** *n* [U] game played by two teams of swimmers who try to throw a ball into a goal. 水球。'~**-power** *n* [U] power obtained from flowing or falling ~, used to drive machinery or generate electric current. 水力(用以推動機器或發電)。'~**·proof** *adj*

W

which does not let ~ through: 不透水的;防水的: *~proof material.* 防水料子;防水布。▭ *n* ~proof coat; raincoat. 雨衣;防水裝。▭ *vt* make ~proof. 使防水;使不透水。'**~-rat / -vole** *n* rat-like animal frequenting ~. 河鼠。'**~-rate** *n* (GB) charge made (usu quarterly) for the use of ~ from a public ~-supply. (英)自來水費(通常按季計算)。'**~·shed** *n* line of high land separating river systems; (fig) dividing line between events which take different courses. 分水線;分水界;(喻)事件的分界線(許多事件間各事件個別發展的基點)。'**~·side** *n* margin of the sea, a river, lake, etc: (海、河、湖等的)水濱;水邊: *go for a stroll along the ~side.* 沿水濱散步。'**~-skiing** *n* the sport of skiing on ~ while being towed at speed by a fast motor-boat. 滑水運動(由汽艇以高速拖着在水上滑行)。'**~-skin** *n* skin bag for carrying ~. (携水用的)革製水袋。'**~-softener** *n* device or substance for removing the causes of hardness in ~. (除去硬水中礦物質的)軟水劑;軟水裝置。'**~-spaniel** *n* kind of spaniel that can be trained to swim out and bring back ~fowl, etc shot down by sportsmen. 水犬(一種長毛垂耳狗,經過訓練後能游水取回射落水面之水鳥等)。'**~-spout** *n* **(a)** pipe or spout from which ~ is discharged, eg rainwater from a roof. 排水管;排水槽;排水口(如用以排除屋頂之雨水)。**(b)** whirlwind over the sea which draws up a whirling mass of ~ so as to look like a funnel-shaped column of ~ going up to the clouds. (海上龍捲風旋起的)旋水柱;海龍捲。'**~-supply** *n* system of providing and storing ~, amount of ~ stored, for a district, town, building, etc. 給水系統;供水;自來水;自來水儲存量。'**~·table** *n* level below which the ground is saturated with ~: 地下水位: *The ~table has been lowered by drought.* 乾旱已使地下水位降低了。'**~-tight** *adj* **1** made, fastened, etc so that ~ cannot get in or out: 不透水的;防水的;水密的;不漏水的: *~-tight boots / joints / compartments in a ship.* 不透水靴(水密接合;水密小船室)。**2** (fig, of an agreement, etc) drawn up so that there can be no escape from any of the provisions; leaving no possibility of misunderstanding. (喻,指合約等)無漏洞的;嚴謹的;無誤解之可能的。'**~-tower** *n* one which supports a large tank which secures pressure for distributing a ~-supply. 自來水塔。'**~-waggon** (US = **-wagon**) *n* = ~-cart: *on the ~-waggon,* ⇨ waggon(1). '**~-way** *n* navigable channel (eg a canal, channel up a river where the ~ is deep enough for ships). 航路;航道;水路。'**~-wheel** *n* one turned by a flow of ~, used to work machinery. (藉水流之力旋轉以推動機器的)水輪。'**~·wings** *n pl* floats worn on the shoulders by a person learning to swim. (學習游泳者套在双肩上的)浮水圈。'**~·works** *n* (with *sing* or *pl v*) (用單數或複數動詞) **1** system of reservoirs, pumping stations, ~-mains, etc for supplying ~. 自來水廠。**2** ornamental fountains. (裝飾性質的)人工噴泉。**3** (colloq) (working of the) bladder: (俗)膀胱(的功能): *Are your ~works all right?* Can you pass urine normally? 你的膀胱功能正常嗎?(你排尿正常嗎?) **4** (colloq) tears: (俗)眼淚: *turn on the ~works,* shed tears. 淌眼淚;哭泣。'**~-worn** *adj* (of rocks, etc) made smooth by the action of ~. (指岩石等)水蝕的(因水的作用而被磨得平滑的)。

water² /ˈwɔːtə(r); ˈwɔtə/ *vt, vi* **1** [VP6A] put water on; sprinkle with water: 澆以水;灑以水: *~ the lawn / the plants / the streets.* 灑水於草地(花木,街道)上。**~·ing-can** /ˈwɔːtərɪŋ kæn; ˈwɔtərɪŋ ˌkæn/ *n* container with a long spout, used for ~ing plants. 噴壺;澆水器。**~·ing-cart** /ˈwɔːtərɪŋ kɑːt; ˈwɔtərɪŋ ˌkɑrt/ *n* one with a tank and a sprinkler for ~ing roads (to settle the dust, clean them). 灑水車。**2** [VP6A] give water to: 供以水;給以飲水: *~ the horses.* 飲馬。**3** [VP2A] (of the eyes or mouth) fill with water; have much liquid: (指眼或嘴)出水;多水;充滿水: *The smoke made my eyes ~.* 煙使我的眼睛流淚。*The smell from the kitchen made my mouth ~,* aroused my appetite. 廚房裏來的香味使我垂涎。Hence, 由此產生, '**mouth-~ing** *adj* highly appetizing. 令人垂涎三尺的;極能引起食欲的。**4** [VP15B] *~ sth down,* add water to: 加水於;冲淡: *This whisky has been ~ed (down).* 這威士忌已加水(冲淡)了。*The story has been ~ed down,* (fig) weakened, eg by making details less vivid. (喻)這故事的生動性已被減弱了。**5** [VP6A] (fin) increase (a company's debt or nominal capital) by issuing new shares without increasing the assets. (財政)藉發行新股票以增加(公司債或名義資本);名義增資。**6** **~ed** (*pp* as *adj*) supplied with water: (過去分詞作形容詞用) 被供以水的: *a country ~ed by numerous rivers.* 河川交錯的國家。**~ed silk,** manufactured so that there are wavy markings on the surface. (面上有波紋的)紋綢。**7** **~·ing-place** /ˈwɔːtərɪŋ pleɪs; ˈwɔtərɪŋ ˌples/ *n* **(a)** water-hole; place to which animals go to drink. 水洞;動物飲水處。**(b)** spa. 有礦泉或溫泉之處。**(c)** seaside resort. 海濱遊憩處。

Wat·er·loo /ˌwɔːtəˈluː; ˌwɔtəˈlu/ *n* ***meet one's ~,*** be finally and crushingly defeated in a contest (esp after a period of success). 最後遭遇慘敗(尤指經過一段成功之後)。

wat·ery /ˈwɔːtərɪ; ˈwɔtərɪ/ *adj* (-ier, -iest) **1** of or like water; (esp of cooked vegetables) containing, cooked in, too much water: 水的;似水的;(尤指煮好的蔬菜)含水太多的;加水太多的: *~ soup / cabbage.* 稀薄的湯(加水太多的包心菜)。**2** (of colour) pale. (指顏色)淡的。**3** (of the eyes or lips) running with, covered with, water. (指眼睛或嘴唇)流着口水的;淚汪汪的。**4** suggesting that there will be rain: 有雨意的;有下雨朕兆的: *a ~ moon / sky.* 有雨意的月亮(天空)。

watt /wɒt; wɑt/ *n* unit of electrical power: 瓦特;瓦(電功率單位): *a 60 ~ light-bulb.* 六十瓦的燈泡。**wat·tage** /ˈwɒtɪdʒ; ˈwɑtɪdʒ/ *n* [U] amount of electrical power expressed in ~s. (電)瓦特數;瓦數。

wattle¹ /ˈwɒtl; ˈwɑtl̩/ *n* **1** structure of sticks or twigs woven over and under thicker upright sticks, used for fences, walls, etc. 編條;枊柵(用作籬笆、圍牆等)。**ˌ~ and ˈdaub,** this structure covered with clay, for walls and roofs. 夾條牆壁或屋頂(由編條外面塗灰泥而成)。**2** kinds of Australian acacia supplying such twigs, with golden flowers adopted as the national emblem. 澳洲產金合歡樹(其枝可作編條,花呈金色,爲澳洲國徽)。

wattle² /ˈwɒtl; ˈwɑtl̩/ *n* red flesh hanging down from the head or throat of a bird, esp a turkey. (禽類,尤指火鷄的)肉垂。⇨ the illus at fowl. 參看 fowl 之挿圖。

wave /weɪv; wev/ *vi, vt* **1** [VP2A, 3A] ***~ (at / to / in),*** (of a fixed object, eg a hand, flag, branch) move regularly to and fro, up and down: (指固定物體,如手、旗、樹枝等)波動;飄揚;揮舞: *flags / branches waving in the wind.* 迎風飄動的旗幟(樹枝)。*Bill ~ed at me,* ie his hand, eg as a signal. 畢爾向我揮手(示意)。*Bill ~ed to me,* ie his hand, eg as a greeting (in meeting or parting). 畢爾向我揮手致意(如相遇或分離時)。**2** [VP6A, 15A, 12A, 13A] cause (sth) to move in this way (eg to make a signal or request, to give a greeting, etc): 使波動、飄揚或揮舞(如作手勢、打招呼等): *~ one's hand at sb;* 向某人揮手; *~ one's umbrella / a flag.* 揮動雨傘(旗幟)。*She ~d (me) a greeting.* 她(向我)揮手致意。*She ~d goodbye to us.* 她向我們揮手告別。**3** [VP15B, 16A] cause (sb) to move in a certain direction by waving: 藉揮舞動作使(某人)向某方向移動: *The officer ~d his men on / ~d them to advance.* 那軍官指揮其士兵(他們)前進。*He ~d us away.* 他揮手叫我們走開。***~ sth aside,*** (fig) dismiss: (喻)不予受理;不予考慮: *My objections were ~d aside.* 我的反對意見未受重視。**4** [VP2A] (of a line or surface, of hair) be in a series of curves (~~~): (指線條或表面,指頭髮)鬈曲;呈波紋狀(如~~~): *Her hair ~s beautifully.* 她的頭髮鬈曲得很漂亮。**5** [VP6A] cause to be in a series of curves: 使鬈曲;使有波紋: *She's had her hair ~d.* 她已把她的頭髮燙鬈了。⇨ perm. □ *n* [C] **1** long ridge of water, esp on the sea, between two hollows (or troughs, furrows); such a ridge curling over and breaking on the shore. 水波;波浪;(尤指)海浪;(拍擊岸邊的)冲浪;碎浪。**the ~s,** (poet) the sea. (詩)海。***in ~s,*** in successive lines like sea-~s: 似海浪般接踵而至地;一波接一波地: *The infantry attacked in ~s.* 步兵一波接一波地攻擊。 **2** act of waving(1) the hand; waving movement: 揮手;揮動;波動;起伏: *with a ~ of his hand,* eg as a signal. 揮動一下手(如作爲信號)。**3** curve like a ~ of the sea: (似海浪般)鬈曲;波紋: *the ~s in a girl's hair.* 一女郎鬈髮上的波紋。*She has a natural ~ in her hair.* 她的頭髮自然鬈曲。 **4** steady increase and spread: 持續的增加及擴散;高潮: *a ~ of enthusiasm/indignation;* 熱情(憤怒)的高潮; *a 'crime ~;* 接踵而來的犯罪事件; *a 'heat ~,* a period of weather with temperatures much higher than usual and over a large area. 熱浪(一段特别炎熱的時期,氣溫比平常高很多,且波及一廣大地區)。**5** ~-like motion by which heat, sound, light, radio, magnetism, etc is spread or carried. (熱,聲,光,無線電,磁等的)波狀運動;波。**'~-length** *n* distance between the highest point (the crest) of one ~ and that of the next (esp with reference to radio telegraphy). (尤指無線電的) 波長。**long/medium/short ~,** ~ used in radio broadcasting: (廣播用的)長(中,短)波: *a short-~ transmitter.* 短波發射機。**wavy** *adj* (-ier, -iest) having ~-like curves: 有波狀曲線的;波形的: *a wavy line;* 波形線; *wavy hair.* 鬈髮。

wa·ver /'weɪvə(r); 'wevɚ/ *vi* [VP2A, C] **1** move uncertainly or unsteadily: 擺動;搖曳: *~ing shadows/flames.* 搖曳的陰影(火焰)。 **2** be or become unsteady; begin to give way: 動搖;開始退讓: *His courage ~ed.* 他的勇氣動搖了。*He ~ed in his resolution.* 他猶豫不定。*The line of troops ~ed and then broke.* 戰線開始動搖,繼而崩潰。**3** hesitate: 躊躇;遲疑: *~ between two opinions.* 遲疑於兩種看法之間。**~er** *n* person who ~s. 動搖者;遲疑者。

wax[1] /wæks; wæks/ *n* [U] soft yellow substance produced by bees (*'beeswax*) and used for making honeycomb cells; kinds of substance similar to beeswax (eg as obtained from petroleum); such material bleached and purified, used for making candles, for modelling, etc: 蜂蠟(亦稱 beeswax); 蠟狀物(如得自石油者);蠟(經過漂白及淨化之蠟狀物,用以製蠟燭、塑像等): (attrib) (形容用法) *a wax candle;* 蠟燭; *a wax doll,* one with the head made of wax; 蠟玩偶; *'paraffin wax;* 石蠟; *'cobblers'-wax,* kind of resin used on thread; 鞋線蠟; *'ear-wax,* substance secreted in the ears. 耳垢。**'wax-chandler** *n* maker or seller of candles. 蠟燭製造商或販賣商。 **'wax·paper** *n* paper that is waterproofed with a layer of wax. 防潮的蠟紙。**'wax·work** *n* object modelled in wax, esp the form of a human being with face and hands in wax, coloured and clothed to look like life and to be exhibited: 蠟製品;蠟人;蠟像: *go to see the waxworks at Madame Tussaud's,* a place in London famous for waxworks. 去倫敦參觀圖梭夫人蠟像館的蠟像。**'sealing-wax,** ⇨ seal *vt*(1). □ *vt* [VP6A] cover, polish or treat with wax: 以蠟塗敷、擦拭或處理: *wax furniture/a wooden floor/linoleum.* 在傢具(木地板,油地氈)上打蠟。 **waxen** /'wæksn; 'wæksn̩/ *adj* **1** (old use; now usu *wax*) made of wax. (舊用法;現通常用 wax)蠟製的。 **2** like wax: 似蠟的: *a waxen complexion.* 蠟黃的面色。**waxy** *adj* like wax; having a smooth, pale surface; like wax in texture: 似蠟的;有光滑而淡色之表面的;結構或質地似蠟的: *waxy potatoes.* 似蠟的馬鈴薯。

wax[2] /wæks; wæks/ *vi* **1** [VP2A] (esp of the moon, contrasted with *wane*) show a larger bright area. (尤指月亮,與 wane 相對)漸滿;變圓。**2** [VP2D] (old use) become: (舊用法)變爲: *wax merry/lyrical/eloquent.* 變得快樂(有詩意,能言善道)。

wax[3] /wæks; wæks/ *n* (sl) fit of anger: (俚)震怒;發怒: *be in/get into/put sb into a wax.* 發怒(震怒;使某人發怒)。**waxy** *adj* angry. 憤怒的。

way[1] /weɪ; we/ *n* **1** road, street, path, etc: 路;街;徑;道路;通路: (in compounds) (用於複合字中) *'highway;* 公路; *'railway;* 鐵路; *'byway;* 小路; *a way across the fields;* 一條横越田野的路; *a covered* (= roofed) *way;* 一條有遮頂的路; *the Appian Way,* a Roman road in Italy. 艾匹亞斯路(義大利古羅馬時期興建的一條道路)。**'clear~,** ⇨ clear[1](5). *There's no way through.* 無路可通。 *My friend lives across/over the way,* on the other side of the street (or road). 我的朋友住在過街那邊。***pave the way for,*** prepare for, prepare people to accept (reforms, etc). 爲…做準備工作;使人民準備接受(改革等)。**the Way of the Cross,** a series of paintings, carvings, etc (usu in or near a church) illustrating the progress of Jesus to Calvary. 苦路(說明耶穌至髑髏地的一系列圖畫、彫刻等,通常展列於教堂內或其附近)。 **2** route, road (to be) used (*from* one place *to* another): 路線;(從一地至他地的)路途(與 from…to…連用): *Which is the best/right/quickest/shortest, etc way there/from A to B?* 哪條路是到該地(由甲地至乙地)最好(正確,最快,最近等)的路? *Can you find your way home?* 你認得你回家的路嗎? *We lost the way/our way in the dark.* 我們在黑夜中迷路了。*Which is the way in/out?* 哪條是進入(出去)的路? *The longest/farthest way round/about is the nearest way home,* (prov) Short cuts are often delusive. (諺)最遠的路才是捷徑;抄小路常靠不住。*We'd better stop and ask someone the way.* 我們最好停下來向人問問路。*He made/pushed/fought/felt his way out/back, etc.* 他走(擠,衝,摸索着走)出去(回來等)。*We had to pick our way along the muddy path.* 我們必須在泥濘的小徑上謹愼前行。***go one's way(s),*** depart. 動身;出發。***go out of one's way (to do sth),*** make a special effort: 特意(花心血,時間等)(做某事);故意(做某事): *He went out of his way to be rude to me/to help me.* 他故意對我粗魯(特意幫助我)。 ***lead the way,*** go in front as leader; show by example how sth may be done. 帶路;帶頭;示範。***make one's 'way in life,*** succeed. 發跡;成功。***make the best of one's way,*** go as fast as one can. 盡量快走。 ***make one's way (to/towards),*** go. (向…)走去。 ***pay one's way,*** **(a)** keep out of debt. 量入爲出;不舉債。 **(b)** pay one's share of expenses instead of letting others pay. 付自己的費用;自掏腰包。***the parting of the ways,*** (fig) the time when an important decision must be made as to future plans, etc. (喻) 對未來的計畫等須做重要决定的時刻。***by way of,*** via; using a route through: 由;經過: *He came by way of Dover.* 他經由多佛來此。⇨ also 14 below. 亦參看下列第 14 義。***out of the way,*** exceptional, uncommon: 奇特的;不尋常的: *He has done nothing out of the way yet.* 他尚未做出不尋常的事。**,out-of-the-'way,** (attrib use) remote: (形容用法)遙遠的;荒僻的: *an out-of-the-way place/corner.* 偏僻的地方(角落)。 **3** ***by the way,*** **(a)** during a journey. 在途中;順路。**(b)** (fig) incidentally; in passing (often used to introduce a remark not connected with the subject of conversation). (喻) 順便說; 却說(常用以引入與當時話題無關的挿語)。***on the/one's way,*** being engaged in going or coming: 在路上;在途中: *They're still on the way.* 他們尙在途中。*I'll buy some on the/my way home.* 我將在回家的途中購買一些。*He's on the way to success.* 他正走向成功的路上。*She's got another*

W

child on the way, (colloq) is pregnant again. (俗)她又懷孕了。***on the way out,*** (fig; colloq) about to become out of date, out of fashion. (喻;俗)行將變得過時或陳舊;快要不流行。 **4** [C] method or plan; course of action: 方法;方式;行動方針: *the right/wrong/best, etc way to do/of doing a thing.* 做某事的正確(錯誤,最好等)的方法。*Is this the way to do it/the way you do it?* 這就是做(你做)那件事的方法嗎? *Do it (in) your own way if you don't like my way.* 如果你不喜歡我的方法,按照你自己的方法做吧。*The work must be finished (in) one way or another.* 這工作必須設法做好。***Where there's a will there's a way,*** (prov) If we want to do sth, we will find a method of doing it. (諺)有志者事竟成。***ways and means,*** methods, esp of providing money. (尤指籌款的)方法。***have/get one's own way,*** get/do what one wants. 爲所欲爲;隨心所欲。***go/take one's own way,*** act independently, esp contrary to the advice of others. 獨斷獨行;我行我素(尤指所爲與他人所進言者相反)。**5** (*sing* only) distance between two points; distance (to be) traversed: (僅用單數) 距離;路程: *It's a long way off/a long way from here.* 那地方距此很遠。*The roots go a long way down.* 這些根入地很深。*Your work is still a long way off perfection,* is far from being perfect. 你的工作距離理想還遠得很。*Your work this week is better by a long way,* much better. 你這個禮拜的工作好多了。*This will go a long way* (=will be very helpful) *in overcoming the difficulty.* 這將很有助於克服困難。 **6** [C] direction: 方向: *He went this/that/the other way.* 他向這(那,另一)邊走。*Look this way, please.* 請向這邊看。*He couldn't look my way,* towards me. 他不可能朝我這方向看。*Such opportunities never come/fall my way,* come to me. 這樣的好機會從不會落到我身上。*You've got your hat on the wrong way,* eg back to front. 你的帽子戴反了。*He's in a fair way to succeed,* is making progress in the right direction. 他正朝著成功的路前進(很有成功的希望)。***put sb in the way of (doing) sth,*** help him to make a start: 幫助某人開始做某事: *A kind friend put him in the way of earning a living.* 一位好心的朋友幫助他走上自立的道路。 **7** (colloq; *sing* only; not stressed) neighbourhood: (俗;僅用單數;不重讀)附近;隣近: *He lives somewhere Lincoln way,* near Lincoln. 他住在林肯市附近。*The crops are looking very well our way,* in our part of the country. 我們這一帶農作物長得很不錯。 **8** [U] advance in some direction; progress (esp of a ship or boat). (向某方向之)行進;(尤指船之)前進。***be under way; have way 'on,*** (of a ship) be moving through the water. (指船)在航行中。***gather/lose way,*** gain/lose speed: 增加(減低)速度: *The boat slowly gathered way.* 船在逐漸增加速度。***get under way,*** start to move forward. 開始前進。***give way,*** (of oarsmen) row hard. (指槳手)努力划。 Also ⇨ give¹(10). ***make way,*** (lit or fig) advance. (字面或喻)前進;進行。 **9** [U] space for forward movement, for passing ahead; freedom to go forward: 向前進的空間;向前進的自由: *Don't stand in the way.* 不要擋住路。*Tell that boy not to get in the way.* 叫那男孩不要擋住路。*Tell him to stand out of the/my way.* 叫他讓開。*Clear the way!* 讓路! ***be/put sth out of harm's way,*** in a safe place. 在(置某物在)安全處。***get sth out of the way,*** settle it, dispose of it. 解決某事;除去某事物。***give way (to sth/sb),*** ⇨ give¹(10). ***make way (for),*** allow space or a free passage: (爲…)讓路: *All traffic has to make way for a fire-engine.* 行人車輛皆應給救火車讓路。***put sb out of the way,*** put him in prison, kill him (secretly), or otherwise get rid of him. 拘禁某人;暗殺或幹掉某人;除去某人。***put sb in the way of sth,*** give him the opportunity of securing, eg a good bargain. 給某人獲得…的機會。***see one's way (clear) to doing sth,*** see how to do it; (esp) feel justified in doing it: 知道如何做某事;(尤指)覺得該做某事;有充分理由做某事: *I don't see my way clear to helping you.* 我不知道怎樣幫助你。*I don't see my way clear to recommending you for the job.* 我不知道該不該推薦你去做那工作。***right of way,*** ⇨ right³(2). **10** [C] custom; manner of behaving; personal peculiarity: 習俗;態度;作風;癖性: *the good old ways;* 良好的古老習俗; *English/Chinese, etc ways of life/living;* 英國人(中國人等)的生活方式; *the way of the world,* what appears to be justified by custom. 世風;世道常情。*It's not his way to be mean,* Meanness is not in his nature. 卑下不是他的本性。*It's disgraceful the way he drinks,* His habit of (excessive) drinking is disgraceful. 他那種縱飲的習慣眞不像話。*I don't like the way* (= manner in which) *he looks at me.* 我不喜歡他那樣看我。 *Don't take offence—it's only his way,* a manner of behaving that has no special significance. 不要生氣 — 他就是那個樣子。***to 'my way of thinking,*** in my opinion. 我認爲。**the way,** (colloq; adverbial use) as; in the manner that: (俗;作副詞用)像;一如: *He doesn't do it the way I do.* 他做那事的方法和我不一樣。***he/she has a way with him/her,*** he/she is persuasive. 他(她)有說服力(講起話來有一套)。***mend one's ways,*** improve one's manners, behaviour, etc. 改善自己的擧止、行爲、方式等。 **11** [C] respect; point or detail: 方面;細節;點: *He's a clever man in some ways.* 他在某些方面很聰明。*Can I help you in any way?* 我能够幫任何忙嗎? *He is in no way* (= not at all) *to blame.* 他決不該受責備。*They are in no way similar.* 他們根本不相似。*The work was well done in one way,* to a limited extent but not on the whole. 那工作在某方面做得很好(整個看來就不然)。*He's an amusing man in his (own) way.* 他是一個很有趣的人。*What have we in the way of food,* What food is there (eg in the house, for the next meal, etc)? 我們有些什麽吃的呢? ***no way,*** (sl) in no way; not at all. (俚)一點也不;不行;決不。 **12** [C] condition, state, degree: 情形;狀態;程度: *Things are in a bad way.* 情勢很糟。*She was in a terrible way,* much agitated. 她異常激動。***'any way,*** in either case; in any case or event. 在任何情況下;兩種情況無論那一種。***each way/both ways,*** (in backing horses) to win, to get a place in the first three. (賭賽馬)獲勝;獲前三名之一。***in the 'family way,*** (colloq) pregnant. (俗)懷孕。***in a big/small way,*** on a big/small scale: 大(小)規模地: *live in a small way,* simply, without ostentation; 過省吃儉用的生活; *a printer in a small way;* 小本經營的印刷商; *advertise in a big way.* 大(規模)做廣告。***have it both ways,*** choose first one and then the other of alternatives in order to suit one's convenience, argument, etc. 左右逢源;脚踏雙船;見風轉舵(二者間先選其一,再選另一,以配合自己的方便、論據等)。 **13** ordinary course: 平常途徑;一般方法: *do sth in the way of business.* 按一般做生意的方式做某事。**14** ***by way of,*** **(a)** as a substitute for or as a kind of: 作爲;當作;代替: *say sth by way of apology/introduction.* 說一點作爲道歉(介紹)的話。**(b)** for the purpose of, with the intention of: 爲了;意在: *make inquiries by way of learning the facts of case.* 爲了獲知該案的眞相而調查。 **(c)** in the course of: 在…之中: *by way of business.* 在營業中。⇨ also 2 above. 亦參看上列第2義。 **15** (*pl*) structure of heavy timber on which a ship is built and down which it slides when launched. (複)造船架;(新船的)下水臺。⇨ *slipway* at slip¹(6). **16** (compounds) (複合字) **'way-bill** *n* list of goods being conveyed by a carrier, with instructions about their destinations, etc. 運貨單(載明運達地點等者)。 **'way-farer** /-feərə(r); -ˌfɛrə/ *n* (liter) traveller, esp on foot. (文)旅人;(尤指)徒步旅行者。 **'way·faring**

/-feərɪŋ ; -ˌfɛrɪŋ/ *adj* travelling: 旅行的;徒步旅行的: *a wayfaring man.* (徒步)旅行者。**'way·side** *n* side of a road: 路旁;道旁: (attrib) (形容用法) *wayside flowers.* 路旁的花。

way² /weɪ ; we/ *adv* far ; by a long way¹(5): 遠;遠離: *The discussion wandered way off the point.* 該項討論遠離了主題。*Bill finished way ahead of me in the 100 metres sprint.* 畢爾在百米賽跑中遠比我先到達終點。*The wage-claim is way above what the firm can afford.* 這項工資要求遠非該公司所能負擔。ˌ**way-'out** *adj* (colloq) strange; eccentric: (俗)奇異的;古怪的: *way-out clothes/ideas.* 奇裝異服(古怪的想法)。

way·lay /ˌweɪ'leɪ ; ˌwe'le/ *vt* (*pt, pp* -laid /-'leɪd ; -'led/) [VP6A] (wait somewhere to) attack, rob (sb); accost (sb) unexpectedly (usu with a request): (在某處等待以)襲擊,搶刼(某人);伏擊;(在路上等候以)攔住(某人)而向其搭訕或招呼: *He was waylaid by bandits.* 他遭到盜匪的伏擊。*He waylaid me with a request for a loan.* 他(在路上)攔住我向我借錢。

way·ward /'weɪwəd ; 'wewɚd/ *adj* self-willed; not easily controlled or guided: 任性的;剛愎的;不易管束的;不聽教導的: *a ~ child;* 頑童; *a child with a ~ disposition.* 性情倔强的小孩。

we /wiː ; wi/ *pron* **1** used by a speaker or writer referring to himself and another or others (with object form *us*). 我們(受格作 us)。**2** used by a King, Pope, etc in proclamations instead of *I*, and by the writer of an unsigned article in a newspaper, etc. 朕(帝王,教皇等在告示中之自稱);報章雜誌文章中不署名時之自稱語。

weak /wiːk ; wik/ *adj* (-er, -est) **1** (opp of *strong*) lacking in strength; easily broken; unable to resist hard wear or use, attack, etc: (爲 strong 的相反字)弱的;虛弱的;脆弱的;易破的;不耐用的;不能抵抗攻擊等的: *too ~ to walk;* 太虛弱不能走動; *~ in the legs;* 兩腿軟弱無力; *a table with ~ legs;* 搖搖晃晃的桌子; *a ~ defence;* 脆弱的防禦工事; *a ~ team;* 弱隊; *the ~ points of an argument/plan.* 論據(計畫)的弱點。ˌ**~-'kneed** *adj* (fig) lacking determination; ~ in character. (喻)無決心的;優柔寡斷的。**2** (of the senses, etc) below the usual standard: (指感官等)不够標準的;衰弱的: ~ (more usu 較常用 *poor*) *sight and hearing;* 視力及聽力不佳; *a ~ heart.* 衰弱的心臟。Hence, 由此產生, *~-eyed;* 視力不佳的; *~-headed;* 低能的; *~-minded;* 懦弱的;優柔寡斷的; *~-sighted.* 視力不佳的。**3** (of mixed liquids or solutions) watery; having little of some substance in relation to the water, etc: (指混合的飲料或溶液)多水的;淡的: *~ tea/beer;* 淡茶(啤酒); *a ~ solution.* 稀薄的溶液。**4** not good; not efficient: 不精的;不擅長的: *~ in spelling/arithmetic/biology.* 不擅長拼字(算術,生物學)。**5** (gram)(文法) **~ verb,** one inflected by additions to the stem, not by vowel change (as *walk, walked,* contrasted with *run, ran* and *come, came*). 弱動詞;規則動詞(詞形變化藉加 ed 或 t 等形成,如 walk, walked; 而非經由改變原字的母音,如 run, ran 及 come, came)。**~ form** (of the pronunciation of some common words), form occurring in an unstressed position, usu by the use of a different vowel sound or by the absence of a vowel sound or consonant (eg /ən ; ən/ or /n ; n/ for /ænd ; ænd/ *and,* as in *bread and butter* /ˌbred n 'bʌtə(r) ; 'brɛdn̩'bʌtɚ/). (指某些常見字的讀音)弱式讀法(用於不重讀的場合,通常不讀原母音,或省去母音或子音,如 bread and butter 中的 and, 讀作 /ən/ 或 /n/)。**~en** /'wiːkən ; 'wikən/ *vt, vi* [PV6A, 2A] make or become ~(er). 使弱;變弱。**~·ling** *n* ~ person or animal. 孱弱的人或動物;弱者。**~·ly** *adv* in a ~ manner. 弱地;虛弱地;脆弱地。□ *adj* delicate in health; not robust: 身體虛弱的;不强壯的: *a ~ly child.* 虛弱的小孩。**~·ness** *n* **1** [U] state of being ~: 弱;虛弱;脆弱: *the ~ness of old age;* 老年的虛弱; *the ~ness of a country's defences.* 一國的脆弱國防。**2** [C] fault or defect of character: 性格的缺點;弱點: *We all have our little ~nesses.* 我們都有一些小缺點。**3** ***have a ~ness for,*** a special or foolish liking for: 特別喜歡…;過於喜歡…: *He has a ~ness for fish and chips/fast cars.* 他特別喜歡吃油炸的魚和馬鈴薯條(開快車)。

weal¹ /wiːl ; wil/ *n* [U] (liter) well-being (chiefly in): (文)幸福;福祉(主要用於): *~ and woe,* good and bad fortune; 禍福; *for the public/general ~,* the welfare of all. 爲公益。

weal² /wiːl ; wil/ *n* [C] mark on the skin made by a blow from a stick, whip, etc. 皮膚上的傷痕、條痕、杖痕、鞭痕等。

weald /wiːld ; wild/ *n* (GB) stretch of open country, formerly forest: (英)原野;曠野;昔日的森林地帶: *the ~ of Kent.* 肯特原野。

wealth /welθ ; wɛlθ/ *n* **1** [U] (possession of a) great amount of property, money, etc; riches: 大量財產(的擁有);財富: *a man of ~;* 富人; *acquire great ~.* 獲得巨大財富。**2** ***a/the ~ of,*** great amount or number of: 多量;大量;豐富;大數目: *a book with a ~ of illustrations;* 一本有大量插圖的書; *the ~ of phrases and sentences to illustrate meanings in this dictionary.* 本字典闡明字義的大量片語及例句。**~y** *adj* (-ier, -iest) having ~(1); rich. 擁有大量財富的;富有的。**~·ily** /-ɪlɪ ; -əlɪ/ *adv*

wean /wiːn ; win/ *vt* **1** [VP6A] accustom (a baby, a young animal) to food other than its mother's milk. 使(嬰兒、幼小動物)斷奶。**2** [VP14] ***~ sb from sth,*** cause (sb) to turn away (from a habit, companions, etc). 使某人戒絕或斷絕某事(如革除某習慣,與人斷絕來往等)。

weapon /'wepən ; 'wɛpən/ *n* sth designed for, or used in, fighting or struggling (eg swords, guns, fists, a strike by workmen): 武器;兵器(如刀、槍、拳、工人的罷工): *Whether a gun is a ~ of offence or a ~ of defence depends upon which end of it you are at.* 槍是攻擊武器還是防禦武器,端視你的目的而定。**~·less** *adj* without ~s. 沒有武器的。

wear¹ /weə(r) ; wɛr/ *n* [U] **1** wearing or being worn; use as clothing: 穿;著;佩;戴: *a suit for everyday ~;* 一套日常穿的衣服; *a coat that has been in constant ~.* 一件經常穿的上裝。*This carpet will stand any amount of hard ~.* 這地氈極其耐用。*This coat is beginning to look the worse for ~,* shows signs of having been worn for a long time, so that it is no longer in a good or useful condition. 這件上裝看起來破舊了。**2** damage or loss of quality from use: 用損;耗損;磨損: *These shoes are showing (signs of) ~.* 這雙鞋子快要穿壞了。***~ and tear,*** damage, loss in value, from normal use. 損耗。**3** capacity to endure: 耐久性;耐用性: *There's not much ~ left in these shoes,* They cannot be worn much longer. 這雙鞋子穿不久了。**4** (chiefly in compounds or in terms used by tradesmen) things to wear: (主要用於複合字或商業用語中)穿的東西;衣著: *'under~;* 內衣; *'foot~;* 鞋襪; *'ladies'/'men's ~;* 女(男)裝; *a shop that specializes in 'children's ~.* 專賣童裝的商店。

W

wear² /weə(r) ; wɛr/ *vt, vi* (*pt* wore /wɔː(r) ; wor/, *pp* worn /wɔːn ; worn/) **1** [VP6A, 22, 15B] have on the body, carry on one's person or on some part of it; (of looks) have on the face: 穿;著;戴;佩;(指面貌)帶着;呈現: *He was ~ing a hat/spectacles/a beard/heavy shoes/a ring on his finger/a troubled look.* 他戴着一頂帽子(戴著一付眼鏡,蓄着鬍子,穿着笨重的鞋子,手指上戴着戒指,面帶憂容)。*This is a style that is much worn now,* that is in fashion now. 這是時下流行的款式。*She never ~s green,* ie green clothes. 她從不穿綠色的衣服。*She used to ~ her hair long,* used to have long hair. 她從前留著長髮。*The house wore* (=had) *a neglected look.* 那房子有一種無人照管的樣子。***~ the crown,*** **(a)** be a monarch. 做國君;做皇帝。**(b)** be a martyr. 做殉道者。**2** [VP2C, D, 22, 15A, B] (cause to) become less useful or to be in a certain condition, by being used: (使)磨損;(使)變舊;用壞: *I have worn my socks into holes.* 我的襪子已磨出洞來了。*This material has worn thin.* 這料子已磨薄了。*The stones were worn by the constant flow of water.* 經常不斷的水流將石頭冲蝕了。*This old overcoat is much worn,* is much the worse for wear. 這件舊大衣已穿得破舊不堪。~ ***away,*** become impaired, thin, weak, as the result of constant use: 磨損;磨去;磨滅: *The inscription on the stone had worn away,* the words were difficult to read. 刻在石頭上的文字已磨損得難以辨認了。 ~ ***sth away,*** consume or impair sth by constant use, etc: 磨損某物: *The footsteps of thousands of visitors had worn away the steps.* 經過萬千遊客長時間的踐踏,臺階磨損了。~ ***down,*** become gradually smaller, thinner, weaker, etc: 磨損;耗損;磨小;磨薄;磨弱等: *The heels of these shoes are ~ing down.* 這雙鞋子的鞋跟已(漸)磨壞了。~ ***sth down,*** cause to ~ down. 使磨損;使耗損;使磨小、磨薄、磨弱。~ ***sb／sth down,*** weaken by constant attack, nervous strain, etc: 藉經常攻擊、騷擾等而使某人或某物衰弱: *These noisy children do ~ me down!* 這些吵鬧的孩子們眞把我煩死了。*We wore down the enemy's resistance.* 我們不斷攻擊敵人而耗弱其抵抗力。~ ***off,*** pass away: 消逝;消失;消滅: *The novelty will soon ~ off.* 這種新鮮感很快就會消逝。~ ***sth off,*** cause to pass away by degrees; be rubbed off by friction: 使磨損;使逐漸消失或消滅;磨掉;磨去: *~ the nap off a piece of velvet.* 磨掉一塊天鵝絨的絨毛。~ ***(sth) out,*** (cause to) become useless, threadbare, exhausted: 使(某物)變得無用、陳舊、枯竭;用壞;穿破;耗盡: *Cheap shoes soon ~ out.* 便宜的鞋子不耐穿。*My shoes are worn out.* 我的鞋子穿壞了。*His patience had／was at last worn out.* 他最後終於忍耐不住了。*He has worn out* (= outstayed) *his welcome.* 他待得太久,以致不受歡迎了。 ~ ***sb out,*** exhaust, tire out: 使某人筋疲力竭;使某人疲憊困乏: *I'm worn out by all this hard work.* 這些艱苦的工作使我疲憊不堪。*That fellow ~s me out with his silly chatter.* 那傢伙喋喋不休,簡直把我煩死了。Hence, 由此產生, ˌ**worn-ˈout** *attrib adj*: *a worn-out coat.* 破舊上衣。 **3** [VP6A] make (a hole, groove, etc) in by rubbing or attrition: 由摩擦而造成(洞,溝等): ~ *holes in a rug／one's socks.* 地毯(短襪)磨破而成洞。*In time a path was worn across the field.* 時間一久,這塊田地上踏出了一條小徑。 **4** [VP2B, 2A, C] endure continued use; remain in a certain condition: 耐用;耐久: *Good leather will ~ for years.* 好的皮革可以耐很多年。*This cloth has worn well／badly.* 這種布很耐穿(不耐穿)。*Old Mr Smith is ~ing well,* still looks well in spite of his advanced age. 史密斯老先生不顯老。 **5** [VP2C] ~ ***on／away, etc,*** (of time) go slowly or tediously; pass gradually: (指時間)緩慢或沉悶地挨過;逐漸過去: *as the evening wore on;* 當夜晚緩緩度過的時候; *as winter wore away;* 當冬季慢慢地過去; *as his life wore towards its close.* 當他的生命漸趨結束的時候。~**er** *n* person who is ~ing sth. 穿戴者;穿某種衣服者;佩帶某物者。 ~**-able** /-əbl ; -əbl/ *adj* that can be, or is fit to be, worn. 可穿着的;可佩帶的;耐磨的。~**·ing** *adj* tiring: 令人疲倦的;使人厭煩的: *a ~ing day.* 令人困乏的一天。

weary /ˈwɪərɪ ; ˈwɪrɪ/ *adj* (-ier, -iest) **1** tired: 疲倦的;勞累的: ~ *in body and mind;* 身心疲勞; *feel ~;* 感到疲倦; *be ~ of someone's constant grumbling.* 對某人經常的抱怨感到厭倦。 **2** causing tiredness: 令人疲倦的;令人厭煩的: *a ~ journey／wait;* 令人厭倦的旅程(等待); *after walking ten ~ miles.* 步行了令人困乏的十哩以後。 **3** showing tiredness: 顯示疲倦的: *a ~ sigh.* 一聲疲倦的歎息。□ *vt, vi* [VP6A, 14, 2A, 3A] ~ ***sb (with sth); ~ of sth,*** make or become ~: (使)疲倦;(使)厭煩: ~ *sb with requests;* 不住的請求使某人厭煩; ~ *of living all alone;* 厭煩獨居; *wearied with marching and climbing.* 因行進和爬山而感到疲倦。**wear·ily** /-əlɪ ; -ɪlɪ/ *adv* **weari·ness** *n* **weari·some** /ˈwɪərɪsəm ; ˈwɪrɪsəm/ *adj* tiring; long and dull. 令人疲倦的;冗長而沉悶的。

wea·sel /ˈwiːzl ; ˈwizl/ *n* small, fierce animal with red-brown fur, living on rats, rabbits, birds' eggs, etc. 伶鼬;黃鼠狼。

weather[1] /ˈweðə(r) ; ˈwɛðə/ *n* **1** [U] conditions over a particular area and at a specific time with reference to sunshine, temperature, wind, rain, etc. (⇨ climate, used with reference to a long period of time, eg a season): 天氣;氣象(參看 climate, 指一季等長時期的天氣狀況): *He stays indoors in wet ~.* 下雨天他常待在家裏。*She goes out in all ~s* (*pl* here = all kinds of ~). 無論天氣如何,她都要外出。*Many crops depend on the ~.* 許多農作物都依靠天氣。 ***be／feel under the ~,*** (colloq) ill. (俗)不適;生病。 ***keep a／one's ˈ~ eye open,*** be on the alert; be on the look-out (for trouble, etc). 警戒;注意(困難、麻煩等)。 ***make good／bad ~,*** (used by sailors) meet with good／bad ~. (水手用語)遇到好(壞)天氣。 ***make heavy ~ of sth,*** find it (unnecessarily) troublesome, difficult. 小題大做。 ***under stress of ~,*** because of storms, etc. 因受惡劣天氣(暴風雨等)的影響。 **2** (compounds) (複合字) ˈ**~-beaten** *adj* bearing marks or signs which come from exposure to the sun, wind, rain, etc: 飽經日曬、風吹、雨打等的;飽經風霜的: *a ~-beaten face.* 飽經風霜的臉。 ˈ**~-boarding／-boards** *nn* horizontal boards each of which overlaps the one below to cause rain to run off and so keep the wall, etc, from becoming damp. 護牆板;封簷板。 ˈ**~-bound** *adj* unable to make or continue a journey because of bad ~. 爲風雨所阻的;因天氣惡劣無法成行或繼續旅程的。 ˈ**~-bureau** *n* office where the ~ is studied and where ~ forecasts are made; meteorological office. 氣象局;氣象所。 ˈ**~-chart／-map** *n* diagram showing details of the ~ over a wide area. 氣象圖;天候圖。 ˈ**~·cock** *n* ~-vane in the shape of a cock. 風標;風信標。 ˈ**~ forecast** *n* ⇨ forecast. ˈ**~-glass** *n* barometer. 晴雨計;氣壓計。 ˈ**~·man** /-mæn ; -ˌmæn/ *n* (*pl* -men) (colloq) man who reports and forecasts the ~. (俗)氣象員;預報天氣者。 ˈ**~-proof** *adj* able to stand exposure to the ~, to keep out rain, snow, wind, etc. 不受氣候影響的;防風雨日晒的;抗風化的。 ˈ**~-ship** *n* one stationed at sea to make observations of the ~. 氣象船。 ˈ**~-station** *n* one where the ~ is observed. 氣象站;測候站。 ˈ**~-vane** *n* = vane(1).

weather[2] /ˈweðə(r) ; ˈwɛðə/ *vt, vi* **1** [VP6A] come through successfully; survive: 平安度過;捱過: ~ *a storm;* 平安度過暴風雨; ~ *a crisis.* 度過一次危機。 **2** [VP6A] sail to the windward of: 航至…的上風: ~ *an island.* 航行至一個島的上風。 **3** [VP 6A] expose to the weather: 晾乾;風乾;曝露: ~ *wood,* leave it in the open air until it is properly shrunk and ready for use. 風乾木材。 ⇨ season, *vt, vi*(1). **4** [VP6A, 2A] discolour, be discoloured, (cause to) become worn by the weather: 褪色;被褪色;(使)因天氣而變磨損;風化;侵蝕: *rocks ~ed by wind and water;* 受風雨侵蝕的岩石; *~ed limestone.* 風化的石灰石。

weave /wiːv ; wiv/ *vt, vi* (*pt* wove /wəʊv ; wov/, *pp* woven /ˈwəʊvn ; ˈwovən/) **1** [VP6A,15A,B,2A] ~ ***sth (up) into sth; ~ sth (from sth),*** make (by hand or by machine) (threads) into cloth, etc; make (cloth, etc) from threads; work at a loom: 織(紗、線)成布等;以紗、線織成(布等);紡織: ~ *cotton yarn into cloth;* 把棉紗織成布; ~ *threads together;* 把紗、線織起來; *woven from／of silk;* 用絲織成的; make (garlands, baskets, etc) by a similar process: 編製(花環、籃等): ~ *flowers into a wreath;* 把花編成花圈; ~ *a garland of flowers.* 編花環。 **2** [VP6A, 15A] (fig) put together, compose (a story, romance, etc): (喻)編排;撰作(故事,傳奇小說等): ~ *a* *story round an incident;* 以某一事件爲中心編撰一個故事; ~ *a plot.* 編排一個情節。***get weaving (on sth),*** (sl) make an energetic start (on a task, etc). (俚)大力開始(一項任務等);幹勁十足地開始(一項事業等)。**3** [VP2C] twist and turn: 迂迴;盤旋;曲折: *The driver was weaving (his way) through the traffic.* 駕車者在行人和車輛中迂迴前進。*The road ~s through the valleys.* 那條路曲折地通過山谷。□ *n* style of weaving: 編法;織法;編織型式: *a loose/tight/coarse/plain, etc ~.* 鬆(緊,粗,平,等)的編織。**~r** *n* person whose trade is weaving cloth at a loom. 織者;織工。**~r-bird** *n* tropical bird that makes its nest by tightly weaving together leaves, grass, twigs, etc. 一種織巢鳥(產於熱帶)。

web /web; wɛb/ *n* [C] **1** network (usu fig): 網;網織品;網狀組織(通常爲比喻用法): *a web of lies/deceit/intrigue.* 謊話連篇(謊話連篇;一套陰謀詭計)。**2** sth made of threads by a spider or other spinning creature: (蜘蛛等結的)網: *a spider's web.* 蜘蛛網。⇨ cobweb. ⇨ the illus at arachnid. 參看 arachnid 之插圖。**3** skin joining the toes of some waterbird, eg ducks, geese, bats and some water-animals (eg frogs). (鴨、鵝等水禽,蝙蝠,以及蛙等水生動物的)蹼;掌皮;翼手。Hence, 由此產生, **ˌweb-ˈfooted/-ˈtoed** *adjj* **webbed** *adj* having the toes joined by webs. 蹼足的;有掌皮的;翼手的。⇨ the illus at fowl. 參看 fowl 之插圖。

web·bing /ˈwebɪŋ; ˈwɛbɪŋ/ *n* [U] strong fabric (usu coarse woven) used in belts, upholstery, binding the edges of rugs, etc. (用作繫帶,室內裝飾品,鑲地毯之邊等的)厚邊;邊帶;結實的帶狀織物。

wed /wed; wɛd/ *vt, vi* (*pt, pp* wedded or wed) [VP6A, 14, 2A] **1** (journalism) marry. (新聞學)結婚;嫁;娶。**2** (liter) unite: (文)結合;合併: *simplicity wed to beauty.* 兼具簡樸和美麗。***wedded to,*** devoted to; unable to give up: 專注於;不能放棄;固執: *He is wedded to his own opinions and nothing can change him.* 他固執己見,什麼也不能使他改變。

we'd /wi:d; wid/ = we had; we would.

wed·ding /ˈwedɪŋ; ˈwɛdɪŋ/ *n* marriage ceremony (and festivities connected with it): 婚禮;婚慶: *invite one's friends to one's ~;* 邀朋友參加其婚禮; *a ~ dress.* 結婚禮服。**ˈ~ breakfast** *n* meal for the bride and bridegroom, their relatives, friends, etc between the ~ ceremony and departure for the honeymoon. 喜宴(在婚禮後蜜月旅行前舉行)。**ˈ~-cake** *n* cake distributed to guests and sent in small portions to absent friends. 結婚蛋糕;喜餅(分送客人及缺席朋友)。**ˈ~-ring** *n* ring placed on the bride's (and in some cases the groom's) finger and worn by her/him afterwards. 結婚戒指。**silver/golden/diamond ~,** 25th/50th/60th (or 75th) anniversary of a ~. 銀(金,鑽石)婚紀念;結婚廿五(五十,六十或七十五)週年。

wedge /wedʒ; wɛdʒ/ *n* **1** V-shaped piece of wood or metal, used to split wood or rock (by being hammered), to widen an opening, or to keep two things separate. 劈;楔;V形木片或金屬片。***the thin end of the ~,*** (fig) a small change or demand likely to lead to big changes or demands. (喻)可能引起重大後果的小事;可能導致重大變化的小變化;可能引發重大需求的小需求。**2** sth shaped like or used like a ~: 形狀或用途似楔之物: *a ~ of cake,* eg cut from a large round cake; 一塊楔形糕餅; *seats arranged in a ~,* so as to form a triangle. 排列成楔形的座位。□ *vt* [VP6A, 15A, 22] fix tightly (as) with a ~; keep in place with a ~: 以楔(等)使之牢固;楔住;嵌;插;擠: *~ packing into a crack;* 把填料楔入裂縫中; *~ a door open,* by placing a ~ under it. 在門下置楔,使之敞開。*I was so tightly ~d between two fat women that it was difficult for me to get up and leave the bus.* 我被兩個肥胖女人緊緊地擠在中間,以致要站起來下公共汽車都很困難。

wed·lock /ˈwedlɒk; ˈwɛdlɑk/ *n* [U] (legal) condition of being married: (法律)結婚的狀態;婚姻;結婚生活: *born in lawful ~,* born of married parents; 婚生的;嫡出的; *born out of ~,* illegitimate. 私生的;庶出的。

Wed·nes·day /ˈwenzdɪ; ˈwɛnzdɪ/ *n* fourth day of the week. 星期三;禮拜三;水曜日。

wee[1] /wi:; wi/ *adj* very small: 很小的;微小的: *just a wee drop of brandy in my coffee.* 我的咖啡中的一小滴白蘭地酒。***a wee bit,*** (adverbial) a little: (作副詞用)少許;些許;有一點: *She's a wee bit jealous.* 她有點妒嫉。***the wee folk,*** the fairies. 小仙人(總稱);仙人們。***the wee hours,*** (US) the hours after midnight. (美)午夜後的一、二、三點鐘。□ *n* (Scot) ***bide a wee,*** stay for a short time. (蘇)待一會兒。

wee[2]**, wee-wee** /(ˈwi:) wi:; (ˈwi) wi/ *n* (used by and to small children) urine: (兒語,對小孩所說的話)小便;撒尿: *do a wee-wee.* 撒尿。□ *vi* urinate. 小便;撒尿。

weed /wi:d; wid/ *n* [U] **1** wild plant growing where it is not wanted (eg in a garden, or in a field of wheat): (園子、麥田等中的)雜草;莠草;野草: *My garden is running to ~s,* is overgrown with ~s. 我的園子裡長滿了雜草。**ˈ~-killer** *n* substance used to kill ~s. 除草劑;除莠劑。**2** (fig) thin, tall, weak-looking person or horse. (喻)高而瘦弱的人或馬;瘦高個子。**3** (dated sl) cigar; cigarette; tobacco; (modern sl) marijuana. (過時俚語)雪茄;香烟;烟草;(現代俚語)大麻烟。□ *vt, vi* **1** [VP6A, 2A] take ~s out of (the ground): 除去(地面)的雜草: *~ the garden;* 除去園子裏的雜草; *be busy ~ing.* 忙於除草。**2** [VP15B] ***~ sth/sb out,*** sort or thin out; remove or get rid of (what is unwanted, or of lower value than the rest): 挑出;揀出;除去;淘汰(不需要者或價值較低者): *~ out the herd,* get rid of the inferior animals. 淘汰劣等牲口。**weedy** *adj* (-ier, -iest) **1** full of, overgrown with, ~s. 多雜草的;長滿雜草的。**2** (sl) tall, thin and weak: (俚)高而瘦弱的: *a ~y young man.* 高而瘦弱的青年男子。

weeds /wi:dz; widz/ *n pl* **widow's ~,** black clothes as formerly worn by a widow for mourning. (昔時的)寡婦的喪服。

week /wi:k; wik/ *n* **1** any period of seven days; (esp) seven days from Saturday midnight to Saturday midnight: 週;星期(尤指自星期六午夜至次一個星期六午夜的七日): *this/last/next ~;* 本(上,下)週; *this day ~,* one week from today; 距今一週; *this Monday ~,* one week from Monday next; 自下一個禮拜一起算一週後; *for the last/next six ~s;* 在過去(未來)的六週間; *a six weeks' holiday;* 六週的假日; *tomorrow ~,* eight days from today; 一週後的明天(八天後); *yesterday ~,* eight days ago; 一週前的昨天(八天前); *three ~s ago yesterday,* twenty-two days ago; 三週前的昨天(二十二天前); *the working ~,* (usu) Monday to Friday or Saturday. 工作週(通常指禮拜一至禮拜五或至禮拜六)。*What day of the ~ is it?* 今天是星期幾? Cf 參較 What's the date? 今天是幾號? ***~ in, ~ out,*** for ~s in succession. 一週又一週地;接連許多星期。**ˌ~·ˈend** *n* Saturday and Sunday (as a period of rest or holiday): 週末(指星期六和星期日,爲休息或度假期間): *a ~end visit to the country;* 週末的鄉間旅行; *spend the ~end with friends.* 和朋友們在一起度週末。□ *vi* spend a ~end: 度週末: *I'm ~ending at Brighton.* 我在布來頓度週末。**ˌ~-ˈender** *n* person spending the ~end away from home. 外出度週末者。**ˌlong ~·ˈend** *n* ~end, together with Friday or Monday as a public holiday. 長週末(自禮拜五開始的週末,或延長至禮拜一的週末)。**2** the working days of the ~. (一週中的)工作日;工作週。**ˈ~·day** /-deɪ; -ˌde/ *n* any day except Sunday: 週日;工作日;除星期天外的任何一天: *I'm always busy on ~days.* 我在週日總是很忙。(attrib) (形容用法) *There are only ~day trains from this sta-*

W

tion. 本站僅工作日有火車開出(週末停駛)。**~·ly** *adj, adv* (happening) once a ~, every ~; of, for a ~: 每週(發生)一次;每週;每週的: *a ~ly wage of £50;* 週薪五十鎊; *~ly visits.* 每週一次的訪問。□ *n* periodical published once a ~. 週刊;週報。

weeny /ˈwiːnɪ ; ˈwinɪ/ *adj* (-ier, -iest) (often 常作 ˌteeny-ˈ~) (colloq) tiny. (俗)極小的;微小的。

weep /wiːp ; wip/ *vi, vt* (*pt, pp* wept /wept ; wɛpt/) [VP2A, B, C, 4B, 3A, 6A] (liter) cry; let tears fall from the eyes: (文)哭泣;流淚: *~ for joy;* 喜極而泣; *~ over one's misfortunes.* 為某人的不幸而哭泣。*She wept to see him in such a terrible state.* 看到他處於那樣的慘境,她哭了。*She wept over her sad fate.* 她為自己悲慘的命運而哀哭。**~·ing** *adj* (of trees, eg the birch and willow) having drooping branches. (指樹,尤指樺樹和柳樹)垂枝的。

wee·vil /ˈwiːvl ; ˈwivl/ *n* small beetle with a hard shell, feeding on and infesting stores of grain, nuts and other seeds. 象鼻蟲;蛄蟹。⇨ boll.

weft /weft ; wɛft/ *n* **the ~,** cross-threads taken over and under the warp in weaving. 緯;緯線。⇨ the illus at warp. 參看 warp 之插圖。

weigh /weɪ ; we/ *vt, vi* **1** [VP6A] measure (by means of a scale, balance, etc) how heavy sth is: 稱…的重量;估量;稱: *He ~ed himself on the scales.* 他在體重器上稱體重。*He ~ed the stone* (= estimated how heavy it was) *in his hands.* 他用手估量這塊石頭的重量。**~ sth out,** distribute in definite quantities; take a definite quantity of: 照定量分配;從…中取出一定的數量: *She ~ed out flour, sugar and butter for a cake.* 她量取麵粉、糖和奶油,要做一塊糕餅。**~ (oneself) in,** (of a jockey, boxer, etc) be ~ed before a race or contest. (指騎師,拳擊師等)比賽前量體重。**~ in (with),** produce (arguments, facts, etc) triumphantly; bring (them) to bear on a discussion. 成功地提出(議論、事實等);把(議論、事實等)運用於討論。ˈ**~-bridge** *n* ~ing-machine with a platform on to which vehicles, etc can be driven to be ~ed. (車輛等可開上去過磅的)地磅;臺秤。ˈ**~·ing-machine** *n* machine for ~ing objects that are too large for a simple balance or scale. 稱量機;衡器。**2** [VP2B] show a certain measure when put on a scale, etc: 重(若干): *~ 10 kilos/a ton/nothing, etc.* 重十公斤(重一噸,無重量等)。*How much do you ~,* How heavy are you? 你的體重是多少? **3** [VP2C] (of a machine, etc) be capable of taking, designed to take, objects up to a specified weight: (指機器等)可處理重達若干的物體: *This machine will ~ up to 5 tons.* 這機器可處理重達五噸的物體。**4** [VP6A, 14, 15B] **~ sth (with/against sth),** compare the importance, value, etc of (one thing and another): 權衡;考量;對比;比較(一物與他物)的重要性或價值: *~ one plan against another.* 評估一計畫與另一計畫的優劣。**~ sth (up),** consider carefully, assess: 仔細估量;慎重考慮: *~ (up) the consequences of an action;* 評估某一行動的後果; *~ one's words,* consider/choose them carefully; 斟酌字句; *~ the pros and cons.* 權衡贊成與反對的理由。**5** [VP15B, 3A] **~ sth down,** pull or bring down; depress: 把某物壓下;使某物沉下;壓低: *The fruit ~ed the branches down.* 果實使樹枝下墜。**~ sb down,** depress; make tired, troubled, etc: 使某人悶悶不樂;使某人困乏、擔心、懸慮等: *~ed down with sorrow/cares/anxieties.* 因憂愁(擔心,焦慮)而悶悶不樂。**~ on sb/sth,** cause concern, anxiety (because of importance, seriousness): 重壓;(因為重要、嚴重等而)使關心、焦慮: *The problem/responsibility ~s heavily on him/on his mind.* 那個難題(那項責任)沉重地壓在他的身上(心上)。**~ with sb,** influence: 影響某人: *evidence that did not ~ with the judges;* 不為法官所重視的證據; *the point that ~s with me.* 對我有重大關係之處。**6 ~ anchor,** raise the anchor and start a voyage. 起錨;啓航。

weight /weɪt ; wet/ *n* **1** [U] gravitational force with which a body tends towards the centre of the earth. 重力。**2** [U] how heavy a thing is; this expressed in some scale (eg tons, kilogrammes) as measured on a scale, weighing-machine, etc (⇨ App 5): (物體的)重量;分量(如噸,公斤)(參看附錄五): *Are bananas sold by ~ or at so much a piece?* 香蕉是論重量賣呢,還是論根賣? *That man is twice my ~.* 那個人的體重是我的兩倍。*My ~ is 70 kilos.* 我的體重是七十公斤。*The two boys are (of) the same ~.* 那兩個男孩體重相等。*He is your superior both in size and in ~.* 他的塊頭和體重都超過你。**under/over ~,** weighing too little/too much. 過輕(過重);不到(超過)分量。**pull one's ~,** ⇨ pull²(2). **put on ~,** (of a person) become heavier. (指人)體重增加;長胖。**throw one's ~ about,** (colloq) be domineering or conceited; try to bully people. (俗)仗勢欺人;濫用權勢。**3 a/the ~ (of),** load to be supported: 負擔;重累;重擔: *The pillars have a great ~ to bear/have to support the ~ of the roof.* 這些柱子須承受重大的壓力(須承受屋頂的重量)。*That's a great ~ off my mind.* 那眞釋去了我心頭的一大重負。*He has a great ~ of responsibility.* 他肩負着重大的責任。**4** [U] (degree of) importance or influence: 重要;勢力;影響力;重要或影響力的程度: *arguments of great ~;* 有力的論據; *considerations that had great ~ with me.* 對我有重大影響的因素。**carry ~,** be important or influential: 具重要性;具影響力: *a man/an opinion that carries ~.* 有影響力的人物(意見)。**5** [C] piece of metal of known ~ used in scales for weighing things: 稱錘;砝碼;秤鉈: *an ounce/100 grammes/2 lb, etc ~;* 一嘝(一百克,兩磅等)的砝碼; heavy object for various purposes: 作各種用途的重物: *a clock worked by ~s;* 利用擺走動的鐘; *keep papers down with a ~ (ˈpaper-~).* 用文鎭(紙壓)把紙壓住。*The doctor said he must not lift ~s.* 醫生說他切不可舉重物。ˈ**~-lifting** *n* gymnastic feat of lifting great ~s. 舉重(體操項目之一)。**6** [U] system of units, scale or notation, for expressing ~: 計重法;衡制: *troy/avoirdupois ~.* 金(常)衡。□ *vt* **1** [VP6A] put a ~ or ~s(5) on; add ~ to; make heavy: 放錘或砝碼於…之上;加重;使重: *~ a walking-stick with lead,* eg to make it useful as a weapon. 加鉛於手杖,使之重量增加(俾用作武器等)。*Circumstances are ~ed in his favour,* (fig) give him an extra advantage. (喻)情況對他尤其有利。**2 ~ sb down,** burden with: 使負重擔: *He was ~ed down with packages.* 他拿着過多的包裹。**3** [VP6A] treat (a fabric) with a mineral substance to make it seem stronger: 用礦物質處理(織物)使之顯得更結實: *~ed silk.* 以礦物質處理過的綢布。**~·less** *adj* having no ~, eg because of absence of gravity. 無重量的;失重的(例如因為沒有地心引力)。**~·less·ness** *n*: 無重量;失重狀態: *become accustomed to ~lessness in a spacecraft.* 習慣於太空船裡的失重狀態。**~y** *adj* (-ier, -iest) **1** of great ~; burdensome. 重的;煩重的;累人的。**2** influential; important: 有影響力的;重要的: *~y considerations/arguments.* 重要的因素(論據)。**~·ily** /-ɪlɪ ; -əlɪ/ *adv* **~i·ness** *n*

weir /wɪə(r) ; wɪr/ *n* [C] wall or barrier across a river to control the flow of water; fence of stakes or broken branches in a stream as a trap for catching fish. 堰(攔河建築之牆或似牆物,用以控制水流);魚梁(溪流中以樁或斷枝構成的柵欄,用以捕魚)。

weird /wɪəd ; wɪrd/ *adj* **1** unnatural; unearthly; mysterious: 不自然的;怪誕的;非人世所有的;神秘的: *~ shrieks from the darkness of the ruined castle.* 從殘破城堡的黑暗處傳來的怪誕尖叫聲。**2** (colloq) strange; difficult to understand or explain: (俗)奇異的;難以瞭解或解釋的: *What ~ shoes women sometimes wear!* 女人穿的鞋子有時多麼怪模怪樣呀! **~ie** /ˈwɪədɪ ; ˈwɪrdɪ/, **~o** /ˈwɪədəʊ ; ˈwɪrdo/ *nn* (sl) eccentric person, esp one who is very unconventional in behaviour, dress and appearance.

(俚) 古怪的人 (尤指行爲、服飾、模樣非常不合習俗者)。 **~·ly** *adv.* **~·ness** *n*

wel·come /ˈwelkəm; ˈwɛlkəm/ *adj* **1** received with, giving, pleasure: 受歡迎的;令人愉快的: *a ~ visitor/rest;* 受歡迎的訪客(休息); *~ news;* 佳音;可喜的消息; *make a friend ~,* show him that his coming is ~. 使朋友覺得受歡迎。*A loan would be very ~ to me just now.* 現在如果誰肯借我錢,我會很高興。 **2 ~ to do sth/to sth,** **(a)** freely permitted: 可隨意做某事;可隨意取用某物: *You are ~ to borrow my bicycle.* 歡迎你借用我的單車。*You are ~ to the use of my car.* 你可以隨意借用我的車。*Anyone is ~ to my share,* may have it. 歡迎任何人用我這一份。**(b)** (ironic) permitted to have sth burdensome or unwanted: (反語)歡迎做(某麻煩事);歡迎取(人家不要之物): *If anyone thinks he can do this job any better, he's ~ to it/~ to try!* I'll gladly let him do it. 如果有人認爲這件事他可以做得更好一點,他不妨來做做看(歡迎他試一試)。**(c)** absolved of the need to express thanks: 不必表示感謝的: *You are ~ to it* (usu shortened to) (通常略作) ***You're ~,*** = Don't mention it. 別客氣。 **3** (as an interjection) (用作感嘆詞) *W~ home!* 歡迎歸來! *W~ to England!* 歡迎到英國來! (歡迎莅臨英國!) □ *n* [C] greeting, response by word or action, when sb arrives, when an offer is received, etc: 歡迎;接待;款待: *They gave us/We received a warm/cold/enthusiastic, etc ~.* 他們給予我們(我們受到)熱烈(冷淡,熱誠等)的歡迎。*The heartiest of ~s awaited us.* 最熱烈的歡迎在等待着我們。□ *vt* [VP6A, 15A] show pleasure or satisfaction at sth, at the arrival of sb or sth; greet (in the manner indicated): 歡迎;(以某種態度)接受: *~ a friend to one's home;* 歡迎朋友到家中; *~ a suggestion warmly/coldly.* 熱烈地(冷淡地)接受一項建議。

weld /weld; wɛld/ *vt, vi* **1** [VP6A, 15A, B] join (pieces of metal) by hammering or pressure (usu when the metal is softened by heat) or fusing by the use of an oxy-acetylene flame or an electric arc; make by doing this: 鎔接;銲接;鍛接: *~ the pieces of a broken axle;* 銲接斷了的車軸; *~ parts together;* 銲接零件; (fig) (喻) *arguments that are closely ~ed.* 嚴謹的論據。⇨ the illus at oxy-acetylene. 參看 oxy-acetylene 之插圖。 **2** [VP 2A] (of iron, etc) be capable of being ~ed: (指鐵等)能鎔接;可被銲接: *Some metals ~ better than others.* 有些金屬比其他金屬容易銲接。□ *n* ~ed joint. 銲接點;鎔接的接頭。**~er** *n* workman who ~s. 鎔銲工人。

wel·fare /ˈwelfeə(r); ˈwɛlˌfɛr/ *n* [U] **1** condition of having good health, comfortable living and working conditions, etc: 平安;安寧;福祉;福利;幸福: *work for the ~ of the nation;* 爲謀求國家的福祉而工作; *be concerned about sb's ~;* 關心某人的幸福; *child/infant ~.* 兒童(嬰兒)的福利; **the W~ State,** name applied to a country with State-financed social services, eg health, insurance, pensions. 福利國家 (以政府財政舉辦衛生、保險、養老金等社會服務的國家)。 **2** (US) social security. (美)社會安全; 社會保障。 **~ work(er),** (US) social work(er). (美) (社會) 福利事業 (工作者)。

wel·kin /ˈwelkɪn; ˈwɛlkɪn/ *n* (poet) sky: (詩)天空;蒼穹: *make the ~ ring,* make the air re-echo with shouts. 呼喊之聲響徹雲霄。

a weir

well¹ /wel; wɛl/ *n* **1** shaft, usu lined with brick or stone, for obtaining water from an underground source: 井: *drive/sink a ~.* 開井;鑿井。**ˈ~-water** *n* water from a ~. 井水。 **2** hole bored for mineral oil: 油井: *the ˈoil-~s of Iran.* 伊朗的油井。 **3** (old use, or in place-names) spring or foundation of water; (fig) source. (舊用法,或用於地名中)泉;水源;(喻)來源。**ˈ~-head** *n* source of a spring or fountain. 泉源;水源。 **4** deep, enclosed space in a building, often from roof to basement, for a staircase of lift. 井孔(建築物中深而封閉的空間,通常自屋頂至底層,以安設樓梯或電梯)。**5** (GB) railed space for barristers, etc in a law court. (英) (法庭上有圍欄的) 律師席。**6** **ˈ~-deck** *n* space on the main deck of a ship, enclosed by bulwarks and higher decks. 凹形甲板(主甲板上由舷牆及較高甲板圍成的部分)。□ *vi* [VP2C] **~ out (from/of),** flow, like water from a ~: 湧出;噴出;流出: *The blood was ~ing out (from the wound).* 血(從傷口)流出。 **~ over,** overflow. 溢流;泛濫。 **~ up (in),** rise, like water in a ~: 湧升;湧出;湧現: *Tears ~ed up in her eyes.* 眼淚從她的眼中湧出。*Their anger ~ed up.* 他們怒火上升。

well² /wel; wɛl/ (comp better, superl best) *adv* **1** in a good, right or satisfactory manner (placed after the *v*, and after the direct object if the *v* is transitive): 好;對;滿意地 (置於動詞後,如果是及物動詞,置於直接受詞後): *The children behaved ~.* 孩子們行爲良好。*They are ~-behaved children.* 他們是乖孩子。*The house is ~ situated.* 那房子地點適中。*He speaks English ~.* 他的英語說得很好。 *W~ done!* 做得好! *W~ run!* 做得好! *W~ played!* (cries indicating satisfaction, praise, etc). 表演得好!(表示滿意、讚美等的喊叫聲)。*I hope everything is going ~* (= satisfactorily) *with you.* 但願你事事如意。*Do these two colours go ~ together,* Do they harmonize, look satisfactory side by side? 這兩種顏色調和嗎? *Does this colour go ~ with that colour?* 這顏色配得上那顏色嗎? **do ~,** succeed; make progress; prosper: 成功;有進步;興旺: *Simon has done ~ at school this term.* 塞孟本學期在學校裏成績很好。 *Peter is doing ~ in Canada.* 彼得在加拿大過得很好。**be doing ~,** (progressive tenses only) making a good recovery (from illness, etc): (僅用於進行式) (生病等後) 復原或恢復情況良好: *Both mother and baby are doing ~.* 母親與嬰兒恢復情況都很好。**do oneself ~,** provide oneself with good things, esp comforts and luxuries. 生活優裕。**do ~ by sb,** treat him with generosity. 善待某人。**do ~ out of,** make a profit from sb or sth. 從(某人或某事物)獲得好處或利益。***wish sb ~,*** hope that he has good fortune, success, etc. 祝某人好運;祝某人成功等。**2** with praise or approval: 誇獎地;稱讚地: *think/speak ~ of sb.* 重視(稱讚)某人。*It speaks ~ for your teaching that all your pupils passed the examination,* This fact is evidence that your teaching was good. 你教的學生考試都及格了,這證明你教學優異。***stand ~ with sb,*** be in his favour: 合某人之意: *He stands ~ with his employers,* They like him, think highly of his abilities, etc. 他的雇主們都喜歡他。 **3** fortunately. 幸運地。 ***be ˌ~ ˈout of sth,*** be out of an affair without loss, etc: 安然脫免;未受損失等而擺脫某事: *You are ~ out of it,* may consider yourself fortunate to be out of the affair. 你有幸而擺脫此事。*I wish I was ~ out of this business,* that I could free myself from it without misfortune. 我希望我能安然擺脫這事務。 ***~ off,*** **(a)** fortunate: 幸運的: *He doesn't know when he is ~ off,* does not realize how fortunate he is. 他不知道他是多麼幸運。**(b)** wealthy. 富裕的;有錢的。***~ ˈoff for,*** ~ provided with: 被充分供以;充分備有: *~ off for food/drink/bright ideas.* 有充分的食物(有充分的飲料;滿腦子的巧妙主意)。***come off ~,*** **(a)** (of a person) have good fortune; be lucky. (指人)有好

W

運;幸運。**(b)** (of an event) have a satisfactory outcome. (指事件)有滿意的結果。***do ~ to + inf,*** used to suggest either good judgement or good luck: 用來表示好的判斷或好運: *He did ~ to leave the country before the revolution started.* 他幸好在革命開始前離開了那個國家。*You would do ~* (= It would be wise for you) *to say nothing about what happened.* 你最好不要提發生了什麼事。*You did ~ to ask my advice.* 你來徵詢我的意見,算是你運氣。**4** (mid position) with good reason, justice or likelihood; advisably: (置於句中助動詞與動詞之間)有理由地;合理地;可能地;適當地: *You may ~ be surprised.* 你可能感到驚訝。*We might ~ make the experiment.* 我們該做那項實驗。*I couldn't very ~ refuse to help them,* It would have been difficult, unreasonable, etc, to have done so. 我(當時)很難拒絕幫助他們。*You may quite ~* (= with good reason) *give illness as an excuse.* 你儘可把生病當作藉口。*We may as ~ begin at once.* 我們還是馬上開始的好。*It may ~ be that...,* It is likely or possible that.... 那很可能就是⋯。**5** ***'may ('just) as ~,*** ⇨ may(4). **(a)** with equal reason, advantage, justification, etc: 不如;等於是;還是⋯好: *You might just as ~ say that white is black* (*as say that...*). 你(說⋯)等於說白的就是黑的。*Our holidays were ruined by the weather—we might just as ~ have stayed at home!* 我們的假期被天氣糟塌了;我們還不如待在家裏! **(b)** without worse consequences: 沒有更壞的結果: *You may as ~ tell me the truth,* ie because if you don't tell me, I shall certainly hear it from others. 你還是把眞相告訴我的好。***be just as ~,*** with no loss of advantage, no need for regret: 無何損失;無須後悔;不妨: *It's just as ~ I didn't lend him the money.* 我不會後悔沒有借錢給他。**6** (end position) thoroughly; completely: (置於動詞之後,或及物動詞的受詞之後)徹底地;充分地: *Examine the account ~ before you pay it.* 在付款以前仔細核對一下帳目。*Shake the bottle ~.* 把這個瓶子徹底搖一搖。**7** to a considerable extent: 至相當的程度;頗;甚: *He was leaning ~ back / forward in his chair.* 他坐著身體靠在椅背上(他坐在椅上,身體前傾著)。*His name is ~ up in the list,* near the top. 他的名字列在相當前面(靠近頂端)。*He must be ~ past forty / ~ over forty years of age.* 他一定超過四十歲很多了。*It's ~ worth trying.* 那很値得一試。**'~ away, (a)** making good progress: 進展良好: *We're ~ away,* have made a good start. 我們已經有了好的開端。**(b)** (colloq) on the way to being slightly drunk, to becoming hilarious, etc. (俗)有點醉意了;玩鬧得快要忘形了。***be ~ up in / on,*** ⇨ up(8). ***leave / let ~ alone,*** leave it as it is; don't interfere. 保持原來的樣子;維持原狀;不介入;不干預。**8** ***as ~ (as),*** in addition (to): 除⋯外;同;和;並;也: *He gave me money as ~ as advice.* 他除了給我忠告外,還給我錢。*He gave me advice, and money as ~.* 他給我忠告,並給我錢。*We shall travel by night as ~ as by day,* both by night and by day. 我們將日夜趕路。*Give me those as ~,* = those, too. 把那些也給我。**9** (with another *adv*) (與另一副詞連用) ***pretty ~,*** almost: 幾乎: *You're pretty ~ the only person who's willing to help.* 你幾乎是唯一願意協助的人。□ *pred adj* **1** in good health: 健康的;安好的: *be / look / feel / get ~.* 是(看起來,感覺到,恢復)健康的。*I'm quite ~, thank you.* 我很好,謝謝你。Cf 參較 *I'm fine, thank you.* **2** in a satisfactory condition: 滿意的;良好的: *All's ~ that ends ~.* 凡事結局好,則全局都好(事業的成敗以結局爲憑,不必計較所經歷的艱苦)。*We're very ~ where we are.* 我們目前情況甚好。*All is not ~ in the world nowadays.* 當前的世界情勢並不令人滿意。***It's all very ~...,*** formula (used ironically) to indicate discontent, dissatisfaction, disagreement, etc: (反語用法)表示不平,不滿,不同意等的套語: *It's all very ~ (for you) to suggest a holiday in Italy, but how am I to find the money?* (你)提議去義大利度假的確很好,但是我如何去籌這筆錢呢? **3** advisable; desirable: 得當的;適宜的: *It would be ~ to start early.* 最好早點動身。*It would be just as ~ for you to ask your employer's permission.* 你最好徵求雇主的同意。**4** lucky; fortunate: 幸運的;有好運的: *It was ~ for you that nobody saw you.* 沒有人看到你,是你的運氣。□ *int* **1** (expressing astonishment): (表示驚愕): *W~, who would have thought it?* 啊,誰會想得到是這樣呢? *W~, ~! I should never have guessed it!* 唉呀!我永遠猜不出來! **2** (expressing relief): (表示慰藉): *W~, here we are at last!* 好了,我們終於到了! **3** (expressing resignation): (表示無可奈何): *W~, it can't be helped.* 唉,這是沒有辦法的事。*W~, there's nothing we can do about it.* 唉,我們無能爲力了。**4** (expressing understanding or agreement): (表示瞭解或同意): *Very ~, then, we'll talk it over again tomorrow.* 很好,那末明天我們再談談吧。**5** (expressing concession): (表示讓步): *W~, you may be right.* 好罷,你也許是對的。**6** (used to resume a story, etc): (用於繼續一個故事等): *W~, as I was saying,....* 唔,當時我談到,⋯。*W~, the next day....* 後來,第二天⋯。

well- /wel; wɛl/ **1** (*pref*) **,~-'being** *n* [U] welfare; health, happiness and prosperity: 平安;健康;幸福;福利;興盛: *have a sense of ~-being,* good bodily health; 覺得健康(快樂); *work for the ~-being of the nation.* 爲國家的福祉而工作。**,~-'doer** *n* (archaic) virtuous person. (古)君子;善人。**,~-'doing** *n* [U] (archaic) virtuous conduct; good deeds. (古)善行;好事。**'~-nigh** *adv* (archaic) almost: (古)幾乎;殆: *It's ~-nigh impossible.* 那幾乎是不可能的。*He was ~-nigh drowned.* 他幾乎被淹死。**,~-to-'do** *adj* wealthy. 富裕的;富有的。**'~-wisher** *n* person who wishes well to one, to a cause, etc. 祝福者。**2** (compounds with numerous participles and words in *-ed,* usu hyphened when attrib (before a *n*), but not hyphened when pred except when the compound has acquired a restricted sense): (與很多分詞及加 -ed 的字構成複合字,作爲形容用法(置於名詞之前)時,通常加短畫,作爲敍述用法時,除有限定含意外,不加短畫): **,~-ad'vised,** prudent; wise: 審愼的;明智的: *a ~-advised action.* 審愼的行爲。**,~-ap'pointed,** having all the necessary equipment, furniture, etc: 配備或裝備齊全的;設備完善的: *a ~-appointed expedition / hotel / office / suite.* 裝備齊全的探險隊;設備完善的旅館(辦公室,套房)。**,~-'balanced,** sane, sensible. 精神正常的;意識健全的;通情達理的。**,~-'born,** of a family with high social position. 出身名門的;家庭背景好的。**,~-'bred,** of good upbringing. 教養良好的。**,~-con'ducted,** characterized by good organization and control: 品行端正的;組織良好的;安排妥當的: *a ~-conducted meeting.* 一次妥爲安排的會議。**,~-con'nected,** connected by blood or marriage with families of good social position or to rich or influential people. 與望族或權貴有血親或姻親關係的。**,~-dis'posed (towards),** having kind feelings (towards); ready to help. (對⋯)懷有好意的;樂於助人的。**,~-'favoured,** (old use) good-looking. (舊用法)樣子好看的;貌美的。**,~-'found,** = ~-appointed. **,~-'founded,** based on facts, having a foundation in fact: 有事實爲依據的;有根據的: *~-founded suspicions.* 有根據的懷疑。**,~-'groomed,** carefully tended; neat; meticulously dressed. 細心照料的;整潔的;穿着考究的。**,~-'grounded, (a)** = ~-founded. **(b)** having a good training in or knowledge of the groundwork of a subject. 具有某學科之良好基礎的;根底好的。**,~-'heeled,** (sl) rich. (俚)有錢的。**,~-in'formed, (a)** having wide knowledge. 見識廣博的;博識的。**(b)** having access to reliable information: 消息靈通的;能獲得可靠消息的: *in ~-informed quarters.* 消息靈通方面。**,~-in'tentioned,** aimed or aiming (often or usu unsuccessfully) at good results. 出自善意的;好心的;指望有好結果的(常常或通常事與願違,未產生好的結果)。**,~-'knit,** compact;

firmly jointed, not loose-made (esp of a person or his body).(尤指人或其身體)結實的;强健的;硬朗的。ˌ~-ˈ**known,** widely known. 出名的; 衆所週知的。ˌ~-ˈ**lined,** (of a purse, colloq) full of money. (指錢包,俗)放滿錢的。ˌ~-ˈ**marked,** definite; distinct. 清楚的; 明顯的。ˌ~-ˈ**meaning,** = ~-intentioned. ˌ~-ˈ**meant,** done, said, etc, with good intentions. 出於善意的。ˌ~-ˈ**read,** having read much; having a mind well stored with information as the result of wide reading. 讀書多的; 博學多聞的; 腹笥寬的。ˌ~-ˈ**rounded,** complete and symmetrical. 完全而對稱的。ˌ~-ˈ**set,** = ~-knit. ˌ~-ˈ**spoken,** **(a)** speaking well, politely, in refined language. 善於辭令的;言語謙恭的;說話漂亮的。**(b)** spoken well. 說得中肯的;得體的。ˌ~-ˈ**timed,** done, said, at the right or a suitable time. 在正確或適當的時間做出或說出的;做得或說得恰合時宜的。ˌ~-ˈ**tried,** (of methods, remedies) tested and proved useful. (指方法,救治法)經過試驗而證明有用的。ˌ~-ˈ**turned,** (of a compliment, phrase, verse) gracefully expressed. (指讚語,片語,詩句)措辭巧妙的;說得妙的。ˌ~-ˈ**worn,** much used; (esp) commonplace; trite. 用得太多的;(尤指)陳腐的;平凡的。

we'll /wiːl ; wil/ = we shall; we will.

wel·ling·ton /ˈwelɪŋtən ; ˈwɛlɪŋtən/ *n* ~ **(boot),** water-proof boot reaching to the knee. 威靈頓長靴(高達膝部的防水靴)。

Welsh /welʃ ; wɛlʃ/ *n, adj* (the language) of the people of Wales. 威爾斯語;威爾斯人的。ˌ~ ˈ**rabbit**/ˈ**rarebit,** ⇨ rarebit.

welsh /welʃ ; wɛlʃ/ *vi* [VP3A] ~ *on sth/sb.* **1** avoid payment of: 賴帳: ~ *on a debt.* 賴債。**2** break one's word to: 對…食言: ~ *on a friend.* 失信於友人。**~er** *n*

welt /welt ; wɛlt/ *n* [C] **1** strip of leather to which the sole and the upper part of a shoe are stitched. (鞋底與鞋面接縫之間的)革條。**2** = weal².

Welt·an·schau·ung /ˌveltˌɑːnˈʃaʊʊŋ ; ˈvɛltˌɑn-ˌʃaʊ·ʊŋ/ *n* (G) philosophy of life; perception of the world. (德)人生觀;世界觀。

wel·ter¹ /ˈweltə(r) ; ˈwɛltə/ *vi* [VP2C] roll; wallow; be soaked or steeped (in blood, etc). 滾動;翻滾;浸浴(於血等中)。□ *n* (*sing* only) general confusion; disorderly mixture or aimless conflict: (祇用單數)混亂;混雜;紛爭: *the ~ of creeds/political beliefs;* 各種宗教信仰(政治信仰)的紛爭; *a ~ of meaningless verbiage.* 一堆無意義的冗詞。

wel·ter² /ˈweltə(r) ; ˈwɛltə/ *adj* ˈ~ **race** *n* race for horses with heavy-weight riders. 重騎師賽馬;重負賽馬。ˈ~-**weight** *n* (esp boxing) boxer weighing 135-147lb/61-66.6kg. (尤指拳擊)次中量級的拳擊者(體重在135至147磅,或61至66.6公斤之間)。

wen /wen ; wɛn/ *n* [C] harmless, usu permanent, tumour on the scalp or other part of the body; (fig) abnormally large or overgrown urban area. (生於頭皮或身體其他部分的)良性腫瘤;(通常爲永久性的)贅疣;(喻)都市之過分擴大或發展的地區。

wench /wentʃ ; wɛntʃ/ *n* (archaic) (古) **1** girl or young woman. 少女;少婦。**2** prostitute. 妓女。□ *vi* [VP2A] associate with prostitutes. 嫖妓。

wend /wend ; wɛnd/ *vt* (old use, only in) (舊用法,僅用於) ~ ***one's way (home),*** go, make one's way. 走;赴;往;回(家)。

went /went ; wɛnt/ *pt* of go¹.

wept /wept ; wɛpt/ *pt, pp* of weep.

were /wɜː(r) ; wɝ; *weak form:* wə(r) ; wɚ/ *pt* of be¹.

we're /wɪə(r) ; wir/ = we are.

weren't /wɜːnt ; wɝnt/ = were not.

were·wolf /ˈwɪəwʊlf ; ˈwɪrˌwʊlf/ *n* (*pl* -wolves /-wʊlvz ; -ˌwʊlvz/) (myth) human being turned into a wolf. (神話)變成狼的人;狼人。

wert /wɜːt ; wɝt/ ***thou ~,*** (archaic) you were. (古)你是。

Wes·leyan /ˈwezlɪən ; ˈwɛslɪən/ *n, adj* (member) of the Methodist Church deriving from John Wesley. 美以美教派(起源於約翰·衞斯理)的;美以美教派信徒。

west /west ; wɛst/ *n* **1 the ~,** point of the horizon where the sun sets; that part of the world, of a country, etc, in this direction: 西;西方;西部: *Bristol is in the ~ of England.* 布里斯托在英格蘭的西部。**the W~, (a)** Europe and the continent of America (contrasted with Asia). 西方;西洋(指歐洲及美洲大陸,與亞洲相對)。**(b)** (world politics) Western Europe and America (contrasted with Eastern Europe, the USSR and China). (國際政治)西方國家;西方集團(指西歐與美國;與東歐,蘇聯及中國相對)。**(c)** the part of the US between the Mississippi River and the Pacific Ocean. 美國西部(介於密西西比河與太平洋之間)。**(d)** ~ern part of any country. 任何國家的西部。ˌ~-**north·ˈwest,** ˌ~-**south·ˈwest,** ⇨ the illus at compass. 參看 compass 之插圖。**2** (attrib) coming from the ~: (形容用法)來自西方的: *a ~ wind;* 西風; towards, at, in the direction of the ~: 向西方的;在西方的;西方的: *on the ~ coast;* 在西海岸; *~ longitude.* 西經。**the W~ End,** part of London with the largest and most fashionable shops, theatres, etc. 倫敦西區(倫敦之最大最時髦的商店,戲院等的所在地)。Hence, 由此產生, ˌ~-ˈ**end** *adj*: *~-end theatres/department stores.* 倫敦西區的戲院(百貨公司)。**the** ˈ~ **country,** part of England ~ of a line from the Isle of Wight to the mouth of the River Severn. 英格蘭西部地方(自威特島至塞汶河口連成一直線,指此線以西的部分)。Hence, 由此產生, ˈ~-**country** *adj* of, from, characteristic of the ~ country. (英格蘭之)西部地方的;來自西部地方的;具有西部地方特徵的。**W~ Central,** (abbr 略作 **WC**) London postal districts. 西中央區(倫敦郵遞區之一)。□ *adv* towards the ~: 向西;向西地: *sail/travel ~.* 向西航行(旅行)。***go ~,*** (sl) be lost, ruined, etc. (俚)歸西;完蛋;失掉;失敗;毁滅;破產等。~ ***of,*** farther ~ than. 在…之西。ˈ~**·ward** /-wəd ; -wɚd/ *adj* towards the ~: 向西的: *in a ~ward direction.* 向西方地。**~·ward(s)** /-wəd(z) ; -wɚd(z)/ *adv*: *travel ~ward(s).* 向西旅行。

west·er·ly /ˈwestəlɪ ; ˈwɛstɚlɪ/ *attrib adj* towards the west; (of winds) from the west. 向西的;(指風)來自西方的。□ *adv* towards the west. 向西。

west·ern /ˈwestən ; ˈwɛstɚn/ *adj* of, in, from, characteristic of, the west: 西方的;在西方的;來自西方的;有西方之特徵的: **the W~ Hemisphere,** N and S America. 西半球(卽南北美洲)。**the W~ Empire,** that part of the old Roman Empire with Rome as its capital. 西羅馬帝國(古羅馬帝國分裂後,以羅馬爲首都的部分)。□ *n* [C] film or novel dealing with life in the ~ part of the US in the times of the wars with the American Indians, or one with cowboys, rustlers, sheriffs, etc. 西部電影或小說(描寫美國西部昔日與印第安人作戰時代之生活,或描寫西部牛仔、偷牛賊或警官等之生活者)。**~er** *n* native of the West, esp of the ~ US. 西方人;泰西人;(尤指美國的)西部人。**~·ize** /-aɪz ; -ˌaɪz/ *vt* [VP6A] introduce ideas, ways of living, working, etc of *the West*(b) into. 引進西方的觀念、生活方式、活動方式等;使西化。**~·iz·ation** /ˌwestənaɪˈzeɪʃn *US:* -nɪˈz- ; ˌwɛstɚnɪˈzeʃən/ *n* ˈ~**·most** /-məʊst ; -ˌmost/ *adj* farthest west. 最西的;極西的。

wet /wet ; wɛt/ *adj* (wetter, wettest) **1** covered or soaked with water or other liquid: 濕的;潮濕的: *wet clothes/roads.* 濕衣服(濕路)。*Her cheeks were wet with tears.* 她的面頰沾滿了淚水。*Did you get wet,* eg in the rain? 你淋濕了嗎? *We got wet to the skin,* Our clothes were soaked through. 我們渾身濕透了。*Your coat is wet through,* from one side to the other. 你的上裝濕透了。ˌ**wet** ˈ**blanket,** ⇨ blanket(1). ˌ**wet** ˈ**dock** *n* one (that can be) filled with water, able to float a ship. 濕塢(有水的或可進水的船塢)。ˈ**wet-nurse** *n* woman employed to suckle another's child. 乳母;奶媽。ˌ**wet**

ˈ**paint,** paint recently applied, not yet dry. 尚未乾的油漆。 **2** rainy: 多雨的;下雨的: *wet weather;* 雨天; *the wettest summer for 20 years.* 二十年來最多雨的夏季。 **3** (US) not prohibiting or opposing the sale and use of alcoholic drinks: (美)不禁酒的: *a wet State.* 不禁酒的州。 **4** (sl, of a person) ineffectual; spiritless. (俚,指人)無效率的;沒精打采的;沒精神的。□ *n* **1 the wet,** rain: 雨: *Come in out of the wet.* 進來免得淋雨。 **2** [U] moisture. 濕氣;潮濕;水分。 □ *vt* (*pt, pp* wetted or wet) (-tt-) [VP6A] make wet: 使濕: *The baby has wet(ted) its bed again.* 嬰兒又尿床了。 ***wet one's whistle,*** ⇨ whistle, *n*(3). **wet·ting** *n* becoming or being made wet: 濕;變濕: *get a wetting,* eg in heavy rain. 淋濕(如在大雨中)。

wether /ˈweðə(r) ; ˈwɛðɚ/ *n* castrated ram. 閹過的公羊;閹羊。

we've /wiːv ; wiv/ = we have.

whack /wæk *US:* hwæk ; hwæk/ *vt* [VP6A] strike (sb or sth) with a hard blow; thwack. 重擊(某人或某物);用力打。□ *n* **1** (sound of a) hard blow. 重擊;重擊聲。 **2** (sl) share: (俚)份: *Have you all had a fair ~?* 你們都已得到公平的一份了嗎? **~ed** *adj* (colloq) (of a person) worn out; tired. (俗)(指人)疲倦的;困乏的。 **~·ing** *n* beating: 毆打;打擊: *give a naughty child a ~ing.* 把頑皮的小孩打一頓。 □ *adj* (colloq) big of its kind: (俗)在同類中甚大的;特大的: *a ~ing lie.* 大謊言。□ *adv* (colloq) very: (俗)非常;甚: *a ~ing great lie.* 彌天大謊。 **~er** *n* sth big of its kind. 同類中的大者;特大物。

whale /weɪl *US:* hweɪl ; hwel/ *n* **1** kinds of large sea-animal some of which are hunted for their oil and flesh (used for pet foods). 鯨。 ⇨ the illus at sea. 參看 sea 之插圖。 ˈ**~-bone** *n* thin, horny springy substance from the upper jaw of some kinds of ~. 鯨鬚(細而有彈性的角質物,生於數類鯨魚的上顎)。 **2** (colloq) ***a ˈ~ of a time,*** an exceedingly good time; no end of a good time. (俗)非常愉快的時光;無窮盡的愉快時光。□ *vi* [VP2A] hunt ~s: 捕鯨: *go whaling;* 去捕鯨; *the whaling industry.* 捕鯨業。 ˈ**whaling-gun** *n* one used for firing harpoons at ~s. 捕鯨砲。 **~r** /ˈweɪlə(r) *US:* ˈhw- ; ˈhwelɚ/ *n* man or ship engaged in hunting ~s. 捕鯨人;捕鯨船。

whang /wæŋ *US:* hwæŋ ; hwæŋ/ *vt* (colloq) strike heavily and loudly. (俗)砰然重擊。□ *n* ~ing sound or blow. 重擊聲;重擊。□ *adv* (colloq) exactly: (俗)恰好;正好: *hit the target ~ in the centre.* 恰好擊中靶心。

wharf /wɔːf *US:* hwɔːrf ; hwɔrf/ *n* (*pl* ~s or wharves /-vz ; -vz/) wooden or stone structure at which ships are moored for (un)loading cargo. 碼頭;埠頭。 ˈ**~·age** /-ɪdʒ ; -ɪdʒ/ *n* [U] (money paid for) accommodation at a ~. 碼頭設備;碼頭費。

what /wɒt *US:* hwɒt ; hwɑt/ *adj* **1** (interr) asking for a selection from an indefinite number (⇨ which): (疑問)什麼;哪一個或哪些個: *W~ books have you read on this subject?* 你讀過哪些有關這方面的書? *Tell me ~ books you have read recently.* 告訴我,你近來讀過什麼書。 *W~ time is it?* 現在幾點鐘了? *Ask him ~ time it is.* 去問問他現在幾點鐘了。 *W~ size/colour/shape, etc do you want?* 你要什麼尺碼(顏色,形狀等)? **2** (exclamatory): (用於感嘆句中): *W~ a good idea!* 多麼好的主意! *W~ genius you have!* 你多麼有才氣啊! **3** the... that; any... that; as much/many... as: …的;任何…的;所…的: *Give me ~ books* (= the books, any books, that) *you have on the subject.* 把你所有關於這方面的書都給我。 *W~ little* (= The little that) *he said on the subject was full of wisdom.* 他就該問題所說的幾句話充滿了智慧。 *W~ few friends* (= The few friends that) *I have here have been very kind to me.* 我在這裡的幾個朋友一直對我很好。□ *pron* (interr) ~ thing(s): (疑問)什麼東西;什麼: *W~ happened?* 發生了什麼事? *Tell me ~ happened.* 告訴我發生了什麼事。 *W~ is he,* W~ is his occupation? 他是做什麼的? ˌ~... ˈ***for,*** for ~ purpose: 爲何;爲何目的: *W~ is this tool used for?* 這工具是做什麼用的? *W~ did you do that for,* (colloq) Why did you do that? (俗)你爲什麼要做那事? ˌ**~-ˈfor** *n* [U] (colloq) punishment: (俗)處罰;懲戒: *give sb ~-for.* 處罰某人。 ˌ~... ˈ***like,*** (used to ask for a description, for details, etc): (用來要求作一番描述,說明細節等): *W~'s the weather like this morning?* 今天早晨的天氣怎麼樣? *W~'s the new neighbour like?* 新搬來的鄰居人怎麼樣? ˈ***~ if,*** ~ will, would, be the result if: 萬一…怎麼辦: *W~ if it rains while we are a long way from shelter?* 萬一天下雨而我們離躲雨的地方又很遠怎麼辦? *W~ if the rumour is true?* 如果謠言是眞的怎麼辦? ˈ***~ though,*** (liter) ~ does it matter if: (文)即使…又有什麼關係: *W~ though we are poor, we still have each other.* 窮算得了什麼,祇要我們還能彼此相守。 ***~ about/of,*** **(a)** ~ news is there about.... 關於…有何消息。 **(b)** ⇨ about³(4), of (10). ˌ***~ ˈof it?*** (or, mod colloq) (在現代口語中亦用) ˌ***So ˈ~?*** (used to admit that sth is true, but questioning the inference (to be) made from it.) 是又怎麼樣? (用於承認某事是眞實的,但質詢由此會推論出何種結論。) ***and ˈ~ not,*** and other things of the same kind. 等等;諸如此類。 ***and/or ˌ~ ˈhave you,*** used to indicate that there are other things, etc: 等等(用來表示還有其他東西等): *Then there are bills for gas and electricity and ~ have you.* 還有瓦斯及電費等的帳單。 ˈ**~-not** *n* unnamed thing; piece of furniture with open shelves for small ornaments, odds and ends. 叫不出名字的東西;陳列小裝飾品及零碎東西的格架。 ˌ***I know ˈ~...,*** I have an idea, a suggestion to make.... 我有意見;我建議…。 ˌ***I/I'll tell you ˈ~...,*** Here's a suggestion.... 我建議…。 ***know ˌ~'s ˈ~,*** have common sense; know how to distinguish useful things from useless, good things from bad, etc. 有常識;有判斷力等。 ˈ**~-d'you-call-him/-her/-it/-them** /ˈwɒt dʒʊ kɔːl ɪm *etc* ; ˈhwɑt dʒʊ kɔl ɪm *etc*/; ˈ**~'s-his/-her/-its/-their-name,** used as substitutes for a name that one cannot recall. 某某;某人;某物;某先生;某女士(用以代替記不起來的名字)。□ *rel pron* that which; the thing(s) which: 兼爲先行詞的關係代名詞: *W~ he says is not important.* 他所說的話並不重要。 *Do ~ you think is right.* 照你認爲對的去做。 *W~ the country needs most is wise leadership.* 國家最需要的是睿智的領導。 *When people say that they know ~ they like, they really mean that they like ~ they know,* They like ~ they are familiar with. 當人們說他們知道他們喜歡什麼的時候,他們眞正的意思是說他們所喜歡的是他們所知道的事物。 *It's a useful book and, ~ is more, not an expensive one.* 這是一本有用的書,而且價錢不貴。 ˈ***~ with... and (ˈ~ with),*** between various causes: 一方面因爲…一方面因爲;因…和: *W~ with one thing and another,...,* as a result of many things,.... 由於種種原因…。 *W~ with overwork and (~ with) undernourishment he fell ill.* 一方面由於工作過度,一方面由於營養不良,他病倒了。

what·e'er /wɒtˈeə(r) *US:* hw- ; hwɑtˈɛr/ (poet for) (詩) whatever.

what·ever /wɒtˈevə(r) *US:* hw- ; hwɑtˈɛvɚ/ *adj* **1** (emphatic for *what*) of any sort, degree, etc: (what 的强勢語)任何種類,程度等的;不論什麼: *W~ nonsense the newspapers print, some people always believe it.* 無論報紙上刊登什麼荒謬的東西,總會有人相信。 *Take ~ measures you consider best.* 採取任何你認爲最好的措施。 **2** (placed after a *n* in a negative context, giving emphasis to the negative): (在否定文句中置於名詞之後,强調否定語氣): *There can be no doubt ~ about it.* 該事是毫無疑問的。 *I have no intention ~* (= not the least intention) *of resigning.* 我毫無辭職的意思。□ *pron* **1**

no matter what: 不論什麼;無論如何: *You are certainly right, ~ others may say.* 不論別人怎麼說,你確實是對的。*Keep calm, ~ happens.* 無論發生什麼事都要保持冷靜。 **2** anything or everything that: 任何…的事物;每一…的事物: *Do ~ you like.* 做任何你喜歡做的事。*W~ I have is at your service.* 我所有的每一樣東西,你都可以任意使用。**3** ***or ~,*** (colloq) (usu at the end of a list of similar *nn* or *adjj*) or anything at all: (俗)(通常置於一系列類似的名詞或形容詞之後)或任何東西;諸如此類: *He'd have difficulty in learning any language—Greek, Chinese, or ~.* 他學習任何語言都會遭遇困難 — 不論是希臘語,漢語,或諸如此類。

what·so·e'er /ˌwɒtsəʊˈeə(r) *US:* ˈhw- ; ˌhwɑtsoˈɛr/ (poet for) (詩) **what·so·ever** /ˌwɒtsəʊˈevə(r) *US:* ˈhw- ; ˌhwɑtsoˈɛvɚ/ (emphatic for) whatever. 爲 whatever 的强勢語。

wheat /wi:t *US:* hw- ; hwit/ *n* [U] (plant producing) grain from which flour (as used for bread and pastry products) is made: 小麥;小麥粒: *a field of ~.* 小麥田。⇨ the illus at cereal. 參看 cereal之挿圖。**~en** /ˈwi:tn *US:* ˈhw- ; ˈhwitn̩/ *adj* of ~: 小麥的: *~en flour/bread.* 麵粉(麵包)。

wheedle /ˈwi:dl *US:* ˈhw- ; ˈhwidl̩/ *vt* [VP6A, 14] ~ ***(into/out of),*** make oneself pleasant to sb, flatter or coax, to get sth one wants: 諂媚;阿諛(以期獲得所需要的東西);哄;騙;(用甜言蜜語)騙取: *The girl ~d a pound out of her father/~d her father into buying her a bicycle.* 那女孩用甜言蜜語從她父親那裡得到了一鎊(使她父親爲她買了一輛脚踏車)。

wheel /wi:l *US:* hwi:l ; hwil/ *n* **1** circular frame or disc which turns on an axle (as on carts, cars, bicycles, etc and for various purposes in machines). 輪;車輪;機輪。⇨ the illus at bicycle. 參看 bicycle 之挿圖。***~s within ~s,*** (fig) complicated motives and influences; indirect and secret agencies, all interacting. (喩)錯綜複雜的動機及影響力;交互作用的間接及隱匿的諸般力量;複雜的情勢,局面,結構等。***put one's shoulder to the ~,*** help a cause or undertaking. 幫助推展某項事業、運動或任務;出一把力。***the man at the ~,*** the driver (at the steering-~ of a car, etc). 駕駛員;舵手。**ˈ~·barrow** *n* small vehicle with one ~ and two handles for moving small loads. 手推車;獨輪手車。**ˈ~·base** *n* distance between the axles of a motor-vehicle. (機動車輛的)軸距(卽汽車等自前輪軸中點至後輪軸中點的距離)。**ˈ~-chair** *n* chair with large ~s for the use of sb unable to walk. (病人等用的)輪椅。**ˈ~·house** *n* small enclosed place on a ship (old style sailing-ship, a small river-launch, a tug, etc), to shelter the pilot or steersman. (舊式帆船、小型內河汽船、拖船等的)舵手室。**ˈ~-wright** *n* man who makes and repairs (esp waggon and cart) ~s. 製造及修理車輪的人;輪匠;車匠。 **2** ***potter's ~,*** ⇨ potter²; **ˈpaddle-~,** ⇨ paddle¹(3). **3** [C] motion like that of a ~; motion of a line of men as on a pivoted end, esp as a military movement: 旋轉運動;旋轉;(尤指軍隊操練時的)方向變換: *a right/left ~.* 向右轉(左轉)。□ *vt, vi* **1** [VP6A, 15A, B] push or pull (a vehicle with ~s): 推動;拉動(車子): *~ a bike up a hill;* 騎脚踏車爬上斜坡; *~ a barrow;* 推動手推車; convey (sb or sth) in a vehicle with ~s: 以車載運: *~ the rubbish out to the dump.* 把垃圾用車運到垃圾場去。 **2** [VP2A, C, 6A, 15B] (cause to) turn in a curve or circle: (使)旋轉;廻旋: *The sails of the windmill were ~ing round.* 風車的車葉正在旋轉。*The seagulls were ~ing in the air above me.* 海鷗正在我的上空盤旋。*Right/Left ~!* (an order given to a column of men, esp troops, to change their line of route to the right (left)). 向右(左)轉走!(隊伍,尤指軍隊,變換方向的口令)。

wheeze /wi:z *US:* hwi:z ; hwiz/ *vi, vt* **1** [VP2A, B, C] breathe noisily, esp with a whistling sound in the chest (as when suffering from asthma); (of a pump, etc) make a similar sound. 有響聲地呼吸;(尤指)喘息;哮喘;(指唧筒等)發出似喘息的聲音。 **2** [VP15B] ~ ***sth out,*** utter with such sounds: 哮喘地說;喘息地發出: *The asthmatic old man ~d out a few words.* 那哮喘的老人喘息地說出幾個字。*A barrel-organ was wheezing out an old tune.* 一架筒風琴正在喝哧喝哧地奏出一首老歌。□ *n* [C] **1** sound of wheezing. 喘息聲;哮喘聲。 **2** (dated school sl) trick; bright idea. (過時的學校俚語)詭計;巧妙的主意。**wheezy** *adj* breathing, speaking, uttered, with ~s: 喘息地呼吸,說話,發聲的: *a fat and wheezy old dog;* 一隻肥胖喘息的老狗; *a wheezy old pump.* 發喝哧聲的舊唧筒。**wheez·ily** /-ɪlɪ ; -ɪlɪ/ *adv* **wheezi·ness** *n*

whelk /welk *US:* hwelk ; hwɛlk/ *n* kinds of marine mollusc (like a snail) with a spiral shell, some used as food. 峨螺;油螺(有的可食用)。⇨ the illus at mollusc. 參看 mollusc 之挿圖。

whelp /welp *US:* hwelp ; hwɛlp/ *n* **1** young dog, lion, tiger, bear, wolf, fox, etc. 幼獸(幼犬,幼獅,幼虎,幼熊,幼狼,幼狐等)。**2** ill-bred boy or youth. 缺乏教養的男孩或青年。□ *vi* give birth to ~s(1). 產幼獸。

when /wen *US:* hwen ; hwɛn/ *interr adv* **1** at what time; on what occasion: 於何時;於何時機;什麼時候: *W~ can you come?* 你什麼時候能來? *W~ did that happen?* 那事是何時發生的? *I don't know ~ that happened.* 我不知道那事是何時發生的。 **2** (after a *prep*) what time: (用於介詞後)何時;什麼時候: *Till ~ can you stay?* 你可以待到什麼時候? *Since ~ has he been missing?* 他從何時起失踪的? □ *rel adv* (with *day, time,* etc as antecedent) at or on which: (以 day, time 這一類字爲先行詞)在那時;其時;斯時: *Sunday is the day ~ I am least busy.* 禮拜天是我最不忙的一天。*There are times ~ joking is not permissible.* 有的時候開玩笑是不許可的。*It was one of those cold, wet evenings ~ most people stay indoors.* 那是一個寒冷陰雨而人們大都會待在家裡的晚上。□ *conj* **1** at or during the time that: 當…時;在…之際;在…的時候: *It was raining ~ we arrived.* 我們到的時候,正在下雨。*He waved ~ he saw her.* 當他看到她的時候,他揮手致意。*W~ speaking French, I often make mistakes.* 我在講法語的時候,時常犯錯。 **2** although: 儘管;雖然: *He walks ~ he might take a taxi.* 雖然他可以坐計程車,他還是步行。 **3** since; considering that: 旣然;鑒於: *How can I help them to understand ~ they won't listen to me?* 旣然他們不願意聽我說,我怎麼能幫助他們瞭解呢? **4** at or during which time: 屆時;在那時;當其時: *The Queen will visit the town in May, ~ she will open the new hospital.* 女王將於五月間訪問該城,屆時她將主持一所新醫院的開幕典禮。

whence /wens *US:* hwens ; hwɛns/ *adv* (formal) (正式用語) **1** (in questions) from what place or cause: (用於問句中)從何處;何以;因何;由何: *Do you know ~ she came?* 你知道她從何處來嗎? *W~ comes it that…,* How is it that…? 怎麼會…? **2** (in statements) from which place: (用於敍述句中)從哪地方;從哪處;從哪裡: *the land ~ they are come.* 他們來的地方。**3** to the place from which: 向或到…的地方: *Return ~ you came.* 回到你來的地方去。**ˌ~·so·ˈever** *adv, conj* from whatever place, cause or origin. 無論從何處;無論由何原因,原由,出處。

when·ever /wenˈevə(r) *US:* hw- ; hwɛnˈɛvɚ/ *adv, conj* **1** at whatever time; no matter when: 在任何時候;無論何時: *I'll discuss it with you ~ you like.* 你什麼時候高興,我都願意同你討論這件事情。 **2** on any occasion; as often as; every time that: 於任何時機;每逢;每當: *W~ that man says 'To tell the truth', I suspect that he's about to tell a lie.* 每逢那個人說'說實在話'的時候,我都在懷疑他要說謊了。**3** ***or ~,*** (colloq) or at any time: (俗)或任何時間;或任何時候: *He might turn up on Monday, or Friday, or ~, and expect to be given a meal.* 他也許禮拜一,或禮拜五,或任何時候來,並可望被招待一餐。

where /weə(r) *US:* hweə(r) ; hwɛr/ *interr adv* **1**

in or to what place or position; in what direction; in what respect: 在何處或何位置;至何處或何位置;在何方向;在何方面: *W~ does he live?* 他住在何處? *I wonder ~ he lives.* 我想知道他住在何處。*W~ shall we be* (ie What will be our situation) *if another world war breaks out?* 如果另一場世界大戰爆發,我們處境如何? **2** (with a *prep* following the *v*) what place: (與接在動詞之後的介詞連用)何處;什麼地方: *W~ does he come from?* 他是哪裏人? *W~ are you going to?* 你到哪裏去? *W~ did we get up to,* ie What point did we reach? 我們到達何種地步了? □ *rel adv* **1** (with *place*, etc as antecedent) in or at which: (以 place 等爲其先行詞)在那裏;在該處: *She would like to live in a country ~ it never snows.* 她喜歡住在不下雪的國家。*That's the place ~ the accident occurred.* 那就是出事的地點。 **2** (with no antecedent) in, at or to the place in which; in the direction in which: (無先行詞)在,於,或至…的地方;在…方向或方面: *W~ there is no rain, farming is difficult or impossible.* 在不下雨的地方,農業是困難的或根本不可能。*I found my books ~ I had left them.* 我在我原來放的地方找到了我的書。*That's ~* (ie the point in respect of which) *you are mistaken.* 那就是你錯誤的地方了。 **ˌ~·a'bouts** *adv* in or near what place: 在何處;近何處: *W~abouts did you find it?* 你在何處找到(它)的? *I wonder ~abouts he put it.* 我不知道他(把它)放在哪裏了。▭ **'~·abouts** *n* (with *sing* or *pl v*) place ~ sb or sth is: (與單數或複數動詞連用)下落;某人或某物所在之處;行踪;所在: *Her present ~abouts is/are unknown.* 她現在行止不明。 **ˌ~·'as** *conj* **1** (esp legal) considering that. (尤作法律用語)鑒於;既然;就…而論。 **2** but in contrast; while on the other hand: 反之;而在另一方面;却;而: *Some people like fatty meat, ~as others hate it.* 有些人喜歡肥肉,而有些人却不喜歡。 **ˌ~·'at** *adv* (old use) at or upon which. (舊用法)在那裏;對於那個;關於那個。 **ˌ~·'by** *adv* by what; by which: 憑什麼;憑那;由是: *He devised a plan ~by he might escape.* 他想出了一個可藉以逃走的辦法。 **'~·fore** *adv* (old use) why. (舊用法)爲何;何故。 ***the whys and the ~fores,*** the reasons, causes. 理由;原因。 **ˌ~·'in** *adv* (formal) in what; in which; in what respect: (正式用語)在那裡面;在其中;在那點上;在那方面;在什麼地方: *W~in am I mistaken?* 我錯在什麼地方? **ˌ~·'of** *adv* (formal) of what; of which. (正式用語)關於什麼;關於那個;關於它。 **ˌ~·'on** *adv* (old use) on which; on what. (舊用法)在其上;在那上面;在什麼上面。 **ˌ~·so·'ever** *adv* (emphatic for) *~ver.* 爲 wherever 的强勢語。 **ˌ~·'to** *adv* (old use) to what; to which; to what end (= purpose). (舊用法)向哪裡;向那個;爲何目的。 **ˌ~·'unto** *adv* (old use) (舊用法) = *~to.* **ˌ~·u'pon** *adv* after which; and then. 因此;於是。 **wher·ever** /ˌweər'evə(r) *US:* ˌhw- ; hwɛr'ɛvɚ/ *adv* in, to, at, whatever place; at those places: 在,到,於任何地方;無論何處;在那些…的地方: *Sit ~ver you like.* 隨便坐在那裡吧。*He comes from Boula, ~ver that may be,* from a place called Boula, and I have no idea where it is. 他的老家是一個叫「布拉」的地方,我不知道這地方在哪裏。 **ˌ~·'with** *adv* (old use) with that; with which. (舊用法)用以;用那個。 **'~·withal** /-wɪðɔ:l ; -wɪðˌɔl/ *adv* (old use) (舊用法) = ~with. ▭ *n* **the ~withal,** (colloq) money needed for a purpose: (俗)爲某項目的而需要的金錢: *I should like to buy a new car but haven't got the ~withal.* 我希望買一部新汽車,但是還沒有籌到那筆錢。

wherry /'werɪ *US:* 'hw- ; 'hwɛrɪ/ *n* (*pl* -ries) light, shallow rowing-boat for carrying passengers and goods on rivers. 擺渡船;舢板;划艇。

whet /wet *US:* hwet ; hwɛt/ *vt* (-tt-) [VP6A] sharpen (a knife, axe, etc); (fig) sharpen or excite (the appetite, a desire). 磨;磨快(刀,斧等);(喻)增强;促進;刺激(胃口,欲望)。 **'~·stone** *n* shaped stone used for sharpening tools, eg scythes. 磨刀石;砥石。

whether /'weðə(r) *US:* 'hw- ; 'hwɛðɚ/ *conj* **1** (introducing an indirect question; ⇨VP10, 21; often replaced by *if* in colloq style except when there is possible confusion with a true conditional clause): (引導間接問句;在口語中常爲 if 所代替,但可能與眞正條件子句混淆時,不可改用if): *I don't know ~/if she will be able to come.* 我不知道她是否能來。*I wonder ~/if it's large enough.* 我想知道它是否够大。(Note that when there are two indirect questions with *or*, ~ is repeated after *or*): (注意:二間接問句由 or 相連時,在 or 之後, whether 再重複一次): *I wonder ~ we shall be in time for the last bus or ~ we shall have to walk home.* 我不知道我們是否趕得上最後一班公車,還是必須步行回家。(Compare ~ and *if* in these sentences): (比較下列各句中 whether 與 if 的用法): *Send me a telegram letting me know ~ I am to come,* ie saying 'Come' or 'Don't come'. 拍一個電報給我,告訴我是否要我來。*Send me a telegram if I am to come,* ie only if I am to come, no telegram being needed if I am not to come. 如果要我來,拍一個電報給我。 **2** (introducing an infinitive phrase; ⇨ VP8, 20): (引導不定詞片語): *I don't know ~ to accept or refuse.* 我不知道該接受還是該拒絕。*Would you advise me ~ to accept the offer* (*or not*)*?* 請教你,我該不該接受那項提議? **3** (Clauses and infinitive phrases introduced by ~ are used with preparatory *it*): (以 whether 引導的子句及不定詞片語,可與虛詞 it 連用): *It's doubtful ~ we shall be able to come.* 我們是否能來,尙未確定。(Such clauses and phrases may be subjects or complements): (這種子句或片語,可作爲主詞或補足語): *The question was ~ to take the children to the funeral or to leave them at home.* 問題是該帶孩子們去參加葬禮呢,還是該把他們留在家裡。*W~ to pay the price demanded was a question that worried him a long time.* 該不該按照(對方)所要的價錢付款,是困擾他很久的一個問題。(Such a clause may be the object of a *prep*): (這種子句也可以作介詞的受詞): *Everything depends upon ~ we have enough money.* 一切端視我們是否有足够的錢。*I am not interested in ~ you like the plan or not.* 我不在乎你是否喜歡那項計畫。(A clause introduced by ~ may be used in apposition to a *n*): (由 whether 引導的子句,可以用作名詞的同位語): *I am in doubt ~ I ought to give this plan my approval.* 我決定不了是否該同意這項計畫。*The question ~ we ought to call in a specialist was answered by the family doctor.* 我們是否應該請一位專家來,這問題由(我們的)家庭醫生答覆了。 **~ or no,** **(a)** = ~ or not. **(b)** in either case: 總之;無論如何: *You may rely upon my help, ~ or no,* eg ~ others agree to help, or refuse to help. 無論如何,你總可以信賴我的幫助(不管旁人是否答應幫忙,我總會幫助你的)。 **~ or not,** (allowing the negative alternative): 是否;無論是不是;不管: *W~ or not it rains, I'm giving a party tomorrow.* 不管下雨不下雨,明天我都要舉行宴會。*Tell me ~ or not I should invite Nick and his wife.* 告訴我,我應不應該邀請尼克夫婦。

whew /hju: ; hwju *or similar sounds roughly breathed out or whistled* 亦可讀作類似此音的粗而猛的呼氣聲或口哨聲/ *int* cry used (often in joke) to express consternation, dismay, fatigue or surprise. 哎呀!唷!(表示恐怖,沮喪,疲勞或驚訝的叫聲;有時係出以玩笑態度)。

whey /weɪ *US:* hweɪ ; hwe/ *n* [U] liquid part of sour milk after separation of curds (for cheese). (酸牛奶在提出製乾酪的凝乳後的)乳漿;乳清。

which /wɪtʃ *US:* hwɪtʃ ; hwɪtʃ/ *interr adj* (asking for selection from two, or from a group, esp from possibilities thought of as limited in number; ⇨ what) (要求從二者或一羣,尤指從有限數目的可能性中,加以選擇) **1** *W~ way shall we go — up the hill or along the river bank?* 我們要走哪一條路——是要爬這個斜坡呢,還是要沿着河岸走? *W~*

way (= How) *shall we do it?* 我們要怎麼做(它)呢？*W～ Jones do you mean—Jones the baker or Jones the postman?* 你說的是哪一位瓊斯先生——做麵包師的瓊斯，還是做郵差的瓊斯？*W～ foreign languages have you studied?* 你已經學過哪幾種外國語？*Tell me ～ ones you want.* 告訴我哪幾個是你所需要的。**2** (*rel adj*, formal, and rare except after a *prep;* preceded by a comma) and this; and these: (關係形容詞，爲正式用語，除置於介詞之後外，不常使用；前面須加逗號)而這一個；而這些個：*I told him to go to a doctor, ～ advice he took,* and this advice he took. 我告訴他該去看醫生，這個意見他採納了。*Don't call between 1 o'clock and 2 o'clock, at ～ time I am usually having lunch.* 不要在一點至兩點之間來訪，我通常在這段時間吃中飯。□ *interr pron* ～ thing(s); ～ person(s): 何物；何人；何者；哪(些)物；哪(些)人：*W～ is taller, Mike or Steve?* 誰比較高，是邁克還是史蒂夫？*W～ of the boys is the tallest?* 這些男孩哪一個最高？*W～ of you wish to go with me?* 你們誰要同我一起去？*Tell me ～ of them is better.* 告訴我，它們當中哪一個比較好。*Please advise me ～ to take.* 請告訴我該選擇哪一個。*The twins are so much alike that I never know ～ is ～,* ie I cannot distinguish one from the other. 這一對雙胞胎太相像了，我分辨不出誰是誰。□ *rel pron* (of things only, not of persons; 僅指事物，不指人；⇨ that) **1** (in defining or restrictive clauses, often replaced by *that;* used with no selective meaning; no pause before the clause and not set off by commas) (在限定子句中常爲 that 所代替；不含選擇的意義；在子句之前不停頓，也不用逗號分開) **(a)** (with the *rel pron* as the subject of the *v* in the clause): (以此關係代名詞作子句中的動詞的主詞)：*Take the book ～ is lying on that table.* 把桌子上的那本書拿去。*The house ～ is for sale is at the end of the street.* 出售的房子在街的盡頭。*The river ～ flows through London is called the Thames.* 流過倫敦的那條河叫做泰晤士河。**(b)** (with the *rel pron* as the object of the *v* in the clause; in spoken English usually suppressed): (以此關係代名詞作子句中的動詞的受詞；在口語英文中，通常略去)：*Was the book* (～) *you were reading a novel?* 你(剛才)讀的那一本書是小說嗎？**(c)** (with the *rel pron* as the object of a *prep;* when replaced by *that,* the *prep* follows the *v;* if ～ is used, the *prep* should precede): (以此關係代名詞作介詞的受詞；如換用 that，介詞須置於動詞後；如用 which，介詞該置於 which 前)：*The photographs at ～ you were looking/The photographs* (*that*) *you were looking at were all taken by my brother.* 你(剛才)看的那些照片，全是我哥哥(弟弟)拍攝的。*The hotel at ～ we stayed/The hotel we stayed at was both cheap and comfortable.* 我們住的那家旅館，既便宜又舒服。*The book to ～ I wanted to refer/The book I wanted to refer to was not in the library.* 我要參考的那本書，不在圖書館裏。*The shop opposite ～ the car is parked is a grocer's.* 對面停着汽車的那家店鋪是一家雜貨店。**2** (in non-defining or non-restrictive clauses, rare in the spoken language but common in the written language; ～ is not replaceable by *that;* the clause is preceded by a pause and is set off by commas) (用於非限定子句中，講話時很少用，書寫文字中很普遍；which 不能用 that 代替；子句前須稍作停頓，並須用逗號分開) **(a)** (referring to an antecedent *n*): (先行詞爲名詞)：(*i*) (with the *rel pron* as the subject of the clause): (以此關係代名詞爲子句的主詞)：*This house, ～ is to be sold by auction next month, was built about fifty years ago.* 這房子大約是五十年前造的，下個月要拍賣。*The meeting, ～ was held in the park, was attended by five hundred people.* 那次集會是在公園裏舉行的，有五百人參加。(*ii*) (with the *rel pron* as the object of the *v* in the clause): (以此關係代名詞作子句中動詞的受詞)：*These apple-trees, ～ I planted three years ago, have not yet borne any fruit.* 這些蘋果樹是我三年前種的，尚未結過果實。*This desk, ～ I bought second-hand, is made of oak.* 我買的這張二手貨桌子，是橡木做的。(*iii*) (with the *rel pron* as the object of a *prep*): (以此關係代名詞作爲介詞的受詞)：*His car, for ～ he paid £8000, is a five-seater saloon.* 他花八千鎊買的那汽車，是一部有五個座位的轎車。*Their house, at ～ I have often stayed, is just outside Dorking.* 他們的房子就在多金市郊外，我常住在那裡。**(b)** (in non-defining clauses that refer to a clause or sentence, not to a *n*): (在非限定子句中，指涉一個子句或句，而非指涉名詞)：*It was raining hard, ～* (= and this) *kept us indoors.* 雨下得很大，把我們困在家裏。*He said he had lost the book, ～* (= but this) *was untrue.* 他說他把那本書遺失了，但這是不確實的。(The clause may occasionally precede the sentence to ～ it refers): (這種子句偶而也可能置於它所指涉的句子之前)：*Moreover, ～ you may hardly believe, the examiners had decided in advance to fail half the candidates!* 還有，你可能很難相信，主試人員事先已經決定要淘汰一半應考人！

which·ever /wɪtʃ'evə(r) *US:* hw- ; hwɪtʃ'ɛvɚ/ *adj, pron* **1** the one which: …的那一個：*Take ～ you like best.* 挑選你最喜歡的那一個。*W～ (of you) comes in first will receive a prize.* (你們之中)哪一個最先到，就可以得到一個獎品。**2** no matter which: 無論哪個或哪些；隨便哪個或哪些：*W～ of the three sisters you choose to marry, you will have a good wife.* 不論你選擇的結婚對象是這三姐妹中的哪一位，你都會娶到一位賢淑的妻子。*Does British foreign policy remain the same, ～ party is in power?* 無論哪一個政黨執政英國的外交政策都不會改變嗎？**,which·so·'ever,** (emphatic for) ～. 爲 whichever 的强勢語。

whiff /wɪf *US:* hwɪf ; hwɪf/ *n* [C] slight puff or breath (*of* sth): (某物的)一噴；一吹；一陣(與 of 連用)：*a ～ of fresh air;* 一陣新鮮空氣；*the ～* (= smell) *of a cigar.* 雪茄烟的氣味。*The dentist gave her another ～ of anaesthetic.* 牙醫再給她一劑麻醉劑。*He stopped work to have a few ～s,* a short smoke (of a pipe, etc). 他停止工作，吸幾口烟。

Whig /wɪg *US:* hwɪg ; hwɪg/ *n* member of a political party in GB which upheld the authority of Parliament (against the sovereign) during the 17th and 18th cc, their place being taken in the 19th c by the Liberals. 英國維新黨黨員(該黨於十七、八世紀時維護國會權力以對抗君主，在十九世紀時，其地位爲自由黨所取代)。

while /waɪl *US:* hwaɪl ; hwaɪl/ *n* (*sing* only) (period of) time: (僅用單數)時；時間；一段時間：*Where have you been all this ～?* 這一陣子你一直在哪兒？*I haven't seen him for a long ～/for this long ～ past.* 我已經很久沒有見到他了。*We're going away for a ～.* 我們要出門一陣子。*I'll be back in a little ～,* soon. 我很快就會回來。*He was here a short ～ ago.* 他剛才還在這兒。***once in a ～,*** occasionally. 偶而；有時。***worth (one's) ～,*** worth the time spent in doing it, etc: 值得(花時間做等)：*It isn't worth ～ going there now,* ie It would be a waste of time to go. 現在去那兒就不值得了。*He will make it worth your ～,* ie will pay or reward you in some way. 他將會酬謝(回報)你的。□ *vt* [VP 15B] (only in) (僅用於) ～ ***sth away,*** pass (the time) in a leisurely way: 消磨(時間)；閒混(時間)：～ *away the time;* 消磨時間；～ *a few hours away.* 閒混幾小時。□ *conj* **1** during the time that; for as long as; at the same time as: 當…的時候；在…之時；和…同時：*He fell asleep ～ (he was) doing his English exercises.* 他在做英文練習的時候睡着了。*W～ in London he studied music.* 他在倫敦的時候研究音樂。*W～* (= As long as) *there is life there is hope.* 祇要有生命就有希望。**2** (implying a contrast) whereas: (含有相對之意)而；却；其實；反之：*Jane was dressed in brown ～ Mary was dressed in blue.* 珍穿的是咖啡色衣服，而瑪莉穿的是藍色衣服。**3**

(implying a concession) although: (含有讓步之意) 雖然: *W~ I admit that the problems are difficult, I don't agree that they cannot be solved.* 雖然我承認這些問題很困難，我不同意它們不能解決。**whilst** /waɪlst *US:* hwaɪlst ; hwaɪlst/ *conj* = ~.

whim /wɪm *US:* hwɪm ; hwɪm/ *n* [C] sudden desire or idea, often sth unusual or unreasonable: 一時的興致；突然的念頭；怪念頭；奇想: *only a passing ~,* an idea, a desire, that will soon pass; 只是一時的想法而已; *full of ~s.* 充滿了怪念頭。*His every ~ is complied with/catered for.* 對他(大家)是百依百順。

whim·per /ˈwɪmpə(r) *US:* ˈhw- ; ˈhwɪmpɚ/ *vi, vt* **1** [VP2A] utter weak, frightened or complaining sounds, eg a baby when ill, a dog when frightened of punishment. 發出虛弱而驚恐或抱怨的聲音；嗚咽；啜泣 (如嬰兒生病，狗怕懲罰時)。 **2** [VP6A] utter in a ~ing voice. 嗚咽而言；抽噎地說出。□ *n* [C] ~ing cry; low sobbing sound. 嗚咽聲；啜泣聲。

whimsy, whim·sey /ˈwɪmzɪ *US:* ˈhw- ; ˈhwɪmzɪ/ *n* (*pl* -sies, -seys) **1** [C] whim; fanciful idea or wish. 一時的興致；怪念頭；奇想。 **2** [U] quaintness; odd or fanciful humour. 古怪；奇癖；怪脾氣。 **whim·si·cal** /ˈwɪmzɪkl *US:* ˈhw- ; ˈhwɪmzɪkl/ *adj* full of whimsies; quaint. 多古怪念頭或奇想的；古怪的。 **whim·si·cally** /-klɪ ; -klɪ/ *adv* **whim·si·cal·ity** /ˌwɪmzɪˈkælətɪ *US:* ˈhw- ; ˌhwɪmzəˈkælətɪ/ *n* [U] quality of being whimsical; [C] (*pl* -ties) caprice; quaint fancy. 古怪；反覆無常；怪念頭。

whin /wɪn *US:* hw- ; hwɪn/ *n* [U] = gorse.

whine /waɪn *US:* hwaɪn ; hwaɪn/ *n* [C] long complaining cry or high-pitched sound (eg as made by a miserable dog, a siren, a motor or a shell in flight). 長的抱怨聲；哀鳴聲；嗚嗚聲(如痛苦中的狗，或汽笛，或汽車，或飛行中的砲彈等所發的聲音)。□ *vi, vt* **1** [VP2A, C, 4A] make such cries; utter complaints, esp about trivial things: 發哀鳴聲；發嗚鳴聲；作悲鳴；抱怨(尤指爲了無關緊要之事): *The dog was whining outside the door/whining to come into the room.* 那隻狗在門外嗚嗚地叫(嗚嗚地叫着要進入室內)。*If that child doesn't stop whining, I'll clobber it!* 如果那孩子再不停止哭叫，我要狠狠地揍他(她)一頓。 **2** [VP6A, 15B] utter with a ~ or ~s: 以哀聲說；抱怨而言；哀訴: *beggars whining (out) requests for alms.* 以哀聲請求施捨的乞丐們。 **~r** *n* animal or person that ~s. 發哀聲或嗚嗚聲的動物或人；哀鳴者；哀訴者。

whinny /ˈwɪnɪ *US:* ˈhw- ; ˈhwɪnɪ/ *n* (*pl* -nies) gentle neigh. 馬嘶聲。□ *vi* (*pt, pp* -nied) make such a sound. 嘶叫。

whip[1] /wɪp *US:* hwɪp ; hwɪp/ *n* [C] **1** lash (length of cord, strip of leather, etc) fastened to a handle, used for urging a horse on, or for punishing. 鞭(用以策馬或懲罰)。***have the ~ hand (over sb),*** have mastery over; be in a position to control. 控制(某人)；居於操縱…的地位。 **ˈ~·cord** *n* [U] **1** tightly twisted cord used for the lashes of ~s. 鞭繩。 **2** kind of hard-wearing worsted fabric. 一種耐穿的毛織品；馬褲呢。 **2** (also 亦作 **ˌ~per-ˈin**) (foxhunting) person who controls the hounds. (獵狐)指揮獵犬的人。 **3** organizing secretary of a political party (in GB and US) with authority over its members to maintain discipline and secure attendance at parliamentary debates and divisions(6); such authority; order given by such a secretary to members of his party to attend a debate and vote: (英美國家政黨的)組織秘書或政黨幹事 (有維持紀律及要求該黨國會議員出席議會及表決之權)；組織秘書或政黨幹事的權威；由其發給該黨議員要求參加辯論及投票的命令: *take the Liberal ~.* 就任自由黨組織秘書。*The ~s are off,* Members may vote as they wish. 議員們可以自由投票(直譯:組織秘書都不在場)。***a ˌthree-line ˈ~,*** urgent order of this kind. (組織秘書或政黨幹事發出的)緊急命令。 **4** preparation of eggs, cream, etc beaten or whipped (2). 攪打鷄蛋、奶油等所製成的食物；一種餐後甜食。**~py** *adj* flexible; springy. 易彎曲的；有彈性的。

whip[2] /wɪp *US:* hwɪp ; hwɪp/ *vt, vi* (-pp-) **1** [VP6A, 15A, B] strike with a whip; beat or flog: 鞭打；笞責；抽打: *~ a horse/a child;* 抽打馬(小孩)； *~ a top,* ⇨ top[3]. *The rain was ~ping the windowpanes,* beating against them. 雨點正打擊着窗子的玻璃。*The driver ~ped the horses on.* 趕車者策馬前進。 **2** [VP6A] beat (eggs, cream, etc) with a fork or other utensil to mix thoroughly or to make stiff: 攪打(鷄蛋，奶油等): *~ped cream.* 攪打過的奶油。 **3** [VP6A] (colloq) defeat. (俗)擊敗。 **4** [VP15B, 2C] take, be taken, move, be moved, suddenly: 突然攫取或被攫取；突然移動或被移動: *He ~ped off his coat.* 他迅速地脫去上衣。*He ~ped out a knife.* 他突然抽出一把刀。*The thief ~ped the jewels off the counter.* 那賊一下子就拿去了櫃臺上的珠寶。*The thief ~ped round the corner and disappeared in the crowd.* 那賊迅速地轉過拐角而消失在人叢中。[VP6A] (GB colloq) steal: (英俗)偷；扒竊: *Someone's ~ped my purse!* 有人偷走了我的錢包！***~ round for money, etc,*** appeal to friends, members of a club, etc for money to buy a gift, etc. 籲請(朋友，俱樂部會員等)捐款。Hence, 由此產生，**ˈ~-round** *n* such an appeal. 捐款呼籲；募捐。 **5** [VP6A] bind (a stick, a rope-end, etc) with a close, tight covering of thread or string; sew (a seam, the edge of a piece of cloth) with stitches that pass over and over. 緊纏線索於(棍、杖、繩端等)；接縫(結口)；包縫(布邊)。 **~·ping** *n* [C] beating with a whip as a punishment. 鞭笞(作爲懲罰)。 **ˈ~·ping-boy** *n* (hist) boy educated with a prince and ~ped when the prince deserved punishment; (hence) scapegoat. (史)陪王子讀書而代他受罰的少年；(由此產生) 代人受罰者。 **ˈ~·ping-post** *n* (hist) post to which persons were tied to be ~ped. (史)綁縛受鞭笞者的柱子。**ˈ~·ping-top** *n* = top[3].

whip·per-in /ˌwɪpər ˈɪn *US:* ˈhw- ; ˈhwɪpɚˈɪn/ ⇨ whip[1](2).

whip·per-snap·per /ˈwɪpə snæpə(r) *US:* ˈhw- ; ˈhwɪpɚˌsnæpɚ/ *n* young insignificant person who intrudes upon people and behaves as if he were important. 妄自尊大的年輕人；自以爲了不起的青年。

whip·pet /ˈwɪpɪt *US:* ˈhw- ; ˈhwɪpɪt/ *n* dog that looks like a small greyhound, used for racing. 一種賽跑用的狗(形似小獵犬)。

whip-poor-will /ˈwɪp pʊə wɪl *US:* ˈhwɪp pər wɪl ; ˌhwɪpɚˈwɪl/ *n* small American bird whose call (made at night or twilight) is imitative of its name. 美國產的一種怪鴟 (夜間或晨昏時發鳴聲，宛如其名的發音)。

whir /wɜ:(r) *US:* hw- ; hwɝ/ = whirr.

whirl /wɜ:l *US:* hw- ; hwɝl/ *vt, vi* **1** [VP15A, B, 2C] (cause to) move quickly round and round: (使)廻旋；旋轉: *The wind ~ed the dead leaves about.* 風吹得枯葉在四處廻旋。*The leaves came ~ing down in the autumn wind.* 樹葉在秋風中旋落。*The dancers ~ed round the room.* 舞者繞室旋轉。 **2** [VP15A, B, 2C] (cause to) move or travel rapidly (*off, away,* etc): (使)急動；急走(與 off，away 等連用): *The telegraph poles ~ed past us as the train gathered speed.* 火車的速度增加時，電線桿急速地在我們面前馳過。*Our friends were ~ed away in Jack's sports-car.* 我們的朋友們迅速地被賈克的跑車載走了。 **3** [VP2A, C] (of the brain, the senses) seem to go round and round; (of thoughts) be confused: (指腦筋，知覺) 暈眩；(指思緒) 紛亂: *His head ~ed.* 他頭昏了。□ *n* (*sing* only) (僅用單數) **1** ~ing movement: 廻旋；旋轉: *a ~ of dust/of dead leaves.* 塵土飛揚(枯葉紛飛)。*His brain was in a ~,* (fig) a confused state. (喻)他的腦筋昏了。 **2** rapid succession of activities, etc: 連續的快速活動，等: *the ~ of modern life in a big city;* 大都市現代生活的忙碌; *a ~ of social engagements,* eg parties, receptions. 一連串的社交活動(宴會，招待會等)。 **3**

(compounds) (複合字) '~·**pool** *n* place where there are ~ing currents (circular eddies) in the sea, etc (usu drawing floating objects towards its centre). (海上等處的)漩渦。 '~·**wind** *n* swift circling current of air in a funnel-shaped column. 旋風。 ***Sow the wind and reap the ~wind,*** (prov) Do wrong and, as a result, bring severe punishment upon oneself. (諺)惡有惡報;爲非做歹終將得到加倍報應。

whirli·gig /'wɜːlɪgɪg *US:* 'hw- ; 'hwɝlɪ,gɪg/ *n* **1** kinds of spinning top, 陀螺, ⇨ top³. **2** revolving motion: 旋轉;旋轉運動: *the ~ of time,* the changes of fortune that come with time. 時運的變遷。

whirr /wɜː(r) *US:* hw- ; hwɝ/ *n* (*sing* only) sound (as) of a bird's wings moving quickly, or of wheels, etc turning fast: (僅用單數)呼呼聲;颼颼聲(如鳥翼迅速鼓動,或輪子快速旋轉的聲音): *the ~ of an aircrafts' propellers.* 飛機螺旋槳的呼呼聲。□ *vi* [VP2A, C] make such sounds: 作呼呼聲;發颼颼聲: *A bird ~ed past.* 一隻鳥颼颼地飛過去了。

whisk /wɪsk *US:* hw- ; hwɪsk/ *n* **1** small brush for removing dust (from clothes, etc). (刷去衣服等灰塵用的)小刷帚;撢帚。 **('fly-)~,** brush made of hair for flapping flies away. 趕走蒼蠅用的毛撢子。 **2** device (eg coiled wire) for whipping eggs, cream, etc. 攪拌蛋、奶油等的金屬器;打蛋器。 **3** light brushing movement (eg of a horse's tail). 輕掃動作(如馬尾之擺拂);撢;揮;拂。□ *vt, vi* **1** [VP15B] ***~ sb/sth off/away,*** brush quickly and lightly: 輕快地掃開或刷去: *~ the flies off.* 趕走蒼蠅。 **2** [VP6A] move or sweep quickly through the air: 在空中快速活動或掃動;拂;撢;揮: *The cow ~ed her tail.* 母牛拂動她的尾巴。 **3** [VP15B] take (sb) quickly and suddenly: 迅速而突然地帶走(某人): *They ~ed him off to prison.* 他們突然把他逮捕下獄。 *I was ~ed up to the top floor in an express lift.* 我被一架快速電梯很快地送至頂層。 **4** [VP6A] = whip²(2): *~ eggs.* 打蛋。

whisker /'wɪskə(r) *US:* 'hw- ; 'hwɪskɚ/ *n* **1** **~s,** hair allowed to grow on the sides of a man's face. 頰鬚;髯;連鬢鬍子。 ⇨ beard(1), moustache. **2** one of the long, stiff hairs growing near the mouth of a cat, rat, etc. (貓,鼠等的)鬚;一根鬚。 ***cat's ~s,*** (sl) fine thing or person: (俚)美好的事物;傑出的人: *He thinks he's the cat's ~s,* He thinks highly of himself. 他自視甚高(自以爲了不起)。 **~ed** *adj* having ~s. 有頰鬚的;有髯的。

whis·key /'wɪskɪ *US:* 'hw- ; 'hwɪskɪ/ *n* (*pl* ~s) US and Irish spelling of whisky. 係 whisky 的美國及愛爾蘭拼法。

whisky /'wɪskɪ *US:* 'hw- ; 'hwɪskɪ/ *n* (*pl* -kies) (GB and Canadian spelling) (英國及加拿大拼法) [C, U] strong alcoholic drink distilled from malted grain (esp barley or rye); drink of this: 威士忌酒;一份或一客威士忌酒: *Two whiskies, please.* 請來兩份威士忌酒。

whis·per /'wɪspə(r) *US:* 'hw- ; 'hwɪspɚ/ *vi, vt* **1** [VP2A, 3A, 6A, 14, 19] ***~ (to),*** speak, say (sth), using the breath but no vibration of the vocal cords: (聲帶不振動而)以氣音說(某事物);低語;耳語;私語: *~ (a word) to sb;* 對某人低聲說(話); *~ (to sb) that.* 低聲(對某人)說。 '~·**ing-gallery,** gallery in which a sound made at one point may be heard at another far off (owing to acoustic peculiarities). 耳語廊;低聲廊(由於特殊的傳音性質,在此廊之一處所發的聲音,可在遠方他處聽到)。 **2** [VP6A, 15B] tell privately or secretly; (esp) put (a story, slander) into circulation: 私下述說;秘密告訴;(尤指)散播(故事,謠言): *The story is being ~ed about the neighbourhood.* 這故事正在附近流傳。 *It is ~ed that he is heavily in debt.* 據秘密傳聞他負債很多。 '~·**ing campaign,** systematic attack on sb by passing from person to person malicious statement, etc. 有計畫地散佈流言以攻擊或誹謗某人。 **3** [VP2A, C] (of leaves, the wind, etc) make soft sounds; rustle: (指葉,風等)作低悄聲;發沙沙聲;颯颯地響: *The wind was ~ing in the pines.* 風在松林中颯颯作響。□ *n* **1** ~ing sound or speech: 低悄的聲音或話語: *He answered in a ~.* 他低聲回答。 *They were talking in ~s.* 他們在悄悄地談話。 **2** ~ed remark; sth ~ed secretly; rumour: 耳語;私語;傳聞: *W~s are going round that the firm is likely to go bankrupt.* 傳聞那家公司可能倒閉。 **~er** *n*

whist /wɪst *US:* hwɪst ; hwɪst/ *n* card-game like bridge² for two pairs of players. 惠斯特(由兩對參加者所玩的一種紙牌戲,類似橋牌)。 '~-**drive** *n* series of games played by several sets of partners at different tables, certain players after each round passing to the next table. 數組合夥人在不同的桌上所玩的一連串的紙牌戲(某些參與者在一局後,轉至次一桌)。

whistle /'wɪsl *US:* 'hw- ; 'hwɪsl/ *n* **1** (usu steady) clear note made by forcing air or steam through a small opening, or made by the wind; tuneful sound made by some kinds of bird (eg the blackbird): (通常爲穩定的)口哨聲;口笛聲;汽笛聲;警笛聲;風嘯聲;(畫眉等的)鳥鳴聲: *We heard the ~ of a steam-engine.* 我們聽到火車頭的汽笛聲。 '~-**stop** *n* (US) short stop (during a journey made by a politician) for electioneering purposes (eg to speak to voters in a rural district): (美)(從政者旅行期間)爲競選活動(如對鄉區選民演講)所作的短暫停留: (attrib) (形容用法) *a ~-stop tour.* 作短暫停留的競選旅行。 **2** instrument for producing such sounds: 口笛;汽笛;警笛;哨子: *the referee's ~;* 裁判的哨子; *a* '*steam-~,* sounded by a jet of steam. 汽笛。 **3** ***wet one's ~,*** (sl) have a drink. (俚)潤喉;喝杯酒。□ *vi, vt* **1** [VP2A, C] make a ~(1) (eg by blowing through the rounded lips or by using a ~(2): 吹口哨;吹哨子;發口笛聲;鳴笛;發嘯聲: *The engine/The driver ~d before reaching the level-crossing.* 火車機車(司機)在抵達平交道之前先鳴汽笛。 *The wind ~d through the rigging/up the chimney, etc.* 風呼呼吹過纜索(烟囱等上)。 ***~ for sth,*** wish in vain for: 空想獲得;徒然希望得到: *I owe my butcher £10, but he can ~ for it,* I shan't pay him. 我欠肉商十鎊,但他休想得到這筆錢。 **2** [VP2A, C, 6A] produce a tune in this way: 用口哨吹奏(曲調): *~ a tune.* 吹出一個曲子。 *The boy was whistling (away) merrily.* 那男孩愉快地吹着口哨(離開了)。 ***~ down the wind,*** abandon sth. 放棄某事物。 ***~ in the dark,*** do sth to overcome one's fears. 做某事給自己壯膽。 **3** [VP6A, 15B, 16A] ***~ (up),*** make a signal (to) by whistling: 用口哨聲、笛聲、嘯聲等(向…)作信號: *He ~d his dog back/~d to his dog to come back to him/~d up his dog.* 他用口哨召喚他的狗回來(召喚他的狗回到他身邊)。 **4** [VP2A, C] pass swiftly with a whistling sound: 發嘯聲快速通過或經過: *The bullets/arrows ~d past our ears.* 槍彈(箭)颼颼地從我們耳邊飛過。

whit /wɪt *US:* hwɪt ; hwɪt/ *n* ***not a ~; no ~,*** not the least, not at all: 一點也沒有;一點也不: *There's not a ~ of truth in the statement.* 該項陳述沒有一點點眞實性。 *I don't care a ~.* 我一點也不介意。

Whit /wɪt *US:* hwɪt ; hwɪt/ *n* ⇨ Whitsun.

white¹ /waɪt *US:* hwaɪt ; hwaɪt/ *adj* **1** of the colour of fresh snow or common salt: 白的;白色的;雪白的: *His hair has turned ~.* 他的頭髮已變白了。 *Her face went ~,* pale. 她的面色變得蒼白。 ***bleed (sb/sth) ~,*** (fig) drain (sb/sth) of wealth, strength, etc. (喻)耗盡(某人,某物)的財富,力量等;榨盡(某人)的血汗;用盡(某物)的物力。 **2** (special uses, compounds) (特殊用法,複合字) '**~ alloy,** any of various alloys that are cheap imitations of silver. 假銀(類似銀的便宜合金)。 '**~ ant,** termite. 白蟻;蟗。 '~·**bait** *n* [U] small fish, the young of several varieties, eaten fried when small (about 2 inches long). 銀魚(數種魚類的幼魚,長約二吋,用油炸食)。 '**~ bear,** polar bear. 北極熊。 '~-**caps** *n pl* waves at sea with ~ foam on their crests. 白帽浪(波峯有白色泡沫的海浪)。 ,~-'**collar,** used as a symbol of non-manual labour: 白領階級(指不從事體力勞動者): *~-collar jobs／workers.* 勞心的工作(工作者); 腦力工作(腦力工作者)。 ⇨ *blue-collared* at blue²(7). **~ coffee,** with milk added. 加牛奶的咖啡。 ,**~ 'elephant／'ensign／'feather,** ⇨ these nouns. 參看這些名詞。 **~ flag,** symbol of surrender. 白旗(投降的標幟)。**~ heat,** high temperature at which metals become ~; (fig) intense passion. 白熱; 熾熱(金屬變爲白色的高溫); (喻)激情; 高度緊張的情緒。 Hence, 由此產生, ,**~-'hot** *adj.* **the 'W~ House,** the official residence of the President of the US, in Washington, DC; (hence) US Government (policy).白宮(美國總統府);(由此產生)美國政府(政策)。 **~ lead** *n* poisonous compound of lead carbonate, used in paints. 白鉛(碳酸鉛,有毒,用於塗料中)。**~ lie,** lie considered to be harmless, esp one told for the sake of being polite: 小謊;無惡意的謊言;(尤指)不實的客氣話: *She tells enough ~ lies to ice a wedding-cake!* 她撒了許多小謊祇爲了在結婚蛋糕上加一層糖霜! ,**~-'lipped** *adj* having ~ lips, esp with fear. (尤指因害怕而) 嘴唇發白的。 ,**~-'livered** *adj* cowardly. 怯懦的;膽小的。,**~ 'magic,** ⇨ magic. **'~ man／woman,** European person. 白種人;歐洲人。 **~ meat,** poultry, veal, pork. 白肉(家禽肉,小牛肉,豬肉)。**~ metal,** ~ alloy. 白色合金; 假銀。**~ paper,** (GB) report issued by the Government to give information. (英) 白皮書 (英國政府的報告書)。**~d sepulchre,** (from Matt 23: 27) person who appears to be righteous but is in fact wicked; hypocrite. 粉飾的墳墓(見新約馬太福音 23 章 27節);僞君子;假冒爲善的人。**~ slave,** ~ girl who is forced to be a prostitute, esp one who is tricked into going to a foreign country by promises of employment: 白奴(指被迫爲娼的白種女子,尤指以工作爲餌被騙至外國者);白種妓女: *the ,~-'slave traffic.* 白奴交易(販賣白種女子爲娼的買賣)。 **'~·thorn** *n* hawthorn. 山楂。**~ tie,** ~ bow tie worn with men's full evening dress; (short for) full evening dress: (男性穿着正式晚禮服時所用的)白色領結;男性正式晚禮服(的簡稱): *Is it dinner jacket or ~ tie?* 那是一般晚禮服還是正式晚禮服? **'~·wash** *n* [U] mixture of powdered lime or chalk and water, used for coating walls, ceilings, etc; (fig) means used to cover or hide sb's errors, faults, etc. 石灰水;白粉水;白塗料(用於粉刷牆壁,天花板等); (喻)掩飾過失、錯誤等的方法。□ *vt* put ~wash on (a wall, etc); (fig) try to make (sb, his reputation, etc) appear blameless by covering up his faults, etc. 粉刷(牆壁等);(喻)粉飾(某人,其名聲等)。

white² /waɪt *US:* hwaɪt ; hwaɪt/ *n* **1** [U] ~ colour: 白;白色: *dressed in ~.* 穿著白衣。 **2** [C] ~ person. 白種人。 **3** [C, U] colourless part round the yolk of an egg: 蛋白: *Take the ~s of two eggs.* 吃兩個蛋的蛋白。*There's too much ~ of egg in this mixture.* 這混合物中的蛋白太多。 **4** [C] the ~ part of the eyeball: 眼白;白眼珠: *Don't fire until you see the ~s of their eyes,* until they are very close. 等他們非常接近時再射擊。**~·ness** *n* **~n** /'waɪtn *US:* 'hw- ; 'hwaɪtn̩/ *vt, vi* [VP6A, 2A] make or become ~. 使白;變白;漂白;刷白。

White·hall /waɪt'hɔ:l *US:* hw- ; 'hwaɪt'hɔl/ *n* (street in London where there are) Government offices; (hence) British Government (policy). 白廳(倫敦的一條街道,爲政府機關所在地);政府機關;(由此產生)英國政府(政策)。

whit·en·ing /'waɪtnɪŋ *US:* 'hw- ; 'hwaɪtnɪŋ/ *n* [U] = whiting².

whither /'wɪðə(r) *US:* 'hw- ; 'hwɪðɚ/ *adv* (old use) to which place; (current use, rhet, or in journalism) what is the likely future of: (舊用法) 向何處; 往何處;(現代用法,修辭或報紙用語)未來可能如何; …的將來可能會怎麼樣; 什麼是…的可能前途: *W~ Ulster?* 阿爾斯特未來可能如何? *W~ the pound sterling?* 英鎊的前途可能會怎樣? ,**~so·'ever** *adv* (old use) to whatever place; anywhere at all. (舊用法) 到或往任何地方;無論何處。

whit·ing¹ /'waɪtɪŋ *US:* 'hw- ; 'hwaɪtɪŋ/ *n* (*pl* unchanged) kinds of small sea-fish used as food. (複數不變)鱈類。

whit·ing² /'waɪtɪŋ *US:* 'hw- ; 'hwaɪtɪŋ/ *n* [U] powdered white chalk used in whitewashing, and for polishing silver, etc. (用於粉刷及擦亮銀器等的)白堊粉;白粉。

whit·low /'wɪtləʊ *US:* 'hw- ; 'hwɪtlo/ *n* small inflamed place on a finger or toe, esp near the nail. 膿性指頭炎(尤指在指甲附近的);指頭疽;瘭疽。

Whit·sun /'wɪtsn *US:* 'hw- ; 'hwɪtsn̩/ *n* (also 亦作 ,*Whit 'Sunday*) 7th Sunday after Easter, the feast of the Pentecost. 聖靈降臨節(復活節後第七個禮拜天)。 **~·tide** /-taɪd ; -,taɪd/ *n* ~ and the weekend or the following week. 聖靈降臨週(包括聖靈降臨節及週末或隨後的一週)。

whittle /'wɪtl *US:* 'hw- ; 'hwɪtl/ *vt, vi* **1** [VP15B, 2C, 3A] **~ *(sth) away,*** cut thin slices or strips off, eg wood; (fig) reduce. 削切或削修(某物,如木材等);(喻)削減;逐漸減少: **~ *(away) at sth,*** cut at sth in this way: 削;切: *He was whittling at a piece of wood.* 他正在削一塊木頭。 **~ *sth down,*** reduce the size of by cutting away slices, etc; (fig) reduce the amount of: 削小;(喻)削減: *They won't dare to ~ down our salaries.* 他們不敢減我們的薪。**2** [VP6A, 15A] make or shape by whittling: 削切成;削製成: *The boy ~d a whip handle from a branch／~d a branch into a whip handle.* 那個男孩把一根樹枝削成一個鞭柄。

whiz /wɪz *US:* hwɪz ; hwɪz/ *vi* [VP2C] (-zz-), *n* [U] (make the) sound of sth rushing through the air: 物體掠過空中的聲音;颼颼聲;發颼颼聲: *The arrows／shells ~zed past.* 箭(砲彈)颼颼地飛過。

whizz-kid /'wɪz kɪd *US:* 'hw- ; 'hwɪz ,kɪd/ *n* (sl) bright, inventive young person with progressive ideas who achieves rapid success. (俚)傑出青年;天才兒童;神童。

who /hu: ; hu/ *interr pron* (used as the subject, and only of persons; object form **whom** /hu:m ; hum/) (用作主詞,且僅用以指人;受格形式爲 whom) **1** *Who is that man?* 那個人是誰? *Who are those men?* 那些人是誰? *I wonder who those people are.* 我想知道那些人是誰。*Who broke the window?* 誰把窗子打破了? *Do you know who broke the window?* 你知道窗子是誰打破的嗎? *Who do you think he is?* 你認爲他是誰? ***(know) ,who's 'who,*** (know) who people are, what they do, etc. (知道)誰是誰; (知道)誰是有影響力的人物等。 **2** (*Whom* is used in formal and literary style, but is usually replaced by *who* in ordinary colloq style): (whom 用於正式的及文學的文體中,一般通俗文體中常可用 who 代替): *To whom did you give it?* 你把它交給誰了? *Who did you give it to?* 你把它交給誰了? *Who(m) did you see?* 你看到誰了? *Who(m) do you think I met in the post-office this morning?* 你猜今天早晨我在郵局遇到誰了? *I don't know to whom I ought to address the request.* 我不曉得該向誰作此請求。 *I don't know who I ought to address the request to.* 我不曉得該向誰作此請求。*Who else did you see?* 你還看見誰了? □ *rel pron* **1** (in defining, or restrictive, clauses; ⇨ that³, which sometimes replaces *who*): (用於限定子句中; 參看有時可代替 who 的 that³): *This is the man who／These are the men who wanted to see you.* 這(這些)就是要見你的那個人(那羣人)。 (After *there + to be* the *rel pron 'who'* may be omitted: 在 there + to be 之後,關係代名詞 who 可省略: *There's somebody (who) wants you on the telephone.* 有人來電話找你。 *There was a man (who) called to see you while you were out.* 你出去的時候,有一個人來看你。) **2** (*Whom* is often replaced by *that* except after a *prep;* the *prep* may be placed at the end and *that* used for *whom*): (whom 常被 that 代替, 但緊接在介詞之後時,不可改用 that; 如將介詞移至句末,

則可用 that 代替 whom): *That is the man (whom) I met in London last year.* 那就是我去年在倫敦碰見的那個人。*That is the man about whom we were speaking.* 那就是我們剛才在談論的那個人。*That's the man (that) we were speaking about.* 那就是我們剛才在談論的那個人。*I know the man (whom) you mean.* 我知道你(的意思)指的是誰。 **3** (in non-defining clauses, not replaceable by *that;* clause set off by the use of commas or placed in parentheses): (在非限定子句中,不可用 that 代替;子句用逗號分開或置於括號中): *My wife, who has been abroad recently, hopes to see you soon.* 內子剛從海外歸來,她希望很快見到你。*My brother, whom you met the other day, has recently written a book on Indian art.* 前幾天你曾遇見家兄 (舍弟),他最近寫了一本關於印度藝術的書。 *Our new neighbours, to whom I was introduced yesterday, have come here from Yorkshire.* 我們的新鄰居是從約克郡搬來的,昨天我被介紹與他們相識。 **4** (independent relative) (獨立關係詞) ***Whom*** (= Those whom) ***the gods love die young,*** Those who are specially favoured by Providence die young. 神所眷愛者常夭折(好人不長壽)。

whoa /wəʊ ; hwo/ *int* ⇨ wo.

who'd /hu:d ; hud/ = who had; who would.

who·dun·it /ˌhu:ˈdʌnɪt ; huˈdʌnɪt/ *n* (sl) (= *who done it,* sl for *who did it*) detective or mystery story. (俚) (= who done it, 在俚語中代替 who did it) 偵探小說;神秘小說。

who·ever /hu:ˈevə(r) ; huˈɛvɚ/ *pron* any person who; the person who: 任何人;不論誰;…的人: *W~ says that is wrong.* 說那話的人是錯誤的。*W~ else may object, I shall approve.* 不管旁人會不會反對,我是贊成的。

whole /həʊl ; hol/ *adj* **1** not injured or damaged; unbroken: 完整的;齊全的;未受傷的;未損壞的;未打破的: *You're lucky to escape with a ~ skin.* 你能安然脫險,眞是幸運。*There isn't a ~ plate* (=a plate that is not chipped, cracked, broken, etc) *in the house.* 這家裡竟沒有一隻完整的盤子。(Because ~(3) means 'all', ~(1) is sometimes placed after the *n.* 因爲 whole 的第 3 義作 'all' 解, whole 作第 1 義解有時可放在名詞後面。 Cf: 參較 *He swallowed the plum ~,* without chewing it. 他把那個梅子整個吞下去了(未咀嚼)。*He ate the ~ loaf,* all of it. 他吃下了一整條麵包。*The ox was roasted ~,* without being cut up into joints. 那條公牛是整條烘烤的。*They ate the ~ ox,* all of it. 他們把那條牛吃得光光。*Snakes swallow their victims ~.* 蛇把捕獲物整個地吞下。) ***go the ~ hog,*** ⇨ hog. **2** entire; complete: 全部;完全: *I waited for a ~ hour.* 我等了整整一個鐘頭。 **ˈ~ food** *n* [U] food that is nutritious and free of artificial substances: (未加人工物質之)營養食品: (attrib) (形容用法) *a ~ food restaurant/shop.* 營養食品餐廳(商店)。 **~ note** *n* [C] (US) semibreve. (美)全音符。 **ˌ~ ˈnumber** *n* [C] undivided quantity; integer. 未分割的量;整數。 **ˈ~-meal, ˌ~-ˈwheat** *nn* [C] flour containing everything in the grain, with nothing extracted. (沒有去麩的)粗麵粉;營養麵粉。 **3** (attrib only, with a *sing n*) (僅作形容用法,置於單數名詞前) **the/one's ~,** all that there is of; complete: 所有…的;全部的: *I want to know the ~ truth about this matter.* 我要知道這件事的全部眞相。*The ~ country* (=Everyone in the country) *was anxious for peace.* 全國上下都渴望和平。*I didn't see him the ~ evening.* 我整晚未見到他。 *He gave his ~ attention* (= all of his attention) *to the problem.* 他全神貫注在那個問題上。*You haven't eaten the ~ lot* (= all of it, all of them), *have you?* 你尙未全部吃光,是不是? ***do sth with one's ~ heart,*** do it with concentrated efforts, undivided attention. 全心全力做某事。Hence, 由此產生, **ˌwhole-ˈhearted(ly),** *adj, adv* **4** (attrib with a *pl n*) not less or fewer than; nothing less than: (形容用法,放在複數名詞前)不少於; 一點也不少;整整的: *It rained for three ~ days.* 整整下了三天雨。*Give your ~ energies to the task.* 把你全副精力用到那件工作上去。*W~* (= Complete) *regiments surrendered to the enemy.* 整團整團的軍隊向敵人投降了。 **5** (old use; biblical) in good health; well: (舊用法;聖經用字)身體好的;健康的;無恙的;治好了的: *They that are ~ need not a physician.* 健康的人不需要醫生。*His hand was made ~.* 他的手被治好了。□ *n* thing that is complete in itself; all that there is of something: 完整事物;整體;整個;全部;全數: *Four quarters make a ~.* 四個四分之一構成全部。*A ~ is greater than any of its parts.* 全量大於分量。*The ~* (= All) *of my money was stolen.* 我全部的錢都被偸走了。 *He spent the ~ of that year in Pakistan.* 他在巴基斯坦度過了那一整年。 *Is the land to be divided up or sold as a ~?* 那塊土地將予以分割,還是整個地出售? ***on the ~,*** taking everything into consideration. 從整體來看;大體上。***(taken) as a ~,*** (considered) all together, not separately. 全部地 (加以考慮);總體上(看來)。 **wholly** /ˈhəʊllɪ ; ˈholɪ/ *adv* completely; entirely: 完全地;全部地: *Few men are wholly bad.* 很少人是完全壞的。*I wholly agree.* 我完全同意。

whole·sale /ˈhəʊlseɪl ; ˈholˌsel/ *n* (usu attrib) selling of goods (esp in large quantities) to shopkeepers, for resale to the public. ⇨ retail: (通常作形容用法)批發;躉售: *sell by ~* (US 美 *at ~*); 批售; *~ prices;* 批發價格; *a ~ dealer.* 批發商。□ *adj, adv* on the ~ plan; (fig) on a large scale: 批發的(地);躉售的(地);(喩)大規模的(地): *Our business is ~ only.* 我們祇做批發生意。*We buy goods ~.* 我們係大批購貨。*There was a ~ slaughter when the police opened fire.* 警察開火造成了大規模屠殺。 **~r** *n* one who sells by ~. 批發商。

whole·some /ˈhəʊlsəm ; ˈholsəm/ *adj* healthy; favourable to the health (bodily or moral); suggesting good health: 健康的;有益於(身心)健康的;顯示健康的;衞生的: *~ food / exercise / surroundings;* 有益於健康的食物(運動,環境); *a ~ appearance;* 健康的外表; *~ advice.* 有益的忠言。

who'll /hu:l ; hul/ = who will.

whom /hu:m ; hum/ ⇨ who.

whoop /hu:p ; hup/ *n* [C] **1** loud cry: 大叫;呼喊;吶喊: *~s of joy.* 歡呼。 **2** gasping sound heard during a fit of coughing. (咳嗽時的)喘息聲;哮喘聲。 **ˈ~ing-cough** *n* [U] children's disease with gasping coughs and long, noisy indrawing of breath. (小兒的)百日咳。□ *vi, vt* utter a loud cry or yell: 高喊;大叫;吶喊;高聲說: *to ~ with joy.* 歡呼。 **~ *it up*** /wu:p *US:* hwʊp ; hup/, (sl) have a hilarious time. (俚)歡鬧;狂歡。

whoopee /ˈwʊpɪ ; ˈhwupi/ *n* ***make ~,*** (sl) take part in noisy rejoicing. (俚)歡鬧;狂歡。

whop /wɒp *US:* hwɒp ; hwɑp/ *vt* (-pp-) [VP6A] (sl) beat; defeat. (俚)打敗;擊敗。 **~·per** *n* anything unusually big, esp a big lie. 特大物;(尤指)漫天大謊。 **~·ping** *adj* very large of its kind: 特大的;極大的: *a ~ping lie.* 大謊。□ *adv* very: 非常;極: *a ~ping big fish.* 非常大的魚。

who're /ˈhu:ə(r) ; hur/ = who are.

whore /hɔ:(r) ; hor/ *n* ⚠ (derog) prostitute. (諱)(貶)娼妓。

whorl /wɜ:l *US:* hw- ; hwɝl/ *n* ring of leaves, petals, etc round a stem of a plant; one turn of a spiral, eg as seen on the shell of a mollusc or on a fingerprint: 輪生體;環生體(環生在植物莖或梗四周的葉或瓣等);螺紋;渦旋: *identify a criminal by the ~s of his fingerprints.* 由指紋的螺紋辨認罪犯。 **~ed** *adj* having ~s; arranged in ~s. 有輪生體或環生體的;有螺紋的;有渦旋的;排列成輪生體或渦旋的。

who's /hu:z ; huz/ = who is; who has.

whose /hu:z ; huz/ *poss pron* (⇨ who) of whom; of which. 誰的;何者的。 **1** *W~ house is that?* 那是誰的房子? *I wonder ~ house that is.* 我想知道那是誰的房子。 **2** (in rel, defining clause): (用於

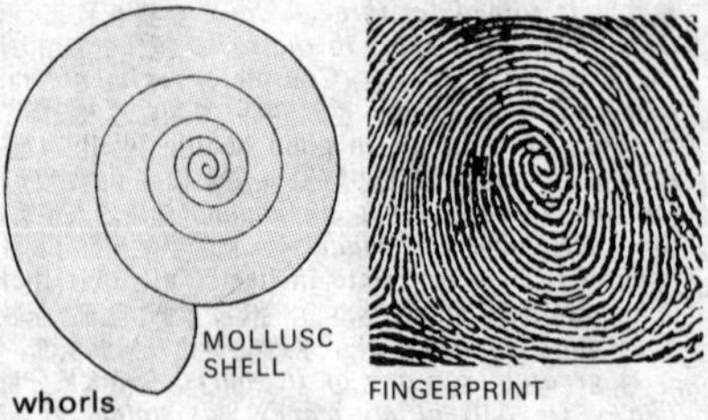

whorls

限定關係子句中): *Is that the man ~ house was broken into by burglars last week?* 那就是上星期遭夜賊侵入其住宅的那個人嗎? *The boy ~ father complained to me is very stupid.* 他父親向我訴過苦的那個男孩非常愚笨。 **3** (*W~* is sometimes used in place of the usual *of which*, but it is often better to use a different construction, as shown below): (whose 有時用來代替通常所使用的 of which, 但是使用另外不同的結構常常更好, 見下列例句): *the house ~ windows are broken*, the house with the broken windows; 窗子破了的房屋; *that dictionary ~/of which the cover has come off*, that dictionary without a cover. 封面脫落的那本字典。 **4** (in rel, nondefining clause): (在非限定關係子句中): *Members of the Fire Service, ~ work is often dangerous, are paid less than members of the Police Force.* 消防人員的待遇比警員低,但是他們的工作時常是很危險的。*Mr Hamilton, ~ car I borrowed for this journey, is a rich lawyer.* 漢彌爾敦先生是一位富有的律師,我這次旅行就是借用他的汽車。

who·so /ˈhuːsəʊ ; ˈhuso/, **who·so·ever** /ˌhuːsəʊˈevə(r); ˌhusoˈɛvɚ/ *pron* (old use) (舊用法) = whoever.

why /waɪ *US:* hwaɪ ; hwaɪ/ *adv* **1** (interr) for what reason; with what purpose: (疑問副詞) 何故; 爲什麼; 有何目的: *Why was he late?* 他爲什麼遲到? *Do you know why he was late?* 你知道他爲什麼遲到嗎? *Tell me why.* 告訴我爲什麼。 *Why not let her do as she likes?* 爲什麼不讓她想怎麼做就怎麼做呢? **2** (rel *adv*): (關係副詞): *The reasons why he did it are obscure.* 他做那事的理由還不清楚。 *This is (the reason) why I left early.* 這就是我早退的原因。*Why you should always arrive late I don't know.* 我不知道你爲什麼總是遲到。□ *int* **1** (expressing surprise) (表示驚訝): *Why, it's quite easy! A child could do it!* 啊,那很容易!小孩子也會(做它)! **2** (expressing protest): (表示異議或抗議): *Why, What's the harm?* ie there's no harm in it, is there? 怎麼,有什麼不好嗎? □ *n* (*pl* whys) reason or cause. 理由或原因。 ***the whys and the wherefores***, the reasons, causes. 原由;理由;原因。

wick /wɪk ; wɪk/ *n* [C, U] (length of) thread through a candle, the top end of which is lit, to burn with a light-giving flame; (strip of) woven material by which oil is drawn up in some cigarette lighters, an oil-lamp or oil-stove to burn: 蠟燭芯;燈芯;燭心頭(燃燒發光部分);(有些打火機,油燈,或油爐的)油繩;吸油繩: *trim the ~ of an oil-lamp.* 修剪油燈的芯子。

wicked /ˈwɪkɪd ; ˈwɪkɪd/ *adj* **1** (of a person, his acts) bad; wrong; immoral: (指人,其行爲)壞的;錯的;不道德的;缺德的;邪惡的: *It was ~ of you to torment the poor cat.* 你折磨那隻可憐的貓眞缺德。 **2** spiteful; intended to injure: 有惡意的;意欲加害的: *a ~ blow.* 惡意的一擊。 **3** roguish; mischievous: 淘氣的;惡作劇的: *She gave me a ~ look.* 她朝我淘氣地看了一眼。 **~·ly** *adv* **~·ness** *n*

wicker /ˈwɪkə(r) ; ˈwɪkɚ/ *n* [U] (usu attrib) twigs or canes woven together, usu for baskets and furniture: (通常作形容用法)編製籃子及傢具的小枝;枝條;柔枝;柳條: *a ~ chair.* 柳條椅。 **ˈ~·work** *n* [U] things made of ~. 柳條製品。

wicket /ˈwɪkɪt ; ˈwɪkɪt/ *n* [C] **1** **ˌ~(-ˈdoor/-ˈgate)**, small door or gate, esp one at the side of, or made in, a larger one. 邊門;便門;(尤指大門旁邊或大門上的)小門。 **2** small opening (eg one with a sliding window) at which tickets are sold. 售票口;售票處(如有拉窗者)。 **3** (cricket) either of the two pairs of three stumps (with crosspieces called *bails*) at which the ball is bowled, ⇨ the illus at cricket; stretch of grass between two ~s: (板球)三柱門(其橫木稱作 bails) (參看 cricket 之挿圖);兩個三柱門之間的球場: *take a ~*, defeat a batsman. 擊敗一個擊球員。 *A soft ~* (= soft ground between ~s) *helps the bowler.* 柔軟的板球場有助於投球手。 *Surrey were four ~s down*, Four of their batsmen were out. 薩里隊有四位擊球員被判出局了。*We won by six ~s*, won with seven of our batsmen not out. 我們因七位擊球員未被判出局而獲勝。 ***keep ~***, act as ~-keeper. 防守三柱門。 **ˈ~-keeper** *n* player who stands behind the ~ to stop balls not struck by the batsman, to catch batsmen out, etc. 三柱門的守門員。 **4** (US) croquet hoop. (美)槌球戲中的弓形小鐵門。

wide /waɪd ; waɪd/ *adj* (-r, -st) **1** measuring much from side to side or in comparison with length; broad: 寬廣的;廣闊的: *a ~ river;* 寬闊的河; *a road twelve feet ~.* 十二呎寬的路。 **2** of great extent; comprehensive: 廣大的;廣泛的;淵博的: *a man with ~ interests*, interested in many subjects; 興趣廣泛的人; *the ~ world;* 廣大的世界; *the ~ Atlantic;* 廣闊的大西洋; *a ~ selection of new books.* 類別繁多供挑選的新書。 **3** fully opened: 張大的;完全張開的: *She stared at him with ~ eyes.* 她睜大了眼睛注視他。*Open your mouth ~.* 張大你的嘴。 **4** far from what is aimed at or from a specific point: 遠離目標的;差得遠的: *a ~ ball*, (in cricket) one judged by the umpire to be out of the batsman's reach. (板球)(裁判員判定的)遠球(擊球員不可能打到者)。 *Your answer was ~ of the mark.* 你的回答離題太遠了。 **5** (sl) shrewdly aware of business chances; unscrupulous. (俚)老奸巨滑的;不擇手段的。 **~ boy**, (sl) such a man. (俚)老奸巨滑的人;不擇手段的人。□ *adv* **1** far from the point aimed at: 遠離目標地;差得遠地: *The arrow fell ~ of the mark.* 那支箭落在距離目標很遠的地方。 **2** fully: 完全地;充分地: *He was ~ awake.* 他完全清醒了。 *The window was ~ open.* 那窗子是大開着的。 **ˌ~-aˈwake** *adj* (fig) alert, vigilant: (喻)機警的;警戒着的: *a ~-awake young woman*, one who realizes what is going on, etc and is not easily deceived. 機警的年輕女子。 **3** over a large area: 廣及地;遼闊地: *travel far and ~.* 到處旅行。 **ˈ~-spread** *adj* (esp) found, distributed, over a large area. (尤指)廣佈的;遍及的;流傳廣的。 **~·ly** *adv* **1** at ~ intervals: 間隔大地: *~ly scattered.* 廣佈的。 Cf 參較 *scattered far and ~.* 分佈遠而廣的。 **2** to a large extent or degree: 達到大範圍或程度;大大地: *~ly different;* 大不相同的; *differing ~ly in opinions.* 意見極不相同。 **3** over a large area: 廣泛地;廣及地: *It is ~ly known that....* 很多人知道…。 **~n** /ˈwaɪdn ; ˈwaɪdn̩/ *vt, vi* [VP6A, 2A] make or become ~(r): 加寬;弄寬;變寬;擴展: *ˈroad-~ning in process.* 正在進行中的道路拓寬工程。

wid·geon /ˈwɪdʒən ; ˈwɪdʒən/ *n* kind of wild freshwater duck. 水鳧;赤頸鳧(一種淡水野鴨)。

widow /ˈwɪdəʊ ; ˈwɪdo/ *n* woman who has not married again after her husband's death. 寡婦;孀婦。**~er** *n* man who has not married again after his wife's death. 鰥夫。 **widowed** /ˈwɪdəʊd ; ˈwɪdod/ *adj* made into a ~ or ~er: 寡居的;鰥居的;喪失配偶的: *~ed by war.* 由於戰爭而喪失配偶的。 **ˈ~·hood** /-hʊd ; -ˌhʊd/ *n* state of, time of being, a ~. 孀居;守寡。

width /wɪtθ ; wɪdθ/ *n* **1** [U] quality or state of being wide: 廣;寬;廣闊的性質或狀態: *a road of great ~;* 很寬的一條路; (fig) (喻) *~ of mind/intellect/views.* 心胸(悟力,見解)的廣闊。 Cf 參較

broadminded, broad views. **2** measurement from side to side: 廣度;寬度: *a ~ of 10 metres;* 十米寬; *10 metres in ~.* 寬十米。 **3** [C] piece of material of a certain ~: 有一定寬度的一幅布料: *join two ~s of cloth;* 接合兩幅布; *curtain material of various ~s.* 寬度不同的窗簾布。

wield /wi:ld ; wild/ *vt* [VP6A] have and use: 使用;揮舞: *~ an axe;* 揮斧; *~ power/authority/control.* 運用權力(權威;控制)。

wife /waɪf ; waɪf/ *n* (*pl* wives /waɪvz ; waɪvz/) married woman, esp in relation to her husband: 妻;已婚婦女: *Smith and his ~;* 史密斯夫婦; *the baker's ~;* 麵包師的妻子; *a club for young wives.* 年輕太太俱樂部。***old wives' tales,*** foolish or superstitious story, usu traditional. 老婦譚;荒誕故事;迷信而愚昧的故事。 ⇨ also *fish~* at fish¹(3), *house~* at house¹(7). **'~·like, ~·ly** *adjj* of, like, suitable for, a ~: 妻子的;已婚婦女的;似妻子的;適於妻子的: *~ly virtues/duties.* 婦德(妻子的職責)。

wig /wɪg ; wɪg/ *n* head-covering of false hair (as worn to hide baldness, and by actors, barristers and judges, and formerly worn as a fashionable ornament in Europe during the 17th and 18th cc). 假髮(禿子,演員,律師,法官等所戴者;在十七、十八世紀時,歐洲流行戴假髮爲時髦裝飾)。 ⇨ the illus at judge. 參看 judge 之插圖。 **wigged** /wɪgd ; wɪgd/ *adj* wearing a wig. 戴假髮的。

wig·ging /'wɪgɪŋ ; 'wɪgɪŋ/ *n* (colloq) scolding: (俗)罵;叱責: *get/give sb a good ~.* 挨(給與某人)一頓痛罵。

wiggle /'wɪgl ; 'wɪgḷ/ *vt, vi* [VP6A, 2A] (cause to) move with quick, short, side-to-side movements: (使)短而快地擺動;快速扭動: *The baby was wiggling its toes.* 那嬰兒正在扭動脚趾。*Stop wiggling and sit still.* 不要搖擺,靜靜地坐着。 □ *n* wiggling movement. 快速擺動或搖動。

wight /waɪt ; waɪt/ *n* (archaic) person; human being: (古)人;傢伙: *a luckless ~.* 不幸的傢伙。

wig·wam /'wɪgwæm *US:* -wɑ:m ; 'wɪgwɑm/ *n* hut or tent made by fastening skins or mats over a framework of poles, as formerly used by N American Indians. (北美印第安人昔時用木棍作架,蒙以獸皮或草蓆的)帳篷;小屋。

wild /waɪld ; waɪld/ *adj* (-er, -est) **1** ⇨ the illus at cat, large, small. 參看 cat, large, small 之插圖。(of animals) not tamed or domesticated; living in natural conditions (eg lions, giraffes, wolves); (of plants) growing in natural conditions; not cultivated: (指動物) 野的; 野性的; 野居的 (如獅,長頸鹿,狼); (指植物) 野生的; 非栽植的: *~ flowers;* 野花; *a reserve for the preservation of ~ life,* area where ~ animals, birds, etc are protected and helped to survive; 野生動物保護區; (attrib): (形容用法): *a ~-life sanctuary.* 野生動植物保護區。 **'~·cat** *attrib adj* reckless, unsound, impracticable: 莽撞的;不健全的;不能實行的: *~cat schemes,* esp in finance and commerce; (尤指在財政及商務方面)不能實行的計畫; *a ~cat strike,* unofficial and irresponsible strike (by workers). 未經工會允許的不負責任的罷工。 **'~-fowl** *n* (esp) birds ordinarily shot or hunted as game, eg ~ ducks and geese, quail, pheasants. (尤指)獵鳥(如野鴨,雁,鵪,雉)。 ***,~-'goose chase,*** foolishly useless enterprise. 荒謬無益的行事;徒勞無益的追求。 ***sow one's ~ oats,*** ⇨ oat(1). **2** (of horses, game birds, etc) easily startled; hard to get near: (指馬,獵鳥等)容易受驚的;怕人的;不易接近的: *The deer/pheasants are rather ~.* 鹿(雉)很容易受驚。 **3** (of persons, tribes, etc) uncivilized; savage. (指人,部族等)未開化的;野蠻的。 **4** (of scenery, areas of land, etc) desolate; waste; unsettled: (指景色,地區等)荒涼的;荒蕪的;無人居住的: *~ scenery;* 荒涼的景色; ~, *mountainous areas.* 荒蕪的山區。 **5** violent; uncontrolled; stormy: 猛烈的;狂暴的;暴風雨的: *You'd better stay indoors on a ~ night like this.* 像這樣暴風雨的夜晚,你還是待在家裡的好。*What ~ weather we're having!* 我們遇着多麼惡劣的天氣! **6** excited; passionate; distracted: 激動的;激昂的;狂亂的: *There were sounds of ~ laughter.* 有狂笑的聲音。 *He was ~ with anger.* 他狂怒。 *It made her ~* (= filled her with anger) *to see such cruelty.* 看到這樣殘酷的行爲,令她極爲憤怒。*The anxiety drove them almost ~,* mad. 焦慮逼得他們幾乎發狂了。 **7** ***be ~ about sth/sb,*** (colloq) have a strong desire for; be madly enthusiastic about: (俗)對某事物(某人)極爲狂熱;極想做某事;熱中於: *~ about strawberries/Prince Charles.* 極想吃草莓(極崇拜查理王子)。 **8** disorderly; out of control: 紊亂的;無秩序的;失去控制的: *a state of ~ confusion;* 混亂的狀態; *a room in ~ disorder;* 極爲紊亂的房間; *settle down after a ~ youth.* 在一段放蕩的青年時期以後安定下來。 ***run ~,*** be without check, restraint or training: 放肆;放蕩;失教養: *They allow their children to run ~,* allow them to amuse themselves in any way they like, with no control of any kind. 他們聽任孩子們冶遊放蕩。 **'~·fire** *n* [U] (chiefly in) (主要用於) ***spread like ~fire,*** (of reports, rumours, etc) very fast. (指傳聞,謠言等)迅速地傳播。 **9** reckless; done or said without reflection or consideration: 胡亂的; 鹵莽的;輕率的; 未加考慮而做或說出的: *a ~ guess/scheme;* 胡亂的猜測 (輕率的計畫); *~ shooting,* without taking aim. 亂射。 **10** (of a playing-card) having any value (as eg a *joker*): (指紙牌)百搭的(如 joker): *a '~ card.* 一張百搭牌。 □ *adv* in a ~ manner: 胡亂地;鹵莽地;輕率地: *shoot ~.* 亂射。 □ *n pl* **the ~s,** uncultivated (and often uninhabited) areas: 荒地;未開發地區: *the ~s of Africa;* 非洲的荒野; *go out into the ~s.* 進入未開發地區。 **~·ly** *adv* in a ~ manner: 狂野地;激動地;紊亂地;鹵莽地;輕率地: *rush about ~ly;* 橫衝直闖; *talk ~ly,* eg in an exaggerated way; 胡扯;瞎吹; *a ~ly exaggerated account.* 極度誇張的敍述。 **~·ness** *n*

wilde·beest /'wɪldɪbi:st ; 'wɪldə,bist/ *n* = gnu. ⇨ the illus at large. 參看 large 之插圖。

wil·der·ness /'wɪldənɪs ; 'wɪldənɪs/ *n* (rarely *pl*) (罕用複數) **1** wild uncultivated waste land. 荒地;荒野。 **2** desolate expanse: 茫茫的一大片;荒涼的一大片: *a ~ of waters.* 一片汪洋。 *From his attic window he looked out over a ~ of roofs.* 從他閣樓的窗子望出去,他看到一大片屋頂。

wile /waɪl ; waɪl/ *n* (usu *pl*) trick; bit of cunning: (通常用複數)詭計;奸計: *fall a victim to the ~s of an unscrupulous rogue;* 中了一個無恥惡棍的詭計; *the ~s of the Devil.* 魔鬼的奸計。

wil·ful (US also **will-**) /'wɪlfl ; 'wɪlfəl/ *adj* **1** (of a person) obstinate; determined to have one's own way: (指人)剛愎的;任性的: *a ~ child.* 任性的孩子。 **2** intentional; for which compulsion, ignorance or accident is no excuse: 故意的;不能用不得已,不知,或巧合作藉口的: *~ murder/negligence/waste/disobedience.* 故意的謀殺(疏忽,浪費,抗命)。 **~ly** /-fəlɪ ; -fəlɪ/ *adv* **~·ness** *n*

will¹ /*weak form:* l ; l; *strong from:* wɪl ; wɪl/ *anom fin* (often shortened to 常略作 'll; *neg* ~ not or won't /wəʊnt ; wont/; *pt,* conditional 過去式及條件句 would /*after 'I, he, she, we, you, they':* 人稱代名詞後: d ; d, *elsewhere:* 用於他處: *weak form:* əd ; əd; *strong form:* wʊd ; wʊd/, *neg* would not or wouldn't /'wʊdnt ; 'wʊdṇt/) [VP5] **1** (used as an auxiliary verb of the future tense): (用作表未來時態的助動詞): *If today is Monday, tomorrow ~ be Tuesday.* 如果今天是禮拜一,明天將是禮拜二。*You'll be in time if you hurry.* 如果你快一點就會來得及。*You won't be in time unless you hurry.* 如果你不趕快,就來不及了。(*Would* replaces ~ to show future in the past). (would 代替 will 表示過去未來)。*I wonder whether it ~ be ready.* 我不知道是否會準備好。*I wondered whether it would be ready.* 我(那時)不知道是不是會準備好。 *You'll be in Oxford this time tomorrow.*

明天這個時候你就到牛津了。*You would have been in Oxford this time yesterday.* 你本來昨天這個時候就可以到牛津的。 **2** (used with the 1st person (*I, we*) to express willingness, consent, an offer or a promise): (與第一人稱 I, we 連用,表示意願,同意,提議或允許): *All right, I'll come.* 好的,我(願意)來。*I won't do it again.* 我不會再做那事了。*We'll pay back the money soon.* 我們很快就會還錢。 (*Would* replaces ~ to show future in the past): (表示過去未來時,用 would 代替 will): *I said I would do it.* 我說過我要做那事。 *We said we would help them.* 我們說過我們願意幫助他們。**3** (used with the 2nd person in questions, marking polite requests, and often equivalent to *please*): (與第二人稱連用,用在問句中,用來表示客氣的請求,並且常常相當於please的用法): '*W~ you* (*please*) *come in?*' 請進來好嗎? '*Would you* (*please*) *come back later?*' 請稍晚回來好嗎? '*Pass the salt, would you?*' 遞給我鹽巴好吧? '*Would you* (*please*) *pass the salt?*' (勞駕)遞給我鹽巴好吧? **4** (used in *affirm* sentences, always with stress (never *'ll* or *'d*), indicating insistence or inevitability): (用於肯定句中,永遠重讀,不可略作 'll 或 'd, 表示堅持或不可避免): *He* '*~ have his own way,* insists on this. 他一意孤行。*Boys* '*~ be boys,* We cannot expect them to behave except as boys naturally behave. 男孩子總歸是男孩子。*Accidents* '*~ happen,* They are to be expected from time to time. 意外事件總是會發生的。*That's just what you* '*would say,* what you might be expected to say. 那正是你可能會說的話。*Of course it* '*would rain on the day we chose for a picnic,* We might expect such treatment from Fate. 當然,我們選定野餐的那天可能會下雨(我們祇好聽天由命)。**5** (used in the neg to indicate refusal): (用於否定句中表示拒絕): *He won't/wouldn't help me.* 他不會幫助我。*This window won't open,* cannot be opened. 這窗子打不開。**6** (used to indicate that sth happens from time to time, that sb is in the habit of doing sth, that sth is natural or to be expected): (用於表示某事時常發生,某人有做某事的習慣,某事自然會如何或在預料之中): *He'll sit there hour after hour looking at the traffic go by.* 他常常坐在那裡好幾個鐘頭,看着來往的車輛行人。*Sometimes the boys would play a trick on their teacher.* 有的時候男孩子們會作弄老師。*Occasionally the machine will go wrong without any apparent cause.* 機器偶而會發生故障而找不出明顯的原因。 **7** (used to indicate probability or likelihood): (用於表示可能性): *This'll be the book you're looking for, I think.* 我想,這本書可能就是你正在找尋的書。*She would be about 60 when she died.* 她死時大概是六十歲左右。'*I want someone to do a lot of typing for me*'—'*Will/Would I do?*' Am I likely to be suitable for the job? '我需要人爲我做許多的打字工作'——'我可以嗎?' **8** (*Would* is used with the 2nd and 3rd persons to form conditional statements and questions): (would 與第二、第三人稱連用,形成條件敍述句及問句): *They'd be killed if the car went over the cliff.* 汽車如果翻落懸崖,他們就沒命了。*They'd have been killed if the car had gone over the cliff.* 當時如果汽車翻落懸崖,他們就沒命了。***would rather,*** ⇨ rather(1). **9** (*Would* is used with the 1st person to form conditional statements expressing the speaker's will or intention): (would 與第一人稱連用,構成條件敍述句,表示說話者的意志或意向): *We would have come if it hadn't rained.* 如果那時沒有下雨,我們就來了。

will² /wɪl; wɪl/ *vt* (*pt* would /wʊd; wʊd/, no other forms used 其他形式不用) (all old uses) (皆爲舊用法) **1** [VP6A] wish: 希望;希冀: *Let him do what he ~.* 他希望做什麼就讓他做什麼。*What would you?* 你希望什麼呢? **2** [VP9] (the subject *I* is often omitted) used to express wishes: (主詞 I 常省略)用於表示願望: *Would* (*that*) *it were otherwise!* 要不是這樣,該多好啊! *Would* (= I would) *to God* (*that*) *I had not agreed!* 天啊,我眞希望我當時未同意! *Would that they were safe home again!* 但願他們還能平安歸來! **3** [VP5] choose; desire: 選擇;欲;想: *the place where he would be.* 他想停留的地方。*Come whenever you ~* (ie ~ or wish to come). 你隨時想來就來。(Cf will³ with which will² is closely connected.) (參較 will³, 該字與 will² 有密切關係。) '**would-be** *attrib adj* used to indicate what is desired, aspired to, or intended: 用於表示所希求,所熱望或所意欲者: *would-be authors,* persons who aspire to be authors. 熱望成爲作家的人。

will³ /wɪl; wɪl/ *vt, vi* (*pt, pp* ~ed) **1** [VP6A] make use of one's mental powers in an attempt to do sth or get sth: 立意做某事或獲得某物;意欲;想要: *We cannot achieve success merely by ~ing it.* 僅僅想要成功,並不能獲得成功。 **2** [VP2A] exercise will-power: 運用意志力; 決意; 決心: *W~ing and wishing are not the same thing.* 決意和願望並非一回事。**3** [VP6A, 9] intend unconditionally: 絕對地意欲: *God has ~ed it so.* 上帝已作如此安排。*God ~s that man should be happy.* 上帝的意旨是要人快樂。 **4** [VP17, 14, 15A] influence, control or compel, by exercising the will: 運用意志力以影響,控制或驅使: *Can you ~ yourself to keep awake/into keeping awake?* 你能以意志力使自己保持清醒嗎? *It would be convenient if we could ~ ourselves across lands and oceans.* 如果我們能够運用意志力駕馭自己越過陸地和海洋,那就方便多了。 **5** [VP12A, 13A] ***~ sth to sb; ~ sb sth,*** leave (property, etc) (to sb) by means of a will and testament: 遺贈(財產等)(給某人): *He ~ed most of his money to charities.* 他把大部分的錢遺贈給慈善機關了。*I hope my uncle has ~ed me that fine painting.* 我希望我叔叔已立遺囑把那幅好畫遺贈給我。

will⁴ /wɪl; wɪl/ *n* **1 the ~,** mental power by which a person can direct his thoughts and actions, and influence those of others: 意志: *the freedom of the ~.* 意志的自由。 **2** [U, C] (*sing* only) (僅用單數) (also 亦作 '**~-power**) control exercised over oneself, one's impulses: 意志力;自制力;自我控制: *He has no ~ of his own,* is easily influenced by others. 他沒有獨立的意志 (易受他人左右)。*W~ can conquer habit.* 意志力可以克服習慣。*He has a strong/weak ~.* 他的意志力堅强(薄弱)。*He showed a strength of ~ that overcame all obstacles.* 他表現出堅强的意志力,克服了所有的障碍。**-willed,** (in compound *adjj*) having the kind of ~ indicated: (用於複合形容詞中)有…意志力的: ˌ*strong-*'*~ed;* 意志堅强的; ˌ*weak-*'*~ed.* 意志薄弱的。 **3** [U, C] (*sing* only) determination; desire or purpose: (僅用單數)決心;意向; 欲望; 目的: *The ~ to live helps a patient to recover.* 求生的欲望有助於病人的康復。*She has a boundless ~ to please,* is full of desire to please. 她極力想討好。***Where there's a ~ there's a way,*** (prov) If one has the determination to achieve sth, a way of doing so will be found. (諺)有志者事竟成。***take the ~ for the deed,*** understand and be grateful for the fact that one wants to help, etc although unable to do so. 以意向判斷行爲; 事雖未成而仍領其心意。 ***of one's own free ~,*** without being required or compelled: 自願;甘心情願: *I did it of my own free ~.* 我做此事乃出於自願。***at ~,*** whenever and however one pleases: 隨意: *You may come and go at ~.* 你可以隨意來去。***tenant at ~,*** (legal) one who can be required to give up (land, a house, etc). (法律) 可隨意令其退租的佃戶; 可隨意令其遷出的房客。**4 a ~,** energy; enthusiasm: 精力;活力;熱心: *work with a ~.* 努力工作。 **5** [U] (with a *possessive*) that which is desired or determined upon: (與所有格連用)所意欲或決心要做的事情: *God's ~ be done.* 願神的旨意能完成。*He has always had his ~* (or, more colloq, *his own way*). 他總是自行其是。*What is your ~* (more usu, *What do you want*)? 你需要什麼? **6 good/ill ~,** kind/unkind disposition or feeling: 善(惡)意: *feel no ill ~ towards anybody.* 對任何人無惡意。 *'Peace on earth and good ~ towards men.'* '願世界有平安,以善意待人。' **7** [C] (also 亦作 ***last ~ and testament***), = testament. 遺囑。 **~·ful** /-fl ; -fəl/ *adj* (US spelling of) wilful. 爲 wilful 的美國拼法。

wil·lies /ˈwɪlɪz ; ˈwɪlɪz/ *n pl* (sl) feeling of unease or nervousness: (俚) 神經緊張; 心驚肉跳: *This gloomy old house gives me the ~.* 這幢幽暗的老房子使我毛骨悚然。

will·ing /ˈwɪlɪŋ ; ˈwɪlɪŋ/ *adj* **1** ready to help, to do what is needed, asked, etc: 願意按照所需,所求等予以幫助或去做的;樂意的: *~ workers.* 自願的工作者。 *He's quite ~ to pay the price I ask.* 他很願意照我的要價付錢。 **2** done, given, etc readily, without hesitation: 願意而不猶豫地做成,給予等的;甘願的: *~ obedience.* 甘心情願的服從。 **~·ly** *adv* **~·ness** *n* [U].

will-o'-the-wisp /ˌwɪl ə ðə ˈwɪsp ; ˌwɪləðəˈwɪsp/ *n* moving light seen at night over marshy ground; (more usu fig) sth or sb that one pursues unsuccessfully because it or he is difficult to grasp or reach. 沼地的燐火;鬼火;(通常多作比喻用法)難於捉摸而令人追逐不到的人或事物。

wil·low /ˈwɪləʊ ; ˈwɪlo/ *n* [C] ⇨ the illus at tree. 參看 tree 之插圖。 **ˈ~-(tree),** kinds of tree and shrub with thin, easily bent branches; [U] twigs of this tree used for weaving into baskets; its wood, used for making cricket bats, etc. 柳;柳樹;柳枝(用以編織籃子等);柳木(用做板球棒等)。 **ˈ~-pattern** *n* Chinese design (with a ~-tree, a river, etc) in blue upon white china (seen on plates, etc). 柳景圖案(中國瓷器上的白地藍花圖案)。 **~y** *adj* (of persons) lithe and slender. (指人) 柔軟而細長的;苗條的。

willy-nilly /ˌwɪlɪ ˈnɪlɪ ; ˈwɪlɪˈnɪlɪ/ *adv* willingly or unwillingly; whether wanted or unwanted. 不管願意不願意;無論需要不需要;强迫地。

wilt[1] /wɪlt ; wɪlt/ *v* (archaic form of will[2]) (爲 will[2] 的古舊形式) ***thou ~,*** = you will.

wilt[2] /wɪlt ; wɪlt/ *vi, vt* [VP6A, 2A] (of plants, flowers) (cause to) droop, lose freshness; (of persons) become limp. (指植物,花)(使)凋謝;枯萎;(指人)變爲頹喪;變得衰弱或無生氣。

Wil·ton /ˈwɪltən ; ˈwɪltn̩/ *n* kind of carpet. 威爾頓地毯。

wily /ˈwaɪlɪ ; ˈwaɪlɪ/ *adj* (-ier, -iest) full of wiles; cunning: 多智謀的;狡詐的: *a ~ old fox.* 狡猾的老狐狸。

wimple /ˈwɪmpl ; ˈwɪmpl̩/ *n* linen covering arranged in folds about the head, cheeks, chin and neck, worn by women in the Middle Ages, and still by some nuns. (中世紀婦女所著,現在有些修女仍用的)頭巾;包頭圍布。

win /wɪn ; wɪn/ *vt, vi* (*pt, pp* won /wʌn ; wʌn/) (-nn-) **1** [VP6A, 12B, 13B, 15A, 2A] get by means of hard work, perseverance, struggle, as the result of competition, gambling, etc; do best (in a fight, etc): 贏;獲勝;得到成功;做得最好: *win a race/a battle/a war/a scholarship/a prize;* 贏得賽跑(戰役,戰爭,獎學金,獎品); *~ fame and fortune.* 名利雙收。 *Which side won?* 那一邊贏了? *She has a nature that quickly won her the friendship of her colleagues.* 她具有一種天性,可以很快地獲得同事們的友誼。 *He soon won a reputation for himself.* 他很快就成名了。 *We've won!* 我們贏了! *He won £5 from me at cards.* 玩紙牌的時候他贏了我十鎊。 ***win the day/the field,*** be victorious. 獲勝;戰勝。 ***win free/clear/out/through,*** make one's way through, out, etc; free oneself, get out of a difficult position, etc by effort. 完成;達成;掙脫;擺脫(困境等)。 ***win hands down,*** (colloq) succeed easily. (俗)輕易地成功。 **ˈwinning-post** *n* post marking the end of a race. (賽跑的)終點標。 **2** [VP6A, 15B, 17] ***win sb over (to sth);*** (less usu 較不常用) ***win sb to do sth,*** persuade (sb) by argument; gain the favour of: 說服(某人)做某事;獲得…的好感;把某人爭取過來: *We won him over to our view.* 我們說服他贊成我們的觀點。 **3** [VP6A] reach by effort: 藉努力而到達: *win the summit/the shore.* 到達山巔(岸上)。 □ *n* [C] success in a game, competition, etc: (遊戲,比賽等中的)贏;勝利: *Our team has had five wins this summer.* 我們的球隊今年夏天已贏了五場。 **win·ner** *n* person, animal, thing, that wins. 獲勝的人,動物,東西;獲勝者。 **win·ning** *adj* **1** that wins: 勝利的;得勝的: *the winning horse.* 獲勝的馬。 **2** persuasive; gaining confidence and friendship: 動人的;能獲得信任和友誼的: *a winning smile.* 動人的微笑。 **win·nings** /ˈwɪnɪŋz ; ˈwɪnɪŋz/ *n pl* (esp) money won in betting, gambling, etc. (尤指在打賭,賭博等中)贏來的錢。

wince /wɪns ; wɪns/ *vi* [VP2A, C] show bodily or mental pain or distress (by a movement or by loss of composure): (因疼痛或苦惱等而)畏縮;退縮;退避;失常態: *He ~d under the blow/at the insult.* 他因受打擊而退縮(因受辱而失常態)。 *He didn't ~ when the knife slipped and cut his thumb.* 小刀滑過割傷他的拇指時,他沒有閃避。 □ *n* wincing movement: 畏縮;退縮: *without a ~.* 不畏縮地。

win·cey·ette /ˌwɪnsɪˈet ; ˌwɪnsɪˈɛt/ *n* [U] strong material of wool and cotton, or wool, used for shirts, etc. 一種棉絨布;絨布(一種結實的棉毛混紡或純毛布料用以做襯衫等)。

winch /wɪntʃ ; wɪntʃ/ *n* windlass; stationary machine for hoisting or pulling. 絞車;(起重或牽引用的)轆轤。 □ *vt* [VP6A, 15B] move by using a ~: 用絞車拉動: *The glider was ~ed off the ground,* pulled along by means of a ~ until it rose into the air: 那滑翔機藉絞車拉起而升空。 *We can ~ out these big tree roots,* get them out by using a ~. 我們可以藉絞車拔出這些巨樹的樹根。

wind[1] /wɪnd ; wɪnd/ *n* **1** [C, U] (often 常作 **the ~**; with *much, little,* etc when the reference is to degree or force; with *indef art* or in *pl* when the reference is to the kind of ~, etc; ⇨ the examples) air in motion as the result of natural forces: 風(說明風的强度或力量時,用 much, little 等;說明風的種類等時,加不定冠詞或用其複數形; 見下面例句): *a north ~,* blowing from the north; 北風; *warm ~s from the south.* 南方吹來的和風。 *The ~ blew my hat off.* 風吹落了我的帽子。 *He ran like the ~,* very fast. 他跑得像風一般快。 *The ~ is rising/falling,* becoming stronger/weaker. 風勢在增强(減弱)。 *There's no/not much/a lot of ~ today.* 今天無風(風不大,風很大)。 ***fling/throw caution/prudence, etc to the ~s,*** abandon it, take no thought of it. 不再顧慮;完全不顧;不再小心謹慎等。 ***get/have the ˈ~ up,*** (sl) become/be frightened. (俚)受驚嚇;害怕。 ***raise the ~,*** (sl) obtain the money needed. (俚)籌款;獲得所需金錢。 ***put the ˈ~ up sb,*** (sl) cause him to feel frightened. (俚)使某人害怕;驚嚇某人。 ***see/find out how the ˈ~ blows,*** what people are thinking, what is likely to happen. 看風頭;觀望情勢。 ***sail close/near to the ~,*** ⇨ sail[2](1). ***take the ˈ~ out of sb's sails,*** prevent him from doing or saying sth by doing it or saying it before him; take away his advantage suddenly. 搶先做或說以阻止某人做或說;先發制人地佔某人上風;突然搶去某人的優勢。 ***There is/was sth in the ~,*** being secretly prepared or plotted. 有什麼事快要發生了(目前正在醞釀中)。 **2** (*pl*) the cardinal points: (複)基本方位: *The house stands on a hilltop, exposed to the four ~s of heaven,* ~s from all directions. 該屋位於山頂,受到四面八方的風吹。 *My papers were blown to the four ~s,* in all directions. 我的文件被吹得到處都是。 **3** [U] breath needed for running or continuous exertion: (跑步或不斷用力所需要的)呼吸;喘息;氣息: *The runner soon lost his ~,* became out of breath. 那跑者很快就喘息不已。 *He stopped to recover/get back his ~.* 他停下來喘一

口氣。***get one's second ~***, recover the ability to breathe regularly after a first period of breathlessness; (fig) get new energy for a task. (第一陣喘息後) 恢復正常呼吸；(喻) 重整旗鼓；獲得新的工作精力。***sound in ~ and limb***, in excellent physical condition. 健康極佳。 **4** [U] scent carried by the ~ (as indicating where sth is): (顯示某物在何處的)氣味: ***get ~ of***, (fig) hear a rumour of, begin to suspect. (喻)風聞；開始覺察。 **5** [U] empty words; meaningless or useless talk: 空話；無聊的或無用的話: *Don't listen to the politicians—they're all ~.* 不要聽那些政客們的話——全是空話。 **6** [U] gas formed in the bowels and causing discomfort: (使人不舒服的)腸中的氣體: *The baby is suffering from ~.* 那嬰兒患腸氣症。***break ~***, expel ~ from the bowels or stomach. 放屁。 **7** **the ~**, orchestral ~ instruments. 管樂器。 **8** (compounds) (複合字) **'~·bag** *n* (colloq) person who talks a lot but says nothing important. (俗)空談者；滿口空話的人。 **'~·break** *n* hedge, fence, line of trees, etc to break the force of the ~ and give protection. 防風籬；防風牆；防風林；防風設備。 **'~-cheater** (US 美 = **'~·breaker**) *n* close-fitting garment for the upper part of the body, designed to give protection against the ~. 防風的緊身上衣。 **'~·fall** *n* [C] **1** fruit (eg an apple) blown off a tree by the ~. 風吹落的果實(如蘋果)。 **2** (fig) unexpected piece of good fortune, esp money coming to sb. (喻)意外的好運；(尤指)意外之財。 **'~-flower** *n* anemone. 白頭翁。 **'~-gauge** *n* instrument for measuring the force of the ~. 風力計；風速計；風壓計。 **'~ instrument** *n* musical instrument in which sound is produced by a current of air (eg an organ, a flute, a cornet). 管樂器；吹樂器(如風琴，笛，短號)。 ⇨ the illus at brass. 參看 brass 之挿圖。 **'~-jammer** *n* (colloq) merchant sailing-ship. (俗)商用帆船。 **'~·mill** *n* mill worked by the action of the ~ on sails which revolve. 風車。***fight/tilt at ~mills***, (from the story of Don Quixote) fight imaginary enemies; try to put right imaginary wrongs. (源於吉訶德先生傳)同幻想中的敵人作戰；試圖改革幻想中的弊端。 **'~·pipe** *n* passage for air from the throat to the lungs. (由喉至肺的)氣管。 ⇨ the illus at respiratory. 參看 respiratory 之挿圖。 **'~-screen** (US 美 = **'~·shield**) *n* screen of glass in front of a motor-vehicle, etc. 風屏；(汽車等的)擋風玻璃；擋風屏。⇨ the illus at motor. 參看 motor 之挿圖。 **'~·screen-wiper** *n* ⇨ *wiper* at wipe. **'~-sock** *n* canvas sleeve flown at the top of a pole (eg on an airfield) to show the direction of the ~. 風向袋；風向標(如飛機場等處者)。 **'~·swept** *adj* exposed to the ~s; blown bare by strong ~s: 當風的；被强風吹光的: *a ~swept hillside.* 當風的山坡。 **'~-tunnel** *n* structure through which air is forced (at controlled speeds) to study its effects on (models of) aircraft, etc. 風洞(爲研究風力對於飛機等的影響而建造的隧道，風速由人控制) **~·less** *adj* without ~: 無風的: *a ~less day.* 一個無風的日子。 **~·ward** /-wəd; -wɚd/ *n, adj* (side) in the direction from which the ~ blows; (side) exposed to the ~: 上風的；當風的；上風側；上風邊；當風面: *Let's get to ~ward of that tannery* (to avoid the bad smell). 讓我們轉到製革廠的上風側去(以躲避臭氣)。 **windy** *adj* (-ier, -iest) **1** with much ~: 多風的: *a ~y day;* 多風的日子; *~y weather;* 多風的天氣; *a ~y hilltop*, open to the ~. 當風的山頂。 **2** wordy, ⇨ 5 above. 空談的；多廢話的(參看上列第5義)。 **3** (sl) frightened. (俚)受驚嚇的；害怕的。 **~·ily** /-ɪlɪ; -ɪlɪ/ *adv* **~i·ness** *n*

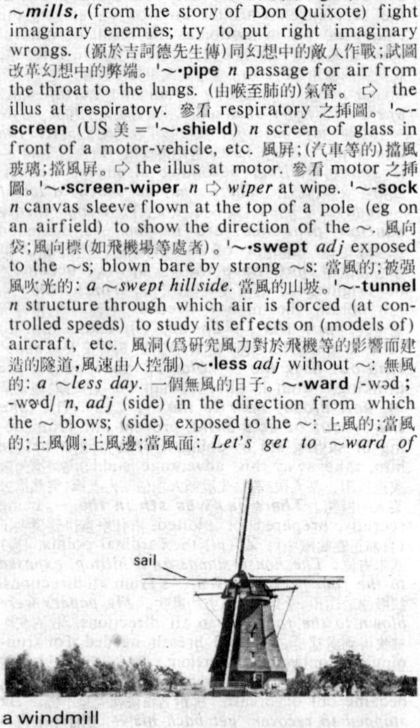

a windmill

wind[2] /wɪnd; wɪnd/ *vt* (from 源於 wind[1]) (*pt, pp* ~ed /ˈwɪndɪd; ˈwɪndɪd/) [VP6A] **1** detect the presence of by scent: 嗅出；聞出: *The hounds ~ed the fox.* 獵犬嗅出了狐狸的踪跡。*The deer ~ed the stalkers.* 那隻鹿嗅出了偷偷接近的獵人。 **2** exhaust the wind(3) of; cause to breathe fast: 使喘息；使呼吸急促: *He was quite ~ed by the long climb/by running to catch the bus.* 他由於長時間的攀爬(跑去趕公車)而呼吸急促。 **3** give an opportunity of recovering the breath to: 使喘口氣；使稍休息: *We stopped to ~ our horses.* 我們停下來使馬稍事休息。

wind[3] /waɪnd; waɪnd/ *vi, vt* (*pt, pp* wound /waʊnd; waʊnd/) **1** [VP2A, B, C, 15A] go, (cause to) move, in a curving, spiral, or twisting manner: 迂迴地走；彎曲前進；(使)蜿蜒；(使)彎曲移動: *The river ~s (its way) to the sea.* 那條河蜿蜒地流入大海。*We climbed the ~ing* (= spiral) *staircase.* 我們爬上螺旋梯。*The path ~s up the hillside.* 那條小徑沿着山坡蜿蜒而上。*She wound herself/her way into his affections*, won his affections by her clever ways. 她以聰明的手段贏得了他的感情。 **2** [VP6A, 15A, B] twist (string, wool yarn, etc) into a ball, or round or on to sth: 捲(帶，細繩，毛線等)成球；纏繞；裹: *~ (up) wool into a ball;* 將毛線捲成球; *~ yarn;* 纏繞紗線; *~ thread on to a reel;* 將線纏繞在線軸上。 *~ in the line*, eg a fishing-line on to a reel. 收線(如把釣線捲在軸上)。 ***~ sth off***, unwind it. 解開；放開；鬆開。***~ sb round one's (little) finger***, make him do whatever one wants him to do. 任意操縱某人；隨意左右或擺布某人。 **3** [VP14, 15A] ***~ sth round sb/sth; ~ sb/sth in sth***, fold or wrap closely; embrace: 包緊；圍緊；環抱；裹: *~ a shawl round a baby;* 以圍巾裹着嬰兒; *~ a baby in a shawl.* 把嬰兒裹在圍巾裡。*She wound her arms round the child.* 她以雙臂環抱那孩子。 **'~ing-sheet** *n* shroud; sheet (to be) wound round a corpse. 裹屍布。 **4** [VP6A, 15B] ***~ sth (up)***, turn (a handle, eg of a windlass); raise (sth) by doing this: 轉動(絞盤等的把手)；絞起；吊起: *~ a handle;* 轉動把手; *~ up ore from a mine/a bucket from a well.* 從礦坑中以絞盤吊出礦石(從井中用轆轤吊出水桶)。 **5** [VP6A, 15B] ***~ sth (up)***, tighten the spring of (a watch or clock); raise the weights that operate a clock (to put or keep the watch or clock in motion): 上(鐘或錶)的絃；上發條: *If you forget to ~ (up) your watch it will stop—unless it is a self-~ing watch*, ie one that is wound up automatically by movements of the wrist. 如果你忘記上錶的絃，錶就會停——除非它是自動(上絃的)錶。 **6** ***be wound up (to)***, be (emotionally) excited (esp in passive), ⇨ unwind: (情緒方面)激動；緊張；振奮(尤用於被動語態中): *He was wound up to a high pitch of excitement.* 他極爲興奮。*Expectation was wound up to a high pitch.* 期待的心情已達到極其緊張的地步。*She was wound up to a fury.* 她極爲憤怒。 **7** [VP2C, 15B] ***~ (sth) up***, come or bring to an end: 結束: *It's time for him to ~ up his speech*, come to a conclusion. 現在是他結束演說的時候了。*He wound up by declaring that his efforts would be continued.* 他最後宣稱他的努力將繼續下去。*They wound up the evening by singing some folksongs.* 他們唱了幾支民謠，結束了那個夜晚。***~ up a business company***, put everything in order before dissolving it. 結束一個公司；解散前清理一個公司。***~ up one's affairs***, put them in order before bringing them to an end. 結束私務；結束個人事務。 □ *n* [C] single turn in ~ing string, ~ing up a clock, etc. (捲線，上鐘錶發條等

的)一次轉動;纏繞;上絃。

wind·lass /ˈwɪndləs ; ˈwɪndləs/ *n* machine for pulling or lifting things (eg water from a well) by means of a rope or chain which is wound round an axle; winch. (起重等用的)絞車;絞盤;轆轤。

win·dow /ˈwɪndəʊ ; ˈwɪndo/ *n* opening in a wall or roof of a building, the side of a ship, carriage, car, etc to let in light and air: 窗;窗口;窗扉: *look out of the ~.* 從窗口望出去。 **ˈ~-box** *n* long narrow box fixed to a ~-sill in which to grow plants. 窗檻花箱;窗台花箱(固定於窗台前的長而窄的部分,栽花用)。 **ˈ~-dressing** *n* art of arranging goods attractively in shop-~s; (fig) (art of) making an impressive display of one's work, abilities, qualities, etc. (商店的)橱窗裝飾術;橱窗佈置;(喻)自我宣傳(術);自我炫耀(術)。 **ˌ~ ˈenvelope** *n* one with a transparent part in the front through which an address on the paper inside may be read. 開窗信封(正面部分透明,可看見信紙上收信人的地址)。 **ˈ~-pane** *n* pane of glass for or in a ~. 窗(子上的)玻璃。 ***go ˈ~-shopping,*** look at goods displayed in shop-~s (for interest, but not necessarily with the idea of buying anything). 瀏覽商店的橱窗(不一定想買東西);逛街。 **ˈ~-sill** *n* ⇨ sill. ***a ~ on the world,*** (fig) means of learning about, or coming into contact with, other countries: (喻)瞭解或接觸其他國家的方法、手段、媒介或工具;世界之窗: *The English language is a ~ on the world.* 英語是瞭解或接觸世界的一種工具。

windy /ˈwɪndɪ ; ˈwɪndɪ/ ⇨ wind¹.

wine /waɪn ; waɪn/ *n* [U] **1** alcoholic drink made from the fermented juice of grapes: 葡萄酒: *a barrel/bottle/glass of ~;* 一桶(瓶,杯)葡萄酒; *French ~(s),* (*pl* for different kinds of ~). 法國(產的)葡萄酒(複數形表示各種葡萄酒)。 ***new ~ in old bottles,*** a new principle that is too strong to be held back by old forms. 舊瓶裝新酒;舊形式包容不了新內容。 **ˈ~·glass** *n* glass designed for drinking ~ from. 酒杯。 **ˈ~·press** *n* one in which grapes are pressed (葡萄)壓汁器。 **ˈ~·skin** *n* whole skin of a goat, etc sewn up and used formerly for holding ~. 皮酒袋(整張羊皮等縫製而成,昔時盛酒用)。 **2** fermented drink resembling ~, made from other fruits or plants: 水果酒;酒: *currant/cowslip/palm, etc ~.* 醋栗(櫻草,棕櫚等)酒。 □ *vt* (esp) (尤用於) ***~ and dine sb,*** entertain at a meal with ~: 以酒宴款待: *We were ~d and dined at the firm's expense.* 公司以酒宴款待我們。

wing /wɪŋ ; wɪŋ/ *n* **1** either of the two organs of a bird by which it flies; one of the similar organs of an insect; one of the surfaces by which an aircraft is supported in the air. (鳥,昆蟲,飛機等的)翼;翅。 ⇨ the illus at air, bird. 參看 air 與 bird 之挿圖。 ***clip a person's ~s*** limit his movements, activities, expenditure, etc. 限制某人的活動,行動,花費等。 ***lend/add ~s to,*** cause to go fast: 使快走;使加速: *Fear lent him ~s,* made him run off fast. 恐懼使他加快了脚步。 ***take (to itself) ~s,*** disappear, vanish: 消失;消逝: *As soon as we go on a holiday, our money seems to take ~s.* 每當我們去度假,錢就飛也似地花掉了。 ***take sb under one's ~,*** take him under one's protection; give him care and guidance. 保護或庇護某人;給予某人照顧與指導。 **ˈ~-nut/-screw,** = thumb-nut. **ˈ~-span/-spread** *nn* measurement across ~s when these are extended. 翼幅;翼展(兩翼張開時的寬度)。 **2** part of an object, building, etc which projects or is extended from one of its sides (eg the part of a motor-vehicle covering a wheel, called a *fender* in US): (物體,建築物等的)側翼;翼;廂房;(汽車的)擋泥板(美國稱作 fender): *a ˈ~ chair,* an upholstered chair with arms as high as the back; 高邊椅(側邊與靠背等高); *add a new ~ to a hospital.* 為醫院的一側增建一排房屋。 *The north ~ of the house was added 50 years ago.* 那房子北面的廂房是五十年前添建的。 **3** (mil) either of the flanks of an

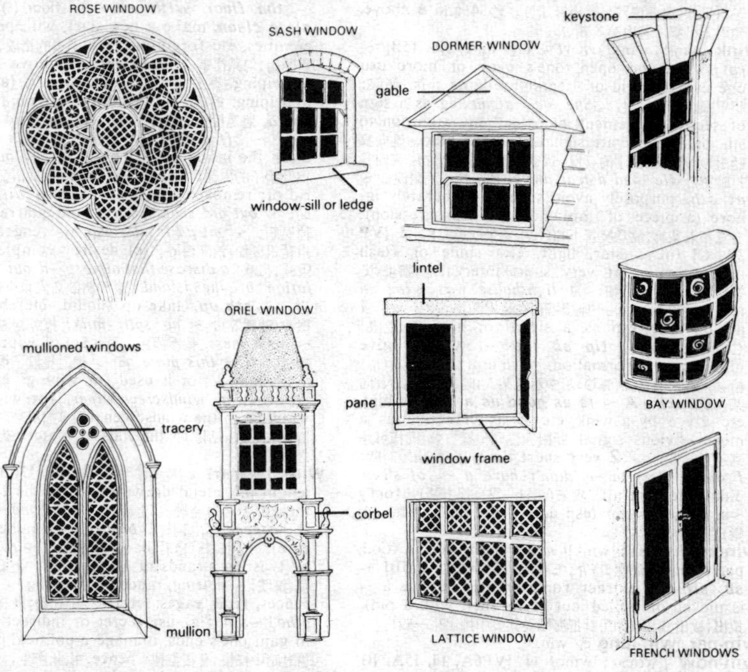

windows

army or fleet; unit placed to guard a flank. (軍)(部隊、艦隊的)翼;側翼;保護側翼的部隊。 **4** those members of a political party holding more extreme views than those of the majority: (政黨中的)派別;翼(所持觀點較大多數黨員極端): *the radical ~ of the Labour Party.* 工黨的激進派。Hence, 由此產生, ˌ**left-** / ˌ**right-**ˈ**~(er).** 左(右)派(分子)。 **5** unseen areas to the right and left of the stage of a theatre; the scenery there: 舞臺的側面;舞臺的側景: *We were allowed to watch the performance from the ~s.* 我們獲准在舞臺的側面看表演。 **6** flying. 飛行;飛翔。 ***on the ~,*** in flight: 在飛行中: *shoot a bird on the ~.* 射擊飛行中的鳥。 ***take ~,*** start flying. 起飛;飛去。 **7** sth like a ~ in appearance or position, eg certain seeds (esp of the maple and sycamore). 形狀或位置似翼之物; (尤指楓樹及大楓樹的)翼形種子;翼瓣。 **8** (also 亦作 **~er**) (football, hockey) forward player whose place is either side of the centre. (足球,曲棍球)翼;邊鋒(球員)。⇨ the illus at football. 參看 football 之插圖。 **9** (GB; RAF) formation of two or more squadrons; (*pl*) pilot's badge: (英;皇家空軍)大隊; (複)飛行徽章: *get one's ~s.* 獲得飛行徽章。ˈ**~-commander,** RAF rank, next below Group Captain. (英國皇家空軍的)空軍中校。□ *vt, vi* **1** [VP6A] give ~s to; lend speed to: 增加…的速度;加快: (usu fig) (通常作喻) *Fear ~ed his steps.* 恐懼使他加快步子。 **2** [VP2C, 15A] fly; travel on ~s: 飛;飛行: *The planes ~ed (their way) over the Alps.* 飛機飛越阿爾卑斯山。 **3** [VP6A] wound (a bird) in the ~; (colloq) wound (a person) in the arm. 傷(鳥)之翼;(俗)傷(人)之臂。 **~ed** *adj* having ~s: 有翼的;有翅膀的: *the ~ed god,* Mercury; (羅馬神話中的)信使神; *a ~ed Victory,* a statue of the goddess of victory with ~s. 有翼的勝利女神彫像。 **~·less** *adj* without ~s. 無翼的;無翅膀的。 **~er** *n* person who acts or plays in a position on the ~s. (政黨中的)激進分子;左(右)派分子;(足球,曲棍球)邊鋒;邊鋒球員。⇨ 4 and 8 above. 參看上列第4義與第8義。

wink /wɪŋk ; wɪŋk/ *vi, vt* **1** [VP2A, 3A, 15B] ~ ***(at),*** close and open (one's eyes, or more usu one eye); get rid of (tears) by doing this: 眨眼;眨單眼;眨掉(眼淚): *She ~ed at me,* eg as a sign of secret amusement, or to call my attention to sth, or as a private signal of some kind. 她向我眨眼(示意某種私下的喜悅,或欲引我注意某事物,或向我打暗號)。 *He ~ed a tear away.* 他眨掉一滴眼淚。 ***~ at sth,*** purposely avoid seeing; deliberately ignore (a piece of misconduct, a transgression). 有意不看某物;故意裝着不知(一項過失或違犯)。 **2** [VP 2A, C] (of a star, light, etc) shine or flash intermittently, at very short intervals: (指星,光等)閃爍;閃動;閃耀: *A lighthouse was ~ing in the far distance.* 一座燈塔正在遠處閃爍。□ *n* **1** act of ~ing, esp as a signal or hint. 瞬;眨眼; (尤指)目語;眼色。 ***tip sb the ~,*** (colloq) give him special information; warn him secretly. (俗)給某人特別消息,情報等;暗中警告某人;向某人眨眼示意。 ***A ~ is as good as a nod,*** A hint, etc given by a wink, etc is as effective as a more obvious signal. 眨眼與點頭一樣有效(同樣可達到示意的目的)。 **2** very short time: 瞬息;極短時間: *I didn't sleep a ~ / didn't have a ~ of sleep,* didn't sleep at all. 我未合眼(一點也沒有睡)。 **forty ~s,** a short sleep (esp during the day). 小眠;(尤指)白天的小睡。

win·kle /ˈwɪŋkl ; ˈwɪŋkl/ *n* sea snail used as food; periwinkle. 海螺;盲介;玉黍螺。□ *vt* [VP15B] ~ ***sb / sth out,*** extract, force or pull out (as a ~ is picked or pulled out of its shell with a pin). 拉出;拔出;剔出(如用針把海螺從其殼中挑出來一般)。

win·ner, win·ning ⇨ win.

win·now /ˈwɪnəʊ ; ˈwɪno/ *vt* [VP6A, 14, 15A, B] use a stream of air to separate dry outer coverings from (grain): 吹,扇(穀物)以除去其糠皮: *~ wheat;* 簸小麥;搧小麥; blow (husks, chaff) away from grain in this way: 簸去或吹去(穀殼,糠皮): *~ the chaff away / out;* 搧或吹去糠皮; (fig) (喻) *~ truth from falsehood.* 分辨眞假。

win·some /ˈwɪnsəm ; ˈwɪnsəm/ *adj* (of a person, his appearance) attractive; pleasing; bright: (指人,其外表)有吸引力的;可愛的;悅目的;活潑的;聰明的: *a ~ smile / manner.* 迷人的微笑(儀態)。 **~·ly** *adv* **~·ness** *n*

win·ter /ˈwɪntə(r) ; ˈwɪntɚ/ *n* [U, C] season between autumn and spring (Nov or Dec to Feb or March in the northern hemisphere): 冬;冬季(北半球從十一月或十二月至二月或三月): *many ~s* (liter, 文 = years) *ago;* 多年前; *~ sports,* eg ice-skating, skiing; 冬季運動(如溜冰,滑雪); *~ wheat,* planted in the autumn and harvested in the following spring or summer; 冬小麥(秋季下種而於來年春季或夏季收割); *~ quarters,* (esp) to which troops retired for the ~ (in former times). (尤指昔時軍隊於冬天駐紮的)冬營。ˈ**~ garden,** glass-enclosed area with plants, etc eg as the lounge of a hotel. 冬園(用玻璃圍繞而且種有植物等的地方,如旅館的大廳等)。□ *vi* [VP2C] pass the ~: 過冬: *~ in the south;* 在南方過冬; *the ~ing quarters of wild geese.* 雁的冬季棲息處。 **~y, win·try** /ˈwɪntrɪ ; ˈwɪntrɪ/ *adjj* of or like ~; cold: 冬天的;像冬季的;寒冷的: *a wintry sky / day;* 寒冬的天空(日子); *wintry weather;* 寒冷的天氣;冬天的天氣; (fig) (喻) *a wintry smile / greeting,* one lacking in warmth or liveliness. 冷淡的微笑(招呼)。

wipe /waɪp ; waɪp/ *vt, vi* [VP6A, 15A, B, 22] clean or dry (sth) by rubbing with a cloth, paper, the hands, etc: 擦;拭;抹;揩: *~ the dishes;* 擦盤子; *~ one's hands on a towel;* 在毛巾上擦手; *~ one's face;* 擦臉; *~ sth dry;* 擦乾某物; *~ one's eyes,* dry the tears. 擦乾眼淚。 *Take this handkerchief and ~ your nose, David.* 拿這塊手帕揩你的鼻子,大衞。 ***~ the floor with sb,*** ⇨ floor¹(1). ***~ the slate clean,*** make a new start, with past errors, enmities, etc forgotten. (忘掉過去的錯誤、仇恨等)重新開始;勾銷往事。 ***~ sth away,*** remove (eg tears) by wiping. 擦去(如眼淚)。 ***~ sth off,*** **(a)** remove by wiping: 擦掉: *~ off a drawing from the blackboard.* 將黑板上的圖畫擦掉。 **(b)** get rid of: 除去;清除: *~ off a debt.* 還清債務。 ***~ sth out,*** **(a)** clean the inside of: 擦洗…的內部: *~ out a jug;* 擦洗罐子的內部; *~ out the bath.* 擦拭浴盆。 **(b)** get rid of; remove: 清除;除去: *~ out a disgrace;* 雪恥; *~ out old scores,* forget old quarrels, etc; 忘掉夙怨; *~ out an insult* (esp by vengeance). (尤指藉報復而)消除侮辱。 **(c)** destroy completely: 澈底毀滅;掃滅: *a disease that almost ~d out the population of the island.* 幾乎將該島人口全部消滅的疾病。 ***~ sth up,*** take up (liquid, etc) by wiping: 擦淨(液體等): *~ up spilt milk;* 擦乾淨濺出的牛奶; *~ up a mess.* 擦淨髒污。□ *n* act of wiping: 擦;拭;揩;抹: *Give this plate a ~.* 把這隻盤子擦一擦。 **~r** *n* sth that ~s or is used for wiping: 擦拭物;擦拭用的東西: *a* ˈ*windscreen-wiper,* for wiping rain-water from the windscreen. (汽車擋風玻璃上的)揩拭器;刮水器;雨刮。⇨ the illus at motor. 參看 motor 之插圖。

wire /ˈwaɪə(r) ; waɪr/ *n* **1** [C, U] (piece or length of) metal drawn out into the form of a thread: (一段)金屬線;金屬絲: ˈ*telephone ~(s);* 電話線; *copper ~;* 銅絲; *barbed ~* (⇨ the illus at barb); 有刺鐵絲(參看 barb 之插圖); *~ rope,* made by twisting strands of ~ together; 金屬繩索;金屬纜;鋼纜; *~ netting,* made by weaving ~ (used for fences, fruit cages, etc). 金屬絲網;鐵絲網。 ***pull (the) ~s,*** (fig) use secret or indirect influence to gain one's ends, manage a political party, etc; (喻)暗中操縱;幕後指揮; hence, 由此產生, ˈ**~-puller** *n.* **live ~, (a)** ~ charged with electric current.

通電的電線。 **(b)** (fig) active, vigorous person. (喻)活潑而有精力的人；精力充沛的人。 **'~-cutters** *n pl* tool for cutting ~. 剪斷金屬絲所用的工具；鋼絲鉗。 **,~-'haired** *adj* (esp of a dog) with stiff or wiry hair. (尤指狗)硬毛的。 **'~ tapping** *n* [U] tapping of telephones, ⇨ tap¹, *vt*(2). 電話竊聽(參看 tap¹, vt. 第2義)。 **~ wool** *n* [C, U] (pad of) fine ~ for cleaning pots and pans. (清洗鍋盤等用的)金屬絲絨(墊等)。 **'~-worm** *n* kinds of worm-like larva destructive to plants. (對植物有害的)切根蟲。 **2** [C] (colloq, esp US) telegram: (俗,尤美)電報： *send sb a ~;* 拍電報給某人； *send off a ~.* 拍發電報。 *Let me know by ~ what time to expect you.* 拍電報告訴我你什麼時候到。 □ *vt, vi* **1** [VP6A, 15A, B] fasten with ~: 用金屬絲綑起： *~ two things together;* 用金屬絲把二物綁在一起； put ~(s) in or on; put (beads, pearls, etc) on fine ~. 加金屬絲於…中；加金屬絲於…上；用細金屬絲穿(珠子、珍珠等)。 **2** [VP6A] install electrical circuits (in a building, to provide lighting, power, etc): 裝置電線於(建築物中，以供給電力、照明等)： *Has the house been ~d for electricity yet?* 這房子已裝好電線了嗎？ **3** [VP6A] catch, snare (birds, rabbits, etc) with ~. 用鐵絲網捕捉，網住(鳥、兔等)。 **4** [VP6A, 16A, 12A, 13A, 11, 2C] (colloq, esp US) telegraph: (俗，尤美)拍電報： *He ~d (to) his brother to buy oil shares.* 他拍電報給他的哥哥(弟弟)購買石油股票。 *He ~d me that he would be delayed.* 他拍電報給我，說他將延期到達。 **wir·ing** *n* [U] (esp) system of ~s for electric current. (尤指)電線系統；佈線；接線。 **wiry** *adj* (-ier, -iest) like ~; (of persons) lean and with strong sinews. 似金屬絲的；(指人)瘦而結實的。

wire·less /ˈwaɪələs ; ˈwaɪrlɪs/ *adj* without the use of wire(s). 不用電線的；無線的。 □ *n* (dated word for) (過時用語，指) **1** [U] radio. 無線電。 **2** [C] radio set. 收音機。

wis·dom /ˈwɪzdəm ; ˈwɪzdəm/ *n* [U] **1** quality of being wise. 智慧；睿智。 **'~-tooth** *n* (*pl* -teeth) back tooth, usu coming through after 20 years of age: 智齒(最後面的臼齒，通常在廿歲以後才長出)： *cut one's ~-teeth,* reach the age when one has discretion, etc. 到達懂事的年齡；開始識世故。⇨ the illus at mouth. 參看 mouth 之插圖。 **2** wise thoughts, sayings, etc: 睿智的思想、言詞等： *the ~ of the ancients/our ancestors.* 古人(我們祖先)的名言、卓識等。

wise¹ /waɪz ; waɪz/ *adj* (-r, -st) having or showing experience, knowledge, good judgement, prudence, etc: 聰明的；明智的；具有或顯示經驗、知識、良好的判斷、審慎等的： *~ men/acts.* 聰明的人(行爲)。 *He was ~ enough not to drive when he was feeling ill.* 他很明智，感覺身體不適的時候便不駕車。 *'I don't agree', he said, with a ~ shake of the head,* ie suggesting that he was ~. '我不同意'，他說，頗有見地地搖搖頭。 *It's easy to be ~ after the event,* to know, after sth has happened, what one failed to see in advance. 事後聰明是很容易的。 ***be none the ~r,*** be no better informed: 仍舊不明白；照樣糊塗： *He came away none the ~r,* knowing no more than before. 他離去時仍舊和以前一樣的不明白。 ***be/get ~ to sb/sth,*** (sl) be/become aware of: (俚)明白；懂得： *get ~ to what's happening/to the ways of business men, etc.* 明白現況(商人的成習和作風等)。 ***put sb ~ to sb/sth,*** inform him of (what is happening, etc). 告訴某人(現況、實情等)。 **'~·acre** *n* dull and boring person who pretends to be much ~r than he is. 自作聰明的人；假聰明人。 **'~-crack** *n* (sl) smart, witty saying or remark. (俚)俏皮話；妙語。 □ *vi* make ~cracks. 說俏皮話；作妙語。 **~·ly** *adv*

wise² /waɪz ; waɪz/ *n* (*sing* only; old use) way, manner: (僅用單數；舊用法)方法；方式： *in no ~;* 一點也不；絕不； *in this ~.* 這樣地。

wish /wɪʃ ; wɪʃ/ *vt, vi* **1** [VP9] ~ ***that...,*** (*that* usu omitted; the *that*-clause usu in the *pt*) have as an unfulfilled desire or a desire that cannot be fulfilled: (that 通常省去；that 子句中，通常用過去時態)有某種未實現或無法實現的欲望或希望；但願： *I ~ I knew what is happening.* 但願我知道現在正在發生什麼事。 *I ~ I were rich.* 我希望我很有錢。 *I ~ I were a bird.* 我希望我是一隻鳥。 *She ~ed she'd stayed at home,* was sorry that she had not stayed at home. 她遺憾當時不在家。 **2** [VP15A] have as a desire: 切望；渴望；希望： *She ~ed herself home* (= ~ed that she was at home) *again.* 她眞希望已經再度回到家裡。 *They ~ed the voyage at an end.* 他們渴望航行告一結束。 *He began to ~ himself* (= ~ that he was) *out of the affair.* 他開始希望自己未介入那事。 **3** [VP22] ~ ***sb well/ill,*** hope that he may have good/ill fortune, etc: 祝某人好運(希望某人倒楣)等： *He ~ed me well.* 他祝我好運。 *I ~ nobody ill.* 我不希望有人遭殃。 **4** [VP12A, 13A] say that one hopes for: 頌；祝： *~ sb a pleasant journey;* 祝某人旅途快樂； *~ happiness to all one's friends;* 祝福所有朋友； express as a greeting: 表示某種問候語；問候；招呼： *~ sb good morning/goodbye.* 向某人道早安(再見)。 **5** [VP7A, 17, rarely VP6A with pron] want: (VP6A 與代名詞連用的用法較少見)想要；需要： *She ~es to be alone.* 她不想被打擾。 *Do you really ~ me to go?* 你眞的要我去嗎？ *I ~ there to be no misunderstanding on this matter.* 關於這件事我不願有所誤會。 *What do you ~?* 你想要什麼？ *Well, if you ~ it...,* if that is what you want me to do, etc. 唔，如果你眞要…。 **6** [VP3A] ~ ***for,*** have a desire for, pray for (esp sth unlikely to be obtained or achieved, or sth that can be obtained only by good fortune or in exceptional circumstances): 欲；願(尤指不大可能獲得或達到的，或有賴於好運或特殊環境才能獲得的某種事物)： *She has everything a woman can ~ for,* (suggesting unusual good fortune). 女人想要獲得的一切，她都有了(顯示她有不尋常的好運)。 *How he ~ed for an opportunity to go abroad!,* (suggesting small likelihood of getting one). 他多麼希望有機會出國啊！(顯示這種機會並不大)。 *The weather was everything they could ~ for,* (suggesting unusual good fortune). 他們遇到的天氣再好沒有了。 *What more can you ~ for?* 你究竟還想得到什麼呢？ (Cf 參較： *He would like a glass of cold water,* and *How he ~ed for a glass of cold water,* the second sentence suggesting that there was little likelihood of his getting one 第二句話表示他獲得一杯冷水的機會很小)。 **7** [VP2A] express a desire: 表示一種欲望： *Doing is better than ~ing.* 行動勝於癡心夢想。 **'~-bone** *n* forked bone above the breastbone of a fowl, pulled in two by two persons, the person getting the longer part having the right to the magic fulfilment of any wish. (鳥胸的)叉骨；如願骨(兩人同時拉扯，據迷信，扯到長的一段的人，無論希望什麼，都會神奇地如願以償)。 **'~·ing-cap** *n* (in fairy tales) cap which secures to the wearer the fulfilment of any wish. (神仙故事中)魔帽(戴者隨心所欲有求必應)。 **8** ~ ***sb/sth on sb,*** (colloq) transfer him/it to sb (esp with the idea of getting rid of sb/sth unwanted or disliked): (俗)把某人或某物轉交給某人(尤指欲擺脫不需要或不喜歡之人或物)；把某人或某物塞給某人： *I wouldn't ~ my mother-in-law on anyone,* suggesting that she is intolerable. 我不會把我丈母娘塞給旁人(意謂其丈母娘叫人受不了)。 *We had the Jones children ~ed on us for the weekend.* 瓊斯家的孩子們在週末被塞到我們這兒來。 □ *n* **1** [C, U] desire; longing: 欲望；願望： *He has no/not much ~ to go.* 他不(不大)想去。 *She expressed a ~ to be alone.* 她表示願意獨處(不願有人打擾)。 *He disregarded his father's ~es.* 他不顧他父親的願望。 *I hope you will grant my ~.* 我希望你答應我的請求。 ***If ~es were horses, beggars might ride,*** (prov) If things could be obtained merely by ~ing for them, poor people would soon be rich. (諺)如果願望是馬，叫化子都可以乘騎；如果夢想皆可成事實，窮人很快就發財了。***The ~ is father to the thought,*** (prov) We are apt to believe sth because we ~ it were true. (諺) 願望是意念之父；人們容易相信他們希望相信的事物。 **2** [C] that which is ~ed for: 被希冀的事物；所願望的事物: *She got her ~.* 她如願以償了。 **~·ful** /-fl ; -fəl/ *adj* having or expressing a ~; desiring. 有願望的；表示願望的；欲望的。***~ful thinking,*** thinking or believing that sth is true because one ~es it were true. 如意的想法或信念；妄想；如意算盤。**~·fully** /-fəlɪ ; -fəlɪ/ *adv*

wishy-washy /ˈwɪʃɪ wɒʃɪ *US:* wɔːʃɪ ; ˈwɪʃɪˌwɑʃɪ/ *adj* (of soup, tea, etc) thin; weak; (of talk, persons) lacking in spirit or vigour; sloppy. (指湯、茶等)淡的；稀薄的；(指談話、人)無力的；軟弱的。

wisp /wɪsp ; wɪsp/ *n* [C] small bundle, bunch or twist: 小綹；小把；小束；小捆: *a ~ of straw/hay;* 一小捆稻草(秣草)；*a ~ of hair;* 一綹頭髮； spiral or ribbon: 螺旋形物；帶；條: *a ~ of smoke/steam.* 一縷烟(蒸氣)。**~y** *adj* like a ~; slight. 似小束、小綹等的；纖細的；輕微的。

wis·teria /wɪˈstɪərɪə ; wɪsˈtɪrɪə/ *n* (kinds of) climbing plant with a woody stem and long drooping clusters of pale purple or white flowers and seeds in long pods, often grown on walls or over pergolas. (植)紫藤。

wist·ful /ˈwɪstfl ; ˈwɪstfəl/ *adj* sad and longing; having, showing, moved by, a rather unsatisfied and often vague desire: 愁悶而渴望的；具有或顯出頗爲不滿足而常爲模糊之欲望的；爲此種欲望所激動的: *~ eyes;* 渴望的眼睛；*a ~ expression;* 渴望的表情；*in a ~ mood.* 心情愁悶的。**~ly** /-fəlɪ ; -fəlɪ/ *adv* in a ~ manner: 愁悶而渴望地: *She looked ~ly at the photographs of herself when she was young and beautiful.* 她若有所思地悵悵然看着她自己年輕漂亮時的照片。

wit[1] /wɪt ; wɪt/ *n* **1** (*sing* or *pl*) intelligence; understanding; quickness of mind: (單數或複數)理智；理解；心智；智力；機智: *He hadn't the wits/hadn't wit enough to realize what to do in the emergency.* 他沒有應付緊急事件的才智。***at one's wit's end,*** not knowing what to do or say. 智窮；窮於應付；不知所措。***out of one's wits,*** greatly upset; distracted; mad: 不知所措；精神錯亂；發瘋: *You'll drive me out of my wits if you go on behaving in this way.* 如果你繼續這樣胡作非爲，你會使我發瘋。***have a ready wit,*** be quick to make clever and amusing remarks. 有捷才；口才機敏。***have/keep one's ˈwits about one,*** be quick to see what is happening, alert and ready to act. 警覺；機警。***live by one's wits,*** live by clever, not always honest, methods (as opportunities arise). 靠耍小聰明過日子。 **2** [U] clever and humorous expression of ideas; liveliness of spirit: 機智的措詞；才智；情趣橫溢: *Our teacher/Our teacher's conversation is full of wit.* 我們的老師(我們老師的談話)很風趣。*His writings sparkle with wit.* 他的作品閃露着才智。 **3** [C] person noted for his wit(2). 有才智者；富於機智的人；才子。 **witty** *adj* (-ier, -iest) full of humour: 詼諧的；諧趣橫生的；風趣的: *a witty girl/remark.* 黠慧風趣的女孩(妙語)。**wit·tily** /-ɪlɪ ; -ɪlɪ/ *adv* **wit·ti·cism** /ˈwɪtɪsɪzəm ; ˈwɪtəˌsɪzəm/ *n* [C] witty remark. 妙語；雋語；詼諧語。 **wit·less** *adj* stupid. 愚笨的；無機智的。

wit[2] /wɪt ; wɪt/ *v* ***to wit,*** (legal) namely; that is to say. (法律)卽；就是。

witch /wɪtʃ ; wɪtʃ/ *n* woman said to use magic, esp for evil purpose; (fig) fascinating or bewitching woman. 女巫；巫婆；(喩)迷人的女子。**ˈ~·craft** *n* [U] sorcery; use of magic. 巫術；魔法。 **ˈ~-doctor** *n* male ~; tribal magician (esp among primitive peoples). 男巫；巫醫(尤指原始民族中的)。**ˈ~-hunt** *n* (fig) searching out and persecution (eg of persons said to be disloyal or untrustworthy). (喩)搜尋迫害(如政治上不忠或可疑分子等)。 **~·ery** /ˈwɪtʃərɪ ; ˈwɪtʃərɪ/ *n* [U] **1** ~craft. 巫術；魔法。 **2** fascination; charm. 魅力；誘惑力；蠱惑。**~·ing** *adj* bewitching: 行巫術的；迷人的；銷魂的: *the ~ing hour of night,* the time when ~es are active; midnight. 女巫出動活躍的時刻；午夜。

witch-elm, witch-hazel ⇨ wych.

with /wɪð ; wɪð/ *prep* **1** (equivalent to constructions with the *v 'have'*) having; carrying; characterized by: (相當於帶動詞 have 的結構)有；帶着；有…的特徵: *a cup ~ a broken handle;* 把手破損的杯子；*a coat ~ two pockets;* 有兩個口袋的外衣；*a girl ~ blue eyes;* 碧眼女郎；*a baby ~ no clothes on;* 未穿衣服的嬰兒；*a woman ~ an angry look in her eyes;* 眼露怒氣的婦人；*~ your permission.* 經你允許。 ***~ child*** (of a woman 指女人)***; ~ young*** (of an animal 指動物), pregnant. 懷孕的；懷胎的。 **2** (to indicate what is used for filling, covering, etc): (表示填充物、覆蓋物等): *Fill the box ~ sand.* 將這個盒子裝滿沙子。*The lorry was loaded ~ timber.* 貨車裝滿了木材。*The sack was stuffed ~ straw.* 袋子裡塞滿了稻草。*The hills were covered ~ snow.* 丘陵被雪覆蓋了。 **3** (to indicate the means or instrument): (表示方式或工具): *write ~ a pen;* 用筆書寫；*take sth ~ both hands;* 用雙手取物；*walk ~ a crutch;* 用拐杖走路；*cut sth ~ a knife;* 用刀切割某物；*see sth ~ your own eyes;* 用你的眼睛看某物；*~ the help of your friends;* 藉你朋友們的幫助； *~ your help.* 靠你的幫助。 **4** (to indicate accompaniment or relationship): (表示伴隨或關係): *live ~ your parents;* 與你的雙親同住；*go for a walk ~ a friend;* 同一位朋友去散步；*discuss a problem ~ somebody;* 與某人討論一個問題； *spend the day ~ one's uncle;* 和叔父在一起度過一日；*mix one substance ~ another;* 把一種物質與另一物質混合；*put one thing ~ others.* 把一物與他物放在一起。*I shall be ~ you in a few minutes.* 我幾分鐘內(一會兒)就來招呼你。*Is there anyone ~ you or are you alone?* 有人陪伴你呢，還是你單獨一個人？*The general, (together) ~ his staff officers, will inspect the camp.* 那位將軍將率同其參謀官們視察營區。***in ~,*** in association ~; mixed up ~: 結交；與…交遊；與…交往: *She's in ~ the wrong crowd,* eg of a girl whose companions are criminals. 她結交了一羣不法之徒。 **5** (to indicate antagonism, opposition): (表示敵對、反對): *fight/argue/struggle/quarrel, etc ~ sb;* 與某人打架(辯論，競爭，吵架等)；*have an argument ~ sb;* 與某人辯論； *in competition ~;* 與…競爭；*a battle ~ savages;* 對抗野蠻人的戰鬥；*at war ~ the Romans.* 與羅馬人作戰。***fall out ~,*** ⇨ fall[2](14). ***have it out ~ sb,*** ⇨ have[4](9). **6** (to indicate cause) because of; owing to: (表示原因)因爲；由於: *silent ~ shame;* 因羞恥而沉默； *trembling ~ fear/rage;* 因恐懼(憤怒)而抖顫；*shaking ~ cold;* 冷得發抖；*a face wet ~ tears.* 眼淚濡濕的臉。 **7** (to indicate manner): (表示方式或樣態): *do sth ~ an effort/~ a light heart/~ one's whole heart/~ joy/~ pleasure;* 努力(心情輕鬆，全心全意，高高興興，甘心情願)地做某事；*standing ~ his hands in his pockets;* 他站着，雙手放在口袋裡；*win ~ ease,* easily; 輕易地獲勝；*fight ~ courage,* courageously; 英勇地戰鬥；*~ a roar/a growl/a shout of triumph;* 大吼(咆哮，歡呼)著；*receive sb ~ open arms.* 熱忱地歡迎某人。 **8** in the same way or direction as; at the same time as: 與…同方向或路徑；與…同時: *A tree's shadow moves ~ the sun.* 樹影隨着太陽移動。*W~ the approach of sunset it becomes chilly.* 到日落時分，天變冷了。*Do you rise ~ the sun,* ie at dawn? 你黎明卽起嗎？ **9** (to indicate care, charge or possession): (表示照顧、管理或保有): *Leave the child ~* (= in the care of) *its aunt.* 把小孩留給他的姑媽照管。*I have no money ~ me.* 我身上沒錢。*The next mover is ~ you.* 下一步該你。*It rests ~ you to decide/The decision rests ~ you,* ie you must decide. 由你作決定。 **10** in regard to; concerning: 對於;關於: *be patient ~ them;* 對他們有耐性; *sympathize ~ her;* 同情她; *bear/put up ~* (= endure) *sb or sth;* 忍受某人或某事; *have dealings/business ~ sb.* 與某人有交往(商業往來)。 *What do you want ~ me?* 你要我做什麼呢?(你找我幹什麼?) *What's your business ~ him?* 你和他有什麼事? *It's a habit ~ some people.* 這是某些人的習慣。 *We can't do anything/can do nothing ~ him,* cannot influence, control, make use of, him. 我們對他毫無辦法(不能影響、控制或利用他)。 *It's holiday time ~ us now.* 對於我們來說現在是假期。 *The first object ~ him* (= His first object) *is always to make a profit.* 他的第一目標永遠是賺錢。 *Away ~ him!* Send or take him away! 帶他走! *Out ~ you!* Get out! 出去! *Off ~ his head!* 砍掉他的頭! (and many other exclamatory sentences in the pattern *adv* + ~ + *n/pron* 另有許多感嘆句亦屬於這類句型,卽:副詞 + with + 名詞或代名詞). **11** (to indicate separation): (表示分離): *Let us dispense ~ ceremony,* ie not be ceremonious. 讓我們免除禮節吧。 *I parted ~ her at the gate.* 我和她在大門口分手。 *He has broken ~ his best friend.* 他已同他的至友絕交。 **12** (to indicate agreement, harmony): (表示同意,和諧): *He that is not ~ me* (= on my side) *is against me.* 不贊成我的人就是反對我。 *I'm ~ you* (= in agreement or sympathy ~ you) *in what you say.* 我同意你說的話。 *I* (dis)*agree ~ you.* 我同意(不同意)你。 *I can't go along ~ you on that question,* can't agree or co-operate with you. 關於那個問題我不能附和你。 *Does this blue go well ~ this green?* 這種藍色和這種綠色相配嗎? **be/get '~ it,** (sl) become aware of what is popular and up to date: (俚)知道或懂得最新或最流行的事物; 懂得時髦: (attrib) (形容用法) *'~-it clothes.* 流行的服裝。 **13** in spite of; notwithstanding (the possession of): 儘管;縱然(有): *W~ all her faults he still liked her.* 儘管她有許多缺點,他還是喜歡她。 *He failed ~ the best of intentions to win the sympathy of his pupils.* 他雖然費盡苦心,依然無法獲得學生們的贊同。

withal /wɪ'ðɔːl ; wɪð'ɔl/ *adv* (archaic) in addition. (古)又;且;此外。

with·draw /wɪð'drɔː ; wɪð'drɔ/ *vt, vi* (*pt* -drew /-'druː ; -'dru/, *pp* -drawn /-'drɔːn ; -'drɔn/) **1** [VP6A, 14] **~ sth/sb (from),** pull or draw back; take out or away: 取回;收回;拿出;拿開: *~ money from the Bank/dirty banknotes from circulation;* 自銀行提款(收回骯髒的鈔票使不再流通); *~ a boy from school,* not allow him to attend. 令一男孩退學。 *The workers threatened to ~ their labour,* to go on strike. 工人們威脅着要罷工。 **2** [VP6A, 2A] take back (a statement, an accusation, an offer): 撤回;撤銷(一項陳述、控告、提議): *He refused to ~* (*the offending expression*), eg after calling sb a liar. 他拒絕道歉(撤回冒犯的話,如稱某人爲說謊者)。 **3** [VP6A, 14, 2A, C] (cause to) move back or away: (使)撤退;退出;脫離;撤出: *~ troops from an exposed position;* 把部隊撤離無掩蔽的地區; *~ from society.* 隱遁。 *Our troops had to ~.* 我們的部隊必須撤退。 (Cf 參較 *The enemy had to retreat.* 敵人不得不退却。) **~al** /-'drɔːəl ; -'drɔəl/ *n* [U] ~ing or being withdrawn; [C] instance of this. 取回; 收回; 撤回; 撤銷; 退出; 此種實例。 **'~al symptom,** physical or mental reaction when steadily deprived of sth to which one is addicted (in order to break the habit). (醫)脫癮徵狀;斷除徵狀(在戒癮過程中,漸次斷除癮物時,所產生的身心反應)。 **~n** *adj* (of persons, their looks) retiring; unsociable; abstracted. (指人、人的外貌)孤獨的;緘默的;不喜交際的;孤僻的;出神的;心不在焉的。

withe /wɪθ ; wɪθ/, **withy** /'wɪðɪ ; 'wɪðɪ/ *nn* [C] tough but easily bent twig or branch, esp of willow or osier used for binding bundles, eg of firewood. 柔枝;(尤指捆柴等用的)柳枝。

wither /'wɪðə(r) ; 'wɪðɚ/ *vt, vi* **1** [VP6A, 15B, 2A, C] **~ (sth) up; ~ (away),** (cause to) become dry, faded or dead: (使)枯萎;凋謝: *The hot summer ~ed* (*up*) *the grass.* 炎熱的夏季(陽光)使草枯萎了。 *Her hopes ~ed* (*away*). 她的希望漸漸凋萎了。 **2** [VP6A] cause (sb) to be covered with shame or confusion: 使(某人)感到羞慚或迷惑: *She ~ed him with a scornful look/gave him a ~ing look.* 她輕蔑的一瞥使他感到羞慚(她向他投注令他自慚形穢的一瞥)。 **~·ing·ly** /'wɪðərɪŋlɪ ; 'wɪðrɪŋlɪ/ *adv*

with·ers /'wɪðəz ; 'wɪðɚz/ *n pl* highest part of the back of a horse, etc between the shoulder-blades (where the strain of the collar is taken). 鬐甲(馬等兩肩骨間的隆起部分,爲軛的着力處)。 ⇨ the illus at dog, domestic. 參看 dog, domestic 之插圖。

with·hold /wɪð'həʊld ; wɪθ'hold/ *vt* (*pt, pp* -held /-'held ; -'hɛld/) [VP6A, 14] **~ sth (from),** keep back; refuse to give: 抑制;制止;隱瞞;保留;扣留: *He tried to ~ the truth from us.* 他試圖隱瞞眞相,不讓我們知道。 *I shall ~ my consent.* 我不會同意。

with·in /wɪ'ðɪn ; wɪð'ɪn/ *prep* inside; not beyond: 在…之內;不越出: *remain ~ call/reach,* near by; 留在附近; *live ~ one's income,* not spend more than one's income; 量入爲出; *~ an hour,* in less than an hour; 不到一小時; *~ a mile of the station.* 距離火車站不到一哩。 □ *adv* (liter) inside. (文)在內;在內部。

with·out /wɪ'ðaʊt ; wɪð'aʊt/ *prep* **1** not having; not with; free from; lacking: 沒有; 缺乏; 無; 不: *You can't buy things ~ money.* 沒有錢買不到東西。 *Do you ever travel ~ a ticket?* 你曾經無票(搭車、船、飛機等)旅行過嗎? *I once did it ~ being caught.* 我試過一次沒被抓到。 *The rumour was ~ foundation.* 那項謠言毫無根據。 *He was working ~ any hope of reward.* 他當時工作不希冀酬勞。 *She went out ~* (= not wearing) *a coat.* 她沒穿外衣就出去了。 *Please don't leave ~ me,* Don't leave until I have joined you. 請等我同你一道去。 **~ fail,** certainly. 必定;無疑;確然。 **do ~,** ⇨ do²(15). **~ doubt,** admittedly; certainly. 無疑;必定;確然。 **2** (before gerunds) (用於動名詞前) *He can't speak German ~ making mistakes,* He speaks German incorrectly. 他每說德語必有錯誤。 *Can you make an omelette ~ breaking eggs?* 不打破蛋你能煎蛋餅嗎? *Can you do it ~ his knowing,* so that he will not know? 你能做此事而不讓他知道嗎? *He passed ~ seeing me,* and did not see me. 他走過去未看見我。 *He passed ~ my seeing him,* and I did not see him. 他走過去我沒看見。 *He left ~ so much as saying* (= left and did not even say) *that he was sorry/~ even a thank-you.* 連一句道歉都沒說,他就離開了(連一聲謝都沒說,他就離開了)。 **go ~ saying,** be too obvious, too well known, etc to need saying. 不消說;自不待言。 **3** (old use) outside. (舊用法)在…之外。 □ *adv* (liter or old use) outside. (文或舊用法)在外面。

with·stand /wɪð'stænd ; wɪθ'stænd/ *vt* (*pt, pp* -stood /-'stʊd ; -'stʊd/) [VP6A] resist; hold out against (pressure, attack): 抵抗;抗拒;經得起(壓力、攻擊): *~ a siege;* 抵抗圍攻; *shoes that will ~ hard wear.* 耐穿的鞋子。

withy /'wɪðɪ ; 'wɪðɪ/ *n* (*pl* -thies) ⇨ withe.

wit·less /'wɪtlɪs ; 'wɪtlɪs/ *adj* ⇨ wit¹.

wit·ness /'wɪtnɪs ; 'wɪtnɪs/ *n* **1** (often 常作 **'eye-~**) person who was actually present at an event and should, for this reason, be able to describe it; person who gives evidence under oath in a law court. 目擊者;(在法庭上經過宣誓的)證人。 **'~-box** (US also 美亦作 **'~-stand**) *n* enclosure in a law court in which ~es stand while giving evidence. (法庭的) 證人席。 **2** [U] evidence; testimony; what is said about sb, an event, etc: 證據;證明;證言: *give ~ on behalf of an accused person at his trial.* 在被告受審時替他作證。 **bear ~ to sb/sth, (a)** speak in support of, eg sb's character. 作證支持某人(某事物)(如證明某人的品格)。**(b)** be evidence of: 爲…的證據;證明: *The tests bear ~ to the quality of this new car.* 這些試驗證明了這輛新(汽)車的品質。 **3** person who adds his own signature to a document to testify that another person's signature on it is genuine. 連署人;證人(在文件上簽名以證明他人的簽名爲親筆所簽者)。**4** sb or sth that is a sign or proof of sth: 作爲…表徵、象徵或證據的某人或某物: *My clothes are a ~ to my poverty.* 我穿的衣服證明我是貧窮的。□ *vt, vi* **1** [VP6A] be present at and see: 親見;目擊: *~ an accident.* 目擊一件意外禍事。 **2** [VP3A] *~ to sth/doing sth,* give evidence (in a law court): (在法庭上)作證: ~ (= testify) *to the truth of a statement.* 證明一項陳述的眞實性。 *Mr X ~ed to having seen the accused near the scene of the crime.* 某先生(當庭)作證說曾看到被告在犯罪現場附近。 **3** [VP6A] be a ~(3) to the signing of (an agreement, a will, etc): 在(合約、遺囑等)上簽名作證;連署: *~ a signature.* 爲一項簽名連署。 **4** [VP6A] give evidence of; show: 證明;顯示: *Her pale face ~ed the agitation she felt.* 她蒼白的臉孔顯示出她所感到的激動。

wit·ti·cism /ˈwɪtɪsɪzəm ; ˈwɪtəˌsɪzəm/ ⇨ wit¹.

wit·ting·ly /ˈwɪtɪŋlɪ ; ˈwɪtɪŋlɪ/ *adv* knowingly; intentionally. 明知地;故意地;有意地。

witty /ˈwɪtɪ ; ˈwɪtɪ/ *adj* (-ier, -iest) ⇨ wit¹.

wive /waɪv ; waɪv/ *vi, vt* [VP6A, 2A] (archaic) marry. (古)娶;嫁;與…結婚。

wives /waɪvz ; waɪvz/ *pl* of wife.

wiz·ard /ˈwɪzəd ; ˈwɪzɚd/ *n* **1** magician. 術士;男巫。 **2** person with amazing abilities: 有傑出才幹的人;奇才;能手: *a financial ~,* person able to make money with amazing ease. 生財有道者。□ *adj* (sl) excellent. (俚)極好的。 **~ry** /-drɪ ; -drɪ/ *n* [U] magic (which is more usu). 魔術;巫術(magic 較常用)。

wiz·ened /ˈwɪznd ; ˈwɪzn̩d/ *adj* having a dried-up appearance; shrivelled: 外形枯槁的;皺縮的: *a ~ old man;* 形容枯槁的老人; *an old man with a ~ face;* 面孔皺縮的老人; *~ apples.* 乾癟的蘋果。

wo, whoa /wəʊ ; wo/ *int* (used chiefly to a horse) stop. (主要用於令馬停住)遏!站住!

woad /wəʊd ; wod/ *n* [U] (plant from which is obtained a) kind of blue dye. 大青;菘藍;大青染料。

wobble /ˈwɒbl ; ˈwɑbl/ *vi, vt* [VP2A, C, 6A] (cause to) move unsteadily from side to side; (fig) be uncertain (in opinions, in making decisions, etc): (使)擺動;搖動;震顫;(喩)(在意見、主張等方面)游移不定: *This table ~s.* 這張桌子不穩。 *The front wheels of that car ~.* 那輛汽車的前輪擺動。 *Don't ~ the desk.* 不要搖動書桌。 *He ~d between two opinions.* 他在兩個意見之間游移不定。 *Her voice sometimes ~s on high notes,* Her high notes are not always steady. 她的高音有時不穩定。 **wob·bler** /ˈwɒblə(r) ; ˈwɑbl̩ɚ/ *n* sb or sth that ~s. 擺動、震顫、游移不定的人或物。 **wob·bly** /ˈwɒblɪ ; ˈwɑblɪ/ *adj* not firm or steady; inclined to ~: 不穩定的;會擺動的;震顫的: *a wobbly chair.* 不穩的椅子。 *He's still a bit wobbly on his legs after his long illness.* 久病之後,他的腿仍然有一點震顫。

woe /wəʊ ; wo/ *n* (chiefly poet; sometimes hum) (主要用於詩歌中;有時爲詼諧用法) **1** [U] sorrow; grief; distress: 悲哀;悲痛;痛苦: *a tale of woe.* 悲哀的故事。 *Woe (be) to ...,* A curse upon .... 願…受難。 **2** (*pl*) causes of woe; troubles: (複)悲哀的因由;災難;憂患: *poverty, illness and other woes.* 貧苦,疾病以及其他災難。 **woe·ful** /-fl ; -fəl/ *adj* sorrowful; causing woe; regrettable: 悲哀的;引起悲哀的;遺憾的;不幸的: *woeful ignorance.* 可悲的無知。 **woe·fully** /-fəlɪ ; -fəlɪ/ *adv* **woe·be·gone** /ˈwəʊbɪgɒn *US:* -gɔːn ; ˈwobɪˌgɔn/ *adj* dismal (-looking): 顯出悲傷的;憂愁的;愁眉苦臉的: *What woebegone looks!* 多麼憂愁的神情!

woke, woken ⇨ wake¹.

wold /wəʊld ; wold/ *n* [C, U] (area of) open uncultivated country; downs or moor. 荒原;荒野。

wolf /wʊlf ; wʊlf/ *n* (*pl* wolves /wʊlvz ; wʊlvz/) wild, flesh-eating animal of the dog family, hunting in packs. 狼。 ***cry ~,*** raise false alarms: 作虛假的警報: *You've cried ~ too often* (suggesting that genuine cries for help will in future be ignored). 你作虛假的警報次數太多了(意謂以後眞有需要請人幫忙時,就沒有人理會了)。 ***a ~ in sheep's clothing,*** person who appears friendly but is really an enemy. 披着羊皮的狼;外貌友善的敵人。***keep the ~ from the door,*** be able to buy enough food for oneself and one's family. 能够免於饑餓;勉强可維持生活。 **ˈ~'s-bane** *n* aconite. 附子;草烏頭。 **ˈ~-cub** *n* **(a)** young ~. 小狼。 **(b)** (former name for) junior Boy Scout (now *Cub Scout*). 幼童軍(Junior Boy Scout 的舊稱,現稱作 Cub Scout)。 **ˈ~-hound** *n* large dog originally bred for hunting wolves. 獵狼犬。 **ˈ~ whistle** *n* whistle expressing sexual admiration. 讚美異性容貌、對異性表示愛慕或作挑逗時吹出的口哨。□ *vt* [VP6A, 15A] eat quickly and greedily: 狼吞虎嚥: *~ (down) one's food.* 狼吞虎嚥地吃東西。 **~·ish** /-ɪʃ ; -ɪʃ/ *adj* of or like a ~: 狼的;似狼的: *a ~ish appetite.* 强烈的食慾。

wolf·ram /ˈwʊlfrəm ; ˈwʊlfrəm/ *n* tungsten; tungsten ore. 鎢;鎢礦石。

woman /ˈwʊmən ; ˈwʊmən/ *n* (*pl* women /ˈwɪmɪn ; ˈwɪmɪn/) **1** adult female human being: 婦女;女人: *men, women and children;* 男人、女人和兒童; *a single* (= unmarried) *~;* 未婚女子;獨身女子; *a ~ of the world,* one with experience of society, not young and innocent; 深通世故的女人; (attrib; to be preferred to *lady*) (形容用法;比 lady 更爲通用) *a ˌ~ ˈdoctor* (*pl* 複數爲 *ˌwomen ˈdoctors*); 女醫生; *a ˌ~ ˈdriver* (*pl* 複數爲 *ˌwomen ˈdrivers*); 女駕駛員; *a caˈreer-~,* with a career; 職業婦女; *a ˈcountry-~,* who lives and works in the country; 鄉下婦女; *a ˈneedle-~,* expert at sewing, etc. 善縫紉的婦女;善女紅的婦女。 **2** [U] (without article) the female sex. (不加冠詞)女性;女流。**3** [U] feminine character: 女子性格;女子特質: *All the ~ in her rebelled against the treatment she was receiving.* 女性的尊嚴使她反抗所受到的待遇。 **ˈ~·hood** /-hʊd ; -ˌhʊd/ *n* [U] **1** (collective) women in general. (集合用法)女人。 **2** the state of being a ~: (女人)成年期;女人的特性: *She had now grown to/reached ~hood.* 她現在已經成年了。 **~·ish** /-ɪʃ ; -ɪʃ/ *adj* of, like, for women. 女人的;像女人的;爲女人的。 **~·ize** /-aɪz ; -ˌaɪz/ *vi* pursue women (esp for casual sexual intercourse). 追求女色;(尤指)玩女人。 **~·izer** *n* man who does this. 追求女色者;玩女人者。 **ˈ~·kind** *n* women in general. 女性;婦女的總稱。 **ˈ~·like, ~·ly** *adjj* like a ~. 像女人的。 **women·folk** /ˈwɪmɪnfəʊk ; ˈwɪmɪnˌfok/ *n pl* women; women of one's family. 婦女;(家中的)女眷。

womb /wuːm ; wum/ *n* (anat) organ in a female mammal in which offspring is carried and nourished while developing before birth: (解剖)子宮: (fig) (喩) *It still lies in the ~ of time,* is sth which the passage of time will reveal. 那仍在醞釀中(經過一段時間才會見分曉)。⇨ the illus at reproduce. 參看 reproduce 之插圖。

wom·bat /ˈwɒmbæt ; ˈwɑmbæt/ *n* Australian animal (looking like a small bear), the female of which has a pouch for its young. (澳洲產)袋熊(形似小熊,雌者生有袋囊,以携其幼仔)。

won /wʌn ; wʌn/ ⇨ win.

won·der /ˈwʌndə(r) ; ˈwʌndɚ/ *n* **1** [U] feeling caused by sth unusual, surprising or inexplicable; surprise combined with admiration, bewilderment, etc: 驚奇;驚嘆;驚愕;驚服: *They were filled with ~.* 他們感到驚奇。 *We looked at the conjurer in silent ~.* 我們目瞪口呆地看着那魔術師。 ***no/little/small ~,*** it is not/hardly surprising: 不(難以,不太)令人吃驚: *No ~ you were so late.* 難怪你來得那

麼遲。*He was taken ill, and no/little ~, considering that he had been overworking for years.* 他病了,以他多年來一直工作過度來看,實在不足怪。'~-land /-lænd; -ˌlænd/ *n* **1** fairyland. 仙境;奇境。**2** [C] country that is remarkable in some way (eg because of abundant natural resources). 在某方面突出的地方(如天然物資豐富)。**'~-struck** *adj* overcome with ~. 深感驚異的。 **2** [C] thing or event that causes such feeling: 奇物;奇蹟;奇觀;奇事: *Walking on the moon is one of the ~s of our times.* 在月球上漫步是現代奇景之一。 ***signs and ~s,*** miracles. 奇蹟;奇事。 ***work ~s,*** work with remarkable results, perform miracles. 創造奇蹟;做奇事。***a nine days' ~,*** sth which arouses great interest or admiration for a short time. 轟動一時的事件(很快就會被人忘記)。***for a ~,*** it is surprising (because unusual, unexpected, etc): 奇怪得很;令人驚奇;說也奇怪(由於不尋常、未料到等): *For a ~ he paid back the money he had borrowed.* 說也奇怪,他居然還了他所借的錢。 ***It is a ~ (that),*** It is surprising that: 奇怪的是;令人驚奇的是: *It's a ~ (that) you didn't lose your way in the dark.* 令人驚奇的是你在黑暗中竟未迷路。 ***What a ~,*** How surprising! 多麼令人驚奇! □ *vi, vt* **1** [VP2A, 3A, B, 4B] ***~ (at sth),*** be filled with ~(1); marvel; feel surprised: 感到驚奇;驚愕;驚嘆;驚訝: *Can you ~ at it,* Isn't it natural, to be expected, etc? 你能(對它)感到驚奇嗎?(那不是很自然,可以預料得到的嗎?) *I don't ~ at her refusing to marry him.* 她拒絕和他結婚,我一點也不感到驚異。 *It's not to be ~ed at,* is sth one might expect. 那不足爲奇。*I ~ (at the fact) (that) he wasn't killed,* am surprised that he wasn't killed. 我感到驚奇他竟未遇難。 *I shouldn't ~ if...,* shouldn't be surprised if.... 如果…,我一點也不覺得奇怪。*I ~ed to hear her voice in the next room.* 我聽到她在隔壁房間的聲音,覺得很奇怪。**2** [VP2A, 3A] ***~ (about sth),*** feel curiosity; ask oneself: 覺得好奇;想要知道;問自己: *I was ~ing about that.* 我對那事覺得好奇。 *I was just ~ing.* 我祇不過好奇而已。**3** [VP8, 10] ask oneself: 自忖;想知道: *I ~ who he is/what he wants/why he is late/whether he will come/whose it is.* 我想知道他是誰(他需要什麼,他爲什麼遲到,他是否會來,那是誰的)。*I was ~ing how to get there quickly/where to spend the weekend, etc.* 我想知道怎麼樣可以很快地到達那裏(在何處度週末等)。 **~·ing·ly** /'wʌndrɪŋlɪ; 'wʌndərɪŋlɪ/ *adv* **~·ful** /-fl; -fəl/ *adj* causing ~; surprising; remarkable; admirable: 令人驚奇的;使人驚服的;奇妙的;了不起的;令人羨慕的: *We've been having ~ful weather recently.* 近來天氣非常好。 *What a ~ful memory she has!* 她的記憶力多麼驚人啊! **~·fully** /-fəlɪ; -fəlɪ/ *adv* **~·ment** /-mənt; -mənt/ *n* [U] surprise. 驚異;驚訝。 **won·drous** /'wʌndrəs; 'wʌndrəs/ *adj* (archaic, or liter) ~ful. (古或文)令人驚奇的;使人驚服的。 □ *adv* (only with *adjj*) ~fully: (祇與形容詞連用)令人驚奇地;使人驚服地: *wondrous kind.* 非常和善的。

wonky /'wɒŋkɪ; 'wɑŋkɪ/ *adj* (GB sl) (英俚) **1** infirm; unreliable: 不穩的;搖擺的;靠不住的: *a ~ chair,* one that might break. 一把不牢固的椅子。**2** tottery; in poor health: 虛弱的;健康不佳的: *She still feels a bit ~ after that attack of flu.* 那次害過流行性感冒以後,她仍舊感到有點虛弱。

wont /wəʊnt *US:* wɔ:nt; wʌnt/ *n* (archaic or liter) (*sing* only) what sb is accustomed to doing: (古或文)(僅用單數)習慣;慣常活動: *He went to bed much earlier than was his ~,* than he usually did. 他(那晚)就寢的時間比平常早了很多。 ***use and ~,*** established custom. 積習;世俗。 □ *pred adj* ***be ~ to,*** be accustomed to. 習慣於。 **~ed** *attrib adj* customary; usual. 慣例的;通常的。

won't /wəʊnt; wont/ = will not. ⇨ will¹.

woo /wu:; wu/ *vt* (*pt, pp* wooed) [VP6A] **1** (old use) try to win (a woman's) hand in marriage; court. (舊用法)向(女子)求婚;求愛。 **2** try to win (fame, fortune, success, sleep). 求取或想要獲得(名譽、財富、成功、睡眠)。 **3** try to get the support of (voters, customers, businessmen). 求取(選民、顧客、商人)的支持。 **wooer** *n* one who woos. 求婚者;求愛者;尋求名譽、財富、成功、選民的支持等者。

wood /wʊd; wʊd/ *n* **1** [U] (with *indef art* and *pl* only when meaning *kind, sort, variety*) hard solid substance of a tree below the bark: (祇有表示種、類、各色各樣等概念時,才可加不定冠詞,或用複數形式)木;木材;木頭;木柴;木料: *Tables are usually made of ~.* 桌子通常是木材做的。*Put some more ~ on the fire.* 在火上添加點木柴。 *He was chopping ~ for the fire.* 他在劈柴生火。 *Teak is a hard (kind of) ~ and pine is a soft (kind of) ~.* 麻栗木是硬材,松木是軟材。(attrib): (形容用法): *~ floors/pavements,* made of blocks of ~. 木磚地板(人行道)。 Cf 參較 *wooden,* used for articles made of ~. 指木製的物件。 **2** [C] (often *pl*) area of land covered with growing trees (not so extensive as a forest): (常用複數)樹林(不如 forest 範圍大): *a ~ of beech(-trees);* 山毛櫸林; *a house in the middle of a ~;* 林中一屋; *go for a walk in the ~(s).* 到林中散步。 ***out of the ~,*** (fig) free from troubles or difficulties: (喻)脫離麻煩或困難: *We're not yet out of the ~,* still have difficulties to face. 我們尙未脫離困難。 ***be unable to see the ~ for the trees,*** (fig) be unable to get a clear view of the whole because of too many details: (喻)見樹不見林(因細節過多而看不清全局)。 **3** ***in/from the ~,*** in/from the cask or barrel: 在(從)木桶中: *wine in the ~;* 木桶中的酒; *drawn from the ~.* 從木桶中取出的。 **4** (compounds, from 1 above) (複合字,來自上列第1義) **~ alcohol** *n* [U] kind of alcohol distilled from ~ (also called *methyl alcohol*) used as a fuel and a solvent. 木醇;甲醇(用作燃料及溶劑,亦稱作 methyl alcohol)。 **'~-block** *n* block of ~ from which ~cuts are made. (木刻用的)版木。**'~·cut** *n* print from a design, drawing, picture, etc cut on a block of ~. 木刻;木刻畫;木版畫。 **'~-louse** *n* (*pl* -lice) kinds of small, wingless, insect-like creature living in decaying ~, damp soil, etc. 土鱉;地鱉(數種無翅而似昆蟲的小生物,生於朽木、濕地等處)。 **'~·pecker** *n* kinds of bird that clings to the bark of trees and taps or pecks it to find insects. 啄木鳥。 **'~·pile** *n* pile of ~, esp for fuel. 木材堆;(尤指)柴堆。 **'~-pulp** *n* [U] ~ shredded to pulp as the material for making paper. (造紙用的)木漿。 **'~-shed** *n* shed for storing ~ (esp for fuel). 存放木材(尤指柴薪)的小棚。 **'~·wind** *n* musical wind instrument made (originally) of ~. 木管樂器(最初以木材製成,故名)。 **'~·work** *n* [U] **1** things made of ~, esp the ~en parts of a building (eg doors, stairs). 木製品;(尤指)房屋之木造部分(如門,梯)。 **2** art of making things of ~; carpentry. 木工手藝;木工活。 **'~·worm** *n* **1** ~-eating larva that bores into ~. 蝕木蟲;蝕船蟲。 **2** [U] damage caused by ~worm. 蝕木蟲或蝕船蟲造成的損害。 **5** (compounds, from 2 above) (複合字,來自上列第2義) **'~·bine** *n* wild honeysuckle. (植)野忍冬。 **'~·cock** *n* (*pl* unchanged) kinds of game bird, brown with a long, straight bill, short legs and tail, found in ~land and valued as food. (複數不變)(動)丘鷸;山鷸。 **'~·craft** *n* [U] knowledge of forest conditions, skill in finding one's way in ~s and forests, esp as used in hunting, etc. (尤指用於打獵等的)森林知識;林中識路技巧。 **'~-cutter** *n* man who cuts down trees. 伐木者。 **'~-land** /-lənd; -ˌlænd/ *n* [U] land covered with trees; ~s: 林地;森林;樹林: (attrib) (形容用法) *~land scenery.* 林景。 **'~·man** /-mən; -mən/ *n* (*pl* -men) forester; ~-cutter. 居於森林之人;看管森林之人;伐木者。 **'~s·man** /-zmən; -zmən/ *n* (*pl* -men) (esp US) (尤美) = ~man. **~ed** *adj* covered with growing trees: 多樹木的;樹木繁茂的: *~ed country,* abounding in trees. 多樹木的地帶。 **~en** /'wʊdn;

ˈwʊdn̩/ *adj* **1** (attrib) made of ~: (形容用法)木製的: *a ~en leg;* 木腿; *~en walls* (fig, of the old ~en warships, thought of as a defence); 木製干城(喻,指昔時的木造軍艦,被視作防衛屏障); *a ˈ~en-head,* ⇨ blockhead. Hence, 由此產生, ˌ**~en-ˈheaded** *adj* stupid. 木頭腦袋的;愚笨的。 **2** stiff, clumsy, awkward (as if made of ~): 生硬的;愚鈍的;笨拙的(宛如木製的): *a ~en* (= inexpressive) *smile.* 呆板的笑容。 *His manners were extremely ~en.* 他的舉止極爲呆笨。 **~y** *adj* (-ier, -iest) **1** ~ed: 多樹木的: *a ~y hillside.* 多樹木的山坡。 **2** of or like ~: 木的;似木的: *the ~y stems of a plant.* 植物的木莖。

wooer /ˈwuːə(r); ˈwuə˞/ *n* ⇨ woo.

woof /wuːf; wuf/ *n* = weft.

woofer /ˈwʊfə(r); ˈwʊfə˞/ *n* loudspeaker designed to produce low notes. 低音揚聲器;低音喇叭。

wool /wʊl; wʊl/ *n* [U] **1** soft hair of sheep, goats and some other animals (eg the llama and alpaca); thread, yarn, cloth, clothing, made from this: 羊毛;駱馬毛;羊駝毛;毛線;絨線;毛織品;毛料衣服: *wear ~* (ie clothing made of ~) *next to the skin;* 貼身穿毛料衣服; *the ˈ~ trade;* 羊毛業; *ˈ~ merchants;* 羊毛商人; *imports of ~ from Australia;* 從澳洲進口羊毛; *ˈknitting-~,* ~ yarn for knitting. 毛線;絨線。 ***dyed in the ~,*** dyed before spinning and weaving; (fig) thorough; complete: 在紡織以前卽染色的;生染的;(喻)澈底的;道地的;不可改變的: *a dyed-in-the-~ Tory,* person who is strongly convinced that Tory principles, etc are the best. 死硬的英國保守黨員。 ***much cry and little ~,*** much talk with little result; fuss about trifles. 說的多做的少;雷聲大雨點小;爲小事而大驚小怪。 ***pull the ˈ~ over sb's eyes,*** deceive or trick him. 欺騙或玩弄某人。 **ˈ~-gathering** *adj, n* absent-minded(ness). 心不在焉(的)。 **the ˈ~·sack,** ~-stuffed cushion on which the Lord Chancellor sits in the House of Lords: 英國上議院議長(兼大法官)的席位: *reach the ~sack,* become Lord Chancellor. 膺任上議院議長(兼大法官)。 **2** material similar in appearance or texture to ~; 似羊毛之物; *cotton-~,* raw cotton (US 美 = *cotton-batting*). 生棉。 **3** (person's) thick curly hair. (人的)捲曲的厚髮。 ***lose one's ~,*** (colloq) get angry. (俗)發怒。 **~·len** (US 美 = **~en**) /ˈwʊlən; ˈwʊlɪn/ *attrib adj* made of ~: 羊毛製的: *~len cloth/blankets;* 呢絨(毛毯); of ~ fabrics: 毛織品的: *~len manufacturers/merchants.* 毛織品製造者(商人)。 **~·lens** (US 美= **~ens**) *n pl* ~len fabrics; cloth, flannel, blankets, etc, made of ~. 毛織品;毛製的絨布、法蘭絨、毯子等。 **~ly** (US also **~y**) /ˈwʊlɪ; ˈwʊlɪ/ *adj* (-ier, -iest) **1** covered with, made of, looking like, ~: 覆滿羊毛或捲曲厚髮的;羊毛製的;像羊毛的: *~ly hair;* 捲曲的厚髮; *a ~ly coat.* 羊毛製的上裝。 **2** (fig, of the mind, ideas, arguments) confused, not clear; not incisive. (喻,指頭腦,觀念,論點)模糊的;不清楚的;不透澈的。 ▭ *n* (*pl* -lies) (colloq) ~len garment, esp a sweater: (俗)毛織衣服;(尤指)毛線衫: *Put an extra ~ly on when you go out.* 外出時多加一件毛線衣。

word /wɜːd; wɝd/ *n* **1** [C] sound or combination of sounds (or the written or printed symbols) forming a unit of the grammar or vocabulary of a language: 語;言;字;詞;(一種語言的)文法單位或字彙單位: *When we speak we put our thoughts into ~s.* 我們說話時,是用言語表達我們的思想。 *I have no ~s to* (= cannot adequately) *express my gratitude.* 我找不到適當的言詞來表達我的謝意。 *W~s failed him,* He could not express his thoughts, his emotion, etc in ~s. 他呐呐不能言。 ***a play on/upon ~s,*** a pun. 雙關語;俏皮話。 ***be not the ~ for it,*** not an adequate or satisfactory description: 非恰當字眼;不是恰當的或令人滿意的描述: *Warm's not the ~ for it* (ie *hot* is perhaps a better ~)! '暖和' 不是恰當的字眼('炎熱' 也許更恰當)! ***not get a ~ in edgeways,*** ⇨ edgeways. ***(repeat sth) ~ for ~,*** exactly, with no changes or omissions. 正確地;不改變亦不省略地(複述某事)。 ***(translate sth) ~ for ~,*** literally. 逐字地(翻譯); 照字面(翻譯); 直譯。 Cf 參較 *a free translation.* ***in a/one ~,*** briefly; to sum up. 簡言之;一句話;總之。 ***by ~ of mouth,*** in spoken, not written, ~s. 口頭地。 **2** [C] sth said; remark or statement: 所說的話;談話;言辭: *He didn't say a ~ about it.* 他對那件事隻字未提。 *I don't believe a ~ of the story.* 這故事我一點也不相信。 *Mr A will now say a few ~s,* make a few remarks, give a short address. A先生現在要說幾句話。 *Don't waste ~s on that fellow,* don't try to persuade, convince, warn, etc him. 不要同那傢伙費口舌(不必想勸告、說服、警告他等)。 ***eat one's ~s,*** admit that one was wrong; take one's ~s back and apologize. 認錯;收回前言並道歉;認錯道歉。 ***have a ~ with sb,*** speak to him. 同某人說一兩句話。 ***have ~s (with sb),*** quarrel: (同某人)口角: *They've had ~s, I hear.* 他們有過爭吵,我聽到的。 ***have the last ~,*** make the final remark in an argument, esp by making a retort to which there is no good answer. 在辯論中作最後的辯駁(尤指說出對方無法回駁的話)。 ***put in/say a good ~ (for sb),*** speak on his behalf (to support or defend). (爲某人)進言或說項。 ***suit the action to the ~,*** do at once what one has said one will do (eg of a threat). 說了就做;說做就做(如威脅)。 ***take sb at his ~,*** act on the belief that he means what he says. 把某人的話信以爲眞;相信某人的話。 ***big ~s,*** boasting. 大話;吹牛。 ***on/with the ~,*** as soon as sth has been said. 說了這話以後(立卽…)。 ***a ~ in/out of season,*** a piece of advice given when it is welcome and helpful/unwelcome and interfering. 合(不合)時宜的忠言。 ***the last ~ on (a subject),*** statement, etc which includes the latest views and information: 有關(某問題)的最近的見解及消息: *The last ~ has not yet been said on this subject,* There will be further facts, views, etc. 這問題尚未成定論(尚有進一步的發現、觀點等)。 ***the last ~ (in sth),*** the latest, most up-to-date, etc, in: 爲(某事物或某方面)的最近或最新式者: *Our coach tours of Scotland are the last ~ in comfort and convenience.* 我們乘長途汽車去蘇格蘭的旅遊,就舒適與方便上的設備而言,是最新式的了。 **3** (*sing,* without *def art*) news; information: (單數,不用定冠詞)消息;音訊: *Please send me ~ of your safe arrival.* 請儘早把你平安到達的消息告訴我。 *Please leave ~ for me at work.* 請在我上班處留言。 *W~ came that I was wanted at home.* 家裏傳來消息要我回去。 **4** (*sing* only, with a possessive) promise; assurance. (僅用單數,與所有格連用)諾言;保證。 ***be as good as one's ~,*** do what one promises: 守信: *Don't worry—I'm sure he'll be as good as his ~.* 不要擔心 —— 我相信他不會食言。 ***give sb one's ~ (that...),*** promise: 允諾;答應;許下諾言: *The goods will arrive on time—I give you my ~.* 那批貨會準時到達 —— 我向你保證。 ***keep/break one's ~,*** do/fail to do what one has promised to do. 守(爽)約;守(失)信。 ***take sb's ˈ~ for it,*** believe what he says: 相信某人的話: *I have no proof, but you may take my ~ for it.* 我沒有證據,不過你可以相信我的話。 ***take sb at his ~,*** believe that he is telling the truth, that he will keep a promise. 相信某人的話是眞的;相信某人會信守諾言。 ***upon my ~,*** **(a)** on my honour. 一定;的確;我向你保證是這樣。 **(b)** used as an exclamation of surprise. (用作驚訝的呼聲)噯呀。 **5** (*sing* only) command; order; spoken signal: (僅用單數)號令;命令;口令;口號: *The officer gave the ~ to fire.* 軍官下令射擊。 *His ~ is law,* His orders must be obeyed. 他的命令就是法律。 *You must give the ~ before you can pass.* 你必須說出口令才能通過。 ⇨ *password* at pass¹(10). **6** (in the Christian religion) (基督教) **the W~ (of God); God's W~, (a)** the Scriptures, esp the Gospel: 聖經;(尤指)福音書: *preach the W~.* 傳福音。

(b) title of Jesus Christ. 耶穌基督之稱謂。**7** (compounds) (複合字) ˈ**~·book** *n* vocabulary; list of ~s with meanings, etc. 字彙;單字表;字典。ˈ**~-division** *n* [U] dividing of the spelling of a ~, eg at the end of a line on a page. 斷字;斷字法(按照音節將某字分開的方法,如在一行的末尾所爲)。ˈ**~-painter** *n* person who can describe vividly in ~s. 擅長以文字作生動描述者。ˌ**~-ˈperfect** *adj* knowing, able to repeat, a poem, a part in a play, etc by heart. 熟記或背誦詩歌、臺詞等的。ˈ**~-picture** *n* vivid description in ~s. 生動的文字描述。ˈ**~-splitting** *n* [U] sophistry; making of distinctions of meaning, etc that are subtle. 詭辯;咬文嚼字;過細的詞義分辨。□ *vt* [VP 6A] express in ~s: 說;言;以言辭表達: *a well-~ed letter.* 措辭得當的信。*The suggestion might be ~ed more politely.* 那項建議的措辭可以更婉轉些。 **~·ing** *n* (*sing* only) way in which sth is expressed; choice of ~s to express meaning: (僅用單數)表達法;語法;措辭;用字: *A different ~ing might make the meaning clearer.* 換一個說法可能使意義更爲明白。**~·less** *adj* without ~s; not put into ~s: 無話的;未明說的: *~less grief.* 無言的悲戚。 **wordy** *adj* (-ier, -iest) using, expressed in, a large number of ~s, esp unnecessary ~s: 多言的;冗長的;(尤指)廢話連篇的; 嘮叨的: *a ~y telegram;* 冗長的電報; *~y warfare,* ie argument. 論戰。 **~·ily** /-ɪlɪ; -ɪlɪ/ *adv* **~i·ness** *n*

wore /wɔː(r); wor/ *pt* of wear².

work¹ /wɜːk; wɝk/ *n* **1** [U] use of bodily or mental powers with the purpose of doing or making sth (esp contrasted with play or recreation); use of energy supplied by steam, electric current, etc: 工作;勞動(尤指與遊戲或娛樂相對而言);(由蒸氣,電流等供給的)能的使用;功: *Are you fond of hard ~?* 你喜歡艱苦的工作嗎? *The ~ of building the new bridge took six months.* 那座新橋樑的工程費時半載。*It was the ~ of a moment* (= Only a moment was needed) *to turn the key in the lock and make him a prisoner.* 把門上鎖,將他囚禁,祇需片刻工夫。*It was very hard ~ getting to the top of the mountain.* 爬到那座山的山頂是一件極爲辛苦的事。*This is the ~ of an enemy,* An enemy has done this. 這是敵人幹的事。*Machines now do much of the ~ formerly done by man.* 以前由人力做的工作現在大部份用機器來做。***make hard ~ of sth,*** make it seem more difficult than it is. 使某事顯得更加困難。***make short ~ of sth,*** finish it quickly. 匆匆做完某事。***set/get to ~ (on sth/to do sth),*** begin; make a start. 開始;着手工作。***set/go about one's ~,*** start doing it: 開始自己的工作: *You're not setting about your ~ in the right way.* 你未以正確的方法開始你的工作。 ***at ~ (on sth),*** busy or occupied with (indicating uncompleted ~, ~ in progress). 在工作;忙於(未完成的工作,進展中的工作)。***all in the day's ~,*** (used to indicate that sth is) normal; what is usual or to be expected. (用於表示某事物是)正常的;一般的;合乎常理的。 **2** [U] what a person does to earn a living; employment: 謀生所做之工作;職業;業務: *What time do you get to (your) ~ every day?* 你每天何時上班? *The men were on their way to ~.* 那些(男)人在上班的途中。*It is difficult to find ~ during a depression.* 經濟蕭條的時候很難找工作。 ***at ~,*** at one's place of employment: 在工作的地方;在工作: *He's at ~ now, but he'll be back at six.* 他工作去了,但他六點鐘會回來。***in/out of ~,*** having/not having employment: 有(無)職業;就(失)業: *He has been out of ~ for a year.* 他已經失業一年了。*He'll be glad to be in regular ~ again.* 他將很高興再從事固定的職業。 Hence, 由此產生, (attrib *adj*) (屬性形容詞) ˌ**out-of-ˈwork.** 失業的。 **3** [U] sth to be done, not necessarily connected with a trade or occupation, not necessarily for payment: 待做之事;工作(不一定與職業有關,亦不一定爲報酬): *I always find plenty of ~ that needs doing in my garden.* 在庭園中我總有許多需要做的事情。*I have some ~ for you to do.* 我有一些事情要你做。 **4** [U] things needed or used for ~: 工作時所需用的東西;工具: *She took her ~* (eg her sewing materials) *out on the verandah.* 她把工作所需用之物 (如縫級所需的布料和用具) 帶到走廊上去工作。ˈ**~-bag/-basket/-box** *nn* bag, etc for holding such things, esp for sewing. 工具袋(籃,匣);(尤指)針線袋(筐,匣)。**5** [U] that which is produced by ~: 製作品;工藝品: *The ~ of famous silversmiths and sculptors may be seen in museums.* 著名的銀匠及雕刻家的製作品可以在博物館中見到。*What a beautiful piece of ~!* 多麼美麗的一件工藝品! *The villagers sell their ~* (eg needlework, wood-carvings, metal articles) *to tourists.* 村民把他們的手工藝品(如刺繡、木雕刻、金屬器具)賣給觀光客。 ⇨ also compounds such as *stone~, wood~* at stone(1), wood(4). **6** [C] product of the intellect or the imagination: 作品;著作: *the ~s of Shakespeare;* 莎士比亞的著作; *the ~s of Beethoven.* 貝多芬的作品。 ⇨ opus; *~s of art;* 藝術品; 美術品; *a new ~* (= musical composition) *by John Lewis;* 約翰·路易斯的新作(卽新作的樂曲); *a new ~* (= book) *on modern art.* 論現代藝術的新著作(卽新書)。 **7** (*pl*) moving parts of a machine: (複)機器的活動部分; (活動)機件: *the ~s of a clock or watch.* 鐘或錶的(活動)機件。*There's something wrong with the ~s.* 機件出毛病了。 **8** (*pl,* with *sing* or *pl v*) building(s) where industrial or manufacturing processes are carried on: (複數形式,可用單數或複數動詞)工廠;工場: *a ˈgas-~s;* 煤氣廠; *an ˈiron-~s;* 鐵工廠; *a ˈbrick-~s.* 磚廠。*The ˈsteel-~s was/were closed for the Christmas holidays.* 那家煉鋼廠歇工以度聖誕假期。 ˈ**~s council/committee,** joint council of representatives of employers and employees to deal with problems of management, labour relations, etc. 工廠委員會(勞資雙方皆有代表的聯合會議,以處理有關管理、勞工關係等方面的問題)。 **9 public ~s,** the building of roads, dams, embankments; other engineering operations (by government departments, etc): 公共工程(政府部門等建築的道路、水壩、堤防及其他工程): *the Ministry of Public Building and W~,* (until 1971) government department (now part of the Department of the Environment) responsible for these operations. (1971年以前之)公共工程部(政府機構,現爲'環境部'的一部分)。**10** (*pl v*) (用複數動詞) (cf 參較 *ˈearth~s, ˈout~s*) defensive structures; fortifications: 防禦工事;堡壘: *The ~s were thought to be impregnable.* 那防禦工事被認爲無法攻破。 **11** (compounds) (複合字) ˈ**~-bench** *n* table at which a mechanic does his ~. 工匠檯;細工檯。ˈ**~·book** *n* book with outlines of a subject of study, with questions to be answered (in blank spaces, in writing), for notes, etc. (輔助)練習簿;習題簿;筆記簿;記事簿;工作手册;業務手册。ˈ**~·day** *n* day for ~; day which is not a Sunday or a holiday. 工作日;非星期日或假日。ˈ**~force** *n* total number of men working in a particular factory, etc. 某一工廠等的工作總人數;勞動力。ˈ**~·house** *n* **1** (GB hist) public institution for homeless people. (英國史)貧民習藝所; 救貧院。 **2** (US) place where those who have committed small crimes are confined and made to work. (美)監犯工廠;感化院(監禁輕微罪犯並使其工作的所在)。ˈ**~·man** /-mən; -mən/ *n* (*pl* -men) **1** man who earns a living by physical labour or at machines, etc. 工人;勞工。 **2** person who works in a specified way: 以某種方式工作的人: *a skilled/quick, etc ~man.* 熟練(敏捷等)的工作者。 ˈ**~·man·like** *adj* characteristic of a good ~man. 工作熟練的;有技巧的。ˈ**~·man·ship** /-mənʃɪp; -mənˌʃɪp/ *n* [U] quality as seen in sth made: (成品中顯出的)手藝;技藝;做工: *articles of poor/excellent ~manship;* 做工拙劣(極好)的物品; person's skill in doing ~. 人的工作技巧。ˈ**~·room** *n* room in which

~ is done. 工作室;作業室。 ˈ~·**shop** *n* room or building in which things (esp machines) are made or repaired. 工廠;工場;修理廠。ˈ~-**shy** *adj* disinclined to work; lazy. 不願工作的;懶惰的。ˈ~-**study** *n* (*pl* -dies) study of how ~ may be done efficiently and economically (eg by observing the sequence of movements in an operation, time needed, etc). 工作效率的研究(例如觀察作業的程序,所需的時間等)。ˈ~·**table** *n* (esp) table with drawers for sewing materials, etc. (尤指)有抽屜的裁縫檯。 ~·**a·day** /ˈwɜːkədeɪ ; ˈwɝkə,de/ *adj* commonplace; dull: 普通的;乏味的: *this ~aday world/life.* 這個乏味的世界(生活)。

work² /wɜːk ; wɝk/ *vi, vt* (*pt, pp* ~ed or wrought /rɔːt ; rɔt/) (For uses with *adverbial particles* and *preps*, ⇨ 10 below. For uses with *wrought*, ⇨ wrought). (與副詞接語及介詞連用的用法,參看下列第10義;wrought 的用法,參看 wrought 條)。 **1** [VP2A, B, C, 3A, 4A] do work; engage in physical or mental activity: 工作;勞動;勞心;做事: *He's been ~ing hard all day.* 他已經辛苦地工作了一整天。*The men in this factory ~ 40 hours a week.* 這個工廠裡的工人每週工作四十小時。*Most people have to ~ in order to live,* ie to earn a living. 大多數人必須工作以維持生活。*He ins't ~ing now,* eg because unemployed or retired. 他現在不做事(如失業,退休等)。*Have British statesmen always ~ed for peace?* 英國的政治家們一直爲和平努力嗎? *He's ~ing at* (= studying) *Physics and Chemistry.* 他正在研習物理學及化學。*Green is ~ing on* (= writing) *a new novel.* 格林目前正在寫一部新小說。*This man ~s in leather,* is a craftsman in leather. 此人是皮匠。*He has always ~ed against* (= opposed) *reform.* 他一直阻撓改革。 ~ ***to rule***, ⇨ rule(1). ˈ~-**in** *n* occasion when workers continue to ~ in a factory to protest against proposed dismissal, closure of the factory, etc. 工作抗議(指工人繼續在工廠工作,以抗議解雇工人、關閉工廠等計畫)。 **2** [VP2A, C] (of a machine, apparatus, bodily organ, plan, method, etc) do what it is designed to do; have the desired result; function; operate: (指機器,機械,儀器,身體器官,計畫,方法等)運轉;運作;發揮正常功能;獲得預期結果: *The lift/elevator/bell/telephone is not ~ing.* 電梯(升降機,門鈴,電話)壞了。*The gears ~ smoothly.* 齒輪運轉靈活。*This machine ~s by electricity.* 這架機器是電力推動的。*My brain doesn't seem to be ~ing well today.* 我的腦筋今天好像不太靈活。 *Will this new plan/scheme/method ~?* 這項新計畫(方案,方法)行得通嗎? *The charm ~ed.* 那符咒奏效了。*It ~ed like a charm.* 它非常靈光。 **3** [VP6A, 15A] cause to ~; set in motion: 使工作;使活動;使運轉: *He ~s his wife/himself too hard.* 他使他的妻子(他自己)工作過度了。*Don't ~ yourself/your poor wife to death.* 不要讓你自己(你那可憐的妻子)過於勞累。 *She was ~ing the treadle of her sewing-machine.* 她正用腳踩動縫紉機的踏板。*This machine is ~ed by steam/electricity.* 這架機器是蒸氣(電力)推動的。 **4** [VP6A] produce or obtain as the result of effort: 努力做成或獲得; 完成; 造成: ~ *wonders/a cure/harm/mischief.* 造成奇蹟(獲得痊癒; 造成傷害; 造成損害)。 ~ ***one's passage,*** earn it by ~ing: 做工賺取旅費: *He ~ed his passage from England to Australia,* by ~ing on the ship. 他從英國到澳洲時在船上工作以賺取旅費。 ~ ***one's way (through college, etc),*** have a paid job, while studying to meet costs: 工讀(完成大學學業等): *He's ~ing his way through medical school.* 他以半工半讀的方式讀醫學院。~ ***one's will (on sb),*** make him do what one wants him to do. 操縱(某人);使(某人)做自己想要他做的事情。 ~ ***it,*** (sl) bring sth about (by scheming, etc): (俚) 完成某事;(藉陰謀,詭計等)使某事發生: *I'll ~ it if I can,* eg by using influence, cajolery, etc. 如果我能够,我會搞出個名堂來。 **5** [VP 6A] operate; control; be employed in the management of: 經營;管理;控制: ~ *a mine.* 經營一個礦場。*This salesman ~s the North Wales area,* travels there as a salesman. 這個推銷員在北威爾斯地區推銷貨物。 **6** [VP2C, D, 15A, B, 22] (cause to) move into, reach, a new state or position, usu by degrees or with a succession of small movements: (使)逐漸地(或藉連續不斷的微小活動而)進入或達到一種新的狀態或位置;(使)逐漸變動;(使)緩慢移動: *Your shirt has ~ed out,* has come out from above the top of your trousers. 你的襯衫跑到褲子外面來了。*One of the screws has ~ed loose.* 有一個螺絲釘已經鬆了。*The rain had ~ed through the roof,* had penetrated it slowly. 雨水漸漸滲過屋頂了。 *Can you ~ the stone into place,* eg when building a stone wall? 你能把這塊石頭移至適當的位置嗎(如建造石牆時)? *The men ~ed their way forward.* 那些(男)人奮力向前擠。*Many months later the splinter ~ed out of her arm,* came out after travelling through the flesh from the point at which it had entered. 好幾個月以後,扎進她手臂的那根刺跑出來了。*The wind has ~ed round to the south,* changed direction by degrees. 風已漸漸轉向南。 **7** [VP6A] make or shape by hammering, kneading, pressure, etc: 藉鎚、搓、捏、壓等而做成或形成;鎚成;捏成;搓成;壓成: ~ *clay,* knead it with water; 捏黏土; ~ *dough,* (when making bread). (做麵包時)揉麵團。 ⇨ wrought for *wrought iron.* **8** [VP2A] ferment; move in an agitated way: 發酵;激動地抽動;顫動: *The yeast began to ~,* to ferment, eg in dough. 酵母開始發酵(如在麵團中)。*His face/features began to ~ violently,* twitch, etc in a way showing agitation. 他的臉孔(面容)開始劇烈地抽搐(因爲感情激動)。 **9** [VP6A, 14] make by stitching; embroider: 縫製;刺繡: ~ *a design on a cushion-cover/one's initials on a handkerchief.* 把一個圖樣繡在墊套上 (把自己的姓名縮寫刺繡在手帕上)。 **10** [VP2C, 3A, 14, 15B] (special uses with *adverbial particles* and *preps*): (與副詞接語及介詞連用的特殊用法):

work away (at sth), continue to ~: 繼續工作: *He's been ~ing away at this job since breakfast.* 從吃過早飯他就一直做這個工作。

work ˈin; ~ into sth, (⇨ 6 above) penetrate; find a way in/into: (參看上列第 6 義)滲透;穿透;進入: *The dust has ~ed in everywhere,* eg into a house during a sandstorm. 灰塵無孔不入遍佈室內各處(如在一次暴風沙中,房舍遭風沙侵入)。 ~ ***sth in/into,*** introduce; find a place for: 引進;挿入;加入: *Can't you ~ in a few jokes/~ a few jokes into your story?* 你不能挿幾個笑話進去(挿幾個笑話到你的故事裏)嗎?

work sth off, get rid of; dispose of; deal with: 除去;排除;處置: ~ *off arrears of correspondence/superfluous energy/one's excess weight.* 處理積壓的信件(發洩過剩的精力;減除過剩體重)。

work on/upon sb/sth, (⇨ 8 above) excite, influence: (參看上列第 8 義)激動;激起;激發;影響: *Will the high figure for unemployment ~ on the conscience of the Government?* 龐大的失業數字會使政府的良心不安嗎? *The sufferings of the refugees ~ed upon our feelings so much that we gave them all the help we could.* 難民們的痛苦令我們如此難過,所以我們給予他們一切可能的幫助。⇨ also 1 above: 亦參看上列第 1 義: ~ *on a new novel, etc.* 從事於一部新小說的寫作等。

work out, **(a)** be capable of being solved: 可以解決,解答等;可以算出: *This sum/problem will not ~ out.* 這一總數(題目)算不出來。 **(b)** be, turn out, in the end: 結局;至最後;結果爲: *How will things ~ out?* 事情將如何變化? *The situation ~ed out quite well.* 情況到最後相當不錯。*The total ~s out at £10.* 金額總計爲十鎊。*How much does it ~ out at,* What's the total? 總共是多少錢? **(c)** ⇨ 6 above. 參看上列第6義。 **(d)** exercise, train (for a contest): (爲參加競賽而)練習;訓練: *The champion is ~ing out in the gym this morning.*

衞晃者今天早晨正在體育館訓練。 Hence, 由此產生, **'~-out** *n* period, form, of training or exercise. 訓練或練習的期間或形式。 **~ *sth out,*** **(a)** calculate: 計算;算出: *I've ~ed out your share of the expenses at £5.* 我已計算出你該分攤的費用是五鎊。 **(b)** get results for: 獲得結果;解答: *I can't ~ out these algebra problems.* 這些代數題目我解不出來。 **(c)** devise; invent; develop in detail: 設計;發明;詳細制定: *a well-~ed out scheme.* 妥善周詳的方案。 *They've ~ed out a method of sending a spacecraft to Mars.* 他們已經設計出一種發射太空船到火星的方法。 *You must ~ out your own salvation,* find a way of saving yourself by your own efforts. 你必須奮力自救。 **(d)** solve: 解決;解出: *He was ~ing out some coded messages.* 他在譯出幾項密碼電訊。 **(e)** (usu passive) exhaust by using, operating, etc: (通常用被動式)用盡;耗盡: *That silver-mine is now ~ed out,* has no more ore. 那銀礦已經枯竭了。

work up to sth, advance steadily to a high level: 逐漸而穩定地達到高的水準或層面: *The orchestra was ~ing up to a crescendo.* 那交響樂團即將演奏到音量漸强的一節。 **~ *sth up,*** **(a)** make by degrees; bring to an efficient or satisfactory condition: 逐漸造成或發展; 使達到有效或滿意的情況; 拓展: *~ up a business.* 拓展一家商店。 **(b)** excite; stir up: 激動;煽動;鼓動: *~ up the feelings of an audience.* 煽動聽衆情緒。 **~ *sb/oneself up (into),*** rouse to a high point (of excitement, etc): 使某人(自己)達到(興奮等)的最高點; 激動;激起;引起: *He ~ed himself/everyone up into a frenzy/rage/state of hysteria.* 他(他使每一個人)激動得發狂(狂怒,發瘋)。 *The audience was really ~ed up by this time.* 這時觀衆已變得非常激動。

work upon sb/sth, ⇨ ~ on sb/sth above. 參看上列 work on sb/sth。

work·able /ˈwɜːkəbl; ˈwɝkəbl/ *adj* that can be worked; that will work; practicable: 可使用的;可操作的;可以塑製的; 可運轉的;可經營的; 行得通的;切實際的: *The silver-mine is no longer ~,* it cannot be worked (eg because it is flooded, or because the ore is exhausted). 那銀礦已無法採掘了(如爲洪水所淹沒,或已枯竭)。 *Is the proposed scheme ~,* feasible? 那項建議的方案可行嗎？

worker /ˈwɜːkə(r); ˈwɝkɚ/ *n* person who works; 工作者;工人; (attrib) (形容用法) *~ bees* (contrasted with the drones). 工蜂(與雄蜂相對)。

work·ing /ˈwɜːkɪŋ; ˈwɝkɪŋ/ *n* **1** [C] mine, quarry, etc or part of it, which is being, or has been, worked: (正在開採,或已開採過的)礦坑;採石場等: *The boys went exploring in some disused ~s,* eg the shafts of an old tin-mine. 那些男孩子到幾個廢棄的礦坑中(如舊錫礦的豎坑)去探索。 **2** [C] the way sth works, or the result of this: 運轉、活動等的方式或結果;運作情況;作用結果: *the ~s of conscience;* 良心的驅策; *the principles that guide the ~s of the human mind.* 指導人類心靈活動的原理原則。 ***in ~ order,*** able to function properly, do what is required; going smoothly: (工作,營業,機能)正常的;(操作,進行,經營)情況良好的: *put a machine in ~ order.* 使機器操作正常。 **3** (attrib) (in various senses of the *v*): (形容用法)(具有動詞諸義): *'~ clothes,* worn while ~; 工作服; *a ~ drawing/plan,* one made as a guide for building, construction, etc. 工作圖;製造圖;建築藍圖;施工圖。 *The Government has a ~ majority,* one that is sufficient. 政府(在議會中)掌有足够的多數(支持票)。 **~ breakfast/lunch/dinner,** one at which persons discuss business, etc: 工作早餐(午餐,正餐)(與餐者於餐席間討論正事): *The Prime Minister and some of his colleagues had a ~ breakfast to discuss the crisis in the docks.* 首相同他幾位同僚共進工作早餐討論碼頭危機。 **~ capital,** money needed for carrying on a business, etc. 流動資本;運用資本;週轉資金;營運資本。 **~ day, (a)** workday (as opposed to a day of rest). 工作日(與休息日相對)。 **(b)** number of hours worked on a normal day: (一工作日的)工作時數: *a ~ day of eight hours.* 一天工作八小時。 **~ hypothesis,** one formulated for a theory, etc. 運作假設(爲求證或研究某一理論,學說等所定的假設)。 **~ knowledge,** knowledge that is sufficient for the purpose. 足夠的實用知識。 **ˌ~-ˈout (a)** calculation of results; elaboration of details: 成果統計;細節的釐定;計算;算出;釐定: *the ~-out of a plan.* 擬定一項計畫。 **(b)** execution: 執行: *Don't interfere with them in the ~-out of their scheme.* 在他們執行其方案時,不要加以干擾。 **'~ party,** (esp) committee appointed to secure efficiency in an industry, or one appointed (eg by a government department) to study and report on a question. (尤指)爲提高某項工業效率,或爲研究及報告某一專題,而任命的委員會;專案委員會;營運委員會。 □ *part adj* engaged in work: 從事工作的: *a hard-~ woman.* 一個勤勞的婦女。 **the ~ class(es),** those engaged in manual work. 勞工階級。 Hence, 由此產生, **'~-class** *adj* of this class: 勞工階級的: *a ~-class family.* 勞工階級的家庭。

world /wɜːld; wɝld/ *n* **1 the ~,** the earth, its countries and people: 世界(地球,地球上的國家及人民): *the Old W~,* Europe, Asia and Africa; 舊世界(歐、亞、非三洲); *the New W~,* America; 新世界(美洲); *the Roman W~,* that part known to the ancient Romans; 古羅馬人(所認識)的世界; *the English-speaking ~,* those parts where English is the mother tongue of the inhabitants; 講英語的地區; *make a journey round the ~;* 作環球旅行; *to the ~'s end,* to the farthest distance possible. 到天涯海角。 *The whole ~/All the ~ knows...,* It is widely or generally known.... 世人皆知…。[C] heavenly body that may resemble our ~: 與地球類似的天體: *Are there any other ~s besides ours?* 宇宙間除地球外，還有其他類似地球的天體嗎？ ***make a 'noise in the ~,*** be widely talked of; become famous. 廣爲人所談論;聲名大噪。 ***a citizen of the ~,*** a cosmopolitan person. 世界公民;四海爲家的人。 ***It's a small ~!*** (said when meeting someone in an unexpected place). 世界眞小(沒想到會在這裏遇見你)！ **2** (as 1 above; used attrib) affecting, used by, intended for, extending over, the ~: (如上列第1義;形容用法)影響世界的;世界所用的;意欲用於世界的;遍及世界的;包括世界的: *a ~ language,* one that is or will be used, or is designed for use, in all or most parts of the ~: 世界語: *English is a ~ language now.* 英語現在是一種世界語。 *Esperanto was designed as a ~ language.* 艾斯帕蘭多是一種製作出來的世界語。 *Which countries today can be called ~ powers,* countries whose policies, etc affect all parts of the ~? 哪些國家在今天稱得上是世界强國呢？ *We've had two ~ wars in this century.* 本世紀我們已經經歷了兩次世界大戰。 **the W~ Bank,** international bank established in 1945 for providing loans for development when private capital is not available (officially the *International Bank for Reconstruction and Development*). 世界銀行(創設於1945年,提供開發貸款給無法籌集民間資金的國家,正式名稱爲'國際重建及開發銀行')。 **ˌ~-ˈwide** *adj* found in, spread over, all parts of the ~: 遍及全世界的: *~-wide fame.* 享譽全球。 **3** time, state or scene of existence: 生存的時間、狀態或景象: *this ~ and the next,* life on earth and existence after death; 今生及來世; *the ~ to come,* existence after death; 來世; *the lower ~,* hell, Hades; 下界;地獄;冥府; *bring a child into the ~,* beget one or give birth to one. 生孩子。 **ˌ~-ˈweary** *adj* tired of living. 厭世的。 **4** the universe; everything: 宇宙;萬有;萬物: *Is this the best of all possible ~s?* 這是宇宙間最好的世界嗎？ ***in the ~,*** at all, in existence: 究竟;到底;世界上: *Nothing in the ~ would please me more.* 世界上沒有別的比這更使我高興的了。 *Who in the ~* (=Who ever, Who on earth) *is that strange man?* 那個

陌生的人究竟是誰？ ***for all the ~ like sb／sth,*** exactly like: 恰似某人(某物)；與某人(某物)一模一樣： *She's for all the ~ like a woman I knew 20 years ago, in looks, behaviour, everything.* 她與我廿年前認識的一個女人一模一樣，外貌、舉止，無論那一方面。***be all the ~ to sb,*** be everything to: 爲某人的一切；某人所最喜愛： *She's all the ~ to him,* He lives for her alone. 她是他的一切(他僅爲她而活)。 ***not for the ~,*** not on any account: 決不；無論如何不會： *I wouldn't hurt her feelings for the ~.* 我決不會傷她的感情。***be／feel on top of the ~,*** elated (because of success, good health, etc). (因爲成功，健康等而)得意洋洋的；興高采烈的。***be out of this ~,*** (sl) (of sth) be sublime, magnificent. (俚)(指某事物)極佳的；特別好的；無與倫比的。 ***carry the ˌ~ beˈfore one,*** have quick and complete success. 獲得迅速而完全的成功。***a ~ of sth,*** a great number or quantity of; very much／many: 大量；許多: *My holiday did me a ~ of good.* 我的假日對我大有益處。*There was a ~ of meaning in the look she gave him.* 她看他的一眼含意無窮。 *There's often a ~ of difference between promise and achievement.* 承諾與履行諾言之間往往相差甚遠。 ***think the ~ of sb／sth,*** admire him／it. 羨慕某人(某物)；看重某人(某物)。 **5** the material things and occupations of life (contrasted with the spiritual). 物質生活(與精神生活相對)。***the ~, the flesh, and the devil,*** the various temptations that face us. 物質，肉慾及魔鬼(我們面臨的各種引誘)。***the best of ˈboth ~s,*** the best of what is offered from two different (perhaps conflicting) sources. 兩全其美(兩不同事物或兩相抵觸事物的長處兼而有之)。 ***forsake／renounce the ~,*** devote one's life to spiritual things. 全心追尋精神生活；出家；遁世。 **6** human affairs; active life: 世事；世態；世務: *know／see the ~,* have experience of life; 通達世故；見過世面; *a man of the ~,* person who has had experience of life, knows the ways of men, is tolerant, etc; 老於世故的人; *take the ~ as one finds it,* adapt oneself to things, not try to reform people, etc. 安於現實；安於現況。*How goes the ~ with you,* How are your affairs going? 近況如何？ **7** persons, institutions, etc connected with a special social class or special interests: 與某一社會階層或特殊利益有關係的人、機構等；界: *the ~ of sport／art;* 運動(藝術)界; *the ˈracing／ˈscientific ~;* 賽馬(科學)界; all that concerns or belongs to a specified sphere: 有關或屬於某範圍的一切; 領域; 界: *the ˈanimal／ˈmineral／ˈvegetable ~.* 動物(礦物, 植物)界。⇨ kingdom(3). **8** ***the ~,*** society, its opinions, customs, etc: 社交界，上流社會；其見解，習俗等: *the great ~,* fashionable society. 時髦的上流社會。*All the ~ and his wife were at the ball,* all those who claim positions in high society. 所有上流社會人士和他們的夫人都參加了該舞會。*What will the ~ say,* What about public opinion; can we defy it, etc? 人們會怎麼說呢(我們能不顧輿論嗎…)？**~·ly** *adj* **1** material: 物質的: *my ~ly goods,* my property. 我的財產。 **2** temporal; of the affairs of this life (esp the pursuit of pleasure, contrasted with spiritual): 世俗的；現世的(尤指追求享樂，與'精神的'相對): *~ly wisdom,* prudence, etc which enables one to obtain material gains and advantages. 處世之才；致富等的本領；世故。 **3** (also 亦作 *ˌ~ly-ˈminded*) concerned with, interested in, material things. 耽於利慾的；汲汲於名利的；世俗的。**~·li·ness** *n*

worm /wɜːm ; wɝm/ *n* **1** kinds of small, boneless, limbless, creeping creature, esp **(ˈearth·~)** the kind living in the ground, or the kinds living as parasites in the intestines, etc of animals. 蟲；蠕蟲；(尤指)蚯蚓；(動物腸等中的)寄生蟲。⇨ the illus at silk. 參看 silk 之插圖。⇨ *hookworm* at hook(1), *tapeworm* at tape. **ˈ~-cast** *n* tubular pile of earth pushed up by an earth~ on the ground. 蚯蚓糞。***the ~ of conscience,*** remorse. 良心的譴責；悔恨。 **2** (in compounds) used as a name for larvae, insects, etc: (用於複合字中)用作幼蟲、昆蟲等的名稱: *ˈsilk~;* 蠶; *ˈglow~.* 螢火蟲。**ˈ~-eaten** *adj* full of ~ holes; (fig) antiquated. 蟲蛀的；多蛀孔的；(喻)過時的；陳舊的。 **ˈ~-hole** *n* hole left in wood, fruit, etc by ~s. (木材、果實等上)蟲蛀之孔；蟲孔；蛀洞。 **3** (fig) insignificant or contemptible person. (喻)小人物；可鄙之人；可憐蟲。 ***Even a ~ will turn,*** (prov) There are limits to patience. (諺)忍耐是有限度的。 **4** spiral part of a screw. 螺紋；蝸桿(螺絲的螺旋部分)。 **ˈ~-gear** *n* arrangement in which a wheel with teeth gears with the ~(4) of a revolving spiral. 蝸輪(聯動)裝置。□ *vt* **1** [VP15A, B] ***~ oneself／one's way in／into／through,*** move slowly, or by patience, or with difficulty: 蠕行；堅忍地或困難地行進: *He ~ed himself／his way through the undergrowth.* 他緩慢地穿過灌木叢。*He ~ed himself into favour／into her confidence.* 他逐漸獲得寵信(她的信任)。 ***~ sth out (of sb),*** extract (by persistent questioning, etc): (藉不斷地詢問等)從某人取得(某物)；迫使某人供出(某事): *He ~ed the secret out of me.* 他從我這裡逐漸探知該項秘密。 **2** [VP6A] rid of parasitic ~s: 除去腸等中的寄生蟲；爲…驅蟲: *I think we'd better ~ the cat,* eg by giving it a powder or pill. 我想我們最好給貓打打蟲(如給它吃一劑藥粉或藥丸)。 **~y** *adj* having many ~s; damaged by ~s; like a ~. 多蟲的；爲蟲所損壞的；似蟲的。

worm·wood /ˈwɜːmwʊd ; ˈwɝmˌwʊd/ *n* [U] kinds of perennial plant with a bitter flavour, used in the preparation of vermouth and absinthe and in medicine; (fig) bitter mortification and its cause. 苦艾；茵蔯(多年生植物，有苦味，用以調製苦艾酒，並用於醫藥)；(喻)苦惱；悔恨；其原由。

worn /wɔːn ; worn/ *pp* of wear².

worri·some /ˈwʌrɪsəm ; ˈwɝɪsəm/ *adj* troublesome; worrying. 煩惱的；令人憂慮的。

worry /ˈwʌrɪ ; ˈwɝɪ/ *vt, vi* (*pt, pp* -ried) **1** [VP 6A, 14, 15A, 17, 22] trouble; give (sb, oneself) no peace of mind; cause anxiety or discomfort to: 困擾；使(某人，自己)不安；使煩惱；使不適: *~ sb with foolish questions;* 用愚蠢的問題困擾某人; *~ oneself sick／be worried sick about sth,* be extremely anxious about it. 爲某事愁出病來；爲某事極端煩惱。*The noise of the traffic worried her.* 交通的嘈雜聲使她不安。*What's ~ing you?* 你在爲何事煩惱？ *Her child has a bad cough and it rather worries her.* 她的孩子咳嗽得很厲害，這使她很煩惱。*I have a bad tooth that is ~ing me.* 我有一顆蛀牙，使我感到不適。 *Don't ~ yourself about the children; they're old enough to take good care of themselves.* 別爲孩子們擔心；他們已經大得會照顧自己了。*He'll ~ himself to death,* kill himself by ~ing. 他會愁死的。 *She was always ~ing her husband for more money／~ing him to give her more money.* 她總是纏着她的丈夫，不斷向他要錢。 **2** [VP 2A, B, C, 3A] ***~ (about／over sth),*** be anxious, uneasy, troubled: 焦慮；不安；煩惱: *Don't ~ about trifles.* 不要爲小事情煩惱。 *You have no cause to ~.* 你沒有理由煩惱。*What's the use of ~ing?* 焦慮有什麼用？ *Don't ~ trying to find it—it'll turn up one day.* 別急着找它 — 它總有一天會出現的。 ***~ along,*** (colloq) manage to get along in spite of troubles. (俗)不顧困難設法進行；熬過；撐持過。 **3** [VP6A] (esp of dogs) seize with the teeth and shake: (尤指狗)銜在口裏搖；咬嚙；撕咬: *The dog was ~ing the rat.* 那隻狗在撕咬那隻老鼠。 **4** [VP15B] ***~ a problem, etc out,*** attack it again and again until one solves it. 絞盡腦汁解決問題等。□ *n* (*pl* -ries) **1** [U] condition of being troubled: 困擾；煩惱；憂愁: *show signs of ~.* 顯出憂愁的樣子。 **2** [C] (usu *pl*) sth that worries; cause of anxiety: (通常用複數)令人煩惱的事物；憂愁的原因: *Is your life full of worries?* 你的生活充滿了令人苦惱的事情嗎？ *Money worries and little domestic worries have* *made him look old.* 由於爲錢以及家庭中的瑣事發愁，他顯得老了。*What a little ~ that child is!* 那孩子是多麼煩人的小傢伙啊！ **wor·ried** *adj* troubled; anxious: 煩惱的；焦慮的；擔心的：*He has a worried look.* 他顯出焦慮的神色。**~·ing** *adj* full of ~; causing ~: 多煩惱的；令人憂慮的：*have a ~ing time.* 度過一段煩惱的時間。**~·ing·ly** *adv*

worse /wɜːs; wɝs/ *adj* (independent comparative; 獨立比較級；⇨ bad, worst) **1** *Your work is bad but mine is much ~.* 你的工作很壞，但我的更糟。*We couldn't have had ~ weather for our journey.* 這次旅行我們所遇到的天氣再壞沒有了。*Is there anything ~ than war/a ~ catastrophe than war/a catastrophe ~ than war?* 還有比戰爭更壞的(災難)嗎？*You are making things ~.* 你把事情弄得更糟了。*He escaped with nothing ~ than a few scratches.* 他安然脫險，僅受到了擦傷。***the ~ for wear,*** badly worn as the result of long wear; (fig) exhausted: 穿得破舊不堪；(喩) 筋疲力盡；枯竭：*He looks the ~ for wear after only a year as President.* 他就任總統才不過一年，就顯得疲憊不堪了。 **2** (*pred* only) having less good health or condition or circumstances: (僅作敍述用法)有較差的健康，狀況或環境的；更壞的；更惡劣的：*The doctor says she is much ~ today.* 醫生說她的病情今天大爲惡化。*I'm glad you don't feel any ~.* 我很高興你沒有覺得更不舒服。***be none the ~ (for sth),*** be unharmed (by it): 未(因…而)受傷害；安然無恙：*He fell into the river but is none the ~ for it.* 他掉入河裏，但是並沒有怎麼樣。□ *adv* (⇨ badly, worst) **1** *He is behaving ~ than ever.* 他的舉止更壞了。*He has been taken ~,* has become more seriously ill. 他的病勢更沉重了。***none the ~,*** not less: 依然；還是；不差：*I like a man none the ~ for being outspoken.* 我不因爲一個人直言無諱而不喜歡他。***~ off,*** (⇨ *badly off* at bad[1]; *better off* at better[2](1); *well off* at well[2](3)) more badly situated; in ~ circumstances. 情況更壞；處境更糟；惡化。 **2** (used to intensify): (用以加强語氣)：*It's raining ~* (= more heavily) *than ever.* 雨下得更大了。*She hates me ~* (= more strongly) *than before.* 她更恨我了。□ *n* [U] ~ thing(s): 更壞的事物：*I have ~ to tell.* 我有更壞的事情奉告。*The first news was bad, but ~ followed.* 最初的消息很壞，但是接著來的更壞。*There has been a change for the ~ in the patient's condition.* 病人的情況更形惡化了。*Things seem to be going from bad to ~ nowadays.* 目前的局勢似乎愈來愈壞了。**~n** /ˈwɜːsn; ˈwɝsn̩/ *vt, vi* [VP6A, 2A] make or become ~. 使壞；變壞；惡化。

wor·ship /ˈwɜːʃɪp; ˈwɝʃəp/ *n* [U] **1** reverence and respect paid to God: (對上帝的)崇拜；禮拜：*places of ~,* churches, mosques, synagogues, temples, etc; 教堂，清眞寺，猶太教會堂，佛教廟宇等；拜神的地方；*hours of ~,* times of church etc services; 禮拜時間；拜神時間；*public ~,* church etc service(s). 教堂崇拜儀式；禮拜；拜神。 **2** admiration and respect shown to or felt for sb or sth: (對某人或某物的)崇拜；敬慕；景仰；尊敬：*the ~ of success;* 仰慕成功；*hero ~.* 英雄崇拜。*She gazed at the film star with ~ in her eyes.* 她注視那電影明星，眼睛裡充滿着仰慕。 **3** ***your/his W~,*** (GB) title of respect used to/of a magistrate or mayor: (英)閣下(對於地方長官或市長的尊稱)：*his W~ the Mayor of Chester.* 赤斯特市長閣下。□ *vt, vi* (-pp-; US -p-) [VP6A, 2A, B] give ~(1, 2) to: 崇拜；尊敬；仰慕：*~ God;* 崇拜上帝；attend church service: 參加禮拜；做禮拜：*the church where she had ~ped for ten years.* 她已經在那兒做了十年禮拜的教堂。**~·per** (US = **~er**) *n* **~·ful** /-fl; -fəl/ *adj* (in GB titles of respect, eg to Justices of the Peace, aldermen) worthy of respect; honourable. (用於英國對治安推事，市議員等的尊稱中)值得尊敬的；可敬的。

worst /wɜːst; wɝst/ *adj* (independent superlative; 獨立最高級；⇨ bad, worse): *the ~ storm for five years;* 五年來最猛烈的暴風雨；*the ~ dinner I've ever eaten;* 我所吃過的最惡劣的正餐；*the ~* (= most intense) *frost this winter.* 今年冬天最嚴烈的霜寒。□ *adv* (independent superlative; 獨立最高級；⇨ badly, worse) most badly: 最壞地；最差地：*Tom played badly, Harry played worse and I played ~.* 湯姆玩得不好，哈利玩得更壞，而我玩得最差。□ *n* ~ part, state, event, etc: 最壞的部分，狀態，事件等：*You must be prepared for the ~,* the ~ possible news, outcome, etc. 你必須爲最壞的情況作準備(或你必須作最壞的打算)。*The ~ of the storm is over.* 暴風雨最猛烈的時候已經過去了。*She keeps cheerful, even when things are at their ~.* 即使是事情最糟的時候，她也能保持愉快的心情。***If the ˌ~ comes to the ˈ~,*** If the ~ happens. 如果最壞的事發生。***get the ~ of it*** (in a fight etc), be defeated. (在打鬥等中)被打敗；敗北。***The ~ of it is that…,*** The most unfortunate part of the affair is that…. 最壞的是；最不幸的是…。***at (the) ~,*** if the ~ happens. 在最壞(最不利)的情況下。***do your ~/let him do his ~,*** used as expressions of defiance. 你有什麼狠處儘管使出來吧(他有什麼狠處讓他儘管使出來吧)(用作挑戰語)。□ *vt* [VP6A] defeat; get the better of: 打敗；擊敗；勝過：*He ~ed his enemy.* 他打敗了他的敵人。

wor·sted /ˈwʊstɪd; ˈwʊstɪd/ *n* [U] twisted woollen yarn or thread; cloth made from this. 絨線；毛紗；絨線或毛紗做成的布料。

worth /wɜːθ; wɝθ/ *pred adj* **1** having a certain value; of value equal to: 值；相等於…的價值：*I paid only £300 for this used car but it's ~ much more.* 我僅僅花了三百鎊買到這部舊車，但是它比這種價格值得多的多呢。*It's not ~ more than two pounds.* 它的價值不會超過兩鎊。*It's not ~ the paper it's printed on.* 它(通常指文章、小說等)的價值比用來印它的紙張還不如。***~ (one's) while,*** ⇨ while. ***for what it is ~,*** without any guarantee or promise concerning it: 無任何擔保或承諾；不論眞僞；照原來樣子：*That's the news I heard—I pass it on to you for what it is ~.* 那是我聽來的消息——不管眞實與否，我照原樣告訴你。**ˌ~·ˈwhile** *adj* that is ~ the time, etc needed: 值得的：*a ~while experiment.* 一項值得做的實驗。⇨ while. **2** possessing; having property to the value of: 擁有的；有…價值的財產的：*What's the old man ~?* 那個老人有多少財產？*He died ~ a million pounds.* 他死時有一百萬鎊財產。***for all one is ~,*** (colloq) with all one's energy; making every effort: (俗)出全力；盡力；拚命：*He was running for all he was ~.* 他正拚命地跑。 **3** ~ + *verb* in ***-ing,*** giving a satisfactory or rewarding return for: (後接 -ing 形動詞)對…有滿意的或有代價的回報；值得：*The book is well ~ reading.* 這本書很值得讀。*It's hardly ~ troubling about.* 這事幾乎不值得去麻煩。*He says life wouldn't be ~ living without friendship.* 他說人生若沒有友情便不值得活下去了。□ *n* [U] **1** value; what sb or sth is ~: 價值；某人或某事物的價值：*books/discoveries, etc of great/little/not much ~;* 極有(極少，不大有)價值的書(發現等)；*know a friend's ~.* 認識一位朋友的價值。 **2** quantity of sth of a specified value: 値某價額的數量：*a pound's ~ of apples;* 一鎊的蘋果；*fifty pence ~ of copper coins;* 値半鎊的銅幣；*a penny~ of sweets.* 一便士的糖果。**~·less** *adj* having no value. 無價值的。**~·less·ly** *adv* **~·less·ness** *n*

worthy /ˈwɜːðɪ; ˈwɝðɪ/ *adj* (-ier, -iest) **1** ~ ***(of sth/to be sth),*** deserving: 值得…的；應…的；足以…的：*a cause ~ of support;* 一項值得支持的主張；*behaviour ~ of praise;* 值得稱道的行爲；*nothing ~ of mention;* 乏善可陳；沒有值得提的事；*a man who is ~ to have a place in the team.* 足以成爲該隊隊員的人。*He found a ~ enemy/an enemy ~ of his sword,* one brave or strong enough. 他遇到了足以和他匹敵(勢均力敵)的敵人。 **2** (often ironic or used with a patronizing effect) having merit; deserving respect: (常用做反語，或帶有傲慢意味)有價值的；

可敬的: *a ~ gentleman.* 可敬的紳士。*She says she helps only the ~ poor* (in contrast to those people who, she thinks, are poor through their own laziness, etc). 她說她祇幫助那些值得她去幫助的窮人(她不幫助那些她認爲好吃懶做的窮人)。□ *n* **1** person of some distinction (in his own country or during a certain period): (在其本國或某一時代)傑出的人;名士: *an Elizabethan ~*, ie during the reign of Queen Elizabeth I. 英國女王伊莉莎白一世時代的傑出人物。 **2** (hum or ironic) person who appears to be distinguished: (諧或反語)顯得了不起的人物;大人物: *Who's the ~ who has just arrived?* 剛到的那位大人物是誰呀? *Who are the worthies on the platform?* 臺上那些大人物是誰呀? **worth·ily** /-ɪlɪ; -ɪlɪ/ *adv* **worthi·ness** *n*

wot /wɒt; wɑt/ ***God wot,*** (archaic or hum) God knows. (古或諧)天曉得。

wot·cher /ˈwɒtʃə(r); ˈwɑtʃɚ/ *int* (GB sl) (as a greeting) Hello! (英俚)(用作問候語)喂!哈囉!

would ⇨ will¹.

wouldst /wʊdst; wʊdst/ *v* old form used with *thou*: 與 thou 連用的舊形式: *Thou ~,* You would.

wound¹ /wuːnd; wund/ *n* [C] **1** hurt or injury to the living tissue of the body, caused by cutting, shooting, tearing, etc, esp as the result of attack (*injury* being more usu for the result of an accident): 傷;創傷(指由割切、射擊、撕扯等,尤指受攻擊所受的傷;意外事件所受的傷,通常多用 injury): *a ˈknife ~ in the arm;* 臂上的刀傷; *a ˈbullet ~.* 子彈傷。*The dog was licking its ~s,* eg after a fight with another dog. 那隻狗在舐它的傷口。 **2** injury to a plant, tree, etc in which the bark is cut or torn. (剝去皮的)草木等的損傷。 **3** pain given to a person's feelings: (加諸感情上的)痛苦: *a ~ to his pride/vanity.* 對於他的自尊心(虛榮心)的傷害。□ *vt* [VP6A] give a ~ to: 傷;傷害: *Ten soldiers were killed and thirty ~ed.* 十名士兵陣亡,三十名負傷。Cf 參較 *hurt* or *injured* in an accident. 意外事件負傷,該用 hurt 或 injured。 *He felt ~ed in his honour/affections.* 他覺得他的榮譽(感情)受到了傷害。

wound² /waʊnd; waʊnd/ *pt, pp* of wind³.

wove, wo·ven ⇨ weave.

wow¹ /waʊ; waʊ/ *n* (sl) tremendous success: (俚)極大的成功;巨大的成就: *The new play at the National Theatre's a wow.* 在國家劇院上演的新劇獲得極大的成功。□ *int* expressing wonder, admiration, etc. (表示驚異,羨慕等的驚嘆聲)哇!

wow² /waʊ; waʊ/ *n* [U] varieties in the pitch of sound reproduced from a disc or tape, caused by fluctuations in speed (from the motor). (由於馬達速度快慢不一,從唱片或錄音帶放出來的)不同的音高;聲音的失眞;(唱片或錄音帶放出的)變質音。⇨ flutter, *n*(3).

wrack /ræk; ræk/ *n* [U] **1** seaweed thrown up on the shore by the waves (and used for manure, etc). (冲到岸上作肥料等用的)海草。 **2** = rack⁴.

wraith /reɪθ; reθ/ *n* apparition of a person seen shortly before or after his death. (人在臨終前或死後不久顯現的)生魂。

wrangle /ˈræŋgl; ˈræŋgl/ *vi* [VP2A, 3A] **~ *(with sb) (about/over sth),*** take part in a noisy or angry argument. 口角;爭吵。□ *n* such an argument. 口角;爭吵。

wrap /ræp; ræp/ *vt, vi* (-pp-) **1** [VP6A, 15A, B] ***~ (up) (in sth),*** cover or roll up (in): 包;捲;纏: *~ a child in a shawl;* 把小孩裹在披巾裏面; *~ up sth in tissue paper;* 用薄紙包起某物; *~ oneself in a blanket.* 把自己裹在毯子裏。*The mountain top was ~ped in mist.* 山頂爲霧所籠罩。*You'd better ~ (yourself) up well before you go out,* put on an overcoat, scarf, etc. 你在外出以前最好把衣服穿妥當(穿厚一點)。 *Why does he ~ up his meaning in such obscure language,* Why doesn't he express his meaning clearly? 他爲什麼不直說呢? ***~ sth up,*** (sl) complete it: (俚)完成某事: *~ up a business deal.* 完成一項交易。 **2** [VP14] ***~ sth round sth,*** put round; wind or fold round as a covering or protection; pack: 包裹;包裝: *W~ plenty of paper round it.* 用很多紙將它包起。*W~ this shawl round your shoulders.* 把這披肩圍在你的肩上。 **3** ***be ~ped up in,*** (a) be packed or enclosed in; (fig) be concealed in: 被包裹於;被包封於…中;(喻)爲…所隱蔽;隱藏於: *The affair is ~ped up in mystery.* 這件事隱蔽於神祕之中。(b) be deeply interested in: 對…有極大興趣: *He is ~ped up in his work/studies.* 他對於他的工作(研究)有極大興趣。 (c) be deeply devoted to: 專心於;全神致力於: *She is ~ped up in her children,* devotes all her time, care, attention, etc to them. 她的全部精神都花在兒女身上了。□ *n* outer garment or covering (eg a scarf, cloak, fur or rug); outer covering. 外套;罩件(如圍巾,披風,皮衣或圍毯)。 (trade uses): (商業用語): ***keep sth under ~s,*** conceal it. 隱藏某事;保密。 ***take off the ~s,*** place on public view (eg a new model of a car). 公開展示(新型汽車等)。 **~·per** *n* (esp) (尤指) **1** piece of paper (to be) ~ped round a newspaper or other periodical, a book etc (esp for sending by post); cover of loose paper, etc for a book. (尤指郵寄書、報、雜誌等的)包紙;書的封皮;書套。 **2** light dressing-gown. 輕便晨衣。 **~·ping** *n* **1** [C] sth used for covering or packing: 用於包裹或包裝之物;包裝紙、布等: *the ~pings of a mummy.* 木乃伊的包裹物。 **2** [U] material for covering or packing sth: 用於包裹或包裝的材料;墊料: *Put plenty of ~ping round the cups and saucers when you pack them.* 包裝杯碟時,在周圍多放些墊料。

wrath /rɒθ *US:* ræθ; ræθ/ *n* [U] (liter) great anger; indignation. (文)暴怒;憤怒;義憤。 **~·ful** /-fl; -fəl/ *adj* **~·fully** /-fəlɪ; -fəlɪ/ *adv*

wreak /riːk; rik/ *vt* [VP6A, 14] **~ *sth (on sb),*** (liter) give expression to; give effect to: (文)發洩;遂行;施: *~ one's fury upon sb;* 對某人發脾氣; *~ havoc/vengeance upon sb.* 對某人加以蹂躪(報復)。

wreath /riːθ; riθ/ *n* (*pl* ~s /riːðz; riðz/) **1** flowers or leaves twisted or woven together into a circle (worn on the head as a garland, or placed on a coffin, a grave, a memorial to the dead, etc). 花環;花圈;花冠。 **2** ring, spiral or curling line (*of* smoke, mist, etc). (烟,霧等的)圈;渦卷(與 of 連用)。

wreathe /riːð; rið/ *vt, vi* **1** [VP6A] (esp in *pp*) cover, encircle: (尤用過去分詞形式)遮蓋;覆蓋;環繞: *~d with flowers;* 覆以花; *hills ~d in mist;* 隱蔽於霧中的丘陵; *a face ~d in smiles.* 微笑的臉。 **2** [VP14] (reflex) (反身) **~ *itself round,*** wind: 盤繞;捲纏: *The snake ~d itself round the branch.* 那條蛇盤繞在樹枝上。 **3** [VP14] **~ *sth into,*** make (flowers, etc) (into a wreath). 把(花等)製作成(花環等)。 **4** [VP2A, C] (of smoke, mist, etc) move in the shape of a wreath. (指烟,霧等)繚繞;盤旋。

wreck /rek; rɛk/ *n* **1** [U] ruin or destruction, esp of a ship by storms: 破壞;毀滅;(尤指船遭受暴風雨襲擊所造成的)船難;失事;遭難: *save a ship from ~;* 營救遇難船隻; (fig) (喻) *the ~ of one's hopes/plans;* 希望(計畫)的破滅; [C] instance of this: 破滅等的實例;失事;船難: *The storm caused ~s all along the coast.* 那次暴風雨沿海岸造成了許多船難。 **2** [C] ship that has suffered ~(1): 遭遇暴風雨而失事的船;遇難船: *Robinson Crusoe obtained food and supplies from the ~.* 魯賓遜•克魯梭從遇難的船上獲得了食物及其他物品。 **3** [C] vehicle, building, etc that has been badly damaged or fallen into ruin; person whose health has been destroyed: 遭受嚴重破壞或完全毀壞的車輛,建築物等;殘骸;廢墟;健康受到損壞的人: *The car was a worthless ~ after the collision.* 撞車以後,那部車成爲無價值的殘骸了。 *He is a mere ~ of his former self.* 他已經形銷骨立。*If these anxieties continue she will become a nervous ~.* 如果她繼續爲這些事焦慮下去,她的神經就會崩潰了。□ *vt* [VP6A] cause the ~ of: 使破

壞;使毁滅;使失事: *The ship/train was ~ed.* 那隻船(那列火車)失事了。 **~·age** /ˈrekɪdʒ; ˈrɛkɪdʒ/ *n* [U] ~ed material, fragments: 殘骸;殘餘物;碎片: *The ~age of the aircraft was scattered over a wide area.* 那架飛機的殘骸散佈在一片廣大的區域。 **~er** *n* **1** person employed to recover a ~ed ship or its contents. 營救難船或其裝載的貨物、乘客等的人;救助難船者。 **2** (US) person employed to demolish old buildings. (美)拆除舊建築者。⇨ *house-breaker* at house¹(7). **3** (hist) person who tried from the shore to bring about shipwreck (eg by showing false lights) in order to plunder the cargo, etc. (史)在岸上誘使船隻失事而加以刼掠的人;爲刼掠而誘使船隻失事者。

wren /ren; rɛn/ *n* kinds of small short-winged songbird. 歐鷦;鷦鷯。

wrench /rentʃ; rɛntʃ/ *n* [C] **1** sudden and violent twist or pull: 猛扭;猛拉;突然的扭轉: *He gave his ankle a ~,* twisted it by accident. 他失足扭傷了足踝。 *He pulled the handle off with a single ~.* 他用力一拉就拉掉了把手。 **2** (pain caused by a) sad parting or separation: 別離的痛苦;傷別: *Separation from her children was a terrible ~.* 同她的孩子們分別是一項很大的痛苦。 **3** tool for gripping and turning nuts, bolts, etc; spanner. 螺旋鉗;扳鉗;扳手。⇨ the illus at tool. 參看 tool 之插圖。□ *vt* **1** [VP6A, 15A, 22] twist or pull violently: 猛扭;猛拉: *~ the door open;* 用力把門扭開; *~ sth from sb;* 從某人處搶取某物; *~ sth out of his hand;* 從他手裡强奪某物; *~ a door off its hinges.* 用力扭脫門的鉸鏈。 *She ~ed herself from the villain's clutches.* 她掙脫了那惡棍的掌握。 **2** [VP6A] injure (eg one's ankle) by twisting. 扭傷(足踝等)。 **3** [VP6A] (fig) distort (facts, the meaning of a sentence, etc). (喻)歪曲;曲解(事實,句義等)。

wrest /rest; rɛst/ *vt* **1** [VP14] ***~ sth from/out of,*** take (sth) violently away: 奪取(某物);扭奪: *~ a knife from sb/~ it out of his hands.* 從某人處(從他手中)奪去一把刀。 **2** [VP14] ***~ sth from,*** get by effort: 費力取得;努力獲致: *~ a confession of guilt from sb;* 費力取得某人的犯罪自白; *~ a living from poor farmland.* 靠貧瘠的農田勉强維持生活。 **3** twist or pervert (facts, the meaning of sth). 歪曲;曲解(事實,某事物的意義)。

wrestle /ˈresl; ˈrɛsl̩/ *vi* [VP2A, C, 3A] ***~ (with sb),*** struggle with sb (as a sport) and try to throw him to the ground without hitting him: (體育)(與某人)角力;摔角: *~ with sb;* 和某人摔角; (fig) (喻) *~ with a problem/a temptation/one's conscience.* 努力解決一個問題(抗拒誘惑;與良心苦鬪)。□ *n* [C] wrestling match; hard struggle. 角力或摔角比賽;艱苦奮鬪。 **wres·tler** /ˈreslə(r); ˈrɛslɚ/ *n* person who ~s. 角力者;摔角者;艱苦奮鬪者。

wretch /retʃ; rɛtʃ/ *n* **1** unfortunate and miserable person. 不幸而可憐的人。 **2** contemptible, mean person. 卑鄙的人。 **3** (playfully or affectionately) rogue. (戲謔或親暱語)壞蛋。

wretched /ˈretʃɪd; ˈrɛtʃɪd/ *adj* **1** miserable: 可憐的;不幸的: *lead a ~ existence in the slums;* 在貧民窟過可憐的生活; *living in ~ poverty.* 過可憐的貧苦生活。 *This aching tooth makes me feel ~.* 這一顆痛的牙使我很苦惱。 **2** causing misery: 致使不幸或悲慘的: *~ houses.* 骯髒破舊的房子。 **3** of poor quality; bad: 劣質的;壞的: *~ weather/food.* 惡劣的天氣(食物)。 **4** (with *nn* implying blame) that causes dismay (because excessive): (與名詞連用,含示責難)(由於過度而)致使狼狽或沮喪的: *the ~ stupidity of the nation's leaders.* 該國領導人物令人沮喪的愚昧。 **~·ly** *adv* **~·ness** *n*

wrick, rick /rɪk; rɪk/ *vt* [VP6A] sprain or twist slightly: 稍微扭傷;扭筋: *~ one's ankle/a muscle in one's back.* 扭了足踝(背部的肌肉)。□ *n* [C] sprain: 扭傷;扭筋: *give one's back a ~;* 扭傷某人的背; *have a ~ in the neck.* 脖子扭筋。

wriggle /ˈrɪgl; ˈrɪgl̩/ *vi, vt* **1** [VP2A, C, 3A] move with quick, short, twistings; move along in this way: 蠕動;扭動;蜿蜒行進: *The worm ~d as Jim put it on the fish-hook.* 當吉姆把蚯蚓放在釣魚鈎上的時候,它在蠕動。 *Small children ~ in their seats when they are bored.* 小孩子們感到厭煩的時候,就會在座位上扭動。 *The eel ~d out of my fingers.* 那條黃鱔從我的指縫間扭動着滑走了。 *He ~d out of* (= escaped from) *the difficulty.* 他千方百計擺脫了困境。 *He ~d (his way) through the thick hedge.* 他穿過濃密的樹籬蜿蜒行進。 *My criticism made him ~,* feel uncomfortable. 我的批評使他很不舒服。 **2** [VP6A, 15B, 22] move with a wriggling motion: 蠕動;扭動;蜿蜒而行: *~ one's toes;* 扭動足趾; *~ oneself free,* get free (eg from ropes round the body); 掙脫束縛(如從捆在身上的繩子中); *~ one's way out.* 設法擺脫。□ *n* wriggling movement. 蠕動;扭動;蜿蜒。 **wrig·gler** /ˈrɪgələ(r); ˈrɪglɚ/ *n* (esp) larva of a mosquito. (尤指)孑孓。

wright /raɪt; raɪt/ *n* (rare except in compounds) workman, maker. (除見於複合字外,罕用)工人;製造者。⇨ *play~* at play¹(5), *ship~* at ship¹(3), *wheel~* at wheel(1).

wring /rɪŋ; rɪŋ/ *vt* (*pt, pp* wrung /rʌŋ; rʌŋ/) **1** [VP6A] twist; squeeze: 擰;扭;絞出: *~ a hen's neck,* to kill it; 宰殺一隻母鷄; *~ a person's hand,* clasp it warmly. (熱情地)緊握某人的手。 ***~ one's hands,*** squeeze them together (indicating despair, sorrow, etc). 絞手;扭手(表示失望,悲哀等)。 **2** [VP15B, 14] ***~ sth out; ~ sth out of/from sth,*** twist and squeeze sth tightly; force out (esp water) by doing this: 扭緊;壓緊;用力絞出(尤指水): *~ out wet clothes;* 絞乾濕衣服; *~ out the water from one's swimming-trunks.* 絞出游泳褲的水。 *They wrung a confession from her,* (fig) forced her to confess, by persuasion, threats, etc. (喻)他們千方百計逼她招供。 ***~ing wet,*** (of clothes, etc) so wet that water can be wrung from them. (指衣服等)濕得可以擰出水來。□ *n* [C] squeeze: 擰;扭;絞: *Give it another ~.* 再把它絞一下。 **~er** /ˈrɪŋə(r); ˈrɪŋɚ/ *n* = mangle¹.

wrinkle¹ /ˈrɪŋkl; ˈrɪŋkl̩/ *n* small fold or line in the skin (esp of the kind produced by age) or on the surface of sth: 皺;皺紋: *She's beginning to get ~s round her eyes.* 她的眼角開始有皺紋了。 *Her new dress fits without a ~.* 她的新衣非常合身,穿起來連一條皺紋也沒有。 *She ironed out the ~s in her dress.* 她熨平了衣服上的皺紋。□ *vt, vi* [VP6A, 15B, 2A, C] ***~ (up),*** make, get, have, ~s in: 使皺;起皺;有皺紋: *~ up one's forehead,* eg in perplexity; 皺起眉頭(如感到困惑時); *~d with age.* 因年老而起皺紋。 *The front of this dress ~s.* 這衣服的前襟起皺紋。 **wrinkly** /ˈrɪŋklɪ; ˈrɪŋklɪ/ *adj*

wrinkle² /ˈrɪŋkl; ˈrɪŋkl̩/ *n* [C] (colloq) useful hint or suggestion: (俗)有用的提示;好主意;妙計: *give sb a ~.* 給某人一個好建議。

wrist /rɪst; rɪst/ *n* joint between the hand and the arm: 腕部;腕關節: *He took me by the ~.* 他握住我的手腕。⇨ the illus at arm. 參看 arm 之插圖。 **ˈ~-band** *n* band of a shirt-sleeve fitting round the ~. (襯衫的)袖口。 **ˈ~-watch** *n* one worn on the ~. 手錶;腕錶。 **~·let** /ˈrɪstlɪt; ˈrɪstlɪt/ *n* band or ornament for the ~. 腕帶;腕飾。

writ /rɪt; rɪt/ *n* **1** written order issued in the name of a ruler or sb in authority to an official to do or not to do sth: 書面命令;令狀: *a ~ of habeas corpus;* 人身保護令; *a ~ for the arrest of sb.* 拘票;逮捕某人的令狀。 **2 Holy W~,** the Bible. 聖經。□ *v* (*pp*) ***~ large,*** ⇨ write(6).

write /raɪt; raɪt/ *vi, vt* (*pt* wrote /rəʊt; rot/, *pp* written /ˈrɪtn; ˈrɪtn̩/) **1** [VP2A, B, C] make letters or other symbols (eg ideographs) on a surface, esp with a pen or pencil on paper: 書寫;寫字: *learn to read and ~;* 學習讀書和寫字; *~ on both sides of the paper.* 在紙的兩面上書寫。 *I've been* *writing (for) three hours.* 我已經寫了三個小時了。*Are we to ~ in ink or in pencil?* 我們該用鋼筆寫，還是該用鉛筆寫？ **2** [VP6A] put down (on paper) by means of words, etc: (在紙上)寫字;書寫;寫下: *~ words／Chinese characters／shorthand;* 寫字(寫中國字;速記)；*~ one's name;* 寫下自己的名字；*~ a cheque／a certificate／an application* (by filling in the spaces with words, figures, etc); 塡寫支票(證書,申請書)；~ (=fill) *three sheets.* 塡寫三張紙。**3** [VP2C, 15B] **~ *sth down,*** **(a)** put down (on paper) in words: (在紙上)寫下;記載: *You'd better ~ down the address／~ it down before you forget it.* 你最好把這地址(它)寫下來,免得忘了。**(b)** (more usu 較常用 *mark down*) reduce the nominal value of (stock, goods, etc); reduce in value or price. 減低(資產,貨物)的帳面價值;減低價值或價格。**~ *sb down as,*** describe as: 描寫爲;看成: *I'd ~ him down as a fool.* 我要把他描寫爲一個笨伯。**~ *in for sth,*** apply by letter for. 寫信要求;寫報告要求。**~ *off (for sth),*** order by post: 郵購;寫信訂購: *~ off for another dozen bottles of rum.* 郵購另一打瓶裝蘭酒。**~ *sth off,*** **(a)** compose quickly and easily: 迅速而容易地撰述;容易地寫成: *~ off an account of a sports meeting.* 迅速而容易地寫成一篇運動會的報導。**(b)** cancel; recognize that sth is a loss or failure: 取消;註銷;勾銷;削減: *~ off a debt;* 註銷一筆債款; *~ off £500 for depreciation of machinery.* 因機器折舊而削減五百鎊。*He has just written off a new car,* damaged it beyond repair, so that the insurers regard it as a loss. 他剛剛報銷了一輛新車(損壞到無法修理,保險公司視爲損失)。Hence, 由此產生, **'~-off** *n* sth that no longer has any value: 報廢物品;不再有任何價值的東西: *The burnt-out airliner was a complete ~-off,* had no value whatever. 被燒毀的班機完全報廢了。**~ *sth out,*** ~ the whole of; ~ in full: 全部寫出;謄淸: *~ out a copy of an agreement;* 謄寫一份合約; *~ out a cheque.* 開出一張支票。**~ *sth up,*** **(a)** bring up to date; complete: 補寫到最近日期;整理: *~ up one's diary.* 逐日補寫日記。*I must ~ up my notes of the lecture.* 我必須整理演講的筆記。**(b)** overstate the value of (assets). 提高(資產)的帳面價值。**(c)** describe, ~ about, (an event) elaborately: 詳細描寫;花心血記述: *The journalist wrote up the wedding for his paper.* 記者爲他的報紙詳細報導那項婚禮。**(d)** ~ a description giving praise: 爲文讚揚: *A friendly critic wrote up the acting of the leading players.* 一位友善的批評家爲文讚揚主角們的演技。Hence, 由此產生, **'~-up** *n* written account or record of an event. 事件的記述、說明或記錄。 **4** [VP6A, 2A] do the work of an author; compose for publication: 寫作;著述: *~ a novel;* 寫一部小說; *~ for the newspapers;* 爲報紙撰寫文章; *make a living by writing.* 以寫作爲生。 **5** [VP2A, B, C, 12A, 13A, 4A] ~ and send a letter (*to*, or colloq without *to*): 寫信給(與 to 連用,在口語中可省去 to): *He promised to ~ (to) me every week.* 他答應每週寫信給我。*He ~s home／~s to his parents regularly.* 他經常寫信回家(給他的雙親)。*He wrote me that he was staying with his brother in York.* 他寫信告訴我說，他正和他哥哥(弟弟)在約克郡小住。*He wrote me an account of his visit.* 他寫信向我報導他參觀的情形。*I wrote to let them know that I was coming.* 我寫信通知他們我就要來了。**6** (usu passive) show clear signs of: (通常用被動語態)顯露: *He had trouble／honesty written on his face.* 他的臉上顯露他的困難(誠實)。***written*** (also ***writ,*** archaic form of the *pp*) ***large,*** easily or clearly recognizable. (亦作 writ large, writ 爲古體的過去分詞)顯而易見;容易識別。

writer /'raɪtə(r) ; 'raɪtɚ/ *n* **1** person who writes: 書寫者: *the ~ of this letter.* 寫這封信的人。**~'s cramp,** cramp of the muscles in the hand, causing difficulty in writing. 書寫痙攣(使人不便書寫)。**2** author. 作家;著者。**3** (GB) clerk in some government offices; naval rating who does office work. (英)某些政府機構中的書記;海軍文書士。

writhe /raɪð ; raɪð/ *vi* [VP2A, C] twist or roll about in pain; (fig) suffer mental agony: 因痛苦而折騰;翻滾;扭動;(喻)遭受精神痛苦: *~ under insults.* 受侮辱而感到痛苦。

writ·ing /'raɪtɪŋ ; 'raɪtɪŋ/ *n* **1** [U] (in the senses of the *v 'write'*): (與動詞 write 的含義同): *busy with his ~;* 忙於寫作; *put sth down in ~.* 記下某事。*His ~ (= 'hand~) is difficult to read.* 他的字跡不易辨認。**'~-desk** *n* desk (usu with drawers) for ~ at. 書桌(通常有抽屜)。**'~-ink** *n* ink for ~ (contrasted with printing-ink). 書寫用墨水(與印刷用的油墨相對)。**'~-paper** *n* [U] (esp) paper cut to the size usual for letters. 寫字紙;(尤指)信紙。**2** (*pl*) literary work: (複)文學作品;著述: *the ~s of Swift.* 斯威夫特的作品。

writ·ten /'rɪtn ; 'rɪtn̩/ ⇨ write.

wrong /rɒŋ *US:* rɔːŋ ; rɔŋ/ *adj* (contrasted with *right*) (與 right 相對) **1** not morally right; unjust: 不正當的;不法的;道德不好的: *It is ~ to steal.* 偷竊是不法的。*It was ~ of you／You were ~ to borrow his bicycle without asking his permission.* 你未得他的允許而借用他的脚踏車是不對的。 **2** mistaken; unsuitable; improper: 錯誤的;不適當的;不合宜的: *He has six ~ answers in his arithmetic.* 他的算術中有六個地方答錯。*Can you prove that I am／that my opinions are ~?* 你能證明我是(我的意見是)錯誤的嗎？ *You're doing it the ~ way.* 你正以錯誤的方法做那事。*We got into the ~ train.* 我們搭錯了火車。*We came the ~ way／took a ~ turning.* 我們走錯路(轉錯彎)了。*This is the ~ side of the tablecloth,* not the side intended to be seen. 這是桌布的反面。**~ *side out,*** with the ~ side outside. 翻轉;反面向外;裡面翻向外。***be caught on the ~ foot,*** be caught when one is not ready. 措手不及。***get out of bed on the ~ side,*** said of sb who is in a bad temper early in the day. 一大早就發脾氣；一大早就心緒不好。***get hold of the ~ end of the stick,*** have a completely mistaken idea or impression. 想法或印象完全錯誤。***in the ~ box,*** in an awkward position. 處境尷尬;爲難。***on the ~ side of fifty, etc,*** over fifty, etc years old. 過了五十歲,等。**,~-'headed** *adj* perverse and obstinate. 頑固的;剛愎的。**,~-'headedly** *adv* **3** out of order; in a bad condition: 失常的;有毛病的;狀況不佳的: *There's nothing ~ with the engine—perhaps there's no petrol in the tank.* 引擎沒有毛病 — 也許油箱裏沒有汽油了。*There's something ~ with my digestion.* 我有一點消化不良。*What's ~ with that?* (colloq, as a rhetorical question, meaning 'That's quite all right, isn't it?') 那有什麼不對嗎？(俗,作爲反語問句,意卽 '那沒有什麼不對,不是嗎？') □ *adv* (usu end position) not correctly; in a ~ manner: (通常置於句末)不正確地;不正當地;錯誤地;失常地: *guess ~.* 猜錯。*You've spelt my name ~.* 你把我的名字拼錯了。Cf 參較 *~ly spelt. They told me ~.* 他們告訴我的話是錯誤的。Cf 參較 *~ly informed.* ***get sth ~,*** miscalculate or misunderstand it. 誤算或誤解某事。***go ~,*** **(a)** take the ~ path or road. 走錯路。**(b)** have a bad or poor result; fail: 獲致不好的結果;失敗: *All our plans went ~.* 我們所有的計畫都失敗了。**(c)** (colloq) (of a machine, etc) break down. (俗)(指機器,等)出毛病;不對頭;壞。□ *n* **1** [U] what is morally ~; [C] ~ action: 道德上的罪;邪惡;罪行: *know the difference between right and ~;* 能辨別是非善惡; *do ~,* do what is ~; sin. 做壞事;犯罪。*Two ~s don't make a right.* 兩個錯並不等於對;寃寃相報,永無了時。**'~·doer** *n* person who does ~. 做壞事者;犯罪行者。**'~·doing** *n* [U] doing ~; crime; sin. 犯罪;加害;罪惡;(道德上或法律上的)罪。 **2** [U] injustice; unjust treatment; [C] instance of this; unjust action: 不義;不公正的對待;其實例;不義的行爲: *suffer ~;* 受寃屈;受虐待; *do ~ to sb.* 寃屈某人;虐待某人。*You do me*

~, treat me unjustly. 你對我不公正(寃屈我)。*They have done me a great* ~. 他們對待我非常不公正。*She complained of the* ~*s she had suffered.* 她抱怨所遭受的虐待。 **3** ***in the*** **~,** in the position of being responsible for an error, for having caused a quarrel, etc: 對錯誤,對引起爭執等應負責任;不對;不正當;犯錯誤: *He admitted that he was in the* ~, that the fault, etc was his. 他承認錯誤在他。*They tried to put me in the* ~, to make it seem that the fault, etc was mine. 他們試圖諉過於我。*You are both in the* ~, Each of you is in error. 你們倆都錯了。□ *vt* [VP6A] treat unjustly; be unfair to: 虐待;寃屈;對…不公正: *He* ~*ed me when he said that I was envious.* 他說我嫉妬,是寃枉我了。*His deeply* ~*ed wife deserves our help and sympathy.* 他那深受虐待的妻子值得我們的幫助和同情。 **~·ful** /-fl; -fəl/ *adj* unjust; unlawful: 不正當的;不公正的;不合法的: ~*ful dismissal* (from employment). 不合法的解雇。 **~·fully** /-fəlɪ; -fəlɪ/ *adv* **~·ly** *adv* in a ~ manner (used esp before a *pp*): 不正當地;錯誤地;失常地(尤用於過去分詞之前): ~*ly informed/directed/accused.* 被錯誤地告知的(被導入歧途的;被誣告的)。

wrote /rəʊt; rot/ ➪ write.

wroth /rəʊθ *US:* rɔ:θ; rɔθ/ *adj* (pred only; poet, biblical, or in mod use hum) angry; indignant. (僅用於述語中;詩,聖經體,或現代用法中作詼諧語)憤怒的;憤慨的;義憤的。

wrought /rɔ:t; rɔt/ *pt, pp* of work² **1** beaten into shape: 被打成形的;敲擊成的;鍛的: ~ *iron.* 鍛鐵;熟鐵。➪ *cast iron* at cast¹(3). **2** (archaic or liter) (古或文) ~ ***on/upon sb/sth,*** excited him/it: 使某人(某物)激動;刺激某人(某物): *Their sufferings* ~ *upon our feelings.* 他們所遭受的痛苦使我們情緒激動。➪ *work on/upon sb/sth* at work²(10). **,~-'up** *adj* over-excited; extremely agitated. 過度興奮的;極度激動的。

wrung /rʌŋ; rʌŋ/ ➪ wring.

wry /raɪ; raɪ/ *adj* (wrier, wriest) pulled or twisted out of shape: 扭歪的;歪斜的: *make a wry face,* usu to show disappointment or disgust; 面孔沮喪;拉長面孔(通常表示失望或厭惡); *a wry smile,* a forced smile that indicates disappointment. 苦笑。 **wry·ly** *adv*

wych- (also **wich-, witch-**) /wɪtʃ; wɪtʃ/ *pref* used in names of trees: 用於樹名中: '~*-elm;* 歐洲山楡; '~*-hazel.* 山楡;金縷梅。

Xx

X, x /eks; ɛks/ *n* (*pl* X's, x's /'eksɪz; 'ɛksɪz/) **1** the 24th letter of the English alphabet. 英文字母的第二十四個字母。 **2** symbol for the Roman numeral 10. 羅馬數字之十。➪ App 4. 參看附錄四。 **3** (algebra) first unknown quantity; (fig) factor or influence about which there is uncertainty. (代數)第一個未知數;(喻)未能確定的因素或影響。

xeno·phobia /ˌzenə'fəʊbɪə; ˌzɛnə'fobɪə/ *n* [U] irrational hatred or fear of strangers or foreigners. 陌生恐怖;生客恐怖(對陌生人或外國人的不合理的憎恨或恐怖)。

Xerox /'zɪərɒks; 'zirɑks/ *n, vt* [VP6A] (P) (商標) = photocopy.

Xhosa /'kɔ:zɑ:; 'kozɑ/ *n, adj* (member or language) of the people of *Transkei* /ˌtræn'skaɪ; ˌtræn'skaɪ/ in Southern Africa. (南非川斯凱共和國的)科薩人(的);科薩語(的)。

Xmas /'krɪsməs; 'krɪsməs/ *n* (common abbr, in writing, for) Christmas. (書寫中常用之略語) Christmas。

X-ray /'eks reɪ; 'ɛks're/ *n* short-wave ray that penetrates solids and makes it possible to see into or through them; photograph taken by this means: 愛克斯光;X光;X光照片: (attrib) (形容用法) *have an X-ray (examination);* 照X光(作X光檢查); *an X-ray diagnosis;* X光診斷; *X-ray photography.* X光照相術。□ *vt* [VP6A] examine, treat, photograph, with X-rays. 用X光檢查,治療或照相。

xylo·phone /'zaɪləfəʊn; 'zaɪləˌfon/ *n* musical instrument of parallel wooden bars, graduated in length, which produce different notes when struck with small wooden hammers. 木琴。➪ the illus at percussion. 參看 percussion 之挿圖。

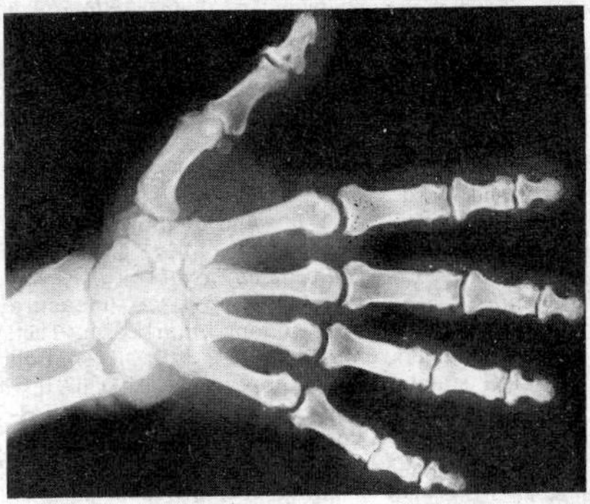

an X-ray photograph of the hand

Yy

Y, y /waɪ; waɪ/ *n* (*pl* Y's, y's /waɪz; waɪz/) the 25th letter of the English alphabet. 英文字母的第二十五個字母。

yacht /jɒt; jɑt/ *n* **1** light sailing-boat built specially for racing. 競賽用的輕快小帆船;輕舟;快艇。 '**~-club** *n* club for ~-owners. 快艇俱樂部。 '**~s·man** /-smən; -smən/ *n* (*pl* -men) person who makes a hobby of sailing. 嗜好駕駛快艇者。 **2** (usu privately-owned, usu motor-driven) vessel kept by a wealthy person for pleasure-cruising. (通常爲私有,由發動機推動)遊艇。□ *vi* [VP2A] travel or race in a ~. 乘遊艇旅遊;作快艇競賽。 **~·ing** *n* [U] the art, practice or sport of sailing ~s. 駕駛快艇或遊艇的技術、實務或競技;快(遊)艇駕駛;快(遊)艇航行。

yah /jɑ:; jɑ/ *int* used to express derision. 呀(用以表示嘲笑)。

ya·hoo /jɑ:'hu:; 'jɑhu/ *n* name given by Swift (in *Gulliver's Travels*) to members of a race of inferior human beings with the habits of animals; hence, detestable person with bestial habits. 雅虎 (Swift 所著 Gulliver's Travels 中的有野獸習性的劣等人); (由此產生)有野獸習性的可惡的人; 人面獸心的人。

yak /jæk; jæk/ *n* long-haired ox, wild or domesticated, of Central Asia. 犛牛(產於中亞,毛長,野生或飼養)。

yam /jæm ; jæm/ *n* [C] **1** (edible tuber of) kinds of tropical climbing plant. 山藥;薯蕷;其可食塊莖。⇨ the illus at vegetable. 參看 vegetable 之插圖。**2** (US) kind of sweet potato. (美)番薯;甘薯。

yam·mer /ˈjæmə(r) ; ˈjæmɚ/ *vi* (colloq) (俗) **1** complain peevishly; whine. 氣憤地抱怨;哭訴。 **2** talk volubly or foolishly. 滔滔不絕地或無聊地談話。

yank /jæŋk ; jæŋk/ (colloq) (俗) *vt* [VP6A, 15A, B] give a sudden sharp pull to: 用力猛拉;突然拉動: *~ out a tooth.* 拔出一顆牙。*Tom ~ed the bedclothes off his young brother and told him to get up.* 湯姆一把拉開他弟弟的被子,叫他起床。□ *n* sudden sharp pull. 突然猛拉。

Yank /jæŋk ; jæŋk/ *n* (sl) (abbr of) Yankee. (俚)爲 Yankee 之略。

Yan·kee /ˈjæŋkɪ ; ˈjæŋkɪ/ *n* **1** native of New England (US). (美國的)新英格蘭人。 **2** (in the American Civil War) native of any of the Northern States. (美國南北戰爭中)北部諸州的人;北方佬。**3** (colloq, in GB, Europe) US citizen: (俗,用於英國、歐洲)美國公民;美國人: (attrib) (形容用法) *~ inventions.* 美國人的發明物。

yap /jæp ; jæp/ *vi* (-pp-) [VP2A] **1** (esp of dogs) utter short, sharp barks. (尤指犬)狂吠;尖聲急吠。 **2** (sl) talk noisily or foolishly: (俚)哇啦哇啦地講;瞎談: *Stop yapping!* 別再瞎談了! □ *n* short, shrill bark. 狂吠;尖聲急吠。

yard[1] /jɑːd ; jɑrd/ *n* **1** (usu unroofed) enclosed or partly enclosed space near or round a building or group of buildings, often paved: (通常無頂篷)房屋附近或周圍的圍地;圍院;院子: *a ˈfarm~;* 農莊的院子; *a ˈcattle-~;* 家畜的圍欄; *the school ~,* used as a playground; (學校的)運動場; (US) area of land laid out as a garden round a house. (美)庭院;庭園。 **2** (usu in compounds) enclosure for a special purpose: (通常用於複合字中)作專門用途的圍地;工作場: *the ˈrailway ~s/ˈmarshalling ~s,* area where trains are made up, where coaches, wagons, etc are stored; 鐵路調車場(貨運火車集結場); *a ˈtan-~,* where tanning is carried on. 製革場。⇨ also *back ~* at back[4](3), *dock~* at dock[1], *ship~* at ship[1](3), *vine~* at vine(2). **3 the Y~,** (colloq abbr for) *New Scotland Y~.* (俗)爲 New Scotland Yard 之略。

yard[2] /jɑːd ; jɑrd/ *n* **1** (⇨ App 5) unit of length, 3 feet or 36 inches: (參看附錄五) 碼 (長度單位,合三呎或卅六吋): *Can you still buy cloth by the ~ in Britain?* 在英國買布仍舊用碼爲單位嗎?**ˌ~-ˈmeasure** *n* rod, tape, etc one ~ long, marked in feet, inches, quarters, etc. 碼尺(指直尺、捲尺等)。**ˈ~·stick** *n* (fig) standard of comparison. (喻)(用作比較的)標準。 **2** long, polelike piece of wood fastened to a mast for supporting and spreading a sail. 帆桁。⇨ the illus at barque. 參看 barque 之插圖。**ˈ~-arm** *n* either end of such a ~. 帆桁的一端;桁端。***man the ~s,*** place men along the ~s, stand along the ~s, as a form of salute. 行進(出)港禮。

yarn /jɑːn ; jɑrn/ *n* **1** [U] fibres (esp of wool) which have been spun for knitting, weaving, etc. 紗;線;(尤指)毛線。**2** [C] (colloq) story; traveller's tale. (俗)故事;奇談;旅行者的故事。***spin a ~,*** tell a story; make up a story: 講故事; 編造故事: *The beggar spun a long ~ about his misfortunes.* 那個乞丐編造了一大篇自己如何遭遇不幸的故事。 □ *vi* [VP2A, C] tell ~s: 講故事: *We stayed up ~ing until midnight.* 我們講故事一直講到午夜才睡。

yar·row /ˈjærəʊ ; ˈjæro/ *n* common perennial herb with flat clusters of small flowers. 西洋蓍草。

yash·mak /ˈjæʃmæk ; jɑʃˈmɑk/ *n* veil worn in public by some Muslim women in some countries. (某些國家回教婦女在公衆場合所戴的)面紗。

yaw /jɔː ; jɔ/ *vi* (of a ship or aircraft) turn unsteadily off the right course. (指船或航空器)偏航;逸出航線。□ *n* such a turn. 偏航;逸出航線。

yawl /jɔːl ; jɔl/ *n* (naut) (航海) **1** sailing-boat with two masts, the second being a short one near the stern. 縱帆快艇(具有二桅,後桅較低)。 **2** ship's boat with four or six oars. (有四或六槳的)船載小艇。

yawn /jɔːn ; jɔn/ *vi* [VP2A, C] **1** take (usu involuntarily) a deep breath with the mouth wide open, as when sleepy or bored. 打呵欠。 **2** be wide open: 張開;裂開: *a ~ing fissure.* 張開的裂縫。*A gulf ~ed at our feet.* 一個深坑在我們腳前豁然展開。□ *n* [C] act of ~ing(1). 打呵欠。

yaws /jɔːz ; jɔz/ *n pl* contagious tropical skin disease. 雅司病;熱帶莓疹。

ye[1] /jiː ; ji/ *pron* (old form of) you: (you 的古字形)你;你們: *Ye fools!* 你們這些傻子! *How d'ye do* /ˌhaʊ djɪˈduː ; ˈhaʊdjəˈdu/? 你好!

ye[2] /jiː ; ji/ *def art* = the (old written form, still seen on signboards over some shops and inns): the 的古書寫形(仍可見於某些商店或旅舍的店招上): *Ye Olde Bull and Bush.* 布爾及布希老店。

yea /jeɪ ; je/ *adv, int* (archaic) yes. (古)是;然。□ *n* aye: 贊成;贊成者: *Yeas and nays,* ayes and noes. 贊成者與反對者。

yeah /jeə ; jɛ/ *adv* (sl) yes. (俚)是。

year /jɜː(r) *US:* jɪər ; jɪr/ *n* **1** time taken by the earth in making one revolution round the sun, about 365¼ days. 太陽年(地球繞行太陽一週所需的時間,約爲 365¼ 天)。 **2** period from 1 January to 31 December (also called 亦稱作 the *calendar ~*): 年;曆年(從一月一日至十二月卅一日): *in the ~ 1865;* 在 1865 年; *last ~;* 去年; *this ~;* 今年; *next ~;* 明年; *the ~ after next;* 後年; *New Y~'s Day,* 1 January. 元旦。***~ in ~ out,*** ~ after ~. 一年一年地;年復一年。***all (the) ~ round,*** at all times of the ~. 一年到頭。***~ of grace...; ~ of our Lord...,*** any named ~ after the birth of Jesus: 耶穌紀元;公元: *in the ~ of our Lord, 1999.* 在公元 1999 年。***the ~ dot,*** (colloq) a very long time ago: (俗)很久很久以前: *I've known her since the ~ dot.* 我認識她很久很久了。 **3** any period of 365 consecutive days: 任何相連的三百六十五天;年;歲;載: *It is just a ~ since I arrived here.* 我到此地恰恰一年了。*He's twenty ~s of age.* 他廿歲了。*He became blind in his twelfth ~,* at the age of 11. 他在十一歲時眼睛瞎了。**ˈ~-book** *n* book issued once a ~ giving information (reports, statistics, etc) esp about trade or commerce. 年鑑。**ˌ~-ˈlong** *adj* continuing for a ~: 連續一年的: *a ~-long struggle.* 連續一年的奮鬪。 **4** period of one ~ associated with sth. 與某事物相關連的一年;…年。***the academic ~,*** for schools, colleges and universities (beginning, in GB and US, in the autumn). 學年(英國和美國始於秋季)。***the financial/fiscal ~,*** (in GB, for making up accounts, etc from the beginning of April). 財政(會計)年度(英國始於四月)。 **5** (*pl*) age; time of life: (複)年齡;年歲: *a boy of ten ~s;* 十歲的男孩; *young for her ~s,* looking young although not young in age; 顯得比她實際年齡年輕; *reach the ~s of discretion.* 達到懂事的年齡。**~·ly** *adj, adv* (taking place) every ~; once a ~. 每年(的);每年一次(的);一年一度(的)。

year·ling /ˈjɜːlɪŋ ; ˈjɪrlɪŋ/ *n* animal between one and two years old: 一歲至兩歲的幼獸: (attrib) (形容用法) *a ~ colt.* 一兩歲的小馬。

yearn /jɜːn ; jɜn/ *vi* [VP3A, 4A] ***~ (for sth/to do sth),*** long for with tender feeling, affection, etc: 渴望;思念;懷念;嚮往: *He ~ed for a sight of the old, familiar faces.* 他渴望一見那些熟悉的老面孔。*He ~ed to return to his native land.* 他渴望返回故鄉。**~·ing** *n* strong desire; tender longing. 渴望;思念。**~·ing·ly** *adv*

yeast /jiːst ; jist/ *n* [U] substance used in brewing beer, and in the making of bread. 酵母;發酵物。**~y** *adj* frothy like ~. 似酵母般多泡沫的。

yell /jel ; jɛl/ *vi, vt* **1** [VP2A, C] utter a loud sharp cry or cries as of pain, excitement, etc:

號叫；呼喊：~ *with fright/laughter.* 驚恐得大聲喊叫(高聲大笑)。 **2** [VP6A, 15B] **~ *sth (out),*** say in a ~ing voice: 喊出；大聲說出；叫着說：~ *(out) an order/oath;* 大聲發布命令(宣誓)；~ *one's defiance.* 大聲抗議。□ *n* loud sharp cry: 大喊；號叫：*a ~ of terror;* 恐怖的叫喊；*the college ~,* (US) particular kind of shout or cheer used at a college to encourage a team, etc. (美)大學啦啦隊助威的喊聲。*They greeted us with ~s of hate.* 他們以憤恨的喊叫聲迎接我們。

yel·low /ˈjeləʊ; ˈjɛlo/ *n, adj* **1** (of) the colour of gold or the yolk of a hen's egg. 黃；黃色；黃色的。**~ fever,** infectious tropical disease causing the skin to turn ~. 黃熱病。**ˈ~-flag** *n* flag coloured ~ displayed by a ship or hospital which is in quarantine. 黃旗(表示船隻或醫院正在檢役期間者)。**the ~ press,** newspapers which present news in a sensational way. 黃色報刊(以聳人聽聞的方式報導新聞者)。 **2** (often 常作 **ˈ~-bellied**) (colloq) cowardly: (俗)懦弱的；卑怯的：*He has a ~ streak in him.* 他有點膽小。□ *vt, vi* [VP6A, 2A] (cause to) become ~: (使)變黃：*The leaves of the book were ~ed/had ~ed with age.* 書葉因年久而變黃了。*The leaves of the trees are ~ing.* 樹上的葉子正變爲黃色。**~·ish** /-ɪʃ; -ɪʃ/ *adj* rather ~. 微黃的；帶黃色的。**~·ness** *n*

yelp /jelp; jɛlp/ *vi* [VP2A], *n* (utter a) short, sharp cry (of pain, anger, excitement, etc): (發出)(痛苦、憤怒、興奮等的)叫嗥：*The dog ~ed/gave a ~ when I trod on its paw.* 當我踩到那隻狗的爪子時，它發出了嗥叫聲。

yen¹ /jen; jɛn/ *n* (*pl* unchanged) unit of currency in Japan. (複數不變)圓(日本的幣制單位)。

yen² /jen; jɛn/ *n* **~ *(for),*** (colloq) yearning (for sth). (俗)熱望；渴望。□ *vi* yearn (*to do* sth). 渴望；熱望(接不定詞)。

yeo·man /ˈjəʊmən; ˈjomən/ *n* (*pl* -men) **1** (hist) working farmer who owned his land (contrasted with tenant farmers and those who own large farms which they did not work themselves). (史)自耕農(與佃農及地主相對)。 **~ service,** long and efficient service; help in time of need. 長期而有效的勤務；緊急時期的援助。 **2 *~ of signals,*** (GB) naval petty officer in the branch concerned with signalling by visual means (flags, etc); (US) petty officer with clerical duties. (英)(海軍的)信號士官；(美)文書士官。 **3 *Y~ of the Guard,*** (GB) member of a royal bodyguard with ceremonial duties at the Tower of London, and else-where on special occasions. (英)英國王室的衛士。**4** member of the ~ry. 義勇騎兵；志願騎兵。**~ry** /-rɪ; -rɪ/ *n* (hist) (collective for) volunteer cavalry force raised from farmers, etc. (史)(集合用法)(從農民等中徵召的)義勇騎兵隊；志願騎兵隊。

yes /jes; jɛs/ *particle* (contrasted with *no*) expressing agreement, affirmation, consent, etc: (與no相對)是；然：*'Can you read this?' 'Yes.'* '你能讀這個嗎？' '我能。' Note that *yes* is used in answer to an interrogative-negative if the complete answer is affirmative: 注意：yes 用於答覆答案是肯定的否定問句：*'Don't you like it?'—'Yes'* (= 'Yes, I do like it') '你不喜歡它嗎？'—'我喜歡。' *'Isn't she beautiful!'—'Yes, isn't she?'* '她不是很漂亮嗎？'—'是的，她很漂亮，不是嗎？' *'Waiter!'—'Yes, sir.'* (= 'What do you want, sir?') '堂倌！'—'是的，先生。' (= '要什麼，先生？') □ *n* [C] affirmation; acceptance: 是；同意；接受；贊成：*Answer with a plain 'Yes' or 'No'.* 明白回答我 '是' 或 '不是' ('同意' 或 '不同意')。

yes·ter- /ˈjestə(r); ˈjɛstɚ/ *pref* (on) the day, year, etc before this, chiefly poet except in *~day* (⇨ below): 表示昨日，去年等義(除下面的 yesterday 外，主要爲詩中用語)：*Where are the snows of ~year?* 去年白雪今何在？

yes·ter·day /ˈjestədɪ; ˈjɛstɚdɪ/ *adv, n* (on) the day just past; (on) the day before today: (在)昨天；昨日：*He arrived ~.* 他昨天到了。*Y~ was Sunday.* 昨天是禮拜天。*Where's ~'s (news)paper?* 昨天的報紙在那裏？*Why were you away from work the day before ~?* 前天你爲何未上班？*Where were you ~ morning/afternoon/evening?* 昨天早晨(下午，晚上)你在何處？ (Cf 參較 *last night.*) *She left home ~ week,* eight days ago. 她是上星期的昨天(八天前)離開家的。

yet /jet; jɛt/ *adv* **1** (in neg and conditional contexts and in contexts indicating ignorance or uncertainty; usu in end position, but also immediately after *not*; ⇨ already(2)) by this or that time; up to now; up to then: (用於否定及條件的文句中，並用於表示不知或不確定的文句中；通常用於句末，亦可緊接在not之後)到此時；到那時；至今；至當時：*They are not here yet/not yet here.* 他們還沒有到(尙未來此)。*We have had no news from him yet.* 我們還沒有接到他的消息。*We have not yet had news from him.* 我們還沒有接到他的消息。*At 2 o'clock they had not yet decided how to spend the afternoon.* 到兩點鐘他們尙未決定如何消磨那個下午。*I wonder whether they have finished the work yet.* 我不知道他們現在是否已做完那件工作。 **2** (in interr and neg contexts; ⇨ already and still) so far; up to this/that time: (用於疑問句及否定句中)到目前爲止；至這時；至那時：*Has your brother arrived yet?* 你哥哥(弟弟)到了嗎？ *Need you go yet?* 你需要去了嗎？*We needn't do it just yet.* 此刻我們無須做那事。 **3** (in affirm sentences) still: (用於肯定句中)還；仍；更；益發：*Be thankful you are yet alive* (*Still* is the more usu word). 你仍然還活着，眞該感謝上蒼(still 比 yet 更常用)。*Go at once while there is yet time,* while it is not too late. 趕快去，還來得及。*This problem is yet* (= still) *more difficult.* 這個問題益發困難了。*I have yet* (= still) *more exciting news for you.* 我還有更令人興奮的消息告訴你。 **4** at some future time; before all is over: 在未來某一時間；遲早；早晚：*The enemy may win yet/may yet win if we relax our efforts.* 如果我們鬆懈下來，敵人遲早會獲得勝利的。*He may surprise us all yet.* 他總有一天會讓我們大家驚奇。 **5 *as yet,*** up to now/then: 到現在(那時)爲止：*As yet we have/had not made any plans for the holidays.* 到目前(那時)爲止，我們還沒有計畫如何度假。*The scheme has worked well as yet.* 到目前爲止，那項計畫進行順利。 ***nor yet,*** (liter) and not even: (文)甚至也不；而且也不：*The book is not well written—nor yet is it accurate.* 那本書寫得不好—而且也不精確。□ *conj* but at the same time; nevertheless: 然而；可是：*She's vain and foolish, and yet people like her.* 她自負而愚蠢，然而人們喜歡她。*He worked hard, yet he failed.* 他努力工作，可是他失敗了。 *It is strange, yet (it is) true.* (它)雖然奇怪，却是眞實的。*He's a wealthy, yet honest, businessman.* 他是一位富有而又正直的商人。

yeti /ˈjetɪ; ˈjɛtɪ/ *n* name of a hairy, man-like animal reported to live in the highest part of the Himalayas. 雪人(傳說生活在喜馬拉雅山最高處，似人而多毛的動物)。

yew /juː; ju/ *n* [C] **ˈyew(-tree),** evergreen, berry-bearing tree with dark-green leaves, often used for garden hedges; [U] wood of this tree (formerly used for making bows). 紫杉；水松(常用做庭園之樹籬)；紫杉木；水松木(昔時用以製弓)。

Yid·dish /ˈjɪdɪʃ; ˈjɪdɪʃ/ *n* [U] international Jewish language, a form of old German with words borrowed from several modern languages, used by Jews in or from Eastern or Central Europe (*note:* the language used in Israel is modern Hebrew). 意地希語(中歐或東歐的猶太人所使用的國際語，爲一種古日耳曼語，並借用數種近代語的字彙。注意：現在以色列使用的語言爲近代希伯來語)。

yield /jiːld; jild/ *vt, vi* **1** [VP6A] give a natural product, a result or profit: 生產；出產；生：*trees* that ~ fruit; 結果的樹; investments ~ing 10 per cent. 生息百分之十的投資。 **2** [VP2A, 3A, 6A, 15A, B] ~ ***(to sb / sth),*** give way (to); cease opposition: 讓步;屈服;不再反對: *We will never ~ to force.* 我們決不會向暴力屈服。 *The disease ~ed to treatment.* 該病經治療後痊癒(減輕)了。 *He ~ed to temptation.* 他屈服於誘惑之下。 ***~ (up) sth (to sb),*** give up; surrender: 放棄;棄守: *~ a fort;* 放棄要塞; *~ ground to the enemy.* 將陣地放棄給敵人。 ***~ up the ghost,*** (liter or rhet) die. (文或修辭)死。 □ *n* [C, U] amount produced: 生產量;獲益率;產出率;收益: *a good ~ of wheat.* 小麥的豐收。*What is the ~ per acre?* 每畝產量若干? *The ~s on his shares have decreased this year,* The dividends are lower. 他的股票今年的紅利降低了。 **~·ing** *adj* easily giving way or bending; (fig) not obstinate. 易變形的; 易彎曲的;(喻)不固執的; 讓步的; 屈從的。 **~·ing·ly** *adv*

yip·pee /ˈjɪpɪ ; ˈjɪpi/ *int* cry of joy or elation. 表示歡欣鼓舞的歡呼聲。

yob /jɒb ; jɑb/, **yobo, yobbo** /ˈjɒbəʊ ; ˈjɑbo/ *n* (GB sl) idle, objectionable person. (英俚)遊手好閒而令人討厭的人。

yodel /ˈjəʊdl ; ˈjodḷ/ *vt, vi* (-ll-; US also -l-) sing (a song), utter a musical call, with frequent changes from the normal voice to high falsetto notes, in the manner of Swiss mountaineers. 用眞假嗓音常常互換而唱或呼喚 (如瑞士高山居民的唱法); 以岳得爾調唱(歌)。□ *n* ~ling song or call. 用此種方式所唱的歌或所作的呼喚;岳得爾調。 **~·ler** (US also **~er**) *n* person who ~s. 用岳得爾調歌唱或呼喚者。

yoga /ˈjəʊgə ; ˈjogə/ *n* [U] **1** Hindu system of meditation and self-control intended to produce mystical experience and the union of the individual soul with the universal spirit. 瑜伽;瑜伽術(印度的冥思及自制法,旨在產生神秘經驗及天人合一)。 **2** system of physical exercises and breathing-control. 瑜伽工夫(一種運動身體及控制呼吸的方法);瑜伽功。 **yogi** /ˈjəʊgɪ ; ˈjogi/ *n* (*pl* ~s) teacher of, expert in, ~(1). 瑜伽派教師;精於瑜伽術者。

yo·gurt, yo·ghurt, yo·ghourt /ˈjɒgət *US:* ˈjəʊgərt ; ˈjogɚt/ *n* [U] thick fermented liquor made from milk. (濃厚的)酵母乳;酸乳酪。

yo-heave-ho /ˌjəʊ ˈhiːv həʊ ; ˈjoˈhivˈho/ *int* cry (formerly) used by sailors when pulling together (eg to raise a sail). 唷唏唷(往昔水手們一同揚帆等時的喊叫聲)。

yoke /jəʊk ; jok/ *n* **1** shaped piece of wood placed across the necks of oxen pulling a cart, plough, etc. 牛軛;軛。⇨ harness. **2** (*pl* unchanged) two oxen working together: (複數不變)共同工作的一對牛;共軛牛: *five ~ of oxen.* 五對共軛牛。**3** (Roman history) arch of three spears (a symbol of the ~ placed on oxen) under which defeated enemies were made to pass; (羅馬史)軛門(三隻矛做成的拱門,做爲軛的象徵,戰敗的敵人被迫從下面穿過); hence, 由此產生, (fig) (喻) *pass / come under the ~,* acknowledge and accept defeat; 承認失敗; 屈從; *throw off the ~* (of servitude, etc), rebel; refuse to obey; 反抗;拒絕服從;擺脫奴役等; *the ~ of a tyrant.* 暴君的奴役。 **4** shaped piece of wood to fit a person's shoulders and support a pail at each end. 軛狀木扁擔。 **5** (dressmaking) part of a garment fitting round the shoulders and from which the rest hangs; top part of a skirt, fitting the hips. (女服縫製)上衣的抵肩; 裙子的腰。□ *vt* [VP6A, 15A] **1** put a ~ on (oxen): 加軛於(牛); 用軛把(牛)連接於: *~ oxen together;* 用軛連起牛; *~ oxen to a plough.* 用軛把牛連接於犂。 **2** unite: 使結合;使聯合: *~d to an unwilling partner;* 與一位不情願的夥伴合作; *~d in marriage.* 結婚;聯姻。

yokel /ˈjəʊkl ; ˈjokḷ/ *n* simple-minded countryman. 頭腦簡單的鄉下人;鄉下佬;土包子。

yolk /jəʊk ; jok/ *n* [C, U] yellow part of an egg: 蛋黃: *Beat up the ~s of three eggs.* 攪勻三個蛋黃。

yon /jɒn ; jɑn/ *adj, adv* (archaic or dial) (古或方) = yonder.

yon·der /ˈjɒndə(r) ; ˈjɑndɚ/ *adj, adv* (liter) (that is, that can be seen) over there: (文) (在,見於)那邊(的);(在,見於)彼處(的);(在,見於)遠處(的): *~ group of trees.* 遠處的樹叢。

yore /jɔː(r) ; jor/ *n* [U] ***of ~,*** long ago: 很久以前: *in days of ~.* 在很久以前的時代。

you /juː ; ju/ *pron* **1** the person(s) addressed: 你;你們: *You are my friend(s).* 你(們)是我的朋友。*Does he know you?* 他認識你嗎? *This is for you.* 這是給你的。 **2** (colloq; used as an *impers pron*) one; anyone: (俗;用作無人稱代名詞)一個人;任何人: *It is much easier to cycle with the wind behind you.* 順着風騎單車容易得多。*You never know,* One can never be certain about things. 事情難以逆料(或:誰也沒法預料)。 **3** (preceding a *n,* esp in vocatives): (置於名詞前,尤其用作直接稱呼語): *You boys!* 你們男孩子們! *You over there!* 喂,你! (in exclamations): (用於驚嘆句中): *You bloody fool!* 你這個大傻瓜!

you'd /juːd ; jud/ = you had; you would.

you'll /juːl ; jul/ = you will.

young /jʌŋ ; jʌŋ/ *adj* (-nger, /-ŋgə(r) ; -ŋgɚ/, -ngest /-ŋgɪst ; -ŋgɪst/) **1** (contrasted with *old*) not far advanced in life, growth, development, etc; of recent birth or origin: (與 old 相對)年幼的;年輕的;幼小的: *a ~ woman / tree / animal / nation, etc.* 年輕的女人(幼小的樹; 小動物; 新興國家等)。 **2** still near its beginning: 仍然接近開始階段的;初期的: *The evening / century is still ~.* 夜還不深(本世紀剛開始不久)。 **3** ***the ~er,*** (used before or after a person's name, to distinguish that person from another; contrasted with *elder*): (用於人名前或後,以便和同姓名的人區別;與 elder 相對): *the ~er Pitt;* 小皮特; *Pliny the Y~er.* 小蒲林尼。 ***be sb's ~er,*** be ~er than him. 較某人年輕。 **4** (used before a person's name to distinguish esp a son from his father): (用於人名之前,尤用以分別父子): *Y~ Jones is always ready to help his old parents.* 小瓊斯時時準備幫助他年老的雙親。 **5** (as a familiar or condescending form of address): (用作親熱或屈尊的稱呼): *Now listen to me, ~ man / my ~ lady!* 現在聽我說,年輕人(我的小姐)! **6** having little practice or experience (in sth): (對某事物)不熟練的;無經驗的: *~ in crime.* 無犯罪經驗的。 **7** ***~ and old,*** everyone. 每一個人; 年輕的和年老的。 **the ~,** ~ people; children: 年輕人;青年;孩子們: *books for the ~.* 青少年讀物。□ *n* [U] offspring; ~ ones (of animals and birds): 後裔;(鳥獸的)雛;仔: *The cat fought fiercely to defend its ~,* its ~ offspring. 那隻貓拚命打鬥以保護其幼仔。*Some animals quickly desert their ~.* 有些動物很快地就不理它們的幼仔了。 ***with ~,*** (of an animal) pregnant. (指動物)有孕的。 **~·ish** /ˈjʌŋɪʃ ; ˈjʌŋɪʃ/ *adj* fairly ~; somewhat ~. 尙年輕的;頗幼小的。 **~·ster** /ˈjʌŋstə(r) ; ˈjʌŋstɚ/ *n* child, youth. 兒童;少年;青年。

your /jɔː(r) *US:* jʊər ; jʊr/ *adj* **1** belonging to, relating to, you: 你(們)的;屬於你(們)的;有關你(們)的: *Show me ~ hands.* 把你兩隻手伸出來讓我看看。

yoked oxen

Y

You'll see the post office on ~ right, ie ~ right side. 你將會在你的右邊看見郵局。 **2** (often indicating polite interest, or disapproval or contempt, or used to suggest that sth is not so good, remarkable, etc as is claimed): (常表示禮貌的關心，或表示不贊成或輕視，或用以含示某事物不如所說的那麼好或那麼出色): *So this is what ~ experts said, is it?* 原來這就是你們專家所說的，是嗎？ *This is ~ famous English beer, is it?* 這就是你們英國著名的啤酒，是嗎？

you're /jʊə(r) ; jur/ = you are.

yours /jɔːz *US:* jʊərz ; jurz/ *pred adj, pron* **1** of you: 你的;你們的: *Is that book ~?* 那本書是你的嗎？ *I borrowed a book of ~.* 我向你借過一本書。 **2** (at the end of a letter): (用於信函的結尾處): *~ truly／sincerely／faithfully.* 信尾套語，相當於中文書信中的'敬啓;敬上' 等。

your·self /jɔːˈself *US:* jʊərˈself ; jurˈsɛlf/ (*pl* -selves /-ˈselvz ; -ˈsɛlvz/ *reflex pron: Did you hurt ~?* 你弄傷了自己嗎？ □ *emphat pron: You ~ said so.* 你自己這樣說的。*You said so ~.* 你自己這樣說的。 ***(all) by ~,*** **(a)** alone. 獨自;單獨。 **(b)** without help. 獨力;靠自己。

youth /juːθ ; juθ/ *n* (*pl* ~s /juːðz ; juðz/) **1** [U] the state or time of being young: 青春;青春期;青少年時代: *the enthusiasm of ~;* 青春時代的熱忱; *the friends of one's ~;* 少年時代的朋友; *in my ~,* when I was young. 當我年輕時。 **2** [C] young man: 少年;青年: *As a ~ he showed no promise of becoming a great pianist.* 他在少年時代未顯示出將來會變成一位偉大的鋼琴家。*Half a dozen ~s were standing at the street corner.* 有六個青年站在街角。 **3** [U] (collective *sing*, with *pl v*) young men and women: (集合單數,與複數動詞連用)青年男女;青年們: *the ~ of the nation;* 全國青年; *a '~ hostel,* ⇨ hostel; 青年招待所; *a '~ centre／club,* club (usu provided by a voluntary organization) for the leisure time activities of young people. 青年活動中心(俱樂部)。 **~·ful** /-fl ; -fəl/ *adj* young; having the qualities, etc, of young people: 年少的;青春的;有青年之性質等的: *a ~ful appearance.* 青春的外貌。 **~·fully** /-fəlɪ ; -fəlɪ/ *adv* **~·ful·ness** *n*

you've /juːv ; juv/ = you have.

yowl /jaʊl ; jaʊl/ *vi* howl; wail. 嚎叫;嚎咷;慟哭。

yo-yo /ˈjəʊjəʊ ; ˈjo,jo/ *n* toy in the shape of a top with a groove for string, the top moving up and down the string by movement of the fingers: 悠悠;空鐘(形似陀螺的玩具,上有溝槽,可使之嵌入細索,以手操縱該索,此玩具卽沿索上下移動): *The exchange rate is going up and down like a ~.* 外滙的滙率就像悠悠一樣忽上忽下。

yule /juːl ; jul/ *n* (also 亦作 **'~-tide**) (archaic) Christmas. (古)聖誕節;聖誕季節。 **'~-log** *n* log of wood burnt on Christmas Eve. 聖誕柴(聖誕前夕焚燒的木柴)。

Zz

Z, z /zed *US:* ziː ; zi/ *n* (*pl* **Z's, z's** /zedz *US:* ziːz ; ziz/) the last letter of the English alphabet. 英文字母的最後一個字母。

zany /ˈzeɪnɪ ; ˈzenɪ/ *n* (*pl* -nies) half-witted person; foolish joker. 遲鈍者;糊塗蟲;愚笨的詼諧者。□ *adj* foolish; mad. 愚笨的;荒唐的。

zap /zæp ; zæp/ *vt* (-pp-) [VP6A] (sl) attack; defeat. (俚)攻擊;打敗。

zeal /ziːl ; zil/ *n* [U] energy and enthusiasm: 熱忱;熱心: *show ~ for a cause;* 顯示對某主義熱心; *work with great ~.* 非常熱心地工作。 **~·ous** /ˈzeləs ; ˈzɛləs/ *adj* full of, acting with, showing, ~: 熱心的;熱忱的;充滿熱心的;熱心行事的;顯示熱心的: *~ous to please one's employer;* 熱中於討好雇主; *~ous for liberty and freedom.* 熱心爭取自由。 **~·ous·ly** *adv*

zealot /ˈzelət ; ˈzɛlət/ *n* person who shows great and uncompromising enthusiasm for a religion, a party, a cause, etc; fanatic. 對宗教、黨派、主義等極爲熱心者;狂熱分子。 **~ry** /-trɪ ; -trɪ/ *n* [U].

zebra /ˈziːbrə ; ˈzibrə/ *n* horse-like wild animal of Africa, with dark stripes on its body. 斑馬。⇨ the illus at large. 參看 large 之挿圖。 **,~ 'crossing,** street-crossing marked with broad white stripes, at which pedestrians have priority over traffic. (行人優先通過的)斑馬線。⇨ panda.

zebu /ˈziːbjuː ; ˈzibju/ *n* domestic animal like an ox, with a hump on its shoulders, used in Asia and E Africa. 瘤牛(似牛家畜,肩上有瘤,亞洲及東非洲用作馱獸)。

zee /ziː ; zi/ *n* (US) name of the letter z. (美)字母 z。

Zen /zen ; zɛn/ *n* [U] form of Buddhism asserting that enlightenment comes from meditation and intuition, with less dependence upon the scriptures. (佛敎的)禪宗(强調打坐及專念卽可修成正果)。

zen·ith /ˈzenɪθ *US:* ˈziːnɪθ ; ˈzinɪθ/ *n* part of the sky directly overhead; (fig) highest point (of one's fame, fortunes, etc): 天空的正上方部分;天頂;(喩)(名譽、幸運等的)最高點;頂點: *at the ~ of his career.* 在他事業的頂點。 **~al** *adj: ~al projection,* map obtained by projecting²(6). 天頂投影(地)圖。⇨ nadir. ⇨ the illus at projection. 參看 projection 之挿圖。

zephyr /ˈzefə(r) ; ˈzɛfə/ *n* west wind; (poet) soft, gentle breeze. 西風;(詩)和風;微風。

zep·pe·lin /ˈzepəlɪn ; ˈzɛpəlɪn/ *n* large dirigible used by the Germans in World War I. 齊柏林飛船(德國人在第一次世界大戰中使用的飛船)。

zero /ˈzɪərəʊ ; ˈzɪro/ *n* **1** the figure 0 ; nought. 數字 '零' ;0。⇨ App 4 (1, *note 2*). 參看附錄四第一項註 2。 **2** the point between the positive (+) and negative (—) on a scale, esp on a thermometer (⇨ App 5): 零點;零位;(尤指溫度計上的)零度(參看附錄五): *The thermometer fell to ~ last night.* 昨天夜裡溫度計降到了零度。*It was ten degrees below ~* (eg —10°C or —10°F). 氣溫是零下十度。 **absolute ~,** ⇨ absolute(5). **'~ hour,** (mil) time at which operations are to begin: (軍)行動或攻擊開始時刻;零時: *Z~ hour was 3am.* 攻擊開始的時刻是淩晨三點鐘。□ *vi* [VP2C] **~ in (on),** (sl) fix attention (on). (俚)集中注意力(於)。

zest /zest ; zɛst/ *n* [U] **1** great interest or pleasure; gusto: 强烈的興趣;熱心: *He entered into our plans with ~.* 他熱心地參加我們的計畫。 **2** (often with *indef art*) pleasing or stimulating quality or flavour: (常與不定冠詞連用)可愛性;刺激性;風味;興味: *The possibility of danger gave (a) ~ to the adventure.* 危險的可能發生增加了那次冒險的刺激性。

zig·zag /ˈzɪgzæg ; ˈzɪgzæg/ *n* [C] line or path which turns right and left alternately at sharp (equal or unequal) angles: 鋸齒形的線或道路;之字形: (attrib) (形容用法) *a ~ path up the hillside.* 山坡上的一條曲折小徑。□ *adv* in a ~. 成鋸齒形地;曲折地。□ *vi* (-gg-) go in a ~: 曲折地前進: *The drunken man ~ged down the street.* 那個醉鬼歪歪倒倒地沿街走去。

zinc /zɪŋk ; zɪŋk/ *n* [U] hard, bluish-white metal (symbol **Zn**) used in alloys and in coating iron sheets and wire to give protection against rust. 鋅(金屬元素,化學符號 Zn, 用來製合金,或鍍於鐵皮或鐵絲外面,以防止生銹)。

zing /zɪŋ ; zɪŋ/ *n* [U] (sl) vigour; energy. (俚)精力;活力;生命力。

Z

zin·nia /ˈzɪnɪə ; ˈzɪnɪə/ *n* kinds of garden plant with bright-coloured flowers. 百日草；魚尾菊(園藝植物)。

Zion /ˈzaɪən ; ˈzaɪən/ *n* the Jewish homeland, esp as a symbol of Judaism; Israel. 錫安山(猶太人故鄉，尤指作爲猶太人之宗教及其文化的象徵)；以色列。**~·ism** /-ɪzəm ; -ˌɪzəm/ *n* (hist) political movement for the establishment of an independent state for the Jews; (mod use) movement concerned with the development of Israel as a Jewish political and religious State. (史)猶太人復國運動；(現代用法)以色列猶太化運動 (使以色列成爲猶太人的政治及宗教國家的運動)。**~·ist** /-ɪst ; -ɪst/ *adj, n*

zip /zɪp ; zɪp/ *n* **1** sound as of a bullet going through the air, or of the sudden tearing of cloth. (如彈丸飛過天空或突然撕裂布帛的)嘶嘶聲；颼颼聲；嘘嘘聲；咻咻聲。 **2** (sl) vigour; energy. (俚)精力；活力；生命力。 □ *vt* (-pp-) [VP6A, 15B, 22] open sth (***zip sth open***) or close sth (***zip sth up***) by means of a zip-fastener: 拉開或拉上(某物上的)拉鍊： *She zipped her bag open/up.* 她拉開(拉上)她袋子的拉鍊。**zip·per, zip-fastener** *nn* device for locking together two toothed metal or plastic edges by means of a sliding tab, used for fastening articles of clothing, bags, etc. 拉鍊。

zip code /ˈzɪp kəʊd ; ˈzɪpˌkod/ *n* (US) (美)＝postcode.

zither /ˈzɪðə(r) ; ˈzɪθɚ/ *n* musical instrument with many strings on a flat sounding-board, played with a plectrum or the fingers. 齊特琴；扁琴(在扁平的共鳴盤上有許多琴絃的樂器，以手指或撥子彈奏)。

zo·diac /ˈzəʊdɪæk ; ˈzodɪˌæk/ *n* **1** belt of the heavens extending about 8° on each side of the path followed by the sun and containing the path of the principal planets, divided into 12 equal parts known as the ***signs of the ~***, named after 12 groups of stars. 黃道帶(天空中太陽行經的路線，向兩側各延伸8度所成的區域，包括主要行星的運行軌道，分爲十二等分，稱爲十二宮 signs of the zodiac, 依十二星羣而得名)。 **2** diagram of the ~, used in astrology. 黃道十二宮圖(用於占星學中)。

zom·bie /ˈzɒmbɪ ; ˈzɑmbɪ/ *n* (colloq) dull, slow, lifeless, mindless person. (俗)呆鈍、遲緩、無生氣、沒腦筋的人；傻瓜；呆子。

zone /zəʊn ; zon/ *n* **1** belt, band or stripe going round, and distinguished by colour, appearance, etc. 環帶；圈。 **2** one of the five parts into which the earth's surface is divided by imaginary lines parallel to the equator (the ˈ*torrid, N & S* ˈ*temperate*, and the ˈ*frigid ~s*). (地球上的)帶；地帶(以想像中與赤道平行之線，分地球爲五個地帶，即熱帶、北溫帶、南溫帶、北寒帶、南寒帶)。 **3** area with particular features, purpose or use: (具有某特徵、目的或用途的)地區；區域： *the war ~;* 戰區； *within the ~ of submarine activity*, ie where, during a war, submarines are active; 在潛水艇活動的區域內； *the* ˈ*danger ~;* 危險區； *a* ˈ*parking ~;* 停車區(場)； *smokeless ~s*, (usu urban) areas in which only smokeless fuels may be used (in homes, factories, etc). 無烟區(通常指城市內禁燃發烟燃料的區域)。 **4** (US) particular area in which certain postal, telephone, etc rates are charged. (美)(便於計算郵費、電話費等的)區；段；郵區。 □ *vt* [VP6A] encircle, mark, with, into, or as with a ~ or ~s; divide into ~s. 用或似用帶圍起或標示出；把…分成若干區域。**zonal** /ˈzəʊnl ; ˈzonl/ *adj* relating to, arranged in, ~s. 環帶的；地帶的；劃分爲區域的；排列或形成環帶的。**zon·ing** *n* [U] (in planning urban areas) designation of areas for various purposes, eg shopping, residential, industrial. (都市計畫中)分區；區域劃分(指定某某地區爲商業區、住宅區、工業區等)。

zonked /zɒŋkt ; zɑŋkt/ *pred adj* ~ ***out***, (US sl) drugged; drunk. (美俚)服過痲醉藥的；喝醉了的。

zoo /zuː ; zu/ *n* zoological gardens: 動物園： *take the children to the zoo.* 帶孩子們去動物園。

zo·ol·ogy /zəʊˈɒlədʒɪ ; zoˈɑlədʒɪ/ *n* [U] science of the structure, forms and distribution of animals. 動物學。 **zo·ol·ogi·cal** /ˌzəʊəˈlɒdʒɪkl ; ˌzoəˈlɑdʒɪkl/ *adj* of ~. 動物學的。 **zoological gardens**, park (usu public) in which many kinds of animals are kept for exhibition. 動物園。 **zo·ol·ogist** /zəʊˈɒlədʒɪst ; zoˈɑlədʒɪst/ *n* expert in ~. 動物學家。

zoom /zuːm ; zum/ *n* **1** [U] (low, deep humming sound of the) sudden upward flight of an aircraft. 飛機的陡直上昇；攢昇；攢昇時發出的低沉嗡嗡聲。 **2** ~ **lens**, (on a camera), one with continuously variable focal length. (照相機上)有連續不同焦距的鏡頭；可變焦距鏡頭。⇨ the illus at camera. 參看 camera 之插圖。 □ *vi* [VP2A, C] **1** (of aircraft) move upwards at high speed: (指飛機)陡直地上昇；攢昇： (fig, colloq) (喻，俗) *Prices ~ed*, rose sharply. 物價直線上昇了。 **2** (of a camera with a ~ lens): (指有可變焦距鏡頭的照相機)： *~ in/out*, cause the object being photographed to appear nearer/further. 將畫面放大(縮小)；使物體形像變近(遠)。

zo·ophyte /ˈzəʊəfaɪt ; ˈzoəˌfaɪt/ *n* plant-like sea animal (eg a sea anemone, coral). 似植物的海生動物(如海葵、珊瑚蟲)。

zoot suit /ˈzuːt suːt ; ˈzut ˌsut/ *n* one with a knee-length jacket and tight-fitting trousers. 阻特裝(一

the signs of the zodiac

種上衣長達膝部而褲子窄狹的服裝)。

zuc·chini /zʊˈkiːnɪ ; zuˈkinɪ/ *n* (*pl* ~s or unchanged 複數加 s 或不變) (esp US) (尤美) = courgette. ⇨ the illus at vegetable. 參看 vegetable 之插圖。

Zulu /ˈzuːluː ; ˈzulu/ *n, adj* (member or language) of the people of *Kwazulu* /ˌkwɑːˈzuːluː;ˌkwɑˈzulu/ (formerly 昔作 *Zululand*) in South Africa. (非洲南部之)祖魯人(的);祖魯語(的)。

Appendix 1 IRREGULAR VERBS
附錄一 不規則動詞表

Note: Full phonetic transcriptions of the irregular past tense and past participle forms are given in the entries on the infinitive forms in the dictionary.

注意：不規則動詞過去式及過去分詞的注音，均列於本辭典各首字之不定詞形式中。

Infinitive 不定詞	**Past Tense** 過去式	**Past Participle** 過去分詞
abide	abode, abided	abode, abided
arise	arose	arisen
awake	awoke	awaked, awoken
be	was	been
bear	bore	borne
beat	beat	beaten
become	became	become
befall	befell	befallen
beget	begot	begotten
begin	began	begun
behold	beheld	beheld
bend	bent	bent
bereave	bereaved, bereft	bereaved, bereft
beseech	besought	besought
beset	beset	beset
bet	bet, betted	bet, betted
betake	betook	betaken
bethink	bethought	bethought
bid	bade, bid	bidden, bid
bind	bound	bound
bite	bit	bitten, bit
bleed	bled	bled
blend	blended, blent	blended, blent
bless	blessed, blest	blessed, blest
blow	blew	blown
break	broke	broken
breed	bred	bred
bring	brought	brought
broadcast	broadcast, broadcasted	broadcast, broadcasted
build	built	built
burn	burnt, burned	burnt, burned
burst	burst	burst
buy	bought	bought
cast	cast	cast
catch	caught	caught
chide	chided, chid	chided, chidden
choose	chose	chosen
cleave	clove, cleft	cloven, cleft
cling	clung	clung
clothe	clothed, clad	clothed, clad
come	came	come
cost	cost	cost
creep	crept	crept
crow	crowed, crew	crowed
cut	cut	cut
dare	dared, durst	dared
deal	dealt	dealt
dig	dug	dug
dive	dived; (US) dove	dived
do	did	done
draw	drew	drawn
dream	dreamt, dreamed	dreamt, dreamed
drink	drank	drunk
drive	drove	driven
dwell	dwelt	dwelt
eat	ate	eaten
fall	fell	fallen
feed	fed	fed
feel	felt	felt
fight	fought	fought
find	found	found
flee	fled	fled

fling	flung	flung
fly	flew	flown
forbear	forbore	forborne
forbid	forbade, forbad	forbidden
forecast	forecast, forecasted	forecast, forecasted
foreknow	foreknew	foreknown
foresee	foresaw	foreseen
foretell	foretold	foretold
forget	forgot	forgotten
forgive	forgave	forgiven
forsake	forsook	forsaken
forswear	forswore	forsworn
freeze	froze	frozen
gainsay	gainsaid	gainsaid
get	got	got; (US) gotten
gild	gilded, gilt	gilded
gird	girded, girt	girded, girt
give	gave	given
go	went	gone
grave	graved	graven, graved
grind	ground	ground
grow	grew	grown
hamstring	hamstringed, hamstrung	hamstringed, hamstrung
hang	hung, hanged	hung, hanged
have	had	had
hear	heard	heard
heave	heaved, hove	heaved, hove
hew	hewed	hewed, hewn
hide	hid	hidden
hit	hit	hit
hold	held	held
hurt	hurt	hurt
inlay	inlaid	inlaid
keep	kept	kept
kneel	knelt	knelt
knit	knitted, knit	knitted, knit
know	knew	known
lade	laded	laden
lay	laid	laid
lead	led	led
lean	leant, leaned	leant, leaned
leap	leapt, leaped	leapt, leaped
learn	learnt, learned	learnt, learned
leave	left	left
lend	lent	lent
let	let	let
lie	lay	lain
light	lit, lighted	lit, lighted
lose	lost	lost
make	made	made
mean	meant	meant
meet	met	met
melt	melted	melted, molten
miscast	miscast	miscast
misdeal	misdealt	misdealt
misgive	misgave	misgiven
mislay	mislaid	mislaid
mislead	misled	misled
misspell	misspelt	misspelt
misspend	misspent	misspent
mistake	mistook	mistaken
misunderstand	misunderstood	misunderstood
mow	mowed	mown; (US) mowed
outbid	outbid	outbid
outdo	outdid	outdone
outgo	outwent	outgone
outgrow	outgrew	outgrown
outride	outrode	outridden
outrun	outran	outrun
outshine	outshone	outshone

overbear	overbore	overborne
overcast	overcast	overcast
overcome	overcame	overcome
overdo	overdid	overdone
overhang	overhung	overhung
overhear	overheard	overheard
overlay	overlaid	overlaid
overleap	overleapt, overleaped	overleapt, overleaped
overlie	overlay	overlain
override	overrode	overridden
overrun	overran	overrun
oversee	oversaw	overseen
overshoot	overshot	overshot
oversleep	overslept	overslept
overtake	overtook	overtaken
overthrow	overthrew	overthrown
partake	partook	partaken
pay	paid	paid
prove	proved	proved, proven
put	put	put
quit	quitted, quit	quitted, quit
read /riːd ; rid/	read /red ; rɛd/	read /red ; rɛd/
rebind	rebound	rebound
rebuild	rebuilt	rebuilt
recast	recast	recast
redo	redid	redone
relay	relaid	relaid
remake	remade	remade
rend	rent	rent
repay	repaid	repaid
rerun	reran	rerun
reset	reset	reset
retell	retold	retold
rewrite	rewrote	rewritten
rid	rid, ridded	rid, ridded
ride	rode	ridden
ring	rang	rung
rise	rose	risen
rive	rived	riven, rived
run	ran	run
saw	sawed	sawn, sawed
say	said	said
see	saw	seen
seek	sought	sought
sell	sold	sold
send	sent	sent
set	set	set
sew	sewed	sewn, sewed
shake	shook	shaken
shave	shaved	shaved, shaven
shear	sheared	sheared, shorn
shed	shed	shed
shine	shone /ʃɒn/; (US) /ʃəun ; ʃon/	shone /ʃɒn/; (US) /ʃəun ; ʃon/
shoe	shod	shod
shoot	shot	shot
show	showed	shown, showed
shrink	shrank, shrunk	shrunk, shrunken
shrive	shrove, shrived	shriven, shrived
shut	shut	shut
sing	sang	sung
sink	sank	sunk, sunken
sit	sat	sat
slay	slew	slain
sleep	slept	slept
slide	slid	slid
sling	slung	slung
slink	slunk	slunk
slit	slit	slit
smell	smelt, smelled	smelt, smelled
smite	smote	smitten

sow	sowed	sown, sowed
speak	spoke	spoken
speed	sped, speeded	sped, speeded
spell	spelt, spelled	spelt, spelled
spend	spent	spent
spill	spilt, spilled	spilt, spilled
spin	spun, span	spun
spit	spat	spat
split	split	split
spoil	spoilt, spoiled	spoilt, spoiled
spread	spread	spread
spring	sprang	sprung
stand	stood	stood
stave	staved, stove	staved, stove
steal	stole	stolen
stick	stuck	stuck
sting	stung	stung
stink	stank, stunk	stunk
strew	strewed	strewn, strewed
stride	strode	stridden
strike	struck	struck, stricken
string	strung	strung
strive	strove	striven
swear	swore	sworn
sweep	swept	swept
swell	swelled	swollen, swelled
swim	swam	swum
swing	swung	swung
take	took	taken
teach	taught	taught
tear	tore	torn
tell	told	told
think	thought	thought
thrive	throve, thrived	thriven, thrived
throw	threw	thrown
thrust	thrust	thrust
tread	trod	trodden, trod
unbend	unbent	unbent
unbind	unbound	unbound
underbid	underbid	underbid
undergo	underwent	undergone
understand	understood	understood
undertake	undertook	undertaken
undo	undid	undone
upset	upset	upset
wake	woke, waked	woken, waked
waylay	waylaid	waylaid
wear	wore	worn
weave	wove	woven
weep	wept	wept
win	won	won
wind	wound	wound
withdraw	withdrew	withdrawn
withhold	withheld	withheld
withstand	withstood	withstood
work	worked, wrought	worked, wrought
wring	wrung	wrung
write	wrote	written

Appendix 2 **COMMON ABBREVIATIONS**
附錄二 通用略語

Note: This list includes abbreviations that occur in newspapers, timetables, etc. For abbreviations of parts of speech etc used in the text of the dictionary, ⇨ the inside covers of this book.
The use of capital or lower case letters indicates the more common usage but some abbreviations can be written in either style. Full points are often used in abbreviations though they are usually omitted in modern style.
Those abbreviations and acronyms that may be spoken, usually in a colloquial context, are given with phonetic transcriptions or stress marks, e g ˌAG'M is pronounced /ˌeɪ dʒiː 'em ; ˏedʒi'ɛm/.
注意：本表所收略語散見於報紙、時間表等。至於本辭典正文中所用詞類等之略語，請參看封面內頁或 lvi 頁之略語表。大寫或小寫字母之使用表示比較常見的用法，不過有的略語可寫作其中任一種形式。雖然在現代文體中略語通常不用句點，但有的略語常常加有句點。
凡是可以說出來的略語和字首組字(通常見於口語體的上下文中)，都加了注音或重音，如 ˌAG'M 讀作 /ˌeɪ dʒiː 'em ; ˏedʒi'ɛm/。

'A-bomb atomic bomb
'A-level advanced level (examination)
ˌA 'A Alcoholics Anonymous; Automobile Association
ˌA A 'A Amateur Athletics Association; American Automobile Association
ˌA 'B (GB) Able Seaman; (US) Bachelor of Arts
ˌA B 'C Australian Broadcasting Commission
ˌa 'c alternating current
a/c account
acc(t) account
ack(n) acknowledge(d)
ad(vt) advertisement
ˌA 'D *Anno Domini* in the year of the Lord
ˌA D 'C Aide-de-camp
add(r) address
Afr Africa(n)
ˌA G 'M Annual General Meeting
ˌA I 'D (US) Agency for International Development
ˌa 'm *ante meridiem* before noon
ˌA M 'A (US) American Medical Association
amp /æmp/ ampere(s)
anon anonymous
ˌA 'P Associated Press
ˌA P 'B (US) All Points Bulletin (for missing or wanted person)
appro /'æprəʊ ; 'æpro/ approval
approx approximately
Apr April
arr arrival; arrives
asap as soon as possible
ASEAN Association of South-East Asian Nations
assoc associate; association
asst assistant
Aug August
ˌA 'V Audio-Visual; Authorised Version (of the Bible)
Av(e) Avenue
ˌAWO'L absent without leave

b born; bowled
ˌb & 'b bed and breakfast
ˌB 'A (GB) Bachelor of Arts; British Airways
Barr Barrister
ˌB B 'C British Broadcasting Corporation
ˌB 'C Before Christ; British Council
ˌB 'D Bachelor of Divinity
bk book
Bldg(s) building(s)
Blvd Boulevard
ˌB 'M British Museum
ˌB M 'A British Medical Association
B Mus /ˌbiː'mʌs ; ˏbi'mʌs/ Bachelor of Music
ˌb 'o body odour; box office
Br Brother
Brig Brigadier
Brit Britain, British
Bro(s) brother(s)
ˌB 'S (US) Bachelor of Science
B Sc /ˌbiːes'siː ; ˏbiɛs'si/ (GB) Bachelor of Science
ˌB S 'T British Summer Time
Bt; Bart Baronet
ˌB Th 'U British Thermal Unit
ˌB V 'M *Beata Virgo Maria* Blessed Virgin Mary

C Centigrade; (Roman) 100
c cent(s); century; *circa* about; cubic
ca *circa* about, approximately
ˌC 'A Chartered Accountant
Cantab /'kæntæb ; 'kænṭæb/ *Cantabrigiensis* of Cambridge University
Capt Captain
CARE /keə(r) ; kɛr/ (US) Co-operative for American Relief Everywhere
Cath Catholic
ˌC B 'C Canadian Broadcasting Corporation
ˌC B 'I Confederation of British Industry
ˌC B 'S (US) Columbia Broadcasting System
ˌc 'c cubic centimetre(s)
cc *capita* chapters; centuries
ˌC 'D *Corps Diplomatique* Diplomatic Service
Cdr Commander
Cdre Commodore
cert certificate; certified
c 'f *confer* compare
cg centigram
c 'h central heating
C 'H Companion of Honour
ch(ap) chapter
Ch B /ˌsiː eɪtʃ 'biː ; ˏsietʃ'bi/ Bachelor of Surgery
C 'I Channel Islands
C I 'A (US) Central Intelligence Agency
C I 'D (GB) Criminal Investigation Department
c i 'f cost, insurance, freight
ˌC-in-'C Commander-in-Chief
cl class; centilitre(s)
cm centimetre(s)
Co (comm) Company
ˌC 'O Commanding Officer
c/o care of
ˌC O 'D Cash on Delivery
ˌC of 'E /ˌsiː əv 'iː ; ˏsiəv'i/ Church of England
ˌC O 'I (GB) Central Office of Information
Col Colonel
Coll College
concl concluded; conclusion
Cons (GB) Conservative (political party)
cont contents; continued
Co-op /'kəʊ ɒp ; ko'ɑp/ Co-operative (Society)
Corp Corporation
Coy (mil) Company
cp compare
ˌC 'P Cape Province; Communist Party
Cpl Corporal
ˌc p 's cycles per second

Cres(c) Crescent
ˌC ˈS Civil Servant; Civil Service
ˌC S ˈE (GB) Certificate of Secondary Education
ˌC SˈT (US) Central Standard Time
cu cubic
cwt hundredweight

D Roman 500
d *denarius* penny; died
D-day day on which a course of action is planned to start; ⇨ D-day in the dictionary
ˌD ˈA (US) District Attorney
dbl double
ˌD ˈC (US) District of Columbia
ˌd ˈc direct current
ˌD ˈD Doctor of Divinity
ˌD D ˈT *Dichloro-diphenyl-trichloroethane* insecticide
Dec December
dec deceased
deg degree(s)
Dem Democrat
dep departs; departure; deputy
Dept Department
ˌD ˈG *Dei Gratia* by the grace of God; Director General
diag diagram
diff difference; different
Dip Diploma
Dip Ed /ˌdɪp ˈed ; ˌdɪpˈɛd/ Diploma in Education
Dir Director
ˌD I ˈY do it yourself
ˌD ˈJ dinner jacket; disc jockey
D Litt /ˌdiː ˈlɪt;ˌdiˈlɪt/ Doctor of Letters/Literature
DM *Deutschmark* /ˈdɔɪtʃmɑːk ; ˈdɔɪtʃmɑrk/ German currency
ˌD N ˈA *deoxyribonucleic acid* basic constituent of the gene
doz dozen
D Phil /ˌdiː ˈfɪl ; ˌdiˈfɪl/ Doctor of Philosophy
Dr Debtor; Doctor; Drive (ie small road)
dr dram(s)
D Sc /ˌdiː es ˈsiː ; ˌdiɛsˈsi/ Doctor of Science
ˌD ˈT; (the) d ts /ˌdiː ˈtiːz ; ˌdiˈtiz/ *delirium tremens* 'trembling delirium' (extreme state of alcoholism)
dupl duplicate
ˌD ˈV *Deo Volente* God being willing

E east
Ed edited by; editor; edition; education; educated
ˌE D ˈP Electronic Data Processing
ˌE E ˈC European Economic Community (the Common Market)
ˌE E ˈG Electro-encephalo-gram/graph
EFTA /ˈeftə ; ˈɛftə/ European Free Trade Association
ˌe ˈg *exempli gratia* for example, for instance
enc(l) enclosed
ENE east-northeast
Eng Engineer(ing); England; English
ˌE ˈP extended-playing (record)
ˌE ˈR *Elizabeth Regina* Queen Elizabeth
ESE east-southeast
ˌE S ˈP Extra-Sensory Perception
Esq Esquire
ˌE S ˈT (US) Eastern Standard Time
ˌe t ˈa estimated time of arrival
et al /ˌet ˈæl ; ˌɛtˈæl/ *et alii* and other people; *et alia* and other things
etc; & c /ˌet ˈsetrə ; ɛtˈsɛtərə/ *et cetera* and the rest, and all the others
ˌe t ˈd estimated time of departure
et seq /ˌet ˈsek ; ˌɛtˈsɛk/ *et sequens* and the following
eve evening
excl excluding; exclusive
ext exterior; external

F Fahrenheit; Fellow
f foot; feet; female; feminine
ˌF ˈA Football Association
ˌF A ˈO Food and Agricultural Organisation
ˌF B ˈA Fellow of the British Academy
ˌF B ˈI (US) Federal Bureau of Investigation
ˌF ˈD *Fidei Defensor* Defender of the Faith
Feb February
Fed Federal; Federated; Federation
fem female; feminine
fig figurative; figure
fl fluid; floor
fm fathom(s)
ˌF ˈM Frequency Modulation
ˌF ˈO (GB) Foreign Office
ˌf o ˈb free on board
fol(l) following
for foreign
Fr Father; Franc; France; French
Fri Friday
ˌF R ˈS Fellow of the Royal Society
ft foot; feet
fur furlong(s)
furn furnished
fwd forward

g acceleration due to gravity; gram(s)
gal(l) gallon(s)
GATT /gæt ; gæt/ General Agreement on Tariffs and Trade
ˌG ˈB Great Britain
ˌG ˈC George Cross
ˌG C ˈE (GB) General Certificate of Education
Gdn(s) Garden(s)
Gen General
Ger German(y)
ˌG H ˈQ General Headquarters
ˌG ˈI (US) enlisted soldier
Gk Greek
ˌG L ˈC Greater London Council
gm gram(s)
ˌG ˈM General Manager
ˌG M ˈT Greenwich Mean Time
ˌG N ˈP Gross National Product
gov(t) government
Gov Governor
ˌG ˈP General Practitioner (Medical Doctor)
ˌG P ˈO General Post Office
gr grade; grain; gross; group
gt great

h height; hour
ha hectare(s)
ˌh & ˈc hot and cold (water)
ˈH-bomb Hydrogen bomb
ˌH ˈE high explosive; His/Her Excellency; His Eminence
ˌH ˈF High Frequency
ˌH ˈH His Holiness
ˌH ˈM His/Her Majesty
ˌH M ˈS His/Her Majesty's Ship
ˌH M S ˈO His/Her Majesty's Stationery Office
Hon Honorary; Honourable
hosp hospital
ˌH ˈP Hire Purchase; Horse Power
ˌH ˈQ Headquarters
hr hour(s)
ˌH R ˈH His/Her Royal Highness

I Island; Roman 1
ib; ibid *ibidem* in the same place

ˌ**I B 'A** (GB) Independent Broadcasting Authority
i/c in charge
ˌ**I C B 'M** Inter-Continental Ballistic Missile
ˌ**i 'e** *id est* which is to say, in other words
ˌ**I H 'S** *Iesous* (Greek for) Jesus (Christ)
ˌ**I L 'O** International Labour Organisation
ˌ**I M 'F** International Monetary Fund
in inch(es)
Inc Incorporated
incl including; inclusive
Ind India(n); Independent
inf *infra* below
info /ˈɪnfəʊ ; ˈɪnfo/ information
infra dig /ˌɪnfrə ˈdɪg ; ˌɪnfrəˈdɪg/ *infra dignitatem* beneath one's social dignity
ˌ**I N R 'I** *Iesus Nazarenus Rex Iudaeorum* Jesus of Nazareth, King of the Jews
Inst Institute
int interior; internal; international
intro /ˈɪntrəʊ ; ˈɪntro/ introduction
ˌ**I O 'U** I owe you
ˌ**I 'Q** *Intelligence Quotient* comparative measure of intelligence
ˌ**I R 'A** Irish Republican Army
Ire Ireland
Is Islands
It(al) Italy, Italian
ˌ**I T 'V** (GB) independent television

Jan January
ˌ**J 'C** Jesus Christ
Jnr; Jr Junior
ˌ**J 'P** Justice of the Peace
Jul July
Jun June; Junior

kg kilogram(s)
ˌ**K G 'B** Intelligence Agency of the USSR
km kilometre(s)
ˌ**K 'O** knock-out
kw kilowatt(s)

L lake; little; Roman 50; (GB) Liberal (political party)
l left; length; line
ˌ**L 'A** Legislative Assembly; Los Angeles
Lab (GB) Labour (political party)
lang language
Lat Latin
lat latitude
lb pound(s) (weight)
ˌ**l b 'w** leg before wicket (cricket term)
Ld Lord
ˌ**L E 'A** Local Education Authority
ˌ**l 'h** left hand
Lib (GB) Liberal (political party); Liberation
lit literal(ly); literature; literary
ll lines
LL B /ˌel el ˈbiː ; ˌɛlɛlˈbi/ Bachelor of Laws
ˌ**L M 'T** (US) Local Mean Time
loc cit /ˌlɒk ˈsɪt ; ˌlakˈsɪt/ *loco citato* in the place mentioned
long longitude
ˌ**L 'P** long-playing (record)
ˌ**L S 'D** *lysergic acid diethylamide* drug inducing hallucinations
£ s d /ˌel es ˈdiː ; ˌɛlɛsˈdi/ *librae, solidi, denarii* pounds, shillings, pence (former GB currency system)
ˌ**L S 'T** (US) Local Standard Time
Lt Lieutenant
Ltd Limited
lux luxury

M Member
m male; married; metre(s); mile(s); million
ˌ**M 'A** Master of Arts
Maj Major
Mans Mansions
Mar March
masc masculine
math /mæθ ; mæθ/ (US) mathematics
maths /mæθs ; mæθs/ (GB) mathematics
max maximum
ˌ**M 'B** Bachelor of Medicine
ˌ**M 'C** (US) Marine Corps; Master of Ceremonies; (US) Member of Congress; (GB) Military Cross
ˌ**M C 'C** (GB) Marylebone Cricket Club (the governing body of English cricket)
Mc Megacycle(s)
ˌ**M 'D** Doctor of Medicine
Med(it) Mediterranean
mg milligram(s)
Mgr Monsignor
ˌ**M I '5** (GB) National Security Division of Military Intelligence
min minimum
misc miscellaneous
mkt market
ml mile(s); millilitre(s)
mm millimetre(s)
M 'O Mail Order; Medical Officer; Money Order
mod moderate; modern
mod cons /ˌmɒd ˈkɒnz ; ˌmadˈkanz/ modern conveniences
Mon Monday
ˌ**M 'P** Member of Parliament (House of Commons); Military Police
ˌ**m p 'g** miles per gallon
ˌ**m p 'h** miles per hour
Mr, Mrs, Ms ⇨ dictionary entries
MS(S) manuscript(s)
M Sc /ˌem es ˈsiː ; ˌɛmɛsˈsi/ Master of Science
Mt Mount

N north
NAAFI /ˈnæfɪ ; ˈnæfɪ/ (GB) Navy, Army and Air Force Institute
nat national; native; natural
NATO /ˈneɪtəʊ ; ˈneto/ North Atlantic Treaty Organisation
ˌ**N 'B** *nota bene* take special note of
ˌ**N C 'O** Non-Commissioned Officer
NE northeast
ˌ**N H 'S** (GB) National Health Service
NNE north-northeast
NNW north-northwest
no(s) number(s)
non-U /ˌnɒn ˈju ; ˌnanˈju/ not upper class; vulgar
Nov November
nr near
ˌ**N S ˌP C 'C** (GB) National Society for the Prevention of Cruelty to Children
ˌ**N 'T** New Testament
NW northwest
ˌ**N 'Y('C)** New York (City)
ˌ**N 'Z** New Zealand

ˌ**O A 'P** (GB) old-age pensioner
ˌ**O A 'S** (US) Organisation of American States
ˌ**O A 'U** Organisation of African Unity
ob *obiit* died
Oct October
ˌ**O E C 'D** Organisation for Economic Co-operation and Development
ˌ**O E 'D** Oxford English Dictionary
ˌ**O H M 'S** (GB) On Her/His Majesty's Service
'O-level (GB) Ordinary level (examination)

ˌo n ˈo or nearest offer
op opus; operation
op cit /ˌɒp ˈsɪt ; ˏɑpˈsɪt/ *opere citato* in the work mentioned
OPEC /ˈəʊpek ; ˈopɛk/ Organisation of Petroleum Exporting Countries
opp opposite
orch orchestra(l); orchestrated
ˌO ˈS Ordinary Seaman
ˌO ˈT Old Testament
Oxon /ˈɒksn ; ˈɑksn̩/ *Oxoniensis* of Oxford University; Oxfordshire
oz ounce(s)

P Parking
p page; penny, pence; per
ˌp ˈa *per annum* per year
ˌP ˈA Personal Assistant; Press Association; Public Address (System)
para(s) paragraph(s)
ˌP A Y ˈE pay as you earn
ˌP ˈC (GB) Police Constable; (GB) Privy Councillor; (US) Peace Corps
pd paid
ˌP D S ˈA People's Dispensary for Sick Animals
ˌP ˈE physical education
PEN /pen ; pɛn/ International Association of Writers
ˌP ˈG Paying Guest
Ph D /ˌpiː eɪtʃ ˈdiː ; ˏpietʃˈdi/ Doctor of Philosophy
Pk Park
pkt packet
Pl Place
ˌP ˈM Prime Minister
ˌp ˈm *post meridiem* after noon; per month
ˌP ˈO Personnel Officer; Petty Officer; Post Office; Postal Order
ˌP ˈO Box Post Office Box
ˌP O ˈE Port of Entry
pop popular; population
poss possible; possibly
ˌP O ˈW Prisoner of War
pp pages
ˌp ˈp *per procurationem* on behalf of (precedes name of person signed for)
ˌP P ˈS *post postscriptum* additional postscript
pr pair; price
ˌP ˈR Public Relations
Pres President
ˌP R ˈO Public Records Office; Public Relations Officer
pro /prəʊ ; pro/ professional
pro tem /ˌprəʊ ˈtem ; ˏproˈtɛm/ *pro tempore* for the time being; temporarily
Prof (*informally* /prɒf ; prɑf/) Professor
pron pronounced; pronunciation
Prot Protestant
Prov Province
Ps Psalm
ˌP ˈS Postscript
ˌP S ˈT (US) Pacific Standard Time
pt part; payment; pint; point
ˌP ˈT Physical Training
ˌP T ˈA Parent-Teacher Association
Pte (GB) Private (soldier)
ˌP T ˈO Please turn over
Pty Proprietary
Pvt (US) Private (soldier)
ˌp ˈw per week
ˌP ˈX post exchange (US equivalent of NAAFI)

ˌQ ˈC Queen's Counsel
ˌQ E ˈD *quod erat demonstrandum* which had to be proved
qt quart
ˌq ˈt ⇨ quiet (5)
Qu Queen; Question
ˌq ˈv *quod vide* which may be referred to

R River; Royal
r radius; right
ˌR ˈA Rear-Admiral; Royal Academy; Royal Academician
RADA /ˈrɑːdə ; ˈrɑdə/ Royal Academy of Dramatic Art
ˌR A ˈF (*also* /ræf ; ræf/) Royal Air Force
ˌR A ˈM Royal Academy of Music
ˌR ˈC Red Cross; Roman Catholic
ˌR C ˈM Royal College of Music
Rd Road
rec(d) received
ref referee /ref ; rɛf/; reference; refer(red)
Rep Repertory /rep ; rɛp/; Representative /rep ; rɛp/; Republic(an)
res residence; resigned; reserved
resp respectively
ret(d) retired
rev revolution
Rev(d) Reverend
ˌr ˈh right hand
ˌR I ˈP *requiescat/requiescant in pace* may he/they rest in peace
rly railway
rm room
ˌR ˈM Royal Marines
ˌR ˈN Royal Navy
ˌr p ˈm revolutions per minute
ˌR S ˈM Regimental Sergeant Major; Royal School of Music
ˌR S V ˈP *répondez s'il vous plaît* please reply
ˌR S ˌP C ˈA Royal Society for the Prevention of Cruelty to Animals
rt right
Rt Hon Right Honourable
Rt Rev Right Reverend
ˌR (S) ˈV Revised (Standard) Version (of the Bible)
ˌR ˈU Rugby Union

S south
s second(s); shilling(s)
ˌS ˈA South Africa
ˌs a ˈe stamped addressed envelope
SALT /sɔːlt ; sɔlt/ Strategic Arms Limitation Talks
Sat Saturday
ˌS A Y ˈE save as you earn
sc *scilicet* namely
s/c self-contained
Sch School
sci science
SE southeast
sec second(ary); secretary
Sen Senate; Senator; Senior
Sept September
ˌS ˈF Science Fiction
sgd signed
Sgt Sergeant
SHAPE /ʃeɪp ; ʃep/ Supreme Headquarters of Allied Powers in Europe
Sn(r) Senior
Soc Society
Sol Solicitor
sp special; spelling
Sp Spain, Spanish
sp gr specific gravity
Sq Square
Sr Senior; Sister
ˌS R ˈN State Registered Nurse
ˌS ˈS Steamship
SSE south-southeast

SSW south-southwest
St Saint; Street
Sta Station
ˌS T ˈD subscriber trunk dialling (telephone)
Str Strait; Street
sub(s) subscription; substitute
Sun Sunday
Supt Superintendent
SW southwest

T temperature
t time; ton(s)
ˌT ˈB Tuberculosis
Tech /tek ; tɛk/ Technical (College)
tel telephone
temp /temp ; tɛmp/ temperature; temporary (secretary)
Ter(r) Terrace; Territory
Thurs Thursday
ˌT K ˈO technical knock-out
ˌT N ˈT *Tri-nitro-toluene* explosive
trans translated
treas treasurer
ˌT ˈU Trade Union
ˌT U ˈC (GB) Trades Union Congress
Tues Tuesday
ˌT ˈV television

U Union; Upper; upper class, fashionable, polite, ⇨ non-U above
ˌU D ˈI unilateral declaration of independence
ˌU F ˈO (*also* /ˈjuːfəʊ ; ˈjufo/) unidentified flying object
ˌU H ˈF ultra high frequency
ˌU ˈK United Kingdom
ˌU ˈN United Nations
UNCTAD /ˈʌŋktæd ; ˈʌŋktæd/ United Nations Conference on Trade and Development
UNESCO /juːˈneskəʊ ; juˈnɛsko/ United Nations Educational, Scientific and Cultural Organisation
UNICEF /ˈjuːnɪsef ; ˈjunɪsɛf/ United Nations Children's Fund
Univ University
UNO /ˈjuːnəʊ ; ˈjuno/ United Nations Organisation
UNRWA /ˈʌnwə ; ˈʌnwə/ United Nations Relief and Works Agency
ˌU P ˈI United Press International
ˌU ˈS United States
ˌU S ˈA United States of America; United States Army
ˌU S A ˈF United States Air Force
ˌU S ˈN United States Navy
ˌU S ˈS United States Ship
ˌU S S ˈR Union of Soviet Socialist Republics

V Roman 5; Victory; Volt
v very; verse; versus; *vide* see, refer to
V & A /ˌviː ən ˈeɪ ; ˌviənˈe/ Victoria and Albert (Museum in London)
vac /væk ; væk/ vacation
ˌV A ˈT (*also* /væt ; væt/) Value Added Tax, ⇨ value (3)
ˌV ˈC Vice Chairman; Vice Chancellor; Vice Consul; Victoria Cross; Vietcong
ˌV ˈD Venereal Disease
ˌV ˈE Day Victory in Europe (end of Second World War in Europe: 8. 5. 1945)
Ven Venerable
ˌV H ˈF very high frequency
ˌV I ˈP very important person
viz /vɪz ; vɪz/ *videlicet* namely
vol volume
ˌV ˈP(res) Vice-President
vs versus
ˌV ˈS (US) Veterinary Surgeon
ˌV S ˈO (GB) Voluntary Service Overseas

W west
w watt(s); week; width; with
WASP /wɒsp ; wɑsp/ (US) White Anglo-Saxon Protestant
ˌw ˈc water closet, ⇨ water¹(7)
ˌW C ˈC World Council of Churches
ˌw e ˈf with effect from
ˌW H ˈO (*also* /huː ; hu/) World Health Organisation
ˌW ˈI West Indian; West Indies; Women's Institute
wk week; work
WNW west-northwest
ˌW ˈO Warrant Officer
ˌw p ˈb waste paper basket
ˌw p ˈm words per minute
ˌW R A ˈC Women's Royal Army Corps
ˌW R A ˈF Women's Royal Air Force
ˌW R N ˈS (*also* /renz ; rɛnz/) Women's Royal Naval Service
WSW west-southwest
wt weight

X Roman 10; a kiss; an unknown number, thing, name, etc
Xmas Christmas

Y Yen (Japanese currency)
ˌY H ˈA Youth Hostels Association
ˌY M C ˈA Young Men's Christian Association
yr year; your
ˌY W C ˈA Young Women's Christian Association

Appendix 3 **AFFIXES**

附錄三 接語

Note: Many affixes have more than one pronunciation form or stress pattern. This often depends on the form of the word to which it is attached. ⇨ the entries in the dictionary for full phonetic transcriptions of the words given as examples in this appendix.

注意：很多接語具有不止一種發音形式或重音型態。這種情形常視所接的詞的形式而定。有關本附錄例字的完整音標，參看本辭典各該字目。

a-[1] /eɪ-, ə-, æ- ; e-, ə-, æ-/ *pref* not, without: 不;非;無: *aseptic; atheist.*

a-[2] /ə- ; ə-/ *pref* **1** (∼+*n*=*adv*) in: (∼+名詞=副詞) 在…裡面: *abed;* on, at: 在…上;在…: *afield; ashore.* **2** (∼+*v*=*adv*) in the state of, in the process of: (∼+動詞=副詞)在…狀態中;在…過程中: *asleep; ablaze.* **3** (old use) (∼+*gerund*=*adv*) in the act of: (舊用法)(∼+動名詞=副詞)正在: *a-running; a-singing.*

ab- /æb-, əb- ; æb-, əb-/ *pref* from, away from: 脫離;離開: *absent; abduct.*

-able (also 亦作 **-ible**) /-əbl ; -əbl/ *suff* **1** (*n*+∼=*adj*) showing qualities of: (名詞+∼=形容詞)顯示…性質或特點的: *fashionable; responsible.* **2** (*v*+∼=*adj*) that can be, fit to be: (動詞+∼=形容詞)可被…的;適於…的: *eatable; reducible.* **-ably, -ibly** /-əblɪ ; -əblɪ/ *adv*

ad- /əd-, æd- ; əd-, æd-/ *pref* to, towards: 向;往;朝: *advance; adjoin.*

-ade /-eɪd, -ɑːd ; -ed, -ɑd/ *suff* (used to form a *n*): (用以構成名詞): *blockade; lemonade; façade.*

aer(o)- /eər(ə- *etc*) ; ɛr(ə- *etc*)/ *pref* of aircraft: 與飛機或飛行有關的: *aerodynamics; aeronaut.*

-age /-ɪdʒ, -ɑːʒ ; -ɪdʒ, -ɑʒ/ *suff* (used to form a *n*): (用以構成名詞): *breakage; postage; sabotage.*

-al /-l, -əl ; -l̩, -əl/ *suff* **1** (*n* + ∼=*adj*): (名詞+∼=形容詞): *magical; verbal.* **-ally** /-lɪ, -əlɪ ; -l̩ɪ, -əlɪ/ *adv* **2** (*v* +∼= *n*): (動詞+∼=名詞): *recital; survival; displayal.*

ambi- /æmbɪ- *etc* ; æmbɪ- *etc*/ *pref* both, double, two: 雙;雙重;兩: *ambiguous; ambidextrous.*

an- /æn-, ən- ; æn-, ən-/ *pref* not, without: 不;非;無: *anaesthetic; anonymous.*

-an /-ən, -n ; -ən, -n̩/ *suff* (*proper n*+∼=*n* or *adj*, ⇨ App 6): (專有名詞+∼=名詞或形容詞,參看附錄六): *Lutheran; Mexican.* ⇨ -ian below. 參看下列的 -ian。

-ana ⇨ -iana

-ance (also 亦作 **-ence**) /-əns, -ns ; -əns, -n̩s/ *suff* (*v* + ∼ = *n*): (動詞+∼=名詞): *assistance; confidence.*

-ant (also 亦作 **-ent**) /-ənt, -nt ; -ənt, -n̩t/ *suff* **1** (*v*+∼= *adj*): (動詞+∼=形容詞): *significant; different.* **2** (*v* + ∼ = *n*): (動詞+∼=名詞): *assistant; deterrent.*

ante- /æntɪ- ; æntɪ-/ *pref* in front of: 在前面的: *anteroom;* before, previous to: 在…之前的;先於…的: *antenatal.*

anthrop(o)- /ænθrəp(ə- *etc*) ; ænθrəp(ə- *etc*)/ *pref* of man, of mankind: 人的;人類的: *anthropoid; anthropology.*

anti- /æntɪ- *US:* æntaɪ- ; æntaɪ-/ *pref* **1** opposed to, against: 反對;反抗;對抗: *antisocial; antiseptic.* **2** instead of: 替代;取代: *anti-hero.*

arch- /ɑːk-, ɑːtʃ- ; ɑrk-, ɑrtʃ-/ *pref* first, chief, head: 第一的;首要的;爲首的: *archetype; archbishop.*

-arian /-eərɪən ; -ɛrɪən/ *suff* practiser of: 實行或實踐…的人: *disciplinarian; vegetarian.*

-ary /-ərɪ, -rɪ *US:* -erɪ ; -ɛrɪ, -ərɪ/ *suff* **1** (used to form an *adj*): (用以構成形容詞): *planetary; reactionary.* **2** (*pl* -aries) (used to form a *n*): (用以構成名詞): *dictionary; functionary.*

astr(o)- /æstr(ə- *etc*) ; æstr(ə- *etc*)/ *pref* of the stars, of outer space: 星球的;天體的;太空的: *astronomy; astronaut.*

-ate *suff* **1** /-ət, -ɪt ; -ət, -ɪt/ (used to form an *adj*): (用以構成形容詞): *affectionate; passionate.* **-ately** /-ətlɪ, -ɪtlɪ ; -ətlɪ, -ɪtlɪ/ *adv* **2** /-ət, -ɪt ; -ət, -ɪt/ (used to form a *n*): (用以構成名詞): *directorate; electorate.* **3** /-eɪt ; -et/ (used to form a *v*): (用以構成動詞): *gyrate; stimulate.* **4** /-eɪt ; -et/ (chem) salt formed by the action of an acid on a base: (化學)酸與鹽基化合而成的鹽: *phosphate; nitrate.*

-ation ⇨ -tion

-ative /-ətɪv ; -ətɪv/ *suff* (used to form an *adj*, usu from an '-ate' *v*): (用以構成形容詞,通常以 ate 結尾的動詞加上本接語而成): *illustrative; quantitative.* **-atively** /-ətɪvlɪ ; -ətɪvlɪ/ *adv*

-ator /-eɪtə(r) ; -etɚ/ *suff* object or person carrying out the action of an '-ate' *v*: 作用物;執行者: *percolator; stimulator.*

audio- /ɔːdɪəʊ- ; ɔdɪo-/ *pref* of hearing, of sound: 聽覺的;聲音的: *audio-visual; audio-frequency.*

aut(o)- /ɔːt(ə- *etc*) ; ɔt(ə- *etc*)/ *pref* **1** of oneself: 自己的: *autobiography; autograph.* **2** without help, independent of others: 自動的;自主的: *automatic; autocrat.*

be- /bɪ- ; bɪ-/ *pref* **1** (∼+*v*=*v*) all over, all around, in all directions: (∼+動詞=動詞)遍及;四周;到處: *bedeck; bespatter.* **2** (∼ + *n* or *adj* = *v*) make, become: (∼+名詞或形容詞=動詞)使成爲;變成: *befriend; belittle.* **3** (∼+*vi* = *vt*): (∼+不及物動詞=及物動詞): *bemoan; bewail.*

bi- /baɪ- ; baɪ-/ *pref* **1** occurring twice in one period: 每…二次的(地): *bi-monthly; bi-annual.* **2** occurring once in a period of two: 兩…一次的(地): *bicentenary; biennial.* **3** having two: 雙…的;兩…的: *bilingual; biped.*

bibli(o)- /bɪblɪ(ə- *etc*) ; bɪblɪ(ə- *etc*)/ *pref* of books: 書籍的: *bibliography; bibliophile.*

bio- /baɪ(ə- *etc*) ; baɪ(ə- *etc*)/ *pref* of life, of living organisms: 生平的;生活的;生物的: *biography; biology; biotic.*

by- (also 亦作 **bye-**) /baɪ- ; baɪ-/ *pref* of secondary importance, incidental: 次要的;附帶的: *by-election; bye-law; by-product.*

cent(i)- /sent(ɪ- *etc*) ; sɛnt(ɪ- *etc*)/ *pref* a hundred, a hundredth part: 一百的;百分之一的: *Centigrade; centimetre.*

chron(o)- /krɒn(ə- *etc*) ; krɑn(ə- *etc*)/ *pref* of time: 時間的: *chronology; chronometer.*

-cide /-saɪd ; -saɪd /*suff* (used to form a *n*) killing, killer: (用以構成名詞)殺害;消滅;殺害者; 消滅…之物: *suicide; insecticide.*

co- /kəʊ- *etc* ; ko- *etc*/ *pref* together, jointly, equally: 一起;共同;同等: *cohabit; co-operate; co-education.*

con- (also 亦作 **col-, com-, cor-**) /kɒn-, kən-, *etc* ; kɑn-, kən-, *etc*/ *pref* with, together: 連同; 一起: *conduct; collaborate; combine; correlate.*

contra- /kɒntrə- ; kɑntrə-/ *pref* against, opposite to: 反對;相反;對立: *contraception; contradict.*

-cracy /-krəsɪ ; -krəsɪ/ *suff* (*pl* -cracies) (used to form a *n*) government or rule by, class characterised by: (用以構成名詞)…政體; …政治; …階級: *democracy; aristocracy.*

-crat /-kræt ; -kræt/ *suff* (used to form a *n*) member or supporter of a '-cracy': (用以構成名詞)某種政體或政治的支持者;某一階級的成員: *democrat; aristocrat.*

-cratic /-krætɪk ; -krætɪk/ *adj*: *democratic; aristocratic.*

-cy (also 亦作 **-acy**) /-(ə)sɪ ; -(ə)sɪ/ *suff* (*pl-* (a)cies) (used to form a *n*) condition, quality: (用以構成名詞)狀態;性質: *accuracy; infancy; supremacy.*

-d ⇨ -ed

de- /diː-, dɪ- ; di-, dɪ-/ *pref* (used with a *v*) the negative, reverse, opposite of: (與動詞連用)…的否定、相對、相反: *depopulate; defrost; defuse.*

demi- /demɪ- ; dɛmɪ-/ *pref* half, partly: 半;部分: *demimonde; demigod.*

di- /daɪ-, dɪ- ; daɪ-, dɪ-/ *pref* twice, double: 兩倍的;雙重的;二的: *dilemma; dioxide.*

dia- /daɪə- ; daɪə-/ *pref* through, across: 穿過;橫過;通過: *diameter; diagonal; diaphragm.*

dis- /dɪs- ; dɪs-/ *pref* (used with a *v*) the negative, reverse, opposite of: (與動詞連用)…的否定、相對、相反: *disbelieve; disorder; disagree.*

-dom /-dəm ; -dəm/ *suff* (used to form a *n*) (用以構成名詞) **1** a condition, state: 狀況;狀態: *boredom; freedom.* **2** domain: 領域;範圍: *kingdom; officialdom.*

-ed (also 亦作 **-d**) /*After* p, k, ʃ, f, θ, s *pronounced* -t; *after* t, d *pronounced* -ɪd; *otherwise pronounced* -d. *Exception* 'used', ⇨ use² 在 p, k, ʃ, f, θ, s 之後讀做 t; 在 t, d 之後讀做 ɪd; 他處讀做 d。used 的讀音例外,參看 use²/ *suff* **1** (used to form *pt* and *pp* of a *v*): (用以構成動詞的過去式及過去分詞): *laughed; acted; washed.* **2** (*n*+～= *adj*) having the characteristics of: (名詞+～=形容詞) 有…特徵的: *diseased; talented; cracked.*

-ee /-iː ; -i/ *suff* (*v*+～=*n*) (動詞+～=名詞) **1** person affected by the action of the *v*: 受…者: *employee; payee.* **2** person acting: 做出…行爲的人: *absentee; refugee.* **3** (*n*+～=*n*) diminutive: (名詞+～=名詞) 小型的: *bootee; coatee.*

-eer /-ɪə(r) ; -ɪr/ *suff* (*n*+～=*n*) person concerned with the *n*: (名詞+～=名詞)與所述名詞有關聯的人: *auctioneer; mountaineer.*

electr(o)- /ɪlektr(ə- *etc*) ; ɪlɛktr(ə- *etc*)/ *pref* concerned with, caused by, electricity: 與電有關的;由電所引起的: *electrocute; electromagnet.*

en- /ɪn-, en- ; ɪn-, ɛn-/ (also 亦作 **em-** /ɪm-, em- ; ɪm-, ɛm-/ *pref* **1** (～+*n* or *v*=*v*) put in, on: (～+名詞或動詞=動詞)置於…中或上: *encase; endanger; emplane.* **2** (～+ *n* or *adj* = *v*) make into, cause to be: (～+名詞或形容詞=動詞)使變成;使成爲: *enlarge; enrich; empower.*

-en /-ən, -n ; -ən, -n̩/ *suff* **1** (used to form the *pp* of some *vv*): (用以構成某些動詞的過去分詞): *broken; eaten; hidden.* **2** (*n* +～= *adj*) made of: (名詞+～=形容詞)用…做成的: *golden; wooden.* **3** (*adj* + ～= *v*) make, cause to be: (形容詞+～=動詞)使變成: *blacken; sadden.*

-ence ⇨ -ance

-ent ⇨ -ant

equi- /iːkwɪ- *etc* ; ikwɪ- *etc*/ *pref* equal, the same: 相等;相同: *equidistant; equivalent.*

-er /-ə(r) ; -ɚ/ *suff* **1** (*v* +～=*n*) person who carries out the action of the *v*: (動詞+～=名詞)執行者;實行者: *runner; sleeper.* **2** (*n*+～=*n*) practiser of: (名詞+～=名詞)從事…的人: *astronomer; philosopher.* **3** (also 亦作 **-r**) (used to form the *comp* of an *adj*): (用以構成形容詞的比較級): *stronger; rarer; thinner.* ⇨ also -ier.

-ery /-ərɪ, -rɪ ; -ərɪ, -ri/ (also 亦作 **-ry** /-rɪ ; -rɪ/ *suff* (*pl* -eries) (*n* or *v* +～= *n*) (名詞或動詞+～=名詞) **1** place where an action is carried out: 做某事的地方或場所: *bakery; fishery.* **2** art of, practice of: …術;…法: *cookery; pottery.* **3** state, quality, character: 狀態;性質;性格: *rivalry; snobbery.*

-es (also 亦作 **-s**) /-ɪz ; -ɪz/ *suff* **1** (used to form *pl* of a *n* ending in /s, z, ʃ, ʒ/): (用以構成以 /s, z, ʃ, ʒ/ 各音結尾的名詞的複數): *pieces; judges.* **2** (used to form *3rd pers sing pres t* of a *v* ending in /s, z, ʃ, ʒ/): (用以構成以 /s, z, ʃ, ʒ/ 各音結尾的動詞之第三人稱單數現在式): *washes; urges.*

-ese /-iːz ; -iz/ *suff* **1** (*proper n* +～= *adj*) of a place or a country: (專有名詞+～=形容詞)…地方的;…國家的: *Burmese;* (the *adj* may also be used as a *n*, ⇨ App 6) person or language: (上述的形容詞也可作名詞用,參看附錄六)…地方或國家的人;…地方或國家的語言: *Japanese.* **2** (used to form a *n*) in the (literary) style of: (用以構成名詞)…的風格,文體或用語: *journalese.*

-esque /-esk ; -ɛsk/ *suff* (*n*+～=*adj*) in the manner, style of: (名詞+～=形容詞)…樣子的;…風格的: *statuesque; picturesque.*

-ess /-ɪs, -es ; -ɪs, -ɛs/ *suff* (*n* or *v*+～=*n*) female: (名詞或動詞+～=名詞)女…;雌…;母…: *lioness; actress.*

-est (also 亦作 **-st**) /-ɪst ; -ɪst/ *suff* (used to form the *superl* of an *adj* or *adv*): (用以構成形容詞或副詞的最高級): *fastest; barest; wettest.*

-ette /-et ; -ɛt/ *suff* (*n* +～= *n*) (名詞+～=名詞) **1** diminutive: 小型的: *cigarette; kitchenette.* **2** female: 女性: *usherette; suffragette.* **3** imitation: 仿造物: *flannelette; leatherette.*

ex- *pref* **1** /ɪks-, eks-, ɪgz-, egz ; ɪks-, ɛks-, ɪgz-, ɛgz-/ out, out of, from: 向外;脫離;離開: *exclaim; extract.* **2** /eks- ; ɛks-/ former, at one time: 從前的;前任的: *ex-wife; ex-president.*

extra- /ekstrə- ; ɛkstrə-/ *pref* **1** outside, beyond: 在…之外; 超出…範圍: *extramarital; extrasensory.* **2** very: 非常;極: *extra-thin.*

-fic /-fɪk ; -fɪk/ *suff* (used with a '-fy' *v* to form an *adj*): (用以構成以 fy 結尾的動詞之形容詞): *horrific; specific.*

-fied /-faɪd ; -faɪd/ ⇨ -fy

-fold /-fəʊld ; -fold/ *suff* (*cardinal numeral* +～= *adj*) (基數+～=形容詞) **1** multiplied by: …倍的: *tenfold; hundredfold.* **2** of (so many) parts: …重的: *twofold.*

fore- /fɔː(r)- ; for-/ *pref* before, in front of: 預先;在前面的: *foretell; foreground.*

-form /-fɔːm ; -fɔrm/ *suff* (used to form an *adj*) having the shape or character of: (用以構成形容詞)具有…形狀或特徵的: *uniform; cuneiform.*

-ful *suff* **1** /-fl ; -fəl/ (*n* or *v* +～= *adj*) full of, having the quality of: (名詞或動詞+～=形容詞)充滿…的;具有…性質的: *eventful; peaceful.* **2** /-fʊl ; -fʊl/ (*n* +～= *n*) amount that fills: (名詞+～=名詞)充滿…的量: *handful; mouthful.*

-gamy /-gəmɪ ; -gəmɪ/ *suff* (used to form a *n*) of marriage: (用以構成名詞)…的婚姻(制度): *monogamy; polygamy.* **-gamous** /-gəməs ; -gəməs/ *adj.*

ge(o)- /dʒiː(ə- *etc*) ; dʒi(ə- *etc*)/ *pref* (used to form a *n*) of the earth: (用以構成名詞)與地球或土地有關的: *geography; geology.*

-gon /-gən, -gɒn ; -gən, -gɑn/ *suff* angle, corner: 角;隅: *polygon; pentagon.*

-gram /-græm ; -græm/ *suff* (used to form a *n*) sth written down or drawn: (用以構成名詞)文字;圖案;圖表: *telegram; monogram; diagram.*

-graph /-grɑːf *US:* -græf ; -græf/ *suff* (used to form a *n*) sth written down, of writing: (用以構成名詞)文字;書寫: *autograph; telegraph.* **-graphy** /-grəfɪ ; -grəfɪ/ *n*: *calligraphy; orthography.*

hem(o)- (also 亦作 **haem(o)-**) /hiːmə-, hemə- ; himə-, hɛmə-/ *pref* of the blood: 血的: *hemoglobin; hemorrhage.*

heter(o)- /hetər(ə- *etc*) ; hɛtər(ə- *etc*)/ *pref* the other, the opposite, different: 其他;相反;不同: *heterogeneous; heterosexual.*

hom(o)- /hɒm(ə- *etc*), həʊm- ; hɑm(ə- *etc*), hom-/ *pref* the same: 相同;同…: *homogeneous; homosexual.*

-hood /-hʊd ; -hʊd/ *suff* (*n*+～=*n*) status, rank, condition of life: (名詞+～=名詞)身分;地位;生活狀況: *boyhood; brotherhood.*

hydr(o)- /haɪdr(ə- *etc*) ; haɪdr(ə- *etc*)/ *pref* of water: 水的: *hydrant; hydroelectric.*

hyper- /haɪpə(r)- ; haɪpɚ-/ *pref* to a large or extreme degree: 非常;過於;極度: *hypercritical; hypersensitive.*

-ial /-ɪəl, -l; -ɪəl, -əl/ *suff* (*n*+～=*adj*) characteristic of: (名詞+～=形容詞)有…特點的: *dictatorial; palatial.* **-ially** /-ɪəlɪ, -lɪ; -ɪəlɪ, -əlɪ/ *adv*

-ian /-ɪən, -n; -ɪən, -ən/ *suff* **1** (*proper n*+～=*n* or *adj*, ⇨ App 6): (專有名詞+～=名詞或形容詞,參看附錄六): *Brazilian; Shakespearian.* **2** (used with an '-ics' *n* to form a *n* ending in -cian /-ʃn; -ʃən/) specialist in: (用在以 ics 結尾的名詞上,以構成由 cian /-ʃn;-ʃən/ 結尾的名詞)…專家: *optician; pediatrician.*

-(i)ana /-(ɪ)ɑːnə; -(i)ænə/ *suff* (used with words ending in '-ian' or '-an' to form a *collective n*) collection of facts, objects, etc relating to: (用在以 ian 或 an 結尾的詞上,以構成集合名詞)與…有關的資料、物件等之總稱,…文物: *Victoriana; Africana.*

-ible ⇨ -able

-ic /-ɪk; -ɪk/ *suff* (*n*+～=*adj*): (名詞+～=形容詞): *poetic; romantic.* **-ical** /-ɪkl; -ɪkḷ/ *adj* **-ically** /-ɪklɪ; -ɪkḷɪ/ *adv*

-ics /-ɪks; -ɪks/ *suff* (used to form a *n*) science or specific activity: (用以構成名詞) 學科或某種活動: *physics; politics; athletics.*

-ide /-aɪd; -aɪd/ *suff* (used to form a *n*) (chem) chemical compound: (用以構成名詞)(化學)化合物: *chloride; sulphide.*

-ie ⇨ -y

-ier ⇨ -y

-ies ⇨ -y

-(i)fy /-(ɪ)faɪ; -(ə)faɪ/ *suff* (*pt* and *pp* -(i)fied /-(ɪ)faɪd; -(ə)faɪd/) (*n* or *adj*+～=*v*) make into, cause to be, bring to a state of: (名詞或形容詞+～=動詞)使成爲;使變成;使進入…狀態: *beautify; terrify; solidify.*

in- (also 亦作 **il-, im-, ir-**) /ɪn-, ɪl-, ɪm-, ɪr-; ɪn-, ɪl-, ɪm-, ɪr-/ *pref* **1** (～+*v*=*v* or *n*) in, on: (～+動詞=動詞或名詞)在內;在上: *intake; imprint.* **2** (～+*adj* =*adj*) not: (～+形容詞=形容詞)不;無: *infinite; illicit; immoral; irrelevant.*

-ing /-ɪŋ; -ɪŋ/ *suff* (*v*+～=*pres p* and *gerund*): (動詞+～=現在分詞及動名詞): *talking; thinking.*

inter- /ɪntə(r)-; ɪntɚ-/ *pref* between, from one to another: 在…之間; 從一個到另一個: *international; interplanetary.*

intra- (also 亦作 **intro-**) /ɪntrə-; ɪntrə-/ *pref* inside: 在內部: *intravenous; intra-uterine; introspection.*

-ise ⇨ -ize

-ish /-ɪʃ; -ɪʃ/ *suff* **1** (*national name*+～=*adj*, ⇨ App 6): (國家名稱+～=形容詞,參看附錄六): *Irish; Spanish.* **2** (*n*+～=*adj*) resembling, in the manner of: (名詞+～=形容詞)像…一樣的;…似的: *childish; devilish.* **3** (*adj*+～=*adj*) somewhat, near to: (形容詞+～=形容詞)有點…的;將近…的: *reddish; twentyish.*

-ism /-ɪzəm; -ɪzəm/ *suff* (used to form a *n*) (用以構成名詞) **1** showing qualities typical of: …的特質或特點: *Americanism; heroism.* **2** specific doctrine, principle or movement: 學說;主義;教義;原理;運動: *Buddhism; Communism.*

-ist /-ɪst; -ɪst/ *suff* (*n*+～=*n*) (名詞+～=名詞) **1** agent of an '-ize' *v*: (表示以 ize 結尾的動詞之)實行者;推動者: *dramatist; publicist.* **2** follower, practiser of an '-ism': (表示以 ism 結尾的名詞之)信徒;黨徒;主義者: *industrialist; fascist.* **3** person concerned with a specific activity or thing: 與某種活動或事物有關的人: *tobacconist; motorist.*

-ite /-aɪt; -aɪt/ *suff* **1** (*proper n*+～=*n*) follower, devotee of a person or organisation: (專有名詞+～=名詞)(某人或某組織的)追隨者;擁護者: *Labourite.* **2** (chem) specific chemical substance: (化學)某種化學物質: *anthracite; dynamite.*

-ities ⇨ -ity

-ition ⇨ -tion

-itis /-aɪtɪs; -aɪtɪs/ *suff* (med) (used to form a *n*) inflammation of: (醫)(用以構成名詞)炎症; …炎: *appendicitis; tonsillitis.*

-ity /-ɪtɪ; -ətɪ/ *suff* (*pl* -ities) (used with an *adj* to form a *n*): (用在形容詞上以構成名詞): *crudity; oddity.*

-ive /-ɪv; -ɪv/ *suff* (*v*+～=*adj*) having a tendency towards, quality of: (動詞+～=形容詞)有…傾向的;有…性質的: *active; constructive.*

-ize (also **-ise**, which is not used in this dictionary, but is equally acceptable) (亦作 -ise, 此拼法雖不用於本辭典,但同樣可接受) /-aɪz; -aɪz/ *suff* (used to form a *v*) (用以構成動詞) **1** cause to be, make like, change into: 使成爲;使像;使變成: *computerize; dramatize.* **2** act with the qualities of: 以…的特點行事: *criticize; deputize.*

-less /-lɪs; -lɪs/ *suff* (*n*+～=*adj*) without: (名詞+～=形容詞)沒有…的: *treeless; spiritless.* **-lessly** /-lɪslɪ; -lɪslɪ/ *adv* **-lessness** /-lɪsnɪs; -lɪsnɪs/ *n*

-let /-lɪt; -lɪt/ *suff* (*n*+～=*n*) diminutive: (名詞+～=名詞)小型的: *piglet; booklet.*

-like /-laɪk; -laɪk/ *suff* (*n*+～=*adj*) resembling, in the manner of: (名詞+～=形容詞)像…的;…般的: *childlike; godlike.*

-ling /-lɪŋ; -lɪŋ/ *suff* **1** (used to form a *n*) diminutive: (用以構成名詞)非常小的: *duckling; fledgeling.* **2** (used to form a *n*) person connected with (often used disparagingly): (用以構成名詞)與…有關的人(常帶貶義): *hireling; underling.*

-logue /-lɒg *US:* -lɔːg; -lɔg/ *suff* (used to form a *n*) sth spoken: (用以構成名詞)話;談話: *dialogue; travelogue; monologue.*

-logy /-lədʒɪ; -lədʒɪ/ *suff* (*pl* -logies) (used to form a *n*) branch of learning: (用以構成名詞)某門學問;…學: *biology; sociology.*

-ly /-lɪ; -lɪ/ *suff* **1** (*n*+～=*adj*) having the qualities of: (名詞+～=形容詞)具有…性質或特點的: *cowardly; scholarly.* **2** (*n*+～=*adj* or *adv*) regular occurrence: (名詞+～=形容詞或副詞)定期發生;每…一次: *hourly; yearly.* **3** (*adj*+～=*adv*) in the manner of the *adj*: (形容詞+～=副詞)(以所述形容詞的方式)…地: *happily; stupidly.*

macro- /mækrə(ʊ)-; mækrə-, mækro-/ *pref* relatively large, extending: 比較大的;延長的: *macrocosm; macrobiotic.*

mal- /mæl-; mæl-/ *pref* bad, wrong, not: 壞;差;不良;錯誤: *maladjusted; malnutrition.*

-man *suff* **1** /-mən; -mən/ (used to form a *n*) dweller in: (用以構成名詞)…的居民: *Irishman; countryman.* **2** /-mən, -mæn; -mən, -mæn/ (*n*+～=*n*) sb connected by a specific activity to: (名詞+～=名詞)與某種活動有關的人: *guardsman; doorman; businessman.*

-mania /-meɪnɪə; -menɪə/ *suff* (used to form a *n*) abnormal behaviour, excessive enthusiasm: (用以構成名詞)反常行爲;狂熱: *kleptomania; bibliomania.* **-maniac** /-meɪnɪæk; -menɪæk/ sb affected by a '-mania': 有…狂者: *kleptomaniac.*

matri- /meɪtrɪ-, mætrɪ-; metrɪ-, mætrə-/ *pref* mother: 母親: *matriarch; matricide.*

mega- /megə-; mɛgə-/ *pref* **1** large: 大: *megalith.* **2** one million: 一百萬: *megaton.*

-ment /-mənt; -mənt/ *suff* (*v*+～=*n*) result or means of an action: (動詞+～=名詞)行爲的結果或方式: *development; government.* **-mental** *adj* **-mentally** *adv*: *governmental(ly).*

-meter /-mɪtə(r); -mətɚ/ *suff* (used to form a *n*) a means of measuring: (用以構成名詞)測量用的工具;計;表: *speedometer.*

-metre /-miːtə(r); -mitɚ/ *suff* (used to form a *n*) a (specified) part of a metre: (用以構成名詞)一公尺的…部分: *centimetre.*

micro- /maɪkr(ə- *etc*); maɪkr(ə- *etc*)/ *pref* **1** relatively small: 比較小的;微: *microfilm; microwave.* **2** of examining or reproducing small quantities: 顯微的;擴大的;放大的: *microscope; microphone.*

milli- /mɪlɪ-; mɪlə-/ *pref* a thousandth part of: 千分

之一;毫: *milligram; millimetre.*

mis- /mɪs- ; mɪs-/ *pref* bad, wrong, not: 不良;錯誤;不: *misconduct; misdirect; mistrust.*

-monger /-mʌŋgə(r) ; -mʌŋgɚ/ *suff* (used to form a *n*) sb who deals in: (用以構成名詞)販賣…的人;經營…的人: *fishmonger; scandalmonger.*

mono- /mɒn(ə- *etc*) ; mɑn(ə- *etc*)/ *pref* one, a single: 一;單一: *monosyllable; monotone.*

-most /-məʊst ; -most/ *suff* (*prep* or *adj of position* +～=*superl adj*): (介詞或方位形容詞+～=最高級形容詞): *inmost; outermost.*

multi- /mʌltɪ- ; mʌltɪ-/ *pref* many: 許多: *multistage; multi-coloured.*

neo- /niː(ə- *etc*) ; ni(ə- *etc*)/ *pref* new, revived, later: 新的;復興的;新近的: *neologism; neo-classical.*

-ness /-nɪs ; -nɪs/ *suff* (*adj*+～=*n*) a quality, state, character: (形容詞+～=名詞)性質;狀態;性格: *dryness; silliness.*

neur(o)- /njʊər(ə- *etc*) *US:* nʊə- ; njʊr(ə- *etc*)/ *pref* of the nervous system: 神經系統的: *neuralgia; neurology.*

non- /nɒn- ; nɑn-/ *pref* not: 非;不: *nonsense; non-stop.*

-oid /-ɔɪd ; -ɔɪd/ *suff* (used to form an *adj* or *n*) resembling in shape: (用以構成形容詞或名詞)…狀的(東西): *asteroid; rhomboid.*

-or /-ə(r), -ɔː(r) ; -ɚ, -ɔr/ *suff* (*v*+～=*n*) sb or sth that carries out the action of the *v*: (動詞+～=名詞)執行或做出…之人或物: *governor; elevator; lessor.*

-ories ⇨ -ory

ortho- /ɔːθ(ə- *etc*) ; ɔrθ(ə- *etc*)/ *pref* correct, standard: 正確的;標準的: *orthodox; orthopaedic.*

-ory /-ərɪ, -rɪ *US:* -ɔːrɪ ; -orɪ, -ərɪ/ *suff* (*pl* -ories) **1** (used to form a *n*) place where specific activity is carried on: (用以構成名詞) 從事某種活動的地方: *laboratory; observatory.* **2** (used to form an *adj*): (用以構成形容詞): *compulsory; illusory.*

-osis /-əʊsɪs *etc* ; -osɪs *etc*/ *suff* (used to form a *n*) a process, change: (用以構成名詞)過程;變化: *hypnosis; metamorphosis.*

-ous /-əs ; -əs/ *suff* (*n*+～=*adj*) having the qualities of: (名詞+～=形容詞)具有…性質的: *poisonous; zealous.* **-ously** /-əslɪ ; -əslɪ/ *adv* **-ousness** /-əsnɪs ; -əsnɪs/ *n*

out- /aʊt- ; aʊt-/ *pref* **1** located outside: 在外面的: *outhouse; outpost.* **2** surpassing, to a greater extent: 超越;在…上超過: *outnumber; outmanoeuvre.* **3** with the various senses of 'out' as defined in the dictionary: 具有本辭典 out 條各種意義: *outcry; outspoken.*

over- /əʊvə(r)- ; ovɚ-/ *pref* **1** across, above: 橫越;在…之上: *overland; overhead.* **2** to excess, too much: 過度;過多: *overcharge; overwork.* **3** with the various senses of 'over' as defined in the dictionary: 具有本辭典 over 條的各種意義: *overthrow; overpower.*

pale(o)- (also 亦作 **palae(o)-** /pælɪ(ə- *etc*) ; pelɪ(ə- *etc*)/ *pref* of ancient times: 古代的: *paleolithic; paleontology.*

pan- /pæn- ; pæn-/ *pref* all, throughout: 全部;遍及;泛: *panchromatic; Pan-African.*

patri- /peɪtrɪ-, pætrɪ- ; petrɪ-, pætrə-/ *pref* father: 父親: *patriarch; patricide.*

-philia /-fɪlɪə ; -fɪlɪə/ *suff* (used to form a *n*) excessive love of: (用以構成名詞)對…過度愛好: *Anglophilia; bibliophilia.* **-phile** /-faɪl ; -faɪl/ *n* lover of. …的愛好者;親…的人。

-phobia /-fəʊbɪə ; -fobɪə/ *suff* (used to form a *n*) excessive fear of: (用以構成名詞)對…過度恐懼: *claustrophobia; xenophobia.* **-phobic** *adj* **-phobe** *n* fearer of. 恐懼…的人;仇視…的人。

-phone /-fəʊn ; -fon/ *suff* (used to form a *n*) means of reproducing sound: (用以構成名詞)重現聲音的工具: *megaphone; telephone.* **-phonic** /-fɒnɪk ; -fɑnɪk/ *adj*: *stereophonic.*

phon(o)- /fə(ʊ)n(ə- *etc*) ; fon(ə- *etc*)/ *pref* of sound: 聲音的;語音的: *phonetic; phonology.*

photo- /fəʊt(ə- *etc*) ; fot(ə- *etc*)/ *pref* **1** of light: 光的: *photoelectric.* **2** of photography: 攝影的;照相的: *photocopy; photogenic.*

physi(o)- /fɪzɪ(ə- *etc*) ; fɪzɪ(ə- *etc*)/ *pref* of the body, of living things: 身體的; 生物的: *physiotherapy; physiology.*

poly- /pɒlɪ- *etc* ; pɑlɪ- *etc*/ *pref* many: 許多的; 多…的: *polygamy; polysyllabic.*

post- /pəʊst- *etc* ; post- *etc*/ *pref* after: 在…之後的: *postscript; posthumous; postgraduate.*

pre- /priː- *etc* ; pri- *etc*/ *pref* before: 預先;在…之前: *prefabricate; premature; prerecorded.*

pro- /prəʊ- ; pro-/ *pref* **1** supporting, in favour of: 支持…的;贊同…的: *pro-Chinese; pro-revolutionary.* **2** acting as: 代理…;臨時…: *pro-Vice-Chancellor.*

proto- /prəʊt(ə- *etc*) ; prot(ə- *etc*)/ *pref* first, original, basic: 最早的;最先的;原始的;基本的: *prototype; protoplasm.*

pseud(o)- /sjuːd(ə- *etc*) *US:* suː- ; sjud(ə- *etc*)/ *pref* false, fake: 假的;偽造的: *pseudonym; pseudo-intellectual.*

psych(o)- /saɪk(ə- *etc*) ; saɪk(ə- *etc*)/ *pref* of the mind: 精神的;心理的: *psychiatry; psycho-analysis.*

quasi- /kweɪsaɪ- ; kwesaɪ-/ *pref* almost, seemingly: 近乎…的;似乎是…的: *quasi-serious; quasi-explanation.*

re- /riː- *etc* ; ri- *etc*/ *pref* again: 再;重新: *re-echo; reinstate.*

retro- /retr(ə- *etc*) ; rɛtr(ə- *etc*)/ *pref* backwards, behind: 向過去;向後: *retrospective; retro-rocket.*

-ry ⇨ -ery

-s /*After* p, t, k, f, θ *pronounced* s; *otherwise* z 在 p, t, k, f, θ 各音後讀做 s; 他處讀做 z/ *suff* **1** (used to form the *pl* of a *n*): (用以構成名詞的複數) *pots; stars.* **2** (used to form *3rd pers sing pres t* of a *v*): (用以構成動詞第三人稱單數現在式): *breaks; sees.*

-scape /-skeɪp ; -skep/ *suff* (*n*+～=*n*) a stretch of scenery: (名詞+～=名詞)一片景色;…景: *landscape; moonscape.*

-scope /-skəʊp ; -skop/ *suff* (used to form a *n*) means of observing or showing: (用以構成名詞)觀察或指示用的工具(或儀器): *microscope; stroboscope.*

self- /self- ; sɛlf-/ *pref* of one's self, alone, independent: 自己; 自力; 自動; 自我; 自主: *self-taught; self-service.*

semi- /semɪ- *US:* semaɪ- ; sɛmə-/ *pref* half, partially, midway: 一半;部分地;在中間: *semicircular; semi-detached; semi-final.*

-ship /-ʃɪp ; -ʃɪp/ *suff* (*n*+～=*n*) (名詞+～=名詞) **1** state of being, status, office: …的狀態、身分、職位或職務: *friendship; ownership; professorship.* **2** skill, proficiency as: 做為…的技能或熟練: *musicianship; scholarship.*

-sion ⇨ -tion

soci(o)- /səʊsɪ(ə- *etc*) ; soʃɪ(ə- *etc*)/ *pref* of society: 社會的: *sociology; socio-economic.*

-some /-səm ; -səm/ *suff* (used to form an *adj*) likely to, productive of: (用以構成形容詞)易於…的;會引起…的: *quarrelsome; meddlesome.*

-sphere /-sfɪə(r) ; -sfɪr/ *suff* (used to form a *n*) spherical, of a sphere: (用以構成名詞)球形的; 球狀的: *hemisphere; atmosphere.*

-ster /-stə(r) ; -stɚ/ *suff* **1** (*n*+～=*n*) sb connected with the *n*: (名詞+～=名詞)與所述名詞有關的人: *songster; gangster.* **2** (*adj*+～=*n*) sb with the qualities of the *adj*: (形容詞+～=名詞)具有所述形容詞的性質的人: *youngster.*

sub- /sʌb- *etc* ; sʌb- *etc*/ *pref* **1** under: 在…下面的: *subway; subsoil.* **2** secondary, lower in rank: 次等;次要;附屬: *sub-committee; sub-species.* **3** not quite: 低於;次於;亞於: *subtropical; subnormal.* **4** (used with a *v*) secondary repetition: (用在動詞上)第二次重複;再: *sublet; subdivide.*

super- /suːpə(r)-; supɚ-/ *pref* **1** above, over: 在…上面: *superstructure; superimpose.* **2** superior to, more than: 超過;過越: *superhuman; supernatural.*

sym- (also 亦作 **syn-**) /sɪm-, sɪn- *etc*; sɪm-, sɪn- *etc*/ *pref* sharing with, together: 共同,聯同: *sympathy; synchronize.*

-t /-t; -t/ *suff* (used to form the *pt* and *pp* of some *vv*): (用以構成某些動詞的過去式和過去分詞): *burnt; lent; slept.*

techn(o)- /tekn(ɒ- *etc*); tɛkn(ɑ- *etc*)/ *pref* of applied science: 與應用科學有關的;與技術有關的: *technocracy; technology.*

tele- /telɪ- *etc*; tɛlə- *etc*/ *pref* of linking across distances: 遠距離的: *telepathy; television.*

theo- /θiː(ɒ- *etc*); θi(ɑ- *etc*)/ *pref* of God: 上帝的;神的: *theocracy; theology.*

thermo- /θɜːm(ə- *etc*); θɝm(ə- *etc*)/ *pref* of heat, of temperature: 與熱有關的;與溫度有關的: *thermostat; thermometer.*

-tion /-ʃn; -ʃən/ (also 亦作 **-sion** /-ʃn, -ʒn; -ʃən, -ʒən/; **-ation** /-eɪʃn; -eʃən/; **-ition** /-ɪʃn; -ɪʃən/) *suff* (*v*+～=*n*): (動詞+～=名詞): *relation; confession; adhesion; hesitation; competition.* **-tional** /-ʃənl; -ʃənl̩/ *adj* **-tionally** /-ʃnəlɪ; -ʃənl̩ɪ/ *adv*

trans- /trænz- *etc*; trænz- *etc*/ *pref* **1** across: 橫越;橫過: *transatlantic; transcontinental.* **2** to a changed state: 轉變;移轉: *transplant; transform.*

tri- /traɪ- *etc*; traɪ- *etc*/ *pref* three: 三;三個: *triangle; tricolour.*

-tude /-tjuːd *US:* -tuːd; -tjud/ *suff* (used to form a *n*) condition: (用以構成名詞)狀況;狀態: *magnitude; exactitude.*

-ule /-juːl; -jul/ *suff* (used to form a *n*) relative smallness: (用以構成名詞)較小;小: *capsule; globule.*

ultra- /ʌltrə-; ʌltrə-/ *pref* beyond, to excess: 在…的那一邊;超過;極度: *ultraviolet; ultra-liberal.*

un- /ʌn-; ʌn-/ *pref* **1** (used with an *adj* or *n*) not: (用在形容詞或名詞上)不; 非: *unable; untruth.* **2** (used with a *v*) negative, reverse, opposite of: (用在動詞上)…的否定、還原、相反: *uncover; unpack.*

under- /ʌndə(r)-; ʌndɚ-/ *pref* **1** located beneath: 在…下面的: *undercurrent; undergrowth.* **2** not enough: 不足;過少;過低: *underestimate; undersized.* **3** lower in rank, importance: 低於;次於;副: *under-secretary; understudy.*

uni- /juːnɪ-; junɪ-/ *pref* one, the same: 單一;同一: *uniform; unisex.*

up- /ʌp-; ʌp-/ *pref* to a higher or better state: 向上;較高;較好: *uphill; upgrade.*

-ure /-jʊə(r), -jə(r) *etc*; -jʊr, -jɚ *etc*/ *suff* (used to form a *n*) act, process, condition: (用以構成名詞)動作;過程;狀況: *closure; legislature.*

vice- /vaɪs-; vaɪs-/ *pref* sb who is next in rank to and may act for another: 次;副: *vice-consul; vice-president.*

-ward /-wəd; -wɚd/ *suff* (used to form an *adj* or *adv*) in the direction of: (用以構成形容詞或副詞)朝向: *backward; eastward; homeward.* **-wards** /-wədz; -wɚdz/ *adv*

well- /wel-; wɛl-/ *pref* (～+*pp* of a *v*=*adj*) (～+動詞的過去分詞=形容詞) **1** fortunately: 幸運地: *well-born.* **2** properly, thoroughly: 適當地;完全地: *well-informed; well-worn.*

-wise /-waɪz; -waɪz/ *suff* (*n* or *adj*+～=*adv*) (名詞或形容詞+～=副詞) **1** in the manner of: 以…的方式;像…般地: *crosswise; crabwise.* **2** (colloq) in connection with: (俗)在…方面: *disciplinewise; accommodationwise.*

-worth /-wɜːθ, -wəθ; -wɝθ, -wɚθ/ *suff* (used to form a *n*) using the amount of: (用以構成名詞)相當於…數目或價值: *poundsworth; daysworth.*

-worthy /-wɜːðɪ; -wɝðɪ/ *suff* (*n*+～=*adj*) deserving of: (名詞+～=形容詞)值得…的;應受…的: *praiseworthy; blameworthy.* **-worthily** *adv*

-y[1] (also 亦作 **-ey**) /-ɪ; -ɪ/ *suff* (*n*+～=*adj*): (名詞+～=形容詞): *dusty; bushy; clayey.* **-ier** /-ɪə(r); -ɪɚ/ *comp* **-iest** /-ɪɪst; -ɪɪst/ *superl* **-ily** /-ɪlɪ; -ɪlɪ/ *adv.*

-y[2] (also 亦作 **-ie**) /-ɪ; -ɪ/ *suff* (*n*+～=*n*) pet name or familiar name: (名詞+～=名詞)親暱或親密的稱呼: *piggy; doggie; daddy; Susie.* ⇨ also App 7. 亦參看附錄七。

Appendix 4 **NUMERICAL EXPRESSIONS**

附錄四 數字表達法

The following section will give you help in the reading, speaking and writing of numbers and expressions which commonly contain numbers.
本附錄就有關數字及通常含有數字的用語之閱讀、口說和書寫三方面提供如下的資料。

1 Numbers 數字

Note. 'a /ə ; ə/ hundred' is a less formal usage than 'one /wʌn ; wʌn/ hundred'.
注意:a hundred 的說法不如 one hundred 正式。

CARDINAL 基數

1 one /wʌn ; wʌn/ 一
2 two /tuː ; tu/ 二
3 three /θriː ; θri/ 三
4 four /fɔː(r) ; for/ 四
5 five /faɪv ; faɪv/ 五
6 six /sɪks ; sɪks/ 六
7 seven /'sevn ; 'sɛvən/ 七
8 eight /eɪt ; et/ 八
9 nine /naɪn ; naɪn/ 九
10 ten /ten ; tɛn/ 十
11 eleven /ɪ'levn ; ɪ'lɛvən/ 十一
12 twelve /twelv ; twɛlv/ 十二
13 thirteen /ˌθɜː'tiːn ; θɝ'tin/ 十三
14 fourteen /ˌfɔː'tiːn ; for'tin/ 十四
15 fifteen /ˌfɪf'tiːn ; fɪf'tin/ 十五
16 sixteen /ˌsɪk'stiːn ; sɪks'tin/ 十六
17 seventeen /ˌsevn'tiːn ; ˌsɛvən'tin/ 十七
18 eighteen /ˌeɪ'tiːn ; e'tin/ 十八
19 nineteen /ˌnaɪn'tiːn ; naɪn'tin/ 十九
20 twenty /'twentɪ ; 'twɛntɪ/ 二十
21 twenty-one /ˌtwentɪ'wʌn ; 'twɛntɪ'wʌn/ 二十一
22 twenty-two /ˌtwentɪ'tuː ; 'twɛntɪ'tu/ 二十二
23 twenty-three /ˌtwentɪ'θriː ; 'twɛntɪ'θri/ 二十三
30 thirty /'θɜːtɪ ; 'θɝtɪ/ 三十
38 thirty-eight /ˌθɜːtɪ'eɪt ; 'θɝtɪ'et/ 三十八
40 forty /'fɔːtɪ ; 'fɔrtɪ/ 四十
50 fifty /'fɪftɪ ; 'fɪftɪ/ 五十
60 sixty /'sɪkstɪ ; 'sɪkstɪ/ 六十
70 seventy /'sevntɪ ; 'sɛvəntɪ/ 七十
80 eighty /'eɪtɪ ; 'etɪ/ 八十
90 ninety /'naɪntɪ ; 'naɪntɪ/ 九十
100 a/one hundred
/ə, wʌn 'hʌndrəd ; ə, wʌn 'hʌndrəd/ 一百
1000 a/one thousand
/ə, wʌn 'θaʊznd ; ə, wʌn 'θaʊzn̩d/ 一千
10 000 ten thousand
/ˌten 'θaʊznd ; 'tɛn'θaʊzn̩d/ 一萬
100 000 a/one hundred thousand
/ə, wʌn ˌhʌndrəd 'θaʊznd ; ə, wʌn 'hʌndrəd 'θaʊzn̩d/ 十萬
1 000 000 a/one million
/ə, wʌn 'mɪlɪən ; ə, wʌn 'mɪljən/ 一百萬

ORDINAL 序數

1st first /fɜːst ; fɝst/ 第一
2nd second /'sekənd ; 'sɛkənd/ 第二
3rd third /θɜːd ; θɝd/ 第三
4th fourth /fɔːθ ; forθ/ 第四
5th fifth /fɪfθ ; fɪfθ/ 第五
6th sixth /sɪksθ ; sɪksθ/ 第六
7th seventh /'sevnθ ; 'sɛvənθ/ 第七
8th eighth /eɪtθ ; etθ/ 第八
9th ninth /naɪnθ ; naɪnθ/ 第九
10th tenth /tenθ ; tɛnθ/ 第十
11th eleventh /ɪ'levnθ ; ɪ'lɛvənθ/ 第十一
12th twelfth /twelfθ ; twɛlfθ/ 第十二
13th thirteenth /ˌθɜː'tiːnθ ; θɝ'tinθ/ 第十三
14th fourteenth /ˌfɔː'tiːnθ ; for'tinθ/ 第十四
15th fifteenth /ˌfɪf'tiːnθ ; fɪf'tinθ/ 第十五
16th sixteenth /ˌsɪk'stiːnθ ; sɪks'tinθ/ 第十六
17th seventeenth /ˌsevn'tiːnθ ; ˌsɛvən'tinθ/ 第十七
18th eighteenth /eɪ'tiːnθ ; e'tinθ/ 第十八
19th nineteenth /ˌnaɪn'tiːnθ ; naɪn'tinθ/ 第十九
20th twentieth /'twentɪəθ ; 'twɛntɪɪθ/ 第二十
21st twenty-first /ˌtwentɪ'fɜːst ; 'twɛntɪ'fɝst/ 第二十一
22nd twenty-second /ˌtwentɪ'sekənd ; 'twɛntɪ'sɛkənd/ 第二十二
23rd twenty-third /ˌtwentɪ'θɜːd ; 'twɛntɪ'θɝd/ 第二十三
30th thirtieth /'θɜːtɪəθ ; 'θɝtɪɪθ/ 第三十
38th thirty-eighth /ˌθɜːtɪ'eɪtθ ; 'θɝtɪ'etθ/ 第三十八
40th fortieth /'fɔːtɪəθ ; 'fɔrtɪɪθ/ 第四十
50th fiftieth /'fɪftɪəθ ; 'fɪftɪɪθ/ 第五十
60th sixtieth /'sɪkstɪəθ ; 'sɪkstɪɪθ/ 第六十
70th seventieth /'sevntɪəθ ; 'sɛvəntɪɪθ/ 第七十
80th eightieth /'eɪtɪəθ ; 'etɪɪθ/ 第八十
90th ninetieth /'naɪntɪəθ ; 'naɪntɪɪθ/ 第九十
100th a/one hundredth
/ə, wʌn 'hʌndrədθ ; ə, wʌn 'hʌndrədθ/ 第一百
1000th a/one thousandth
/ə, wʌn 'θaʊznθ ; ə, wʌn 'θaʊznθ/ 第一千
10 000th ten thousandth
/ˌten 'θaʊznθ ; 'tɛn 'θaʊzn̩θ/ 第一萬
100 000th a/one hundred thousandth
/ə, wʌn ˌhʌndrəd 'θaʊznθ ; ə, wʌn 'hʌndrəd 'θaʊzn̩θ/ 第十萬
1 000 000th a/one millionth
/ə, wʌn 'mɪlɪənθ ; ə, wʌn 'mɪljənθ/ 第一百萬

SOME MORE COMPLEX NUMBERS 比較複雜的數字

101 a/one hundred and one /ə, wʌn ˌhʌndrəd n 'wʌn ; ə, wʌn 'hʌndrəd n̩ 'wʌn/ 一百零一
152 a/one hundred and fifty-two /ə, wʌn ˌhʌndrəd n ˌfɪftɪ 'tuː ; ə, wʌn 'hʌndrəd n̩ 'fɪftɪ 'tu/ 一百五十二
1 001 a/one thousand and one /ə, wʌn ˌθaʊznd ən 'wʌn ; ə, wʌn 'θaʊzn̩d ən 'wʌn/ 一千零一
2 325 two thousand, three hundred and twenty-five /ˌtuː ˌθaʊznd, ˌθriː ˌhʌndrəd n ˌtwentɪ 'faɪv ; 'tu 'θaʊzn̩d, 'θri 'hʌndrəd n̩ 'twɛntɪ 'faɪv/ 二千三百二十五
15 972 fifteen thousand, nine hundred and seventy-two /ˌfɪftiːn ˌθaʊznd, ˌnaɪn ˌhʌndrəd n ˌsevntɪ 'tuː ; 'fɪftin 'θaʊzn̩d, 'naɪn 'hʌndrəd n̩ 'sɛvəntɪ 'tu/ 一萬五千九百七十二
234 753 two hundred and thirty-four thousand, seven hundred and fifty-three /ˌtuː ˌhʌndrəd n ˌθɜːtɪ ˌfɔː ˌθaʊznd, ˌsevn ˌhʌndrəd n ˌfɪftɪ 'θriː ; 'tu 'hʌndrəd n̩ 'θɝtɪ 'for 'θaʊznd, 'sɛvən 'hʌndrəd n̩ 'fɪftɪ 'θri/ 二十三萬四千七百五十三

		US 美國	GB and other European countries 英國及其他歐洲國家
1 000 000 000	10^9	a/one billion /ə, wʌn 'bɪlɪən ; ə, wʌn 'bɪljən/ 十億	a/one thousand million(s) /ə, wʌn 'θaʊznd 'mɪlɪən(z) ; ə, wʌn 'θaʊzn̩d 'mɪljən(z)/ 十億
1 000 000 000 000	10^{12}	a/one trillion /ə, wʌn 'trɪlɪən ; ə, wʌn 'trɪljən/ 萬億,兆	a/one billion /ə, wʌn 'bɪlɪən ; ə, wʌn 'bɪljən/ 萬億,兆

1 000 000 000 000 000	10^{15}	a／one quadrillion /ə, wʌn kwɒ'drɪlɪən ; ə, wʌn kwɑ'drɪljən/ 千萬億,千兆	a／one thousand billion(s) /ə, wʌn 'θaʊznd 'bɪlɪən(z) ; ə, wʌn 'θaʊznd 'bɪljən(z)/ 千萬億,千兆
1 000 000 000 000 000 000	10^{18}	a／one quintillion /ə, wʌn kwɪn'tɪlɪən ; ə, wʌn kwɪn'tɪljən/ 百億億,百萬兆	a／one trillion /ə, wʌn 'trɪlɪən ; ə, wʌn 'trɪljən/ 百億億,百萬兆

VULGAR FRACTIONS 分數

$\frac{1}{8}$ an／one eighth /ən, wʌn 'eɪtθ ; ən, wʌn 'etθ/ 八分之一

$\frac{1}{4}$ a／one quarter /ə, wʌn 'kwɔːtə(r) ; ə, wʌn 'kwɔrtɚ/ 四分之一

$\frac{1}{3}$ a／one third /ə, wʌn 'θɜːd ; ə, wʌn 'θɝd/ 三分之一

$\frac{1}{2}$ a／one half /ə, wʌn 'hɑːf *US:* 'hæf ; ə, wʌn 'hæf/ 二分之一

$\frac{3}{4}$ three quarters /ˌθriː 'kwɔːtəz ; 'θri 'kwɔrtɚz/ 四分之三

DECIMAL FRACTIONS 小數

0·125 (nought) point one two five /(ˌnɔːt) pɔɪnt ˌwʌn tuː 'faɪv ; (ˌnɔt) pɔɪnt ˌwʌn tu 'faɪv/ 零點一二五

0·25 (nought) point two five /(ˌnɔːt) pɔɪnt ˌtuː 'faɪv ; (ˌnɔt) pɔɪnt ˌtu 'faɪv/ 零點二五

0·33 (ˌnought) point ˌthree 'three 零點三三

0·5 (ˌnought) point 'five 零點五

0·75 (ˌnought) point ˌseven 'five 零點七五

Notes. 注意:

1 In the spoken forms of vulgar fractions, the versions 'and a half／quarter／third' are preferred to 'and one half／quarter／third' whether the measurement is approximate or precise. With more obviously precise fractions like $\frac{1}{8}$, $\frac{1}{16}$, 'and one eighth／sixteenth' is normal. Complex fractions like 3／462, 20／83 are spoken as 'three over four-six-two; twenty over eighty-three', especially in mathematical expressions, eg 'twenty-two over seven' for 22／7.

用口語表達分數時, and a half／quarter／third 的説法比 and one half／quarter／third 更爲人所喜用,不論所指的數量是近似的或精確的。至於像 $\frac{1}{8}$, $\frac{1}{16}$ 這些更清楚而精確的分數,則常用 and one eighth／sixteenth 的説法。像 3／462, 20／83 複雜的分數,則分別讀做 three over four-six-two 和 twenty over eighty-three, 在數學用語中尤其如此,例如 22／7 讀做 twenty-two over seven。

2 When speaking ordinary numbers we can use 'zero', 'nought' or 'oh' /əʊ ; o/ for the number 0; 'zero' is the most common US usage and the most technical or precise form, 'oh' is the least technical or precise. In using decimals, to say 'nought point five' for 0·5 is a more precise usage than 'point five'.

口說一般的數目時,我們可以用 zero, nought 或 oh 來指數字 0; zero 是最普通的美國用法,也是最專門或最精確的說法, 而 oh 的說法則是最不專門或是最不精確的。在使用小數時, 0·5 讀做 nought point five 比讀做 point five 來得精確。

3 In most continental European countries a comma is used in place of the GB／US decimal point. Thus 6·014 is written 6,014 in France. A space is used to separate off the thousands in numbers larger than 9999, eg 10 000 or 875 380. GB／US usage can also have a comma in this place, eg 7,500,000. This comma is replaced by a full point in continental European countries, eg 7.500.000. Thus 23,500·75 (GB／US) will be written 23.500,75 in France.

在大多數歐洲大陸上的國家,逗號用來替代英美的小數點。因此,在法國 6·014 寫做 6,014。在比 9999 大的數目裡,千的倍數皆以間隔隔開,例如 10 000 或 875 380。在此位置上,英美的用法也可有逗號,例如 7,500,000。在歐洲大陸上的國家裡,逗號以句點來替代,例如 7.500.000。因此 23,500·75 (英美寫法)在法國就寫成 23.500,75。

COLLECTIVE NUMBERS 集合數字

6 a half dozen／half a dozen 半打

12 a／one dozen (24 is two dozen *not* two dozens) 一打 (24 寫做 two dozen 而非 two dozens)

20 a／one score 廿,念

144 a／one gross /grəʊs ; gros/ 一羅,籮;十二打

three score years and ten (Biblical 聖經用語) = 70 years, the traditional average life-span of man. 七十歲(傳統上人之平均壽命)。

ROMAN 羅馬		ARABIC 阿拉伯	ROMAN 羅馬		ARABIC 阿拉伯	ROMAN 羅馬	ARABIC 阿拉伯	ROMAN 羅馬	ARABIC 阿拉伯
I	i	1	XVI	xvi	16	LX	60	DCC	700
II	ii	2	XVII	xvii	17	LXV	65	DCCC	800
III	iii	3	XVIII	xviii	18	LXX	70	CM	900
IV(IIII)	iv(iiii)	4	XIX	xix	19	LXXX	80	M	1000
V	v	5	XX	xx	20	XC	90	MC	1100
VI	vi	6	XXI	xxi	21	XCII	92	MCD	1400
VII	vii	7	XXV	xxv	25	XCV	95	MDC	1600
VIII	viii	8	XXIX	xxix	29	XCVIII	98	MDCLXVI	1666
IX	ix	9	XXX	xxx	30	IC	99	MDCCCLXXXVIII	1888
X	x	10	XXXI	xxxi	31	C	100		
XI	xi	11	XXXIV	xxxiv	34	CC	200	MDCCCXCIX	1899
XII	xii	12	XXXIX	xxxix	39	CCC	300	MCM	1900
XIII	xiii	13	XL	xl	40	CD	400	MCMLXXVI	1976
XIV	xiv	14	L	l	50	D	500	MCMLXXXIV	1984
XV	xv	15	LV	lv	55	DC	600	MM	2000

A letter placed after another letter of greater value adds, eg VI = 5+1 = 6. A letter placed before a letter of greater value subtracts, eg IV = 5−1 = 4. A dash placed over a letter multiplies the value by 1 000; thus $\overline{X}$ = 10 000 and $\overline{M}$ = 1 000 000. The alternative IIII is seen only on some clock faces (⇨ the illus at dial), and iiii is seen only in the preliminary pages of some books.

一個字母置於另一個數值較大的字母之後表示'加', VI = 5 + 1 = 6。一個字母置於另一個數值較大的字母之前表示'減',例如 IV=5−1=4。一短橫加於一字母上表示'乘上 1 000'; 因此 $\overline{X}$=10 000 而 $\overline{M}$=1 000 000。IV 的另一寫法 'IIII' 只見於某些鐘面上(參看 dial 之插圖), 而 'iiii' 的寫法只見於某些書籍的卷首數頁上。

2 Mathematical Expressions 數學用語

Below are some of the more common symbols and expressions used in mathematics, geometry and statistics; in the cases where alternative ways of saying the expressions are given, both are equally common but generally the first is more formal or technical and the second less formal or technical.
下列爲若干在數學、幾何及統計學上較常用的符號和說法；在列有兩種可供選擇的說法之情形中，此兩者皆同樣普遍，不過通常前列者比較正式或專門，而後列者則爲較不正式或不專門的說法。

- $+$ plus／and 加(上)
- $-$ minus／take away 減(去)
- $\pm$ plus or minus／approximately 正負，加(上)或減(去)；大約，…左右
- $\times$ (is) multiplied by／times (*or when giving dimensions* 或在表示面積、體積時說成) by 乘(以)
- $\div$ (is) divided by 除以
- $=$ is equal to／equals 等於
- $\neq$ is not equal to／does not equal 不等於
- $\simeq$ is approximately equal to (大)約等於
- $\equiv$ is equivalent to／is identical with 全等於
- $<$ is less than 小於
- $\nless$ is not less than 不小於
- $\leqslant$ is less than or equal to 小於或等於
- $>$ is more than 大於
- $\ngtr$ is not more than 不大於
- $\geqslant$ is more than or equal to 大於或等於
- % per cent 百分之…
- ∞ infinity 無限大
- $\propto$ varies as／is proportional to 隨…起變化，與…成比例
- 3:9::4:12 three is to nine, as four is to twelve, ⇨ proportion (5) 3比9等於4比12
- $\in$ is an element of (a set) 屬於
- $\notin$ is not an element of (a set) 不屬於
- $\emptyset$ *or* {} is an empty set 空集合
- $\cap$ intersection 交集
- $\cup$ union 聯集
- $\subset$ is a subset of 爲…的子集
- $\Rightarrow$ implies 蘊含；若…則…
- $\log_e$ natural logarithm *or* logarithm to the base e /i；i/ 自然對數(或以 e 爲底的對數)
- $\sqrt{}$ (square) root 平方根
- $\sqrt[3]{}$ cube root 立方根
- x^2 x /eks；ɛks/ squared x 平方
- x^3 x /eks；ɛks/ cubed x 立方
- x^4 x /eks；ɛks/ to the power four／to the fourth x 的四次方(或四次冪)
- π pi /paɪ；paɪ/ 圓周率
- r /ɑ:(r)；ɑr/ = radius of circle 半徑
- πr^2 pi r squared /ˌpaɪ ɑ: ˈskweəd；ˌpaɪ ɑr ˈskwɛrd/ (formula for area of circle) 圓周率乘半徑平方(圓面積的公式)
- n! n /en；ɛn/ factorial n 的階乘
- $\int$ the integral of …的積分
- $\angle$ angle 角
- ∟ right angle 直角
- $\triangle$ triangle 三角形
- $\parallel$ is parallel to 平行於
- $\perp$ is perpendicular to 垂直於
- ° degree, ⇨ degree(1) 度
- ′ minute (of an arc), ⇨ minute¹(2); foot *or* feet (unit of length) (弧之)分；呎，英尺(長度單位)
- ″ second (of an arc), ⇨ second³(1); inch *or* inches (unit of length) (弧之)秒；吋，英寸(長度單位)

THE GREEK ALPHABET 希臘字母

Many letters of the Greek alphabet are commonly used in statistics and other branches of mathematics. Here is a complete list of the letters:
希臘字母中有許多常用於統計學及其他種類的數學。以下是完整的希臘字母表：

capitals 大寫	*small letters* 小寫	*name* 名稱
Α	α	alpha /ˈælfə；ˈælfə/
Β	β	beta /ˈbi:tə *US:* ˈbeɪtə；ˈbetə/
Γ	γ	gamma /ˈgæmə；ˈgæmə/
Δ	δ	delta /ˈdeltə；ˈdɛltə/
Ε	ε	epsilon /epˈsaɪlən *US:* ˈepsɪlɒn；ˈɛpsəˌlɑn/
Ζ	ζ	zeta /ˈzi:tə *US:* ˈzeɪtə；ˈzetə/
Η	η	eta /ˈi:tə *US:* ˈeɪtə；ˈetə/
Θ	θ	theta /ˈθi:tə *US:* ˈθeɪtə；ˈθetə/
Ι	ι	iota /aɪˈəʊtə；aɪˈotə/
Κ	κ	kappa /ˈkæpə；ˈkæpə/
Λ	λ	lambda /ˈlæmdə；ˈlæmdə/
Μ	μ	mu /mju:；m(j)u/
Ν	ν	nu /nju: *US:* nu:；nu/
Ξ	ξ	xi /ksaɪ；zaɪ/
Ο	ο	omicron /əʊˈmaɪkrən *US:* ˈɒmɪkrɒn；ˈɑmɪˌkrɑn/
Π	π	pi /paɪ；paɪ/
Ρ	ρ	rho /rəʊ；ro/
Σ	σ,ς	sigma /ˈsɪgmə；ˈsɪgmə/
Τ	τ	tau /taʊ；taʊ/
Υ	υ	upsilon /ju:pˈsaɪlən *US:* ˈju:psɪlɒn；ˈjupsəˌlɑn/
Φ	φ	phi /faɪ；faɪ/
Χ	χ	chi /kaɪ；kaɪ/
Ψ	ψ	psi /psaɪ；saɪ/
Ω	ω	omega /ˈəʊmɪgə *US:* əʊˈmegə；oˈmɛgə/

3 Computer Numbers 電腦數字

Cheque books, business accounts, etc have long strings of numerals. If such a number has to be read aloud, the numerals are spoken as separate digits (1–9, 0=/əʊ；o/) grouped rhythmically into pairs. Doubled numerals may be read separately or as eg 'double six'. For example, '05216472' is ˌoh ˌfive／ˌtwo ˌone／ˌsix ˌfour／ˌseven ˈtwo. As mentioned earlier, 0 can also be read as 'zero' (formal) or 'nought' (informal). ⇨ also binary.
支票簿、帳簿等上常會有長串的數字。如要大聲讀出這種數目，則以兩個數字 (即 1–9, 0 讀作 /əʊ；o/) 爲一組有節奏地讀出。兩個相同的數字可分別讀出，或讀作，如 'double six'。例：'05216472' 讀作 ˌoh ˌfive／ˌtwo ˌone／ˌsix ˌfour／ˌseven ˈtwo。如前面所提過的，0 可讀成 'zero' (正式)或 'nought' (非正式)。亦參看 binary。

4 Measurements (Inanimate) 量度(指事物)

Traditionally GB and US measurements have been made in inches, feet, yards, miles, etc, but there is now a gradual move towards the metric system of millimetres, metres, kilometres, etc. Examples of

both are given below. (For tables of weight, measurement, etc and conversion tables, ➪ App 5.) Even if the move towards metrication is completed in the near future, there will remain a vast amount of literature in which the other units are used.
傳統上，英美的測量制度是以吋、呎、碼、哩等爲單位的，但目前逐漸有使用公釐、公尺、公里等公制單位的趨勢。(度量衡表及換算表參看附錄五)。即使在最近的將來完全改用公制，依然會留下大量的文獻是採用其他的單位。

in	inch(es) 吋	sq in	square inch(es) 平方吋	cu in	cubic inch(es) 立方吋
ft	foot/feet 呎	sq ft	square foot/feet 平方呎	cu ft	cubic foot/feet 立方呎
yd	yard(s) 碼	sq yd	square yard(s) 平方碼	cu yd	cubic yard(s) 立方碼
—	mile(s) 哩	—	square mile(s) 平方哩	—	—
mm	millimetre(s) 公釐	mm^2	square millimetre(s) 平方公釐	mm^3	cubic millimetre(s) 立方公釐
cm	centimetre(s) 公分	cm^2	square centimetre(s) 平方公分	cm^3, cc	cubic centimetre(s) 立方公分
m	metre(s) 公尺	m^2	square metre(s) 平方公尺	m^3	cubic metre(s) 立方公尺
km	kilometre(s) 公里	km^2	square kilometre(s) 平方公里	—	—

(➪ square¹(4) for the difference between eg 'four square feet' and 'four feet square')
(像 'four square feet' 與 'four feet square' 之差別，參看 square¹(4))

DISTANCE 距離

London to New York is three thousand, four hundred and forty-one miles. (3 441 miles)
從倫敦到紐約有三千四百四十一哩的距離。

London to New York is five thousand, five hundred and six kilometres. (5 506 km)
從倫敦到紐約有五千五百零六公里的距離。

There is a speed limit of thirty miles per/an hour. (30 mph)
限制時速爲30哩。

There is a speed limit of fifty kilometres per/an hour. (50 kph)
限制時速爲50公里。

That ship has a top speed of fifteen knots.
(1 knot=1 nautical mile per hour)
該船最高的速度爲15節。(1節＝每小時1海哩)

HEIGHT/DEPTH 高度/深度

Mount Everest is twenty-nine thousand and twenty-eight feet high. (29 028 ft)
埃佛勒斯峯是兩萬九千零二十八呎高。

Mount Everest is eight thousand, eight hundred and forty-eight metres high. (8 848 m)
埃佛勒斯峯是八千八百四十八公尺高。

The airliner is flying at a height/an altitude of twenty thousand feet. (20 000 ft)
該架客機在(海拔)二萬呎的高空飛行。

The airliner is flying at a height/an altitude of six thousand metres. (6 000 m)
該架客機在(海拔)六千公尺的高空飛行。

The sea's average depth is twelve thousand feet or two and half miles. (12 000 ft)
該海的平均深度爲一萬二千呎或二哩半。

The sea's average depth is three thousand seven hundred metres. (3 700 m)
該海的平均深度爲三千七百公尺。

DIMENSION 大小

This room is sixteen foot/feet (wide) by twenty-five (foot/feet) (long). (16ft × 25ft *or* 或 16′ × 25′)
這個房間是十六呎寬二十五呎長。

This room is three metres (wide) by eight and half (metres) (long). (3m×8.5m)
這個房間是三公尺寬八點五公尺長。

AREA 面積

We need five thousand square foot/feet of office space. (5 000 sq ft)
我們需要五千平方呎的空間作辦公處所。

We need six hundred square metres of office space. (600 sq m)
我們需要六百平方公尺的空間作辦公處所。

Scotland has an area of thirty thousand, four hundred and five square miles. (30 405 sq miles)
➪ square¹(4)
蘇格蘭的面積爲三萬零四百零五平方哩。

Scotland has an area of seventy-six thousand, two hundred and thirty-five square kilometres. (76 235 sq km)
蘇格蘭的面積爲七萬六千二百三十五平方公里。

The house is for sale with ten acres of grounds.
此屋連同十畝庭園出售。

The house is for sale with four hectares of grounds.
此屋連同四公頃庭園出售。

VOLUME 容量

You'll need thirty (cubic) feet/foot of sand to mix with the cement. (30 cu ft)
➪ cubic
你需要三十立方呎的沙與水泥拌合。

You'll need a (cubic) metre of sand to mix with the cement. ($1\ m^3$)
你需要一立方公尺的沙與水泥拌合。

TEMPERATURE 溫度

The ordinary GB temperature scale for everyday use has been Fahrenheit. With metrication, the use of Centigrade (which has long been common in scientific usage) is becoming widespread.
英國日常用以量溫度的單位向來是華氏。隨著公制的使用，攝氏度量法日漸普及(攝氏度量法早已普遍使用於科學中)。

FAHRENHEIT 華氏

Water freezes at thirty-two degrees Fahrenheit. (32°F)
水在華氏三十二度時結冰。

Last night we had nine degrees of frost. (23°F)
昨夜溫度是冰點下九度(即華氏二十三度)。

It was ninety-five in the shade this morning. (95°F)
今晨在陰處溫度爲華氏九十五度。

CENTIGRADE 攝氏

Water freezes at nought drgrees Centigrade. (0°C)
水在攝氏零度時結冰。

Last night the temperature was five degrees below zero. (-5°C)
昨夜溫度是(攝氏)零下五度。

It was thirty-five in the shade this morning. (35°C)
今晨在陰處溫度爲攝氏三十五度。

ATHLETICS 田徑

He holds the record for the fifteen hundred metres (colloq 俗 '*the metric mile*'). (1 500 m)
他保持一千五百公尺的記錄。

She ran for her country in the two hundred metres women's hurdles. (200 m)
她代表她的國家參加兩百公尺女子跳欄賽跑。

Our team was narrowly beaten in the four by four hundred metres relay. (4 × 400 m)
我們隊在一千六百公尺接力賽跑中以極小之差被擊敗。

Our captain won the high jump with a jump of two point oh five metres (2.05 m), *and threw the javelin a national record of eighty-three point four four metres* (83.44 m).
我們隊長以二點零五公尺的高度贏得跳高冠軍，並以八十三點四四公尺的成績刷新擲標槍的全國記錄。

SWIMMING 游泳
I swam for Britain in the eight hundred metres freestyle. (800 m)
我代表英國參加八百公尺自由式泳賽。
She came second in the women's hundred metres back-stroke. (100 m)
她在女子一百公尺仰泳賽中得第二名。

TENNIS 網球
Smith won the first set six four/by six games to four (6–4). *The scoring in the final game was: fifteen love* (15–0), *fifteen all* (15–15), *thirty fifteen* (30–15), *forty fifteen* (40–15), *forty thirty* (40–30), *deuce* (40–40), *advantage Smith, game to Smith. Smith went on to win the match by three sets to two* (3–2).
史密斯以六比四贏得第一盤。最後一局的得分爲十五比零(卽一比零)，十五比十五(卽一比一)，三十比十五(卽二比一)，四十比十五(卽三比一)，四十比三十(卽三比二)，(四十比四十)平手，史密斯得分，史密斯贏得此局。史密斯最後以三盤對二盤(卽三比二)贏得此次比賽。

ASSOCIATION FOOTBALL (SOCCER) 英式足球
In the first leg the half-time score was one all (1–1). *In the second half only Italy scored and won the match two one/by two goals to one* (2–1). *The full time score in the return match was nil all/a goalless draw/a no goal draw* (0–0), *but Brazil scored two magnificent goals in extra time to win the Cup two nil* (2–0).
初賽上半場的比數是一比一。下半場只有義大利隊得分而以二比一贏得此賽。複賽全場的比數是零比零，但巴西隊在加賽時踢進兩個漂亮的球而得分，以二比零贏得獎杯。

RUGBY FOOTBALL (RUGGER) 橄欖球
Wales beat Scotland sixteen six/by sixteen points to six (16–6). *For Wales, Owen scored two tries* (8 points), *Price converted one* (2 points), *and kicked two penalty goals* (6 points). *Scotland's score came from a penalty* (3 points) *and a dropped goal* (3 points), *both kicked by Frazer.*
威爾斯隊以十六比六擊敗蘇格蘭隊。威爾斯隊中，歐文以兩次觸地球得八分，普萊斯踢入一球得兩分，踢兩次罰球得六分。蘇格蘭隊之得分來自一次罰球得三分，一次碰踢得三分，兩次皆爲弗雷熱所踢。

HORSE-RACING 賽馬
The Derby is run over a distance of twelve furlongs/one mile four furlongs/one and a half miles/a mile and a half. (12 fur = $1\frac{1}{2}$ miles)
英國大賽馬之全程爲十二浪(一哩又四浪，一哩半)。(12 浪＝$1\frac{1}{2}$哩)

The favourite in the Grand National was Never Say Die *at five to two.* (5–2, betting stake; *The odds on* Never Say Die *were five to two.*)
全英障礙賽馬中的熱門馬是人們以五比二的賭注看好的‘甭灰心’。(‘五比二’爲打賭方式，卽對‘甭灰心’的賠率爲賠五贏二。)

5 Measurements (Human) 量度(指人)

HEIGHT, ETC 身高等

i Note that 'tall', not 'high', is used. Feet and inches are used, or metres and centimetres if the metric system is employed.
注意：用 tall 不用 high。用呎和吋爲單位，如使用公制則以公尺和公分爲單位。

My wife is five foot/feet six (inches) (tall). (5ft 6in/5′6″) 我的太太身高五呎六(吋)。	*My wife is one metre sixty-eight (centimetres) (tall).* (1 m 68cm/1.68m) 我的太太身高一公尺六十八(公分)。

ii Measurements round parts of the body are in inches or centimetres:
量度身體各部的單位用吋或公分：

She is 36-24-36. (ie 36 inches round the bust, 24 round the waist, 36 round the hips) 她的三圍是 36-24-36。(卽胸圍 36 吋，腰圍 24 吋，臀圍 36 吋)	*She is 91-61-91.* (ie 91 centimetres round the bust, 61 round the waist, 91 round the hips) 她的三圍是 91-61-91。(卽胸圍 91 公分，腰圍 61 公分，臀圍 91 公分)

WEIGHT 體重
In GB weight has traditionally been given in stones and pounds, and in the US in pounds only. The metric system uses kilos/kilograms.
在英國，重量的單位傳統上用石與磅，在美國只用磅。公制則用公斤。

I weigh twelve stone eleven (pounds)/a hundred and seventy-nine pounds. (12st 11lb/179lb) 我重十二石十一磅(一百七十九磅)。	*I weigh eighty-one kilos* (81 kg). 我重八十一公斤。

AGE 年齡
I have three children. The eldest is nine (years old), the middle one is five and a half and the youngest is four. I'm thirty-three. How old are you?
我有三個孩子。最大的九歲，中間的五歲半，最小的四歲。我三十三歲。你幾歲？

6 Time of Day 時刻

Note When times are quoted, specified precisely or 'read' from a digital clock, the second form given below is more common.
注意：報時的時候，精確報時或根據數字鐘說出時，下列的第二種形式較爲常用。

GB 英國
7.00 seven o'clock/a m/p m /ə'klɒk, ˌeɪ'em, ˌpiː-'em ; ə'klɑk, ˌe'ɛm, ˌpi'ɛm/
(上午,下午)七點
8.15 a quarter past eight/eight fifteen
八點一刻/八點十五分
9.45 a quarter to ten/nine forty-five
差一刻十點/九點四十五分

US 美國
The system used is similar to that used in GB except that *after* is usual where GB has *past:*
與英國用法類似，只是英國用 past 之處，美國通常用 after:

5.10 ten after five
五點十分

4.30 half past four／four thirty／(colloq 俗) half four
四點半／四點卅分
5.10 ten (minutes) past five／five ten
五點十分
6.25 twenty-five (minutes) past six／six twenty-five
六點二十五分
6.35 twenty-five (minutes) to seven／six thirty-five
差廿五分七點／六點三十五分
9.57 three minutes to ten／nine fifty-seven
差三分十點／九點五十七分
2.03 three minutes past two／two oh three
兩點零三分

5.15 a quarter after five
五點一刻

9.30 'nine thirty' is more usual than 'half past nine'
'nine thirty' 較 'half past nine' 爲常用
九點半／九點卅分

of is common where GB has *to*:
英國用 to 之處，美國常用 of:

7.45 a quarter of eight
差一刻八點
7.55 five of eight
差五分八點

TWENTY-FOUR HOUR CLOCK 標示廿四小時之鐘

Used originally in military orders etc, but now increasingly used in travel timetables.
原用於軍事命令等，但今於旅行時刻表中漸多使用。

07.00 (ˌoh) ˌseven ˈhundred hours = 7.00 a m
七點(指上午)
10.30 ˌten ˈthirty = 10.30 a m
十點三十分(指上午)
12.00 ˌtwelve ˈhundred hours = midday／noon
十二點(卽正午)
13.45 ˌthirteen ˌforty-ˈfive = 1.45 p m
十三點四十五分(卽下午一點四十五分)
15.15 ˌfifteen ˌfifˈteen = 3.15 p m
十五點十五分(卽下午三點十五分)

19.00 ˌnineteen ˈhundred hours = 7.00 p m
十九點(卽下午七點)
22.50 ˌtwenty-ˌtwo ˈfifty = 10.50 p m
二十二點五十分(卽下午十點五十分)
23.05 ˌtwenty-ˌthree ˌoh ˈfive = 11.05 p m
二十三點零五分(卽下午十一點零五分)
24.00 ˌtwenty-ˌfour ˈhundred hours = midnight
二十四點(卽午夜)

7 Dates 日期

2000 BC 讀作 'two thousand /ˌbiːˈsiː ; ˌbiˈsi/'
公元前 2000 年
55 BC 讀作 'fifty-five /ˌbiːˈsiː ; ˌbiˈsi/' 公元前 55 年

AD is usually reserved only for the earlier years:
AD 通常只用於較早的年代:
AD 55 '/ˌeɪˈdiː ; ˌeˈdi/ fifty-five'; but 1066, not AD 1066.
公元 55 年寫作 AD 55; 但公元 1066 年則不加 AD。

Queen Elizabeth I 1558–1603: 'Queen Elizabeth the first reigned from fifteen (hundred and) fifty-eight to sixteen (hundred and) three／sixteen oh three.'
'伊麗莎白女王一世 1558–1603' 讀作: 伊麗莎白女王一世在位期間從 1558 年到 1603 年。

GB 英國
3(rd) January 1985: 1985 年1月3日，讀作 'the third of January nineteen eighty-five', often abbreviated to 常略作 3 Jan '85 (其餘各月略作 Feb, Mar, Apr, May, Jun, July, Aug, Sept, Oct, Nov, Dec) or to numbers only eg 或只以數字表示，如 3／1／85. Sometimes Roman numbers are used for the month, eg 有時用羅馬數字表示月份，如 27 ii 40.

US 美國
May 4, 1985: 1985 年 5 月 4 日，讀作 'May fourth, nineteen eighty-five.' In numbers only 只以數字表示，則爲: 5.4.85 (GB 英 = 4.5.85).

8 Money 錢幣

For monetary tables ⇨ Appendix 5
幣制表參看附錄五

GB 英國
I paid a penny／one p for it. (1p)
我付了一辨士買它。
It's ten pence／ten p a cup. (10p)
一杯十辨士。
The cheapest seats are fifty pence／fifty p each. (50p)
最便宜的座位每個五十辨士。
They'll charge you a pound／(sl 俚) *a quid membership fee.* (£1)
他們會收你一鎊的會費。

US 美國
I bought it for a cent. (1¢)
我以一分錢買了它。
It's ten cents a cup. (10¢)
一杯十分錢。
The cheapest seats are half a dollar／(sl 俚) *half a buck each.* (50¢)
最便宜的座位每個半塊錢。
They'll charge you a dollar／(sl 俚) *a buck membership fee.* ($1)
他們會收你一元的會費。

I was given one (pound) fifty (pence) change. (£1.50)
找了我一鎊五十辨士的零錢。
The return ticket is thirteen (pounds) twenty-seven (pence). (£13.27)
來回票是十三鎊二十七辨士。

I was given a dollar fifty／one fifty／(sl 俚) *one and a half bucks change.* ($1.50)
找了我一塊錢五角的零錢。
The return ticket is thirteen (dollars) twenty-seven (cents). ($13.27)
來回票是十三元二十七分。

Note: The penny and cent signs (p, ¢) are *never* shown with the pound and dollar signs (£, $) when writing down a sum of money:
eg £6.25 and $6.25 are right
£6.25p and $6.25¢ are wrong
注意：在寫一筆款項時，辨士與分的記號(p, ¢)'絕不' 與鎊與元的記號(£, $)同時標出: 如 £6.25 與 $6.25 是正確的，£6.25p 與 $6.25¢ 是錯誤的。

9 Telephoning 打電話

Each digit is spoken separately, ie no figure above nine is used. 0 is pronounced /əʊ ; o/. In US usage, 'zero' (and sometimes 'nought') may replace 'oh'. The figures are usually grouped rhythmically in pairs (pairing from the right), though there is a tendency to use rhythmic triplets, especially for six-figure numbers. If the two digits of a pair are the same, it is usually spoken as 'double three' etc. An exception is the GB emergency call 999 which is always *ˌnine ˌnine ˈnine.*
每個數字分別讀出，亦卽大於九的數字不用。0 讀成 /əʊ ; o/。美國用法中，0 可讀做 zero (有時讀成 nought)。所有的數字通常是兩個一組（由右至左計算）有節奏地讀出，雖然目前有使用三個爲一組讀法的趨勢，尤其是具有六個數字的號碼。如果一組中兩個數字都相同時，通常讀成如 double three 等。例外：英國緊急電話號碼 999 總是讀作 ˌnine ˌnine ˈnine。

6638 讀作 ˌdouble ˌsix, ˌthree ˈeight

but 但是

3668 讀作 ˌthree ˌsix, ˌsix ˈeight (or 或 ˌthree, ˌdouble ˌsix, ˈeight)

677 讀作 ˌsix, ˌdouble ˈseven

but 但是

667 讀作 ˌsix, ˌsix ˈseven (or 或 ˌdouble ˌsix, ˈseven)
In numbers which include a code number, the code is to be separated by a pause:
在包括區域代號的電話號碼中，念區域代號之後要稍作停頓：

01-629 8495 讀作 ˌoh ˈone ‖ ˌsix ˌtwo ˈnine ‖ ˌeight ˌfour, ˌnine ˈfive.

10 Chemical Formulae 化學式

In chemical formulae full-size and reduced-size numbers, and capital and lower case letters are not distinguished orally.
在化學式中，普通寫法的數字與縮小的數字，以及大寫字母和小寫字母，口語上均無分別。

NaCl 讀作 /ˌen eɪ siː ˈel ; ˏɛn e si ˈɛl/
$2H_2+O_2 = 2H_2O$ 讀作 /ˌtuː eɪtʃ ˌtuː ‖ plʌs ˌəʊ ˈtuː ‖ ˌiːkwəlz ˌtuː eɪtʃ tuː ˈəʊ ; ˏtu etʃ ˏtu ‖ plʌs ˏoˈtu ‖ ˏikwəlz ˏtu etʃ tu ˈo/

Appendix 5 **WEIGHTS AND MEASURES**

附錄五 度量衡表

The Metric System 公制

METRIC 公制	*length* 長度	GB & US 英美制
10 millimetres (mm) 公釐	= 1 centimetre (cm) 公分	= 0.3937 inches (in) 吋
100 centimetres 公分	= 1 metre (m) 公尺	= 39.37 inches 吋 or 或 1.094 yards (yd) 碼
1000 metres 公尺	= 1 kilometre (km) 公里	= 0.62137 miles 哩 or about 或約 ⅝ mile 哩
	surface 面積	
100 square metres (m^2) 平方公尺	= 1 are (a) 公畝	= 0.0247 acres 畝
100 ares 公畝	= 1 hectare (ha) 公頃	= 2.471 acres 畝
100 hectares 公頃	= 1 square kilometre (km^2) 平方公里	= 0.386 square miles 平方哩
	weight 重量	
10 milligrams (mg) 公絲	= 1 centigram (cg) 公毫	= 0.1543 grains 喱
100 centigrams 公毫	= 1 gram (g) (公)克	= 15.4323 grains 喱
1000 grams (公)克	= 1 kilogram (kg) 公斤	= 2.2046 pounds 磅
1000 kilograms 公斤	= 1 tonne 公噸	= 19.684 cwt 英擔
	capacity 容量	
1000 millilitres (ml) 公撮	= 1 litre (l) 公升	= 1.75 pints 品脫 (2.101 US pints 美國品脫)
10 litres 公升	= 1 decalitre (dl) 公斗	= 2.1997 gallons 加侖 (2.63 US gallons 美國加侖)

Avoirdupois Weight 常衡

GB & US 英美制		METRIC 公制
	1 grain (gr) 喱	= 0.0648 grams (g) (公)克
437½ grains 喱	= 1 ounce (oz) 啢,盎斯	= 28.35 grams 公克
16 drams (dr) 特拉姆,英錢	= 1 ounce 啢,盎斯	= 28.35 grams 公克
16 ounces 啢,盎斯	= 1 pound (lb) 磅	= 0.454 kilograms (kg) 公斤
14 pounds 磅	= 1 stone 呏	= 6.356 kilograms 公斤
2 stone 呏	= 1 quarter 夸特	= 12.7 kilograms 公斤
4 quarters 夸特	= 1 hundredweight (cwt) 英擔	= 50.8 kilograms 公斤
112 pounds 磅	= 1 cwt 英擔	= 50.8 kilograms 公斤
100 pounds 磅	= 1 short cwt 短擔	= 45.4 kilograms 公斤
20 cwt 英擔	= 1 ton 噸	= 1016.04 kilograms 公斤
2000 pounds 磅	= 1 short ton 短噸	= 0.907 metric tons 公噸
2240 pounds 磅	= 1 long ton 長噸	= 1.016 metric tons 公噸

Troy Weight 金衡

system of weights used in England for gold, silver and precious stones
英國金、銀及寶石之計量單位

GB & US 英美制		METRIC 公制
24 grains 喱	= 1 pennyweight (dwt) 英錢	= 1.555 grams (公)克
20 pennyweights 英錢	= 1 ounce 啢,盎斯	= 31.1 grams (公)克
12 ounces 啢,盎斯	= 1 pound 磅 (5760 grains 喱)	= 0.373 kilograms 公斤

Apothecaries' Weight 藥衡

used by pharmacists for mixing their medicines; they buy and sell drugs by Avoirdupois weight
藥劑師配藥之計量單位;買賣藥物則用常衡

GB & US 英美制		METRIC 公制
20 grains 喱	= 1 scruple 司克陸布,吩	= 1.296 grams (公)克
3 scruples 司克陸布,吩	= 1 dram 特拉姆,英錢	= 3.888 grams (公)克
8 drams 特拉姆,英錢	= 1 ounce 啢,盎斯	= 31.1035 grams (公)克
12 ounces 啢,盎斯	= 1 pound 磅	= 373.24 grams (公)克

Linear Measure 長度單位

GB & US 英美制		METRIC 公制
	1 inch (in) 吋	= 25.3995 millimetres (mm) 公釐
12 inches 吋	= 1 foot (ft) 呎	= 30.479 centimetres (cm) 公分
3 feet 呎	= 1 yard (yd) 碼	= 0.9144 metres (m) 公尺
5½ yards 碼	= 1 rod, pole, or 或 perch 桿	= 5.0292 metres 公尺
22 yards 碼	= 1 chain (ch) (測)鏈	= 20.1168 metres 公尺
220 yards 碼	= 1 furlong (fur) 浪	= 201.168 metres 公尺
8 furlongs 浪	= 1 mile 哩	= 1.6093 kilometres (km) 公里
1760 yards 碼	= 1 mile 哩	= 1.6093 kilometres 公里
3 miles 哩	= 1 league 里格	= 4.8279 kilometres 公里

Square Measure 面積單位

GB & US 英美制		METRIC 公制
	1 square inch 平方吋	= 6.4516 sq centimetres 平方公分
144 sq inches 平方吋	= 1 sq foot 平方呎	= 929.030 sq centimetres 平方公分
9 sq feet 平方呎	= 1 sq yard 平方碼	= 0.836 sq metres 平方公尺
484 sq yards 平方碼	= 1 sq chain 平方鏈	= 404.624 sq metres 平方公尺
4840 sq yards 平方碼	= 1 acre 畝	= 0.405 hectares 公頃
40 sq rods 平方桿	= 1 rood 路得	= 10.1168 ares 公畝
4 roods 路得	= 1 acre 畝	= 0.405 hectares 公頃
640 acres 畝	= 1 sq mile 平方哩	= 2.599 sq kilometres 平方公里

Cubic Measure 體積單位

GB & US 英美制		METRIC 公制
	1 cubic inch 立方吋	= 16.387 cu centimetres 立方公分
1728 cu inches 立方吋	= 1 cu foot 立方呎	= 0.028 cu metres 立方公尺
27 cu feet 立方呎	= 1 cu yard 立方碼	= 0.765 cu metres 立方公尺

Surveyors' Measure 丈量單位

GB & US 英美制		METRIC 公制
7.92 inches 吋	= 1 link 令	= 20.1168 centimetres 公分
100 links 令	= 1 chain 鏈	= 20.1168 metres 公尺
10 chains 鏈	= 1 furlong 浪	= 201.168 metres 公尺
80 chains 鏈	= 1 mile 哩	= 1.6093 kilometres 公里
10 square chains 平方鏈	= 1 acre 畝	= 0.405 hectares 公頃

Nautical Measure 海程單位

used for measuring the depth and surface distance of seas, rivers, etc
測量海洋、河流等的深度及水面距離所用

GB & US 英美制		METRIC 公制
6 feet 呎	= 1 fathom 嘚	= 1.8288 metres 公尺
608 feet 呎	= 1 cable 錨鏈	= 185.313 metres 公尺
6080 feet 呎	= 1 sea (or 或 nautical) mile 浬 (1.151 statute miles 法定哩)	= 1.852 kilometres 公里
3 sea miles 浬	= 1 sea league 海里格	= 5.550 kilometres 公里
60 sea miles 浬	= 1 degree 度	
360 degrees 度	= 1 circle 圓周	

The speed of one sea mile per hour is called a *knot*
每小時一浬的速率稱作一'節'

Liquid Measure of Capacity 液量單位

	GB 英制	US 美制	METRIC 公制
4 gills 吉爾,及耳	= 1 pint (pt) 品脫	= 1.201 pints 品脫	= 0.5679 litres 公升
2 pints 品脫	= 1 quart (qt) 夸脫	= 1.201 quarts 夸脫	= 1.1359 litres 公升
4 quarts 夸脫	= 1 gallon (gal) 加侖	= 1.201 gallons 加侖	= 4.5435 litres 公升

Apothecaries' Fluid Measure 液體藥量單位

used by pharmacists for measuring medicines
藥劑師量藥所用

GB & US 英美制		METRIC 公制
60 minims 量滴	= 1 fluid dram 液特拉姆	= 3.552 millilitres 公撮
8 fluid drams 液特拉姆	= 1 fluid ounce 液兩	= 2.841 centilitres 公勺
20 fluid ounces 液兩	= 1 pint 品脫	= 0.568 litres 公升
8 pints 品脫	= 1 gallon 加侖	= 4.546 litres 公升

Dry Measure of Capacity 乾量單位

GB & US 英美制		METRIC 公制 GB 英國	METRIC 公制 US 美國
	1 gallon 加侖	= 4.5435 litres 公升	= 4.404 liters 公升
2 gallons 加侖	= 1 peck 配克	= 9.0870 litres 公升	= 8.810 liters 公升
4 pecks 配克	= 1 bushel 蒲式耳	= 36.3477 litres 公升	= 35.238 liters 公升
8 bushels 蒲式耳	= 1 quarter 夸特	= 290.7816 litres 公升	= 281.904 liters 公升

Circular or Angular Measure 圓弧或角度單位

60 seconds (″) 秒 = 1 minute (′) 分

60 minutes 分 = 1 degree (°) 度

90 degrees 度 = 1 quadrant or right angle (L) 象限或直角

360 degrees 度 = 1 circle or circumference 圓(周)

the diameter of a circle = the straight line passing through its centre
圓的直徑＝過圓心的直線

the radius of a circle = ½ × the diameter
圓的半徑＝ ½ ×直徑

the circumference of a circle = ²²⁄₇ × the diameter
圓周(長)＝ ²²⁄₇ ×直徑

Temperature Equivalents 溫度等值

	FAHRENHEIT (F) 華氏	CENTIGRADE (C) 攝氏
Boiling Point 沸點	212°	100°
	194°	90°
	176°	80°
	158°	70°
	140°	60°
	122°	50°
	104°	40°
	86°	30°
	68°	20°
	50°	10°
Freezing Point 冰點	32°	0°
	14°	−10°
	0°	−17.8°
Absolute Zero 絕對零度	−459.67°	−273.15°

To convert Fahrenheit temperature into Centigrade: subtract 32 and multiply by 5/9 (five-ninths).
華氏溫度換算成攝氏溫度:減去 32 再乘以 5/9 (九分之五)。
To convert Centigrade temperature into Fahrenheit: multiply by 9/5 (nine-fifths) and add 32.
攝氏溫度換算成華氏溫度:乘以 9/5 (五分之九)再加上 32。

Money 錢幣

also ⇨ App 4(8) 亦參看附錄四第八節

GB: £ p (pounds and pence) 英國: £ p (鎊和辨士)

100 pence (100p) 辨士 = 1 pound (£1) 鎊

	(amount) (數額)	(coin) (硬幣)
½p	a halfpenny /ˈheɪpnɪ ; ˈhepənɪ/, half a penny 半辨士	a halfpenny /ˈheɪpnɪ ; ˈhepənɪ/ 半辨士硬幣
1p	a penny, (colloq 俗) one p /piː ; pi/ 一辨士	a penny 一辨士硬幣
2p	twopence /ˈtʌpəns ; ˈtʌpəns/, two pence, (colloq 俗) two p /piː ; pi/ 兩辨士	a twopenny /ˈtʌpnɪ ; ˈtuˌpɛnɪ/ piece 兩辨士硬幣
5p	five pence /ˈfaɪfpəns ; ˈfaɪvˈpens/ 五辨士	a fivepenny /ˈfaɪfpənɪ;ˈfaɪvˌpɛnɪ/ piece 五辨士硬幣
10p	ten pence /ˈtenpəns ; ˈtɛnˈpɛns/ 十辨士	a tenpenny /ˈtenpənɪ ; ˈtɛnˌpɛnɪ/ piece 十辨士硬幣
50p	fifty pence 五十辨士	a fifty pence piece 五十辨士硬幣
		(note) (紙幣)
£1	a pound, (sl 俚) a quid 一鎊	a pound note 一鎊面額鈔票
£5, £10, £20	five／ten／twenty pounds, (sl 俚) five／ten／twenty quid 五(十,廿)鎊	a five／ten／twenty pound note, (sl 俚) a fiver／tenner 五(十,廿)鎊面額鈔票
£3.82	three pounds eighty-two (pence) 3.82 鎊(即 3 鎊 82 辨士)	

US: $¢ (dollars and cents) 美國: $¢:(元和分)
100 cents (100¢) 分 = 1 dollar ($1) 元

	(amount) (數額)	(coin) (硬幣)
1¢	a cent 一分	a penny 一分硬幣
5¢	five cents 五分	a nickel 五分硬幣
10¢	ten cents 十分	a dime 十分硬幣
25¢	twenty-five cents 廿五分	a quarter 廿五分硬幣
50¢	half a dollar, (sl 俚) half a buck 五角	a half-dollar 五角硬幣
		(note) (紙幣)
$1	a dollar, (sl 俚) a buck 一元	a dollar bill 一元面額鈔票
$5, $10, $20	five/ten/twenty dollars, (sl 俚) five/ten/twenty bucks 五(十,廿)元	a five/ten/twenty dollar bill 五(十,廿)元面額鈔票
$3.82	three dollars eighty-two (cents) 3.82 元(卽 3 元 82 分)	

Time 時間

60 seconds 60 秒	= 1 minute = 1 分	4 weeks, or 28 days 4 週或 28 日	= 1 lunar month = 1 太陰月
60 minutes 60 分	= 1 hour = 1 小時	52 weeks, 1 day; or 13 lunar months, 1 day 52 週又 1 日,或 13 太陰月又 1 日	= 1 year = 1 年
24 hours 24 小時	= 1 day = 1 日		
7 days 7日	= 1 week = 1 週	365 days, 6 hours 365 日又 6 小時	= 1 (Julian) year = 1 (凱撒曆)年

Number of Days in the Month 日數歌

30 days have September,	四、六、九、十一,
April, June and November;	皆爲三十日;
All the rest have 31,	其餘三十一,
Excepting February alone,	唯有二月奇,
Which has but 28 days clear	常年二十八,
And 29 in each leap year.	閏年添一日。

Speed 速度

Light travels at 186 300 miles per second; 300 000 kilometres per second.
光的速度每秒 186,300 哩,或 300,000 公里。

Sound travels at 1130 feet per second; 330 metres per second; 770 miles per hour (the 'sound barrier').
聲音的速度每秒1,130 呎,或 330 公尺;每小時則是 770 哩(卽'音障')。

Appendix 6 GEOGRAPHICAL NAMES
附錄六　地名

A(a)lborg /'ɔ:lbɔ:g; 'ɔlbɔrg/ 阿爾堡(丹麥北部一港市)。
Abadan /ˌɑ:bɑ:'dɑ:n; ˌɑbə'dɑn/ 阿巴丹(伊朗西南部一港市)。
Aberdeen /æbə'di:n; 'æbɚˌdin/ 亞伯丁(美國華盛頓州西部一港埠)。
Aberdeenshire /ˌæbə'di:nʃə(r); ˌæbɚ'dinˌʃɪr/ 亞伯丁夏(昔爲蘇格蘭東北部一郡)。
Abidjan /ˌæbɪ'dʒɑ:n; ˌæbɪ'dʒɑn/ 阿必尙 (Ivory Coast 之首都)。
Abilene /'æbɪli:n; 'æbəˌlin/ 亞平倫(美國德克薩斯州西北部一城市)。
Abu Dhabi /'æbu:'ðæbi:; ˌɑbu'dæbɪ/ 阿布達比(United Arab Emirates 之首都)。
Abyssinia /ˌæbɪ'sɪnjə; ˌæbə'sɪnɪə/ 阿比西尼亞(參看 Ethiopia)。
Accra, Akkra /æ'krɑ:; ə'krɑ/ 阿克拉 (Ghana 之首都)。
Aconcagua /ˌækɒŋ'kɑ:gwə; ˌækən'kɑgwə/ 阿空加瓜山(在阿根廷西部)。
Acropolis /ə'krɒpəlɪs; ə'krɑpəlɪs/ 亞克羅玻利 (爲希臘雅典城之一部，多古跡)。
Adana /'ædənə; 'ɑdənə/ 亞達那(土耳其南部一城市)。
Addis Ababa /'ædɪs 'æbəbə; 'ædə 'sæbəbə/ 阿廸斯阿貝巴(Ethiopia 之首都)。
Adelaide /'ædəleɪd; 'ædḷˌed/ 阿得雷德(澳洲一城市)。
Aden /'eɪdn; 'ɑdṇ/ 亞丁 (Southern Yemen 之首都)。
Adirondacks /ˌædɪ'rɒndæks; ˌædə'rɑnˌdæks/ 阿第倫達克山脈(在美國紐約州東北部)。
Adriatic /ˌeɪdrɪ'ætɪk; ˌedrɪ'ætɪk/ 亞得里亞海(在義大利之東)。
Aegean /i:'dʒi:ən; ɪ'dʒiən/ 愛琴海(在希臘之東)。
Aetna = Etna。
Afghanistan /æfˌgænɪ'stɑ:n; æf'gænəˌstæn/ 阿富汗(亞洲西部一國家，首都 Kabul)。
Africa /'æfrɪkə; 'æfrɪkə/ 非洲。
Agra /'ɑ:grə; 'ɑgrə/ 亞格拉(印度北部一城市)。
Ahaggar /ə'hægə(r); ə'hɑgɚ/ 阿哈革山脈 (在阿爾及利亞南部)。
Aigun /aɪ'gʊn; aɪ'gun/ 瑷琿(中國黑龍江西岸一邊城，與蘇聯交界)。
Ajaccio /ə'jætʃɪəʊ; ɑ'jɑtʃo/ 阿雅丘(法國科西嘉島之首府)。
Akkra = Accra.
Akron /'ækrɒn; 'ækrən/ 亞克朗 (美國俄亥俄州東北部一城市，爲橡膠工業中心)。
Alabama /ˌælə'bæmə; ˌælə'bæmə/ 阿拉巴馬 (美國東南部一州，略作 *AL*)。
Alameda /ˌælə'mi:də; ˌælə'midə/ 阿拉美達 (美國加州舊金山灣東岸一城市)。
Alaska /ə'læskə; ə'læskə/ 阿拉斯加 (在北美洲西北部，爲美國之一州，略作 *AK*)。
Albania /æl'beɪnɪə; æl'benɪə/ 阿爾巴尼亞(國名，在歐洲南部巴爾幹半島上，首都 Tirana)。
Albany /'ɔ:lbənɪ; 'ɔlbənɪ/ 奥爾班尼 (**1** 美國紐約州之首府; **2** 美國喬治亞州西南部一城市; **3** 加拿大中部一河流)。
Alberta /æl'bɜ:tə; æl'bɝtə/ 亞伯達(加拿大西部之一省，略作 *Alta*)。
Albuquerque /'ælbəˌkɜ:kɪ; 'ælbəˌkɝkɪ/ 阿布圭基(美國新墨西哥州中部一城市)。
Aldan /ɑ:l'dɑ:n; ɑl'dɑn/ 阿耳丹河 (蘇聯亞洲部分之東部一河流)。
Aleutians /ə'lu:ʃɪənz; ə'luʃənz/ 阿留申羣島 (在阿拉斯加西南方，亦稱 Aleutian Islands)。
Alexander /ˌælɪg'zɑ:ndə; ˌælɪg'zændɚ/ 亞力山大羣島(在阿拉斯加東南方太平洋中)。
Alexandria /ˌælɪg'zɑ:ndrɪə; ˌælɪg'zændrɪə/ 亞歷山大(埃及北部一港市)。
Algeria /æl'dʒɪərɪə; æl'dʒɪrɪə/ 阿爾及利亞(國名，在非洲西北部，1962 年 7 月獨立，首都 Algiers)。
Algiers /æl'dʒɪəz; æl'dʒɪrz/ 阿爾及爾 (Algeria 之首都)。
Alicante /ˌælɪ'kæntɪ; ˌælə'kæntɪ/ 亞利坎第(西班牙東南部一港埠)。
(Al) Kuwait /(ˌæl)ku'weɪt; (ˌæl)kə'wet/ 科威特市 (Kuwait 之首都)。
Allahabad /ˌæləhə'bæd; 'æləhəˌbæd/ 阿拉哈巴(印度北部一城市，爲印度教之聖地)。
Allegheny /ˌælə'geɪnɪ; 'æləgenɪ/ **1** 阿利根尼河(在美國賓夕凡尼亞州西部)。**2** 阿利根尼山脈(在美國東部)。
Allentown /'ælɪntaʊn; 'ælənˌtaʊn/ 亞林鎮(美國賓夕凡尼亞州東部一城市)。
Alma-Ata /ˌælmə-ə'tɑ:; ˌælmə-ə'tɑ/ 阿拉木圖(蘇聯哈薩克共和國之首府)。
Almadén /ˌælmə'deɪn; ˌælmə'den/ 阿馬達(西班牙中南部一城市)。
Alps /ælps; ælps/ 阿爾卑斯山脈(歐洲最重要山脈，分全洲爲南北兩部)。
Alsace /'ælsæs; 'ælsæs/ 阿耳沙斯(法國東北部一地區)。
Altai /æl'teɪaɪ; 'ælˌtaɪ/ 阿爾泰山脈(在外蒙古、新疆及西伯利亞中南部境內)。
Amazon /'æməzən; 'æməˌzɑn/ 亞馬遜河(在南美洲之北部)。
Ambrose Channel /'æmbrəʊz-; 'æmbroz-/ 恩布路斯海峽(在美國紐約港進口處)。
America /ə'merɪkə; ə'mɛrəkə/ **1** 美洲。**2** 美國之通稱(參看 United States)。
American Samoa 美屬薩摩亞羣島 (亦稱 Eastern Samoa, 在 Samoa 之東部)。
Amiens /'æmjæŋ; 'æmɪənz/ 亞眠(法國北部一城市)。
Amman /ə'mɑ:n; æ'mɑn/ 安曼(Jordan 之首都)。
Amoy /ə'mɔɪ; ɑ'mɔɪ/ 厦門(中國福建省一海港城市)。
Amritsar /ʌm'rɪtsə(r); ʌm'rɪtsɚ/ 阿木里查(印度北部一城市)。
Amsterdam /'æmstə'dæm; 'æmstɚˌdæm/ 阿姆斯特丹(Netherlands 之首都)。
Amsterdam Ship Canal 阿姆斯特丹運河(在荷蘭西部，亦稱 North Sea Canal)。
Amu Darya /'ɑ:mu:'dɑ:rjə; ˌɑmu'dɑrjə/ 阿母河(在蘇聯中亞細亞南部，亦稱 Oxus /'ɑ:ksəs; 'ɑksəs/)。
Amur /ə'mʊə(r); ɑ'mʊr/ 黑龍江 (中國東北一河流，亦稱 Heilungkiang)。
Anatolia /ˌænə'təʊljə; ˌænə'tolɪə/ 安那托利亞(今土耳其之亞洲部分)。
Anchorage /'æŋkərɪdʒ; 'æŋkərɪdʒ/ 安克治 (美國阿拉斯加州中南部一港埠)。
Ancohuma /ˌæŋkə'hu:mə; ˌæŋkə'humə/ 安克休馬峯(玻利維亞西部一山峯)。
Andalusia /ˌændə'lu:ʒɪə; ˌændə'luʒə/ 安達魯西亞(西班牙南部一地區)。
Andaman /'ændəmæn; 'ændəmən/ **1** 安達曼羣島(在孟加拉灣內，屬印度)。**2** 安達曼海(在安達曼羣島與尼古巴羣島之東)。
Andes /'ændi:z; 'ændiz/ 安地斯山脈(在南美洲西部)。
Andizhan /ˌændɪ'ʒæn; ˌændɪ'ʒæn/ 安集延(蘇聯烏玆別克東部一城市)。
Andorra /æn'dɔ:rə; æn'dɔrə/ **1** 安道爾(歐洲國名，在法西交界之庇里牛斯山中)。**2** 安道爾市(安道爾之首都，參看 Andorra la Vella)。
Andorra la Vella /-lə'velə; -lə'vɛlə/ 安道爾市(Andorra 之首都，亦簡稱 Andorra)。
Andros /'ændrɒs; 'ændrəs/ 安得羅斯島 (**1** 大西洋巴哈馬羣島中之最大島嶼; **2** 希臘昔克蘭羣島北部之一島)。
Aneto, Pico de /'pi:kɔ:ðeɪɑ:'neɪtəʊ; 'pikoˌdeə'neto/ 阿內多峯(在西班牙東北部，爲庇里牛斯山脈最高峯，亦稱 Pic de Néthou)。
Angara /æn'gærə; ˌɑŋgə'rɑ/ 安加拉河 (蘇聯亞洲部分中部一河流，注於葉尼塞河)。
Angkor /'æŋˌkɔ:(r); 'æŋˌkɔr/ 吳哥 (柬埔寨西北部一古城)。
Anglesey, Anglesea /'æŋglsɪ; 'æŋgḷsɪ/ 安格西島(在英國威爾斯西北，昔爲其一郡)。
Anglo-Egyptian Sudan 參看 Sudan。
Angola /æŋ'gəʊlə; æŋ'golə/ 安哥拉 (昔爲葡屬西非洲，

1975年11月獨立,首都 Luanda)。
Angora /æŋ'gɔːrə ; æŋ'gorə/ Ankara 之舊稱。
Anguilla /æŋ'gwɪlə ; æŋ'gwɪlə/ 安圭拉島(英屬西印度羣島中之一島)。
Angus /'æŋgəs ; 'æŋgəs/ 安加斯(昔蘇格蘭東部一郡)。
Anhwei, Anhui /'ɑːn'hweɪ ; 'ɑn'hweɪ/ 安徽(中國之一省)。
Anjou /ɑːŋ'ʒuː ; 'æn,dʒu/ 安如(法國西北部一地區,在 Loire 河谷)。
Ankara /'æŋkərə ; 'æŋkərə/ 安卡拉(自1923年起爲 Turkey 的首都,舊稱 Angora)。
Anking /'ɑːn'kɪŋ ; 'ɑn'kɪŋ/ 安慶(中國安徽省西南部一城市,亦稱 Hwaining '懷寧')。
Annam /'ænæm ; æ'næm/ 安南(越南中部地區,亦稱中圻)。
Annapolis /ə'næpəlɪs ; ə'næp(ə)ləs/ 安那波里斯(美國馬利蘭州之首府)。
An(n)apurna /,ænə'pɜːnə ; ,ænə'pɝnə/ 安那波那山(在尼泊爾北部)。
Ann Arbor /æ'nɑːbə ; æ'nɑrbɚ/ 安亞伯(美國密西根州東南部一城市)。
Anshan /'ɑːn'ʃɑːn ; 'ɑn'ʃɑn/ 鞍山(中國遼寧省一城市,以產鐵著名)。
Antananarivo /'æntə,nænə'riːvəʊ ; ,æntə,nænə'rivo/ 安塔那那利佛(昔稱 Tananarive, Madagascar 之首都)。
Antarctic /ænt'ɑːktɪk ; ænt'ɑrktɪk/ 南極區;南極地方。
Antarctica /ænt'ɑːktɪkə ; ænt'ɑrktɪkə/ 南極洲(亦稱 Antarctic Continent)。
Antigua /æn'tiːgə ; æn'tigə/ 安提瓜(原英屬西印度羣島中之一島,於1981年11月1日與 Barbuda 聯合宣佈獨立,稱爲 Antigua and Barbuda, 首都爲 St. Johns)。
Antigua and Barbuda /æn'tiːgə ən bɑː'buːdə ; æn'tigə ən bɑr'budə/ 安提瓜和巴爾布達(參看 Antigua)。
Anti-Lebanon /'æntɪ'lebənən ; 'æntɪ'lɛbənən/ 安替黎巴嫩山脈(在黎巴嫩,敍利亞間)。
Antilles /æn'tɪliːz ; æn'tɪliz/ 安地列斯羣島(西印度羣島中之兩大羣島,即 Greater ~ 和 Lesser ~)。
Antioch /'æntɪɒk ; 'æntɪ,ɑk/ 安提阿(小亞細亞之古城,其遺址在今土耳其西部)。
Antofagasta /,æntəfə'gɑːstə ; ,æntəfə'gɑstə/ 安多法加斯大(智利北部一港埠)。
Antrim /'æntrɪm;'æntrɪm/ 安特令(北愛爾蘭東部一郡)。
Antung /'ɑːn'dʊŋ ; 'ɑn'dʊŋ/ 安東(**1** 中國東北一省; **2** 安東省最大的工業城市)。
Antwerp /'æntwɜːp ; 'ænt,wɝp/ 安特衞普(比利時北部一省,又其首府名)。
Apennines /'æpɪnaɪnz ; 'æpə,naɪnz/ 亞平寧山脈(在義大利中部)。
Apia /ɑː'piːɑː ; ə'piə/ 阿比亞(Western Samoa 之首都)。
Apo, Mount /'ɑːpəʊ ; 'ɑpo/ 阿坡火山(在菲律賓民答那峨島之東南部)。
Appalachian /,æpə'leɪtʃɪən ; ,æpə'letʃən/ 阿帕拉契山脈(在北美洲之東部)。
Arabia /ə'reɪbɪə ; ə'rebɪə/ 阿拉伯半島(在亞洲西南部)。
Arabian Desert 阿拉伯沙漠(在埃及東部,亦稱 Eastern Desert)。
Arabian Sea 阿拉伯海(在印度和阿拉伯半島之間)。
Aragon /'ærəgən ; 'ærə,gɑn/ 亞拉岡(西班牙東北部一地區;昔爲一王國)。
Araguaia, Araguaya /,ærə'gwaɪə ; ,ærə'gwaɪə/ 阿拉圭河(在巴西中部,注於托肯丁斯河)。
Aral Sea /'ɑːrəl ; 'ɛrəl/ 鹹海(在蘇聯亞洲部分西南)。
Ararat /'ærəræt;'ærə,ræt/ 亞拉拉特山(在土耳其東部)。
Archangel /'ɑːkeɪndʒəl ; 'ɑr,kendʒəl/ 阿干折(蘇聯歐洲部分之北部一港市,亦稱 Arkhangelsk /ɑː'kæn,gelsk ; ɑr'kæn,gɛlsk/)。
Arctic Sea 北極海。
Arden /'ɑːdn ; 'ɑrdn̩/ 阿爾丁(英格蘭中部瓦立克郡內一區,昔爲林地)。
Ardennes /ɑː'den ; ɑr'dɛn/ 亞耳丁(綿亙於法國、比利時、盧森堡三國間之高原森林地區)。
Arequipa /,ærɪ'kiːpə ; ,ærə'kipə/ 阿累奇帕(秘魯南部一城市)。
Argentina /,ɑːdʒən'tiːnə ; ,ɑrdʒən'tinə/ 阿根廷(亦稱 *The Argentine* /'ɑːdʒəntaɪn ; 'ɑrdʒən,tin/, 南美洲南部一國,首都 Buenos Aires)。
Argyllshire /ɑː'gaɪlʃə(r) ; ɑr'gaɪl,ʃɪr/ 亞蓋爾夏(昔爲蘇格蘭西部一郡)。
Arizona /,ærɪ'zəʊnə ; ,ærə'zonə/ 亞利桑那(美國西南部一州,略作 *AZ*)。
Arkansas /'ɑːkənsɔː ; 'ɑrkən,sɔ/ 阿肯色(**1** 州名,在美國中南部,略作 *AR*; **2** 河名,爲美國密西西比河之大支流)。
Arlington /'ɑːlɪŋtən ; 'ɑrlɪŋtən/ 阿靈頓(**1** 美國維吉尼亞州之一郡,在華盛頓之郊區,該處有無名英雄墓; **2** 美國麻薩諸塞州東部之一城市)。
Armagh /ɑː'mɑː ; ɑr'mɑ/ 亞爾馬(北愛爾蘭南部一郡)。
Armenia /ɑː'miːnjə ; ɑr'minɪə/ 亞美尼亞(**1** 高加索山脈以南、亞洲西南一古國; **2** 蘇聯之一加盟共和國,或稱 Armenian Republic)。
Arno /'ɑːnəʊ ; 'ɑrno/ 亞諾河(在義大利中部)。
Arras /'ærəs ; ə'rɑs/ 阿拉斯(法國北部一城市)。
Arthur's Pass /'ɑːθəz- ; 'ɑrθɚz-/ 阿瑟山隘(在紐西蘭的南島之中部)。
Ascension /ə'senʃn ; ə'sɛnʃən/ 亞森欣島(在南大西洋,屬英國)。
Ashanti /ə'ʃæntɪ ; ə'ʃæntɪ/ 阿善提(非洲迦納共和國中部一地區)。
Asia /'eɪʃə ; 'eʒə/ 亞洲。
Asia Minor 小亞細亞(黑海與地中海間之亞洲部分)。
Asmara /æz'mɑːrə ; æz'mɑrə/ 阿斯馬拉(非洲衣索比亞 Eritrea 省之首府)。
Assam /'æsæm ; ə'sæm/ 阿薩密(印度東北部一邦)。
Assyria /ə'sɪrɪə ; ə'sɪrɪə/ 亞述(古國名,在今亞洲之西南部,約盛於 750-612 B. C.)。
Asunción /ə,sʊnsɪ'əʊn ; ə,sunsi'on/ 亞松森(Paraguay 之首都)。
Aswân, Ass(o)uan /,æsʊ'æn ; æ'swɑn/ 阿斯安(非洲埃及南部一城市)。
Atbara /æt'bɑːrə ; 'ætbərə/ 阿特巴拉河(非洲尼羅河之一大支流)。
Athabasca, Athabaska /,æθə'bæskə ; ,æθə'bæskə/ 亞大巴斯卡河(在加拿大亞伯達省,注於亞大巴斯卡湖)。
Athens /'æθɪnz ; 'æθɪnz/ 雅典(Greece 之首都)。
Athos /'æθɒs ; 'æθ,ɑs/ 阿陀斯山(在希臘之東北境)。
Atlanta /ət'læntə ; ət'læntə/ 亞特蘭大(美國喬治亞州之首府)。
Atlantic, the /ət'læntɪk ; ət'læntɪk/ 大西洋(亦稱 Atlantic Ocean)。
Atlantic City 大西洋城(美國新澤西洲東南部一城市)。
Atlas /'ætləs;'ætləs/ 亞特拉斯山脈(非洲西北境一山脈)。
Attica /'ætɪkə ; 'ætɪkə/ 阿提喀(希臘東部一地區,古爲一城邦)。
Auckland /'ɔːklənd ; 'ɔklənd/ 奧克蘭(紐西蘭之北島一省區;又該省區之首府)。
Augusta /ɔː'gʌstə ; ɔ'gʌstə/ 奧古斯特(美國緬因州之首府)。
Austin /'ɔːstɪn ; 'ɔstɪn/ 奧斯丁(美國德克薩斯州之首府)。
Australasia /,ɔːstrə'leɪʒɪə ; ,ɔstrə'leʒə/ 澳大拉西亞(澳洲、紐西蘭及附近南太平洋諸島之總稱)。
Australia /ɒ'streɪlɪə ; ɔ'streljə/ **1** 澳洲(在南太平洋與印度洋之間)。**2** 澳大利亞聯邦(國名,全名爲 Commonwealth of Australia, 含整個澳洲及塔斯曼尼亞島,首都 Canberra)。
Australian Alps 澳洲大山脈(在澳洲新南威爾士州東南部)。
Austria /'ɒstrɪə ; 'ɔstrɪə/ 奧地利(亦稱奧國,在歐洲中部,首都 Vienna)。
Austria-Hungary 奧匈帝國(1867-1918 中歐之一國,包括奧地利帝國及匈牙利王國)。
Austronesia /,ɒstrəʊ'niːʒə ; ,ɔstrə'niʒə/ 澳斯特羅尼西亞(南太平洋諸島嶼之總稱)。
Aux Sources, Mont /,mɒn,təʊ'sʊəs ; ,mɑn,to'surs/ 蘇爾斯山(在南非賴索托國北部)。
Avernus /ə'vɜːnəs ; ə'vɝnəs/ 亞維努斯湖(在義大利那不勒斯附近,古人認係地獄之入口)。
Avon /'eɪvən ; 'evən/ **1** 亞芬河(在英格蘭中部,流經莎士比亞出生地 Stratford)。**2** 亞芬郡(在英格蘭西南部,首府爲 Bristol)。
Ayrshire /'eəʃə(r) ; 'ɛr,ʃɪr/ 亞爾夏(昔蘇格蘭西南部一

郡)。

Ayutthaya /ɑːˈjuːtɑːjɑː; ɑˈjutəjə/ 猶地亞(亦作 Ayudhya, 泰國南部一城市,昔爲泰國首都)。

Azerbaijan (Republic) /ˌæzəˌbaɪˈdʒɑːn; ˌæzəˌbaɪˈdʒɑn/ 亞塞拜然(亦作 Azerbaidzhan, 蘇聯一加盟共和國,在亞洲外高加索東南部,首府爲 Baku)。

Azores /əˈzɔːz; ˈeˌzorz/ 亞速爾羣島(在北大西洋,屬葡萄牙)。

Azov, Sea of /ˈɑːzɒv; ˈæzˌɔf/ 亞速海(在蘇聯境內,位於黑海東北)。

Babylon/ ˈbæbɪlən; ˈbæbələn/ 巴比倫(古代Babylonia之首都)。

Babylonia /ˌbæbɪˈləʊnjə; ˌbæbəˈlonɪə/ 巴比倫尼亞(古國名,卽巴比倫王國,在今亞洲西南部幼發拉底河之下游,首都爲 Babylon)。

Back /bæk; bæk/ 北克河 (在加拿大北部,舊稱 Great Fish River)。

Badajoz /ˈbædəhɒz; ˌbadəˈhoz/ 巴達和斯(西班牙西南部一省;又該省之首府)。

Baden /ˈbɑːdn; ˈbadn̩/ 巴登(德國西南部一地區)。

Baffin /ˈbæfɪn; ˈbæfɪn/ 巴芬島(在加拿大東北部)。

Bag(h)dad /ˈbægdæd; ˈbægˌdæd/ 巴格達 (Iraq 之首都)。

Baguio /ˈbɑːgɪˌəʊ; ˌbagɪˈo/ 碧瑤(菲律賓呂宋島西北部一城市,爲其夏都)。

Bahamas, the /bəˈhɑːməz; bəˈhaməz/ 巴哈馬(美國佛羅里達州東南大西洋中一羣島, 亦稱 Bahama Islands, 於 1973 年 7 月獨立,稱爲 Commonwealth of ~, 首都 Nassau)。

Bahia Blanca /bəˈhiːə ˈblɑːŋkə; bəˌhiə ˈblæŋkə/ 布蘭加港(阿根廷東部一海港)。

Bahrain, Bahrein /bɑːˈreɪn; baˈren/ 巴林(波斯灣一島國, 1971 年 8 月獨立,首都 Manama)。

Baikal, Lake /baɪˈkɔːl; baɪˈkɔl/ 貝加爾湖(亦作 Baykal, 在蘇聯亞洲部分之南部)。

Baku /bɑːˈkuː; baˈku/ 巴庫(在裏海西岸, 爲蘇聯 Azerbaijan 之首府)。

Balbi /ˈbɑːlbɪ; ˈbalbɪ/ 巴比火山(在西太平洋布干維島之西北)。

Balearic /ˌbælɪˈærɪk; ˌbælɪˈærɪk/ 巴利亞利羣島(在西地中海,屬西班牙)。

Bali /ˈbɑːlɪ; ˈbalɪ/ 巴里島(屬印尼,在爪哇之東)。

Balikpapan /ˌbɑːlɪkˈpɑːˌpɑːn; ˌbalɪkˈpapˌan/ 巴里把板(婆羅洲東南部一港埠,屬印尼,產石油)。

Balkan /ˈbɔːlkən; ˈbɔlkən/ 巴爾幹半島 (在歐洲東南,西臨亞得里亞海及愛奧尼亞海,南臨地中海,東臨愛琴海及黑海)。

Balkans, the /ˈbɔːlkənz; ˈbɔlkənz/ 巴爾幹半島諸國(亦稱 Balkan States, 包括南斯拉夫,羅馬尼亞,保加利亞,阿爾巴尼亞,希臘及土耳其之歐洲部分)。

Balk(h)ash, Lake /bælˈkæʃ; bælˈkæʃ/ 巴爾喀什湖(在蘇聯中亞部分)。

Baltic Sea /ˈbɔːltɪk; ˈbɔltɪk/ 波羅的海(在歐洲北部,與北海相連)。

Baltic States 波羅的海諸國(指過去波羅的海東岸之愛沙尼亞、拉脫維亞及立陶宛,有時也包括芬蘭和波蘭)。

Baltimore /ˈbɔːltɪmɔː(r); ˈbɔltəˌmor/ 巴的摩爾(美國馬里蘭州北部一港埠)。

Baluchistan /bəˈluːtʃɪstæn; bəˌlutʃəˈstæn/ 俾路支(巴基斯坦西南部一省)。

Bamako /ˈbɑːməkəʊ; ˌbaməˈko/ 巴馬科(Mali 之首都)。

Banda /ˈbændə; ˈbændə/ 班達(印度北部一城鎭)。

Bandar Seri Begawan /bænˈdɑː ˈsɪəriː bəˈgɑːwæn; ˌbʌndɚ ˌsɛrɪ bəˈgawən/ 斯里巴加萬港(Brunei 之首府,舊稱 Brunei)。

Ban(d)jarmasin /ˌbændʒəˈmɑːsn; ˌbændʒɚˈmasn̩/ 馬辰(婆羅洲南部一城鎭,屬印尼)。

Bandung, Bandoeng /ˈbɑːndʊŋ; ˈbanˌdʊŋ/ 萬隆(印尼爪哇島西部一城市)。

Banffshire /ˈbænfʃə(r); ˈbæmfˌʃɪr/ 班夫夏(昔爲蘇格蘭東北部一郡)。

Bangalore /ˌbæŋgəˈlɔː(r); ˈbæŋgəˌlor/ 邦加羅爾(印度南部一城市)。

Ban(g)ka /ˈbæŋkə; ˈbæŋkə/ 邦加島(在爪哇海西北,屬印尼)。

Bangkok /bæŋˈkɒk; ˈbæŋˌkak/ 曼谷 (Thailand 之首都)。

Bangladesh /ˌbæŋgləˈdeʃ; ˌbaŋgləˈdɛʃ/ 孟加拉共和國(位於亞洲南部,濱孟加拉灣,原爲東巴基斯坦,於 1971 年 3 月獨立,首都 Dacca)。

Bang(u)i /ˈbɑːŋgiː; baŋˈgi/ 班基 (Central African Republic 之首都)。

Bani(y)as /ˌbænɪˈjæs; ˌbænɪˈ(j)æs/ 巴尼雅斯(敍利亞臨海一城鎭)。

Banjul /ˈbændʒuːl; ˈbanˌdʒul/ 班竹(Gambia 之首都, 舊稱 Bathurst)。

Barbados /bɑːˈbeɪdəs; barˈbedəs/ 巴貝多(英屬西印度羣島之一島,於 1966 年 11月獨立,首都 Bridgetown)。

Barbuda /bɑːˈbuːdə; barˈbudə/ 巴爾布達島(英屬西印度羣島中一島,參看 Antigua)。

Barcelona /ˌbɑːsɪˈləʊnə; ˌbarsl̩ˈonə/ 巴塞隆納(西班牙東北部一省,又其首府名)。

Barisan Mountains /ˌbɑːrɪˈsɑːn-; ˌbarɪˈsan-/ 巴利桑山脈(在印尼之蘇門答臘島)。

Baroda /bəˈrəʊdə; bəˈrodə/ 巴洛達(印度西部一城市)。

Barranquilla /ˌbærənˈkiːjə; ˌbærənˈki(j)ə/ 巴蘭吉亞(哥倫比亞北部一港市)。

Bartle Frere, Mount /ˈbɑːtlfriːə; ˈbartl̩ˌfrir/ 巴特弗里山(在澳洲東北部)。

Basel /ˈbɑːzəl; ˈbazəl/ 巴塞爾(瑞士西北部一城市, 舊稱 Basle /bɑːl; bal/)。

Bashi Channel /ˈbɑːʃɪ-; ˈbaʃɪ-/ 巴士海峽(介於菲律賓巴旦島與中國臺灣的南端之間)。

Basra /ˈbæzrə; ˈbasrə/ 巴斯拉(伊拉克南部一海港)。

Basutoland /bəˈsuːtəʊlænd; bəˈsutəˌlænd/ 巴蘇陀蘭(現稱 Lesotho)。

Bataan /bəˈtæn; bəˈtæn/ 巴丹 (**1** 菲律賓呂宋島西部一半島,亦爲其一省; **2** 菲律賓馬尼拉之南一城鎭)。

Batan /bɑːˈtɑːn; bəˈtan/ 巴旦 (**1** 菲律賓呂宋島以北一羣島; **2** 巴旦羣島中之主島)。

Batangas /bəˈtæŋgəs; bəˈtæŋgəs/ 八打雁(菲律賓呂宋島南部一省,又其首府名)。

Batavia /bəˈteɪvɪə; bəˈtevɪə/ 巴達維亞 (Jakarta 之舊稱)。

Bath /bɑːθ; bæθ/ 巴斯(英格蘭西南部一城市)。

Bathurst /ˈbæθɜːst; ˈbæθɚst/ 巴得斯特 (Banjul 之舊稱)。

Battersea /ˈbætəsɪ; ˈbætɚsɪ/ 巴特西(倫敦泰晤士河南岸一市區)。

Batumi /bɑːˈtuːmɪ; bəˈtumɪ/ 巴統米(蘇聯黑海東岸之海港,舊稱 Batum)。

Bavaria /bəˈveərɪə; bəˈvɛrɪə/ 巴伐利亞(德國南部一地區)。

Bavarian Alps /bəˈveərɪən-; bəˈvɛrɪən-/ 巴伐利亞山脈(在歐洲德、奧間)。

Bayankara Mts /ˌbɑːjænˈkɑːrə-; ˌbajænˈkarə-/ 巴顏喀喇山(在中國青海省)。

Bayrut = **Beirut**

Bear Lake /beə-; bɛr-/ 熊湖(在美國猶他州與愛達和州之間)。

Beaufort /ˈbəʊfət; ˈbofɚt/ 波福海 (在美國阿拉斯加州東北,爲北極海之一部)。

Beaumont /ˈbəʊmənt; ˈboˌmant/ 波蒙特(美國德克薩斯州東南部一港埠)。

Bechuanaland /ˌbetʃʊˈɑːnəlænd; ˌbɛtʃ(ə)ˈwanəˌlænd/ 貝專納蘭(現名 Botswana)。

Bedfordshire /ˈbedfədʃə(r); ˈbɛdfɚdˌʃɪr/ 貝德福郡(英格蘭東南部一郡,略作 *Beds*)。

Beirut, Bayrut /beɪˈruːt; beˈrut/ 貝魯特(Lebanon 之首都)。

Belém /bəˈlem; bəˈlɛm/ 貝倫(巴西北部一城市)。

Belfast /belˈfɑːst; ˈbɛlˌfæst/ 貝爾發斯特(北愛爾蘭之首府)。

Belgian Congo 比屬剛果(參看 Zaire)。

Belgium /ˈbeldʒəm; ˈbɛldʒəm/ 比利時(歐洲西部一王國,首都 Brussels)。

Belgrade /belˈgreɪd; ˈbɛlˌgred/ 貝爾格萊德 (Yugoslavia 之首都)。

Benares, Banaras /bəˈnɑːrəs; bəˈnarəs/ 貝那拉斯(印度北部一城市,爲印度教之聖地)。

Bengal /ben'gɔːl ; bɛn'gɔl/ 孟加拉(劃爲東孟加拉及西孟加拉,分屬巴基斯坦和印度,東孟加拉現已獨立爲孟加拉共和國)。
Bengal, Bay of 孟加拉灣(爲印度洋之一部,界於印度,緬甸與馬來半島之間)。
Benin /be'niːn ; bə'nɪn/ 貝南(國名,舊稱 Dahomey, 在非洲西部, 1960 年 8 月獨立,首都 Porto-Novo)。
Berchtesgaden /'beəktəsgɑːdən ; 'bɛrktəs,gadən/ 柏特斯加登(德國東南部一城鎮)。
Bergen /'bɜːgən ; 'bɝgən/ 卑爾根(挪威西南部一海港)。
Bering /'berɪŋ ; 'bɪrɪŋ/ **1** 白令海(太平洋之最北部分)。**2** 白令海峽(位於美國阿拉斯加州與蘇聯西伯利亞之間)。
Berkeley /'bɜːklɪ;'bɝklɪ/ 伯克萊(美國加州西部一港埠)。
Berkshire /'bɑːkʃə(r) *US:* 'bɜːrk- ; 'bɝk,ʃɪr/ 波克郡(英格蘭中南部一郡,略作 *Berks*)。
Berlin /bɜː'lɪn ; 'bɝlɪn/ 柏林(爲第二次大戰前德國之國都,自 1949 年後柏林分爲東西兩部,東柏林爲東德之首都,西柏林爲西德之一部)。
Bermuda /bə'mjuːdə ; bɚ'mjudə/ 百慕達羣島(位於北大西洋西部,爲英屬自治領,首府 Hamilton)。
Bern(e) /bɜːn ; bɝn/ 伯恩(Switzerland 之首都)。
Berwickshire /'berɪkʃə(r) ; 'bɛrɪk,ʃɪr/ 伯立克夏(昔爲蘇格蘭東南部一郡)。
Bessarabia /ˌbesə'reɪbjə ; ˌbɛsə'rebɪə/ 比薩拉比亞(歐洲東南部一地區,原屬土耳其,現爲蘇聯所據)。
Bethlehem /'beθlɪhem ; 'bɛθlɪ,hɛm/ 伯利恆 (**1** 約旦國一市鎮,在耶路撒冷南方六哩之處,爲耶穌之降生地; **2** 美國賓夕法尼亞州東部一城市)。
Bhamo /bə'mɔː ; bə'mɔ/ 八莫(緬甸北部一城鎮)。
Bhutan /buː'tɑːn ; bu'tæn/ 不丹(印度東北喜馬拉雅山之麓一王國,首都 Thimbu)。
Bialystok /bɪ'ɑːlɪˌstɔːk ; bɪ'alɪ,stɔk/ 畢亞維斯托(波蘭東北部一城市)。
Bilbao /bɪl'bɑːəʊ ; bɪl'bao/ 畢爾包(西班牙北部一城市)。
Billiton /bə'liːˌtɑːn ; bə'li,tan/ 勿里洞島(印尼蘇門答臘東南海中一島,亦作 Belitung)。
Birkenhead /'bɜːkənhed ; 'bɝkən,hɛd/ 伯肯赫德(英格蘭西北部一城市)。
Birmingham /'bɜːmɪŋəm ; 'bɝmɪŋ,hæm/ 伯明罕 (**1** 美國阿拉巴馬州中北部一城市; **2** 英格蘭中部一城市,爲英國鋼鐵工業之中心)。
Biscay, Bay of /'bɪskeɪ ; 'bɪs,ke/ 比斯開灣(在法國以西、西班牙以北之海灣)。
Bisley /'bɪzlɪ ; 'bɪzlɪ/ 比斯利 (英國薩里郡一鄉村,爲 National Rifle Association 之靶場)。
Bismarck /'bɪzmɑːk ; 'bɪzmark/ **1** 俾斯麥羣島(在西太平洋新幾內亞之東北)。**2** 俾斯麥海(俾斯麥羣島所包圍之海面)。
Bismarck Range /'bɪzmɑːk- ; 'bɪzmark-/ 俾斯麥山脈(在新幾內亞東北部)。
Bissau /bɪ'saʊ ; bɪs'aʊ/ 比索(亦作 Bissão, Guinea-Bissau 之首都)。
Bithynia /bɪ'θɪnɪə ; bə'θɪnɪə/ 俾斯尼亞(古國名,在今小亞細亞西北部)。
Bizerte /bə'zɜːtɪ ; bə'zɝtɪ/ 比塞大(非洲突尼西亞北部一港埠)。
Blackburn /'blækbɜːn ; 'blækbɝn/ 布拉克本(英格蘭西北部一城市)。
Blackburn, Mount /'blækbɜːn ; 'blækbɝn/ 布拉克本山(在美國阿拉斯加州東南部)。
Black Hills 黑丘(在美國南達科他州之西與懷俄明州之東北)。
Blackpool /'blækpuːl ; 'blæk,pul/ 黑潭 (英格蘭西北部一城市)。
Black Sea 黑海(界於歐亞兩洲之間)。
Blagoveshchensk /ˌblɑːgə'veʃˌtʃensk ; ˌblagə'vɛʃ-tʃənsk/ 海蘭泡(蘇聯亞洲部分東部一城市)。
Blanc, Cape /blæŋk ; blæŋk/ 白朗角(在非洲突尼西亞北部,爲非洲之最北點)。
Blanc, Mont /mɔːm'blɑːŋ ; mant'blæŋk/ 白朗峯(在法國東南與義大利接界處,爲阿爾卑斯山之最高峯)。
Blanca Peak /'blæŋkə- ; 'blæŋkə-/ 白朗卡峯(在美國科羅拉多州南部)。
Bloemfontein /'bluːmfənteɪn ; 'blumfən,ten/ 布隆芬田(南非共和國中部一城市,爲其司法首都)。
Blue Mts. 藍山 (**1** 在西印度羣島牙買加島東部; **2** 在美國俄勒岡州東北部及華盛頓州東南部)。
Bogong /'bəʊgɑːŋ ; 'bo,gaŋ/ 波岡山(在澳洲維多利亞州東南部)。
Bogotá /ˌbəʊgə'tɑː ; ˌbogə'tɔ/ 波哥大 (Colombia 之首都)。
Bohemia /bəʊ'hiːmjə ; bo'himɪə/ 波希米(以前中歐一國家,現爲捷克斯拉夫之一省)。
Bohemian Plateau 波希米高原 (在捷克波希米省之東南)。
Bokhara /bəʊ'kɑːrə ; bo'karə/ 布卡拉(蘇聯烏玆別克西部一城市,亦作 Bukhara)。
Bolivia /bə'lɪvɪə ; bə'lɪvɪə/ 玻利維亞 (南美洲西部一國家,首都 La Paz)。
Bologna /bə'ləʊnjə ; bə'lonjə/ 波隆那(義大利北部一城市)。
Bolton /'bəʊltn ; 'boltən/ 波爾頓(英格蘭西北部一城市)。
Bombay /bɒm'beɪ ; bam'be/ 孟買 (**1** 印度西部一邦; **2** 該邦之首府)。
Bonin Islands /'bəʊnɪn- ; 'bonən-/ 波檸羣島 (參看 Ogasawara Islands)。
Bonn /bɒn ; ban/ 波昂(West Germany 之首都,位於萊因河畔)。
Bophuthatswana /ˌbəʊpuːtɑːt'swɑːnə ; ˌboputat-'swanə/ 波布那共和國(在南非共和國境內, 1977 年 12 月宣佈獨立,首都爲 Mmabatho)。
Borah Peak /'bəʊrə ; 'borə/ 波拉峯 (在美國愛達荷州中部)。
Bordeaux /bɔː'dəʊ ; bɔr'do/ 波爾多(法國西南部一港埠)。
Borders/ 'bɔːdəz ; 'bɔrdɚz/ 波德玆(蘇格蘭南部一區,首府爲 Newtown St. Boswells)。
Borneo /'bɔːnɪəʊ ; 'bornɪ,o/ 婆羅洲(南洋羣島一島,一部屬馬來西亞一部屬印尼)。
Bosnia /'bɒznɪə ; 'baznɪə/ 波士尼亞(南斯拉夫中部一地區)。
Bosporus /'bɒsprəs ; 'baspərəs/ 博斯普魯斯海峽(亦作 Bosphorus 介於歐、亞兩洲之間,北接黑海,南通馬爾馬拉海)。
Boston /'bɒstn ; 'bɔstən/ 波士頓(美國麻薩諸塞州之首府)。
Botany Bay /'bɒtənɪ ; 'batənɪ/ 植物灣(澳洲東南海岸一海灣,在雪梨附近)。
Bothnia, Gulf of /'bɒθnɪə ; 'baθnɪə/ 波斯尼亞灣(波羅的海一海灣,在瑞典與芬蘭之間)。
Botswana /bɒ'tswɑːnə; bat'swanə/ 波札那(昔名 Bechuanaland, 南非一共和國,原爲英國保護地,於 1966 年 9 月獨立,首都 Gaborone)。
Bougainville /'buːgənvɪl ; 'bugən,vɪl/ 布干維爾島(南太平洋所羅門羣島中最大之島)。
Boulder /'bəʊldə ; 'boldɚ/ 波爾德(美國內華達州與亞利桑那州間一水壩名,亦作 Hoover Dam)。
Boulogne /bʊ'ləʊn ; bʊ'lon/ 布倫(法國北部一海港)。
Boundary Peak /'baʊndərɪ ; 'baʊndərɪ/ 龐德峯(在美國內華達州西南部)。
Bournemouth /'bɔːnməθ ; 'bornməθ/ 波茅斯(英格蘭南部一城市)。
Bow River /bəʊ ; bo/ 布河(在加拿大亞伯達省西南部)。
Bradford /'brædfəd ; 'brædfɚd/ 布拉福(英格蘭北部一城市)。
Brahmaputra /ˌbrɑːmə'puːtrə ; ˌbramə'putrə/ 雅魯藏布江(在印度東北部及中國西藏南部)。
Brandenburg /'brændənbɜːg ; 'brændən,bɝg/ 勃蘭登堡(德國柏林以西一城市)。
Brasilia /brə'ziːljə ; brə'zɪljə/ 巴西利亞 (Brazil 之首都)。
Bratislava /ˌbrætɪ'slɑːvə ; ˌbrætə'slavə/ 伯拉第斯拉瓦(捷克一城市,臨多瑙河)。
Brazil /brə'zɪl ; brə'zɪl/ 巴西(國名,在南美洲東部,首都 Brasilia)。
Brazos /'bræzəs ; 'bræzəs/ 布拉佐斯河(在美國德州中部,注於墨西哥灣)。
Brazzaville /'bræzəvɪl ; 'bræzə,vɪl/ 布拉薩市(Congo 之首都)。
Brecknockshire /'breknɒkʃə(r) ; 'brɛknak,ʃɪr/ 布勒

克諾夏(昔爲威爾斯東南部一郡)。

Bremen /ˈbreɪmən ; ˈbremən/ 不來梅(**1** 德國西北部一邦; **2** 該邦之首府)。

Breslau /ˈbreslaʊ ; ˈbrɛs,laʊ/ 布勒斯勞(波蘭西南部一城市,亦作 Wroclaw)。

Brest /brest ; brɛst/ 布勒斯特(**1** 法國西北部一城市; **2** 蘇聯歐洲部分之西一城市)。

Bretagne /brəˈtɑːnɪ ; brəˈtɑn/ 不列塔尼(法國西部一半島,亦作 Brittany)。

Bridgetown /ˈbrɪdʒtaʊn ; ˈbrɪdʒ,taʊn/ 橋鎮(Barbados 之首都)。

Brighton /ˈbraɪtn ; ˈbraɪtn̩/ 布來頓(英國南部一城市)。

Brisbane /ˈbrɪzbən ; ˈbrɪzbən/ 布利斯班(澳洲東北部摩頓灣之東一城市)。

Bristol /ˈbrɪstl ; ˈbrɪstl̩/ 布里斯托(英國西南部一城市)。

Britain /ˈbrɪtn ; ˈbrɪtn̩/ 不列顛島(包括 England, Scotland, Wales 三部分;亦稱 Great Britain)。

British Columbia /-kəˈlʌmbɪə ; -kəˈlʌmbiə/ 英屬哥倫比亞(加拿大西部之一省,略作 *BC*)。

British Guiana /-gɪˈɑːnə ; -gɪˈænə/ 英屬圭亞那(參看 Guyana)。

Brno /ˈbɜːnəʊ ; ˈbɝno/ 布爾諾(捷克中部一城市)。

Bronx /brɒŋks ; brɑŋks/ 布隆克斯(紐約市一區)。

Brooklyn /ˈbrʊklɪn;ˈbrʊklɪn/ 布魯克林(紐約市一區)。

Brunei /ˈbruːnaɪ ; ˈbru,naɪ/ 文萊(英之保護國,在南洋婆羅洲西北部,首都 Bandar Seri Begawan)。

Brunswick /ˈbrʌnzwɪk ; ˈbrʌnzwɪk/ 布倫玆維克(德國中部一行政區)。

Brussels /ˈbrʌslz ; ˈbrʌsl̩z/ 布魯塞爾(Belgium 之首都)。

Bucharest /ˈbjuːkərest ; ˈb(j)ukə,rɛst/ 布加勒斯特(Romania 之首都)。

Buckingham /ˈbʌkɪŋəm ; ˈbʌkɪŋ,hæm/ 白金汗 (**1** 美國維吉尼亞州中部一地名; **2** 加拿大魁北克省西南部一城鎮)。

Buckinghamshire /ˈbʌkɪŋəmʃə(r) ; ˈbʌkɪŋəm,ʃɪr/ 白金漢郡(英格蘭中南部一郡,略作 *Bucks*)。

Budapest /ˈbjuːdəˈpest ; ˈbjudə,pɛst/ 布達佩斯(Hungary 之首都)。

Buenaventura /ˌbwenə,venˈtjʊrə ; ,bwenə,vɛnˈturə/ 布維那文土拉(哥倫比亞西部一城市)。

Buenos Aires /ˈbwenəs ˈaɪərɪz ; ,bweɪnəˈsæriz/ 布艾諾賽利斯 (Argentina 之首都)。

Buffalo /ˈbʌfələʊ ; ˈbʌfə,lo/ 布法羅(美國紐約州西部一城市,亦稱水牛城)。

Bug River /buːg- ; bug-/ 布格河(在蘇聯烏克蘭中部,注於聶伯河)。

Bujumbura /ˌbuːdʒəmˈbʊrə ; ,budʒəmˈbʊrə/ 布松布拉(舊名 Usumbura, Burundi 之首都)。

Bulgaria /bʌlˈgeərɪə ; bʌlˈgɛrɪə/ 保加利亞(國名,在歐洲東南部,爲巴爾幹半島諸國之一,首都 Sofia)。

Bungay /ˈbʌŋgɪ ; ˈbʌŋgɪ/ 邦加(英格蘭東南部一城鎮)。

Burgundy /ˈbɜːgəndɪ ; ˈbɝgəndɪ/ 勃艮地(法國東部一地區)。

Burma /ˈbɜːmə ; ˈbɝmə/ 緬甸(國名,在亞洲東南部,首都 Rangoon)。

Burundi /bʊˈrʊndɪ ; bʊˈrundi/ 蒲隆地(舊稱 Urundi, 國名,在非洲中東部,原爲比利時託管地,1962 年 7月獨立,首都 Bujumbura)。

Bute /bjuːt ; bjut/ 標得島(在蘇格蘭之西南)。

Bute(shire) /ˈbjuːt(ʃə(r)) ; ˈbjut(,ʃɪr)/ 標得夏(昔爲蘇格蘭西南部一郡)。

Byelorussia /bɪˌeləʊˈrʌʃə ; bɪ,ɛloˈrʌʃə/ 白俄羅斯(亦作 Belorussia, 國名,在歐洲東部,爲蘇聯一加盟共和國,全名作白俄羅斯蘇維埃社會主義共和國 'Byelorussian Soviet Socialist Republic', 首府 Minsk)。

Cádiz /ˈkeɪdɪz ; ˈkedɪz/ 加地斯(西班牙西南部一海港)。

Caernarvonshire /kəˈnɑːvənʃə(r) ; kəˈnɑrvən,ʃɪr/ 喀那芬夏(昔爲威爾斯西北部一郡)。

Cagliari /kæˈljɑːrɪ ; ˈkɑljərɪ/ 卡拉里(義大利薩丁尼亞之首府)。

Cairo /ˈkaɪərəʊ ; ˈkaɪro/ 開羅 (Egypt 之首都)。

Caithness /ˈkeɪθnes ; ˈkeθnəs/ 開斯納斯 (昔爲蘇格蘭北部一郡)。

Calais /ˈkæleɪ ; ˈkæle/ 加來(法國北部一海港)。

Calcutta /kælˈkʌtə ; kælˈkʌtə/ 加爾各答(印度東北部一城市)。

Calgary /ˈkælgərɪ ; ˈkælgərɪ/ 卡加立(加拿大亞伯達省南部一城市)。

Cali /ˈkɑːlɪ ; ˈkɑlɪ/ 卡利(哥倫比亞西南部一城市)。

Calicut /ˈkælɪkət ; ˈkælɪkət/ 卡利刻特 (印度南部一城市,亦稱 Kozhikode /ˈkəʊʒəˌkəʊd ; ˈkoʒə,kod/)。

California /ˌkælɪˈfɔːnɪə ; ,kæləˈfɔrnjə/ 加利福尼亞(簡稱加州,在美國西海岸,略作 *CA*)。

California, Gulf of 加利福尼亞灣(在墨西哥西北海岸)。

Callao /kəˈjɑː,əʊ ; kəˈjɑ,o/ 卡耀(秘魯首都利瑪之外港)。

Calvary /ˈkælvərɪ ; ˈkælvərɪ/ 髑髏地(在巴勒斯坦耶路撒冷之郊外,爲耶穌被害地)。

Cambodia /kæmˈbəʊdɪə ; kæmˈbodɪə/ 柬埔寨(亦稱高棉, 爲中南半島上一國家, 1975 年起稱爲 Democratic Kampuchea, 首都 Phnom Penh)。

Cambridge /ˈkeɪmbrɪdʒ ; ˈkembrɪdʒ/ 劍橋 (**1** 英格蘭東部一城市,爲 Cambridgeshire 之首府,因劍橋大學而著名; **2** 美國波士頓附近一城市,爲哈佛大學所在地)。

Cambridgeshire /ˈkeɪmbrɪdʒʃə(r) ; ˈkembrɪdʒ,ʃɪr/ 劍橋郡(英格蘭東部一郡,略作 *Cambs*)。

Camden /ˈkæmdən ; ˈkæmdən/ 康登 (美國新澤西州西南部一城市)。

Cameroon /ˈkæməruːn ; ,kæməˈrun/ 喀麥隆山(在西非喀麥隆境內)。

Cameroun /ˌkæməˈruːn ; ,kæməˈrun/ 喀麥隆(國名,在非洲西部,原爲法國託管地及英屬喀麥隆的南半部,1960年1月獨立,首都 Yaoundé, 亦作 Cameroon)。

Campania /kæmˈpeɪnjə ; kæmˈpenjə/ 坎佩尼亞(義大利南部一地區)。

Canada /ˈkænədə ; ˈkænədə/ 加拿大(北美洲一國家,爲大英國協之一員,首都 Ottawa)。

Canadian /kəˈneɪdjən ; kəˈnedɪən/ 加那丁河(在美國中南部,注於阿肯色河)。

Canal Zone /kəˈnæl- ; kəˈnæl-/ 運河區(在中美洲巴拿馬共和國中部)。

Canary Islands /kəˈneərɪ- ; kəˈnɛrɪ-/ 加那利群島(在非洲西北之大西洋中,屬西班牙)。

Canaveral, Cape /kəˈnævərəl ; kəˈnævərəl/ 加那維爾角(在美國佛羅里達州東海岸外加那維爾半島之東部,亦稱 Cape Kennedy 甘迺迪角)。

Canaveral Peninsula 加那維爾半島(在美國佛羅里達州東海岸)。

Canberra /ˈkænb(ə)rə ; ˈkænb(ə)rə/ 坎培拉 (Australia 之首都,位於雪梨西南)。

Candia /ˈkændɪə ; ˈkændɪə/ 干地亞 (**1** 地中海東部一島,一名 Crete 克里特; **2** 干地亞島北部一港埠)。

Cannes /kæn ; kæn/ 坎內(法國東南部一港埠)。

Cantabrian /kænˈteɪbrɪən ; kænˈtebrɪən/ 坎退布連山(在西班牙北境)。

Canterbury /ˈkæntəbrɪ *US:* -berɪ ; ˈkæntə,bɛrɪ/ 坎特布里(英格蘭東南部肯特郡中一城市)。

Canton /ˈkænˈtɒn;ˈkæn,tɑn/ **1** 廣州(中國廣東省省會)。 **2** /ˈkæntn ; ˈkæntn̩/ 坎吞(美國俄亥俄州東北部一城市)。

Cape Cod 鱈角(美國麻州東南部一半島)。

Cape Hatteras /-ˈhætərəs ; -ˈhætərəs/ 哈特拉斯角(在美國北卡羅來納州東海岸外,哈特拉斯島之東南端)。

Cape Horn 合恩角(在智利南部,南美洲之極南端)。

Cape of Good Hope 好望角(非洲南端一海角)。

Cape Town, Capetown /ˈkeɪptaʊn ; ˈkep,taʊn/ 開普敦(南非共和國西南部一港埠,爲其立法首都)。

Cape Verde Islands /-vɜːd- ; -vɝd-/ 維德角群島(在西非海岸外之大西洋中,原屬葡萄牙,於 1975 年 7 月獨立,首都 Praia)。

Capri Island /kæˈpriː- ; kæˈpri-/ 喀普里島(在義大利西南部拿坡里灣中)。

Caracas /kəˈrækəs ; kəˈrækəs/ 卡拉卡斯 (Venezuela 之首都)。

Cardiff /ˈkɑːdɪf;ˈkɑrdɪf/ 加地夫(威爾斯東南部一海港)。

Cardiganshire /ˈkɑːdɪgənʃə(r) ; ˈkɑrdɪgən,ʃɪr/ 喀地干夏(昔爲威爾斯西部一郡)。

Caribbean, the /ˌkærɪˈbiː(ː)ən ; ,kærəˈbiən/ 加勒比海(在中南美洲東部,介於南美洲,中美洲及西印度羣島之間)。

Carlow /'kɑːləʊ ; 'kɑr,lo/ 喀羅(愛爾蘭東南部一郡,又其首府名)。
Carmarthenshire /kə'mɑːðənʃə(r) ; kɑr'mɑrðən,ʃɪr/ 喀麥登夏(昔爲威爾斯南部一郡)。
Carolina /,kærə'laɪnə ; ,kærə'laɪnə/ 卡羅來納 (**1** 南非共和國東南部一城鎮; **2** 西印度羣島波多黎各島東北部一城鎮; **3** 巴西中東部一城鎮)。
Caroline /'kærəlaɪn ; 'kærə,laɪn/ 加羅林羣島(在西太平洋,由美國託管)。
Carpathian /kɑː'peɪθjən ; kɑr'peθɪən/ 喀爾巴阡山(在歐洲中部,介於捷克與波蘭之間)。
Carstensz /'kɑːstənz ; 'kɑrstənz/ 卡爾斯登峯(在新幾內亞西部,今稱 Djaja /'dʒɑːjə ; 'dʒɑjə/)。
Cartagena /,kɑːtə'dʒiːnə ; ,kɑrtə'dʒinə/ 喀他基那 (**1** 哥倫比亞西北部一海港; **2** 西班牙東南部一海港)。
Casablanca /,kæsə'blæŋkə ; ,kæsə'blæŋkə/ 卡薩布蘭加(非洲摩洛哥西部一港埠)。
Cascade Range /kæs'keɪd ; kæs'ked/ 喀斯開山脈(在美國西北部)。
Caspian, the /'kæspɪən ; 'kæspɪən/ 裏海(歐亞兩洲間之內海)。
Castries /'kæstriːz ; 'kæs,triz/ 卡斯翠 (亦稱 Port Castries, 爲 Saint Lucia 之首都及港口)。
Catalonia /,kætə'ləʊnɪə ; ,kætə'lonɪə/ 加泰隆尼亞(西班牙東北部一地區)。
Catania /kə'teɪnjə ; kə'tenjə/ 卡塔尼亞 (**1** 西西里島東部一地區; **2** 西西里島東部一城市)。
Catskill Mountains /'kætskɪl ; 'kæt,skɪl/ 卡兹奇山脈(在美國紐約州之東南部)。
Caucasia /kɔː'keɪzɪə ; kɔ'keʒə/ 高加索(亦稱 Caucasus, 蘇聯黑海與裏海間之一地區,分內高加索及外高加索二部)。
Caucasus /'kɔːkəsəs ; 'kɔkəsəs/ **1** 高加索山脈(在蘇聯歐洲部分之高加索境內)。**2** = Caucasia.
Cavan /'kævən ; 'kævən/ 卡凡(愛爾蘭東北部一郡,又其首府名)。
Cavite /kə'viːtɪ ; kə'vitɪ/ 加維特 (**1** 菲律賓呂宋島之西南部一省; **2** 加維特省之首府,在馬尼拉西南)。
Cayman (Islands) /keɪ'mæn ; ke'mæn/ 開曼羣島(在加勒比海西北部,屬英領西印度羣島)。
Cebu /seɪ'buː ; se'bu/ 宿霧 (**1** 菲律賓羣島中部一島; **2** 宿霧島東岸一城市,爲宿霧島之首府)。
Celebes /se'liːbɪz ; 'sɛlə,biz/ **1** 西里伯島(在婆羅洲以東菲律賓以南,屬印尼)。**2** 西里伯海(在印尼北部)。
Cenis /sə'niː ; sə'ni/ 塞尼峯(在法、義之間,有隧道貫通)。
Central /'sentrəl ; 'sɛntrəl/ 中區(蘇格蘭中部一地區,首府 Stirling)。
Central African Republic 中非共和國(非洲中部一國家,1960 年 8 月獨立,首都 Bangui)。
Central America 中美洲(爲北美洲之南端,北接北美洲之墨西哥,南連南美洲之哥倫比亞)。
Central Asia 中亞細亞(亞洲西部一地區)。
Central Provinces and Benar 中央省(在印度中部,今名 Madhya Pradesh /,mɑːdjə prə'deʃ ; ,mɑdjə prə'dɛʃ/)。
Ceuta /'sjuːtə ; 'se,utə/ 休達(摩洛哥北部一海港,與直布羅陀隔海相望)。
Ceylon /sɪ'lɒn ; sɪ'lɑn/ 錫蘭(參看 Sri Lanka)。
Chad /tʃæd ; tʃæd/ 查德 (非洲中北部一國家, 1960 年 8 月獨立,首都 Ndjamena)。
Chahar /'tʃɑː'hɑː ; 'tʃɑ'hɑr/ 察哈爾(中國北部一省)。
Chaldea, Chaldaea /kæl'di(ː)ə ; kæl'diə/ 古巴比倫南部一地區(位於波斯灣之西北)。
Chamonix /'ʃæmənɪ ; 'ʃæmənɪ/ 沙木尼(法國東部一遊覽中心)。
Champagne /ʃæm'peɪn ; ʃæm'pen/ 香檳(法國東北部一地區,以產香檳酒聞名全球)。
Changan /'tʃɑːŋ'ɑːn ; 'tʃɑŋ'ɑn/ 長安(參看 Sian)。
Changchun /'tʃɑːŋ'tʃʊn ; 'tʃɑŋ'tʃʊn/ 長春(中國吉林省一城市)。
Changhua /'tʃɑːŋ'hwɑː ; 'tʃɑŋ'hwɑ/ 彰化(中國臺灣省中西部一縣,亦爲其縣治名)。
Changkiakow /'dʒɑːŋdʒɪ'ɑː'kəʊ ; 'dʒɑŋdʒɪ'ɑ'ko/ 張家口(舊稱 Wanchuan 或 Kalgan, 中國察哈爾省省會)。
Chang-pai Shan /'tʃɑːŋ 'baɪ 'ʃɑːn ; ,tʃɑŋ ,baɪ 'ʃɑn/ 長白山(在中國東北境內)。
Changsha /'tʃɑːŋ'ʃɑː ; 'tʃɑŋ'ʃɑ/ 長沙(中國湖南省省會)。
Changshu /'tʃɑːŋ'ʃuː ; 'tʃɑŋ'ʃu/ 常熟(中國江蘇省境內一城市)。
Changyeh /'tʃɑːŋ'iː ; 'tʃɑŋ'i/ 張掖(在中國甘肅省境內)。
Chankiang /'tʃɑːndʒɪ'ɑːŋ ; 'tʃɑndʒɪ'ɑŋ/ 湛江市(在中國廣東省雷州半島東北岸)。
Channel Islands 海峽羣島(在英吉利海峽,屬英)。
Chantrey Inlet /'tʃɑːntrɪ- ; 'tʃæntrɪ-/ 查得來灣(在加拿大西北地方之東南海岸)。
Charleston /'tʃɑːlstən ; 'tʃɑrlstən/ 查理斯敦 (**1** 美國南卡羅來納州一海港; **2** 美國西維吉尼亞州之首府)。
Charlotte /'ʃɑːlət ; 'ʃɑrlət/ 沙羅特 (美國北卡羅來納州南部一城市,爲棉花及煙草大市場)。
Chartres /ʃɑːt ; ʃɑrt/ 沙特爾(法國中北部一城市)。
Chatham /'tʃætəm ; 'tʃætəm/ **1** 占松羣島(在南太平洋,屬紐西蘭)。**2** 占松(英格蘭東南部一城市,爲英國海、陸軍重地)。
Chaudoc /'tʃʌʊ'dəʊk ; 'tʃʌʊ'dɔk/ 朱篤(越南南部一城鎮)。
Chautauqua /ʃə'tɔːkwə ; ʃə'tɔkwə/ 朱太奎 (**1** 湖名,在美國紐約州西南部; **2** 美國堪薩斯州東南部之一郡; **3** 美國紐約州西南部之一郡)。
Chefoo /'dʒʌ'fuː ; 'dʒə'fu/ 煙臺(亦稱 Yentai, 中國山東省一漁港)。
Chekiang /'dʒʌdʒɪ'ɑːŋ ; 'dʒʌdʒɪ'ɑŋ/ 浙江(中國東部一省)。
Chemnitz /'kemnɪts ; 'kɛmnɪts/ 肯尼支(德國東部之工業城市)。
Chemulpo /tʃɪ'mʌlpəʊ ; dʒə'mʊlpo/ 濟物浦(今名 Inchon)。
Chengteh /'tʃʌŋ'dʌ ; 'tʃʌŋ'də/ 承德(中國熱河省省會)。
Chengtu /'tʃʌŋ'duː ; 'tʃʌŋ'du/ 成都(中國四川省省會)。
Cherrapunji /,tʃerə'pʊndʒɪ ; ,tʃɛrə'pʊndʒɪ/ 乞拉朋吉(在印度東北部,爲世界雨量最多之地)。
Chesapeake Bay /'tʃesəpiːk ; 'tʃɛsə,pik/ 乞沙比克灣(大西洋一海灣,突入美國維吉尼亞州及馬里蘭州)。
Cheshire /'tʃeʃə(r) ; 'tʃɛʃɚ/ 赤郡(英格蘭西北部一郡,略作 *Ches*)。
Chester /'tʃestə(r) ; 'tʃɛstɚ/ 赤斯特(英格蘭西北部一城市)。
Chesterfield /'tʃestəfiːld ; 'tʃɛstɚ,fild/ 赤斯特非(英格蘭中北部一城市)。
Cheyenne /ʃaɪ'æn ; ʃaɪ'æn/ 斜陽河 (在美國南達科他州西部,注於密蘇里河)。
Chiai /dʒɪ'ɑː'iː ; dʒɪ'ɑ'i/ 嘉義(中國臺灣省中西部一縣,亦爲其縣治名)。
Chicago /ʃɪ'kɑːgəʊ ; ʃə'kɑgo/ 芝加哥(在美國中西部,爲美國第二大城)。
Chihfeng /'tʃɪ'feŋ ; 'tʃɪ'fɛŋ/ 赤峯(中國熱河省中部一商業中心)。
Chihuahua /tʃʌ'wɑːwə ; tʃə'wɑwɑ/ 濟華花(北美墨西哥西北部一城市)。
Chile /'tʃɪlɪ ; 'tʃɪlɪ/ 智利(南美洲西南部一國,首都 Santiago)。
Chimborazo /,tʃɪmbə'rɑːzəʊ ; ,tʃɪmbə'rɑzo/ 青坡拉索山(在厄瓜多爾之中西部)。
China /'tʃaɪnə ; 'tʃaɪnə/ 中國。
Chinchow /'dʒɪn'dʒəʊ ; 'dʒɪn'dʒo/ 錦州(中國遼寧省西部交通要道)。
Chinghai /'tʃɪŋ'haɪ ; 'tʃɪŋ'haɪ/ 青海(亦作 Tsinghai, 中國西部一省)。
Chinhai /'dʒɪn'haɪ ; 'dʒɪn'haɪ/ 鎮海 (中國浙江省甬江之河口港)。
Chinju /'dʒɪn'dʒuː ; 'dʒɪn'dʒu/ 青州(韓國南部一城鎮)。
Chinkiang /'dʒɪndʒiː'ɑːŋ ; 'dʒɪndʒɪ'ɑŋ/ 鎮江(中國江蘇省省會)。
Chinmen = **Kinmen**
Chinnampo /'dʒɪn,nɑːm,pəʊ ; 'dʒɪn,nɑm,po/ 鎮南浦(北韓一港市)。
Chinwangtao /'tʃɪn'hwɑːŋ'daʊ ; 'tʃɪn'hwɑŋ'daʊ/ 秦皇島(中國河北省一海港)。
Chiriquí /,tʃɪrɪ'kiː ; ,tʃɪrɪ'ki/ 捷瑞奇峯(在巴拿馬西部)。
Chirripó Grande /,tʃɪrɪ'pəʊ 'grɑːndə ; ,tʃɪrɪ,po 'grɑndɪ/ 奇里波格蘭德山(在哥斯達黎加東南部)。

Chita /tʃɪ'tɑː; tʃɪ'tɑ/ 赤塔(蘇聯亞洲部分中南部一城市)。
Chittagong /'tʃɪtəˌɡɑːŋ; 'tʃɪtəˌɡɑŋ/ 吉大港(孟加拉共和國東南部一城鎮)。
Chkalov /tʃə'kɑːləf; tʃə'kaləf/ 乍加洛夫(蘇聯歐洲部分之東部一城市,現稱 Orenburg /'ɒrənˌbɜːɡ; 'ɔrənˌbɝɡ/)。
Cholon /ʃə'ləʊn; ʃə'lon/ 堤岸(南越東部一城市,在西貢對岸)。
Chongjin /'tʃɔːŋˌdʒɪn; 'tʃɔŋˌdʒɪn/ 清津(北韓一商港)。
Chosen /'tʃəʊ'sen; 'tʃo'sɛn/ 朝鮮 (**1** 卽今韓國; **2** 半島名,卽韓國全部; **3** 韓國與日本間之海峽名)。
Christchurch /'kraɪstʃɜːtʃ; 'kraɪsˌtʃɝtʃ/ 基督城(紐西蘭之南島東岸一城市)。
Christmas Island /'krɪsməs-; 'krɪsməs-/ 聖誕島 (**1** 在印度洋東部,爪哇之西南; **2** 在太平洋中部,夏威夷之南)。
Chuckchee Sea /'tʃʌktʃɪ; 'tʃʌktʃɪ/ 楚克芝海(或作 Chukchi Sea, 爲北極海之一部分,位於白令海峽以北)。
Chu Kiang /'dʒuːdʒɪ'ɑːŋ; 'dʒudʒɪ'ɑŋ/ 珠江(中國廣東省境內,注入南海,亦作 Pearl River)。
Chunchon /'tʃʊnˌtʃɔːn; 'tʃʊnˌtʃɔn/ 春川(韓國漢城之東北一城市)。
Chungking /'tʃʊŋ'kɪŋ; 'tʃʊŋ'kɪŋ/ 重慶(中國四川省東南部一城市)。
Chungshan /'dʒʊŋ'ʃɑːn; 'dʒʊŋ'ʃɑn/ 中山(中國廣東省珠江西岸一縣,爲 國父孫中山先生故鄉)。
Churchill /'tʃɜːtʃɪl; 'tʃɝˌtʃɪl/ 邱吉爾河(在加拿大境內)。
Chu River /tʃuː-; tʃu-/ 楚河(在蘇聯中亞哈薩克之東南)。
Cimarron /'sɪmərəʊn; 'sɪməˌrɑn/ 西馬隆河(在美國境內,注於阿肯色河)。
Cimone, Monte /ˌmɒntɪ tʃɪ'məʊnə; ˌmɔntɪ tʃɪ'monɪ/ 祈孟那山(在義大利北部)。
Cincinnati /ˌsɪnsɪ'nætɪ; ˌsɪnsə'nætɪ/ 辛辛那提(美國俄亥俄州西南部一城市)。
Cinto /'tʃɪntəʊ; 'tʃinto/ 欽多山(在歐洲科西嘉島西北部)。
Ciscaucasia /ˌsɪskɒ'keɪʒə; ˌsɪskɔ'keʒə/ 內高加索(蘇聯黑海與裏海間之一地區,在高加索山以北)。
Clackmannanshire /klæk'mænənʃə(r); klæk'mænənˌʃɪr/ 克拉克曼南夏(昔爲蘇格蘭中部一郡)。
Clare /kleə(r); klɛr/ 克雷(愛爾蘭西部一郡)。
Cleveland /'kliːvlənd; 'klivlənd/ 克利夫蘭 (**1** 美國俄亥俄州北部一城市; **2** 英格蘭北部一郡)。
Clifton /'klɪftən; 'klɪftən/ 克利夫頓(美國新澤西州東北部一城市)。
Clingmans Dome /'klɪŋmənz; ˌklɪŋmənz/ 克林曼山(在美國田納西州與北卡羅來納州之交界處)。
Cloud Peak 雲峯(在美國懷俄明州北部)。
Clwyd /'kluːɪd; 'kluɪd/ 克魯依德(威爾斯東北部一郡)。
Coast Range 海岸山脈(在北美洲大陸西部之太平洋岸)。
Coats Island /kəʊts-; kots-/ 科玆島(在加拿大哈得孫灣北部)。
Cochin China /'kəʊtʃən-; ˌkotʃən-/ 交趾支那(越南南部一地區)。
Cocos Islands /'kəʊkəs-; 'kokəs-/ 可可斯羣島(在印度洋東部,爪哇島之西南,屬澳洲)。
Cologne /kə'ləʊn; kə'lon/ 科倫(德國西部一城市,濱萊茵河)。
Colombia /kə'lɒmbɪə; kə'lʌmbɪə/ 哥倫比亞(南美洲西北部之一國,首都 Bogotá)。
Colombo /kə'lʌmbəʊ; kə'lʌmbo/ 可倫坡(Sri Lanka 之首都,爲東西洋航路之要衝)。
Colorado /ˌkɒlə'rɑːdəʊ; ˌkɑlə'rædo/ 科羅拉多(美國西部之一州,略作 *CO*)。
Columbia /kə'lʌmbɪə; kə'lʌmbɪə/ 哥倫比亞 (**1** 美國西北部一河流; **2** 美國南卡羅來納州之首府; **3** 美國密蘇里州中部一城市)。
Columbia, Mount 哥倫比亞峯 (**1** 在美國科羅拉多州之咖啡郡; **2** 在加拿大亞伯達省之西南部,與英屬哥倫比亞省之東南部)。
Columbus /kə'lʌmbəs; kə'lʌmbəs/ 哥倫布(美國俄亥俄州之首府,在辛辛那提之東北)。
Como /'kəʊməʊ; 'komo/ 科木 (**1** 義大利北部一城市; **2** 湖名,在義大利北部,爲著名之遊覽地)。
Comoro Islands /'kɒmərəʊ-; 'kɑməˌro-/ 科摩羅羣島(在非洲東南方,莫三比克海峽之北口,原屬法國,於1975年7月獨立,稱爲 Federal and Islamic Republic of Comoros 科摩羅伊斯蘭聯邦共和國,首都 Moroni)。
Compiègne /kəʊmp'jeɪn; komp'jen/ 康白尼(法國北部一城市)。
Conakry /'kɒnəkrɪ; 'kɑnəkrɪ/ 柯那克里(Guinea 之首都,亦作 Konakry)。
Concepción /kənˌsepsɪ'əʊn; kənˌsɛpsɪ'on/ 康塞普森(智利西南部一城市)。
Coney Island /'kəʊnɪ-; 'konɪ-/ 科尼島(紐約市一小島,爲一遊樂地)。
Congo, the /'kɒŋɡəʊ; 'kɑŋɡo/ **1** People's Republic of ～ 剛果人民共和國(在非洲中西部,昔稱 Middle Congo, 爲法屬赤道非洲一部分,1960年8月獨立,首都 Brazzaville)。**2** 參看 Zaire。**3** 剛果河(亦稱 Zaire, 在中非,注入大西洋)。
Connacht /'kɒnɔːt; 'kɑˌnɔt/ 康瑙特(昔作 Connaught, 愛爾蘭西部一省)。
Connecticut /kə'netɪkət; kə'nɛtɪkət/ 康乃狄格(美國東北部之一州,略作 *CT*)。
Constance, Mount /'kɒnstəns; 'kɑnstəns/ 康士坦士峯(在美國華盛頓州西部)。
Constantine /'kɒnstəntaɪn; 'kɑnstənˌtin/ 君士坦丁(阿爾及利亞東北部一城市)。
Constantinople /ˌkɒnstæntɪ'nəʊpl; ˌkɑnˌstæntə'nopl̩/ 君士坦丁堡(Istanbul 之舊稱)。
Constantsa /kən'stɑːntsɑː; kən'stɑntsɑ/ 康士坦沙(羅馬尼亞東南部一城市)。
Cook /kʊk; kʊk/ 科克 (**1** 美國阿拉斯加州東南部一山峯; **2** 南太平洋一羣島,屬紐西蘭)。
Coolgardie /kuːl'ɡɑːdɪ; kul'ɡɑrdɪ/ 古耳加底(澳洲西南部一城市)。
Copenhagen /ˌkəʊpn'heɪɡn; ˌkopən'heɡən/ 哥本哈根(Denmark 之首都)。
Coral Sea /'kɒrəl-; 'kɔrəl-/ 珊瑚海(在澳洲昆士蘭之東北)。
Cordillera Mts. /ˌkɔːdɪ'ljeərə; ˌkɔrdɪ'ljɛrə/ 科地勒拉山(在南美秘魯中北部)。
Cordoba /'kɔːdəʊbɑː; 'kɔrdəbə/ 哥多華 (**1** 阿根廷中部一城市,爲該國第二大城; **2** 西班牙南部一城市)。
Corfu /kɔː'fuː; kɔr'fu/ 科孚島(希臘西北部一海島)。
Corinth /'kɒrɪnθ; 'kɔrənθ/ 科林斯(希臘南部一城市)。
Cork /kɔːk; kɔrk/ 科克(愛爾蘭西南部一郡,又該郡之首府)。
Corno /'kɔːnə; 'kɔrno/ 考奴山(在義大利中部)。
Cornwall /'kɔːnwɔːl; 'kɔrnˌwɔl/ 康瓦耳(英格蘭西南部一郡,略作 *Corn*)。
Corrientes /ˌkɒrɪ'enti(ː)z; ˌkɔrɪ'ɛnˌtɛs/ 可林特斯(阿根廷東北部一城市)。
Corsica /'kɔːsɪkə; 'kɔrsɪkə/ 科西嘉島(法國在地中海中之一島,拿破崙之誕生地)。
Costa Rica /ˌkɒstə 'riːkə; ˌkɑstə 'rikə/ 哥斯大黎加(中美洲之一國,首都 San José)。
Côte d'Azur /ˌkəʊdə'zʊə; ˌkodə'zʊr/ 蔚藍海岸(在法國東南部,臨地中海)。
Cotonou /ˌkəʊtə'nuː; ˌkotə'nu/ 柯都努(Benin 南部一港市,爲其中央政府所在地)。
Cotopaxi /ˌkɒtə'pæksɪ; ˌkotə'pæksɪ/ 科多伯西山(厄瓜多爾中北部一火山)。
Coventry /'kɒvəntrɪ; 'kʌvəntrɪ/ 科芬特里(英格蘭中部一城市)。
Cradle Mount /'kreɪdl; 'kredl̩/ 搖籃峯(在澳洲塔斯曼尼亞島西北部)。
Cranston /'krænstən; 'krænstən/ 克蘭斯敦(美國羅得島州東北部一城市)。
Crefeld /'kreɪfeld; 'kreˌfɛlt/ 克雷非耳(德國西部一城市,亦作 Krefeld)。
Crete /kriːt; krit/ 克里特島(地中海東部一島,屬希臘,亦稱 Candia)。
Crewe /kruː; kru/ 克魯(英格蘭西北部一城鎮)。
Crimea /kraɪ'mɪə; kraɪ'miə/ 克里米亞(蘇聯西南部黑海中一半島)。
Croatia /krəʊ'eɪʃɪə; kro'eʃə/ 克羅埃西亞(歐洲東南部一地區,屬南斯拉夫)。
Cro-Magnon /ˌkrəʊmə'njɔ̃ː; ˌkromæ'njõ/ 克魯麥農(在法國西南部,該地於1868年以發現歐洲史前人骸而聞名)。

Crosby /ˈkrɒzbɪ ; ˈkrɔzbɪ/ 克勞士貝(英格蘭西北部蘭開郡一城市)。

Croydon /ˈkrɔɪdn; ˈkrɔɪdn̩/ 克洛頓(英格蘭南部一城市)。

Cuba /ˈkjuːbə ; ˈkjubə/ 古巴(西印度羣島中最大之島國,首都 Havana)。

Cumberland /ˈkʌmbələnd ; ˈkʌmbɚlənd/ **1** 昆布蘭(昔爲英格蘭西北部一郡,略作 *Cumb*, 今併入 Cumbria)。**2** 昆布蘭(美國馬里蘭州西北部一城市)。**3** 昆布蘭河(從美國肯塔基州東南,經田納西州北部,流入俄亥俄河)。

Cumbria /ˈkʌmbrɪə ; ˈkʌmbrɪə/ 康布里亞(英格蘭西北部一郡)。

Cumbrian Mountains /ˈkʌmbrɪən- ; ˈkʌmbrɪən-/ 康布連山(在英格蘭西北部康布里亞郡)。

Cushing /ˈkʊʃɪŋ ; ˈkʊʃɪŋ/ 刻興山(在加拿大英屬哥倫比亞省北部)。

Cyclades /ˈsɪklədiːz ; ˈsɪklə,diz/ 昔克蘭羣島(在南愛琴海,屬希臘)。

Cyprus /ˈsaɪprəs ; ˈsaɪprəs/ 賽普勒斯(地中海東部一島國,原屬英,1960年8月獨立,首都 Nicosia)。

Cyrenaica /ˌsaɪrəˈneɪkə ; ˌsaɪrəˈneəkə/ 昔蘭尼加(北非利比亞東部一地區)。

Czechoslovakia /ˌtʃekəʊsləˈvækɪə ; ˌtʃɛkəsloˈvɑkɪə/ 捷克斯拉夫(簡稱捷克,歐洲中部一國,首都 Prague)。

Dacca /ˈdækə ; ˈdækə/ 達卡(Bangladesh 之首都)。

Dagenham /ˈdægənəm ; ˈdægənəm/ 達根安(英格蘭東南部一城市)。

Dahomey /dəˈhəʊmɪ ; dəˈhomɪ/ 達荷美(參看 Benin)。

Dairen /ˈdaɪˈren ; ˈdaɪˈrɛn/ 大連(中國東北部一港市,在遼寧省境內,與旅順合稱旅大)。

Dai-Sen /ˈdaɪˈsen ; ˈdaɪˈsɛn/ 大森峯(在日本本州島西部)。

Dakar /ˈdækə(r) ; ˈdæk,ɑr/ 達喀爾(Senegal 之首都)。

Dakota /dəˈkəʊtə ; dəˈkotə/ 達科塔(昔爲美國北部之一地,1889年分爲南、北達科塔二州)。

Dallas /ˈdæləs ; ˈdæləs/ 達拉斯(美國德克薩斯州東北部一城市,美國甘迺廸總統遇刺於此)。

Damar /ˈdɑːmɑː(r) ; ˈdɑm,ɑr/ 大馬羣島(印尼希蘭島之南一羣島)。

Damascus /dəˈmɑːskəs ; dəˈmæskəs/ 大馬士革(Syria 之首都)。

Dampier Strait /ˈdæmpjə- ; ˈdæmpjɚ-/ 丹頗海峽(**1** 介於俾斯麥羣島中之新不列顛島與烏寶島之間; **2** 在新幾內亞西端與威谷島之間)。

Danger Islands /ˈdeɪndʒə- ; ˈdendʒɚ-/ 危險羣島(在太平洋中部)。

Danube /ˈdænjuːb ; ˈdænjub/ 多瑙河(在歐洲中部,由德國經奧國,匈牙利,南斯拉夫,保加利亞,羅馬尼亞流入黑海)。

Danzig /ˈdæntsɪg ; ˈdæntsɪg/ 但澤(波蘭北部一港埠,亦作 Gdansk /gəˈdɑːnsk ; gəˈdɑnsk/)。

Dardanelles, the /ˌdɑːdəˈnelz ; ˌdɑrdəˈnɛlz/ 達達尼爾海峽(在土耳其歐亞兩部分之間,連接馬爾馬拉海與愛琴海)。

Dar es Salaam /ˈdɑːres səˈlɑːm ; ˌdɑr,ɛs səˈlɑm/ 達萊撒蘭(Tanzania 之首都)。

Darien /ˌdærɪˈen ; ˌdærɪˈɛn/ 達連海灣(介於巴拿馬與哥倫比亞間)。

Darjeeling /dɑːˈdʒiːlɪŋ ; dɑrˈdʒilɪŋ/ 大吉嶺(亦作 Darjiling, 印度東北部一市鎮,爲印度入中國西藏之要道)。

Darling R. /ˈdɑːlɪŋ ; ˈdɑrlɪŋ/ 大令河(在澳洲東南部,注於墨累河)。

Darlington /ˈdɑːlɪŋtən ; ˈdɑrlɪŋtən/ 達令敦(英格蘭北部一城市)。

Darmstadt /ˈdɑːmstæt ; ˈdɑrm,stæt/ 達木士塔(德國西南部一城市)。

Darwin /ˈdɑːwɪn ; ˈdɑrwən/ 達爾文(澳洲北部一海港)。

Dauphiné Alps /ˌdəʊfɪˈneɪ- ; ˌdofɪˈne-/ 多芬尼山脈(法國東南部近義大利邊境一山脈)。

Davenport /ˈdævnpɔːt ; ˈdævən,port/ 達分波特(美國愛俄華州東部一城市,工商業及鐵路中心)

Davis Strait /ˈdeɪvɪs- ; ˈdevəs-/ 大衞斯海峽(在格陵蘭與巴芬島之間)。

Dawna Range /ˈdɔːnə- ; ˈdɔnə-/ 道納山(在亞洲南部,介於緬甸與泰國之間)。

Dawson /ˈdɔːsn ; ˈdɔsn̩/ 道生河(澳洲昆士蘭州東部一河流)。

Dayton /ˈdeɪtn ; ˈdetn̩/ 達頓(美國俄亥俄州西南部一城市)。

Dead Sea 死海(亞洲西部一鹽水湖,介於約旦與以色列之間)。

Dearborn /ˈdɪə,bɔːn ; ˈdɪr,bɔrn/ 臺奔(美國密西根州東南部一城市)。

Deccan /ˈdekən ; ˈdɛkən/ 德干(亦作 Dekkan, 印度南部一高原)。

Delano Peak /ˈdelə,nəʊ- ; ˈdɛlə,no-/ 德來諾峯(美國猶他州中部一山峯)。

Delaware /ˈdeləweə(r) ; ˈdɛlə,wɛr/ 德拉瓦(美國東部濱大西洋之一州,略作 *DE*)。

Delhi /ˈdelɪ ; ˈdɛlɪ/ 德里(印度北部德里地方之首府,其南端之新市區稱做 New Delhi, 卽印度之首都)。

Delphi /ˈdelfaɪ ; ˈdɛl,faɪ/ 特耳菲(古希臘一都城)。

Demavend /ˈdemə,vend ; ˈdɛmə,vɛnd/ 德馬溫峯(在伊朗北部)。

Denbighshire /ˈdenbɪʃə(r) ; ˈdɛnbɪ,ʃɪr/ 但比夏(昔爲威爾斯北部一郡,現已併入 Clwyd)。

Denmark /ˈdenmɑːk ; ˈdɛn,mɑrk/ 丹麥(北歐之一國,首都 Copenhagen)。

Denmark Strait 丹麥海峽(介於格陵蘭與冰島間)。

Denver /ˈdenvə(r) ; ˈdɛnvɚ/ 丹佛(美國科羅拉多州之首府)。

Derbyshire /ˈdɑːbɪʃə(r) *US:* ˈdɜːrbɪ- ; ˈdɑrbɪ,ʃɪr/ 德貝郡(英格蘭中部一郡)。

Des Moines /dɪˈmɔɪn ; dɪˈmɔɪn/ 第蒙(**1** 美國愛俄華州中南部一城市; **2** 美國愛俄華州中部一河流,注於密西西比河)。

Detroit /dəˈtrɔɪt ; dɪˈtrɔɪt/ 底特律(美國密西根州東南部一城市,爲汽車工業中心)。

Devon Island /ˈdevn- ; ˈdɛvən-/ 得文島(在加拿大北部)。

Devonport /ˈdevnpɔːt ; ˈdɛvən,port/ 得文港(在紐西蘭北島威得曼他港之北岸)。

Devon(shire) /ˈdevn(ʃə(r)) ; ˈdɛvən(,ʃɪr)/ 得文郡(英格蘭西南部一郡)。

Dhaulagiri /ˌdaʊləˈgɪərɪ ; ˌdaʊləˈgɪrɪ/ 刀拉吉利峯(在印度之北,尼泊爾之中西部)。

Diamond Peak /ˈdaɪəmənd- ; ˈdaɪəmənd-/ 鑽石峯(**1** 在美國加州中南部; **2** 在美國俄勒岡州西部)。

Dien Bien Phu /ˌdjenˌbjenˈfuː ; ˌdjɛn,bjɛnˈfu/ 奠邊府(越南西北部一城鎮)。

Dijon /ˈdiːʒɔ̃ŋ ; ˈdiʒɑn/ 第戎(法國東部一城市)。

District of Columbia /-kəˈlʌmbɪə ; -kəˈlʌmbɪə/ 哥倫比亞特區(美國聯邦地區,與美首都華盛頓同其範圍,略作 *DC*)。

Djibouti /dʒɪˈbuːtɪ ; dʒəˈbutɪ/ **1** 吉布地共和國(在非洲東部,臨亞丁灣,原係法屬阿法及依薩地區,1977年6月獨立,首都 Djibouti)。**2** 吉布地(其首都,亦作 Jibuti)。

Dnieper /ˈniːpə(r) ; ˈnipɚ/ 聶伯河(在蘇聯歐洲部分境內,流入黑海)。

Dniester /ˈniːstə(r) ; ˈnistɚ/ 聶斯特河(在蘇聯東南部,注於黑海)。

Doha /ˈdəʊhə ; ˈdohɑ/ 杜哈(Qatar 之首都)。

Dominica /dəˈmɪnɪkə ; ˌdɑməˈnikə/ 多米尼克(原英屬西印度羣島之島嶼,於1978年11月獨立,首都 Roseau)。

Dominican Republic /dəˈmɪnɪkən- ; dəˈmɪnɪkən-/ 多明尼加共和國(昔名 San(to) Domingo, 西印度羣島諸國之一,首都 Santo Domingo)。

Doncaster /ˈdɒŋkəstə(r) ; ˈdɑŋkəstɚ/ 頓卡斯特(英格蘭中部一城市)。

Donegal /ˈdɒnɪgɔːl (in Ireland 愛爾蘭讀音), ˌdʌnɪˈgɔːl ; ˌdɑnɪˈgɔl/ 多尼哥(愛爾蘭西北部一郡)。

Donets /dəˈnets ; dəˈnɛts/ 頓內次河(在蘇聯烏克蘭東部,流入頓河)。

Don River /dɒn- ; dɑn-/ 頓河(在蘇聯歐洲部分之東南部,流入亞速海)。

Dorset(shire) /ˈdɔːsɪt(ʃə(r)) ; ˈdɔrsət(,ʃɪr)/ 多塞特郡(英格蘭南部一郡,略作 *Dors*)。

Douglas /ˈdʌgləs ; ˈdʌgləs/ 道格拉斯(英國愛爾蘭海中人島之首府)。

Douro /ˈdʊərəʊ ; ˈdoru/ 斗羅河(在西、葡兩國境內,流入大西洋)。

Dover /ˈdəuvə(r) ; ˈdovɚ/ 多佛 (**1** 英國東南部之一海港; **2** 美國德拉瓦州之首府)。
Dovrefjell /ˈdɔːvrəˌfjel ; ˈdɔvrəˌfjɛl/ 多甫勒高原(在挪威中部)。
Down /daʊn ; daʊn/ 道恩(北愛爾蘭東南部一郡)。
Drakensberg /ˈdrɑːkənzˌbɜːg ; ˈdrɑkənzˌbɝg/ 龍山(在南非共和國境內)。
Dresden /ˈdrezdən ; ˈdrɛzdən/ 德勒斯登(德國東部一城市,為 Saxony 邦之首府)。
Duala /duːˈɑːlɑː ; dʊˈɑlə/ 杜亞拉(非洲喀麥隆西部一城市,亦作 Douala)。
Dublin /ˈdʌblɪn ; ˈdʌblɪn/ 都柏林(Ireland 之首都,又其東部一郡)。
Dubrovnik /ˈdubrɒvnɪk ; ˈduˌbrɔvnɪk/ 杜布洛尼(南斯拉夫西南部一港市)。
Dudley /ˈdʌdlɪ ; ˈdʌdlɪ/ 杜德里(英格蘭中西部一城市)。
Duff /dʌf ; dʌf/ 都夫羣島(太平洋西南部一羣島)。
Duluth /djuːˈluːθ ; dəˈluθ/ 杜魯司(美國明尼蘇達州東部一城市)。
Dumbarton Oaks /dʌmˈbɑːtn ; ˌdʌmˈbɑrtn̩/ 敦巴頓橡園(在美京華盛頓郊外,1944 年曾舉行國際會議於此)。
Dumbartonshire /dʌmˈbɑːtnʃə(r) ; ˌdʌmˈbɑrtn̩ˌʃɪr/ 敦巴頓夏(昔為蘇格蘭中西部一郡)。
Dumfries and Galloway /dʌmˌfriːs ən ˈgæləweɪ ; ˌdʌmˌfris ən ˈgæləˌwe/ 敦夫里斯及加拉威(蘇格蘭南部一地區)。
Dumfries-shire /dʌmˈfriːʃʃə(r) ; ˌdʌmˈfriʃˌʃɪr/ 敦夫里斯夏(昔為蘇格蘭南部一部)。
Dundee /dʌnˈdiː ; ˌdʌnˈdi/ 丹地(蘇格蘭東部一海港)。
Dunedin /dʌˈniːdɪn ; ˌdʌˈnidn̩/ 丹尼丁(紐西蘭南島東南部一城市)。
Dunkirk /dʌnˈkɜːk ; ˈdʌnˌkɝk/ 敦克爾克(法國北部一港埠,亦作 Dunkerque)。
Durban /ˈdɜːbən ; ˈdɝbən/ 德爾班(南非共和國東部一海港)。
Durham /ˈdʌrəm ; ˈdʌrəm/ 達拉謨 (**1** 英格蘭北部一郡,略作 *Dur*; 其首府; **2** 美國北卡羅來納州北部一城市)。
Düsseldorf /ˈduːsəlˌdɔːf ; ˈdusəlˌdɔrf/ 杜塞爾多夫(德國西部一城市)。
Dutch East Indies /-ˈɪndiːz ; -ˈɪndiz/ 荷屬東印度羣島(或稱 Netherlands East Indies, 即現今之印尼共和國國土)。
Dutch Guiana 荷屬圭亞那(參看 Surinam)。
Dutch Harbor 荷蘭港(在美國阿拉斯加州西部,恩那拉斯加島之東端)。
Dutch West Indies 荷屬西印度羣島(亦稱 Netherlands Antilles)。
Dvina /dəˌvɪˈnɑː ; dəˌviˈnɑ/ 杜味拿河(蘇聯歐洲部分之西一河流,注於里加灣)。
Dvina, Northern 北杜味拿河(在蘇聯歐洲部分之北,注於地文斯克灣)。
Dyfed /ˈdʌvɪd ; ˈdʌvɛd/ 德維得(威爾斯西南部一郡)。
Dykh Tau /ˈdɪk taʊ ; ˈdɪkˌtaʊ/ 狄克山(亦作 Dikh Tau, 在蘇聯歐洲部分之南部)。
Ealing /ˈiːlɪŋ ; ˈilɪŋ/ 伊令(英格蘭東南部一鎮,為大倫敦之一部)。
East Berlin 東柏林(East Germany 之首都,參看 Berlin)。
Eastbourne /ˈiːstbɔːn ; ˈistˌbɔrn/ 伊斯特本(英格蘭南部一鎮)。
Easter Island 伊斯特島 (或稱復活島,在東南太平洋,屬智利)。
East Germany 東德(參看 German Democratic Republic 和 Germany)。
East Ham 伊斯哈木(昔為英格蘭東南部一城鎮)。
East Lothian 東樓甸(昔為蘇格蘭東南部一郡,又名 Haddington(shire) /ˈhædɪŋtənʃə(r) ; ˈhædɪŋtənˌʃɪr/)。
East Pakistan 東巴基斯坦(參看 Bangladesh)。
Ecuador /ˈekwədɔː(r) ; ˈɛkwəˌdɔr/ 厄瓜多爾(南美洲西北部一國家,首都 Quito)。
Edinburg /ˈednˌbɜːg ; ˈɛdn̩ˌbɝg/ 愛登伯(美國德克薩斯州南部一城市)。
Edinburgh /ˈedɪnbrə ; ˈɛdn̩ˌbərə/ 愛丁堡(Scotland 之首府)。
Edmonton /ˈedməntən ; ˈɛdməntən/ 艾德蒙吞 (**1** 加拿大西南部一城市; **2** 昔為英格蘭東南部一鎮)。
Edward, Lake /ˈedwəd ; ˈɛdwɚd/ 愛德華湖(在非洲東部烏干達與薩伊之間)。
Egypt /ˈiːdʒɪpt ; ˈidʒəpt/ 埃及(非洲東北部一國,首都 Cairo, 1958-61 與敍利亞合併而成阿拉伯聯合共和國, 1971 年改為埃及阿拉伯共和國)。
Eire /ˈeərə ; ˈɛrə/ 愛爾蘭共和國(亦稱 Republic of Ireland 或 Irish Republic, 歐洲西北部一國,首都Dublin)。
Elba /ˈelbə ; ˈɛlbə/ 厄爾巴島(屬義大利,在地中海北部,介於義大利本土與科西嘉島之間)。
Elbe /elb; ˈɛlbə/ 易北河(自捷克西部流經德國,注入北海)。
Elbert, Mount /ˈelbət ; ˈɛlbɚt/ 易北特峯(在美國科羅拉多州中部)。
Elborus /ˌelbəʊˈruːz ; ˌɛlbəˈruz/ 艾布魯斯峯(在蘇聯喬治亞共和國北部)。
Elburz Mts. /elˈbʊəz ; ɛlˈbʊrz/ 艾布士山脈(在伊朗北部,自西而東與裏海南岸並行)。
Eleusis /eˈljuːsɪs ; ɪˈlusəs/ 艾留西斯(古希臘一城市,在雅典西北)。
Elisabethville /ɪˈlɪzəbəθvɪl ; ɪˈlɪzəbəθˌvɪl/ 伊利薩白市(現稱 Lubumbashi)。
Ellice Islands /ˈelɪs- ; ˈɛlɪs-/ 艾利斯羣島(參看 Tuvalu)。
El Misti /elˈmiːstɪ ; ɛlˈmistɪ/ 米斯替火山(在秘魯南部,亦稱 Misti)。
El Salvador /elˈsælvədɔː(r) ; ɛl ˈsælvəˌdɔr/ 薩爾瓦多(中美洲太平洋岸一共和國,首都 San Salvador)。
Emden /ˈemdən ; ˈɛmdən/ 恩登(德國西北部一港市)。
Emi Koussi /ˈeɪmɪ ˈkuːsɪ ; ˌemɪ ˈkusə/ 愛米哥西峯(在非洲查德共和國北部)。
Emperor Range /ˈempərə- ; ˈɛmpərɚ-/ 帝王山脈(在所羅門羣島之布干維爾島之北)。
Enderby Land /ˈendɜːbɪ- ; ˈɛndɚbɪ-/ 恩德比地(南極洲一地區)。
England /ˈɪŋglənd ; ˈɪŋglənd/ **1** 英格蘭(英國一地區,在大不列顛島南部)。**2** 英國之通稱。
English Channel 英吉利海峽(介於英國南部與法國北部之間)。
Entebbe /enˈtebə; ɛnˈtɛbə/ 恩德培(烏干達南部一城鎮)。
Ephesus /ˈefɪsəs ; ˈɛfəsəs/ 以弗所 (小亞細亞西部一古城)。
Epsom and Ewell /ˈepsəm ən ˈjuːəl ; ˌɛpsəmənˈjuəl/ 艾普孫(英格蘭東南部一市鎮)。
Equatorial Guinea 赤道幾內亞 (西非一共和國, 原為 Spanish Guinea, 1968 年 10 月獨立,首都 Malabo)。
Erebus, Mount /ˈerəbəs ; ˈɛrəbəs/ 伊里布斯峯(在南極洲羅斯島上,為一活火山)。
Erie /ˈɪərɪ ; ˈɪrɪ/ **1** 伊利湖(在美國與加拿大之間)。**2** 伊利城(在美國賓夕凡尼亞州西北境)。**3** 伊利運河(在美國紐約州北部)。
Eritrea /ˌerɪˈtreɪə ; ˌɛrəˈtriə/ 厄立特里亞 (在非洲東北部,為衣索比亞一自治省,首府 Asmara)。
Esdraelon, Plain of /ˌezdreɪˈiːlɒn ; ˌɛzdrəˈilən/ 厄斯垂伊倫(以色列北部一平原)。
Essen /ˈesn ; ˈɛsn̩/ 埃森(德國西部一城市)。
Essex /ˈesɪks ; ˈɛsɪks/ 艾色克斯(英格蘭東海岸一郡,略作 *Ess*)。
Estonia, Esthonia /esˈtəunjə ; ɛsˈtonɪə/ 愛沙尼亞(蘇聯一加盟共和國,在波羅的海沿岸, 亦稱 Estonian Republic)。
Ethiopia /ˌiːθɪˈəupɪə ; ˌiθɪˈopɪə/ 衣索比亞(即 Abyssinia, 非洲東部一國家,首都 Addis Ababa)。
Etna /ˈetnə ; ˈɛtnə/ 埃特納火山(在義大利西西里島之東北部,亦作 Aetna)。
Eton /ˈiːtn ; ˈitn̩/ 伊頓(英國倫敦以西一城市)。
Euboea /juːˈbɪə ; juˈbɪə/ 尤比亞島(屬希臘,在愛琴海中)。
Euphrates /juːˈfreɪtiːz ; juˈfretiz/ 幼發拉底河(在亞洲西南部)。
Eurasia /juərˈeɪʒə ; jʊˈreʒə/ 歐亞大陸。
Europe /ˈjuərəp ; ˈjʊrəp/ 歐羅巴洲(簡稱歐洲)。
Evans, Mount /ˈevənz ; ˈɛvənz/ 艾凡山(在美國科羅拉多州中北部)。
Evanston /ˈevnstən ; ˈɛvənstən/ 艾凡斯頓(美國伊利諾州東北部一城市)。
Everest, Mount /ˈevərɪst ; ˈɛvərəst/ 埃佛勒斯峯(世界最高峯,屬喜馬拉雅山脈,亦稱 Chomolungma /ˌtʃɒmə-

'lʊŋmə ; ˌtʃɔmə'lʊŋmə/, 藏語‘聖母峯’之意)。

Everett /'evərɪt ; 'ɛvərət/ 艾威雷特 (**1** 美國麻薩諸塞州東部一城市; **2** 美國華盛頓州西北部一城市)。

Exeter /'eksətə(r) ; 'ɛksətɚ/ 愛塞特 (英格蘭西南部一城市)。

Eyre, Lake /eə(r) ; ɛr/ 艾耳湖(澳大利亞南澳州東北部一鹹水湖)。

Fairweather, Mount /'feəˌweðə(r) ; 'fɛrˌweðɚ/ 費委德山(在加拿大與阿拉斯加之間)。

Falkland /'fɔːklənd ; 'fɔklənd/ 福克蘭羣島(在阿根廷東南方,屬英,首府爲 Stanley)。

Fanning Island /'fænɪŋ- ; 'fænɪŋ-/ 芬寧島(在夏威夷之南,屬英)。

Federal Republic of Germany /-'dʒɜːmənɪ ; -'dʒɝm(ə)nɪ/ 德意志聯邦共和國 (卽西德, 1949 年成立, 首都 Bonn, 參看 Germany)。

Fenghwa /'fʌŋ'hwɑː ; 'fʌŋ'hwɑ/ 奉化 (中國浙江省一縣)。

Fen (Ho) /'fʌn 'hʌ ; 'fɛn 'ho/ 汾河(在中國山西省)。

Fenyang /'fʌn'jɑːŋ;'fʌn'jɑŋ/ 汾陽(中國山西省一城市)。

Ferg(h)ana /feə'gɑːnɑː ; fɚ'gɑnə/ 費加那 (蘇聯烏玆別克東部一城市)。

Fermanagh /fə'mænə ; fɚ'mænə/ 非曼那(北愛爾蘭西南部一郡)。

Fernando Po(o) /fə'nændəʊ 'pəʊ ; fɚˌnændo 'po/ 非南多波 (非洲西部一島, 屬赤道幾內亞, 現稱 Bioko /bɪ'əʊkəʊ ; bɪ'oko/)。

Fertile Crescent 肥沃半月形(亦稱‘肥腴月彎’,在西亞)。

Fife /faɪf ; faɪf/ 伐夫(蘇格蘭東部一區)。

Fifeshire /'faɪfʃə(r) ; 'faɪfˌʃɪr/ 伐夫夏(昔爲蘇格蘭東部一郡)。

Fiji /ˌfiː'dʒiː ; 'fidʒi/ 斐濟(西南太平洋之一國,原爲英屬飛枝羣島, 1970 年 10 月獨立,首都 Suva)。

Finchley /'fɪntʃlɪ ; 'fɪntʃlɪ/ 芬赤利 (昔爲英格蘭東南部一鎭)。

Finisterre, Cape /ˌfɪnəs'teə(r) ; ˌfɪnə'stɛr/ 天涯角(在西班牙之西北端)。

Finland /'fɪnlənd ; 'fɪnlənd/ 芬蘭 (歐洲北部一國家,首都爲 Helsinki)。

Finsteraarhorn /ˌfɪnstər'ɑːhɔːn ; ˌfɪnstɚ'ɑˌhɔrn/ 芬斯特瓦山(瑞士西南部一山名)。

Flanders /'flɑːndəz ; 'flændɚz/ 法蘭德斯 (比利時西部及法國北部一地區)。

Flattery, Cape /'flætərɪ ; 'flætərɪ/ 夫拉特黎角(在美國華盛頓州西北部)。

Flint(shire) /'flɪnt(ʃə(r)) ; 'flɪnt(ˌʃɪr)/ 夫林特夏(昔爲威爾斯東北部一郡)。

Florence /'flɒrəns ; 'flɔrəns/ 佛羅倫斯 (**1** 義大利中部一城市; **2** 美國阿拉巴馬州西北部一城市)。

Flores /'flɔːrɪz ; 'florəz/ 弗洛勒斯島 (印尼小巽他羣島內之一島)。

Florida /'flɒrɪdə *US:* 'flɔːr- ; 'flɔrədə/ 佛羅里達(美國東南部一州,略作 *FL*)。

Folkestone /'fəʊkstən ; 'fokstən/ 福克斯頓 (英格蘭東南部一港埠)。

Foochow /'fuː'dʒəʊ ; 'fu'dʒo/ 福州(中國福建省省會)。

Foraker, Mount /'fɒrəkə ; 'fɔrɪkɚ/ 福拉克山(在美國阿拉斯加州南部)。

Formosa /fɔː'məʊsə ; fɔr'mosə/ 參看 Taiwan。

Fort-Lamy /ˌfɔːˌlɑː'miː ; ˌfɔrlə'mi/ 拉米堡(Nďjamena 之舊稱)。

Fowliang /'fuːlɪ'ɑːŋ ; 'fulɪ'ɑŋ/ 浮梁(中國江西省一縣,所轄景德鎭以出產精美瓷器著名)。

France /frɑːns ; fræns/ 法國; 法蘭西(西歐國名, 首都 Paris)。

Frankfort /'fræŋkfət ; 'fræŋkfɚt/ 法蘭克佛(美國肯塔基州首府)。

Frankfurt /'fræŋkfət ; 'fræŋkfɚt/ 法蘭克福 (德國西部一城市)。

Franklin /'fræŋklɪn ; 'fræŋklɪn/ 富蘭克林(加拿大西北邊區北部一區)。

Fraser /'freɪzə(r);'frezɚ/ 夫拉則河(在加拿大西南境)。

Freetown /'friːtaʊn ; 'friˌtaʊn/ 自由城 (Sierra Leone 之首都)。

Freiburg /'fraɪbɜːg ; 'fraɪˌbʊrg/ 夫來堡 (德國西南部一城市)。

Fremantle /fre'mæntl ; frɪ'mæntl̩/ 弗利曼特(澳洲西南部一海港)。

French Guiana /-gɪ'ɑːnə ; -gɪ'ænə/ 法屬圭亞那(在南美洲北部,首府爲 Cayenne /kaɪ'en ; kaɪ'ɛn/)。

Fresno /'freznəʊ ; 'frɛzno/ 夫勒斯諾 (美國加利福尼亞州中部一城市)。

Friendly Islands = Tonga Islands

Frisian Islands /'frɪzɪən- ; 'frɪʒən-/ 弗利然羣島(北歐荷蘭、德國及丹麥沿海之羣島)。

Front Range /frʌnt- ; frʌnt-/ 福蘭特山脈(在美國科羅拉多州北部)。

Fuji(yama) /ˌfuːdʒɪ'jɑːmɑː ; ˌfudʒɪ'jɑmə/ 富士山(在日本本州島中南部)。

Fukien /'fuː'kjen ; 'fu'kjɛn/ 福建(中國東南一省)。

Fukuoka /ˌfuːku'əʊkə ; ˌfukə'wokə/ 福岡 (日本九州島北部一港市)。

Funafuti /ˌfuːnə'fuːtiː ; ˌfunə'futi/ 富那富提 (Tuvalu 之首都)。

Fundy, Bay of /'fʌndɪ;'fʌndɪ/ 芬地灣(在加拿大東南)。

Fushun /'fuː'ʃʊn ; 'fu'ʃʊn/ 撫順(中國遼寧省一城市,以產煤著名)。

Gaberones /ˌgɑːbə'rəʊnes ; ˌgɑbə'ronəs/ 嘉柏樓尼斯 (Gaborone 之舊稱)。

Gabon /gæ'bɒn ; gæ'bon/ 加彭(非洲西部一共和國,原爲法國屬地, 1960 年 8 月獨立,首都 Libreville)。

Gaborone /ˌgɑːbə'rəʊn ; ˌgɑbə'ron/ 嘉柏隆(Botswana 之首都,舊稱 Gaberones)。

Galápagos /gə'lɑːpəgəs ; gə'lɑpəgəs/ 加拉巴哥羣島(在厄瓜多爾以西之太平洋中)。

Galdhöpiggen /'gɑːlhɜːˌpɪgən ; 'gɑlhɚˌpɪgən/ 加赫皮根山(在挪威中南部)。

Galicia /gə'lɪʃɪə ; gə'lɪʃ(ɪ)ə/ 加里西亞(原爲奧匈帝國領土,二次大戰間屬波蘭,今分屬波蘭與蘇聯)。

Galilee/ 'gælɪliː;'gæləˌli/ 加里利(以色列北部一丘陵區)。

Galveston /'gælvəstn ; 'gælvəstən/ 加爾維斯敦(美國德克薩斯州東南部一海港)。

Galway /'gɔːlweɪ ; 'gɔlˌwe/ 哥耳威(愛爾蘭西部一郡,亦爲其首府)。

Gambia /'gæmbɪə ; 'gæmbɪə/ 甘比亞 (**1** 亦稱 The ~, 西非一共和國, 1965 年 2 月獨立,首都爲 Banjul; **2**非洲西部一河流)。

Gambier /'gæmbɪə(r) ; 'gæmˌbɪr/ 岡必爾羣島(在南太平洋 Tuamotu Archipelago 之東南,屬法國)。

Ganges /'gændʒiːz ; 'gænˌdʒiz/ 恆河(在印度北部)。

Gangtok /'gʌgtɒk ; 'gæŋ'tɑk/ 干托(Sikkim 之首府)。

Gannett Peak /'gænɪt- ; 'gænət-/ 干尼峯(在美國懷俄明州中部)。

Garonne /gə'rɒn ; gə'rɑn/ 加倫河(在法國西南部)。

Gary /'gerɪ ; 'gɛrɪ/ 噶里(美國印第安納州西北部一城市)。

Gascony /'gæskənɪ ; 'gæskənɪ/ 卡斯肯尼(法國西南部一地區)。

Gasherbrum /'gʌʃəbrʊm ; 'gʌʃɚˌbrum/ 加歇布龍山(在印度北部)。

Gateshead /'geɪtshed ; 'getsˌhɛd/ 加玆海得 (英格蘭北部一城市)。

Gdynia /gə'dɪnɪə; gə'dɪnɪə/ 格地尼亞(波蘭北部一港市)。

Geneva /dʒɪ'niːvə ; dʒə'nivə/ 日內瓦 (瑞士西南部一城市)。

Genoa /'dʒenəʊə ; 'dʒɛnəwə/ 熱那瓦(義大利西北部一海港)。

Genzan /'genˌzɑːn ; 'gɛnˌsɑn/ 元山(北韓東北部一港市,現稱 Wonsan /'wʌnˌsɑːn ; 'wʌnˌsɑn/)。

Georgetown /'dʒɔːdʒtaʊn ; 'dʒɔrdʒˌtaʊn/ **1** 喬治城(美國華盛頓市西部一區)。**2** 佐治敦(Guyana 之首都)。

Georgia /'dʒɔːdʒə ; 'dʒɔrdʒ(j)ə/ 喬治亞 (**1** 美國東南部之一州,略作 *GA*; **2** 蘇聯一加盟共和國,在外高加索之西部,瀕臨黑海,亦稱 Georgian Republic, 首府 Tiflis)。

German Democratic Republic 德意志民主共和國(卽東德, 1949 年成立, 首都爲 East Berlin, 參看 Germany)。

Germany /'dʒɜːmənɪ ; 'dʒɝm(ə)nɪ/ 德國(歐洲中部一國, 1949 年分爲 East ~ 和 West ~)。

Ghana /'gɑːnə ; 'gɑnə/ 迦納(非洲西部一國家,舊稱 Gold Coast, 1957 年 3 月獨立,首都爲 Accra)。

Ghats /gɔːts ; gɔts/ 高止山脈(在印度南部)。
Ghent /gent ; gɛnt/ 根特(比利時西北部一城市)。
Gibraltar /dʒɪˈbrɔːltə(r) ; dʒəˈbrɔltɚ/ 直布羅陀(在西班牙南端,包括 the Rock of Gibraltar 地區,爲英國之殖民地及要塞)。
Gila /ˈhiːlə ; ˈhilə/ 希拉河(在美國亞利桑那州南部,注於科羅拉多河)。
Gilbert Islands /ˈgɪlbət- ; ˈgɪlbɚt-/ 吉耳貝特羣島(在西太平洋,原屬英,1979 年獨立,改名 Kiribati)。
Gillingham /ˈdʒɪlɪŋəm ; ˈdʒɪlɪŋəm/ 吉令安(英格蘭肯特郡一城市)。
Gironde /dʒɪˈrɒnd ; dʒəˈrand/ 吉倫特灣(在法國西南岸)。
Glamorgan(shire) /gləˈmɔːgən(ʃə(r)) ; gləˈmɔrgən(ˌʃɪr)/ 格拉馬干夏(昔爲威爾斯東南部一郡;今分爲 Mid Glamorgan, South Glamorgan 及 West Glamorgan 三郡)。
Glasgow /ˈglɑːsgəʊ ; ˈglæsgo/ 格拉斯哥(蘇格蘭中南部主要港埠)。
Gloucester /ˈglɒstə(r) ; ˈglɑstɚ/ 格洛斯特(英格蘭西南部格洛斯特郡之首府)。
Gloucestershire /ˈglɒstəʃə(r) ; ˈglɑstɚˌʃɪr/ 格洛斯特郡(在英格蘭西南部,略作 *Glos*)。
Gobi, Desert of /ˈgəʊbɪ ; ˈgobɪ/ 戈壁沙漠(在蒙古境內)。
Godavari /gəˈdɑːvəriː ; gəˈdɑvərɪ/ 哥達維利河(在印度中部,注於孟加拉灣)。
Godwin Austen /ˈgɒdwɪn ˈɔːstən ; ˌgɑdwəˈnɔstən/ 哥德文奧斯騰峯(亦稱 K² /ˈkeɪˈtuː ; ˈkeˈtu/ (葵土峯),爲喀拉崑崙山之最高峯,在喀什米爾北部)。
Gold Coast 黃金海岸(參看 Ghana)。
Gorki, Gorky /ˈgɔːkɪ ; ˈgɔrkɪ/ 高爾基(蘇聯莫斯科東北一城市)。
Gosainthan /ˈgəʊsaɪnˈtɑːn ; ˌgoˌsaɪnˈtɑn/ 哥杉塘峯(在中國西藏南部,近尼泊爾)。
Gosport /ˈgɒspɔːt ; ˈgɑsˌport/ 哥斯波(英格蘭南部漢普郡一城市)。
Göteborg /ˌjɜːtəˈbɔə(jə) ; ˌjɝtəˈbɔrɪ/ 越特堡(瑞典西南部一港市)。
Gothenburg /ˈgɒθənbɜːg ; ˈgɑθənˌbɝg/ 哥森堡(美國內布拉斯加州中南部一城市; Göteborg 之別稱)。
Grampian /ˈgræmpɪən ; ˈgræmpɪən/ 格蘭屛(蘇格蘭東北一區)。
Grampian Hills /ˈgræmpɪən- ; ˈgræmpɪən-/ 格蘭屛山脈(在蘇格蘭中北部,亦稱 The Grampians)。
Granada /grəˈnɑːdə ; grəˈnɑdə/ 格拉那達(西班牙南部一省,亦爲其首府)。
Grand Teton /-ˈtiːtɑːn ; -ˈtiˌtɑn/ 大梯頓山(在美國懷俄明州西北)。
Granite Peak /ˈgrænɪt- ; ˈgrænɪt-/ 格蘭尼峯(在美國蒙他拿州南部)。
Grays Peak /greɪz- ; grez-/ 格雷斯峯(在美國科羅拉多州之中部)。
Great Bear Lake 大熊湖(在加拿大西北部)。
(Great) Britain **1** 大不列顛島(在歐洲西部)。**2** 英國之別稱(參看 Britain)。
Great Dividing Range 大分水山脈(在澳洲東部)。
Greater Antilles /-ænˈtɪliːz ; -ænˈtɪliz/ 大安地列斯羣島(西印度羣島中三大羣島之一)。
Great Slave Lake 大奴湖(在加拿大西北部)。
Great Smoky Mountains 大煙山(亦稱 Great Smokies, 在美國田納西州與北卡羅來納州之邊境,部份地方劃爲國家公園)。
Greece /griːs ; gris/ 希臘(歐洲南部一國家,首都爲 Athens)。
Green /griːn ; grin/ 格陵河(在美國西部,注於科羅拉多河)。
Greenland /ˈgriːnlənd ; ˈgrinlənd/ 格林蘭島(大西洋北部一島,在北美洲之東北,屬丹麥,爲世界最大之島)。
Greenock /ˈgriːnək ; ˈgrinək/ 格陵諾克(蘇格蘭西南部一港埠)。
Greenwich /ˈgrɪnɪdʒ ; ˈgrɪnɪdʒ/ 格林尼治(倫敦東南一市鎮,爲英國國立天文臺所在地)。
Grenada /grɪˈneɪdə ; grəˈnedə/ 格瑞那達(原英屬西印度羣島中之一島,1974 年 2 月獨立,首都爲 St. George's)。
Grenadines /ˌgrenəˈdiːnz ; ˌgrɛnəˈdinz/ 格林那定羣島(原英屬西印度羣島中之一部,今分屬 Grenada 和 St. Vincent)。
Grenoble /grəˈnəʊbl ; grəˈnobl/ 格勒諾勃(法國東南部一城市)。
Grimsby /ˈgrɪmzbɪ ; ˈgrɪmzbɪ/ 格林斯比(英格蘭東部一海港)。
Grossglockner, Gross Glockner /grəʊs ˈglɔːknə ; ˈgrosˈglɑknɚ/ 大格洛克納峯(在奧地利西南部)。
Grozny /ˈgrɔːznɪ ; ˈgrɔznɪ/ 格洛斯尼(蘇聯歐洲部分之南部一城市,產石油)。
Guadalupe Mountains /ˌgwɑːðɑːˈluːpə- ; ˈgwɑdəˌlup-/ 瓜達鹿白山脈(在西班牙中部)。
Guadeloupe /ˌgwɑːdəˈluːp ; ˈgwɑdəˌlup/ 哥德洛普(法屬西印度羣島內 Basse-Terre 和 Grande-Terre 二島之合稱)。
Guam /gwɒm ; gwɑm/ 關島(屬美,在西太平洋,爲馬里亞納羣島中之最大島,位於該羣島之極南端)。
Guantánamo /gwɑːnˈtɑːnɑːməʊ ; gwɑnˈtɑnəˌmo/ 關達那摩灣(古巴東部一海灣,爲美國在古巴之海軍基地)。
Guatemala /ˌgwɑːtəˈmɑːlə ; ˌgwɑtəˈmɑlə/ 瓜地馬拉(中美洲西北部一國家,首都爲 ～ City)。
Guatemala (City) 瓜地馬拉市(Guatemala 之首都)。
Guayaquil /ˌgwɑːjɑːˈkiːl ; ˌgwaɪəˈkil/ 瓜亞基爾(厄瓜多爾西南部一港市)。
Guiana /gɪˈɑːnə ; gɪˈænə/ 圭亞那(南美洲北部一地區,分屬英、荷、法三國,其中之英屬圭亞那於 1966 年獨立,改名 Guyana, 荷屬圭亞那於 1975 年獨立,改名 Surinam)。
Guinea /ˈgɪnɪ ; ˈgɪnɪ/ 幾內亞(西非一國家,原爲 French Guinea, 1958 年 10 月獨立,首都 Conakry)。
Guinea-Bissau /ˌgɪnɪbɪˈsaʊ ; ˌgɪnibɪsˈaʊ/ 幾內亞比索(西非一國家,原爲 Portuguese Guinea, 1974 年 9 月獨立,首都 Bissau)。
Gunong Tahan /ˈguːnɒŋ ˈtɑːhɑːn ; ˌgunɔŋ ˈtɑhɑn/ 大漢峯(在馬來西亞彭亨州之北)。
Guyana /gaɪˈænə ; gaɪˈænə/ 蓋亞納(南美洲北部一國,原係 British Guiana, 於 1966 年 5 月獨立,首都爲 Georgetown)。
Gwent /gwent ; gwɛnt/ 貫特(威爾斯東南部一郡)。
Gwynedd /ˈgwɪnəð ; ˈgwɪnɛð/ 圭那特(威爾斯西北部一郡)。
Hague, The /heɪg ; heg/ 海牙(荷蘭西南部一城市,爲荷蘭王室及國際法庭所在地)。
Haifa /ˈhaɪfə ; ˈhaɪfə/ 海法(以色列西北部一港埠)。
Hailar /ˈhaɪˈlɑː(r) ; ˈhaɪˈlɑr/ 海拉爾(中國興安省省會,舊作 Hulun '呼倫')。
Hainan /ˈhaɪˈnɑːn ; ˈhaɪˈnɑn/ 海南島(在中國南海)。
Haiphong /ˈhaɪˈfɔːŋ ; ˈhaɪˈfɔŋ/ 海防(越南北部一港市)。
Haiti /ˈheɪtɪ ; ˈhetɪ/ 海地(西印度羣島中一黑人共和國,首都爲 Port-au-Prince)。
Hakodate /ˌhækəˈdɑːtɪ ; ˌhɑkəˈdɑtɪ/ 函舘(日本北海道一海港)。
Haleakala /ˌhɑːliːˌɑːkəˈlɑː ; ˌhɑlɪˌɑkəˈlɑ/ 哈里阿克拉山(死火山,在夏威夷茂伊島東部)。
Halifax /ˈhæləfæks ; ˈhæləˌfæks/ 哈利法克斯(加拿大東部一港口)。
Halmstad /ˈhɑːlmstɑːd ; ˈhɑlmˌstɑd/ 哈母市(在瑞典西南部)。
Hamburg /ˈhæmbɜːg ; ˈhæmˌbɝg/ 漢堡(德國西北部一港市)。
Hami /ˈhɑːˈmiː ; ˈhɑˈmi/ 哈密(中國新疆省東部一城市)。
Hamilton /ˈhæməltən ; ˈhæməltən/ 漢米敦(**1** 加拿大安大略省東南部一港市; **2** 英屬 Bermuda 之首府)。
Hammerfest /ˈhæməˌfest ; ˈhæmɚˌfɛst/ 亨墨菲斯(挪威北部一港市)。
Hammond /ˈhæmənd ; ˈhæmənd/ 哈蒙德(美國印第安納州西北部一城市)。
Hampshire /ˈhæmpʃə(r) ; ˈhæmpˌʃɪr/ 漢普郡(在英格蘭南部,略作 *Hants* /hænts ; hænts/)。
Hampstead /ˈhæmpstɪd ; ˈhæmpstəd/ 漢普斯特(倫敦西北部一區)。
Hangchow /ˈhæŋˈdʒəʊ ; ˈhɑŋˈdʒo/ 杭州(中國浙江省省會)。
Hankow /ˈhænˈkaʊ ; ˈhæŋˈkaʊ/ 漢口(中國中東部一城市,位於長江中游)。

Han(n)over /ˈhænəʊvə(r) ; ˈhæn,ovɚ/ 漢諾威(德國西北部一城市)。
Hanoi /hæˈnɔɪ ; hæˈnɔɪ/ 河內(Vietnam 之首都,原爲北越首府)。
Harbin /ˈhɑːˈbɪn ; hɑrˈbɪn/ 哈爾濱(在中國東北部一城市)。
Harney Peak /ˈhɑːnɪ- ; ˈhɑrnɪ-/ 哈尼峯(在美國南達科他州西南部)。
Hartford /ˈhɑːtfəd ; ˈhɑrtfɚd/ 哈特福特(美國康乃狄格州首府)。
Harvard, Mount /ˈhɑːvəd ; ˈhɑrvɚd/ 哈佛山(在美國科羅拉多州中部)。
Harz /hɑːts ; hɑrts/ 哈次山脈(在德國中部)。
Hastings /ˈheɪstɪŋz ; ˈhestɪŋz/ 哈斯丁斯(英格蘭南部一城市)。
Havana /həˈvænə ; həˈvænə/ 哈瓦那(Cuba 之首都)。
Hawaii /həˈwaɪiː ; həˈwaɪi/ 夏威夷 (美國之一州，除 Midway 島外,統轄整個夏威夷羣島,略作 *HI*)。
Hawaiian Islands /həˈwaɪɪən- ; həˈwaɪɪən-/ 夏威夷羣島(位於太平洋中部,爲構成美國夏威夷州之一羣島嶼)。
Hawke's Bay /ˌhɔːksˈbeɪ ; ˈhɔksˈbe/ 和克灣(紐西蘭北部一省區)。
Hebrides /ˈhebrɪdiːz ; ˈhɛbrə,diz/ 海布里地羣島(屬英,在大西洋中,蘇格蘭以西,分內外二羣島)。
Hecate Strait /ˈhekətɪ- ; ˈhɛkət-/ 赫卡提海峽(在加拿大西部英屬哥倫比亞與沙羅特羣島之間)。
Heidelberg /ˈhaɪdlbɜːg ; ˈhaɪdḷ,bɝg/ 海德堡(德國西部一城市)。
Heijo /ˈheɪdʒəʊ ; ˈhe,dʒo/ 平壤(現稱 Pyongyang)。
Heilungkiang /ˈheɪˈlʊŋdʒɪˈɑːŋ ; ˈheˈlʊŋdʒɪˈɑŋ/ 黑龍江(**1** 中國東北一河流,亦稱 Amur; **2** 中國東北之一省)。
Helicon /ˈhelɪkən; ˈhɛlə,kɑn/ 赫利孔山(在希臘中東部)。
Helsingör /ˌhelsɪŋˈɜː(r) ; ˌhɛlsɪŋˈɝ/ 赫新革(丹麥西蘭島北部一港埠)。
Helsinki /ˈhelsɪŋkɪ ; ˈhɛl,sɪŋkɪ/ 赫爾辛基(Finland 之首都)。
Helvetia /helˈviːʃɪə ; hɛlˈviʃ(ɪ)ə/ 赫爾維希亞(Switzerland 之古稱)。
Hendon /ˈhendən ; ˈhɛndən/ 亨頓 (英國倫敦之西北郊區)。
Heng (Shan) /ˈhʌŋ ˈʃɑːn ; ˈhɛŋ ˈʃɑn/ 衡山(在中國湖南省中部,爲五嶽中之南嶽)。
Hengyang /ˈhʌŋˈjɑːŋ ; ˈhʌŋˈjɑŋ/ 衡陽市 (中國湖南省東南一工商業中心)。
Hereford and Worcester /ˌherɪfəd n ˈwʊstə(r) ; ˌhɛrəfɚd ṇ ˈwʊstɚ/ 赫勒福與霧斯特(英格蘭西部一郡)。
Herefordshire /ˈherɪfədʃə(r) ; ˈhɛrəfɚd,ʃɪr/ 赫勒福夏(昔爲英格蘭西部一郡)。
Hermon, Mount /ˈhɜːmən ; ˈhɝmən/ 哈蒙峯(在敍利亞大馬士革之西南方)。
Hertfordshire /ˈhɑː(t)fədʃə(r) ; ˈhɑrfɚd,ʃɪr/ 哈德福郡(英格蘭東南部一郡,略作 *Herts* /hɑːts ; hɑrts/)。
Hesse /ˈhesɪ ; ˈhɛsɪ/ 赫斯(德國西南部一區)。
Highland /ˈhaɪlənd; ˈhaɪlənd/ 高地(蘇格蘭北部一地區)。
Himalaya(s), The /ˌhɪməˈleɪə(z) ; ˌhɪməˈleə(z)/ 喜馬拉雅山脈(在亞洲南部,位於中國之西藏與印度和尼泊爾之間)。
Hindu Kush /ˈhɪnˈduːˈkuːʃ ; ˌhɪndu ˈkʊʃ/ 興都庫什山脈(在阿富汗東北部及印度西北部)。
Hindustan, Hindostan /ˌhɪndʊˈstæn ; ˌhɪndʊˈstæn/ 印度斯坦 (**1** 印度德干高原以北之地區; **2** 指印度次大陸; **3** 指印度)。
Hiroshima /ˌhiːrəʊˈʃiːmə ; ˌhɪrəˈʃimə/ 廣島(日本本州西南海岸一港市)。
Hobart /ˈhəʊbɑːt ; ˈho,bɑrt/ 荷巴特 (澳洲塔斯曼尼亞之首府)。
Hoboken /ˈhəʊˌbəʊkən ; ˈho,bokən/ 后波肯(美國新澤西州東北部一城市)。
Ho Chi Minh City /ˈhəʊ tʃiː ˌmɪn- ; ˈho tʃi ˌmɪn-/ 胡志明市(越南南部一港市,昔爲南越首都 Saigon '西貢')。
Hofei /ˈhʌˈfeɪ ; ˈhəˈfe/ 合肥(中國安徽省之省會)。
Hokiang /ˈhʌdʒɪˈɑːŋ ; ˈhədʒɪˈɑŋ/ 合江(中國東北一省)。
Hokkaido /hɒˈkaɪdəʊ ; hɑˈkaɪdo/ 北海道(日本第二大島,位於日本北部,舊稱 Yezo /ˈjezəʊ ; ˈjɛzo/)。
Holland /ˈhɒlənd ; ˈhɑlənd/ 荷蘭(參看 Netherlands)。
Hollywood /ˈhɒlɪwʊd ; ˈhɑlɪ,wʊd/ 好萊塢 (在美國洛杉磯市)。
Holstein /ˈhəʊlstaɪn ; ˈhol,staɪn/ 好斯坦(德國西北部一地區)。
Holyoke /ˈhəʊljəʊk ; ˈhol,jok/ 荷由克(美國麻薩諸塞州西南部一城市)。
Holy See 教廷(位於梵蒂岡)。
Honan /ˈhəʊˈnæn ; ˈhoˈnæn/ 河南(中國中部一省)。
Honduras /hɒnˈdjʊərəs ; hɑnˈd(j)ʊrəs/ 宏都拉斯(中美洲北部一國家,首都爲 Tegucigalpa)。
Hong Kong, Hongkong /ˌhɒŋˈkɒŋ ; ˈhɑŋ,kɑŋ/ 香港(中國東南部珠江口外之海島)。
Honiara /ˌhəʊniːˈɑːrə ; ˌhoniˈɑrə/ 荷尼阿拉 (Solomon Islands 之首都)。
Honolulu /ˌhɒnəˈluːluː ; ˌhɑnəˈlulu/ 檀香山(美國夏威夷州之首府,在歐胡島之東南部)。
Honshu /ˈhɒnʃuː ; ˈhɑnʃu/ 本州(日本最大之島)。
Hood, Mount /hʊd ; hʊd/ 胡德峯(在美國俄勒岡州西北部)。
Hopei, Hopeh /ˈhəʊˈpeɪ ; ˈhoˈpe/ 河北(中國北部一省)。
Hornsey /ˈhɔːnzɪ ; ˈhɔrnzɪ/ 合恩賽(英格蘭東南部一城市)。
Hsinchu /ˈʃɪnˈtʃʊ ; ˈʃɪnˈtʃu/ 新竹(中國臺灣省西北部一縣,亦爲其縣治名)。
Hsingan /ˈʃɪŋˈɑːn ; ˈʃɪŋˈɑn/ 興安(中國東北一省)。
Hsingan Shan /ˈʃɪŋˈɑːnˈʃɑːn ; ˈʃɪŋˈɑnˈʃɑn/ 興安山(在熱河省境內)。
Huascarán /ˌwɑːskɑːˈrɑːn ; ˌwɑskəˈrɑn/ 瓦斯卡蘭峯(在秘魯西部)。
Huddersfield /ˈhʌdəzfiːld ; ˈhʌdɚz,fild/ 哈得玆菲爾(英格蘭北部一城市)。
Hudson /ˈhʌdsn; ˈhʌdsṇ/ 哈得孫河(在美國紐約州東部)。
Hue, Hué /hjuːˈeɪ ; hjuˈe/ 順化(越南中部一港市,昔爲國都)。
Huila /ˈwiːlɑː ; ˈwilɑ/ 韋拉火山(在南美哥倫比亞中部)。
Hull /hʌl ; hʌl/ 赫爾 (**1** 英格蘭北部一港埠; **2** 加拿大渥太華附近一城市)。
Hulutao /ˈhuːˈluːˈdaʊ ; ˈhuˈluˈdaʊ/ 葫蘆島(中國遼東灣西岸之不凍港)。
Humberside /ˈhʌmbəsaɪd ; ˈhʌmbɚ,saɪd/ 韓柏塞(英格蘭東部一郡)。
Hunan /ˈhuːˈnɑːn ; ˈhuˈnɑn/ 湖南(中國中南部一省)。
Hungary /ˈhʌŋgərɪ ; ˈhʌŋg(ə)rɪ/ 匈牙利(中歐一國家,首都爲 Budapest)。
Hungtze Hu /ˈhʊŋˈdzʌ ˈhuː ; ˈhʊŋˈdzə ˈhu/ 洪澤湖(在中國蘇、皖交界處)。
Huntingdon /ˈhʌntɪŋdən ; ˈhʌntɪŋdən/ 亨丁頓(美國賓夕法尼亞州一城市)。
Huntingdonshire /ˈhʌntɪŋdənʃə(r) ; ˈhʌntɪŋdən,ʃɪr/ 亨丁頓夏(昔爲英格蘭東部一郡,略作 *Hunts* /hʌnts ; hʌnts/, 自1974年爲 Cambridgeshire 之一部分)。
Hupei, Hupeh /ˈhuːˈpeɪ ; ˈhuˈpe/ 湖北(中國中部一省)。
Huron, Lake /ˈhjʊərn ; ˈhjʊrən/ 休倫湖(爲美國與加拿大間五大湖之一)。
Hwalien /ˈhwɑːˈljən ; ˈhwɑˈljən/ 花蓮(中國臺灣省東部一縣,亦爲此縣內一港口)。
Hwang Hai /ˈhwɑːŋ ˈhaɪ ; ˈhwɑŋ ˈhaɪ/ 黃海(中國東岸一緣海,亦稱 Yellow Sea)。
Hwang Ho /ˈhwɑːŋ ˈhəʊ ; ˈhwɑŋ ˈho/ 黃河(中國境內第二大河,亦稱 Yellow River)。
Hwa Shan, Hua Shan /ˈhwɑː ˈʃɑːn ; ˈhwɑ ˈʃɑn/ 華山(在中國陝西省東部,爲五嶽中的西嶽)。
Hyderabad /ˈhaɪdrə,bæd ; ˈhaɪdərə,bæd/ 海得拉巴 (**1** 印度中南部一城市; **2** 巴基斯坦南部一城市)。
Iberia /aɪˈbɪərɪə ; aɪˈbɪrɪə/ 伊伯利亞半島(在歐洲西南部,爲西、葡兩國所在地)。
Iceland /ˈaɪslənd ; ˈaɪslənd/ 冰島(大西洋東北一島,1918年獨立,首都 Reykjavik)。
Ida /ˈaɪdə ; ˈaɪdə/ 愛達山 (**1** 在地中海克里特島; **2** 在亞洲土耳其之西北)。
Idaho /ˈaɪdəhəʊ ; ˈaɪdə,ho/ 愛達荷 (美國西北部之一州,略作 *ID*)。
Igarka /ɪˈgɑːkə ; ɪˈgarkə/ 易加卡(蘇聯亞洲部分之西北部一城鎮)。
Ilan /ˈiːˈlɑːn ; ˈiˈlɑn/ 宜蘭(中國臺灣省東北部一縣,亦爲其

縣治名)。
Illampu /ɪ'jɑːmpuː ; ɪ'jɑmpu/ 伊央普山(在玻利維亞西部)。
Illinois /ˌɪlə'nɔɪ ; ˌɪlə'nɔɪ/ 伊利諾(美國中部之一州,略作 *IL*)。
Incahuasi /ˌiːŋkɑː'wɑːsɪ ; ˌiŋkə'wɑsɪ/ 英加瓦錫山(在阿根廷西北部)。
Inchon /'ɪnˌtʃɒn ; 'ɪnˌtʃɑn/ 仁川(韓國漢城以西一港市)。
India /'ɪndɪə ; 'ɪndɪə/ 印度(亞洲南部一國家,首都爲 New Delhi)。
Indiana /ˌɪndɪ'ænə ; ˌɪndɪ'ænə/ 印第安納(美國中東部之一州,略作 *IN*)。
Indianapolis /ˌɪndɪə'næpəlɪs ; ˌɪndɪə'næp(ə)lɪs/ 印第安納波里(美國印第安納州之首府)。
Indian Ocean /'ɪndjən 'əʊʃən ; 'ɪndɪən 'oʃən/ 印度洋(位於非洲以東,亞洲以南,澳洲以西,南極洲以北)。
Indochina /'ɪndəʊ'tʃaɪnə ; 'ɪndo'tʃaɪnə/ **1** 中南半島(位於亞洲東南部,包括緬甸,泰國,馬來亞,柬埔寨,寮國,及越南)。**2** 前法屬印度支那(含越南、柬埔寨及寮國)。
Indonesia /ˌɪndə'niːzɪə ; ˌɪndə'niʒə/ **1** 馬來羣島。**2** 印度尼西亞(簡稱印尼,亞洲東南部一島國,首都 Jakarta)。
Indore /ɪn'dɔː(r) ; ɪn'dor/ 茵多爾(印度中部一城市)。
Indus /'ɪndəs ; 'ɪndəs/ 印度河(在印度西北部)。
Inner Mongolia 內蒙古(中國北部一地區)。
Innsbruck /'ɪnzbrʊk ; 'ɪnzˌbrʊk/ 因斯布魯克(奧地利西部一城市)。
Inverness-shire /ˌɪnvə'neʃə(r) ; ˌɪnvə'nɛˌʃɪr/ 印威內斯夏(昔爲蘇格蘭西北部一郡)。
Iona /aɪ'əʊnə ; aɪ'onə/ 愛奧那島(在蘇格蘭西部莫耳島之西南)。
Ionia /aɪ'əʊnjə ; aɪ'onɪə/ 愛奧尼亞(小亞細亞愛琴海沿岸古地名)。
Iowa /'aɪəwə ; 'aɪəwə/ 愛俄華(美國中部之一州,略作 *IA*)。
Iowa City 愛俄華城(在美國愛俄華州東部)。
Ipoh /'iːpəʊ ; 'ipo/ 怡保(馬來西亞西北部一城市)。
Ipswich /'ɪpswɪtʃ ; 'ɪpswɪtʃ/ 易普威治(英格蘭東南部一城市)。
Iran /ɪ'rɑːn ; ɪ'ræn/ 伊朗(昔稱 Persia, 亞洲西南部一國家,首都爲 Teheran)。
Iraq, Irak /ɪ'rɑːk ; ɪ'rɑk/ 伊拉克(亞洲西南部一國家,首都爲 Baghdad)。
Ireland /'aɪələnd ; 'aɪrlənd/ **1** 愛爾蘭島(不列顛羣島中之一島,分爲北愛爾蘭 Northern Ireland 及愛爾蘭共和國 Republic of Ireland)。**2** 愛爾蘭共和國(參看 Eire)。
Irish Republic = Eire
Irkutsk /ɜː'kuːtsk ; ɪr'kutsk/ 伊爾庫次克(蘇聯亞洲部分南境貝加爾湖附近一城市)。
Irrawaddy /ˌɪrə'wɒdɪ ; ˌɪrə'wɑdɪ/ 伊洛瓦底江(在緬甸中部)。
Irtysh, Irtish /ɪə'tɪʃ ; ɪr'tɪʃ/ 額爾濟斯河(在蘇聯哈薩克東北部)。
Ischia /'ɪskɪə ; 'ɪskɪə/ 伊斯其亞島(在義大利那不勒斯之西南)。
Islamabad /ɪs'lɑːməbɑːd ; ɪs'lɑməˌbɑd/ 伊斯蘭馬巴德(Pakistan 之首都)。
Isle of Wight /ˌaɪl əv 'waɪt ; ˌaɪl əv 'waɪt/ 威特島(英吉利海峽中之一島,爲英格蘭一郡,略作 *I of W*)。
Israel /'ɪzreɪl ; 'ɪzrɪəl/ 以色列(原爲中東巴勒斯坦之一部,現爲一猶太國家,首都爲 Jerusalem)。
Istanbul /ˌɪstæn'buːl ; ˌɪstəm'bul/ 伊斯坦堡(土耳其歐洲部分之東部一城市,昔稱 Constantinople)。
Italy /'ɪtəlɪ ; 'ɪtl̩ɪ/ 義大利(歐洲地中海岸一國家,首都爲 Rome)。
Ivanovo /ɪ'vɑːnəvə ; ɪ'vanəvə/ 伊凡諾弗(蘇聯歐洲部分之中部,窩瓦河之南一城市)。
Ivory Coast 象牙海岸(非洲西部一共和國,原爲法國屬地,1960 年 8 月獨立,首都 Abidjan)。
Izmir /ɪz'mɪə(r) ; ɪz'mɪr/ 伊士麥(土耳其西部一港埠)。
Iztaccihuatl /ˌiːstɑː'k'siːwɑːtl ; ˌistɑk'siˌwɑtl̩/ 伊斯塔西瓦脫山(在墨西哥之墨西哥城東南)。
Jackson /'dʒæksn ; 'dʒæksn̩/ 傑克遜 (**1** 美國密西西比州之首府; **2** 美國密西根州南部一都市)。
Jadotville /ˌʒɑːˌdəʊ'viːl ; ˌʒædo'vil/ 查多市(非洲薩依共和國東南部一城市,現稱 Likasi /lɪ'kɑːsɪ ; lɪ'kɑsɪ/)。
Jaffa /'dʒæfə ; 'dʒæfə/ 雅法(以色列特拉維夫市一區,昔爲海港)。
Jaipur /dʒaɪ'pʊə(r) ; 'dʒaɪˌpʊr/ 齋浦爾(印度西北部一城市)。
Jakarta, Djakarta /dʒə'kɑːtə ; dʒə'kɑrtə/ 雅加達(Indonesia 之首都)。
Jamaica /dʒə'meɪkə ; dʒə'mekə/ 牙買加(原爲西印度羣島中英國一殖民地,於 1962 年 8月獨立,首都爲 Kingston)。
James /dʒeɪmz ; dʒemz/ 詹姆斯河(在美國中北部,注於密蘇里河,亦稱 Dakota)。
Jamshedpur /'dʒɑːmʃedˌpʊə ; 'dʒɑmˌʃɛdˌpʊr/ 哲雪鋪(印度東北部一城市)。
Japan /dʒə'pæn ; dʒə'pæn/ 日本(亞洲東部一國家,首都爲 Tokyo)。
Japan, Sea of 日本海(在蘇聯、韓國與日本之間)。
Japurá /ˌʒɑːpuː'rɑː ; ˌʒɑpə'rɑ/ 甲浦拉河(南美洲西北部一河流)。
Jarvis (或 Jervis) Island /'dʒɑːvɪs ; 'dʒɑrvəs/ 查維斯島(在中太平洋,屬美國)。
Jassy /'dʒæsɪ ; 'jɑsɪ/ 雅西 (亦稱 Iaşi /'jɑːʃɪ ; 'jɑʃɪ/, 爲羅馬尼亞東北部一城市)。
Java /'dʒɑːvə ; 'dʒɑvə/ 爪哇(南洋羣島之一,屬印尼)。
Jefferson City /'dʒefəsn- ; 'dʒɛfɚsn̩-/ 傑佛遜城(美國密蘇里州之首府)。
Jehol /dʒə'həʊl ; dʒə'hol/ 熱河(中國北部一省)。
Jena /'jeɪnə ; 'jenə/ 耶拿(德國東部一城市)。
Jerusalem /dʒə'ruːsləm ; dʒə'rus(ə)ləm/ 耶路撒冷(Israel 之首都)。
Jervis Bay /'dʒɑːvɪs- ; 'dʒɑrvəs-/ 查維斯灣(在澳洲東南部)。
Jesselton /'dʒesltən ; 'dʒɛsl̩tən/ 亞庇(位於北婆羅洲,爲馬來西亞沙巴之首府,現稱 Kota Kinabalu /'kəʊtəˌkɪnəbə'luː ; 'kotəˌkɪnəbə'lu/)。
Jibuti 參看 Djibouti(2)。
Jinsen /'dʒɪnsen ; 'dʒɪnˌsɛn/ 仁川(今稱 Inchon)。
Johannesburg /dʒəʊ'hænɪsbɜːg ; dʒo'hænɪsˌbɝg/ 約翰尼斯堡(南非共和國東北部一城市)。
Johore /dʒəʊ'hɔː(r) ; dʒə'hor/ 柔佛(馬來西亞之一邦,位於馬來半島之南端)。
Jönköping /'jɜːnˌtʃɜːpɪŋ ; 'jɝnˌtʃɝpɪŋ/ 顏哥平(瑞典南部一城市)。
Jordan /'dʒɔːdn ; 'dʒɔrdn̩/ 約旦 (**1** 亞洲西南部一王國,首都爲 Amman; **2** 巴勒斯坦境內一河流)。
Julian Alps /'dʒuːljən- ; 'dʒuljən-/ 侏利安阿爾卑斯山(在南斯拉夫西北部)。
Jungfrau /'jʊŋˌfraʊ ; 'jʊŋˌfraʊ/ 少女峯(在瑞士中部)。
Juruá /ʒuː'rwɑː ; ʒʊ'rwɑ/ 佐魯亞河(在南美洲中部,注入亞馬遜河上游)。
Kabul /'kɔːbl ; 'kabʊl/ 喀布爾(Afghanistan 之首都)。
Kaifeng /'kaɪ'fəŋ ; 'kaɪ'fəŋ/ 開封(中國河南省省會)。
Kalahari Desert /ˌkɑːlɑː'hɑːrɪ- ; ˌkælə'harɪ-/ 喀拉哈利沙漠(介於南非和波札那之間)。
Kalgan /'kɑːl'gɑːn ; 'kæl'gæn/ 參看 Changkiakow。
Kalgoorlie /kɑːl'gʊəlɪ ; kæl'gʊrlɪ/ 卡谷力(澳洲西部一城市)。
Kaliningrad /kə'liːnɪngræd ; kə'linənˌgræd/ 加里寧格勒(蘇聯歐洲部分之西部一港埠)。
Kama /'kɑːmə ; 'kɑmə/ 卡馬河(在蘇聯歐洲部分之東部)。
Kamchatka Peninsula /kæm'tʃætkə-;kæm'tʃætkə-/ 堪察加半島(在蘇聯亞洲部分之東北部,介於鄂霍次克海與白令海之間)。
Kamet /'kʌmeɪt ; 'kʌmet/ 喀美特峯(爲喜馬拉雅山之一峯,位於印度與西藏之邊境)。
Kampala /kɑːm'pɑːlə ; kɑm'pɑlə/ 坎帕拉(Uganda 之首都)。
Kampuchea /kæmpʊ'tʃɪə ; ˌkæmpə'tʃɪə/ 參看 Cambodia。
Kanchenjunga /ˌkʌntʃən'dʒʌŋgə ; ˌkæntʃən'dʒʌŋgə/ 肯欽眞加山(在尼泊爾與錫金之間,爲世界第三高峯)。
Kangting /'kɑːŋ'dɪŋ ; 'kɑŋ'dɪŋ/ 康定(中國西康省省會)。
Kansas /'kænzəs ; 'kænzəs/ 堪薩斯(美國中部之一州,略作 *KS*)。
Kansu /'kæn'suː ; 'kæn'su/ 甘肅(中國西北部一省,省會 Lanchow)。

Kaohsiung /ˈgaʊˈʃjʊŋ ; ˈgaʊʃɪˈʊŋ/ **1** 高雄市(中國臺灣省南部一港市)。**2** 高雄縣(中國臺灣省南部一縣)。
Karachi /kəˈrɑːtʃɪ ; kəˈrɑtʃɪ/ 喀拉蚩(巴基斯坦南部一港埠,爲其舊都)。
Karaganda /ˌkɑːrɑːgɑːnˈdɑː ; ˌkɑrəgənˈdɑ/ 加拉干達(蘇聯哈薩克中部一城市)。
Karakoram Range /ˌkærəˈkɔːrəm- ; ˌkærəˈkorəm-/ 喀拉崑崙山脈(在中國新疆與喀什米爾邊境)。
Karelia, Carelia /kəˈriːlɪə ; kəˈrilɪə/ 卡累里亞(在蘇聯歐洲部分之西北部,爲其自治共和國之一)。
Kariba /kəˈriːbə ; kəˈribə/ 加里巴湖(在羅得西亞北部與尙比亞東南之間)。
Kashmir /kæʃˈmɪə(r) ; ˈkæʃˌmɪr/ 喀什米爾(印度西北部一地區)。
Katahdin, Mount /kəˈtɑːdɪn ; kəˈtɑdn/ 克大定山(在美國緬因州中北部)。
Katanga /kəˈtɑːŋgə ; kəˈtɑŋgə/ 喀坦加(非洲薩伊共和國東南部一地區,現稱 Shaba /ˈʃɑːbə ; ˈʃɑbə/)。
Katar = Qatar
Kat(h)mandu, Khatmandu /ˈkɑːtmɑːnˈduː ; ˌkæt-ˌmænˈdu/ 加德滿都(Nepal 之首都)。
Katowice /ˌkɑːtɔːˈviːtse ; ˌkɑtəˈvitsə/ 卡托維治(波蘭南部一城市)。
Kawaikini /kɑːwaɪˈkiːnɪ ; ˌkɑwaɪˈkinɪ/ 加外基尼山(在夏威夷之考艾島上)。
Kazak(h)stan /ˌkɑːzɑːkˈstɑːn ; kəˌzækˈstæn/ 哈薩克(在蘇聯亞洲部分之中部,爲其加盟共和國之一)。
Kazbek, Kasbek /kʌzˈbjek ; kɑzˈbɛk/ 刻玆柏克峯(在蘇聯高加索山脈之中部)。
Kebnekaise /ˌkebnəˈkaɪsə ; ˌkɛbnəˈkaɪsə/ 刻奈啓塞峯(在瑞典北部)。
Keelung /ˈkiːˈlʊŋ ; ˈkiˈlʊŋ/ 基隆(中國臺灣省北部一港市)。
Keewatin /kiːˈweɪtn ; kiˈwetn̩/ 基威丁(加拿大西北邊區東部一區)。
Keighley /ˈkiːθlɪ ; ˈkiθlɪ/ 奇利(英格蘭北部一城市)。
Kelantan /kəˈlæntən ; kəˈlænˌtæn/ 吉蘭丹(馬來西亞北部一邦)。
Kent /kent ; kɛnt/ 肯特(英格蘭東南部一郡)。
Kentucky /kenˈtʌkɪ ; kənˈtʌkɪ/ 肯塔基(美國中東部一州,略作 *KY*)。
Kenya /ˈkenjə ; ˈkɛnjə/ 肯亞 (**1** 東非一共和國,原爲英國殖民地,1963 年12月獨立,首都爲 Nairobi; **2** 肯亞中部一死火山)。
Kerch /keətʃ ; kɛrtʃ/ 克赤 (蘇聯克里米亞半島東端一港市)。
Kerguelen /ˈkɜːgɪlɪn ; ˈkɝgələn/ 克革倫羣島(在印度洋南部,屬法國)。
Kerintji /kəˈrɪntʃɪ ; kəˈrɪntʃɪ/ 克令奇峯(在印尼蘇門答臘中西部)。
Kerry /ˈkerɪ ; ˈkɛrɪ/ 克立(愛爾蘭西南部一郡)。
Kew /kjuː ; kju/ 克佑 (**1** 澳洲東南部一城市; **2** 倫敦西郊一村鎭)。
Key West /ˈkiː ˈwest ; ˈki ˈwɛst/ 基維斯 (**1** 美國佛羅里達州西南墨西哥灣中一小島; **2** 該島上一城市)。
Khabarovsk /kəˈbɑːrəfsk ; kəˈbɑrəfsk/ 伯力(蘇聯亞洲部分之東部一城市)。
Kharkov /ˈkɑːkɔːf ; ˈkɑrˌkɔf/ 卡爾可夫(蘇聯烏克蘭東北部一城市)。
Khart(o)um /kɑːˈtuːm ; kɑrˈtum/ 卡土穆(Sudan 之首都)。
Khiva /ˈkiːvə ; ˈkivə/ 基發(蘇聯烏玆別克中部一城市)。
Khyber Pass /ˈkaɪbə- ; ˈkaɪbɚ-/ 開伯爾山口(在阿富汗與巴基斯坦之間)。
Kiamusze /dʒiːˈɑːˈmuːˈsuː ; dʒiˈɑˈmuˈsu/ 佳木斯(中國合江省省會)。
Kiangsi /dʒiːˈɑːŋˈsiː ; dʒiˈɑŋˈsi/ 江西(中國東南部一省)。
Kiangsu /dʒiːˈɑːŋˈsuː ; dʒiˈɑŋˈsu/ 江蘇(中國東部一省)。
Kiaochow Bay /dʒɪˈaʊˈdʒəʊ- ; dʒɪˈaʊˈdʒo-/ 膠州灣(中國山東省一海灣)。
Kiel /kiːl ; kil/ 基爾 (**1** 德國北部一海港; **2** 德國北部一運河)。
Kielce /ˈkjeltse ; kɪˈɛltse/ 開耳策(波蘭華沙之南一城市)。
Kiev, Kiyev /ˈkiːev ; ˈkiˌ(j)ɛf/ 基輔(蘇聯烏克蘭共和國之首府)。
Kigali /kɪˈgɑːlɪ ; kɪˈgɑlɪ/ 吉佳利(Rwanda 之首都)。
Kildare /kɪlˈdeə(r) ; kɪlˈdɛr/ 啓耳達(愛爾蘭東部一郡)。
Kilimanjaro /ˌkɪlɪmənˈdʒɑːrəʊ ; ˌkɪləmənˈdʒɑro/ 吉力曼札羅山(在非洲坦尙尼亞之東北部)。
Kilkenny /kɪlˈkenɪ ; kɪlˈkɛnɪ/ 啓耳肯尼(愛爾蘭東南部一郡,又其首府名)。
Kimberley /ˈkɪmbəlɪ ; ˈkɪmbɚlɪ/ 慶伯利(南非共和國一城市,爲世界最大鑽石市場)。
Kinabalu, Kinabulu /ˌkɪnəbəˈluː ; ˌkɪnəbəˈlu/ 金乃巴羅山(在婆羅洲北部之沙巴境內)。
Kincardineshire /kɪnˈkɑːdɪnʃə(r) ; kɪnˈkɑrdɪnˌʃɪr/ 琴喀丁夏(昔爲蘇格蘭東部一郡)。
Kings Peak /kɪŋz- ; kɪŋz-/ 京斯峯(在美國猶他州東北部)。
Kingston /ˈkɪŋstən ; ˈkɪŋstən/ 京斯敦(Jamaica 之首都)。
Kingstown /ˈkɪŋstən ; ˈkɪŋˌstaʊn/ 京斯頓(St. Vincent and the Grenadines 之首都)。
Kinmen, Chinmen /ˈdʒɪnˈmən ; ˈdʒɪnˈmən/ 金門(中國臺灣海峽中一島,在厦門以東,亦稱 Quemoy)。
Kinross-shire /kɪnˈrɒʃʃə(r) ; kɪnˈrɔˌʃɪr/ 琴洛斯夏(昔爲蘇格蘭中東部一郡)。
Kinshasa /kɪnˈʃɑːsə ; kɪnˈʃɑsə/ 金夏沙(Zaire 之首都,前稱 Léopoldville)。
Kintyre /kɪnˈtaɪə(r) ; kɪnˈtaɪr/ 琴泰半島(在蘇格蘭西南海岸)。
Kirg(h)iz Republic /ˈkɜːgɪz- ; kɪrˈgiz-/ 吉爾吉斯(在蘇聯亞洲部分之中部,爲其加盟共和國之一)。
Kiribati /ˈkɪərəˌbɑːs;ˈkɪrəˌbæs/ 吉里巴斯(昔稱 Gilbert, 西太平洋一群島, 原屬英, 於 1979 年 7 月獨立, 首都爲 Tarawa)。
Kirin /ˈkiːˈrɪn ; ˈkiˈrɪn/ 吉林(中國東北部一省,又該省之省會)。
Kirkcudbrightshire /kɜːˈkuːbrɪʃə(r) ; kɝˈkubrɪˌʃɪr/ 刻古布立夏(昔爲蘇格蘭南部一郡)。
Kirkpatrick, Mount /kəkˈpætrɪk ; ˌkɝkˈpætrɪk/ 寇克帕特雷克峯(在南極洲)。
Kirkuk /kɪəˈkuːk ; kɪrˈkuk/ 吉爾庫克(伊拉克東北部一城市)。
Kitchener /ˈkɪtʃɪnə(r) ; ˈkɪtʃ(ə)nɚ/ 啓赤奈(加拿大安大略省東南部一城市)。
Kiukiang /dʒɪˈuːdʒɪˈɑːŋ ; dʒɪˈudʒɪˈɑŋ/ 九江(中國江西省內,長江沿岸一重要河港)。
Kjölen Mts. /ˈtʃɜːlən ; ˈtʃɝlən/ 基阿連山脈(在歐洲挪威和瑞典交界處)。
Klondike /ˈklɒndaɪk ; ˈklɑnˌdaɪk/ 克命代克 (**1** 加拿大一地區; **2** 加拿大一河流)。
Klyuchevskaya /kljuːˈtʃefskəjə ; klɪuˈtʃɛfskəjə/ 克羅契夫山(在蘇聯堪察加半島之東部)。
Kobe /ˈkəʊbɪ ; ˈkobɪ/ 神戶(日本本州南海岸一海港)。
Kokand /kəʊˈkænd ; koˈkænd/ 浩罕(蘇聯烏玆別克東部一城市)。
Kola /ˈkəʊlə ; ˈkolə/ 可拉半島(蘇聯歐洲部西北一半島)。
Kolyma, Kolima /kəʊˈliːmə ; kəˈlimə/ 科力馬河(在蘇聯雅庫次克之東北部,注於北極海)。
Komsomolsk /ˈkɒmsəˈmɔːlsk ; ˌkɑmsəˈmolsk/ 青年城(蘇聯亞洲部分,黑龍江左岸一城市)。
Konakry = Conakry
Korea /kəˈrɪə ; kəˈrɪə/ 韓國(1948 年分爲南韓與北韓,參看 North ~ 和 South ~)。
Koror /ˈkɔːˌrɔː ; ˈkɔˌrɔ/ 高羅(Palau 之首都)。
Kosciusko, Mount /ˌkɒsɪˈʌskəʊ ; ˌkɑzɪˈʌsko/ 科修斯古峯(在澳洲新南威爾士州東南)。
Kowait = Kuwait
Kowloon /ˈkaʊˈluːn ; ˈkaʊˈlun/ 九龍(香港對面一半島)。
Krasnovodsk /ˈkræsnəvɒtsk ; ˌkræsnəˈvɔtsk/ 克拉斯諾夫斯克(蘇聯土庫曼西北部一港市)。
Krasnoyarsk /ˈkræsnəjɑːsk ; ˌkræsnəˈjɑrsk/ 克拉斯諾雅斯克(蘇聯亞洲部西南一城市)。
Kristiansand /ˈkrɪstʃənˌsænd ; ˈkrɪstʃənˌsænd/ 克欣桑(挪威西南部一港埠)。
Krivoi (或 Krivoy) Rog /ˈkrɪvɔɪ ˈrəʊg ; ˌkrɪvɔɪ ˈrog/ 克利福洛(蘇聯烏克蘭中部一城市)。
Krons(h)tadt /ˈkrɒnstæt ; ˈkronˌstæt/ 克倫斯塔(蘇聯列寧格勒以西一海島要塞)。

Kuala Lumpur /'kwɑːlə'lʊmpʊə(r); ˌkwɑlə'lʊmpʊr/ 吉隆坡(Malaysia 之首都)。
Kuching /'kuːtʃɪŋ; 'kutʃɪŋ/ 古晉(馬來西亞沙撈越之首府)。
Kuibyshev, Kuybyshev /'kwiːbɪʃef; 'kwibəˌʃef/ 古比雪夫(蘇聯莫斯科東南一城市)。
Kunlun, Kuenlun /'kʊnlʊn; 'kun'lun/ 崑崙山脈(在中國西藏高原與新疆之間)。
Kunming /'kʊn'mɪŋ; 'kʊn'mɪŋ/ 昆明(中國雲南省省會)。
Kuril(e) /'kuːrɪl; 'kjʊrˌil/ 千島羣島(在日本之東北,二次大戰後爲蘇聯所佔領)。
Kursk /kʊəsk; kʊrsk/ 庫斯克(蘇聯歐洲部中南一城市)。
Kuwait, Kuweit, Kowait /kʊ'weɪt; kə'wet/ 科威特(亞洲西南部一國家,位於波斯灣西北隅,首都爲 Al Kuwait)。
Kuznetsk /kʊz'netsk; kʊz'nɛtsk/ 庫斯內次(蘇聯歐洲部分中南部一城市)。
Kwangsi /'gwɑːŋ'siː; 'gwɑŋ'si/ 廣西(中國南部一省)。
Kwangtung /'gwɑːŋ'dʊŋ; 'gwɑŋ'dʊŋ/ 廣東(中國南部一省)。
Kweichow /'gweɪ'dʒəʊ; 'gwe'dʒo/ 貴州(中國南部一省)。
Kweilin /'gweɪ'lɪn; 'gwe'lɪn/ 桂林(中國廣西省省會)。
Kweisui /'gweɪ'sweɪ'; 'gwe'swe/ 歸綏(中國綏遠省省會)。
Kweiyang /'gweɪ'jɑːŋ; 'gwe'jɑŋ/ 貴陽(中國貴州省省會)。
Kyoto /'kjəʊtəʊ; ki'oto/ 京都(日本本州中西部一城市)。
Kyushu /'kjuːʃuː; ki'uʃu/ 九州(日本南部一島)。
Labrador /'læbrədɔː(r); 'læbrəˌdɔr/ 拉布拉多(加拿大一地區,位於東北部之 Labrador 半島上,略作 *Lab*)。
Labuan /lə'buːən; lə'buən/ 納閩島(在婆羅洲北部沙巴之西海岸外)。
Laccadive Islands /'lækədaɪv-; 'lækəˌdɪv-/ 拉克代夫羣島(在阿拉伯海,屬印度)。
Lachlan /'læklən; 'lɑklən/ 拉克蘭河(在澳洲東南部)。
Ladoga /'lɑːdəʊgə; 'lædəgə/ 拉多加湖(在蘇聯西北部,爲歐洲最大湖)。
Lagos /'leɪgɒs; 'leˌgɑs/ 拉哥斯(Nigeria 之首都)。
La Guaira /lə'gwaɪrə; lə'gwaɪrə/ 拉奎拉(委內瑞拉首都卡拉卡斯之外港)。
Lahore /lə'hɔː(r); lə'hor/ 拉合爾(巴基斯坦東北部一城市)。
Lanarkshire /'lænəkʃə(r); 'lænəkˌʃɪr/ 蘭那克夏(昔爲蘇格蘭南部一郡)。
Lancashire /'læŋkəʃə(r); 'læŋkəˌʃɪr/ 蘭開郡(英格蘭西北部一郡,略作 *Lancs* /læŋks; læŋks/)。
Lanchow /'lɑːn'dʒəʊ; 'lɑn'dʒo/ 蘭州(中國甘肅省省會)。
Langson, Lang Son /'læŋ'sɒn; 'læŋ'sɑn/ 諒山(越南北部一市鎮,毗連中國廣西省)。
Laos /'lɑːɒs; laʊs/ 寮國(中南半島一國,首都爲 Vientiane)。
La Paz /lɑː'pæz; lə'pæz/ 拉巴斯(Bolivia 之首都)。
Lapland /'læplænd; 'læpˌlænd/ 拉布蘭(北歐一地區,包括挪威、瑞典、芬蘭之北部及蘇聯之可拉半島)。
La Plata /lə'plɑːtə; lə'plɑtə/ 拉布拉他(阿根廷東部一海港)。
La Selle /lə'sel; lə'sɛl/ 拉賽爾山脈(在海地東南部)。
Lashio /lə'ʃəʊ; lə'ʃo/ 臘戌(緬甸中東部一市鎮)。
Las Palmas /læs'pælməs; lɑ'spɑlməs/ 拉斯帕馬 (**1** 西班牙一省; **2** 西班牙大加那利島上一海港)。
Lassen Peak, Mount Lassen /'læsn-; 'læsn̩-/ 拉孫峯(在美國加州東北)。
Las Vegas /lɑːs 'veɪgəs; lɑs 'vegəs/ 拉斯維加斯(美國內華達州東南部一城市,爲一著名賭城)。
Latakia /ˌlætə'kiː(ː)ə; ˌlætə'kiə/ 拉塔基亞(敍利亞西北部一海港,古名 Laodicea /ˌleɪədɪ'sɪə; leˌɑdə'siə/)。
Latium /'leɪʃəm; 'leʃ(ɪ)əm/ 拉丁姆(義大利中部一地區)。
Latvia /'lætvɪə; 'lætvɪə/ 拉脫維亞(原爲波羅的海沿岸一獨立國,1940 年起爲蘇聯一加盟共和國,稱作 Latvian Republic, 首府爲 Riga)。
Lausanne /ləʊ'zæn; lo'zɑn/ 洛桑(瑞士西部一城市)。
Lawrence /'lɒrəns; 'lɔrəns/ 羅倫斯(美國麻薩諸塞州東北部一城市)。
Lebanon /'lebənən; 'lɛbənən/ 黎巴嫩(地中海東岸一國家,首都爲 Beirut)。
Leeds /liːdz; lidz/ 里玆(英格蘭北部一城市)。
Leghorn /'leg'hɔːn; 'lɛgˌ(h)ɔrn/ 來亨(義大利中部一港埠)。
(Le) Havre /lə'hɑːvə(r); lə'hɑvə/ 哈佛爾(法國北部一港埠)。
Leicester /'lestə(r); 'lɛstə/ 列斯特(英格蘭列斯特郡之首府)。
Leicestershire /'lestəʃə(r); 'lɛstəˌʃɪr/ 列斯特郡(在英格蘭中部,略作 *Leics*)。
Leinster /'lenstə(r); 'lɛnstə/ 倫斯特(愛爾蘭東南部一省)。
Leipzig /'laɪpzɪg; 'laɪpsɪg/ 來比錫(德國東部一城市,亦稱 Leipsic /'laɪpsɪk; 'laɪpsɪk/)。
Leitrim /'liːtrɪm; 'litrəm/ 利特令(愛爾蘭西北部一郡)。
Leix, Laoighis /liːʃ; leɪʃ/ 雷斯(愛爾蘭中部一郡)。
Lena /'liːnə; 'linə/ 勒拿河(在蘇聯亞洲部分西伯利亞之中東部)。
Leningrad /'lenɪngræd; 'lɛnənˌgræd/ 列寧格勒(蘇聯西北部一城市)。
Léopoldville /'lɪəpəʊldvɪl; 'liəˌpoldˌvɪl/ 雷堡市(現稱 Kinshasa)。
Lepontine Alps /lɪ'pɒntaɪn-; lɪ'pɑnˌtaɪn-/ 利旁廷阿爾卑斯山(在瑞士與義大利邊境)。
Lesbos /'lezbɒs; 'lɛzˌbɑs/ 來玆波斯島(亦稱 Mytilene, 在愛琴海中,位於土耳其西北,屬希臘)。
Lesotho /lə'suːtuː; lə'soto/ 賴索托(非洲一王國,在南非共和國境內,原名 Basutoland, 爲英國殖民地,1966 年10 月獨立,首都爲 Maseru)。
Lesser Antilles /-æn'tɪliːz; -æn'tɪliz/ 小安地列斯羣島(南美洲東北海岸外,西印度羣島中三大羣島之一)。
Levant /lɪ'vænt; lə'vænt/ 地中海東部及愛琴海沿岸之國家和島嶼。
Leven, Loch /'lɒk 'liːvn; 'lɑk'livn̩/ 利文湖(在蘇格蘭東部)。
Lexington /'leksɪŋtən; 'lɛksɪŋtən/ 勒星頓 (**1** 美國肯塔基州中北部一城市; **2** 美國麻薩諸塞州東北部一城市)。
Leyton /'leɪtn; 'letn/ 雷敦(昔爲英格蘭東南部一城市)。
Lhasa, Lassa /'lɑːsə; 'lɑsə/ 拉薩(中國西藏首府)。
Liaoning /liː'aʊ'nɪŋ; lɪ'aʊ'nɪŋ/ 遼寧(中國東北一省)。
Liaopei /liː'aʊ'peɪ; li'aʊ'pe/ 遼北(中國東北一省)。
Liaoyüan /liː'aʊ'jʊɑːn; li'aʊ'jʊɑn/ 遼源(中國遼北省省會)。
Liberia /laɪ'bɪərɪə; laɪ'bɪrɪə/ 賴比瑞亞(西非一國家,首都爲 Monrovia)。
Libreville /'liːbrəvɪl; 'librəˌvɪl/ 自由市(Gabon 之首都)。
Libya /'lɪbɪə; 'lɪbɪə/ 利比亞(北非一國家, 1951 年 12 月獨立,首都爲 Tripoli)。
Lido /'liːdəʊ; 'lido/ 里度(義大利威尼斯附近一小島)。
Liechtenstein /'lɪktənstaɪn; 'lɪktənˌstaɪn/ 列支敦斯登(瑞士與奧國之間一小侯國,首都爲 Vaduz)。
Liège /lɪ'eɪʒ; li'ɛʒ/ 列日(比利時東部一省,又該省之省會)。
Lille /liːl; lil/ 里耳(法國北部一城市)。
Lilongwe /lɪ'lɔːŋweɪ; lɪ'lɔŋwe/ 里郎威 (Malawi 之首都)。
Lima¹ /'liːmə; 'limə/ 利瑪(Peru 之首都)。
Lima² /'laɪmə; 'laɪmə/ 賴馬(美國俄亥俄州西北部一城市)。
Limerick /'lɪmərɪk; 'lɪm(ə)rɪk/ 利麥立克(愛爾蘭西南部一郡,又該郡之首府)。
Limpopo /lɪm'pəʊpəʊ; lɪm'popo/ 林坡坡河(在非洲東南部,亦稱 Crocodile)。
Lincolnshire /'lɪŋkənʃə(r); 'lɪŋkənˌʃɪr/ 林肯郡(英格蘭東海岸一郡,略作 *Lincs* /lɪŋks; lɪŋks/)。
Lingayen Gulf /ˌlɪŋgə'jen-; ˌlɪŋgə'jɛn-/ 仁牙因灣(在菲律賓呂宋島之西北岸)。
Lipari Islands /'lɪpərɪ-; 'lɪpərɪ-/ 利巴里羣島(在西西里島東北,屬義大利)。
Lisbon /'lɪzbən; 'lɪzbən/ 里斯本(Portugal 之首都)。
Lithuania /ˌlɪθjuː(ː)'eɪnjə; ˌlɪθ(j)ə'wenɪə/ 立陶宛(昔爲歐洲波羅的海沿岸一國,現爲蘇聯一加盟共和國,稱作 Lithuanian Republic)。
Little Missouri 小密蘇里河(在美國西部,注於密蘇里河)。
Liverpool /'lɪvəpuːl; 'lɪvəˌpul/ 利物浦 (**1** 英格蘭西北

部一海港；2 澳洲新南威爾士州東北部一山脈）。
Loanda /ləʊ'ændə ; lo'ændə/ 參看 Luanda。
Locarno /ləʊ'kɑːnəʊ ; lo'kɑrno/ 羅加諾（瑞士中部一市鎮）。
Lodz /luːdʒ ; ludʒ/ 洛次（波蘭中部一城市）。
Logan, Mount /'ləʊgən ; 'logən/ 羅干山（在加拿大西北部）。
Loire /lə'wɑː(r) ; lə'wɑr/ 羅亞爾河（在法國中部，注於比斯開灣）。
Lombok /'lɑːmˌbɑːk ; 'lɑmˌbɑk/ 龍目島（屬印尼小巽他羣島，在巴里島之東）。
Lomé /ləʊ'meɪ ; lo'me/ 洛梅（Togo 之首都）。
Lomond, Loch /'ləʊmənd ; 'lomənd/ 羅蒙湖（在蘇格蘭中南部）。
London /'lʌndən ; 'lʌndən/ 倫敦（**1** United Kingdom 之首都；**2** 加拿大安大略省東南一城市）。
Londonderry /'lʌndənderɪ ; ˌlʌndən'dɛrɪ/ 倫登德立（北愛爾蘭西北部一郡，又該郡首府）。
Longford /'lɒŋfəd *US:* 'lɔːŋ- ; 'lɔŋfəd/ 長津（愛爾蘭中部一郡，又該郡首府）。
Longs Peak /'lɒŋz- ; 'lɔŋz-/ 隆峯（在美國科羅拉多州中北部）。
Lorain /lə'reɪn ; lə'ren/ 羅藍（美國俄亥俄州北部一城市）。
Lorne, Firth of /lɔːn ; lɔrn/ 羅恩灣（在蘇格蘭西部）。
Lorraine /lə'reɪn ; lə'ren/ 洛林（法國東北部一地區）。
Los Angeles /lɒs'ændʒɪlɪs ; lɔ'sændʒələs/ 洛杉磯（美國加州西南部一港埠）。
Lost River Range 迷河山脈（在美國愛達荷州東部）。
Lothian /'ləʊðɪən ; 'loðɪən/ 樓甸（蘇格蘭南部一區）。
Louisiana /luːˌiːzɪ'ænə ; luˌizɪ'ænə/ 路易西安那（美國南部之一州，略作 *LA*）。
Lourenço Marques /lə'rensəʊ'mɑːk ; ləˌrɛnsoˌmɑr-'kɛs/ 洛朗索馬克（現稱 Maputo）。
Louth /laʊð ; laʊð/ 勞司（愛爾蘭東部一郡）。
Lowell /'ləʊəl ; 'loəl/ 羅厄耳（美國麻薩諸塞州東北部一城市）。
Loyang /'ləʊ'jɑːŋ ; 'lo'jɑŋ/ 洛陽（中國河南省一城市，爲著名之古都）。
Luanda /luː'ɑːndə ; lʊ'ændə/ 羅安達（Angola 之首都，亦稱 Loanda）。
Luang Prabang /luˌɑːŋprə'bɑːŋ ; luˌɑŋprə'bɑŋ/ 琅勃拉邦（寮國王城）。
Lübeck /'luːbek ; 'luˌbɛk/ 盧比克（德國北部一港市）。
Lublin /'luːblɪn ; 'lublən/ 盧布令（波蘭東部一城市）。
Lubumbashi /ˌluːbuːm'bɑːʃiː ; ˌlubum'bɑʃɪ/ 盧佈巴西（薩依共和國東南部一城市，昔稱 Elisabethville）。
Lucerne /luː'sɜːn ; lu'sɝn/ 琉森（瑞士中部一城市）。
Lucknow /'lʌknaʊ ; 'lʌkˌnaʊ/ 勒克腦（印度北部一城市）。
Luleå /'luːləˌəʊ ; 'luləˌo/ 魯勒（瑞典北部一港埠）。
Lupin /'luː'pɪn ; 'lu'pɪn/ 臚濱（中國興安省一邊城，舊名滿洲里）。
Lusaka /luː'sɑːkə ; lu'sɑkə/ 路沙卡（Zambia 之首都）。
Lüshun /'ljuː'ʃʊn ; 'lu'ʃʊn/ 旅順（中國遼寧省南部一海港，舊稱 Port Arthur）。
Luton /'luːtn ; 'lutn̩/ 琉頓（英格蘭中部一城市）。
Luxemb(o)urg /'lʌksəmbɜːg ; 'lʌksəmˌbɝg/ 盧森堡（**1** 西歐一公國，位於德、法、比之間，首都亦稱 Luxembourg；**2** 比利時東南部一省）。
Luzon /luː'zɒn ; lu'zɑn/ 呂宋島（菲律賓羣島中之最大島）。
Lydia /'lɪdɪə ; 'lɪdɪə/ 呂底亞（小亞細亞西部一古國，臨愛琴海，首都 Sardis）。
Lynn /lɪn ; lɪn/ 林城（美國麻薩諸塞州東北部一城市）。
Lyons /'laɪənz ; 'laɪənz/ 里昂（法國東南部一城市）。
Maas /mɑːs ; mɑs/ 馬士河（源於法國東北部，注入北海，亦稱 Meuse /mjuːz ; mjuz/）。
Macao, Macau /mə'kaʊ ; mə'kaʊ/ 澳門（中國東南一海島，位於香港以西）。
Macassar, Maka(s)sar /mə'kæsə(r) ; mə'kæsɚ/ 馬加撒（在西里伯島西南岸，爲印尼東部的大商港）。
Mackenzie /mə'kenzɪ ; mə'kɛnzɪ/ 馬更些（**1** 加拿大西北部一河流；**2** 加拿大西北邊區之西部一區）。
Madagascar /ˌmædə'gæskə(r) ; ˌmædə'gæskɚ/ 馬達加斯加（非洲東南印度洋中一島，原屬法國，1960 年 6 月獨立，名爲馬拉加西共和國 the Malagasy Republic, 1975 年改爲 Democratic Republic of ～，首都 Antananarivo）。
Madeira /mə'dɪərə ; mə'dɪrə/ **1** 馬得拉羣島（位於大西洋北部，屬葡萄牙）。**2** 馬得拉河（在巴西西部，流入亞馬遜河）。
Madras /mə'dræs ; mə'dræs/ 馬德拉斯（印度東南部一邦，又該邦之首府）。
Madrid /mə'drɪd ; mə'drɪd/ 馬德里（Spain 之首都）。
Madura /'mædjʊrə ; mə'dʊrə/ 馬杜拉島（屬印尼，位於爪哇東北）。
Maebashi, Mayebashi /ˌmɑːje'bɑːʃɪ ; ˌmɑjə'bɑʃɪ/ 前橋（日本本州山區中一城市）。
Mafeking /'mæfɪkɪŋ ; 'mæfəkɪŋ/ 馬菲金（南非共和國南部一市鎮）。
Magdalen /'mægdəlɪn ; 'mægdələn/ 馬達蘭羣島（在加拿大聖羅倫斯灣內）。
Magdalena /ˌmægdə'leɪnə ; ˌmægdə'lenə/ 馬格達琳那河（在南美洲哥倫比亞北部，注於加勒比海）。
Magdeburg /'mægdəbɜːg ; 'mægdəˌbɝg/ 馬德堡（德國東部一城市）。
Magellan, Strait of /mə'gelən ; mə'dʒelən/ 麥哲倫海峽（在智利南部）。
Maggiore, Lake /ˌmædʒɪ'ɔːrɪ ; mə'dʒorɪ/ 馬奏列湖（在義大利北部及瑞士南部）。
Magnitogorsk /mæg'netəˌgɒsk ; mæg'nitəˌgɔrsk/ 馬克尼土哥斯克（蘇聯亞洲部之西一城市，又名鋼城）。
Maidstone /'meɪdstən ; 'medstən/ 美斯頓（英格蘭東南部一城市）。
Maikop /maɪ'kɒp ; maɪ'kɔp/ 邁科普（蘇聯歐洲部南部一城市）。
Maine /meɪn ; men/ 緬因（美國東北部一州，略作 *ME*）。
Mainz /maɪnts ; maɪn(t)s/ 梅因斯（德國西部一城市）。
Majorca /mə'dʒɔːkə ; mə'dʒɔrkə/ 馬約卡島（屬西班牙，在西地中海）。
Makalu /'mʌkəluː ; 'mʌkəˌlu/ 麥卡魯山（世界第五高峯，在尼泊爾東北）。
Makun(g) /'mɑː'gʊŋ ; 'mɑ'guŋ/ 馬公（中國澎湖羣島之主要市鎮）。
Malabar Coast /ˌmælə'bɑː- ; 'mæləˌbɑr-/ 馬拉巴海岸（印度西南海岸地區）。
Malabo /'mɑːlɑːbəʊ ; mɑ'lɑbo/ 馬拉博（昔稱 Santa Isabel, 爲 Equatorial Guinea 之首都）。
Malacca, Malakka /mə'lækə ; mə'lækə/ 麻六甲（馬來西亞之一邦，又該邦之首府）。
Malacca, Strait of 麻六甲海峽（位於馬來半島南端與蘇門答臘之間）。
Málaga /'mæləgə ; 'mæləgə/ 馬拉加（西班牙南部一省，又該省之首府）。
Malagasy Republic /ˌmælə'gæsɪ- ; ˌmælə'gæsɪ-/ 馬拉加西共和國（參看 Madagascar）。
Malakka = Malacca
Malawi /mə'lɑːwɪ ; mə'lɑwɪ/ 馬拉威（非洲東南一國家，昔爲英國之保護領 Nyasaland, 1964 年 7 月獨立，首都 Lilongwe）。
Malaya /mə'leɪə ; mə'leə/ 馬來半島（亦稱 Malay Peninsula, 在亞洲大陸之南端）。
Malay Archipelago /mə'leɪ- ; mə'le-/ 馬來羣島（昔稱 Malaysia, 在亞洲東南部，介於太平洋與印度洋之間，包括蘇門答臘、爪哇、婆羅洲、西里伯、摩鹿加及帝汶等）。
Malaysia, (Federation of) /mə'leɪzɪə ; mə'leʒ(ɪ)ə/ 馬來西亞（東南亞一聯邦國家，首都爲 Kuala Lumpur）。
Maldives /'mældaɪvz ; 'mɔlˌdivz/ 馬爾地夫（印度洋中一羣島，位於錫蘭之西南，昔稱 Maldive Islands, 原爲英之保護國，於 1965 年 7 月獨立，首都爲 Male）。
Male /'mɑːleɪ ; 'mɑlɪ/ 瑪律（Maldives 之首都）。
Mali /'mɑːlɪ ; 'mɑlɪ/ 馬利（非洲西部一共和國，昔稱 Sudanese Republic, 昔爲法屬蘇丹 French Sudan, 1960 年 9 月獨立，首都爲 Bamako）。
Malmö /'mælmə ; 'mælˌmə/ 馬耳摩（瑞典西南部一港埠）。
Malta /'mɔːltə ; 'mɔltə/ 馬爾他（地中海中一羣島，位於西西里之南，原爲英國殖民地，於 1964 年 9 月獨立，首都爲 Valletta）。
Man, Isle of /'mæn ; 'mæn/ 曼島（在愛爾蘭海中，屬英）。
Managua /mə'nɑːgwə ; mə'nɑgwə/ 馬拿瓜（Nicaragua 之首都）。

Manama /məˈnæmə ; məˈnæmə/ 麥納瑪(Bahrain 之首都)。
Manaus /məˈnaʊs ; məˈnaus/ 瑪瑙斯(巴西西部一城市)。
Manchester /ˈmæntʃɪstə(r) ; ˈmæn,tʃɛstɚ/ 曼徹斯特(**1** 英格蘭西北部一郡;又該郡之首府; **2** 美國新罕布夏州南部一城市; **3** 美國康乃狄格州中部一城市)。
Manchuria /mænˈtʃʊərɪə ; mænˈtʃurɪə/ 中國東北部;東北九省。
Mandalay /ˌmændəˈleɪ ; ˌmændəˈle/ 瓦城(又譯曼德勒,緬甸中部一城市)。
Manhattan /mænˈhætn ; mænˈhætn̩/ **1** 曼哈坦島(在美國紐約灣內)。 **2** 曼哈坦區(美國紐約市一區,包括曼哈坦島及其附近地區)。
Manila /məˈnɪlə ; məˈnɪlə/ 馬尼拉(Philippines 之首都)。
Manitoba /ˌmænɪˈtəʊbə ; ˌmænəˈtobə/ 曼尼托巴(加拿大中南部一省,略作 *Man*)。
Mannheim /ˈmænhaɪm ; ˈmæn,haɪm/ 曼漢(西德南部一城市)。
Mansfield /ˈmænsfiːld ; ˈmæns,fild/ 曼斯菲爾 (**1** 美國俄亥俄州中北部一城市; **2** 英格蘭諾丁安郡北部一城市)。
Mantua /ˈmæntjʊə ; ˈmæntʃ(ə)wə/ 曼求亞(義大利北部一城市)。
Maputo /mɑːˈpuːtəʊ ; mɑˈputo/ 馬布多(Mozambique 之首都)。
Maracaibo /ˌmærəˈkaɪbəʊ ; ˌmærəˈkaɪbo/ 馬拉開波(**1** 委內瑞拉西北部一城市; **2** 委內瑞拉西北部一湖名)。
Marañón /ˌmɑːrɑːˈnjɔːn ; ˌmɑrəˈnjon/ 馬藍雲河(在秘魯北部)。
Marcus Island /ˈmɑːkəs- ; ˈmɑrkəs-/ 馬卡斯島(又譯南鳥島,在西太平洋,屬日本,曾爲美國佔領)。
Marcy, Mount /ˈmɑːsɪ ; ˈmɑrsɪ/ 馬西峯(在美國紐約州東北部)。
Mariana Islands /ˌmeərɪˈænə- ; ˌmɛrɪˈænə-/ 馬里亞納羣島(在西太平洋,由美國託管)。
(Marie) Byrd Land /mə,riːˈbɜːd- ; mə,riˈbɝd-/ 馬利伯德地(南極洲西部一地區)。
Maritime Territory 沿海州(在蘇聯亞洲部分之東部,瀕日本海)。
Markham, Mount /ˈmɑːkəm ; ˈmɑrkəm/ 馬坎山(在南極洲維多利亞地東部)。
Marlborough /ˈmɑːlbrə ; ˈmɑrl,bərə/ 馬堡 (**1** 美國麻薩諸塞州東部一城市; **2** 紐西蘭中部一省區)。
Marquesas Islands /mɑːˈkeɪsæs- ; mɑrˈkezəz-/ 馬貴斯羣島(在南太平洋,屬法國)。
Marsala /mɑːˈsɑːlə ; mɑrˈsɑlə/ 馬沙拉(義大利西西里島西海岸一港埠)。
Marseilles /mɑːˈseɪlz ; mɑrˈse(lz)/ 馬賽(法國東南部一港埠)。
Marshall Islands /ˈmɑːʃəl- ; ˈmɑrʃəl-/ 馬紹爾羣島(在西太平洋,由美國託管)。
Martha's Vineyard /ˈmɑːθəz- ; ˈmɑrθəz-/ 漫沙文雅島(在大西洋中,位於美國麻薩諸塞州之東南方)。
Martinique /ˌmɑːtɪˈniːk ; ˌmɑrtn̩ˈik/ 馬丁尼克島(西印度羣島中一島,屬法國)。
Maryland /ˈmeərɪlənd ; ˈmɛrələnd/ 馬里蘭(美國東部大西洋岸一州,略作 *MD*)。
Maseru /ˈmæzəruː ; ˈmæzə,ru/ 馬塞魯(Lesotho 之首都)。
Maskat, Masqat＝Muscat
Massachusetts /ˌmæsəˈtʃuːsɪts ; ˌmæs(ə)ˈtʃusəts/ 麻薩諸塞(美國東北部一州,位於新英格蘭地區,略作 *MA*)。
Massive, Mount /ˈmæsɪv ; ˈmæsɪv/ 馬西梧山(在美國科羅拉多州中部)。
Matsu /ˈmɑːˈtsuː ; ˈmɑˈtsu/ 馬祖(中國臺灣海峽中一島,在福州以東)。
Matterhorn /ˈmætəhɔːn ; ˈmætɚ,hɔrn/ 馬特合恩峯(阿爾卑斯山中一高峯,在義大利及瑞士邊境)。
Mauga Sili /ˈmaʊgəˈsiːlɪ ; ˌmaʊgəˈsilɪ/ 莫加希里山(在中太平洋薩瓦伊島中央)。
Mauna Kea /ˈmaʊnɑː ˈkeɪɑː ; ˌmaʊnəˈkeə/ 冒納開亞山(夏威夷島中部北一死火山)。
Mauna Loa /ˈmaʊnɑːˈləʊɑː ; ˌmaʊnəˈloə/ 冒納羅亞山(夏威夷島中南部一活火山)。
Mauritania /ˌmɒrɪˈteɪnɪə ; ˌmɔrəˈtenɪə/ 茅利塔尼亞(非洲西北部一國家,原爲法國屬地,1960 年 11 月獨立,首都爲 Nouakchott)。
Mauritius /məˈrɪʃəs ; mɔˈrɪʃ(ɪ)əs/ 模里西斯(印度洋中一島,曾爲英國屬地,於1968 年 3月獨立,首都 Port Louis)。
Mayo /ˈmeɪəʊ ; ˈmeo/ 馬由(愛爾蘭西北部一郡)。
Mbabane /mbɑːˈbɑːn ; ˌɛmbəˈbɑn/ 墨巴本(Swaziland 之首都)。
McKinley, Mount /məˈkɪnlɪ ; məˈkɪnlɪ/ 馬金利山(在美國阿拉斯加州中部,爲北美洲之最高峯)。
M'Clure Strait /məˈkluə- ; məˈklur-/ 馬克盧海峽(在加拿大北部 Banks 與 Melville 兩島之間)。
Meath /miːθ ; mið/ 米司(愛爾蘭東部一郡)。
Mecca, Mekka /ˈmekə ; ˈmɛkə/ 麥加(沙烏地阿拉伯西部一城市,爲回教之聖地)。
Medina /məˈdiːnə ; məˈdinə/ 麥地那(沙烏地阿拉伯西部一城市)。
Mediterranean (Sea) /ˌmedɪtəˈreɪnjən ; ˌmɛdətəˈrenɪən/ 地中海(在歐、非兩洲之間)。
Mekong /ˈmeɪkɑːŋ ; ˈmeˈkɔŋ/ 湄公河(發源於中國之青海省,向東南流,經西康、雲南,在越南注入南中國海)。
Melanesia /ˌmeləˈniːʒə ; ˌmɛləˈniʒə/ 美拉尼西亞(在澳洲東北和 Micronesia 以南太平洋中諸島嶼之總稱)。
Melbourne /ˈmelbən ; ˈmɛlbɚn/ 新金山(音譯墨爾本,澳洲東南部一港市)。
Memphis /ˈmemfɪs ; ˈmɛmfəs/ 孟斐斯 (**1** 埃及尼羅河畔一古城; **2** 美國田納西州西南部一城市)。
Menai Strait /ˈmenaɪ- ; ˈmɛn,aɪ-/ 麥奈海峽(在威爾斯北部)。
Me Nam, Menam /meˈnɑːm ; meˈnɑm/ 湄南河(在泰國中西部)。
Mendoza /menˈdəʊzə ; mɛnˈdozə/ 門多薩(阿根廷西部一城市)。
Mercedario /ˌmeəsəˈdɑːriːəʊ ; ˌmɛrsəˈdɑrio/ 麻塞達里歐山(在阿根廷西部)。
Merionethshire /ˌmerɪˈɒnɪθʃə(r) ; ˌmɛrɪˈɑnəθ,ʃɪr/ 麥立昂斯夏(昔爲威爾斯西北部一郡)。
Meroë /ˈmerəʊɪ ; ˈmɛrə,wɪ/ 梅羅伊(非洲蘇丹境內尼羅河畔一古都)。
Merseyside /ˈmɜːzɪsaɪd ; ˈmɝzɪ,saɪd/ 莫日塞德(英格蘭西北部一郡)。
Merthyr Tydfil /ˈmɜːθə ˈtɪdvɪl ; ˌmɝθɚ ˈtɪd,vɪl/ 莫色提維(威爾斯東南部一城市)。
Meshed /ˈmeʃed ; məˈʃɛd/ 麥什德(伊朗東北部一城市)。
Mesopotamia /ˌmespəˈteɪmjə ; ˌmɛs(ə)pəˈtemɪə/ 美索不達米亞(亞洲西南部一地區,在底格里斯與幼發拉底兩河之間)。
Messina /meˈsiːnə ; məˈsinə/ 墨西拿(義大利西西里島東北部一海港)。
Metz /mets ; mɛts/ 麥次(法國東北部一城市)。
Mexico /ˈmeksɪkəʊ ; ˈmɛksɪ,ko/ 墨西哥(北美洲南部一國家,首都爲 Mexico City)。
Mexico (City) 墨西哥城(Mexico 之首都)。
Mexico, Gulf of 墨西哥灣(位於美國,古巴與墨西哥之間)。
Miami /maɪˈæmɪ ; maɪˈæmɪ/ 邁阿密(美國佛羅里達州東南部一港埠)。
Miaoli /ˈmjaʊˈliː ; ˈmjaʊˈli/ 苗栗(中國臺灣省西北部一縣,又其縣治名)。
Michigan /ˈmɪʃɪgən ; ˈmɪʃɪgən/ 密西根(美國中北部一州,略作 *MI*)。
Micronesia /ˌmaɪkrəˈniːʒə ; ˌmaɪkrəˈniʒə/ 密克羅尼西亞(西太平洋諸島嶼之總稱)。
Middlesex /ˈmɪdlseks ; ˈmɪdl̩,sɛks/ 密得塞斯(昔爲英格蘭東南部一郡,略作 *Middx*)。
Mid Glamorgan 中格拉馬干(威爾斯東南部一郡)。
Midlothian /mɪdˈləʊðɪən ; mɪdˈloðɪən/ 中樓甸(昔爲蘇格蘭東南部一郡)。
Midway /ˈmɪdweɪ ; ˈmɪd,we/ 中途島(在太平洋中部,屬美國)。
Mieres /mɪˈeɪrəs ; mɪˈɛrəs/ 美雷斯(西班牙西北部一城市)。
Milan /mɪˈlæn ; məˈlæn/ 米蘭(義大利北部一城市)。
Milk /mɪlk ; mɪlk/ 密耳克河(在美國北部及加拿大南部,注於密蘇里河)。
Milwaukee /mɪlˈwɔːkɪ ; mɪlˈwɔkɪ/ 密耳瓦基(美國威斯

康辛州密西根湖西岸一港市)。

Mindanao /ˌmɪndəˈnɑːəʊ ; ˌmɪndəˈnɑˌo/ 民答那峨(菲律賓羣島南部一島,包括其附近島嶼)。

Min (Kong) /ˈmɪnˈkɔːŋ ; ˈmɪnˈkɔŋ/ 閩江(在中國福建省中北部)。

Minneapolis /ˌmɪnɪˈæpəlɪs ; ˌmɪnɪˈæp(ə)ləs/ 明尼亞波利斯(美國明尼蘇達州東南部一城市)。

Minnesota /ˌmɪnɪˈsəʊtə ; ˌmɪnəˈsotə/ 明尼蘇達(美國中北部一州,略作 *MN*)。

Minorca /mɪˈnɔːkə ; məˈnɔrkə/ 米諾卡島(在地中海西部,屬西班牙)。

Minsk /mɪnsk ; mɪnsk/ 明斯克(蘇聯白俄羅斯之首府)。

Mississippi /ˌmɪsɪˈsɪpɪ ; ˌmɪs(ə)ˈsɪpɪ/ 密西西比 (**1** 美國南部一州,略作 *MS*; **2** 美國一河名,注入墨西哥灣)。

Missouri /mɪˈzʊərɪ ; məˈzʊrɪ/ 密蘇里 (**1** 美國中部一州,略作 *MO*; **2** 美國西部一河流)。

Mitchell, Mount /ˈmɪtʃl ; ˈmɪtʃəl/ 密契耳山(在美國北卡羅來納州西部)。

Mobile /ˈməʊbiːl ; moˈbil/ 木比耳(美國阿拉巴馬州西南部一港埠)。

Mogadishu /ˌmɒgəˈdɪʃuː ; ˌmɑgəˈdɪʃu/ 摩加迪休(Somalia 之首都)。

Moldavia /mɒlˈdeɪvjə ; mɑlˈdevɪə/ 摩爾達維亞(蘇聯一加盟共和國,在其西南部)。

Molokai /məʊləˈkaɪ ; ˌmɑləˈkaɪ/ 毛洛開島(在夏威夷中部)。

Molotov /ˈmɔːlətɔːf ; ˈmɑləˌtɔf/ 莫洛托夫(今名 Perm)。

Moluccas /məˈlʌkəz ; məˈlʌkəz/ 摩鹿加羣島(在印尼東部,又名 Spice Islands)。

Mombasa /mɒmˈbæsə ; mɑmˈbɑsə/ 蒙巴薩島(在非洲東海岸,屬肯亞)。

Monaco /ˈmɒnəkəʊ ; ˈmɑnəˌko/ 摩納哥 (**1** 法國東南地中海岸一侯國; **2** 該國首都)。

Monaghan /ˈmɒnəhən ; ˈmɑnəhən/ 蒙納干(愛爾蘭東北部一郡)。

Mongolia /mɒŋˈgəʊlɪə ; mɑŋˈgolɪə/ 蒙古(亞洲東部一地區,在興安嶺以西和阿爾泰山以東,包括內、外蒙古)。

Monmouthshire /ˈmɒnməθʃə(r) ; ˈmɑnməθˌʃɪr/ 蒙茅斯夏(昔威爾斯東南部一郡)。

Monrovia /mənˈrəʊvɪə ; mənˈrovɪə/ 蒙羅維亞(Liberia 之首都)。

Montana /mɒnˈtænə ; mɑnˈtænə/ 蒙大拿(美國西北部一州,略作 *MT*)。

Monte Carlo /ˌmɒntɪˈkɑːləʊ ; ˌmɑntɪˈkɑrlo/ 蒙地卡羅(摩納哥一城市,俗稱賭城)。

Montenegro /ˌmɒntɪˈniːgrəʊ ; ˌmɑntəˈnigro/ 蒙特尼哥羅(南斯拉夫一省,在其南部)。

Montevideo /ˌmɒntɪvɪˈdeɪəʊ ; ˌmɑntəvəˈdeo/ 孟特維得亞(Uruguay 之首都)。

Montgomeryshire /məntˈgʌmrɪʃə(r); mən(t)ˈgʌm(ə)rɪˌʃɪr/ 蒙哥馬利夏(昔爲威爾斯東部一郡)。

Montmartre /mɔ̃ˈmɑːtə ; mɔ̃ˈmɑrtɚ/ 蒙馬特區(巴黎中北部一區)。

Montpelier /mɒntˈpiːljə(r) ; mɑntˈpiljɚ/ 蒙皮立(美國佛蒙特州首府)。

Montreal /ˌmɒntrɪˈɔːl ; ˌmɑntrɪˈɔl/ 蒙特利爾(加拿大魁北克省南部一港市)。

Montserrat /ˌmɒntsəˈræt ; ˌmɑn(t)səˈræt/ 蒙特色拉島(英屬西印度羣島中一島)。

Morava /ˈmɒrəvə ; ˈmɔrəvə/ 摩拉瓦河(亦稱 March, 在捷克中部)。

Morayshire /ˈmʌrɪʃə(r) ; ˈmʌrɪˌʃɪr/ 莫立夏(昔爲蘇格蘭東北部一郡)。

Morocco /məˈrɒkəʊ ; məˈrɑko/ 摩洛哥(非洲西北部一王國, 1956 年 3 月獨立,首都爲 Rabat)。

Moroni /məˈrɒnɪ ; moˈronɪ/ 莫洛尼(Comoro 之首都)。

Moscow /ˈmɒskəʊ ; ˈmɑsko/ 莫斯科(Soviet Union 之首都)。

Mosul /ˈməʊsl ; ˈmosl̩/ 摩蘇爾(伊拉克北部一城市)。

Moulmein /ˈmʊlˈmeɪn ; mulˈmen/ 毛淡棉(緬甸南部一都市)。

Mozambique /ˌməʊzæmˈbiːk ; ˌmozəmˈbik/ 莫三比克(位於東南非,原爲葡屬東非洲,於1975 年 6月獨立,首都 Maputo)。

Mukden /ˈmʊkdn ; ˈmʊkdən/ 瀋陽(參看 Shenyang)。

Mulhacén /ˌmuːlɒˈseɪn ; ˌmulɑˈsen/ 木拉森山(在西班牙南部)。

Munich /ˈmjuːnɪk ; ˈmjunɪk/ 慕尼黑(德國南部一城市)。

Munko Sardik /ˈmʌŋkəʊ ˈsɑːdɪk ; ˈmʌŋko ˈsɑrdɪk/ 門科薩地克峯(在蒙古與蘇聯之布里亞特間)。

Munster /ˈmʌnstə(r) ; ˈmʌnstɚ/ 蒙斯特(愛爾蘭南部一省)。

Murchison /ˈmɜːtʃɪsn ; ˈmɝtʃəsn̩/ 莫契生河(在澳洲西部)。

Murmansk /mɜːˈmɑːnsk ; mɚˈmænsk/ 莫曼斯克(蘇聯歐洲部西北一港埠)。

Murray /ˈmɜːrɪ ; ˈmɝɪ/ 墨累河(在澳洲東南部)。

Musala /muːsəˈlɑː ; ˌmusəˈlɑ/ 摩沙拉峯(在歐洲保加利亞西南部)。

Muscat /ˈmʌskət ; ˈmʌsˌkæt/ 馬斯喀特(Oman 之首都,亦作 Masqat 或 Maskat)。

Muztagh Ata /muːsˈtɑː ɑːˈtɑː ; musˈtɑ əˈtɑ/ 木斯塔阿塔山(在中國新疆省西部)。

Mycenae /maɪˈsiːniː ; maɪˈsinɪ/ 美錫尼(希臘南部一古都)。

Myitkyina /ˈmjɪˈtʃiːˈnɑː ; ˌmitʃɪˈnɔ/ 密支那 (緬甸北部一城鎮)。

Mysia /ˈmɪsɪə ; ˈmɪʃ(ɪ)ə/ 米西亞(小亞細亞西北一古國)。

Mytilene /ˌmɪtɪˈliːnɪ; ˌmɪtl̩ˈinɪ/ 密特里尼(參看 Lesbos)。

Nagasaki /ˌnægəˈsɑːkɪ ; ˌnɑgəˈsɑkɪ/ 長崎(日本九州西部一港埠)。

Nagoya /nɑːˈgəʊjɑː ; nəˈgɔɪə/ 名古屋 (日本本州南部一城市)。

Nagpur /ˈnɑːgpʊə(r) ; ˈnɑgˌpʊr/ 那格坡爾(印度東部一城市)。

Naha /ˈnɑːhɑː ; ˈnɑhɑ/ 那霸(琉球之首府)。

Nairnshire /ˈneənʃə(r) ; ˈnɛrnˌʃɪr/ 那恩夏(昔爲蘇格蘭東北部一郡)。

Nairobi /ˌnaɪˈrəʊbɪ ; naɪˈrobɪ/ 奈洛比(Kenya 之首都)。

Namibia /nəˈmɪbɪə ; nəˈmɪbɪə/ 那米比亞(又名 South-West Africa, 在非洲西南部,臨大西洋,原屬德國, 1919 年國際聯盟委託南非聯邦管理, 1966 年聯合國決定終止託管,但不爲南非聯邦接受)。

Nanchang /ˈnɑːnˈtʃɑːŋ ; ˈnɑnˈtʃɑŋ/ 南昌(中國江西省省會)。

Nancy /ˈnænsɪ ; ˈnænsɪ/ 南錫(法國東北部一城市)。

Nanda Devi /ˌnʌndə ˈdeɪviː ; ˌnʌndəˈdevɪ/ 楠達代維峯(在印度北部)。

Nanga Parbat /ˌnʌŋgəˈpɜːbət ; ˌnʌŋgəˈpɝbət/ 楠加帕巴峯(在印度北部,喀什米爾之西北)。

Nanking /ˈnænˈkɪŋ ; ˈnænˈkɪŋ/ 南京(中國東部揚子江畔一城市)。

Nanning /ˈnɑːnˈnɪŋ ; ˈnɑnˈnɪŋ/ 南寧(中國廣西省之交通與軍事中心)。

Nantes /nænts ; nænts/ 南特(法國西北部一城市)。

Nantow /ˈnɑːnˈtəʊ ; ˈnɑnˈto/ 南投(中國臺灣省中部一縣,又其縣治名)。

Nantucket /nænˈtʌket ; nænˈtʌkət/ 南塔克特島(在美國麻薩諸塞州東南)。

Naples /ˈneɪplz ; ˈnepl̩z/ 拿玻里(又譯那不勒斯,義大利南部一海港)。

Narbada /nɑːˈbʌdə ; nɚˈbʌdə/ 那巴達河 (在印度中部,注於康貝灣)。

Narvik /ˈnɑːvɪk ; ˈnɑrvɪk/ 那維克(挪威北部一港市)。

Nassau /ˈnæsɔː ; ˈnæsˌɔ/ 拿索(Bahamas 之首都)。

Nassau Range /ˈnæsɔː- ; ˈnæsˌɔ-/ 拿索山脈(在新幾內亞中西部,現稱 Sudirman /suːˈdɪəmən ; suˈdɪrmən/)。

Natal /nəˈtæl ; nəˈtæl/ 納塔耳 (**1** 巴西東北部一海港; **2** 南非共和國東部一省)。

Nauru /ˌnaʊˈruː ; nɑˈuru/ 諾魯(西太平洋一島,於 1968年 1 月獨立)。

Navarre /nəˈvɑː(r) ; nəˈvɑr/ 那瓦爾(西班牙北部一省)。

Nazareth /ˈnæzərɪθ ; ˈnæz(ə)rəθ/ 拿撒勒(以色列北部一小城)。

Ndjamena /enˈdʒɑːmenɑː ; ɛnˈdʒɑmənə/ 恩將納(Chad 之首都)。

Nebraska /nəˈbræskə ; nəˈbræskə/ 內布拉斯加(美國中部一州,略作 *NE*)。

Negoiul /neˈgɔɪuːl ; nɛˈgɔɪˌul/ 那果佑勒山(在羅馬尼亞中部)。

Negri Sembilan /ˈnegrɪsemˈbi:lən ; nəˌgrɪsəmˈbilən/ 森美蘭(馬來西亞南部一州)。
Negro /ˈneɪgrəʊ ; ˈnegro/ 內革羅河 (**1** 在南美洲西北部; **2** 在南美洲阿根廷中南部)。
Neiges, Piton des /ˌpi:ˈtɒn deɪ ˈnæʒ ; pɪˌtonde ˈneʒ/ 納士峯(在印度洋留尼旺島中部)。
Neisse /ˈnaɪsə ; ˈnaɪsə/ 奈塞河(在捷克北部)。
Nelson /ˈnelsn ; ˈnelsn̩/ 納爾遜(紐西蘭南島北部一省區,又該省區之首府)。
Nepal /nɪˈpɔ:l ; nəˈpɔl/ 尼泊爾(印度與西藏之間一小王國,首都爲 Katmandu)。
Netherlands, The /ˈneðələndz ; ˈneðɚlən(d)z/ 荷蘭(卽 Holland, 歐洲西北部一王國,首都爲 Amsterdam)。
Netherlands Guiana = Dutch Guiana
Néthou, Pic de /ˌpi:k də neɪˈtu: ; ˌpik də neˈtu/ 參看 Pico de Aneto。
Neva /ˈneɪvə ; ˈnivə/ 尼瓦河(在蘇聯列寧格勒西北)。
Nevada /nəˈvɑ:də *US:* -ˈvædə ; nəˈvædə/ 內華達(美國西部一洲,略作 *NV*)。
Newark /ˈnju:ək ; ˈn(j)uɚk/ 紐華克 (**1** 美國新澤西州東北部一港市; **2** 美國俄亥俄州中部一城市)。
New Britain 新不列顛(美國康乃狄格州中部一城市)。
New Brunswick 新伯倫瑞克(加拿大東南部一省,略作 *NB*)。
New Caledonia /-ˌkæləˈdəʊnjə ; -ˌkæləˈdonjə/ 新喀里多尼亞島(西南太平洋之一島,屬法國)。
Newcastle /ˈnju:ˌkɑ:sl ; ˈn(j)uˌkæsl/ 紐加塞耳(英國諾森伯蘭郡之首府)。
New Delhi 新德里(India 之首都)。
New England 新英格蘭 (**1** 美國東北部諸州之總名; **2** 澳洲新南威爾士州東北部一山脈)。
Newfoundland /ˈnju:fənlənd *US:* ˈnu:- ; ˈn(j)ufənlənd/ 紐芬蘭(大西洋一大島,近加拿大東岸,爲其一行省,略作 *ND* 或 *Nfd*)。
New Guinea 新幾內亞島(又名 Papua, 馬來羣島中之一大島,位於澳洲以北,分屬 Indonesia 及 Papua New Guinea 兩國; 又本島之東北部及附近島嶼亦名 New Guinea, 而東南部亦名 Papua)。
New Hampshire /-ˈhæmpʃə(r) ; -ˈhæm(p)ʃɚ/ 新罕布夏(美國東北部一州,略作 *NH*)。
New Haven /-ˈheɪvn ; -ˈhevn̩/ 新哈芬(美國康乃狄格州南部一海港)。
New Jersey /-ˈdʒɜ:zɪ ; -ˈdʒɝzɪ/ 新澤西(美國東部一州,略作 *NJ*)。
New Mexico 新墨西哥(美國西南部一州,略作 *NM*)。
New Orleans /-ˈɔ:lɪənz ; -ˈɔrlɪənz/ 新奧爾良(美國路易西安那州東南部一港市)。
New South Wales 新南威爾士(澳洲東南部一邦,略作 *NSW*)。
New York /-ˈjɔ:k ; -ˈjɔrk/ 紐約 (**1** 美國東北部一州,略作 *NY*; **2** 紐約州東南部一港市,亦稱 ~ City 略作 *N.Y.C.*)。
New Zealand 紐西蘭(西南太平洋一國,爲大英國協之一員,首都爲 Wellington)。
Niagara /naɪˈægərə ; naɪˈæg(ə)rə/ 尼加拉河(在加拿大與美國之邊境)。
Niagara Falls 尼加拉瀑布(在美加邊境之尼加拉河上)。
Niamey /ˌnjɑ:ˈmeɪ ; ˌnɪˈɑme/ 尼阿美(Niger 之首都)。
Nicaragua /ˌnɪkəˈrægjʊə ; ˌnɪkəˈrɑgwə/ 尼加拉瓜(中美一國家,首都爲 Managua)。
Nice /ni:s ; nis/ 尼斯(法國東南部一港埠)。
Nicobar Islands /ˈnɪkoˌbɑ:(r)- ; ˈnɪkəˌbɑr-/ 尼古巴羣島(亦稱 Nicobars, 屬印度,在孟加拉灣東南部)。
Nicosia /ˌnɪkəʊˈsi:ə ; ˌnɪkəˈsiə/ 尼古西亞(Cyprus 之首都)。
Niger /ni:ˈʒeə(r) ; ˈnaɪdʒɚ/ **1** 尼日(西非一共和國,原爲法國屬地,1960 年 8 月獨立,首都爲 Niamey)。 **2** 尼日河(在非洲西部)。
Nigeria /naɪˈdʒɪərɪə ; naɪˈdʒɪrɪə/ 奈及利亞(西非一國家,原爲英國屬地,1960 年 10 月獨立,首都爲 Lagos)。
Nijmegen, Nimeguen /ˈnaɪˌmeɪgən ; ˈnaɪˌmegən/ 奈美根(荷蘭東部一城市)。
Nile /naɪl ; naɪl/ 尼羅河(在非洲東部)。
Ningpo /ˈnɪŋˈpəʊ ; ˈnɪŋˈpo/ 寧波(中國浙江省甬江下游一城市)。
Ningsia, Ninghsia /ˈnɪŋʃɪˈɑ: ; ˈnɪŋʃɪˈɑ/ 寧夏(中國北部一省)。
Nizhni Tagil /ˈnɪʒnɪ təˈgɪl ; ˌnɪʒnɪ təˈgɪl/ 下塔吉爾(蘇聯烏拉山脈東麓一城市)。
Norfolk /ˈnɔ:fək ; ˈnɔrfək/ 諾福克(英格蘭東部一郡,略作 *Norf*)。
Normandy /ˈnɔ:məndɪ ; ˈnɔrməndɪ/ 諾曼第(法國西北部一地區)。
Norrköping /ˈnɔ:ˌtʃɜ:pɪŋ ; ˈnɔrˌtʃɝpɪŋ/ 諾庫平(瑞典東南部一港埠)。
Northampton /nɔ:ˈθæmptən ; nɔrθˈ(h)æmptən/ 諾坦普頓 (**1** 英國諾坦普頓郡之首府; **2** 美國麻薩諸塞州西部一城市)。
Northamptonshire /nɔ:ˈθæmptənʃə(r); nɔrθˈ(h)æmptənˌʃɪr/ 諾坦普頓郡 (英格蘭中部一郡,略作 *Northants* /nɔ:ˈθænts ; nɔrθˈ(h)ænts/)。
North Borneo 北婆羅洲(今稱 Sabah)。
North Carolina 北卡羅來納(美國東部大西洋岸一州,略作 *NC*)。
North Dakota 北達科他(美國西北部一州,略作 *ND*)。
Northern Ireland 北愛爾蘭(愛爾蘭島之東北部,爲英國之一區,首府爲 Belfast)。
Northern Territory 北領土(澳洲中北部一地區,略作 *NT*)。
North Korea 北韓(亞洲朝鮮半島北部一國,首都 Pyongyang)。
North Platte /-ˈplæt ; -ˈplæt/ 北普拉特河(在美國科羅拉多,懷俄明與內布拉斯加三州之間)。
North Sea 北海(爲大西洋之一部,在英國與歐洲大陸之間,亦稱 German Ocean)。
Northumberland /nɔ:ˈθʌmbələnd ; nɔrˈθʌmbɚlənd/ 諾森伯蘭(英格蘭北部一郡,略作 *Northd*)。
North West Territories 西北邊區(加拿大北部一地區,分爲 Mackenzie, Keewatin, 和 Franklin 三區,略作 *NWT*)。
North Yorkshire 北約克郡(英格蘭北部一郡)。
Norton Sound /ˈnɔ:tn- ; ˈnɔrtn̩-/ 諾頓灣(在美國阿拉斯加州以西)。
Norway /ˈnɔ:weɪ ; ˈnɔrˌwe/ 挪威(歐洲西北部一王國,首都爲 Oslo)。
Norwegian Sea 挪威海(在挪威以西)。
Norwich[1] /ˈnɒrɪdʒ ; ˈnɑrɪdʒ/ 挪利其(英格蘭東部 Norfolk 郡之首府)。
Norwich[2] /ˈnɔ:wɪtʃ ; ˈnɔrwɪtʃ/ 挪維其(美國康乃狄格州東南部一城市)。
Nottingham /ˈnɒtɪŋəm ; ˈnɑtɪŋəm/ 諾丁安(英格蘭中北部諾丁安郡之首府)。
Nottinghamshire /ˈnɒtɪŋəmʃə(r) ; ˈnɑtɪŋəmˌʃɪr/ 諾丁安郡(在英格蘭中北部,略作 *Notts* /nɒts ; nɑts/)。
Nouakchott /nʊˈɑ:kʃɒt ; nuˈɑkˌʃɑt/ 諾克少(Mauritania 之首都)。
Nova Scotia /ˌnəʊvə ˈskəʊʃə ; ˌnovə ˈskoʃə/ 新斯科夏(加拿大東南部沿海一省,略作 *NS*)。
Novosibirsk /ˌnəʊvəsəˈbɪəsk ; ˌnovosəˈbɪrsk/ 新西伯利亞(蘇聯亞洲部分南部一城市)。
Nukualofa /ˌnu:kʊəˈlɔ:fə ; ˌnukəwəˈlɔfə/ 努瓜婁發(Tonga 之首都)。
Nuneaton /nʌˈni:tn ; ˌnʌˈnitn̩/ 努尼頓(英格蘭中部一城市)。
Nunkiang /ˈnʊndʒi:ˈɑ:ŋ ; ˈnundʒiˈɑŋ/ 嫩江(中國東北一省)。
Nyasa, Lake /nɪˈæsə ; naɪˈæsə/ 尼亞沙湖(在非洲東南部,亦稱 Lake Malawi)。
Nyasaland /ˈnjæsəlænd ; naɪˈæsəˌlænd/ 尼亞沙蘭(Malawi 之舊稱)。
Oahu /əʊˈɑ:hu: ; əˈwɑhu/ 歐胡島(夏威夷羣島中之主要島嶼)。
Oakland /ˈəʊklənd ; ˈoklənd/ 奧克蘭(美國加利福尼亞州西部一港埠)。
Ob /ɔ:b ; ɑb/ 鄂畢河(在蘇聯亞洲部分之西部)。
Oceania /ˌəʊʃɪˈeɪnɪə ; ˌoʃɪˈænɪə/ 大洋洲 (中南太平洋諸島之總稱)。
Odense /ˈəʊðənsə ; ˈodn̩sə/ 奧登色(丹麥菲英島北部一城市)。
Oder /ˈəʊdə(r) ; ˈodɚ/ 奧德河 (在東德和波蘭之邊界上,

注入波羅的海)。
Odessa /əʊ'desə ; o'dɛsə/ 敖得薩 (**1** 美國德克薩斯州西部一城市; **2** 蘇聯烏克蘭南部一海港)。
Offaly /'ɒfəlɪ ; 'ɔfəlɪ/ 奧法利(愛爾蘭中部一郡)。
Offenbach /'ɒfənbɑ:k ; 'ɔfən,bɑk/ 奧芬巴克(德國西部一城市)。
Ogasawara Islands /'ogɑ:sɑ:'wɑ:rɑ:- ; o,gɑsə'wɑrə-/ 小笠原羣島(屬日本,在東京東南,亦稱 Bonin Islands)。
Ohio /əʊ'haɪəʊ ; o'haɪo/ 俄亥俄 (**1** 美國中東部一州,略作 *OH*; **2** 美國東部一河名,注入密西西比河)。
Ojos del Salado /,əʊhəʊz,del sə'lɑ:dəʊ ; 'ohoz,dɛl sə'lɑdo/ 歐霍士德而塞拉多山(在阿根廷西北部)。
Oka /ʌ'kɑ: ; o'kɑ/ 俄咯河(在蘇聯亞洲部之南)。
Okhotsk, Sea of /əʊ'kɒtsk ; o'kɑtsk/ 鄂霍次克海(位於西伯利亞以東,堪察加半島以西)。
Okinawa /,əʊkə'nɑ:wə ; ,okə'nɑwə/ 冲繩島(在琉球羣島之中部)。
Oklahoma /,əʊklə'həʊmə ; ,oklə'homə/ 俄克拉荷馬(美國中南部一州,略作 *OK*)。
Oldham /'əʊldəm ; 'oldəm/ 奧耳丹(英格蘭西北部一城市)。
Olympic Peninsula 奧林匹克半島(在美國華盛頓州西北部)。
Olympus /ə'lɪmpəs ; ə'lɪmpəs/ 奧林帕斯 (**1** 希臘東北部一山脈; **2** 美國華盛頓州西北部一山峯)。
Omaha /'əʊməhɑ: ; 'omə,hɔ/ 俄馬哈(美國內布拉斯加州東部一城市)。
Oman /əʊ'mɑ:n ; o'mɑn/ 阿曼(阿拉伯半島東南部一回教王國, 1951 年 12 月獨立,首都爲 Muscat)。
Omdurman /,ɒmdɜ:'mæn ; ,ɑmdɚ'mæn/ 恩圖曼(非洲蘇丹共和國中部一城市)。
Omei /'əʊ'meɪ ; 'o'me/ 峨眉山(在中國四川省西南部,爲中國三大佛教聖地之一)。
Omsk /ɒmsk ; ɔmsk/ 鄂木斯克(蘇聯亞洲部分西南部一城市)。
Onega /əʊ'nɪgə ; o'nɛgə/ 阿尼加湖(在蘇聯歐洲部分之西北部)。
Ontario /ɒn'teərɪəʊ ; ɑn'tɛrɪ,o/ 安大略 (**1** 加拿大東部一省,略作 *Ont*; **2** 美國和加拿大間一湖)。
Oporto /əʊ'pɔ:təʊ ; o'porto/ 奧波多(葡萄牙西北部一海港)。
Öraefajökull /'ɜ:,raɪvɑ:,jɜ:ku:tl ; 'ɜ,raɪvə'jɜ,kjutl/ 奧來瓦峯(在冰島東南海岸)。
Oran /ɔ:'rɑ:n ; ɔ'rɑn/ 奧倫(阿爾及利亞西北部一港埠)。
Orange /'ɒrɪndʒ ; 'ɔrɪndʒ/ 奧倫治河(在南非,流入大西洋)。
Oregon /'ɒrɪgən *US:* 'ɔ:r- ; 'ɔrɪgən/ 俄勒岡(美國西北部太平洋沿岸一州,略作 *OR*)。
Orinoco /,ɒrɪ'nəʊkəʊ ; ,orə'noko/ 奧利諾科河(在委內瑞拉境內,流入大西洋)。
Orissa /ɒ'rɪsə ; ɔ'rɪsə/ 奧立沙(印度東部一省)。
Orizaba /,ɒrə'zɑ:bə ; ,orə'zɑbə/ 俄利薩巴山(在墨西哥東南部)。
Orkney /'ɔ:knɪ ; 'ɔrknɪ/ 奧克尼羣島(在蘇格蘭東北,原爲其一郡,現爲一區)。
Orléans /ɔ:'lɪənz ; 'ɔrlɪənz/ 奧爾良(法國中北部一城市)。
Orohena, Mount /,əʊrɒ'heɪnə ; ,orə'henə/ 歐拉赫那山(在南太平洋大溪地島之中央)。
Orpington /'ɔ:pɪŋtən ; 'ɔrpɪŋtən/ 奧屏頓(昔爲英格蘭肯特郡西部一市鎮)。
Osage /əʊ'seɪdʒ ; o'sedʒ/ 奧撒奇河(在美國密蘇里州西部,注於密蘇里河)。
Osaka /'ɔ:səkə ; o'sɑkə/ 大阪(日本本州南部一港埠)。
Oslo /'ɒzləʊ ; 'ɑzlo/ 奧斯陸(Norway 之首都)。
Ossa /'ɒsə ; 'ɑsə/ 奧塞山(在希臘東北部)。
Ostrava /'ɔ:strəvə ; 'ɔstrəvə/ 奧斯特拉瓦(捷克中部一城市)。
Otago /əʊ'tɑ:gəʊ ; o'tɑgo/ 奧塔哥(紐西蘭南部一省區)。
Otranto, Strait of /ɒ'træntəʊ ; o'trænto/ 奧特蘭托海峽(在義大利東南與阿爾巴尼亞西部之間)。
Ottawa /'ɒtəwə ; 'ɑtəwə/ 渥太華 (**1** Canada 之首都; **2** 河名,在加拿大安大略省東南部與魁北克省南部,注於聖羅倫斯河)。
Ouachita /'wɒʃətɔ: ; 'wɑʃə,tɔ/ 烏時塔河(亦作 Washita, 在美國阿肯色州西南部及路易西安那州東部,注於黑河)。
Ouagadougou /,wɑ:gə'du:gu: ; ,wɑgə'dugu/ 瓦加杜古 (Upper Volta 之首都)。
Oviedo /,ɒvɪ'eɪdəʊ ; ,ovɪ'eðo/ 奧威多(西班牙西北部一省,又該省之首府)。
Owen Stanley Range /,əʊɪn 'stænlɪ- ; ,oən 'stænlɪ-/ 歐文斯坦利山脈(在新幾內亞東部)。
Oxfordshire /'ɒksfədʃə(r) ; 'ɑksfɚd,ʃɪr/ 牛津郡(英格蘭中南部一郡,略作 *Oxon* /'ɒksn ; 'ɑksn̩/)。
Pacific, the 太平洋(亦稱 Pacific Ocean, 介於美、亞、澳三洲與北極之間)。
Padua /'pædjʊə ; 'pædʒəwə/ 帕度亞(義大利東北部一城市)。
Pakistan /,pɑ:kɪ'stɑ:n ; ,pækɪ'stæn/ 巴基斯坦(亞洲南部一國家,爲大英國協之一員,首都 Islamabad; 原包括東、西巴基斯坦兩部,但東巴已於 1971 年獨立,改名 Bangladesh)。
Palau /pɑ:'laʊ ; pə'laʊ/ 帛琉(太平洋西部菲律賓東南一羣島, 1981 年 1 月獨立,首都 Koror)。
Palembang /,pɑ:lem'bɑ:ŋ ; ,pɑləm'bɑŋ/ 巴鄰旁(又名巨港,印尼蘇門答臘東南岸一港埠)。
Palermo /pə'lɜ:məʊ ; pə'lɝmo/ 巴勒摩(義大利西西里島之首府)。
Palestine /'pæləstaɪn ; 'pælə,staɪn/ 巴勒斯坦(昔爲一國家,位於西南亞,瀕地中海;今分屬以色列、約旦和埃及)。
Palma (de Mallorca) /'pælmə di: mə'jɔ:kə ; 'pɑlmə ,de mə'jɔrkə/ 帕耳馬(在地中海西班牙之馬約卡島西部,爲該島最大都市)。
Palmerston /'pɑ:məstn ; 'pɑmɚstən/ 帕麥斯頓島(在中太平洋,屬紐西蘭)。
Palmyra Island /pæl'maɪərə- ; pæl'maɪrə-/ 巴美拉島(在中太平洋之來因羣島中,屬吉里巴斯)。
Pamir /pə'mɪə(r) ; pə'mɪr/ 帕米爾高原(在亞洲中部,亦稱 The Pamirs)。
Panama /,pænə'mɑ: ; 'pænə,mɑ/ 巴拿馬(中美洲一國家,首都爲 Panama (City) 巴拿馬市)。
Panié, Mount /,pæ'njeɪ ; ,pæ'nje/ 帕尼艾山(在太平洋西南之新喀里多尼亞島)。
Paoting /'baʊ'dɪŋ ; 'baʊ'dɪŋ/ 保定(舊稱清苑,中國河北省之省會)。
Paotow /'baʊ'təʊ ; 'baʊ'to/ 包頭(在中國綏遠省內,爲塞北交通中心之一)。
Papua /'pæpjʊə;'pæpjəwə/ 巴布亞(見 New Guinea)。
Papua New Guinea 巴布亞紐幾內亞(國名,領土包括新幾內亞島之東部及附近之島嶼,原爲澳洲託管地,於1975年 9 月獨立,首都 Port Moresby)。
Paraguay /'pærəgwaɪ ; 'pærə,gwaɪ/ 巴拉圭 (**1** 南美洲中部一國家,首都爲 Asunción; **2** 南美洲中部一河流)。
Paramaribo /,pærə'mærɪbəʊ ; ,pærə'mɑrə,bo/ 巴拉馬利波(Surinam 之首都)。
Paraná /,pɑ:rɑ:'nɑ: ; ,pærə'nɑ/ 巴拉那河(在南美洲東南部)。
Paranaíba /,pærənə'i:bə ; ,pærənə'ibə/ 帕拉納伊巴河(在巴西南部,注於大西洋)。
Paricutin /pɑ:'ri:ku:ti:n ; pə'rikə,tin/ 帕里庫亭山(在墨西哥墨西哥城以西)。
Paris /'pærɪs ; 'pærɪs/ 巴黎(France 之首都)。
Parma /'pɑ:mə ; 'pɑrmə/ 巴馬(義大利北部一城市)。
Parnassus /pɑ:'næsəs ; pɑr'næsəs/ 巴納塞斯山(在希臘中部)。
Paros /'peərɒs ; 'pɛr,ɑs/ 派洛斯島(在愛琴海中,屬希臘)。
Parthia /'pɑ:θɪə ; 'pɑrθɪə/ 安息(古國名,位於今伊朗東北部)。
Patagonia /,pætə'gəʊnjə ; ,pætə'gonjə/ 巴塔哥尼亞(南美一地區,在阿根廷及智利之南部)。
Paterson /'pætəsn ; 'pætɚsn̩/ 帕特生(美國新澤西州東北部一城市)。
Patna /'pætnə ; 'pʌtnə/ 巴特那(印度東北部一城市)。
Pavia /pə'vi:ə ; pə'viə/ 帕維亞(義大利北部一城市)。
Peace /pi:s ; pis/ 和平河(在加拿大西部)。
Pearl Harbor 珍珠港(在美國夏威夷之歐胡島南海岸)。
Pechenga /'petʃəŋgə ; 'pɛtʃəŋgə/ 百成加(蘇聯歐洲部分西北部一港市)。
Pechora /pə'tʃəʊrə ; pə'tʃorə/ 白紹拉河(在蘇聯歐洲部東北)。
Pecos /'peɪkəs ; 'pekəs/ 貝可斯河(在美國新墨西哥州東

部與德克薩斯州西部,注於格蘭河)。

Peebles-shire /ˈpiːblʃə(r) ; ˈpibl̩ˌʃɪr/ 皮布斯夏(昔爲蘇格蘭東南部一郡)。

Peian /ˈbeɪˈɑːn ; ˈbeˈɑn/ 北安(中國黑龍江省省會)。

Peking /ˈpiːˈkɪŋ ; ˈpiˈkɪŋ/ 北京(中國北部一城市)。

Peipus, Lake /ˈpaɪpʊs ; ˈpaɪpəs/ 帛布斯湖(在蘇聯之愛沙尼亞東部)。

Peloponnesus, Peloponnesos /ˌpeləpəˈniːsəs ; ˌpɛləpəˈnisəs/ 伯羅奔尼撒(希臘南部之一大半島)。

Pembrokeshire /ˈpembrʊkʃə(r) ; ˈpɛmbrʊkˌʃɪr/ 朋布洛克夏(昔爲威爾斯西南部一郡)。

Penang /peˈnæŋ ; pəˈnæŋ/ **1** 檳榔嶼(在馬來半島西海岸外,麻六甲海峽之北端)。**2** 檳州(馬來西亞西北部一州)。

Penghu /ˈpʌŋˈhuː ; ˈpəŋˈhu/ 澎湖(亦稱 Pescadores, 爲中國臺灣海峽中一羣島,又指該羣島中之最大島)。

Pennine Alps /ˈpenaɪn- ; ˈpɛnˌaɪn-/ 本寧阿爾卑斯山(在瑞士與義大利之交界處)。

Pennsylvania /ˌpenslˈveɪnɪə ; ˌpɛnsəlˈvenjə/ 賓夕法尼亞(美國東北部一州,俗譯賓州,略作 *PA*)。

Perak /ˈpeərə ; ˈpɛrə/ 霹靂(馬來西亞西部一州)。

Perlis /ˈpɜːlɪs ; ˈpɝlɪs/ 玻璃市(馬來西亞北部一州)。

Perm /peəm ; pɝm/ 白爾姆(蘇聯歐洲部分東部一城市)。

Persia /ˈpɜːʃə ; ˈpɝʒə/ 波斯(參看 Iran)。

Persian Gulf 波斯灣(在伊朗與阿拉伯半島之間)。

Perth /pɜːθ ; pɝθ/ 伯斯(澳洲西部一城市)。

Perthshire /ˈpɜːθʃə(r) ; ˈpɝθˌʃɪr/ 伯斯夏(昔爲蘇格蘭中部一郡)。

Peru /pəˈruː; pəˈru/ 秘魯(南美西部一國家,首都爲 Lima)。

Pescadores /ˌpeskəˈdɔːrɪz ; ˌpɛskəˈdoriz/ 澎湖羣島(參看 Penghu)。

Peshawar /pəˈʃɔːə(r) ; pəˈʃawɚ/ 白夏瓦(巴基斯坦北部一城市)。

Petersburg /ˈpiːtəzbɜːg ; ˈpitɚzˌbɝg/ 彼得斯堡(美國維吉尼亞州東南部一城市)。

Petsamo /ˈpetsəməʊ ; ˈpɛtsəˌmo/ 百沙摩(現稱 Pechenga)。

Philadelphia /ˌfɪləˈdelfjə ; ˌfɪləˈdɛlfjə/ 費城(美國賓夕法尼亞州東南部一港市)。

Philippines, the /ˈfɪlɪpiːnz ; ˈfɪləˌpinz/ **1** 菲律賓羣島(亦稱 Philippine Islands, 在西太平洋,位於婆羅洲東北)。**2** 菲律賓共和國(含整個菲律賓羣島,首都爲 Manila)。

Phnom Penh, Pnompenh /ˈpnɒm ˈpen; ˈ(p)nɔmˈpɛn/ 金邊(Cambodia 之首都)。

Ph(o)enicia /fɪˈnɪʃɪə ; fɪˈnɪʃ(ɪ)ə/ 腓尼基(敘利亞西部瀕地中海之古國名)。

Phoenix /ˈfiːnɪks ; ˈfinɪks/ 費尼克斯(美國亞利桑那州之首府)。

Pidurutalagala /ˌpɪdəruːtəˈlɑːgələ ; ˌpɪdəˌrutl̩ˈɑgələ/ 彼德路特拉格勒山(在斯里蘭卡中央省南部)。

Pietermaritzburg /ˌpiːtəˈmærɪtsbɜːg ; ˌpitɚˈmærɪtsˌbɝg/ 彼得馬利堡(南非共和國納塔耳省之首府)。

Pikes Peak /paɪks- ; paɪks-/ 皮克峯(在美國科羅拉多州中東部)。

Pilcomayo /ˌpiːlkəʊˈmɑːjəʊ ; ˌpɪlkəˈmaɪo/ 比可馬約河(在南美洲中南部,注於巴拉圭河)。

Pilsen /ˈpɪlzən ; ˈpɪlzən/ 皮耳森(亦稱 Plzen /ˈpʌlzen ; ˈpʌlˌzɛn/, 捷克西部一城市)。

Pingtung /ˈpɪŋˈtʌŋ ; ˈpɪŋˈtʌŋ/ 屏東(中國臺灣省南部一縣,又其縣治名)。

Pisa /ˈpiːzə ; ˈpizə/ 比薩(義大利中西部一城市)。

Pittsburg /ˈpɪtsbɜːg ; ˈpɪtsˌbɝg/ 匹次堡(美國加利福尼亞州西部一城市)。

Pittsburgh /ˈpɪtsbɜːg ; ˈpɪtsˌbɝg/ 匹玆堡(美國賓夕法尼亞州西南部一城市)。

Plata, Río de la /ˈriːəʊdələˈplɑːtə ; ˌrioˌdɛləˈplatə/ 拉巴拉他河口(在烏拉圭與阿根廷之間,亦稱 River Plate)。

Ploesti /plɔːˈjeʃt ; plɔˈ(j)ɛʃt(ɪ)/ 普洛什特(羅馬尼亞東南部一城市)。

Plymouth /ˈplɪməθ ; ˈplɪməθ/ 普里茅斯(英格蘭西南部一港市)。

Po /pəʊ ; po/ 波河(在義大利北部,注入地中海)。

Poitiers /pwɑːˈtjeɪ ; pwɑˈtje/ 普瓦泰(法國中西部一城市)。

Poland /ˈpəʊlənd ; ˈpolənd/ 波蘭(歐洲中東部一國家,首都爲 Warsaw)。

Polynesia /ˌpɒlɪˈniːzjə ; ˌpaləˈniʒə/ 玻里尼西亞(西太平洋諸島之總稱)。

Pomona /pəˈməʊnə ; pəˈmonə/ 波姆那(美國加利福尼亞州西南部一城市)。

Pompeii /pɒmˈpiːaɪ ; pamˈpe/ 龐貝(義大利西南部一古城,於公元 79 年因維蘇威火山爆發而埋入地下)。

Pondicherry /ˌpɒndɪˈtʃerɪ ; ˌpandəˈtʃɛrɪ/ 彭地治利(印度東南部一地區,又該區之首府)。

Poole /puːl ; pul/ 浦耳(英格蘭南部一城市)。

Poona /ˈpuːnə ; ˈpunə/ 波那(印度西部一城市)。

Popocatepetl /ˈpɒpəˌkætɪˈpetl ; ˌpopəˌkætəˈpɛtl̩/ 煙峯(墨西哥東南部一火山)。

Pori /ˈpɔːrɪ ; ˈpɔrɪ/ 波里(芬蘭西南部一港埠)。

Porkkala Peninsula /ˈpɔːkələ- ; ˈpɔrkələ-/ 包加拉半島(在芬蘭南部)。

Port Arthur /-ˈɑːθə(r) ; -ˈɑrθɚ/ **1** 旅順港(現稱 Lüshun)。**2** 阿瑟港(在美國德克薩斯州東南部)。

Port-au-Prince /ˌpɔːtəʊˈprɪns ; ˌportoˈprɪns/ 太子港(Haiti 之首都)。

Port Louis /-ˈluːɪs ; -ˈluɪs/ 路易士港(Mauritius 之首都)。

Port Moresby /-ˈmɔːzbɪ;-ˈmorzbɪ/ 摩爾斯貝港(Papua New Guinea 之首都)。

Port of Spain, Port-of-Spain 西班牙港 (Trinidad and Tobago 之首都)。

Porto-Novo /ˈpɔːtəʊ ˈnəʊvəʊ ; ˌportə ˈnovo/ 新港(Benin 之首都)。

Porto Rico /ˌpɔːtəʊ ˈriːkəʊ ; ˌportə ˈriko/ 見 Puerto Rico。

Port Said /-ˈsaɪd ; -sɑˈid/ 塞得港(在埃及東北部,蘇伊士運河之北端)。

Portsmouth /ˈpɔːtsməθ ; ˈportsməθ/ 朴次茅斯 (**1** 英格蘭南部一城市; **2** 美國維吉尼亞州東南部一港埠; **3** 美國新罕布夏州東南部一港埠)。

Portugal /ˈpɔːtʃʊgl ; ˈportʃəgl/ 葡萄牙(歐洲西南部一國家,濱大西洋,首都爲 Lisbon)。

Portuguese East Africa 葡屬東非洲 (參看 Mozambique)。

Portuguese Guinea 葡屬幾內亞(參看 Guinea-Bissau)。

Portuguese West Africa 葡屬西非洲(參看 Angola)。

Posen /ˈpəʊzən ; ˈpozn̩/ 坡森(波蘭中西部一城市,波蘭名 Poznań)。

Potomac /pəˈtəʊmæk ; pəˈtomək/ 波多馬克河(自美國西維吉尼亞州流入乞沙比克灣)。

Potosi /ˌpɒtəʊˈsiː ; ˌpotəˈsi/ 波多西(玻利維亞南部一城市)。

Potsdam /ˈpɒtsdæm ; ˈpatsˌdæm/ 波茨坦(德國柏林西南一城市)。

Powys /ˈpaʊɪs ; ˈpoəs/ 泡易斯(威爾斯中東部一郡)。

Poyang Hu /ˈpəʊˈjɑːŋ ˈhuː ; ˈpoˈjaŋ ˈhu/ 鄱陽湖(在中國江西省北部)。

Poznań /ˈpɔːznɑːnjə ; ˈpozˌnæn(jə)/ 波玆蘭 (參看 Posen)。

Prague /prɑːg; prag/ 布拉格(Czechoslovakia 之首都)。

Praia /ˈpraɪɑː ; ˈpraɪə/ 培賴亞(Cape Verde 之首都)。

Preston /ˈprestən ; ˈprɛstən/ 普勒斯頓(英格蘭西北部一城市)。

Pretoria /prɪˈtɔːrɪə ; prɪˈtorɪə/ 普利托里亞 (South Africa 之行政首都)。

Prince Edward Island 愛德華島(加拿大一省,在其東南之聖羅倫斯灣中,略作 *PEI*)。

Princeton /ˈprɪnstən ; ˈprɪnstən/ 普林斯頓(美國新澤西州中西部一城市)。

Providence /ˈprɒvɪdəns ; ˈpravədəns/ 普洛維頓斯(美國羅德島州一港埠,爲該州之首府)。

Prussia /ˈprʌʃə ; ˈprʌʃə/ 普魯士(德國北部一地區,昔爲一王國)。

Puerto Rico /ˈpwɜːtəʊ ˈriːkəʊ ; ˌpwɛrtə ˈriko/ 波多黎各(西印度羣島東部一島,屬美國,首府爲 San Juan)。

Pulog /ˈpuːlɔːg ; ˈpuˌlɔg/ 普洛山(在菲律賓呂宋島北部)。

Punakha /ˈpʊnəkə ; ˈpunəkə/ 普那卡(不丹之多都)。

Punjab, Panjab /ˈpʌnˈdʒɑːb ; ˌpʌnˈdʒab/ 旁遮普(印度次大陸西北一地區)。

Purbeck, Isle of /ˈpɜːbek ; ˈpɝˌbɛk/ 波白克半島(在英

格蘭南部)。
Purus /pu:'ru:s ; pə'rus/ 普魯司河(在南美洲中部)。
Pusan /'pu:sɑ:n ; 'pu,san/ 釜山(韓國東南部一港市)。
Puto Shan /'pu:'tɔ: 'ʃɑ:n ; 'pu'to 'ʃan/ 普陀山(中國舟山羣島中一小島,爲中國三大佛教聖地之一)。
Pyongyang /'pjɒŋ'jæŋ ; pɪ'ɔŋ,jaŋ/ 平壤(North Korea之首都)。
Pyrenees /,pɪrə'ni:z ; 'pɪrə,niz/ 庇里牛斯山脈(在法、西兩國邊境)。
Qatar /'kʌtɑ:(r) ; 'katɚ/ 卡達(亦作 Katar, 阿拉伯半島東部波斯灣沿岸一小酋長國, 於 1971 年 9 月獨立, 首都爲 Doha)。
Qatif, Katif /kɒ'ti:f ; ka'tif/ 卡提夫(沙烏地阿拉伯東部一海港,瀕波斯灣)。
Quebec /kwɪ'bek ; kwɪ'bɛk/ 魁北克(加拿大東部一省,略作 *Que*, 又該省之首府)。
Queen Alexandra Range /-,ælɪg'zɑ:ndrə- ; -,ælɪg-'zændrə-/ 亞歷山竹山脈(在南極洲)。
Queen Maud Mountains /-mɔ:d- ; -mɔd-/ 莫德山脈(在南極洲)。
Queensland /'kwi:nzlənd ; 'kwinz,lænd/ 昆士蘭(澳洲東北部一邦,略作 *Qld*)。
Quemoy /'kweɪ'mɒɪ ; k(w)ɪ'mɔɪ/ = Kinmen。
Quincy[1] /'kwɪnsɪ ; 'kwɪnsɪ/ 昆西(美國伊利諾州西部一城市)。
Quincy[2] /'kwɪnzɪ ; 'kwɪnzɪ/ 昆依(美國麻薩諸塞州東部一城市)。
Quito /'ki:təʊ ; 'kito/ 基多(Ecuador 之首都)。
Rabat /rə'bɑ:t ; rə'bɑt/ 拉巴特(Morocco 之首都)。
Racine /rə'si:n ; rə'sin/ 拉辛(美國威斯康辛州東南部一城市)。
Radnorshire /'rædnəʃə(r) ; 'rædnɚ,ʃɪr/ 拉德奈夏(昔爲威爾斯東部一郡)。
Rainier, Mount /reɪ'ni:ə(r) ; rə'nir/ 來尼爾峯(在美國華盛頓州中西部)。
Rakaposhi /,rʌkə'pɔ:ʃɪ ; ,rʌkə'pɔʃɪ/ 勒卡泡歇峯(在喀什米爾北部之喀拉崑崙山脈中)。
Raleigh /'rɔ:lɪ ; 'rɔlɪ/ 洛利(美國北卡羅來納州之首府)。
Rangoon /ræŋ'gu:n ; ræŋ'gun/ 仰光(Burma 之首都)。
Rantemario /,rɑ:ntə'mɑ:rɪəʊ ; ,rantə'marɪ,o/ 蘭特馬里奧山(在印尼西里伯島西南部)。
Ras Dashan /'rɑ:s dɑ:'ʃɑ:n ; ,ras də'ʃan/ 大祥山(在非洲衣索比亞北部)。
Ravenna /rə'venə ; rə'vɛnə/ 拉溫那(義大利北部一城市)。
Rawalpindi /,rɑ:vəl'pɪndi: ; ,rawəl'pɪndɪ/ 洛瓦平第(巴基斯坦東北部一城市)。
Red River 紅河 (**1** 在美國中南部,發源於新墨西哥州,流經德克薩斯等州,注入密西西比河; **2** 在越南北部,注入東京灣)。
Red Sea 紅海(介於非洲與阿拉伯半島間)。
Regina /rɪ'dʒaɪnə ; rɪ'dʒaɪnə/ 利宅那(加拿大南部一城市)。
Reims, Rheims /ri:mz ; rimz/ 理姆斯(法國東北部一城市)。
Renfrewshire /'renfru:ʃə(r) ; 'rɛnfru,ʃɪr/ 藍夫魯夏(昔爲蘇格蘭西南部一郡)。
Reunion /ri:'ju:njən ; ri'junjən/ 留尼旺島(在印度洋西部,馬達加斯加島以東,屬法國)。
Reykjavik /'reɪkjə,vɪk ; 'rek(j)ə,vɪk/ 雷克雅維克(Iceland 之首都)。
Rhaetian Alps /'ri:ʃɪən- ; 'riʃən-/ 里申阿爾卑斯山(在瑞士東南部)。
Rhine /raɪn ; raɪn/ 萊茵河(自瑞士東南部經德國流入北海)。
Rhode Island /,rəʊd'aɪlənd ; rod'aɪlənd/ 羅德島(美國東北部一州,略作 *RI*)。
Rhodesia /rəʊ'di:zjə ; ro'diʒ(ɪ)ə/ 羅德西亞(非洲中南部一地區,包括 Northern Rhodesia 和 Southern Rhodesia 兩部分, 前者已於 1964 年獨立, 易名爲 Zambia; 後者於 1970 年自行宣佈獨立, 並於 1980 年改組新政府易名爲 Zimbabwe)。
Rhodope /'rɒdəpɪ ; 'rɑdəpɪ/ 洛多皮山脈(在保加利亞西南部)。
Rhone /rəʊn ; ron/ 隆河(在法國東南部,注於地中海)。
Richmond /'rɪtʃmənd ; 'rɪtʃmənd/ 里乞蒙 (**1** 美國維吉尼亞州之首府; **2** 美國印第安納州東部一城市; **3** 美國加利福尼亞州西部一海港)。
Riga /'ri:gə ; 'rigə/ 里加(蘇聯拉脫維亞北部一城市,爲其首府)。
Rindjani /rɪn'jɑ:nɪ ; rɪn'janɪ/ 潤亞尼峯(在印尼龍目島北部)。
Rio de Janeiro /'ri:əʊ də dʒə'nɪərəʊ ; 'rio ,de ʒə-'nero/ 里約熱內盧(在巴西瓜那白拉灣之西南部,爲巴西舊都)。
Rio Grande /'ri:əʊ 'grɑ:ndə ; ,rio 'grænd(ɪ)/ 里奧格蘭河(在美國與墨西哥之間)。
Riviera /,rɪvɪ'eərə ; ,rɪvɪ'ɛrə/ 里維耶拉(法國東南部及義大利西北部之海岸地區,濱地中海)。
Riyadh /ri:'jɑ:d ; ri'jad/ 利雅德(Saudi Arabia 之首都)。
Roanoke /,rəʊə'nəʊk ; 'ro(ə),nok/ 洛亞諾克(美國維吉尼亞州中西部一城市)。
Robson, Mount /'rɒbsn ; 'rɑbsn̩/ 洛布孫峯(在加拿大西南部)。
Rochdale /'rɒtʃdeɪl ; 'ratʃ,del/ 洛支旦(英格蘭西北部一城市)。
Rochester /'rɒtʃɪstə(r) ; 'ratʃəstɚ/ 羅契斯特(美國紐約州西部一城市)。
Rocky Mountains /'rɒkɪ ; 'rakɪ/ 落磯山脈(北美洲西部一山脈)。
Romania /rə'meɪnɪə ; ru'menɪə/ 羅馬尼亞(亦作 Rumania 或 Roumania, 歐洲東南部一國家,濱黑海,首都 Bucharest)。
Rome /rəʊm ; rom/ 羅馬(Italy 之首都)。
Romford /'rɒmfəd ; 'ramfɚd/ 羅木福得(昔爲英格蘭東南部一城市)。
Rosa, Monte /'rəʊzə ; 'rozə/ 羅沙峯(在瑞士與義大利邊境)。
Roscommon /rɒs'kɒmən ; rɑs'kɑmən/ 羅斯哥蒙(愛爾蘭中部一郡,又該郡之首府)。
Roseau /rəʊ'zəʊ ; ro'zo/ 羅梭(Dominica 之首都)。
Ross and Cromarty /,rɒs ən 'krɒmətɪ ; 'rɔs ən 'kramɚtɪ/ 羅斯可麥提(昔爲蘇格蘭北部一郡)。
Ross Sea /rɒs- ; rɔs-/ 羅斯海(南冰洋一海灣)。
Rostov /'rɒstɒv ; rə'stɔf/ 羅斯托夫(蘇聯歐洲部分東南部一城市)。
Rotherham /'rɒðərəm ; 'raðərəm/ 羅塞蘭(英格蘭北部一城市)。
Rotterdam /'rɒtədæm ; 'ratɚ,dæm/ 鹿特丹(荷蘭西南部一港埠)。
Rouen /'ru:ɑ:ŋ ; ru'an/ 盧昂(法國北部一港市)。
Roumania = Romania。
Rovaniemi /'rɔ:vɑ:ni:emi: ; 'rovən,iəmɪ/ 洛瓦奈密(芬蘭北部一城市)。
Roxburghshire /'rɒksbrəʃə(r) ; 'raksbərə,ʃɪr/ 羅斯勃洛夏(昔爲蘇格蘭東南部一郡)。
Ruanda 參看 Rwanda。
Ruapehu /,ru:ə'peɪhu: ; ,ruə'pehu/ 魯亞帕和峯(在紐西蘭北島中南部)。
Rubicon /'ru:bɪkən ; 'rubɪ,kan/ 盧比孔河(在義大利中北部)。
Rudolf, Lake /'ru:dɒlf ; 'ru,dalf/ 羅多夫湖(在非洲肯亞北部)。
Rugby /'rʌgbɪ ; 'rʌgbɪ/ 拉格比(英格蘭中部一城市)。
Ruhr /rʊə(r) ; rʊr/ **1** 魯爾河(在德國西部)。**2** 魯爾區(沿魯爾河之礦業及工業區)。
Rumania = Romania。
Russia /'rʌʃə ; 'rʌʃə/ **1** 俄羅斯(蘇聯一加盟共和國)。**2** 蘇聯之通稱。
Ruthenia /ru:'θi:njə ; ru'θinɪə/ 羅塞尼亞(蘇聯一地區,在烏克蘭西部,昔爲捷克斯拉夫之一省)。
Rutland /'rʌtlənd ; 'rʌtlənd/ 拉特蘭(美國佛蒙特州中西部一城市)。
Rutland(shire) /'rʌtlənd(ʃə(r)) ; 'rʌtlənd(,ʃɪr)/ 拉特蘭夏(昔爲英格蘭中東部一郡)。
Ruwenzori /,ru:wən'zəʊrɪ ; ,ru(w)ən'zorɪ/ 羅溫乍里山脈(在非洲中東部)。
Rwanda /rʊ'ændə ; rʊ'ɑndə/ 盧安達(非洲中東部一共和國, 1962 年 7 月獨立,首都爲 Kigali)。
Rye /raɪ ; raɪ/ 瑞埃(英格蘭東南部一城市)。

Ryukyu /riːˈuːkuː ; riˈ(j)uk(j)u/ 琉球(西太平洋一羣島嶼,在臺灣之東北,日本之西南)。
Saarland /ˈsɑːlænd ; ˈsɑrˌlænd/ 薩爾區(德國西南部一地區,現爲西德一州)。
Sabah /ˈsʌbə ; ˈsɑbə/ 沙巴(在婆羅洲東北部,昔爲英國殖民地,1963年成爲馬來西亞一州)。
Sabine /sæˈbiːn ; səˈbin/ 色賓河(源於美國德克薩斯州東北部,沿路易西安那和德克薩斯邊境流入墨西哥灣)。
Sacramento /ˌsækrəˈmentəʊ ; ˌsækrəˈmɛnto/ **1** 薩克拉曼多(美國加利福尼亞州之首府)。 **2** 薩克拉曼多河(在加州北部)。**3** 薩克拉曼多山脈(在美國新墨西哥州南部)。
Saghalien /ˌsægəˈliːn ; ˈsægəˌlin/ 參看 Sakhalin。
Sahara, the /səˈhɑːrə ; səˈhærə/ 撒哈拉(非洲北部之大沙漠)。
Saigon /saɪˈgɒn ; saɪˈgɑn/ 西貢(參看 Ho Chi Minh City)。
Saint-Étienne /ˌsenteɪˈtjen ; ˌsænteˈtjɛn/ 聖德堅(法國東南部一城市)。
Sakhalin /ˌsɑːkɑːˈliːn ; ˈsækəˌlin/ 庫頁島(舊稱 Saghalien, 在日本北海道以北,屬蘇聯)。
Salado /sɑːˈlɑːðəʊ ; səˈlɑdo/ 沙拉索河(**1** 在阿根廷北部,注於巴拉那河; **2** 在阿根廷東部,注入拉布拉他河)。
Salamanca /ˌsæləˈmæŋkə ; ˌsæləˈmæŋkə/ 塞拉曼加(西班牙西部一省,又該省之首府)。
Salem /ˈseɪlem ; ˈseləm/ 賽倫 (**1** 美國麻薩諸塞州東北部一港市; **2** 美國俄勒岡州之首府)。
Salford /ˈsɔːlfəd ; ˈsɔlfɚd/ 索福特(英格蘭西北部一城市)。
Salisbury /ˈsɔːlzbrɪ ; ˈsɔlzˌbɛrɪ/ **1** 索爾斯堡(英格蘭南部一城市)。**2** 索斯柏里(Zimbabwe 之首都)。
Salonika, Salonica /səˈlɒnɪkə ; səˈlɑnɪkə/ 薩羅尼加(希臘東北部一海港)。
Salop /ˈsæləp ; ˈsæləp/ 塞洛浦(英格蘭西部一郡)。
Salvador /ˈsælvədɔː(r) ; ˈsælvəˌdɔr/ 薩爾瓦多 (**1** 參看 El Salvador; **2** 巴西東北部一海港)。
Salween /ˈsælwiːn ; ˈsælˌwin/ 薩爾溫江(卽怒江,在亞洲東南部,源於西藏,流入緬甸之瑪打萬灣)。
Salzburg /ˈsæltsbɜːg ; ˈsɔlzˌbɝg/ 薩爾斯堡(奧國西部一城市)。
Samaria /səˈmeərɪə ; səˈmɛrɪə/ 撒馬利亞 (**1** 巴勒斯坦北部一古國; **2** 其首都)。
Samarkand /sæməˈkænd ; ˈsæmɚˌkænd/ 撒馬爾罕(蘇聯烏玆別克東部一城市)。
Samoa /səˈməʊə ; səˈmoə/ 薩摩亞羣島(在中太平洋西南部,分爲 American ~ 和 Western ~ 二部分)。
Samos /ˈseɪmɒs ; ˈseˌmɑs/ 薩摩斯島(在愛琴海中,屬希臘)。
Samothrace /ˈsæməθreɪs ; ˈsæməˌθres/ 撒摩得拉斯島(在愛琴海東北部,屬希臘)。
San'a, Sanaa /sɑːˈnɑː ; ˈsænˌɑ/ 沙那(Yemen Arab Republic 之首都)。
San Bernardino /ˈsænˌbɜːnəˈdiːnəʊ ; ˈsænˌbɝnɚˈdino/ 聖布那的諾山脈(在美國加州南部)。
San Diego /ˌsændɪˈeɪgəʊ ; ˌsændiˈego/ 聖地牙哥(美國加州西南部一港市)。
Sanford, Mount /ˈsænfəd ; ˈsænfɚd/ 聖福峯(在阿拉斯加南境)。
San Francisco /ˌsænfrənˈsɪskəʊ ; ˌsænfrənˈsɪsko/ 舊金山;三藩市(美國加州太平洋岸之大城)。
San Gorgonio /ˌsæŋgɔːˈgəʊnɪəʊ ; ˌsæŋgɔrˈgonɪo/ 桑哥弓尼奧峯(在美國加州南部)。
Sangre de Cristo /ˈsæŋgrɪdəˈkrɪstəʊ ; ˌsæŋgrɪdəˈkrɪsto/ 桑格累得克利斯托山脈(在美國科羅拉多州南部與新墨西哥州北部)。
San José /sɑːnhəʊˈseɪ ; ˌsæn(h)oˈze/ 聖約瑟 (Costa Rica 之首都)。
San Juan /sæn ˈhwɑːn ; sæn ˈ(h)wɑn/ 聖胡安(Puerto Rico 之首府)。
San Marino /ˌsænməˈriːnəʊ ; ˌsænməˈrino/ 聖馬利諾(義大利半島東部一小共和國,首都 San Marino)。
San Remo /sænˈreɪməʊ ; sænˈremo/ 聖利摩(義大利西北部一海港)。
San Salvador /sænˈsælvədɔː(r) ; sænˈsælvəˌdɔr/ 聖薩爾瓦多(El Salvador 之首都)。
Santa Ana /ˈsæntə ˈænə ; ˌsæntə ˈænə/ 聖大阿那(美國加州西南部一城市)。
Santa Isabel /ˌsæntə ˈɪzəbel ; ˌsæntəˈɪzəˌbɛl/ 聖伊斯貝爾(Malabo 之舊稱)。
Santiago /ˌsæntɪˈɑːgəʊ ; ˌsæntɪˈɑgo/ 聖地牙哥(Chile 之首都)。
Santo Domingo /ˌsæntəʊ dəˈmɪŋgəʊ ; ˌsæntə dəˈmɪŋgo/ 聖多明哥(Dominican Republic 之舊稱,亦爲其首都名)。
Santos /ˈsæntəs ; ˈsæntəs/ 聖多斯(巴西東南部一港市)。
São Francisco /ˌsaʊnfrənˈsiːskuː ; ˌsaʊnfrənˈsɪsko/ 三藩河(在巴西東部)。
São Paulo /saʊn ˈpaʊləʊ ; saʊn ˈpaʊlʊ/ 聖保羅(巴西東南部一省;又該省之首府)。
São Tomé /ˌsaʊntəˈmeɪ ; ˌsaʊntəˈme/ 聖多美 (São Tomé and Principe 之首都)。
São Tomé and Principe /ˌsaʊntəˈmeɪ ənd ˈprɪnsəpə; ˌsaʊntəˈme ənd ˈprɪnsəpə/ 聖多美及普林西比共和國(西非一島國,原屬葡萄牙,於1975年7月獨立,首都爲 São Tomé)。
Sapporo /səˈpəʊrəʊ ; ˈsɑpəˌro/ 札幌(日本北海道西部一城市)。
Saragossa /ˌsærəˈgɒsə ; ˌsærəˈgɑsə/ 撒拉哥沙(亦稱 Zaragoza, 西班牙東北部一省,又該省之首府)。
Saratoga /ˌsærəˈtəʊgə ; ˌsærəˈtogə/ 薩拉多加(美國紐約州東部一村鎮, 1777年 Gates 敗 Burgoyne 於此)。
Saratov /sʌˈrɑːtəf ; səˈrɑtəf/ 薩拉多夫(蘇聯歐洲部東南一城市)。
Sarawak /səˈrɑːwæk ; səˈrɑwɑk/ 沙撈越(在婆羅洲西北部,爲馬來西亞之一州,首府 Kuching)。
Sardinia /sɑːˈdɪnjə ; sɑrˈdɪnjə/ 薩丁尼亞(義大利一島嶼,在科西嘉島以南)。
Sardis /ˈsɑːdɪs ; ˈsɑrdɪs/ 薩狄斯(古代 Lydia 之首都)。
Sasebo /ˈsɑːsəˌbəʊ ; ˈsɑsəˌbo/ 佐世保(日本九州西北部一港埠)。
Saskatchewan /səˈskætʃəwən ; səsˈkætʃəwən/ 薩斯克其萬 (**1** 加拿大西南部一省,略作 *Sask*; **2** 加拿大中南部一河流)。
Saudi Arabia /ˌsaʊdɪ- ; ˌsaʊdɪ-/ 沙烏地阿拉伯(阿拉伯半島上一王國, 1927年5月獨立,首都爲 Riyadh)。
Sawatch Range /səˈwɒtʃ- ; səˈwɑtʃ-/ 撒瓦琪山脈(亦作 Saguache ~, 在美國科羅拉多州中部)。
Saxony /ˈsæksnɪ ; ˈsæks(ə)nɪ/ 薩克森 (**1** 德國西北部一地區; **2** 德國東部一地區)。
Sayan /sɑːˈjɑːn ; səˈjɑn/ 薩彥山脈(在中國之蒙古與西伯利亞之間)。
Scafell Pike /ˈskɔːˈfel ˈpaɪk ; ˈskɔˈfɛl ˈpaɪk/ 斯可斐峯(在英格蘭之西北部)。
Scandinavia /ˌskændɪˈneɪvjə ; ˌskændəˈnevjə/ **1** 斯堪的那維亞(挪威,瑞典,丹麥,冰島和芬蘭之總稱)。 **2** 斯堪的那維亞半島(在北歐,爲挪威及瑞典之所在地)。
Scapa Flow /ˈskæpəˈfləʊ ; ˌskæpəˈflo/ 斯卡帕佛洛(蘇格蘭北部 Orkney 羣島間一內海)。
Schenectady /skɪˈnektədɪ ; skəˈnɛktədɪ/ 斯克奈塔第(美國紐約州東部一城市)。
Schiedam /ˈskiːdæm ; skiˈdæm/ 斯奇丹(荷蘭西南部一城市)。
Schleswig /ˈʃlezwɪg ; ˈʃlɛzwɪg/ 什列斯威格(德國西北部一地區)。
Schouten /ˈskaʊtən ; ˈskaʊtn̩/ 叔騰羣島(在新幾內亞之西北,屬印尼)。
Schuylkill /ˈskuːlkɪl ; ˈskulˌkɪl/ 斯古吉爾河(在美國賓夕法尼亞州東南部)。
Scilly /ˈsɪlɪ ; ˈsɪlɪ/ 夕利羣島(在英格蘭西南)。
Scotland /ˈskɒtlənd ; ˈskɑtlənd/ 蘇格蘭(英國一區,在大不列顛島北部,首府爲 Edinburgh)。
Scythia /ˈsɪðɪə ; ˈsɪθɪə/ 塞西亞(歐亞兩洲間一古國)。
Seattle /sɪˈætl ; siˈætl̩/ 西雅圖(美國華盛頓州西部一海港)。
Sedan /sɪˈdæn ; sɪˈdæn/ 色當(法國東北部一城市)。
Seine /seɪn ; sen/ 塞納河(在法國北部,向西北流入英吉利海峽)。
Selangor /səˈlæŋə(r) ; səˈlæŋɚ/ 雪蘭峨(馬來西亞一州,在麻六甲海峽)。
Selkirk /ˈselkɜːk ; ˈsɛlˌkɝk/ 塞扣克山(落磯山一支脈,在加拿大西南境)。

Selkirkshire /ˈselkɜːkʃə(r) ; ˈsɛlkɚk,ʃɪr/ 塞扣克夏(昔爲蘇格蘭東南部一郡)。
Semarang /səˈmɑːrɑːŋ ; səˈmɑr,ɑŋ/ 三寶壠(印尼爪哇北部海岸一大商港)。
Senegal /ˌsenɪˈgɔːl ; ˌsɛnɪˈgɔl/ 塞內加爾 (**1** 非洲西海岸一共和國,原爲法國屬地,1960 年 8 月獨立,首都 Dakar; **2** 非洲西部一河流,注於大西洋)。
Seoul /səul ; sol/ 漢城(South Korea 之首都)。
Serbia /ˈsɜːbjə ; ˈsɝbɪə/ 塞爾維亞(昔爲巴爾幹半島上一王國,今爲南斯拉夫東南部一地區)。
Seville /ˈsevɪl ; səˈvɪl/ 塞維爾(西班牙西南部一省,又該省之首府)。
Sèvres /ˈseɪvə(r) ; ˈsevɚ/ 塞弗爾(法國北部一城市,在巴黎之西南方)。
Seward Peninsula /ˈsiːwəd- ; ˈsuɚd-/ 西華德半島(在白令海峽,阿拉斯加西部)。
Seychelles, (The) /ˈseɪʃelz ; seˈʃɛl(z)/ 塞席爾(印度洋西部,馬達加斯加島之東北一羣島,原屬英,於 1976 年 6 月獨立,首都爲 Victoria)。
Sham, Jebel /ˈdʒebl ˈʃæm ; ˌdʒɛbl̩ ˈʃæm/ 夏姆峯(阿拉伯半島東南部阿曼之最高峯)。
Shanghai /ˈʃæŋˈhaɪ ; ˈʃæŋ ˈhaɪ/ 上海(中國東部一港市,近長江口)。
Shanhaikwan /ˈʃɑːnˈhaɪˈgwɑːn ; ˈʃɑn ˈhaɪ ˈgwɑn/ 山海關(亦稱 Linyu, 在河北省東北部,爲萬里長城之起點)。
Shansi /ˈʃɑːnˈsiː ; ˈʃɑn ˈsi/ 山西(中國北部一省)。
Shantung /ˈʃɑːnˈtʌŋ ; ˈʃæn ˈtʌŋ/ 山東(中國東部一省)。
Sharon /ˈʃeərɒn ; ˈʃɛrən/ 沙倫(美國賓夕法尼亞州西北部一城市)。
Shasta, Mount /ˈʃæstə ; ˈʃæstə/ 沙斯塔峯(在美國加州北部)。
Shawnee /ˈʃɔːniː ; ʃɔˈni/ 雪里(美國俄克拉荷馬州中部一城市)。
Sheba /ˈʃiːbə ; ˈʃibə/ 希巴(阿拉伯半島南部一古國,卽今之 Yemen 地方)。
Sheffield /ˈʃefiːld;ˈʃɛf,ild/ 雪非耳(英格蘭北部一城市)。
Shensi /ˈʃenˈsiː ; ˈʃɛnˈsi/ 陝西(中國中北部一省)。
Shenyang /ˈʃənˈjɑːŋ ; ˈʃənˈjɑŋ/ 瀋陽(亦稱 Mukden, 中國遼寧省省會)。
Shetland /ˈʃetlənd ; ˈʃɛtlənd/ 謝德蘭羣島(位於蘇格蘭北方,自成一區)。
Shikoku /ʃɪˈkəukuː ; ʃɪˈkoku/ 四國(日本南部一島嶼,位於九州之東)。
Shimonoseki /ˌʃɪməunəuˈsekɪ ; ˌʃɪmənoˈsɛkɪ/ 下關(日本本州西南部一港市,舊名馬關)。
Shiraz /ˈʃɪəræz ; ʃɪˈrɑz/ 夕拉玆(伊朗西南部一城市)。
Shkara Tau /ˈʃkɑːrəˈtau ; ˌʃəkərəˈtau/ 希卡拉陶山(在蘇聯歐洲部之南部)。
Shrewsbury /ˈʃruːzbrɪ ; ˈʃruz,bɛrɪ/ 舒玆伯利 (英格蘭西部一城市,爲 Salop 之首府)。
Shropshire /ˈʃrɒpʃə(r);ˈʃrɑp,ʃɪr/ 什羅浦郡(參看Salop)。
Shuri /ˈʃurɪ ; ˈʃurɪ/ 首里(琉球南端一城市)。
Siam /ˈsaɪæm ; saɪˈæm/ 暹羅(參看 Thailand)。
Sian /ˈʃiːˈɑːn;ˈʃiˈɑn/ 西安(中國陝西省省會,舊名Changan長安)。
Siberia /saɪˈbɪərɪə ; saɪˈbɪrɪə/ 西伯利亞(蘇聯亞洲部分自烏拉山以迄太平洋之間的地區)。
Sicily /ˈsɪsɪlɪ ; ˈsɪs(ɪ)lɪ/ 西西里島(屬義大利,在其南端)。
Sidon /ˈsaɪdn ; ˈsaɪdn̩/ 希登(黎巴嫩西南部一港埠)。
Siena, Sienna /sɪˈenə ; sɪˈɛnə/ 西恩那(義大利中部一城市)。
Sierra Leone /sɪˌerə lɪˈəun ; sɪˌɛrəlɪˈon/ 獅子山國(西非一國,1961 年 4 月獨立,首都爲 Freetown)。
Sierra Madre Oriental /-ˈmædre ˌɔːrɪˈentl ; -ˌmædrɪ ˌorɪ,ɛnˈtal/ 東塞拉馬德雷山脈(在北美墨西哥東部)。
Sierra Nevada /-nəˈvædə ; -nəˈvædə/ 內華達山脈 (**1** 在美國加州東部; **2** 在西班牙南部)。
Sikang /ˈʃiːˈkɑːŋ ; ˈʃiˈkɑŋ/ 西康(中國西南一省)。
Si-kiang /ˈʃiːdʒɪˈɑːŋ;ˈʃidʒɪˈɑŋ/ 西江(中國東南部一河流)。
Sikkim /ˈsɪkɪm ; ˈsɪkəm/ 錫金(原印度之保護國,位於西藏與印度之間,於1975年成爲印度一省,首府爲 Gangtok)。
Silesia /saɪˈliːzjə ; saɪˈliʒ(ɪ)ə/ 西利西亞 (東歐中部一地區,在捷克北部及波蘭西南部)。
Simla /ˈsɪmlə ; ˈsɪmlə/ 西姆拉(印度北部一城市)。
Simplon /ˈsɪmplən ; ˈsɪm,plɑn/ 辛普倫(瑞士與義大利間一大隧道)。
Simyen Mountains /sɪˈmjeɪn- ; sɪˈmjen-/ 西米恩山脈(亦作 Semien mountains, 在東非衣索比亞北部)。
Sinai /ˈsaɪnaɪ ; ˈsaɪ,naɪ/ 西奈半島(在埃及之東北)。
Singapore /ˌsɪŋgəˈpɔː(r) ; ˈsɪŋ(g)ə,por/ 新加坡(馬來羣島中之一島,原爲馬來西亞一部分,1965 年 8 月宣佈獨立,首都亦稱 Singapore)。
Singkep /ˈsɪŋkep ; ˈsɪŋ,kɛp/ 新開(印尼林加羣島西南部一島)。
Sining /ˈʃiːˈnɪŋ ; ˈʃiˈnɪŋ/ 西寧(中國青海省省會)。
Sinkiang /ˈʃɪndʒiːˈɑːŋ ; ˈʃɪndʒiˈɑŋ/ 新疆(中國西北一省)。
Sinuiju /ˈʃiniː,dʒuː ; ˈʃini,dʒu/ 新義州(韓國西北部一城市)。
Sioux City /suː-;su-/ 蘇城(美國愛阿華州西北部一城市)。
Skye /skaɪ ; skaɪ/ 斯開島(在蘇格蘭西北)。
Sligo /ˈslaɪgəu ; ˈslaɪgo/ 斯來哥(愛爾蘭共和國北部一郡,又該郡之首府)。
Slovakia /sləuˈvækɪə ; sloˈvɑkɪə/ 斯洛伐克(捷克東部一地區)。
Smethwick /ˈsmeðɪk ; ˈsmɛðɪk/ 斯麥細克(英格蘭中西部一城市)。
Smoky Hill 煙山河(在美國堪薩斯州中部,注於堪薩斯河)。
Snake 蛇河(在美國西北部,注於哥倫比亞河)。
Society Islands 社會羣島(在南太平洋,屬法國)。
Socotra, Sokotra /səˈkəutrə ; səˈkotrə/ 索科得拉島(在印度洋中,位於阿拉伯半島以南)。
Sofia /ˈsəufjə ; ˈsofɪə/ 索非亞(Bulgaria 之首都)。
Solomon Islands /ˈsɒləmən- ; ˈsɑləmən-/ 所羅門羣島(位於西太平洋,原屬英國,於 1978 年 7 月獨立,首都爲 Honiara)。
Solway Firth /ˈsɒlweɪ- ; ˈsɑlwe-/ 索耳威灣(在英格蘭與蘇格蘭之間)。
Somalia /səˈmɑːlɪə ; soˈmɑlɪə/ 索馬利亞(非洲東部一國家,1960 年 7 月獨立,首都爲 Mogadishu)。
Somaliland /səˈmɑːlɪlænd ; soˈmɑlɪ,lænd/ 索馬利蘭(東非一地區)。
Somali Republic /səˈmɑːlɪ- ; soˈmɑlɪ-/ 參看 Somalia。
Somerset(shire) /ˈsʌməsət(ʃə(r)) ; ˈsʌmɚsɛt(,ʃɪr)/ 索美塞得郡(英格蘭西南部一郡,略作 *Som*)。
Somerville /ˈsʌməvɪl ; ˈsʌmɚ,vɪl/ 薩莫維耳(美國麻薩諸塞州東部一城市)。
Soochow, Suchou /ˈsuːˈdʒəu ; ˈsuˈdʒo/ 蘇州 (參看 Wuhsien)。
Sound, the 松得海峽(亦稱 Öresund, 介於丹麥西蘭島與瑞典南部之間)。
South Africa, Republic of 南非共和國(昔稱南非聯邦,爲大英國協一自治領,1961 年成爲獨立共和國,首都爲 Pretoria, Capetown 和 Bloemfontein)。
South Australia 南澳大利亞(澳洲南部一邦,略作 *S Aus* 或 *S Austr*)。
South Carolina 南卡羅來納(美國東南部一州,略作 *SC*)。
South Dakota 南達科他(美國西北部一州,略作 *SD*)。
South(ern) Yemen 南葉門(參看 Yemen)。
South Glamorgan 南格拉馬干(威爾斯東南部一郡)。
South Korea 南韓(正式名稱爲 Republic of Korea 大韓民國,亞洲朝鮮半島南部一國,首都 Seoul)。
South-West Africa 西南非洲(參看 Namibia)。
South Yorkshire 南約克郡(英格蘭北部一郡)。
Soviet Union 蘇聯(歐洲東部及亞洲北部一國,正式名稱爲 Union of Soviet Socialist Republics 蘇維埃社會主義共和國聯邦,略作 U.S.S.R., 首都爲 Moscow)。
Spain /speɪn ; spen/ 西班牙(西南歐一國家,首都爲 Madrid)。
Spanish Guinea 西屬幾內亞(參看Equatorial Guinea)。
Sparta /ˈspɑːtə ; ˈspɑrtə/ 斯巴達(古希臘南部一重要城市)。
Spitsbergen /ˈspɪts,bɜːgən ; ˈspɪts,bɝgən/ 斯匹玆卑爾根羣島(位於北冰洋,屬挪威)。
Sri Lanka /ˌsrɪ ˈlæŋkə;srɪˈlɑŋkə/ 斯里蘭卡(昔稱Ceylon,印度洋上一島國,首都 Colombo)。
Srinagar /srɪˈnʌgə(r) ; srɪˈnʌgɚ/ 斯利那加(印度北部一城市)。
Stafford /ˈstæfəd ; ˈstæfɚd/ 斯塔福(英格蘭中西部斯塔福郡之首府)。
Staffordshire /ˈstæfədʃə(r) ; ˈstæfɚd,ʃɪr/ 斯塔福郡

(英格蘭中西部一郡,略作 *Staffs* /stæfs ; stæfs/)。
Stalingrad /ˈstɑːlɪngræd ; ˈstɑlɪn,græd/ 史太林格勒(蘇聯歐洲部分窩瓦河畔一城市,自 1961 年起更名爲 Volgograd)。
Stalino /ˈstɑːljɪnə ; ˈstɑlɪ,no/ 史太林諾(現稱 Donetsk, 蘇聯烏克蘭東部一城市)。
Stalin Peak /ˈstɑːlɪn- ; ˈstɑlɪn-/ 史太林峯(在蘇聯中亞塔吉克之東南,現稱 Communism Peak)。
Stalinsk /ˈstɑːlɪnsk ; ˈstɑlɪnsk/ 史太林斯克(蘇聯亞洲部分之西南部一城市,自1961年起更名爲 Novokuznetsk)。
Stamford /ˈstæmfəd ; ˈstæmfɚd/ 斯坦福(美國康乃狄格州西南部一城市)。
Stanley /ˈstænlɪ ; ˈstænlɪ/ **1** 斯坦萊峯(在非洲中東部,爲羅溫乍里山脈之最高峯)。**2** 斯坦萊(亦稱 Port ~, 英國福克蘭羣島之首府)。
Stassfurt /ˈʃtɑːsfʊət ; ˈstɑs,fʊrt/ 司塔斯弗(德國東部一城市)。
Stavanger /stɑːˈvɑːŋə(r) ; stəˈvɑŋɚ/ 斯塔凡格(挪威西南部一海港)。
St. Bernard /-ˈbɜːnəd ; -bɚˈnɑrd/ 聖伯納山隘(阿爾卑斯山兩山隘:一爲大聖伯納山隘,介於義大利與瑞士之間;一爲小聖伯納山隘,介於義大利與法國之間)。
St. Christopher /-ˈkrɪstəfə(r) ; -ˈkrɪstəfɚ/ 聖克利斯托弗(英屬西印度羣島中之一島,亦稱 St. Kitts)。
St. Clair, Lake /-kleə(r) ; -klɛr/ 聖克萊爾湖(介於美國之密西根州與加拿大之安大略省之間)。
St. Elias Range /-ɪˈlaɪəs- ; -əˈlaɪəs-/ 聖夷耐厄斯山脈(在加拿大與阿拉斯加間)。
Stettin /ʃteˈtiːn ; ʃtɛˈtin/ 斯德丁(波蘭西北部一港市,亦稱 Szczecin)。
Stewart Island /stjʊət- ; ˈst(j)uɚt-/ 司徒華島(在紐西蘭南島以南)。
St. George's /-ˈdʒɔːdʒɪz ; -ˈdʒɔrdʒɪz/ 聖喬治(Grenada 之首都)。
St. Got(t)hard Tunnel /-ˈgɒtəd- ; -ˈgɑtɚd-/ 聖哥達隧道(在瑞士南部)。
St. Helena /-ˈhelɪnə ; -həˈlinə/ 聖赫勒拿島(大西洋南部一英屬小島)。
Stirlingshire /ˈstɜːlɪŋʃə(r) ; ˈstɝlɪŋ,ʃɪr/ 斯特林夏(昔爲蘇格蘭中部一郡)。
St. Johns /sntˈdʒɒnz ; sentˈdʒɑnz/ 聖專斯(Antigua and Barbuda 之首都)。
St. Lawrence /-ˈlɒrəns ; -ˈlɔrəns/ 聖羅倫斯河(在加拿大東南部,自安大略湖流入聖羅倫斯灣)。
St. Lawrence, Gulf of 聖羅倫斯灣(在加拿大東南部)。
St. Louis /-ˈlʊɪs ; -ˈlʊɪs/ 聖路易(美國密蘇里州東部,密西西比河畔一城市)。
St. Lucia /-ˈluːʃə ; -ˈluʃə/ 聖露西亞(英屬西印度羣島中之一島,於 1979 年 2 月獨立,首都 Castries)。
Stockholm /ˈstɒkhəʊm ; ˈstɑk,hom/ 斯德哥爾摩(Sweden 之首都)。
Stockport /ˈstɒkpɔːt ; ˈstɑk,port/ 斯托克波特(英格蘭西北部一城鎮)。
Stockton /ˈstɒktən ; ˈstɑktən/ 斯托克頓 (**1** 美國加州中部一城市; **2** 英格蘭北部一城市)。
St. Paul /-ˈpɔːl ; -ˈpɔl/ 聖保羅(美國明尼蘇達州之首府)。
St. Petersburg /-ˈpiːtəzbɜːg ; -ˈpitɚz,bɝg/ 聖彼得堡(沙皇時代之俄國首都,現稱 Leningrad)。
Strasbourg /ˈstræzbɜːg ; ˈstrɑs,bʊrg/ 斯特拉斯堡(法國東北部一城市)。
Stratford-(up)on-Avon /ˈstrætfəd(əp)ɒnˈeɪvən ; ˈstrætfɚd(əp)ɑnˈevən/ 斯特拉福(英格蘭瓦立克郡內一小城,濱亞芬河,爲莎士比亞出生與埋葬之地)。
Strathclyde /stræθˈklaɪd ; stræθˈklaɪd/ 斯特科來(蘇格蘭西南部一區)。
Stuttgart /ˈstʊtgɑːt ; ˈstʊt,gɑrt/ 司徒加(西德西南部一城市)。
St. Vincent and the Grenadines /-ˈvɪnsənt--ˌgrenəˈdiːnz ; -ˈvɪnsənt--ˌgrɛnəˈdinz/ 聖文森 (西印度羣島中之一國,於 1979 年 10 月獨立,領土包括聖文森島及格里那汀羣島北部,首都 Kingstown)。
Sûchow, Hsû-chou /ˈsuːˈdʒəʊ ; ˈsuˈdʒo/ 徐州(中國江蘇省西北部一城市)。
Sudan, (The) /suːˈdɑːn ; suˈdæn/ 蘇丹(非洲東北部一共和國,昔爲 Anglo-Egyptian Sudan 英埃蘇丹,1956 年1月獨立,首都爲 Khartoum)。
Sudbury /ˈsʌdbərɪ ; ˈsʌd,bɛrɪ/ 索德柏立(加拿大安大略省東南部一城市)。
Sudeten /səʊˈdeɪtn ; suˈdetn̩/ 蘇臺德山脈(在捷克北部,介於波蘭、捷克之間)。
Suez /ˈsuːɪz ; suˈɛz/ **1** 蘇伊士港(在埃及東北部,蘇伊士運河南端)。**2** 蘇伊士運河(在埃及東北部,橫貫蘇伊士地峽)。
Suez, Isthmus of 蘇伊士地峽(連接亞非兩洲,爲蘇伊士運河所在地)。
Suffolk /ˈsʌfək ; ˈsʌfək/ 索夫克(英格蘭東海岸一郡,略作 *Suff*)。
Suiyuan /ˈsweɪjuːˈɑːn;ˈswe juˈɑn/ 綏遠(中國北部一省)。
Sulu Archipelago /ˈsuːluː- ; ˈsulu-/ 蘇祿羣島(位於菲律賓羣島西南)。
Sumatra /suːˈmɑːtrə ; sʊˈmɑtrə/ 蘇門答臘(印尼西部一大島)。
Sunda Isles /ˈsʌndə- ; ˈsundə-/ 巽他羣島(分爲大巽他羣島與小巽他羣島二部;前者包括 Java, Sumatra, Borneo 及 Celebes; 後者包括 Bali 以東至 Timor 之各島;其中除 Borneo 之北部外,均屬印尼)。
Sunderland /ˈsʌndələnd ; ˈsʌndɚlənd/ 巽得蘭(英格蘭北部一城市)。
Sungkiang /ˈsʊŋdʒɪˈɑːŋ ; ˈsʊŋdʒɪˈɑŋ/ 松江(中國東北一省,省會爲牡丹江市)。
Sung Shan /ˈsʊŋ ˈʃɑːn ; ˈsʊŋ ˈʃɑn/ 嵩山(在中國河南省,爲五嶽中之中嶽)。
Sun-moon Lake 日月潭(在中國臺灣省中部)。
Superior, Lake 蘇必略湖(位於美國與加拿大之間,爲北美五大湖中之最大者)。
Surabaja, Surabaya /sʊrəˈbɑːjə ; ˌsʊrəˈbaɪə/ 泗水(印尼爪哇東北角一港埠)。
Surat /ˈsʊərət ; ˈsʊrət/ 蘇拉特(印度西部一城市)。
Surbiton /ˈsɜːbɪtn ; ˈsɝbɪtn̩/ 索比頓(昔爲英格蘭南部一城市)。
Surinam /ˌsʊərɪˈnæm ; ˌsʊrəˈnɑm/ 蘇利南(南美北部一國,原爲 Dutch Guiana 或 Netherlands Guiana, 於 1975 年 11 月獨立,首都爲 Paramaribo)。
Surrey /ˈsʌrɪ ; ˈsʌrɪ/ 薩里(英格蘭東南部一郡,略作 *Sy*)。
Susquehanna /ˌsʌskwəˈhænə ; ˌsʌskwəˈhænə/ 沙士魁海納河(在美國東北部)。
Sussex /ˈsʌsɪks ; ˈsʌsɪks/ 索塞克斯(英格蘭東南海岸一郡,略作 *Sx*)。
Sutherland /ˈsʌðələnd ; ˈsʌðɚlənd/ 索色蘭(昔爲蘇格蘭北部一郡)。
Sutherland Falls 索色蘭瀑布(在紐西蘭南島西南部)。
Sutlej /ˈsʌtledʒ ; ˈsʌt,lɛdʒ/ 薩特來治河(在印度北部)。
Suva /ˈsuːvə ; ˈsuvə/ 蘇瓦(Fiji 之首都)。
Svalbard /ˈsvɑːlbɑː ; ˈsfɑl,bɑr/ 冷岸羣島(屬挪威,在北極海中)。
Sverdlovsk /svɜːdˈlɔːfsk ; sfɛrdˈlɔfsk/ 斯弗羅夫斯克(蘇聯烏拉山東麓一城市)。
Swatow /ˈswɑːˈtaʊ ; ˈswɑˈtaʊ/ 汕頭(中國廣東省韓江流域一海港)。
Swaziland /ˈswɑːzɪlænd ; ˈswɑzɪ,lænd/ 史瓦濟蘭(非洲東南部一王國,原爲英之保護國,於 1968 年 9 月獨立,首都 Mbabane)。
Sweden /ˈswiːdn ; ˈswidn̩/ 瑞典(北歐斯堪的那維亞半島東部一王國,首都爲 Stockholm)。
Swindon /ˈswɪndən ; ˈswɪndən/ 斯文頓(英格蘭南部一城市)。
Switzerland /ˈswɪtsələnd ; ˈswɪtsɚlənd/ 瑞士(西歐一共和國,首都爲 Bern)。
Sybaris /ˈsɪbərɪs ; ˈsɪbərɪs/ 希巴利斯(古希臘一城市,在義大利南部)。
Sydney /ˈsɪdnɪ ; ˈsɪdnɪ/ 雪梨(澳洲東南部一港埠)。
Syracuse /ˈsaɪərəkjuːz ; ˈsɪrə,kjus/ 敍拉古 (**1** 美國紐約州中部一城市; **2** 義大利西西里島東南部一海港)。
Syr Darya /ˈsɪə dɑːˈjɑː ; sɪrˈdɑrjə/ 錫爾河(在蘇聯亞洲部分之中部)。
Syria /ˈsɪrɪə ; ˈsɪrɪə/ 敍利亞(西南亞地中海岸一共和國,首都爲 Damascus)。
Szechwan /ˈseˈtʃwɑːn ; ˈsɛˈtʃwɑn/ 四川(中國中西部一省)。
Szeping /ˈsuːˈpɪŋ ; ˈsuˈpɪŋ/ 四平市(中國遼北省之鐵路中

心)。

Tabriz /təˈbriːz ; təˈbriz/ 大布里士(伊朗西北部一城市)。

Tadzhikistan, Tajikistan /tɑːˌdʒɪkɪˈstɑːn ; tɑˌdʒɪkɪˈstæn/ 塔吉克(蘇聯一加盟共和國,在其亞洲部分之中部)。

Taegu /tæˈguː ; tæˈgu/ 大邱(韓國東南部一城市)。

Tagus /ˈteɪgəs ; ˈtegəs/ 太加斯河(在西班牙與葡萄牙之間,注於大西洋)。

Tahiti /tɑːˈhiːtɪ ; təˈhitɪ/ 大溪地(南太平洋法屬社會羣島中之一島)。

Taichung /ˈtaɪˈtʃʊŋ ; ˈtaɪˈtʃʊŋ/ **1** 臺中市(中國臺灣省中西部一城市)。**2** 臺中縣(中國臺灣省中西部一縣)。

Tai Hu /ˈtaɪ ˈhuː ; ˈtaɪ ˈhu/ 太湖(中國江蘇省和浙江省交界處一大湖)。

Tainan /ˈtaɪˈnɑːn ; ˈtaɪˈnɑn/ **1** 臺南市(中國臺灣省西南部一城市)。**2** 臺南縣(中國臺灣省西南部一縣)。

Taipei /ˈtaɪˈpeɪ ; ˈtaɪˈpe/ **1** 臺北市(中國臺灣省北部一城市)。**2** 臺北縣(中國臺灣省北部一縣)。

Tai Shan /ˈtaɪ ˈʃɑːn ; ˈtaɪ ˈʃɑn/ 泰山(在中國山東省西部,爲五嶽中之東嶽)。

Taitung /ˈtaɪˈdʊŋ ; ˈtaɪˈdʊŋ/ 臺東(中國臺灣省東南部一縣,又其縣治名)。

Taiwan /taɪˈwɑːn ; ˈtaɪˈwɑn/ 臺灣(舊稱 Formosa, 中國東南海岸外一島,自成一省)。

Taiwan Strait 臺灣海峽(位於中國福建省與臺灣省之間)。

Taiyuan /ˈtaɪjuːˈɑːn ; ˈtaɪjʊˈɑn/ 太原(中國山西省省會)。

Tallin(n) /ˈtælɪn ; ˈtælɪn/ 塔林(蘇聯愛沙尼亞共和國之首府)。

Tamatave /ˌtɑːmɑːˈtɑːv ; ˌtæməˈtɑv/ 塔馬達夫(馬達加斯加島東海岸一港埠)。

Tampere /ˈtɑːmpere ; ˈtæmpəˌre/ 坦派勒(芬蘭西南部一城市)。

Tampico /tæmˈpiːkəʊ ; tæmˈpiko/ 坦比哥(墨西哥東部一港市)。

Tananarive /ˌtɑːnɑːnɑːˈriːv ; təˈnænəˌriv/ 塔那那利佛(參看 Antananarivo)。

Tanganyika /ˌtæŋgəˈnjiːkə ; ˌtæŋgənˈjikə/ 坦干伊喀(在非洲東部,昔爲英國託管地,於 1961 年獨立,1964 年與 Zanzibar 聯合組成 Tanzania)。

Tangier /tænˈdʒɪə(r) ; tænˈdʒɪr/ 丹吉爾(非洲摩洛哥北部一港埠)。

Tannu Ola /ˈtænuː ˈəʊlə ; ˌtænʊ ˈolə/ 唐努山脈(位於外蒙古西北與唐努烏梁海南部之間)。

Tan-shui, Tansui /ˈtɑːnˈsuːɪ ; ˈdɑnˈʃwe/ 淡水(中國臺灣省北部一海港)。

Tanzania /ˌtænzəˈnɪə ; ˌtænzəˈnɪə/ 坦尙尼亞(東非一國家,於 1964 年 4 月由 Tanganyika 和 Zanzibar 合併而成,首都爲 Dar es Salaam)。

Taoyuan /ˈtaʊjuːˈɑːn ; ˈtaʊjuˈɑn/ 桃園(中國臺灣省西北部一縣,又其縣治名)。

Taranaki /ˌtærəˈnɑːkɪ ; ˌtærəˈnækɪ/ 塔拉納基(紐西蘭北島西部一省區)。

Taranto /təˈræntəʊ ; təˈrænto/ 大蘭多(義大利東南部一港埠)。

Tarawa /təˈrɑːwə ; təˈrɑwə/ 塔拉瓦(中太平洋之一島,爲 Kiribati 之首都)。

Tashkent, Tashkend /tæʃˈkent ; tæʃˈkɛnt/ 塔什干(蘇聯中亞烏玆別克之首府)。

Tasmania /tæzˈmeɪnɪə ; tæzˈmenɪə/ 塔斯曼尼亞(澳洲東南一島,爲澳洲一邦,略作 *Tas*)。

Tasman Sea /ˈtæzmən- ; ˈtæzmən-/ 塔斯曼海(在澳洲東南與紐西蘭西部之間)。

Tatung /ˈdɑːˈtʊŋ; ˈdɑ ˈtʊŋ/ 大同(中國山西省北部一城市)。

Taunton /ˈtɔːntən ; ˈtɔntən/ 陶頓(美國麻薩諸塞州東南部一城市)。

Taurus /ˈtɔːrəs ; ˈtɔrəs/ 托魯斯山脈(在土耳其南部)。

Tayeh /ˈdɑːˈje ; ˈdɑˈjɛ/ 大冶(中國湖北省東南一縣城,以產鐵著名)。

Tayside /ˈteɪsaɪd; ˈteˌsaɪd/ 提塞德(蘇格蘭中東部一區)。

Tayu Ling /ˈdɑːˈjʊ ˈlɪŋ ; ˈdɑˈjʊ ˈlɪŋ/ 大庾嶺(亦稱 Mei-ling, 在中國江西省南部,以產鎢著名)。

Tegucigalpa /təˌguːsɪˈgælpə ; təˌgusəˈgælpə/ 德古斯加巴(Honduras 之首都)。

Tehran, Teheran /tɪəˈrɑːn ; ˌteəˈræn/ 德黑蘭(Iran 之首都)。

Tel Aviv /ˈteləˈviːv ; ˌtɛləˈviv/ 臺拉維夫(以色列西部一城市,曾爲其國都)。

Tenerife /ˌtenəˈriːf ; ˌtɛnəˈrif/ 特納利夫島(屬西班牙,爲加那利羣島中之最大島嶼)。

Tennessee /ˌtenəˈsiː ; ˌtɛnəˈsi/ 田納西 (**1** 美國東南部一州,略作 *TN*; **2** 美國東南部一河流)。

Texas /ˈteksəs ; ˈtɛksəs/ 德克薩斯(美國南部一州,略作 *TX*)。

Thailand /ˈtaɪlænd ; ˈtaɪˌlænd/ 泰國(舊稱 Siam, 東南亞一王國,首都爲 Bangkok)。

Thames /temz ; temz/ 泰晤士河(在英格蘭南部,倫敦即位於其畔)。

Thar Desert /tɑː- ; tɑr-/ 塔爾沙漠(在印度西北部,又名印度沙漠)。

Thebes /θiːbz ; θibz/ 底比斯 (**1** 埃及南部一古城; **2** 希臘東部一古城)。

Thimbu /ˈθɪmbuː ; ˈθɪmbu/ 辛布(Bhutan 之首都)。

Thohoyandou /təʊˌhɔɪ ænˈduː ; toˌhɔɪænˈdu/ 托赫揚度(Venda 之首都)。

Thousand Islands 千島羣島(位於美加之間的聖羅倫斯灣中)。

Thrace /θreɪs ; θres/ 色雷斯(歐洲巴爾幹半島上一地區,分屬希臘及土耳其)。

Thule /ˈtuːlɪ ; ˈtulɪ/ 杜里(丹麥格陵蘭島西北部一地區)。

Thun, Lake of /tuːn ; tun/ 土恩湖(在瑞士中部,由阿爾河形成)。

Thuringian Plateau /θjʊˈrɪndʒɪən- ; θ(j)ʊˈrɪndʒ(ɪ)ən-/ 紹林吉高原(在德國中部)。

Tiber /ˈtaɪbə(r) ; ˈtaɪbɚ/ 臺伯河(在義大利中部)。

Tibesti /tɪˈbestɪ ; tɪˈbɛstɪ/ 提柏斯提山脈(在非洲查德共和國西北部)。

Tibet, Thibet /tɪˈbet ; tɪˈbɛt/ 西藏(中國西南部一地區)。

Tien Shan, Tian Shan /tɪˈen ˈʃɑːn ; tɪˈɛn ˈʃɑn/ 天山(在中國新疆省)。

Tientsin /ˈtjenˈtsɪn ; tɪˈɛnˈtsɪn/ 天津(中國東北部河北省一港市)。

Tiflis /ˈtɪflɪs ; ˈtɪflɪs/ 提弗利司(蘇聯喬治亞之首府)。

Tigris /ˈtaɪgrɪs ; ˈtaɪgrɪs/ 底格里斯河(自土耳其東南部,流經伊拉克,與幼發拉底河滙合而注入波斯灣)。

Tihwa /ˈdiːˈhwɑː ; ˈdiˈhwɑ/ 廸化(中國新疆省省會,亦稱 Urumchi)。

Timor /ˈtiːmɔː(r) ; ˈtiˌmɔr/ 帝汶 (小巽他羣島中之最大島,原分屬荷蘭及葡萄牙,現屬印尼)。

Tintagel Head /tɪnˈtædʒəl- ; tɪnˈtædʒəl-/ 廷塔哲岬(在英格蘭西南部)。

Tipperary /ˌtɪpəˈreərɪ ; ˌtɪpəˈrɛrɪ/ 提派累立(愛爾蘭南部一郡)。

Tirana /tɪˈrɑːnɑː ; tɪˈrɑnə/ 地拉那(Albania 之首都,亦作 Tirane)。

Tisza /ˈtɪsɒ ; ˈtɪsˌɔ/ 提蘇河(在歐洲東部,注於多瑙河)。

Tobago /təˈbeɪgəʊ ; təˈbego/ 托貝哥島(爲千里達共和國一部分)。

Tobol /təʊˈbɔːl ; təˈbɔl/ 托包河(在蘇聯亞洲部分西部)。

Tocantins /ˌtəʊkænˈtiːns ; ˌtokənˈtinz/ 托肯丁斯江(在巴西東部)。

Togo /ˈtəʊgəʊ ; ˈtogo/ 多哥(西非一共和國,昔爲French Togo, 1960 年 4 月獨立,首都爲 Lomé)。

Tokyo /ˈtəʊkɪəʊ ; ˈtokɪˌo/ 東京(Japan 之首都)。

Toledo /tɒˈleɪdəʊ ; təˈledo/ 托利多(西班牙中部一省,又該省之首府)。

Tomsk /tɒmsk ; tɑmsk/ 托木斯克(蘇聯亞洲部分東南部一城市)。

Tonga /ˈtɒŋə ; ˈtɑŋ(g)ə/ 東加王國(位於西南太平洋之羣島國,於 1970 年 6 月獨立,首都爲 Nukualofa)。

Tonga Islands 東加羣島(亦稱 Friendly Islands, 現已獨立成爲東加王國,參看 Tonga)。

Tongking /ˈtɒŋˈkɪŋ ; ˈtɑŋˈkɪŋ/ 東京(亦稱 Tonkin, 爲越南北部一地區)。

Toronto /təˈrɒntəʊ ; təˈrɑnto/ 多倫多(加拿大安大略省之首府)。

Torquay /ˈtɔːˈkiː ; ˈtɔrˈki/ 托基 (昔爲英格蘭西南部一城市)。

Torres Strait /ˈtɒrɪs- ; ˈtɔrɪs-/ 托列斯海峽(在澳洲與新幾內亞之間)。

Toubkal /ˈtuːbkæl ; tubˈkɑl/ 土白克爾峯(在非洲摩洛哥西部)。

Toulon /tuːˈlɔːŋ ; tuˈlɑn/ 土倫(法國東南部一港口)。
Toulouse /tuːˈluːz ; tuˈluz/ 土魯斯(法國西南部一城市)。
Tours /tʊə(r) ; tʊr/ 都爾(法國西北部一城市)。
Trafalgar, Cape /trəˈfælgə(r) ; trəˈfælgɚ/ 特拉法加角(在西班牙西南部,直布羅陀海峽之西端)。
Transcaucasia /ˌtrænzkɔːˈkeɪzɪə ; ˌtrænskɔˈkeʒə/ 外高加索(蘇聯高加索山脈以南一地區)。
Transkei /trænsˈkaɪ ; trænsˈkaɪ/ 川斯凱共和國(原係南非共和國之黑人自治區,於 1976 年 10 月宣佈獨立,首都爲 Umtata)。
Transvaal /ˈtrænzvɑːl ; trænsˈvɑl/ 特蘭斯瓦爾(南非共和國東北部一省)。
Trengganu /treŋˈgɑːnuː ; trɛŋˈgɑnu/ 丁家奴(馬來西亞一州)。
Trier /ˈtriːə(r) ; trɪr/ 特里爾(德國西部一城市)。
Trieste /triːˈest ; triˈɛst/ **1** 的里雅斯德港(在義大利東北部)。**2** 的里雅斯德區(爲包括此港在內之一地區,1919-47年屬義,1947-54 年由聯合國治理,1954 年以後分爲兩部,北部屬義大利,南部屬南斯拉夫)。
Trinidad /ˈtrɪnɪdæd ; ˈtrɪnəˌdæd/ 千里達島(千里達共和國之組成部分,在委內瑞拉之東北方)。
Trinidad and Tobago 千里達共和國(西印度羣島一國,1962 年 8 月獨立,現爲大英國協之一員,首都 Port of Spain)。
Tripoli /ˈtrɪpəlɪ ; ˈtrɪpəlɪ/ 的黎波里 (**1** Libya 之首都; **2** 黎巴嫩西北部一港埠)。
Trondheim /ˈtrɒnheɪm ; ˈtrɑnˌhem/ 特倫汗(挪威中部一海港)。
Troy /trɔɪ ; trɔɪ/ 特洛伊 (**1** 小亞細亞西北部一古城; **2** 美國紐約州東部一城市)。
Tsinan /ˈdʒiːˈnɑːn ; ˈdʒiˈnɑn/ 濟南(中國山東省省會)。
Tsinghai = Chinghai
Tsingtao /ˈtʃɪŋˈdaʊ ; ˈtʃɪŋˈdaʊ/ 青島(中國東部山東省一港市)。
Tsitsihar /ˈtsiːtsiːhɑː(r) ; ˈtsi tsiˌhɑr/ 齊齊哈爾(中國嫩江省省會)。
Tsushima Strait /tsʊˈʃiːmɑː- ; tsuˈʃimə-/ 對馬海峽(介於日本對馬島與九州之間)。
Tuapse /tʊʌpˈsje ; tʊˌɑpˈse/ 土普塞(蘇聯南部一港,濱黑海)。
Tucson /ˈtuːsɒn ; tuˈsɑn/ 土孫(美國亞利桑那州東南部一城市)。
Tula /ˈtuːlə ; ˈtulə/ 杜拉(蘇聯莫斯科以南一城市)。
Tunghwa /ˈtʊŋˈhwɑː ; ˈtʊŋˈhwɑ/ 通化(中國安東省省會)。
Tungkwan /ˈtʊŋˈgwɑːn ; ˈtʊŋˈgwɑn/ 潼關(在中國陝西省東部,爲一交通孔道)。
Tungting Hu /ˈdʊŋˈtɪŋ ˈhuː ; ˈdʊŋˈtɪŋ ˈhu/ 洞庭湖 (中國湖南省境內一大湖)。
Tunis /ˈtjuːnɪs ; ˈt(j)unɪs/ 突尼斯(Tunisia 之首都,在古代迦太基舊址附近)。
Tunisia /tjuːˈnɪzɪə ; t(j)uˈnɪʒ(ɪ)ə/ 突尼西亞(北非一共和國,濱地中海,1956 年 3 月獨立,首都爲 Tunis)。
Turin /tjʊˈrɪn ; ˈt(j)ʊrɪn/ 杜林(義大利西北部一城市)。
Turkey /ˈtɜːkɪ ; ˈtɝkɪ/ 土耳其(橫跨西亞與東南歐一國家,首都爲 Ankara)。
Turkmenistan /ˌtɜːkmenɪˈstɑːn ; ˌtɝkˈmɛnɪˌstæn/ 土庫曼(蘇聯一加盟共和國,位於中亞)。
Turku /ˈtʊəkʊ ; ˈtʊrku/ 土庫(芬蘭西南部一港埠)。
Tuscany /ˈtʌskənɪ ; ˈtʌskənɪ/ 多斯加尼(義大利西北部一地區)。
Tuvalu /tuːˈvɑːluː ; tuˈvɑlu/ 吐瓦魯(昔稱 Ellice Islands,在西太平洋之羣島,原爲英屬地,於 1978 年 10 月獨立,並爲大英國協的一員,首都 Funafuti)。
Tyler /ˈtaɪlə(r) ; ˈtaɪlɚ/ 泰勒(美國德克薩斯州東部一城市)。
Tyne and Wear /ˌtaɪn ən ˈwɪə(r) ; ˌtaɪn ən ˈwɪr/ 泰恩與威爾(英格蘭北部一郡)。
Tynemouth /ˈtaɪnmaʊθ ; ˈtaɪnˌmaʊθ/ 泰因茅斯(英格蘭北部一城市)。
Tyrol, Tirol /ˈtɪrəl ; ˈtɪrəl/ 提洛爾(奧國西部與義大利北部一地區,在阿爾卑斯山中)。
Tyrone /tɪˈrəʊn ; tɪˈron/ 替隆(北愛爾蘭中西部一郡)。
Tyrrhenian Sea /tɪˈriːnɪən- ; tɪˈrinɪən-/ 第勒尼安海(爲地中海之一部,在義大利西南,西西里島以北)。

Ucayali /ˌuːkɑːˈjɑːlɪ ; ˌukəˈjɑlɪ/ 烏卡雅利河(在秘魯中北部)。
Uganda /juːˈgændə ; juˈgændə/ 烏干達(東非一共和國,1962 年 10 月獨立,爲大英國協之一員,首都 Kampala)。
Ukraine /juːˈkreɪn ; juˈkren/ 烏克蘭(蘇聯歐洲部分一加盟共和國,首府爲 Kiev)。
Ulan Ude /ˈuːlɑːn uːˈde ; ˌulɑn ʊˈde/ 烏蘭烏德(蘇聯亞洲部分布里亞特之首府)。
Ulawun /uːˈlɑːwʊn ; uˈlɑwun/ 烏拉武山(亦稱 The Father, 在太平洋西部,新不列顛島東北端)。
Ulster /ˈʌlstə(r) ; ˈʌlstɚ/ 阿爾斯特(愛爾蘭共和國北部一省)。
Umbria /ˈʌmbrɪə ; ˈʌmbrɪə/ 安布利亞(義大利中部一地區)。
Umtata /ʊmˈtɑːtə;ʊmˈtɑtə/ 翁塔達(Transkei 之首都)。
Union of Soviet Socialist Republics, (The) 蘇聯(參看 Soviet Union)。
United Arab Emirates 阿拉伯聯合大公國(在阿拉伯半島東北部,原爲英國保護地,1971 年 12 月獨立,首都 Abu Dhabi)。
United Arab Republic 阿拉伯聯合共和國(原由埃及與敍利亞於 1958 年2月1日合併而成,1961 年敍利亞退出,僅餘埃及部份,略作 U.A.R., 1971年起改爲 Arab Republic of Egypt, 首都爲 Cairo)。
United Kingdom (of Great Britain and Northern Ireland) 大不列顛與北愛爾蘭聯合王國 (卽英國, 通稱 England, 在西歐,包括大不列顛島和愛爾蘭島北部,首都爲 London)。
United States (of America) 美利堅合衆國;美國(略作 U.S.A. 或 U.S., 在北美洲, 首都爲 Washington, D.C.)。
Upper Volta /-ˈvɒltə ; -ˈvɑltə/ 上伏塔 (西非一共和國,原爲法國屬地,1960年8月獨立,首都爲 Ouagadougou)。
Up(p)sala /ˈʌpsɑːlə ; ˈʌpˌsɑlə/ 烏普沙拉(瑞典東部一城市)。
Ural /ˈjʊərəl ; ˈjʊrəl/ 烏拉 (**1** 蘇聯亞洲部份西北部一山脈; **2** 蘇聯亞洲部份西部一河流)。
Urmia, Lake /ˈɜːmɪə ; ˈɝmɪə/ 烏爾米亞湖(亦稱 Rizaiyeh, 在伊朗西北部)。
Uruguay /ˈjʊərəgwaɪ ; ˈ(j)ʊrəˌgwaɪ/ 烏拉圭 (**1** 南美東南部一國家,首都爲 Montevideo; **2** 南美洲東南部一河流,注於拉布拉他河)。
Urumchi /ʊˈrʊmtʃɪ ; ʊˈrʊmtʃɪ/ 烏魯木齊(參看 Tihwa)。
Usumbura /ˌuːsʊmˈbʊrə ; ˌusəmˈbʊrə/ 烏蘇布拉(參看 Bujumbura)。
Utah /ˈjuːtɔː ; ˈjuˌtɔ/ 猶他(美國西部一州,略作 *UT*)。
Utica /ˈjuːtɪkə ; ˈjutɪkə/ 由提卡(美國紐約州中東部一城市)。
Utrecht /ˈjuːtrekt ; ˈjuˌtrɛkt/ 烏特勒克(荷蘭中部一省,又該省之首府)。
Uzbekistan /ˌʊzbekɪˈstɑːn ; ˌʊzbɛkɪˈstæn/ 烏玆別克(蘇聯一加盟共和國,在中亞)。
Vaasa /ˈvɑːsɑː ; ˈvɑsə/ 瓦沙 (**1** 芬蘭西部一地區; **2** 芬蘭西部一港市,爲該區之首府)。
Vaduz /fɑːˈduːts ; vɑˈduts/ 瓦都玆(Liechtenstein 之首都)。
Valdai Hills /vʌlˈdaɪ-; vɑlˈdaɪ-/ 瓦耳代山(在蘇聯西部)。
Valencia /vəˈlenʃɪə ; vəˈlɛnʃɪə/ 瓦倫西亞 (西班牙東部一省,又該省之首府)。
Valenciennes /ˌvælənsɪˈen ; vəˌlɛnsɪˈɛn(z)/ 華倫西安(法國北部一城市)。
Valladolid /ˌvælədəˈlɪd ; ˌvælədəˈlɪd/ 法來多利(西班牙西北部一省,又該省之首府)。
Va(l)letta /vəˈletə ; vəˈlɛtə/ 法勅他(Malta 之首都)。
Valparaiso /ˌvælpəˈraɪzəʊ ; ˌvælpəˈraɪzo/ 法耳巴拉索(智利中部一港埠)。
Vancouver /vænˈkuːvə(r) ; vænˈkuvɚ/ 溫哥華 (**1** 加拿大西南部一港市; **2** 美國華盛頓州西南部一城市)。
Vatican City (State) /ˈvætɪkən- ; ˈvætɪkən-/ 梵蒂岡(羅馬天主敎敎廷所在地,在義大利羅馬市內)。
Vatnajökull /ˈvɑːtnɑːˌjɜːkuːtl ; ˈvɑtnɑˌjəkutl̩/ 瓦那冰嶺(冰島東南部一地區)。
Vaud /vəʊ ; vo/ 弗州(瑞士西部一州)。
Venda /ˈvendə ; ˈvɛndə/ 溫達共和國(原南非共和國之黑人區,於 1979 年 9 月獨立,首都爲 Thohoyandou)。

Venezuela /ˌvenɪ'zweɪlə ; ˌvɛnə'zwelə/ 委內瑞拉(南美洲北部一國家,首都爲 Caracas)。
Venice /'venɪs ; 'vɛnɪs/ 威尼斯(義大利東北海岸一港市)。
Verdun /'veədʌn ; vɝ'dʌn/ 凡爾登 (**1** 法國東北部一城市; **2** 加拿大東南部蒙特利爾島上一城市)。
Vermont /və'mɒnt ; vɚ'mɑnt/ 佛蒙特(美國東北部一州,略作 *VT*)。
Versailles /veə'saɪ ; vɚ'saɪ/ 凡爾賽(法國北部一城市,在巴黎西南郊)。
Vesuvius /vɪ'su:vɪəs ; və'suvɪəs/ 維蘇威火山(義大利西南部一活火山,近那不勒斯灣)。
Viborg, Vyborg /'vi:bɔ:g ; 'viˌbɔrg/ 維堡(蘇聯歐洲部分一港埠,在芬蘭灣)。
Vichy /'vi:ʃi: ; 'viʃɪ/ 維琪(法國中部一城市)。
Vicksburg /'vɪksbɜ:g ; 'vɪksˌbɝg/ 維克斯堡(美國密西西比州西部一城市)。
Victoria /vɪk'tɔ:rɪə ; vɪk'torɪə/ 維多利亞 (**1** 澳洲東南部一邦,略作 *Vic*; **2** 加拿大英屬哥倫比亞省之首府; **3** Seychelles 之首都)。
Victoria, Mount 維多利亞山 (**1** 在新幾內亞島東南部; **2** 在加拿大亞伯達省與英屬哥倫比亞省之間; **3** 在加拿大溫哥華島中北部; **4** 在緬甸北部)。
Vienna /vɪ'enə ; vɪ'ɛnə/ 維也納(Austria 之首都)。
Vientiane /ˌvjen'tjɑ:n ; ˌvjɛn'tjɑn/ 永珍(Laos 之首都)。
Vietnam, Viet-Nam /ˌvɪet'næm ; vɪ'ɛt'nɑm/ 越南(東南亞中南半島上一國家,1954-1975年分裂爲北越與南越,1975年復歸統一,首都爲 Hanoi)。
Vigo /'vi:gəʊ ; 'vigo/ 維哥(西班牙西北部一港埠)。
Virginia /və'dʒɪnɪə ; vɚ'dʒɪnjə/ 維吉尼亞(美國東部一州,略作 *VA*)。
Virgin Islands 維爾京羣島(在西印度羣島,分屬英、美兩國)。
Vistula /'vɪstjʊlə ; 'vɪstʃələ/ 維斯杜拉河(在波蘭境內)。
Vitim /vɪ'ti:m ; vɪ'tim/ 味地謨河(在蘇聯西伯利亞南部)。
Vitória /vɪ'tɔʊrɪə ; vɪ'torɪə/ 維多利亞(巴西東部一港市)。
Vladivostok /ˌvlædɪ'vɒstɒk ; ˌvlædəvə'stɑk/ 海參崴(蘇聯亞洲部分東南部一港埠,爲沿海州之首府)。
Volcano Islands 琉璜羣島(在西太平洋,小笠原羣島以南)。
Volga /'vɒlgə ; 'vɑlgə/ 窩瓦河(亦譯作伏爾加河,發源於蘇聯西部,東流入裏海)。
Vorkuta /vɔ:'ku:tə ; vɔr'kutə/ 伏可他(蘇聯歐洲部分一市鎮,在烏拉山之北端)。
Vosges /vəʊʒ ; voʒ/ 佛日山脈(在法國東北境)。
Wake /weɪk ; wek/ 威克島(在太平洋北部,屬美國)。
Wales /weɪlz ; welz/ 威爾斯(英國一區,在大不列顛島西南部)。
Walsall /'wɔ:lsɔ:l ; 'wɔlˌsɔl/ 瓦索耳(英格蘭中西部一城市)。
Waltham /'wɔ:ltəm ; 'wɔlˌθæm/ 瓦爾珊(美國麻薩諸塞州東部一城市)。
Wanchuan /'wɑ:ntʃʊ'ɑ:n ; 'wɑntʃu'ɑn/ 萬全 (參看 Changkiakow)。
Wanganui /ˌwɒŋə'nʊɪ ; ˌwɑŋ(g)ə'nuɪ/ 汪加奴(紐西蘭北島一海港)。
Warrington /'wɒrɪŋtən ; 'wɔrɪŋtən/ 瓦令頓(英格蘭西北部一城市)。
Warsaw /'wɔ:sɔ: ; 'wɔrˌsɔ/ 華沙(Poland 之首都)。
Warwickshire /'wɒrɪkʃə(r) *US:* 'wɔ:r- ; 'wɑrɪkˌʃɪr/ 瓦立克郡(英格蘭中部一郡,略作 *Warks*)。
Washington /'wɒʃɪŋtən ; 'wɑʃɪŋtən/ **1** 華盛頓州(在美國西北部,略作 *WA*)。**2** 華盛頓(美國首都,即哥倫比亞特區 District of Columbia)。
Waterbury /'wɔ:təbrɪ ; 'wɔtɚˌbɛrɪ/ 瓦特伯利(美國康乃狄格州中西部一城市)。
Waterford /'wɔ:təfəd ; 'wɔtɚfɚd/ 窩特福(愛爾蘭南部一郡,又該郡之首府)。
Weihaiwei /'weɪhaɪ'weɪ ; ˌweˌhaɪ'we/ 威海衞(中國山東省東北部一海港)。
Weimar /'vaɪmɑ:(r) ; 'vaɪˌmɑr/ 威瑪(德國東部一城市)。
Welland /'welənd ; 'wɛlənd/ 威蘭 (**1** 加拿大安大略省東南部一城市; **2** 加拿大安大略省東南部一運河,連接伊利湖與安大略湖)。
Wellesley /'welzlɪ ; 'wɛlzlɪ/ 威爾斯利(美國麻薩諸塞州東部一城市)。
Wellington /'welɪŋtən ; 'wɛlɪŋtən/ 威靈頓 (**1** New Zealand 之首都; **2** 紐西蘭一省區)。
West Berlin 西柏林(參看 Berlin)。
Western Australia 西澳大利亞(澳洲西部一邦,略作 *W Aus* 或 *W Austr*)。
Western Isles 西島區(即外海布里地羣島 Outer Hebrides, 在蘇格蘭以西的大西洋中,1975年起爲蘇格蘭一區)。
Western Samoa 西薩摩亞(南太平洋一國家,在薩摩亞羣島之西部,1962年1月獨立,首都爲 Apia)。
West Germany 西德(參看 Federal Republic of Germany 和 Germany)。
West Glamorgan 西格拉馬干(威爾斯東南部一郡)。
West Indies, (The) /-'ɪndɪz ; -'ɪndɪz/ 西印度羣島(介於北美洲東南與南美洲以北之間)。
West Lothian 西樓甸(昔爲蘇格蘭東南部一郡)。
Westmeath /west'mi:θ ; wɛs(t)'mið/ 威斯米司(愛爾蘭中東部一郡)。
West Midlands 威斯特米蘭(英格蘭中西部一郡,首府爲 Birmingham)。
Westmorland /'westmələnd ; 'wɛs(t)mɚlənd/ 威斯特麥蘭(昔爲英格蘭西北部一郡)。
West Pakistan 西巴基斯坦(參看 Pakistan)。
Westphalia /west'feɪljə ; wɛs(t)'feljə/ 西發里亞(德國西部一地區)。
West Virginia 西維吉尼亞(美國東部一州,略作 *WV*)。
West Yorkshire 西約克郡(英格蘭西北部一郡)。
Wexford /'weksfəd ; 'wɛksfɚd/ 威克斯福(愛爾蘭東南部一郡)。
Weymouth /'weɪməθ ; 'weməθ/ 威茅斯(美國麻薩諸塞州東部一市鎮)。
Whales, Bay of 鯨魚灣(在南極洲羅斯海南部)。
White 白河(在美國阿肯色州,注於密西西比河)。
Whitney, Mount /'hwɪtnɪ ; 'hwɪtnɪ/ 輝特尼峯(在美國加州東南部)。
Wicklow /'wɪkləʊ ; 'wɪklo/ 維克羅(愛爾蘭東部一郡)。
Wigan /'wɪgən ; 'wɪgən/ 維干(英格蘭西北部一城市)。
Wigtownshire /'wɪgtənʃə(r) ; 'wɪgtənˌʃɪr/ 維格頓夏(昔爲蘇格蘭西南部一郡)。
Wilmington /'wɪlmɪŋtən ; 'wɪlmɪŋtən/ 維明頓 (**1** 美國德拉瓦州北部一港市; **2** 美國北卡羅來納州東南部一港市)。
Wiltshire /'wɪltʃə(r) ; 'wɪltˌʃɪr/ 維特郡(英格蘭南部一郡,略作 *Wilts* /wɪlts ; wɪlts/)。
Wimbledon /'wɪmbldən ; 'wɪmbḷdən/ 溫布頓(昔爲英格蘭 Surrey 郡之市鎮)。
Winchester /'wɪntʃɪstə(r) ; 'wɪnˌtʃɛstɚ/ 文契斯特 (**1** 英格蘭南部漢普郡之首府; **2** 美國維吉尼亞州北部一城市)。
Windhoek /'vɪnthʊk ; 'vɪntˌhʊk/ 文特胡克(Namibia 之首府)。
Windsor /'wɪnzə(r) ; 'wɪnzɚ/ 溫莎 (**1** 加拿大安大略省東南部一城市; **2** 英格蘭南部波克郡一城市)。
Windward Islands 迎風羣島(在西印度羣島,爲組成小安地列斯羣島的一部分島嶼)。
Winnipeg /'wɪnɪpeg ; 'wɪnəˌpɛg/ 溫尼伯(加拿大南部一城市)。
Wisconsin /wɪs'kɒnsn ; wɪs'kɑnsṇ/ 威斯康辛(美國中北部一州,略作 *WI*)。
Witwatersrand /wɪt'wɔ:təzrænd ; 'wɪtˌwɔtɚzˌrænd/ 維瓦特斯蘭(南非共和國東北部一含金礦之岩嶺)。
Wolverhampton /'wʊlvəˌhæmtən; 'wʊlvɚˌhæmptən/ 烏未罕普頓(英格蘭中西部一都市)。
Worcestershire /'wʊstəʃə(r) ; 'wʊstɚˌʃɪr/ 烏斯特夏(昔爲英格蘭中西部一郡,略作 *Worcs*)。
Wrath, Cape /rɔ:θ ; rɑθ/ 拉斯角(在蘇格蘭之西北端)。
Wuchang /'wu:'tʃɑ:ŋ;'wu'tʃɑŋ/ 武昌(中國湖北省省會)。
Wuhsien /'wu:ʃɪ'en ; 'wuʃɪ'ɛn/ 吳縣(亦稱 Soochow 蘇州,中國江蘇省第一大城市)。
Wuhu /'wu:'hu: ; 'wu'hu/ 蕪湖(在中國安徽省東部,爲重要米市)。
Wusih /'wu:'ʃi: ; 'wu'ʃi/ 無錫(中國江蘇省南部一城市)。
Wu Tai Shan /'wu: 'taɪ 'ʃɑ:n ; 'wu 'taɪ 'ʃɑn/ 五臺山(在中國山西省東北部,爲中國三大佛教聖地之一)。
Wyoming /waɪ'əʊmɪŋ ; waɪ'omɪŋ/ 懷俄明(美國西北部

一州,略作 *WY*)。

Xanthus /ˈzænθəs ; ˈzænθəs/ 贊塔斯 (**1** 土耳其南部一河流; **2** 小亞細亞南部一古城)。

Xingu /ʃɪŋˈguː ; ʃiŋˈgu/ 申古河 (在南美洲巴西中部與北部)。

Yakutsk /jɑːˈkʊtsk ; jəˈkutsk/ 雅庫次克(蘇聯亞洲部分東部一自治共和國,又其首府)。

Yalta /ˈjæltə ; ˈjɔltə/ 雅爾達(蘇聯歐洲部分一港埠,在克里米亞南海岸)。

Yalu /ˈjɑːˈluː ; ˈjɑˈlu/ 鴨綠江(在中國與韓國邊境)。

Yangtze, Yangtse /ˈjæŋtsiː ; ˈjæŋˌtsi/ 長江(中國第一大河)。

Yaoundé, Yaunde /ˌjɑːuːnˈdeɪ ; jaʊnˈde/ 雅恩德(Cameroun 之首都)。

Yarmouth /ˈjɑːməθ ; ˈjɑrməθ/ 雅茅斯(英格蘭東部一港埠,濒北海)。

Yaunde = Yaoundé

Yawata /ˈjɑːwɑːtɑː ; jəˈwɑtə/ 八幡(日本九州北部一城市,亦稱 Yahata)。

Yellow Sea 黃海(介於中國山東半島與韓國之間)。

Yellowstone /ˈjeləʊstəʊn ; ˈjeloˌston/ **1** 黃石河(在美國懷俄明州西北部,經黃石公園往東北流,在蒙大拿州與密蘇里河滙合)。 **2** 黃石公園(美國之國立公園,在懷俄明與蒙大拿兩州之間,或稱 ～ National Park)。

Yemen /ˈjemən ; ˈjɛmən/ **1** ～ Arab Republic 葉門阿拉伯共和國(在阿拉伯半島西南部,濱紅海,1962年9月獨立,首都 San'a)。**2** People's Democratic Republic of ～ 葉門人民民主共和國(亦稱 Southern ～ 南葉門,在阿拉伯半島南部, 濱亞丁灣, 1967年11月獨立, 首都 Aden)。

Yenangyaung /ˈjeɪnɑːnˈdʒaʊŋ ; ˈjenɑnˈdʒaʊŋ/ 仁安羌(緬甸北部一市鎮)。

Yenisey, Yenisei /ˌjenɪˈseɪɪ ; ˌjɛnɪˈseɪ/ 葉尼塞河(在蘇聯之亞洲部分,流入北極海)。

Yinchwan /ˈjɪntʃʊˈɑːn ; ˈjɪntʃʊˈɑn/ 銀川(中國寧夏省省會)。

Yingkow /ˈjɪŋˈkaʊ ; ˈjɪŋˈko/ 營口(中國遼寧省遼河口一港市)。

Yokohama /ˌjəʊkəˈhɑːmə ; ˌjokəˈhɑmə/ 橫濱(日本本州東南部一海港)。

Yokosuka /ˌjəʊkəˈsʊkə ; joˈkɔsəkə/ 橫須賀(日本本州東京灣口一海港)。

York /jɔːk ; jɔrk/ 約克(美國賓夕法尼亞州東南部一城市)。

Yorkshire /ˈjɔːkʃə(r) ; ˈjɔrkˌʃɪr/ 約克夏(昔爲英格蘭北部一郡,略作 *Yorks*, 今分爲 North ～, South ～, 及 West ～ 三郡)。

Yuanlin /ˈjuːɑːnˈliːn ; ˈjuɑnˈlin/ 員林(中國臺灣省中部一市鎮)。

Yucatán /ˌjuːkəˈtɑːn ; ˌjukəˈtæn/ 猶加敦 (**1** 墨西哥東南部與中美北部一半島; **2** 墨西哥東南部一州)。

Yugoslavia, Jugoslavia /ˌjuːgəʊˈslɑːvɪə ; ˌjugoˈslɑvɪə/ 南斯拉夫(歐洲南部一國家,首都爲 Belgrade)。

Yukon /ˈjuːkɒn ; ˈjuˌkɑn/ 育康河(在北美洲西北部)。

Yukon Territory 育康地區(在加拿大西北部)。

Yulin /ˈjuːˈlɪn ; ˈjuˈlɪn/ 榆林港(中國海南島南部一天然良港)。

Yungan /ˈjʊŋˈɑːn ; ˈjʊŋˈɑn/ 永安(中國閩西大城,抗日戰爭時福建省會所在地)。

Yunlin /ˈjuːnˈliːn ; ˈjunˈlin/ 雲林(中國臺灣省中西部一縣)。

Yunnan, Yünnan /ˈjuːˈnɑːn ; ˈjuˈnɑn/ 雲南(中國西南一省)。

Zagreb /ˈzɑːgreb ; ˈzɑgˌrɛb/ 札格拉布(南斯拉夫西北部一城市)。

Zagros /ˈzægrəs ; ˈzægrəs/ 札格洛斯山脈(在伊朗西南部)。

Zaire /zɑːˈɪə(r) ; zɑˈɪr/ 薩伊(中非一共和國,昔爲 Belgian Congo, 1960年6月獨立,稱爲 Democratic Republic of the Congo, 1971年10月改用現稱,首都 Kinshasa)。

Zama /ˈzɑːmə ; ˈzɑmə/ 札馬(北非一古城)。

Zambezi, Zambesi /zæmˈbiːzɪ ; zæmˈbizɪ/ 三比西河(在非洲東南部,自尙比亞流入莫三鼻克海峽)。

Zambia /ˈzæmbɪə ; ˈzæmbɪə/ 尙比亞(南非一共和國,昔爲英屬北羅德西亞,於1964年10月獨立,首都 Lusaka)。

Zanzibar /ˌzænzɪˈbɑː(r) ; ˈzænzəˌbɑr/ 尙西巴(東非一島,原爲英之保護地,於1963年獨立,現爲坦尙尼亞一部分)。

Zaporozhe /ˌzɑːpəˈrɔːʒə ; ˌzɑpəˈrɔʒə/ 札波羅結(蘇聯烏克蘭東南部一城市)。

Zealand /ˈziːlənd ; ˈzilənd/ 西蘭島(亦稱 Sjaelland, 在丹麥東部,爲丹京哥本哈根之所在地)。

Zetland /ˈzetlənd ; ˈzɛtlənd/ 昔得蘭(昔爲蘇格蘭一郡,參看 Shetland)。

Zimbabwe /zɪmˈbɑːbwɪ ; zɪmˈbɑbwɪ/ 辛巴威(南非一共和國,原英屬南羅德西亞,於1970年自行宣佈獨立,稱爲 Rhodesia, 1980年4月改組新政府並改用此名,首都 Salisbury)。

Zomba /ˈzɒmbə ; ˈzɑmbə/ 松巴(非洲馬拉威東南部一城市)。

Zugspitze /ˈtsuːkˌʃpɪtsə ; ˈtsukˌʃpɪtsə/ 組格峯(在德國南部)。

Zuider Zee /ˈzaɪdə ˈzeɪ ; ˌzaɪdɚ ˈze/ 須德海(亦稱 IJsselmeer, 荷蘭北部一湖泊,與北海僅一堤之隔)。

Zurich /ˈzjʊərɪk ; ˈzʊrɪk/ 蘇黎克(瑞士東北部一城市)。

COUNTRIES OF THE WORLD 世界各國和地區

Notes: 注意:

1 The list consists of both sovereign independent countries and dependent states forming such countries: eg *Malaysia*, a sovereign nation, is a federation of *Malaya, Sabah* and *Sarawak; England, Scotland* and *Wales* make up *Great Britain;* the *United Kingdom* is the union of *Great Britain* and *Northern Ireland*.

本附錄包含有主權獨立之國家和組成此等國家之屬地: 例如主權國家 Malaysia 是由 Malaya, Sabah 和 Sarawak 組成之聯邦; England, Scotland 和 Wales 構成 Great Britain; United Kingdom 是由 Great Britain 和 Northern Ireland 聯合而成。

2 Some countries have different words for the *adjective* and the *person:* in these cases both are given, eg *Swedish; Swede.*

某些國家或地區的形容詞和表人之名詞並不相同;遇到這種情形,二者皆列出,例如 Swedish; Swede。

Adjective: 形容詞: I admire *Swedish* architecture. 我欣賞瑞典的建築。
He sang a *Japanese* song. 他唱了一首日本歌。
Person: 人: My mother is a *Swede*. 我母親是瑞典人。
A *Japanese* has joined our class. 一位日本人加入了我們的班級。

3 Words for the *person* ending in '-ese', and *Swiss*, remain unchanged in the plural:
以 -ese 結尾表人之字以及名詞 Swiss, 其複數和單數相同:
I know many *Japanese*. 我認識很多日本人。
The *Swiss* have arrived. 那些瑞士人已經到達。

4 In some cases, the *adjective* is also the word for the country's language:
在若干情形中,某國家或地區的形容詞也是表該國或地區之語言之字:
I am learning to speak *Malay*. 我在學講馬來話。

COUNTRY 國家和地區	ADJECTIVE; PERSON 形容詞;人
Afghanistan /æfˌgænɪ'stɑːn *US:* -'stæn ; æf'gænəˌstæn/ 阿富汗	**Afghan** /'æfgæn ; 'æfˌgæn/ 阿富汗的; **Afghanistani** /-nɪ ; -nɪ/ 阿富汗人
Albania /æl'beɪnɪə ; æl'benɪə/ 阿爾巴尼亞	**Albanian** /-nɪən ; -nɪən/ 阿爾巴尼亞的;阿爾巴尼亞人
Algeria /æl'dʒɪərɪə ; æl'dʒɪrɪə/ 阿爾及利亞	**Algerian** /-rɪən ; -rɪən/ 阿爾及利亞的;阿爾及利亞人
Andorra /æn'dɔːrə ; æn'dɔrə/ 安道爾	**Andorran** /-rən ; -rən/ 安道爾的;安道爾人
Angola /æŋ'gəʊlə ; æŋ'golə/ 安哥拉	**Angolan** /-lən ; -lən/ 安哥拉的;安哥拉人
Anguilla /æŋ'gwɪlə ; æŋ'gwɪlə/ 安圭拉	**Anguillan** /-lən ; -lən/ 安圭拉的;安圭拉人
Antigua /æn'tiːgə ; æn'tigə/ 安提瓜	**Antiguan** /-gən ; -gən/ 安提瓜的;安提瓜人
Argentina /ˌɑːdʒən'tiːnə ; ˌɑrdʒən'tinə/ (also 亦稱 *The Argentine* /'ɑːdʒəntaɪn ; 'ɑrdʒənˌtin/) 阿根廷	**Argentinian** /-'tɪnɪən ; -'tɪnɪən/, **Argentine** 阿根廷的;阿根廷人
Australia /ɒ'streɪlɪə *US:* ɔː's- ; ɔ'streljə/ 澳大利亞	**Australian** /-lɪən ; -lɪən/ 澳大利亞的;澳大利亞人
Austria /'ɒstrɪə *US:* 'ɔːs- ; 'ɔstrɪə/ 奧地利	**Austrian** /-strɪən ; -strɪən/ 奧地利的;奧地利人
(The) Bahamas /bə'hɑːməz *US:* -'heɪm- ; bə'hɑməz/ 巴哈馬	**Bahamian** /bə'heɪmɪən ; bə'hemɪən/ 巴哈馬的; 巴哈馬人
Bahrain /bɑː'reɪn ; bɑ'ren/ 巴林	**Bahraini** /-'reɪnɪ ; -'renɪ/ 巴林的;巴林人
Bangladesh /ˌbæŋglə'deʃ ; ˌbɑŋglə'dɛʃ/ 孟加拉	**Bangladeshi** /-'deʃɪ ; -'dɛʃɪ/ 孟加拉的;孟加拉人
Barbados /bɑː'beɪdəs ; bɑr'bedəs/ 巴貝多	**Barbadian** /-dɪən ; -dɪən/ 巴貝多的;巴貝多人
Belgium /'beldʒəm ; 'bɛldʒəm/ 比利時	**Belgian** /-dʒən ; -dʒən/ 比利時的;比利時人
Benin (formerly 舊稱 *Dahomey*) /be'niːn ; bə'nɪn/ 貝南	**Beninese** /benɪ'niːz ; bəˌnɪn'iz/ 貝南的;貝南人
Bermuda /bə'mjuːdə ; bɚ'mjudə/ 百慕達	**Bermudan** /-dən ; -dən/ 百慕達的;百慕達人
Bhutan /buː'tɑːn ; bu'tæn/ 不丹	**Bhutani** /-nɪ ; -nɪ/ 不丹的;不丹人
Bolivia /bə'lɪvɪə ; bə'lɪvɪə/ 玻利維亞	**Bolivian** /-vɪən ; -vɪən/ 玻利維亞的;玻利維亞人
Botswana /bɒ'tswɑːnə ; bɑt'swɑnə/ 波札那	**Tswana** /'tswɑːnə ; 'tswɑnə/ 波札那的;波札那人
Brazil /brə'zɪl ; brə'zɪl/ 巴西	**Brazilian** /-lɪən ; -ljən/ 巴西的;巴西人
Brunei /'bruːnaɪ ; 'bruˌnaɪ/ 文萊	**Bruneian** /bruː'naɪən ; bru'naɪən/ 文萊的;文萊人
Bulgaria /bʌl'geərɪə ; bʌl'gɛrɪə/ 保加利亞	**Bulgarian** /-rɪən ; -rɪən/ 保加利亞的;保加利亞人
Burma /'bɜːmə ; 'bɝmə/ 緬甸	**Burmese** /ˌbɜː'miːz ; ˌbɝ'miz/ 緬甸的;緬甸人
Burundi /bʊ'rʊndɪ ; bʊ'rundɪ/ 蒲隆地	**Burundian** /-dɪən ; -dɪən/ 蒲隆地的;蒲隆地人
Cambodia /kæm'bəʊdɪə ; kæm'bodɪə/ 柬埔寨	**Cambodian** /-dɪən ; -dɪən/ 柬埔寨的;柬埔寨人
Cameroon /ˌkæmə'ruːn ; ˌkæmə'run/ 喀麥隆	**Cameroonian** /-nɪən ; -nɪən/ 喀麥隆的;喀麥隆人
Canada /'kænədə ; 'kænədə/ 加拿大	**Canadian** /kə'neɪdɪən ; kə'nedɪən/ 加拿大的;加拿大人
Chad /tʃæd ; tʃæd/ 查德	**Chadian** /-dɪən ; -dɪən/ 查德的;查德人
Chile /'tʃɪlɪ ; 'tʃɪlɪ/ 智利	**Chilean** /-lɪən ; -lɪən/ 智利的;智利人
China /'tʃaɪnə ; 'tʃaɪnə/ 中國	**Chinese** /ˌtʃaɪ'niːz ; tʃaɪ'niz/ 中國的;中國人
Colombia /kə'lɒmbɪə ; kə'lʌmbɪə/ 哥倫比亞	**Colombian** /-bɪən ; -bɪən/ 哥倫比亞的;哥倫比亞人
Congo /'kɒŋgəʊ ; 'kɑŋgo/ 剛果	**Congolese** /ˌkɒŋgə'liːz ; ˌkɑŋgə'liz/ 剛果的;剛果人
Costa Rica /ˌkɒstə 'riːkə ; ˌkɑstə 'rikə/ 哥斯大黎加	**Costa Rican** /-kən ; -kən/ 哥斯大黎加的;哥斯大黎加人
Cuba /'kjuːbə ; 'kjubə/ 古巴	**Cuban** /-bən ; -bən/ 古巴的;古巴人
Cyprus /'saɪprəs ; 'saɪprəs/ 賽普勒斯	**Cyprian** /'sɪprɪən ; 'sɪprɪən/ 賽普勒斯的; **Cypriot** /'sɪprɪət ; 'sɪprɪət/ 賽普勒斯人
Czechoslovakia /ˌtʃekəʊslə'vækɪə ; ˌtʃɛkoslo'vɑkɪə/ 捷克	**Czech** /tʃek ; tʃɛk/, **Czechoslovak** /ˌtʃekəʊ'sləʊvæk ; ˌtʃɛkə'sloˌvɑk/, **Czechoslovakian** /ˌtʃekəʊslə'vækɪən ; ˌtʃɛkoslo'vɑkɪən/ 捷克的;捷克人
Denmark /'denmɑːk ; 'dɛnˌmɑrk/ 丹麥	**Danish** /'deɪnɪʃ ; 'denɪʃ/ 丹麥的; **Dane** /deɪn ; den/ 丹麥人
Djibouti /dʒɪ'buːtɪ ; dʒə'butɪ/ 吉布地	**Djiboutian** /-tɪən ; -ʃən/ 吉布地的;吉布地人
Dominica /də'mɪnɪkə ; ˌdɑmə'nikə/ 多米尼克	**Dominican** /-kən ; -kən/ 多米尼克的;多米尼克人
Ecuador /'ekwədɔː(r) ; 'ɛkwəˌdɔr/ 厄瓜多爾	**Ecuadorian** /ˌekwə'dɔːrɪən ; ˌɛkwə'dɔrɪən/ 厄瓜多爾的;厄瓜多爾人
Egypt /'iːdʒɪpt ; 'idʒəpt/ 埃及	**Egyptian** /ɪ'dʒɪpʃn ; ɪ'dʒɪpʃən/ 埃及的;埃及人
El Salvador /el 'sælvədɔː(r) ; ɛl 'sælvəˌdɔr/ 薩爾瓦多	**Salvadorean** /ˌsælvə'dɔːrɪən ; ˌsælvə'dɔrɪən/ 薩爾瓦多的;薩爾瓦多人
Eritrea /ˌerɪ'treɪə ; ˌɛrə'triə/ 厄立特里亞	**Eritrean** /-eɪən ; -iən/ 厄立特里亞的;厄立特里亞人
Ethiopia /ˌiːθɪ'əʊpɪə ; ˌiθɪ'opɪə/ 衣索比亞	**Ethiopian** /-pɪən ; -pɪən/ 衣索比亞的;衣索比亞人
Fiji /ˌfiː'dʒiː *US:* 'fiːdʒiː ; 'fidʒi/ 斐濟	**Fijian** /ˌfiː'dʒiːən *US:* 'fiːdʒɪən ; 'fidʒɪən/ 斐濟的;斐濟人
Finland /'fɪnlənd ; 'fɪnlənd/ 芬蘭	**Finnish** /'fɪnɪʃ ; 'fɪnɪʃ/ 芬蘭的; **Finn** /fɪn ; fɪn/ 芬蘭人
France /frɑːns ; fræns/ 法國	**French** /frentʃ ; frɛntʃ/ 法國的; **Frenchman** /'frentʃmən ; 'frɛntʃmən/ 法國人
Gabon /gæ'bɒn ; gæ'bon/ 加彭	**Gabonese** /ˌgæbə'niːz ; ˌgæbə'niz/ 加彭的;加彭人
(The) Gambia /'gæmbɪə ; 'gæmbɪə/ 甘比亞	**Gambian** /-bɪən ; -bɪən/ 甘比亞的;甘比亞人
German Democratic Republic /ˌdʒɜːmən deməˌkrætɪk rɪ'pʌblɪk ; ˌdʒɝmən ˌdɛmə'krætɪk rɪ'pʌblɪk/ 東德	**(East) German** /'dʒɜːmən ; 'dʒɝmən/ 東德的;東德人
(Federal Republic of) Germany /ˌfedərəl rɪˌpʌblɪk əv 'dʒɜːmənɪ ; ˌfɛdərəl rɪˌpʌblɪk əv 'dʒɝmənɪ/ 西德	**(West) German** /'dʒɜːmən ; 'dʒɝmən/ 西德的;西德人
Ghana /'gɑːnə ; 'gɑnə/ 迦納	**Ghanaian** /gɑː'neɪən ; gɑ'ne(j)ən/ 迦納的;迦納人
Gibraltar /dʒɪ'brɔːltə(r) ; dʒə'brɔltɚ/ 直布羅陀	**Gibraltarian** /ˌdʒɪbrɔːl'teərɪən ; dʒəˌbrɔl'tɛrɪən/ 直布羅陀的;直布羅陀人
Great Britain /ˌgreɪt 'brɪtn ; ˌgret 'brɪtn̩/ 英國	**British** /'brɪtɪʃ ; 'brɪtɪʃ/ 英國的; **Briton** /'brɪtn ; 'brɪtn̩/ 英國人
Greece /griːs ; gris/ 希臘	**Greek** /griːk ; grik/ 希臘的;希臘人

Grenada /grɪˈneɪdə ; grəˈnedə/ 格瑞那達
Guatemala /ˌgwɑːtəˈmɑːlə ; ˌgwɑtəˈmɑlə/ 瓜地馬拉
Guinea /ˈgɪnɪ ; ˈgɪnɪ/ 幾內亞
Guyana /gaɪˈænə ; gaɪˈænə/ 蓋亞納
Haiti /ˈheɪtɪ ; ˈhetɪ/ 海地
Holland /ˈhɒlənd ; ˈhɑlənd/ (also 亦稱 *The Netherlands* /ˈneðələndz ; ˈnɛðɚləndz/) 荷蘭
Honduras /hɒnˈdjʊərəs *US:* -ˈdʊə- ; hɑnˈd(j)ʊrəs/ 宏都拉斯
Hong Kong /ˌhɒŋ ˈkɒŋ ; ˈhɑŋ ˌkɑŋ/ 香港
Hungary /ˈhʌŋgərɪ ; ˈhʌŋg(ə)rɪ/ 匈牙利

Iceland /ˈaɪslənd ; ˈaɪslənd/ 冰島

India /ˈɪndɪə ; ˈɪndɪə/ 印度
Indonesia /ˌɪndəˈniːzɪə *US:* -ˈniːʒə ; ˌɪndəˈniʒə/ 印尼
Iran (formerly 舊稱 *Persia*) /ɪˈrɑːn ; ɪˈræn/ 伊朗
Iraq /ɪˈrɑːk ; ɪˈrɑk/ 伊拉克
(The Republic of) Ireland /ˈaɪələnd ; ˈaɪrlənd/ 愛爾蘭
Israel /ˈɪzreɪl ; ˈɪzrɪəl/ 以色列
Italy /ˈɪtəlɪ ; ˈɪtl̩ɪ/ 義大利
Jamaica /dʒəˈmeɪkə ; dʒəˈmekə/ 牙買加
Japan /dʒəˈpæn ; dʒəˈpæn/ 日本
Java /ˈdʒɑːvə ; ˈdʒɑvə/ 爪哇
Jordan /ˈdʒɔːdn ; ˈdʒɔrdn̩/ 約旦
Kampuchea /kæmpuˈtʃɪə ; ˌkæmpəˈtʃɪə/ 柬埔寨
Kashmir /kæʃˈmɪə(r) *US:* ˈkæʃmɪər ; ˈkæʃˌmɪr/ 喀什米爾
Kenya /ˈkenjə *US:* ˈkiːnjə ; ˈkɛnjə/ 肯亞
Korea /kəˈrɪə ; kəˈrɪə/ 韓國
Kuwait /kuˈweɪt *US:* -ˈwaɪt ; kəˈwet/ 科威特
Laos /ˈlɑːɒs ; laʊs/ 寮國
Lebanon /ˈlebənən ; ˈlɛbənən/ 黎巴嫩
Lesotho /ləˈsuːtuː ; ləˈsoto/ 賴索托
Liberia /laɪˈbɪərɪə ; laɪˈbɪrɪə/ 賴比瑞亞
Libya /ˈlɪbɪə ; ˈlɪbɪə/ 利比亞
Liechtenstein /ˈlɪktənstaɪn ; ˈlɪktənˌstaɪn/ 列支敦斯登

Luxemburg /ˈlʌksəmbɜːg ; ˈlʌksəmˌbɝg/ 盧森堡

Madagascar /ˌmædəˈgæskə(r) ; ˌmædəˈgæskɚ/ 馬達加斯加
Malawi /məˈlɑːwɪ ; məˈlɑwɪ/ 馬拉威
Malaya /məˈleɪə ; məˈleə/ 馬來亞
Malaysia /məˈleɪzɪə *US:* -ˈleɪʒə ; məˈleʒ(ɪ)ə/ 馬來西亞

Mali /ˈmɑːlɪ ; ˈmɑlɪ/ 馬利
Malta /ˈmɔːltə ; ˈmɔltə/ 馬爾他
Mauritania /ˌmɒrɪˈteɪnɪə *US:* ˌmɔːr- ; ˌmɔrəˈtenɪə/ 茅利塔尼亞
Mauritius /məˈrɪʃəs *US:* mɔː- ; mɔˈrɪʃ(ɪ)əs/ 模里西斯
Mexico /ˈmeksɪkəʊ ; ˈmɛksɪˌko/ 墨西哥
Monaco /ˈmɒnəkəʊ ; ˈmɑnəˌko/ 摩納哥

Mongolia /mɒŋˈgəʊlɪə ; mɑŋˈgolɪə/ 蒙古

Montserrat /ˌmɒntsəˈræt ; ˌmɑn(t)səˈræt/ 蒙特色拉

Morocco /məˈrɒkəʊ ; məˈrɑko/ 摩洛哥
Mozambique /ˌməʊzæmˈbiːk ; ˌmozəmˈbik/ 莫三比克
Namibia /nəˈmɪbɪə ; nəˈmɪbɪə/ 那米比亞
Nauru /ˌnaʊˈruː ; nɑˈuru/ 諾魯
Nepal /nɪˈpɔːl ; nəˈpɔl/ 尼泊爾
New Zealand /ˌnjuː ˈziːlənd *US:* ˌnuː- ; ˌn(j)uˈzilənd/ 紐西蘭
Nicaragua /ˌnɪkəˈrægjʊə *US:* -ˈrɑːgwə ; ˌnɪkəˈrɑgwə/ 尼加拉瓜
Niger /niːˈʒeə(r) ; ˈnaɪdʒɚ/ 尼日
Nigeria /naɪˈdʒɪərɪə ; naɪˈdʒɪrɪə/ 奈及利亞

Norway /ˈnɔːweɪ ; ˈnɔrˌwe/ 挪威
Oman /əʊˈmɑːn ; oˈmɑn/ 阿曼

Grenadian /-dɪən ; -dɪən/ 格瑞那達的;格瑞那達人
Guatemalan /-lən ; -lən/ 瓜地馬拉的;瓜地馬拉人
Guinean /-nɪən ; -nɪən/ 幾內亞的;幾內亞人
Guyanese /ˌgaɪəˈniːz ; ˌgaɪəˈniz/ 蓋亞納的;蓋亞納人
Haitian /ˈheɪʃn ; ˈheʃən/ 海地的;海地人
Dutch /dʌtʃ ; dʌtʃ/ 荷蘭的; **Hollander** /ˈhɒləndə(r); ˈhɑləndɚ/, **Dutchman** /ˈdʌtʃmən ; ˈdʌtʃmən/ 荷蘭人
Honduran /-rən ; -rən/ 宏都拉斯的;宏都拉斯人

—
Hungarian /hʌŋˈgeərɪən ; hʌŋˈgɛrɪən/ 匈牙利的;匈牙利人
Icelandic /aɪsˈlændɪk; aɪsˈlændɪk/冰島的; **Icelander** /ˈaɪsləndə(r) ; ˈaɪˌslændɚ/ 冰島人
Indian /-dɪən ; -dɪən/ 印度的;印度人
Indonesian /-zɪən *US:* -ʒn ; -ʒən/ 印尼的;印尼人
Iranian /ɪˈreɪnɪən ; ɪˈrenɪən/ 伊朗的;伊朗人
Iraqi /ɪˈrɑːkɪ ; ɪˈrɑkɪ/ 伊拉克的;伊拉克人
Irish /ˈaɪərɪʃ ; ˈaɪrɪʃ/ 愛爾蘭的; **Irishman** /ˈaɪərɪʃmən ; ˈaɪrɪʃmən/ 愛爾蘭人
Israeli /ɪzˈreɪlɪ ; ɪzˈrelɪ/ 以色列的;以色列人
Italian /ɪˈtælɪən ; ɪˈtæljən/ 義大利的;義大利人
Jamaican /-kən ; -kən/ 牙買加的;牙買加人
Japanese /ˌdʒæpəˈniːz ; ˌdʒæpəˈniz/ 日本的;日本人
Javanese /ˌdʒɑːvəˈniːz ; ˌdʒævəˈniz/ 爪哇的;爪哇人
Jordanian /dʒɔːˈdeɪnɪən ; dʒɔrˈdenɪən/ 約旦的;約旦人
Kampuchean /-ˈtʃɪən ; -ˈtʃɪən/ 柬埔寨的;柬埔寨人
Kashmiri /kæʃˈmɪərɪ ; kæʃˈmɪrɪ/ 喀什米爾的; 喀什米爾人
Kenyan /-jən ; -jən/ 肯亞的;肯亞人
Korean /-ˈrɪən ; -ˈrɪən/ 韓國的;韓國人
Kuwaiti /-tɪ ; -tɪ/ 科威特的;科威特人
Laotian /ˈlɑːɒʃn *US:* leɪˈəʊʃn ; leˈoʃən/ 寮國的;寮國人
Lebanese /ˌlebəˈniːz ; ˌlɛbəˈniz/ 黎巴嫩的;黎巴嫩人
Sotho /ˈsuːtuː ; ˈsoto/ 賴索托的;賴索托人
Liberian /-rɪən ; -rɪən/ 賴比瑞亞的;賴比瑞亞人
Libyan /-bɪən ; -bɪən/ 利比亞的;利比亞人
Liechtenstein; 列支敦斯登的; **Liechtensteiner** /-nə(r) ; -nɚ/ 列支敦斯登人
Luxemburg; 盧森堡的; **Luxemburger** /-gə(r) ; -gɚ/ 盧森堡人
Madagascan /-kən ; -kən/ 馬達加斯加的;馬達加斯加人
Malawian /-wɪən ; -wɪən/ 馬拉威的;馬拉威人
Malay /məˈleɪ ; məˈle/ 馬來亞的;馬來人
Malaysian /-zɪən *US:* -ʒn ; -ʒən/ 馬來西亞的; 馬來西亞人
Malian /-lɪən ; -lɪən/ 馬利的;馬利人
Maltese /mɔːlˈtiːz ; mɔlˈtiz/ 馬爾他的;馬爾他人
Mauritanian /-nɪən; -nɪən/ 茅利塔尼亞的;茅利塔尼亞人
Mauritian /-ˈrɪʃn ; -ˈrɪʃən/ 模里西斯的;模里西斯人
Mexican /-kən ; -kən/ 墨西哥的;墨西哥人
Monegasque /ˌmɒnəˈgæsk ; ˌmɑnɪˈgæsk/ 摩納哥的; 摩納哥人
Mongolian /-lɪən ; -lɪən/ 蒙古的; **Mongol** /ˈmɒŋgl ; ˈmɑŋgəl/ 蒙古人
Montserratian /-ˈræʃn ; -ˈræʃən/ 蒙特色拉的; 蒙特色拉人
Moroccan /-kən ; -kən/ 摩洛哥的;摩洛哥人
Mozambican /-ˈbiːkən ; -ˈbikən/ 莫三比克的; 莫三比克人
Namibian /-bɪən ; -bɪən/ 那米比亞的;那米比亞人
Nauruan /-ˈruːən ; -ˈrəwən/ 諾魯的;諾魯人
Nepalese /ˌnepəˈliːz ; ˌnɛpəˈliz/ 尼泊爾的;尼泊爾人
New Zealand 紐西蘭的; **New Zealander** /-də(r) ; -dɚ/ 紐西蘭人
Nicaraguan /-ən ; -ən/ 尼加拉瓜的;尼加拉瓜人
Nigerien /niːˈʒeərɪən ; naɪˈdʒɛrɪən/ 尼日的;尼日人
Nigerian /naɪˈdʒɪərɪən ; naɪˈdʒɪrɪən/ 奈及利亞的;奈及利亞人
Norwegian /nɔːˈwiːdʒən ; nɔrˈwidʒən/ 挪威的;挪威人
Omani /əʊˈmɑːnɪ ; oˈmɑnɪ/ 阿曼的;阿曼人

Pakistan /ˌpɑːkɪˈstɑːn *US:* ˈpækɪstæn ; ˌpækɪˈstæn/ 巴基斯坦	**Pakistani** /-nɪ *US:* ˌpækɪˈstænɪ ; -nɪ/ 巴基斯坦的；巴基斯坦人
Palestine /ˈpæləstaɪn ; ˈpæləˌstaɪn/ 巴勒斯坦	**Palestinian** /ˌpæləˈstɪnɪən ; ˌpæləˈstɪnɪən/ 巴勒斯坦的；巴勒斯坦人
Panama /ˌpænəˈmɑː *US:* ˈpænəmɑː ; ˈpænəˌmɑ/ 巴拿馬	**Panamanian** /ˌpænəˈmeɪnɪən ; ˌpænəˈmenɪən/ 巴拿馬的；巴拿馬人
Papua /ˈpæpjʊə ; ˈpæpjəwə/ 巴布亞	**Papuan** /-ən ; -ən/ 巴布亞的；巴布亞人
Paraguay /ˈpærəgwaɪ *US:* -gweɪ ; ˈpærəˌgwaɪ/ 巴拉圭	**Paraguayan** /ˌpærəˈgwaɪən *US:* -ˈgweɪən ; ˌpærəˈgwaɪən/ 巴拉圭的；巴拉圭人
Peru /pəˈruː ; pəˈru/ 秘魯	**Peruvian** /-ˈruːvɪən ; -ˈruvɪən/ 秘魯的；秘魯人
(The) Philippines /ˈfɪlɪpiːnz ; ˈfɪləˌpinz/ 菲律賓	**Philippine** /ˈfɪlɪpiːn ; ˈfɪləˌpin/ 菲律賓的； **Filipino** /ˌfɪlɪˈpiːnəʊ ; ˌfɪləˈpino/ 菲律賓人
Poland /ˈpəʊlənd ; ˈpolənd/ 波蘭	**Polish** /ˈpəʊlɪʃ ; ˈpolɪʃ/ 波蘭的； Pole /pəʊl ; pol/ 波蘭人
Portugal /ˈpɔːtʃʊgl ; ˈportʃəgl/ 葡萄牙	**Portuguese** /ˌpɔːtʃʊˈgiːz ; ˌportʃəˈgiz/ 葡萄牙的；葡萄牙人
Qatar /ˈkʌtɑː(r) ; ˈkɑtɚ/ 卡達	**Qatari** /-ɑːrɪ ; -ərɪ/ 卡達的；卡達人
Romania /rəˈmeɪnɪə ; rʊˈmenɪə/ 羅馬尼亞	**Romanian** /-nɪən ; -nɪən/ 羅馬尼亞的；羅馬尼亞人
Russia /ˈrʌʃə ; ˈrʌʃə/ 俄羅斯	**Russian** /-ʃn ; -ʃən/ 俄羅斯的；俄羅斯人
Rwanda /rʊˈændə ; rʊˈɑndə/ 盧安達	**Rwandan** /-dən ; -dən/ 盧安達的；盧安達人
Sabah /ˈsʌbə ; ˈsɑbə/ 沙巴	**Sabahan** /ˈsʌbəhən ; ˈsɑbəhən/ 沙巴的；沙巴人
Samoa /səˈməʊə ; səˈmoə/ 薩摩亞	**Samoan** /-ən ; -ən/ 薩摩亞的；薩摩亞人
San Marino /ˌsæn məˈriːnəʊ ; ˌsæn məˈrino/ 聖馬利諾	**San Marinese** /ˌsæn ˌmærɪˈniːz ; ˌsæn ˌmærəˈniz/ 聖馬利諾的；聖馬利諾人
Sarawak /səˈrɑːwæk ; səˈrɑwɑk/ 沙撈越	**Sarawakian** /ˌsærəˈwækɪən ; ˌsærəˈwækɪən/ 沙撈越的；沙撈越人
Saudi Arabia /ˌsaʊdɪ əˈreɪbɪə ; ˌsaʊdɪ əˈrebɪə/ 沙烏地阿拉伯	**Saudi Arabian** /-bɪən ; -bɪən/ 沙烏地阿拉伯的；沙烏地阿拉伯人
Senegal /ˌsenɪˈgɔːl ; ˌsɛnɪˈgɔl/ 塞內加爾	**Senegalese** /ˌsenɪgəˈliːz ; ˌsɛnɪgəˈliz/ 塞內加爾的；塞內加爾人
(The) Seychelles /ˈseɪʃelz ; seˈʃɛl(z)/ 塞席爾	**Seychellois** /seɪˈʃelwɑː ; ˌseʃəlˈwɑ/ 塞席爾的；塞席爾人
Sierra Leone /sɪˌerə lɪˈəʊn ; sɪˌɛrəlɪˈon/ 獅子山國	**Sierra Leonean** /-nɪən ; -nɪən/ 獅子山國的；獅子山國人
Singapore /ˌsɪŋgəˈpɔː(r) *US:* ˈsɪŋəpɔːr ; ˈsɪŋ(g)əˌpor/ 新加坡	**Singaporean** /ˌsɪŋgəˈpɔːrɪən *US:* -ŋə-;ˌsɪŋ(g)əˈporɪən/ 新加坡的；新加坡人
Somalia /səˈmɑːlɪə ; soˈmɑlɪə/ 索馬利亞	**Somalian** /-lɪən ; -lɪən/ 索馬利亞的； **Somali** /-lɪ ; -lɪ/ 索馬利亞人
South Africa /ˌsaʊθ ˈæfrɪkə ; ˌsaʊθ ˈæfrɪkə/ 南非	**South African** /-kən ; -kən/ 南非的；南非人
Spain /speɪn ; spen/ 西班牙	**Spanish** /ˈspænɪʃ ; ˈspænɪʃ/ 西班牙的； **Spaniard** /ˈspænɪəd ; ˈspænjɚd/ 西班牙人
Sri Lanka (formerly 舊稱 *Ceylon*) /ˌsrɪ ˈlæŋkə ; srɪˈlɑŋkə/ 斯里蘭卡	**Sri Lankan** /ˌsrɪ ˈlæŋkən ; srɪ ˈlɑŋkən/ 斯里蘭卡的；斯里蘭卡人
(The) Sudan /suːˈdɑːn ; suˈdæn/ 蘇丹	**Sudanese** /ˌsuːdəˈniːz ; ˌsudəˈniz/ 蘇丹的；蘇丹人
Sumatra /suːˈmɑːtrə ; sʊˈmɑtrə/ 蘇門答臘	**Sumatran** /-trən ; -trən/ 蘇門答臘的；蘇門答臘人
Swaziland /ˈswɑːzɪlænd ; ˈswɑzɪˌlænd/ 史瓦濟蘭	**Swazi** /ˈswɑːzɪ ; ˈswɑzɪ/ 史瓦濟蘭的；史瓦濟蘭人
Sweden /ˈswiːdn ; ˈswidn̩/ 瑞典	**Swedish** /ˈswiːdɪʃ ; ˈswidɪʃ/ 瑞典的； **Swede** /swiːd ; swid/ 瑞典人
Switzerland /ˈswɪtsələnd ; ˈswɪtsɚlənd/ 瑞士	**Swiss** /swɪs ; swɪs/ 瑞士的；瑞士人
Syria /ˈsɪrɪə ; ˈsɪrɪə/ 敍利亞	**Syrian** /-rɪən ; -rɪən/ 敍利亞的；敍利亞人
Tahiti /tɑːˈhiːtɪ ; təˈhitɪ/ 大溪地	**Tahitian** /-ˈhiːʃn ; -ˈhiʃən/ 大溪地的；大溪地人
Taiwan (formerly 舊稱 *Formosa*) /taɪˈwɑːn ; ˈtaɪˈwɑn/ 臺灣	**Taiwanese** /ˌtaɪwəˈniːz ; ˌtaɪwɑˈniz/ 臺灣的；臺灣人
Tanzania /ˌtænzəˈnɪə ; ˌtænzəˈnɪə/ 坦尚尼亞	**Tanzanian** /-ˈnɪən ; -ˈnɪən/ 坦尚尼亞的；坦尚尼亞人
Thailand (formerly 舊稱 *Siam*) /ˈtaɪlænd ; ˈtaɪˌlænd/ 泰國	**Thai** /taɪ ; taɪ/ 泰國的；泰國人
Tibet /tɪˈbet ; tɪˈbɛt/ 西藏	**Tibetan** /-tn ; -tn̩/ 西藏的；西藏人
Tobago /təˈbeɪgəʊ ; təˈbego/ 托貝哥	**Tobagonian** /ˌtəʊbəˈgəʊnɪən ; ˌtobəˈgonɪən/ 托貝哥的；托貝哥人
Togo /ˈtəʊgəʊ ; ˈtogo/ 多哥	**Togolese** /ˌtəʊgəˈliːz ; ˌtogəˈliz/ 多哥的；多哥人
Tonga /ˈtɒŋə ; ˈtɑŋ(g)ə/ 東加	**Tongan** /-ən ; -ən/ 東加的；東加人
Trinidad /ˈtrɪnɪdæd ; ˈtrɪnəˌdæd/ 千里達	**Trinidadian** /ˌtrɪnɪˈdeɪdɪən ; ˌtrɪnəˈdedɪən/ 千里達的；千里達人
Tunisia /tjuːˈnɪzɪə *US:* tuːˈnɪʒə;t(j)uˈnɪʒ(ɪ)ə/ 突尼西亞	**Tunisian** /-ən ; -ən/ 突尼西亞的；突尼西亞人
Turkey /ˈtɜːkɪ ; ˈtɝkɪ/ 土耳其	**Turkish** /ˈtɜːkɪʃ ; ˈtɝkɪʃ/ 土耳其的； **Turk** /tɜːk ; tɝk/ 土耳其人
Uganda /juːˈgændə ; juˈgændə/ 烏干達	**Ugandan** /-dən ; -dən/ 烏干達的；烏干達人
(The) Union of Soviet Socialist Republics /ˌjuːnɪən əv ˌsəʊvɪət ˌsəʊʃəlɪst rɪˈpʌblɪks ; ˌjunjən əv ˌsovɪət ˌsoʃəlɪst rɪˈpʌblɪks/ 蘇聯	**Soviet** /ˈsəʊvɪət ; ˈsovɪət/ 蘇聯的；—
(The) United States of America /juːˌnaɪtɪd ˌsteɪts əv əˈmerɪkə ; jʊˌnaɪtədˌstets əv əˈmɛrɪkə/ 美國	**American** /-kən ; -kən/ 美國的；美國人
Uruguay /ˈjʊərəgwaɪ *US:* -gweɪ;ˈ(j)ʊrəˌgwaɪ/ 烏拉圭	**Uruguayan** /ˌjʊərəˈgwaɪən *US:* -ˈgweɪən ; ˌ(j)ʊrəˈgwaɪən/ 烏拉圭的；烏拉圭人
Venezuela /ˌvenɪˈzweɪlə ; ˌvɛnəˈzwelə/ 委內瑞拉	**Venezuelan** /-lən ; -lən/ 委內瑞拉的；委內瑞拉人
Vietnam /ˌvietˈnæm *US:* -ˈnɑːm ; vɪˈɛtˈnɑm/ 越南	**Vietnamese** /ˌvɪetnəˈmiːz;vɪˌɛtnəˈmiz/ 越南的；越南人

(The) West Indies /ˌwest ˈɪndɪz ; ˌwɛst ˈɪndiz/ 西印度羣島 — **West Indian** /-dɪən ; -dɪən/ 西印度羣島的;西印度羣島人

Yemen /ˈjemən ; ˈjɛmən/ 葉門 — **Yemeni** /-nɪ ; -nɪ/ 葉門的;葉門人

Yugoslavia /ˌjuːgəʊˈslɑːvɪə ; ˌjugoˈslɑvɪə/ 南斯拉夫 — **Yugoslavian** /-vɪən ; -vɪən/ 南斯拉夫的; **Yugoslav** /ˈjuːgəʊslɑːv ; ˌjugoˈslɑv/ 南斯拉夫人

Zaire /zɑːˈɪə(r) ; zɑˈɪr/ 薩伊 — **Zairean** /-rɪən ; -rɪən/ 薩伊的;薩伊人

Zambia /ˈzæmbɪə ; ˈzæmbrə/ 尙比亞 — **Zambian** /-bɪən ; -bɪən/ 尙比亞的;尙比亞人

Zimbabwe /zɪmˈbɑːbwɪ ; zɪmˈbɑbwɪ/ 辛巴威 — **Zimbabwean** /-wɪən ; -wɪən/ 辛巴威的;辛巴威人

Appendix 7 **BIOGRAPHICAL NAMES**

附錄七 人名

Abel /ˈeɪbl ; ˈebl̩/ 阿培爾 (Sir Frederick Augustus, 1827-1902, 英國化學家)。

Adams /ˈædəmz ; ˈædəmz/ 亞當斯 (**1** Charles Francis, 1807-1886, 美國律師及外交家; **2** Henry Brooks, 1838-1918, 美國歷史學家; **3** James Truslow, 1878-1949, 美國歷史學家; **4** John, 1735-1826, 美國律師及第二任總統(1797-1801); **5** John Quincy, 1767-1848, 美國第六任總統 (1825-29); **6** Samuel, 1722-1803, 美國革命家及政治家)。

Addams /ˈædəmz ; ˈædəmz/ 亞當斯 (Jane, 1860-1935, 美國女社會工作者, 與 N. M. Butler 同獲 1931 年諾貝爾和平獎)。

Addison /ˈædɪsn ; ˈædəsn̩/ 阿狄生 (Joseph, 1672-1719, 英國詩人及散文家)。

Adler /ˈædlə ; ˈædlɚ/ 阿德勒 (**1** Alfred, 1870-1937, 奧國精神病學家; **2** Cyrus, 1863-1940, 美國教育家及作家; **3** Felix, 1851-1933, 美國教育家及改革家)。

Adrian /ˈeɪdrɪən ; ˈedrɪən/ 亞德連 (Edgar Douglas, 1889-1977, 英國生理學家,與 Sir C. Sherrington 同獲 1932 年諾貝爾醫學獎)。

Aeschylus /ˈeskələs ; ˈɛskələs/ 埃斯奇勒斯 (525-456 B. C., 希臘詩人及劇作家)。

Aesop /ˈiːsɒp ; ˈisəp/ 伊索(約 620-560 B. C., 希臘寓言作家)。

Agassiz /ˈægəsiː ; ˈægəsɪ/ 阿加西 (Alexander, 1835-1910, 美國動物學家)。

Agesilaus II /əˌdʒesɪˈleɪəs ; əˏdʒɛsəˈleəs/ 阿傑西雷斯二世 (?-?360 B. C., 約於 400-360 B. C. 為斯巴達國王)。

Agnes /ˈægnɪs ; ˈægnɪs/ 聖女埃格尼斯 (Saint, 三世紀人,守護西方教會之四大女聖徒之一,一月廿一日爲其紀念日)。

Agnon /ˈægnɒn ; ˈægnɑn/ 艾格農 (Shmuel Yosef, 1888-1970, 生於奧地利的以色列作家, 與 N. Sachs 同獲 1966 年諾貝爾文學獎)。

Agricola /əˈgrɪkələ ; əˈgrɪkələ/ 阿古利可拉 (Gnaeus Julius, 37-93, 羅馬大將)。

Agrippa /əˈgrɪpə ; əˈgrɪpə/ 阿古利巴 (Marcus Vipsanius, 63-12 B. C., 羅馬政治家)。

Aiken /ˈeɪkɪn ; ˈekɪn/ 艾坎 (Conrad Potter, 1889-1973, 美國詩人及小說家)。

Ainsworth /ˈeɪnzwɜːθ ; ˈenzwɝθ/ 恩玆韋斯 (William Harrison, 1805-1882, 英國小說家)。

Aitken /ˈeɪtkɪn ; ˈetkɪn/ 艾特坎 (Robert Ingersoll, 1878-1949, 美國雕刻家)。

Alaric /ˈælərɪk ; ˈælərɪk/ 阿拉列 (370?-410, 西哥德王, 紀元 410 年征服羅馬)。

Albert I /ˈælbət ; ˈælbɚt/ 阿伯特一世 (1875-1934, 比利時國王, 在位期間 1909-34)。

Alcott /ˈɔːlkət ; ˈɔlkət/ 奧爾科特 (**1** Amos Bronson, 1799-1888, 美國教育家及哲學家; **2** Louisa May, 1832-1888, 美國女作家)。

Alcuin /ˈælkwɪn ; ˈælkwɪn/ 阿昆 (735-804, 英國神學家及學者)。

Alder /ˈɔːldə ; ˈɑldɚ/ 奧爾德 (Kurt, 1902-1958, 德國化學家, 與 O. P. H. Diels 同獲 1950 年諾貝爾化學獎)。

Aldrich /ˈɔːldrɪtʃ ; ˈɔldrɪtʃ/ 奧爾德利奇 (Thomas Bailey, 1836-1907, 美國作家)。

Aleixandre /ˌɒlekˈsɒndre ; ˏɑlɛkˈsɑndrɛ/ 阿歷山大 (Vicente, 1898-, 西班牙詩人,曾獲 1977 年諾貝爾文學獎)。

Alexander the Great /ˌælɪgˈzɑːndə ; ˏælɪgˈzændɚ/ 亞歷山大大帝 (356-323 B. C., 即亞歷山大三世,爲馬其頓國王)。

Alfonso (or **Alphonso) XIII** /ælˈfɒnzəʊ ; ælˈfɑnzo/ 阿豐索十三世 (1886-1941, 西班牙國王,在位期間 1902-31)。

Alfred /ˈælfrɪd ; ˈælfrɪd/ 阿佛列 (849-899, West Saxons 之王,在位期間 871-899)。

Alger /ˈældʒə ; ˈældʒɚ/ 阿傑 (Horatio, 1832-1899, 美國作家)。

Ali /ɑːˈliː ; ɑˈli/ 阿利 (600?-661, 回教第四任教主,在位期間 656-661)。

Allen /ˈælən ; ˈælən/ 阿倫 (Charles Grant Blairfindie, 1848-1899, 英國作家)。

Ampère /ˈæmpeə ; ˈæmpɛr/ 安培 (André Marie, 1775-1836, 法國物理學家)。

Amundsen /ˈɑːmʊndsən ; ˈɑmənsn̩/ 阿孟森 (Roald, 1872-1928, 挪威探險家, 於 1911 年發現南極)。

Anacreon /əˈnækrɪən ; əˈnækrɪən/ 亞奈科雷昂 (572?-?488 B. C., 希臘詩人)。

Anaxagoras /ˌænækˈsægəræs ; ˏænækˈsægərəs/ 亞拿薩哥拉 (500?-428 B. C., 希臘哲學家)。

Andersen /ˈændəsn ; ˈændɚsn̩/ 安徒生 (Hans Christian, 1805-1875, 丹麥童話作家)。

Anderson /ˈændəsn ; ˈændɚsn̩/ 安德生 (**1** Carl David, 1905-, 美國物理學家,與 V. F. Hess 同獲 1936 年諾貝爾物理獎; **2** Sherwood, 1876-1941, 美國作家)。

Andrić /ˈɑːndrɪtʃ ; ˈɑndrɪtʃ/ 安瑞奇 (Ivo, 1892-1975, 南斯拉夫詩人及小說家, 曾獲 1961 年諾貝爾文學獎)。

Angell /ˈeɪndʒəl ; ˈendʒəl/ 安傑爾 (Sir Norman, 1872-1967, 原名 Ralph Norman Angell Lane, 英國作家及演說家,曾獲 1933 年諾貝爾和平獎)。

Anna Ivanovna /ˈænə ɪˈvɑːnəvnə ; ˈænə ɪˈvɑnəvnə/ 安娜 (1693-1740, 於 1730-40 爲俄國女皇)。

Anne /æn ; æn/ 安 (1665-1714, 詹姆斯二世之女,於 1702-14 爲英國女王)。

Anthony /ˈæntənɪ ; ˈæntənɪ/ 安東尼 (**1** Saint, 約 250-350, 埃及僧侶, 一般認係基督教修道制度之創建者; **2** Susan Brownell, 1820-1906, 美國女權運動倡導者)。

Antigonus I /ænˈtɪgənəs ; ænˈtɪgənəs/ 安提哥那一世 (全名 Antigonus Cyclops, 382-301 B. C., 亞歷山大大帝麾下大將,於 306-301 B. C. 爲馬其頓國王)。

Antipater /ænˈtɪpətə ; ænˈtɪpətɚ/ 安堤巴特 (398?-319 B. C., 馬其頓將軍及政治家)。

Antoninus /ˌæntəˈnaɪnəs ; ˏæntəˈnaɪnəs/ 安多耐諾斯 (Marcus Aurelius, 121-180, 斯多噶學派哲學家, 於 161-180 爲羅馬帝國皇帝)。

Antonius /ænˈtəʊnɪəs ; ænˈtonɪəs/ 安東尼 (Marcus, 英文稱作 Mark Ant(h)ony, 83?-30 B. C., 羅馬演說家、將軍及三執政之一)。

Apelles /əˈpeliːz ; əˈpɛliz/ 阿培里玆(紀元前四世紀之希臘畫家)。

Apollonius /ˌæpəˈləʊnɪəs ; ˏæpəˈlonɪəs/ **of Rhodes** 阿波羅尼(或稱 Apollonius Rhodius, 紀元前三世紀之希臘詩人)。

Appleton /ˈæpltən ; ˈæpl̩tən/ 阿波敦 (Sir Edward Victor, 1892-1965, 英國物理學家, 曾獲 1947 年諾貝爾物理獎)。

Aquinas /əˈkwaɪnəs ; əˈkwaɪnəs/ 阿奎奈 (Saint Thomas, 1225-1274, 義大利神學家)。

Archer /ˈɑːtʃə ; ˈɑrtʃɚ/ 阿契爾 (William, 1856-1924, 蘇格蘭批評家及劇作家)。

Archimedes /ˌɑːkɪˈmiːdiːz ; ˏɑrkəˈmidiz/ 阿基米德 (287?-212 B. C., 希臘數學家, 物理學家及發明家)。

Ariosto /ˌærɪˈɒstəʊ ; ˏɑrɪˈɑsto/ 阿里奧斯多 (Lodovico, 1474-1533, 義大利詩人)。

Aristarchus /ˌærɪsˈtɑːkəs ; ˏærəˈstarkəs/ 阿里斯塔克斯 (**1** 220?-150 B. C., 希臘文法家; **2** ~ of Samos, 紀元前三世紀之希臘天文學家)。

Aristides, Aristeides /ˌærɪsˈtaɪdiːz ; ˏærɪsˈtaɪdiz/ 阿里斯臺底斯 (530?-?468 B. C., 雅典政治家, 被尊爲 ~ the Just)。

Aristophanes /ˌærɪsˈtɒfəniːz ; ˏærɪsˈtɑfəniz/ 阿里斯多芬尼斯 (448?-?380 B. C., 雅典詩人及劇作家)。

Aristotle /ˈærɪstɒtl ; ˈærəˏstɑtl̩/ 亞里斯多德 (384-322 B. C., 希臘哲學家)。

Arkwright /ˈɑːkraɪt ; ˈɑrkˏraɪt/ 阿克萊特 (Sir Richard, 1732-1792, 英人,爲紡織機發明者)。

Armstrong /ˈɑːmstrɒŋ ; ˈɑrmstrɔŋ/ 阿姆斯壯 (Neil Alden, 1930-, 美國太空人, 爲第一位登陸月球者)。

Arne /ɑːn ; ɑrn/ 阿恩 (Thomas Augustine, 1710-1778, 英國作曲家)。

Arnold /ˈɑːnld ; ˈɑrnl̩d/ 阿諾德 (**1** Sir Edwin, 1832-1904, 英國詩人; **2** Matthew, 1822-1888, 英國詩人及批評家; **3** Thomas, 1795-1842, 英國教育家)。

Arnoldson /ˈɑːnldsn ; ˈɑrnl̩dsn̩/ 阿諾生 (Klas Pontus,

1844–1916, 瑞典和平主義者，與 F. Bajer 同獲 1908 年諾貝爾和平獎)。
Arrhenius /əˈriːnɪəs ; əˈrinɪəs/ 阿倫尼亞斯 (Svante August, 1859–1927, 瑞典物理學家及化學家，曾獲 1903 年諾貝爾化學獎)。
Artaxerxes /ˌɑːtəgˈzɜːksiːz ; ˌɑrtəˈzɝksiz/ 阿塔塞克西斯(三位波斯王之名，在位期間：一世，464–424 B.C.；二世，404–359 B.C.；三世，359–338 B.C.)。
Arthur /ˈɑːθə ; ˈɑrθɚ/ 亞瑟 (Chester Alan, 1829–1886, 美國第廿一任總統，任期爲 1881–85)。
Ascham /ˈæskəm ; ˈæskəm/ 阿斯堪 (Roger, 1515–1568, 英國學者及作家)。
Ashton /ˈæʃtən ; ˈæʃtən/ 艾錫頓 (Winifred, 參看 C. Dane)。
Asoka, Açoka /əˈsəʊkə ; əˈsokə/ 阿育王 (?–232 B.C., 古印度北部 Magadha 國之國王，在位期間 273–232 B.C.)。
Asser /ˈæsə ; ˈæsɚ/ 亞塞 (Tobias Michael Carel, 1838–1913, 荷蘭法學家，與 A. H. Fried 同獲 1911 年諾貝爾和平獎)。
Astor /ˈæstə ; ˈæstɚ/ 艾斯特 (Viscountess Nancy Langhorne, 1879–1964, 英國議院第一位女議員，任期 1919–45)。
Asturias /əˈstjʊərɪəs ; əˈst(j)ʊrɪəs/ 阿斯杜利亞斯 (Miguel Angel, 1899–1974, 瓜地馬拉作家，曾獲 1967 年諾貝爾文學獎)。
Attar /ˈætə ; ˈætɚ/ 阿特 (1119–?1229, 波斯詩人)。
Attila /ˈætɪlə ; ˈætḷə/ 阿提拉 (406?–453, 於 433?–53 爲匈奴之王，被稱爲 the Scourge of God, 意爲'上帝之鞭'或'天罰')。
Attlee /ˈætlɪ ; ˈætlɪ/ 艾德禮 (Clement Richard, 1883–1967, 英國從政者，於 1945–51 任首相)。
Aubrey /ˈɔːbrɪ ; ˈɔbrɪ/ 奧布雷 (John, 1626–1697, 英國古物研究家及收藏家)。
Auden /ˈɔːdn ; ˈɔdṇ/ 奧登 (Wystan Hugh, 1907–1973, 生於英國的美國詩人)。
Augustus /ɔːˈgʌstəs ; ɔˈgʌstəs/ 奧古斯都 (63 B. C.–A. D. 14, 羅馬帝國第一任皇帝，在位期間 27 B. C.–A. D. 14)。
Aurelian /ɔːˈriːljən ; ɔˈriljən/ 奧理安 (212?–275, 羅馬帝國皇帝，在位期間 270–275)。
Austen /ˈɔːstɪn ; ˈɔstɪn/ 奧斯汀 (Jane, 1775–1817, 英國女小說家)。
Austin /ˈɔːstɪn ; ˈɔstɪn/ 奧斯丁 (**1** Alfred, 1835–1913, 英國詩人，於 1896–1913 榮膺桂冠詩人； **2** John, 1790–1859 英國法學家； **3** Mary, 1868–1934, 美國女小說家，本姓 Hunter)。
Babbitt /ˈbæbɪt ; ˈbæbɪt/ 白璧德 (Irving, 1865–1933, 美國學者及教育家)。
Babington /ˈbæbɪŋtən ; ˈbæbɪŋtṇ/ 巴賓頓 (Anthony, 1561–1586, 英國天主教徒，因陰謀反抗伊利莎白女皇一世而被處死)。
Bach /bɑːk ; bɑk/ 巴哈 (Johann Sebastian, 1685–1750, 德國風琴家及作曲家)。
Bacon /ˈbeɪkən ; ˈbekən/ 培根 (**1** Francis, 1561–1626, 英國作家及哲學家； **2** Roger, 1214?–1294, 英國僧侶及哲學家)。
Baden-Powell /ˈbeɪdnˈpəʊəl ; ˈbedṇˈpoəl/ 貝登堡 (Sir Robert Stephenson Smyth, 1857–1941, 英國將軍，童子軍運動創始者)。
Baeyer, von /fənˈbeɪjə ; fənˈbejɚ/ 馮拜爾 (Adolf, 1835–1917, 德國化學家，曾獲 1905 年諾貝爾化學獎)。
Baffin /ˈbæfɪn ; ˈbæfɪn/ 巴芬 (William, 1584–1622, 英國航海家)。
Bahaullah /bɑːˌhɑːuːˈlɑː ; bɑˌhauˈlɑ/ 巴哈烏拉 (本名 Mirza Husayn Ali, 1817–1892, 波斯人，巴海大同教之創始人)。
Bailey /ˈbeɪlɪ ; ˈbelɪ/ 貝利 (Liberty Hyde, 1858–1954, 美國植物學家及作家)。
Baillie /ˈbeɪlɪ ; ˈbelɪ/ 貝里 (Joanna, 1762–1851, 蘇格蘭女劇作家及詩人)。
Bain /beɪn ; ben/ 貝恩 (Alexander, 1818–1903, 蘇格蘭心理學家)。
Baird /bɛəd ; bɛrd/ 貝爾德 (John Logie, 1888–1946, 蘇格蘭發明家，有'電視之父'之稱)。
Bajer /ˈbaɪə ; ˈbaɪɚ/ 拜爾 (Fredrik, 1837–1922, 丹麥政治家及作家，與 K. P. Arnoldson 同獲 1908 年諾貝爾和平獎)。
Baker /ˈbeɪkə ; ˈbekɚ/ 貝克爾 (**1** Newton Diehl, 1871–1937, 美國律師及政治家； **2** Ray Stannard, 1870–1946, 筆名 David Grayson, 美國作家)。
Balboa /bælˈbəʊə ; bælˈboə/ 貝爾波爾 (Vasco Núñez de, 1475–1519, 西班牙探險家，於 1513 年發現太平洋)。
Balch /bɒltʃ ; bɔltʃ/ 鮑爾奇 (Emily Greene, 1867–1961, 美國女經濟學家及社會學家，與 J. R. Mott 同獲 1946 年諾貝爾和平獎)。
Baldwin I /ˈbɔːldwɪn ; ˈbɔldwɪn/ 包爾文一世 (1058–1118, 耶路撒冷國王，在位期間 1100–18)。
Balfour /ˈbælfʊə ; ˈbælfʊr/ 巴爾福 (Arthur James, 1848–1930, 英國哲學家及政治家，於 1902–05 任首相)。
Baliol, de /də ˈbeɪljəl ; dəˈbeljəl/ 戴貝亞 (John, 1249–1315, 蘇格蘭國王，在位期間 1292–96)。
Balzac, de /də ˈbælzæk ; dəˈbælzæk/ 巴爾札克 (Honoré, 1799–1850, 法國小說家)。
Bancroft /ˈbænkrɒft ; ˈbænkrɔft/ 班克勞夫 (George, 1800–1891, 美國歷史學家)。
Banks /bæŋks ; bæŋks/ 班克斯 (Sir Joseph, 1743–1820, 英國博物學家)。
Banting /ˈbæntɪŋ ; ˈbæntɪŋ/ 班亭 (Sir Frederick Grant, 1891–1941, 加拿大醫生，用胰島素治療糖尿病之發現者，與 J. J. R. Macleod 同獲 1923 年諾貝爾醫學獎)。
Bárány /ˈbɑːrɑːnjə ; ˈbɑranjə/ 巴雷尼 (Robert, 1876–1936, 奧國醫生，曾獲 1914 年諾貝爾醫學獎)。
Bardeen /bɑːˈdiːn ; bɑrˈdin/ 巴丁 (John, 1908–, 美國物理學家，與 W. H. Brattain 及 W. B. Shockley 同獲 1956 年諾貝爾物理獎，又與 L. N. Cooper 及 J. R. Schrieffer 同獲 1972 年諾貝爾物理獎)。
Barkla /ˈbɑːklə ; ˈbɑrklə/ 巴克拉 (Charles Glover 1877–1944, 英國物理學家，曾獲 1917 年諾貝爾物理獎)。
Barlow /ˈbɑːləʊ ; ˈbɑrlo/ 巴羅 (Joel, 1754–1812, 美國詩人及外交家)。
Barnard /ˈbɑːnəd ; ˈbɑrnɚd/ 巴納 (George Grey, 1863–1938, 美國雕刻家)。
Barnes /bɑːnz ; bɑrnz/ 巴恩斯 (Harry Elmer, 1889–1968, 美國社會學家及教育家)。
Barrie /ˈbærɪ ; ˈbærɪ/ 巴利 (Sir James Matthew, 1860–1937, 蘇格蘭小說家及劇作家)。
Barrow /ˈbærəʊ ; ˈbæro/ 巴魯 (Isaac, 1630–1677, 英國數學家及神學家)。
Barry /ˈbærɪ ; ˈbærɪ/ 白利 (Philip, 1896–1949, 美國劇作家)。
Barth /bɑːt ; bɑrt/ 巴特 (Karl, 1886–1968, 瑞士神學家)。
Bartlett /ˈbɑːtlɪt ; ˈbɑrtlɪt/ 巴特利 (John, 1820–1905, 美國出版家及編輯)。
Bartók /ˈbɑːtɒk ; ˈbɑrtɑk/ 巴托克 (Béla, 1881–1945, 匈牙利作曲家)。
Barton /ˈbɑːtn ; ˈbɑrtṇ/ 巴頓 (Clara, 全名爲 Clarissa Harlowe ～, 1821–1912, 女性，美國紅十字會創始者)。
Basov /ˈbɑːsɒf ; ˈbɑsɔf/ 巴瑟夫 (Nikolai Gennadievich, 1922–, 俄國物理學家，與 C. H. Townes 及 A. M. Prokhorov 同獲 1964 年諾貝爾物理獎)。
Bates /beɪts ; bets/ 貝玆 (Katharine Lee, 1859–1929, 美國女詩人及教育家)。
Baudelaire /bəʊdˈlɛə ; bodˈlær/ 波德來爾 (Charles Pierre, 1821–1867, 法國詩人)。
Bayle /beɪl ; bel/ 貝爾 (Pierre, 1647–1706, 法國哲學家及批評家)。
Beadle /ˈbiːdl ; ˈbidḷ/ 畢德爾 (George Wells, 1903–, 美國生物學家及教育家，與 J. Lederberg 及 E. L. Tatum 同獲 1958 年諾貝爾醫學獎)。
Beattie /ˈbiːtɪ ; ˈbitɪ/ 畢替 (James, 1735–1803, 蘇格蘭詩人)。
Beaumont /ˈbəʊmənt ; ˈbomɑnt/ 包蒙 (Francis, 1584–1616, 英國劇作家)。
Becket, à /əˈbekɪt ; əˈbɛkət/ 阿拜基特 (Saint Thomas, 1118?–1170, 英國 Canterbury 大主教，因反對 Henry II 而被殺)。
Beckett /ˈbekɪt ; ˈbɛkɪt/ 貝克特 (Samuel, 1906–, 旅居法國之愛爾蘭作家及劇作家，曾獲 1969 年諾貝爾文學獎)。

Becquerel /bek'rel ; bɛk'rɛl/ 白克勒爾(法國研究理化科學最傑出的世家: **1** Antoine César, 1788-1878, 創結晶體重組學說; **2** Alexandre Edmond, 1820-1891, Antoine César 之子; **3** Antoine Henri, 1852-1908, 爲放射能的發現者，與居里夫婦同獲 1903 年諾貝爾物理獎)。

Bede /biːd ; bid/ 比得 (Saint, 673-735, 英國學者、歷史學家及神學家)。

Beerbohm /'bɪəbəʊm ; 'bɪrbom/ 畢爾本 (Sir Max, 1872-1956, 英國批評家及漫畫家)。

Beernaert /'beənɑːt ; 'bɛrˌnɑrt/ 貝爾納特 (Auguste Marie François, 1829-1912, 比利時政治家，與 Estournelles de Constant 同獲 1909 年諾貝爾和平獎)。

Beethoven /'beɪtəʊvn ; 'betovən/ 貝多芬 (Ludwig van, 1770-1827, 德國大作曲家)。

Begin /bə'giːn ; bə'gin/ 比金 (Menachem, 1913-, 於 1977 年起任以色列總理，與 A. el Sadat 同獲 1978 年諾貝爾和平獎)。

Behring, von /fɒn'berɪŋ ; fɑn'bɛrɪŋ/ 方貝令 (Emil, 1854-1917, 德國細菌學家，曾獲 1901 年首屆諾貝爾醫學獎)。

Békésy /'beɪkeɪʃɪ ; 'bekəʃɪ/ 貝凱西 (Georg von, 1899-1972, 生於匈牙利之美國生理學家及物理學家，曾獲 1961 年諾貝爾醫學獎)。

Bell /bel ; bɛl/ 貝爾 (Alexander Graham, 1847-1922, 生於蘇格蘭的美國人，爲電話發明者)。

Bellamy /'beləmɪ ; 'bɛləmɪ/ 貝拉米 (Edward, 1850-1898, 美國作家)。

Bellini /bə'liːnɪ ; bə'linɪ/ 貝里尼 (Vincenzo, 1801-1835, 義大利歌劇作曲家)。

Bellow /'beləʊ ; 'bɛlo/ 貝婁 (Saul, 1915-, 生於加拿大的美國作家，曾獲 1976 年諾貝爾文學獎)。

Bellows /'beləʊz ; 'bɛloz/ 貝羅玆 (George Wesley, 1882-1925, 美國畫家及平版印刷家)。

Benavente y Martínez /ˌbenəˌventɪ iːmɑː'tiːnəs ; ˌbɛnəˌvɛntɪˌimɑr'tinəs/ 貝納溫第 (Jacinto, 1866-1954, 西班牙劇作家，曾獲 1922 年諾貝爾文學獎)。

Benét /bə'neɪ ; bə'ne/ 貝內 (**1** Stephen Vincent, 1898-1943, 美國詩人及小說家; **2** William Rose, 1886-1950, 美國詩人、小說家及編輯)。

Bennett /'benɪt ; 'bɛnɪt/ 貝湼特 ((Enoch) Arnold, 1867-1931, 英國小說家)。

Benson /'bensn ; 'bɛnsn̩/ 彭生 (Arthur Christopher, 1862-1925, 英國教育家及作家)。

Bentham /'benθəm ; 'bɛnθəm/ 邊沁 (Jeremy, 1748-1832, 英國法學家及哲學家)。

Bentinck /'bentɪŋk ; 'bɛntɪŋk/ 彭廷克 (William Henry Cavendish, 1738-1809, 英國政治家，曾於 1783 及 1807-09 任首相)。

Bergius /'beəgɪəs ; 'bɛrgɪəs/ 柏吉斯 (Friedrich, 1884-1949, 德國化學家，與 K. Bosch 同獲 1931 年諾貝爾化學獎)。

Bergson /'bɜːgsn ; 'bɛrgsn̩/ 柏克森 (Henri, 1859-1941, 法國哲學家，曾獲 1927 年諾貝爾文學獎)。

Bering /'berɪŋ ; 'bɛrɪŋ/ 白令 (Vitus, 1680-1741, 丹麥航海家，白令海峽及白令海之發現者)。

Berkeley /'bɑːklɪ ; 'bɝklɪ/ 伯克里 (Ceorge, 1685-1753, 愛爾蘭主教及哲學家)。

Berlioz /'beəlɪəʊz ; 'bɛrlɪˌoz/ 白遼士 ((Louis) Hector, 1803-1869, 法國作曲家)。

Bernard /beə'nɑː ; bɛr'nɑr/ 伯納 (Claude, 1813-1878, 法國生理學家)。

Bessemer /'besəmə ; 'bɛsəmɚ/ 貝瑟摩 (Sir Henry, 1813-1898, 英國工程師。)

Beveridge /'bevərɪdʒ ; 'bɛv(ə)rɪdʒ/ 柏衞基 (Albert Jeremiah, 1862-1927, 美國從政者及歷史學家)。

Birrell /'bɪrəl ; 'bɪrəl/ 畢雷爾 (Augustine, 1850-1933, 英國作家)。

Bismarck, von /'bɪzmɑːk ; 'bɪzmɑrk/ 俾斯麥 (Prince Otto Eduard Leopold, 1815-1898, 普魯士政治家，德意志帝國第一任首相)。

Björnson /'bjɜːnsn ; 'bjɝnsn̩/ 邊爾生 (Björnstjerne, 1832-1910, 挪威詩人、劇作家及小說家，曾獲 1903 年諾貝爾文學獎)。

Black /blæk ; blæk/ 布拉克 (Hugo Lafayette, 1886-1971, 美國法學家及從政者)。

Blackett /'blækət ; 'blækət/ 伯來克特 (Patrick Maynard Stuart, 1897-1974, 英國物理學家，曾獲 1948 年諾貝爾物理獎)。

Blackmore /'blækmɔː ; 'blækmor/ 布拉克摩爾 (Richard Doddridge, 1825-1900, 英國小說家)。

Blackstone /'blækstən ; 'blækˌston/ 布拉克斯東 (Sir William, 1723-1780, 英國法學家)。

Blake /bleɪk ; blek/ 布雷克 (**1** Robert, 1599-1657, 英國海軍上將; **2** William, 1757-1827, 英國詩人及藝術家)。

Blériot /'blerɪəʊ ; 'blɛrɪo/ 布雷里奧 (Louis, 1872-1936, 法國飛行家及工程師，發明單翼飛機)。

Bloch /blɒk ; blɑk/ 布洛克 (**1** Ernest, 1880-1959, 生於瑞士之美國作曲家; **2** Felix, 1905-, 美國物理學家，與 E. M. Purcell 同獲 1952 年諾貝爾物理獎; **3** Konrad E., 1912-, 生於德國之美國生物化學家，1964 年獲諾貝爾醫學獎)。

Bloomfield /'bluːmfiːld ; 'blumˌfild/ 布隆費德 (Leonard, 1887-1949, 美國語言學家及教育家)。

Blücher /'bluːkə;'blukɚ/ 布魯克 (Gebhard Leberecht von, 1742-1819, 普魯士元帥)。

Boadicea /ˌbəʊədɪ'sɪə ; ˌboədɪ'siə/ 波阿狄西亞 (?-A. D. 62, 英國古代 Iceni 族女王，曾反抗羅馬)。

Boas /'bəʊæz ; 'boæz/ 包艾斯 (Franz, 1858-1942, 生於德國之美國人類學家及民族學家)。

Boccaccio /bəʊ'kɑːtʃɪəʊ ; bo 'kɑtʃɪo/ 包伽邱 (Giovanni, 1313-1375, 義大利作家)。

Boethius /bəʊ'iːθɪəs ; bo'iθɪəs/ 包伊夏斯 (Anicius Manlius Severinus, 480?-?524, 羅馬哲學家)。

Bohr /'bəʊə ; bor/ 鮑爾 (Niels, 1885-1962, 丹麥物理學家，曾獲 1922 年諾貝爾物理獎)。

Boleyn /'bʊlɪn ; 'bʊlɪn/ 布林 (Anne, 1507-1536, 英王亨利八世之次妻，伊利莎白女王一世之母)。

Böll /bʌl ; bʌl/ 鮑爾 (Heinrich Theodor, 1917-, 德國作家，曾獲 1972 年諾貝爾文學獎)。

Bonaparte /'bəʊnəpɑːt ; 'bonəˌpɑrt/ 拿破崙之姓 (參看 Napoleon 各條，亦作 Buonaparte)。

Boniface VIII /'bɒnɪfeɪs ; 'bɑnəˌfes/ 龐尼菲斯八世 (1235?-1303, 羅馬教皇，在位期間 1294-1303)。

Bonnet /bɔː'neɪ ; bɔ'ne/ 鮑奈 (**1** Georges, 1889-1973, 法國從政者及外交家; **2** Henri, 1888-1978, 法國歷史學家及外交家)。

Bordet /bɔː'deɪ ; bɔr'de/ 包爾蒂 (Jules, 1870-1961, 比利時細菌學家，曾獲 1919 年諾貝爾醫學獎)。

Born /bɔːn ; bɔrn/ 波恩 (Max, 1882-1970, 德國物理學家，與 W. Bothe 同獲 1954 年諾貝爾物理獎)。

Bosch /bɑːʃ ; bɑʃ/ 包士 (Karl, 1874-1940, 德國工業化學家，與 F. Bergius 同獲 1931 年諾貝爾化學獎)。

Boswell /'bɒzwəl ; 'bɑzwɛl/ 包斯威爾 (James, 1740-1795, 蘇格蘭律師及作家，曾著 'Samuel Johnson 傳')。

Bothe /'bəʊtə ; 'botə/ 波特 (Walther, 1891-1957, 德國物理學家，與 M. Born 同獲 1954 年諾貝爾物理獎)。

Botticelli /ˌbɒtɪ'tʃelɪ ; ˌbɑtɪ'tʃɛlɪ/ 包提柴里 (Sandro, 1444?-1510, 義大利畫家)。

Bougainville /'buːgənvɪl ; 'bugənˌvɪl/ 蒲干維爾 (Louis Antoine de, 1729-1811, 法國航海家)。

Bourgeois /bʊə'ʒwɑː;bʊr'ʒwɑ/ 布爾喬亞 (Léon Victor Auguste, 1851-1925, 法國政治家，曾獲 1920 年諾貝爾和平獎)。

Bovet /bəʊ've ; bo've/ 波費 (Daniel, 1907-, 生於瑞士之義大利生理學家，曾獲 1957 年諾貝爾醫學獎)。

Boyd-Orr /'bɔɪd 'ɔə ; 'bɔɪd'ɔr/ 波義奧爾 (Sir John, 1880-1971, 蘇格蘭農學家，曾獲 1949 年諾貝爾和平獎)。

Boyle /bɔɪl ; bɔɪl/ 波義耳 (Robert, 1627-1691, 英國物理學家及化學家)。

Bradford /'brædfəd ; 'brædfɚd/ 布萊德福 (**1** Gamaliel, 1863-1932, 美國傳記作家; **2** Roark, 1896-1948, 美國作家)。

Bragg /bræg ; bræg/ 布萊格 (Sir William (Henry), 1862-1942, 與其子 Sir (William) Lawrence 1890-1971, 同爲英國物理學家，並同獲 1915 年諾貝爾物理學獎)。

Brahms /brɑːmz ; brɑmz/ 布拉姆斯 (Johannes, 1833-1897, 德國作曲家及鋼琴家)。

Braille /breɪl ; brel/ 布雷爾 (Louis, 1809-1852, 法國盲人教師,目失明,發明點字法)。
Branting /ˈbræntɪŋ ; ˈbræntɪŋ/ 布蘭庭 (Karl Hjalmar, 1860-1925, 瑞典政治家,與 C. L. Lange 同獲 1921年諾貝爾和平獎)。
Brattain /ˈbrætən ; ˈbrætn̩/ 布拉敦 (Walter Houser, 1902-, 美國物理學家,與 J. Bardeen 及 W. B. Shockley 同獲 1956年諾貝爾物理獎)。
Braun /brɔːn ; braʊn/ 布朗 (Karl Ferdinand, 1850-1918, 德國物理學家,與 M. G. Marconi 同獲 1909年諾貝爾物理獎)。
Breasted /ˈbrestɪd ; ˈbrɛstɪd/ 布萊斯堤德 (James Henry, 1865-1935, 美國東方學家、歷史學家及考古學家)。
Breton /ˈbretn ; ˈbrɛtn̩/ 布萊頓 (André, 1896-1966, 法國超現實主義詩人)。
Brewster /ˈbruːstə ; ˈbrustɚ/ 布魯斯德 (William, 1567-1644, 開發美國之清教徒)。
Brezhnev /ˈbreʒnef ; ˈbrɛʒˌnɛf/ 布里玆涅夫 (Leonid Ilyich, 1906-82, 蘇俄共產黨總書記, 並於 1960-64 和 1977-82 爲蘇俄元首)。
Briand /ˈbriːɒnd ; ˈbriɑnd/ 白里安 (Aristide, 1862-1932, 法國政治家, 與 G. Stresemann 同獲 1926年諾貝爾和平獎)。
Bridges /ˈbrɪdʒɪz ; ˈbrɪdʒɪz/ 布立基玆 (Robert Seymour, 1844-1930, 英國詩人,於 1913-30 榮膺桂冠詩人)。
Bridgman /ˈbrɪdʒmən ; ˈbrɪdʒmən/ 布立基曼 (Percy Williams, 1882-1961, 美國物理學家, 曾獲 1946年諾貝爾物理獎)。
Briggs /brɪgz ; brɪgz/ 布立格玆 (Lyman James, 1874-1963, 美國物理學家)。
Bright /braɪt ; braɪt/ 布萊特 (John, 1811-1889, 英國演說家及政治家)。
Britten /ˈbrɪtən ; ˈbrɪtn/ 布立頓 ((Edward) Benjamin, 1913-1976, 英國作曲家)。
Broglie, de /brɔɪ ; brɔɪ/ 戴布勞格利 (Louis Victor, 1892-, 法國物理學家,曾獲 1929年諾貝爾物理獎)。
Brontë /ˈbrɒntɪ ; ˈbrɑntɪ/ 布朗蒂 (**1** Charlotte, 1816-1855, 筆名 Currer Bell; **2** Emily Jane, 1818-1848, 筆名 Ellis Bell; **3** Anne, 1820-1849, 筆名 Acton Bell; 三姊妹均爲英國小說家)。
Brooke /brʊk ; brʊk/ 布魯克 (Rupert, 1887-1915, 英國詩人)。
Brown /braʊn ; braʊn/ 布朗 (**1** Charles Brockden, 1771-1810, 美國小說家; **2** Ford Madox, 1821-1893, 英國畫家; **3** John, 1800-1859, 美國主張廢除奴隸制度者)。
Browne /braʊn ; braʊn/ 布朗 (Sir Thomas, 1605-1682, 英國醫生及作家)。
Browning /ˈbraʊnɪŋ ; ˈbraʊnɪŋ/ 布朗寧 (**1** Elizabeth Barrett, 1806-1861, Robert 之妻, 英國女詩人; **2** Robert, 1812-1889, 英國詩人)。
Broz(ovitch) /ˈbrəʊz(əvɪtʃ) ; ˈbroz(əvɪtʃ)/ 布樓尤維奇 (Josip, 1892-1980, 通稱 Tito '狄托', 南斯拉夫元帥, 1945-53 任總理, 1953-80 任總統)。
Bruce /bruːs ; brus/ 普魯斯 (**1** Sir David, 1855-1931, 英國醫生及細菌學家; **2** Robert, 1274-1329, 蘇格蘭國王, 在位期間 1306-29, 1314年領導蘇格蘭人民在 Bannockburn 擊敗英國,而使蘇格蘭獲得獨立; **3** Stanley Melbourne, 1883-1967, 澳大利亞政治家, 於 1923-29 任總理)。
Bryan /ˈbraɪən ; ˈbraɪən/ 布萊安 (William Jennings, 1860-1925, 美國律師及從政者)。
Bryant /ˈbraɪənt ; ˈbraɪənt/ 布萊安特 (William Cullen, 1794-1878, 美國詩人及編輯)。
Bryce /braɪs ; braɪs/ 布萊斯 (Viscount James, 1838-1922, 英國法學家、歷史學家及外交家)。
Buchanan /bjuːˈkænən ; bjuˈkænən/ 布坎南 (James, 1791-1868, 美國從政者及外交家,爲美第十五任總統,任期 1857-61)。
Buchner /ˈbuːknə ; ˈbuknɚ/ 布克納 (Eduard, 1860-1917, 德國化學家, 曾獲 1907年諾貝爾化學獎)。
Buck /bʌk ; bʌk/ 賽珍珠 (Pearl, 1892-1973, 本姓 Sydenstricker, 美國女小說家,曾獲 1938年諾貝爾文學獎)。
Buckle /ˈbʌkl ; ˈbʌkl̩/ 巴克爾 (Henry Thomas, 1821-1862, 英國歷史學家)。
Buddha 參看 Gautama ～。
Buisson /bwiːˈsɒn ; bwiˈsɔn/ 布易生 (Ferdinand, 1841-1932, 法國教育家,與 L. Quidde 同獲 1927年諾貝爾和平獎)。
Bunche /bʌntʃ ; bʌntʃ/ 彭區 (Ralph Johnson, 1904-1971, 美國政治學家及外交家,曾獲1950年諾貝爾和平獎)。
Bunin /ˈbuːnjən ; ˈbun(j)ən/ 布延 (Ivan Alekseevich, 1870-1953, 俄國詩人及小說家, 曾獲 1933年諾貝爾文學獎)。
Bunsen /ˈbʊnsn ; ˈbʌnsn̩/ 本生 (Robert Wilhelm, 1811-1899, 德國化學家)。
Bunyan /ˈbʌnjən ; ˈbʌnjən/ 班揚 (John, 1628-1688, 英國傳教士及作家)。
Burgess /ˈbɜːdʒɪs ; ˈbɝdʒɪs/ 柏基斯 ((Frank) Gelett, 1866-1951, 美國插畫家及幽默作家)。
Burke /bɜːk ; bɝk/ 柏克 (Edmund, 1729-1797, 英國政治家及演說家)。
Burne-Jones /ˈbɜːn-ˈdʒəʊnz ; ˈbɝn-ˈdʒonz/ 柏恩瓊斯 (Sir Edward Coley, 1833-1898, 英國畫家及設計家)。
Burnet /bəˈnet ; bɚˈnɛt/ 白奈特 (Sir (Frank) Macfarlane, 1899-, 澳大利亞醫生,與 P. B. Medawar 同獲 1960年諾貝爾醫學獎)。
Burnett /bəˈnet ; bɚˈnɛt/ 貝妮特 (Frances Eliza, 本姓 Hodgson, 1849-1924, 生於英國之美國女作家)。
Burns /bɜːnz ; bɝnz/ 柏恩斯 (Robert, 1759-1796, 蘇格蘭詩人)。
Burroughs /ˈbʌrəʊz ; ˈbɝoz/ 柏洛玆 (John, 1837-1921, 美國博物學家)。
Burton /ˈbɜːtn ; ˈbɝtn̩/ 柏頓 (**1** Harold Hitz, 1888-1964, 美國法學家; **2** Sir Richard Francis, 1821-1890, 英國探險家及東方學家; **3** Robert, 1577-1640, 英國傳教士及作家)。
Bush /bʊʃ ; bʊʃ/ 布西 (Vannevar, 1890-1974, 美國電機工程師)。
Butenandt /ˈbuːtənɑːnt ; ˈbutn̩ˌɑnt/ 布特南 (Adolph, 1903-, 德國化學家,與 L. Ružička 同獲 1939年諾貝爾化學獎)。
Butler /ˈbʌtlə ; ˈbʌtlɚ/ 巴特勒 (**1** Benjamin Franklin, 1818-1893, 美國律師, 將軍及從政者; **2** Joseph, 1692-1752, 英國神學家; **3** Nicholas Murray, 1862-1947, 美國教育家,與 J. Addams 同獲 1931年諾貝爾和平獎; **4** Samuel, 1612-1680, 英國諷刺詩人; **5** Samuel, 1835-1902, 英國諷刺小說家)。
Byron /ˈbaɪrən ; ˈbaɪrən/ 拜倫 (George Gordon, 1788-1824, 英國詩人)。
Cabell /ˈkæbəl ; ˈkæbl̩/ 喀拜爾 (James Branch, 1879-1958, 美國小說家及散文家)。
Cable /ˈkeɪbl ; ˈkebl̩/ 蓋博 (George Washington, 1844-1925, 美國小說家)。
Cabot /ˈkæbət ; ˈkæbət/ 喀波特 (John, 1450-1498, 威尼斯航海家,北美之發現者)。
Caesar /ˈsiːzə ; ˈsizɚ/ 凱撒 (Gaius Julius, 100-44 B.C., 羅馬將軍、政治家及作家)。
Caine /keɪn ; ken/ 克恩 (Sir (Thomas Henry) Hall, 1853-1931, 英國小說家)。
Caius 參看 Gaius。
Calderón de la Barca /ˈkɔːldərən ˌdeləˈbɑːkə ; ˈkɔldərən ˌdɛləˈbɑrkə/ 喀爾德隆 (Pedro, 1600-1681, 西班牙劇作家及詩人)。
Caldwell /ˈkɔːldwəl ; ˈkɔldwəl/ 考德威爾 (Erskine, 1903-, 美國小說家)。
Caligula /kəˈlɪgjʊlə ; kəˈlɪgjʊlə/ 喀利古拉 (眞名 Gaius Caesar, 12-41, 羅馬皇帝, 在位期間 37-41)。
Callisthenes /kæˈlɪsθəniːz ; kæˈlɪsθəˌniz/ 凱利斯尼玆 (360?-?328 B.C., 希臘哲學家及歷史學家)。
Callistratus /kæˈlɪstrətəs ; kæˈlɪstrətəs/ 凱利斯屈塔斯 (?-355 B.C., 雅典演說家及將軍)。
Calvin /ˈkælvɪn ; ˈkælvɪn/ 喀爾文 (**1** John, 原名 Jean Chauvin, 1509-1564, 法國神學家及宗教改革者; **2** Melvin, 1911-, 美國化學家,曾獲 1961年諾貝爾化學獎)。
Camden /ˈkæmdən ; ˈkæmdən/ 康登 (William, 1551-1623, 英國古物學家、古物收藏家及歷史學家)。
Campbell /ˈkæmbl ; ˈkæmbl̩/ 甘貝爾 (Thomas, 1777-1844, 英國詩人)。
Campion /ˈkæmpjən ; ˈkæmpɪən/ 甘萍 (Thomas, 1567-1620, 英國詩人及音樂家)。

Camus /kɑ:'mu: ; kɑ'mu/ 卡繆 (Albert, 1913–1960, 法國小說家、散文家及劇作家,曾獲 1957 年諾貝爾文學獎)。
Canetti /'kɑ:netɪ ; 'kɑnɛtɪ/ 卡內提 (Elias, 1905–, 德國作家,曾獲 1981 年諾貝爾文學獎)。
Canning /'kænɪŋ ; 'kænɪŋ/ 甘寧 (**1** George, 1770–1827, 英國政治家,於 1827 年任首相; **2** Stratford, 1786–1880, 英國外交家)。
Cannon /'kænən ; 'kænən/ 甘農 (Joseph Gurney, 1836–1926, 美國律師及從政者)。
Canute II /kə'nju:t ; kə'njut/ 喀奴特二世 (994?–1035, 亦稱Canute the Great, 英王,在位期間 1016–35, 並於 1018–35 爲丹麥國王, 1028–35 爲挪威國王)。
Carducci /kɑ:'du:tʃɪ ; kɑr'dutʃɪ/ 賈多祺 (Giosuè, 1835–1907, 義大利詩人,曾獲 1906 年諾貝爾文學獎)。
Carew /kə'ru: ; kə'ru/ 加露 (Thomas, 1595?–?1645, 英國詩人)。
Carlos /'kɑ:lɒs ; 'kɑrləs/ 卡勒斯 (Don, 1788–1855, 西班牙 Charles IV 之次子,曾力謀篡取王位)。
Carlyle /kɑ:'laɪl ; kɑr'laɪl/ 喀萊爾 (Thomas, 1795–1881, 蘇格蘭散文家及歷史學家)。
Carman /'kɑ:mən ; 'kɑrmən/ 喀曼 ((William) Bliss, 1861–1929, 加拿大詩人)。
Carnegie /kɑ:'negɪ ; kɑr'nɛgɪ/ 卡內基 (Andrew, 1835–1919, 生於蘇格蘭之美國鋼鐵工業家及慈善家)。
Carol II /'kærəl ; 'kærəl/ 加羅爾二世 (1893–1953, 羅馬尼亞國王,在位期間 1930–40)。
Carrel /kə'rel ; kə'rɛl/ 喀雷爾 (Alexis, 1873–1944, 法國外科醫生及生物學家,曾獲 1912 年諾貝爾醫學獎)。
Carter /'kɑ:tə ; 'kɑrtɚ/ 卡特 (**1** Howard, 1873–1939, 英國考古學家; **2** Jimmy, 全名 James Earl ~, Jr., 1924–, 美國從政者, 於 1977–80 任美國第三十九任總統)。
Carteret /'kɑ:təret ; 'kɑrtərɛt/ 加特利 (John, 1690–1763, 英國政治家)。
Cartwright /'kɑ:traɪt ; 'kɑrt,raɪt/ 喀特萊特 (Edmund, 1743–1823, 英國發明家,水力紡織機發明者)。
Caruso /kə'ru:səʊ ; kə'ruso/ 卡羅素 (Enrico, 1873–1921, 義大利男高音歌唱家)。
Carver /'kɑ:və ; 'kɑrvɚ/ 喀威爾 (**1** George Washington, 1864–1943, 美國植物學家; **2** John, 1576?–1621, 英國清教徒, Plymouth 殖民地之首任總督)。
Cary /'keərɪ ; 'kɛrɪ/ 喀利 (Henry Francis, 1772–1844, 英國教士,但丁神曲之英文翻譯者)。
Cassius Longinus /'kæʃɪəs lɒn'dʒaɪnəs ; 'kæʃəs lɑn'dʒaɪnəs/ 加西阿斯 (Gaius, ?–42 B.C., 羅馬大將,謀殺凱撒之主要刺客)。
Catesby /'keɪtsbɪ ; 'ketsbɪ/ 凱次比 (Mark, 1679?–1749, 英國博物學家)。
Catherine I /'kæθrɪn ; 'kæθ(ə)rɪn/ 加德琳一世 (1684?–1727, 彼得大帝之妻,俄女皇,在位期間 1725–27)。
Catherine II 加德琳二世 (1729–1796, 俄國女皇, 在位期間 1762–96, 被稱爲 Catherine the Great)。
Catiline /'kætɪlaɪn ; 'kætḷ,aɪn/ 加蒂藍 (全名 Lucius Sergius Catilina, 108?–62 B.C., 羅馬政客及謀叛者)。
Cato /'keɪtəʊ ; 'keto/ 加圖 (**1** Marcus Porcius, 234–149 B.C., 稱爲 ~ the Elder, 羅馬政治家; **2** Marcus Porcius, 95–46 B.C., 稱爲 ~ the Younger, 羅馬斯多噶派哲學家,爲老加圖之曾孫)。
Cattell /kæ'tel ; kə'tɛl/ 加太爾 (James McKeen, 1860–1944, 美國心理學家及編輯)。
Catullus /kə'tʌləs ; kə'tʌləs/ 加塔拉斯 (Gaius Valerius, 84?–54 B.C., 羅馬詩人)。
Cavendish /'kævəndɪʃ ; 'kævəndɪʃ/ 加文狄希 (Henry, 1731–1810, 英國化學家及物理學家)。
Caxton /'kækstən ; 'kækstən/ 卡克斯頓 (William 1422?–1491, 英國第一位印刷家)。
Cecil /'sesl ; 'sɛsl/ 塞梭 (**1** (Edgar Algernon) Robert, 1864–1958, 英國政治家, 曾獲 1937 年諾貝爾和平獎; **2** William, 1520–1598, 英國政治家)。
Celsius /'selsɪəs ; 'sɛlsɪəs/ 攝爾夏斯 (Anders, 1701–1744, 瑞典天文學家,首創溫度計百度計法)。
Cervantes Saavedra, de /sɜ:'vænti:z sɑ:'veɪdrə ; sɚ'væn,tiz sɑ'vedrə/ 塞凡蒂斯 (Miguel, 1547–1616, 西班牙小說家,'唐・吉訶德'之作者)。
Cézanne /seɪ'zæn ; se'zæn/ 塞尚 (Paul, 1839–1906, 法國畫家)。
Chadwick /'tʃædwɪk ; 'tʃædwɪk/ 查特威克 (Sir James, 1891–1974, 英國物理學家,曾獲 1935 年諾貝爾物理獎)。
Chain /tʃeɪn ; tʃen/ 柴恩 (Ernst Boris, 1906–1979, 生於德國之英國生物化學家,與 A. Fleming 及 H. W. Florey 同獲 1945 年諾貝爾醫學獎)。
Chaliapin /ʃə'ljɑ:pi:n ; ʃə'ljɑpin/ 沙利亞賓 (Feodor Ivanovitch, 1873–1938, 俄國男低音歌唱家)。
Chalmers /'tʃɑ:məz ; 'tʃælmɚz/ 查麥玆 (Alexander, 1759–1834, 蘇格蘭傳記作家及編輯)。
Chamberlain /'tʃeɪmbəlɪn ; 'tʃembɚlɪn/ 張伯倫 (**1** (Arthur) Neville, 1869–1940, 英國政治家, 於 1937–40 任首相; **2** Sir (Joseph) Austen, 1863–1937, 英國政治家,與 C. G. Dawes 同獲 1925 年諾貝爾和平獎; **3** Owen, 1920–, 美國物理學家, 與 E. Segrè 同獲 1959 年諾貝爾物理獎)。
Chang Ch'ien /'dʒɑ:ŋ'tʃjen ; 'dʒɑŋ'tʃjɛn/ 張騫 (中國西漢之外交家)。
Chao K'uang-yin /'dʒaʊ 'kwɑ:ŋ'jɪn ; 'dʒaʊ 'kwɑŋ'jɪn/ 趙匡胤 (927–976, 中國宋朝開國之主,即宋太祖,在位十七年)。
Chao Yuen Ren /'dʒaʊ'jwen'rən ; dʒaʊ'jwɛn'rən/ 趙元任 (1893–1982, 中國語言學家,有'漢語語言學之父'之稱)。
Chapman /'tʃæpmən ; 'tʃæpmən/ 查浦曼 (**1** Frank Michler, 1864–1945, 美國鳥類學家; **2** George 1559?–1634, 英國劇作家及翻譯家)。
Charlemagne /'ʃɑ:ləmeɪn ; 'ʃɑrlə,men/ 查理曼 (742–814, 世稱 Charles the Great 或 Charles I, 於 768–814 爲法蘭克王,並於 800–814 爲西羅馬帝國皇帝)。
Charles I /tʃɑ:lz ; tʃɑrlz/ 查理一世 (**1** 全名 Charles Stuart, 1600–1649, 於 1625–49 爲英王; **2** 全名 Charles Francis Joseph, 1887–1922, 於 1916–18 爲奧國皇帝及匈牙利國王)。
Charles I or II 查理一世 (823–877, 世稱 Charles the Bald, 於 840–877 爲法王,稱查理一世; 875–877 爲神聖羅馬帝國皇帝,改稱二世)。
Charles II 查理二世 (1630–1685, 於 1660–85 爲英王)。
Charles IV 查理四世 (1294–1328, 世稱 Charles the Fair, 於 1322–28 爲法王)。
Charles V 查理五世 (**1** 1337–1380, 世稱 Charles the Wise, 於 1364–80 爲法王; **2** 1500–1558, 於 1519–56 爲神聖羅馬帝國皇帝, 1516–56 以查理一世稱號爲西班牙國王)。
Charles VI 查理六世 (1368–1422, 世稱 Charles the Mad 或 Charles the Beloved, 於 1380–1422 爲法王)。
Charles VII 查理七世 (1403–1461, 世稱 Charles the Victorious, 於 1422–61 爲法王)。
Charles IX 查理九世 (1550–1574, 於 1560–74 爲法王)。
Charles X 查理十世 (1757–1836, 於 1824–30 爲法王)。
Charles XII 查理十二世 (1682–1718, 於 1697–1718 爲瑞典國王)。
Chase /tʃeɪs ; tʃes/ 蔡斯 (Salmon Portland, 1808–1873, 美國政治家及法學家,於 1864–73 爲美國最高法院大法官)。
Chatterton /'tʃætətn ; 'tʃætɚtn̩/ 查特頓 (Thomas, 1752–1770, 英國詩人)。
Chaucer /'tʃɔ:sə ; 'tʃɔsɚ/ 喬塞 (Geoffrey, 1340?–1400, 英國詩人, Canterbury Tales 之作者)。
Chek(h)ov, Tchekhov /'tʃekɒf ; 'tʃɛk,ɔf/ 契可夫 (Anton Pavlovich, 1860–1904, 俄國作家及劇作家)。
Cheng Ho /'dʒeŋ 'hɔ: ; 'dʒɛŋ 'hɔ/ 鄭和 (中國明朝之航海家)。
Ch'eng T'ang /'tʃeŋ 'tɑ:ŋ ; 'tʃɛŋ 'tɑŋ/ 成湯 (姓子,名履,中國商朝開國帝王,在位三十年)。
Cherenkov /tʃə'reŋkəf ; tʃə'rɛŋkəf/ 齊蘭可夫 (Pavel Alekseevich, 1904–, 俄國物理學家, 與 I. M. Frank 及 I. E. Tamm 同獲 1958 年諾貝爾物理獎)。
Cherubini /,keru'bi:ni: ; ,kɛrʊ'bini/ 凱路比尼 (Luigi Carlo Zenobio Salvatore, 1760–1842, 義大利作曲家)。
Chesterfield /'tʃestəfi:ld ; 'tʃɛstɚ,fild/ 柴斯特菲爾德 (原名 Philip Dormer Stanhope, 1694–1773, 英國政治家及作家)。
Chiang Kai-shek /dʒɪ'ɑ:ŋ 'kaɪ'ʃek ; dʒɪ'ɑŋ'kaɪ'ʃɛk/ 蔣介石 (1887–1975, 即蔣中正,中國大軍事家及政治家,中華民國行憲後第一、二、三、四、五任總統)。

Ch'ien Lung, Kien Lung /tʃɪ'en 'lʊŋ ; tʃɪ'ɛn'lʊŋ/ 乾隆 (1711–1799, 中國清朝皇帝,卽清高宗,原爲年號名,在位期間 1736–96)。
Chi Fa /'dʒiː'fɑː ; 'dʒi'fɑ/ 姬發(中國周朝開國帝王,卽周武王,在位十九年)。
Child /tʃaɪld ; tʃaɪld/ 柴爾德 (Francis James, 1825–1896, 美國語言學家及民謠研究專家)。
Chippendale /'tʃɪpəndeɪl ; 'tʃɪpəndel/ 齊本德耳 (Thomas, 1718?–1779, 英國傢具專家及設計家)。
Chopin /'ʃɒpæŋ ; 'ʃopæn/ 蕭邦 (Frédéric Francois, 1810–1849, 波蘭鋼琴家及作曲家)。
Christian X /'krɪstʃən ; 'krɪstʃən/ 克里斯欽十世 (1870–1947, 丹麥國王,在位期間 1912–47)。
Christie /'krɪstɪ ; 'krɪstɪ/ 克里斯蒂 (Dame Agatha, 1891–1976, 本姓 Miller, 英國女偵探小說家)。
Christina /krɪs'tiːnə ; krɪs'tinə/ 克里斯蒂納 (1626–1689, 瑞典女王,在位期間 1632–54)。
Chuang-tzu /'dʒwɑːŋ 'dzʊ ; 'dʒwɑŋ 'dzʊ/ 莊子 (約公元前四世紀之中國哲學家,本名莊周)。
Chu Hsi /'dʒuː 'ʃiː ; 'dʒu 'ʃi/ 朱熹 (1130–1200, 中國宋朝理學家)。
Churchill /'tʃɜːtʃɪl ; 'tʃɝtʃɪl/ 邱吉爾 (**1** Sir Winston Leonard Spencer, 1874–1965, 英國政治家及作家, 於 1940–45, 1951–55 任首相, 並於 1953 獲諾貝爾文學獎; **2** John, 1650–1722, 英國將軍, 爲首位 Marlborough 公爵)。
Ch'ü Yüan /'tʃjuː'juːɑːn ; 'tʃɪu 'juɑn/ 屈原 (343–290 B.C., 中國戰國時代大詩人)。
Chu Yüan-chang /'dʒuː 'juːɑːn 'dʒɑːŋ ; 'dʒu 'juɑn 'dʒɑŋ/ 朱元璋 (1328–1398, 中國明朝開國君主,卽明太祖,在位三十一年)。
Cicero /'sɪsərəʊ ; 'sɪsə,ro/ 西塞羅 (Marcus Tullius, 106–43 B.C., 羅馬政治家、演說家及作家)。
Clark /klɑːk ; klɑrk/ 克拉克 (**1** Champ, 1850–1921, 美國政治家; **2** Mark Wayne, 1896–, 美國將軍; **3** Thomas Campbell, 1899–1977, 美國法學家; **4** William, 1770–1838, 美國探險家)。
Clay /kleɪ ; kle/ 克雷 (Henry, 1777–1852, 美國政治家及演說家)。
Clemenceau /,klemən'səʊ ; ,klɛmən'so/ 克里孟梭 (Georges, 1841–1929, 有 the Tiger 之稱,法國政治家)。
Clemens /'klemənz ; 'klɛmənz/ 克里門斯 (Samuel Langhorne, 1835–1910, 筆名 Mark Twain, 美國幽默作家)。
Clement VII /'klemənt ; 'klɛmənt/ 克里門七世(原名 Giulio de' Medici, 1478–1534, 羅馬教皇, 在位期間 1523–34)。
Cleopatra /klɪə'pætrə;,kliə'pætrə/ 克利歐佩特拉 (69–30 B.C., 古埃及最後女王,在位期間 51–49 B.C., 48–30 B.C.)。
Cleveland /'kliːvlənd ; 'klivlənd/ 克里夫蘭 ((Stephen) Grover, 1837–1908, 美國第 22 任(1885–89)及 24 任(1893–97)總統)。
Clinton /'klɪntən ; 'klɪntn̩/ 克林頓 (**1** De Witt, 1769–1828, 美國政治家; **2** George, 1739–1812, 美國政治家, 於 1805–12 任副總統)。
Clive /klaɪv ; klaɪv/ 克萊夫 (Robert, 1725–1774, 英國將軍)。
Clough /klʌf ; klʌf/ 克勒夫 (Arthur Hugh, 1819–1861, 英國詩人)。
Clovis I /'kləʊvɪs ; 'klovɪs/ 克洛維一世 (466?–511, 於 481–511 爲法蘭克國王)。
Cobb /kɒb ; kɑb/ 柯布 (Irvin Shrewsbury, 1876–1944, 美國新聞記者及幽默作家)。
Cobbett /'kɒbɪt ; 'kɑbɪt/ 柯貝特 (William, 1763–1835, 筆名 Peter Porcupine, 英國新聞記者及政論作家)。
Cobden /'kɒbdən ; 'kɑbdən/ 柯布敦 (Richard, 1804–1865, 英國政治家及經濟學家)。
Cockcroft /'kɒkrɒft ; 'kɑkrɔft/ 科克勞佛 (Sir John Douglas, 1897–1967, 英國物理學家,與 E. T. S. Walton 同獲 1951 年諾貝爾物理獎)。
Coffin /'kɒfɪn ; 'kɔfɪn/ 柯芬 (Robert Peter Tristram, 1892–1955, 美國作家)。
Cole /kəʊl ; kol/ 柯爾 (Thomas, 1801–1848, 生於英國之美國畫家)。
Coleridge /'kəʊlrɪdʒ ; 'kolrɪdʒ/ 柯爾雷基 (Samuel Taylor, 1772–1834, 英國詩人、評論家及哲學家)。
Collier /'kɒlɪə ; 'kɑljɚ/ 柯里爾 (**1** Jeremy, 1650–1726, 英國傳教士及作家; **2** Peter Fenelon, 1849–1909, 美國出版家)。
Colman /'kəʊlmən ; 'kolmən/ 柯爾曼 (George, 1732–1794, 英國劇作家)。
Columbus /kə'lʌmbəs ; kə'lʌmbəs/ 哥倫布 (Christopher, 1451–1506, 義大利航海家,於 1492 發現美洲)。
Comenius /kə'miːnjəs ; kə'minɪəs/ 柯米尼亞斯 (John Amos, 1592–1670, 捷克神學家及教育家)。
Compton /'kɒmptən ; 'kɑmptən/ 康普頓 (**1** Arthur Holly, 1892–1962, 美國物理學家,與 C. T. R. Wilson 同獲 1927 年諾貝爾物理獎; **2** Karl Taylor, 1887–1954, 美國物理學家)。
Comte /kɔːnt ; kɔnt/ 孔德 (Auguste, 1798–1857, 法國數學家及哲學家)。
Condon /'kɒndən ; 'kɑndən/ 康敦 (Edward Uhler, 1902–1974, 美國物理學家)。
Confucius /kən'fjuːʃɪəs ; kən'fjuʃəs/ 孔子 (本名孔丘, 約 551–479 B.C., 中國春秋時代哲學家及教育家)。
Coningham /'kʌnɪŋəm ; 'kʌnɪŋ,hæm/ 肯寧漢 (Sir Arthur, 1895–1948, 英國空軍中將)。
Conrad /'kɒnræd ; 'kɑnræd/ 康拉德 (Joseph, 1857–1924, 英籍波蘭裔小說家)。
Constable /'kʌnstəbl ; 'kʌnstəbl̩/ 康斯塔伯 (John, 1776–1837, 英國畫家)。
Constant /kɒn'stɑːn ; kɔn'stɑn/ 康斯丹 (Benjamin, 1845–1902, 法國畫家)。
Constantine I /'kɒnstəntaɪn ; 'kɑnstən,taɪn/ **1** 君士坦丁大帝 (280?–337, 羅馬皇帝, 在位期間 306–337)。**2** 君士坦丁一世 (1868–1923, 希臘國王, 在位期間 1913–17 及 1920–22)。
Cook /kʊk ; kʊk/ 科克 (James, 1728–1779, 英國航海家及探險家)。
Cooke /kʊk ; kʊk/ 柯克 (Jay, 1821–1905, 美國金融家)。
Coolidge /'kuːlɪdʒ ; 'kulɪdʒ/ 柯立芝 (**1** (John) Calvin, 1872–1933, 美國第三十任總統,任期爲1923–29; **2** Julian Lowell, 1873–1954, 美國數學家)。
Cooper /'kuːpə ; 'kupɚ/ 庫柏 (**1** James Fenimore, 1789–1851, 美國小說家; **2** Leon N., 1930–, 美國物理學家, 與 J. Bardeen 及 J. R. Schrieffer 同獲 1972 年諾貝爾物理獎)。
Copernicus /kəʊ'pɜːnɪkəs ; ko'pɝnɪkəs/ 哥白尼 (Nicolaus, 1473–1543, 波蘭天文學家,近代天文學之創始者)。
Cori /'kɔːrɪ ; 'kɔrɪ/ 葛里 (Carl Ferdinand, 1896–, 與其妻 Gerty Theresa ～, 1896–1957, 皆爲生於捷克之美國生物化學家,並和 B. A. Houssay 三人同獲 1947 年諾貝爾醫學獎)。
Corneille /kɔː'neɪ ; kɔr'ne/ 柯奈 (Pierre, 1606–1684, 法國劇作家)。
Cornelius /kɔː'niːljəs ; kɔr'niljəs/ 葛尼路斯 (Peter von, 1783–1867, 德國畫家)。
Coulomb /'kuːlɒm ; 'kulɑm/ 庫倫 (Charles Augustin de, 1736–1806, 法國物理學家)。
Cournand /'kʊənæn ; 'kʊrnɑnd/ 庫爾南 (André Frédéric, 1895–, 美籍法裔生理學家, 與 D. W. Richards, Jr. 及 W. Forssmann 同獲 1956 年諾貝爾醫學獎)。
Cousin /kuː'zæn ; ku'zæn/ 古霑 (Victor, 1792–1867, 法國哲學家)。
Cowley /'kaʊlɪ ; 'kaʊlɪ/ 科里 (Abraham, 1618–1667, 英國詩人)。
Cowper /'kuːpə ; 'kupɚ/ 科伯 (William, 1731–1800, 英國詩人)。
Crabbe /kræb ; kræb/ 克拉卜(George, 1754–1832, 英國詩人)。
Craigie /'kreɪgɪ ; 'kregɪ/ 克雷基 (Sir William Alexander, 1867–1957, 英國語言學家及辭典編纂家)。
Craik /kreɪk ; krek/ 克雷克 (Dinah Maria, 1826–1887, 本姓 Mulock, 英國女小說家)。
Crane /kreɪn ; kren/ 克倫 (Stephen, 1871–1900, 美國作家)。
Cremer /'kriːmə ; 'krimɚ/ 葛禮默 (Sir William Randal, 1838–1908, 英國和平主義者, 曾獲 1903 年諾貝

爾和平獎)。

Crick /krɪk ; krɪk/ 克里克 (Francis Harry Compton, 1916–, 英國生物物理學家,與 J. D. Watson 及 M. H. F. Wilkins 同獲 1962 年諾貝爾醫學獎)。

Croesus /ˈkriːsəs ; ˈkrisəs/ 克里薩斯 (?–546 B.C., 爲 Lydia 王,極爲富有,在位期間 560–546 B.C.)。

Croker /ˈkrəʊkə ; ˈkrokɚ/ 克羅科 (John Wilson, 1780–1857, 英國散文家及編輯)。

Crompton /ˈkrʌmptən ; ˈkrɑmptən/ 克倫頓 (Samuel, 1753–1827, 英國發明家)。

Cromwell /ˈkrɒmwəl ; ˈkrɑmwəl/ 克倫威爾 (Oliver, 1599–1658, 英國將軍及政治家,於 1653–58 任攝政)。

Crookes /krʊks ; krʊks/ 克魯克斯 (Sir William, 1832–1919, 英國物理學家及化學家)。

Cross /krɒs ; krɔs/ 克勞斯 (Wilbur Lucius, 1862–1948, 美國教育家及從政者)。

Cudworth /ˈkʌdwəθ ; ˈkʌdwɚθ/ 寇德華斯 (Ralph, 1617–1688, 英國哲學家)。

Cunningham /ˈkʌnɪŋəm ; ˈkʌnɪŋˌhæm/ 康寧安 (Allan, 1784–1842, 蘇格蘭作家)。

Curie /ˈkjʊərɪ ; ˈkjʊrɪ/ 居禮 (Pierre, 1859–1906, 與夫人 Marie ~, 1867–1934, 同爲法國物理學家及化學家,與 A. H. Becquerel 三人同獲 1903 年諾貝爾物理獎;居禮夫人並於 1911 年再得諾貝爾化學獎)。

Curry /ˈkʌrɪ ; ˈkʌrɪ/ 寇里 (John Steuart, 1897–1946, 美國畫家)。

Curtiss /ˈkɜːtɪs ; ˈkɝtɪs/ 寇蒂斯 (Glenn Hammond, 1878–1930, 美國航空家及發明家)。

Cushing /ˈkʊʃɪŋ ; ˈkʊʃɪŋ/ 顧盛 (Caleb, 1800–1879, 美國律師及外交家)。

Cuvier /ˈkjuːvɪeɪ ; ˈkjuvɪe/ 邱維埃 (Georges, 1769–1832, 法國博物學家)。

Cyrus /ˈsaɪərəs ; ˈsaɪrəs/ 塞魯士 (600?–529 B.C., 世稱 ~ the Great 或 the Elder, 波斯王,在位期間 550–529 B.C.)。

Dale /deɪl ; del/ 德爾 (Sir Henry Hallett, 1875–1968, 英國生理學家,與 O. Loewi 同獲 1936年諾貝爾醫學獎)。

Dalén /dəˈleɪn ; dəˈlen/ 達倫 (Nils Gustaf, 1869–1937, 瑞典發明家,曾獲 1912 年諾貝爾物理獎)。

Dalrymple /dælˈrɪmpl ; dælˈrɪmpḷ/ 道爾林普 (Sir James, 1619–1695, 蘇格蘭法學家)。

Dalton /ˈdɔːltən ; ˈdɔltṇ/ 道爾頓 (John, 1766–1844, 英國化學家及物理學家)。

Dam /dɑːm ; dɑm/ 達姆 ((Carl Peter) Henrik, 1895–1976, 丹麥生物化學家,與 E. A. Doisy 同獲 1943 年諾貝爾醫學獎)。

Dana /ˈdeɪnə ; ˈdenə/ 德納 (**1** Edward Salisbury, 1849–1935, 美國礦物學家; **2** James Dwight, 1813–1895, 美國地質學家)。

Dane /deɪn ; den/ 德恩 (Clemence, 1888–1965, 爲 Winifred Ashton 之筆名,英國小說家)。

Daniel /ˈdænjəl ; ˈdænjəl/ 但尼爾 (Samuel, 1562?–1619, 英國詩人及歷史學家,於 1599–1619 榮膺桂冠詩人)。

Dante /ˈdæntɪ ; ˈdæntɪ/ 但丁 (全名 ~ Alighieri, 1265–1321, 義大利詩人)。

Darius I /dəˈraɪəs ; dəˈraɪəs/ 大流士一世(全名 Darius Hystaspis, 558?–486 B.C., 古波斯王,在位期間 521–486 B.C., 世稱 Darius the Great)。

Darwin /ˈdɑːwɪn ; ˈdɑrwɪn/ 達爾文 (**1** Charles Robert, 1809–1882, 英國博物學家,進化論之創立者; **2** Erasmus, 1731–1802, 前者之祖父,英國生理學家及詩人)。

Daudet /ˈdəʊˈdeɪ ; doˈde/ 都德 (Alphonse, 1840–1897, 法國小說家。)

David[1] /dɑːˈviːd ; dɑˈvid/ 大衛 (Jacques Louis, 1748–1825, 法國畫家)。

David[2] /ˈdeɪvɪd ; ˈdevɪd/ 大衛 (**1** 1013?–?973 B.C., 以色列王; **2** ~ I, 1084–1153, 蘇格蘭王,在位期間 1124–53; **3** Saint, 紀元六世紀之聖者,爲威爾斯之守護神,亦稱 Saint Dewi)。

David d'Angers /dɑːˈviːd dɑːnˈʒeɪ ; dɑˈvid dɑnˌʒe/ 大衛當葉 (Pierre Jean, 1788–1856, 法國雕刻家)。

Davidson /ˈdeɪvɪdsn ; ˈdevɪdsṇ/ 大衛生 (Jo, 1883–1952, 美國雕刻家)。

Davisson /ˈdeɪvɪsn ; ˈdevɪsṇ/ 大衛森 (Clinton Joseph, 1881–1958, 美國物理學家,與 G. P. Thomson 同獲 1937 年諾貝爾物理獎)。

Davy /ˈdeɪvɪ ; ˈdevɪ/ 德維 (Sir Humphrey, 1778–1829, 英國化學家)。

Dawes /dɔːz ; dɔz/ 道斯 (Charles Gates, 1865–1951, 美國律師及財政家,於 1925–29 任美國副總統,與 Sir J. A. Chamberlain 同獲 1925 年諾貝爾和平獎)。

Dawson /ˈdɔːsn ; ˈdɔsṇ/ 道生 (Sir John William, 1820–1899, 加拿大地質學家)。

Day /deɪ ; de/ 戴伊 (**1** Thomas, 1748–1789, 英國作家; **2** William Rufus, 1849–1923, 美國政治家及法學家)。

Day-Lewis /ˈdeɪ ˈluːɪs ; ˈde ˈluəs/ 戴路易斯 (Cecil, 1904–1972, 筆名爲 Nicholas Blake, 英國作家,於 1968–72 榮膺桂冠詩人)。

Debussy /dəˈbusɪ ; dəˈbjusɪ/ 德布西 (Claude Achille, 1862–1918, 法國作曲家)。

Debye /dəˈbaɪ ; dəˈbaɪ/ 狄白 (Peter Joseph Wilhelm, 1884–1966, 荷蘭物理學家,曾獲 1936 年諾貝爾化學獎)。

Decius /ˈdiːʃɪəs ; ˈdiʃ(ɪ)əs/ 狄希阿斯 (201–251, 羅馬皇帝,在位期間 249–51)。

Defoe /dəˈfəʊ ; dəˈfo/ 狄福 (Daniel, 1660?–1731, 英國記者及小說家)。

De Forest /dəˈfɒrɪst ; dəˈfɔrɪst/ 德福來斯特 (Lee, 1873–1961, 美國發明家)。

Degas /dəˈgɑː ; dəˈgɑ/ 狄加 ((Hilaire Germain) Edgar, 1834–1917, 法國印象派畫家)。

de Gaulle /də ˈgəʊl ; dɪˈgol/ 戴高樂 (Charles André Joseph Marie, 1890–1970 法國將軍及政治家,於 1959–69 任法國總統)。

de la Mare /ˌdeləˈmeə ; ˌdɛləˈmɛr/ 狄拉麥爾 (Walter John, 1873–1956, 英國詩人及小說家)。

Deland /ˈdiːlənd ; dɪˈlænd/ 狄蘭德 (Margaret, 1857–1945, 本姓 Campbell, 美國女小說家)。

Deledda /dəˈledə ; dəˈlɛdə/ 戴麗達 (Grazia, 1875–1936, 義大利女小說家,曾獲 1926 年諾貝爾文學獎)。

Delius /ˈdiːlɪəs ; ˈdilɪəs/ 狄里雅斯 (Frederick, 1862–1934, 英國作曲家)。

Democritus /dɪˈmɒkrɪtəs ; dɪˈmɑkrɪtəs/ 德謨克里脫 (460?–362? B.C., 希臘哲學家,有 'the Laughing Philosopher' 之稱)。

De Morgan /dəˈmɔːgən ; dəˈmɔrgən/ 狄摩甘 (William Frend, 1839–1917, 英國藝術家及小說家)。

Depew /dɪˈpjuː ; dɪˈpju/ 德普 (Chauncey Mitchell, 1834–1928, 美國律師及從政者)。

De Quincey /dəˈkwɪnsɪ ; dɪˈkwɪnsɪ/ 戴昆西 (Thomas, 1785–1859, 英國作家)。

Descartes /deɪˈkɑːt ; deˈkɑrt/ 笛卡爾 (René, 1596–1650, 法國哲學家及數學家)。

de Vere /dəˈvɪə ; dəˈvɪɚ/ 德威爾 (Aubrey Thomas, 1814–1902, 愛爾蘭詩人)。

Dewar /ˈdjuːə ; ˈdjuɚ/ 杜爾 (Sir James, 1842–1923, 蘇格蘭化學家及物理學家)。

Dewey /ˈdjuːɪ ; ˈdjuɪ/ 杜威 (**1** George, 1837–1917, 美國海軍上將; **2** John, 1859–1952, 美國教育家及哲學家; **3** Melvil, 1851–1931, 美國圖書館專家; **4** Thomas Edmund, 1902–1971, 美國律師及從政者)。

Dickens /ˈdɪkɪnz ; ˈdɪkɪnz/ 狄更斯 (Charles, 1812–1870, 英國小說家)。

Dickinson /ˈdɪkɪnsn ; ˈdɪkɪnsṇ/ 狄勤生 (Emily Elizabeth, 1830–1886, 美國女詩人)。

Diderot /ˈdiːdərəʊ ; ˈdidəro/ 狄德羅 (Denis, 1713–1784, 法國哲學家及百科全書編纂者。)

Diels /ˈdiːəlz ; ˈdiəlz/ 戴爾士 (Otto Paul Hermann, 1876–1954, 德國化學家,與 K. Alder 同獲 1950 年諾貝爾化學獎)。

Diesel /ˈdiːzəl ; ˈdizəl/ 狄塞爾 (Rudolf, 1858–1913, 德國機械工程師,發明柴油引擎)。

Diocletian /ˌdaɪəˈkliːʃɪən ; ˌdaɪəˈkliʃən/ 戴克里先(245–313, 於 284–305 爲羅馬皇帝)。

Diogenes /daɪˈɒdʒɪniːz ; daɪˈɑdʒəˌniz/ 戴奧眞尼斯 (412?–323 B.C., 希臘大儒學派哲學家)。

Dionysius /ˌdaɪəˈnɪsɪəs ; ˌdaɪəˈnɪʃɪəs/ 戴奧尼夏 (**1** 430?–?367 B.C., 稱爲 ~ the Elder, 古希臘 Syracuse 之暴君,在位期間 405–367 B.C.; **2** 其子,稱爲 ~ the Younger, 古希臘 Syracuse 之暴君, 在位期間 367–356 B.C. 及 347–344 B.C.)。

Dirac /dɪˈræk ; dɪˈræk/ 狄雷克 (Paul Adrien Maurice, 1902–, 英國物理學家,與 E. Schrödinger 同獲 1933 年諾貝爾物理獎)。

Disney /ˈdɪznɪ ; ˈdɪznɪ/ 狄斯耐 (Walter Elias, 1901–1966, 美國電影製片人,卡通電影家)。

Disraeli /dɪzˈreɪlɪ;dɪzˈrelɪ/ 狄斯雷利 (Benjamin, 1804–1881, 英國從政者及作家,於 1868 及 1874–80 任首相)。

Dixon /ˈdɪksn ; ˈdɪksn̩/ 狄克森 (Jeremiah, 十八世紀之英國測量家, 與 C. Mason 共同測定 Mason-Dixon line)。

Dobie /ˈdəʊbɪ ; ˈdobɪ/ 道比 (James Frank, 1888–1964, 美國民俗學家)。

Dobrée /ˈdəʊbreɪ ; ˈdobre/ 道卜雷 (Bonamy, 1891–1974, 英國學者)。

Dobson /ˈdɒbsn ; ˈdɑbsn̩/ 多卜生 ((Henry) Austin, 1840–1921, 英國詩人及散文家)。

Dodgson /ˈdɒdʒsn ; ˈdɑdʒsən/ 多治生 (Charles Lutwidge, 1832–1898, 筆名 Lewis Carroll, 英國數學家及小說家)。

Doisy /ˈdɔɪzɪ ; ˈdɔɪzɪ/ 杜伊基 (Edward Adelbert, 1893–, 美國生物化學家,與 C. P. H. Dam 同獲 1943 年諾貝爾醫學獎)。

Domagk /ˈdəʊmɑːk ; ˈdoˌmɑk/ 杜馬克 (Gerhard, 1895–1964, 德國化學家,曾獲 1939 年諾貝爾醫學獎)。

Dominic /ˈdɒmɪnɪk ; ˈdɑmɪnɪk/ 聖・多明尼克 (Saint, 1170–1221, 西班牙修士, Dominican 教派之創始人)。

Domitian /dəˈmɪʃɪən ; dəˈmɪʃən/ 杜米仙 (51–96, 羅馬皇帝,在位期間 81–96)。

Donatello /ˌdɒnəˈteləʊ ; ˌdɑnəˈtɛlo/ 道納太羅 (1386?–1466, 義大利雕刻家)。

Donizetti /ˌdɒnɪˈzetɪ ; ˌdɑnɪˈzɛtɪ/ 唐尼才第 (Gaetano, 1797–1848, 義大利作曲家)。

Donne /dʌn ; dʌn/ 但恩 (John, 約 1572–1631, 英國詩人及教士)。

Doré /dəˈreɪ ; doˈre/ 杜雷 (Paul Gustave, 1833–1883, 法國畫家)。

Dostoevski /ˌdɒstəˈjefskiː ; ˌdɑstəˈjɛfskɪ/ 杜斯妥也夫斯基 (Fëdor Mikhailovich, 1821–1881, 俄國小說家)。

Doughty /ˈdaʊtɪ ; ˈdaʊtɪ/ 道蒂 (Charles Montagu, 1843–1926, 英國詩人及旅行家)。

Douglas /ˈdʌgləs;ˈdʌgləs/ 道格拉斯 (William Orville, 1898–1980, 美國法學家)。

Downes /daʊnz ; daʊnz/ 黨玆 ((Edwin) Olin, 1886–1955, 美國音樂批評家)。

Dowson /ˈdaʊsn ; ˈdaʊsn̩/ 道生 (Ernest Christopher, 1867–1900, 英國抒情詩人)。

Doyle /dɔɪl ; dɔɪl/ 道爾 (Sir Arthur Conan, 1859–1930, 英國醫生及偵探小說作家, 塑造名偵探福爾摩斯一角色)。

Drake /dreɪk ; drek/ 杜雷克 (Sir Francis, 1540?–1596, 英國航海家及海軍將軍)。

Draper /ˈdreɪpə ; ˈdrepɚ/ 杜雷波 (**1** Henry, 1837–1882, 美國天文學家; **2** John William, 1811–1882, 生於英國之美國科學家及作家)。

Drayton /ˈdreɪtn ; ˈdretn/ 杜雷頓 (Michael, 1563–1631, 英國詩人)。

Dreiser /ˈdraɪsə ; ˈdraɪsɚ/ 德萊塞 (Theodore Herman Albert, 1871–1945, 美國編輯及小說家)。

Drinkwater /ˈdrɪŋkˌwɔːtə ; ˈdrɪŋkˌwɔtɚ/ 杜林克華特 (John, 1882–1937, 英國詩人及劇作家)。

Drummond /ˈdrʌmənd ; ˈdrʌmənd/ 杜倫孟德 (**1** William, 1585–1649, 蘇格蘭詩人; **2** William Henry, 1854–1907, 生於愛爾蘭之加拿大詩人)。

Dryden /ˈdraɪdn ; ˈdraɪdn̩/ 德萊敦 (John, 1631–1700, 英國詩人及劇作家,於 1670–88 榮膺桂冠詩人)。

Ducommun /ˌdjuːkəˈmɜːn ; ˌdjukəˈmɝn/ 杜康默 (Élie, 1833–1906, 瑞士作家,與 C. A. Gobat 同獲 1902 年諾貝爾和平獎)。

Du Gard /duːˈgɑː ; duˈgɑr/ 杜嘉 (Roger Martin, 1881–1958, 法國小說家,曾獲 1937 年諾貝爾文學獎)。

Dumas /ˈdjuːmɑː ; djuˈmɑ/ 仲馬 (**1** Alexandre, 1802–70, 法國小說家及劇作家,世稱 '大仲馬'; **2** Alexandre, 1824–1895, 法國小說家及劇作家,爲大仲馬之子,世稱 '小仲馬')。

du Maurier /djuːˈmɔːrɪeɪ ; djuˈmɔrɪe/ 杜莫里哀 (George Louis Palmella Busson, 1834–1896, 英國藝術家及小說家)。

Dunant /d(j)uːˈnɑːn ; d(j)uˈnɑn/ 杜南 (Jean Henri, 1828–1910, 瑞士慈善家,爲紅十字會創始者,與 F. Passy 同獲 1901 年首屆諾貝爾和平獎)。

Dunbar /ˈdʌnbɑː ; ˈdʌnbar/ 唐巴爾 (**1** Paul Laurence, 1872–1906, 美國詩人; **2** William, 1460?–?1520, 蘇格蘭詩人)。

Duncan /ˈdʌŋkən ; ˈdʌŋkən/ 鄧肯 (Isadora, 1878–1927, 美國女舞蹈家)。

Dunlop /dʌnˈlɒp ; dʌnˈlɑp/ 唐洛普 (John Boyd, 1840–1921, 蘇格蘭發明家)。

Dunne /dʌn ; dʌn/ 德昂 (Finley Peter, 1867–1936, 美國幽默作家)。

Dunsany /dʌnˈseɪnɪ ; dʌnˈsenɪ/ 唐西尼 (Edward John Moreton Drax Plunkett, 1878–1957, 愛爾蘭詩人及劇作家)。

Du Pont /d(j)uːˈpɒnt ; d(j)uˈpɑnt/ 杜邦 (Éleuthère Irénée, 1771–1834, 出生於法國之美國實業家)。

Durant /d(j)ʊˈrænt;d(j)ʊˈrænt/ 杜蘭 (William James, 1885–, 美國教育家及作家)。

du Vigneaud /duːˈviːnjəʊ ; duˈvinjo/ 杜芬友 (Vincent, 1901–, 美國生物化學家,曾獲 1955 年諾貝爾化學獎)。

Dyer /ˈdaɪə ; ˈdaɪɚ/ 戴爾 (1700?–1758, 英國詩人)。

Eads /iːdz ; idz/ 伊玆 (James Buchanan, 1820–1887, 美國工程師及發明家)。

Eastman /ˈiːstmən ; ˈistmən/ 伊士曼 (**1** George, 1854–1932, 美國發明家及實業家; **2** Max Forrester, 1883–1969, 美國作家及編輯)。

Eccles /ˈekəlz ; ˈɛkəlz/ 阿克斯 (Sir John Carew, 1903–, 澳大利亞生理學家,與 A. L. Hodgkin 及 A. F. Huxley 同獲 1963 年諾貝爾醫學獎)。

Echegaray y Eizaguirre /ˌeɪtʃəgəˈraɪ ˌiː ˌeɪθəˈgwɪəreɪ ; ˌetʃəgəˈraɪˌi ˌeθəˈgwɪre/ 艾契加來 (José, 1832–1916, 西班牙劇作家,與 F. Mistral 同獲 1904 年諾貝爾文學獎)。

Eddington /ˈedɪŋtən ; ˈɛdɪŋtən/ 愛丁頓 (Sir Arthur Stanley, 1882–1944, 英國天文學家)。

Eddy /ˈedɪ ; ˈɛdɪ/ 愛迪 (Mary Morse, 1821–1910, 本姓 Baker, 美國女宗教領袖, 爲 Christian Science Church 的創始人)。

Eden /ˈiːdn ; ˈidn̩/ 艾登 ((Robert) Anthony, 1897–1977, 英國政治家,於 1955–57 任首相)。

Edgeworth /ˈedʒwɜːθ ; ˈɛdʒwɝθ/ 艾吉渥玆 (Maria, 1767–1849, 英國小說家)。

Edison /ˈedɪsn ; ˈɛdəsn̩/ 愛迪生 (Thomas Alva, 1847–1931, 美國發明家)。

Edmund (or Eadmund) II /ˈedmənd ; ˈɛdmənd/ 愛德蒙二世 (980?–1016, 英王,在位期間 1016, 世稱 Ironside, 意爲 '毅力堅强者')。

Edward, Eadward /ˈedwəd ; ˈɛdwɚd/ 愛德華 (1002?–1066, 英王,在位期間 1042–66, 世稱 the Confessor)。

Edward /ˈedwəd ; ˈɛdwɚd/ 愛德華 (1330–1376, Wales 親王, Edward III 之子,世稱 the Black Prince)。

Edward I 愛德華一世 (1239–1307, 英王,在位期間 1272–1307)。

Edward II 愛德華二世 (1284–1327, 英王,在位期間 1307–27)。

Edward III 愛德華三世 (1312–1377, 英王,在位期間 1327–77)。

Edward IV 愛德華四世 (1442–1483, 英王,在位期間 1461–70 及 1471–83)。

Edward V 愛德華五世 (1470–1483, 英王,在位期間 1483)。

Edward VI 愛德華六世 (1537–1553, 英王,在位期間 1547–53, 亨利八世之子)。

Edward VII 愛德華七世 (1841–1910, 英王, 在位期間 1901–10, 維多利亞女王之子,全名 Albert Edward)。

Edward VIII 愛德華八世 (1894–1972, 英王, 在位期間 1936, 遜位後稱溫莎公爵)。

Egbert /ˈegbɜːt ; ˈɛgbɝt/ 愛格伯 (775?–839, West Saxons 王,在位期間 802–839, 及第一位英王,在位期間 828–839)。

Eggleston /ˈeglstən ; ˈɛgl̩stən/ 愛格斯頓 (Edward, 1837–1902; 其弟 George Cary, 1839–1911, 同爲美國作家)。

Ehrlich /ˈeəlɪk ; ˈɛrlɪk/ 愛利克 (Paul, 1854-1915, 德國細菌學家,與 E. Metchnikoff 同獲 1908 年諾貝爾醫學獎)。

Eiffel /ˈaɪfəl ; ˈaɪfl̩/ 愛費爾 (Alexandre Gustave, 1832-1923, 法國工程師)。

Eijkman /ˈaɪkˌmɑːn ; ˈaɪkˌmɑn/ 愛克曼 (Christiaan, 1858-1930, 荷蘭衞生學家,與 F. G. Hopkins 同獲 1929 年諾貝爾醫學獎)。

Einstein /ˈaɪnstaɪn ; ˈaɪnˌstaɪn/ 愛因斯坦 (Albert, 1879-1955, 生於德國之美國物理學家,爲相對論之提出者,曾獲 1921 年諾貝爾物理獎)。

Einthoven /ˈaɪntˌhəʊvn ; ˈaɪntˌhovn̩/ 恩特霍文 (Willem, 1860-1927, 荷蘭生理學家,曾獲 1924 年諾貝爾醫學獎)。

Eisenhower /ˈaɪznˌhaʊə ; ˈaɪznˌhaʊɚ/ 艾森豪 (Dwight David, 1890-1969, 美國將領,於 1953-61 任美國第三十四任總統)。

Eldon /ˈeldən ; ˈɛldn̩/ 艾爾登 (John Scott, 1751-1838, 英國法學家)。

Eleanor /ˈelɪnə ; ˈɛlənɚ/ **1 ~ of Castile**, ?-1290, 英王 Edward I 之后; **2 ~ of Provence**, ?-1291, 英王 Henry III 之后。

Elgar /ˈelgə ; ˈɛlgɚ/ 艾爾加 (Sir Edward, 1857-1934, 英國作曲家)。

Eliot /ˈeljət ; ˈɛljət/ 艾略特 (**1** Charles William, 1834-1926, 美國教育家; **2** George, 1819-1880, 本名 Mary Ann Evans, 英國女小說家; **3** Thomas Stearns, 1888-1965, 生於美國之英國詩人及批評家,曾獲 1948 年諾貝爾文學獎)。

Elizabeth /ɪˈlɪzəbəθ ; ɪˈlɪzəbəθ/ **1** ~ I, 伊利莎白一世 (1533-1603, 於 1558-1603 爲英女王)。**2** ~ II, 伊利莎白二世 (1926-, 英女王,於 1952 即位)。

Ellsworth /ˈelzwɜːθ ; ˈɛlzwɝθ/ 艾爾斯渥玆 (Lincoln, 1880-1951, 美國探險家)。

Elyot /ˈeljət ; ˈɛljət/ 艾略特 (Sir Thomas, 1490?-1546, 英國學者及外交家)。

Elytis /ˈelɪtiːs ; ˈɛlɪtis/ 艾利廸斯 (Odysseus, 1911-, 希臘詩人,曾獲 1979 年諾貝爾文學獎)。

Emerson /ˈeməsn ; ˈɛmɚsn̩/ 愛默生 (Ralph Waldo, 1803-1882, 美國散文家及詩人)。

Empedocles /emˈpedəkliːz ; ɛmˈpɛdəˌkliz/ 恩貝多克利(紀元前五世紀之希臘哲學家及政治家)。

Enders /ˈendəz ; ˈɛndɚz/ 安德斯 (John Franklin, 1897-, 美國細菌學家,與 F. C. Robbins 及 T. H. Weller 同獲 1954 年諾貝爾醫學獎)。

Epaminondas /eˌpæmɪˈnɒndæs ; ɛˌpæməˈnɑndəs/ 義巴敏諾達 (418?-362 B.C., 古 Thebes 之將軍及政治家)。

Epictetus /ˌepɪkˈtiːtəs ; ˌɛpɪkˈtitəs/ 艾匹克蒂塔 (60?-120? A.D., 希臘斯多噶學派哲學家)。

Epicurus /ˌepɪˈkjʊərəs ; ˌɛpɪˈkjʊrəs/ 艾庇顧拉斯 (342?-270 B.C., 希臘哲學家)。

Epstein /ˈepstaɪn ; ˈɛpstaɪn/ 艾普斯坦 (Sir Jacob, 1880-1959, 生於美國之英國雕刻家)。

Erasmus /ɪˈræzməs ; ɪˈræzməs/ 伊拉斯莫斯 (Desiderius, 1466?-1536, 荷蘭學者)。

Erlanger /ˈɜːˌlæŋə ; ˈɝˌlæŋɚ/ 歐蘭格 (Joseph, 1874-1965, 美國生理學家,與 H. S. Gasser 同獲 1944 年諾貝爾醫學獎)。

Erskine /ˈɜːskɪn ; ˈɝskɪn/ 歐斯金 (**1** John, 1695-1768, 蘇格蘭法學家; **2** John, 1879-1951, 美國教育家及作家)。

Ervine /ˈɜːvɪn ; ˈɝvɪn/ 歐文 (St. John Greer, 1883-1971, 愛爾蘭劇作家及小說家)。

Estournelles de Constant, d' /ˌdesˌtʊəˈnel də kɒnˈstɑːn ; ˌdɛsˌtʊrˈnɛl də konˈstɑn/ 戴思鐸尼爾 (Paul Henri Benjamin Balluat, 1852-1924, 法國外交家及政治家,與 A. M. F. Beernaert 同獲 1909 年諾貝爾和平獎)。

Ethelred II /ˈeθəlred ; ˈɛθəlˌrɛd/ 艾思雷德二世 (968?-1016, 英王,在位期間 978-1016)。

Eucken /ˈɔɪkn ; ˈɔɪkn̩/ 歐鏗 (Rudolf Christoph, 1846-1926, 德國哲學家,曾獲 1908 年諾貝爾文學獎)。

Euclid /ˈjuːklɪd ; ˈjuklɪd/ 歐幾里德(希臘幾何學家, 330?-?275 B.C., 被稱爲幾何學之父)。

Eugene or **Eugène** /ˈjuːdʒiːn ; ˈjudʒin/ 尤金 (1663-1736, 奧國將軍及 Savoy 地方之君侯)。

Euler /ˈɔɪlə ; ˈɔɪlɚ/ 奧伊勒 (Leonhard, 1707-1783, 瑞士數學家及物理學家)。

Euler-Chelpin /ˌɔɪləˈkelpən ; ˌɔɪlɚˈkɛlpən/ 歐伊勒凱賓 (Hans August Simon von, 1873-1964, 生於德國之瑞典化學家,與 A. Harden 同獲 1929 年諾貝爾化學獎)。

Euripides /jʊəˈrɪpɪdiːz ; jʊˈrɪpəˌdiz/ 尤里披帝 (480?-?406 B.C., 希臘劇作家)。

Evelyn /ˈiːvlɪn ; ˈivlɪn/ 伊夫林 (John, 1620-1706, 英國日記作家)。

Everett /ˈevərɪt ; ˈɛv(ə)rɪt/ 愛維利特 (Edward, 1794-1865, 美國教士、演說家及政治家)。

Eyck /aɪk ; aɪk/ 艾克 (Hubert 或 Huybrecht van, 1366?-1426; 其弟 Jan van, 1370?-1440, 均爲法蘭德斯畫家)。

Ezekiel /ɪˈziːkjəl ; ɪˈzikjəl/ 伊西吉爾 (Moses Jacob, 1844-1917, 美國雕刻家)。

Fabius /ˈfeɪbɪəs ; ˈfebɪəs/ 費畢阿斯 (?-203 B.C., 羅馬帝國大將)。

Fahrenheit /ˈfærənhaɪt ; ˈfærənˌhaɪt/ 華倫海特 (Gabriel Daniel, 1686-1736, 德國物理學家,華氏寒暑表的設計者)。

Falkner 參看 Faulkner。

Faraday /ˈfærədɪ ; ˈfærədɪ/ 法拉第 (Michael, 1791-1867, 英國化學家及物理學家)。

Farina /fəˈriːnə ; fəˈrinə/ 法雷納 (Salvatore, 1846-1918, 義大利小說家)。

Farquhar /ˈfɑːk(w)ə ; ˈfɑrk(w)ɚ/ 法科 (George, 1678-1707, 英國劇作家)。

Fa(u)lkner /ˈfɔːknə ; ˈfɔknɚ/ 佛克納 (William Cuthbert, 1897-1962, 美國小說家, 1949 年獲諾貝爾文學獎)。

Fāy /faɪ ; faɪ/ 法伊 (Bernard, 1893-, 法國歷史學者及傳記作家)。

Fel(l)tham /ˈfelθəm ; ˈfɛlθəm/ 費爾贊 (Owen, 1602?-1668, 英國作家)。

Ferdinand I /ˈfɜːdɪnænd ; ˈfɝdn̩ænd/ 斐迪南一世 (**1** 1503-1564, 神聖羅馬帝國皇帝, 在位期間 1556-64; **2** 1861-1948, 全名 Maximilian Karl Leopold Maria, 保加利亞國王,在位期間 1908-18)。

Ferdinand II 斐迪南二世 (1578-1637, 波希米亞國王,在位期間 1617-37, 並於 1621-37 爲匈牙利國王,於 1619-37 爲神聖羅馬帝國皇帝)。

Ferdinand III 斐迪南三世 (1608-1657, 匈牙利國王,在位期間 1625-57, 並於 1637-57 爲神聖羅馬帝國皇帝)。

Ferdinand VII 斐迪南七世 (1784-1833, 西班牙國王,在位期間 1808 及 1814-33)。

Fermi /ˈfeəmɪ ; ˈfɛrmɪ/ 費爾米 (Enrico, 1901-1954, 生於義大利之美國物理學家,曾獲 1938 年諾貝爾物理獎)。

Feynman /ˈfaɪnmən ; ˈfaɪnmən/ 淮曼 (Richard Phillips, 1918-, 美國物理學家, 與 J. S. Schwinger 及 Shinichiro Tomonaga 同獲 1965 年諾貝爾物理獎)。

Fibiger /ˈfiːbiːgə ; ˈfibigɚ/ 費比格 (Johannes, 1867-1928, 丹麥病理學家,曾獲 1926 年諾貝爾醫學獎)。

Fielding /ˈfiːldɪŋ ; ˈfildɪŋ/ 費爾丁 (**1** Henry, 1707-1754, 英國小說家; **2** 其妹 Sarah, 1710-1768, 英國女作家)。

Fillmore /ˈfɪlmɔː ; ˈfɪlmɔr/ 費爾摩 (Millard, 1800-1874, 美國第十三任總統,任期 1850-53)。

Finlay /fɪnˈlaɪ ; fɪnˈlaɪ/ 芬萊 (Carlos Juan, 1833-1915, 古巴醫生及生物學家)。

Finsen /ˈfɪnsn ; ˈfɪnsn̩/ 芬生 (Niels Ryberg, 1860-1904, 丹麥醫師, 曾獲 1903 年諾貝爾醫學獎)。

Fischer /ˈfɪʃə ; ˈfɪʃɚ/ 費雪 (**1** Emil, 1852-1919, 德國化學家,曾獲 1902 年諾貝爾化學獎; **2** Hans, 1881-1945, 德國化學家,曾獲 1930 年諾貝爾化學獎)。

Fiske /fɪsk ; fɪsk/ 費斯克 (John, 1842-1901, 美國哲學家及歷史學家)。

Fitch /fɪtʃ ; fɪtʃ/ 費區 (John, 1743-1798, 美國發明家)。

Fitzgerald /fɪtsˈdʒerəld ; fɪtsˈdʒɛrəld/ 費玆哲羅 (Francis Scott Key, 1896-1940, 美國作家)。

FitzGerald /fɪtsˈdʒerəld ; fɪtsˈdʒɛrəld/ 費玆哲羅 (Edward, 1809-1883, 英國詩人及翻譯家)。

Flaubert /fləʊˈbeə ; floˈbɛr/ 福樓拜 (Gustave, 1821-1880, 法國小說家)。

Flaxman /ˈflæksmən ; ˈflæksmən/ 福萊克斯曼 (John, 1755-1826, 英國雕刻家)。

Fleming /ˈflemɪŋ ; ˈflɛmɪŋ/ 佛來明 (Sir Alexander, 1881-1955, 英國細菌學家, 於 1928 年發現盤尼西林, 與 E. B. Chain 和 H. W. Florey 同獲 1945 年諾貝爾醫學獎)。

Florey /ˈflɔːrɪ ; ˈflorɪ/ 富樂禮 (Sir Howard Walter, 1898-1968, 英國病理學家,與 E. B. Chain 及 A. Fleming 同獲 1945 年諾貝爾醫學獎)。

Florio /ˈflɔːrɪəʊ ; ˈflɔrɪo/ 福羅里歐 (John, 1553?-1625, 英國辭典編纂家及翻譯家)。

Foley /ˈfəʊlɪ ; ˈfolɪ/ 福里 (John Henry, 1818-1874, 愛爾蘭雕刻家)。

Ford /fɔːd ; fɔrd/ 福特 (**1** Henry, 1863-1947, 美國汽車製造商; **2** John, 1586?-?1639, 英國劇作家; **3** Paul Leicester, 1865-1902, 美國歷史學家及小說家; **4** Gerald Rudolph, 1913-, 美國第 38 任總統,任期 1974-77)。

Forester /ˈfɒrɪstə ; ˈfɑrɪstɚ/ 福雷斯特 (Cecil Scott, 1899-1966, 英國小說家)。

Forssmann /ˈfɔːsmɑːn ; ˈforsmɑn/ 福爾斯曼 (Werner Theodor Otto, 1904-1979, 德國外科醫生,與 D. W. Richards 及 A. F. Cournand 同獲 1956 年諾貝爾醫學獎)。

Forster /ˈfɔːstə ; ˈfɔrstɚ/ 福斯特 (Edward Morgan, 1879-1970, 英國小說家)。

Fourier /ˈfʊrɪeɪ ; ˈfʊrɪe/ 傅立業 (François Marie Charles, 1772-1837, 法國社會學家及改革者)。

Fowler /ˈfaʊlə ; ˈfaʊlɚ/ 福勒 (Henry Watson, 1858-1933, 英國辭典編纂家)。

Fox /fɒks ; fɑks/ 福克斯 (**1** Charles James, 1749-1806, 英國政治家及演說家; **2** Dixon Ryan, 1887-1945, 美國教育家及歷史學家; **3** John William, 1863-1919, 美國小說家)。

France /frɑːns ; fræns/ 法朗士 (Anatole, 本名 Jacques Anatole François Thibault, 1844-1924, 法國小說家及諷刺文家,曾獲 1921 年諾貝爾文學獎)。

Francesca /frænˈtʃeskə ; frænˈtʃɛskə/ 法朗契斯卡 (Piero della, 1420?-1492, 義大利畫家)。

Francis of Assisi /ˈfrɑːnsɪs əv əˈsiːzɪ ; ˈfrænsɪs əv əˈsizɪ/ 聖芳濟 (Saint, 1182-1226, 本名 Giovanni Francesco Bernardone, 義大利修道士, 聖芳濟修會之創始者)。

Franck /frɑːŋk ; frɑŋk/ 佛朗克 (James, 1882-1964, 美籍德裔物理學家, 與 G. Hertz 同獲 1925 年諾貝爾物理獎)。

Francke /ˈfrɑːŋkə ; ˈfrɑŋkə/ 佛朗柯 (Kuno, 1855-1930, 生於德國之美國歷史學家及教育家)。

Franco /ˈfræŋkəʊ ; ˈfræŋko/ 佛朗哥 (Francisco, 1892-1975, 西班牙將軍, 1936-75 爲元首)。

Frank /frɑːŋk ; frɑŋk/ 佛蘭克 (Ilya Mikhailovich, 1908-, 俄國物理學家, 與 P. A. Cherenkov 及 I. E. Tamm 同獲 1958 年諾貝爾物理獎)。

Franklin /ˈfræŋklɪn ; ˈfræŋklɪn/ 富蘭克林 (**1** Benjamin, 1706-1790, 美國政治家及哲學家; **2** Sir John, 1786-1847, 英國北極探險家)。

Frazer /ˈfreɪzə ; ˈfrezɚ/ 佛萊則 (Sir James George, 1854-1941, 蘇格蘭人類學家)。

Frederick I /ˈfredrɪk ; ˈfrɛdrɪk/ 腓特烈一世 (**1** 1123?-1190, 稱爲 Frederick Barbarossa, 神聖羅馬帝國皇帝,在位期間 1152-90; **2** 1657-1713, 普魯士國王,在位期間 1701-13)。

Frederick II **1** 腓特烈大帝 (1712-1786, 世稱 Frederick the Great, 普魯士國王,在位期間 1740-86); **2** 腓特烈二世 (1194-1250, 西西里王,在位期間 1198-1250, 及神聖羅馬帝國皇帝,在位期間 1215-50)。

Frederick IX 腓特烈九世 (1899-1972, 丹麥國王,在位期間 1947-72)。

Freeman /ˈfriːmən ; ˈfrimən/ 佛里門 (**1** Douglas Southall, 1886-1953, 美國歷史學家及編輯; **2** Edward Augustus, 1823-1892, 英國歷史學家; **3** Mary Eleanor, 1852-1930, 本姓 Wilkins, 美國女作家)。

French /frentʃ ; frɛntʃ/ 佛蘭奇 (**1** Alice, 1850-1934, 筆名爲 Octave Thanet, 美國女小說家; **2** Daniel Chester, 1850-1931, 美國雕刻家)。

Freud /frɔɪd ; frɔɪd/ 佛洛伊德 (Sigmund, 1856-1939, 奧國神經病學家,首創精神分析)。

Fried /friːt ; frit/ 富禮德 (Alfred Hermann, 1864-1921, 奧地利和平主義者,與 T. M. C. Asser 同獲 1911 年諾貝爾和平獎)。

Frobisher /ˈfrəʊbɪʃə ; ˈfrobɪʃɚ/ 佛洛比西爾 (Sir Martin, 1535?-1594, 英國航海家)。

Froebel or **Fröbel** /ˈfreɪbəl ; ˈfrebl̩/ 福祿貝爾 (Friedrich, 1782-1852, 德國教育家,爲幼稚園制度的創始人)。

Frost /frɔːst ; frɔst/ 佛洛斯特 (Robert Lee, 1874-1963, 美國詩人)。

Froude /fruːd ; frud/ 佛洛德 (James Anthony, 1818-1894, 英國歷史學家)。

Fuad I /fʊˈɑːd ; fʊˈɑd/ 福阿德一世(本名 Ahmed Fuad Pasha, 1868-1936, 埃及王,在位期間 1922-1936)。

Fu Lin /ˈfuː ˈlɪn ; ˈfu ˈlɪn/ 福臨 (1638-1661, 中國清朝開國之主,卽清世祖,年號順治,在位十八年)。

Fulton /ˈfʊltən ; ˈfʊltn̩/ 福爾敦 (Robert, 1765-1815, 美國發明家及工程師)。

Funk /fʌŋk ; fʌŋk/ 豐克 (Casimir, 1884-1967, 生於波蘭之美國生物化學家)。

Furness /ˈfɜːnɪs ; ˈfɝnɪs/ 佛奈斯 (Horace Howard, 1833-1912, 與其子, 1865-1930, 同爲美國莎士比亞學者)。

Furnivall /ˈfɜːnɪvəl ; ˈfɝnəvl̩/ 佛尼法 (Frederick James, 1825-1910, 英國語言學家)。

Gaius /ˈgaɪəs ; ˈgaɪəs/ or **Caius** /ˈkaɪəs ; ˈkaɪəs/ 蓋阿斯(二世紀時之羅馬法學家)。

Galba /ˈgælbə ; ˈgælbə/ 蓋爾巴 (Servius Sulpicius, 5B.C.?-A.D. 69, 於 68-69 爲羅馬皇帝)。

Galen /ˈgeɪlɪn ; ˈgelən/ 伽林 (130?-?200, 古希臘醫生及作家)。

Galerius /gəˈlɪərɪəs ; gəˈlɪrɪəs/ 伽勒利 (死於 311, 羅馬皇帝,在位期間 305-311)。

Galileo /ˌgælɪˈleɪəʊ ; ˌgæləˈleo/ 伽利略 (全名 Galileo Galilei, 1564-1642, 義大利物理學家及天文學家)。

Gallup /ˈgæləp ; ˈgæləp/ 蓋洛普 (George Horace, 1901-, 美國統計學家)。

Galsworthy /ˈgɔːlzwɜːðɪ ; ˈgɔlzˌwɝðɪ/ 高爾斯華迪 (John, 1867-1933, 英國小說家及劇作家, 曾獲 1932 年諾貝爾文學獎)。

Galt /gɔːlt ; gɔlt/ 高爾特 (John, 1779-1839, 蘇格蘭小說家)。

Galton /ˈgɔːltn ; ˈgɔltn̩/ 高爾頓 (Sir Francis, 1822-1911, 英國科學家)。

Galvani /gælˈvɑːnɪ ; gælˈvɑnɪ/ 伽凡尼 (Luigi 或 Aloisio, 1737-1798, 義大利醫生及物理學家)。

Gama /ˈgɑːmə ; ˈgɑmə/ 伽馬 (Vasco da, 1469?-1524, 葡萄牙航海家)。

Gambetta /gæmˈbetə ; gæmˈbɛtə/ 甘必大 (Léon, 1838-1882, 法國律師及政治家)。

Gandhi[1] /ˈgændiː ; ˈgændi/ 甘地 (Mohandas Karamchand, 世稱 Mahatma ～, 1869-1948, 印度民族獨立運動領袖)。

Gandhi[2] 甘地夫人 (Indira Nehru, 1917-, 印度政治領袖,尼赫魯之女, 1966-77; 1980- 爲總理)。

Gardiner /ˈgɑːdnə ; ˈgardnɚ/ 伽德納 (Samuel Rawson, 1829-1902, 英國歷史學者)。

Garfield /ˈgɑːfiːld ; ˈgarˌfild/ 伽菲爾德 (James Abram, 1831-1881, 於 1881 年任美國第二十任總統)。

Garibaldi /ˌgærɪˈbɔːldɪ ; ˌgærɪˈbɔldɪ/ 加里波的 (Giuseppe, 1807-1882, 義大利愛國者及將軍)。

Garner /ˈgɑːnə ; ˈgarnɚ/ 伽納 (John Nance, 1868-1967, 美國從政者,於 1933-41 任副總統)。

Garros /gɑːˈrɒs ; gɑˈrɔs/ 加羅斯 (Roland, 1888-1918, 法國飛行家)。

Gascoigne /ˈgæskɔɪn ; ˈgæskɔɪn/ 蓋斯柯恩 (George, 1525?-1577, 英國詩人)。

Gaskell /ˈgæskəl ; ˈgæskəl/ 蓋斯凱爾 (Elizabeth Cleghorn, 1810-1865, 本姓 Stevenson, 英國女小說家)。

Gasser /ˈgæsə ; ˈgæsɚ/ 蓋塞 (Herbert Spencer, 1888-1963, 美國生理學家,與 J. Erlanger 同獲 1944 年諾貝爾醫學獎)。

Gauguin /ˌgəʊˈgæn ; ˌgoˈgæn/ 高更 ((Eugène Henri) Paul, 1848-1903, 法國畫家)。

Gauss /gaʊs ; gaʊs/ 高斯 (Karl Friedrich, 1777-1855, 德國數學家及天文學家)。

Gautama Buddha /ˈgaʊtəmə ˈbʊdə ; ˌgaʊtəmə ˈbʊdə/

釋伽牟尼 (563?-?483 B.C., 印度哲學家,佛教創始者)。
Gay /geɪ ; ge/ 蓋伊 (John, 1685-1732, 英國詩人及劇作家)。
Geikie /ˈgiːkɪ ; ˈgikɪ/ 格基 (Sir Archibald, 1835-1924, 蘇格蘭地質學家)。
Genghis Khan /ˌdʒeŋgəsˈkɑːn ; ˌdʒɛŋgəsˈkɑn/ 成吉思汗(亦作 Jenghiz Khan, 1162-1227, 蒙古帝國開國之主,即元太祖)。
Gentile da Fabriano /dʒenˈtiːliː də ˌfɑːbriːˈɑːnəʊ ; dʒɛnˈtili də ˌfɑbriˈɑno/ 眞蒂利(原名 Gentile Massi, 1370?-?1427, 義大利畫家)。
George I /dʒɔːdʒ ; dʒɔrdʒ/ 喬治一世 (**1** 1660-1727, 英王,在位期間 1714-27; **2** 1845-1913, 希臘國王,在位期間 1863-1913)。
George II 喬治二世 (**1** 1683-1760, 英王,在位期間 1727-60; **2** 1890-1947, 希臘國王,在位期間 1922-23 及 1935-47)。
George III 喬治三世 (1738-1820, 英王,在位期間 1760-1820)。
George IV 喬治四世 (1762-1830, 英王,在位期間 1820-30)。
George V 喬治五世 (1865-1936, 英王,在位期間 1910-36)。
George VI 喬治六世 (1895-1952, 英王,在位期間 1936-52)。
Giauque /dʒiːˈəʊk ; dʒiˈok/ 吉奧克 (William Francis, 1895-, 美國化學家,曾獲 1949 年諾貝爾化學獎)。
Gibbon /ˈgɪbən ; ˈgɪbən/ 吉朋 (Edward, 1737-1794, 英國歷史學家)。
Gibbs /gɪbz ; gɪbz/ 吉布斯 (Josiah Willard, 1839-1903, 美國數學家及物理學家)。
Gide /ʒiːd ; ʒid/ 紀德 (André Paul Guillaume 1869-1951, 法國小說家、批評家及散文家,曾獲 1947 年諾貝爾文學獎)。
Gilbert /ˈgɪlbət ; ˈgɪlbɚt/ 吉柏特 (**1** Sir Humphrey, 1539?-1583, 英國航海家; **2** William, 1540-1603, 英國醫師及物理學家; **3** Sir William Schwenck, 1836-1911, 英國詩人及歌詞與歌劇詞作家)。
Gilder /ˈgɪldə ; ˈgɪldɚ/ 吉爾德 (Richard Watson, 1844-1909, 美國詩人及編輯)。
Gillette /dʒɪˈlet ; dʒɪˈlɛt/ 吉勒特 (King Camp, 1855-1932, 美國發明家及製造家)。
Gilman /ˈgɪlmən ; ˈgɪlmən/ 吉爾曼 (Daniel Coit, 1831-1908, 美國教育家)。
Girtin /ˈgɜːtɪn ; ˈgɝtn̩/ 格爾丁 (Thomas, 1775-1802, 英國風景畫家,爲現代水彩畫之創始者)。
Giscard d'Estaing /ʒɪsˌkɑːr desˈtæŋ ; ʒɪsˌkɑr dɛsˈtæŋ/ 季斯卡 (Valéry, 1926-, 於 1974-81 任法國總統)。
Gissing /ˈgɪsɪŋ ; ˈgɪsɪŋ/ 吉興 (George Robert, 1857-1903, 英國小說家)。
Gjellerup /ˈgelərʊp ; ˈgɛləˌrʊp/ 蓋萊洛普 (Karl, 1857-1919, 丹麥作家, 與 H. Pontoppidan 同獲 1917 年諾貝爾文學獎)。
Gladstone /ˈglædstən ; ˈglædˌston/ 格萊斯頓 (William Ewart, 1809-1898, 英國政治家,於 1868-94 年間四度任英國首相)。
Glaser /ˈgleɪzə ; ˈglezɚ/ 格雷色 (Donald Arthur, 1926-, 美國物理學家,曾獲 1960 年諾貝爾物理獎)。
Glasgow /ˈglɑːsgəʊ ; ˈglæsgo/ 格拉斯谷 (Ellen Anderson Gholson, 1874-1945, 美國女小說家)。
Glover /ˈglʌvə ; ˈglʌvɚ/ 格洛威 (John, 1732-1797, 美國大革命時代之將軍)。
Glyn /glɪn ; glɪn/ 格林 (Elinor, 1864-1943, 本姓 Sutherland, 英國女小說家)。
Gobat /gəʊˈbɑː ; goˈbɑ/ 戈巴 (Charles Albert, 1843-1914, 瑞士政治家,與 E. Ducommun 同獲 1902 年諾貝爾和平獎)。
Goddard /ˈgɒdəd ; ˈgɑdɚd/ 哥大德 (Robert Hutchings, 1882-1945, 美國物理學家)。
Godfrey of Bouillon /ˌgɒdfrɪ əv ˌbuːˈjɔːŋ ; ˌgɑdfrɪ əv ˌbuˈjɔn/ 哥弗雷 (1061?-1100, 法國十字軍領袖)。
Godwin /ˈgɒdwɪn ; ˈgɑdwɪn/ 哥德文 (William, 1756-1836, 英國哲學家及小說家)。
Godwin-Austen /ˈgɒdwɪnˈɔːstɪn ; ˈgɑdwɪnˈɔstɪn/ 哥德文奧斯汀 (Henry Haversham, 1834-1923, 英國探險家及地質學家)。
Goethe /ˈgɜːtə ; ˈgɝtə/ 哥德 (Johann Wolfgang von, 1749-1832, 德國詩人及劇作家)。
Gogh, van /vænˈgəʊ ; vænˈgo/ 梵谷 (Vincent, 1853-1890, 荷蘭畫家)。
Gogol /ˈgəʊgɒl ; ˈgogəl/ 果戈里 (Nikolai Vasilievich, 1809-1852, 俄國作家)。
Goldsmith /ˈgəʊldsmɪθ ; ˈgoldsmɪθ/ 哥德斯密 (Oliver, 1728-1774, 英國作家)。
Golgi /ˈgɔːldʒɪ ; ˈgɔldʒɪ/ 高爾基 (Camillo, 1844-1926, 義大利醫生,與 Ramón y Cajal 同獲 1906 年諾貝爾醫學獎)。
Goodrich /ˈgʊdrɪtʃ ; ˈgʊdrɪtʃ/ 古德利奇 (Samuel Griswold, 1793-1860, 筆名 Peter Parley, 美國作家)。
Goodyear /ˈgʊdjə ; ˈgʊdˌjɪr/ 古德伊爾 (Charles, 1800-1860, 美國發明家)。
Gosse /gɒs ; gɑs/ 戈斯 (Sir Edmund William, 1849-1928, 英國詩人及批評家)。
Gounod /ˈguːnəʊ ; ˈguno/ 古諾 (Charles François, 1818-1893, 法國作曲家)。
Gower /ˈgaʊə ; ˈgaʊɚ/ 古爾 (John, 1325?-1408, 英國詩人)。
Goya y Lucientes /ˈgɔɪə ˌiː ˌluːsɪˈenteɪs ; ˈgɔɪə ˌi ˌlusɪˈɛntes/ 戈耶 (Francisco José de, 1746-1828, 西班牙畫家)。
Graham /ˈgreɪəm ; ˈgreəm/ 格雷姆 (Thomas, 1805-1869, 蘇格蘭化學家)。
Grahame /ˈgreɪəm ; ˈgreəm/ 格雷姆 (Kenneth, 1859-1932, 英國作家)。
Gramme /græm ; græm/ 格拉姆 (Zénobe Théophile, 1826-1901, 比利時電學家)。
Grant /grɑːnt ; grænt/ 格蘭特 (Ulysses Simpson, 1822-1885, 美國將軍,於 1869-77 任美國第十八任總統)。
Gratian /ˈgreɪʃɪən ; ˈgreʃən/ 格雷先 (359-383, 羅馬皇帝,在位期間 375-383)。
Grattan /ˈgrætn ; ˈgrætn̩/ 格萊敦 (Henry, 1746-1820, 愛爾蘭政治家及演說家)。
Graves /greɪvz ; grevz/ 格雷夫斯 (Robert Ranke, 1895-, 愛爾蘭作家)。
Gray /greɪ ; gre/ 格雷 (Thomas, 1716-1771, 英國詩人)。
Grayson, David 參看 Baker (2)。
Greely /ˈgriːlɪ ; ˈgrilɪ/ 格利列 (Adolphus Washington, 1844-1935, 美國將軍及北極探險家)。
Green /griːn ; grin/ 格林 (**1** John Richard, 1837-1883, 英國歷史學家; **2** Julian, 1900-, 出生於法國之美國小說家)。
Greenaway /ˈgriːnəweɪ ; ˈgrinəˌwe/ 格林納維 (Catherine, 1846-1901, 英國女畫家及插圖畫家)。
Greene /griːn ; grin/ 格林 (Graham, 1904-, 英國小說家)。
Greenough /ˈgriːnəʊ ; ˈgrino/ 格雷諾 (Horatio, 1805-1852, 美國雕刻家)。
Gregory I /ˈgregərɪ ; ˈgrɛgərɪ/ 格列高里一世 (Saint, 540?-604, 於 590-604 任教皇)。
Gregory VII 格列高里七世 (Saint, 1020?-1085, 於1073-85 任教皇)。
Gregory XIII 格列高里十三世 (Saint, 1502-1585, 於 1572-85 任教皇)。
Gregory, Lady Augusta 格列高里夫人 (1852-1932, 本姓 Persse, 愛爾蘭女劇作家)。
Grenville /ˈgrenvɪl ; ˈgrɛnˌvɪl/ 格倫維爾 (George, 1712-1770, 英國政治家)。
Gresham /ˈgreʃəm ; ˈgrɛʃəm/ 葛雷賢 (Sir Thomas, 1519?-1579, 英國財政家)。
Greuze /grɜːz ; grɝz/ 格樂玆 (Jean Baptiste, 1725-1805, 法國畫家)。
Grey /greɪ ; gre/ 格雷 (**1** Charles, 1764-1845, 英國政治家,於 1830-34 任首相; **2** Lady Jane, 1537-1554, 愛德華六世死後任英女王僅九日,退位後被弑; **3** (Pearl) Zane, 1875-1939, 美國小說家)。
Grieg /griːg ; grig/ 格雷哥 (Edvard Hagerup, 1843-1907, 威挪作曲家)。
Grierson /ˈgrɪəsn ; ˈgrɪəsn̩/ 格列爾遜 (Sir Herbert John Clifford, 1866-1960, 英國學者)。

Grignard /ˌgriːˈnjɑː ; ˌgrinˈjɑr/ 格雷尼亞 (Victor, 1871–1935, 法國化學家,與 P. Sabatier 同獲 1912 年諾貝爾化學獎)。
Grimm /grɪm ; grɪm/ 格利姆 (Jacob, 1785–1863, 與其弟 Wilhelm, 1786–1859, 均爲德國語言學家及童話故事作家)。
Grosvenor /ˈgrəʊvnə ; ˈgrovnɚ/ 格洛維諾 (Gilbert Hovey, 1875–1966, 美國地理學家及編輯)。
Grote /grəʊt ; grot/ 格魯特 (George, 1794–1871, 英國歷史學家)。
Guillaume /ˌgiːˈjəʊm ; ˌgiˈjom/ 吉永 (Charles Édouard, 1861–1938, 法國物理學家,曾獲 1920 年諾貝爾物理獎)。
Gullstrand /ˈgʌlstrænd ; ˈgʌlstrænd/ 伽爾士德蘭 (Allvar, 1862–1930, 瑞典眼科專家,曾獲 1911 年諾貝爾醫學獎)。
Gunter /ˈgʌntə ; ˈgʌntɚ/ 甘特 (Edmund, 1581–1626, 英國數學家)。
Gutenberg /ˈguːtnbɜːg ; ˈgutn̩ˌbɝg/ 古騰堡 (Johann, 1400?–?1468, 德國發明家,發明活版印刷術)。
Haakon VII /ˈhɔːkɒn ; ˈhɔkən/ 哈康七世 (1872–1957, 挪威國王,在位期間 1905–57)。
Haber /ˈhɑːbə ; ˈhɑbɚ/ 哈勃 (Fritz, 1868–1934, 德國化學家,曾獲 1918 年諾貝爾化學獎)。
Hadfield /ˈhædfiːld ; ˈhædˌfild/ 哈德菲德 (Sir Robert Abbott, 1858–1940, 英國礦冶學家)。
Hadley /ˈhædlɪ ; ˈhædlɪ/ 哈德里 (Henry Kimball, 1871–1937, 美國作曲家)。
Hadrian /ˈheɪdrɪən ; ˈhedrɪən/ 哈德連 (76–138, 羅馬皇帝,在位期間 117–138)。
Haggard /ˈhægəd ; ˈhægɚd/ 哈葛德 (Sir (Henry) Rider, 1856–1925, 英國小說家)。
Hahn /hɑːn ; hɑn/ 哈恩 (Otto, 1879–1968, 德國物理化學家,曾獲 1944 年諾貝爾化學獎)。
Hakluyt /ˈhækluːt ; ˈhæklut/ 哈克路特 (Richard, 1552?–1616, 英國地理學家及歷史學家)。
Haldane /ˈhɔːldeɪn ; ˈhɔlden/ 哈爾登 (**1** John Burdon Sanderson, 1892–1964, 英國科學家; **2** John Scott, 1860–1936, 英國生理學家; **3** Richard Burdon, 1856–1928, 英國律師、哲學家及政治家)。
Hale /heɪl ; hel/ 赫爾 (**1** George Ellery, 1868–1938, 美國天文學家; **2** Sir Matthew, 1609–1676, 英國法學家)。
Hall /hɔːl ; hɔl/ 賀爾 (**1** Charles Francis, 1821–1871, 美國北極探險家; **2** Charles Martin, 1863–1914, 美國化學家及製造商; **3** Granville Stanley, 1846–1924, 美國心理學家及教育家; **4** James Norman, 1887–1951, 美國小說家)。
Hallam /ˈhæləm ; ˈhæləm/ 賀萊姆 (Henry, 1777–1859, 英國歷史學家)。
Halley /ˈhælɪ ; ˈhælɪ/ 賀萊 (Edmund, 1656–1742, 英國天文學家)。
Hals /hæls ; hɑls/ 哈爾斯 (Frans, 1580?–1666 荷蘭畫家)。
Halsted /ˈhɔːlstɪd ; ˈhɔlstɪd/ 哈爾斯特 (William Stewart, 1852–1922, 美國外科醫生)。
Hamilcar Barca /ˈhæmɪlkɑː ˈbɑːkə ; ˈhæmɪlkɑr ˈbɑrkə/ 哈密爾加 (270?–228 B.C., 迦太基大將, Hannibal 之父)。
Hamilton /ˈhæməltən ; ˈhæml̩tən/ 哈密爾敦 (Alexander, 1755–1804, 美國政治家)。
Hammarskjöld /ˈhæməˌʃʌld ; ˈhæmɚˌʃʌld/ 哈瑪紹 (Dag Hjalmar Agné Carl, 1905–1961, 瑞典政治經濟學家, 於 1953–61 任聯合國秘書長, 曾獲 1961 年諾貝爾和平獎)。
Hammond /ˈhæmənd ; ˈhæmənd/ 漢孟 (John Hays, 1888–1965, 美國電機工程師及發明家)。
Hamsun /ˈhɑːmsn ; ˈhɑmsn̩/ 哈姆遜 (Knut, 1859–1952, 本名 Knut Pedersen, 挪威作家,曾獲 1920 年諾貝爾文學獎)。
Handel /ˈhændl ; ˈhændl̩/ 韓德爾 (George Frederick, 1685–1759, 生於德國之英國作曲家)。
Hannibal /ˈhænɪbl ; ˈhænəbl̩/ 漢尼拔 (247–183 B.C., 迦太基大將)。
Han Wu-ti /ˈhæn ˈuː ˈdiː ; ˈhæn ˈu ˈdi/ 漢武帝 (157–87 B.C., 名徹,中國漢朝皇帝,在位五十四年)。
Han Yü /ˈhɑːn ˈyuː ; ˈhɑn ˈyu/ 韓愈 (768–824, 中國唐代詩人、散文家及哲學家)。
Harden /ˈhɑːdn ; ˈhɑrdn̩/ 哈登 (Sir Arthur, 1865–1940, 英國化學家,與 Euler-Chelpin 同獲 1929 年諾貝爾化學獎)。
Harding /ˈhɑːdɪŋ ; ˈhɑrdɪŋ/ 哈定 (Warren Gamaliel, 1865–1923, 於 1921–23 任美國第二十九任總統)。
Hardy /ˈhɑːdɪ ; ˈhɑrdɪ/ 哈代 (Thomas, 1840–1928, 英國小說家及詩人)。
Hargreaves /ˈhɑːgriːvz ; ˈhɑrgrivz/ 哈格里夫 (James, ?–1778, 英國發明家,曾發明紡織機)。
Harley /ˈhɑːlɪ ; ˈhɑrlɪ/ 哈利 (Robert, 1661–1724, 英國政治家)。
Harold I /ˈhærəld ; ˈhærəld/ 哈羅德一世 (?–1040, 英王,在位期間 1035–40)。
Harold II 哈羅德二世 (1022?–1066, 英王,在位期間 1066)。
Harold III 哈羅德三世 (1015–1066, 挪威國王, 在位期間 1047–66)。
Harriman /ˈhærɪmən ; ˈhærɪmən/ 哈里曼 (William Averell, 1891–, 美國商人、外交家及從政者)。
Harris /ˈhærɪs ; ˈhærɪs/ 哈利斯 (William Torrey, 1835–1909, 美國哲學家及教育家)。
Harrison /ˈhærɪsn ; ˈhærəsn̩/ 哈利生 (**1** Benjamin, 1833–1901, 於 1889–93 任美國第二十三任總統; **2** Frederic, 1831–1923, 英國作家及哲學家; **3** William Henry, 1773–1841, 於 1841 任美國第九任總統)。
Hart /hɑːt ; hɑrt/ 哈特 (Sir Robert, 1835–1911, 英國外交家)。
Harte /hɑːt ; hɑrt/ 哈特 (Francis Brett, 1836–1902, 美國作家)。
Harvard /ˈhɑːvəd ; ˈhɑrvɚd/ 哈佛 (John, 1607–1638, 移居美國之英國牧師,爲哈佛大學之主要創辦人)。
Harvey /ˈhɑːvɪ ; ˈhɑrvɪ/ 哈維 (William, 1578–1657, 英國醫生及解剖學家,血液循環之發現者)。
Hasdrubal /ˈhæzdruːbəl ; ˈhæzdrubl̩/ 哈玆魯勃 (?–207 B.C., 迦太基將軍, Hannibal 之弟)。
Hastings /ˈheɪstɪŋz ; ˈhestɪŋz/ 哈斯丁斯 (Warren, 1732–1818, 英國政治家,印度第一任英國總督)。
Hauptmann /ˈhaʊp(t)mɑːn ; ˈhaʊp(t)ˌmɑn/ 霍普曼 (Gerhart, 1862–1946, 德國作家,曾獲 1912 年諾貝爾文學獎)。
Hawkins /ˈhɔːkɪnz ; ˈhɔkɪnz/ 霍金斯 (**1** Sir Anthony Hope, 1863–1933, 筆名 Anthony Hope, 英國小說家及劇作家; **2** Sir John, 1532–1595, 英國海軍上將)。
Haworth /ˈhɔːəθ ; ˈhaʊɚθ/ 哈爾斯 (Sir (Walter) Norman, 1883–1950, 英國化學家,與 P. Karrer 同獲 1937 年諾貝爾化學獎)。
Hawthorne /ˈhɔːθɔːn ; ˈhɔˌθɔrn/ 霍桑 (Nathaniel, 1804–1864, 美國作家)。
Hay /heɪ ; he/ 海約翰 (John Milton, 1838–1905, 美國政治家)。
Haydn /ˈhaɪdn ; ˈhaɪdn̩/ 海頓 ((Franz) Joseph, 1732–1809, 奧國作曲家)。
Hayes /heɪz ; hez/ 海斯 (**1** Carlton Joseph Huntley, 1882–1964, 美國歷史學家及外交家; **2** Isaac Israel, 1832–1881, 美國北極探險家; **3** Rutherford Birchard, 1822–1893, 於 1877–81 任美國第十九任總統)。
Haynes /heɪns ; henz/ 海恩斯 (Elwood, 1857–1925, 美國發明家)。
Hazard /ˈhæzəd ; ˈhæzɚd/ 哈沙德 (Caroline, 1856–1945, 美國女教育家)。
Hazlitt /ˈhæzlɪt ; ˈhæzlɪt/ 海斯利特 (William, 1778–1830, 英國散文家)。
Hearn /hɜːn ; hɝn/ 小泉八雲 (Lafcadio, 1850–1904, 日名 Yakumo Koizumi, 入日本籍之美國作家)。
Heaviside /ˈhevɪsaɪd ; ˈhɛvɪˌsaɪd/ 海維塞 (Oliver, 1850–1925, 英國物理學家及電學家)。
Hegel /ˈheɪgl ; ˈhegl̩/ 黑格爾 (Georg Wilhelm Friedrich, 1770–1831, 德國哲學家)。
Heidenstam /ˈheɪdnstæm ; ˈhedn̩ˌstæm/ 海丹斯坦 (Verner von, 1859–1940, 瑞典作家,曾獲 1916 年諾貝爾文學獎)。
Heisenberg /ˈhaɪznbeəg ; ˈhaɪzn̩bɛrg/ 海森堡 (Werner, 1901–1976, 德國物理學家,曾獲 1932 年諾貝爾物理獎)。

Heliogabalus /ˌhiːlɪəʊ'gæbələs ; ˌhilɪo'gæbələs/ 希利伽巴拉 (204-222, 羅馬皇帝, 在位期間 218-222)。
Helmholtz, von /'helmˌhəʊlts ; 'hɛlmˌholts/ 赫爾姆霍茲 (Hermann Ludwig Ferdinand, 1821-1894, 德國物理學家、解剖學家及生理學家)。
Hemans /'hemənz ; 'hɛmənz/ 海曼斯 (Felicia Dorothea, 1793-1835, 本姓 Browne, 英國女詩人)。
Hemingway /'hemɪŋweɪ ; 'hɛmɪŋwe/ 海明威 (Ernest Miller, 1899-1961, 美國小說家及記者, 曾獲 1954 年諾貝爾文學獎)。
Hench /hentʃ ; hɛntʃ/ 韓奇 (Philip Showalter, 1896-1965, 美國醫生, 與 E. C. Kendall 及 T. Reichstein 同獲 1950 年諾貝爾醫學獎)。
Henderson /'hendəsn ; 'hɛndɚsn̩/ 韓德遜 (Arthur, 1863-1935, 英國工黨領袖及政治家, 曾獲 1934 年諾貝爾和平獎)。
Henley /'henlɪ ; 'hɛnlɪ/ 韓里 (William Ernest, 1849-1903, 英國作家及編輯)。
Henry /'henrɪ ; 'hɛnrɪ/ 亨利 (**1** Joseph, 1797-1878, 美國物理學家; **2** Patrick, 1736-1799, 美國政治家及演說家)。
Henry I 亨利一世 (**1** 1068-1135, 英王, 在位期間 1100-35; **2** 1008-1060, 法國國王, 在位期間 1031-60)。
Henry II 亨利二世 (**1** 1133-1189, 英王, 在位期間 1154-89; **2** 1519-1559, 法國國王, 在位期間 1547-59)。
Henry III 亨利三世 (**1** 1207-1272, 英王, 在位期間 1216-72; **2** 1551-1589, 法國國王, 在位期間 1574-89)。
Henry IV 亨利四世 (**1** 1367-1413, 英王, 在位期間 1399-1413; **2** 1553-1610, 世稱 Henry of Navarre, 法國 Bourbon 王朝第一代國王, 在位期間 1589-1610)。
Henry V 亨利五世 (1387-1422, 英王, 在位期間 1413-22)。
Henry VI 亨利六世 (1421-1471, 英王, 在位期間 1422-61 及 1470-71)。
Henry VII 亨利七世 (1457-1509, 英國 Tudor 王朝第一代國王, 在位期間 1485-1509)。
Henry VIII 亨利八世 (1491-1547, 英王, 在位期間 1509-47)。
Heraclitus /ˌherə'klaɪtəs ; ˌhɛrə'klaɪtəs/ 赫拉克賴脫 (紀元前五世紀之希臘哲學家)。
Heraclius /ˌherə'klaɪəs ; ˌhɛrə'klaɪəs/ 赫勒克留 (575?-641, 東羅馬帝國皇帝, 在位期間 610-641)。
Herbert /'hɜːbət ; 'hɝbɚt/ 赫伯特 (**1** George, 1593-1633, 英國牧師及詩人; **2** Victor, 1859-1924, 生於愛爾蘭之美國作曲家及樂隊指揮)。
Hero /'hɪərəʊ ; 'hɪro/ or **Heron** /'hɪərɒn ; 'hɪrɑn/ 希羅 (三世紀時之希臘科學家)。
Herodotus /he'rɒdətəs ; hə'rɑdətəs/ 希羅多德 (紀元前五世紀之希臘歷史學家, 被稱爲史學之父)。
Herrick /'herɪk ; 'hɛrɪk/ 赫里克 (**1** Myron Timothy, 1854-1929, 美國外交家; **2** Robert, 1591-1674, 英國詩人; **3** Robert, 1868-1938, 美國教育家及小說家)。
Herschel /'hɜːʃəl ; 'hɝʃəl/ 赫瑟爾 (Sir John Frederick William, 1792-1871, 與其父 Sir William, 1738-1822, 皆爲英國天文學家)。
Hertz /hɜːts ; hɝts/ 赫芝 (**1** Gustav Ludwig, 1887-1975, 德國物理學家, 與 J. Franck 同獲 1925 年諾貝爾物理獎; **2** Heinrich Rudolf, 1857-1894 德國物理學家)。
Hesiod /'hiːsɪɒd ; 'hisɪəd/ 海希奧德 (紀元前八世紀之希臘詩人)。
Hess /hes ; hɛs/ 希斯 (**1** Victor Franz, 1883-1964, 奧國物理學家, 與 C. D. Anderson 同獲 1936 年諾貝爾物理獎; **2** Walter Rudolf, 1881-1973, 瑞士生理學家, 與 E. Moniz 同獲 1949 年諾貝爾醫學獎)。
Hesse /'hesə ; 'hɛsə/ 赫塞 (Hermann, 1877-1962, 德國作家, 曾獲 1946 年諾貝爾文學獎)。
Hevesy, de /'hevəʃɪ ; 'hɛvəʃɪ/ 海威希 (George, 1885-1966, 匈牙利化學家, 曾獲 1943 年諾貝爾化學獎)。
Heymans /eɪ'mɑːns ; e'mɑns/ 海孟茲 (Corneille, 1892-1968, 比利時生理學家, 曾獲 1938 年諾貝爾醫學獎)。
Heyrovsky /'heɪrɒfskɪ ; 'herɔfskɪ/ 海洛斯基 (Jaroslav, 1890-1967, 捷克化學家, 曾獲1959年諾貝爾化學獎)。
Heyse /'haɪzə ; 'haɪzə/ 海塞 (Paul von, 1830-1914, 德國小說家、劇作家及詩人, 曾獲 1910 年諾貝爾文學獎)。
Heywood /'heɪwʊd ; 'hewʊd/ 海伍德 (**1** John, 1497?-?1580, 英國作家; **2** Thomas, 1574?-1641, 英國劇作家)。
Hichens /'hɪtʃɪnz ; 'hɪtʃɪnz/ 希勤茲 (Robert Smythe, 1864-1950, 英國小說家)。
Hill /hɪl ; hɪl/ 希爾 (**1** Archibald Vivian, 1886-1977, 英國生理學家, 與 O. Meyerhof 同獲 1922 年諾貝爾醫學獎; **2** Sir Rowland, 1795-1879, 英國郵政改革者)。
Hillman /'hɪlmən ; 'hɪlmən/ 希爾曼 (Sidney, 1887-1946, 美國勞工領袖)。
Hindenburg, von /'hɪndənbɜːg ; 'hɪndənˌbɝg/ 興登卜 (Paul, 1847-1934, 德國元帥, 於 1925-34 任總統)。
Hinshelwood /'hɪnʃəlˌwʊd ; 'hɪnʃəlˌwʊd/ 興歇伍德 (Sir Cyril Norman, 1897-1967, 英國化學家, 與 N. N. Semënov 同獲 1956 年諾貝爾化學獎)。
Hipparchus /hɪ'pɑːkəs ; hɪ'pɑrkəs/ 希巴克斯 (**1** 雅典暴君, 在位期間 527-514 B.C.; **2** 紀元前二世紀時之希臘天文學家)。
Hippocrates /hɪ'pɒkrətiːz ; hɪ'pɑkrətiz/ 希波克拉底 (460?-?377 B.C., 希臘醫生, 世稱醫學之父)。
Hitchcock /'hɪtʃkɒk ; 'hɪtʃkɑk/ 希區考克 (Edward, 1793-1864, 美國地質學家)。
Hitler /'hɪtlə ; 'hɪtlɚ/ 希特勒 (Adolf, 1889-1945, 德國納粹黨魁, 於 1933-45 任德國總理)。
Hobbema /'hɒbɪmə ; 'hɑbɪmə/ 霍白瑪 (Meindert, 1638-1709, 荷蘭畫家)。
Hobbes /hɒbz ; hɑbz/ 霍布士 (Thomas, 1588-1679, 英國哲學家)。
Hocking /'hɒkɪŋ ; 'hɑkɪŋ/ 霍京 (William Ernest, 1873-1966, 美國哲學家)。
Hodgkin /'hɒdʒkɪn ; 'hɑdʒkɪn/ 霍治京 (**1** Sir Alan Lloyd, 1914-, 英國生理學家, 與 J. C. Eccles 及 A. F. Huxley 同獲 1963 年諾貝爾醫學獎; **2** Dorothy Mary Crowfoot, 1910-, 英國化學家, 曾獲 1964 年諾貝爾化學獎)。
Hoe /həʊ ; ho/ 何歐 (Richard March, 1812-1886, 美國發明家及製造商)。
Hofstadter /'hɒf stætə ; 'hofˌstætɚ/ 郝夫斯臺特 (**1** Robert, 1915-, 美國物理學家, 與 R. L. Mössbauer 同獲 1961 年諾貝爾物理獎; **2** Richard, 1916-, 美國歷史學家)。
Hogarth /'həʊgɑːθ ; 'hogɑrθ/ 霍迦斯 (William, 1697-1764, 英國畫家及雕版家)。
Hogg /hɒg ; hɔg/ 霍格 (James, 1770-1835, 世稱 the Ettrick Shepherd, 蘇格蘭詩人)。
Holbein /'hɒlbaɪn ; 'hɔlbaɪn/ 霍爾班 (Hans, the Elder, 1465?-1524, 與其子 Hans, the Younger, 1497?-1543, 均爲德國畫家)。
Holland /'hɒlənd ; 'hɑlənd/ 霍蘭 (John Philip, 1840-1914, 生於愛爾蘭之美國發明家)。
Holmes /həʊmz ; homz/ 霍姆茲 (Oliver Wendell, 1809-1894, 美國醫生及作家; 其子, 同名, 1841-1935, 美國法學家)。
Homer /'həʊmə ; 'homɚ/ 荷馬 (**1** 紀元前九世紀之古希臘詩人; **2** Winslow, 1836-1910, 美國畫家)。
Honorius /həʊ'nɔːrɪəs ; ho'nɔrɪəs/ 霍諾留斯 (Flavius, 384-423, 西羅馬帝國皇帝, 在位期間 395-423)。
Hood /hʊd ; hʊd/ 胡德 (Thomas, 1799-1845, 英國詩人)。
Hooke /hʊk ; hʊk/ 胡克 (Robert, 1635-1703, 英國實驗主義哲學家)。
Hooker /'hʊkə ; 'hʊkɚ/ 胡克爾 (Sir Joseph Dalton, 1817-1911, 英國植物學家)。
Hoover /'huːvə ; 'huvɚ/ 胡佛 (**1** Herbert Clark, 1874-1964, 於 1929-33 任美國第 31 任總統; **2** John Edgar, 1895-1972, 美國犯罪學家, 於 1924-72 任聯邦調查局局長)。
Hopkins /'hɒpkɪnz ; 'hɑpkɪnz/ 霍布金斯 (**1** Sir Frederick Gowland, 1861-1947, 英國生物化學家, 與 C. Eijkman 同獲 1929 年諾貝爾醫學獎; **2** Gerard Manley, 1844-1889, 英國詩人; **3** Mark, 1802-1887, 美國教育家)。
Horace /'hɒrəs ; 'hɑrəs/ 賀瑞斯 (65-8 B.C., 原名 Quintus Horatius Flaccus, 羅馬詩人及諷刺文家)。
Housman /'haʊsmən ; 'haʊsmən/ 霍斯曼 (Alfred Edward, 1859-1936, 英國古典文學家及詩人)。

Houssay /uːˈsaɪ ; uˈsaɪ/ 吳賽 (Bernardo Alberto, 1887–1971, 阿根廷生理學家，與 Cori 夫婦同獲 1947 年諾貝爾醫學獎)。

Houston /ˈhjuːstən ; ˈhjustən/ 休斯頓 (Samuel, 1793–1863, 美國政治家及將軍，於 1836–38 及 1841–44, 任 Texas 共和國總統)。

Howard /ˈhaʊəd ; ˈhaʊɚd/ 何爾德 (Henry, 亦稱 Earl of Surrey, 1517?–1547, 英國軍人及詩人)。

Howe /haʊ ; haʊ/ 何奧 (Elias, 1819–1867, 美國發明家)。

Howells /ˈhaʊəlz ; ˈhaʊəlz/ 郝爾斯 (William Dean, 1837–1920, 美國作家及批評家)。

Hsia Yü /ˈʃjɑːˈjuː ; ˈʃjɑˈju/ 夏禹(中國夏朝開國帝王，姓姒，治洪水有功，在位八年)。

Hsüan Tsang /ˈʃuːɑːn ˈdzɑːŋ ; ˈʃuɑn ˈdzɑŋ/ 玄奘 (596–664, 中國唐朝佛教高僧)。

Hsüan Tsung /ˈʃuːɑːn ˈdzʊŋ ; ˈʃuɑn ˈdzʊŋ/ 唐玄宗 (685–762, 中國唐朝皇帝，即位後宇內昇平，世稱開元之治，在位年間 713–755)。

Huangti /ˈhwɑːŋˈdiː ; ˈhwɑŋ ˈdi/ 黃帝(中國上古聖王，姓公孫，長於姬水，又姓姬，生於軒轅之丘，故曰軒轅氏；國於有熊，故亦稱有熊氏，在位一百年)。

Hudson /ˈhʌdsn ; ˈhʌdsn̩/ 哈德生 (**1** Henry, ?–1611, 英國航海家及探險家; **2** Manley Ottmer, 1886–1960, 美國法學家; **3** William Henry, 1841–1922, 英國博物學家及作家)。

Huggins /ˈhʌɡɪnz ; ˈhʌɡɪnz/ 赫金斯 (Sir William, 1824–1910, 英國天文學家)。

Hughes /hjuːz ; hjuz/ 休斯 (**1** Charles Evans, 1862–1948, 美國法學家，於 1930–41 任最高法院院長; **2** Thomas, 1822–1896, 英國法學家、改革者及作家)。

Hugo /ˈhjuːɡəʊ ; ˈhjugo/ 雨果 (Victor Marie, 1802–1885, 法國詩人、小說家及劇作家)。

Hull /hʌl ; hʌl/ 赫爾 (Cordell, 1871–1955, 美國政治家，於 1933–44 任美國國務卿，曾獲 1945 年諾貝爾和平獎)。

Humbert I /ˈhʌmbət ; ˈhʌmbɚt/ 洪柏特一世 (1844–1900, 義大利國王，在位期間 1878–1900)。

Humbert II 洪柏特二世 (1904–, 義大利國王，在位期間 1946)。

Humboldt, von /ˈhʌmbəult ; ˈhʌmbolt/ 洪保德 (**1** Baron (Friedrich Heinrich) Alexander, 1769–1859, 德國博物學家、旅行家及政治家; **2** 其兄 Baron Wilhelm, 1767–1835, 德國語言學家及外交家)。

Hume /hjuːm ; hjum/ 休姆 (David, 1711–1776, 蘇格蘭哲學家及歷史學家)。

Hunt /hʌnt ; hʌnt/ 韓特 (**1** (James Henry) Leigh, 1784–1859, 英國散文家及詩人; **2** (William) Holman, 1827–1910, 英國畫家)。

Hunter /ˈhʌntə ; ˈhʌntɚ/ 韓特爾 (John, 1728–1793, 英國解剖學家及外科醫生)。

Hunyadi or **Hunyady** /ˈhʊnjɑːdɪ ; ˈhʊnjɑdɪ/ 洪亞底 (János, 1387?–1456, 匈牙利英雄)。

Hurst /hɜːst ; hɝst/ 赫斯特 (Fannie, 1889–1968, 美國女作家)。

Hu Shih /ˈhuːˈʃiː ; ˈhuˈʃi/ 胡適 (1891–1962, 中國哲學家、外交家及作家)。

Husserl /ˈhʊsəl ; ˈhʊsɚl/ 胡塞爾 (Edmund, 1859–1938, 德國哲學家)。

Huxley /ˈhʌkslɪ ; ˈhʌkslɪ/ 赫胥黎 (**1** Aldous Leonard, 1894–1963, J. S. ～之弟，英國小說家及批評家; **2** Sir Julian Sorell, 1887–1975, T. H. ～之孫，英國生物學家; **3** Thomas Henry, 1825–1895, 英國生物學家; **4** Andrew Fielding, 1917–, 英國生理學家及教育家，與 A. L. Hodgkin 及 J. C. Eccles 同獲 1963 年諾貝爾醫學獎)。

Huyg(h)ens /ˈhaɪɡənz ; ˈhaɪɡənz/ 海更斯 (Christian, 1629–1695, 荷蘭數學家、物理學家及天文學家)。

Hyde /haɪd ; haɪd/ 海德 (**1** Douglas, 1860–1949, 愛爾蘭作家，於 1938–45 任愛爾蘭共和國總統; **2** Edward, 1609–1674, 英國政治家及歷史學家)。

Ibsen /ˈɪbsn ; ˈɪbsn̩/ 易卜生 (Henrik, 1828–1906, 挪威詩人及劇作家)。

Ignatius /ɪɡˈneɪʃɪəs ; ɪɡˈneʃ(ɪ)əs/ 伊格那修 (Saint, 西元 1–2 世紀之安提阿 (Antioch) 大主教)。

Ingersoll /ˈɪŋɡəsɒl ; ˈɪŋɡɚsɔl/ 殷格索 (Robert Green, 1833–1899, 美國律師及不可知論者)。

Inness /ˈɪnɪs ; ˈɪnɪs/ 殷奈斯 (George, 1825–1894, 與其子，同名, 1854–1926, 均爲美國畫家)。

Innocent II /ˈɪnəsnt ; ˈɪnəsn̩t/ 英諾森二世 (?–1143, 於 1130–43 爲教皇)。

Innocent III 英諾森三世 (1161–1216, 於 1198–1216 爲教皇)。

Innocent IV 英諾森四世 (?–1254, 於 1243–54 任教皇)。

Innocent XI 英諾森十一世 (1611–1689, 於 1676–89 任教皇)。

Iredell /ˈaɪədel ; ˈaɪrdɛl/ 艾代爾 (James, 1751–1799, 美國法學家)。

Irving /ˈɜːvɪŋ ; ˈɝvɪŋ/ 歐文 (Washington, 1783–1859, 美國散文家、小說家及歷史學家)。

Isaacs /ˈaɪzəks ; ˈaɪzəks/ 艾薩克斯 (Sir Isaac Alfred, 1855–1948, 澳大利亞法學家及政治家，於 1931–36 任澳洲總督)。

Isabella I /ˌɪzəˈbelə ; ˌɪzəˈbɛlə/ 伊薩伯拉一世 (1451–1504, Ferdinand II (of Aragon) 之妻, 1474–1504 爲 Castile 女王，哥倫布的贊助人)。

Isherwood /ˈɪʃəwʊd ; ˈɪʃɚwʊd/ 伊塞伍德 (Christopher William Bradshaw, 1904–, 生於英國之美國作家)。

Isocrates /aɪˈsɒkrətiːz ; aɪˈsɑkrətiz/ 艾索克拉底 (436–338 B.C., 雅典演說家)。

Ivan III /ɪˈvɑːn ; ɪˈvɑn/ 伊凡三世 (1440–1505, 世稱 Ivan the Great, 俄國大公，在位期間 1462–1505)。

Ivan IV 伊凡四世 (1530–1584, 世稱 Ivan the Terrible, 於 1533–84 統治俄國，於 1547–84 任俄國第一位沙皇)。

Ives /aɪvz ; aɪvz/ 艾伍玆 (James Merritt, 1824–1895, 美國平版印刷家)。

Jackson /ˈdʒæksn ; ˈdʒæksn̩/ 傑克生 (**1** Andrew, 1767–1845, 美國將軍，於 1829–37 任美國第七任總統; **2** Helen Maria Hunt, 1830–1885, 本姓Fiske, 美國女小說家; **3** Robert Houghwout, 1892–1954, 美國法學家)。

James /dʒeɪmz ; dʒemz/ 詹姆斯 (**1** Henry, 1811–1882, 美國哲學家; **2** 其子 Henry, 1843–1916, 生於美國之英國作家; **3** 前者之兄 William, 1842–1910, 美國心理學家及哲學家)。

James I 詹姆斯一世 (1566–1625, 英王，在位期間 1603–25, 並於 1567–1603 爲蘇格蘭王，稱做詹姆斯六世)。

James II 詹姆斯二世 (1633–1701, 英王，在位期間 1685–88)。

Jansen /ˈdʒænsn ; ˈdʒænsn̩/ 詹生 (Cornelis, 1585–1638, 荷蘭天主教神學家)。

Jay /dʒeɪ ; dʒe/ 傑伊 (John, 1745–1829, 美國法學家及政治家，於 1789–95 任美國第一任最高法院院長)。

Jeans /dʒiːnz ; dʒinz/ 金斯 (Sir James Hopwood, 1877–1946, 英國物理學家、天文學家及作家)。

Jebb /dʒeb ; dʒɛb/ 傑卜 (Sir Richard Claverhouse, 1841–1905, 蘇格蘭古典學者)。

Jefferson /ˈdʒefəsn ; ˈdʒɛfɚsn̩/ 傑佛遜 (Thomas, 1743–1826, 美國政治家，於 1801–09 任第三任總統)。

Jeffrey /ˈdʒefrɪ ; ˈdʒɛfrɪ/ 傑佛利 (Lord Francis, 1773–1850, 蘇格蘭批評家及法學家)。

Jeffreys /ˈdʒefrɪz ; ˈdʒɛfrɪz/ 傑佛利斯 (George, 1648–1689, 英國法學家)。

Jenghiz Khan /ˌdʒeŋɡɪz ˈkɑːn ; ˌdʒɛŋɡəzˈkɑn/ 參看 Genghis Khan。

Jenner /ˈdʒenə ; ˈdʒɛnɚ/ 金納 (**1** Edward, 1749–1823, 英國醫生; **2** Sir William, 1815–1898, 英國醫生)。

Jensen /ˈjensn, ˈjenzn ; ˈjɛnsn̩, ˈjɛnzn̩/ 顏生 (**1** Johannes Vilhelm, 1873–1950, 丹麥詩人及小說家，曾獲 1944 年諾貝爾文學獎; **2** (Johannes) Hans (Daniel) 1906–1973, 德國物理學家，與 M. G. Mayer 及 E. P. Wigner 同獲 1963 年諾貝爾物理獎)。

Jespersen /ˈjespəsn ; ˈjɛspɚsn̩/ 耶斯波生 ((Jens) Otto (Harry), 1860–1943, 丹麥語言學家)。

Jesus (Christ) /ˈdʒiːzəs(kraɪst) ; ˈdʒizəs(kraɪst)/ 耶穌(基督) (或稱 Christ Jesus, 4–8? B.C.—A.D. ?29, 基督教之創始人)。

Jevons /ˈdʒevənz ; ˈdʒɛvənz/ 傑文玆 (William Stanley, 1835–1882, 英國經濟學家及邏輯學家)。

Jiménez /hɪˈmeɪneɪθ ; hɪˈmeˌneθ/ 希梅內斯 (Juan Ramón, 1881–1958, 西班牙詩人，曾獲 1956 年諾貝爾文學獎)。

Joan of Arc /ˌdʒəʊnə ˈvɑːk ; ˌdʒonə ˈvɑrk/ 貞德

(Saint, 1412–1431, 世稱 the Maid of Orleans, 法國民族女英雄, 法文作 **Jeanne d'Arc** /ʒɑːnˈdɑːk ; ʒɑnˈdɑrk/)。

John /dʒɒn ; dʒɑn/ 約翰 (1167?–1216, 亦稱 John Lackland, 英王, 在位期間 1199–1216)。

John I 約翰一世 (1357–1433, the Great, 葡萄牙國王, 在位期間 1385–1433)。

John III 約翰三世 (1629–1696, John Sobieski, 波蘭國王, 在位期間 1674–96)。

Johnson[1] /ˈdʒɒnsn ; ˈdʒɑnsn̩/ 約翰生 (**1** Andrew, 1808–1875, 於 1865–69 任美國第十七任總統; **2** James Weldon, 1871–1938, 美國作家; **3** Samuel, 1709–1784, 被稱爲 Dr. Johnson, 美國辭典編纂家及作家)。

Johnson[2] 詹森 (Lyndon Baines, 1908–1973, 美國從政者, 1963–69 任美國第三十六任總統)。

Johnson[3] /ˈjuːnsɒn ; ˈjunsɔn/ 雍松 (Eyvind, 1900–1976, 瑞典作家, 與 H. E. Martinson 同獲 1974 年諾貝爾文學獎)。

Johnston /ˈdʒɒnstən ; ˈdʒɑnstən/ 詹斯頓 (Mary, 1870–1936, 美國女小說家)。

Joliot-Curie /ˈʒəulɪəʊ kjʊˈriː ; ˈʒolɪˌo kjʊˈri/ 若利歐居里 (**1** Frédéric, 本姓 Joliot, 1900–1958, 法國物理學家; **2** 其妻 Irène, 1897–1956, 居里夫婦之女, 法國物理學家, 二人同獲 1935 年諾貝爾化學獎)。

Jones /dʒəʊnz ; dʒonz/ 仲斯 (**1** Daniel, 1881–1967, 英國語音學家; **2** Henry Arthur, 1851–1929, 英國劇作家; **3** Inigo, 1573–1652, 英國建築家)。

Jonson /ˈdʒɒnsn ; ˈdʒɑnsn̩/ 章生 (Ben, 1573?–1637, 英國詩人及劇作家, 於 1619–37 榮膺桂冠詩人)。

Jordan /ˈdʒɔːdn ; ˈdʒɔrdn̩/ 焦爾敦 (David Starr, 1851–1931, 美國生物學家及教育家)。

Joseph II /ˈdʒəʊzɪf ; ˈdʒozɪf/ 約瑟二世 (1741–1790, 德國國王, 在位期間 1764–90, 於 1765–90 爲神聖羅馬帝國皇帝)。

Josephus /dʒəʊˈsiːfəs ; dʒoˈsifəs/ 周瑟法斯 (Flavius, 37–?100, 猶太歷史學家)。

Jouhaux /ʒuːˈəʊ ; ʒuˈo/ 儒歐 (Léon, 1879–1954, 法國工會領袖, 曾獲 1951 年諾貝爾和平獎)。

Joule /dʒaʊl ; dʒaʊl/ 焦耳 (James Prescott, 1818–1889, 英國物理學家)。

Jowett /ˈdʒaʊɪt ; ˈdʒaʊɪt/ 喬義特 (Benjamin, 1817–1893, 英國古典學者)。

Joyce /dʒɔɪs ; dʒɔɪs/ 喬伊斯 (James, 1882–1941, 愛爾蘭作家)。

Jugurtha /dʒʊˈgɜːθə ; dʒʊˈgɝθə/ 朱古達 (?–104 B.C. Numidia 國王, 在位期間 113–104 B.C.)。

Julian /ˈdʒuːljən ; ˈdʒuljən/ 朱利安 (331–363, 世稱 ~ the Apostate, 羅馬帝國皇帝, 在位期間 361–363)。

Juliana /ˌdʒuːlɪˈɑːnə ; ˌdʒulɪˈænə/ 朱莉安娜 (1909–, 荷蘭女王, 在位期間 1948–80)。

Junkers /ˈjʊŋkəz ; ˈjʊŋkɚz/ 容克斯 (Hugo, 1859–1935, 德國飛機設計家及建造家)。

Justinian I /dʒʌsˈtɪnɪən ; dʒʌsˈtɪnɪən/ 賈斯丁尼安一世 (483–565, 世稱 Justinian the Great, 東羅馬帝國皇帝, 在位期間 527–565)。

Juvenal /ˈdʒuːvɪnl ; ˈdʒuvɪnl̩/ 朱文諾 (60?–?140, 羅馬詩人及諷刺文家)。

Kamerlingh Onnes /ˌkɑːməlɪŋˈɒnəs ; ˌkamɚlɪŋˈɑnəs/ 卡麥琳翁奈 (Heike, 1853–1926, 荷蘭物理學家, 曾獲 1913 年諾貝爾物理獎)。

Kane /keɪn ; ken/ 克恩 (Elisha Kent, 1820–1857, 美國北極探險家)。

K'ang Hsi /ˈkɑːŋˈʃiː ; ˈkɑŋˈʃi/ 康熙 (1654–1722, 中國清朝皇帝, 原爲年號名, 卽清聖祖, 在位期間 1662–1722)。

Kant /kænt ; kænt/ 康德 (Immanuel, 1724–1804, 德國哲學家)。

Karlfeldt /ˈkɑːlfelt ; ˈkarlˌfɛlt/ 喀爾菲爾特 (Erik Axel, 1864–1931, 瑞典詩人, 曾獲 1931 年諾貝爾文學獎)。

Karlgren /ˈkɑːlgrən ; ˈkarlgren/ 高本漢 ((Klas) Bernhard (Johannes), 1889–1978, 瑞典漢學家)。

Karrer /ˈkɑːrə ; ˈkarɚ/ 喀拉 (Paul, 1889–1971, 瑞士化學家, 與 W. N. Haworth 同獲 1937 年諾貝爾化學獎)。

Kawabata /ˌkɑːwɑːˈbɑːtɑː ; ˌkawəˈbatə/ 川端康成 (Yasunari, 1899–1972, 日本作家, 曾獲 1968 年諾貝爾文學獎)。

Keats /kiːts ; kits/ 濟慈 (John, 1795–1821, 英國詩人)。

Keble /ˈkiːbl ; ˈkibl̩/ 吉卜爾 (John, 1792–1866, 英國牧師及詩人)。

Kelland /ˈkelənd ; ˈkɛlənd/ 凱蘭德 (Clarence Budington, 1881–1964, 美國小說家)。

Keller /ˈkelə ; ˈkɛlɚ/ 凱勒 (Helen Adams, 1880–1968, 美國盲聾女教師及作家)。

Kellogg /ˈkelɒg ; ˈkɛlˌɑg/ 凱洛格 (Frank Billings, 1856–1937, 美國政治家, 曾獲 1929 年諾貝爾和平獎)。

Kelly /ˈkelɪ ; ˈkɛlɪ/ 凱利 (James Edward, 1855–1933, 美國雕刻家)。

Kelvin /ˈkelvɪn ; ˈkɛlvɪn/ 克爾文 (William Thomson, 1824–1907, 英國數學家及物理學家)。

Kemal Atatürk /kəˌmæl ˈætətɜːk ; kəˌmæl ˈætəˌtɝk/ 凱末爾 (1881–1938, 原名 Mustafa (或 Mustapha) Kemal, 土耳其將軍, 於 1923–38 任第一任總統)。

Kendall /ˈkendl ; ˈkɛndl̩/ 甘德爾 (**1** Edward Calvin, 1886–1972, 美國生物化學家, 與 P. S. Hench 及 T. Reichstein 同獲 1950 年諾貝爾醫學獎; **2** (William) Sergeant, 1869–1938, 美國畫家及雕刻家)。

Kendrew /ˈkendruː ; ˈkɛndru/ 甘諾 (Sir John Cowdery, 1917–, 英國科學家, 與 M. F. Perutz 同獲 1962 年諾貝爾化學獎)。

Kennedy /ˈkenədɪ ; ˈkɛnədɪ/ 甘廼迪 (John Fitzgerald, 1917–1963, 美國從政者, 於 1961–63 任美國第三十五任總統)。

Kent /kent ; kɛnt/ 甘特 (**1** James, 1763–1847, 美國法學家; **2** Rockwell, 1882–1971, 美國畫家及插圖畫家)。

Kepler /ˈkeplə ; ˈkɛplɚ/ 開普勒 (Johannes, 1571–1630, 德國天文學家)。

Kern /kɜːn ; kɝn/ 克恩 (Jerome David, 1885–1945, 美國作曲家)。

Kettering /ˈketərɪŋ ; ˈkɛtərɪŋ/ 克德林 (Charles Franklin, 1876–1958, 美國電機工程師及發明家)。

Keynes /keɪnz ; kenz/ 凱因斯 (John Maynard, 1883–1946, 英國經濟學家)。

Khrushchev /krʊʃˈ(tʃ)ɒf ; krʊʃˈ(tʃ)ɔf/ 赫魯雪夫 (Nikita Sergeevich, 1894–1971, 於 1953–64 任蘇共總書記, 1958–64 任蘇聯總理)。

Kierkegaard /ˈkɪəkə gɑːd; ˈkɪrkəˌgɑrd/ 齊克果 (Sören Aabye, 1813–1855, 丹麥哲學家及神學家)。

King /kɪŋ ; kɪŋ/ 金 (**1** Rufus, 1755–1827, 美國從政者及外交家; **2** William Lyon Mackenzie, 1874–1950, 加拿大政治家, 於 1921–26, 1926–30 及 1935–48 任首相; **3** Martin Luther, 1929–1968, 美國牧師, 黑人民權運動領袖, 曾獲 1964 年諾貝爾和平獎)。

Kingsley /ˈkɪŋzlɪ ; ˈkɪŋzlɪ/ 金斯利 (Charles, 1819–1875, 英國牧師及小說家)。

Kipling /ˈkɪplɪŋ ; ˈkɪplɪŋ/ 吉普林 (Rudyard, 1865–1936, 英國作家, 曾獲 1907 年諾貝爾文學獎)。

Kissinger /ˈkɪsndʒə; ˈkɪsn̩dʒɚ/ 季辛吉 (Henry Alfred, 1923–, 美國政治學家, 1973–77 任美國國務卿, 並獲 1973 年諾貝爾和平獎)。

Kitchener /ˈkɪtʃɪnə ; ˈkɪtʃɪnɚ/ 吉青納 (Horatio Herbert, 1850–1916, 英國陸軍元帥)。

Kittredge /ˈkɪtrɪdʒ ; ˈkɪtrɪdʒ/ 吉特律幾 (George Lyman, 1860–1941, 美國語言學家及教育家)。

Koch /kɒk ; kɔk/ 高訶 (Robert, 1843–1910, 德國醫生及細菌學家, 曾獲 1905 年諾貝爾醫學獎)。

Kocher /ˈkɒkə ; ˈkɔkɚ/ 考克爾 (Emil Theodor, 1841–1917, 瑞士外科醫生, 曾獲 1909 年諾貝爾醫學獎)。

Kornberg /ˈkɔːnbəg ; ˈkɔrnˌbɝg/ 考恩柏格 (Arthur, 1918–, 美國生物化學家, 與 S. Ochoa 同獲 1959 年諾貝爾醫學獎)。

Kossel /ˈkɒsəl ; ˈkɔsəl/ 考塞爾 (Albrecht, 1853–1927, 德國生理化學家, 曾獲 1910 年諾貝爾醫學獎)。

Krebs /krebz ; krɛbz/ 克萊普斯 (Sir Hans (Adolf), 1900–, 英籍德裔生物化學家, 與 F. A. Lipmann 同獲 1953 年諾貝爾醫學獎)。

Krogh /krɒg ; krɔg/ 柯勞格 (August, 1874–1949, 丹麥生理學家, 曾獲 1920 年諾貝爾醫學獎)。

Kruger /ˈkruːgə ; ˈkrugɚ/ 柯魯格 (Stephanus Johannes Paulus, 1825–1904, 南非政治家, 於 1883–1900 任 Transvaal 總統)。

Krutch /kruːtʃ ; krutʃ/ 克魯芝 (Joseph Wood, 1893–

1970, 美國作家及批評家)。

Kublai Khan /ˈkʊblaɪˈkɑːn ; ˌkublaɪˈkɑn/ 忽必烈汗 (1216–1294, 中國元朝開國者, 即元世祖)。

Kuhn /kuːn ; kun/ 庫恩 (Richard, 1900–1967, 奧國化學家, 曾獲 1938 年諾貝爾化學獎)。

Kusch /kʊʃ ; kʊʃ/ 庫士 (Polykarp, 1911–, 生於德國之美國物理學家, 與 W. E. Lamb 同獲 1955 年諾貝爾物理獎)。

Kyd or **Kid** /kɪd ; kɪd/ 吉德 (Thomas, 1558–1594, 英國劇作家)。

Lafayette, de /ˌlɑːfaɪˈet ; ˌlɑfɪˈɛt/ 拉法埃脫 (Marquis, 1757–1834, 法國將軍與政治家, 於美國獨立戰爭時曾統率法軍協助美軍作戰)。

Lafontaine /ləˌfɑːnˈteɪn ; ləˌfɑnˈten/ 拉豐田 (Henri, 1854–1943, 比利時律師及政治家, 曾獲 1913 年諾貝爾和平獎)。

La Fontaine /ləˌfɑːnˈteɪn ; ləˌfɑnˈten/ 拉豐田 (Jean de, 1621–1695, 法國寓言作家)。

Lagerkvist /ˈlɑːgəkfɪst ; ˈlɑgɚˌkfɪst/ 拉格維斯 (Pär Fabian, 1891–1974, 瑞典劇作家、詩人及小說家, 曾獲1951年諾貝爾文學獎)。

Lagerlöf /ˈlɑːgəlʌv ; ˈlɑgɚˌlʌv/ 拉格勒夫 (Selma Ottiliana Lovisa, 1858–1940, 瑞典女小說家及詩人, 曾獲 1909 年諾貝爾文學獎)。

Lamb /læm ; læm/ 蘭姆 (**1** Charles, 1775–1834, 英國散文家及批評家; **2** Willis Eugene, 1913–, 美國物理學家, 與 P. Kusch 同獲 1955 年諾貝爾物理獎)。

Lampson /ˈlæmpsn ; ˈlæmpsn̩/ 藍普生 (Sir Miles Wedderburn, 1880–1964, 英國外交家, 1926–33 任駐華公使。)

Landau /lɑːnˈdaʊ ; lɑnˈdaʊ/ 藍道 (Lev Davidovich 1908–1968, 俄國物理學家, 曾獲 1962 年諾貝爾物理獎)。

Landseer /ˈlænsɪə;ˈlænsɪr/ 藍塞爾 (Sir Edwin Henry, 1802–1873, 英國畫家)。

Landsteiner /ˈlæn(d)staɪnə ; ˈlæn(d)ˌstaɪnɚ/ 藍士台納 (Karl, 1868–1943, 生於奧國之美國病理學家, 曾獲 1930 年諾貝爾醫學獎)。

Lane /leɪn ; len/ 雷恩 (Edward William, 1801–1876, 英國東方學者)。

Lang /læŋ ; læŋ/ 藍恩 (Andrew, 1844–1912, 蘇格蘭學者及作家)。

Lange /ˈlæŋə ; ˈlɑŋə/ 藍格 (Christian Louis, 1869–1938, 挪威歷史學家及和平主義者, 與 K. H. Branting 同獲 1921 年諾貝爾和平獎)。

Langland /ˈlæŋlənd ; ˈlæŋlənd/ or **Langley** /ˈlæŋlɪ ; ˈlæŋlɪ/ 朗蘭 (William, 1332?–?1400, 英國詩人)。

Langley /ˈlæŋlɪ ; ˈlæŋlɪ/ 藍利 (Samuel Pierpont, 1834–1906, 美國天文學家並爲飛機發明史上之先驅者)。

Langmuir /ˈlæŋmjʊə ; ˈlæŋˌmjʊɚ/ 藍穆爾 (Irving, 1881–1957, 美國化學家, 曾獲 1932 年諾貝爾化學獎)。

Langton /ˈlæŋtən ; ˈlæŋtən/ 藍敦 (Stephen, ?–1228, 英國神學家、歷史學家及詩人)。

Lansing /ˈlænsɪŋ ; ˈlænsɪŋ/ 藍辛 (Robert, 1864–1928, 美國律師及政治家, 於 1915–20 任國務卿)。

Lao-tzu or **Lao-tse** or **Lao-tze** /ˈlaʊˈtsiː ; ˈlaʊˈdzə/ 老子 (604?–?531 B.C., 中國大哲學家)。

Laue /ˈlaʊə ; ˈlaʊə/ 勞厄 (Max von, 1879–1960, 德國物理學家, 曾獲 1914 年諾貝爾物理獎)。

Laveran /ˌlævəˈrɑːn ; ˌlævəˈrɑn/ 拉佛蘭 (Charles Louis Alphonse, 1845–1922, 法國生理學家及細菌學家, 曾獲 1907 年諾貝爾醫學獎)。

Lavery /ˈleɪvərɪ ; ˈlev(ə)rɪ/ 拉威利 (Sir John, 1856–1941, 英國畫家)。

Lawes /lɔːz ; lɔz/ 勞斯 (Henry, 1596–1662, 英國作曲家)。

Lawrence /ˈlɔːrəns ; ˈlɔrəns/ 勞倫斯 (**1** David Herbert, 1885–1930, 英國小說家; **2** Ernest Orlando, 1901–1958, 美國物理學家, 曾獲 1939 年諾貝爾物理獎; **3** Sir Thomas, 1769–1830, 英國畫家; **4** Thomas Edward, 1888–1935, 世稱 Lawrence of Arabia, 英國考古學家、軍人及作家)。

Laxness /ˈlɑːksnes ; ˈlɑksnɛs/ 拉克斯內斯 (Halldór Kiljan, 1902–, 冰島作家, 曾獲 1955 年諾貝爾文學獎)。

Layamon /ˈleɪəmən ; ˈleəmən/ 雷亞孟 (十三世紀之英國詩人)。

Layard /leəd ; ˈleɚd/ 賴爾德 (Sir Austen Henry, 1817–1894, 英國考古學家及外交家)。

Leacock /ˈliːkɒk ; ˈlikɑk/ 李科克 (Stephen Butler, 1869–1944, 加拿大經濟學家及幽默作家)。

Lear /lɪə ; lɪr/ 李耳 (Edward, 1812–1888, 英國畫家及胡謅詩人)。

Lecky /ˈlekɪ ; ˈlɛkɪ/ 賴基 (William Edward Hartpole, 1838–1903, 愛爾蘭歷史學家及散文家)。

Lederberg /ˈleɪdəbɜːg ; ˈledɚˌbɝg/ 雷德柏格 (Joshua, 1925–, 美國遺傳學家, 與 G. W. Beadle 及 E. L. Tatum 同獲 1958 年諾貝爾醫學獎)。

Lee /liː ; li/ 李 (Robert Edward, 1807–1870, 美國將軍)。

Lee Tsung-Dao /ˈliːˈdʒʌŋˈdaʊ ; ˈliˈdʒʌŋˈdaʊ/ 李政道 (1926–, 中國物理學家, 與楊振寧同獲 1957 年諾貝爾物理獎)。

Léger /leɪˈʒeɪ ; leˈʒe/ 雷傑 (Alexis Saint-Léger, 1887–1975, 筆名 St. John Perse, 法國外交家及詩人, 曾獲 1960 年諾貝爾文學獎)。

Leighton /ˈleɪtn ; ˈletn̩/ 雷頓 (Frederick, 1830–1896, 英國畫家)。

Lely /ˈliːlɪ ; ˈlilɪ/ 李里 (Sir Peter, 1618–1680, 旅居英國之荷蘭畫家)。

Lenard /ˈleɪnɑːt ; ˈleˌnɑrt/ 雷納德 (Philipp, 1862–1947, 德國物理學家, 曾獲 1905 年諾貝爾物理獎)。

Lenin /ˈlenɪn ; ˈlɛnɪn/ 列寧 (Nikolai, 本名 Vladimir Ilyich Ulyanov, 1870–1924, 蘇俄共產黨領袖, 建立蘇維埃政府)。

Leo I /ˈliːəʊ ; ˈlio/ 利奧一世 (Saint, 390?–461, 羅馬教皇, 在位期間 440–61)。

Leonard /ˈlenəd ; ˈlɛnɚd/ 賴納德 (William Ellery, 1876–1944, 美國教育家及詩人)。

Leonidas /liːˈɒnɪdæs ; lɪˈɑnədəs/ 李奧尼大 (紀元前五世紀之希臘英雄, 於 490?–480 B.C. 任斯巴達國王)。

Leopold I /ˈliːəpəʊld ; ˈliəˌpold/ 利奧波德一世 (**1** 1640–1705, 匈牙利國王, 在位期間 1655–1705, 並於 1658–1705 爲神聖羅馬帝國皇帝; **2** 1790–1865, 比利時國王, 在位期間 1831–65)。

Leopold II 利奧波德二世 (**1** 1747–1792, 神聖羅馬帝國皇帝, 在位期間 1790–92; **2** 1835–1909, 比利時國王, 在位期間 1865–1909)。

Leopold III 利奧波德三世 (1901–, 比利時國王, 在位期間 1934–51)。

Lepidus /ˈlepɪdəs ; ˈlɛpɪdəs/ 雷比達 (Marcus Aemilius, ?–13 B.C., 古羅馬三執政之一)。

Lesseps, de /leˈseps ; lɛˈsɛps/ 雷賽 (Vicomte Ferdinand Marie, 1805–1894, 法國外交家, 蘇彝士運河建造之發起人)。

Lessing /ˈlesɪŋ ; ˈlɛsɪŋ/ 萊興 (Gotthold Ephraim, 1729–1781, 德國批評家及劇作家)。

Lever /ˈliːvə ; ˈlivɚ/ 利威爾 (Charles James, 1806–1872, 英國小說家)。

Lewes /ˈluːɪs ; ˈlʊɪs/ 劉易斯 (George Henry, 1817–1878, 英國哲學家及批評家)。

Lewis /ˈluːɪs ; ˈlʊɪs/ 劉易士 (**1** Cecil Day, 參看 Day-Lewis; **2** Isaac Newton, 1858–1931, 美國陸軍軍官及發明家; **3** Matthew Gregory, 1775–1818, 別稱 *Monk Lewis*, 英國作家; **4** Meriwether, 1774–1809, 美國探險家; **5** (Percy) Wyndham, 1884–1957, 英國畫家及作家; **6** (Harry) Sinclair, 1885–1951, 美國小說家及劇作家, 曾獲 1930 年諾貝爾文學獎)。

Liang Ch'i-ch'ao /ˈljɑːŋ ˈtʃiː ˈtʃaʊ ; ˈljɑŋ ˈtʃi ˈtʃaʊ/ 梁啓超 (1873–1929, 號任公, 中國近代學者)。

Libby /ˈlɪbɪ ; ˈlɪbɪ/ 李比 (Willard Frank, 1908–1980, 美國化學家, 曾獲 1960 年諾貝爾化學獎)。

Li Ch'ing-chao /ˈliː ˈtʃɪŋ ˈdʒaʊ ; ˈli ˈtʃɪŋ ˈdʒaʊ/ 李清照 (1081–?, 號易安居士, 中國宋朝女詞人)。

Licinius /lɪˈsɪnɪəs ; lɪˈsɪnɪəs/ 李西尼 (270?–325, 羅馬皇帝, 在位期間 308–324)。

Liddell Hart /ˈlɪdl ˈhɑːt ; ˈlɪdl̩ ˈhɑrt/ 李德哈特 (Basil Henry, 1895–1970, 英國軍事科學家)。

Lie /liː ; li/ 賴伊 (**1** Jonas, 1833–1909, 挪威小說家及劇作家; **2** Trygve, 1896–1968, 挪威律師及政治家, 於 1946–53 任聯合國秘書長)。

Liebig, von /ˈliːbɪg ; ˈlibɪg/ 利比克 (Baron Justus, 1803–1873, 德國化學家)。

Li Hung-chang /ˈliː hʊŋ ˈtʃæŋ ; ˈli ˈhʊŋ ˈdʒɑŋ/ 李鴻章

(1823-1901, 中國清朝政治家)。

Linacre /'lɪnəkə ; 'lɪnəkɚ/ 林納克 (Thomas, 1460?-1524, 英國人文學家及醫生)。

Lincoln /'lɪŋkən ; 'lɪŋkən/ 林肯 (Abraham, 1809-1865, 美國第十六任總統,任期 1861-65, 以解放黑奴著稱於世)。

Lindbergh /'lɪn(d)bɜːg ; 'lɪn(d),bɝg/ 林白 (Charles Augustus, 1902-1974, 美國飛行家)。

Lindley /'lɪndlɪ ; 'lɪndlɪ/ 林黎 (John, 1799-1865, 英國植物學家)。

Linnaeus /lɪ'niːəs ; lɪ'niəs/ 林奈 (Carolus, 1707-1778, 瑞典植物學家)。

Lin Sên /'lɪn 'sen ; 'lɪn 'sɛn/ or **Lin Shen** /-'ʃen ; -'ʃɛn/ 林森 (1867?-1943, 中國政治家,於 1932-43 任國民政府主席)。

Lin Yutang /'lɪn 'juː 'tɑːŋ ; 'lɪn 'ju 'tɑŋ/ 林語堂 (1895-1976, 中國作家及語言學家)。

Li Pai /'liː 'baɪ ; 'li 'baɪ/ or **Li Po** /-'bɔː ; -'bɔ/ 李白 (字太白, 701?-762, 中國唐代詩人)。

Lipmann /'lɪpmən ; 'lɪpmən/ 李普曼 (Fritz Albert, 1899-, 生於德國之美國生物化學家,與 H. A. Krebs 同獲 1953 年諾貝爾醫學獎)。

Lippmann /lɪp'mɑːn ; lip'mɑn/ 李普曼 (Gabriel, 1845-1921, 法國物理學家,曾獲 1908 年諾貝爾物理獎)。

Li Shih-min /'liː 'ʃiː 'mɪn ; 'li 'ʃi 'min/ 李世民 (597-649, 中國唐朝皇帝,即唐太宗,在位期間 626-649)。

Lister /'lɪstə ; 'lɪstɚ/ 李斯特 (Joseph, 1827-1912, 英國外科醫生)。

Liszt /lɪst ; lɪst/ 李斯特 (Franz, 1811-1886, 匈牙利鋼琴家及作曲家)。

Littleton /'lɪtltən ; 'lɪtl̩tən/ 李特爾頓 (Sir Thomas, 1407?-1481, 英國法學家)。

Liu Hsiu /'ljuː 'ʃjuː ; 'lju 'ʃju/ 劉秀 (6 B.C.-A.D. 57, 中國東漢中興之君主,即漢光武帝,在位三十三年)。

Liu Pang /'ljuː 'bɑːŋ ; 'lju 'bɑŋ/ 劉邦 (247-195 B.C., 中國漢朝開國之主,即漢高祖,在位十二年)。

Livingstone /'lɪvɪŋstən ; 'lɪvɪŋstən/ 李文斯頓 (David, 1813-1873, 旅居非洲之蘇格蘭探險家)。

Livy /'lɪvɪ ; 'lɪvɪ/ 李維 (原名 Titus Livius, 59 B.C.-A.D. 17, 羅馬歷史學家)。

Li Yüan /'liː 'juːɑːn ; 'li 'juɑn/ 李淵 (565-635, 中國唐朝開國之主,即唐高祖,在位九年)。

Lloyd George /'lɔɪd 'dʒɔːdʒ ; 'lɔɪd'dʒɔrdʒ/ 勞埃喬治 (David, 1863-1945, 英國政治家,於 1916-22 任首相)。

Locke /lɒk ; lɑk/ 洛克 (John, 1632-1704, 英國哲學家)。

Locker-Lampson /'lɒkə 'læmpsn ; 'lɑkɚ 'læmpsn̩/ 洛克蘭生 (Frederick, 1821-1895, 英國詩人)。

Lockhart /'lɒkət ; 'lɑkɚt/ 洛克哈特 (John Gibson, 1794-1854, 蘇格蘭小說家及傳記作家)。

Lockyer /'lɒkjə ; 'lɑkjɚ/ 洛克伊爾 (Sir Joseph Norman, 1836-1920, 英國天文學家)。

Lodge /lɒdʒ ; lɑdʒ/ 洛吉 (**1** Sir Oliver Joseph, 1851-1940, 英國物理學家; **2** Thomas, 1558-1625, 英國詩人及劇作家)。

Loewi /'ləʊɪ ; 'loɪ/ 羅威 (Otto, 1873-1961, 生於德國之美國藥物學家,與 H. H. Dale 同獲 1936 年諾貝爾醫學獎)。

Lombard /'lɒmbəd ; 'lɑmbɚd/ 郎巴德 (Peter, 1100?-1160 或 1164, 義大利神學家)。

London /'lʌndən ; 'lʌndən/ 倫敦 (Jack, 全名 John Griffith ~, 1876-1916, 美國小說家)。

Longfellow /'lɒŋfeləʊ ; 'lɔŋ,fɛlo/ 朗非羅 (Henry Wadsworth, 1807-1882, 美國詩人)。

Longinus /lɒn'dʒaɪnəs ; lɑn'dʒaɪnəs/ 朗吉納斯 (Dionysius Cassius, ?-273, 希臘哲學家)。

López /'ləʊpez ; 'lopɛz/ 羅培斯 (**1** Carlos Antonio, 1790-1862, 於1844-62任巴拉圭總統; **2** 其子 Francisco Solano, 1827-1870, 於 1862-70 任巴拉圭總統)。

Lorentz /'ləʊrents ; 'lorɛnts/ 勞倫茨 (Hendrik Antoon, 1853-1928, 荷蘭物理學家,與 P. Zeeman 同獲 1902 年諾貝爾物理獎)。

Lothair I /ləʊ'θeə ; lo'θɛr/ 羅塞爾一世 (795?-855, 德國國王,在位期間 840-43, 並於 840-55 任神聖羅馬帝國皇帝)。

Louis I /'luːɪ ; 'luɪ/ 路易一世 (778-840, 世稱 le Débonnair, 法國國王及神聖羅馬帝國皇帝,在位期間 814-40)。

Louis IV 路易四世 (1287?-1347, 德國國王及神聖羅馬帝國皇帝,在位期間 1314-47)。

Louis V 路易五世 (966?-987, 世稱 le Fainéant, 法國國王,在位期間 986-987)。

Louis IX 路易九世 (1214-1270, 法國國王, 在位期間 1226-70)。

Louis XI 路易十一世 (1423-1483, 法國國王,在位期間 1461-83)。

Louis XII 路易十二世 (1462-1515, 世稱 the Father of the People, 法國國王,在位期間 1498-1515)。

Louis XIII 路易十三世 (1601-1643, 法國國王,在位期間 1610-43)。

Louis XIV 路易十四世 (1638-1715, 世稱 the Great, 法國國王,在位期間 1643-1715)。

Louis XV 路易十五世 (1710-1774, 法國國王,在位期間 1715-74)。

Louis XVI 路易十六世 (1754-1793, 大革命時之法國國王,在位期間 1774-92, 1793 年被送上斷頭臺處死)。

Louis XVII 路易十七世 (1785-1795, 法國國王,實未卽王位,但 1793-95 年間保皇黨稱之爲王)。

Louis XVIII 路易十八世 (1755-1824, 法國國王,在位期間 1814-24)。

Louis Napoleon 路易拿破崙 (參看 Napoleon III)。

Lounsbury /'laʊnzbərɪ ; 'laʊnz,bɛrɪ/ 朗玆伯里 (Thomas Raynesford, 1838-1915, 美國學者及教育家)。

Lovelace /'lʌvleɪs ; 'lʌvles/ 拉夫累斯 (Richard, 1618-1658, 英國詩人)。

Lowell /'ləʊəl ; 'loəl/ 羅厄爾 (**1** Amy, 1874-1925, 美國女詩人及批評家; **2** James Russell, 1819-1891, 美國詩人、散文家及劇作家; **3** Percival, 1855-1916, Amy 之兄,美國天文學家)。

Lowes /ləʊz ; loz/ 羅玆 (John Livingston, 1867-1945, 美國教育家)。

Loyola /lɔɪ'əʊlə ; lɔɪ'olə/ 聖・羅耀拉 (St. Ignatius of, 1491-1556, 西班牙軍人及天主教教士,耶穌會 (Society of Jesus) 之創始者)。

Lubbock /'lʌbək ; 'lʌbək/ 拉布克 (**1** Sir John, 1834-1913, Sir J. W. 之子,英國財政學家及作家; **2** Sir John William, 1803-1865, 英國天文學家及數學家)。

Lucan /'luːkən ; 'lukən/ 魯堪 (39-65, 本名 Marcus Annaeus Lucanus, 羅馬詩人)。

Luce /luːs ; lus/ 魯斯 (**1** Henry Robinson, 1898-1967, 美國編輯及出版家; **2** 其妻 Clare 1903-, 本姓 Boothe, 美國劇作家、從政者及外交家)。

Lucretius /luː'kriːʃɪəs ; lu'kriʃəs/ 留克利希阿斯 (96?-55 B.C. 羅馬哲學家及詩人)。

Lucullus /luː'kʌləs ; lu'kʌləs/ 盧加拉斯 (Lucius Licinius, 公元前一世紀之羅馬將軍及美食主義者)。

Luther /'luːθə ; 'luθɚ/ 路德 (Martin, 1483-1546, 德國宗教改革領袖)。

Luthuli /luː'tuːlɪ ; lu'tulɪ/ 魯吐黎 (Albert John, 1898-1967, 南非改革者,原爲組魯族酋長,曾獲 1960 年諾貝爾和平獎)。

Lycurgus /laɪ'kɜːgəs ; laɪ'kɝgəs/ 萊克爾加斯 (紀元前九世紀之斯巴達政治家,爲斯巴達立法者)。

Lyell /'laɪəl ; 'laɪəl/ 萊伊爾 (Sir Charles, 1797-1875, 英國地質學家)。

Lyly /'lɪlɪ ; 'lɪlɪ/ 李里 (John, 1554?-1606, 英國作家)。

Lyon /'laɪən ; 'laɪən/ 萊昂 (Mary, 1797-1849, 美國女教育家)。

Lyons /'laɪənz ; 'laɪənz/ 萊昂玆 (Joseph Aloysius, 1879-1939, 澳大利亞政治家,於 1932-39 任首相)。

Lysander /laɪ'sændə ; laɪ'sændɚ/ 賴山德 (?-395 B.C. 斯巴達將軍及政治家)。

Lysias /'lɪsɪæs ; 'lɪsɪəs/ 李西亞斯 (450?-?380 B.C. 雅典雄辯家)。

Lysippus /laɪ'sɪpəs ; laɪ'sɪpəs/ 賴西帕斯 (紀元前四世紀之希臘雕刻家)。

Lytton /'lɪtn ; 'lɪtn̩/ 李頓 (**1** 全名 Edward Robert Bulwer-Lytton, 1831-1891, 筆名 Owen Meredith, 英國政治家及詩人; **2** 其父, 全名 Edward George Earle Lytton Bulwer-Lytton, 1803-1873, 英國小說家及劇作家)。

MacArthur /mək'ɑːθə ; mək'ɑrθɚ/ 麥克阿瑟 (**1** Arthur, 1845-1912, 美國將軍; **2** Douglas, 1880-1964, Arthur

之子，美國五星上將）。
Macaulay /məˈkɔːlɪ ; məˈkɔlɪ/ 麥考萊 (**1** Dame Rose, 1881-1958, 英國女小說家; **2** Thomas Babington, 1800-1859, 英國歷史學家、作家及政治家)。
Macbeth /mækˈbeθ ; mækˈbɛθ/ 馬克白 (?-1057, 蘇格蘭國王，在位期間 1040-57)。
Macdonald /məkˈdɒnəld ; məkˈdɑnəld/ 麥克唐納 (George, 1824-1905, 蘇格蘭小說家及詩人)。
Machiavelli /ˌmækɪəˈvelɪ ; ˌmækɪəˈvɛlɪ/ 馬基亞維利 (Niccolò, 1469-1527, 義大利政治家及政治哲學家)。
Mackenzie /məˈkenzɪ ; məˈkɛnzɪ/ 馬坎玆 (**1** Alexander, 1822-1892, 生於蘇格蘭之加拿大政治家, 1873-78 任總理; **2** Sir Compton, 1883-1972, 英國小說家)。
Mackintosh /ˈmækɪntɒʃ ; ˈmækɪnˌtɑʃ/ 麥金陶西 (Sir James, 1765-1832, 蘇格蘭哲學家及歷史學家)。
Macleod /məˈklaʊd ; məˈklaʊd/ 麥克勞德 (John James Rickard, 1876-1935, 蘇格蘭生理學家，與 Sir F. G. Banting 同獲 1923 年諾貝爾醫學獎)。
MacMahon (或 Macmahon), de /məkˈmɑːən ; məkˈmæən/ 麥馬韓 (Comte Marie Edme Patrice Maurice, 1808-1893, 法國元帥及政治家，於 1873-79 任總統)。
MacMillan /məkˈmɪlən ; məkˈmɪlən/ 麥米倫 (Donald Baxter, 1874-1970, 美國北極探險家)。
Macmillan 麥米倫 (Harold, 1894-, 英國從政者，於 1957-63 任首相)。
Macpherson /məkˈfɜːsn; məkˈfɝsn̩/ 麥克佛生 (James, 1736-1796, 蘇格蘭作家)。
Madison /ˈmædɪsn ; ˈmædɪsn̩/ 麥迪生 (James, 1751-1836, 於 1809-17 任美國第四任總統)。
Maecenas /miːˈsiːnæs ; mɪˈsinəs/ 米西奈斯 (Gaius, 70?-8 B.C., 羅馬政治家及文藝支持者)。
Maeterlinck /ˈmeɪtəlɪŋk; ˈmetɚlɪŋk/ 梅特林克 (Count Maurice, 1862-1949, 比利時詩人、劇作家及散文家，曾獲 1911 年諾貝爾文學獎)。
Magellan /məˈgelən ; məˈdʒɛlən/ 麥哲倫 (Ferdinand, 1480?-1521, 葡萄牙航海家)。
Maginot /ˌmæʒəˈnəʊ ; ˌmæʒəˈno/ 馬奇諾 (André, 1877-1932, 法國從政者，於 1922-24, 1926-31 任國防部長)。
Mahan /məˈhæn ; məˈhæn/ 馬漢 (Alfred Thayer, 1840-1914, 美國海軍少將及歷史學家)。
Mahmud II /mɑːˈmuːd ; mɑˈmud/ 馬穆德二世 (1785-1839, 土耳其國王，在位期間 1808-39)。
Mailer /ˈmeɪlə ; ˈmelɚ/ 梅樂 (Norman, 1923-, 美國作家)。
Maine /meɪn ; men/ 梅恩 (Sir Henry James Sumner, 1822-1888, 英國法學家)。
Maitland /ˈmeɪtlənd ; ˈmetlənd/ 梅特蘭 (Frederic William, 1850-1906, 英國法學家及歷史學家)。
Malone /məˈləʊn ; məˈlon/ 馬倫 (Edmund 或 Edmond, 1741-1812, 愛爾蘭研究莎士比亞之學者)。
Malthus /ˈmælθəs ; ˈmælθəs/ 馬爾薩斯 (Thomas Robert, 1766-1834, 英國經濟學家)。
Manes /ˈmɑːneɪz ; ˈmeniz/ 摩尼斯 (亦稱 Mani 或 Manichaeus, 216?-?276, 波斯哲人，摩尼教 (Manichaeism) 之創始者)。
Manet /məˈneɪ ; məˈne/ 馬奈 (Édouard, 1832-1883, 法國畫家)。
Mani /ˈmɑːnɪ ; ˈmɑnɪ/, **Manichaeus** /ˌmænɪˈkiːəs ; ˌmænɪˈkiəs/ 參看 Manes。
Mann /mæn ; mæn/ 麥恩 (**1** Horace, 1796-1859, 美國教育家; **2** Thomas, 1875-1955, 美籍德裔作家，曾獲 1929 年諾貝爾文學獎)。
Mansfield /ˈmænsfiːld ; ˈmænsfild/ 曼斯菲爾 (Katherine, 1888-1923, 本名 Kathleen Beauchamp, 英國女作家)。
Manutius /məˈnjuːʃɪəs; məˈn(j)uʃəs/ 馬紐夏斯 (Aldus, 1450-1515, 義大利印刷家及古典學者)。
Marcellus /mɑːˈseləs ; mɑrˈsɛləs/ 馬賽拉斯 (Marcus Claudius, 268?-208 B.C., 羅馬大將)。
Marconi /mɑːˈkəʊnɪ ; mɑrˈkonɪ/ 馬可尼 (Marchese Guglielmo, 1874-1937, 義大利電機工程師，無線電報發明者，與 K. F. Braun 同獲 1909 年諾貝爾物理獎)。
Marco Polo 參看 Polo。
Marcus Aurelius /ˈmɑːkəs ɔːˈriːljəs; ˈmɑrkəs ɔˈriljəs/ 馬卡斯・奧里留斯 (參看 Antoninus)。
Margaret of Anjou /ˈmɑːgərɪt əv ɒŋˈʒuː ; ˈmɑrgrɪt əv ˈændʒu/ 安珠瑪格麗特 (1430-1482, 英王亨利六世之后)。
Marie /məˈriː ; məˈri/ 瑪利 (1875-1938, 羅馬尼亞女王，在位期間 1914-27; 1927-38 爲太后)。
Marius /ˈmeərɪəs ; ˈmɛrɪəs/ 馬留 (Gaius, 155?-86 B.C., 羅馬將軍)。
Markham /ˈmɑːkəm ; ˈmɑrkəm/ 馬爾侃 ((Charles) Edwin, 1852-1940, 美國詩人)。
Marlowe /ˈmɑːləʊ ; ˈmɑrlo/ 馬婁 (Christopher, 1564-1593, 英國劇作家)。
Márquez /ˈmɑːkeɪs ; ˈmɑrkes/ 馬爾格思 (Gabriel García, 1928-, 哥倫比亞作家，曾獲 1982 年諾貝爾文學獎)。
Marshall /ˈmɑːʃəl ; ˈmɑrʃəl/ 馬歇爾 (**1** George Catlett, 1880-1959, 美國將軍及外交家，曾獲 1953 年諾貝爾和平獎; **2** John, 1755-1835, 美國法學家)。
Marston /ˈmɑːstən ; ˈmɑrstən/ 馬斯敦 (John, 1575?-1634, 英國劇作家)。
Martial /ˈmɑːʃəl ; ˈmɑrʃəl 馬休爾 (40?-102?, 羅馬諷刺詩人)。
Martin /ˈmɑːtɪn ; ˈmɑrtɪn/ 馬丁 (**1** Homer Dodge, 1836-1897, 美國畫家; **2** Sir Theodore, 1816-1909, 英國詩人、翻譯家及散文家; **3** Archer John Porter, 1910-, 英國生物化學家，與 R. L. M. Synge 同獲 1952 年諾貝爾化學獎)。
Martin du Gard, Roger 參看 Du Gard。
Martineau /ˈmɑːtɪnəʊ ; ˈmɑrtɪno/ 馬蒂諾 (**1** Harriet, 1802-1876, 英國小說家及經濟學家; **2** 其弟 James, 1805-1900, 英國神學家及哲學家)。
Martini /mɑːˈtiːnɪ ; mɑrˈtinɪ/ 馬蒂尼 (Simone, 1283?-1344, 義大利畫家)。
Martinson /ˈmɑːtiːnsɒn ; ˈmɑrtinsɔn/ 馬汀生 (Harry Edmund, 1904-1978, 瑞典作家及詩人，與 E. Johnson 同獲 1974 年諾貝爾文學獎)。
Marx /mɑːks ; mɑrks/ 馬克斯 (Karl, 1818-1883, 德國政治哲學家、經濟學家及社會主義者，1847 與恩格斯聯合發表'共產主義宣言')。
Mary /ˈmeərɪ; ˈmɛrɪ/ 瑪利 (1867-1953, 全稱爲 Princess Victoria Mary of Teck, 英國喬治五世之后)。
Mary I 瑪利一世 (1516-1558, 英國女王，在位期間 1553-58)。
Mary II 瑪利二世 (1662-1694, 英國女王，與夫 William III 共同治理英國，在位期間 1689-94)。
Mary Stuart /-ˈstjʊət; -ˈstjuɚt/ 瑪利・斯圖亞特 (1542-1587, 蘇格蘭女王，在位期間 1542-67, 被 Elizabeth I 斬首)。
Mascagni /mæsˈkɑːnjɪ; mæsˈkɑnjɪ/ 馬斯卡尼 (Pietro, 1863-1945, 義大利作曲家)。
Masefield /ˈmeɪsfiːld ; ˈmesfild/ 梅斯菲爾德 (John, 1878-1967, 英國詩人及作家, 1930-67 爲桂冠詩人)。
Mason /ˈmeɪsn ; ˈmesn̩/ 梅遜 (Charles, 1730-1787, 英國天文學家及測量家，與 J. Dixon 共同測定 Mason-Dixon line)。
Massenet /mæsˈneɪ ; mæsˈne/ 馬斯奈 (Jules Emile Frédéric, 1842-1912, 法國作曲家)。
Masters /ˈmɑːstəz ; ˈmæstɚz/ 馬斯特玆 (Edgar Lee, 1869-1950, 美國作家)。
Matthews /ˈmæθjuːz ; ˈmæθjuz/ 馬休玆 ((James) Brander, 1852-1929, 美國教育家及作家)。
Maugham /mɔːm ; mɔm/ 毛姆 (William Somerset, 1874-1965, 英國小說家及劇作家)。
Maupassant /ˌməʊpəˈsɑːŋ ; ˈmopəˌsɑnt/ 莫泊桑 ((Henri René Albert) Guy de, 1850-1893, 法國短篇小說作家)。
Mauriac /mɔːˈrjɑːk ; ˌmɔrɪˈɑk/ 摩里亞克 (François 1885-1970, 法國詩人及小說家，曾獲 1952 年諾貝爾文學獎)。
Maurice of Nassau /ˈmɔːrɪs əv ˈnæsɔː ; ˈmɔrɪs əv ˈnæsɔ/ 摩利士 (1567-1625, 荷蘭將軍及政治家)。
Mauser /ˈmaʊzə ; ˈmaʊzɚ/ 毛瑟 (Peter Paul, 1838-1914, 其兄 Wilhelm, 1834-1882, 均爲德國發明家)。
Maxim /ˈmæksɪm ; ˈmæksɪm/ 馬克沁 (**1** Sir Hiram

Stevens, 1840-1916, 生於美國之英國發明家; **2** 其弟 Hudson, 1853-1927, 美國發明家及火藥專家)。

Maximilian I /ˌmæksɪˈmɪljən ; ˌmæksɪˈmɪljən/ 馬克西米連一世 (1459-1519, 神聖羅馬帝國皇帝, 在位期間 1493-1519)。

Maximilian II 馬克西米連二世 (1527-1576, 神聖羅馬帝國皇帝,在位期間 1564-76)。

Maxwell /ˈmækswəl ; ˈmækswɛl/ 馬克士威 (James Clerk, 1831-1879, 蘇格蘭物理學家)。

Mayer /ˈmaɪə ; ˈmaɪɚ/ 麥爾 (Maria Goeppert 1906-1972, 生於德國之美國物理學家,與 E. P. Wigner 及 J. H. D. Jensen 同獲 1963 年諾貝爾物理獎)。

Mayo /ˈmeɪəʊ ; ˈmeo/ 梅歐 (Charles Horace, 1865-1939, 其兄 William James, 1861-1939, 均爲美國外科醫生)。

Mazzini /mædˈziːnɪ ; mædˈzinɪ/ 馬志尼 (Giuseppe, 1805-1872, 義大利愛國者及革命家)。

McCarthy /məˈkɑːθɪ ; məˈkɑrθɪ/ 麥卡錫 (Joseph Raymond, 1908-1957, 美國從政者)。

McCrae /məˈkreɪ ; məˈkre/ 馬克雷 (John, 1872-1918, 加拿大醫生及詩人)。

McKinley /məˈkɪnlɪ ; məˈkɪnlɪ/ 麥金萊 (William, 1843-1901, 於 1897-1901 任美國第廿五任總統)。

McMillan /məkˈmɪlən ; məkˈmɪlən/ 麥克米倫 (Edwin Mattison, 1907-, 美國化學家,與 G. T. Seaborg 同獲 1951 年諾貝爾化學獎)。

Medawar /ˈmedəwə;ˈmɛdəwɚ/ 梅德瓦 (Peter Brian, 1915-, 生於巴西之英國動物學家及解剖學家, 與 F. M. Burnet 同獲 1960 年諾貝爾醫學獎)。

Meir /meˈɪə ; mɛˈɪr/ 梅爾夫人 (Golda, 1898-1978, 以色列女政治家, 1969-74 任總理)。

Melanchthon /meˈlæŋkθən ; məˈlæŋkθən/ 米郎克孫 (本名 Philipp Schwarzert, 1497-1560, 德國學者及宗教改革家)。

Melville /ˈmelvɪl ; ˈmɛlvɪl/ 梅威爾 (Herman, 1819-1891, 美國小說家)。

Menander /mɪˈnændə;mɪˈnændɚ/ 米南德 (343?-?291 B.C., 希臘劇作家)。

Mencius /ˈmentʃəs ; ˈmɛntʃəs/ 孟子 (372?-?289 B.C., 亦譯作 Mêng-tzŭ 或 Meng-tse, 中國哲學家)。

Mendel /ˈmendl ; ˈmɛndl̩/ 孟德爾 (Gregor Johann, 1822-1884, 奧國植物學家)。

Mendelssohn /ˈmendlsn ; ˈmɛndl̩sn̩/ 孟德爾遜 (**1** Moses, 1729-1786, 德國哲學家; **2** Felix, 全名 Jakob Ludwig Felix Mendelssohn-Bartholdy, 1809-1847, 德國作曲家、鋼琴家及音樂指揮)。

Mercator /mɜːˈkeɪtɔː ; mɝˈketɚ/ 麥卡托 (Gerhardus, 1512-1594, 法蘭德斯 (Flanders) 之地理學家)。

Mesmer /ˈmezmə ; ˈmɛzmɚ/ 梅斯美爾 (Franz 或 Friedrich Anton, 1734-1815, 奧國醫生, 發明催眠術)。

Metchnikoff /ˈmetʃnɪkɒf ; ˈmɛtʃnɪˌkɔf/ 梅奇尼可夫 (Élie, 1845-1916, 旅居法國之俄國動物學家及細菌學家, 與 P. Ehrlich 同獲 1908 年諾貝爾醫學獎)。

Metternich, von /ˈmetənɪk ; ˈmɛtɚnɪk/ 梅特涅 (Prince Klemens Wenzel Nepomuk Lothar, 1773-1859, 奧國政治家)。

Meyer /ˈmaɪə ; ˈmaɪɚ/ 梅爾 (Annie, 1867-1951, 本姓 Nathan, 美國女教育家及作家)。

Meyerbeer /ˈmaɪəbɪə ; ˈmaɪɚˌbɪr/ 梅爾貝亞 (Giacomo, 1791-1864, 德國作曲家)。

Meyerhof /ˈmaɪəhəʊf ; ˈmaɪɚˌhof/ 梅爾霍夫 (Otto, 1884-1951, 德國生理學家,與 A. V. Hill 同獲 1922 年諾貝爾醫學獎)。

Michael /ˈmaɪkl ; ˈmaɪkl̩/ 邁克爾(本名 ~ Hohenzollern, 1921-, 羅馬尼亞文名 Mihai, 羅馬尼亞國王,在位期間 1927-30 及 1940-47)。

Michelangelo Buonarroti /ˌmaɪkəlˈændʒɪləʊ bwɔːnəˈrɔːtɪ ; ˌmaɪkl̩ˈændʒəˌlo ˌbwɔnəˈrɔtɪ/ 米開蘭基羅 (1475-1564, 義大利雕刻家、畫家、建築家及詩人)。

Michelson /ˈmaɪkəlsn ; ˈmaɪkl̩sn̩/ 邁克爾生 (Albert Abraham, 1852-1931, 生於德國之美國物理學家,曾獲 1907 年諾貝爾物理獎)。

Middleton /ˈmɪdltən ; ˈmɪdl̩tən/ 梅得爾敦 (Thomas, 1570?-1627, 英國劇作家)。

Mill /mɪl ; mɪl/ 米爾 (**1** James, 1773-1836, 蘇格蘭哲學家、歷史學家及經濟學家; **2** 其子 John Stuart, 1806-1873, 英國哲學家及經濟學家)。

Millais /mɪˈleɪ ; mɪˈle/ 米雷 (Sir John Everett, 1829-1896, 英國畫家)。

Millet /mɪˈleɪ ; mɪˈle/ 米列 (Jean François, 1814-1875, 法國畫家)。

Millikan /ˈmɪlɪkən ; ˈmɪləkən/ 米里坎 (Robert Andrew, 1868-1953, 美國物理學家,曾獲 1923 年諾貝爾物理獎)。

Milne /mɪl(n) ; mɪl(n)/ 米爾恩 (Alan Alexander, 1882-1956, 英國詩人及劇作家)。

Milosz /ˈmiːlɒʃ ; ˈmiləʃ/ 密瓦時 (Czeslaw, 1911-, 波蘭作家,曾獲 1980 年諾貝爾文學獎)。

Milton /ˈmɪltən ; ˈmɪltn̩/ 密爾頓 (John, 1608-1674, 英國詩人)。

Minot /ˈmaɪnət ; ˈmaɪnət/ 邁諾德 (George Richards, 1885-1950, 美國醫生, 與 W. P. Murphy 及 G. H. Whipple 同獲 1934 年諾貝爾醫學獎)。

Mistral /mɪˈstrɑːl ; mɪˈstrɑl/ 米斯特拉爾 (**1** Frédéric, 1830-1914, 法國 Provençal 語詩人,與 Echegaray y Eizaguirre 同獲 1904 年諾貝爾文學獎; **2** Gabriela, 本名 Lucila Godoy de Alcayaga, 1889-1957, 智利女詩人及教育家,曾獲 1945 年諾貝爾文學獎)。

Mitchell /ˈmɪtʃəl ; ˈmɪtʃəl/ 米契爾 (Maria, 1818-1889, 美國女天文學家)。

Mitford /ˈmɪtfəd ; ˈmɪtfɚd/ 米特福德 (Mary Russell, 1787-1855, 英國女小說家及劇作家)。

Mohammed = Muhammad

Moissan /mwɒˈsɒŋ ; mwɑˈsɑn/ 莫瓦桑 (Henri, 1852-1907, 法國化學家,曾獲 1906 年諾貝爾化學獎)。

Molière /ˈmɒlɪeə ; ˌmolɪˈɛr/ 莫里哀 (1622-1673, 本名 Jean Baptiste Poquelin, 法國演員及劇作家)。

Mommsen /ˈməʊmzn ; ˈmomzn̩/ 牟姆森 (Theodor, 1817-1903, 德國古典學者及歷史學家, 曾獲 1902 年諾貝爾文學獎)。

Monet /məʊˈneɪ ; moˈne/ 莫內 (Claude, 1840-1926, 法國畫家)。

Moneta /məʊˈneɪtə ; moˈnetə/ 莫納達 (Ernesto Teodoro, 1833-1918, 義大利新聞記者及和平主義者,與 L. Renault 同獲 1907 年諾貝爾和平獎)。

Moniz /mʊˈniːʃ ; mʊˈniʃ/ 莫尼慈 (Antonio Caetano de Abrere Freire Egas, 1874-1955, 葡萄牙神經外科醫生,與 W. R. Hess 同獲 1949 年諾貝爾醫學獎)。

Monroe /mənˈrəʊ ; mənˈro/ 門羅 (James, 1758-1831, 於 1817-25 任美國第五任總統)。

Montagu /ˈmɒntəgjuː ; ˈmɑntəgju/ 孟塔古 (Lady Mary Wortley, 1689-1762, 英國女作家)。

Montaigne, de /mɒnˈteɪn ; mɑnˈten/ 蒙田 (Michel Eyquem, 1533-1592, 法國散文家)。

Montale /məʊnˈtɑːleɪ ; monˈtɑle/ 蒙太雷 (Eugenio, 1896-, 義大利詩人,曾獲 1975 年諾貝爾文學獎)。

Montesquieu, de /ˌmɒntesˈkjuː ; ˌmɑntəˈskju/ 孟德斯鳩 (本名 Charles de Secondat, 1689-1755, 法國律師及政治哲學家)。

Montessori /ˌmɒnteˈsɔːrɪ ; ˌmɑntəˈsorɪ/ 蒙臺梭利 (Maria, 1870-1952, 義大利女醫師及教育家)。

Montfort, de /ˈmɒntfət ; ˈmɑntfɚt/ 孟德福 (Simon, 1208?-1265, 英國軍人及政治家)。

Montgolfier /mɒntˈgɒlfɪə ; mɑntˈgɑlfɪr/ 孟高爾費 (Joseph Michel, 1740-1810, 及其弟 Jacques Étienne, 1745-1799, 均爲法國發明家及航空界先驅)。

Montgomery /mən(t)ˈgʌmərɪ ; mɑn(t)ˈgʌmrɪ/ 蒙哥馬利 (Bernard Law, 1887-1976, 英國陸軍元帥)。

Moody /ˈmuːdɪ ; ˈmudɪ/ 穆地 (William Vaughn, 1869-1910, 美國詩人及劇作家)。

Moore /mʊə ; mʊr/ 摩爾 (**1** George, 1852-1933, 愛爾蘭作家; **2** John Bassett, 1860-1947, 美國法學家; **3** Thomas, 1779-1852, 愛爾蘭詩人)。

More /mɔː ; mɔr/ 摩爾 (**1** Hannah, 1745-1833, 英國宗教方面之女作家; **2** Henry, 1614-1687, 英國哲學家; **3** Paul Elmer, 1864-1937, 美國散文家及批評家; **4** Sir Thomas, 1478-1535, 英國政治家及作家)。

Morgan /ˈmɔːgən ; ˈmɔrgən/ 摩爾根 (**1** Conway Lloyd, 1852-1936, 英國動物學家及心理學家; **2** John Pierpont, 1837-1913, 美國財政家; **3** Thomas Hunt,

1866–1945, 美國動物學家,曾獲 1933 年諾貝爾醫學獎)。
Morison /ˈmɔːrɪsn ; ˈmɔrɪsn̩/ 摩禮遜 (Samuel Eliot, 1887–1976, 美國歷史學家)。
Morley /ˈmɔːlɪ ; ˈmɔrlɪ/ 摩爾利 (**1** Christopher Darlington, 1890–1957, 美國作家; **2** John, 1838–1923, 英國政治家及作家)。
Morohashi /ˌmɒrɒˈhɑːʃɪ ; ˌmɔrɔˈhɑʃɪ/ 諸橋轍次 (Tetsuji, 1883–1982, 日本著名漢學家)。
Morris /ˈmɔːrɪs ; ˈmɔrɪs/ 毛禮斯 (**1** Gouverneur, 1752–1816, 美國政治家及外交家; **2** William, 1834–1896, 英國詩人、藝術家及社會主義者)。
Morse /mɔːs ; mɔrs/ 摩爾斯 (Samuel Finley Breese, 1791–1872, 美國藝術家及發明家,發明摩爾斯電碼)。
Morton /ˈmɔːtn ; ˈmɔrtn̩/ 摩頓 (William Thomas Green, 1819–1868, 美國牙科醫生)。
Moses /ˈməʊzɪz ; ˈmozəz/ 摩西 (古代希伯來人之先知,據聖經記載,曾領導以色列人脫離埃及人之奴役)。
Mosley /ˈmɒzlɪ ; ˈmozlɪ/ 摩兹利 (Sir Oswald Ernald, 1896–, 英國從政者)。
Mössbauer /ˈmɜːsbaʊə;ˈmɝsbaʊɚ/ 摩斯包爾 (Rudolf Ludwig, 1929–, 德國物理學家,與 R. Hofstadter 同獲 1961 年諾貝爾物理獎)。
Mo Ti /ˈməʊˈdiː ; ˈmoˈdi/ or **Mo-tzu** /-ˈdzə ; -ˈdzə/ 墨翟(即墨子,公元前五至四世紀之中國哲學家)。
Motley /ˈmɒtlɪ ; ˈmɑtlɪ/ 馬特利 (John Lothrop, 1814–1877, 美國歷史學家)。
Mott /mɒt ; mɑt/ 馬特 (**1** Lucretia, 1793–1880, 本姓 Coffin, 美國女社會改革者; **2** John Raleigh, 1865–1955, 美國基督教青年會領袖,與 E. G. Balch 同獲 1946 年諾貝爾和平獎)。
Moulton /ˈməʊltən ; ˈmoltn̩/ 摩爾頓 (Forest Ray, 1872–1952, 美國天文學家)。
Mozart /ˈməʊtsɑːt ; ˈmotˌsɑrt/ 莫札特 (Wolfgang Amadeus, 1756–1791, 奥國作曲家)。
Muhammad, Mohammed /məˈhæmɪd ; moˈhæməd/ 穆罕默德 (570–632, 阿拉伯先知及回教創始者)。
Muir /mjʊə ; mjur/ 繆爾 (John, 1838–1914, 生於蘇格蘭之美國博物學家)。
Muller /ˈmʌlə ; ˈmʌlɚ/ 墨勒 (Hermann Joseph, 1890–1967, 美國遺傳學家,曾獲 1946 年諾貝爾醫學獎)。
Müller /ˈmjuːlə ; ˈmjulɚ/ 穆勒 (Paul Hermann, 1899–1965, 瑞士化學家,曾獲 1948 年諾貝爾醫學獎)。
Murillo /mjʊəˈrɪləʊ ; mjuˈrɪlo/ 穆律羅 (Bartolomé Esteban, 1617–1682, 西班牙畫家)。
Murphy /ˈmɜːfɪ ; ˈmɝfɪ/ 摩菲 (**1** Frank, 1890–1949, 美國法學家; **2** William Parry, 1892–, 美國醫生,與 G.R. Minot 及 G. H. Whipple 同獲 1934 年諾貝爾醫學獎)。
Murray /ˈmʌrɪ ; ˈmʌrɪ/ 摩雷 (**1** (George) Gilbert (Aimé), 1866–1957, 英國古典學者; **2** Sir James Augustus Henry, 1837–1915, 英國辭典編纂家; **3** Lindley, 1745–1826, 美國語法學家)。
Mussolini /ˌmʊsəˈliːnɪ ; ˌmʊsəˈlinɪ/ 墨索里尼 (Benito, 1883–1945, 義大利法西斯首相及獨裁者,當權期間 1922–45)。
Nabokov /nəˈbɔːkəf ; nəˈbɔkəf/ 納伯可夫 (Vladimir Vladimirovich, 1899–1977, 出生於俄國的美國小說家及詩人)。
Nansen /ˈnænsn ; ˈnænsən/ 南森 (Fridtjof, 1861–1930, 挪威北極探險家、動物學家及政治家, 曾獲 1922 年諾貝爾和平獎)。
Napier /ˈneɪpɪə ; ˈnepɪr/ 納皮爾 (John, 1550–1617, 蘇格蘭數學家)。
Napoleon I /nəˈpəʊljən ; nəˈpoljən/ 拿破崙一世 (全名 Napoleon Bonaparte, 1769–1821, 法國皇帝,在位期間 1804–15)。
Napoleon II 拿破崙二世 (1811–1832, Napoleon I 與 Marie Louise 之子,爲名義上之法國皇帝)。
Napoleon III 拿破崙三世 (1808–1873, 亦稱 Louis Napoleon, 法國皇帝,在位期間 1852–70)。
Nash /næʃ ; næʃ/ 納西 (Ogden, 1902–1971, 美國詩人)。
Nasmyth /ˈneɪzmɪθ ; ˈnezmɪθ/ 納玆米 (Alexander, 1758–1840, 蘇格蘭畫家)。
Nast /ˈnɑːst ; ˈnæst/ 納斯特 (Thomas, 1840–1902, 生於德國之美國卡通畫家)。
Nathan /ˈneɪθən;ˈneθən/ 納森 (**1** George Jean, 1882–1958, 美國編輯及戲劇批評家; **2** Robert, 1894–, 美國小說家)。
Natta /ˈnɑːtɑː ; ˈnɑtɑ/ 納塔 (Giulio, 1903–1979, 義大利化學家及工程師,與 C. Ziegler 同獲 1963 年諾貝爾化學獎)。
Nebuchadnezzar /ˌnebjʊkədˈnezə ; ˌnɛbjʊkədˈnɛzɚ/ 尼布加尼撒 (?–562 B.C., 巴比倫國王,在位期間 605–562 B.C.)。
Nehru /ˈneəruː ; ˈneru/ 尼赫魯 (**1** Motilal, 1861–1931, 印度民族主義者及律師; **2** 其子 Jawaharlal, 1889–1964, 印度民族主義者;甘地夫人之父, 1947–64 任總理)。
Neilson /ˈniːlsn ; ˈnilsn̩/ 尼爾遜 (William Allan, 1869–1946, 生於蘇格蘭之美國教育家)。
Nelson /ˈnelsn ; ˈnɛlsn̩/ 納爾遜 (Horatio, 1758–1805, 英國海軍大將)。
Nepos /ˈniːpɒs ; ˈnipɑs/ 尼波斯 (Cornelius, 紀元前一世紀之羅馬歷史學家)。
Nernst /ˈneənst ; ˈnɛrnst/ 納恩斯德 (Walther Hermann, 1864–1941, 德國物理學家及化學家,曾獲 1920 年諾貝爾化學獎)。
Nero /ˈnɪərəʊ ; ˈnɪro/ 尼祿 (37–68, 羅馬暴君,在位期間 54–68)。
Neruda /neɪˈruːdə ; neˈrudə/ 涅魯達 (Pablo, 1904–1973, 原名 Neftalí Ricardo Reyes Basoalto, 智利詩人及外交家,曾獲 1971 年諾貝爾文學獎)。
Nestorius /nesˈtɔːrɪəs ; nɛsˈtorɪəs/ 聶斯托里 (?–?451, 景教 (Nestorianism) 之創始人,於 428–431 任君士坦丁堡之主教)。
Nevin /ˈnevɪn ; ˈnɛvɪn/ 尼文 (Ethelbert Woodbridge, 1862–1901, 美國作曲家)。
Newbolt /ˈnjuːbəʊlt ; ˈn(j)ubolt/ 牛波特 (Sir Henry John, 1862–1938, 英國作家)。
Newman /ˈnjuːmən ; ˈn(j)umən/ 牛曼 (John Henry, 1801–1890, 英國紅衣主教及作家)。
Newton /ˈnjuːtn ; ˈn(j)utn̩/ 牛頓 (Sir Isaac, 1642–1727, 英國數學家及自然哲學家,發現萬有引力)。
Nicholas I /ˈnɪkələs ; ˈnɪk(ə)ləs/ 尼古拉一世 (1796–1855, 俄國沙皇,在位期間 1825–55)。
Nicholas II 尼古拉二世 (1868–1918, 俄國沙皇,在位期間 1894–1917)。
Nicolle /ˌniːˈkɔːl ; ˌniˈkɔl/ 尼考爾 (Charles Jean Henri, 1866–1936, 法國醫生及細菌學家,曾獲 1928 年諾貝爾醫學獎)。
Nietzsche /ˈniːtʃə ; ˈnitʃə/ 尼采 (Friedrich Wilhelm, 1844–1900, 德國哲學家)。
Nightingale /ˈnaɪtɪŋgeɪl ; ˈnaɪtɪŋˌgel/ 南丁格爾 (Florence, 1820–1910, 英國女護士,近代護理制度之創始人)。
Nixon /ˈnɪksən ; ˈnɪksən/ 尼克森 (Richard Milhous, 1913–, 美國律師,於 1969–74 任美國第三十七屆總統)。
Nobel /nəʊˈbel ; noˈbɛl/ 諾貝爾 (Alfred Bernhard, 1833–1896, 瑞典製造家、發明家及慈善家,創設諾貝爾獎)。
Noel-Baker /ˌnəʊəlˈbeɪkə ; ˌnoəlˈbekɚ/ 諾爾貝克 (Philip John, 1889–, 英國政治家及作家,曾獲 1959 年諾貝爾和平獎)。
Norris /ˈnɔːrɪs ; ˈnɔrɪs/ 諾利斯 (**1** Charles Gilman, 1881–1945, 美國小說家; **2** 其兄 Benjamin Franklin, 通稱 Frank, 1870–1902, 美國小說家; **3** Kathleen, 1880–1966, Charles 之妻,美國女小說家)。
North /nɔːθ ; nɔrθ/ 諾斯 (Frederick, 1732–1792, 英國政治家,於 1770–82 任首相)。
Northrop /ˈnɔːθrəp ; ˈnɔrθrəp/ 諾斯洛普 (John Howard, 1891–, 美國科學家,與 W. M. Stanley 及 J. B. Sumner 同獲 1946 年諾貝爾化學獎)。
Norton /ˈnɔːtn ; ˈnɔrtn̩/ 諾頓 (**1** Charles Eliot, 1827–1908, 美國作家及教育家; **2** Thomas, 1532–1584, 英國律師及詩人)。
Noyes /nɔɪz ; nɔɪz/ 諾伊斯 (Alfred, 1880–1958, 英國詩人)。
Ochoa /əʊˈtʃəʊə ; oˈtʃoə/ 歐綢亞 (Severo, 1905–, 生於西班牙之美國生物化學家,與 A. Kornberg 同獲 1959 年諾貝爾醫學獎)。
Ockham or **Occam** /ˈɒkəm ; ˈɑkəm/ 奥坎 (William of, 1300?–?1349, 英國哲學家)。
Offenbach /ˈɔːfənbɑːk;ˈɔfənbɑk/ 奥芬巴赫 (Jacques,

1819–1880, 法國作曲家)。

O'Flaherty /əʊ'fleətɪ;o'flæ(h)ɚtɪ/ 歐福拉赫蒂 (Liam, 1896–, 愛爾蘭小說家)。

Ogden /'ɒgdən ; 'ɔgdən/ 歐格登 (Charles Kay, 1889–1957, 英國心理學家及教育家)。

Oglethorpe /'əʊglθɔ:p ; 'oglθɔrp/ 歐格紹普 (James Edward, 1696–1785, 英國將軍及慈善家,美洲 Georgia 殖民地之建立者)。

Ohm /əʊm ; om/ 歐姆 (Georg Simon, 1787–1854, 德國物理學家)。

Olaf I /'əʊləf ; 'oləf/ 奧拉夫一世 (969–1000, 挪威國王, 在位期間 995–1000)。

Olaf II 奧拉夫二世 (995?–1030, 挪威國王, 在位期間 1016–28)。

Omar Khayyám /'əʊmɑ: kaɪ'jɑ:m ; 'omɑr kaɪ'jɑm/ 奧瑪開陽 (1025?–1123?, 波斯詩人及天文學家)。

O'Neill /əʊ'ni:l ; o'nil/ 歐尼爾 (Eugene Gladstone, 1888–1953, 美國劇作家,曾獲 1936 年諾貝爾文學獎)。

Onions /'ʌnjənz ; 'ʌnjənz/ 安年思 (Charles Talbut, 1873–1965, 英國語言學家及辭典編纂家)。

Oppenheim /'ɒpənhaɪm ; 'ɑpənhaɪm/ 歐本海姆 (Edward Phillips, 1866–1946, 英國小說家)。

Oppenheimer /'ɒpənhaɪmə ; 'ɑpənhaɪmɚ/ 歐本海默 (Julius Robert, 1904–1967, 美國物理學家)。

Orczy /'ɔ:tsɪ ; 'ɔrtsɪ/ 奧特西 (Baroness Emmuska, 1865–1947, 生於匈牙利之英國女小說家及劇作家)。

Orlando /ɔ:'lændəʊ ; ɔr'lændo/ 奧蘭多 (Vittorio Emanuele, 1860–1952, 義大利政治家)。

Orwell /'ɔ:wel ; 'ɔr,wɛl/ 歐威爾 (George, 1903–1950, 本名 Eric Blair, 英國作家)。

Osborn /'ɒzbən ; 'ɑzbɚn/ 奧斯本 (Henry Fairfield, 1857–1935, 美國古生物學家)。

Oscar II /'ɒskə ; 'ɑskɚ/ 奧斯卡二世 (1829–1907, 於 1872–1907 爲瑞典國王,並於 1872–1905 兼挪威國王)。

Osler /'əʊzlə ; 'ozlɚ/ 奧斯勒 (Sir William, 1849–1919, 加拿大醫生)。

Osman /ɒz'mɑ:n ; 'ɑzmɑn/ or **Othman** /ɒθ'mɑ:n; 'ɑθmɑn/ 奧斯曼 (1259–1326, Ottoman 帝國開國者)。

Ossietzky, von /,ɑ:sɪ'etskɪ ; ,ɑsɪ'ɛtskɪ/ 奧錫厄慈吉 (Carl, 1889–1938, 德國作家及和平主義者,曾獲 1935 年諾貝爾和平獎)。

Ostwald /'əʊstwɔ:ld ; 'os,twɔld/ 奧士德華 (Wilhelm, 1853–1932, 德國物理化學家及哲學家,曾獲 1909 年諾貝爾化學獎)。

Otto I /'ɒtəʊ;'ɑto/ 鄂圖一世 (912–973, 世稱 the Great, 神聖羅馬帝國皇帝,在位期間 936–973)。

Otway /'ɒtweɪ ; 'ɑtwe/ 奧特維 (Thomas, 1652–1685, 英國劇作家)。

Ovid /'ɒvɪd ; 'ɑvɪd/ 奧維德 (全名 Publius Ovidius Naso, 43 B.C.–?A. D. 17, 羅馬詩人)。

Owen /əʊɪn ; 'oɪn/ 歐文 (Robert, 1771–1858, 英國威爾斯社會改革者)。

Paderewski /,pædə'revskɪ ; ,pædə'rɛvskɪ/ 帕德列夫斯基 (Ignace Jan, 1860–1941, 波蘭鋼琴家及政治家)。

Paganini /,pægə'ni:nɪ ; ,pægə'ninɪ/ 帕格尼尼 (Niccolò, 1782–1840, 義大利小提琴家)。

Page /peɪdʒ ; pedʒ/ 佩基 (Thomas Nelson, 1853–1922, 美國小說家及外交家)。

Paget /'pædʒɪt ; 'pædʒɪt/ 派吉特 (Sir James, 1814–1899, 英國外科醫生及病理學家)。

Pai Chü-yi /'baɪ 'dʒju: 'i: ; 'baɪ 'dʒju 'i/ 白居易 (772–846, 中國唐朝詩人)。

Paine /peɪn ; pen/ 佩恩 (**1** Albert Bigelow, 1861–1937, 美國作家; **2** Thomas, 1737–1809, 生於英國之美國政治哲學家及作家)。

Paley /'peɪlɪ ; 'pelɪ/ 佩利 (William, 1743–1805, 英國神學家及哲學家)。

Palgrave /'pælgreɪv ; 'pælgrev/ 帕爾格雷夫 (Francis Turner, 1824–1897, 英國詩人及詩文編選家)。

Palma /'pɑ:lmə ; 'pɑlmə/ 帕爾瑪 (Tomás Estrada, 1835–1908, 於 1902–06 任古巴第一任總統)。

Palmer /'pɑ:mə ; 'pɑmɚ/ 帕麥爾 (**1** Alice Elvira, 1855–1902, 本姓 Freeman, G. H. 之妻,美國女教育家; **2** George Herbert, 1842–1933, 美國學者及教育家)。

Palmerston /'pɑ:məstən ; 'pɑmɚstən/ 帕麥爾斯頓 (Henry John Temple, 1784–1865, 英國政治家,於 1855–58 及 1859–65 任首相)。

Pan Ch'ao /'bæn 'tʃaʊ ; 'bɑn 'tʃaʊ/ 班超 (約 32–102, 中國東漢之外交家)。

Pan Ku /'bæn 'gu: ; 'bɑn 'gu/ 班固 (32–92, 中國漢朝史學家)。

Paracelsus /,pærə'selsəs ; ,pærə'sɛlsəs/ 巴拉塞爾士 (Philippus Aureolus, 1493–1541, 瑞士煉金家及醫生)。

Pares /peəz ; pɛrz/ 派爾茲 (Sir Bernard, 1876–1949, 英國歷史學家)。

Paris[1] /'pærɪs;'pærɪs/ 巴利斯 (Matthew, 1200?–1259, 英國僧侶及歷史學家)。

Paris[2] /pɑ:'ri:s ; pɑ'ris/ 巴利斯 (Gaston, 1839–1903, 法國語言學家)。

Park /pɑ:k ; pɑrk/ 巴克 (Mungo, 1771–1806, 蘇格蘭籍非洲探險家)。

Parker /'pɑ:kə ; 'pɑrkɚ/ 巴克爾 (**1** Dorothy, 1893–1967, 本姓 Rothschild, 美國女作家; **2** Matthew, 1504–1575, 英國神學家)。

Parkinson /'pɑ:kɪnsn ; 'pɑrkɪnsn̩/ 巴金生 (James, 1755–1824, 英國外科醫生及古生物學家)。

Parnell /pɑ:'nel ; pɑr'nɛl/ 巴奈爾 (Charles Stewart, 1846–1891, 愛爾蘭政治家及民族主義者)。

Parry /'pærɪ ; 'pærɪ/ 巴利 (Sir William Edward, 1790–1855, 英國北極探險家)。

Parsons /'pɑ:snz ; 'pɑrsn̩z/ 巴森茲 (William, 1800–1867, 英國天文學家)。

Passy /pæ'si: ; pæ'si/ 柏西 (**1** Frédéric, 1822–1912, 法國經濟學家及政治家, 與 J. H. Dunant 同獲 1901 年首屆諾貝爾和平獎; **2** 其子 Paul Édouard, 1859–1940, 法國語音學家)。

Pasternak /'pæstənæk ; 'pæstɚ,næk/ 巴斯特納克 (Boris Leonidovich, 1890–1960, 蘇聯詩人及小說家, 曾獲 1958 年諾貝爾文學獎)。

Pasteur /pæs'tɜ: ; pæs'tɝ/ 巴斯德 (Louis, 1822–1895, 法國化學家)。

Pater /'peɪtə ; 'petɚ/ 裴特爾 (Walter Horatio, 1839–1894, 英國散文家及批評家)。

Patrick /'pætrɪk ; 'pætrɪk/ 巴特瑞克 (Saint, 389?–?461, 愛爾蘭之守護聖徒)。

Paul /pɔ:l ; pɔl/ 聖・保羅 (Saint, ?–? A. D. 67, 耶穌門徒之一,傳基督教於非猶太人者)。

Paul I 保羅一世 (**1** 1754–1801, 俄國皇帝,在位期間 1796–1801; **2** 1901–1964, 希臘國王,在位期間 1947–64)。

Paul III 保羅三世 (1468–1549, 羅馬教皇,在位期間 1534–49)。

Paul V 保羅五世 (1552–1621, 羅馬教皇,在位期間 1605–21)。

Pauli /'paʊlɪ ; 'paʊlɪ/ 寶立 (Wolfgang, 1900–1958, 旅居美國的奧國物理學家,曾獲 1945 年諾貝爾物理獎)。

Pauling /'pɔ:lɪŋ ; 'pɔlɪŋ/ 鮑林 (Linus Carl, 1901–, 美國化學家, 曾獲 1954 年諾貝爾化學獎及 1963 年諾貝爾和平獎)。

Paulus /'pɔ:ləs ; 'pɔləs/ 保魯斯 (Julius, 二至三世紀時之羅馬法學家)。

Pausanias /pɔ:'seɪnɪæs ; pɔ'senɪəs/ 保塞尼亞斯 (二世紀時之希臘旅行家及地理學家)。

Pavlov /'pævlɒf ; 'pɑv,lɔf/ 巴夫洛夫 (Ivan Petrovich, 1849–1936, 俄國生理學家,曾獲 1904年諾貝爾醫學獎)。

Pavlova /'pævləvə ; 'pævləvə/ 巴夫洛瓦 (Anna, 1885–1931, 俄國女芭蕾舞蹈家)。

Peabody /'pi:bɒdɪ ; 'pibɑdɪ/ 皮巴蒂 (Endicott, 1857–1944, 美國教育家)。

Peacock /'pi:kɒk ; 'pikɑk/ 皮考克 (Thomas Love, 1785–1866, 英國小說家及詩人)。

Pearson /'pɪəsn ; 'pɪrsn̩/ 皮爾生 (**1** Karl, 1857–1936, 英國科學家; **2** Lester Bowles, 1897–1972, 加拿大外交家及政治家, 1963–68 任總理,曾獲 1957 年諾貝爾和平獎)。

Peary /'pɪərɪ ; 'pɪrɪ/ 皮列 (Robert Edwin, 1856–1920, 美國北極探險家)。

Peel /pi:l ; pil/ 皮爾 (Sir Robert, 1788–1850, 英國政治家)。

Pegram /'pi:grəm ; 'pigrəm/ 皮格拉姆 (George Brax-

ton, 1876–1958, 美國物理學家)。
Pepin the Short /ˈpepɪn- ; ˈpɛpɪn-/ 丕平 (714?–768, 法蘭克國王,在位期間 751–768)。
Pepys /piːps ; pips/ 丕普斯 (Samuel, 1633–1703, 英國日記作家)。
Percy /ˈpɜːsɪ ; ˈpɝsɪ/ 柏西 (Thomas, 1729–1811, 英國詩人及古物專家)。
Pérez Galdós /ˈpeərəs gɑːlˈdəʊs ; ˈpɛrəs gɑlˈdos/ 裴雷加道斯 (Benito, 1843–1920, 西班牙小說家及劇作家)。
Pericles /ˈperɪkliːz;ˈpɛrɪkliz/ 培里克里斯 (?–429 B.C., 雅典政治家、將軍及演說家)。
Perrault /peˈrəʊ ; pɛˈro/ 伯羅 (Charles, 1628–1703, 法國童話作家)。
Perrin /ˈperɪn ; pɛˈræn/ 伯蘭 (Jean Baptiste, 1870–1942, 法國物理學家及化學家,曾獲1926年諾貝爾物理獎)。
Perry /ˈperɪ ; ˈpɛrɪ/ 培理 (**1** Bliss, 1860–1954, 美國教育家及批評家; **2** Matthew Calbraith, 1794–1858, 美國海軍代將; **3** Ralph Barton, 1876–1957, 美國哲學家及教育家)。
Perse /pɜːs ; pɝs/ 波思 (St. John, 參看 Léger)。
Perugino /ˌperuːˈdʒiːnəʊ ; ˌpɛruˈdʒino/ 裴路几諾 (Il, 本名 Pietro Vannucci, 1446–1523, 義大利畫家)。
Perutz /pəˈruːts ; pəˈruts/ 裴路玆 (Max Ferdinand, 1914–, 生於奧國之英國化學家,與 J. C. Kendrew 同獲 1962 年諾貝爾化學獎)。
Pestalozzi /ˌpestəˈlɒtsɪ ; ˌpɛstəˈlɑtsɪ/ 裴斯太洛西 (Johann Heinrich, 1746–1827, 瑞士教育家)。
Peter /ˈpiːtə ; ˈpitɚ/ 彼得 (Saint, ?–? A.D. 67, 耶穌十二門徒之一)。
Peter I 彼得大帝 (1672–1725, 世稱 Peter the Great, 俄國沙皇,在位期間 1682–1725)。
Peter II 彼得二世 (1923–1970, 南斯拉夫國王,在位期間 1934–45)。
Peters /ˈpeɪtəz ; ˈpetɚz/ 彼得斯 (Carl, 1856–1918, 德籍非洲探險家)。
Petrarch /ˈpiːtrɑːk;ˈpitrɑrk/ or **Petrarca** /peɪˈtrɑːkə; peˈtrɑrkə/ 彼脫拉克 (Francesco, 1304–1374, 義大利詩人)。
Phaedrus /ˈfiːdrəs ; ˈfidrəs/ 菲德拉斯(紀元前五世紀之希臘哲學家)。
Phidias /ˈpɪdɪæs ; ˈfɪdɪəs/ 菲狄亞斯(紀元前五世紀之希臘雕刻家)。
Philip /ˈfɪlɪp ; ˈfɪlɪp/ 菲力普 (**1** 本名 Metacomet, 1639?–1676, 印地安 Wampanoag 族酋長; **2** Prince, 1921–, 英女王伊利莎白二世之夫,自 1947 年爲愛丁堡公爵)。
Philip II 菲力普二世 (**1** 1165–1223, 法國國王,在位期間 1180–1223; **2** 1527–1598, 西班牙國王,在位期間 1556–98; **3** 382–336 B. C., 馬其頓國王,在位期間 359–336 B.C.)。
Philip IV 菲力普四世 (1268–1314, 法國國王,在位期間 1285–1314, 世稱 the Fair)。
Philip V 菲力普五世 (1683–1746, 西班牙國王,在位期間 1700–46)。
Philip VI 菲力普六世 (1293–1350, 法國國王,在位期間 1328–50)。
Philips /ˈfɪlɪps ; ˈfɪlɪps/ 菲力普斯 (Ambrose, 1675?–1749, 綽號 Namby-Pamby, 英國詩人及劇作家)。
Phillips /ˈfɪlɪps ; ˈfɪlɪps/ 菲力普斯 (Stephen, 1868–1915, 英國詩人及劇作家)。
Phocion /ˈfəʊsɪən ; ˈfosɪɑn/ 福西昂 (402?–317 B.C., 雅典將軍及政治家)。
Picasso /pɪˈkɑːsəʊ ; pɪˈkɑso/ 畢加索 (Pablo, 1881–1973, 旅居法國的西班牙畫家及雕刻家)。
Pickering /ˈpɪkərɪŋ ; ˈpɪk(ə)rɪŋ/ 皮克令 (Edward Charles, 1846–1919, 其弟 William Henry, 1858–1938, 均爲美國天文學家)。
Pierce /pɪəs ; pɪrs/ 皮爾斯 (Franklin, 1804–1869, 於 1853–57 任美國第十四任總統)。
Pilate /ˈpaɪlət ; ˈpaɪlət/ 比拉多 (Pontius, 紀元一世紀審判耶穌之 Judea 總督)。
Pindar /ˈpɪndə ; ˈpɪndɚ/ 平德爾 (522?–443 B.C., 希臘詩人)。
Pinero /pɪˈnɪərəʊ ; pɪˈnɪro/ 皮尼洛 (Sir Arthur Wing, 1855–1934, 英國劇作家)。
Pirandello /ˌpɪrənˈdeləʊ ; ˌpɪrənˈdɛlo/ 皮藍德羅 (Luigi, 1867–1936, 義大利小說家及劇作家,曾獲 1934 年諾貝爾文學獎)。
Pire /pɪə ; pɪr/ 皮爾 (Dominique-Georges, 1910–1969, 比利時教士,曾獲 1958 年諾貝爾和平獎)。
Pisistratus or **Peisistratus** /paɪˈsɪstrətəs ; paɪˈsɪstrətəs/ 皮西斯特拉妥 (?–527 B.C., 雅典暴君)。
Pitt /pɪt ; pɪt/ 庇特 (**1** William, 1708–1778, 稱做 the Elder Pitt, 英國政治家; **2** 其子 William, 1759–1806, 稱做 the Younger Pitt, 英國政治家)。
Pius II /ˈpaɪəs;ˈpaɪəs/ 庇護二世 (1405–1464, 羅馬教皇, 任期 1458–64)。
Pius VII 庇護七世 (1742–1823, 羅馬教皇,任期1800–23)。
Pius IX 庇護九世 (1792–1878, 羅馬教皇,任期 1846–78)。
Pius X 庇護十世 (1835–1914, 羅馬教皇,任期 1903–14)。
Pius XI 庇護十一世 (1857–1939, 羅馬教皇,任期1922–39)。
Pius XII 庇護十二世 (1876–1958, 羅馬教皇,任期 1939–58)。
Planck /plɑːŋk ; plɑŋk/ 浦朗克 (Max Karl Ernst Ludwig, 1858–1947, 德國物理學家,曾獲 1918 年諾貝爾物理獎)。
Plato /ˈpleɪtəʊ ; ˈpleto/ 柏拉圖 (427?–347 B.C., 希臘哲學家)。
Plautus /ˈplɔːtəs ; ˈplɔtəs/ 浦勞塔斯 (Titus Maccius, 254?–184 B.C., 羅馬喜劇作家)。
Plimsoll /ˈplɪmsəl ; ˈplɪmsəl/ 普林索 (Samuel, 1824–1898, 英國船運改革者,世稱 the Sailor's Friend)。
Pliny /ˈplɪnɪ ; ˈplɪnɪ/ 蒲林尼 (本名 Gaius Plinius Secundus, 23–79, 羅馬學者)。
Plutarch /ˈpluːtɑːk ; ˈplutɑrk/ 蒲魯塔克 (46?–?120, 希臘傳記作家及道德家)。
Poe /pəʊ ; po/ 愛倫・坡 (Edgar Allan, 1809–1849, 美國詩人、小說家及批評家)。
Pole /pəʊl ; pol/ 波爾 (Reginald, 1500–1558, 英國紅衣主教, 1556 年任 Canterbury 之大主教)。
Polk /pəʊk ; pok/ 波克 (James Knox, 1795–1849, 於 1845–49 任美國第十一任總統)。
Polo /ˈpəʊləʊ ; ˈpolo/ 馬哥孛羅 (Marco, 1254?–?1324, 義大利旅行家)。
Polybius /pəˈlɪbɪəs ; pəˈlɪbɪəs/ 波力比阿 (205?–?125 B.C., 希臘歷史學家)。
Pompey /ˈpɒmpɪ;ˈpɑmpɪ/ 龐培大帝 (拉丁全名 Gnaeus Pompeius Magnus, 106–48 B.C., 世稱 ~ the Great, 羅馬大將及政治家)。
Pontoppidan /pɑːnˈtɑːpədæn ; pɑnˈtɑpəˌdæn/ 龐陶皮丹 (Henrik, 1857–1943, 丹麥小說家,與 K. Gjellerup 同獲 1917 年諾貝爾文學獎)。
Porson /ˈpɔːsn ; ˈpɔrsn̩/ 波生 (Richard, 1759–1808, 英國學者)。
Porter /ˈpɔːtə ; ˈpɔrtɚ/ 波忒 (**1** Gene, 1868–1924, 本姓 Stratton, 美國女小說家; **2** Noah, 1811–1892, 美國哲學家及辭典編纂家; **3** William Sydney, 1862–1910, 筆名 O. Henry, 美國短篇小說家)。
Potter /ˈpɒtə ; ˈpɑtɚ/ 波特爾 (Paul, 1625–1654, 荷蘭畫家)。
Pound /paʊnd ; paʊnd/ 龐德 (**1** Ezra Loomis, 1885–1972, 美國詩人; **2** Roscoe, 1870–1964, 美國法學家)。
Powell /ˈpaʊəl ; ˈpaʊəl/ 鮑威爾 (Cecil Frank, 1903–1969, 英國物理學家,曾獲 1950 年諾貝爾物理獎)。
Pratt /præt ; præt/ 蒲拉特 (Bela Lyon, 1867–1917, 美國雕刻家)。
Praxiteles /prækˈsɪtəliːz ; prækˈsɪtl̩ˌiz/ 蒲拉克西蒂利 (紀元前四世紀之雅典雕刻家)。
Pregl /ˈpreɪgl ; ˈpregl̩/ 浦瑞格爾 (Fritz, 1869–1930, 奧國化學家,曾獲 1923 年諾貝爾化學獎)。
Prescott /ˈpreskət ; ˈprɛskət/ 蒲萊斯考特 (William Hickling, 1796–1859, 美國歷史學家)。
Prior /ˈpraɪə ; ˈpraɪɚ/ 蒲萊爾 (Matthew, 1664–1721, 英國詩人)。
Prokhorov /ˌprɒhəˈrɒf;ˌprɔhəˈrɔf/ 普洛柴諾夫 (Aleksandr Mikhailovich, 1916–, 俄國物理學家,與 G. H. Townes 及 N. G. Basov 同獲 1964 年諾貝爾物理獎)。
Propertius /prəˈpɜːʃɪəs ; prəˈpɝʃəs/ 浦洛柏夏斯 (Sextus, 50?–?15 B.C., 羅馬詩人)。
Protagoras /prəʊˈtægəræs ; proˈtægərəs/ 普洛塔高勒

斯(紀元前五世紀之希臘哲學家)。

Proust /pruːst ; prust/ 蒲魯斯特 (Marcel, 1871-1922, 法國小說家)。

Puccini /puːˈtʃiːnɪ ; puˈtʃinɪ/ 普契尼 (Giacomo, 1858-1924, 義大利作曲家)。

Pulitzer /ˈpʊlɪtsə ; ˈpʊlɪtsɚ/ 普立玆 (Joseph, 1847-1911, 生於匈牙利之美國報人)。

Pullman /ˈpʊlmən ; ˈpʊlmən/ 蒲爾曼 (George Mortimer, 1831-1897, 美國發明家)。

Purcell 柏塞爾 (**1** /ˈpɜːsl ; ˈpɝsl̩/ Henry, 1658?-1695, 英國作曲家; **2** /pɜːˈsel ; pɝˈsɛl/ Edward Mills, 1912-, 美國物理學家,與 F. Block 同獲 1952 年諾貝爾物理獎)。

Pusey /ˈpjuːzɪ ; ˈpjuzɪ/ 蒲賽 (Edward Bouverie, 1800-1882, 英國神學家)。

Pushkin /ˈpʊʃkɪn ; ˈpʊʃkɪn/ 普希金 (Aleksander Sergeevich, 1799-1837, 俄國詩人)。

P'u-yi /ˈpuː ˈjiː ; ˈpu ˈji/ 溥儀 (Henry, 1906-1967, 即清宣統帝,爲中國最後一個皇帝,在位期間 1908-12)。

Pye /paɪ ; paɪ/ 蒲艾 (Henry James, 1745-1813, 英國詩人,於 1790-1813 榮膺桂冠詩人)。

Pyrrhus /ˈpɪrəs ; ˈpɪrəs/ 皮拉斯 (318?-272 B.C., 古希臘 Epirus 之國王,在位期間 306-272 B.C.)。

Pythagoras /paɪˈθægəræs ; paɪˈθægərəs/ 畢達哥拉斯 (?-? 497 B.C., 希臘哲學家及數學家)。

Quasimodo/ ˌkwɑːzɪˈməʊdəʊ;ˌkwɑzɪˈmodo/ 瓜析莫多 (Salvatore, 1901-1968, 義大利詩人及批評家,曾獲 1959 年諾貝爾文學獎)。

Quidde /ˈkwɪdə ; ˈkwɪdə/ 桂德 (Ludwig, 1858-1941, 德國歷史學家及和平主義者,與 F. Buisson 同獲 1927年諾貝爾和平獎)。

Quiller-Couch /ˈkwɪləˈkuːtʃ ; ˈkwɪlɚˌkutʃ/ 奎勒枯赤 (Sir Arthur Thomas, 1863-1944, 英國作家)。

Quincy /ˈkwɪnsɪ ; ˈkwɪnsɪ/ 昆西 (Josiah, 1744-1775, 美國律師及從政者)。

Quintilian /kwɪnˈtɪljən ; kwɪnˈtɪljən/ 昆提連 (本名 Marcus Fabius Quintilianus, 一世紀時之羅馬修辭學家)。

Rabelais /ˈræbəleɪ ; ˈræbəˌle/ 拉伯雷 (François, 1494?-1553, 法國幽默文及諷刺文作家)。

Rabi /ˈrɑːbɪ ; ˈrɑbi/ 拉比 (Isidor Isaac, 1898-, 生於奧國之美國物理學家,曾獲 1944 年諾貝爾物理獎)。

Rachmaninoff /rækˈmænɪnɒf ; rækˈmænɪnɔf/ 拉克瑪尼諾夫 (Sergei Wassilievitch, 1873-1943, 俄國鋼琴家、作曲家及指揮家)。

Racine /ræˈsiːn ; ræˈsin/ 拉辛 (Jean Baptiste, 1639-1699, 法國劇作家)。

Radcliffe /ˈrædklɪf ; ˈrædklɪf/ 賴德克利芙 (Ann, 1764-1823, 本姓 Ward, 英國女小說家)。

Rae /reɪ ; re/ 雷依 (John, 1813-1893, 蘇格蘭北極探險家)。

Raeburn /ˈreɪbɜːn ; ˈrebɚn/ 雷本 (Sir Henry, 1756-1823, 蘇格蘭畫家)。

Rale(i)gh /ˈrɔːlɪ ; ˈrɔlɪ/ 饒列 (Sir Walter, 1552?-1618, 英國朝臣、歷史學家及航海家)。

Raman /ˈrɑːmən ; ˈrɑmən/ 拉曼 (Sir Chandrasekhara Venkata, 1888-1970, 印度物理學家,曾獲 1930 年諾貝爾物理獎)。

Ramón y Cajal /rəˌməʊnɪkəˈhɑːl ; rəˌmonɪkəˈhɑl/ 拉孟伊卡哈 (Santiago, 1852-1934, 西班牙組織學家,與 C. Golgi 同獲 1906 年諾貝爾醫學獎)。

Ramsay /ˈræmzɪ ; ˈræmzɪ/ 雷姆塞 (**1** Allan, 1686-1758, 蘇格蘭詩人; **2** James Andrew Broun, 1812-1860, 英國政治家,1848-56任印度總督; **3** Sir William, 1852-1916, 英國化學家,曾獲 1904 年諾貝爾化學獎)。

Raphael /ˈræfeɪəl ; ˈræfɪəl/ 拉斐爾 (本名 Raffaello Santi 或 Sanzio, 1483-1520, 義大利畫家)。

Ravel /ræˈvel ; ræˈvɛl/ 拉維爾 (Maurice Joseph, 1875-1937, 法國作曲家)。

Rawlinson /ˈrɔːlɪnsn ; ˈrɔlɪnsn̩/ 勞林森 (George, 1812-1902, 英國歷史學家及東方學家)。

Ray /reɪ ; re/ 雷伊 (John, 1627?-1705, 英國博物學家)。

Rayleigh /ˈreɪlɪ ; ˈrelɪ/ 雷利 (本名 John William Strutt, 1842-1919, 英國物理學家及數學家,獲 1904 年諾貝爾物理獎)。

Read /riːd ; rid/ 利德 (Thomas Buchanan, 1822-1872, 美國詩人及畫家)。

Reade /riːd ; rid/ 利德 (Charles, 1814-1884, 英國小說家及劇作家)。

Reading /ˈredɪŋ ; ˈrɛdɪŋ/ 列丁 (John, 1677-1764, 英國風琴家)。

Reagan /ˈreɪgən ; ˈregən/ 雷根 (Ronald, 1911-, 美國演員及從政者, 1981- 任美國第四十任總統)。

Réaumur, de /ˈreɪəmjʊə ; ˈreəmjʊr/ 列歐穆 (René Antoine Ferchault, 1683-1757, 法國博物學家及物理學家,列氏溫度計之設計者)。

Redmond /ˈredmənd ; ˈrɛdmənd/ 列德蒙 (John Edward, 1856-1918, 愛爾蘭政治家)。

Reed /riːd ; rid/ 列德 (**1** Stanley Forman, 1884-1980, 美國法學家; **2** Thomas Brackett, 1839-1902, 美國從政者; **3** Walter, 1851-1902, 美國陸軍外科醫生)。

Regulus /ˈregjʊləs ; ˈrɛgjʊləs/ 雷古拉斯 (Marcus Atilius, ?-?250 B.C., 羅馬將軍)。

Reichstein /ˈraɪkstaɪn ; ˈraɪkˌstaɪn/ 萊克斯坦 (Tadeus, 1897-, 生於波蘭之瑞士化學家,與 P. S. Hench 及 E. C. Kendall 同獲 1950 年諾貝爾醫學獎)。

Reid /riːd ; rid/ 利德 (Thomas, 1710-1796, 蘇格蘭哲學家)。

Remarque /rəˈmɑːk ; rəˈmɑrk/ 雷馬克 (Erich Maria, 1898-1970, 出生於德國的美國小說家)。

Rembrandt van Rijn (or Ryn) /ˈrembrænt vɑːn ˈraɪn ; ˈrɛmbrænt vɑn ˈraɪn/ 倫布蘭特 (1606-1669, 荷蘭畫家)。

Remington /ˈremɪŋtən ; ˈrɛmɪŋtən/ 雷明頓 (Frederic, 1861-1909, 美國藝術家)。

Renault /rəˈnəʊ ; rəˈno/ 雷諾 (Louis, 1843-1918, 法國法學家及和平主義者,與 E. T. Moneta 同獲 1907 年諾貝爾和平獎)。

Renoir /ˈrenwɑː ; ˈrɛnˌwɑr/ 雷諾瓦 (Pierre Auguste, 1841-1919, 法國畫家)。

Revere /rɪˈvɪə ; rɪˈvɪr/ 列維爾 (Paul, 1735-1818, 美國愛國志士及銀匠)。

Reymont /ˈreɪmɑːnt ; ˈreˌmɑnt/ 雷孟德 (Wladyslaw Stanislaw, 1867-1925, 波蘭小說家,曾獲 1924 年諾貝爾文學獎)。

Reynolds /ˈrenldz ; ˈrɛnl̩(d)z/ 藍諾玆 (Sir Joshua, 1723-1792, 英國畫家)。

Rhodes /rəʊdz ; rodz/ 羅玆 (Cecil John, 1853-1902, 英國南非行政長官及財政家)。

Rice /raɪs ; raɪs/ 萊斯 (Elmer L. 1892-1967, 美國劇作家)。

Richard I /ˈrɪtʃəd ; ˈrɪtʃɚd/ 利查一世 (1157-1199, 英王,在位期間 1189-99, 第三次十字軍東征的領袖之一,世稱 Richard Coeur de Lion 或 Richard the Lion-Hearted)。

Richard II 利查二世 (1367-1400, 英王,在位期間 1377-99, 爲 Plantagenet 王朝最後一主,後被黜)。

Richard III 利查三世 (1452-1485, 英王,在位期間 1483-85)。

Richards /ˈrɪtʃədz ; ˈrɪtʃɚdz/ 利查玆 (**1** Theodore William, 1868-1928, 美國化學家,於 1914 年獲諾貝爾化學獎; **2** Dickinson Woodruff, 1895-1973, 美國醫生,與 W. Forssmann 及 A. F. Cournand 同獲 1956 年諾貝爾醫學獎)。

Richardson /ˈrɪtʃədsn ; ˈrɪtʃɚdsn̩/ 利查生 (**1** Henry Handel, 本名 Ethel Florence Lindesay ～, 1870-1946, 澳大利亞小說家; **2** Sir Owen Willans, 1879-1959, 英國物理學家,曾獲1928年諾貝爾物理獎; **3** Samuel, 1689-1761, 英國小說家)。

Richelieu, de /ˈrɪʃəljuː ; ˈrɪʃəlju/ 黎希留 (Duc, 1585-1642, 本名 Armand Jean du Plessis, 法國政治家及紅衣主教)。

Richet /rɪˈʃeɪ ; rɪˈʃe/ 黎歇 (Charles Robert, 1850-1935, 法國生理學家,曾獲 1913 年諾貝爾醫學獎)。

Richter /ˈrɪktə ; ˈrɪktɚ/ 立克特 (Burton, 1931-, 美國物理學家,與丁肇中同獲 1976 年諾貝爾物理獎)。

Ridley /ˈrɪdlɪ ; ˈrɪdlɪ/ 黎德利 (Nicholas, 1500?-1555, 英國主教及宗教改革家,後被焚殉道)。

Riley /ˈraɪlɪ ; ˈraɪlɪ/ 萊黎 (James Whitcomb, 1849-1916, 美國詩人)。

Rimski-Korsakov /ˈrɪmskɪˈkɔːsəkɒf ; ˈrɪmskɪˈkɔrsəkɔf/ 黎姆斯基・考薩科夫 (Nikolai Andreevich, 1844–1908, 俄國作曲家)。
Ripley /ˈrɪplɪ ; ˈrɪplɪ/ 黎普列 (George, 1802–1880, 美國文學批評家及社會主義者)。
Robbins /ˈrɒbɪnz ; ˈrɑbɪnz/ 羅賓斯 (Frederick Chapman, 1916–, 美國醫生, 與 J. F. Enders 及 T. H. Weller 同獲 1954 年諾貝爾醫學獎)。
Roberts /ˈrɒbəts ; ˈrɑbɚts/ 羅伯次 (**1** Frederick Sleigh, 1832–1914, 英國陸軍元帥; **2** Kenneth, 1885–1957, 美國小說家; **3** Owen Josephus, 1875–1955, 美國法學家)。
Robespierre, de /ˈrəʊbzpjeə ; ˈrobzpjɛr/ 羅伯斯比 (Maximilien François Marie Isidore, 1758–1794, 法國革命家)。
Robinson /ˈrɒbɪnsn ; ˈrɑbɪnsn̩/ 魯賓遜 (Sir Robert, 1886–1975, 英國化學家,曾獲 1947 年諾貝爾化學獎)。
Rockefeller /ˈrɒkɪfelə ; ˈrɑkɪfɛlɚ/ 洛克菲勒 (John Davison, 1839–1937, 其子,同名, 1874–1960, 均爲美國石油大王及慈善家)。
Rockingham /ˈrɒkɪŋəm ; ˈrɑkɪŋəm/ 羅京安 (本名 Charles Watson-Wentworth, 1730–1782, 英國政治家)。
Rode /ˈrəʊðə ; ˈroðə/ 羅澤 (Helge, 1870–1937, 丹麥詩人)。
Rodgers /ˈrɒdʒəz ; ˈrɑdʒɚz/ 羅傑斯 (Richard, 1902–1979, 美國作曲家)。
Roentgen or **Röntgen** /ˈrentgən ; ˈrɛntgən/ 樂勤 (Wilhelm Conrad, 1845–1923, 德國物理學家,曾獲 1901 年諾貝爾物理獎)。
Rogers /ˈrɒdʒəz ; ˈrɑdʒɚz/ 羅傑妶 (**1** James Gamble, 1867–1947, 美國建築家; **2** Samuel, 1763–1855, 英國詩人)。
Roget /ˈrəʊʒeɪ ; ˈroʒe/ 羅傑 (Peter Mark, 1779–1869, 英國醫生及學者)。
Rolland /ˌrɔːˈlɒŋ ; ˏrɔˈlɔŋ/ 羅朗 (Romain, 1866–1944, 法國作家,曾獲 1915 年諾貝爾文學獎)。
Romney /ˈrɒmnɪ ; ˈrɑmnɪ/ 隆尼 (George, 1734–1802, 英國畫家)。
Roosevelt /ˈrəʊzəvelt;ˈrozəvɛlt/ 羅斯福 (**1** Franklin Delano, 1882–1945, 於 1933–45 任美國第三十二任總統; **2** Theodore, 1858–1919, 於 1901–09 任美國第二十六任總統,曾獲 1906 年諾貝爾和平獎)。
Root /ruːt ; rut/ 羅德 (Elihu, 1845–1937, 美國律師及政治家,曾獲 1912 年諾貝爾和平獎)。
Rosa /ˈrəʊzə ; ˈrozə/ 羅莎 (Salvator, 1615–1673, 義大利畫家及詩人)。
Ross /rɒs ; rɔs/ 羅斯 (**1** Betsy, 1752–1836, 女性,本姓 Griscom, 設計與製造第一面美國國旗者; **2** Sir James Clark, 1800–1862, 蘇格蘭南北極探險家; **3** Sir John, 1777–1856, 蘇格蘭北極探險家; **4** Sir Ronald, 1857–1932, 英國醫生,曾獲 1902 年諾貝爾醫學獎)。
Rossetti /rəʊˈsetɪ ; roˈsɛtɪ/ 羅塞蒂 (**1** Christina Georgina, 1830–1894, 英國女詩人; **2** Dante Gabriel, 1828–1882, 英國畫家及詩人)。
Rossini /rɒˈsiːnɪ ; rɔˈsinɪ/ 羅西尼 (Gioacchino Antonio, 1792–1868, 義大利作曲家)。
Rousseau /ˈruːsəʊ ; ˈruso/ 盧梭 (Jean Jacques, 1712–1778, 生於瑞士之法國哲學家及作家)。
Rowe /rəʊ ; ro/ 羅歐 (Nicholas, 1674–1718, 英國詩人及劇作家,於 1715–18 榮膺桂冠詩人)。
Royce /rɔɪs ; rɔɪs/ 羅伊斯 (Josiah, 1855–1916, 美國哲學家)。
Rubens /ˈruːbɪnz ; ˈrubɪnz/ 魯賓斯 (Peter Paul, 1577–1640, 法蘭德斯 (Flanders) 畫家)。
Rubinstein /ˈruːbɪnstaɪn ; ˈrubɪnstaɪn/ 盧賓斯坦 (**1** Anton, 1829–1894, 俄國作曲家及鋼琴家; **2** Arthur, 1886–1983, 生於波蘭之美國鋼琴家)。
Rudolf I of Hapsburg /ˈruːdɒlf ðəˈfɜːst əv ˈhæpsbɜːg ; ˈrudɑlf ðəˈfɝst əv ˈhæpsbɝg/ 魯道夫一世 (1218–1291, 神聖羅馬帝國皇帝,在位期間 1273–91, 爲 Hapsburg 王朝之始祖)。
Rupert /ˈruːpət ; ˈrupɚt/ 路柏王子 (Prince, 1619–1682, 德國將軍及海軍上將,在英國內戰中協助其舅父查理一世)。
Rusk /rʌsk ; rʌsk/ 魯斯克 ((David) Dean, 1909–, 於 1961–69 任美國國務卿)。
Ruskin /ˈrʌskɪn ; ˈrʌskɪn/ 羅斯金 (John, 1819–1900, 英國散文家、批評家及社會改革者)。
Russell /ˈrʌsl ; ˈrʌsl̩/ 羅素 (**1** Bertrand Arthur William, 1872–1970, 英國數學家及哲學家,曾獲 1950 年諾貝爾文學獎; **2** George William, 1867–1935, 筆名 Æ, 愛爾蘭作家; **3** Lord John, 1792–1878, 英國政治家)。
Rutherford /ˈrʌðəfəd ; ˈrʌðɚfɚd/ 羅塞福 (Ernest, 1871–1937, 英國物理學家,曾獲 1908 年諾貝爾化學獎)。
Ružička /ˈruːʒɪtʃkə ; ˈruˏʒɪtʃkə/ 盧基伽 (Leopold, 1887–1976, 南斯拉夫化學家,與 A. Butenandt 同獲 1939 年諾貝爾化學獎)。
Saavedra Lamas /sɑːˌveɪdrə ˈlɑːməs;sɑˏvedrə ˈlɑməs/ 薩維妶拉 (Carlos, 1880–1959, 阿根廷律師及外交家,曾獲 1936 年諾貝爾和平獎)。
Sabatier /ˌsæbəˈtjeɪ ; ˏsæbəˈtje/ 薩巴提 (Paul, 1854–1941, 法國化學家,與 V. Grignard 同獲 1912 年諾貝爾化學獎)。
Sachs /sæks ; sæks/ 薩克斯 (Nelly, 1891–1970, 出生於德國之瑞典女劇作家及詩人,與 S. Y. Agnon 同獲 1966 年諾貝爾文學獎)。
Sackville /ˈsækvɪl ; ˈsækvɪl/ 塞克維爾 (Thomas, 1536–1608, 英國詩人及外交家)。
Sadat, el /səˈdæt ; səˈdæt/ 沙達特 (Anwar, 1918–1981, 埃及總統,任期爲 1970–81, 與 Menachem Begin 同獲 1978 年諾貝爾和平獎)。
Saint-Saëns /sæŋˈsɑːŋs ; sænˈsɑns/ 聖桑 ((Charles) Camille, 1835–1921, 法國作曲家)。
Saintsbury /ˈseɪntsbərɪ;ˈsentsbərɪ/ 聖次勃利 (George Edward Bateman, 1845–1933, 英國作家及文學批評家)。
Sakharov /ˈsɑːkərɒf ; ˈsɑkəˏrɔf/ 沙卡洛夫 (Andrei Dimitrievich, 1921–, 俄國物理學家及公民自由論者,曾獲 1975 年諾貝爾和平獎)。
Saladin /ˈsælədɪn ; ˈsælədɪn/ 薩拉丁 (1138–1193, 埃及和敍利亞之(回教)君主)。
Sallust /ˈsæləst ; ˈsæləst/ 塞勒斯特 (全名 Gaius Sallustius Crispus, 86–34 B.C., 羅馬歷史學家及從政者)。
Sand /sænd ; sænd/ 桑德 (George, 1804–1876, 爲 Amandine Aurore Lucie 之筆名,本姓 Dupin, 法國女作家)。
Sandburg /ˈsændbɜːg ; ˈsændˏbɝg/ 桑德堡 (Carl, 1878–1967, 本名 Carl August ～, 美國作家)。
Sanger /ˈsæŋgə ; ˈsæŋ(g)ɚ/ **1** 桑格 (Frederick, 1918–, 英國生物化學家,曾獲 1958 年諾貝爾化學獎)。 **2** 桑格夫人 (Margaret, 1883–1966, 本姓 Higgins, 美國護士及作家,爲節育運動之領袖)。
Santa A(n)na, de /ˌsæntə ˈænə ; ˏsæntə ˈænə/ 聖大安納 (Antonio López, 1795?–1876, 墨西哥將軍及獨裁者)。
Santayana /ˌsæntəˈjɑːnə ; ˏsæntəˈjɑnə/ 桑塔雅納 (George, 1863–1952, 出生於西班牙的美國詩人及哲學家)。
Sapir /səˈpɪə ; səˈpɪr/ 沙比爾 (Edward, 1884–1939, 生於德國之美國人類學家及語言學家)。
Sappho /ˈsæfəʊ ; ˈsæfo/ 莎孚 (紀元前 600 年左右之希臘女詩人)。
Sargent /ˈsɑːdʒənt ; ˈsɑrdʒənt/ 薩爾金特 (John Singer, 1856–1925, 美國畫家)。
Saroyan /səˈrɔɪən ; səˈrɔɪən/ 薩洛楊 (William, 1908–, 美國作家)。
Sartre /ˈsɑːtrə ; ˈsɑrtrə/ 沙特 (Jean-Paul, 1905–1980, 法國哲學家、劇作家及小說家,曾獲 1964 年諾貝爾文學獎)。
Sassoon /səˈsuːn ; səˈsun/ 薩松 (Siegfried Lorraine, 1886–1967, 英國詩人及小說家)。
Savage /ˈsævɪdʒ ; ˈsævɪdʒ/ 薩維基 (Richard, 1697?–1743, 英國詩人)。
Savonarola /ˌsævənəˈrəʊlə ; ˏsævənəˈrolə/ 薩佛納羅拉 (Girolamo, 1452–1498, 義大利宗教改革者)。
Sayers /ˈseɪəz ; ˈseɚz/ 塞爾妶 (Dorothy Leigh, 1893–1957, 英國散文家、劇作家及小說家)。
Scaliger /ˈskælɪdʒə ; ˈskælɪdʒɚ/ 斯卡利哲 (**1** Joseph Justus, 1540–1609, 寄居法國之義大利醫生及學者; **2** 其

父 Julius Caesar, 1484–1558, 義大利醫生)。
Scarlatti /skɑːˈlætɪ ; skɑrˈlɑtɪ/ 史卡拉第 (Alessandro, 1659–1725, 義大利作曲家,近代歌劇之父)。
Scharwenka /ʃɑːˈveŋkə ; ʃɑrˈvɛŋkə/ 夏文卡 (**1** Philipp, 1847–1917; **2** 其弟 Xaver, 1850–1924, 皆爲德國鋼琴家及作曲家)。
Schiller, von /ˈʃɪlə ; ˈʃɪlɚ/ 席勒 (Johann Christoph Friedrich, 1759–1805, 德國詩人及劇作家)。
Schopenhauer /ˈʃəʊpənhaʊə ; ˈʃopən,haʊɚ/ 叔本華 (Arthur, 1788–1860, 德國悲觀主義哲學家)。
Schrieffer /ˈʃriːfə ; ˈʃrifɚ/ 施立非 (John Robert, 1931–, 美國物理學家,與 J. Bardeen 及 L. N. Cooper 同獲 1972 年諾貝爾物理獎)。
Schrödinger /ˈʃreɪdɪŋə ; ˈʃredɪŋɚ/ 施洛丁格 (Erwin, 1887–1961, 奧國物理學家,與 P. A. M. Dirac 同獲 1933 年諾貝爾物理獎)。
Schubert /ˈʃuːbɜːt ; ˈʃubɚt/ 舒伯特 (Franz Peter, 1797–1828, 奧國作曲家)。
Schumann /ˈʃuːmən ; ˈʃumən/ 舒曼 (Robert, 1810–1856, 德國作曲家)。
Schweitzer /ˈʃvaɪtsə ; ˈʃvaɪtsɚ/ 史懷徹 (Albert, 1875–1965, 法國基督教牧師、哲學家、醫生及音樂家,曾獲 1952 年諾貝爾和平獎)。
Schwinger /ˈʃwɪŋgə ; ˈʃwɪŋ(g)ɚ/ 史文格 (Julian Seymour, 1918–, 美國物理學家,與 R. P. Feynman 及 Tomonaga 同獲 1965 年諾貝爾物理獎)。
Scipio Africanus /ˈsɪpɪəʊ ˌæfrɪˈkeɪnəs ; ˈsɪpɪo ˌæfrɪˈkenəs/ 西比奧 (Publius Cornelius, 237–183 B.C., 羅馬將軍)。
Scott /skɒt ; skɑt/ 司各脫 (**1** Sir George Gilbert, 1811–1878, 英國建築家; **2** Robert Falcon, 1868–1912, 英國南極探險家; **3** Sir Walter, 1771–1832, 蘇格蘭詩人及小說家)。
Scriabin or **Scriabine** /ˈskrɪəbɪn ; skriˈɑbɪn/ 司克力亞賓 (Alexander, 1872–1915, 俄國作曲家)。
Scribe /skriːb ; skrib/ 司克利卜 (Augustin Eugène, 1791–1861, 法國劇作家)。
Seaborg /ˈsiːbɔːg ; ˈsibɔrg/ 西堡 (Glenn Theodore, 1912–, 美國化學家,與 E. M. McMillan 同獲 1951 年諾貝爾化學獎)。
See /siː ; si/ 西伊 (Thomas Jefferson Jackson, 1866–1962, 美國天文學家及數學家)。
Seferiades /seˌferiːˈɑːðiːs ; ˌsɛ,fɛrɪˈɑðis/ 賽飛雷阿西 (Giorgos Stylianou, 1900–1971, 筆名 George Seferis, 希臘詩人及外交家,曾獲 1963 年諾貝爾文學獎)。
Segrè /səˈgreɪ ; səˈgre/ 薩格雷 (Emilio, 1905–, 生於義大利之美國物理學家,與 O. Chamberlain 同獲 1959 年諾貝爾物理獎)。
Selden /ˈseldən ; ˈsɛldən/ 塞爾丹 (George Baldwin, 1846–1922, 美國律師及發明家)。
Semënov /səˈmjɒnəf ; səˈmjɔnəf/ 西淼諾夫 (Nikolai Nikolaevich, 1896–, 俄國化學家,與 C. N. Hinshelwood 同獲 1956 年諾貝爾化學獎)。
Seneca /ˈsenɪkə ; ˈsɛnɪkə/ 塞尼加 (Lucius Annaeus, 4 B.C. ?–A.D. 65, 羅馬政治家及哲學家)。
Service /ˈsɜːvɪs ; ˈsɝvɪs/ 塞維斯 (Robert William, 1874–1958, 加拿大作家)。
Severus /sɪˈvɪərəs ; sɪˈvɪrəs/ 塞佛留 (Lucius Septimius, 146–211, 羅馬皇帝,在位期間 193–211)。
Shackleton /ˈʃækltən ; ˈʃækl̩tən/ 沙克爾頓 (Sir Ernest Henry, 1874–1922, 英國南極探險家)。
Shadwell /ˈʃædwəl ; ˈʃædwəl/ 沙德威爾 (Thomas, 1642?–1692, 英國劇作家,於 1688–92 榮膺桂冠詩人)。
Shaftesbury /ˈʃɑːftsbərɪ ; ˈʃæfts,bɛrɪ/ 沙佛玆伯里(本名 Anthony Ashley Cooper, 1621–1683, 英國政治家)。
Shakespeare or **Shakspere** /ˈʃeɪkspɪə ; ˈʃekspɪr/ 莎士比亞 (William, 1564–1616, 英國劇作家及詩人)。
Shaw /ʃɔː ; ʃɔ/ 蕭伯納 (George Bernard, 1856–1950, 生於愛爾蘭之英國作家及社會主義者,曾獲 1925 年諾貝爾文學獎)。
Shelley /ˈʃelɪ ; ˈʃɛlɪ/ 雪萊 (Percy Bysshe, 1792–1822, 英國詩人)。
Shepard /ˈʃepəd ; ˈʃɛpɚd/ 謝波德 (Alan Bartlett, 1923–, 美國太空人,爲美國第一個進入太空者 (1961))。
Sheraton /ˈʃerətn ; ˈʃɛrətn̩/ 雪里頓 (Thomas, 1751–1806, 英國傢具設計及製造家)。
Sheridan /ˈʃerɪdn ; ˈʃɛrɪdn̩/ 雪利敦 (**1** Philip Henry, 1831–1888, 美國將軍; **2** Richard Brinsley, 1751–1816, 愛爾蘭劇作家及演說家)。
Sherriff /ˈʃerəf ; ˈʃɛrəf/ 雪利夫 (Robert Cedric, 1896–1975, 英國作家)。
Sherrington /ˈʃerɪŋtn ; ˈʃɛrɪŋtn̩/ 謝領頓 (Sir Charles Scott, 1861–1952, 英國生理學家,與 E. D. Adrian 同獲 1932 年諾貝爾醫學獎)。
Sherwood /ˈʃɜːwʊd ; ˈʃɝwʊd/ 雪伍德 (Robert Emmet, 1896–1955, 美國劇作家)。
Shih Huang Ti /ˈʃiː ˈhwɑːŋ ˈtiː ; ˈʃi ˈhwɑŋ ˈti/ 始皇帝 (卽嬴政, 259–210 B.C., 中國秦朝開國帝王,在位三十七年)。
Shirley /ˈʃɜːlɪ ; ˈʃɝlɪ/ 雪萊 (James, 1596–1666, 英國劇作家)。
Shockley /ˈʃɒklɪ ; ˈʃɑklɪ/ 沙克利 (William Bradford, 1910–, 美國物理學家,與 J. Bardeen 及 W. H. Brattain 同獲 1956 年諾貝爾物理獎)。
Sholokhov /ˈʃɔːləkɒf ; ˈʃɔlə,kɔf/ 蕭勒可夫 (Mikhail Aleksandrovich, 1905–, 俄國小說家,曾獲 1965 年諾貝爾文學獎)。
Sidney /ˈsɪdnɪ ; ˈsɪdnɪ/ 西德尼 (Sir Philip, 1554–1586, 英國詩人、軍人及政治家)。
Siegbahn /ˈsiːgbɑːn ; ˈsig,bɑn/ 西格班 (Karl Manne Georg, 1886–1978, 瑞典物理學家,曾獲 1924 年諾貝爾物理獎)。
Sienkiewicz /ʃenˈkjeɪvɪtʃ ; ʃɛnˈkjevɪtʃ/ 顯克維支 (Henryk, 1846–1916, 波蘭小說家,曾獲 1905 年諾貝爾文學獎)。
Sigismund /ˈsɪgəsmənd ; ˈsɪgəsmənd/ 西格門 (1368–1437, 神聖羅馬帝國皇帝,在位期間 1411–37)。
Sillanpää /ˈsɪlənpɑː ; ˈsɪlən,pæ/ 西藍排 (Frans Eemil, 1888–1964, 芬蘭小說家,曾獲 1939 年諾貝爾文學獎)。
Simon /ˈsaɪmən ; ˈsaɪmən/ 塞門 (John Allsebrook, 1873–1954, 英國法學家及政治家)。
Sinclair /ˈsɪŋkleə ; ˈsɪŋklɛr/ 辛克萊 (May, 1865?–1946, 英國女小說家)。
Singer /ˈsɪŋə ; ˈsɪŋɚ/ 辛爾 (**1** Isaac Merrit, 1811–1875, 美國發明家; **2** Isaac Bashevis, 1904–, 生於波蘭之美籍猶太作家,曾獲 1978 年諾貝爾文學獎)。
Skeat /skiːt ; skit/ 斯基特 (Walter William, 1835–1912, 英國語言學家)。
Skelton /ˈskeltn ; ˈskɛltn̩/ 斯凱爾頓 (John, 1460?–1529, 英國詩人)。
Smetana /ˈsmetənə ; ˈsmɛtənə/ 史麥塔高 (Bedřich, 1824–1884, 捷克鋼琴家、作曲家及指揮家)。
Smith /smɪθ ; smɪθ/ 斯密 (**1** Adam, 1723–1790, 蘇格蘭經濟學家; **2** Alfred Emanuel, 1873–1944, 美國從政者; **3** Goldwin, 1823–1910, 英國歷史學家及國際法專家; **4** Joseph, 1805–1844, 美國 Mormon 教會創始人; **5** Sydney, 1771–1845, 英國散文家; **6** William, 1769–1839, 英國地質學家; **7** Winchell, 1871–1933, 美國劇作家)。
Smithson /ˈsmɪθsn ; ˈsmɪθsn̩/ 斯密生 (James, 1765–1829, 英國化學家及礦物學家)。
Smollett /ˈsmɒlɪt;ˈsmɑlɪt/ 斯摩里特 (Tobias George, 1721–1771, 英國作家)。
Smyth /smaɪθ ; smaɪθ/ 史邁司 (Henry De Wolf, 1898–, 美國物理學家)。
Snowden /ˈsnəʊdn ; ˈsnodn̩/ 斯諾登 (Philip, 1864–1937, 英國經濟學家及從政者)。
Socinus /səʊˈsaɪnəs ; soˈsaɪnəs/ 蘇塞納斯 (Faustus, 1539–1604, 原名 Fausto Sozzini, 義大利宗教改革家)。
Socrates /ˈsɒkrətiːz ; ˈsɑkrətiz/ 蘇格拉底 (470?–399 B.C., 希臘哲學家)。
Soddy /ˈsɒdɪ ; ˈsɑdɪ/ 蘇第 (Frederick, 1877–1956, 英國化學家,曾獲 1921 年諾貝爾化學獎)。
Söderblom /ˈsʌdəblʊm ; ˈsʌdɚ,blʊm/ 蘇德卜龍 (Nathan, 1866–1931, 瑞典神學家,曾獲 1930 年諾貝爾和平獎)。
Solon /ˈsəʊlɒn ; ˈsolən/ 梭倫 (638?–?559 B.C., 雅典立法者)。
Solzhenitsyn /ˌsəʊlʒəˈniːtsən ; ˌsolʒəˈnitsən/ 索忍尼辛

(Aleksandr Isayevich, 1918–, 俄國小說家,曾獲 1970 年諾貝爾文學獎)。
Sophocles /ˈsɒfəkliːz ; ˈsafəkliz/ 沙孚克里斯 (496?–406 B.C., 希臘悲劇作家)。
Southey /ˈsaʊðɪ ; ˈsaʊðɪ/ 索迪 (Robert, 1774–1843, 英國作家,於 1813–34 榮膺桂冠詩人)。
Sparks /spɑːks ; sparks/ 史巴克斯 (Jared, 1789–1866, 美國歷史學家)。
Spemann /ˈʃpeɪmɑːn; ˈʃpe,man/ 施培曼 (Hans, 1869–1941, 德國動物學家,曾獲 1935 年諾貝爾醫學獎)。
Spencer /ˈspensə ; ˈspɛnsɚ/ 斯賓塞 (Herbert, 1820–1903, 英國哲學家)。
Spender /ˈspendə; ˈspɛndɚ/ 斯賓德 (Stephen Harold, 1909–, 英國詩人及批評家)。
Spengler /ˈspeŋlə ; ˈspɛŋ(g)lɚ/ 史賓勒 (Oswald, 1880–1936, 德國哲學家)。
Spenser /ˈspensə ; ˈspɛnsɚ/ 斯賓塞 (Edmund, 1552–1599, 英國詩人,於 1591–99 榮膺桂冠詩人)。
Spinoza /spɪˈnəʊzə ; spɪˈnozə/ 斯賓諾莎 (Baruch 或 Benedict, 1632–1677, 荷蘭哲學家)。
Spitteler /ˈʃpɪtlə ; ˈʃpɪt(ə)lɚ/ 斯比特勒 (Carl, 1845–1924, 筆名 Felix Tandem, 瑞士作家,曾獲 1919 年諾貝爾文學獎)。
Ssŭ-ma Ch'ien /ˈsʊ ˈmɑː ˈtʃjæn ; ˈsʊ ˈma ˈtʃjɛn/ 司馬遷 (145–?86 B.C., 中國漢朝編史家)。
Ssŭ-ma Kuang /ˈsʊ ˈmɑː ˈgwɑːŋ ; ˈsʊ ˈma ˈgwaŋ/ 司馬光 (1019–1086, 中國宋朝編史家)。
Ssŭ-ma Yen /ˈsʊ ˈmɑː ˈjen ; ˈsʊ ˈma ˈjɛn/ 司馬炎 (236–290, 中國晉朝開國之主,即晉武帝,在位二十五年)。
Stalin /ˈstɑːlɪn ; ˈstalɪn/ 史達林 (Joseph, 原名 Iosif Vissarionovich Dzhugashvili, 1879–1953, 蘇聯政治領袖)。
Stanley /ˈstænlɪ ; ˈstænlɪ/ 斯坦萊 (**1** Sir Henry Morton, 1841–1904, 英國非洲探險家; **2** Wendell Meredith, 1904–1971, 美國生物化學家,與 J. H. Northrop 及 J. B. Sumner 同獲 1946 年諾貝爾化學獎)。
Stanton /ˈstɑːntən ; ˈstæntən/ 斯坦東 (Edwin McMasters, 1814–1869, 美國律師及政治家)。
Stark /stɑːk ; stark/ 施塔克 (**1** Johannes, 1874–1957, 德國物理學家, 曾獲 1919 年諾貝爾物理獎; **2** John, 1728–1822, 美國獨立戰爭時之將軍)。
Staudinger /ˈstaʊdɪŋgə ; ˈstaʊdɪŋ(g)ɚ/ 史滔丁格 (Hermann, 1881–1965, 德國化學家,曾獲 1953 年諾貝爾化學獎)。
Steele /stiːl ; stil/ 斯蒂爾 (Sir Richard, 1672–1729, 英國散文家及劇作家)。
Stein /staɪn ; staɪn/ 斯坦因 (Gertrude, 1874–1946, 美國女作家)。
Steinbeck /ˈstaɪnbek ; ˈstaɪnbɛk/ 史坦培克 (John Ernst, 1902–1968, 美國小說家,曾獲 1962 年諾貝爾文學獎)。
Stendhal /stenˈdɑːl ; stɛnˈdal/ 史湯達爾 (Marie Henrie Beyle 之筆名, 1783–1842, 法國作家)。
Stephen /ˈstiːvn ; ˈstivn̩/ 史蒂芬 (**1** 1097?–1154, 亦稱 ~ of Blois, 英王,在位期間 1135–54; **2** Sir Leslie, 1832–1904, 英國哲學家、批評家及傳記作家)。
Stephens /ˈstiːvnz ; ˈstivn̩z/ 史蒂芬斯 (**1** Alexander Hamilton, 1812–1883, 美國從政者; **2** James, 1882–1950, 愛爾蘭詩人及小說家)。
Stephenson /ˈstiːvnsn; ˈstivn̩sn̩/ 史蒂芬生 (**1** George, 1781–1848, 英國發明家,發明蒸汽機車,於 1825 年首先造成載運客貨的火車; **2** 其子 Robert, 1803–1859, 英國工程師)。
Stern /stɜːn ; stɝn/ 史德因 (Otto, 1888–1969, 生於德國之美國物理學家,曾獲 1943 年諾貝爾物理獎)。
Sterne /stɜːn ; stɝn/ 史特恩 (Laurence, 1713–1768, 英國小說家)。
Stevens /ˈstiːvnz ; ˈstivn̩z/ 史蒂文斯 (**1** John, 1749–1838, 美國發明家; **2** Thaddeus, 1792–1868, 美國律師及從政者)。
Stewart /ˈstjuːət ; ˈst(j)ʊɚt/ 史圖爾特 (**1** Dugald, 1753–1828, 蘇格蘭哲學家; **2** Robert, 1769–1822, 英國政治家)。
Stoddard /ˈstɒdəd ; ˈstadɚd/ 史達德爾 (Richard Henry, 1825–1903, 美國詩人及批評家)。
Stone /stəʊn ; ston/ 史頓 (Harlan Fiske, 1872–1946, 美國法學家)。
Story /ˈstɔːrɪ ; ˈstɔrɪ/ 史多里 (**1** Joseph, 1779–1845, 美國法學家; **2** 其子 William Wetmore, 1819–1895, 美國雕刻家及作家)。
Stow /stəʊ ; sto/ 史陀 (John, 1525?–1605, 英國歷史學家及古物專家)。
Stowe /stəʊ ; sto/ 史陀 (Harriet Elizabeth, 1811–1896, 本姓Beecher, 美國女作家)。
Strabo /ˈstreɪbəʊ ; ˈstrebo/ 史特雷波 (63 B.C. ?–? A.D. 24, 希臘地理學家)。
Strafford /ˈstræfəd ; ˈstræfɚd/ 史特拉佛 (本名 Sir Thomas Wentworth, 1593–1641, 英國政治家)。
Straus /straʊs ; straʊs/ 史特勞士 (Oskar, 1870–1954, 生於奧國之法國作曲家)。
Strauss /straʊs ; straʊs/ 史特勞士 (**1** David Friedrich, 1808–1874, 德國神學家及哲學家; **2** Johann, 1804–1849, 其子 Johann, 1825–1899, 及 Josef, 1827–1870, 均爲奧國作曲家; **3** Richard, 1864–1949, 德國作曲家)。
Stravinsky /strəˈvɪnskɪ ; strəˈvɪnskɪ/ 史特拉芬斯基 (Igor Fëdorovich, 1882–1971, 生於俄國之美國作曲家)。
Stresemann /ˈstreɪzəmɑːn ; ˈstrezə,man/ 施德萊斯曼 (Gustav, 1878–1929, 德國政治家,與 A. Briand 同獲 1926 年諾貝爾和平獎)。
Strindberg /ˈstrɪndbɜːg ; ˈstrɪn(d)bɝg/ 史特林柏 (August, 1849–1912, 瑞典劇作家及小說家,被認爲是現代瑞典最偉大的作家,有 'the Shakespeare of Sweden' 之稱)。
Stuart /ˈstjuːət ; ˈst(j)ʊɚt/ 史圖爾特 (Gilbert Charles, 1755–1828, 美國畫家)。
Stubbs /stʌbz ; stʌbz/ 史塔卜斯 (William, 1825–1901, 英國歷史學家)。
Suckling /ˈsʌklɪŋ ; ˈsʌklɪŋ/ 索克令 (Sir John, 1609–1642, 英國詩人)。
Sue /suː ; su/ 蘇 (Eugène, 1804–1857, 本名 Marie Joseph, 法國小說家)。
Suetonius /swiːˈtəʊnjəs; swiˈtonjəs/ 史維都尼亞斯(全名 Gaius Suetonius Tranquillus, 二世紀時之羅馬傳記作家及歷史學家)。
Sukarno /suːˈkɑːnəʊ ; suˈkarno/ 蘇加諾 (Achmed, 1901–1970, 印尼政治家, 1945–67 任總統)。
Suleiman I /ˈsuːleɪmɑːn; ˈsuleman/ 蘇利曼一世 (1496?–1566, 世稱 the Magnificent, Ottoman 蘇丹,在位期間 1520–66)。
Sulla /ˈsʌlə ; ˈsʌlə/ 索拉 (138–78 B.C., 全名 Lucius Cornelius Sulla Felix, 羅馬將軍及政治家)。
Sullivan /ˈsʌlɪvən ; ˈsʌlɪvən/ 索利凡 (Sir Arthur Seymour, 1842–1900, 英國作曲家)。
Sully /ˈsʌlɪ ; ˈsʌlɪ/ 索列 (**1** 本名 Maximilien de Béthune, 1560–1641, 法國政治家; **2** Thomas, 1783–1872, 旅居美國之英國畫家)。
Sully Prudhomme /ˈsʌlɪpruːˈdʌm ; ˈsʌlɪpruˈdʌm/ 蘇里普魯敦 (René François Armand, 1839–1907, 法國詩人及批評家,曾獲 1901 年首屆諾貝爾文學獎)。
Sumner /ˈsʌmnə ; ˈsʌmnɚ/ 索姆奈 (**1** Charles, 1811–1874, 美國政治家及演說家; **2** James Batcheller, 1887–1955, 美國生物化學家,與 J. H. Northrop 及 W. M. Stanley 同獲 1946 年諾貝爾化學獎)。
Sun Yat-sen /ˈsuːn ˈjɑːt ˈsen ; ˈsun ˈjat ˈsɛn/ 孫逸仙 (1866–1925, 即孫中山先生,中國政治家,中華民國國父)。
Surrey /ˈsʌrɪ ; ˈsʌrɪ/ 薩里 (參看 H. Howard)。
Su Shih/ ˈsuː ˈʃɪ ; ˈsu ˈʃɪ/ 蘇軾 (1036–1101, 自號東坡居士,中國宋朝文學家)。
Suttner, von /ˈzʊtnə ; ˈzʊtnɚ/ 蘇德納夫人 (Bertha, 1843–1914, 本姓 Kinsky, 奧國作家及和平主義者,曾獲 1905 年諾貝爾和平獎)。
Svedberg /ˈsfedbɜːg ; ˈsfɛd,bɝg/ 史維德堡 (Theodor 或 The, 1884–1971, 瑞典化學家,曾獲 1926 年諾貝爾化學獎)。
Swedenborg /ˈswiːdnbɔːg ; ˈswidn̩bɔrg/ 史維東堡 (Emanuel, 1688–1772, 瑞典哲學家及宗教類作家)。
Sweet /swiːt ; swit/ 史威特 (Henry, 1845–1912, 英國語音學家及語言學家)。

Swift /swɪft ; swɪft/ 史威夫特 (Jonathan, 1667–1745, 生於愛爾蘭之英國諷刺文家)。
Swinburne /ˈswɪnbən ; ˈswɪnbɚn/ 史文本恩 (Algernon Charles, 1837–1909, 英國詩人及批評家)。
Symonds /ˈsaɪmən(d)z ; ˈsaɪmən(d)z/ 塞門玆 (John Addington, 1840–1893, 英國學者、詩人及作家)。
Symons /ˈsaɪmənz ; ˈsaɪmənz/ 塞門玆 (Arthur, 1865–1945, 英國詩人及批評家)。
Synge /sɪŋ ; sɪŋ/ 辛 (**1** John Millington, 1871–1909, 愛爾蘭詩人及劇作家; **2** Richard Laurence Millington, 1914–, 英國生物化學家,與 A. J. P. Martin 同獲 1952 年諾貝爾化學獎)。
Szent-Györgyi von Nagyrapolt /sentˈdʒɜːdʒ(ɪ) fən ˈnɑːdʒˈrɑːpəʊlt ; sɛntˈdʒɝdʒ(ɪ) fən ˈnɑdʒˈrɑpolt/ 桑德哲基 (Albert, 1893–, 匈牙利化學家,曾獲 1937 年諾貝爾醫學獎)。
Tacitus /ˈtæsɪtəs ; ˈtæsɪtəs/ 泰西塔斯 (Cornelius, 55?–?117, 羅馬歷史學家)。
Taft /tɑːft ; tæft/ 塔虎特 (**1** Lorado, 1860–1936, 美國雕刻家; **2** Robert Alphonso, 1889–1953, 美國律師及從政者; **3** R. A. 之父 William Howard, 1857–1930, 於 1909–13 任美國第廿七任總統)。
Tagore /təˈgɔː ; təˈgɔr/ 泰戈爾 (Sir Rabindranath, 1861–1941, 印度詩人,曾獲 1913 年諾貝爾文學獎)。
Taine /teɪn ; ten/ 泰恩 (Hippolyte Adolphe, 1828–1893, 法國哲學家及批評家)。
Tamm /tɑːm ; tɑm/ 坦姆 (Igor Yevgenievich, 1895–1971, 俄國物理學家, 與 P. A. Cherenkov 及 I. M. Frank 同獲 1958 年諾貝爾物理獎)。
Tancred /ˈtæŋkred ; ˈtæŋkrɪd/ 唐克列德 (1078?–1112, 第一次十字軍東征之 Norman 領袖)。
Tarkington /ˈtɑːkɪŋtən ; ˈtɑrkɪŋtən/ 塔金頓 ((Newton) Booth, 1869–1946, 美國小說家)。
Tasman /ˈtæzmən ; ˈtæzmən/ 塔斯曼 (Abel Janszoon, 1603–1659, 荷蘭航海家)。
Tasso /ˈtæsəʊ ; ˈtæso/ 塔索 (Torquato, 1544–1595, 義大利詩人)。
Tate /teɪt ; tet/ 泰特 (Nahum, 1652–1715, 英國劇作家, 於 1692–1715 榮膺桂冠詩人)。
Tatum /ˈteɪtəm ; ˈtetəm/ 泰塔姆 (Edward Lawrie, 1909–1975, 美國生物化學家, 與 G. W. Beadle 及 J. Lederberg 同獲 1958 年諾貝爾醫學獎)。
Taylor /ˈteɪlə ; ˈtelɚ/ 泰勒 (**1** (James) Bayard, 1825–1878, 美國作家; **2** (Joseph) Deems, 1885–1966, 美國作曲家及音樂批評家; **3** Jeremy, 1613–1667, 英國主教及作家; **4** Tom, 1817–1880, 英國劇作家; **5** Zachary, 1784–1850, 綽號 Old Rough-and-Ready, 於 1849–50 任美國第十二任總統)。
Tchaikovsky, Tschaikovsky /tʃaɪˈkɒfskɪ;tʃaɪˈkɔfskɪ/ 柴可夫斯基 (Pëtr Ilich, 1840–1893, 俄國作曲家)。
Tchekhov = Chekhov
Teller /ˈtelə ; ˈtɛlɚ/ 泰勒 (Edward, 1908–, 生於匈牙利之美國物理學家,有'氫彈之父'之稱)。
Temple /ˈtempl ; ˈtɛmpl̩/ 譚普爾 (Sir William, 1628–1699, 英國政治家及散文家)。
Teniers /ˈtenɪəz ; tɛˈnirs/ 但耶斯 (David, 1582–1649, 與其子 David, 1610–1690, 均爲法蘭德斯畫家)。
Tenniel /ˈtenjəl ; ˈtɛnjəl/ 但涅爾 (Sir John, 1820–1914, 英國卡通畫家及插畫家)。
Tennyson /ˈtenɪsn ; ˈtɛnɪsn̩/ 但尼生 (Alfred, 1809–1892, 英國詩人,於 1850–92 爲桂冠詩人)。
Terence /ˈterəns ; ˈtɛrəns/ 德倫西 (185?–159 B.C., 全名 Publius Terentius Afer, 羅馬劇作家)。
Tesla /ˈteslə ; ˈtɛslə/ 臺斯拉 (Nikola, 1856–1943, 生於克羅埃西亞之美國電學家及發明家)。
Thackeray /ˈθækərɪ ; ˈθæk(ə)rɪ/ 薩克萊 (William Makepeace, 1811–1863, 英國小說家)。
Thales /ˈθeɪliːz ; ˈθeliz/ 臺利斯 (640?–546 B.C., 希臘哲學家)。
Thatcher /ˈθætʃə ; ˈθætʃɚ/ 柴契爾夫人 (Margaret Hilda, 本姓 Roberts, 1925–, 自 1975 年起任英國保守黨黨魁, 1979 當選首相)。
Theiler /ˈtaɪlə ; ˈtaɪlɚ/ 翟易樓 (Max, 1899–1972, 旅居美國之南非熱帶醫學專家,曾獲 1951 年諾貝爾醫學獎)。
Themistocles /θɪˈmɪstəkliːz ; θɪˈmɪstəkliz/ 狄密斯托克利 (527?–?460 B.C., 雅典將軍及政治家)。
Theocritus /θɪˈɒkrɪtəs ; θiˈɑkrɪtəs/ 狄奧克里塔(紀元前三世紀之希臘詩人)。
Theodosius I /θɪəˈdəʊsjəs ; ˌθiəˈdoʃ(ɪ)əs/ 狄奧多西一世 (346?–395, 世稱 the Great, 羅馬將軍及皇帝,在位期間 379–395)。
Theophrastus /θɪəˈfræstəs ; ˌθiəˈfræstəs/ 狄奧佛拉斯塔 (371?–287 B.C., 希臘哲學家及博物學家)。
Theorell /ˈteɪərel ; ˌteəˈrɛl/ 泰歐洛 (Axel Hugo Theodor, 1903–, 瑞典生物化學家,曾獲 1955 年諾貝爾醫學獎)。
Thespis /ˈθespɪs ; ˈθɛspɪs/ 狄斯比斯(紀元前六世紀之希臘詩人,被尊爲悲劇之始祖)。
Thomas /ˈtɒməs ; ˈtɑməs/ 湯瑪斯 (Norman Mattoon, 1884–1968, 美國社會主義從政者)。
Thomas à Becket 參看 Becket。
Thomas a Kempis /-əˈkempɪs ; -əˈkɛmpɪs/ 湯瑪斯阿肯披斯 (1380–1471, 德國修士及作家,咸認其爲 The Imitation of Christ 一書之作者)。
Thompson /ˈtɒm(p)sn ; ˈtɑm(p)sn̩/ 湯普生 (**1** Benjamin, 1753–1814, 生於美國之英國物理學家與政治家; **2** Francis, 1859–1907, 英國詩人)。
Thomson /ˈtɒmsn ; ˈtɑmsn̩/ 湯姆生 (**1** Sir George Paget, 1892–1975, 英國物理學家,與 C. J. Davisson 同獲 1937 年諾貝爾物理獎; **2** James, 1700–1748, 蘇格蘭詩人; **3** John Arthur, 1861–1933, 蘇格蘭生物學家; **4** Sir Joseph John, 1856–1940, G. P. 之父,英國物理學家)。
Thoreau /ˈθɔːrəʊ ; ˈθɔro/ 索洛 (Henry David, 1817–1862, 美國作家)。
Thornton /ˈθɔːntən ; ˈθɔrntən/ 桑頓 (William, 1759–1828, 美國建築家)。
Thucydides /θjuːˈsɪdɪdiːz ; θjuˈsɪdədiz/ 修西狄底斯 (471?–?400 B.C., 希臘歷史學家)。
Tiberius /taɪˈbɪərɪəs ; taɪˈbɪrɪəs/ 臺比留 (42 B.C.–A.D. 37, 全名 ~ Claudius Nero Caesar, 羅馬皇帝, 在位期間 14–37)。
Tibullus /tɪˈbʌləs ; tɪˈbʌləs/ 狄巴拉斯 (Albius, 54?–?18 B.C., 羅馬詩人)。
Tiglath-pileser III /ˈtɪglæθpaɪˈliːzə ; ˈtɪglæθpaɪˈlizɚ/ 狄格拉派立玆三世 (?–727 B.C., 亞述 (Assyria) 國王, 在位期間 745–727 B.C.)。
Ting /tɪŋ ; tɪŋ/ 丁肇中 (Samuel Chao Chung, 1936–, 美籍華裔物理學家,與 B. Richter 同獲 1976 年諾貝爾物理獎)。
Tintoretto /ˌtɪntəˈretəʊ ; ˌtɪntəˈrɛto/ 丁都萊多 (Il, 1518–1594, 本名 Jacopo Robusti, 義大利畫家)。
Tiselius /təˈseɪlɪəs ; təˈselɪəs/ 狄西樓 (Arne Wilhelm Kaurin, 1902–1971, 瑞典生物化學家,曾獲 1948 年諾貝爾化學獎)。
Titian /ˈtɪʃən ; ˈtɪʃən/ 提申 (1477–1576, 本名 Tiziano Vecelli(o) 義大利畫家)。
Tito /ˈtiːtəʊ ; ˈtito/ 狄托 (參看 J. Broz)。
Titus /ˈtaɪtəs ; ˈtaɪtəs/ 臺塔斯 (40?–81, 全名 ~ Flavius Sabinus Vespasianus, 羅馬皇帝,在位期間 79–81)。
Todd /tɒd ; tɑd/ 陶德 (**1** David, 1855–1939, 美國天文學家; **2** Sir Alexander Robertus, 1907–, 英國化學家,曾獲 1957 年諾貝爾化學獎)。
Tolstoy, Tolstoi /ˈtɒlstɔɪ ; ˈtɑlstɔɪ/ 托爾斯泰 (Count Lev Nikolaevich, 1828–1910, 俄國小說家、哲學家及神秘主義者)。
Tomonaga /ˌtɒmɒˈnɑːgɑː ; ˌtoməˈnɑgə/ 朝永振一郎 (Shinichiro 1906–1979, 日本物理學家,與 R. P. Feynman 及 J. S. Schwinger 同獲 1965 年諾貝爾物理獎)。
Tone /təʊn ; ton/ 托恩 ((Theobald) Wolfe, 1763–1798, 愛爾蘭革命家)。
Tooke /tʊk ; tʊk/ 托克 ((John) Horne, 1736–1812, 英國急進派從政者及語言學家)。
Torricelli /ˌtɒrɪˈtʃelɪ ; ˌtɑrɪˈtʃɛlɪ/ 托里拆利 (Evangelista, 1608–1647, 義大利數學家及物理學家)。
Townes /taʊnz ; taʊnz/ 唐玆 (Charles Hard, 1915–, 美國物理學家及教育家, 與 N. G. Basov 及 A. M. Prokhorov 同獲 1964 年諾貝爾物理獎)。
Toynbee /ˈtɔɪnbɪ ; ˈtɔɪnbɪ/ 湯恩比 (Arnold Joseph, 1889–1975, 英國歷史學家)。

Trajan /ˈtreɪdʒən ; ˈtredʒən/ 圖雷眞 (52?-117, 本名 Marcus Ulpius Trajanus, 羅馬皇帝,在位期間 98-117)。
Trench /trentʃ ; trɛntʃ/ 脫蘭契 (Richard Chenevix, 1807-1886, 英國詩人及大主教)。
Trevelyan /trɪˈveljən;trɪˈvɛljən/ 脫利衞連 (**1** George Macaulay, 1876-1962, 英國歷史學家; **2** 其父 Sir George Otto, 1838-1928, 英國政治家、傳記作家及歷史學家)。
Trollope /ˈtrɒləp ; ˈtrɑləp/ 脫洛勒普 (Anthony, 1815-1882, 英國小說家)。
Truman /ˈtru:mən ; ˈtrumən/ 杜魯門 (Harry S., 1884-1973, 美國第三十三任總統,任期爲 1945-53)。
T'sai Lun /ˈtsaɪ ˈlʊn ; ˈtsaɪˈlʊn/ 蔡倫 (50?-?118 中國漢朝發明家,發明製紙方法)。
Tschaikovsky = Tchaikovsky
Tso-ch'iu Ming /ˈdzwɔ: ˈtʃjəʊ ˈmi:ŋ ; ˈdzwɔ ˈtʃɪu ˈmɪŋ/ 左丘明(中國周朝史學家)。
Tu Fu /ˈdu: ˈfu: ; ˈdu ˈfu/ 杜甫 (712-770, 中國唐代詩人)。
Turenne, de /tjʊˈren ; t(j)ʊˈrɛn/ 替倫 (Vicomte, 1611-1675, 本名 Henri de la Tour d'Auvergne, 法國元帥)。
Turner /ˈtɜ:nə ; ˈtɝnɚ/ 脫爾諾 (**1** Frederick Jackson, 1861-1932, 美國歷史學家; **2** Joseph Mallord William, 1775-1851, 英國畫家)。
Twain /tweɪn ; twen/ 馬克吐溫 (Mark, 爲 S. L. Clemens 之筆名)。
Tweed /twi:d ; twid/ 脫衞得 (William Marcy, 1823-1878, 美國從政者)。
Tyler /ˈtaɪlə ; ˈtaɪlɚ/ 泰勒 (John, 1790-1862, 於 1841-45 任美國第十任總統)。
Tyndale /ˈtɪndl ; ˈtɪndl̩/ 丁道爾 (William, 1492?-1536, 英國宗教改革家)。
Tyndall /ˈtɪndl ; ˈtɪndl̩/ 丁鐸爾 (John, 1820-1893, 英國物理學家)。
Tyrwhitt-Wilson /ˈtɪrɪt-ˈwɪlsn ; ˈtɪrɪt-ˈ wɪlsn̩/ 狄利特・威爾遜 (Gerald Hugh, 1883-1950, 英國作曲家及畫家)。
Uhland /ˈu:lənd ; ˈulənd/ 烏蘭特 (Johann Ludwig, 1787-1862, 德國詩人及歷史學家)。
Undset /ˈʊnset ; ˈʊnˌsɛt/ 翁塞特 (Sigrid, 1882-1949, 挪威女小說家,曾獲 1928 年諾貝爾文學獎)。
Upton /ˈʌptən ; ˈʌptən/ 額普頓 (Emory, 1839-1881, 美國將軍及作家)。
Urban II /ˈɜ:bən ; ˈɝbən/ 烏爾班二世 (1042?-1099, 於 1088-99 任羅馬教皇)。
Urey /ˈjʊərɪ ; ˈjʊrɪ/ 尤雷 (Harold Clayton, 1893-, 美國化學家,曾獲 1934 年諾貝爾化學獎)。
Urquhart /ˈɜ:kət ; ˈɝkɚt/ 烏爾喀特 (Sir Thomas, 1611-1660, 蘇格蘭作家及翻譯家)。
Valentinian /ˌvælənˈtɪnɪən;ˌvælənˈtɪnɪən/ 發蘭廷尼安 (羅馬三皇帝之名: **1** 一世, 321-375, 在位期間 364-375; **2** 二世, 372-392, 在位期間 375-392; **3** 三世, 419-455, 在位期間 425-455)。
Valerian /vəˈlɪərɪən ; vəˈlɪrɪən/ 瓦勒利安 (?-?269, 全名 Publius Licinius Valerianus, 羅馬皇帝, 在位期間 253-260)。
Vanbrugh /vænˈbru: ; vænˈbru/ 凡布魯 (Sir John, 1664-1726, 英國劇作家及建築家)。
Van Buren /væn ˈbjʊərən ; væn ˈbjʊrən/ 范標倫 (Martin, 1782-1862, 美國第八任總統,任期 1837-41)。
Vancouver /vænˈku:və ; vænˈkuvɚ/ 溫哥華 (George, 1757-1798, 英國航海家及探險家)。
Vandyke or **Van Dyck** /vænˈdaɪk ; vænˈdaɪk/ 范大克 (Sir Anthony, 1599-1641, 旅居英國之法蘭德斯 (Flanders) 畫家)。
Van't Hoff /vɑ:nt ˈhɒf ; vɑntˈhɔf/ 范特霍夫 (Jacobus Hendricus, 1852-1911, 荷蘭物理化學家,曾獲 1901 年首屆諾貝爾化學獎)。
Varro /ˈværəʊ ; ˈværo/ 瓦羅 (Marcus Terentius, 116-27 B.C., 羅馬學者及作家)。
Vaughan /vɔ:n ; vɔn/ 豐恩 (Henry, 1622-1695, 英國詩人)。
Vega, de /ˈveɪgə ; ˈvegə/ 威加 (Lope, 1562-1635, 全名 Lope Félix de Vega Carpio, 西班牙劇作家)。
Verdi /ˈveədɪ ; ˈvɛrdɪ/ 威爾第 (Giuseppe, 1813-1901, 義大利作曲家)。
Vergil or **Virgil** /ˈvɜ:dʒɪl ; ˈvɝdʒəl/ 威吉爾 (70-19 B.C., 全名 Publius Vergilius Maro, 羅馬詩人)。
Verne /veən ; vɛrn/ 威恩 (Jules, 1828-1905, 法國作家)。
Verner /ˈvɜ:nə ; ˈvɝnɚ/ 威爾納 (Karl Adolph, 1846-1896, 丹麥語言學家)。
Vernier /ˈvɜ:nɪə ; ˈvɝnɪɚ/ 威尼爾 (Pierre, 1580-1637, 法國數學家)。
Veronese /ˌverəˈneɪzɪ ; ˌvɛrəˈnezɪ/ 維洛內塞 (Paolo, 1528-1588, 本名 Paolo Cagliari, 義大利畫家)。
Vespasian /vesˈpeɪʒɪən ; vɛsˈpeʒ(ɪ)ən/ 維斯佩西安 (9-79, Titus Flavius Sabinus Vespasianus, 羅馬皇帝,在位期間 69-79)。
Victor Emmanuel I /ˈvɪktə ɪˈmænjʊəl ; ˈvɪktɚ ɪˈmænjʊəl/ 維多伊曼紐一世 (1759-1824, 於 1802-21 爲 Sardinia 國王)。
Victoria /vɪkˈtɔ:rɪə;vɪkˈtɔrɪə/ 維多利亞 (Alexandrina, 1819-1901, 英國女王,在位期間 1837-1901)。
Vinci, da /ˈvɪntʃɪ ; ˈvɪntʃɪ/ 達文西 (Leonardo, 1452-1519, 義大利畫家、雕刻家、建築家及工程師)。
Virchow /ˈfɪəkəʊ ; ˈfɪrko/ 斐爾科 (Rudolf, 1821-1902, 德國病理學家)。
Virgil = Vergil
Virtanen /ˈvɪətənen ; ˈvɪrtəˌnɛn/ 魏爾塔南 (Artturi Ilmari, 1895-1973, 芬蘭生物化學家,曾獲 1945 年諾貝爾化學獎)。
Vitruvius Pollio /vɪˈtru:vɪəs ˈpɔ:ljəʊ ; vɪˈtruvɪəs ˈpɑlɪo/ 維特魯維亞 (Marcus, 紀元前一世紀時之羅馬建築家及工程師)。
Vladimir /ˈvlædɪmɪə ; ˈvlædɪmɪr/ 烏拉底米爾 (956?-1015, 世稱 ～ the Great, 980-1015 之俄國統治者)。
Volta /ˈvɒltə ; ˈvɑltə/ 伏特 (Count Alessandro, 1745-1827, 義大利物理學家)。
Voltaire /ˈvɒlteə ; vɑlˈtɛr/ 瓦爾泰 (1694-1778, 本名 François Marie Arouet, 法國作家)。
Waals, van der /ˈvændəwɒlz ; ˈvændɚˌwɔlz/ 凡德瓦爾斯 (Johannes Diderik, 1837-1923, 荷蘭物理學家, 曾獲 1910 年諾貝爾物理獎)。
Wagner /ˈvɑ:gnə ; ˈvɑgnɚ/ 華格納 ((Wilhelm) Richard, 1813-1883, 德國詩人及作曲家)。
Wagner von Jauregg /-fɒn ˈjaʊrek ; -fɔn ˈjaʊˌrɛk/ 華格納耀雷格 (Julius, 1857-1940, 奧國神經學專家及精神病專家,曾獲 1927 年諾貝爾醫學獎)。
Waksman /ˈwɑ:ksmən ; ˈwɑksmən/ 瓦克斯曼 (Selman Abraham, 1888-1973, 生於烏克蘭之美國微生物學家,曾獲 1952 年諾貝爾醫學獎)。
Waldemar (or Valdemar) I /ˈvældəmɑ: ; ˈwɔldəmɑr/ 瓦德瑪一世 (1131-1182, 丹麥國王,世稱 the Great, 在位期間 1157-82)。
Waldersee, von /ˈvɑ:ldəzeɪ;ˈvɑldɚze/ 瓦德西 (Count Alfred, 1832-1904, 德國陸軍元帥)。
Walker /ˈwɔ:kə ; ˈwɔkɚ/ 瓦克爾 (Francis Amasa, 1840-1897, 美國經濟學家)。
Wallace /ˈwɒləs ; ˈwɑləs/ 華萊士 (**1** Alfred Russel, 1823-1913, 英國博物學家; **2** Henry Agard, 1888-1965, 美國農學家及從政者,於 1941-45 任副總統)。
Wallach /ˈwɒlək ; ˈwɑlək/ 瓦拉克 (Otto, 1847-1931, 德國化學家,曾獲 1910 年諾貝爾化學獎)。
Walpole /ˈwɔ:lpəʊl ; ˈwɔlpol/ 華爾波爾 (**1** Horace 或 Horatio, 1717-1797, 英國作家; **2** Sir Hugh Seymour, 1884-1941, 英國小說家; **3** Sir Robert, 1676-1745, 英國政治家, Horace 之父)。
Walter /ˈwɔ:ltə ; ˈwɔltɚ/ 華爾德 (John, 1739-1812, 英國新聞記者)。
Walton /ˈwɒltn ; ˈwɔltn̩/ 華爾頓 (Ernest Thomas Sinton, 1903-, 愛爾蘭物理學家,與 J. D. Cockcroft 同獲 1951 年諾貝爾物理獎; 2 Izaak, 1593-1683, 英國作家)。
Warburg /ˈwɔ:bɜ:g ; ˈwɔrˌbɝg/ 華爾堡 (Otto Heinrich, 1883-1970, 德國生理學家,曾獲 1931 年諾貝爾醫學獎)。
Ward /wɔ:d ; wɔrd/ 華德 (**1** Sir Adolphus William,

1837–1924, 英國歷史學家; **2** Mary Augusta, 1851–1920, 亦稱 Mrs. Humphry Ward, 本姓 Arnold, 英國女小說家)。

Warner /ˈwɔːnə ; ˈwɔrnɚ/ 華納 (Charles Dudley, 1829–1900, 美國編輯及散文家)。

Warren /ˈwɒrɪn ; ˈwɑrɪn/ 華倫 (**1** Earl, 1891–1974, 美國律師及從政者, 1953–69, 任最高法院院長; **2** Joseph, 1741–1775, 美國醫生及將軍; **3** Robert Penn, 1905–, 美國作家及教育家; **4** Whitney, 1864–1943, 美國建築家)。

Warton /ˈwɔːtn ; ˈwɔrtn̩/ 華頓 (Thomas, 1728–1790, 英國文學史專家及批評家, 於 1785–90 爲桂冠詩人)。

Warwick /ˈwɒrɪk ; ˈwɑrɪk/ 華瑞克 (Earl of, 本名 Richard Neville, 1428–1471, 世稱 the Kingmaker, 英國軍人及政治家)。

Washington /ˈwɒʃɪŋtən; ˈwɑʃɪŋtən/ 華盛頓 (**1** Booker Taliaferro, 1856–1915, 美國教育家; **2** George, 1732–1799, 美國將軍, 於 1789–97 任美國第一任總統)。

Watson /ˈwɒtsn ; ˈwɑtsn̩/ 華特生 (**1** John, 1850–1907, 筆名 Ian Maclaren, 蘇格蘭牧師及作家; **2** John Broadus, 1878–1958, 美國心理學家; **3** Sir William, 1858–1935, 英國詩人; **4** James Dewey, 1928–, 美國遺傳學家, 與 F. H. C. Crick 及 M. H. F. Wilkins 同獲 1962 年諾貝爾醫學獎)。

Watson-Watt /-ˈwɒt ; -ˈwɑt/ 華特森瓦特 (Sir Robert Alexander, 1892–1973, 蘇格蘭物理學家)。

Watt /wɒt ; wɑt/ 瓦特 (James, 1736–1819, 蘇格蘭發明家)。

Watteau /ˈwɒtəʊ ; wɑˈto/ 瓦都 (Jean Antoine, 1684–1721, 法國畫家)。

Waugh /wɔː ; wɔ/ 瓦渥 (Evelyn Arthur St. John, 1903–1966, 英國作家)。

Wayne /weɪn ; wen/ 威恩 (Anthony, 1745–1796, 世稱 Mad Anthony, 美國革命時期之將軍)。

Webb /web ; wɛb/ 韋布 (**1** Beatrice, 1858–1943, 本姓 Potter, 英國女經濟學家及社會主義者; **2** 其夫 Sidney James, 1859–1947, 英國經濟學家及社會主義者)。

Weber /ˈveɪbə ; ˈvebɚ/ 韋伯 (1 Ernst Heinrich, 1795–1878, 德國生理學家; **2** Baron, Karl Maria Friedrich Ernst von, 1786–1826, 德國作曲家及指揮家; **3** Wilhelm Eduard, 1804–1891, E. H. 之弟, 德國物理學家; **4** Max, 1864–1920, 德國社會學家及經濟學家)。

Webster /ˈwebstə ; ˈwɛbstɚ/ 韋伯斯特 (**1** Daniel, 1782–1852, 美國政治家及演說家; **2** John, 1580?–?1625, 英國劇作家; **3** Noah, 1758–1843, 美國作家及辭典編纂家)。

Wedgwood /ˈwedʒwʊd ; ˈwɛdʒwʊd/ 威基伍 (Josiah, 1730–1795, 英國陶器製造家)。

Weems /wiːmz ; wimz/ 韋姆茲 (Mason Locke, 1759–1825, 亦稱 Parson ～, 美國牧師及傳記作家)。

Weir /wɪə ; wɪr/ 韋爾 (Robert Walter, 1803–1889, 與其二子, John Ferguson, 1841–1926, 與 Julian Alden, 1852–1919, 皆爲美國畫家)。

Welch /welʃ ; wɛl(t)ʃ/ 韋爾契 (William Henry, 1850–1934, 美國病理學家)。

Weller /ˈwelə ; ˈwɛlɚ/ 魏勒 (Thomas Huckle, 1915–, 美國公共衞生專家及醫生, 與 F. C. Robbins 及 J. F. Enders 同獲 1954 年諾貝爾醫學獎)。

Wellesley /ˈwelzlɪ ; ˈwɛlzlɪ/ 威爾斯利 (Richard Colley, 1760–1842, 英國政治家, 於 1797–1805 任印度總督)。

Wellington /ˈwelɪŋtən ; ˈwɛlɪŋtən/ 威靈頓 (Duke of, 本名 Arthur Wellesley, 1769–1852, 英國將軍及政治家)。

Wells /welz ; wɛlz/ 威爾斯 (Herbert George, 1866–1946, 英國小說家、歷史學家及社會學家)。

Wendell /ˈwendl ; ˈwɛndl̩/ 溫德爾 (Barrett, 1855–1921, 美國學者)。

Wentworth /ˈwentwɜːθ ; ˈwɛntˌwɝθ/ 溫特渥 (William Charles, 1793–1872, 澳大利亞政治家)。

Werner /ˈveənə ; ˈvɛrnɚ/ 魏納 (Alfred, 1866–1919, 瑞士化學家, 曾獲 1913 年諾貝爾化學獎)。

Wesley /ˈwezlɪ ; ˈwɛzlɪ/ 衞斯理 (**1** Charles, 1707–1788, 英國美以美教會傳教士及聖詩作家; **2** 其兄 John, 1703–1791, 英國神學家、傳教士及美以美教會 (Methodism) 創始人)。

West /west ; wɛst/ 威斯特 (**1** Benjamin, 1738–1820, 旅居英國之美國畫家; **2** Dame Rebecca, 1892–, 眞名爲 Cicily Isabel Fairfield, 英國女批評家及小說家)。

Westcott /ˈwes(t)kət ; ˈwɛs(t)kət/ 威斯考特 (Edward Noyes, 1846–1898, 美國銀行家及小說家)。

Weyman /ˈweɪmən ; ˈwemən/ 魏曼 (Stanley John, 1855–1928, 英國小說家)。

Wharton /ˈwɔːtn ; ˈ(h)wɔrtn̩/ 華爾敦 (Edith Newbold, 1862–1937, 本姓 Jones, 美國女小說家)。

Wheatstone /ˈwiːtstən ; ˈ(h)witstən/ 惠斯登 (Sir Charles, 1802–1875, 英國物理學家及發明家)。

Whipple /ˈwɪpl ; ˈ(h)wɪpl̩/ 惠普爾 (George Hoyt, 1878–1976, 美國病理學家, 與 G. R. Minot 及 W. P. Murphy 同獲 1934 年諾貝爾醫學獎)。

Whistler /ˈwɪslə ; ˈ(h)wɪslɚ/ 惠斯勒 (James Abbott McNeill, 1834–1903, 美國畫家及蝕刻家)。

White /waɪt ; (h)waɪt/ 懷特 (**1** Andrew Dickson, 1832–1918, 美國教育家及外交家; **2** Edward Douglass, 1845–1921, 美國法學家; **3** Gilbert, 1720–1793, 英國傳教士及博物學家; **4** Patrick Victor Martindale, 1912–, 澳洲作家, 曾獲 1973 年諾貝爾文學獎; **5** Stanford, 1853–1906, 美國建築家; **6** Stewart Edward, 1873–1946, 美國小說家; **7** William Allen, 1868–1944, 美國新聞記者及作家)。

Whitehead /ˈwaɪthed; ˈ(h)waɪtˌhɛd/ 懷特海 (**1** Alfred North, 1861–1947, 英國數學家及哲學家; **2** William, 1715–1785, 英國劇作家, 於 1757–85 爲桂冠詩人)。

Whitman /ˈwɪtmən ; ˈ(h)wɪtmən/ 惠特曼 (Walt, 原稱 Walter, 1819–1892, 美國詩人)。

Whitney /ˈwɪtnɪ ; ˈ(h)wɪtnɪ/ 惠特尼 (**1** Eli, 1765–1825, 美國發明家; **2** Josiah Dwight, 1819–1896, 美國科學家; **3** William Dwight, 1827–1894, J. D. 之弟, 美國語言學家)。

Whittier /ˈwɪtɪə ; ˈ(h)wɪtɪɚ/ 惠蒂爾 (John Greenleaf, 1807–1892, 有 the Quaker Poet 之稱, 美國詩人)。

Wieland /ˈviːlɑːnt ; ˈviˌlɑnt/ 魏蘭德 (Heinrich, 1877–1957, 德國化學家, 曾獲 1927 年諾貝爾化學獎)。

Wien /viːn ; vin/ 韋恩 (Wilhelm, 1864–1928, 德國物理學家, 曾獲 1911 年諾貝爾物理獎)。

Wiggins /ˈwɪgɪnz ; ˈwɪgɪnz/ 威金茲 (Carleton, 1848–1932; 其子 Guy Carleton, 1883–1962, 皆爲美國畫家)。

Wigner /ˈwɪgnə ; ˈwɪgnɚ/ 魏格納 (Eugene Paul, 1902–, 生於匈牙利之美國物理學家, 與 M. G. Mayer 及 J. H. D. Jensen 同獲 1963 年諾貝爾物理獎)。

Wilberforce /ˈwɪlbəfɔːs; ˈwɪlbɚfɔrs/ 韋爾伯佛思 (William, 1759–1833, 英國慈善家及主張廢除奴隸制度者)。

Wilde /waɪld ; waɪld/ 王爾德 (Oscar Fingal O'Flahertie Wills, 1854–1900, 生於愛爾蘭之英國戲劇家、詩人、小說家、散文家及批評家)。

Wilder /ˈwaɪldə ; ˈwaɪldɚ/ 威爾德 (Thornton Niven, 1897–1975, 美國小說家及劇作家)。

Wilkins /ˈwɪlkɪnz ; ˈwɪlkɪnz/ 威爾金斯 (Maurice Hugh Frederick, 1916–, 生於紐西蘭之英國生物物理學家, 與 J. D. Watson 及 F. H. C. Crick 同獲 1962 年諾貝爾醫學獎)。

Willard /ˈwɪlɑːd ; ˈwɪlɚd/ 威勒德 (**1** Emma, 1787–1870, 本姓 Hart, 美國女教育家; **2** Frances Elizabeth Caroline, 1839–1898, 美國女教育家及改革家)。

Willcocks /ˈwɪlkɑks ; ˈwɪlkɑks/ 威爾考克 (Sir William, 1852–1932, 英國工程師)。

William I /ˈwɪljəm ; ˈwɪljəm/ 威廉一世 (**1** 1027–1087, 世稱 William the Conqueror, 英國國王, 在位期間 1066–87; **2** 1533–1584, 世稱 William the Silent, 荷蘭獨立戰爭之領袖; **3** 1797–1888, 於 1861–88 爲普魯士王, 並於 1871–88 爲德國皇帝)。

William II 威廉二世 (**1** 1056?–1100, 亦稱 William Rufus, 英國國王, 在位期間 1087–1100; 2 1859–1941, 德國皇帝及普魯士王, 在位期間1888–1918)。

William III 威廉三世 (1650–1702, 於 1689–1702 爲英國國王, 1694 以前與其后 Mary II 共同秉政)。

William IV 威廉四世 (1765–1837, 世稱 Sailor-King, 英國國王, 在位期間 1830–37)。

Willis /ˈwɪlɪs ; ˈwɪlɪs/ 韋利斯 (Nathaniel Parker, 1806–1867, 美國編輯及作家)。

Willstätter /ˈvɪlʃtetə ; ˈvɪl͵ʃtɛtɚ/ 韋爾施泰德 (Richard, 1872–1942, 德國化學家，曾獲 1915 年諾貝爾化學獎)。

Wilson /ˈwɪlsn ; ˈwɪlsn̩/ 威爾遜 (**1** Charles Thomson Rees, 1869–1959, 蘇格蘭物理學家,與 A. H. Compton 同獲 1927 年諾貝爾物理獎; **2** Sir Henry Hughes, 1864–1922, 英國陸軍元帥; **3** (Thomas) Woodrow, 1856–1924, 於 1913–21 任美國第廿八任總統，曾獲 1919 年諾貝爾和平獎)。

Windaus /ˈvɪndaʊs ; ˈvɪndaʊs/ 溫道斯 (Adolf, 1876–1959, 德國化學家,曾獲 1928 年諾貝爾化學獎)。

Wister /ˈwɪstə ; ˈwɪstɚ/ 威斯特 (Owen, 1860–1938, 美國小說家)。

Wither(s) /ˈwɪðə(z) ; ˈwɪðɚ(z)/ 韋娍爾 (George, 1588–1667, 英國詩人)。

Wittgenstein /ˈvɪtgənstaɪn ; ˈvɪtgən͵staɪn/ 維根斯坦 (Ludwig Josef Johan, 1889–1951, 生於奧國之英國哲學家)。

Wodehouse /ˈwʊdhaʊs ; ˈwʊd͵haʊs/ 伍德霍斯 (Pelham Grenville, 1881–1975, 生於英國之美國小說家)。

Wolf /vɔːlf ; vɔlf/ 渥爾夫 (Friedrich August, 1759–1824, 德國語言學家)。

Wolfe /wʊlf ; wʊlf/ 渥爾夫 (**1** Charles, 1791–1823, 愛爾蘭詩人; **2** James, 1727–1759, 英國將軍; **3** Thomas Clayton, 1900–1938, 美國小說家)。

Wolff[1] /vɒlf ; vɔlf/ 渥爾夫 (Kaspar Friedrich, 1733–1794, 德國解剖學家)。

Wolf(f)[2]**, von** 渥爾夫 (Baron Christian, 1679–1754, 德國哲學家及數學家)。

Wolfram von Eschenbach /ˈwʊlfrəm fɒn ˈeʃənbɑːk ; ˈwʊlfrəm fɔn ˈɛʃənbɑk/ 渥爾夫拉姆 (1170?–?1220, 德國詩人)。

Wollaston /ˈwʊləstən ; ˈwʊləstən/ 渥拉斯頓 (William Hyde, 1766–1828, 英國化學家及物理學家)。

Wood /wʊd ; wʊd/ 伍德 (Grant, 1892–1942, 美國畫家)。

Woodward /ˈwʊdwəd ; ˈwʊdwɚd/ 伍德華德 (Robert Burns, 1917–1979, 美國化學家,曾獲 1965 年諾貝爾化學獎)。

Woolf /wʊlf ; wʊlf/ 吳爾芙 (Virginia, 1882–1941, 本姓 Stephen, 英國女作家)。

Woolley /ˈwʊlɪ ; ˈwʊlɪ/ 伍理 (Sir Charles Leonard, 1880–1960, 英國考古學家)。

Worcester /ˈwʊstə ; ˈwʊstɚ/ 渥斯特 (Joseph Emerson, 1784–1865, 美國辭典編纂家)。

Wordsworth /ˈwɜːdzwəθ ; ˈwɝdzwɚθ/ 華茨華斯 (William, 1770–1850, 英國詩人,於 1843–50 爲桂冠詩人)。

Wotton /ˈwɒtn ; ˈwʊtn̩/ 渥敦 (Sir Henry, 1568–1639, 英國外交家及詩人)。

Wren /ren ; rɛn/ 列恩 (Sir Christopher, 1632–1723, 英國建築家)。

Wright /raɪt ; raɪt/ 萊特 (**1** Frank Lloyd, 1869–1959, 美國建築家; **2** Joseph, 1855–1930, 英國語言學家; **3** Orville, 1871–1948, 及其兄 Wilbur, 1867–1912, 皆爲美國飛行先驅)。

Wu Tsê-t'ien /ˈwuː ˈdzɜː ˈtjen ; ˈwu ˈdzə ˈtjɛn/ 武則天 (624–705, 中國唐代之女皇帝,改國號爲周)。

Wyat(t) /ˈwaɪət ; ˈwaɪət/ 韋艾特 (Sir Thomas, 1503?–1542, 英國詩人及外交家)。

Wycherley /ˈwɪtʃəlɪ ; ˈwɪtʃɚlɪ/ 韋策利 (William, 1640?–1716, 英國劇作家)。

Wycliffe /ˈwɪklɪf ; ˈwɪklɪf/ 威克利夫 (John, 1320?–1384, 英國宗教改革家及聖經譯者)。

Wyld /waɪld ; waɪld/ 偉爾德 (Henry Cecil Kennedy, 1870–1945, 英國語言學家及辭典編纂家)。

Wylie /ˈwaɪlɪ ; ˈwaɪlɪ/ 偉利 (Elinor Morton, 1885–1928, 本姓 Hoyt, 美國女詩人及小說家)。

Wyndham /ˈwɪndəm ; ˈwɪndəm/ 溫丹 (George, 1863–1913, 英國從政者及作家)。

Xavier /ˈzævɪə ; ˈzævɪɚ/ 聖・查威爾 (Saint Francis, 1506–1552, 世稱 Apostle of the Indies, 西班牙天主教耶穌會之傳教士)。

Xenophon /ˈzenəfən ; ˈzɛnəfən/ 贊諾芬 (434?–?355 B.C., 希臘歷史學家、散文家及軍人)。

Xerxes I /ˈzɜːksiːz ; ˈzɝksiz/ 澤克西斯一世 (519?–465 B.C., 世稱 the Great, 波斯國王,在位期間 486–465 B.C.)。

Yale /jeɪl ; jel/ 耶魯 (Elihu, 1649–1721, 英國在美洲之殖民地行政官,爲美國耶魯大學之創始人)。

Yang Chen Ning /ˈjɑːŋ ˈdʒən ˈnɪŋ ; ˈjɑŋ ˈdʒən ˈnɪŋ/ 楊振寧 (1922–, 中國物理學家,與李政道同獲1957年諾貝爾物理獎)。

Yang Chien /ˈjɑːŋ ˈdʒjen ; ˈjɑŋ ˈdʒjɛn/ 楊堅 (541–604, 中國隋朝開國之主,即隋文帝,在位二十四年)。

Yao /jaʊ ; jaʊ/ 堯(中國上古帝王,史稱唐堯,又稱放勳,在位一百年,禪位於帝舜)。

Yeats /jeɪts ; jets/ 葉芝 (william Butler, 1865–1939, 愛爾蘭詩人及劇作家,曾獲 1923 年諾貝爾文學獎)。

Young /jʌŋ ; jʌŋ/ 楊格 (**1** Edward, 1683–1765, 英國詩人; **2** Francis Brett, 1884–1954, 英國小說家)。

Younghusband /ˈjʌŋ͵hʌzbənd ; ˈjʌŋ͵hʌzbənd/ 楊赫斯班 (Sir Francis Edward, 1863–1942, 英國探險家及作家)。

Yüan Shih-k'ai /juˈɑːn ˈʃɪ ˈkaɪ ; juˈɑn ˈʃi ˈkaɪ/ 袁世凱 (1859–1916, 中國政治家,於 1913–16 任總統)。

Yukawa /juːˈkɑːwə ; juˈkɑwə/ 湯川秀樹 (Hideki, 1907–, 日本物理學家,曾獲 1949 年諾貝爾物理獎)。

Yü Shun /ˈjuː ˈʃʌn ; ˈju ˈʃʌn/ 虞舜(中國上古帝王,姓姚名重華,在位四十八年,禪位於夏禹)。

Zamenhof /ˈzɑːmənhɒf ; ˈzɑmənhɔf/ 亞門霍夫 (Lazarus Ludwig, 1859–1917, 波蘭眼科醫生及語言學家, 1887 年創製'世界語')。

Zangwill /ˈzæŋgwɪl ; ˈzæŋ(g)wɪl/ 桑桂爾 (Israel, 1864–1926, 英國劇作家及小說家)。

Zarathustra 參看 Zoroaster。

Zeeman /ˈzeɪmɑːn ; ˈze͵mɑn/ 吉曼 (Pieter, 1865–1943, 荷蘭物理學家,與 H. A. Lorentz 同獲 1902 年諾貝爾物理獎)。

Zeno /ˈziːnəʊ ; ˈzino/ 季諾(紀元前四至三世紀之希臘哲學家,斯多噶學派之創始者)。

Zeno of Elea /-ˈiːlɪə ; -ˈilɪə/ 以利亞的季諾(紀元前五世紀之希臘哲學家)。

Zenobia /zɪˈnəʊbɪə ; zɪˈnobɪə/ 季諾碧亞 (?–?272, 古代 Palmyra 之女王,在位期間 267–272)。

Zeppelin, von /ˈzepəlɪn ; ˈzɛp(ə)lɪn/ 齊柏林 (Count Ferdinand, 1838–1917, 德國將軍及飛船專家)。

Zernike /ˈzeənɪkə ; ˈzɛrnɪkə/ 賽尼加 (Frits, 1888–1966, 荷蘭物理學家,曾獲 1953 年諾貝爾物理獎)。

Ziegler /ˈziːglə ; ˈziglɚ/ 齊格拉 (Karl, 1898–1973, 德國化學家,與 G. Natta 同獲 1963 年諾貝爾化學獎)。

Zola /ˈzəʊlə ; ˈzolə/ 左拉 (Émile, 1840–1902, 法國小說家)。

Zoroaster /͵zɒrəʊˈæstə ; ͵zoroˈæstɚ/ or **Zarathustra** /͵zærəˈθuːstrə ; ͵zærəˈθustrə/ 索羅亞斯德(紀元前六世紀之波斯宗教家,爲古波斯祆教 (Zoroastrianism) 之創始人)。

Zsigmondy /ˈʒɪgmɒndɪ ; ˈʒɪg͵mɔndɪ/ 季格孟德 (Richard, 1865–1929, 德國化學家，曾獲 1925 年諾貝爾化學獎)。

COMMON FORENAMES 常見的名字

Note. Pet-names are either shown after the name from which they are formed or listed separately with a note on their origins. Many of the names listed which consist of a single syllable have pet-name forms produced by adding /ɪ/ to the pronunciation and -y or -ie to the spelling, and doubling the final consonant if the preceding vowel is short:
注意：暱稱列在自其衍生的名字之後，或單獨列出並註明其出處。表內很多單音節的名字都有暱稱，這些暱稱是在音標之後加 /ɪ ; ɪ/ 音，在拼法上加 -y 或 -ie 而構成的，如果最後一個子音前面的母音是短母音，則重複該子音：
eg 例如: Fred, Freddy /'fredɪ ; 'frɛdɪ/; Hugh, Hughie /'hju:ɪ ; 'hjuɪ/;
Liz, Lizzie /'lɪzɪ ; 'lɪzɪ/; Rose, Rosie /'rəuzɪ ; 'rozɪ/.

Men 男子名

Abraham /'eɪbrəhæm ; 'ebrə,hæm/ 亞伯拉罕
Adam /'ædəm ; 'ædəm/ 亞當
Adrian /'eɪdrɪən ; 'edrɪən/ 亞德里恩
Alan, Allan, Allen /'ælən ; 'ælən/ 艾倫
Albert /'ælbət ; 'ælbɚt/ 艾爾伯特; **Al** /æl ; æl/ 艾爾
Alexander /ˌælɪg'zɑ:ndə(r) *US*: -'zæn- ; ˌælɪg'zændɚ/ 亞歷山大; **Alex** /'ælɪks ; 'ælɪks/ 亞歷士
Alfred /'ælfrɪd ; 'ælfrɪd/ 艾夫列; **Alf** /ælf ; ælf/ 艾夫
Andrew /'ændru: ; 'ændru/ 安德魯; **Andy** /'ændɪ ; 'ændɪ/ 安迪
Angus /'æŋgəs ; 'æŋgəs/ 安格斯
Anthony, Antony /'æntənɪ ; 'æntənɪ/ 安東尼
Arnold /'ɑ:nld ; 'ɑrnḷd/ 阿諾德
Arthur /'ɑ:θə(r) ; 'ɑrθɚ/ 亞瑟
Barry /'bærɪ ; 'bærɪ/ 巴利
Bartholomew /bɑ:'θɒləmju: ; bɑr'θɑlədmju/ 巴梭羅繆; **Bart** /bɑ:t ; bɑrt/ 巴特
Basil /'bæzl ; 'bæzḷ/ 巴澤爾
Benjamin /'bendʒəmɪn ; 'bɛndʒəmən/ 本傑明; **Ben** /ben ; bɛn/ 本恩
Bernard /'bɜ:nəd *US:* bər'nɑ:rd ; 'bɝnɚd/ 伯納; **Bernie** /'bɜ:nɪ ; 'bɝnɪ/ 伯倪
Bert /bɜ:t ; bɝt/ (from 出自 *Albert, Gilbert, Herbert, Hubert*) 伯特
Bill /bɪl ; bɪl/ (from 出自 *William*) 比爾
Bob /bɒb ; bɑb/ (from 出自 *Robert*) 鮑布
Boris /'bɒrɪs *US:* 'bɔ:r- ; 'borɪs/ 伯里斯
Brian, Bryan /'braɪən ; 'braɪən/ 布萊恩
Bruce /bru:s ; brus/ 布魯斯
Carl /kɑ:l ; kɑrl/ 卡爾
Cecil /'sesl *US:* 'si:sl ; 'sisḷ/ 塞西爾
Cedric /'sedrɪk ; 'sɛdrɪk/ 賽德里克
Charles /tʃɑ:lz ; tʃɑrlz/ 查理; **Chas** /tʃæz ; tʃæz/ 查士
Christian /'krɪstʃən ; 'krɪstʃən/ 克里斯辰
Christopher /'Krɪstəfə(r) ; 'krɪstəfɚ/ 克利斯多夫; **Chris** /krɪs ; krɪs/ 克利斯
Claud(e) /klɔ:d ; klɔd/ 克勞德
Clement /'klemənt ; 'klɛmənt/ 克雷孟特
Clifford /'klɪfəd ; 'klɪfɚd/ 柯利弗德; **Cliff** /klɪf ; klɪf/ 柯利弗
Clive /klaɪv ; klaɪv/ 克萊夫
Colin /'kɒlɪn ; 'kɑlɪn/ 科林
Cyril /'sɪrəl ; 'sɪrəl/ 西瑞爾
Daniel /'dænɪəl ; 'dænjəl/ 丹尼爾; **Dan** /dæn ; dæn/ 丹(恩)
David /'deɪvɪd ; 'devɪd/ 大衛; **Dave** /deɪv ; dev/ 迪夫
Dean /di:n ; din/ 迪恩
Dennis, Denis /'denɪs ; 'dɛnɪs/ 鄧尼斯
Derek /'derɪk ; 'dɛrɪk/ 德立克
Desmond /'dezmənd ; 'dɛzmənd/ 德妶門; **Des** /dez ; dɛz/ 德妶
Dick /dɪk ; dɪk/ (from 出自 *Richard*) 狄克
Dominic /'dɒmɪnɪk ; 'dɑmənɪk/ 多明尼克
Donald /'dɒnld ; 'dɑnḷd/ 唐納德; **Don** /dɒn ; dɑn/ 唐
Douglas /'dʌgləs ; 'dʌgləs/ 道格拉斯; **Doug** /dʌg ; dʌg/ 道格
Duncan /'dʌŋkən ; 'dʌŋkən/ 鄧肯
Edgar /'edgə(r) ; 'ɛdgɚ/ 艾德嘉
Edmund /'edmənd ; 'ɛdmənd/ 艾德門
Edward /'edwəd ; 'ɛdwɚd/ 艾德華; **Ed** /ed ; ɛd/ 艾德
Enoch /'i:nɒk ; 'inək/ 伊諾克
Eric /'erɪk ; 'ɛrɪk/ 艾立克
Ernest /'ɜ:nɪst ; 'ɝnɪst/ 鄂倪斯特; **Ernie** /'ɜ:nɪ ; 'ɝnɪ/ 鄂倪
Eugene /ju:'dʒi:n ; ju'dʒin/ 尤金
Felix /'fi:lɪks ; 'filɪks/ 菲里克斯
Francis /'frɑ:nsɪs *US:* 'fræn- ; 'frænsɪs/ 法蘭西斯
Frank /fræŋk ; fræŋk/ 富蘭克
Frederick /'fredrɪk ; 'frɛd(ə)rɪk/ 弗雷德里克; **Fred** /fred ; frɛd/ 弗雷德
Gareth /'gærəθ ; 'gærɪθ/ 蓋勒斯
Gary /'gærɪ ; 'gɛrɪ/ 蓋里
Gavin /'gævɪn ; 'gævɪn/ 蓋文
Gene /dʒi:n ; dʒin/ (from 出自 *Eugene*) 吉恩
Geoffrey /'dʒefrɪ ; 'dʒɛfrɪ/ 傑佛瑞; **Geoff** /dʒef ; dʒɛf/ 傑夫
George /dʒɔ:dʒ ; dʒɔrdʒ/ 喬治
Gerald /'dʒerəld ; 'dʒɛrəld/ 吉拉爾德; **Gerry** /'geri ; 'gɛrɪ/ 吉瑞
Gerard /'dʒerəd ; dʒə'rɑrd/ 吉拉德
Gilbert /'gɪlbət ; 'gɪlbɚt/ 吉伯特
Giles /dʒaɪlz ; dʒaɪlz/ 翟爾斯
Glen /glen ; glɛn/ 格倫
Godfrey /'gɒdfrɪ ; 'gɑdfrɪ/ 高德弗里
Gordon /'gɔ:dn ; 'gɔrdṇ/ 郭登
Graham /'greɪəm ; 'greəm/ 葛雷恩
Gregory /'gregərɪ ; 'grɛgərɪ/ 葛列格里; **Greg** /greg ; grɛg/ 葛列格
Guy /gaɪ ; gaɪ/ 蓋伊
Harold /'hærəld ; 'hærəld/ 哈樂德; **Harry** /'hærɪ ; 'hærɪ/ 哈里; **Hal** /hæl ; hæl/ 哈爾
Harvey /'hɑ:vɪ ; 'hɑrvɪ/ 哈維
Henry /'henrɪ ; 'hɛnrɪ/ 亨利
Herbert /'hɜ:bət ; 'hɝbɚt/ 赫伯特
Hilary /'hɪlərɪ ; 'hɪlərɪ/ 希拉里
Horace /'hɒrɪs *US:* 'hɔ:r- ; 'hɔrɪs/ 賀利斯
Howard /'haʊəd ; 'haʊɚd/ 豪爾德
Hubert /'hju:bət ; 'hjubɚt/ 休伯特
Hugh /hju: ; hju/ 修
Humphrey /'hʌmfrɪ ; 'hʌmfrɪ/ 韓弗里
Ian /'i:ən ; 'iən/ 毅恩
Isaac /'aɪzək ; 'aɪzək/ 艾薩克
Ivan /'aɪvən ; 'aɪvən/ 艾凡
Ivor /'aɪvə(r) ; 'aɪvɚ/ 艾維爾
Jack /dʒæk ; dʒæk/ (from 出自 *John*) 傑克
Jacob /'dʒeɪkəb ; 'dʒekəb/ 傑科卜
James /dʒeɪmz ; dʒemz/ 詹姆斯
Jason /'dʒeɪsn ; 'dʒesṇ/ 傑森
Jeffrey /'dʒefrɪ ; 'dʒɛfrɪ/ 傑弗里; **Jeff** /dʒef ; dʒɛf/ 傑夫
Jeremy /'dʒerəmɪ ; 'dʒɛrəmɪ/ 哲里米; **Jerry** /'dʒerɪ ; 'dʒɛrɪ/ 哲里
Jerome /dʒə'rəum ; dʒə'rom/ 哲羅姆
Jim /dʒɪm ; dʒɪm/ (from 出自 *James*) 吉姆
John /dʒɒn ; dʒɑn/ 約翰
Jonathan /'dʒɒnəθən ; 'dʒɑnəθən/ 卓納森
Joseph /'dʒəuzɪf ; 'dʒozəf/ 約瑟; **Jo, Joe** /dʒəu ; dʒo/ 喬
Joshua /'dʒɒʃuə ; 'dʒɑʃuə/ 卓曙瓦
Julian /'dʒu:lɪən ; 'dʒuljən/ 朱里恩
Justin /'dʒʌstɪn ; 'dʒʌstɪn/ 札斯廷
Keith /ki:θ ; kiθ/ 契斯
Kenneth /'kenɪθ ; 'kɛnɪθ/ 肯尼斯; **Ken** /ken ; kɛn/ 肯恩
Kevin /'kevɪn ; 'kɛvɪn/ 凱文
Laurence, Lawrence /'lɒrəns *US:* 'lɔ:rəns ; 'lɔrəns/ 羅倫斯; **Larry** /'lærɪ ; 'lærɪ/ 賴里
Leo /'li:əu ; 'lio/ 利歐

Leonard /ˈlenəd ; ˈlɛnɚd/ 倫納德; **Len** /len ; lɛn/ 倫恩
Leslie /ˈlezlɪ ; ˈlɛslɪ/ 勒斯里; **Les** /lez ; lɛs/ 勒斯
Lewis /ˈluːɪs ; ˈlʊɪs/ 路易斯
Lionel /ˈlaɪənl ; ˈlaɪənl̩/ 賴恩內爾
Louis /ˈluːɪ *US:* ˈluːɪs ; ˈlʊɪs/ 路易; **Lou** /luː ; lu/ 路
Luke /luːk ; luk/ 陸克
Malcolm /ˈmælkəm ; ˈmælkəm/ 麥爾肯
Mark /mɑːk ; mɑrk/ 馬克
Martin /ˈmɑːtɪn *US:* -tn ; ˈmɑrtɪn/ 馬丁
Matthew /ˈmæθjuː ; ˈmæθju/ 馬修; **Matt** /mæt ; mæt/ 馬特
Maurice /ˈmɒrɪs *US:* ˈmɔːr- ; ˈmɔrɪs/ 摩里斯
Max /mæks ; mæks/ 麥克斯
Michael /ˈmaɪkl ; ˈmaɪkl̩/ 邁克爾; **Mick** /mɪk ; mɪk/ 密克; **Mike** /maɪk ; maɪk/ 邁克
Miles /maɪlz ; maɪlz/ 麥爾斯
Nathaniel /nəˈθænɪəl ; nəˈθænjəl/ 納旦尼爾; **Nat** /næt ; næt/ 納特
Ned /ned ; nɛd/ (from 出自 *Edward*) 奈德
Neil /niːl ; nil/ 尼爾
Neville /ˈnevl ; ˈnɛvl̩/ 奈維爾
Nicholas /ˈnɪkələs ; ˈnɪk(ə)ləs/ 尼可勒斯; **Nick** /nɪk ; nɪk/ 尼克
Nigel /ˈnaɪdʒl ; ˈnaɪdʒəl/ 奈哲爾
Noel /ˈnəʊəl ; ˈnoəl/ 諾爾
Norman /ˈnɔːmən ; ˈnɔrmən/ 諾曼
Oliver /ˈɒlɪvə(r) ; ˈɑləvɚ/ 奥立弗
Oscar /ˈɒskə(r) ; ˈɔskɚ/ 奥斯卡
Oswald /ˈɒzwəld ; ˈɑzwəld/ 奥斯維德
Patrick /ˈpætrɪk ; ˈpætrɪk/ 培特里克; **Pat** /pæt ; pæt/ 培特; **Paddy** /ˈpædɪ ; ˈpædɪ/ 培迪
Paul /pɔːl ; pɔl/ 保羅
Percy /ˈpɜːsɪ ; ˈpɝsɪ/ 伯西
Peter /ˈpiːtə(r) ; ˈpitɚ/ 彼得; **Pete** /piːt ; pit/ 皮特
Philip /ˈfɪlɪp ; ˈfɪləp/ 菲力普; **Phil** /fɪl ; fɪl/ 菲爾
Quentin /ˈkwentɪn *US:* -tn ; ˈkwɛntn̩/ 昆廷
Ralph /rælf ; rælf/ 拉爾夫
Randolph /ˈrændɒlf ; ˈrændɑlf/ 藍道夫
Raymond /ˈreɪmənd ; ˈremənd/ 雷孟德; **Ray** /reɪ ; re/ 雷伊
Reginald /ˈredʒɪnld ; ˈrɛdʒɪnl̩d/ 雷哲諾德; **Reg** /redʒ ; rɛdʒ/ 雷哲
Rex /reks ; rɛks/ 雷克斯
Richard /ˈrɪtʃəd ; ˈrɪtʃɚd/ 理查
Robert /ˈrɒbət ; ˈrɑbɚt/ 羅伯特
Robin /ˈrɒbɪn ; ˈrɑbɪn/ 拉賓
Rodney /ˈrɒdnɪ ; ˈrɑdnɪ/ 羅德尼; **Rod** /rɒd ; rɑd/ 羅德
Roger /ˈrɒdʒə(r) ; ˈrɑdʒɚ/ 羅哲爾
Ronald /ˈrɒnld ; ˈrɑnl̩d/ 羅諾德; **Ron** /rɒn ; rɑn/ 羅恩
Roy /rɔɪ ; rɔɪ/ 羅伊
Rudolf /ˈruːdɒlf ; ˈrudɑlf/ 魯道夫
Rupert /ˈruːpət ; ˈrupɚt/ 魯伯特
Samuel /ˈsæmjʊəl ; ˈsæmjʊəl/ 撒姆爾; **Sam** /sæm ; sæm/ 山姆
Sandy /ˈsændɪ ; ˈsændɪ/ (from 出自 *Alexander*) 山迪
Seamus /ˈʃeɪməs ; ˈʃeməs/ 謝摩斯
Sean /ʃɔːn ; ʃɔn/ 朔恩
Sidney /ˈsɪdnɪ ; ˈsɪdnɪ/ 錫德尼; **Sid** /sɪd ; sɪd/ 錫德
Simon /ˈsaɪmən ; ˈsaɪmən/ 賽門
Stanley /ˈstænlɪ ; ˈstænlɪ/ 斯旦里; **Stan** /stæn ; stæn/ 斯旦
Stephen, Steven /ˈstiːvn ; ˈstivən/ 史迪文; **Steve** /stiːv ; stiv/ 史迪夫
Stewart, Stuart /ˈstjuːət *US:* ˈstuː-; ˈst(j)uɚt/ 史都華
Ted /ted ; tɛd/ (from 出自 *Edward*) 泰德
Terence /ˈterəns ; ˈtɛrəns/ 泰倫斯; **Terry** /ˈterɪ ; ˈtɛrɪ/ 泰里
Theodore /ˈθiːədɔ(r); ˈθiəˌdor/ 希歐多爾; **Theo** /ˈθiːəʊ; ˈθio/ 希歐
Thomas /ˈtɒməs ; ˈtɑməs/ 湯瑪斯; **Tom** /tɒm ; tɑm/ 湯姆
Timothy /ˈtɪməθɪ ; ˈtɪməθɪ/ 提摩西; **Tim** /tɪm ; tɪm/ 提姆
Toby /ˈtəʊbɪ ; ˈtobɪ/ 托比
Tony /ˈtəʊnɪ ; ˈtonɪ/ (from 出自 *Anthony*) 東尼
Trevor /ˈtrevə(r) ; ˈtrɛvɚ/ 特雷弗爾
Vernon /ˈvɜːnən ; ˈvɝnən/ 維能
Victor /ˈvɪktə(r) ; ˈvɪktɚ/ 維克多爾; **Vic** /vɪk ; vɪk/ 維克
Vincent /ˈvɪnsnt ; ˈvɪnsn̩t/ 文森特
Vivian /ˈvɪvɪən ; ˈvɪvɪən/ 衞維恩
Walter /ˈwɔːltə(r) ; ˈwɔltɚ/ 華爾特
Wayne /weɪn ; wen/ 韋恩
Wilfred /ˈwɪlfrɪd ; ˈwɪlfrɪd/ 威(爾)弗列德
William /ˈwɪlɪəm ; ˈwɪljəm/ 威廉; **Will** /wɪl ; wɪl/ 威爾

Women 女子名

Ada /ˈeɪdə ; ˈedə/ 愛達
Agatha /ˈægəθə ; ˈægəθə/ 愛佳莎
Agnes /ˈægnɪs ; ˈægnɪs/ 艾格妮絲; **Aggie** /ˈægɪ ; ˈægɪ/ 艾姬
Alexandra /ˌælɪgˈzɑːndrə *US:* -ˈzæn- ; ˌælɪgˈzændrə/ 愛麗珊德拉
Alice /ˈælɪs ; ˈælɪs/ 愛麗絲
Alison /ˈælɪsn ; ˈæləsn̩/ 愛麗蓀
Amanda /əˈmændə ; əˈmændə/ 娥曼達
Amy /ˈeɪmɪ ; ˈemɪ/ 艾美
Angela /ˈændʒələ ; ˈændʒələ/ 安琪拉
Anita /əˈniːtə ; əˈnitə/ 艾妮塔
Ann, Anne /æn ; æn/ 安
Annabel /ˈænəbel ; ˈænəˌbɛl/ 愛娜蓓
Anthea /ˈænθɪə ; ænˈθɪə/ 安喜雅
Audrey /ˈɔːdrɪ ; ˈɔdrɪ/ 奥德莉
Barbara /ˈbɑːbrə ; ˈbɑrb(ə)rə/ 芭芭拉; **Babs** /bæbz ; bæbz/ 芭布絲
Beatrice /ˈbɪətrɪs ; ˈbiətrɪs/ 碧翠絲
Belinda /bəˈlɪndə ; bəˈlɪndə/ 碧琳達
Bella /ˈbelə ; ˈbɛlə/ (from 出自 *Isabella*) 貝拉
Beryl /ˈberəl ; ˈbɛrəl/ 白麗兒
Bess /bes ; bɛs/ (from 出自 *Elizabeth*) 貝絲
Betsy /ˈbetsɪ ; ˈbɛtsɪ/ (from 出自 *Elizabeth*) 貝琪
Betty /ˈbetɪ ; ˈbɛtɪ/ (from 出自 *Elizabeth*) 貝蒂
Brenda /ˈbrendə ; ˈbrɛndə/ 布倫黛
Bridget /ˈbrɪdʒɪt ; ˈbrɪdʒɪt/ 布麗姬(特)
Carol, Carole /ˈkærəl ; ˈkærəl/ 凱洛爾
Caroline /ˈkærəlaɪn ; ˈkærəˌlaɪn/ 卡珞萊
Carolyn /ˈkærəlɪn ; ˈkærəlɪn/ 卡珞琳
Catherine /ˈkæθrɪn ; ˈkæθ(ə)rɪn/ 凱塞琳; **Cathy** /ˈkæθɪ ; ˈkæθɪ/ 凱絲
Cecilia /səˈsiːlɪə ; sɪˈsɪljə/ 西西莉亞
Cecily /ˈsesəlɪ ; ˈsɛsl̩ɪ/ 西西莉
Celia /ˈsiːlɪə ; ˈsiljə/ 西莉亞
Charlotte /ˈʃɑːlət ; ˈʃɑrlət/ 夏綠蒂
Chloe /ˈkləʊɪ ; ˈklo•ɪ/ 克樂怡
Christina /krɪˈstiːnə ; krɪsˈtinə/ 克莉絲婷娜
Christine /ˈkrɪstiːn ; krɪsˈtin/ 克莉絲婷; **Chris** /krɪs ; krɪs/ 克莉絲
Clare /kleə(r) ; klɛr/ 克萊兒
Constance /ˈkɒnstəns ; ˈkɑnstəns/ 康絲妲; **Connie** /ˈkɒnɪ ; ˈkɑnɪ/ 康妮
Cynthia /ˈsɪnθɪə ; ˈsɪnθɪə/ 莘喜雅
Daisy /ˈdeɪzɪ ; ˈdezɪ/ 黛西
Daphne /ˈdæfnɪ ; ˈdæfnɪ/ 黛芙妮
Dawn /dɔːn ; dɔn/ 妲恩
Deborah /ˈdebərə ; ˈdɛbərə/ 黛博拉; **Debby** /ˈdebɪ ; ˈdɛbɪ/ 黛碧
Deirdre /ˈdɪədrɪ ; ˈdɪrdrɪ/ 狄德莉
Denise /dəˈniːz ; dəˈniz/ 德妮絲
Diana /daɪˈænə ; daɪˈænə/ 黛安娜
Dolly /ˈdɒlɪ ; ˈdɑlɪ/ (from 出自 *Dorothy*) 多麗
Dora /ˈdɔːrə ; ˈdorə/ 朵拉
Doreen /ˈdɔːriːn ; ˈdorin/ 多琳
Doris /ˈdɒrɪs *US:* ˈdɔːr- ; ˈdɔrɪs/ 朵麗絲
Dorothy /ˈdɒrəθɪ *US:* ˈdɔːr- ; ˈdɔrəθɪ/ 桃樂西
Edith /ˈiːdɪθ ; ˈidɪθ/ 伊蒂絲
Eileen /ˈaɪliːn ; aɪˈlin/ 愛琳
Elaine /ɪˈleɪn ; ɪˈlen/ 怡蓮
Eleanor /ˈelənə(r) ; ˈɛlənɚ/ 愛麗諾
Eliza /ɪˈlaɪzə ; ɪˈlaɪzə/ (from 出自 *Elizabeth*) 伊萊莎
Elizabeth /ɪˈlɪzəbəθ ; ɪˈlɪzəbəθ/ 伊麗莎白

Ellen /ˈelən ; ˈɛlən/ 愛倫
Elsie /ˈelsɪ ; ˈɛlsɪ/ (from 出自 *Elizabeth*) 愛喜
Emily /ˈeməlɪ ; ˈɛmḷɪ/ 愛彌麗
Emma /ˈemə ; ˈɛmə/ 愛瑪
Erica /ˈerɪkə ; ˈɛrɪkə/ 艾麗嘉
Ethel /ˈeθl ; ˈɛθəl/ 愛瑟兒
Eunice /ˈjuːnɪs ; ˈjuːnɪs/ 尤妮絲
Eva /ˈiːvə ; ˈivə/ 伊娃
Eve /iːv ; iv/ 伊芙
Evelyn /ˈiːvlɪn ; ˈɛv(ə)lɪn/ 伊芙琳
Fanny /ˈfænɪ ; ˈfænɪ/ (from 出自 *Frances*) 芬妮
Felicity /fəˈlɪsətɪ ; fəˈlɪsətɪ/ 菲莉思蒂
Fiona /fɪˈəʊnə ; fɪˈonə/ 翡歐娜
Flora /ˈflɔːrə ; ˈflorə/ 弗蘿拉
Florence /ˈflɒrəns *US:* ˈflɔːr- ; ˈflɔrəns/ 弗蘿倫絲
Frances /ˈfrɑːnsɪs *US:* ˈfræn- ; ˈfrænsɪs/ 法蘭西絲; **Fran** /fræn ; fræn/ 法蘭
Freda /ˈfriːdə ; ˈfridə/ 弗麗達
Geraldine /ˈdʒerəldiːn ; ˈdʒɛrəldˌin/ 吉樂爾汀
Gertrude /ˈgɜːtruːd ; ˈgɝtrud/ 葛特璐(德); **Gertie** /ˈgɜːtɪ ; ˈgɝtɪ/ 葛蒂
Gillian /ˈdʒɪlɪən ; ˈdʒɪlɪən/ 姬蓮; **Gill** /dʒɪl ; dʒɪl/ 姬兒
Gladys /ˈglædɪs ; ˈglædɪs/ 葛萊蒂絲
Gloria /ˈglɔːrɪə ; ˈglorɪə/ 葛羅瑞亞
Grace /greɪs ; gres/ 葛瑞絲
Gwendoline /ˈgwendəlɪn;ˈgwɛndḷɪn/ 葛雯德琳; **Gwen** /gwen ; gwɛn/ 葛雯
Harriet /ˈhærɪət ; ˈhærɪət/ 海麗特
Hazel /ˈheɪzl ; ˈhezḷ/ 海柔
Heather /ˈheðə(r) ; ˈhɛðɚ/ 荷姿
Helen /ˈhelən ; ˈhɛlən/ 海倫
Hilary /ˈhɪlərɪ ; ˈhɪlərɪ/ 希拉瑞
Hilda /ˈhɪldə ; ˈhɪldə/ 希爾達
Ida /ˈaɪdə ; ˈaɪdə/ 愛達
Ingrid /ˈɪŋgrɪd ; ˈɪŋgrɪd/ 英格麗
Irene /aɪəˈriːnɪ *US:* ˈaɪəriːn ; aɪˈrin/ 艾琳
Iris /ˈaɪərɪs ; ˈaɪrɪs/ 艾莉絲
Isabel, Isobel /ˈɪzəbel ; ˈɪzəˌbɛl/ 伊莎蓓
Isabella /ˌɪzəˈbelə ; ˌɪzəˈbɛlə/ 伊莎蓓拉
Ivy /ˈaɪvɪ ; ˈaɪvɪ/ 艾薇
Jacqueline /ˈdʒækəlɪn ; ˈdʒækəlɪn/ 賈桂琳; **Jackie** /ˈdʒækɪ ; ˈdʒækɪ/ 賈姬
Jane /dʒeɪn ; dʒen/ 珍
Janet /ˈdʒænɪt ; ˈdʒænɪt/ 珍尼特
Janice /ˈdʒænɪs ; ˈdʒænɪs/ 珍尼絲
Jean /dʒiːn ; dʒin/ 琴
Jennifer /ˈdʒenɪfə(r) ; ˈdʒɛnəfɚ/ 珍尼佛; **Jenny** /ˈdʒenɪ ; ˈdʒɛnɪ/ 珍尼
Jessica /ˈdʒesɪkə ; ˈdʒɛsəkə/ 傑西嘉; **Jess** /dʒes ; dʒɛs/ 傑絲
Jill /dʒɪl ; dʒɪl/ (from 出自 *Gillian*) 姬兒
Joan /dʒəʊn ; dʒon/ 瓊
Joanna /dʒəʊˈænə ; dʒoˈænə/ 瓊安娜
Jocelyn /ˈdʒɒslɪn ; ˈdʒɑs(ə)lɪn/ 賈思琳
Josephine /ˈdʒəʊzəfiːn;ˈdʒozəˌfin/ 約瑟芬; **Jo** /dʒəʊ; dʒo/ 喬
Joy /dʒɔɪ ; dʒɔɪ/ 喬伊
Joyce /dʒɔɪs ; dʒɔɪs/ 喬伊絲
Judith /ˈdʒuːdɪθ ; ˈdʒudɪθ/ 朱蒂絲; **Judy** /ˈdʒuːdɪ ; ˈdʒudɪ/ 朱蒂
Julia /ˈdʒuːlɪə ; ˈdʒuljə/ 朱麗亞
Julie /ˈdʒuːlɪ ; ˈdʒulɪ/ 朱莉
Juliet /ˈdʒuːlɪət ; ˈdʒuljət/ 朱麗葉
June /dʒuːn ; dʒun/ 朱恩
Karen /ˈkærən ; ˈkærən/ 凱琳
Katherine /ˈkæθrɪn;ˈkæθ(ə)rɪn/ 凱瑟琳; **Kate** /keɪt ; ket/ 凱特; **Kathy** /ˈkæθɪ ; ˈkæθɪ/ 凱絲
Kay /keɪ ; ke/ 凱伊
Kitty /ˈkɪtɪ ; ˈkɪtɪ/ (from 出自 *Katherine*) 吉蒂
Laura /ˈlɔːrə ; ˈlɔrə/ 珞拉
Lesley /ˈlezlɪ ; ˈlɛslɪ/ 雷思麗
Lilian /ˈlɪlɪən ; ˈlɪlɪən/ 麗蓮
Lily /ˈlɪlɪ ; ˈlɪlɪ/ 莉莉
Linda /ˈlɪndə ; ˈlɪndə/ 琳達
Lisa /ˈliːsə ; ˈlisə/ 麗莎; **Liza** /ˈlaɪzə ; ˈlaɪzə/ (from 出自 *Elizabeth*) 萊莎
Liz /lɪz ; lɪz/ (from 出自 *Elizabeth*) 麗絲
Lois /ˈləʊɪs ; ˈlo•ɪs/ 路易絲
Lorna /ˈlɔːnə ; ˈlɔrnə/ 羅娜
Louise /luːˈiːz ; luˈiz/ 盧伊絲
Lucy /ˈluːsɪ ; ˈlusɪ/ 露西
Lydia /ˈlɪdɪə ; ˈlɪdɪə/ 麗迪亞
Lynn /lɪn ; lɪn/ 琳
Mabel /ˈmeɪbl ; ˈmebḷ/ 梅伯兒
Madeleine /ˈmædəlɪn ; ˈmædḷɪn/ 瑪德琳
Madge /mædʒ ; mædʒ/ (from 出自 *Margaret*) 瑪琪
Maggie /ˈmægɪ;ˈmægɪ/ (from 出自 *Margaret*) 瑪姬
Mamie /ˈmeɪmɪ ; ˈmemɪ/ (from 出自 *Mary*) 梅蜜
Mandy /ˈmændɪ ; ˈmændɪ/ (from 出自 *Amanda*) 曼蒂
Margaret /ˈmɑːgrɪt ; ˈmɑrg(ə)rɪt/ 瑪格麗特
Margery /ˈmɑːdʒərɪ ; ˈmɑrdʒərɪ/ 瑪芝莉; **Margie** /ˈmɑːdʒɪ ; ˈmɑrdʒɪ/ 瑪芝
Maria /məˈrɪə ; məˈriə/ 瑪麗亞
Marian, Marion /ˈmærɪən ; ˈmɛrɪən/ 瑪麗安
Marie /məˈriː, ˈmɑːrɪ ; məˈri, ˈmɑrɪ/ 瑪麗
Marilyn /ˈmærəlɪn ; ˈmærəlɪn/ 瑪麗琳
Marjorie /ˈmɑːdʒərɪ ; ˈmɑrdʒərɪ/ 瑪芝麗
Marlene /mɑːˈliːn ; mɑrˈlin/ 瑪琳
Martha /ˈmɑːθə ; ˈmɑrθə/ 瑪莎
Mary /ˈmeərɪ ; ˈmɛrɪ/ 瑪莉
Maud /mɔːd ; mɔd/ 穆德
Maureen /ˈmɔːriːn ; mɔˈrin/ 穆琳
Mavis /ˈmeɪvɪs ; ˈmevɪs/ 梅薇思
Maxine /ˈmæksiːn ; mækˈsin/ 麥可馨
May /meɪ ; me/ (from 出自 *Mary*) 玫
Meg /meg ; mɛg/ (from 出自 *Margaret*) 麥格
Michelle /mɪˈʃel ; mɪˈʃɛl/ 蜜筱
Mildred /ˈmɪldrɪd ; ˈmɪldrɪd/ 繆德莉
Millicent /ˈmɪlɪsnt ; ˈmɪləsn̩t/ 蜜莉生; **Milly** /ˈmɪlɪ ; ˈmɪlɪ/ 蜜莉
Miranda /mɪˈrændə ; məˈrændə/ 米蘭達
Miriam /ˈmɪrɪəm ; ˈmɪrɪəm/ 米瑞安
Moira /ˈmɔɪrə ; ˈmɔɪrə/ 茉怡拉
Molly /ˈmɒlɪ ; ˈmɑlɪ/ (from 出自 *Mary*) 茉莉
Monica /ˈmɒnɪkə ; ˈmɑnɪkə/ 茉妮卡
Muriel /ˈmjʊərɪəl ; ˈmjʊrɪəl/ 繆麗兒
Myra /ˈmaɪərə ; ˈmaɪrə/ 瑪伊拉
Nancy /ˈnænsɪ ; ˈnænsɪ/ 南希
Naomi /ˈneɪəmɪ ; neˈomɪ/ 內娥米
Natalie /ˈnætəlɪ ; ˈnætḷɪ/ 娜特莉
Nelly /ˈnelɪ ; ˈnɛlɪ/ (from 出自 *Eleanor* or 或 *Helen*) 乃麗
Nora /ˈnɔːrə ; ˈnorə/ 娜拉
Olive /ˈɒlɪv ; ˈɑlɪv/ 奧麗芙
Olivia /əˈlɪvɪə ; oˈlɪvɪə/ 歐莉薇亞
Pamela /ˈpæmələ ; ˈpæmələ/ 巴美拉; **Pam** /pæm ; pæm/ 巴美
Patience /ˈpeɪʃns ; ˈpeʃəns/ 裴欣絲
Patricia /pəˈtrɪʃə ; pəˈtrɪʃə/ 珮特麗莎; **Pat** /pæt;pæt/ 珮特
Paula /ˈpɔːlə ; ˈpɔlə/ 珀拉
Pauline /ˈpɔːliːn ; pɔˈlin/ 珀琳
Pearl /pɜːl ; pɝl/ 珮兒
Peg /peg ; pɛg/ (from 出自 *Margaret*) 珮格
Penelope /pəˈneləpɪ ; pəˈnɛləpɪ/ 珮內珞碧; **Penny** /ˈpenɪ ; ˈpɛnɪ/ 珮妮
Philippa /ˈfɪlɪpə ; fɪˈlɪpə/ 菲麗帕
Phoebe /ˈfiːbɪ ; ˈfibɪ/ 菲碧
Phyllis /ˈfɪlɪs ; ˈfɪlɪs/ 菲麗絲
Polly /ˈpɒlɪ ; ˈpɑlɪ/ 珀莉
Priscilla /prɪˈsɪlə ; prɪˈsɪlə/ 普露西拉
Prudence /ˈpruːdns ; ˈprudn̩s/ 普露登絲
Rachel /ˈreɪtʃl ; ˈretʃəl/ 瑞琪兒
Rebecca /rəˈbekə ; rɪˈbɛkə/ 麗蓓嘉
Rita /ˈriːtə ; ˈritə/ 麗達
Rosalie /ˈrəʊzəlɪ ; ˈrozəlɪ/ 羅莎莉
Rosalind /ˈrɒzəlɪnd ; ˈrɑz(ə)lɪnd/ 羅莎琳
Rose /rəʊz ; roz/ 羅絲
Rosemary /ˈrəʊzmərɪ *US:* -merɪ ; ˈrozˌmɛrɪ/ 露絲瑪莉
Ruth /ruːθ ; ruθ/ 露絲

Sally /ˈsælɪ ; ˈsælɪ/ (from 出自 *Sarah*) 莎莉
Samantha /səˈmænθə ; səˈmænθə/ 塞曼莎
Sandra /ˈsɑːndrə *US:* ˈsæn- ; ˈsændrə/ 珊德拉
Sarah /ˈseərə ; ˈsɛrə/ 賽拉
Sharon /ˈʃærən ; ˈʃɛrən/ 雪倫
Sheila /ˈʃiːlə ; ˈʃilə/ 希拉
Shirley /ˈʃɜːlɪ ; ˈʃɝlɪ/ 雪莉
Sonia /ˈsɒnɪə ; ˈsonɪə/ 蘇妮亞
Sophia /səˈfaɪə ; səˈfaɪə/ 蘇菲亞
Sophie /ˈsəʊfɪ ; ˈsofɪ/ 蘇菲
Stella /ˈstelə ; ˈstɛlə/ 史黛拉
Stephanie /ˈstefənɪ ; ˈstɛfənɪ/ 史黛芬妮
Susan /ˈsuːzn ; ˈsuzn̩/ 蘇珊; **Sue** /suː ; su/ 蘇; **Susie** /ˈsuːzɪ ; ˈsuzɪ/ 蘇西
Suzanne /suːˈzæn ; suˈzæn/ 蘇善
Sylvia, Silvia /ˈsɪlvɪə ; ˈsɪlvɪə/ 西維亞
Teresa, Theresa /təˈriːzə ; təˈrisə/ 黛麗莎; **Tess** /tes ; tɛs/ 黛絲; **Tessa** /ˈtesə ; ˈtɛsə/ 黛莎
Tina /ˈtiːnə ; ˈtinə/ (from 出自 *Christina*) 婷娜
Tracy /ˈtreɪsɪ ; ˈtresɪ/ 翠西
Ursula /ˈɜːsjʊlə ; ˈɝsjʊlə/ 歐秀拉
Vanessa /vəˈnesə ; vəˈnɛsə/ 溫內莎
Vera /ˈvɪərə ; ˈvɪrə/ 維拉
Veronica /vəˈrɒnɪkə ; vəˈrɑnɪkə/ 維倫妮嘉
Victoria /vɪkˈtɔːrɪə; vɪkˈtorɪə/ 維多利亞; **Vicky** /ˈvɪkɪ ; ˈvɪkɪ/ 維琪
Viola /ˈvaɪələ ; ˈvaɪələ/ 懷娥拉
Violet /ˈvaɪələt ; ˈvaɪəlɪt/ 懷娥麗特
Virginia /vəˈdʒɪnɪə ; vɚˈdʒɪnjə/ 維琴尼亞
Vivien(ne) /ˈvɪvɪən ; ˈvɪvɪən/ 維文
Wendy /ˈwendɪ ; ˈwɛndɪ/ 溫蒂
Winifred /ˈwɪnɪfrɪd ; ˈwɪnəfrɪd/ 溫妮弗瑞; **Winnie** /ˈwɪnɪ ; ˈwɪnɪ/ 溫妮
Yvonne /ɪˈvɒn ; ɪˈvɑn/ 伊芳
Zoe /ˈzəʊɪ ; ˈzo•ɪ/ 若漪

Appendix 8 THE WORKS OF WILLIAM SHAKESPEARE (1564-1616)

附錄八 莎士比亞 (1564-1616) 的作品

Note. The list below includes the approximate date of composition, full title and common abbreviation; phonetic transcriptions are provided where necessary.
注意：下列之表包括作品完成的大約年代，作品的全名及普通的縮寫；必要時並注有音標。

Plays 劇目

1590–1 The First Part of King Henry VI (*1 Hen VI*) 亨利六世(上)
The Second Part of King Henry VI (*2 Hen VI*) 亨利六世(中)
The Third Part of King Henry VI (*3 Hen VI*) 亨利六世(下)
1592–3 The Tragedy of King Richard III (*Rich III*) 利查三世
The Comedy of Errors (*Com Err*) 錯中錯
1593–4 Titus Andronicus (*Titus A*) /ˌtaɪtəs ænˈdrɒnɪkəs ; ˏtaɪtəs ænˈdrɑnɪkəs/ 泰特斯•安莊尼克斯
The Taming of the Shrew (*Tam Shr*) 馴悍婦
1594–5 The Two Gentlemen of Verona (*Two Gent*) /vəˈrəʊnə ; vəˈronə/ 維洛那二紳士
Love's Labour's Lost (*Love's L L*) 空愛一場
Romeo and Juliet (*Rom & Jul*) /ˌrəʊmɪəʊ ən ˈdʒuːlɪət ; ˏromɪo ən ˈdʒuljət/ 羅密歐與朱麗葉
1595–6 The Tragedy of King Richard II (*Rich II*) 利查二世
A Midsummer Night's Dream (*Mid N D*) 仲夏夜夢
1596–7 The Life and Death of King John (*K John*) 約翰王
The Merchant of Venice (*Mer of Ven*) /ˈvenɪs ; ˈvɛnəs/ 威尼斯商人
1597–8 The First Part of King Henry IV (*1 Hen IV*) 亨利四世(上)
The Second Part of King Henry IV (*2 Hen IV*) 亨利四世(下)
1598–1600 Much Ado about Nothing (*M Ado*) 無事自擾
As You Like It (*As You L It*) 如願
Twelfth Night, or, What You Will (*Tw N*) 第十二夜
The Life of King Henry V (*Hen V*) 亨利五世
Julius Caesar (*Jul Caes*) /ˈdʒuːlɪəs ˈsiːzə(r) ; ˈdʒuljəs ˈsizɚ/ 朱利阿斯•西撒
1600–1 Hamlet, Prince of Denmark (*Haml*) /ˈhæmlɪt ; ˈhæmlət/ 哈姆雷特
The Merry Wives of Windsor (*Merry W*) /ˈwɪnzə(r) ; ˈwɪnzɚ/ 溫莎的風流婦人
1601–2 Troilus and Cressida (*Tro & Cr*) /ˌtrɔɪləs n ˈkresɪdə ; ˏtrɔɪləs n̩ ˈkrɛsədə/ 脫愛勒斯與克萊西達
All's Well that Ends Well (*All's Well*) 皆大歡喜
1604–5 Measure for Measure (*Meas for Meas*) 惡有惡報
Othello, the Moor of Venice (*Oth*) /əˈθeləʊ ; əˈθɛlo/ 奧賽羅
1605–6 King Lear (*K Lear*) /lɪə(r) ; lɪr/ 李爾王
Macbeth (*Macb*) /mækˈbeθ ; məkˈbɛθ/ 馬克白
1606–7 Antony and Cleopatra (*Ant & Cleop*) /ˌæntənɪ ən ˌklɪəˈpætrə ; ˏæntənɪ ən ˏklɪəˈpætrə/ 安東尼與克利歐佩特拉
1607–8 Coriolanus (*Cor*) /ˌkɒrɪəˈleɪnəs *US:* ˌkɔːr- ; ˏkɔrɪəˈlenəs/ 考利歐雷諾斯
Timon of Athens (*Tim of Ath*) /ˌtaɪmən əv ˈæθənz ; ˏtaɪmən əv ˈæθənz/ 雅典的泰蒙
1608–10 Pericles, Prince of Tyre (*Per*) /ˈperɪkliːz ; ˈpɛrəˏkliz/ 波里克利斯
Cymbeline (*Cymb*) /ˈsɪmbəliːn ; ˈsɪmbl̩ˏin/ 辛伯林
The Winter's Tale (*Wint T*) 多天的故事
1611–12 The Tempest (*Temp*) 暴風雨
1612–13 The Famous History of the Life of King Henry VIII (*Hen VIII*) 亨利八世

Poems 詩集

(Date given is that of first printing) (年代係根據初版)

1593 Venus and Adonis (*Ven & Ad*) /ˌviːnəs n əˈdəʊnɪs *US:* əˈdɒnɪs ; ˏvinəs n̩ əˈdɑnəs/ 維納斯與亞東尼斯
1594 The Rape of Lucrece (*Lucr*) /luːˈkriːs ; luˈkris/ 路克麗絲的被姦
1601 The Phoenix and the Turtle (*Phoen & T*) 鳳凰與斑鳩
1609 Sonnets (*Sonn*) 十四行詩
1609 A Lover's Complaint (*Lover's Comp*) 情人怨

Appendix 9 **PUNCTUATION**

附錄九 標點使用法

. Full Stop (US = Period) 句點

Used to mark the end of a sentence: 用以表示一個句子的結束:

Edward walked briskly into the hotel. The receptionist looked at him coldly. 愛德華輕快地走入旅館。接待員冷淡地望着他。

Also ⇨ Letters and Abbreviations below. 亦參看下列之 '書信' 與 '略語'。

? Question Mark 問號

1 Used at the end of a *direct question:* 用於'直接問句'之尾:

Who was the first to arrive? 誰是最先到達的？

(*Note.* It is not used at the end of an *indirect question:* 注意:問號不用於 '間接問句' 之尾:
He asked who had been the first to arrive. 他問誰是最先到達的)。

2 Used in parentheses to express doubt: 用於括弧內表示懷疑:

He was born in 1550(?) and died in 1613. 他生於 1550(？)年,卒於 1613 年。

! Exclamation Mark (US also 美亦稱 Exclamation Point) 感嘆號

Used at the end of a sentence or remark expressing a high degree of anger, amazement or other strong emotion: 用於句尾或語尾表示高度的憤怒、驚異或其他强烈的感情:

'*What a wonderful surprise!*' *she cried.* '這眞是一件令人驚喜的事！' 她大聲說。
Get out of here and never come back! 滾出去,永遠不要再回來！

(*Note:* Beware of over-using exclamation marks, or including them where the emotion is only mild.)
(注意:當心不要過度使用感嘆號,或在僅表達平和感情的句中使用。)

, Comma 逗點

1 Used to separate the items in lists of words, phrases or clauses: 用以分開一系列的字、片語或子句:

Red, pink, yellow and white roses filled the huge vases. 那些大花瓶裡裝滿了紅的、粉紅的、黃的和白的玫瑰花。
If you take your time, stay calm, concentrate and think ahead, you'll pass your driving test. 如果你不着急,保持鎮定,集中精神注意前面,你會通過駕駛考試的。

2 Sometimes used after a subordinate adverbial clause or after a phrase which comes before the main clause. It is essential after longer clauses and phrases, and to avoid ambiguity: 有時用於主要子句前面的附屬副詞子句或片語之後。在較長的子句或片語之後及爲了避免意義含糊,用逗點是必要的:

When the sun is shining brightly above, the world seems a happier place. 當太陽在天空中照耀的時候,這個世界似乎是一個更快樂的地方。
In the summer of 1984, many trees died. 1984 年的夏季,許多樹木死去了。

3 Used after a non-finite or verbless clause at the beginning of a sentence:
用於句首帶非限定動詞形式的子句或無動詞子句之後:

To get there on time, she left half an hour early. 爲了準時到達那裡,她提早半小時離開。
Happy and contented, the cat fell asleep. 又快樂又滿足,那隻貓睡着了。

4 Used to separate an introductory or transitional word or phrase (eg *therefore, however, by the way, for instance*) from the rest of the sentence: 用以將一導言的或轉變語氣的詞或片語(如 therefore, however, by the way, for instance)與句中其餘部分隔開:

Yes, it certainly had been an eventful day. 是的,那確實是一個多事之日。
In fact, I don't even know her name. 說實在的,我甚至不知道她的姓名。
Driving on icy roads can be dangerous and one should, therefore, be very careful. 在覆蓋着冰的道路上駕駛有發生危險的可能性,因此我們應當十分小心。

5 Used before and after any element (eg a dependent clause, a comment) which interrupts the sentence: 用於任何打斷一句的部分(例如一附屬子句,評論)之前後:

The fire, although it had been burning for several hours, was still blazing fiercely. 雖然燃燒了好幾個小時,但火勢仍很兇猛。
You should, indeed you must, report the matter to the police. 你應該,說實在的你必須,把這事向警方報告。

6 Used before and after a non-defining relative clause, or a phrase in apposition, which gives more information about the noun it follows: 用於進一步說明其前之名詞的非限制關係子句或同位片語之前後:

The Pennine Hills, which have been a favourite with hikers for many years, are situated between Lancashire and Yorkshire. 賓南山脈位於蘭開郡與約克郡之間,許多年來是一個遠足者所喜愛的地方。
Queen Elizabeth II, a very popular monarch, celebrated her Silver Jubilee in 1977. 伊麗莎白女王二世爲一深受人民愛戴的女王,在 1977 年慶祝她在位二十五週年紀念。

(*Note:* No commas are used around a relative clause that *defines* the noun it follows: 注意:在'限制'其前之名詞的關係子句之前後不用逗點: *The hills that separate Lancashire from Yorkshire are called The Pennines.* 把蘭開郡和約克郡分開的山巒叫做賓南山脈)。

7 Sometimes used to separate main clauses linked by a conjunction (eg *and, as, but, for, or*), especially when the first clause is long: 有時用來分隔由一連接詞(例如 and, as, but, for, or)連接的主要子句,尤其當第一個子句過長時:

We had been looking forward to meeting Sarah's husband, but discovered tha the was not as pleasant as we had hoped. 我們曾一直盼望能見到莎拉的丈夫，然而却發現他並不像我們所期望的那樣討人喜歡。

Also ⇨ Conversation and Letters below. 亦參看下列之'會話'與'書信'。

: Colon 冒號

1 (Formal) Used after a main clause where the following statement illustrates or explains the content of that clause. It may be replaced by a semicolon or a full stop: (正式用法)用於一主要子句後，其後的陳述進一步說明該主要子句的含義。冒號可由一分號或句點代替：

The garden had been neglected for a long time: it was overgrown and full of weeds. 那花園曾長期乏人照料：裡面植物蔓生而且還長滿了雜草。

2 Used before a long list, and often introduced by phrases such as: *such as: for example: for instance: in the following examples: as follows:* 用於一長列項目前，並常在 such as: for example: for instance: in the following examples: as follows: 等片語之後：

Your first aid kit should include the following items: cotton wool, lint, antiseptic lotion, sticking plaster, bandages and safety pins. 你的急救工具應包括下列各項：棉花，繃帶麻布，消毒藥水，橡皮膏，繃帶和安全別針。

Also ⇨ Letters and Quotations below. 亦參看下列之'書信'及'引用文'。

; Semicolon 分號

1 (Formal) Used to separate main clauses, not (usually) joined by a conjunction, which are considered so closely connected as to belong to one sentence: (正式用法)用來分隔(通常)沒有連接詞連接的主要子句，這些主要子句被認爲關係密切而屬於一個句子：

The sun was setting now; the shadows were long. 太陽正在沉落；陰影顯得很長。
He had never been to Russia before; however, it had always been one of his life-long ambitions. 他以前從未去過蘇俄；然而，這一直是他的終生目標之一。

2 Used instead of a comma to separate from each other parts of a sentence that are already separated by commas: 用來代替逗點，分隔業經由逗點分開的句中部分：

There are two facts to consider: first, the weather; second, the expense. 有兩項事實要考慮：第一，天氣；第二，費用。

— Dash 破折號

1 (Colloq) Used instead of a colon or a semicolon to make the writing more vivid or dramatic: (俗)用以代替冒號或分號，使寫作較生動或動人：

Sirens blared, men shouted, and people crowded in to witness the scene—it was chaos. 號笛響起，人們在叫喊，而一大堆人湧進來目覩這景像——那是一團混亂。
So you've been lying to me for years and years—how can I ever trust you again? 既然這些年來你一直在騙我——我怎能再信任你呢？

2 (Colloq) Used singly or in pairs to separate extra information, an after-thought or a comment, in a vivid or dramatic way, from the rest of the sentence: (俗)單一或成雙使用，將一額外說明，事後想起的解釋或評論生動地與句中其餘部分隔開：

Schooldays are the happiest days of our lives—or so we are told. 求學時代是我們一生中最幸福的日子——或者據說是如此。
Schooldays—or so we are told—are the happiest days of our lives. 求學時代——或者據說是如此——是我們一生中最幸福的日子。

(*Note:* In more formal usage, parentheses or commas replace dashes.) (注意：在較正式用法中，以括弧或逗點代替破折號。)

Also ⇨ Conversation below. 亦參看下列之'會話'。

( ) Parentheses (GB also 英亦稱 Brackets) 括弧

1 Used to separate extra information, an after-thought or a comment from the rest of the sentence: 用來將一額外說明，事後想起的解釋或評論與句中其餘部分隔開：

Schooldays (*so we are told*) *are the happiest days of our lives.* 求學時代(據說是如此)是我們一生中最幸福的日子。
He said he'd never seen the sea before (*but I think he was joking*). 他說他以前從未看到過海(不過我想他是在開玩笑)。

2 Used to enclose cross-references: 用以括起表示互相參照之說明：

The abacus (*see the picture on page* 1) *is used for teaching numbers to children.* 算盤(參看第一頁之插圖)是用來教兒童算術的。

' ' Quotation Marks (GB also 英亦稱 Inverted Commas) 引號

(*Note:* In GB usage they are usually single: *'Fire!'* In US usage they are usually double: *"Fire!"*) (注意：英國通常是用單引號：'Fire!' 美國通常是用雙引號："Fire!")

Used around a slang or technical term when it is in a context in which it is not usually found, or around a word to which the writer wishes to draw particular attention: 用來括起不常出現在上下文中之俚語或專門用語，或括起作者希望特別引起注意的字：

Next, the clay pot had to be 'fired'. 其次,土罐必須加以'烘燒'。
He called himself a 'gentleman', but you would never have thought so from the way he behaved. 他自認爲是一個'紳士',但是從他的行爲看來,你絕不會認爲他是紳士。

Also ⇨ Conversation and Quotations below. 亦參看下列之'會話'與'引用文'。

- Hyphen 連字號

(*Note:* It must not be confused with the dash, which separates parts of a sentence. The hyphen is half the length of the dash.) (注意:連字號不可與破折號相混,後者分隔句中的若干部分。連字號的長度爲破折號的一半。)

1 Sometimes used to form a compound word from two other words: 有時用以連接兩個字形成一複合字:

hard-hearted; 無情的; *radio-telescope;* 無線電望遠鏡; *fork-lift truck.* 叉式起重車。

2 Used to form a compound word from a prefix and a proper name: 用以連接一字首和一專有名詞而形成一複合字:

pre-Raphaelite; 前拉斐爾派的; *pro-Soviet;* 親蘇的; *anti-Nazi.* 反納粹的。

3 Used to form a compound word from two other words which are separated by a preposition: 用以連接中間加一介詞的兩個字,而形成一複合字:

mother-in-law; 岳母; *mother-to-be;* 孕婦; *mother-of-pearl;* 眞珠母; *out-of-date.* 過時的。

4 (Esp GB) Sometimes used to separate a prefix ending in a vowel from a word beginning with that same vowel: (尤用於英國)有時用以分隔一字首與一字,若該字首的末尾字母與該字起首的字母爲相同的母音:

co-ordination; 同等; *re-elect;* 再選; *pre-eminent.* 超羣的。

Also ⇨ Introduction: page xvi (*A compound*); page xxiii (*How to divide a word*). 亦參看'緒論'第 xvi 頁(複合字);第 xxiii 頁(怎樣斷字)。

' Apostrophe 省略號;所有格符號

1 Used with 's' to indicate the possessive: 與's'連用表示所有格:

Singular noun: 單數名詞: *the dog's* /dɒgz ; dɔgz/ *bone.* 狗的骨頭。
Singular noun ending in 's': 字尾爲's'的單數名詞: *the princess's* /prɪn'sesɪz ; 'prɪnsɪsɪz/ *smile.* 公主的微笑。
Singular proper noun ending in 's' (two possible forms): 字尾爲's'的單數專有名詞(兩種可能的形式): *King Charles's* /'tʃɑːlzɪz ; 'tʃɑrlzɪz/ *crown; King Charles'* /'tʃɑːlzɪz ; 'tʃɑrlzɪz/ *crown.* 查理王的王冠。
Plural noun: 複數名詞: *students'* /'stjuːdənts ; 'stjudn̩ts/ *books.* 學生們的書。
Irregular plural: 不規則的複數: *men's* /menz ; mɛnz/ *jackets.* 男人的夾克。

2 Used in a *contracted form* to indicate the omission of letters or figures: 用於'縮寫式'表示省略字母或數字:

I'm (= I am); *he's* (= he is/has); *they'd* (= they would/had). *In '87* (= 1987).

3 Used with 's' to form the plural of a letter, a figure or an abbreviation, when these are used as proper words. In modern usage it is often omitted after a figure or a capital letter: 當某一字母、數字或略語作普通字用時,與's'連用形成複數。在現代用法中,在一數字或大寫字母後,此號常被省去:

in the 1960's or 或 *in the 1960s.* 在二十世紀六十年代。*MP's* or 或 *MPs.*
He can't pronounce his r's. 他的 r 音發不出來。

4 Used with 's' to form the plural of a word (eg a preposition or a conjunction) that does not usually have a plural: 與's'連用形成一個通常沒有複數的字(如介詞或連接詞)之複數:

No if's or but's—just do as I say. 不要'假如'或'但是'——祇是照我說的去做。

Abbreviations 略語

1 A full stop may end an abbreviation or a person's initials, although this is becoming less common, especially in GB usage: 在一略語或姓名的起首字母略語後可用句點,不過這種用法,尤其是在英國,越來越不常見:

Mr. R. S.H. Smith or 或 *Mr R S H Smith.*

2 When the abbreviation consists of capitals, it is common GB usage to omit the full stops: 略語由大寫字母構成時,英國的普遍用法是省去句點:

UN WHO BBC

3 The omission of full stops in a lower case abbreviation is less common: 在小寫字母構成的略語中省去句點較不常見:

i.e. p.m. e.g. or 或 *ie pm eg*

4 If the abbreviation includes the last letter of the word, it is usual in GB usage to omit the full stop: 一字之略語如包括該字最後一個字母時,在英國的用法通常是省去句點:

Mr Dr St Rd

5 To form the plural of capital letter abbreviations, add a lower case *'s* or *s*: 大寫字母構成的略語,其複數是加一小寫的 's 或 s:

MP's or 或 *MPs TV's* or 或 *TVs*

Also ⇨ Appendix 2 (*Abbreviations*). 亦參看附錄二(略語表)。

Conversation 會話

1 A new indented paragraph is begun with each new speaker. 每當換一說話者時，要新起一段，並且第一行應縮進排印或書寫。

2 Quotation marks enclose all words and punctuation in direct speech: 直接敍述時，引號將所有的字及標點括進：

'*What on earth did you do that for?*' *he asked.* '你做那事究竟是爲了什麼？' 他問道。

3 Introductory words (eg *he said, she cried, they answered*) are separated from the actual words spoken by commas if no other punctuation mark (eg question mark, exclamation mark) is used: 如無其他標點(例如問號，感嘆號)時，引導的字(例如 he said, she cried, they answered)與實際說的話之間用逗點分開：

John said, 'That's all I know.' 約翰說，'那就是我所知道的一切。' '*That's all I know,' said John.* '那就是我所知道的一切，'約翰說。'*That,' said John, 'is all I know.*' '那些，' 約翰說，'就是我所知道的一切。' '*Why?' asked John.* '爲什麼？' 約翰問道。

4 A comma separates a question tag from the rest of the sentence: 附加問句與句中其餘部分之間用逗點分開：

'*You knew he'd come, didn't you?*' '你知道他會來，是不是？'

5 A mild interjection or the direct use of a name is separated from the rest of the sentence by a comma: 不强烈的感嘆語或直呼的姓名與句中其餘部分用逗點分開：

'*Oh, so that's what he wanted.*' '噢，那麼那就是他所要的了。' (Cf 參較 '*Oh no! I don't believe you!*' '啊不！我不相信你！')
'*Well, Peter, I did my best.*' '唔，彼得，我盡了我的力了。' (Cf 參較 '*Peter! Look out!*' '彼得！當心！')

6 Hesitant or interrupted speech can be indicated by dashes: 猶豫或打斷的話可用破折號表示：

'*Can I—I mean, would you mind if I came too?*' '我可以—我是說，我也來你會介意嗎？'
'*You'll find it in—' were his dying words.* '你會發現它在—' 他臨終時如此說。

7 Speech within speech is shown by (GB usage) double quotation marks inside single marks, or (US usage) single quotation marks within double marks: 直接敍述中如再有直接敍述是由單引號中加雙引號表示(英國用法)，或雙引號中加單引號(美國用法)：

'*When the judge said, "Not guilty," I could have hugged him.*' (GB)
'當那法官說"無罪"時，我眞想擁抱他。' (英)
"*When the judge said, 'Not guilty,' I could have hugged him.*" (US)
"當那法官說'無罪'時，我眞想擁抱他。" (美)

Letters 書信

1 A business letter is set out as shown below. The punctuation marks are optional. The address of the person who is writing the letter is in the top right-hand corner; the address of the person to whom the letter is being written is in the top left-hand corner, but below the address of the sender: 商業書信的格式如下列所示。其標點符號可用可不用。寫信人的地址在右上角；收信人的地址在左上角，但在寫信人的地址之下：

3 Willow Street,
Frambleton,
Suffolk.
SF5 9PK.
6th June, 1984.

Mr D. B. Taylor,
Metalwork Ltd,
Booth Street,
Ormton,
Lancashire.
LC14 3JQ.

Dear Mr Taylor,

Thank you for . . .

Yours faithfully/sincerely/(US) truly,

[signature]

Mary Burton.

2 In US usage, a colon is substituted for the comma in the salutation, except informally: 美國用法中，信頭之稱呼是以冒號代替逗點，但非正式的信函不在此例：

Dear Ms Burton: but 但 *Dear Mary,*

3 In an informal letter, only the address of the sender is necessary, the optional punctuation is more likely to be omitted, and *Yours sincerely* etc is replaced by a more friendly or personal phrase, eg *Yours, Yours affectionately, With best/warm wishes, With love.* 非正式書信中，僅須寫發信人的地址，可以不使用的標點省去的機會更大，而 Yours sincerely 等則由較友好或親切的片語如 Yours, Yours affectionately, With best/warm wishes, With love 等代替。

Quotations 引用文

1 The quotation is separated from its introduction by a colon and is enclosed by quotation marks: 引用文置於引導語及冒號之後,並由引號括起:

It was Disraeli who said: 'Little things affect little minds.' 狄斯雷利說過:'小事情會影響小心眼的人。'

2 If a word or phrase is omitted from the quotation, this is indicated by a row of three dots (...): 如果引用文中省略字或片語,用連續三點(…)表示:

'The condition of man . . . is a condition of war of everyone against everyone.' (Thomas Hobbes) '人類的性格 . . . 即是你爭我奪。'(湯瑪斯・霍布士)

Also ⇨ Conversation above. 亦參看上列之'會話'。

附錄十　聖經目錄

The Old Testament 舊約全書

Genesis (*Gen*) /ˈdʒenəsɪs ; ˈdʒɛnəsəs/ 創世記
Exodus (*Exod*) /ˈeksədəs ; ˈɛksədəs/ 出埃及記
Leviticus (*Lev*) /lɪˈvɪtɪkəs ; lɪˈvɪtɪkəs/ 利未記
Numbers (*Num*) /ˈnʌmbəz ; ˈnʌmbɚz/ 民數記
Deuteronomy (*Deut*) /ˌdjuːtəˈrɒnəmɪ *US:* ˌduː- ; ˌdutəˈrɑnəmɪ/ 申命記
Joshua (*Josh*) /ˈdʒɒʃʊə ; ˈdʒɑʃʊə/ 約書亞記
Judges (*Judg*) /ˈdʒʌdʒɪz ; ˈdʒʌdʒəz/ 士師記
Ruth /ruːθ ; ruθ/ 路得記
I Samuel (*I Sam*) /ˈsæmjʊəl ; ˈsæmj(ʊ)əl/ 撒母耳記上
II Samuel (*II Sam*) /ˈsæmjʊəl ; ˈsæmj(ʊ)əl/ 撒母耳記下
I Kings (*I Kgs*) /kɪŋz ; kɪŋz/ 列王紀上
II Kings (*II Kgs*) /kɪŋz ; kɪŋz/ 列王紀下
I Chronicles (*I Chron*) /ˈkrɒnɪklz ; ˈkrɑnɪklz/ 歷代志上
II Chronicles (*II Chron*) /ˈkrɒnɪklz ; ˈkrɑnɪklz/ 歷代志下
Ezra /ˈezrə ; ˈɛzrə/ 以斯拉記
Nehemiah (*Neh*) /ˌniːəˈmaɪə ; ˌniəˈmaɪə/ 尼希米記
Esther /ˈestə(r) ; ˈɛstɚ/ 以斯帖記
Job /dʒəʊb ; dʒob/ 約伯記
Psalms (*Ps*) /sɑːmz ; sɑmz/ 詩篇
Proverbs (*Prov*) /ˈprɒvɜːbz ; ˈprɑvɝbz/ 箴言
Ecclesiastes (*Eccles*) /ɪˌkliːzɪˈæstiːz ; ɪkˌlizɪˈæstiz/ 傳道書
Song of Solomon /ˌsɒŋ əv ˈsɒləmən *US:* ˌsɔːŋ ; ˌsɔŋ əv ˈsɑləmən/ *or* 或 Song of Songs (*S of S*) 雅歌
Isaiah (*Isa*) /aɪˈzaɪə *US:* aɪˈzeɪə ; aɪˈzeə/ 以賽亞書
Jeremiah (*Jer*) /ˌdʒerɪˈmaɪə ; ˌdʒɛrəˈmaɪə/ 耶利米書
Lamentations (*Lam*) /ˌlæmənˈteɪʃnz ; ˌlæmənˈteʃənz/ 耶利米哀歌
Ezekiel (*Ezek*) /ɪˈziːkɪəl ; ɪˈzikɪəl/ 以西結書
Daniel (*Dan*) /ˈdænɪəl ; ˈdænjəl/ 但以理書
Hosea (*Hos*) /həʊˈziːə ; hoˈziə/ 何西阿書
Joel /ˈdʒəʊəl ; ˈdʒoəl/ 約珥書
Amos /ˈeɪmɒs *US:* -məs ; ˈeməs/ 阿摩司書
Obadiah (*Obad*) /ˌəʊbəˈdaɪə ; ˌobəˈdaɪə/ 俄巴底亞書
Jonah /ˈdʒəʊnə ; ˈdʒonə/ 約拿書
Micah /ˈmaɪkə ; ˈmaɪkə/ 彌迦書
Nahum /ˈneɪhəm ; ˈne(h)əm/ 那鴻書
Habakkuk (*Hab*) /ˈhæbəkək *US:* həˈbækək ; həˈbækək/ 哈巴谷書
Zephaniah (*Zeph*) /ˌzefəˈnaɪə ; ˌzɛfəˈnaɪə/ 西番雅書
Haggai (*Hag*) /ˈhægeɪaɪ *US:* ˈhægɪaɪ ; ˈhægɪˌaɪ/ 哈該書
Zechariah (*Zech*) /ˌzekəˈraɪə ; ˌzɛkəˈraɪə/ 撒迦利亞書
Malachi (*Mal*) /ˈmæləkaɪ ; ˈmæləˌkaɪ/ 瑪拉基書

The Apocrypha /əˈpɒkrɪfə ; əˈpɑkrəfə/ 僞經

Tobit /ˈtəʊbɪt ; ˈtobət/ 透比書
Judith /ˈdʒuːdɪθ ; ˈdʒudəθ/ 朱迪絲書
Wisdom /ˈwɪzdəm ; ˈwɪzdəm/ 智慧論
Ecclesiasticus /ɪˌkliːzɪˈæstɪkəs ; ɪkˌlizɪˈæstɪkəs/ 不經之書
Baruch /ˈbeərək ; ˈbɛrək/ 巴魯書
I Maccabees /ˈmækəbiːz ; ˈmækəbiz/ 麥克比斯前書
II Maccabees /ˈmækəbiːz ; ˈmækəbiz/ 麥克比斯後書

The New Testament 新約全書

St Matthew (*Matt*) /ˈmæθjuː ; ˈmæθju/ 馬太福音
St Mark /mɑːk ; mɑrk/ 馬可福音
St Luke /luːk ; luk/ 路加福音
St John /dʒɒn ; dʒɑn/ 約翰福音
Acts /ækts ; ækts/ 使徒行傳
Romans (*Rom*) /ˈrəʊmənz ; ˈromənz/ 羅馬書
I Corinthians (*I Cor*) /kəˈrɪnθɪənz ; kəˈrɪnθɪənz/ 哥林多前書
II Corinthians (*II Cor*) /kəˈrɪnθɪənz ; kəˈrɪnθɪənz/ 哥林多後書
Galatians (*Gal*) /gəˈleɪʃnz ; gəˈleʃənz/ 加拉太書
Ephesians (*Eph*) /ɪˈfiːʒnz ; ɪˈfiʒənz/ 以弗所書
Philippians (*Phil*) /fɪˈlɪpɪənz ; fəˈlɪpɪənz/ 腓立比書
Colossians (*Col*) /kəˈlɒʃnz ; kəˈlɑʃənz/ 哥羅西書
I Thessalonians (*I Thess*) /ˌθesəˈləʊnɪənz ; ˌθɛsəˈlonɪənz/ 帖撒羅尼迦前書
II Thessalonians (*II Thess*) /ˌθesəˈləʊnɪənz ; ˌθɛsəˈlonɪənz/ 帖撒羅尼迦後書
I Timothy (*I Tim*) /ˈtɪməθɪ ; ˈtɪməθɪ/ 提摩太前書
II Timothy (*II Tim*) /ˈtɪməθɪ ; ˈtɪməθɪ/ 提摩太後書
Titus (*Tit*) /ˈtaɪtəs ; ˈtaɪtəs/ 提多書
Philemon (*Philem*) /fɪˈliːmən ; fəˈlimən/ 腓利門書
Hebrews (*Heb*) /ˈhiːbruz ; ˈhibruz/ 希伯來書
James (*Jas*) /dʒeɪmz ; dʒemz/ 雅各書
I Peter (*I Pet*) /ˈpiːtə(r) ; ˈpitɚ/ 彼得前書
II Peter (*II Pet*) /ˈpiːtə(r) ; ˈpitɚ/ 彼得後書
I John /dʒɒn ; dʒɑn/ 約翰一書
II John /dʒɒn ; dʒɑn/ 約翰二書
III John /dʒɒn ; dʒɑn/ 約翰三書
Jude /dʒuːd ; dʒud/ 猶大書
Revelation (*Rev*) /ˌrevəˈleɪʃn ; ˌrɛvəˈleʃən/ *or* 或 Apocalypse /əˈpɒkəlɪps ; əˈpɑkəˌlɪps/ 啓示錄

Appendix 11 **TABLE OF CHEMICAL ELEMENTS**

附錄十一 化學元素表

Element 元 素	Symbol 符 號	Atomic number 原子序	Relative★ Atomic mass 原子量
Actinium 錒	Ac	89	227*
Aluminium 鋁	Al	13	26·981 5
Americium 鋂	Am	95	243*
Antimony 銻	Sb	51	121·75
Argon 氬	Ar	18	39·948
Arsenic 砷	As	33	74·921 6
Astatine 砹	At	85	210*
Barium 鋇	Ba	56	137·34
Berkelium 錇	Bk	97	249*
Beryllium 鈹	Be	4	9·012 2
Bismuth 鉍	Bi	83	208·980 6
Boron 硼	B	5	10·81
Bromine 溴	Br	35	79·904
Cadmium 鎘	Cd	48	112·40
Caesium 銫	Cs	55	132·905 5
Calcium 鈣	Ca	20	40·08
Californium 鐦	Cf	98	251*
Carbon 碳	C	6	12·011
Cerium 鈰	Ce	58	140·12
Chlorine 氯	Cl	17	35·453
Chromium 鉻	Cr	24	51·996
Cobalt 鈷	Co	27	58·933 2
Copper 銅	Cu	29	63·546
Curium 鋦	Cm	96	247*
Dysprosium 鏑	Dy	66	162·50
Einsteinium 鑀	Es	99	254*
Erbium 鉺	Er	68	167·26
Europium 銪	Eu	63	151·96
Fermium 鐨	Fm	100	257*
Fluorine 氟	F	9	18·998 4
Francium 鈁	Fr	87	223*
Gadolinium 釓	Gd	64	157·25
Gallium 鎵	Ga	31	69·72
Germanium 鍺	Ge	32	72·59
Gold 金	Au	79	196·966 5
Hafnium 鉿	Hf	72	178·49
Hahnium [illegible]	Ha	105	262*
Helium 氦	He	2	4·002 6
Holmium 鈥	Ho	67	164·930 3
Hydrogen 氫	H	1	1·008
Indium 銦	In	49	114·82
Iodine 碘	I	53	126·904 5
Iridium 銥	Ir	77	192·22
Iron 鐵	Fe	26	55·847
Krypton 氪	Kr	36	83·80
Lanthanum 鑭	La	57	138·905 5
Lawrencium 鐒	Lw/Lr	103	260*
Lead 鉛	Pb	82	207·19
Lithium 鋰	Li	3	6·939
Lutetium 鑥	Lu	71	174·97
Magnesium 鎂	Mg	12	24·312
Manganese 錳	Mn	25	54·938 0
Mendelevium 鍆	Md	101	258*

Element 元 素	Symbol 符 號	Atomic number 原子序	Relative★ Atomic mass 原子量
Mercury 汞	Hg	80	200·59
Molybdenum 鉬	Mo	42	95·94
Neodymium 釹	Nd	60	144·24
Neon 氖	Ne	10	20·183
Neptunium 錼	Np	93	237*
Nickel 鎳	Ni	28	58·71
Niobium 鈮	Nb	41	92·906 4
Nitrogen 氮	N	7	14·006 7
Nobelium 鍩	No	102	259*
Osmium 鋨	Os	76	190·2
Oxygen 氧	O	8	15·999 4
Palladium 鈀	Pd	46	106·4
Phosphorus 磷	P	15	30·973 8
Platinum 鉑	Pt	78	195·09
Plutonium 鈈	Pu	94	244*
Polonium 釙	Po	84	210*
Potassium 鉀	K	19	39·102
Praseodymium 鐠	Pr	59	140·907 7
Promethium 鉕	Pm	61	145*
Protactinium 鏷	Pa	91	231·035 9
Radium 鐳	Ra	88	226·025 4
Radon 氡	Rn	86	222*
Rhenium 錸	Re	75	186·2
Rhodium 銠	Rh	45	102·905 5
Rubidium 銣	Rb	37	85·467 8
Ruthenium 釕	Ru	44	101·07
Rutherfordium 鑪	Rf	104	261*
Samarium 釤	Sm	62	150·4
Scandium 鈧	Sc	21	44·955 9
Selenium 硒	Se	34	78·96
Silicon 硅	Si	14	28·086
Silver 銀	Ag	47	107·868
Sodium 鈉	Na	11	22·989 8
Strontium 鍶	Sr	38	87·62
Sulphur 硫	S	16	32·06
Tantalum 鉭	Ta	73	180·947 9
Technetium 鎝	Tc	43	99*
Tellurium 碲	Te	52	127·60
Terbium 鋱	Tb	65	158·925 4
Thallium 鉈	Tl	81	204·37
Thorium 釷	Th	90	232·038 1
Thulium 銩	Tm	69	168·934 2
Tin 錫	Sn	50	118·69
Titanium 鈦	Ti	22	47·90
Tungsten 鎢	W	74	183·85
Uranium 鈾	U	92	238·029
Vanadium 釩	V	23	50·941 4
Xenon 氙	Xe	54	131·30
Ytterbium 鐿	Yb	70	173·04
Yttrium 釔	Y	39	88·905 9
Zinc 鋅	Zn	30	65·37
Zirconium 鋯	Zr	40	91·22

★ These values are based on the carbon–12 isotope as the standard. 數值以碳 12 同位數爲標準。

*These are the values of the most stable isotope. 最穩定同位數的數值。

Letter 字 母	Name 名 稱	Pronunciation 讀 音	
		Jones	**Kenyon & Knott**
Α α	alpha	'ælfə	\`ælfə
Β β	beta	'bi:tə, 'beɪtə	\`bitə, \`betə
Γ γ	gamma	'gæmə	\`gæmə
Δ δ	delta	'deltə	\`dɛltə
Ε ε	epsilon	ep'saɪlən, 'epsɪlən	ɛp\`saɪlən, \`ɛpsɪlən
Ζ ζ	zeta	'zi:tə	\`zitə
Η η	eta	'i:tə, 'eɪtə	\`itə, \`etə
Θ θ	theta	'θi:tə, 'θeɪtə	\`θitə, \`θetə
Ι ι	iota	aɪ'əʊtə	aɪ\`otə
Κ κ	kappa	'kæpə	\`kæpə
Λ λ	lambda	'læmdə	\`læmdə
Μ μ	mu	mju:	mju
Ν ν	nu	nju:	nju
Ξ ξ	xi	saɪ, gzaɪ, ksaɪ, zaɪ	saɪ, gzaɪ, ksaɪ, zaɪ
Ο ο	omicron	əʊ'maɪkr*ə*n	*o*\`maɪkr*ə*n
Π π	pi	paɪ	paɪ
Ρ ρ	rho	rəʊ	ro
Σ σ	sigma	'sɪgmə	\`sɪgmə
Τ τ	tau	taʊ, tɔ:	tau, tɔ
Υ υ	upsilon	ju:p'saɪlən, 'ju:psɪlən	jup\`saɪlən, \`jupsɪlən
Φ φ	phi	faɪ	faɪ
Χ χ	chi	kaɪ	kaɪ
Ψ ψ	psi	*p*saɪ	*p*saɪ
Ω ω	omega	'əʊmɪgə, 'əʊmegə	\`omɪgə, \`omɛgə

A sectional view of the earth showing the main structural elements. The lithosphere consists of the crust and the solid outer-most layer of the upper mantle. This zone of rigid material is underlain by the asthenosphere within the upper mantle. The density of the mantle increases with depth until a sudden sharp increase, the Gutenberg discontinuity, marks the boundary with the liquid outer core.

剖視圖顯示地球的主要構成部分。岩石圈所繪包括地殼和上地幔的固態外層，這層堅硬的物質爲軟流圈所覆蓋，軟流圈爲上地幔內一薄層岩石。地幔的密度隨深度漸增，達至某深度密度銳增，該處爲顧維不連續面，爲呈液態狀的外地心外緣。

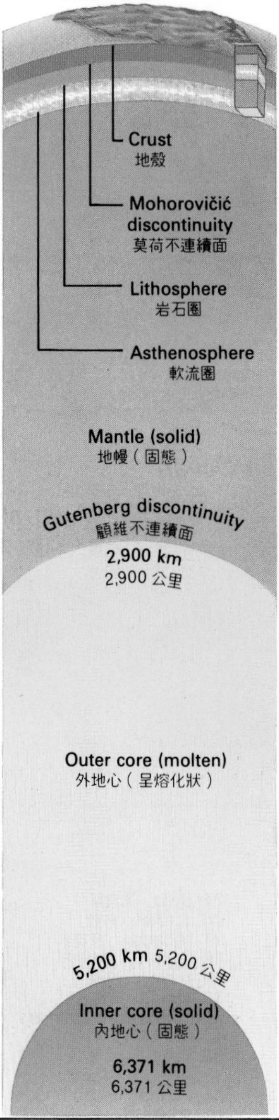

The light granitic rocks of the continental crust 'float' on the denser basaltic material below, the upstanding masses of mountain ranges being compensated by deep 'roots'.

大陸地殼的輕質花崗質岩「浮」在下層含玄武岩的物質之上，而高聳的山脈之下相應地有較深的「根部」。

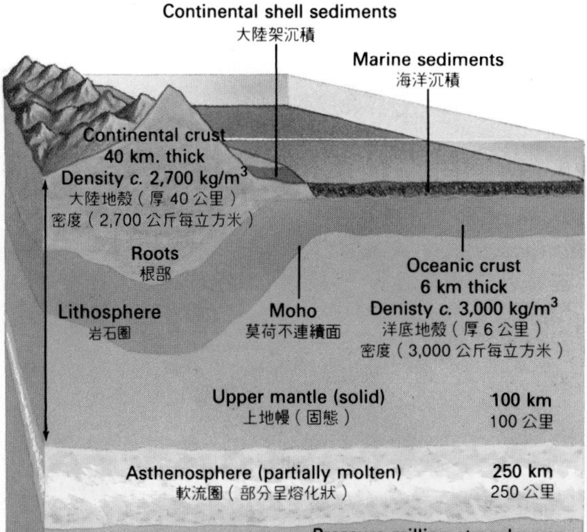

Graphs represent the changes in temperature, density, and pressure with increasing depth.
圖表顯示深度增加對溫度、密度、壓力的影響。

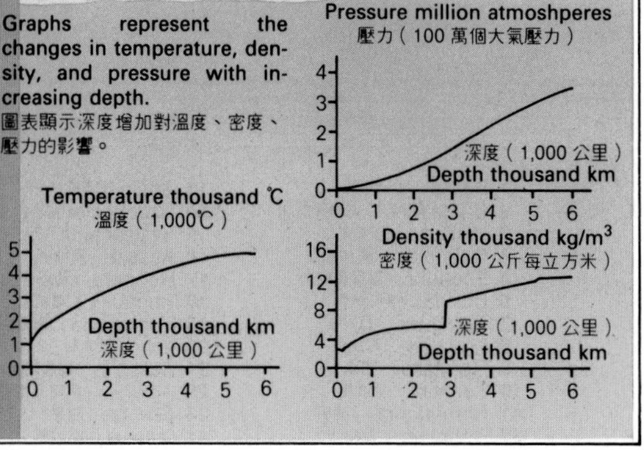

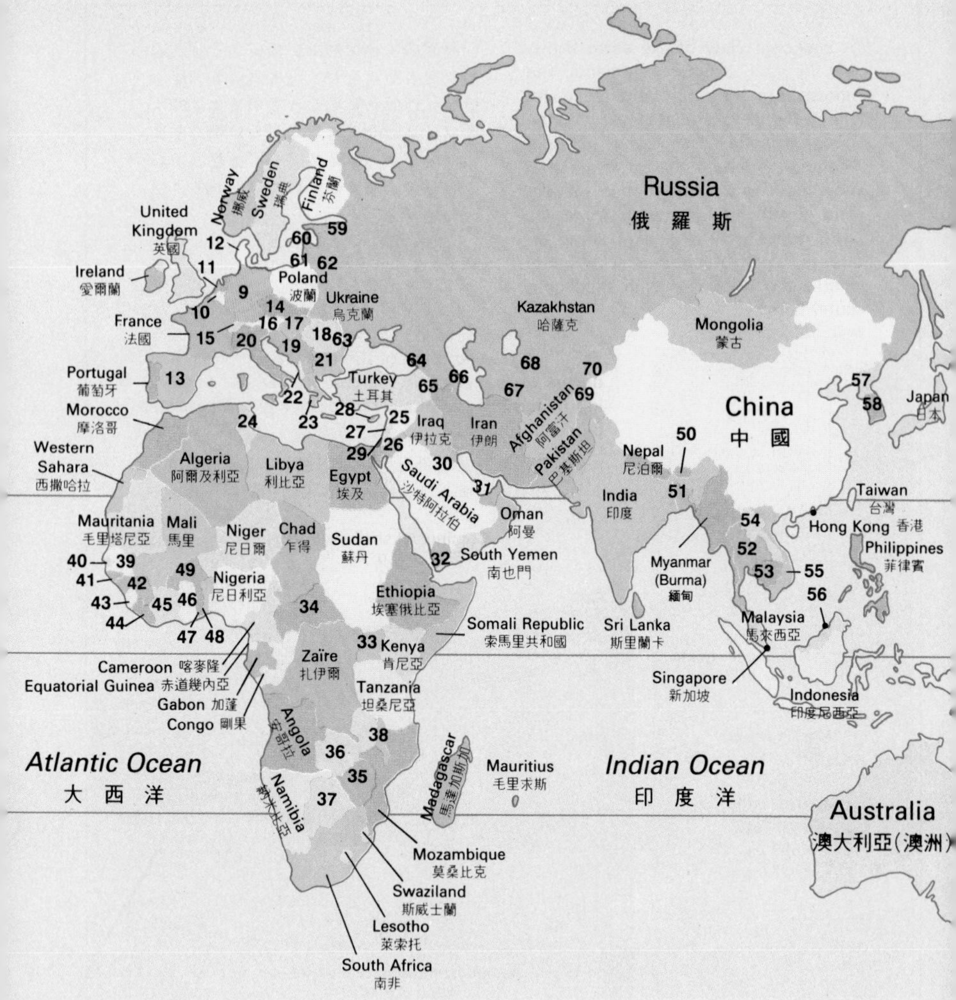

1 Belize 伯利茲
2 Costa Rica 哥斯達黎加
3 Panama 巴拿馬
4 Colombia 哥倫比亞
5 Ecuador 厄瓜多爾
6 Bolivia 玻利維亞
7 Paraguay 巴拉圭
8 Uruguay 烏拉圭
9 Germany 德國
10 Belgium 比利時
11 Netherlands 荷蘭
12 Denmark 丹麥
13 Spain 西班牙
14 Czechoslovakia 捷克
15 Switzerland 瑞士
16 Austria 奧地利
17 Hungary 匈牙利
18 Romania 羅馬尼亞
19 Yugoslavia 南斯拉夫
20 Italy 意大利
21 Bulgaria 保加利亞
22 Albania 阿爾巴尼亞
23 Greece 希臘
24 Tunisia 突尼斯
25 Syria 敍利亞
26 Jordan 約旦
27 Lebanon 黎巴嫩
28 Cyprus 塞浦路斯
29 Israel 以色列
30 Kuwait 科威特
31 United Arab Emirates 阿拉伯聯合酋長國
32 Yemen 也門
33 Uganda 烏干達
34 Central African Rep. 中非共和國

35 Zimbabwe 津巴布韋
36 Zambia 贊比亞
37 Botswana 博茨瓦納
38 Malawi 馬拉維
39 Senegal 塞內加爾
40 Gambia 岡比亞
41 Guinea-Bissau 幾內亞比紹
42 Guinea 幾內亞
43 Sierra Leone 塞拉利昂
44 Liberia 利比里亞
45 Ivory Coast 象牙海岸
46 Ghana 加納
47 Togo 多哥
48 Benin 貝寧
49 Burkina Faso 伯基納法索
50 Bhutan 不丹
51 Bangladesh 孟加拉
52 Thailand 泰國
53 Cambodia 柬埔寨
54 Laos 寮國
55 Vietnam 越南
56 Brunei 文萊
57 North Korea 北韓
58 South Korea 南韓
59 Estonia 愛沙尼亞
60 Latvia 拉脱維亞
61 Lithuania 立陶宛
62 Belorussia 白俄羅斯
63 Moldavia 摩爾多瓦
64 Georgia 格魯吉亞
65 Armenia 亞美尼亞
66 Azerbaijan 阿塞拜疆
67 Turkmenistan 土庫曼
68 Uzbekistan 烏茲別克
69 Tadzhikistan 塔吉克
70 Kirghizia 吉爾吉斯

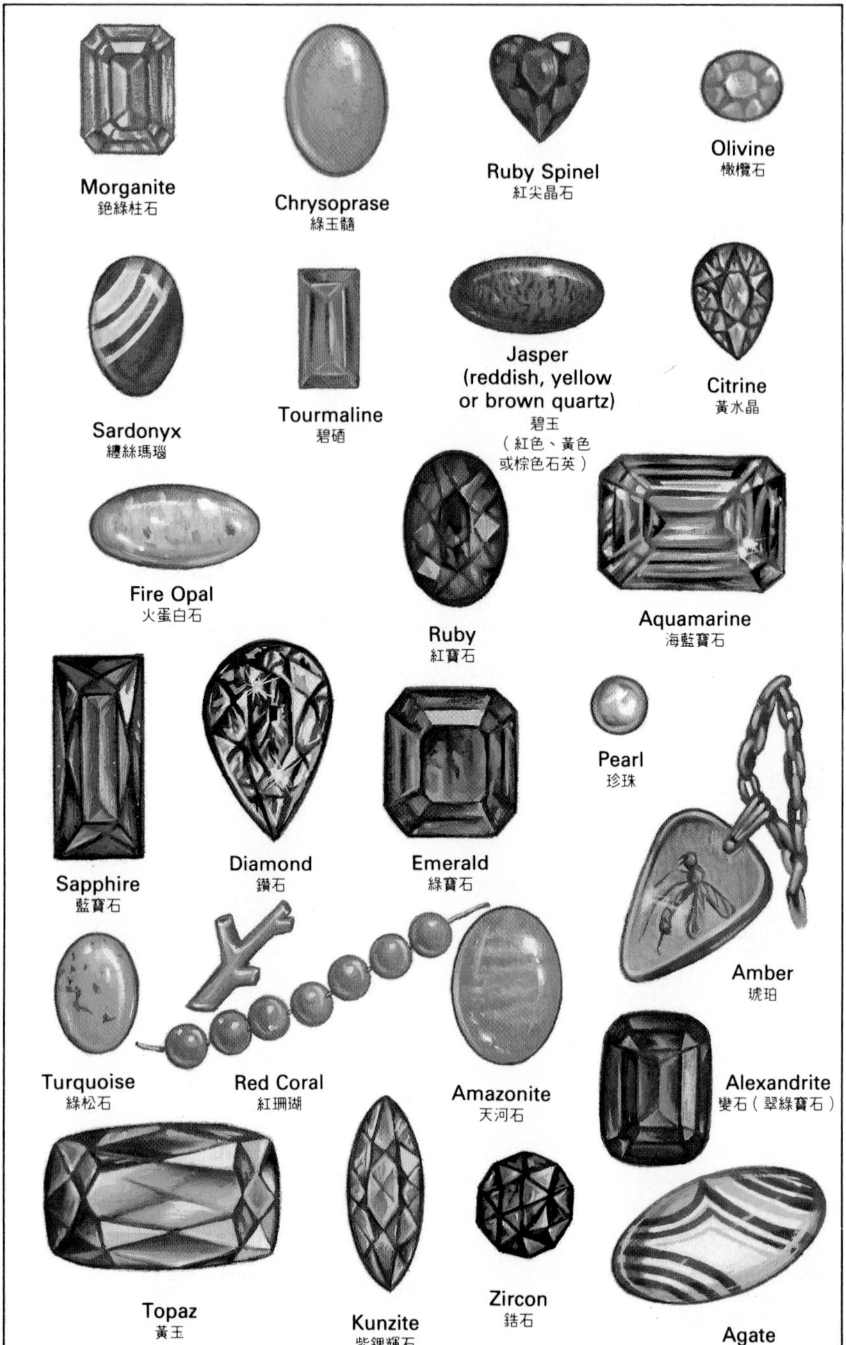
Morganite
銫綠柱石
Chrysoprase
綠玉髓
Ruby Spinel
紅尖晶石
Olivine
橄欖石
Sardonyx
纏絲瑪瑙
Tourmaline
碧硒
Jasper
(reddish, yellow
or brown quartz)
碧玉
（紅色、黃色
或棕色石英）
Citrine
黃水晶
Fire Opal
火蛋白石
Ruby
紅寶石
Aquamarine
海藍寶石
Sapphire
藍寶石
Diamond
鑽石
Emerald
綠寶石
Pearl
珍珠
Amber
琥珀
Turquoise
綠松石
Red Coral
紅珊瑚
Amazonite
天河石
Alexandrite
變石（翠綠寶石）
Topaz
黃玉
Kunzite
紫鋰輝石
Zircon
鋯石
Agate
瑪瑙

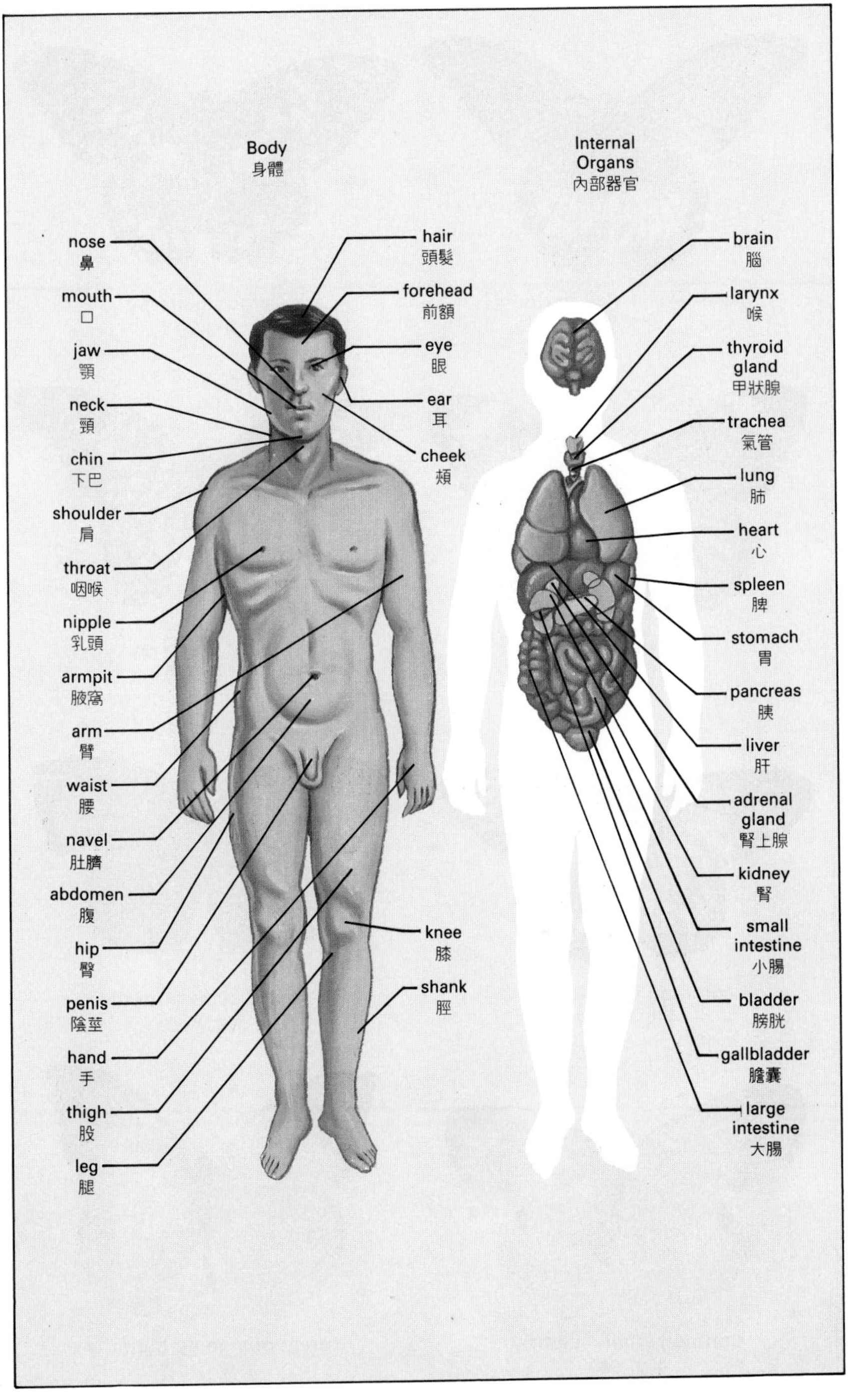
Body
身體
nose
鼻
mouth
口
jaw
顎
neck
頸
chin
下巴
shoulder
肩
throat
咽喉
nipple
乳頭
armpit
腋窩
arm
臂
waist
腰
navel
肚臍
abdomen
腹
hip
臀
penis
陰莖
hand
手
thigh
股
leg
腿
hair
頭髮
forehead
前額
eye
眼
ear
耳
cheek
頰
knee
膝
shank
脛
Internal Organs
內部器官
brain
腦
larynx
喉
thyroid gland
甲狀腺
trachea
氣管
lung
肺
heart
心
spleen
脾
stomach
胃
pancreas
胰
liver
肝
adrenal gland
腎上腺
kidney
腎
small intestine
小腸
bladder
膀胱
gallbladder
膽囊
large intestine
大腸

citrus swallowtail butterfly
柑桔鳳蝶

lemon butterfly
黃花鳳蝶

dark veined tiger
虎紋藍斑蝶

tailed green jay
綠斑鳳蝶

common black jezebel
花點褐粉蝶

small yellow butterfly
銀歡粉蝶

common white butterfly
東方粉蝶

great orange tip butterfly
赤翅頂粉蝶

stream loach
溪鰍

wild carp
白條

common carp
鯉魚

grey mullet
烏頭鯔

six-banded barb
花斑刺鲃

Tilapia
金山鯽

puffer fish
河豚

snakehead
生魚

scat
金鼓

goldfish
金魚

Torenia
藍豬耳

Oleander
夾竹桃

sunshine tree
黃槐

Chinese New Year flower
吊鐘

bamboo orchid
竹葉蘭

Chinese hibiscus
大紅花

cactus
仙人掌

maize
玉蜀黍

Key to the verb patterns 動詞類型例釋（詳見xxxv—li頁）

S = Subject 主詞 *vi* = intransitive verb 不及物動詞 *vt* = transitive verb 及物動詞
DO = Direct Object 直接受詞 IO = Indirect Object 簡接受詞

[VP1]	S + BE + subject complement/adjunct *This is a book/where I work.*
[VP2A]	S + *vi* *The moon rose.*
[VP2B]	S + *vi* + (*for*) + adverbial adjunct *We walked (for) five miles.*
[VP2C]	S + *vi* + adverbial adjunct *Go away/Come in.*
[VP2D]	S + *vi* + adjective/noun/pronoun *She married young.*
[VP2E]	S + *vi* + present participle *They've gone dancing.*
[VP3A]	S + *vi* + preposition + noun/pronoun *You can rely on me.*
[VP3B]	S + *vi* + (preposition (+ *it*)) + clause *Have you decided (on) what to do next?*
[VP4A]	S + *vi* + *to*-infinitive *We stopped to rest.*
[VP4B]	S + *vi* + *to*-infinitive *He awoke to find the house on fire.*
[VP4C]	S + *vi* + *to*-infinitive *He agreed to come at once.*
[VP4D]	S + SEEM/APPEAR + (*to be*) + adjective/noun *He seemed (to be) surprised at the news.*
[VP4E]	S + SEEM/APPEAR/HAPPEN/CHANCE + *to*-infinitive *She appears to have left already.*
[VP4F]	S + BE + *to*-infinitive *At what time am I to come?*
[VP5]	S + anomalous finite + infinitive *You needn't wait.*
[VP6A]	S + *vt* + noun/pronoun *Everyone likes her.*
[VP6B]	S + *vt* + noun/pronoun *She has green eyes.*
[VP6C]	S + *vt* + gerund *She enjoys playing tennis.*
[VP6D]	S + *vt* + gerund *He began talking about his family.*
[VP6E]	S + NEED/WANT/BEAR + gerund *He needs looking after.*
[VP7A]	S + *vt* + (*not*) + *to*-infinitive *I forgot to post your letter.*
[VP7B]	S + HAVE/OUGHT + (*not*) + *to*-infinitive *He often has to work overtime.*
[VP8]	S + *vt* + interrogative pronoun/adverb + *to*-infinitive *I couldn't decide what to do next.*
[VP9]	S + *vt* + *that*-clause *Do you think (that) it will rain?*
[VP10]	S + *vt* + dependent clause/question *Does anyone know how it happened?*